Chambers Crossword Companion

Chambers

CHAMBERS
An imprint of Chambers Harrap Publishers Ltd
7 Hopetoun Crescent
Edinburgh
EH7 4AY

www.chambers.co.uk

First published by Chambers Harrap Publishers Ltd 2007

A CIP catalogue record for this book is available from the British Library.

ISBN 978 0550 10382 6

Sources and Permissions

Crosswords

New York World crossword, p12, reproduced from *New York World*; *The Crossword Puzzle Book (First Series)* extract, pp13–14, reproduced by permission of Simon and Schuster; Quixote crossword, p86, by Don Manley from *The Independent on Sunday* © *The Independent*, reproduced by permission of Independent News & Media.

Photographs

Azed and solvers, p65, reproduced by permission of Susan Manley; Torquemada, p65, from *112 Best Crossword Puzzles* reproduced by permission of Joan M Rodker; Afrit, p65, reproduced by permission of Wells Cathedral School; Ximenes, p65, by Jane Bown, reproduced by permission of *The Observer*; Azed, p65, reproduced by permission of David Harry; *The Times* setters, p66, reproduced by permission of *The Times*; Zander/Custos, p66, reproduced by permission of Anne Robins; Rufus/Dante/Hodge, p66, by Anna Squires, reproduced by permission of Roger Squires; Apex, p66, reproduced by permission of Chris Rutter; Araucaria/Cinephile, p66, reproduced by permission of John Graham; Mark Goodliffe, p77, reproduced by permission of Derek Harrison; Barbara Hall, p89, by Kevin Dutton, reproduced by permission of *The Sunday Times*; Ross Beresford, p96, reproduced by permission of Ross Beresford; Antony Lewis, p96, reproduced by permission of Antony Lewis.

Thanks are also due to *The Observer* and Colin Dexter for the poem about Ximenes on p71.

Designed and typeset by Chambers Harrap Publishers Ltd, Edinburgh
Printed by Clays Ltd, St Ives plc

Contents

Contributors

Chambers Editor
Hazel Norris

Prepress
Nicolas Echallier

Crossword Manual

Author
Don Manley

Chambers Editor
Hazel Norris

Crossword Checker
Ross Beresford

Prepress
Heather Macpherson

Crossword Dictionary

Chambers Editor
Hazel Norris

Editors
Derek Arthur
Ross Beresford

Consultants
Derek Arthur
Ross Beresford
Jonathan Crowther
Don Manley
Tim Moorey

Contributors
Vicky Aldus
Katie Brooks

Crossword Essays
Jonathan Crowther
Don Manley
Tim Moorey

Data Management
Patrick Gaherty

Prepress
Nicolas Echallier
Susan Lawrie
Isla MacLean

Crossword Completer

Chambers Editor
Hazel Norris

Editorial Assistance
Pat Bulhosen

Data Management
Patrick Gaherty

Prepress
Isla MacLean

Preface

Solving crosswords is, by all accounts, an enjoyable way of spending one's leisure hours. More than 80 years after crosswords first appeared in the newspapers, and despite the temptations of Sudoku and other puzzles, the crossword is still our favourite pastime. Yet so often crossword-solving can become a frustrating experience, accompanied by the gritting of teeth, the tearing-out of hair and the grumpy tossing aside of pens, as the clues prove baffling and the squares remain mockingly empty. *Chambers Crossword Companion* is a balm and a help for exactly those moments, providing as it does a wealth of potential solutions to even the thorniest and most apparently impenetrable clues, alongside practical advice on how to solve a diverse array of clues and crossword types.

The *Crossword Companion* brings together, in a single volume, everything the crossword lover needs for successful solving. Firstly, there is a wealth of advice and expertise taken from the latest edition of *Chambers Crossword Manual* by Don Manley. Here, Don explains the history and development of crosswords, the language of crossword clues and the various clue types that may be encountered. He provides tips on solving and plenty of clue examples, many of which are broken down to explain exactly how the clue works. The various types of crossword, from concise and general knowledge through to the most advanced cryptics, are discussed and illuminated, with plenty of encouragement and practical assistance to help solvers of all abilities. As one of the world's foremost setters, Don is superbly placed to help the novice begin to learn, and the experienced solver progress into the realms of the toughest puzzles.

Then follows the complete text of the latest edition of *Chambers Crossword Dictionary*, which includes more than 500,000 possible solutions to quick and cryptic clues, arranged in over 19,600 entries. The entries comprise not only thesaurus-style synonyms, but also more than 1,200 reference lists of encyclopedic information, from famous pirates to ancient cities, baseball terms to types of grass. The Crossword Dictionary section draws on material from across the authoritative Chambers reference range, and notably contains many thousands of terms from *The Chambers Dictionary*, including those archaic, literary and obscure words so beloved of cryptic crossword compilers. It also makes use of the Chambers clue database, a huge and ever-growing record of the way words are actually used in crosswords, and includes abbreviations, symbols, codes and typical crossword jargon, such as 'AB' for 'sailor', or 'flower' to mean 'river'. Another invaluable feature is the inclusion of 'indicators', denoting terms that may be used in a cryptic clue to show that a word or words should be reversed, anagrammatized or otherwise manipulated. A detailed introduction explains how to get the most from this part of the book.

And finally, the *Crossword Companion* also includes the complete text of the latest edition of *Chambers Crossword Completer*, which lets the solver complete solutions from letters already filled in. It includes over 370,000 entries, from 4 to 15 letters long, arranged alphabetically in order of alternate letters. Thousands of words from *The Chambers Dictionary* are augmented with encyclopedic terms, ensuring unrivalled coverage for everything from concise crosswords to advanced cryptics. When inspiration fails, this section allows beleaguered solvers to fill in those last few blank squares in seconds. Again, the section is preceded by a detailed explanation of how to use this part of the book to best effect.

Additional insights into the world of cruciverbalism are given in the highly-regarded introductory essays which follow this preface. 'The Art of the Crossword Setter' by Jonathan Crowther offers an insight into the creation of these puzzles, while 'Crossword English' by Don Manley explores the language of cryptics and offers advice on how to approach solving. Tim Moorey writes on 'The Art of the Crossword Clue', discussing the qualities that make for a memorable clue and offering examples of the finest clues so far devised. And for those new to cryptic crosswords, or wishing to brush up on their understanding, he goes on to explain how indicators are used in cryptic crossword clues; there follows a list of words that may be used as indicators.

We would like to thank all those people who have been involved in the preparation of this book and its constituent volumes, notably the Chambers team of crossword consultants: Ross Beresford and Derek Arthur, respectively a former and current co-editor of *The Listener* crossword in *The Times*, and top setters Jonathan Crowther, Don Manley and Tim Moorey.

We warmly welcome all comments and suggestions from members of the public, which will be considered for incorporation in future editions. These should be sent to The Editor, *Chambers Crossword Companion*, Chambers Harrap Publishers Ltd, 7 Hopetoun Crescent, Edinburgh, EH7 4AY.

The Publishers
Edinburgh, 2007

The Art of the Crossword Setter

Jonathan Crowther (Azed of *The Observer*)

I am regularly asked – as often by people who habitually solve crosswords as by those who never do – how I set about compiling a puzzle, and especially what order I do things in. (The other commonly-asked question is how long each puzzle takes me, but I usually hedge when answering this one. A puzzle is best constructed over several sittings, and I have never bothered to calculate accurately the total time involved.) For most normal crosswords there are three distinct stages, each more time-consuming than the last: (i) constructing the grid pattern, (ii) filling this with words and (iii) writing the clues. The three stages demand different skills, and for this reason I often compartmentalize the first two, constructing several grid patterns at a sitting and then filling all of these with words before returning to the first grid to start the lengthier and more creative process of writing the clues. Let us now look at each stage in turn.

Crossword grids

There is no absolute rule that crosswords should be symmetrical in design, ie with their blocked squares or bars arranged so that they look the same if the grid is turned upside down or if it is given a quarter-turn. The fact is that most are, and this is the widely-accepted norm. It is also aesthetically pleasing, by no means a negligible consideration. Most importantly, the grid design should ensure a range of entries of varying lengths and a fair distribution of unchecked letters (those which belong to only one word, across or down, and are not 'checked' by a word entered in the other direction). In general the number of unchecked letters is greater in a blocked grid than in a barred one. As a rule of thumb (though one that is regularly infringed by puzzles in a number of our national dailies), no more than half the letters of a solution should be unchecked in a blocked grid. In barred grids, like mine in *The Observer*, the solver can expect a more generous quota of cross-checked letters because such puzzles tend to use more rare and unusual words. In both types of puzzle the inclusion of consecutive unchecked letters in answers is considered bad practice and generally frowned on. It is all a question of fairness to the solver.

There is a fundamental difference in standard grid design between British-style and American-style crosswords. British crosswords, with their tradition of cryptic clues and unchecked letters, normally require the solver to solve every clue in order to complete the puzzle. In most American crosswords, whose clues are not cryptic in the British sense, there are proportionally far fewer blocked squares and they are arranged in such a way that *every* letter is cross-checked, so that, in theory at least, it is possible to complete a puzzle by solving only about half its clues.

In practice, setters of most normal blocked grids in daily or Sunday newspapers in both Britain and the US do not have to concern themselves with grid construction. Each paper uses a limited number of basic patterned grids to which the setter is restricted. In an age of ever-greater standardization this is perhaps inevitable, and it reduces the risk of error, but I still regard it as regrettable and am pleased that no such restriction is placed on me. I derive much satisfaction from exploring the many different grid designs possible within the established parameters: grid size (normally 12 × 12 in my case), number of entries (usually 36), a good spread of entry lengths, and a fair number of unchecked letters. My predecessor Derrick Macnutt (the legendary Ximenes) preferred to let his patterns grow, organically as it were, around the words he wanted to include in his puzzles, effectively merging my first two stages of crossword construction into a single process. My own routine is as I have described, since I start with no preconceptions as to the words I want to use, and this only goes to show that there is no universally prescribed method. There are also no Mosaic laws governing the *size* of crosswords. Blocked grids in daily papers are usually 15 × 15, with about 32 answers (16 across and 16 down), but recent years have seen a growth in the number of 'jumbo' puzzles (typically 27 × 27, with 76 answers), presenting new challenges to solvers and setters alike by the inclusion of longer words and multi-word phrases. In a more modest way, the Azed crossword is now sometimes 13 × 11, enabling me to include 13-letter words on a regular basis. More specialized crosswords explore other designs, including circular diagrams with entries arranged circularly and radially, but these will probably remain the exception and the domain of the seriously dedicated solver.

Word choice

Having completed the grid, or having chosen it from the available range, the setter moves on to fill it with words. There are computer programs which can do this in the twinkling of an eye, though they are limited to the word-lists in the program's memory. The human brain takes much longer but it can select or reject words according to their suitability for cluing and its own real-world knowledge, a crucial factor in the writing of clues. Which words does one choose, and where does one start? I personally start from what seems the natural place, the top left-hand corner of the grid, extending down and across more or less at the same time while keeping a weather eye open for potential problem areas. Anything in the dictionary is fair game, and for me this means *The Chambers Dictionary*. My task is made easier by *Chambers Words* and *Chambers Back-Words for Crosswords*, books which present words alphabetically (or reverse-alphabetically) by length, so that I can see at a glance, say, all the 7-letter words beginning or ending with L. These aids are available to the solver as well as the setter, of course, but I like to think that whereas they are an invaluable tool for the hard-pressed setter, the solver will turn to them only as a last resort. Solving clues should be a contest of minds between setter and solver, not a series of conundrums to be resolved by reference to a published word-list. I also think the setter should be free to include non-dictionary words and phrases, especially topical ones, if these are sufficiently well known. Assessing what is and is not familiar enough to include here is of course a matter of fine judgement. Some newspapers have a policy of not allowing certain taboo words to be used as answers in their crosswords. In these liberated days such bowdlerization strikes me as rather old-fashioned. Crossword setters, like journalists and other writers, should be trusted to know where to draw the line.

The task of filling a grid with words is naturally easier in blocked diagrams than in barred ones, since the number of unchecked letters is significantly greater in blocked diagrams. In both types the setter develops with experience a feel for the 'shape' of words: common letter-clusters, the distribution of consonants and vowels, 'danger' letters (especially at the ends of words), helpful affixes and inflections, and so on. He or she must think ahead to avoid getting boxed into an awkward corner which will involve undoing part of the grid construction, an agonizing waste of time when deadlines are tight. The *Chambers Crossword Completer* is another valuable tool in this context, especially when setting blocked puzzles. This time words are arranged alphabetically by word length according to the alternate letters of each word, first the odd letters (first, third, fifth, etc) and then the even ones (second, fourth, sixth, etc). Special care needs to be taken with shorter words, especially those of four or five letters. There are comparatively few of these in the language (and of these far fewer begin with vowels than with consonants), so most will have been clued many times already. Good setters try to avoid reusing old clues, however proud of them they may be, and they should also not reuse *words* too often. Guarding against this is not easy, and inevitably, there being no copyright in good ideas, similar or identical clues to the same word will recur, but I do make a conscious effort not to repeat myself and think other setters should do likewise. (As a matter of passing interest, there are more different words in the language of eight letters than of any other word length.)

I have already mentioned fair play between setter and solver. This is an important principle in grid construction, just as much as in the writing of clues. Consonants, especially the less common ones, are generally more helpful to the solver as cross-checking letters than vowels are (with obvious exceptions like I or U in final position), and the setter should recognize this. I know that as a solver I feel hard done by if faced by _A_E, one of the most frequent four-letter-word patterns, especially if the setter has made matters worse by giving the word an extra-difficult clue!

Clues

The writing of the clues for a crossword is the last and much the most important task for the setter, for it is here that one stamps one's character and personal style on the puzzle. Seasoned solvers develop clear preferences for the style of this or that setter, and satisfied solvers usually remain loyal to a particular puzzle (even, sometimes, if they are less than happy with other aspects of the paper in which it appears). I firmly believe that an impersonal style of cluing can be boring, and there is no harm at all in letting one's own interests, sense of humour, even prejudices, emerge through one's clues, provided always that these are fair and accurate. Don Manley in his essay on 'Crossword English' describes in detail the range of different clue types regularly used by setters. As a setter myself, I follow a method which has not changed greatly over the years. I always write clues in the order in which they appear in the puzzle. Taking the more colourful words first means leaving a 'sump' of less interesting ones till last, an encouragement to treat the latter as second-class citizens and produce second-class clues as a result. I write no more than nine or ten clues at a sitting, having found that if I try to do more staleness sets in and pedestrian clues result. The restorative effects of even quite a short break doing other things can be truly remarkable! At the same time it is important to see the puzzle as a whole and to present a reasonable variety of clue types (not too many anagrams, for example) to ensure a balanced fare for the solver. This can be tricky when a word cries out for one particular treatment but that treatment has already been used for other words in the puzzle (or for the same word in an earlier puzzle), but the principle is sound. The aim must be to divert the solver, not to massage the setter's ego, so variety is important.

Some words are much more difficult to clue interestingly than others. Scientific terms come high on my list of unfavourite words, mainly because their meaning is very specific and does not lend itself to the sort of wordplay that is at the heart of cryptic clue-writing. A word with many meanings offers far greater scope for punning and similar red herrings to strew in the solver's path. But whichever word I am cluing I always strive (with varying success, I'm sure) for three key ingredients in a clue: accuracy, economy and wit. Every clue should lead accurately and unmistakably to its solution, saying precisely and grammatically what it means (though it may not always mean what it appears to say – taking advantage of the manifold ambiguities of our language is an essential part of cryptic clue-writing). It should do this in as few words as are consistent with fair play, avoiding all superfluous verbiage or mere padding. And it should if at all possible be enjoyable to solve, leaving successful solvers feeling both satisfied at their success and pleasurably diverted by the experience.

About the author

Jonathan Crowther is better known to many cryptic crossword solvers as Azed of *The Observer*. He has also set puzzles under the pseudonyms Gong and Ozymandias. His *Book of Azed Crosswords* is published by Chambers.

Crossword English

Don Manley (crossword setter and author of *Chambers Crossword Manual*)

I am a monoglot, more or less. Although I studied French at school, I can't say I use it much – except when I have to on holiday, and even then it's a sort of pidgin French. But at least I feel I know English, and since (as Bernard Shaw put it) England and America are two countries divided by a common language, maybe one can be a polyglot just by watching television. Or maybe I can be a polyglot just by coming from Devon, where 'thistles' used to be called 'dashels'.

So what has this to do with crosswords? Well, in a sense Crossword English is rather like a foreign language – and it is a language that must be learnt. What may seem odd (if the cross-section of crossword setters I know is anything to go by) is that the polyglots who can speak French and English are not necessarily polyglots in the sense of knowing English and Crossword English. You're more likely to find that a crossword setter is a computer scientist, a physicist or a mathematician than a French teacher these days.

The irritating thing – to anyone who has not yet learnt Crossword English – is that it looks so like Everyday English. For the crossword which offers definitions only, this is perfectly obvious. So if the clue reads 'Cry of an ass (4)' you can write in BRAY straight away. You might have a few alternative answers for 'River (5)', and if you are living in Nottinghamshire you may be disposed to write in TRENT, but when faced with 'River in Paris (5)' you'll know that anything other than SEINE just isn't sane. So for the definition puzzle we're looking at a test of our ability to recognize synonyms or at a quiz with questions that would crop up early on in *Who Wants To Be A Millionaire?*. This is as far as most people get with solving crosswords – the verbal quiz solved with a little help from reference books: a dictionary, an atlas and possibly an encyclopedia. They know English but not Crossword English.

So what is Crossword English? It is the language of the cryptic crossword, a language which looks like ordinary English but which has its own strange rules of grammar and construction and which has its own vocabulary. Crossword English is a series of mini-statements, mini-pictures, and mini-stories even, but the statements, the pictures, and the stories are each designed to hide a sort of riddle. So a riddle isn't a bad place to start with as an example of a cryptic clue:

> My first is in Cornwall but isn't in Devon
> For my second shun Hell and start looking in Heaven
> My third you may find in this or in that
> My whole is a creature that sits on the mat

Thus in a woeful verse of 39 words we have written a cryptic clue for CAT, and at each stage along the way we are spoon-fed with a letter at a time. It's obviously a puzzle, even if it's a pretty heavy-handed one.

Now look at these little riddles and see what you make of them:

1. Lady I rather fancy (7)
2. There's nothing in Basildon I like (3)
3. Delightful tea with the best china (8)
4. It's best to have cold sheets (5)
5. Delicate proposal (6)
6. The clock's put back? Relax! (5)
7. Company car? (3-6)
8. It could deflect battle spear (11)
9. Writer gathers wood as something that'll burn quickly (8)

10. Marsh plant enthrals artist (6)
11. Defeat brought by bowling gaining wicket – something captain controls? (9)
12. Amuse the French after a short time (6)
13. Did he have spelling lessons? (3,9,10)
14. Who you'd expect to find at gay weddings in the Isles?! (8)
15. Female beheaded in the sultanate (4)
16. Lab in, Tory out would suit him (4,5)
17. Boyfriend tied ribbon from what we hear (4)
18. Rejected young troublemaker longed to be free (8)
19. Fool about fifty, one not altogether bright (6)
20. 014? (6,5)

Here are twenty 'portrayals' – perfectly sensible 'portrayals' in generally understandable English – though 20 looks a bit odd. All of these were written by myself at some stage over the past fifteen years or so, and as I look at them I see not only Crossword English but a certain kind of Englishness. There is romance in 1 and 17 (and perhaps 5); there is an austere and rather snooty middle-Englishness about 2, 3 and 4; a concern with cricket in 11; hints of a threatening world outside modern England in 8 and 15; and so on. There may even be a touch of humour here and there. This is English language and English culture.

There are twenty puzzles to solve, so how are these clues different from those for BRAY and SEINE? The answer is (fairly) simple, though the implications of the answer may be complicated. It is this. In each cryptic clue there will still be a definition but the clue writer will have done one of two things. He (sometimes she – and, to be honest, we could do with more 'shes') will have either wrapped up the definition in 'cryptic language' or will have provided a definition plus some indication of the letters in the answer. Sometimes the crossword setter will have done both. In most cryptic clues there will be what we call a 'definition' followed by what we call a 'subsidiary indication' (sometimes also called 'wordplay'), or a subsidiary indication followed by a definition, or even an indication and a definition rolled into one. The secret in decoding a clue lies in trying to solve the answer from either or both of these components while using any letters that are already filled in.

If that all sounds horrible, it's because I've tried to give you a grammar lesson, and (as we all know) it's really much better to start learning a language by speaking it or writing it. No one ever really taught me 'all that grammar stuff' when I was a fledgling cruciverbalist (someone who 'does' crosswords). I was lucky enough to have a father who taught me how to solve clues when I was barely out of short trousers, and the best way I can explain Crossword English is to take you through the clues one by one.

1. *Lady I rather fancy (7)*
   The word 'fancy' is one of a huge set of **anagram indicators**. It tells us that the letters next to it are to be made 'fancy' or jumbled up. If you jumble up 'I rather' you get HARRIET, a lady. This clue, then is an **anagram**, perhaps the one form of cryptic clue everyone knows.

2. *There's nothing in Basildon I like (3)*
   If you look carefully, you'll see that there is indeed a word meaning nothing in the sequence of letters 'Basildon I like' and it's NIL. This is a **hidden word**.

3. *Delightful tea with the best china (8)*
   If you put a word for 'tea' and add it to a word for 'the best china', you will add 'char' to 'Ming' to form CHARMING, meaning 'delightful'. This is a **charade clue**.

4. *It's best to have cold sheets (5)*
   As it happens, this is another charade, but this time we join an **abbreviation** 'c' to the sheets (= ream) to form CREAM (the best). Abbreviations are common in subsidiary indications.

5. *Delicate proposal (6)*
   This is a **double-definition** clue, so you can look upon one definition as the official 'definition' and the other one as the 'subsidiary indication' – or vice versa. What word means both 'delicate' and 'proposal'? Answer: TENDER.

6. *The clock's put back? Relax! (5)*
   This suggests (quite rightly) that you'll get an extra hour in bed when the clocks go back. But if you put back a 'timer' you will get REMIT, which means 'relax'. This is a **reversal** clue. In down clues you may see the word 'up' suggesting a reversal. And here the definition is at the end.

7. *Company car? (3-6)*
   You may be tempted to think of this as another double-definition clue and look for a word that means both 'company' and 'car'. In fact the setter is inviting you to think of 'two's company, three's none', and so the answer is TWO-SEATER. There is no indication of letters in this clue, but we have noticed that it has a **cryptic definition**.

8. *It could deflect battle spear (11)*
   We're looking for an anagram of 'battle spear' and find it in BREASTPLATE, but we notice that the clue as a whole is a definition. Every word in the clue is serving as a definition and as part of the subsidiary indication. We call this an **&lit.** clue. This particular type is **anag. &lit.**

9. *Writer gathers wood as something that'll burn quickly (8)*
   The word 'gathers' suggests that a word for 'wood' might be inside a writer. Put 'fir' inside 'Wilde' and you'll find WILDFIRE. This is known as a **container-and-contents** clue.

10. *Marsh plant enthrals artist (6)*
    This is another container-and contents clue. This time we have an abbreviation for artist (RA) inside a plant (moss) to give MORASS.

11. *Defeat brought by bowling gaining wicket – something captain controls? (9)*
    If you solve crosswords you'll need to get used to **cricket vocabulary**. In this charade bowling is 'over', wicket is 'w', and something the captain controls is 'helm'. Put the three together to get OVERWHELM (defeat).

12. *Amuse the French after a short time (6)*
    Although we're talking about Crossword English, we do allow a few **foreign words** to creep in, especially definite and indefinite articles of common European languages. In this charade a short time is 'tick' added to 'the French', which in this case is 'le', giving the answer TICKLE (amuse).

13. *Did he have spelling lessons? (3,9,10)*
    The setter is tempting you to think about spelling in the sense of getting the right letters in sequence. In fact you should think about spelling in the sense of magic. The answer is THE SORCERER'S APPRENTICE, another cryptic definition, this one being set in what we call a **misleading context** occasioned by the **double-meaning** of 'spelling'. You'll find many other double meanings including 'flower' which can mean river. One of the delights of learning Crossword English is to work these out for yourself!

14. *Who you'd expect to find at gay weddings in the Isles?! (8)*
    This is an outrageous charade, the answer being 'he brides' (ie HEBRIDES). No one ever seems to have taken offence. Every crossword should have at least one clue with an element of **humour**.

15. *Female beheaded in the sultanate (4)*
    This is a particular type of **subtractive** clue. Take the head letter off 'woman' to give the sultanate OMAN. If you take up cryptic crosswords you will also learn about 'endless' and 'heartless'.

16. *Lab in, Tory out would suit him (4,5)*
    This is another **anag. &lit.** Note that 'out' is a very common anagram indicator. You should be able to see TONY BLAIR quite easily.

17. *Boyfriend tied ribbon from what we hear (4)*
When you see words like 'we hear' or 'they say' you almost certainly have a **homophone** clue. Here 'tied ribbon' is 'bow' and BEAU is bow 'from what we hear', ie 'beau' and 'bow' are homophones.

18. *Rejected young troublemaker longed to be free (8)*
This is a **complex** clue in that it consists of the reverse of one word in a charade with another. A rejected troublemaker is 'Ted' backwards ('det') and longed is 'ached', which when attached makes DETACHED. Who ever calls unruly troublemakers 'teddy-boys' or 'teds' these days? Well, we do in crosswords. This is one example of **preserved obsolescence** in an area of language where we still have an extended-play record (EP) and sex appeal is still 'it'.

19. *Fool about fifty, one not altogether bright (6)*
In this container-and-contents clue we make use of our knowledge of **Roman numerals**. Fifty is 'L' and 'twit' about 'L, I' is TWILIT. And there's a slightly misleading context here, isn't there?

20. *014? (6,5)*
This last clue is what one might call a **zany** or **improvised** clue – a sort of one-off cryptic definition. It depends on the solver seeing that 014 = 2 x 007. Since 007 is the agent James Bond, the answer must be DOUBLE AGENT.

With these twenty clues we have touched on all of the most important aspects of Crossword English, and maybe I have already been rather too 'English English' for some. What about other Englishes? Well, I'm writing this article for a Scottish publisher with a very special dictionary, *The Chambers Dictionary*. This is of course an excellent 'English English' dictionary but it also contains some excellent English words from the past and some highly unusual Scottish words. *Chambers* should be in every self-respecting crossworder's library, but its greatest treasures tend to come into play in the more difficult puzzles where Edmund (Spenser) and Jock (the archetypal Scot) make frequent appearances.

Across the Atlantic, in the USA and Canada, 'American Crossword English' is developing as cryptic puzzles, based on British puzzles, become more popular. British solvers will find one or two unfamiliar abbreviations, maybe, and the contexts will be more American – but the similarities tend to contradict Shaw's assertion mentioned earlier.

It has often been pointed out that English is ideal for the crossword because words split up so agreeably. How convenient that 'astronomer' is an anagram of 'moon-starer' and how nicely 'bestride' splits into 'best ride'. Clearly it would be difficult to imagine Crossword Urdu, and yet cryptic crosswords do exist in Hebrew, Bengali, Welsh and Dutch – and other languages too, I dare say.

It's time for a final word about the 'custodians' of Crossword English and what they are trying to do. The word 'custodian' may suggest conservatism and a grammar rule-book. There's more to it than that, of course, but there is a necessary element of grammar in crosswords which needs to be preserved. There are, after all, limits to what is acceptable in Everyday English, and it is the same in Crossword English.

In our language the strict grammarians call themselves **Ximeneans** after Ximenes, *The Observer* crossword setter who died in 1971. There is no space here for a digression into the grammar over which crossword setters and their editors argue, but there is an ongoing debate about what is acceptable and what is not. Today the tradition of Ximenes is upheld by his successor Azed, who tells us about his approach to crossword setting elsewhere in this book. Many of today's crossword setters have been competitors in Azed's clue-writing competitions, and so it is no surprise that many of the crossword setters in our national dailies are Ximenean – as are their crossword editors. Puzzles will inevitably vary in style and in level of difficulty. Crossword setters are turning Crossword English Language into Crossword English Literature and different 'readers' (solvers) will inevitably have their own favourite 'authors' (setters). But there are rules within which the custodians make sure that Crossword English operates – rules not just of grammar, but rules of taste. Practitioners of this language don't have to be absolutely politically correct, but their language is still that of the polite drawing-room, not that of the gutter. We can gently poke fun at pompous bishops and politicians (though not by name specifically!), and we can make wry comments about modern society, but we aim to entertain and not to give offence.

We want to give pleasure and intellectual challenge. Crossword English began as a sort of 20th-century poetry for all to enjoy. Long may it continue into the 21st century and beyond.

About the author

Don Manley sets crosswords under a variety of pseudonyms (Bradman, Duck, Quixote, Pasquale and Giovanni) for many national newspapers (including *The Times, The Guardian, The Independent on Sunday,* the *Financial Times* and *The Sunday Telegraph*). He is the author of the authoritative *Chambers Crossword Manual,* much of which is reproduced here in the Crossword Manual section of this *Crossword Companion.*

The Art of the Crossword Clue

Tim Moorey (Mephisto of *The Sunday Times*)

What is it that makes certain clues stay in the memory when the vast majority are forgotten as soon as their solutions are discovered? I will try to answer the question by identifying characteristics and qualities that setters strive to find and solvers tend to appreciate. Each is illustrated with my choice of clue examples based on over 50 years of crossword solving, and also with choices made by fellow setters from their own past clues and those of other setters. In addition, having had the task of selecting a 'Clue of the Week' for *The Week* magazine since its inception, I regularly have to consider what constitutes a good clue, and my focus there – and here – is on what solvers are likely to have found satisfying. To an increasing extent, it is also based on actual feedback from *The Sunday Times* and *The Week* solvers, following the introduction several years ago of invitations to respond by email.

It is fairly clear which qualities are enjoyed in favoured clues: in a nutshell, short, simple, well-crafted sentences that paint a coherent and believable but misleading picture are well regarded. If these can be supplemented with topicality and wit, so much the better. Technical soundness is taken for granted, albeit that crossword professionals sometimes heatedly debate exactly what is technically sound. Solvers, I think, are unconcerned with this aspect; if a warm glow of recognition on uncovering the answer is obtained, they will value a clue that some professionals (including this one) rate as 'unsound'.

So here are four things I look for in clue selection:

1. **Definition**
   My test is whether the word or words used in the clue could be substituted for the solution in a normal English sentence.

2. **Ease of solving**
   The clue answer should not be immediately apparent; and the penny should drop after not too long an interval of puzzlement.

3. **Clue length**
   Anything over ten words can make for indigestibility, but I wouldn't rule out clues that are slightly longer.

4. **Artificiality in wording**
   There should be no strain evident, and especially no sign that the clue-writer would ideally have preferred to use a different word or words, but was unable to do so in the interest of clueing integrity.

The clues chosen as examples for this essay include what may be regarded as 'classics', that is to say that they are spoken of and quoted still, in most cases despite having appeared some years ago. I also include more recent clues that have featured as 'Clue of the Week'. In most cases, to give readers a better chance of solving, the solutions are fairly common words.

Now for the qualities and characteristics of memorable clues, with illustrations. Hints are given in italics alongside clues, with solutions provided at the end of the essay.

1. Short and succinct

Cryptic definition clues fit this category best, albeit that they may have the disadvantage of not conveying a picture. However, their neatness and deviousness appeal. Ideally, there can only be a unique solution to each of these; note that the bracketed number of letters can sometimes rule out possible alternatives, as in the last of the examples.

Art master (8) *Think old English*

Stiff examination (4,6) *Think Latin*

This cylinder is jammed (5,4) *Think food*

A pound of sultanas (8) *Nothing to do with food*

Bar of soap (6,6) *Two of the three words mislead*

Double definitions – where either word could define the answer – can also be mentioned here. Perhaps the two best known are:

Let rip (4) *Ideas associated with a tear mustn't be shed here*

Driving licence (2-5) *Think of driving in the 'pushy' sense*

2. Well-crafted, painting a believable picture

If these qualities can be included in a totally misleading sentence, then you may have a fine clue.

Neglectful having left off dicky bow (9) *Dicky and bow mislead*

Seems a hip replacement brings about stress (9) *Anagram*

Licking for Persians is a prolonged exercise (8) *Two definitions; think ancient battles*

Amazon order mailed with shrink wrapping (6-3) *A very tough but wonderful clue for a rare word; shrink = shy*

In autumn, we're piling up the last of the leaves (8) *Partial anagram*

Tumbler, nuts, smoke, rapture! (7-5) *Anagram*

3. Topicality

The references in these clues, in order, are: an infamous fatwa issued against an English novelist; a disastrous attempt in 1980 to rescue US hostages from Iran; fears before the 1990 World Cup relating to unruly English soccer fans; and finally the Iraq war.

He's rued his novel (7) *Anagram*

Carter coup tails off in disarray – prepare for war? (8) *Adjusted anagram*

Trouble Italy has looming? (11) *Anagram*

War's started by Bush? Completely! (6) *W is the answer's first letter*

Also topical was this prize-winning effort to celebrate puzzle number 1000 by Ximenes (or X as he was often known) in 1968; C refers to Chambers.

Up to date product of X and C (8) *Think multiplication*

4. Wit and humour

Undoubtedly appreciated by the solver, this is probably the category hardest for setters to achieve, and thus most rarely found. The fine first example won a prize in a Ximenes competition in *The Observer* in 1967, when the recently-coined solution word had not yet made it into the dictionary.

Abbreviations not in Chambers but should not be looked up anyway (4-6) *Think feminine clothes*

Silicone valley! (8) *Think feminine*

Roman marbles lost (3,6,6) *Think Latin*

In which three couples get together for sex (5) *Last word is the key*

Odd if no males could be found here (4,2,3) *Anagram*

Variety of *English* pastry – Dane would look down on it! (7) *Anagram*

Stiff collaring's my trade – it shows what can be done by starch (4,8) *Anagram*

5. Definition and secondary indications being the same ('& lit.' type clues)

Often considered as the pinnacle of the clue-writer's art, the best of this type have a conciseness of wording and do not reveal their charms too easily.

We'll get excited with Ring seat (10) *Anagram*
No fellow for mixing (4,4) *Anagram*
I rifle tubs at sea (10) *Anagram*
What you might find in Lechtal overlooking lake? (6) *Overlook here means 'ignore'*
What's tea passed round in? (5) *Tea is 'cha'*
Waitress with large bust could model as this (7-4) *Bust here means 'broken'*
Names I must jot endlessly (8) *Must here means 'in a frenzy'*
What grass is (even for a fool) (5) *Substitute one word for another*
By it 'truth' and 'lie' looked alternately interchangeable (6-5) *Anagram*

6. Subtlety of language

This type often requires a second, careful reading of a word or words, not necessarily prominent ones.

Lass I love moving upwards you may find well beneath this (3,3) *Down clue*
A chap could attend this celebration but never does (4,5) *Read it again*
Drink causing a problem? What if it is! (9) *An additive clue*
Item Gran arranged family slides in (5,7) *Family is 'clan'*
Shot with craft on course (9) *Golf and poetry cleverly in play*
A murder suspect, one hears (7) *Last two words especially mislead*
Dive made from upturned punts? (7) *A down clue; think Ireland*

7. Technical virtuosity

Long anagrams, as in the first two examples, are often quoted by solvers. This shows that work by setters (whether by computer or not) is appreciated. The third example of virtuosity is also one of the most deceptive clues ever published.

Ground with the Arsenal not getting the least bit of sympathy (5,4,4) *Ground, the past tense of grind*
Poetical scene with surprisingly chaste Lord Archer vegetating (3,3,8,12) *Brooke*
Some job at hand? We'll soon see (4,3,5) *Last word misleads*

8. Highly original clues not obviously fitting into any category

These typically require a leap of imagination on the part of the solver and maybe raise an especially wide smile when the penny drops. Even though the first two of the following clues are often considered 'unsound', they do get plaudits from solvers.

HIJKLMNO (5) *Chemistry; no direct definition included*
ONMLKJIH (9) *No direct definition included*
I can identify vehicles here (5) *IVR code knowledge needed*
014? (6,5) *Think spooks*
His, for example (9) *Plural answer*

Finally, the clue most suggested by fellow setters, and my own favourite, goes back over 25 years. It was originated by Les May, who won first prize in *The Observer*'s Azed competition, and could have been included in several of the other categories. A tough one to crack but solving it for real would be highly satisfying nonetheless.

Bust down reason (9) *Solution splits into three separate words for the purposes of the secondary reading*

Solutions and (where known) authors

Where the clue originally appeared under a pseudonym, the pseudonym is shown in brackets after the author's real name. Where there is no pseudonym or no name at all, the clue's author is unknown to me, or it may have featured either in clue-writing competitions or in publications such as *The Times* or *The Daily Telegraph* where setters are unnamed (though in three instances where names are known to me, due credit is given below).

1. TEACHEST; POST MORTEM; SWISS ROLL Adrian Bell *The Times*; SERAGLIO Valerie Coleman; ROVER'S RETURN; RENT; GO-AHEAD Norman Goddard;

2. GENUFLECT; EMPHASISE John Halpern (Mudd); MARATHON and SHIELD-MAY Ross Beresford; FAREWELL *anag we're in fall* H S Tribe; POSTURE-MAKER I M Raab;

3. RUSHDIE John Grimshaw; ACCOUTRE Tim Moorey; HOOLIGANISM Malcolm Barley; WHOLLY Michael Curl (Orlando); THOUSAND Sir Jeremy Morse;

4. MINI-SKIRTS M C Raphael; CLEAVAGE Roy Dean *The Times*; NON COMPOS MENTIS; LATIN *three times two is six* Brian Greer; ISLE OF MAN; YAPSTER Paul Henderson; BODY SNATCHER Sir Jeremy Morse;

5. WAGNERITES Derrick Macnutt (Ximenes); LONE WOLF Don Manley (Quixote); FILIBUSTER A N Clark; CHALET John Tozer; CHINA; SWEATER-GIRL Tim Moorey (Mephisto); AMNESIAC Kathleen Bissett; GREEN *een for ass* Richard Morse; DOUBLE-THINK Colin Dexter;

6. OIL RIG Jonathan Crowther (Azed); STAG PARTY; SUPPOSING; MAGIC LANTERN Colin Dexter; ALBATROSS; EARDRUM; NITERIE *Eire tin reversed* Roger Hooper;

7. WHITE HART LANE Richard Palmer (Merlin); THE OLD VICARAGE GRANTCHESTER John Graham (Araucaria); BATH AND WELLS *hidden clue* Brian Greer;

8. WATER; BACKWATER John Grimshaw *The Times*; ITALY; DOUBLE AGENT *007* Don Manley (Quixote); GREETINGS; BRAINWASH *bra in wash* Les May.

About the author

Tim Moorey sets crosswords as one of the three-strong Mephisto team for *The Sunday Times*, for which he also regularly contributes *The Sunday Times* crossword. He has additionally appeared as Owzat in newspapers such as *The Independent*, *The Sunday Telegraph* and *The Listener* crossword in *The Times*. He is the crossword editor of *The Week* magazine, gives talks on crosswords and runs regular crossword workshops.

Indicators in Cryptic Crossword Clues

Tim Moorey (Mephisto of *The Sunday Times*)

Why do crosswords have 'indicators'?

As compared to definition-only crosswords (general knowledge, quick, easy and the like) which have clues offering only one means of arriving at each solution, cryptic crossword clues usually have two. These are a definition and a secondary way, often termed 'wordplay'. This, in effect, acts as a check on the definition, or vice versa if the solver finds the definition elusive. Wordplay relies on 'indicators', of which there are many types. In effect, an indicator shows how the setter has manipulated the solution, in that a whole word (or part) may have been subject to one or more tricks, such as the following:

	Type of indicator
Changed into another word by a letter mix	Anagram
Split into parts with one part inside another	Containment/Insertion
Letter(s) chosen for subtraction	Deletion
Concealed inside the rest of the clue	Hidden
Considered as spoken, giving a different word	Homophone
Linked to other part(s)	Juxtaposition
Written backwards (or upwards for a Down clue)	Reversal
Letter(s) chosen for manipulation	Selection

How are indicators used?

Indicators are designed to signal to solvers:

- which type of wordplay is to be unravelled
- how to adjust a letter or letters within the clue
- how the whole clue sentence fits together

What are the main types of indicator?

In the clue examples that follow, the indicator is denoted in bold type.

1 Anagram

In nearly all cryptic crosswords solvers are expected to unravel some solutions from a mix of letters, and there is a need for this wordplay to be flagged up. Hence the anagram indicator, of which there are a huge number. Most – but not all – imply some form of movement, lack of order, change, uncertainty or instability (especially in assumed mental or physical state) in their meanings, albeit often in a concealed surface reading. Anagram indicators such as 'ground' being the past tense of 'grind', and 'bananas' and 'potty' with their double meanings, show such concealment.

There are also some indicators that can only be fully justified by well-established convention. For example, the many synonyms of 'drunk' such as 'pickled', 'stoned' and the like are commonly used, it being assumed that cruciverbal tipplers are wobbly rather than flat out! Nor are setters static in their usages: a modern synonym for 'crazy' such as 'out to lunch' makes a highly misleading anagram indicator, as does 'supply' in the second example.

People seen **working** in Basra (5)

The indicator 'working' for this purpose is in the sense of 'being in action' and it signals a letter mix for the solution ARABS.

Monn (Caterers) **supply** beef and grouse (12)

Here the adverb of 'supple' meaning 'pliant' shows that the first two words must be anagrammatized into REMONSTRANCE meaning complaint, or 'beef' and 'grouse'. Note that as well as wordplay there are two definitions here, a practice often found in advanced puzzles such as Azed or Mephisto.

2 Containment

A solution may be split such that one part of it can be seen as being 'outside' another, duly shown by the many indicators of this type. Containment and insertion indicators have the same effect.

Opportunity to **go round** one Italian city (5)

'Opportunity' is 'turn', and when that is put outside 'I' for 'one' you get the Italian city TURIN. Here 'to go round' is the indicator and 'one' for '1' for 'I' is a common crossword convention.

Saw dog **wearing** lead (7)

This requires 'Rover' for 'dog' to be placed inside 'lead' – or rather the metal's abbreviation 'Pb' – to give PROVERB, or 'saw'.

Is **trapped in** burning lift (5)

The indicator 'trapped in' signals that 'is' has to be contained by, ie put inside, 'burning' meaning 'hot' for the solution HOIST, which defines 'lift'.

3 Insertion

These have the same effect as containment indicators. A solution may be split such that one part is viewed as being 'inside' another.

Disreputable type in favour of **cutting** discount (9)

If you put 'pro', meaning 'in favour of', inside (ie 'cutting') the term 'rebate' meaning 'discount', the solution REPROBATE, a 'disreputable type', appears.

Crumpet may be so to speak **in** bed (8)

Here the well-concealed definition ends at the word 'so'. The wordplay is then 'utter' meaning 'to speak' in 'bed' leading us nicely to BUTTERED. (Note that the 'to' is to be ignored, as is commonly the practice with verbs in wordplay).

4 Deletion

These indicators signal the deletion of a letter or letters (as in the first example), or a whole word within a clue (as in the second example).

Applause left **out** in graduation ceremony (7)

'Applause' is 'clapping' and the indicator demands that its L for 'left' be taken out to leave CAPPING, a 'graduation ceremony'.

Surgeon **fails to get** on in this swell (5)

Take 'on' from 'surgeon' to get to SURGE which is the definition for 'swell'.

Note that the word 'in' here in both deletion examples is being used not as an indicator but as common crossword shorthand, in effect for 'leading to …' or 'coming from …'.

Other specific deletion indicators are discussed in Ends deletion indicators, Head deletion indicators, Middle deletion indicators and Tail deletion indicators.

5 Ends indicators

5a Ends selection

The first and last letters of a word within a clue are indicated for addition to some other letters, or to a whole word, in order to form the solution.

Urges for example, **both sides** in games (4)

The indicator 'both sides' when applied to 'games' gives two letters G and S. Put these together with 'eg', meaning 'for example', and you have EGGS as in to egg or urge someone on.

5b Ends deletion

The first and last letters of a word within a clue are indicated for deletion in order to form the solution.

Shell prawn uncooked (3)

'Shell' in the sense of 'separate from the shell or covering' implies removing the first and last letters of 'prawn' to give RAW meaning 'uncooked'.

6 Head indicators

There is a common (but not universally applied) convention that Down solutions should be indicated as the word appears in the completed grid. This means that a distinction is sometimes made between Across and Down clues as regards what constitutes 'heads'. For example, head selection indicators such as 'summit' or 'top' are sometimes said to be applicable to Down clues only.

6a Head selection

The first letter of a word within a clue is indicated for addition to some other letters or, as below, to a whole word to form the solution.

Starter with pork and mild pickle (6)

Here the indicator 'starter' is applied to 'pork' to give 'P'. Added to 'light' meaning 'mild' this provides the solution PLIGHT, or a 'pickle' – a predicament if you are in one.

6b Head deletion

The first letter of a word is indicated for deletion in order to form the solution.

Colleague in Monte Carlo event **failing to start** (4)

A 'Monte Carlo event' is a 'rally' which 'fails to start', ie it loses its initial letter. This leaves the answer ALLY, meaning 'colleague'.

7 Middle indicators

7a Middle selection

The middle letter (or letters) of a word within a clue is indicated for addition to some other letters, or to a whole word, in order to form the solution.

Plastic building toy on **centre** of floor (4)

'On' for 'leg' (as in cricket) plus the middle letter of floor, 'O', makes LEGO, the required toy.

7b Middle deletion

The middle letter (or letters) of a word within a clue is indicated for deletion in order to form the solution.

Royal Artillery really **disheartened**? Seldom (6)

The central two letters 'AL' are eliminated from 'really' to give 'RELY', which put after 'RA' (an abbreviation of 'Royal Artillery') gives RARELY, 'seldom'.

8 Tail indicators

8a Tail selection

The last letter (or letters) of a word within a clue is indicated for addition to some other letters, or to a whole word, in order to form the solution.

Dull **back** of road could be a cul-de-sac (4,3)

'Dull' is 'deaden', to which an added 'D' from 'back of road' provides DEAD END, a 'cul-de-sac'.

8b Tail selection down

This is similar to that above, but this indicator is for a Down clue only (see Head indicators above for an explanation of this convention). The above Across clue could be adapted as follows, with 'bottom' as the Tail Selection Down indicator.

Dull **bottom** of road could be a cul-de-sac (4,3)

This gives a Down clue with the same solution DEAD END, a 'cul-de-sac'.

8c Tail deletion

The last letter (or letters) of a word is indicated for deletion in order to form the solution.

English poet messing around **endlessly** (6)

'Messing around' is 'larking' which becomes (Philip) LARKIN, the poet, when its last letter is taken off.

8d Tail deletion down

This is similar to that above, but this indicator is for a Down clue only.

Baseless worry for vehicle (3)

If the final letter of 'care' for 'worry' is ignored, CAR, a 'vehicle', comes out as the Down clue answer.

9 Hidden

9a Hidden

The indicator instructs solvers to look for the solution within the clue sentence, or wholly within one of the clue's words.

In Amritsar it's a common habit (4)

Indicated by 'in', the challenge is to uncover a hidden but defined four-letter word. This is SARI – formed from the last three letters of 'Amritsar' and the first letter of 'it's' – a common habit with the final word in its 'dress' sense.

Sensation **concealed by** Chopin, Sand – needlessly (4,3,7)

Not quite so easy to spot, as a result of its misleading punctuation, is the hidden phrase PINS AND NEEDLES, a sensation.

9b Hidden alternately

A second form of this indicator applies where every other letter has to be taken to form the solution word. The indicator will not necessarily always signal whether it's the even or odd letters to be used. For example, the indicator 'regularly' may refer to either even or odd letters.

Select **even parts** of strongest gear (4)

The instruction 'select' indicates taking the even letters in 'strongest' to form a word meaning 'gear'. Hence the solution is TOGS.

10 Homophone

In this type, the definition when spoken becomes another word which forms the wordplay. Sometimes with careless word placement, setters do not make clear which is the solution and which the homophone, though this may be established from the word-length. It can also be a problem for solvers as to which part of the English-speaking world, with its many differing pronunciations, is deemed to be speaking the homophone.

It's cold in a S American country **reportedly** (6)

'Reportedly' is an indicator that the solver is looking for a word that sounds like another meaning of 'cold'. 'Chile' clearly fits the bill as a homonym of CHILLY, the answer.

Check **on radio** for weather forecast? (4)

If listening to the radio, 'rein' (meaning 'check') would sound like RAIN, the solution.

11 Juxtaposition

11a Juxtaposition

The indicator shows that the two words or parts of words need to be placed together for the solution.

Endeavour perhaps to be **alongside** learner in a scrap (6)

Morse ('Endeavour', the first name of Inspector Morse in the novels by Colin Dexter) is juxtaposed with 'L' for 'learner' to make 'scrap', a MORSEL.

11b Juxtaposition down

This is similar to that above, but this indicator is for a Down clue only (see Head indicators above for an explanation of this convention).

One **above** Bishop given the answer: forgiveness (10)

'A' for 'one' put on top of 'B' for 'bishop' and 'solution' for 'answer' makes ABSOLUTION, meaning 'forgiveness'. Actually there are two juxtaposition indicators here, in that as well as 'above', the word 'given' also shows that some words are to be placed together.

12 Reversal

12a Reversal

The whole of a solution word can sometimes be reversed to form another different word (or the same word in the case of a palindrome – see below). It's the job of reversal indicators to show this, and sometimes also reversals of only part of a word which is then subject to more wordplay, as in the second example.

Huge flans **all round** – that's the plan (9)

'Huge flans' are 'mega tarts', which when reversed gives STRATAGEM or 'plan'.

Optimistic US president admitting bad **back** (7)

Reversing 'ill' for 'bad' and putting this inside (further wordplay signalled by 'admitting') Bush gives BULLISH, or 'optimistic'.

12b Reversal down

Reversal indicators used in Down clues will often be, for example, 'rising' or 'brought up' rather than those used in Across clues implying reversal horizontally such as 'all round' (as above) or as 'backwards' (see Head indicators above for further explanation of this convention). Using this in the preceding example, a Down clue could have been:

Huge flans **served up** – that's the plan (9)

It's 'served up' showing the necessary upwards movement in 'mega tarts' to lead to the same STRATEGEM solution.

12c Reversal palindrome

The third type of reversal indicator applies to palindromic solutions, for which there are a small number of indicators.

> This note is small **whichever way you look at it** (5)

The indicator signals that the solution is the same as its reversal, in this case MINIM, the 'small note' of the clue.

Other indicators

In addition to the most important indicators already covered above, there are some others met in cryptic puzzles that can be mentioned briefly. They tend to be self-explanatory.

Foreign

Many European languages, especially French, can be indicated, usually obviously but occasionally not so, as in this example:

> **Nice** girl has time for a piece of beef (6)

The indicator refers to the French city of Nice, where the word for 'girl' would be 'fille'. Put next to 'T' for 'time', you have FILLET, a piece of beef.

Archaic

Rather than use the mundane 'archaic' or 'obsolete' as indicators, setters find more interesting and misleading ways of expressing words that are no longer in general usage.

> Mark **antique** articles rubbish! (2,3)

'M' for 'mark' (as in Germany before the euro), plus 'ye ye' or two archaic definite 'articles' will show as MY EYE, meaning 'rubbish!'

Dialect

Different regional words and accents may be referred to, especially British ones such as Scottish and Cockney.

> The **Yorkshire** beer in fiction (4)

The solution TALE, meaning 'fiction' in the sense of a lie, comes from 'T' for 'the' as supposedly used in 'Yorkshire' plus 'ALE' for 'beer'.

Repetition

A small number of indicators show, nearly always self-evidently, when letters or words need to be included more than once in a solution.

> The Queen **repeatedly** behind grown-up man of affairs (9)

Thus 'grown-up' is 'adult' which when preceding 'ER' (the Queen) twice gives 'ADULTERER', the 'man of affairs' being sought.

Conclusion

In the foregoing examples there is mostly only one type of indicator used in any one example. However, it is not uncommon in advanced puzzles to find one or more indicators of the same or different type being used in one clue. For example:

> Clever wordplay recalled Thomas Mann's last book about love (3,3)

Here the solver is asked to do all the following:

	Indicator (and type)
Abbreviate *Thomas* to TOM	none given
Take *Mann's last* as N	*last* (tail selection)
Abbreviate *book* to B	none given
Abbreviate *love* to O	none given
Put TOM N B outside O	*about* (containment)
Amongst other possibilities, this gives TOMNOB.	
Reverse this to get BONMOT	*recalled* (reversal)
And finally split it (3,3) to get BONMOT, meaning 'clever wordplay'.	

Note that, as is almost always the case, abbreviations have to be identified without the aid of indicators. The clue is perhaps over-complex and you may or not agree that it offers clever wordplay!

About the author

Tim Moorey sets crosswords as one of the three-strong Mephisto team for *The Sunday Times*, for which he also regularly contributes *The Sunday Times* crossword. He has additionally appeared as Owzat in newspapers such as *The Independent*, *The Sunday Telegraph* and *The Listener* crossword in *The Times*. He is the crossword editor of *The Week* magazine, gives talks on crosswords and runs regular crossword workshops.

Indicator Lists

The following lists show those headwords, phrasal verbs and idioms that are denoted in the Crossword Dictionary section of this book as being indicators of cryptic crossword clue wordplay.

The lists have been compiled on the basis of those indicators most commonly seen in crosswords. They are not, and never could be, definitive. The lists reflect the way that these words have been used in actual cryptic clues. Appearance in a list does not mean that such a usage is considered acceptable by all crossword setters and editors.

Indicators may not appear in a cryptic clue in the way in which they appear here, but rather may be encountered in an inflected form – for example the anagram indicator 'digest' is more frequently encountered as 'digested' – or as part of a phrase, for example 'not reaching a conclusion' to indicate a tail deletion. As the lists given here reflect the headwords in the Crossword Dictionary section, not every form of every indicator is included.

Additionally, there are some indicators which may be encountered in cryptic clues, but which are not denoted in the text or in the following lists. Examples of these include:

Type	**Indicator example**
Abbreviation to be used	short
Colloquial usage	commonly
First half, second half of word selected	left half, right half
Insertion between letters SS	aboard ship, on board
Move first letter to end	brings first to last, runs down
Move internal letter to front	puts foremost
Not all letters used	not entirely
One of two central letters deleted	half-heartedly
Only limited wordplay	slightly
Only two, three, etc letters selected	two of, three of, etc
Plural word loses final S	singular
Proportion of letters in a word selected	half, two-thirds
Selection of second, third, fourth, etc letter	second, third, fourth, etc
Selection of two letters	couple of
Single letter instead of double	just one
Substitute letters	replace, take instead, change, changing
Unusual homophone	drunkard says (*for a homophone that sounds slurred, eg 'mesh' for 'mess'*)

It should also be noted that as the number of foreign word indicators is potentially unlimited – any person or place might be used – only the most general have been included here. For example, 'article from Paris', 'day in Calais', 'Renoir's here', 'lake in Savoie' or 'of Chirac's' could all indicate that a French word is required (in these instances, 'la' or 'le', 'jour', 'ici', 'lac' and 'de' respectively).

Anagram indicators

Anagram indicators include:

abandon
abandoned
aberrant
abnormal
abominable
about
abroad
absurd
abuse
abysmal
abysmally
accident
accidentally
acrobatics
acting
action
activate
active
activity
adapt
adaptable
adaptation
adjust
adjustment
administer
adrift
affected
afflicted
afresh
after injury
aggrieved
agile
agitate
agitated
ague
alarm
allocate
allocation
all over the place
alloy
alter
alteration
alternative
alternatively
amazing
amend
amendment
amiss
amok
analyse
analysis
anarchic
anew
angrily
angry
animated
animatedly
anomalous
anomaly
another
anxious
anyhow
anyway
apart
appalling
appallingly
appliance
applied
appointed
appraisal
arch
around
arousal
arouse
arrange
arrangement
array
artefact
artful
artfully
articulate
articulated
askew
assassinate
assassination
assemble
assorted
astonishing
astray
at fault
at random
atrocious
at sea
away
awful
awfully
awkward
awkwardly
awry
bad
badly
baffle
baffling
bake
bamboozle
bananas
bandy
barbaric
barbarous
barge
barking
baroque
bastard
bats
batter
battered
batting
batty
beaten
beat up
become
bedevil
bedlam
befuddle
belabour
belt
bemuse
bemused
bend
bendy
bent
berserk
bespoke
bewildered
biased
bizarre
bizarrely
blast
blasted
blazing
blend
blessed
blight
blotchy
blow up
blue
blunder
blur
blurred
body
bogus
boil
boiled
boiling
boisterous
bomb
boozy
boss
botch
bother
bottle
bouncing
bouncy
brain
break
break up
breeze
brew
brittle
broach
broadcast
broke
broken
broth
bruise
bubbly
buck
buckle
buffeted
building
built
bully
bum
bumble
bumbling
bundle
bungle
burst
bust
bustle
bustling
busy
butcher
Byzantine
calamitous
camouflage
capricious
career
careless
carelessly
carve
carve up
cast
cavort
change
changeable
chaotic
chew
choppy
chop up
churn
circulate
clobber
clumsy
cocktail
cock up
cock-up
code
collapse
collected
collection
combustible
compilation
compile
complex
complicate
complicated
complication
component
compose
composed
composition
compound
compromise
concerned
concoct
condemn
condemnation
condition
confection
confound
confuse
confused
confusing
confusion
constituent
construct
construe
contaminate
contamination
contort
contrive
contrived
conversion
convert
convertible
convoluted
convulse
cook
cooked
cook up
correct
correction
corrupt
could be
could become
crack
cracked
crackers
crackpot
crack up
craft
craftily
crafty
cranky
crash
crazed
crazily
crazy
creation
criminal
crocked
crook
crooked
cross
crude
crudely
cruel
crumble
crumbly
crush
cuckoo
cultivate
cure
curious

curiously
cut
daft
damage
damaged
dance
dash
dashing
dazed
debris
decompose
defective
deficient
defile
deform
deformed
delirious
deliriously
demented
demolish
deplorable
deploy
deranged
desecrate
design
desperate
desperately
destabilize
destroy
destruction
desultory
deterioration
detour
devastate
devastated
develop
deviant
deviate
deviation
devilish
devious
diabolical
dicky
different
differently
digest
dilapidated
dire
direct
disarrange
disarray
disastrous
disband
discomfit
discompose
disconcert
disconcerting
discord
discordant
discover
diseased
disfigure
disgruntled
disguise
disguised
dish
dishevelled
dish out
disintegrate
disintegration
disjointed
dislocate
dislocation
dismantle
disorder
disordered
disorderly
disorganization
disorganize
disorganized
disorientate
disorientated
disorientation
dispel
disperse
dispersion
disport
dispose
disposed
disposition
disrupt
disruption
dissipate
dissipated
dissolute
dissonant
distillation
distort
distorted
distract
distracted
distraught
distribute
distribution
disturb
disturbance
disturbed
disturbing
dither
diverse
divert
diverting
dizzy
do
doctor
doddering
doddery
dodgy
done
dotty
doubtfully
drastic
drawn
dreadful
dreadfully
dress
dressing
dress up
drift
drunk
drunken
dubious
duff
dynamic
easily
easy
eccentric
edit
effervescent
elaborate
elastic
elevated
embarrass
embarrassed
embroil
emend
emendation
emerge
employ
engineer
enigmatic
enliven
entangle
entanglement
entwine
err
errant
erratic
erratically
erring
erroneous
error
erupt
eruption
evolution
evolve
exchange
excite
excited
excruciate
exercise
exotic
explode
explosive
extract
extraordinarily
extraordinary
extravagant
fabricate
fake
fall
false
faltering
fan
fanciful
fancy
fantastic
fashion
fault
faulty
fearful
ferment
fettle
feverish
fickle
find in
finesse
finicky
fishy
fit
fix
fixed
flabbergasted
flail
flake
flaky
flap
flash
flawed
flexible
flighty
flit
floating
flog
flop
floppy
flounder
flourish
flourished
flourishing
flow
fluctuate
fluff
fluid
flurried
flurry
fluster
flutter
fly
fly open
fog
foolish
foolishly
force
forced
foreign
forge
forged
forlorn
form
foul
founder
found in
fracture
frantic
frantically
freak
freak out
free
freely
frenetic
frenetically
frenzy
fresh
freshen
freshly
frightful
frightfully
frilly
frisky
frolic
frolicsome
fuddled
fudge
full
fumble
funnily
funny
furious
fussy
fuzzy
gaffe
gambol
garble
garbled
generate
giddily
giddy
ginger
gnarled
go crazy
gone
go off
grim
groggy
groom
gross
grotesque
ground
hairy
ham
hammer
hammered
hammer out
hamper
haphazard
haphazardly
happy
harass
harassed
harm
hash
hatch
havoc
haywire
hazy
head over heels
heat
hectic
hellish

helter-skelter
hideous
higgledy-piggledy
high
hit
hopeless
hopelessly
horrible
horribly
horrid
horrific
hotchpotch
hurl
hurt
hybrid
idiotic
ill
ill-assorted
ill at ease
ill-bred
ill-treat
imbecile
impair
impaired
imperfect
implicate
implicated
improper
improperly
inaccurate
incapable
in circulation
incorrect
indecent
indiscriminate
inebriated
inept
ingredient
injure
injured
inky
in motion
inordinate
in pieces
insane
insanely
insanity
insecure
intoxicate
intoxicated
intricate
invalid
invention
involve
involved
irregular
irritated
itinerant
jagged
jangle
jar
jaunty
jazz
jerk
jerky
jig
jiggle
jitters
jittery
jockey
jog
jolt
jostle
judder
juggle
jumble
jumbled
jump
junk
kick
kind of
kink
kinky
knead
knock
knock over
knot
knotty
labour
laboured
labyrinthine
lace
lamentable
lark
launder
lawless
lax
layout
lazily
leap
liberal
light
lit
lively
loaded
loony
loose
loosely
lost
lousy
ludicrous
lunatic
mad
madden
maddening
made-up
madly
madness
make
make up
make-up
maladjusted
malformed
malfunction
malleable
maltreat
mangle
manic
manically
manifest
manifestation
manipulate
manipulation
manoeuvre
manufacture
mar
marshal
mash
masquerade
massage
maul
maybe
mayhem
maze
meandering
meddle
medley
melange
mêlée
melt
mental
merry
mess
messy
metamorphose
metamorphosis
mill
mince
mint
misbehave
misbehaviour
mischievous
mischievously
misconduct
misconstrue
misdirect
miserable
miserably
misfit
misguided
mishandle
mishap
misinterpret
mislead
misleading
mismanage
mismanagement
misplace
misprint
misread
misrepresent
misrepresentation
misshapen
misspell
mistake
mistaken
mistakenly
mistreat
misuse
mix
mixed
mixed up
mix in
mixture
mix up
mix-up
mobile
mobilize
model
modification
modify
mongrel
mortal
mould
mouldy
move
movement
moving
muddle
muddled
muddy
muff
mushy
muss
must
musty
mutate
mutation
mutilate
mutilation
mutinous
mysterious
mysteriously
nastily
nasty
naughty
neaten
neglect
neglected
negligence
negligent
negotiate
negotiation
nervous
nervously
new
newly
nobble
nonsensical
not
novel
nuts
obfuscate
oblique
obscure
obstreperous
odd
oddball
oddly
off
off-colour
on
on the rampage
operate
order
orderly
organization
organize
organized
original
ornate
other
otherwise
out
outlandish
out of hand
out of order
out of place
out of sorts
output
outrageous
outré
outside
overthrow
overturn
painfully
panic
paranormal
pastiche
patchy
pathetic
peculiar
peculiarly
peddle
pell-mell
perform
perhaps
perplex
perturb
perturbed
perverse
perversely
perversion
perversity
pervert
perverted
phoney
pickle
pie
piece
plan
plastered
plastic
play
play around with
play with
ply
police
pollute

pollution
poor
poorly
pop
possible
possibly
potential
potentially
potty
prance
precarious
precariously
preparation
prepare
prepared
preposterous
problem
problematic
process
produce
production
promiscuous
protean
provide
pulverize
pummel
punish
puzzle
quaint
quake
queer
questionable
quirky
quiver
raddled
rag
rage
ragged
ramble
rambling
rampage
rampant
ramshackle
random
randomly
rare
rash
rattle
ravage
ravaged
rave
raving
react
reactionary
realign
rearrange
reassemble
rebel
rebellious
rebuild
recast
reckless
recklessly
recollect
recollection
recondition
reconfigure
reconstitute
reconstruct
recover
recreate
recycle
red
redeploy
redevelop
redevelopment
redistribute
redistribution
redraft
re-edit
reel
refashion
refine
refit
reform
reformat
reformation
refurbish
refurbishment
refuse
regenerate
regenerated
regulate
rehash
rejig
relax
relaxed
relay
remake
remarkable
remedy
remodel
render
renegade
renegotiate
renew
renovate
rent
reorder
reorganize
repackage
repair
replace
reposition
represent
representation
reprocess
reproduce
resettle
reshape
reshuffle
resolution
resolve
resort
restless
restoration
restore
re-use
revamp
reveal
revel
review
revise
revolt
revolting
revolution
revolutionary
rework
rewrite
rickety
ridiculous
ridiculously
rifle
rig
rile
riot
riotous
riotously
rip
ripple
rock
rocky
rogue
roll
rollicking
rolling
rot
rotten
rough
roughen
roughly
round
rouse
rove
rub
rubbish
rude
ruffle
ruin
ruined
rum
run
running
runny
run riot
run wild
rupture
rustic
sabotage
sack
sad
sadly
salad
scatter
scatty
scheme
scour
scraggy
scramble
scrappy
scratch
screw
screwy
scruffy
scuffle
sculpt
sculpture
scuttle
seedy
seethe
serve
set
set out
settlement
shake
shaky
sham
shape
shapeless
shatter
shattered
shell
shift
shifty
shimmer
shimmering
shiver
shock
shoddy
shot
shower
show off
shuffle
sick
signal
silliness
silly
sink
sketchy
skip
slack
slapdash
slaughtered
slide
slip
slippery
slipshod
sloppy
slosh
slovenly
slyly
smash
snarl
solution
solve
somehow
sorry
sort
soup
sozzled
spasmodic
spatter
special
specially
speech
spin
splash
splice
spoil
spongy
sport
sporting
spray
spread
spring
sprinkle
spurious
squiffy
squirm
stagger
staggered
staggering
steaming
stew
stir
stirring
storm
stormy
straighten
strange
strangely
stray
stress
structure
struggle
stumble
stupid
stupidly
style
subtle
subtly
suffer
suffering
sunk
supply
surprising
suspect
suspicious
swap
swill
swim
swimming
swing
swinging
swirl
switch
swop
synthetic
tailor
taint

tangle
tangled
tattered
tease
teeter
terrible
terribly
throb
throw
tidy
tight
tipsy
topple
topsy-turvy
torment
torn
tortuous
torture
toss
totter
tour
tragic
train
trammel
transfer
transfigure
transform
transformation
translate
translation
transmute
transport
transported
transpose
trash
travelling
treat
treatment
tremble
trembling
tremulous
trick
tricky
trip
trouble
troubled
troublesome
tumble
tumbledown
tumult
turbulence
turbulent
turmoil
turn
turning
tweak
twiddle
twinkle
twinkling
twirl
twirling
twist
twisted
twitch
type
ugly
unbalanced
uncertain
uncommon
uncommonly
uncomplicated
uncontrolled
unconventional
unco-ordinated
uncouth
undisciplined
undo
undoing
undone
unduly
uneasy
uneven
unexpected
unexpectedly
unfair
unfairly
unfamiliar
unfit
unfortunate
unfortunately
ungainly
unhappily
unhappy
unholy
unkempt
unnatural
unnaturally
unorthodox
unpredictable
unravel
unreliable
unrest
unrestrained
unrestricted
unruly
unscramble
unseemly
unsettle
unsettled
unsound
unstable
unsteady
untidy
untrue
unusual
unusually
unwind
unwise
upset
upsetting
upturn
use
used
useless
vacillate
vacillating
vacillation
vagrant
vague
vaguely
vandalize
variant
variation
varied
variegated
variety
various
vary
vault
versatile
version
vibrate
vigorous
vigorously
vile
violate
violation
violent
violently
volatile
vulnerable
wacky
wag
waggle
wander
wanton
warp
warring
waste
wasted
wave
waver
wavering
way
weave
weird
whip
whip up
whirl
whisk
wicked
wild
wildly
wind
winding
wobble
wobbly
woeful
work
working
worried
worry
wound
wrack
wreck
wreckage
wrestling
wretched
writhe
wrong
wrongly
wrought
yank
yearning
yield
yielding
zany

Containment indicators

Containment indicators include:

about
absorb
absorbed
accept
accommodate
accommodating
accommodation
acquire
admit
adopt
around
arrest
assimilate
assume
astride
ate
bag
bear
bearing
beset
besiege
bewilder
bite
biting
box
bracket
break up
bring in
bring round
bury
capture
carry
casing
catch
catching
caught
circle
clasp
cleft
clutch
collect
come to grips with
comprehend
comprise
conceal
concealed
consume
consuming
contain
cover
crossing
custody
describe
detectable
drape
draw in
eat
embody
embrace
encapsulate
encircle
enclose
encompass
enfold
engulf
ensnare
entertain
entertaining
enthral
enthralling
envelop
fence
flank
found in
frame
framework
gather
gathering
get around

get hold of
get round
get to grips with
go about
go around
gobble
go round
grab
grasp
grasping
grip
gripping
guard
gulp
hamper
harbour
hedge
herein
hide
hiding
hold
host
house
housing
hug
imbibe
imprison
include
including
incorporate
in possession
introduce
keep
limit
lock up
net
nurse
obstruct
occlude
outside
over
overshadow
pen
pinch
pocket
possess
protect
purse
receive
repress
restrain
restrict
retain
round
sandwich
secure
see around
seize
shelter
snare
squeeze
stow
stuffing
superficial
surround
surrounding
swallow
tackle
take in
trap
trapped
wearing
welcome
without
wrap

Insertion indicators

Insertion indicators include:

aboard
amid
amidst
among
at heart
between
bisect
block
break
cleave
collected
cut
cutting
devour
divide
don
during
engage in
enter
feed
fill
filling
find in
get into
go into
half
halve
held by
held in
imprisoned
in
infuse
inside
intercept
interception
interrupt
interruption
invest
involve
occupy
part
parting
penetrate
penetrating
pierce
piercing
puncture
seduce
set in
split
tuck in
tuck into
wear
within

Deletion indicators

Deletion indicators include:

abandon
absent
cut
disappear
disappearance
dismiss
dismissal
disregard
drop
edit
elude
excision
excluding
fail to get
heave
ignore
junk
lack
lacking
leave
left
lose
missing
nearly
no
not
out
regardless
sack
sacrifice
scratch
scrub
shed
shun
skip
small
take off
withdraw
withhold

Ends indicators

Ends selection indicators include:

banks
borders of
both sides
bounds
casing
determination
edge
extreme
fringe
limit
side

Ends deletion indicators include:

limited
limitless
peel
shell
top and tail
unlimited
wingless

Head indicators

Head selection indicators include:

at first
beginner
beginning
capital
extreme
first
foremost
front
head
heading
initial
initially
introduction
lead
leader
leadership
leading
minimum
opener
opening
primarily
start
starter
summit
tip
top

Head deletion indicators include:

behead
decapitate
deface
fail to start
headless
head off
leaderless
limitless
tip-off
topless
trim

Middle indicators

Middle selection indicators include:

at heart
central
centre
heart
heartily
innards
middle
nucleus

Middle deletion indicators include:

disembowel
disheartened
empty
gutless
heartless
heartlessly

Tail indicators

Tail selection indicators include:

at last
at the end of
back
behind
end
ending
endmost
extreme
far end
far side
final
finale
finally
finish
foundation
last
lastly
rear
tail
terminal
ultimate
ultimately

Tail selection down indicators include:

base of
bottom
south
abbreviate
abridged
abrupt

Tail deletion indicators include:

almost
brief
briefly
clip
contract
curtail
curtailment
cut short
detail
detailed
dock
endless
endlessly
immature
incomplete
limit
limitless
Manx
most
nearly
reduce
reduction
short
shorten
shortened
shortly
trim
unfinished

Tail deletion down indicators include:

baseless
bottom

Hidden indicators

Hidden indicators include:

amid
amidst
among
apparent
belonging to
bit
bottle
central
characters in
concealed
contain
content
continuous
continuously
cover
cover up
deposit
discover
embrace
emerge
extract
find in
found in
fragment
from
held by
held in
hidden
hide
immerse
immersed
in
include
in part
inside
keep
lock up
part
part of
piece
sample
show
slice
some
stuffing
within

Hidden alternately indicators include:

alternate
even
evenly
even parts
ignore the odds
odd
oddly
odd parts

Homophone indicators

Homophone indicators include:

aloud
announce
articulate
articulated
audible
aural
broadcast
conversation
conversational
converse
ear
hear
hearing
hearsay
inform
list
listen
listen in
murmur
mutter
narrate
on radio
on telephone
oral
orally
pronounce
pronounced
read aloud
report
reportedly
said
say
saying
sound
speak
speech
spoken
state
told
utter
verbal
vocal

Juxtaposition indicators

Juxtaposition indicators include:

abut
add
adjacent
adjoin
adjoining
after
against
ahead
also
alongside
altogether
and
append
approach
arrive
associate
associated
at the end of
before
behind
beside
by
chase
come first
continuous
continuously
first
follow
following
given
go together
in front
in front of
join
meet
take on
trail
with

Juxtaposition down indicators include:

above
below
beneath
go under
on
over
subordinate
support
supporter
topping
under
about
all round
around

Reversal indicators

Reversal indicators include:

back
backfire
backing
backslide
backsliding
backtrack
backward
backwards
boomerang
bring back
capsize
come back
contrary
cutback
east
fall
flip
go around
go back
go back on
go round
go west
head over heels
hinge
in retrospect
in return
inversion
invert
keep back
knock back

make a comeback
on the contrary
preposterous
raise
rampant
reactionary
rear
rebellious
recall
recede
recess
recoil
recollect
recurrent
reflect
reflection
regress
reject
repel
retire
retired
retiring
retreat
retrograde
retrogress
retrospective
return
reversal
reverse
reversion
revert
review
revolution
revolutionary
rotate
round
set back
setback
switch
turn
turn back
turned
turning
turnover
volte-face
wheel

Reversal down indicators include:

arise
ascend
ascendant
bring up
climb
come up
elevate
elevated
give rise to
hold up
keel over
mount
over
overturn
put up
raised
rise
rising
send up
serve up
set up
set-up
take up
turn over
turn up
up
uplift
uprising
upset
upside down
upturn
upward
use up

Palindrome indicators include:

back and forth
either way
to and fro
up and down
whichever way you look at it

Foreign indicators

Foreign word indicators include:

European
foreign
French
in France
local
translate

Archaic indicators

Archaic indicators include:

antique
old
old-fashioned
once

Dialect indicators

Dialect indicators include:

American
Cockney
Cumbrian
East End
local
New York
Sandy
Scot
Scottish
US
Yorkshire

Repetition indicators

Repetition indicators include:

couple
double
repeat
repeated
repeatedly
repetition
twice

Crossword Manual

Don Manley

Contents of the Crossword Manual

Solutions

Appendix

About Don Manley and the Crossword Manual

Where I'm coming from

People often tell me that they would like to solve cryptic crosswords if only they could understand them, and before I can answer they as likely add 'someone should write a book'. When I tell them that I have already done so they look at me quizzically and I hope for a further sale.

After that I am asked one of the following questions: 'how long does it take you to produce a puzzle?', 'what is your favourite clue?', 'how did you get started?'. I shall now answer the first two very quickly: 'a few hours' and 'I don't have a favourite, but here's one I'm proud of ...'. The third question is perhaps more interesting, so I'll attempt an answer here.

I grew up in Cullompton, a small Devon town on the A38 as it then was. We had newsagents but the nearest bookshops were in Tiverton (8 miles away) and Exeter (13 miles away) and Taunton (20 miles away and visited in the cricket lunch interval as a respite from the sufferings of Somerset County Cricket Club). My father was the last in the line of a family of commercial travellers trying (often in vain) to sell cattle medicine to farmers. Lunch for him was usually a few sandwiches and a Guinness in the pub – accompanied by one of his three daily cryptic crosswords, *The Daily Express*, *The Daily Mail* and *The Daily Telegraph*. All were delivered, and on Sunday we took *The Sunday Express* (delivered from a private house rather than the usual newsagent). When, after retirement, my father decided he could no longer afford *The Daily Telegraph* the lady next door cut the crossword out each day for him and placed it in an old Elastoplast tin and hung it on a string over the garden wall.

I saw *The Times* at Blundell's School (and looked at the crossword), but *The Observer* was unknown to me until I went to university. My first experiences of solving (as I recall) were with children's crossword books bought at Wheaton's in Exeter and with *The Daily Telegraph* 'quick' puzzle – often with the help of my older sister Jean.

By the age of 16 I was reasonably competent at *The Daily Telegraph* cryptic puzzle thanks largely to my father's coaching, and in 1963, in the gap between school and university, I managed to obtain a cheque for £2.2s from the *London Evening News* for a definition puzzle – the first time I had heard of Coutt's, the bankers.

My first cryptic breakthrough came in 1964 when I made my debut in the *Radio Times* – and crosswords really did seem much easier than university physics. Diversifying from the *Radio Times* was not so easy and *The Daily Telegraph* crossword editor Miss M R K Binstead told me not to expect to make a sudden leap into Fleet Street. I produced one puzzle for the Morley Adams agency for *The Daily Express* but it was not an encouraging experience. Then, after a night watching Neil Armstrong land on the Moon, I received a letter saying that the new editor of the *Radio Times* had decided to jettison the crossword, so it looked as though my short crossword-setting career had come to an end.

At the end of the sixties I discovered Ximenes of *The Observer* through buying a Penguin book at Paddington station. The purchase of a *Chambers's Twentieth Century Dictionary* and a monthly copy of *The Observer* to enter his competitions followed soon after. I was just about good enough to get the odd mention in the Very Highly Commended list for the clue-writing competition by the time Ximenes died in 1971, while admiring the consistent performances of N C Dexter, C J Morse, R Postill and a few others. When Azed took over *The Observer* I found that a new office colleague, one R J Palmer, was outperforming me, and the competition between us undoubtedly spurred me to new heights (and, I suspect, Richard as well).

Settled into married family life by the mid-1970s I was performing well in the Azed competitions and had begun a new setting career as Duck in *Games and Puzzles*. In 1976 I made my debut in *The Listener* (still open to all-comers by the way) and the following year was contracted for some everyday cryptics by Gyles Brandreth. (He phoned me hours before my daughter was born.)

In the early eighties I found myself drawn into a crossword network through my contacts with other crossworders at various social occasions. At a crossword dinner in Oxford I met Betty Kirkpatrick of Chambers, and by the mid-eighties I had persuaded her to commission *Chambers Crossword Manual*. At about this time I moved to Oxford and was soon signed up by *The Oxford Times* as a colleague of Colin Dexter (that N C Dexter of Ximenes fame, who had also written some Morse detective novels). Colin didn't think that 'Duck' carried much gravitas, so I adopted the name 'Quixote' (we crossword setters love pseudonyms with Q, X, J and Z!). Then in 1986 the breakthrough into the national press happened when I was asked to write clues only at short notice for the new *Today* newspaper. The breaking-up of the print unions opened up new possibilities for dailies, and a friend in Oxford told me about the forthcoming *Independent*. By the time I had phoned that paper I discovered that they had a full complement of setters but that the *Manual* was the recommended text. It wasn't too hard, therefore, to persuade them to take me on when a vacancy occurred in 1987, and I decided to call myself Quixote again. The advent of a Saturday magazine also offered an outlet for advanced cryptic puzzles. I remained a weekday regular on *The Independent* until I was transferred to *The Independent on Sunday* in 1989 – my puzzle has been in every issue and I am closing in on 1000.

At the end of 1988 I suffered a redundancy and decided that whatever future job I took in publishing I had better extend my crossword career as a second string. By the time I had settled in a new publishing job I was also setting for *The Times* and *The Guardian* (choosing another Don name, 'Pasquale'). I had also taken on the new role of *Church Times* crossword editor which I continue to enjoy – we have a wonderful mix which includes semi-professional setters and retired canons.

My fourth (and, I thought, final!) pseudonym, Giovanni, emerged when I started to set the occasional puzzle for *The Sunday Telegraph*'s Enigmatic Variations in the nineties. A demanding full-time job combined with several hours' work each week for the newspapers was certainly stressful, but in 2002 I suffered a second redundancy and at 57 I knew that I had no choice but to set crosswords full-time. I phoned Val Gilbert at *The Daily Telegraph* just at the moment when she was looking for a 'floater' (an occasional setter) – so my patience had paid off! My fifth pseudonym, Bradman, had occurred to me previously, especially since I am a pretty lousy batsman. I put it to use when I was taken on by the *Financial Times*. In 2004 I also began to set the occasional puzzle for *The Sunday Times*.

So my career has come from a hobby. There was certainly a breakthrough when those new papers appeared in the mid-eighties, but the real breakthrough came when I strove assiduously to write good clues each month for the Ximenes and Azed competitions. As my good friend Colin Dexter has suggested, the top clues are written only 'after much fasting and prayer'. To this day I am what they call a Ximenean. I accept that there are differences of opinion about what is a grammatically acceptable clue but what success I have owes a lot to a school with hard training. This is why I recommend that all would-be crossword setters enter the Azed competitions, and it is no surprise that many of my contemporaries have done just that.

Naturally I have made many friends over the years – and I hope not too many enemies! But that's enough about my 'cruciverbal journey'. Perhaps I can take you on yours.

Where I'm taking you to

I'm working on the assumption that you might be a bit interested in cryptic crosswords but want to know more – or maybe you just don't understand anything about what 'cryptic' really means. The idea of the *Crossword Manual* is to start off with quite a bit of history, then to learn about the different types of clue you are likely to encounter. I've also given some hints on how to tackle crosswords and which ones to try in the British national dailies. Later we move beyond the daily cryptic to the advanced cryptic – and some readers may well opt to join the journey here. I've also given a case study of how I set one particular puzzle, showing how the grid was constructed and how I wrote the clues. At some point you may wish to leave me and settle down with the daily or weekly puzzle of your choice.

At the end of the section I will certainly have to leave you – unless, of course, you settle down with one of those five Dons in the dailies.

Don Manley
Oxford, 2006

Chambers Crossword Manual

The material in this part of the *Crossword Companion* is taken from Don Manley's *Crossword Manual* (ISBN 978 0550 10220 1), widely recognized as the definitive work on modern cruciverbalism. If you enjoy the help Don offers here, and would like to try out what you've learned, the original *Crossword Manual* includes nearly 100 practice crosswords, many with annotated solutions, taken from a wide range of publications.

From Definition to Cryptic

1 The Crossword Emerges

Before the crossword

The Victorian age is commonly portrayed in terms of unmitigated gloom; and yet it was also an age of fun and invention, and certainly it was the age of the word puzzle. In 1892 you might have bought *Everybody's Illustrated Book of Puzzles* (selected by a certain Don Lemon) for 6d. That Don of yesteryear offered you 794 puzzles complete with answers, and if we look at a few we shall see hints of what was to come when the crossword emerged in the 20th century. We shall also greatly regret, in passing, the attitude of our forebears implicit in the clue at the eighth line of the acrostic. Clues have advanced over a hundred years in more ways than one.

No. 6.—Anagrams

For the benefit of very young readers we will explain that making an anagram consists in forming a new word or words from the letters of other words. An illustration is: Cheer sick lands—the anagram for Charles Dickens. We now invite you, with the permission of Good Housekeeping, to an anagrammatical Dickens party, the guests of which are prominent characters in Dickens' writings: Blame Crumple; We debtor to toys; Clever fop I did pad; Pair my ages; His by a linen clock; Toy lily blows; Canny Skyes; Mere Walls; O, feel my corn bed; We kill red vics; Over it wilts; Bug ran by dear.

No. 200.—Double Acrostic

Two words are here to be found out,
Both you have heard of, I've no doubt;
One is a thing that gives its aid
to ships engaged in peaceful trade.
The other thing is often found
To war's chief weapon closely bound.
These stars replace with letters true,
And both the things will look at you.
In the first letters, downwards read,
Is that by which the vessel's sped;
And in the last, if downwards spelt,
That which adorns the soldier's belt.

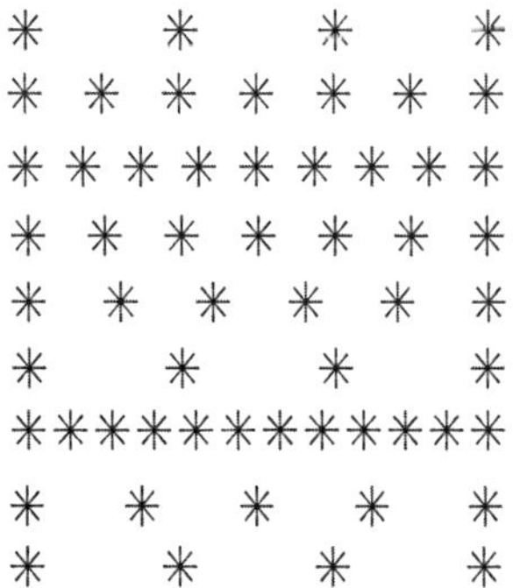

1st line – What a bull does, if he can.
2nd line – What is the most beauteous span.
3rd line – Hog in armor is my third.
4th line – Boy in barracks often heard.
5th line – What the street boys often run.
6th line – What gives light, not like the sun.
7th line – What makes doctors oft despair.
8th line – What is black, with curly hair.
9th line – What is very hard to bear.

The word square was so well established that it evidently didn't need a diagram to explain it, but just in case you don't know what one looks like, here is the puzzle followed by its answer:

No. 420.—Easy Squares

(a) 1. A crippled. [*sic*]
2. Hot and dry.
3. A deposit of mineral.
4. Paradise.

(b) 1. An article of food that appears early on the bill of fare.
2. To glance sideways.
3. A Turkish soldier.
4. The plural of an article used in writing.

```
(a) L A M E      (b) S O U P
    A R I D          O G L E
    M I N E          U L A N
    E D E N          P E N S
```

Some of the puzzles are even given titles like the one below, but this is not yet the true crossword:

No. 541.—Cross Word Enigma

My first is in cotton, but not in silk;
My second in coffee, but not in milk;
My third is in wet, but not in dry;
My fourth is in scream, but not in cry;
My fifth is in lark, but not in sparrow;
My sixth is in wide, but not in narrow;
My seventh in pain, but not in sting;
My whole is a flower that blooms in spring.

We can trace anagrams, acrostics and word squares back to ancient times. For example, Psalm 119 was an acrostic based on the Hebrew alphabet, and the most remarkable early word square is this reversible one found on a Roman site at Cirencester:

```
R O T A S
O P E R A
T E N E T
A R E P O
S A T O R
```

which is Latin for 'The sower Arepo controls the wheels with force' and which can be rearranged in 'crossword' form as:

```
            A
            P
            A
            T
            E
            R
A P A T E R N O S T E R O
            O
            S
            T
            E
            R
            O
```

'Could this be an early Christian crossword with A for alpha and O for omega?' some have asked.

The earliest crosswords

So when was the first 'proper' crossword published? In 1904 a puzzle called 'Blended Squares' appeared in *People's Home Journal*, and some have claimed that it is a crossword in all but name. However, it took another nine years for something called a 'Word-Cross' to appear in a newspaper.

Then, in 1913, a certain Arthur Wynne produced the following puzzle for the *New York World*. With it the true crossword era began.

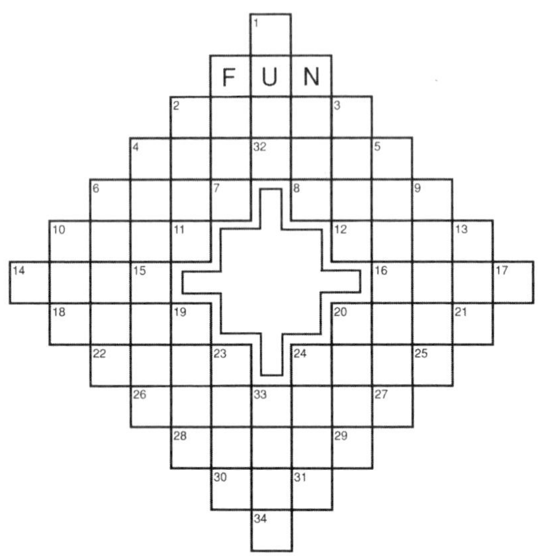

2-3	What bargain hunters enjoy
4-5	A written acknowledgement
6-7	Such and nothing more
10-11	A bird
14-15	Opposed to less
18-19	What this puzzle is
22-23	An animal of prey
26-27	The close of a day
28-29	To elude
30-31	The plural of is
8-9	To cultivate
12-13	A bar of wood or iron
16-17	What artists learn to do
20-21	Fastened
24-25	Found on the seashore
10-18	The fibre of the gomuti palm

6-22	What we all should be
4-26	A day dream
2-11	A talon
19-28	A pigeon
F-7	Part of your head
23-30	A river in Russia
1-32	To govern
33-34	An aromatic plant
N-8	A fist
24-31	To agree with
3-12	Part of a ship
20-29	One
5-27	Exchanging
9-25	To sink in mud [*sic*]
13-21	A boy

Wynne, an immigrant from Liverpool, remained a leading crossword setter for about ten years, and then (sad to say) he faded into obscurity.

It wasn't until the 1920s that crosswords took off in a really big way. Messrs Simon and Schuster launched an amazingly successful publishing company in the USA and their *Cross Word Puzzle Book* was published in England by Hodder and Stoughton (a copy of which I purchased second-hand in the 1960s for 6d!). The book begins with a detailed account of how to do a crossword. For the benefit of my one reader who has never seen any crossword and the entertainment of the others here is how the book started:

THE CROSS WORD PUZZLE BOOK
FIRST SERIES

Cross word puzzles are a great deal simpler to explain than to solve. And as the quickest and clearest way to explain any game is by demonstration, let us do a typical, if rather easy, example together.

Here is the puzzle:

1		2	3	4		5
	■	6			■	
7	8	■		■	9	
10			■	11		
12		■	13	■	14	
	■	15		16	■	
17						

HORIZONTAL

1 A pasty composition
6 Prefix, meaning new
7 Exist
9 Sixth note of the musical scale
10 A domestic animal
11 Affirmative particle
12 Indefinite article
14 In
15 Fuss
17 Went into

VERTICAL

1 Pacify
2 Indefinite article
3 Large body of water
4 Toward
5 Cooked before a fire
8 Male human being
9 Meadow
13 Short poem
15 Near
16 Alternative

All the puzzles are not the same square shape as this, but all have one thing in common: the black squares among the white make a symmetrical pattern, so that the whole looks like a piece of cross-stitch needlework, as for instance an old-fashioned 'sampler'.

What have we to do?

Each white square represents a single letter. The puzzle is—to find out what letter belongs in each white square. And you determine this by working out the words from the definitions, which you will see beside the puzzle. When you have completed the puzzle correctly you will find that it consists of a number of words *which read both horizontally and vertically*, interlocking round the pattern made by the black squares.

You will notice numbers in many of the white squares, corresponding to numbers in the lists of 'horizontals' and 'verticals'. These show the starting-points of words, sometimes a horizontal word (*e.g.* 6), sometimes a vertical word (*e.g.* 2), sometimes both horizontal and vertical words (*e.g.* 1). Each word starts in the first space to the *right* of a black square if it is a horizontal, and in the first space *below* a black square if it is a vertical. Some words of both kinds of course start on the outside squares, i.e., we imagine a ring of black squares all round the puzzle.

We now know where the words begin. How long are they to be? Each will consist of just as many letters, one letter to a square, as it will take to reach the next black square (or the edge of the puzzle where no black square intervenes) in whichever direction we are going. For example, '1 horizontal' will be 7 letters long, and so will '1 vertical'. But '6 horizontal' will have only 3 letters; '2 vertical' will have only 2 letters; '7 horizontal' will have only 2 letters; and '13 vertical' will have 3: and so on.

Sometimes a letter will come between two blacks in the pattern. In this case it will only be used in making one word, either a horizontal or a vertical one: for instance, the last letter of '3 vertical' or the first of '13 vertical'. But generally a letter has got to fit into two words—one horizontal and one vertical. For instance, the second letter of '6 horizontal' must also be right for the second letter of '3 vertical'.

And then the fun begins.

Now let us work out this puzzle. (It's a very simple one; you won't have such an easy time again, I warn you!). Start with '1 horizontal'.

'A pasty composition'. How many letters? Seven—since there is no black square right the way across the top line. 'A pasty composition' of seven letters? Let us try PLASTER. (Write it in lightly. You'll soon find you need india-rubber at this game.)

Now is this the right word? We can soon find out; for if it is the right word, it has given us some splendid clues for no less than five of our 'verticals' (1–5).

1 P	L	2 A	3 S	4 T	E	5 R
	■	6			■	
7	8	■		■	9	
10			■	11		
12		■	13	■	14	
	■	15		16	■	
17						

What about 'vertical 1'? 'Pacify', seven letters beginning (apparently) with 'P'. How about PLACATE? Yes, it fits. Write it in lightly. One check is not enough. But we can soon get proof positive that we are on the right track. For it looks as if '2 vertical', which as you see has two letters only (and therefore ought to be easy to guess), ought to begin with 'A'.

What is '2 vertical'? 'Indefinite article'. Obviously AN. It fits, and it begins with 'A'. Write it in. But we can check again. For '3 vertical' presumably begins with 'S'. It has three letters. It is a 'large body of water'. Exultantly, we write in SEA.

And so it goes on. You may like to note incidentally that the practice of putting the number of letters in brackets after a clue had not yet been introduced.

Newspapers also latched on to crosswords in the 1920s, and by 1930 crosswords were commonplace. Indeed dictionaries were torn apart in libraries, worries were expressed about eyesight, and crosswords were increasingly regarded as an 'unsociable habit' (how little times have changed!). One of the developments in the 20s and 30s was the big-money puzzle with alternative answers. A clue to a word with a seven-letter answer might be offered as follows with the (7) denoting the length of the answer:

[1.1] A yellow addition to your food (7)

with a corresponding answer in the diagram printed as:

	U	S	T	A	R	D

Solvers were invited to use their skill to choose between MUSTARD and CUSTARD and see if they could reach the same set of answers as the panel of experts. Lotteries like this thrived in *Titbits* and other magazines until well after World War II, but they have little appeal for the true aficionado, so we can forget them without further mention.

Numbers in brackets

In the clue for CUSTARD/MUSTARD above we met the convention of using a number in brackets to denote the length of an answer. For an answer of HEDGE-MUSTARD we would be given (5-7) and for CUSTARD PIE (7,3). This seems straightforward enough and looks like a matter of common sense, surely?

Ah yes – but is that COMMON-SENSE, COMMONSENSE or COMMON SENSE? And what if different dictionaries give different versions? For a clue giving this eleven-letter answer we could be faced with (6-5), (11) or (6,5). In advanced cryptic puzzles you could also meet (11, hyphenated) and (11,2 words).

Clearly you may sometimes find a number in brackets that does not conform to your dictionary, and even your favourite dictionary can change between editions since there is a tendency to reduce the number of hyphenated words. For example, SEA SALT in the current edition of *The Chambers Dictionary* was SEA-SALT once in earlier versions of *Chambers's Twentieth Century Dictionary*.

In this book you will find a mix of all the possibilities, and no attempt has been made to rewrite lexicographical history. (The author does, however, confess that history has been rewritten in respect of one or two inaccurate clues!)

2 Definition-type Puzzles

The basic crossword grid

In this section we will explore some more crosswords that rely on definitions only. We're interested primarily in cryptic puzzles, but there is much to be learnt from definition-type puzzles. Before we consider these puzzles and their clues, please have a look at the clueless puzzle below.

We can use this to define certain terms:

1 The 3 × 3 matrix is referred to as the *grid*, or sometimes the *diagram*.
2 This particular grid, with its use of a black square, is a *blocked grid*.
3 The letters C, T, W and N are in squares that belong to both across and down answers. These are called *checked squares*.
4 The letters A, O, E and I belong to only one answer each and these are in *unchecked squares* or *unches*.
5 The words CAT, WIN, COW and TEN are of course the *answers*.
6 Individual answers are sometimes called *lights*, but this is a term better avoided as *lights* can also mean individual squares.

In British puzzles it is unusual to have every letter 'checked', although this is more common in American puzzles.

Now look at the completed grid below:

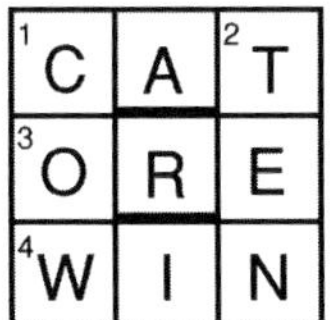

Here the checked squares contain C, T, O, E, W and N, and the unchecked squares contain A, R and I. Letters are kept apart by a bar rather than a block and this is known as a *barred grid*.

Most crosswords are in fact blocked puzzles, but the 'Small Crossword' of *The Daily Express* is a definition-type puzzle with a barred grid. As we shall see, most advanced puzzles use barred grids, and the reasons for this will become clear later.

The *alternate-letter grid*, in which alternate letters are checked, is the basis of many puzzles in Britain, including the cryptic puzzles in the daily newspapers. The crossword that follows is rather trickier than many cryptic puzzles, though. If you have a go, you'll see why.

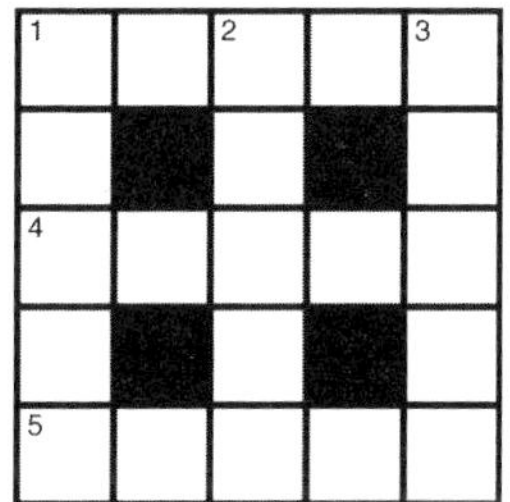

	ACROSS		DOWN
1	Country (5)	1	Mammal (5)
4	College (5)	2	River (5)
5	River (5)	3	Fish (5)

The problem here, as you may have discovered, lies in the clues. How many five-letter fish are there? How many five-letter rivers? One thing you will learn is that a cryptic clue gives you *two* clues, so it can actually be *easier* to finish than a definition puzzle. The amount of help that should be given with a definition in a cryptic puzzle is a matter to be pursued later, but I feel I should offer a more helpful set of clues:

	ACROSS		DOWN
1	Arab country (5)	1	Mammal related to weasel (5)
4	Oxford college (5)	2	European river (5)
5	English river (5)	3	The bleak (5)

I guess you may still have to search a dictionary for the answer to 3 Down (*The Chambers Dictionary* for this one – but more about dictionaries, anon).

Crossword grids, by convention, usually have a high level of symmetry. Think of the grid as follows:

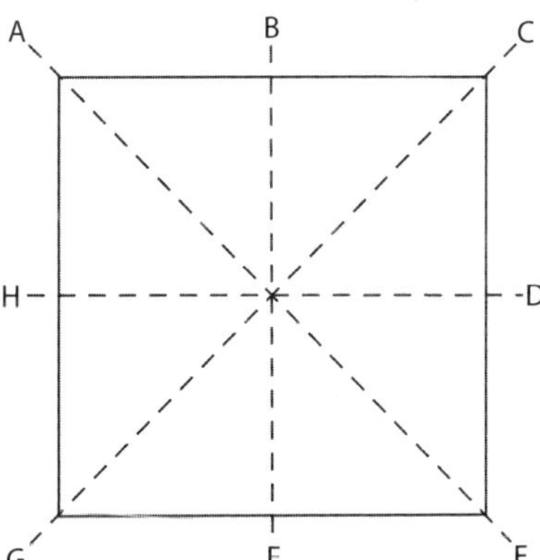

This grid shows mirror symmetry about the lines BF, DH, AE and CG. In most modern grids we find rotational symmetry only, about the diagonals AE and CG. Grids don't *have* to be symmetrical but diagonal symmetry gives a pleasing appearance and has become a standard convention.

We would also expect a grid to show total *connectedness* with no *isolated portions*.

Quiz and general knowledge puzzles

People who enjoy quizzes often enjoy clues which depend on knowledge that may not be found in an everyday dictionary. A clue like the one below (from *The Daily Telegraph* of 25 May 1967) is one which will send many happily scurrying to a dictionary of quotations:

[2.3] 'Had, having, and in quest to have, _______' (Shakespeare *Sonnets*) (7)

Did you know that the answer is EXTREME? If you didn't know, you might have worked it out from E_T_E_E.

This is a *quotation clue*, which could be regarded as a particular type of *quiz clue* or *general knowledge clue*. Here is another quiz clue, which relies on the solver's general knowledge:

[2.4] Wife of Ahab, King of Israel (7)

You probably won't need a concordance to arrive at JEZEBEL.

General knowledge puzzles are very popular and allow families the opportunity to take an otherwise little-used atlas from the bookshelf. Those in *The Daily Telegraph* and *The Sunday Telegraph* are particularly popular and the answers are accessible using a variety of reference books. One of the hardest general knowledge puzzles is the 'Polymath' published in the *Financial Times* each Saturday. This deliberately caters for those who like obscure words and relish searches using the Internet.

Cruciverbalism

The 'cross word puzzle' has become the 'crossword puzzle' or plain 'crossword'. But what about the 'realm' of crosswords and the people who participate in it? Could we agree on 'crosswording' and 'crossworders'? Maybe, but neither of these words has found a regular place in the dictionaries.

A word that was coined in the 1970s was 'cruciverbalism' (from the Latin *crux, crucis*, a cross, and *verbum*, a word). This means 'the realm of crosswords', and a 'cruciverbalist' would be someone interested in crosswords. The adjective is 'cruciverbal'. Happily all three words have made it into *The Chambers Dictionary*.

Cruciverbalists are of course in two categories: those who make up the crosswords and those who solve them. The latter are clearly 'solvers', but what about the former? The word 'compiler' has been much used, but suggests that puzzle construction only involves collecting the material together and underplays the aspect of creativity. What about 'composer'? This is quite good, but would be viewed by some as too grandiose. Many crossword contributors like to be called 'setters', since anyone making up a crossword is 'setting' a puzzle for the solver. 'Setter' therefore seems the ideal word.

3 Beyond the Simple Definition

What makes a crossword cryptic

We have already seen that the definition 'river' for a five-letter word can pose a difficult problem for the solver. We got around this problem by providing a more specific definition and one of the tricks of the trade for writers of definition clues is to know how specific to be. Suppose we wanted to write a clue for SEINE. 'River' would be too vague and 'River in Paris' perhaps too specific. 'River in France' might at least make the solver think about entering LOIRE. In a cryptic crossword we try to give a clue which leads to a unique answer, but in a subtle way, and very often a clue actually consists of two clues put together so the solver has two chances to work out the answer.

There are essentially two ways in which a clue can be made cryptic:

1. It can be given a *cryptic definition*. We shall be looking at what this means shortly.
2. It can be given a *definition (cryptic or otherwise) and some additional indications*. There are lots of ways in which the additional indication can be given and later on we will start to explain these.

Each clue will have a definition and sometimes this will help lead the solver to the correct answer almost immediately, but usually the solver will need to decode the additional indication to work out the answer.

It is time to take a look at cryptic definitions.

Cryptic definitions

A cryptic definition is a bit like a joke. Here is an example:

[3.1] A Parisian flower (5)

You may be thinking of FLEUR (or even LILAC, I suppose) but the answer is in fact SEINE, because 'flower' is interpreted as 'flow-er' or 'something which flows'. It is a curious fact, known to very few crossworders, that this meaning is not even found in the *Oxford English Dictionary*, but the joke lives on. Well, I hope you find that marginally more interesting than 'French river'.

We have noticed that, at first sight, this clue suggests petalled plants rather than a river. The solver who thinks of the Jardin du Luxembourg has been the victim of a *misleading context* and we refer to the naive reading of the clue as *surface meaning*. The ways in which surface meaning can entertainingly lead a solver up the garden path (flowers again!) will become apparent as we go along.

Here are a couple of clues derived from my children's joke book:

[3.2] You take the lid off it before putting the bottom on! (6)

Because this is an outrageous definition we allow ourselves an exclamation mark to warn the solver. The answer? TOILET!

[3.3] Will doing them make a scout or guide dizzy? (4,5)

Answer: GOOD TURNS. What about this one?

[3.4] An extremely distressed youngster (8)

Who has minimal tresses? The SKINHEAD. A definition such as:

[3.5] A letter demanding money for accommodation (8)

may suggest an unpleasant communication through the post until we remember that it is the LANDLORD (or LANDLADY) who lets out the accommodation. 'Letter' is another *-er* word (like 'flower') which is often used in a misleading sense.

Here are some cryptic definitions, including one or two old chestnuts:

[3.6] A wicked thing (6)

[3.7] A jammed cylinder (5,4)

[3.8] Keen observer of gulls? (8)

[3.9] Presumably one doesn't run after it? (4,5)

[3.10] He was rushed almost from the start (5)

[3.11] 014? (6,5)

[3.12] Having no batteries provided (4-5)

[3.13] You won't necessarily see anyone till after this meal (10,5)

The answers to the last eight clues? CANDLE, SWISS ROLL, SWINDLER, LAST TRAIN, MOSES, DOUBLE AGENT (=2×007!), FREE-RANGE and PLOUGHMAN'S LUNCH.

Notice how in [3.13] 'till' is a verb, not a preposition (a *misleading part of speech*).

The Times crossword has always been notable for its cryptic definitions. Here is one that gives the same answer as the last clue:

[3.14] What expert in share movement wants from the board (10,5)

And here are some, from *The Times* 'Jumbo', for long answers (which often have to rely on cryptic definitions if their clues are to be cryptic):

[3.15] Did he have spelling lessons? (3,9,10)

[3.16] Paper chain (10,10)

[3.17] Honest but careless, these famous last words (7,2,4,1,4,4,1,4)

[3.18] Factory skip? (7,2,8)

The answers are: THE SORCERER'S APPRENTICE, CONTINUOUS STATIONERY, FRANKLY MY DEAR I DON'T GIVE A DAMN (from *Gone With the Wind*) and CAPTAIN OF INDUSTRY.

Healthy crosswords

Did you know that solving crosswords can help keep your brain healthy into old age?

For a long time it has been suspected that crosswords can help ward off Alzheimer's and other degenerative diseases, and now scientists at Edinburgh University claim to have found 'survival genes' that can be switched on by problem-solving. So keep solving those puzzles, but don't sit in the armchair or at the computer all day because your body needs exercise as well as your brain!

4 Multiple Definitions

A second definition as an 'additional indication'

The earliest crosswords had lots of short words of the type that quickly became hackneyed. The solver of the 20s must soon have realized that 'poems' = ODES, 'thank you' = TA and 'before' = ERE. Yet sometimes there was a hint of the cryptic, as in this clue from the very first *Daily Telegraph* crossword in 1925: 'A seat of learning is the key to this'. The setter is inviting us to think of Yale University and a Yale lock; and he has offered us something a little more interesting than 'An American university'. Now, as it happens, I don't find this a very sound clue because Yale University can't really be the key to a Yale lock – but the setter's heart was in the right place! The Yale clue has a descendant in the modern puzzle called the *double definition*.

An example of the double definition clue might be this:

[4.1] University name on key (4)

The answer is YALE because it is both a university and the name on certain keys. This may not be a very exciting clue, but it shows a degree of trickery absent from the definition clue. Had we wanted simply to offer two definitions on a plate we might have written 'University, name on key', but the omission of the comma is a legitimate trick and we might just be led astray for an instant to think of some poor Oxbridge undergraduate returning home after midnight unable to enter his college. In this clue 'name on key' has given us an additional indication in the form of a second definition.

Further examples

Now here are some more examples of double definitions which you might like to try for yourselves:

[4.2] Broken part of body (4)

[4.3] Take notice of Gospel writer (4)

[4.4] Sombre mausoleum? (5)

[4.5] Tumblers producing spectacles (7)

The answers are BUST, MARK, GRAVE and GLASSES. In [4.5] the two definitions are joined by a *linkword*: 'producing'. This linkword helps the clue make sense, and it is justified because the word for 'tumblers' produces the word for 'spectacles'. More about linkwords in due course. Notice again how this clue gives a surface meaning connected with the circus, but how the answer has nothing whatsoever to do with the big top. This is another example of a misleading context.

There is no reason why we should not string together a whole series of definitions, as the following clue shows:

[4.6] Left harbour gate bearing drink (4)

The solver may have visions of a sailor sloping off with his rum, but this is simply a series of five definitions for the word PORT.

Here is a double definition, using a cryptic allusion which we have already come across:

[4.7] Sad like the girl who's had a haircut? (10)

This girl, like the skinhead earlier, is DISTRESSED. Because this usage is fanciful the clue finishes with a question mark.

Here are two examples that yield phrases:

[4.8] Feeling very happy like the mountaineer who's climbed Everest? (2,3,2,3,5)

What phrase suggests that someone is either 'very happy' or at the highest point on Earth? Answer: ON TOP OF THE WORLD.

[4.9] Dismantle slate (4,5)

Another misleading context, because 'slate' here means 'criticize', which like 'dismantle' means TAKE APART.

Finally, a rather tricky clue:

[4.10] Red wine in excess (4)

At first sight this looks as though it might be a double definition, one definition being 'red wine' and the other being 'in excess' or possibly 'excess' (in which case 'in' would be a linkword meaning 'consisting of'). Once you've decided that 'port' cannot mean 'excess' or 'in excess', you need to think again. In fact the two definitions are 'red' and 'wine in excess', and the second definition is more likely to give the game away since the answer is LAKE. Lake is also a reddish pigment of course. Because 'red wine' is a familiar phrase we have put together two elements which in terms of the clue structure need to be separate. We are victims of the *misleading split*. Sophisticated stuff at this stage, but be prepared to meet this phenomenon again.

We are now leaving definition-only puzzles behind.

Cross-references to other clues

A reference to another clue can avoid the use of 'Across' or 'Down' if the clue is in the same (Across or Down) section. Something like 'See 6' will do. If the clue is in the other section expect to see 'Across', 'across', 'Ac' or 'A' – or 'Down', 'down', 'Dn' or 'D'.

5 The Anagram and an Introduction to Clue Analysis

'Playing with the letters'

So far we have only been concerned with definitions. We noted that a cryptic clue often had an 'additional indication' and for the double-definition clue this was a second definition. It is now time to look at all the other ways of giving an additional indication and all these involve 'playing with the letters' of the answer. One very common way of doing this is by jumbling the letters into an *anagram*.

From 'anag.' to anagram indicator

We are 40 years on from Don Lemon and his book of puzzles, and we are looking at *The Daily Telegraph* crossword for 21 July 1932. Here is 7 Down:

[5.1] 'Meet tired Pa' (anag.)

Although there are millions of ways of arranging these letters, it will only take a minute or two to come up with PREMEDITATE – and of course it may well prove easier if we already know some of the checked letters. Even so, there is something unsatisfactory about this clue because we aren't given any definition of the answer.

However, we must not be unfairly critical when considering clues from more than 50 years ago – some progress has been made. The next clue appeared in 1947:

[5.2] Atom plaint farce (anag.) (Yet power can be controlled by it) (3,2,10)

This clue offers us an anagram and a definition – and it is a definition that tries to link up with the theme of the letters to be anagrammed (however vaguely!). The answer is ACT OF PARLIAMENT. An improvement, yes, but this is still a bit on the clumsy side. How much more elegant is this 1973 *Daily Telegraph* clue:

[5.3] Pure ice broken up for the fussy diner (7)

Remember that most cryptic clues contain a definition, and some additional indication of the answer. In an anagram clue this will consist of a definition, something to be made into an anagram, and some word or phrase indicating that an anagram must be formed. In this clue the words 'pure ice' must be 'broken up' for an answer defined by 'fussy diner'. When we look for an anagram of 'pure ice' we can find the answer is EPICURE. The phrase 'broken up' is called an *anagram indicator*.

In a 1960 puzzle we have this clue:

[5.4] Arrange to send port (6)

Here the anagram indicator is the imperative verb 'arrange'. We are told to arrange 'to send' so that we can get a word meaning 'port'. We've already seen that port has at least five meanings (p21), and from the way the clue is worded we're probably thinking of an alcoholic Christmas gift. In fact, however, the port is a harbour and the answer is OSTEND.

Anagram indicators are many and varied. Any words or phrases that indicate a jumbling of the letters will do, so long as the clues are grammatical and make sense: 'excited', 'mixed up', 'disturbed' and 'out of order' are all warnings to the solver that an anagram might be afoot. Now try this:

[5.5] Dicky came top (4)

The surface meaning suggests a clever boy called Richard who beat his classmates in the examination. However, this is another example of the misleading context because the *cryptic reading* of the clue has nothing whatever to do with a successful male. In the cryptic reading 'Dicky' is an adjective (not a proper noun) meaning shaky and shaky 'came' means an anagram of came. The answer therefore is ACME, meaning 'top'. Again we see an example of how a cryptic clue presents you with a series of words which are ostensibly about a particular theme, but you must ignore the theme and concentrate on the words as a series of cryptic instructions to lead you to the answer.

Introduction to clue analysis

Before we look at some more anagrams we are going to have a foretaste of 'clueology' to see how the coded instructions are put together. We are going to analyse all the bits and pieces that actually make up a cryptic clue and label them.

We shan't be doing this for *all* our clues, but if we do it now and then, you will see that there is some sense in the cryptic clue, even if it looks like gobbledegook at first sight! Once you appreciate this, you will know what to look for in a clue when you try to solve it – and this is important.

Into clueology we go then, and first of all we take a look again at clue [5.3] and under its different parts you will see that I have placed some letters:

[5.3] Pure ice broken up for the fussy diner (7)

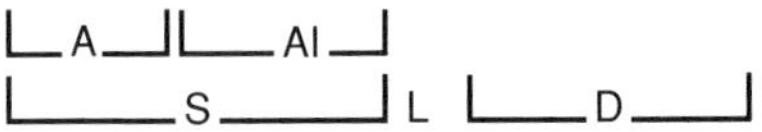

```
|_A_||__AI_|
|_____S_____| L |___D___|
```

There are two main sections to this clue. One is 'D', the definition, and other is 'S'. So what is S? This is the *subsidiary indication*, the traditional term for what I have so far called the 'additional indication'. It is also sometimes called the *wordplay* but since 'wordplay' is involved in the whole of a crossword clue we will keep to the 'S' term in this book.

Joining the S and the D is a linkword 'L' (the subsidiary indication serves here as a purpose *for* the definition). Within the S for an anagram clue there is an A, the actual *anagram*, and an AI, the *anagram indicator*.

Already in the clues we have seen that A and AI can be the other way round and that L need not always exist, as is the case with:

[5.5] Dicky came top (4)

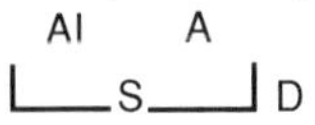

```
 AI    A
|___S___| D
```

Now, it is also possible for D to come before S, as in this example:

[5.6] Fungus in a crag, I fancy (6)

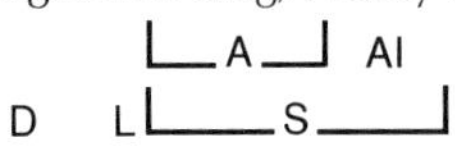

```
          |_A_|  AI
D      L|____S____|
```

The linkword 'in' means 'consisting of', so we are being asked to find a fungus which consists of the six letters of 'a crag I' being fancy ('capriciously departing from the ordinary, the simple, or the plain' as *The Chambers Dictionary* so nicely puts it). The answer is AGARIC.

Further examples

Here are some more anagrams for you to sort out. In each case, look for the D and look for the S. There might be an L or there might not. You can often identify the A by counting letters, and the AI telling you to do the jumbling should be next to it.

[5.7] More wrath upset gardener's friend (9)

[5.8] Percy lies when in trouble? Exactly! (9)

[5.9] Attack from aircraft moving faster (6)

[5.10] Constable perhaps is 'sad' – can prattle uncontrollably (9,6)

[5.11] Student of the past to split hairs? Not I! (9)

The answers are EARTHWORM, PRECISELY, STRAFE, LANDSCAPE ARTIST and HISTORIAN.

Clue [5.10] uses an adverb as an anagram indicator and you will meet many more ('terribly' and 'dreadfully' to name but two). This clue also gives a totally misleading surface meaning of course.

A tip for finding anagrams

Suppose you are faced with this clue:

Mad tirades becoming silly and exaggerated (10)

You suspect that the answer is an anagram of MAD TIRADES, but maybe jumbling these letters in your head isn't easy. If that is the case, you can always write them in a two-dimensional jumble at random, and you may come up with something like this:

If you then let your eyes wander over the pattern, you just might see DRAMATISED that bit more easily.

6 Charades

Putting parts together

In the last section we saw how the anagram and its indicator could be used as a subsidiary indication to a definition. We now start to look at a few ways in which a crossword setter can indicate the letters in the answer. For the moment we must leave the history of crosswords behind, and look at some modern examples.

Have you ever played the game of charades? In Act 1 someone drops the word 'hat' into the conversation; in Act 2 the word 'red' is dropped in; then in Act 3 someone tries to mention the word 'hatred' without you noticing. You have played this parlour game? Well, the *charade clue* is just like that; you define 'hatred' as 'hat' and 'red' and tell the solver to put the parts together.

[6.1] Headgear on communist evokes intense dislike (6)

```
 (hat)    CI   (red)       L
|________S__________|        |___D____|
```

CI is a *charade indicator*; the word 'on' is suitable for a down word. The *linkword* L means 'draws out' (ie 'provides').

Before we pass on to other examples note how the word 'red' is defined by 'communist'. This is a bit of *crossword jargon* and there are a number of such words that are great favourites with crossword setters. Another favourite is 'ant', which is often defined by 'worker'. You will pick these up as you go, but many are included in the Crossword Dictionary section of this *Crossword Companion*.

Now here are some more examples of charades:

[6.2] Man needs essential animal (6)

```
(Don)    CI    (key)
|_______S_______|    D
```

giving don + key = DONKEY. Here is an alternative clue giving the same answer:

[6.3] Stupid person a university lecturer provided with solution (6)

What about this one?

[6.4] Discharge of lightning on a Lancashire town (6)

Here the 'discharge of lightning' equals 'bolt'; 'on' is simply equal to itself, 'on'; and the 'Lancashire town' is BOLTON. There is no CI in the clue; the parts just follow on. Here is another clue with no CI:

[6.5] Expose record waste (8)

'Disc' ('record') plus 'lose' ('waste') equals DISCLOSE ('expose').

[6.6] Dental deposit? Use salt repeatedly (6)

You may use a salt water rinse for that stain on your teeth, but think too much along those lines and you'd be a victim of the misleading context. Think instead of 'salt' as a sailor and use 'tar' repeatedly to get TARTAR.

[6.7] Bridge over loch? That's cunning (8)

This is a down clue and 'arch' (= bridge) is 'over' (CI) 'Ness' (a loch). Such ARCHNESS from the crossword setter!

[6.8] It's very warm, the Spanish inn (5)

'Very warm' is 'hot', 'the Spanish' is 'el' (ie 'the' in Spanish) and an 'inn' is a HOTEL. Again there is no

CI. This is a good moment to warn you that you can expect some simple *foreign words* in subsidiary indications. EL is often used by clue-writers. In addition, LE, LA and LES can all be denoted by 'the French'; 'of the French' would be DU; 'the German' is DIE, DER or DAS. Expect also to meet other common foreign words such as TRES ('very French') and MIT ('with German'). We are concentrating on the grammar, but we are also picking up some vocabulary.

Further examples

Now try these:

[6.9] Delightful tea with the best china (8)

[6.10] Fighting the German guard (6)

[6.11] Lamb batting? He was responsible for some good scores (6)

[6.12] Animal at back of vehicle may have a shaggy pile (6)

How did you get on? Clue [6.9] gives CHARMING ('char' plus 'Ming'). [6.10] gives 'war' and 'der' which makes WARDER (I warned you about 'der'!). [6.11] introduces us to cricket and the surface meaning suggests former England player Allan Lamb. However 'chop' (which could be lamb) plus 'in' (which means batting) gives CHOPIN. In [6.12] the definition is 'may have a shaggy pile' (with the 'it' before 'may' understood). Put 'pet' at the back of 'car' to get CARPET.

Three amazing stories

The Times did not decide until 1930 to include a daily crossword, and when the go-ahead was given there was no one readily to hand to produce the puzzle. Robert Bell of *The Observer* was approached (he was producing the Everyman puzzle) and he delegated the task to his 28-year-old son Adrian. Adrian had never solved a puzzle before, let alone set one! He had ten days to learn and continued setting for over 40 years. Bell's identity was kept secret until a BBC interview in 1970. (Adrian's son Martin achieved fame as a broadcaster and white-suited MP.)

One of the early *Daily Telegraph* setters was L S Dawe. In 1944 he was visited by members of MI5 who pointed to six suspicious words in his recent puzzles: MULBERRY, NEPTUNE, OMAHA, OVERLORD, PLUTO and UTAH. These words just happened to be code-words for the impending D-Day. Dawe persuaded MI5 that this was a coincidence, but in the mid-1980s 'the true story came to light' (as described by Val Gilbert in *The Daily Telegraph: 80 Years of Cryptic Crosswords*). A former pupil of Dawe's, Ronald French, claimed that his teacher often asked his pupils to fill his blank puzzle grids, and it just happened that there were some Canadian and US servicemen in the area waiting for D-Day to happen. The pupils met these men and heard the words without realizing their significance, and it seems that French used them innocently. A conspiracy of silence was established by Dawe when French found out the truth, but French confessed 40 years later.

A lady in Fiji completed a *Times* crossword in May 1966. The puzzle was published on 4 April 1932 and she had been working on it for 34 years!

7 Container and Contents

Something inside something

The charade clue gave us a formula A *plus* B equals C; the *container-and-contents clue* gives us a new formula A *in* B equals C:

[7.1] Vegetable to stick in the shelter (6)
CCI

Stop thinking about the wilting lettuce and start getting word-conscious! 'To stick' is a definition for 'gum'; 'the shelter' is 'lee'; 'gum' in 'lee' gives LEGUME.

[7.2] Finishing with a boxed ear – charming! (9)
CCI

When 'ear' is *boxed* by 'ending' we have ENDEARING. Have you guessed what I mean by CCI? It's the *container-and-contents indicator*! 'Holds' is a popular CCI and will often tell you what sort of clue you are dealing with:

[7.3] Girl holds information for business programme (6)

'Ada' holds the 'gen' for the AGENDA.

'Clutching' is another giveaway CCI:

[7.4] Members clutching a rota – they insist on proper procedure (9)

'Members' here are 'legs' because we're thinking about members of the body, not MPs in the chamber – a nice piece of crossword jargon in a misleading context. 'A rota' is 'a list' and 'legs' clutching 'a list' becomes LEGALISTS.

[7.5] A jeer about music club being below par (2,1,8)

The word 'about' is a very common CCI. Put 'a taunt' about 'disco' and you have AT A DISCOUNT.

Another common CCI is 'around'. So too is 'outside'.

[7.6] Rubbish outside lair may suit this creature (6)

'Rot' outside 'den' is RODENT.

Sometimes a container-and-contents clue using the word 'in' can be misread. Consider:

[7.7] Prisoner with worker in part of Switzerland (6)

One is tempted to read this as:

Prisoner with worker in part of Switzerland
CCI
D L S

whereas the correct reading is:

Prisoner with worker in part of Switzerland
CCI
S D

A prisoner ('con') with worker ('ant') in gives CANTON. You'll soon recognize 'ant' for worker, but of course you might have solved this clue just from the *giveaway definition*. If you did misread the clue initially you were a victim of *ambiguous construction*. In future you must find traps like this for yourself.

Now it's your turn again:

[7.8] A lady one's observed in pubs (8)

[7.9] Criticizing crooner – about the worst (8)

[7.10] Part-time soldier makes mistake coming into range (7)

[7.11] Call out disapprovingly when trapped in crate in guard's van (7)

[7.12] Abandoned cat in torment (9)

The answers are: BARONESS ('one's' in 'bars'), BLASTING ('last' in 'Bing' – Crosby, of course), TERRIER ('err' in 'tier'), CABOOSE ('boo' in 'case') and RENOUNCED ('ounce' in 'rend'). Perhaps you didn't know that an 'ounce' was a snow leopard – you do now!

A filler on fillers

This little article is a filler, an extra topic slotted in to fill an awkward gap. Some words in crossword grids could also be described as 'fillers'.

Imagine the crossword setter filling in the grid. At the outset, everything looks possible – nice long phrases (OVER THE MOON, OUT FOR THE COUNT), long and interesting words (STAGE WHISPER, POWER STATION). All too soon, though, the setter is faced with E_T_A. It has to be EXTRA, a word he or she has written a clue for several times before (usually something to do with an extra run at cricket or a jobbing actor). EXTRA is a filler, a word that the crossworder can't escape from. Here are some more five-letter words beginning with E in the same category: EASEL, ELAND, ELOPE, ENSUE, ERASE, ERATO and EVOKE. And what can you do with I_A_E? IMAGE, INANE, IRATE (and IRADE, if that isn't too hard a word). And look – here's R_D_O. Last time it was RADIO, so this time we'll fill in RODEO (oh, not 'rode + O' again, please!). If you are a setter, beware of the five-letter words beginning with E! No one likes coming up with a sixth clue for ENSUE – one is bad enough.

Grids are, of course, to blame – but, as we have already noted, _A_E_ and _R_T_ would seem to offer the solver too many possibilities. No doubt about it – five-letter words are a problem.

There are fillers of other lengths too. Expect to find ELEMENT and EVEREST frequently, especially along the edge. And in barred puzzles you'll soon learn about EATH (an old word meaning 'easy') and the noun EALE (from Shakespeare's *Hamlet* I.iv.36, with various conjectures, generally supposed to be for evil, but perhaps a misprint).

Dear solver, forgive the setters their fillers. Learn to regard them as old friends.

8 Reversals

Back to front, upside down

Turn around the word 'peek' and you get 'keep'. This simple fact can be made the basis for a *reversal clue*:

[8.1] Have a little look round part of fortification (4)
RI

RI is the *reversal indicator*, telling us that when 'peek' (to have a little look) is put around (backwards) we get KEEP (part of the castle). You mean 'around' is an RI? I thought it was a CCI. Well yes, it could be either: ambiguity is what cryptic clues are all about!

Here are some more:

[8.2] Effort made by nocturnal animals heading west (4)

We often regard the crossword grid as a map, so 'heading west' in an across clue means 'backwards'. 'Bats' going backwards makes STAB, an informal word for 'effort'.

[8.3] Exist the wrong way? That's bad (4)

Put 'live' the wrong way and you get EVIL.

[8.4] Performer wants despicable people sent back (4)

The reverse of 'rats' (despicable people) is STAR.

For down clues we often use 'upset' or 'up' or even 'heading north' as RIs. Here are three examples using these:

[8.5] This walk makes domestic animals upset (4)

Reverse 'pets' to obtain STEP.

[8.6] Bear up: here's a ring (4)

Not 'Cheer up, darling, have a bit of jewellery!', but Pooh (Winnie-the-!) up to give HOOP.

[8.7] Ensnare division heading north (4)

In this clue, suggestive of an unsuccessful military campaign, 'part' goes up the grid map to become TRAP.

Some words are of course palindromes, and so we could have a clue like this:

[8.8] To-and-fro action (4)

Write the word DEED 'to' (forwards) or 'fro' (backwards) and it is the same.

Sometimes the reversed clue can be ambiguous:

[8.9] Expert turned evil (3)

Read this as D, S and the answer is DAB; read it as S, D and it's BAD! (If the setter has offered you _A_ with the first and third letters unchecked, he is no dab and is most certainly very bad!)

You now know about six types of cryptic clue:

- cryptic definition
- double definitions
- anagrams
- charades
- container and contents
- reversals

We've still got a long way to go, however, before we've covered all the weaponry at the setter's disposal.

9 Hidden Words

Letter by letter

If you take the letters of a sentence in order, a word will often be found lurking. To show what I mean, I invite you to consider the very sentence you have just read. Look at 'order, a word' and you may see ERA spanning the first two words and RAW spanning all three. Look at 'will often' and you can see LOFT. This phenomenon is the basis of the *hidden clue*, and it may best be illustrated by an example:

[9.1] Pub in Pinner (3)
D HI HW

'Pub' is INN and it may be found in 'Pinner'. The word 'in' is our HI (*hidden indicator*) and HW is the *hiding word*.

The word 'in' is also part of the HI in this clue, where the hidden word spans more than one word (HP = *hiding phrase*):

[9.2] Rat getting in among children? Egad – exterminate! (8)
D HI HP

The hidden word, meaning 'rat', is RENEGADE.

Another common HI is 'some':

[9.3] Some overenthusiastic kissing – one draws blood (4)

This is nothing whatever to do with a romantic love scene. 'Some (ie part of) overenthusiastic kissing' is TICK, a bloodsucker (defined by 'one draws blood').

A very long phrase is revealed in this *Times* clue written by Brian Greer:

[9.4] Some job at hand? We'll soon see (4,3,5)

The 'see' in question is BATH AND WELLS.

Further examples

You shouldn't have too much difficulty with these extra clues:

[9.5] Bad-tempered outburst brought by instant rumour (7)

[9.6] Powder used in ancient alchemy (4)

[9.7] Those Norwegians can entertain this foreigner (5)

[9.8] Plutonium partially destroyed town (5)

The answers with their HIs are: TANTRUM ('brought by'), TALC ('used in'), SENOR ('can entertain') and LUTON ('partially destroyed' – ie only some of the hidden letters have survived).

But what about this one?

[9.9] Ruler wants artistic bottle (4)

Here the HI is subtly disguised at the end of the sentence. The ruler that the words 'wants artistic' bottle (ie contain) is TSAR. An equally valid alternative clue would have been:

[9.10] Ruler wants artistic bottles (4)

Here we are regarding the two-word collection 'wants artistic' as a single entity which 'bottles' the ruler. Quite why the great Russian was so particular about his glassware is beside the point.

We still have a number of clue types to learn, so let's press on.

10 Vocal Clues

What we hear

Vocal clues depend on how the answer sounds when it is spoken. There are two sub-categories.

Pun clues

The *pun clue* relies on the fact that some words sound like others, eg PAIR and PEAR, HEIR and AIR. They are 'homophones', to use the technical jargon. Here is a pun clue:

[10.1] Feature of Scotland where there was a vicar, we hear (4)

The two words 'we hear' form a very common *pun indicator* (PI). Where was there 'a vicar'? Bray of course, and it's 'Bray' that we hear when we get the answer which is a feature of Scotland – BRAE. Can you find the PI in the following clue?

[10.2] Such a range of food is said to be satisfactory (4)

It is the phrase 'is said to be'. FARE sounds like 'fair' ('satisfactory'). One more:

[10.3] Shakespeare in speech? It should be precluded (6)

'Shakespeare' is the 'Bard'. What sounds like 'Bard'? BARRED, meaning 'precluded'. (Would you have spotted the PI?)

Accent clues

The *accent clue* relies on oddities of speech. Such a clue could also be regarded as a special type of two-definition clue. Here are some examples:

[10.4] Animal is warmer according to 'Arry (5)

[10.5] Correct, but in a refaned way? Scold angrily (4)

[10.6] A f-fellow somewhere in Jordan (5)

[10.7] Bird gettin' dressed for ceremony (5)

[10.8] Not thin and thuffering from a complaint (5)

In [10.4] 'Arry is an aitch-dropping cockney who talks about things being 'otter (hence OTTER). In [10.5] our awfully 'nace' person is never 'right' but 'rate', which prompts us to RATE him. [10.6] is a combination of an accent clue with a simple charade. Our unfortunate stutterer is unable to talk about 'a man'; instead he refers to 'a m-man' (AMMAN is Jordan's capital). In [10.7] 'robing' without the final 'g' leads to a bird (ROBIN) and in [10.8] our lisping (or 'lithping') friend is 'sick' (THICK). Your author is quite fond of stammering and lisping clues, but some crossword editors eschew them, wishing not to cause offence – I think that is being a little oversensitive.

Spoonerisms

Archibald Spooner had his own vocal problem which led to the term 'spoonerism'. We will talk about this later – but if you want to have a look at p44 now, why not?

11 Subtractive Clues

Reverse charades

In several of our clue types we have been involved in adding words to other words or putting words into other words. In a charade, for example, the formula has been A + B = C. Well, equally we can use the idea that B = C – A, which is a sort of *'reverse charade'*.

In the average daily cryptic the most common way of subtracting is by removing a head or a tail and the indicator is usually fairly obvious. Thus:

[11.1] Mama, topless, is something else! (5)

Concentrate on the words please, reader, not the misleading nudity! 'Mama' is mother. Remove the 'top' letter and we get OTHER. 'Topless' is a giveaway *beheading indicator*; 'headless' is another. (The suggestion of 'top' means that this clue would probably be suitable for a down word rather than an across one, by the way.)

Here's a clue involving truncation at the other end:

[11.2] Endlessly talk about the field event (6)

This may conjure up a picture of a boring commentator, but you need to decode the words regardless of that unappealing image. Again, concentrate on the words, please. When 'discuss' is presented 'endlessly' it becomes DISCUS. 'Endlessly' and 'endless' are giveaways for this type of clue.

If words can lose their first and last letters, they can also lose their hearts:

[11.3] Get the better of the heartless monster (4)

The 'monster' is a 'beast' – remove the heart ('a') to give BEST, a verb meaning 'to get the better of'.

You might come across something like this:

[11.4] University lecturer is an ass ignoring the solution (3)

D L (Donkey) SI (key)

'Donkey' minus 'key' = DON (SI = subtraction indicator), or even:

[11.5] Arousing affection, having had ear removed, dying (6)

(Endearing) SI(i) (ear) SI(ii) D

Answer: ENDING.

Further examples

See if you've got the idea by trying these fishy clues.

[11.6] Chippy – but you don't get to go in for fish! (4)

[11.7] Celebrity has a bird but not a fish (4)

[11.8] Fish had to leave harbour (4)

Clue [11.6] suggests a fish and chip shop but take 'enter' from 'carpenter' to find CARP. In [11.7] the definition is really a giveaway but 'starling' minus 'ling' confirms STAR. Take 'haddock' in [11.8] and follow the instruction 'had to leave' and you will find DOCK.

12 Non-word Elements in Subsidiary Indications

Up to now we have looked at all the main clue types, but so far we have used whole words as building-blocks for the clues. We can, however, use letters or clusters of letters as we shall see below.

Abbreviations and symbols

Consider the word PRATTLED. This may suggest 'p + rattled', but can the setter indicate 'p' in a subsidiary indication? The answer is yes, because 'p' is short for 'piano' or 'quietly', so a charade clue might read as follows:

[12.1] Gossiped quietly in a fluster (8)

(p) (rattled)

D S

In the world of crosswords there are a vast number of common abbreviations, and you will find a fair number in the Crossword Dictionary section of this *Crossword Companion*. This list is by no means exhaustive though, and one of the joys of learning how to solve is in coming to recognize the language of abbreviations and symbols.

In the clues that follow we can introduce only a small number in various types of clue.

[12.2] Miss West embraces novice man (4)

Answer: MALE: 'Mae' embraces 'L' (= learner, novice).

[12.3] Good man, a sailor lying on bed, wounded (7)

A 'good man' is a saint (ST); a 'sailor' on this occasion is an AB (on other occasions he's a 'tar' or something else!). Put it all together (in a down clue) to give STABBED.

[12.4] Old Bob has to study for the exam – buzz off! (5)

A 'bob' is (or was!) a shilling (= s); 's' + 'cram' = SCRAM.

[12.5] Slant in Conservative policy (7)

A simple charade: 'in' + 'C' + 'line' = INCLINE.

[12.6] Poet has edited religious education book (6)

This is a bit trickier. 'Religious education' = RE and an (edited) anagram of 'RE book' is BROOKE.

Asking the solver to form an abbreviation which is then incorporated into an anagram is regarded as fair only where the abbreviation is obvious. Even so it is a technique better left to the more advanced cryptics. On fairness and advanced puzzles, more anon!

Numbers

In crossword land we still use Roman numbers when convenient. Thus I (the roman letter) = 1 (the number), V = 5, X = 10, L = 50, C = 100, D = 500 and M = 1000, with of course the possibility of combinations. Thus:

[12.7] 100, very old and shut in (5)

And glad to get the Queen's telegram? Forget it! 'C' is a hundred; 'very old' becomes 'aged'. Answer: CAGED.

[12.8] Five hundred taking beer in the valley (4)

Just the sort of outdoor festival that might appeal to me! 'D' is five hundred. Add to 'ale' to get DALE.

[12.9] Around 50, it takes courage to get a sweetheart (7)

Just as well some of us are happily married. 'L' in 'daring' gives DARLING.

'Love' (from tennis) and 'duck' (from cricket) are useful sporting terms for zero which is regarded as the shape of O. Thus:

[12.10] The lady's love is a very brave man (4)

Answer: 'her' + 'O' gives HERO.

[12.11] Cricket ground where there's a duck, 5 and a 50 (4)

Answer: 'O' + 'V' + 'a L' = OVAL.

Bits and pieces

In this section we've seen two ways in which the crossword setter can get rid of odd letters. There remains a third, very important way. A letter can be defined by the position it occupies in another word. A few examples will suffice to illustrate this:

[12.12] Look at bee for example round end of cowslip (7)

The words 'end of' will tell us that we want the last letter in the word that follows, ie 'p'. Put 'insect' around 'p' to get INSPECT.

[12.13] Craftsman is good initially – then not working so hard (7)

'Initially' is a tell-tale word and 'good initially' gives 'g'. When the craftsman is not working so hard he is 'lazier'. Answer: GLAZIER.

'Finally' is also a tell-tale word:

[12.14] Climbing plant with flower finally providing fruit (4)

'Climbing plant' is 'pea'; 'flower finally' is 'r' ('r' being the last letter of 'flower'). Answer: PEAR.

Expect also to meet 'extremely' as in:

[12.15] Keep silent about extremely unmerciful prison system (5)

from *The Times*. Here 'extremely' denotes the first and last letters of 'unmerciful' which put inside 'gag' leads to GULAG. Not everyone approves of such a use of 'extremely', but its use is widespread.

[12.16] Head of school, many years a wise man (4)

'Head of school' is 's'; add 'age' to get the answer: SAGE.

Initial letters can often be put together in a charade, as follows:

[12.17] Leaders of firm are terribly obese (3)

Take the three 'leaders' (leading letters) to get FAT. (Alternatively final letters may be joined together, but this is much less common.)

Now try this one:

[12.18] A bit of trouble with relation's reproach (5)

Not all crossword editors like 'bit of', but those who do take it to mean 'the first bit of', so 'a bit of trouble' is by convention 't'. Add 't' to 'aunt' and you get TAUNT. There's one other thing to notice about this clue. The apostrophe-plus-s combination denotes a possessive to give the clue sense, but means 'is' when we're thinking about the construction of the clue ('t' with 'aunt' is TAUNT).

Though bits, a head and an end always have single letters, a heart may have one letter or more:

[12.19] Chap with heart of steel, bit of a lion? (4)

The 'heart of steel' is 'e'; add it on to 'man' and you have MANE.

[12.20] Stupid fool in middle of road beginning to fluster (3)

The 'beginning' to the word 'fluster' is 'f' and the 'middle' of the word 'road' is 'oa', giving OAF.

Half-words can be useful to the crossword setter:

[12.21] Famous performer is semi-naked (4)

'Semi-starkers' is STAR.

Sometimes the phrase 'not half' is used, as in:

[12.22] Household worker is delightful, not half (4)

Take 'charming' but not one half of it and you are left with CHAR.

So too can pairs of letters, as in:

[12.23] Leading couples in Chelsea actually hated dance music (3-3)

Add 'Ch' from 'Chelsea' to 'ac' from 'actually' to 'ha' from 'hated' and you have CHA-CHA.

Further examples

Here are a few more for practice:

[12.24] Previous hits were played, including Elvis's No 2 (9)

[12.25] Sailor, a rower, died on ship (6)

[12.26] Grand way in for the nobs (6)

[12.27] Four or six in a test? It's unimportant (7)

[12.28] Legal action – defendant's first in the box (5)

[12.29] What's found in Devon maybe is a very soft stone (8)

In [12.24] we have brought Elvis's No 2, the letter 'l', into an anagram of 'hits were' to give ERSTWHILE. Clue [12.25] is a charade: 'AB' plus 'oar' + 'd' equals ABOARD. [12.26] gives G (for grand) plus 'entry': GENTRY. [12.27] suggests that a boundary of IV or VI in a test (= trial) is TRIVIAL. In [12.28] we put 'd' after 'case' to produce CASED. Then in [12.29] a 'pp' (a very soft) inside 'shire' (as in Devonshire) gives you SAPPHIRE.

Bits and pieces offer all sorts of possibilities. The clue-writer can, for example, take third letters from words, substitute one bit for another, or even move bits around. It would be impossible to catalogue all the various possibilities, especially since inventive clue-writers will find new ones. Some of the techniques are covered in a later section, Other Types of Clue, where we will look at further improvisations.

13 The Orchestration of Subsidiary Parts

Summary of clue types

You now should be able to solve the following clues, recognizing a different type of subsidiary indication in each one:

(a)	[13.1] Put up with a rude person (4)
(b)	[13.2] Goose's mate ruined garden (6)
(c)	[13.3] The French shelter is hidden (6)
(d)	[13.4] Fast and quiet in sudden attack (5)
(e)	[13.5] Show contempt perhaps – gratuities sent back (4)
(f)	[13.6] Sea-eagle in her nest (4)
(g)	[13.7] Despatched perfume we hear (4)
(h)	[13.8] Senior is more daring, losing head (5)

The clue types are:

(a)	*Multiple definitions*	(answer: BEAR)
(b)	*Anagram*	(answer: GANDER)
(c)	*Charade*	(answer: LATENT)
(d)	*Container and contents*	(answer: RAPID)
(e)	*Reversal*	(answer: SPIT)
(f)	*Hidden*	(answer: ERNE)
(g)	*Vocal*	(answer: SENT)
(h)	*Subtractive*	(answer: OLDER)

Complex clues

Each of the eight clues above could be described as a *simple* cryptic clue (however hard it is to solve!). A *complex* cryptic clue on the other hand, includes some combination of more than one technique. Here is a random selection (keyed by the letters above):

(b,c) [13.9] Trails along with legs collapsing after wearisome task (8)

An anagram of 'legs' is 'gles'. Add it to 'drag' and we get DRAGGLES. If you like you can add the S/D notation to see how the clue works, but it's about time you understood the shorthand way that setters use to explain a solution. In this case the solution note would read (drag + anag.). Other notes will be explained as we go along.

(c,h) [13.10] The man has almost finished paved area around a plant (7)

Here the charade incorporates a subsidiary component which has been clued 'subtractively'. The man is 'he'; and 'almost finished paved area' is 'pati' (not quite a patio!) and around is 'c'. The answer is therefore HEPATIC (a liverwort). The note would read (he + pati(o) + c).

(c,d) [13.11] You get dry around bottom of tongue with an American disease (7)

You get 'TT' around 'e' ('bottom' because it is a down clue) with 'an' plus 'US': (e in TT + an + US) gives TETANUS.

(b,d) [13.12] Secular lot are somehow besieging politician (8)

Here we have an abbreviation inside an anagram: (MP in anag.) gives TEMPORAL. Alternatively we could have an anagram inside something else:

(b,d) [13.13] Palatable fruit nasty lice will get into (8)

Here 'nasty lice' = 'elic', and so (anag. in date) gives us DELICATE.

(b,c,d) [13.14] Sweetmeat – kitchenware contains a small amount, cool possibly (5,9)

'Plate' contains 'a' plus 'inch' plus an anagram of cool, 'ocol': (a + inch + anag.) in plate gives PLAIN CHOCOLATE. In this clue we have the formula A contains BC, with both B and C placed inside A. However it is quite possible for A contains BC to mean 'A contains B, then add C' as in this example:

(b,c,d) [13.15] Mathematician worries terribly about Northern fisherman (6,8)

A strange bringing together of concerns? No matter – put an anagram of 'worries' around N, then add 'angler': (N in anag. + angler) gives SENIOR WRANGLER, Cambridge's best maths graduate. You, the solver, would have to sort out whether to put the fisherman inside the anagram or outside. This sort of ambiguity adds a distinct spice to a crossword clue.

(b,c,e) [13.16] Signified dire need after doctor returned (6)

Signified means OMENED and the clue works like this: (MO, rev. + anag.).

(e,f) [13.17] Fairy coming back in dire pantomime (4)

Here we have to look for a word hidden in reverse, and it isn't too hard to spot PERI (hidden, rev.).

(b,h) [13.18] Bread in short supply – unusually scanty (4)

Take (anag. of brea(d)), ie an unusual presentation of a short rendering of 'bread', and you get BARE.

(d,e) [13.19] Chaps turned up in the American agency – it should be entertaining (6)

Our note would read (men, rev. in CIA) and the answer is CINEMA.

(c,d,e) [13.20] Women's Libber swallows man up, one man who'd fight (9)

Poor chap! The man is Dan (he could be Les or anybody else, but he isn't). When one (1) is added on and (Ms) Greer does her swallowing, the answer is GRENADIER. Our note would read (Dan, rev. + 1 in (Germaine) Greer). We add the bracketed Germaine, because Ms Greer may not be found in the dictionary.

Clearly we could find yet other combinations of our eight clue techniques, and you can expect to meet others not given here. Deciphering a complex clue is one of the joys of crossword solving.

Linking clues together

In most daily puzzles each clue is separate and independent. The solver has to manage (say) 28 or 32 clues and any linking occurs in the checking of the letters. Sometimes though a setter will attempt to find connections between *clues*. For example, successive clues may be linked together by three dots to suggest a common theme:

[13.21] Now for the give away (7) ...

[13.22] ... from me, perhaps, a Spaniard with gold (5)

The answer to the first clue is PRESENT, a simple double-definition clue with two meanings – which we would explain in the notes as (2 defs) or (2 mngs). Who does a present come from? Answer: a DONOR (don + or). You may not yet have learnt that gold = or (the heraldic colour) or possibly Au (the chemical symbol), but I can't tell you everything at once!

Answers may spread across several words at different sites in the puzzle. This was a clue I used in the *Birmingham Evening Mail* (starting at 9 Across):

[13.23] 9, 5 down, 1 across, 25 down, 27 across, 22 across Claim of our paper – exceptional deal, this fine blend reveals many great things (2,3,3,7,7,4,2,3,8)

An anagram of the last eight words gives the catchline on the front page: BY FAR THE LARGEST EVENING SALE IN THE MIDLANDS.

Sometimes there will be cross-referencing between clues all linked by a common theme. Thus, 30 Across and 9 Down could be linked as follows and the solver may be (mildly) misled into treating 9 as a number in its own right rather than a clue reference:

[13.24] 30 Looked after 9 somehow (6)

[13.25] 9 Separate revolutionary students in rising (6)

9 gives the answer SUNDER (red NUS, rev.) which can somehow give NURSED (anag.), the answer to 30.

This is a simple example. In some puzzles the cross-references can cover half the clues. Before we move on, here's an additional challenge.

Additional challenge

Take the word PALE and see if you can use each of the clue types listed on p37 to write a clue for it. The reverse clue can be a reverse charade (e,c). For good measure, try two charades and a reverse hidden. Then compare your list with mine on p46.

14 The & Lit. Clue

What is an 'and lit.'?

Unless you solve advanced crosswords and look at the solution notes, you are unlikely to come across the expression 'and lit.', which is conventionally written with an ampersand. This does not mean, however, that you are unlikely to meet an '& lit.' clue – and it is something rather special. Take a good look at this clue:

[14.1] No fellow for mixing (4,4)

Can you solve it? Where is the definition? Well, it reads like one, doesn't it? In that case, where's the subsidiary indication? Well, it could be that as well – perhaps an anagram of 'no fellow' (with 'for mixing' as the anagram indicator). In fact, all four words serve as both a definition and a subsidiary indication. This is indeed an anagram clue and the answer is LONE WOLF. If we use our S/D notation we can analyse the clue thus:

[14.1] No fellow for mixing (4,4)

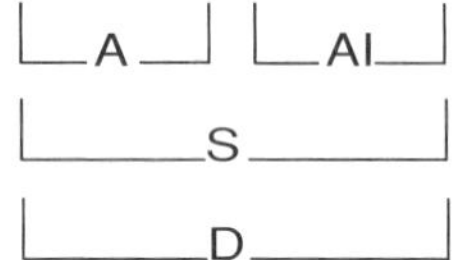

A clue like this, where S and D span the whole length, is known as an '& lit.'. Clue [14.1] is an 'anag. & lit.'. Here are two more:

[14.2] I'm one involved with cost (9)

[14.3] What could give bang out at sea? (7)

The answers are ECONOMIST and GUNBOAT ('at sea' suggests confusion and is a very useful anagram indicator). The & lit. doesn't have to be an anagram, though, as the following examples show:

[14.4] Part of it 'it an iceberg (7)

The 'hidden & lit.' gives us TITANIC.

[14.5] Leaders of various individual congregations (alternatively rectors sometimes) (6)

'Leaders' are first letters here. This 'initials & lit.' clue leads to VICARS. A somewhat overused old chestnut is:

[14.6] One has gone into the church (8)

'I in minster' & lit. gives MINISTER. For a 'rev. & lit.' try:

[14.7] The reverse of a divine fellow (3)

DOG is the reverse of a god in more ways than one.

The 'semi & lit.'

Let's have a look at this clue:

[14.8] Denomination spreading abroad 'Christ doeth much'? (9,6)

The last three words may be spread abroad and we see that they are an anagram of METHODIST CHURCH. The first word is clearly a definition and yet the whole clue also gives a definition – an 'enhanced definition', in fact. We could analyse the clue as follows:

[14.8] Denomination spreading abroad 'Christ doeth much'? (9,6)

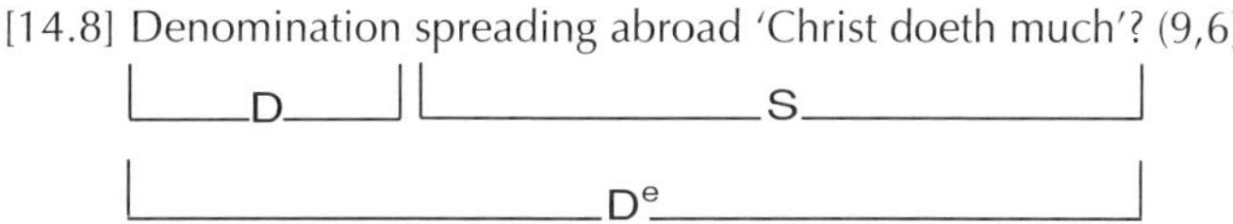

where De stands for 'enhanced definition'. Since in this clue De and S overlap for much of the clue I will term this a 'semi & lit.' We could attempt to turn this into a 'pure & lit.' by rewording it as follows:

[14.9] It spreads abroad 'Christ doeth much' (9,6)

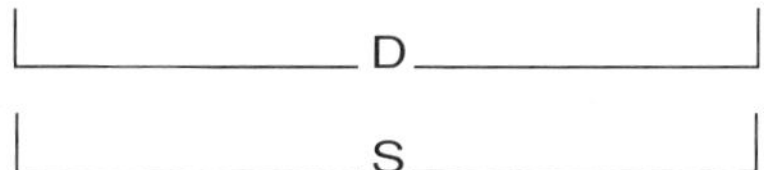

Both clues are acceptable, although [14.8] is perhaps a little more helpful to the solver.

Some 'non & lits.'

Here is an attempt at an & lit. clue where there is no real definition:

[14.10] Andrew could become this (6)

This is a very bad attempt at an anag. & lit. to give WARDEN. Little Andy could become a bus conductor or a brain surgeon (or even a crossword setter!). The definition is somewhat remote, to say the least! But the clue becomes perfectly respectable (even if uninspired) when we stop trying to be too clever and put in a definition:

[14.11] Andrew could become a guard (6)

To finish, a word on what & lit. *doesn't* mean! The origin of the phrase is much debated but it seems to stand for 'and literally'. This clue, & lit. tells us, is a configuration of letters *and* a literal definition. What & lit. does *not* mean is: here is a clue which simply gives you a piece of information which is literally true. Here is such a clue:

[14.12] Mint perhaps in gel? It can be refreshing (7)

The answer is SHERBET (herb in set). Anyone who has eaten a glacier mint can bear testimony to the truth of the clue, but anyone who understands the S/D analysis knows that this is *not* an & lit. clue.

Further examples

It's time for you to have a go at some & lits.

[14.13] What can make trade tricky, extremes of 'procedure'? (3,4)

[14.14] When it's wielded you might find there's nothing left wet (5)

[14.15] Unreliable date, yes? Not 'e! (6)

[14.16] In Rome that is the time to get bumped off (4)

[14.17] ABC is somehow … this! (5)

[14.18] Who does able act for kitchen when given order (5,4,3,6-6)

Clue [14.13] gives us an anagram of 'trade' plus the extreme letters of procedure – hence RED TAPE. In [14.14] we incorporate 'O' for 'nothing' and 'L' for 'left' into the anag. & lit. to give TOWEL. Then in [14.15] we take the letter 'e' away from an anagram to give us a *reliable* boyfriend, STEADY. The Latin for 'that is' is 'id est' and if we remove 't' (an abbreviation for 'time') we find IDES (a bad day for Caesar) in [14.16]. [14.17] is simple – in fact BASIC, and the long anag. & lit. for [14.18] gives CHIEF COOK AND BOTTLE-WASHER.

15 Other Types of Clue

In this section we look at some other types of clue which are more common in advanced cryptic puzzles. You will meet more of this kind of thing later, but since *The Times* (for instance) is quite fond of alternate-letter clues and I've spotted a spoonerism clue or two in *The Guardian*, there's no harm in your making the acquaintance of these relatively rare devices straight away.

The examples here come mostly from *The Observer's* Azed puzzles and Azed clue-writing competition, so you have a foretaste of the harder stuff to come later on.

The moving letter(s)

In this clue type the solver is invited to find a word and then move a particular letter (or letters) to discover a new word:

[15.1] See me in N European water, tail moving? (6)

N European water is 'wasser': move the tail (ie the final letter, which is 'r') to get WRASSE. Note that an '& lit.' effect is also achieved since a wrasse is a fish.

[15.2] I disapproved of the unseemly skunk, tail foremost (4)

Move the c of 'atoc' (a skunk) to the front to obtain the censor CATO.

The substituted letter(s)

Here you are invited to find a word and substitute one letter (or set of letters) for another. Thus in this clue:

[15.3] Vigorous? Love yielding to East in source of drowsiness (5)

We find a source of 'drowsiness' (poppy) and substitute 'e' for 'o' ('love') to arrive at PEPPY (meaning 'vigorous').

Alternate letters

The solver is asked to discard every other letter in a clue such as the following:

[15.4] Outings in which you find chain keeps losing odd bits (5)

A ride on a shaky bicycle? Maybe – but forget the misleading context and remove the odd letters ('bits') from the 'chain keeps'. The result is HIKES.

The words 'odd bits' and 'even bits' usually give the game away but here is the technique given a new subtlety by Azed:

[15.5] Ancient Syrian one regularly placed among king and troops (8)

Place A alternately among R and MEN and you'll get ARAMAEAN.

In the following clue (which won a first prize for N C Dexter in a 1984 Azed competition) the alternate letters are anagrammed:

[15.6] By it 'truth' and 'lie' looked alternately interchangeable (11)

An anagram of BITUHNLEOKD is DOUBLE-THINK (another & lit. of course).

The missing-words charade

This type of charade is best illustrated by some examples:

[15.7] Opening gambit at parties is hard if shyness ____ inhibits one (7)

The first word here provides the definition. The remainder is a sentence into which you must insert some words which make sense. The words required are 'or if ice' ('ice' meaning 'reserve'). Put them together in a charade and the answer is ORIFICE.

[15.8] 'Adam's ____ ', said archaic Eve, very old crone? (6)

The answer is RIBIBE (an old crone). Can you see why?

Sometimes the charade provides a 'letter formula' telling you how to get from one group of letters to another:

[15.9] Highland cattle put with this will become quiet (4)

The answer is NOUT (Highland cattle) because 'put with no ut' equals 'p' (an abbreviation for 'quiet'). A relatively unusual type of clue this, and the example given threw more than one solver when perpetrated by Azed.

The subtractive container-and-contents

This type of clue can be seen as a 'container and contents in reverse'. Here's an example of my own:

[15.10] This minor when put in bed is happy (4)

It's nothing to do with a compliant child when you read the clue cryptically. You want a word which when put in bed gives you 'blessed': hence LESS.

Here's one from Azed:

[15.11] What'll those enthralled like us in Market get? Mare's-nest (5)

The word you want, hidden in the 'mart' (or market) in 'mare's nest' is ESNES, who are enthralled as slaves. Quite simple really!

The composite anagram

The composite anagram was revived by Don Putnam in the (now-defunct) *Games and Puzzles* magazine in 1975. He quoted the following clue by the pioneer crossword setter Afrit:

[15.12] You could make this whale seem quarrelsome, but hold it up by its tail and it begins to laugh (7)

Forget the words after 'quarrelsome' and concentrate on the first seven words. Afrit is saying take 'this word for whale' plus 'seem' and you could make 'quarrelsome'. The answer is RORQUAL (hence the 'lau' in the reversal, the beginning (!) of 'laugh'). Quite soon after Putnam's article Azed and *Listener* puzzlers were faced with the rediscovery of the composite anagram. The clue-writer was saying in effect 'If A won't form a decent anagram, I'll add B and define it as an anagram of C.' A way had been rediscovered of combining the anagram with the subtractive clue.

This type of clue normally appears as an & lit., as the following examples illustrate:

[15.13] Ecuadorans, broke, might produce a ____ and nothing else (5)

ECUADORANS is an anagram of 'a, ____ and, o'. The missing word is SUCRE.

[15.14] Some sprinkling with this could give a tame meal gusto (9)

This won B Franco a first prize from Azed in 1977. The word 'some' has to be sprinkled with a word to give 'a tame meal gusto'. Answer: MALAGUETTA (look up its meaning in *Chambers* if you don't know it).

My own prize-winning Azed clue for PICKLE (which can mean 'steal') read as follows:

[15.15] Kleptomaniac: a man to ____ indiscriminately? (6)

(Incidentally 'A man to pickle indiscriminately' is a rather good clue for KLEPTOMANIAC, don't you think?)

The composite anagram does not have to be part of an & lit. clue; as in this case of mine 'very highly commended' by Azed near St Valentine's Day:

[15.16] A little romance? Such fun with cryptic letters may show it is fourteenth (11)

In other words take a word possibly meaning 'a little romance', combine it with 'fun' cryptically to give 'it is fourteenth'. The answer comes out as HISTORIETTE (a short story). Quite often though you won't find a single example of any of them, even in an Azed. Remember, too, that the setter will always be looking for a new and subtle way of telling you how to deal with the letters in front of you.

Spoonerisms

The English clergyman Archibald Spooner (1844–1930) had a 'nervous tendency to transpose initial letters or half-syllables', the *Chambers Biographical Dictionary* tells us. He was liable to say something like 'half-warmed fish' instead of 'half-formed wish', and such a lapse is now known as a *spoonerism*. Spoonerism clues make use of this, so here's one I've just thought of as I write:

[15.17] An insect to flit past, according to Spooner (9)

'To flit past' is to 'flutter by' which is of course a spoonerism of BUTTERFLY.

Common crossword mistakes

There's enough space here for me to list some things that can go wrong. Here are ten off the top of my head:

1. The wrong grid in the newspaper
2. The solution to a puzzle alongside the puzzle itself
3. Missing clues
4. Clues that don't work – especially inaccurate anagrams, and letters not properly indicated in subsidiary indications
5. A repeat of last week's puzzle
6. Numbers wrong in brackets
7. Clues and grid entries for misspelt words
8. Definitions that are totally inaccurate
9. Computer errors cutting off parts of the grid
10. Late corrections being misinterpreted and leading to nonsensical clues

Maybe you can think of more. Let's just hope that none of them are in evidence in this book!

16 The Grid for 15 × 15 Cryptics

Earlier we defined what we meant by checked and unchecked squares and I mentioned that the alternate-letter grid was the basis for many British puzzles. It is time to look at grids in a little more detail.

The most common size for an everyday cryptic is 15 × 15 and the grid will usually be based on the lattice shown below:

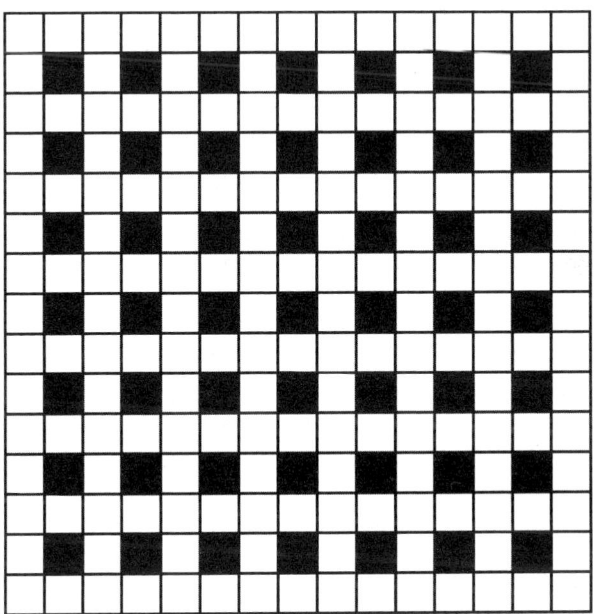

Extra squares will then be blocked out to divide words off and the result will usually be a puzzle of 28, 30 or 32 clues. The 28 formula is regarded as ideal because it offers four long words or phrases and a range of answer lengths. The *Times* crossword championship, however, uses puzzles of 30 clues, so that each clue can be assigned an equivalence of one minute during a 30-minute solving period. It is also possible to blank out the squares in either of these ways:

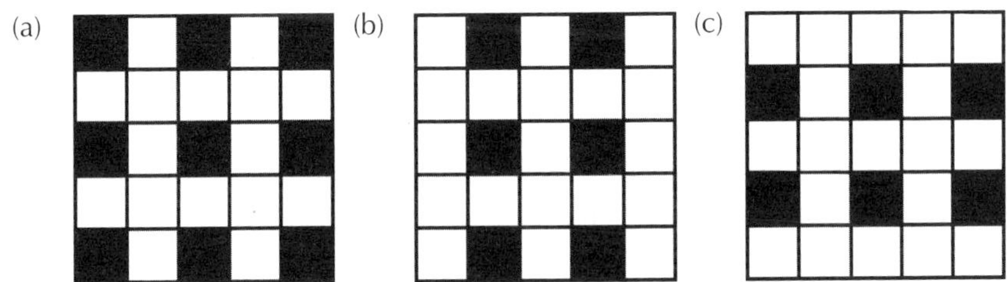

(Grid (c) amounts to the same thing as Grid (b) turned through 90 degrees.)

Sometimes a pattern will have different lattices clashing into one another, so that rows and columns appear to be dislocated. Here is an example in a 9 × 9 grid:

1		2		3	■	4	■	■
	■		■	5				6
7					■		■	
■	■		■	8				
9	■	■	■		■	■	■	
10		11			■	12	■	■
	■		■	13				14
15					■		■	
■	■		■	16				

Whatever basic grid is used the setter should try to keep to certain standards of fairness:

1. *No part of the grid should be completely cut off* from another part of the grid.
2. *The number of unchecked letters (unches) in an answer should be half of the total or less.* It won't matter much if seven letters out of thirteen are left unchecked, as here: _R_S_O_R_V_R_. Knowing that the answer should give you a football team (7,6) you will soon get BRISTOL ROVERS. In some grids, though, one may be left trying to solve a clue leading to _A_E_ and this can simply pose too many possibilities for comfort.
3. *There should never be three or more successive unchecked letters*. This means that no answer should contain three consecutive letters not checked by crossing letters.
4. *Normally the grid should be symmetrical if given a half-turn* (ie through 180 degrees). Some grids also give symmetry if turned through 90 degrees. Sometimes a mirror symmetry will be preferred to a half-turn symmetry.

Ten clues for pale

(see 'Additional challenge' on p39)

- *(a)* Whitish stake of wood.
- *(b)* Leap frantically looking ill?
- *(c)* Soft drink wanting in colour (p+ale). Friend needs a bit of expertise to make part of fence (pal+e).
- *(d)* Albert in Physical Education is not looking well, maybe (Al in PE).
- *(e,c)* Eastern circuit goes around wooden post ((E + lap), rev.)
- *(f)* Sup ales – partly making you lose colour? (pale, verb).
- *(f,e)* Wooden post in hotel apparently rejected (rejected = sent back).
- *(g)* Whitish bucket, we hear ('pail').
- *(h)* Bill coming out of palace looking ashen (palace minus a/c, a/c = account, bill).

17 Back to Definitions

How precise?

Now that we have looked at all the main clue types, it is time to look again at definitions. We saw earlier that it is quite easy in a definition puzzle to be too helpful ('River in Paris' for SEINE) and equally easy to be too vague ('River' could make you think of RHINE, RHONE, TRENT or TWEED). In that type of puzzle 'River in France' seemed about right.

In cryptic puzzles it is equally important to be fair and accurate but in clues where there is a subsidiary indication 'river' will be enough of a definition for SEINE. We could use the 'flower' idea (see p19) or we could try something like:

> [17.1] What sounds like a reasonable river (5)

Well, I suppose a river can be 'reasonable' in size, if not in mind. SEINE sounds like 'sane'. You get the point.

What would not be fair, I think, would be to define SEINE by 'water'. While it is true that the Seine is indeed a watercourse, the water definition is too vague. Similarly it would be rather unfair to define 'sparrow' by 'animal'. A sparrow may be a member of the animal kingdom but we would want a definition to suggest a bird – and if 'bird' was thought to be too obvious 'flighty creature' might do the job.

Some crossword setters try to get around the problem of a giveaway definition by making the definition too vague:

> [17.2] Must assume Dada is wandering around in London (6,8)

The anagram is clear enough, but 'in London' is wholly inadequate as a definition for MADAME TUSSAUDS.

An alternative using the same anagram is:

> [17.3] Must assume Dada will go astray in London establishment (6,8)

I could have suggested 'London waxworks' but you wouldn't have needed to look at the subsidiary indication at all. The definition here strikes a nice balance between vagueness and obviousness. Achieving that balance has to be part of the setter's skill.

You can see that we are now delving into matters of fairness. There will be a lot more discussion about what is fair and what isn't when we come to look at 'crossword grammar' later on.

Three ways of defining a word

The three ways of defining a word can best be illustrated by an example. Take the word CAPTAIN. A dictionary definition begins thus: 'a head or chief officer; the commander of a troop of horse, a company of infantry, a ship, or a portion of a ship's company.' In providing a definition for a cryptic clue we can either: (i) provide a *straight definition*:

> [17.4] Commander with army in awful panic (7)

(TA in anag.) or

(ii) provide a *cryptic description* (based here on a cricket captain's function):

> [17.5] 'Pa, I can't! That's wrong!' he may declare (7)

(anag. with the misleading context of George Washington?) or

(iii) provide a *definition by example*:

[17.6] Cook? Starts to prepare the added ingredients to be put into container (7)

('ptai' in 'can' with another misleading context – think of Captain Cook). Clue [17.6] shows us how the crossword setter's lingo often relies on *double meanings*. Vocabulary may be specially selected to mislead – but the clue is nevertheless fair.

Why do setters have pseudonyms?

I am often asked this question, and I suppose it really began with Torquemada. Historically many authors took pseudonyms, and this practice spread into the world of puzzles. Hubert Phillips was a famous general problems setter as well as an early crossword setter and he had (at least?) four pseudonyms: Caliban, T O Hare, the Doc and Dogberry. Today publications tend either to use pseudonyms or let setters remain anonymous, and relatively few publish puzzles under 'real' names. Some of this has to do with 'branding'. A pseudonym gives the individual setter (with all his or her own 'quirks') a high profile, but some papers like to emphasize the uniformity of their own style and to play down any variation between their contributors.

18 Crossword Vocabulary

Crossword English

It is time to turn our attention at a broader level to what may be called 'Crossword English'. First we shall look at vocabulary and in the next section we shall consider the very contentious matter of crossword grammar.

There are two aspects to vocabulary. One is the vocabulary of the clues and the other the vocabulary of the answers. You will have been picking up a lot of experience in both aspects, but let's start with the clues themselves.

Components of clue answers

Within a clue you need to recognize words and phrases that represent the components of the clue and it is particularly important to be able to decode the small components of just a few letters.

Attempt a daily cryptic and you will enter a world preoccupied with directions (north = N, etc), numbers (hundred = C, etc) and a more-than-usual interest in the French (LA, LE, LES). American soldiers may have gone home after World War II, but the good old GI still appears in the back pages of our papers. Indeed there is something of a military preoccupation with gunners (RA), engineers (RE), volunteers (TA) and so on. Crosswords may be square, but they often have sex-appeal (IT or SA) which may please a sailor (AB or TAR usually). A worker is regarded as less than human (ANT), but great consideration is shown to the doctor (DR, GP, MB, MD, MO – a health centre practice where you don't know which one you will get). Political neutrality is achieved with a fair balance between left (L) and right (R), though the Conservative (C) party has more seats in the grid than Labour (LAB) which still lags behind the Liberal (L) party.

You probably need to know something about cricket too. The ON side is also known as the LEG side – as opposed to the OFF side. M for maiden (or maidens) is very common, as featured in bowling analysis, and the component OVER is often defined by something like 'Maiden perhaps'.

Popular culture often comes in handy with EVITA (the show) being the reverse of '-ative' and the weepy film ET has often made an appearance. Quite where to draw the line with culture is difficult, but over a period of time solvers become familiar with an eclectic subculture in the language of the clues. Don't worry if you don't know that 'Rugby' equals 'RU' or that 'Abraham's old city' is UR – you'll learn these things fairly quickly and in any case I must leave you some things to find out for yourself!

Anagram and other indicators

It is not long before a crossword solver learns to recognize *anagram indicators*. There are hundreds of words at a crossword setter's disposal: 'strange', 'unusual' and 'terrible' are common adjectives; also used are the corresponding adverbs ('strangely', etc). A setter may refer to 'a mixture of' something or talk about something being 'cooked' or 'ruined'. And so on. But beware of 'upset' which can indicate reversal in a down word.

'Upset' is indeed an ambiguous word as the following examples show:

> [18.1] Light at night has upset these rodents (4)

Answer: RATS (star, rev.).

> [18.2] Rats upset Russian emperor (4)

Answer: TSAR (anag.).

We learned earlier that 'around' and 'about' are likewise ambiguous – even more so in fact. Consider these clues with 'about'.

[18.3] Banter about a fibber (4)

Answer: LIAR (rev. of rail).

[18.4] The manner shown by chaps about one (4)

Answer: MIEN (I in men).

[18.5] Fastening device about source of light (5)

Answer: CLAMP (c. + lamp).

[18.6] About to get single girl, being lax (6)

Answer: REMISS (re + miss).

In these four examples we see how the word 'about' can indicate two types of clue or be part of a subsidiary indication.

'In' is another troublesome little word, which the solver must learn to interpret:

[18.7] Girl found in cloisters (4)

Answer: LOIS (hidden).

[18.8] Mean not to go in the river (6)

Answer: DENOTE (not in Dee).

[18.9] Setter let loose in thoroughfare (6)

Answer: STREET (anag.) with 'in' simply acting as a linkword between the subsidiary indication and the definition.

You know now that 'we hear' means a pun and you will spot reversal indicators such as 'returning' and 'coming back' quite easily. Something 'getting' something might suggest a charade and something 'outside' something could suggest a container-and-contents clue. Recognizing the indicators, like everything else, comes with practice.

Before we stop thinking about abbreviations, solvers should be warned that they differ from dictionary to dictionary and the newspapers use different dictionaries. For example *The Daily Telegraph* uses *The Chambers Dictionary* whereas *The Times* tends to use the *Concise Oxford Dictionary*. You may therefore expect to meet 'sun' for 's' in *The Daily Telegraph* but 'son' for 's' in *The Times*. You will get to know what to expect over time but why not buy a copy of *XWD* (the Chambers abbreviations book) to get a list of virtually all the possibilities? In the meantime, you will find some of the more common abbreviations listed in the Crossword Dictionary section of the *Crossword Companion*.

Linkwords

If you can spot linkwords in the middle of a clue, you can often work out more easily what is the definition and what is the subsidiary indication. The little word 'in' is often used as a link since it means 'consisting of' or 'contained in' so you may often find clues that are 'S in D' or 'D in S'. 'For' is another linkword, so expect 'S for D' (though some do not like 'D for S'). Sometimes you will find 'S gives D', 'S produces D' or 'D from S' and 'D is shown by S'. The construction 'D of S' is generally acceptable but 'S of D' seems more dubious (expect to see it though).

There isn't space here to give you all the possible linkwords and you will enjoy finding them for yourself. Just look for them and you should more easily appreciate how the clue is constructed.

Vocabulary of the solution

The level of vocabulary used in most crosswords is that of a standard dictionary or reference book, but this needs a bit of spelling out since what is 'standard' for one crossword is by no means 'standard' for another – and the solver may have different ideas again!

For words that are not proper nouns *The Chambers Dictionary* should supply everything you need. Many of its words are rare or old or both, but the solver will find everything needed. Many crosswords will use other dictionaries as a 'sieve' – so if a word is in *Chambers* but not in the *Concise Oxford Dictionary* or *Collins English Dictionary* it may be deemed too obscure. *The Oxford Dictionary of English* contains an excellent range of proper nouns, as does *Collins English Dictionary* (although the most recent edition omits names of people). No dictionary will give you every Shakespearean character or geographical place you might come across, so a copy of the Bard's works and a good atlas will always come in handy.

For looking up answers from definitions, try the Crossword Dictionary section of this *Crossword Companion*.

I mentioned earlier the vexed matter of culture, and there is always a healthy debate about what is fair and what isn't. Could one include the title of a popular record, for instance – possibly in an attempt to attract youth interest? In this respect the puzzles in *The Guardian* probably offer the greatest range of vocabulary of any daily paper, other newspapers being more conservative in their tastes. References to living people are generally (but not universally) eschewed on the basis that libel cases may be risked. However, the Queen as ER is a definite exception to this rule.

There is no doubt that the vocabulary of crosswords does tend to reflect the interests of the middle-class middle-aged male, and doubtless this will long continue – but over the course of time new words have crept in and many of an older generation are bemused by the possibility of GARAGE being something other than a shelter for the car. And in the USA you will obviously meet baseball terminology beyond that of the simple HOME RUN. At their best, crosswords don't simply echo the past age of the empire. They accommodate all that, but their vocabulary moves on as the language moves on – and through our involvement with them we extend our delight in the riches of the English language.

19 Basic Principles of Crossword Grammar

Fair play

The *Crossword Manual* is all about crossword English. Learning about different clue types is rather like learning about parts of speech – nouns, verbs, adjectives and so on. By doing some analysis of definitions and subsidiary indications, we've learnt how to 'parse' a cryptic clue. Now it's time to look at 'crossword grammar'. Normal English has its grammar; so too does crossword English. Normal English has some rules and some areas of dispute; crossword English is the same.

To trace the history of crossword grammar we must resume the historical account we left a while ago. It is now time to introduce three famous names. The first is Torquemada of *The Observer*. He is the setter credited with the invention of the cryptic clue. Born Edward Powys Mathers, he dominated the scene in the 1930s so far as very hard cryptics are concerned, but at times his puzzles were unsolvable. Torquemada was a genius who invented much of crossword English, but it was left to others to codify crossword grammar. We shall return to him later.

While Torquemada was teasing *The Observer*'s readers in the 1930s, another crossword setter was exploring new crossword possibilities in *The Listener*. Prebendary A F Ritchie of Wells Cathedral took the pseudonym Afrit (an Arabian demon), and he too on occasion was able to produce puzzles that attracted no correct entries! But Afrit was a pioneer, and when after World War II he turned his attention to the theory of crosswords he laid the foundation on which another great pioneer, Ximenes, was to build so successfully.

Torquemada died in 1939 and his eventual successor was Derrick Somerset Macnutt, a classics master at Christ's Hospital, Horsham, who took another inquisitorial name, Ximenes. Afrit and Ximenes can be regarded as the 'lawmakers', the codifiers who brought order and discipline to a pastime that might otherwise have got out of hand. Their campaign began with Afrit's book of *Armchair Crosswords* which was published in 1949. In a preface Ximenes commends Afrit thus: 'The crossword world may be trivial, but like greater worlds it needs standards, and Afrit is the man to set them.' The next few pages contain an Introduction by Afrit which mentions *The Book of the Crossword*, an 'exhaustive treatise' which 'has not been written'. In his section on clues we discover Afrit's Injunction, appropriately culled from Alice (how appropriate indeed when Lewis Carroll was such a marvellous forerunner of the modern crossword setter!). This is what Afrit says:

> We must expect the composer to play tricks, but we shall insist that he play fair. *The Book of the Crossword* lays this injunction upon him: 'You need not mean what you say, but you must say what you mean.' This is a superior way of saying that he can't have it both ways. He may attempt to mislead by employing a form of words which can be taken in more than one way, and it is your fault if you take it the wrong way, *but it is his fault if you can't logically take it the right way*. The solver, for his part, is enjoined to read the clues in an anti-Pickwickian sense. This also requires explanation. To take a remark in a Pickwickian sense is not to take it literally; therefore, to read a clue in an anti-Pickwickian sense is to close the mind to the acquired metaphorical meaning of the words and to concentrate upon their bald literal significance. If you do so, you may find you are being presented with an anagram of the solution, or the solution is 'hidden' in the clue, or a bit of jugglery with its component parts is being done.

In other words: the solver who follows the structure of a clue literally should expect to discover a grammatical set of coded instructions leading to the answer.

A crossword clue is rather like a mathematical sum. The symbolism must be fair to lead the solver to the correct answer. The concept of fairness was further developed by Ximenes through his clue-writing competitions in *The Observer* and his book *Ximenes on the Art of the Crossword*. In fact the post-1949 developments now make many of Afrit's own clues in *Armchair Crosswords* look suspect!

The debates about crossword grammar are still ongoing (and the *Crossword Manual* undoubtedly contributes to them). Modern followers of the principles laid down by Ximenes sometimes call themselves 'Ximeneans'. The successor to Ximenes, Azed (about whom more anon) is certainly one of these. For Ximeneans there are definite rules of grammar that make a clue fair and they point the finger at crosswords who produce 'unsound', 'unfair' or 'non-Ximenean' clues. Your author is a Ximenean, but realizes that *some* non-Ximenean practices are not necessarily all bad.

It's time to look at some examples of fair and unfair clues.

Fair and unfair clues

Let's start with this one:

[19.1] Small pebbles – English (7)

This is supposed to give an anagram of 'English', namely SHINGLE, but the clue is a breach of Afrit's Injunction because the clue-writer has omitted an anagram indicator. This is a case of the *unindicated anagram*. The clue may be rendered sound by the addition of a suitable indicator:

[19.2] Small pebbles – possibly English (7)

might do. 'Possibly' is an anagram indicator. Here is an alternative:

[19.3] Broken English pebbles on the beach (7)

By no means a great clue, but a sound one, and this is important.

Here is a clue which may look all right at first sight, but which a Ximenean would regard as unacceptable:

[19.4] English mixture on the beach (7)

Two things are wrong here. For the Ximenean 'English mixture' cannot mean 'mixture of English' – it is simply ungrammatical. This is an example of an *unsatisfactory nounal anagram indicator*. Secondly 'on the beach' is an *inaccurate definition* leading to the wrong part of speech. An adverbial phrase (which this is) cannot be used to define a noun. Here is [19.4] rewritten:

[19.5] Mixture of English pebbles on the beach (7)

A clue such as the one following has all sorts of problems!

[19.6] Small pebbles possibly coming from the country (7)

This sort of structure has often been referred to as a clue to a clue and this particular example is an indirect anagram. The solver is expected to equate 'coming from the country' with 'English' and then work out an anagram. He may get the right answer from the definition and the checked letters, but to deduce 'English' and then work out an anagram is too much, because there are simply so many interpretations of 'from the country': 'Turkish' and 'bucolic' are just two! And of course any letters already in the diagram cannot easily be fed into the working-out of the subsidiary indication. However, some would find the following clue quite defensible:

[19.7] Concerning what diet might become, it's seasonal (5)

Written by your author for the *Radio Times*, this clue was meant to suggest TIDAL (ie of 'tide', which is an anagram of 'diet'). Since 'diet' can only become two different words ('tide' and 'edit'), perhaps the clue may be deemed fair. [19.7] may perhaps be termed an *indirect definition*.

Here are three more indirect clues sanctioned by *The Times*:

[19.8] Country with its capital in Czechoslovakia (6)

[19.9] Novel sounds as if it will never be read (7,5)

[19.10] Half-hearted robber found in kitchen (7)

The answers are NORWAY (the capital in 'Czechoslovakia' being Oslo); FOREVER AMBER (it will never be 'red'); DRESSER ('robber' becomes 'rober').

Are these fair? Perhaps they are if you consider that they lead to unique solutions. I am not personally very keen on the indirect homophone (eg [19.9]), but it is common, and an unexpected clue type can add spice.

There is no excuse whatever for the following clue if the answer is supposed to be SHINGLE:

[19.11] What English could produce (7)

Here we have no indication of the definition – an *undefined answer*! Nor would there be any excuse if the length indication were (6) and the answer were supposed to be GRAVEL! The inexperienced clue-writer might argue thus: 'English could produce shingle, and gravel means shingle. What's wrong with that?' Let me tell you: (i) there is no definition to the clue, and (ii) the subsidiary indication leads not to the answer but to a clue to the answer. All very unsatisfactory!

Here are two further clues with unsatisfactory definitions:

[19.12] Brief affair with a lassie? (8,5)

The answer is supposed to be HIGHLAND FLING. This would be a clever idea for a subsidiary indication but the true meaning of Highland fling is Scottish dance and the clue presents an *inadequate cryptic definition*. It could be remedied by turning it into a double definition thus:

[19.13] Jock pursuing an illicit affair in a Scottish dance (8,5)

Here's an old chestnut, usually attributed to Torquemada:

[19.14] HIJKLMNO (5)

This clue consists of the sequence H to O. Say 'H to O' and it sounds like 'H_2O', which everyone knows is WATER. This may seem ingenious, but to my mind this *indirect pun* is simply a nonsense. I know that one or two crossword editors have quoted [19.14] as their favourite clue, but I must part company with them.

Sometimes a clue-writer will provide an *inaccurate definition*. One way of doing this is by *false generalization*. A couple of examples will suffice to illustrate this:

[19.15] Month in East for the saint (9)

clearly gives Augustine (August + in + E), but now look at this clue:

[19.16] Dreadful stain produced by Augustine (5)

The intended answer is SAINT, but this won't do because while 'saint' can define a particular saint (ie Augustine), 'Augustine' cannot define 'saint'. Because the saint (who produced this mysterious stain!) might have been Matthew, Mark, Luke or John, we must qualify 'Augustine'. Three common ways of doing this are:

[19.17] Dreadful stain produced by Augustine? (5)

[19.18] Dreadful stain produced by Augustine maybe (5)

[19.19] Dreadful stain produced by Augustine perhaps (5)

Another way of providing an inaccurate definition is by indicating an *incorrect part of speech*, and we saw an example of this in [19.4]. Here is another example:

[19.20] What's hidden by Fred afterwards? He must be stupid! (4)

The S part of this clue is straightforward. The answer is DAFT. But what about the last few words? They suggest a definition that is a noun rather than an adjective – say TWIT or FOOL. A clue-writer will often want to dress up his clue to make sense but won't know how to tie in the D with the S. In difficulty he adds extra words ('He must be'), then tries to convince himself that the clue is really quite good by sticking an *unnecessary exclamation mark* at the end (an additional fault in itself). When you think about it, clue [19.20] is indeed daft. If we must stick with this idea, though, and we want to produce a sound clue we could try this version:

[19.21] What Fred afterwards conceals is stupid (4)

Clearly an adjective must define an adjective, so presumably a noun must define a noun? Well, it's not quite that simple, sorry. Hold tight for the next few clues – we're about to get into deep water.

By convention, it *is* permissible for a noun to be defined by a verb, as in this clue:

[19.22] One party after another is really dead (4)

S D

('do' plus 'do' equals DODO). Here the definition is understood to be '[It] is really dead' with the 'it' understood.

However the clue could be unacceptable to Ximeneans without the 'is' since taking 'It is' on trust is simply too unfair – an adjective cannot define a noun. Similarly unacceptable would be this attempt at a hidden & lit. clue for SIMKIN:

[19.23] Among wines I'm king (6)

An adverbial phrase is being used to define a noun and the clue should be recast to make it acceptable:

[19.24] It is among wines I'm king (6)

This 1981 ruling was given by Azed, the successor to Ximenes, about whom we will hear more anon. What is interesting is that the 1972 Azed had no problem with clues like [19.23] (even awarding one a prize). I warned you about deep water!

It's time to move on, but first please look back to clue [19.20]. It gives evidence of the *redundant word syndrome*. Here is another clue that suffers from the same syndrome, and it is supposed to give the answer DORSET.

[19.25] Strode out to where Hardy lived (6)

S D

The trouble is that 'to' fulfils no syntactical function in the clue. It is not a legitimate linkword between the S and D parts denoting equivalence (such as 'for' or 'in'); it is merely there to make the whole clue read better. A better version is:

[19.26] Strode out where Hardy lived (6)

Before we leave the subject of redundant words, let's take a fresh look at two clues from an earlier section:

[12.3] Good man, a sailor lying on bed, wounded (7)

The answer, remember, is STABBED (ST + AB + bed). Isn't the 'a' redundant? In a sense it is, but by a long-standing convention we may allow ourselves to introduce an article when defining a noun.

[12.4] Old Bob has to study for the exam – buzz off! (5)

SCRAM consists of 's' + 'cram', and here we have defined cram by 'to study' in the way that a dictionary might. In fact the 'to' in the infinitive could be deemed redundant, but convention allows us to use it.

Now to another type of unfair clue. I call this the *overhidden clue*:

[19.27] Idle in the United States of America (4)

This hidden clue to ERIC (he of *Monty Python* fame) can't justify all those extra words where our comedian isn't lurking, so let's make it snappier:

[19.28] Idle in America (4)

If a crossword setter can put too many words in his clue he can also put in too few:

[19.29] Fred in a bad way? A mate is required (6)

An anagram of 'Fred in' suggests itself fairly quickly: FRIEND which means mate. But look carefully. The word 'in' is doing *double duty* as part of the phrase to be anagrammed and the anagram indicator. The clue should really read 'Fred in in a bad way' – it is 'Fred in' that is 'in a bad way', not just Fred. What about the right-hand side of the clue? After all I have said about redundant words, wouldn't 'mate' suffice? Yes – but the extra words can be justified syntactically. The setter is telling you 'You require a word meaning mate,' so the extra words do fulfil a function as a legitimate instruction to the solver. If we want to rewrite the clue soundly let's try this version:

[19.30] Fred in muddle. A mate is required (6)

At first sight this may look like another example of double duty: 'Fred in' in (a) muddle. Or it may look as though we have an unsatisfactory noun as the anagram indicator (see [19.4] above). But this clue can be justified: 'muddle' is an acceptable intransitive verb: the words 'Fred in' muddle, ie they 'potter about', to produce the answer.

Contrast [19.30] with this:

[19.31] Fred in difficulty – a mate is required (6)

A clue-writer might try to argue that 'in' is not doing double duty. The clue is meant to suggest that there is difficulty with the words 'Fred in'. This is not Mr Macmillan's 'little local' difficulty but a 'Fred in' difficulty. A true Ximenean will regard this as stretching the language too far: the clue suffers from the same fault as [19.4].

Here is another way in which an anagram could be improperly indicated:

[19.32] The East has lad striking a bargain (4)

The word 'striking' is the anagram indicator and we are supposedly asked to form an anagram from 'E' and 'lad' to give DEAL. The word 'has' is quite unfairly misleading however. It is true that East is somehow involved with lad in the anagram, but 'has' is grammatically misleading. It's easy to make the clue sound:

[19.33] Eastern lad striking a bargain (4)

[19.34] Lad involved with Eastern bargain (4)

are both possible.

In [19.33] we have treated 'has' as a redundant word; in [19.34] we have integrated the anagram letters with the anagram indicator in a syntactically accurate way.

The unsatisfactory anagram indicator is a particular example of what we might call *word abuse* (for want of a better phrase). Types of word abuse are best illustrated by individual examples.

[19.35] An accomplishment indeed to be beaten (8)

This is supposed to give 'feat' in 'deed' = DEFEATED. Ximeneans say that 'indeed' in a clue does not equal 'in deed' (two separate words). Not all setters agree (alas).

Here are two clues with similar difficulties:

[19.36] Peruse in Gateshead – or somewhere in Berkshire (7)

The intended answer is READING ('read in g'), but Gateshead = G is taking too great a liberty with the language say Ximeneans (even if 'g' is head of the word 'gate'). Let's call this *unacceptable initial indication*. Here is a different form of the same problem:

[19.37] First man to have cut grass (4)

Here 'first man' is supposed to indicate 'm', so that 'm' + 'own' = MOWN, but for a Ximenean this is unsound – 'first man' simply cannot mean 'first letter of man', unlike 'man initially'. But there is another problem with this clue: 'mown' is defined as 'cut grass' whereas it really means 'cut'. This is another example of the redundant word syndrome. This time we have a *redundant object associated with a verb*.

What about this one from a daily newspaper:

[19.38] In chair first, one's getting gold tooth (7)

This is supposed to yield in + c + 1's + or = INCISOR, but can 'chair first' indicate 'c'? I don't think so.

This clue shows another offence against the spirit of Ximenes:

[19.39] Last girl joining German boy for game (5)

This time 'last girl' is supposed to indicate 'L', but grammatically this just doesn't work – 'last girl' cannot mean the 'last letter of girl'.

[19.40] Girl finally joining German boy for game (5)

Not exciting, but an accurate clue giving us 'l' + 'Otto': LOTTO.

Continuing on the theme of word abuse, let's look at the following clue:

[19.41] The cold season now in Bury (5)

This is supposed to suggest INTER ('winter' with no 'w'). The Ximeneans rightly assert that 'now' cannot equal 'no w' in a clue. Notice too that Bury has a capital B which it shouldn't really have. The false capital is a very minor offence (if it is an offence at all), but see how we can overcome the difficulty and the 'now' problem by putting Bury at the beginning of the clue:

[19.42] Bury in the cold season, no hint of warmth (5)

The 'cold season' (winter) with no 'hint of warmth' (w) gives INTER.

The same convention applies to 'hint' and words of that type as applies to 'bit' (see p35). It should indicate only the first letter. Similarly with the tail. Ximenes has an amusing example of an unsound clue where this is not so:

[19.43] There's a horse in the stable with a lion's tail (8)

The answer is STALLION (stall + (l)ion), but as Ximenes says, 'Why should a lion have a tail three times as long as the rest of him?' Middles must be precisely middles, too, says Ximenes, so this would not pass muster:

[19.44] Active learner at heart of Universe (4)

The supposed answer is LIVE (L + (Un)ive(rse)) but the heart of UNIVERSE is 've' or even 'iver', not 'ive'.

The next example is perhaps the most oft-quoted of all clues adjudged unsound by Ximenes:

[19.45] I am in the plot, that's clear (5)

The intended answer is PLAIN ('i' in 'plan'), but 'I' is the letter, not the pronoun. To overcome the deliberate ambiguity we can change the form of the verb and of course we can change 'I' to 'One'. Here are just some of the ways by which [19.45] can be rendered sound:

[19.46]

{ I / One } { will be / must be / can be seen / should be } in the plot, that's clear (5)

Curiously enough, though Ximeneans do not allow the word 'I' to assume a personal status, a word or cluster of words can develop human characteristics:

[19.47] Rescue reviled drunk (7)

The word 'reviled' is 'drunk', ie in a disorderly condition, giving the answer DELIVER. Notice how 'reviled' is an adjective in the surface meaning of the clue and 'drunk' is a noun – but in the actual cryptic reading these parts of speech are reversed. This is a nice example of Afrit's Injunction.

Sometimes a setter will produce a double definition clue using meanings derived from the same dictionary headword:

[19.48] Leave vehicle in enclosed piece of land (4)

gives PARK using verbal and nounal definitions but this is a *spurious double definition* since the clue relies essentially on one word (unlike the clue for the many 'ports' we met on p21). Similarly it would be less than ideal to use 'park' as a partial subsidiary indicator within a clue for 'park-keepers'.

One very common error is that of the *wrong direction*. Consider this clue for example:

[19.49] Dull poet coming back (4)

This is all right for an across clue but not for a down clue. The letters of 'bard' are reversed to form the answer DRAB, but they should go back in an across word and up in a down word. So a better version for a down clue would be:

[19.50] Dull poet turned up (4)

If for some reason a crossword setter had a brilliant clue involving 'up' (and 'back' would not do), he could change the grid by making all the across words down and down words across. A drastic measure, but one which your author has resorted to a few times.

In some crosswords you will find almost any Roman numeral defined by 'many' (L possibly, C, D and M certainly). Thus:

[19.51] Many aged suffering from hypothermia (4)

Here, 'many' is supposed to suggest C (= 100); C + old = COLD. But by what criterion is a hundred equal to 'many'? Ximenes certainly didn't like this practice, and I don't think he would have liked this clue either:

[19.52] Note ancient brave (4)

Here you are presumably invited to take cognizance of a revered figure by his tepee, and B + old = BOLD. But a 'note' could be A, B, C, D, E, F or G (not to mention DO, RE, MI, FA, SO, LA, TI with all their variant spellings!). If notes are plentiful, so too are directions:

[19.53] Direction to have a meal – get a chair (4)

It's quite easy (S + eat = SEAT), but there are lots of directions if you box the compass from N, NE, round to NW. I haven't got a name for what is wrong with these last three clues. Shall we call it the *many/note/direction syndrome*?

Less common these days is a tendency to provide a *partial subsidiary indication*, as in:

[19.54] Can be inside what's mythical (6)

Here 'can be' is supposed to be a definition of 'able' (which it isn't!) and 'able' is found in FABLED, but the 'f' and the 'd' are left unclued – which is unfair. This clue appeared in a national daily in the British Isles in August 2000. Can you believe it?

Next a few words on *punctuation*. You will already have noticed how the D and S parts of a clue can be juxtaposed without any punctuation (as in [19.47]). The Ximenean convention is to allow the omission of punctuation but not to allow inaccurate punctuation. This would amount to word abuse. The presentation of 'Gateshead' for 'gate's head' could be deemed an example of this, but there are other dreadful possibilities usually reserved for the more difficult cryptics with the words 'Punctuation may be misleading' in the preamble.

Watch out for this sort of thing:

[19.55] Stage love-in – Shakespeare setting initially? (6)

'Stage' is the definition for BOARDS (O in bard + s). The addition of the hyphen and the dash undoubtedly helps to make sense of the sequence of words, but this constitutes a case of unfair punctuation in breach of Afrit's Injunction. The clue must be recast to make it sound.

I have left until last the type of clue that is sound but meaningless. It is quite possible to write a clue which is fair under the conditions laid down in this chapter but which is still unsatisfactory.

[19.56] Floor covering fish – and Parisian! (6)

The answer is CARPET (carp + et). Yes, this is fair in terms of its construction, but in what context would this gibberish mean anything – and does the clue-writer hope we will enjoy this nonsense by adding an exclamation mark? The surface meaning makes this a *nonsensical clue*, and it is a type that many crossword clue-writers (especially novices) find difficult to avoid. Clues must make sense, or even semi-sense, but not *non*sense.

Challenges to Ximenean standards

I have dwelt on the matter of fair and unfair clues at some length, and I'd like to think that I've said all that needs to be said. Alas this cannot be so, for two good reasons that apply as much to crossword grammar as to English grammar generally: (i) grammar can never be a fixed prescription in any language and ideas will change; (ii) not everyone agrees with the rules laid down. Most of the principles I have outlined in this chapter would be taken on board by virtually every clue-writer, but not everyone will be bound by all the rules, whether those rules be laid down by Ximenes, Azed or even Don Manley. Here then is an outline of where the main challenges to Ximenean standards lie:

1. *The nounal anagram indicator.* Some would see 'English mixture' (see [19.4]) as an acceptable tatpurusha to denote 'mixture of English'. Expect to find this construction in *The Times*, for instance, where it is regarded as an acceptable grammatical construction. Incidentally Ximenes himself was happy with 'gin cocktail' for ING and 'train crash' for RIANT, on the grounds that these two-word constructions had a meaning in terms of things being involved in a jumbling action, but some have suggested that in making this distinction the great man was guilty of a *categorical error*, since clues have to do with letters being mixed, not objects. More deep water, I'm afraid!
2. *Other anagram indicators.* Although we haven't mentioned it, Ximeneans are happy with 'possibly' as an anagram indicator, but find 'perhaps' and 'maybe' too weak. Expect to find both these words, though, in the papers. There is also disagreement about other individual candidates for anagram indication with a number of marginal candidates such as: 'sort of' (no, say Ximeneans?), 'form of' (yes, say Ximeneans?), 'playful' (Ximeneans perhaps divided!).
3. *Indirect clues.* While the extreme form of a clue to a clue would be shunned by all, some indirect clues, such as [19.8] to [19.10], might be deemed to add a little spice. Even Ximeneans might turn a blind eye.
4. *Definition by part of speech.* In practice many clue-writers would be happy to have 'in India' as a definition written within a clue to BOMBAY even if Ximeneans would prefer 'somewhere in India'.
5. *Gateshead and suchlike.* Expect Gateshead = G. As a Ximenean, I'd be reluctant to give in on this one – but expect to see it. And expect 'many' for 'C' and 'note' for 'te' (the latter perhaps a very minor offence!).
6. *Direction conventions.* Some would argue that clue [19.49] was quite satisfactory for a down clue on the grounds that clues are always written horizontally with verticality being introduced only when a solution is reconfigured on the grid. They have a point, *pace* Ximenes.

Why does crossword grammar matter?

We've spent a long time on crossword grammar and what constitutes a fair or an unfair clue. Does it all matter, you may ask? Well I think it does. To quote the master in *Ximenes on The Art of the Crossword* in his chapter on Cluemanship: '...I believe the principles laid down in this chapter can, if followed, make crosswords more satisfying.' Ximenes was a prescriptive grammarian, and prescriptive grammar hasn't been hugely in fashion these past 30 years. Isn't it the case, though, that the best writers of English have a command of English grammar? That grammar may well not be noticed by the reader, but a grammatically correct work will be more helpful to the reader than an ungrammatical one. Grammar may not be entirely prescriptive and it may not be absolutely rigid, but the best writers know what it's all about and how it can help their readers. The same goes for crossword setters and their solvers.

Ten clues to edit

Here are ten clues from published crosswords but they are far from sound grammatically. Can you take the setter's ideas and turn these into sound clues? If you can, you might have the makings of a crossword setter or even a crossword editor. You can see how I would have edited them by looking at p90.

1. Ate nuts in a way that produced lockjaw (7)
   (Answer: TETANUS)
2. Is that you among the cargo with the cat? (6)
   (Answer: COUGAR)
3. Salvia may be such a help in this way (6)
   (Answer: AVAILS)
4. Please sound like a victim (4)
   (Answer: PRAY)
5. A famous conqueror at the beginning (6)
   (Answer: ATTILA)
6. Ego clue provided by short poem (7)
   (Answer: ECLOGUE)
7. How Henry plays on board with his mother (5)
   (Answer: HALMA)
8. A six-foot long caper, I see (5)
   (Answer: ANTIC)
9. A Dior creation in most homes (5)
   (Answer: RADIO)
10. Bid a run to be used to free locks (7)
    (Answer: UNBRAID)

20 Clues to Savour

Speed isn't everything

Ever since crosswords began, some solvers have delighted in telling others about how quickly they can solve puzzles. Letters to *The Times* told readers that in the 30s Sir Josiah Stamp had solved a puzzle in 50 minutes and that the Provost of Eton managed a puzzle while his egg boiled. In the 70s solvers such as Roy Dean and John Sykes managed to beat the four-minute crossword, and in several competitions over the past three or four decades solvers have sat in examination rooms trying to see if they could solve *The Times* or *The Daily Telegraph* puzzles faster than anyone else.

Speed of solving can be impressive, but one of the delights of solving a puzzle ought to be taking some time to enjoy the clues. Very able solvers can read a clue cryptically and hardly notice the surface meaning. Fast decoding is fine, but sometimes the crossword setter might like you to sit back and enjoy his or her work.

On that principle I've pulled a few crossword books off my shelf and am asking you to enjoy a few of the clues I've found there. These don't have to be 'all-time favourites' (my 'favourite clue' is inevitably the masterpiece I've just written) but I hope you will enjoy them.

Gleanings from my library

> [20.1] Bar of soap (6,6)

This one comes from Rufus (Roger F Squires) of *The Guardian*, and the answer is that well-known *Coronation Street* pub, ROVERS RETURN. Pause a while to ponder on how the bath misled you – and admire!

> [20.2] Burglar jokes with servant (9)

This comes from a *Daily Telegraph* book. Not a very complicated clue and you should be able to see why the answer is CRACKSMAN. But I hope the solver was able to enjoy the mental image of a collusion in the manor house.

> [20.3] Medical expert giving unfortunate tot a grim dose – *litre* to be swallowed! (13)

This is one of mine from an *Independent* Quixote puzzle and I leave you to understand why the answer is DERMATOLOGIST. I also leave you with the image of trying to make a youngster take that amount of medicine.

> [20.4] Climb into apartment with female, interrupted by dad? It won't happen again! (5,2,3,3)

This enchanting picture comes from *The Times Crossword Book 6*. Enjoy this clever clue for FLASH IN THE PAN. Great stuff!

> [20.5] I say nothing (3)

This isn't in my library, but I remember it for its neatness. Enigmatist (John Henderson) of *The Guardian* came up with this beauty for EGO. And that reminds me of another *Guardian* clue from John Halpern, who calls himself Paul:

> [20.6] Play featuring Adam and Eve relaxing at home with their two beautiful children? (7)

Can you imagine an early edition of the magazine *Hello* – an OT *Hello*, in fact? The anachronistic incongruity of this clue for OTHELLO made me laugh when I first saw it.

This *Times* clue is all about two fairy stories:

> [20.7] Pea told about that grew to be noticed by princess in story? (7)

You could decode the anagram into TADPOLE quite easily and pass on to the next clue, but just notice how this clue reminds us of (i) *The Princess and the Pea* by Hans Christian Andersen and (ii) what the kissed frog must have begun life as. It's worthwhile spending a couple of seconds to admire this.

[20.8] ____ ! ____ ____ ! he heard the widow cry, smelling burning (6,3,5)

This clue of Merlin's relies on a pun. Can you imagine ALFRED THE GREAT being asked to pay attention to the grate? A pleasing clue that reminds some of us of an old story we learnt at school.

Araucaria (Revd John Graham) of *The Guardian* is well-known for painting interesting word pictures. This clue for PARALLEL BARS presents a lovely picture of a boozer who can't sit still:

[20.9] Pubs either side of the road will give you exercise (8,4)

An example from *The Times* effectively gives us an answer and asks for the clue:

[20.10] Could be seen as A-level film? (3,5,3)

The film is ALL ABOUT EVE, which could indeed be a construction for 'A-level'. The realization of this is indeed something to make the solver stop and think 'Aha!'.

Finally, enjoy the misleading surface meanings of these two:

[20.11] Corresponding but never meeting (8)

[20.12] My son's or my daughter's invention? (9)

I hope you can work out PARALLEL and NECESSITY.

So there you have it – a dozen clues that I've managed to dig out or remember. As I've said it wouldn't be easy for me to settle on my absolute favourite clues, but a good clue is always worth a second look. Don't just gobble your meal – appreciate the delicate tastes as well!

What makes a good clue?

Here's a checklist for what might help to make a good clue:

1. The clue must be sound in its construction.
2. The clue must have surface meaning (even if it is surrealistic).
3. The definition may be well disguised.
4. The construction as a whole may be well disguised. For example:
   - it may not be easy for the solver to spot the type of clue
   - the join between the subsidiary indication and the definition may be disguised
   - there may be a shift in a word's part of speech between the cryptic construction and the surface meaning
   - the surface meaning may distract the solver
5. There may be a novel element within the subsidiary indication. For example:
   - there may be an unusual indicator – for indicating a charade or hidden word, say
   - there may be an unusual way of indicating individual letters within the subsidiary indication
6. A good clue is often short and pithy.
7. Perhaps the best clues will make the solver laugh.

At this point you may like to analyse some of the many clues in this book and see how they measure up to these criteria – and you may like to look at your own clues, should you decide to write any.

21 Further Guidance to Solvers of Everyday Cryptics

Ten tips for solvers

Here are ten tips for solvers:

1. Don't spend all day on 1 Across! If I am solving a 15 × 15 standard cryptic, I read through the clues in order, spending no more than 15 seconds (roughly) on each and solving where I can. As I start on the down clues I can expect help from checking letters. After this first run-through I concentrate on clues relevant to a particular part of the diagram and follow wherever that leads.
2. Remember that the definition *should* always be at the beginning of the clue or at the end. If you can separate it out easily, the remaining words in the clue may suggest the clue type.
3. Hidden words and anagrams offer beginners the easiest start. Some crossword jargon shouts 'Anagram!'
4. Look out for other crossword jargon. Something 'going around' something may alert you to a container-and-contents clue. The 'worker' may well be an 'ant'.
5. Look out for opportunities to fill in individual letters on the diagram in pencil. The definition of a plural may allow you to fill in an 's'. Similarly you may see opportunities for 'ing', 'ed' and other common endings.
6. Learn to work backwards from the letters already filled in, ie solve *inductively*! Say to yourself 'The answer could be GRAMOPHONE, so will the clue give this answer?
7. Don't be afraid to use a dictionary, especially when you are learning. It is *not* 'cheating'! In addition to a dictionary you may find other reference books helpful, especially a one-volume encyclopedia and an atlas.
8. If you get desperately stuck, have a break. Let your brain tick over on 'automatic pilot' and after a night's sleep the answer may be obvious.
9. If you fail to finish a puzzle, try to learn something by reading the answers.
10. Keep a sense of proportion, and don't let solving crosswords dominate your entire existence!

Reference books

We have already mentioned dictionaries in the chapter about vocabulary. For my money there are two front-runners and I would recommend that you buy both: *The Chambers Dictionary* will give you all the everyday words plus some unusual ones; the *Oxford Dictionary of English* will give you all the everyday words plus a wide range of proper nouns. Sometimes a word or phrase will crop up which is only in *Collins English Dictionary*. By all means buy this as a third dictionary but you may find the absence of any biographical entries a serious handicap in some editions.

It is also useful to have a good world atlas, but one that also gives you extra detail for the UK – you are spoilt for choice. There are lots of crossword reference books, published by Chambers. For everything cryptic the *Crossword Completer*, with words organized by alternate letters, is particularly useful. As mentioned earlier, a copy of Shakespeare may come in handy, and one other useful work is the *Oxford Dictionary of Quotations*.

For more on crossword books see the Appendix at the end of this part of the book.

Electronic help

The Internet provides reference material on virtually every topic, of course, and the existence of Google means that you no longer need a vast library of reference books.

For finding a full word from known letters there are a number of hand-held devices. I still use my Franklin Spellmaster using a database from Collins and there is also a range from Seiko using dictionary material from Oxford and from Franklin using material from Chambers.

Again, there is more on 'electronic help' in the Appendix.

Which newspapers?

All the national dailies have crosswords and all undoubtedly have something to recommend them. However, I shall confine myself to the five 'broadsheet' groups, to all of which I have contributed – not that *The Times*, *The Guardian* and *The Independent* are in broadsheet format any longer. As a group, all these papers provide sound entertaining puzzles (I would have to say that!) but there are often some deviations from Ximenean principles that you will get used to. And all are worth buying for the crossword alone if you find that it suits you. I am saddened by people who say 'That sounds like a really good crossword but I don't take that paper' but am equally cheered to know that the crossword is high on the list of key factors for consumer choice.

I always suggest *The Daily Telegraph* as a starting point – and you can buy lots of their books of puzzles too. Usually one (unattributed) crossword setter occupies one day of the week – on Friday it's my turn. Two Sunday puzzles which are avowedly Ximenean and not all that hard are my Quixote puzzles in *The Independent on Sunday* and the Everyman in *The Observer*. For both puzzles (and for *The Independent*) setters can use their own grids. Like *The Daily Telegraph*, *The Times* does not name its setters, but the crossword editor ensures a fairly uniform style with consistent high standards of clueing; on Saturday there is an additional 23 × 23 jumbo (as well as *The Listener* crossword, of course). *The Independent* names its setters and there you will meet, among others, Virgilius (Brian Greer), Mass (Harold Massingham), Merlin (Richard Palmer), Phi (Paul Henderson) and Nimrod (John Henderson), all of whom have considerable experience with a number of other newspapers. *The Guardian* too has high standards, but styles and levels of difficulty vary significantly from setter to setter. At the easiest end of the spectrum is Rufus – one Roger F Squires, who has set puzzles for the five broadsheet groups and who also holds the world record for the number of puzzles published. For a stiffer challenge try Paul (John Halpern, who also sets slightly easier puzzles for other newspapers).

I contribute to *The Guardian* as Pasquale, but the leading brand name in that paper is Araucaria, a mark for the Revd John Graham, an octogenarian clergyman of the Church of England who was awarded an MBE for his work in crosswords. His thematic puzzles often contain outrageously non-Ximenean clues but they are great fun and he is hugely respected as one of the crossword doyens. Araucaria is found as Cinephile (an anagram of 'Chile pine', which is another name for the araucaria) in the *Financial Times*, where a number of other *Guardian* setters also appear. There are of course many collections of crossword books, so it is not a bad idea to settle down with a selection of these before you decide which one is for you. You might even find yourself liking them all, and buying more than one paper for that long train journey.

Azed and some of his solvers: Chris Brougham and Richard Palmer (far left) watch Azed (centre left) present the Azed Champions' Salver to Don Manley, Colin Dexter and Tim Moorey on a summer's day in Don Manley's garden, 2005.

Two early pioneers: Torquemada (Edward Powys Mathers) and Afrit (Prebendary A F Ritchie). Torquemada is generally regarded as the father of the cryptic clue. Afrit in turn may be thought of as the father of the *fair* cryptic clue.

The two since Torquemada: Ximenes (Derrick Somerset Macnutt) and Azed (Jonathan Crowther). Ximenes developed the idea of the fair clue through his long stay at *The Observer*. His principles have been upheld and developed yet further by his successor Azed.

The Times setters meeting the editor at The Garrick Club in 2005. Left to right at back: Bob Hesketh, Paul Henderson, Dave Crossland, John Grimshaw, Don Manley, Mark Kelmanson, Roger Phillips, John Halpern. Left to right at front: Richard Rogan, Wadham Sutton, Richard Browne (also crossword editor), Robert Thomson (editor of *The Times*), Joyce Cansfield, John Grant, Roy Dean (with his trophy from a solving competition). Allan Scott was absent.

Two stalwarts: Zander/Custos/half of Everyman (the late Alec Robins) and Rufus/Dante/Hodge (Roger Squires). Alec Robins, who worked closely with Ximenes, is here seen holding the Azed cup which he won as L F Leason. Roger Squires has produced more cryptic puzzles than anyone else.

Two setters awarded the MBE: Apex (the late Eric Chalkley) and Araucaria/Cinephile (the Revd John Graham). Apex sought to 'ape X(imenes)' whereas Araucaria has managed to entertain generations of solvers without strict adherence to the Ximenean code.

Advanced Cryptics

22 The Basic Advanced Cryptic Crossword

The transition

We now move to the 'advanced' cryptic crossword. Maybe you can meet all the challenges of the everyday cryptic without too much trouble and are looking for an additional challenge. Or maybe you have got stuck already trying to move from *The Guardian* to Azed of *The Observer*. I hope I can help.

There are generally three features that distinguish the advanced puzzle from the everyday one:

(i) The vocabulary includes lesser-known words

(ii) The clues are generally more difficult

(iii) Barred grids are used rather than blocked grids

We'll look at these three features in turn.

The vocabulary

You should already have *The Chambers Dictionary* for your everyday cryptics. However, it's just possible that you've been managing with the dictionary your grandmother used at school (with the covers now falling off). If that is the case, you really need to buy *Chambers* right now, because it is the basic reference dictionary for virtually every advanced cryptic. I've opened my *Chambers* (2003 edition) at random at p609.

There are lots of words I know: GARISH, GARLIC, GARRET, GARTER and GAS, for instance. But there are lots of words I cannot remember meeting before in over 30 years of solving advanced cryptics: GARJAN (an alternative spelling of GURJUN, an East Indian tree), GARRIGUE (Mediterranean scrub), GARRYOWEN (a rugby kick) and GARUM (a thick sauce prepared from pickled fish, very popular amongst the ancient Romans).

In *Chambers* you will meet a supposed 'cross between a male yak and a common horned cow' with ten different spellings (though some are male only, some female only). If you don't believe me, look under ZHO in the 'big red book' where you will also find: ZO, DSO, DZHO, DZO, ZHOMO, DSOMO, JOMO, ZOBO, ZOBU and DSOBO... You will also come across some ancient words for 'grievous' (DEAR, DEARE, DEERE) and a Scotticism for a hanging clock (WAG-AT-THE-WA'). If you pause to read *Chambers* while solving a puzzle, you may also find some quirky definitions in the best Johnsonian tradition: try ÉCLAIR and MIDDLE-AGED, for example.

As you progress to the barred puzzle you will need to learn the abbreviations in *Chambers*. You will still be meeting MA indicated by 'master', but that abbreviation may also be clued by Morocco, the International Vehicle Registration. Copper may still be Cu, but you had also better know that beryllium has the symbol Be. And so on.

The clues

The clues are harder because they incorporate more obscure words and abbreviations in the subsidiary indications *and* because the constructions themselves are more devious. To give a flavour of what to expect, here are some examples and answers, all from Azed and those who compete in his clue-writing competitions (we shall look at the Azed competition again later):

[22.1] Pour out Jock's shin-bone soup (5)

Answer: SKINK which has two meanings – hence the note reads (2 mngs). 'Skink' is a Scottish word for that form of soup – hence the label 'Jock's'. Jock is a familiar person in Azed.

[22.2] Zinc sulphide to mix with einsteinium (6)

Answer: BLENDE (blend + E). You've been warned about abbreviations. (In fact, einsteinium is now abbreviated as Es.)

This clue was the very first first-prizewinner in an Azed competition and was written by S L Paton in 1972:

[22.3] Before the heart ensnares one, one likes to go on a binge (7)

Answer: ORGIAST (a in or + gist). Note two things: that 'before' = 'or', a rare usage which would be too obscure for the average cryptic, and that 'one' = 'a' (quite justifiable, but in less advanced cryptics 'one' usually means 'I').

[22.4] Campaigner in old company holding steadfast to right (8)

Answer: CRUSADER (sad in crue + r, 'semi & lit.'). This is another Azed first-prizewinner, from M L Perkins. Note the use of 'old' to denote the obsolescence of the word 'crue'. Many words in *Chambers* can be labelled 'obsolete', 'stale', 'traditional' or 'as before'. In this clue also note 'to' meaning 'beside', a useful throwaway in a charade.

[22.5] Gee surrounded by at least four more dashes (6)

Answer: SPANGS (g in spans). 'Gee' is a spelling of the letter 'g' (as well as a suggestion of a horse). Look out for 'el', 'em', 'es' and others!

[22.6] Oily swimmer has success on lake – goodness me, born genius (9)

Answer: GOLOMYNKA for a down clue (go + L + o my! + n + ka). An interesting assemblage of obscure bits and pieces combining to make an obscure word – but 'genius' = 'ka' is soon learnt with experience!

Sometimes the answer describes itself in the first person. This prize-winning clue from C O Butcher uses this convention to achieve an & lit:

[22.7] I form bulges erected on a defence's sides (9)

The answer is GABIONADE (I bag (rev.) + on a d e & lit.).

This *personification* goes back to the Victorian riddle (see p11). This is definitely allowed, even if the personal I cannot be allowed in the plot (see p57)!

Solvers of an Azed puzzle will need to know that familiar words can take on unfamiliar meanings when used as indicators. If you are familiar with the hymn 'There is a green hill far away', you will know that 'without' can mean 'outside' as well as 'lacking'. Here's an example from Ximenes:

[22.8] Rural spot without excitement (8)

giving MOFUSSIL ('fuss' in 'moil'). However, even while I was reading the proofs for this book, Azed expressed a dislike for this archaic usage.

Did you know that 'on' can mean 'getting drunk' and that 'over' can suggest a word being rolled over (ie reversed)? No examples here, but you will meet them soon enough!

From unusual words and unusual usages of usual words to unusual word order. Most of us think and write like this:

I hate most of all the lie that flatters.

But a poet does not always write his or her sentences in the order 'subject/verb/object'. Thus William Cowper:

The lie that flatters I abhor the most.

And thus Will (W J M) Scotland, an Azed prizewinner demonstrating another verbal art form, that of clue-writing:

[22.9] The jungly mass one cleaves? (7)

The answer is MACHETE (anag. in m ace, because in fact 'the jungly' is cleaving 'mass one').

Finally a subtle pair of clues from Azed linked by leader dots:

[22.10] Cunning but timorous if losing head ... (5)

[22.11] ...to these fools, given which they would have heads (5)

[22.10] gives LEERY and [22.11] OAVES. Transfer the L from the answer to the first clue to the second and you would have 'eery' (timorous) and 'loaves' (heads). Clever stuff!

[22.12] Cut away; as W's partner I —— (8)

Here is the missing-letters charade again. The missing phrase is 'am put at E' and the answer is AMPUTATE.

[22.13] Pro-war? A mere child (but no ninny) back I go (11)

The explanation given is picca (rev.) + I + trine. In other words you need to reverse 'piccaninny' without the ninny, then add I, then add trine (= go). The answer is ACCIPITRINE, which means hawk-like (so presumably 'pro-war'). This clue is difficult in the construction and the solution is an obscure word. Quite often in Azed there is a reasonably straightforward clue for a hard word or a hard clue for a straightforward word – but not this time.

This clue recalls a favourite Old Testament story:

[22.14] Eg Jonah with nasty chills a whole lot of fish swallowed (10)

This consists of 'maze' (= mease, a measure of herrings) inside an anagram of 'chills'. The answer is SCHLIMAZEL, an American slang word for a persistently unlucky person.

By now you should be getting the flavour of what to expect.

The barred grid

The tradition of using bars was established in the early days of British crosswords and became the hallmark of Torquemada.

A typical 12 × 12 Azed grid is shown below:

The basic permitted parameters for the 12 × 12 plain puzzle were laid down by Ximenes in his book *On the Art of the Crossword*:

1 Number of unches in a word:

4 and 5 letters, 1 unch

6 and 7 letters, 1 or 2 unches

8 and 9 letters, 2 or 3 unches

10, 11 and 12 letters, 3 or 4 unches

2 Number of words in a barred puzzle: 36, usually with six rows and six columns containing one word and the other twelve two words. Four of the twelve one-word rows and columns will contain your four long words: the other eight will be reduced in length by bars to fit shorter words.

(In recent times however some setters of 12 × 12 puzzles have prided themselves on managing with as few as 32, 28 or even 24 clues.)

Note how the Ximenean formula leads to a tidy, balanced-looking grid with no multiple unches. You can see that there is more checking in a Ximenean grid than in a blocked grid, and this is a distinct asset for the solver. Suppose you are faced with a clue such as this:

[22.15] Vegetable, very black inside – it grows in the tropics (6)

and you have all the crossing words to give you LEB_E_.

By the time you get that far you should be able to work out 'BB' in 'leek' = LEBBEK, but if you cannot you can always look up *Chambers*, find the only word that will fit and work backwards to see how the clue works. With L_B_E_ or _E_B_K it would be significantly harder.

We must now look at some of the more sophisticated clue types common to barred puzzles.

Letter to The Observer, 11 July 1971

XIMENES

'It just won't do,' said the angel crew,
'To go on with our present compilers:
It's getting much harder for Torquemada
And Afrit can no longer beguile us.'

'The judging, too, has gone all askew;
And the lists grow quite absurd;
A crafty sinner was last month's winner,
With God's clue only third.'

'I'm on your side,' St Peter cried,
'I'd hoped for a VHC,
And the last bit of luck for old Habakkuk
Was in 1953.'

So loud and long the heavenly throng
Debated some fresh nominees:
Then with one voice they agreed on a choice –
And sent for Ximenes.

N C Dexter (Oxford)

This letter was published shortly after the death of Ximenes.

23 Special Advanced Crosswords

All the crosswords so far have had normal clues (however complex) and the words have been entered in a normal grid. In a special advanced crossword something is abnormal – either the form of clue or the grid. In extreme cases you may be faced with several forms of abnormality. There are a number of standard special crossword types and beyond that there are the 'special specials'! In this section we shall look at some of the well-known specials. In each case we shall look at the standard rubric which accompanies that type of puzzle and then illustrate it with a tutorial.

Printer's Devilry

This form of puzzle was invented by Afrit. Here is the rubric in its classical Ximenean form:

> Each clue is a passage from which the printer has removed a hidden answer, closing the gap, taking liberties sometimes with punctuation and spacing, but not disturbing the order of the remaining letters. Thus in the sentence *Now that it's so much warmer, can't I let the boiler go out?* MERCANTILE is hidden. The printer might offer as a clue: *Now that – it's so much wart, the boil: ergo, out!* Each passage when complete makes some sort of sense.

The clue Ximenes chose has an extreme case of shifting word breaks along the line. A Printer's Devilry clue with a simple break and no shifting letters is also possible, as in this beautiful example which won Mrs E M Pardo a first prize from Ximenes:

> [23.1] Children taking piano lessons soon learn the sign ff (6)

The break occurs in 'ff' giving the undevilled version '... for a clef', and the answer is therefore ORACLE. In Azed competitions this additional advice is given to PD clue-writers:

> NB: Preference is given to PD clues in which breaks before and after the word omitted (before and after omission) do not occur at the ends or beginnings of words in the clue.

Hints to solvers: Sort out any obvious space shifts. Then try to find the point at which the clue looks strained and insert a pencil stroke. See if you can add new letters to the stranded letters either side of the stroke to produce a word which fits in with the theme of the clue. In the Ximenean example above you should be able to see 'the boiler go out'. In that context a 'wart' doesn't make much sense. By trial and error you might decide to break thus: war/t. In the context of the clue and perhaps with some help from checking letters you should arrive at 'warm' and 'warmer'. Then if all else fails, you can look up the ten-letter MER words in *Chambers Words for Crosswords and Wordgames* and work backwards.

Misprints

Misprints is a form of puzzle invented by Ximenes, and the rubric explains all:

> Half the clues, both across and down, contain a misprint of one letter only in each, occurring always in the definition part of the clue: their answers are to appear in the diagram correctly spelt. The other half, both across and down, are correctly printed: all their answers are to appear in the diagram with a misprint of one letter only in each. No unchecked letter in the diagram is to be misprinted; each twice used letter is to appear as required by the correct form of at least one of the words to which it belongs. All indications such as anagrams, etc, in clues lead to the correct forms of words required, not to the misprinted forms.

The Ximenean rubric does not give an example of a misprinted clue, but we can illustrate from Ximenes himself:

> [23.2] Rummy sort of girl – see the old-fashioned bun (6)

The answer is GINGAL (gin + gal), and the misprinted word is 'bun' which should be 'gun'. It is a curious feature of the misprinted clue that it always makes much better sense than the so-called correct version!

Correctly-printed clues are like any other clue but you need to work out by process of elimination where the misprint occurs in the answer.

Hints to solvers: Fill in unchecked squares in ink, but divide the checked squares diagonally, putting the across letter in pencil in the top corner and the down letter in pencil in the bottom, thus:

When you have settled the priority, work out the implication for the crossing words, inking in where possible. And if two letters agree, use ink straight away. Put a pencil line through each misprint in the clues, and beside the number of each misprint clue mark C (for *clue* misprint). If the misprint is in the grid or diagram, mark D (for *diagram* misprint). Thus a sequence may read as follows (supposing that 'work' is a misprint for 'word'):

> *Down*
>
> C 1 ......work......
>
> D 2 ....
>
> D 3 ....

In each section of clues you will probably be looking for nine Cs and nine Ds. This may help you categorize some of the clues as you tussle with the last one or two.

Playfair

The Playfair code was invented by the famous Victorian scientist Charles Wheatstone (you may remember his electrical bridge for measuring resistance if you took physics at school), but it was his friend Lyon Playfair who publicized it: hence the name. Used by the British army in World War I, this code is rather more difficult than the simple substitution code where one letter is replaced by another. It was Afrit who introduced Playfair codes to crosswords, and this is the now-familiar rubric using the sample code-word favoured by Azed:

> In a Playfair word square the code-word (in which no letter recurs) is followed by the remaining letters of the alphabet, I doing duty for I and J (see below).
>
> O R A N G
> E S T I C
> K B D F H
> L M P Q U
> V W X Y Z
>
> To encode a word split it into pairs of letters, eg CR IT IC AL. Each pair is then seen as forming the opposite corners of a rectangle within the word square, the other two letters [at the corners of the rectangle] being the coded form. Thus CR gives SG (not GS which RC would give). When a pair of letters appears in the same row or column, the coded form is produced from the letters immediately to the right of or below each respectively. For last letters in a row or column, use the first letter of the same row or column. When all pairs are encoded the word is joined up again, thus: SGCICEOP. Answers to clues are to be encoded thus in the diagram. Solvers must deduce the code-word from pairings determinable by cross-checking letters, thus enabling them to complete the diagram.

This rubric nowhere states that the remaining letters are in alphabetical order, but this is always evident from the example. In a typical Playfair puzzle there are four words to be encoded. Often they are of six letters each with two pairs of letters checked for coding and one pair unchecked.

Hints to solvers: The first stage is to solve the Playfair clues – without help from any checked letters! Because of the lack of checking the setter should give you easy clues (eg a hidden word, a simple anagram or a two-part charade all help). For solving these codes Scrabble® tiles can be a great help, enabling you to shift around the letters more quickly than with pencil and paper. The setter should give you some straight line coding and once you can decide whether the straight line is a row or column you are well on the way. Remember always to point your diagonals consistently upwards or downwards rather than sideways (see the note about CR above).

If you come across a sequence such as PQR, you may reasonably assume that it comes horizontally among the remaining letters. This can be a great help.

Letters Latent

Here is the appropriate rubric:

> From the answer to each clue one letter must be omitted whenever it occurs in the word, before entry in the diagram. Definitions in the clues refer to the full unmutilated answers; subsidiary indications refer to mutilated forms to be entered in the diagram. Numbers in brackets show the full lengths of unmutilated words.

Then usually is added something like this:

> The letters omitted, read in the order in which the clues are printed, form an appropriate message/quotation from the *Oxford Dictionary of Quotations*.

Curiously a sample clue is rarely provided, but that is no reason for you to be deprived:

> [23.3] Politicians monkey with society repeatedly (8)

The diagram for this crossword (from Azed) showed that the mutilated form had five letters, so we are looking for a word with three letters the same, all missed out. The subsidiary indication consisting of the last four words gives us 'sai' + S + S = SAISS and since '-ists' looks like a possible ending for a word meaning politicians, we try to find some way of constructing a word with three t's. There is one, STATISTS, so we put a T in the margin to contribute to the message or quotation.

The Common Theme

Perhaps this is the most common of all special puzzles. The rubric simply reads as follows:

> The unclued answers have something in common.

(Sometimes the word 'lights' is used instead of 'answers', but since this word has also been used on occasion for actual letters, I have avoided using it in this book.) If you finish solving all the clues you might be left with a set of unfilled answers as follows:

CAL_IO_E
CLI_
ER_TO
EUT_RP_
_ELP_MENE
PO_YH__NIA
TE_PSI_HOR_
THA_IA
RANI

It should not be difficult to spot that these are the nine muses (Calliope, Clio, Erato, Euterpe, Melpomene, Polyhymnia, Terpsichore, Thalia and Urania).

Theme and Variations

A development of the thematic puzzle is the theme and variations puzzle, for which the rubric is as follows (the numbers may vary):

Four theme words have something in common. Each of them has two variations connected to it, though the nature of the connection differs with each set of variations.

In the puzzle some of the clues read 'Theme word A', 'Variation of A' and so on. To give you some idea of how this works, here is a listing of some answers from an early Azed puzzle:

Theme: Four stomachs of ruminants

Theme word A:	Rumen Variations: Lions, Wasps (RU men)
Theme word B:	Reticulum Variations: Bonnet, King's hood (alternative names, see *Chambers*)
Theme word C:	Bible Variations: Vinegar, Breeches (names of famous Bibles)
Theme word D:	Read Variations: Solve, Study (definitions)

Carte Blanche

With this sort of puzzle you are presented with a blank grid or diagram, usually 12 × 12, and asked to fill in the bars as well as the letters. Instructions are in the form:

> The symmetry of the diagram is such that it would be the same if turned upside down, but not if given a quarter turn. The proportion of checked to unchecked letters is about normal. The clues are in their correct order.

In other words you have a normal Ximenes/Azed grid of 36 clues with the usual conventions on the number of checked letters (see p71).

Hints to solvers: You would be well advised to avoid using the printed grid initially. Start solving the puzzle on a large sheet of squared paper, until you have defined the tops of the grid's two sides. Concentrate very carefully on the first three or four across clues, and a few down answers will suggest themselves. When you are able to fill in a bar, fill in the one symmetrically opposite. Remember the *n*th across clue will be in a symmetrical position with the *n*th counting from the end, but the same is not true of the downs. By the end of the sixth row of the grid there should be space for nine across clues since there are usually 18 in total.

Right and Left

This type of puzzle was invented by Ximenes, who also set several examples under his other pseudonym Tesremos for *The Listener* (for the uninitiated, Tesremos is the reverse of Somerset, Macnutt's middle name). The rubric says all:

> Apart from 1 Across, which is normal, each clue is really two clues, side by side but not overlapping, leading to two answers, one for the numbered space on the left of the central line and one for that on the right: the clue for either side may come first. The division between clues is not necessarily marked by punctuation.

Hints to solvers: It is worth spending several minutes on 1 Across. Quite often it is a straightforward anagram clue and it may be related to the peculiarity of the right-and-left puzzle. Solve as many clues as you can in the upper half of the puzzle and expect the break to be cunningly concealed in many cases. If the worst comes to the worst, arrange clusters of answers together on one side of the central divide and be prepared to transpose the letters across the divide when everything becomes clearer. Alternatively you might consider using a copied grid before working on the printed one.

Definition and Letter-Mixture

In a DLM puzzle each clue consists of a sentence which contains a definition of the answer and a mixture of the letters (beginning with the beginning or ending with the end of a word in the clue) of the required word.

That, more or less, is the normal rubric. A typical clue might read as follows (without the bold, of course!).

> [23.4] I can't sleep **'cos I'm an in**secure sort of person (9)

The first three words here give the definition and 'cosimanin' is a mixture of INSOMNIAC.

Here is a DLM clue where the mixture ends at the end of a word:

> [23.5] Tan**go theme is** rendered by octet (9)

Can you see a mixture of EIGHTSOME working back from the 's'?

Unlike the strictly hidden clues, a certain amount of verbal 'cotton wool' is encouraged to produce an interesting context.

Wrong Number

This, perhaps, is the least common of the standard specials, and it is very hard to start off. Here is the rubric:

> Each clue includes a one-word definition of the word required at the number where it stands but belongs as a whole to a word of the same length elsewhere. Method recommended is to find, after solving a clue, a definition of the solution in one of the other clues to words of its length: this will show where the word is to go.

Here is a set of four clues with answers of the same length from a puzzle by Azed:

> [23.6] 10 Across Insects in cabbage – picker's covering one? (10)
>
> 30 Across After round grimace, show start of husbandly love, iron crumpled vestment (10)
>
> 8 Down Man, what bugs us in a love? Essentially the same (10)
>
> 11 Down Like believer in thrift, aim on nil return in silver, take pounds (10)

The answer to the clue at 10 Across is COLEOPTERA (cole + opter + a), and this is placed at 8 Down, where 'bugs' is the definition. The answer to the clue at 8 Down is HOMOOUSIAN (homo + anag.) which in turn is placed at 11 Down, where 'believer' is the definition. The answer to the clue at 11 Down is AGRONOMIAL (aim on O, rev. in Ag r L), which is placed at 30 Across, 'husbandly' being the definition. The answer to the clue at 30 Across is OMOPHORION (o + mop + h + o + anag.), and the only ten-letter slot left is at 10 Across, which is confirmed by the definition 'covering'.

Hints to solvers: Focus on a set of clues of the same length and look for pairs of synonyms (eg insects/bugs in the example above), but be warned that the synonyms are sometimes well disguised.

Other special gimmicks

Azed, Mephisto in *The Sunday Times* (currently three different setters) and Beelzebub in *The Independent on Sunday* (currently two) offer a regular fare of 12 × 12 advanced cryptics. In addition Azed offers a range of special puzzles, some of which are repeated regularly. Some of these also require solvers to produce special clues. Yet other newspapers in the UK seek to offer a different gimmick each week. All sorts of techniques are used including:

- (i) A different clue type. One of these is the clue with a redundant word, the initial letters of which spell out a message.
- (ii) Entering letters on the grid in a special way (eg anagrammatically).
- (iii) Hiding a message in the grid which needs to be highlighted.
- (iv) Using other movements around the grid (eg movement through a maze or a knight's move) to spell out a message.
- (v) Using a special shape of grid (eg a circle).

The Listener and other advanced cryptics

Some advanced puzzles are extremely difficult and take experienced solvers hours or even days, especially those in the Saturday edition of *The Times* under the banner of '*The Listener* crossword', which is produced by a different setter every week.

The Listener crossword began unpromisingly on 2 April 1930 with a 'musical crossword'. One clue was 'Last three letters of Christian name of a great composer'. The answer (without notes) was IAN – presumably from the Sebastian of J S Bach. Mr I Cresswell of 40 Hamilton Road, Colchester, provided the only correct solution but he didn't get a prize. The first pseudonymous setter appears to have been Doggerel, but the running was soon taken up by Proton (A McIntyre) and Afrit. Before World War II prizes were given to all entrants who submitted a correct solution, but the setters of a pre-Ximenean era confessed in print that they could not always gauge the appropriate level of difficulty.

After the war the puzzle settled down and was solved by a few hundred each week, as were the Ximenes puzzles. On a difficult week, however, entries could still be in double (or even single) figures. In 1991 when *The Listener* folded, the two 'vetters' of the puzzles, John Grimshaw and the late Mike Rich, persuaded *The Times* to take it on, and since then it has thrived more than ever.

Listener solvers are obsessive about trying to achieve 100% solving success since this guarantees them a free place at an annual dinner (there are easier ways of earning a meal, that's for sure!). At the dinner the champion solver receives the Solver Silver Salver (there is a system to ensure a single winner if more than one solver achieves 100%) and those with 100% success can choose the best puzzle of the year and award the Ascot Gold Cup to its setter. 'Ascot' is the pseudonym of Allan Scott, who donated the trophy (not gold and not a cup, incidentally!).

An accomplished solver, setter and magazine editor: Mark Goodliffe displays the Solver Silver Salver at The Listener Setters' Dinner in 2006. As a setter he has the pseudonym Mr Magoo, and he is one of the editors of *The Magpie* (see below and p95).

The Listener is generally the hardest puzzle currently on offer and many solvers only reach it after several years (or decades!) solving easier puzzles. For an easier puzzle on a Saturday the one in the *The Independent*'s Magazine can be recommended, and on a Sunday you can attempt 'Enigmatic Variations' in *The Sunday Telegraph*. Each of these publications can on occasion produce a puzzle to rival the easier *Listener* crosswords. Azed himself produces 'special specials' from time to time, especially at Christmas.

Two subscription magazines that provide these puzzles are *Crossword* for the Crossword Club and *The Magpie* (the latter often attempts to produce puzzles even harder than *The Listener*). Details of these publications are given in the Appendix.

One common complaint against the 'special special' is that it tilts the balance too far against the solver. For example, the checking of letters is often less straightforward, especially if some answers are to be entered anagrammatically. While this can be a justifiable complaint there is no doubt that many enjoy the challenge of a cruciverbal Everest. If, however, you find the blizzards blowing too hard in your face or your mental oxygen running low, there is no disgrace in enjoying the lesser peaks.

24 Azed's Clue-writing School

I learnt my clue-writing in the schools of Ximenes and Azed. It is hard to underestimate the significance of *The Observer's* clue-writing competition. Started in 1945 by Ximenes, it continued until his death in 1971, then resumed under Azed in 1972. Solvers are required to solve the puzzle, then write a cryptic clue for a specified word (usually replacing a definition-only clue in the puzzle itself). Through the competition Ximenes developed the theory of cluemanship from Afrit's basic ideas to a fine art (culminating with the publication of *Ximenes on the Art of the Crossword*). Azed is the pseudonym of Jonathan Crowther, who for many years was also an editor at Oxford University Press. He has carried on where Ximenes left off, and although he takes his name from the reverse of the Spanish inquisitor called Deza he is no more tolerant of latter-day 'heretics'!

Associated with *The Observer's* competition have been annual honours lists and periodic celebrations to salute the setter. As the competition now stands, the submitters of the three clues judged best by Azed are rewarded with book tokens and two honours points; the next 20 or so are labelled VHC (very highly commended) and gain one honours point; and a further 50 or so are deemed HC (highly commended). A cup passes between first-prizewinners and a silver salver between annual champions. Prizewinners and VHCs are listed in *The Observer*, and in a competing year there are 13 competitions (twelve monthly, plus one at Christmas when VHCs are awarded 'extra prizes'). Solvers can subscribe to a newsletter (called the 'slip') detailing successful clues plus a commentary from Azed on the competition, often with details of clues that didn't make it and why they didn't. Would-be clue-writers and crossword setters are heartily advised to study the Azed slip, as it is invaluable for advice on honing one's clue-writing skills. Recently a website has been established for an Azed slip archive: www.andlit.org.uk. This is a fantastic innovation developed by John Tozer, one of Azed's most successful solvers.

Azed champions since 1972–73

The following initials are inscribed on the Azed Champions' Salver:

72–73	NCD, LFL, RJP	90–91	RJH
73–74	CAB, COB, FRP	91–92	DFM
74–75	JRK	92–93	DFM
75–76	FRP	93–94	DFM
76–77	DFM, CJM, WKMS	94–95	CRG
77–78	CJ & RSM	95–96	CJM
78–79	FRP	96–97	CJM
79–80	NCD, DFM, RJP	97–98	CRG
80–81	CJM	98–99	CRG
81–82	DFM	99–00	CRG
82–83	DFM	00–01	CRG
83–84	DFM	01–02	DFM
84–85	RJH	02–03	CRG
85–86	RJH	03–04	DFM
86–87	EJB, NCD	04–05	NCD, DFM, TJM
87–88	MB	05–06	MB
88–89	DFM	06–07	MB
89–90	FRP		

Key (in order of appearance): NC Dexter, LF Leason (=A Robins under pseudonym), RJ Palmer, C Allen Baker, CO Butcher, FR Palmer, JR Kirby, DF Manley, CJ Morse, WKM Slimmings, CJ & RS Morse (father and son), RJ Hooper, EJ Burge, M Barley, CR Gumbrell, TJ Moorey

Setting and Editing

25 Crossword Setting: A Case Study

Where to start?

'How do you go about making up a crossword?', people ask. 'Do you start with the clues or must you fill in the diagram? Where do you get your diagrams from?'

I shall now try to answer these questions. For most daily newspapers I am presented with a choice of grids and having filled them in I write the clues. However, *The Independent on Sunday* allows me to construct my own grids, so here is how I set No. 827.

Using software

Although I still occasionally use pencil and paper (especially for advanced cryptics) I now use a computer to help me with grids and clues. There are two excellent products on the market. One which is particularly good for advanced cryptics is Ross Beresford's Sympathy and the other is Antony Lewis's Crossword Compiler (for details of both see the Appendix). This is the one I used for the puzzle that follows.

Constructing the grid

While I am driving along listening to Radio 3 one day (or was it Classic FM?) I am put in a good mood by the post-storm movement of Beethoven's PASTORAL SYMPHONY. Funny, I think – I've never clued that. A little while later Stravinsky's THE RITE OF SPRING is mentioned. Those two phrases give me my starting point for this particular puzzle. (On another occasion I might have simply picked a phrase out of a dictionary or even seen what 13-lettered phrase I could slot in at a particular place – but not this time.) How I will clue these I have no idea. That can wait.

I decide to begin with the basic 15 × 15 grid with all white squares around the edge.

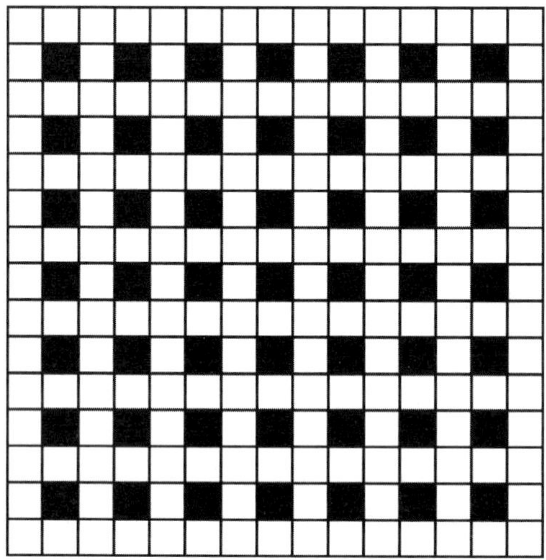

Clearly PASTORAL SYMPHONY is (8,8) so I decide that I will put the first word at the top and the second one symmetrically opposite at the bottom. Then I would like to use that T at the top for my 15-letter phrase THE RITE OF SPRING. That takes me to the diagram opposite.

I put in SHRUG on the bottom line and then decide I would like two long crossing words or phrases. Rows 5 and 11 look promising. I provisionally block out the last square of Row 5 and the first one in Row 11 and use the Autofind facility of the computer.

'Compounds and phrases' finds me COME DOWN TO EARTH, SIMPLE INTEREST and LOLLIPOP LADIES. After filling in LAST LAP in the 9th column and POWERED in the 7th row I decide to use a central black cross and fill in a few more words to arrive at the grid below.

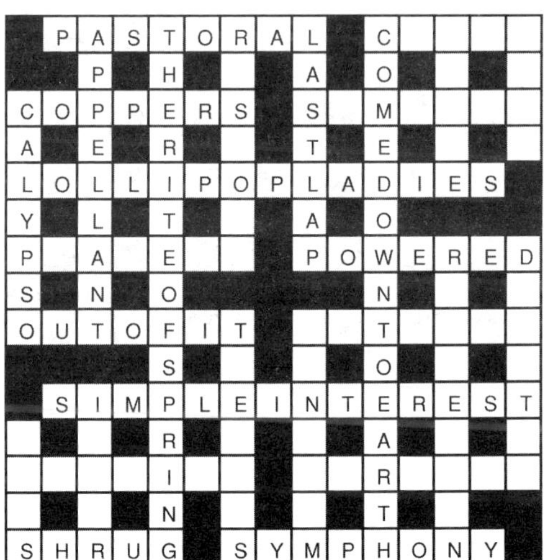

The bottom left corner now fills in nicely with THESEUS, IDLER, SALTIRE and AS IS (I could have used ISIS but I've written a clue for that *so* many times). Now I have three more isolated corners to work on but on using Autofind I discover that the SE corner is awkward – and the NW corner doesn't fill either, so I block out another square and everything fits nicely. I choose RAISE CAIN rather than RHODESIAN at one point.

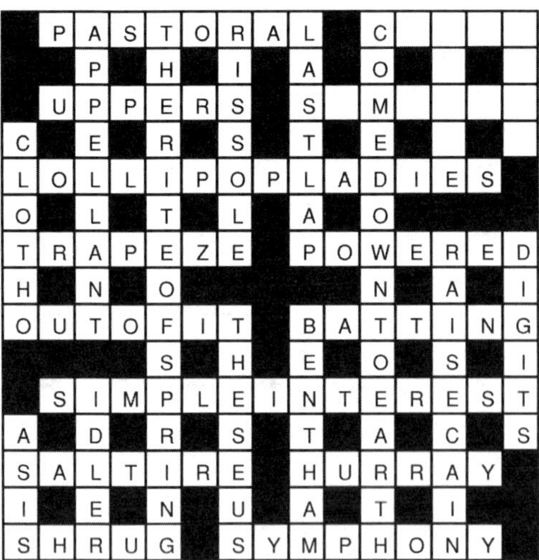

Getting to the final grid is then a doddle.

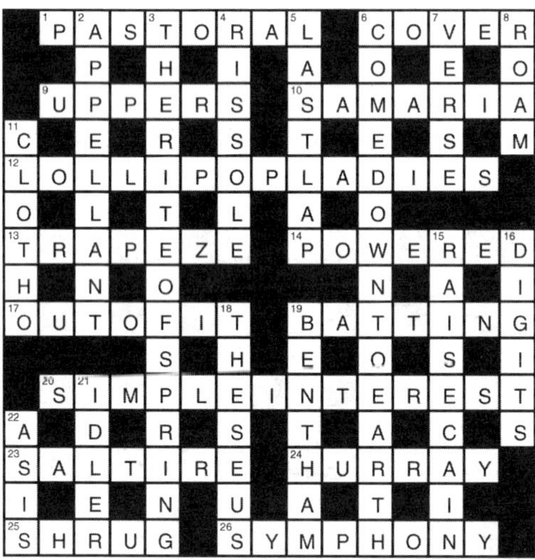

Writing the clues

Now comes the hard bit: writing the clues. Usually I take them in order, but PASTORAL SYMPHONY is a brute. The Anagram facility in Crossword Compiler offers me PROTOPLASM ANY SHY, SPORTSMAN HOY PLY A, and much else that is of no use whatsoever. Never mind – let's crack on with the rest:

6 Across: COVER.

This suggests 'c + over' or 'cove + r'. To disguise the definition I'd use 'insurance' and link it to 'claim': **Insurance claim initially too much**.

9 Across: UPPERS.

Parts of shoes or drugs? The latter, I think and I'll link it to meal times by moving the 's' of 'supper': **Drugs character's taken at end of meal rather than at beginning**.

10 Across: SAMARIA.

Obviously 'Sam' + 'aria', so: **Fellow with song from old biblical region**. Some people don't like using 'fellow' or 'man' for the many different possible names – but it's not unfair, I think.

12 Across: LOLLIPOP LADIES.

Let's go for a fairly obvious double meaning: **Sweet women – they help schoolchildren cross the road**.

13 Across: TRAPEZE.

I've used 'trap' + 'sound of ease' before, so let's go for a cryptic definition: **It makes for some swinging entertainment**.

14 Across: POWERED.

'We're' in 'pod' looks obvious and did you know that a 'pod' is a 'school' (as in a school of whales)? So: **In school you and I are equipped for doing work**. Note how I have written 'in A B' to mean 'in A you will find B'.

17 Across: OUT OF IT.

Lacking Information Technology? Maybe. But 'O' in 'outfit' also screams at me, so here's a clue which maybe suggests social exclusion for a scantily clad young lady: **Dress hiding nothing gets one excluded from participation**. Here 'gets one' serves as a nice link phrase to give us the surface meaning we want.

19 Across: BATTING.

In cricket terms 'in' means 'batting' and the batsman stands between the on side and the off side, so what about this: **In between on and off**. Not too obvious, I hope!

20 Across: SIMPLE INTEREST.

Another gift for a double definition: **Extra money made by modest concern**.

23 Across: SALTIRE.

A sort of cross, this, and we can use the word 'cross' to give a surface meaning about anger, especially since 'ire' is there: **Anger shown by sailor getting cross**.

24 Across: HURRAY.

I mentioned 'without' meaning 'outside' in the context of advanced cryptics, but I confess that I often use it in everyday puzzles. Here I see 'a' in 'hurry', so my clue becomes: **Make haste without a word of encouragement from the crowd**.

25 Across: SHRUG.

We haven't had a hidden lately, and with the British Lions looking past their best I have a tease: **Gesture suggesting uncertainty of belief in British rugby**.

26 Across is the second half of PASTORAL SYMPHONY and I'll carry on ducking it.

At this stage I've had enough of ploughing through clues in order, so I'll pick a few here and there as I fancy, once I've had a coffee break.

21 Down: IDLER.

This breaks up nicely in 'I'd + l + er' and if I define 'er' by 'a little hesitation' (a very common definition) I come up with: **As a lazy person, I had left with little hesitation**.

22 Down: AS IS.

My thesaurus suggests 'unchanged' as a definition so let's put 'one' in 'ass': **Fool, one inwardly unchanged**.

11 Down: CLOTHO.

I've used 'clot + ho' and 'cloth + o' before, my clue database tells me, but there's still 'loth' in 'Co'. Clotho is one of the Fates, so I produce: **Fateful person unwilling to appear in company**.

18 Down: THESEUS.

Another word which splits up nicely (there are several in this puzzle), so 'these + us' can be exploited as: **The people here meeting American hero**.

19 Down: BENTHAM.

'Bent' + 'ham' looks obvious: **Philosopher establishing trend with overacting**.

15 Down: RAISE CAIN.

Cain was the murderous son of Adam and Eve, Abel being his victim. I want to avoid the suggestion that the two in the Garden of Eden had to bring this lad up, an idea I (and doubtless countless other setters) have used, so I'll try: **Get very angry when salary increase is given to murderer**.

8 Down: ROAM.

Sounds like ROME, but if we use 'round' (a round shape) for 'O' we can conjure up an unlikely pastoral scene: **Wander round, hemmed in by sheep**. One sheep in the clue construction, but dozens in the surface meaning.

6 Down: COME DOWN TO EARTH

I can define this in two ways – once literally and once metaphorically: **Land to reconnect with reality**. The surface meaning could suggest that the nation needs reform. How useful that land is both a noun and a verb!

5 Down: LAST LAP

Working backwards at this point I hope to reach my own last lap soon. Time for an anagram I think: **Pat's all excited – it's the end of the race**.

4 Down: RISSOLE.

We haven't reversed anything yet, so let's add the reverse of 'sir' to sole: **Gentleman upset when given only fried food**. (A problem with his cholesterol, maybe?)

2 Down: APPELLANT.

I have to look this one up in the dictionary to find out exactly what it means. It's a legal term and I have some difficulty managing to convey its meaning in a few words. Using a + pp + Ella + NT (National Trust) I come up with: **A very quiet lady with national organisation is someone wanting decision reversed**.

I'm still ducking THE RITE OF SPRING and hoping it will anagram nicely – unusually I have only used one anagram so far.

7 Down: VERSE.

I've used V + Erse before but not quite in this way: **Five at the forefront of Irish poetry**.

16 Down: DIGITS.

This is another one that is hard to define in an interesting way. I put 'It' in 'digs' and hope to deceive with a surface meaning of 'guesses': **Figures Italian will be housed in lodgings**.

Everything has now been given a clue except the two phrases I began with. They prove to be the most intractable.

3 Down: THE RITE OF SPRING.

I use the Find Anagram device, but nothing looks obvious. Using trial and error, I eventually take away the final 'ing' and look at how the rest of the letters break down. After many minutes of effort I come up with: **There's profit possibly in good musical composition** (And in composing rubbish too, did I hear you say?)

1, 26 Across: PASTORAL SYMPHONY.

Anagrams are no good and I can't think of any cryptic definition. I must see if I can split up the different components and then try to make sense of them. What I see is past + orals + my, rev + phony. Even then it's not easy but I think I've got a picture of a nervous student consoling himself in a pre-iPod era the night before finals: **Tense before exams, this person's spinning 'unreal' piece of music**.

So – all done at last, and you can turn over to see how the puzzle looked when it was published on 11 December 2005.

Ninas

Sometimes a crossword setter will incorporate a feature in the completed grid that is completely independent of the clues. This feature is sometimes referred to as a 'nina'. The American artist Al Hirschfield always liked to incorporate the name of his daughter Nina into his sketches. Setters often do something similar to announce a personal landmark. Sometimes a setter will use all the letters of the alphabet in the completed grid to create a pangrammatic puzzle. This too is a type of nina.

By Quixote from *The Independent on Sunday*

ACROSS

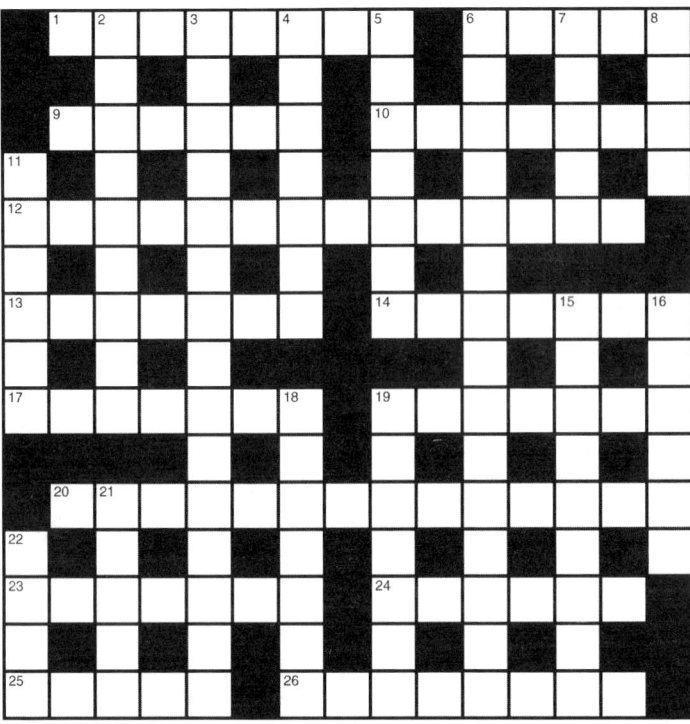

1/26 Tense before exams, this person's spinning 'unreal' piece of music (8,8)
6 Insurance claim initially too much (5)
9 Drugs character's taken at end of meal rather than at beginning (6)
10 Fellow with song from old biblical region (7)
12 Sweet women – they help schoolchildren cross the road (8,6)
13 It makes for some swinging entertainment (7)
14 In school you and I are equipped for doing work (7)
17 Dress hiding nothing gets one excluded from participation (3,2,2)
19 In between on and off (7)
20 Extra money made by modest concern (6,8)
23 Anger shown by sailor getting cross (7)
24 Make haste without a word of encouragement from the crowd (6)
25 Gesture suggesting uncertainty of belief in British rugby (5)
26 See 1

DOWN

2 A very quiet lady with national organisation is someone wanting decision reversed (9)
3 There's profit possibly in good musical composition (3,4,2,6)
4 Gentleman upset when given only fried food (7)
5 Pat's all excited – it's the end of the race (4,3)
6 Land to reconnect with reality (4,4,2,5)
7 Five at the forefront of Irish poetry (5)
8 Wander round, hemmed in by sheep (4)
11 Fateful person unwilling to appear in company (6)
15 Get very angry when salary increase is given to murderer (5,4)
16 Figures Italian will be housed in lodgings (6)
18 The people here meeting American hero (7)
19 Philosopher establishing trend with overacting (7)
21 As a lazy person, I had left with little hesitation (5)
22 Fool, one inwardly unchanged (2,2)

26 Tips for Setters and Editors

The complete setter

The would-be crossword setter has to face two challenges: (i) locating an outlet for puzzles, and (ii) doing a decent job.

I must say a word about (i) first. When I was a teenager setting puzzles for the *Radio Times* I received a letter from the crossword editor of *The Daily Telegraph* returning my puzzle and telling me that 'Fleet Street is not normally reached in one leap'. Quite so. There have been one or two spectacular under-20 crossword setters since then, but on the whole you must work your way up. It is just possible that *The Modern Lady's Weekly* (my invention) may want a puzzle, or the *Agricultural News*, but don't think you can start with *The Times*. That way lies disappointment. Look for openings, local and national, but recognize that you're at the bottom of the ladder. If the only way to get on the ladder is to set a definition puzzle for *The Barchester News*, go for it.

Let's suppose that you're going to set a 15 × 15 puzzle. Perhaps it's for the good folk of Barchester or perhaps it's for your college mag. I suggest that you (like the solver) need ten tips.

Ten tips for setters

1 Get the grid settled first. If you want to devise your own grid, take note of the points I made earlier about grids for 15 × 15 cryptics. As a novice, though, you would do better to use a grid from one of the dailies (but preferably not one of those which has five-letter words with only the second and fourth letters checked). Experienced setters can make up the grids as they go along and choose them to fit the selection of long words and phrases they want to use. This is the ideal situation – something the complete setter should eventually aim for. Ideally your grid should have answers with several different lengths. Words with three letters are not often used but they do provide an opportunity for the eleven-letter answer that is otherwise likely to be forgotten.

2 Keep a good stock of resources, including dictionaries, encyclopedias and reference books. Have access to the Internet, if possible.

3 Be careful about word endings. There aren't many nine-letter words ending in J, so be prepared to start again and don't be stubborn.

4 Use an interesting variety of words and phrases and fill in the long answers first. Avoid words that are boring to define and/or difficult to break up (eg STRENGTHLESS). You will often be forced to have dull words, but there is no need for you to make life difficult for yourself. Make sure that any phrase used is standard, ie either in the dictionary, in common parlance or well known as a title. YELLOW SHIRT is not acceptable, but YELLOW FEVER is. YELLOW SUBMARINE wouldn't have been acceptable before it became a Beatles hit, but it could be appropriate in some crosswords (if the crossword editor allows song titles).

5 If you are setting for a periodical and dealing with a crossword editor, you must know what he or she does and doesn't allow on the grid. Several dailies will not allow the names of living people on the grid, for instance, and *The Times* doesn't like names of products or 'words with unpleasant or non-drawing-room associations (eg leprosy, semen, carcinoma, incontinent)'. For a 15 × 15 puzzle you will want your *Chambers*, but also use the *Oxford Dictionary of English* (or the *Concise Oxford Dictionary*) to check that you have an 'everyday' word if in doubt.

6 As you write in your words and phrases, log up a few ideas on how you will clue them later on. If you have ten words that can only be clued by anagrams, you could be in trouble. For the sake of variety you will only want about half a dozen anagrams at most.

7 When you write your clues, put into effect all the principles outlined in the *Manual*. Ask yourself these questions for each clue:

Is the definition fair?
(Could I substitute the answer for the definition in a sentence?)

Is the subsidiary indication fair?
Can all the words in the clue be justified?
(What about the linkword(s)?)

Does the clue as a whole make some sort of sense or is it only a zany mixture of subject, verb and object?
Am I trying to be too clever?
(Err on the side of simplicity, and don't write a 'clue to a clue'.)

8 Check your crossword carefully and get it checked by others if possible. If you know someone else who is a 15 × 15 solver, ask that friend to try and solve the puzzle. When you check your puzzle, check one thing at a time – the clue numbers, the clues, the numbers in brackets. You can easily make mistakes by trying to check everything at once.

9 If you are having your crossword published by a crossword editor, try to establish a dialogue if possible. The editor may be able to help you, but (if you've read this *Manual* carefully) you might even be able to help the editor. If an editor doesn't like your clue, do not allow him or her to inflict a non-Ximenean alternative if you can help it. Instead suggest a new clue yourself. You may want to ask to see proofs.

10 If you publish crosswords regularly, you may get much less reaction than you had hoped for. Solvers often overlook mistakes, so don't get too many hang-ups about them. They are much more likely to complain that a puzzle is too hard. It's one thing to set a really hard 'advanced' puzzle, another to set a 15 × 15 standard. You don't want your puzzles to be a push-over, but in the contest between setter and solver you must expect to lose graciously.

It is just possible that some readers of this *Manual* will want to go on to set advanced puzzles. If you do set advanced puzzles for a periodical, you will almost certainly be able to choose your own grid and you will have the freedom to shift bars around to get the words to fit – this can be a great help. If you move on to advanced specials, you will need to have lots of original ideas or gimmicks. You will have the opportunity to construct imaginative new grids with letters entered in fanciful new ways, and you may even invent your own type of clue. Not many of you may get that far, but specialist publications such as that of the Crossword Club will take puzzles from all comers solely on merit – and *The Listener* puzzle in *The Times* is still open to all. There will always be room for new talent.

The crossword editor

Not many readers, I guess, will become crossword editors, but a few at least will become crossword setters who have to deal with editors, so it may be useful to reflect on the editor's role. The job of the editor is twofold:

(i) to ensure that a fair and accurate puzzle appears in print;

(ii) to keep everyone happy (as far as possible).

To take point (ii) first. There are, of course, the solvers to be kept happy. Inevitably some will from time to time complain about a puzzle being too easy or too hard, so it is a matter of keeping most of the solvers happy for most of the time. But it is also a matter of keeping the setters happy too. As an editor one may well need to rewrite clues, but one needs to be sensitive to the feelings of the setter. As in all areas of publishing (and this is something I have learnt in the day job!) authors and editors need to establish mutual respect. So let's have ten tips for crossword editors, shall we?

Ten tips for editors

1 Establish ground rules with your setters about your channels of communication. How would you like your puzzles submitted? Do you want the setters to provide notes? Do you want submissions by e-mail? Will you send proofs? And so on.

2 Establish ground rules with your setters about matters of style by providing written notes. You may wish to give guidance about such matters as which dictionaries to use, and you may wish to discourage certain practices. Many crossword editors now recommend *Chambers Crossword Manual* rather than attempting to write their own book about types of clue, etc!

3 Establish an understanding about 'ownership' of the final puzzle. Will you wish to rewrite clues or ask the setter to? Will you want to put your rewritten clues in print under the setter's name or pseudonym and will the setter be happy if you do? Do you want a protracted dialogue with your setters, or is time so short that you have to impose 'the editor's decision is final' at a fairly early stage?

4 Look after your setters by representing them to the periodical for which you are working. This may mean asking for a pay rise for them or making sure that they receive a free copy. One essential requirement is that you have the courtesy to tell your setters when their puzzles will appear.

5 When you receive a puzzle you can do one of two things: either (i) try to solve it on a blank grid (something you should always ask for by the way) or (ii) check out the clues against the solution. Option (i) is the ideal but you may find yourself wasting time if the setter is new and unreliable. A quick inspection using option (ii) can often (alas!) lead to a rejection with minimal time loss.

6 Even if you go for option (i) above, you should check out the puzzle using option (ii) subsequently. Before you look at the clues look at the grid. If it offends you, you must decide whether it is redeemable or not and who is to do any redeeming – you or the setter.

7 After looking at the grid look at the words on the grid. Again, face the redemption issue. You may decide, for example, that a crossing of a junction at the N of TENOR and NO HAIR can be redeemed by changing NO HAIR to MOHAIR and TENOR to TIMER. (And, yes, I have seen NO HAIR as a phrase in a puzzle!)

8 Faced with a clue you have three options: (i) leave it, (ii) amend it slightly, or (iii) rewrite it. If a clue is sound and sensible (and hasn't appeared recently), you are best to leave it (option (i)) unless you can think of a small amendment which will add a touch of gloss (option (ii)); you may prefer someone to 'shelter' in a tent, for example, rather than to 'be located' in a tent. Only make the change if (a) it adds finesse or (b) it renders an unsound clue sound. Go for option (iii) if the clue is grossly unsound or doesn't make sense. Try to avoid substituting your own clue just because you think it's better than the perfectly adequate one submitted – save that for your own puzzles.

9 When you have been through the whole puzzle, look at the clues as a whole. Are there more anagrams than you would like and if so might you want to replace some of the clues? Do you really want right = R to be used *three* times? And so on.

10 Know your solvers. Know your setters. Know the editor of the periodical you are working for. Talk to them. Meet them. Be nice to them.

A crossword editor with vast experience: Barbara Hall of *The Sunday Times* has been setting cryptic crosswords since 1938. She has also been a crossword editor for over 30 years.

If you accepted my earlier challenge, you will have been a crossword editor already. Now you can see how I edited those clues. How did you get on?

Ten clues edited

On p60 I challenged you to edit ten clues. How did you get on? Here is how I would have dealt with them.

1 The clue would be sounder with 'that produced' changed to 'that's produced' or 'that produces'. Even then it makes little sense and 'lockjaw' is a *giveaway definition*. To preserve the idea behind the clue the editor might change this to: Eat nuts? From such one might get disease (7)

2 There's a lot wrong with this clue: for starters, 'you' does not equal 'u', nor is there an anagram indicator. To preserve the cat and the cargo I would suggest: Cat you finally found hiding in cargo – naughty! (6)

3 Here the definition suggests a noun (some sort of help) rather than a verb. How can 'salvia' be linked to 'avails'? Perhaps through some idea of an aromatherapeutic preparation, so let's try: Preparation of salvia is effectual (6)

4 When I attempted this clue I didn't know whether to put in PRAY or PREY. And is the definition accurate anyway? I don't think so. Let's try this: Victim is heard to make supplication (4)

5 This is an example of a *partial subsidiary indication*. It's all very well to indicate the 'at' bit of ATTILA but what about the rest of the clue? Perhaps the clue should be rewritten, but let's try to preserve the 'at' with: Invader at front of tower – one starts to look anxious (6)

6 Is 'provided by' strong enough as an anagram indicator? I'm not convinced – and I'm not convinced by the sense of the clue either. But perhaps this edited version is *slightly* more plausible: Damaged ego – clue provided by short poem (6)

7 Try doing an S/D analysis on this one! The definition is sandwiched between bits of subsidiary indication and the 'How' at the front is supposed to make the clue more readable and the definition stronger. I think the author intended Hal + ma, rather than H + Alma (my mother's name!), so let's try: Henry faces mother in a board game (5)

8 An 'ant' is sometimes a 'six-footer' but again the definition has been sandwiched in the middle. Also note that 'see' and 'C' is a bit advanced for a daily paper (in which this clue was found). Let's try: Six-footer, one about to join in caper (5)

9 You know my views on nounal anagram indicators, but I am sure many crossword editors would let this through because soundness will inevitably increase inelegance – and after all, we've all clued RADIO (and RODEO!) every possible way, haven't we? Well, let's preserve 'Dior' at any rate with this: Special creation of Dior includes a device that has people talking (5)

10 I'm not at all sure what this clue means, but apart from that it is also victim of the *unwanted-object-of-the-verb syndrome*. 'To unbraid' means 'to separate the strands of' according to my *Webster*, the only one of my non-OED dictionaries to include the word. So 'to free locks' is 'to unbraid locks', not simply 'to unbraid'. 'Locks' is the 'unwanted object'. It's a marginal word, but let's say we allow it. Let's try: Free from entanglement – bird Una released (7)

Not a brilliant clue, but notice how useful 'free' is here as a word that is a verb in the definition but appears to be an adjective in the overall context of the clue. 'Multi-part-of-speech' words are extraordinarily useful, as are words like 'put' and 'set' which retain the same form in the past tense and as past participles. Some things I must leave you to discover!

Solutions

27 Solutions

DON LEMON'S PUZZLE 6

Caleb Plummer; Betsey Trotwood; David Copperfield; Sairey Gamp; Nicholas Nickleby; Tilly Slowboy; Nancy Sykes; Sam Weller; Florence Dombey; Dick Swiveller; Oliver Twist; Barnaby Rudge

(But I have my doubts about 'Sykes')

DON LEMON'S PUZZLE 420

'Crippled' would have been a better clue for 1, although some today may find the word itself unacceptable.

DON LEMON'S PUZZLE 541

COWSLIP

DON LEMON'S PUZZLE 200

T O S S
R A I N B O W
A R M A D I L L O
D R U M M E R
E R R A N D
W I C K
I N F L A M M A T I O N
N E G R O
D E B T

ARTHUR WYNNE'S *NEW YORK WORLD* CROSSWORD

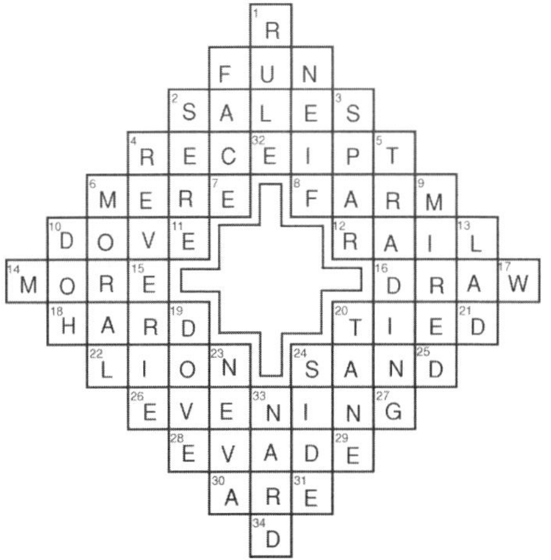

Not too demanding, but 9-25 shows the first error in the first crossword. Why wasn't the clue 'Sunk in mud'?

THE CROSS WORD PUZZLE BOOK FIRST SERIES

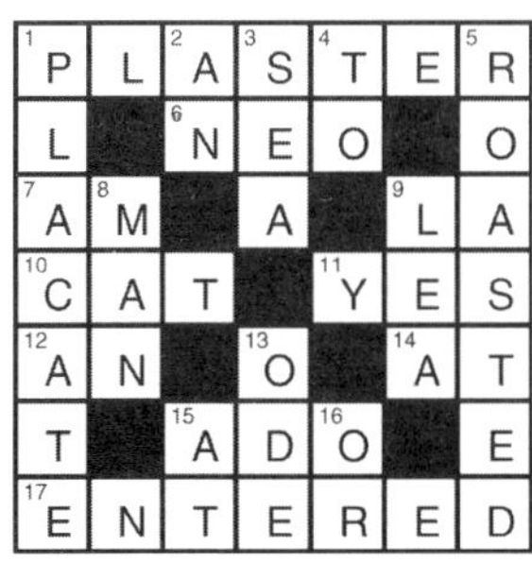

Did *you* use a pencil?!

Appendix

Crossword Resources

Books on crossword theory and history

Chambers Crossword Manual is the successor to three significant books (all out of print except for the Ximenes book which was reissued in 2001):

> *Armchair Crosswords* by Afrit (Warne, 1949) – the preface is short and the most significant section is reproduced in this *Manual* section on p52
>
> *Ximenes on the Art of the Crossword* by D S Macnutt (Methuen, 1966; reissued in 2001 by Swallowtail Books, 3 Danesbrook, Claverley, Shropshire WV5 7BB)
>
> *Crosswords* by Alec Robins (Teach Yourself Books, Hodder and Stoughton, 1975), subsequently revised as *The ABC of Crosswords* (Corgi, 1981)

For a very good introduction to American cryptics try:

> *Random House Guide to Cryptic Crosswords* by Emily Cox and Henry Rathvon (Random House, 2003)

A number of books have been written that are linked to specific newspapers. Among these are:

> *How to do The Times Crossword* by Brian Greer (Times Books, 2001)
>
> *How to Crack the Cryptic Crossword* by Val Gilbert (Pan Books, 2001)
>
> *The Daily Telegraph: 80 Years of Cryptic Crosswords* by Val Gilbert (Macmillan, 2004)
>
> *75 Years of The Times Crossword* (with a foreword by Colin Dexter) (Times Books, 2005)
>
> *Secrets of the Setters: How to Solve the Guardian Crossword* by Hugh Stephenson (Guardian Books, 2005)

Two out-of-print crossword history books are:

> *The Strange World of the Crossword* by Roger Millington (Hobbs/Joseph, 1974)
>
> *A History of the Crossword Puzzle* by Michelle Arnot (Random House, 1981; Macmillan Papermac, 1982)

One book in a category of its own (also out of print, alas) is:

> *Lost for Words* by Jon Riley and Ozymandias (the latter being Jonathan Crowther, Azed) (Angus and Robertson, 1988)

For books that lift the lid on the personalities of crossword setters (including your author) try:

> *Pretty Girl in Crimson Rose (8): A Memoir of Love, Exile and Crosswords* by Sandy Balfour (Atlantic Books, 2004)

and:

> *A–Z of Crosswords* by Jonathan Crowther (Collins, 2006)

For an insight into the minds of American setters I can recommend:

> *The Crossword Obsession* by Coral Amende (Berkley Books, 2001)

Dictionaries

I've already mentioned the main 'English English' dictionaries on p63.

For American words and spellings I use Webster's *Third International Dictionary*. And for the ultimate English dictionary I recommend the *Oxford English Dictionary* online, which you may be able to obtain via your local library.

If you are visiting a public library looking for old proper nouns keep an eye open for *The New Century Cyclopedia of Names,* a three-volume masterpiece dating from over a hundred years ago – it is wonderful!

Thesauruses

Two very good thesauruses are:

The Chambers Thesaurus (Chambers, 2004)

The New Oxford Thesaurus of English (OUP, 2000)

Both contain useful lists as well as synonyms and antonyms.

Other information books

There are many good books of quotations, but the one referred to by crossword setters is *The Oxford Dictionary of Quotations*. Another book much used by setters of crossword puzzles is *Brewer's Dictionary of Phrase and Fable*. For solvers of advanced cryptics these are both 'musts'.

For a single-volume encyclopedia, I have *The Cambridge Encylopedia* but there are a number of other titles on the market. You are spoilt for choice with atlases. One which will not be too expensive is *The Times Concise Atlas*.

After that you may want a *Cruden's Concordance* and of course the Bible itself. A few specialist reference books on history, literature, music and even pop music can be useful. And you'll want a complete Shakespeare too maybe.

Other crossword 'cribs': books and electronic devices

For lists of words organized in particular ways, Chambers offers a whole range of books, including:

Anagrams (alphabetically arranged anagrams of words)

Words for Crosswords and Wordgames (listings by number of letters and then alphabetically)

XWD: A Dictionary of Crossword Abbreviations (abbreviations, symbols and codes used as building blocks in cryptic crosswords)

There are also several hand-held electronic devices that can help you find all the possibilities for (say) ??A?E?T and some useful synonyms. Among these are the Seiko/Oxford Desktop Crossword Solver, the Sharp Electronic Dictionary (which also uses Oxford reference books) and the Franklin Chambers Crossword Dictionary. Products such as these are frequently advertised in newspapers and displayed in office supply shops.

Periodicals

You will, of course, have your daily and Sunday papers in your 'library' (by the way be careful lest your whole house becomes one extended crossword library – it can happen!). You will know by now what papers you might buy to have a go at the cryptic puzzle. If you are a new cryptic solver, I suggest you start with *The Daily Telegraph* (as I've already said). If you want to get in a lot of practice at a relatively low cost, you can buy lots of books of crosswords. The range is always changing and there are too many different ones to mention here. For rude and cheeky clues try *Private Eye*. Clues from that periodical have often featured as 'clue of the week' in a news magazine called *The Week*.

For a club magazine (*Crossword*) which will take you into advanced cryptics I suggest you seriously consider joining *The Crossword Club* (at Coombe Farm, Awbridge, Romsey, Hants SO51 0HF). For 15 × 15 specials (many by Araucaria) try *1 Across* (write to Christine Jones, The Old Chapel, Middleton Tyas, Richmond, North Yorks DL10 6QX).

For those who want crosswords as hard as *The Listener* puzzle or even harder (and can't get enough of them) there is a subscription magazine called *The Magpie*. Details are available from *The Magpie*, Court Lodge, 3 Layhams Road, West Wickham, Kent BR4 9HJ.

Crossword puzzles on the Internet

When I last put 'crossword' into Google I discovered that there were 48,000,000 sites. As it happened, the first one of these is www.crossword-puzzles.co.uk and it gives links to many other useful sites, including several subscription sites for daily newspapers. Among these I recommend:

The Times Crossword Club at www.timesonline.co.uk/crossword

This offers a vast array of puzzles (including *The Listener* crossword), a monthly clue-writing competition and a bulletin board for comments.

Guardian Unlimited Crosswords at www.guardian.co.uk/crossword

This covers all the latest *Observer* crosswords (including Azed) as well as *Guardian* puzzles. There is a monthly article by the crossword editor. The crossword talk threads are not for the faint-hearted.

Enigmatist at www.enigmatist.com

A number of *Guardian* setters also appear on this website managed by the setter John Henderson, also known as Enigmatist.

Telegraph Crossword Society at www.telegraph.co.uk

This covers puzzles for *The Daily Telegraph* and *The Sunday Telegraph* (including Enigmatic Variations). There are also 'tips and pointers' among the other features.

For those who want to progress to advanced cryptics there is a free site run by Derek Harrison at the Crossword Centre. Go to www.crossword.org.uk. There are many crosswords and competitions. The message board tends to focus largely on solvers' experience with *The Listener* crossword.

I also like a site run by Peter Biddlecombe, *The Times* crossword champion in 2000. Entitled Peter's Cryptic Crossword Corner, you'll find it at www.biddlecombe.demon.co.uk/puzzles.html.

Two new blogs for solvers are 'Times for *The Times*' and 'Fifteensquared'. Links to both can be found on Peter Biddlecombe's website.

Crossword setting via the computer

As mentioned on p80, there are two particularly good products on the market for crossword setters. One is Sympathy, along with its TEA Crossword Helper (TEA being The Electronic Alveary). This has been devised by Ross Beresford and details may be found on his website at www.crosswordman.com. The other product, devised by Antony Lewis, is called Crossword Compiler and the website for this is www.crossword-compiler.com.

Two devisers of impressive crossword software: Ross Beresford and Antony Lewis

Crossword solving via the computer

Using a computer to set a puzzle is one thing; using it to solve clues is surely another! A very bold attempt, however, has been made by William Tunstall-Pedoe with his Crossword Maestro (available from PO Box 395, Cambridge CB3 9PJ and featured at www.genius2000.com). One keys in a puzzle and tries out the clues, with varying degrees of success. I tried out a crossword. After a few outright failures it solved 5 across correctly as HAZARD with a confidence level of 95% and told me that 'az' placed inside 'hard' is 'hazard'. I wasn't convinced with the 31% confidence level for a clue for PAPER TOWELLING at 13 across, but a nice straightforward clue at 17 down gave GRANDEE with a 99% confidence level. As letters were filled in, the suggestions became better but the puzzle needed a human brain for completion. The program is excellent on simple clues, though, and could be recommended to beginners as a way of trying to understand some of the basics. Crossword Maestro is great fun and an impressive achievement.

Solvers of difficult puzzles have also been known to subject unfinished grids to Sympathy and see what words might fit.

If you simply wish to find as many possibilities as you can for ??A?E?T you could try the CD ROM version of *The Chambers Dictionary and Thesaurus,* visit the One Look Dictionary Search website at www.onelook.com or use the 'Word Wizard' feature on the Chambers website at www.chambers.co.uk.

Finally, something to write with ...

If you solve crosswords online, you won't need a pen or a pencil of course, but for now there will be quite a few of you sitting in an armchair writing on old-fashioned paper. A pencil *with an eraser* is most useful! Otherwise I use a biro. The one implement I never use is a fountain pen – because it smudges! Should you win that fountain pen when your crossword comes 'out of the hat' I suggest you save it for those thank you letters to auntie.

So you've got your crossword, your books, your electronic gadgets and maybe your computer – and now your pen and pencil. Off you go!

Postscript

The *Inspector Morse* author Colin Dexter is a renowned clue-writer and set crosswords for *The Oxford Times* for many years. In *The Wench is Dead* he attributed a clue to me, as Quixote of *The Oxford Times*, although it was in fact his own. Here it is:

Bradman's famous duck (6)

The answer is of course DONALD, referring to Sir Donald Bradman (the cricketer) and the famous Donald Duck.

The clue is of course extremely elegant, but it is also a brilliant one because of its context. In his last test innings at The Oval in 1948 (as all cricket lovers will know) Bradman scored a duck when he only needed four runs to finish with a test match batting average of 100.

Oh that I *had* written it!

Clues such as this provide us all with magic moments.

Crossword Dictionary

How to Use the Crossword Dictionary

The Crossword Dictionary section of this book contains more than 500,000 possible solutions to quick and cryptic crossword clues. It draws on *The Chambers Dictionary, The Chambers Thesaurus* and other books in the Chambers reference range; it also uses the Chambers crossword clue database.

It does not contain definitions, parts of speech, usage labels or similar material. To check the exact meaning of a word or phrase, a dictionary such as *The Chambers Dictionary* is recommended.

Content

Entries in the Crossword Dictionary section include both single words and phrases. Also included are abbreviations, short forms, acronyms, symbols, codes and the like, for the answers to crossword clues are often built up from these small pieces. Solvers will also find crossword jargon, such as 'tar' under 'sailor' and 'goat' under 'butter'. Anagrams, however, have not been included; so, for example, an entry for 'rotten time' would not list 'emit'.

Consideration has been given to the differing needs of various kinds of crosswords, from concise to advanced cryptics, and nothing has been excluded simply on the grounds of obscurity. Archaic, dialect, literary and uncommon words have been included, as these are often found in a variety of crosswords, not just (although undoubtedly most frequently) in advanced cryptics such as Azed in *The Observer* and *The Listener* in *The Times*. An emphasis has been placed on unusual short words with helpful letter sequences – for example 'tana' under 'police station' – as these often form the 'building blocks' which make up a cryptic solution. Variant spellings listed in *The Chambers Dictionary* have often been included. Where a usage is dubious but technically possible, as with an archaic variant of a synonym where it is unclear whether the variant is also synonymous with the headword, a degree of leniency has been employed.

The content of the Crossword Dictionary section is broadly international in scope, with words from British regional dialects, Scots, Australian, New Zealand, North American, Anglo-Indian and other varieties of English included. Some common short foreign words sometimes found in crosswords are included too, such as 'mer' under 'sea' or 'ici' under 'here'.

Synonyms which are only loosely associated with the headword have not been included (for example 'twelfth' will not be found at 'grouse'). However, some names are included, as crossword convention allows references to people by first name or surname; for example 'Berlin' with the synonym 'Irving', 'Lincoln' for 'Abe' or 'Milne' for 'AA'. While a smattering of those most commonly found have been included, the list is not exhaustive and there will be others.

There is debate in crossword circles over what constitutes a 'sound' clue, and some crossword setters and editors do not employ particular uses of words or senses which others consider to be permissible. So as to be of maximum use to solvers of crosswords from a variety of sources, terms have been included here even if frowned upon by some. However, some usages considered to be especially contentious (usually as a result of word spacing and grammatical links having been ignored) have not been included, such as 'G' for 'Gateshead', 'm' for 'topmast' or 'fats' for 'breakfast'.

No attempt has been made to ensure that entries are 'symmetrical', ie that a synonym found under one headword (for example 'lucky') will also be found under another broadly synonymous entry (for example 'fortunate'). Since it is impossible to anticipate every reference a clue-writer will come up with, there are bound to be gaps. This deficiency can be mitigated by searching under different headwords, and there may be hints to be picked up from what is given. For example, the entry for 'swimmer' lists 'fish' as a synonym, which suggests that looking at the main entry for 'fish' may be helpful; here the intended solution, say 'eel', may be found.

Plural and inflected forms of words have generally not been given. Solvers should remember that if the wording of a cryptic clue suggests that a plural or verb form is required, they may need to pluralize or otherwise inflect a possible solution found in this Dictionary section. Some abbreviations listed in the Dictionary section stand for both singular and plural forms of a word (for example 'kg' can be kilogram or kilograms). For parts of cryptic solutions, plural and other forms may not be straightforward; for example, where 'duck' can conventionally be 'O', then 'ducks' in a clue may indicate 'Os' or 'OO'. This may also be encountered with the reference list of collective nouns, as setters may use 'crows', for example, for 'murder'.

This is also true for comparatives and superlatives; if a clue says 'more' or 'most', for example, it may be that an -er or -est ending needs to be added (for example 'more sensible' for 'saner' or 'most stupid' for 'dopiest'). Similarly, solvers should bear in mind that 'not' may be used in a clue to indicate the prefix 'un-' (for example 'not hidden' for 'unconcealed'), that 'again' may be used for the prefix 're-' (for example 'publish again' for 'reissue'), and so on.

Numbers, and terms which include both numbers and letters, have been included in many instances as some – although not all – setters and editors allow the number 1 to be converted to the letter I (as in the Roman numeral). Thus, 'M1' may be rendered as part of a solution as 'MI', and '1st' as 'IST'.

Word forms

The forms -ize and -ization are used throughout, but the alternative -ise or -isation spellings may be needed for the solutions to some crossword clues.

Similarly, the form 'your' is used in place of 'one's' in phrases such as 'put your foot down'. Solvers should remember that 'one's' may be required instead for a crossword solution. In some instances this may be reflected in the indication of word-length given in a clue: for example, 'sure of yourself' would be denoted as (4,2,8), hence listed here under **14**, whereas 'sure of oneself' would be (4,2,7), which would have been **13**.

Italics have not been used, even where conventionally a word or letter is italicized. This may be noted especially in relation to physics terms, for example, under 'Boltzmann constant' the symbol 'k' is given in roman type, whereas in *The Chambers Dictionary* it is italicized as '*k*'. Similarly, titles of novels and films, names of ships and other similar instances will all be found in roman type.

Where words can be hyphenated (as a noun) or unhyphenated (as a phrasal verb) both forms are usually included in synonym lists (for example 'back-up' and 'back up' at 'second').

Word length

The words and phrases given contain 15 letters or fewer, reflecting the most commonly used crossword grids. However, where a list represents a closed set, that is, where a list is clearly defined and limited, then all relevant terms have been included regardless of length. For example, all of the US states and all of the plays of Shakespeare have been included, even though some of these are longer than 15 letters in length.

Organization of entries

Within the Dictionary section, words have been sorted into over 19,600 one-stop alphabetical entries by meaning or subject category. Entries provide a range of words that are relevant to the headword, in two types of list:

- synonym lists, which present words with similar meanings to the headword
- reference lists, which present encyclopedic information related to the headword, such as people's names, place names and types of item

Some entries include only one type of list, whereas others include a range of synonyms plus one or more reference lists. For example:

abbey
03 Abb **06** abbacy, friary, priory **07** convent, minster, nunnery **08** cloister, seminary **09** cathedral, monastery

Abbeys include:

04 Bath, Iona
05 Cluny, Kelso, Meaux, Roche, Royal
06 Bolton, Byland, Hexham, Whitby, Woburn
07 Citeaux, Furness, Melrose, Tintern, Waltham
08 Buckfast, Crowland, Dryburgh, Fontenay, Fonthill, Holyrood, Jedburgh, Newstead, Rievaulx
09 Clairvaux, Fountains, Holy Cross, Kirkstall, Nightmare, Sherborne
10 Malmesbury, Northanger
11 Westminster

Reference lists always follow thesaurus-style lists.

Within entries, words are grouped firstly by length, that is by the total number of letters in each word or phrase, and then ordered alphabetically within these word-length sections:

aisle
04 lane, path **07** gangway, passage, walkway **08** alleyway, corridor **10** passageway **12** deambulatory

Alphabetization is strictly by letter, and some stylistic conventions have been disregarded: for example, 'Mc' will be found at 'Mc' rather than mingled with 'Mac'.

No distinction is made between parts of speech, or between homonyms (words spelled the same but with different meanings), as crossword setters play on multiple meanings and possible ambiguity in clues. For example, the entry for 'rebel' lists synonyms for the adjective, verb and noun senses:

rebel
◇ *anagram indicator*
04 defy, riot **06** flinch, mutine, mutiny, oppose, recoil, resist, revolt, rise up, shrink **07** aginner, beatnik, defiant, disobey, dissent, heretic, run riot, shy away **08** agitator, apostate, mutineer, mutinous, pull back, recusant, revolter **09** dissenter, guerrilla, insurgent **10** malcontent, rebellious, schismatic **11** disobedient, turn against **12** malcontented, paramilitary **13** insubordinate, nonconformist, revolutionary **14** freedom fighter **15** insurrectionary

and the entry for 'dock' presents synonyms for what are, in fact, three separate words, one being a type of plant, another meaning a wharf or to land at a wharf and the third meaning to cut short:

dock
◇ *tail deletion indicator*
02 dk **03** bob, cut, pen **04** clip, crop, land, moor, pier, quay, rump **05** basin, berth, jetty, put in, Rumex, tie up, wharf
06 anchor, deduct, detail, lessen, marina, reduce, remove, sorrel
07 bistort, curtail, harbour, shorten
08 boat yard, canaigre, decrease, diminish, patience, quayside, subtract, truncate, withhold **09** grapetree, polygonum **10** drop anchor, tidal basin, waterfront **12** monk's rhubarb, submarine pen **15** fitting-out basin

Synonym lists for idioms and phrasal verbs derived from many of the headwords are also included and are marked by •:

vouch
• vouch for
04 back **06** affirm, assert, assure, avouch, uphold, verify **07** certify, confirm, endorse, support, swear to, warrant **08** attest to, speak for
09 answer for, guarantee **10** asseverate

There may be more than one entry in the Crossword Dictionary section for a word or phrasal verb. For example, 'shake up' appears as a phrasal verb at the entry for 'shake', but there is also an entry for the noun 'shake-up' as a headword in its own right.

Phrases, idioms and phrasal verbs have been located under the key headword contained and so should be found in an appropriate and intuitive place; *The Chambers Dictionary* has been followed in most instances. However, if a term cannot be found in the first place sought, solvers should try under other likely headwords.

Expressions of ...

Interjections and similar terms related to emotions are often found in cryptic crossword clues and introduced by 'expression of...' or a similar phrase. In this Dictionary section these are listed under the relevant headword; for example 'expression of hesitation' may require 'um' or 'er', and these can be found under the headword 'hesitation'.

If expressions relating to a particular emotion cannot be found in the first place sought, solvers should look under a likely alternative; for example, if seeking an 'expression of disapprobation' but finding nothing under 'disapprobation', solvers should then try 'disapproval'.

Lists of interjections, cries, shouts and expressions may be found at the following headwords:

admiration
agreement
annoyance
appreciation
approval
attention
concession
contempt
defiance
derision
disagreement
disappointment
disapproval
disbelief
discovery
disdain
disgust
dismay
dismissal
dissatisfaction
distaste
doubt
drinking
emotion
emphasis
encouragement
enthusiasm
excitement
farewell
frenzy
fright
gratitude
greeting
grief
hesitation
hunting
impatience
invocation
joy
misfortune
pain
pleasure
praise
protest
puzzlement
realization
regret
relief
reproof
resignation
sarcasm
scepticism
silence
stop
stupidity
success
support
surprise
sympathy
triumph
warning
weariness
wonder
worry

Indicators

Terms which are often used as wordplay indicators in cryptic crossword clues are denoted with a diamond

adrift
◇ *anagram indicator*
04 lost **05** at sea **07** aimless
08 drifting, goalless, insecure, rootless
09 off course, unsettled **10** anchorless, unanchored **11** disoriented
13 directionless, disorientated

icon and the type of indicator – anagram, hidden, reversal, etc – is given:

oddly
◇ *anagram indicator*
◇ *hidden alternately indicator*
07 weirdly **09** curiously, strangely, unusually **10** abnormally, remarkably
11 irregularly

Some words can be used as indicators of more than one kind of word play:
Indicators always follow the headword, idiom or phrasal verb. There may be instances in which an idiom or phrasal verb is followed only by an indicator, and not by synonym entries; this is because it was felt helpful to include the term for its usefulness as an indicator, but where it does not have synonyms in the usual way.

Indicators may not always appear in a cryptic clue in the way in which they appear in the Dictionary section, but rather may be encountered in an inflected form: for example, 'digest' is marked as an anagram indicator, but solvers may be more likely to encounter it in a cryptic clue as 'digested'. While efforts have been made to denote all common indicators, the lists can never be exhaustive.

More information on the use of indicators in cryptic clues, and lists of words that may be used as indicators, can be found in the introductory material at the start of the book.

Reference lists

The reference lists have been derived from *Chambers Crossword Lists* and from other authoritative Chambers reference databases. Lists are entered in the Dictionary section at the appropriate headword.

The reference lists are not intended to be all-inclusive, but to strike a balance between comprehensiveness and the likelihood of the words and phrases actually occurring as the solutions to crossword clues. For more comprehensive reference lists, *Chambers Crossword Lists* is recommended.

The reference lists include both historical and current information; for example, in the list of actors are not only contemporary figures like Sir Ian McKellen and Robin Williams, but also notable actors from the past like Richard Burbage and Edward Alleyn. Similarly, the lists may contain both real and fictional or legendary items. For example, the list of heroes includes the legendary Robin Hood, the literary D'Artagnan, the historical William Wallace, the cinematic Indiana Jones and the comic strip Superman.

Reference lists have been subdivided to make finding information easier. For example, there is not one list of singers, but separate lists of classical, folk, jazz, opera, pop and other singers.

Some of the reference lists contain additional information in brackets following core information. For example, first names or nicknames are given in brackets following a surname. In such lists, the core term (the unbracketed term) is presented in bold type to make browsing easier:

Pirates include:

03 **Tew** (Thomas)
04 **Bart** (Jean), **Gunn** (Ben), **Hook** (Captain), **Kidd** (William), **Otto**, **Read** (Mary), **Smee**
05 **Barth** (Jean), **Bones** (Billy), **Bonny** (Anne), **Bunce** (Jack), **Drake** (Sir Francis), **Every** (Henry), **Ewart** (Nanty), **Flint** (Captain), **Tache** (Edward), **Teach** (Edward)
06 **Aubery** (Jean-Benoit), **Conrad**, **Jonsen** (Captain), **Morgan** (Sir Henry), **Silver** (Long John), **Thatch** (Edward), **Walker** (William)
07 **Dampier** (William), **Lafitte** (Jean), **O'Malley** (Grace), **Rackham** (John), **Roberts** (Bartholomew), **Sparrow** (Captain Jack), **Trumpet** (Solomon)
08 **Altamont** (Frederick), **Black Dog**, **Blackett** (Nancy), **Blackett** (Peggy), **Blind Pew**, **Redbeard**, **Ringrose** (Basil)
09 **Black Bart**, **Cleveland** (Clement)
10 **Barbarossa** (Khair-ed-din), **Blackbeard**, **Calico Jack**
14 **Long John Silver**

Additional bracketed information is not included in the word-length count although it may form part of the solution to some crossword clues. The regnal numbers of individual popes, queens and kings have generally been omitted.

Common generic terms have often been omitted from the names and terms presented in reference lists, to avoid unwieldy and unnecessary repetition. For example, the word 'abbey' has not been included in names in the list of abbeys, and the word 'saw' has been omitted from the list of saws. Users should be aware that these terms may form part of the solution to some crossword clues.

The reference material has been selected to be as wide-ranging in scope as possible. Solvers should note that:

- numbers may be found in solutions in some instances, as numbers may be encountered or referenced in some form in cryptic puzzles. For example, the list of films includes *2001: A Space Odyssey* and *Apollo 13*.
- some items are included under a certain headword on the grounds of usefulness, even if they are not strictly types of the headword. For example, 'Washington DC' is included in the list of US states and 'tomato' is included in the list of vegetables. Similarly, items which are related to the headword may be included; succulents in the list of cacti, for example. Items which have been officially reclassified but which are still popularly thought of in their earlier category are also given, for example Pluto in the list of planets.
- variant spellings have been included, for example 'topi' and 'topee' in the list of hats.

In some entries without a distinct reference list, both synonyms and reference list type information may be found intermingled.

Cross-references

The Crossword Dictionary section is extensively cross-referenced to make finding solutions easy. There are two forms of cross-reference; those at main headwords directing users elsewhere:

lough *see* **lake**

and those which suggest that additional information may be found at other entries:

petrol
03 gas, LRP **05** ethyl, juice, super
08 gasolene, gasoline
See also **fuel**

In many of the latter instances, the cross-reference directs solvers to a relevant reference list. It may also direct solvers to a similar but longer entry with additional synonyms, or may make explicit some crossword jargon or other slang; for example, a cross-reference at 'bloomer' to 'flower', or a cross-reference at 'stir' to 'prison'.

a
02 an **03** ane, one, per **05** alpha
• **a French**
02 un **03** une
• **a German**
03 ein **04** eine

aardvark
07 antbear **08** anteater, earth-hog
09 groundhog

aback
• **take aback**
04 stun **05** shock, upset **06** dismay **07** astound, set back, stagger, startle **08** astonish, bewilder, knock out, surprise **09** dumbfound **10** disconcert **11** flabbergast

abalone
04 paua, pawa

abandon
◇ *anagram indicator*
◇ *deletion indicator*
04 cede, drop, dump, jilt, quit, sink, stop **05** abort, cease, chuck, ditch, forgo, leave, let go, scrap, waive, yield **06** banish, desert, desist, escape, forego, forhow, get out, give up, jack in, maroon, pack in, resign, strand, vacate **07** bail out, forsake, yield to **08** abdicate, evacuate, forswear, jettison, jump ship, part with, renounce, run out on, wildness **09** break away, give way to, sacrifice, stop doing, surrender, walk out on **10** break loose, depart from, go away from, relinquish, resign from **11** discontinue, impetuosity, leave behind, unrestraint **12** be overcome by, break off with, carelessness, dispense with, kick the habit, leave for dead, recklessness, withdraw from **13** break free from, impulsiveness, leave it at that **14** break it off with, give the elbow to, lose yourself in **15** leave high and dry, leave in the lurch, thoughtlessness, uninhibitedness

abandoned
◇ *anagram indicator*
03 mad, old **04** left, wild **05** crazy, empty **06** unused, vacant, wanton, wicked **07** corrupt, disused, forlorn, immoral **08** derelict, deserted, desolate, forsaken, reckless **09** debauched, dissolute, neglected, reprobate **10** profligate, unoccupied **11** uninhibited **12** unrestrained

abandonment
05 drift, loose **07** cession, discard, Dunkirk, jilting, leaving, neglect, waiving **08** ditching, dropping, giving-up, stopping **09** cessation, desertion, forsaking, marooning, sacrifice, scrapping, stranding, surrender **10** abdication, decampment, exposition **11** dereliction, reprobation, resignation **12** renunciation, running out on **13** leaving behind **14** discontinuance, relinquishment **15** discontinuation, resignation from

abase
05 crawl, lower **06** debase, demean, humble, kowtow, malign **07** degrade, mortify, put down **08** belittle, cast down, suck up to **09** disparage, humiliate

abasement
08 crawling, humility **09** demeaning **10** debasement, humbleness **11** humiliation, sucking up to **13** disparagement, mortification

abash
03 cow **05** quell, shame **06** humble **07** astound **08** confound, face down **09** embarrass, humiliate **10** disconcert **14** discountenance

abashed
07 ashamed, floored, humbled **08** confused **09** affronted, mortified, perturbed, shamefast **10** bewildered, confounded, humiliated, nonplussed, remorseful, shamefaced, taken aback **11** discomfited, discomposed, dumbfounded, embarrassed **12** disconcerted **15** discountenanced

abate
04 alay, ease, fade, faik, fall, sink, slow, vail, wane **05** aleye, allay, allow, appal, let up, quell, remit, slake **06** lessen, pacify, rebate, reduce, relent, soothe, weaken **07** assuage, decline, detract, die down, drop off, dwindle, fall off, qualify, relieve, slacken, subside **08** decrease, diminish, mitigate, moderate, peter out, pluck off, taper off **09** alleviate, attenuate

abatement
04 wane **05** let-up, lysis **06** easing, relief **07** decline **08** decrease, lowering **09** allowance, deduction, dwindling, dying-down, lessening, reduction, remission, weakening **10** diminution, mitigation, moderation, palliation, slackening, subsidence **11** alleviation, assuagement, attenuation, dropping-off

abattoir
08 butchery, shambles
14 slaughterhouse

abbess
03 Abb **09** prelatess

abbey
03 Abb **06** abbacy, friary, priory **07** convent, minster, nunnery **08** cloister, seminary **09** cathedral, monastery

Abbeys include:

04 Bath, Iona
05 Cluny, Kelso, Meaux, Roche, Royal
06 Bolton, Byland, Hexham, Whitby, Woburn
07 Citeaux, Furness, Melrose, Tintern, Waltham
08 Buckfast, Crowland, Dryburgh, Fontenay, Fonthill, Holyrood, Jedburgh, Newstead, Rievaulx
09 Clairvaux, Fountains, Holy Cross, Kirkstall, Nightmare, Sherborne
10 Malmesbury, Northanger
11 Westminster

abbot
03 Abb **07** prelate **11** commendator **13** archimandrite

abbreviate
◇ *tail deletion indicator*
03 cut **04** clip, trim **06** digest, lessen, précis, reduce, shrink **07** abridge, curtail, cut down, shorten **08** abstract, compress, condense, contract, truncate **09** constrict, summarize

abbreviated
03 cut **05** short **07** clipped, compact, reduced, summary **08** abridged **09** condensed, shortened, truncated **10** contracted

abbreviation
05 short **06** digest, précis, résumé **07** acronym, summary **08** abstract, clipping, mnemonic, synopsis **09** reduction, short form **10** initialism, shortening, truncation **11** abridgement, compression, contraction, curtailment **13** shortened form, summarization, truncated form

See also **county**; **United States of America**

abdicate
04 cede, quit **05** forgo, shirk, yield **06** abjure, disown, forego, give up, reject, resign, retire **07** abandon, forsake **08** abnegate, renounce, step down **09** repudiate, stand down, surrender **10** relinquish **14** turn your back on **15** give up the throne, wash your hands of

abdication
07 refusal **08** giving-up **09** disowning, rejection, surrender **10** abjuration, abnegation, retirement
11 abandonment, repudiation, resignation **12** renunciation, standing-down, stepping-down
14 relinquishment

abdomen
03 maw, tum **04** guts, puku, womb
05 belly, bingy, heart, pleon, tummy
06 gaster, middle, paunch, venter
07 beer gut, insides, midriff, stomach
08 pot belly **09** beer belly, ventricle
10 little Mary **11** bread-basket, corporation, opisthosoma

abdominal
02 ab **05** belly **07** coeliac, gastric, ventral **08** visceral **10** intestinal
11 ventricular

abduct
05 seize **06** kidnap, ravish, snatch
07 capture **08** carry off, shanghai
09 lay hold of **10** run off with, spirit away **11** appropriate, make off with, run away with, take by force **12** hold to ransom **13** take as hostage **15** take away by force

abduction
04 rape **06** kidnap **07** capture, seizure
09 ravishing, seduction, snatching
10 enlevement, kidnapping
11 carrying off **15** taking as hostage

aberrant
◇ *anagram indicator*
03 odd **05** rogue **06** quirky
07 corrupt, deviant **08** abnormal, atypical, freakish, peculiar, straying
09 anomalous, defective, deviating, different, divergent, eccentric, irregular, wandering **11** incongruous

aberration
05 lapse **06** oddity **07** anomaly, mistake **08** delusion, straying
09 deviation, oversight, variation, wandering **10** deliration, divergence
11 abnormality, instability, peculiarity
12 eccentricity, irregularity
13 nonconformity

abet
03 aid **04** back, help, spur **05** egg on
06 assist, back up, incite, second
07 condone, endorse, promote, succour, support **08** sanction **09** encourage, lend a hand **11** collude with

abeyance
• in abeyance
05 on ice **06** on hold **07** disused, dormant, pending, shelved
09 postponed, suspended **11** hanging fire **12** in suspension **13** no longer in use **14** not in operation

abhor
04 hate, shun **05** spurn **06** detest, loathe, reject **07** despise **08** execrate
09 abominate, shudder at **10** cannot bear, recoil from, shrink from **11** cannot abide, cannot stand

abhorrence
04 hate **05** odium **06** enmity, hatred, horror, malice **07** disgust **08** aversion, contempt, distaste, loathing
09 animosity, revulsion **10** execration, repugnance **11** abomination, detestation

abhorrent
05 hated, yucky **06** horrid, odious
07 hateful, heinous **08** absonant, detested, horrible **09** detesting, execrable, loathsome, obnoxious, offensive, repellent, repugnant, repulsive, revolting **10** abominable, detestable, disgusting, nauseating
11 distasteful

abide
03 lie, won **04** bear, hack, last, stay, take **05** brook, dwell, stand, thole
06 accept, endure, live on, remain, reside **07** persist, stomach, survive
08 continue, tolerate **09** put up with
• abide by
04 obey **05** stand **06** accept, follow, fulfil, hold to, keep to, uphold **07** agree to, observe, respect, stand by
08 adhere to, carry out, submit to
09 conform to, discharge **10** comply with, toe the line **11** go along with, go by the book **15** stick to the rules

abiding
04 firm **05** fixed **06** stable **07** chronic, durable, eternal, lasting **08** constant, enduring, immortal, lifelong, long-term, standing, unending **09** continual, immutable, permanent **10** continuous, persistent, persisting, unchanging
11 continuance, everlasting, long-lasting, long-running **12** unchangeable

ability
04 gift **05** flair, forte, knack, means, power, savvy, skill, touch **06** genius, powers, talent **07** calibre, faculty, knowhow, prowess, the hang
08 aptitude, capacity, deftness, facility, strength, the knack **09** adeptness, dexterity, endowment, expertise, potential, resources **10** adroitness, capability, competence, competency, motivation, propensity **11** proficiency, savoir-faire, what it takes, wherewithal
12 potentiality **13** qualification

ab initio
07 at first, firstly **09** initially, primarily
10 at the start, originally **11** to begin with, to start with **12** from the start
14 at the beginning

abject
03 low **04** base, mean, vile **05** awful
06 sordid, woeful **07** debased, forlorn, ignoble, outcast, pitiful, servile, slavish
08 degraded, hopeless, pathetic, pitiable, shameful, wretched
09 execrable, miserable, worthless
10 degenerate, deplorable, despicable, grovelling, submissive
11 humiliating, ignominious
12 contemptible, ingratiating
13 dishonourable

abjure
04 deny, reny **05** renay, reney
06 disown, eschew, recant, reject
07 abandon, disavow, forsake, retract
08 abdicate, abnegate, disclaim, forswear, renege on, renounce
09 repudiate **10** relinquish
12 dispense with

ablaze
03 lit **04** alow **05** afire, aglow, alowe, angry, fiery, lit up **06** aflame, alight, ardent, fuming, on fire, raging
07 aroused, blazing, burning, excited, fervent, flaming, furious, glowing, ignited, intense, lighted, radiant
08 flashing, frenzied, gleaming, incensed, in flames, luminous
09 brilliant, sparkling **10** passionate, shimmering, stimulated **11** exhilarated, illuminated, impassioned
12 enthusiastic, incandescent

able
03 fit **04** deft, fere **05** adept **06** adroit, clever, expert, fitted, gifted, strong, up to it **07** capable, clued up, skilful, skilled **08** all there, masterly, powerful, talented **09** competent, cut out for, dexterous, effective, efficient, ingenious, on the ball, practised, qualified **10** proficient **11** experienced, intelligent **12** accomplished
• able to
05 fit to **06** free to **09** allowed to, capable of **10** prepared to
11 competent to, qualified to

able-bodied
02 AB **03** fit **04** fine, hale **05** burly, hardy, lusty, sound, stout, tough
06 hearty, robust, rugged, strong, sturdy **07** healthy, staunch
08 powerful, stalwart, vigorous
09 strapping **12** in good health **13** hale and hearty **14** as fit as a fiddle

ablution
05 laver **07** bathing, rinsing, soaking, washing **08** cleaning **09** cleansing, scrubbing, showering

abnegate
04 deny **06** abjure, eschew, give up, refuse, reject **07** abandon, abstain, disavow, forbear **08** forswear, renounce **09** repudiate, surrender
10 relinquish

abnegation
08 eschewal, giving-up **09** surrender
10 abjuration, abstinence, self-denial, temperance **11** forbearance, repudiation **12** renunciation **13** self-sacrifice **14** relinquishment

abnormal
◇ *anagram indicator*
03 odd **04** para- **05** outré, queer, weird **07** curious, deviant, erratic, oddball, strange, uncanny, unusual, wayward **08** aberrant, atypical, peculiar, singular, uncommon
09 anomalous, different, divergent, eccentric, irregular, unnatural
10 paranormal, unexpected

11 exceptional **13** extraordinary, funny peculiar, idiosyncratic, preternatural

abnormality
04 flaw **06** oddity **07** anomaly **08** enormity, vitiligo **09** deformity, deviation, exception, palilalia, water-core **10** aberration, difference, divergence **11** atypicality, bizarreness, dysfunction, monstrosity, pathography, peculiarity, singularity, strangeness, unusualness **12** eccentricity, irregularity, malformation, monstruosity, uncommonness **13** unnaturalness

abnormally
09 extremely, unusually **10** especially, remarkably, uncommonly **12** particularly **13** exceptionally **15** extraordinarily, preternaturally

aboard
◇ *insertion indicator*
02 in, on **04** into, onto **07** on board **09** alongside **11** on board ship

abode
02 in **03** inn, pad, won **04** home, seat, stay **05** lodge, whare **06** libken, remain **07** domicil, habitat, mansion, presage **08** domicile, dwelling, lodgings **09** residence, residency **10** habitation **11** inhabitance, inhabitancy **13** dwelling-place

abolish
03 axe, ban, end **04** chop, dump, sink, stop **05** annul, quash, scrap **06** cancel, repeal, revoke **07** blot out, destroy, expunge, nullify, rescind, subvert, vitiate, wipe out **08** abrogate, down with, get rid of, overturn, stamp out, suppress **09** eliminate, eradicate, overthrow, terminate **10** annihilate, do away with, invalidate, obliterate, put an end to **11** discontinue, exterminate

abolition
03 axe **04** chop **06** ending, repeal **07** dumping, voiding **08** chopping, quashing, stopping **09** annulment, overthrow, scrapping, vitiation **10** abrogation, extinction, rescission, revocation, subversion, withdrawal **11** blotting-out, destruction, dissolution, elimination, eradication, extirpation, rescindment, suppression, termination **12** annihilation, cancellation, invalidation, obliteration **13** doing-away with, extermination, nullification

abomasum
04 read

abominable
◇ *anagram indicator*
04 base, foul, vile **06** cursed, horrid, nefast, odious **07** hateful, heinous **08** damnable, dreadful, god-awful, horrible, terrible, wretched **09** abhorrent, appalling, atrocious, execrable, loathsome, nefandous, obnoxious, offensive, repellent, repugnant, repulsive, revolting **10** despicable, detestable, disgusting, nauseating **12** contemptible **13** reprehensible

abominably
07 beastly **08** horribly, odiously, terribly **09** execrably **10** dreadfully **11** appallingly, obnoxiously **12** disgustingly **13** reprehensibly

abominate
04 hate **05** abhor **06** detest, loathe **07** condemn, despise **08** execrate

abomination
04 evil, hate **05** curse, odium **06** hatred, horror, plague **07** disgust, offence, outrage, torment **08** anathema, atrocity, aversion, disgrace, distaste, loathing **09** hostility, revulsion **10** abhorrence, execration, repugnance **11** detestation

aboriginal
05 first, Koori, local, Murri, Nunga **06** Anangu, native, primal **07** ancient, initial **08** earliest, original, primeval **09** primaeval, primitive **10** indigenous **13** autochthonous, tangata whenua

Aboriginal activists include:

04 Mabo (Eddie)
05 Scott (Evelyn)
06 Dodson (Mick), Dodson (Patrick), O'Shane (Pat)
07 Bandler (Faith), Gilbert (Kevin), Pearson (Noel), Perkins (Charles)
09 Yunupingu (Galarrwuy)
12 Burnum Burnum

Aboriginal tribes include:

03 Wik
04 Tiwi
05 Bardi, Yanda
06 Aranda, Dharug
07 Noongar, Nyungar
08 Gurindji, Warlpiri
09 Kuring-gai, Wiradjuri
10 Bundjalung, Pitta Pitta, Wemba Wemba
14 Pitjantjatjara

aborigine
03 gin **05** koori, Maori, myall **06** native **08** indigene **11** black-fellow **15** first inhabitant

abort
03 axe, end **04** fail, halt, stop **05** check **06** thwart **07** call off, nullify, suspend **08** cut short, miscarry **09** frustrate, terminate **11** come to an end, discontinue **12** bring to an end **13** pull the plug on

abortion
08 misbirth **09** foeticide **10** aborticide **11** miscarriage, termination

abortive
04 idle, vain **06** barren, failed, futile **07** misborn, sterile, useless **08** bootless, thwarted **09** fruitless **10** unavailing **11** ineffective, ineffectual **12** unproductive, unsuccessful **13** inefficacious

abound
04 flow, teem **05** crowd, swarm, swell **06** be full, thrive **07** bristle **08** brim over, flourish, increase, overflow **09** exuberate, luxuriate **10** be abundant **11** be plentiful, proliferate, superabound

about
◇ *anagram indicator*
◇ *containment indicator*
◇ *reversal indicator*
01 a, c **02** ca, on, re **03** cir **04** circ, near, over **05** anent, circa, close, round **06** almost, approx, around, beside, nearby, nearly **07** all over, close by, close to, nearing, roughly **08** to and fro **09** apropos of, as regards, regarding **10** adjacent to, concerning, encircling, more or less, relating to, throughout **11** approaching, dealing with, referring to, surrounding, within reach **12** encompassing, here and there, with regard to **13** approximately, concerned with, connected with, in the matter of, in the region of, with respect to **14** on the subject of **15** in the vicinity of, with reference to

• **about to**
06 all but, soon to **07** going to, ready to **08** all set to **11** intending to, preparing to **12** on the point of, on the verge of

about-turn
03 uey **05** U-turn **08** reversal **09** about-face, turnabout, volte-face **10** turnaround **13** enantiodromia

above
◇ *juxtaposition down indicator*
03 sup, sur **04** atop, over, owre, upon **05** aloft, prior, sopra, super-, supra- **06** before, beyond, higher, high up, on high **07** earlier, on top of **08** immune to, overhead, previous, senior to **09** aforesaid, exceeding, foregoing, not open to, preceding **10** exempt from, higher than, in excess of, prevenient, previously, superior to, surpassing **11** above-stated, greater than, not liable to **12** not exposed to **14** above-mentioned, aforementioned

• **above all**
07 chiefly, firstly, notably **09** most of all, primarily **10** first of all **15** most importantly

• **above yourself**
04 smug, vain **05** cocky, proud **07** haughty, stuck-up **08** arrogant, boastful, immodest, puffed-up **09** bigheaded, conceited **10** complacent **11** egotistical, toffee-nosed **12** narcissistic, supercilious, vainglorious **13** self-important, self-satisfied, swollen-headed **14** full of yourself

• **as above**
02 us **07** ut supra

above-board
04 open, true **05** frank, legit **06** candid, dinkum, honest, kosher, square **07** upright **08** straight, truthful **09** guileless, reputable, veracious

10 forthright, honourable, legitimate, on the level 11 trustworthy 13 fair and square 15 straightforward

abracadabra
05 spell 09 gibberish, magic word 10 hocus pocus, mumbo-jumbo, open sesame

abrade
03 rub 04 stun 05 awake, chafe, erode, grate, graze, grind, rouse, scour, start 06 scrape 07 scratch, wear off 08 wear away, wear down 10 scrape away

abrasion
03 cut 05 chafe, graze 06 scrape 07 chafing, erosion, grating, rubbing, scratch 08 abrading, friction, grinding, scouring, scraping 10 scratching 11 excoriation, wearing-away, wearing-down

abrasive
04 bort 05 boart, emery, harsh, nasty, rough, sharp 06 biting 07 brusque, caustic, chafing, erodent, erosive, grating, hurtful 08 annoying, grinding, scraping 09 corrosive, sandpaper 10 frictional, glasspaper, irritating, scratching, unpleasant 11 attritional, garnet-paper, ground glass 14 silicon carbide

abreast
02 up 03 hep 05 level 06 afront, au fait, well up 07 in touch 08 familiar, informed, up to date 09 au courant, on the ball 10 acquainted, conversant, side by side 11 cheek by jowl 12 in the picture 13 knowledgeable 15 beside each other, next to each other

abridge
03 cut, lop 04 clip 05 elide, prune 06 digest, lessen, précis, reduce 07 curtail, cut down, shorten 08 abstract, compress, condense, contract, cut short, decrease, truncate 09 epitomize, summarize, synopsize 10 abbreviate 11 concentrate 12 circumscribe

abridged
◇ *tail deletion indicator*
03 abd, abr 05 short 06 potted 07 clipped, cut down, reduced, shorter 08 cut short, digested 10 contracted, summarized 11 abbreviated

abridgement
03 abr 06 abrégé, digest, précis, résumé 07 compend, cutting, epitome, outline, pastime, summary 08 abstract, decrease, synopsis 09 reduction 10 compendium, conspectus, diminution, shortening, truncation 11 contraction, curtailment, diminishing, restriction 12 abbreviation, abbreviature, short version 13 concentration

abroad
◇ *anagram indicator*
◇ *foreign word indicator*
03 out 04 away 05 about, forth 06 around, astray, widely 07 at large, current 08 offshore, overseas, publicly 10 far and wide 11 circulating, extensively 14 doing your OE, in foreign parts, to foreign parts 15 out of the country

• go abroad
08 emigrate

abrogate
03 axe, end 04 chop, dump, stop 05 annul, scrap 06 cancel, repeal, revoke 07 abolish, rescind, retract, reverse, vitiate 08 disenact, dissolve 09 disaffirm, repudiate 10 do away with, invalidate 11 countermand

abrogation
03 axe 04 chop 06 repeal 07 dumping 08 recision, reversal 09 abolition, annulment, repealing, scrapping, vitiation 10 overruling, rescinding, rescission, revocation 11 dissolution, repudiation, rescindment 12 cancellation, invalidation 14 countermanding, disaffirmation

abrupt
◇ *tail deletion indicator*
03 off 04 bold, curt, rude, snap 05 blunt, brisk, gruff, hasty, quick, rapid, rough, sharp, sheer, short, squab, steep, swift, terse 06 direct, snappy, sudden 07 brusque, hurried, instant, offhand, prerupt, uncivil 08 dramatic, impolite, snappish, vertical 09 immediate, startling 10 dismissive, surprising, unexpected, unforeseen, unfriendly 11 declivitous, precipitate, precipitous, unannounced 12 discourteous 13 instantaneous, unceremonious

abruptly
04 bang 05 short 06 curtly, rudely 07 bluntly, briskly, gruffly, hastily, offhand, quickly, rapidly, roughly, shortly, swiftly, tersely 08 directly, snappily, suddenly 09 brusquely, hurriedly, instantly 10 impolitely, snappishly 11 immediately 12 dismissively, unexpectedly 13 precipitately 14 discourteously 15 instantaneously, unceremoniously

abscess
04 boil, noma, sore 05 ulcer 06 canker 07 gumboil 08 swelling 09 gathering, impostume, infection 10 imposthume, ulceration 12 inflammation

abscond
03 fly 04 bolt, flee, quit 05 scram 06 beat it, decamp, escape, run off, vanish 07 do a bunk, make off, run away, scarper, vamoose 08 clear off, clear out, jump bail, run for it 09 disappear, do a runner, skedaddle 12 absquatulate 15 take French leave

absence
03 abs 04 lack, need, want 06 dearth 07 default, paucity, skiving, truancy, vacancy, vacuity 08 omission, scarcity 09 privation 10 bunking off, deficiency 11 absenteeism, abstraction, inattention 12 non-existence 13 non-appearance, non-attendance, playing hookey 14 unavailability

• feel absence
04 miss

absent
◇ *deletion indicator*
01 a 03 abs, MIA, off, out 04 away, AWOL, gone 05 blank 06 dreamy, truant, vacant 07 faraway, lacking, missing, not here, unaware 08 not there 09 elsewhere, miles away, not around, oblivious, unheeding 10 distracted, in absentia, not present 11 daydreaming, inattentive, preoccupied, unavailable 12 absent-minded

• absent yourself
04 exit 06 depart, retire 07 back out, retreat 08 slip away, withdraw 13 take your leave

absentee
06 no-show, truant 11 non-attender

absently
07 blankly 08 dreamily 12 abstractedly 13 inattentively 14 absent-mindedly

absent-minded
06 absent, dreamy, musing, scatty 07 faraway, pensive, unaware 08 absorbed, distrait, dreaming, heedless, yonderly 09 distraite, engrossed, forgetful, miles away, oblivious, unheeding, withdrawn 10 abstracted, distracted, unthinking 11 impractical, inattentive, not all there, preoccupied, unconscious 13 somewhere else, wool-gathering 14 dead to the world, scatterbrained

absent-mindedly
07 blankly 08 absently 12 abstractedly 13 inattentively

absolute
01 A 03 abs, set 04 dead, firm, full, meer, mere, pure, rank, sure, true 05 final, fixed, rigid, sheer, total, utter 06 entire 07 certain, decided, genuine, perfect, settled, supreme, unmixed 08 almighty, complete, decisive, definite, despotic, outright, positive, thorough 09 autarchic, boundless, downright, out-and-out, sovereign, undivided, universal, unlimited 10 autocratic, conclusive, consummate, definitive, exhaustive, high-handed, omnipotent, peremptory, tyrannical 11 autarchical, categorical, dictatorial, established, indubitable, non-variable, unalterable, unambiguous, unequivocal, unmitigated, unqualified 12 totalitarian, unrestrained, unrestricted 13 authoritarian, non-negotiable, unadulterated, unconditional 14 unquestionable

absolutely
03 abs, yes 04 bang, dead, just, mere, very 05 fully, quite, truly 06 fairly,

purely, surely, wholly **07** clearly, exactly, finally, for sure, no doubt, plainly, quite so, totally, utterly **08** entirely, of course **09** assuredly, certainly, decidedly, doubtless, genuinely, naturally, obviously, perfectly, precisely, supremely **10** by all means, completely, decisively, definitely, in every way, infallibly, positively, separately, thoroughly, undeniably **11** à toute force, doubtlessly, undoubtedly **12** conclusively, despotically, exhaustively, high-handedly, tyrannically **13** categorically, dictatorially, unambiguously, unequivocally, without a doubt **14** autocratically, in every respect, unquestionably, wholeheartedly **15** unconditionally

absolution
05 mercy **06** pardon, shrift **07** amnesty, freedom, release **09** acquittal, discharge, pardoning, purgation, remission **10** assoilment, letting off, liberation, redemption **11** deliverance, exculpation, exoneration, forgiveness, vindication **12** emancipation **13** justification

absolve
04 free, quit **05** clear, loose, quite, quyte, remit **06** acquit, assoil, excuse, let off, pardon, quight **07** deliver, forgive, justify, release, set free **08** liberate **09** assoilzie, discharge, exculpate, exonerate, vindicate **10** accomplish, emancipate **11** have mercy on

absorb
◇ *containment indicator*
04 fill, hold, soak, sorb, suck, wrap **05** eat up, mop up, use up **06** blot up, devour, digest, draw in, engage, engulf, fill up, imbibe, ingest, occupy, retain, soak up, suck up, take in, take up **07** consume, drink in, engross, enthral, involve, receive **08** sponge up **09** captivate, fascinate, integrate, preoccupy, swallow up **10** assimilate, monopolize, understand **11** incorporate

absorbed
◇ *containment indicator*
04 rapt **07** riveted **08** involved, occupied **09** engrossed **10** captivated, enthralled, fascinated, interested, spellbound **11** preoccupied, taken up with

absorbent
03 abs **04** dope **06** porous, spongy **07** soaking **08** bibulous, blotting, pervious **09** permeable, receptive, resorbent, retentive **10** absorptive, spongiform **12** assimilative, sorbefacient

absorbing
07 amusing **08** gripping, riveting **09** diverting, enjoyable **10** compelling, compulsive, engrossing, intriguing **11** captivating, enthralling, fascinating, interesting **12** entertaining, preoccupying, spellbinding **13** unputdownable

absorption
07 holding, osmosis **08** monopoly, raptness, riveting, taking-in **09** devouring, drawing-in, immersion, ingestion, soaking-up **10** engagement, engrossing, intentness, occupation **11** captivating, consumption, involvement **12** assimilation **13** attentiveness, concentration, preoccupation

abstain
04 fast, pass, quit, shun, stop **05** avoid, forgo, spare **06** cut out, desist, eschew, forego, give up, jack in, refuse, reject, resist **07** decline, forbear, not vote, refrain **08** hold back, renounce, restrain **09** be neutral, do without, go without **11** stop short of **12** deny yourself, refuse to vote **13** sit on the fence

abstainer
02 TT **06** tee-tee, wowser **08** teetotal **09** Rechabite **11** teetotaller **12** water-drinker

• abstainers
02 AA, TT

abstemious
02 TT **05** sober **06** frugal **07** ascetic, austere, sparing **08** moderate, teetotal **09** abstinent, temperate **10** restrained **11** disciplined, self-denying **14** self-abnegating **15** self-disciplined

abstention
08 celibacy **09** not voting **10** neutrality **13** refusal to vote **15** declining to vote

abstinence
04 fast **07** fasting, refusal **08** eschewal, giving-up, sobriety **09** avoidance, frugality, nephalism, restraint **10** abjuration, abstaining, asceticism, continence, continency, declension, desistance, moderation, refraining, self-denial, temperance, water wagon **11** forbearance, self-control, teetotalism **12** going-without, renunciation **13** non-indulgence, self-restraint **14** abstemiousness, self-discipline
See also **fast**

abstinent
05 sober **06** frugal **07** ascetic **08** moderate, teetotal **09** continent, temperate **10** abstaining, abstemious, forbearing, restrained **11** self-denying **12** non-indulgent **14** self-controlled, self-restrained **15** self-disciplined

abstract
03 abs, cut, tap **04** deep **06** arcane, detach, digest, précis, remove, résumé, subtle **07** abridge, complex, cut down, draw off, epitome, extract, general, isolate, outline, shorten, subduce, subduct, summary, take out **08** abstruse, academic, compress, condense, discrete, ideative, notional, prescind, profound, separate, syllabus, symbolic, synopsis, take away, withdraw **09** contrived, recondite, summarize **10** abbreviate, compendium, conceptual, conspectus, dissociate, ideational, indefinite **11** abridgement, compression, generalized, non-concrete, suppositive, theoretical, unpractical, unrealistic **12** hypothetical, intellectual, metaphysical, non-realistic **13** philosophical, suppositional **14** recapitulation

• in the abstract
07 on paper **08** in theory **09** generally **10** notionally **11** in abstracto **12** conceptually **13** theoretically **14** hypothetically **15** philosophically

abstracted
06 absent, dreamy, musing, scatty **07** bemused, faraway, pensive, unaware **08** absorbed, dreaming, heedless **09** engrossed, forgetful, miles away, oblivious, unheeding, withdrawn **10** distracted, unthinking **11** impractical, inattentive, inconscient, preoccupied, unconscious **12** absent-minded **13** wool-gathering **14** scatterbrained

abstractedly
07 blankly **08** absently **13** inattentively **14** absent-mindedly

abstraction
04 idea **05** dream **06** entity, notion, revery, theory **07** absence, concept, formula, removal, reverie, theorem, thought **09** isolation **10** absorption, conception, conjecture, dreaminess, extraction, generality, hypothesis, remoteness, separation, withdrawal **11** bemusedness, distraction, inattention, pensiveness **13** preoccupation **14** generalization

abstruse
04 deep, high, long **06** arcane, hidden, subtle **07** complex, cryptic, Delphic, obscure **08** esoteric, hermetic, profound, puzzling **09** enigmatic, exquisite, recherché, recondite **10** hermetical, mysterious, perplexing **11** inscrutable **12** unfathomable

absurd
◇ *anagram indicator*
04 daft **05** crazy, funny, gonzo, inane, silly **06** stupid **07** asinine, comical, foolish, idiotic, Laputan, risible **08** cockeyed, derisory, farcical, humorous, Laputian **09** fantastic, grotesque, illogical, laughable, ludicrous, priceless, senseless, unearthly, untenable **10** irrational, ridiculous **11** harebrained, implausible, incongruous, meaningless, nonsensical, paradoxical **12** preposterous, unreasonable

absurdity
04 joke **05** farce, folly **06** drivel, humour, idiocy **07** charade, inanity, paradox, rubbish, twaddle

08 claptrap, daftness, malarkey, nonsense, ridicule, solecism, travesty **09** craziness, gibberish, silliness, stupidity **10** balderdash, caricature **11** fatuousness, foolishness, incongruity **12** illogicality **13** irrationality, ludicrousness, senselessness **14** implausibility, ridiculousness **15** meaninglessness

absurdly
07 crazily, funnily, inanely **08** stupidly **09** comically, foolishly, laughably, untenably **10** farcically, humorously **11** idiotically, implausibly, ludicrously, senselessly **12** irrationally, ridiculously, unreasonably **13** fantastically, incongruously, meaninglessly, nonsensically, paradoxically **14** preposterously

abundance
04 bags, glut, load, lots **05** feast, flush, fouth, fowth, heaps, loads, piles, routh, rowth, scads, sonce, sonse, store **06** bounty, excess, masses, oodles, plenty, riches, stacks, wealth **07** bonanza, fortune, lashing, oodlins, pleroma, tallent **08** fullness, lashings, opulence, overflow, plethora, richness **09** affluence, amplitude, fertility, plenitude, profusion **10** exuberance, generosity, lavishness, luxuriance, profligacy **11** copiousness, corn in Egypt, great supply, munificence, prodigality **12** extravagance, milk and honey **13** plentifulness, rack and manger **14** stouth and routh

abundant
04 full, rank, rich **05** ample, hefty, large, thick **06** filled, galore, lavish, strong **07** copious, opulent, profuse, teeming **08** affluent, generous, in plenty, prolific **09** bounteous, bountiful, exuberant, luxuriant, plenteous, plentiful **11** overflowing **12** well-supplied **14** more than enough

abundantly
04 very, well **05** amply, jolly **06** highly, plenty, really **07** acutely, awfully, greatly, utterly **08** severely, terribly **09** copiously, decidedly, extremely, intensely, profusely, unusually **10** completely, dreadfully, remarkably, thoroughly, uncommonly **11** exceedingly, excessively, extensively, exuberantly, frightfully, in abundance, in profusion, plentifully **12** immoderately, inordinately, prolifically, terrifically, unreasonably **13** exceptionally **15** extraordinarily

abuse
◇ *anagram indicator*
03 hit, mud **04** beat, harm, hurt, rail, rape **05** bully, curse, libel, scold, serve, slate, smear, snash, wrong **06** batter, damage, defame, impugn, injure, injury, insult, jawing, malign, misuse, molest, oppugn, pick on, revile, tirade, verbal **07** affront, beating, calumny, censure, cruelty, cursing, exploit, insults, jobbery, miscall, offence, oppress, slag off, slander, swear at, torture, upbraid, violate, vitriol **08** be rude to, bullyrag, chuck off, derision, diatribe, ill-treat, maltreat, misapply, mistreat, reproach, scolding, swearing **09** call names, castigate, contumely, denigrate, disparage, invective, misemploy, swear-word, victimize **10** calumniate, chuck off at, defamation, imposition, oppression, upbraiding, vituperate **11** castigation, clapperclaw, denigration, hurl abuse at, malediction, molestation, mud-slinging, name-calling **12** billingsgate, calumniation, exploitation, ill-treatment, interference, maltreatment, mistreatment, vilification, vituperation **13** disparagement, interfere with, misemployment, sexual assault, treat like dirt **14** harass sexually, misapplication **15** assault sexually, take advantage of

abusive
04 rude **05** cruel **06** bitchy, brutal **07** harmful, hurtful, railing, satiric **08** reviling, scathing, scolding, scornful **09** injurious, insulting, invective, libellous, maligning, offensive, satirical, vilifying **10** censorious, defamatory, derogatory, pejorative, scurrilous, slanderous, upbraiding **11** blasphemous, castigating, denigrating, destructive, disparaging, opprobrious, reproachful **12** calumniating, contumelious, vituperative

abusively
06 rudely **07** cruelly **08** bitchily, brutally **10** revilingly, scathingly, scoldingly, scornfully **11** injuriously, insultingly, offensively **12** calumniously, censoriously, pejoratively, scurrilously, upbraidingly **13** blasphemously, denigratingly, disparagingly, opprobriously, reproachfully **14** contumeliously, vituperatively

abut
◇ *juxtaposition indicator*
04 join, lean **05** touch **06** adjoin, border **07** conjoin, impinge, verge on **08** be next to

abysmal
◇ *anagram indicator*
05 awful, utter **06** dismal **08** complete, dreadful, shocking, terrible **09** appalling, frightful **10** bottomless **11** disgraceful **12** unfathomable

abysmally
◇ *anagram indicator*
07 awfully **08** terribly **10** dreadfully **11** appallingly, frightfully **13** disgracefully

abyss
03 pit **04** gulf, hell, void **05** abysm, chasm, depth, gorge, gulph **06** abrupt, canyon, crater, depths, ravine **07** Avernus, fissure, swallow **08** crevasse, profound, Tartarus **09** barathrum **13** bottomless pit

acacia
03 koa **05** babul, boree, mulga, myall, sally **06** bablah, gidgee, gidjee, mimosa, sallee **07** robinia, shittah **08** brigalow **09** blackwood, doornboom, fever tree, flame-tree **10** locust tree **11** shittah tree **12** golden wattle **13** kangaroo-thorn

academic
03 don **04** acca **05** smart, tutor **06** brainy, fellow, master, pedant **07** bookish, donnish, erudite, learned, scholar, serious, student, teacher, trainer **08** abstract, bookworm, educated, educator, highbrow, lecturer, literary, notional, studious, well-read **09** pedagogue, professor, scholarly **10** conceptual, instructor, irrelevant, ivory-tower, scholastic **11** conjectural, educational, impractical, pedagogical, speculative, theoretical **12** hypothetical, intellectual, man of letters, well-educated **13** instructional, suppositional **14** woman of letters

academician
01 A **02** RA **03** ARA, RSA

academy
01 A **02** RA **03** RAM **04** RADA **05** forty **06** school **07** academe, college **08** immortal, seminary **09** institute **10** university **11** charm school

acanthus
07 ruellia **08** many-root **10** thunbergia **11** bear's-breech, brankursine, shrimp plant

accede
05 admit, agree, bow to **06** accept, assume, attain, come to, concur, give in **07** agree to, consent, inherit, succeed **08** assent to, back down, take over **09** acquiesce, consent to, succeed to **10** comply with

accelerate
05 hurry, speed **06** hasten, open up, spur on, step up **07** advance, forward, further, promote, quicken, speed up **08** antedate, expedite, go faster, step on it **09** festinate, stimulate **10** facilitate **11** drive faster, gather speed, pick up speed, precipitate, put on a spurt **12** gain momentum, step on the gas **14** step on the juice **15** put your foot down

acceleration
01 a, g **07** speed-up **08** momentum **09** hastening, promotion **10** expedition, forwarding, speeding-up, stepping-up **11** advancement, furtherance, stimulation **14** gathering speed, rate of increase

accent
04 beat, dash, tone **05** acute, force, grave, ictus, pitch, pulse, twang **06** brogue, rhythm, stress, timbre, tittle

07 cadence, diction **08** emphasis, priority **09** diacritic, intensity, pulsation **10** circumflex, importance, inflection, intonation, modulation, prominence **11** enunciation, underlining **12** accentuation, articulation, highlighting **13** pronunciation **15** diacritical mark

accentuate
06 accent, deepen, show up, stress **07** point up **08** heighten **09** emphasize, highlight, intensify, spotlight, underline **10** strengthen, underscore **15** make great play of

accept
◇ *containment indicator*
03 buy, get **04** bear, gain, have, take, wear **05** abide, admit, adopt, allow, bow to, grasp, stand, trust **06** come by, credit, endure, give in, honour, jump at, obtain, pocket, secure, suffer, take on, take up **07** abide by, acquire, agree to, approve, believe, embrace, fall for, let go of, receive, stomach, swallow, welcome, yield to **08** accede to, back down, face up to, say yes to, tolerate **09** approbate, believe in, consent to, integrate, put up with, recognize, undertake **10** comply with, concur with, not say no to **11** acknowledge, acquiesce in, be certain of, go along with, take on board **12** be resigned to **13** make the best of, receive warmly **15** come to terms with

acceptable
01 U **02** OK, on **04** so-so **06** not bad **07** welcome **08** adequate, all right, moderate, passable, pleasant, pleasing **09** agreeable, allowable, desirable, tolerable **10** admissible, delightful, gratifying, reasonable **11** appreciated, appropriate, permissible **12** satisfactory, the done thing **15** unexceptionable

• make acceptable
04 sell

acceptably
08 passably, suitably **09** agreeably, desirably, tolerably **10** adequately, moderately, reasonably **13** appropriately **14** satisfactorily

acceptance
02 OK **03** acc, nod **04** acpt **05** faith, trust **06** assent, belief, buying, taking **07** bearing, consent, gaining, getting, receipt, welcome **08** adoption, approval, credence, currency, giving-in, securing, taking on, taking-up **09** accepting, accession, acquiring, admission, agreement, embracing, endurance, obtaining, receiving, tolerance, welcoming **10** admittance, assumption, compliance, facing up to, falling for **11** affirmation, backing-down, concurrence, endorsement, integration, recognition, resignation, undertaking **12** acquiescence, ratification **13** putting up with, taking on board **14** going along with, seal of approval **15** acknowledgement, making the best of, stamp of approval

accepted
01 a **04** taen **05** taken, usual **06** agreed, common, normal **07** correct, regular **08** admitted, approved, orthodox, ratified, received, standard **09** confirmed, customary, universal **10** acceptable, authorized, recognized, sanctioned **11** appropriate, established, traditional **12** acknowledged, conventional, time-honoured

access
03 key, use **04** door, path, read, road **05** drive, entry, log on, way in **06** course, entrée, locate **07** gateway, ingress, passage **08** approach, driveway, entering, entrance, retrieve **09** admission **10** admittance **12** gain access to, means of entry, right of entry **13** accessibility **15** means of approach, permission to see

accessibility
11 convenience **12** availability, ease of access **13** attainability, obtainability **15** approachability, intelligibility

accessible
04 near, open **05** handy, ready **06** nearby, on hand, patent **07** general **09** available, get-at-able, reachable **10** achievable, attainable, come-at-able, convenient, easy to read, obtainable, procurable **11** close at hand, close to hand, within cooee **12** approachable, easy to follow, intelligible, user-friendly **14** comprehensible, understandable

accession
04 gain, gift **06** afflux, influx **08** addition, increase, purchase **09** affluxion, attaining **10** assumption, possession, succession, taking over **11** acquisition, inheritance

accessorize
04 trim **05** add to, adorn **06** bedaub, set off **07** augment, bedizen, enhance **08** contrast, decorate, round off **10** complement, supplement

accessory
03 aid, hat **04** belt, help **05** add-in, add-on, extra, frill, shoes **06** gloves, helper **07** abettor, adjunct, cathead, fitting, handbag, partner **08** addition, conniver, ornament, trimming **09** adornment, ancillary, appendage, assistant, associate, attribute, auxiliary, colleague, component, extension, jewellery, secondary **10** accomplice, additional, attachment, complement, decoration, incidental, peripheral, subsidiary, supplement **11** confederate, subordinate **12** appurtenance, contributory, supplemental **13** embellishment, supplementary

accident
◇ *anagram indicator*
03 cva, hap, RTA **04** blow, fate, luck **05** crash, fluke, freak, prang, shunt, smash, wreck **06** bingle, chance, hazard, mishap, pile-up, upcast **07** fortune, smash-up, tragedy **08** blowdown, calamity, casualty, disaster, fatality, fortuity, good luck **09** collision, mischance **10** misfortune **11** coincidence, contingency, contretemps, good fortune, serendipity **12** circumstance, happenstance, misadventure

accidental
04 flat **05** fluky, sharp **06** casual, chance, flukey, random **07** natural, outward **08** aleatory, external **09** adventive, dividuous, haphazard, uncertain, unplanned, unwitting **10** contingent, fortuitous, incidental, unexpected, unforeseen, unintended **11** inadvertent, promiscuous, unlooked-for **12** adventitious, uncalculated **13** serendipitous, unanticipated, unintentional **14** unpremeditated

accidentally
◇ *anagram indicator*
08 bechance, by chance, randomly **09** by mistake **10** by accident **11** ex accidenti, haphazardly, unwittingly **12** fortuitously, incidentally, unexpectedly **13** inadvertently **14** adventitiously **15** serendipitously, unintentionally

acclaim
04 clap, hail, laud **05** cheer, exalt, extol, toast, voice **06** cheers, eulogy, homage, honour, praise, salute **07** applaud, commend, fanfare, ovation, tribute, welcome **08** applause, approval, bouquets, cheering, clapping, eulogium, eulogize, plaudits, shouting **09** celebrate, extolment, laudation, publicity, rave about **10** exaltation **11** acclamation, approbation, celebration **12** commendation

acclaimed
05 famed, great, noted **06** famous **07** admired, eminent, exalted, notable, revered **08** honoured, renowned **09** legendary, prominent **10** celebrated **11** illustrious, outstanding **13** distinguished

acclamation
03 rap **04** wrap **05** paean **06** bravos, eulogy, homage, honour, praise **07** fanfare, ovation, tribute, welcome **08** applause, approval, cheering, clapping, shouting **09** panegyric **10** enthusiasm, exaltation, laudations **11** approbation, celebration **12** commendation **13** felicitations **15** congratulations

acclimatization
10 adaptation, adjustment **11** acclimation, habituation, orientation **13** accommodation, acculturation **14** naturalization **15** familiarization

acclimatize
04 salt **05** adapt, inure **06** adjust, attune **07** conform **08** accustom

09 acclimate, get used to, habituate 10 naturalize 11 accommodate, acculturate, familiarize 12 find your feet 15 get your bearings

accolade
05 award 06 homage, honour, praise 07 dubbing, embrace, tribute 11 recognition, testimonial 12 pat on the back

accommodate
◇ *containment indicator*
03 aid, fit 04 help, hold, seat, take 05 adapt, board, house, lodge, put up, serve 06 adjust, assist, attune, bestow, billet, comply, modify, oblige, settle, supply, take in 07 compose, conform, provide, quarter, shelter 08 accustom, cater for, domicile 09 fit in with, habituate, harmonize, reconcile 11 acclimatize, be helpful to, give a hand to, have room for, lend a hand to 12 have space for

accommodating
◇ *containment indicator*
04 kind 07 helpful, pliable, willing 08 friendly, obliging 09 agreeable, compliant, indulgent, unselfish 10 hospitable 11 complaisant, considerate, co-operative, sympathetic

accommodation
◇ *containment indicator*
04 home 05 abode, board, place, rooms 07 harmony, housing, lodging, quarter, storage 08 dwelling, lodgings, quarters 09 agreement, residence 10 compromise, conformity, settlement 11 negotiation 12 negotiations 13 understanding 14 reconciliation

Accommodation types include:

03 inn, pad, pod
04 camp, digs, flat, gaff, gite, tent, yurt
05 b and b, cabin, hotel, house, igloo, lodge, motel, squat, villa
06 bedsit, billet, camper, duplex, flotel, hostel, jack-up, refuge, studio, succah, sukkah
07 caravan, cottage, dockage, floatel, lairage, parador, pension, shelter, taverna
08 barracks, berthage, crashpad, pod hotel, roomette, shipping, stabling, tenement, wharfage
09 apartment, bedsitter, bunkhouse, camper van, dormitory, full board, half board, penthouse, residence, rooming-in, timeshare
10 guardhouse, guest house, labour camp, mobile home
11 bachelor pad, bed and board, youth hostel
12 halfway house, hunting-lodge, room and board, self-catering
13 boarding-house, habitat module
14 loft conversion
15 bed and breakfast, hall of residence, married quarters

See also **building**; **house**; **tent**

accompaniment
04 vamp 06 backup, patter 07 adjunct, backing, bourdon, descant, support 08 addition, obligato 09 accessory, obbligato, orchestra, side order 10 background, complement, supplement 11 coexistence, concomitant, tracklement
• **provide accompaniment**
04 la-la

accompanist
04 comp 11 accompanier 12 backing group 15 instrumentalist

accompany
04 back, chum 05 usher 06 assist, attend, convoy, escort, follow, go with, squire, wait on 07 coexist, conduct, consort, partner, support 08 belong to, chaperon, coincide, come with, play with, tag along, wait upon, walk with 09 associate, chaperone, companion, occur with 10 complement, supplement, travel with 11 go along with 12 tag along with 13 associate with, come along with 14 go together with, hang around with

accomplice
04 aide, ally, mate 05 shill, stale 06 bonnet, button, helper 07 abettor, fedarie, nobbler, partner 08 approver, complice, copemate, federary, foedarie, henchman, sidekick, swagsman 09 accessory, assistant, associate, colleague, copesmate, federarie 11 confederate, conspirator 12 collaborator, participator, right-hand man 14 right-hand woman

accomplish
02 do 06 attain, effect, finish, fulfil, hack it, manage, obtain, wangle 07 achieve, compass, execute, perform, produce, realize 08 bring off, carry out, complete, complish, conclude, engineer 09 discharge, pull it off 10 bring about, consummate, effectuate 15 carry into effect, deliver the goods

accomplished
03 ace 04 arch, done, over 05 adept 06 adroit, expert, gifted, savant, wicked 07 learned, savante, skilful, skilled 08 compleat, masterly, polished, talented 09 practised 10 consummate, cultivated, proficient 11 experienced 12 professional

accomplishment
03 act, art 04 deed, feat, gift 05 doing, forte, knack, skill 06 stroke, talent, virtue 07 ability, exploit, faculty, finesse, prowess, quality, triumph 08 aptitude, exercise, fruition 09 discharge, effecting, execution, finishing, operation 10 attainment, capability, completion, conclusion, fulfilling, fulfilment, futurition, management, perfection, production 11 achievement, carrying-out, performance, proficiency, realization 12 consummation 13 qualification 14 stroke of genius

accord
04 deal, give, jibe, pact, sort, suit 05 agree, allow, chime, endow, grant, match, unity, yield 06 assent, bestow, concur, confer, extend, square, tender, treaty 07 compact, concert, conform, congree, consort, harmony, present 08 contract, sympathy 09 agreement, concordat, congruity, consensus, harmonize, unanimity, vouchsafe 10 accordance, conformity, congruence, convention, correspond, settlement 11 be in harmony, concurrence 13 be in agreement 14 correspondence
• **of your own accord**
06 freely 09 willingly 11 voluntarily
• **with one accord**
09 of one mind 11 unanimously

accordance
• **in accordance with**
02 by 05 after, under 10 in line with, obedient to 12 in relation to, in the light of 13 in concert with, in keeping with, in the manner of 14 consistent with, in proportion to 15 in agreement with

according
03 acc
• **according to**
03 per 05 after, as per 08 as said by, secundum 10 as stated by, in line with, obedient to 11 as claimed by, depending on 12 in relation to, in the light of 13 in keeping with, in the manner of, on the report of 14 consistent with, in proportion to

accordingly
02 so 04 duly, ergo, thus 05 fitly, hence 08 properly, suitably 09 agreeably, as a result, therefore 10 sure enough, thereafter 12 consequently, consistently 13 appropriately, for that reason, in consequence 15 correspondingly

accost
04 bord, hail, halt, stop 05 abord, assay, board, boord, borde 06 attack, boorde, detain, molest, nobble, waylay 07 address, solicit 08 approach, confront 09 importune 10 buttonhole

account
02 a/c 03 acc, tab 04 acct, bill, deem, hold, sake, tale 05 books, count, story, value 06 assess, behalf, detail, esteem, import, ledger, memoir, moment, reckon, record, regard, report, sketch, view as 07 adjudge, believe, charges, details, history, invoice, journal, version, write up 08 appraise, consider, look upon, regard as, register 09 chronicle, inventory, narration, narrative, portrayal, statement 10 commentary, importance 11 consequence, description, distinction, explanation 12 presentation, significance
• **account for**
04 give, kill 06 defeat, make up, say

why, supply **07** clear up, destroy, explain, justify, provide **08** comprise **09** answer for, eliminate, elucidate, represent, vindicate **10** constitute, illuminate **11** rationalize **14** give reasons for

• **falsify accounts**
04 cook, rort **12** cook the books

• **give an account of**
04 tell **06** relate

• **on account of**
02 o/a **03** for **04** over **05** along **07** because, owing to, through **08** in view of **09** because of **10** by virtue of, in virtue of **11** the reason is **12** for the sake of

• **on no account**
05 never, no way **12** certainly not **13** not on your life

accountability
09 liability, reporting **10** obligation **11** amenability **13** answerability **14** responsibility

accountable
05 bound **06** liable **07** obliged **08** amenable **09** comptable, comptible, obligated **10** answerable, chargeable, explicable **11** charged with, responsible

accountant
02 CA **03** ACA, acc, CPA **06** bookie **09** bookmaker **11** bean counter

accoutrements
03 kit **04** gear **05** stuff **06** outfit, things **07** clobber **08** fittings, fixtures **09** caparison, equipment, trimmings **10** adornments **11** decorations, furnishings, odds and ends **12** appointments **13** appurtenances, bits and pieces, paraphernalia

accredit
06 depute **07** approve, certify, endorse, license, warrant **09** attribute, authorize, recognize **10** commission **11** certificate

accredited
07 deputed **08** approved, endorsed, licensed, official **09** appointed, certified, qualified **10** authorized, recognized **12** certificated, commissioned

accretion
05 add-on **06** growth **07** build-up **08** addition, increase **09** gathering, increment **10** collecting, cumulation, supplement **12** accumulation, augmentation

accrue
05 amass, mount **07** augment, be added, build up, collect, mount up **08** increase **10** accumulate

accumulate
04 gain, grow, pile, pool **05** amass, hoard, stash, store, tot up **06** accrue, distil, garner, gather, pile up **07** acquire, augment, build up, collect, congest, distill **08** assemble, cumulate, increase, multiply, snowball **09** aggregate, stockpile

accumulation
04 gain, heap, mass, pile **05** hoard, stack, stock, store **06** growth **07** accrual, build-up, reserve **08** assembly, increase **09** accretion, aggregate, gathering, stockpile **10** building-up, collection, cumulation **11** acquisition **12** augmentation **14** conglomeration, multiplication

accumulative
07 growing **08** mounting **09** enlarging **10** increasing **11** multiplying, snowballing

accuracy
05 truth **06** verity **08** fidelity, veracity **09** closeness, exactness, precision **10** exactitude **11** carefulness, correctness **12** authenticity, faithfulness, scrupulosity, truthfulness, veridicality **14** meticulousness

accurate
04 fair, nice, true **05** close, exact, right, sound, valid **06** bang on, dead-on, spot-on, strict **07** correct, factual, literal, perfect, precise **08** faithful, on target, rigorous, truthful, unerring **09** authentic, faultless, on the mark, veracious, veridical, well-aimed **10** meticulous **11** word-for-word, word-perfect **12** well-directed **13** letter-perfect

accurately
05 truly **07** closely, exactly **08** strictly **09** correctly, literally, perfectly, precisely **10** faithfully, rigorously, truthfully, unerringly **11** faultlessly, veraciously, veridically **12** meticulously

accursed
05 blest, hated **06** damned, doomed, goddam, sacred **07** blessed, goddamn, hateful **08** maledict, wretched **09** bewitched, condemned, execrable, goddamned, loathsome **10** abominable, bedevilled, despicable, detestable **13** anathematized

accusation
03 tax **04** bill **05** blame, cause, libel, smear **06** charge, threap, threep **08** citation, delation, gravamen **09** challenge, complaint, invective **10** allegation, imputation, indictment **11** arraignment, crimination, impeachment, inculpation, information, prosecution **12** denunciation **13** incrimination, recrimination

accuse
03 tax **04** book, cite **05** blame, frame, peach **06** allege, appeal, charge, detect, impugn, impute, indict **07** appeach, arraign, asperse, attaint, censure, impeach, reprove **08** confront, denounce **09** attribute, challenge, criminate, implicate, prosecute **10** put on trial **11** incriminate, recriminate **12** bring charges, press charges **13** inform against **14** throw the book at **15** hold responsible, make accusations, make allegations

accustom
03 use **05** adapt, enure, inure, teach **06** adjust, attune **07** conform **08** occasion **09** acclimate, climatize, get used to, habituate **11** acclimatize, accommodate, familiarize **15** get familiar with

accustomed
03 old **04** tame, used, wont **05** fixed, given, usual **06** at home, inured, normal, wonted **07** general, regular, routine **08** everyday, familiar, frequent, habitual, ordinary **09** customary **10** acquainted, habituated, prevailing **11** established, traditional **12** acclimatized, conventional, in the habit of **14** consuetudinary

ace
01 A **03** jot, one, Tib **04** cool, neat, unit **05** basto, brill, great, whizz **06** expert, genius, grouse, master, superb, wicked, winner **07** dab hand, hotshot, maestro, perfect **08** champion, spadille, terrific, top-notch, very good, virtuoso **09** brilliant, excellent **10** first-class **11** outstanding

acerbic
05 harsh, sharp, spiky **06** biting **07** caustic, mordant **08** abrasive, stinging **09** rancorous, sarcastic, trenchant, vitriolic **10** astringent **11** acrimonious

ache
01 H **03** die, yen **04** hurt, itch, kill, long, pain, pang, pine, work **05** agony, aitch, crave, pound, smart, sting, throb, yearn **06** be sore, desire, hanker, hunger, play up, stound, stownd, suffer, thirst, twinge **07** agonize, anguish, craving, longing **08** pounding, smarting, soreness, stinging, yearning **09** be in agony, be painful, hankering, suffering, throbbing

achieve
02 do **03** get, win **04** earn, gain **05** reach **06** attain, effect, finish, fulfil, manage, obtain, wrap up **07** acquire, execute, perform, procure, produce, realize, succeed **08** carry out, complete **09** polish off **10** accomplish, bring about, consummate, effectuate

achievement
03 act **04** deed, feat **06** action, effort, stroke **07** exploit, success, triumph **08** activity, fruition **09** execution **10** attainment, chevisance, completion, fulfilment **11** acquirement, performance, procurement, realization **12** consummation, effectuation **14** accomplishment, stroke of genius

achiever
04 doer **08** go-getter, live wire, whizz kid **09** high-flyer, performer, succeeder **12** success story

Achilles' heel
05 fault **07** failing **08** weakness, weak spot **09** weak point **12** imperfection **15** vulnerable point

acid
04 keen, sour, tart **05** catty, harsh, sharp, sugar **06** acidic, biting, bitter, morose, unkind **07** acerbic, acetous, caustic, cutting, hurtful, mordant, pungent **08** critical, incisive, stinging, vinegary **09** acidulous, corrosive, sarcastic, trenchant, vitriolic **10** astringent, ill-natured **11** unsweetened

Acids include:

03 DNA, LSD, RNA
04 acyl, EDTA, uric
05 amino, boric, fatty, folic
06 acetic, citric, formic, lactic, nitric, oxalic, phenol, tannic
07 acrylic, benzoic, boracic, chloric, nitrous, nucleic, prussic, pyruvic, silicic, stearic
08 abscisic, ascorbic, carbolic, carbonic, ethanoic, lysergic, palmitic, periodic, retinoic, tartaric
09 methanoic, nicotinic, propionic, salicylic, sulphonic, sulphuric
10 aqua fortis, barbituric, carboxylic, phosphoric, sulphurous
11 hydrocyanic, ribonucleic
12 hydrochloric, hydrofluoric
13 thiosulphuric, tricarboxylic

See also **amino acid**

• **acid test**
02 pH

• **work with acid**
04 etch

acknowledge
03 con, own **04** avow, hail, mark **05** admit, allow, grant, greet, thank **06** accede, accept, affirm, agnize, answer, avouch, honour, notice, salute, wave to **07** address, agree to, concede, confess, confirm, declare, own up to, react to, reply to **08** signal to **09** acquiesce, celebrate, recognize, respond to **10** be grateful **11** say thank you, write back to **13** give thanks for

acknowledged
06 avowed **08** accepted, admitted, approved, attested, declared **09** confirmed, professed **10** accredited, recognized

acknowledgement
03 nod **04** wave **05** reply, smile **06** answer, avowal, credit, homage, notice, praise, thanks **07** tribute, welcome **08** bouquets, cognovit, comeback, granting, greeting, reaction, response **09** admission, allowance, deference, gratitude **10** acceptance, confession, profession, salutation **11** declaration, recognition **12** appreciation, gratefulness, recognizance

acme
04 apex, peak **05** crown, prick **06** apogee, climax, comble, height, summit, zenith **07** optimum **08** pinnacle **09** high point **11** culmination, sublimation **12** highest point

acolyte
06 helper **08** adherent, altar boy, follower, hanger-on, sidekick, thurifer **09** assistant, attendant **11** acolouthite

acorn
04 mast **05** glans **07** oak mast, valonea, valonia **08** racahout, vallonia **09** raccahout

acoustic
05 aural, sound **06** audile **07** hearing **08** auditory

acquaint
04 tell **05** brief **06** advise, inform, notify, reveal **07** apprise, divulge, let know, possess **08** accustom, announce, disclose **09** enlighten **11** familiarize, make aware of **14** make conversant **15** put in the picture

acquaintance
04 mate **06** friend, pick-up **07** contact, homeboy **08** confrère, habitude, hanger-on, intimacy **09** associate, awareness, colleague, companion, knowledge **10** cognizance, connection, experience, fellowship **11** association, conversance, familiarity **12** relationship **13** companionship, social contact, understanding

acquainted
05 aware **06** au fait, versed **07** abreast **08** apprised, familiar, friendly, intimate **09** au courant, cognizant, in the know, up to speed **10** conversant, well-versed **11** on good terms **13** knowledgeable **15** on friendly terms

• **be acquainted with**
03 ken **04** know

acquiesce
05 agree, allow, defer **06** accede, accept, assent, concur, give in, permit, submit **07** approve, consent **12** give the nod to

acquiescence
03 nod **05** say-so **06** assent **07** consent, go-ahead **08** approval, thumbs-up, yielding **09** agreement, deference **10** acceptance, compliance, green-light, submission **11** concurrence, countenance

acquiescent
07 servile **08** acceding, agreeing, amenable, obedient, yielding **09** accepting, agreeable, approving, compliant **10** concurring, consenting, submissive **11** complaisant, deferential

acquire
◇ *containment indicator*
03 bag, buy, cop, ern, get, net, win **04** earn, gain, grab **05** amass **06** attain, collar, come by, gather, obtain, pick up, secure, snap up, take on **07** achieve, collect, procure, realize, receive, snaffle, usucapt **08** purchase **10** accumulate **11** appropriate, splash out on

acquisition
03 buy **04** gain **05** prize **07** acquest, gaining **08** property, purchase, securing, takeover **09** accession, obtaining, usucapion **10** attainment, investment, possession, usucaption **11** achievement, procurement **13** appropriation

acquisitive
04 avid **06** greedy **08** covetous, grasping, hoarding **09** predatory, rapacious, voracious **10** avaricious **12** accumulative

acquisitiveness
05 greed **07** avarice, avidity **08** cupidity, rapacity, voracity **12** covetousness, graspingness **13** predatoriness

acquit
02 do **03** act **04** bear, free **05** clear, prove, repay **06** assoil, behave, bestow, excuse, let off, settle **07** absolve, comport, conduct, deliver, dismiss, perform, release, relieve, satisfy, set free **08** liberate, reprieve, uncharge **09** discharge, exculpate, exonerate, vindicate **11** make a bad job **12** make a good job **13** let off the hook

acquittal
06 relief **07** freeing, release **08** clearing, excusing, reprieve **09** clearance, discharge, dismissal **10** absolution, liberation **11** deliverance, exculpation, exoneration, vindication **12** compurgation

acre
01 a **02** ac

acrid
04 acid, sour, tart **05** harsh, nasty, sharp **06** biting, bitter **07** acerbic, burning, caustic, cutting, mordant, pungent **08** incisive, sardonic, stinging, venomous, virulent **09** malicious, sarcastic, trenchant, vitriolic **10** astringent **11** acrimonious

acrimonious
05 sharp **06** bitchy, biting, bitter, severe **07** abusive, acerbic, caustic, crabbed, cutting, waspish **08** petulant, spiteful, venomous, virulent **09** irascible, rancorous, splenetic, trenchant, vitriolic **10** astringent, censorious **11** atrabilious, ill-tempered

acrimony
04 gall **05** spite, venom **06** spleen **07** ill will, rancour, sarcasm, vitriol **08** acerbity, acridity, asperity, mordancy **09** harshness, ill temper, petulance, virulence **10** bitterness, causticity, ill feeling, resentment, trenchancy **11** astringency **12** irascibility

acrobat
05 speel **07** gymnast, speeler, tumbler **08** balancer, posturer, stuntman

09 aerialist, posturist 10 rope-dancer, rope-walker, stuntwoman, wing-walker 11 equilibrist, funambulist 12 somersaulter, trick cyclist 13 contortionist, trapeze artist 15 tightrope-walker

acrobatics

◇ *anagram indicator*

06 stunts 09 balancing 10 gymnastics 11 equilibrity, funambulism, rope-walking, wire-walking 13 somersaulting

across

01 a 02 ac 03 dia-, tra- 04 over, tran- 05 trans- 06 thwart 07 athwart 08 à travers

act

02 be, do 03 bit, gig, kid, law 04 bill, deal, deed, fake, feat, item, mime, move, part, play, sham, show, skit, step, turn, work 05 canon, doing, edict, enact, feign, front, mimic, put on, react, serve 06 action, affect, assume, be busy, behave, decree, number, ruling, sketch, stroke 07 episode, exploit, go about, imitate, measure, operate, perform, portray, pretend, respond, routine, section, statute 08 be active, division, feigning, function, pretence, put-up job, simulate 09 dissemble, execution, manoeuvre, operation, ordinance, represent, take steps 10 do the job of, enterprise, resolution, subsection, take action, take effect 11 achievement, affectation, counterfeit, dissimulate, impersonate, make-believe, performance, undertaking 12 characterize, dissemblance, go on the stage, have an effect, take measures 13 be efficacious, dissimulation, exert yourself 14 accomplishment, acquit yourself 15 comport yourself, conduct yourself

See also **law**

• **act badly**

03 ham

• **act on**

04 heed, obey, take 05 alter 06 affect, change, follow, fulfil, modify, work on 08 carry out 09 conform to, influence, transform 10 comply with

• **act the part of**

04 come

• **act up**

04 fail 06 pack up, play up 07 carry on, conk out, go kaput, go wrong, not work 09 break down, mess about, misbehave 10 give bother, muck around 11 behave badly, malfunction, stop working 12 cause trouble

acting

◇ *anagram indicator*

01 a 03 act 04 actg 05 drama 06 action, deputy, fill-in, pro tem, relief, supply 07 interim, reserve, showbiz, stand-by, stand-in, stopgap, theatre 08 artistry, covering 09 dramatics, imitating, in place of, luvviedom, melodrama, portrayal, short-term, surrogate, temporary 10 footlights, performing, play-acting, stagecraft, substitute 11 histrionics, performance, provisional, theatricals, Thespianism 12 show business 13 impersonation, standing in for 14 performing arts

actinium

02 Ac

actinon

02 an

action

◇ *anagram indicator*

03 act, pas 04 case, deed, feat, fray, move, step, suit, work 05 clash, doing, fight, force, power 06 affray, battle, combat, effect, effort, energy, events, motion, result, spirit, vigour 07 exploit, lawsuit, measure, pizzazz, process, warfare 08 activity, conflict, exercise, exertion, fighting, goings-on, movement, practice, skirmish, vitality 09 encounter, endeavour, influence, mechanism, operation 10 activities, engagement, enterprise, excitement, get-up-and-go, happenings, litigation, liveliness, proceeding 11 achievement, functioning, hostilities, performance, proceedings, prosecution, stimulation, undertaking 12 exhilaration, forcefulness 14 accomplishment, course of action

• **check action**

04 stay

• **course of action**

04 path

• **critical time of action**

04 D-day

activate

◇ *anagram indicator*

04 fire, move, stir, trip 05 impel, put on, rouse, start 06 arouse, bestir, excite, prompt, propel, set off, turn on 07 actuate, animate, trigger 08 energize, get going, initiate, mobilize, motivate, set going, switch on 09 derepress, galvanize, kick-start, stimulate 10 trigger off 11 set in motion 12 start working 13 push the button 14 press the button, throw the switch

active

◇ *anagram indicator*

01 a 03 act 04 at it, busy, go-go, spry 05 agile, alert, astir, manic, quick, vital, yauld, zippy 06 birkie, lively, mobile, nimble, quiver, wimble 07 devoted, engaged, forward, in force, on the go, running, springe, vibrant, working 08 activist, animated, diligent, forceful, frenetic, involved, militant, occupied, practive, spirited, vigorous 09 committed, effectual, energetic, operative, sprightly, stirabout 11 functioning, hard-working, hyperactive, industrious, in operation, light-footed, operational 12 contributing, enterprising, enthusiastic 13 indefatigable

• **be active**

02 do 03 hum

activist

07 inciter, stirrer 08 agitator, fomenter, henchman, militant 09 firebrand 10 incendiary, subversive 12 troublemaker 13 revolutionary

Activists include:

04 **Bono**, **King** (Martin Luther)
05 **Nader** (Ralph), **Parks** (Rosa)
06 **Gandhi** (Mahatma), **Geldof** (Bob)
07 **Angelou** (Maya), **Chomsky** (Noam), **Guevara** (Che), **Jackson** (Jesse), **Mandela** (Nelson), **Mandela** (Winnie)
08 **Malcolm X**, **Silkwood** (Karen)
09 **Pankhurst** (Christabel), **Pankhurst** (Emmeline), **Pankhurst** (Sylvia)

See also **aboriginal**

activity

◇ *anagram indicator*

02 do, go 03 act, job 04 deed, life, play, stir, task, work 05 hobby 06 action, bustle, labour, motion, scheme 07 pastime, project, pursuit, venture 08 business, exercise, exertion, industry, interest, movement 09 avocation, commotion, diversion, endeavour 10 activeness, enterprise, hurly-burly, liveliness, occupation 11 distraction, undertaking 13 something to do 14 toing and froing 15 a hive of activity, a hive of industry, hustle and bustle

• **bustling activity**

04 rush 06 bustle 07 beehive

• **focus of activity**

03 hub

• **furious activity**

04 rage

• **increase in activity**

04 boom

actor, actress

03 ham 04 feed, mime, mute, supe 05 buffa, buffo, comic, extra, luvvy, super, thesp 06 artist, luvvie, mummer, player, stager, stooge, walk-on 07 artiste, comique, histrio, ingénue, Roscius, starlet, support, trouper 08 comedian, epilogue, film star, histrion, juvenile, thespian 09 bit player, film actor, hamfatter, movie star, performer, play actor, principal, tragedian 10 leading man, mime artist, movie actor, understudy, utility man 11 leading lady, matinée idol, pantomimist, protagonist, straight man, tragedienne, tritagonist 12 impersonator, spear carrier 13 deuteragonist, supernumerary 14 character actor, dramatic artist, stage performer 15 strolling player

Actors include:

03 **Cox** (Brian), **Fox** (James), **Fox** (Michael J), **Fry** (Stephen), **Law** (Jude), **Lee** (Bruce), **Lee** (Christopher), **Lee** (Spike), **Lom** (Herbert), **Sim** (Alastair)
04 **Cage** (Nicolas), **Chan** (Jackie), **Chow** (Yun-Fat), **Dean** (James), **Depp** (Johnny), **Ford** (Harrison), **Gere** (Richard), **Holm** (Sir Ian), **Hope** (Bob), **Hurt** (John), **Kaye** (Danny),

actor, actress

Kean (Edmund), **Lowe** (Rob), **Peck** (Gregory), **Penn** (Sean), **Pitt** (Brad), **Reed** (Oliver), **Sher** (Sir Antony), **Tati** (Jacques), **Thaw** (John), **Tree** (Sir Herbert Beerbohm), **Wood** (Elijah)

05 **Allen** (Woody), **Bacon** (Kevin), **Bates** (Alan), **Brody** (Adrien), **Caine** (Sir Michael), **Clift** (Montgomery), **Craig** (Daniel), **Crowe** (Russell), **Dafoe** (Willem), **Damon** (Matt), **Dance** (Charles), **Firth** (Colin), **Flynn** (Errol), **Fonda** (Henry), **Gable** (Clark), **Grant** (Cary), **Grant** (Hugh), **Grant** (Richard E), **Hanks** (Tom), **Hardy** (Oliver), **Irons** (Jeremy), **Kelly** (Gene), **Kempe** (Will), **Kline** (Kevin), **Leung** (Tony), **Lewis** (Jerry), **Lloyd** (Harold), **Lorre** (Peter), **Mason** (James), **Mills** (Sir John), **Moore** (Roger), **Neill** (Sam), **Nimoy** (Leonard), **Niven** (David), **Nolte** (Nick), **Price** (Vincent), **Quinn** (Anthony), **Reeve** (Christopher), **Robey** (Sir George), **Scott** (George C), **Sheen** (Charlie), **Sheen** (Martin), **Smith** (Will), **Spall** (Timothy), **Stamp** (Terence), **Sydow** (Max von), **Tracy** (Spencer), **Wayne** (John)

06 **Alleyn** (Edward), **Beatty** (Warren), **Bogart** (Humphrey), **Brando** (Marlon), **Brooks** (Mel), **Burton** (Richard), **Cagney** (James), **Carrey** (Jim), **Chaney** (Lon), **Coburn** (James), **Cooper** (Gary), **Cruise** (Tom), **Curtis** (Tony), **De Niro** (Robert), **DeVito** (Danny), **Dillon** (Matt), **Finney** (Albert), **Gambon** (Sir Michael), **Gibson** (Mel), **Glover** (Danny), **Harris** (Richard), **Heston** (Charlton), **Hopper** (Dennis), **Howard** (Trevor), **Hudson** (Rock), **Irving** (Sir Henry), **Jacobi** (Sir Derek), **Jolson** (Al), **Jouvet** (Louis), **Keaton** (Buster), **Keitel** (Harvey), **Kemble** (John Philip), **Laurel** (Stan), **Laurie** (Hugh), **Lemmon** (Jack), **Lugosi** (Bela), **Martin** (Steve), **Murphy** (Eddie), **Murray** (Bill), **Neeson** (Liam), **Newman** (Paul), **Oldman** (Gary), **O'Toole** (Peter), **Pacino** (Al), **Phelps** (Samuel), **Quayle** (Sir Anthony), **Reagan** (Ronald), **Reeves** (Keanu), **Rooney** (Mickey), **Rourke** (Mickey), **Sharif** (Omar), **Sinden** (Sir Donald), **Slater** (Christian), **Spacey** (Kevin), **Swayze** (Patrick), **Walken** (Christopher), **Welles** (Orson), **Wilder** (Gene), **Willis** (Bruce), **Wolfit** (Sir Donald)

07 **Astaire** (Fred), **Auteuil** (Daniel), **Aykroyd** (Dan), **Benigni** (Roberto), **Berkoff** (Steven), **Bogarde** (Sir Dirk), **Branagh** (Kenneth), **Bridges** (Jeff), **Bridges** (Lloyd), **Bronson** (Charles), **Brosnan** (Pierce), **Brynner** (Yul), **Burbage** (Richard), **Carlyle** (Robert), **Chaplin** (Charlie), **Clooney** (George), **Connery** (Sir Sean), **Costner** (Kevin), **Crystal** (Billy), **Cushing** (Peter), **Douglas** (Kirk), **Douglas** (Michael), **Everett** (Rupert), **Fiennes** (Joseph), **Fiennes** (Ralph), **Forrest** (Edwin), **Freeman** (Morgan), **Garrick** (David), **Gielgud** (Sir John), **Hoffman** (Dustin), **Hopkins** (Sir Anthony), **Hordern** (Sir Michael), **Jackson** (Samuel L), **Karloff** (Boris), **Marceau** (Marcel), **Matthau** (Walter), **McQueen** (Steve), **Mitchum** (Robert), **Montand** (Yves), **Nielsen** (Leslie), **Olivier** (Laurence, Lord), **Poitier** (Sidney), **Redford** (Robert), **Rickman** (Alan), **Robbins** (Tim), **Robeson** (Paul), **Roscius**, **Russell** (Kurt), **Savalas** (Telly), **Selleck** (Tom), **Sellers** (Peter), **Shatner** (William), **Steiger** (Rod), **Stewart** (James), **Ustinov** (Sir Peter)

08 **Atkinson** (Rowan), **Barrault** (Jean-Louis), **Day-Lewis** (Daniel), **DiCaprio** (Leonardo), **Dreyfuss** (Richard), **Eastwood** (Clint), **Goldblum** (Jeff), **Guinness** (Sir Alec), **Harrison** (Sir Rex), **Kingsley** (Ben), **Laughton** (Charles), **Macready** (William Charles), **McGregor** (Ewan), **McKellen** (Sir Ian), **Redgrave** (Sir Michael), **Reynolds** (Burt), **Robinson** (Edward G), **Scofield** (Paul), **Stallone** (Sylvester), **Travolta** (John), **Van Cleef** (Lee), **Van Damme** (Jean-Claude), **von Sydow** (Max), **Williams** (Robin), **Woodward** (Edward)

09 **Barrymore** (Lionel), **Broadbent** (Jim), **Broderick** (Matthew), **Chevalier** (Maurice), **Courtenay** (Sir Tom), **Depardieu** (Gérard), **Fairbanks** (Douglas), **Fernandel**, **Hawthorne** (Sir Nigel), **Lancaster** (Burt), **Malkovich** (John), **Nicholson** (Jack), **Pleasence** (Donald), **Strasberg** (Lee), **Valentino** (Rudolph)

10 **Richardson** (Sir Ralph), **Sutherland** (Donald), **Sutherland** (Kiefer), **Washington** (Denzel)

11 **Mastroianni** (Marcello), **Weissmuller** (Johnny)

12 **Attenborough** (Richard, Lord), **Garcia Bernal** (Gael), **Stanislavsky** (Konstantin)

14 **Schwarzenegger** (Arnold)

See also **comedian**

Actresses include:

03 **Bow** (Clara), **Cox** (Courteney), **Day** (Doris), **Loy** (Myrna)

04 **Ball** (Lucille), **Dern** (Laura), **Diaz** (Cameron), **Dors** (Diana), **Duse** (Eleonora), **Gish** (Lillian), **Gwyn** (Nell), **Hawn** (Goldie), **Hird** (Dame Thora), **Rigg** (Dame Diana), **Ryan** (Meg), **West** (Mae), **Wood** (Natalie), **York** (Susannah)

05 **Allen** (Gracie), **Berry** (Halle), **Bloom** (Claire), **Close** (Glenn), **Davis** (Bette), **Davis** (Geena), **Dench** (Dame Judi), **Derek** (Bo), **Evans** (Dame Edith), **Fonda** (Jane), **Gabor** (Zsa Zsa), **Garbo** (Greta), **Jolie** (Angelina), **Kelly** (Grace), **Lange** (Jessica), **Leigh** (Janet), **Leigh** (Vivien), **Lopez** (Jennifer), **Loren** (Sophia), **Mills** (Hayley), **Moore** (Demi), **Ryder** (Winona), **Smith** (Dame Maggie), **Stone** (Sharon), **Swank** (Hilary), **Terry** (Dame Ellen), **Welch** (Raquel)

06 **Adjani** (Isabelle), **Bacall** (Lauren), **Bardot** (Brigitte), **Bisset** (Jacqueline), **Cheung** (Maggie), **Curtis** (Jamie Lee), **Farrow** (Mia), **Fisher** (Carrie), **Foster** (Jodie), **Grable** (Betty), **Hannah** (Daryl), **Harlow** (Jean), **Hedren** (Tippi), **Hunter** (Holly), **Huston** (Anjelica), **Keaton** (Diane), **Kemble** (Fanny), **Kidman** (Nicole), **Kinski** (Nastassja), **Lamarr** (Hedy), **Lumley** (Joanna), **Midler** (Bette), **Mirren** (Helen), **Monroe** (Marilyn), **Moreau** (Jeanne), **Robson** (Dame Flora), **Rogers** (Ginger), **Spacek** (Sissy), **Streep** (Meryl), **Suzman** (Janet), **Tautou** (Audrey), **Taylor** (Dame Elizabeth), **Temple** (Shirley), **Turner** (Kathleen), **Turner** (Lana), **Ullman** (Tracey), **Weaver** (Sigourney), **Winger** (Debra)

07 **Andress** (Ursula), **Andrews** (Dame Julie), **Aniston** (Jennifer), **Bergman** (Ingrid), **Binoche** (Juliette), **Colbert** (Claudette), **Deneuve** (Catherine), **Gardner** (Ava), **Garland** (Judy), **Hepburn** (Audrey), **Hepburn** (Katharine), **Jackson** (Glenda), **Johnson** (Dame Celia), **Langtry** (Lillie), **Lombard** (Carole), **Paltrow** (Gwyneth), **Roberts** (Julia), **Russell** (Jane), **Seymour** (Jane), **Siddons** (Sarah), **Swanson** (Gloria), **Walters** (Julie), **Winslet** (Kate)

08 **Ashcroft** (Dame Peggy), **Bancroft** (Anne), **Bankhead** (Tallulah), **Basinger** (Kim), **Campbell** (Mrs Patrick), **Charisse** (Cyd), **Christie** (Julie), **Crawford** (Joan), **Dietrich** (Marlene), **Fontaine** (Joan), **Goldberg** (Whoopi), **Griffith** (Melanie), **Hayworth** (Rita), **MacLaine** (Shirley), **Minnelli** (Liza), **Pfeiffer** (Michelle), **Pickford** (Mary), **Rampling** (Charlotte), **Redgrave** (Vanessa), **Sarandon** (Susan), **Shepherd** (Cybill), **Signoret** (Simone), **Stanwyck** (Barbara), **Thompson** (Emma)

09 **Barrymore** (Drew), **Bernhardt** (Sarah), **Blanchett** (Cate), **Johansson** (Scarlett), **MacDowell** (Andie), **Mansfield** (Jayne), **Plowright** (Joan Ann), **Streisand** (Barbra), **Thorndike** (Dame Sybil), **Zellweger** (Renée), **Zeta Jones** (Catherine)

10 **Rossellini** (Isabella), **Rutherford** (Dame Margaret)

11 **Bracegirdle** (Anne), **de Havilland** (Olivia), **Mistinguett**, **Scott-Thomas** (Kristin)

12 **Bonham Carter** (Helena), **Lollobrigida** (Gina)

See also **comedian**

• actor's portrayal
04 part, role
• bad actor
03 ham

actors
04 cast **07** company

actress *see* **actor, actress**

actual
04 real, true, very **07** certain, de facto, factual, genuine **08** absolute, bona fide, concrete, definite, existent, material, physical, positive, real life, tangible, truthful, verified
09 authentic, confirmed, realistic
10 legitimate **11** substantial
12 indisputable **14** unquestionable

actuality
03 ens **04** fact **05** truth **07** realism, reality **08** solidity **09** entelechy, existence, substance **10** factuality
11 historicity, materiality
12 corporeality **14** substantiality

actually
04 even **05** truly **06** indeed, in fact, really **07** de facto, insooth, in truth, soothly **09** in reality **10** absolutely
11 as it happens **12** surprisingly
14 believe it or not **15** as a matter of fact

actuate
04 move, stir **05** rouse, start
06 arouse, kindle, prompt, set off, turn on **07** animate, trigger **08** activate, motivate, set going, switch on
09 instigate, stimulate **10** trigger off
11 set in motion **12** start working

acumen
03 wit **05** sense **06** wisdom **07** insight
08 gumption, keenness, sagacity, sapience **09** ingenuity, intuition, judgement, quickness, sharpness, smartness **10** astuteness, cleverness, perception, shrewdness
11 discernment, penetration, percipience, perspicuity
12 intelligence, perspicacity
13 judiciousness **14** discrimination

acupressure
04 do-in **07** shiatsu, shiatzu **09** Jin Shin Do®

acute
04 dire, keen **05** canny, grave, sharp, smart, vital **06** astute, clever, severe, shrewd, urgent **07** crucial, cutting, drastic, extreme, intense, sapient, serious, violent **08** critical, decisive, incisive, peracute, piercing, poignant
09 dangerous, judicious, observant, sensitive **10** discerning, insightful, perceptive, percipient, unbearable
11 distressing, penetrating, sharp-witted **13** perspicacious

acutely
04 very **06** keenly **07** gravely, sharply **08** markedly, severely, strongly **09** extremely, intensely, seriously

adage
03 saw **05** axiom, gnome, maxim
06 byword, saying **07** precept, proverb **08** aphorism, paroemia
10 apophthegm, whakatauki

adamant
03 set **04** firm, hard **05** fixed, rigid, stiff, tough **07** diamond **08** obdurate, resolute, stubborn **09** immovable, insistent, lodestone, unbending
10 determined, inflexible, unshakable, unwavering, unyielding **11** unrelenting, unshakeable **12** intransigent
14 uncompromising

Adamson
04 Abel, Cain, Seth

adapt
◇ *anagram indicator*
03 apt, fit **04** suit **05** alter, apply, frame, match, shape, tally **06** adjust, change, comply, modify, reduce, tailor
07 arrange, conform, convert, exploit, fashion, get used, prepare, qualify, remodel **08** attemper, settle in
09 contemper, customize, harmonize
10 specialize **11** accommodate **13** get accustomed

adaptable
◇ *anagram indicator*
07 open-end, plastic, pliable
08 amenable, flexible, variable
09 alterable, compliant, easy-going, malleable, open-ended, versatile
10 adjustable, changeable, modifiable
11 conformable, convertible

adaptation
◇ *anagram indicator*
05 shift **06** change **07** fitting, shaping
08 matching, revision **09** refitting, reshaping, reworking, variation
10 adjustment, alteration, conformity, conversion, fashioning **11** getting used, habituation, preparation, remodelling
12 conformation, modification, refashioning **13** accommodation, customization, harmonization
14 transformation **15** acclimatization, familiarization

add
◇ *juxtaposition indicator*
03 eik, eke, put, sum, tot **04** go on, join, tote **05** affix, annex, boost, count, put in, put on, raise, top up, total, tot up
06 adjoin, append, attach, deepen, extend, hike up, prefix, suffix, tack on
07 augment, build on, carry on, combine, count up, enhance, improve, include, postfix, summate, throw in
08 complete, continue, heighten, increase **09** aggravate, go on to say, increment, intensify, introduce
10 supplement **15** work out the total
• add up
03 fit **04** cast, make, mean **05** count, run to, spell, sum up, tally, total, tot up
06 amount, come to, reckon
07 compute, count up, include, signify, stack up **08** figure up, indicate, ring true
09 calculate, make sense **10** constitute
11 add together, be plausible **12** be consistent, be reasonable, hang together **13** stand to reason

added
03 new **04** more **05** extra, fresh, spare
07 adjunct, another, further
10 additional **13** supplementary

addendum
02 PS **03** add **05** annex **07** adjunct, allonge, codicil **08** addition, appendix
09 appendage **10** attachment, postscript, supplement
11 endorsement **12** augmentation

addict
03 fan **04** buff, head, hype, user
05 fiend, freak, hound, junky
06 junkie, stoner **07** devotee, druggie, fanatic, hop-head, tripper
08 adherent, coke head, drug user, follower, snowbird **09** clay eater, crackhead, dope-fiend, drug fiend, drug taker, mainliner, smackhead
10 enthusiast **14** cruciverbalist

addicted
04 daft, fond, nuts, wild **05** crazy, given, potty **06** hooked **07** devoted
08 absorbed, bibulous, frequent, inclined, obsessed **09** confirmed, dedicated, dependent, fanatical, strung out **10** dissipated **13** drug-dependent

addiction
04 need **05** habit, mania, thing
06 monkey **07** craving **08** caffeism, opiumism, vinosity **09** cocainism, ergomania, obsession **10** caffeinism, compulsion, dependence, dependency, femininism **11** a colt's tooth, etheromania

addictive
09 obsessive **10** compulsive **12** habit-forming, irresistible **14** uncontrollable

addition
02 PS **03** eik, eke, PPS **04** also, gain, plus **05** extra, rider **06** adding, annexe
07 adjunct, codicil **08** addendum, additive, appendix, counting, increase
09 accession, accessory, accretion, appendage, extension, inclusion, increment, reckoning, summing-up, totalling, totting-up **10** annexation, attachment, increasing, postscript, supplement **11** computation, enlargement **12** afterthought, appurtenance, augmentation
• in addition
03 too **04** also **05** forby **06** as well, to boot, withal **07** besides, further, thereto **08** as well as, moreover
09 thereunto **11** furthermore
12 additionally, not to mention, over and above **14** for good measure, into the bargain

additional
03 new, odd **04** more, plus **05** added, extra, fresh, other, spare **07** another, further **09** increased **10** excrescent
12 adscititious, adventitious, supervenient, supplemental
13 supplementary

additionally
03 too **04** also **05** forby **06** as well, to boot, withal **07** besides, further
08 moreover **10** in addition
11 furthermore **12** over and above
14 for good measure, into the bargain

additive
04 MTBE **05** extra **07** E-number
08 addition **09** oxygenate, summative
10 emulsifier, stabilizer, supplement
12 preservative **13** canthaxanthin
14 canthaxanthine

addle
03 bad **04** daze, faze **05** empty
06 barren, muddle, putrid **07** confuse, fluster, muddled, perplex **08** befuddle, bewilder

addled
04 lost **05** fazed **07** mixed-up, muddled **08** confused **09** befuddled, flustered, perplexed **10** bewildered

address
03 add **04** call, flat, hail, home, lord, mail, post, send, talk **05** abode, greet, house, label, orate, place, remit, spiel, uncle **06** accost, convey, direct, invoke, mister, prayer, sermon, speech, talk to **07** accoast, bespeak, lecture, lodging, oration, speak to, welcome, write to **08** diatribe, dwelling, greeting, harangue, location, mistress, petition, preach to **09** apartment, designate, discourse, epirrhema, inaugural, intend for, monologue, philippic, residence, rhetorize, sermonize, situation, soliloquy
10 allocution, apostrophe, directions, invocation, salutation
11 communicate, give a talk to, inscription, make a speech, superscribe, superscript, valedictory, whereabouts **12** disquisition, dissertation **13** give a speech to, poste restante **14** deliver a speech

• **address yourself to**
06 tackle **07** focus on **08** attend to, deal with, engage in **09** undertake
10 take care of **12** buckle down to
13 concentrate on **15** apply yourself to

adduce
04 cite, lead, name **05** quote
06 assign, object **07** mention, present, proffer, refer to, trot out, upbraid
08 allude to, evidence, point out
10 put forward

adept
03 ace, don **04** able, deft, good
05 handy, sharp, swell **06** adroit, clever, deacon, expert, genius, master, nimble, versed, wicked, wizard
07 capable, dab hand, maestro, mahatma, skilled, veteran **08** hot stuff, masterly, polished **09** competent, practised **10** proficient
11 experienced, nobody's fool
12 accomplished

adequacy
07 ability, fitness, measure **08** fairness
10 capability, competence, mediocrity
11 passability, sufficiency, suitability
12 indifference, tolerability
13 acceptability, requisiteness, tolerableness **14** reasonableness, serviceability

adequate
02 OK **03** fit **04** able, enow, good
05 equal, ho-hum, valid **06** enough, patchy, will do, worthy **07** average, capable, working **08** all right, passable, suitable **09** competent, requisite, tolerable **10** acceptable, reasonable, sufficient **11** appropriate, indifferent, serviceable
12 commensurate, could be worse, run of the mill, satisfactory **13** could be better, no great shakes, unexceptional
14 fair to middling **15** undistinguished

adequately
08 passably, suitably **09** tolerably
10 acceptably, reasonably
12 sufficiently **13** appropriately
14 satisfactorily

adhere
03 fix **04** bond, glue, grip, heed, hold, join, keep, link, obey **05** cling, paste, stick **06** attach, cement, cleave, cohere, defend, fasten, follow, fulfil, solder **07** abide by, accrete, combine, espouse, observe, respect, stand by, support **08** cleave to, coalesce, hold fast **10** comply with, stick up for **11** go along with **13** stick together

adherence
05 cling **07** defence, respect, support
08 advocacy, fidelity **10** compliance, fulfilment, observance

adherent
03 bur, fan, nut **04** buff, burr, Jain, Sikh, Sofi, Sufi **05** Bahai, child, freak, Hindu, Jaina **06** Hindoo, Maoist, Sabean, votary **07** admirer, devotee, engager, Genevan, gnostic, Patarin, Sabaean, sceptic, sectary, skeptic **08** advocate, believer, catholic, disciple, follower, groupist, hanger-on, henchman, Jacobite, loyalist, partisan, partizan, Patarine, rightist, royalist, sectator, servitor, sticking, upholder, Vichyite, Wesleyan **09** Caesarean, Caesarian, Communard, Gothicist, ideologue, Oliverian, Samaritan, satellite, socialist, Spinozist, supporter, Wagnerist, Wagnerite **10** aficionado, Bourbonist, enthusiast, Protestant **12** episcopalian, hereditarian **13** sun worshipper
14 restorationist **15** hereditarianist, parliamentarian

adhesion
04 bond, grip **08** cohesion, purchase, sticking, synechia **09** adherence
10 attachment **12** adhesiveness
15 holding together

adhesive
03 gum **04** bond, glue, tape **05** glair, gluey, gummy, paste, tacky **06** Blu-tak®, cement, clammy, Cow Gum®, gummed, sticky **07** Band-aid®, Blu-tack®, holding, hot melt, stick-on
08 adherent, adhering, clinging, cohesive, fixative, goldsize, mountant, mucilage, sticking **09** attaching, emplastic, glutinous, Sellotape®, Superglue® **10** sticky tape
11 Elastoplast®, hot-melt glue
12 mucilaginous, passe-partout, rubber cement, self-adhesive

ad hoc
05 ad-lib **09** extempore, makeshift
10 improvised, off the cuff, unprepared, unscripted
11 spontaneous, unrehearsed
13 spontaneously

adieu
03 bye **04** ciao, ta-ta **05** adios **06** bye-bye, cheers, kia ora, see you, so long
07 cheerio, goodbye, haere ra **08** au revoir, farewell, take care **10** all the best **11** arrivederci, be seeing you, leave-taking, see you later, valediction, valedictory **12** have a nice day, mind how you go, see you around **14** auf Wiedersehen

ad infinitum
03 aye **07** for ever **08** evermore
09 endlessly, eternally **10** at all times, constantly **11** continually, incessantly, permanently, perpetually **12** till doomsday

adjacent
◇ *juxtaposition indicator*
04 near, next, nigh **05** close **06** beside
07 closest, nearest, vicinal
08 abutting, next-door, touching
09 adjoining, alongside, bordering, proximate **10** contiguous, coterminal, juxtaposed **11** conterminal, coterminant, coterminate, coterminous **12** conterminant, conterminate, conterminous, neighbouring

adjective
01 a **03** adj

adjoin
◇ *juxtaposition indicator*
03 add **04** abut, join, link, meet
05 annex, touch, unite, verge
06 append, attach, be next, border, couple **07** combine, connect
09 juxtapose, neighbour
12 interconnect

adjoining
◇ *juxtaposition indicator*
04 near, next **07** joining, linking, uniting, verging, vicinal **08** abutting, adjacent, next door, touching
09 bordering, combining, impinging, proximate **10** conjoining, connecting, contiguous, juxtaposed
12 neighbouring **15** interconnecting

adjourn
04 stay **05** defer, delay, pause **06** put off, recess, repair, retire **07** retreat, suspend **08** break off, continue, postpone, prorogue, withdraw
09 interrupt **11** discontinue **14** betake yourself **15** stop temporarily

adjournment
04 stay **05** break, delay, let-up, pause **06** recess **08** deferral, interval **09** deferment **10** moratorium, putting-off, suspension **11** continuance, dissolution, prorogation **12** intermission, interruption, postponement **15** discontinuation

adjudge
04 aret, cide, deem, side **05** aread, arede, arett, award, judge **06** addeem, addoom, assign, decide, decree, reckon, regard **07** arreede **08** consider **09** determine

adjudicate
04 pass **05** award, judge **06** decide, settle, umpire **07** adjudge, referee **09** arbitrate, determine, pronounce

adjudication
06 decree, ruling **07** verdict **08** decision **09** judgement **10** conclusion, settlement **11** arbitration **13** determination, pronouncement

adjudicator
03 ref, ump **05** judge **06** umpire **07** arbiter, referee **08** mediator **10** arbitrator

adjunct
05 added **06** joined **07** apanage **08** addition, appanage **09** accessory, appendage, appendant **10** complement, supplement **11** concomitant **13** accompaniment

adjust
◇ *anagram indicator*
03 fit, fix, set **04** gang, sort, suit, tram, true, tune **05** adapt, align, alter, amend, coapt, frame, shape, tweak **06** change, modify, reduce, repair, revise, settle, square, temper **07** arrange, balance, compose, concert, conform, convert, dispose, measure, rectify, remodel, reshape **08** fine-tune, modulate, register, regulate **09** get used to, harmonize, reconcile, refashion **11** accommodate **14** grow accustomed **15** make adjustments

adjustable
07 movable **08** flexible **09** adaptable, alterable, versatile **10** modifiable **11** convertible

adjustment
◇ *anagram indicator*
03 adj **04** COLA **06** change, fixing, tuning **07** fitting, setting, shaping **08** ordering, revision, tweaking **09** amendment, arranging **10** adaptation, alteration, coaptation, conforming, conversion, fine-tuning, regulation, settlement, settling in **11** arrangement, habituation, orientation, rearranging, remodelling **12** modification, settling down **13** accommodation, getting used to, harmonization, rearrangement, rectification **14** naturalization, reconciliation **15** acclimatization

adjutant
03 adj **04** adjt **06** argala **07** marabou **08** marabout

ad-lib
06 freely, invent, made-up, make up, wing it **09** extempore, impromptu, improvise **10** improvised, off the cuff, unprepared **11** extemporize, impulsively, play it by ear, spontaneous, unrehearsed **12** extemporized **13** spontaneously **14** extemporaneous, unpremeditated **15** speak off the cuff

administer
◇ *anagram indicator*
03 run **04** drug, give, head, lead, rule **05** anele, apply, fetch, guide **06** direct, govern, impose, manage, supply **07** adhibit, conduct, control, deliver, dole out, execute, exhibit, give out, mete out, oversee, provide **08** disburse, dispense, organize, regulate **09** discharge, officiate, supervise **10** distribute, measure out **11** preside over, superintend

administration
05 admin **06** regime, ruling, senate **07** cabinet, command, control, council, red tape, running **08** congress, ministry **09** direction, discharge, execution, executive, governing, paperwork, provision, supplying **10** government, imposition, leadership, management, overseeing, parliament **11** application, supervision **12** directorship, dispensation, organization, powers that be, term of office **13** administering, governing body **15** superintendence

administrative
09 executive **10** management, managerial, regulatory **11** directorial, legislative, supervisory **12** governmental **13** authoritative, gubernatorial **14** organizational

Administrative areas include:

04 area, city, town, ward, zila, zone
05 shire, state, theme
06 county, oblast, parish, region, sector, zillah
07 borough, commune, enclave, pargana, village
08 district, division, precinct, province, township
09 pergunnah, territory
11 conurbation
12 constituency, municipality

See also **borough**; **council**; **county**; **department**; **district**; **province**; **state**

administrator
04 boss, head **05** chief, elder, ruler **06** bigwig, leader, top dog **07** manager, trustee **08** big noise, chairman, director, governor, guardian, overseer **09** big cheese, commander, custodian, executive, organizer, patrician, president **10** controller, supervisor **11** dispensator **14** chief executive, judicial factor, superintendent **15** director-general, judicial trustee

admirable
04 cool, fine, rare **05** brill **06** choice, wicked, worthy **07** slammin' **08** laudable, masterly, slamming, superior, terrific, valuable **09** deserving, estimable, excellent, exquisite, respected, wonderful **10** creditable **11** commendable, exceptional, magnificent, meritorious **12** praiseworthy, second to none **14** out of this world

admirably
09 eminently, supremely **11** commendably, deservingly, excellently, wonderfully **13** exceptionally, magnificently

admiral
02 AF, RA, VA **03** Adm **07** capitan, navarch, vanessa

Admirals include:

04 Byng (George, Viscount Torrington), Hood (Samuel, Viscount), Howe (Richard, Earl), Togo (Heihachiro, Count)
05 Blake (Robert), Croft, Doria (Andrea), Hawke (Edward, Lord), Rooke (Sir George)
06 Beatty (David, Earl), Benbow (John), Dönitz (Karl), Fisher (John, Lord), Grasse (François, Comte de), Halsey (William F, Jnr), Nelson (Horatio, Lord), Nimitz (Chester), Raeder (Erich), Vernon (Edward)
07 Old Grog, Tirpitz (Alfred von), Wrangel (Ferdinand, Baron von)
08 Cochrane (Thomas), Jellicoe (John, Earl)
09 Artemisia
10 Villeneuve (Pierre Charles)
11 Collingwood (Cuthbert, Lord), Mountbatten (Louis, Earl)

admiration
03 yen **04** mana **05** kudos **06** esteem, fureur, praise, regard, wonder **07** acclaim, delight, idolism, respect, worship **08** approval, pleasure, surprise **09** adoration, adulation, affection, amazement, reverence **10** high esteem, high regard, veneration **11** approbation, hero-worship **12** appreciation, astonishment, commendation

• **expression of admiration**
01 O **02** oh **03** man, wow **05** golly, wowee **06** by Jove **07** caramba, gee whiz, respect

admire
04 laud, like **05** adore, prize, value **06** esteem, praise, revere, wonder **07** applaud, approve, iconize, idolize, respect, worship **08** look up to, venerate **09** approve of **10** appreciate **11** hero-worship **12** esteem highly, like very much **13** think highly of **14** put on a pedestal **15** think the world of

admirer
03 fan **04** beau, buff **05** fiend, freak, lover, wooer **06** suitor **07** amateur,

beloved, devotee, gallant
08 adherent, disciple, follower, idolater, idolator, idolizer
09 boyfriend, supporter
10 aficionado, enthusiast, girlfriend, sweetheart, worshipper

admissible
02 OK **05** legit, licit **06** lawful
07 allowed **08** passable **09** allowable, permitted, tolerable, tolerated
10 acceptable, legitimate **11** justifiable, permissible

admission
06 access, avowal, entrée, exposé
07 ingress, peccavi **08** entrance, granting, mea culpa **09** allowance
10 acceptance, admittance, concession, confession, confidence, disclosure, divulgence, ordination, permission, profession, revelation
11 affirmation, declaration, entrance fee, entry charge, recognition
12 admission fee, asseveration, grande entrée, right of entry **13** right of access
14 acknowledgment
15 acknowledgement, enfranchisement

admit
◇ *containment indicator*
03 gie, own **04** give, take **05** adopt, agree, allow, enter, grant, let in, own up, yield **06** accept, affirm, fess up, ordain, reveal, take in **07** adhibit, concede, confess, declare, divulge, embrace, profess, receive, swear in, welcome
08 blurt out, disclose, initiate, intromit
09 come clean, introduce, recognize
10 allow entry, give access
11 acknowledge, matriculate **12** allow to enter, eat your words **13** give admission

admittance
05 entry **06** access, entrée **07** ingress
08 audience, entrance **09** admission, admitting, letting in, reception
10 acceptance, initiation
12 introduction, right of entry **13** right of access

admitted
05 given **07** confest, granted
08 accepted, affirmed, declared
09 confessed, confirmed, professed
10 recognized **12** acknowledged

admittedly
07 granted **08** avowedly **09** allowedly, certainly **11** confessedly

admitting
03 tho' **06** though

admixture
03 mix **05** alloy, blend **06** fusion
07 amalgam, mixture **08** compound, tincture **10** commixture
11 combination **12** amalgamation, intermixture

admonish
04 warn **05** chide, scold **06** berate, exhort, rebuke, school **07** censure, correct, counsel, reprove, tell off, upbraid **09** reprimand **10** discipline
13 tear a strip off

admonition
05 pi-jaw **06** advice, earful, rebuke
07 censure, counsel, reproof, warning, wigging **08** berating, moniment, monument, scolding **09** reprimand
10 correction, telling-off, ticking-off
11 exhortation **12** dressing-down, reprehension

ad nauseam
08 boringly **09** endlessly
10 constantly **11** continually, perpetually **12** continuously, interminably, monotonously

ado
04 flap, fuss, stir, to-do **05** hoo-ha, tizzy **06** bother, bustle, hassle
07 stashie, stishie, stushie, trouble
08 stooshie **09** commotion
10 difficulty, hurly-burly **11** piece of work **12** song and dance

adolescence
05 teens, youth **07** boyhood, puberty
08 girlhood, minority **10** boyishness, immaturity, juvenility, pubescence
11 development, girlishness
12 juvenescence, teenage years, youthfulness **14** young adulthood

adolescent
03 ned, Ted **04** teen **05** minor, young, youth **06** boyish, neanic **07** girlish, growing, puerile, teenage **08** childish, immature, juvenile, subadult, Teddy boy, teenager, youthful **09** infantile, pubescent, Teddy girl **10** bobbysoxer, developing, young adult
11 juvenescent, young person

adopt
◇ *containment indicator*
04 back, take, vote **05** elect **06** accept, assume, borrow, choose, father, follow, foster, mother, ratify, select, take in, take on, take up **07** appoint, approve, embrace, endorse, espouse, support
08 arrogate, decide on, maintain, nominate, settle on **10** naturalize
11 appropriate **13** take as your own

adoption
04 vote **06** choice **07** backing, support
08 approval, election, espousal, taking-in, taking-on, taking-up **09** embracing, fostering, selection **10** acceptance, nomination **11** appointment, approbation, embracement, endorsement **12** ratification
13 appropriation **15** taking as your own

adorable
04 dear **05** sweet **07** darling, lovable, winning, winsome **08** charming, fetching, pleasing, precious
09 appealing, wonderful **10** attractive, bewitching, delightful, enchanting
11 captivating

adoration
04 love **06** esteem, homage, praise, regard **07** worship **08** devotion, doting on, idolatry **09** laudation, reverence **10** admiration, cherishing, exaltation, high regard, veneration
11 idolization **12** thanksgiving
13 glorification, magnification

adore
04 love **05** enjoy **06** admire, dote on, esteem, honour, relish, revere, savour
07 cherish, worship **08** be fond of, hold dear, venerate **10** idolatrize **11** be devoted to, be partial to **12** enjoy greatly, esteem highly, like very much
15 think the world of

adorn
04 deck, dink, do up, gild, trim
05 array, begem, besee, crown, dight, dress, grace, paint **06** aguise, attire, attrap, bedeck, doll up, enrich, honour, invest, ornate, set out, tart up
07 adonize, apparel, bedight, bedizen, bejewel, bestick, commend, emblaze, enhance, festoon, furbish, garnish, impearl, miniate **08** beautify, decorate, emblazon, ornament **09** bespangle, embellish **10** illustrate

adornment
05 frill **06** fallal **07** decking, falbala, figgery, flounce, garnish, gilding
08 frippery, furbelow, ornament
09 accessory, fallalery, fandangle, garnishry, garniture, jewellery, trappings, trimmings **10** decorating, decoration, enrichment, ornateness, tawdry lace **11** bedizenment
13 embellishment, ornamentation
14 beautification

adrift
◇ *anagram indicator*
04 lost **05** at sea **07** aimless
08 drifting, goalless, insecure, rootless
09 off course, unsettled **10** anchorless, unanchored **11** disoriented
13 directionless, disorientated

adroit
04 able, deft, neat, pert **05** adept, slick, trick **06** clever, expert, habile
07 skilful **08** dextrous, tactical
09 dexterous, ingenious, masterful
10 proficient **11** resourceful

adroitly
04 ably **06** deftly **08** cleverly, expertly
09 skilfully **11** dexterously, masterfully
12 proficiently **13** resourcefully

adroitness
05 skill **07** ability, address, finesse, mastery **08** deftness, facility
09 adeptness, dexterity, expertise
10 cleverness, competence
11 proficiency, skilfulness
15 resourcefulness

adulation
06 praise **07** fawning, incense
08 flattery **10** admiration, sycophancy
11 assentation, bootlicking, hero worship, idolization **12** blandishment
13 pats on the back **15** personality cult

adulatory
07 fawning, fulsome, servile
08 praising, unctuous **10** flattering,

obsequious **11** blandishing, bootlicking, sycophantic **13** complimentary

adult
01 A, X **03** man **04** blue, ripe **05** of age, woman **06** fruity, mature, sleazy, X-rated **07** grown-up, obscene, raunchy, ripened **08** hard-core, indecent **09** developed, full-grown **10** fully-grown **11** grown person, near the bone **12** fully-fledged, pornographic **14** near the knuckle

adulterate
04 card, lime, load **05** taint, water **06** debase, defile, dilute, weaken **07** corrupt, degrade, devalue, falsify, pollute, vitiate **09** attenuate, water down **10** bastardize, make impure **11** contaminate, deteriorate **12** sophisticate

adulteration
08 dilution **09** pollution, vitiation, weakening **10** corruption, debasement, defilement **13** contamination, deterioration

adulterer
03 cad **04** rake, roué, stud, wolf **05** flirt **06** lecher **07** Don Juan, playboy **08** Casanova, deceiver **09** avouterer, ladies' man, libertine, womanizer **10** lady-killer, profligate **11** philanderer

adulterous
05 false **08** cheating, disloyal **09** deceitful, faithless, two-timing **10** inconstant, unfaithful

adultery
06 affair **07** avoutry, liaison **08** cheating **09** two-timing **10** flirtation, infidelity, misconduct, unchastity **11** fornication **12** entanglement **13** a bit on the side, playing around **14** unfaithfulness **15** extramarital sex, playing the field

advance
01 a **03** pay, sub **04** ante, cite, give, grow, help, lend, loan, pass, push, rise, seek, step **05** early, march, offer, prior, raise **06** adduce, allege, assist, avaunt, better, come on, credit, foster, growth, incede, move on, submit, supply, thrive **07** benefit, deposit, develop, forward, furnish, further, go ahead, headway, impress, improve, leading, present, proceed, proffer, promote, prosper, provide, suggest, support, upgrade **08** flourish, get ahead, increase, move in on, progress, retainer, vanguard **09** go forward **10** betterment, facilitate, forge ahead, gain ground, prepayment, put forward **11** advancement, come forward, development, down payment, furtherance, improvement, make earlier, make headway, move forward, preliminary, progression, step forward **12** amelioration, breakthrough, bring forward, going forward, make progress, pay in advance, surge forward **13** expeditionary, moving forward, pay beforehand **14** onward movement **15** forward movement, marching forward

• **in advance**
02 on **05** ahead, early **06** sooner **07** earlier, forward, in front, up front **09** aforehand, in the lead **10** beforehand, previously **11** ahead of time **14** in the forefront

advanced
01 a **03** far **04** high, lent, shot **05** ahead, early **06** higher, hi-tech, onward **07** complex, forward, leading **08** foremost, high-tech, up-to-date **09** high-level **10** avant-garde, precocious **11** progressive, ultra-modern **13** sophisticated, state-of-the art **14** forward-looking **15** ahead of the times

advancement
04 gain, rise **06** ascent, growth **07** advance, headway **08** progress **09** evolution, promotion, upgrading **10** betterment, furthering, preferment, proceeding, upward step **11** development, furtherance, improvement **12** kick upstairs

advances
05 moves, offer **08** approach **09** addresses, overtures **10** approaches, attentions, suggestion **11** proposition

advantage
02 ad **03** aid, pro, use, van **04** boon, boot, edge, gain, good, head, help, lead, odds, plus, pull, sake, sted, sway **05** asset, avail, cause, favor, fruit, prise, prize, stead, value **06** beauty, favour, ground, pay-off, profit, reward, virtue **07** account, benefit, box-seat, service, utility, vantage, welfare **08** blessing, eminence, interest, leverage, whip hand **09** dominance, emolument, good point, head start, obvention, plus point, privilege, upper hand **10** assistance, percentage, perquisite, precedence, proceeding, usefulness, whip handle **11** convenience, helpfulness, pre-eminence, superiority, weather gage **12** weather gauge **14** on the windy side

advantageous
04 plus **06** useful **07** gainful, helpful **08** valuable **09** favorable, of service, opportune, rewarding **10** beneficial, convenient, favourable, profitable, propitious, worthwhile **11** furthersome, serviceable **12** of assistance, remunerative

advent
03 adv **04** dawn **05** birth, onset **06** coming **07** arrival, looming **08** approach, entrance **09** accession, beginning, emergence, inception **10** appearance, occurrence **12** introduction

adventitious
07 foreign **09** unplanned **10** accidental, additional, fortuitous, unexpected, unforeseen, unintended **12** uncalculated

adventure
04 gest, kick, risk **05** kicks, peril, quest **06** aunter, chance, danger, hazard, thrill **07** exploit, romance, venture **08** escapade, incident **09** happening **10** enterprise, excitement, experience, occurrence **11** speculation, undertaking

adventurer
04 hero **06** pirate **07** heroine, Ulysses, voyager **08** Argonaut, Odysseus, venturer, wanderer **09** daredevil, traveller **10** filibuster, speculator **11** bandeirante, enterpriser, opportunist **12** carpetbagger, swashbuckler

adventurous
04 bold, rash **05** gutsy, risky **06** daring, spunky **07** dareful **08** exciting, intrepid, perilous, reckless, romantic **09** audacious, dangerous, daredevil, hazardous, impetuous **10** headstrong, precarious **11** venturesome **12** enterprising **13** swashbuckling

adversary
03 foe **05** enemy, rival, Satan **07** opposer **08** attacker, copemate, opponent **09** assailant, copes-mate **10** antagonist, competitor, contestant

adverse
05 cross **06** thwart **07** awkward, counter, harmful, hostile, hurtful, opposed, unlucky **08** contrary, negative, opposing, opposite, perverse, untoward **09** injurious **10** unfriendly **11** conflicting, detrimental, inexpedient, inopportune, uncongenial, unfortunate **12** antagonistic, inauspicious, unfavourable, unpropitious **15** disadvantageous

adversely
09 harmfully, unluckily **10** negatively **12** unfavourably **13** detrimentally, unfortunately **14** inauspiciously, unpropitiously

adversity
03 woe **04** hell **05** cross, trial **06** misery, sorrow **07** bad luck, ill luck, reverse, the pits, trouble **08** calamity, disaster, distress, hardship, traverse **09** hard times, suffering **10** affliction, ill fortune, living hell, misfortune, perversity **11** catastrophe, tribulation **12** wretchedness

advertise
04 bark, bill, hype, plug, post, puff, push, sell, tout **05** boost, quack, trail **06** inform, market, notify, poster, praise, talk up **07** declare, display, promote, publish **08** announce, proclaim **09** broadcast, make known, publicize **10** make public, promulgate **11** merchandize

advertisement
02 ad, PR **04** bill, hype, plug, puff **05** blurb, promo **06** advert, jingle, notice, poster, teaser, tele-ad, want ad **07** display, handout, leaflet, placard, trailer **08** banner ad, bulletin, circular, handbill **09** marketing, promotion, publicity, throwaway **10** commercial, propaganda **12** announcement

advice
03 tip **04** help, rede, reed, view, word **05** reede **06** notice, wisdom **07** caution, conseil, counsel, opinion, warning **08** guidance **09** direction **10** admonition, injunction, memorandum, suggestion **11** counselling, dos and don'ts, information, instruction **12** notification **13** communication, encouragement **14** recommendation
• **source of advice**
03 CAB **10** counsellor

advisability
06 wisdom **07** aptness **08** prudence **09** soundness **10** expediency **11** suitability **12** desirability **13** judiciousness, preferability **15** appropriateness

advisable
03 apt, fit **04** best, well, wise **05** sound **06** proper, wisest **07** correct, fitting, politic, prudent **08** sensible, suitable **09** desirable, expedient, judicious, suggested **10** beneficial, preferable, profitable **11** appropriate, recommended

advise
04 read, rede, tell, urge, vise, warn **05** guide, reede, teach, tutor **06** enjoin, inform, notify, preach, report **07** apprise, caution, commend, counsel, suggest **08** acquaint, fill in on, forewarn, instruct **09** make known, recommend **10** give notice **11** give counsel **12** give guidance **14** give the low-down **15** give suggestions, make suggestions

advisedly
06 wisely **09** carefully, prudently **10** cautiously **11** judiciously **13** intentionally

adviser
03 IFA **04** aide, guru **05** angel, coach, guide, tutor **06** Egeria, helper, lawyer, mentor, minder **07** counsel, monitor, starets, staretz, teacher **08** assessor **09** agony aunt, authority, confidant, therapist, town clerk **10** confidante, consultant, counsellor, instructor, law-officer, pensionary **12** amicus curiae, right-hand man **13** company doctor **14** right-hand woman **15** Attorney-General

advisory
03 adv **07** helping **08** advising **10** consulting **11** counselling **12** consultative, consultatory, recommending

advocacy
06 avowry **07** backing, defence, pushing, support **08** adoption, espousal, proposal **09** patronage, promotion, upholding **11** advancement, campaigning, championing, propagation **12** promulgation **13** encouragement, justification **14** recommendation

advocate
02 KC, QC **03** adv **04** back, peat, plug, urge **05** adopt, be pro, lobby **06** advise, back up, defend, favour, lawyer, preach, syndic, uphold **07** counsel, endorse, espouse, justify, pleader, promote, propose, push for, speaker, support **08** argue for, attorney, be behind, champion, defender, exponent, plead for, preacher, press for, promoter, upholder **09** barrister, believe in, encourage, paraclete, patronize, prescribe, proponent, recommend, solicitor, spokesman, supporter **10** campaigner, evangelist, vindicator **11** campaign for, countenance, protagonist, spokeswoman, subscribe to **12** King's Counsel, spokesperson **13** Queen's Counsel **14** sympathize with

aegis
04 wing **06** favour **07** backing, support **08** advocacy, auspices **09** patronage **10** protection **11** sponsorship **12** championship, guardianship

aeon
03 age, eon, era **04** span, time, year **05** epoch, years **08** duration, eternity **10** generation

aerate
06 excite, gasify **07** lighten, perturb, refresh **09** oxygenate, ventilate **10** put air into **13** charge with air, charge with gas

aerial
04 aery, dish, yagi **05** aerie **06** dipole, duplex, midair **07** aeolian, antenna, booster, scanner **08** air-to-air, in the air, radiator, receiver, squarial **13** satellite dish **14** above the ground

aeroplane
03 bus **04** kite **05** crate
See also **aircraft**

aesthetic
04 arty, fine **07** elegant, stylish **08** adorning, artistic, tasteful **10** decorative, ornamental **11** beautifying **12** embellishing **15** greenery-yallery

afar
06 far off **07** far away **08** a long way **09** distantly **13** a long distance

affability
06 warmth **08** courtesy, facility, matiness, mildness, openness **09** benignity, geniality, palliness **10** amiability, chumminess, cordiality, good humour, good nature, kindliness **11** amicability, benevolence, sociability **12** congeniality, friendliness, graciousness, obligingness, pleasantness **15** approachability, conversableness

affable
04 maty, mild, open, warm **05** matey, pally, suave **06** chummy, facile, genial, kindly **07** amiable, cordial **08** amicable, friendly, gracious, obliging, pleasant, sociable **09** agreeable, congenial, courteous, expansive **10** benevolent, soft-spoken **11** good-natured **12** approachable, good-humoured

affair
02 go **03** biz **04** gear, love, ploy, shew, show **05** amour, cause, event, fling, issue, thing, topic **06** effeir, effere, matter, pidgin, pigeon **07** affaire, carry-on, concern, episode, funeral, liaison, pidgeon, project, romance, shebang, subject **08** activity, amour fou, business, hypothec, incident, interest, intrigue, question **09** happening, operation **10** love affair, occurrence, proceeding **11** transaction, undertaking **12** circumstance, relationship **13** affaire d'amour, grande passion **14** affaire de coeur, responsibility

affect
03 hit **04** do to, fake, faze, move, sham, stir, sway, take **05** act on, adopt, alter, amove, assay, feign, pinch, put on, taint, throw, touch, up-end, upset **06** assume, attack, change, impact, modify, regard, salute, strike **07** apply to, concern, disturb, imitate, impress, involve, perturb, pretend, profess, trouble **08** bear upon, come home, interest, overcome, relate to, simulate **09** influence, transform **10** do things to, take hold of **11** counterfeit, impinge upon, prevail over **14** have an effect on

affectation
03 act **04** airs, pose, sham, show **06** façade **07** charade, foppery, ladyism **08** pretence, pretense **09** affection, imitation, mannerism **10** appearance, minauderie, simulation **11** insincerity, theatricism **12** false display **13** airs and graces, artificiality **15** pretentiousness

affected
◇ *anagram indicator*
04 camp, fake, posy, sham, twee **05** ditsy, ditzy, posey, put-on, stiff **06** chichi, la-di-da, phoney **07** assumed, feigned, foppish, mincing, minikin, pompous, stuck up, studied **08** literose, mannered, precious **09** contrived, insincere, simpering, simulated, unnatural **10** artificial, euphuistic, histrionic, hoity-toity **11** counterfeit, highfalutin, pretentious **12** highfaluting, histrionical, niminy-piminy

affecting
03 sad **06** moving **07** piteous, pitiful **08** pathetic, pitiable, poignant,

powerful, stirring, touching
09 troubling **10** impressive **12** heart-rending **13** heartbreaking

affection
03 luv **04** care, love **05** amity
06 caring, desire, favour, liking, storge, warmth **07** feeling, passion, worship
08 calf-love, devotion, fondness, goodwill, kindness, localism, penchant
10 attachment, endearment, partiality, proclivity, propensity, tenderness, topophilia **11** inclination
12 friendliness, predilection
14 predisposition

affectionate
04 fond, kind, warm **05** eager
06 caring, doting, loving, tender
07 adoring, amiable, cordial, devoted, fervent, fulsome **08** attached, friendly, Platonic, sisterly **09** brotherly
10 passionate **11** warm-hearted

affectionately
06 dearly, fondly, kindly, warmly
07 amiably **08** lovingly, tenderly
09 adoringly, cordially, devotedly

affiliate
04 ally, join **05** annex, merge, unite
06 team up **07** combine, conjoin, connect, filiate **09** associate, syndicate
10 amalgamate, fraternize
11 confederate, incorporate **12** band together

affiliated
06 allied **07** related **08** in league
09 connected **10** associated, integrated **11** amalgamated
12 incorporated **13** in partnership

affiliation
03 tie **04** bond, link **05** union
06 league, merger **07** joining
08 alliance **09** coalition, filiation
10 connection, federation, membership **11** association, combination **12** amalgamation, relationship **13** confederation, incorporation

affinity
03 kin **04** bond **06** kinred, liking
07 analogy, empathy, kindred, kinship, rapport **08** affiance, fondness, homology, likeness, sympathy
09 chemistry, good terms
10 attraction, partiality, propensity, similarity, similitude **11** resemblance
12 relationship **13** comparability, compatibility **14** correspondence, predisposition

affirm
03 say **04** aver, avow **05** state, swear
06 adhere, assert, attest, avouch, ratify, uphold **07** certify, confirm, declare, endorse, support, testify, witness
08 maintain **09** predicate, pronounce
10 asseverate **11** corroborate

affirmation
02 ay **03** aye, yes **04** oath **06** avowal
07 protest, witness **08** averment
09 assertion, statement, testimony
10 affirmance, avouchment, deposition **11** attestation, declaration, endorsement **12** asseveration, confirmation, ratification
13 certification, corroboration, pronouncement

affirmative
02 ay, OK **03** aye, yea, yes
08 agreeing, dogmatic, emphatic, positive **09** agreement, approving, assenting, asserting, assertory
10 acceptance, concurring, confirming, consenting
11 concurrence, predicatory
12 acquiescence, confirmation, ratification **13** corroborative

affix
03 add, put, tag **04** bind, glue, join, tack **05** annex, paste, pin on, set to, stick **06** adhere, adjoin, append, attach, fasten, prefix, suffix
07 connect, subjoin **09** privative
13 frequentative

afflict
03 ail, try **04** harm, hurt, pain, prey
05 assay, beset, curse, gripe, smite, visit, wound **06** bother, burden, grieve, harass, plague, strain, stress, strike
07 anguish, inflict, oppress, scourge, torment, torture, trouble **08** distress, lacerate **09** persecute **12** bear hard upon

afflicted
◇ *anagram indicator*
03 ill, sad **04** hurt, sick, sore **05** beset, woful **06** cursed, humble, pained, struck, woeful **07** injured, laid low, plagued, wounded, wracked
08 affected, bothered, burdened, harassed, strained, stricken, tortured, troubled **09** aggrieved, anguished, depressed, disturbed, miserable, oppressed, sorrowful, suffering, tormented **10** distressed, overthrown
11 traumatized **13** grief-stricken

affliction
03 woe **04** care, pain, sore, teen, tene, tine, tyne **05** anger, cross, curse, grief, night, teene, trial **06** misery, ordeal, plague, sorrow, unweal **07** disease, furnace, illness, languor, scourge, torment, trouble **08** calamity, disaster, distress, hardship, sickness
09 adversity, suffering **10** depression, heart-grief, misfortune, visitation
11 tribulation **12** wretchedness

affluence
06 inflow, plenty, riches, wealth
07 fortune, tidy sum **08** opulence, property **09** abundance, megabucks, profusion, substance **10** easy street, prosperity **11** wealthiness

affluent
04 rich **05** flush **06** loaded
07 moneyed, opulent, wealthy, well-off **08** well-to-do **09** abounding, inflowing **10** in the money, prosperous, well-heeled **11** comfortable, rolling in it **12** on easy street

afford
04 bear, give **05** allow, grant, offer, spare, yield **06** answer, impart, manage, pay for, supply **07** furnish, present, produce, provide, sustain
08 generate **09** stretch to **11** be able to pay **13** have enough for **15** have the money for

affordable
05 cheap **06** budget **07** low-cost
08 moderate **09** dirt cheap, low-priced **10** economical, manageable, reasonable **11** inexpensive, sustainable

affray
03 row **04** fear, feud, fray, riot
05 brawl, brush, fight, mêlée, scrap, set-to **06** fracas, tussle **07** contest, disturb, punch-up, quarrel, scuffle, startle, wrangle **08** frighten, skirmish, squabble **10** fisticuffs, free-for-all
11 disturbance

affront
03 vex **04** face, slur, snub **05** abuse, anger, annoy, facer, pique, wrong
06 injury, insult, offend, slight
07 incense, offence, outrage, provoke
08 confront, dishonor, irritate, rudeness, vexation **09** aspersion, dishonour, displease, indignity
10 disrespect **11** discourtesy, provocation **13** slap in the face **14** kick in the teeth

affronted
05 angry, vexed **06** piqued
07 annoyed, injured **08** incensed, insulted, offended, outraged, slighted
09 irritated **10** displeased

Afghanistan
03 AFG

aficionado
03 fan, nut **04** buff **05** fiend, freak
06 expert **07** admirer, devotee
09 authority **10** enthusiast, specialist
11 connoisseur

aflame
02 in **03** lit **05** aglow, lit up **06** ablaze, alight, bright, on fire **07** burning, ignited, lighted, radiant, shining
11 illuminated

afloat
05 aswim, at sea, awash, sound
06 viable **07** buoyant, solvent, unfixed
08 drifting, floating, swimming, watching **09** out of debt **10** in the black, unsinkable

afoot
02 up **05** about, agate, astir
06 abroad, around **07** brewing, current, going on **08** in the air **09** in the wind **10** going about **11** circulating
13 in the pipeline

aforementioned
04 this **07** the same **09** aforesaid
10 aforenamed

afraid
03 rad **04** nesh **05** adrad, adred, afear, sorry, timid **06** afeard, aghast, craven,

feared, scared **07** affeard, alarmed, anxious, daunted, fearful, nervous **08** affrayed, cowardly, effraide, timorous **09** concerned, petrified, regretful, reluctant, terrified, tremulous **10** apologetic, frightened, suspicious **11** distrustful, in a blue funk, intimidated **12** apprehensive, faint-hearted, in a cold sweat **13** having kittens, panic-stricken, scared to death

• **be afraid**

05 quake

afresh

◇ *anagram indicator*

04 anew **05** again, newly **08** once more **09** once again, over again

Africa

African countries include:

04 Chad, Mali, Togo
05 Benin, Congo, Egypt, Gabon, Ghana, Kenya, Libya, Niger, Sudan
06 Angola, Guinea, Malawi, Rwanda, Uganda, Zambia
07 Algeria, Burundi, Comoros, Eritrea, Lesotho, Liberia, Morocco, Namibia, Nigeria, Senegal, Somalia, Tunisia
08 Botswana, Cameroon, Djibouti, Ethiopia, Tanzania, Zimbabwe
09 Cape Verde, Mauritius, Swaziland, The Gambia
10 Madagascar, Mauritania, Mozambique, Seychelles
11 Burkina Faso, Côte d'Ivoire, Sierra Leone, South Africa
12 Guinea-Bissau
13 Western Sahara
16 Equatorial Guinea
18 São Tomé and Príncipe
22 Central African Republic
28 Democratic Republic of the Congo

African landmarks include:

04 Giza, Nile
05 Congo, Luxor
06 Karnak, Sphinx
07 Zambezi
08 Aswan Dam, Kalahari, Lake Chad, Okavango, Pyramids
09 Lake Nyasa, Masai Mara, River Nile, Serengeti, Suez Canal
10 Lake Malawi, Lake Nasser, River Congo, River Niger
11 Drakensberg, Great Sphinx, Kilimanjaro, Luxor Temple
12 Aswan High Dam, Great Pyramid, Lake Victoria, Sahara Desert, Zambezi River
13 Mt Kilimanjaro, Okavango Delta, Table Mountain, Victoria Falls
14 Atlas Mountains, Cape of Good Hope, Kalahari Desert, Lake Tanganyika
15 Great Rift Valley

African

Africans include:

03 Ibo, Kru, Twi
04 Boer, Efik, Igbo, Kroo, Moor, Susu, Tshi, Zulu
05 Masai, Swazi, Temne, Tonga
06 Griqua, Herero, Kenyan, Kikuyu, Libyan, Malian, Somali, Tuareg, Yoruba
07 Angolan, Basotho, Chadian, Gambian, Guinean, Ivorian, Mosotho, Rwandan, Sahrawi, Swahili, Ugandan, Zambian
08 Algerian, Batswana, Beninese, Egyptian, Eritrean, Gabonese, Ghanaian, Liberian, Malagasy, Malawian, Moroccan, Motswana, Namibian, Nigerian, Nigerien, Sahraoui, Sudanese, Togolese, Tunisian
09 Burkinabé, Burundian, Congolese, Ethiopian, Sahrawian, Santoméan, São Toméan, Tanzanian
10 Djiboutian, Mozambican, Sahraouian, Senegalese, Zimbabwean
11 Cameroonian, Cape Verdean, Mauritanian
12 South African
13 Equatoguinean, Sierra Leonean
14 Central African, Guinea-Bissauan

after

◇ *juxtaposition indicator*

02 on **03** epi-, for **04** past **05** about, since **06** behind **07** chasing, owing to, wanting **09** because of, following, posterior, regarding **10** concerning, in honour of **11** as a result of, in pursuit of, on account of, trying to get **12** subsequent to, with regard to **15** in consequence of

• **after all**

08 in the end **09** most of all, primarily **10** first of all **12** nevertheless **15** most importantly

• **after that**

04 then **05** later

• **after which**

04 when

• **immediately after**

04 next

• **not after**

02 by

• **until after**

04 over

after-effect

06 result, upshot **07** spin-off **09** aftermath **11** consequence **12** repercussion

aftermath

03 end **04** rawn, wake **05** rowan **06** rawing, rowing, upshot **07** effects, fallout, outcome, results **08** backwash **10** lattermath **11** aftergrowth **12** after-effects, consequences **13** repercussions

afternoon

01 a **02** pm **04** arvo **06** undern **07** evening **12** postmeridian

• **pleasant Sunday afternoon**

03 PSA

afterpiece

03 jig **05** exode

afterthought

02 PS **03** PPS **05** rider **07** codicil **10** postscript

afterwards

03 eft **04** next, syne, then **05** later **07** later on **09** after that, thereupon **12** subsequently

again

02 do, re **03** eft **04** anew, back, more, over, then **05** ditto **06** afresh, encore, iterum **07** further **08** once more, yet again **09** once again, over again **11** another time, one more time

• **again and again**

05 often **10** constantly, frequently, repeatedly **11** continually **12** time and again

against

◇ *juxtaposition indicator*

01 v **02** on, to, vs **03** con **04** anti **06** facing, versus **07** harmful **08** abutting, fronting, in case of, opposing, touching **09** close up to, hostile to, opposed to, resisting **10** adjacent to, opposite to **11** confronting, detrimental, in the face of, prejudicial **12** in contrast to, in defiance of, unfavourable **13** in contact with **14** antagonistic to, in opposition to **15** disadvantageous

agate

04 onyx **05** afoot, astir, murra **06** astray, murrha, pebble **10** Mocha stone **11** chalcedonyx, dendrachate **12** Scotch pebble

agave

05 sisal **06** maguey **08** henequen, henequin, heniquin **12** American aloe, century plant

age

03 day, eon, era, yug **04** aeon, date, days, span, time, yuga **05** epoch, ripen, years **06** dotage, grow up, mature, mellow, old age, period, season, wither **07** century, decline, grow old **08** duration, maturity, senility **09** become old, come of age, seniority **10** degenerate, generation, senescence **11** decrepitude, deteriorate, elderliness **14** advancing years, declining years

See also **old age**

aged

02 ae, of **03** aet, old **04** grey **05** aging, hoary **06** ageing, mature, past it, senior **07** ancient, doddery, elderly **08** advanced, wintered **09** geriatric, getting on, senescent **11** over the hill, patriarchal **13** superannuated **15** advanced in years, no spring chicken

agency

04 firm, work **05** force, means, power **06** action, bureau, effect, medium, office **07** company, vehicle **08** activity, business, workings **09** influence, mechanism, operation **10** department **11** involvement **12** intervention, organization **15** instrumentality

See also **news**; **spy**

agenda
04 list, menu, plan **05** diary **06** scheme **08** calendar, schedule, to-do list **09** programme, timetable **12** scheme of work

agent
03 agt, Fed, rep, spy, way **04** Bond, doer, G-man, mole, narc, nark, root, spie, wait **05** cause, envoy, force, means, mover, narco, plant, proxy, route, spial, spook **06** agency, beagle, broker, deputy, engine, factor, medium, setter, shadow, source, worker **07** channel, liaison, sleeper, trustee, vehicle **08** assignee, delegate, emissary, Mata Hari, minister, mouchard, operator **09** go-between, middleman, operative, performer **10** instrument, negotiator, substitute **11** double agent, functionary **12** intermediary **14** representative
See also **publicity**

age-old
03 old **04** aged **07** ancient, antique, very old **08** primeval, time-worn **09** long-lived, primaeval

agglomeration
04 mass **05** stash, store **07** build-up **08** increase **09** aggregate, gathering, stockpile **10** collection **11** aggregation **12** accumulation, augmentation

aggrandize
05 exalt, widen **06** enrich **07** advance, amplify, dignify, elevate, enhance, enlarge, ennoble, glorify, inflate, magnify, promote, upgrade **09** glamorize **10** exaggerate, make richer

aggrandizement
09 elevation, promotion **10** exaltation **11** advancement, enhancement, enlargement **12** exaggeration **13** magnification

aggravate
03 irk, try, vex **05** annoy, get at, tease **06** harass, needle, pester, wind up, worsen **07** incense, inflame, magnify, provoke **08** compound, heighten, increase, irritate **09** intensify, make worse **10** exacerbate, exaggerate, exasperate

aggravation
05 aggro **06** hassle **07** teasing **08** vexation **09** annoyance **10** irritation **11** irksomeness, provocation **12** exasperation **15** thorn in the flesh

aggregate
03 ore, ped, sum **04** full, mass **05** gross, total, whole **06** amount, domain, entire **08** assemble, combined, complete, dendrite, detritus, entirety, manifold, point set, potstone, sum total, totality **09** complexus, inclusive, summation **10** collection, generality, grand total **11** accumulated, combination, total amount, whole amount **12** accumulation **13** comprehensive, hypersthenite

aggression
04 rage, raid **06** attack, injury, strike **07** air rage, assault, offence **08** invasion, road rage **09** hostility, incursion, intrusion, militancy, offensive, onslaught, pugnacity **10** antagonism **11** bellicosity, provocation **12** belligerence, encroachment, forcefulness, infringement **13** combativeness **14** aggressiveness

aggressive
04 bold **05** lairy, pushy **06** bad-ass, brutal, chippy, feisty, full-on, savage **07** bullish, go-ahead, hostile, kick-ass, zealous **08** forceful, invasive, ruthless, vigorous **09** assertive, bellicose, combative, cut-throat, ferocious, incursive, intrusive, in-yer-face, offensive, truculent **10** in-your-face, pugnacious **11** bareknuckle, belligerent, competitive, contentious, destructive, provocative, quarrelsome **12** bareknuckled **13** argumentative

aggressor
07 invader **08** attacker, intruder, offender, provoker **09** assailant, assaulter **10** instigator

aggrieved
◇ *anagram indicator*
04 hurt, sore **05** angry, upset **06** bitter, miffed, pained, peeved **07** annoyed, ill-used, injured, unhappy, wronged **08** insulted, offended, saddened **09** pissed off, resentful **10** distressed, maltreated **11** disgruntled

aghast
06 amazed **07** shocked, stunned **08** appalled, dismayed, startled **09** astounded, horrified, stupefied **10** astonished, confounded **12** horror-struck **13** thunderstruck

agile
◇ *anagram indicator*
04 deft, spry **05** acute, alert, brisk, fleet, lithe, nifty, quick, sharp, swank, swift, withy **06** active, astute, clever, limber, lissom, lively, mobile, nimble, supple **07** lissome **08** athletic, flexible **09** dexterous, sprightly **11** quick-witted

agility
08 deftness, mobility **09** alertness, briskness, quickness, sharpness, swiftness **10** activeness, astuteness, liveliness, nimbleness, suppleness **11** flexibility **15** quick-wittedness

agitate
◇ *anagram indicator*
03 vex **04** beat, faze, fuss, heat, poss, rile, rock, stir, toss **05** alarm, argue, blend, churn, fight, rouse, shake, upset, whisk, worry **06** arouse, battle, betoss, dither, excite, flurry, incite, rattle, ruffle, rumble, stir up, wind up, work up **07** commove, confuse, disturb, ferment, fluster, inflame, perturb, torment, trouble, unnerve **08** campaign, convulse, disquiet, distract, kefuffle, unsettle **09** carfuffle, curfuffle, kerfuffle, stimulate **10** discompose, disconcert, perturbate

agitated
◇ *anagram indicator*
04 wild **05** het up, upset **06** heated, hectic, mobled, stormy **07** agitato, anxious, excited, nervous, ruffled, worried **08** hopped-up, in a tizzy, troubled, unnerved **09** disturbed, ebullient, flustered, in a lather, steamed up, troublous, unsettled, wrought up **10** distraught, tumultuous **11** highwrought **12** all of a dither, all of a doodah, disconcerted **14** hot and bothered

agitation
04 fret **05** alarm, tweak, worry **06** battle, flurry, frenzy, jabble, lather, motion, moving, pucker, ruffle, taking **07** anxiety, beating, concern, crusade, emotion, fanteeg, ferment, fluster, flutter, shaking, tempest, tension, tossing, trouble, turning **08** blending, disquiet, distress, fantigue, fighting, kefuffle, movement, stirring, striving, struggle, whisking **09** carfuffle, commotion, curfuffle, kerfuffle **10** ebullition, excitement **11** campaigning, distraction, disturbance, jactitation, trepidation **12** perturbation, restlessness

agitator
07 inciter, stirrer **08** activist, fomenter **09** Bolshevik, firebrand **10** instigator, subversive **12** rabble-rouser, troublemaker **13** revolutionary

agnostic
07 doubter, sceptic **08** doubting **09** sceptical **10** questioner, unbeliever **11** questioning, unbelieving **12** disbelieving **14** doubting Thomas

ago
04 back, gone, past, syne **05** since **06** before **07** earlier **09** in the past **10** previously **12** from that time

agog
04 avid, keen **05** eager **07** anxious, curious, excited, pop-eyed **09** impatient **10** enthralled, in suspense **12** enthusiastic **13** on tenterhooks

agonize
04 fret **05** worry **06** labour, strain, strive **07** contend, trouble, wrestle **08** struggle

agonizing
07 painful, racking **08** piercing, worrying **09** harrowing, torturous **10** tormenting **11** distressing **12** excruciating, heart-rending

agony
03 woe **04** hurt, pain **05** spasm **06** misery, throes **07** anguish, torment, torture **08** distress **09** suffering **10** affliction **11** tribulation **12** wretchedness

agrarian
07 bucolic, farming, georgic, predial **08** geoponic, praedial **09** agronomic **10** cultivated **12** agricultural

agree
02 OK **03** fit, yes **04** gree, jibe, jump, okay, sort, suit **05** admit, align, aline, allow, apply, atone, chime, close, fadge, get on, grant, match, tally, yield **06** accede, accept, accord, adhere, assent, assort, attone, clinch, comply, concur, cotton, decide, go with, permit, settle, square **07** be at one, comport, concede, concord, conform, congree, congrue, consent, consort, paction **08** coincide, compound, hit it off, say yes to, strike in **09** determine, harmonize, subscribe, symbolize **10** compromise, condescend, correspond, fall in with, homologate, underwrite **11** acquiesce in, be of one mind, go along with, meet halfway, rubber-stamp, see eye to eye **12** be consistent, share the view **14** give the go-ahead, strike a bargain **15** give the thumbs-up, make concessions

agreeable
04 fine, kind, nice **05** jolly, sapid **07** likable, willing **08** amenable, amicable, charming, euphonic, friendly, likeable, pleasant **09** compliant, congenial, desirable, enjoyable, toothsome **10** acceptable, attractive, delightful, euphonical, euphonious **11** complaisant, conformable, good-natured, sympathetic **12** approachable **13** companionable, consentaneous

agreeably
09 enjoyably **10** acceptably, pleasantly, pleasingly **11** accordingly **12** attractively, delightfully

agreement
03 agt, FTA **04** amen, band, deal, deed, GATT, pact, repo, whiz **05** chime, covin, NAFTA, tally, union, whizz **06** accord, assent, comart, covyne, pre-nup, treaty, unison **07** analogy, bargain, closing, compact, concert, concord, consent, consort, contrat, entente, fitting, harmony, syntony **08** affinity, contract, covenant, matching, Mercosur, sortance, sponsion, sympathy **09** Ausgleich, collusion, community, concordat, consensus, indenture, unanimity **10** compliance, conformity, congruence, congruency, consonance, convention, settlement, similarity, uniformity **11** arrangement, concordance, concurrence, consistence, consistency, respondence, supersedere, transaction **12** complaisance **13** compatibility, embellishment, understanding **14** correspondence, correspondency

See also **treaty**

• **expression of agreement**
01 I **02** ay, OK **03** aye, oke, olé **04** amen, done, good, okay, sure **05** right, uh-huh, wilco **06** quotha, rather, righto **07** d'accord, right-ho

agricultural
05 rural **06** farmed **07** bucolic, farming, georgic **08** agrarian, geoponic, pastoral, praedial **09** agronomic **10** cultivated, geoponical **11** countryside

See also **farm**

agriculture
03 agr **04** plow **06** plough **07** farming, tillage, tilling **08** agronomy **09** geoponics, husbandry **10** agronomics **11** agroscience, cultivation **12** agribusiness

Agriculturists include:

04 Coke (Thomas William), **Tull** (Jethro)
05 Lawes (Sir John Bennet), **Young** (Arthur)
06 Carver (George Washington)
07 Borlaug (Norman), **Burbank** (Luther)
08 Bakewell (Robert)
09 McCormick (Cyrus)
12 Boussingault (Jean-Baptiste)

aground
05 stuck **06** ashore, neaped **07** beached, wrecked **08** grounded, marooned, stranded **09** foundered **10** high and dry, on the rocks

ague
◇ *anagram indicator*
05 exies, fever **07** malaria **10** the shivers

ah
02 ay, la **10** alas the day **12** alas the while

ahead
◇ *juxtaposition indicator*
02 up **05** forth **06** before, onward **07** forward, in front, leading, onwards, winning **08** advanced, forwards, headlong, superior **09** at the head, earlier on, in advance, in the lead, to the fore **13** at an advantage, in the vanguard **14** in the forefront

aid
04 ease, gift, hand, help, prop **05** boost, grant, serve **06** a leg up, assist, backup, favour, hasten, oblige, relief, second **07** backing, benefit, charity, funding, promote, relieve, service, speed up, subsidy, succour, support, sustain **08** donation, expedite **09** encourage, patronage, subsidize **10** assistance, facilitate, rally round, subvention **11** accommodate, helping hand, sponsorship **12** contribution **13** a shot in the arm, co-operate with, encouragement

aide
02 PA **06** minder, Sherpa **07** adviser, attaché **08** adjutant, advocate, disciple, follower **09** assistant, confidant, supporter **10** aide-de-camp, confidante **12** right-hand man **14** right-hand woman

ail
04 fail, pain **05** upset, worry **06** bother, sicken, weaken **07** afflict, trouble **08** distress, irritate **13** indisposition

ailing
03 ill **04** poor, sick, weak **05** frail, unfit **06** feeble, infirm, poorly, sickly, unwell **07** failing, invalid, unsound **08** diseased **09** deficient, insolvent, off-colour, suffering **10** foundering, inadequate, indisposed, out of sorts **11** debilitated, languishing **12** in poor health **15** under the weather

ailment
03 ill, pip **04** waff, worm **05** cough **06** malady **07** disease, illness, passion **08** disorder, sickness, weakness **09** complaint, infection, infirmity **10** affliction, disability **11** dog's disease **13** indisposition

aim
03 end, eye, try **04** bend, goal, gole, hope, mark, mean, plan, sake, seek, vizy, want, wish **05** dream, ettle, level, point, sight, telos, train, visie **06** aspire, course, design, desire, direct, intend, intent, line up, motive, object, scheme, strive, target, vizzie **07** attempt, mission, propose, purpose, resolve, shoot at, take aim **08** ambition, zero in on **09** direction, endeavour, intention, objective **10** aspiration **11** work towards **15** set your sights on

aimless
05 stray **06** chance, futile, random **07** erratic, wayward **08** drifting, goalless, rambling, unguided **09** haphazard, pointless, shiftless, unsettled, wandering **10** irresolute, undirected **11** purposeless, unmotivated **13** directionless, unpredictable

air
03 sky **04** aero-, aria, aura, ayre, lift, lilt, look, mien, puff, song, tell, tune, waft, wind **05** blast, dirge, ditty, ether, ozone, state, utter, voice, whiff **06** aerate, allure, aspect, breath, breeze, demean, effect, expose, manner, oxygen, reveal, screen, zephyr **07** arietta, bearing, canzona, canzone, declare, demaine, demayne, demeane, divulge, draught, express, feeling, freshen, heavens, publish **08** ambience, carriage, cavatina, disclose, fresh air, serenade **09** broadcast, character, circulate, demeanour, make known, publicize, ventilate **10** appearance, atmosphere, expression, give vent to, impression, make public **11** chansonette, communicate, disseminate, have your say **13** speak your mind

• **air defence**
02 AD

• **Air Transport Association**
03 ATA

airbed
04 Lilo®

airborne
02 a/b **06** flying **07** winging
08 hovering, in flight, in the air

aircraft

Aircraft include:

01 B, F
03 jet, MiG
04 Hawk, kite, Moth, STOL, VTOL
05 blimp, Comet, jumbo, Piper, plane, Stuka
06 Airbus®, Boeing, bomber, Cessna, copter, Fokker, glider, Mirage, Nimrod
07 airship, air taxi, balloon, biplane, Chinook, chopper, fighter, Halifax, Harrier, jump-jet, prop-jet, Tornado, Tristar, Typhoon
08 airliner, Blenheim, Concorde, Hercules, jumbo jet, Mosquito, seaplane, Spitfire, spy plane, superjet, triplane, turbojet, warplane, Zeppelin
09 aeroplane, amphibian, aquaplane, Boeing 747, delta-wing, dirigible, freighter, Gipsy Moth, Hurricane, Lancaster, monoplane, swing-wing, Tiger Moth, turboprop, two-seater
10 dive-bomber, hang-glider, helicopter, microlight, Sunderland, Wellington, whirlybird
11 battleplane, de Havilland, Flying Tiger, intercepter, rocket plane, Thunderbolt
12 air ambulance, single-seater, Sopwith Camel, troop-carrier
13 hot-air balloon, Messerschmitt, Stealth Bomber

Aircraft include:

04 R101
06 Bell X-1
07 Voyager
08 Enola Gay
09 Winnie Mae
10 Hindenburg
11 Air Force One, Lucky Lady II, Spruce Goose, Wright Flyer
12 Graf Zeppelin, Memphis Belle
15 Spirit of St Louis

Aircraft parts include:

03 fin, rib
04 cowl, flap, hood, skid, wing
05 cabin, radar, radio, stick
06 canopy, engine, rudder
07 aileron, ammeter, cockpit, cowling, fairing, tail fin, winglet
08 elevator, fuselage, intercom, joystick, tail boom, turbojet, wing flap
09 altimeter, nose wheel, propeller, tailplane, tail wheel
10 flight deck
11 chronometer, landing flap, landing gear, vertical fin
12 control stick, equilibrator, radio compass, rudder pedals
13 accelerometer, control column, undercarriage
14 radar altimeter
15 landing-carriage, magnetic compass

aircraftsman, aircraftswoman
02 AC **03** ACW, erk, LAC **04** LACW

air force
03 RAF **04** RAAF, RCAF, USAF, WAAF, WRAF **05** RNZAF, WRAAF
06 RAuxAF **09** Luftwaffe **11** Flying Corps
See also **rank**

airily
07 lightly, readily **08** breezily, casually, jauntily **10** flippantly **12** nonchalantly **14** light-heartedly

airing
07 venting, voicing **08** aeration, exposure, uttering **09** broadcast, statement **10** disclosure, divulgence, expression, freshening, refreshing, revelation **11** circulation, declaration, making known, publication, ventilation **13** communication, dissemination

airless
05 close, heavy, muggy, musty, stale
06 stuffy, sultry **08** stifling
10 breathless, oppressive
11 suffocating **12** unventilated
15 badly ventilated

airline

Airlines include:

02 BA, UA
03 BEA, BMI, JAL, KLM, PIA, SAS, TWA
04 BOAC, El Al
05 Pan Am
06 Qantas
07 EasyJet, Ryanair
08 Aeroflot, Alitalia
09 Aer Lingus, Air Canada, Air France, Lufthansa
13 Air New Zealand, Cathay Pacific
14 British Airways, British Midland, United Airlines, Virgin Atlantic

airman
02 AC, AR **03** ace, erk, LAC

airport
08 STOLport **09** aerodrome, vertiport

Airports include:

03 JFK, Zia
04 Orly
05 Luton, McCoy, O'Hare
06 Cannon, Changi, Dulles, Midway, V C Bird
07 Ataturk, Bradley, D F Malan, Entebbe, Gatwick, Hopkins, Lincoln, Lubbock, Roberts
08 Ciampino, El Dorado, G Marconi, Heathrow, Jan Smuts, La Aurora, McCarran, Mohamed V, Sangster, Schiphol, Stansted
09 Ben Gurion, Charleroi, Fiumicino, James M Cox, J F Kennedy, Jose Marti, Lindbergh, Marco Polo, Queen Alia
10 George Bush, Golden Rock, Hellenikon, John Lennon, King Khaled, Louis Botha, Sky Harbour, Will Rogers
11 Berlin-Tegel, Capodichino, Jorge Chavez, Las Americas, Ninoy Aquino, Owen Roberts, Pointe Noire, Tito Menniti
12 Benito Juarez, Eduardo Gomes, Hancock Field, Indira Gandhi, Jomo Kenyatta, Norman Manley, Queen Beatrix, Simon Bolivar
13 Château Bougon, Chiang Kai Shek, Grantley Adams, King Abdul Aziz, Mariscal Sucre, Robert Mueller
14 Galileo Galilei, Juan Santa Maria, Kingsford Smith, Lester B Pearson, Murtala Mohamed
15 Augusto C Sandino, Charles de Gaulle, General Mitchell, Hamilton Kindley, Leonardo da Vinci, Theodore Francis

airs
05 swank **06** frills, posing **07** hauteur
09 arrogance, pomposity
10 snootiness **11** affectation, haughtiness, pretensions
12 affectedness **13** artificiality
15 pretentiousness

airtight
06 closed, sealed **08** flawless
09 windtight **10** conclusive
11 impermeable, indubitable, irrefutable **12** impenetrable, indisputable, tight-fitting **13** beyond dispute, incontestable **14** beyond question, unquestionable

airy
04 open **05** blowy, fresh, gusty, happy, roomy, windy **06** aerial, breezy, casual, jaunty, lively **07** offhand **08** cheerful, draughty, ethereal, etherial, flippant, spacious **09** spiritual, sprightly
10 immaterial, intangible, nonchalant, spirit-like **11** incorporeal **12** high-spirited, light-hearted **13** unsubstantial
14 well-ventilated

aisle
04 lane, path **07** gangway, passage, walkway **08** alleyway, corridor
10 passageway **12** deambulatory

ajar
04 agee, ajee, open **08** half open, unbolted, unclosed, unlocked
09 unlatched **10** unfastened
12 slightly open

akin
03 sib **04** like, near, sibb **05** close, sybbe **07** related, similar **08** congener
10 comparable, equivalent
13 corresponding

Alabama
02 AL **03** Ala

alacrity
06 ardour **07** fervour **08** keenness
09 briskness, eagerness, readiness
10 enthusiasm, impatience, promptness **11** willingness

alarm
◇ *anagram indicator*
03 din **04** bell, fear, horn **05** alert, daunt, larum, panic, scare, shock, siren **06** arouse, beat up, dismay, fright, horror, rattle, terror, tirrit, tocsin **07** agitate, anxiety, perturb, startle, terrify, unnerve, warning, whistle **08** affright, distress, frighten, Teasmade® **09** alarm-bell **10** make afraid, uneasiness **11** nervousness, trepidation **12** apprehension, danger signal, perturbation, put the wind up **13** consternation, smoke detector **14** distress signal

alarming
05 scary **07** ominous **08** daunting, dreadful, shocking, worrying **09** dismaying, startling, unnerving **10** disturbing, perturbing, terrifying **11** distressing, frightening, threatening

alarmist
09 doomsayer, jitterbug, pessimist **11** doomwatcher, scaremonger **12** doom-merchant **13** prophet of doom

alas
02 ay **03** out **04** haro, waly **06** harrow **07** welaway **08** waesucks, welladay, wellaway **09** alack-a-day, wellanear

Alaska
02 AK

Albania
02 AL **03** ALB

albatross
10 gooneybird, Quaker-bird

Alberta
02 AB

album
04 disc

albumin
05 ricin **06** myogen **08** leucosin

alchemist
05 adept **06** chemic **08** spagyric **09** spagyrist

alcohol
03 jar **04** bowl, diol, grog, lush, slug **05** booze, drink, juice, mahua, mahwa, sauce, skink, tinct **06** fuddle, gutrot, liquor, sterol, strunt, tiddly, tipple **07** butanol, ethanol, liqueur, mannite, shebeen, spirits, xylitol **08** catechol, farnesol, geraniol, glycerin, glycerol, linalool, mannitol, methanol, propanol, stimulus **09** aqua vitae, firewater, glycerine, hard stuff, the bottle **10** intoxicant **11** jungle juice, sphingosine, strong drink, the creature, tickle-brain **12** Dutch courage, spirit of wine

See also **drink**

• low in alcohol
04 lite

alcoholic
03 sot **04** alky, hard, lush, soak, wino **05** alkie, bloat, dipso, drunk, souse, toper **06** ardent, boozer, brewed, sponge, strong **07** Bacchus, drinker, tippler, tosspot **08** drunkard, habitual **09** distilled, fermented, inebriate **10** spirituous, wine-bibber **11** dipsomaniac, hard drinker, inebriating **12** heavy drinker, intoxicating

See also **drink**

• very alcoholic
04 hard

alcove
03 bay **04** nook **05** booth, niche **06** carrel, corner, recess, shrine **07** carrell, cubicle, dinette, opening **09** cubbyhole, ingleneuk, inglenook **11** compartment

alderman
02 CA **03** Ald **09** ealdorman

Alderney
03 GBA

ale
03 nog **04** beer, mild, nogg, purl **05** nappy, swats **06** alegar, tipper **07** morocco, October **08** heavy wet, twopenny **10** barley-bree, barley-broo **11** barley-broth

alehouse *see* **pub**

alert
04 gleg, warn, wary **05** agile, alarm, awake, brisk, quick, ready, shake, sharp **06** active, inform, lively, nimble, notice, notify, signal, sprack, tip off, tip-off **07** apprise, careful, caution, heedful, warning **08** all there, forewarn, prepared, spirited, vigilant, watchful **09** attentive, observant, on the ball, on the spot, sharp-eyed, up to snuff, wide-awake **10** on your toes, perceptive, presential, wake-up call **11** circumspect, sharp-witted **12** notification, on the lookout, on the qui vive

alertness
08 wariness **09** vigilance **10** observance **12** watchfulness **14** attentivenenss, perceptiveness **15** sharp-wittedness

alga, algae

Algae and lichens include:

05 chara, manna, usnea
06 archil, corkir, crotal, desmid, diatom, korkir, nostoc, volvox
07 crottle, cup moss, euglena, oak lump, parella, seaweed, Valonia
08 anabaena, conferva, frustule, lecanora, lungwort, pond scum, red algae, sea ivory, stonerag, stoneraw, tree moss, Ulothrix, wall moss, wartwort
09 chlorella, cup lichen, Isokontae, rock tripe, spirogyra, stonewort
10 brown algae, Conjugatae, cyanophyte, fallen star, green algae, heterocont, heterokont, rock violet, water bloom
11 blanketweed, Iceland moss, manna-lichen, Protococcus
12 Cyanophyceae, Phaeophyceae, reindeer moss, Rhodophyceae, stromatolite, water flowers
13 chlamydomonas, Protococcales, Schizophyceae, witches' butter
14 blue-green algae, cyanobacterium, dinoflagellate

See also **seaweed**

Algeria
02 DZ **03** Alg, DZA

alias
03 aka, née **06** anonym **07** allonym, moniker, pen name **08** formerly, monicker, nickname **09** false name, otherwise, pseudonym, sobriquet, stage name **10** also called, nom de plume, soubriquet **11** also known as, assumed name, nom de guerre **14** under the name of

alibi
05 story **06** excuse, reason **07** cover-up, defence, pretext **11** explanation, vindication **13** justification

alien
02 ET **03** LGM, odd **05** metic **06** exotic, remote **07** foreign, incomer, Martian, opposed, strange, unusual **08** contrary, forinsec, inimical, newcomer, outsider, peculiar, stranger **09** estranged, foreigner, immigrant, non-native, offensive, repugnant **10** extraneous, forinsecal, outlandish, unfamiliar **11** conflicting, incongruous **12** antagonistic, incompatible **14** little green man

alienate
05 sever **06** cut off, devest **07** divorce, turn off **08** amortize, estrange, separate, turn away **09** disaffect **10** antagonize, set against **11** make hostile

alienation
07 divorce, rupture **08** disunion **09** diversion, isolation, severance **10** detachment, remoteness, separation **11** turning away **12** disaffection, estrangement, indifference **14** antagonization

alight
02 in **03** lit, pop **04** fall, land, rest **05** alive, avail, avale, fiery, light, lit up, perch, pitch **06** ablaze, aflame, availe, bright, debark, get off, lively, on fire, settle, strike **07** blazing, burning, descend, detrain, flaming, get down, ignited, lighted, radiant, shining **08** come down, dismount, gleaming **09** brilliant, disembark, touch down **10** come to rest, disentrain **11** illuminated

align
04 ally, even, join, side, tram **05** agree, order, range, unite **06** adjust, even up, line up **07** arrange, combine **08** regulate **09** affiliate, associate, co-operate, orientate **10** co-ordinate, join forces, regularize, straighten, sympathize **12** make parallel

alignment
04 line **05** order **06** lining, siding **07** ranging **08** alliance, lining up, sympathy **09** agreement **10** alineation **11** affiliation, allineation, arrangement, association, co-operation **13** straightening

alike
04 akin, even **05** equal, samey **06** at once **07** cognate, equally, similar, the same, uniform **08** in common, matching, parallel **09** analogous, duplicate, identical, similarly **10** comparable, equivalent, resembling **11** analogously, much the same **12** in the same way **13** corresponding **15** correspondingly

alimony
06 upkeep **07** aliment, support **08** palimony **09** allowance **11** maintenance **12** child support

alive
04 live, vive **05** alert, awake, brisk, quick, vital **06** active, chirpy, extant, full of, lively, living **07** alert to, animate, awake to, aware of, in force, running, vibrant, working, zestful **08** animated, existent, spirited, vigorous **09** breathing, energetic, heedful of, on the hoof, surviving, to the fore, vivacious **10** carrying on, full of life, having life, in the flesh **11** abounding in, above-ground, cognizant of, conscious of, functioning, going strong, in existence, in operation, sensitive to, teeming with **12** crawling with, swarming with, thronged with **15** overflowing with

alkaloid
06 emetin, harmin, theine **07** atropin, betaine, brucine, caffein, cocaine, codeine, coniine, emetine, harmine, morphia, narceen **08** atropine, caffeine, curarine, cytisine, daturine, harmalin, hyoscine, ibogaine, lobeline, mescalin, morphine, narceine, nicotine, piperine, thebaine, veratrin **09** aconitine, bebeerine, berberine, chaconine, ephedrine, gelsemine, harmaline, mescaline, muscarine, narcotine, quinidine, rhoeadine, sparteine, veratrine, yohimbine **10** apomorphia, cinchonine, colchicine, corydaline, ergotamine, papaverine, pilocarpin, strychnine **11** apomorphine, gelseminine, hyoscyamine, pilocarpine, scopolamine, theobromine, vincristine **15** castanospermine

all
01 a' **03** sum **04** each, even, full, just **05** every, fully, quite, total, tutti, utter, whole **06** apiece, entire, the lot, utmost, wholly **07** perfect, totally, utterly **08** complete, entirely, entirety, everyone, greatest, outright **09** aggregate, everybody, wholesale **10** altogether, completely, every bit of, every one of, everything, infinitely, the whole of **11** every single, total amount, whole amount **12** each and every, universality **13** in its entirety

• **at all**
03 any, ava, eer **04** ever **10** oughtlings **14** in the slightest

allay
04 calm, cool, ease, stay **05** blunt, check, quell, quiet, slake **06** alegge, allege, lessen, pacify, reduce, smooth, soften, solace, soothe, stanch, subdew, subdue **07** allegge, appease, assuage, compose, mollify, relieve, smoothe, staunch **08** decrease, diminish, moderate **09** alleviate **12** tranquillize

allegation
04 plea **05** claim, story **06** avowal, charge **07** surmise **08** averment, citation **09** assertion, statement, testimony **10** accusation, deposition, profession **11** affirmation, declaration **12** asseveration

allege
04 aver, hold, urge **05** allay, claim, plead, state, trump **06** affirm, assert, attest, insist, obtend **07** contend, declare, profess **08** maintain **09** alleviate, represent **10** asseverate, put forward

alleged
06 stated **07** claimed, dubious, reputed, suspect **08** declared, doubtful, inferred, putative, so-called, supposed **09** described, professed, purported **10** designated, ostensible

allegedly
09 dubiously **10** apparently, doubtfully, ostensibly, putatively, reportedly, supposedly **11** purportedly **13** by all accounts

allegiance
03 foy **04** duty **06** fealty **07** loyalty, support **08** devotion, fidelity, liegedom **09** adherence, constancy, obedience **10** friendship, obligation, solidarity **12** faithfulness

allegorical
06 mystic **07** typical **08** symbolic **09** parabolic **10** emblematic, figurative **11** symbolizing **12** metaphorical **13** significative **14** representative

allegory
04 myth, tale **05** fable, story **06** emblem, legend, symbol **07** analogy, parable **08** apologue, metaphor **09** symbolism **10** comparison

allergic
06 averse **07** hostile, opposed **08** affected **09** sensitive **11** disinclined, dyspathetic, susceptible **12** antagonistic **14** hypersensitive

allergy
08 aversion, dyspathy **09** antipathy, hostility **10** antagonism, opposition **11** sensitivity **14** disinclination, susceptibility

alleviate
04 alay, dull, ease, kill **05** abate, aleye, allay, check **06** alegge, allege, deaden, lessen, reduce, soften, soothe, subdue, temper **07** allegge, assuage, cushion, mollify, relieve **08** diminish, mitigate, moderate, palliate **14** take the edge off

alleviation
06 easing, relief **07** dulling **08** soothing **09** abatement, deadening, lessening, reduction **10** allegeance, diminution, mitigation, moderation, palliation **11** aleggeaunce, assuagement, consolation **13** mollification

alley
03 taw **04** gate, lane, mall, road, walk, wynd **05** close **06** ginnel, marble, street, vennel **07** dead end, passage, pathway **08** alleyway, cul-de-sac, pall-mall, rope-walk **10** back street, passageway

alliance
04 axis, bloc, bond, NATO, pact **05** Anzus, guild, union **06** cartel, league, treaty **07** compact, kinship **08** marriage **09** agreement, coalition, concordat, syndicate **10** connection, consortium, federation, Warsaw Pact **11** affiliation, association, combination, confederacy, partnership **12** conglomerate, consociation, popular front **13** confederation

allied
03 wed **05** bound, joint **06** agnate, joined, linked, united **07** cognate, connate, coupled, kindred, married, related, unified **08** combined, in league **09** connected, federated, in cahoots **10** affiliated, associated **11** amalgamated, confederate, hand in glove **12** confederated

allocate
04 mete, task **05** allot, allow, issue **06** assign, budget, divide, ration **07** deal out, dole out, earmark, mete out **08** dispense, set aside, share out **09** admeasure, apportion, designate, parcel out **10** distribute

allocation
03 cut, lot **05** grant, quota, share, stint, whack **06** budget, ration **07** measure, portion **09** allotment, allowance, giving-out **10** sharing-out **12** distribution **13** apportionment **14** slice of the cake

allot
03 lot **04** aret, mete, rate, sort **05** allow, arett, grant, stint, teene **06** affect, assign, budget, divide, ration **07** dole out, earmark, mete out, portion **08** allocate, dispense, set aside, share out **09** admeasure, apportion, designate **10** distribute

allotment
03 cut, lot **04** land, plot **05** grant, quota, share, stint, whack **06** ration **07** measure, portion **08** division **09** allowance, partition **10** allocation,

percentage, plot of land **12** distribution **13** apportionment **14** slice of the cake

all-out
04 full **05** total **06** utmost **07** maximum **08** complete, forceful, powerful, resolute, thorough, vigorous **09** energetic, full-scale, intensive, undivided, unlimited, unstinted, wholesale **10** determined, exhaustive, forcefully, powerfully, resolutely, thoroughly, vigorously **11** intensively, unremitting **12** determinedly, exhaustively, unrestrained **13** comprehensive, energetically, no-holds-barred, thoroughgoing, unremittingly

allow
02 OK **03** let, own **04** give, okay **05** admit, agree, allot, grant, spare **06** afford, assign, beteem, enable, endure, permit, suffer **07** agree to, approve, beteeme, concede, confess, consent, earmark, provide, warrant **08** allocate, sanction, say yes to, set aside, tolerate **09** apportion, authorize, consent to, give leave, put up with **11** acknowledge **15** give your consent

• **allow for**
07 foresee, include, plan for **08** consider **09** budget for **10** arrange for, bear in mind, keep in mind, provide for **15** take into account

allowable
02 OK **04** okay **05** legal, legit, licit **06** lawful **07** rulable **08** all right, approved **09** excusable **10** acceptable, admissible, legitimate **11** appropriate, justifiable, permissible **12** sanctionable

allowance
03 DLA, fya, ICA, JSA, law, lot, RDA **04** diet, feed, mags, size, tare, tret **05** batta, cloff, grant, maggs, quota, ratio, share, stint **06** amount, budget, corody, income, livery, milage, ration, rebate, sequel **07** aliment, alimony, annuity, benefit, bursary, charter, corrody, dietary, leakage, mileage, payment, pension, portion, provand, provend, stipend, subsidy, windage **08** discount, expenses, latitude, pittance, proviant **09** baby bonus, deduction, reduction, risk money, salt-money, strike pay, weighting **10** allocation, assistance, concession, exhibition, husbandage, percentage, privy purse, remittance, table money, toleration **11** appointment, deferred pay, maintenance, pocket money **12** child benefit, contribution, severance pay **15** capitation grant

• **make allowances**
06 excuse, pardon **07** condone, forgive **08** bear with, consider, overlook **10** bear in mind, keep in mind **15** take into account

allowed
02 OK **03** let **04** luit, okay **05** legal, legit, licit **06** lawful **08** accepted, all right, approved **09** of warrant, permitted, tolerated **10** authorized

alloy
◇ *anagram indicator*
04 bras **05** blend, brass, Invar®, metal, potin, terne **06** Alnico®, Babbit, billon, bronze, eureka, fusion, latten, Magnox®, occamy, ormolu, oroide, pewter, solder, tambac, tombac, tombak **07** amalgam, Babbitt, chromel, mixture, Nitinol, shakudo, similor, tinfoil, tutenag **08** cast iron, compound, electron, gunmetal, Manganin®, Nichrome®, orichalc, pot metal, zircaloy, Zircoloy® **09** admixture, bell-metal, composite, Duralumin®, Dutch gold, Dutch leaf, eutectoid, magnalium, oricalche, pinchbeck, platinoid, shibuichi, type metal **10** constantan, Dutch metal, iridosmine, iridosmium, mischmetal, Monel metal®, mosaic gold, nicrosilal **11** coalescence, combination, cupronickel, white copper **12** fusible metal, German silver, prince's metal **13** Babbitt's metal, speculum metal **14** Britannia metal, high-speed steel, phosphor bronze **15** aluminium bronze, Corinthian brass

See also **metal**

all-powerful
05 great **07** supreme **08** absolute, almighty **10** omnipotent, pre-eminent **12** totalitarian

all-purpose
08 all-round, flexible **09** adaptable, versatile **12** multi-purpose **14** general-purpose

all right
02 OK **03** A-OK, yes **04** fair, fine, okay, safe, well **05** hunky, right, sound, sweet, whole **06** agreed, indeed, secure, unhurt **07** average, healthy, no doubt **08** adequate, passable, passably, suitable, suitably, unharmed, very well **09** allowable, all serene, certainly, hunky-dory, uninjured **10** absolutely, acceptable, acceptably, adequately, definitely, good enough, reasonable, reasonably, unimpaired, well enough **11** right as rain **12** satisfactory **13** appropriately **14** satisfactorily **15** unobjectionable, unobjectionably, without question

allspice
07 pimento **11** calycanthus **13** Jamaica pepper

allude
04 hint **05** imply, infer, refer **06** remark **07** mention, speak of, suggest, touch on **08** intimate **09** adumbrate, insinuate, touch upon

allure
02 it, SA **03** air, win **04** coax, draw, gait, lure, mien, pull **05** charm, decoy, tempt, train, troll **06** appeal, cajole, disarm, entice, lead on, seduce, work on **07** attract, beguile, enchant, glamour, win over **08** entrance, interest, persuade, sirenize **09** captivate, fascinate, magnetism, seduction **10** attraction, come-hither, enticement, temptation **11** captivation, enchantment, fascination **13** give the come-on

alluring
04 sexy **05** siren **06** taking **07** agaçant, winning **08** agaçante, arousing, engaging, enticing, fetching, inviting, sensuous, tempting, to die for **09** beguiling, desirable, glamorous, seductive **10** attractive, bewitching, come-hither, enchanting, intriguing **11** captivating, fascinating, interesting

allusion
04 hint **06** glance, remark **07** comment, mention **08** citation **09** quotation, reference **10** intimation, side glance, suggestion **11** implication, insinuation, observation

ally
03 taw **04** join, link, side **05** marry, unify, unite **06** friend, helper, league, marble, team up **07** combine, connect, consort, partner **08** co-worker, sidekick **09** accessory, affiliate, associate, colleague, supporter **10** accomplice, amalgamate, foederatus, fraternize, join forces **11** collaborate, confederate **12** band together, collaborator

almanac
06 annual, Wisden **08** calendar, register, yearbook **09** ephemeris, Whitaker's

almighty
04 huge **05** awful, great **06** severe **07** immense, intense, supreme **08** absolute, enormous, terrible **09** desperate, very great **10** invincible, omnipotent **11** all-powerful, exceedingly, plenipotent **12** irresistible, overpowering, overwhelming

almond
06 comfit **07** amygdal, praline

almost
◇ *tail deletion indicator*
03 nie, sub- **04** near, nigh **05** about, quasi- **06** all but, nearly, next to, nighly, nigh on, uneath **07** close on, close to, nearing **08** as good as, nigh-hand, not quite, well-nigh **09** just about, virtually **10** more or less, not far from, pretty much, pretty well **11** approaching, practically **12** pretty nearly **13** approximately

alms
05 gifts **06** awmous **07** charity **08** devotion, handouts, largesse **09** donations, endowment **13** contributions

aloft
02 up **04** high **05** above **06** high up **07** ahceight **08** in the air, in the sky, overhead **12** off the ground

alone
03 sad **04** just, only, sola, sole, solo **05** apart, solus **06** lonely, simply,

single, singly, solely, unique **07** forlorn, herself, himself, insular, private, unaided, unhappy **08** by itself, deserted, desolate, detached, forsaken, high-lone, isolated, lonesome, rejected, separate, solitary, uniquely **09** destitute, miserable, on your own, on your tod **10** by yourself, cloistered, unassisted, unattended, unescorted **11** exclusively, sequestered, without help **12** single-handed **13** companionless, independently, off your own bat, unaccompanied

along
02 on, up **04** down, near **05** ahead **06** beside, next to **07** close to, further, onwards, with you **09** alongside, as company **10** adjacent to, as a partner **11** at the side of

• all along
06 always **07** for ever **10** all the time, constantly **11** continually

• along with
09 including **12** in addition to, not to mention, over and above, together with **14** to say nothing of

alongside
◇ *juxtaposition indicator*
02 by **04** near **05** aside **06** beside **08** adjacent

aloof
03 off **04** cold, cool **05** chill **06** abeigh, chilly, formal, offish, remote, skeigh **07** distant, haughty, insular, stuck-up **08** detached, reserved **09** exclusive **10** antisocial, forbidding, unfriendly, unsociable **11** indifferent, standoffish **12** inaccessible, supercilious, uninterested, unresponsive **13** unforthcoming, unsympathetic **14** unapproachable

aloud
◇ *homophone indicator*
06 loudly **07** audibly, clearly, noisily, out loud, plainly **10** à haute voix, distinctly, sonorously **12** for all to hear, intelligibly, resoundingly, vociferously

alpha
01 A

alphabet
05 abcee, absey **06** script **13** criss-cross-row **14** Christ-cross-row

Alphabets and writing systems include:

03 ABC, IPA, ITA
04 Cree, kana, ogam
05 Greek, kanji, Kufic, Latin, ogham, Roman, runic
06 Arabic, Brahmi, finger, Glagol, Hebrew, nagari, naskhi, Pinyin, romaji
07 Braille, futhark, futhorc, futhork, Glossic, linear A, linear B
08 Cyrillic, Georgian, Gurmukhi, hiragana, katakana, phonetic
09 Byzantine, cuneiform, ideograph, logograph, syllabary
10 Chalcidian, devanagari, estrangelo, pictograph
11 estranghelo, hieroglyphs
14 Augmented Roman
15 Initial Teaching

Letters of the Arabic alphabet:

02 ba, fa, ha, ra, ta, ya, za
03 ayn, dad, dai, jim, kaf, kha, lam, mim, nun, qaf, sad, sin, tha, waw, zay
04 alif, dhai, shin
05 ghayn

Letters of the English alphabet:

01 A, B, C, D, E, F, G, H, I, J, K, L, M, N, O, P, Q, R, S, T, U, V, W, X, Y, Z
02 ar, ay, ee, ef, el, em, en, es, ex, oh, wy
03 bee, cee, cue, dee, eff, eks, ell, enn, ess, eye, gee, jay, kay, kew, pee, see, tee, vee, you, zed, zee
05 aitch
06 haitch
07 double-u
09 double-you

Letters of the Greek alphabet:

02 mu, nu, pi, xi
03 chi, eta, phi, psi, rho, san, tau, vau
04 beta, iota, zeta
05 alpha, delta, gamma, kappa, koppa, omega, sampi, sigma, theta
06 lambda
07 digamma, epsilon, omicron, upsilon, ypsilon
08 episemon

Letters of the Hebrew alphabet:

02 fe, he, pe
03 bet, heh, het, kaf, mem, nun, peh, qof, sin, tav, taw, tet, vav, waw, yod
04 alef, ayin, beth, chaf, heth, kaph, khaf, koph, qoph, resh, sade, shin, teth, yodh
05 aleph, cheth, dalet, gimel, lamed, sadhe, tsadi, tzade, zayin
06 daleth, lamedh, saddhe, samech, samekh

Letters of the NATO phonetic alphabet:

04 echo, golf, kilo, lima, mike, papa, xray, zulu
05 alpha, bravo, delta, hotel, india, oscar, romeo, tango
06 juliet, quebec, sierra, victor, yankee
07 charlie, foxtrot, uniform, whiskey
08 november

already
05 by now **06** by then, so soon **07** even now, just now, so early, thus far **08** even then, hitherto **09** before now **10** beforehand, by that time, by this time, heretofore, previously **12** so soon as this

alright *see* **all right**

also
◇ *juxtaposition indicator*
03 and, eke, too **04** item, plus **06** as well **07** besides, further **08** as well as, likewise, moreover **09** along with, including **10** in addition **11** furthermore **12** additionally

alter
◇ *anagram indicator*
04 turn, vary **05** adapt, amend, emend, shift, tweak **06** adjust, bushel, change, deform, modify, recast, reform, revise, rework **07** antique, convert, disform, distort, improve, qualify, remodel, reshape **08** airbrush, innovate **09** diversify, transform, transmute, transpose **10** manipulate, metaphrase **12** metamorphose **13** make different

• alter ego
04 Hyde (Mr)

alteration
◇ *anagram indicator*
05 shift, tweak **06** change **07** massage **08** revision, variance **09** amendment, reshaping, reworking, variation **10** adaptation, adjustment, conversion, difference, emendation **11** reformation, remodelling, vicissitude **12** modification **13** metamorphosis, transmutation, transposition **14** transformation **15** diversification, transfiguration

altercation
03 row, wap **04** beef, miff, whid, yike **05** broil, clash, scrap, set-to **06** barney, bicker, breach, breeze, bust-up, dust-up, fracas, fratch, ruffle, square **07** brattle, discord, dispute, punch-up, quarrel, wrangle **08** argument, squabble **09** high words, logomachy **10** dependence, difference, difficulty, dissension **12** disagreement **13** slanging match

alternate
◇ *hidden alternately indicator*
03 alt **04** vary **05** alter, other **06** change, rotate, second **07** in turns **08** rotating **09** fluctuate, oscillate, take turns **10** every other, reciprocal, substitute **11** alternating, consecutive, every second, interchange, intersperse, reciprocate **13** chop and change, interchanging, take it in turns

alternative
◇ *anagram indicator*
02 or **05** other, wacky **06** back-up, choice, fringe, option, second **07** another, oddball, unusual **08** alterant, fall-back, recourse, uncommon **09** different, duplicate, selection, surrogate **10** preference, substitute, unorthodox **12** second string **14** nontraditional, unconventional

alternatively
◇ *anagram indicator*
02 or **06** or else **07** instead **09** otherwise **13** as a substitute **14** on the other hand **15** as another option

although
03 and **04** albe, as if, when **05** while **06** albeit, even if, much as, though, whilst **07** howbeit **08** as much as

09 howsoever 10 even though
11 granted that 13 even supposing
15 notwithstanding

altitude
03 alt 05 depth 06 height 07 stature 08 tallness 09 elevation, loftiness

alto
01 a 03 alt

altogether
◇ *juxtaposition indicator*
04 alto 05 all-to, fully, in all, joint, quite, slick, whole 06 algate, in toto, wholly 07 algates, all told, in total, overall, totally, utterly 08 all in all, all to one, entirely 09 perfectly 10 absolutely, completely, holus-bolus, thoroughly 12 first and last

altruism
06 unself 10 generosity
11 benevolence, disinterest, magnanimity 12 selflessness 13 self-sacrifice, unselfishness
15 considerateness

altruistic
06 humane 08 generous, selfless
09 unselfish 10 benevolent, charitable
11 considerate, magnanimous
12 humanitarian 13 disinterested, philanthropic 14 public-spirited
15 self-sacrificing

aluminium
02 Al

alumnus
02 OB 06 old boy 07 old girl

always
02 ay 03 aye, e'er 04 ever 05 still
06 algate, semper, sempre 07 algates, forever 08 evermore 09 endlessly, eternally, every time, regularly 10 all the time, constantly, habitually, invariably, repeatedly 11 continually, in perpetuum, perpetually, unceasingly, unfailingly 12 consistently 13 again and again 14 on each occasion 15 on every occasion

amalgam
05 alloy, blend, union 06 fusion, merger 07 mixture 08 compound
09 admixture, aggregate, synthesis
10 commixture 11 coalescence, combination

amalgamate
04 ally, fuse 05 alloy, blend, merge, unify, unite 06 mingle 07 combine
08 coalesce, compound, intermix
09 commingle, integrate
10 homogenize, synthesize
11 incorporate

amalgamation
05 blend, union, unity 06 fusion, merger 07 joining, merging
08 alliance, blending, compound
09 admixture, synthesis
11 coalescence, combination, commingling, integration, unification 13 incorporation
14 homogenization

amass
04 gain, heap, pile 05 hoard, store
06 accrue, garner, gather, heap up, pile up 07 acquire, collect, store up
08 assemble 09 aggregate
10 accumulate, foregather
11 agglomerate, agglutinate

amateur
01 A 02 Am 03 DIY, ham 04 buff
06 layman 07 admirer, dabbler, fancier, varment, varmint 08 armchair
09 lay person 10 aficionado, Corinthian, dilettante, enthusiast
11 afficionado 12 do-it-yourself
15 non-professional

amateurish
03 lay 05 crude, hammy, inept
06 clumsy, unpaid 08 bungling, inexpert 09 unskilful, untrained
10 blundering 11 incompetent, unqualified 14 unprofessional 15 non-professional

amatory
04 fond 05 randy 06 erotic, loving, sexual, tender 07 amorous, lesbian
10 passionate 11 impassioned
12 affectionate

amaze
03 wow 04 daze, kill, stun 05 floor, panic, shock 06 awhape, dazzle, dismay 07 astound, flatten, stagger, startle, stupefy 08 astonish, bewilder, bowl over, confound, gobsmack, surprise 09 dumbfound 10 disconcert, strike dumb 11 flabbergast, knock for six 12 blow your mind

amazed
05 dazed 06 agazed 07 floored, stunned 08 startled 09 astounded, surprised 10 astonished, bewildered, gobsmacked, speechless
11 dumbfounded, open-mouthed
13 flabbergasted, thunderstruck

amazement
04 maze 05 shock 06 dismay, marvel, wonder 08 surprise 09 confusion
10 admiration, perplexity, wonderment 11 incredulity
12 astonishment, bewilderment, stupefaction 13 consternation

amazing
◇ *anagram indicator*
06 awsome, far-out, unreal
07 awesome 08 dazzling, exciting, fabulous, stunning 09 thrilling, wonderful 10 astounding, formidable, impressive, incredible, marvellous, monumental, staggering, surprising
11 astonishing, bewildering, jaw-dropping, magnificent, spectacular
12 awe-inspiring, overwhelming
13 disconcerting

amazon
06 virago 09 shield-may 10 shield-maid 12 shield-maiden

ambassador
05 agent, elchi, envoy 06 backer, consul, deputy, elchee, eltchi, ledger, legate, leiger, lieger, nuncio 07 leaguer, leidger 08 advocate, delegate, diplomat, emissary, minister
09 pronuncio, supporter
10 campaigner 14 representative
15 plenipotentiary

ambience
03 air 04 aura, feel, mood, tone
05 tenor, vibes 06 milieu, spirit
07 climate, feeling, flavour
09 character 10 atmosphere, impression, vibrations 11 environment
12 surroundings

ambiguity
05 doubt 06 enigma, puzzle
07 dubiety, paradox 08 polysemy
09 confusion, obscurity, vagueness
10 double-talk, woolliness
11 ambivalence, double-speak, dubiousness, imprecision, uncertainty, unclearness 12 doubtfulness, equivocality, equivocation 13 double meaning 14 double entendre

ambiguous
05 vague 06 double, louche, woolly
07 cryptic, dubious, obscure, unclear
08 confused, doubtful, oracular, puzzling, two-edged 09 confusing, enigmatic, equivocal, imprecise, oraculous, uncertain 10 back-handed, homonymous, indefinite, multivocal
11 double-edged, paradoxical
12 inconclusive 13 double-meaning, indeterminate

ambit
04 area 05 range, realm, scope, sweep
06 bounds, extent, sphere 07 breadth, compass 08 confines

ambition
03 aim 04 goal, hope, push, wish, zeal
05 dream, drive, graal, grail, ideal
06 design, desire, grayle, hunger, intent, object, target, thrust 07 craving, longing, purpose 08 striving, yearning
09 eagerness, hankering, holy grail, objective 10 aspiration, commitment, enterprise, get-up-and-go, initiative
11 what it takes 13 determination
15 fire in your belly

ambitious
04 bold, hard, keen 05 eager, pushy
06 driven, intent 07 arduous, driving, emulate, go-ahead, hopeful, zealous
08 aspirant, aspiring, desirous, exacting, full of go, striving
09 assertive, demanding, difficult, elaborate, energetic, go-getting, grandiose, strenuous 10 determined, formidable, impressive, purposeful
11 challenging, industrious, power-hungry, pretentious 12 enterprising, enthusiastic

ambivalence
05 clash, doubt 08 conflict, wavering
09 confusion 10 hesitation, opposition, unsureness 11 fluctuation, uncertainty, vacillation
12 equivocation 13 contradiction, inconsistency 14 irresoluteness

ambivalent
05 mixed **06** unsure **07** opposed, warring **08** clashing, confused, doubtful, hesitant, wavering
09 debatable, equivocal, uncertain, undecided, unsettled **10** irresolute, unresolved **11** conflicting, fluctuating, vacillating **12** inconclusive, inconsistent **13** contradictory

amble
04 pace, walk **05** drift **06** dawdle, ramble, stroll, toddle, wander
07 meander, saunter **09** promenade
10 mosey along, single-foot
11 perambulate

ambulance
07 pannier **09** meat wagon **10** blood-wagon

ambush
04 jump, trap, wait **05** await, lurch, snare **06** attack, entrap, turn on, waylay
07 ensnare, forelay, lay wait
08 embusqué, lie perdu, pounce on, surprise **09** ambuscade, bushwhack, emboscata, lie in wait, lie perdue, waylaying **11** lay a trap for **14** surprise attack

ameliorate
04 ease, mend **05** amend **06** better, remedy **07** benefit, elevate, enhance, improve, promote, rectify, relieve
08 mitigate **09** alleviate **10** make better

amelioration
04 help **07** benefit **09** amendment, bettering **10** mitigation, refinement
11 alleviation, enhancement, improvement **13** rectification

amenable
04 open **06** docile **07** pliable, subject, willing **08** biddable, flexible
09 agreeable, compliant, tractable
10 responsive, submissive
11 acquiescent, complaisant, persuadable, responsible, susceptible
13 accommodating

amend
◇ *anagram indicator*
03 fix **04** cure, heal, mend **05** alter, emend **06** adjust, better, change, modify, reform, remedy, repair, revise
07 correct, enhance, improve, qualify, recover, rectify, redress **08** emendate
10 ameliorate

amendment
◇ *anagram indicator*
03 ERA **05** Fifth **06** change, reform, remedy **07** adjunct **08** addendum, addition, revision **10** adjustment, alteration, attachment, correction, emendation **11** corrigendum, enhancement, improvement, reformation **12** modification
13 clarification, qualification, rectification

amends
07 redress **08** requital **09** atonement, expiation, indemnity **10** recompense, reparation **11** restitution, restoration
12 compensation, satisfaction
15 indemnification

• **make amends**
05 atone

amenity
07 service, utility **08** civility, facility, resource **09** advantage
11 arrangement, convenience, opportunity

America
01 A **02** Am, US **03** USA **04** Amer
See also **United States of America**

Countries of the Americas include:

04 Cuba, Peru
05 Chile, Haiti
06 Belize, Brazil, Canada, Guyana, Mexico, Panama
07 Bolivia, Ecuador, Grenada, Jamaica, St Lucia, Uruguay
08 Colombia, Dominica, Honduras, Paraguay, Suriname
09 Argentina, Costa Rica, Guatemala, Nicaragua, Venezuela
10 El Salvador, The Bahamas
15 St Kitts and Nevis
17 Antigua and Barbuda, Dominican Republic, Trinidad and Tobago
21 United States of America
25 St Vincent and the Grenadines

South American landmarks include:

04 moai
05 Andes, Colca, llano, Plata, Plate, selva
06 Amazon, Iguaçu, Itaipu, Osorno, pampas, Paraná
07 Atacama, Ipanema, Orinoco
08 Cape Horn, Cotopaxi, Titicaca
09 Aconcagua, Cartagena, Galápagos, Gran Chaco, Itaipu Dam, Patagonia
10 Angel Falls, Copacabana, Mato Grosso, River Plate, Salto ángel
11 Colca Canyon, Iguaçu Falls, Machu Picchu, Mt Aconcagua, Pico Bolívar
12 Easter Island, Lake Titicaca, Perito Moreno, Río de la Plata
13 Atacama Desert, Kaieteur Falls
14 Cristo Redentor, Tierra del Fuego
15 Guiana Highlands

• **Central America**
02 CA

• **South America**
02 SA

American
◇ *dialect word indicator*
01 A **02** Am, US **04** Amer, Yank
06 Yankee, yanqui **08** Jonathan
09 stateside
See also **president**; **United States of America**

Native American peoples include:

02 Ge
03 Fox, Han, Mam, Ofo, Ute, Zia
04 Adai, Coos, Cree, Crow, Erie, Hopi, Hupa, Inca, Innu, Iowa, Maya, Pomo, Suma, Tewa, Yana, Yuit, Yuma, Zuñi
05 Aztec, Carib, Creek, Haida, Huron, Inuit, Kaska, Mayan, Olmec, Omaha, Opata, Osage, Sioux, Tache, Wappo, Wiyot, Yupik
06 Apache, Arawak, Beaver, Bororo, Cayuga, Chiaha, Dakota, Haihai, Haisla, Iquito, Jumano, Kitsai, Konkow, Lakota, Micmac, Mixtec, Mohawk, Mojave, Nakipa, Navaho, Navajo, Nootka, Ojibwa, Oneida, Ottawa, Paipai, Paiute, Pawnee, Pueblo, Quapaw, Santee, Seneca, Toltec, Yakama, Yamana
07 Arapaho, Atakapa, Bannock, Chibcha, Chinook, Choctaw, Hohokam, Huastec, Ingalik, Koskimo, Koyukon, Kwatami, Mahican, Miskito, Mohegan, Mohican, Nahuatl, Natchez, Secotan, Shawnee, Tlingit, Walapai, Wanapum, Zapotec
08 Algonkin, Cherokee, Cheyenne, Comanche, Delaware, Iroquois, Kwakiutl, Menomini, Onondaga, Seminole, Shoshone, Shoshoni, Squamish, Tarascan, Yanomamo
09 Algonquin, Blackfoot, Chickasaw, Menominee, Tuscarora, Winnebago
10 Athabascan, Athabaskan, Potawatomi, Wallawalla

• **North American**
04 Yank **06** Yankee **08** Canadian

American football

American football teams:

11 New York Jets, St Louis Rams
12 Buffalo Bills, Chicago Bears, Detroit Lions
13 Dallas Cowboys, Denver Broncos, Houston Texans, Miami Dolphins, New York Giants
14 Atlanta Falcons, Oakland Raiders
15 Baltimore Ravens, Cleveland Browns, Green Bay Packers, Seattle Seahawks, Tennessee Titans
16 Arizona Cardinals, Carolina Panthers, Kansas City Chiefs, Minnesota Vikings, New Orleans Saints, San Diego Chargers
17 Cincinnati Bengals, Indianapolis Colts, San Francisco 49ers
18 New England Patriots, Philadelphia Eagles, Pittsburgh Steelers, Tampa Bay Buccaneers, Washington Redskins
19 Jacksonville Jaguars

American football-related terms include:

03 AFC, NFC, NFL
04 down, flag, pass, play, punt, sack, snap
05 blitz, block, drive, field, guard, sneak
06 center, fumble, huddle, pocket, punter, safety, tackle
07 defense, end zone, lateral, lineman, offense, quarter, rushing, shotgun, time out
08 fullback, gridiron, halfback, linesman, overtime, receiver, scramble, tailback, tight end

09 field goal, reception, secondary, Super Bowl, touchdown
10 completion, cornerback, extra point, linebacker, nose tackle
11 quarterback, running back
12 defensive end, interception, interference, special teams, wide receiver
13 defensive back
15 run interference

American footballers include:

04 **Camp** (Walter Chauncy), **Monk** (Art), **Rice** (Jerry)
05 **Allen** (Marcus), **Baugh** (Sammy), **Brown** (Jim), **Brown** (Paul), **Craig** (Roger), **Elway** (John), **Favre** (Brett), **Fouts** (Dan), **Halas** (George), **Perry** (Joe), **Perry** (William), **Shula** (Don), **Smith** (Emmitt), **White** (Reggie)
06 **Blanda** (Frederick), **Butkus** (Dick), **Graham** (Otto), **Grange** (Red), **Greene** (Joe), **Hutson** (Don), **Landry** (Tom), **Madden** (John), **Marino** (Dan), **Namath** (Joe Willie), **Payton** (Walter), **Rockne** (Knute), **Sayers** (Gale), **Taylor** (Lawrence), **Thorpe** (Jim), **Unitas** (Johnny Constantine)
07 **Lambeau** (Curly), **Montana** (Joe), **Sanders** (Barry), **Sanders** (Deion), **Simpson** (OJ)
08 **Campbell** (Earl), **Lombardi** (Vince), **Staubach** (Roger)
09 **Tarkenton** (Frank)

American Samoa
03 ASM

americium
02 Am

amiability
06 warmth **08** kindness **10** cordiality, likability **11** likeability **12** cheerfulness, friendliness, pleasantness **15** warm-heartedness

amiable
04 kind, maty, warm **05** matey, pally, sweet **06** chummy, genial, gentle **07** affable, cordial, likable, lovable **08** charming, cheerful, engaging, friendly, likeable, loveable, obliging, pleasant, sociable **09** agreeable, clubbable, congenial, gemütlich **11** good-natured, warm-hearted **12** approachable, good-tempered **13** companionable **15** easy to get on with

amicable
05 civil **07** cordial **08** friendly, peaceful **09** civilized **10** harmonious **11** good-natured

amicably
07 civilly **09** cordially, peaceably **12** harmoniously **13** good-naturedly

amid, amidst
◇ *hidden indicator*
◇ *insertion indicator*
05 among, midst **06** amidst **07** amongst **12** in the midst of, in the thick of, surrounded by **13** in the middle of

Amin
03 Idi

amino acid

Amino acids include:

04 dopa
06 glycin, leucin, lysine, serine, valine
07 alanine, glycine, leucine, proline
08 arginine, cysteine, tyrosine
09 glutamine, histidine, ornithine, threonine
10 asparagine, citrulline, domoic acid, isoleucine, methionine, tryptophan
11 tryptophane
12 aspartic acid, glutamic acid, phenylalanin
13 phenylalanine
14 glutaminic acid

amiss
◇ *anagram indicator*
02 up **03** ill **04** awry, evil **05** false, wonky, wrong **06** astray, faulty **07** misdeed, wrongly **08** faultily, improper, untoward **09** defective, imperfect, incorrect **10** improperly, inaccurate, out of order, unsuitable **11** out of kilter **13** inappropriate

amity
05 peace **06** accord, comity **07** concord, harmony **08** goodwill, kindness, sympathy **10** cordiality, fellowship, fraternity, friendship **12** friendliness, peacefulness **13** brotherliness, understanding

ammo *see* **ammunition**

ammonia
• **derivative of ammonia**
05 amide, amine

ammunition
04 ammo, mine, shot **05** bombs, round, slugs **06** rounds, shells **07** bullets, rockets **08** grenades, missiles **09** gunpowder **10** cartridges, explosives **11** projectiles

amnesty
05 mercy **06** pardon **07** freedom, liberty, release **08** immunity, lenience, oblivion, reprieve **09** discharge, remission **10** absolution, indulgence **11** forgiveness **12** dispensation

amok
◇ *anagram indicator*
05 crazy, madly **06** wildly **07** berserk **08** frenzied, insanely **09** in a frenzy, violently **12** like a lunatic, on the rampage, out of control **14** uncontrollably

among
◇ *hidden indicator*
◇ *insertion indicator*
02 in, of **04** amid, with **05** midst **06** amidst **07** amongst, between **12** in the midst of, in the thick of, surrounded by, together with **13** in the middle of **14** in the company of

amorous
04 fond, warm **05** kissy, nutty, randy **06** erotic, in love, lovely, loving, sexual, tender, wanton **07** amatory, gallant, lustful **08** lovesick **10** cupidinous, passionate **11** flirtatious, impassioned **12** affectionate

amorphous
05 vague **08** formless, inchoate, nebulous, unformed, unshapen **09** irregular, shapeless, undefined **10** indistinct **11** featureless **12** unstructured **13** indeterminate

amount
03 lot, sum **04** bulk, come, mass **05** quota, total, whole **06** degree, extent, figure, number, supply, volume **07** expanse, measure, quantum **08** entirety, quantity, sum total **09** aggregate, magnitude
• **amount to**
04 come, make, mean **05** equal, run to, spell, total, tot up **06** come to, number **07** add up to, run into, tot up to **09** aggregate, inventory **10** boil down to, come down to **12** correspond to **14** be equivalent to, be tantamount to
• **large amount**
03 lot **04** peck, slew, slue, tons
• **small amount**
03 tad **04** haet, ha'it, hate, iota, whit

amphetamine
04 whiz **05** benny, crank, speed, whizz **06** bomber **07** crystal **10** Benzedrine®, Methedrine®

amphibian
04 duck **06** weasel **07** amtrack
See also **animal**

Amphibians include:

03 ask, eft, olm
04 frog, hyla, newt, pipa, Rana, toad
05 Anura
06 Anoura, peeper
07 axolotl, paddock, proteus, puddock, tadpole
08 bullfrog, cane-toad, mudpuppy, platanna, tree frog, tree toad
09 Ambystoma, caecilian, green toad, marsh frog, Nototrema, warty newt
10 Amblystoma, common frog, common toad, edible frog, flying frog, hellbender, horned toad, natterjack, salamander, smooth newt
11 midwife toad, painted frog, Surinam toad
12 springkeeper, spring peeper
14 common treefrog, fire salamander, natterjack toad
15 arrow-poison frog, common spadefoot

amphitheatre
04 bowl, ring **05** arena **06** circus

ample
03 big **04** full, good, rich, wide **05** broad, great, large, roomy, wally **06** enough, plenty **07** copious, liberal, profuse **08** abundant, adequate, generous, handsome, spacious **09** expansive, extensive, plenteous, plentiful **10** commodious, sufficient,

voluminous **11** substantial **12** considerable, unrestricted **14** more than enough

amplification
07 raising **08** addition, boosting, increase **09** expansion, loudening **10** supplement **11** development, elaboration, enlargement **12** augmentation, making louder **13** strengthening **15** intensification

amplify
05 add to, boost, raise, widen **06** deepen, expand, extend, louden **07** augment, broaden, bulk out, develop, enhance, enlarge, fill out **08** enlargen, flesh out, heighten, increase, lengthen **09** enlarge on, intensify **10** make louder, strengthen, supplement **11** elaborate on, expatiate on **13** go into details

amplitude
04 bulk, mass, size **05** throw, width **06** extent, volume **07** expanse **08** capacity, fullness, vastness **09** greatness, largeness, magnitude, plenitude, profusion **11** copiousness **12** spaciousness **13** capaciousness

ampoule
04 vial

amputate
03 lop **04** dock **05** sever **06** cut off, lop off, remove **07** chop off, curtail, hack off **08** dissever, separate, truncate

amulet
04 juju, tiki **05** charm **06** fetish, grigri, mascot, scarab **07** abraxas, periapt, sea bean **08** churinga, greegree, grisgris, pentacle, talisman **09** toadstone **10** lucky charm, phylactery

amuse
04 play, slay **05** charm, cheer, crack, jolly, relax, sport, swing **06** absorb, crease, divert, engage, occupy, please, popjoy, regale, tickle, trifle **07** cheer up, delight, disport, engross, enthral, gladden **08** distract, interest, recreate **09** entertain, make laugh

amusement
03 fun, toy **04** game, play **05** flume, hobby, mirth, R and R, sport, swing **06** solace **07** cockshy, delight, Dodgems®, pastime **08** cottabus, flip-flop, hilarity, interest, laughter, pleasure **09** big dipper, diversion, enjoyment, merriment, parish top **10** recreation **11** distraction **12** fruit machine **13** entertainment, scenic railway **15** shooting gallery

amusing
03 fun **04** zany **05** a hoot, drôle, droll, funny, jolly, light, witty **07** a scream, comical, jocular, killing, waggish **08** charming, humorous, pleasant **09** diverting, enjoyable, facetious, funny ha-ha, hilarious, laughable, ludicrous, quizzical **10** delightful, recreative **11** interesting **12** entertaining

amusingly
07 wittily **09** comically, enjoyably **10** humorously, pleasantly **11** hilariously **12** delightfully **13** interestingly **14** entertainingly

anaconda
04 boma **08** sucurujú, water boa

anaemic
03 wan **04** lame, pale, poor, tame, weak **05** ashen, bland, frail, livid, pasty, stale **06** chalky, feeble, infirm, pallid, sallow, sickly **07** insipid **09** bloodless, enervated, hackneyed, whey-faced **10** colourless, exsanguine, uninspired, unoriginal **11** ineffective, ineffectual **12** exsanguinous **13** unimaginative

anaesthetic
05 local **06** number, opiate, premed **07** anodyne, general **08** epidural, narcotic, sedative **09** analgesic, soporific **10** nerve block, painkiller, palliative **12** stupefacient, stupefactive **13** premedication

Anaesthetics include:

03 gas, PCP
05 ether, trike
06 eucain, Evipan®, spinal
07 Avertin®, cocaine, eucaine, urethan
08 ketamine, metopryl, procaine, stovaine, urethane
09 Fluothane®, halothane, lidocaine, Pentothal®
10 benzocaine, chloroform, lignocaine, nerve block, orthocaine, thiopental
11 Dutch liquid, laughing gas, thiopentone
12 cyclopropane, hexobarbital, nitrous oxide
13 hexobarbitone, phencyclidine
14 methyl chloride
15 tribromoethanol

anaesthetize
04 dope, drug, dull, numb **06** deaden, freeze **07** stupefy **09** cocainize **10** put to sleep **11** desensitize

analgesic
10 painkiller

Analgesics include:

06 Calpol®
07 aspirin, codeine, Disprin®, Disprol®, menthol, metopon, morphia, Nurofen®, Panadol®, quinine, salicin
08 Cuprofen®, fentanyl, ketamine, morphine, salicine, stovaine
09 Calprofen®, co-codamol, ibuprofen, pethidine
10 diclofenac
11 aminobutene, Distalgesic®, indometacin, paracetamol, pentazocine
12 indomethacin, salicylamide
13 carbamazepine, phencyclidine
14 phenylbutazone

analogous
04 like **07** kindred, similar **08** agreeing, matching, parallel, relative **10** comparable, equivalent, resembling **11** correlative **13** corresponding

analogy
06 simile **08** likeness, metaphor, parallel, relation **09** agreement, semblance **10** comparison, similarity, similitude **11** correlation, equivalence, resemblance **14** correspondence

analyse
◇ *anagram indicator*
04 scan, sift, test **05** assay, judge, parse, study **06** divide, reduce, review **07** dissect, examine, inquire, process, resolve **08** calendar, consider, construe, critique, estimate, evaluate, separate **09** anatomize, break down, criticize, interpret, metricize, take apart **10** scrutinize **11** investigate, phonemicize

analysis
◇ *anagram indicator*
04 test **05** assay, check, study **06** review **07** anatomy, check-up, inquiry, opinion, sifting **08** division, scrutiny **09** blood test, breakdown, judgement, reasoning, reduction **10** dissection, estimation, evaluation, exposition, inspection, resolution, separation **11** examination, explanation, explication, navel-gazing **13** anatomization, introspection, investigation **14** interpretation

analyst
06 prober, tester **07** assayer, chemist **08** analyser, inquirer **09** dissector **10** researcher **12** experimenter **15** experimentalist

analytical
07 in-depth, logical **08** analytic, clinical, critical, detailed, rational, studious **09** inquiring, searching **10** diagnostic, dissecting, expository, methodical, systematic **11** explanatory, inquisitive, questioning **13** investigative **14** interpretative

anarchic
◇ *anagram indicator*
07 chaotic, lawless, riotous **08** confused, mutinous, nihilist **10** disordered, rebellious, ungoverned **11** anarchistic, libertarian **12** disorganized **13** revolutionary

anarchism
05 chaos **07** mob-rule **08** disorder, rent-a-mob, sedition **09** mobocracy, rebellion **10** insurgency, ochlocracy, revolution **11** lawlessness **12** insurrection, racketeering

anarchist
05 rebel **08** nihilist **09** Bolshevik, insurgent, terrorist **11** libertarian **13** revolutionary

anarchy
04 riot **05** chaos **06** mutiny, unrule **07** misrule **08** disorder, nihilism

09 anarchism, confusion, rebellion
10 revolution 11 lawlessness, pandemonium 12 insurrection

anathema
04 bane 05 curse, taboo 07 bugbear
08 aversion 09 bête noire
10 abhorrence 11 abomination
12 proscription

anatomy
05 build, frame 06 make-up
07 zootomy 08 analysis, topology
09 framework, phytotomy, sarcology, structure 10 dissection
11 composition, vivisection
12 anthropotomy, constitution, construction

Anatomical terms include:

04 bone, hock, limb, oral, vein, womb
05 aorta, aural, bowel, digit, elbow, gland, groin, helix, ileum, nasal, pedal, renal, spine, uvula, volar, vulva
06 artery, axilla, biceps, buccal, carpal, carpus, dental, dermal, dorsal, gullet, lumbar, muscle, neural, ocular, septum, tendon, thymus, uterus
07 abdomen, alveoli, auricle, cardiac, cochlea, gastric, glottis, gristle, hepatic, jugular, mammary, membral, optical, patella, sternum, thyroid, triceps
08 cerebral, duodenal, foreskin, gingival, ligament, mandible, pectoral, thoracic, vena cava, vertebra, voice-box, windpipe
09 capillary, cartilage, diaphragm, epidermis, funny bone, genitalia, hamstring, lachrymal, lymph node, pulmonary, sphincter, umbilicus, ventricle
10 cerebellum, epiglottis, oesophagus
11 intercostal, solar plexus
14 Fallopian tubes

See also **bone**; **brain**; **ear**; **eye**; **gland**; **heart**; **hormone**; **mouth**; **muscle**; **teeth**; **vein**

Anatomists include:

04 **Baer** (Karl), **Bell** (Sir Charles), **Dart** (Raymond), **Knox** (Robert)
05 **Clark** (Sir Wifred le Gros), **Graaf** (Regnier de), **Monro** (Alexander)
06 **Adrian** (Edgar, Lord), **Cowper** (William), **Cuvier** (Georges, Lord), **Haller** (Albrecht von), **Stubbs** (George), **Tobias** (Phillip)
07 **Colombo** (Matteo Realdo), **Galvani** (Luigi)
08 **Alcmaeon**, **Malpighi** (Marcello), **Vesalius** (Andreas)
09 **Bartholin** (Caspar), **Eustachio** (Bartolomeo), **Fallopius** (Gabriel), **Zuckerman** (Solly, Lord)
10 **Herophilus**
13 **Waldeyer-Hartz** (Wilhelm)

ancestor
04 sire 05 elder 06 father, mother, tipuna, tupuna 07 forbear 08 forebear
09 ascendant, ascendent, grandsire, precursor 10 antecedent, antecessor, forefather, forerunner, progenitor
11 predecessor 12 primogenitor
13 primogenitrix

ancestral
06 avital, lineal 07 genetic 08 familial, parental 09 inherited 10 hereditary
12 genealogical

• ancestral image
04 tiki

ancestry
04 line, race 05 blood, roots, stock
06 family, linage, lynage, origin, stirps
07 descent, lignage, lineage
08 breeding, heredity, heritage, pedigree 09 ancestors, ancientry, forebears, genealogy, offspring, parentage, whakapapa 10 derivation, extraction, family tree 11 forefathers, progenitors

anchor
03 fix 04 hook, host, moor 05 affix, berth, tie up 06 attach, fasten
07 bulwark, compère, mooring, mudhook, recluse, support
08 backbone, linchpin, mainstay, make fast 09 anchorman, announcer, presenter 10 foundation, newsreader
11 anchorwoman 15 tower of strength

Anchors include:

03 car, CQR, ice, sea
04 navy, rond
05 bower, drift, kedge, sheet, waist
06 drogue, plough, stream
07 grapnel, killick, killock, stocked, weather
08 mushroom
09 admiralty, stockless, yachtsman
12 double fluked

• lie at anchor
04 ride

anchorage
04 cell, road, rode 06 riding

anchorite
04 monk 05 loner 06 anchor, hermit
07 ascetic, eremite, recluse, stylite
08 solitary 09 anchoress 10 solitarian

ancient
03 old 04 aged 05 early, first, hoary, passé 06 age-old, antick, bygone, démodé 07 antique, archaic
08 earliest, obsolete, original, outmoded, primeval, pristine, time-worn, world-old 09 antiquary, atavistic, auld-warld, out-of-date, primaeval, primitive 10 antiquated, fossilized, immemorial, primordial
11 prehistoric 12 antediluvian, old-fashioned 13 superannuated 15 as old as the hills

See also **city**; **Egyptian**; **festival**

ancillary
05 extra 07 helping 08 adjuvant
09 accessory, auxiliary, secondary
10 additional, subserving, subsidiary, supporting 11 adminicular, ministering, subordinate
12 contributory 13 supplementary

and
◇ *juxtaposition indicator*
01 'n' 02 an' 03 too 04 also, plus, then, with 06 as well 07 ampassy, besides 08 as well as, by the way, moreover, together 09 along with, ampersand, amperzand, including, what's more 10 ampussy-and, in addition 11 furthermore 12 in addition to, together with

andiron
03 dog 06 chenet 07 firedog

Andorra
03 AND

androgynous
08 bisexual 09 polygamic
10 monoecious 11 monoclinous, protogynous 12 heterogamous
13 gynodioecious, hermaphrodite, male and female 14 androdioecious

anecdotal
08 everyday, informal 09 narrative
10 unofficial 11 reminiscing
12 storytelling, unscientific

anecdote
04 tale, yarn 05 story 06 sketch
08 exemplum 09 narrative, urban myth 11 urban legend 12 reminiscence

anecdotes
03 ana

anew
◇ *anagram indicator*
05 again 06 afresh, de novo, iterum
07 freshly 08 once more 09 de integro, once again 12 all over again

angel
03 gem 05 ideal, saint 07 darling, paragon, watcher 08 guardian, treasure 09 nonpareil 13 heavenly being 14 messenger of God 15 divine messenger

Angels include:

05 Ariel, Eblis, Iblis, Satan, Uriel
06 Abdiel, Arioch, Azrael, Belial, Mammon, Moloch, Zephon
07 Gabriel, Israfel, Lucifer, Michael, Raphael, Zadkiel
08 Ithuriel
09 Beelzebub

Orders of angel include:

05 angel, power
06 cherub, seraph, throne, virtue
08 dominion
09 archangel
10 domination
12 principality

angelic
04 holy, pure 05 pious 06 divine, lovely 07 saintly 08 adorable, beatific, cherubic, empyrean, ethereal, heavenly, innocent, seraphic, virtuous
09 beautiful, celestial, unworldly
10 cherubical, cherubimic

anger
03 bug, ire, irk, vex, wax 04 face, fuff, fury, gall, gram, huff, miff, mood, move,

nark, pelt, rage, rile, roil, teen, tene **05** annoy, blood, flake, get at, pique, teene, wrath **06** bother, choler, dander, emboil, enrage, madden, monkey, needle, nettle, offend, ruffle, temper, wind up **07** affront, air rage, bluster, chagrin, dudgeon, incense, inflame, kippage, offence, offense, outrage, provoke, rancour **08** bad blood, drive mad, irritate, paroxysm, road rage, vexation **09** aggravate, annoyance, infuriate, make angry **10** antagonism, antagonize, bitterness, conniption, drive crazy, exasperate, fit of anger, irritation, resentment **11** displeasure, indignation **12** boiling-point, drive bananas, exasperation, irritability **13** make sparks fly **14** drive up the wall

• **show anger**
06 bridle

angle
03 aim **04** bend, edge, face, fish, fork, hook, knee, nook, side, spin, take, tilt, turn **05** crook, elbow, facet, point, slant **06** aspect, corner, crotch, direct **07** flexure, outlook **08** approach, gradient, position **09** direction, viewpoint **10** projection, standpoint **11** inclination, perspective, point of view **12** intersection

• **angle for**
03 aim **04** seek **05** go for **07** fish for **08** shoot for, try to get **11** make a bid for **12** seek to obtain

• **angle in botany**
04 axil

• **angle in mining**
04 hade

• **angle of 45°**
05 mitre

• **reflex angle**
02 in

angler
03 rod **06** fisher, Walton **07** rodster, wide-gab **08** frogfish, monkfish, piscator **09** devilfish, fisherman, goose-fish, piscatrix, Waltonian

Anglican
02 CE

angling *see* **fishing**

Anglo-French
02 AF

Angola
02 AN **03** AGO

angrily
◇ *anagram indicator*
05 hotly **06** warmly **07** crossly, irately **08** bitterly **09** furiously, stroppily **10** wrathfully **11** indignantly, rancorously, resentfully **12** passionately

angry
◇ *anagram indicator*
03 hot, mad **04** evil, high, warm, wild, yond **05** black, cross, het up, irate, livid, moody, radge, ratty, spewy, wrath **06** bitter, choked, heated, raging, sullen, sultry **07** annoyed, berserk, blazing, crooked, enraged, furious, ropable, stroppy, uptight **08** burned up, choleric, foribund, hairless, in a paddy, incensed, moody-mad, outraged, ropeable, seething, steaming, up in arms, wrathful **09** in a lather, in a temper, indignant, infuriate, irritated, pissed off, rancorous, raving mad, resentful, seeing red, splenetic, ticked off **10** aggravated, displeased, hopping mad, infuriated, passionate, stomachful, up in the air **11** disgruntled, exasperated, fit to be tied **12** on the rampage, on the warpath **14** beside yourself

• **make angry**
07 incense

angst
05 dread, worry **06** stress **07** anguish, anxiety, tension **08** distress **09** worriment **10** foreboding, uneasiness **11** disquietude **12** apprehension

angstrom
01 A

Anguilla
03 AIA

anguish
03 woe **04** dole, pain, pang, rack **05** agony, dolor, grief **06** dolour, misery, sorrow **07** anxiety, torment, torture **08** distress **09** heartache, suffering **10** affliction, desolation, heartbreak **11** tribulation **12** wretchedness

anguished
08 dolorous, harrowed, stressed, stricken, tortured, wretched **09** afflicted, miserable, suffering, tormented **10** distressed

angular
04 bony, lank, lean, thin **05** gaunt, gawky, lanky, spare **06** skinny **07** scrawny **08** rawboned **12** sharp-pointed

animal
03 pig **04** wild, zoic **05** beast, brute, swine **06** bodily, carnal, mammal, savage **07** bestial, brutish, critter, fleshly, inhuman, monster, sensual **08** animalic, creature, physical **09** barbarian **11** furry friend, instinctive **13** theriomorphic

Animals include:

02 ai, ox, zo
03 ape, asp, ass, bay, boa, bok, cat, cow, dog, dso, eft, elk, ewe, ewt, fox, gnu, hob, kob, olm, pig, ram, rat, roe, roo, sai, wat, yak
04 anoa, anta, arna, atoc, axis, balu, bear, boma, bull, cavy, colt, cony, deer, dieb, douc, emys, euro, eyra, foal, frog, gila, goat, hare, hart, hyen, ibex, lion, mara, mare, mico, mink, mohr, mole, moyl, mule, naga, newt, oont, oryx, paca, paco, peba, pipa, pudu, puma, quey, rana, rusa, saki, scut, seal, seps, skug, stag, tahr, tegu, tehr, thar, titi, toad, unau, ursa, urus, urva, wolf
05 adder, bison, camel, civet, coney, eland, horse, hyena, koala, lemur, llama, loris, moose, mouse, otter, panda, ratel, sheep, skunk, tiger, whale, zebra
06 baboon, badger, beaver, cougar, ermine, ferret, gerbil, gibbon, impala, jaguar, monkey, ocelot, rabbit, racoon, walrus, weasel, wombat
07 buffalo, caribou, cheetah, dolphin, gazelle, giraffe, gorilla, hamster, leopard, panther, polecat, sealion, wallaby
08 aardvark, antelope, elephant, hedgehog, kangaroo, kinkajou, mongoose, platypus, reindeer, sea otter, squirrel
09 armadillo, orang-utan, polar bear, wolverine
10 camelopard, chimpanzee, giant panda, rhinoceros
11 grizzly bear
12 hippopotamus

See also **amphibian**; **ape**; **beetle**; **bird**; **butterfly**; **cat**; **cattle**; **chicken**; **collective**; **crustacean**; **deer**; **dinosaur**; **disease**; **dog**; **duck**; **farm**; **fish**; **game**; **horse**; **insect**; **invertebrate**; **lair**; **lizard**; **mammal**; **marsupial**; **mollusc**; **monkey**; **moth**; **pig**; **poultry**; **reptile**; **rodent**; **shark**; **sheep**; **snake**; **sound**; **spider**; **whale**; **worm**

Animal lairs, nests and homes include:

03 den, nid, pen, sty
04 bike, bink, byre, cage, coop, drey, fold, form, hive, hole, holt, nest, sett
05 earth, eyrie, lodge, shell
06 burrow, warren, wurley
08 dovecote, fortress, vespiary
09 formicary
11 formicarium, termitarium

Adjectives relating to animals include:

05 apian, avian, avine, ovine
06 bovine, canine, equine, feline, hippic, larine, lupine, murine, simian, ursine
07 acarine, anguine, asinine, caprine, cervine, corvine, hircine, leonine, milvine, otarine, pardine, phocine, piscine, porcine, saurian, sebrine, taurine, tigrine, turdine, vespine, vulpine
08 anserine, aquiline, bubaline, cameline, chthyoid, elaphine, ichthyic, lemurine, leporine, limacine, ophidian, pavonine, sciurine, soricine, suilline, viperine, vituline
09 caballine, chelonian, colubrine, columbine, crotaline, falconine, hirundine, musteline, ornithoid, viverrine, volucrine, vulturine
10 psittacine, serpentine
11 accipitrine, elephantine, fringilline, lacertilian

12 gallinaceous, oryctolagine
13 rhopalocerous
14 papilionaceous

Animal-related terms include:

03 ear, egg, eye, fin, fur, leg, paw, pet
04 beak, bill, bite, claw, coat, crop, dock, gill, gula, hoof, horn, hump, jowl, loin, mane, mate, prey, rump, tail, teat, tusk, wild, wing, wool
05 chine, crest, fangs, feral, moult, pouch, scale, shell, snout, spine, sting, trunk, udder, venom
06 antler, barrel, dewlap, jubate, mantle, muzzle, thorax, ungula
07 abdomen, antenna, feather, flehmen, flipper, gizzard, habitat, migrate, mimicry, pallium, segment, withers
08 coupling, domestic, forefoot, forewing, halteres, hindfoot, hindwing, predator, torquate, ungulate, whiskers
09 marsupium, oviparous, prehallux, proboscis, pygostyle, syndactyl, taligrade
10 camouflage, gressorial, ovipositor, viviparous, webbed feet
11 compound eye, lateral line, search image, swim bladder, waggle dance
12 forked tongue
13 electric organ, metamorphosis
14 startle colours
15 prehensile thumb

Female animals include:

03 cow, doe, ewe, hen, pen, ree, sow
04 duck, gill, hind, jill, jomo, mare
05 bitch, dsomo, jenny, nanny, queen, reeve, vixen, zhomo
06 peahen
07 greyhen, lioness, tigress
08 water cow
09 dolphinet, guinea hen, turkey hen
10 leopardess, weasel coot

Male animals include:

03 cob, dog, hob, nun, ram, tom, tup
04 boar, buck, bull, cock, hart, jack, stag, zobo, zobu
05 billy, drake, drone, dsobo
06 gander, musket, old man, ramcat
08 seecatch, stallion
09 blackcock
10 turkey cock
12 throstle-cock

Young animals include:

03 cub, elt, fry, kid, kit, nit
04 brit, calf, colt, eyas, fawn, foal, gilt, grig, joey, lamb, maid, parr, peal, sild, slip, yelt
05 chick, elver, owlet, piper, puppy, scrod, shote, smolt, squab, steer, whelp
06 alevin, cygnet, eaglet, gimmer, grilse, heifer, hidder, kitten, lionet, piglet, pullet, samlet, weaner
07 codling, eelfare, gosling, leveret, pigling, sardine, skegger, sounder, tadpole, wolfkin
08 brancher, duckling, goatling, nestling, pea-chick
09 fledgling

Animals representing years in the Chinese calendar:

02 ox
03 dog, pig, rat
04 boar, cock, goat, hare
05 horse, sheep, snake, tiger
06 dragon, monkey, rabbit
07 buffalo, rooster, serpent

• **animal display**
03 zoo **09** menagerie
• **animal's body**
04 soma
• **stock of animals**
04 team, teme
• **tame animal**
03 pet
• **unsuitable animal**
04 cull

animate

04 fire, goad, live, move, spur, stir, urge, wake **05** alive, impel, quick, rouse, spark, vital **06** arouse, buck up, ensoul, excite, incite, inform, insoul, kindle, living, revive, vivify **07** enliven, inspire, quicken **08** activate, embolden, energize, inspirit, vitalize
09 breathing, conscious, encourage, galvanize, instigate, stimulate
10 invigorate, reactivate **11** bring to life

animated

◇ *anagram indicator*
03 hot **05** alive, brisk, eager, peppy, quick, vital, zappy **06** active, ardent, chirpy, lively **07** buoyant, chipper, excited, fervent, glowing, radiant, vibrant **08** instinct, spirited, vehement, vigorous **09** ebullient, energetic, sparkling, sprightly, vivacious
10 passionate **11** full of beans, impassioned **12** enthusiastic **15** bright and breezy

animatedly

◇ *anagram indicator*
05 mosso **07** briskly, eagerly
08 actively, ardently **09** excitedly, fervently, radiantly, vibrantly
10 vehemently, vigorously
11 vivaciously **12** passionately
13 energetically

animation

02 go **03** pep **04** fire, heat, life, zeal, zest, zing **05** verve **06** action, energy, spirit, vigour **07** elation, fervour, passion, sparkle **08** activity, radiance, vibrancy, vitality, vivacity **10** claymation, ebullience, enthusiasm, excitement, liveliness **11** high spirits **12** exhilaration
13 sprightliness, vivaciousness

animosity

04 feud, hate **05** odium, pique, spite
06 animus, enmity, hatred, malice **07** ill will, rancour **08** acrimony, friction, loathing **09** antipathy, hostility, malignity **10** abhorrence, antagonism, bitterness, ill feeling, race hatred, resentment **11** malevolence

ankle

04 coot, cuit, cute, hock **05** hough, talus **06** tarsus

annals

04 acta **05** fasti **07** history, memoirs, records, reports **08** accounts, archives, journals **09** registers
10 chronicles

annex

03 add **04** join **05** affix, seize, unite, usurp **06** adjoin, append, attach, fasten, occupy, take in **07** acquire, connect, conquer, purloin
08 arrogate, take over **09** extension, mediatize **11** appropriate, incorporate

annexation

07 seizure **08** conquest, takeover, usurping **10** arrogation, occupation
11 acquisition **13** appropriation

annexe

04 wing **08** addition **09** expansion, extension **10** attachment, supplement

annihilate

04 raze, rout **05** erase **06** defeat, murder, rub out, thrash **07** abolish, conquer, destroy, take out, trounce, wipe out **09** eliminate, eradicate, extirpate, liquidate **10** extinguish, obliterate **11** assassinate, exterminate

annihilation

03 end **06** defeat, murder **07** erasure
09 abolition **10** extinction
11 destruction, elimination, eradication, extirpation, liquidation
12 obliteration **13** assassination, extermination

anniversary

04 obit **07** jubilee **08** birthday, yahrzeit **09** centenary, millenary
10 birthnight, centennial, millennium, wedding day **11** bicentenary, bimillenary, octingenary, semi-jubilee
12 bicentennial, quinquennial, sexcentenary, tercentenary
13 novocentenary, octocentenary, quincentenary, tercentennial
14 octingentenary
15 quatercentenary, sesquicentenary

Anniversaries include:

04 D-Day
05 VE Day, VJ Day
07 Flag Day
08 Anzac Day
09 Canada Day, Empire Day
10 Burns Night, Victory Day
11 Bastille Day, Columbus Day, Dominion Day, Oak-apple Day, Republic Day, Waitangi Day
12 Armistice Day, Australia Day, Discovery Day, Fourth of July, Thanksgiving
13 King's Birthday, Liberation Day, Revolution Day
14 Guy Fawkes Night, Queen's Birthday, Remembrance Day, Unification Day
15 Constitution Day, Emancipation Day, Independence Day

Wedding anniversaries include:

03 fur, tin
04 gold, iron, jade, lace, ruby, silk, wood, wool
05 china, coral, fruit, glass, ivory, linen, paper, pearl, steel, sugar
06 bronze, clocks, copper, cotton, silver, willow
07 crystal, diamond, emerald, flowers, leather, pottery, watches
08 desk sets, platinum, sapphire, textiles
09 aluminium
10 appliances, silverware
13 gold jewellery

annotate
04 note **05** gloss **07** comment, explain **09** elucidate, explicate, interpret **10** add notes to
11 marginalize

annotation
04 note **05** gloss **07** comment
08 exegesis, footnote, scholion, scholium **10** commentary
11 elucidation, explanation, explication
12 commentation

announce
◇ *homophone indicator*
04 bill, post **05** sound, state **06** advise, blazon, notify, report, reveal
07 betoken, declare, divulge, gazette, give out, publish **08** denounce, disclose, intimate, proclaim, propound
09 advertise, broadcast, make known, preconize, publicize **10** make public, promulgate **12** blazon abroad **14** make a statement **15** issue a statement

announcement
04 card **06** notice, report **07** message, release **08** bulletin, dispatch, handbill, obituary **09** broadcast, giving-out, ipse dixit, publicity, reporting, statement **10** communiqué, disclosure, divulgence, intimation, revelation **11** declaration, information, making known, publication, publicizing **12** making public, notification, proclamation, promulgation **13** advertisement
14 pronunciamento

announcer
02 MC **04** host **06** anchor, herald
07 compère **09** anchorman, messenger, presenter, town crier
10 newscaster, newsreader, speakerine **11** anchorwoman, annunciator, broadcaster, commentator

annoy
03 bug, din, hip, hyp, irk, nag, noy, try, vex **04** fash, gall, hump, miff, nark, ride, rile, roil **05** anger, cross, sturt, tease
06 bother, harass, hassle, hatter, hector, madden, molest, nettle, pester, plague, ruffle, tee off, wind up
07 chagrin, disturb, hack off, provoke, tick off, trouble **08** brass off, contrary, irritate **09** aggravate, cheese off, displease, drive nuts, importune
10 drive crazy, exasperate **11** get your goat **12** drive bananas **13** get on your wick, get up your nose, get your back up, make sparks fly **14** drive up the wall, get your blood up, give you the hump, piss someone off, take the michael **15** get on your nerves, get your dander up

annoyance
04 bind, bore, drag, fash, hump, pain, pest **05** anger, sturt, tease **06** bother, injury, molest, pester, ruffle
07 bugbear, chagrin, noyance, trouble
08 headache, irritant, mischief, nuisance, vexation **09** bête noire
10 harassment, irritation
11 aggravation, displeasure, disturbance, provocation
12 exasperation, excruciation **13** pain in the butt, pain in the neck **14** thorn in the side

• **expression of annoyance**
03 dam, dee, god, hey, sod, tut
04 damn, drat, heck, hell, hoot, phew, rats **05** blast, blimy, damme, devil, Jesus, my God!, shoot, waugh
06 blimey, bother, Christ, dammit, shucks, zounds **07** caramba, doggone **08** honestly, hoot-toot
09 cor blimey, do you mind?, good grief, gorblimey **10** hell's bells, hell's teeth, hoots-toots **11** botheration, for God's sake, for pete's sake, that's torn it **12** Donnerwetter
13 Gordon Bennett **14** for Christ's sake, for heaven's sake **15** for goodness sake

annoyed
04 sore **05** angry, cross, fed up, upset, vexed **06** bugged, hipped, miffed, narked, peeved, piqued, shirty
07 chocker, hassled, in a huff, pig sick, stroppy **08** harassed, in a paddy, provoked **09** indignant, irritated, pissed off, ticked off **10** brassed off, cheesed off, displeased, driven nuts, got the hump **11** driven crazy, exasperated

annoying
05 pesky **06** trying **07** galling, irksome, teasing **08** infernal, niggling, tiresome **09** harassing, intrusive, maddening, offensive, provoking, unwelcome, vexatious
10 bothersome, disturbing, irritating, plaguesome **11** aggravating, importunate, infuriating, pestiferous, troublesome **12** exasperating

annual
06 yearly **07** almanac **08** calendar, register, yearbook

• **annual return**
02 AR

annul
04 undo, void **05** quash **06** cancel, defeat, negate, recall, reduce, repeal, revoke, vacate **07** abolish, cashier, nullify, rescind, retract, reverse, suspend, vacuate **08** abrogate, disannul, dissolve, overrule, set aside
10 invalidate **11** countermand

annulment
06 defeat, recall, repeal **07** reverse, voiding **08** negation, quashing
09 abolition, cassation **10** abrogation, rescission, revocation, suspension
11 countermand, dissolution, rescindment **12** cancellation, invalidation **13** nullification

anodyne
04 dull **05** bland **07** neutral
08 harmless, innocent **09** analgesic, deadening, innocuous **11** inoffensive

anoint
03 oil, rub **04** balm, daub, nard, oint
05 anele, bless, salve, smear
06 grease, hallow, ordain, pomade
08 dedicate, sanctify, set apart
09 embrocate, lubricate **10** apply oil to, consecrate

anomalous
◇ *anagram indicator*
03 odd **04** rare **05** freak **07** deviant, unusual **08** abnormal, atypical, freakish, peculiar, singular
09 eccentric, irregular **11** exceptional, incongruous **12** inconsistent

anomaly
◇ *anagram indicator*
05 freak **06** misfit, oddity, rarity
09 departure, deviation, exception
10 aberration, divergence
11 abnormality, incongruity, peculiarity
12 eccentricity, irregularity
13 inconsistency

anon
04 soon **06** coming **07** by and by, shortly **09** quite soon **10** before long
11 immediately **14** in a little while **15** in the near future

anonymous
01 a **02** an **04** anon, gray, grey
07 unknown, unnamed **08** faceless, nameless, unsigned **09** incognito
10 authorless, impersonal, innominate, unattested
11 nondescript, unspecified
12 unattributed, unidentified, unremarkable **13** unexceptional
14 unacknowledged

anorak
04 nerd, nurd, spod, wonk **06** cagoul, kagool, kagoul **07** cagoule, kagoule
11 windcheater **12** trainspotter

another
◇ *anagram indicator*
04 more **05** added, extra, other, spare
06 second **07** further, variant
09 different, some other **10** additional, not the same **11** alternative

answer
01 a **03** ans, fit, get, key **04** fill, meet, pass, rein, suit **05** agree, match, react, reply, serve **06** fulfil, pick up, refute, result, retort, return **07** conform, resolve, respond, riposte, satisfy
08 comeback, quick fix, reaction, rebuttal, rescript, response, solution
09 correlate, get back to, match up to,

rejoinder, retaliate, write back **10** come back to, resolution **11** acknowledge, explanation, replication, retaliation, unravelling **12** correspond to **15** acknowledgement

• **answer back**

04 sass **05** argue, rebut **06** retort **07** dispute, riposte **08** backchat, disagree, talk back **09** retaliate **10** be cheeky to, contradict

• **answer for**

06 pay for **08** speak for, vouch for **09** engage for, suffer for **11** be liable for **13** be punished for

• **answer to**

08 report to **09** work under **15** be accountable to, be responsible to

answerable

06 liable **07** to blame **08** suitable **10** chargeable, equivalent **11** accountable, blameworthy, responsible

ant

05 emmet, nurse **06** ergate, nasute, neuter **07** ergates, pismire, termite

Ants include:

03 red
04 army, fire, leaf, wood
05 black, crazy
06 Amazon, driver, weaver
07 bulldog, forager, pharaoh, soldier
08 honeydew
09 black lawn, carpenter, harvester
10 leaf-cutter
12 red harvester

antagonism

06 enmity **07** discord, ill will, rivalry **08** conflict, friction **09** animosity, antipathy, hostility **10** antibiosis, contention, dissension, ill feeling, opposition, oppugnancy

antagonist

03 foe **04** peer **05** enemy, rival **08** opponent **09** adversary, contender **10** competitor, contestant

antagonistic

06 averse **07** adverse, hostile, opposed **08** opponent **10** at variance, unfriendly **11** adversarial, belligerent, conflicting, contentious, ill-disposed **12** incompatible

antagonize

03 bug **04** miff, rile **05** anger, annoy, get at, repel **06** insult, needle, nettle, offend, wind up **07** incense, provoke **08** alienate, drive mad, embitter, estrange, irritate **09** aggravate, disaffect **10** drive crazy **12** drive bananas **13** make sparks fly **14** drive up the wall

Antarctica

03 ATA

Antarctic animal

07 Penguin

antbear

08 aardvark, tamanoir **12** Myrmecophaga

anteater

05 Manis **07** echidna, tamandu **08** aardvark, pangolin, tamandua

antecedent

04 race **05** blood, roots, stock **06** stirps, tipuna, tupuna **09** ancestors, forebears, genealogy, precedent, preceding, precursor **10** extraction, forerunner, prevenient **11** forefathers, preparatory, progenitors

antedate

07 precede, predate, prevene **08** antecede, go before **10** come before

antediluvian

03 old **05** early, passé **06** bygone, old hat **07** archaic **08** outmoded **10** antiquated **11** out of the Ark **15** as old as the hills

antelope

Antelopes include:

03 bok, doe, gnu, kid, kob
04 kudu, oryx, puku, suni, thar, topi
05 addax, bubal, chiru, eland, goral, nagor, nyala, oribi, sable, saiga, sasin, serow
06 bosbok, dik-dik, duiker, duyker, dzeren, impala, inyala, koodoo, lechwe, nilgai, nilgau, pygarg, reebok
07 blaubok, blesbok, bloubok, bubalis, chamois, chikara, gazelle, gemsbok, gerenuk, grysbok, madoqua, nylghau, sassaby
08 Antilope, bontebok, boschbok, bushbuck, palebuck, reedbuck, steenbok, tsessebe
09 blackbuck, sitatunga, situtunga, springbok, steinbock, tragelaph, waterbuck
10 Alcelaphus, hartebeest, ox-antelope, wildebeest
11 zebra duiker
12 goat-antelope, klipspringer
13 sable antelope

antenna

04 horn **06** aerial, feeler

anteroom

04 hall **05** foyer, lobby, porch **09** vestibule **11** antechamber, waiting-room **12** entrance hall, voiding-lobby

anthem

04 hymn, song **05** chant, motet, paean, psalm **06** motett, waiata **07** chorale, introit **08** antiphon, canticle, isodicon **10** responsory **12** Marseillaise, song of praise

anthology

06 digest **07** omnibus **08** treasury **09** selection, spicilege **10** collection, compendium, miscellany **11** compilation, florilegium **12** chrestomathy

Anthony

04 Tony

anthrax

04 sang

anthropology

09 ethnology

Anthropologists include:

04 **Boas** (Franz), **Buck** (Sir Peter), **Mead** (Margaret)
05 **Hiroa** (Te Rangi), **Tylor** (Sir Edward)
06 **Frazer** (Sir J G), **Leakey** (Louis), **Marett** (R R)
07 **Métraux** (Albert)
09 **Heyerdahl** (Thor)
10 **Malinowski** (Bronislaw)
11 **Lévi-Strauss** (Claude)
14 **Radcliffe-Brown** (Alfred)

antibiotic

Antibiotics include:

05 Cipro®
08 neomycin, nystatin
09 avoparcin, kanamycin, Neosporin®, polymyxin, quinolone
10 ampicillin, Aureomycin®, bacitracin, gramicidin, lincomycin, meticillin, penicillin, polymyxin B, rifampicin, Terramycin®, vancomycin
11 amoxicillin, amoxycillin, clindamycin, cloxacillin, cycloserine, doxorubicin, doxycycline, fusidic acid, methicillin
12 erythromycin, griseofulvin, streptomycin, tetracycline, trimethoprim
13 cephalosporin, ciprofloxacin, co-trimoxazole, metronidazole, spectinomycin, virginiamycin
15 chloramphenicol, oxytetracycline

antibody

03 MAB **06** reagin **10** agglutinin, amboceptor, immune body, precipitin **13** isoagglutinin

antic

04 dido **05** caper, clown **07** buffoon **09** fantastic, grotesque **10** mountebank

Antichrist

08 man of sin, the Beast **10** lawless one

anticipate

05 await, guess **06** bank on, expect **07** count on, foresee, hope for, look for, obviate, precede, predict, pre-empt, prepare, prevene, prevent **08** antedate, beat to it, figure on, forecast, preclude, reckon on **09** apprehend, count upon, forestall, intercept **10** prepare for **11** preoccupate, second-guess, think likely **13** look forward to

anticipation

04 hope, type **08** forecast **09** foretaste, intuition, prejudice, prolepsis **10** excitement, expectancy, prediction, prevention **11** bated breath, expectation, preparation **12** apprehension, presentiment

anticlimax

06 bathos, fiasco **07** let-down

08 comedown, non-event 09 damp squib 14 disappointment

antics
06 capers, doings, pranks, stunts, tricks 07 foolery, frolics 08 clowning, mischief 09 horseplay, silliness 10 buffoonery, shenanigan, skylarking, tomfoolery 11 playfulness, shenanigans 12 monkey-tricks

antidote
04 cure 05 serum 06 bezoar, remedy, senega 07 theriac, treacle 08 naloxone, Orvietan, theriaca 09 antitoxin, antivenin 10 corrective, mithridate 11 contrayerva, dimercaprol, neutralizer 12 alexipharmic, counter-agent 13 counter-poison, Venice treacle 14 alexipharmakon, countermeasure

Antigua and Barbuda
03 ATG

antimony
02 Sb

antipathy
04 hate 05 odium 06 animus, enmity, hatred 07 allergy, disgust, dislike, ill will 08 aversion, bad blood, distaste, dyspathy, loathing 09 animosity, hostility, repulsion 10 abhorrence, antagonism, opposition, repugnance 15 incompatibility

antiquated
05 dated, passé 06 bygone, démodé, fogram, fossil, old hat 07 ancient, archaic, outworn 08 obsolete, outdated, outmoded 09 out-of-date, primitive 10 fossilized 11 on the way out, prehistoric 12 antediluvian, old-fashioned 13 anachronistic, prehistorical

antique
◇ *archaic word indicator*
03 old 05 curio, relic 06 bygone, quaint, rarity 07 ancient, archaic, veteran, vintage 08 Egyptian, heirloom, obsolete, outdated 09 antiquity, curiosity 10 antiquated 11 antiquarian, museum piece, period piece 12 old-fashioned 13 object of virtu 14 collector's item

Antiques-related terms include:

04 Goss, Ming, ring, T'ang
05 glaze, ivory
06 barock, dealer, empire, Gothic, lustre, patina, period, rococo
07 art deco, auction, barocco, baroque, ceramic, federal, impasto, opaline, pilgrim, pottery, Tiffany
08 filigree, Georgian, Jacobean, majolica, Sheraton, trecento
09 bone china, collector, Delftware, Edwardian, porcelain, Queen Anne, soft paste, stoneware, valuation, Victorian
10 art nouveau, millefiori
11 chinoiserie, Chippendale, cinquecento, haute époque, Hepplewhite, period piece, restoration
12 antiques fair, arts and craft, blanc de Chine, blue and white, reproduction, transitional
13 willow pattern
15 churrigueresque

antiquity
03 age, eld 06 old age 07 oldness 08 agedness 09 ancientry, olden days 10 days of yore 11 ancientness, distant past 12 ancient times 14 time immemorial

antiseptic
04 pure 05 clean 07 aseptic, sterile 08 cleanser, germ-free, hygienic, purifier, sanitary 09 germicide, medicated, mouthwash, sanitized 10 sterilized, unpolluted 11 bactericide 12 disinfectant 14 uncontaminated

Antiseptics include:

03 TCP®
05 eupad, eusol
06 cresol, Dettol®, flavin, formol, phenol, Savlon®, thymol
07 benzoin, flavine
08 creasote, creosote, formalin, iodoform
09 cassareep, cassaripe, cetrimide, Germolene®, Listerine®, merbromin, zinc oxide
10 acriflavin
11 acriflavine
12 carbolic acid, methyl violet
13 chlorhexidine, crystal violet, flowers of zinc, gentian violet, silver nitrate
14 Dakin's solution, rubbing alcohol, sodium benzoate, sodium chlorate
15 hexachlorophane, hexachlorophene

antisocial
07 asocial, hostile, lawless 08 anarchic, reserved, retiring 09 alienated, withdrawn 10 disorderly, disruptive, rebellious, unfriendly, unsociable 11 belligerent 12 antagonistic, misanthropic, unacceptable 13 unforthcoming 14 unapproachable 15 uncommunicative

antisubmarine
02 AS

antithesis
07 reverse 08 contrast, converse, opposite, reversal 10 opposition 13 contradiction 15 opposite extreme

antithetical
07 opposed 08 clashing, contrary, opposing 11 conflicting 12 incompatible, in opposition 13 contradictory 14 irreconcilable

antler
04 horn 08 staghorn 09 hartshorn

antler
04 horn 08 staghorn 09 hartshorn

Antony
04 Tony

anxiety
03 tiz 04 care, cark, fear, rack, stew 05 angst, dread, sweat, tizzy, worry 06 fantad, fantod, hang-up, nerves, strain, stress 07 anguish, concern, fantads, fanteeg, fantods, jitters, tension, thought, willies 08 disquiet, distress, fantigue, suspense 09 dysthymia, misgiving, worriment 10 foreboding, impatience, solicitude, uneasiness 11 butterflies, disquietude, fretfulness, nervousness 12 apprehension, collywobbles, hypochondria, restlessness 13 consternation, heebie-jeebies 14 solicitousness

See also **phobia**

• free from anxiety
04 ease

anxious
◇ *anagram indicator*
04 keen, taut, toey 05 eager, het up, tense, upset 06 afraid, uneasy 07 careful, fearful, fretful, in a stew, jittery, longing, nervous, uptight, worried 08 desirous, dismayed, in a tizzy, insecure, restless, tortured, troubled, yearning 09 concerned, desperate, disturbed, expectant, ill at ease, impatient, on the rack, tormented 10 distressed, in suspense, solicitous 11 overwrought 12 apprehensive, enthusiastic 13 grandmotherly, on tenterhooks 14 hot and bothered, valetudinarian 15 a bundle of nerves

anxiously
07 tensely 08 uneasily 09 fearfully, fretfully, nervously 10 restlessly 11 impatiently, tormentedly 12 solicitously 14 apprehensively

any
03 ary, one 04 a few, some 05 arrow, at all 06 a bit of 09 whichever 10 a single one, in the least 11 the least bit, to any extent 12 to some extent

anybody
03 one

anyhow
◇ *anagram indicator*
06 anyway 07 anyways 08 at random, untidily 09 at any rate, in any case 10 carelessly, in any event, not in order, regardless 11 at all events, haphazardly 12 nevertheless, no matter what 13 indifferently

anyone
03 you

anything
03 owt 05 ought

anyway
◇ *anagram indicator*
06 anyhow 07 anyroad 09 in any case 10 in any event, regardless 11 at all events 12 nevertheless, no matter what

apace
04 fast 07 hastily, quickly, rapidly, swiftly 08 speedily 10 at top speed 11 at full speed, double-quick 12 without delay

apart
◇ *anagram indicator*
04 afar, away **05** alone, aloof, aside **06** beside, cut off, in bits, singly, to bits **07** asunder, distant **08** by itself, distinct, divorced, excluded, in pieces, isolated, separate, to pieces **09** into parts, on your own, piecemeal, privately, separated, to one side **10** by yourself, separately **11** not together **12** individually **13** independently

• apart from
04 save **06** beyond, but for, except **07** besides, outside **08** excepted **09** aside from, except for, excluding **11** not counting

apartment
03 apt, pad **04** flat, gaff, room, unit **05** bower, condo, split **06** duplex, walk-up **07** chamber, mansion **08** home unit, paradise, tenement **11** condominium **12** privy chamber **13** accommodation **15** duplex apartment
See also **room**

apathetic
04 cold, cool, numb **05** blasé, ho-hum **07** passive, unmoved **08** listless, lukewarm **09** impassive, lethargic, unfeeling **10** insouciant, uninvolved **11** emotionless, half-hearted, indifferent, unambitious, unconcerned, unemotional **12** uninterested, unresponsive

apathy
06 acedia, torpor **07** accidie, inertia, languor **08** coldness, coolness, lethargy **09** passivity, unconcern **11** impassivity **12** indifference, listlessness, sluggishness **13** insensibility, lack of concern **14** lack of interest

ape
04 copy, echo, mock **05** magot, mimic **06** affect, mirror, parody, parrot, send up, simian **07** imitate, take off **09** proconsul **10** anthropoid, caricature, jackanapes, troglodyte **11** counterfeit
See also **animal**; **monkey**; **primate**

Apes include:

05 chimp, drill, jocko, orang, pigmy, pongo, pygmy, satyr
06 baboon, bonobo, chacma, dog-ape, gelada, gibbon, monkey, wou-wou, wow-wow
07 gorilla, hoolock, macaque, siamang
08 hylobate, mandrill
09 hamadryad, orang-utan
10 chimpanzee, silverback
11 orang-outang
12 Cynocephalus, ourang-outang, paranthropus
13 Kenyapithecus
15 pygmy chimpanzee

aperture
03 eye, gap **04** hole, rent, slit, slot, vent **05** chink, cleft, crack, light, mouth, space **06** breach, choana, oscule, rictus, throat, window **07** fissure, foramen, opening, orifice, osculum, passage, punctum, swallow **08** fenestra, overture, punctule **09** sight-hole **10** interstice **11** perforation **14** counter-opening

apex
03 tip, top **04** acme, peak **05** crest, crown, point **06** apogee, climax, height, summit, vertex, zenith **08** pinnacle **09** fastigium, high point **10** apotheosis, pyramidion **11** culmination **12** consummation **13** crowning point

aphid, aphis
06 ant cow **08** blackfly, greenfly **09** bark-louse **10** dolphin-fly, plant louse, smother-fly

aphorism
03 saw **05** adage, axiom, gnome, maxim **06** dictum, saying **07** epigram, precept, proverb **08** sentence **09** witticism **10** apophthegm, whakatauki

aphrodisiac
06 erotic **07** amative, amatory, philter, philtre **08** venerous **09** cantharis, erogenous, stimulant, venereous **10** love potion, Spanish fly **11** erotogenous, stimulative

Aphrodite
05 Venus

apiece
03 all **04** each **06** singly **07** per head **09** per capita, per person **10** separately **12** individually, respectively

aplomb
05 poise **08** calmness, coolness **09** assurance, composure, sangfroid **10** confidence, equanimity **11** savoir-faire **13** self-assurance **14** self-confidence, self-possession, unflappability

apocryphal
06 made-up **07** dubious **08** doubtful, fabulous, mythical, spurious **09** concocted, equivocal, imaginary, legendary **10** fabricated, fictitious, unverified **11** unsupported **12** questionable **15** unauthenticated, unsubstantiated

Apocryphal books of the Bible include:

03 Bar, Esd, Jud, Sir, Sus, Tob
04 Macc, Wisd
05 Bel&Dr, Tobit (Book of)
06 Baruch (Book of), Ecclus, Esdras (Books of), Judith (Book of)
07 Pr of Man, Susanna (History of)
08 Manasseh (Prayer of)
09 Maccabees
14 Ecclesiasticus (Book of)
15 Bel and the Dragon, Wisdom of Solomon (Book of)

See also **Bible**

apologetic
05 sorry **06** rueful **08** contrite, penitent **09** regretful, repentant **10** excusatory, remorseful

apologetically
08 ruefully **10** contritely, penitently **11** regretfully, repentantly **12** remorsefully

apologia
07 defence **08** argument **11** explanation, explication, vindication

apologist
06 backer **08** advocate, defender, endorser, upholder **09** supporter **10** vindicator

apologize
05 plead **06** grovel, regret **07** confess, explain, justify **08** say sorry **09** ask pardon **11** acknowledge **12** be apologetic, eat humble pie, eat your words **14** ask forgiveness, say you are sorry

apology
04 oops, plea **05** sorry **06** excuse **07** defence, mockery, regrets **08** excuse me, pardon me, travesty **10** caricature, confession, corruption, distortion, palliation **11** explanation, saying sorry, vindication **12** poor specimen **13** justification **14** poor substitute **15** acknowledgement

apoplectic
03 mad **04** high **05** cross, irate, livid, moody, radge, ratty, spewy, wrath, wroth **06** bitter, choked, raging, sullen, sultry **07** annoyed, crooked, enraged, furious, ropable, stroppy, uptight **08** burned up, choleric, foribund, hairless, in a paddy, incensed, outraged, seething, up in arms, wrathful **09** in a lather, in a temper, indignant, irritated, pissed off, rancorous, raving mad, resentful, seeing red, splenetic, ticked off, very angry **10** hopping mad, infuriated, passionate, up in the air **11** disgruntled, exasperated, fit to be tied **12** on the rampage, on the warpath **14** beside yourself

apostasy
06 heresy **07** perfidy, rattery, ratting **09** defection, desertion, falseness, recreance, recreancy, treachery **10** disloyalty, renegation **12** renunciation **13** faithlessness **14** unfaithfulness

apostate
03 rat **07** heretic, traitor **08** defector, deserter, recreant, renegade, runagate, turncoat **10** recidivist **13** tergiversator

apostle
07 pioneer, teacher **08** advocate, champion, crusader, disciple, preacher, reformer **09** apologist, messenger, proponent, supporter **10** evangelist, missionary **12** proselytizer

Apostles of Jesus Christ:

04 John
05 James, Judas, Peter, Simon
06 Andrew, Philip, Thomas
07 Matthew
08 Matthias, Thaddeus
11 Bartholomew
13 Judas Iscariot
14 Simon the Zealot
15 James of Alphaeus
17 Simon the Canaanite

apotheosis
03 tip **04** acme, apex, peak **05** crest, crown, point **06** apogee, climax, height, summit, vertex, zenith **08** pinnacle **09** fastigium, high point **11** culmination, deification **12** consummation **13** crowning point, glorification

appal
05 alarm, daunt, scare, shock **06** dismay **07** disgust, horrify, outrage, terrify, unnerve **08** frighten **10** disconcert, intimidate

appalling
◇ *anagram indicator*
04 dire, grim, naff, poor, ropy **05** awful, lousy, pants, ropey **06** horrid **07** ghastly, hideous, the pits, very bad **08** alarming, daunting, dreadful, hopeless, horrible, horrific, inferior, pathetic, shocking, terrible **09** atrocious, frightful, harrowing, loathsome, unnerving **10** disgusting, horrifying, inadequate, outrageous, terrifying **11** frightening, nightmarish **12** intimidating, unacceptable **14** unsatisfactory

appallingly
◇ *anagram indicator*
07 awfully **08** horribly, terribly **09** hideously **10** dreadfully, hopelessly, shockingly **11** frightfully **12** horrifically, pathetically, unacceptably

apparatus
03 rig **04** bank, gear, tool **05** means, set-up, tools **06** device, gadget, outfit, system, tackle **07** machine, network **08** utensils **09** appliance, equipment, framework, implement, machinery, materials, mechanism, structure **10** implements, instrument **11** contraption
See also **laboratory**

apparel
03 kit **04** garb, gear, tire, togs **05** besee, dress, get-up, weeds **06** attire, outfit, robing, vestry **07** clobber, clothes, costume, raiment, vesture **08** clothing, garments, wardrobe **09** garniture **11** habiliments

apparent
◇ *hidden indicator*
02 ap **03** app **04** open **05** clear, overt, plain **06** marked, patent **07** evident, obvious, outward, seeming, visible **08** declared, distinct, manifest **10** detectable, noticeable, ostensible **11** conspicuous, perceptible, superficial **12** unmistakable **13** be standing out

apparently
02 ap **03** app **07** clearly, plainly **08** patently **09** evidently, obviously, outwardly, reputedly, seemingly **10** manifestly, ostensibly **12** on the surface **13** on the face of it, superficially

apparition
05 fetch, ghost, shape, spook, taish **06** double, spirit, taisch, vision, wraith **07** chimera, eidolon, gytrash, phantom, specter, spectre **08** illusion, manifest, phantasm, presence, visitant **09** hobgoblin, semblance **10** appearance **12** doppelgänger **13** manifestation **15** materialization

appeal
02 it, SA **03** ask, beg, cry, SOS, sue **04** call, draw, lure, peal, pele, plea, pray, suit **05** apply, charm, claim, oomph, plead, tempt **06** allure, ask for, avouch, beauty, call on, engage, entice, invite, invoke, orison, please, prayer, review **07** address, attract, beseech, entreat, implore, provoke, reclaim, request, retrial, solicit **08** approach, call upon, charisma, entreaty, interest, petition **09** fascinate, magnetism **10** adjuration, attraction, invocation, recusation, supplicate **11** application, conjuration, enchantment, fascination, imploration, winsomeness **12** re-evaluation, solicitation, supplication **13** re-examination **14** attractiveness **15** reconsideration
• **solemn appeal**
04 oath

appealing
07 winning, winsome **08** alluring, charming, engaging, enticing, inviting, magnetic, pleasing, tempting **10** attractive, enchanting **11** charismatic, fascinating, interesting

appear
◇ *homophone indicator*
03 act, eye **04** go on, look, loom, peer, play, rise, seem, shew, show, star **05** arise, bob up, break, enter, issue, kithe, kythe, occur, pop up **06** arrive, attend, cast up, co-star, crop up, emerge, figure, show up, spring, turn up **07** come out, compear, develop, perform, surface, topline, turn out **08** platform, take part **09** be on stage, be present, come along **10** be a guest in **11** be published, come to light, materialize, show signs of **12** come across as, come into view, show your face **13** become visible, come into sight **14** take the guise of **15** become available
• **begin to appear**
03 ope **04** open

appearance
03 air, hew, hue **04** broo, brow, face, form, garb, look, mien, rise, show, view **05** debut, front, ghost, guise, image, looks **06** advent, aspect, coming, effeir, effere, façade, figure, manner, ostent, visage **07** arrival, bearing, outward **08** exterior, illusion, presence, pretence **09** appearing, demeanour, emergence, semblance **10** apparition, attendance, complexion, expression, impression **11** outward form **12** introduction **14** coming into view
• **final appearance**
08 swansong
• **personal appearance**
02 PA

appease
04 stay **05** allay, atone, quiet, still **06** aslake, attone, defray, pacify, soothe **07** mollify, placate, qualify, satisfy **08** mitigate **09** reconcile **10** conciliate, propitiate **13** make peace with

appeasement
09 placation **11** peacemaking **12** conciliation, pacification, satisfaction **14** reconciliation

appellation
04 name **05** title **07** epithet **08** monicker, nickname **09** most noble, sobriquet **10** soubriquet **11** description, designation **12** compellation, denomination

append
◇ *juxtaposition indicator*
03 add, put, tag **04** join **05** affix, annex **06** adjoin, attach, fasten, tack on **07** conjoin, subjoin **08** pickback **09** pickaback, pickapack, piggyback

appendage
03 lug **04** aril **05** affix, aglet, whisk **06** aiglet, arista, barbel, cercus, stipel, uropod **07** adjunct, arillus, auricle, foretop, maxilla, stipule **08** addendum, addition, appendix, gnathite, nose-leaf, pedipalp, pendicle **09** allantois, chelicera, swimmeret, tailpiece **10** paraglossa, parapodium, supplement **11** aiguillette **12** appurtenance

appendix
03 app **05** annex, rider **07** adjunct, codicil, pendant, pendent **08** addendum, addition, epilogue, schedule **09** appendage **10** postscript, supplement

appertain
05 apply, refer **06** bear on, effeir, effere, regard, relate **07** concern, pertain **10** be relevant **14** have a bearing on

appetite
03 maw, yen **04** lust, urge, zeal, zest **05** taste, tooth, twist **06** desire, hunger, liking, orexis, relish, thirst **07** craving, longing, malacia, passion, stomach **08** inner man, yearning **09** eagerness **10** inner woman, propensity **11** inclination **13** concupiscence
• **sharpness of appetite**
04 edge

appetizer
04 meze, tapa, whet **05** bhaji, mezze, tapas **06** bhagee, bhajee, canapé, dim sum, relish **07** starter **08** antepast, apéritif, cocktail **09** antipasto
11 amuse-bouche, amuse-gueule, first course, hors d'oeuvre **13** prawn cocktail

appetizing
05 tasty, yummy **06** morish
07 moreish, piquant, savoury, scrummy **08** inviting, tempting
09 appealing, delicious, palatable, succulent, toothsome **11** lip-smacking, scrumptious **13** mouthwatering

applaud
03 hum **04** clap, laud, root, ruff
05 cheer, extol **06** cry aim, praise
07 acclaim, approve, commend
08 eulogize **10** compliment
12 congratulate **14** cheer to the echo, give a big hand to **15** give an ovation to

applause
04 hand, ruff **05** éclat, salvo, vivat
06 bravos, cheers, praise **07** acclaim, ovation, plaudit **08** a big hand, accolade, approval, cheering, clapping, encomium, plaudits
11 acclamation, Kentish fire
12 commendation **14** congratulation
15 standing ovation

apple
04 pome

Apples include:

03 Cox
04 Cox's, crab, snow
05 Coxes, eater
06 biffin, codlin, cooker, eating, idared, pippin, russet
07 Baldwin, Bramley, codling, cooking, costard, crispin, ribston, Sturmer, wine-sap
08 Braeburn, Jonathan, McIntosh, pearmain, Pink Lady, queening, ribstone, sweeting
09 delicious, jenneting, king-apple, nonpareil, Royal gala
11 Granny Smith, McIntosh red, russet apple
12 Red Delicious
13 Ribston pippin, Sturmer Pippin
15 Golden Delicious

• **apple core**
04 runt
• **big apple**
02 NY **03** NYC

appliance
03 use **04** iron, tool **05** gizmo, truss, value, waldo **06** device, gadget, praxis
07 machine **08** function
09 apparatus, implement, mechanism, relevance **10** fire engine, instrument
11 application, carrying-out, contraption, contrivance
See also **domestic**; **utensil**

applicable
03 apt, fit **04** live **05** valid **06** proper, suited, useful **07** fitting **08** apposite, relevant, suitable **09** pertinent
10 legitimate **11** appropriate
• **not applicable**
02 n/a

applicant
06 suitor **08** aspirant, claimant, inquirer **09** candidate, postulant
10 competitor, contestant, petitioner
11 interviewee

application
03 use **04** suit **05** claim, study, value
06 appeal, demand, effort, praxis
07 aptness, bearing, inquiry, program, purpose, request, rubbing
08 function, hard work, industry, keenness, petition, smearing, software **09** anointing, assiduity, diligence, putting on, relevance, spreading, treatment **10** commitment, dedication, pertinence
11 germaneness **12** perseverance, sedulousness, significance
13 attentiveness **15** industriousness
• **make application**
03 sue

applied
◇ *anagram indicator*
04 real **06** actual, useful **07** hands-on **08** relevant **09** practical
10 functional
• **applied to**
02 on

apply
03 fit, lay, ply, put, rub, set, sue, use
04 give, suit, turn **05** brush, claim, exert, lay on, order, paint, put on, refer, smear, study, wield **06** affect, anoint, appeal, appose, ask for, assign, bestow, betake, commit, devote, direct, draw on, employ, engage, relate, resort
07 address, adhibit, execute, harness, inquire, involve, pertain, present, request, solicit, utilize **08** dedicate, exercise, petition, practise, put in for, resort to, spread on, work hard
09 appertain, cover with, implement, persevere, treat with **10** administer, be diligent, be relevant, buckle down, settle down **11** bring to bear, concentrate, knuckle down, requisition, write off for **12** make an effort, write away for **13** be industrious, be significant, bring into play **14** commit yourself, devote yourself, fill in a form for **15** put into practice
• **apply carelessly**
04 slap

appoint
03 fix, set **04** cast, hire, make, name, pick, post **05** allot, co-opt, elect, limit, place, put in, voice **06** assign, charge, choose, decide, decree, depute, detail, direct, employ, engage, ordain, select, settle, take on **07** arrange, command, destine, install, present, recruit, specify, station **08** delegate, nominate
09 designate, determine, establish
10 commission, constitute **13** be shortlisted

appointed
◇ *anagram indicator*
03 due, set **05** fixed **06** chosen
07 decided, decreed, settled
08 allotted, arranged, assigned, destined, ordained **09** scheduled
10 designated, determined
11 established, pre-arranged, preordained

appointment
03 job **04** date, post, room **05** place, tryst **06** choice, naming, office
07 meeting **08** choosing, election, position **09** interview, selection, situation **10** delegation, engagement, nomination, rendezvous
11 arrangement, assignation
12 consultation **13** commissioning
• **keep an appointment**
04 meet

apportion
04 deal, mete **05** allot, carve, grant, share, stint, weigh **06** assign, divide, morsel, number, ration **07** deal out, dole out, hand out, mete out
08 allocate, dispense, share out
09 admeasure, ration out **10** distribute, measure out

apportionment
05 grant, share **06** ration **07** dealing, handout, sharing **08** division
09 allotment, rationing **10** allocation, assignment **12** dispensation, distribution

apposite
03 apt **06** suited **07** apropos, germane, in point **08** relevant, suitable
09 befitting, pertinent **10** applicable, to the point **11** appropriate **12** to the purpose

appraisal
◇ *anagram indicator*
05 assay, prise, prize **06** rating, review, survey **07** opinion **08** estimate, once-over **09** judgement, reckoning, valuation **10** assessment, estimation, evaluation, inspection **11** examination
12 appreciation

appraise
04 rate **05** assay, judge, sum up, value
06 assess, review, size up, survey
07 examine, inspect, valuate
08 estimate, evaluate, once-over

appreciable
04 vast **08** definite, sensible
10 noticeable, ponderable
11 discernible, perceptible, significant, substantial **12** considerable, recognizable

appreciably
08 markedly **10** definitely, noticeably
11 perceptibly **12** considerably
13 significantly, substantially

appreciate
03 see **04** gain, go up, grow, know, like, rise **05** enjoy, grasp, mount, prize, sense, thank, value **06** admire, esteem, regard, relish, savour **07** apprise,

apprize, cherish, enhance, improve, inflate, realize, respect, welcome **08** increase, perceive, treasure **09** be aware of, recognize **10** comprehend, strengthen, understand **11** acknowledge **12** be indebted to, take kindly to **13** be conscious of, be grateful for, be sensitive to, give thanks for, think highly of **14** be appreciative, sympathize with

appreciation
04 gain, rise **05** grasp, sense **06** esteem, growth, liking, notice, praise, regard, relish, review, thanks **07** feeling, respect, valuing **08** analysis, critique, increase, sympathy **09** awareness, enjoyment, gratitude, inflation, judgement, knowledge, valuation **10** admiration, assessment, cognizance, commentary, escalation, estimation, evaluation, obligation, perception, respecting **11** enhancement, high opinion, improvement, realization, recognition, sensitivity **12** gratefulness, indebtedness, thankfulness **13** comprehension, understanding **14** responsiveness **15** acknowledgement
• **expression of appreciation**
02 ta **05** merci, mercy, super **06** cheers!, phwoah, phwoar, thanks **08** thank you **10** danke schon

appreciative
07 mindful, obliged, pleased **08** admiring, beholden, grateful, indebted, thankful **09** conscious, sensitive **10** perceptive, respectful, responsive, supportive **11** encouraging **12** enthusiastic **13** knowledgeable

apprehend
03 nab, see **04** bust, grab, nick, take, twig **05** catch, grasp, run in, seize **06** arrest, collar, detain, pick up, pull in **07** believe, capture, realize **08** conceive, consider, perceive **09** deprehend, recognize **10** comprehend, understand

apprehension
04 fear **05** alarm, doubt, dread, grasp, qualm, worry **06** arrest, belief, noesis, taking, unease, uptake **07** anxiety, capture, concern, jitters, seizure, willies **08** disquiet, mistrust **09** detention, misgiving, suspicion **10** cognizance, conception, foreboding, perception, the willies, uneasiness **11** butterflies, discernment, nervousness, realization, recognition, trepidation **12** collywobbles, intellection, perturbation **13** comprehension, heebie-jeebies, understanding

apprehensive
04 toey **06** afraid, uneasy **07** alarmed, anxious, fearful, nervous, worried **08** bothered, doubtful, insecure **09** concerned **10** suspicious **11** distrustful, mistrustful **13** on tenterhooks

apprehensively
08 uneasily **09** anxiously, fearfully, nervously **10** doubtfully **12** suspiciously **13** distrustfully, mistrustfully

apprentice
01 L **03** app, cub **04** snob, tiro, tyro **05** cadet, maiko, pupil **06** commis, indent, intern, novice, rookie **07** flat cap, learner, recruit, starter, student, trainee **08** beginner, improver, newcomer, prentice, servitor, turnover **11** probationer **13** printer's devil

apprenticeship
09 Lehrjahre, novitiate **11** studentship, traineeship, trial period **14** training period

apprise
04 tell, warn **05** brief **06** advise, inform, notify, tip off **08** acquaint, intimate **09** ascertain, enlighten **11** communicate

approach
◇ *juxtaposition indicator*
03 nie, way **04** cost, draw, meet, near, nigh, plea, road **05** abord, anear, angle, begin, close, coast, coste, drive, greet, knock, means, reach, run-in, slant, style, treat **06** access, accost, advent, appeal, arrive, avenue, broach, coming, gain on, go near, invite, manner, method, stance, system, tackle, talk to **07** accoast, address, advance, apply to, arrival, catch up, contact, doorway, get onto, mention, opinion, passage, request, speak to, succeed, tactics **08** advances, appeal to, attitude, bear down, border on, commence, deal with, draw near, driveway, embark on, entrance, go nearer, landfall, oncoming, overture, position, proposal, set about, sound out, strategy **09** introduce, overtures, procedure, technique, threshold, undertake, viewpoint **10** buttonhole, come closer, come nearer, come near to, coming near, invitation, launch into, standpoint, suggestion **11** application, appropinque, approximate, come close to, coming close, compare with, get closer to, move towards, perspective, point of view, proposition, suggestions **12** make advances **13** appropinquate, make overtures, modus operandi **14** advance towards, course of action, get in touch with, proceed towards

approachable
04 open, warm **07** affable **08** friendly, informal, pleasant, sociable **09** agreeable, congenial, get-at-able, reachable, welcoming **10** accessible, attainable **15** easy to get on with

approbation
06 esteem, favour, praise **07** respect **08** applause, approval **09** allowance, laudation **10** acceptance, well-liking **11** countenance, endorsement, good opinion, recognition **12** commendation **13** encouragement

appropriate
03 apt, fit, nab **04** jump, lift, meet, nick, sink, take **05** annex, filch, pinch, right, seize, steal, swipe, usurp **06** assume, choice, pilfer, pocket, proper, seemly, spot-on, suited, thieve, timely **07** apropos, correct, fitting, germane, impound, in order, pre-empt, purloin, trouser **08** accepted, arrogate, becoming, embezzle, glom on to, knock off, liberate, peculate, property, relevant, suitable **09** befitting, congruous, expedient, opportune, pertinent, well-timed **10** applicable, commandeer, confiscate, felicitous, seasonable, to the point, well-chosen **11** appurtenant, expropriate, in character, make off with, requisition **12** appertaining **14** misappropriate

appropriately
07 apropos **08** properly, suitably **09** correctly, fittingly **10** relevantly **12** felicitously

approval
02 OK **03** nod **04** okay, wink **05** favor, leave, voice **06** assent, esteem, favour, honour, liking, praise, regard **07** acclaim, approof, consent, go-ahead, licence, mandate, plaudit, respect, support **08** agrément, applause, blessing, sanction, thumbs-up **09** agreement **10** acceptance, admiration, green light, imprimatur, permission, validation **11** acclamation, approbation, concurrence, endorsement, good opinion, rubber stamp **12** appreciation, commendation, confirmation, ratification **13** authorization, certification **14** recommendation
• **expression of approval**
02 ay, OK **03** aye, oke, olé, rah, yay **04** good, hear, okay, viva, vive **05** bravo, hurra, huzza, there, vivat **06** beauty, hooray, hurrah, hurray **07** attaboy, too much, top-hole, way to go! **08** attagirl, long live, zindabad **09** full marks, good on you **10** good for you, hubba hubba

approve
02 OK **03** buy, dig **04** amen, back, like, pass **05** adopt, allow, bless, carry **06** accept, admire, concur, esteem, favour, permit, praise, ratify, regard, second, uphold **07** acclaim, agree to, applaud, commend, confirm, endorse, mandate, support **08** accede to, assent to, hold with, sanction, validate **09** authorize, consent to, recommend **10** appreciate, homologate **11** countenance, rubber-stamp, think well of **12** give the nod to **13** be pleased with, think highly of

approved
03 app **06** proper **07** correct **08** accepted, favoured, official, orthodox **09** permitted, preferred **10** authorized, recognized, sanctioned **11** comme il faut, permissible, recommended **13** authoritative

approving
08 admiring, praising **09** laudatory **10** favourable, respectful, supportive **12** appreciative, commendatory

approvingly
10 admiringly, favourably **12** with pleasure **14** appreciatively

approximate
03 app **04** like, near, wild **05** close, loose, rough, round **06** coarse **07** guessed, inexact, similar, verge on **08** approach, ballpark, border on, relative, resemble **09** estimated, imprecise **10** come near to **11** be similar to, come close to **14** be tantamount to

approximately
01 c **02** ca **03** odd, say **04** or so, some **05** about, circa **06** around, nearly **07** close to, loosely, roughly **09** just about, not far off, rounded up **10** give or take, more or less, round about **11** approaching, rounded down **13** in the region of, or thereabouts, something like **14** in round figures, in round numbers **15** in the vicinity of

approximation
05 guess **08** approach, estimate, likeness **09** rough idea, semblance **10** conjecture, estimation, similarity **11** guesstimate, resemblance **14** ballpark figure, correspondence

appurtenance
09 equipment, trappings **10** belongings **11** accessories, impedimenta **13** paraphernalia

April
03 Apr

a priori
07 deduced **08** inferred **11** conjectural, theoretical **12** hypothetical **13** suppositional

apron
03 bay, bib, rim **04** brat, edge, tier **05** dicky, skirt **06** border, dickey, dickie, fringe, napron, pinnie, tabard **07** placket, tablier **08** pinafore, standing **09** barm-cloth, forecourt, periphery **10** loading bay **12** hard-standing

apropos
02 re **03** apt **05** right **06** proper, seemly, timely **07** correct, fitting **08** accepted, becoming, relevant, suitable **09** befitting, opportune, pertinent, regarding **10** applicable, felicitous, respecting, seasonable, to the point, well-chosen **11** in respect of **12** in relation to, with regard to **13** with respect to **14** on the subject of **15** with reference to

apse
04 bema **06** concha, exedra **07** exhedra **09** apsidiole, prothesis

apt
03 fit **04** gleg **05** given, happy, prone, ready **06** liable, likely, proper, seemly, spot-on, timely, toward **07** correct, fitting, germane, subject, tending **08** accurate, apposite, disposed, inclined, relevant, suitable **10** acceptable, applicable, seasonable **11** appropriate

aptitude
04 bent, gift, turn **05** flair, skill **06** talent **07** ability, faculty, fitness, leaning **08** capacity, facility, tendency **09** endowment, quickness **10** capability, cleverness **11** disposition, inclination, proficiency **12** intelligence **14** natural ability

aptly
05 fitly **08** suitably **09** fittingly **10** appositely, relevantly, to the point **13** appropriately

aquatic
03 sea **05** fluid, river, water **06** liquid, marine, watery **07** fluvial **08** maritime, nautical

aquiline
06 hooked **10** hooknosed

Arab
02 Ar

Arab League countries:

03 UAE
04 Iraq, Oman
05 Egypt, Libya, Qatar, Sudan, Syria, Yemen
06 Jordan, Kuwait
07 Algeria, Bahrain, Comoros, Lebanon, Morocco, Somalia, Tunisia
08 Djibouti
09 Palestine
10 Mauritania
11 Saudi Arabia
18 United Arab Emirates

Arabic
02 Ar **04** Arab
See also **alphabet**

arable
03 lay, lea, lee, ley **06** fecund **07** fertile **08** farmable, fruitful, tillable **10** cultivable, ploughable, productive
See also **crop**

arachnid *see* **spider**

arbiter
05 judge **06** expert, master, pundit, umpire **07** oddsman, referee **08** governor **09** authority, birlieman, byrlaw-man **10** controller **11** adjudicator

arbitrarily
08 by chance, randomly **11** illogically **12** irrationally, subjectively, unreasonably **14** inconsistently

arbitrary
06 chance, random **08** absolute, despotic, dogmatic, personal **09** illogical, imperious, whimsical **10** autocratic, capricious, dominative, high-handed, irrational, subjective, tyrannical, unreasoned **11** dictatorial, domineering, instinctive, magisterial, overbearing **12** conventional, inconsistent, unreasonable **13** discretionary

arbitrate
05 judge **06** decide, settle, umpire **07** mediate, referee **09** determine **10** adjudicate **13** pass judgement **14** sit in judgement

arbitration
08 decision **09** arbitrage, judgement, mediation **10** compromise, settlement **11** arbitrament, negotiation **12** adjudication, intervention **13** determination

arbitrator
03 ref, ump **05** judge **06** umpire **07** arbiter, referee **08** mediator **09** go-between, moderator **10** negotiator **11** adjudicator **12** intermediary

arbour
03 bay **05** bower **06** alcove, grotto, herbar, recess **07** pergola, retreat, shelter **09** sanctuary

arc
03 bow **04** arch, bend, spin, turn **05** curve, round **06** swerve **09** curvature **10** curved line, semicircle

arcade
04 mall, stoa **05** plaza **06** loggia, piazza **07** gallery, portico **08** cloister, galleria, precinct **09** colonnade, peristyle, triforium **10** covered way **12** shopping mall

arcane
06 hidden, occult, secret **07** cryptic, obscure **08** abstruse, esoteric, mystical, profound **09** concealed, enigmatic, recondite **10** mysterious

arch
◇ *anagram indicator*
03 arc, bow, hog, sly **04** bend, dome, hoop, span **05** chief, curve, embow, ogive, roach, vault **06** bridge, camber, diadem, girdle, invert, portal, shrewd, zygoma **07** archway, concave, cunning, playful, roguish, squinch, waggish **08** cross-rib, espiègle, platband **09** curvature, principal **10** manteltree, mysterious, semicircle **11** counterfort, mischievous **13** arc de triomphe

Arches include:

04 keel, ogee, skew
05 round, Tudor
06 convex, corbel, Gothic, lancet, Norman, tented
07 pointed, stilted, trefoil
09 Ctesiphon, horseshoe, parabolic, segmental, triumphal
10 four-centre, proscenium, shouldered
11 equilateral
12 basket handle

archaeology

Archaeological terms include:

03 cup, dig, jar, jug, tor, urn
04 adze, bowl, celt, cist, core, kist, site, tell
05 blade, burin, cairn, ditch, flake, flask, flint, henge, hoard, mound, mummy, shard, sherd, stele, whorl
06 barrow, beaker, bogman, dolmen, dromos, eolith, menhir, midden, mosaic, patina, strata, trench
07 amphora, anomaly, cave art, crannog, handaxe, Iron Age, neolith, obelisk, papyrus, rock art, sondage, stratum, tumulus
08 artefact, artifact, cromlech, excavate, hill fort, knapping, ley lines, megalith, post hole, Stone Age
09 arrowhead, Bronze Age, cartouche, crop-marks, earthwork, enclosure, hypocaust, longhouse, Neolithic
10 Anglo-Saxon, assemblage, excavation, geophysics, grave goods, inhumation, roundhouse, tear bottle
11 burial mound, rock shelter, stone circle
12 amphitheatre, archaeometry, carbon dating, field walking, Interglacial, Palaeolithic, stratigraphy
13 kitchen-midden, standing stone, treasure trove, wattle and daub
14 hunter-gatherer

Archaeologists include:

04 **Uhle** (Max)
05 **Clark** (Grahame), **Evans** (Sir Arthur)
06 **Anning** (Mary), **Breuil** (Henri), **Carter** (Howard), **Childe** (Gordon), **Clarke** (David L), **Daniel** (Glyn), **Hawkes** (Jacquetta), **Kidder** (A V), **Layard** (Sir Austen), **Leakey** (Louis), **Leakey** (Mary), **Petrie** (Sir Flinders), **Putnam** (Frederic Ward)
07 **Binford** (Lewis), **Renfrew** (Colin, Lord), **Thomsen** (Christian), **Wheeler** (Sir Mortimer), **Woolley** (Sir Leonard), **Worsaae** (Jens Jacob)
08 **Breasted** (J H), **Cunliffe** (Barry), **Fiorelli** (Giuseppe), **Koldewey** (Robert), **Mallowan** (Sir Max), **Mariette** (Auguste), **Marshall** (Sir John)
09 **Andersson** (Johan Gunnar)
10 **Pitt-Rivers** (Augustus), **Schliemann** (Heinrich)
11 **Champollion** (Jean François)

archaic

03 old **05** passé **06** bygone, old hat, quaint **07** ancient, antique **08** medieval, obsolete, outdated, outmoded **09** mediaeval, out-of-date, primitive **10** antiquated
11 obsolescent, out of the ark
12 antediluvian, old-fashioned

archangel

08 hierarch **10** dead-nettle **14** garden angelica

See also **angel**

archbishop

03 abp **07** primate **12** metropolitan

See also **cardinal**

Archbishops include:

04 **Gray** (Gordon), **Hope** (David), **Hume** (Basil), **Kemp** (John), **Lang** (Cosmo), **Laud** (William), **Tutu** (Desmond)
05 **Beran** (Josef), **Carey** (George), **Glemp** (Jozef)
06 **Anselm**, **Beaton** (David), **Becket** (Thomas à), **Benson** (Edward White), **Blanch** (Stuart), **Coggan** (Donald), **Edmund** (St), **Fisher** (Geoffrey), **Heenan** (John Carmel), **Hilary** (of Poitiers, St), **Mannix** (Daniel), **Morton** (John), **Parker** (Matthew), **Potter** (John), **Ramsay** (Michael), **Runcie** (Robert), **Temple** (Frederick), **Temple** (William), **Trench** (Richard Chenevix), **Ussher** (James), **Walter** (Hubert), **Warham** (William), **Wolsey** (Thomas)
07 **Arundel** (Thomas), **Cranmer** (Thomas), **Dunstan** (St), **Habgood** (John), **Langton** (Stephen), **Mendoza** (Pedro Gonzalez de), **Sentamu** (John), **Sheldon** (Gilbert), **Wiseman** (Nicholas)
08 **Adalbert**, **Cuthbert**, **Davidson** (Randall), **Ethelred**, **Makarios**, **Whitgift** (John), **Williams** (Rowan)
09 **Augustine** (St), **Wyszynski** (Stefan)
10 **Damaskinos**, **Huddleston** (Trevor)

archdiocese *see* diocese

archer

04 Eros, Tell **05** Cupid **06** bow-boy, bowman **09** sagittary **11** Sagittarius, toxophilite

archetypal

05 ideal, model, stock **07** classic, typical **08** original, standard
09 exemplary **12** paradigmatic
14 characteristic, quintessential, representative

archetype

04 form, idea, type **05** ideal, model
06 entity **07** classic, epitome, pattern
08 exemplar, original, paradigm, standard **09** precursor, prototype
10 stereotype **12** quintessence, typification

archipelago

Archipelagoes include:

04 Cuba, Fiji, Sulu
05 Åland, Gulag, Japan, Malay, Malta, Tonga
06 Arctic, Azores, Chagos, Kosrae, Tuvalu
07 Bahamas, Mayotte, Tuamotu
08 Bismarck, Cyclades, Kiribati, Maldives, Moluccas, Svalbard
09 Alexander, Antarctic, Cape Verde, Catherine, Galápagos, Indonesia, Louisiade, Marquesas, North Land
10 Ahvenanmaa, Les Iles d'Or, Seychelles, Vesterålen, West Indies
11 Iles d'Hyères, Line Islands, Philippines, Spitsbergen, Vesteraalen
12 Kuril Islands, Novaya Zemlya, Pearl Islands, Spice Islands, Sunda Islands
13 Aegean Islands, Caicos Islands, Canary Islands, Ellice Islands, Ionian Islands, Tubuai Islands
14 Austral Islands, Bijagos Islands, Channel Islands, Franz Josef Land, Gilbert Islands, Leeward Islands, Lofoten Islands, Nicholas II Land, Oki Archipelago, Papua New Guinea, Phoenix Islands, Solomon Islands, Tierra del Fuego, Visayan Islands
15 Balearic Islands, Friendly Islands, Marshall Islands, Pitcairn Islands, Severnaya Zemlya, Wallis and Futuna, Windward Islands

architect

05 maker **06** author, shaper
07 creator, founder, planner
08 designer, engineer, inventor
10 instigator, mastermind, originator, prime mover **11** constructor, draughtsman **13** master builder

Architects include:

04 **Adam** (Robert), **Drew** (Dame Jane), **Loos** (Adolf), **Nash** (John), **Shaw** (Norman), **Wren** (Sir Christopher)
05 **Aalto** (Alvar), **Barry** (Sir Charles), **Costa** (Lucio), **Dudok** (Willem), **Gaudí** (Antonio), **Jones** (Inigo), **Meier** (Richard), **Nervi** (Pier Luigi), **Piano** (Renzo), **Pugin** (Augustus), **Scott** (Sir George Gilbert), **Scott** (Sir Giles Gilbert), **Soane** (Sir John), **Speer** (Albert), **Velde** (Henri van de)
06 **Casson** (Sir Hugh), **Cubitt** (Thomas), **Foster** (Sir Norman), **Giotto**, **Howard** (Sir Ebenezer), **Lescot** (Pierre), **Morris** (William), **Paxton** (Sir Joseph), **Pisano** (Giovanni), **Rogers** (Sir Richard), **Semper** (Gottfried), **Serlio** (Sebastiano), **Spence** (Sir Basil), **Wright** (Frank Lloyd)
07 **Alberti** (Leon Battista), **Asplund** (Erik Gunnar), **Behrens** (Peter), **Bernini** (Gian Lorenzo), **Gropius** (Walter), **Ictinus**, **Imhotep**, **Lutyens** (Sir Edwin), **Olmsted** (Frederick Law), **Vignola** (Giacomo da)
08 **Bramante** (Donato), **Jacobsen** (Arne), **Miralles** (Enric), **Niemeyer** (Oscar), **Palladio** (Andrea), **Piranesi** (Giambattista), **Saarinen** (Eero), **Sottsass** (Ettore), **Stirling** (James), **Sullivan** (Louis), **Vanbrugh** (Sir John)
09 **Borromini** (Francesco), **Haussmann** (Georges, Baron), **Hawksmoor** (Nicholas), **Libeskind** (Daniel), **Mackmurdo** (Arthur), **Vitruvius**
10 **Mackintosh** (Charles Rennie)
11 **Le Corbusier**
12 **Brunelleschi** (Filippo), **Viollet-Le-Duc** (Eugène)
14 **Mies van der Rohe** (Ludwig)
15 **Leonardo da Vinci**

architecture
04 form **05** frame, set-up, style **06** design, make-up, system **08** building, planning **09** designing, framework, structure **11** arrangement, composition **12** conformation, constitution, construction, organization **13** configuration **14** architectonics

Architecture styles include:

04 Adam
05 Greek, Saxon
06 Gothic, modern, Norman, rococo
07 barocco, baroque, Italian, Lombard, mission, mudéjar
08 baronial, high tech
09 beaux arts, brutalism, Byzantine, Cape Dutch, decorated, Palladian, Queen Anne
10 art nouveau, Corinthian, Romanesque
11 Elizabethan, Renaissance
13 Gothic revival, international, neoclassicism, Perpendicular, post-modernism
15 churrigueresque

Architectural features include:

03 orb, web
04 anta, apse, arch, base, bell, boss, cove, crop, cusp, cyma, dado, drum, list, neck, ribs, vase, void
05 antae, attic, congé, crown, flute, gable, gavel, glyph, groin, gutta, hance, helix, mould, nerve, ogive, print, pylon, quirk, scape, socle, spire, stria, talon, tenia, tondo, torus, tower, truss, vault
06 abacus, atrium, canton, caulis, chevet, cinque, cippus, column, concha, congee, coping, corona, coving, crenel, dentil, facade, fascia, fillet, finial, flèche, fornix, frieze, haunch, impost, lierne, metope, patera, patten, pillar, podium, portal, reglet, regula, rosace, scotia, severy, striae, taenia, turret, wreath
07 aileron, annulet, balloon, bandrol, capital, cavetti, cavetto, conchae, corbeil, cornice, crocket, diglyph, doucine, echinus, fantail, festoon, fronton, fusarol, grecque, larmier, mullion, necking, nervure, pannier, parapet, Persian, pilotis, portico, rosette, solidum, squinch, surbase, tambour, telamon, tondino
08 abutment, accolade, apophyge, astragal, baguette, bandelet, banderol, bannerol, bellcote, buttress, canephor, cartouch, chapiter, chaptrel, ciborium, cincture, crenelle, diastyle, dipteral, dipteros, entresol, epistyle, frontoon, fusarole, gorgerin, imperial, intrados, mascaron, moulding, pediment, pilaster, prostyle, pulpitum, rockwork, sept-foil, skewback, spandrel, spandril, terminus, triglyph, tympanum, voussoir
09 apsidiole, archivolt, balection, banderole, bolection, cartouche, crossette, cul-de-four, decastyle, embrasure, embrazure, foliation, guilloche, hypostyle, mezzanine, modillion, octastyle, octostyle, peristyle, strap work, stylobate, tierceron, triforium, water leaf
10 acroterion, architrave, ball-flower, bratticing, cauliculus, chambranle, clearstory, clerestory, demicupola, ditriglyph, egg-and-dart, eye-catcher, feathering, jerkinhead, pendentive, quatrefoil, subarcuate, water table, weathering
11 brattishing, entablature, paternoster
12 egg-and-anchor, egg-and-tongue, frontispiece
13 chain moulding, interpilaster, quatrefeuille, vermiculation
14 Catherine-wheel, flying buttress

See also **arch**

Architectural and building terms include:

04 dado, dome, jamb, roof
05 Doric, eaves, groin, Ionic, ridge, Tudor
06 alcove, annexe, coving, duplex, façade, fascia, fillet, finial, frieze, Gothic, lintel, Norman, pagoda, plinth, reveal, rococo, scroll, soffit, stucco, Tuscan
07 baroque, cornice, festoon, fletton, fluting, mullion, pantile, parapet, rafters, Regency, rotunda
08 baluster, capstone, dogtooth, dry-stone, gargoyle, Georgian, pinnacle, sacristy, terrazzo, wainscot
09 bas relief, classical, Edwardian, elevation, gatehouse, Queen Anne, roughcast
10 architrave, barge-board, Corinthian, drawbridge, flamboyant, groundplan, Romanesque, weathering
11 coping stone, corner-stone, Elizabethan, Flemish bond
12 Early English, frontispiece, half-timbered

archives
04 roll **05** deeds **06** annals, papers **07** ledgers, records **09** documents, memorials, registers **10** chronicles **11** memorabilia

arctic
05 polar **06** boreal, frosty, frozen **07** glacial, subzero **08** Far North, freezing, Siberian **11** far northern, hyperborean **12** bitterly cold, freezing cold
• **arctic animal**
09 polar bear

ardent
03 hot **04** avid, keen, warm **05** eager, fiery **06** fervid, fierce, strong **07** burning, devoted, fervent, intense, mettled, zealous **08** sanguine, spirited, vehement **09** dedicated, perfervid, spiritous **10** mettlesome, passionate **11** empassioned, evangelical, impassioned, warm-blooded **12** enthusiastic **14** enthusiastical
• **be ardent**
04 glow

ardently
05 hotly **06** avidly, warmly **07** eagerly **08** strongly **09** devotedly, fervently, intensely, zealously **10** vehemently **12** passionately

ardour
04 fire, heat, lust, rage, zeal, zest **05** flame, wrath **06** duende, fervor, spirit, warmth **07** avidity, fervour, passion **08** covetise, devotion, keenness **09** animation, eagerness, intensity, vehemence **10** dedication, enthusiasm **12** empressement

arduous
04 hard **05** chore, harsh, heavy, steep, stiff, tough **06** severe, taxing, tiring, uphill **07** be a slog, onerous **08** be murder, daunting, rigorous, wearying **09** difficult, fatiguing, gruelling, laborious, punishing, strenuous **10** burdensome, exhausting, formidable **12** backbreaking

are
01 A **04** live **05** exist

area
01 A **04** beat, part, size, zone **05** field, manor, patch, place, range, realm, scope, tract, width, world **06** branch, domain, extent, parish, region, sector, sphere **07** breadth, compass, enclave, expanse, portion, quarter, section, stretch, terrain **08** district, environs, locality, precinct, province **09** territory **10** department **11** environment, reserve area **13** catchment area, neighbourhood

See also **administrative**; **council**; **county**; **district**

arena
04 area, bowl, ring **05** field, realm, scene, world **06** domain, ground, sphere **07** stadium, theatre **08** coliseum, province **10** department, hippodrome **11** battlefield **12** amphitheatre, battleground **14** area of conflict

Ares
04 Mars

Argentina
02 RA **03** ARG

argon
02 Ar

argot
04 cant **05** idiom, slang **06** jargon **08** parlance

arguable
04 moot **09** debatable, uncertain, undecided **10** disputable **11** contentious, open to doubt **12** questionable **14** controvertible, open to question

arguably
05 maybe **08** possibly, probably **10** most likely **15** in all likelihood

argue
03 rag, row **04** feud, hold, moot, show, spar **05** claim, fight, imply, nyaff, plead, prove **06** assert, bicker, cangle, debate, denote, haggle, hassle, reason **07** accurse, contend, declare, discuss, display, dispute, exhibit, fall out, quarrel, quibble, suggest, wrangle, wrestle **08** convince, disagree, dissuade, have a row, indicate, logicize, maintain, manifest, persuade, question, squabble **09** altercate, chop logic, have it out, have words, join issue, take issue, talk out of **10** chew the fat, chew the rag, contradict, hold a brief **11** cross swords, demonstrate, expostulate, remonstrate **13** be evidence for, have it out with
15 be at loggerheads, have a bone to pick

argument
03 pro, row **04** beef, blue, case, feud, plot, spat, tiff, yike **05** claim, clash, fight, lemma, logic, run-in, set-to, theme, topic, yikes **06** barney, bust-up, contra, debate, dust-up, hassle, reason, ruckus, rumpus, tangle, thesis
07 contest, defence, dispute, fallacy, outline, polemic, quarrel, summary, wrangle **08** conflict, ding-dong, evidence, exchange, squabble, synopsis, trilemma **09** argy-bargy, assertion, enthymeme, objection, quodlibet, rationale, reasoning, syllogism **10** contention, discussion
11 altercation, controverse, controversy, declaration
12 antistrophon, disagreement
13 argumentation, demonstration, expostulation, justification, running battle, shouting-match, slanging-match **14** heated exchange

argumentation
04 case **05** claim, logic **06** debate
07 defence **08** argument, disproof, evidence **09** rationale, reasoning
10 contention **13** expostulation, justification

argumentative
06 chippy **07** stroppy **08** captious, contrary, perverse **09** litigious, polemical, truculent **11** belligerent, contentious, dissentious, opinionated, quarrelsome **12** cantankerous, disputatious

arid
03 dry **04** drab, dull, flat **05** baked, vapid, waste **06** barren, boring, desert, dreary, jejune, meagre, torrid
07 parched, sterile, tedious **08** lifeless
09 infertile, torrefied, waterless
10 colourless, dehydrated, desiccated, monotonous, spiritless, uninspired **12** moistureless, shrivelled up, unproductive
13 uninteresting

aright
02 OK **05** aptly, fitly, truly **07** exactly, rightly **08** properly, suitably
09 correctly **10** accurately

arise
◇ *reversal down indicator*
04 come, flow, go up, lift, rise, soar, stem **05** begin, climb, ensue, get up, issue, mount, occur, start, tower
06 appear, ascend, come up, crop up, derive, emerge, follow, happen, result, rise up, spring **07** emanate, proceed, stand up **08** commence **10** be caused by **11** be a result of, come to light
12 straighten up **13** come into being, get to your feet, present itself

aristocracy
04 nobs, rank **05** élite, lords, peers, toffs **06** gentry, ladies **07** peerage
08 nobility, noblemen **09** gentility, optimates, top drawer **10** haute monde, noblewomen, patricians, patriciate, upper class, upper crust
11 aristocrats, high society, ruling class
15 privileged class

aristocrat
03 nob **04** lady, lord, peer, toff
05 noble **06** Junker **07** grandee, high-hat, peeress **08** eupatrid, nobleman, optimate **09** patrician
10 grande dame, noblewoman
13 grand seigneur
See also **nobility**

aristocratic
01 U **05** élite, noble **06** lordly, titled
07 courtly, elegant, refined
08 highborn, well-born **09** dignified, patrician **10** upper-class, upper-crust
11 blue-blooded **12** thoroughbred

arithmetic
07 algebra **08** algorism, logistic
11 computation

Arizona
02 AZ **04** Ariz

Arkansas
02 AR **03** Ark

Arkwright
04 Noah

arm
03 bay, fin, rig **04** barb, cove, gird, heel, iron, limb, loch, prop, whip, wing
05 array, brace, crank, creek, equip, firth, force, index, inlet, issue, might, power, prime, rearm, steel, wiper
06 branch, outfit, sleeve, supply, weapon **07** channel, estuary, euripus, forearm, fortify, furnish, passage, prepare, protect, provide, quillon, sea loch, section **08** accoutre, brachium, division, embattle, offshoot, strength
09 appendage, authority, extension, reinforce, upper limb **10** department, detachment, projection, strengthen
12 embranchment **15** windscreen-wiper

armada
04 navy **05** fleet **08** flotilla, squadron
10 naval force

armadillo
04 peba **05** tatou **07** Dasypus, tatouay
10 pichiciego

armaments
04 arms, guns **06** cannon **07** weapons
08 ordnance, weaponry **09** artillery, munitions **10** ammunition

armed
06 fitted **07** packing **08** tooled up
• armed man
03 gun

armed services *see* **army**; **air force**; **military**; **navy**; **rank**

Armenia
02 AM **03** ARM

armistice
04 pact **05** peace, truce **09** ceasefire
10 still-stand **11** peace treaty

armour
04 gear, gere, mail, weed **05** plate, proof, stand **06** corium, shield
07 panoply **08** armature **12** iron-cladding

Armour includes:

04 cush, jack, jamb, lame, mail, suit, tace
05 armet, brace, cuish, culet, curat, jambe, salet, tasse, visor
06 beaver, byrnie, casque, couter, crinet, cuisse, curiet, faulds, gorget, greave, grille, gusset, helmet, jamber, morion, poleyn, rondel, salade, sallet, taslet, tasset, tonlet, tuille, voider
07 ailette, barding, basinet, besagew, brasset, buckler, cap-à-pie, corslet, cuirass, harness, hauberk, jambeau, jambeux, jambier, lamboys, morrion, palette, placcat, placket, poitrel, puldron, sabaton, surcoat, ventail
08 aventail, bascinet, brassard, brassart, chaffron, chamfron, chausses, corselet, gauntlet, giambeux, jambeaux, jazerant, pauldron, pectoral, placcate, pouldron, shynbald, solleret, spaulder, vambrace, ventaile, ventayle
09 aventaile, backpiece, backplate, chain mail, chamfrain, garniture, habergeon, jesserant, mandilion, mandylion, nosepiece, rerebrace, vantbrace, vantbrass
10 body armour, cataphract, coat-armour, coat of mail
11 breastplate, genouillère, mentonnière, plate armour, scale armour
12 splint armour

armoured
06 plated **08** iron-clad, loricate
09 bomb-proof, protected, toughened
10 reinforced **11** bullet-proof, steel-plated **12** armour-plated

armoury
05 depot, stock **07** arsenal
08 magazine **09** arms depot, garderobe, stockpile **10** repository
13 ordnance depot **14** ammunition dump

armpit
05 oxter **06** axilla

arms
04 guns **05** crest **06** cannon, emblem, shield **07** weapons **08** blazonry, firearms, heraldry, insignia, missiles, ordnance, weaponry **09** armaments, artillery, munitions **10** ammunition, coat-of-arms, escutcheon
11 projectiles **14** heraldic device

army
03 mob **04** host, pack, sena **05** crowd, horde, swarm **06** throng, troops
07 cohorts, legions, militia
08 brachial, infantry, military, soldiers, soldiery **09** multitude **10** armed force, arrière-ban, land forces **11** thin red line

Armies include:

02 AA, SA, TA
03 AVR, GAR, IRA, USA, WLA
04 BAOR, INLA
05 Sally
06 Church, Tartan
08 New Model
09 Eurocorps, Salvation
10 Blue Ribbon, Women's Land
11 Grande Armée, Territorial

See also **rank**; **regiment**
- **army corps** *see* **regiment**
- **army regulation**

02 AR

aroma
04 nose **05** fumet, odour, scent, smell
06 savour **07** bouquet, fumette, perfume **09** fragrance, redolence

aromatic
05 balmy, fresh, spicy **07** pungent, savoury, scented **08** fragrant, perfumed, redolent **11** odoriferous
12 sweet-scented **13** sweet-smelling

around
◇ *anagram indicator*
◇ *containment indicator*
◇ *reversal indicator*
01 c **02** ca **04** near **05** about, circa, close, round **06** at hand, nearby, nearly
07 all over, close by, close to, roughly
08 framed by, to and fro **09** enclosing
10 encircling, everywhere, more or less, on all sides, throughout
11 surrounding, within reach
12 circumjacent, encompassing, everywhere in, here and there, on all sides of, to all parts of
13 approximately, circumambient, on every side of **15** in all directions

arousal
◇ *anagram indicator*
06 firing **08** stirring **09** agitation, evocation **10** excitement
11 provocation, titillation **12** getting going, inflammation

arouse
◇ *anagram indicator*
04 fire, goad, move, spur, whet
05 alarm, cause, evoke, incur, pique, rouse, spark, tease, waken **06** awaken, beat up, bestir, excite, incite, induce, kindle, prompt, stir up, turn on, wake up, whip up **07** agitate, animate, inflame, knock up, provoke, quicken, sharpen, startle, trigger, upraise **08** get going, summon up **09** call forth, eroticize, galvanize, impassion, instigate, stimulate, suscitate, titillate
11 disentrance

arraign
06 accuse, charge, impugn, indict
07 appoint, empeach, impeach
09 prosecute **11** incriminate **13** call to account

arraignment
04 case **05** trial **06** charge
07 summons **10** accusation, indictment **11** impeachment, legal action **13** incrimination

arrange
◇ *anagram indicator*
02 do **03** fix, set **04** cast, comb, file, gang, list, make, plan, sift, size, sort, stow, tidy, tile, trim **05** adapt, agree, align, aline, array, braid, class, dress, fix up, grade, group, ink in, order, place, preen, range, score, set up, swing
06 adjust, blouse, codify, decide, design, devise, digest, fettle, format, gather, lay out, line up, make up, ordain, set out, settle **07** address, article, blow-dry, concert, dispose, echelon, enrange, marshal, prepare, process, project, rummage, seriate, sort out, windrow **08** alphabet, classify, conclude, contrive, embattle, engineer, enraunge, organize, pencil in, position, regulate, rustle up, settle on, stratify **09** catalogue, collocate, determine, harmonize, methodize, negotiate, serialize **10** categorize, co-ordinate, distribute, foreordain, instrument, put in order, transcribe
11 choreograph, configurate, orchestrate, systematize
12 chronologize

arranged
03 arr

arrangement
◇ *anagram indicator*
03 lay **04** form, pack, plan **05** array, order, plans, score, set-up, taxis, terms
06 design, detail, fixing, format, layout, line-up, method, scheme, system
07 details, display, setting, version
08 contract, disposal, grouping, ordnance, planning, position, schedule **09** agreement, Ausgleich, bandobast, bundobust, digestion, formation, preparing, structure
10 adaptation, compromise, groundwork, schematism, settlement
11 disposition, positioning, preparation
12 modus vivendi, organization, preparations **13** configuration, harmonization, orchestration
14 classification, interpretation
15 instrumentation

arranger
03 arr

arrant
04 rank, vile **05** gross, utter **06** brazen
07 blatant, extreme **08** absolute, complete, flagrant, infamous, outright, rascally, thorough **09** barefaced, downright, egregious, notorious, out-and-out **11** unmitigated **12** incorrigible
13 thoroughgoing

array
◇ *anagram indicator*
03 set **04** deck, garb, robe, show, trim
05 adorn, align, dress, group, herse, order, range **06** attire, attrap, clothe, draw up, effeir, effere, lay out, line up, line-up, matrix, muster, parade, plight, spread **07** apparel, arrange, bedight, bedizen, display, dispose, exhibit, marshal, panoply **08** accoutre, assemble, decorate, position
09 formation **10** assemblage, assortment, collection, exhibition, exposition, habilitate **11** arrangement, disposition, marshalling

arrears
04 debt **05** debts **07** balance, deficit
10 amount owed, money owing
11 liabilities **14** sum of money owed
- **in arrears**

04 late **05** owing **06** behind, in debt
07 overdue **10** behindhand **11** back-ganging, outstanding

arrest
◇ *containment indicator*
02 do **03** cop, lag, nab, nip, sus
04 book, bust, grab, grip, halt, hold, lift, nail, nick, slow, stem, stop, suss
05 block, catch, check, delay, pinch, rivet, run in, seize, stall **06** absorb, attach, collar, detain, engage, fixate, hinder, impede, nobble, pick up, pull in, retard, stasis, take up **07** attract, caption, capture, engross, inhibit, seizure, snabble, snaffle **08** intrigue, obstruct, restrain, slow down **09** apprehend, detention, epistasis, fascinate, interrupt
11 nip in the bud **12** apprehension
15 take into custody
- **under arrest**

06 copped **09** in custody **11** in captivity

arresting
07 amazing, notable **08** engaging, riveting, striking, stunning
10 impressive, noteworthy, noticeable, remarkable, surprising **11** conspicuous, eye-catching, outstanding
13 extraordinary

arrival
03 arr **04** dawn **05** birth, comer, entry, guest, start **06** advent, blow-in, coming, income, origin **07** entrant, fresher, incomer, visitor **08** approach, debutant, entrance, freshman, newcomer, visitant **09** debutante, emergence, invention **10** appearance, homecoming, occurrence
11 development

arrive
◇ *juxtaposition indicator*
03 arr, get, hit **04** come, dock, gain, land, make, show **05** enter, fetch, get

to, occur, reach **06** accede, appear, attain, become, blow in, come in, come to, drop in, happen, make it, obtain, pull in, roll in, roll up, show up, swan in, swan up, turn up **07** achieve, check in, clock in, get here, pitch up, succeed, surface **08** get there **09** be present, hammer out, thrash out, touch down **10** accomplish, be a success, be produced, come to hand **11** get to the top, materialize **12** become famous **14** come on the scene **15** become available, come on the market

arrogance
04 side **05** nerve, pride, scorn
06 hubris, hybris, morgue, vanity
07 conceit, disdain, egotism, hauteur, opinion **08** assuming, boasting, contempt, high hand, surquedy
09 contumely, insolence, lordiness, pomposity, surquedry **11** haughtiness, presumption, superiority
12 snobbishness **13** condescension, imperiousness **14** high-handedness, self-importance

arrogant
04 high **05** cobby, proud, stout
06 lordly, uppity, wanton **07** haughty, stuck-up, topping **08** assuming, boastful, insolent, jumped-up, scornful, snobbish, superior
09 bigheaded, conceited, dangerous, egotistic, hubristic, imperious
10 disdainful, high-handed, hoity-toity
11 overbearing, overweening, patronizing, toffee-nosed
12 contemptuous, presumptuous, supercilious **13** condescending, high and mighty, self-important **14** full of yourself, on the high ropes

arrogantly
04 high **07** proudly **09** haughtily
10 boastfully, insolently, scornfully, snobbishly **11** conceitedly, imperiously
12 disdainfully, high-handedly
13 hubristically, overbearingly, overweeningly, patronizingly
14 contemptuously, presumptuously, superciliously **15** condescendingly, self-importantly

arrogate
05 seize, usurp **06** assume
07 presume **08** take over
10 commandeer **11** appropriate
14 misappropriate

arrogation
07 seizure **10** assumption, possession, taking over **13** appropriation, commandeering

arrow
03 any, ary **04** bolt, dart **05** shaft
06 flight, marker, quar'le **07** dogbolt, pointer, quarrel, sagitta **08** bird-bolt
09 butt-shaft, indicator **11** swallowtail
13 grey-goose wing **14** cloth-yard shaft, grey-goose quill, grey-goose shaft

arrowhead
04 fork

arrowroot
03 pia **07** Maranta

arsenal
05 depot, stock **06** armory
07 armoury, weapons **08** magazine, weaponry **09** arms depot, garderobe, stockpile **10** repository **13** ordnance depot **14** ammunition dump

arsenic
02 As

arson
09 pyromania, saddlebow
11 firebombing, fire-raising
12 incendiarism

arsonist
05 torch **07** firebug **10** firebomber, fire-raiser, incendiary, pyromaniac

art
04 feat, gift **05** craft, flair, guile, knack, skill, trade **06** Arthur, deceit, design, method, talent **07** artwork, cunning, daubery, finesse, knowhow, mastery, sleight, slyness **08** aptitude, artistry, facility, strategy, trickery, wiliness
09 dexterity, expertise, ingenuity, technique **10** adroitness, artfulness, astuteness, craftiness, profession, shrewdness, virtuosity **12** creative work **13** craftsmanship
15 draughtsmanship

See also **Japanese**; **painting**; **sculpture**

Arts and crafts include:

04 film
05 batik, video
06 fresco, mosaic, saikei
07 carving, collage, crochet, drawing, etching, ikebana, origami, pottery, weaving
08 ceramics, graphics, knitting, painting, pencraft, spinning, tapestry, tsutsumu
09 animation, cloisonné, engraving, jewellery, marquetry, metalwork, modelling, patchwork, sculpture, sketching, woodcraft
10 basketwork, caricature, embroidery, enamelling, needlework, xylography
11 calligraphy, lithography, needlecraft, oil painting, photography, portraiture, psaligraphy, stitchcraft, watercolour, woodcarving, wood cutting
12 animatronics, architecture, chalcography, illustration, stained glass
13 digital design, graphic design, wood engraving
14 relief printing, screenprinting

See also **picture**

Schools, movements and styles of art include:

05 Nabis, Op Art, video
06 Cubism, Gothic, Pop Art, Purism, Rococo
07 Art Brut, Art Deco, Baroque, Bauhaus, Brit art, Dadaism, digital, Fauvism, folk art, Realism
08 abstract, Barbizon, Bohemian, Futurism, Japonism, Venetian
09 Byzantine, formalism, Mannerism, Modernism, Symbolism, Vorticism
10 arte povera, Art Nouveau, automatism, classicism, Florentine, literalism, Minimal Art, Naturalism, New Realism, Romanesque, Surrealism
11 Hellenistic, Pointillism, Primitivism, renaissance, Romanticism, Suprematism
12 Aestheticism, magic realism, Quattrocento, Superrealism
13 Arts and Crafts, Conceptual Art, Expressionism, Impressionism, Neoclassicism, Neo-Plasticism, Post-Modernism, Preraphaelite
14 action painting, Constructivism

Art materials and art-related terms include:

03 ink
04 term, wash
05 cameo, easel, fitch, liner, sable, smock, turps, video
06 badger, crayon, fusain, pastel, pencil, relief, sketch, tusche
07 atelier, cartoon, digital, modello, organic, palette, scumble, torchon
08 abstract, alfresco, charcoal, gumption, intaglio, Luminism, monotint, paintbox, pastille
09 lay-figure, pen and ink, stretcher
10 delineavit, from nature, paint brush, sketchbook
11 perspective, trompe l'oeil, wash drawing
12 installation, underdrawing
13 social realism
15 oil of turpentine

• **work of art**
06 doodle **09** Old Master

artefact
◇ *anagram indicator*
04 item, tool **05** thing **06** object
07 neolith **09** something
10 palaeolith

Artemis
05 Diana

artery
02 M1 **04** duct, road, tube **06** vessel
07 channel, conduit **11** blood vessel
See also **vein**

artful
◇ *anagram indicator*
03 sly **04** foxy, rusé, wily **05** dodgy, sharp, smart **06** cautel, clever, crafty, shrewd, subtle, tricky **07** cunning, devious, skilful, vulpine **08** masterly, scheming **09** cautelous, deceitful, designing, dexterous, ingenious
11 resourceful

artfully
◇ *anagram indicator*
05 slyly **08** cleverly, craftily, shrewdly
09 cunningly, deviously, skilfully
11 deceitfully, ingeniously

arthropod

Arthropods include:

09 trilobite, water bear
10 tardigrade
14 bear-animalcule

See also **crustacean**; **insect**; **invertebrate**; **spider**

Arthurian legend *see* **knight**; **legend**

article
01 a **02** an, el, il, la, le, un **03** art, ein, les, the, une **04** eine, item, part, term, unit **05** curio, essay, paper, piece, point, story, thing **06** clause, exposé, object, report, review **07** account, exhibit, feature, portion, section, whatsit, write-up **08** artefact, offprint **09** commodity, editorial, monograph, paragraph, something, thingummy **10** boondoggle, commentary, subsection
11 composition, constituent
12 thingummybob, thingummyjig
14 what-d'you-call-it

articulate
◇ *homophone indicator*
◇ *anagram indicator*
03 say **04** talk **05** clear, frame, lucid, speak, state, utter, vocal, voice
06 fluent, tongue, verbal **07** breathe, enounce, express, jointed, realize
08 coherent, distinct, eloquent, vocalize **09** enunciate, pronounce, verbalize **10** expressive, meaningful, well-spoken **12** intelligible
13 communicative
14 comprehensible, understandable

articulated
◇ *homophone indicator*
◇ *anagram indicator*
05 joint **06** hinged, joined, linked
07 coupled, jointed **08** attached, fastened **09** connected, segmented
10 vertebrate **11** interlocked **14** fitted together

articulately
07 clearly, lucidly **08** fluently
10 coherently, distinctly, eloquently
12 expressively, intelligibly
14 comprehensibly

articulation
05 joint **06** saying **07** diction, segment, talking, voicing **08** coupling, delivery, jointing, junction, speaking, tonguing **09** arthrosis, clavation, consonant, gomphosis, utterance
10 connection, expression
11 diarthrosis, enunciation
12 schindylesis, synarthrosis, vocalization **13** pronunciation, verbalization

artifice
03 art, con, gin **04** ruse, scam, wile
05 craft, dodge, fraud, guile, reach, set-up, shift, trick **06** deceit, device, scheme, tactic **07** cunning, shuffle, slyness **08** strategy, subtlety, trickery
09 chicanery, deception, stratagem
10 artfulness, cleverness, craftiness, subterfuge **11** contrivance, deviousness **12** contrivement
14 davenport-trick

artificial
03 art **04** fake, faux, mock, sham
05 bogus, false, paste, pseud
06 ersatz, forced, made-up, phoney, pseudo **07** assumed, feigned, man-made, plastic, studied **08** affected, mannered, specious, spurious
09 contrived, imitation, insincere, pretended, processed, simulated, synthetic, unnatural **10** non-natural
11 counterfeit **12** manufactured

artificiality
04 sham **07** falsity **08** pretence
10 simulation **11** insincerity
12 speciousness, spuriousness
13 theatricalism, theatricality, unnaturalness

artificially
07 falsely **10** speciously, spuriously
11 insincerely, unnaturally
13 synthetically

artillery
02 RA **03** AAA, art, RHA **04** arty, guns
05 train **07** cannons, gunnery, weapons **08** cannonry, missiles, ordnance **09** heavy guns, munitions
12 heavy weapons

artisan
06 expert **07** pioneer **08** mechanic
09 artificer, craftsman, operative
10 journeyman, technician
11 craftswoman **12** craftsperson
13 skilled worker **14** handicraftsman

artist
02 RA **03** ace, ARA, pro **04** poet
05 actor, maker, maven, mavin
06 author, dancer, expert, writer
07 creator, dab hand, founder, maestro
08 Bohemian, composer, inventor, musician **09** authority, mannerist, performer **10** originator, specialist, trecentist **12** professional
13 perspectivist

Artists, craftsmen and craftswomen include:

06 etcher, master, potter, weaver
07 painter, printer
08 animator, designer, engraver, sculptor
09 architect, carpenter, goldsmith
10 blacksmith, cartoonist, oil painter
11 coppersmith, draughtsman, illustrator, miniaturist, portraitist, silversmith, web designer
12 caricaturist, lithographer, photographer
13 draughtswoman, graphic artist, screenprinter
14 graffiti artist, pavement artist, watercolourist
15 graphic designer

See also **painter**; **photograph**; **sculpture**

• **great artist**
09 Old Master

artiste
05 actor, comic **06** dancer, player, singer **07** actress, trouper
08 comedian, musician **09** performer
10 comedienne **11** entertainer
12 vaudevillian **13** variety artist

artistic
04 fine **06** gifted **07** elegant, refined, skilled, stylish **08** creative, cultured, graceful, original, talented, tasteful
09 aesthetic, beautiful, exquisite, sensitive **10** attractive, cultivated, decorative, expressive, harmonious, ornamental **11** imaginative

artistry
05 craft, flair, skill, style, touch
06 genius, talent **07** ability, finesse, mastery **08** deftness **09** expertise
10 brilliance, creativity **11** proficiency, sensitivity, workmanship
13 craftsmanship **14** accomplishment

artless
04 open, pure, true **05** frank, naive, naked, plain **06** candid, direct, honest, simple, unwary **07** genuine, natural, sincere **08** homespun, innocent, trusting **09** childlike, guileless, ingenuous, unworldly
10 unaffected **11** undesigning
13 unpretentious **15** straightforward, unsophisticated

artlessly
05 truly **06** openly, purely, simply
07 frankly, naively, plainly **08** candidly, directly **09** naturally, sincerely
10 innocently **11** ingenuously
15 unpretentiously

Aruba
03 ABW

as
02 eg, so, ut **03** als, qua **04** kame, like, when **05** being, esker, since, while
06 just as, such as, whilst **07** arsenic, because, owing to, through
09 forasmuch, similar to **10** for example, inasmuch as, seeing that
11 as a result of, for instance, in the role of, on account of **12** in the guise of
13 at the same time, functioning as, with the part of **14** simultaneously
15 at the same time as, considering that

• **as for**
07 apropos **09** as regards
10 concerning, respecting **12** in relation to, with regard to **13** with respect to **14** on the subject of, with relation to **15** with reference to

• **as it were**
05 quasi **06** in a way, kind of, second, sort of **07** so to say **09** in some way, so to speak **10** in some sort **11** as it might be

asafoetida
04 hing

asbestos
07 amosite **08** amiantus, rock wood
09 amianthus, earthflax **10** chrysotile
11 crocidolite **12** mountain wood

ascend
◇ *reversal down indicator*
03 sty **04** go up, rise, soar, upgo **05** arise, climb, fly up, get up, mount, scale, tower **06** climax, come up, move up **07** float up, lift off, take off **10** gain height **12** slope upwards

ascendancy
04 edge, sway **05** power
07 command, control, mastery
08 dominion, hegemony, lordship, prestige **09** authority, dominance, dominancy, influence, mobocracy, supremacy, upper hand
10 domination, prevalence **11** pre-eminence, superiority
12 predominance

ascendant
◇ *reversal down indicator*
07 growing **08** dominant, powerful, superior **09** prevalent **10** developing **11** predominant **12** on the up and up **13** rising in power

ascending
02 up

ascent
04 hill, pull, ramp, rise **05** climb, slope **06** rising, uphill **07** advance, incline, scaling **08** anabasis, climbing, gradient, mounting, progress **09** acclivity, ascending, ascension, elevation **10** escalation **11** advancement

ascertain
03 fix, see **04** twig **05** learn, prove **06** detect, locate, settle, verify **07** confirm, find out, pin down, suss out **08** discover, identify, make sure **09** determine, establish, get to know **10** come to know, make sure of **11** make certain

ascetic
03 nun **04** Jain, monk, yogi **05** fakir, harsh, Jaina, plain, sadhu, stern **06** Essene, hermit, saddhu, severe, strict **07** austere, dervish, Jainist, puritan, recluse, spartan, stylite **08** celibate, Nazarite, rigorous, sannyasi, solitary **09** abstainer, abstinent, anchorite, Montanist, pillarist **10** abstemious **11** pillar-saint, puritanical, self-denying **14** self-controlled **15** self-disciplined

asceticism
07 ascesis **08** severity **09** austerity, harshness **10** abstinence, self-denial **11** monasticism, self-control **14** self-discipline

ascidian
08 tunicate **09** sea squirt
15 appendicularian

ascribe
05 apply **06** assign, charge, credit, impute **07** put down, set down **08** accredit, arrogate **09** attribute **12** give credit to

ash
04 kali, kelp, kilp **05** aizle, easle, rowan **06** embers, tephra **07** cinders, clinker, residue, witchen **08** charcoal, Ygdrasil **09** xanthoxyl, Yggdrasil **10** Yggdrasill **11** nuée ardente **13** toothache tree **15** Pharaoh's serpent

ashamed
05 loath, sorry **06** guilty, modest
07 abashed, bashful, humbled
08 blushing, contrite, hesitant, penitent, red-faced, sheepish **09** mortified, reluctant, unwilling **10** apologetic, distressed, humiliated, remorseful, shamefaced **11** crestfallen, discomfited, discomposed, embarrassed **12** on a guilt trip **13** self-conscious

ashen
03 wan **04** grey, pale **05** livid, pasty, white **06** leaden, pallid **07** anaemic, ghastly **08** blanched, bleached **09** pale-faced **10** colourless

ashore
05 aland **11** onto the land **12** onto the beach, onto the shore **15** towards the shore

Asia

Asian countries include:

04 Laos
05 Burma, China, India, Japan, Nepal
06 Bhutan, Taiwan
07 Myanmar, Vietnam
08 Cambodia, Malaysia, Maldives, Mongolia, Pakistan, Sri Lanka, Thailand
09 East Timor, Indonesia, Singapore
10 Bangladesh, Kazakhstan, Kyrgyzstan, North Korea, South Korea, Tajikistan, Uzbekistan
11 Afghanistan, Philippines
12 Turkmenistan
16 Brunei Darussalam

Asian landmarks include:

05 Indus
06 Ganges, Mekong, Mt Fuji
07 Everest, Yangtze
08 Krakatoa, Lake Sebu, Red River, Taj Mahal
09 Angkor Wat, Annapurna, Great Wall, Himalayas, Hiroshima, Ming Tombs, Mt Everest
10 Gobi Desert, River Indus, Sagarmatha, Sea of Japan, Thar Desert
11 Brahmaputra, Mekong River, Three Gorges, Yellow River
12 Golden Temple, Potala Palace, Raffles Hotel
13 Forbidden City, Kangchenjunga
14 Jaganath Temple
15 Tiananmen Square

Asian

Asians include:

03 Han, Lao
04 Ainu, Cham, Nair, Shan, Sulu, Thai
05 Bajau, Karen, Kazak, Nayar, Tajik, Tamil, Uzbeg, Uzbek, Vedda
06 Afghan, Baluch, Gurkha, Indian, Kazakh, Kyrgyz, Manchu, Mongol, Pathan, Tadjik, Telugu
07 Baluchi, Burmese, Chinese, Goanese, Goorkha, Karenni, Kirghiz, Laotian, Manchoo, Maratha, Russian, Tadzhik, Tagálog, Turkish, Turkmen
08 Bruneian, Canarese, Filipina, Filipino, Japanese, Kanarese, Mahratta, Nepalese
09 Bhutanese, Cambodian, Malaysian, Mongolian, Pakistani, Sri Lankan, Taiwanese
10 Indonesian, Myanmarese, Vietnamese
11 Azerbaijani, Bangladeshi, Kazakhstani, North Korean, Singaporean, South Korean, Tajikistani

aside
02 by **04** away **05** alone, apart
07 whisper **08** secretly **09** alongside, departure, monologue, on one side, privately, soliloquy, to one side
10 apostrophe, digression, separately
11 in isolation, out of the way, parenthesis **12** obiter dictum, stage whisper **13** cursory remark
15 notwithstanding

asinine
04 daft **05** crazy, inane, potty, silly
06 absurd, stupid **07** fatuous, foolish, idiotic, moronic **08** gormless
09 imbecilic, ludicrous, senseless
10 half-witted **11** nonsensical

ask
03 beg, bid, eft, sue **04** evet, newt, poll, pose, pray, pump, quiz, seek
05 crave, grill, order, plead, posit, press, query, speer, speir, yearn
06 appeal, demand, desire, invite, summon **07** beseech, bespeak, canvass, clamour, enquire, entreat, fire off, implore, inquire, propose, request, require, solicit, suggest **08** approach, have over, petition, propound, question **09** entertain, have round, interview, postulate **10** put forward, supplicate **11** interrogate, requisition
12 cross-examine, put on the spot
13 cross-question **14** put a question to
15 give a grilling to

askance
04 awry **07** asconce **08** sideways
09 dubiously, obliquely **10** doubtfully, indirectly, scornfully **11** sceptically
12 disdainfully, suspiciously
13 distrustfully, mistrustfully
14 contemptuously, disapprovingly

askew
◇ *anagram indicator*
04 awry, skew **05** aglee, agley, tipsy
06 skivie, squint **07** crooked, oblique
08 lopsided, sideways **09** crookedly, obliquely, off-centre, out of line, skew-whiff **10** lopsidedly **12** asymmetrical
14 asymmetrically

asleep
04 numb **05** inert **06** dozing
07 dormant, napping, resting
08 comatose, inactive, reposing,

sleeping, snoozing **09** conked out, flaked out, nodded off, popped off **10** crashed out, fast asleep, sparked out **11** sound asleep, unconscious **13** out like a light **14** dead to the world, in the land of Nod, out for the count

asparagus
05 sprew, sprue **06** smilax

aspect
03 air **04** brow, face, look, side, view **05** angle, facet, light, phase, point, trine, visor, vizor **06** facies, factor, manner, phasis **07** bearing, contour, feature, outlook, respect, sextile **08** position, quartile, quincunx, quintile **09** dimension, direction, landscape **10** apparition, appearance, biquintile, complexion, expression, standpoint **11** conjunction, countenance, physiognomy, point of view **13** configuration

asperity
08 acerbity, acrimony, severity, sourness **09** crossness, harshness, roughness, sharpness **10** bitterness, causticity **11** astringency, crabbedness, peevishness **12** abrasiveness, churlishness, irascibility, irritability

aspersion
04 slur **07** calumny, slander
• **cast aspersions on**
04 slur **05** knock, slate, smear **06** defame, vilify **07** censure, run down, slander **08** reproach **09** criticize, denigrate, deprecate, disparage **10** calumniate, sling mud at, throw mud at

asphalt
08 uintaite **09** gilsonite, Jew's-pitch, uintahite **12** mineral pitch

asphyxiate
03 gas **05** choke **06** stifle **07** smother **08** strangle, throttle **09** suffocate **11** strangulate

asphyxiation
07 choking **08** stifling **10** smothering **11** suffocation **13** strangulation

aspirant
06 donzel, squire **09** candidate

aspirate
05 rough

aspiration
03 aim, yen **04** goal, hope, wish **05** dream, ideal **06** desire, intent, object **07** craving, longing, purpose **08** ambition, yearning **09** breathing, endeavour, hankering, objective **10** pretension

aspire
03 aim, yen **04** hope, long, mint, seek, wish **05** crave, dream, ettle, yearn **06** desire, hanker, intend, pursue **07** pretend, purpose **11** have as a goal, have as an aim

aspiring
04 keen **05** eager **07** budding, hopeful, longing, wishful, would-be **08** aspirant, striving **09** ambitious, intending **10** optimistic **12** endeavouring, enterprising

ass
03 fon, git, mug, nit, oaf, sot, yap **04** berk, cake, clot, cony, coof, dill, dope, dork, fool, geek, goop, gowk, gull, joss, moke, mule, nana, nerd, nerk, nong, pony, prat, soft, twit, yo-yo **05** burro, cluck, cuddy, dicky, dweeb, galah, hinny, idiot, Jenny, kiang, klutz, kulan, kyang, neddy, ninny, patch, schmo, snipe, sumph, twerp, wally **06** bampot, cretin, dickey, dimwit, donkey, dottle, drongo, koulan, nidget, nitwit, numpty, onager, quagga, sawney, turkey, wigeon **07** airhead, asinico, buffoon, gubbins, halfwit, jackass, jughead, lemming, muggins, natural, plonker, saphead, want-wit **08** dipstick, flathead, fondling, imbecile, innocent, lunkhead, mooncalf, numskull, omadhaun, Tom-noddy **09** blockhead, capocchia, dumb-cluck, dziggetai, lack-brain, lame brain, mumchance, schlemiel **10** nincompoop **11** jenny donkey, knuckle-head **13** Jerusalem pony, proper Charlie
See also **fool**

assail
03 din, rag, row **04** peal, pelt, slam **05** assay, beset, go for, slate, worry **06** attack, invade, malign, plague, rattle, revile, strafe, straff, strike **07** barrage, bedevil, belabor, bestorm, bombard, disturb, lay into, perplex, rubbish, run down, set upon, slag off, torment, trouble **08** badmouth, ballyrag, belabour, bludgeon, bullyrag, maltreat, overfall, set about, tear into **09** criticize, pitch into **10** fall foul of, set against

assailant
05 enemy **06** abuser, mugger **07** invader, reviler **08** assailer, attacker, onsetter, opponent **09** adversary, aggressor, assaulter

assassin
04 thug **05** bravo, ninja **06** gunman, hit-man, killer, slayer **07** sworder **08** murderer **09** cut-throat **10** hatchet man, liquidator **11** contract man, executioner
See also **murderer**

assassinate
◇ *anagram indicator*
03 hit **04** do in, kill, slay **06** murder **07** bump off, execute **08** dispatch **09** eliminate, liquidate, slaughter

assassination
◇ *anagram indicator*
06 murder **07** killing **09** execution, slaughter, taking-off **11** termination

assault
02 do **03** GBH, hit, mug **04** raid, rape **05** abuse, assay, blitz, feint, go for, onset, smite, stoor, storm, stour **06** affray, attack, beat up, charge, do over, fall on, insult, invade, molest, stound, stownd, stowre, strike **07** attempt, battery, bombard, lay into, mugging, offence, offense, set upon **08** invasion, storming **09** fusillade, incursion, offensive, onslaught **10** hamesucken, violent act **11** molestation **13** interfere with **15** act of aggression, throw yourself on

assay
04 test **05** check, cupel, ELISA **08** analysis **09** appraisal, judgement **10** assessment, evaluation, inspection **11** examination

assemblage
04 mass **05** crowd, flock, group, rally, shoal, strew **06** galaxy, school, throng **07** montage **09** aggregate, gathering, multitude **10** collection, collective, parliament **12** accumulation

assemble
◇ *anagram indicator*
04 band, join, make, mass, meet **05** amass, build, flock, group, rally, relie, set up, troop **06** accoil, cobble, gather, join up, muster, relide, roll up, summon **07** collate, collect, compose, connect, convene, convoke, marshal, round up, summons **08** mobilize **09** aggregate, construct, fabricate **10** accumulate, congregate, rendezvous **11** fit together, get together, manufacture, put together **12** come together **13** bring together, piece together

assembly
03 hui, mob **04** body, Dáil, diet, feis, meet, moot, Sejm **05** agora, bench, court, crowd, divan, flock, gemot, group, jirga, rally, synod, thing **06** indaba, kgotla, Majlis, Mejlis, muster, plenum, throng **07** chamber, chapter, company, council, gorsedd, Knesset, Landtag, meeting, squeeze, turnout, zemstvo **08** audience, building, bun fight, conclave, congress, ecclesia, folkmoot, panegyry, presence, Sobranje, Sobranye, Storting **09** Aula Regis, concourse, frequence, gathering, multitude, Skupstina, Storthing, synagogue, synedrion, synedrium, volksraad **10** assemblage, bear garden, collection, conference, consistory, convention, Curia Regis, Donnybrook, masquerade, Oireachtas, Skupshtina **11** church court, convocation, Dáil Eireann, fabrication, manufacture, Pandemonium **12** body of people, common vestry, congregation, construction, Pandaemonium **15** piecing together, putting together
See also **parliament**
• **General Assembly**
02 GA

assent
03 buy **05** agree, allow, grant, yield **06** accede, accept, accord, comply, concur, permit, submit **07** approve, concede, consent, go-ahead

08 approval, sanction, thumbs-up **09** accession, acquiesce, agreement, subscribe **10** acceptance, compliance, concession, green light, permission, submission **11** approbation, concurrence **12** acquiescence, capitulation **14** give the go-ahead **15** give the thumbs-up

• **expression of assent**
01 I **02** ay, OK **03** aye, oke, olé **04** done, good, okay **07** d'accord **09** I am agreed **10** I am content

assert
03 put, say **04** have, hold, pose **05** argue, claim, state, swear, vouch **06** affirm, attest, avouch, defend, stress, uphold **07** confirm, contend, declare, lay down, profess, protest **08** constate, insist on, maintain **09** establish, predicate, pronounce, testify to, vindicate **10** stand up for **12** crack the whip

assertion
03 vow **04** word **05** claim, vouch **06** avowal, threap, threep **08** averment, pretence, pretense, sentence **09** statement **10** affirmance, allegation, contention, insistence, profession **11** affirmation, attestation, declaration, jactitation, predication, testificate, vindication **12** constatation, gratis dictum **13** pronouncement

assertive
04 bold, firm **05** perky, pushy **07** decided, forward **08** assuming, dogmatic, dominant, emphatic, forceful, immodest, positive **09** confident, insistent **10** aggressive, determined **11** domineering, opinionated, overbearing, self-assured **12** presumptuous, strong-willed **13** self-confident **14** sure of yourself **15** feeling your oats

assertively
06 boldly, firmly **10** dominantly, forcefully, positively **11** confidently, insistently **12** aggressively **14** presumptuously **15** self-confidently

assess
03 fix, tax **04** levy, rate **05** cense, gauge, Jenny, judge, stent, sum up, teind, value, weigh **06** affeer, assize, demand, extend, impose, modify, review, size up **07** compute **08** appraise, check out, consider, estimate, evaluate **09** calculate, determine **11** jenny donkey

assessment
04 levy, rate, toll **05** recce, stent **06** demand, review, tariff **07** opinion, testing **09** appraisal, judgement, valuation **10** estimation, evaluation, imposition **11** computation **12** appraisement **13** consideration

assessor
05 judge **06** expert, gauger, umpire, valuer **07** adviser, arbiter, referee **08** examiner, measurer, recorder, reviewer, valuator **09** appraiser, estimator, inspector **10** arbitrator, consultant, counsellor **11** adjudicator **12** loss adjuster **15** average adjuster

asset
03 aid **04** boon, help, plus **05** funds, goods, means, money **06** estate, virtue, wealth **07** benefit, capital, savings **08** blessing, holdings, property, reserves, resource, seed corn, strength, tangible **09** advantage, liability, plus point, resources, valuables **10** securities **11** hot property, possessions, receivables, strong point

asseverate
04 aver, avow **05** claim, state **06** affirm, assert, attest **07** confirm, declare, profess **08** maintain

assiduity
08 devotion, hard work, industry, sedulity **09** constancy, diligence **10** dedication **11** persistence **12** perseverance **14** meticulousness **15** industriousness

assiduous
06 steady **07** careful, devoted **08** constant, diligent, sedulous, studious, thorough, untiring **09** attentive, dedicated **10** meticulous, persistent, unflagging **11** hard-working, industrious, persevering **13** conscientious, indefatigable

assign
03 fix, put, set **04** aret, cast, give, name, rank, sort **05** allot, allow, apply, arett, grant, range **06** affect, choose, convey, detail, impute, ordain, select **07** adjudge, appoint, ascribe, consign, endorse, hive off, indorse, install, put down, specify, station **08** accredit, allocate, arrogate, delegate, dispense, hand over, make over, nominate, relegate, transfer, transmit **09** apportion, attribute, chalk up to, designate, determine, stipulate **10** commission, distribute **11** appropriate

assignation
04 date **05** tryst **10** engagement, rendezvous **11** appointment, arrangement **13** secret meeting

assignment
03 job **04** duty, post, task **05** grant **06** charge, errand **07** project **08** position, transfer **09** selection **10** allocation, commission, conveyance, delegation, nomination, obligation **11** appointment, consignment, designation, disposition **12** distribution **14** responsibility

assimilate
◇ *containment indicator*
03 mix **05** adapt, blend, grasp, learn, unite **06** absorb, adjust, imbibe, mingle, pick up, take in **08** accustom **09** integrate **11** acclimatize, accommodate, incorporate, internalize

assimilation
07 osmosis **08** blending, grasping, learning, mixing in, taking in **09** digestion **10** absorption, adaptation, adjustment, resorption **11** integration **13** accommodation, incorporation **15** acclimatization, internalization

assist
03 aid **04** abet, back, help **05** serve **06** back up, enable, second **07** advance, benefit, further, pitch in, relieve, succour, support, sustain **08** expedite **09** co-operate, do your bit, encourage, give a hand, lend a hand, reinforce **10** facilitate, make easier, rally round **11** collaborate **12** give a leg up to

assistance
03 aid **04** hand, help **05** boost **06** a leg up, relief **07** backing, benefit, service, subsidy, succour, support **08** easement **09** adjutancy **10** friendship **11** co-operation, furtherance **12** a helping hand **13** collaboration, reinforcement

assistant
02 PA **03** cad, PDA **04** aide, ally, mate **05** clerk, usher **06** backer, curate, deputy, helper, intern, leg-man, nipper, second, yeoman **07** abettor, acolyte, acolyth, best boy, fireman, matross, nobbler, omnibus, partner **08** chainman, leg-woman, mud-clerk, right arm, salesman, servitor **09** accessory, ancillary, associate, auxiliary, coadjutor, colleague, land-reeve, midinette, prorector, secretary, suffragan, supporter, toad-eater, whipper-in **10** accomplice, aide-de-camp, amanuensis, copyholder, evangelist, proproctor, reading-boy, roughrider, sales clerk, saleswoman, subsidiary **11** confederate, merry-andrew, salesperson, subordinate **12** brigade major, collaborator, demonstrator, driving force, right-hand man **13** counter-jumper **14** boatswain's mate, checkout person, Common Serjeant, counter-skipper **15** second-in-command, vice-chamberlain

associate
◇ *juxtaposition indicator*
01 A **03** Ass, mix, pal **04** ally, band, chum, gang, herd, join, link, mate, mell, pair, peer, yoke **05** crony, haunt, unite **06** attach, couple, fellow, friend, helper, hobnob, league, mingle, relate **07** combine, company, compeer, comrade, connect, consort, goombah, hang out, partner, sociate **08** complice, confrère, co-worker, follower, identify, sidekick, sororize, yoke-mate **09** accompany, affiliate, assistant, coadjutor, colleague, companion, correlate, hang about, neighbour, socialize, syndicate **10** accomplice, amalgamate, be involved, coadjutrix, consociate, fraternize, hang around, yokefellow

11 coadjutress, confederate, keep company 12 band together, collaborator, go hand in hand, rub shoulders 15 think of together

associated
◇ *juxtaposition indicator*
03 Ass 05 alike 06 allied, linked
07 coupled, related, similar
08 combined, in league
09 connected, consorted 10 affiliated, correlated, syndicated
11 amalgamated 12 confederated
13 corresponding, in partnership

association
03 Ass, tie 04 band, bond, club, gild, hunt, link 05 group, guild, tie-up, union 06 cartel, chapel, clique, league, Probus, thrift, Verein 07 combine, company, contact, job club, society
08 alliance, clanship, intimacy, relation, sodality 09 coalition, goose-club, syndicate 10 connection, consortium, craft guild, federation, fellowship, fraternity, friendship, Jockey Club, Land League, propaganda, Young Italy
11 affiliation, confederacy, corporation, correlation, familiarity, involvement, partnership, triumvirate
12 consociation, Gesellschaft, organization, relationship
13 companionship, confederation, incorporation, interrelation
14 Burschenschaft, identification, Primrose League 15 friendly society

assorted
◇ *anagram indicator*
05 mixed 06 divers, motley, sundry, varied 07 diverse, several, various
08 manifold, sortable 09 different, differing 10 variegated 11 farraginous
12 multifarious 13 heterogeneous, miscellaneous

assortment
03 lot, mix 05 array, bunch, group
06 choice, jumble, medley 07 farrago, mixture, variety 08 grouping, mixed bag 09 diversity, menagerie, potpourri, selection 10 collection, miscellany, salmagundi
11 arrangement, olla-podrida, smörgåsbord 13 bits and pieces

assuage
04 beet, bete, calm, ease, lull 05 allay, lower, mease, slake, swage 06 lenify, lessen, pacify, quench, reduce, soften, soothe 07 appease, lighten, mollify, relieve, satisfy 08 mitigate, moderate, palliate 09 alleviate

assume
◇ *containment indicator*
03 don 04 bear, take 05 adopt, fancy, feign, guess, infer, posit, put on, seize, think, usurp 06 accept, affect, deduce, expect, strike, take it, take on
07 acquire, believe, embrace, imagine, pre-empt, presume, pretend, suppose, surmise 08 arrogate, shoulder, simulate, take over 09 enter upon, postulate, undertake 10 come to have, commandeer, presuppose, take as read, understand 11 appropriate, counterfeit 14 take for granted

assumed
04 fake, sham 05 bogus, false
06 made-up, phoney 07 feigned
08 affected, borrowed, putative, supposed 09 pretended, simulated
10 fictitious 11 counterfeit
12 adscititious, hypothetical, pseudonymous 14 supposititious

assumption
04 idea 05 axiom, donné, fancy, guess
06 belief, donnée, notion, theory
07 embrace, premise, seizure, surmise
08 adoption, takeover 09 inference, postulate 10 acceptance, arrogation, conclusion, conjecture, hypothesis, pre-emption, usurpation
11 embarkation, expectation, postulation, presumption, shouldering, supposition, undertaking
13 appropriation, commandeering
14 presupposition

assurance
03 vow 04 gall, oath, word 05 nerve, poise 06 aplomb, pledge 07 courage, promise, surance, warrant 08 audacity, boldness, security, sureness
09 assertion, certainty, guarantee
10 confidence, conviction, positivism
11 affirmation, assuredness, declaration, undertaking 12 self-reliance 13 self-assurance 14 self-confidence, unflappability

assure
03 vow 04 affy, hete, seal, tell
05 hecht, hight, swear 06 affirm, attest, avouch, ensure, pledge, secure, soothe 07 certify, comfort, confirm, hearten, promise, resolve, warrant 08 convince, persuade, reassure 09 ascertain, encourage, guarantee

assured
04 bold, calm, sure 05 fixed 06 secure
07 certain, ensured, settled
08 definite, positive, promised
09 assertive, audacious, confident, confirmed, thoughten 10 guaranteed
11 cut and dried, irrefutable, self-assured 12 indisputable 13 self-confident, self-possessed 14 sure of yourself

• **be assured of**
04 know

assuredly
05 pardi, pardy, perdy 06 pardie, perdie, surely 07 my certy 08 my certie 09 by my certy, certainly, of a verity 10 by my certie, definitely, for certain 12 and no mistake, indisputably, without doubt
14 unquestionably 15 without question

astatine
02 At

astern
03 aft 04 baft 05 abaft, apoop

asteroid
09 planetoid 11 minor planet

Asteroids include:

04 Eros, Hebe, Iris, Juno
05 Ceres, Flora, Metis, Vesta
06 Apollo, Cybele, Davida, Europa, Hygiea, Icarus, Pallas, Psyche, Trojan
07 Eunomia
10 Interamnia

astir
05 afoot, agate 07 abroach, humming
09 in the wind

astonish
03 wow 04 daze, stun 05 amaze, floor, shock, stony 07 astound, flummox, stagger, startle, stupefy
08 bewilder, bowl over, confound, dumfound, gobsmack, surprise
09 dumbfound, electrify, take aback
11 flabbergast, knock for six 12 blow your mind

astonished
05 dazed 06 amazed 07 shocked, stunned 08 open-eyed, startled, wide-eyed 09 astounded, staggered, surprised 10 bewildered, bowled over, confounded, gobsmacked, taken aback 11 dumbfounded 12 lost for words 13 flabbergasted, knocked for six, thunderstruck

astonishing
◇ *anagram indicator*
07 amazing 08 shocking, striking, stunning 09 startling 10 astounding, impressive, marvellous, prodigious, staggering, surprising 11 bewildering, mind-blowing 12 awe-inspiring, breathtaking, mind-boggling, unbelievable

astonishment
05 shock 06 dismay, marvel, wonder
08 surprise 09 amazement, confusion, disbelief 10 admiration, wonderment
12 bewilderment, stupefaction
13 consternation

astound
04 stun 05 abash, amaze, floor, shock
06 stound 07 flummox, startle, stupefy
08 astonish, bewilder, bowl over, surprise 09 overwhelm 11 knock for six

astounding
07 amazing 08 shocking, stunning
09 startling 10 staggering, stupefying, stupendous, surprising 11 astonishing, bewildering 12 breathtaking, overwhelming

astray
◇ *anagram indicator*
04 awry, lost, miss, will, wull 05 abord, agate, amiss, wrong 06 abroad, adrift, errant, erring 07 missing 09 off course
10 miswandred, off the mark 11 off the rails

astride
◇ *containment indicator*
08 straddle 10 en cavalier 12 colossus-wise

astringent
04 acid, hard, kino **05** harsh, rough, stern **06** biting, gambir, severe **07** acerbic, austere, caustic, gambier, guaraná, mordant, puckery, rhatany, styptic **08** alum-root, critical, krameria, scathing **09** obstruent, tormentil, trenchant, zinc oxide **10** astrictive, witch-hazel **11** restringent

astrologer
09 stargazer **10** genethliac **11** horoscopist, Nostradamus **12** figure-caster **14** archgenethliac

astronaut
08 lunanaut, spaceman **09** cosmonaut, lunarnaut, taikonaut **10** spacewoman **14** space traveller

Astronauts and space travellers include:

03 Ham
04 **Bean** (Alan), **Ride** (Sally), **Tito** (Dennis)
05 **Foale** (Michael), **Glenn** (John), **Irwin** (James), **Laika**, **Scott** (David), **Titov** (Gherman), **White** (Edward)
06 **Aldrin** (Buzz), **Conrad** (Pete), **Leonov** (Aleksei), **Lovell** (Jim)
07 **Chaffee** (Roger), **Collins** (Michael), **Gagarin** (Yuri), **Grissom** (Gus), **Schirra** (Wally), **Sharman** (Helen), **Shepard** (Alan)
08 **Mitchell** (Edgar)
09 **Armstrong** (Neil)
10 **Tereshkova** (Valentina)

• **would-be astronaut**
10 space cadet

astronomer
04 astr **06** astron **09** stargazer

Astronomers and astrophysicists include:

04 **Airy** (Sir George), **Biot** (Jean-Baptiste), **Gold** (Thomas), **Hale** (George), **Lyot** (Bernard), **Oort** (Jan), **Pond** (John), **Rees** (Sir Martin), **Ryle** (Sir Martin), **Saha** (Meghnad), **Webb** (James E)
05 **Adams** (John Couch), **Adams** (Walter S), **Baade** (Walter), **Baily** (Francis), **Bliss** (Nathaniel), **Brahe** (Tycho), **Dyson** (Sir Frank), **Gauss** (Carl Friedrich), **Hoyle** (Sir Fred), **Jeans** (Sir James), **Jones** (Sir Harold Spencer), **Moore** (Sir Patrick), **Sagan** (Carl), **Smith** (Sir Francis), **Vogel** (Hermann Carl)
06 **Bessel** (Friedrich), **Halley** (Edmond), **Hewish** (Antony), **Hubble** (Edwin), **Jansky** (Karl), **Kepler** (Johannes), **Kuiper** (Gerard), **Lovell** (Sir Bernard), **Olbers** (Heinrich), **Piazzi** (Giuseppe), **Roemer** (Olaus)
07 **Babcock** (Harold D), **Barnard** (Edward Emerson), **Bradley** (James), **Cassini** (Giovanni), **Celsius** (Anders), **Galilei** (Galileo), **Galileo**, **Hawking** (Stephen), **Huggins** (Sir William), **Langley** (Samuel), **Laplace** (Pierre), **Lockyer** (Sir Norman), **Maunder** (E W), **Penrose** (Roger), **Penzias** (Arno), **Ptolemy**, **Russell** (Henry Norris), **Sandage** (Allan), **Schmidt** (Maarten), **Seyfert** (Carl), **Shapley** (Harlow), **Whipple** (Fred), **Woolley** (Sir Richard)
08 **Burbidge** (Geoffrey), **Burbidge** (Margaret), **Chandler** (Seth Carlo), **Christie** (Sir William), **Friedman** (Herbert), **Herschel** (Caroline), **Herschel** (Sir John), **Herschel** (Sir William), **Lemaître** (Georges), **Tombaugh** (Clyde W)
09 **Eddington** (Sir Arthur), **Fabricius** (David), **Flamsteed** (John), **Maskelyne** (Nevil), **Sosigenes**
10 **Carrington** (Richard), **Copernicus** (Nicolas), **Hipparchos**, **Wolfendale** (Sir Arnold)
11 **Bell Burnell** (Jocelyn), **Graham-Smith** (Sir Francis), **Hertzsprung** (Ejnar), **Tsiolkovsky** (Konstantin)
12 **Schiaparelli** (Giovanni)
13 **Chandrasekhar** (Subrahmanyan), **Schwarzschild** (Karl)
14 **Galileo Galilei**

astronomical
04 astr, huge, vast **06** astron, cosmic **07** immense, mammoth, massive, stellar **08** colossal, enormous, gigantic, heavenly, infinite, thumping, whopping **09** celestial, planetary **10** tremendous **11** substantial **12** considerable, cosmological, immeasurable, interstellar

• **astronomical model**
06 orrery

astronomy
04 astr **06** astron **08** star-read **09** uranology

astrophysicist *see* **astronomer**

astute
03 sly **04** cute, keen, sage, wide, wily, wise **05** canny, sharp **06** clever, crafty, shrewd, subtle **07** cunning, knowing, prudent **09** sagacious **10** discerning, perceptive **11** intelligent, penetrating, sharp-witted **13** perspicacious

astutely
06 keenly, wisely **08** craftily, shrewdly **12** perceptively **13** intelligently, sharp-wittedly

asunder
02 up **05** apart, in two **06** atwain **07** in twain **08** in pieces, to pieces

asylum
03 bin **05** girth, grith, haven **06** bedlam, refuge **07** retreat, shelter **08** madhouse, Magdalen, nuthouse **09** dark-house, funny farm, sanctuary **10** frithsoken **11** institution **12** penitentiary, port in a storm **13** place of safety **14** mental hospital

asymmetrical
04 awry, skew **06** uneven **07** anaxial, crooked, oblique, unequal **08** lopsided **09** distorted, irregular, malformed **10** unbalanced **13** unsymmetrical

asymmetry
09 imbalance **10** distortion, handedness, inequality, unevenness, unsymmetry **11** crookedness **12** irregularity, lopsidedness, malformation

at
02 in, to **08** astatine

ate
◇ *containment indicator*

atheism
07 impiety **08** nihilism, paganism, unbelief **09** disbelief, non-belief **10** heathenism, infidelity, irreligion, scepticism **11** godlessness, rationalism, ungodliness **12** freethinking

atheist
05 pagan **07** heathen, heretic, infidel, sceptic **08** humanist, nihilist **10** unbeliever **11** disbeliever, freethinker, non-believer, nullifidian, rationalist

Athene
07 Minerva

athlete
04 jock **05** miler **06** player, runner **07** gymnast, hurdler **09** contender, sportsman **10** competitor, contestant **11** sportswoman **12** quarter-miler

Athletes include:

03 **Coe** (Sebastian, Lord)
04 **Budd** (Zola), **Cram** (Steve), **Koch** (Marita), **Mota** (Rosa)
05 **Bubka** (Sergey), **Jones** (Marion), **Keino** (Kip), **Lewis** (Carl), **Lewis** (Denise), **Moses** (Ed), **Nurmi** (Paavo), **Ottey** (Merlene), **Ovett** (Steve), **Owens** (Jesse), **Waitz** (Grete), **Wells** (Allan)
06 **Aouita** (Said), **Barber** (Eunice), **Beamon** (Bob), **Devers** (Gail), **Foster** (Brendan), **Greene** (Maurice), **Holmes** (Kelly), **Mutola** (Maria), **Oerter** (Al), **Peters** (Mary)
07 **Backley** (Steve), **Edwards** (Jonathan), **Fosbury** (Dick), **Freeman** (Cathy), **Gunnell** (Sally), **Jackson** (Colin), **Johnson** (Ben), **Johnson** (Michael), **Liddell** (Eric), **Zatopek** (Emil), **Zelezny** (Jan)
08 **Christie** (Linford), **Guerrouj** (Hicham el-), **Kipketer** (Wilson), **McColgan** (Liz), **Pieterse** (Zola), **Thompson** (Daley)
09 **Bannister** (Sir Roger), **O'Sullivan** (Sonia), **Radcliffe** (Paula), **Sanderson** (Tessa), **Whitbread** (Fatima)
12 **Blankers-Koen** (Fanny), **Gebrselassie** (Haile), **Grey-Thompson** (Dame Tanni)
14 **Griffith Joyner** (Florence 'Flo-Jo')

athletic
01 A **03** fit **04** wiry **05** games, leish **06** active, brawny, muscly, robust, sinewy, sports, sporty, strong, sturdy

08 muscular, powerful, sporting, vigorous, well-knit 09 energetic, gymnastic, strapping

athletics
05 games, races 06 sports 07 matches 08 aerobics 09 exercises 10 gymnastics 11 field events, track events 13 callisthenics

See also **sport**

Athletics events include:

04 ball, shot, walk
05 relay
06 discus, hammer, sprint
07 hurdles, javelin, shot put
08 biathlon, high jump, long jump, marathon, tug-of-war
09 broad jump, caber toss, decathlon, pole vault, sheaf toss, triathlon
10 heptathlon, pentathlon, tetrathlon, triple jump
11 discus throw, fell running, fifty metres, hammer throw, race walking
12 cross-country, half marathon, javelin throw, steeplechase
14 hop, step and jump
15 tossing the caber

athwart
04 awry 06 across, aslant 07 asklent

atmosphere
03 air, atm, fug, sky 04 aura, feel, mood, tone 05 ether, miasm, tenor, vibes 06 miasma, milieu, spirit, welkin 07 climate, feeling, flavour, heavens, quality, setting 08 ambience, empyrean 09 aerospace, character, firmament 10 background 11 environment 12 surroundings 13 vault of heaven

Atmosphere layers include:

09 exosphere, ionopause, mesopause
10 ionosphere, mesosphere, ozone layer, tropopause
11 stratopause, troposphere
12 stratosphere, thermosphere

atom
03 bit, jot 04 hint, iota, mite, spot, whit 05 crumb, grain, scrap, shred, speck, trace 06 morsel 08 fragment, molecule, particle 09 scintilla

See also **particle**

atomic
01 A
• **atomic mass unit**
03 amu
• **atomic number**
04 at no 06 at numb
• **atomic weight**
01 A 03 AWU 04 at wt

atone
03 aby 04 abye 06 offset, pay for, ransom, redeem, remedy, repent 07 appease, expiate, redress, satisfy 08 make good 09 indemnify, make right, make up for, reconcile 10 compensate, make amends, propitiate, recompense 14 make reparation

atonement
06 amends, ransom 07 payment, penance, redress 08 requital 09 expiation, indemnity, repayment 10 recompense, redemption, reparation 11 appeasement, eye for an eye, restitution, restoration 12 compensation, propitiation, satisfaction 13 acceptilation, reimbursement

atrocious
◇ *anagram indicator*
05 awful, cruel, enorm 06 brutal, savage, wicked 07 ghastly, heinous, hideous, vicious 08 dreadful, enormous, fiendish, grievous, horrible, ruthless, shocking, terrible 09 appalling, frightful, merciless, monstrous, nefarious 10 abominable, diabolical, disgusting, flagitious, horrendous

atrociously
07 cruelly 08 brutally, horribly, terribly, wickedly 09 heinously 10 abominably, dreadfully, fiendishly, ruthlessly, shockingly 11 appallingly, monstrously

atrocity
04 evil 06 horror 07 cruelty, outrage 08 enormity, savagery, vileness, villainy 09 barbarity, brutality, violation 10 wickedness 11 abomination, heinousness, hideousness, monstrosity, viciousness 13 atrociousness 14 flagitiousness

atrophy
04 fade 05 decay, waste 06 shrink, sweeny, tabefy, wither 07 decline, dwindle, shrivel, wasting 08 diminish, emaciate, marasmus 09 waste away, withering 10 amyotrophy, degenerate, diminution, emaciation, involution 11 deteriorate, shrivelling, tabefaction, wasting away 12 degeneration 13 deterioration

attach
03 add, fix, lay, pin, put, sew, tag, tie 04 ally, bind, join, link, nail, send, tack, weld 05 add on, affix, annex, cling, place, put on, snell, stick, unite 06 adhere, append, assign, belong, couple, detail, fasten, impute, limber, second, secure, solder 07 adhibit, ascribe, Blu-Tack®, connect, harness, plaster 08 allocate, relate to 09 affiliate, align with, associate, attribute, factorize, latch onto, piggyback 10 articulate, make secure 11 combine with 13 affiliate with, associate with

attached
04 fond 06 liking, loving, tender 07 devoted, engaged, married 08 friendly 09 affianced, appendant, spoken for 11 going steady 12 affectionate 15 in a relationship

attachment
03 tie 04 bond, frog, link, love 05 extra 06 fetich, fetish, liking 07 adapter, adaptor, adjunct, codicil, fetiche, fitment, fitting, fixture, loyalty 08 addition, adhesion, affinity, calf-love, devotion, fixation, fondness 09 accessory, affection, appendage, closeness, extension 10 attraction, commitment, friendship, partiality, supplement, tenderness 12 accoutrement, appurtenance 13 grande passion

attack
03 fit, gas, get, lam, mob, mug, pan, pin, TIA 04 bash, bomb, bout, chin, fake, flak, fork, gang, go at, jump, Mace®, nuke, prey, push, raid, rear, roll, rush, Scud, slam, tilt 05 abuse, alert, begin, blame, blast, blitz, board, brash, decry, fling, fly at, foray, glass, go for, ictus, knock, prang, sally, scrag, siege, slate, snipe, spasm, start, storm, touch 06 access, affect, ambush, assail, batter, beat up, berate, bodrag, bottle, charge, come at, do over, duff up, extent, fall on, hold-up, impugn, infect, insult, invade, jump on, malign, molest, napalm, oppugn, pounce, rebuke, revile, rocket, savage, send in, shower, sortie, strafe, strike, stroke, tackle, tongue, vilify, wade in, waylay 07 address, aggress, air-raid, assault, attempt, battery, besiege, blister, bombard, bulldog, censure, clobber, destroy, fly upon, focus on, handbag, hiccups, inveigh, kicking, lampoon, lay into, reprove, round on, rubbish, run down, sandbag, seizure, set upon, slag off, slating, torpedo 08 attend to, camisade, camisado, commence, deal with, denounce, dive-bomb, embark on, firebomb, invasion, knocking, paroxysm, pounce on, roasting, set about, slamming, storming, strike at, tear into, tomahawk 09 broadside, cannonade, criticism, criticize, go wilding, have a go at, hiccoughs, incursion, invective, irruption, light into, obsession, offensive, onslaught, pull apart, stand upon, submarine, undertake, weigh into 10 bitch about, calumniate, chuck off at, convulsion, coup de main, crise de foi, get stuck in, hatchet job, have a pop at, impugnment, revilement, take a pop at, vituperate, weight into 11 bombardment, infestation, pick holes in 12 crise de nerfs, get started on, get stuck into, go over the top, leave for dead, Pearl Harbour, pull to pieces, put in the boot, put the boot in, tear to pieces, tear to shreds, vilification 13 feeding frenzy, find fault with 14 a warm reception, make a dead set at 15 act of aggression, apply yourself to, go for the jugular, throw yourself on

attacker
06 abuser, critic, mugger, raider 07 invader, reviler, striker 09 aggressor, assailant, assaulter, detractor 10 persecutor

attain
03 get, hit, net, win 04 earn, find, gain 05 fetch, grasp, reach, seize, touch

06 effect, fulfil, obtain, secure
07 achieve, acquire, possess, procure, realize, recover **08** arrive at, complete
10 accomplish

attainable
06 at hand, doable, viable **08** feasible, possible, probable **09** potential, reachable, realistic **10** accessible, achievable, imaginable, manageable, obtainable **11** conceivable, practicable, within reach

attainment
03 art **04** feat, gift **05** skill **06** talent
07 ability, mastery, success
08 aptitude, facility **10** capability, competence, completion, fulfilment
11 achievement, acquirement, procurement, proficiency, realization
12 consummation **14** accomplishment

attempt
02 go **03** aim, bid, shy, try **04** bash, burl, fand, fond, make, mint, push, seek, shot, stab, trie **05** assay, crack, essay, foray, offer, trial, whack
06 aspire, effort, set out, strive, tackle
07 have a go, pretend, venture
08 attentat, endeavor, have a try, struggle **09** endeavour, give it a go, have a bash, have a shot, have a stab, tentative, undertake **10** coup d'essai, experiment, give it a try, have a crack
11 have a stab at, try your hand, undertaking **12** give it a whirl **13** see if you can do, try your hand at **15** do your level best

attend
04 go to, hear, heed, help, mark, mind, note, page, show, stay, tend, wait
05 audit, await, guard, holla, nurse, serve, usher, visit, watch **06** appear, assist, be here, escort, follow, listen, notice, show up, squire, turn up **07** be there, care for, give ear, go along, observe **08** chaperon, frequent, take note, wait upon **09** accompany, chaperone, come along, look after
10 minister to, take care of, take notice, take part in **11** be present at, concentrate **12** pay attention

• attend to
03 fix **04** heed, mind, sort, tent **05** see to, valet **06** direct, handle, manage, notice **07** control, oversee, process
08 consider, cope with, deal with, follow up, see about **09** look after, supervise **10** follow up on, take care of
11 give an eye to

attendance
04 duty, gate **05** crowd, house
06 escort, roll-up **07** showing, turnout
08 audience, courting, presence
09 appearing, showing up
10 appearance

attendant
03 man **04** aide, jack, mute, page, sice, syce **05** angel, gilly, guard, guide, jäger, saice, sowar, usher, woman
06 batman, bedral, escort, gillie, helper, jaeger, keeper, porter, varlet, verger, waiter **07** acolyte, acolyth, bederal, best man, bulldog, checker, custrel, equerry, esquire, famulus, footboy, footman, ghillie, janitor, linkboy, linkman, marshal, orderly, related, servant, snuffer, steward
08 attached, batwoman, beach boy, chaperon, chasseur, follower, footpage, handmaid, janitrix, retainer, waitress **09** assistant, auxiliary, boxkeeper, chaperone, chaprassi, chaprassy, chuprassy, companion, custodian, groomsman, janitress, kennelman, lady's-maid, observant, pew-opener, resultant, satellite
10 associated, conclavist, consequent, handmaiden, incidental, kennelmaid, led captain, lock-keeper, ministrant, pursuivant, subsequent, vivandière
11 apple-squire, body servant, concomitant, gentlewoman, loblolly-boy **12** accompanying, bottle-holder, shield-bearer **13** church officer, gillie-wetfoot **14** gentleman usher, valet de chambre **15** gillie-white-foot

attention
03 ear, eye **04** care, gaum, gorm, heed, help, mind, 'shun **06** notice, regard **07** concern, respect, service, therapy, thought **08** civility, courtesy, scrutiny **09** alertness, awareness, gallantry, limelight, treatment, vigilance **10** advertence, advertency, attendance, politeness
11 compliments, high profile, mindfulness, observation, recognition
13 concentration, consideration, contemplation, preoccupation

• expressions relating to attracting or directing attention
02 hi, ho, la, lo, oi, 'st, yo **03** hem, hey, hoa, hoh, hoi, hoy, pst, say, see, why
04 ahem, ecce, ecco, here, hist, look, oyes, oyez, psst, 'shun, soho, what, yo-ho **05** cooee, cooey, hallo, hello, holla, hollo, hullo, voilà **06** behold, halloa, halloo, yo-ho-ho, yoo-hoo **07** whoa-hoa **08** whoa-ho-ho **10** view-halloo

• pay attention
04 gaum, gorm, heed **06** listen
07 focus on, hearken, observe **10** get a load of, take notice **13** concentrate on
14 watch carefully **15** focus your mind on, listen carefully

attentive
04 kind **05** alert, awake, aware, civil, tenty, whist **06** polite, tentie **07** all ears, careful, devoted, dutiful, gallant, heedful, listful, mindful **08** gracious, noticing, obliging, vigilant, watchful, watching **09** advertent, adviceful, avizefull, courteous, listening, observant, on the ball, regardant
10 chivalrous, particular, thoughtful
11 advertising, considerate, punctilious **12** on the qui vive
13 accommodating, concentrating, conscientious

attentively
09 carefully, mindfully **10** watchfully
11 observantly **15** conscientiously

attenuated
04 bony, fine, slim, thin **06** narrow, skinny, slight **07** scraggy, scrawny, slender

attest
04 aver, show **05** prove **06** adjure, affirm, assert, depose, evince, verify
07 certify, confirm, declare, display, endorse, witness **08** evidence, manifest, proclaim, vouch for
10 asseverate **11** corroborate, demonstrate **13** bear witness to

attic
04 loft **06** garret **07** mansard **10** sky parlour

attire
04 garb, gear, suit, tire, togs, wear
05 dress, habit **06** finery, outfit, rig-out
07 apparel, clobber, clothes, costume
08 clothing, garments **10** habiliment, habilitate **11** habiliments
13 accoutrements

attired
05 ready **07** adorned, arrayed, clothed, dressed **09** decked out, rigged out, turned out **11** habilitated

attitude
04 mood, pose, song, view **05** piety, sense, stand **06** aspect, manner, stance **07** bearing, feeling, mindset, opinion, outlook, posture
08 approach, carriage, position
09 mentality, sentiment, viewpoint, world-view **10** Anschauung, deportment **11** disposition, perspective, point of view **13** way of thinking **14** Weltanschauung

attorney
02 AG, DA, QC **03** Att **04** Atty **05** brief
06 lawyer **07** counsel, proctor
08 advocate **09** barrister, solicitor
12 legal adviser

attract
04 draw, hook, lure, pull **05** charm, rivet, swing, tempt **06** allure, engage, entice, excite, induce, invite, pull in, seduce **07** bewitch, bring in, enchant, incline **08** appeal to, interest
09 captivate, fascinate, magnetize

attraction
02 it, SA **04** bait, bond, draw, hook, lure, pull **05** charm, sight **06** allure, appeal, favour **07** draught, feature, glamour **08** activity, affinity, building, cohesion, interest **09** box office, diversion, magnetism, seduction
10 enticement, inducement, invitation, temptation **11** captivation, enchantment, fascination, Ferris wheel
13 entertainment

• centre of attraction
04 clou

attractive
03 bad, fit, hot **04** cute, fair, foxy, sexy, taky **05** bonny, dishy, hunky, tasty, triff
06 catchy, comely, glossy, lovely, nubile, pretty, snazzy **07** dashing, elegant, nymphic, shapely, triffic,

winning, winsome **08** all right, beddable, catching, charming, engaging, enticing, epigamic, fetching, gorgeous, handsome, hot stuff, inviting, knockout, luscious, magnetic, pleasant, pleasing, striking, stunning, tempting, terrific **09** agreeable, appealing, appetible, beautiful, desirable, fanciable, glamorous, insidious, seductive, toothsome **10** adamantine, personable, photogenic, voluptuous **11** captivating, charismatic, fascinating, good-looking, interesting, picturesque **12** irresistible **13** prepossessing **14** a bit of all right

attribute
03 lay **04** mark, note, side, sign **05** apply, blame, facet, point, quirk, refer, trait **06** aspect, assign, charge, credit, impute, reckon, streak, symbol, virtue **07** adjunct, apanage, ascribe, feature, put down, quality, set down **08** accredit, appanage, arrogate, property **09** affection, indicator **11** peculiarity **12** idiosyncrasy **14** characteristic

attrition
07 chafing, erosion, rubbing **08** abrasion, friction, grinding, scraping **09** detrition, weakening **10** harassment **11** attenuation, wearing away, wearing down

attuned
03 set **05** tuned **07** adapted **08** adjusted **09** regulated **10** accustomed, harmonized **11** assimilated, co-ordinated **12** acclimatized, familiarized

atypical
07 deviant, unusual **08** aberrant, abnormal, freakish, uncommon **09** anomalous, divergent, eccentric, untypical **11** exceptional **13** extraordinary **14** unconventional

aubergine
07 brinjal **08** eggplant, mad-apple

auburn
04 rust **05** henna, tawny **06** copper, russet, Titian **07** dark-red **08** chestnut **12** reddish-brown

auction
04 cant, roup, sale **06** outcry, vendue **07** outroop **09** trade sale **11** warrant sale **12** subhastation

auctioneer
09 outrooper **11** rouping-wife

audacious
04 bold, pert, rash, rude **05** brave, fresh, lippy, nervy, risky, saucy **06** brazen, cheeky, daring, plucky **07** assured, forward, valiant **08** assuming, fearless, impudent, insolent, intrepid, reckless **09** dauntless, shameless, unabashed **10** courageous **11** adventurous, impertinent, venturesome **12** devil-may-care, enterprising, presumptuous **13** disrespectful

audacity
04 grit, guts, neck, risk **05** cheek, nerve, pluck **06** bottle, daring, valour **07** bravery, courage **08** boldness, defiance, forehead, pertness, rashness, rudeness **09** assurance, hardihead, hardihood, impudence, insolence **10** brazenness, effrontery, enterprise **11** forwardness, intrepidity, presumption **12** fearlessness, impertinence, recklessness **13** dauntlessness, shamelessness **15** adventurousness

audible
◇ *homophone indicator*
05 clear, heard **08** distinct, hearable **10** detectable **11** appreciable, discernible, perceptible **12** recognizable

audience
04 fans **05** audit, crowd, house **06** public **07** hearing, meeting, patrons, ratings, theater, theatre, turnout, viewers **08** assembly, auditory, devotees, regulars **09** followers, following, gathering, interview, listeners, onlookers, reception **10** auditorium, conference, discussion, spectators **11** bums on seats **12** congregation, consultation

audit
05 check **06** go over, review, survey, verify **07** analyse, balance, examine, inspect **08** analysis, scrutiny **09** balancing, go through, statement **10** inspection, scrutinize **11** examination, investigate, work through **12** verification **13** investigation

audition
05 trial **07** hearing

auditorium
04 hall **05** front, house **07** chamber, theatre **09** playhouse, sphendone **10** opera house **11** concert hall **12** assembly room **14** conference hall

au fait
05 aware **06** versed **07** abreast, in touch **08** familiar, up to date **09** au courant **10** conversant **13** knowledgeable

augment
03 ech, ich **04** eche, eech, grow **05** add to, boost, put on, raise, swell **06** expand, extend **07** amplify, build up, enhance, enlarge, inflate, magnify **08** heighten, increase, multiply **09** intensify, reinforce **10** strengthen **11** make greater

augmentation
05 boost **06** growth **07** build-up **08** increase **09** expansion, extension **11** enlargement **13** amplification, magnification, strengthening **15** intensification

augur
04 bode, spae **06** herald **07** betoken, portend, predict, presage, promise, signify **08** forebode, foretell, prophesy **09** auspicate, be a sign of, harbinger

augury
04 omen, sign **05** sooth, token **06** herald **07** portent, promise, warning **08** prodrome, prophecy **09** harbinger **10** foreboding, forerunner, prediction **11** forewarning **12** ornithoscopy **13** haruspication **15** prognostication

august
03 Aug **05** grand, lofty, noble **06** solemn **07** exalted, stately, sublime **08** glorious, imperial, imposing, majestic **09** dignified, respected, venerable **10** impressive **11** magnificent **12** awe-inspiring **13** distinguished

Augustines
03 OSA

auk
04 roch **05** rotch **06** rotche **07** Alcidae, dovekie, penguin, rotchie, sea dove **08** garefowl **09** razorbill

Auntie
03 BBC **04** Beeb

aura
03 air **04** feel, hint, mood **05** vibes **06** nimbus **07** feeling, quality **08** ambience, mystique **09** emanation **10** atmosphere, genius loci, suggestion, vibrations

aural
◇ *homophone indicator*

aurora
03 Eos **11** polar lights **12** merry dancers **14** northern lights, southern lights

auspices
• under the auspices of
11 in the care of **13** in the charge of **15** under the aegis of

auspicious
04 rosy **05** happy, lucky, white **06** bright, timely **07** hopeful **08** cheerful **09** fortunate, opportune, promising **10** fair-boding, favourable, felicitous, optimistic, propitious, prosperous **11** encouraging

austere
04 cold, grim, hard **05** basic, bleak, grave, harsh, plain, rigid, sober, stark, stern, stoic, stoor, stour, sture **06** chaste, formal, frugal, severe, simple, solemn, sombre, stowre, strict **07** ascetic, Dantean, distant, killjoy, serious, spartan **08** exacting, rigorous **09** stringent, unadorned, unbending, unfeeling **10** abstemious, astringent, economical, forbidding, functional, inflexible, restrained, Waldensian **11** puritanical, self-denying **12** unornamented **14** self-abnegating **15** self-disciplined

austerity
06 rigour **07** economy **08** coldness, hardness, severity **09** formality, harshness, plainness, solemnity

10 abstinence, asceticism, puritanism, self-denial, simplicity **13** inflexibility **14** abstemiousness, self-discipline

Australia

01 A **02** Oz **03** AUS **04** Aust **05** Austr **09** down under

See also **electorate**; **governor**; **Prime Minister**; **state**; **team**

Australian cities and notable towns include:

05 Perth
06 Cairns, Darwin, Hobart, Sydney
08 Adelaide, Brisbane, Canberra
09 Fremantle, Melbourne
12 Alice Springs

Australian landmarks include:

05 Uluru
08 Lake Eyre, Shark Bay
09 Ayers Rock, Botany Bay, Pinnacles, Purnululu
10 Bondi Beach, Yarra River
11 Barrier Reef, Mt Kosciusko, Murray River
12 Darling River, Fraser Island, Gibson Desert, Hunter Valley, Rialto Towers
13 Barossa Valley, Blue Mountains, Bungle Bungles, Devil's Marbles, Dividing Range, Flinders Range, Harbour Bridge, Simpson Desert
14 Australian Alps, Nullarbor Plain, Pinnacle Desert, Snowy Mountains, Twelve Apostles, Uluru–Kata Tjuta, Victoria Desert

Australian

01 A **02** Oz **03** gin **05** koori, myall, ocker **06** Aussie, Strine

See also **Aboriginal**; **state**

Australian football

Australian football-related terms include:

03 AFL
04 goal, mark, ruck, wing
05 rover
06 ball up, behind, centre, tackle, time on, umpire
07 dispose, kick out, quarter, ruckman
08 follower, free kick, full back, half back, handball, handpass, left wing, screamer, stab pass
09 playfield, right wing, ruck rover
10 back pocket, banana kick, behind post, centre line, goal square, goal umpire, off the boot
11 Aussie Rules, daisy cutter, full forward, half forward
12 boundary line, centre bounce, centre square, Magarey Medal
13 Brownlow Medal, checkside punt, fifty-metre arc, forward pocket, half-back flank, Sandover Medal
14 aerial pingpong, boundary umpire, centre half back
15 chewy on your boot

Australian football players include:

04 **Dyer** (Jack)
05 **Carey** (Wayne)
06 **Ablett** (Gary), **Blight** (Malcolm), **Bunton** (Haydn), **Capper** (Warwick), **Cazaly** (Roy), **Farmer** (Graham 'Polly')
07 **Barassi** (Ron), **Jackson** (Mark), **Lockett** (Tony), **Whitten** (Ted)
08 **Bartlett** (Kevin), **Brereton** (Dermot), **Brownlow** (Charles), **Matthews** (Leigh), **Richards** (Lou)
10 **Jesaulenko** (Alex)

Australian Football League team nicknames include:

04 Cats
05 Blues, Crows, Hawks, Lions, Power, Swans
06 Demons, Eagles, Saints, Tigers
07 Bombers, Dockers, Magpies
08 Bulldogs
09 Kangaroos

Austria

01 A **03** AUT

authentic

04 echt, real, true **05** legal, valid **06** actual, dinkum, honest, kosher, lawful **07** certain, correct, factual, genuine **08** accurate, attested, bona fide, credible, faithful, reliable, sterling **10** dependable, historical, legitimate, true-to-life, undisputed **11** trustworthy **12** the real McCoy, the real thing

authentically

04 echt **06** really **08** actually, credibly, lawfully, reliably **09** genuinely **10** accurately, faithfully **12** historically, legitimately

authenticate

04 test **05** prove **06** attest, ratify, signet, verify **07** certify, confirm, endorse, warrant **08** accredit, notarize, validate, vouch for **09** authorize, guarantee **11** corroborate **12** substantiate

authentication

10 validation **11** attestation, endorsement **12** confirmation, ratification, verification **13** accreditation, authorization, corroboration **14** substantiation

authenticity

05 truth **07** honesty **08** accuracy, fidelity, legality, validity, veracity **09** certainty **10** legitimacy **11** correctness, credibility, genuineness, reliability **12** faithfulness, truthfulness **13** dependability **15** trustworthiness

author

03 pen **04** hand, poet **05** maker, mover **06** parent, penman, writer **07** creator, founder, planner **08** composer, designer, essayist, inventor, lyricist, novelist, penwoman, producer, reporter, volumist **09** architect, dramatist, garreteer, initiator, ink-jerker, scribbler **10** biographer, ink-slinger, journalist, librettist, originator, playwright, prime mover, songwriter, trecentist **11** contributor, hedge-writer **12** man of letters, paper-stainer, screenwriter **13** Deuteronomist, revelationist **14** woman of letters

See also **writer**

Authors include:

03 **Eco** (Umberto), **Kee** (Robert), **Lee** (Harper), **Lee** (Laurie), **Poe** (Edgar Allan), **Pym** (Barbara), **RLS**, **Roy** (Arundhati)
04 **Amis** (Kingsley), **Amis** (Martin), **Behn** (Aphra), **Böll** (Heinrich), **Boyd** (William), **Buck** (Pearl S), **Cary** (Joyce), **Dahl** (Roald), **Dane** (Clemence), **Fine** (Anne), **Ford** (Ford Madox), **Gide** (André), **Grey** (Zane), **Hogg** (James), **Hope** (Anthony), **Hugo** (Victor), **Jane** (Fred T), **King** (Stephen), **Levi** (Primo), **Loos** (Anita), **Mann** (Thomas), **Okri** (Ben), **Puzo** (Mario), **Rhys** (Jean), **Roth** (Philip), **Sade** (Marquis de), **Saki**, **Sand** (George), **Seth** (Vikram), **Shah** (Eddy), **Snow** (C P), **Wain** (John), **West** (Dame Rebecca), **Wood** (Mrs Henry), **Zola** (Emile)
05 **Adams** (Douglas), **Adams** (Richard), **Agnon** (Shmuel Yosef), **Banks** (Iain), **Banks** (Lynne Reid), **Bates** (H E), **Behan** (Brendan), **Benét** (Stephen), **Bowen** (Elizabeth), **Bragg** (Melvyn), **Brink** (André), **Brown** (George Mackay), **Bunin** (Ivan), **Byatt** (A S), **Camus** (Albert), **Chase** (James Hadley), **Craik** (Dinah), **Crane** (Stephen), **Dante**, **Defoe** (Daniel), **Desai** (Anita), **Doyle** (Roddy), **Doyle** (Sir Arthur Conan), **Dumas** (Alexandre, fils), **Dumas** (Alexandre, père), **Eliot** (George), **Ellis** (Alice Thomas), **Elton** (Ben), **Faure** (Edgar), **Frayn** (Michael), **Genet** (Jean), **Gogol** (Nikolai), **Gorky** (Maxim), **Grass** (Günter), **Hardy** (Thomas), **Hasek** (Jaroslav), **Hesse** (Hermann), **Heyer** (Georgette), **Innes** (Hammond), **James** (Henry), **James** (P D), **Joyce** (James), **Kafka** (Franz), **Keane** (Molly), **Kesey** (Ken), **Laski** (Marghanita), **Lewis** (C S), **Lewis** (M G 'Monk'), **Lewis** (Sinclair), **Lewis** (Wyndham), **Lodge** (David), **Lowry** (Malcolm), **Marsh** (Dame Ngaio), **Milne** (A A), **Moore** (Brian), **Moore** (Thomas), **Munro** (H H), **O'Hara** (John), **Paton** (Alan), **Peake** (Mervyn), **Plath** (Sylvia), **Powys** (John), **Queen** (Ellery), **Reade** (Charles), **Sagan** (Françoise), **Scott** (Paul), **Scott** (Sir Walter), **Shute** (Nevil), **Simon** (Claude), **Smith** (Dodie), **Smith** (Stevie), **Smith** (Wilbur), **Spark** (Dame Muriel), **Staël** (Madame de), **Stowe** (Harriet Beecher), **Swift** (Graham), **Swift** (Jonathan), **Twain** (Mark), **Tyler** (Anne), **Verne** (Jules), **Vidal** (Gore), **Waugh** (Auberon), **Waugh** (Evelyn), **Wells** (H G), **White** (Patrick), **White**

(T H), **Wilde** (Oscar), **Wolfe** (Thomas Clayton), **Wolfe** (Tom), **Woolf** (Virginia), **Yates** (Dornford), **Yonge** (Charlotte)

06 **Achebe** (Chinua), **Alcott** (Louisa May), **Aldiss** (Brian), **Ambler** (Eric), **Aragon** (Louis), **Archer** (Jeffrey), **Asimov** (Isaac), **Atwood** (Margaret), **Austen** (Jane), **Auster** (Paul), **Balzac** (Honoré de), **Barker** (Pat), **Barnes** (Julian), **Barrie** (Sir J M), **Bellow** (Saul), **Binchy** (Maeve), **Blixen** (Karen, Lady), **Blyton** (Enid), **Borges** (Jorge Luis), **Braine** (John), **Bratby** (John), **Brazil** (Angela), **Brontë** (Anne), **Brontë** (Charlotte), **Brontë** (Emily), **Bryson** (Bill), **Buchan** (John), **Bunyan** (John), **Burney** (Fanny), **Butler** (Samuel), **Capote** (Truman), **Carter** (Angela), **Cather** (Willa), **Chopin** (Kate), **Clancy** (Tom), **Clarke** (Arthur C), **Conrad** (Joseph), **Cooper** (James Fenimore), **Cooper** (Jilly), **Cronin** (A J), **Faulks** (Sebastian), **Fowles** (John), **France** (Anatole), **Fuller** (Margaret), **Gibbon** (Lewis Grassic), **Godden** (Rumer), **Godwin** (William), **Goethe** (Johann Wolfgang von), **Graham** (Winston), **Graves** (Robert), **Greene** (Graham), **Haddon** (Mark), **Hamsun** (Knut), **Heller** (Joseph), **Hilton** (James), **Holtby** (Winifred), **Hornby** (Nick), **Hughes** (Thomas), **Huxley** (Aldous), **Ibáñez** (Vicente Blasco), **Jensen** (Johannes V), **Jerome** (Jerome K), **Keller** (Gottfried), **Kelman** (James), **Laclos** (Pierre Choderlos de), **Larkin** (Philip), **Le Fanu** (Sheridan), **Lively** (Penelope), **London** (Jack), **Mailer** (Norman), **Malouf** (David), **McEwan** (Ian), **Miller** (Henry), **Morgan** (Charles), **Nesbit** (E), **O'Brien** (Edna), **O'Brien** (Flann), **Orwell** (George), **Porter** (Katherine Anne), **Powell** (Anthony), **Proulx** (E Annie), **Proust** (Marcel), **Rankin** (Ian), **Sapper**, **Sartre** (Jean-Paul), **Sayers** (Dorothy L), **Sewell** (Anna), **Sharpe** (Tom), **Singer** (Isaac Bashevis), **Steele** (Danielle), **Sterne** (Laurence), **Stoker** (Bram), **Storey** (David), **Tagore** (Rabindranath), **Thomas** (Dylan), **Traven** (B), **Undset** (Sigrid), **Updike** (John), **Walker** (Alice), **Warner** (Marina), **Warren** (Robert Penn), **Weldon** (Fay), **Wesley** (Mary), **Wilder** (Thornton), **Wilson** (Sir Angus), **Wright** (Richard)

07 **Ackroyd** (Peter), **Aksakov** (Sergei), **Angelou** (Maya), **Arrabal** (Fernando), **Baldwin** (James), **Ballard** (J G), **Beckett** (Samuel), **Bennett** (Arnold), **Bentine** (Michael), **Burgess** (Anthony), **Burnett** (Frances Hodgson), **Calvino** (Italo), **Canetti** (Elias), **Carroll** (Lewis), **Chatwin** (Bruce), **Chekhov** (Anton), **Clavell** (James), **Cleland** (John), **Cocteau** (Jean), **Coetzee** (J M), **Colette**, **Collins** (Wilkie), **Cookson** (Catherine), **Deledda** (Grazia), **Dickens** (Charles), **Diderot** (Denis), **Dineson** (Isaac), **Douglas** (Norman), **Drabble** (Margaret), **Durrell** (Gerald), **Durrell** (Lawrence), **Fleming** (Ian), **Forster** (E M), **Forster** (Margaret), **Forsyth** (Frederick), **Francis** (Dick), **Gaskell** (Mrs Elizabeth), **Gautier** (Théophile), **Gibbons** (Stella), **Gissing** (George), **Golding** (William), **Grahame** (Kenneth), **Grisham** (John), **Haggard** (Sir H Rider), **Hammett** (Dashiell), **Hartley** (L P), **Kerouac** (Jack), **Kipling** (Rudyard), **Kundera** (Milan), **Lardner** (Ring), **Laxness** (Halldór), **Le Carré** (John), **Lehmann** (Rosamond), **Lessing** (Doris), **Maclean** (Alistair), **Mahfouz** (Naguib), **Malamud** (Bernard), **Malraux** (André), **Manning** (Olivia), **Manzoni** (Alessandro), **Marryat** (Captain Frederick), **Maugham** (W Somerset), **Mauriac** (François), **Mérimée** (Prosper), **Mishima** (Yukio), **Mitford** (Nancy), **Moravia** (Alberto), **Murdoch** (Dame Iris), **Nabokov** (Vladimir), **Naipaul** (V S), **Peacock** (Thomas Love), **Prévost** (l'Abbé), **Pullman** (Philip), **Pushkin** (Alexander), **Pynchon** (Thomas), **Ransome** (Arthur), **Raphael** (Frederic), **Renault** (Mary), **Rendell** (Ruth), **Richler** (Mordecai), **Robbins** (Harold), **Rolland** (Romain), **Rowling** (J K), **Rushdie** (Salman), **Sassoon** (Siegfried), **Shelley** (Mary), **Shields** (Carol), **Simenon** (Georges), **Sitwell** (Sir Osbert), **Soyinka** (Wole), **Spender** (Sir Stephen), **Surtees** (Robert Smith), **Theroux** (Paul), **Tolkien** (J R R), **Tolstoy** (Leo, Count), **Tremain** (Rose), **Wallace** (Lewis), **Walpole** (Sir Hugh), **Wharton** (Edith), **Wyndham** (John)

08 **Andersen** (Hans Christian), **Apuleius** (Lucius), **Asturias** (Miguel), **Barbusse** (Henri), **Beckford** (William Thomas), **Beerbohm** (Sir Max), **Björnson** (Björnstjerne), **Bradbury** (Malcolm), **Bradbury** (Ray), **Bradford** (Barbara Taylor), **Brittain** (Vera), **Brookner** (Anita), **Bulgakov** (Mikhail), **Caldwell** (Erskine), **Cartland** (Barbara), **Chandler** (Raymond), **Christie** (Dame Agatha), **Constant** (Benjamin), **Cornwell** (Patricia), **Crompton** (Richmal), **Day-Lewis** (Cecil), **Deighton** (Len), **De La Mare** (Walter), **Disraeli** (Benjamin), **Donleavy** (J P), **Faulkner** (William), **Fielding** (Henry), **Flaubert** (Gustave), **Forester** (C S), **Francome** (John), **Goncourt** (Edmond de), **Gordimer** (Nadine), **Hochhuth** (Rolf), **Huysmans** (J K), **Ishiguro** (Kazuo), **Jhabvala** (Ruth Prawer), **Kawabata** (Yasunari), **Keneally** (Thomas), **Kingsley** (Charles), **Koestler** (Arthur), **Lagerlöf** (Selma), **Lawrence** (D H), **Lockhart** (John Gibson), **Macaulay** (Dame Rose), **McCarthy** (Mary), **Melville** (Herman), **Meredith** (George), **Michener** (James A), **Milligan** (Spike), **Mitchell** (Margaret), **Morrison** (Toni), **Mortimer** (John), **Murasaki** (Shikibu), **Oliphant** (Margaret), **Ondaatje** (Michael), **Remarque** (Erich Maria), **Rousseau** (Jean Jacques), **Salinger** (J D), **Sillitoe** (Alan), **Sinclair** (Upton), **Smollett** (Tobias), **Spillane** (Mickey), **Stendhal**, **Tanizaki** (Junichiro), **Trollope** (Anthony), **Trollope** (Joanna), **Turgenev** (Ivan), **Voltaire**, **Vonnegut** (Kurt, Junior)

09 **Allingham** (Margery), **Bernières** (Louis de), **Bleasdale** (Alan), **Burroughs** (Edgar Rice), **Burroughs** (William S), **Cervantes** (Miguel de), **Charteris** (Leslie), **Chatterji** (Bankim), **D'Annunzio** (Gabriele), **Delafield** (E M), **De La Roche** (Mazo), **De Quincey** (Thomas), **Dos Passos** (John), **Du Maurier** (Dame Daphne), **Du Maurier** (George), **Edgeworth** (Maria), **Gerhardie** (William), **Goldsmith** (Oliver), **Greenwood** (Walter), **Grossmith** (George), **Grossmith** (Weedon), **Guareschi** (Giovanni), **Hauptmann** (Gerhart), **Hawthorne** (Nathaniel), **Hemingway** (Ernest), **Highsmith** (Patricia), **Hölderlin** (Friedrich), **Hopkinson** (Sir Tom), **Isherwood** (Christopher), **Lampedusa** (Giuseppe Tomasi de), **Lermontov** (Mikhail), **Linklater** (Eric), **Llewellyn** (Richard), **Mackenzie** (Sir Compton), **Mankowitz** (Wolf), **Mansfield** (Katherine), **Marinetti** (Filippo Tommaso), **Masefield** (John), **McCullers** (Carson), **Mitchison** (Naomi), **Monsarrat** (Nicholas), **Pasternak** (Boris), **Pratchett** (Terry), **Priestley** (J B), **Radcliffe** (Ann), **Santayana** (George), **Sholokhov** (Mikhail), **Steinbeck** (John), **Stevenson** (Robert Louis), **Thackeray** (William Makepeace), **Wodehouse** (Sir P G)

10 **Bainbridge** (Beryl), **Ballantyne** (R M), **Chesterton** (G K), **De Beauvoir** (Simone), **Dostoevsky** (Fyodor), **Fairbairns** (Zoë), **Fitzgerald** (F Scott), **Galsworthy** (John), **Lagerkvist** (Pär), **Maupassant** (Guy de), **Pirandello** (Luigi), **Richardson** (Dorothy M), **Richardson** (Samuel), **Strindberg** (August), **Van der Post** (Sir Laurens), **Waterhouse** (Keith)

11 **Kazantzakis** (Nikos), **Sienkiewicz** (Henryk), **Vargas Llosa** (Mario)

12 **Quiller-Couch** (Sir Arthur), **Robbe-Grillet** (Alain), **Saint-Exupéry** (Antoine de), **Solzhenitsyn** (Aleksandr)

13 Alain-Fournier (Henri), García Márquez (Gabriel), Sackville-West (Vita)
14 Compton-Burnett (Dame Ivy)
15 Somerset Maugham (William)

See also **playwright**; **poet**

authoritarian
05 harsh, rigid, tough **06** despot, severe, strict, tyrant **08** absolute, autocrat, despotic, dictator, dogmatic **09** imperious, Orwellian **10** absolutist, autocratic, inflexible, oppressive, tyrannical, unyielding **11** dictatorial, doctrinaire, domineering, magisterial **12** totalitarian **14** disciplinarian

authoritarianism
06 Nazism **07** Fascism **09** autocracy, despotism **10** absolutism, oppression, repression **12** dictatorship **15** totalitarianism

authoritative
04 bold, true **05** crisp, sound, valid **07** factual, learned **08** accepted, accurate, approved, decisive, faithful, imposing, official, reliable, truthful **09** assertive, audacious, authentic, confident, masterful, scholarly **10** authorized, commanding, convincing, definitive, dependable, imperative, legitimate, sanctioned **11** cathedratic, magisterial, self-assured, trustworthy **13** self-confident, self-possessed **14** sure of yourself

authoritatively
06 boldly **08** reliably **09** factually **10** accurately, decisively, dependably, ex cathedra, faithfully **11** assertively, audaciously, confidently **12** convincingly, definitively **13** authentically **15** self-confidently

authority
03 bar **04** buff, mana, name, rule, sage, sway, them, they **05** adept, bible, clout, force, leave, power, right, say-so, state **06** expert, master, muscle, permit, pundit **07** command, consent, control, council, faculty, go-ahead, licence, prelacy, royalty, scepter, sceptre, scholar, Vatican, warrant **08** dominion, lordship, sanction, thumbs-up **09** influence, provostry, supremacy, vicariate **10** domination, fatherhood, government, green light, inquirendo, management, permission, specialist **11** bureaucracy, connoisseur, credentials, imperialism, landlordism, officialdom, prerogative, sovereignty **12** carte blanche, jurisdiction, professional, protectorate **13** authorization, establishment **14** administration, patria potestas **15** the powers that be

• **emblem of authority**
03 rod **04** vare, wand **05** sword **07** scepter, sceptre

• **post of authority**
04 seat

authorization
02 OK **04** okay, pass **05** leave, stamp **06** permit **07** consent, go-ahead, licence, mandate, warrant **08** approval, passport, retainer, sanction, thumbs-up, warranty **09** authority **10** commission, empowering, green light, permission, validation, warrantise **11** credentials, entitlement, procuratory **12** confirmation, ratification **13** accreditation

authorize
02 OK **03** let **04** okay **05** allow **06** enable, permit, ratify **07** approve, confirm, empower, entitle, licence, license, mandate, warrant **08** accredit, legalize, sanction, validate **09** consent to, make legal, privilege **10** commission **15** give authority to

authorized
05 legal, legit **06** lawful **08** approved, licensed, official **09** permitted, warranted **10** accredited, recognized **12** commissioned, under licence

autobahn
02 AB

autobiography
02 CV **05** diary **06** memoir **07** journal, memoirs **09** life story **15** story of your life

autocracy
07 fascism, tyranny **08** autarchy **09** despotism **10** absolutism **12** dictatorship **15** totalitarianism

autocrat
04 cham **06** Caesar, despot, Hitler, tyrant **08** dictator **10** absolutist, panjandrum **12** little Hitler, totalitarian **13** authoritarian

autocratic
08 absolute, despotic **09** autarchic, imperious **10** tyrannical **11** all-powerful, dictatorial, domineering, overbearing **12** totalitarian **13** authoritarian

autograph
04 mark, name, sign **07** endorse, initial **08** initials, monicker **09** signature **11** countersign, endorsement, inscription, put your mark **13** write your name

automatic
06 reflex **07** certain, natural, robotic, routine **08** knee-jerk, unmanned, unwilled **09** automated, necessary, Pavlovian **10** inevitable, mechanical, mechanized, programmed, push-button, self-acting, unthinking **11** inescapable, instinctive, involuntary, spontaneous, unavoidable, unconscious **12** computerized **14** self-activating, self-propelling, self-regulating, uncontrollable

See also **gun**

automatically
09 certainly, naturally, routinely **10** inevitably **11** inescapably, necessarily, robotically, unavoidably **12** mechanically, unthinkingly **13** instinctively, involuntarily, spontaneously, unconsciously **14** uncontrollably

automobile
03 car **05** motor **07** vehicle **08** motor car **12** motor vehicle

See also **car**

autonomous
04 free **09** sovereign **11** independent **13** self-directing, self-governing **15** self-determining

autonomy
07 autarky, freedom **08** free will, home rule, self-rule **11** sovereignty **12** independence **14** rangatiratanga, self-government **15** self-sufficiency

autopsy
08 necropsy **10** dissection, post-mortem

autumn
04 fall **07** back-end, harvest **08** leaf-fall

auxiliary
03 aid **05** extra, spare **06** aiding, backer, back-up, helper, second **07** helping, partner, reserve **09** accessory, adminicle, ancillary, assistant, assisting, emergency, secondary, supporter **10** additional, peripheral, subsidiary, substitute, supporting, supportive **11** subordinate **12** right-hand man **13** supplementary **14** right-hand woman **15** second-in-command

avail
03 dow, use **04** doff, vail **05** lower, serve, stead **06** accept, alight, draw on **07** bestead, prevail, succeed, utilize **08** exercise, resort to **09** make use of **15** take advantage of

• **to no avail**
06 in vain, vainly **11** fruitlessly **13** ineffectually **14** unsuccessfully, without success

available
02 on **04** free, open **05** handy, on tap, ready, to let **06** at hand, on hand, single, to hand, usable, vacant **07** not busy, untaken **09** at liberty **10** accessible, convenient, disposable, obtainable, procurable, unoccupied, up for grabs **11** contactable, forthcoming, off the shelf, within reach **12** up your sleeve **13** at your command **14** at your disposal

avalanche
04 wave **05** flood **06** deluge **07** barrage, cascade, lauwine, torrent **08** landslip, snowslip **09** landslide **10** inundation

avant-garde
06 far-out, modern, way-out **07** go-ahead **08** advanced, original **09** inventive **10** futuristic, innovative, innovatory, pioneering **11** progressive **12** contemporary, enterprising,

experimental **14** forward-looking, ground-breaking, unconventional

avarice
05 greed **06** misery **07** avidity
08 meanness **09** pleonexia, the gimmes **10** greediness
11 gourmandise, materialism, miserliness, selfishness
12 covetousness **15** acquisitiveness

avaricious
04 avid, gare, mean **06** greedy, grippy, sordid **07** griping, gripple, miserly
08 covetous, grasping **09** mercenary, rapacious **10** pleonectic **11** acquisitive
12 curmudgeonly

avatar *see* **incarnation**

avenge
05 repay, right, venge, wreak
06 punish **07** pay back, requite **09** get back at, retaliate, vindicate **11** get even with **14** get your own back, take revenge for

avenger
04 goel

avenue
02 Av **03** ave, way **04** line, road, walk
05 allée, corso, drive, grove, vista
06 dromos, method, midway, scheme, street **07** Madison, passage
08 approach, broadway **09** boulevard
10 cradlewalk **12** thoroughfare
13 modus operandi **14** course of action

aver
04 avow **05** state **06** affirm, attest, cattle **07** confirm, declare **08** maintain
09 make known **11** possessions

average
02 av **03** ave, par, run **04** fair, mean, mode, norm, rule, so-so **05** usual
06 centre, common, medial, median, medium, middle, Nikkei, normal
07 regular, routine, typical **08** Dow-Jones, everyday, mediocre, middling, mid-point, moderate, ordinary, passable, standard **09** tolerable **10** not much cop **11** indifferent, not up to much **12** intermediate, run-of-the-mill, satisfactory **13** no great shakes, unexceptional **14** common-or-garden, fair to middling, nothing special **15** undistinguished
• **on average**
06 mainly, mostly **07** as a rule, chiefly, usually **08** normally **09** generally, in the main, routinely, typically **10** by and large, on the whole, ordinarily

averse
05 loath **07** hostile, opposed
09 reluctant, unwilling **10** indisposed
11 disinclined, ill-disposed
12 antagonistic, antipathetic, unfavourable

aversion
04 hate **06** hatred, horror, phobia
07 disgust, dislike **08** distaste, loathing
09 antipathy, hostility, repulsion, revulsion **10** abhorrence, antagonism, opposition, reluctance, repugnance
11 abomination, detestation
13 unwillingness **14** disinclination
See also **phobia**

avert
03 wry **04** stop **05** avoid, evade, parry
07 deflect, fend off, forfend, head off, obviate, prevent, ward off **08** preclude, stave off, turn away **09** forestall, frustrate, turn aside

aviary
06 volary

aviation
06 flight, flying **11** aeronautics

Aviation-related terms include:

04 dive, drag, flap, taxi
05 fly-by, pilot, plane, prang
06 airway, hangar, runway, thrust
07 airline, air miss, airport, airship, captain, console, fly-past, landing, lift-off, spoiler, take-off
08 aircraft, airfield, airplane, airspace, airstrip, altitude, black box, nose dive, subsonic, windsock, wingspan
09 aeroplane, aerospace, crash dive, fixed-wing, fly-by-wire, jetstream, overshoot, parachute, sonic boom, test pilot, touchdown
10 chocks away, flight crew, Mach number, solo flight, supersonic, test flight, undershoot
11 ground speed, loop-the-loop, night-flying, vapour trail
12 control tower, crash-landing, landing strip, maiden flight, sound barrier
13 ground control, jet propulsion
14 automatic pilot, flight recorder, holding pattern

aviator
05 flyer, pilot **06** airman **08** airwoman
12 aircraftsman **14** aircraftswoman

Aviators include:

04 **Byrd** (Richard Evelyn), **Rust** (Mathias), **Udet** (Ernst)
05 **Bader** (Sir Douglas), **Balbo** (Italo, Count), **Brown** (Sir Arthur Whitten), **Johns** (Captain W E), **Smith** (Sir Ross)
06 **Alcock** (Sir John), **Cessna** (Clyde), **Gibson** (Guy), **Harris** (Sir Arthur 'Bomber'), **Hughes** (Howard), **Nobile** (Umberto), **Wright** (Orville), **Wright** (Wilbur), **Yeager** (Chuck)
07 **Bennett** (Floyd), **Blériot** (Louis), **Branson** (Richard), **Cochran** (Jacqueline), **Dornier** (Claudius), **Douglas** (Donald Wills), **Earhart** (Amelia), **Fossett** (Steve), **Giffard** (Henri), **Goering** (Hermann), **Hinkler** (Bert), **Johnson** (Amy), **Korolev** (Sergei), **Piccard** (Auguste), **Sopwith** (Sir Thomas)
08 **Brabazon** (John, Lord), **Cheshire** (Leonard, Lord), **Zeppelin** (Count Ferdinand von)
09 **Blanchard** (Jean Pierre), **Lindbergh** (Charles), **McDonnell** (James Smith)
10 **Lindstrand** (Per), **Richthofen** (Manfred, Baron von)
11 **Montgolfier** (Jacques), **Montgolfier** (Joseph)
12 **Saint-Exupéry** (Antoine de)
13 **Messerschmitt** (Willy)

avid
03 mad **04** keen **05** crazy, eager, great
06 ardent, greedy, hungry **07** athirst, devoted, earnest, fervent, intense, thirsty, zealous **08** covetous, grasping, ravenous **09** dedicated, fanatical
10 insatiable, passionate
12 enthusiastic

avidly
05 madly **06** keenly **07** eagerly
08 ardently, greedily, hungrily
09 devotedly, earnestly, fervently, intensely, thirstily, zealously
10 covetously, insatiably, ravenously
11 fanatically **12** passionately

avocado
08 aguacate **09** guacamole
13 alligator pear

avocet
07 awlbird, scooper

avoid
03 fly **04** balk, duck, miss, shun
05 avert, dodge, elude, evade, evite, hedge, shirk **06** bypass, escape, eschew **07** decline, evitate, forbear, prevent **08** get out of, get round, sidestep **09** give a miss **10** circumvent
11 abstain from, make a detour, refrain from, run away from, shy away from
12 hold back from, keep away from, stay away from, steer clear of

avoidable
08 eludible, evitable **09** avertible, escapable, stoppable **11** preventable

avow
03 vow **04** aver **05** admit, state, swear
06 assert, attest, avouch **07** confess, declare, profess **08** maintain
11 acknowledge

avowed
04 open **05** overt, sworn **07** confest
08 admitted, declared **09** barefaced, confessed, professed **10** professing
12 acknowledged **13** self-confessed
14 self-proclaimed

await
04 bide, stay **05** tarry **06** expect, remain **07** hope for, look for, wait for
10 anticipate **12** be in store for, lie in wait for **13** look forward to

awake
04 stir, wake **05** abray, alert, alive, aware, rouse, waken **06** abrade, abraid, arouse, awaken, wake up
07 aroused, mindful, wakeful
08 stirring, vigilant, watchful
09 attentive, conscious, observant, sensitive, wide awake **12** appreciative

awaken
04 stir, wake **05** awake, rouse, waken
06 abraid, excite, wake up **07** inspire

08 engender, generate 09 stimulate 11 disentrance 14 cause to realize

awakening
05 birth 06 waking 07 arousal, awaking, revival, rousing 08 wakening 09 animating 10 activation, enlivening 11 reanimating, revivifying, stimulation 12 vivification

award
03 cup 04 aret, gift, give, gong 05 allot, allow, arett, endow, grant, medal, order, prize 06 accord, addeem, addoom, adward, assign, bestow, confer, modify, reward, trophy 07 adjudge, bursary, honours, payment, present, rosette 08 accolade, allocate, bestowal, citation, decision, decorate, dispense 09 allotment, allowance, apportion, conferral, determine, endowment, judgement 10 adjudicate, decoration, distribute, palatinate, settlement, subvention 11 certificate, scholarship 12 adjudication, commendation, dispensation, presentation

Awards and prizes include:

02 CH, MM, OM
03 CBE, OBE
04 Brit, Emmy, Tony
05 Bafta, César, Nobel, Oscar
06 Booker, Grammy, Orange, Turner
07 Academy, Olivier
08 Palme d'Or, Pulitzer, Stirling
09 Grand Jury, Grand Prix, Man Booker, Templeton
10 Golden Bear, Golden Palm
11 Fields Medal, Golden Globe
12 Prix Goncourt
13 Whitbread Book

See also **honour**; **military**

aware
03 hip 05 alert, awake, sharp 06 shrewd, sussed 07 alive to, clued up, heedful, knowing, mindful 08 apprised, familiar, informed, sensible, sentient, vigilant 09 attentive, au courant, cognizant, conscient, conscious, in the know, observant, on the ball, sensitive 10 acquainted, conversant 11 enlightened, recognizant 12 appreciative 13 knowledgeable
• **aware of**
04 on to
• **be aware of**
03 ken 04 feel, know

awareness
03 sus 04 suss 05 grasp 06 vision 07 insight, samadhi 09 knowledge 10 cognizance, perception 11 familiarity, panesthesia, recognition, sensitivity 12 acquaintance, appreciation, panaesthesia 13 consciousness, sensitiveness, understanding

awash
04 full 05 alive 06 packed, soaked 07 flooded, replete, teeming 08 crawling, drenched, swarming 09 inundated, saturated, submerged

away
◇ *anagram indicator*
02 by 03 far, fro, off, out 04 from 05 apart, aside, hence 06 abroad, absent 08 from here 09 elsewhere, from there, not at home, not at work, on holiday 10 on vacation 11 at a distance

awe
04 fear 05 dread 06 honour, terror, wonder 07 respect 09 amazement, reverence 10 admiration, veneration, wonderment 12 apprehension, astonishment, stupefaction

awed
06 amazed, solemn 07 fearful, stunned 09 awe-struck 10 astonished 11 reverential 12 lost for words

awe-inspiring
06 moving, solemn 07 amazing, awesome, exalted, sublime 08 daunting, dazzling, fearsome, imposing, majestic, numinous, striking, stunning 09 wonderful 10 formidable, impressive, stupefying, stupendous 11 astonishing, magnificent, spectacular 12 breathtaking, intimidating, mind-boggling, overwhelming

awesome
07 amazing 08 daunting, stunning 10 formidable, impressive 11 astonishing, jaw-dropping, spectacular 12 breathtaking, intimidating, mind-boggling, overwhelming 13 extraordinary

awestruck
04 awed 06 amazed 09 awe-struck, impressed 10 astonished 12 lost for words

awful
◇ *anagram indicator*
03 ill 04 crap, dire, naff, sick 05 lousy, nasty, pants, rough, seedy, spewy 06 crummy, horrid, in pain, poorly, unwell 07 abysmal, fearful, ghastly, heinous, the pits 08 alarming, dreadful, gruesome, horrible, horrific, inferior, pathetic, shocking, terrible, very poor 09 appalling, atrocious, frightful, third-rate, washed out 10 disgusting, horrifying, inadequate, second-rate, unpleasant 11 distressing 14 a load of rubbish, unsatisfactory 15 under the weather

awfully
◇ *anagram indicator*
04 very 06 deeply, really 07 greatly 08 terribly 09 extremely, immensely 10 absolutely, dreadfully, remarkably 12 particularly, tremendously, unbelievably

awhile
10 for a moment 11 for some time 13 for a short time

awkward
◇ *anagram indicator*
03 shy 04 rude 05 blate, gawky, inept, nasty 06 clumsy, clunky, fiddly, gauche, rustic, thumby, touchy, tricky, ungain 07 bashful, boorish, cubbish, loutish, prickly, spastic, stroppy, uncouth 08 annoying, bungling, clownish, delicate, handless, inexpert, lubberly, stubborn, ungainly, untoward, unwieldy 09 all thumbs, difficult, graceless, ham-fisted, ill at ease, inelegant, irritable, maladroit, obstinate, unskilful 10 cumbersome, left-handed, perplexing, ungraceful, unpleasant 11 disobliging, embarrassed, heavy-handed, obstructive, problematic, troublesome 12 bloody-minded, embarrassing, inconvenient 13 chuckle-headed, oversensitive, uncomfortable, unco-operative, unco-ordinated 15 unaccommodating

awkwardly
◇ *anagram indicator*
05 shyly 07 ineptly 08 clumsily, uneasily, ungainly 09 bashfully 10 inexpertly 11 gracelessly, ham-fistedly, inelegantly, maladroitly, unskilfully 12 ungracefully 13 heavy-handedly, uncomfortably

awkwardness
09 confusion, gawkiness, inaptness 10 clumsiness, inaptitude, inelegance, maladdress, uneasiness 11 bashfulness 12 discomfiture, ungainliness 13 embarrassment, gracelessness, left-handiness 15 heavy-handedness

awl
04 brog, prod, stob 05 elsin 06 elshin

awn
05 beard

awning
04 tilt 05 blind, cover, shade 06 canopy 07 shelter 08 covering, shamiana, sunblind, sunshade, velarium 09 shamianah

awry
◇ *anagram indicator*
03 cam, kam 04 skew 05 aglee, agley, amiss, askew, kamme, tipsy, wonky, wrong 06 skivie, uneven 07 askance, athwart, crooked, haywire, oblique, tortive, twisted 08 cockeyed 09 off-centre, skew-whiff 10 misaligned, out of joint 12 asymmetrical, by transverse

axe
03 cut, hew 04 bill, celt, chop, fell, fire, sack 05 split 06 cancel, cleave, guitar, labrys, piolet, remove, sparth 07 chopper, cleaver, cut down, dismiss, gisarme, halberd, hatchet, sparthe, twibill 08 get rid of, palstaff, palstave, partisan, throw out, tomahawk, withdraw 09 battle-axe, discharge, eliminate, saxophone, terminate 11 coup de poing, discontinue, thunderbolt 12 Jeddart staff
• **get the axe**
10 get the boot, get the chop, get the sack 11 be cancelled

axiom
02 ax **05** adage, maxim, truth **06** byword, dictum, truism **07** precept **08** aphorism, petition **09** postulate, principle **11** fundamental

axiomatic
05 given **06** gnomic **07** assumed, certain, granted **08** accepted, manifest **10** aphoristic, proverbial, understood **11** fundamental, indubitable, presupposed, self-evident **12** unquestioned **14** apophthegmatic, unquestionable

axis
01 X, Y, Z **03** cob **04** axle **05** henge, hinge, pivot **06** chital, rachis **07** rhachis **08** backbone, modiolus, vertical **10** centre-line, horizontal **13** macrodiagonal **14** brachydiagonal

• end of axis
04 pole

axle
03 pin, rod **04** axis **05** pivot, shaft, truck **07** mandrel, mandril, spindle **11** paddle-shaft

Azerbaijan
02 AZ **03** AZE

azure
04 Saxe **07** sky-blue **08** cerulean, pale blue **09** light blue **11** nattier blue **13** Cambridge blue

B

B
04 beta **05** bravo

babble
03 gab, jaw **05** babel, prate **06** burble, cackle, gabble, gibber, gurgle, hubbub, jabber, jawing, mumble, murmur, mutter, waffle, witter **07** blabber, brabble, chatter, clamour, prattle, twaddle, twattle **08** rabbit on **09** gibberish, wittering **10** tongue-work **12** bibble-babble

babe
03 sis, tot **04** baby **05** child **06** infant **07** newborn, tiny tot **08** suckling **10** babe in arms **11** newborn baby

babel
03 din **05** chaos **06** babble, bedlam, hubbub, tumult, uproar **07** clamour, turmoil **08** disorder **09** commotion, confusion **10** hullabaloo **11** pandemonium

baboon
05 drill **06** chacma, dog-ape, gelada **08** mandrill **09** hamadryad **12** Cynocephalus

baby
03 bub, sis, tot, wee **04** babe, dear, love, mini, mite, tiny **05** bairn, bubby, child, dwarf, honey, small, sprog, teeny **06** infant, little, midget, minute **07** darling, dearest, neonate, newborn, papoose, sweetie, tiny tot, toddler **08** killcrop, pint-size, suckling **09** miniature, pint-sized **10** diminutive, small-scale, sweetheart **11** newborn baby

babyish
04 baby, soft **05** naive, silly, sissy, young **07** foolish, puerile **08** childish, immature, juvenile **09** infantile

Babylonian *see* **god, goddess**

bacchanalian
• **bacchanalian expression**
04 euoi, evoe, upsy **05** evhoe, evohe, upsee, upsey

Bacchus
08 Dionysus

bachelor
01 B **02** BA **04** Bach **05** batch

bacillus
02 TB **03** bcg **07** anthrax **08** coliform **11** micrococcus

back
◇ *reversal indicator*
◇ *tail selection indicator*
03 aft, ago, aid, bet, bid, end, off **04** abet, ante, away, help, hind, past, rear, risk, tail **05** boost, other, spine, stake, stern, wager **06** assist, before, behind, bygone, chance, dorsum, far end, favour, former, gamble, rachis, recede, recoil, retire, second, tergum **07** bolster, confirm, earlier, elapsed, endorse, finance, promote, rear end, regress, retreat, reverse, sponsor, support, sustain, tail end, venture **08** advocate, back away, backbone, backside, be behind, champion, hindmost, hind part, obsolete, outdated, previous, sanction, side with, withdraw **09** backtrack, backwards, encourage, get behind, other side, out of date, posterior, speculate, subsidize, to the rear **10** previously, underwrite **11** countenance, countersign, go backwards, reverse side **12** hindquarters **13** move backwards

• **back and forth**
◇ *palindrome indicator*

• **back away**
06 recede, recoil **07** retreat **08** draw back, fall back, move back, step back, withdraw **10** give ground

• **back down**
05 yield **06** give in, submit **07** abandon, concede, retreat **08** withdraw **09** back-pedal, backtrack, climb down, surrender

• **back out**
◇ *reversal indicator*
06 cancel, cry off, give up, recant, resign, resile **07** abandon, call off, pull out, retreat **08** crawfish, go back on, withdraw **10** chicken out **11** get cold feet

• **back up**
03 aid **04** abet **06** assist, second, soothe, verify **07** bear out, bolster, confirm, endorse, reserve, stand by, stand to, support **08** champion, validate **09** reinforce **11** corroborate **12** substantiate

• **behind your back**
05 slyly **08** covertly, secretly, sneakily **09** furtively **11** deceitfully **15** surreptitiously

• **turn your back on**
04 quit **05** leave **06** ignore, reject **07** abandon, exclude **08** throw out **09** repudiate **15** wash your hands of

backbiting
05 abuse, catty, libel, slurs, spite **06** bitchy, gossip, malice **07** abusive, calumny, cattish, insults, slander **08** spiteful **09** aspersion, cattiness, criticism, libellous, malicious, vilifying **10** bitchiness, defamation, detraction, revilement, rubbishing, slanderous **11** denigration, disparaging, mud-slinging, slagging off **12** back-wounding, spitefulness, vilification, vituperation **13** disparagement

backbone
04 core, grit, guts **05** basis, chine, nerve, pluck, power, spine **06** bottle, mettle **07** courage, nucleus, resolve, stamina, support **08** firmness, mainstay, strength, tenacity **09** character, toughness, vertebrae, willpower **10** foundation, resolution **11** cornerstone **12** spinal column, vertebration **13** determination, steadfastness **15** vertebral column

backbreaking
04 hard **05** heavy **07** arduous, killing, onerous **08** crushing, grueling **09** gruelling, laborious, punishing, strenuous **10** exhausting

backchat
03 lip **04** face **05** cheek, mouth, nerve, snash **08** back talk, repartee, rudeness **09** brass neck, cross-talk, impudence, insolence, sauciness **12** impertinence

backer
05 angel **06** friend, funder, patron, second **07** sponsor **08** advocate, champion, investor, promoter, seconder, stickler **09** supporter **10** benefactor, subscriber, subsidizer, well-wisher **11** underwriter **12** bottle-holder

backfire
◇ *reversal indicator*
04 fail, flop **06** blow up, recoil **07** explode, misfire, rebound **08** detonate, miscarry, ricochet **09** boomerang, discharge **10** strike back **12** defeat itself **14** score an own goal **15** be self-defeating, come home to roost

backgammon
08 tick-tack, tric-trac, verquere **10** trick-track

background
04 fond **05** field, scene **06** canvas, family, milieu, record, status **07** context, culture, factors, history, origins, setting **08** backdrop, breeding, surround **09** backcloth, cyclorama, education, framework, grounding, tradition **10** experience, influences, upbringing **11** credentials, environment, preparation **12** surroundings **13** circumstances **14** qualifications, social standing

backhanded
06 ironic **07** awkward, dubious, oblique, reverse **08** indirect, sardonic, two-edged **09** ambiguous, equivocal, insincere, sarcastic **11** double-edged

backing
◇ *reversal indicator*
03 aid **04** help, vamp **05** funds, grant **06** backup, facing, favour, lining **07** finance, funding, helpers, padding, subsidy, support **08** advocacy, approval, sanction **09** obbligato, patronage, promotion, seconding **10** assistance, stiffening **11** championing, co-operation, endorsement, interlining, sponsorship **12** commendation, moral support **13** accompaniment, encouragement, reinforcement

backlash
06 recoil **08** backfire, kickback, reaction, reprisal, response **09** boomerang **11** retaliation **12** repercussion **13** counteraction

backlog
04 heap, pile **05** hoard, stock **06** excess, supply **07** reserve **08** mountain, reserves **09** resources **12** accumulation

back-pedal
05 yield **06** give in, renege, submit **07** abandon, concede, retract, retreat **08** do a U-turn, go back on, take back, withdraw **09** about-face, about-turn, backtrack, climb down, surrender **12** tergiversate **14** change your mind

backslide
◇ *reversal indicator*
03 sin **04** slip **05** lapse, stray **06** defect, desert, go back, renege, revert **07** default, regress, relapse **08** go astray, turn away **10** apostatize **12** tergiversate, turn your back **13** fall from grace

backslider
07 reneger **08** apostate, defector, deserter, recreant, renegade, turncoat **09** defaulter **10** recidivist **13** tergiversator

backsliding
◇ *reversal indicator*
05 lapse **07** relapse **08** apostasy **09** defection, desertion **10** defaulting, regression **14** tergiversation

backtrack
◇ *reversal indicator*
06 renege **08** do a U-turn, go back on, withdraw **09** back-pedal, climb down **12** tergiversate **14** change your mind

backup
03 aid **04** help **07** support **10** assistance **11** endorsement **12** confirmation **13** encouragement, reinforcement

backward
◇ *reversal indicator*
03 shy **04** hind, slow **05** timid **06** arrear, averse, behind **07** arriéré, bashful, reverse **08** hesitant, immature, rearward, retarded, reticent, retiring, wavering **09** reluctant, shrinking, subnormal, to the back, unwilling **10** hesitating, regressive, retrograde **11** undeveloped **13** retrogressive **14** underdeveloped **15** unsophisticated

backwards
◇ *reversal indicator*
05 aback, retro- **09** rearwards, to the back **12** regressively **15** retrogressively

backwash
04 flow, path, wake, wash **05** swell, waves **06** result **07** results **08** reaction **09** aftermath **11** after effect, consequence **12** after effects, consequences, repercussion **13** repercussions **14** reverberations

backwater
05 bogan, scrub **06** slough **08** Woop Woop **11** remote place **13** isolated place

backwoods
04 bush **05** brush **07** outback **08** backveld **09** backwater, the sticks **10** back-blocks, the boonies **11** remote place **12** back of beyond, the boondocks **13** isolated place **15** middle of nowhere

bacon
04 bard, spek **05** Roger, speck **06** collar, gammon, lardon, rasher **07** Francis, lardoon **08** forehock, pancetta

bacteria *see* **bacterium**

bacteriology

Bacteriologists include:

04 Cohn (Ferdinand), Gram (Hans), Koch (Robert), Roux (Émile)
05 Avery (Oswald), Smith (Theobald), Twort (Frederick)
06 Enders (John)
07 Behring (Emil von), Buchner (Hans), Ehrlich (Paul), Fleming (Sir Alexander), Löffler (Friedrich)
08 Calmette (Albert), Kitasato (Shibasaburo)
10 Wassermann (August von)

See also **biology**

bacterium
03 bug, rod **04** cell, germ **06** mother, packet, strain **07** microbe **08** parasite, serotype, superbug **13** micro-organism

Bacteria include:

04 MRSA
06 coccus, vibrio
07 Proteus
08 bacillus, listeria, Shigella, yersinia, zoogloea
09 Azobacter, peritrich, ray fungus, Rhizobium, spirillum, treponema, treponeme
10 gonococcus, Klebsiella, Leptospira, salmonella, saprophyte
11 acidophilus, Actinomyces, Azotobacter, Bacillaceae, clostridium, Escherichia, Pasteurella, Penicillium, pseudomonad, pseudomonas, spirochaete
12 enterococcus, helicobacter, pneumococcus, vinegar plant
13 campylobacter, Eubacteriales, fission fungus, lactobacillus, Mycobacterium, streptococcus
14 actinobacillus, Corynebacteria, staphylococcus, trichobacteria, Vibrio cholerae, Yersinia pestis
15 Escherichia coli, intestinal flora, sulphur bacteria

bad
◇ *anagram indicator*
03 hot, ill, mal-, off **04** blue, eale, edgy, evil, foul, high, hurt, lewd, mean, naff, nice, poor, poxy, ropy, rude, sick, sour, vile, wack, weak **05** acute, angry, awful, black, cross, crude, dirty, gammy, grave, gross, harsh, humpy, juicy, lousy, narky, nasty, onkus, pants, ratty, sorry, testy **06** aching, coarse, crabby, crummy, faulty, feisty, filthy, gallus, gloomy, grumpy, guilty, in pain, mouldy, poorly, putrid, rancid, rotten, severe, shirty, shoddy, sinful, smutty, snappy, spoilt, stingy, tetchy, unruly, unwell, vulgar, wicked **07** abusive, adverse, ashamed, bilious, bolshie, botched, corrupt, crabbed, decayed, gnarled, grouchy, harmful, hurtful, immoral, in a huff, in a sulk, injured, intense, naughty, obscene, painful, peppery, prickly, profane, raunchy, ruinous, serious, stroppy, tainted, the pits, unhappy, useless, wayward, wounded **08** choleric, contrite, criminal, critical, damaging, diseased, dreadful, hopeless, impaired, impolite, indecent, inferior, mediocre, pathetic, petulant, shameful, terrible **09** appalling, atrocious, crotchety, dangerous, defective, deficient, difficult, dishonest, dyspeptic, fractious, impatient, imperfect, injurious, insulting, irascible, irritable, offensive, querulous, reprobate, splenetic, third-rate, unhealthy **10** apologetic, capernoity, degenerate, deplorable, despondent, ill-behaved, inadequate, mismanaged, outrageous, putrescent, refractory, remorseful, second-rate, shamefaced, unpleasant, unsuitable **11** a load of crap, bad-tempered, blasphemous, carnaptious, deleterious, destructive, detrimental, disobedient, distressing, incompetent, ineffective, ineffectual, mischievous, substandard, thin-skinned, undesirable, unfortunate, unwholesome **12** badly-behaved, cantankerous, contaminated, disagreeable, discourteous, inauspicious, inconvenient, putrefactive, unacceptable, unfavourable **13** inappropriate, quick-tempered, reprehensible **14** a load of garbage, a load of rubbish,

uncontrollable, unsatisfactory
15 under the weather

• not bad

02 OK **04** fair, so-so **07** average
08 adequate, all right, passable
09 quite good, tolerable
10 acceptable, reasonable
12 satisfactory

badge

03 mon **04** blue, logo, mark, sign, star **05** brand, crest, eagle, patch, stamp, token, wings **06** button, device, emblem, ensign, rondel, shield, symbol
07 cockade, insigne, kikumon, rosette
08 episemon, insignia, numerals, vernicle **09** indicator, trademark
10 cognizance, escutcheon, indication
14 identification

badger

03 nag **04** bait, goad, ride **05** brock, bully, harry, hound, ratel **06** chivvy, go on at, harass, hassle, keep at, pester, plague, teledu **07** torment **08** ballyrag, bullyrag, keep on at **09** importune

• badger-like animal

05 ratel

• badgers

04 cete

badinage

05 borak, chaff **06** banter, humour
07 mockery, ribbing, teasing, waggery
08 dicacity, drollery, raillery, repartee, wordplay **10** jocularity, persiflage
11 give and take

badly

◇ *anagram indicator*

03 ill, mis- **06** deeply, evilly, poorly
07 acutely, awfully, cruelly, gravely, greatly, ineptly, wrongly **08** bitterly, faultily, severely, sinfully, terribly, unfairly, very much, wickedly
09 adversely, crucially, extremely, immorally, intensely, painfully, seriously, unhappily, uselessly **10** carelessly, criminally, critically, enormously, improperly, shamefully **11** appallingly, dangerously, defectively, desperately, dishonestly, exceedingly, imperfectly, incorrectly, negligently, offensively
12 inadequately, pathetically, tremendously, unacceptably, unfavourably **13** incompetently, ineffectually, unfortunately
14 unsuccessfully

• badly off

04 poor **05** needy **06** in need

bad-mannered

04 rude **05** crude **06** coarse
07 boorish, cubbish, ill-bred, loutish, uncivil, uncouth **08** churlish, impolite, insolent **10** ill-behaved, unmannerly
11 ill-mannered, insensitive **12** badly-behaved, discourteous

badminton

Badminton-related terms include:

03 net, set
04 bird, kill
05 clear, court, drive, flick, rally, serve, smash
06 racket
07 doubles, racquet, singles
08 drop shot, wood shot
11 shuttlecock
12 service court
13 underarm clear

badness

03 sin **04** evil **07** cruelty **08** foulness, vileness **09** depravity, nastiness
10 corruption, dishonesty, immorality, wickedness **12** shamefulness
14 unpleasantness

bad-tempered

04 edgy, mean **05** black, cross, humpy, narky, ratty, sulky, testy, vixen **06** crabby, feisty, gnarly, grumpy, shirty, snappy, stingy, tetchy **07** bilious, crabbed, crabbit, gnarled, grouchy, in a huff, in a mood, in a sulk, peppery, prickly, stroppy, vicious, vixenly **08** choleric, petulant, scratchy, vixenish
09 crotchety, dyspeptic, fractious, impatient, irascible, irritable, querulous, splenetic **10** capernoity, ill-natured, in a bad mood **11** carnaptious, curnaptious, dyspeptical, ill-humoured, thin-skinned
12 cantankerous **13** quick-tempered

baffle

◇ *anagram indicator*

03 bar, fox, get **04** daze, faze, foil, mate
05 block, check, elude, evade, stump, throw, upset **06** bemuse, defeat, fickle, hinder, puzzle, thwart **07** bumbaze, confuse, flummox, mystify, nonplus, perplex **08** bewilder, confound
09 bamboozle, dumbfound, frustrate
10 disconcert **13** bring to naught

baffling

◇ *anagram indicator*

07 amazing, cryptic **08** bemusing, puzzling **09** confusing, enigmatic
10 astounding, mysterious, perplexing, stupefying, surprising **11** bewildering
12 unfathomable **13** disconcerting, extraordinary

bag

◇ *containment indicator*

03 cod, get, net, pot, sac **04** gain, grab, kill, land, pock, poke, port, take, trap
05 catch, pouch, shoot **06** come by, corner, obtain, pocket, secure
07 acquire, capture, reserve
09 container **10** commandeer, receptacle **11** appropriate

Bags include:

03 bum, jag, kit, pod
04 caba, case, grip, hand, mail, pack, sack, tote, wash
05 bulse, cabas, dilli, dilly, ditty, money, purse, scrip
06 carpet, clutch, duffel, flight, sachel, saddle, tucker, valise, vanity, wallet
07 carrier, evening, holdall, satchel, shopper, utricle
08 backpack, carry-all, gripsack, knapsack, mailsack, meal-poke, pochette, reticule, rucksack, shopping, shoulder, suitcase, wineskin, woolpack
09 briefcase, fanny pack, Gladstone, haversack, moneybelt, overnight
10 sabretache
11 attaché-case, portmanteau

baggage

04 bags, gear, swag **05** cases
06 things **07** clobber, dunnage, effects, luggage **08** carriage, materiel
09 equipment, suitcases, viaticals
10 belongings **11** impedimenta
13 accoutrements, paraphernalia

See also **prostitute**

baggy

05 kneed, loose, roomy, slack
06 bulged, droopy, floppy, pouchy, sloppy **07** bulging, sagging
08 oversize **09** billowing, shapeless
10 ballooning, extra large, ill-fitting
12 loose-fitting

bagpipe

05 gaita, pipes **07** musette, piffero
08 dulcimer, zampogna
09 cornemuse **10** small-pipes, sourdeline **12** uillean pipes **13** uilleann pipes

• bagpipe composition

04 port **07** pibroch

Bahamas

02 BS **03** BHS

Bahrain

03 BHR, BRN

bail

04 bond, hoop **05** ladle **06** pledge, surety **07** caution, custody, replevy
08 security, warranty **09** guarantee
10 collateral **12** jurisdiction

• bail out

03 aid **04** help, quit, save **05** eject, ladle, scoop **06** assist, escape, get out, rescue **07** back out, finance, relieve, retreat **08** get clear, withdraw

bailiff

04 foud **05** agent, reeve **06** beagle
07 nut-hook **08** huissier **09** bum-baylie, hundreder, hundredor
10 philistine **11** land-steward
12 shoulder knot **15** shoulder-clapper

bait

03 dap, irk, lug **04** goad, lure, rage
05 annoy, bribe, decoy, harry, hound, leger, slate, snare, squid, taunt, tease, tie-up, yabby **06** badger, berley, burley, caplin, gentle, harass, hassle, ledger, lidger, needle, plague, yabbie
07 capelin, catworm, lugworm, provoke, ragworm, torment **08** irritate
09 anchoveta, angleworm, brandling, incentive, killifish, persecute, propeller, white worm **10** allurement, attraction, enticement, incitement, inducement, temptation **11** hellgramite, refreshment
12 hellgrammite, night crawler **15** give a hard time to

bake

◇ *anagram indicator*

03 dry **04** burn, cake, cook, fire, heat, shir **05** brown, parch, roast, shirr
06 harden, scorch, wither **07** shrivel

08 pot-roast 09 oven-roast, spit-roast 12 porcellanize

balance
03 bal, set 04 meet, rest, trim, tron 05 agree, level, Libra, match, pease, peaze, peise, peize, peyse, poise, pound, tally, weigh 06 adjust, aplomb, equate, equity, even up, excess, juggle, launce, make up, offset, parity, review, square, stasis, steady 07 compare, even out, librate, residue, surplus, weigh up 08 appraise, calmness, consider, equality, equalize, estimate, evaluate, evenness, symmetry 09 assurance, composure, equipoise, remainder, sangfroid, stability, stabilize 10 correspond, counteract, difference, equanimity, neutralize, set against, steadiness, uniformity 11 equilibrate, equilibrium, equivalence, self-control 12 counterweigh 13 compensate for, equiponderate 14 cool-headedness, correspondence, counterbalance, self-possession, unflappability 15 level-headedness
• **balance sheet**
02 bs
• **in the balance**
04 iffy 06 unsure 07 unknown 08 in the air 09 knife-edge, uncertain, undecided, unsettled 10 indefinite, touch and go 12 undetermined 13 unpredictable
• **on balance**
07 overall 08 all in all 09 generally 12 in conclusion

balanced
04 calm, even, fair 05 equal, level, sound 06 poised 07 assured, healthy, weighed 08 complete, sensible, straight, unbiased 09 equitable, impartial, objective 10 cool-headed, even-handed 11 level-headed, well-rounded 12 unprejudiced 13 dispassionate, self-possessed

balcony
04 gods 06 loggia 07 gallery, portico, sundeck, terrace, veranda 09 mezzanine 10 moucharaby 11 upper circle 14 quarter-gallery

bald
04 bare 05 bleak, blunt, naked, plain, stark 06 barren, direct, paltry, peeled, severe, simple, smooth 07 exposed, obvious, pollard, trivial 08 glabrate, glabrous, hairless, outright, straight, tonsured, treeless 09 depilated, downright, outspoken, unadorned, uncovered 10 bald-headed, forthright 11 bald as a coot, unambiguous, undisguised, unsheltered 15 straightforward

balderdash
03 rot 04 blah, bosh, bull, bunk, crap, guff, jazz 05 bilge, borak, hooey, trash, tripe 06 blague, bunkum, drivel, faddle, havers, hot air, piffle 07 baloney, eyewash, hogwash, rhubarb, rubbish, twaddle 08 blethers, bulldust, claptrap, cobblers, doggerel, malarkey, nonsense, tommyrot 09 bull's wool, gibberish, moonshine, poppycock 10 codswallop, galimatias 12 clamjamphrie

balding
04 bald 08 receding 09 thin on top 14 losing your hair

baldmoney
03 meu 07 spignel

baldness
07 fox-evil 08 alopecia, bareness, hair loss, psilosis 09 calvities, madarosis, starkness 12 glabrousness, hairlessness 14 alopecia areata, bald-headedness

bale
02 bl 04 lave, pack 05 ladle, seron, truss 06 bundle, parcel, seroon 07 confine, package 08 woolpack
• **bale out**
04 quit 06 escape, get out 07 back out, retreat 08 get clear, withdraw

baleful
04 evil 05 swart 06 deadly, malign, sullen, swarth 07 harmful, hurtful, malefic, noxious, ominous, painful, ruinous 08 menacing, mournful, sinister, venomous 09 injurious, malignant, sorrowful 10 lugubrious, malevolent, pernicious 11 destructive, threatening

balefully
09 harmfully, hurtfully 10 menacingly 11 dangerously 13 destructively, detrimentally, threateningly

balk, baulk
03 bar, hen, jib 04 chop, foil 05 avoid, check, demur, dodge, evade, reest, reist, shirk, stall 06 baffle, boggle, defeat, eschew, flinch, hinder, ignore, impede, pull up, recoil, refuse, resist, shrink, thwart 07 decline, prevent 08 hesitate, obstruct 09 discomfit, forestall, frustrate 10 counteract, disconcert 11 frustration 14 disappointment

ball
01 O 02 ba 03 cop, nur, orb 04 clew, clue, drop, knur, nurr, pill, shot, slug, tice 05 dance, fungo, globe, Jaffa, knurr, party 06 beamer, bullet, googly, pellet, soirée, sphere, strike, yorker 07 bouncer, globule, long hop, shooter, swinger 08 assembly, carnival, Chinaman, delivery, full toss, gazunder, leg break, off break 09 inswinger 10 masquerade, outswinger, projectile 11 daisy-cutter, dinner-dance 14 conglomeration
• **high ball**
03 lob
• **play ball**
07 go along, respond 09 co-operate, play along 11 collaborate, reciprocate, show willing
• **position of ball**
03 lie

ballad
03 jig 04 poem, song 05 carol, ditty, mento 06 shanty 07 ballant, calypso, romance 08 folk-song, singsong 09 cantilena 10 forebitter 12 Lillibullero

ballet
07 dancing 11 leg-business 13 ballet-dancing

See also **choreography**; **dance**; **dancer**

Ballets include:

05 Manon, Rodeo, Rooms
06 Apollo, Boléro, Carmen, Façade, Ondine, Onegin, Parade
07 Giselle, La Valse, Orpheus, Requiem
08 Coppélia, Les Noces, Nocturne, Swan Lake
09 Anastasia, Les Biches, Mayerling
10 Cinderella, Don Quixote, La Sylphide, Petroushka, Prince Igor, Pulcinella
11 Billy the Kid, Las Hermanas, The Firebird
12 Les Sylphides, Schéhérazade
13 Pineapple Poll, The Nutcracker
14 Daphnis et Chloé, Romeo and Juliet, The Prodigal Son
15 The Rite of Spring

Ballet-related terms include:

03 bar, pas
04 jeté, plié, posé, tutu
05 barre, battu
06 à terre, attack, ballon, chassé, écarté, en face, en l'air, pointe, school, splits
07 à pointe, bourrée, bras bas, ciseaux, company, danseur, en avant, fouetté, leotard, maillot, pointes, premier
08 attitude, batterie, cabriole, capriole, coryphée, couronne, danseuse, en pointe, ensemble, fish dive, glissade, première, stulchak
09 arabesque, ballerina, battement, cou de pied, elevation, entrechat, pas de chat, pas de deux, pas de seul, pirouette, point shoe, promenade, régisseur
10 ballet shoe, répétiteur
11 Laban system, ports de bras
12 ballet-dancer, ballet-master, choreography, labanotation
13 corps de ballet, five positions, sur les pointes
14 divertissement, maître de ballet, petit battement, premier danseur, prima ballerina
15 grande battement, principal dancer

balloon
03 bag 04 soar 05 belly, bulge, swell 06 billow, blow up, dilate, expand, rocket 07 distend, enlarge, fumetto, inflate, puff out 08 aerostat, escalate, snowball 09 dirigible, skyrocket 11 grow rapidly, montgolfier 12 ballon d'essai 15 increase rapidly

ballot
04 poll, vote 06 voting 07 polling 08 election 10 plebiscite, referendum
• **ballot-box**
03 urn

ballyhoo
04 fuss, hype, to-do **05** noise **06** hubbub, racket, tumult **07** build-up, clamour **09** agitation, commotion, hue and cry, kerfuffle, promotion, publicity **10** excitement, hullabaloo, propaganda **11** advertising, disturbance

balm
04 nard, tolu **05** cream, salve **06** balsam, lotion, relief **07** anodyne, bromide, comfort, unguent **08** curative, lenitive, ointment, sedative **09** calmative, emollient, opobalsam **10** palliative **11** consolation, embrocation, restorative

balmy
04 mild, soft, warm **06** gentle **07** clement, summery **08** pleasant, soothing **09** temperate

balsam
04 heal, Tolu **06** embalm **07** wood oil **09** impatiens, spikenard **13** noli-me-tangere

Balt
04 Esth, Lett

bamboozle
◇ *anagram indicator*
03 con **04** daze, dupe, fool, gull, rook **05** cheat, trick, upset **06** bemuse, diddle, puzzle **07** bumbaze, confuse, deceive, mystify, nonplus, perplex, swindle **08** bewilder, confound, hoodwink **09** dumbfound **10** disconcert **14** pull a fast one on

ban
03 bar **04** band, tabu, tapu, veto **05** black, curse, taboo **06** banish, censor, forbid, outlaw **07** abolish, boycott, embargo, exclude **08** disallow, outlawry, prohibit, restrict, stoppage, suppress **09** ostracize, proscribe, sanctions **10** banishment, censorship, disqualify, injunction, moratorium **11** prohibition, restriction, suppression **12** anathematize, condemnation, denunciation, interdiction, proclamation, proscription

banal
04 dull, flat **05** bland, corny, empty, inane, stale, stock, tired, trite, vapid **06** boring, old hat **07** cliché'd, humdrum, mundane, trivial **08** clichéed, cornball, everyday, ordinary, overused **09** hackneyed **10** threadbare, unoriginal **11** commonplace, nondescript, stereotyped, wearing thin **13** unimaginative

banality
06 cliché, truism **07** bromide, fatuity **08** cornball, dullness, vapidity **09** emptiness, inaneness, platitude, staleness, tiredness, triteness **10** prosaicism, triviality **11** commonplace, old chestnut **12** ordinariness **13** unoriginality

banana
08 plantain

bananas
◇ *anagram indicator*
03 mad **04** hand, Musa **05** bunch, crazy

• go bananas
04 flip **05** freak **08** freak out

band
02 CB **03** bar, rib, rim, tie **04** ally, belt, body, bond, club, cord, core, crew, fess, frog, gang, ging, herd, hoop, join, line, link, ring, sash, tape, team, teme, tire, tyre, welt, with, zona, zone **05** chain, crowd, fesse, flock, group, horde, merge, music, party, strap, strip, thong, troop, unite, withe **06** clique, fetter, gather, girdle, ribbon, streak, stripe, swathe, team up, throng **07** bandage, binding, company, manacle, shackle, society **08** ensemble, federate, ligature, pop group **09** affiliate, gathering, orchestra **10** amalgamate, close ranks, connection, contingent, join forces, music group **11** association, collaborate, consolidate **12** club together, musical group, pull together **13** stand together, stick together

See also **singer**

• raised band
03 rib

• twisted band
04 torc, with **05** withe **06** torque

bandage
01 T **04** bind, lint, wrap **05** cover, dress, gauze, spica **06** binder, bind up, swathe **07** Band-aid®, bandeau, plaster, scapula, swaddle **08** capeline, compress, dressing, ligature, Tubigrip® **09** capelline, suspensor **10** tourniquet **11** Elastoplast®

bandicoot
05 bilby **06** pig-rat **10** Malabar-rat

bandit
05 crook, thief **06** cowboy, gunman, mugger, outlaw, pirate, raider, robber **07** brigand **08** criminal, gangster, hijacker, marauder **09** buccaneer, desperado, plunderer, racketeer **10** highwayman

bandsman
04 wait

bandy
◇ *anagram indicator*
04 bent, pass, swap, toss **05** bowed, fight, fling, throw, trade **06** barter, curved, spread, strive **07** chaffer, crooked **08** exchange **09** bow-legged, misshapen **11** interchange, reciprocate

bane
03 woe **04** evil, harm, pest, ruin **05** curse, death, trial **06** blight, burden, misery, ordeal, plague, poison **07** scourge, torment, trouble **08** calamity, disaster, distress, downfall, mischief, nuisance, vexation **09** adversity, annoyance, bête noire **10** affliction, irritation, misfortune, pestilence **11** destruction **14** thorn in the side **15** thorn in the flesh

baneful
07 harmful, noxious, painful, ruinous **08** annoying **09** poisonous **10** disastrous, pernicious **11** destructive, distressing, troublesome **12** pestilential

bang
03 hit, pop, rap **04** bash, benj, blow, boom, bump, clap, dead, drum, echo, hard, peal, shot, slam, slap, sock, thud, wham **05** burst, clang, clash, crack, crash, knock, noise, pound, punch, right, smack, spang, stamp, thump, whack **06** blow up, hammer, report, strike, stroke, thwack, wallop **07** clatter, exactly, explode, noisily, resound, thunder **08** abruptly, bump into, cannabis, detonate, directly, headlong, slap-bang, straight, suddenly **09** collision, crash into, explosion, precisely **10** absolutely, detonation

banger
04 bomb, heap **05** crate **06** jalopy **07** clunker, jaloppy, sausage **09** tin lizzie

Bangladesh
02 BD **03** BGD

bangle
04 band, kara **06** anklet **07** circlet **08** bracelet, wristlet

banish
03 ban, bar **04** band, oust **05** debar, eject, evict, exile, expel **06** deport, dispel, forsay, outlaw, remove **07** abandon, cast out, discard, dismiss, exclude, foresay, shut out **08** dislodge, get rid of, relegate, send away, throw out **09** drive away, eliminate, eradicate, extradite, ostracize, rusticate, transport **10** disimagine, expatriate, repatriate **13** excommunicate

banishment
03 ban **05** exile **08** eviction, outlawry **09** exclusion, exilement, expulsion, ostracism **11** deportation, extradition **12** expatriation **14** transportation **15** excommunication

banisters
04 rail **07** railing **08** handrail **10** balustrade

bank
02 as, bk **03** bar, dam, row, tip **04** bink, brae, edge, fund, heap, keep, line, link, mass, pile, pool, rank, reef, rise, rive, save, side, sunk, tier, tilt **05** amass, array, bench, bluff, cache, drift, group, hoard, hurst, knoll, lay by, levee, mound, panel, pitch, ridge, shore, slant, slope, stack, stock, store, train **06** heap up, margin, pile up, rivage, save up, series, supply **07** deposit, hillock, incline, parados, pottery, rampart, reserve, savings, stack up **08** put aside, sequence, treasury **09** earthwork,

reservoir, stash away, stockpile **10** accumulate, depository, embankment, repository, succession **11** put together, savings bank **12** accumulation, clearing bank, finance house, merchant bank **14** finance company, high-street bank **15** building society

• **banking system**
04 giro

• **bank on**
05 bet on, trust **06** rely on **07** count on **08** depend on **09** bargain on, believe in **14** pin your hopes on

• **bank rate**
02 br

• **banks**
◇ *ends selection indicator*

• **bank up**
04 hele, hill

banker
05 gnome **06** shroff **07** Lombard **09** exchanger
See also **river**

banknote
03 fin **04** bill, note **05** fiver, scrip **06** flimsy, greeny, single, tenner, twenty **07** greenie, iron man, sawbuck **09** greenback **10** paper money **12** treasury note

bankrupt
04 bung, bust, duck, ruin **05** break, broke, spent **06** beggar, bereft, broken, debtor, dyvour, failed, folded, hard up, pauper, ruined **07** cripple, lacking, wanting, without **08** beggared, depleted, deprived, in the red, lame duck **09** deficient, destitute, exhausted, gone under, insolvent, penurious, sequester **10** impoverish, on the rocks, stony broke, trade-falne **11** impecunious, trade-fallen **12** impoverished, on your uppers **13** gone to the wall, in liquidation

bankruptcy
04 lack, ruin **05** smash **06** penury, stumer **07** beggary, dyvoury, failure **08** disaster **09** ruination **10** exhaustion, insolvency **11** Carey Street, liquidation **12** indebtedness **13** financial ruin, sequestration

• **to bankruptcy**
04 scat **05** skatt

banner
04 flag, sign **06** burgee, ensign, fanion, pennon **07** bandrol, colours, labarum, pennant, placard **08** banderol, bannerol, gonfalon, gumphion, standard, streamer, vexillum **09** banderole, bannerall, oriflamme

banquet
04 dine, meal **05** feast, party, treat **06** dinner, junket, spread **11** dinner party **13** entertainment

banter
03 kid, pun, rag, rib **04** jest, joke, josh, mock, quiz, rail **05** borak, borax, chaff, rally, roast, tease **06** deride, joking **07** jesting, kidding, mockery, ribbing **08** badinage, chaffing, derision, dicacity, raillery, repartee, ridicule, word play **09** make fun of **10** persiflage, pleasantry

Bantu
04 Hutu, Xosa, Zulu **05** Nguni, Sotho, Swazi, Tonga, Tutsi, Xhosa **06** Herero, Nyanja, Tswana **07** Basotho, Lingala, Sesotho, Swahili **08** Congoese **09** Congolese

baptism
05 debut **06** launch, naming **07** mersion **08** affusion **09** aspersion, beginning, immersion, launching **10** dedication, initiation, sprinkling **11** christening, parabaptism **12** inauguration, introduction, paedobaptism, purification

baptize
03 dip **04** call, name, term **05** admit, enrol, style, title **06** purify **07** cleanse, immerse, recruit **08** christen, initiate, sprinkle **09** introduce

bar
01 T, Z **03** ban, fen, fid, gad, inn, pub, rib, rod, zed, zee **04** bolt, cake, dive, howf, hunk, lock, lump, pole, rail, risp, rung, save, shet, shut, slab, slot, snug, spar, stop, swee, toll **05** block, check, chunk, court, debar, estop, grill, ingot, latch, lever, shaft, stake, stick, table, wedge **06** batten, bistro, boozer, but for, except, fasten, forbid, hinder, lounge, nugget, paling, saloon, secure, tavern **07** barrier, counsel, counter, exclude, lawyers, padlock, prevent, railing, suspend, taproom **08** blockade, drawback, hostelry, obstacle, obstruct, omitting, preclude, prohibit, restrain, snuggery, tribunal **09** advocates, apart from, aside from, barricade, brasserie, deterrent, except for, excepting, excluding, hindrance, lounge bar, stanchion **10** barristers, beer-parlor, crosspiece, disqualify, impediment **11** obstruction, public house **12** beverage room, watering-hole

barb
03 dig, mow **04** gibe, harl, herl, tang, trim **05** arrow, beard, fluke, point, prong, ramus, scorn, shave, sneer, spike, sting, thorn **06** insult, needle, rebuff **07** affront, bristle, killick, killock, prickle

Barbados
03 BDS, BRB

barbarian
03 Hun, oaf **04** boor, Goth, lout, wild **05** brute, crude, rough **06** coarse, savage, vandal, vulgar **07** brutish, loutish, ruffian, uncouth **08** hooligan **09** Hottentot, ignoramus **10** illiterate, philistine, tramontane, uncultured, wild person **11** Neanderthal, uncivilized **12** uncultivated **15** unsophisticated

barbaric
◇ *anagram indicator*
04 rude, wild **05** crude, cruel **06** brutal, coarse, fierce, savage, vulgar **07** bestial, brutish, foreign, inhuman, uncouth, vicious **08** ruthless **09** barbarous, ferocious, murderous, primitive **11** uncivilized

barbarism
07 cruelty **08** enormity, ferocity, rudeness, savagery, wildness **09** brutality, crudeness, vulgarity **10** bestiality, coarseness, corruption, fierceness, heathenism **11** brutishness, inhumanness, uncouthness, viciousness **12** ruthlessness **13** murderousness **15** uncivilizedness

barbarity
07 cruelty, outrage **08** atrocity, enormity, ferocity, savagery, wildness **09** brutality **10** inhumanity, savageness **11** brutishness, viciousness **12** ruthlessness **13** barbarousness

barbarous
◇ *anagram indicator*
04 rude, wild **05** crude, cruel, harsh, rough **06** brutal, fierce, Gothic, savage, vulgar **07** bestial, brutish, corrupt, inhuman, vicious **08** barbaric, ignorant, ruthless **09** barbarian, ferocious, heartless, murderous, primitive, unrefined **10** uncultured, unlettered **11** uncivilized, unscholarly **15** unsophisticated

barbecue
03 BBQ **04** bake, cook **05** braai, broil, brown, grill, roast **06** barbie **07** cookout, griddle, hibachi, stir-fry **09** spit-roast **10** braaivleis

barbed
04 acid **05** armed, catty, jaggy, nasty, snide, spiky, spiny **06** bitchy, hooked, jagged, spiked, tanged, thorny, unkind **07** bearded, caustic, cutting, hostile, hurtful, pointed, prickly, pronged, toothed **08** barbated, critical, spiteful, wounding **09** sarcastic

barber
04 Todd **05** shave, strap **06** Figaro, shaver, tonsor **07** scraper **11** hairdresser, Sweeney Todd

bard *see* **poet**

bare
04 bald, cold, hard, lewd, mere, nude, peel, pure, very **05** basic, bleak, clear, empty, naked, plain, sheer, stark, strip, utter **06** barren, expose, reveal, simple, unmask, unveil, vacant **07** denuded, display, exposed, lay bare, uncover, undress **08** absolute, complete, desolate, in the nip, in the raw, stripped, treeless, unclothe, unwooded, woodless **09** essential, in the buff, in the nude, in the scud, unadorned, unclothed, uncovered, undressed, very least **10** defoliated, no more than, stark-naked, unforested **11** unfurnished, unsheltered **13** with nothing on **15** straightforward

barefaced
04 bald, bold, open **05** brash, naked **06** arrant, avowed, brazen, patent **07** blatant, glaring, obvious **08** flagrant, impudent, insolent, manifest, palpable **09** audacious, bald-faced, beardless, shameless, unabashed **11** transparent, unconcealed, undisguised

barefooted
06 unshod **08** barefoot, shoeless **09** discalced

barely
04 just, only **05** scant **06** almost, hardly, openly, scrimp **07** halfway, nakedly, none too, plainly **08** narrowly, no sooner, only just, scarcely **10** by a whisker, explicitly **12** be a near thing, by a short head **13** be a close thing

bargain
02 go **03** buy **04** deal, pact, sell, snip, whiz **05** broke, cheap, steal, trade, truck, whizz **06** barter, broker, clinch, haggle, indent, market, pledge, settle, treaty **07** chaffer, cheapen, good buy, promise, traffic **08** beat down, cheap buy, contract, covenant, discount, giveaway, purchase, transact, wanworth **09** agreement, bon marché, concordat, negotiate, reduction **11** arrangement, negotiation, transaction **12** special offer **13** understanding, value for money

• **bargain for**
06 expect **07** foresee, imagine, include, look for, plan for **08** consider, contract, figure on, reckon on **10** anticipate **11** contemplate **13** be prepared for **15** take into account

• **into the bargain**
04 also **06** as well **07** besides **10** in addition **11** furthermore **12** additionally

bargaining
05 trade **06** barter, buying, dicker, outcry **07** chaffer, dealing, selling **08** dealings, haggling **09** bartering **11** negotiation, trafficking, transaction **12** horsetrading **14** wheeler-dealing

barge
◇ *anagram indicator*
03 hit **04** bump, keel, pram, push, rush, scow **05** barca, butty, casco, elbow, praam, press, shove, smash **06** galley, hopper, jostle, plough, push in, wherry **07** birlinn, budgero, collide, gabbard, gabbart, lighter, piragua, pirogue, pontoon **08** budgerow, flatboat, keelboat, periagua **09** Bucentaur, canal-boat, houseboat **10** narrowboat **11** galley-foist, push your way **12** force your way

• **barge in**
05 cut in **06** butt in **07** break in, burst in, intrude **09** gatecrash, interfere, interrupt

baritone
03 bar

barium
02 Ba

bark
03 bay, cry, tan, wow, yap **04** bass, bast, bawl, cork, hide, howl, husk, kina, peel, rind, skin, snap, tapa, waff, woof, yaff, yawp, yell, yelp **05** china, cough, crust, growl, quest, quill, quina, shell, shout, snarl, suber, tappa **06** bellow, bowwow, casing, cortex **07** cascara, encrust, pereira, thunder **08** calisaya, cinchona, cinnamon, covering, simaruba, tan balls **09** bull's wool, quebracho, sassafras, simarouba, xanthoxyl **10** cascarilla, integument, quercitron **11** slippery elm **13** cascara amarga **14** cascara sagrada

barking
◇ *anagram indicator*
03 bay, mad, odd **04** daft, nuts **05** barmy, batty, crazy, dippy, dotty, loony, loopy, nutty, potty **06** cuckoo, insane **07** bananas, bonkers **08** crackers **09** latration **10** off your nut, unbalanced **11** off your head **12** mad as a hatter, round the bend **13** off your rocker, round the twist **14** off your trolley

barley
04 bear, bere, bigg, malt **07** Hordeum

barmy
03 mad, odd **04** daft, nuts **05** batty, crazy, dippy, dotty, loony, loopy, nutty, silly **06** cuckoo, frothy, insane, stupid **07** foolish, idiotic **08** crackers **10** fermenting, off your nut, out to lunch, unbalanced **11** off your head **12** round the bend **13** off your rocker, round the twist **14** off your trolley

barn
06 grange **07** skipper

barometer
07 aneroid **09** barograph **10** statoscope **12** weather glass **13** sympiesometer

baron
01 B **02** Bn **04** lord, peer **05** mogul **06** bigwig, fat cat, tycoon **07** big shot, magnate **08** nobleman **09** big cheese, executive **10** aristocrat, Münchausen **12** entrepreneur **13** industrialist

baroness
04 lady, peer **07** baronne **10** aristocrat, noblewoman

baronet
02 Bt **04** Bart

baroque
◇ *anagram indicator*
04 bold **05** showy **06** florid, ornate, rococo **07** flowery **08** fanciful, vigorous **09** decorated, elaborate, exuberant, fantastic, grotesque, whimsical **10** convoluted, flamboyant **11** embellished, extravagant, overwrought **13** overdecorated, overelaborate **15** churrigueresque

barrack
03 boo **04** hiss, jeer **05** taunt **06** casern, heckle **07** caserne **09** interrupt, shout down

barracking
04 boos **07** hissing, jeering **08** heckling **12** interruption **13** interruptions

barracks
03 bks **04** camp, fort **06** billet, casern **07** lodging **08** garrison, quarters **10** encampment, glasshouse, guardhouse **11** gendarmerie **13** accommodation

barrage
03 dam **04** dyke, hail, mass, rain, wall **05** burst, flood, onset, salvo, storm **06** attack, deluge, shower, stream, volley **07** assault, barrier, battery, gunfire, torrent **08** shelling **09** abundance, barricade, broadside, cannonade, fusillade, onslaught, profusion **10** embankment **11** bombardment, obstruction

barrel
01 b **02** bl **03** bbl, but, keg, tub, tun **04** butt, cade, cask, drum, pipe, wood **05** pièce **06** clavie, firkin, runlet, tierce, tumble **07** oil drum, rundlet **08** hogshead **09** water-butt **10** Morris-tube

barren
03 dry **04** arid, dull, eild, flat, yeld, yell **05** addle, bleak, blunt, empty, gaunt, vapid, waste **06** desert, effete, meagre **07** hirstie, sterile, useless **08** desolate, infecund, teemless **09** childless, fruitless, infertile, pointless, unbearing, valueless **10** profitless, unfruitful, unprolific **11** purposeless, uninspiring, unrewarding **12** inhospitable, uncultivable, unproductive **13** uninformative, uninstructive, uninteresting

barrenness
06 dearth **07** aridity, dryness **08** dullness **09** emptiness, sterility **11** infecundity, infertility, uselessness **13** pointlessness **14** unfruitfulness

barricade
03 bar **04** shut **05** block, close, fence **06** defend **07** barrier, bulwark, close up, defence, fortify, protect, rampart, shut off **08** blockade, obstacle, obstruct, palisade, stockade **10** protection, strengthen **11** obstruction

Barrie
02 JM

barrier
03 bar, dam **04** bail, boom, doll, gate, ha-ha, wall **05** block, check, ditch, fence, hedge, rails, spina **06** haw-haw, hurdle **07** barrage, curtain, railing, rampart **08** blockade, boundary, bulkhead, division, drawback, frontier, handicap, obstacle, railings, stockade, tick gate, traverse, turnpike

09 barricade, enclosure, hindrance, inclosure, partition, restraint, ring-fence, roadblock **10** breakwater, difficulty, dingo fence, impediment, limitation, tariff wall **11** iron curtain, mental block, obstruction, restriction **12** glass ceiling **13** bamboo curtain, fortification, kangaroo fence **14** stumbling-block **15** cordon sanitaire, dingo-proof fence

barring
02 if **03** bar **06** except, unless **09** except for

barrister
02 KC, QC **03** Bar **04** silk **05** brief **06** lawyer **07** counsel, Rumpole **08** advocate, attorney, recorder, serjeant **09** counselor, solicitor **10** counsellor **12** King's Counsel **13** Queen's Counsel, serjeant-at-law
See also **lawyer**

barrow
03 how **04** cart, howe, tump **05** hurly, truck **07** tumulus **08** push-cart **11** horned cairn

bartender
06 barman **07** barkeep, barmaid **08** publican **09** barkeeper **10** mixologist

barter
04 chop, cope, coup, deal, sell, swap, swop **05** trade, truck **06** dicker, haggle, niffer **07** bargain, dealing, trading, traffic **08** exchange, haggling, swapping, truckage **09** negotiate **10** bargaining **11** negotiation, permutation, trafficking

basalt
04 trap, whin **05** wacke **07** diabase **08** basanite, traprock **09** toadstone, whinstone

base
01 e **02** HQ **03** bed, dog, key, low, ten **04** camp, core, evil, foot, home, mean, poor, post, prop, rest, root, seat, site, stay, vile **05** basis, build, depot, found, heart, hinge, layer, lowly, stand **06** abject, bottom, centre, depend, derive, fundus, ground, locate, origin, plinth, sordid, source, vulgar, wicked **07** bedrock, coating, corrupt, essence, immoral, install, pitiful, situate, station, support **08** backbone, covering, depraved, infamous, keystone, pedestal, position, shameful, wretched **09** component, construct, essential, establish, low-minded, miserable, principal, reprobate, thickness, valueless, worthless **10** despicable, foundation, groundwork, scandalous, settlement, substratum, underneath **11** disgraceful, fundamental, ignominious **12** contemptible, disreputable, have as a basis, headquarters, substructure, unprincipled **13** starting-point **14** understructure **15** foundation stone

• **base of**
◇ *tail selection down indicator*

baseball

Baseball players include:

03 **Ott** (Mel)
04 **Cobb** (Ty), **Mack** (Connie), **Mays** (Willie), **Ruth** (Babe), **Ryan** (Nolan)
05 **Aaron** (Hank), **Bench** (Johnny), **Berra** (Yogi), **Paige** (Satchel), **Spahn** (Warren), **Young** (Cy)
06 **Gehrig** (Lou), **Gibson** (Bob), **Gibson** (Josh), **Koufax** (Sandy), **Mantle** (Mickey), **Musial** (Stan), **Ripken** (Cal)
07 **Clemens** (Roger), **Jackson** (Reggie), **McGwire** (Mark), **Stengel** (Casey)
08 **Clemente** (Roberto), **DiMaggio** (Joe), **Robinson** (Brooks), **Robinson** (Jackie), **Williams** (Ted)
09 **Alexander** (Grover Cleveland), **Mathewson** (Christy)

Major league baseball teams:

11 Chicago Cubs, New York Mets
12 Boston Red Sox, Texas Rangers
13 Atlanta Braves, Detroit Tigers, Houston Astros
14 Cincinnati Reds, Florida Marlins, Minnesota Twins, New York Yankees, San Diego Padres
15 Chicago White Sox, Colorado Rockies, Seattle Mariners, Toronto Blue Jays
16 Baltimore Orioles, Cleveland Indians, Kansas City Royals, Milwaukee Brewers, Oakland Athletics, St Louis Cardinals
17 Los Angeles Dodgers, Pittsburgh Pirates, Tampa Bay Devil Rays
18 San Francisco Giants
19 Arizona Diamondbacks, Washington Nationals
20 Philadelphia Phillies
25 Los Angeles Angels of Anaheim

Baseball terms include:

03 ace, ERA, hit, out, RBI, run, tag
04 balk, ball, base, bunt, cage, mitt, safe, walk
05 alley, bench, error, mound, pitch, plate
06 assist, batter, bottom, closer, double, dugout, fly out, inning, on deck, single, sinker, slider, strike, triple, wind-up
07 all-star, base hit, battery, bull pen, catcher, chopper, diamond, fly ball, home run, infield, pennant, pitcher, rundown, shutout
08 ballpark, baseline, fair ball, fastball, foul ball, foul pole, nightcap, no-hitter, outfield, set-up man
09 cut-off man, earned run, first base, gold glove, grand slam, ground out, hit-and-run, home plate, infielder, in the hole, left field, line drive, sacrifice, screwball, strike out, third base, wild pitch
10 baserunner, batter's box, double play, ground ball, outfielder, passed ball, right field, second base, strike zone
11 base on balls, basket catch, centre field, knuckleball, left fielder, perfect game, pinch hitter, pinch runner, run batted in, unearned run
12 breaking ball, double-header, extra innings, load the bases, right fielder, warning track
13 centre fielder, foul territory, relief pitcher, safety squeeze
14 American League, backdoor slider, batting average, fielder's choice, National League, suicide squeeze
15 starting pitcher

• **baseball statistic**
03 ERA, RBI

baseless
◇ *tail deletion down indicator*
04 idle **06** untrue **09** unfounded **10** fabricated, gratuitous, groundless, ill-founded, unattested **11** uncalled-for, unconfirmed, unjustified, unsupported **15** unauthenticated, unsubstantiated

basement
05 crypt, dunny, vault **06** cellar

bash
02 go **03** box, hit, ram, try **04** bang, beat, belt, biff, blow, bump, clip, dent, rave, shot, slug, sock, stab **05** blast, break, crack, crash, knock, party, punch, smack, smash, thump, whack, whirl **06** batter, rave-up, strike, thrash, wallop **07** attempt, clobber **11** celebration

bashful
03 coy, shy **05** blate, timid **06** modest **07** abashed, laithfu', nervous **08** backward, blushing, hesitant, reserved, reticent, retiring, sheepish, timorous **09** diffident, inhibited, shamefast, shrinking **10** shamefaced, sheep-faced **11** embarrassed **12** self-effacing **13** self-conscious, unforthcoming

bashfully
05 shyly **07** timidly **08** modestly **09** nervously **10** hesitantly, reticently, sheepishly **11** diffidently **14** self-effacingly **15** self-consciously

bashfulness
05 shame **07** blushes, coyness, modesty, reserve, shyness **08** timidity **09** hesitancy, reticence **10** diffidence, inhibition **11** nervousness **12** sheepishness **13** embarrassment, mauvaise honte **14** self-effacement, shamefacedness

basic
03 gut, key **04** bare, root **05** crude, first, plain, stark, vital **06** simple, staple **07** austere, bedrock, central, minimal, minimum, primary, radical, spartan **08** inherent, no-frills, standard, starting **09** essential, important, intrinsic, necessary, primitive, unadorned **10** elementary, underlying **11** bog standard, fundamental, lowest level, preparatory, rudimentary **12** down-and-dirty **13** indispensable **14** unsophisticate **15** unsophisticated

basically
06 mainly **07** at heart **08** at bottom **09** in essence, in the main, primarily, radically **10** inherently **11** essentially, in principle, principally **13** fundamentally, intrinsically, substantially

basics
03 ABC **04** core **05** abcee, absey, facts **07** bedrock **08** alphabet, elements **09** realities, rudiments **10** brass tacks, essentials, principles, rock bottom **11** necessaries, nitty-gritty **12** fundamentals, introduction, nuts and bolts **14** practicalities **15** first principles

basin
03 bed, dip, pan, pot **04** bowl, dish, dock, park, sink, tank **05** bidet, docks, gully, laver, playa **06** cavity, crater, hollow, lavabo, valley **07** channel, piscina **08** birdbath, washbowl **09** impluvium, reservoir **10** aquamanale, aquamanile, depression

basis
03 key, way **04** base, core, fond, root **05** heart, radix, terms **06** bottom, ground, method, reason, status, system, thrust **07** bedrock, essence, footing, grounds, keynote, premise, reasons, support **08** approach, pedestal, platform **09** condition, essential, principle, procedure, rationale **10** conditions, essentials, foundation, grass-roots, groundwork, hypostasis, substratum **11** arrangement, cornerstone, fundamental **12** fundamentals, quintessence **13** alpha and omega, starting-point **14** main ingredient **15** first principles

bask
03 lie, sun **04** laze, loll **05** bathe, enjoy, lap up, relax, revel **06** lounge, relish, savour, sprawl, wallow **08** apricate, sunbathe **09** delight in, luxuriate **14** take pleasure in

basket
03 bin, box, cob, fan, rip, van, wpb **04** case, cauf, chip, coop, corf, crib, goal, hask, kipe, leap, skep, trug **05** cabas, creel, frail, maund, scull, skull, willy **06** gabion, hamper, holder, junket, mocock, mocuck, murlan, murlin, petara, pottle, punnet, willey, wisket **07** corbeil, cresset, flasket, murlain, pannier, scuttle, seedlip, shopper, trolley **08** bassinet, calathus **09** container, corbeille, fish-creel, peat-creel **10** receptacle **12** wagger-pagger

basketball

Basketball teams:

08 Utah Jazz
09 Miami Heat
11 Phoenix Suns
12 Atlanta Hawks, Chicago Bulls, Orlando Magic
13 Boston Celtics, Denver Nuggets, Indiana Pacers, New Jersey Nets, New York Knicks
14 Detroit Pistons, Houston Rockets, Milwaukee Bucks, Toronto Raptors
15 Dallas Mavericks, Sacramento Kings, San Antonio Spurs
16 Charlotte Bobcats, Los Angeles Lakers, Memphis Grizzlies
17 New Orleans Hornets, Philadelphia 76ers, Washington Wizards
18 Cleveland Cavaliers, Los Angeles Clippers, Seattle SuperSonics
19 Golden State Warriors
20 Portland Trail Blazers
21 Minnesota Timberwolves

Basketball players and associated figures include:

04 **Bird** (Larry)
05 **Belov** (Sergei), **Cousy** (Bob), **Lemon** (Meadowlark), **Mikan** (George), **O'Neal** (Shaquille)
06 **Bryant** (Kobe), **Erving** (Julius), **Jordan** (Michael), **Malone** (Karl), **Miller** (Cheryl), **Pippen** (Scottie), **Rodman** (Dennis)
07 **Barkley** (Charles), **Bradley** (Bill), **Iverson** (Allen), **Jackson** (Phil), **Johnson** (Earvin 'Magic'), **Russell** (Bill)
08 **Auerbach** (Arnold 'Red'), **Olajuwon** (Hakeem), **Petrovic** (Drazen), **Stockton** (John)
09 **Robertson** (Oscar)
11 **Abdul-Jabbar** (Kareem), **Chamberlain** (Wilt)

Basketball-related terms include:

03 key, NBA
04 dunk, hoop, trap
05 block, drive, guard, lay-up, pivot, steal, tap-in
06 assist, basket, box out, centre, post up, rim out, screen, tip-off
07 dribble, forward, foul out, kick out, low post, rebound, sky hook, time-out
08 alley oop, bank shot, charging, fadeaway, foul lane, foul line, hang time, high post, hook shot, inbounds, jump ball, jump hook, jump shot, slam dunk, turnover
09 backboard, chest pass, fast break, field goal, free throw, perimeter, shot clock, violation
10 bounce pass, double pump, foul circle, point guard, transition, travelling
11 goal-tending, pick and roll, zone defence
12 baseball pass, power forward, small forward
13 shooting guard

bass
01 B **03** low **04** base, bast, deep, full, rich **05** fibre, grave **06** burden, phloem **07** bourdon, burthen, matting, sea dace, sea wolf **08** continuo, diapason, low-toned, resonant, sea perch, sonorous **09** deep-toned, full-toned, loup de mer, succentor **10** low-pitched **11** deep-pitched

bast
04 bass **05** fibre, liber **06** phloem, raffia **07** leptome, matting

bastard
◇ *anagram indicator*
03 git **05** slink **06** basket, by-blow, mamzer **07** buzzard **08** sideslip, spurious **09** come-o'-will, love child **10** lucky-piece, misfortune **12** come-by-chance, illegitimate, natural child **13** filius nullius

bastardize
06 debase, defile, demean **07** cheapen, corrupt, degrade, devalue, distort, pervert, vitiate **10** adulterate, degenerate, depreciate **11** contaminate

bastion
04 prop, rock **06** pillar **07** bulwark, citadel, defence, lunette, moineau, redoubt, support **08** defender, fortress, mainstay **10** protection, stronghold

bat
04 blow, club, lath, rate **05** fungo, lingo, speed, spree, stick **06** paddle, racket, willow **07** batsman, battery, flutter **09** battalion, rearmouse, reremouse, trap stick **10** battledoor, battledore, Scotch hand **12** flitter-mouse

Bats include:

03 fox, red
05 fruit, guano, hoary
06 kalong, yellow
07 leisler, mastiff, noctule, spectre, vampire
08 big brown, big-eared, Leisler's, noctilio, serotine
09 barbastel, flying fox, horseshoe, leaf-nosed, roussette
10 free-tailed, frog-eating, mouse-eared
11 barbastelle, little brown, pipistrelle
12 false vampire
14 Kitti's hog-nosed
15 Mexican freetail

batch
03 lot, set **04** mass, pack **05** bunch, crowd, group **06** amount, parcel **07** cluster **08** quantity **09** aggregate **10** assemblage, assortment, collection, contingent **11** consignment **12** accumulation **14** conglomeration

bath
03 dip, spa, tub **04** soak, stew, wash **05** banya, bathe, clean, sauna, scrub, stove, therm **06** douche, hammam, hot tub, hummum, mikvah, mikveh, shower, therms **07** bathtub, hummaum, Jacuzzi®, spa pool, thermae **08** aerotone, balneary **09** bain-marie, freshen up, have a bath, steam bath, steam room, take a bath, whirlpool **10** Aquae Sulis **11** slipper bath, Turkish bath

bathe
03 bay, dip, tub, wet **04** bath, baye, dook, lave, soak, stew, surf, swim, wash

05 beath, clean, cover, embay, flood, rinse, steep 06 paddle 07 cleanse, embathe, imbathe, immerse, Jacuzzi®, moisten, suffuse 08 permeate, saturate, take a dip 09 encompass, skinny-dip

bathos
07 let-down 08 comedown
10 anticlimax 14 disappointment

baton
03 rod 05 staff, stick 06 cudgel, warder 07 scepter, sceptre
09 truncheon

bats
◇ *anagram indicator*
03 mad 04 nuts 05 crazy
07 Mormops 15 Megacheiroptera, Microchiroptera

batsman
• **first batsman**
06 opener
• **weaker batsmen**
04 tail

battalion
02 bn 03 bat, mob 04 army, herd, host, mass, unit 05 crowd, force, horde
06 battle, legion, throng, troops
07 brigade, company, platoon, section
08 division, garrison, regiment, squadron 09 multitude 10 contingent, detachment

batten
03 bar, fix 04 bolt 05 board, strip
06 fasten, secure 07 board up, tighten
08 nail down 09 barricade, clamp down

batter
◇ *anagram indicator*
03 hit, lam, ram 04 bash, beat, club, dash, hurt, lash, maul, pelt 05 abuse, erode, pound, smash, whack 06 beat up, bruise, buffet, damage, hatter, injure, mangle, pummel, strike, thrash, wallop 07 assault, bombard, destroy, lay into, rough up, wear out
08 demolish, ill-treat, maltreat, wear down 09 cannonade, disfigure
10 knock about 11 overweather
• **batter down**
04 ruin 05 smash, wreck 07 destroy
08 demolish 09 break down

battered
◇ *anagram indicator*
03 hit 06 abused, beaten, shabby
07 bruised, crushed, damaged, injured, run-down 09 crumbling
10 ill-treated, maltreated, ramshackle, tumbledown 11 dilapidated
13 weather-beaten

battery
03 bat, row, set 04 bank, cell, guns, pram 05 array, cycle, force, group, nicad, praam 06 attack, cannon, series
07 assault, beating, mugging
08 cannonry, ordnance, sequence, striking, violence 09 artillery, thrashing
10 button cell, succession
12 emplacements

batting
◇ *anagram indicator*
02 in

battle
02 by 03 bye, row, war 04 feud, fray, race, wage 05 argue, brawl, clash, drive, field, fight, scrap, set-to, stoor, stour 06 action, affair, attack, buffet, combat, debate, engage, stoush, stowre, strife, strive 07 agitate, clamour, contend, contest, crusade, dispute, fertile, hosting, quarrel, warfare 08 campaign, conflict, darraign, disagree, naumachy, sea-fight, skirmish, struggle 09 battalion, encounter, naumachia
10 Armageddon, engagement, free-for-all, nourishing, tournament
11 altercation, competition, controversy, final battle, hostilities, turkey-shoot 12 disagreement
13 armed conflict, confrontation

See also **siege**; **war**

Battles include:

04 Jena, Loos, Neva, Nile, Zama
05 Alamo, Anzio, Boyne, Bulge, Crécy, Issus, Liège, Maipó, Maipú, Marne, Mylae, Pavia, Rhine, Sedan, Sluys, Somme, Spurs, Valmy, Varna, Ypres
06 Actium, Amiens, Arnhem, Cannae, Crimea, Harlaw, Kosovo, Lützen, Midway, Mohács, Mycale, Naseby, Pinkie, Quebec, Shiloh, Tobruk, Towton, Verdun, Wagram
07 Antwerp, Britain, Bull Run, Cambrai, Cassino, Colenso, Corunna, Cowpens, Dresden, Dunkirk, Flodden, Iwo Jima, Jutland, Leipzig, Lepanto, Leuctra, Marengo, Okinawa, Plassey, Salamis, Salerno, Thapsus
08 Atlantic, Ayacucho, Blenheim, Carabobo, Culloden, Fontenoy, Formigny, Granicus, Hastings, Mafeking, Marathon, Monmouth, Omdurman, Philippi, Poitiers, Pyramids, Saratoga, Spion Kop, St Albans, Waterloo, Yorktown
09 Agincourt, Balaclava, Bay of Pigs, Chaeronea, El Alamein, Pharsalus, Ramillies, Sedgemoor, Seven Days, Solferino, Trafalgar, Vicksburg
10 Aboukir Bay, Adrianople, Austerlitz, Brandywine, Bunker Hill, Charleston, Cold Harbor, Copenhagen, Gettysburg, Malplaquet, Oudenaarde, River Plate, Stalingrad, Tannenberg, Tel-El-Kebir, Wilderness
11 Bannockburn, Guadalcanal, Hohenlinden, Marston Moor, Navarino Bay, Pearl Harbor, Prestonpans, Wounded Knee
12 Mons Graupius, Monte Cassino, Tet offensive
13 Bosworth Field, Cape St Vincent, Killiecrankie, Little Bighorn, Magersfontein, Passchendaele
14 Fredericksburg

battle-axe
03 axe, hag 04 bill, fury, wife 05 shrew, witch 06 dragon, poleax, sparth, Tartar, virago 07 gisarme, poleaxe, sparthe
08 harridan, martinet 09 termagant
12 Jeddart staff 14 disciplinarian

battle-cry
05 motto 06 banzai, slogan, war cry
07 war song 09 catchword, watchword 11 catchphrase, rallying cry
12 rallying call

battlefield
05 arena, field, front, place 07 war zone 09 front line 10 Armageddon, combat zone 12 battleground 13 field of battle

battlement
07 barmkin 08 bartisan, bartizan

batty
◇ *anagram indicator*
03 mad, odd 04 bats, daft, nuts
05 barmy, buggy, crazy, dippy, dotty, loony, loopy, nutty, silly 06 insane, stupid 07 bonkers, foolish, idiotic
08 crackers, demented, peculiar
09 eccentric 10 off your nut, out to lunch 11 off your head 12 round the bend 13 off your rocker, round the twist

bauble
03 toy 06 gewgaw, tinsel, trifle
07 bibelot, flamfew, trinket
08 gimcrack, kickshaw, ornament
09 bagatelle, plaything 10 knick-knack

baulk *see* **balk, baulk**

bawd
04 pimp 05 madam 08 procurer
09 panderess, procuress 13 brothel-keeper

bawdy
04 blue, lewd, rude 05 adult, dirty, gross 06 coarse, erotic, ribald, risqué, smutty, vulgar, X-rated 07 lustful, obscene, raunchy 08 improper, indecent, prurient 09 lecherous, salacious 10 indecorous, indelicate, lascivious, libidinous, licentious, sculduddry, suggestive 11 sculduddery, skulduddery 12 pornographic 14 near the knuckle

bawl
03 cry, sob 04 call, gape, howl, roar, wail, weep, yell, yowl 05 shout
06 bellow, cry out, gollar, goller, holler, scream, snivel, squall 07 blubber, call out, screech 10 vociferate
• **bawl out**
05 scold 06 rebuke, yell at 07 rouse on, tell off 09 dress down, reprimand

bay
03 arm, cry, vae, voe 04 bark, bawl, bell, cove, gulf, howl, loch, nook, roar, yelp, yowl 05 bathe, bight, booth, creek, firth, fleet, inlet, niche, reach, sound, stall 06 alcove, bellow, carrel, holler, lagoon, laurel, recess
07 clamour, classis, cubicle, estuary,

opening **09** cubbyhole, embayment **11** compartment, indentation

Bays include:

04 Acre, Clew, Daya, Kiel, Luce, Lyme, Pigs, Tees
05 Algoa, Blind, Cloud, Enard, Evans, False, Fundy, Hawke, Shark, Table
06 Baffin, Bantry, Bengal, Biscay, Botany, Broken, Colwyn, Dingle, Dublin, Galway, Hervey, Hudson, Lubeck, Mounts, Naples, Plenty, Tasman, Torbay, Walvis
07 Bustard, Chaleur, Donegal, Dundalk, Fortune, Halifax, Hudson's, Montego, Moreton, Pegasus, Prudhoe, Thunder, Trinity, Volcano
08 Campeche, Cardigan, Delaware, Georgian, Hang-Chow, Portland, Quiberon, San Pablo, Tremadog, Weymouth
09 Admiralty, Discovery, Encounter, Frobisher, Galveston, Geographe, Hermitage, Mackenzie, Morecambe, Notre Dame, Placentia
10 Barnstaple, Bridgwater, Carmarthen, Chesapeake, Conception, Heligoland, Providence, Robin Hood's
11 Port Jackson, Port Phillip, Saint Bride's, Saint Magnus
12 Saint George's, San Francisco

• bay with spots
04 roan

bayonet
04 pike, stab **05** blade, knife, spear, spike, stick, sword **06** dagger, impale, pierce **07** poniard **08** white arm

bazaar
04 fair, fête, mart, sale, souk **06** market **07** alcázar **08** exchange **10** alcaicería, jumble sale **11** bring-and-buy, marketplace **13** nearly-new sale

BBC
04 Beeb **06** Auntie

be
03 lie **04** form, last, live, make, stay **05** abide, arise, dwell, exist, occur, stand **06** befall, endure, happen, make up, obtain, remain, reside **07** add up to, be alive, breathe, develop, inhabit, persist, prevail, survive **08** amount to, continue **09** be located, be present, beryllium, come about, represent, take place, transpire **10** account for, be situated, come to pass, constitute

beach
04 hard, land, lido, sand **05** coast, plage, sands, shore **06** ground, strand **07** machair, seaside, shingle **08** go ashore, littoral, seaboard, seashore **09** coastline, run ashore **10** be grounded, be stranded, run aground, water's edge

Beaches include:

04 Gold, Juno, Long, Palm, Utah
05 Bells, Bondi, Cable, Manly, Miami, Omaha, Sword
06 Chesil, Malibu, Sunset, Tahiti, Venice
07 Daytona, Glenelg, Ipanema, Pattaya, Waikiki
08 Hotwater, St Tropez, Virginia
09 Blackpool
10 Copacabana, Ninety Mile
11 Coney Island
13 Skeleton Coast
15 Surfers Paradise

beachcomber
06 loafer **07** forager **08** loiterer, wayfarer **09** scavenger

beacon
04 beam, fire, sign **05** fanal, flare, light, racon **06** pharos, rocket, signal **07** bonfire **08** bale-fire, needfire **09** watch fire **10** lighthouse, watchtower **12** danger signal, warning light

bead
03 dot **04** ball, bede, blob, drip, drop, gaud, glob, nurl, tear **05** bugle, jewel, knurl, ojime, pearl **06** bubble, pellet, prayer **07** cabling, droplet, globule **08** moulding, spheroid **10** adderstone **11** paternoster, spacer plate **13** cable-moulding

beadle
06 bedral, Bumble **07** bederal **09** apparitor **10** bluebottle **13** church officer

beak
02 JP **03** neb, nib, ram **04** bill, nose **05** becke, snout **07** rostrum **09** mandibles, proboscis, rostellum **10** magistrate **12** schoolmaster **14** schoolmistress

beaker
03 cup, jar, mug **05** glass **07** tankard, tumbler

beam
03 aim, bar, ray, RSJ, tie **04** balk, boom, emit, glow, grin, lath, send, spar, yard **05** baulk, board, chink, flare, flash, glare, gleam, glint, joist, laugh, plank, relay, shaft, shine, smile, smirk, stock, strut, trave **06** binder, bumkin, direct, gibbet, girder, hurter, lintel, needle, pencil, purlin, rafter, solive, streak, stream, summer, timber **07** bumpkin, carling, effulge, glimmer, glitter, radiate, sleeper, sparkle, support, transom, trimmer **08** herisson, kingpost, stanchel, stancher, streamer, stringer, transmit **09** broadcast, crosshead, outrigger, principal, queen post, scantling, stanchion, weigh-bauk **10** bressummer, cantilever **12** breastsummer

• off beam
05 wrong **08** mistaken **09** incorrect, misguided, off target **10** inaccurate **11** wrong-headed **13** wide of the mark

bean

Beans and pulses include:

03 dal, Goa, pea, soy, urd, wax
04 dahl, dhal, fava, gram, guar, jack, Lens, lima, loco, mung, navy, okra, snap, soja, soya
05 aduki, berry, black, broad, carob, dholl, green, horse, moong, pinto, sugar, tonga, tonka
06 adsuki, adzuki, butter, cherry, chilli, coffee, cowpea, French, frijol, kidney, lablab, legume, lentil, locust, runner, string, winged
07 alfalfa, Calabar, fasolia, frijole, haricot, jumping, Molucca, scarlet, snow pea, tonquin
08 black-eye, borlotti, chickpea, garbanzo, pichurim, snuffbox, split pea, sugar pea, yard-long
09 black-eyed, black gram, flageolet, green gram, jequirity, mangetout, pigeon pea, puy lentil, red kidney, red lentil
10 cannellini, golden gram, prayer bead
11 black-eye pea, garbanzo pea, green lentil
12 asparagus pea, black-eyed pea, marrowfat pea, sassafras nut, St John's bread
13 scarlet runner

bear
◇ *containment indicator*
02 go **03** act, hae, owe, pay, sit **04** bend, dree, hack, have, hold, hump, keep, like, move, show, take, teem, tote, turn, veer **05** abear, abide, admit, allow, beget, breed, bring, brook, carry, curve, drive, fetch, stand, thole, yield **06** accept, acquit, behave, convey, endure, foster, give up, hold up, keep up, permit, suffer, swerve, uphold **07** abrooke, cherish, comport, conduct, deliver, develop, deviate, display, diverge, endorse, exhibit, harbour, produce, stomach, support, sustain **08** engender, fructify, generate, live with, maintain, shoulder, tolerate **09** entertain, propagate, put up with, transport **10** bring forth **11** give birth to **13** grin and bear it

Bears include:

03 sea, sun
04 balu, cave, Pooh, Yogi
05 baloo, black, brown, Bruin, Great, honey, koala, Nandi, polar, sloth, teddy, water, white
06 Little, native, Rupert, woolly
07 grizzly, Malayan
08 cinnamon
09 Ursa Major, Ursa Minor
10 giant panda, Paddington
13 Teddy Robinson, Winnie the Pooh

• bear down on
08 approach, browbeat, move in on
09 advance on, close in on

• bear in mind
04 mind, note **06** keep in **08** consider, remember **10** keep in mind **11** be mindful of **15** make a mental note, take into account

• bear out
05 prove **06** back up, ratify, uphold, verify **07** confirm, endorse, justify, support, warrant **08** validate **09** vindicate **11** corroborate, demonstrate **12** substantiate

• bear up
04 buoy, cope **06** endure, suffer **07** carry on, survive **09** persevere, soldier on, withstand **13** grin and bear it

• bear with
06 endure, suffer **07** forbear **08** tolerate **09** put up with **13** be patient with

bearable
07 livable **08** liveable, passable, portable **09** endurable, tolerable **10** acceptable, admissible, manageable, sufferable **11** supportable, sustainable

beard
03 awn **04** dare, defy, face, kesh, peak, tuft, ziff **05** brave **06** beaver, goatee, oppose, pappus **07** bristle, Charley, Charlie, stubble, vandyke **08** confront, imperial, whiskers **09** challenge, moustache, sideburns **10** face-fungus, facial hair, sideboards **11** mutton chops **12** Newgate frill **13** Newgate fringe **14** stand up against

bearded
05 awned, bushy, hairy **06** barbed, shaggy, tufted **07** bristly, hirsute, prickly, stubbly **08** barbated, unshaven **09** pogoniate, whiskered **11** bewhiskered

bearer
05 agent, owner, payee **06** holder, porter, runner **07** carrier, courier, jampani **08** chairman, conveyor, jampanee **09** consignee, messenger, possessor **11** beneficiary, transporter

bearing
◇ *containment indicator*
01 E, N, S, W **03** aim, air, way **04** east, gait, gest, mien, port, west **05** geste, north, poise, south, track **06** aspect, course, manner **07** concern, posture, stature **08** attitude, carriage, location, portance, position, relation **09** behaviour, demeanour, direction, influence, reference, relevance, situation **10** connection, deportment, pertinence **11** comportment, orientation, whereabouts **12** significance

• strewn with bearings
04 semé **05** semée

beast
03 pig **04** bête, ogre **05** brute, devil, fiend, swine **06** animal, savage, tarand **07** monster, salvage **08** behemoth, creature, opinicus **09** barbarian
See also **animal**

• mark of the Beast
02 mb

beastly
04 foul, mean, vile **05** awful, cruel, nasty **06** brutal, horrid, rotten **07** swinish **08** horrible, terrible **09** brutishly, repulsive **10** abominably, unpleasant **11** frightfully **12** disagreeable

beat
02 do **03** box, gub, hit, lam, mix, pug, ram, tan, tap, way, wop **04** bang, bash, belt, best, biff, blow, cane, club, cuff, dash, ding, drub, dust, firk, flap, flay, flog, form, lash, lick, mall, maul, path, pelt, race, rout, ruin, slap, slat, stir, thud, tick, time, tund, walk, welt, wham, whip, whop, work, yerk, yirk **05** all in, birch, blend, clout, crush, excel, forge, knock, knout, metre, mould, outdo, paste, pound, pulse, punch, quake, quell, repel, rhyme, round, route, shake, shape, smack, smash, stamp, strap, swing, swipe, tempo, throb, thump, tired, whack, whisk, worst **06** accent, batter, bruise, buffet, bushed, course, cudgel, done in, exceed, fill in, granny, hammer, outrun, outwit, pooped, pummel, quiver, reject, rhythm, rounds, stress, strike, stroke, subdue, thrash, thresh, thwack, wallop, zonked **07** banging, cadence, circuit, clobber, combine, conquer, contuse, eclipse, fashion, flutter, journey, knubble, lambast, lay into, measure, outplay, pulsate, surpass, tremble, trounce, vibrate, wearied, whacked, worn out **08** dead-beat, dog-tired, fatigued, jiggered, knocking, malleate, outmatch, outscore, outsmart, outstrip, overcome, pounding, rib-roast, striking, throw out, tired out, vanquish, vapulate **09** devastate, discomfit, exhausted, knackered, marmelize, overpower, overthrow, overwhelm, palpitate, pooped out, pulsation, pulverize, slaughter, subjugate, territory, transcend, vibration, zonked out **10** annihilate, clapped-out, knock about **11** palpitation, tuckered out **13** have the edge on, put to the worse, run rings round **14** get the better of **15** make mincemeat of

• beat against the wind
03 ply

• beat off
05 repel **07** hold off, repulse, ward off **08** beat back, fight off, overcome, push back **09** drive back, force back, keep at bay

• beats per minute
03 BPM **05** pulse **09** pulse rate

• beat up
◇ *anagram indicator*
02 do **03** mug **05** scrag **06** arouse, attack, bang up, batter, donder, do over, duff up, switch **07** assault, clobber, disturb, rough up, scare up **08** duff over, work over **10** knock about **11** knock around

beaten
◇ *anagram indicator*
04 flat, ybet **05** foamy, mixed, trite **06** forged, formed, frothy, shaped, worked **07** blended, moulded, stamped, stirred, trodden, whipped, whisked, wrought **08** foliated, hammered, trampled, well-used, well-worn **09** exhausted, fashioned, stonkered **11** well-trodden

beatific
06 divine, joyful **07** angelic, blessed, exalted, sublime **08** blissful, ecstatic, glorious, heavenly, seraphic **09** rapturous

beatification
10 exaltation **12** canonization **13** glorification **14** sanctification

beatify
05 bless, exalt **07** glorify **08** canonize, macarize, sanctify

beating
04 loss, rout, ruin, warm **05** laldy, pandy, pulse, socks **06** caning, defeat, hiding, lacing, laldie **07** battery, belting, duffing, hitting, lashing, pasting, pugging, tanning, the cane, warming **08** bruising, clubbing, conquest, downfall, drubbing, flogging, knocking, once-over, punching, slapping, smacking, the birch, the strap, thumping, whacking, whipping, whupping **09** bastinade, bastinado, battering, doing-over, duffing-up, going-over, hammering, overthrow, pulsation, pulsatory, slaughter, thrashing, trouncing, walloping **10** clobbering, loundering, outwitting, paddy-whack **11** duffing-over, outsmarting, vanquishing **12** annihilation, chastisement, overpowering, overwhelming

beatitude
07 delight, ecstasy, elation, rapture **08** macarism **09** happiness **11** blessedness **13** contentedness

beau
03 fop, guy **04** buck **05** dandy, lover, spark **06** Adonis, escort, fiancé, suitor **07** admirer, coxcomb **08** muscadin, popinjay **09** boyfriend **10** sweetheart

beautician
07 friseur **09** visagiste **11** cosmetician, hairdresser **12** aesthetician

beautiful
04 fair, fine **05** bonny, sheen **06** bright, comely, lovely, pretty, seemly **07** auroral, radiant, smicker **08** alluring, aurorean, becoming, charming, gorgeous, graceful, handsome, pleasing, smashing, specious, striking, stunning **09** appealing, exquisite, fair-faced, fairytale, ravishing **10** attractive, delightful, voluptuous **11** good-looking, hyacinthine, magnificent **14** out of this world, poetry in motion **15** pulchritudinous

beautifully
06 fairly, lovely **09** radiantly
10 charmingly, gracefully, pleasantly, pleasingly, strikingly, stunningly
12 attractively, delightfully

beautify
04 deck, gild **05** adorn, array, grace
06 bedeck, doll up, tart up
07 enhance, garnish, improve, smarten
08 decorate, flourish, ornament, spruce up, titivate **09** embellish, glamorize, smarten up

beauty
04 boon, dish, fair, form **05** asset, belle, bonus, charm, doozy, glory, grace, looks, merit, peach, pride, siren, Venus **06** allure, appeal, corker, doozer, glamor, virtue **07** benefit, charmer, cracker, delight, feature, glamour, harmony, smasher, stunner
08 blessing, dividend, Greek god, knockout, radiance, strength, symmetry **09** advantage, beau ideal, good looks, good point, good thing, plus point **10** attraction, excellence, good-looker, loveliness, prettiness, seemliness **11** femme fatale, pulchritude **12** gorgeousness, gracefulness, handsomeness
13 exquisiteness **14** attractiveness, beauté du diable

beaver
04 flix **05** beard **06** castor **08** sewellel

• **beaver away**
04 slog **06** work at **07** persist **08** plug away, work hard **09** persevere, slave away

becalmed
04 idle **05** still, stuck **07** at a halt
08 marooned, stranded **10** motionless
13 at a standstill

because
02 as **03** 'cos, for **05** due to, since
06 for why **07** owing to, through
08 seeing as, thanks to **09** forasmuch
10 by reason of, by virtue of **11** as a result of, on account of

• **because of**
02 in **07** owing to **08** what with **10** by virtue of, in virtue of **11** on account of

beckon
03 nod **04** call, coax, draw, lure, pull, waft, wave **05** tempt **06** allure, entice, induce, invite, motion, signal, summon
07 attract, gesture **08** persuade
11 gesticulate

become
◇ *anagram indicator*
02 go **03** get, run, set, wax, won
04 come, fall, grow, suit, take, turn
05 befit, grace, worth **06** beseem, besort, set off **07** enhance, flatter
08 come to be, grow into, ornament, pass into **09** embellish, harmonize
10 change into, look good on, mature into **11** develop into, turn out to be
13 be changed into

• **become of**
06 befall **08** happen to **11** be the fate of

becoming
03 fit **06** comely, decent, pretty, seemly **07** elegant, fitting
08 charming, decorous, fetching, graceful, gracious, handsome, suitable, tasteful **09** befitting, besitting, congruous **10** attractive, compatible, consistent, flattering **11** appropriate

becomingly
09 elegantly **10** charmingly, fetchingly, gracefully, tastefully **12** attractively

bed
03 fix, hay, kip, mat, pad, pit, row, set
04 area, base, bury, doss, plot, sack
05 basis, embed, floor, found, inlay, layer, patch, plant, space, strip
06 border, bottom, garden, ground, insert, matrix, settle **07** channel, implant, stratum **09** establish
10 foundation, groundwork, substratum **11** watercourse

Beds include:

01 Z
03 box, cot, day
04 bunk, camp, cott, crib, sofa, twin
05 berth, couch, divan, futon, water
06 cradle, double, litter, pallet, Put-u-up®, single
07 folding, hammock, trestle, truckle, trundle
08 bassinet, foldaway, king-size, mattress, platform, put-you-up
09 couchette, king-sized, lit bateau, palliasse, queen-size, shakedown
10 adjustable, four-poster, mid sleeper, queen-sized
11 high sleeper
12 chaise longue

• **bed down**
03 kip **05** sleep **06** turn in **07** go to bed, kip down **08** doss down **09** hit the hay **10** call it a day, get some kip, hit the sack, settle down

• **dry bed**
04 wadi, wady

• **get out of bed**
04 rise **07** surface, turn out **08** show a leg, tumble up **10** hit the deck **12** rise and shine

• **out of bed**
02 up **05** astir, risen

bedaub
04 clag, moil **05** smear **06** parget
07 besmear, plaster **08** slaister
09 beslubber

bedbug
01 B **05** B flat **06** chinch

bedclothes
06 covers **07** bedding **08** bed-linen

Bedclothes include:

05 doona, duvet, quilt, sheet
06 downie, pillow
07 bedroll, blanket, bolster, valance
08 coverlet
09 bed canopy, bedspread, comforter, eiderdown, throwover
10 duvet cover, pillowcase, pillow sham, pillowslip, quilt cover
11 counterpane, fitted sheet, sleeping bag
13 mattress cover, valanced sheet, Witney blanket
14 patchwork quilt
15 cellular blanket, electric blanket

bedeck
04 deck, trim **05** adorn, array
07 festoon, garnish, trick up
08 beautify, decorate, ornament, trick out **09** embellish

bedevil
◇ *anagram indicator*
03 irk, vex **04** fret **05** annoy, beset, tease, worry **06** harass, pester, plague
07 afflict, besiege, torment, torture, trouble **08** confound, distress, irritate
09 frustrate

bedfellow
04 ally **06** fellow, friend **07** partner
09 associate, colleague, companion

bedlam
◇ *anagram indicator*
05 babel, chaos, noise **06** furore, hubbub, madman, tumult, uproar
07 anarchy, clamour, turmoil
08 madhouse **09** commotion, confusion **10** hullabaloo
11 pandemonium

bedraggled
03 wet **05** dirty, messy, muddy
06 soaked, sodden, soiled, untidy
07 muddied, scruffy, soaking, unkempt
08 drenched, dripping, slovenly
10 disordered, soaking wet
11 dishevelled

bedridden
06 bedrid, laid up **07** worn-out
10 housebound **13** confined to bed, incapacitated **14** flat on your back

bedrock
04 base, core **05** basis, heart
06 basics, bottom, reason **07** essence, footing, premise, reasons, support
09 rationale **10** essentials, foundation, rock bottom **12** fundamentals
13 starting-point **15** first principles

bedroom
02 br **06** dormer **07** cubicle
08 roomette **09** bed-closet
10 bedchamber

bee
01 B **04** king **05** drone, nurse, queen
06 hummer, neuter, worker **07** royalty
10 drumbledor, dumbledore, leaf-cutter

beech
05 Fagus **06** myrtle **15** Tasmanian myrtle

beef
03 gag, sey **04** moan, rump, shin
05 bully, chuck, filet, flank, gripe, keema, mouse, round, skink, steak, T-bone **06** grouse, object, runner
07 charqui, dispute, grumble, sirloin, surloin, topside **08** bresaola, complain, disagree, pastrami, salt-junk

09 aitchbone, criticize, rump steak, salt horse, tournedos **10** mousepiece, silverside **11** filet mignon, sauerbraten **12** mouse-buttock **13** Chateaubriand, Scotch collops **15** scotched collops

• beef up
07 build up, toughen **08** flesh out **09** establish, reinforce, toughen up **10** invigorate, strengthen **11** consolidate **12** substantiate **15** give new energy to

beefeater
04 exon **06** ox-bird, yeoman **07** Buphaga **08** oxpecker

beefy
03 fat **05** bulky, burly, heavy, hefty, tubby **06** brawny, fleshy, robust, stocky, stolid, sturdy **07** hulking **08** muscular, stalwart **09** corpulent

beehive
03 gum **04** skep

beer
04 brew, grog, half, pint **06** liquor **07** brewski **11** amber liquid

Beers include:

03 ale, dry, ice, IPA, keg
04 bock, mild, Pils, rice
05 black, fruit, guest, heavy, honey, kvass, lager, plain, sixty, stout, wheat, white
06 bitter, eighty, export, old ale, porter, shandy, Stella®
07 bottled, draught, pale ale, Pilsner, real ale, seventy
08 amber ale, brown ale, Guinness®, home brew, light ale, Pilsener, trappist
09 microbrew, milk stout, snakebite, wheat beer
10 barley wine, low-alcohol, malt liquor, sweet stout, Weisse Bier
11 black-and-tan
12 Christmas ale, India Pale Ale
13 sixty shilling
14 eighty shilling
15 cask-conditioned, seventy shilling

See also **glass**

beetle
03 nip, run, zip **04** dash, maul, rush, tear **05** hurry, scoot **06** batler, batlet, bustle, mallet, scurry **07** scamper

See also **animal**; **insect**

Beetles include:

03 dor, may, oil
04 bark, dorr, dung, leaf, musk, pine, rove, stag
05 black, click, clock, shard, tiger, water
06 carpet, chafer, dor-fly, ground, may bug, sacred, scarab, sexton, weevil
07 burying, cadelle, carabid, carrion, goliath, hop-flea, hornbug, rose bug
08 bum-clock, cardinal, Colorado, glow-worm, Hercules, Japanese, ladybird, longhorn, wireworm, woodworm
09 furniture, goldsmith, longicorn, tumblebug, whirligig
10 bombardier, cockchafer, deathwatch, rhinoceros, rose chafer, scarabaean, scarabaeid, tumbledung, turnip flea
11 coprophagan, typographer

• beetle-crusher
03 cop **09** policeman **11** infantryman

beetling
07 jutting, pendent **09** poking out, prominent **10** projecting, protruding **11** leaning over, overhanging, sticking out

befall
04 fall **05** ensue, occur **06** arrive, astart, betide, chance, follow, happen, result, strike **07** fortune **08** bechance, come over, come upon, fall upon, happen to **09** befortune, overwhelm, supervene, take place **11** materialize

befit
03 set, sit **04** seem, sort, suit **05** match **06** become, befall, behove, beseem, besort **10** complement **13** harmonize with

befitting
03 apt, fit **04** like, meet **05** right **06** decent, proper, seemly **07** correct, fitting **08** becoming, sortable, suitable **11** appropriate **12** well-becoming **13** well-beseeming

before
◇ *juxtaposition indicator*
01 a **02** an, or, to **03** bef, ere, pre, pro- **04** ante, once, onst, prae- **05** ahead **07** ahead of, already, earlier, in front, prior to **08** formerly **09** in advance, in front of **10** on the eve of, previously, previous to, sooner than **11** earlier than **12** in the sight of, not later than **15** in the presence of

• as before
02 do **05** ditto

beforehand
03 pre- **04** fore-, prae- **05** afore, early **06** before, former, sooner **07** already, earlier **08** paravant **09** aforehand, in advance, paravaunt **10** previously **11** ahead of time **13** preliminarily

befriend
03 aid **04** back, help **06** assist, defend, favour, uphold **07** benefit, comfort, protect, stand by, succour, support, sustain, welcome **09** encourage, get to know, look after **10** fall in with, stick up for **11** keep an eye on **13** make a friend of **15** make friends with

befuddle
◇ *anagram indicator*
04 daze, faze **06** baffle, muddle, puzzle **07** confuse, nonplus, perplex, stupefy **08** bewilder **09** disorient

beg
03 ask, bum **04** pray, prog, thig **05** cadge, crave, maund, mooch, mouch, plead **06** appeal, ask for, desire, fleech, sponge, turn to **07** beseech, beseeke, entreat, implore, intreat, maunder, request, require, schnorr, skelder, solicit **08** governor, mooch off, petition, scrounge, stand pad **09** importune, panhandle **10** supplicate **11** ask for money **13** touch for money

beget
03 get **04** kind, sire **05** breed, cause, spawn **06** create, effect, father, gender, lead to **07** produce, propage **08** engender, generate, occasion, result in **09** procreate, propagate **10** bring about, give rise to

beggar
03 bum **04** defy **05** randy, tramp **06** baffle, blowse, blowze, cadger, canter, craver, exceed, mumper, pauper, randie, toerag **07** bludger, jarkman, maunder, moocher, ruffler, sponger, surpass, vagrant **08** Abram-man, beadsman, bedesman, besognio, besonian, bezonian, blighter, glassman, palliard, vagabond, whipjack **09** challenge, lazzarone, mendicant, schnorrer, scrounger, sundowner, transcend **10** Abraham-man, beadswoman, down-and-out, freeloader, panhandler, supplicant, upright-man **11** gaberlunzie **12** down-and-outer, hallan-shaker

beggarly
03 low **04** mean, poor **05** needy **06** abject, meagre, modest, paltry, slight, stingy **07** miserly, pitiful **08** pathetic, wretched **09** niggardly, worthless **10** despicable, inadequate **12** contemptible **13** insubstantial

begin
02 go **03** gin, ope **04** open, take **05** arise, enter, found, get at, set in, set up, shoot, spark, start **06** appear, broach, come on, crop up, embark, emerge, incept, set off, set out, spring **07** actuate, do first, enter on, kick off, take off **08** activate, commence, embark on, fire away, get going, inchoate, initiate, set about, shoot off, strike up **09** enter upon, instigate, institute, introduce, originate **10** launch into **11** get cracking, give birth to, open the ball, set in motion **13** take the plunge

beginner
◇ *head selection indicator*
01 L **03** cub, deb **04** tiro, tyro **05** pupil, rooky **06** author, newbie, novice, rookie **07** fresher, learner, new chum, recruit, starter, student, trainee **08** freshman, initiate, neophyte, newcomer **09** fledgling, greenhorn, Johnny-raw **10** apprentice, raw recruit, tenderfoot **11** abecedarian, probationer **13** alphabetarian

beginning
◇ *head selection indicator*
03 ord **04** dawn, germ, rise, root, seed **05** birth, debut, get-go, intro, onset, start **06** day one, launch, origin, outset, source **07** genesis, kick-off, new leaf, opening, preface, prelude **09** emergence, first base, first part,

inception, square one, the word go **10** conception, fresh start, inchoation, incipience, initiation **11** institution, opening part, pastures new **12** commencement, fountainhead, inauguration, introduction **13** establishment, new beginnings, starting-point

• **from beginning to end**
04 over **07** through **08** from A to Z

begone
04 away **05** hence **06** avaunt **10** aroint thee **11** allez-vous-en

begrudge
04 envy, mind **05** covet, stint **06** grudge, resent **08** object to **11** be jealous of **13** be resentful of

beguile
04 dupe, fool, gull, wile **05** amuse, blend, charm, cheat, cozen, guile, guyle, trick **06** delude, divert, occupy, seduce **07** attract, bewitch, deceive, delight, enchant, engross, mislead **08** distract, hoodwink **09** captivate, entertain

beguiling
08 alluring, charming, enticing **09** appealing, diverting, seductive **10** attractive, bewitching, delightful, enchanting, intriguing **11** captivating, interesting **12** entertaining

behalf
04 name, part, sake **07** account, benefit **08** interest

• **on behalf of**
02 pp **03** for **06** per pro **09** acting for **11** in support of, in the name of **12** for account of, for the good of, for the sake of, representing **13** to the profit of **15** for the benefit of

behave
02 be, do **03** act, use **04** bear, go on, quit, walk, work **05** abear, carry, quite, quyte, react **06** acquit, be good, demean, deport, quight **07** comport, conduct, operate, perform, respond **08** function **10** act your age **11** act politely, act properly **12** not mess about, not muck about **13** be well-behaved **14** acquit yourself **15** comport yourself, conduct yourself, mind your manners, mind your p's and q's

behaviour
04 form, ways **06** action, doings, habits, manner **07** conduct, manners **08** dealings, reaction, response **09** attitudes, demeanour, operation **10** deportment **11** comportment, functioning, performance, way of acting

behead
◇ *head deletion indicator*
04 head, kill **07** execute **09** decollate **10** decapitate, guillotine, put to death

behest
• **at the behest of**
11 at the hest of **12** at the order of **13** on the wishes of **14** at the bidding of, at the command of, at the request of

behind
◇ *juxtaposition indicator*
◇ *tail selection indicator*
03 aft, ass, bum, for **04** back, baft, butt, late, next, post, rear, rump, slow **05** abaft, after, ahind, ahint, retro-, stern **06** arrear, astern, back of, bottom, heinie, in debt **07** backing, causing, close on, delayed, overdue **08** backside, buttocks, derrière, in back of **09** at the back, at the rear, endorsing, following, in arrears, in the rear, later than, posterior **10** behindhand, explaining, initiating, supporting **11** at the back of, at the rear of, instigating, on the side of, running late **12** giving rise to, subsequently **13** accounting for, at the bottom of **14** responsible for **15** slower than usual

behindhand
03 lag **04** down, late, slow **05** tardy **06** behind, remiss **07** delayed **08** backward, dilatory **09** in arrears, out of date **14** behind schedule

behold
02 la, lo **03** see **04** ecce, ecco, espy, look, mark, note, scan, view **05** voici, voilà, watch **06** descry, gaze at, look at, regard, survey **07** discern, observe, witness **08** consider, perceive **11** contemplate

beholden
05 bound, owing **07** obliged **08** addebted, grateful, indebted, thankful **09** obligated **12** appreciative **15** under obligation

behove
05 befit **06** import, profit **07** benefit, stand on **08** be proper, be seemly **11** be essential, be necessary **13** be suitable for **14** be advantageous

beige
03 tan **04** buff, ecru, fawn **05** camel, khaki, sandy, suede, taupe **06** coffee, greige, oyster **07** neutral, oatmeal **08** mushroom

being
03 ens, man **04** esse, life, soul, will **05** beast, heart, human, thing, woman **06** animal, entity, living, mortal, nature, person, psyche, spirit **07** essence, reality **08** creature, emotions **09** actuality, animation, existence, haecceity, inner self, substance **10** human being, individual, inner being **11** personality **13** heart of hearts

belabour
◇ *anagram indicator*
03 hit **04** beat, belt, flay, flog, whip **05** sauce **06** attack, pummel, strike, thrash **07** dwell on **09** lay on load, reiterate **11** flog to death, harp on about **14** go on and on about

Belarus
02 BY, SU **03** BLR

belated
04 late **05** lated, tardy **07** delayed, overdue **09** benighted, out of date **10** behindhand, unpunctual **14** behind schedule

belatedly
07 tardily **12** unpunctually **14** behind schedule

belch
03 yex **04** boak, bock, boke, burp, emit, gush, rift, spew, vent, yesk **05** eject, eruct, issue **06** hiccup **07** give off, give out **08** disgorge, eructate **09** discharge **10** eructation **11** bring up wind

beleaguered
05 beset, vexed **07** plagued, worried **08** badgered, besieged, bothered, harassed, pestered, troubled **09** blockaded, tormented **10** persecuted, surrounded, under siege

Belgium
01 B **03** BEL **04** Belg

belie
04 deny **06** negate, refute **07** conceal, confute, cover up, deceive, falsify, gainsay, mislead **08** disguise, disprove **10** contradict **12** misrepresent, run counter to

belief
03 ism **04** idea, view **05** creed, dogma, ethic, faith, ideal, tenet, trust **06** credit, notion, theory, threap, threep **07** feeling, opinion **08** credence, doctrine, ideology, reliance, sureness, teaching **09** assurance, certainty, intuition, judgement, knowledge, principle, tradition, viewpoint **10** confidence, conviction, impression, persuasion **11** expectation, point of view, presumption

Beliefs include:

06 holism, malism, racism
07 animism, atheism, elitism
08 demonism, feminism, hedonism, humanism, nihilism, Satanism
09 pantheism, physicism, tritheism
10 liberalism, Manicheism, monotheism, polytheism
11 agnosticism, parallelism, supremacism, tetratheism
12 Manicheanism
13 ethnocentrism, individualism, structuralism
14 fundamentalism, traditionalism, tripersonalism
15 supernaturalism

See also **religion**

believable
06 likely **07** credent **08** credible, possible, probable, reliable **09** plausible **10** acceptable, imaginable **11** conceivable, trustworthy **13** authoritative

believe
03 buy, wis **04** deem, feel, hold, trow, wear, ween, wish, wist **05** faith, guess,

judge, opine, think, trust **06** accept, assume, credit, figure, gather, reckon **07** fall for, imagine, suppose, swallow **08** consider, maintain, perceive **09** postulate, speculate **10** Adam and Eve, conjecture, understand **11** be certain of, take on board **13** be convinced by, be persuaded by

• believe in

04 rate **05** trust **06** favour, follow, hold by, rely on **07** swear by **08** depend on **09** approve of, encourage, recommend **11** value highly **12** be in favour of **13** be convinced of, be persuaded by **15** set great store by

• hard to believe

04 tall

believer

06 zealot **07** convert, devotee **08** adherent, disciple, follower, upholder **09** proselyte, supporter

Believers include:

03 Jew
04 Babi, Jain, Sikh, Sofi, Sufi
05 Babee, Hindu, Jaina
06 holist, Muslim
07 Alawite, animist, Bahaist, Genevan, Lollard, Scotist
08 Arminian, Buddhist, Calixtin, Catholic, demonist, Erastian, Glassite, humanist, Lutheran, Nazarean, Nazarene, Pelagian, Salesian, Satanist, Wesleyan
09 animalist, Calixtine, Christian, Confucian, Eutychian, Gregorian, Methodist, Nestorian, Origenist, pantheist, Sabellian, Simeonite, Wyclifite
10 Bergsonian, Berkeleian, Cameronian, Capernaite, Holy Roller, Marcionite, polytheist, Wycliffite
11 Sandemanian, Valentinian
12 Apollinarian, Southcottian
13 Hutchinsonian, Roman Catholic, Swedenborgian
14 fundamentalist, the Oxford group
15 supernaturalist

belittle

04 slag, slam **05** abase, decry, knock, scorn, slate **06** demean, deride, do down, dump on, lessen **07** dismiss, rubbish, run down, slag off **08** diminish, minimize, play down, ridicule **09** deprecate, disparage, downgrade, sell short, underrate **10** trivialize, understate, undervalue **11** detract from, pick holes in **12** pull to pieces, tear to shreds **13** underestimate **15** do a hatchet job on

Belize

02 BH, BZ **03** BLZ

bell

03 tom **04** gong, horn, peal, ring **05** bleep, chime, knell, larum, siren **06** alarum, curfew, hooter, signal, tocsin, vesper **07** angelus, bleeper, tinkler, warning **08** pavilion **13** tintinnabulum

• sound of bell, sound of bells

04 clam, dong, peal, ring, ting, tink, toll **05** chime, knell **06** firing, tinkle **08** ding-dong **09** ding-a-ling

bellbird

08 araponga, arapunga **09** campanero

belle

05 peach, siren, Venus **06** beauty, corker **07** charmer, cracker, smasher, stunner **08** knockout **10** good-looker **11** femme fatale

bellicose

07 violent, warlike, warring **08** bullying, militant **09** combative **10** aggressive, pugnacious **11** belligerent, contentious, quarrelsome **12** antagonistic **13** argumentative

belligerence

03 war **08** bullying, violence **09** militancy, pugnacity **10** aggression, antagonism **11** provocation **12** warmongering **13** combativeness, sabre-rattling **14** unfriendliness **15** contentiousness, quarrelsomeness

belligerent

06 chippy **07** hostile, scrappy, violent, warlike, warring **08** bullying, militant **09** combative, truculent **10** aggressive, pugnacious **11** contentious, provocative, quarrelsome **12** antagonistic, disputatious, warmongering **13** argumentative, sabre-rattling

bellow

03 cry **04** bawl, howl, roar, rout, yell **05** shout, troat **06** buller, holler, scream, shriek **07** clamour, thunder **14** raise your voice

belly

03 gut, pot, tum, wem **04** bulk, bunt, guts, kite, kyte, puku, wame, wemb **05** gastr-, tummy, weamb **06** gastro-, paunch, venter **07** abdomen, gastero-, insides, stomach **08** pot-belly **09** beer belly **10** intestines **11** bread basket, corporation

belong

02 go **03** fit **04** be in, long **05** fit in **06** go with **07** be found, be yours, pertain **08** attach to, be part of, be sorted, relate to **09** appertain, be owned by, tie up with **10** be included, be situated, link up with **11** be a member of **12** be classified **13** be categorized, have as its home **14** be affiliated to, be an adherent of, have as its place **15** be connected with, be the property of

belonging

04 link **05** links **07** kinship, loyalty, rapport **08** affinity **09** closeness **10** acceptance, attachment, fellowship **11** affiliation, association **12** relationship **13** compatibility, fellow-feeling

• belonging to

◇ *hidden indicator*

belongings

03 kit **04** gear **05** goods, stuff, traps **06** tackle, things **07** clobber, effects **08** chattels, property **11** possessions **13** accoutrements, appurtenances, paraphernalia

beloved

02 jo **03** joe, joy, pet **04** baby, bird, dear, duck, leve, lief, love, wife **05** angel, fella, honey, lieve, loved, lover, sweet **06** adored, fiancé, liking, prized, spouse, tender **07** admired, darling, dearest, fiancée, husband, partner, revered, sweetie **08** endeared, lady-love, loved one, precious, true-love **09** belamoure, betrothed, boyfriend, cherished, favourite, heart-dear, inamorata, inamorato, much loved, treasured **10** bellamoure, girlfriend, sweetheart, worshipped **12** alder-liefest **13** special friend

below

◇ *juxtaposition down indicator*

03 inf, sub- **04** down **05** infra, later, lower, under **07** beneath **09** further on, hereunder, lower down, lower than, subject to **10** inferior to, lesser than, underneath **13** at a later place, subordinate to **15** lower in rank than

belt

◇ *anagram indicator*

03 box, fly, hit, tan, zip **04** area, band, bang, bash, biff, blow, cane, cord, dash, flay, flog, lash, loop, pelt, rush, sash, slap, tear, whip, zona, zone **05** apron, birch, chain, clout, girth, knock, layer, mitre, punch, slosh, smack, speed, strap, strip, swipe, thump, tract, wanty, whack **06** bruise, career, cestus, charge, corset, extent, girdle, region, sector, strike, swathe, thwack, wallop, waspie **07** baldric, bashing, clobber, harness, stretch, zonulet **08** baldrick, ceinture, cincture, cingulum, district **09** bandoleer, bandolier, hip-girdle, Sam Browne, waistband **10** cummerbund

See also **karate**

• below the belt

05 dirty **06** unfair, unjust **09** dishonest, underhand, unethical **10** out of order **11** uncalled-for, unjustified **12** unscrupulous

• belt up

02 sh, st **03** shh **04** hist **05** shush, whish, whist **06** shut up, whisht, wrap up **07** be quiet, wheesht **08** button up, cut it out, pipe down **10** keep shtoom, stay shtoom **12** put a sock in it, shut your face **13** button your lip, shut your mouth

belvedere

06 gazebo **07** mirador

bemoan

03 rue **04** moan, pity, wail **05** mourn **06** bewail, lament, regret **07** deplore, sigh for, weep for **09** grieve for **10** sorrow over

bemuse
◇ *anagram indicator*
04 daze, faze **05** floor, throw
06 baffle, muddle, puzzle **07** confuse, perplex, stupefy **08** befuddle, bewilder **09** bamboozle

bemused
◇ *anagram indicator*
05 dazed, fazed, mused **07** baffled, floored, muddled, puzzled
08 confused **09** astounded, befuddled, perplexed, pixilated, stupefied **10** astonished, bamboozled, bewildered, pixillated
11 overwhelmed **12** disconcerted

bemusement
04 daze **09** confusion **10** bafflement, perplexity, puzzlement
12 bewilderment, stupefaction
14 disorientation

Ben
03 Hur

bench
03 pew **04** banc, bank, bink, form, seat **05** board, court, judge, ledge, stall, table, thoft **06** banker, exedra, settle, thwart **07** counter, exhedra, tribune **08** rout-seat, tribunal
09 courtroom, judiciary, shopboard, workbench, worktable **10** judicature, knife-board, magistrate **13** judgement-seat

benchmark
04 norm **05** basis, gauge, level, model, scale **07** example, pattern **08** standard
09 criterion, guideline, reference, yardstick **10** guidelines, touchstone
14 reference-point

bend
◇ *anagram indicator*
01 S, U, Z **02** es **03** arc, bow, ess, out, ply, sag **04** arch, curb, flex, genu, hook, hump, kink, knot, lean, loop, ramp, sway, trap, turn, veer, warp, wind
05 angle, bight, courb, crimp, crook, curve, elbow, embow, hinge, hunch, kneel, mould, ox-bow, plash, round, shape, squat, stoop, trend, twist, wring
06 affect, bought, buckle, compel, corner, crouch, cut-off, deflex, direct, dog-leg, recede, reflex, spring, swerve, wimple, zigzag **07** compass, contort, crankle, decline, deflect, deviate, dip-trap, diverge, flexion, flexure, incline, incurve, inflect, meander, recline, recurve, reflect, turning, whimple, wriggle **08** persuade, swan neck
09 curvature, genuflect, incurvate, inflexure, influence, prostrate, retroflex
10 circumflex, deflection, divergence, make curved, manipulate
11 circumflect, hairpin bend, inclination, incurvation
• **bend over**
04 lean **08** double up
• **bend over backwards**
08 go all out **10** do your best **11** try very hard **13** exert yourself **14** put yourself out **15** trouble yourself

bendy
◇ *anagram indicator*
08 flexible

beneath
◇ *juxtaposition down indicator*
03 sub **05** below, lower, neath, under
06 aneath **09** lower down, lower than
10 unbecoming, underneath, unworthy of **11** unbefitting

Benedictines
03 OSB

benediction
05 grace **06** favour, prayer **07** benison
08 blessing **10** invocation
11 blessedness **12** consecration, thanksgiving

benefactor
05 angel, donor, giver **06** backer, friend, helper, patron **07** sponsor
08 promoter, provider **09** supporter
10 subscriber, subsidizer, well-wisher
11 contributor **14** fairy godmother, philanthropist

beneficent
04 kind **06** benign **07** benefic, helpful, liberal **08** generous **09** bountiful, unselfish **10** altruistic, benevolent, charitable, munificent
12 Grandisonian **13** compassionate

beneficial
04 good **06** useful **07** helpful
08 edifying, salutary, valuable
09 benignant, improving, promising, rewarding, wholesome **10** favourable, profitable, propitious, worthwhile
11 serviceable **12** advantageous
• **beneficial to**
03 for

beneficiary
04 heir **05** payee **07** heiress, legatee
08 receiver **09** inheritor, recipient, successor **10** the assured

benefit
03 ACC, aid, DPB, pay, use **04** boon, broo, dole, gain, good, help, perk, sake
05 asset, avail, bonus, buroo, compo, merit, serve **06** assist, behalf, behoof, better, credit, favour, income, milage, pay-off, profit, reward **07** advance, bespeak, enhance, further, improve, mileage, payment, pension, promote, service, sick pay, spin-off, support, vantage, welfare **08** blessing, dividend, do good to, interest, kindness
09 advantage, allowance, good point
10 assistance, perquisite
11 benefaction **13** be of service to, fringe benefit, income support
14 social security **15** be of advantage to

benevolence
04 care, pity **05** grace, mercy
08 altruism, goodness, goodwill, kindness **09** tolerance **10** compassion, generosity, humaneness, liberality
11 magnanimity, munificence
12 friendliness, philanthropy
14 charitableness **15** considerateness, humanitarianism, kind-heartedness

benevolent
04 good, guid, kind **06** benign, caring, humane, kindly **07** liberal **08** friendly, generous, gracious, merciful, tolerant
10 altruistic, charitable, munificent
11 considerate, kind-hearted, magnanimous, soft-hearted
12 humanitarian, well-disposed
13 compassionate, philanthropic
15 philanthropical

benevolently
06 kindly **08** benignly, humanely
09 liberally **10** charitably, generously, graciously, mercifully, tolerantly
13 considerately, kind-heartedly, magnanimously, soft-heartedly
14 altruistically **15** compassionately

benighted
07 belated, nighted **08** backward, ignorant **09** unknowing **10** illiterate, uncultured, uneducated, unlettered, unschooled **11** unfortunate
13 inexperienced, unenlightened

benign
04 good, kind, mild, warm **05** sweet, trine **06** genial, gentle, kindly
07 affable, amiable, benefic, cordial, curable, healthy, liberal **08** benedict, friendly, generous, gracious, harmless, innocent, obliging **09** agreeable, avuncular, opportune, temperate, treatable, wholesome **10** auspicious, beneficial, benevolent, charitable, favourable, propitious, refreshing, salubrious **11** restorative, sympathetic, warm-hearted
12 advantageous, non-malignant, providential

benignly
06 kindly **07** affably, amiably
08 genially **10** charitably, generously, graciously, obligingly **12** benevolently
15 sympathetically

Benin
02 DY, RB **03** BEN

bent
◇ *anagram indicator*
04 curb, gift, turn **05** bowed, corbe, courb, dodgy, flair, forte, knack, wrong
06 angled, arched, curved, fiorin, folded, redtop, reflex, talent, warped
07 ability, corrupt, crooked, curvate, doubled, embowed, faculty, falcate, hunched, illegal, leaning, stooped, strepto-, twafald, twisted **08** aptitude, capacity, criminal, cup of tea, curvated, facility, falcated, fondness, inclined, inflexed, penchant, reflexed, retorted, tendency **09** contorted, dishonest, infracted, refracted, retroflex, swindling **10** fraudulent, geniculate, preference, proclivity, propensity
11 disposition, geniculated, inclination
12 predilection **13** untrustworthy
14 predisposition
• **bent on**
05 set on **07** fixed on **08** intent on
10 disposed to, inclined to, resolved to
11 insistent on **12** determined to

bequeath
04 give, will **05** endow, grant, leave **06** assign, bestow, commit, demise, devise, impart, pass on **07** consign, entrust **08** hand down, make over, transfer, transmit

bequest
04 gift **05** trust **06** estate, legacy **07** devisal **08** bestowal, donation, heritage, pittance **09** endowment **10** bequeathal, settlement **11** inheritance **13** mortification

berate
05 blast, chide, scold, slate **06** rail at, rebuke, revile **07** censure, chew out, reprove, start on, tell off, upbraid **08** chastise, give hell, reproach **09** castigate, criticize, dress down, fulminate, reprimand, start in on **10** vituperate **13** give a rocket to, tear a strip off

bereaved
03 orb **04** lost **06** robbed **07** widowed **08** deprived, divested, grieving, orphaned **12** dispossessed

bereavement
04 loss **05** death, grief **06** orbity, sorrow **07** passing, sadness **08** deprival **11** deprivation, passing-away **13** dispossession

bereft
• bereft of
05 minus **07** lacking, wanting **08** devoid of, robbed of **10** cut off from, deprived of, parted from, stripped of **11** destitute of

berkelium
02 Bk

Berlin
06 Irving

Bermuda
03 BMU

berry
05 bacca **06** acinus

Berries include:

05 lichi
06 lichee, litchi, lychee
07 bramble, leechee
08 bilberry, dewberry, goosegog, mulberry, tayberry
09 blaeberry, blueberry, cranberry, raspberry, whimberry
10 blackberry, cloudberry, elderberry, gooseberry, loganberry, redcurrant, strawberry
11 boysenberry, huckleberry
12 blackcurrant, serviceberry, whitecurrant, whortleberry

berserk
◇ *anagram indicator*
03 mad **04** nuts, wild **05** angry, barmy, batty, berko, crazy, manic, rabid **06** crazed, insane, raging, raving **07** frantic, furious, violent **08** baresark, demented, deranged, frenzied, maniacal **10** hysterical **11** off your head **13** off the deep end, out of your mind **14** beside yourself, uncontrollable

berth
03 bed **04** bunk, dock, land, moor, port, quay **05** tie up, wharf **06** anchor, billet **07** hammock, harbour, mooring, sleeper **09** anchorage, couchette **10** cast anchor, drop anchor
• give a wide berth to
04 shun **05** avoid, dodge, evade **06** eschew **09** give a miss **12** steer clear of

beryl
07 emerald **08** emeraude, heliodor **09** morganite **10** aquamarine

beryllium
02 Be

beseech
03 ask, beg, sue **04** pray **05** crave, plead **06** adjure, call on, desire, exhort **07** entreat, implore, intreat, solicit **08** appeal to, petition **09** deprecate, importune, obsecrate **10** supplicate

beset
◇ *containment indicator*
03 lay, rag **04** bego **05** belay, hem in, press, worry **06** assail, attack, bestad, bested, harass, hassle, obsess, pester, plague, preace, prease **07** bedevil, besiege, bestead, preasse, torment **08** bestadde, entangle, scabrous, surround

besetting
08 constant, dominant, habitual **09** harassing, obsessive, prevalent, recurring **10** compulsive, inveterate, persistent **11** troublesome **12** irresistible **14** uncontrollable

beside
◇ *juxtaposition indicator*
02 by, on, to **04** near **06** next to **07** close to, upsides **08** abutting, adjacent **09** abreast of, alongside, bordering **10** next door to **11** by the side of, overlooking **12** neighbouring
• beside yourself
03 mad **05** crazy **06** crazed, insane **07** berserk, frantic **08** demented, deranged, frenetic, frenzied, overcome, unhinged **09** delirious **10** distraught, unbalanced **13** out of your mind

besides
02 by **03** too, yet **04** also, else **05** forby **06** as well, either, forbye, foreby, withal **07** au reste, further **08** as well as, moreover **09** apart from, aside from, excluding, other than, otherwise, what's more **10** in addition **11** furthermore **12** additionally, in addition to, over and above

besiege
◇ *containment indicator*
03 nag **05** belay, beset, besit, hem in, hound, worry **06** assail, badger, bother, harass, invest, obsess, pester, plague, shut in **07** assiege, confine, oppress, torment, trouble **08** blockade, encircle, surround **09** beleaguer, encompass, importune, overwhelm **10** lay siege to

besmirch
04 slur, soil **05** dirty, smear, stain, sully **06** damage, defame, defile **07** besmear, blacken, slander, tarnish **08** besmutch **09** dishonour

besom
03 cow, kow **05** broom

besotted
03 mad **04** wild **05** crazy, potty **06** doting, sotted, stupid **07** bedazed, drunken, smitten **08** obsessed **09** bedazzled, bewitched, stupefied **10** bowled over, hypnotized, infatuated, spellbound **11** intoxicated

bespatter
04 dash, drop, soil **05** bemud, dirty, smear, spray, stain **06** bedash, befoam, defame, shower, splash **07** asperse, scatter, spatter, splodge **08** splatter, sprinkle

bespeak
04 show **05** imply **06** attest, denote, engage, evince, reveal **07** betoken, display, exhibit, signify, suggest **08** evidence, indicate, proclaim, speak for **11** demonstrate

bespoke
◇ *anagram indicator*
09 dedicated **10** tailor-made

best
02 A1 **03** ace, cap, top **04** beat, lick, most, pick, plum, rout, star, tops **05** cream, élite, first, ideal, jewel, prime, worst **06** choice, defeat, finest, flower, hammer, outwit, subdue, thrash, utmost **07** clobber, conquer, greatly, hardest, highest, largest, leading, optimal, optimum, outplay, perfect, premium, supreme, the tops, trounce **08** foremost, greatest, outsmart, overcome, peerless, ultimate, vanquish **09** damnedest, excellent, extremely, favourite, first-rate, highlight, matchless, nonpareil, number one, overpower, overwhelm, slaughter, supremely, top-drawer, worthiest **10** annihilate, first-class, pre-eminent, unbeatable, unequalled, unrivalled **11** excellently, matchlessly, outstanding, superlative, unsurpassed **12** incomparable, incomparably, second to none **13** exceptionally, have the edge on, one in a million, outstandingly, superlatively, unsurpassedly **14** crème de la crème, get the better of, greatest effort, record-breaking

bestial
04 rude, vile **05** cruel, feral, gross **06** animal, brutal, carnal, savage, sordid **07** beastly, brutish, inhuman, sensual **08** barbaric, degraded, depraved **09** barbarous, unrefined

bestiality
07 cruelty **08** savagery **09** barbarism

10 inhumanity, sordidness 15 animal behaviour

bestir
05 exert 06 arouse, awaken, incite 07 actuate, animate 08 activate, energize, motivate 09 galvanize, stimulate

bestow
02 do 04 give 05 allot, award, endow, grant, spend, wreak 06 accord, commit, confer, donate, estate, impart, lavish 07 dispose, entrust, present 08 bequeath, transmit 09 apportion 11 communicate

bestride
05 cross 06 defend 07 command, protect 08 dominate, straddle 10 bestraddle, overshadow, sit astride 12 stand astride

bestseller
03 hit 07 success, triumph 08 smash hit 11 blockbuster, brand leader

bestselling
03 top 06 famous 07 leading, popular 08 unbeaten

bet
02 go 03 bid, lay, pot, put 04 ante, back, hold, punt, risk, view 05 place, pound, stake, wager 06 be sure, chance, choice, expect, gamble, hazard, notion, option, pledge, theory 07 feeling, flutter, lottery, opinion, venture 09 be certain, intuition, judgement, speculate, viewpoint 10 conviction, impression, prediction 11 alternative, be convinced, point of view, speculation 12 have a flutter, play for money 14 course of action, not be surprised

See also **gambling**

Bets and betting systems include:

03 TAB
04 tote
06 double, parlay, roll-up, tierce, treble, triple, Yankee
07 à cheval, each way
08 ante-post, forecast, perfecta, quinella, trifecta
09 on the nose, quadrella
10 martingale, pari-mutuel, superfecta, sweepstake
11 accumulator, daily double
13 double or quits

• **accept bet**
03 see

betel
03 pan 04 paan, pawn, siri 05 sirih

bête noire
04 bane 05 curse 07 bugbear, pet hate 08 anathema, aversion 11 abomination, pet aversion 14 thorn in the side 15 thorn in the flesh

betide
05 ensue, occur 06 befall, betime, chance, happen 07 develop 08 overtake 09 supervene, take place

betoken
04 bode, mark, mean, sign 05 augur, token 06 betide, denote, signal 07 bespeak, declare, portend, presage, promise, signify, suggest 08 evidence, forebode, indicate, manifest 09 represent, symbolize 13 prognosticate

betray
03 dob 04 dupe, sell, shop, show, tell 05 abuse, cross, dob in, grass, peach, rat on 06 bewray, delude, desert, expose, reveal, rumble, tell on, unmask 07 abandon, confess, deceive, divulge, forsake, let down, let slip, mislead, sell out, split on, stool on 08 disclose, give away, go back on, inform on, manifest, renege on, squeal on 09 play false, walk out on 11 double-cross, turn traitor 12 be disloyal to, bring to light 13 stab in the back 14 be unfaithful to, break faith with

betrayal
05 abuse 06 duping 07 perfidy, sell-out, treason 08 giveaway, trickery 09 deception, duplicity, falseness, treachery 10 disloyalty 11 double-cross 13 breaking faith, double-dealing, stab in the back 14 double-crossing, traitorousness, unfaithfulness

betrayer
05 grass, Judas 07 stoolie, traitor 08 apostate, deceiver, informer, renegade, traditor, treacher 09 treachour 10 supergrass 11 backstabber, conspirator, stool pigeon 13 double-crosser, whistle-blower

betrothal
03 vow 04 vows 05 troth 07 promise 08 affiance, contract, espousal, handfast 09 assurance 10 engagement 11 fiançailles, handfasting, hand-promise, subarration, trothplight 12 subarrhation

betrothed
05 troth 07 assured, engaged, pledged 08 espoused, promised 09 affianced, combinate 10 contracted 11 trothplight 13 trothplighted

better
03 cap, top 04 beat, best, mend, well 05 cured, finer, outdo, raise 06 bigger, enrich, exceed, fitter, healed, larger, longer, punter, reform 07 correct, enhance, forward, further, gambler, greater, improve, promote, rectify, surpass 08 improved, outstrip, overtake, restored, stronger, superior, worthier 09 a cut above, healthier, improve on, improving, on the mend, recovered 10 ameliorate, make better, preferable, recovering, speculator, surpassing 11 more fitting, progressing 12 more valuable 14 fully recovered, more acceptable 15 go one better than, of higher quality

betterment
10 enrichment 11 advancement, edification, enhancement, furtherance, improvement, melioration 12 amelioration

betting *see* **bet**

between
◇ *insertion indicator*
03 bet, mid 04 amid 05 among, inter- 06 amidst 07 amongst, halfway 11 in the middle 13 in the middle of

bevel
04 bias, cant, tilt 05 angle, basil, bezel, mitre, slant, slope, splay 07 chamfer, oblique 08 diagonal

beverage
04 brew 05 drink 06 liquid, liquor 07 draught, potable 08 ambrosia, potation 11 refreshment

See also **drink**

bevy
04 band, gang, pack 05 bunch, crowd, flock, group, troop 06 gaggle, throng, troupe 07 company 08 assembly 09 gathering 10 collection

bewail
03 rue 04 keen, moan 05 mourn 06 bemoan, lament, regret, repent 07 cry over, deplore 08 sigh over 10 grieve over, sorrow over 14 beat your breast

beware
04 cave, mind, shun, ware 05 avoid, watch 06 be wary, caveat 07 look out, mind out 08 take heed, watch out 09 be careful 10 be cautious 12 guard against, steer clear of 13 be on your guard

bewilder
◇ *containment indicator*
04 daze, faze, lose, maze 05 amaze, floor, mix up, stump 06 baffle, bemuse, fickle, muddle, puzzle, wander, wilder 07 buffalo, bumbaze, confuse, flummox, mystify, nonplus, perplex, stupefy 08 confound 09 bamboozle, disorient, obfuscate 10 disconcert, take to town 12 tie up in knots

bewildered
◇ *anagram indicator*
04 lost, will, wull 05 at sea, dizzy, fazed, muzzy 06 fogged, tavert 07 baffled, bemazed, bemused, floored, mixed up, muddled, pixy-led, puzzled, stunned, taivert 08 all at sea, confused, jiggered, pathless, wandered 09 flummoxed, mystified, perplexed, pixilated, surprised, trackless, uncertain 10 bamboozled, distracted, nonplussed, pixillated, speechless, taken aback 11 disoriented

bewildering
05 dizzy 07 amazing, cryptic 08 baffling, puzzling 09 confusing, enigmatic 10 astounding, mysterious, mystifying, perplexing, surprising 12 unfathomable

bewilderment
03 awe, fog **04** daze, maze **05** amaze **06** muddle, puzzle **07** mizmaze **08** surprise **09** amazement, confusion, égarement, puzzledom **10** amazedness, perplexity, puzzlement **11** uncertainty **12** stupefaction **13** disconcertion, mystification **14** disorientation

bewitch
03 hex, obi **04** obia, take, wish **05** charm, obeah, witch **06** allure, hoodoo, obsess, seduce, strike, voodoo, voudou **07** beguile, delight, enchant, enthral, glamour, possess **08** elf-shoot, entrance, forspeak, intrigue, overlook, sirenize, transfix **09** captivate, enrapture, ensorcell, fascinate, forespeak, hypnotize, mesmerize, spellbind, tantalize

beyond
04 over, past **05** above, after, ayont, trans- **08** away from **09** apart from, later than, upwards of **10** remote from **11** further than, greater than **12** out of range of, out of reach of **14** on the far side of

Bhutan
03 BTN

bias
04 bent, load, sway, warp **05** angle, cross, poise, slant, twist **06** colour, earwig, weight **07** bigotry, distort, leaning, oblique **08** diagonal, jaundice, penchant, tendency **09** influence, parti pris, prejudice, preoccupy, slantwise **10** distortion, partiality, partialize, predispose, prepossess, proclivity, propensity, unfairness **11** favouritism, inclination, intolerance, load the dice, prejudicate **12** one-sidedness, predilection, stereotyping **13** prepossession

biased
◇ *anagram indicator*
04 skew **06** angled, loaded, skewed, swayed, unfair, warped **07** bigoted, partial, slanted, twisted **08** one-sided, partisan, partizan, weighted **09** blinkered, distorted, jaundiced **10** influenced, interested, prejudiced, subjective, tendential **11** predisposed, prejudicate, tendencious, tendentious **12** prepossessed **14** discriminatory

bib
04 pout **05** Bible, blain **06** brassy, feeder

Bible
02 NT, OT **03** ABC, Bib, law **05** canon **06** fardel, manual, omasum, primer **07** Gospels, letters, lexicon **08** epistles, good book, handbook, holy writ, prophets, textbook, writings **09** Apocrypha, authority, companion, directory, guidebook, Holy Bible, manyplies **10** dictionary, Pentateuch, psalterium, revelation, Scriptures **12** encyclopedia, New Testament, Old Testament **13** reference book **14** holy Scriptures

See also **plague**; **scripture**

Versions of the Bible include:

02 AV, EV, RV
03 NEB, RSV
05 Douai, Douay, Itala, Reims
06 Geneva, Gideon, Italic, Wyclif
07 Matthew, Peshito, Tyndale, Vulgate
08 Breeches, Peshitta, Peshitto, Wycliffe
09 Coverdale, King James
10 New English, Septuagint
14 English Version, Revised Version

Books of the Bible include:

02 Am, Ch, Dt, Ec, Ex, Ez, Is, Jg, Jl, Jn, Kg, Lk, Mk, Mt, Ob, Pr, Ps, Ru, Th
03 Bar, Chr, Col, Cor, Dan, Eph, Esd, Est, Gal, Gen, Hab, Hag, Heb, Hos, Isa, Jas, Jer, Job (Book of), Jon, Jos, Jud, Lam, Lev, Mal, Mic, Nah, Neh, Num, Pet, Rev, Rom, Sam, Sir, Sus, Tim, Tit, Tob
04 Acts, Amos (Book of), Deut, Eccl, Epis, Esth, Exod, Ezek, Ezra (Book of), Hebr, Joel (Book of), John (Gospel according to), John (Letters of), Josh, Jude (Letter of), Luke (Gospel according to), Macc, Mark (Gospel according to), Numb, Obad, Phil, Prov, Ruth (Book of), S of S, Wisd, Zech, Zeph
05 Bel&Dr, Hosea (Book of), James (Letter of), Jonah (Book of), Kings (Books of), Levit, Micah (Book of), Nahum (Book of), Peter (Letters of), Thess, Titus (Letter of Paul to), Tobit (Book of)
06 Baruch (Book of), Coloss, Daniel (Book of), Eccles, Ecclus, Esdras (Books of), Esther (Book of), Exodus (Book of), Haggai (Book of), Isaiah (Book of), Joshua (Book of), Judges (Book of), Judith (Book of), Philem, Psalms (Book of), Romans (Letter of Paul to the), Samuel (Books of), Sirach (Book of)
07 Ezekiel (Book of), Genesis (Book of), Gospels, Hebrews (Letter of Paul to the), Malachi (Book of), Matthew (Gospel according to), Numbers (Book of), Obadiah (Book of), Pr of Man, Susanna (History of), Timothy (Letters of Paul to)
08 Habakkuk (Book of), Jeremiah (Book of), Jeremiah (Letter of), Nehemiah (Book of), Philemon (Letter of Paul to), Proverbs (Book of)
09 Apocrypha, Ephesians (Letter of Paul to the), Galatians (Letter of Paul to the), Hexateuch, Leviticus (Book of), Maccabees, Zechariah (Book of), Zephaniah (Book of)
10 Apocalypse, Chronicles (Books of), Colossians (Letter of Paul to the), Heptateuch, Pentateuch, Revelation
11 Corinthians (Letters of Paul to the), Deuteronomy (Book of), Philippians (Letter of Paul to the)
12 Ecclesiastes (Book of), Lamentations, New Testament, Old Testament
13 Song of Solomon, Thessalonians (Letters of Paul to the)
14 Ecclesiasticus (Book of), Pauline Letters
15 Bel and the Dragon, Pastoral Letters, Prayer of Azariah, Wisdom of Solomon
16 Prayer of Manasseh, Revelation of John
17 Acts of the Apostles
22 Song of the Three Young Men

Biblical characters include:

03 Dan, Eve, Gad, Ham, Job, Lot
04 Abel, Adam, Ahab, Amos, Anna, Baal, Cain, Esau, Ezra, Joel, John, Leah, Levi, Luke, Mark, Mary, Noah, Paul, Ruth, Saul, Seth, Shem
05 Aaron, Abner, Asher, Caleb, David, Enoch, Hagar, Herod (the Great), Hosea, Isaac, Jacob, James, Jesus, Jonah, Judah, Judas, Magog, Micah, Moses, Nahum, Naomi, Peter, Rhoda, Sarah, Sheba (Queen of), Simon, Titus, Tobit, Uriah
06 Andrew, Baruch, Christ, Daniel, Elijah, Elisha, Esther, Gideon, Isaiah, Joseph, Joshua, Josiah, Judith, Martha, Miriam, Nathan, Nimrod, Philip, Pilate, Rachel, Reuben, Salome, Samson, Samuel, Simeon, Thomas, Uzziah
07 Abigail, Abraham, Absalom, Azariah, Delilah, Ephraim, Ezekiel, Gabriel, Goliath, Ishmael, Japheth, Jezebel, Lazarus, Malachi, Matthew, Michael, Obadiah, Rebecca, Rebekah, Solomon, Stephen, Susanna, Tabitha, Timothy, Zebedee, Zebulun
08 Barabbas, Barnabus, Benjamin, Caiaphas, Habbakuk, Hezekiah, Issachar, Jeremiah, Jeroboam, Jonathan, Manasseh, Matthias, Mordecai, Naphtali, Nehemiah, Thaddeus, Zedekiah
09 Bathsheba, Beelzebub, Nathanael, Nathaniel, Nicodemus, Priscilla, Zechariah, Zephaniah
10 Adam and Eve, Bartimaeus, Belshazzar, Methuselah, Simon Magus, Simon Peter
11 Bartholomew, Gog and Magog, Jehoshaphat, Jesus Christ
12 Herod Agrippa, Herod Antipas, Queen of Sheba
13 Judas Iscariot, Mary Magdalene, Pontius Pilate, Simon of Cyrene
14 John the Baptist, Nebuchadnezzar, Simon the Zealot

Biblical placenames include:

03 Nod
04 Eden, Gaza, Rome, Zion
05 Babel, Egypt, Judah, Sinai, Sodom
06 Ararat, Canaan, Cyrene, Israel, Jordan, Judaea, Mt Zion, Red Sea
07 Babylon, Calvary, Galilee, Jericho, Mt Sinai, Nineveh

08 Bethesda, Dalmatia, Damascus, Golgotha, Gomorrah, Mt Ararat, Nazareth
09 Bethlehem, Jerusalem, Palestine
10 Alexandria, Gethsemane
11 River Jordan
12 Garden of Eden, Sea of Galilee

See also **apocryphal**

bibliography
06 record **08** book list **09** catalogue **10** bibliology **11** bibliotheca, list of books

bicker
03 row **04** spar, spat **05** argue, clash, fight, scrap **06** patter, quiver **07** dispute, fall out, glitter, quarrel, wrangle **08** disagree, squabble **09** altercate

bickering
06 at odds **07** arguing **08** clashing **09** scrapping **10** squabbling **11** disagreeing, quarrelling **13** at loggerheads **15** like cats and dogs

bicycle
04 bike **05** cycle, wheel **10** pedal cycle

Bicycles include:

03 BMX
04 push, quad, solo
05 hobby, racer
06 safety, tandem
07 chopper, Raleigh®, touring
08 draisene, draisine, exercise, kangaroo, mountain, ordinary, push-bike, tricycle, unicycle
09 recumbent
10 all-terrain, boneshaker, dandy-horse, fairy-cycle, fixed-wheel, stationary, two-wheeler, velocipede
12 mountain bike
13 penny farthing
14 all-terrain bike

Bicycle parts include:

03 hub
04 bell, fork, gear, lamp, pump, tire, tyre
05 brake, chain, crank, frame, pedal, spoke, wheel
06 dynamo, fender, hanger, pulley, saddle, spokes
07 bar ends, carrier, headset, hub gear, pannier, rim tape, toe clip, tool bag, top tube
08 aero bars, cassette, chainset, crankset, crossbar, down tube, head tube, mudguard, rim brake, rod brake, seat post, seat tube, sprocket, wheel nut, wheel rim
09 brake shoe, chain link, chain ring, disc brake, drum brake, gear cable, gear lever, gearwheel, inner tube, kickstand, prop stand, reflector, seat stays, tyre valve, wheel lock
10 brake block, brake cable, brake lever, chain guard, chain guide, chain stays, chain wheel, crank lever, derailleur, drive train, handlebars, seat pillar, stabilizer, Woods® valve
11 gear shifter, lamp bracket, Presta® valve, roller chain, speedometer
12 brake caliper, coaster brake, diamond frame, spoke nipples, steering head, steering tube, stirrup guide, wheel bearing, wheel spindle
13 bottom bracket, clipless pedal, freewheel unit, handlebar stem, Schrader® valve, shock absorber, sprocket wheel
14 drop handlebars, side-pull brakes

bid
02 go **03** ask, say, sum, try, vie **04** bode, call, pray, tell, wave, wish **05** greet, offer, order, price, put up **06** amount, charge, demand, desire, direct, effort, enjoin, invite, submit, summon, tender **07** advance, attempt, call for, command, proffer, propose, request, require, solicit, venture **08** instruct, proposal **09** endeavour **10** put forward, submission

• no bid
04 pass

biddable
04 meek **08** amenable, obedient **09** compliant, easy-going, malleable, tractable **10** submitting **11** subservient

bidding
04 call **05** order **06** behest, charge, demand, desire **07** command, request, summons **09** direction **10** injunction, invitation **11** instruction, requirement

• bidding system
04 Acol **06** canapé **09** blackwood

big
02 OS **03** fat **04** huge, loud, main, mega, tall, vast **05** adult, beefy, build, bulky, burly, elder, giant, great, hefty, jumbo, large, major, obese, older, stout **06** brawny, bumper, famous, mature, pile up, valued **07** eminent, grown-up, hulking, immense, leading, mammoth, massive, pompous, radical, salient, serious, sizable, weighty **08** boastful, colossal, critical, enormous, generous, gigantic, gracious, muscular, powerful, sizeable, spacious, whopping **09** cavernous, corpulent, extensive, ginormous, humungous, important, momentous, principal, prominent, unselfish, well-built, well-known **10** benevolent, extra large, munificent, noteworthy, voluminous **11** fundamental, influential, kind-hearted, magnanimous, outstanding, pretentious, significant, substantial **12** considerable **13** distinguished

bigheaded
04 vain **05** cocky **07** haughty, stuck-up **08** arrogant **09** conceited **11** swell-headed **12** vainglorious **13** self-important, self-satisfied, swollen-headed **14** full of yourself

bigot
03 MCP **06** racist, sexist, zealot **07** fanatic **08** partisan **09** dogmatist, homophobe, sectarian **10** chauvinist **11** religionist

bigoted
06 biased, closed, narrow, swayed, warped **07** partial, twisted **08** dogmatic, one-sided **09** blinkered, fanatical, hidebound, illiberal, jaundiced, obstinate **10** influenced, intolerant, prejudiced **11** opinionated **12** narrow-minded

bigotry
04 bias **06** racism, sexism **08** jingoism **09** dogmatism, injustice, prejudice, racialism **10** chauvinism, fanaticism, partiality, unfairness **11** intolerance, religionism **12** sectarianism **14** discrimination

bigwig
03 nob, VIP **04** tuan **05** mogul, swell **06** big gun, honcho, worthy **07** big shot, notable **08** big noise, somebody **09** big cheese, celebrity, dignitary, personage **10** panjandrum **11** heavyweight

bijou
03 wee **04** tiny **05** jewel, small **06** little, minute, petite, pocket **07** compact, trinket **10** diminutive

bile
04 gall **05** anger **06** choler, spleen **07** rancour **09** bad temper, ill-humour, testiness **10** bitterness, melancholy **11** peevishness, short temper **12** irascibility, irritability

bilge
03 rot **04** crap **05** balls, trash, tripe **06** drivel, faddle, hot air, piffle **07** rubbish, twaddle **08** blethers, claptrap, cobblers, nonsense, tommyrot **09** gibberish, poppycock **10** codswallop **12** clamjamphrie

bilious
04 edgy, sick **05** cross, lurid, testy **06** crabby, garish, grumpy, queasy, sickly **07** grouchy, peevish **08** choleric **09** crotchety, irritable, nauseated **10** disgusting, nauseating, out of sorts **11** bad-tempered, ill-humoured, ill-tempered **13** short-tempered

bilk
02 do **03** con **05** cheat, elude, sting, trick **06** diddle, fleece **07** deceive, defraud, do out of, swindle **09** bamboozle **14** pull a fast one on

bill
02 a/c, ad, ax **03** acc, act, axe, fin, IOU, neb, nib, tab **04** acct, beak, chit, note, post **05** check, debit, flyer, score, tally **06** advert, charge, notice, poster **07** account, charges, handout, invoice, leaflet, measure, placard, promote, rostrum, statute, William **08** announce, banknote, bulletin, circular, handbill, mandible, playbill, proposal **09** advertise, list costs, programme, reckoning, statement **10** broadsheet,

give notice **11** legislation
12 announcement **13** advertisement, send an account, send an invoice
14 send a statement

- **bill of sale**

02 bs

billet

03 job **04** post **05** berth, lodge, put up, rooms **06** casern, coupon, office
07 caserne, housing, lodging, quarter, station **08** barracks, position, quarters
09 situation **10** employment, occupation **11** accommodate
13 accommodation **14** living quarters

billow

04 mass, rise, roil, roll, rush, wave
05 bulge, cloud, flood, heave, surge, swell **06** expand **07** balloon, breaker, fill out, puff out **08** undulate

billowy

06 waving **07** heaving, rolling, surging, tossing **08** rippling, swelling, swirling
09 billowing **10** undulating

Billy

06 Bunter

bin

03 box **04** bing, bunk **05** chest
06 basket, bucket, holder **07** wheelie
09 container **10** garbage can, receptacle **11** waste basket

bind

03 oop, oup, tie, wap **04** bond, bore, gage, gird, hold, hole, join, lash, pain, rope, spot, tape, whip, wrap, yoke
05 chain, clamp, cover, dress, force, impel, leash, stick, strap, thirl, tie up, truss, unify, unite **06** attach, compel, embale, fasten, fetter, hamper, objure, oblige, secure, swathe, tether
07 astrict, bandage, combine, confine, dilemma, embrace, impasse, require, shackle **08** astringe, enfetter, nuisance, quandary, restrain, restrict **09** colligate, constrain, tight spot **10** close ranks, difficulty, irritation **11** necessitate, predicament **12** knit together, pull together **13** embarrassment, inconvenience, pain in the neck, stand together

binding

04 tape, yapp **05** cover, tight, valid
06 border, edging, strict **07** bandage
08 covering, ligation, rigorous, trimming, wrapping **09** mandatory, necessary, permanent, requisite, stringent **10** compulsory, conclusive, obligatory **11** irrevocable, unalterable, unbreakable
12 indissoluble

bindweed

08 bearbine, bellbind, withwind, woodbind, woodbine **09** withywind
11 convolvulus

binge

02 do **03** jag **04** bout, orgy, sesh, toot, tout **05** beano, blind, fling, spree
06 bender, guzzle **07** blow-out, session

biochemistry

Biochemists include:

04 **Abel** (John Jacob), **Cori** (Carl), **Duve** (Christian de)
05 **Boyer** (Herbert), **Brown** (Rachel Fuller), **Chain** (Sir Ernst B), **Doisy** (Edward A), **Krebs** (Sir Edwin G), **Krebs** (Sir Hans), **Monod** (Jacques), **Moore** (Stanford)
06 **Asimov** (Isaac), **Beadle** (George), **Domagk** (Gerhard), **Martin** (Archer), **Mullis** (Kary B), **Oparin** (Alexandr), **Perutz** (Max), **Porter** (Rodney R), **Sanger** (Frederick)
07 **Edelman** (Gerald M), **Fischer** (Edmond H), **Hopkins** (Sir Frederick), **Khorana** (Har Gobind), **Stanley** (Wendell M), **Waksman** (Selman), **Warburg** (Otto)
08 **Anfinsen** (Christian B), **Chargaff** (Erwin), **Kornberg** (Arthur), **Meyerhof** (Otto), **Northrop** (John H), **Weinberg** (Robert)
09 **Bergström** (Sune), **Butenandt** (Adolf), **Michaelis** (Leonor)
11 **Hoppe-Seyler** (Felix)
12 **Szent-Györgyi** (Albert von)

See also **biology**

biography

02 CV **03** bio **04** biog, life **05** diary
06 biopic, letter, memoir, record, résumé **07** account, diaries, history, journal, letters, memoirs, profile
08 journals **09** life story
11 hagiography **12** recollection
13 autobiography, prosopography, recollections **15** curriculum vitae

Biographers include:

05 **Spark** (Dame Muriel), **Weems** (Mason Locke)
06 **Aubrey** (John), **Morley** (John, Viscount), **Motion** (Andrew), **Napier** (Mark), **Wilson** (Andrew Norman)
07 **Ackroyd** (Peter), **Bedford** (Sybille), **Bolitho** (Hector), **Boswell** (James), **Debrett** (John), **Ellmann** (Richard), **Holroyd** (Michael), **Lubbock** (Percy), **Pearson** (Hesketh), **Sitwell** (Sacheverell)
08 **Lockhart** (John Gibson), **Plutarch**, **Strachey** (Lytton)
09 **Aldington** (Richard), **Kingsmill** (Hugh), **Suetonius**

biology

Biological terms include:

02 GM
03 DNA, RNA
04 cell, gene
05 class, genus, virus
06 coccus, enzyme, family, fossil, tissue
07 meiosis, microbe, mitosis, nucleus, osmosis, protein, species
08 bacillus, bacteria, cultivar, genetics, membrane, molecule, mutation, organism, parasite, ribosome, stem cell
09 amino acid, cell cycle, corpuscle, cytoplasm, diffusion, ecosystem, ectoplasm, evolution, food chain, Mendelism, pollution, reticulum, symbiosis
10 alpha helix, chromosome, extinction, Lamarckism, metabolism, parasitism, protoplasm
11 Haeckel's law, homeostasis, respiration
12 conservation, mitochondria, reproduction
13 flora and fauna, micro-organism, mitochondrion
14 Golgi apparatus, photosynthesis
15 nuclear membrane, ribonucleic acid

Biologists and naturalists include:

03 **His** (Wilhelm)
04 **Axel** (Richard), **Baer** (Karl Ernst von), **Berg** (Paul), **Hess** (Walter), **Hunt** (Tim), **Katz** (Sir Bernard), **Koch** (Ludwig), **Lyon** (Mary)
05 **Arber** (Werner), **Bacon** (Francis, Viscount), **Bates** (Henry Walter), **Beebe** (William), **Bruce** (Sir David), **Crick** (Francis), **Golgi** (Camillo), **Lewis** (Edward B), **Luria** (Salvador), **Lwoff** (André), **Nurse** (Sir Paul M), **Sabin** (Albert), **Scott** (Sir Peter), **Sharp** (Phillip), **Smith** (Hamilton), **White** (Gilbert)
06 **Altman** (Sidney), **Anning** (Mary), **Bishop** (Michael), **Blobel** (Günter), **Boveri** (Theodor), **Buffon** (George-Louis, Comte de), **Cairns** (Hugh), **Cannon** (Walter), **Carson** (Rachel), **Claude** (Albert), **Darwin** (Charles), **Friend** (Charlotte), **Huxley** (Sir Julian), **Huxley** (T H), **Isaacs** (Alick), **Kandel** (Eric), **Lartet** (Edouard), **Morgan** (Thomas Hunt), **Palade** (George), **Sloane** (Sir Hans), **Varmus** (Harold), **Watson** (James), **Wilson** (Edward)
07 **Adamson** (Joy), **Agassiz** (Louis), **Andrews** (Roy), **Beneden** (Edouard), **Brenner** (Sydney), **Dawkins** (Richard), **Driesch** (Hans), **Durrell** (Gerald), **Epstein** (Sir Anthony), **Flavell** (Richard), **Gilbert** (Walter), **Haeckel** (Ernst), **Haldane** (J B S), **Hershey** (A D), **Jackson** (Barbara, Lady), **Kendrew** (Sir John), **Lamarck** (Jean), **Lubbock** (Sir John), **Nathans** (Daniel), **Pasteur** (Louis), **Roberts** (Richard), **Steptoe** (Patrick), **Wallace** (Alfred)
08 **Cousteau** (Jacques), **Delbrück** (Max), **Flemming** (Walther), **Franklin** (Rosalind), **Hartwell** (Lee), **Humboldt** (Alexander, Baron von), **Jeffreys** (Sir Alec), **Linnaeus** (Carl), **Li Shizen**, **Margulis** (Lynn), **Meselson** (Matthew), **Milstein** (Cesar), **Purkinje** (Jan), **Sielmann** (Heinz), **Starling** (Ernest), **Tonegawa** (Susumu), **Weismann** (August)
09 **Lederberg** (Joshua), **Schaudinn** (Fritz), **Wieschaus** (Eric)

10 Ingen-Housz (Jan)
11 Deisenhofer (Johan), Leeuwenhoek (Antoni van), Metchnikoff (Elie), Ramón y Cajal (Santiago), Spallanzani (Lazaro)
12 Attenborough (Sir David), Maynard Smith (John)
13 Du Bois-Reymond (Emil Heinrich)
14 Levi-Montalcini (Rita)
15 Nusslein-Volhard (Christiane)

See also **bacteriology**; **biochemistry**; **palaeontologist**; **physiology**

birch

03 rod **04** birk, flog, twig **05** swish
06 Betula

bird

03 jug **04** avis, babe, gaol, girl, jail, nick, quod, shop, stir, time **05** choky, clink **06** chokey, lumber, prison
07 college, slammer **10** girlfriend

See also **animal**; **chicken**; **duck**; **game**; **hen**; **poultry**

Birds include:

02 ka
03 ani, auk, bat, cob, daw, doo, emu, hae, hen, jay, kea, kia, mag, maw, mew, moa, owl, pie, roc, tit, tui
04 barb, chat, cirl, cobb, cock, coot, crow, dodo, dove, duck, emeu, erne, eyas, fowl, gled, guan, gull, hawk, hern, huia, ibis, jynx, kagu, kaka, kite, kiwi, knot, kora, kuku, lark, loom, loon, lory, mina, myna, nene, nyas, pavo, pern, pica, piet, pyat, pyet, pyot, rail, rhea, rook, ruff, runt, ruru, rype, shag, skua, smee, sora, swan, taha, teal, tern, tody, weka, wren, xema, yite
05 agami, ariel, booby, capon, chick, crane, diver, eagle, egret, eider, finch, fleet, flier, galah, glede, goose, grebe, heron, hobby, macaw, mynah, ousel, piper, pipit, pitta, potoo, quail, raven, robin, scops, snipe, solan, squab, stilt, stork, swift, tewit, twite, vireo, wader
06 avocet, bantam, barbet, budgie, bulbul, canary, chough, condor, cuckoo, curlew, cushat, darter, dipper, drongo, dunlin, falcon, fulmar, gannet, godwit, grouse, hoopoe, houdan, jabiru, jacana, kakapo, linnet, magpie, martin, merlin, mesite, motmot, oriole, osprey, parrot, peahen, peewit, petrel, pigeon, plover, puffin, pullet, raptor, redcap, roller, sea-mew, shrike, siskin, takahe, thrush, tom-tit, toucan, trogon, turaco, turkey, yaffle, zoozoo
07 antbird, apteryx, babbler, barn owl, bittern, bluecap, blue jay, bluetit, bullbat, bunting, bustard, buzzard, chicken, coal-tit, cotinga, courser, cowbird, creeper, dottrel, dunnock, fantail, finfoot, goshawk, grackle, halcyon, harrier, hoatzin, jacamar, jackdaw, kestrel, lapwing, leghorn, limpkin, mallard, manakin, moorhen, mudlark, oilbird, ostrich, peacock, pelican, penguin, phoenix, pintail, poultry, quetzal, redpoll, redwing, rooster, ruddock, seagull, seriema, skimmer, skylark, spadger, sparrow, sunbird, swallow, tanager, tiercel, tinamou, titlark, touraco, vulture, wagtail, warbler, waxbill, wrybill, wryneck
08 aasvogel, accentor, adjutant, aigrette, bee-eater, bellbird, blackcap, bobolink, cockatoo, currasow, dabchick, dotterel, fish-hawk, flamingo, great tit, grosbeak, hernshaw, hornbill, landrail, laverock, leafbird, lorikeet, lovebird, lyrebird, megapode, myna bird, nightjar, nuthatch, ovenbird, ox-pecker, palmchat, parakeet, pheasant, puffbird, rainbird, redshank, redstart, ringtail, screamer, sea eagle, shoebill, starling, tapaculo, water-hen, whimbrel, white-eye, woodcock
09 aepyornis, albatross, bald eagle, bergander, blackbird, blackhead, bowerbird, broadbill, bullfinch, cassowary, chaffinch, chickadee, cockatiel, cormorant, corncrake, eider duck, fairy tern, fieldfare, frogmouth, gerfalcon, gnateater, goldfinch, goosander, guillemot, jack-snipe, kittiwake, little owl, merganser, mollymawk, mousebird, mynah bird, nighthawk, ossifrage, partridge, peregrine, phalarope, ptarmigan, razorbill, sandpiper, scrub-bird, sheldrake, thornbill, trumpeter, turnstone, wind-hover
10 budgerigar, chiff-chaff, fledgeling, flycatcher, goatsucker, gobemouche, greenfinch, greenshank, guinea fowl, hammerhead, harpy eagle, honeyeater, honeyguide, kingfisher, kookaburra, nutcracker, sanderling, sandgrouse, shearwater, sheathbill, song thrush, sunbittern, tropicbird, turtledove, wattlebird, woodpecker, wood pigeon
11 butcherbird, frigatebird, golden eagle, hummingbird, mockingbird, nightingale, plantcutter, reed-warbler, snow bunting, song sparrow, sparrowhawk, stone-curlew, storm petrel, thunderbird, tree-creeper, woodcreeper, wood-swallow
12 adjutant bird, cuckoo-roller, diving petrel, flowerpecker, golden plover, honeycreeper, missel-thrush, mistle-thrush, sedge warbler, yellowhammer
13 archaeopteryx, barnacle goose, oystercatcher, secretary bird, willow warbler
14 bird of paradise, plains wanderer
15 blue-footed booby, passenger pigeon, peregrine falcon

Birds of prey include:

03 owl
04 erne, hawk, kite, pern
05 eagle, hobby
06 falcon, lanner, merlin, osprey, raptor
07 barn owl, buzzard, goshawk, harrier, hawk owl, kestrel, red kite
08 bateleur, berghaan, duck-hawk, eagle owl, fish-hawk, Scops owl, sea eagle, spar-hawk, tawny owl
09 bald eagle, black kite, eagle-hawk, fish eagle, gyrfalcon, little owl, marsh hawk, peregrine, stone hawk
10 harpy eagle, hen harrier, tawny eagle
11 booted eagle, chicken hawk, Cooper's hawk, golden eagle, sparrowhawk, stone falcon
12 great grey owl, honey buzzard, long-eared owl, marsh harrier
13 American eagle, Iceland falcon, imperial eagle, lesser kestrel, pallid harrier, secretary bird, short-eared owl
14 short-toed eagle
15 Montagu's harrier, peregrine falcon, red-footed falcon

Flightless birds include:

03 emu
04 dodo, emeu, kiwi, rhea, weka
06 kakapo, ratite, takahe
07 ostrich, penguin
08 great auk, notornis
09 cassowary, owl-parrot, solitaire

Mythical birds include:

03 fum, roc, rok, ruc
04 fung, huma, rukh
07 phoenix
08 whistler
09 impundulu
11 thunderbird
12 bird of wonder

Seabirds include:

03 auk, cob, maw, mew
04 cobb, guga, gull, shag, skua, tern, Xema
05 solan
06 fulmar, gannet, petrel, puffin
07 pickmaw, seagull
08 comorant
09 black tern, great skua, guillemot, kittiwake, little auk, mallemuck, razorbill, swart-back
10 Arctic skua, Arctic tern, common gull, common tern, little gull, little tern, saddleback, solan goose
11 herring gull, Iceland gull, roseate tern, Sabine's gull, storm petrel
12 glaucous gull, Leach's petrel, pomarine skua, sandwich tern
14 black guillemot, long-tailed skua, Manx shearwater
15 black-backed gull, black-headed gull

Wading birds include:

03 ree
04 hern, ibis, knot, ruff
05 crake, crane, heron, reeve, snipe, stilt, stint, stork

06 avocet, curlew, dunlin, godwit, plover
07 bittern, bustard, lapwing
08 dotterel, flamingo, redshank, whimbrel, woodcock
09 dowitcher, grey heron, phalarope, sandpiper, turnstone
10 greenshank, sanderling
11 little stint, stone curlew
12 golden plover, great bustard, ringed plover
13 little bustard, oystercatcher

• birds
04 Aves **05** ornis

birth
04 dawn, line, race, rise, root, seed
05 blood, house, start, stock
06 advent, family, labour, origin, source, strain **07** arrival, descent, genesis, lineage, origins **08** ancestry, breeding, delivery, nativity, pedigree
09 beginning, emergence, genealogy, parentage **10** appearance, background, childbirth, derivation, extraction **11** confinement, parturition
12 commencement, fountainhead
13 starting-point

Birth flowers:

04 rose
05 aster, daisy, holly, poppy
06 cosmos, violet
07 jonquil
08 hawthorn, larkspur, primrose, snowdrop, sweet pea
09 calendula, carnation, gladiolus, narcissus, water lily
10 poinsettia
11 honeysuckle
12 morning glory
13 chrysanthemum
15 lily of the valley

Birth stones:

04 opal, ruby
05 pearl, topaz
06 garnet, zircon
07 diamond, emerald, peridot
08 amethyst, sapphire, sardonyx
09 moonstone, turquoise
10 aquamarine, bloodstone, tourmaline
11 alexandrite

• give birth to
03 cub, ean, kid, lay, pig, pup **04** bear, drop, fawn, foal, have, lamb, yean
05 calve, found, throw **06** create, farrow, kitten, litter, mother **08** initiate
09 establish **10** bring forth, give rise to, inaugurate **12** cause to exist

birthday
03 dob **10** day of birth **11** anniversary

birthmark
04 mole **05** naeve, nevus, patch
06 naevus **07** blemish **10** beauty spot, mother spot **13** discoloration, port-wine stain **14** strawberry mark

birthplace
02 bp **03** b pl **04** home, root **05** fount, roots **06** cradle, source **08** home town
10 fatherland, incunables, incunabula, native town, provenance **12** place of birth **13** mother country, native country, place of origin

birthright
03 due **06** legacy **08** birthdom
09 privilege **11** inheritance, prerogative

biscuit
04 bake, cake **05** biccy **06** bickie

Biscuits include:

03 dog, nut, sea, tea
04 kiss, Nice, puff, rice, rusk, ship, snap, tack, thin, Twix®, wine
05 Marie, ship's, wafer, water
06 cookie, hob-nob, Kit-Kat®, parkin, perkin
07 Bourbon, cracker, fig roll, Gold Bar®, iced gem, Lincoln, oatcake, Penguin®, pretzel, ratafia, rich tea, saltine
08 biscotto, captain's, cracknel, flapjack, hardtack, macaroon, Zwieback
09 Abernethy, Breakaway®, chocolate, digestive, four-by-two, garibaldi, ginger nut, jaffa cake, party ring, petit four, pink wafer, shortcake
10 Bath Oliver, Blue Riband®, brandy snap, butter-bake, crispbread, dunderfunk, florentine, gingersnap, malted milk, shortbread, Wagon Wheel®
11 brown George, fly cemetery, soda cracker, squashed fly
12 cream cracker, custard cream, jammie dodger, langue de chat
14 gingerbread man

• soften biscuit
04 dunk

bisect
◇ *insertion indicator*
04 fork **05** cross, halve, split **06** divide
08 cut in two, separate **09** bifurcate, cut in half, intersect **13** divide into two

bisexual
02 bi **04** AC/DC **07** epicene
11 androgynous, monoclinous
12 ambidextrous, switch hitter
13 hermaphrodite
15 gynandromorphic

bishop
01 B **02** Bp, DD, RR **04** abba, lord
06 exarch, magpie, primus **07** pontiff, prelate, primate **08** diocesan
09 coadjutor, patriarch, suffragan
10 archbishop, episcopant, metropolis
11 intercessor **12** metropolitan
13 spiritual peer **14** vicar-apostolic

Bishops include:

05 Aidan (St), Peter (St)
06 Blaise, Ninian (St), Osmund (St)
07 Ambrose (St), Carroll (John), Hadrian, Patrick (St)
08 Geoffrey (of Monmouth), Holloway (Richard), Nicholas (St), Sheppard (David)
11 Elphinstone (William), Odo of Bayeux

See also **archbishop**

bishopric
03 see **07** diocese, Holy See
10 episcopacy, episcopate
See also **diocese**

bismuth
02 Bi

bison
04 gaur **06** wisent **07** aurochs, bonasus, buffalo **08** bonassus

bit
◇ *hidden indicator*
03 ate, dot, jot, ort, tad **04** atom, chip, curb, dash, doit, drap, drop, haet, hint, iota, lump, mite, part, what, whit
05 chunk, crumb, drill, flake, fleck, grain, piece, scrap, shred, slice, speck, touch, trace **06** cannon, morsel, nibble, pelham, sliver, tittle
07 kenning, portion, segment, snaffle, soupçon, vestige **08** fragment, mouthful, particle **09** scintilla **10** small piece **12** small portion

• a bit
04 tick **05** jiffy **06** a while, fairly, minute, moment, rather **07** a little, a moment, not much, not very
08 slightly **10** a short time, few minutes, few moments **12** a little while

• bit by bit
06 slowly **08** in stages **09** gradually, piecemeal **10** step by step **14** little by little

• bit of
◇ *head selection indicator*

• last bit of
◇ *tail selection indicator*

bitch
03 cat, cow, pig **04** moan, slut
05 brach, gripe, harpy, shrew, swine, trial, vixen, whine **06** ordeal, virago, whinge **07** doggess, grumble, torment
08 badmouth, complain **09** criticize, female dog, nightmare **13** find fault with **15** be spiteful about

bitchiness
05 spite, venom **06** malice **07** cruelty
08 meanness **09** cattiness, nastiness
13 maliciousness

bitchy
04 mean **05** catty, cruel, nasty, snide
07 cutting, vicious **08** shrewish, spiteful, venomous, vixenish
09 malicious, rancorous
10 backbiting, vindictive

bite
◇ *containment indicator*
03 bit, eat, nip **04** chew, crop, gnaw, grip, hold, kick, peck, pick, rend, snap, take, tang, tear, work **05** champ, chomp, crush, force, gnash, munch, piece, pinch, power, prick, punch, seize, smart, snack, spice, sting, taste, wound **06** begnaw, crunch, effect, impact, lesion, morsel, nibble, pierce, tingle **07** morsure, remorse

08 mouthful, piquancy, puncture, pungency, smarting, strength
09 influence, light meal, masticate, sharpness, spiciness **10** impression, take effect **11** refreshment

biting
◇ *containment indicator*
03 raw **04** acid, cold, keen, tart
05 acrid, harsh, nippy, sharp **06** bitter, severe, shrewd, toothy **07** caustic, cutting, cynical, hurtful, mordant, nipping, pointed, pungent, vicious
08 freezing, incisive, piercing, scathing, stinging **09** sarcastic, trenchant, vitriolic **10** astringent, mordacious **11** penetrating

bitter
03 ale, raw, sad, wry **04** acid, keen, sore, sour, tart **05** acerb, acidy, acrid, angry, aygre, cruel, eager, harsh, nippy, parky, sharp, tangy, wersh **06** arctic, biting, fierce, morose, porter, savage, severe, sullen, tragic **07** acerbic, caustic, cynical, hostile, intense, painful, pungent, unhappy
08 freezing, piercing, sardonic, scathing, spiteful, stinging, venomous, vinegary, virulent **09** aggrieved, harrowing, indignant, jaundiced, merciless, rancorous, resentful, vitriolic
10 astringent, begrudging, embittered, malevolent, vindictive, wry-mouthed
11 acrimonious, disgruntled, distressing, penetrating, unsweetened
12 freezing cold, gut-wrenching, heart-rending, vituperative
13 disappointing, heartbreaking

bitterly
05 wryly **06** sourly **07** angrily, cruelly
08 bitingly, morosely, savagely, severely, sullenly **09** cynically, hostilely, intensely, painfully **10** grievously, grudgingly, piercingly, scathingly, spitefully, venomously **11** acerbically, caustically, indignantly, rancorously, resentfully, with vitriol **12** begrudgingly, embitteredly, malevolently, sardonically, vindictively **13** acrimoniously, penetratingly **14** vituperatively

bittern
05 Ardea **06** bittor, bittur **07** bittour
08 mire-drum **10** butter-bump
11 mossbluiter **12** bull-of-the-bog

bitterness
04 bite, edge, fell, gall, pain **05** anger, marah, spite, venom **06** enmity, grudge, rancor, spleen **07** acidity, cruelty, iciness, rancour, rawness, sadness, tragedy, vinegar **08** acrimony, coldness, cynicism, distress, ferocity, jaundice, pungency, severity, sourness, tartness, wormwood **09** harshness, hostility, intensity, sharpness, tanginess, virulence **10** acerbicity, antagonism, chilliness, frostiness, moroseness, resentment, sullenness **11** indignation, malevolence, painfulness, penetration, unhappiness **12** embitterment, heart-rending **13** heartbreaking
14 disappointment, vindictiveness

bitty
06 broken, fitful **07** scrappy
09 piecemeal **10** disjointed, fragmented, incoherent
12 disconnected

bitumen
03 tar **05** slime **09** albertite, elaterite
11 pissasphalt

bivalve
06 cockle, oyster, tellen, tellin
07 geoduck, scallop, scollop **08** ark-shell **10** otter shell

bizarre
◇ *anagram indicator*
03 odd **05** funny, gonzo, outré, queer, wacky, weird **06** way-out **07** comical, curious, deviant, oddball, offbeat, strange, surreal, unusual **08** abnormal, freakish, peculiar, uncommon
09 eccentric, fantastic, grotesque, left-field, ludicrous **10** off the wall, outlandish, ridiculous **11** extravagant, Pythonesque **13** extraordinary
14 unconventional

bizarrely
◇ *anagram indicator*
05 oddly **07** weirdly **09** comically, curiously, strangely, unusually
10 abnormally, freakishly, peculiarly
11 ludicrously **12** outlandishly, ridiculously **13** extravagantly

blab
04 blat, leak, tell **05** prate **06** gossip, reveal, squeal, tattle **07** blister, divulge, let slip, tattler **08** blurt out, disclose, tattling **11** blow the gaff **15** give the game away

blabber
04 chat **06** babble, gabble, gossip, jabber, witter **07** blather, blether, chatter, prattle, swollen, twattle, twitter

black
01 B **03** bad, dim, sad **04** dark, evil, inky, sick, slae, sloe, vile **05** angry, awful, bleak, cruel, dingy, dirty, dusky, grimy, gross, gungy, muddy, raven, sooty, unlit, wrong **06** bitter, dismal, filthy, gloomy, grotty, grubby, odious, soiled, sombre, sullen, tragic, vulgar, wicked **07** cynical, demonic, heinous, immoral, satanic, stained, Stygian, subfusc, swarthy, unclean, unhappy
08 coloured, devilish, funereal, hopeless, menacing, moonless, mournful, overcast, starless
09 Cimmerian, depressed, malicious, miserable, nefarious, resentful, tasteless, tenebrous **10** depressing, diabolical, fuliginous, in bad taste, lugubrious, malevolent, melancholy, melanistic, nigrescent, pitch-black
11 black as coal, crepuscular, dark-skinned, distressing, threatening
13 unilluminated

Blacks include:

03 jet
04 blae, ebon, jeat
05 dwale, ebony, sable
08 jet-black
09 coal-black

• **black and white**
02 b/w **04** gray, grey **05** plain
07 brocked, brockit, on paper, piebald, printed, pyebald, written **08** clear-cut, definite, distinct, on record
11 categorical, unambiguous, unequivocal, well-defined, written down **12** monochromist **13** pepper-and-salt
• **black eye** *see* **eye**
• **black out**
03 gag **05** faint **06** censor, darken
07 conceal, cover up, eclipse, pass out
08 collapse, flake out, keel over, suppress, withhold
• **in the black**
03 ban, bar, hit **05** punch, taboo
06 bruise, injure **07** blacken, boycott, embargo, solvent **08** in credit
09 blacklist, out of debt **11** without debt
• **very black**
02 BB **04** inky

blackball
03 ban, bar, pip **04** oust, pill, snub, veto
05 debar, expel **06** reject **07** drum out, exclude, shut out **08** throw out
09 blacklist, ostracize, repudiate
11 vote against

blacken
03 ink, tar **04** cork, soil **05** black, cloud, decry, dirty, libel, smear, smoke, stain, sully, taint **06** besmut, darken, defame, defile, impugn, malign, revile, smudge, vilify **07** detract, nigrify, run down, slander, tarnish **08** besmirch
09 denigrate, discredit, dishonour, make dirty **10** calumniate

blackguard
05 crook, devil, knave, rogue, sweep, swine **06** rascal, rotter, wretch
07 bleeder, bounder, scumbag, stinker, villain **08** blighter **09** miscreant, reprobate, scoundrel **10** vituperate

blackleg
03 leg **04** fink, scab, snob
09 knobstick

blacklist
03 ban, bar **04** snub, veto **05** debar, expel, taboo **06** outlaw, reject
07 boycott, exclude, shut out
08 disallow, preclude **09** ostracize, proscribe, repudiate

blackmail
04 milk **05** black, bleed, chout, exact, force **06** coerce, compel, demand, extort, lean on, ransom, strike
07 bribery, squeeze **08** chantage, exaction, threaten **09** extortion, greenmail, hush money, shakedown
10 pressurize **12** hold to ransom, intimidation **14** put the screws on

blackmailer
07 vampire **08** hijacker **10** highbinder, highjacker **11** bloodsucker, extortioner
12 extortionist

blackout
04 coma **05** faint, swoon **07** cover-up, embargo, secrecy, silence, syncope **08** brownout, oblivion, power cut **10** censorship, flaking-out, passing out **11** concealment, suppression, withholding **12** power failure **15** unconsciousness

blacksmith
06 vulcan **09** hammerman, ironsmith **11** burn-the-wind

bladder
04 swim **05** sound **06** vesica **07** blister, utricle, vesicle **09** cholecyst

blade
03 fan, oar **04** edge, peel, vane, wash **05** float, knife, lance, razor, skate, spear, sword **06** dagger, lamina, paddle, scythe, Toledo **07** bayonet, scalpel, spatula **10** cream-slice, paperknife **11** cutting edge

See also **dagger**; **sword**

blame
03 rap, tax **04** onus, wite, wyte **05** chide, decry, fault, guilt, odium, stick, thank, wight **06** accuse, berate, charge, dirdam, dirdum, injury, rebuke **07** appoint, censure, condemn, pin it on, reproof, reprove, upbraid **08** admonish, berating, reproach, tear into **09** criticism, criticize, dispraise, inculpate, liability, name names, reprehend, reprimand, scapegoat **10** accusation, confounded, disapprove, discommend, find guilty, hold liable **11** culpability **12** condemnation, name and shame **13** find fault with, incrimination, recrimination **14** accountability, responsibility **15** hold accountable, hold responsible

blameless
05 clear **07** perfect, sinless, upright **08** innocent, virtuous, witeless **09** faultless, guiltless, lily-white, stainless **10** inculpable, unblamable, unreproved **11** unblemished **12** irreprovable, without fault **13** above reproach, unimpeachable **14** irreproachable **15** irreprehensible

blameworthy
06 guilty **07** at fault **08** culpable, shameful, unworthy **10** flagitious **11** inexcusable, responsible **12** disreputable, indefensible, reproachable **13** discreditable, reprehensible

blanch
04 boil **05** scald **06** blench, whiten **07** go white, lighten **08** etiolate, grow pale, turn pale **09** turn white **10** become pale, grow pallid **11** become white **12** become pallid

blancmange
04 mold **05** mould **08** flummery

bland
04 dull, flat, mild, weak **05** suave **06** boring, smooth, spammy **07** anodyne, humdrum, insipid, mundane, tedious, vanilla **08** ordinary **09** tasteless **10** antiseptic, monotonous, unexciting **11** flavourless, inoffensive, nondescript, uninspiring **13** characterless, uninteresting

blandishments
05 sooth, spiel **07** blarney, coaxing, fawning, flannel, treacle **08** cajolery, flattery, lipsalve, soft soap **09** agréments, sweet talk, wheedling **10** sycophancy **11** compliments, enticements, inducements **12** ingratiation, inveiglement **14** persuasiveness

blank
03 gap **04** bare, void **05** break, clean, clear, empty, plain, space, white **06** glazed, vacant, vacuum **07** deadpan, vacancy, vacuity, vacuous **08** lifeless, unfilled, unmarked **09** apathetic, emptiness, impassive, unwritten **10** empty space, poker-faced **11** emotionless, indifferent, inscrutable, nothingness **12** uninterested **14** expressionless, without feeling **15** uncomprehending

blanket
04 coat, film, hide, mask **05** bluey, cloak, cloud, cover, layer, manta, quilt, sheet, total **06** afghan, carpet, deaden, global, mantle, muffle, poncho, sarape, serape, stroud **07** coating, conceal, eclipse, obscure, overall, overlay, whittle, wrapper **08** bedcover, coverage, covering, coverlet, envelope, mackinaw, suppress, surround, sweeping, wrapping **09** bedspread, eiderdown, inclusive, wholesale **11** wide-ranging **12** all-embracing, all-inclusive, underblanket **13** comprehensive **14** across-the-board, indiscriminate

blankly
08 vacantly **09** vacuously **10** lifelessly **11** impassively **13** apathetically, emotionlessly, indifferently **14** uninterestedly, without feeling

blare
04 boom, honk, hoot, peal, ring, roar, toot **05** blast, clang **07** boom out, clamour, resound, thunder, trumpet **08** blast out **11** sound loudly

blarney
05 spiel, taffy **06** cajole, sawder **07** coaxing, flannel **08** cajolery, flattery, soft soap **09** sweet talk, wheedling **10** soft sawder, soft sowder **13** blandishments **14** persuasiveness

blasé
04 cool **05** bored, jaded, weary **07** offhand, unmoved **08** lukewarm **09** apathetic, impassive, unexcited **10** nonchalant, phlegmatic, uninspired **11** indifferent, unconcerned, unimpressed **12** uninterested

blaspheme
04 cuss, damn **05** abuse, curse, swear **06** revile **07** profane **08** execrate **09** desecrate, imprecate **10** utter oaths **12** anathematize

blasphemous
07 godless, impious, profane, ungodly **10** irreverent, sulphurous **11** imprecatory, irreligious **12** sacrilegious

blasphemously
09 profanely **12** irreverently **14** sacrilegiously **15** disrespectfully

blasphemy
05 curse, oaths **07** cursing, impiety, outrage **08** swearing **09** expletive, profanity, sacrilege, violation **10** execration, unholiness **11** desecration, impiousness, imprecation, irreverence, profaneness, ungodliness

blast
◇ *anagram indicator*
03 dee, wap **04** bang, blow, bomb, boom, clap, dang, drat, gale, gust, honk, hoot, parp, peal, puff, roar, ruin, rush, shot, slam, toot, tout, waff, wail, zonk **05** blare, burst, clang, crack, crash, pryse, scath, slate, sound, storm, trump, whiff, whift **06** assail, attack, bellow, berate, blow up, blow-up, flatus, flurry, jigger, rebuke, scaith, scathe, scream, shriek, skaith, squall, strike, volley, wuther **07** blaring, blatter, bluster, booming, boom out, clamour, destroy, draught, explode, gun down, reprove, roaring, shatter, tantara, tell off, tempest, thunder, upbraid, whither **08** blare out, demolish, outburst, siderate **09** criticize, discharge, explosion, reprimand, shoot down, tantarara **10** detonation, sideration **12** blow to pieces **13** thunder-stroke

• **blast off**
07 lift off, take off **10** be launched

blasted
◇ *anagram indicator*
05 ruddy **06** cursed, damned, darned **07** flaming **08** annoying, blighted, blooming, dratting, flipping, infernal **10** confounded, unpleasant **12** planet-struck **14** planet-stricken

blatant
04 bald, open **05** naked, overt, sheer **06** arrant, brazen, coarse, full-on, patent **07** glaring, obvious **08** flagrant, hard-core, manifest, outright **09** bald-faced, barefaced, clamorous, obtrusive, out-and-out, prominent, shameless, unashamed **10** pronounced **11** conspicuous, undisguised, unmitigated **12** ostentatious

blatantly
06 openly **08** brazenly, patently **09** glaringly, obviously, out-and-out **10** flagrantly, manifestly **11** shamelessly, unashamedly **13** conspicuously

blaze
03 low **04** beam, boil, burn, fire, glow, lowe, lunt, rage **05** blast, burst, erupt,

flame, flare, flash, glare, gleam, light, shine, shoot **06** blow up, flames, ignite, let fly, let off, see red, seethe, set off **07** bonfire, explode, flare up, flare-up, glitter, inferno **08** be alight, be on fire, outburst, radiance **09** be radiant, catch fire, discharge, explosion, fire-storm **10** brilliance **11** be brilliant **13** conflagration **15** burst into flames

blazing
◇ *anagram indicator*
05 angry **06** on fire **07** burning

blazon
05 vaunt **06** flaunt, herald **07** trumpet **08** announce, flourish, proclaim **09** broadcast, celebrate, make known, publicize

bleach
04 fade, pale **06** blanch, whiten **07** lighten **08** decolour, etiolate, make pale, peroxide, turn pale **09** make white, turn white **10** decolorize

bleak
03 raw **04** arid, bare, blae, blay, bley, cold, dark, drab, dull, grim, open **05** ablet, empty, harsh, windy **06** barren, chilly, dismal, dreary, gloomy, leaden, sombre **07** exposed, joyless, spartan **08** desolate, hopeless, soulless, wretched **09** cheerless, desperate, miserable, windswept **10** depressing **11** comfortless, unpromising, unsheltered **12** discouraging, unfavourable **13** disheartening, weather-beaten

bleakly
06 grimly **08** dismally, drearily, gloomily, sombrely **09** joylessly, miserably **10** wretchedly **11** cheerlessly **12** unfavourably **13** unpromisingly

bleary
03 dim **05** tired **06** blurry, cloudy, drowsy, rheumy, watery **07** blurred **09** unfocused **10** bleary-eyed

bleat
03 baa, cry, maa **04** beef, blat, bray, call, moan **05** gripe, whine **06** grouse, kvetch, whinge **07** grumble, whicker **08** complain **09** complaint

bleed
03 run, sap **04** flow, gush, melt, milk, ooze, seep, weep **05** blood, drain, exude, flood, glide, merge, spurt **06** extort, reduce **07** deplete, exhaust, extract, squeeze, suck dry, trickle **08** let blood **09** lose blood, shed blood **10** bleed white **11** extravasate, haemorrhage **12** exsanguinate, phlebotomize

blemish
03 mar **04** blot, blur, flaw, mark, mote, tash, vice, want **05** botch, fault, speck, spoil, stain, sully, taint, touch **06** blotch, damage, deface, defame, defect, impair, smudge **07** tarnish **08** disgrace **09** deformity, disfigure, dishonour **10** compromise **12** imperfection **13** discoloration, disfigurement

Blemishes include:

03 zit
04 acne, boil, bump, corn, mole, scab, scar, spot, wart
06 bunion, callus, naevus, pimple
07 blister, freckle, pustule, verruca
08 pockmark
09 birthmark, blackhead, carbuncle, chilblain, whitehead
14 strawberry mark

blench
03 shy **05** cower, quail, quake, start, wince **06** falter, flinch, quiver, recoil, shrink **07** shudder **08** draw back, hesitate, pull back

blend
◇ *anagram indicator*
03 fit, mix **04** beat, fuse, meld, melt, stir, suit **05** admix, alloy, match, merge, union, unite, whisk **06** commix, fusion, go with, mingle, set off **07** amalgam, combine, merging, mixture, uniting **08** coalesce, compound, intermix **09** admixture, commingle, composite, contemper, harmonize, synthesis **10** amalgamate, commixture, complement, concoction, go together, go well with, homogenize, intertwine, interweave, synthesize **11** combination, portmanteau, run together **12** amalgamation

bless
04 laud **05** exalt, extol, thank, wound **06** anoint, favour, hallow, honour, ordain, praise, thrash **07** glorify, magnify, worship **08** brandish, dedicate, sanctify **10** consecrate, lay hands on **13** be grateful for, be thankful for, give thanks for

• **bless you**
10 benedicite, Gesundheit

blessed
◇ *anagram indicator*
04 glad, holy **05** happy, lucky **06** adored, divine, graced, joyful, joyous, sacred **07** endowed, revered **08** benedict, favoured, hallowed, heavenly, provided **09** benedight, contented, fortunate **10** prosperous, sanctified **11** consecrated

blessing
02 OK **04** boon, gain, gift, help **05** grace, leave **06** bounty, favour, profit **07** backing, benefit, benison, consent, darshan, go-ahead, godsend, kiddush, service, support **08** approval, felicity, sanction, thumbs-up, windfall **09** advantage, agreement, authority, good thing **10** benedicite, dedication, green light, invocation, permission **11** approbation, benediction, concurrence, good fortune **12** commendation, consecration, thanksgiving

blight
◇ *anagram indicator*
03 mar, rot, woe **04** bane, dash, evil, kill, ruin, take **05** blast, check, crush, curse, decay, spoil, wreck **06** cancer, canker, damage, fungus, injure, mildew, strike, wither **07** destroy, disease, scourge, scowder, setback, shatter, shrivel, trouble **08** calamity, scouther, scowther **09** blastment, fire-blast, frustrate, pollution, undermine **10** affliction, annihilate, corruption, disappoint, misfortune, sideration **11** infestation **13** contamination

blimey
03 coo, lor

blind
03 mad **04** hood, mask, rash, seal, seel, slow, trap, wild **05** blend, chick, cloak, cover, front, hasty, shade, trick **06** bisson, closed, dazzle, façade, hidden, screen **07** confuse, cover-up, curtain, deceive, eyeless, mislead, shutter, unaware, winking **08** careless, heedless, ignorant, mindless, obscured, reckless, unseeing, Venetian **09** concealed, impetuous, impulsive, make blind, oblivious, sightless, unmindful, unsighted **10** beetle-eyed, camouflage, intimidate, irrational, masquerade, neglectful, obstructed, out of sight, uncritical, unthinking, visionless **11** distraction, inattentive, indifferent, injudicious, insensitive, roller blind, smokescreen, thoughtless, unconscious, unobservant, unreasoning, window shade **12** festoon blind, imperceptive **13** Austrian blind, inconsiderate, Venetian blind **14** deprive of sight, indiscriminate **15** block your vision, deprive of vision, put the eyes out of

See also **sight**

blindly
05 madly **06** rashly, wildly **10** carelessly, mindlessly, recklessly, unseeingly **11** impetuously, impulsively, senselessly, sightlessly **12** incautiously, irrationally, uncritically, unthinkingly, without sight **13** thoughtlessly, without vision

blink
04 peep, pink, wink **05** flash, gleam, shine, twink **06** glance, wapper **07** flicker, flutter, glimmer, glimpse, glitter, nictate, sparkle, twinkle **09** nictitate **11** scintillate

blip
03 pip **04** buzz **05** bleep **06** glitch, hiccup, squeal **07** screech

bliss
03 joy **06** heaven, utopia **07** ecstasy, elation, nirvana, rapture **08** euphoria, gladness, paradise **09** happiness **11** blessedness **12** blissfulness **13** seventh heaven

blissful
05 happy **06** elated, joyful, joyous **07** idyllic **08** ecstatic, euphoric, seraphic **09** delighted, enchanted, rapturous **10** enraptured, seraphical

blister
03 wen **04** blab, bleb, boil, cyst, sore **05** blain, bulla, ulcer **06** canker,

papula, pimple **07** abscess, measles, papilla, pustule, vesicle **08** cold sore, furuncle, overgall, swelling, vesicate, vesicula **09** carbuncle, phlyctena, pompholyx **10** phlyctaena

blistering
03 hot **05** cruel **06** fierce, savage **07** caustic, extreme, intense, vicious **08** scathing, vesicant, virulent **09** ferocious, sarcastic, scorching, withering **10** epispastic

blithe
05 happy, merry **06** casual, cheery **08** carefree, careless, cheerful, heedless, uncaring **10** unthinking, untroubled **11** thoughtless, unconcerned **12** light-hearted

blithely
08 casually **10** carelessly **12** unthinkingly **13** thoughtlessly

blitz
04 raid **06** attack, effort, strike **07** attempt **08** campaign, exertion **09** endeavour, offensive, onslaught **10** blitzkrieg **11** bombardment **12** all-out effort

blizzard
05 buran, storm **06** squall **07** tempest **08** white-out **09** snowstorm

bloated
04 full **05** puffy **06** sodden **07** blown up, dilated, stuffed, swollen **08** enlarged, expanded, inflated, puffed up **09** distended, puffed out

blob
01 O **03** dab, gob **04** ball, bead, drop, duck, glob, lump, mass, pill, spot, tear **05** pearl **06** bubble, pellet, splash **07** droplet, globule

bloc
04 axis, ring **05** block, cabal, group, union **06** cartel, clique, league **07** entente, faction **08** alliance **09** coalition, syndicate **10** federation **11** association

block
◇ *insertion indicator*
03 bar, dam, dit, jam, let, ped **04** cake, clog, cube, halt, hunk, lump, mass, plug, seal, slab, stop **05** batch, brick, check, choke, chunk, close, dam up, delay, deter, group, piece, wedge **06** arrest, bung up, clog up, hamper, hinder, impede, scotch, series, square, stop up, thwart **07** barrier, cluster, complex, occlude, section **08** blockage, building, drawback, obstacle, obstruct, quantity, stoppage **09** deterrent, frustrate, hindrance, stonewall, structure **10** be in the way, impediment, resistance **11** development, obstruction **14** stumbling-block

• **block off**
04 seal, stop **05** close **06** stop up **07** close up, shut off

• **block out**
04 hide, mask, veil **06** screen **07** blot out, conceal, eclipse, obscure, repress, shut out **08** blank out, suppress **10** obliterate

• **block up**
03 ram **04** cloy

blockade
03 ram **04** cloy, stop **05** block, check, siege **06** hinder **07** barrier, besiege, choke up, closure, prevent **08** encircle, keep from, obstacle, obstruct, oppilate, stoppage, surround **09** barricade **10** investment **11** obstruction, restriction **12** encirclement, prevent using **15** prevent entering, prevent reaching

blockage
03 jam **04** clot **05** block **06** log jam **08** blocking, snifters, stoppage **09** hindrance, occlusion **10** bottleneck, congestion, impediment **11** obstruction

blockhead
03 git **04** dope, dork, fool, geek, jerk, mome, mutt, nerd, prat, twit **05** chump, dunce, goosy, idiot, ninny, twerp, wally **06** dimwit, goosey, nitwit, noodle, oxhead, tumphy **07** dizzard, jackass, log-head, plonker **08** bonehead, clotpoll, dipstick, imbecile, jolthead, lunkhead, numskull **09** besom-head, doddipoll, doddypoll, dottipoll, numbskull, pigsconce, thickhead, thickskin **10** bufflehead, jolterhead, loggerhead, muddle-head, nincompoop, thick-skull, woodenhead **11** chuckle-head, leather-head

bloke
03 boy, guy, man, oik **04** chap, male **05** fella **06** fellow **09** character **10** individual

See also **boy**

blond, blonde
04 fair **05** light **06** cendré, flaxen, golden **08** bleached **10** fair-haired **11** tow-coloured **12** golden-haired **13** light-coloured

blood
03 nut **04** Blut, gore, knut, ruby, sang **05** birth **06** claret, family **07** descent, kindred, kinship, lineage **08** ancestry **09** lifeblood, relations **10** extraction, vital fluid **11** descendants **12** relationship

• **draw blood**
03 cup **05** bleed

• **mass of blood**
04 clot

bloodcurdling
05 scary **06** horrid **07** fearful **08** chilling, dreadful, horrible, horrific **09** appalling **10** horrendous, horrifying, terrifying **11** frightening, hair-raising **13** spine-chilling

bloodgroup
01 A, B, O **02** AB

bloodhound
04 lime, lyam, lyme **06** sleuth **07** coondog **09** coonhound, detective, lime-hound, lyam-hound, lyme-hound **11** sleuth-hound

bloodless
03 wan **04** cold, dead, pale **05** ashen, pasty, white **06** chalky, feeble, pallid, sallow, sickly, torpid **07** anaemic, drained, insipid, languid **08** lifeless, listless, peaceful **09** unfeeling, unwarlike **10** colourless, non-violent, spiritless, strife-free **11** passionless, unemotional

bloodshed
04 gore **06** murder, pogrom **07** carnage, killing, slaying **08** butchery, massacre **09** bloodbath, slaughter **10** decimation **12** bloodletting

bloodsucker
04 flea, gnat, tick **05** lamia, leech **06** gadfly **07** deer fly, sponger, tabanid, vampire **08** birch fly, black fly, mosquito, parasite, simulium **09** stable fly **10** horseleech, vampire bat **11** blackmailer, buffalo gnat, extortioner **12** extortionist, sucking louse

bloodthirsty
05 cruel **06** brutal, savage **07** inhuman, vicious, warlike **08** barbaric, ruthless **09** barbarous, ferocious, homicidal, murderous **10** sanguinary

bloody
03 red **04** gory, rare **05** bally, cruel, ruddy **06** bluggy, brutal, fierce, purple, savage **08** bleeding, blinking, blooming, sanguine **09** ferocious, homicidal, murderous **10** sanguinary **11** ensanguined, sanguineous **12** bloodstained, bloodthirsty, sanguinolent **13** ensanguinated

bloody-minded
05 cruel **06** touchy **07** awkward, stroppy **08** stubborn **09** difficult, irritable, obstinate, unhelpful **11** obstructive **13** unco-operative

bloom
03 bud **04** blow, glow, grow, open **05** blush, chill, flush, prime **06** beauty, flower, health, heyday, lustre, mature, pruina, sprout, thrive, vigour **07** blossom, develop, prosper, red tide **08** flourish, radiance, rosiness, strength **09** freshness **10** perfection **11** florescence **13** efflorescence

• **in bloom**
03 out

bloomer *see* **flower**; **mistake**

blooming
04 rosy **05** bonny, primy, ruddy **07** healthy **09** flowering **10** blossoming, florescent

blossom
03 bud, may, pip **04** blow, grow **05** bloom **06** flower, mature, pruina, thrive **07** bloosme, burgeon, develop,

prosper, succeed **08** flourish, progress **10** effloresce **11** florescence **13** efflorescence

blot

03 dot, dry, mar **04** blur, flaw, mark, soak, spot **05** dry up, fault, smear, spawn, speck, spoil, stain, sully, taint **06** absorb, blotch, defect, smudge, soak up **07** blacken, blemish, splodge, tarnish **08** disgrace **09** black mark, disfigure **10** tarnishing **12** imperfection, obliteration

• blot out

04 bury, hide **05** blank, erase **06** cancel, darken, delete, efface, screen, shadow **07** conceal, eclipse, expunge, obscure **08** black out **10** obliterate

blotch

04 blot, dash, mark, monk, spot **05** patch, stain **06** smudge, splash **07** blemish, pustule, splodge, splotch **08** heatspot

blotched

06 marked, pimply, spotty **07** blotchy, freckly, scarred, spotted, stained **09** blemished, centonate, scratched

blotchy

◇ *anagram indicator*

06 patchy, smeary, spotty, uneven **07** spotted **08** inflamed, reddened **09** blemished

blouse

05 middy, shirt, smock, tunic, waist **09** garibaldi **10** shirtwaist

blow

03 bat, bob, bop, box, cut, dad, fan, hit, rap, tip, wap **04** bang, bash, belt, biff, buff, butt, chop, clap, clip, conk, cuff, daud, dint, flow, flub, fuse, gale, gust, hook, jolt, lick, melt, oner, paik, pant, pash, pelt, pipe, play, plug, puff, ruin, rush, scat, slap, snot, sock, stot, swat, tear, toot, waff, waft, welt, whop, wind, wipe, yank **05** appel, blare, blast, botch, break, burst, carry, clout, drift, drive, fling, float, fluff, knock, one-er, peise, punch, shock, skiff, smack, sound, souse, spang, split, spoil, sweep, swipe, thump, upset, waste, whack, whang, whirl, whisk, wreck **06** buffet, bungle, cock up, devvel, exhale, flurry, inhale, stream, stroke, thwack, wallop, whammy, wunner, wuther **07** blow out, breathe, flutter, lounder, puff out, reverse, rupture, screw up, setback, shocker, trumpet, whample, whirret **08** calamity, comedown, disaster, misspend, puncture, squander, surprise **09** bombshell, dissipate, miss out on **10** affliction, breathe out, concussion, exsufflate, insufflate, misfortune **11** catastrophe, fritter away, make a mess of, miss the boat, spend freely **12** short-circuit **13** rude awakening **14** disappointment, spend like water **15** bolt from the blue

• blow out

04 tear **05** burst, snift, split **06** put out **07** rupture, smother **08** puncture, snuff out **10** extinguish

• blow over

03 end **04** pass **05** abate, cease **06** finish, vanish **07** die down, subside **08** peter out **09** disappear, dissipate, fizzle out **10** settle down **11** be forgotten

• blow up

◇ *anagram indicator*

04 bomb, fill, flip, gale, go up, gust, puff, wind **05** blast, bloat, blore, burst, go ape, go mad, go off, scold, storm, swell **06** dilate, expand, flurry, puff up, pump up, squall **07** balloon, distend, draught, enlarge, explode, fill out, inflate, magnify, tempest **08** detonate **09** overstate **10** exaggerate, hit the roof **11** become angry, blow your top, flip your lid, go ballistic **12** get into a rage **14** lose your temper **15** fly off the handle

• gentle blow

03 tip **04** peck

• heavy blow

02 KO **04** bang, bash, bump, oner, slog, slug, swat **05** douse, dowse, one-er, slosh, souse, swash, thump **06** lander, wallop, wunner **07** lounder **08** knockout **11** neck-herring

blow-out

04 bash, flat, rave **05** binge, feast, party **06** rave-up **07** knees-up **08** flat tyre, puncture **09** beanfeast, burst tyre **11** celebration

blowpipe

03 hod **06** sumpit **07** blowgun **08** sumpitan **09** sarbacane

blowy

05 fresh, gusty, windy **06** breezy, stormy **07** squally **08** blustery

blowzy

05 messy **06** sloppy, untidy **07** tousled, unkempt **08** slipshod, slovenly **09** ungroomed **10** bedraggled **11** dishevelled

blubber

03 cry, sob **04** blub, spek, weep **05** speck **06** bubble, snivel **07** sniffle, snotter, whimper **09** jellyfish

bludgeon

03 hit, sap **04** beat, club, cosh **05** baton, bully, force **06** badger, batter, coerce, compel, cudgel, harass, hector, strike **07** clobber, dragoon **08** browbeat, bulldoze **09** terrorize, truncheon **10** intimidate, pressurize

blue

◇ *anagram indicator*

03 low, sad **04** down, glum, lewd, rude, Tory **05** adult, bawdy, dirty, fed up, saucy **06** coarse, dismal, erotic, fruity, gloomy, morose, risqué, smutty, steamy, vulgar, X-rated **07** obscene, raunchy, unhappy **08** dejected, downcast, improper, indecent **09** depressed, miserable, off-colour, offensive **10** despondent, dispirited, melancholy **11** downhearted, near the bone **12** Conservative, pornographic **14** down in the dumps, near the knuckle

Blues include:

03 sky
04 anil, aqua, bice, blae, cyan, navy, Saxe, teal
05 azure, perse, smalt
06 cerule, cobalt, haüyne, indigo
07 caerule, gentian, ice-blue, jacinth, sea-blue, sky-blue, watchet
08 baby blue, cerulean, dark blue, mazarine, navy blue, Nile blue, sapphire, Saxe blue
09 caerulean, royal blue, steel-blue, turquoise
10 aquamarine, Berlin blue, cornflower, kingfisher, Oxford blue, periwinkle, petrol blue, powder blue
11 duck-egg blue, lapis lazuli, nattier blue, peacock-blue, ultramarine
12 air-force blue, dumortierite, electric blue, midnight blue, Prussian blue, Wedgwood blue
13 Cambridge blue, robin's-egg blue
15 lapis lazuli blue

bluebottle

06 beadle **07** blawort, blewart, blowfly, brommer **09** policeman

blueprint

04 plan **05** draft, guide, model, pilot **06** design, scheme, sketch **07** outline, pattern, project **08** strategy **09** archetype, cyanotype, programme, prototype **14** representation

blues

05 dumps, gloom **06** cafard **07** sadness **08** doldrums, glumness, miseries **09** dejection, moodiness **10** depression, gloominess, melancholy **11** despondency, unhappiness

bluff

03 lie **04** bank, brow, crag, fake, fool, open, peak, sham, show **05** blind, blunt, cliff, feign, feint, frank, fraud, ridge, scarp, surly, trick **06** candid, deceit, delude, direct, escarp, genial, hearty, height, humbug **07** affable, bravado, deceive, leg-pull, mislead, pretend **08** foreland, headland, hoodwink, pretence **09** bamboozle, deception, downright, four-flush, idle boast, outspoken, precipice **10** blustering, escarpment, promontory, subterfuge **11** braggadocio, good-natured, plain-spoken **15** straightforward

blunder

◇ *anagram indicator*

03 err **04** bish, boob, flub, gaff, goof, slip **05** bevue, boner, botch, break, error, fault, fluff, gaffe **06** bêtise, booboo, bumble, bungle, cock up, cock-up, goof up, howler, mess up, muck up, muddle, ricket, slip up, slip-up **07** bloomer, clanger, faux pas, floater, go wrong, mistake, screw up,

stumble **08** flounder, get wrong, misjudge, pratfall, solecism
09 mismanage, oversight
10 inaccuracy **12** drop a clanger, indiscretion, make a mistake, miscalculate, misjudgement

blunt
04 bald, bate, curt, dull, numb, rude, worn **05** abate, allay, frank, stark
06 abrupt, candid, dampen, deaden, direct, honest, obtund, obtuse, rebate, retund, soften, unedge, weaken
07 brusque, disedge, rounded, stubbed, uncivil **08** edgeless, explicit, hebetate, impolite, not sharp, tactless
09 alleviate, downright, outspoken, pointless **10** forthright, point-blank
11 insensitive, plain-spoken, unsharpened **12** anaesthetize
13 unceremonious **14** take the edge off **15** straightforward

bluntly
06 rudely **07** frankly, roundly
08 candidly, directly **09** brusquely
10 explicitly, impolitely, point-blank, tactlessly **12** forthrightly
13 insensitively **15** unceremoniously

blur
◇ *anagram indicator*
03 dim, fog **04** dull, fuzz, haze, mask, mist, muzz, slur, spot, veil **05** befog, blear, cloud, mudge, smear, stain
06 blotch, darken, mackle, muddle, smudge, soften **07** becloud, blemish, conceal, confuse, dimness, obscure
09 confusion, disfigure, fuzziness, make vague, obscurity **10** cloudiness
14 indistinctness, make indistinct

blurb
04 copy, hype, puff **05** spiel
12 commendation **13** advertisement

blurred
◇ *anagram indicator*
03 dim **04** hazy, soft **05** blear, faint, foggy, fuzzy, misty, muzzy, vague, woozy **06** bleary, cloudy **07** clouded, obscure, unclear **08** confused **10** ill-defined, indistinct, out of focus

blurt
• **blurt out**
03 cry **04** blab, blat, gush, leak, tell
05 plump, spout, utter **06** cry out, let out, reveal **07** call out, divulge, exclaim, let slip **08** disclose
09 ejaculate **11** come out with **13** spill the beans **15** give the game away

blush
03 red **04** glow **05** flush, go red, rouge **06** colour, mantle, redden
07 crimson, scarlet, turn red
08 colour up, rosiness **09** reddening, ruddiness

blushing
03 red **04** rosy **06** modest
07 ashamed, flushed, glowing, red face **08** confused **09** rubescent
10 erubescent **11** embarrassed
12 apple-cheeked

bluster
04 brag, crow, huff, rage, rant, roar
05 bluff, boast, bully, storm, strut, vaunt
06 hector, ruffle **07** bravado, crowing, roister, royster, show off, swagger, talk big **08** boasting, harangue
11 braggadocio, domineering, fanfaronade, rodomontade

blustery
04 wild **05** gusty, windy **06** stormy
07 squally, violent **10** boisterous, swaggering **11** tempestuous

boar
03 hog **05** brawn **06** barrow, tusker
07 sounder **08** sanglier

board
02 bd **04** beam, deal, food, grub, jury, nosh, slab, slat, tray **05** catch, embus, enter, get in, get on, meals, mount, Ouija®, panel, plank, sheet
06 embark, timber **07** council, emplane, entrain, get into, rations
08 advisers, trustees, victuals
09 committee, directors, governors
10 commission, head office, management, provisions, step aboard, sustenance **11** directorate **12** working party **13** advisory group
• **board up**
04 seal, shut **05** close, cover **06** shut up **07** close up, cover up
• **on board**
02 SS
• **put on board**
04 lade **06** embark
• **remove from board**
04 bear

boarder
02 PG **09** pensioner

board game *see* **game**

boast
03 gab, gem, joy **04** blow, brag, crow, have, yelp **05** claim, crack, crake, enjoy, glory, prate, pride, skite, strut, swank, vapor, vaunt **06** avaunt, bounce, hot air, vapour **07** big-note, bluster, crowing, exhibit, possess, show off, swagger, talk big, trumpet
08 mouth off, sound off, talk tall, treasure **09** gasconade, gasconism, jactation, loudmouth, overstate, vainglory **10** blustering, exaggerate, self-praise **11** fanfaronade, rodomontade **12** cry roast-meat
13 overstatement **15** blow your own horn, pride yourself on

boastful
03 big **04** vain **05** cocky, proud, windy
06 hot-air, swanky **07** crowing
08 arrogant, braggart, bragging, glorious, immodest, puffed up
09 bigheaded, blustrous, cock-a-hoop, conceited, thrasonic **10** blusterous, swaggering **11** egotistical, spread-eagle, swell-headed, thrasonical
12 self-glorious, vainglorious
13 swollen-headed **14** self-flattering
• **boastful talk**
03 gas **05** mouth

boastfully
03 big **07** cockily, proudly
09 crowingly **10** arrogantly
11 conceitedly **13** egotistically
14 vaingloriously

boat
03 tub
See also **sail**; **ship**

boatman
05 rower **06** bargee, sailor
07 oarsman **08** ferryman, hoveller, voyageur, waterman, water rat
09 gondolier, oarswoman, yachtsman
11 yachtswoman

bob
01 s **03** bow, dop, hod, hop, nod, tap
04 dock, jerk, jolt, jump, leap, skip
05 float **06** bobble, bounce, curtsy, popple, quiver, Robert, spring, twitch, wobble **08** shilling **09** oscillate
• **bob up**
04 rise **05** arise, pop up **06** appear, arrive, crop up, emerge, show up
07 surface **08** spring up **11** materialize

bobbin
04 bone, pirn, reel **05** quill, spool

bobby *see* **police officer**

bobsleigh run
04 lauf

bode
03 bid **04** sign, warn **05** augur, dwelt, offer **06** herald, waited **07** betoken, endured, portend, predict, presage, purport, signify **08** forebode, foreshow, foretell, forewarn, indicate, intimate, prophesy, remained, threaten
09 adumbrate, foretoken
10 foreshadow **13** prognosticate

bodge
04 flub, goof, mess, ruin **05** botch, fluff, spoil **06** bungle, foul up, goof up, mess up, muck up **07** blunder, louse up, screw up **11** make a hash of

bodice
04 body **05** choli, gilet, jumps, waist
06 Basque, corset, halter **07** bustier, corsage **08** camisole, jirkinet, overslip
10 chemisette

bodily
04 real **05** as one, fully **06** actual, carnal, in toto, wholly **07** en masse, fleshly, totally **08** as a whole, concrete, entirely, material, physical, tangible
09 corporeal **10** altogether, completely **11** substantial
12 collectively
See also **humour**

body
◇ *anagram indicator*
03 bod, lot, mob, nub **04** area, band, bloc, bouk, buik, buke, bulk, clay, core, form, lich, mass, soma **05** build, crowd, frame, group, heart, range, shell, stiff, torso, trunk **06** amount, cartel, casing, corpse, extent, figure, kernel, throng, volume, weight **07** anatomy, cadaver, carcase, chassis, company, council,

density, essence, expanse, phalanx, society, stretch **08** congress, dead body, firmness, fullness, main part, physique, quantity, richness, skeleton, solidity **09** authority, framework, multitude, structure, substance, syndicate **10** collection **11** association, central part, consistency, corporation, largest part **12** organization **13** confederation

• body odour
02 BO

bodyguard
02 SS **05** guard **06** minder **08** defender, guardian **09** lifeguard, protector **10** triggerman **11** Swiss Guards **13** Schutzstaffel **15** praetorian guard

boffin
05 brain **06** expert, genius, wizard **07** egghead, planner, thinker **08** designer, engineer, inventor **09** intellect, scientist **10** mastermind **11** backroom-boy **12** intellectual

bog
02 WC **03** can, fen, lav, loo **04** dike, dyke, john, kazi, mire, moss, quag, sink, spew, spue, sump **05** dunny, gents, karsy, karzy, khazi, lavvy, marsh, privy, swamp, yarfa **06** carsey, karsey, ladies', lavabo, morass, muskeg, office, petary, slough, stodge, throne, toilet, yarpha **07** cludgie, latrine **08** bathroom, dunnakin, quagmire, washroom, wetlands **09** cloakroom, marshland, swampland **10** facilities, quicksands **11** convenience, water closet **12** smallest room

• bog down
04 halt, mire, sink, trap **05** delay, stall, stick **06** deluge, hinder, hold up, impede, retard, slow up **07** set back **08** encumber, slow down **09** overwhelm

• bog myrtle
04 gale **06** Myrica **09** sweet-gale

• hole in bog
03 hag **04** hagg

boggle
03 jib **05** alarm, amaze, demur **06** bungle, marvel, wonder **07** astound, confuse, scruple, stagger, startle **08** bowl over, hesitate, surprise **09** objection, overwhelm **11** flabbergast

boggy
04 miry, oozy, soft **05** fenny, moory, mossy, muddy, soggy, spewy **06** marshy, quaggy, sodden, spongy, swampy **07** moorish, morassy, paludal, queachy, queechy **11** waterlogged

bogus
◇ *anagram indicator*
03 bad **04** fake, sham **05** dummy, false, pseud, spoof **06** forged, phoney, pseudo **08** spurious **09** imitation **10** artificial, fraudulent **11** counterfeit, make-believe **13** disappointing

bohemian
04 arty, boho **06** exotic, hippie, way-out **07** beatnik, bizarre, drop-out, oddball, offbeat **08** artistic, original **09** eccentric **10** avant-garde, off-the-wall, unorthodox **11** alternative **12** trustafarian **13** nonconformist **14** unconventional

bohrium
02 Bh

boil
◇ *anagram indicator*
03 jug **04** brew, cook, fizz, foam, fume, heat, leep, rage, rave, sore, stew **05** blain, botch, erupt, froth, steam, storm, ulcer **06** bubble, bunion, decoct, growth, gurgle, pimple, see red, seethe, simmer, tumour, wallop **07** abscess, anthrax, blister, explode, gumboil, parboil, pustule **08** furuncle, ganglion, swelling **09** blow a fuse, carbuncle, fulminate, gathering **10** effervesce, hit the roof **11** blow your top **12** fly into a rage, inflammation **13** come to the boil **14** bring to the boil **15** fly off the handle, go off the deep end

• boil down
06 amount, digest, distil, reduce **07** abridge **08** abstract, condense **09** summarize **11** concentrate

boiled
◇ *anagram indicator*
03 sod **06** sodden

boiler
06 kettle

boiling
◇ *anagram indicator*
03 hot **05** angry, surge **06** baking, fuming, torrid **07** coction, enraged, flaming, furious **08** broiling, bubbling, gurgling, incensed, roasting, scalding, steaming **09** indignant, scorching, turbulent **10** blistering, ebullition, infuriated, sweltering **12** effervescent

boisterous
◇ *anagram indicator*
04 loud, wild **05** noisy, randy, rough, rowdy **06** active, bouncy, lively, randie, stormy, unruly **07** laddish, riotous, romping **08** animated, roisting, roysting, spirited **09** clamorous, energetic, exuberant, goustrous, turbulent **10** disorderly, knockabout, rollicking, strepitoso, tumultuous **11** dithyrambic, hyperactive, rumbustious **12** obstreperous, rambunctious, unrestrained

boisterously
06 loudly, wildly **07** noisily, roughly, rowdily **08** actively **09** riotously **10** animatedly, spiritedly **11** clamorously, exuberantly, turbulently **12** tumultuously **13** energetically, hyperactively **14** obstreperously, unrestrainedly

bold
02 bf **04** free, loud, pert **05** brash, brave, heavy, saucy, showy, steep, thick, vivid **06** abrupt, brassy, brazen, bright, cheeky, daring, flashy, heroic, manful, plucky, strong **07** assured, defiant, forward, gallant, haughty, naughty, valiant **08** definite, distinct, fearless, impudent, insolent, intrepid, malapert, outgoing, spirited, striking, valorous **09** audacious, bald-faced, barefaced, chivalric, colourful, confident, dauntless, foolhardy, prominent, shameless, unabashed, undaunted **10** chivalrous, courageous, diastaltic, flamboyant, in-your-face, noticeable, pronounced **11** adventurous, bold as a lion, bold as brass, conspicuous, eye-catching, venturesome **12** enterprising, high-spirited, presumptuous

• be bold
04 dare

boldly
06 crouse **07** bravely, vividly **08** brightly, daringly, pluckily, risoluto, strongly **09** valiantly **10** definitely, distinctly, fearlessly, heroically, intrepidly, strikingly **11** audaciously, confidently, prominently **12** courageously **13** adventurously

Bolivia
03 BOL

bolshie
04 rude **06** touchy **07** awkward, prickly, problem, stroppy **08** stubborn **09** difficult, irritable, obstinate, unhelpful **10** unpleasant **12** bloody-minded **13** oversensitive, unco-operative

bolster
03 aid, pad **04** help, prop, stay **05** boost, brace **06** assist, buoy up, firm up, pillow **07** augment, cushion, shore up, stiffen, support **08** buttress, maintain **09** Dutch wife, reinforce **10** invigorate, revitalize, strengthen, supplement

bolt
01 U **03** bar, fly, peg, pin, rat, ray, rod, run **04** cram, dart, dash, flee, gulp, lock, rush, slot, sneb, snib, stud, wolf **05** arrow, blaze, burst, catch, elope, flare, flash, gorge, latch, rivet, scoff, screw, shaft, shoot, spark, stuff **06** devour, escape, fasten, gobble, guzzle, hurtle, pintle, run off, secure, sperre, sprint, streak **07** abscond, run away, scarper **08** fastener, wolf down

Boltzmann constant
01 k

bomb
◇ *anagram indicator*
03 egg **05** prang, speed **06** attack, blow up, device, mortar **07** bombard, destroy **09** bombshell, explosive **10** projectile

Bombs include:

01 A, H
02 V-1, V-2
03 car

04 aero, atom, buzz, dumb, fire, mine, MOAB, nail, pipe, time
05 dirty, E-bomb, Mills, shell, smart, smoke, stink
06 binary, candle, cobalt, drogue, flying, fusion, letter, parcel, petrol, radium, rocket
07 bomblet, cluster, fission, grenade, missile, neutron, nuclear, plastic, tallboy, torpedo
08 bouncing, firebomb, hydrogen, landmine
09 doodlebug, Grand Slam, pineapple
10 incendiary
11 blockbuster, daisy-cutter, depth charge, penetration, sensor fuzed, stun grenade, thermobaric
12 bunker buster, rifle grenade
13 fragmentation, thermonuclear
15 Molotov cocktail

bombard
04 bomb, pelt, raid 05 blast, blitz, flood, hound, pound, shell, stone, swamp 06 assail, attack, batter, bother, deluge, harass, mortar, pellet, pester, strafe, straff 07 besiege, torpedo 08 inundate 09 blackjack

bombardment
04 fire, flak, hail 05 blitz, salvo, stonk 06 attack 07 air raid, assault, barrage, bombing, stonker 08 hounding, pounding, shelling 09 besieging, bothering, cannonade, fusillade, harassing, onslaught, pestering, shellfire

bombast
03 pad 04 rant 05 stuff 06 hot air 07 bluster, fustian, heroics, inflate, padding 08 euphuism, inflated, stuffing 09 dithyramb, pomposity, verbosity, wordiness 10 sophomoric, turgidness 11 ampullosity 13 magniloquence 14 grandiloquence 15 pretentiousness

bombastic
04 tall 05 puffy, tumid, windy, wordy 06 turgid 07 bloated, fustian, pompous, verbose 08 affected, inflated 09 grandiose, high-flown 10 euphuistic, portentous, sophomoric 11 pretentious, spread-eagle 12 magniloquent, ostentatious, sophomorical 13 grandiloquent

bomber
01 B

Bombers include:

03 B-10, B-17, B-19, B-52, MB-1
04 dive
05 Stuka
06 Gotha G, Harris, Sukhoi
07 Avenger, Heinkel, Junkers, stealth, suicide, Tupolev, Warthog
08 Mitchell
09 Lancaster, Liberator
13 Superfortress
14 Flying Fortress

bona fide
04 real, true 05 legal, valid 06 actual, dinkum, honest, kosher, lawful 07 genuine 09 authentic 10 legitimate 12 the real McCoy

bonanza
04 boon 07 godsend 08 blessing, windfall 12 stroke of luck, sudden wealth

bond
02 bd 03 gum, tie, vow 04 band, bind, cord, deal, fuse, glue, join, knot, link, pact, seal, ties, weld, word, yoke 05 chain, nexus, noose, paste, starr, stick, union, unite 06 attach, cement, copula, fasten, fetter, league, pledge, treaty 07 binding, connect, liaison, linkage, manacle, promise, rapport, shackle, statute, valence 08 affinity, contract, covenant, ligament, mateship, relation, vinculum, yearling 09 agreement, chemistry 10 attachment, connection, friendship, obligation 11 affiliation, transaction 12 relationship

bondage
04 yoke 06 thrall 07 serfdom, slavery 08 nativity, thraldom 09 captivity, restraint, servitude, thralldom, vassalage 10 subjection, villeinage 11 confinement, enslavement, subjugation 12 imprisonment, subservience 13 incarceration

bone
03 nab, tot 05 seize 06 bobbin

Bones include:

01 T
02 os
03 hip, jaw, luz, rib
04 back, coxa, knee, shin, ulna
05 ankle, anvil, cheek, costa, femur, funny, hyoid, ilium, incus, jugal, pubis, skull, spine, talus, thigh, thumb, tibia, vomer, wrist
06 breast, carpal, coccyx, collar, fibula, hammer, pecten, pelvis, radius, sacrum, saddle, stapes, tarsus
07 cranium, ethmoid, humerus, ischium, kneecap, knuckle, malleus, ossicle, patella, phalanx, scapula, sternum, stirrup
08 clavicle, lower jaw, mandible, parietal, scaphoid, shoulder, upper jaw, vertebra
09 calcaneum, calcaneus, occipital, trapezium, zygomatic
10 metacarpal, metatarsal
12 pelvic girdle
13 shoulder-blade

bones
02 Dr, GP, MO 03 doc 04 dice, ossa 06 doctor 08 skeleton

bonfire
04 pyre 08 bale-fire 09 feu de joie

bonhomie
08 sympathy 09 geniality 10 affability, amiability, good nature, tenderness 12 conviviality, friendliness 15 kind-heartedness, warm-heartedness

bon mot
04 quip 07 riposte 08 one-liner, repartee 09 wisecrack, witticism 10 pleasantry

bonnet
03 cap 04 hood, poke 06 kiss-me, toorie, tourie 08 balmoral, bongrace 11 kiss-me-quick

• bonnet monkey
04 zati

bonny
04 fair, fine 05 bonie, merry, plump 06 cheery, comely, joyful, lovely, pretty 07 smiling 08 blooming, bouncing, cheerful, handsome 09 beautiful 10 attractive, sweetheart

bonus
03 tip 04 gain, gift, perk, plus 05 bribe, extra, prize 06 reward 07 benefit, handout, premium 08 dividend, gratuity 09 advantage, lagniappe 10 commission, honorarium, perquisite 14 fringe benefits

bony
04 lean, thin 05 drawn, gaunt, gawky, lanky 06 skinny 07 angular, osseous, scraggy, scrawny 08 gangling, rawboned, sclerous, skeletal 09 emaciated

book
01 b 02 bk 03 bag, lib, log, vol 04 text, tome, work 05 Bible, blame, enter, folio, order, tract 06 accuse, arrest, charge, engage, script, volume 07 arrange, booklet, charter, procure, reserve 08 accuse of, libretto, organize, schedule 09 programme 10 prearrange 11 publication

Books include:

03 pad
04 A to Z, bath, chap, cook, copy, days, hand, hymn, note, text, work, year
05 album, atlas, audio, board, cloth, comic, diary, e-book, guide, novel, pop-up, scrap, story
06 annual, gradus, hymnal, jotter, ledger, manual, missal, phrase, prayer, primer, sketch
07 almanac, fiction, Filofax®, journal, lexicon, omnibus, picture, psalter
08 exercise, grimoire, hardback, libretto, self-help, softback, thriller
09 anthology, biography, catalogue, children's, detective, directory, gazetteer, paperback, reference, thesaurus
10 bestseller, compendium, dictionary, large print, lectionary, manuscript
11 coffee-table, concordance, instruction, travel guide
12 encyclopedia
13 penny dreadful, travel journal
15 pocket companion

See also **apocryphal**; **Bible**

• book in
05 enrol 07 check in 08 register

• book of rules
03 pie, pye 07 ordinal 11 penitential

bookbinding
10 bibliopegy

Bookbinding terms include:

03 aeg
04 case, head, limp, tail, yapp
05 bolts, hinge, spine
06 boards, gather, jacket, lining, Linson®, sewing
07 binding, buckram, drawn-on, flyleaf, headcap, morocco
08 backbone, blocking, casing-in, doublure, drilling, endpaper, fore edge, hardback, headband, open-flat, shoulder, smashing, stamping, tailband
09 backboard, book block, casebound, debossing, dust cover, embossing, full bound, half bound, loose-leaf, millboard, paperback, signature, soft-cover
10 back lining, binder's die, front board, laminating, pasteboard, raised band, side-stitch, square back, stab-stitch, strawboard, varnishing, whole bound
11 comb binding, ring binding, velo binding, wire binding, wiro binding
12 all edges gilt, binder's board, binder's brass, cloth binding, flexi binding, notch binding, quarter bound, saddle-stitch, thread sewing
13 back cornering, blind blocking, spiral binding, unsewn binding, wire stitching
14 library binding, perfect binding
15 adhesive binding, cloth-lined board, hot foil stamping

booking
11 appointment, arrangement, reservation

bookish
07 donnish, erudite, inkhorn, learned **08** academic, cultured, highbrow, lettered, literary, pedantic, studious, well-read **09** scholarly **10** scholastic **12** bluestocking, intellectual

booklet
06 folder, notice **07** handout, leaflet **08** brochure, circular, pamphlet **09** programme

books
02 bb, NT, OT **03** bks **07** ledgers, records **08** accounts **12** balance sheet

boom
03 jib **04** bang, clap, gain, grow, jump, leap, roar, roll, spar **05** blare, blast, boost, burst, crash, spurt, surge, swell **06** bellow, do well, expand, growth, rumble, thrive, upturn **07** advance, burgeon, develop, explode, prosper, resound, succeed, success, thunder, upsurge, upswing **08** escalate, flourish, increase, mushroom, progress, snowball **09** bombilate, bombinate, expansion, explosion, intensify, loud noise, resonance, skyrocket **10** escalation, strengthen **11** development, improvement, reverberate **13** reverberation

boomerang
◇ *reversal indicator*
05 kiley, kylie **06** recoil **07** rebound, reverse **08** backfire, ricochet **10** bounce back, spring back, throw stick

boon
04 bene, gift, help, plus **05** bonus, grant **06** favour, jovial **07** benefit, godsend, present, request **08** blessing, gratuity, intimate, kindness, petition, windfall **09** advantage, convivial

• **boon companion**
06 cupman, Trojan **07** franion **09** confidant **10** best friend, confidante, dear friend **11** bosom friend, close friend **13** special friend

boor
03 hog, lob, oaf, oik, yob **04** clod, Jack, kern, lout, pleb, slob **05** chuff, clown, kerne, ocker, yahoo, yobbo, yokel **06** chough, keelie, rustic **07** Grobian, peasant **08** plebeian **09** barbarian, lager lout, vulgarian **10** clodhopper, philistine **14** country bumpkin

boorish
04 rude **05** borel, crass, crude, gross, gruff, ocker, rough, swain **06** borrel, coarse, jungli, lumpen, oafish, rustic, vulgar **07** borrell, ill-bred, loutish, uncouth **08** ignorant, impolite, swainish **09** unrefined **10** uneducated **11** clodhopping, ill-mannered, uncivilized

boost
03 aid, rap **04** boom, help, hype, lift, plug, rise, spur, wrap **05** put up, raise, steal **06** assist, expand, fillip, foster, play up, praise, talk up, uplift
07 advance, amplify, augment, bolster, develop, ego-trip, enhance, enlarge, further, improve, inspire, promote, support **08** addition, heighten, increase, maximize, shoplift, stimulus **09** advertise, encourage, expansion, increment, promotion, publicity, publicize, stimulate **10** assistance, potentiate, supplement
11 development, enhancement, enlargement, furtherance, improvement, inspiration
12 augmentation, shot in the arm
13 advertisement, amplification, encouragement

boot
04 kick **05** shove, trunk **06** profit **09** advantage

Boots include:

03 gum, top, ugg
04 crow, half, jack, lace, moon, snow
05 ankle, kamik, rugby, thigh, wader, welly
06 bootee, buskin, chukka, combat, finsko, galosh, golosh, hiking, jemima, mucluc, mukluk, riding
07 blucher, bottine, Chelsea, cracowe, finnsko, galoche, Hessian, walking
08 balmoral, bootikin, climbing, finnesko, football, high shoe, larrigan, muckluck, overshoe
09 scarpetto
10 Doc Martens®, wellington
13 beetle-crusher

• **boot out**
04 fire, sack, shed **05** eject, expel **06** lay off **07** dismiss, kick out, suspend **10** give notice **12** give the heave **13** make redundant

• **to boot**
03 too **06** as well **07** besides **10** in addition **14** into the bargain

booth
03 box, hut **05** crame, kiosk, stall, stand **06** bothan, carrel **07** cubicle **11** compartment, luckenbooth

bootleg
05 wrong **06** banned, barred, pirate **07** illegal, illicit, pirated, smuggle **08** criminal, outlawed, smuggled, unlawful **09** forbidden **10** prohibited, proscribed **11** black-market, interdicted **12** unauthorized **15** under-the-counter

bootless
04 vain **06** barren, futile **07** sterile, useless **09** fruitless, pointless **10** profitless, unavailing **11** ineffective **12** unprofitable, unsuccessful

booty
04 haul, loot, prey, swag **05** bribe, gains, prize, spoil **06** bottom, creach, creagh, shikar, spoils **07** pillage, plunder, profits, takings **08** pickings, purchase, winnings

booze
03 jar **04** grog, slug, tank **05** drink, juice, skink, tinct **06** fuddle, liquor, strunt, tiddly, tipple **07** alcohol, indulge, liqueur, spirits **08** stimulus **09** firewater, get pissed, hard stuff, the bottle, the cratur **10** have a drink, intoxicant **11** jungle juice, strong drink, the creature **12** Dutch courage, hit the bottle **14** drink like a fish

See also **beer**; **cocktail**; **drink**; **liqueur**; **liquor**; **spirits**; **wine**

boozer
03 bar, inn, pub, sot **04** howf, lush, soak, wino **05** alkie, bloat, dipso, drunk, local, souse, toper **06** lounge, saloon, sponge, tavern **07** Bacchus, drinker, tippler, tosspot **08** drunkard, habitual, hostelry **09** alcoholic, inebriate, lounge bar **10** wine-bibber **11** dipsomaniac, hard drinker, public house **12** heavy drinker, watering-hole

boozy
◇ *anagram indicator*
See **drunken**

bop
03 hop, jig **04** blow, jive, jump, leap, rock, spin, sway **05** dance, stomp, twirl, twist, whirl **06** boogie, gyrate, hoof it, strike **09** pirouette, shake a leg **11** move to music

borage
07 alkanet, anchusa, bugloss, comfrey, manjack, myosote **08** gromwell, lungwort, myosotis, sebesten
09 stickseed, Symphytum **10** dog's-tongue, heliotrope, Pulmonaria
11 cool-tankard, oyster plant
12 hound's-tongue, lithospermum
13 viper's bugloss

border
03 bed, hem, mat, rim **04** abut, bank, bord, brim, cost, curb, dado, edge, join, kerb, limb, line, list, mark, mete, orle, rand, roon, rund, side, trim, welt
05 apron, board, boord, borde, bound, brink, coast, coste, flank, frill, limit, march, skirt, swage, touch, verge
06 accost, adjoin, boorde, bounds, cotise, frieze, fringe, margin, purfle, screed, trench, weeper **07** accoast, bordure, confine, connect, cottise, enclose, engrail, impinge, marches, margent, selvage, valance, valence, wayside **08** be next to, boundary, confines, dentelle, emborder, frontier, furbelow, headland, roadside, selvedge, surround, trimming
09 cartouche, guilloche, lie next to, perimeter, periphery, state line
10 borderline, limitrophe, marchlands
11 demarcation **12** be adjacent to, circumscribe **13** circumference

Borders and boundaries include:

07 Rubicon
09 Green Line
10 Berlin Wall, no-man's-land
11 Iron Curtain, Maginot Line
13 Bamboo Curtain
14 Mason–Dixon line
15 cordon sanitaire

• **border on**
07 verge on **08** approach, be almost, be nearly, resemble **13** approximate to
14 be tantamount to

• **borders of**
◇ *ends selection indicator*
08 purlieus

borderline
04 iffy, line **05** limit **06** divide
08 boundary, division, doubtful, marginal **09** uncertain **10** ambivalent, indecisive, indefinite **11** problematic
12 dividing-line **13** indeterminate
15 demarcation line, differentiation

See also **border**

bore
03 awl, dig, irk, sap, sat, tap, vex
04 bare, bind, drag, eger, jade, mine, pain, sink, tire **05** annoy, drill, eager, eagre, ennui, grind, weary, worry
06 bother, burrow, dig out, hollow, jostle, pall on, pierce, tunnel
07 exhaust, fatigue, sondage, trouble, turn off, turn-off, wear out
08 headache, irritate, nuisance, puncture **09** hollow out, make tired, penetrate, perforate, terebrant, terebrate, undermine **11** be tedious to, send to sleep **13** pain in the neck
15 bore the pants off

• **enlarge bore**
04 ream, rime

bored
05 fed up, tired **06** ennuyé, in a rut
07 ennuied, wearied **09** exhausted, turned off, unexcited **10** bored stiff, brassed off, browned off, cheesed off
12 bored to tears, sick and tired, uninterested

boredom
05 ennui **06** acedia, apathy, tedium
07 humdrum, malaise, taedium, vapours **08** dullness, flatness, monotony, sameness **09** weariness
11 frustration, tediousness
12 listlessness **14** world-weariness

boring
03 dry **04** dull, flat, slow, tedy **05** dully, ho-hum, samey, stale, trite **06** draggy, dreary, flatly, jejune, stupid, tiring
07 humdrum, insipid, mundane, prosaic, routine, tedious, tritely
08 drearily, tiresome, unvaried
09 insipidly, tediously **10** long-winded, monotonous, tiresomely, uneventful, unexciting, uninspired
11 commonplace, prosaically, repetitious, stultifying, uninspiring
12 long-windedly, monotonously, uneventfully, unexcitingly
13 repetitiously, stultifyingly, unimaginative, uninteresting **14** soul-destroying **15** unimaginatively, uninterestingly

• **boring piece**
05 drill

born
01 b, n **02** né **03** nat, née **05** natus

boron
01 B

borough
03 bor **04** area, port, town **05** borgo, burgh **06** parish **08** district
09 community **12** constituency
See also **London**; **New York**

borrow
03 use **04** draw, hire, rent, take
05 adopt, cadge, lease, lever, usurp
06 derive, obtain, pledge, scunge, sponge, surety, take up **07** acquire, charter **08** scrounge, take over
10 have on loan, take on loan
11 appropriate **12** have the use of, take out a loan **14** use temporarily

borrowing
03 IOU, use **04** debt, hire, loan
06 calque, rental **07** charter, leasing
08 adoption, loan-word, takeover
10 derivation **11** acquisition
12 temporary use **15** loan-translation

Bosnia and Herzegovina
03 BIH

bosom
03 pap, tit **04** boob, boon, bust, core, dear **05** booby, chest, close, diddy, heart, midst **06** breast, centre, desire, loving **07** breasts, devoted, shelter
08 faithful, intimate **09** sanctuary
10 protection **12** confidential

boss
◇ *anagram indicator*
03 cow, don, gov, guv **04** calf, head, knob, knot, stud, umbo **05** bully, chief, empty, jewel, owner, stock **06** bigwig, gaffer, hollow, honcho, leader, manage, master, oubaas, pellet, top dog, top man **07** cacique, captain, cazique, control, foreman, manager, mistake, supremo **08** browbeat, bulldoze, bull's-eye, chairman, director, dominate, domineer, employer, governor, omphalos, overseer, superior, top woman **09** big cheese, excellent, executive, top banana, tyrannize **10** chairwoman, order about, push around, supervisor
11 chairperson, order around **12** give orders to **13** administrator, lay down the law **14** superintendent

bossiness
07 tyranny **09** autocracy, despotism
13 assertiveness, imperiousness
14 high-handedness

bossy
03 cow **04** calf **06** lordly **08** despotic, exacting **09** assertive, demanding, imperious, insistent **10** autocratic, dominating, high-handed, oppressive, tyrannical **11** dictatorial, domineering, overbearing **13** authoritarian

botany
03 bot **09** phytology **11** phytography

Botanists include:

03 **Mee** (Margaret Ursula), **Ray** (John)
04 **Bary** (Heinrich Anton de), **Bose** (Sir Jagadis Chandra), **Cohn** (Ferdinand Julius), **Gray** (Asa)
05 **Banks** (Sir Joseph), **Brown** (Robert), **Hales** (Stephen), **Sachs** (Julius von), **Vries** (Hugo de)
06 **Biffen** (Sir Rowland Harry), **Carver** (George Washington), **Haller** (Albrecht von), **Hooker** (Sir Joseph Dalton), **Hudson** (William), **Mendel** (Gregor Johann), **Nägeli** (Karl Wilhelm von), **Torrey** (John)
07 **Bartram** (John), **Bellamy** (David), **Bentham** (George), **De Vries** (Hugo Marie), **Pfeffer** (Wilhelm), **Tansley** (Sir Arthur George), **Vavilov** (Nikolai)
08 **Blackman** (Frederick Frost), **Candolle** (Augustin Pyrame de), **Linnaeus** (Carolus)
09 **Boerhaave** (Hermann), **Schleiden** (Matthias Jakob)
10 **Camerarius** (Rudolph Jacob), **Hofmeister** (Wilhelm Friedrich Benedikt), **Pringsheim** (Nathaniel)

botch
◇ *anagram indicator*
03 mar, mux **04** boil, flop, flub, goof, hash, mess, muff, ruin, sore **05** bodge, farce, fluff, patch, spoil **06** bungle, clatch, cock up, cock-up, foul up, goof up, mess up, muck up, muddle, pimple

07 blemish, blunder, butcher, clamper, failure, louse up, screw up
08 shambles 09 mismanage 11 make a hash of, make a mess of, miscarriage
13 make a bad job of

both

04 each 06 as well, the two 07 the pair

bother

◇ *anagram indicator*

03 ado, bug, irk, nag, vex 04 drat, fash, fuss, pest 05 aggro, alarm, annoy, deave, deeve, grief, grind, pains, tease, upset, worry 06 bovver, bustle, dismay, effort, flurry, harass, hassle, molest, pester, plague, put out, rumpus, shtook, shtuck, strain, unrest
07 concern, disturb, fluster, perplex, problem, schtook, schtuck, trouble
08 disorder, distress, exertion, fighting, irritate, nuisance, vexation
09 annoyance, incommode
10 aggravate, difficulty, irritation
11 disturbance 12 make an effort
13 inconvenience, make the effort, pain in the neck 14 think necessary
15 concern yourself

bothersome

05 pesky 06 boring, vexing 07 brickle, irksome, tedious 08 annoying, fashious, tiresome 09 laborious, vexatious, wearisome 10 irritating
11 aggravating, distressing, infuriating, troublesome 12 exasperating, inconvenient

Botswana

02 BW, RB 03 BWA

bottle

◇ *anagram indicator*
◇ *hidden indicator*

03 bot 04 grit, guts 05 nerve, spunk
06 daring, valour 07 bravery, courage
08 boldness 09 container
11 intrepidity 12 Dutch courage

Bottles include:

03 bed, gas, ink, pig
04 beer, case, codd, jack, junk, mick, milk, tear, vial, wash, wine
05 bidon, cruet, cruse, dumpy, flask, gourd, Klein, phial, scent, snuff, water
06 carafe, carboy, cutter, feeder, fiasco, flacon, flagon, hottie, inkpot, lagena, magnum, poison, pooter, siphon, stubby, syphon, Woulfe
07 amphora, ampulla, costrel, feeding, flacket, pilgrim, pitcher, squeezy, sucking, torpedo, vinegar, washing
08 calabash, decanter, demijohn, hip flask, hot-water, magnetic, medicine, screwtop, smelling, weighing
09 Aristotle
10 apothecary, lachrymary, winchester
11 vinaigrette, water bouget
12 Bologna phial, lachrymatory, Thermos® flask

See also **wine**

• **bottle up**

04 curb, hide 06 cork up, shut in
07 conceal, confine, contain, enclose, inhibit, repress 08 disguise, hold back, keep back, restrain, restrict, suppress
11 keep in check

bottleneck

05 block 06 hold-up 07 snarl-up
08 blockage, clogging, gridlock, obstacle 09 narrowing 10 congestion, traffic jam 11 obstruction, restriction
12 constriction

bottom

◇ *tail selection down indicator*

03 ass, bed, bum, end 04 base, butt, coit, foot, prat, rear, rump, seat, sill, sole, tail, tush 05 basis, batty, booty, botty, floor, lower, nadir, quoit, tushy
06 behind, depths, far end, fundus, ground, heinie, lowest, plinth, seabed, tushie 07 bedrock, staddle, support
08 backside, buttocks, pedestal, sea floor 09 posterior, undermost, underside 10 foundation, underneath
11 farthest end, furthest end, lowest level 12 substructure, underpinning

See also **buttocks**

bottomless

◇ *tail deletion down indicator*

04 deep 07 abysmal, abyssal
08 infinite, profound 09 boundless, depthless, limitless, subjacent, unfounded, unlimited, unplumbed
10 fathomless, unbottomed, unfathomed
11 measureless 12 immeasurable, unfathomable 13 inexhaustible

bough

04 limb 06 branch 07 gallows, roughie

bought

04 coft

boulder

04 rock 05 stone 06 gibber
07 bowlder 10 niggerhead

boulevard

04 Blvd, Boul, mall, road 05 drive
06 avenue, parade, street 08 corniche, prospect 09 promenade
12 thoroughfare

bounce

02 go 03 bob, dap, lie, zip 04 bang, beat, give, jump, leap, stot, thud
05 boast, boing, boink, bound, pitch, stoit, styte, throw 06 energy, morgay, recoil, spring, vigour 07 dogfish, rebound 08 boasting, dynamism, ricochet, vitality, vivacity
09 animation, dismissal 10 ebullience, elasticity, exaggerate, exuberance, get-up-and-go, liveliness, resilience, spring back 11 springiness 12 spiritedness

• **bounce back**

07 improve, recover 09 get better
13 make a comeback 15 get back to normal

bouncer

03 dud 04 liar 05 bully 06 bumper
10 chucker-out

bouncing

◇ *anagram indicator*

05 bonny 06 hearty, lively, robust, strong
07 healthy 08 blooming, thriving, vigorous 09 energetic, walloping

bouncy

◇ *anagram indicator*

04 spry 05 alive 06 active, lively, spongy 07 dynamic, elastic, rubbery, springy 08 flexible, spirited, stretchy, vigorous 09 energetic, resilient, sprightly, vivacious 11 full of beans

bound

◇ *containment indicator*

02 bd 03 bob, hop, lep, off 04 curb, edge, held, jump, leap, line, mere, skip, sten, stot, sure, tied, tyde 05 brink, caper, check, dance, fated, fixed, flank, frisk, going, limit, off to, roped, scoup, scowp, skelp, skirt, sling, spang, stend, sworn, vault, verge 06 border, bounce, cavort, coming, doomed, forced, fringe, frolic, gambol, headed, hurdle, lashed, liable, limits, lollop, margin, prance, spring, tied up 07 affined, certain, chained, clamped, confine, contain, control, enclose, galumph, gambado, heading, obliged, outline, pledged, secured, trussed 08 articled, attached, bandaged, beholden, confines, definite, destined, fastened, fettered, gallumph, handfast, moderate, regulate, required, restrain, restrict, shackled, strapped, surround, tethered 09 committed, compelled, duty-bound, extremity, perimeter, restraint 10 borderline, covenanted, limitation, proceeding, restricted, travelling 11 constrained, demarcation, on your way to, restriction, termination
12 circumscribe 13 circumference

• **bound up with**

07 involve 09 related to 10 linked with, tied up with 11 dependent on
13 connected with 14 associated with, hand in hand with

boundary

02 IV, VI 03 six 04 edge, four, goal, gole, limb, line, list, mark, mere, mete, pale, term 05 bourn, brink, limes, limit, march, meith, score, verge 06 border, bounds, bourne, fringe, limits, margin
07 barrier, confine, marches, Rubicon, surface 08 confines, frontier
09 extremity, parameter, perimeter, periphery 10 borderline
11 demarcation, termination 15 point of no return

See also **border**

bounded

05 edged 07 cramped, defined, limited 08 bordered, confined, enclosed, hemmed in, walled in
09 delimited, encircled 10 controlled, demarcated, restrained, restricted, surrounded 11 encompassed
13 circumscribed

bounder

03 cad, cur, pig, rat, roo 04 euro
05 cheat, knave, rogue, swine

06 hopper, jumper, rotter 07 dastard, wallaby 08 blighter, dirty dog
09 miscreant 10 blackguard

boundless
04 vast 06 untold 07 endless, immense 08 infinite, unending
09 countless, limitless, shoreless, unbounded, unlimited 10 numberless, unconfined, unflagging 11 everlasting, illimitable, innumerable, measureless, never-ending 12 immeasurable, incalculable, interminable
13 indefatigable, inexhaustible

bounds
◇ *ends selection indicator*
05 edges, scope 06 limits 07 borders, fringes, marches, margins 08 confines
09 perimeter, periphery
10 boundaries, parameters
11 extremities 12 demarcations, restrictions 13 circumference

• out of bounds
02 OB 04 tapu 05 taboo 06 banned, barred 09 forbidden, off limits
10 disallowed, not allowed, prohibited

bountiful
05 ample 06 lavish 07 copious, liberal, profuse 08 abundant, generous, princely, prolific 09 boundless, bounteous, exuberant, luxuriant, plenteous, plentiful 10 munificent, open-handed, ungrudging, unstinting
11 magnanimous, overflowing

bounty
03 tip 04 gift 05 bonus, grant
06 reward 07 charity, premium, present 08 donation, gratuity, kindness, largesse 09 allowance
10 almsgiving, generosity, liberality, recompense 11 beneficence, magnanimity, munificence
12 philanthropy

bouquet
04 nose, posy 05 aroma, bunch, odour, scent, smell, spray 06 eulogy, favour, honour, praise, wreath
07 corsage, garland, nosegay, perfume, tribute 08 accolade, approval 09 fragrance, redolence
10 buttonhole, compliment
11 boutonnière 12 commendation, felicitation, pat on the back
15 congratulations, odoriferousness

bourgeois
04 dull 05 banal, trite 06 square
07 humdrum 08 ordinary
09 hidebound, Pooterish 10 capitalist, conformist, pedestrian, uncreative, uncultured, uninspired, unoriginal
11 Biedermeier, commonplace, middle-class, traditional
12 conservative, conventional
13 materialistic, unadventurous, unimaginative 15 money-orientated

bout
02 go 03 fit, jag, run 04 bend, bust, dose, fall, game, heat, lush, sesh, term, time, turn 05 binge, boose, booze, bouse, brash, burst, drunk, fight, match, round, set-to, spasm, spell, spree, stint, touch, veney, venue
06 attack, battle, beer-up, bottle, course, fuddle, period, screed, venewe
07 booze-up, carouse, contest, session, splurge, stretch, wassail, wrestle 08 struggle 09 encounter
10 engagement, makunouchi
11 competition

bovine
04 dull, dumb, slow 05 dense, thick
06 stupid 07 cowlike, doltish 09 dim-witted 10 cattlelike, slow-witted

• bovine animals
04 cows, neat 06 cattle

bow
03 arc, bob, nod, tie, yew 04 arch, arco, beak, beck, bend, duck, eugh, head, jook, jouk, knot, loop, lout, lowt, move, prow, ring, stem 05 crook, crush, curve, defer, dicky, drail, front, slope, stick, stoop, yield 06 accede, accept, circle, comply, crouch, curtsy, dickey, dickie, give in, humble, kowtow, salaam, subdue, submit 07 bending, concede, conquer, consent, incline, namaste, rostrum, succumb
08 forepart, namaskar, vanquish
09 acquiesce, genuflect, give way to, humiliate, lavaliere, obeisance, overpower, subjugate, surrender
10 capitulate, lavallière, salutation
11 fiddlestick, genuflexion, inclination, prostration 12 dorsiflexion 13 make obeisance 15 acknowledgement

• bow out
04 quit 05 leave 06 defect, desert, give up, resign, retire 07 abandon, back out, pull out 08 step down, withdraw 09 stand down 10 chicken out

• part of bow
03 nut 04 frog, heel, luff

• with bow
04 arco

bowdlerize
03 cut 04 edit 05 purge 06 censor, excise, modify, purify 07 clean up, expunge 09 expurgate 10 blue-pencil

bowels
04 core, guts 05 belly, colon, heart
06 cavity, centre, depths, inside, middle 07 innards, insides, viscera
08 entrails, interior 09 entralles
10 intestines

bower
03 bay 05 arbor 06 alcove, arbour, grotto, recess 07 retreat, shelter
09 sanctuary

bowl
03 cap, cog, pan 04 caup, dish, hurl, race, roll, rush, sink, spin, wood
05 basin, cogie, fling, hurry, joram, jorum, mazer, motor, pitch, speed, tazza, throw, whirl 06 beaker, bicker, career, coggie, crater, goblet, krater, piggin, propel, rotate, vessel
07 brimmer, cage-cup, chalice, écuelle, revolve 08 jeroboam, monteith 09 container, porringer, posset cup, pottinger 10 receptacle
11 fingerglass 12 move steadily

• bowled
01 b

• bowl over
03 wow 04 fell, stun 05 amaze, floor, shock 06 topple 07 astound, stagger, startle 08 astonish, push into, surprise
09 dumbfound, knock down, overwhelm, unbalance 11 flabbergast
12 affect deeply 14 impress greatly

bowler
03 hat 04 skip 05 Derby 06 pot hat, seamer 07 Christy, hard hat, spinner
08 Christie

box
◇ *containment indicator*
02 tv 03 ark, dan, hit, pew, pix, pyx, urn 04 butt, case, cuff, etui, fist, fund, inro, loge, mill, pack, slap, slug, sock, spar, tele, wrap 05 bijou, chest, clout, fight, lodge, punch, pyxis, telly, thump, whack 06 batter, buffet, carton, casket, coffin, encase, packet, parcel, strike, wallop 07 coffret, package, present 09 baignoire, container
10 receptacle, television

• box in
04 cage, trap 05 hem in 06 bail up, coop up, corner, shut in 07 block in, confine, contain, enclose, fence in
08 imprison, restrain, restrict, surround
09 cordon off 12 circumscribe

boxer
03 ham, pug 07 cruiser, fighter
08 pugilist, southpaw 12 prizefighter
15 sparring partner

Boxers, managers and promoters include:

03 Ali (Muhammad)
04 Benn (Nigel), Clay (Cassius), Khan (Amir), King (Don)
05 Bruno (Frank), Duran (Roberto), Hamed ('Prince' Naseem), Lewis (Lennox), Louis (Joe), Moore (Archie), Tyson (Mike)
06 Cooper (Henry), Dundee (Angelo), Eubank (Chris), Holmes (Larry), Liston (Sonny), Spinks (Leon)
07 Dempsey (Jack), Foreman (George), Frazier (Joe), Leonard (Sugar Ray)
08 Marciano (Rocky), McGuigan (Barry), Robinson (Sugar Ray)
09 Armstrong (Henry), Holyfield (Evander), Honeyghan (Lloyd)
11 Fitzsimmons (Bob), Queensberry (Sir John Sholto Douglas, Marquis of)

boxing
04 ring 06 savate 08 fighting, pugilism, sparring 10 fisticuffs, infighting, the science 11 the noble art
13 prizefighting 15 the noble science

See also **sport**

Professional boxing weight divisions include:

09 flyweight
11 heavyweight, lightweight, strawweight

12 bantamweight, middleweight, welterweight
13 cruiserweight, featherweight, mini flyweight, minimum weight
14 light flyweight, super flyweight
15 junior flyweight

• boxing match
04 bout, mill, spar **10** glove-fight, prizefight

boy
03 bub, cub, kid, lad, son, tad **04** boyo, loon, lown, male, tama **05** bubby, bucko, child, gilpy, groom, knave, lowne, sprog, youth **06** chield, chokra, chummy, fellow, garçon, junior, loonie, nickum, nipper, shaver **07** galopin, gorsoon, gossoon **08** man-child, spalpeen, teenager, young man
09 dandiprat, dandyprat, Jack-a-Lent, schoolboy, stripling, youngster
10 adolescent, knave-bairn
11 guttersnipe, kinchin-cove
14 whippersnapper

Boys' names include:

02 Al, Cy, Ed, Ik, Jo
03 Abe, Alf, Ali, Asa, Bat, Baz, Ben, Bob, Dai, Dan, Deb, Dee, Del, Den, Dev, Dob, Don, Gay, Gaz, Gil, Gus, Guy, Hew, Huw, Ian, Ike, Iky, Ira, Ivo, Jay, Jem, Jim, Joe, Jon, Jos, Ken, Kim, Kit, Lal, Lee, Len, Leo, Lew, Mat, Max, Nat, Ned, Nye, Pat, Pip, Rab, Rae, Ray, Reg, Rex, Rob, Rod, Ron, Roy, Sam, Sim, Sol, Tam, Ted, Tim, Tom, Val, Vic, Viv, Wat, Wyn, Zia
04 Adam, Adil, Alan, Alec, Aled, Alex, Algy, Alun, Amin, Andy, Anil, Arch, Arun, Bart, Bert, Bill, Bram, Bryn, Carl, Ceri, Chad, Chae, Chay, Clem, Colm, Dave, Davy, Dean, Dewi, Dick, Dirk, Doug, Drew, Eddy, Egon, Eoin, Eric, Eryl, Euan, Evan, Ewan, Ewen, Ezra, Finn, Fred, Gabi, Gary, Gaye, Gene, Glen, Glyn, Gwyn, Hani, Hank, Hari, Hope, Huey, Hugh, Hugo, Iain, Ifor, Ivan, Ivon, Ivor, Jack, Jake, Jeff, Jock, Joel, Joey, John, Josh, Joss, Jude, Jule, Karl, Kirk, Kurt, Liam, Luke, Mark, Matt, Mick, Mike, Neal, Neil, Nick, Noam, Noel, Omar, Owen, Ozzy, Paul, Pete, Phil, Rana, Ravi, Raza, René, Rhys, Rick, Rolf, Rory, Ross, Ryan, Saul, Sean, Seth, Siôn, Theo, Thos, Toby, Tony, Trev, Umar, Walt, Will, Yves, Zach, Zack
05 Aaron, Abd-al, Abdul, Abram, Adeel, Adnan, Ahmad, Ahmed, Aidan, Aiden, Alfie, Allan, Allen, Alwin, Alwyn, Amrit, Andie, Angel, Angus, Anwar, Archy, Arran, Barry, Basil, Bazza, Benny, Billy, Bobby, Boris, Brent, Brett, Brian, Bruce, Bruno, Bryan, Bunny, Cahal, Calum, Cecil, Chaim, Chris, Chuck, Claud, Clint, Clive, Clyde, Colin, Colum, Conor, Corin, Cosmo, Craig, Cyril, Cyrus, Damon, Danny, David, Davie, Denis, Denny, Denys, Derek, Dicky, Dilip, Dipak, Donal, Duane, Dwane, Dylan, Eddie, Edgar, Edwin, Elroy, Elton, Elvis, Elwyn, Emlyn, Emrys, Enoch, Ernie, Errol, Farid, Faruq, Felix, Fionn, Floyd, Frank, Gabby, Gamal, Garry, Gavin, Geoff, Gerry, Giles, Glenn, Gopal, Hamza, Harry, Harun, Hasan, Haydn, Henry, Homer, Howel, Humph, Husni, Hywel, Idris, Ieuan, Inigo, Isaac, Jacob, Jamal, James, Jamie, Jamil, Jared, Jason, Jerry, Jesse, Jimmy, Jools, Kamal, Kasim, Keith, Kelly, Kenny, Kerry, Kevan, Kevin, Kiran, Kumar, Lance, Larry, Leigh, Lenny, Leroy, Lewie, Lewis, Linus, Lloyd, Logan, Lorne, Louie, Louis, Lucas, Madoc, Manny, Micky, Miles, Moray, Moses, Moshe, Mungo, Murdo, Myles, Neale, Neddy, Niall, Nicky, Nicol, Nigel, Ollie, Orson, Oscar, Ozzie, Paddy, Patsy, Percy, Perry, Peter, Piers, Qasim, Rajiv, Ralph, Randy, Ricky, Roald, Robin, Roddy, Roger, Rowan, Rufus, Sacha, Salim, Sammy, Sandy, Sasha, Scott, Shane, Shaun, Shawn, Silas, Simon, Solly, Steve, Sunil, Taffy, Tariq, Teddy, Terry, Tommy, Tudor, Ulric, Ultan, Vijay, Vinay, Waldo, Walid, Wally, Wasim, Wayne, Willy, Wynne
06 Adrian, Albert, Alexei, Alexej, Alexis, Alfred, Andrew, Antony, Archie, Arnold, Arthur, Ashley, Ashraf, Aubrey, Austin, Barney, Benjie, Bernie, Bertie, Bharat, Billie, Blaise, Bobbie, Callum, Calvin, Caspar, Cathal, Cedric, Ciaran, Clancy, Claude, Clovis, Colley, Connor, Conrad, Dafydd, Damian, Damien, Daniel, Darren, Declan, Deepak, Delroy, Dennis, Denzil, Dermot, Deryck, Devdan, Dicken, Dickie, Dickon, Dilwyn, Dobbin, Donald, Donnie, Dougal, Dudley, Dugald, Duggie, Duncan, Dustin, Eamonn, Eamunn, Edmund, Edward, Ernest, Esmond, Eugene, Faisal, Fareed, Faysal, Fergus, Finbar, Fingal, Finlay, Finley, Fintan, Freddy, Gareth, Garret, George, Georgy, Gerald, Gerard, Gerrie, Gideon, Gobind, Gordon, Govind, Graeme, Graham, Gussie, Hamish, Harold, Haroun, Harvey, Hassan, Hayden, Haydon, Hector, Herbie, Hervey, Hilary, Horace, Howard, Howell, Hubert, Hughie, Husain, Isaiah, Iseult, Ismail, Israel, Jarvis, Jasper, Jeremy, Jerome, Jervis, Jethro, Jimmie, Jolyon, Jordan, Joseph, Joshua, Julian, Julius, Justin, Kelvin, Kennie, Kieran, Kieron, Laurie, Lawrie, Lennie, Leslie, Lester, Lionel, Lorcan, Lucius, Luther, Lynsey, Magnus, Mahmud, Marcel, Marcus, Marlon, Martin, Martyn, Marvin, Melvin, Melvyn, Mervyn, Milton, Morgan, Morris, Murray, Nathan, Neddie, Nichol, Ninian, Norman, Oliver, Osbert, Oswald, Pascal, Pearce, Philip, Pierce, Rajesh, Randal, Ranulf, Reggie, Reuben, Richie, Robbie, Robert, Rodney, Roland, Ronald, Rudolf, Rupert, Saleem, Samuel, Sanjay, Seamas, Seamus, Seumas, Shamus, Sharif, Sidney, Sorley, Steven, Stevie, St John, Stuart, Sydney, Teddie, Thomas, Timmie, Tobias, Trevor, Tyrone, Vernon, Victor, Vikram, Virgil, Vivian, Vyvian, Vyvyan, Walter, Willie, Xavier
07 Abraham, Alister, Ambrose, Aneurin, Anthony, Auberon, Barnaby, Bernard, Bertram, Brendan, Chandra, Charles, Charley, Charlie, Christy, Clement, Crispin, Derrick, Desmond, Dominic, Douglas, Eustace, Feargal, Finbarr, Francie, Francis, Frankie, Freddie, Gabriel, Geordie, Georgie, Geraint, Gervase, Gilbert, Godfrey, Grahame, Gwillym, Herbert, Humphry, Hussain, Hussein, Ibrahim, Isadore, Isidore, Isodore, Jeffrey, Johnnie, Kenneth, Killian, Krishna, Lachlan, Leonard, Leopold, Lindsay, Lindsey, Ludovic, Malcolm, Matthew, Maurice, Michael, Murdoch, Mustafa, Neville, Nicolas, Orlando, Patrick, Peredur, Phillip, Quentin, Quintin, Quinton, Randall, Randolf, Ranulph, Raymond, Reynold, Richard, Rowland, Rudolph, Russell, Shankar, Shelley, Solomon, Stanley, Stephen, Stewart, Terence, Timothy, Torquil, Tristan, Vaughan, Vincent, Wilfred, Wilfrid, William, Winston, Zachary
08 Alasdair, Alastair, Algernon, Alistair, Augustus, Barnabas, Benedick, Benedict, Benjamin, Beverley, Christie, Clarence, Clifford, Crispian, Cuthbert, Dominick, Emmanuel, Frederic, Geoffrey, Humphrey, Jonathan, Jonathon, Kimberly, Kingsley, Lancelot, Laurence, Lawrence, Llewelyn, Matthias, Meredith, Mordecai, Muhammad, Nicholas, Perceval, Percival, Randolph, Reginald, Roderick, Ruaidhri, Ruairidh, Ruaraidh, Rupinder, Terrance, Theodore, Tristram
09 Alexander, Archibald, Augustine, Christian, Ferdinand, Frederick, Kimberley, Launcelot, Nathaniel, Peregrine, Sebastian, Siegfried, Somhairle, Sylvester, Valentine
10 Maximilian
11 Bartholomew, Christopher

boycott
03 ban, bar **04** snub **05** avoid, black, spurn **06** eschew, ignore, outlaw, refuse, reject **07** embargo, exclude, refusal **08** disallow, prohibit, spurning **09** blacklist, exclusion, ostracism, ostracize, proscribe, rejection **11** prohibition **12** cold-shoulder, proscription **14** send to Coventry

boyfriend
03 ami, guy, man **04** beau, date **05** bloke, fella, lover **06** fellow, fiancé, steady, suitor, toyboy **07** admirer, best

boy, partner, squeeze **08** young man **09** cohabitee **10** sweetheart **11** live-in lover **15** common-law spouse

boyish
05 gamin, green, young **06** gamine, tomboy **07** puerile **08** childish, immature, innocent, juvenile, youthful **09** childlike **10** adolescent, unfeminine, unmaidenly

brace
02 II, PR **03** duo, tie, two **04** beam, bend, bind, pair, prop, stay, vice **05** clamp, nerve, shore, steel, strap, strut, truss **06** couple, fasten, gear up, hold up, prop up, secure, steady, wimble **07** bandage, bolster, compose, fortify, prepare, psych up, shore up, shoring, support, tighten, twosome **08** accolade, bridging, buttress, fastener, get ready **09** reinforce, stanchion, undergird **10** strengthen **13** reinforcement

bracelet
04 band **05** armil **06** bangle **07** armilla, circlet **08** handcuff, wristlet

bracing
05 brisk, crisp, fresh, tonic **07** rousing **08** reviving, vigorous **09** energetic **10** energizing, enlivening, fortifying, refreshing **11** stimulating **12** exhilarating, invigorating **13** strengthening

bracken
04 tara **05** brake

bracket
◇ *containment indicator*
03 lot **04** prop, rest, stay **05** batch, brace, class, frame, group **06** becket, cohort, corbel, gusset, holder, mutule, trivet **07** cripple, potence, support **08** category, grouping **09** goose-neck, modillion **10** cantilever, misericord **11** misericorde, parenthesis **14** classification

brackish
04 brak, salt **05** briny, salty **06** bitter, saline **07** saltish **11** salsuginous

bract
05 glume, palea **06** spathe **08** phyllary **10** hypsophyll

brad
04 nail

brag
03 gab **04** bull, crow **05** boast, proud, vapor, vaunt **06** vapour **07** big-note, bluster, proudly, show off, swagger, talk big **08** mouth off **10** shoot a line **11** hyperbolize, rodomontade **12** cry roast-meat, lay it on thick **15** blow your own horn

braggart
06 gascon **07** bluffer, boaster, show-off, swasher, windbag **08** bangster, big mouth, boastful, fanfaron, puckfist **09** blusterer, loud-mouth, swaggerer **11** braggadocio **12** rodomontader, swashbuckler

bragging
06 hot air **07** bluster, bravado **08** boasting, vauntery **09** thrasonic **10** showing-off **11** jactitation, thrasonical **12** boastfulness, exaggeration **13** tongue-doubtie

braid
04 cord, lace, tail, wind, yarn **05** plait, pleat, queue, ravel, tress, twine, twist, weave **06** caddis, ric-rac, sennit, sinnet, thread **07** caddice, embraid, entwine **08** reproach, rick-rack, soutache **09** interlace, passement **10** intertwine, interweave **13** scrambled eggs

brain
◇ *anagram indicator*
03 wit **04** head, mind, nous **05** savvy, sense **06** acumen, boffin, brains, expert, genius, pundit, reason **07** egghead, prodigy, scholar **08** brainbox, highbrow, pia mater, sagacity **09** intellect, sensorium **10** encephalon, grey matter, mastermind, shrewdness **11** cleverclogs, common sense, upper storey **12** intellectual, intelligence **13** understanding

Brain parts include:

04 falx, lobe, lobi, pons
06 cortex
07 cinerea
08 amygdala, cerebrum, meninges, midbrain, thalamus
09 brainstem, forebrain, hindbrain, ventricle
10 Broca's area, cerebellum, grey matter, pineal body, spinal cord
11 frontal lobe, hippocampus, white matter
12 hypothalamus, limbic system, parietal lobe, Purkinje cell, temporal lobe, visual cortex
13 choroid plexus, mesencephalon, occipital lobe, olfactory bulb, optic thalamus, Wernicke's area
14 cerebral cortex, corpus callosum, left hemisphere, pituitary gland
15 right hemisphere, substantia nigra

brainless
04 daft **05** crazy, inept, silly **06** stupid **07** foolish, idiotic **08** mindless **09** hen-witted, senseless **10** half-witted **11** incompetent, thoughtless **12** simple-minded

brains
02 IQ **03** wit **04** loaf, nous **05** harns, savey, savvy **06** common, savvey, sconce, wisdom **08** gumption **10** grey matter

brainteaser
05 poser **06** puzzle, riddle **07** problem **09** conundrum **10** mind-bender **12** brain-twister

brainwashing
08 grilling **09** menticide **10** persuasion **11** mind-bending, re-education **12** conditioning, pressurizing **14** indoctrination

brainy
04 wise **05** smart **06** bright, clever, gifted **07** sapient **09** brilliant **11** intelligent **12** intellectual

brake
04 curb, drag, fern, halt, rein, slow, stop **05** check **06** harrow, pull up, retard **07** bracken, control, slacken, thicket **08** moderate, slow down **09** restraint **10** constraint, decelerate, retardment **11** reduce speed, restriction

• **braking system**
03 ABS

bramble
05 Rubus **06** lawyer **08** dewberry **10** blackberry, cloudberry **12** Penang-lawyer

bran
06 chesil, chisel, shorts **07** pollard **08** roughage

branch
02 br **03** arm, cow, leg, lye **04** axis, fork, limb, lobe, loop, part, reis, rice, stem, whip, wing **05** bough, corps, prong, ramus, scrog, shoot, sprig, withy **06** agency, bureau, office **07** braunch, cladode, section **08** division, offshoot **09** affiliate, succursal, tributary **10** department, discipline, subsection, subsidiary **11** local office, phylloclade, subdivision **12** ramification **14** regional office

• **branch off**
04 fork **06** divide, offset, spring **07** deviate, diverge, furcate **08** separate **09** bifurcate

• **branch out**
04 vary **05** add to **06** expand, extend, ramify **07** develop, enlarge **08** increase, multiply **09** diversify, spread out, subdivide **10** broaden out **11** proliferate

brand
03 tag **04** burn, chop, kind, line, logo, make, mark, sear, sere, sign, sort, type, wipe **05** class, grill, label, stain, stamp, taint **06** burn in, emblem, marque, symbol **07** censure, quality, species, variety **08** besmirch, denounce, disgrace, hallmark, typecast **09** brand-name, discredit, trademark, tradename **10** stigmatize **14** identification **15** identifying mark

brandish
03 wag **04** wave **05** bless, flash, raise, shake, swing, wield **06** flaunt, hurtle, parade, waving **07** display, exhibit, vibrate, wampish **08** flourish

brandy
03 dop **04** fine, marc **05** bingo, mobby, Nantz, peach, smoke **06** Cognac, grappa, mobbie **07** quetsch **08** Armagnac, Calvados, eau de vie, mahogany, slivovic **09** apple-jack, aqua vitae, Cape smoke, mirabelle, slivovica, slivovitz, slivowitz **10** ball of fire **11** aguardiente, cold-without, water of life **12** cherry bounce **13** fine Champagne

brash
04 bold, rash, rude **05** cocky, crude, hasty, pushy **06** brazen, flashy
07 assured, brittle, forward
08 impudent, insolent, reckless
09 assertive, audacious, bumptious, foolhardy, heartburn, impetuous, impulsive **10** incautious, indiscreet
11 impertinent, precipitate **13** self-confident

brashly
06 boldly, rashly, rudely **07** cockily, hastily, pushily **08** brazenly
09 assuredly, forwardly **10** impudently, insolently, recklessly **11** assertively, audaciously, foolhardily, impetuously, impulsively **12** incautiously, indiscreetly **13** impertinently, precipitately **15** self-confidently

brashness
08 audacity, boldness, rashness, rudeness **09** hastiness, impudence, incaution, insolence, pushiness
10 brazenness **12** impertinence, recklessness **13** assertiveness, foolhardiness **14** self-confidence

brass
04 gall, loot, sass **05** cheek, money, nerve **06** latten **08** audacity, chutzpah, orichalc, rudeness, temerity
09 brass neck, impudence, insolence, necessary, oricalche **10** brass nerve, brazenness, effrontery **11** presumption
12 impertinence
• **top brass**
04 VIPs

brassy
04 bold, hard, loud **05** brash, cocky, harsh, noisy, pushy, sassy, saucy
06 brazen **07** blaring, forward, grating, jarring, raucous **08** insolent, jangling, piercing, strident **09** dissonant, shameless **11** loud-mouthed

brat
03 get, imp, kid **04** gait, geit, gyte
05 brach, puppy **06** nipper, rascal
07 brachet **08** bantling, bratchet
09 youngster **10** jackanapes
11 guttersnipe **14** whippersnapper

bravado
04 show, talk **05** boast, brave
06 parade **07** bluster, bombast, bravery, swagger **08** boasting, bragging, pretence, vaunting
09 swaggerer **10** showing-off
11 braggadocio, fanfaronade, rodomontade

brave
04 bear, bold, dare, defy, face
05 bravo, bully, gutsy, hardy, manly, noble, showy **06** daring, endure, feisty, gritty, heroic, plucky, spunky, suffer
07 doughty, gallant, stoical, valiant
08 confront, face up to, fearless, handsome, intrepid, resolute, stalwart, unafraid, valorous, yeomanly
09 audacious, challenge, dauntless, excellent, put up with, stand up to, undaunted, withstand **10** courageous
11 indomitable, lion-hearted, unflinching **12** face the music, not turn a hair, stout-hearted **14** game as Ned Kelly, keep your chin up

bravely
06 boldly **07** hardily **08** daringly, pluckily, yeomanly **09** doughtily, gallantly, stoically, valiantly
10 fearlessly, heroically, intrepidly, resolutely, stalwartly, valorously
11 audaciously, dauntlessly, indomitably, undauntedly
12 courageously **13** unflinchingly
14 stout-heartedly

bravery
04 grit, guts **05** pluck, spunk, valor
06 daring, finery, mettle, spirit, valour
07 bravado, courage, heroism, prowess **08** audacity, boldness, chivalry, tenacity, valiance
09 fortitude, gallantry, hardiness
10 resolution **11** intrepidity
12 fearlessness, stalwartness
13 dauntlessness **14** courageousness, indomitability

bravo
01 B **03** olé **04** euge **08** well done
09 excellent, spadassin

bravura
04 dash, élan **06** spirit **07** sparkle
10 brilliance **12** magnificence

brawl
03 row **04** dust, fray, rout **05** argue, broil, clash, fight, flite, flyte, mêlée, scold, scrap **06** affray, bundle, bust-up, dust-up, fracas, fratch, ruckus, rumpus, stoush, tussle **07** bagarre, brabble, brangle, dispute, punch-up, quarrel, scuffle, tuilyie, tuilzie, wrangle, wrestle
08 argument, disorder, skirmish, squabble **09** altercate
10 Donnybrook, fisticuffs, free-for-all, rough-house **11** altercation

brawn
04 beef, boar, bulk **05** might, power
06 muscle, sinews **07** muscles
08 beefcake, strength **09** beefiness, bulkiness **10** headcheese, robustness
11 muscularity

brawny
05 beefy, bulky, burly, hardy, hefty, hunky, husky, meaty, solid **06** fleshy, robust, sinewy, strong, sturdy
07 hulking, massive **08** athletic, muscular, powerful, stalwart, vigorous
09 strapping, well-built

bray
04 bell, hoot, roar **05** blare, neigh
06 bellow, heehaw, whinny
07 screech, trumpet

brazen
04 bold, pert **05** brash, pushy, saucy
06 brassy **07** blatant, defiant, forward
08 flagrant, immodest, impudent, insolent **09** audacious, bald-faced, barefaced, shameless, unabashed, unashamed **10** hard-boiled, in-your-face
• **brazen it out**
04 defy **09** be defiant **11** be unashamed **12** be impenitent

brazenly
06 boldly **09** blatantly, defiantly
10 flagrantly, immodestly, impudently, insolently **11** audaciously, shamelessly, unashamedly

brazier
06 hearth, mangal **07** brasero
08 scaldino **10** fire-basket

Brazil
02 BR **03** BRA **04** Braz

breach
03 gap **04** gulf, hole, rift, slap
05 break, chasm, cleft, crack, lapse, space, split, unlaw **06** open up, saltus, schism **07** crevice, fissure, offence, offense, opening, parting, quarrel, rupture, violate **08** aperture, breakers, breaking, division, fraction, infringe, solution, trespass, variance **09** break open, severance, violation
10 alienation, contravene, difference, disruption, dissension, infraction, separation **12** break through, burst through, disaffection, disagreement, disobedience, dissociation, estrangement, infringement
13 contravention, transgression

bread
03 fat, tin **04** cash, diet, dosh, fare, food, pane **05** dough, dumps, funds, lolly, money, sugar **06** crusts
07 shekels **08** sandwich, victuals
09 nutriment **10** livelihood, provisions, sustenance **11** necessities, nourishment, spondulicks, subsistence
12 the necessary

Bread and rolls include:

03 bap, cob, nan, rye, tea
04 azym, cake, corn, diet, farl, flat, loaf, milk, naan, pita, pone, roti, soda
05 arepa, azyme, bagel, black, brown, cheat, fancy, horse, matza, matzo, pitta, plait, poori, ravel, white
06 burger, damper, French, garlic, graham, hoagie, hot dog, Indian, injera, lavash, matzah, matzoh, panini, panino, simnel, stotty, wastel
07 bannock, bloomer, brioche, brownie, buttery, challah, chapati, currant, ficelle, granary, jannock, manchet, paratha, pretzel, stollen, stottie, wheaten
08 baguette, barm cake, chapatti, ciabatta, corn pone, focaccia, grissini, leavened, milk loaf, ravelled, ryebread, schnecke, standard, tortilla
09 bara brith, barmbrack, batch loaf, burger bun, cornbread, croissant, flatbread, hamburger, petit pain, schnecken, shewbread, showbread, sourdough, wholemeal
10 breadstick, bridge roll, finger roll, French loaf, stotty cake, unleavened, vienna loaf, wholewheat

11 cottage loaf, French stick, morning roll, potato bread, potato scone
12 pumpernickel
13 farmhouse loaf
14 pain au chocolat

• **bread and butter**
11 maintenance
• **bread in milk**
03 sop

breadbasket
03 tum **05** tummy **07** stomach

breadth
01 b **04** beam, size, span **05** range, reach, scale, scope, sweep, width **06** extent, spread **07** compass, expanse, measure **08** latitude, vastness, wideness **09** amplitude, beaminess, broadness, dimension, magnitude, thickness **10** distension **13** extensiveness

break
◇ *anagram indicator*
◇ *insertion indicator*
03 gap, vac **04** beat, bust, dash, dawn, fail, gash, halt, hole, kick, lash, luck, lull, open, part, quit, rend, rest, rift, rise, ruin, snap, stop, tame, tear, tell, vary **05** begin, cleft, crack, crash, crush, excel, flout, let-up, outdo, pause, pound, sever, smash, solve, split **06** appear, be born, better, breach, chance, change, cut off, cut out, decode, divide, emerge, exceed, falter, give up, go phut, impair, impart, inform, lessen, open up, pack up, pierce, reduce, reveal, schism, shiver, soften, strike, subdue, weaken, worsen **07** abandon, conk out, crevice, cushion, decrypt, destroy, disobey, disturb, divulge, fissure, fortune, go kaput, holiday, improve, lighten, opening, respite, rupture, shatter, smoke-ho, stammer, stumble, stutter, surpass, suspend, time off, time-out, unravel, violate, work out **08** announce, breather, decipher, demolish, diminish, disclose, enfeeble, fracture, infringe, interval, outstrip, overcome, puncture, separate, shake off, splinter, vacation **09** advantage, dishonour, figure out, interlude, interrupt, perforate, undermine **10** contravene, demoralize, relinquish, separation **11** discontinue, malfunction, opportunity, stop working **12** bring to an end, disintegrate, estrangement, go on the blink, intermission, interruption, stroke of luck **13** interfere with
• **break away**
03 fly **04** flee, quit **05** leave, split, start **06** depart, detach, escape, secede **07** run away **08** separate, split off **11** part company **13** make a run for it
• **break down**
02 go **04** cark, conk, fail, kark, stop **05** crash, crock, crush, plash, smash **06** detail, go down, go phut, pack up **07** analyse, burn out, conk out, crack up, crock up, destroy, dissect, founder, give way, itemize, seize up **08** collapse, demolish, separate **09** attenuate, decompose, knock down **10** be overcome, categorize, go to pieces **11** fall through, lose control, stop working **13** come to nothing
• **break in**
03 rob **04** raid, tame, wear **05** cut in, prime, start, train **06** burgle, butt in, irrupt **07** impinge, intrude **08** accustom, encroach **09** condition, cultivate, get used to, interject, interpose, interrupt, intervene **14** enter illegally
• **break off**
03 end **04** halt, part, stop **05** cease, pause, sever **06** detach, divide, finish **07** snap off, suspend **08** dissever, separate **09** interrupt, terminate **10** disconnect **11** discontinue **12** bring to an end
• **break out**
03 rip **04** bolt, flee **05** arise, begin, erupt, occur, shout, start **06** blow up, emerge, escape, happen **07** abscond, exclaim, flare up **08** burst out, commence **09** come out in, interject **13** begin suddenly
• **break through**
04 pass **06** emerge **07** succeed **08** fracture, overcome, progress **09** penetrate **10** gain ground **11** leap forward, make headway
• **break up**
◇ *anagram indicator*
◇ *containment indicator*
04 part, stop **05** sever, split, stave **06** divide, finish, reduce, reform **07** adjourn, destroy, disband, divorce, resolve, split up, suspend **08** demolish, diffract, disperse, dissolve, separate, splinter, to-bruise **09** dismantle, dismember, take apart, terminate **11** come to an end, discontinue, part company **12** bring to an end, disintegrate
• **break with**
04 drop, jilt **05** ditch **06** reject **08** part with, renounce **09** repudiate **10** finish with **12** separate from

breakable
05 frail **06** flimsy **07** brittle, fragile, friable **08** delicate **09** frangible **10** jerry-built **12** easily broken **13** insubstantial

breakaway
05 rebel **06** escape, revolt **08** apostate, renegade, seceding **09** defection, heretical, secession **10** dissenting, schismatic, separatist, withdrawal **12** secessionist

breakdown
07 failure **08** analysis, collapse, stoppage **10** cracking-up, dissection **11** itemization, malfunction **12** interruption **13** going to pieces **14** categorization, classification, disintegration
• **breakdown service**
02 AA **03** RAC

breaker
04 wave **06** billow, buster, roller **10** roughrider **11** white horses

breakfast
07 dejeune, disjune **08** déjeuner **10** chota hazri **13** petit déjeuner
See also **cereal**

break-in
04 raid **07** larceny, robbery **08** burglary, invasion, trespass **09** intrusion **13** house-breaking

breakneck
05 rapid, swift **06** speedy **07** express **08** headlong, very fast **09** very quick **11** precipitate **13** like lightning

breakthrough
04 find, gain, leap, step **07** advance, finding, headway **08** progress **09** discovery, invention, milestone **10** innovation **11** development, improvement, leap forward, quantum leap, step forward

break-up
03 end **04** rift **05** split **06** finish **07** debacle, divorce, parting, upbreak **09** crumbling, dispersal **10** separation **11** dissolution, splitting-up, termination **14** disintegration

breakwater
04 dock, mole, pier, quay, spur **05** jetty, wharf **06** groyne **07** bulwark, sea wall

bream
03 tai **05** porgy **06** braise, braize, porgie, sargos, sargus **08** tarwhine

breast
03 dug, pap, tit **04** boob, bust, stem, teat **05** booby, bosom, chest, diddy, front, heart, mamma, titty **06** nipple, thorax **07** brisket, bristol, knocker **08** breaskit

breastplate
06 byrnie, thorax **07** cuirass, placket **08** pectoral, plastron, rational

breath
03 air **04** gasp, gulp, gust, hint, pant, puff, sigh, waft, wind **05** aroma, odour, prana, smell, whiff **06** breeze, flatus, murmur, pneuma, spirit **07** whisper **09** breathing, suspicion, undertone **10** exhalation, inhalation, suggestion **11** inspiration, respiration

breathe
04 gasp, pant, puff, sigh, tell **05** imbue, snore, utter, voice **06** exhale, expire, impart, infuse, inhale, inject, instil, murmur **07** express, inspire, respire, suspire, whisper **09** embreathe, inbreathe, transfuse **10** articulate, insufflate

breather
04 gill, halt, lung, nare, rest, walk **05** break, pause **06** recess **07** respite **10** relaxation **14** breathing space, constitutional

breathless
04 agog, dead **05** eager **06** pooped,

puffed, winded **07** airless, anxious, choking, excited, gasping, panting, puffing **08** feverish, wheezing **09** exhausted, expectant, impatient, pooped out, puffed out **10** in suspense **11** open-mouthed, out of breath, short-winded, tuckered out

breathtaking
06 moving **07** amazing **08** drop-dead, exciting, stirring, stunning **09** thrilling **10** astounding, impressive, stupendous **11** astonishing, magnificent, spectacular **12** awe-inspiring, overwhelming

breathtakingly
09 amazingly **10** excitingly, stirringly, stunningly **11** thrillingly **12** impressively, stupendously **13** astonishingly, spectacularly **14** awe-inspiringly, overwhelmingly

breeches
04 hose **05** slops **06** breeks, tights, trouse, trunks **07** plushes, trusses **08** chausses, jodhpurs, leathers, trossers, trousers **09** buckskins, knee-cords, strossers, trunk hose **12** galligaskins, pedal pushers, small-clothes **14** knickerbockers

breed
04 bear, kind, line, make, race, rear, sort, type **05** cause, class, hatch, raise, stamp, stock **06** arouse, create, family, foster, hybrid, strain **07** bring up, calibre, develop, lineage, nourish, nurture, produce, progeny, species, variety **08** engender, generate, multiply, occasion, pedigree **09** cultivate, originate, procreate, propagate, pullulate, reproduce **10** bring about, bring forth, give rise to **11** give birth to

breeding
05 stock **06** polish **07** culture, lineage, manners, nurture, raising, rearing **08** ancestry, civility, gentrice, training, urbanity **09** education, gentility **10** politeness, refinement, upbringing **11** cultivation, development, good manners, procreation, savoir-vivre **12** reproduction

• **breeding establishment**
04 stud

breeding-ground
04 nest **06** cradle, hotbed, school **07** nursery **08** hothouse **14** training ground

breeze
◇ *anagram indicator*
03 air **04** flit, gust, puff, sail, trip, waft, wind **05** glide, hurry, sally, slant, snift, sweep **06** breath, doctor, flurry, wander, zephyr **07** cat's paw, draught, saunter, snifter **08** sniffler **12** periodic wind

breezy
04 airy **05** blowy, brisk, fresh, gusty, light, windy **06** blithe, bright, casual, jaunty, lively **07** blowing, buoyant, relaxed, squally **08** animated, blustery, carefree, cheerful, debonair, informal **09** confident, easy-going, vivacious **12** exhilarating, light-hearted

Brenda
02 ER

brevity
07 economy, fewness **08** curtness, laconism **09** briefness, concision, crispness, pithiness, shortness, terseness **10** abruptness, transience **11** compactness, conciseness **12** ephemerality, impermanence, incisiveness, succinctness **14** transitoriness

brew
◇ *anagram indicator*
04 boil, cook, loom, make, mash, plan, plot, soak, stew **05** blend, drink, hatch, steep **06** devise, excite, foment, gather, infuse, liquor, potion, scheme, seethe **07** build up, concoct, develop, ferment, mixture, prepare, project **08** beverage, compound, contrive, infusion **10** be on its way, concoction **11** combination, preparation **12** distillation, fermentation **13** be in the offing **15** be in preparation

bribe
03 buy, fix, sop **04** bung, dash, gift, palm, vail, wage **05** bonus, booty, drink, sling, spoil, touch, vails, vales **06** boodle, buy off, carrot, grease, hamper, nobble, pay off, pay-off, payola, reward, square, suborn **07** buy over, corrupt, douceur, palm-oil, pension **08** kickback, the drink **09** hush money, incentive, keep sweet, lubricate, refresher, slush fund, sweetener **10** allurement, back-hander, enticement, inducement, palm-grease, take care of **12** straightener **13** gratification **15** protection money

bribery
05 graft **09** embracery **10** corruption, inducement, protection **11** subornation **12** malversation, palm-greasing

bric-à-brac
06 curios **07** baubles, gewgaws **08** antiques, bibelots, trinkets, trumpery **09** gimcracks, ornaments **10** Japanesery, rattletrap, Victoriana **11** knick-knacks, odds and ends **13** bits and pieces

brick
03 bar, bur, pal **04** burr, chum, lump, mass, mate, rock, slab **05** adobe, block, buddy, gault, piece, stone, wedge **06** header, rubber, rustic **07** clinker, fletton, klinker, nogging, soldier **09** briquette, firebrick, stretcher **10** real friend **11** breeze block **12** Dutch clinker

• **brick waste**
04 grog

• **piece of brick**
03 bat

bridal
07 marital, nuptial, wedding **08** conjugal, marriage **09** connubial **11** matrimonial

bride
04 wife **06** spouse **07** GI bride **08** newly-wed, war bride, wife-to-be **09** bride-to-be **11** honeymooner **15** marriage partner

bridegroom
05 groom **06** spouse **07** husband **08** newly-wed **11** honeymooner, husband-to-be **15** marriage partner

bridge
02 br **03** tie **04** bind, bond, fill, join, link, pons, rest, span **05** cross, unite **06** couple, go over **07** connect, spanner **08** traverse **10** connection **11** reach across

Bridge types include:

03 air, fly
04 arch, beam, deck, draw, foot, leaf, over, raft, road, rope, skew, toll, wire
05 chain, pivot, swing
06 Bailey, flying, girder
07 bascule, flyover, lattice, lifting, pontoon, railway, through, viaduct
08 aqueduct, causeway, floating, humpback, overpass
09 box girder
10 cantilever, suspension, traversing
11 cable-stayed

Bridges include:

03 Tay
04 Skye, Tyne
05 Forth, Sighs, Tower
06 Bailey, Humber, Kintai, London, Rialto, Severn
07 Bifrost, Clifton, Rainbow, Tsing Ma, Yichang
08 Bosporus, Brooklyn, Jiangyin, Mackinac, Waterloo
09 Evergreen, Forth Road, Kurushima, River Kwai
10 Bosporus II, Golden Gate, Höga Kusten, Ironbridge, Millennium, Pont du Gard, Storebaelt
11 Brocade Sash
12 Akashi-Kaikyo, Pont d'Avignon, Ponte Vecchio
13 Great Belt East, Kita Bisan-seto, Millau Viaduct, Sydney Harbour
14 Ponte 25 de Abril, Quebec Railroad
15 Minami Bisan-Seto

• **bridge player**
01 e, n, s, w **04** east, west **05** north, south

• **bridge support**
04 pier

• **bridge system**
04 Acol **06** canapé **09** blackwood

bridle
05 check **06** branks, govern, halter, master, subdue **07** bristle, contain, control, repress **08** hold back, moderate, restrain **09** hackamore, restraint **12** be offended by **15** become indignant

Bridle parts include:

03 bit
04 curb
05 cheek
06 musrol, pelham
07 bridoon, eye-flap, snaffle
08 browband, noseband
09 headstall
10 cheekpiece

See also **horse**

brief
◇ *tail deletion indicator*
02 KC, QC **04** case, curt, data, tell **05** blunt, breve, crisp, gen up, guide, hasty, pithy, prime, quick, remit, sharp, short, surly, swift, terse **06** abrupt, advice, advise, digest, direct, fill in, flying, inform, lawyer, orders, précis **07** brusque, compact, concise, cursory, defence, dossier, explain, laconic, limited, mandate, outline, passing, prepare, summary **08** abridged, abstract, argument, breviate, briefing, capsular, evidence, fleeting, instruct, succinct **09** barrister, condensed, directive, ephemeral, fugacious, laconical, momentary, temporary, thumbnail, tout court, transient **10** aphoristic, compressed, directions, evanescent, short-lived, transitory **11** abridgement, information **12** instructions **13** bring up to date, short and sweet **14** responsibility

briefing
03 gen **06** advice, orders **07** low-down, meeting, priming, run-down **08** guidance **09** filling-in **10** conference, directions, intimation **11** information, preparation **12** instructions

briefly
◇ *tail deletion indicator*
05 in few, short **07** in a word, in brief, in short, quickly, shortly, tersely **09** concisely, cursorily, precisely, summarily **10** succinctly, to the point **11** in a few words, in a nutshell

brigade
03 Bde **04** band, body, crew, team, unit **05** corps, force, group, party, squad, troop **07** company **10** contingent
• **Boys' Brigade**
02 BB

brigand
06 bandit, haiduk, outlaw, robber **07** cateran, heyduck, ruffian **08** gangster, marauder **09** desperado, plunderer **10** bushranger, freebooter, highwayman **11** trailbaston

bright
03 gay, lit, net **04** fine, glad, keen, nett, rosy **05** acute, clear, happy, jolly, light, merry, quick, sharp, smart, sunny, vivid **06** astute, brainy, clever, genial, joyful, lively **07** beaming, blazing, glaring, glowing, hopeful, intense, radiant, shining **08** blinding, cheerful, dazzling, flashing, gleaming, glorious, luminous, lustrous, pleasant, splendid **09** beautiful, brilliant, cloudless, effulgent, promising, refulgent, sparkling, twinkling, unclouded, vivacious **10** auspicious, favourable, glistening, glittering, optimistic, perceptive, propitious, shimmering **11** encouraging, illuminated, illustrious, intelligent, quick-witted, resplendent **12** incandescent **15** bright as a button

brighten
03 rub **04** glow, jazz **05** gleam, pep up, rub up, shine **06** buck up, buoy up, jazz up, perk up, polish **07** burnish, cheer up, clear up, enhance, enliven, gladden, hearten, lighten, light up, liven up **09** encourage, irradiate, refurbish, smarten up **10** illuminate, make bright

brightly
06 ablaze, gladly **07** happily **08** joyfully **09** glaringly, glowingly, intensely, radiantly **10** blindingly, cheerfully, dazzlingly, splendidly **11** brilliantly, vivaciously

brilliance
04 tone **05** glare, glory, gloss, sheen **06** dazzle, genius, lustre, talent **07** bravura, glamour, prowess, sparkle **08** aptitude, fulgency, radiance, splendor **09** greatness, intensity, splendour, vividness **10** brightness, cleverness, effulgence, excellence, refulgence, virtuosity **11** coruscation, distinction **12** magnificence, resplendence

brilliant
03 ace, def **04** cool, hard, mega, neat, pear, star **05** brill, gemmy, great, quick, showy, vivid **06** astute, brainy, bright, clever, expert, famous, gifted, glossy, superb, wicked **07** blazing, crucial, erudite, fulgent, glaring, intense, lambent, radical, shining, skilful **08** dazzling, glorious, masterly, smashing, splendid, talented, terrific, top-notch **09** effulgent, excellent, fantastic, refulgent, sparkling, splendent, sunbright, wonderful **10** brightsome, celebrated, glittering, remarkable **11** exceptional, illustrious, intelligent, magnificent, outstanding, resourceful, resplendent **12** accomplished, enterprising, second to none **13** scintillating **14** out of this world

brilliantly
07 vividly **08** brightly, cleverly, superbly **09** intensely, skilfully **10** dazzlingly, gloriously, splendidly **11** masterfully, wonderfully **13** magnificently, resplendently

brim
03 lip, rim, top **04** edge, poke **05** brink, limit, verge **06** border, margin **09** perimeter **10** be full with **12** be filled with, overflow with **13** circumference

brimful
04 full **05** abrim **06** filled, jammed **07** bulging, crammed, stuffed **09** packed out **11** chock-a-block, overflowing

brindled
04 pied **05** tabby **06** dotted **07** dappled, flecked, mottled, piebald **08** speckled, stippled, streaked **10** variegated

bring
03 fet, get, lay **04** bear, lead, take **05** carry, cause, fetch, force, guide, usher **06** convey, create, escort, prompt, submit **07** conduct, deliver, present, produce, provoke **08** engender, initiate, result in **09** accompany, transport **10** make happen, put forward
• **bring about**
04 make **05** cause, frame, wreak **06** create, effect, fulfil, manage **07** achieve, compass, inspire, operate, perform, procure, produce, provoke, realize **08** contrive, generate, occasion, purchase **09** encompass, instigate **10** accomplish
• **bring back**
◇ *reversal indicator*
05 evoke, recal **06** call up, recall, reduce, relate, remind **07** recover, reverse, suggest **13** take you back to **14** make you think of
• **bring down**
04 drop, oust, pull, stop **05** abate, lower, shoot **06** defeat, depose, derive, embace, embase, humble, imbase, reduce, sadden, topple, unsea **07** destroy **08** decrease, dismount, vanquish **09** knock down, overthrow, shoot down **11** cause to drop, cause to fall
• **bring forward**
05 raise **06** adduce, allege, object **07** advance, prepone, present, produce, propose, suggest, trot out **10** put forward **11** make earlier
• **bring in**
◇ *containment indicator*
03 net **04** earn, make, wind **05** fetch, gross, set up, yield **06** accrue, import, induce, launch, return **07** pioneer, produce, realize, usher in **08** initiate **09** introduce, originate, pronounce **10** inaugurate
• **bring off**
03 win **06** fulfil, rescue **07** achieve, execute, perform, pull off **09** discharge, put across, succeed in **10** accomplish, consummate
• **bring on**
05 cause, infer **06** foster, induce, lead to, prompt **07** advance, improve, inspire, nurture, provoke **08** expedite, generate, occasion **10** accelerate, give rise to, make happen **11** precipitate
• **bring out**
05 issue, print **06** launch, stress **07** draw out, enhance, produce, publish **09** emphasize, highlight, introduce **10** accentuate
• **bring round**
◇ *containment indicator*
04 coax **05** rouse **06** awaken, cajole, revive, wake up **07** bring to, convert,

win over **08** convince, persuade **11** resuscitate

• bring up

◇ *reversal down indicator*

03 cat **04** barf, form, puke, rear **05** breed, nurse, raise, teach, train, vomit **06** broach, foster, nousle, nuzzle, submit **07** care for, educate, mention, nourish, noursle, nousell, nurture, propose, throw up, touch on **09** introduce **11** regurgitate

brink

03 lip, rim **04** bank, brim, edge **05** limit, marge, verge **06** border, fringe, margin **08** boundary **09** extremity, threshold

brio

03 pep, zip **04** dash **05** force, gusto, oomph, verve **06** energy, spirit, vigour **08** dynamism, vivacity **09** animation **10** liveliness

brisk

04 busy, cant, cold, fast, good, perk, pert, yare **05** agile, alert, cobby, crisp, fresh, kedge, kedgy, kidge, quick, rapid, sharp, smart **06** active, crouse, lively, nimble, snappy **07** allegro, bracing **08** brushing, bustling, friskful, galliard, spirited, vigorous **09** energetic, sprightly **10** no-nonsense, refreshing **11** stimulating **12** businesslike, exhilarating, invigorating

briskly

04 well **06** busily, nimbly **07** allegro, con moto, quickly, rapidly, sharply **08** abruptly **09** brusquely **10** decisively, vigorously **13** energetically

bristle

03 awn **04** barb, hair, rise, seta **05** birse, quill, spine, thorn **06** arista, bridle, chaeta, seethe, setule, stilet, striga, stylet **07** hum with, prickle, stubble, whisker **08** abound in, bridle at, teem with, vibrissa **09** swarm with **10** seethe with, stand on end, vibraculum **11** be thick with, horripilate **12** be incensed at **14** draw yourself up

bristly

05 hairy, rough, spiky, spiny **06** hispid, thorny **07** bearded, hirsute, prickly, stubbly **08** echinate, unshaven **09** echinated, whiskered **10** barbellate

British

01 B **02** Br, GB, UK **03** pom **04** Brit **05** pommy

See also **monarch**

• British Columbia

02 BC

brittle

◇ *anagram indicator*

04 curt, edgy, hard **05** birsy, brash, crisp, frail, frowy, frush, harsh, nervy, sharp, short, spall, spalt, tense **06** frowie **07** bruckle, crackly, crumbly, fragile, friable, froughy, grating, nervous, redsear, shivery **08** delicate, hot-short, redshare, redshire, redshort, shattery, unstable **09** breakable, cold-short, crumbling, frangible, irritable, sensitive **12** easily broken

broach

◇ *anagram indicator*

03 tap **04** open, spit **05** begin, raise **06** hint at, open up, pierce, strike **07** bring up, mention, propose, refer to, suggest **08** allude to **09** introduce

broad

04 free, open, vast, wide **05** ample, clear, large, plain, roomy, vague **06** coarse, direct, marked, strong, vulgar **07** evident, general, obvious **08** catholic, eclectic, spacious, sweeping, unsubtle **09** capacious, extensive, inclusive, outspoken, universal, unlimited **10** noticeable, widespread **11** compendious, far-reaching, not detailed, unconcealed, undisguised, wide-ranging **12** all-embracing, encyclopedic, latitudinous **13** comprehensive

broadcast

◇ *anagram indicator*

◇ *homophone indicator*

03 air, sow **04** beam, show **05** aired, cable, relay **06** repeat, report, spread **07** network, publish, radiate, scatter, trailer, webcast **08** announce, newscast, teletext, televise, transmit **09** advertise, cablecast, circulate, make known, programme, publicize, simulcast, soap opera **10** promulgate, sportscast, telebridge **11** disseminate **12** transmission **15** access broadcast

• outside broadcast

02 OB **06** remote

broaden

05 widen **06** expand, extend, open up, spread **07** augment, develop, enlarge, stretch **08** increase **09** branch out, diversify

broadly

05 fully **06** mainly, mostly, widely **07** as a rule, largely, usually **08** commonly, normally **09** generally **10** by and large, more or less, on the whole, thoroughly **11** extensively, in most cases, in principle **14** for the most part **15** comprehensively

broad-minded

07 liberal **08** tolerant, unbiased **09** impartial, indulgent, receptive **10** forbearing, open-minded, permissive **11** enlightened, progressive **12** free-thinking, unprejudiced **13** dispassionate

broadside

04 tire **05** blast, salvo, stick **06** attack, volley **07** assault, censure **08** brickbat, diatribe, harangue **09** battering, cannonade, criticism, invective, philippic **11** bombardment, fulmination **12** counterblast, denunciation

brochure

05 flyer **06** folder **07** booklet, handout, leaflet **08** circular, handbill, pamphlet **09** throwaway **10** broadsheet, prospectus

broil

03 fry **04** cook **05** grill, roast, toast **08** barbecue, stramash

broiling

03 hot **06** baking **07** boiling **08** roasting **09** scorching **10** blistering, sweltering

broke

◇ *anagram indicator*

04 bust, poor **05** skint, stony **06** hard up, ruined **07** bargain **08** bankrupt, indigent, strapped **09** destitute, insolvent, negotiate, penniless, penurious **10** cleaned out, stony-broke **11** impecunious **12** impoverished, on your uppers **14** on your beam ends **15** poverty-stricken, strapped for cash

broken

◇ *anagram indicator*

04 bust, down, duff, rent, weak **05** burst, ended, kaput, tamed, wonky **06** beaten, failed, faulty, feeble, fitful, pakaru **07** crushed, damaged, erratic, halting, severed, smashed, subdued **08** defeated, divorced, ruptured **09** defective, destroyed, disturbed, exhausted, faltering, fractured, gone wrong, imperfect, knackered, oppressed, separated, shattered, spasmodic **10** demolished, disjointed, dispirited, hesitating, not working, on the blink, on the fritz, out of order, stammering, vanquished **11** demoralized, fragmentary, inoperative, interrupted, out of action **12** disconnected, intermittent **13** discontinuous **14** malfunctioning

• not to be broken

04 iron

broken-down

03 ill **04** bust, duff **05** kaput **06** broken, faulty, ruined **07** damaged, decayed, rickety, worn-out **08** decrepit **09** collapsed, defective **10** on the blink, on the fritz, out of order, ramshackle **11** dilapidated, in disrepair, inoperative

broken-hearted

03 sad **04** down **07** forlorn, unhappy **08** dejected, desolate, dolorous, mournful, wretched **09** miserable, sorrowful **10** despairing, despondent, devastated, prostrated **11** crestfallen, heartbroken **12** disappointed, disconsolate, inconsolable **13** grief-stricken **14** down in the dumps

broker

03 job **04** deal **05** agent, agree, bania **06** banian, banyan, clinch, dealer, factor, jobber, settle **07** arrange, bargain, execute, handler, mediate **08** complete, conclude, organize **09** arbitrate, go-between, land agent, middleman, negotiate **10** negotiator **11** arbitrageur, stockbroker, stockjobber **12** intermediary

bromide
06 cliché, downer, opiate, truism **07** anodyne **08** banality, narcotic, sedative **09** calmative, platitude **10** stereotype **11** barbiturate, commonplace **12** sleeping pill **13** tranquillizer

bromine
02 Br

bronze
02 br **03** tan **04** rust **05** brass **06** auburn, copper, Titian **07** aeneous, vermeil **08** chestnut **09** impudence **10** horseflesh **12** reddish-brown **14** copper-coloured

bronzed
05 brown **06** bronze, tanned **07** browned **08** hardened, sunburnt **09** sunburned, suntanned

brooch
03 pin **04** clip, ouch, prop **05** badge, broch, clasp **06** fibula, tiepin **08** lapel pin **09** breastpin

brood
03 eye, nid, nye, sit **04** aery, clan, eyry, fret, kind, mope, muse, nest, nide, race, sulk, team **05** aerie, ayrie, breed, cleck, clock, cover, covey, eyrie, hatch, issue, spawn, sperm, tribe, young **06** chicks, clutch, family, go over, kindle, litter, ponder **07** agonize, dwell on, eelfare, progeny **08** children, clecking, incubate, meditate, mull over, rehearse, ruminate **09** bairn-team, bairn-time, fret about, household, offspring, parentage **10** extraction, worry about

brook
04 bear, beck, burn, gill, kill, purl, rill **05** allow, creek, fleet, ghyll, inlet, stand **06** accept, branch, endure, permit, runnel, stream **07** abrooke, channel, rivulet, stomach, support **08** tolerate **09** put up with, withstand **11** countenance, watercourse

broom
04 wisp **05** besom, scrub, spart **06** retama **07** cytisus, hag-weed **09** knee-holly, Turk's head **10** Jew's-myrtle **15** shepherd's myrtle

broth
◇ *anagram indicator*
04 kail, kale, soup **05** ramen **06** brewis, cullis **08** bouillon, hotchpot **09** pot liquor **10** beef-brewis, hodgepodge, hotchpotch, muslin-kale

brothel
03 kip **04** crib, stew **05** stews **06** bagnio, bordel **07** Corinth **08** bordello, cathouse, hothouse, red light **10** bawdy-house, flash-house, whorehouse **12** knocking-shop, leaping-house **13** sporting house, vaulting-house **14** house of ill fame, massage parlour **15** disorderly house

brother
02 br **03** bro, fra, pal, sib **04** bhai, brer, chum, mate, monk, sibb **05** billy, buddy, frère, friar **06** billie, fellow, friend, german **07** comrade, partner, sibling **08** relation, relative **09** associate, colleague, companion **11** full brother, half-brother, twin-brother **12** blood-brother **13** brother-german

• big brother
05 prior **08** dictator

brotherhood
03 PRB **05** guild, union **06** clique, league **07** society **08** alliance, confrère **09** community, confrérie, Félibrige **10** fellowship, fraternity, friendship **11** association, cameraderie, comradeship, confederacy **12** fraternalism, friendliness **13** confederation, confraternity

brotherly
04 kind **05** loyal **06** caring, loving **08** amicable, friendly **09** fraternal **10** benevolent **11** sympathetic **12** affectionate **13** philanthropic

brow
03 tip, top **04** peak **05** brink, cliff, ridge, verge **06** summit **07** pit-head, temples **08** forehead

browbeat
05 bully, force, hound **06** coerce, hector **07** dragoon, oppress **08** bulldoze, domineer, overbear, threaten **09** tyrannize **10** intimidate

brown
02 br **03** fry **04** cook, fusc, seal **05** grill, singe, toast **06** tanned **07** bronzed, browned, embrown, fuscous **08** sunburnt **09** infuscate

Browns include:

03 bay, dun, tan
04 buff, drab, ecru, fawn, pine, rust, sand, teak
05 beige, camel, cocoa, dusky, hazel, honey, khaki, mocha, ochre, rusty, sepia, taupe, tawny, tenné, umber
06 auburn, bister, bistre, bronze, burnet, coffee, copper, ginger, russet, sorrel, walnut
07 biscuit, caramel, chamois, filemot, oatmeal, oxblood
08 brunette, chestnut, cinnamon, mahogany, mushroom, nut-brown, philamot, raw umber
09 chocolate, earth-tone
10 burnt umber, café au lait, terracotta
11 burnt sienna, orange-tawny
12 vandyke brown

browned off
05 bored, fed up, weary **07** annoyed **09** hacked off, irritated, pissed off **10** bored stiff, brassed off, cheesed off, dispirited **11** discouraged, disgruntled, downhearted, exasperated **12** discontented, disheartened

brownie
03 hob, nis **05** nisse

browse
03 eat **04** feed, look, scan, skim, surf **05** graze **06** nibble, peruse, survey **07** dip into, pasture **09** quick read **11** leaf through **12** flick through, flick-through

bruise
◇ *anagram indicator*
04 beat, hurt, mark, stun **05** break, clour, crush, frush, pound, spoil, upset, wound **06** damage, grieve, injure, injury, insult, intuse, lesion, offend, shiner **07** blacken, blemish, contuse, rainbow, surbate **08** black eye, to-bruise **09** contusion, discolour **10** ecchymosis **13** discoloration

bruiser
04 thug **05** bully, rough, tough **07** hoodlum, ruffian **08** bully boy **09** bovver boy, roughneck **12** prize-fighter

Brunei
03 BRN, BRU

brunt
05 force, shock **06** burden, impact, strain, thrust, weight **07** impetus **08** pressure **09** main force **10** full weight

brush
03 hog, rub **04** bush, dust, kiss, swab, wipe **05** besom, broom, clash, clean, clear, fight, fitch, flick, frith, graze, scrap, scrub, scuff, set-to, shine, sweep, touch, whisk **06** badger, bushes, caress, duster, dust-up, fracas, pallet, polish, putois, scrape, shrubs, stroke, tussle **07** burnish, contact, fox-tail, stipple, sweeper, thicket, tickler **08** argument, conflict, skirmish **09** brushwood, currycomb, encounter, pope's head, underwood **10** hair-pencil **11** ground cover, overgrainer, undergrowth **12** disagreement **13** confrontation

• brush aside
05 flout **06** ignore **07** dismiss **08** belittle, override, pooh-pooh **09** disregard

• brush off
04 snub **05** spurn **06** disown, ignore, rebuff, reject, slight **07** dismiss, repulse **09** disregard, repudiate **12** cold-shoulder

• brush up
04 cram, swot, tidy **05** clean, study **06** go over, read up, revise, tidy up **07** improve, refresh, relearn **08** bone up on, polish up **09** freshen up **15** clean yourself up, refresh yourself

brush-off
04 snub **06** rebuff, slight **07** kiss-off, refusal, repulse **09** dismissal, rejection **11** repudiation **12** cold shoulder **14** discouragement

brushwood
03 hag **04** hagg, reis, rice **05** bavin, firth, frith, scrub **06** jungle **07** fascine **08** mattress, ovenwood **09** chaparral **10** underscrub

brusque
04 curt **05** blunt, brief, gruff, sharp, short, surly, terse **06** abrupt **07** uncivil **08** impolite, tactless **09** downright **12** discourteous, undiplomatic

brutal
05 cruel, frank, harsh, plain, tough **06** animal, coarse, savage, severe **07** beastly, bestial, boarish, brutish, callous, doggish, inhuman, ruffian, vicious, violent **08** inhumane, pitiless, ruthless **09** barbarous, ferocious, heartless, merciless, unfeeling, unsparing **10** Rottweiler **11** insensitive, iron-hearted, remorseless **12** bloodthirsty, down-and-dirty **15** straightforward

brutality
07 cruelty **08** atrocity, ferocity, savagery, violence **09** barbarism, barbarity, callosity, roughness **10** coarseness, inhumanity **11** brutishness, callousness, viciousness **12** ruthlessness

brutalize
03 hit **04** beat, flog **05** inure, pound **06** attack, batter, deaden, harden, thrash **07** assault, degrade **09** animalize **10** dehumanize **11** desensitize

brutally
07 cruelly, frankly, harshly **08** savagely, severely **09** brutishly, callously, viciously **10** inhumanely, pitilessly, ruthlessly **11** barbarously, ferociously, heartlessly, mercilessly, unfeelingly **13** insensitively

brute
04 bête, lout, ogre **05** beast, bully, crude, devil, fiend, gross, swine, yahoo **06** animal, bodily, carnal, coarse, sadist, savage, stupid **07** Caliban, fleshly, monster, ruffian, sensual **08** creature, depraved, mindless, physical **09** senseless **10** irrational, Rottweiler, unthinking **11** instinctive

brutish
05 crass, crude, cruel, feral, gross **06** animal, brutal, coarse, ferine, savage, stupid, vulgar **07** bestial, loutish, uncouth **08** barbaric **09** barbarian, barbarous **11** uncivilized

bubble
04 ball, bead, bell, bleb, boil, drop, fizz, foam, head, lock, seed, suds **05** fraud, froth, gloop, spume **06** bounce, burble, dimple, gurgle, lather, mantle, seethe, trifle, vanity, wallop **07** air-bell, air-lock, blister, blubber, droplet, fantasy, globule, sparkle, vesicle **08** be elated, be filled, blowhole, delusion, fleeting, illusion, rowndell **09** ball of air, be excited, deceptive, transient **10** depression, effervesce **13** effervescence, insubstantial

bubbly
◇ *anagram indicator*
04 fizz **05** fizzy, happy, merry, sudsy **06** bouncy, elated, frothy, lively **07** excited, foaming **08** animated, champers **09** champagne, ebullient, exuberant, sparkling, vivacious **10** carbonated **12** effervescent

buccaneer
06 pirate **07** corsair, sea wolf **08** sea rover **09** privateer, sea robber **10** filibuster, freebooter

buck
◇ *anagram indicator*
03 bok **04** soar, sore **05** cheer, dandy, soare, sorel **06** buoy up, dollar, ignore, marker, oppose, resist, sorell, sorrel **07** counter, hearten, pricket **08** reassure **09** encourage **10** contradict **13** break the rules

• **buck up**
05 cheer, gee up, hurry, rally **06** hasten, perk up **07** cheer up, enliven, hearten, hurry up, improve **08** inspirit, step on it **09** encourage, stimulate, take heart **10** get a move on **14** rattle your dags **15** get your skates on

bucket
03 can, dip, tub **04** bail, bale, pail **05** ladle, stoop, stope, stoup **06** dipper, kibble, situla, stoope, vessel **07** pitcher, scuttle **09** clamshell

• **bucket down**
04 pour **08** pelt down, pour down **11** rain heavily **15** rain cats and dogs

• **bucket chain**
05 noria **12** Jacob's ladder

buckle
◇ *anagram indicator*
04 bend, clip, fold, hasp, hook, kink, warp **05** bulge, catch, clasp, close, hitch, twist **06** cave in, fasten, secure **07** connect, crumple, distort, wrinkle **08** collapse, fastener **10** contortion, distortion

• **buckle down**
08 go all out **11** get down to it, knuckle down **15** start to work hard

buckler
05 pelta **06** target **08** rondache **09** protector **10** protection

bucolic
05 rural **06** rustic **07** country **08** agrarian, pastoral **11** countrified **12** agricultural

bud
03 eye, gem **04** bulb, germ, grow, knop, knot **05** caper, clove, gemma, knosp, shoot, sprig **06** bulbel, bulbil, button, embryo, friend, sprout, turion **07** brother, burgeon, cabbage, develop, plumule **09** débutante, pullulate **11** heart of palm, palm-cabbage **12** hibernaculum

Buddhist
03 Zen **04** lama **05** bonze **08** talapoin **09** Dalai Lama

• **Buddhist dome**
04 tope **05** stupa **06** dagaba, dagoba

budding
07 growing, nascent **09** embryonic, fledgling, flowering, gemmation, germinant, incipient, potential, promising **10** burgeoning, developing **11** up-and-coming

buddy
03 pal **04** chum, mate **05** crony **06** cobber, friend **07** brother, comrade **09** companion **10** buddy-buddy, good friend

budge
03 jee **04** bend, give, move, push, roll, stir, sway **05** bodge, bouge, shift, slide, stiff, yield **06** change, give in, remove **07** give way, pompous **08** convince, dislodge, persuade **09** influence **13** not compromise **14** change your mind

budget
04 plan **05** allot, allow, funds, means, quota **06** afford, bouget, bowget, ration **08** allocate, estimate, finances, schedule, set aside **09** allotment, allowance, apportion, economics, resources **10** allocation **13** financial plan

buff
03 fan, rub, tan **04** blow, fawn **05** beige, brush, fiend, freak, khaki, maven, rub up, sandy, shine, straw **06** addict, expert, nankin, polish, smooth, stroke **07** admirer, burnish, devotee, fanatic, nankeen, natural **09** yellowish **10** aficionado, enthusiast **11** connoisseur **14** yellowish-brown

• **in the buff**
04 bare, nude **05** naked **08** in the raw, starkers, stripped **09** unclothed, uncovered, undressed **10** stark-naked **12** not a stitch on **13** with nothing on **15** in the altogether

buffalo
04 anoa, arna **05** bison, bugle **07** Bubalus, carabao, overawe, tamarao, tamarau, timarau, zamouse **08** bewilder, water cow

buffer
03 pad **06** absorb, bumper, deaden, fender, lessen, pillow, reduce, screen, shield, soften **07** bulwark, cushion, protect **08** diminish, mitigate, polisher, suppress **12** intermediary **13** shock absorber

buffet
03 box, hit, jar, tax **04** bang, beat, blow, buff, bump, café, cuff, harm, jolt, push, slap **05** clout, knock, pound, shove, smack, thump, weigh **06** batter, battle, blight, burden, pummel, strike **07** afflict, counter, disturb, oppress, trouble **08** cold meal, distress, snackbar **09** cafeteria, cold table, weigh down **11** self-service, smorgasbord **12** help yourself

buffeted
◇ *anagram indicator*

buffoon
03 wag **04** fool, mime, mome, Vice, zany **05** antic, clown, comic, droll, joker **06** antick, jester, Scogan

07 anticke, antique, farceur, Scoggin, tomfool 08 comedian, farceuse, Iniquity 09 harlequin 10 mountebank, Scaramouch 11 Jack-pudding, merry-andrew, Punchinello, Scaramouche

buffoonery
05 farce 07 jesting, zanyism
08 clowning, drollery, nonsense
09 pantomime, silliness 10 tomfoolery
11 waggishness 12 harlequinade, pantaloonery 13 Pantagruelism

bug
03 fad, irk, tap, vex, wog 04 flaw, flea, germ, mite, snag 05 annoy, craze, error, fault, mania, thing, virus
06 bother, cootie, defect, harass, insect, needle, pester, wind up
07 blemish, disease, disturb, failing, gremlin, illness, microbe, monitor, wiretap 08 irritate, listen in, phone-tap
09 aggravate, bacterium, eavesdrop, infection, obsession 10 listen in on, listen in to 11 eavesdrop on 12 creepy-crawly, imperfection 13 micro-organism 15 listening device

bugbear
03 bug 04 bane, bogy 05 bogey, bogle, dread, fiend, poker 06 horror 07 pet hate, rawhead 08 anathema 09 bête noire, nightmare 10 Mumbo-jumbo

bugle
10 flügelhorn 11 hunting-horn

bugle-call
04 post, taps 07 hallali, retreat 08 last post, reveille 09 first post, lights out
15 boots and saddles

build
03 big, set 04 body, form, make, rear, size 05 begin, edify, erect, frame, mason, put up, raise, shape, start
06 extend, figure, timber 07 augment, develop, enlarge, fashion, upbuild
08 assemble, escalate, increase, initiate, physique, throw out
09 construct, fabricate, institute, intensify, overbuild, structure, substruct
10 constitute, inaugurate 11 put together 13 knock together

• **build up**
03 add 04 grow, hype, plug, rear
05 amass, boost, mount, set up
06 expand, extend, gather
07 aggrade, amplify, augment, collect, develop, enhance, enlarge, fortify, improve, mount up, promote
08 assemble, escalate, heighten, increase, snowball 09 advertise, construct, elaborate, establish, intensify, publicize, reinforce, structure
10 accumulate, strengthen 11 put together 13 piece together

builder
05 jerry, mason 06 waller 08 labourer
09 craftsman 11 craftswoman
12 craftsperson, manual worker
13 skilled worker

building
◇ *anagram indicator*
04 pile 07 edifice 08 dwelling, erection 09 structure 11 development, fabrication 12 architecture, construction

See also **architecture**

Building types include:

03 inn, pub
04 barn, café, fort, mews, mill, pier, shed, shop, silo
05 abbey, arena, cabin, hotel, house, store, villa
06 castle, chapel, church, cinema, garage, gazebo, mandir, mosque, museum, pagoda, palace, prison, school, stable, temple
07 chateau, college, cottage, factory, library, low-rise, mansion, theatre
08 barracks, beach hut, bungalow, dovecote, fortress, gurdwara, high-rise, hospital, monument, outhouse, pavilion, showroom, skilling, skillion, windmill
09 apartment, boathouse, cathedral, farmhouse, gymnasium, mausoleum, monastery, multiplex, synagogue, warehouse
10 lighthouse, maisonette, restaurant, skyscraper, sports hall, tower block, university
11 condominium, observatory, office block, public house, summerhouse
12 block of flats, power station
14 apartment house, sliver building

See also **accommodation**; **house**; **tent**

Buildings include:

05 Duomo
07 BT Tower, CN Tower, Kremlin, La Scala, St Paul's, UN Plaza
08 Casa Milà, Cenotaph, Chrysler, Flatiron, Pantheon, St Peter's, Taj Mahal
09 Acropolis, Coit Tower, Colosseum, Notre Dame, Old Bailey, Parthenon, Reichstag, St Pancras, Taipei 101, The Louvre, US Capitol
10 Guggenheim, Sears Tower, Tate Modern, The Gherkin, Trump Tower, Versailles, White House
11 Canary Wharf, Eden Project, Eiffel Tower, Empire State, Musée d'Orsay, Space Needle, The Alhambra, The Panthéon, The Pentagon, Tower Bridge, Tower of Pisa
12 Globe Theatre, Great Pyramid, Mont St Michel, Telecom Tower, The Parthenon, Winter Palace
13 Crystal Palace, Dome of the Rock, Musée du Louvre, Royal Crescent, Somerset House, Tower of London
14 Balmoral Castle, Barbican Centre, Blenheim Palace, Centre Pompidou, Hoover Building, Millennium Dome, Petronas Towers, Pompidou Centre, Sagrada Familia, UN Headquarters, Wells Cathedral
15 Ashmolean Museum, Banqueting House, Brandenburg Gate, Capitol Building, Edinburgh Castle, Lincoln Memorial, Post Office Tower, Royal Opera House, Statue of Liberty, Westminster Hall

See also **religious**; **tower**

Building materials include:

03 MDF
04 clay, sand, tile, wood
05 brick, glass, grout, slate, steel, stone
06 ashlar, cement, girder, gravel, gypsum, lintel, lumber, marble, mastic, mortar, pavior, siding, tarmac, thatch, timber
07 asphalt, bitumen, decking, drywall, fixings, granite, lagging, plaster, plastic, plywood, sarking, shingle
08 asbestos, cast iron, cladding, concrete, hard core, roof tile, wall tile
09 aggregate, aluminium, chipboard, clapboard, flagstone, floor tile, hardboard, sandstone, steel beam
10 glass fibre, insulation, matchboard
11 breeze block, paving stone, roofing felt
12 plasterboard
13 building block, wattle and daub
14 foam insulation, stainless steel

• **building area**
04 site

build-up
04 gain, heap, hype, load, mass, plug, puff 05 drift, stack, store 06 growth
08 increase 09 accretion, expansion, marketing, promotion, publicity, stockpile 10 escalation 11 advertising, development, enlargement
12 accumulation

built
◇ *anagram indicator*

built-in
05 fixed 06 fitted 07 in-built
08 implicit, included, inherent, integral
09 essential, intrinsic, necessary
11 fundamental, inseparable
12 incorporated

bulb
03 set 05 globe 11 Rupert's drop

Plants grown from bulbs and corms include:

04 cive, eddo, iris, ixia, lily, taro
05 camas, chive, onion, tulip
06 allium, camash, camass, chives, crinum, crocus, garlic, nerine, scilla, squill
07 anenome, jonquil, muscari, peacock, quamash
08 amarylis, bluebell, camassia, curtonis, cyclamen, daffodil, endymion, galtonia, gladioli, harebell, hyacinth, scallion, snowdrop, sparaxis
09 amaryllis, colchicum, crocosmia, galanthus, gladiolus, narcissus, snowflake, tiger lily
10 agapanthus, chionodoxa, fritillary, giant rouge, montbretia, ranunculus, snake's head, solfaterre, wand flower

11 acidanthera, African lily, erythronium, fritillaria, hippeastrum, lapeirousia, naked ladies, spring onion, sternbergia, tiger flower
12 autumn crocus, ornithogalum, Solomon's seal, wild hyacinth
13 crown imperial, grape hyacinth, lily-of-the-Nile, striped squill, winter aconite
14 belladonna lily, chincherinchee, glory of the snow, Ithuriel's spear
15 dog's tooth violet, lily-of-the-valley

bulbous
06 convex, puffed **07** bloated, bulging, rounded, swollen
08 swelling, tuberous **09** distended, puffed out, pulvinate **10** pulvinated

Bulgaria
02 BG **03** BGR **04** Bulg

bulge
03 bag, bug, sag **04** bias, bulb, bump, hump, lump, rise **05** belly, pouch, strut, surge, swell **06** billow, dilate, expand, strout **07** blister, distend, enlarge, project, puff out, upsurge **08** increase, protrude, shoulder, swelling
10 distension, projection
12 protuberance **15** intensification

bulk
04 body, bouk, feck, hold, hull, mass, most, size **05** cargo, great, gross
06 extent, volume, weight **07** bigness
08 majority, quantity, roughage
09 amplitude, immensity, largeness, magnitude, nearly all, substance
10 dimensions, lion's share
13 preponderance
• bulk out, bulk up
04 fill **06** expand, extend, fill up, pad out **07** fill out **08** increase **10** make bigger

bulky
03 big **04** huge **05** ample, gross, heavy, hefty, large, lofty, lusty
07 awkward, hulking, immense, lumping, mammoth, massive, volumed, weighty **08** colossal, enormous, unwieldy **10** cumbersome, voluminous **11** substantial
12 unmanageable

bull
02 ox **03** rot **04** brag, male, mick, neat
05 micky **06** mickey, strong, Taurus
07 massive **08** nonsense
09 policeman **10** Unigenitus
11 Hibernicism **12** Hibernianism

bulldoze
04 push, raze **05** bully, clear, force, level **06** coerce **07** flatten
08 browbeat, demolish **09** knock down **10** intimidate **11** push through, steamroller

bullet
04 ball, shot, slug **06** dumdum, pellet
07 missile **08** Biscayan **09** cartouche, cartridge, lead towel, Minié ball
10 projectile, propellant

bulletin
06 report, update **07** leaflet, message, release **08** dispatch **09** newsflash, newspaper, news sheet, statement
10 communiqué, newsletter
12 announcement, notification
13 communication

bullfight
07 corrida **10** tauromachy **14** corrida de toros

bullfighter
07 matador, picador **08** matadore, toreador **10** rejoneador
12 banderillero

bullish
06 upbeat **07** buoyant, hopeful
08 cheerful, positive, sanguine
09 confident, obstinate **10** aggressive, optimistic

bully
◇ *anagram indicator*
03 cow **04** good, haze, huff, prey, thug
05 brave, bucko, great, heavy, tough, tyran **06** coerce, cuttle, hector, pick on, tyrant **07** bluster, bouncer, hoodlum, killcow, oppress, ruffian, torment **08** browbeat, bulldoze, bully-boy, bullyrag, domineer, overbear
09 excellent, persecute, souteneur, terrorize, tormentor, tyrannize, victimize **10** blustering, browbeater, Drawcansir, intimidate, persecutor, push around **11** intimidator
12 swashbuckler

bulrush
04 tule **08** cat's-tail

bulwark
04 wall **05** guard **06** buffer
07 bastion, defence, outwork, rampart, redoubt, sea-wall, support
08 buttress, mainstay, security
09 partition, safeguard **10** breakwater, embankment, protection
13 fortification

bum
◇ *anagram indicator*
03 ass, bad, beg, dud, low **04** butt, coit, duff, hobo, hurl, loaf, naff, poor, rear, rump, seat, tail, toss **05** awful, booty, cadge, false, quoit, spree, tramp, wrong **06** behind, borrow, bottom, crummy, dosser, sponge **07** adverse, gangrel, rubbish, sponger, useless, vagrant **08** backside, beach boy, buttocks, scrounge, terrible, vagabond
09 imperfect, worthless
10 despicable, inadequate, unpleasant
12 disagreeable, unacceptable
14 unsatisfactory

bumble
◇ *anagram indicator*
05 drone, idler, lurch **06** beadle, bungle, falter, teeter, totter **07** blunder, bungler, stagger, stumble

bumbling
◇ *anagram indicator*
05 inept **06** clumsy **07** awkward, muddled **08** botching, bungling
09 lumbering, maladroit, stumbling
10 blundering **11** incompetent, inefficient

bump
03 hit, jar **04** bang, blow, hump, jerk, jole, joll, jolt, jowl, knur, lump, slam, thud, whap, whop **05** barge, bulge, crash, dunch, dunsh, joule, knock, prang, shake, shock, shove, smash, thump **06** bounce, impact, injury, jostle, jounce, nodule, rattle, strike
07 collide, papilla **08** dislodge, swelling **09** collision, speed bump
10 protrusion, tumescence **11** collide with **12** irregularity, protuberance
• bump into
04 meet **07** run into **09** encounter, light upon **10** chance upon, come across, happen upon **12** meet by chance
• bump off
03 top **04** do in, kill **06** murder, remove, rub out **08** blow away
09 eliminate, liquidate **11** assassinate

bumper
03 big **04** rich **05** great, jumbo, kelty, large, rouse **06** keltie **07** bouncer, massive **08** abundant, enormous, whopping **09** excellent, ginormous, plentiful **11** exceptional
12 supernaculum

bumpkin
03 oaf, put, yap **04** boor, hick, lout, lowt, putt, rube **05** clown, yokel
06 rustic **07** hawbuck, hayseed, peasant **08** clodpate, clodpole, clodpoll **09** hillbilly **10** clodhopper, provincial **11** bushwhacker **12** country yokel **14** country bumpkin

bumptious
04 coxy **05** brash, cocky, pushy
06 cocksy, uppish **07** forward, pompous **08** arrogant, boastful, impudent **09** assertive, conceited, egotistic, officious **10** swaggering
11 overbearing **12** presumptuous
13 over-confident, self-important
14 full of yourself

bumpy
05 jerky, lumpy, rough **06** bouncy, choppy, knobby, uneven **07** jolting, knobbly **08** pot-holed **09** irregular

bun
03 wad **04** chou **05** brick **06** cookie
07 Bath bun, huffkin, teacake **08** black bun, cream bun, crescent, cross bun, rock cake **09** burger bun **10** Chelsea bun, currant bun, Eccles cake **11** hot cross bun **12** mosbolletjie

bunch
03 bob, lot, mob, wad **04** band, club, crew, gang, heap, herd, hump, lump, mass, pack, pile, posy, team, tuft, wisp
05 batch, clump, crowd, flock, group, party, sheaf, spray, stack, swarm, troop
06 bundle, gather, huddle, number, string **07** bouquet, cluster, collect, corsage, nosegay **08** assemble, boughpot, fascicle, quantity, swelling

09 fascicule, gathering, multitude **10** assortment, châtelaine, collection, congregate, fasciculus, racemation **11** concentrate **12** tussie mussie **13** agglomeration

bundle
◇ *anagram indicator*
03 bag, box, jag, kit, set, tie, wad, wap **04** bale, bind, drum, heap, mass, pack, pile, roll, rush, swag, wisp, wrap, yelm **05** batch, bavin, bluey, brawl, bunch, group, hurry, sheaf, shook, shove, skein, stack, truss, whisk **06** bottle, carton, faggot, fasces, fasten, gather, huddle, hustle, knitch, packet, parcel, tumble **07** cluster, dorlach, fascine, package **08** fascicle, quantity, shiralee, woolpack **09** fascicule, shirralee, trousseau **10** assortment, collection, fasciculus **11** consignment, push roughly **12** accumulation

bung
03 pay, tip **04** cork, dead, dook, plug, seal **05** bribe, purse, shive **06** spigot **07** stopper, useless **08** bankrupt, cutpurse **10** pickpocket

bungle
◇ *anagram indicator*
03 mar **04** boob, duff, flub, goof, mash, mess, muff, mull, ruin **05** blunk, bodge, botch, fluff, fudge, spoil **06** bobble, boggle, bumble, bummle, cock up, foozle, foul up, goof up, mangle, mess up, muck up, muddle **07** bauchle, blunder, louse up, screw up **09** misguggle, mishandle, mismanage **10** mishguggle **11** make a mess of

bungler
04 muff **05** blunk **06** bumble, bummle, duffer, tinker **07** blunker, botcher, bumbler **08** shlemiel **09** blunderer, schlemiel, schlemihl **11** incompetent **13** butterfingers

bungling
05 inept, messy **06** clumsy **07** awkward **08** botching **09** ham-fisted, ham-handed, maladroit, unskilful **10** amateurish, blundering, cack-handed **11** incompetent

bunk
04 flee **05** berth, sleep **06** humbug **08** claptrap

bunker
03 bin **04** fuel, trap **06** hazard **07** shelter **08** sand trap

bunkum
02 BS **03** rot **04** blah, bosh, bull, bunk **05** balls, bilge, hooey, trash, tripe **06** humbug, piffle **07** baloney, garbage, hogwash, rubbish, twaddle **08** blah-blah, bulldust, claptrap, cobblers, malarkey, nonsense, tommyrot **09** poppycock **10** balderdash, codswallop **12** blah-blah-blah **13** horsefeathers

bunting
04 cirl **05** flags, junco **07** ortolan **08** longspur **09** snowflake, snowfleck, snowflick **10** dickcissel **11** decorations, reed-sparrow, yellow-ammer **12** yellowhammer **13** writing-master

buoy
03 dan **04** rise **05** float **06** beacon, marker, signal **07** dolphin, mooring
• **buoy up**
04 lift **05** boost, cheer, raise **06** bear up **07** cheer up, hearten, support, sustain **09** encourage

buoyancy
03 joy, pep **06** bounce, growth, vigour **07** flotage **08** floatage, gladness, optimism, strength **09** geniality, happiness, jolliness, lightness, toughness **10** brightness, confidence, enthusiasm, resilience **11** development, good spirits **12** cheerfulness, floatability

buoyant
05 happy, hardy, light, peppy, tough **06** afloat, blithe, bouncy, bright, joyful, lively, strong **07** bullish, growing **08** animated, carefree, cheerful, debonair, floating, thriving, youthful **09** adaptable, floatable, resilient, vivacious **10** developing, optimistic, weightless **12** light-hearted

burble
03 lap **04** purl **06** babble, gurgle, murmur, tangle **07** confuse

burden
03 bob, tax **04** bear, care, cark, duty, lade, load, onus, task, tote, yoke **05** beare, cargo, cross, crush, drone, trial, worry **06** bother, charge, fading, impose, lumber, monkey, saddle, sorrow, strain, stress, weight **07** anxiety, burthen, holding, oppress, present, refrain, trouble **08** carriage, encumber, handicap, incumber, land with, overbulk, overload, pressure **09** agistment, cumbrance, grievance, lie hard on, millstone, overpress, overwhelm, undersong, weigh down **10** affliction, dead-weight, imposition, lie heavy on, obligation, overburden, overextend, overstress **11** encumbrance **14** responsibility

burdensome
05 heavy **06** taxing, trying **07** irksome, onerous, weighty **08** crushing, exacting, grievous **09** chargeful, difficult, importune, wearisome **10** chargeable, oppressive **11** importunate, troublesome

burdock
04 gobo **05** clote **07** clotbur, hardoke **08** clotebur **09** cocklebur

bureau
04 desk **06** agency, branch, office **07** counter, service **08** division **10** department **11** writing-desk

bureaucracy
07 red tape **08** city hall, ministry **09** beadledom, paperwork, the system **10** government **11** officialdom **12** civil service **13** officiousness **14** administration, the authorities

bureaucrat
04 suit **07** officer **08** Eurocrat, mandarin, minister, official **09** chinovnik **11** apparatchik, functionary **12** civil servant, office-holder **13** administrator **15** committee member

bureaucratic
05 rigid **08** official **10** inflexible, procedural **11** complicated, ministerial **12** governmental **14** administrative

burgeon
04 grow **05** swell **06** expand, extend **07** develop, enlarge **08** escalate, increase, snowball **11** proliferate

burglar
04 yegg **05** thief **06** robber **07** yeggman **08** pilferer **09** cracksman **10** cat-burglar, trespasser **12** housebreaker

burglary
05 heist, theft **07** break-in, larceny, robbery **08** stealing, trespass **09** pilferage **13** housebreaking

burgle
03 rob **05** screw **09** break into, burst into, steal from **10** burglarize

burial
07 burying, funeral **08** exequies **09** committal, interment, obsequies, sepulchre **10** entombment, inhumation

burial place
05 crypt, grave, vault **06** kurgan **07** charnel, tumulus **08** catacomb, cemetery, God's acre, Golgotha, Pantheon **09** graveyard, mausoleum, sepulcher, sepulchre **10** churchyard, necropolis **12** potter's field
See also **cemetery**

Burkina Faso
02 BF **03** BFA

burlesque
04 mock **05** comic, spoof **06** parody, satire, send-up **07** mockery, mocking, take-off **08** derisive, farcical, ridicule, travesty **09** parodying, satirical **10** caricature, heroi-comic **11** caricatural, hudibrastic **12** heroi-comical, mickey-taking **13** Pantagruelism

burly
03 big **05** beefy, heavy, hefty **06** brawny, knotty, stocky, strong, sturdy **07** buirdly, hulking **08** athletic, muscular, powerful, thickset **09** strapping, well-built

burn
03 fry, gut **04** bite, bren, char, fume, glow, hurt, itch, long, plot, sear, sere **05** blaze, brand, brook, cense, chark, flame, flare, flash, grill, inure, light, parch, ploat, scald, singe, smart, smoke, sting, swale, swayl, sweal, sweel, toast, yearn **06** brenne, desire,

emboil, ignite, kindle, scorch, seethe, simmer, stream, tingle **07** be eager, combust, consume, corrode, cremate, destroy, flare up, flicker, glimmer, inflame, scowder, shrivel **08** be ablaze, be on fire, burn down, scouther, scowther, smoulder **09** catch fire, cauterize, incremate, set alight, set fire to **10** be in flames, deflagrate, incinerate **11** catch ablaze, conflagrate, go up in smoke, put a match to **12** be consumed by, go up in flames **13** put to the torch **15** burst into flames

burning
02 in **03** hot, lit **04** live, sear **05** acrid, acute, afire, eager, fiery, quick, seare, urent, vital **06** ablaze, aflame, alight, ardent, biting, cauter, fervid, urgent, ustion **07** blazing, caustic, cautery, crucial, earnest, fervent, flaming, frantic, glowing, intense, pungent, searing **08** flagrant, flashing, frenzied, gleaming, piercing, pressing, scalding, smarting, stinging, swealing, tingling, vehement **09** consuming, essential, important, inburning, prickling, scorching **10** passionate
11 conflagrant, illuminated, impassioned, significant, smouldering
12 incendiarism **13** conflagration

burnish
04 buff **05** glaze, shine **06** lustre, polish **08** brighten, polish up

burp
04 wind **05** belch **08** eructate
10 eructation **11** bring up wind

burrow
03 den, dig, set **04** bury, hole, howk, lair, mine, root, sett **05** delve, earth, wroot **06** gopher, nuzzle, search, tunnel, warren **07** retreat, rummage, shelter **08** excavate, fox-earth
09 undermine **10** rabbit hole

bursar
06 purser **07** cashier **09** treasurer

bursary
05 award, grant **09** endowment
10 exhibition, fellowship **11** scholarship

burst
◇ *anagram indicator*
03 fit, fly, pop, run **04** bang, blow, clap, dart, gush, gust, loup, part, race, rush, tear **05** barge, blaze, blitz, brash, break, crack, erupt, flash, go off, go pop, hurry, plump, salvo, spate, split, spout, spurt, start, surge **06** blow up, bounce, go bang, shiver, spring, volley
07 blow-out, dehisce, disrupt, explode, rupture, shatter, torrent
08 distrain, fragment, outbreak, outburst, puncture **09** break in on, break open, discharge, fusillade, pull apart, split open **10** outpouring
11 push your way **12** disintegrate
• **burst out**
03 cry **04** buff **05** begin, flash, start, utter **06** cry out, irrupt **07** call out, exclaim, explode **08** blurt out, commence **10** break forth

Burundi
02 RU **03** BDI

bury
◇ *containment indicator*
04 eard, hide, sink, tomb, yerd, yird
05 cover, earth, embed, grave, inter, plant, yeard **06** absorb, burrow, engage, engulf, entomb, inhume, occupy, shroud **07** conceal, enclose, engross, immerse, implant, inearth, inherce **08** enshroud, inhearse, submerge **09** lay to rest, sepulchre
15 put six feet under

bus
03 ISA, PCI, USB **05** coach, trunk
06 jitney, pirate **09** two-decker, vaporetto **10** mammy-wagon, service car **11** park-and-ride **12** double-decker, single-decker

bush
03 tod **05** brush, crude, hedge, plant, scrog, scrub, shrub, todde, wilds
06 busket, tavern **07** bramble, outback, thicket **09** backwoods, makeshift, primitive, scrubland
11 uncivilized **13** rough and ready
• **not beat about the bush**
11 speak openly **12** speak plainly
14 come to the point, commit yourself

bushbaby
06 galago **07** nagapie **08** night-ape

bushel
02 bu **03** fou

bushranger
06 outlaw **07** brigand **10** highwayman
12 backwoodsman

Bushrangers include:

04 **Cash** (Martin), **Hall** (Ben), **Howe** (Michael)
05 **Brady** (Matthew), **Kelly** (Ned)
06 **Caesar** (John 'Black Caesar'), **Morgan** (Dan 'Mad Dog'), **Palmer** (George)
07 **Donohoe** (Jack), **Gilbert** (Johnny)
08 **Flash Dan** (Daniel Charters), **Gardiner** (Frank), **Governor** (Jimmy), **Governor** (Joe), **Melville** (Frank McCallum, 'Captain'), **Moonlite** (Andrew Scott, 'Captain')
09 **Armstrong** (George), **Starlight** (Frank Pearson, 'Captain')
11 **Thunderbolt** (Frederick Ward, 'Captain')
12 **Jackey Jackey** (William Westwood)

bushy
04 wiry **05** bosky, fuzzy, rough, stiff, thick, woody **06** dumose, dumous, fluffy, shaggy, unruly **07** bristly
09 bristling, luxuriant, spreading
12 dasyphyllous

busily
04 hard **07** briskly **08** actively, speedily **09** earnestly **10** diligently
11 assiduously, strenuously
12 purposefully **13** energetically, industriously

business
02 co **03** biz, bus, job **04** baby, deal, duty, firm, gear, line, task, work
05 issue, point, topic, trade **06** affair, buying, career, matter, métier, outfit, pigeon **07** calling, company, concern, problem, selling, subject, trading, venture **08** commerce, dealings, flagship, industry, question, vocation
09 franchise, operation, syndicate
10 bargaining, consortium, employment, enterprise, occupation, profession **11** corporation, partnership
12 conglomerate, organization, transactions **13** establishment, manufacturing, merchandizing, multinational, parent company
14 holding company, responsibility

Businesses include:

02 BA, BP
03 BAA, BAE, BAT, BHS, BMW, BSB, EMI, HMV, IBM, ICI, MFI, NCP, NEC, RAC, RBS
04 Asda, BASF, Esso, Fiat, HBOS, HSBC, Rank, Sony
05 Abbey, Alcan, Bayer, Boots, Canon, Corus, Enron, Exxon, Heinz, Honda, Intel, Mazda, Nokia, Ricoh, Sharp, Shell, Tesco, Volvo
06 Adecco, Arriva, Boeing, Diageo, Dixons, Du Pont, Hanson, L'Oreal, Nestlé, Nissan, Pfizer, Suzuki, Texaco, Toyota, Virgin, Wimpey
07 Alcatel, Arcadia, Aventis, Chevron, EasyJet, Fujitsu, Harrods, Hitachi, Hyundai, Lafarge, Marconi, Matalan, Minerva, Pearson, Pepsico, Peugeot, Renault, Reuters, Samsung, Siemens, Toshiba, Wal-Mart, W H Smith
08 AXA Group, Barclays, Burberry, Centrica, Chrysler, Coca-Cola, Goodyear, JP Morgan, Michelin, Olivetti, Rentokil, Rio Tinto, Unilever, Vodafone, Waitrose
09 Akzo Nobel, John Laing, Ladbrokes, Lloyds TSB, McDonald's, Microsoft, Morrisons, Schroders, Whitbread
10 Exxon Mobil, Greene King, J Sainsbury, Kingfisher, Mitsubishi, Nationwide, Pilkington, Prudential, Rolls-Royce, Sainsbury's, Somerfield, Stagecoach, Telefonica, Volkswagen, Walt Disney, Woolworths
11 AstraZeneca, Caterpillar, Isuzu Motors, Nippon Steel, Standard Oil, William Hill
12 Allied Domecq, Eastman Kodak, Hilton Hotels, Merrill Lynch, Northern Rock, Philip Morris, Philips Group, Reed Elsevier, Sears Roebuck, Total Fina Elf, Union Carbide, Union Pacific, Western Union
13 Abbey National, Anglo American, Balfour Beatty, General Motors, Harvey Nichols, Lever Brothers, Sanyo Electric, Taylor Woodrow, Travis Perkins
14 Alfred McAlpine, British Airways, Credit Agricole, Hewlett-Packard, Virgin Atlantic

15 American Express, DaimlerChrysler, Deutsche Telekom, Electrolux Group, General Electric, GlaxoSmithKline, Legal and General, Marks and Spencer, National Express, News Corporation

• **business centre**
04 city
• **do business**
04 deal, sell
• **go out of business**
04 fold

businesslike
05 slick **06** formal **07** correct, orderly, precise **08** thorough **09** efficient, organized, practical, pragmatic
10 impersonal, methodical, systematic
11 painstaking, well-ordered
12 matter-of-fact, professional

businessman, businesswoman
06 trader, tycoon, wallah **07** Babbitt, magnate **08** city gent, employer, merchant **09** boxwallah, executive, financier **10** capitalist **12** entrepreneur, manufacturer **13** industrialist

Businesspeople include:

04 **Benz** (Karl Friedrich), **Bond** (Alan), **Boot** (Sir Jesse), **Cook** (Thomas), **Ford** (Henry), **Jobs** (Steven), **Mond** (Ludwig), **Shah** (Eddy), **Tate** (Sir Henry), **Wang** (An)
05 **Arden** (Elizabeth), **Astor** (John, Lord), **Bosch** (Carl), **Fayed** (Mohamed al-), **Forte** (Charles, Lord), **Gates** (Bill), **Getty** (Jean Paul), **Grade** (Michael), **Heinz** (Henry John), **Honda** (Soichiro), **Krupp** (Friedrich), **Laker** (Sir Freddie), **Leahy** (Sir Terry), **Lyons** (Sir Joseph), **Marks** (Simon, Lord), **Nobel** (Alfred), **Rolls** (Charles), **Royce** (Sir Henry), **Sugar** (Sir Alan), **Trump** (Donald), **Zeiss** (Carl)
06 **Ansett** (Sir Reg), **Boeing** (William Edward), **Browne** (John, Lord), **Butlin** (Billy), **Conran** (Sir Terence), **Cunard** (Sir Samuel), **Dunlop** (John Boyd), **du Pont** (Pierre Samuel), **Fugger** (Johannes), **Gamble** (Josias), **Hammer** (Armand), **Hilton** (Conrad Nicholson), **Hoover** (William Henry), **Hughes** (Howard), **Mellon** (Andrew William), **Morgan** (J Pierpont), **Packer** (Kerry), **Turner** (Ted)
07 **Agnelli** (Giovanni), **Barclay** (Robert), **Branson** (Sir Richard), **Bugatti** (Ettore), **Cadbury** (George), **Cadbury** (John), **Citroën** (André Gustave), **Iacocca** (Lee), **Kennedy** (Joseph P), **Maxwell** (Robert), **Murdoch** (Rupert), **Onassis** (Aristotle), **Roddick** (Anita), **Sotheby** (John), **Tiffany** (Charles Lewis)
08 **Birdseye** (Clarence), **Carnegie** (Andrew), **Christie** (James), **Gillette** (King Camp), **Guinness** (Sir Benjamin Lee), **Michelin** (André), **Nuffield** (William Richard Morris, Viscount), **Olivetti** (Adriano), **Pulitzer** (Joseph), **Rathenau** (Walther), **Rowntree** (Joseph), **Sinclair** (Sir Clive)
09 **Arkwright** (Sir Richard), **Carothers** (Wallace), **Firestone** (Harvey Samuel), **Sainsbury** (Alan John, Lord), **Selfridge** (Harry Gordon), **Woolworth** (Frank Winfield)
10 **Berlusconi** (Silvio), **Guggenheim** (Meyer), **Leverhulme** (William Hesketh Lever, Viscount), **Pilkington** (Sir Alastair), **Rothschild** (Meyer Amschel), **Vanderbilt** (Cornelius)
11 **Beaverbrook** (Max, Lord), **Harvey-Jones** (Sir John), **Rockefeller** (John D)

busker
14 street-musician

bust
◇ *anagram indicator*
04 duff, head, herm, phut, raid, term
05 boobs, bosom, break, chest, crack, herma, kaput, punch, smash, spree, torso, wonky **06** arrest, breast, broken, damage, demote, faulty, ruined, statue
07 breasts, destroy, shatter
08 terminus **09** defective, penniless, sculpture **10** on the blink, on the fritz, out of order **11** out of action
• **go bust**
04 fail, flop, fold **05** crash **06** go bung
07 founder **08** collapse **09** close down **11** go to the wall **14** become bankrupt **15** become insolvent

bustle
◇ *anagram indicator*
03 ado **04** belt, buzz, dash, fuss, rush, stir, tear, to-do, trot, whew **05** haste, hurry **06** bestir, bumble, bummle, flurry, hasten, pother, ruffle, rustle, scurry, tumult **07** fluster, scamper, the rush **08** activity, rush hour, scramble, to and fro, tournure **09** agitation, commotion, stirabout **10** excitement, hurly-burly **11** hurry-scurry, hurry-skurry **12** rush to and fro **13** dress-improver **15** a hive of activity, hustle and bustle

bustling
◇ *anagram indicator*
04 busy, full **05** astir **06** active, hectic, lively **07** abustle, buzzing, crowded, humming, rushing, teeming
08 eventful, restless, stirring, swarming, thronged **09** energetic, on the trot

busy
◇ *anagram indicator*
04 at it, full **05** manic **06** absorb, active, bustle, eident, embusy, employ, engage, hectic, lively, occupy, red-hot, throng, tied up, tiring **07** concern, crowded, engaged, engross, frantic, go about, immerse, involve, on the go, teeming, vibrant, working **08** bustling, diligent, employed, eventful, hard at it, interest, involved, meddling, occupied, on the job, restless, sedulous, swarming, tireless **09** assiduous, detective, energetic, engrossed, on the trot, stirabout, strenuous **10** busy as a bee **11** industrious, snowed under, unavailable **12** having a lot on, in conference **13** under pressure **14** fully stretched, having a lot to do, in the thick of it
• **be busy**
03 hum

busybody
03 pry **05** snoop **06** gossip
07 meddler, snooper **08** intruder, quidnunc **09** pragmatic **10** interferer
11 Nosey Parker **12** eavesdropper, troublemaker **13** mischief-maker, scandalmonger **14** pantopragmatic

but
03 bar, nay, sed **04** just, only, save
06 anyway, at most, even so, except, merely, purely, simply **07** barring, besides, however **08** omitting
09 apart from, aside from, excepting, excluding, objection, other than **10** all the same, for all that, leaving out, no more than **11** just the same, nonetheless **12** nevertheless
15 notwithstanding
• **all but**
04 near **06** almost

butch
04 male **05** macho, tough **06** virile
07 manlike, mannish **09** masculine

butcher
◇ *anagram indicator*
04 kill, slay **05** botch, spoil **06** killer, slayer **07** destroy, flesher **08** massacre, murderer, mutilate **09** destroyer, liquidate, slaughter **10** meat trader
11 assassinate, exterminate, meat counter, slaughterer, supermarket
12 mass murderer, meat retailer

butchery
06 murder **07** carnage, killing
08 abattoir, butcher's, massacre, shambles **09** bloodshed, meat trade, slaughter **10** mass murder **11** meat-selling **12** blood-letting **13** meat retailing **14** slaughterhouse **15** mass destruction

butler
03 RAB **08** khansama **09** khansamah, sommelier **12** bread-chipper

butt
03 box, bum, but, end, hit, jab, keg, nip, nut, ram, tip, tun **04** base, bump, bunt, cask, dout, dupe, foot, haft, horn, mark, pipe, poke, prod, push, stub
05 dunch, dunsh, knock, punch, roach, shaft, shove, snipe, stock, stump
06 barrel, bottom, buffet, bumper, dog-end, fag end, firkin, handle, object, stooge, target, thrust, tierce, victim **07** butt end, remnant, rundlet, subject, tail end **08** buttocks, hogshead **09** posterior, scapegoat
10 table-sport **12** jesting-stock
13 laughing-stock

• butt in
05 cut in **06** horn in, meddle **07** break in, intrude **09** interfere, interject, interpose, interrupt **12** put your oar in **15** stick your nose in

butter
03 ghi, ram **04** drop, ghee, goat **06** beurre **08** flattery

• butter producer
04 mowa, shea **05** mahua, mahwa, mowra

• butter up
04 coax **06** cajole, kowtow, praise **07** blarney, flatter, wheedle **08** kowtow to, pander to, soft-soap, suck up to **14** be obsequious to

buttercup
06 gilcup **07** giltcup, kingcup **08** crowfoot **10** goldilocks, ranunculus

butterfingers
04 muff

butterfly
05 light **07** flighty **10** dilettante
See also **animal**; **insect**; **moth**

Butterflies include:

03 map
04 blue, wall
05 argus, comma, elfin, heath, satyr, white
06 apollo, copper, hermit, morpho, pierid, psyche
07 admiral, cabbage, monarch, Papilio, peacock, ringlet, satyrid, skipper, thistle, Ulysses, vanessa
08 birdwing, cardinal, grayling, hesperid, milk-weed
09 brimstone, cleopatra, Hesperian, holly-blue, nymphalid, orange-tip, wall brown, wood white
10 brown argus, common blue, fritillary, gatekeeper, hairstreak, red admiral
11 large copper, meadow-brown, painted lady, Scotch argus, swallowtail
12 cabbage-white, dingy skipper, Essex skipper, marbled-white, white admiral
13 chalkhill blue, clouded yellow, mourning cloak, purple emperor, tortoiseshell
15 black hairstreak, brown hairstreak, green hairstreak, grizzled skipper, heath fritillary, Lulworth skipper, marsh fritillary, mountain ringlet

buttocks
03 ass, bum, can, fud **04** buns, butt, coit, doup, duff, prat, rear, rump, seat, tail, tush **05** booty, fanny, nates, pratt, quoit, tushy **06** behind, bottom, breech, cheeks, heinie, tushie **07** crouper, croupon, gluteus, hurdies, keister, sit-upon **08** backside, derrière, haunches **09** fundament, hinder-end, posterior **10** hinderlans, hinderlins **11** hinderlands, hinderlings **12** hindquarters
See also **bottom**

button
04 disc, frog, knob, link, stud **05** catch, clasp, lever **06** barrel, olivet, switch, toggle **08** bell push, fastener **09** fastening

buttonhole
03 nab **04** grab **05** catch **06** accost, collar, corner, detain, waylay **09** importune, take aside **11** boutonnière

buttress
04 pier, prop, stay **05** brace, shore, strut **06** back up, hold up, prop up **07** shore up, support, sustain, tambour **08** abutment, mainstay, underpin **09** bolster up, reinforce, stanchion **10** strengthen **11** counterfort **13** reinforcement

buxom
05 ample, busty, jolly, plump, sonsy **06** bosomy, chesty, comely, lively, sonsie, zaftig **07** bucksom, elastic **08** yielding **09** Junoesque, pneumatic **10** Rubenesque, voluptuous **11** full-figured, well-endowed, well-rounded, well-stacked **12** full-breasted **13** large-breasted

buy
03 fix, get, job **04** chop, coff, deal, take **05** bribe, hedge, scalp, trade **06** buy off, market, nobble, obtain, pay for, pick up, redeem, snap up, suborn **07** acquire, bargain, emption, engross, overbuy, procure, shop for **08** invest in, panic-buy, purchase, underbuy **09** speculate, stock up on, subsidize **10** go shopping, shop around **11** acquisition, merchandize, splash out on **13** do the shopping

buyer
06 broker, client, dealer, emptor, patron, vendee **07** shopper **08** consumer, customer **09** purchaser

buzz
03 fad, hum **04** call, high, kick, purr, race, ring, zing **05** craze, drone, kicks, pulse, throb, throw, whirr **06** bustle, gossip, latest, murmur, rumour, thrill **07** buzzing, hearsay, resound, scandal **08** resonate, susurrus, tinnitus **09** bombilate, bombinate, phone call, susurrate **10** enthusiasm, excitement **11** bombilation, bombination, reverberate, stimulation, susurration **15** word on the street

buzzard
04 pern **05** buteo **07** bee-kite, puttock **08** zopilote **09** gallinazo

buzzer
03 bee **08** telltale **09** whisperer

by
◇ *juxtaposition indicator*
01 X **02** at, in, of, on **03** gin, per, via **04** away, near, over, past, with **05** along, aside, close, forby, handy, times, using **06** at hand, before, beside, beyond, next to **07** close by, close to, through **09** alongside, by means of **11** according to, no later than **12** in relation to **15** under the aegis of

bygone
04 lost, past **05** olden **06** former **07** ancient, antique, one-time **08** departed, forepast, previous **09** erstwhile, forgotten **10** antiquated, dinosauric

bypass
04 CABG, omit **05** avoid, dodge, evade, shunt, skirt **06** detour, ignore **07** neglect **08** ring road, sidestep, slip road **09** diversion, sidetrack **10** circumvent **12** steer clear of **13** find a way round

by-product
06 result **07** fallout, spin-off **10** derivative, entailment, side effect **11** after-effect, concomitant, consequence **12** repercussion **13** epiphenomenon, knock-on effect

bystander
07 watcher, witness **08** looker-on, observer, onlooker, passer-by, talesman **09** spectator **10** eyewitness, rubberneck

byword
03 saw **05** adage, ideal, maxim, model, motto **06** ayword, dictum, saying, slogan **07** epitome, example, nayword, paragon, precept, proverb **08** aphorism, exemplar, overcome, standard **09** catchword, watchword **10** apophthegm, embodiment **14** perfect example

Byzantine
◇ *anagram indicator*
06 knotty **07** complex **08** tortuous **09** intricate **11** complicated **12** labyrinthine

C

c
03 cee, san, see **07** Charlie

cab
04 taxi **05** cabin, noddy **06** drosky, fiacre, hansom **07** droshky, growler, minicab, taxicab, vettura **08** quarters **10** two-wheeler **11** compartment, four-wheeler **15** hackney carriage

cabal
03 set **04** plot **05** junta, junto, party **06** clique, league **07** coterie, faction **08** conclave, intrigue, plotters **09** camarilla, coalition

cabaret
04 acts, club, show **05** turns **06** comedy **07** dancing, singing, variety **09** night club **10** restaurant **11** performance **13** entertainment

cabbage
04 chou, cole, gobi, kail, kale, wort **05** savoy, steal **06** greens **07** bok choy, castock, custock, pak choi, purloin **08** colewort, drumhead, kohlrabi **09** banknotes **10** choucroute, greenstuff, paper money, sauerkraut **11** cauliflower, sea colewort **13** Chinese leaves **14** Brussels sprout

cabbage-head
04 loaf

cabin
03 hut **04** room, shed **05** berth, bothy, coach, cuddy, lodge, shack **06** cabana, chalet, refuge, saloon, shanty **07** cottage, gondola, shelter **08** log-house, quarters **09** signal box, stateroom **10** roundhouse **11** compartment

cabinet
04 case **05** bahut, chest, filer, store **06** closet, locker, senate, shrine **07** almirah, console, dresser **08** cupboard, vargueño **09** executive, ministers **10** chiffonier, encoignure, government, leadership, secretaire **11** chiffonnier **12** Privy Council **14** administration, official family

cable
03 fax, guy **04** co-ax, cord, flex, lead, line, rope, stay, wire **05** chain, e-mail, radio **06** feeder, halser, hawser **07** coaxial **08** telegram, transmit **09** facsimile, send a wire, telegraph **11** Telemessage® **13** send a telegram **15** send by telegraph

cache
04 fund, hide **05** hoard, stash, stock, store **06** garner, supply **07** reserve **09** stockpile **10** collection, repository, storehouse **12** accumulation **13** treasure-store **14** hidden treasure

cachet
06 esteem, favour, status **08** approval, eminence, prestige **10** estimation, reputation, street cred **11** distinction

cack-handed
05 gawky, inept **06** clumsy **07** awkward **08** bungling **09** all thumbs, ham-fisted, unskilful **10** blundering, left-handed, ungraceful **11** heavy-handed **13** unco-ordinated

cackle
04 crow **05** clack **06** gabble, gaggle, giggle, keckle, titter **07** chortle, chuckle, snigger **09** loud laugh **11** laugh loudly **15** unpleasant laugh

cacophonous
04 loud **05** harsh **07** grating, jarring, raucous **08** strident **09** dissonant **10** discordant **11** horrisonant **12** inharmonious

cacophony
03 din **06** racket **07** discord, jarring **09** charivari, harshness, stridency **10** disharmony, dissonance **11** raucousness **12** caterwauling

cactus

Cacti include:

04 crab, toad, tuna
05 dildo, nopal
06 barrel, cereus, cholla, Easter, mescal, old man, orchid, peanut, peyote
07 jointed, old lady, opuntia, rainbow, saguaro
08 dumpling, gold lace, hedgehog, rat's tail, snowball, starfish, Turk's cap
09 bunny ears, Christmas, goat's horn, gold charm, Indian fig, mistletoe, sea-urchin
10 cotton-pole, sand dollar, silver ball, strawberry, zygocactus
11 grizzly bear, mammillaria, prickly pear, scarlet ball, silver torch
12 golden barrel
13 Bristol beauty, schlumbergera
14 drunkard's dream
15 queen of the night, snowball cushion

cad
03 oik, rat **04** heel **05** devil, knave, rogue, swine **06** rascal, rotter, wretch **07** bleeder, bounder, scumbag, stinker, villain **08** blighter, deceiver **09** miscreant, reprobate, scoundrel **10** blackguard

cadaver
04 body **05** stiff **06** corpse **07** carcase, remains **08** dead body

cadaverous
03 wan **04** pale, thin **05** ashen, gaunt **07** ghostly, haggard **08** skeletal **09** death-like, emaciated **10** corpse-like

caddy
05 chest

cadence
04 beat, fall, lilt, rate **05** close, metre, pulse, swing, tempo, throb, trope **06** accent, euouae, evovae, rhythm, stress **07** falling, measure, pattern, sinking **09** half-close **10** inflection, intonation, modulation

cadge
03 beg, bot, bum **05** mooch, mouch, ponce **06** sponge **08** scrounge

cadmium
02 Cd

cadre
03 set **04** band, crew, gang, team **05** corps, squad **10** small group

caesium
02 Cs

café
04 caff **06** bistro, buffet, pull-in **07** noshery, tea room, tea shop, wine bar **08** snackbar **09** brasserie, cafeteria, coffee bar, cybercafé, estaminet, truck stop **10** coffee shop, restaurant **11** greasy spoon

cafeteria
04 café, caff **06** buffet **07** canteen **10** restaurant **15** self-service café

cage
03 mew, pen **04** coop, corf, dray, drey **05** cavie, grate, hutch, pound **06** aviary, corral, keavie, lock-up **07** tumbler **09** enclosure

caged
05 mewed **06** shut up **07** encaged **08** confined, cooped up, fenced in, locked up **09** impounded **10** imprisoned, restrained **12** incarcerated

cagey
04 wary, wily **05** chary **06** shrewd **07** careful, guarded **08** cautious, discreet **09** secretive **11** circumspect **12** non-committal

cahoots

• in cahoots

08 in league **09** colluding
10 conspiring, in alliance **11** hand in glove, in collusion **13** collaborating

cairn

03 man **04** barp **05** raise

cajole

04 coax, dupe, lure, wile, work
05 moody, tempt **06** beflum, chat up, diddle, entice, humbug, seduce, soothe, whilly **07** beguile, blarney, cuittle, flatter, mislead, wheedle
08 blandish, butter up, get round, inveigle, persuade, soft-soap
09 sweet-talk, whillywha
10 whillywhaw **12** work yourself

cajolery

05 wiles **06** duping **07** blarney, coaxing **08** flattery, soft soap **09** sweet talk, wheedling, whillywha
10 cajolement, enticement, inducement, inveigling, misleading, persuasion, whillywhaw
11 beguilement, inducements
12 blandishment, inveiglement
13 blandishments

cake

03 bar, dry, pan **04** coat, cube, farl, loaf, lump, mass, pone, slab **05** block, chunk, cover, fancy, farle **06** harden, pastry, tablet **07** congeal, encrust, plaster, thicken **08** solidify
09 coagulate **11** consolidate

Cakes, pastries and puddings include:

03 bun, pie
04 baba, flan, fool, puri, roti, tart
05 bombe, crêpe, jelly, poori, scone, sweet, torte
06 éclair, gateau, junket, mousse, muffin, parkin, sponge, trifle, waffle, yum-yum
07 baklava, Banbury, bannock, Bath bun, brioche, brownie, crumble, crumpet, cupcake, fig roll, fritter, iced bun, jam roll, jam tart, oatcake, pancake, Pavlova, plum pie, ratafia, rum baba, saffron, savarin, soufflé, stollen, strudel, tartlet, teacake, wedding, Yule log
08 apple pie, black bun, doughnut, flummery, macaroon, malt loaf, meringue, mince pie, pecan pie, plum-cake, rock cake, sandwich, seedcake, syllabub, tiramisu, turnover, whim-wham
09 angel cake, cherry-pie, clafoutis, cranachan, cream cake, cream horn, cream puff, drop scone, fairy cake, fruitcake, fruit tart, fudge cake, Genoa cake, lamington, lardy cake, lemon tart, madeleine, panettone, pound cake, queen cake, Sally Lunn, shortcake, Swiss roll
10 banana cake, Battenburg, carrot cake, cheesecake, Chelsea bun, coffee cake, Dundee cake, Eccles cake, ginger cake, girdle cake, key lime pie, marble cake, panna cotta, pumpkin pie, simnel cake, sponge cake, tarte tatin
11 baked Alaska, banana bread, banoffee pie, crème brulée, currant cake, custard tart, gingerbread, hot cross bun, jam roly-poly, lady's finger, Linzertorte, Madeira cake, plum pudding, profiterole, rice pudding, Sachertorte, sago pudding, spotted dick, treacle tart, wedding cake
12 apfel strudel, Bakewell tart, birthday cake, chocolate log, custard slice, Danish pastry, figgy pudding, hasty pudding, pease pudding, sandwich cake
13 apple dumpling, apple turnover, chocolate cake, Christmas cake, Scotch pancake, sponge pudding, summer pudding
14 apple charlotte, charlotte russe, Pontefract cake, steamed pudding, toasted teacake, upside-down cake, Victoria sponge
15 chocolate éclair, queen of puddings

See also **bun**

calamitous

◇ *anagram indicator*
04 dire **05** fatal **06** deadly, tragic, woeful **07** ghastly, ruinous
08 dreadful, grievous, wretched
10 disastrous **11** cataclysmic, devastating **12** catastrophic

calamity

02 wo **03** wae, woe **04** blow, Jane, ruin, ruth, woes **05** trial **06** mishap
07 reverse, scourge, tragedy, trouble
08 disaster, distress, downfall
09 adversity, mischance **10** affliction, misfortune **11** catastrophe, tribulation
12 misadventure **15** sword of Damocles

calcium

02 Ca

calculate

03 aim **04** cast, make, plan, rate, work
05 add up, count, gauge, judge, tally, think, value, weigh **06** assess, cipher, cypher, derive, design, figure, intend, reckon **07** compute, measure, purpose, suppose, work out
08 consider, estimate, reckon up
09 determine, enumerate

calculated

06 wilful **07** planned **08** computed, intended, measured, purposed, reckoned, tactical **10** considered, deliberate, purposeful, well-judged
11 intentional **12** premeditated

calculating

03 sly **04** wily **05** sharp **06** crafty, shrewd **07** cunning, devious
08 scheming **09** designing
10 contriving **11** circumspect
12 manipulative **13** Machiavellian

• calculating aid

03 log **04** abac **06** abacus **07** soroban
08 computer, isopleth, nomogram
09 nomograph, slide rule **10** calculator
12 arithmometer **14** alignment chart
15 digital computer

calculation

03 sum **06** answer, result **08** estimate, figuring, forecast, logistic, planning
09 evolution, judgement, reckoning
10 alligation, arithmetic, assessment, estimation, figurework, working-out
11 computation, mensuration
12 deliberation

calculus

04 lith- **06** tartar **07** urolith
08 fluxions **09** sialolith
11 quaternions

calendar

Calendars include:

05 Bahà'í, Hindu, lunar, Roman, solar
06 Coptic, Hebrew, Jewish, Julian
07 Chinese, Islamic, Persian
09 arbitrary, Gregorian, lunisolar
10 republican
13 revolutionary

See also **animal**; **month**

calf

04 boss, dogy, veal **05** bossy, dogie, poddy, slink **06** vealer **08** maverick

calibre

03 cal **04** bore, gage, size **05** gauge, gifts, merit, worth **06** league, talent
07 ability, faculty, measure, quality, stature **08** capacity, diameter, strength
09 character **10** competence, endowments, excellence
11 distinction

California

02 CA **05** Calif

californium

02 Cf

call

02 ca', go **03** bid, caa', cap, cry, dub, mot, run **04** bawl, bell, buzz, caul, cite, hail, name, need, nemn, pink, plea, ring, roar, term, toll, yell **05** brand, cause, claim, cleep, clepe, cooee, cooey, hight, label, order, phone, pop in, right, shout, style, title, visit
06 appeal, ask for, bellow, call in, come by, cry out, demand, drop in, excuse, invite, market, reason, reckon, rename, ring up, scream, shriek, signal, stop by, summon, tinkle **07** baptize, command, contact, convene, enstyle, entitle, exclaim, grounds, hallali, phone up, request, send for, summons, warning
08 assemble, christen, occasion
09 call round, designate, pay a visit, telephone **10** denominate, describe as, invitation **11** ask to come in, exclamation **12** announcement
13 justification **14** ask to come round

• call for

04 levy, need, take **05** claim, fetch, go for **06** demand, entail, pick up
07 collect, involve, justify, push for, require, solicit, suggest, warrant
08 occasion, press for **11** necessitate
13 make necessary

• call off
04 drop **05** scrub **06** cancel, revoke, shelve **07** abandon, rescind **08** break off, withdraw **11** discontinue

• call on
03 ask, bid, gam, put, see **04** urge **05** plead, visit **06** appeal, demand, invoke, summon, wait on **07** entreat, request **08** appeal to, go and see, look in on, press for, wait upon **10** supplicate

• call up
04 buzz, pick, ring **05** phone, raise **06** choose, enlist, invite, ring up, select, sign up, summon, take on **07** contact, display, phone up, recruit **08** settle on **09** conscript, telephone

• on call
05 ready **06** on duty **09** on standby **10** standing by

called
03 hot **04** hote **05** nempt

call girl
04 tart **05** whore **06** harlot, hooker **07** hustler **10** loose woman, prostitute **12** street-walker **14** lady of the night

calling
03 job **04** line, work **05** field, trade **06** career, métier **07** mission, pursuit **08** business, province, vocation **10** employment, line of work, occupation, profession **14** line of business

callous
04 cold **05** cruel, harsh, horny, stony, tough **06** seared **08** hardened, indurate, obdurate, uncaring **09** heartless, insensate, unfeeling **10** hard-bitten, hard-boiled, insensible, iron-headed **11** cold-blooded, cold-hearted, hard as nails, hard-hearted, indifferent, insensitive **12** case-hardened, stony-hearted, thick-skinned **13** unsympathetic

callously
06 coldly **07** harshly **11** heartlessly, unfeelingly **13** cold-bloodedly, hard-heartedly, insensitively

callow
03 raw **05** green, naive **06** jejune, rookie **07** puerile, untried **08** immature, innocent, juvenile **09** fledgling, guileless, unbearded, unfledged **11** uninitiated **13** inexperienced **15** unsophisticated

calm
03 cam **04** alay, came, caum, cool, ease, even, hush, loun, lown, lull, mild **05** aleye, allay, lound, lownd, peace, quiet, relax, sleek, still **06** becalm, pacify, placid, poised, repose, sedate, serene, settle, smooth, soothe, steady, stilly **07** appease, assuage, compose, halcyon, mollify, placate, quieten, relaxed, reposed, restful, unmoved **08** ataraxia, calmness, composed, cool down, dead-wind, laid-back, peaceful, pipeclay, quietude, serenity, tranquil, waveless, windless **09** collected, composure, impassive, lighten up, limestone, nerveless, placidity, sangfroid, stillness, supercool, unclouded, unexcited, unruffled **10** cool-headed, equanimity, phlegmatic, settle down, simmer down, untroubled **11** contentment, impassivity, restfulness, undisturbed, unemotional, unexcitable, unflappable, unflustered, unpassioned, unperturbed **12** even-tempered, keep your head, on an even keel, peacefulness, tranquillity, tranquillize, unpassionate **13** dispassionate, impassiveness, imperturbable, self-possessed, unimpassioned **14** presence of mind, self-controlled, unapprehensive, unflappability **15** cool as a cucumber

calmly
08 steadily **11** impassively **12** on an even keel **13** unemotionally **14** phlegmatically **15** dispassionately

calorie
03 cal

calumny
05 abuse, libel, lying, smear **06** attack, insult, mud pie **07** obloquy, slander **09** aspersion **10** backbiting, defamation, derogation, detraction, revilement **11** denigration, slagging-off **12** vilification, vituperation **13** disparagement

camaraderie
08 affinity, intimacy **09** closeness **10** fellowship, friendship **11** brotherhood, comradeship, sociability **12** togetherness **13** brotherliness, companionship, esprit de corps **14** fraternization, good fellowship

Cambodia
01 K **03** KHM

Cambridge University *see* **college**

camel
04 oont **08** Bactrian **09** dromedare, dromedary **15** ship of the desert

camera

Cameras include:

02 TV
03 APS, SLR, TLR
04 CCTV, cine, disc, film, Fuji®, view
05 Canon®, Kodak®, Leica®, Nikon®, plate, press, sound, still, video
06 Konica®, Pentax®, reflex, Rollei®, stereo, Super 8®, Webcam
07 bellows, compact, digital, Minolta®, obscura, Olympus®, pinhole, Yashica®
08 dry-plate, Polaroid®, Praktica®, security, wet-plate
09 automatic, binocular, camcorder, half-plate, miniature, panoramic, Rolliflex®, single use, Steadicam®
10 box Brownie®, disposable, Instamatic®, sliding box
11 large-format
12 quarter-plate, subminiature, surveillance
13 daguerreotype, folding reflex, point-and-press
14 twin-lens reflex
15 cinematographic

• move camera
03 pan **05** track

Cameroon
03 CAM, CMR

camouflage
◇ *anagram indicator*
04 hide, mask, veil **05** blind, cloak, cover, front, guise **06** façade, screen **07** conceal, cover up, cover-up, deceive, obscure **08** disguise **09** deception **10** maskirovka, masquerade **11** concealment, counterfeit

camp
03 set **04** duar, laer, side, tent **05** campy, crowd, douar, dowar, group, gypsy, party, tents **06** caucus, clique, encamp, laager, outlie **07** bivouac, faction, leaguer, rough it, section **08** affected, campsite, mannered **09** pitch camp, posturing, set up camp **10** artificial, effeminate, encampment, over the top, pitch tents, theatrical **11** camping-site, exaggerated **12** ostentatious **13** camping-ground, sleep outdoors

• confined to camp
02 CC

campaign
03 war **04** push, work **05** blitz, drive, fight, jehad, jihad, lobby **06** attack, battle, strive **07** canvass, crusade, journey, promote **08** advocate, movement, strategy, struggle **09** offensive, operation, promotion **10** expedition **14** course of action

campaigner
06 zealot **07** fighter **08** activist, advocate, champion, crusader, promoter, reformer **10** enthusiast

camp-follower
03 boy **05** toady **06** bummer, lackey, lascar **08** hanger-on, henchman **11** leaguer-lady, leaguer-lass

can
03 dow, jar, jug, lav, loo, mug, tin **04** dows, jail, pail, stir **06** prison, toilet **08** canister, jerrycan, lavatory, preserve **09** container **10** chimney pot, receptacle **11** depth charge
See also **prison**; **toilet**

• can it *see* **quiet**; **shut up** *under* **shut**

Canada
03 CAN, CDN
See also **Prime Minister**; **province**

Canadian cities and notable towns include:

06 Ottawa, Quebec, Regina
07 Calgary, Halifax, Toronto
08 Edmonton, Montreal, Victoria, Winnipeg
09 Saskatoon, Vancouver

Canadian landmarks include:

06 Mt Thor
07 CN Tower, Mt Logan, Niagara, Rockies, Sky Dome
08 Lake Erie
09 Hudson Bay, Lake Huron, Mt Seymour
10 Great Lakes, St Lawrence
11 Lake Ontario
12 Lake Superior, Niagara Falls
13 Algonquin Park, Parc Olympique
14 Horseshoe Falls, Rocky Mountains

Canadian
03 Can, Cdn **06** Canuck

canal
03 Can, gut **04** duct, foss, moat, tube **05** ditch, fosse, zanja **06** groove, trench **07** channel, enteron, passage, shipway **08** waterway **10** navigation **11** watercourse **14** digestive tract

Canals include:

04 Erie, Kiel, Suez
05 Grand
06 Panama, Rideau
07 Corinth, Midland, Welland
10 Caledonian, Mittelland
11 Welland Ship
14 Manchester Ship

cancel
03 axe, nix **04** drop, kill, stop, undo, wipe **05** abort, adeem, annul, erase, quash, scrap, scrub **06** delete, offset, repeal, revoke, shelve, strike **07** abandon, abolish, call off, nullify, red-line, rescind, retract, vitiate, wash out **08** abrogate, break off, cross out, dissolve, override, postpone, suppress, withdraw, write off **09** eliminate, strike out **10** declare off, invalidate, obliterate, scrub round **11** countermand, discontinue **14** counterbalance

• cancel out
06 offset, redeem **07** balance, nullify **09** make up for **10** compensate, counteract, neutralize **14** counterbalance

cancellation
06 repeal **08** deletion, dropping, quashing, shelving, stopping **09** abolition, annulment, scrubbing **10** abandoning, calling-off, nullifying, revocation **11** abandonment, elimination **12** invalidation **14** neutralization

cancer
03 rot **04** Big C, Crab, evil **06** blight, canker, growth, plague, tumour **07** disease, scourge, the Big C, the Crab **08** cancroid, sickness **09** carcinoma **10** corruption, malignancy, pestilence **15** malignant growth

candelabrum
07 menorah **09** lampadary **11** candlestick

candid
04 fair, open **05** blunt, clear, frank, plain, round, white **06** honest, simple **07** liberal, shining, sincere, unposed **08** informal, truthful, unbiased **09** guileless, impartial, ingenuous, outspoken **10** forthright **11** plain-spoken, unequivocal, unrehearsed **12** heart-to-heart **15** straightforward

candidate
03 PPC **06** runner, seeker **07** entrant, nominee **08** aspirant, examinee **09** applicant, contender, postulant, pretender **10** competitor, contestant **11** possibility

• candidate list
04 leet **06** ticket

candidly
06 openly, simply **07** bluntly, clearly, frankly, plainly, roundly, up-front **08** honestly **09** liberally, sincerely **10** truthfully **11** guilelessly, ingenuously, outspokenly **12** forthrightly **13** unequivocally

candle
03 dip **04** slut **05** cerge, sperm, taper, torch **06** bougie, ulicon, ulikon **07** oolakan, oulakan, shammes, ulichon **08** amandine, eulachan, eulachon, luminary, oulachon, shammash, wax light **09** tallow dip **10** night-light **12** tallow candle

candour
06 purity **07** honesty, naivety **08** kindness, openness **09** bluntness, franchise, frankness, plainness, sincerity, whiteness **10** directness, liberality, simplicity **11** artlessness, brusqueness **12** impartiality, plain-dealing, truthfulness **13** guilelessness, ingenuousness, outspokenness **14** forthrightness **15** unequivocalness

candy
05 glacé, kandy **06** candie, sweets **07** cocaine, encrust, toffees **10** chocolates **11** crystallize **13** confectionery

cane
03 rod **05** crook, ratan, staff, stick, swish, swits **06** ferule, jambee, rattan, switch **07** tickler, whangee **09** riding rod **10** alpenstock, supplejack **12** swagger-stick, walking-stick

canine
01 c **04** tush **06** cuspid **08** dogtooth, eye tooth
See also **dog**

canker
03 rot **04** bane, boil, evil, sore **05** decay, ulcer **06** blight, cancer, infect, lesion, plague **07** corrupt, destroy, disease, pollute, scourge **08** sickness **09** corrosion, infection **10** cankerworm, corruption, pestilence, ulceration

cannabis
03 kef, kif, pot, tea **04** benj, blow, dope, gage, hash, hemp, kaif, leaf, puff, punk, toke, weed **05** bhang, blunt, ganja, gauge, grass, joint, roach, skunk, splay **06** bomber, greens, reefer, spliff **07** hashish **08** locoweed, Mary Jane **09** marihuana, marijuana, substance **10** sinsemilla, wacky baccy **12** electric puha

cannibal
08 man-eater **09** Thyestean, Thyestian **11** people-eater **15** anthropophagite

cannibalism
08 exophagy **09** endophagy, man-eating **12** people-eating **13** anthropophagy

cannibalistic
09 man-eating, Thyestean **10** exophagous **11** endophagous **12** people-eating **15** anthropophagous

cannily
06 subtly **07** acutely, sharply **08** astutely, cleverly, shrewdly **09** knowingly, skilfully

cannon
03 gun **05** carom, saker **06** barker, big gun, curtal, falcon, monkey, mortar, Quaker **07** battery, bombard, chamber, nursery **08** basilisk, culverin, field gun, great gun, howitzer, murderer, oerlikon, ordnance, spitfire **09** artillery, carambole, carronade, Quaker gun, zumbooruk **10** fieldpiece, serpentine **11** stern-chaser **12** demi-culverin **14** murdering-piece

cannonade
05 salvo **06** volley **07** barrage **08** pounding, shelling **09** broadside **11** bombardment

canny
03 sly **04** good, nice, wice, wise **05** acute, lucky, pawky, sharp **06** artful, astute, clever, gentle, shrewd, subtle **07** careful, knowing, prudent, skilful **08** cautious, innocent **09** fortunate, judicious, sagacious **11** circumspect, worldly-wise **13** perspicacious

canoe
04 waka **05** kaiak, kayak **06** dugout **07** piragua **08** montaria, woodskin **09** monoxylon

canon
03 can, law **04** line, rota, rule **05** round, vicar **06** priest, square, squier, squire **07** brocard, dictate, precept, statute **08** Mathurin, minister, reverend, standard, vice-dean **09** clergyman, criterion, Mathurine, principle, yardstick **10** prebendary, regulation **12** residentiary

canonical
07 regular **08** accepted, approved, orthodox **10** authorized, recognized, sanctioned **13** authoritative

• canonical hours

Canonical hours include:

04 none, sext
05 lauds, nones, prime, terce
06 matins, tierce

07 complin, orthros, vespers
08 compline, evensong

canonize
05 bless, saint **07** beatify, besaint
08 sanctify

canopy
03 sky **04** dais, tilt **05** cover, herse, shade, state **06** awning, estate, hearse, huppah, tester **07** chuppah, majesty, marquee, shelter, veranda
08 ciborium, covering, marquise, pavilion, shamiana, sunshade, umbrella, verandah **09** baldachin, baldaquin, clamshell, parachute, shamianah **10** cooker hood, tabernacle **11** baldacchino **12** cloth of state

cant
04 kant, tilt **05** argot, brisk, lingo, merry, slang, slope **06** jargon, lively, snivel **07** snuffle **09** hypocrisy
10 vernacular **11** insincerity, rogues' Latin **12** thieves' Latin
15 pretentiousness

cantankerous
05 cross, testy **06** crabby, crusty, grumpy, ornery **07** crabbed, grouchy, peevish, piggish **08** contrary, perverse, stubborn **09** crotchety, difficult, irascible, irritable **11** bad-tempered, carnaptious, curnaptious, ill-humoured, quarrelsome **13** quick-tempered

canteen
04 café **05** flask, Naafi **06** buffet
08 snackbar **09** cafeteria, refectory
10 commissary, restaurant

canter
03 jog, ren, rin, run **04** lope, trot
05 amble, titup **06** gallop, tittup
07 jogtrot, tripple **11** false gallop

canton
03 can **04** Vaud **05** space **06** corner
08 division, ordinary

canvas
04 tent **05** Binca®, sails, tents
06 burlap, muslin **08** oilcloth

canvass
04 poll, scan, sift **05** study **06** debate, survey **07** agitate, analyse, discuss, examine, explore, find out, inspect
08 campaign, evaluate **09** seek votes
10 scrutinize **11** ask for votes, electioneer, inquire into, investigate
12 solicit votes **13** drum up support

canyon
05 abyss, cañon, chasm, gorge, gully
06 cañada, ravine, valley

cap
03 hat, lid, mob, taj, tam, top **04** beat, bung, call, caul, coat, coif, curb, kepi, plug **05** beret, chaco, cover, crown, excel, kippa, limit, mutch, outdo, quoif, shako, tammy, toque, tuque
06 amorce, barret, berret, better, biggin, bonnet, bunnet, calpac, chapka, czapka, exceed, granny, kalpak, pileus, shacko **07** biretta, bycoket, calotte, calpack, control, eclipse, ferrule, grannie, montero, stopper, surpass **08** capeline, chaperon, gorblimy, outshine, outstrip, restrain, restrict, schapska, trencher, yarmulka, yarmulke, zuchetta, zuchetto **09** capelline, chaperone, cock's-comb, crown cork, glengarry, gorblimey, transcend, trenchard, zucchetto **10** cockernony, Kilmarnock
11 bonnet-rouge, mortarboard, Tam o' Shanter **12** cheesecutter
13 international **15** go one better than

See also **hat**

capability
05 means, power, skill **06** talent
07 ability, faculty **08** aptitude, capacity, facility **09** potential
10 competence, efficiency
11 proficiency, skilfulness
13 qualification **14** accomplishment

capable
04 able **05** adept, apt to, smart
06 clever, fitted, gifted, suited
07 needing, notable, skilful
08 allowing, liable to, masterly, talented **09** competent, efficient, qualified, tending to **10** disposed to, inclined to, proficient **11** experienced, intelligent **12** accomplished, businesslike **13** comprehensive

capably
04 ably **07** adeptly **08** cleverly
09 skilfully **11** competently, efficiently
12 proficiently **13** intelligently

capacious
03 big **04** huge, vast, wide **05** ample, broad, large, roomy, womby **07** liberal, sizable **08** generous, spacious
09 expansive, extensive
10 commodious, voluminous
11 comfortable, elephantine, substantial **13** comprehensive

capacity
03 cap, job **04** bind, gift, post, role, room, size **05** power, range, scope, skill, space **06** extent, genius, office, talent, volume **07** ability, compass, content, faculty **08** aptitude, function, position **09** largeness, magnitude, potential, readiness, resources
10 capability, cleverness, competence, competency, dimensions, efficiency
11 appointment, proficiency, proportions, sufficience
12 intelligence

• **in the capacity of**
03 qua

cape
01 C **03** ras **04** coat, head, naze, neck, ness, robe, scaw, skaw, wrap **05** amice, cloak, fanon, fichu, point, shawl, talma
06 almuce, domino, mantle, muleta, poncho, sontag, tippet, tongue
07 burnous, manteel, mozetta, pelisse
08 burnouse, headland, pelerine
09 peninsula **10** promontory

See also **cloak**; **peninsula**

Capes include:

03 Cod
04 Fear, Horn, York
05 Wrath
06 Cretin, Orange
07 Kennedy, Leeuwin, Lookout
08 Farewell, Foulwind, Good Hope, Suckling
09 Canaveral, Carbonara, St Vincent, Trafalgar, Van Diemen
10 Finisterre, Kidnappers, Providence
11 Three Points, Tribulation
12 Hopes Advance
13 Prince of Wales

caper
03 hop **04** dido, jape, jest, jump, lark, leap, romp, skip **05** antic, bound, crime, dance, flisk, frisk, prank, scoup, scowp, stunt **06** affair, antics, bounce, cavort, frolic, gambol, prance, spring
07 gambado **08** business, capriole, escapade, mischief **09** high jinks
10 pigeon-wing

Cape Verde
03 CPV

capital
◇ *head selection indicator*
02 A1, uc **03** cap **04** cash, head, main, seat **05** chief, first, fonds, funds, major, means, money, prime, stock **06** assets, uncial, wealth **07** central, finance, leading, primary, savings, serious
08 cardinal, foremost, main city, property, reserves **09** excellent, important, majuscule, principal, resources **10** investment **11** block letter, investments, wherewithal
12 block capital, liquid assets
13 capital letter **15** upper-case letter

See also **city**; **currency**

• **small capitals**
02 sc

capitalism
12 laissez-faire **14** free enterprise

capitalist
05 mogul **06** banker, fat cat, tycoon
07 magnate, moneyer **08** investor, moneyman **09** bourgeois, financier, moneybags, plutocrat **12** money-spinner **13** person of means

capitalize
• **capitalize on**
07 exploit **08** cash in on **10** profit from
13 make the most of **15** take advantage of

capitulate
05 yield **06** give in, give up, relent, submit **07** succumb **08** back down
09 surrender **15** throw in the towel

capitulation
08 giving-in, giving-up, yielding
09 relenting, surrender **10** submission, succumbing **11** backing-down

caprice
03 fad **04** whim **05** fancy, freak, humor, quirk **06** humour, megrim,

notion, spleen, vagary, vapour, whimsy **07** fantasy, impulse **08** humoresk, migraine, phantasy **09** capriccio **10** fickleness, fitfulness, humoresque **11** inconstancy **14** changeableness

capricious
◇ *anagram indicator*
03 odd **05** freak, queer **06** fickle, fitful, kittle, quirky, wanton **07** erratic, wayward **08** fanciful, freakish, humorous, perverse, petulant, variable **09** arbitrary, fantastic, impulsive, mercurial, uncertain, whimsical **10** capernoity, changeable, humoursome, inconstant **11** capernoitie, cappernoity, fantastical **13** unpredictable

capsize
◇ *reversal indicator*
04 purl **05** upset **06** invert **07** tip over, whemmle, whomble, whommle, whummle **08** keel over, overturn, roll over, turn over **10** turn turtle **11** overturning

capsule
03 pod, urn **04** boll, pill **05** craft, jelly, probe, shell **06** bomber, caplet, cocoon, module, ovisac, sheath, tablet **07** habitat, lozenge, sandbox **08** pyxidium, spansule **09** container, poppy-head, radio pill **10** nidamentum, receptacle **11** sporogonium

captain
03 cid **04** boss, head, lead, skip **05** chief, owner, pilot **06** direct, guider, leader, manage, master, old man, patron **07** command, control, officer, patroon, skipper **08** capitayn **09** commander, commodore, supervise **10** ritt-master, shipmaster **12** be in charge of **13** master-mariner, protospataire, whaling-master **14** protospathaire **15** protospatharius

Captains include:

04 **Ahab**, **Cook** (James), **Hook**, **Kidd** (William), **Nemo**
05 **Bligh** (William), **Flint** (Jim Turner), **Johns** (W E), **Queeg**, **Smith** (John), **Swing**
07 **Corelli** (Antonio), **Marryat** (Frederick)
08 **Bobadill**, **Hastings** (Arthur), **MacHeath**
09 **Singleton**
10 **Hornblower** (Horatio)

caption
04 note **05** title **06** arrest, legend, titles **07** cutline, heading, wording **08** headline **09** underline **11** inscription

captious
07 carping, peevish **08** critical, niggling **09** quibbling **10** nit-picking, scrupulous **13** hair-splitting, hypercritical

captivate
03 get, win **04** lure, take **05** charm **06** allure, dazzle, seduce **07** attract, beguile, bewitch, delight, enamour, enchant, enthral **09** enrapture, fascinate, hypnotize, infatuate, mesmerize **11** take by storm

captivating
06 taking **07** winsome **08** alluring, catching, charming, dazzling **09** beautiful, beguiling, seductive **10** attractive, bewitching, delightful, enchanting **11** enthralling, fascinating

captive
03 POW **05** caged, slave **06** secure, shut up **07** caitive, convict, hostage, subject, triumph **08** confined, detained, detainee, enslaved, ensnared, interned, internee, jailbird, locked up, prisoner **09** enchained, in bondage **10** imprisoned, locked away, restrained, restricted **12** incarcerated **13** held in custody

captivity
05 bonds, exile **06** duress **07** bondage, custody, slavery **09** detention, endurance, restraint, servitude **10** constraint, internment **11** confinement, enslavement **12** imprisonment **13** incarceration

captor
05 guard **06** jailor, keeper, warder **09** custodian **12** incarcerator

capture
◇ *containment indicator*
03 cop, nab, net, win **04** land, nick, rush, take, trap, with **05** carry, catch, mop up, seize, snare, withe **06** arrest, collar, cut out, entrap, occupy, pick up, record, secure, taking **07** embrace, ensnare, express, nabbing, nicking, run down, seizure, snabble, snaffle **08** catching, hit a blot, hunt down, imprison, surprise, trapping **09** apprehend, collaring, recapture, represent, reproduce **11** encapsulate **12** imprisonment, take prisoner **13** taking captive **14** taking prisoner
• **be captured**
04 fall

capuchin
03 sai **05** Cebus, sajou **07** sapajou

car
04 auto, cart, heap **05** motor **07** chariot, clunker, vehicle, vettura **08** motor car **09** speedster **10** automobile, rust bucket **12** motor vehicle **13** shooting brake

Car manufacturers include:

02 MG, RR, VW
03 BMW, Kia
04 Audi, Fiat, Ford, Jeep, Lada, Mini, Saab, Seat, Yugo
05 Buick, Dodge, Honda, Isuzu, Lexus, Lotus, Mazda, Riley, Rover, Skoda, Smart, Volvo
06 Austin, Daewoo, Datsun, Jaguar, Lancia, Morgan, Morris, Nissan, Proton, Subaru, Talbot, Toyota
07 Bentley, Bugatti, Citroen, Daimler, Ferrari, Hillman, Hyundai, Peugeot, Pontiac, Porsche, Reliant, Renault, Trabant, Triumph
08 Cadillac, Chrysler, Daihatsu, De Lorean, Maserati, Mercedes, Standard, Vauxhall, Wolseley
09 Alfa Romeo, Chevrolet, Land Rover
10 Mitsubishi, Oldsmobile, Rolls Royce, Vanden Plas, Volkswagen
11 Aston Martin, Lamborghini
12 Mercedes-Benz

Car types include:

02 RR
03 cab, MPV, SUV
04 jeep, limo, Mini®, taxi
05 brake, break, buggy, coupé, sedan
06 banger, Beetle®, estate, hearse, jalopy, kit-car, saloon, tourer
07 jaloppy, minivan
08 fastback, hot hatch, panda car, roadster, runabout, Smart car®, stock car
09 all-roader, bubble-car, cabriolet, hatchback, Land Rover®, limousine, off-roader, patrol car, sports car
10 Model T Ford®, Range Rover®, Sinclair C5, subcompact, veteran car, vintage car
11 convertible
12 station wagon
13 people carrier, shooting brake
14 four-wheel drive

Famous cars include:

04 FAB1
08 Blue Bird
09 Batmobile, Christine, Genevieve
11 Flintmobile

Car and motor vehicle parts include:

03 ABS
04 axle, boot, door, gear, hood, horn, jack, sill, tyre, vent, wing
05 bezel, clock, grill, shaft, trunk, wheel
06 airbag, bonnet, bumper, clutch, dimmer, engine, fender, heater, hub-cap, towbar
07 battery, chassis, fog lamp, gas tank, gearbox, kingpin, spoiler, sunroof
08 air brake, air inlet, bodywork, brake pad, door-lock, fog light, headrest, ignition, jump lead, lift gate, oil gauge, roof rack, seat belt, silencer, solenoid, sun visor, track rod
09 brake drum, brake shoe, crankcase, dashboard, disc brake, drum brake, filler cap, fuel gauge, gear-lever, gearshift, gear-stick, handbrake, headlight, indicator, monocoque, overrider, prop shaft, rear light, reflector, sidelight, spare tyre, stoplight, wheel arch
10 brake light, drive shaft, petrol tank, power brake, rev counter, side mirror, stick shift, suspension, windscreen, windshield, wing mirror

11 accelerator, anti-roll bar, exhaust pipe, ignition key, number plate, parcel shelf, speedometer
12 licence plate, parking-light, quarterlight, transmission
13 centre console, courtesy light, cruise control, flasher switch, pneumatic tyre, rack and pinion, radial-ply tyre, reclining seat, shock absorber, side-impact bar, steering-wheel
14 air-conditioner, central locking, electric window, emergency light, four-wheel drive, hydraulic brake, rear-view mirror, reversing light, steering-column
15 windscreen-wiper

Car and motoring-related terms include:

02 AA
03 dip, GPS, LRP, map, MOT, RAC, tow
04 exit, park, skid, SORN, stop
05 amber, brake, crash, cut up, flash, layby, on tow, prang, shunt
06 diesel, fill up, filter, garage, hold-up, L-plate, octane, petrol, pile-up, pull in
07 blowout, bollard, bus lane, car park, car wash, cat's-eye, give way, logbook, MOT test, neutral, pull out, reverse, road map, snarl-up, tax disc, traffic
08 accident, change up, coasting, declutch, fast lane, flat tyre, gridlock, indicate, junction, main beam, overtake, puncture, red light, road rage, services, slip road, slow lane, speeding, tailback, taxi rank, turn left, unleaded
09 blind spot, breakdown, collision, cycle lane, fifth gear, first gear, green card, hit-and-run, radar trap, road atlas, road studs, roadworks, sixth gear, third gear, T junction, turn right, wheelspin, white line
10 accelerate, amber light, arm signals, bottleneck, change down, change gear, change lane, contraflow, crossroads, fourth gear, green light, inside lane, middle lane, pedestrian, petrol pump, roundabout, second gear, speed limit, stay in lane, straight on, tailgating, traffic jam, yellow line
11 box junction, crawler lane, drink-driver, driving test, hand signals, highway code, outside lane, speed camera, traffic cone, traffic cops, traffic news, zigzag lines
12 drink-driving, hard shoulder, left-hand lane, motorway toll, one-way system, parking meter, passing place, road junction, speeding fine, tyre pressure
13 Belisha beacon, drink and drive, driving lesson, driving school, flashing amber, handbrake turn, jump the lights, left-hand drive, level crossing, no-claims bonus, parking ticket, pay and display, penalty points, petrol station, power steering, right-hand lane, super unleaded, traffic lights, traffic police, zebra crossing
14 cadence braking, double declutch, driving licence, four-wheel drive, mini-roundabout, MOT certificate, motorway pile-up, overtaking lane, poor visibility, puffin crossing, right-hand drive, service station, speeding ticket, unleaded petrol
15 pelican crossing, put your foot down, road fund licence, test certificate, traction control, warning triangle

See also **motor vehicle**

carafe
03 jug **05** flask **06** bottle, flagon **07** pitcher **08** decanter

caravan
02 RV **03** van **04** line **05** group, train **06** cafila, convoy, kafila **07** caffila, trailer **09** camper van, Dormobile®, motor home, Winnebago® **10** mobile home

carbon
01 C **04** copy **07** diamond **08** graphite **09** buckyball

• **carbon copy**
02 cc **03** bcc **06** flimsy **08** manifold

carbuncle
04 boil, bump, lump, sore **06** bunion, pimple **07** anthrax, blister **12** inflammation

carcase, carcass
04 body, hulk **05** shell **06** corpse, cutter **07** cadaver, remains **08** dead body, skeleton **09** framework, structure

See also **meat**

card
03 ace, map, mix **04** Amex, club, comb, jack, king, tose, toze **05** deuce, heart, joker, knave, queen, spade, toaze **06** domino, master, meishi **07** diamond **10** adulterate **13** carte-de-visite

See also **eccentric**; **game**

• **cards suits**
01 c, d, h, s **05** clubs **06** hearts, spades **08** diamonds

• **on the cards**
06 likely **08** possible, probable **11** looking as if, looking like **13** the chances are

• **playing cards**
04 deck, hand **11** devil's books

cardinal
02 HE **03** key **04** main **05** basic, chief, first, pivot, prime **06** number, red hat **07** capital, central, highest, leading, primary **08** foremost, greatest, grosbeak **09** essential, important, paramount, principal **10** pre-eminent **11** fundamental **14** apostolic vicar

See also **archbishop**; **number**

Cardinals include:

03 **Sin** (Jaime)
04 **Gray** (Gordon), **Hume** (Basil), **Pole** (Reginald), **Retz** (Jean Françoise de)
05 **Chigi** (Fabio)
06 **Beaton** (David), **Borgia** (Rodrigo), **Fisher** (John), **Heenan** (John Carmel), **Medici** (Giovanni de'), **Newman** (John Henry), **Rovere** (Francesco della), **Stuart** (Henry, Duke of York), **Wolsey** (Thomas)
07 **Bethune** (David), **Langham** (Simon), **Langton** (Stephen), **Mazarin** (Jules), **Mendoza** (Pedro Gonzalez de), **Pandulf**, **Vaughan** (Herbert), **Wiseman** (Nicholas), **Ximenes** (Francisco)
08 **Alberoni** (Giulio), **Aubusson** (Pierre d'), **Beaufort** (Henry), **Stepinac**
09 **Richelieu** (Armand Jean Duplessis, Duc de), **Wyszynski** (Stefan)
10 **Bellarmine** (Robert), **Breakspear** (Nicolas), **Mindszenty** (József)
13 **Murphy-O'Connor** (Cormac)

• **cardinal's office**
03 hat

care
04 cark, fear, heed, mind, reck, reke, ward **05** kaugh, pains, worry **06** bother, burden, charge, hang-up, kiaugh, regard, strain, stress, tender **07** anxiety, caution, concern, control, custody, keeping, minding, tending, thought, trouble **08** accuracy, disquiet, distress, interest, pressure, prudence, tutelage, vexation **09** attention, give a damn, oversight, vigilance **10** affliction, attendance, protection **11** be concerned, carefulness, forethought, heedfulness, safekeeping, supervision, tribulation **12** be interested, guardianship, looking-after, watchfulness, watching over **13** consideration **14** circumspection, meticulousness, responsibility

• **care for**
04 like, love, mind, tend, want **05** enjoy, nurse **06** attend, desire **07** cherish, protect **08** be fond of, be keen on, maintain **09** be close to, delight in, look after, watch over **10** minister to, provide for, take care of **12** be in love with

• **care of**
01 c/- **02** c/o

career
◇ *anagram indicator*
03 job, ren, rin, run **04** bolt, dash, life, past, race, rush, tear **05** shoot, speed, trade, whang **06** gallop, hurtle, métier **07** calling, cariere, pursuit **08** life-work, vocation **10** employment, livelihood, occupation, profession

carefree
05 happy **06** blithe, breezy, cheery **07** halcyon **08** cheerful, debonair, laid-back **09** easy-going, fancy-free, unworried **10** debonnaire, insouciant, nonchalant, rollicking, untroubled **11** thoughtless, unconcerned **12** happy-go-lucky, light-hearted **13** irresponsible

careful
04 mean, wary, wise **05** alert, aware, chary, close, heedy, tight **06** eyeful, frugal, stingy **07** anxious, guarded, heedful, mindful, miserly, precise, prudent, sparing, tactful, thrifty **08** accurate, cautious, detailed, diligent, discreet, rigorous, sensible, thorough, vigilant, watchful **09** assiduous, attentive, judicious, niggardly, penny-wise **10** deliberate, economical, fast-handed, fastidious, hard-fisted, methodical, meticulous, particular, scrupulous, solicitous, systematic, thoughtful **11** circumspect, close-fisted, close-handed, painstaking, punctilious, tight-fisted **12** parsimonious, softly-softly **13** conscientious, penny-pinching

carefully
05 hooly **06** warily **07** charily, closely **09** guardedly, heedfully, mindfully, precisely, prudently, tactfully **10** accurately, cautiously, diligently, discreetly, handsomely, rigorously, solicitous, thoroughly, vigilantly, watchfully **11** assiduously, attentively, judiciously, punctilious **12** deliberately, fastidiously, methodically, meticulously, scrupulously, thoughtfully **13** circumspectly, painstakingly **14** systematically **15** conscientiously

careless
◇ *anagram indicator*
03 lax **04** nice **05** hasty, messy, slack **06** breezy, casual, remiss, secure, shoddy, simple, sloppy, untidy **07** artless, cursory, négligé, offhand, untenty **08** carefree, cheerful, heedless, laid-back, reckless, slapdash, slipshod, tactless, uncaring **09** easy-going, forgetful, negligent, unguarded, unmindful, unworried **10** disorderly, inaccurate, incautious, indiscreet, insouciant, neglectful, nonchalant, regardless, unthinking, untroubled **11** inattentive, perfunctory, superficial, thoughtless, unconcerned **12** absent-minded, disorganized, happy as a clam, happy-go-lucky, light-hearted **13** inconsiderate, irresponsible **15** happy as a sandboy

carelessly
◇ *anagram indicator*
06 anyhow **07** hastily **08** casually, remissly, shoddily, slam-bang, slapdash, sloppily **09** cursorily **10** heedlessly, recklessly, tactlessly, uncaringly **11** forgetfully, negligently, offhandedly, unguardedly, unmindfully **12** incautiously, indiscreetly, neglectingly, unthinkingly **13** inattentively, irresponsibly, perfunctorily, superficially, thoughtlessly, unconcernedly **14** absent-mindedly **15** inconsiderately

caress
03 coy, hug, pat, pet, rub **04** bill, kiss **05** grope, touch **06** cuddle, feel up, fondle, nuzzle, stroke **07** embrace, petting, touch up **08** canoodle, lallygag, lollygag **10** endearment **13** butterfly kiss, slap and tickle

caretaker
06 acting, fill-in, keeper, porter, pro tem, sexton, verger, warden **07** curator, dvornik, janitor, ostiary, shammes, stand-in, steward **08** janitrix, shammash, watchman **09** concierge, custodian, janitress, short-term, temporary **10** doorkeeper, substitute **11** provisional **14** superintendent

careworn
04 worn **05** gaunt, tired, weary **07** anxious, haggard, worn-out, worried **08** fatigued **09** exhausted

cargo
04 bulk, haul, last, load **05** goods **06** lading **07** baggage, fraught, freight, payload, tonnage **08** contents, deck-load, frautage, shipment **10** fraughtage **11** consignment, merchandise

Caribbean
02 WI **10** West Indies

caricature
04 mock **05** mimic **06** parody, satire, send up, send-up **07** cartoon, distort, lampoon, mimicry, take off, take-off **08** ridicule, satirize, travesty **09** burlesque, imitation **10** distortion, exaggerate **14** representation

caring
04 fond, kind, warm **06** loving, tender **07** devoted, helpful **08** friendly **10** altruistic, benevolent, thoughtful **11** good-natured, kind-hearted, sympathetic **12** affectionate **13** compassionate, philanthropic, tender-hearted

carnage
06 murder **07** killing **08** butchery, genocide, massacre **09** bloodbath, bloodshed, holocaust, slaughter **10** mass murder **15** ethnic cleansing

carnal
04 lewd **05** belly, human **06** animal, bodily, erotic, impure, sexual **07** fleshly, lustful, natural, outward, sensual **08** physical **09** corporeal, lecherous, murderous **10** lascivious, libidinous, licentious **11** flesh-eating, unspiritual

carnival
04 fair, fête, gala **05** carny **06** carney, fiesta **07** holiday, jubilee, revelry **08** Fasching, festival, jamboree **09** amusement, Mardi Gras, merriment **11** celebration, merrymaking

carnivorous
10 meat-eating, zoophagous **11** creophagous, flesh-eating

carol
04 hymn, noel, sing, song **06** carrel, chorus, strain **07** carrell, wassail **13** Christmas song

carousal
04 upsy **05** feast, rouse, upsee, upsey

carouse
04 birl **05** birle, booze, drink, party, quaff, revel, spree **06** imbibe **07** roister, wassail **09** celebrate, make merry **11** drink freely, wassail bout

carousing
08 drinking, partying **11** celebrating, compotation, merrymaking **13** mallemaroking

carp
02 id **03** ide, koi, nag **04** yerk **05** gibel, knock, pinch **06** go on at, twitch **07** censure, crucian, crusian, nit-pick, quibble **08** complain, cyprinid, goldfish, reproach **09** criticize, find fault, round fish **10** find faults, silverfish **11** have a shot at **14** ultracrepidate

carpenter
05 chips **06** chippy, joiner, Joseph, Quince, wright **10** cartwright, shipwright, woodworker **12** cabinet-maker

carpet
03 bed, mat, rug **04** cake, coat, wrap **05** cover, dress, layer **06** clothe, encase, spread **07** blanket, matting, overlay **08** covering **10** tablecloth **13** floor-covering

Carpets and rugs include:

03 rag, red, rya
04 kali
05 Dutch, kelim, kilim, magic, pilch, stair, throw
06 hearth, hooked, khilim, Kirman, numdah, runner, prayer, Turkey, Wilton
07 bergama, flokati, Persian, Turkish
08 Aubusson, bergamot, Brussels, moquette
09 Axminster, prayer rug, sheepskin
10 travelling
11 Bessarabian, buffalo robe
13 Kidderminster

carping
07 nagging, Zoilism **08** captious **09** cavilling, quibbling **10** nit-picking **11** complaining, criticizing **12** fault-finding

carriage
03 air, car, cge, job, set **04** gait, mien, port **05** guise, poise, tenue **06** burden, clatch, manner, stance **07** baggage, bearing, conduct, freight, portage, postage, posture, turnout, vehicle, voiture **08** attitude, carrying, delivery, equipage, portance, presence, truckage **09** behaviour, demeanour, porterage, transport **10** conveyance, deportment **14** transportation

Carriages include:

03 cab, fly, gig
04 arba, baby, chay, drag, dray, ekka, mail, pony, pram, rath, shay, trap

05 araba, aroba, bandy, buggy, coach, coupé, dilly, ratha, stage, sulky, T-cart, wagon
06 berlin, calash, chaise, drosky, go-cart, hansom, herdic, landau, pochay, purdah, spider, spring, surrey
07 britska, britzka, cariole, caroche, chariot, dogcart, droshky, hackney, phaeton, pillbox, ricksha, tilbury, vettura, vis-à-vis
08 barouche, britzska, brougham, carriole, carryall, clarence, diligent, jump-seat, po'chaise, rickshaw, rockaway, sociable, stanhope, victoria
09 britschka, cabriolet, landaulet, wagonette
10 four-in hand, post chaise, stagecoach
11 family coach, hurly-hacket, village cart
13 désobligeante, mourning coach, spider phaeton, thoroughbrace

carried away

04 rapt **06** enlevé, way-out

• **get carried away**

06 lose it **13** become excited

See also **carry**

carrier

06 bearer, porter, runner, telfer, vector
07 airline, telpher, tranter, vehicle
08 conveyor, horseman, kurveyor
09 messenger **10** plastic bag
11 transmitter, transporter
12 roundsperson **13** dispatch rider
14 delivery-person, transport rider

carrion

03 ket

• **carrion feeder**

04 hyen **05** hyena **06** hyaena
07 vulture **08** aardwolf **09** scavenger

carry

◇ *containment indicator*

03 act, lug **04** bear, cart, gain, haul, have, hold, hump, lead, mean, move, pass, pipe, sell, show, take, tote, wain **05** adopt, bring, cover, drive, fetch, mount, print, reach, relay, shift, stand, stock **06** accept, acquit, behave, convey, effect, entail, hold up, lead to, pass on, ratify, retail, suffer, travel, uphold, wheech **07** approve, be heard, comport, conduct, contain, deliver, display, involve, present, publish, release, support, sustain, vote for **08** hand over, maintain, result in, sanction, shoulder, transfer, transmit, underpin **09** authorize, be audible, broadcast, transport **11** communicate, disseminate, have for sale, keep in stock **12** vote in favour **14** be infected with

• **carry away**

03 rap **04** lift **06** asport, ravish
08 bear away **09** transport

• **carry off**

03 lag, net, rob, win **04** gain, hent, land, rape **05** crack **06** abduct, kidnap, pick up, secure **07** achieve **08** complete **09** succeed in, transport **12** come away with

• **carry on**

03 ren, rin, run **04** go on, hold, keep, last, wage **06** bash on, endure, keep on, keep up, manage, play up, pursue, resume **07** conduct, operate, persist, proceed, restart **08** continue, engage in, maintain, progress, return to **09** misbehave, persevere **10** administer, be involved, mess around, play around **12** have an affair **15** behave foolishly

• **carry out**

02 do **04** fill **05** mount **06** effect, fulfil **07** achieve, conduct, deliver, execute, perform, realize **08** bring off **09** discharge, implement, undertake **10** accomplish **12** give effect to **13** put into effect **15** deliver the goods, put into practice

carry-on

04 flap, fuss, stir, to-do **05** hoo-ha
06 bother, hassle **07** trouble
09 commotion, kerfuffle

cart

03 car, jag, lug **04** bear, dray, gill, haul, hump, jill, lead, move, pram, tote **05** bandy, carry, float, furby, gambo, shift, truck, wagon **06** barrow, convey, furphy, gurney **07** cariole, hackery, shandry, trailer, tumbrel, tumbril **08** carriole, democrat, handcart, transfer **09** transport **11** wheelbarrow

cartilage

07 cricoid, gristle **08** chondrus, meniscus

carton

03 box, tub **04** case, pack **06** packet, parcel **07** package **09** container

cartoon

04 toon **05** anime, manga **06** bubble, parody, send-up, sketch **07** balloon, drawing, fumetto, lampoon, picture, take-off **09** animation, burlesque **10** caricature, comic strip **12** animated film, strip cartoon

Cartoon characters include:

03 PHB, Ren, Tom
04 Bart, Fred, Huey, Kyle, Lisa, Stan
05 Alice, Bluto, Dewey, Dumbo, Goofy, Homer, Jerry, Kenny, Louey, Marge, Mr Men, Robin, Rocky, Snowy, Wally
06 Batman, Beavis, Boo Boo, Calvin, Daphne, Droopy, Hobbes, Maggie, Obelix, Popeye, Shaggy, Snoopy, Stimpy, Thelma, Tintin, Top Cat
07 Asterix, Cartman, Custard, Dilbert, Gnasher, Muttley, Penfold, Roobarb
08 Andy Capp, Butthead, Clouseau, Garfield, Krazy Kat, Olive Oyl, Super Man, Superted, Tank Girl, The Joker, Yogi Bear
09 Betty Boop, Bugs Bunny, Chip 'n' Dale, Daffy Duck, Daisy Duck, Dastardly, Dick Tracy, Elmer Fudd, Marmaduke, Oor Wullie, Pepe le Pew, Scooby Doo, Spider Man, Sylvester, The Broons, Tweety Pie
10 Bullwinkle, Donald Duck, Judge Dredd, Road Runner, Scrappy Doo, The Riddler
11 Bart Simpson, Betty Rubble, Danger Mouse, Felix the Cat, Flash Gordon, Fred Bassett, Korky the Cat, Lisa Simpson, Mickey Mouse, Minnie Mouse, The Simpsons, Wile E Coyote
12 Barney Rubble, Charlie Brown, Desperate Dan, Homer Simpson, Little Misses, Marge Simpson, Ren and Stimpy
13 Dick Dastardly, Maggie Simpson, Modesty Blaise, Rupert the Bear, Scrooge McDuck
14 Bash Street Kids, Foghorn Leghorn, Fred Flintstone, Incredible Hulk, The Pink Panther
15 Calvin and Hobbes, Dennis the Menace, Penelope Pitstop, Steamboat Willie, Wilma Flintstone

Cartoonists include:

02 HB
03 **Low** (Sir David)
04 **Capp** (Al), **Kane** (Bob), **Rémi** (Georges)
05 **Adams** (Scott), **Avery** (Tex), **Block** (Herbert L), **Davis** (Jim), **Doyle** (John), **Giles**, **Hanna** (William), **Hergé**, **Jones** (Chuck), **Lantz** (Walter), **McCay** (Winsor), **Segar** (Elzie), **Silas**
06 **Addams** (Charles), **Disney** (Walt), **Fisher** (Bud), **Iwerks** (Ub), **Larson** (Gary), **Scarfe** (Gerald), **Schulz** (Charles M), **Searle** (Ronald), **Siegel** (Jerry), **Smythe** (Reg)
07 **Barbera** (Joseph), **Shuster** (Joseph), **Tenniel** (Sir John), **Trudeau** (Garry), **Watkins** (Dudley D), **Webster** (Tom)
08 **Goldberg** (Rube), **Groening** (Matt), **Herblock**, **Herriman** (George), **Robinson** (Heath)
09 **Baxendale** (Leo), **Fleischer** (Max), **Watterson** (Bill)
12 **Bairnsfather** (Bruce), **Hanna-Barbera**

cartridge

04 case, tube **05** blank, round, shell
06 charge **07** capsule, torpedo
08 canister, cassette, cylinder, magazine, streamer **09** container
11 central fire

caruncle

04 aril **08** arillode **10** strophiole

carve

◇ *anagram indicator*

03 cut, hew **04** chip, chop, etch, form, hack **05** cut up, kerve, mould, notch, sculp, shape, slice, write **06** chisel, entail, incise, indent, sculpt, unlace **07** engrave, entayle, fashion, insculp, whittle **09** apportion, dismember, sculpture, truncheon **10** distribute **11** insculpture

• **carve up**

◇ *anagram indicator*

05 share, split **06** divide **07** split up **08** separate, share out **09** parcel out, partition **10** distribute

carving
03 cut **04** bust **05** model, round, tondo **06** statue **08** incision, knotwork, tympanum **09** scrimshaw, sculpture, statuette **10** lithoglyph, petroglyph, rosemaling **11** dendroglyph, scrimshandy **12** mezzo-relievo, mezzo-rilievo, scrimshander

cascade
03 lin **04** fall, gush, linn, pour, rush **05** chute, falls, flood, pitch, spill, surge **06** deluge, plunge, shower, tumble **07** descend, torrent, trickle **08** cataract, fountain, overflow **09** avalanche, waterfall **10** outpouring, water chute, waterworks

case
◇ *ends selection indicator*
03 bag, box **04** étui, sted, suit **05** cause, chest, cover, crate, crime, event, point, shell, state, stead, stede, trial, trunk **06** action, affair, carton, casing, casket, client, dative, essive, holder, jacket, sheath, valise, victim **07** attaché, cabinet, capsule, context, defence, dispute, elative, examine, example, grounds, holdall, inquiry, invalid, keister, lawsuit, patient, process, wrapper **08** abessive, ablative, adessive, allative, argument, canister, evidence, genitive, illative, incident, inessive, instance, kalamdan, locative, occasion, position, showcase, specimen, suitcase, vasculum, vocative **09** briefcase, cartridge, chrysalid, chrysalis, condition, container, flight bag, papeterie, portfolio, reasoning, situation, travel bag **10** accusative, comitative, nominative, occurrence, receptacle, subjective, vanity-case **11** attaché case, contingency, hand luggage, portmanteau, proceedings, reconnoitre, translative, writing desk **12** illustration, overnight bag **13** circumstances, investigation, particularity

cases
02 ca

cash
03 tin **04** cent, dime, dosh, loot **05** blunt, brass, bread, coins, dough, funds, gravy, lolly, money, notes, Oscar, ready, rhino, smash **06** change, encash, greens, moolah, stumpy **07** bullion, capital, finance, readies, realize, scratch, shekels **08** currency, exchange, greenies **09** banknotes, hard money, liquidate, megabucks, resources **10** ready money **11** legal tender, spondulicks, wherewithal **12** hard currency, turn into cash
• **cash return**
07 jackpot

cashier
04 fire, sack **05** annul, break, clerk, expel **06** banker, bursar, purser, teller **07** checker, discard, dismiss, drum out, unfrock **08** get rid of, throw out **09** bank clerk, discharge, treasurer **10** accountant

casing
◇ *containment indicator*
◇ *ends selection indicator*
03 cup, tub **04** cast, core **05** cover, shell **06** jacket, sheath **07** cowling, housing **08** binnacle, covering, envelope, pair case, trunking, wrapping **09** air-jacket, crankcase, oil string, sheathing **10** protection **11** bell-housing, junction box, steam jacket, water jacket **13** cylinder block

cask
03 but, keg, pin, tub, tun, vat **04** butt, cade, pipe, wood **05** flask **06** barrel, casket, casque, firkin, octave, tierce **07** barrico, breaker, leaguer **08** hogshead, puncheon **09** kilderkin **11** scuttlebutt

casket
03 box **04** case, kist **05** chest, pyxis, shell **06** coffer, coffin, larnax **08** cassette, jewel-box **11** sarcophagus **12** pine overcoat, wooden kimono **14** wooden overcoat

cassava
04 yuca **05** yucca **06** manioc **07** mandioc, manihoc, tapioca **08** mandioca **09** mandiocca

casserole
04 stew **06** diable **07** cocotte, stew-pan, terrine, tzimmes **08** pot-au-feu **09** Dutch oven **10** slow cooker

cast
◇ *anagram indicator*
03 die, lob, mew, put, see, shy **04** drop, emit, form, hurl, look, putt, seek, shed, slip, toss, turn, veer, view, vote, warp **05** add up, drive, fling, found, fusil, heave, impel, model, mould, moult, pitch, place, shape, shoot, sling, stamp, throw **06** actors, assign, chance, create, direct, fusile, glance, launch, look at, manner, record, reject, spread, thrown, troupe **07** appoint, casting, company, condemn, diffuse, discard, dismiss, fashion, give off, give out, glimpse, moulded, players, predict, project, quality, radiate, redound, reflect, scatter **08** covering, register, rejected **09** calculate, formulate **10** catch sight, characters, performers **12** entertainers **13** put in jeopardy **14** mark with a cross
• **cast aside**
06 reject **07** discard, say no to **08** get rid of, turn down **12** dispense with
• **cast down**
05 abase, crush **06** abattu, deject, sadden **07** depress **08** dejected, desolate **10** discourage, dishearten
• **cast out**
09 ostracize

caste
04 race, rank **05** class, grade, group, order **06** degree, estate, status **07** lineage, station, stratum **08** position **10** background **11** social class **14** social standing

castigate
03 rap **04** slam **05** chide, emend, scold **06** berate, punish, rebuke **07** censure, chasten, correct, reprove, upbraid **08** admonish, chastise **09** criticize, dress down, reprimand **10** discipline **13** tear a strip off **15** give someone hell

castle
01 R **04** fort, keep, rook **05** tower, villa **06** kasbah, palace **07** château, citadel, mansion, schloss **08** fastness, fortress **10** stronghold **11** stately home **12** country house

Castles include:

03 Doe, Eye, Lea, Mey
04 Clun, Drum, Leap, Peel, Trim, Ward, York
05 Black, Burgh, Corfe, Croft, Doune, Flint, Knock, Leeds, Skibo, White
06 Cawdor, Durham, Fraser, Glamis, Howard, Ludlow, Maiden, Sandal, Swords
07 Alnwick, Arundel, Braemar, Caister, Culzean, Dunster, Harlech, Lismore, Old Wick, Peveril, Scotney, Warwick, Windsor
08 Balmoral, Bamburgh, Bastille, Broughty, Corgarff, Dunottar, Dunvegan, Egremont, Elsinore, Goodrich, Jedburgh, Kilkenny, Monmouth, Pembroke, Stirling, Stokesay, Tintagel, Urquhart
09 Beaumaris, Blackrock, Chipchase, Dunsinane, Edinburgh, Hermitage, Inverness, Lancaster, Lochleven, St Andrews, Tantallon
10 Bridgnorth, Caernarvon, Caerphilly, Carmarthen, Jewel Tower, Kenilworth, Montgomery, Okehampton, Pontefract, Rockingham
11 Castell Coch, Chillingham, Craigmillar, Eilean Donan, Fotheringay, Lindisfarne, Narrow Water, Ravenscraig, Scarborough, Tattershall, Thirlestane
12 Conisborough
13 Carrickfergus
15 St Michael's Mount

Castle parts include:

04 berm, keep, moat, ward
05 ditch, fosse, motte, mound, scarp, tower
06 bailey, chapel, corbel, crenel, donjon, merlon, turret
07 bastion, dungeon, parados, parapet, postern, rampart
08 approach, barbican, bartizan, brattice, buttress, crosslet, loophole, stockade, wall walk
09 arrow-slit, courtyard, embrasure, gatehouse, inner wall
10 drawbridge, murder hole, portcullis, watchtower
11 battlements, curtain wall, outer bailey
12 crenellation, lookout tower
13 enclosure wall

• **castles**
02 O-O **03** O-O-O

castrate
03 cut, fix **04** geld, glib, swig **05** alter, unman, unsex **06** doctor, neuter
07 evirate, knacker **10** emasculate

casual
03 odd **04** orra **05** blasé, stray
06 chance, random **07** cursory, leisure, offhand, passing, relaxed, scratch **08** careless, informal, laid-back, lukewarm, part-time
09 apathetic, easy-going, irregular, negligent, short-term, temporary, throwaway **10** accidental, fortuitous, incidental, insouciant, nonchalant, occasional, unexpected, unforeseen
11 comfortable, free-and-easy, indifferent, promiscuous, provisional, spontaneous, superficial, unconcerned **12** happy-go-lucky, intermittent **13** lackadaisical, serendipitous, unceremonious, unintentional **14** unpremeditated

casually
06 overly **08** sportily **10** informally, off the cuff **11** comfortably
12 occasionally **13** spontaneously
15 parenthetically

casualty
04 loss **05** death **06** caduac, injury, victim **07** injured, missing, wounded
08 accident, fatality, sufferer **10** dead person, misfortune **13** injured person

casuistry
07 sophism **09** chicanery, sophistry
12 equivocation, speciousness

cat
03 man, mog, tom **04** chap, puss
05 moggy, pussy, queen, rumpy
06 feline, kitten, mouser, neuter, tomcat **08** baudrons, pussy cat
09 catamaran, grimalkin
See also **animal**; **vomit**

Domestic cats include:

03 rex
04 Manx
05 Korat, tabby
06 Angora, Bengal, Birman, Bombay, Cymric, Havana, LaPerm, Ocicat, Somali
07 Burmese, Persian, rag-doll, Siamese, Tiffany
08 Balinese, Burmilla, Devon rex, Snowshoe, Tiffanie
09 Himalayan, Maine Coon, Singapura, Tonkinese
10 Abyssinian, Carthusian, chinchilla, Cornish rex, Selkirk Rex, Turkish Van
11 Egyptian Mau, Foreign Blue, Russian Blue, silver tabby
12 Foreign White, Scottish Fold
13 domestic tabby, Tortoiseshell, Turkish Angora
15 British longhair, Exotic shorthair, Japanese Bobtail, Norwegian Forest

Wild and big cats include:

03 bob
04 eyra, lion, lynx, pard, puma
05 feral, tiger
06 cougar, jaguar, kodkod, margay, ocelot, pampas
07 cheetah, leopard
08 mountain
09 Geoffroy's
10 jaguarundi
11 snow leopard
12 mountain lion, Scottish wild
13 little spotted
14 clouded leopard

Famous cats include:

03 Tom
04 Bast, Jess
05 Dinah, Felix, Korky
06 Arthur, Bastet, Ginger, Kaspar, Top Cat, Ubasti
07 Bagpuss, Custard, Simpkin
08 Beerbohm, Garfield, Humphrey, Krazy Kat, Macavity
09 Mehitabel, Mrs Norris, Sylvester, Thomasina, Tom Kitten
10 El Brooshna, Heathcliff
11 Cat in the Hat, Cheshire Cat, Crookshanks, Korky the Cat, Pink Panther, Puss in Boots
14 Bustopher Jones, Mr Mistoffelees, Old Deuteronomy, The Cat in the Hat

cataclysm
04 blow **07** debacle **08** calamity, collapse, disaster, upheaval
10 convulsion **11** catastrophe, devastation

cataclysmic
05 awful, fatal **06** tragic **08** dreadful, terrible **10** calamitous, disastrous
11 catastrophe, devastating

catacomb
04 tomb **05** crypt, vault **07** ossuary
09 mausoleum **11** burial-vault

catalogue
03 cat **04** file, list, roll **05** guide, index, table **06** litany, ragman, record, roster
07 catelog, magalog, notitia, ragment
08 brochure, bulletin, calendar, classify, manifest, register, schedule, tabulate **09** checklist, directory, gazetteer, inventory, make a list
10 categorize, prospectus
11 alphabetize, iconography, specialogue **12** compile a list
14 classification, Durchmusterung

catapult
01 Y **04** fire, hurl, toss **05** fling, pitch, shoot, sling, throw **06** hurtle, launch, propel **07** balista, bricole **08** ballista, scorpion, shanghai **09** slingshot

cataract
03 lin **04** linn **05** falls, force, pearl
06 deluge, rapids **07** cascade, torrent
08 downpour, overfall, pearl-eye
09 floodgate, pin and web, waterfall
10 portcullis, waterspout

catastrophe
04 blow, doom, rear, ruin **06** fiasco
07 debacle, failure, reverse, tragedy, trouble **08** calamity, disaster, upheaval **09** adversity, cataclysm, mischance **10** affliction, misfortune
11 devastation

catastrophic
05 awful, fatal **06** tragic **08** dreadful, terrible **10** calamitous, disastrous
11 cataclysmic, devastating

catcall
03 boo **04** gibe, hiss, jeer, jibe
07 whistle **09** raspberry
10 barracking, Bronx cheer

catch
◇ *containment indicator*
03 bag, cop, get, kep, nab, net **04** bolt, clip, draw, fang, find, fish, grab, grip, hank, hasp, haul, hear, hold, hook, lock, make, nail, nick, pawl, rope, sear, snag, sneb, snib, tack, take, trap, twig
05 board, clasp, get it, get on, grasp, hitch, latch, phang, seize, snare, sneck, watch **06** arrest, clutch, collar, corner, detect, detent, engage, entrap, expose, fathom, follow, pick up, snatch, take in, unmask **07** attract, capture, develop, discern, ensnare, find out, make out, problem, round up, seizure, startle
08 contract, discover, drawback, fastener, holdfast, hunt down, obstacle, overtake, perceive, surprise
09 apprehend, deprehend, lay hold of, recapture, recognize, succumb to
10 comprehend, difficulty, go down with, understand **11** be in time for
12 disadvantage, get the hang of
13 become ill with, catch in the act
14 catch red-handed
See also **haul**; **song**

• **catch on**
05 grasp **06** fathom, follow, take in
10 comprehend, understand
13 become popular

• **catch up**
06 gain on **08** overtake **09** draw level

catching
◇ *containment indicator*
06 taking **10** attractive, contagious, infectious **11** captivating
12 communicable **13** transmissible, transmittable

catchphrase
05 motto **06** byword, jingle, saying, slogan, wheeze **07** formula
08 password **09** catchword, parrot-cry, watchword **10** shibboleth

catchy
07 melodic, popular, tuneful
08 haunting **09** appealing, deceptive, memorable **10** attractive
11 captivating **13** unforgettable

catechize
04 test **05** drill, grill **07** examine
08 instruct, question **11** interrogate
12 cross-examine

categorical
05 clear, total, utter **06** direct
07 express **08** absolute, definite, emphatic, explicit, positive
09 downright **10** conclusive,

unreserved **11** unequivocal, unqualified **13** unconditional

categorically
07 clearly, utterly **08** directly **09** expressly **10** absolutely, definitely, explicitly, positively **12** emphatically, unreservedly **13** unequivocally **15** unconditionally

categorization
07 listing, ranking, sorting **08** grouping, ordering **11** arrangement **14** classification

categorize
03 peg **04** list, rank, sort **05** class, grade, group, order **06** docket **07** arrange, docquet **08** classify, tabulate **09** phenotype **10** pigeonhole, stereotype

category
04 head, kind, list, rank, sort, type **05** class, genre, grade, group, order, stirp, stuff, taxon, title **06** rubric, stirps **07** bracket, chapter, heading, listing, section, variety **08** division, grouping **10** department, superclass, superorder **11** superphylum **14** classification

cater
05 serve **06** pander, supply **07** furnish, indulge, provide, satisfy, victual **09** provision

caterwaul
03 cry **04** bawl, howl, wail, yowl **05** miaow, wrawl **06** scream, shriek, squall **07** screech

catharsis
07 purging, release **09** cleansing, epuration, purifying **10** abreaction, abstersion, lustration **12** purification

cathartic
07 lustral, purging, release, scourer **09** cleansing, purgative, purifying **10** abreactive, abstersive, eccoprotic

cathedral
04 dome **05** duomo **07** minster **12** procathedral
See also **church**

Cathedrals in the UK include:

03 Ely
05 Derby, Isles, Leeds, Ripon, Truro, Wells
06 Bangor, Brecon, Dundee, Durham, Exeter, Oxford
07 Arundel, Bristol, Cardiff, Chester, Clifton, Dornoch, Glasgow, Lincoln, Newport, Norwich, Salford, St Asaph, St John's, St Mary's, St Paul's, Swansea, Wrexham
08 Aberdeen, Bradford, Carlisle, Coventry, Hereford, Llandaff, Plymouth, St Albans, St Davids
09 Blackburn, Brentwood, Edinburgh, Guildford, Inverness, Lancaster, Leicester, Lichfield, Liverpool, Newcastle, Rochester, Salisbury, Sheffield, Southwark, St Andrews, Wakefield, Worcester
10 Birmingham, Canterbury, Chelmsford, Chichester, Gloucester, Manchester, Nottingham, Portsmouth, Shrewsbury, Winchester
11 Northampton, York Minster
12 Christ Church, Peterborough
13 Middlesbrough, St Edmundsbury

Cathedrals worldwide include:

04 Lund
05 Milan
06 Aachen, Rheims
07 Cologne, Córdoba, Orvieto, St Mark's
08 Chartres, Florence, St Basil's, St Peter's
09 Notre-Dame
10 Strasbourg
11 Hagia Sophia

• **cathedral city**
03 see

catholic
01 C **02** RC **04** Tory, wide **05** broad, Latin, Roman **06** global, varied **07** diverse, general, liberal **08** eclectic, Jebusite, Romanish, Romanist, tolerant **09** inclusive, universal **10** broad-based, left-footer, open-minded, Tridentine, widespread **11** broad-minded, wide-ranging **12** all-embracing, all-inclusive **13** comprehensive **15** all-encompassing

catholicism
04 Rome **06** popery **08** Romanism

catmint
03 nep, nip **06** catnep, catnip, nepeta

cats and dogs
04 rain

cattle
02 ky **03** fee, kye **04** aver, cows, kine, kyne, neat, nout, nowt, oxen **05** bulls, stock **06** beasts, beeves **09** livestock
See also **animal**

Cattle include:

02 zo
03 dso, dzo, gir, gur, gyr, zho
04 dzho, jomo, tuli, zebu, zobo, zobu
05 Angus, black, Devon, dsobo, dsomo, Kerry, Luing, sanga, wagyu, white, zhomo
06 ankole, dexter, Durham, Jersey, Salers, Sussex, watusi
07 beefalo, brahman, brahmin, brangus, cattabu, cattalo, Latvian, red poll
08 Alderney, Ayrshire, Chianina, Friesian, Galloway, gelbvieh, Guernsey, Hereford, Highland, Holstein, illawara, Limousin, longhorn, Shetland
09 Afrikaner, braunvieh, Charolais, Corriente, Romagnola, shorthorn, Simmental, Teeswater, Ukrainian, white park
10 Africander, beefmaster, Brown Swiss, Canadienne, Charollais, Lincoln Red, Murray grey, Piemontese, Simmenthal, South Devon, Tarentaise, Welsh Black
11 Belgian Blue, Chillingham, Piedmontese
12 British White, Simmenthaler
13 Aberdeen Angus, droughtmaster, Texas longhorn
14 Belted Galloway, Santa Gertrudis

catty
03 kin **04** kati, mean **05** katti **06** bitchy **07** vicious **08** spiteful, venomous **09** malicious, rancorous **10** backbiting, ill-natured, malevolent

caucus
03 set **06** clique, parley **07** meeting, session **08** assembly, conclave **09** gathering **10** convention **11** get-together

caught
◇ *containment indicator*
01 c **02** ct **03** had **04** held **06** keight, netted **11** in by the week

cauliflower
04 gobi
• **head of cauliflower**
04 curd

causative
04 root **07** causing, factive **09** factitive

cause
03 aim, end, gar **04** call, make, root, sake **05** agent, basis, beget, begin, breed, causa, force, garre, ideal, maker, mover **06** agency, author, belief, compel, create, effect, factor, incite, induce, lead to, motive, object, origin, parent, prompt, reason, render, source, spring **07** because, creator, grounds, impulse, produce, provoke, purpose, trigger **08** generate, motivate, movement, occasion, producer, result in, stimulus **09** beginning, incentive, originate, principle, stimulate, wherefore **10** accusation, bring about, conviction, enterprise, give rise to, inducement, mainspring, make happen, motivation, originator, prime mover, trigger off **11** explanation, precipitate, undertaking **12** be the cause of **13** be at the root of, justification

caustic
04 acid, keen, tart **05** snide **06** biting, bitter, severe **07** burning, cutting, erodent, mordant, pungent **08** scathing, stinging, virulent **09** acidulent, acidulous, corroding, corrosive, sarcastic, trenchant, vitriolic **10** astringent, escharotic **11** acrimonious, destructive

caustically
08 bitterly, severely **10** scathingly, virulently **11** trenchantly **13** acrimoniously, sarcastically, vitriolically

cauterize
04 burn, fire, sear **05** singe **06** scorch **09** carbonize, disinfect, sterilize

caution
04 bail, care, heed, urge, warn **05** alert, deter, guard **06** advice, advise, cautel, caveat, surety, tip off, tip-off **07** counsel, warning **08** admonish, prudence, security, wariness **09** alertness, reprimand, vigilance **10** admonition, discretion, injunction **11** carefulness, forethought, heedfulness, mindfulness **12** deliberation, watchfulness **14** circumspection

• **lacking caution**
04 rash

cautious
04 safe, ware, wary **05** alert, cagey, chary **06** Fabian, shrewd **07** careful, guarded, heedful, prudent, tactful **08** discreet, gingerly, vigilant, watchful **09** cautelous, defensive, judicious, tentative **10** deliberate **11** circumspect **12** conservative, softly-softly **13** unadventurous

cautiously
08 gingerly **09** carefully, prudently, tactfully **10** discreetly **11** defensively, judiciously, tentatively **12** deliberately **13** circumspectly **14** conservatively

cavalcade
05 array, train, troop **06** parade **07** cortège, retinue, sowarry **08** sowarree **09** march-past, motorcade **10** procession

cavalier
04 curt **05** lofty, spahi **06** casual, escort, knight, lordly **07** gallant, haughty, offhand, partner, warlike **08** arrogant, chasseur, horseman, insolent, Ironside, royalist, scornful **09** chevalier, gentleman, Malignant **10** cavalryman, disdainful, equestrian, incautious, swaggering **11** Bashi-Bazouk, free-and-easy, patronizing **12** devil-may-care, horse soldier, supercilious **13** condescending

cavalry
05 horse **07** hussars, lancers, reiters **08** dragoons, horsemen, sabreurs, troopers **09** chasseurs, Ironsides, risaldars **10** cavalrymen, light-horse, the heavies **11** equestrians, ritt-masters **13** horse soldiers, mounted troops

cave
03 den **04** grot, hole **05** antar, antre, delve **06** beware, cavern, cavity, dugout, grotto, hollow, tunnel **07** pothole **09** Domdaniel

Caves include:

04 Zitu
06 Berger, Vqerdi
08 Badalona
09 G E S Malaga, Snezhnaya
10 Schneeloch
11 Batmanhöhle, Jean Bernard
14 Lamprechstofen, Pierre-St-Martin, Sistema Huautla

• **cave in**
04 fall, slip **05** yield **06** fall in **07** give way, subside **08** collapse

caveat
05 alarm **06** notice **07** caution, proviso, warning **10** admonition

cavern
03 den **04** cave, cove **05** vault **06** cavity, dugout, Erebus, grotto, hollow, tunnel **07** pothole **08** catacomb, vaultage

cavernous
04 dark, deep, huge, vast **05** large **06** gaping, gloomy, hollow, sunken **07** concave, echoing, immense, yawning **08** resonant, spacious **09** depressed **10** bottomless **12** unfathomable

cavil
03 nag **04** carp **06** haggle **07** censure, nit-pick, quarrel, quibble **08** complain, reproach **09** criticize **10** find faults

cavity
03 gap, pit, sac, vug **04** bore, cell, dent, hole, mine, tear, vein, well, womb **05** celom, crypt, druse, geode, lumen, purse, sinus, vitta **06** antrum, atrium, camera, coelom, concha, cotyle, crater, hollow, lacuna, pelvis, pocket **07** chamber, cochlea, coelome, eardrum, glenoid, orifice, vacuole, vesicle **08** aperture, brood-sac **09** ventricle, vestibule **10** acetabulum, blastocoel, brood-pouch, cavitation, excavation, hollowness, thunder-egg **11** conceptacle, haematocele, mediastinum, rhynchocoel **13** neuroblastoma, splanchnocele

cavort
◇ *anagram indicator*
04 romp, skip **05** caper, dance, frisk, sport **06** frolic, gambol, prance

cavy *see* **guinea pig**

Cayman Islands
03 CYM

cease
03 die, end, lin **04** blin, fail, halt, poop, quit, stay, stop, unbe **05** abate, cesse, leave, let up, stint **06** desist, devall, finish, lay off, pack in **07** poop out, refrain, suspend **08** break off, conclude, give over, leave off, peter out, surcease **09** call a halt, cessation, fizzle out, terminate **11** come to a halt, come to an end, discontinue **12** bring to a halt, bring to an end

ceaseless
07 endless, eternal, non-stop **08** constant, unending, untiring **09** continual, incessant, perpetual, unceasing **10** continuous, persistent **11** everlasting, never-ending, unremitting **12** interminable **13** uninterrupted

ceaselessly
07 for ever **09** endlessly, eternally **10** constantly, unendingly **11** day in day out, incessantly, unceasingly **12** continuously, interminably **13** everlastingly, unremittingly **14** for ever and ever **15** uninterruptedly

cedar
06 arolla, deodar **11** cryptomeria

cede
05 allow, grant, yield **06** convey, give up, resign **07** abandon, concede, deliver **08** abdicate, hand over, renounce, transfer, turn over **09** surrender **10** relinquish

ceiling
04 loft, most, roof **05** beams, limit, vault **06** awning, canopy, cupola, soffit **07** lacunar, maximum, plafond, rafters, seeling **08** overhead **09** laquearia **10** upper limit **11** cut-off point

celebrate
03 wet **04** hold, hymn, keep, laud, mark, rave, sing, tune **05** binge, bless, carol, chant, extol, go out, revel, sound, toast **06** besing, chaunt, honour, record, renown, repeat, shrove, sonnet **07** drink to, emblaze, have fun, maffick, observe, perform, poetize, rejoice, triumph, trumpet **08** emblazon, live it up, memorize, remember **09** have a ball, solemnize, whoop it up **10** have a party, procession **11** commemorate, throw a party **12** concelebrate **13** enjoy yourself, go on the razzle **14** go out on the town, push the boat out, put the flags out **15** paint the town red

celebrated
03 cel **05** famed, great, noted **06** famous **07** admired, eminent, exalted, notable, popular, revered **08** fabulous, glorious, renowned **09** acclaimed, legendary, prominent, well-known **11** illustrious, outstanding **13** distinguished

celebration
02 do **03** ale, jol **04** fete, gala, orgy, rave **05** beano, binge, feast, jolly, spree **06** hooley, junket, rave-up **07** jubilee, revelry, shindig **08** festival, jamboree, occasion, Olympiad **09** festivity, gaudeamus **10** observance **11** merrymaking **13** jollification

See also **festival**

Celebrations include:

04 fête, gala
05 feast, party
06 May Day
07 banquet, baptism, jubilee, name-day, reunion, tribute, wedding
08 birthday, festival, hen night, marriage
09 centenary, Labour Day, reception, saint's day, stag night
10 bar mitzvah, bat mitzvah, dedication, graduation, homecoming, retirement
11 anniversary, christening, coming-of-age, harvest-home
12 thanksgiving
13 commemoration
15 harvest festival, Independence Day

celebratory
06 festal

celebrity
03 VIP **04** fame, lion, name, note, star **05** celeb **06** bigwig, esteem, legend, renown, worthy **07** big name, big shot, notable, stardom **08** eminence, luminary **09** dignitary, greatness, notoriety, personage, superstar
10 notability, prominence, reputation
11 distinction, personality **12** famous person, living legend **13** household name **15** illustriousness

celerity
05 haste, speed **08** dispatch, fastness, rapidity, velocity **09** fleetness, quickness, swiftness **10** expedition, promptness

celestial
06 astral, divine, starry, uranic
07 angelic, Chinese, elysian, eternal, godlike, sublime **08** empyrean, ethereal, heavenly, immortal, seraphic, supernal
09 spiritual, unearthly **10** paradisaic, superlunar **11** superlunary, translunary
12 supernatural **14** transcendental

celestially
08 divinely **09** eternally, sublimely
10 immortally **11** angelically, spiritually
14 supernaturally

celibacy
06 purity **08** chastity **09** virginity
10 abnegation, abstinence, continence, maidenhood, self-denial, singleness **12** bachelorhood, spinsterhood **13** self-restraint

celibate
04 pure **05** unwed **06** chaste, single, virgin **08** bachelor, spinster
09 abstinent, unmarried

cell
03 set **04** coop, cyte, jail, room, unit
05 ascus, crowd, crypt, group, party, peter, spore **06** caucus, clique, lock-up, matrix, prison, zygote **07** battery, chamber, cubicle, dungeon, faction, nucleus, section **08** organism
09 anchorage, black hole, cytoplasm, enclosure, hermitage, reclusory
10 protoplasm, protoplast
11 compartment, electric eye

Cells include:

01 B, T
03 egg, PEC, red, rod, sex, wet
04 cone, fuel, germ, HeLa, mast, ovum, stem
05 blood, guard, nerve, plant, solar, sperm, water, white
06 animal, cancer, collar, diaxon, gamete, goblet, Hadley, killer, memory, mother, neuron, oocyte, plasma, target, tumour
07 cadmium, Daniell, gravity, helper T, initial, neurone, primary, Schwann, Sertoli, somatic, voltaic
08 akaryote, basophil, daughter, galvanic, gonidium, gonocyte, monocyte, myoblast, neoblast, parietal, platelet, Purkinje, red blood, retinula, sclereid, selenium, tracheid, zooblast
09 acidophil, antipodal, astrocyte, coenocyte, corpuscle, fibrocyte, haemocyte, hybridoma, idioblast, Leclanché, leucocyte, leukocyte, macrocyte, microcyte, myofibril, phagocyte, photocell, prokaryon, sclereide, secondary, spermatid, syncytium, thymocyte, tracheide
10 choanocyte, cnidoblast, enterocyte, eosinophil, fibroblast, gametocyte, hepatocyte, histiocyte, histoblast, leucoblast, leukoblast, lymphocyte, macrophage, melanocyte, myeloblast, neuroblast, neutrophil, osteoblast, osteoclast, spherocyte, suppressor, thread-cell, white blood
11 B lymphocyte, erythrocyte, granulocyte, lymphoblast, megaloblast, odontoblast, poikilocyte, thrombocyte, T lymphocyte
12 chondroblast, erythroblast, haematoblast, red corpuscle, reticulocyte, spermatocyte, spermatozoid, spermatozoon
13 chromatophore, natural killer, photoelectric, spermatoblast
14 blood corpuscle, spermatogonium, white corpuscle

• mass of cells
05 nodus **06** morula

cellar
04 vaut **05** crypt, dunny, vault, vaute
08 basement, coal hole, vaultage
09 storeroom, wine vault **10** wine cellar, wine vaults

Celtic *see* **mythology**

cement
03 fix, gum **04** bind, bond, glue, join, lime, lute, weld **05** affix, compo, grout, paste, putty, stick, trass, union, unite
06 attach, cohere, fasten, gunite, maltha, mastic, matrix, mortar, screed, slurry, solder, stucco **07** bonding, combine, mastich, plaster
08 adhesive, concrete, fixative, grouting, pointing, rice glue, solution
11 ciment fondu

cemetery
05 tombs **06** graves **08** boneyard, God's acre, urnfield **09** graveyard
10 burial site, campo santo, churchyard, necropolis **11** burial place
12 burial ground, charnel house

Cemeteries and burial places include:

07 Nunhead
08 Brompton, Highgate, Panthéon
09 Abney Park, Arlington
10 El Escorial, La Almudena, Montmartre, Mount Holly, San Michele, Weissensee
11 Kensal Green, Mount Olivet, West Norwood
12 Golders Green, Les Invalides, Montparnasse, Père Lachaise, Tower Hamlets
13 Mount of Olives
15 Island of the Dead

censor
03 ban, cut **04** Cato, edit **06** delete, editor **08** examiner, make cuts
09 expurgate, inspector **10** blue-pencil, bowdlerize, expurgater
11 bowdlerizer

censorious
06 severe **07** carping **08** captious, critical, negative **09** cavilling
10 fuddy-duddy **11** disparaging
12 condemnatory, disapproving, fault-finding, overcritical
13 hypercritical

censoriously
08 severely **10** captiously, critically
13 disparagingly **14** disapprovingly, overcritically **15** hypercritically

censure
03 rap **04** damn, Hell, slam **05** blame, chide, fault, judge, scold, strop, taunt
06 jump on, rebuke, taxing
07 appeach, condemn, obloquy, reproof, reprove, scandal, tell off, trounce, upbraid **08** admonish, denounce, reproach, scolding, sentence **09** castigate, criticism, criticize, dispraise, reprehend, reprimand, reprobate, syndicate
10 admonition, imputation, perstringe, reflection, telling-off, upbraiding
11 castigation, disapproval, remonstrate, reprobation
12 admonishment, condemnation, denunciation, disapprove of, pull to pieces, remonstrance, reprehension, vituperation **15** come down heavy on

cent
01 c **02** ct **03** red **05** penny

centimes
01 c

centipede
08 scutiger **11** scolopendra
12 scolopendrid, thousand-legs

central
◇ *hidden indicator*
◇ *middle selection indicator*
03 cen, key, mid **04** cent, core, main
05 basic, chief, focal, inner, major, prime, vital **06** centre, medial, median, middle **07** crucial, pivotal, primary
08 dominant, foremost, interior
09 essential, principal **11** fundamental, significant **13** most important

• central heating
02 ch

Central African Republic
03 CAF, RCA

Central America *see* **America**; **god, goddess**

centralization
08 focusing **11** convergence, unification **12** amalgamation, streamlining **13** concentration, consolidation, incorporation
15 rationalization

centralize
05 focus, unify **07** compact
08 condense, converge
10 amalgamate, streamline
11 concentrate, consolidate, incorporate, rationalize **13** bring together **14** gather together

centre
◇ *middle selection indicator*
03 hub, mid **04** core, crux **05** arena, focus, heart, hinge, pivot **06** kernel, middle, resort **07** nucleus, revolve
08 bull's-eye, converge, linchpin, midpoint, omphalos **09** gravitate
10 focal point, metropolis, stronghold
11 concentrate
• **in centre**
◇ *hidden indicator*

centre-forward
02 cf

centre-half
02 ch

centrepiece
04 best, peak **05** cream **06** climax
07 epergne **08** duchesse, high spot
09 highlight, high point **13** duchesse cover

century
01 c **03** age, cen, ton **04** cent
09 centenary
• **half century**
01 l

cephalopod
05 Sepia, squid **06** cuttle, loligo
07 octopus **08** ammonite, nautilus
09 goniatite, nautiloid **10** cuttlefish
13 paper nautilus **14** pearly nautilus

ceramics
04 raku, ware **06** bisque **07** faience, pottery **09** ironstone, porcelain
11 earthenware

cereal
05 grain

Cereals include:

03 oat, rye, tef, zea
04 bear, bere, corn, oats, rice, sago, teff, yuca
05 bajra, emmer, maize, spelt, wheat
06 barley, bulgur, manioc, millet
07 bulghur, cassava, mandioc, manihoc, oatmeal, sorghum, tapioca
08 amaranth, amelcorn, couscous, mandioca, semolina
09 buckwheat, mandiocca, sweetcorn, triticale
10 guinea corn, Indian corn, Kaffir corn
11 pearl millet
12 common millet
13 bulrush millet, foxtail millet, grain amaranth, Italian millet

Breakfast cereals include:

04 bran
05 Alpen®
06 muesli
07 All Bran®, granola
08 Cheerios®, Coco Pops®, Frosties®, porridge, Ricicles®, Special K®, Weetabix®
09 Ready Brek®, Shreddies®
10 Bran Flakes®, cornflakes, Quaker Oats®, Sugar Puffs®
11 Fruit'n'Fibre®, Puffed Wheat®, Sultana Bran®
12 Country Crisp®, Rice Krispies®
13 Fruit and Fibre®, Golden Grahams®, Honey Nut Loops®, Shredded Wheat®

ceremonial
04 rite **05** state **06** custom, formal, ritual, solemn **07** mummery, stately
08 ceremony, official, protocol
09 dignified, formality, solemnity
11 ritualistic

ceremonially
08 formally, ritually, solemnly
10 officially

ceremonious
05 civil, exact, grand, stiff **06** formal, polite, ritual, solemn **07** courtly, precise, starchy, stately **08** imposing, majestic, official **09** courteous, dignified **10** scrupulous **11** deferential, punctilious

ceremoniously
07 civilly, exactly, grandly, stiffly
08 formally, politely, solemnly
09 precisely, starchily **10** officially
11 courteously **12** scrupulously
13 deferentially, punctiliously
15 ritualistically

ceremony
04 form, gaud, pomp, rite, show
05 order **06** custom, parade, ritual
07 decorum, liturgy, service
08 exercise, festival, function, niceties, occasion, protocol **09** etiquette, formality, induction, ordinance, pageantry, propriety, punctilio, sacrament, solemnity, tradition, unveiling **10** ceremonial, coronation, dedication, graduation, initiation, observance **11** anniversary, celebration, investiture
12 circumstance, commencement, inauguration **13** commemoration, spit and polish

Ceremonies include:

05 amrit, doseh, tangi
06 maundy, nipter
07 baptism, capping, chanoyu, chuppah, matsuri, wedding
08 marriage, nuptials
09 committal, matrimony
10 bar mitzvah, bat mitzvah, corroboree, graduation, initiation
11 christening, fire-walking
12 confirmation

• **funeral ceremonies**
04 obit

Ceres
07 Demeter

cerium
02 Ce

certain
04 safe, some, sure, true **05** bound, clear, fated, fixed, plain, small
06 doomed, siccar, sicker **07** assured, dead set, decided, evident, express, limited, obvious, partial, perfect, precise, regular, settled, special
08 absolute, definite, destined, in the bag, positive, reliable, resolved, specific **09** confident, convinced, indubious, persuaded, undoubted, unfailing **10** conclusive, convincing, dependable, determined, home and dry, individual, inevitable, inexorable, particular, undeniable **11** cut and dried, established, indubitable, ineluctable, inescapable, irrefutable, open-and-shut, unavoidable
12 indisputable, no ifs and buts
13 bound to happen, meant to happen
14 unquestionable
• **a certain**
03 one **04** some
• **make certain**
06 ensure

certainly
02 OK **03** oke, yes **04** iwis, okay, sure, ywis **06** and how!, certes, siccar, sicker, surely, you bet **07** clearly, for sure, no doubt, plainly **08** forsooth, of course, to be sure **09** assuredly, doubtless, naturally, obviously, sure thing **10** absolutely, by all means, definitely, in very deed, positively, undeniably **11** beyond doubt, doubtlessly, if you please, indubitably, past dispute, undoubtedly **12** as sure as a gun, bang to rights, questionless, without doubt **13** beyond dispute, without a doubt **14** beyond question, unquestionably, without dispute **15** in all conscience

certainty
03 nap **04** cert, fact, lock, snip
05 cinch, faith, moral, trust, truth
06 banker, surety **07** natural, reality, safe bet **08** dead cert, security, sureness, validity **09** assurance, constancy, sure thing **10** confidence, conviction, positivism **11** assuredness
12 positiveness **13** inevitability
14 matter of course

certificate
04 pass **05** award, lines, proof, scrip, title **06** cocket, docket, patent, ticket
07 diploma, licence, voucher, warrant
08 aegrotat, document, navicert, register, testamur **09** clearance, debenture, guarantee, land-scrip
10 securities **11** credentials, endorsement, smart-ticket, testimonial
12 bill of health, Tyburn-ticket
13 authorization, certificatory, marriage-lines, qualification

certify
04 aver **05** vouch **06** assure, attest, inform, ratify, verify **07** confirm, declare, endorse, license, testify, warrant, witness **08** accredit, validate
09 authorize, guarantee, pronounce, recognize **11** corroborate

12 authenticate, substantiate 13 bear witness to

certitude
08 sureness 09 assurance, certainty 10 confidence, conviction, plerophory 11 assuredness, plerophoria 12 positiveness 13 full assurance

cessation
02 ho 03 end, hoa, hoh 04 blin, halt, rest, stay, stop 05 break, cease, let-up, pause, stint 06 ending, hiatus, recess 07 ceasing, failure, halting, respite 08 abeyance, breakoff, interval, stoppage, stopping, surcease, suspense 09 remission 10 conclusion, desistance, standstill, suspension 11 termination 12 intermission, interruption 13 discontinuing 14 discontinuance 15 discontinuation

Chad
03 TCD, TCH

chafe
03 rub, vex 04 bind, fret, rasp, wear 05 anger, annoy, grate, peeve 06 abrade, chaufe, chauff, enrage, scrape 07 be angry, incense, inflame, provoke, scratch 08 irritate, wear away, wear down 09 excoriate 10 exasperate

chaff
03 kid, rag, rib, rot 04 chip, jest, joke, josh, mock, pods 05 cases, husks, tease 06 banter, have-on, joking, shells 07 jesting, kidding, ribbing, rubbish, teasing 08 badinage, repartee 09 make fun of

chagrin
03 irk, vex 05 annoy, peeve, shame 07 mortify 08 disquiet, irritate, shagreen, vexation, wormwood 09 annoyance, displease, embarrass, humiliate 10 disappoint, dissatisfy, exasperate, irritation 11 displeasure, fretfulness, humiliation, indignation 12 discomfiture, discomposure, exasperation 13 embarrassment, mortification 14 disappointment 15 dissatisfaction

chain
02 ch 03 row, set, tie 04 bind, bond, boom, curb, firm, line, link, rode, seal, team 05 group, guard, hitch, range, slang, train, union 06 albert, catena, fasten, fetter, secure, series, string, tether, traces 07 company, confine, creeper, enslave, manacle, measure, shackle, trammel 08 coupling, handcuff, restrain, sequence 09 fanfarona, restraint 10 succession, watchguard 11 progression 13 concatenation

chair
02 MC 04 lead, seat 05 emcee 06 direct 07 convene, speaker 08 chairman, convenor, director, moderate 09 organizer, president, supervise 10 chairwoman 11 chairperson, preside over, toastmaster 13 act as chairman, professorship 15 act as chairwoman

Chairs include:

03 arm, lug, pew
04 Bath, camp, cane, deck, easy, form, high, push, wing
05 bench, elbow, king's, night, potty, sedan, stool, wheel
06 basket, carver, curule, dining, estate, jampan, Morris, pouffe, rocker, sag bag, sledge, swivel, throne, wicker
07 beanbag, Berbice, bergère, commode, guérite, kitchen, lounger, nursing, rocking, Windsor
08 captain's, electric, fauteuil, prie-dieu, recliner, wainscot
09 director's
10 boatswain's, fiddle-back, frithstool, ladder-back
11 Cromwellian, gestatorial
12 ducking-stool

See also **seat**

chairman, chairwoman
02 MC 03 Chm 04 chmn, prof 05 emcee 06 preses 07 praeses 08 convenor, director 09 organizer, president, professor, spokesman 10 prolocutor 11 chairperson, spokeswoman 12 spokesperson

chalcedony
04 sard 05 agate 06 plasma 07 sardius 09 hornstone, moss agate 10 bloodstone 11 chrysoprase

chalk
• chalk up
03 log 04 gain 05 score, tally 06 attain, charge, credit, record 07 achieve, ascribe, put down 08 register 09 attribute 10 accumulate

chalky
03 wan 04 pale 05 ashen, dusty, white 06 ground, pallid 07 crushed, powdery 10 calcareous, colourless, cretaceous, granulated

challenge
03 hen, tax, try, vie 04 call, dare, defy, gage, risk, test 05 assay, brave, claim, demur, query, stand, stump, trial 06 accost, accuse, appeal, cartel, charge, hazard, henner, hurdle, invite, strain, summon, tackle, why-not 07 bidding, darrain, darrayn, deraign, dispute, problem, protest, provoke, stretch, summons 08 champion, confront, darraign, darraine, defiance, object to, obstacle, question 09 darraigne, objection, stimulate, ultimatum 10 accusation, opposition 11 opportunity, provocation, questioning 12 disagreement, disagree with 13 confrontation, interrogation 14 call in question 15 take exception to

challenging
06 gnarly, taxing 07 testing 08 exacting, exciting 09 demanding 10 stretching

chamber
02 po 03 pot 04 hall, room, silo 05 divan, fogou, house, jerry, potty, vault 06 camera, cavern, cavity, chanty, durbar, hollow, jordan, serdab, urinal 07 bedroom, boudoir, confine, council 08 assembly, casemate, gazunder, hypogeum, moot-hall, thalamus 09 apartment, combustor, hypogaeum, mattamore, stokehold, ventricle 10 auditorium, close-stool, parliament, souterrain, subterrain, subterrane, thunderbox 11 compartment, legislature 12 assembly room, meeting-place

See also **room**

champagne
03 fiz, pop 04 fizz 06 bubbly, simkin 07 Sillery, simpkin 08 champers, the Widow 10 gooseberry

See also **wine**

champion
02 Ch 03 ace, Cid, gun 04 back, hero, kemp 05 angel, champ, ozeki 06 backer, defend, expert, kemper, knight, patron, uphold, victor, winner 07 apostle, espouse, messiah, promote, protect, saviour, support, tribune 08 advocate, asserter, assertor, defender, douzeper, guardian, maintain, Palmerin, stand for, upholder, yokozuna 09 campeador, challenge, conqueror, deliverer, doucepere, excellent, promachos, proponent, protector, supporter 10 kemperyman, stand up for, vindicator 11 excellently, protagonist, title-holder 13 hold a brief for

See also **seven**

chance
03 hap, run, try 04 cast, fate, luck, odds, risk, show, time 05 arise, break, essay, fluke, occur, stake, wager 06 crop up, fair go, flukey, follow, gamble, happen, hazard, random, result, strike, upcast 07 destiny, develop, fortune, opening, venture 08 accident, Buckley's, fortuity, occasion, prospect 09 arbitrary, come about, haphazard, speculate, take place 10 likelihood, play a hunch, providence 11 bet your life, coincidence, contingency, opportunity, possibility, probability, serendipity, speculation, take a chance 12 bet your boots, happenstance, push your luck, your best shot 14 Buckley's chance, chance your luck
• by chance
07 happily 08 bechance, randomly 09 by mistake 10 by accident 11 haphazardly, unwittingly 12 accidentally, fortuitously, incidentally, peradventure, unexpectedly 13 inadvertently 14 adventitiously 15 serendipitously, unintentionally
• chance on, chance upon
04 meet 06 casual, flukey, random 07 run into 08 bump into, discover 09 arbitrary, haphazard, run across, stumble on 10 accidental, come across, fortuitous, incidental,

unexpected, unforeseen, unintended **11** inadvertent, unlooked-for **12** find by chance **13** serendipitous, unanticipated, unintentional

• **decision by chance**

03 lot **04** draw **07** lottery

Chancellor of the Exchequer

02 CE

chancy

04 safe **05** dicey, dodgy, lucky, risky **06** tricky **07** fraught **09** dangerous, hazardous, uncertain **11** speculative **13** problematical, unpredictable

chandelier

06 corona, lustre **09** girandola, girandole **11** corona lucis, electrolier

change

◇ *anagram indicator*

02 go **03** mew **04** cash, chop, move, pass, peal, swap, turn, vary **05** adapt, alter, amend, coins, renew, shift, trade, trend, U-turn, waver **06** adjust, barter, become, evolve, modify, mutate, reform, revise, rotate, silver, switch **07** commute, connect, convert, coppers, develop, novelty, remodel, renewal, replace, shake-up, variate, variety **08** do a U-turn, exchange, movement, mutation, reversal, revision, rotation, transfer, upheaval **09** about-face, about-turn, alternate, amendment, customize, diversion, evolution, fluctuate, transform, transpose, turnabout, vacillate, variation, volte-face **10** adaptation, adjustment, alteration, conversion, difference, ebb and flow, innovation, reorganize, revolution, substitute, transition **11** alternation, development, fluctuation, interchange, remodelling, replacement, restructure, state of flux, transfigure, transmutate, vacillation, vicissitude **12** metamorphose, modification, substitution **13** chop and change, customization, make different, metamorphosis, restructuring, transmutation, transposition **14** reconstruction, reorganization, transformation **15** become different, make a connection, transfiguration

changeable

◇ *anagram indicator*

05 fluid, windy **06** fickle, labile, mobile, wankle, whimsy **07** erratic, flighty, movable, mutable, Protean, various, varying, voluble, whimsey **08** moveable, shifting, skittish, unstable, unsteady, variable, volatile, wavering **09** changeful, irregular, mercurial, uncertain, unsettled, versatile **10** capricious, inconstant, unreliable **11** chameleonic, fluctuating, vacillating **12** inconsistent **13** chameleon-like, kaleidoscopic, unpredictable **15** vicissitudinous

changeless

05 final, fixed **06** static **07** eternal **08** constant, timeless **09** immutable, permanent **10** invariable, unchanging **11** unalterable **12** unchangeable

changeling

03 auf, oaf **08** elf-child, killcrop

channel

02 ea **03** bed, eau, gut, sny, sow, use, way **04** duct, feed, gate, kill, lake, lane, lead, main, neck, path, race, send, snye, sure, tube **05** agent, canal, chime, ditch, drain, falaj, flume, focus, force, glyph, guide, gully, latch, letch, level, major, means, radio, rigol, route, sewer, sloot, sluit, sound, stank, trunk **06** agency, airway, artery, avenue, convey, course, cut-off, direct, furrow, gravel, groove, grough, gullet, gulley, gutter, hollow, limber, medium, narrow, rigoll, sheuch, siphon, sluice, strait, trench, trough **07** chamfer, conduct, conduit, culvert, fairway, limbers, narrows, offtake, passage, raceway, shingle, station, wireway **08** approach, aqueduct, headrace, millrace, overflow, tailrace, transmit, wash-away, waterway **11** canaliculus, concentrate, katabothron, katavothron, spill-stream, watercourse

Channels include:

03 Kii
04 Foxe
05 Bashi, Bungo, Kaiwi, Kauai, Lamma, Minas, Minch, North
06 Akashi, Kalohi, Manche, Queens
07 Babuyan, Bristol, English, Jamaica, Massawa, Pailolo, Sandwip, St Lucia, Yucatán
08 Dominica, La Manche, Nicholas, Santaren, Sicilian, St Andrew, The Minch
09 Balintang, Capricorn, East Lamma, Geographe, Kaulakahi, Northwest, Old Bahama, Skagerrak, St George's, West Lamma
10 Alalakeiki, Alenuihaha, McClintock, Mozambique, North Minch
11 Little Minch
12 Kealaikahiki, Santa Barbara

See also **television**

• **Channel Islands**

02 CI

The Channel Islands:

04 Herm, Sark
06 Jersey, Jethou
07 Brechou
08 Alderney, Guernsey
10 the Caskets
11 the Chauseys
12 the Minquiers

chant

03 cry **04** haka, sing, song, yo-ho **05** ditty, psalm, shout **06** cantus, chorus, incant, intone, mantra, melody, recite, slogan, warcry, yo-ho-ho **07** refrain **09** decantate, plainsong, yo-heave-ho **10** cantillate, intonation, recitation **11** Hare Krishna, incantation

chaos

◇ *anagram indicator*

04 mess, muss, riot **05** abyss, havoc, musse, snafu **06** bedlam, mayhem, tumult, uproar **07** anarchy **08** disarray, disorder, madhouse, shambles, tohu bohu, upheaval **09** confusion **10** disruption, dog's dinner **11** lawlessness, pandemonium **13** pig's breakfast **14** Rafferty's rules **15** disorganization

chaotic

◇ *anagram indicator*

05 snafu **06** unruly **07** lawless, riotous **08** anarchic, confused, deranged **09** disrupted, orderless, shambolic **10** disordered, disorderly, topsy-turvy, tumultuary, tumultuous **12** disorganized, uncontrolled **14** all over the shop **15** all over the place

chap

03 boy, cat, cod, guy, jaw, man, mun, oik, sod **04** boyo, chop, cove, hack, sort, type **05** bloke, bucko, cheek, crack, knock, spray **06** codger, fellow, Johnny, shaver, strike **07** bastard, Johnnie, spreaze, spreeze **08** spreathe, spreethe **09** character **10** individual, male person

chapel

05 crypt **06** Beulah **07** chantry, galilee, martyry, oratory **08** chauntry, feretory, parabema, sacellum **09** bead-house, prothesis **13** Nonconformist **15** chapelle ardente

chaperon, chaperone

04 mind **05** guard **06** attend, duenna, escort **07** protect **08** sheepdog, shepherd **09** accompany, companion, look after, matronize, safeguard, watch over **10** take care of

chapped

03 raw **04** sore **06** chafed **07** cracked, sprayed

chapter

01 c **02** ch **03** cap **04** chap, part, sura, time **05** caput, phase, stage, surah, topic **06** branch, clause, period **07** capital, episode, portion, section **08** division **10** department

char

02 do **03** tea **04** burn, coal, sear **05** brown, singe, togue, woman **06** Mrs Mop, scorch **07** blacken, Mrs Mopp, torgoch **08** redbelly, saibling **09** carbonize, cauterize **10** accomplish, brook trout **11** Dolly Varden

character

04 aura, card, case, hair, logo, mark, part, role, rune, sign, sort, tone, type **05** charm, ethos, image, stamp, style, trait, write **06** appeal, cipher, device, emblem, figure, honour, letter, make-up, nature, oddity, person, psyche, status, symbol, temper **07** calibre, courage, engrave, essence, feature, honesty, imprint, oddball, persona, quality **08** backbone, describe, identity, interest, original, position, property, strength **09** delineate, eccentric, ideograph, integrity, reference, represent **10** attributes, hieroglyph, human being, individual, moral fibre, reputation **11** disposition, peculiarity, personality, specialness, temperament, uprightness **12** constitution **13** determination, individuality **14** attractiveness **15** characteristics, eccentric person

See also **alphabet**; **Bible**; **cartoon**; **fairy tale**; **legend**; **letter**; **literary**; **mythology**; **opera**; **pantomine**; **Shakespeare**

• character part
04 role

• characters in
◇ *hidden indicator*

• proper character
03 him

characteristic
04 mark, note **05** point, right, trait **06** factor **07** feature, quality, special, symptom, typical **08** hallmark, peculiar, property, specific, symbolic **09** attribute, mannerism, trademark **10** individual **11** distinctive, peculiarity, symptomatic **12** idiosyncrasy **13** idiosyncratic **14** discriminative, distinguishing, representative

characteristically
09 typically **10** peculiarly **12** individually **13** distinctively

characterization
09 depiction, portrayal **11** description **12** presentation **14** representation

characterize
04 mark **05** brand, stamp **06** depict, typify **07** portray, present, qualify, specify **08** describe, identify, indicate **09** designate, represent **10** stereotype **11** distinguish

• be characterized by
04 have

characterless
05 inane **12** invertebrate

charade
04 fake, sham **05** farce **06** parody, riddle **07** mockery **08** pretence, travesty **09** pantomime

charge
01 Q **03** ask, chg, due, fee, ion, rap, tax **04** bill, care, cost, debt, dues, duty, fill, levy, load, mine, rate, rent, rush, shot, tear, tilt, toll, ward **05** blame, debit, exact, imbue, onset, order, price, prime, storm, terms, trust **06** accuse, affect, amount, ask for, assail, attack, burden, demand, dittay, impose, impute, indict, infuse, onrush, outlay, rental, sortie, tariff, thrill **07** arraign, assault, command, custody, expense, impeach, keeping, mandate, payment, pervade, suffuse **08** godchild, saturate, storming **09** challenge, fix a price, inculpate, incursion, offensive, onslaught, overwhelm, put down to, set a price **10** accusation, accusement, allegation, imputation, indictment, objuration, obligation, protection **11** arraignment, expenditure, impeachment, incriminate, rush forward, safekeeping **12** guardianship **13** incrimination **14** responsibility **15** ask someone to pay, demand in payment

See also **heraldry**

• clear of charges
03 net **04** nett

• in charge of
02 i/c **07** leading **08** managing **09** directing, heading up **10** overseeing **11** controlling, supervising **12** looking after, taking care of **14** responsible for

charged
04 live **08** instinct

chariot
03 car **04** biga, rath, wain **05** ratha, wagon **06** charet, vimana, waggon **08** quadriga

charioteer
03 Hur **04** Jehu **06** Ben-Hur **07** wagoner **08** waggoner

charisma
04 draw, lure, pull **05** charm **06** allure, appeal **09** magnetism **10** attraction **12** drawing-power

charismatic
08 charming, magnetic **09** appealing, glamorous **10** attractive **11** captivating, fascinating **12** irresistible

charitable
04 kind **06** benign, kindly **07** lenient, liberal **08** generous, gracious, tolerant **09** bounteous, forgiving, indulgent **10** beneficent, benevolent, open-handed **11** broad-minded, considerate, magnanimous, sympathetic **12** eleemosynary, humanitarian **13** compassionate, philanthropic, understanding

• charitable person
04 Lion

charitably
06 kindly **09** liberally **10** generously, graciously, tolerantly **11** bounteously **12** open-mindedly **13** considerately **15** compassionately, sympathetically

charity
03 aid **04** alms, fund, gift, love **05** trust **06** relief **07** caritas, concern, funding, handout, mission **08** altruism, clemency, donation, goodness, goodwill, hospital, humanity, kindness, leniency, sympathy **09** affection, tolerance **10** almsgiving, assistance, benignness, compassion, foundation, generosity, indulgence **11** beneficence, benevolence, institution, munificence **12** contribution, graciousness, philanthropy **13** bountifulness, confraternity, consideration, unselfishness **14** thoughtfulness **15** considerateness, kind-heartedness

Charities include:

03 DEC, NCH
04 PDSA, RNIB, RNLI, RSPB, WRVS
05 CAFOD, NSPCC, Oxfam, RSPCA, Scope
09 ActionAid, Barnardo's
10 Greenpeace
11 Comic Relief, Help the Aged
12 Christian Aid
13 National Trust, Wellcome Trust, Woodland Trust
15 Leonard Cheshire, Save the Children, St John Ambulance

Charity fundraising events include:

06 fun run, raffle
08 telethon
09 radiothon, swimathon
10 jumble sale
12 slave auction
13 coffee morning, sponsored swim, sponsored walk
14 charity auction
15 bring-and-buy sale

charlatan
04 fake, sham **05** cheat, fraud, quack **06** con man, phoney **08** impostor, swindler **09** pretender, trickster **10** confidence, mountebank **11** bogus caller, illywhacker **13** bogus official

charlie
01 C

See also **fool**

charm
02 it **03** obi, win **04** draw, idol, ju-ju, mojo, obia, take, tiki **05** aroma, magic, obeah, spell, weird **06** allure, amulet, appeal, cajole, enamor, fetish, glamor, grigri, mascot, please, seduce **07** abraxas, attract, becharm, beguile, bewitch, delight, enamour, enchant, encharm, glamour, hei tiki, periapt, sorcery, trinket, windbag **08** comether, greegree, grisgris, intrigue, medicine, nephrite, ornament, prestige, talisman **09** captivate, cramp-bone, enrapture, fascinate, magnetism, mesmerize **10** allurement, attraction, night-spell, phylactery **11** abracadabra, captivation, enchantment, fascination, hand of glory, what it takes **12** desirability, porte-bonheur **14** attractiveness, delightfulness

charming
04 cute, nice **05** elfin, sweet **06** lovely, pretty, quaint, smooth **07** winning, winsome **08** adorable, alluring, engaging, fetching, pleasant, pleasing, tasteful, tempting **09** appealing, disarming, glamorous, seductive **10** attractive, bewitching, delectable, delightful, enchanting, entrancing **11** captivating, fascinating **12** chocolate-box, irresistible

charmingly
07 sweetly **09** winsomely **10** alluringly, delectably, pleasantly, pleasingly **11** glamorously **12** attractively, delightfully, enchantingly, irresistibly

chart
02 ch **03** map **04** abac, draw, list, mark, note, plan, plot **05** draft, graph,

place, table **06** follow, league, map out, record, sketch **07** diagram, monitor, observe, outline, sea card **08** bar chart, document, isopleth, nomogram, pie chart, register **09** blueprint, delineate, flow chart, flow sheet, hit parade, modulator, nomograph, sociogram, top twenty **10** hyetograph, organogram **11** put on record **13** keep a record of

charter
04 bond, deed, hire, rent **05** carta, grant, lease, right **06** charta, employ, engage, patent, permit **07** licence, license, warrant **08** contract, covenant, document, sanction **09** allowance, authority, authorize, franchise, indenture, novodamus, privilege **10** commission, concession **11** prerogative **13** accreditation, authorization

chary
03 shy **04** cagy, slow, wary **05** cagey, leery **06** tender, uneasy **07** careful, guarded, heedful, prudent **08** cautious, precious **09** reluctant, unwilling **10** fastidious, suspicious **11** circumspect

chase
◇ *juxtaposition indicator*
03 sic **04** fall, hunt, rush, seek, sick, tail **05** chevy, chivy, drive, expel, hound, hurry, track, trail **06** chivvy, course, follow, groove, pursue, quarry, scorse, shadow **07** engrave, hot-trod, hunting, pursuit **08** coursing, run after, send away **09** give chase, prosecute **12** running after **13** hare and hounds

chasm
03 gap **04** gape, gulf, rift, void, yawn **05** abyss, cleft, crack, gorge, split **06** breach, canyon, cavity, crater, hollow, ravine **07** divorce, fissure, opening, quarrel **08** crevasse **10** alienation, separation **12** disagreement, estrangement

chassis
05 frame **08** bodywork, fuselage, skeleton **09** framework, structure **12** substructure **13** undercarriage

chaste
03 ren, rin, run **04** bare, pure, sick **05** moral, plain, worry **06** decent, demure, graced, honest, modest, scorse, simple, single, vestal **07** austere, classic **08** celibate, innocent, virginal, virtuous **09** abstinent, continent, unadorned, undefiled, unmarried, unsullied **10** immaculate, restrained **13** unembellished

chasten
04 curb, tame **06** humble, punish, purify, refine, soften, subdue, temper **07** correct, repress, reprove **08** chastise, moderate, restrain **09** castigate, humiliate **10** discipline

chastise
03 fix **04** beat, cane, flog, lash, whip **05** scold, smack, spank, strap **06** berate, disple, punish, purify, refine, reform, swinge, wallop **07** censure, correct, reprove, scourge, upbraid **08** admonish, moderate, restrain **09** castigate, dress down, reprimand **10** discipline, take to task

chastisement
07 beating, censure, what for **08** flogging, scolding, smacking, spanking, whipping **09** walloping **10** admonition, correction, discipline, punishment **11** castigation **12** dressing-down

chastity
05 honor **06** honour, purity, virtue **07** honesty, modesty **08** celibacy **09** innocence, virginity **10** abstinence, continence, continency, maidenhood, moderation, singleness **13** temperateness **14** immaculateness, unmarried state

chat
03 gas, jaw, rap **04** coze, talk **05** crack, louse, visit, wongi **06** babble, confab, cosher, gossip, jabber, natter, rabbit, waffle, yabber **07** blather, blether, chatter, chinwag, prattle, schmooz, shmoose, shmooze **08** causerie, chitchat, converse, cosy chat, rabbit on, schmooze **09** small talk, tête-à-tête **10** chew the fat, chew the rag **11** confabulate **12** conversation, heart-to-heart, tittle-tattle **13** confabulation **14** clash-ma-clavers, shoot the breeze

• chat up
03 eye **04** ogle **06** leer at **08** come on to **09** flirt with **11** make a pass at **14** make advances to **15** try to get off with

chatter
03 gab, gas, jaw, mag, yap **04** chat, talk **05** clack, clash, froth, skite **06** babble, cackle, confab, gabble, gammon, gossip, jabber, jargon, natter, patter, rabbit, rattle, tattle, waffle, witter, yatter **07** blether, chinwag, chitter, chunder, chunner, chunter, clatter, earbash, gabnash, nashgab, palaver, prattle, twattle **08** chitchat, chounter, rabbit on, rattle on **09** tête-à-tête **10** talky-talky, tongue-work **12** conversation, gibble-gabble, talkee-talkee, tittle-tattle, yada yada yada **14** clitter-clatter **15** yadda yadda yadda

chatterbox
06 gabber, gasbag, gasser, gossip, talker **07** babbler, gabnash, tattler, windbag **08** big mouth, jabberer, natterer **09** chatterer, gossipper, loudmouth **12** blabbermouth **13** tittle-tattler **14** telephone kiosk

chatterer
03 pie **06** chewet, gabber, tatler **07** gabnash, nashgab, tattler

chatty
04 glib **05** dirty, gabby, lousy, newsy **06** casual, mouthy **07** gossipy, gushing, verbose **08** effusive, familiar, friendly, informal **09** garrulous, talkative **10** colloquial, long-winded, loquacious **13** communicative **14** conversational

chauvinism
04 bias **06** sexism **08** jingoism **09** prejudice **10** flag-waving **11** nationalism **12** partisanship **14** male chauvinism

chauvinist
03 MCP **05** jingo **06** biased, sexist **08** jingoist **10** flag-waving, prejudiced **11** nationalist **14** male chauvinist

chauvinistic
06 biased, sexist **10** jingoistic, prejudiced **13** nationalistic

cheap
03 low **04** mean, poor, sale **05** a snip, tacky, tatty **06** a steal, budget, cheapo, chintz, common, jitney, paltry, shoddy, sordid, tawdry, two-bit, vulgar **07** bargain, chintzy, economy, low-cost, reduced, slashed **08** a good buy, cut-price, dog-cheap, giveaway, inferior, low-price, no-frills, sixpenny, twopenny **09** bon marché, cheapjack, cheap-rate, dirt-cheap, good-cheap, knock-down, rinky-dink, tasteless, ten a penny, throwaway, worthless **10** à bon marché, affordable, despicable, discounted, economical, improvised, marked-down, ramshackle, reasonable, rock-bottom, second-rate **11** a dime a dozen, gingerbread, inexpensive, reduced-rate **12** contemptible **13** cheap and nasty, going for a song, on a shoestring, value-for-money **14** on special offer **15** bargain-basement

cheapen
05 lower **06** demean **07** degrade, devalue **08** belittle, derogate **09** denigrate, discredit, disparage, downgrade **10** depreciate

cheaply
09 at low cost, bon marché **10** à bon marché, affordably, reasonably **12** at a cheap rate, economically, with no frills **13** inexpensively **14** at a reduced rate, on special offer

cheat
02 do **03** bam, bob, cog, con, fix, fob, fox, gum, gyp, jew, rig **04** bilk, chiz, clip, colt, deny, dupe, fake, fool, gull, have, jink, mump, slur, snap, swiz, take, trim **05** biter, bluff, check, chess, chizz, cozen, crook, cully, dingo, fraud, fudge, hocus, queer, rogue, screw, shark, stiff, sting, touch, trick, welsh **06** baffle, begunk, cajole, chisel, chouse, con man, diddle, dodger, do down, fiddle, fleece, intake, rip off, smouch, take in, thwart **07** beguile, cheater, cozener, deceive, defraud, deprive, escheat, forfeit, gudgeon, mislead, prevent, sharper, skelder, swindle, swizzle, twister, two-time **08** deceiver, hoodwink, impostor, picaroon, swindler **09** bamboozle, charlatan,

chiseller, cony-catch, deception, duckshove, frustrate, trickster, victimize **10** do a flanker **11** cony-catcher, do one over on, double-cross, extortioner, gull-catcher, hornswoggle, short-change **12** do the dirty on, take for a ride **13** double-crosser

check
02 ch **03** bar, nip, tab **04** balk, bill, curb, damp, foil, halt, rein, scan, slow, sneb, snub, stem, stop, test, tick **05** audit, baulk, crush, delay, limit, pinch, probe, punch, sneap, study, stunt, tally, token **06** arrest, blight, bridle, coupon, hinder, impede, look at, police, rebuff, rebuke, rein in, retard, screen, tartan, thwart, ticket, verify **07** account, analyse, charges, check-up, compare, confirm, contain, control, examine, inhibit, inquiry, inspect, invoice, monitor, repress, repulse, setback, shorten, staunch **08** analysis, holdback, make sure, obstruct, once-over, research, restrain, scrutiny, slow down, suppress, validate **09** going-over, go through, reckoning, reprimand, restraint, statement, take stock **10** cross-check, inspection, monitoring, scrutinize **11** corroborate, counterfoil, examination, inquire into, investigate **12** confirmation, substantiate, verification **13** investigation, look at closely **15** give the once-over

• check in
05 enrol **06** book in **08** register

• check out
04 case, test **05** leave, recce, study **06** depart **07** examine, inspect **08** look into, settle up **10** pay the bill **11** investigate

• check up
04 test **05** probe **06** assess, verify **07** analyse, confirm, examine, inspect **08** evaluate, make sure **09** ascertain **11** inquire into, investigate

• hold in check, keep in check
04 curb, stop **06** arrest, bridle, hinder, impede, rein in **07** control, prevent, repress **08** hold back, keep back, obstruct, restrain, suppress

check-up
04 test **05** audit, probe **07** inquiry **08** analysis, research, scrutiny **09** appraisal **10** evaluation, inspection, monitoring **11** examination **12** confirmation, verification **13** investigation

cheek
03 jaw, lip **04** chap, chop, gall, gena, jole, joll, jowl, neck, sass, wang **05** chaft, mouth, nerve, sauce **06** chafts, dimple **08** attitude, audacity, chutzpah, temerity **09** brass neck, impudence, insolence **10** brazenness, disrespect, effrontery **12** impertinence

cheekily
06 pertly **10** impudently, insolently **13** impertinently **15** disrespectfully

cheeky
04 pert, rude **05** fresh, lippy, sassy, saucy **06** brazen, mouthy **07** forward **08** impudent, insolent **09** audacious **11** impertinent **12** overfamiliar **13** disrespectful

cheep
04 peep, pipe, sing **05** chirp, trill, tweet **06** warble **07** chirrup, twitter, whistle

cheer
03 hip, joy, olé, rah **04** buck, buoy, clap, face, fare, food, glad, hail, hoop, warm, yell **05** bravo, elate, shout, whoop **06** buck up, buoy up, cherry, hurrah, perk up, salute, solace, spirit, uplift **07** acclaim, applaud, comfort, console, enliven, fanfare, gladden, hearten, ovation, revelry, root for, support, welcome **08** applause, brighten, clapping, gladness, inspirit, plaudits, semblant **09** celebrate, encourage, enhearten, happiness, merriment **10** barrack for, exhilarate, joyfulness **11** acclamation, high spirits, hopefulness, merrymaking **12** cheerfulness **13** entertainment

• cheer up
05 liven, rally **06** buck up, perk up **07** chirrup, comfort, console, hearten, liven up **08** brighten **09** encourage, take heart **10** brighten up

• be cheered
04 rise

cheerful
03 gay **04** glad, joco, warm **05** bonny, cadgy, canty, happy, jolly, light, merry, riant, sunny **06** blithe, bonnie, breezy, bright, bubbly, cheery, chirpy, genial, hearty, jaunty, jocund, jovial, joyful, joyous, kidgie, lively, smiley, upbeat **07** buoyant, chipper, holiday, smiling, winsome **08** animated, carefree, chirrupy, eupeptic, laughing, pleasant, pleasing, spirited, stirring **09** agreeable, contented, exuberant, inspiring, lightsome, sparkling **10** attractive, comforting, delightful, heartening, optimistic **11** encouraging **12** enthusiastic, good-humoured, high-spirited, light-hearted **13** in good spirits

cheerily
06 gladly **07** happily **08** brightly, jovially **10** cheerfully **14** light-heartedly

cheerio
03 bye **04** ta-ta **05** adieu **06** bye-bye, cheers, hooray, hooroo, see you, so long **07** goodbye, haere ra **08** au revoir, farewell **11** see you later

See also **farewell**

cheerless
03 sad **04** cold, dank, dark, dead, drab, dull, grim **05** bleak, dingy **06** barren, dismal, dreary, gloomy, lonely, sombre, sullen, wintry **07** austere, forlorn, joyless, sunless, unhappy, wintery **08** dejected, desolate, dolorous, mournful, winterly **09** miserable, sorrowful **10** depressing, despondent, melancholy, uninviting **11** comfortless **12** disconsolate

cheers
02 ta **03** bye **04** rivo, skol, ta-ta, tope **05** adieu, skoal **06** bye-bye, health, prosit, see you, so long **07** cheerio, goodbye, haere ra, slàinte, wassail **08** au revoir, bless you, chin-chin, farewell, thank you, waes hail **09** bottoms up, drink hail **10** all the best, here's to you, many thanks, thanks a lot **11** much obliged, see you later **12** down the hatch, mud in your eye **13** happy landings **14** your good health **15** to absent friends

cheery
03 gay **04** glad **05** happy, jolly, merry **06** breezy, bright, chirpy, genial, hearty, jaunty, jovial, joyful, lively **07** buoyant, smiling **08** animated, carefree, cheerful, laughing, spirited **09** contented, exuberant, sparkling **10** optimistic **12** back-slapping, enthusiastic, light-hearted **13** in good spirits

cheese

Cheeses include:

03 ewe, Oka
04 Brie, curd, Edam, feta, goat, hard, skyr, soft
05 Caboc, Carré, Derby, Gouda, quark
06 Cantal, chèvre, Dunlop, junket, Orkney, paneer, Romano, Tilsit
07 Boursin, Cheddar, crottin, crowdie, Fontina, Gruyère, kebbock, kebbuck, Limburg, Münster, ricotta, sapsago, Stilton®
08 bel paese, Cheshire, Churnton, Emmental, halloumi, Huntsman, manchego, Parmesan, pecorino, raclette, Taleggio, vacherin
09 Amsterdam, Blue Vinny, Cambozola®, Camembert, chevreton, Emmenthal, ewe-cheese, Ilchester, Jarlsberg®, Killarney, Leicester, Limburger, Lymeswold®, mouse-trap, Port Salut, processed, provolone, reblochon, Roquefort, sage Derby
10 blue cheese, Caerphilly, curd cheese, Danish blue, dolcelatte, Emmentaler, Gloucester, Gorgonzola, hard cheese, Lancashire, mascarpone, mozzarella, Neufchâtel, Red Windsor, soft cheese, stracchino, vegetarian
11 Coulommiers, cream cheese, Petit Suisse, Pont l'Évêque, Saint-Paulin, Wensleydale
12 Blue Cheshire, fromage frais, Monterey Jack, Philadelphia®, Red Leicester
13 Bleu d'Auvergne, cottage cheese

• big cheese
03 nob, VIP **04** tuan **05** mogul, swell **06** big gun, bigwig, honcho, worthy **07** big shot, notable **08** big noise,

somebody **09** celebrity, dignitary, personage **10** panjandrum
11 heavyweight

cheesed off

05 bored, fed up **07** annoyed
09 depressed, disgusted, hacked off, pissed off **10** brassed off, browned off
11 disgruntled **12** disappointed, discontented, dissatisfied, sick and tired

chef

Chefs, restaurateurs and cookery writers include:

03 **Hom** (Ken)
04 **Gray** (Rose), **Roux** (Albert), **Roux** (Michel), **Spry** (Constance)
05 **Allen** (Betty), **Blanc** (Raymond René), **David** (Elizabeth), **Delia**, **Floyd** (Keith), **Leith** (Prue), **Roden** (Claudia), **Smith** (Delia), **Soyer** (Alexis), **Stein** (Rick), **White** (Marco Pierre)
06 **Appert** (Nicolas François), **Beeton** (Mrs Isabella Mary), **Carême** (Marie Antoine), **Farmer** (Fannie), **Lawson** (Nigella), **Oliver** (Jamie), **Ramsay** (Gordon), **Rhodes** (Gary), **Rogers** (Ruth), **Slater** (Nigel), **Wilson** (David)
07 **Cradock** (Fanny), **Erikson** (Gunn), **Grigson** (Jane), **Grigson** (Sophie), **Jaffrey** (Madhur), **Ladenis** (Nico)
08 **Dimbleby** (Josceline), **Grossman** (Loyd), **Harriott** (Ainsley), **Mosimann** (Anton), **Paterson** (Jennifer)
09 **Carluccio** (Antonio), **Escoffier** (Auguste), **McCartney** (Linda)
12 **Two Fat Ladies**
13 **Dickson Wright** (Clarissa)
14 **Brillat-Savarin** (Anthelme)
15 **Worrall Thompson** (Antony)

chemical

Chemical compounds include:

03 PVC
04 alum, DEET, urea
05 epoxy
06 phenol
07 ammonia, borazon, chloral, ethanol, styrene, toluene
08 kerosene, methanol, paraffin
10 chloramine, chloroform
12 benzaldehyde, borosilicate
13 carbon dioxide, chlorhexidine, chlorobromide
14 carbon monoxide, chloral hydrate
15 organophosphate, sodium hydroxide

See also **element**

chemist

Chemists include:

03 **Lee** (Yuan T)
04 **Abel** (Sir Frederick), **Davy** (Sir Humphry), **Hess** (Germain Henri), **Kuhn** (Richard), **Mond** (Ludwig), **Urey** (Harold Clayton)
05 **Abegg** (Richard), **Black** (Joseph), **Boyle** (Robert), **Curie** (Marie), **Darby** (Abraham), **Dewar** (Sir James), **Haber** (Fritz), **Hooke** (Robert), **Kroto** (Sir Harold), **Libby** (Willard Frank), **Meyer** (Lothar), **Nobel** (Alfred), **Soddy** (Frederick)
06 **Baeyer** (Adolf von), **Barton** (Sir Derek), **Bunsen** (Robert Wilhelm), **Dalton** (John), **Eyring** (Henry), **Hevesy** (George Charles von), **Liebig** (Justus von), **Miller** (Stanley Lloyd), **Nernst** (Walther), **Porter** (George, Lord), **Ramsay** (Sir William)
07 **Abelson** (Philip H), **Bergius** (Friedrich), **Buchner** (Eduard), **Faraday** (Michael), **Fischer** (Emil Hermann), **Fischer** (Hans), **Hodgkin** (Dorothy), **Pasteur** (Louis), **Pauling** (Linus Carl), **Scheele** (Carl Wilhelm), **Seaborg** (Glenn Theodore)
08 **Avogadro** (Amedeo), **Chevreul** (Michel Eugène), **Hadfield** (Sir Robert Abbott), **Klaproth** (Martin Heinrich), **Langmuir** (Irving), **Lonsdale** (Dame Kathleen), **Lovelock** (James), **Mulliken** (Robert Sanderson), **Regnault** (Henri Victor), **Robinson** (Sir Robert), **Sidgwick** (Nevil Vincent), **Svedberg** (Theodor), **Tiselius** (Arne Wilhelm Kaurin)
09 **Arrhenius** (Svante August), **Baekeland** (Leo Hendrik), **Berzelius** (Jöns Jacob), **Cavendish** (Henry), **Gay-Lussac** (Joseph Louis), **Lavoisier** (Antoine Laurent), **Priestley** (Joseph), **Prigogine** (Ilya, Vicomte)
10 **Cannizzaro** (Stanislao), **Mendeleyev** (Dmitri)
12 **Boussingault** (Jean Baptiste Joseph)

• chemists

03 ICI, RSC **04** BASF **06** IChemE

chemistry

Chemistry terms include:

02 IR, pH
03 cis, gas, ion
04 acid, atom, base, bond, mass, mole, rate, salt, weak
05 assay, block, cycle, ester, group, IUPAC, lipid, order, phase, polar, redox, shell, solid, trans, yield
06 alkali, alkane, alkene, buffer, chiral, dalton, dilute, dipole, fusion, halide, isomer, ketone, ligand, liquid, matter, period, phenyl, pi bond, proton, strong, symbol
07 chelate, chemist, colloid, crystal, element, entropy, fission, formula, halogen, isotope, lattice, mixture, neutral, neutron, nucleus, orbital, organic, polymer, product, racemic, reagent, soluble, solvent, valency
08 analysis, aromatic, catalyst, compound, cracking, dialysis, electron, emulsion, end point, enthalpy, fixation, half life, inert gas, miscible, molecule, noble gas, reactant, reaction, solution
09 aliphatic, allotrope, anhydrous, catalysis, corrosion, diffusion, electrode, empirical, hydroxide, indicator, inorganic, insoluble, ionic bond, oxidation, reduction, saturated, side chain, sigma bond, substance, synthesis, titration
10 amphoteric, atomic mass, combustion, curly arrow, double bond, exothermic, free energy, hydrolysis, immiscible, litmus test, reversible, single bond, suspension, triple bond, zwitterion
11 crystallize, diffraction, electrolyte, endothermic, equilibrium, evaporation, free radical, ground state, hydrocarbon, litmus paper, precipitate, respiration, sublimation
12 atomic number, atomic radius, atomic weight, biochemistry, chemical bond, chlorination, concentrated, condensation, covalent bond, dissociation, distillation, electrolysis, fermentation, hydrogen bond, melting point, metallic bond, spectroscopy
13 chain reaction, decomposition, fractionation, periodic table, radioactivity, stoichiometry
14 Avogadro number, Brownian motion, buffer solution, chromatography, saponification
15 atomic structure, aufbau principle, chemical element, collision theory, transition metal, transition state

cheque

03 dud **04** giro **06** stumer **07** bouncer
11 counterfoil

chequer

04 dice **09** interrupt, variegate
10 chessboard **13** counterchange

chequered

05 diced, mixed **06** checky, chequy, varied **07** checked, diverse, striped
08 eventful **10** variegated
13 multicoloured, particoloured
15 with ups and downs

cherish

03 hug **04** love **05** adore, brood, nurse, prize, value **06** foster, nestle, tender **07** brood on, care for, harbour, nourish, nurture, shelter, support, sustain **08** enshrine, hold dear, treasure **09** encourage, entertain, look after **10** make much of, take care of
11 have at heart, refocillate **14** take good care of

cherished

03 pet **08** precious

cherry

04 gean **05** cheer, morel, ruddy
06 cornel, mazard **07** may-duke, mazzard, morello **08** hagberry
09 Malpighia **10** blackheart

cherub

05 angel **06** seraph

cherubic
04 cute **05** sweet **06** lovely
07 angelic, lovable **08** adorable, heavenly, innocent, loveable, seraphic
09 appealing

chess

Chess players include:

03 Tal (Mikhail), Xie (Jun)
04 Euwe (Max)
05 Anand (Viswanathan), Short (Nigel)
06 Karpov (Anatoli), Lasker (Emanuel), Morphy (Paul), Polgar (Judit), Polgar (Zsuzsa),Thomas (Sir George),Timman (Jan), Xie Jun
07 Fischer (Bobby), Kramnik (Vladimir), Smyslov (Vasili), Spassky (Boris)
08 Alekhine (Alexander), Deep Blue, Kasparov (Garry), Korchnoi (Viktor), Philidor (François André), Steinitz (Wilhelm)
09 Botvinnik (Mikhail), Khalifman (Alexander), Petrosian (Tigran)
10 Capablanca (José)
13 Chiburdanidze (Maya)

Chess pieces include:

04 king, pawn, rook
05 queen
06 bishop, castle, knight

Chess-related terms include:

01 R
03 man, pin, row
04 bind, FIDE, fork, move, play
05 black, board, check, flank, march, piece, white
06 attack, centre, double, gambit, master, patzer, square
07 chequer, defence, endgame, en prise, j'adoube, opening, promote, retract, squeeze
08 back rank, castling, diagonal, exchange, kingside, opponent, queening, zugzwang
09 bad bishop, checkmate, Elo rating, en passant, fool's mate, miniature, promotion, queenside, stalemate
10 fianchetto, good bishop, major piece, middle game, minor piece, passed pawn
11 counterplay, grandmaster, zwischenzug
12 backward pawn, problem child
13 counter attack, fifty move rule
14 perpetual check
15 knight's progress

chest
03 ark, box, cub **04** case, kist
05 bahut, caddy, crate, hutch, trunk
06 breast, bunker, bureau, casket, coffer, girnel, larnax, scrine, shrine, thorax **07** cap-case, cassone, commode, dresser, meal-ark, sternum, tallboy **08** corn-kist, treasury, wakahuia **09** slop-chest, strongbox
10 chiffonier

chestnut
02 ch **05** favel **06** cliché, conker, favell, sorrel **07** badious, buckeye, caltrop, horn-nut, saligot **08** bean tree, Castanea **09** chincapin, chinkapin
10 chinquapin **14** Castanospermum

chevron
01 V **06** stripe **08** dancette

chew
◇ *anagram indicator*
03 eat **04** bite, chaw, gnaw, quid
05 champ, chomp, grind, munch
06 crunch **07** reflect **08** meditate, ruminate **09** manducate, masticate
• **chew over**
06 muse on, ponder **07** weigh up
08 consider, mull over **10** meditate on, ruminate on **14** deliberate upon

chic
05 smart, style **06** chichi, dapper, modish, snazzy, trendy, with it **07** à la mode, elegant, stylish **08** elegance
11 fashionable **13** sophisticated

chicanery
05 dodge, fraud, guile, wiles
08 artifice, cheating, intrigue, trickery
09 deception, duplicity, quibbling, sophistry **10** dishonesty, subterfuge
11 deviousness, hoodwinking
13 deceitfulness, double-dealing, jiggery-pokery, sharp practice
15 underhandedness

chick
04 bird

chicken
03 hen **04** poot, pout **05** biddy, chook, chuck, poule, poult, rumpy, squab **06** scared **07** broiler, chookie, chuckie, poussin **08** coq au vin, cowardly, springer, yakitori
09 howtowdie **10** frightened
See also **animal**; **cowardly**; **hen**

Chickens include:

06 Ancona, bantam, Cochin, houdan, sultan
07 Dorking, Hamburg, leghorn, Minorca
08 Hamburgh, Langshan
09 Orpington,Welsummer, wyandotte
10 Andalusian, Australorp, chittagong, jungle fowl
11 Cochin-China, Spanish fowl
12 Plymouth Rock
14 Rhode Island Red

chickpea
04 gram **05** chana, chich **08** garbanzo

chide
03 row **04** rate, twit **05** blame, dress, scold, shend **06** berate, rebuke
07 censure, lecture, quarrel, reprove, tell off, upbraid **08** admonish, chastise, reproach **09** criticize, objurgate, reprehend, reprimand

chief
02 Ch **03** cid, key, oba **04** arch, boss, cock, head, jarl, kaid, khan, lead, lord, main, raja, ratu **05** ariki, chair, first, grand, great, major, prime, rajah, ratoo, ruler, sheik, vital **06** big gun, gaffer, honcho, leader, master, primal, sachem, sheikh, sudder, top dog
07 cacique, captain, cazique, central, headman, highest, leading, manager, mugwump, premier, primary, supreme, supremo **08** big noise, cardinal, chairman, director, dominant, foremost, governor, intimate, overlord, sagamore, superior, suzerain **09** big cheese, chieftain, commander, directing, essential, head-woman, important, number one, paramount, pendragon, president, principal, rangatira, top banana, uppermost
10 chairwoman, coryphaeus, head bummer, pre-eminent, prevailing, ringleader **11** chairperson, controlling, outstanding, predominant, supervising
13 most important, prime minister
14 chief executive, superintendent
See also **emperor**; **empress**; **governor**; **king**; **president**; **queen**; **ruler**

chiefly
06 mainly, mostly **07** usually
09 capitally, generally, in the main, primarily **10** especially, on the whole
11 essentially, principally
13 predominantly **14** for the most part

child
02 ch, it **03** boy, elf, get, imp, kid, son, tot **04** babe, baby, brat, chit, dalt, gait, geit, girl, gyte, mite, puss, tama, tike, tiny, trot, tyke, waif, wean **05** bairn, chick, dault, elfin, issue, mardy, minor, scamp, slink, smout, smowt, sprog, totty, wench, youth **06** cherub, enfant, infant, kidlet, moppet, nipper, pledge, rug rat, toddle, tottie, urchin, wanton
07 bambino, dilling, gangrel, hellion, kinchin, littlin, name-son, neonate, papoose, preteen, prodigy, progeny, subteen, tiny tot, toddler, young 'un
08 adherent, bantling, Benjamin, daughter, disciple, godchild, innocent, juvenile, little 'un, littling, munchkin, suckling, tamariki, teenager, weanling, young one **09** kiddywink, littleane, little boy, little one, monthling, offspring, stepchild, underfive, youngster **10** adolescent, ankle-biter, changeling, descendant, eyas-musket, fosterling, grandchild, inhabitant, jackanapes, kiddiewink, knave-bairn, little girl, orphanmite, ragamuffin, wunderkind, young adult **11** ankle-nipper, butter-print, encumbrance, guttersnipe, olive branch, preschooler, schoolchild, weeny-bopper, young person **12** kiddiewinkie
• **only child**
02 oc

childbirth
05 pains **06** labour **07** lying-in, travail
08 delivery **09** maternity, pregnancy, puerperal **11** confinement, parturition
12 accouchement, child-bearing

childhood
05 youth **07** boyhood, infancy
08 babyhood, girlhood, minority
09 early days **10** early years,

immaturity, schooldays
11 adolescence

childish
05 silly **06** boyish **07** babyish, foolish, girlish, puerile **08** immature, juvenile, trifling **09** frivolous, infantile
10 namby-pamby **13** irresponsible

childishly
09 foolishly **10** immaturely
13 irresponsibly

childless *see* **without issue** *under* **issue**

childlike
05 naive **06** docile, simple **07** artless, natural **08** innocent, trustful, trusting
09 credulous, guileless, ingenuous
10 unaffected

children
05 issue

Chile
03 CHL, RCH

chill
03 flu, ice, icy, nip, raw **04** bite, cold, cool, fear **05** algid, aloof, bleak, dread, fever, nippy, oorie, ourie, owrie, parky, relax, scare, sharp, virus **06** biting, chilly, dampen, dismay, freeze, frigid, frosty, shiver, wintry **07** anxiety, depress, iciness, petrify, rawness, terrify **08** coldness, cool down, coolness, freezing, frighten, make cold **09** crispness, influenza **10** become cold, depressing, discourage, dishearten, make colder, unfriendly
11 refrigerate **12** apprehension, become colder
• **chilled**
05 on ice **07** relaxed
• **chill out**
05 relax **06** unwind **08** calm down
09 have a rest **10** take it easy

chilly
03 icy, raw **04** cold, cool **05** aloof, bleak, brisk, crisp, fresh, gelid, nippy, parky, sharp, stony **06** biting, frigid, wintry **07** distant, hostile **08** freezing
10 unfriendly **11** unwelcoming
12 unresponsive **13** unsympathetic
14 unenthusiastic

chime
04 boom, ding, dong, peal, ring, tink, toll **05** agree, clang, rhyme, sound
06 accord, jingle, strike, tinkle
07 harmony, resound **11** reverberate
13 reverberation **14** tintinnabulate
• **chime in**
05 agree, blend, cut in, fit in **06** butt in, chip in **09** be similar, harmonize, interject, interpose, interrupt
10 correspond **12** be consistent

chimera
05 dream, fancy **07** fantasy, ratfish, spectre **08** delusion, illusion **09** idle fancy **12** will-o'-the-wisp
13 hallucination

chimney
03 lum **04** flue, vent **05** cleft, shaft, stack, stalk **06** funnel, tunnel
07 chimley, chumley, crevice
08 femerall **10** flare stack, smokestack
12 chimney stalk
• **chimney pot**
03 can **06** top-hat

china
02 Ch, RC **03** CHN, TWN **04** Chin, kina, mate **05** quina **06** dishes, plates
07 ceramic, pottery, quinine
08 crockery **09** porcelain, tableware
10 terracotta **11** earthenware
13 dinner service **14** cups and saucers, the flowery land **15** Celestial Empire, People's Republic
See also **friend**; **porcelain**

Chinese
02 Ch **03** Han **04** Chin, Sino-
05 Seric, Sinic **07** Cataian, Catayan, Sinaean **08** Cathaian, Cathayan
See also **animal**; **dynasty**
• **Chinese society**
04 tong

chink
03 cut, gap **04** gasp, rift, rima, rime, slit, slot **05** cleft, crack, money, space, split **06** cavity, cranny, rictus
07 crevice, fissure, opening
08 aperture

chip
03 bit, fry **04** dent, disc, EROM, flaw, gash, nick, pare **05** break, chaff, crack, crisp, EPROM, flake, nacho, notch, piece, scrap, shard, shred, slice, snick, spale, spall, tease, token, wafer
06 chisel, damage, gallet, paring, sliver
07 blitter, counter, crumble, Pentium®, pinning, scratch, shaving, whittle
08 break off, fragment, splinter
09 French fry **10** transputer **11** fried potato **14** microprocessor
See also **computer**
• **chip in**
03 pay **05** cut in **06** butt in, donate
07 chime in **09** interject, interpose, interrupt, subscribe **10** contribute
12 club together **13** make a donation
14 have a whip-round **15** have a collection

chirp
03 pip **04** peep, pipe, sing **05** cheep, chirk, chirm, chirr, trill, tweet **06** chirre, warble **07** chirrup, chitter, twitter, whistle **10** tweet-tweet

chirpy
03 gay **04** glad **05** happy, jolly, merry, perky **06** blithe, bright, cheery, jaunty, lively **08** cheerful

chisel
03 gad **04** bran, burr **05** burin, cheat, drove, gouge **06** firmer, gravel
07 boaster, bolster, scauper, scorper, shingle **12** pitching tool
See also **carve**; **cheat**; **sculpt**

chit-chat
04 chat, talk **06** confab, gossip, natter
07 chatter, chinwag, prattle **08** cosy chat **09** small talk, tête-à-tête **10** idle gossip **12** conversation, heart-to-heart, tittle-tattle

chivalrous
04 bold **05** brave, noble **06** heroic, polite **07** gallant, valiant **08** gracious, knightly **09** courteous **10** courageous, honourable **11** gentlemanly **12** well-mannered

chivalry
06 honour **07** bravery, bushido, courage **08** boldness, courtesy, noblemen **09** gallantry, integrity
10 politeness **11** courtliness, good manners **12** graciousness, truthfulness
15 gentlemanliness

chivvy
03 bug, nag **04** goad, hunt, prod, urge
05 annoy, chase, hound, hurry
06 badger, harass, hassle, pester, plague **07** hurry up, pursuit, torment
08 pressure **09** importune

chlorine
02 Cl

chock-a-block
04 full **06** jammed, packed **07** brimful, chocker, crammed, crowded
08 overfull **09** congested, jam-packed
14 full to bursting

choice
03 try **04** best, fine, list, plum, rare, trye, wale, will **05** prime, prize, range, taste **06** answer, dainty, finest, opting, option, select **07** Auslese, picking, special, variety **08** choosing, decision, druthers, election, precious, solution, superior, valuable **09** excellent, exclusive, exquisite, first-rate, selection
10 first-class, hand-picked, preference
11 alternative, appropriate
14 discrimination

choke
03 bar, dam, gag **04** clog, glut, plug, silt, stap, stop **05** block, close, cough, dam up, retch, worry **06** accloy, silt up, stifle **07** congest, occlude, smother
08 obstruct, strangle, suppress, throttle
09 constrict, overpower, overwhelm, suffocate **10** asphyxiate
• **choke back**
04 curb **05** check **07** contain, control, inhibit, repress **08** restrain, strangle, suppress **09** fight back

chokey, choky *see* **prison**

choleric
05 angry, fiery, testy **06** crabby, touchy
07 crabbed, peppery **08** petulant
09 crotchety, irascible, irritable
10 passionate **11** bad-tempered, hot-tempered, ill-tempered **13** quick-tempered

choose
03 opt **04** list, pick, take, wale, want, will, wish **05** adopt, chuse, elect, fix on, go for **06** decide, desire, favour, opt for, prefer, see fit, select, take up
07 appoint, espouse, extract, pick out, vote for **08** decide on, plump for, settle on **09** designate, determine,

single out **10** predestine **14** make up your mind

choosy
05 faddy, fussy, picky **07** finicky **08** exacting **09** selective **10** fastidious, particular, pernickety **11** persnickety **14** discriminating

chop
02 ax **03** axe, cut, eat, hew, jaw, lop, saw **04** chap, clap, dice, fell, food, hack, hash, seal, snap **05** brand, carve, crack, cut up, mince, sever, share, slash, slice, split **06** barter, change, cleave, divide, thrust **07** dissect, fissure **08** exchange, truncate **09** côtelette

• **chop up**
◇ *anagram indicator*
03 cut **04** cube, dice **05** cut up, grate, grind, mince, shred, slice **06** divide **07** slice up **13** cut into pieces

choppy
◇ *anagram indicator*
04 wavy **05** rough **06** broken, stormy, uneven **07** ruffled, squally **08** blustery **09** turbulent **11** tempestuous

chore
03 job **04** duty, task **05** truck **06** burden, errand **07** routine **11** piece of work

choreography

Choreographers include:

04 **Bolm** (Adolph), **Dean** (Laura), **Feld** (Eliot), **Kidd** (Michael)
05 **Bruce** (Christopher), **Cohan** (Robert), **Dolin** (Anton), **Jooss** (Kurt), **Laban** (Rudolf von), **Lifar** (Serge), **North** (Robert), **Sleep** (Wayne), **Tharp** (Twyla)
06 **Ashton** (Sir Frederick), **Béjart** (Maurice), **Blasis** (Carlo), **Bourne** (Matthew), **Clarke** (Michael), **Cranko** (John), **Davies** (Siobhan), **Duncan** (Isadora), **Fokine** (Michel), **Graham** (Martha), **Morris** (Mark), **Petipa** (Marius), **Valois** (Dame Ninette de), **Wigman** (Mary)
07 **Darrell** (Peter), **de Mille** (Agnes George), **Joffrey** (Robert), **Massine** (Léonide)
08 **Berkeley** (Busby), **de Valois** (Dame Ninette), **Helpmann** (Sir Robert), **Humphrey** (Doris), **Nijinska** (Bronislava), **Nijinsky** (Vaslav)
09 **Beauchamp** (Pierre), **Macmillan** (Sir Kenneth)
10 **Balanchine** (George), **Cunningham** (Merce)
11 **Baryshnikov** (Mikhail)

choristers
05 choir

chortle
04 crow **05** laugh, snort **06** cackle, guffaw **07** chuckle, snigger

chorus
04 call **05** choir, shout **06** burden, strain **07** refrain, singers **08** ensemble, response **09** vocalists **10** choristers **11** choral group

Christ
01 X **02** Ch, JC, XP, Xt **03** Chr, I am **04** Lord **06** the Son **07** Holy One, Messiah, Saviour **08** Immanuel, Redeemer, Son of God, Son of Man **09** deliverer, Lamb of God, Word of God **11** King of kings, Lord of lords, the Redeemer **12** Good Shepherd **13** Prince of Peace

christen
03 dub **04** call, name, term **05** style, title **07** baptize, immerse **08** sprinkle **09** designate **10** begin using, inaugurate **11** give a name to

Christian
02 Xn **03** Chr **04** Copt, Xian **05** Xtian

Christmas
02 Xm **04** Noel, Xmas, Yule **05** Nowel **06** Crimbo, Nowell **08** Chrissie, Nativity, Yuletide

Gifts for the Twelve Days of Christmas:

09 gold rings
10 French hens
11 turtle doves
12 calling birds, geese a-laying, pipers piping
13 ladies dancing, lords a-leaping, maids a-milking
14 swans a-swimming
16 drummers drumming
20 partridge in a pear tree

Gifts from the Three Wise Men:

04 gold
05 myrrh
12 frankincense

See also **wise man** *under* **wise**

Christmas Island
03 CXR

Christ's-thorn
04 nabk

chromium
02 Cr

chromosome
• **part of chromosome**
02 id **07** cistron

chronic
04 naff, ropy **05** awful, pants **07** abysmal, the pits **08** constant, dreadful, habitual, hardened, long-term, terrible **09** appalling, atrocious, confirmed, continual, frightful, incessant, ingrained, recurring **10** deep-rooted, deep-seated, deplorable, inveterate, persistent **11** long-lasting **12** incorrigible, long-standing **14** a load of rubbish

chronically
08 long-term **10** constantly, habitually **11** continually, incessantly, recurrently **12** deep-rootedly, incorrigibly, inveterately, persistently

chronicle
04 epic, list, saga, tell **05** chron, diary, enter, story **06** annals, record, relate, report **07** account, history, journal, narrate, recount, set down **08** archives, calendar, register **09** narrative, write down **11** put on record

• **entry in chronicle**
05 annal

chronicler
06 scribe **07** diarist **08** annalist, narrator, recorder, reporter **09** archivist, historian **11** chronologer **13** chronographer **15** historiographer

chronological
06 serial **07** in order, ordered **10** historical, in sequence, sequential **11** consecutive, progressive

chubby
03 fat **04** full **05** fubby, fubsy, plump, podgy, round, stout, tubby **06** flabby, fleshy, portly, rotund **07** paunchy **08** roly-poly

chuck
03 put, shy **04** cast, dump, food, hurl, jilt, lump, quit, toss **05** chunk, fling, heave, pitch, sling, throw **06** give up, pack in, pebble, reject **07** abandon, chicken, discard, dismiss, forsake **08** get rid of, jettison **12** give the elbow **15** give the brush-off

chuckle
04 crow **05** laugh, snort **06** cackle, clumsy, giggle, titter **07** chortle, snigger **12** laugh quietly

chum
03 pal **04** mate, tosh **05** buddy, butty, crony **06** cobber, friend **07** comrade **09** accompany, associate, companion

See also **friend**

chummy
04 maty **05** close, matey, pally, thick **08** criminal, friendly, intimate, sociable **12** affectionate

chunk
03 nub **04** hunk, junk, lump, mass, slab **05** block, chuck, piece, wedge, wodge **06** dollop **07** portion

chunky
05 broad, bulky, dumpy, heavy, large, solid, thick **06** blocky, stocky **07** awkward, weighty **08** thickset, unwieldy **09** well-built **10** cumbersome **11** substantial

church
02 CE, Ch **04** cult, fold, kirk, sect **05** abbey, flock **06** bethel, chapel, shrine, temple **07** chantry, minster **08** assembly, basilica, Bethesda, ecclesia, grouping **09** cathedral, community, tradition **10** fellowship, house of God, Lord's house, tabernacle **11** people of God **12** body of Christ, congregation, denomination, meeting-house, procathedral **13** bride of Christ, house of prayer **14** house of worship, place of worship, preaching-house

See also **cathedral**

Church and cathedral parts include:

03 pew
04 apse, arch, font, nave, rood, tomb
05 aisle, altar, choir, crypt, porch, slype, spire, stall, stoup, tower, vault
06 adytum, arcade, atrium, belfry, chapel, chevet, corona, parvis, portal, pulpit, sedile, shrine, squint, vestry
07 almonry, chancel, frontal, gallery, lectern, lucarne, narthex, piscina, reredos, steeple, tambour
08 cloister, credence, crossing, keystone, parclose, pinnacle, predella, sacellum, sacristy, transept
09 antechoir, bell tower, sacrarium, sanctuary, sepulchre, stasidion, triforium
10 ambulatory, baptistery, bell screen, clerestory, diaconicon, fenestella, frithstool, misericord, presbytery, retrochoir, rood screen
12 chapterhouse, confessional, deambulatory
14 ringing chamber, schola cantorum

churchman *see* **clergyman, clergywoman**

churchyard
05 house **07** charnel **08** boneyard, cemetery, God's acre, kirkyard **09** graveyard, kirkyaird **10** burial site, necropolis **11** burial place **12** burial ground

churlish
04 rude **05** harsh, rough, surly **06** morose, oafish, sullen **07** boorish, brusque, carlish, crabbed, doggish, ill-bred, loutish, uncivil **08** impolite **10** ungracious, unmannerly, unsociable **11** bad-tempered, ill-mannered, ill-tempered **12** discourteous **13** unneighbourly **14** ill-conditioned

churn
◇ *anagram indicator*
04 beat, boil, foam, kirn, puke, stir, toss, turn **05** froth, heave, retch, swirl, vomit **06** be sick, seethe, writhe **07** agitate, disturb, throw up **08** convulse

• **churn out**
07 knock up, pump out, turn out **13** throw together

chute
03 lin **04** linn, ramp **05** flume, rapid, shaft, shoot, shute, slide, slope, spout, trunk **06** funnel, gutter, runway, trough **07** channel, incline **09** parachute, waterfall **10** water shoot

chutzpah
03 lip **04** gall **05** cheek, mouth, nerve, sauce **08** audacity **09** brass neck, impudence, insolence **10** brazenness, disrespect, effrontery **12** impertinence

cicada
06 tettix **10** harvest-fly **11** balm-cricket

Cicadas include:

05 Myer's
06 red-eye
09 Union Jack
10 blue prince
11 black prince, floury baker, greengrocer, green Monday, masked devil
12 floury miller, yellow Monday
13 double drummer

cigarette
03 cig, fag, tab **04** weed **05** cigar **06** dog end, fag end **10** coffin-nail, paper-cigar **11** cancer-stick

Cigarettes and cigars include:

04 bidi, burn
05 beedi, blunt, ciggy, claro, joint, paper, roach, segar, smoke, snout, stogy, whiff
06 beedie, bomber, ciggie, concha, gasper, Havana, low-tar, manila, reefer, roll-up, spliff, stogey, stogie
07 cheroot, high-tar, manilla, menthol, regalia
08 king-size, long-nine, perfecto
09 cigarillo, filter tip, panatella
10 tailor-made
11 corona lucis, roll-your-own

cinch
04 snip **06** doddle, scoosh, stroll **08** cakewalk, duck soup, pushover, walkover **09** certainty **10** child's play **11** piece of cake

cinders
04 coal, coke, slag **05** ashes **06** dander, embers **07** clinker **08** charcoal

cinema
05 films, scope **06** flicks, movies **07** drive-in, fleapit, theatre **08** bioscope, bughouse, pictures **09** big screen, multiplex **10** movie house **11** film theatre, nickelodeon **12** movie theatre, picture-house, silver screen **13** picture-palace **14** motion pictures, moving pictures

Cinema and theatre names include:

03 ABC, MGM, Rex, Rio, UCI, UGC
04 Gala, IMAX, Ritz, Roxy
05 Byron, Cameo, Forum, Grand, Kings, Lyric, Metro, Odeon, Orion, Plaza, Regal, Royal, Savoy, Scala, Tower
06 Albany, Apollo, Cannon, Casino, Curzon, Empire, Gaiety, Lyceum, Marina, New Vic, Old Vic, Palace, Queens, Regent, Rialto, Robins, Tivoli, Virgin
07 Adelphi, Almeida, Arcadia, Astoria, Capitol, Carlton, Central, Century, Circuit, Classic, Coronet, Embassy, Essoldo, Gaumont, Granada, La Scala, Locarno, Mayfair, Orpheum, Paragon, Phoenix, Picardy
08 Alhambra, Broadway, Charlton, Cineplex, Citizens, Coliseum, Colonial, Dominion, Electric, Everyman, Festival, Imperial, Landmark, Majestic, Memorial, Pavilion, Windmill
09 Alexandra, Cineworld, Filmhouse, Hollywood, Palladium, Paramount, Playhouse
10 Ambassador, Hippodrome, Lighthouse
11 Her Majesty's, His Majesty's, New Victoria, Ster Century
12 Metropolitan, Picturedrome, Picturehouse, Thefilmworks
13 Lyceum Theatre, Picture Palace, Warner Village
14 Electric Palace
15 Screen on the Hill

cipher
01 O **03** nil **04** code, null, zero **05** zilch **06** Enigma, naught, nobody, nought, yes-man **07** nothing **09** calculate, character, nonentity **10** cryptogram **11** cryptograph **12** coded message, secret system **13** secret writing

circa
01 c **02** ca **03** cir, odd **04** circ, some **05** about **06** around, nearly **07** close to, loosely, roughly **09** just about, not far off **10** more or less, round about **11** approaching **13** approximately, in the region of, or thereabouts, something like **15** in the vicinity of

circle
◇ *containment indicator*
01 O **03** set **04** club, gang, gird, wind **05** crowd, group, hem in, pivot, whirl **06** clique, gyrate, rotate, swivel **07** circlet, company, coterie, cycloid, enclose, envelop, hedge in, revolve, rondure, rounder, society **08** assembly, encircle, surround **09** circulate, encompass, move round **10** fellowship, fraternity **12** circumscribe **14** circumnavigate

Circles include:

03 lap, orb
04 ball, band, belt, coil, corn, crop, curl, disc, eddy, gyre, halo, hoop, hour, loop, oval, ring, turn, tyre
05 crown, cycle, dress, globe, grand, great, magic, mural, orbit, pitch, plate, polar, round, stone, upper, wheel
06 Arctic, circus, cordon, discus, girdle, rundle, saucer, sphere, spiral, tropic, vortex, wreath
07 annulet, annulus, circuit, compass, coronet, ellipse, equator, roundel, traffic, transit, turning, vicious
08 epicycle, gyration, meridian, rotation, roundure, striking, virtuous
09 Antarctic, perimeter, whirlpool, whirlwind
10 almacantar, almucantar, Circassian, revolution
13 circumference

• **stone circle**
08 cromlech **09** cyclolith **10** Stonehenge **11** peristalith

circuit
02 IC **03** lap **04** area, beat, eyre, tour **05** ambit, limit, orbit, range, round, route, track **06** bounds, course, diadem, region **07** compass, rondure, rounder **08** boundary, district, progress, roundure **09** perimeter, race track **10** revolution **12** running-track **13** circumference, perambulation

• **closed circuit**
02 CC

• **logic circuit**
02 OR **03** AND, NOR, NOT, XOR
04 NAND

circuitous
07 devious, oblique, winding
08 indirect, rambling, tortuous
09 meandrian, meandrous
10 meandering, roundabout
11 anfractuous **12** labyrinthine, periphrastic

circular
05 flyer, orbed, round **06** folder, letter, notice **07** annular, leaflet **08** handbill, pamphlet **09** spherical **10** disc-shaped, hoop-shaped, ring-shaped, round robin **12** announcement
13 advertisement

circulate
◇ *anagram indicator*
04 flow, pass, walk **05** float, issue, rumor, swirl, troll, utter, whirl
06 gyrate, report, rotate, rumour, spread **07** diffuse, give out, go about, go round, publish, revolve **08** go abroad, go around, put about, transmit
09 broadcast, get around, pass round, propagate, publicize, send round
10 distribute, promulgate
11 disseminate, go the rounds, spread about **12** spread around **13** make the rounds

circulation
04 flow **05** cycle **06** motion, spread
07 issuing **08** circling, currency, cyclosis, movement, rotation
09 blood-flow, publicity **10** readership
11 propagation, publication
12 distribution, transmission
13 dissemination

• **in circulation**
◇ *anagram indicator*
05 in use **06** afloat, around, issued
07 current, printed **09** available, published **11** distributed, spread about
12 spread around

circumference
03 arc, rim **04** edge **05** girth, round, verge **06** border, bounds, circle, fringe, limits, margin **07** circuit, compass, outline **08** boundary, confines
09 extremity, perimeter, periphery

circumlocution
06 ambage **08** pleonasm
09 euphemism, prolixity, tautology, verbosity, wordiness **10** periphrase, redundancy **11** convolution, diffuseness, periphrasis
12 indirectness **14** discursiveness, roundaboutness

circumlocutory
05 wordy **06** prolix **07** diffuse, verbose **08** elliptic, indirect
09 ambagious, redundant
10 convoluted, discursive, elliptical, long-winded, pleonastic, roundabout
11 euphemistic **12** periphrastic, tautological

circumscribe
04 trim **05** bound, hem in, limit, pen in
06 define **07** abridge, confine, curtail, delimit, enclose **08** encircle, restrain, restrict, surround **09** delineate, demarcate, encompass

circumspect
04 wary, wise **05** canny **07** careful, guarded, politic, prudent **08** cautious, discreet, vigilant, watchful
09 attentive, judicious, observant, sagacious **10** deliberate **11** calculating
14 discriminating

circumspection
04 care **07** caution **08** prudence, wariness **09** canniness, chariness, examining, vigilance **10** discretion
11 carefulness, guardedness
12 deliberation, watchfulness

circumstance
03 lot **04** case, fact, fate, item, nark, this **05** event, means, state, thing
06 detail, factor, plight, status
07 element, fortune, respect, situate
08 accident, ceremony, position
09 condition, happening, lifestyle, resources, situation **10** background, occurrence, particular
11 arrangement, environment **12** lie of the land **14** how the land lies, state of affairs

circumstantial
04 tiny **06** minute **07** deduced, hearsay **08** indirect, inferred, presumed **10** contingent, evidential, incidental **11** conjectural, inferential, presumptive, provisional

circumvent
04 dish **05** avoid, dodge, evade
06 bypass, outwit, thwart **07** get past
08 get out of, get round, go beyond, outflank, sidestep **09** encompass
12 steer clear of

circumvention
07 dodging, evasion **09** avoidance, bypassing, thwarting **12** sidestepping
13 steering clear

circus
06 cirque **10** hippodrome

Circus-related terms include:

03 top
04 geek, ring, tent
05 clown
06 big top, pie car
07 acrobat, balloon, juggler, sawdust, trapeze, tumbler
08 carnival, conjurer, conjuror, drum roll, high wire, magician, sideshow, unicycle
09 aerialist, fire-eater, lion tamer, menagerie, safety net, strongman, tightrope
10 acrobatics, acrobatism, candy floss, custard pie, ringmaster, roustabout, somersault, trick-rider, unicyclist
11 funambulist, greasepaint
12 escape artist, roll up! roll up!, stiltwalking, trick cyclist
13 bareback rider, contortionist, trapeze artist

cissy
03 wet **04** baby, soft, tonk, weak, wimp, wuss **05** pansy, softy
06 coward, feeble **07** crybaby, milksop, unmanly, wimpish
08 cowardly, weakling **09** mummy's boy **10** effeminate, namby-pamby

cistern
03 vat **04** sink, tank **05** basin **08** feed-head, flush-box **09** reservoir

citadel
04 fort, keep **05** tower **06** castle
07 bastion, kremlin **08** fortress
09 acropolis **10** stronghold
13 fortification

citation
03 cit **05** award, quote **06** honour, source **07** cutting, excerpt, mention, passage **08** allusion, epigraph
09 quotation, reference **10** allegation
12 commendation, illustration

cite
04 call, name **05** bring, quote, state, vouch **06** adduce, allege, summon
07 advance, bring up, convent, mention, refer to, specify **08** allude to, evidence **09** enumerate, exemplify
13 give an example

citizen
03 cit **05** local, voter **07** burgher, denizen, freeman, oppidan, subject
08 civilian, national, resident, taxpayer, townsman, urbanite **10** inhabitant, townswoman **11** city-dweller, householder

city
02 EC **04** seat, town **08** big smoke, downtown, precinct **09** inner city, metroplex, Weltstadt **10** city centre, cosmopolis, metropolis, micropolis, pentapolis **11** conurbation, megalopolis, urban sprawl
12 municipality **13** urban district
14 concrete jungle

Ancient cities include:

02 Ur
04 Acre, Axum, Ebla, Nuzi, Rome, Susa, Troy, Tula, Tyre, Uruk
05 Aksum, Argos, Bosra, Bursa, Copán, Cuzco, Eridu, Hatra, Huari, Mitla, Moche, Petra, Saida, Sidon, Tikal, Uxmal
06 Athens, Byblos, Cyrene, Jabneh, Jamnia, Napata, Nippur, Sardis, Shiloh, Sparta, Thebes, Ugarit
07 Antioch, Babylon, Bukhara, Corinth, El Tajin, Ephesus, Megiddo, Miletus, Mycenae, Nineveh, Paestum,

Plataea, Pompeii, Samaria, Sybaris, Vergina
08 Carthage, Damascus, Hattusas, Hattusha, Kerkuane, Palenque, Pergamon, Pergamum, Sigiriya, Tashkent, Thysdrus
09 Byzantium, Cartagena, Epidaurus, Sukhothai
10 Alexandria, Angkor Thom, Carchemish, Heliopolis, Hierapolis, Monte Albán, Persepolis
11 Chichén Itzá, Herculaneum, Machu Picchu, Polonnaruwa, Teotihuacán
12 Anuradhapura
13 Halicarnassus
14 Constantinople

Capital cities include:

04 Apia, Baku, Bern, Dili, Doha, Kiev, Lima, Lomé, Malé, Oslo, Riga, Rome, San'a, Suva
05 Abuja, Accra, Amman, Berne, Cairo, Dacca, Dakar, Dhaka, Hanoi, Kabul, Koror, La Paz, Minsk, Paris, Praia, Quito, Rabat, Sana'a, Seoul, Sofia, Sucre, Tokyo, Tunis, Vaduz
06 Akmola, Ankara, Asmara, Astana, Athens, Bamako, Bangui, Banjul, Beirut, Berlin, Bissau, Bogotá, Dodoma, Dublin, Harare, Havana, Kigali, Lisbon, London, Luanda, Lusaka, Madrid, Majuro, Malabo, Manama, Manila, Maputo, Maseru, Monaco, Moroni, Moscow, Muscat, Nassau, Niamey, Ottawa, Peking, Prague, Riyadh, Roseau, Skopje, T'aipei, Tarawa, Tehran, Tirana, Vienna, Warsaw, Yangon, Zagreb
07 Abidjan, Algiers, Alma-Ata, Baghdad, Bangkok, Beijing, Belfast, Bishkek, Caracas, Cardiff, Cayenne, Colombo, Conakry, Cotonou, El Aaiún, Godthab, Honiara, Jakarta, Kampala, Lobamba, Managua, Mbabane, Nairobi, Nicosia, Palikir, Papeete, Rangoon, San José, San Juan, São Tomé, St John's, Tallinn, Tbilisi, Teheran, Thimphu, Tripoli, Valetta, Vilnius, Yaoundé, Yerevan
08 Abu Dhabi, Ashgabat, Asunción, Belgrade, Belmopan, Brasília, Brussels, Budapest, Canberra, Cape Town, Castries, Chisinau, Damascus, Djibouti, Dushanbe, Freetown, Gaborone, Helsinki, Khartoum, Kingston, Kinshasa, Kishinev, Lilongwe, Monrovia, N'Djamena, New Delhi, Port-Vila, Pretoria, Santiago, Sarajevo, Tashkent, The Hague, Tórshavn, Valletta, Victoria, Windhoek
09 Amsterdam, Ashkhabad, Bucharest, Bujumbura, Edinburgh, Fongafale, Islamabad, Jerusalem, Kathmandu, Kingstown, Ljubljana, Mogadishu, Nuku'alofa, Phnom Penh, Port Louis, Porto Novo, Pyongyang, Reykjavík, San Marino, Singapore, St George's, Stockholm, Ulan Bator, Vientiane
10 Addis Ababa, Basseterre, Bratislava, Bridgetown, Copenhagen, Georgetown, Kuwait City, Libreville, Luxembourg, Mexico City, Montevideo, Nouakchott, Panama City, Paramaribo, Wellington, Willemstad
11 Brazzaville, Buenos Aires, Kuala Lumpur, Monaco-Ville, Ouagadougou, Port Moresby, Port of Spain, San Salvador, Tegucigalpa, Vatican City
12 Antananarivo, Bloemfontein, Fort-de-France, Port-au-Prince, Santo Domingo, Tel Aviv-Jaffa, Washington DC, Yamoussoukro
13 Guatemala City, Yaren District
14 Andorra la Vella
17 Bandar Seri Begawan
23 Sri Jayawardenepura Kotte

Cities and towns include:

02 Bo, LA, NY
03 Åbo, Ayr, Ely, Fès, Fez, Gao, Hué, Lae, Nis, NYC, Pau, Qom, Ufa, Ulm, Vac, Zug
04 Acre, Aden, Agra, Ajme, Amoy, Bari, Bath, Bonn, Brno, Bury, Caen, Cali, Cebu, Como, Cork, Dazu, Deal, Edam, Elat, Eton, Faro, Gand, Gent, Gifu, Graz, Györ, Homs, Hove, Hull, Iasi, Icel, Ipoh, Jima, Jixi, Kano, Kiel, Kobe, Köln, Kota, La-sa, León, Linz, Lódz, Lugo, Luik, Lund, Lvov, Metz, Mold, Mons, Naas, Naha, Nara, Nice, Nuuk, Oban, Oita, Omsk, Oran, Oulu, Pécs, Pegu, Perm, Pisa, Pula, Pune, Rand, Reno, Rhyl, Ruse, Ryde, Safi, Sale, Salt, Sfax, Sian, Sion, Soul, St-Lô, Suez, Sumy, Tema, Thun, Tula, Tyre, Umeå, Vasa, Vigo, Waco, Wick, Wien, Wuhu, Wuxi, Xi'an, York, Zibo, Zörs
05 Adana, Ahvaz, Åland, Al Ayn, Aosta, Aqaba, Argos, Århus, Arica, Arles, Arras, Aspen, Aswan, Ávila, Baden, Banff, Baoji, Basle, Basra, Beira, Belém, Benxi, Blida, Blyth, Boise, Bondi, Borga, Bouar, Breda, Brest, Braga, Bursa, Busan, Cádiz, Canea, Cavan, Ceuta, Chiba, Chita, Colón, Conwy, Cowes, Crewe, Cuzco, Davao, Davos, Delft, Delhi, Derby, Dijon, Dover, Duala, Dubai, Dukou, Eilat, Elche, Epsom, Essen, Eupen, Évora, Fiume, Frome, Fuxin, Genoa, Ghent, Gijón, Gomel, Gorky, Gouda, Gweru, Hagen, Haifa, Halle, Hefei, Hohot, Honan, Ichun, Ieper, Iwaki, Izmir, Jaffa, Jedda, Jilin, Jinan, Jinja, Kaédi, Kandy, Karaj, Kazan, Kelso, Kirov, Kitwe, Kochi, Konya, Köseg, Kursk, Kyoto, Lagos, Leeds, Lewes, Lhasa, Liège, Lille, Limbe, Luton, Luxor, Lyons, Mâcon, Mainz, Malmö, Masan, Mecca, Medan, Miami, Milan, Mitla, Mopti, Mosul, Namen, Namur, Nancy, Nasik, Natal, Ndola, Nîmes, Ohrid, Omagh, Omaha, Omiya, Oryol, Osaka, Otley, Oujda, Padua, Parma, Patan, Patna, Pavia, Penza, Perth, Plzen, Ponce, Poole, Poona, Pusan, Reims, Resit, Ripon, Ronda, Rouen, Rovno, Rugby, Sakai, Salem, Salta, Sebha, Ségou, Sidon, Siena, Skien, Sochi, Sopot, Split, Suita, Surat, Suwon, Taegu, Talca, Tampa, Tanga, Tanta, Tempe, Thane, Thiès, Tomar, Tomsk, Torun, Tours, Trier, Troon, Truro, Tulsa, Tunja, Turin, Turku, Tzupo, Udine, Ulsan, Urawa, Utica, Vaasa, Varna, Vejle, Vlorë, Wells, Wigan, Worms, Wuhan, Ypres, Zadar, Zaria, Zarqa
06 Aachen, Aarhus, Agadez, Agadir, Albany, Aleppo, Amiens, Annaba, Annecy, Anshan, Anvers, Anyang, Arezzo, Armagh, Arnhem, Arusha, Ashdod, Atbara, At Taif, Austin, Avarua, Baguio, Bangor, Baotou, Bastia, Bengpu, Bergen, Bhopal, Bilbao, Biloxi, Bitola, Bochum, Bolton, Bombay, Bootle, Boston, Brasov, Bremen, Bruges, Brugge, Burgos, Buxton, Cairns, Calais, Callao, Calmar, Camden, Campos, Cancún, Cannes, Canton, Carlow, Casper, Chania, Chi-nan, Chonju, Cochin, Cracow, Crosby, Cuenca, Dalian, Dallas, Da Nang, Danzig, Daqing, Darhan, Darwin, Datong, Dayton, Denver, Dieppe, Douala, Dudley, Duluth, Dundee, Durban, Durham, Durrës, El Gîza, El Paso, Eugene, Evreux, Exeter, Fatima, Fresno, Frunze, Fu-chou, Fushun, Fuzhou, Galway, Gdansk, Gdynia, Geneva, Gitega, Grodno, Grozny, Guelph, Guilin, Guimar, Gujrat, Guntur, Ha'apai, Hamina, Handan, Han-kou, Harbin, Harlem, Harlow, Harrow, Hebron, Hegang, Himeji, Hobart, Howrah, Ibadan, Inchon, Indore, Jaffna, Jaipur, Jarash, Jarrow, Jeddah, Jiddah, Jilong, Juneau, Kalmar, Kaluga, Kankan, Kanpur, Kaolan, Kassel, Kaunas, Kendal, Khulna, Kirkby, Kirkuk, Kosice, Kraków, Kumasi, Kurgan, Lahore, Lanark, Leiden, Le Mans, Leshan, Leuven, Leyden, Lübeck, Lublin, Ludlow, Lugano, Maceio, Madras, Makale, Málaga, Malang, Manaus, Mantua, Matrah, Medina, Meerut, Mekele, Meknès, Meshed, Mobile, Mukden, Multan, Muncie, Munich, Murcia, Mysore, Nablus, Nagano, Nagoya, Nagpur, Nantes, Napier, Naples, Narvik, Newark, Ningbo, Nouméa, Odense, Odessa, Oldham, Olinda, Oporto, Örebro, Osasco, Osijek, Ostend, Oviedo, Oxford, Padang, Paphos, Phuket, Piatra, Pierre, Pilsen, Porvoo, Potosí, Poznan, Presov, Puebla, Quebec, Queluz, Quetta, Raipur, Rajkat, Ranchi, Recife, Redcar, Reggio, Regina, Rennes, Rheims, Rijeka, Ryazan, Saigon, Salala, Samara, Santos, Schwyz, Sefadu, Sendai, Shiraz, Silves, Sining, Sintra, Skikda, Sliema, Slough, Smyrna, Sokodé, Sousse, Soweto, Sparta, St Ives, St John, St Malo, St Paul, Stroud, Stuart, Suchow, Sukkur, Suzhou,

Sydney, Szeged, Tabriz, Tacoma, Tadmur, Taejon, Tahoua, Tainan, Tamale, Tambov, Tarbes, Tarsus, Ta-t'ung, Teruel, Thurso, Tipasa, Tobruk, Toledo, Toluca, Topeka, Torbay, Toulon, Toyama, Toyota, Tralee, Trento, Treves, Tromsø, Troyes, Tsinan, Tubruq, Tucson, Tyumen, Urumqi, Vannes, Vargas, Venice, Verona, Viborg, Weimar, Whitby, Widnes, Woking, Xiamen, Xining, Xuzhou, Yangku, Yantai, Yeovil, Yichun, Yunnan, Zabrze, Zigong, Zinder, Zurich, Zwolle

07 Aberfan, Airdrie, Aligarh, Alnwick, Antibes, Antioch, Antwerp, Aracaju, Atlanta, Augusta, Auxerre, Avignon, Baalbek, Badajoz, Bairiki, Banares, Banbury, Bandung, Baoding, Barnaul, Barossa, Bayamón, Bedford, Beeston, Benares, Bendigo, Berbera, Bergama, Bergamo, Bexhill, Bizerta, Blarney, Bologna, Bolzano, Boulder, Bourges, Braemar, Brescia, Bristol, Bryansk, Buffalo, Burnley, Cáceres, Calgary, Calicut, Cardiff, Catania, Chalcis, Changan, Cheadle, Cheddar, Chelsea, Chengde, Chengdu, Cheng-tu, Chester, Chicago, Chifeng, Chi-lung, Chongju, Chungho, Clonmel, Coblenz, Coimbra, Cologne, Concord, Córdoba, Corinth, Corinto, Corunna, Crawley, Dandong, Detroit, Devizes, Donetsk, Douglas, Dresden, Dundalk, Dunedin, Dunkirk, Durango, Entebbe, Erdenet, Esbjerg, Evesham, Exmouth, Falkirk, Fareham, Ferrara, Foochow, Fukuoka, Funchal, Ganzhou, Geelong, Glasgow, Goiânia, Gosport, Granada, Grimsby, Guiyang, Gwalior, Gwangju, Haerbin, Halifax, Hamburg, Hamhung, Hanover, Harwich, Henzada, Heredia, Houston, Huaibai, Huainan, Ipswich, Iquique, Iquitos, Irkutsk, Isfahan, Ivanovo, Izhevsk, Jackson, Jericho, Jiamusi, Jinzhou, Jodhpur, Kaesong, Kaifeng, Kalinin, Kananga, Karachi, Kassala, Kayseri, Keelung, Kenitra, Keswick, Kharkov, Kherson, Koblenz, Kolding, Kuching, Kunming, Kutaisi, Lansing, Lanzhou, La Plata, Larnaca, Latakia, Leghorn, Le Havre, Leipzig, Lerwick, Liberia, Limoges, Lincoln, Lipetsk, Liuzhou, Livorno, Logroño, Louvain, Lucerne, Lucknow, Lugansk, Lumbini, Luoyang, Machida, Madison, Madurai, Malvern, Manzini, Maracay, Marburg, Margate, Mashhad, Massawa, Matlock, Matsudo, Melilla, Memphis, Mendoza, Mildura, Mindelo, Miskolc, Mitsiwa, Mogilev, Mombasa, Morpeth, Münster, Nanjing, Nanking, Nanning, Nantong, Newbury, Newport, Newquay, New Ross, New York, Niigata, Niterói, Norfolk, Norwich, Novi Sad, Oakland, Okayama, Okinawa, Olympia, Orlando, Orleans, Ostrava, Pahsien, Paisley, Palermo, Panshan, Pattaya, Peebles, Penrith, Perugia, Phoenix, Piraeus, Pistoia, Pitesti, Plovdiv, Poltava, Popayán, Portree, Potsdam, Preston, Prizren, Qingdao, Qiqihar, Quimper, Raleigh, Randers, Ravenna, Reading, Redwood, Reigate, Roanoke, Rosario, Rostock, Rotorua, Runcorn, Sagunto, Salamis, Salerno, Salford, Sandown, Santa Fe, São Luis, Sapporo, Saransk, Saratov, Sassari, Seattle, Segovia, Setúbal, Seville, Shannon, Shantou, Shihezi, Shikoku, Shkodër, Sialkot, Sinuiju, Songnam, Spokane, Spoleto, Staines, Stanley, St Denis, St Louis, Sudbury, Swansea, Swindon, Taiyuan, Tampere, Tampico, Tangier, Taunton, Tel Aviv, Telford, Tétouan, Tianjin, Tijuana, Tilburg, Tilbury, Toronto, Torquay, Tournai, Trenton, Trieste, Tucumán, Ulan-Ude, Uppsala, Utrecht, Ventnor, Vicenza, Vitebsk, Vitosha, Walsall, Warwick, Watford, Weifang, Wenzhou, Wexford, Wichita, Windsor, Wrexham, Wroclaw, Wuhsien, Yakeshi, Yichang, Yingkou, Yonkers, Zermatt, Zhuzhou, Zwickau

08 Aberdeen, Acapulco, Adelaide, Akureyri, Alajuela, Albacete, Alicante, Amarillo, Amritsar, Arbroath, Arequipa, Auckland, Augsburg, Aviemore, Ayia Napa, Ballarat, Banghazi, Bareilly, Barnsley, Bathurst, Bayreuth, Beauvais, Belgorod, Benghazi, Benguela, Benidorm, Besançon, Bhadgaon, Biarritz, Bismarck, Blantyre, Bobruysk, Bordeaux, Boulogne, Bradford, Braganza, Brighton, Brindisi, Brisbane, Bulawayo, Burgundy, Cagliari, Calcutta, Campinas, Carlisle, Changsha, Chartres, Chemnitz, Chepstow, Cheyenne, Chiclayo, Chimbote, Chimkent, Ching-tao, Chongjin, Clevedon, Columbia, Columbus, Contagem, Coventry, Culiacán, Curitiba, Dartford, Dearborn, Debrecen, Djakarta, Dortmund, Drogheda, Duisburg, Dumfries, Dunhuang, Dunleary, Durgapur, Dzhambul, Ebbw Vale, Edmonton, El Kharga, Elsinore, Europort, Falmouth, Florence, Flushing, Freeport, Fribourg, Fujisawa, Fukuyama, Gaoxiong, Gisborne, Gorlovka, Grantham, Grasmere, Greenock, Grenoble, Guernica, Hachioji, Haiphong, Hakodate, Hamilton, Hangchow, Hangzhou, Hannover, Hartford, Hastings, Hengyang, Hereford, Hertford, Hirakata, Holyhead, Holywell, Hong Kong, Honolulu, Huangshi, Hunjiang, Ichikawa, Iowa City, Istanbul, Jabalpur, Jaboatoa, Kairouan, Kanazawa, Kandahar, Karlsbad, Katowice, Kawasaki, Keflavik, Kemerovo, Kilkenny, Kirkwall, Kismaayo, Klosters, Kolhapur, Konstanz, Koriyama, Kuei-yang, Kumamoto, Laâyoune, La Laguna, Las Vegas, Lausanne, Legoland, Leskovac, Liaoyang, Liaoyuan, Limassol, Limerick, Londrina, Longford, Lüderitz, Ludhiana, Lyallpur, Makassar, Mandalay, Mannheim, Marbella, Mariupal, Mariupol, Mayaguez, Mazatlán, Medellín, Mercedes, Mexicali, Montreal, Montreux, Montrose, Mufulira, Mulhouse, Murmansk, Myingyan, Nagasaki, Namangan, Nanchang, Nazareth, New Haven, Newhaven, Nijmegen, Novgorod, Nuneaton, Nürnberg, Oak Ridge, Omdurman, Oostende, Orenburg, Oswestry, Pago Pago, Pamplona, Panchiao, Pasadena, Pavlodar, Penzance, Peshawar, Piacenza, Ploiesti, Plymouth, Poitiers, Portland, Portrush, Port Said, Pristina, Ramsgate, Rancagua, Randstad, Redditch, Richmond, Road Town, Rochdale, Rockford, Roskilde, Rosslare, Sabadell, Salonica, Salonika, Saltillo, Salvador, Salzburg, San Diego, Santa Ana, Santarém, São Paulo, Satu Mare, Savannah, Schwerin, Semarang, Shanghai, Shanklin, Shaoguan, Shenyang, Shizuoka, Sholapur, Silk Road, Simbirsk, Skegness, Smolensk, Solihull, Solingen, Sorocaba, Southend, Srinagar, Stafford, St Albans, Stamford, St David's, St Gallen, St Helens, St Helier, Stirling, St Moritz, Stockton, Strabane, St-Tropez, Subotica, Suicheng, Surabaya, Swan Hill, Syracuse, Szczecin, Taganrog, Taichung, Tamworth, Tangshan, Teresina, Thetford, Thonburi, Tiberias, Tientsin, Timbuktu, Titograd, Tolyatti, Tongeren, Toulouse, Toyohasi, Toyonaka, Trujillo, Tsingtao, Tübingen, Uleaborg, Ullapool, Vadodara, Valencia, Valletta, Varanasi, Veracruz, Vila Real, Vinnitsa, Vittoria, Vladimir, Voronezh, Wakayama, Wallasey, Wallsend, Warangal, Weymouth, Winnipeg, Worthing, Würzburg, Xiangfan, Xiangtan, Xinxiang, Yangchow, Yangquan, Yangzhou, Yinchuan, Yin-hsien, Yokohama, Yokosuko, Yorktown, Zakopane, Zanzibar, Zhitomir

09 Adis Abeba, Ahmadabad, Alba Iulia, Albufeira, Aldershot, Algeciras, Allahabad, Amagasaki, Ambleside, Anchorage, Annapolis, Archangel, Asahikawa, Astrakhan, Audenarde, Aylesbury, Bakhtaran, Baltimore, Bangalore, Barcelona, Beersheba, Berbérati, Bethlehem, Bhavnagar, Bialystok, Blackburn,

Blackpool, Bossangoa, Botany Bay, Brunswick, Bydgoszcz, Cambridge, Cartagena, Castlebar, Changchun, Changzhou, Charleroi, Charlotte, Chengchow, Cherbourg, Chernobyl, Chiang Mai, Chihuahua, Choluteca, Chongqing, Chungking, Cleveland, Colwyn Bay, Constance, Constanta, Des Moines, Doncaster, Dordrecht, Dubrovnik, Dudelange, Dumbarton, Dungannon, Dunstable, Eastleigh, Eindhoven, Eskisehir, Esztergom, Fairbanks, Famagusta, Faridabad, Fishguard, Fleetwood, Fortaleza, Fort Worth, Frankfort, Frankfurt, Fremantle, Funabashi, Galveston, Gateshead, Gaziantep, Gippsland, Gold Coast, Gorakhpur, Gravesend, Greenwich, Groningen, Guangzhou, Guarulhos, Guayaquil, Guildford, Hallstatt, Hamamatsu, Harrogate, Haslemere, Helsingør, Heraklion, Hilversum, Hiroshima, Humpty Doo, Hyderabad, Immingham, Innsbruck, Inverness, Ismailiya, Jalandhar, Jamestown, Johnstone, Jönköping, Kagoshima, Kamchatka, Kaohsiung, Karaganda, Karlsruhe, Kawaguchi, Killarney, Kimberley, King's Lynn, Kirkcaldy, Kisangani, Kishinyov, Kitzbühel, Kórinthos, Kozhikode, Krasnodar, Krivoy Rog, Kurashiki, Kuybyshev, Kwang-chow, Lancaster, Las Cruces, Leicester, Lexington, Lichfield, Liverpool, Llangefni, Long Beach, Lowestoft, Lymington, Magdeburg, Mahajanga, Maidstone, Makeyevka, Mamoudzan, Manizales, Mansfield, Maracaibo, Maralinga, Marrakesh, Matsuyama, Melbourne, Middleton, Milwaukee, Monterrey, Moradabad, Morecambe, Mullingar, Nashville, Neuchâtel, Newcastle, Newmarket, Nikolayev, Nuremberg, Ogbomosho, Osnabrück, Palembang, Pamporovo, Perpignan, Peterhead, Pingxiang, Pontianak, Port Natal, Port Sudan, Pressburg, Prestwick, Princeton, Qinghai Hu, Querétaro, Riverside, Rochester, Rotherham, Rotterdam, Rovaniemi, Salisbury, Samarkand, San Miguel, Santa Cruz, Santander, Saragossa, Saskatoon, Shanchung, Sheerness, Sheffield, Sioux City, South Bend, Southport, Southwark, St Andrews, Stavanger, Stavropol, St-Étienne, Stevenage, St-Nazaire, Stockport, Stornoway, St-Quentin, Stranraer, Stuttgart, Sukhothai, Sundsvall, Surakarta, Takamatsu, Takatsuki, Tarragona, Tenkodogo, T'ien-ching, Timisoara, Toamasina, Togliatti, Toowoomba, Trondheim, Tullamore, Ulyanovsk, Vancouver, Velingrad, Vicksburg, Volgograd, Wakefield, Walvis Bay, Waterford, Wiesbaden, Wimbledon, Wolfsburg, Worcester, Wuppertal, Xiangyang, Yaroslavl, Zamboanga, Zaozhuang, Zhengzhou, Zhenjiang, Zrenjanin

10 Alexandria, Baton Rouge, Belize City, Birkenhead, Birmingham, Bridgeport, Bridgwater, Broken Hill, Caernarvon, Caerphilly, Canterbury, Carmarthen, Carnoustie, Carson City, Casablanca, Chandigarh, Charleston, Cheboksary, Chelmsford, Cheltenham, Cheng-hsien, Chichester, Chittagong, Cienfuegos, Cincinnati, Cluj-Napoca, Coatbridge, Cochabamba, Coimbatore, Colchester, Concepción, Darjeeling, Darlington, Diyarbakir, Dorchester, Düsseldorf, Dzerzhinsk, Eastbourne, El Mansoura, Faisalabad, Felixstowe, Folkestone, Fray Bentos, Galashiels, George Town, Gillingham, Glenrothes, Gloucester, Goose Green, Gothenburg, Gujranwala, Haddington, Harrisburg, Hartlepool, Heidelberg, Hermosillo, Hildesheim, Huntingdon, Huntsville, Jamshedpur, Jingdezhen, Joao Pessoa, Juiz de Fora, Kakopetria, Kalgoorlie, Kansas City, Kenilworth, Khabarovsk, Kilmarnock, Kita-Kyushu, Kompong Som, Lake Placid, Las Piedras, Launceston, Leeuwarden, Letchworth, Linlithgow, Little Rock, Liupanshui, Livingston, Llangollen, Los Angeles, Louisville, Lubumbashi, Luluabourg, Maastricht, Maidenhead, Manchester, Marseilles, Medjugorje, Miami Beach, Monte Carlo, Montego Bay, Montgomery, Montpelier, Mostaganem, Motherwell, Mudanjiang, New Orleans, Nottingham, Nouadhibou, Nova Iguacu, Oranjestad, Oudenaarde, Palmerston, Petersburg, Pittsburgh, Pontefract, Portishead, Portsmouth, Providence, Quezon City, Quinnipiac, Rawalpindi, Regensburg, Sacramento, Sagamihara, San Antonio, San Ignacio, Santa Marta, Santo André, São Gonçalo, Scunthorpe, Sebastopol, Shepparton, Shreveport, Shrewsbury, Simferapol, Sioux Falls, Södertälje, Strasbourg, Sunderland, Sverdlovsk, Talcahuano, Tammerfors, Tananarive, Thunder Bay, Townsville, Trivandrum, Trowbridge, Tsaochuang, Utsunomiya, Valladolid, Valparaíso, Vijayawada, Viña del Mar, Vlissingen, Wadi Medani, Wagga Wagga, Warrington, Washington, Whitehorse, Wilmington, Winchester, Windermere, Winterthur, Wittenberg, Wollongong, Workington, Yogyakarta, Yoshkar Ola, Zaporozhye

11 Aberystwyth, Albuquerque, Antofagasta, Bahía Blanca, Banjarmasin, Basingstoke, Bhilai Nagar, Bognor Regis, Bournemouth, Brandenburg, Bremerhaven, Bridlington, Broadstairs, Brownsville, Bucaramanga, Campo Grande, Carcassonne, Charlestown, Chattanooga, Chelyabinsk, Cherepovets, Cirencester, Cleethorpes, Cockermouth, Coney Island, Conisbrough, Constantine, Cumbernauld, Dar es Salaam, Differdange, Downpatrick, Dunfermline, Enniskillen, Farnborough, Fort William, Francistown, Fraserburgh, Fredericton, Glastonbury, Grangemouth, Guadalajara, Guisborough, Hälsingborg, Helsingborg, Helsingfors, High Wycombe, Johor Baharu, Juan-les-Pins, Kaliningrad, Kampong Saom, Karlovy Vary, Kompong Saom, Komsomolosk, Krasnoyarsk, Lianyungang, Londonderry, Lossiemouth, Makhachkala, Mar del Plata, Medicine Hat, Medway Towns, Minneapolis, Montpellier, Narayanganj, Newport News, New York City, Nishinomiya, Northampton, Novosibirsk, Palm Springs, Pointe-Noire, Polonnaruwa, Port Augusta, Porto Alegre, Prestonpans, Punta Arenas, Qinhuangdao, Resistencia, Rockhampton, Rostov-on-Don, Saarbrücken, Scarborough, Southampton, Spanish Town, Springfield, Stourbridge, Szombathely, Tallahassee, Trincomalee, Tselinograd, Vladivostok, Westminster, White Plains, Wu-lu-k'o-mu-shi, Yellowknife, Zhangjiakou

12 Alice Springs, Anuradhapura, Atlantic City, Barquisimeto, Barranquilla, Beverly Hills, Bloemfontein, Buenaventura, Caloocan City, Chesterfield, Christchurch, Ciudad Juárez, East Kilbride, Great Malvern, Higashiosaka, Hubli-Dharwar, Huddersfield, Indianapolis, Jacksonville, Johannesburg, Keetmanshoop, Kota Kinabalu, Kristianstad, Léopoldville, Lisdoonvarna, Loughborough, Luang Prabang, Ludwigshafen, Macclesfield, Magnitogorsk, Mazar-e-Sharif, Milton Keynes, New Amsterdam, Nizhniy Tagil, Novokuznetsk, Oklahoma City, Petaling Jaya, Peterborough, Philadelphia, Pingdingshan, Pointe-à-Pitre, Ponta Delgada, Port Harcourt, Puerto Cortes, Rio de Janeiro, Salt Lake City, San Cristobal, San Francisco, San Pedro Sula, San Sebastian, Santa Barbara, Schaffhausen, Shijiazhuang,

Shuangyashan, Sidi bel Abbès, Skelmersdale, South Shields, Speightstown, Stanleyville, St Catherines, Stoke-on-Trent, St Petersburg, Tel Aviv-Jaffa, Tennant Creek, Thessaloníki, Trichinopoly, Ujung Pandang, Villahermosa, West Bromwich, Williamsburg, Winston-Salem

13 Aix-en-Provence, Belo Horizonte, Bobo-Dioulasso, Charlottetown, Ciudad Guayana, Duque de Caxias, Ellesmere Port, Epsom and Ewell, Great Yarmouth, Ho Chi Minh City, Jefferson City, Kidderminster, Kirkcudbright, Kirkintilloch, Leamington Spa, Lytham St Anne's, Middlesbrough, Ordzhonikidze, Port Elizabeth, Portlaoighise, Quezaltenango, Ribeirao Preto, San Bernardino, San Luis Potosí, Semipalatinsk, Sihanoukville, Veliko Turnovo, Virginia Beach, Visakhapatnam, Wolverhampton, Yekaterinburg, Zlatni Pyasaci

14 Andorra-la-Vella, Dnepropetrovsk, Elisabethville, Feira de Santana, Hemel Hempstead, Henley-on-Thames, Louangphrabang, Santiago de Cuba, Shihchiachuang, Stockton-on-Tees, Székesfehérvár, Tunbridge Wells, Ust-Kamenogorsk, Voroshilovgrad

15 Alcalá de Henares, Angra do Heroísmo, Barrow-in-Furness, Burton-upon-Trent, Charlotte Amalie, Charlottesville, Chester-le-Street, Clermont-Ferrand, Colorado Springs, Frankfurt am Main, Netzahaulcoyotl, Nizhniy Novgorod, Palma de Mallorca, Palmerston North, São João de Meriti, Sekondi-Takoradi, Shoubra el-Kheima, Sutton Coldfield, Weston-super-Mare

See also **Australia**; **Canada**; **Ireland**; **New Zealand**; **Russia**; **United Kingdom**; **United States of America**

• city area
02 EC

civet
05 genet, rasse, zibet **07** genette, linsang, nandine, Viverra
08 mongoose, suricate, toddy cat
09 binturong, delundung, ichneumon, weasel cat **10** paradoxure

civic
04 city, town **05** local, urban **06** public
07 borough **08** communal
09 community, municipal
12 metropolitan

civil
03 civ, lay **04** fair, home **05** civic, local, state **06** polite, public, urbane
07 affable, courtly, refined, secular
08 civilian, communal, domestic, interior, internal, mannerly, national, obliging, polished, temporal, well-bred **09** civilized, community, compliant, courteous, municipal
10 cultivated, respectful
11 complaisant **12** well-mannered
13 accommodating, parliamentary

civilian
03 civ **05** civvy, mufti **07** citizen, gownman **08** gownsman **12** non-combatant

civility
04 tact **06** comity, notice **07** amenity, manners, respect **08** breeding, courtesy, urbanity **09** attention
10 affability, politeness, refinement
11 good manners **12** graciousness, pleasantness **13** courteousness

civilization
06 Kultur, people **07** culture, customs, society **08** progress, urbanity
09 community, education
10 refinement **11** advancement, cultivation, development **12** human society **13** enlightenment
14 sophistication

civilize
04 tame **05** edify **06** polish, refine
07 educate, improve, perfect
08 humanize, instruct **09** cultivate, enlighten, socialize **12** sophisticate

civilized
06 polite, urbane **07** refined
08 advanced, cultured, educated, sensible, sociable **09** courteous, developed **10** cultivated, reasonable
11 enlightened **12** well-mannered
13 sophisticated

civilly
07 courtly **08** mannerly, politely, urbanely **10** obligingly **11** courteously
12 respectfully

clad
06 vested **07** attired, clothed, covered, dressed, wearing

claim
03 ask, bag, own, sue **04** aver, avow, call, hold, kill, need, plea, pose, take
05 cause, clame, exact, right, shout, state **06** affirm, allege, assert, assume, avowal, demand, insist **07** collect, contend, darrain, darrayn, declare, deraign, deserve, pretend, profess, purport, request, require **08** averment, darraign, darraine, maintain, petition, put in for **09** assertion, challenge, darraigne, postulate, privilege
10 allegation, contention, insistence, lay claim to, pretension, profession
11 affirmation, application, declaration, entitlement, requirement, requisition **12** asseveration, be entitled to, have a right to

claimant
06 titler **08** litigant **09** applicant, candidate, pretender, suppliant
10 challenger, petitioner, pretendant, pretendent, supplicant

clairvoyance
03 ESP **09** telepathy **11** second sight
13 psychic powers **14** cryptaesthesia, fortune-telling, hyperaesthesia

clairvoyant
04 seer **05** augur **06** oracle **07** diviner, prophet, psychic **08** telepath
09 prophetic, visionary **10** prophetess, soothsayer, telepathic **12** extrasensory
13 fortune-teller

clam
03 Mya **05** cohog **06** quahog
07 quahaug, scallop **08** tridacna
11 black quahog

clamber
04 claw, shin **05** climb, mount, scale
06 ascend, shinny **08** scrabble, scramble, sprackle **09** spraickle

clammy
04 damp, dank **05** close, heavy, moist, muggy, slimy **06** sticky, sweaty, viscid
08 sweating

clamorous
04 loud **05** lusty, noisy, vocal
07 blaring, blatant, riotous **08** blattant, vehement **09** deafening, insistent
10 boisterous, strepitant, tumultuous, uproarious, vociferant, vociferous
11 open-mouthed **12** obstreperous

clamour
03 cry, din, hue **04** bark, rout, urge, utis
05 blare, claim, noise, raird, reird, rumor **06** demand, hubbub, insist, outcry, racket, rumour, uproar
07 brabble, call for, outrage
08 brouhaha, press for, shouting, stramash **09** agitation, commotion, hue and cry **10** complaints
11 vociferance **12** katzenjammer, vociferation **13** ask for noisily

clamp
03 fix **04** grip, heap, hold, vice
05 brace, clasp, press, stack, tread
06 clench, clinch, fasten, secure
07 bracket, squeeze **08** fastener
09 hand-screw, pinchcock, potato pit
10 Denver boot, immobilize
11 immobilizer

• clamp down on
04 stop **05** limit **07** confine, control, prevent **08** restrain, restrict, suppress
10 put a stop to **11** crack down on
14 come down hard on

clampdown
04 stop **05** limit **07** control
09 crackdown, restraint **10** prevention
11 restriction, suppression

clan
03 set **04** band, gens, hapu, line, name, race, sect, sept **05** group, horde, house, tribe **06** circle, clique, family, kinred **07** coterie, faction, kindred, society **10** fraternity **11** brotherhood
13 confraternity

See also **Scottish**

clandestine
03 sly **06** closet, covert, hidden, secret, sneaky **07** furtive, private
08 backdoor, backroom, stealthy
09 concealed, underhand **10** behind-door, fraudulent, undercover
11 underground **13** surreptitious

14 cloak-and-dagger 15 under-the-counter

clandestinely
05 slyly 07 on the QT 08 covertly, secretly, sneakily 09 furtively, privately 10 on the quiet, stealthily 12 fraudulently 15 surreptitiously, under the counter

clang
04 bong, peal, ring, toll 05 chime, clank, clash, clink, clunk, klang 06 jangle, timbre 07 clatter, resound 11 reverberate 13 reverberation

clanger
04 boob, flub, goof, slip 05 boner, error, fault, gaffe 06 booboo, cock-up, howler, slip-up, stumer 07 bloomer, blunder, faux pas, mistake 08 solecism 09 oversight 10 inaccuracy 12 indiscretion, misjudgement

clank
04 ring, toll 05 clang, clash, clink, clunk 06 jangle 07 clatter, resound 10 resounding 11 reverberate 13 reverberation

clannish
06 narrow, select 07 cliquey, insular 08 cliquish 09 exclusive, parochial, sectarian 10 unfriendly

clap
03 hit, pat, ray 04 bang, bolt, chop, slap 05 blaze, burst, cheer, crack, flare, flash, shaft, smack, spark, whack 06 streak, strike, wallop 07 acclaim, applaud, ovation 08 applause, handclap, plaudite 11 thunderbolt 15 round of applause, standing ovation

claptrap
03 rot 04 blah, bosh, bull, bunk, guff 05 balls, bilge, hokum, trash, tripe 06 bunkum, drivel, faddle, hot air, piffle 07 baloney, blarney, eyewash, hogwash, rhubarb, rubbish, twaddle 08 blethers, buncombe, cobblers, nonsense, tommyrot 09 gibberish, poppycock 10 codswallop

clarification
05 gloss 10 definition, exposition 11 elucidation, explanation 12 illumination 14 interpretation, simplification

clarify
05 clear, gloss, purge 06 define, filter, purify, refine 07 clear up, explain, resolve 08 simplify, spell out 09 elucidate, make clear, make plain 10 illuminate 11 shed light on 12 throw light on

clarity
08 lucidity 09 chiarezza, clearness, plainness, precision, sharpness 10 definition, simplicity, visibility 11 obviousness 12 explicitness, transparency 15 intelligibility, unambiguousness

clash
03 jar, war 04 bang, feud, slam, snap 05 brush, clang, clank, crash, fight, noise, swash 06 gossip, hurtle, jangle, rattle, scream, strike 07 chatter, clatter, collide, contend, co-occur, grapple, jarring, quarrel, warring, wrangle 08 argument, coincide, conflict, disagree, fall foul, fighting, mismatch, not match, showdown, striking 09 collision, not go with 10 fall foul of 11 altercation, discordance, misalliance 12 be discordant, disagreement, irregularity 13 confrontation, not go together 14 be incompatible, look unpleasant 15 incompatibility

clasp
◇ *containment indicator*
03 hug, pin 04 clip, grip, hasp, hold, hook, tach 05 bosom, catch, grasp, press, slide, spang, tache, unite 06 attach, brooch, buckle, clutch, cuddle, enfold, fasten, preace, prease, tassel 07 agraffe, cling to, connect, embosom, embrace, enclasp, grapple, preasse, squeeze 08 fastener 09 fastening, hair slide, interlock, safety pin 10 infibulate

class
03 set 04 chic, form, kind, race, rank, rate, sort, type, year 05 brand, caste, genre, genus, grade, group, level, order, style, taste 06 course, league, lesson, period, phylum, reckon, sphere, status, stream 07 arrange, lecture, quality, section, seminar, species, teach-in 08 category, classify, division, elegance, grouping, standing, tutorial, workshop 09 designate 10 background, categorize, department, pigeonhole, study group 11 distinction, social order, stylishness 12 denomination, pecking order, social status 14 classification, social division, social standing, sophistication

See also **classification**

classic
04 best, Oaks, true 05 Derby, great, ideal, model, prime, usual 06 finest, simple 07 abiding, ageless, elegant, lasting, regular, St Leger, The Oaks, typical, undying 08 Augustan, enduring, exemplar, immortal, masterly, standard, timeless 09 brilliant, excellent, exemplary, first-rate, prototype 10 archetypal, consummate, definitive, first-class, masterwork 11 established, masterpiece, outstanding, traditional, undecorated, understated 12 paradigmatic, time-honoured 13 authoritative 14 characteristic, quintessential, representative 15 established work, unsophisticated

classical
04 pure 05 Attic, Latin, plain 06 humane, simple 07 concert, elegant, Grecian, refined, serious 08 Hellenic 09 excellent, symphonic 10 harmonious, restrained 11 symmetrical, traditional 12 ancient Greek, ancient Roman

See also **musician**; **singer**

classically
06 purely, simply 07 as a rule, plainly, usually 08 normally 09 elegantly, typically 10 ordinarily, originally 11 customarily 12 harmoniously, historically 13 symmetrically, traditionally

classification
05 group 06 method 07 grading, sorting 08 classing, grouping, taxonomy 10 tabulation 11 arrangement, cataloguing 12 codification, distribution 14 categorization 15 systematization

Classifications of living organisms include:

05 class, genus, order
06 domain, empire, family, phylum
07 kingdom, species
08 division

Kingdoms, domains and empires include:

05 fungi
06 monera, plants
07 animals, archaea
08 bacteria, protista
10 eubacteria, eukaryotes
11 prokaryotes
14 archaebacteria

Classes include:

04 Aves
07 Insecta
08 Amphibia, Bivalvia, Mammalia
09 Arachnida, Bryopsida, Pinopsida
10 Gastropoda, Liliopsida
11 Cephalopoda
12 Malacostraca
13 Magnoliopsida

classify
03 peg 04 file, rank, sort, type 05 class, grade, group, order, range 06 assort, codify, divide 07 arrange, dispose, include, sort out 08 regiment, serotype, stratify, tabulate 09 catalogue 10 categorize, distribute, pigeonhole 11 systematize

classy
04 fine, posh 05 grand, ritzy 06 select, smooth, swanky 07 elegant, stylish 08 gorgeous, superior, up-market 09 exclusive, expensive, exquisite, high-class 13 sophisticated

clatter
03 jar 04 bang 05 clang, clank, clunk, crash 06 gossip, hotter, jangle, rattle, strike 07 blatter, chatter

clause
04 item, part 05 point, rider, salvo 06 phrase 07 adjunct, article, chapter, heading, passage, proviso, section 08 clausula, loophole, particle, tenendum 09 condition, novodamus, paragraph, provision, reddendum 10 subsection 13 specification

claw
03 rip **04** clat, crab, fang, maul, nail, sere, tear **05** chela, claut, cloye, graze, griff, seize, talon **06** clutch, griffe, mangle, nipper, pincer, pounce, scrape, unguis **07** falcula, flatter, gripper, scratch **08** lacerate, scrabble **11** clapperclaw

clay
03 cam, pug, wax **04** bole, calm, caum, glei, gley, loam, lute, marl, pisé, slip, soil, tile, till **05** argil, blaes, brick, cloam, earth, fango **06** blaise, blaize, clunch, ground, kaolin **07** kaoline, pottery **08** ceramics, cimolite, illuvium, laterite **09** bentonite **10** lithomarge, meerschaum, plastilina
• **clay-chalk mixture**
04 malm

clean
03 net, new, rub **04** char, even, fair, good, just, neat, nett, pure, tidy, wash, wipe **05** blank, crisp, empty, final, fresh, fully, moral, quite, rinse, scour, sweep, total, utter, whole **06** chaste, decent, emunge, hollow, honest, modest, proper, scrape, simple, smooth, soogee, soogie, unused, washed **07** aseptic, elegant, ethical, launder, perfect, regular, sterile, totally, upright **08** clean-cut, cleansed, clear-cut, complete, decisive, directly, entirely, flawless, graceful, hygienic, innocent, pristine, purified, sanitary, smoothly, spotless, straight, unerring, unmarked, unsoiled, virtuous **09** faultless, guiltless, laundered, reputable, righteous, speckless, unspotted, unstained, unsullied, wholesome **10** above board, antiseptic, completely, conclusive, even-handed, honourable, immaculate, sterilized, unpolluted, upstanding **11** appropriate, respectable, unblemished, uncorrupted, well-defined **12** spick and span, squeaky-clean **13** unadulterated **14** clean as a new pin, decontaminated, uncontaminated

Cleaning products include:

04 soap
06 bleach, polish
07 shampoo, solvent
09 detergent, shower gel
10 bubble bath, soap powder
12 disinfectant
13 washing powder
14 scouring powder
15 washing-up liquid

• **clean out**
03 fay, fey
• **come clean**
05 admit, own up **06** fess up, reveal **07** confess, tell all **11** acknowledge **13** spill the beans

clean-cut
04 neat, tidy, trim **05** fresh, natty, smart, terse **06** spruce **07** orderly **11** uncluttered

cleaner
03 vac **04** char **05** daily, wiper **06** Hoover®, Mrs Mop, vacuum **07** Mrs Mopp, orderly **08** charlady **09** charwoman

cleanliness
06 purity **09** cleanness, freshness **10** perfection **12** spotlessness

cleanse
04 pure, wash **05** bathe, clean, clear, flush, porge, purge, rinse, scour **06** garble, purify **07** absolve, deterge, launder, mundify **08** absterge, lustrate, scavenge **09** disinfect, sterilize **12** make free from

cleanser
04 soap **07** cleaner, scourer, solvent **08** purifier **09** detergent **10** soap powder **12** disinfectant **14** scouring powder

clear
02 go **03** net, rid **04** earn, fair, fine, free, full, gain, jump, keen, land, make, move, neat, nett, open, pass, pure, quit, sure, tidy, void, wipe **05** allow, bring, clean, empty, erase, let go, light, lucid, overt, plain, quick, quite, sharp, sheer, shift, sunny, vault **06** acquit, bright, decode, excuse, filter, glassy, go over, limpid, liquid, loosen, pardon, patent, permit, pocket, refine, remble, remove, serene, settle, unclog, unload, unstop, vacate, vanish, wholly **07** absolve, approve, audible, bring in, certain, cleanse, evident, express, fogless, hyaline, justify, logical, obvious, plainly, precise, release, through, unblock **08** apparent, coherent, definite, distinct, evacuate, evanesce, explicit, get rid of, innocent, jump over, leap over, liberate, luculent, luminous, manifest, melt away, pellucid, positive, pregnant, sanction, sensible, take away, take home, undimmed, undulled **09** authorize, blameless, cloudless, convinced, decongest, disappear, discharge, evaporate, exculpate, exonerate, extricate, guiltless, unblocked, unclouded, unimpeded, vindicate **10** articulate, colourless, diaphonous, disengaged, in the clear, perceptive, pronounced, reasonable, see-through, unhindered, unscramble, untroubled **11** acquittance, beyond doubt, conspicuous, crystalline, disentangle, make a profit, penetrating, perceptible, translucent, transparent, unambiguous, unequivocal, well-defined **12** clear as a bell, crystal-clear, intelligible, recognizable, twenty-twenty, unmistakable, unobstructed **13** find not guilty **14** beyond question, comprehensible, give permission, give the go-ahead, having no qualms, understandable, unquestionable
• **all clear**
09 copacetic, copasetic, kopasetic
• **clear away**
03 mop
• **clear off**
04 quit **06** get out, go away **07** buzz off, gertcha, push off **08** cheese it, run along, shove off
• **clear out**
03 get **04** sort, tidy **05** empty, hop it, leave, scour **06** beat it, depart, get out, go away, tidy up, vacate **07** get lost, push off, sort out **08** clear off, shove off, throw out, withdraw
• **clear up**
03 red **04** fair, redd, sort, tidy **05** crack, order, salve, solve **06** answer, remove **07** clarify, explain, improve, iron out, resolve, sort out, unravel **08** brighten **09** elucidate, liquidate, rearrange **10** become fine, brighten up, put in order, straighten **11** become sunny, stop raining **12** straighten up **13** straighten out
• **not clear**
02 nl **09** non liquet

clearance
02 OK **03** gap **04** room **05** leave, say-so, space, sweep **06** margin, moving **07** consent, freeing, go-ahead, removal **08** clearing, emptying, headroom, riddance, sanction, shifting, vacating **09** allowance, cleansing, unloading **10** demolition, evacuation, green light, permission, taking-away **11** endorsement **13** authorization

clear-cut
05 clean, clear, plain, sharp **07** precise **08** definite, distinct, explicit, sharp-cut, specific **09** trenchant **11** cut and dried, unambiguous, unequivocal, well-defined **13** black and white **15** straightforward

clear-headed
04 wise **05** sober **08** rational, sensible **09** practical, realistic **11** intelligent

clearing
03 gap **04** dell **05** glade, slash, space **06** assart **07** opening **08** scouring, slashing

clearly
04 well **05** plain **06** bright, openly **07** lucidly, plainly **08** markedly, patently **09** evidently, obviously **10** coherently, distinctly, explicitly, manifestly, undeniably **11** undoubtedly **12** indisputably, intelligibly, unmistakably, without doubt **13** conspicuously, incontestably **14** comprehensibly

cleave
◇ *insertion indicator*
03 cut, hew **04** chop, hold, open, part, rend, rift **05** cling, crack, halve, sever, share, slice, split, stick, unite **06** adhere, attach, cohere, divide, pierce, remain, sunder **07** fissure **08** dissever, disunite, separate **09** crack open, split open

cleft
◇ *containment indicator*
03 gap, jag **04** rent, rift, riva **05** break, chasm, chink, cloff, crack, slack, split

06 breach, cranny, parted, sexfid
07 chimney, crevice, divided, fissure, octofid, opening, pharynx
08 cleaving, crevasse, fissured, fracture, scissure 09 bisulcate, quadrifid, septemfid 13 quadripartite

clemency
04 pity 05 mercy 06 lenity
08 humanity, kindness, leniency, mildness, sympathy 10 compassion, generosity, indulgence, moderation, tenderness 11 forbearance, forgiveness, magnanimity
12 mercifulness 15 soft-heartedness

clench
04 grip, grit, hold, seal, shut 05 clasp, close, grasp, press 06 clinch, clutch, double, fasten 07 squeeze 08 double up 12 close tightly 13 press together

clergy
06 church 07 clerics 08 learning, ministry, the cloth 09 churchmen, clergymen, education, the church
10 holy orders, priesthood
11 churchwomen, clergywomen, spiritualty 12 spirituality

clergyman, clergywoman
02 DD, RR 03 Rev 04 dean, imam, papa 05 canon, clerk, padre, rabbi, vicar 06 bishop, cleric, curate, deacon, divine, father, josser, Levite, mother, mullah, parson, pastor, priest, rector
07 diocese, dominie, muezzin, prelate, secular 08 cardinal, chaplain, man of God, minister, Nonjuror, preacher, reverend, sky pilot, spintext, squarson, vartabed 09 churchman, deaconess, presbyter, rural dean 10 arch-priest, prebendary, woman of God
11 churchwoman 12 ecclesiastic
13 man of the cloth 14 superintendent
15 woman of the cloth

clerical
06 filing, office, typing 08 official, pastoral, priestly, reverend
09 canonical, episcopal 10 pen-pushing, sacerdotal 11 keyboarding, ministerial, secretarial, white-collar
14 administrative, ecclesiastical
See also **vestment**

clerk
04 babu 05 baboo 06 circar, notary, priest, scribe, sircar, sirkar, teller, typist, writer 07 actuary, copyist, scholar
08 cursitor, official, Petty Bag, quillman, servitor 09 assistant, clergyman, pen-driver, pen-pusher, secretary 10 book-keeper 11 paper-pusher, protocolist, protonotary, quill-driver 12 prothonotary, receptionist, record-keeper, stenographer
13 account-keeper, administrator, shop-assistant

clever
03 apt 04 able, cute, deft, gleg, keen
05 natty, quick, sharp, smart, witty
06 adroit, artful, brainy, bright, expert, gifted, pretty, shrewd, souple
07 capable, cunning, knowing, notable, sapient, skilful 08 rational, sensible, talented 09 brilliant, conceited, dexterous, ingenious, inventive, sagacious, spiritual
10 discerning, perceptive
11 intelligent, quick-witted, resourceful, sharp-witted
12 apprehensive 13 knowledgeable

cleverly
04 ably 07 capably 08 artfully, astutely, craftily, expertly, shrewdly
09 skilfully 11 ingeniously
12 discerningly 13 intelligently, knowledgeably, quick-wittedly

cliché
06 truism 07 bromide 08 banality, chestnut 09 platitude 10 stereotype
11 commonplace, old chestnut
15 hackneyed phrase

cliché'd, clichéed
04 dull, worn 05 banal, corny, stale, stock, tired, trite 06 common
07 routine, worn-out 08 overused, time-worn 09 hackneyed
10 overworked, pedestrian, threadbare 11 commonplace, stereotyped, wearing thin 12 run-of-the-mill 13 platitudinous, unimaginative

click
04 beat, snap, snip, tick, twig 05 clack, clink, forge, get on, snick 08 cotton on, get along, hit it off 09 get on well, implosive, make sense 10 understand
11 become clear, suction stop 13 fall into place, suctional stop

client
04 user 05 buyer 06 patron, punter, vassal 07 patient, regular, shopper
08 consumer, customer, hanger-on
09 applicant, dependant, purchaser

clientèle
05 trade, users 06 buyers, market
07 clients, patrons 08 business, regulars, shoppers 09 consumers, customers, following, patronage
10 purchasers

cliff
03 tor 04 clef, crag, face, scar 05 bluff, cleve, scarp, scaur 06 cleeve
08 overhang, rock-face 09 precipice
10 escarpment, promontory

climactic
05 final 07 crucial 08 critical, decisive, exciting 09 paramount

climate
04 mood 05 trend 06 milieu, region, spirit, temper 07 feeling, setting, weather 08 ambience, tendency
10 atmosphere 11 disposition, environment, temperament, temperature

climax
03 top 04 acme, apex, head, peak
06 apogee, finale, height, summit, zenith 08 pinnacle 09 crescendo, highlight, high point 11 catastrophe, culmination

climb
◇ *reversal down indicator*
03 sty, top 04 go up, move, ramp, rise, scan, shin, soar, stie, stir, stye 05 jumar, mount, scale, sclim, shift, sklim, speel, swarm 06 ascend, ascent, prusik, shin up 07 clamber, going up, shoot up
08 increase, scramble, surmount
11 herringbone, mountaineer, upward slope 14 uphill struggle

• **climb down**
05 yield 07 concede, descend, retract, retreat 08 back down 09 surrender
12 eat your words

• **climbing party**
04 rope

climb-down
07 retreat 08 yielding 09 surrender
10 concession, retraction, withdrawal

climber
03 ivy 04 Jack, Jill, vine 07 speeler
10 nasturtium 11 balloon-vine, honeysuckle, Jack and Jill, mountaineer
12 kangaroo vine, morning glory
13 scarlet runner 14 Scotch attorney

clinch
03 pun 04 land, seal 05 clink, close, rivet 06 clench, decide, secure, settle, verify 07 confirm, embrace, grapple
08 conclude 09 determine

cling
03 hug 04 grip, hold 05 clasp, grasp, stick 06 adhere, attach, cleave, clutch, defend, fasten, hold on, shrink
07 embrace, shrivel, stand by, support
08 hold on to, stay true 09 adherence
10 be faithful

clinic
07 doctor's 08 hospital 09 infirmary
10 sanatorium 12 health centre
13 medical centre

clinical
04 cold 05 basic, plain, stark
06 simple 07 austere, medical, patient
08 analytic, detached, hospital
09 impassive, objective, unadorned, unfeeling 10 analytical, antiseptic, impersonal, scientific, uninvolved
11 emotionless, unemotional
12 businesslike 13 disinterested, dispassionate

clinically
09 medically 14 scientifically

clink *see* **prison**

clip
◇ *tail deletion indicator*
03 box, cut, dod, fix, hit, pin 04 crop, cuff, dock, hold, mute, pare, poll, slap, snip, trim 05 cheat, clout, D-ring, graze, jumar, prune, punch, shear, smack, thump, tough, whack
06 attach, crutch, cut off, cut out, fasten, reduce, staple, strike, tingle, wallop 07 Bulldog®, curtail, cutting, embrace, excerpt, extract, passage, pollard, run into, section, shorten, snippet 08 citation, cut short, encircle, fastener, truncate 09 crash into,

quotation **10** abbreviate, clothes-peg, clothes-pin, jumar clamp, overcharge **11** collide with, music holder

See also **cut**

clipping

04 clip **05** scrow, shear, shred **06** paring **07** cutting, excerpt, extract, passage, section, snippet, topiary **08** citation, snipping, trimming **09** quotation

clique

03 set **04** band, clan, club, gang, pack, ring **05** bunch, crowd, group **06** circle, set-out **07** coterie, faction, in-crowd, society **08** grouplet **10** fraternity

cloak

04 cape, coat, hide, mask, pall, rail, robe, veil, wrap **05** blind, cloke, cover, front **06** mantle, screen, shield, shroud **07** conceal, obscure, pretext **08** covering, disguise **10** camouflage

Cloaks include:

04 capa
05 amice, grego, jelab, manta, pilch, sagum, shawl, talma
06 abolla, capote, dolman, domino, poncho, visite
07 chlamys, galabea, galabia, jellaba, korowai, manteel, mantlet, paenula, pelisse, pluvial, rocklay, rokelay, sarafan
08 capuchin, cardinal, djellaba, galabeah, galabiah, gallabea, gallabia, himation, mantelet, mantilla, palliate
09 djellabah, gabardine, gaberdine, gallabeah, gallabiah, gallabieh, gallabiya
10 gallabiyah, gallabiyeh, paludament, roquelaure
11 buffalo robe
12 mousquetaire, paludamentum

clobber

◇ *anagram indicator*

03 hit, kit, zap **04** bash, beat, belt, capa, garb, gear, lick, rout, ruin, slap, sock, togs **05** clout, crush, knock, punch, stuff, thump, whack **06** attack, defeat, hammer, strike, tackle, things, thrash, wallop **07** baggage, conquer, trounce **08** clothing, garments **09** equipment, overpaint, overwhelm **10** belongings **11** bits and bobs, possessions **13** bits and pieces, paraphernalia

clock

03 hit, sit **04** face **05** brood, cluck **06** beetle, notice **07** observe **08** ornament **10** mileometer, timekeeper **11** speedometer

Clocks and watches include:

03 fob, Tim
04 ring, stop
05 alarm, wrist
06 atomic, cuckoo, mantel, quartz
07 bracket, digital, pendant, sundial
08 analogue, carriage, longcase, speaking
09 repeating
10 travelling
11 chronograph, chronometer, grandfather, grandmother

• clock up

03 log **05** reach **06** attain, record **07** achieve, archive, chalk up, notch up **08** register

• round the clock

10 constantly **11** ceaselessly, day and night **12** continuously **15** twenty-four seven, without stopping

clod

04 hunk, lump, mass, mool, pelt, slab **05** block, chunk, clump, glebe, throw, wedge **06** ground

clog

03 dam, jam, log, mud **04** ball, gaum, gorm **05** block, choke, dam up, sabot **06** accloy, ball up, bung up, burden, chopin, galosh, golosh, hamper, hinder, hobble, impede, patten, pester, stop up **07** chopine, clutter, congest, galoche, occlude **08** encumber, obstruct

cloister

05 aisle **06** arcade **07** portico, walkway **08** corridor, pavement **10** ambulatory

cloistered

08 confined, enclosed, hermitic, isolated, secluded, shielded **09** cloistral, insulated, protected, reclusive, sheltered, withdrawn **10** restricted **11** sequestered

close

03 bar, Clo, end, row **04** best, bolt, clog, cork, dear, fail, fill, flop, fold, fuse, good, hard, join, keen, lane, like, lock, mean, mews, mure, near, plug, road, seal, shet, shut, slam, stop, true **05** block, bosom, cease, court, dense, exact, fixed, fuggy, heavy, humid, muggy, pause, place, quiet, solid, tight, union, unite **06** at hand, clinch, decide, direct, ending, fasten, finale, finish, gain on, go bust, hidden, lessen, lock up, loving, marked, narrow, nearby, nearly, not far, packed, secret, secure, settle, shut up, square, sticky, stingy, stop up, strait, street, strict, strong, stuffy, sultry, verify, wind up **07** adjourn, airless, block up, cadence, careful, close by, compact, confirm, cramped, crowded, densely, devoted, grapple, intense, literal, miserly, occlude, padlock, precise, private, similar, terrace, tightly **08** accurate, adjacent, approach, attached, block off, collapse, complete, conclude, conflict, cul-de-sac, detailed, distinct, faithful, familiar, imminent, intimate, junction, obstruct, reserved, reticent, rigorous, round off, secluded, secretly, shut down, stifling, straight, streight, taciturn, thorough **09** adjoining, cessation, close down, close-knit, condensed, courtyard, determine, enclosure, encounter, establish, immediate, impending, niggardly, searching, secretive, terminate, winding-up **10** come closer, comparable, completion, conclusion, dénouement, go bankrupt, hard-fought, methodical, oppressive, quadrangle, sweltering **11** adjournment, approaching, catch up with, culmination, discontinue, draw to an end, get closer to, go to the wall, inseparable, neck and neck, painstaking, suffocating, termination, well-matched **12** a stone's throw, bring to an end, concentrated, confidential, neighbouring, on the brink of, on the verge of, parsimonious, unventilated **13** corresponding, evenly matched, in the vicinity, penny-pinching, unforthcoming **14** cease operating, on your doorstep **15** cease operations, uncommunicative

• close in

04 shut **08** approach, draw near, encircle, surround **10** come nearer

• close to

02 on **04** near, nigh **06** fast by, nearby

• keep close to

03 hug

closed

02 to **04** dark, shut **05** drawn **06** lucken

• not closed

04 agee, ajar, ajee, open

closet

04 zeta **05** press, privy **06** covert, hidden, recess, secret **07** cabinet, confine, furtive, isolate, private, seclude **08** cloister, cupboard, shut away, wardrobe **10** undercover, unrevealed **11** storage room, underground **13** surreptitious

closure

03 gag **05** block **07** cloture, failure, folding **08** blocking, shutdown, shutting **09** stricture, winding-up **10** bankruptcy, guillotine, stopping-up **11** closing-down, obstruction **12** laryngospasm

clot

03 gel, git, mug, nit, set **04** clag, dope, dork, fool, glob, lump, mass, nerd, prat, twit **05** clump, cruor, grume, idiot, twerp, wally **06** curdle, gobbet, lapper, lopper **07** congeal, embolus, plonker, splatch, thicken **08** clotting, coalesce, imbecile, solidify, thrombus **09** blockhead, coagulate **10** bufflehead, nincompoop, thrombosis **11** coagulation, obstruction **12** crassamentum

cloth

03 lap, rag **05** sails, stuff, towel **06** duster, fabric, lappie **07** flannel, textile **08** material **09** churchmen, clergymen, dishcloth, facecloth, the church, the clergy **10** floorcloth, holy orders, upholstery **11** churchwomen, clergywomen, the ministry

See also **fabric**

• measure of cloth

03 ell, end

• piece of cloth
03 lap, rag **04** fent, gair, pane, sash **05** clout, godet, lapje **06** lappie **07** remnant

clothe
03 rig **04** coat, cour, deck, gird, robe, vest, wrap **05** cover, drape, dress, endew, endue, equip, habit, indew, indue, put on **06** attire, carpet, emboss, enrobe, fit out, invest, outfit **07** apparel, bedizen, blanket, envelop, garment, overlay, vesture **08** accoutre **09** caparison

clothes, clothing
03 kit **04** drag, duds, garb, gear, togs, wear, weed **05** braws, claes, dress, get-up **06** attire, outfit **07** apparel, clobber, costume, raiment, threads, toggery, uniform, vesture **08** cast-offs, clothing, dressing, garments, glad rags, wardrobe **09** trousseau, vestiture, vestments **11** habiliments, hand-me-downs

See also **boot**; **cloak**; **coat**; **dress**; **footwear**; **hat**; **headdress**; **jacket**; **scarf**; **vestment**

Clothes include:

02 gi
03 aba, boa, bra, fur, gie, obi, PJs, tie, top
04 501s®, abba, belt, body, buff, capa, cape, coat, furs, gown, kilt, maud, midi, mink, mitt, muff, rami, ruff, sack, sari, sash, slip, slop, sock, spat, suit, sulu, toga, toge, veil, vest, wrap
05 abaya, burka, cloak, cords, dhoti, dress, frock, glove, ihram, jeans, kanzu, Levis®, lungi, pants, parka, ruana, scarf, shawl, shift, shirt, shrug, skirt, smock, stole, teddy, thong, tunic
06 basque, bikini, blouse, bodice, boorka, bow-tie, boxers, braces, briefs, caftan, corset, cravat, denims, dirndl, fleece, garter, girdle, jersey, jubbah, jumper, kaross, kimono, mitten, poncho, sacque, samfoo, sarong, shorts, slacks, tabard, tights, T-shirt
07 catsuit, crop top, doublet, g-string, hosiery, jimjams, leotard, muffler, necktie, nightie, overall, panties, pyjamas, singlet, spattee, sweater, tank top, twin-set, uniform, vest top, wet suit, yashmak, Y-fronts
08 bathrobe, bedsocks, breeches, camisole, cardigan, culottes, earmuffs, flannels, guernsey, hipsters, hot pants, jodhpurs, jumpsuit, leggings, lingerie, negligee, pashmina, pinafore, polo-neck, pullover, raincoat, swimsuit, tee-shirt, trousers
09 balaclava, bed-jacket, brassière, coveralls, dress suit, dungarees, hair shirt, housecoat, jockstrap, mini skirt, outerwear, pantihose, petticoat, plus-fours, polo shirt, salopette, separates, shahtoosh, shell suit, Sloppy Joe, stockings, tracksuit, underwear, waistcoat
10 boiler suit, Capri pants, cummerbund, dinner-gown, drainpipes, dress-shirt, flying suit, leg-warmers, lounge suit, nightdress, nightshirt, romper suit, rugby shirt, string vest, suspenders, sweat-shirt, turtle-neck, underpants
11 bell-bottoms, boiled shirt, boxer-shorts, leisure suit, morning suit, pencil-skirt, thermal vest, trouser suit
12 body stocking, camiknickers, divided-skirt, dressing-gown, evening-dress, palazzo pants, pedal-pushers, shirtwaister
13 Bermuda shorts, cycling shorts, liberty bodice, pinafore skirt, shalwar-kameez, suspender belt
14 bathing-costume, combat trousers, double-breasted, French knickers, jogging bottoms, single-breasted, swimming trunks, three-piece suit
15 swimming costume

• plain clothes
05 mufti

• shabby clothes
03 tat

cloud
03 dim, fog **04** blur, dull, mist, puff, rack, veil, weft **05** chill, cover, shade **06** billow, darken, defame, mantle, muddle, shadow, shroud **07** confuse, eclipse, obscure **08** dullness, woolpack **09** obfuscate **10** overshadow

Clouds include:

06 cirrus, nimbus
07 cumulus, stratus
10 mare's-tails
11 altocumulus, altostratus
12 cirrocumulus, cirrostratus, cumulonimbus, nimbostratus
13 fractocumulus, fractostratus, stratocumulus

cloudless
03 dry **04** fair, fine **05** clear, sunny **06** bright **08** pleasant **09** unclouded

cloudy
01 c **03** dim **04** dark, dull, grey, hazy **05** foggy, heavy, milky, misty, muddy, murky, vague **06** blurry, gloomy, leaden, opaque, sombre **07** blurred, muddled, obscure, sunless **08** confused, lowering, nebulous, nubilous, overcast **10** indistinct

clout
03 box, hit **04** blow, cuff, pull, slap, slug, sock **05** patch, power, punch, smack, thump, whack **06** muscle, strike, wallop, weight **07** garment **08** prestige, standing **09** authority, influence

cloven
05 cleft, split **07** divided **08** bisected

clown
04 dork, fool, geek, jerk, jest, joke, nerd, twit, zany **05** antic, chuff, comic, idiot, joker, ninny, twerp, wally **06** antick, august, chough, dimwit, jester, joskin, nitwit, Pompey, rustic **07** anticke, antique, auguste, buffoon, bumpkin, Costard **08** comedian, dipstick, gracioso, imbecile, numskull **09** blockhead, grotesque, harlequin, muck about, patchocke, Whiteface **10** act the fool, fool around, goof around, mess around, nincompoop, patchcocke, Touchstone **11** carpet clown, merry-andrew, play the fool **12** act foolishly **13** pickle-herring

Clowns include:

04 Bozo, Coco, Hobo, Joey
05 Tramp
07 Pierrot
08 Grimaldi, Owl-glass, Trinculo
09 Owle-glass
10 Howleglass, Owlspiegle
14 Joseph Grimaldi

cloying
04 icky **06** sickly **07** choking, fulsome **08** luscious **09** excessive, oversweet, sickening **10** disgusting, nauseating

club
03 hit, set **04** bash, beat **05** bunch, clout, group, guild, order, union **06** batter, beat up, circle, clique, fascio, league, priest, pummel, strike **07** chapter, clobber, combine, company, society, sorosis **08** hetairia **09** auxiliary **10** federation, fraternity, sisterhood **11** association, brotherhood, combination, free-and-easy **12** organization **13** life-preserver

See also **football**; **golf club**

Clubs include:

03 bar, bat
04 cosh, mace, patu, polt
05 bandy, billy, caman, nulla, staff, stick, waddy
06 cudgel, hurley
07 bourdon
08 bludgeon, trunnion
09 blackjack, truncheon
10 knobkerrie, nulla-nulla
12 shinty-stick

Club types include:

03 fan, job
04 boat, book, glee, golf
05 disco, field, goose, night, slate, strip, yacht, youth
06 bridge, health, social, tennis
07 cabaret, country, singles
09 warehouse
10 investment
11 discotheque
12 Darby and Joan

Club names include:

03 MCC, RAC, Ski
04 Arts, Turf
05 Buck's, Naval
06 Alpine, Cotton, Drones, Jockey, Kennel, Kitcat, Pratt's, Queen's, Reform, Rotary, Savage, Savile, United, White's

07 Almack's, Authors', Boodle's, Brooks's, Canning, Carlton, Country, Farmers, Garrick, Groucho, Kiwanis, Leander, Railway, Variety
08 Hell-fire, National, Oriental, Portland
09 Athenaeum, Beefsteak, East India, Green Room, Lansdowne, Wig and Pen
10 Caledonian, City Livery, Crockford's, Flyfishers', Hurlingham, Oddfellows, Roehampton, Travellers
11 Army and Navy, Arts Theatre, Chelsea Arts
12 Anglo-Belgian, City of London, London Rowing, New Cavendish, Thames Rowing
13 Royal Air Force
14 American Women's, City University
15 National Liberal, Royal Automobile, Victory Services

• club together
06 chip in **09** give money **10** contribute, join forces **12** share the cost **14** have a whip-round
• in the club *see* **pregnant**

clubhouse
02 ch **14** nineteenth hole

clubs
01 C
• jack of clubs
03 pam

clue
03 tip **04** hint, idea, lead, sign **05** fix up, light, trace **06** clavis, notion, thread, tip-off **07** inkling, pointer **08** evidence, signpost **09** master-key, suspicion **10** indication, intimation, suggestion

clueless
04 dumb **05** dense, thick **06** stupid **08** helpless, ignorant **09** unlearned **10** uninformed, unschooled **11** not all there, uninitiated **13** inexperienced

clump
03 lot, mot **04** beat, blow, clot, knot, mass, mott, plod, thud, tuft, tump **05** amass, bluff, bunch, clomp, group, motte, plump, stamp, stomp, thump, tramp **06** bundle, lumber, spinny, trudge **07** cluster, spinney, stumble, thicket, tussock **10** accumulate, collection **11** agglutinate **12** accumulation **13** agglomeration, agglutination

clumsy
◇ *anagram indicator*
03 ham **04** rude **05** bulky, crude, Dutch, gawky, heavy, hulky, inept, looby, rough, squab **06** clunky, gauche, oafish, thumby, wooden **07** awkward, chuckle, hulking, ill-made, spastic, uncouth, unhandy **08** bungling, clumping, tactless, ungainly, unheppen, unwieldy **09** all thumbs, ham-fisted, ham-handed, lumbering, maladroit, shapeless, two-fisted, unskilful **10** blundering, cack-handed, cumbersome, Dutch-built, kack-handed, ungraceful, unhandsome **11** heavy-handed, insensitive **12** hippopotamic, unmanageable **13** accident-prone, chuckle-headed, hippopotamian, unco-ordinated **14** banana-fingered

cluster
03 bob **04** band, knot, mass, tuft **05** batch, bunch, clump, crowd, flock, group, plump, strap, truss **06** gather, huddle, raceme **07** collect, panicle **08** assemble, assembly **09** gathering **10** assemblage, assortment, collection, congregate, racemation **11** constellate **12** come together **13** agglomeration, group together, inflorescence

clustered
06 massed **07** bunched, grouped **08** gathered **09** assembled, glomerate **11** agglomerate

clutch
◇ *containment indicator*
03 set **04** claw, grab, grip, hold, jaws, sway **05** brood, catch, clasp, claws, grasp, gripe, group, hands, hatch, mercy, power, seize **06** clench, graple, number, snatch **07** claucht, claught, cling to, control, custody, embrace, grapple, gripper, keeping, setting, sitting **08** dominion, hang on to, hatching **09** get hold of **10** incubation, possession, take hold of

clutter
04 fill, mess, stir **05** chaos, cover, noise, strew **06** jumble, litter, mess up, midden, muddle **07** scatter **08** disarray, disorder, encumber **09** confusion, make a mess **10** make untidy, untidiness **12** fill untidily

coach
03 bus, cab, car, gig **04** coch, cram, drag, post, trap **05** drill, prime, teach, train, tutor, wagon **06** fiacre, hansom, landau, mentor, school **07** droshky, grinder, hackney, minibus, prepare, railbus, rattler, tally-ho, teacher, trainer **08** barouche, brougham, carriage, educator, instruct, motor-bus **09** battlebus, buffet car, cabriolet, charabanc, Greyhound **10** four-in-hand, griddle car, instructor, motor-coach, répétiteur **12** express coach
See also **carriage**

coagulate
03 gel, ren, rin, run, set **04** cake, clot, melt **06** curdle **07** clotted, clotter, congeal, curdled, thicken **08** solidify

coagulation
08 clotting **10** congealing, thickening **11** solidifying

coal
03 jet, jud, nut **04** char, jeat, smut **05** dross, ember, small **06** cinder, splint **07** lignite **10** anthracite **13** black diamonds
• coal dust
04 coom, culm, duff
• coal scuttle
03 hod **09** purdonium
• coal yard
03 ree **04** reed

coalesce
03 mix **04** fuse, join **05** blend, merge, unite **06** cohere, commix **07** combine **09** affiliate, commingle, integrate **10** amalgamate **11** consolidate, incorporate **12** join together

coalescence
06 fusion, merger **07** mixture **08** blending **09** immixture **11** affiliation, combination, integration **12** amalgamation, concrescence **13** consolidation, incorporation

coalition
04 bloc **05** union **06** fusion, league, merger **07** compact, joining **08** alliance **10** federation **11** affiliation, association, combination, confederacy, conjunction, integration, partnership **12** amalgamation **13** confederation

coarse
03 ham **04** base, blue, rank, rude **05** bawdy, broad, brute, crass, crude, gross, hairy, harsh, lumpy, rough, rudas, scaly **06** blowsy, blowzy, brutal, common, earthy, incult, ribald, ribaud, rugged, shaggy, smutty, uneven, vulgar **07** abusive, boorish, bristly, loutish, obscene, prickly, raunchy, rybauld, uncivil **08** gorblimy, immodest, impolite, improper, indecent, inferior, porterly, unbolted **09** gorblimey, off-colour, offensive, unrefined **10** indelicate, unfinished, unpolished, unpurified **11** foul-mouthed, ill-mannered, unprocessed

coarsely
06 rudely **07** bawdily, crudely, roughly **08** ruggedly, unevenly, vulgarly **09** boorishly, loutishly, obscenely **10** immodestly, impolitely, improperly, indecently **11** irregularly, offensively

coarsen
04 dull **05** blunt **06** deaden, harden **07** roughen, thicken **08** indurate **11** desensitize

coarseness
04 smut **06** raunch **07** crudity, hoggery **08** ribaldry **09** bawdiness, hairiness, immodesty, indecency, obscenity, roughness, vulgarism, vulgarity **10** crassitude, earthiness, indelicacy, ruggedness, smuttiness, unevenness **11** grossièreté, prickliness **12** irregularity **13** offensiveness

coast
04 cost, sail, side, taxi **05** beach, coste, drift, glide, limit, shore, slide, terms **06** border, cruise, region, strand **07** footing, seaside **08** littoral, seaboard, seashore **09** coastline, direction, foreshore, freewheel
• coast road
04 prom

coaster
04 grab **05** doily, doyly, smack
07 beermat

coat
04 cake, daub, film, hair, hide, mack, pave, pelt, skin, wool **05** apply, cover, glaze, layer, paint, put on, quote, sheet, skirt, smear **06** clothe, enamel, finish, mantle, spread, veneer **07** coating, encrust, overlay, plaster, put over, varnish **08** cladding, covering, laminate, pellicle **10** integument, lamination

Coats include:

03 box, car, fur, mac
04 baju, buff, cape, jack, jump, maxi, midi, over, pink, rain, sack, tail, warm
05 acton, cimar, cloak, cymar, drape, dress, frock, gilet, great, grego, jupon, lammy, loden, parka, sayon, wamus
06 achkan, Afghan, anorak, Basque, blazer, bolero, cagoul, covert, dolman, duffel, fleece, jacket, jerkin, kagool, kagoul, kirtle, lammie, poncho, reefer, riding, sacque, sports, tabard, taberd, trench, tuxedo, Zouave
07 Barbour®, blanket, blouson, cagoule, cutaway, kagoule, Mae West, matinée, morning, overall, snorkel, surtout, swagger, vareuse, zamarra, zamarro
08 Burberry®, camisole, gambeson, haqueton, mackinaw, sherwani
09 bed jacket, gabardine, gaberdine, hacqueton, macintosh, Mao-jacket, newmarket, pea-jacket, petticoat, redingote, shortgown
10 body-warmer, bumfreezer, bush jacket, carmagnole, claw-hammer, Eton jacket, flak jacket, half-kirtle, life jacket, mackintosh, mess jacket, roundabout, windjammer
11 biker jacket, puffa jacket, shell jacket, swallowtail, Windbreaker®, windcheater
12 bomber jacket, combat jacket, dinner jacket, donkey jacket, lumberjacket, monkey jacket, Prince Albert, pyjama jacket, safari jacket, sports jacket, straitjacket
13 hacking jacket, matinee jacket, Norfolk jacket, reefing-jacket
14 shooting jacket

coating
03 fur **04** coat, film, skin, wash **05** crust, glaze, layer, sheet **06** crusta, enamel, finish, patina, resist, slough, veneer **07** blanket, dusting, overlay, varnish, washing **08** covering, membrane **10** colourwash, lamination, pebbledash

coax
03 pet **04** draw, wile **05** carny, tempt **06** allure, cajole, carney, entice, fleech, humour, induce, soothe **07** beguile, cuittle, flatter, wheedle, win over **08** blandish, collogue, get round, inveigle, persuade, soft-soap, talk into, win round **09** sweet-talk, whillywha **10** whillywhaw **11** prevail upon

cobalt
02 Co

cobber *see* **friend**

cobble
04 pave
• **cobble together**
07 knock up **09** improvise **11** make quickly, make roughly, put together **13** throw together **14** prepare quickly, prepare roughly, produce quickly, produce roughly

cobbler
04 snab, snob **05** sutor **06** cosier, cozier, soutar, souter, sowter

cobblers *see* **rubbish**

cobra
03 asp **04** naga, Naia, Naja **05** aspic
09 hamadryad

cocaine
01 C **04** blow, coke, snow **05** candy, crack **07** charlie, crystal **08** freebase **09** nose candy, ready-wash **10** white stuff

cock
03 dog, tap, tip **04** bend, lift, tilt
05 capon, henny, point, raise, slant, strut **07** chicken, gobbler, incline, rooster, swagger **08** cockerel, nonsense, shake-bag **10** bubbly-jock, roadrunner **11** chanticleer, game-chicken
• **cock up**
◇ *anagram indicator*
04 hash, muff, ruin **05** bodge, farce, fluff **06** bungle, foul up, mess up, muck up **07** blunder, screw up **08** shambles **11** make a hash of, make a mess of

cockeyed
04 awry, daft **05** askew, barmy, crazy, tipsy **06** absurd **07** crooked
08 lopsided **09** half-baked, ludicrous, senseless, skew-whiff **11** nonsensical
12 asymmetrical, preposterous

cockily
08 cheekily **10** impudently, insolently
13 impertinently **15** disrespectfully

Cockney
◇ *dialect indicator*
04 'Arry **06** 'Arriet **09** Londonese
10 pearly king **11** pearly queen

cocksure
04 vain **05** brash, cocky **08** arrogant
09 conceited **10** swaggering
11 egotistical, self-assured, swell-headed **13** overconfident, self-confident, self-important, swollen-headed

cocktail
◇ *anagram indicator*

Cocktails include:

04 Sour
05 Bronx
06 eggnog, Gimlet, Mai tai, mojito, Rickey, Rob Roy
07 Bellini, Collins, Martini®, negroni, pink gin, Sazerac®, Sidecar, Slammer, Stinger
08 Acapulco, Brown Cow, Bullshot, Daiquiri, Pink Lady, salty dog, snowball
09 buck's fizz, Kir Royale, long vodka, Manhattan, Margarita, Rusty Nail, Sea Breeze, whisky mac, White Lady
10 Bloody Mary, blue lagoon, Caipirinha, Horse's Neck, margharita, Moscow Mule, piña colada, Tom Collins, whisky sour
11 black velvet, gin-and-tonic, gloom raiser, Screwdriver
12 Black Russian, Cosmopolitan, Old Fashioned, White Russian
13 Planter's Punch
14 American Beauty, Singapore Sling, tequila slammer, Tequila Sunrise
15 Brandy Alexander

See also **liqueur**; **spirits**

cocky
04 pert, vain **05** brash, perky
06 bouncy **08** arrogant, cocksure, jumped-up **09** bumptious, conceited, hubristic **10** swaggering **11** egotistical, self-assured **13** overconfident, self-confident, self-important, swollen-headed

cocoon
03 pod **04** wrap **05** cover **06** defend, dupion, swathe **07** cushion, envelop, isolate, protect **08** cloister, insulate, preserve **11** overprotect

coddle
03 pet **04** baby **05** spoil **06** cosher, cosset, humour, pamper **07** indulge, protect **11** mollycoddle, overprotect

code
◇ *anagram indicator*
03 law **04** laws **05** codex, fuero, Morse, rules, signs **06** cipher, codify, custom, cypher, ethics, morals, system, volume **07** bar code, conduct, letters, manners, numbers, symbols, zip code
08 morality, postcode, practice
09 etiquette, iddy-umpty, local code, Morse code **10** convention, cryptogram, postal code, principles
11 cryptograph, machine code, regulations **12** dialling code, national code **13** secret message, secret writing
14 secret language

codify
05 group, order **06** digest **07** marshal, sort out **08** classify, organize
09 catalogue **11** systematize

coerce
05 bully, drive, force **06** compel, lean on **07** dragoon **08** bludgeon, browbeat, bulldoze, pressure, railroad, threaten, use force **09** constrain, pressgang, strongarm **10** intimidate, pressurize **14** put the screws on

coercion
04 heat **05** force **06** duress
07 duresse, threats **08** big stick,

bullying, pressure **09** restraint **10** compulsion, constraint **11** arm-twisting, browbeating **12** direct action, intimidation

coffee
03 joe

Coffee roasts and blends include:

04 Java
05 decaf
06 filter, ground, Kenyan
07 Arabica, instant
09 Colombian, dark roast
10 Costa Rican, light roast, percolated
11 French roast
12 Blue Mountain
13 decaffeinated

Coffees include:

05 black, Irish, latte, milky, Mocha, white
06 filter, Gaelic
07 Turkish
08 café noir, espresso
09 Americano, cafetière, demitasse
10 café au lait, café filtre, cappuccino
11 skinny latte

• coffee house
04 cafe, caff

coffer
03 ark, box **04** case, cash, safe **05** chest, funds, hoard, means, money, store, trunk **06** assets, casket, wealth **07** backing, capital, coffret, finance, lacunar **08** moneybox, treasury **09** resources, strongbox **10** repository

coffin
03 box **04** kist **05** flask, shell **06** casket, larnax **11** sarcophagus **12** pine overcoat, wooden kimono **14** wooden overcoat

cogency
05 force, power **06** weight **07** potency, urgency **08** strength **09** influence **12** forcefulness, plausibility **13** effectiveness

cogent
06 potent, strong, urgent **07** weighty **08** forceful, forcible, powerful, pregnant **09** effective **10** compelling, conclusive, convincing, persuasive **11** influential **12** irresistible, unanswerable

cogently
08 forcibly, potently, strongly, urgently **10** forcefully, powerfully **11** effectively **12** compellingly, conclusively, convincingly, persuasively

cogitate
04 mull, muse **06** ponder **07** reflect **08** consider, meditate, mull over, ruminate **09** cerebrate **10** deliberate **11** contemplate, think deeply

cognate
03 cog **04** akin **05** alike **06** agnate, allied, kinred **07** kindred, related, similar **09** analogous, conjugate, connected **10** affiliated, associated, congeneric **11** consanguine **13** corresponding

cognition
06 reason **07** insight **08** learning, thinking **09** awareness, knowledge, reasoning **10** perception **11** discernment, rationality **12** apprehension, intelligence **13** comprehension, consciousness, enlightenment, understanding

cognizance
• take cognizance of
06 accept, regard **09** recognize **11** acknowledge **12** take notice of **13** become aware of

cognizant
05 aware **06** versed **07** witting **08** acknowne, apprised, familiar, informed **09** conscious **10** acquainted, conversant **13** knowledgeable

cohabit
03 bed **06** occupy **07** company, shack up **08** live with **09** live in sin, live tally **12** live together **13** sleep together

cohere
04 bind, fuse, hold **05** add up, agree, cling, stick, unite **06** adhere, square **07** combine **08** coalesce **09** harmonize, make sense **10** correspond **11** consolidate **12** be consistent, hang together, hold together

coherence
05 sense, union, unity **07** harmony **09** agreement, congruity, connexion **10** connection, consonance, logicality **11** concordance, consistency **14** correspondence

coherent
05 clear, lucid **07** logical, orderly **08** joined-up, rational, reasoned, sensible **09** connected, organized **10** articulate, consistent, meaningful, systematic **11** well-planned **12** intelligible **14** comprehensible, well-structured

cohesion
05 sense, union, unity, whole **07** harmony **09** agreement **10** connection, solidarity **11** consistency **12** togetherness **14** correspondence

cohesive
05 close **06** joined, united **08** coherent, together **09** connected, tenacious **10** continuous **12** interrelated

cohort
03 lot, set **04** band, body, mate, unit **05** batch, buddy, class, group, squad, troop **06** column, legion **07** bracket, brigade, company, partner **08** category, division, follower, myrmidon, regiment, sidekick, squadron **09** assistant, associate, companion, supporter **10** accomplice, contingent **11** combination **14** categorization, classification

coil
04 clew, clue, curl, fake, fank, fuss, hank, loop, ring, roll, turn, wind **05** bight, choke, helix, noise, round, skein, snake, spire, twine, twirl, twist, whorl, wring **06** bought, hubbub, spiral, toroid, tumult, wreath, writhe **07** entwine, primary, rouleau, wreathe **08** solenoid, volution **09** convolute, corkscrew **11** convolution

coin
04 bean, cash, cast, dump, mint **05** forge, money, piece, quoin, stamp **06** change, create, devise, invent, make up, silver, specie, strike **07** dream up, produce, think up **08** brockage, conceive, hard cash **09** fabricate, formulate, hard money, neologize, originate **10** lucky-piece **11** cornerstone, loose change, small change

See also **currency**

Coins include:

02 as, at, xu
03 bit, bob, cob, dam, écu, esc, fen, hao, joe, mag, mil, mna, moy, ore, pul, pya, rap, sen, sol, sou, ure, zuz
04 anna, buck, cent, chon, dime, doit, duro, fals, fils, jane, jiao, joey, kuru, lion, lwei, maik, make, merk, mina, mite, mule, obol, para, paul, peni, quid, real, rial, ryal, sent, tael, zack
05 angel, baisa, bodle, brock, brown, butut, conto, copec, crown, ducat, eagle, gerah, gopik, groat, khoum, kopek, laari, lepta, livre, louis, mopus, noble, obang, paolo, pence, penny, piece, pound, royal, scudo, scute, stamp, taler, thebe, unite
06 aureus, bezant, boddle, copeck, copper, denier, dirham, dollar, double, escudo, florin, guinea, hansel, kopeck, nickel, obolus, pagoda, pesewa, satang, sequin, stater, talent, tanner, thaler
07 austral, carolus, centavo, centime, centimo, chetrum, crusado, drachma, guilder, ha'penny, jacobus, moidore, Pfennig, piastre, pistole, pollard, quarter, sextant, solidus, spanker
08 denarius, doubloon, ducatoon, farthing, Groschen, half anna, half mark, imperial, louis d'or, millième, napoleon, new penny, picayune, qindarka, sesterce, shilling, sixpence, solidare, stotinka, ten pence, two pence, two pound
09 centesimo, dandiprat, five pence, gold crown, gold penny, half-crown, half groat, halfpenny, pound coin, sovereign, yellow-boy
10 broadpiece, fifty pence, half florin, half guinea, krugerrand, sestertius
11 bonnet-piece, double eagle, sixpenny bit, spade guinea, twenty pence, twopenny bit

12 antoninianus, silver dollar, two pound coin
13 brass farthing, half sovereign, quarter dollar, sixpenny piece, ten pence piece, tenpenny piece, threepenny bit, two pence piece, twopenny piece
14 five pence piece
15 fifty pence piece, threepenny piece

• **counterfeit coin**
03 rag 04 shan, slip 05 shand
06 doctor, duffer, stumer
• **material for coin**
04 flan
• **supposed coin**
03 moy

coincide
05 agree, clash, match, tally 06 accord, concur, square 07 coexist 09 be the same, harmonize 10 correspond
11 synchronize 14 happen together

coincidence
04 luck, step 05 clash, fluke
06 chance 08 accident, clashing, conflict, fortuity, synastry
11 coexistence, concurrence, conjunction, consilience, correlation, eventuality, serendipity, synchronism
12 simultaneity 13 synchronicity
14 correspondence
15 synchronization

coincident
04 like 05 alike, close 07 related, similar, the same 09 in harmony
10 coexisting, coinciding, comparable, concurrent, consistent, equivalent
11 coterminous, in agreement
12 conterminous, simultaneous
13 corresponding
15 contemporaneous

coincidental
05 lucky 06 casual, chance, flukey
09 unplanned 10 accidental, fortuitous 13 serendipitous, unintentional

coincidentally
07 luckily 08 by chance
12 accidentally 15 unintentionally

coke *see* **cocaine**

cold
01 c 03 ice, icy, raw 04 brrr, cool, dead, jeel, keen, numb, rimy, rume, snow
05 agued, aloof, bleak, cauld, chill, fremd, fresh, frore, frost, gelid, nippy, parky, polar, rheum, stony 06 arctic, biting, bitter, brumal, chilly, frigid, frosty, frozen, numbed, remote, winter, wintry 07 brumous, callous, catarrh, chilled, cutting, distant, glacial, hostile, ice-cold, iciness, rawness, shivery, unmoved 08 clinical, coldness, coolness, freezing, lukewarm, reserved, Siberian, uncaring, unheated
09 chillness, frigidity, heartless, repulsive, unfeeling 10 chilliness, Decemberly, impersonal, phlegmatic, spiritless, unfriendly 11 Decemberish, indifferent, insensitive, passionless, standoffish, unemotional, unexcitable
12 antagonistic, unresponsive
13 unsympathetic 15 undemonstrative
• **cold and wet**
04 sour

cold-blooded
05 cruel 06 brutal, savage 07 callous, inhuman 08 barbaric, pitiless, ruthless
09 barbarous, heartless, merciless, unfeeling 10 iron-headed
14 poikilothermal, poikilothermic

cold-hearted
04 cold 06 flinty, unkind 07 callous, inhuman 08 detached, uncaring
09 heartless, unfeeling 10 iron-headed 11 indifferent, insensitive
12 stony-hearted 13 unsympathetic
15 uncompassionate

coldly
09 callously 11 heartlessly, unfeelingly
13 insensitively, unemotionally

colic
03 bot 04 bott 05 batts 10 mulligrubs

collaborate
04 join 05 unite 06 assist, betray, team up 07 collude 08 conspire 09 co-operate 10 fraternize, join forces
11 participate, turn traitor, work jointly
12 work together 13 associate with, combine forces 14 work as partners

collaboration
05 union 08 alliance, teamwork
09 collusion 10 conspiring
11 association, co-operation, joint effort, partnership 12 fraternizing
13 participation 14 combined effort

collaborator
07 partner, traitor 08 betrayer, colluder, co-worker, quisling, renegade, teammate, turncoat
09 assistant, associate, colleague
10 accomplice 11 conspirator, fraternizer 12 fellow worker

collapse
◇ *anagram indicator*
03 rot 04 blow, bust, fail, fall, flop, fold, ruin, sink 05 break, close, faint, slump, swoon 06 attack, cave in, cave-in, fall in, finish, fold up, go bung, tumble
07 burst-up, crack up, crumble, crumple, debacle, deflate, failure, founder, give way, pancake, pass out, sinking, subside 08 black out, blackout, downfall, fainting, fall down, flake out, keel over 09 break down, breakdown, come apart, fall about, fall apart, falling-in, giving way
10 concertina, foundering, go to pieces, passing-out, subsidence
11 come to an end, coming apart, falling-down, fall through, go to the wall, keeling-over, lose control
12 disintegrate, fall to pieces 13 come to nothing, loss of control
14 disintegration, falling-through, have a breakdown 15 falling to pieces

collar
03 bag, nab 04 band, bust, grab, nick, ring, stop 05 catch, seize 06 arrest, haul in 07 capture 08 neckband
09 apprehend

Collars include:

03 dog
04 Eton, flea, roll, ruff, wing
05 horse, ox-bow, shawl, steel, storm, whisk
06 bertha, choker, collet, gorget, jampot, rabato, rebato
07 brecham, partlet, rebater, stick-up, tie-neck, vandyke
08 carcanet, clerical, granddad, mandarin, Peter Pan, polo neck, rabatine, turn-down
09 holderbat, piccadell, piccadill
10 chevesaile, piccadillo, piccadilly
11 falling band
12 mousquetaire

collate
04 edit, sort 05 order 06 gather
07 arrange, collect, compare, compile, compose 08 organize 10 put in order
11 put together

collateral
05 funds, rival 06 pledge, surety
07 deposit 08 security 09 assurance, guarantee 10 additional, subsidiary
12 contemporary 13 corresponding

collation
07 editing 08 ordering 09 gathering
11 arrangement, compilation, composition 12 organization
15 putting together

colleague
04 aide, ally 06 helper, winger
07 comrade, partner 08 confrère, conspire, co-worker, teammate, workmate 09 assistant, associate, auxiliary, bedfellow, companion
11 confederate 12 collaborator, fellow worker

collect
◇ *containment indicator*
03 get 04 form, heap, mass, meet, save
05 amass, fetch, hoard, rally 06 gather, make up, muster, pick up, pile up, semble, take up, uplift 07 acquire, call for, come for, compose, convene, prepare, recover, solicit 08 assemble, converge, go and get 09 aggregate, go and take, stockpile 10 accumulate, congregate, go and bring, raise money
11 ask for money 12 come together, have as a hobby 14 be interested in, gather together 15 ask people to give

collected
◇ *anagram indicator*
◇ *insertion indicator*
04 calm, cool 06 placid, poised, serene 07 unfazed 08 composed, unshaken 09 unruffled 10 controlled
11 unflappable, unperturbed
13 imperturbable, self-possessed
14 self-controlled

collection
◇ *anagram indicator*
03 set 04 gift, heap, mass, pack, pile, sort 05 gifts, group, hoard, plate, store

06 basket, job-lot, rickle, series
07 boiling, cluster, variety
08 assembly, caboodle, donation, jingbang, offering **09** anthology, composure, congeries, donations, gathering, offertory, selection, stockpile, whip-round **10** assemblage, assortment **11** compilation, ingathering, olla-podrida
12 accumulation, conglomerate, contribution, subscription
13 contributions **14** collected works, conglomeration, omnium-gatherum

collective

05 joint **06** common, moshav, shared, united **07** commune, kibbutz, kolkhoz
08 combined **09** aggregate, community, composite, concerted, corporate, gathering, unanimous
10 assemblage, cumulative, democratic **11** congregated, co-operative **13** collaborative

Collective nouns for animals include:

03 **bed** (clams, oysters), **cry** (hounds), **gam** (whales), **mob** (kangaroos), **nid** (pheasants), **nye** (pheasants), **pod** (seals, whales)
04 **army** (caterpillars, frogs), **bale** (turtles), **band** (gorillas), **bask** (crocodiles), **bevy** (larks, pheasants, quail, swans), **cete** (badgers), **dole** (doves, turtles), **erst** (bees), **herd** (buffalo, cattle, deer, elephants, goats, horses, kangaroos, oxen, seals, whales), **hive** (bees), **pace** (asses), **pack** (dogs, grouse, hounds, wolves), **romp** (otters), **rout** (wolves), **safe** (ducks), **span** (mules), **team** (ducks), **trip** (goats, sheep), **zeal** (zebras)
05 **bloat** (hippopotami), **brace** (ducks), **brood** (chickens, hens), **charm** (finches, goldfinches), **covey** (partridges, quail), **crash** (rhinoceros), **drift** (hogs, swine), **drove** (cattle, horses, oxen, sheep), **flock** (birds, ducks, geese, sheep), **grist** (bees), **shoal** (fish), **siege** (cranes, herons), **skein** (geese), **swarm** (ants, bees, flies, locusts), **tower** (giraffes), **tribe** (goats), **troop** (baboons, kangaroos, monkeys), **watch** (nightingales), **wedge** (swans)
06 **ambush** (tigers), **cackle** (hyenas), **colony** (ants, bees, penguins, rats), **gaggle** (geese), **kindle** (kittens), **labour** (moles), **litter** (kittens, pigs), **murder** (crows), **muster** (peacocks, penguins), **parade** (elephants), **parcel** (penguins), **rafter** (turkeys), **school** (dolphins, fish, porpoises, whales), **string** (horses, ponies), **tiding** (magpies)
07 **bouquet** (pheasants), **clowder** (cats), **company** (parrots), **prickle** (porcupines), **turmoil** (porpoises)
08 **building** (rooks), **paddling** (ducks)
09 **intrusion** (cockroaches), **mustering** (storks), **obstinacy** (buffalo)
10 **exaltation** (larks), **parliament** (owls, rooks), **shrewdness** (apes), **unkindness** (ravens)
11 **convocation** (eagles), **murmuration** (starlings), **ostentation** (peacocks), **pandemonium** (parrots)
12 **congregation** (plovers)

collector

Collectors and enthusiasts include:

05 gamer
07 gourmet
08 neophile, zoophile
09 antiquary, cinephile, ex-librist, logophile, oenophile, philomath, xenophile
10 arctophile, audiophile, cartophile, discophile, ephemerist, gastronome, hippophile, monarchist
11 ailurophile, balletomane, bibliophile, canophilist, etymologist, notaphilist, numismatist, oenophilist, philatelist, scripophile, technophile, toxophilite
12 ailourophile, cartophilist, coleopterist, Dantophilist, deltiologist, entomologist, incunabulist, ophiophilist, phillumenist, stegophilist
13 arachnologist, campanologist, chirographist, lepidopterist, ornithologist, tegestologist, timbrophilist
14 cruciverbalist
15 conservationist, stigmatophilist

college

01 c **04** coll, Eton, hall, poly, tech
06 lyceum, prison, school
07 academy, madrasa **08** madrasah, madrassa, seminary **09** institute, madrassah, medresseh **10** university
11 polytechnic

See also **educational**; **university**

Colleges and halls of Cambridge University:

05 Clare, Jesus, King's
06 Darwin, Girton, Queens', Selwyn
07 Christ's, Downing, New Hall, Newnham, St John's, Trinity, Wolfson
08 Emmanuel, Homerton, Pembroke, Robinson
09 Churchill, Clare Hall, Magdalene, St Edmund's
10 Hughes Hall, Peterhouse
11 Fitzwilliam, Trinity Hall
12 Sidney Sussex, St Catharine's
13 Corpus Christi, Lucy Cavendish
16 Gonville and Caius

Colleges and halls of Oxford University:

03 New
05 Green, Jesus, Keble, Oriel
06 Exeter, Merton, Queen's, Wadham
07 Balliol, Kellogg, Linacre, Lincoln, St Anne's, St Cross, St Hugh's, St John's, Trinity, Wolfson
08 All Souls, Hertford, Magdalen, Nuffield, Pembroke, St Hilda's, St Peter's
09 Brasenose, Mansfield, St Antony's, Templeton, The Queen's, Worcester
10 Somerville, University
11 Campion Hall, Regent's Park
12 Christ Church, St Benet's Hall, St Catherine's, St Edmund Hall, Wycliffe Hall
13 Corpus Christi
14 Greyfriars Hall
15 Blackfriars Hall, St Stephen's House
16 Harris Manchester, Lady Margaret Hall

• at college

02 up

• college head

04 dean

• college square

04 quad

collide

03 hit, war **04** bump, feud, foul
05 clash, crash, fight, prang, smash
06 cannon, go into **07** contend, grapple, quarrel, run into, wrangle
08 bump into, conflict, disagree
09 crash into, smash into **10** meet head on, plough into **12** be in conflict

collision

04 bump, feud **05** brush, clash, crash, fight, prang, shunt, smash, wreck
06 impact, pile-up **07** quarrel, warring, wrangle **08** accident, clashing, conflict, disaster, fighting, showdown **09** rencontre
10 opposition, rencounter
12 disagreement, fender bender
13 confrontation

colloid

03 gel, sol **08** emulsoid **10** suspensoid
11 carrageenan, carrageenin
12 carragheenin

colloquial

06 casual, chatty **07** demotic, popular
08 everyday, familiar, informal
09 idiomatic **10** vernacular
14 conversational

colloquially

09 popularly **10** familiarly, informally

collude

04 plot **06** scheme **07** connive
08 conspire, intrigue **09** machinate
11 be in cahoots, collaborate

collusion

04 plot **06** deceit, league, scheme
07 cahoots **08** artifice, intrigue, scheming **10** complicity, connivance, conspiracy **11** machination
13 collaboration

Colombia

02 CO **03** COL

colonist

04 boor **05** colon **07** pioneer, planter, settler **08** colonial, emigrant, Siceliot, Sikeliot **09** colonizer, immigrant, inhabiter **12** Australasian
See also **governor**

colonize
05 found, plant **06** occupy, people, settle **07** pioneer **08** populate

colonnade
04 stoa **05** porch **06** arcade, xystus
07 eustyle, portico **08** diastyle
09 areostyle, cloisters, peristyle
10 araeostyle **11** covered walk
12 columniation

colony
04 hive **05** apery, group, swarm
07 outpost **08** dominion, province
09 coenobium, community, formicary, hydrosoma, hydrosome, polyzoary, satellite, territory **10** dependency, plantation, possession, settlement
11 association, formicarium, polyzoarium **12** protectorate
14 satellite state

Colorado
02 CO **04** Colo

colossal
04 huge, vast **05** great, jumbo
07 immense, mammoth, massive
08 enormous, gigantic, whopping
09 herculean, monstrous
10 gargantuan, monumental
14 Brobdingnagian

colossus
04 ogre **05** giant, titan **07** Cyclops, Goliath, monster **08** Hercules

colour
03 dye, hew, hue, ink, kit **04** bias, flag, glow, kick, leer, life, race, sway, tint, tone, wash **05** badge, blush, flush, get-up, go red, oomph, paint, shade, slant, stain, strip, taint, tinge **06** affect, banner, crayon, emblem, ensign, reason, redden, tackle, timbre
07 distort, falsify, pervert, pigment, pizzazz, pretext, redness, turn red, variety **08** clothing, colorant, disguise, insignia, pinkness, richness, rosiness, standard, tincture **09** animation, highlight, influence, overstate, prejudice, ruddiness, vividness
10 appearance, brilliance, coloration, complexion, exaggerate, liveliness, skin colour **11** ethnic group, nationality, racial group **12** misrepresent, pigmentation, plausibility

Colours include:

03 dun, jet, red, sky, tan
04 anil, blae, blue, buff, cyan, dove, drab, ecru, fawn, gold, gray, grey, guly, hoar, jade, navy, opal, pink, plum, puce, roan, rose, rosy, ruby, rust, sage, sand, wine
05 amber, beige, black, brown, coral, cream, ebony, green, khaki, lemon, lilac, mauve, milky, ochre, peach, sepia, taupe, topaz, umber, white
06 auburn, bottle, bronze, canary, cerise, cherry, cobalt, copper, indigo, maroon, orange, purple, salmon, silver, violet, yellow
07 apricot, avocado, crimson, emerald, gentian, magenta, saffron, scarlet
08 burgundy, charcoal, chestnut, cinnamon, eau de nil, lavender, magnolia, mahogany, sapphire
09 aubergine, chocolate, nile green, tangerine, turquoise, vermilion
10 aquamarine, chartreuse, cobalt blue, grass-green
11 burnt sienna, lemon yellow

See also **black**; **blue**; **dye**; **green**; **grey**; **orange**; **pigment**; **pink**; **purple**; **rainbow**; **red**; **white**; **yellow**

• lose colour
04 fade, pale

coloured
01 C **09** chromatic

colourful
03 gay **04** deep, rich **05** gaudy, vivid
06 bright, garish, lively **07** graphic, intense, vibrant **08** animated, exciting
09 brilliant **10** flamboyant, polychrome, variegated **11** interesting, picturesque, stimulating **12** many-coloured **13** kaleidoscopic, multicoloured, parti-coloured

colourfully
08 brightly **09** intensely, vibrantly
11 brilliantly

colourless
03 wan **04** drab, dull, fade, grey, pale, tame **05** ashen, bleak, faded, plain, white **06** boring, dreary, sickly
07 anaemic, insipid, neutral
08 bleached **09** washed out
10 lacklustre, monochrome, uncoloured **11** transparent, unmemorable **13** characterless, uninteresting **14** complexionless **15** in black and white

colt
01 c **04** beat, cade, stag **05** staig
06 hogget

Columbia *see* **British**; **District of Columbia** *under* **district**

column
03 col, row **04** anta, file, item, line, list, pier, pole, post, rank **05** Atlas, piece, queue, shaft, story **06** parade, pillar, string **07** article, columel, feature, obelisk, support, telamon, upright
08 caryatid, pilaster **10** procession

• shaft of column
04 fust, tige **05** scape, trunk
06 scapus

columnist
06 critic, editor, writer **08** reporter, reviewer **10** journalist **11** contributor
13 correspondent

coma
03 PVS **05** sopor **06** stupor, torpor, trance **08** hypnosis, lethargy, oblivion
09 catalepsy **10** drowsiness, somnolence **13** insensibility
15 unconsciousness

comatose
03 out **05** dazed **06** drowsy, sleepy, torpid **07** in a coma, out cold, stunned
08 sluggish, soporose **09** lethargic, somnolent, stupefied **10** cataleptic, insensible **11** unconscious

comb
03 red **04** card, hunt, kaim, kame, kemb, rake, redd, sift, tidy, tose, toze
05 combe, coomb, crest, dress, groom, scour, sweep, tease, toaze, trawl **06** coombe, hackle, kangha, neaten, screen, search **07** arrange, explore, ransack, rummage
08 scribble, untangle **09** go through
11 disentangle **14** turn upside down

combat
03 war **04** agon, bout, defy, duel
05 clash, fight, lists **06** action, battle, debate, oppose, resist, strive
07 contend, contest, wage war, warfare **08** conflict, do battle, fighting, skirmish, struggle **09** encounter, monomachy, rencontre, withstand
10 engagement, rencounter, take up arms **11** hostilities

• unarmed combat
04 judo **06** karate **07** ju-jitsu **08** jiu-jitsu

combatant
05 enemy **07** fighter, soldier, warrior
08 opponent **09** adversary, contender, gladiator **10** antagonist, batteilant, serviceman **11** belligerent, protagonist
12 servicewoman

combative
06 bantam **07** hawkish, warlike, warring **08** militant **09** agonistic, bellicose, truculent **10** aggressive, pugnacious **11** adversarial, belligerent, contentious, quarrelsome
12 antagonistic **13** argumentative

combination
03 mix **04** club **05** blend, cross, group, union **06** fusion, merger **07** amalgam, combine, mixture, synergy
08 alliance, clubbing, compound, junction, solution **09** coalition, composite, syndicate, synthesis
10 collection, conflation, connection, consortium, federation **11** association, coalescence, composition, confederacy, conjunction, co-operation, integration, unification
12 amalgamation, co-ordination
13 confederation

combine
03 mix **04** ally, bind, bond, club, fuse, join, link, meld, pool, stir, weld
05 admix, alloy, blend, marry, merge, piece, trust, unify, unite **06** mingle, team up **07** conjoin, connect
08 compound, conflate, cumulate, restrict **09** associate, coadunate, co-operate, integrate, syndicate
10 amalgamate, homogenize, join forces, synthesize **11** incorporate, put together **12** club together **13** bring together

• combined
08 together

• combined with
03 cum

combustible
◇ *anagram indicator*
05 tense **06** ardent, stormy
07 charged **08** volatile **09** excitable, explosive, flammable, ignitable, sensitive **10** incendiary, phlogistic
11 inflammable

combustion
06 firing **07** burning **08** igniting, ignition
• **internal combustion**
02 IC

come
02 be **04** gain, hail, near, stem, turn
05 arise, enter, issue, occur, reach, yield **06** allons, appear, arrive, attain, attend, become, climax, dawn on, evolve, follow, happen, secure, show up, strike, turn up **07** achieve, advance, barge in, burst in, develop, get here, occur to, surface, think of
08 approach, draw near, get there, pass into, remember **09** be on offer, come about, go as far as, originate, take place, transpire **10** be caused by, be produced, come to pass, evolve into, move nearer, result from **11** be a native of, be available, develop into, materialize, move forward, move towards **13** be on the market, present itself, reach an orgasm, travel towards
14 have as your home **15** come to the mind of, have as its origin, have as its source
• **come about**
04 fall, sort **05** arise, occur **06** arrive, befall, happen, result **09** take place, transpire **10** come to pass
• **come across**
04 find, meet, seem **06** appear, notice
07 run into **08** bump into, come over, discover, meet in wi' **09** encounter
10 chance upon, happen upon, meet in with **11** communicate **12** find by chance, meet by chance **13** stumble across
• **come along**
04 mend **05** rally **06** arrive
07 advance, develop, hurry up, improve, recover **08** progress **09** get better, shake a leg **10** get a move on, recuperate **11** get cracking, make headway **12** make progress **15** get your skates on
• **come apart**
04 tear **05** break, split **07** break up, crumble **08** collapse, separate **10** fall to bits **12** disintegrate, fall to pieces
• **come back**
◇ *reversal indicator*
06 go back, remind, return **07** get back
08 come home, reappear **10** be recalled **11** be suggested **12** be remembered **13** be recollected
• **come between**
04 part **06** divide **07** split up
08 alienate, disunite, estrange, separate **09** interpose
• **come by**
03 get **05** visit **06** obtain, secure
07 acquire, procure **09** get hold of
• **come down**
04 drop, fall **05** avail, avale, light
06 availe, reduce, worsen **07** decline, descend **08** decrease, dismount
10 degenerate **11** deteriorate
• **come down on**
05 blame, chide, knock, slate
06 berate, rebuke **07** reprove, upbraid
08 admonish, tear into **09** criticize, reprehend, reprimand **13** find fault with
• **come down to**
04 mean **07** add up to **08** amount to
10 boil down to **12** correspond to
14 be equivalent to, be tantamount to
• **come down with**
03 get **05** catch **06** pick up
07 develop **08** contract **09** succumb to **10** go down with **11** fall ill with
13 become ill with
• **come forward**
05 offer **06** accede, step up
09 volunteer **11** step forward **13** offer yourself
• **come in**
05 enter **06** appear, arrive, entrez, finish, show up **07** receive
• **come in for**
03 get **04** bear **06** endure, suffer
07 receive, sustain, undergo
10 experience **13** be subjected to
• **come into**
04 heir **06** be left **07** acquire, inherit, receive **08** be heir to, contract
• **come off**
04 mend, work **05** end up, occur, rally, strip **06** appear, go well, happen, pay off, thrive **07** advance, develop, improve, proceed, recover, succeed, work out **08** progress **09** get better, take place **10** recuperate, take effect
11 be effective **12** be successful, make progress
• **come on**
03 via **04** mend **05** begin, rally
06 allons, appear, thrive **07** advance, develop, improve, proceed, recover, succeed **08** progress **09** get better
10 recuperate **12** make progress
• **come out**
03 end **05** admit, end up, erupt, issue
06 appear, emerge, finish, result, strike
07 leak out **08** conclude **09** terminate
10 be produced, be released, be revealed **11** become known, be published, come to light **12** be made public **13** declare openly **15** become available
• **come out with**
03 say **05** state, utter **06** affirm
07 declare, divulge, exclaim **08** blurt out, disclose
• **come round**
04 veer, wake **05** agree, allow, awake, grant, occur, recur, visit, yield
06 accede, come to, happen, relent
07 concede, recover **08** reappear
09 be won over, take place **11** be persuaded **13** be converted to
14 change your mind
• **come through**
04 pass, ride **06** endure **07** achieve, prevail, ride out, succeed, survive, triumph **09** withstand **10** accomplish
11 pull through
• **come to**
04 make, stop, wake **05** awake, equal, run to, total **06** obtain **07** add up to, recover **08** amount to **09** aggregate, come round
• **come together**
03 gel **04** jell, meet **05** close, rally
07 collect, convene
• **come up**
◇ *reversal down indicator*
04 rise **05** arise, occur **06** appear, crop up, happen, turn up **13** present itself
• **come up to**
04 meet **05** equal, reach
08 approach, live up to **09** match up to
11 compare with, measure up to
12 make the grade
• **come up with**
05 offer **06** devise, submit
07 advance, dream up, present, produce, propose, suggest, think of
08 conceive **10** put forward

comeback
05 rally **06** retort, return **07** revival
08 recovery **09** rejoinder
10 resurgence **12** reappearance
13 recrimination
• **make a comeback**
◇ *reversal indicator*

comedian
03 wag, wit **05** clown, comic, joker
06 gagman **07** gagster **08** funny man, humorist **10** comedienne, funny woman **11** entertainer

Comedians include:

03 **Dee** (Jack), **Fry** (Stephen), **Lom** (Herbert), **Sim** (Alastair), **Wax** (Ruby)
04 **Cook** (Peter), **Dodd** (Ken), **Hill** (Benny), **Hill** (Harry), **Hope** (Bob), **Idle** (Eric), **Kaye** (Danny), **Marx** (Chico), **Marx** (Groucho), **Marx** (Harpo), **Marx** (Zeppo), **Sims** (Joan), **Tati** (Jacques), **Wise** (Ernie), **Wood** (Victoria)
05 **Abbot** (Russ), **Allen** (Dave), **Allen** (Woody), **Brand** (Jo), **Bruce** (Lenny), **Burns** (George), **Cosby** (Bill), **Davro** (Bobby), **Elton** (Ben), **Emery** (Dick), **Hardy** (Oliver), **Henry** (Lenny), **Inman** (John), **James** (Sid), **Jones** (Griff Rhys), **Jones** (Terry), **Kempe** (Will), **Lewis** (Jerry), **Lloyd** (Harold), **Lucas** (Matt), **Moore** (Dudley), **Oddie** (Bill), **Palin** (Michael), **Pryor** (Richard), **Robey** (Sir George), **Sayle** (Alexei), **Smith** (Mel), **Starr** (Freddie), **Sykes** (Eric)
06 **Abbott** (Bud), **Bailey** (Bill), **Barker** (Ronnie), **Brooks** (Mel), **Cleese** (John), **Coogan** (Steve), **Cooper** (Tommy), **Dawson** (Les), **Fields** (W C), **French** (Dawn), **Garden** (Graeme), **Howerd** (Frankie), **Jordan** (Dorothy), **Keaton** (Buster), **Lauder** (Sir Harry), **Laurel** (Stan), **Laurie** (Hugh), **Martin** (Steve),

Mayall (Rik), Merton (Paul), Murphy (Eddie), Murray (Bill), Reeves (Vic), Ullman (Tracey), Wilder (Gene), Wisdom (Norman)
07 Aykroyd (Dan), Baddiel (David), Bentine (Michael), Bremner (Rory), Carrott (Jasper), Chaplin (Charlie), Chapman (Graham), Corbett (Ronnie), Deayton (Angus), Enfield (Harry), Everett (Kenny), Feldman (Marty), Gervais (Ricky), Hancock (Tony), Handley (Tommy), Jacques (Hattie), Manning (Bernard), Matthau (Walter), Newhart (Bob), Roscius, Secombe (Harry), Sellers (Peter), Tarbuck (Jimmy), Ustinov (Sir Peter)
08 Atkinson (Rowan), Coltrane (Robbie), Connolly (Billy), Coquelin (Benoît Constant), Costello (Lou), Grimaldi (Joseph), Milligan (Spike), Mitchell (Warren), Mortimer (Bob), Roseanne, Saunders (Jennifer), Seinfeld (Jerry), Sessions (John), The Goons, Walliams (David), Williams (Kenneth), Williams (Robin)
09 Edmondson (Adrian), Fernandel, Grossmith (George), Morecambe (Eric), Rhys Jones (Griff), Whitfield (June)
10 The Goodies, Whitehouse (Paul)
11 Monty Python, Terry-Thomas
12 Brooke-Taylor (Tim)
14 Laurel and Hardy, Little and Large
15 The Marx Brothers

See also **actor, actress**

comedown
04 blow **06** bathos **07** decline, descent, let-down, reverse **08** demotion, reversal **09** deflation **10** anticlimax **11** degradation, humiliation **14** disappointment

comedy
03 com, fun **06** humour, joking **07** jesting **08** clowning, drollery, hilarity **09** funniness, pantomime **13** entertainment, facetiousness

Comedy types include:

03 gag, low, pun, wit
04 high, joke, sick
05 black, farce, Greek
06 modern, satire, sitcom, visual
07 musical, stand-up
08 romantic
09 burlesque, satirical, screwball, situation, slapstick
10 comic opera, sketch show, television, theatrical, vaudeville
11 alternative, Pythonesque, restoration, tragicomedy
12 Chaplinesque, neoclassical
13 Shakespearian
15 comedy of humours, comedy of manners, improvisational, situation comedy

comely
04 fair, fine, tidy **05** ample, bonny, buxom, sonsy **06** bonnie, gainly, goodly, likely, lovely, pretty, proper, sonsie **07** sightly, winsome **08** blooming, graceful, handsome, pleasing **09** beautiful, excellent **10** attractive **11** good-looking **15** pulchritudinous

come-on
04 lure **10** allurement, attraction, enticement, inducement, persuasion, temptation **13** encouragement

comet

Comets include:

04 West, Wolf
05 Cruls, Encke, Kirch, Mrkos, Tycho
06 Donati, Halley, Lexell, Newton
07 Bennett, Humason, Tebbutt
08 Daylight, Hale-Bopp, Kohoutek
09 Hyakutake, Ikeya-Seki, Morehouse, Seki-Lines
10 De Chéseaux, Flauergues, Great Comet
11 Arend-Roland, Swift-Tuttle
12 Pons-Winnecke
13 Shoemaker-Levy
14 Tago-Sato-Kosaka

comeuppance
04 dues **05** merit **06** rebuke **07** deserts **08** requital **10** chastening, punishment, recompense **11** just deserts, retribution **14** what you deserve

comfort
03 aid **04** cosy, cozy, ease, help, stay **05** cheer **06** luxury, plenty, relief, repose, solace, soothe **07** assuage, console, encheer, enliven, gladden, hearten, refresh, relieve, succour, support **08** cosiness, opulence, reassure, snugness **09** alleviate, empathize, encourage, enjoyment, recomfort, wellbeing **10** condolence, easy street, invigorate, relaxation, strengthen, sympathize **11** alleviation, consolation, contentment, reassurance **12** compensation, satisfaction **13** bring solace to, encouragement, Gemütlichkeit **15** freedom from pain, speak to the heart

comfortable
04 bein, bien, cosy, cozy, easy, lazy, safe, slow, snug, tosh, warm, well **05** comfy, cushy, happy, loose, roomy **06** at ease, couthy, gentle, homely, kindly, secure **07** couthie, opulent, relaxed, restful, well-off **08** affluent, armchair, carefree, homelike, laid-back, pleasant, relaxing, well-to-do **09** agreeable, confident, contented, enjoyable, gemütlich, leisurely, luxurious, rosewater, unhurried **10** commodious, convenient, delightful, prosperous **11** well-fitting **12** loose-fitting **13** unembarrassed

• **make yourself comfortable**
04 cose

comforting
07 helpful **08** cheering, soothing **09** analeptic, consoling **10** heartening, reassuring **11** consolatory, encouraging, inspiriting **12** heartwarming

comic
03 wag, wit **04** card, rich, zany **05** buffo, clown, droll, funny, joker, light, witty **06** absurd, gagman, joking **07** amusing, buffoon, comical, gagster, jocular **08** comedian, farcical, funny man, humorist, humorous **09** diverting, facetious, hilarious, laughable, ludicrous, priceless **10** funny woman, ridiculous **11** entertainer **12** entertaining, knee-slapping **13** side-splitting

Comics include:

03 Viz
05 Beano, Bunty, Dandy
08 The Beano, The Dandy, The Eagle

comical
05 droll, funny, witty **06** absurd **07** amusing **08** farcical, humorous **09** diverting, hilarious, laughable, ludicrous, quizzical **10** ridiculous **12** entertaining

comically
07 funnily, wittily **08** absurdly **09** amusingly **10** farcically, humorously **11** hilariously, ludicrously **12** ridiculously

coming
03 due **04** anon, dawn, near, next **05** birth **06** advent, future, rising **07** arrival, nearing **08** approach, aspiring, imminent, upcoming **09** accession, advancing, impending, promising **11** approaching, forthcoming, up-and-coming

• **coming out**
09 emergence

command
03 bid, get **04** fiat, gain, head, hest, lead, rule, sway, warn, will **05** edict, heast, order, power, reign **06** adjure, behest, behote, charge, compel, decree, demand, direct, enjoin, govern, heaste, impose, manage, obtain, secure **07** be given, behight, bidding, control, dictate, mandate, mastery, precept, receive, require **08** dominate, dominion, instruct, pleasure **09** authority, direction, directive, supervise **10** ascendancy, domination, government, injunction, leadership, management **11** commandment, instruction, preside over, requirement, superintend, supervision **12** be in charge of, give orders to **13** be in control of **15** superintendence

Commands include:

03 hie, hup, hye
04 easy, halt, high, mush
05 be off, enter, gee up
06 come by, entrez, gee hup, huddup
07 give way
09 stand easy
10 quick march
12 be off with you
15 stand and deliver

commandeer
04 take **05** press, seize, usurp
06 hijack **07** impound **08** arrogate
09 sequester **10** confiscate
11 appropriate, expropriate, requisition, sequestrate

commander
03 Cdr, Com **04** boss, Cmdr, comm, head **05** bloke, chief, Comdr
06 leader, master

Commanders include:
03 aga, mir
04 agha, meer
06 sardar, sirdar
07 admiral, captain, general, officer, prefect, warlord
08 director, governor, hipparch, phylarch, risaldar, taxiarch, tetrarch
09 chieftain, chiliarch, imperator, polemarch, privateer, seraskier, trierarch
11 encomendero, turcopolier
13 generalissimo
14 superintendent

See also **admiral**; **field marshal**; **general**

commanding
05 lofty **06** strong **08** dominant, forceful, imperial, imposing, powerful, superior **09** assertive, confident, directing, strategic **10** autocratic, dominating, impressive, peremptory
11 controlling **12** advantageous
13 authoritative

commemorate
04 keep, mark **06** honour, salute
07 observe **08** remember
09 celebrate, recognize, solemnize
11 immortalize, memorialize **12** pay tribute to

commemoration
04 mind, obit **06** honour, memory, salute **07** tribute **08** ceremony
09 honouring **10** dedication, observance **11** celebration, recognition, recordation, remembrance

commemorative
07 marking **08** memorial, saluting
09 honouring **10** dedicatory, in honour of, in memoriam, in memory of
11 celebratory, remembering **12** as a tribute to **15** in recognition of, in remembrance of

commence
04 open **05** begin, start **06** launch
07 go ahead **08** embark on, initiate
09 originate **10** inaugurate, make a start **14** make a beginning

commencement
05 onset, start **06** launch, origin, outset **07** kick-off, opening
09 beginning **10** initiation

commend
03 rap **04** give, laud, wrap **05** adorn, extol, trust, yield **06** commit, praise, set off **07** acclaim, applaud, approve, confide, consign, deliver, entrust, propose, suggest **08** advocate, eulogize, hand over **09** recommend
10 compliment **13** speak highly of

commendable
04 good **05** noble **06** pretty, worthy
08 laudable **09** admirable, deserving, estimable, excellent, exemplary, well-found **10** creditable **11** meritorious
12 praiseworthy

commendation
06 credit, praise **07** acclaim
08 accolade, applause, approval, encomion, encomium, good word
09 panegyric **10** approvance
11 acclamation, approbation, good opinion, high opinion, recognition
13 brownie points, encouragement
14 congratulation, recommendation, seal of approval, special mention
15 stamp of approval

commensurate
03 due **05** equal **07** fitting
08 adequate **10** acceptable, comparable, equivalent, sufficient
11 according to **13** appropriate to, corresponding, proportionate
14 compatible with, consistent with, in proportion to **15** corresponding to

comment
03 say **04** note, view **05** gloss, gloze, opine **06** remark **07** descant, explain, mention, observe, opinion, speak to
08 annotate, footnote, point out, scholion, scholium, sidenote
09 criticism, elucidate, interject, interpose, interpret, statement
10 annotation, commentary, exposition **11** elucidation, explanation, observation **12** illustration, marginal note, obiter dictum **13** give an opinion

commentary
04 comm **05** notes **06** Gemara, postil, remark, report, review **07** account
08 analysis, Brahmana, critique, exegesis, treatise **09** narration, voice-over **10** annotation, exposition, play-by-play **11** description, elucidation, explanation **14** interpretation

commentator
05 hakam **06** critic **07** exegete, glosser **08** narrator, reporter
09 annotator, commenter, expositor, glossator, scholiast **10** newscaster
11 broadcaster, interpreter
12 sportscaster **13** correspondent
See also **cricket**

commerce
03 com **05** trade **07** dealing, traffic
08 business, dealings, exchange, industry **09** marketing, relations
11 intercourse, trafficking
13 merchandizing

commercial
02 ad **04** bill, hype, plug **05** blurb, trade, venal **06** advert, jingle, notice, poster, shoppy **07** display, handout, leaflet, placard, popular, trading
08 business, circular, handbill, merchant, monetary, saleable, sellable
09 financial, lucrative, marketing, mercenary, promotion, publicity
10 industrial, mercantile, profitable, propaganda **11** moneymaking
12 announcement, profit-making
13 advertisement, materialistic, money-spinning **15** entrepreneurial

commiserate
07 comfort, console, feel for
10 sympathize, understand **12** feel sorry for **13** offer sympathy **15** express sympathy, send condolences

commiseration
04 pity **06** solace **07** comfort
08 sympathy **10** compassion, condolence **11** condolences, consolation **13** consideration, understanding

commission
03 cut, fee, job **04** duty, send, task, work **05** board, order, share, trust
06 ask for, assign, charge, depute, employ, engage, errand, select
07 appoint, arrange, council, empower, mandate, mission, rake-off, request, royalty, warrant **08** contract, delegate, function, nominate, poundage **09** allowance, authority, authorize, brokerage, committee
10 assignment, delegation, deputation, employment, percentage
11 appointment, piece of work
12 advisory body, compensation
13 advisory group **14** representative, responsibility **15** put in an order for

commit
02 do **03** put, sin **04** aret, bind, give, hete, send **05** admit, arett, enact, enure, hecht, hight, inure, trust
06 assign, decide, effect, engage, pledge **07** commend, confide, confine, consign, deliver, deposit, entrust, execute, get up to, intrust, perform, promise, put away
08 bequeath, carry out, covenant, dedicate, delegate, hand over, obligate
09 indulge in, recommend
10 perpetrate **15** cross the Rubicon

commitment
03 tie, vow **04** duty, word **06** effort, pledge **07** loyalty, promise
08 covenant, devotion, hard work
09 adherence, assurance, guarantee, liability **10** allegiance, dedication, engagement, obligation
11 involvement, undertaking
12 imprisonment **14** responsibility

committal
06 pledge **07** sending **09** admission
11 confinement, consignment
12 imprisonment

committed
05 loyal **06** active, engagé, paid up, red-hot **07** devoted, engaged, fervent, sold out, zealous **08** diligent, involved, studious **09** dedicated, sold out on
11 evangelical, hardworking, industrious **12** card-carrying, enthusiastic

committee
03 com **05** board, table **08** delegacy **09** Politburo **10** Propaganda **11** Politbureau

commodious
05 ample, large, roomy **08** spacious, suitable **09** capacious, expansive, extensive **10** convenient **11** comfortable, serviceable

commodity
04 item **05** goods, stock, thing, wares **06** output, profit **07** article, produce, product **08** material **09** advantage, privilege **10** expediency **11** convenience, merchandise

common
03 com, low **05** crude, daily, joint, plain, sense, share, stray, usual **06** coarse, mutual, normal, public, shared, simple, vulgar **07** average, general, ill-bred, loutish, popular, regular, routine, uncouth **08** accepted, communal, everyday, familiar, frequent, habitual, inferior, ordinary, plebeian, standard, tritical, workaday **09** community, customary, prevalent, ten a penny, two a penny, universal, unrefined **10** collective, customable, dime a dozen, prevailing, widespread **11** bog standard, commonplace **12** common as muck, conventional, run-of-the-mill **13** unexceptional **15** undistinguished

commoner
02 MP **04** pleb **07** plebean **08** plebeian

common land
03 tie, tye **04** mark

commonly
05 often, vulgo **07** as a rule, usually **08** normally **09** generally, regularly, routinely, typically **10** frequently **14** for the most part

commonplace
05 banal, stale, stock, trite, usual **06** boring, common, modern, ornery, vulgar **07** humdrum, mundane, obvious, ordinar, prosaic, routine, worn out **08** bromidic, copybook, everyday, exoteric, frequent, ordinary, overused **09** hackneyed, prosaical, quotidian **10** pedestrian, threadbare, widespread **11** a dime a dozen **13** unexceptional, uninteresting

common sense
04 nous **05** savey, savvy, sense **06** brains, reason, sanity, savvey, wisdom **07** realism **08** gumption, prudence **09** good sense, judgement, mother wit, soundness **10** astuteness, experience, pragmatism, shrewdness **11** discernment, rumgumption **12** practicality, sensibleness **13** judiciousness, rumelgumption, rumlegumption **14** hard-headedness, rumblegumption, rummelgumption, rummlegumption **15** level-headedness

commonsense
04 sane, wise **05** sound **06** astute, shrewd **07** prudent **08** sensible **09** judicious, practical, pragmatic, realistic **10** discerning, hard-headed, reasonable **11** down-to-earth, experienced, level-headed **12** matter-of-fact **14** commonsensical

commonwealth
03 Com **04** weal **12** Protectorate

Commonwealth member countries:

04 Fiji
05 Ghana, India, Kenya, Malta, Nauru, Samoa, Tonga
06 Belize, Brunei, Canada, Cyprus, Guyana, Malawi, Tuvalu, Uganda, Zambia
07 Grenada, Jamaica, Lesotho, Namibia, Nigeria, St Lucia, Vanuatu
08 Barbados, Botswana, Cameroon, Dominica, Kiribati, Malaysia, Maldives, Pakistan, Sri Lanka, Tanzania, Zimbabwe
09 Australia, Mauritius, Singapore, Swaziland, The Gambia
10 Bangladesh, Mozambique, New Zealand, Seychelles, The Bahamas
11 Sierra Leone, South Africa
13 United Kingdom
14 Papua New Guinea, Solomon Islands
15 St Kitts and Nevis
16 Brunei Darussalam
17 Antigua and Barbuda, Trinidad and Tobago
21 St Christopher and Nevis
24 United Republic of Tanzania
25 St Vincent and the Grenadines

Commonwealth of Independent States members:

06 Russia
07 Armenia, Belarus, Georgia, Moldova, Ukraine
10 Azerbaijan, Kazakhstan, Kyrgyzstan, Tajikistan, Uzbekistan
12 Turkmenistan

commotion
03 ado, row **04** fuss, Hell, riot, stir, to-do, toss **05** hurly, hurry, noise, steer, stire, storm, styre, whirl **06** bustle, bust-up, flurry, fracas, fraise, furore, hotter, hubbub, pother, pudder, racket, romage, rumpus, steery, tiswas, tizwas, tumult, uproar **07** burst-up, clamour, ferment, rummage, tempest, turmoil **08** ballyhoo, brouhaha, disorder, disquiet, kefuffle, tirrivee, tirrivie, upheaval **09** agitation, carfuffle, confusion, curfuffle, hurricane, kerfuffle, stirabout **10** excitement, hullabaloo, hurly-burly **11** disturbance

communal
05 joint **06** common, public, shared **07** general **09** community **10** collective

communally
07 jointly **08** commonly **09** community, generally **12** collectively

commune
03 com, mir **06** colony **07** kibbutz **08** converse **09** community, discourse **10** collective, fellowship, get close to, get in touch, settlement **11** communicate, co-operative, feel close to, feel in touch, make contact **12** municipality

communicable
08 catching **09** infective **10** contagious, conveyable, infectious, spreadable **12** transferable **13** transmissible, transmittable

communicate
04 talk **05** phone, reach, relay, speak, write **06** bestow, convey, empart, impart, inform, liaise, notify, pass on, report, reveal, spread, unfold **07** commune, contact, declare, deliver, diffuse, divulge, express, get over, mediate, publish, put over **08** acquaint, announce, converse, disclose, intimate, proclaim, transmit **09** be in touch, broadcast, get across, make known, put across, telephone **10** correspond, get in touch **11** demonstrate, disseminate

communication
05 touch **07** contact, message **09** telephony **10** connection, disclosure, intimation **11** information, intercourse **12** intelligence, transmission **13** dissemination **14** correspondence

Communication forms include:

02 IT, TV
03 fax, MMS, Net, PDA, SMS
04 memo, Moon, news, note, post, wire, word
05 cable, e-mail, media, pager, pay TV, press, radar, radio, telex, video
06 gossip, letter, notice, poster, report, speech, tannoy, the net
07 bleeper, Braille, cable TV, journal, leaflet, message, Prestel®, webcast, website
08 access TV, aerogram, brochure, bulletin, circular, computer, dialogue, dispatch, Intelsat, intercom, Internet, junk mail, magazine, mailshot, pamphlet, postcard, telegram, teletext, wireless
09 broadband, catalogue, digital TV, facsimile, grapevine, mass media, megaphone, Morse code, newsflash, newspaper, publicity, satellite, semaphore, statement, telephone, voice mail
10 communiqué, dictaphone, loud-hailer, pay-per-view, television, typewriter
11 advertising, chain letter, satellite TV, Telemessage®, teleprinter, text message, the Internet
12 announcement, broadcasting, conversation, press release, sign language, walkie-talkie, World Wide Web
13 video-on-demand, word processor
14 correspondence, subscription TV

communicative
04 free, open **05** frank **06** candid, chatty **07** voluble **08** friendly, outgoing, sociable **09** expansive, extrovert, talkative **10** unreserved **11** forthcoming, informative, intelligent

communion
02 HC **04** Mass **05** agape, unity **06** accord **07** concord, empathy, harmony, rapport **08** affinity, occasion, sympathy **09** closeness, communing, community, Eucharist, Sacrament **10** fellowship **11** intercourse, Lord's Supper **12** togetherness **13** participation **15** sharing feelings, sharing thoughts

communiqué
06 report **07** message **08** bulletin, dispatch **09** newsflash, statement **12** announcement, press release **13** communication

communism
06 Maoism **07** Marxism, Titoism **08** Leninism **09** socialism, sovietism, Stalinism **10** Bolshevism, Trotskyism **11** revisionism **12** collectivism **15** totalitarianism

communist
03 com, red **04** Trot **05** commo, commy, tanky **06** commie, Maoist, soviet **07** comrade, leftist, Marxist **08** Leninist, Viet Cong **09** communard, socialist, Stalinist **10** Bolshevist, Spartacist, Spartakist, Trotskyist, Trotskyite **11** revisionist **12** collectivist

community
04 body, town, umma **05** biome, group, order, state, tribe, ummah **06** ashram, colony, locale, nation, people, public, region, sangha **07** commune, dogtown, kibbutz, phalanx, section, society **08** district, Greekdom, locality, populace **09** Agapemone, agreement, coenobium, residents, sociation **10** commonness, fellowship, fraternity, population, settlement, sisterhood **11** association, brotherhood **13** neighbourhood

commute
05 remit **06** adjust, lessen, modify, reduce, soften **07** curtail, journey, lighten, shorten, shuttle **08** decrease, exchange, mitigate **10** substitute **12** travel to work

commuter
09 passenger, traveller **11** strap-hanger, suburbanite

Comoros
03 COM

compact
03 ram **04** bond, cram, deal, firm, neat, pact, snug, tamp **05** brief, close, dense, pithy, short, small, solid, terse, tight, union **06** accord, league, little, pocket, settle, treaty **07** bargain, concise, entente, flatten, squeeze **08** alliance, compress, condense, contract, covenant, flapjack, pack down, smallish, succinct, well-knit **09** agreement, concordat, condensed, indenture, press down, telescope **10** compressed, settlement **11** arrangement, close-packed, consolidate, transaction **12** close-grained, close-pressed, impenetrable **13** press together, understanding **15** pressed together

companion
03 lad, pal **04** aide, ally, feer, fere, mate **05** buddy, crony, feare, fiere **06** cohort, co-mate, cupman, escort, fellow, friend, marrow, pheere, potman, shadow, Trojan **07** compeer, comrade, consort, convive, franion, partner **08** barnacle, beau pere, book-mate, chaperon, compadre, copemate, Ephesian, follower, intimate, playmate, sidekick, workmate **09** assistant, associate, attendant, bon vivant, chaperone, colleague, confidant, copes-mate, pew-fellow **10** accomplice, bon vivante, compotator, confidante, goodfellow **11** compotation, confederate, inseparable, skaines mate

See also **boon**

companionable
06 genial **07** affable, amiable, cordial **08** familiar, fellowly, friendly, informal, outgoing, sociable **09** agreeable, congenial, convivial, extrovert **10** gregarious **11** neighbourly, sympathetic **12** approachable

companionship
07 company, rapport, society, support **08** intimacy, sympathy **09** closeness **10** fellowship, friendship **11** association, camaraderie, comradeship **12** consociation, conviviality, togetherness **13** esprit de corps

company
02 AG, BV, Co, SA **03** Cia, Cie, Coy, PLC, set **04** band, body, cast, core, crew, firm, gang, ging, GmbH, heap, push, sort, team **05** crowd, group, house, party, troop, trust **06** cartel, circle, guests, throng, troupe **07** callers, concern, contact, society, support **08** assembly, business, ensemble, jingbang, presence, visitors **09** closeness, community, gathering, syndicate **10** attendance, consortium, fellowship, friendship, subsidiary **11** association, comradeship, corporation, partnership **12** conglomerate, conviviality, togetherness **13** companionship, establishment, multinational **14** holding company, limited company

See also **business**; **dance company** *under* **dance**

comparable
04 akin, like, near **05** alike, close, equal **07** cognate, related, similar **08** parallel **09** analogous **10** equivalent, tantamount **12** commensurate, proportional **13** corresponding, proportionate

comparably
07 equally **09** similarly **11** analogously **14** proportionally **15** correspondingly, proportionately

comparative
02 -er **03** -est **08** relative **12** by comparison, in comparison

comparatively
10 relatively **12** by comparison, in comparison

compare
02 cf, cp **03** get, vie **04** even, like, link **05** equal, liken, match, touch, weigh **06** confer, equate **07** balance, compeer, compete, measure, paragon, provide, stack up **08** confront, contrast, parallel, resemble **09** analogize, correlate, juxtapose **10** be as good as, comparison, set against **13** hold a candle to, set side by side **14** bear comparison, be comparable to **15** regard as the same

• **beyond compare**
06 superb **07** supreme **08** peerless **09** brilliant, matchless, nonpareil, unmatched **10** unequalled, unrivalled **11** superlative, unsurpassed **12** incomparable, without equal **15** without parallel

comparison
07 analogy, parable **08** contrast, likeness, parallel **10** similarity, similitude **11** correlation, differences, distinction, parallelism, resemblance **12** relationship **13** comparability, juxtaposition **15** differentiation

compartment
03 bay, box, pew, pod **04** area, cage, cell, pane, part, room, till **05** berth, booth, niche, panel, stall **06** alcove, carrel, locker, locule **07** chamber, cubicle, loculus, section, sleeper **08** carriage, casemate, category, division, traverse **09** cubbyhole, partition **10** pigeonhole **11** subdivision

compartmentalize
03 tag **04** file, slot, sort **05** group **08** classify **09** catalogue **10** categorize, pigeonhole **11** alphabetize **12** sectionalize

compass
04 area, bend, dial, plot, zone **05** ambit, curve, field, gamut, grasp, limit, range, reach, realm, round, scale, scope, space, sweep, swing **06** bounds, circle, extent, limits, obtain, realms, sphere, spread **07** achieve, circuit, enclose, pelorus, stretch, trammel **08** boundary, contrive, diapason, register, surround **09** enclosure **10** accomplish, comprehend **13** circumference

Compass points:

01 E, N, S, W
02 NE, NW, SE, SW

03 ENE, ESE, NNE, NNW, SSE, SSW, WNW,WSW
04 east, E by N, E by S, N by E, N by W, S by E, S by W,W by N,W by S, west
05 NE by E, NE by N, north, NW by N, NW by W, SE by E, SE by S, south, SW by S, SW by W
09 north-east, north-west, south-east, south-west
11 east by north, east by south, north by east, north by west, south by east, south by west, west by north, west by south
13 east-north-east, east-south-east, west-north-west, west-south-west
14 north-north-east, north-north-west, south-south-east, south-south-west
15 north-east by east, north-west by west, south-east by east, south-west by west
16 north-east by north, north-west by north, south-east by south, south-west by south

compassion
04 care, pity **05** heart, mercy
06 bowels, sorrow, ubuntu
07 concern, remorse **08** humanity, kindness, leniency, sympathy
10 condolence, gentleness, tenderness **11** benevolence
13 commiseration, consideration, fellow-feeling, understanding

compassionate
06 benign, caring, gentle, humane, kindly, tender **07** clement, feeling, lenient, piteous, pitiful, pitying
08 bleeding, merciful **09** forgiving
10 benevolent, charitable, forbearing, passionate, remorseful, supportive
11 kind-hearted, sympathetic, warm-hearted **12** humanitarian **13** tender-hearted, understanding

compatibility
05 match **07** harmony, rapport
08 sympathy **11** consistence, consistency, suitability **12** adaptability
14 like-mindedness

compatible
06 suited **07** similar **08** matching, suitable **09** accordant, adaptable, congruent, congruous, consonant, in harmony **10** consistent, harmonious, like-minded, well-suited
11 conformable, sympathetic, well-matched **12** reconcilable **13** having rapport

compatriot
10 countryman **12** countrywoman
13 fellow citizen **14** fellow national

compel
03 gar **04** make, urge **05** bully, coact, drive, force, garre, impel **06** coerce, hustle, lean on, oblige **07** dragoon, efforce, enforce **08** browbeat, bulldoze, compulse, insist on, pressure
09 constrain, press-gang, strongarm
10 intimidate, pressurize
11 necessitate **14** put the screws on

compelling
06 cogent, urgent **07** weighty
08 coercive, forceful, gripping, mesmeric, powerful, pressing, riveting
09 absorbing **10** compulsive, compulsory, conclusive, convincing, imperative, overriding, persuasive
11 enthralling, fascinating, irrefutable
12 irresistible, spellbinding
13 unputdownable

compendious
05 brief, crisp, short, terse
07 compact, concise, summary
08 complete, succinct **09** condensed
10 to the point **12** all-embracing
13 comprehensive

compendium
06 digest, manual, symbol
07 summary **08** abstract, breviate, handbook, synopsis **09** anthology, companion, vade-mecum
10 abridgment, collection, shortening
11 abridgement, compilation

compensate
05 atone, repay **06** cancel, make up, offset, recoup, redeem, refund, reward
07 balance, nullify, redress, requite, restore, satisfy **08** make good, make up to **09** indemnify, make up for, reimburse **10** balance out, counteract, make amends, neutralize, recompense, remunerate
11 countervail **12** counterpoise
14 counterbalance, make reparation

compensation
04 boot, bote **05** compo **06** amends, refund, return, reward **07** comfort, damages, payment, redress
08 reprisal, requital, solatium
09 atonement, demurrage, indemnity, repayment **10** blood money, correction, recompense, reparation
11 consolation, restitution, restoration
12 remuneration, satisfaction
13 reimbursement **15** conscience money, indemnification

compère
02 MC **04** host **05** emcee, front
06 anchor **07** present **09** anchorman, announcer, presenter **10** link person
11 anchorwoman

compete
03 ren, rin, run, vie **04** play, race
05 enter, fight, match, rival **06** battle, jostle, oppose, strive **07** compare, contend, contest, go in for **08** struggle, take part **09** challenge **11** participate, pit yourself

competence
05 power, skill **07** ability, fitness, purview **08** aptitude, capacity, facility
09 authority, expertise, technique
10 capability, efficiency, experience
11 proficiency, sufficience, sufficiency, suitability **12** jurisdiction **13** legal capacity

competent
03 fit **04** able, good **05** adept, equal, tight **06** expert, habile, strong, useful
07 capable, skilful, skilled, trained
08 adequate, masterly, passable, suitable **09** efficient, qualified
10 acceptable, consummate, legitimate, proficient, reasonable, sufficient **11** appropriate, experienced, respectable **12** accomplished, satisfactory **13** well-qualified

competition
03 bee, cup **04** bout, game, goal, gole, meet, open, quiz, race **05** event, field, match, vying **06** rivals, strife, trials
07 contest, cook off, rivalry
08 concours, conflict, knockout, struggle **09** challenge, emulation, encounter, opponents, spelldown
10 contention, opposition, tournament **11** challengers, competitors, spelling bee
12 championship, cross-country
13 combativeness **15** competitiveness

Sporting competitions include:

02 TT
05 Ashes, Derby, FA Cup
06 Le Mans
07 Grey Cup, Masters, Uber Cup, UEFA Cup
08 Rose Bowl, Ryder Cup, Speedway, World Cup
09 Motocross, Super Bowl, Thomas Cup, World Bowl
10 Asian Games, Formula One, Solheim Cup, Stanley Cup
11 Admiral's Cup, America's Cup, Kinnaird Cup, World Series
12 Iditarod Race, Olympic Games, Tour de France
13 Grand National, Kentucky Derby, Leonard Trophy
15 Paralympic Games
17 Commonwealth Games

competitive
03 low **04** fair, just, keen **05** pushy
06 modest **07** average, cut-rate
08 moderate **09** ambitious, combative, cut-throat, dog-eat-dog
10 aggressive, reasonable
11 contentious, inexpensive
12 antagonistic **15** bargain-basement

competitively
03 low **06** fairly **08** modestly
10 moderately, reasonably
13 inexpensively

competitiveness
07 rat race, rivalry **08** ambition, keenness **09** challenge, pugnacity, pushiness **10** aggression, antagonism
13 ambitiousness, assertiveness, combativeness **14** aggressiveness
15 contentiousness

competitor
05 rival **06** player **07** agonist, entrant, roadman **08** corrival, emulator, Olympian, opponent, trialist
09 adversary, candidate, contender, triallist **10** antagonist, challenger, contestant, opposition
11 competition, pancratiast, participant, pentathlete

compilation
◇ *anagram indicator*
04 opus, work **05** album, segue
06 corpus **07** omnibus **08** treasury
09 amassment, anthology, collation, potpourri, selection, thesaurus
10 assemblage, collection, compendium, miscellany
11 arrangement, collectanea, composition, florilegium
12 accumulation, chrestomathy, organization

compile
◇ *anagram indicator*
04 cull, edit **05** amass **06** garner, gather **07** arrange, collate, collect, compose, marshal **08** assemble, organize **09** construct **10** accumulate
11 put together

• **compiler**
01 I **02** me

• **compiler's**
04 mine

complacency
05 pride **07** triumph **08** gloating, pleasure, serenity, smugness
11 contentment, self-content
12 complaisance, satisfaction
13 gratification, self-assurance

complacent
04 smug, vain **05** proud **06** serene
07 pleased **08** gloating, serenity
09 contented, gratified, satisfied
10 triumphant **11** complaisant, self-assured, unconcerned **13** self-contented, self-righteous, self-satisfied

complain
03 nag **04** ache, beef, bind, carp, fuss, girn, hurt, mean, mein, mene, moan, mump **05** bitch, bleat, gripe, groan, growl, grump, meane, plain, whine
06 bemoan, bewail, endure, grouse, grutch, kvetch, lament, object, repine, snivel, squawk, squeal, whinge
07 carry on, grumble, protest, wheenge **08** be in pain, feel pain
09 bellyache, criticize, find fault, make a fuss **10** make a noise, suffer from
11 expostulate, kick up a fuss, raise a stink, remonstrate **12** moan and groan
14 file a complaint **15** have a bone to pick, lodge a complaint

complainer
04 nark **06** kvetch, moaner, whiner
07 bleater, fusspot, grouser, niggler, whinger **08** grumbler, kvetcher **09** nit-picker **10** bellyacher, fussbudget
11 fault-finder

complaint
04 beef, moan **05** bleat, gripe, groan, plain, upset **06** charge, grouch, grouse, grutch, malady, plaint, squawk, whinge
07 ailment, beefing, carping, censure, disease, grumble, illness, malaise, protest, quarrel, quibble, trouble, wheenge **08** bleating, disorder, plaining, sickness **09** annoyance, bellyache, condition, criticism, grievance, infection, objection, querimony, whingeing **10** accusation, affliction **11** bellyaching **12** fault-finding, inflammation **13** indisposition
14 representation **15** dissatisfaction
See also **disease**; **inflammation**

• **expression of complaint**
02 ah

complaisant
06 docile **07** amiable, willing
08 amenable, biddable, obedient, obliging **09** agreeable, compliant, tractable **10** complacent, solicitous
11 conformable, deferential
12 conciliatory **13** accommodating

complement
03 set, sum **05** crown, match, quota, total **06** alexin, amount, number, set off **08** addition, capacity, complete, contrast, entirety, fullness, round off, strength, totality **09** accessory, accompany, aggregate, allowance, companion **10** completion, go well with **11** counterpart **12** consummation
13 accompaniment **14** go well together **15** combine well with

complementary
04 twin **06** fellow **08** matching
09 companion, finishing
10 compatible, completing, harmonious, perfecting, reciprocal, supporting **11** correlative
12 interrelated **13** corresponding
14 interdependent
See also **medicine**

complete
02 do **03** all, cap, end **04** done, full, over, real **05** clean, close, crown, ended, pakka, pucka, pukka, total, utter, whole **06** answer, clinch, damned, entire, fill in, finish, fulfil, intact, make up, settle, wind up
07 achieve, execute, fill out, fulfill, perfect, perform, plenary, realize, settled **08** absolute, achieved, conclude, detailed, finalize, finished, integral, outright, round off, thorough, unbroken, unedited **09** completed, concluded, discharge, downright, finalized, integrate, out-and-out, polish off, terminate, undivided
10 accomplish, consummate, exhaustive, terminated, unabridged
11 unmitigated, unqualified, unshortened **12** accomplished, unexpurgated **13** comprehensive, thoroughgoing, unabbreviated, unconditional

completely
02 up **03** all, out **05** fully, quite, right, whole **06** hollow, in full, wholly
07 good and, sheerly, solidly, totally, utterly **08** entirely, outright **09** all ends up, all the way, every inch, perfectly, to the hilt, to the wide **10** absolutely, abundantly, altogether, thoroughly
11 back to front, neck and crop, up to the hilt **12** from top to toe, heart and soul, stoop and roop, stoup and roup, well and truly **13** bag and baggage, head over heels, root and branch **14** in every respect **15** down to the ground, from first to last

completion
03 end, sum **05** close, crown **06** finish
08 fruition **09** discharge, execution
10 attainment, conclusion, fulfilling, fulfilment, perfection, settlement
11 achievement, culmination, realization, termination
12 consummation, finalization
14 accomplishment

complex
◇ *anagram indicator*
05 mixed, thing **06** hang-up, phobia, scheme, system, varied **07** devious, diverse, network **08** compound, disorder, fixation, involved, multiple, neurosis, ramified, tortuous
09 Byzantine, composite, difficult, elaborate, institute, intricate, obsession, plexiform, structure **10** circuitous, complicate, convoluted **11** aggregation, complicated, development
12 organization **13** establishment, preoccupation, sophisticated

complexion
03 rud **04** blee, cast, kind, leer, look, skin, sort, tone, type **05** guise, light, stamp **06** aspect, colour, nature
07 texture **08** attitude **09** character, colouring **10** appearance
11 perspective **12** pigmentation

complexity
07 variety **09** intricacy **10** complicacy, complicity **11** convolution, deviousness, diverseness, elaboration, involvement **12** complication, entanglement, multiplicity, ramification, repercussion, tortuousness **13** compositeness
14 circuitousness **15** complicatedness

compliance
01 C **06** assent **07** keeping **08** yielding
09 agreement, appliance, deference, obedience, passivity **10** accordance, conformity, submission **11** application, concurrence **12** acquiescence, complaisance **14** conformability, submissiveness

compliant
05 civil **06** docile **07** passive, pliable
08 amenable, biddable, flexible, obedient, yielding **09** agreeable, appliable, indulgent, tractable
10 obsequious, sequacious, submissive **11** acquiescent, complaisant, conformable, deferential, subservient **13** accommodating

complicate
◇ *anagram indicator*
05 mix up **06** jumble, muddle, puzzle, tangle **07** complex, confuse, involve, inweave, perplex **08** compound, entangle **09** elaborate **12** make involved **13** make difficult

complicated
◇ *anagram indicator*
06 fiddly, implex, tricky **07** complex, cryptic **08** confused, involved,

puzzling, tortuous **09** Byzantine, difficult, elaborate, intricate **10** convoluted, perplexing **11** problematic **12** labyrinthine

complication
◇ *anagram indicator*
03 web **04** node, snag **05** nodus **06** tangle **07** mixture, problem **08** drawback, obstacle **09** confusion, intricacy **10** complexity, difficulty **11** complexness, convolution, elaboration **12** ramification, repercussion **13** complexedness

complicity
08 abetment, approval **09** agreement, collusion, knowledge **10** complexity, connivance **11** concurrence, involvement **13** collaboration **14** being in cahoots

compliment
04 laud **05** extol **06** admire, eulogy, favour, homage, honour, praise, salute **07** applaud, bouquet, commend, devoirs, douceur, flatter, regards, tribute **08** accolade, approval, encomium, eulogize, flattery, respects **09** baisemain, greetings, laudation, sugarplum, trade-last **10** admiration, best wishes, felicitate, good wishes, salutation **11** speak well of **12** commendation, congratulate, felicitation, pat on the back, remembrances **13** speak highly of **15** congratulations

• **looking for compliments**
07 angling, fishing

complimentary
04 free **06** gratis **07** glowing **08** admiring, courtesy, honorary **09** approving **10** eulogistic, favourable, flattering, for nothing, on the house **11** meliorative, panegyrical **12** appreciative, commendatory **14** congratulatory

comply
04 meet, obey **05** agree, all in, defer, yield **06** accede, accord, assent, follow, fulfil, oblige, submit **07** abide by, conform, consent, observe, perform, respect, satisfy **09** acquiesce, discharge **10** condescend **11** accommodate

component
◇ *anagram indicator*
03 bit **04** item, part, unit **05** basic, piece **06** factor, module, widget **07** element, partial, section **08** inherent, integral **09** essential, intrinsic, spare part **10** ingredient **11** constituent **12** constitutive, integral part **15** constituent part

See also **electrical**

comport
03 act, use **04** bear **05** abear, carry **06** acquit, behave, demean, deport **07** conduct, perform

compose
◇ *anagram indicator*
03 pen, set **04** calm, dite, form, lull, make **05** build, frame, quell, quiet, still, write **06** create, devise, draw up, indite, invent, make up, pacify, settle, soothe, steady **07** arrange, assuage, collect, compile, concoct, control, fashion, produce, stickle, think of, think up **08** assemble, calm down, comprise **09** construct, reconcile **10** constitute **11** choreograph, orchestrate, put together **12** tranquillize

composed
◇ *anagram indicator*
04 calm, cool **05** quite **06** at ease, placid, sedate, serene **07** relaxed **08** together, tranquil **09** collected, confident, unruffled, unworried **10** calmed down, controlled **11** level-headed, unflappable **13** imperturbable, quietened down, self-possessed **14** self-controlled **15** cool as a cucumber

composer
04 bard, poet **05** lyric, maker **06** author, master, writer **07** creator, maestro **08** arranger, melodist, musician, producer, psalmist, triadist **09** epitapher, songsmith, tunesmith **10** epitaphist, operettist, originator, songwriter, symphonist **12** balladmonger, variationist, vaudevillist **13** contrapuntist, dodecaphonist, orchestralist

Composers include:

03 **Bax** (Sir Arnold), **Sor** (Fernando)
04 **Adam** (Adolphe), **Arne** (Thomas), **Bach** (Carl Philipp Emanuel), **Bach** (Johann Christian), **Bach** (Johann Sebastian), **Berg** (Alban), **Bull** (John), **Byrd** (William), **Cage** (John), **Ives** (Charles), **Orff** (Carl), **Pärt** (Arvo), **Weir** (Judith)
05 **Adams** (John), **Auric** (Georges), **Berio** (Luciano), **Bizet** (Georges), **Bliss** (Sir Arthur), **Boito** (Arrigo), **Boyce** (William), **Bruch** (Max), **D'Indy** (Vincent), **Dufay** (Guillaume), **Dukas** (Paul), **Durey** (Louis), **Elgar** (Sir Edward), **Falla** (Manuel de), **Fauré** (Gabriel), **Glass** (Philip), **Gluck** (Christoph), **Grieg** (Edvard), **Haydn** (Joseph), **Holst** (Gustav), **Lehár** (Franz), **Liszt** (Franz), **Lully** (Jean Baptiste), **Ogdon** (John), **Parry** (Sir Hubert), **Ravel** (Maurice), **Satie** (Erik), **Verdi** (Giuseppe), **Weber** (Carl Maria von)
06 **Barber** (Samuel), **Bartók** (Béla), **Bishop** (Sir Henry Rowley), **Boulez** (Pierre), **Brahms** (Johannes), **Busoni** (Ferruccio), **Casals** (Pablo), **Chopin** (Frédéric), **Clarke** (Jeremiah), **Coates** (Eric), **Delius** (Frederick), **Dvorák** (Antonín), **Franck** (César), **German** (Sir Edward), **Glinka** (Mikhail), **Gounod** (Charles), **Gurney** (Ivor), **Handel** (George Frideric), **Kodály** (Zoltán), **Ligeti** (György), **Mahler** (Gustav), **Morley** (Thomas), **Mozart** (Wolfgang Amadeus), **Previn** (André), **Rameau** (Jean Philippe), **Rubbra** (Edmund), **Tallis** (Thomas), **Varèse** (Edgard), **Wagner** (Richard), **Walton** (Sir William), **Webern** (Anton von), **Wilbye** (John)
07 **Albéniz** (Isaac), **Allegri** (Gregorio), **Bellini** (Vincenzo), **Bennett** (Sir Richard Rodney), **Berlioz** (Hector), **Borodin** (Alexander), **Britten** (Benjamin), **Campion** (Thomas), **Copland** (Aaron), **Corelli** (Arcangelo), **Debussy** (Claude), **Delibes** (Léo), **Dowland** (John), **Duruflé** (Maurice), **Fricker** (Peter), **Gibbons** (Orlando), **Górecki** (Henryk), **Janácek** (Leos), **Menotti** (Gian-Carlo), **Milhaud** (Darius), **Nicolai** (Otto), **Nielsen** (Carl), **Poulenc** (Francis), **Puccini** (Giacomo), **Purcell** (Henry), **Rossini** (Gioacchino), **Salieri** (Antonio), **Shankar** (Ravi), **Smetana** (Bedrich), **Strauss** (Johann), **Strauss** (Richard), **Tavener** (John), **Tippett** (Sir Michael), **Vivaldi** (Antonio), **Xenakis** (Iannis)
08 **Berkeley** (Sir Lennox), **Bruckner** (Anton), **Couperin** (François), **Goossens** (Sir Eugene), **Grainger** (Percy), **Hoffmann** (Ernst Theodor Wilhelm), **Holliger** (Heinz), **Honegger** (Arthur), **Maconchy** (Dame Elizabeth), **Mascagni** (Pietro), **Massenet** (Jules), **Messiaen** (Olivier), **Respighi** (Ottorino), **Schubert** (Franz), **Schumann** (Robert), **Scriabin** (Aleksandr), **Sibelius** (Jean), **Sondheim** (Steven), **Stanford** (Sir Charles Villiers), **Sullivan** (Sir Arthur), **Telemann** (Georg Philipp), **Victoria** (Tomás Luis de), **Williams** (John)
09 **Beethoven** (Ludwig van), **Boulanger** (Nadia), **Buxtehude** (Diderik), **Donizetti** (Gaetano), **Hindemith** (Paul), **Meyerbeer** (Giacomo), **Offenbach** (Jacques), **Pachelbel** (Johann), **Prokofiev** (Sergei), **Scarlatti** (Alessandro), **Scarlatti** (Domenico), **Tortelier** (Paul)
10 **Birtwistle** (Sir Harrison), **Boccherini** (Luigi), **Kabalevsky** (Dmitri), **Monteverdi** (Claudio), **Mussorgsky** (Modeste), **Praetorius** (Michael), **Rubinstein** (Anton), **Saint-Saëns** (Camille), **Schoenberg** (Arnold), **Stravinsky** (Igor), **Villa-Lobos** (Hector)
11 **Humperdinck** (Engelbert), **Leoncavallo** (Ruggiero), **Mendelssohn** (Felix), **Rachmaninov** (Sergei), **Stockhausen** (Karlheinz), **Tchaikovsky** (Piotr), **Theodorakis** (Mikis)
12 **Shostakovich** (Dmitri)
13 **Khatchaturian** (Aram), **Maxwell Davies** (Sir Peter)
14 **Rimsky-Korsakov** (Nikolai)
15 **Vaughan Williams** (Ralph)

See also **libretto**

composite
05 alloy, blend, fused, mixed **06** fusion **07** amalgam, blended, complex, mixture **08** combined, compound, pastiche **09** patchwork, synthesis **10** conflation **11** agglutinate, combination, synthesized **12** amalgamation, conglomerate **13** agglutination, heterogeneous

composition
◇ *anagram indicator*
02 op **04** book, dite, fine, form, opus, poem, port, task, text, work **05** compo, essay, motet, novel, opera, paper, piece, story, study, thing, verse **06** design, erotic, layout, make-up, making, motett, review, satire, sonata, thesis **07** article, balance, drawing, harmony, mixture, morceau, picture, writing **08** creation, devising, exercise, oratorio, painting, pencraft, rhapsody, symmetry, symphony, treatise **09** album-leaf, arranging, capriccio, character, exaration, formation, impromptu, invention, structure, work of art **10** adaptation, assignment, compromise, concoction, confection, consonance, mock-heroic, production, proportion, whipstitch **11** arrangement, combination, compilation, formulation **12** conformation, constitution, dissertation, organization **13** accompaniment, choral prelude, configuration **15** putting together

See also **musical**

compost
04 peat **05** humus, mulch **06** manure **07** grow-bag, mixture **08** dressing, leaf-soil **09** leaf-mould **10** fertilizer, growing-bag

composure
04 calm, ease **05** poise **06** aplomb, temper **07** dignity **08** calmness, coolness, serenity **09** assurance, character, placidity, sangfroid **10** collection, confidence, dispassion, equanimity **11** composition, impassivity, self-control, temperament **12** tranquillity **13** self-assurance **14** self-possession **15** level-headedness

compound
◇ *anagram indicator*
03 Cpd, mix, pen **04** fold, fuse, yard **05** add to, alloy, blend, court, fused, mixed, pound, put up, unite **06** corral, fusion, hybrid, make up, medley, mingle, worsen **07** amalgam, augment, blended, combine, complex, magnify, mixture, paddock **08** coalesce, combined, dispense, heighten, increase, multiple, stockade **09** admixture, aggravate, composite, enclosure, intensify, intricate, synthesis **10** amalgamate, complicate, exacerbate, synthesize **11** combination, complicated, composition, intermingle, put together, synthesized **12** amalgamation, conglomerate

See also **chemical**

comprehend
◇ *containment indicator*
03 see **04** know, twig **05** catch, cover, get it, grasp, sense **06** fathom, take in, tumble **07** catch on, compass, contain, discern, embrace, include, involve, make out, realize **08** comprise, conceive, perceive, tumble to **09** apprehend, encompass, penetrate **10** appreciate, assimilate, generalize, understand **11** make sense of **15** put your finger on

comprehensible
05 clear, lucid, plain **06** simple **08** coherent, explicit **09** graspable **10** accessible **11** conceivable, discernible **12** intelligible **14** understandable **15** straightforward

comprehension
03 ken **05** grasp, sense **07** insight **09** judgement, knowledge **10** conception, perception **11** discernment, realization **12** appreciation, apprehension, intelligence **13** understanding

comprehensive
04 full, wide **05** all-in, broad **06** global **07** blanket, capable, general, overall **08** complete, elliptic, sweeping, thorough **09** extensive, inclusive, universal **10** elliptical, exhaustive, widespread **11** compendious **12** all-embracing, all-inclusive, encyclopedic **14** across-the-board, encyclopedical

comprehensively
05 fully **06** widely **07** broadly **10** completely, thoroughly, widespread **11** extensively **12** exhaustively

compress
03 jam, ram, zip **04** cram, lace, pack, pump, tamp **05** crowd, crush, pinch, press, screw, stuff, wedge **06** impact, reduce, squash, strain **07** abridge, astrict, compact, embrace, flatten, shorten, squeeze **08** astringe, condense, contract, shoehorn **09** coarctate, constrict, summarize, synopsize, telescope **10** abbreviate, pressurize **11** concentrate, consolidate, strangulate

compression
07 packing, pumping **08** pinching, pressing, stuffing, thlipsis **09** squashing **10** condensing, flattening **12** constriction **13** concentration, consolidation

comprise
◇ *containment indicator*
04 form **05** cover **06** embody, make up, take in **07** compose, contain, embrace, include, involve **09** consist of, encompass **10** comprehend, constitute **11** incorporate **12** be composed of

compromise
◇ *anagram indicator*
04 deal, risk **05** adapt, agree, shame **06** adjust, damage, expose, settle, weaken **07** balance, bargain, concede, imperil, involve **08** endanger, trade-off **09** agreement, arbitrate, discredit, dishonour, embarrass, implicate, mediation, middle way, negotiate, prejudice, settle for, undermine **10** adjustment, concession, jeopardize, settlement **11** arbitration, composition, co-operation, give and take, meet halfway, negotiation, temperament **12** bring shame to, modus vivendi **13** accommodation, understanding **15** make concessions

compulsion
04 need, urge **05** drive, force **06** demand, desire, duress **07** duresse, impulse, longing **08** coaction, coercion, distress, pressure **09** necessity, obsession **10** constraint, insistence, obligation, temptation **11** enforcement **13** preoccupation

compulsive
06 hooked, urgent **07** chronic, driving **08** addicted, gripping, habitual, hardened, hopeless, mesmeric, riveting **09** absorbing, besetting, dependent, incurable, obsessive **10** compelling, inveterate **11** enthralling, fascinating, unavoidable **12** incorrigible, irredeemable, irresistible, overpowering, overwhelming, pathological, spellbinding **14** uncontrollable

compulsively
09 incurably **10** habitually, inevitably **11** chronically, obsessively, unavoidably **12** incorrigibly, irresistibly **13** involuntarily **14** pathologically

compulsory
03 set **06** forced **07** binding **08** coactive, required **09** de rigueur, essential, mandatory, necessary, requisite **10** compelling, imperative, obligatory, stipulated **11** contractual

compunction
05 guilt, qualm, shame **06** qualms, regret, sorrow, unease **07** remorse **09** misgiving, penitence **10** contrition, hesitation, misgivings, reluctance, repentance, uneasiness

computation
03 sum **06** answer, result **08** estimate, figuring, forecast **09** reckoning **10** arithmetic, estimation, working-out **11** calculation, forecasting

compute
03 sum **04** rate **05** add up, count, tally, total **06** assess, figure, reckon **07** count up, measure, work out **08** estimate, evaluate **09** calculate, enumerate

computer
02 NC, PC **03** MPC **10** calculator **15** electronic brain

Computers include:

03 HAL, IBM, Mac, SAL
04 iMac, VIKI
05 Eddie, ENIAC, Holly, iBook
06 UNIVAC

08 Colossus, Deep Blue, Spectrum
09 The Matrix
11 DeepThought
12 Commodore Pet

Computer scientists include:

04 **Bell** (Gordon), **Bush** (Vannevar), **Cray** (Seymour), **Hurd** (Cuthbert Corwin), **Jobs** (Steven), **Zuse** (Konrad)
05 **Aiken** (Howard Hathaway), **Burks** (Arthur Walter), **Gates** (William Henry 'Bill'), **Olsen** (Kenneth Harry), **Sugar** (Alan)
06 **Amdahl** (Gene Myron), **Backus** (John), **Comrie** (Leslie John), **Eckert** (John Presper), **Hopper** (Grace Murray), **Huskey** (Harry Douglas), **Michie** (Donald), **Milner** (Robin Gorell), **Porter** (Arthur), **Turing** (Alan), **Wilkes** (Maurice Vincent)
07 **Babbage** (Charles), **Kilburn** (Tom), **Mauchly** (John William), **Shannon** (Claude Elwood), **Stibitz** (George Robert), **Wheeler** (David John)
08 **Lovelace** (Ada, Countess), **Shockley** (William Bradford), **Sinclair** (Sir Clive), **Williams** (Sir Frederic Calland)
09 **Atanasoff** (John Vincent), **Forrester** (Jay Wright), **Goldstine** (Herman Heine), **Hollerith** (Herman), **Wilkinson** (James Hardy)
10 **Berners-Lee** (Tim), **Fairclough** (John Whitaker), **Michaelson** (Sidney), **Von Neumann** (John)

Computing and Internet terms include:

02 CD, IT, PC, VR
03 bit, bot, bug, bus, CD-R, CPU, DOS, DTP, DVD, FAQ, FTP, GUI, hit, IDE, ISP, Mac®, net, P2P, PDF, RAM, ROM, RTF, URL, VDU, WAN, Web, WWW
04 BIOS, boot, byte, card, CD-RW, cell, chip, data, disk, dump, file, game, HTML, icon, iMac®, ISDN, menu, port, ring, SGML, Unix®, worm
05 ASCII, BASIC, cache, CD-ROM, e-mail, iBook®, JANET®, Linux, login, log on, Mac OS, macro, modem, mouse, MS-DOS®, pixel, shell, virus
06 access, backup, binary, bitmap, buffer, cursor, DVD-ROM, editor, format, Google®, laptop, log off, memory, plug-in, reboot, screen, script, server, the Net, the Web, toggle, window
07 browser, crawler, default, desktop, hacking, monitor, network, palmtop, Pentium®, pointer, printer, program, scanner, toolbar, Unicode, upgrade, Web page, Web site, Windows®, WYSIWYG, zip disk
08 Apple Mac®, autosave, bookmark, chat room, database, emoticon, firewall, freeware, gigabyte, graphics, handheld, hard disk, hardware, home page, Internet, joystick, keyboard, kilobyte, megabyte, mouse mat, notebook, password, platform, protocol, software, template, terabyte, terminal, user name
09 character, debugging, directory, disk drive, e-commerce, hard drive, hyperlink, hypertext, interface, mainframe, newsgroup, shareware, sound card, utilities, video card
10 domain name, floppy disk, multimedia, netiquette, peer-to-peer, peripheral, rewritable, serial port
11 abandonware, application, compact disc, compression, cut and paste, floppy drive, motherboard, optical disk, screen saver, silicon chip, spreadsheet, Trojan horse, workstation
12 circuit board, graphics card, installation, laser printer, parallel port, search engine, spellchecker, subdirectory, World Wide Web
13 file extension, ink-jet printer, microcomputer, user interface
14 electronic mail, internal memory, microprocessor, read only memory, rich text format, virtual reality, word processing
15 operating system, wide area network

See also **key**; **language**

• **connected computers**
03 net, web **07** network

comrade
03 pal **04** aide, ally, mate **05** billy, buddy, butty, crony **06** billie, escort, fellow, frater, friend **07** Achates, consort, partner **08** chaperon, follower, intimate, sidekick, tovarich, tovarish **09** assistant, associate, attendant, bully-rook, chaperone, colleague, communist, companion, confidant, tovarisch **10** accomplice, confidante **11** bon camarade, confederate **12** pot companion

comradeship
08 affinity **09** closeness **10** fellowship, friendship, sisterhood **11** brotherhood, camaraderie, sociability **12** sisterliness, togetherness **13** brotherliness, companionship, esprit de corps

con
02 do **04** dupe, hoax, know, rook, scam, scan, show **05** bluff, cheat, fraud, knock, learn, teach, trick **06** fiddle, fleece, racket, rip off **07** against, deceive, defraud, mislead, swindle, tweedle **08** cheating, hoodwink, inveigle, prisoner **09** bamboozle, deception **11** acknowledge, double-cross **15** confidence trick

concatenation
05 chain, nexus, trail, train **06** course, series, string, thread **07** linking **08** progress, sequence **10** connection, procession, succession **11** progression **12** interlinking, interlocking

concave
04 arch **05** vault **06** cupped, hollow, sunken **07** invexed, scooped **08** curved in, hollowed, incurved, indented **09** depressed, excavated, incurvate **14** bending inwards

conceal
◇ *containment indicator*
◇ *hidden indicator*
04 bury, feal, heal, heel, hele, hide, mask, sink, veil **05** cloak, cloke, cover, stash **06** closet, hush up, keep in, pocket, screen, shroud, vizard **07** cover up, obscure, secrete, smother **08** disguise, keep dark, submerge, suppress, tuck away **09** dissemble, keep quiet, overgreen, whitewash **10** camouflage, keep hidden, keep secret, subterfuge **11** dissimulate, put the lid on **14** keep out of sight, keep under wraps

concealed
◇ *containment indicator*
◇ *hidden indicator*
05 perdu **06** covert, hidden, latent, masked, perdue, unseen **07** covered **08** screened **09** disguised, submerged **10** tucked away **11** clandestine **13** inconspicuous

concealment
◇ *containment indicator*
◇ *hidden indicator*
04 mask, veil **05** cloak, cover, wraps **06** hiding, screen, shroud **07** cover-up, hideout, mystery, privacy, secrecy, shelter **08** disguise, hideaway **09** secretion, whitewash **10** camouflage, protection **11** keeping dark, smokescreen, suppression **13** keeping secret

concede
03 owe, own **04** cede **05** admit, allow, grant, own up, yield **06** accede, accept, give up **07** confess, forfeit **08** hand over **09** recognize, sacrifice, surrender **10** condescend, relinquish **11** acknowledge

conceit
03 ego **04** fume, wind **05** image, pride, think **06** device, simile, vanity **07** bighead, egotism, imagine, swagger, thought **08** conceive, concetto, metaphor, puppyism, self-love **09** arrogance, cockiness, immodesty, vainglory **10** comparison, narcissism **11** complacency, haughtiness **12** boastfulness **13** bigheadedness, conceitedness, understanding **14** figure of speech, self-admiration, self-assumption, self-importance

conceited
04 smug, vain **05** cocky, flory, proud, windy, witty **06** clever, snotty **07** haughty, stuck-up **08** arrogant, boastful, immodest, puffed up **09** bigheaded, cat-witted, egotistic, upsetting **10** complacent, toffee-nose **11** egotistical, fantastical, overweening, swell-headed, toffee-nosed

12 narcissistic, supercilious, vainglorious **13** above yourself, self-important, self-satisfied, swelled-headed, swollen-headed **14** full of yourself

conceivable
06 likely **07** tenable **08** credible, possible, probable **09** cogitable, plausible, thinkable **10** believable, imaginable

conceivably
08 possibly, probably **09** plausibly **10** imaginably

conceive
03 see **04** form, take **05** brain, fancy, grasp, guess, start, think **06** create, design, devise, enwomb, invent **07** believe, conceit, develop, express, fantasy, gestate, imagine, picture, produce, realize, suppose, think of, think up **08** contrive, envisage, perceive **09** apprehend, be fertile, formulate, originate, reproduce, visualize **10** appreciate, come up with, comprehend, understand **11** get pregnant, give birth to **14** become pregnant **15** get into your head

concentrate
04 mind **05** amass, bunch, crowd, focus, juice, rivet, think **06** apozem, attend, centre, direct, distil, elixir, gather, reduce **07** cluster, collect, essence, extract, thicken **08** boil down, compress, condense, consider, converge **09** decoction, decocture, evaporate, intensify **10** accumulate, centralize, congregate **11** consolidate, dephlegmate, put your mind **12** distillation, keep your mind, pay attention, quintessence **13** apply yourself **15** devote attention

concentrated
04 conc, deep, hard, rich **05** dense **06** all-out, strong **07** intense, reduced **08** vigorous **09** concerted, condensed, distilled, intensive, strenuous, thickened, undiluted, undivided **10** compressed, evaporated

concentration
04 conc, heed, mass, mind **05** crowd **07** cluster **08** devotion, focusing, grouping **09** attention, denseness, intensity, reduction, thickness **10** absorption, collection **11** application, boiling-down, compression, convergence, deep thought, engrossment, evaporation **12** accumulation, close thought, congregation, distillation **13** agglomeration, consolidation **14** centralization, conglomeration

concept
04 idea, idée, plan, view **05** image **06** notion, theory, vision **07** picture, thought **09** dimension, intention, universal **10** conception, hypothesis, impression **11** abstraction **13** visualization

conception
04 clue, idea, plan, view **05** birth, image **06** design, notion, origin, outset, theory, vision **07** concept, genesis, inkling, picture, thought **09** beginning, formation, inception, intention, invention, knowledge, launching, pregnancy **10** conceiving, hypothesis, impression, initiation, perception **11** abstraction, fecundation, origination **12** appreciation, impregnation, inauguration, insemination, reproduction **13** comprehension, fertilization, understanding, visualization

conceptual
05 ideal **08** abstract, notional, thematic **11** speculative, theoretical **12** hypothetical **14** classificatory

concern
03 job **04** baby, busy, care, cern, duty, firm, heed, part, reck, reke, task **05** alarm, cover, field, issue, point, stake, topic, touch, upset, worry **06** affair, affect, bear on, bother, charge, debate, devote, indaba, matter, meddle, pidgin, pigeon, reckon, regard, sorrow, strain, tender, unease **07** anguish, anxiety, apply to, be about, company, disturb, involve, lookout, perturb, pidgeon, problem, refer to, subject, thought, trouble **08** argument, business, deal with, disquiet, distress, interest, pressure, question, relate to **09** attention, pertain to, syndicate **10** enterprise, solicitude **11** appertain to, association, concernment, corporation, disturbance, involvement, make anxious, make worried, partnership **12** apprehension, have to do with, organization, perturbation **13** attentiveness, consideration, establishment **14** prey on your mind, responsibility **15** be connected with

See also **company**; **business**

concerned
◇ *anagram indicator*
04 kind **05** upset **06** caring, uneasy **07** anxious, helpful, related, unhappy, versant, worried **08** affected, bothered, gracious, involved, troubled **09** attentive, connected, disturbed, perturbed, sensitive, unselfish **10** altruistic, charitable, distressed, implicated, interested, solicitous, thoughtful **11** considerate **12** apprehensive

• be concerned
04 care, mell

• concerned with
02 in, re **05** about

concerning
02 of, on, re **04** in re, over **05** about, after, anent **07** apropos **08** to do with, touching **09** as regards, regarding **10** relating to, relevant to, respecting **11** referring to **12** with regard to **13** in the matter of, with respect to **14** on the subject of **15** with reference to

concert
03 gig **04** prom, show **05** quill, union **06** accord, smoker, soirée, unison **07** concord, harmony, recital **09** agreement, rendering, rendition, unanimity **10** appearance, consonance, engagement, hootenanny, jam session, production **11** concordance, co-operation, partnership, performance **12** presentation **13** collaboration, entertainment

concerted
05 joint **06** shared, united **07** planned **08** combined **09** organized **10** collective **11** co-operative, co-ordinated, interactive, prearranged **12** concentrated **13** collaborative

concession
03 cut, sop **05** grant, right **06** ceding, favour **07** forfeit **08** decrease, discount, giving-up, handover, yielding **09** admission, allowance, exception, franchise, privilege, reduction, sacrifice, surrender **10** acceptance, adjustment, compromise **11** recognition, synchoresis **12** special right **14** relinquishment **15** acknowledgement

• expression of concession
02 ou, ow

conciliate
06 disarm, pacify, soften, soothe **07** appease, mollify, placate, satisfy **09** reconcile **10** propitiate **11** disembitter

conciliation
09 placation **11** appeasement, peacemaking **12** pacification, propitiation **13** mollification **14** reconciliation

conciliator
04 dove **06** broker **08** mediator **09** go-between, middleman **10** negotiator, peacemaker, reconciler **11** intercessor **12** intermediary

conciliatory
06 irenic **07** pacific **09** appeasing, assuaging, disarming, peaceable, placatory **10** mollifying **11** peacemaking **12** pacificatory, propitiative, propitiatory, smooth-spoken **13** smooth-talking, smooth-tongued **14** reconciliatory

concise
04 curt **05** brief, crisp, pithy, short, terse, tight **07** compact, laconic, summary **08** abridged, elliptic, mutilate, succinct, synoptic **09** condensed, thumbnail **10** aphoristic, compressed, elliptical, to the point **11** abbreviated, compendious **12** epigrammatic **14** epigrammatical

concisely
06 curtly **07** briefly, crisply, in a word, in brief, in short, pithily, tersely

10 succinctly, to the point 11 in a nutshell, laconically

conclave
05 cabal 06 parley, powwow
07 cabinet, council, meeting, session
08 assembly 09 gathering
10 conference 13 confabulation, secret meeting

conclude
03 end 04 amen, make 05 agree, allow, cease, close, debar, infer, judge, uptie 06 assume, clinch, decide, deduce, effect, finish, gather, reason, reckon, settle, top off, wind up, wrap up
07 arrange, enclose, pull off, resolve, suppose, surmise, work out 08 bring off, complete, restrain 09 culminate, determine, establish, negotiate, polish off, terminate 10 accomplish, conjecture, consummate 11 come to an end, discontinue, draw to an end
12 bring to an end

conclusion
03 con, end 04 coda, fine 05 close, finis, issue, omega, point 06 answer, ending, finale, finish, result, riddle, upshot 07 come-off, finding, opinion, outcome, problem, verdict 08 decision, epilogue, explicit, illation, pirlicue, settling, solution 09 agreement, brokering, cessation, clinching, deduction, effecting, inference, judgement, punchline 10 assumption, completion, consectary, conviction, experiment, peroration, pulling-off, resolution, settlement, working-out
11 arrangement, consequence, culmination, negotiation, termination
12 consummation 13 determination, establishment 14 accomplishment, discontinuance

• **in conclusion**
04 ergo 06 in fine 07 finally, to sum up
09 in closing 10 to conclude

conclusive
03 net 04 nett 05 clear, final
08 decisive, definite, ultimate
10 convincing, definitive, unarguable, undeniable 11 irrefutable
12 indisputable, unanswerable, unappealable

conclusively
07 clearly, finally 10 decisively, definitely, ultimately, unarguably, undeniably 11 irrefutably
12 convincingly, definitively, indisputably

concoct
◇ *anagram indicator*
03 fix, mix 04 brew, cook, make, plan, plot 05 blend, frame, hatch 06 cook up, decoct, devise, invent, make up, mature 07 develop, dream up, prepare, think up 08 contrive, rustle up
09 fabricate, formulate
11 manufacture, put together

concoction
◇ *anagram indicator*
04 brew, myth 05 blend, fable, story 06 potion 07 fiction, mixture, untruth
08 compound, creation 09 hell-broth, love-juice 10 fairy story
11 combination, fabrication, preparation, witches' brew

concomitant
07 symptom 09 attendant, by-product, conjoined, secondary, syndromic 10 co-existent, concurrent, incidental, side effect 11 associative, synchronous 12 accompanying, coincidental, conterminous, contributing, simultaneous
13 accompaniment, complementary, epiphenomenon
15 contemporaneous

concord
04 pact 05 agree, amity, peace, union
06 accord, treaty, unison 07 compact, concent, entente, harmony, rapport
09 agreement, concentus, consensus, harmonize, unanimity 10 consonance, friendship 11 amicability

concourse
04 hall 05 crowd, crush, foyer, lobby, plaza, press, swarm 06 lounge, piazza, repair, resort, throng 07 meeting
08 assembly, entrance 09 gathering, multitude 10 collection, confluence

concrete
04 firm, real 05 béton, solid 06 actual
07 factual, genuine, Siporex®, visible
08 definite, explicit, material, physical, positive, specific, tangible
09 touchable 11 perceptible, substantial

concubine
05 leman, lover, madam 07 lorette, sultana 08 mistress, paramour
09 courtesan, guinea-hen, kept woman 11 apple-squire

concupiscence
04 lust 06 desire, libido 07 concupy, lechery 08 appetite, lewdness
09 horniness, lubricity, randiness
11 lustfulness 12 sexual desire
14 lasciviousness, libidinousness

concupiscent
04 lewd 05 horny, randy 07 lustful
09 lecherous 10 lascivious, libidinous, lubricious

concur
05 agree 06 accede, accord, assent, comply 07 approve, consent
08 coincide 09 acquiesce, co-operate, harmonize 11 be in harmony

concurrence
06 assent 07 consent 08 approval, syndrome 09 agreement, synchrony
10 acceptance, conspiracy
11 association, coexistence, coincidence, consilience, convergence
12 acquiescence, common ground, simultaneity 13 juxtaposition
15 contemporaneity

concurrent
10 coexistent, coexisting, coincident, coinciding 11 concomitant, synchronous 12 accompanying, simultaneous 15 contemporaneous

concussion
10 head injury 11 brain injury, water hammer 15 unconsciousness

condemn
◇ *anagram indicator*
03 ban, bar 04 cast, damn, doom, hiss, kest, slam 05 blame, decry, force, judge, knock, slate 06 berate, coerce, compel, ordain, punish, revile
07 accurse, censure, consign, convict, deplore, destine, destroy, reprove, run down, upbraid 08 demolish, denounce, reproach, sentence
09 castigate, criticize, deprecate, disparage, reprehend 10 disapprove, find guilty 12 declare unfit 13 declare unsafe, give a sentence, pass a sentence

condemnation
◇ *anagram indicator*
03 ban 04 doom 05 blame
07 censure, reproof 08 judgment, reproach, sentence 09 criticism, damnation, judgement 10 conviction, thumbs-down 11 castigation, deprecation, disapproval, reprobation
12 denunciation 13 disparagement

condemnatory
08 accusing, critical 09 damnatory, reprobate 10 accusatory, censorious
11 deprecatory, judgemental, reprobative, reprobatory
12 denunciatory, disapproving, discouraging, proscriptive, unfavourable 13 incriminating

condensation
05 steam 06 digest, précis
07 summary 08 moisture, synopsis
09 reduction 11 abridgement, boiling-down, compression, contraction, curtailment, evaporation
12 distillation, liquefaction
13 concentration, consolidation, deliquescence, precipitation

condense
03 cut 06 distil, précis, reduce
07 abridge, compact, curtail, cut down, shorten, thicken 08 boil down, compress, contract, solidify
09 capsulize, coagulate, epitomize, evaporate, intensify, summarize
10 abbreviate, condensate, deliquesce, inspissate 11 concentrate, encapsulate, precipitate

condensed
03 cut 04 rich 05 dense 06 potted, strong 07 capsule, clotted, compact, concise, cut down, reduced, summary
08 capsular 09 curtailed, shortened, thickened, undiluted 10 abstracted, coagulated, compressed, contracted, evaporated, summarized
12 concentrated

condescend
04 bend 05 agree, deign, grant, stoop
06 comply, see fit 07 concede, consent, decline, descend, specify

09 patronize, vouchsafe **10** talk down to **12** be snobbish to **13** lower yourself **14** demean yourself, humble yourself

condescending
05 lofty **06** lordly, snooty **07** haughty, stuck-up **08** gracious, snobbish, superior **09** imperious **10** disdainful **11** patronizing, toffee-nosed **12** supercilious

condescendingly
10 snobbishly **11** imperiously **12** disdainfully **13** patronizingly **14** superciliously

condescension
04 airs **05** stoop **07** disdain **09** loftiness **10** lordliness **11** haughtiness, superiority **12** snobbishness

condiment
04 salt **05** spice **06** ginger, pepper, relish, season **07** caraway, chutney, mustard, pickles, vinegar **08** carraway, chow-chow **09** seasoning **11** horseradish, tracklement **13** French mustard **14** English mustard

condition
◇ *anagram indicator*
02 do, if **03** -dom, ply **04** case, form, nick, pass, rule, sted, tone, trim, tune **05** adapt, equip, groom, limit, mould, order, prime, set-up, shape, state, stead, stedd, stede, steed, teach, terms, train, treat **06** adjust, defect, demand, factor, fettle, health, kilter, malady, milieu, plight, revive, season, stedde, temper **07** ailment, climate, context, disease, educate, factors, fitness, illness, improve, nourish, prepare, problem, proviso, restore, setting **08** accustom, disorder, position, quandary, restrict, weakness **09** brainwash, complaint, essential, infirmity, influence, necessity, provision, situation, transform, way of life **10** atmosphere, background, limitation, obligation **11** environment, familiarize, make healthy, predicament, requirement, restriction, stipulation **12** indoctrinate, precondition, prerequisite, surroundings, working order **13** circumstances, qualification, state of health

See also **disease**; **psychological**; **skin**

• **in good condition**
02 OK **03** fit **04** okay, taut, tidy, well **05** sound **07** in flesh, in shape, thrifty **13** well-preserved

• **in perfect condition**
02 go **06** groovy **12** sound as a bell

• **in such condition**
02 so

• **in what condition**
03 how

conditional
04 tied **05** based **07** limited, subject **08** relative **09** dependent, provisory, qualified **10** contingent, restricted **11** provisional

conditionally
09 limitedly **10** relatively **11** qualifiedly **13** provisionally

conditioning
07 shaping **08** moulding **09** influence **10** adaptation, adjustment **11** preparation **12** transforming

condolence
04 pity **07** comfort, support **08** sympathy **10** compassion **11** consolation **13** commiseration

condom
04 safe **06** johnny, rubber, sheath **07** Femidom®, johnnie, scumbag **10** protective **12** female condom, French letter, prophylactic **13** contraceptive

condone
05 allow, brook **06** accept, excuse, ignore, pardon **07** forgive, let pass **08** overlook, tolerate **09** disregard **15** turn a blind eye to

conducive
06 useful **07** helpful, leading, tending **09** promoting **10** beneficial, favourable, productive **11** encouraging, ministerial **12** advantageous, contributing, contributory, instrumental

conduct
02 do **03** act, ren, rin, run **04** bear, hold, keep, lead, show, take, ways **05** bring, carry, chair, guide, pilot, steer, usher **06** acquit, behave, convey, direct, escort, handle, manage **07** actions, bearing, comport, control, manners, operate, perform, running, solicit **08** attitude, behavior, carry out, guidance, organize, practice, regulate, transmit **09** accompany, behaviour, demeanour, direction, operation **10** administer, deportment, leadership, management **11** comportment, orchestrate, supervision **12** be in charge of, organization **14** administration

conductance
01 G

conductor
06 leader **07** clippie, maestro, manager **11** non-electric

Conductors include:

04 **Böhm** (Karl), **Wood** (Sir Henry)
05 **Boult** (Sir Adrian), **Bülow** (Hans von), **Davis** (Sir Andrew), **Davis** (Sir Colin), **Elgar** (Sir Edward), **Hallé** (Sir Charles), **Kempe** (Rudolf), **Solti** (Sir Georg), **Sousa** (John Philip)
06 **Abbado** (Claudio), **Boulez** (Pierre), **Casals** (Pablo), **Gibson** (Sir Alexander), **Maazel** (Lorin), **Mahler** (Gustav), **Previn** (André), **Rattle** (Sir Simon), **Walter** (Bruno)
07 **Beecham** (Sir Thomas), **Gergiev** (Valery), **Haitink** (Bernard), **Harding** (Daniel), **Jansons** (Mariss), **Karajan** (Herbert von), **Lambert** (Constant), **Nicolai** (Otto), **Richter** (Hans), **Sargent** (Sir Malcolm), **Smetana** (Bedrich), **Strauss** (Johann), **Strauss** (Richard)
08 **Goossens** (Sir Eugene)
09 **Ashkenazy** (Vladimir), **Barenboim** (Daniel), **Bernstein** (Leonard), **Boulanger** (Nadia), **Klemperer** (Otto), **Mackerras** (Sir Charles), **Stokowski** (Leopold), **Tortelier** (Paul), **Toscanini** (Arturo)
10 **Barbirolli** (Sir John), **Villa-Lobos** (Heitor)
11 **Furtwängler** (Wilhelm)
12 **Rostropovich** (Mstislav)

conduit
04 duct, main, pipe, tube **05** canal, chute, ditch, drain, flume, trunk **06** gutter, trough, tunnel **07** channel, culvert, passage, wireway **08** fountain, penstock, waterway **10** passageway **11** watercourse

cone
03 puy **05** spire **06** cornet, funnel **09** monticule, strobilus

confection
◇ *anagram indicator*
See **dessert**

confectionery
05 candy **06** sweets **07** bonbons, goodies, junkets, toffees **08** licorice, sweeties **09** liquorice **10** chocolates, confiserie, sweetmeats, sweet-stuff
See also **sweet**

confederacy
04 band, Bund **05** junta, junto, union **06** league **07** compact **08** alliance **09** coalition **10** conspiracy, federation **11** Five Nations, partnership **13** confederation

confederate
04 ally, band **05** cover **06** allied, friend, united **07** abettor, fedarie, federal, partner **08** combined, federary, federate, foedarie **09** accessory, assistant, associate, colleague, federarie, supporter **10** accomplice, associated **11** conspirator **12** collaborator

confederation
04 zupa **05** union **06** league **07** compact **08** alliance **09** coalition, hermandad **10** federation **11** association, confederacy, partnership **12** amalgamation

confer
02 cf, do **03** pay **04** give, lend, talk **05** award, grant, parle, pawaw **06** accord, bestow, debate, impart, parley, powwow **07** compare, consult, discuss, give out, present **08** converse **10** deliberate **13** exchange views

conference
03 hui **04** diet, pear **05** forum **06** debate, huddle, indaba, parley, powwow, summit **07** meeting, palaver, seminar **08** colloquy, congress, dialogue **09** symposium **10** colloquium, convention,

discussion, imparlance, pourparler **11** convocation, emparlaunce, get-together **12** consultation, council of war

confess
03 own **04** avow, sing **05** admit, cough, grant, own up **06** affirm, agnize, assert, expose, fess up, reveal, shrive, squeak **07** concede, confide, declare, divulge, profess, tell all, unbosom **08** disclose, unburden **09** come clean, make known, recognize **11** accept blame, acknowledge **13** come out with it, spill the beans, spill your guts **15** get off your chest

confession
06 avowal, shrift **08** exposure, owning-up **09** admission, assertion **10** disclosure, divulgence, profession, revelation, submission, unbosoming **11** affirmation, declaration, making known, short shrift, unburdening **14** acknowledgment **15** acknowledgement, amende honorable

confidant, confidante
03 pal **04** chum, mate **05** buddy, crony **06** friend **08** alter ego, intimate **09** companion **10** best friend, bosom buddy, repository **11** bosom friend, close friend

confide
04 affy, tell **05** admit **06** impart, reveal **07** breathe, confess, divulge, entrust, unbosom, whisper **08** disclose, intimate, unburden **11** tell a secret **15** get off your chest

confidence
03 con **04** hope **05** faith, poise, trust **06** aplomb, belief, secret **07** courage **08** boldness, calmness, credence, forehead, intimacy, reliance **09** assurance, certainty, composure **10** conviction, dependence, self-belief **11** assuredness **12** positiveness, self-reliance **13** private matter, self-assurance **14** self-confidence, self-possession

• **in confidence**
08 in secret, secretly **09** entre nous, in privacy, in private, privately **10** personally **11** just quietly **12** under the rose **14** confidentially **15** between you and me

confident
04 bold, calm, cool, sure **05** happy, hardy **06** crouse, secure, upbeat **07** assured, certain **08** composed, definite, fearless, positive, sanguine **09** convinced, dauntless, unabashed **10** courageous, optimistic, sure-footed **11** comfortable, self-assured, self-reliant **12** unhesitating **13** self-confident, self-possessed **14** sure of yourself **15** unselfconscious

confidential
04 pack **05** bosom, privy **06** inward, secret **07** a latere, private **08** hush-hush, intimate, man-to-man, personal **09** sensitive, tête-à-tête, top secret **10** classified, restricted **12** off-the-record, woman-to-woman

confidentially
07 privily, sub rosa **08** in camera, in secret **09** entre nous, in privacy, in private, privately **10** on the quiet, personally **12** in confidence **15** between you and me

confidently
06 boldly, calmly, coolly, surely **09** assuredly **10** composedly, fearlessly, positively **11** comfortably **12** courageously **14** optimistically, unhesitatingly

configuration
04 cast, face, form **05** shape **06** figure **07** contour, outline **11** arrangement, composition, disposition **12** conformation

confine
03 fix, mew, pen **04** bail, bale, bind, cage, coop, crib, edge, gate, hold, keep, mure, shut **05** bound, cramp, emmew, enmew, immew, limit, pound, scope, stick, thirl **06** border, coop up, immure, inhoop, intern, keep in, lock up, narrow, prison, shut in, shut up **07** chamber, control, delimit, enclose, impound, inclose, inhibit, repress, shackle, trammel **08** bottle up, boundary, frontier, imprison, lock away, regulate, restrain, restrict, shut away **09** constrain, immanacle, parameter, perimeter, prescribe **10** limitation **11** hold captive, incarcerate, restriction **12** circumscribe, hold prisoner **13** circumference, hold in custody

confined
04 pent, poky **05** caged, close, pokey, small **06** narrow, penned, poking **07** captive, cramped, limited, squeezy **08** enclosed **09** chambered **10** controlled, housebound, imprisoned, restricted **11** constrained, constricted **13** circumscribed

confinement
05 birth **06** burden, labour **07** custody, lying-in **08** delivery, solitary **09** captivity, detention, restraint **10** childbirth, constraint, internment, prisonment **11** house arrest, parturition **12** imprisonment **13** incarceration

confirm
03 fix, tie **04** aver, back **05** check, prove **06** affirm, assert, assure, bishop, clinch, harden, obsign, pledge, ratify, settle, soothe, uphold, verify **07** approve, certify, endorse, fortify, gazette, promise, qualify, support, warrant **08** evidence, reassure, sanction, validate **09** authorize, establish, guarantee, obsignate, reinforce **10** asseverate, homologate, strengthen **11** corroborate, demonstrate **12** authenticate, substantiate **14** give credence to

confirmation
05 proof **06** assent, chrism **07** backing, support **08** approval, evidence, sanction **09** agreement, testimony **10** acceptance, affirmance, validation **11** affirmation, approbation, endorsement **12** ratification, verification **13** accreditation, corroboration **14** authentication, substantiation

confirmed
03 set **04** firm **05** fixed, sworn, vowe **06** inured, rooted **07** affear'd, chronic, settled **08** addicted, affeered, habitual, hardened, seasoned **09** incurable **10** double-dyed, entrenched, inveterate **11** corroborate, established **12** incorrigible, long-standing **13** dyed-in-the-wool **15** long-established

confiscate
05 seize **06** remove **07** escheat, forfeit, impound **08** arrogate, take away **09** forfeited, sequester **10** commandeer **11** appropriate, expropriate

confiscation
07 escheat, removal, seizure **08** takeover **09** distraint **10** forfeiture, impounding **12** distrainment **13** appropriation, commandeering, expropriation, sequestration

conflagration
04 fire **05** blaze **06** flames **07** burning, inferno **09** holocaust **12** deflagration

conflate
04 fuse **05** blend, merge **07** combine **08** compound **09** integrate **10** amalgamate, synthesize **11** incorporate, put together **13** bring together

conflict
03 jar, row, war **04** agon, camp, feud, muss **05** agony, brawl, clash, close, fight, mêlée, musse, scrap, set-to **06** battle, bust-up, combat, differ, dust up, fracas, oppose, scrape, strife, strive, tangle, thwart, unrest **07** collide, contend, contest, discord, dispute, ill-will, quarrel, warfare **08** antinomy, be at odds, clashing, disagree, friction, skirmish, struggle, variance **09** antipathy, collision, encounter, fron line, go against, hostility **10** antagonism, contention, contradic dissension, dissonance, engagement, opposition **12** be at variance, disagreement **13** be incongruous, confrontation **14** be in opposition **15** be at loggerheads, incompatibility
See also **battle**; **war**

conflicting
06 at odds, off-key **08** clashing, contrary, opposing **09**

conflicting
06 at odds, off-key **08** clashing, contrary, opposing **09** competing, dissonant **10** at variance

11 incongruous **12** antithetical, incompatible, inconsistent **13** contradictory

confluence
05 union **06** infall **07** conflux, meeting **08** junction **09** concourse **10** watersmeet **11** concurrence, convergence **12** meeting-point

conform
03 fit **04** obey, suit **05** adapt, agree, match, tally **06** accord, adjust, comply, follow, square **07** abide by, observe **08** parallel, quadrate **09** be uniform, harmonize **10** comply with, correspond, fall in with, toe the line **11** accommodate **12** fall into line **13** go with the flow **14** be conventional, do the same thing, follow the crowd **15** go with the stream

conformist
03 Con **06** yes-man **11** rubber-stamp **13** stick-in-the-mud **14** traditionalist **15** conventionalist

conformity
07 harmony **08** affinity, likeness **09** agreement, congruity, obedience, orthodoxy **10** accordance, accordancy, adjustment, compliance, consonance, observance, similarity, uniformity **11** resemblance **13** accommodation **14** correspondence, traditionalism **15** conventionality

confound
◇ *anagram indicator*
03 mix **04** beat, dash, faze, mate, ruin, stun **05** abash, amaze, floor, knock, stump, throw, upset **06** awhape, baffle, defeat, puzzle, rabbit, thwart **07** astound, confuse, destroy, flummox, mystify, nonplus, perplex, stagger, startle, stupefy, unshape **08** astonish, bewilder, demolish, surprise **09** bamboozle, discomfit, dumbfound, frustrate, overthrow, overwhelm **10** spiflicate **11** flabbergast, spifflicate

confront
04 defy, face, meet, show **05** brave, cross **06** accost, appose, attack, oppose, resist, tackle **07** address, affront, assault, compare, eyeball, present **08** cope with, deal with, face down, face up to **09** challenge, encounter, stand up to, withstand **10** meet head on, reckon with **11** contend with **12** face the music **15** come to grips with, come to terms with

confrontation
05 brush, clash, fight, set-to **06** battle **07** contest, face-off, quarrel **08** conflict, showdown **09** collision, encounter **10** engagement **12** disagreement

confuse
◇ *anagram indicator*
03 fog **04** faze, lose, maze **05** addle, bemud, dizzy, floor, mix up, mudge, stump, throw, upset **06** baffle, bemuse, burble, didder, dither, fickle, flurry, fuddle, jumble, mess up, mingle, mither, mizzle, moider, muddle, puzzle, tangle **07** bumbaze, flummox, fluster, involve, mistake, moither, mortify, mystify, perplex **08** bemuddle, bewilder, compound, confound, disorder, distract, dumfound, entangle, surprise **09** bamboozle, disorient, dumbfound, elaborate, embarrass, embrangle, imbrangle, obfuscate **10** complicate, disarrange, discompose, disconcert, tie in knots **12** disorientate, make involved, mingle-mangle **13** make difficult

See also **baffle**; **tangle**

confused
◇ *anagram indicator*
04 hazy, lost, mazy, mixt, mixy **05** dazed, dizzy, messy, mixed, muddy **06** addled, untidy **07** baffled, bemused, chaotic, floored, in a flap, jumbled, maffled, mixed-up, muddled, puzzled **08** all at sea, flustery **09** delirious, disturbed, flummoxed, flustered, mystified, perplexed **10** bamboozled, bewildered, confounded, désorienté, disordered, disorderly, distracted, hurly-burly, indistinct, nonplussed, out of order, topsy-turvy, unbalanced, up a gumtree **11** complicated, disarranged, in a flat spin, muddy-headed **12** disconcerted, disorganized, inextricable **13** disorientated, helter-skelter, muddle-brained **15** all over the place

confusing
◇ *anagram indicator*
05 dizzy **07** cryptic, unclear **08** baffling, involved, muddling, puzzling, tortuous **09** ambiguous, difficult **10** misleading, perplexing **11** bewildering, complicated **12** inconclusive, inconsistent **13** contradictory

confusion
◇ *anagram indicator*
02 pi **03** fog, pie, pye **04** mess, muss, toss **05** chaos, lurry, mix-up, musse, shame **06** baffle, bumble, bummle, cock-up, dudder, fuddle, guddle, huddle, jumble, mess-up, muddle **07** clutter, flutter, turmoil, whemmle, whomble, whommle, whummle **08** disarray, disorder, mish-mash, shambles, upheaval **09** commotion, égarement, overthrow, perdition **10** bafflement, hurly-burly, perplexity, puzzlement, topsy-turvy, untidiness **12** bewilderment, entanglement, hubble-bubble, hugger-mugger **13** disconcertion, embarrassment, indistinction, mystification **14** disarrangement **15** disorganization

confute
05 rebut, refel **06** debunk, negate, refute **07** put down **08** disprove, redargue **09** discredit **10** contradict, controvert, prove false

congeal
03 gel, set **04** cake, clot, fuse, geal, jeel **05** jelly **06** curdle, freeze, harden **07** pectize, stiffen, thicken **08** coalesce, solidify **09** coagulate **11** concentrate

congenial
04 cosy **06** genial, homely, kinred **07** kindred **08** friendly, pleasant, pleasing, relaxing, suitable **09** agreeable, simpatico **10** compatible, delightful, favourable, like-minded, well-suited **11** complaisant, sympathetic, sympathique **13** companionable

congenital
05 utter **06** inborn, inbred, innate, inured **07** chronic, connate, natural **08** complete, habitual, hardened, inherent, seasoned, thorough **09** incurable, inherited **10** compulsive, connatural, entrenched, hereditary, inveterate **12** incorrigible **14** constitutional

congested
04 full **06** choked, jammed, packed **07** blocked, clogged, crammed, crowded, stuffed, teeming **08** engorged **11** overcharged, overcrowded, overflowing

congestion
03 jam **07** choking, snarl-up **08** blockage, blocking, clogging, crowding, gridlock **10** bottleneck, pinchpoint, traffic jam **12** overcrowding

conglomerate
04 firm **05** group, trust **06** cartel, merger **07** combine, company, concern **08** business, fullness **10** consortium, traffic jam **11** association, corporation, engorgement, partnership **13** establishment, multinational

conglomeration
04 mass **06** medley **09** composite **10** assemblage, assortment, collection, hotchpotch **11** aggregation **12** accumulation **13** agglomeration

Congo
03 COD, COG, RCB, ZRE

congratulate
05 greet **06** praise **08** wish well **09** gratulate **10** compliment, felicitate **12** pat on the back **13** say well done to **15** wish happiness to
• **congratulate yourself**
05 plume, preen, pride **09** delight in

congratulations
04 euge **07** bouquet **08** bouquets, congrats, mazeltov, well done **09** good on you, greetings **10** best wishes, good for you, good wishes **11** compliments **12** pat on the back **13** felicitations

congregate
04 form, mass, meet **05** clump, crowd, flock, rally **06** gather, muster, throng **07** cluster, collect, convene

08 assemble, converge
10 accumulate, rendezvous 12 come together

congregation
04 fold, host, mass 05 crowd, flock, group, laity 06 parish, people, throng 07 meeting 08 assembly 09 multitude 10 fellowship 12 parishioners

congress
03 hui 04 diet 05 forum, synod 07 council, meeting 08 assembly, conclave 09 gathering 10 conference, convention, parliament
11 convocation, legislature

congruence
05 match 07 harmony 08 identity 09 agreement 10 concinnity, conformity, consonance, similarity
11 coincidence, concurrence, consistency, parallelism, resemblance
13 compatibility 14 correspondence

congruent
07 similar 08 parallel, suitable
09 consonant 10 compatible, concurrent, consistent, harmonious
13 corresponding

conical
06 spired 07 pointed, tapered
08 tapering 09 pyramidal, turbinate
10 cone-shaped, fastigiate 12 funnel-shaped, infundibular 13 infundibulate, pyramid-shaped

conifer *see* **pine**; **tree**

conjectural
07 assumed, posited 08 academic, supposed, surmised 09 tentative
10 divinatory, postulated, stochastic
11 speculative, theoretical
12 divinatorial, hypothetical
13 suppositional

conjecture
03 aim 05 augur, fancy, guess, infer
06 assume, notion, reckon, theory
07 imagine, presume, suppose, surmise, suspect 08 estimate, theorize
09 guesswork, inference, speculate, suspicion 10 assumption, conclusion, divination, estimation, hypothesis, presuppose, projection
11 guesstimate, hypothesize, presumption, speculation, supposition
13 extrapolation 14 presupposition

conjoin
04 join, link 05 match, unify, unite
06 concur 07 combine, connect
08 alligate 10 amalgamate, synthesize
12 join together

conjugal
06 bridal, wedded 07 marital, married, nuptial, spousal 08 hymeneal
09 connubial 11 epithalamic, matrimonial

• **conjugal union**
03 bed

conjunction
05 synod, union 06 syzygy 07 unition
10 alligation, connection, copulative, injunction 11 association, coexistence, coincidence, colligation, combination, concurrence, unification
12 amalgamation, co-occurrence
13 juxtaposition

• **in conjunction with**
04 with 09 alongside, along with
12 combined with, together with 13 in company with

conjure
05 charm, evoke, raise, rouse 06 call up, compel, invoke, juggle, summon
07 bewitch, do magic 08 do tricks
09 fascinate 10 make appear
11 materialize 12 perform magic
13 perform tricks

• **conjure up**
05 evoke 06 awaken, create, excite, invoke, recall 07 produce 08 summon up 09 recollect 10 call to mind
11 bring to mind

conjurer
06 wizard 08 magician, sorcerer
10 mystery-man 11 illusionist, thaumaturge 12 prestigiator
13 miracle-worker 15 prestidigitator

• **conjurer's skill**
11 legerdemain 13 sleight of hand

• **conjurer's words**
09 hey presto 10 hocus-pocus
11 abracadabra

conk
04 head, nose

• **conk out**
03 die 04 fail 06 go bust, go phut, pack up 07 go kaput 08 collapse
09 break down, go haywire 12 go on the blink

con man
04 liar 05 bunco, cheat, crook
06 rorter, usurer 07 blagger, grifter, hustler 08 deceiver, swindler, tweedler 09 con artist 11 bunco artist, illy whacker, overcharger 12 bunko-steerer, extortionist, rip-off artist

connect
03 put, tie 04 ally, bolt, bond, fuse, join, link 05 affix, clamp, unite
06 attach, bridge, couple, equate, fasten, relate, secure 07 bracket, combine 08 identify, relate to
09 associate, correlate 10 articulate
11 compaginate, concatenate 12 hang together

connected
04 akin, tied 06 allied, joined, linked, united 07 coupled, related, secured
08 coherent, combined, fastened
09 associate, conjugate 10 affiliated, associated

Connecticut
02 CT 04 Conn

connection
03 tie 04 bond, link, pons 05 clasp, joint, tie-in, tie-up 06 friend, hook-up, link-up 07 analogy, contact, context, liaison, linkage, rapport, sponsor
08 alliance, coupling, intimacy, junction, parallel, relation, relative
09 coherence, fastening, reference, relevance 10 attachment
11 association, colligation, conjunction, correlation, intercourse
12 acquaintance, relationship
13 communication, consanguinity, interrelation 14 correspondence

• **in connection with**
02 re 04 as to 05 about 07 apropos
09 as regards, regarding
10 concerning, in regard to 12 in relation to, with regard to 13 with respect to 14 on the subject of 15 with reference to

conning-tower
04 sail

connivance
07 consent 08 abetment, abetting
09 collusion, condoning
10 complicity, conspiracy, lenocinium

connive
04 plot, wink 05 allow, brook, cabal, coact, let go 06 ignore, scheme, wink at 07 collude, complot, condone, let pass 08 conspire, intrigue, overlook, pass over, tolerate 09 disregard, gloss over 11 collaborate 15 turn a blind eye to

conniving
05 nasty 07 corrupt, immoral
08 plotting, scheming 09 colluding
10 conspiring 12 manipulative, unscrupulous

connoisseur
04 buff 05 judge 06 expert, pundit
07 arbiter, devotee, epicure, gourmet
08 aesthete, oenophil, virtuoso
09 authority 10 aficionado, gastronome, specialist
11 cognoscente, gastronomer, oenophilist 12 iconophilist

connotation
04 hint 06 intent, nuance 08 allusion, overtone 09 colouring, undertone
10 intimation, suggestion
11 association, implication, insinuation
12 undercurrent 13 comprehension

connote
05 imply 06 hint at, import
07 betoken, purport, signify, suggest
08 allude to, indicate, intimate
09 associate, connotate, insinuate

conquer
03 win 04 beat, best, rout, take
05 annex, crush, debel, quell, seize, worst 06 defeat, humble, master, obtain, occupy, subdew, subdue
07 acquire, control, overrun, possess, succeed, trounce 08 overcome, suppress, surmount, vanquish
09 overpower, overthrow, rise above, subjugate 11 appropriate, prevail over, triumph over 14 get the better of

conqueror
04 hero, lord, Moor 05 champ, Mogul
06 master, victor, winner 08 champion
10 subjugator, vanquisher
12 conquistador

conquest
03 win **04** coup, rout **05** catch, lover **06** defeat **07** beating, captive, capture, mastery, seizing, success, triumph, victory **08** crushing, invasion **09** overthrow, trouncing **10** annexation, occupation, possession, subjection **11** acquisition, overrunning, subjugation **12** overpowering, vanquishment **13** appropriation

conscience
05 inwit **06** ethics, morals, qualms **08** scruples **09** diligence, moral code, standards **10** moral sense, principles, syneidesis, synteresis **11** voice within **12** sense of right **14** scrupulousness **15** still small voice

conscience-stricken
05 sorry **06** guilty **07** ashamed **08** contrite, penitent, troubled **09** disturbed, regretful, repentant **10** remorseful **11** guilt-ridden **12** compunctious, on a guilt trip

conscientious
06 honest **07** careful, dutiful, upright **08** diligent, faithful, thorough **09** assiduous, attentive, dedicated **10** methodical, meticulous, particular, scrupulous **11** hard-working, industrious, painstaking, punctilious, responsible

conscious
05 alert, alive, awake, aware **06** wilful **07** heedful, knowing, mindful, studied, witting **08** rational, sensible, sentient **09** cognizant, conscient, on purpose, reasoning, voluntary **10** calculated, deliberate, percipient, responsive, volitional **11** intentional, recognizant **12** premeditated **13** self-conscious
• **be conscious of**
04 feel **06** savour

consciously
08 wilfully **09** knowingly, on purpose **11** voluntarily **12** deliberately **13** intentionally

consciousness
04 mind **06** psyche **07** thought **09** alertness, awareness, intuition, knowledge, sentience **10** being awake, cognizance, perception **11** cenesthesia, cenesthesis, realization, recognition, sensibility, wakefulness **12** apprehension **13** coenaesthesia, coenaesthesis

conscript
05 draft **06** call up, enlist, induct, muster, take on **07** draftee, recruit, round up **08** enlistee, enrolled, inductee **10** registered

conscription
05 draft **08** drafting

consecrate
03 vow **05** bless, exalt **06** anoint, devote, hallow, ordain, revere **07** devoted **08** dedicate, make holy, sanctify, venerate **10** sanctified

consecutive
06 in a row, in turn, serial **07** running, sequent, seriate **08** parallel, straight, unbroken **09** following, on the trot **10** back to back, continuous, sequential, succeeding, successive **13** uninterrupted

consecutively
06 in a row, in turn **09** on the trot **10** back to back **11** hand-running **12** continuously, sequentially, successively **15** uninterruptedly

consensus
05 unity **07** concord, consent, harmony **09** agreement, unanimity **10** consension **11** concurrence **12** consentience, majority view

consent
05 admit, agree, allow, grant, yield **06** accede, accept, afford, assent, comply, concur, permit, submit **07** affoord, approve, concede, go-ahead **08** approval, sanction **09** acquiesce, agreement, authorize, clearance **10** acceptance, compliance, concession, condescend, green light, homologate, permission **11** concurrence, go along with **12** acquiescence **13** authorization **14** give the go-ahead **15** give the thumbs-up

consequence
03 end **04** note **05** issue, value **06** effect, import, moment, result, upshot, weight **07** concern, outcome **08** eminence, sequence **09** aftermath, inference, substance **10** importance, importancy, prominence, side effect **11** distinction, eventuality, implication **12** repercussion, significance **13** reverberation

consequent
07 ensuing, sequent **09** appendant, corollary, following, resultant, resulting **10** consectary, sequential, subsequent, successive

consequential
03 key **05** vital **07** crucial, ensuing, serious, weighty **08** material, relevant, valuable **09** following, important, momentous, prominent, resultant, resulting **10** noteworthy, sequential, subsequent, successive **11** far-reaching, significant, substantial

consequently
04 ergo, then, thus **05** hence **06** so that **09** as a result, therefore **11** accordingly, necessarily **12** subsequently **13** inferentially **15** consequentially

conservation
03 con **04** care **06** saving, upkeep **07** custody, ecology, economy, keeping **09** husbandry **10** protection **11** maintenance, safe-keeping **12** preservation, safeguarding

conservationist
05 green **06** econut **07** greenie **08** ecofreak **09** ecologist **10** tree-hugger **15** preservationist
• **conservationists**
02 NT **03** WWF

conservatism
09 orthodoxy **14** traditionalism **15** conventionalism

conservative
01 C **03** Con **04** blue, cons, Tory **05** right, sober **06** hunker **07** careful, diehard, guarded, old-line **08** cautious, moderate, old-liner, orthodox, Unionist, verkramp **09** bourgeois, hidebound, right-wing **10** inflexible **11** reactionary, right-winger, traditional **12** buttoned-down, conventional **13** set in your ways, stick-in-the-mud, unprogressive **14** traditionalist **15** backward-looking, middle-of-the-road

conservatory
06 school **07** academy, college **08** hothouse **09** institute **10** glasshouse, greenhouse, storehouse **11** music school **12** drama college, preservative **13** conservatoire

conserve
03 jam **04** keep, save **05** guard, gumbo, hoard, jelly **06** retain **07** husband, protect, store up **08** keep back, maintain, preserve **09** comfiture, marmalade, safeguard **10** take care of **13** keep in reserve

consider
03 see **04** deem, feel, hold, muse, note, rate, view, vise **05** count, judge, study, think, weigh **06** debate, devise, esteem, ponder, regard, reward **07** believe, bethink, examine, reflect, respect, toy with, weigh up **08** chew over, cogitate, envisage, meditate, mull over, prepense, regard as, remember, ruminate, see about **09** apprehend, kick about **10** animadvert, bear in mind, deliberate, keep in mind, kick around **11** contemplate **13** give thought to **15** take into account

considerable
03 big, gay, gey **04** some, tidy, vast **05** ample, great, large, smart **06** lavish, marked, pretty **07** healthy, notable, serious, sizable **08** abundant, generous, sizeable **09** important, plentiful, tolerable **10** noteworthy, noticeable, reasonable **11** appreciable, influential, perceptible, respectable, significant, substantial, substantive **13** distinguished

considerably
03 gay, gey **04** much **07** greatly **08** markedly **10** abundantly, noticeably, remarkably **11** appreciably **13** significantly, substantially

considerate
04 kind **06** caring **07** helpful, tactful **08** discreet, generous, gracious, obliging, selfless **09** attentive, concerned, courteous, sensitive, unselfish **10** altruistic, charitable,

deliberate, respective, solicitous, thoughtful **11** sympathetic **13** compassionate

consideration
04 care, fact, heed, tact **05** count, issue, point **06** factor, motive, notice, reason, regard, review **07** account, concern, payment, respect, thought **08** altruism, analysis, kindness, scrutiny, sympathy **09** attention, reckoning **10** cogitation, compassion, discretion, generosity, importance, inspection, meditation, recompense, reflection, rumination **11** examination, helpfulness, sensitivity **12** circumstance, deliberation, graciousness, selflessness **13** contemplation, unselfishness **14** thoughtfulness
• **lacking consideration**
04 nude
• **take into consideration**
05 study **07** plan for **08** allow for, consider **10** bear in mind, keep in mind **13** give thought to **15** take into account

considering
08 all in all, in view of **10** respecting **12** in the light of **13** bearing in mind

consign
04 seal, send, ship, sign **06** assign, banish, commit, convey, devote **07** commend, deliver, entrust **08** give over, hand over, relegate, transfer, transmit **09** recommend

consignment
04 load **05** batch, cargo, goods **08** delivery, shipment

consist
03 lie **05** exist **06** embody, inhere, reside **07** contain, embrace, include, involve, subsist **08** amount to, be formed, be made up, comprise **10** be composed **11** be contained, incorporate

consistency
07 density, harmony, keeping **08** cohesion, evenness, firmness, identity, sameness **09** agreement, coherence, coherency, congruity, constancy, stability, substance, thickness, viscosity **10** accordance, conformity, consonance, continuity, regularity, smoothness, steadiness, uniformity **11** persistence, reliability **12** lack of change **13** compatibility, dependability, steadfastness **14** correspondence

consistent
04 same **06** stable, steady **07** logical, regular, uniform **08** agreeing, coherent, constant, matching, straight **09** accordant, congruous, consonant, unfailing **10** coinciding, compatible, conforming, dependable, harmonious, persistent, unchanging **11** predictable, undeviating **13** consentaneous, corresponding **15** hanging together

consistently
09 regularly, uniformly **10** constantly, dependably **11** predictably, unfailingly **12** persistently

consolation
03 aid **04** ease, help **05** cheer **06** relief, solace **07** comfort, succour, support **08** soothing, sympathy **11** alleviation, assuagement, reassurance **12** recomforture **13** commiseration, encouragement

console
04 calm, help, Xbox® **05** ancon, board, cheer, dials, knobs, panel **06** levers, solace, soothe **07** buttons, comfort, hearten, relieve, succour, support **08** controls, Gamecube®, keyboard, Nintendo®, reassure, switches **09** consolate, dashboard, encourage, recomfort **11** instruments, PlayStation® **12** control panel **14** sympathize with **15** commiserate with

consolidate
03 pun **04** fuse, join **05** merge, unify, unite **06** cement, secure, united **07** combine, compact, fortify **09** reinforce, stabilize **10** amalgamate, make secure, make stable, make strong, strengthen **12** make stronger **14** make more secure, make more stable

consolidation
06 fusion, merger **07** joining, uniting **08** alliance, securing **09** cementing **10** federation **11** affiliation, association, combination, unification **12** amalgamation **13** confederation, fortification, reinforcement, stabilization, strengthening

consonance
07 concord, harmony **09** agreement, congruity **10** accordance, conformity **11** consistency, suitability **13** compatibility **14** correspondence

consonant
05 lenis, velar **06** fortis, sonant, uvular **08** agreeing, alveolar, bilabial, ejective, emphatic, suitable **09** accordant, according, congruous, implosive, in harmony **10** compatible, conforming, consistent, harmonious **11** in agreement **12** articulation, in accordance **13** correspondent

consort
03 mix **04** lady, maik, make, mate, wife **05** agree, troop **06** accord, escort, mingle, spouse **07** husband, partner **09** accompany, agreement, associate, companion, spend time **10** fraternize **11** keep company

consortium
04 bloc, bond, pact **05** guild, union **06** cartel, league, treaty **07** compact, company **08** alliance, marriage **09** agreement, coalition, syndicate **10** federation, fellowship **11** affiliation, association, combination, corporation, partnership **12** conglomerate, organization **13** confederation

conspicuous
05 clear, showy **06** flashy, garish, marked, patent **07** blatant, eminent, evident, glaring, obvious, shining, visible **08** apparent, flagrant, kenspeck, manifest, remarked, striking **09** prominent **10** easily seen, kenspeckle, noticeable, observable, remarkable **11** discernible, perceptible **12** ostentatious, recognizable **13** easily noticed

conspicuously
07 clearly, showily, visibly **08** flashily, garishly, markedly, patently **09** blatantly, evidently, glaringly, obviously **10** flagrantly, manifestly, noticeably, observably, remarkably, strikingly **11** discernibly, perceptibly, prominently **12** recognizably **14** ostentatiously

conspiracy
03 fix **04** plot **05** cabal, covin, set-up **06** covyne, league, scheme **07** complot, consult, frame-up, treason **08** intrigue **09** collusion, stratagem **10** connivance **11** concurrence, confederacy, machination **13** collaboration

conspirator
05 Casca, Cinna **06** Brutus **07** Cassius, plotter, schemer, traitor **08** Catiline, colluder **09** conspirer, intriguer **10** highbinder, practisant **12** collaborator
• **group of conspirators**
04 band **05** cabal

conspire
04 ally, join, link, plan, plot **05** unite **06** devise, scheme **07** collude, combine, complot, conjure, connect, connive **08** intrigue **09** associate, colleague, co-operate, machinate, manoeuvre **10** hatch a plot, join forces **11** act together, collaborate **12** work together

constable
02 PC, SC **03** cop, WPC **04** Dull **05** jawan, wolly **06** cotwal, harman, kotwal **09** catchpole, catchpoll **10** harman-beck **11** headborough **12** thirdborough

See also **police officer**

constancy
05 truth **07** loyalty **08** devotion, fidelity, firmness, tenacity **09** certainty, fixedness, stability **10** permanence, regularity, resolution, steadiness, uniformity **11** consistency, persistence **12** faithfulness, perseverance **13** dependability, steadfastness **15** trustworthiness, unchangeability

constant
01 c, G, h, k **04** even, firm, trew, true **05** daily, fixed, loyal **06** stable, stanch, steady **07** chronic, devoted, endless, eternal, non-stop, regular, staunch, uniform **08** faithful, resolute, unbroken **09** ceaseless, continual, immutable, incessant, permanent, perpetual,

steadfast, unfailing, unvarying **10** changeless, consistent, continuous, dependable, invariable, persistent, relentless, unchanging, unflagging, unwavering **11** everlasting, never-ending, persevering, trustworthy, unalterable, unremitting **12** interminable, unchangeable **13** uninterrupted **14** without respite

constantly
03 aye **05** daily, still **06** always **07** for ever, non-stop, on and on **09** ad nauseam, endlessly **10** all the time, invariably **11** ceaselessly, continually, day in day out, incessantly, perennially, permanently, perpetually **12** continuously, interminably, relentlessly **13** everlastingly **15** twenty-four seven

constellation

Constellations include:

03 Ara, Cup, dog, Fly, Fox, Leo, Net, Ram
04 Apus, Argo, Bull, Crab, Crow, Crux, Dove, Grus, Hare, Harp, Keel, Lion, Lynx, Lyra, Pavo, Swan, Vela, Wolf
05 Altar, Aries, Arrow, Cetus, Clock, Crane, Draco, Eagle, Easel, Hydra, Indus, Lepus, Level, Libra, Lupus, Mensa, Musca, Norma, Orion, Pyxis, Sails, Table, Twins, Virgo, Whale
06 Antlia, Aquila, Archer, Auriga, Boötes, Caelum, Cancer, Carina, Chisel, Corvus, Crater, Cygnus, Dorado, Dragon, Fishes, Fornax, Gemini, Hydrus, Indian, Lizard, Octans, Octant, Pictor, Pisces, Puppis, Scales, Scutum, Shield, Taurus, Toucan, Tucana, Virgin, Volans
07 Air Pump, Centaur, Cepheus, Columba, Dolphin, Furnace, Giraffe, Lacerta, Peacock, Pegasus, Perseus, Phoenix, Sagitta, Sea Goat, Serpens, Serpent, Sextans, Sextant, Unicorn
08 Aquarius, Circinus, Equuleus, Eridanus, Great Dog, Hercules, Herdsman, Leo Minor, Scorpion, Scorpius, Sculptor, Triangle
09 Andromeda, Centaurus, Chameleon, Compasses, Delphinus, Great Bear, Little Dog, Monoceros, Ophiuchus, Reticulum, Swordfish, Telescope, Ursa Major, Ursa Minor, Vulpecula
10 Canis Major, Canis Minor, Cassiopeia, Chamaeleon, Charioteer, Flying Fish, Horologium, Little Bear, Little Lion, Microscope, Sea Serpent, Ship's Stern, Triangulum, Water Snake
11 Capricornus, Hunting Dogs, Little Horse, Sagittarius, Telescopium, Water Bearer, Winged Horse
12 Microscopium, Southern Fish
13 Berenice's Hair, Canes Venatici, Coma Berenices, Northern Crown, River Eridanus, Serpent Bearer, Southern Cross, Southern Crown
14 Bird of Paradise, Camelopardalis, Corona Borealis
15 Corona Australis, Mariner's Compass, Piscis Austrinus

consternation
03 awe **04** fear **05** alarm, dread, panic, shock **06** dismay, fright, horror, terror **07** anxiety **08** distress **11** disquietude, trepidation **12** bewilderment, perturbation

constipated
05 bound

constituency
04 area, seat, ward, zone **05** burgh, shire **06** parish, region, Riding **07** borough **08** district, division, Euroseat, marginal, precinct **09** community **10** electorate

constituent
◇ *anagram indicator*
03 bit **04** part, unit **05** basic, voter **06** factor **07** content, elector, element, section **08** electing, inherent, integral **09** component, essential, intrinsic, principle **10** ingredient **12** constitution **13** component part

constitute
02 be **04** form, make, mean **05** found, set up **06** create, make up, strike **07** add up to, appoint, charter, compose, empower **08** amount to, comprise, initiate **09** authorize, establish, institute, represent **10** commission, inaugurate **12** be regarded as **14** be equivalent to, be tantamount to

constitution
03 set **04** code, laws **05** fuero, habit, rules, state **06** health, make-up, nature, policy, polity, temper, upmake **07** charter **08** habitude, physique, statutes **09** character, condition, formation, structure **10** social code **11** codified law, composition, disposition, temperament, temperature **12** bill of rights, idiosyncrasy, organization **13** configuration **15** basic principles

constitutional
04 turn, walk **05** amble, by law, legal **06** airing, lawful, stroll, vested **07** politic, saunter **08** codified, ratified **09** promenade, statutory **10** authorized, legitimate **11** legislative **12** governmental

constrain
03 put **04** bind, curb, rein, urge **05** check, drive, force, impel, limit **06** coerce, compel, hinder, oblige, strain **07** confine **08** hold back, obligate, pressure, restrain, restrict **09** constrict **10** perstringe, pressurize **11** necessitate

constrained
04 hard **05** stiff **06** forced, uneasy **07** awkward, guarded **08** reserved, reticent **09** compelled, inhibited, unnatural **11** embarrassed

constraint
04 curb, rein **05** check, force **06** damper, demand, duress **07** duresse, shackle **08** coercion, pressure **09** hindrance, necessity, restraint, reticence, stiffness **10** compulsion, forcedness, impediment, inhibition, insistence, limitation, obligation **11** awkwardness, confinement, guardedness, restriction, self-control **13** embarrassment, unnaturalness

constrict
04 bind, curb **05** check, choke, close, cramp, limit, pinch **06** hamper, hinder, impede, narrow, shrink **07** confine, inhibit, squeeze, tighten **08** compress, contract, hold back, obstruct, restrict, strangle **09** constrain **10** make narrow **11** strangulate

constriction
04 curb **05** check, choke, cramp **07** isthmus **08** blockage, pressure, stenosis, thlipsis **09** hindrance, narrowing, reduction, squeezing, stegnosis, stricture, tightness **10** constraint, impediment, limitation, tightening **11** compression, contraction, restriction **13** constringency, incarceration

construct
◇ *anagram indicator*
04 form, make **05** build, craft, erect, found, model, patch, put up, raise, set up, shape, weave **06** create, design, devise, fabric **07** compile, compose, elevate, fashion, knock up, throw up **08** assemble, engineer **09** carpenter, establish, fabricate, formulate, structure **11** manufacture, put together **13** knock together, throw together

construction
04 form **05** model, order, shape **06** fabric, figure, make-up, making **07** edifice, meaning, reading **08** assembly, building, erection **09** deduction, elevation, formation, framework, inference, structure **11** arrangement, composition, disposition, fabrication, manufacture **12** organization **13** configuration, establishment **14** interpretation

constructive
06 useful **07** helpful **08** inferred, positive, valuable **09** practical **10** beneficial, productive **12** advantageous **13** architectonic

constructively
08 usefully **09** helpfully **10** positively **11** practically **12** beneficially, productively **14** advantageously

construe
◇ *anagram indicator*
04 read **05** infer, see as **06** deduce, render **07** analyse, explain, expound **08** regard as **09** interpret **10** take to mean, understand

consul
03 Con **05** agent, elchi, envoy

06 ledger, legate, nuncio **07** leaguer **08** delegate, diplomat, emissary, minister **10** ambassador **14** representative **15** plenipotentiary

consult
03 see **04** talk, vide **06** confer, debate, look up, turn to **07** discuss, refer to **08** question **09** ask advice **10** deliberate, seek advice **11** interrogate **14** ask information **15** seek information

consultant
06 expert **07** adviser **09** associate, authority **10** specialist

consultation
04 talk **05** forum **07** counsel, hearing, meeting, session **08** dialogue **09** interview **10** conference, discussion **11** appointment, examination **12** deliberation

consultative
07 helping **08** advising, advisory **10** consulting **11** counselling **12** consultatory, recommending

consume
◇ *containment indicator*
03 eat, gut, use **04** burn, grip, kill, pine, take, wear **05** drain, drink, eat up, scoff, shift, snarf, spend, touch, use up, waste **06** absorb, bezzle, burn up, damage, devour, expend, gobble, guzzle, ingest, murder, obsess, punish, ravage, tuck in **07** deplete, destroy, discuss, drink up, engross, exhaust, swallow, torment, utilize **08** demolish, dominate, lay waste, mainline, squander, wear down **09** devastate, dispose of, dissipate, go through, overwhelm, polish off, preoccupy **10** annihilate, get through, monopolize **11** fritter away **12** get stuck into

consumer
04 user **05** buyer, mouth **06** client, patron **07** end-user, shopper **08** customer **09** purchaser

consuming
◇ *containment indicator*
07 wasting, wearing **08** gripping **09** absorbing, devouring, obsessive **10** compelling, destroying, dominating, engrossing, immoderate, tormenting **12** monopolizing, overwhelming, preoccupying

consummate
03 cap, end **05** crown, exact, total, utter **06** finish, fulfil, gifted, made up, superb **07** achieve, execute, perfect, perform, realize, skilled, supreme **08** absolute, complete, conclude, finished, polished, superior, ultimate **09** competent, exemplary, matchless, practised, terminate **10** accomplish, effectuate, proficient **11** replenished, unqualified **12** accomplished, transcendent **13** distinguished

consummation
03 end **04** pass **06** finish **07** capping **08** crowning **09** execution **10** completion, conclusion, fulfilment, perfection **11** achievement, culmination, performance, realization, termination **12** effectuation **13** actualization **14** accomplishment

consumption
02 TB **05** waste **06** eating **07** decline, using-up **08** draining, drinking, guzzling, scoffing, spending **09** depletion, devouring, expending, ingestion, tucking-in **10** absorption, exhaustion, swallowing **11** expenditure, squandering, utilization **12** going-through, tuberculosis **14** getting-through

contact
03 fax **04** call, ring **05** e-mail, phone, reach, touch, union **06** friend, impact, notify **07** apply to, get onto, meeting, speak to, sponsor, taction, write to **08** approach, junction, relation, relative, tangency, touching **09** get hold of, proximity, telephone **10** connection, contiguity **11** association, contingence **12** acquaintance, get through to **13** communication, juxtaposition **14** get in touch with **15** communicate with

• **in contact with**
02 to **04** into

contagion
06 poison **08** tainting **09** infection, pollution **10** corruption, defilement **13** contamination

contagious
07 noxious **08** catching, epidemic, pandemic **09** spreading **10** compelling, infectious **12** communicable, irresistible **13** transmissible, transmittable

contain
◇ *containment indicator*
◇ *hidden indicator*
04 curb, hold, seat, stop, take **05** carry, check, limit **06** embody, enseam, enwomb, hold in, rein in, retain, stifle, take in **07** control, embrace, enclose, include, involve, repress **08** comprise, keep back, restrain, suppress **09** keep under **10** have inside **11** accommodate, incorporate, keep in check

container
◇ *hidden indicator*
06 holder, vessel **10** receptacle, repository

Containers include:

03 bag, bin, box, can, cup, jar, jug, keg, mug, pan, pot, tin, tub, urn, vat
04 bowl, case, cask, dish, drum, Esky®, pack, pail, sack, silo, tank, tube, vase, vial, well
05 basin, chest, churn, crate, crock, glass, purse, trunk
06 barrel, basket, beaker, bottle, bucket, carton, casket, hamper, kettle, locker, packet, punnet, teapot, trough, tureen
07 cistern, dustbin, pannier, pitcher, tumbler
08 canister, cauldron, cylinder, suitcase, tea caddy, tea chest, waste bin
09 water-butt

containment
04 curb **05** check **07** control **08** stifling **09** restraint **10** limitation, repression **11** suppression

contaminate
◇ *anagram indicator*
04 foul, harm, soil **05** decay, spike, spoil, stain, sully, taint **06** debase, defile, infect **07** corrupt, deprave, pollute, tarnish, vitiate **10** adulterate, make impure

contamination
◇ *anagram indicator*
04 harm **05** decay, filth, stain, taint **07** soiling, tarnish **08** foulness, impurity, spoiling, sullying **09** infection, pollution, vitiation **10** corruption, debasement, defilement, rottenness **11** desecration **12** adulteration

contemplate
04 muse, plan, view **05** spell, study, weigh **06** behold, design, expect, intend, look at, ponder, regard, survey **07** dwell on, examine, foresee, inspect, observe, propose, weigh up **08** cogitate, consider, envisage, meditate, mull over, ruminate **09** reflect on **10** deliberate, have in mind, have in view, scrutinize, think about **11** have an eye to **13** give thought to

contemplation
04 muse, view **05** dwell, study **06** gazing, musing, regard, survey **07** purpose, thought, viewing **08** mind's eye, scrutiny, weighing **09** beholding, pondering, regarding **10** cogitation, inspection, meditation, reflection, rumination, weighing up **11** cerebration, examination, mulling-over, observation **12** deliberation, recollection **13** consideration

contemplative
04 rapt **06** intent, musing **07** pensive **08** cerebral **10** meditative, reflective, ruminative, thoughtful **13** deep in thought, introspective

contemporaneous
06 coeval **10** coetaneous, coexistent, concurrent **11** synchronous **12** simultaneous

contemporary
02 AD **03** now **04** peer **05** equal **06** coeval, fellow, latest, modern, recent, today's, trendy, with it **07** current, partner, present, topical **08** confrère, co-worker, parallel, up-to-date **09** associate, colleague **10** avant-garde, coetaneous, coexistent, collateral, concurrent, futuristic, new-fangled, present-day

11 counterpart, fashionable, present-time, synchronous, ultra-modern
12 simultaneous 13 up-to-the-minute
14 contemporanean
15 contemporaneous

contempt
05 scorn 06 hatred 07 disdain, dislike, mockery, neglect 08 derision, despisal, disgrace, loathing, ridicule
09 contumely, dishonour, disregard
10 disrespect 11 detestation
13 condescension
• **expression of contempt**
02 ho 03 ach, aha, bah, boo, foh, gup, hoa, hoh, mew, och, pho, poh, rot, sis, yah 04 booh, nuts, phew, phoh, pish, poof, pooh, push, quep, rats, tush, yech
05 pshaw, snoot, sucks! 06 phooey
10 sucks to you!
• **sign of contempt**
04 fico, figo 05 sneer 11 Harvey Smith
• **term of contempt**
03 cit, dog, nit 05 sprat 06 monkey
07 jive-ass 08 whipster

contemptible
03 low 04 base, mean, vile 05 petty
06 abject, cruddy, ornery, paltry, scurvy, shabby 07 hateful, pelting, pitiful 08 pitiable, shameful, unworthy, wretched 09 loathsome, miserable, worthless 10 degenerate, despicable, detestable, lamentable 11 ignominious
• **contemptible person**
04 crud, scut, snot, toad 05 crumb, diddy, droob, snipe, squit, twerp
06 fellow, louser 07 dogbolt, hangdog
08 dirty dog, scullion, whiffler

contemptuous
05 tossy 06 snorty 07 cynical, haughty, jeering, mocking
08 arrogant, derisive, derisory, insolent, scornful, sneering
09 insulting, withering 10 despiteful, disdainful, dispiteous
12 contumelious, supercilious
13 condescending, disrespectful, high and mighty

contend
03 vie, war 04 aver, cope, deal, face, hold, wage 05 argue, brave, claim, clash, fight, rival, state 06 affirm, allege, assert, battle, combat, debate, oppose, reckon, strive, tackle, tussle
07 address, agonize, compete, contest, declare, dispute, grapple, profess, wrestle 08 conflict, face up to, maintain, militate, struggle
09 challenge 10 asseverate, meet head on 11 come to grips, come to terms

content
◇ *hidden indicator*
04 ease, gist, glad, load, size, text
05 happy, ideas, items, parts, peace, theme, topic 06 amount, at ease, be glad, burden, humour, matter, pacify, please, soothe, volume 07 appease, be happy, chapter, comfort, delight, essence, gratify, indulge, meaning, measure, placate, pleased, satisfy, section, subject, willing 08 capacity, cheerful, contents, division, elements, gladness, material, pleasure, serenity
09 be pleased, contented, fulfilled, happiness, satisfied, substance, unworried 10 components, equanimity, fulfilment, proportion, untroubled 11 comfortable, contentment, ingredients
12 cheerfulness, constituents, peacefulness, satisfaction, significance, things inside
13 gratification, subject matter
14 component parts 15 what is contained
• **remove contents**
03 gut 05 empty 10 disembowel

contented
04 glad 05 happy 07 content, perfect, pleased, relaxed 08 cheerful
09 fulfilled, satisfied, unworried
10 untroubled 11 comfortable

contention
04 bate, case, plea, toil, view 05 claim, stand, sturt, words 06 belief, debate, enmity, jangle, notion, strife, theory, thesis 07 discord, dispute, feeling, feuding, opinion, rivalry 08 argument, position, struggle 09 assertion, hostility, intuition, judgement, logomachy, viewpoint, wrangling
10 conviction, difference, differency, dissension, impression, persuasion
11 controversy, point of view
12 disagreement

contentious
07 hostile 08 captious, disputed, doubtful, perverse 09 bellicose, bickering, debatable, polemical, querulous 10 debateable, disputable, pugnacious 11 dissentious, quarrelsome, tendentious
12 antagonistic, questionable
13 argumentative, controversial

contentment
04 ease 05 peace 07 comfort, content 08 gladness, pleasure, serenity 09 happiness 10 equanimity, fulfilment 11 complacency
12 cheerfulness, peacefulness, satisfaction 13 contentedness, gratification

contest
03 vie, war 04 bout, deny, game, jump, race 05 doubt, event, fight, match, pairs, set-to, vying 06 battle, combat, debate, defend, oppose, pingle, refute, strife, strive, tussle
07 brabble, compete, contend, dispute, matchup 08 argument, concours, conflict, litigate, object to, question, skirmish, struggle
09 challenge, emulation, encounter, try to beat 10 tournament
11 competition, controversy 12 argue against, championship, contestation
• **in contest against**
04 with
• **part of contest**
03 leg

contestant
05 rival 06 player, prizer 07 entrant
08 aspirant, opponent 09 adversary, candidate, contender, disputant
10 competitor 11 participant

context
07 factors, setting 08 position
09 connexion, framework, situation
10 background, conditions, connection 12 surroundings
13 circumstances 14 state of affairs

contiguous
04 near, next 05 close 06 beside
07 vicinal 08 abutting, adjacent, touching 09 adjoining, bordering
10 coadjacent, conjoining, juxtaposed, tangential
12 conterminous, neighbouring
15 juxtapositional

continent
08 mainland, virtuous 09 temperate
10 terra firma

Continents:

04 Asia
06 Africa, Europe
07 Oceania
10 Antarctica
11 Australasia
12 North America, South America

contingency
05 event 06 chance 07 contact
08 accident, fortuity, incident, juncture
09 emergency, happening
10 incidental, randomness 11 chance event, eventuality, possibility, uncertainty 13 arbitrariness

contingent
03 set 04 band, body 05 based, batch, group, party, quota, share
07 company, mission, section, subject
08 division, relative 09 dependant, dependent 10 accidental, complement, delegation, deputation, detachment 11 conditional
15 representatives

continual
05 still 07 abiding, eternal, regular
08 constant, frequent, repeated
09 incessant, perpetual, recurrent, unceasing 10 persistent, repetitive
11 everlasting 12 interminable

continually
03 e'er 04 ever 06 always 07 forever, non-stop, on and on 09 endlessly, eternally, regularly 10 all the time, constantly, frequently, habitually, repeatedly 11 ceaselessly, incessantly, perpetually, recurrently
12 interminably, persistently
13 everlastingly

continuance
04 stay, term 06 period 07 abiding, durance 08 duration, dwelling, standing 09 endurance
10 permanence 11 adjournment, maintenance, persistence, protraction
12 continuation

continuation
06 return, sequel **07** renewal
08 addition, progress **09** extension
10 carrying-on, resumption, supplement **11** development, furtherance, lengthening, maintenance, persistence, protraction
12 prolongation **13** starting again
14 recommencement
• in continuance
02 on

continue
02 on **04** dure, go on, hold, keep, last, rest, stay **05** abide, renew **06** endure, extend, hold on, keep on, keep up, move on, pursue, remain, resume
07 adjourn, carry on, hold out, not stop, persist, press on, proceed, project, prolong, stick at, subsist, survive, sustain **08** lengthen, maintain, progress **09** keep going, persevere, persist in, soldier on **10** begin again, keep moving, keep on with, press ahead, recommence, start again
11 keep walking, persevere in, take up again **12** proceed again **14** keep travelling

continuity
04 flow **07** linkage **08** cohesion, sequence, synaphea **09** synapheia
10 connection, succession
11 progression **14** continuousness

continuous
◇ *hidden indicator*
◇ *juxtaposition indicator*
05 solid **07** endless, flowing, lasting, non-stop, running **08** constant, extended, seamless, unbroken, unending **09** ceaseless, continued, prolonged, unceasing **10** persistent, relentless **11** consecutive, never-ending, not stopping, unremitting, with no let-up **12** interminable
13 uninterrupted, without a break

continuously
◇ *hidden indicator*
◇ *juxtaposition indicator*
04 away **08** together **09** endlessly
10 all the time, at a stretch, constantly
11 ceaselessly **12** interminably, persistently, relentlessly
13 consecutively, unremittingly
15 twenty-four seven, uninterruptedly

contort
◇ *anagram indicator*
03 wry **04** knot, warp **05** gnarl, twist
06 deform, squirm, wrench, writhe
07 distort, screw up, wreathe, wriggle
08 misshape **09** convolute, disfigure
14 bend out of shape

contortionist
07 acrobat, gymnast, tumbler
08 balancer, stuntman **09** aerialist
10 rope-dancer, rope-walker, stuntwoman **11** equilibrist, funambulist
12 posture-maker, somersaulter
13 posture-master, trapeze artist

contour
04 form **05** curve, lines, shape
06 aspect, figure, relief **07** isobase, isobath, outline, profile, surface
08 contorno, tournure **09** character
10 silhouette

contraband
08 hot goods, smuggled **09** smuggling
10 prohibited **11** banned goods, bootlegging **13** unlawful goods
14 illegal traffic **15** prohibited goods, proscribed goods

contraceptive

Contraceptives include:

03 cap, IUD
04 coil, IUCD, loop, pill, safe
06 condom, johnny, rubber, sheath, Vimule®
07 Femidom®, johnnie, the pill
08 Dutch cap, minipill
09 birth pill, diaphragm, prolactin
10 Lippes loop, protective
11 Depo-Provera®
12 female condom, French letter, prophylactic

contract
◇ *tail deletion indicator*
03 get **04** bond, deal, knit, make, pact
05 agree, catch, purse, tense **06** draw in, engage, lessen, narrow, pick up, pledge, reduce, settle, shrink, take in, treaty **07** abridge, appalto, arrange, bargain, betroth, compact, curtail, develop, promise, shorten, shrivel, tighten, wrinkle **08** compress, condense, covenant, decrease, diminish, handfast **09** agreement, betrothal, champerty, concordat, constrict, indenture, negotiate, stipulate, succumb to, undertake
10 abbreviate, agree terms, commitment, constringe, convention, engagement, go down with, settlement **11** arrangement, make shorter, make smaller, stipulation, transaction **12** come down with
13 become ill with, become shorter, become smaller, understanding **14** be taken ill with
• contract out
06 get out **07** drop out, farm out
08 delegate, withdraw **09** outsource
11 subcontract **12** give to others, pass to others

contraction
06 shrink **07** systole, tensing
09 drawing-in, lessening, narrowing, reduction, shrinkage **10** abridgment, shortening, tightening
11 abridgement, astringency, compression, curtailment, shrivelling
12 abbreviation, constriction
13 shortened form

contradict
03 nay **04** deny **05** argue, belie, rebut
06 impugn, naysay, negate, oppose, refute, threap, threep **07** confute, counter, dispute, gainsay, outface, sublate **08** contrary, traverse **09** argue with, challenge, clash with, disaffirm, go against **12** be at odds with, conflict with, contrast with, disagree with
14 fly in the face of

contradiction
04 odds **05** clash **06** denial
07 démenti, dispute, paradox
08 antilogy, antinomy, conflict, negation, rebuttal, traverse, variance
09 challenge **10** antithesis, opposition, refutation **11** confutation, incongruity
12 disagreement **13** disaffirmance, inconsistency **14** disaffirmation
15 counter-argument

contradictory
07 opposed **08** clashing, contrary, opposing, opposite **09** dissonant, repugnant **10** discordant, discrepant
11 conflicting, dissentient, incongruous, paradoxical
12 antagonistic, antithetical, incompatible, inconsistent
14 irreconcilable

contralto
01 c **04** alto

contraption
03 rig **05** gizmo, waldo **06** device, doodad, doodah, doofer, gadget, widget **07** machine **08** thingamy
09 apparatus, invention, mechanism
11 contrivance, thingamybob, thingamyjig **12** what's-its-name

contrary
◇ *reversal indicator*
05 annoy **06** oppose **07** adverse, awkward, counter, hostile, opposed, reverse, stroppy, wayward **08** clashing, converse, opposing, opposite, perverse, stubborn **09** difficult, obstinate **10** antipathic, antithesis, discrepant, headstrong, overthwart, refractory **11** conflicting, disobliging, intractable **12** antagonistic, cantankerous, cross-grained, incompatible, inconsistent **13** unco-operative **14** irreconcilable
• contrary to
10 at odds with **14** at variance with, in conflict with, in opposition to
• on the contrary
◇ *reversal indicator*
08 not at all **09** far from it, per contra
10 conversely, e contrario **11** al contrario, au contraire **14** just the reverse **15** just the opposite, quite the reverse, tout au contraire

contrast
04 foil **05** clash **06** differ, oppose, relief, set-off **07** compare **08** be at odds, chiasmus, conflict, disagree, opposite **09** disparity, go against
10 antithesis, comparison, contradict, difference, divergence, opposition
11 counter-view, distinction, distinguish **12** be at variance, be in conflict, discriminate
13 counterchange, differentiate, dissimilarity, dissimilitude
14 contraposition **15** differentiation
• in contrast to
09 as against, opposed to **10** rather than **14** in opposition to

contravene
04 defy **05** break, flout **06** breach, oppose **07** disobey, violate **08** infringe **10** transgress

contravention
06 breach **08** breaking **09** violation **11** dereliction **12** infringement **13** transgression

contretemps
04 tiff **05** brush, clash, hitch **06** mishap **08** accident, argument, squabble **10** difficulty, misfortune **11** predicament **12** disagreement, misadventure

contribute
04 edit, give, help, make **05** add to, cause, endow, grant, write **06** bestow, chip in, create, donate, kick in, lead to, submit, supply **07** chuck in, compile, compose, conduce, furnish, prepare, present, produce, promote, provide **08** generate, occasion, result in **09** originate, subscribe **10** bring about, give rise to, make happen **11** be a factor in, play a part in **13** give a donation

contribution
03 tax **04** gift, item, koha, levy, mite, shot **05** grant, input, paper, piece, story **06** column, report, review **07** article, feature, handout, present **08** addition, bestowal, donation, gratuity, offering **09** endowment **10** feuilleton, proportion, submission **11** Peter's pence **12** subscription **14** superannuation

contributor
05 donor, giver **06** author, backer, critic, patron, writer **07** sponsor **08** compiler, reporter, reviewer **09** columnist, freelance, supporter **10** benefactor, journalist, subscriber **13** correspondent

contrite
05 sorry **06** humble **07** ashamed **08** penitent, red-faced **09** chastened, regretful, repentant **10** remorseful **11** guilt-ridden, penitential

contrition
05 shame **06** regret, sorrow **07** remorse **09** penitence **10** repentance **11** compunction, humiliation **12** self-reproach

contrivance
03 art, gin **04** gear, plan, plot, ploy, ruse, tool **05** dodge, gizmo, shift, trick **06** design, device, doodad, doodah, doofer, engine, gadget, scheme, tactic, widget **07** machine, project **08** artifice, intrigue, thingamy **09** apparatus, appliance, equipment, expedient, implement, invention, mechanism, stratagem **10** compassing **11** contraption, imagination, machination, thingamybob, thingamyjig **12** excogitation, what's-its-name

contrive
◇ *anagram indicator*
04 brew, cook, form, plan, plot, work **05** frame, set up, spend, weave **06** create, cut out, design, devise, effect, engine, invent, manage, scheme, tamper, wangle **07** arrange, compass, concoct, imagine, succeed **08** conceive, engineer, find a way **09** construct, fabricate, manoeuvre **10** bring about, understand **11** orchestrate, stage-manage

contrived
◇ *anagram indicator*
05 false, hokey, set-up **06** forced **08** laboured, mannered, overdone, strained **09** elaborate, unnatural **10** artificial, factitious

control
03 ren, rin, run **04** curb, dial, head, keep, knob, lead, rein, ride, rule, sway, work **05** brake, check, lever, limit, power, reign **06** adjust, button, charge, direct, govern, make go, manage, reduce, subdue, switch, verify **07** command, contain, mastery, monitor, operate, oversee, repress **08** dominate, guidance, hold back, modulate, regulate, restrain, restrict **09** authority, be the boss, constrain, constrict, direction, dominance, hindrance, influence, oversight, reduction, restraint, supervise, supremacy **10** constraint, discipline, government, impediment, instrument, limitation, management, perstringe, regulation, repression, run the show **11** call the tune, keep in check, preside over, restriction, self-control, superintend, supervision **12** be in charge of, call the shots, jurisdiction, rule the roost **13** be in the saddle, self-restraint **14** pull the strings, put the brakes on, self-discipline **15** superintendence, wear the trousers

• **lose control**
04 slip, spaz **05** spazz **07** flip out

• **numerical control**
02 NC

controversial
04 moot **07** at issue, eristic, polemic **08** disputed, doubtful **09** debatable, polemical **10** disputable **11** contentious, tendentious **12** questionable **13** argumentative

controversy
06 debate, strife **07** discord, dispute, polemic, quarrel, wrangle **08** argument, friction, squabble **10** contention, debatement, discussion, dissension, war of words **11** altercation **12** cause célèbre, disagreement

contusion
04 bump, lump, mark **05** knock **06** bruise, injury **07** blemish **08** swelling **10** ecchymosis **13** discoloration

conundrum
05 guess, poser **06** enigma, puzzle, riddle, teaser **07** anagram, problem **08** quandary, word game **10** difficulty **11** brainteaser **12** brain-twister

conurbation
04 city, town **06** ghetto **08** big smoke, downtown, precinct, suburbia **09** inner city, metroplex, urban area **10** city centre, cosmopolis, metropolis, micropolis, pentapolis **11** megalopolis, urban sprawl **12** municipality **13** urban district **14** concrete jungle

convalesce
05 rally **06** pick up, revive **07** get well, improve, recover **09** get better **10** recuperate **11** get stronger, pull through

convalescence
08 recovery **09** anastasis **11** improvement, restoration **12** recuperation **13** getting better **14** rehabilitation

convene
04 call, meet **05** bring, rally **06** gather, muster, summon **07** collect, convoke **08** assemble **10** congregate **12** call together, come together **13** bring together

convenience
03 bog, lav, loo, use **04** help **06** behoof, device, gadget, toilet **07** amenity, benefit, fitness, service, utility **08** facility, lavatory, resource **09** advantage, appliance, commodity, ease of use, handiness, usability **10** expediency, usefulness **11** propinquity, suitability, water closet **12** availability **13** accessibility, accommodation, opportuneness **14** propitiousness, serviceability **15** appropriateness

See also **toilet**

convenient
03 fit **04** easy, gain, hend **05** handy **06** at hand, fitted, nearby, suited, timely, useful **07** adapted, favored, fitting, helpful **08** favoured, handsome, suitable **09** available, expedient, opportune, well-timed **10** accessible, beneficial, commodious, near at hand **11** appropriate, close at hand, within reach **12** labour-saving **13** advantageable **14** at your disposal

conveniently
04 well **05** patly **06** at hand, nearby **08** suitably, usefully **09** helpfully **10** accessibly, near at hand **11** close at hand, within reach **13** appropriately

convent
04 cite **05** abbey, house **06** fratry, friary, priory, summon **07** convene, fratery, nunnery **08** cloister **09** monastery

See also **monastery**

convention
03 use **04** bond, code, deal, pact **05** ethos, mores, synod, usage **06** accord, custom, treaty **07** bargain, compact, council, fashion, meeting **08** assembly, ceremony, conclave, congress, contract, covenant, practice,

protocol **09** agreement, Blackwood, concordat, delegates, etiquette, formality, gathering, propriety, punctilio, tradition **10** commitment, conference, engagement, settlement **11** arrangement, convocation, transaction **12** matter of form **13** understanding **15** representatives

conventional
04 lame **05** nomic, trite, usual **06** common, formal, normal, proper, ritual **07** correct, pompier, regular, routine, uptight **08** accepted, copybook, expected, ordinary, orthodox, received, standard, straight **09** bourgeois, customary, hidebound, prevalent **10** conformist, mainstream, pedestrian, prevailing, unoriginal **11** commonplace, respectable, stereotyped, traditional **12** conservative, run-of-the-mill **14** common-or-garden

conventionally
07 usually **08** commonly, formally, normally **09** regularly, routinely **10** ordinarily **13** traditionally

converge
04 form, join, mass, meet **05** focus, merge, unite **06** gather **07** close in, combine **08** approach, coincide **09** intersect **11** concentrate, move towards **12** come together

convergence
05 union **07** meeting, merging **08** approach, blending, junction **10** confluence **11** coincidence, combination **12** intersection **13** concentration

conversant
• conversant with
08 versed in **09** skilled in **10** apprised of, au fait with **11** practised in **12** familiar with, proficient in **13** experienced in, informed about **14** acquainted with

conversation
◇ *homophone indicator*
03 rap **04** chat, talk **05** board, convo, crack, craic, wongi **06** confab, gossip, natter, yabber **07** chinwag, purpose **08** chitchat, colloquy, cosy chat, dialogue, exchange, parlance, question, speaking **09** discourse, small talk, table talk, tête-à-tête **10** discussion, pillow talk **12** heart-to-heart **13** communication, interlocution

conversational
◇ *homophone indicator*
06 casual, chatty **07** relaxed **08** informal **09** talkative **10** colloquial **13** communicative

converse
◇ *homophone indicator*
04 chat, talk **05** speak, wongi **06** confer, dialog, gossip, natter, reason, relate **07** chatter, commune, counter, discuss, obverse, propose, purpose, reverse **08** chitchat, collogue, colloquy, contrary, dialogue, opposing, opposite, question, reversed **09** discourse **10** antithesis, chew the fat, chew the rag, colloquize, transposed **11** communicate **12** antithetical **13** other way round

conversely
09 e converso, obversely **10** contrarily **12** contrariwise **13** on the contrary **14** antithetically, on the other hand

conversion
◇ *anagram indicator*
06 change, switch **07** rebirth, turning **08** exchange, metanoia, mutation **09** preaching, reshaping **10** adaptation, adjustment, alteration, conviction, persuasion **11** proselytism, reformation, remodelling, translation **12** modification, regeneration, substitution **13** customization, metamorphosis, transmutation **14** evangelization, reconstruction, reorganization, transformation **15** proselytization, transfiguration

convert
◇ *anagram indicator*
03 put **04** goal, make, turn **05** adapt, alter **06** adjust, change, modify, mutate, reform, revise, switch **07** rebuild, remodel, reshape, restyle, win over **08** adherent, believer, convince, disciple, exchange, go over to, move over, neophyte, persuade, transfer, turn into **09** bring over, customize, new person, proselyte, refashion, transform, transmute **10** evangelize, reorganize, substitute, switch from **11** jump the dyke, loup the dyke, proselytize, reconstruct, restructure, transfigure **12** metamorphose **13** change beliefs, changed person **14** change religion

convertible
◇ *anagram indicator*
06 ragtop **07** soft top **09** adaptable, landaulet **10** adjustable, changeable, modifiable, permutable **11** landaulette **12** exchangeable **15** interchangeable

convex
04 nowy **05** bombé **07** bulging, gibbous, rounded **08** swelling **09** curved out **10** bow-fronted **11** protuberant **15** bending outwards

convey
03 put, tip **04** bear, have, lead, move, pipe, send, take, tell, wain **05** bring, carry, drive, fetch, guide, shift, steal **06** hand on, impart, import, pass on, relate, reveal **07** channel, conduct, deliver, express, forward, mediate, present **08** announce, disclose, transfer, transmit **09** make known, transport **11** communicate

conveyance
03 bus, cab, car, sac, van **04** cart, taxi **05** coach, grant, lorry, truck, wagon **06** ceding **07** bicycle, express, transit, vehicle **08** carriage, delivery, granting, mortgage, movement, transfer **09** transport **10** bequeathal, motorcycle **11** consignment **12** transference, transmission **13** transportance **14** transportation
See also **aircraft**; **bicycle**; **car**; **carriage**; **ship**

convict
03 con, lag **05** crime, crook, felon, judge **06** canary, forçat, inmate **07** approve, attaint, condemn, culprit, old hand, reprove, villain **08** criminal, imprison, jailbird, offender, prisoner, sentence, yardbird **09** wrongdoer **10** canary-bird, emancipist, find guilty, lawbreaker

conviction
04 view **05** creed, faith, prior, tenet **06** belief **07** fervour, opinion **08** firmness, sentence **09** assurance, certainty, certitude, judgement, principle **10** confidence, persuasion, plerophory **11** earnestness, plerophoria **12** condemnation, imprisonment, satisfaction

convince
04 sell, sway **06** assure, induce, prompt **07** prove to, resolve, satisfy, win over **08** persuade, perswade, talk into, talk over **09** bring home, influence **10** bring round **11** prevail upon

convincing
06 cogent, likely **07** certain, telling **08** credible, forceful, luculent, positive, powerful, pregnant, probable **09** plausible **10** compelling, conclusive, conclusory, impressive, persuasive **12** satisfactory

convincingly
08 cogently, credibly **09** all ends up, plausibly, tellingly **10** forcefully, powerfully **12** compellingly, conclusively, impressively, persuasively

convivial
04 boon **05** jolly, merry **06** genial, hearty, jovial, lively, social **07** affable, cordial, festive **08** cheerful, friendly, sociable **09** fun-loving **11** Anacreontic

conviviality
03 fun **05** cheer, mirth **06** gaiety **07** jollity **08** bonhomie **09** festivity, geniality, joviality **10** cordiality, liveliness **11** good feeling, merrymaking, sociability **12** friendliness **14** goodfellowship

convocation
04 diet **05** forum, synod **07** council, meeting **08** assembly, conclave, congress **10** assemblage, conference, convention **12** congregation, forgathering

convoluted
◇ *anagram indicator*
04 mazy **07** complex, unclear, winding, writhen, wrythen **08** involved, tortuous, twisting **09** convolute, intricate, Vitruvian **10** meandering **11** complicated

convolution
04 coil, fold, loop, turn **05** gyrus, helix, twist, whorl **06** spiral **07** coiling, winding **08** curlicue **09** intricacy, sinuosity **10** complexity
11 involvement, sinuousness
12 complication, entanglement, tortuousness

convoy
04 line **05** fleet, group, guard, train
06 escort **07** company **10** attendance, protection

convulse
◇ *anagram indicator*
04 jerk **05** seize **07** disturb, shudder
08 unsettle **10** suffer a fit **14** shake violently, suffer a seizure

convulsion
03 fit, tic **05** cramp, ictus, spasm
06 attack, furore, tremor, tumult, unrest **07** seizure, turmoil **08** disorder, eruption, laughter, outburst, paroxysm, upheaval **09** agitation, commotion
10 turbulence **11** contraction, disturbance **13** electric shock

convulsive
05 jerky **06** fitful **07** violent
08 sporadic **09** spasmodic
11 spasmodical **12** uncontrolled
• **convulsive disorder**
03 DTs **15** delirium tremens

cook
◇ *anagram indicator*
02 do **03** pan **04** burn, chef, fake, heat, make, peep, ruin, warm **05** fryer, put on, spoil **06** doctor, greasy, overdo
07 babbler, concoct, falsify, prepare, scare up, underdo **08** overcook, rustle up **09** cuisinier, improvise, undercook
11 put together **13** throw together
See also **chef**

Cooking methods include:
03 fry
04 bake, boil, sear, stew
05 broil, brown, curry, grill, poach, roast, sauté, steam, toast
06 braise, coddle, flambé, pan-fry, simmer
07 deep-fry, parboil, stir-fry
08 barbecue, pot-roast, scramble
09 casserole, char-grill, fricassee, microwave, oven-roast, spit-roast
10 flame-grill

• **cook up**
◇ *anagram indicator*
04 brew, edit, plan, plot **06** devise, invent, make up, scheme **07** concoct, falsify, prepare **08** contrive **09** fabricate

cooked
◇ *anagram indicator*
• **lightly cooked**
04 rare, rear

cookery

Cookery styles include:
04 Thai
05 Greek, halal, Irish, mezze, rural, tapas, vegan, Welsh
06 French, fusion, German, Indian, kosher, Tex-Mex
07 African, British, Chinese, Eastern, English, Italian, Mexican, seafood, Spanish, Turkish
08 American, fast food, Japanese, Scottish
09 Cantonese, Caribbean, Malaysian, Provençal
10 cordon bleu, Far Eastern, gluten-free, Indonesian, Pacific Rim, vegetarian
11 home cooking, lean cuisine
12 haute cuisine
13 Mediterranean, Middle Eastern
14 cuisine minceur
15 nouvelle cuisine

Cookery-related terms include:
03 Aga, dip, gut, hob, ice
04 chef, chop, cook, cure, dice, mash, oven, rise, whip
05 baste, brown, carve, chill, chump, curry, daube, devil, dress, glaze, grate, knead, mince, mould, press, purée, score, shave, smoke, steep, stuff, whisk
06 batter, blanch, de-bone, entrée, fillet, fondue, infuse, kosher, leaven, recipe, reduce, season, spread
07 garnish, nibbles, proving, starter, tandoor, topping
08 cookbook, devilled, marinade, marinate, preserve
09 antipasto, percolate, reduction, tenderize
10 caramelize
11 hors d'oeuvre

Cook Islands
03 COK

cool
03 ace, fan, ice **04** calm, chic, cold, iced, keel, mega, neat **05** abate, allay, aloof, brill, chill, crisp, fresh, great, nervy, nippy, parky, poise, quiet, smart, tepid **06** breeze, breezy, caller, chilly, dampen, freeze, frigid, frosty, lessen, placid, poised, quench, reduce, sedate, temper, trendy, wicked **07** assuage, bracing, chilled, control, distant, draught, elegant, get cold, ice-cold, relaxed, stylish, subside, unmoved
08 calmness, coldness, composed, coolness, diminish, draughty, impudent, laid-back, lukewarm, make cold, moderate, reserved, smashing, terrific, turn cold **09** admirable, apathetic, collected, composure, crispness, excellent, fantastic, freshness, get colder, impassive, nippiness, sangfroid, unexcited, unruffled, wonderful **10** acceptable, become cold, chilliness, make colder, marvellous, refreshing, streetwise, turn colder, unfriendly, untroubled
11 fashionable, half-hearted, indifferent, level-headed, refrigerate, self-control, standoffish, undisturbed, unemotional, unexcitable, unflappable, unflustered, unperturbed, unwelcoming **12** air-condition, become colder, second to none, uninterested, unresponsive
13 collectedness, defervescence, defervescency, disinterested, dispassionate, imperturbable, self-possessed, sophisticated **14** out of this world, self-discipline, self-possession, unapprehensive, unenthusiastic
15 cool as a cucumber, uncommunicative, undemonstrative

cooler *see* **jail, gaol**

cooling
08 chilling, freezing **10** refreshing
11 refrigerant, ventilation
13 defervescence, defervescency, refrigeration, refrigerative, refrigeratory **15** air-conditioning

coolly
06 calmly, coldly **07** quietly **08** frostily, placidly, sedately **09** distantly
10 composedly, impudently, reservedly **11** collectedly, impassively, unexcitably, unexcitedly
13 apathetically, half-heartedly, imperturbably, indifferently, level-headedly, standoffishly, unemotionally
14 uninterestedly, unresponsively
15 dispassionately

coop
03 box, mew, pen, ren, rin, rip, run
04 cage **05** cavie, hutch, pound
06 keavie **09** enclosure
• **coop up**
03 pen **04** cage, shut **06** bail up, immure, keep in, lock up, shut in, shut up **07** close in, confine, enclose, impound **08** imprison, lock away
11 incarcerate

Cooper
04 Gary

co-operate
03 aid **04** ally, help, play, pool
05 share, unite **06** assist, team up
07 combine, pitch in **08** conspire, play ball **09** play along **10** contribute, join forces **11** collaborate, participate, string along **12** band together, pull together, work together **14** pull your weight, work side by side

co-operation
03 aid **04** help **05** unity **08** teamwork
10 assistance, team spirit **11** give-and-take, helpfulness, helping hand, joint action **12** contribution, co-ordination
13 collaboration, esprit de corps, participation **15** concerted action, concerted effort, working together

co-operative
05 joint **06** shared, united **07** helpful, helping, willing **08** coactive, combined, obliging **09** assisting, compliant, concerted **10** collective, responsive, supportive **11** co-ordinated **13** accommodating, collaborative **15** working together

co-ordinate
01 x, y, z **02** go **04** mesh **05** adapt, blend, match, order **06** go well, join up

07 abscis, arrange, blend in **08** abscissa, abscisse, ordinate, organize, regulate, tabulate **09** co-operate, correlate, harmonize, integrate, mix 'n' match
10 complement, go together
11 collaborate, synchronize, systematize **12** be compatible, work together **14** make compatible

co-ordination
07 harmony **08** blending, matching, ordering **10** ordonnance
11 arrangement, co-operation, integration **12** organization
13 collaboration, compatibility
15 complementation

cop
02 PC **03** get, pig, top **04** bull, head, nark **05** bizzy, bobby, catch **06** arrest, copper, obtain, rozzer **07** acquire, capture, officer **08** flatfoot
09 constable, policeman **10** bluebottle
11 policewoman **13** police officer

See also **police officer**

• **cop out**
04 balk, duck, shun **05** avert, avoid, dodge, elude, evade, hedge, shirk
06 bypass, escape **07** prevent **08** get out of, get round, sidestep **09** give a miss **11** abstain from, make a detour, run away from, shy away from **12** hold back from, keep away from, stay away from, steer clear of

cope
04 meet **05** get by, match **06** barter, make do, manage **07** carry on, chlamys, contend, pluvial, subsist, succeed, survive **08** exchange
09 encounter **10** get through

• **cope with**
04 hack **05** touch, treat **06** endure, handle, manage, take up **07** weather
08 deal with **09** encounter **11** contend with, grapple with, wrestle with
12 struggle with

coping
04 skew

copious
04 full, huge, rich **05** ample, great, large **06** bags of, lavish **07** fulsome, liberal, profuse, teeming **08** abundant, generous, numerous **09** abounding, bounteous, bountiful, extensive, luxuriant, plenteous, plentiful, redundant **11** overflowing
13 inexhaustible

cop-out
05 alibi, dodge, fraud **06** excuse, get-out **07** evasion, pretext **08** pretence, shirking **14** passing the buck

copper
01 p **02** Cu

See also **coin**; **police officer**

cops *see* **police**

copse
04 bush, carr, wood **05** brush, grove
06 spinny, spring **07** coppice, spinney, thicket

copulate
03 tup **04** mate **07** have sex **08** make love **10** fool around, get off with, make it with **11** go all the way, go to bed with

copulation
03 sex **06** coitus, mating **07** coition
08 congress, coupling, embraces, intimacy **09** relations **10** commixtion, love-making **15** carnal knowledge

copy
02 cc **03** ape, bcc, CRC, fax **04** crib, echo, fake, scan **05** clone, forge, image, issue, mimic, model, print, stuff, trace, Xerox® **06** borrow, carbon, ectype, follow, mirror, parrot, pirate, repeat, sample **07** emulate, estreat, example, forgery, imitate, pattern, replica, tracing, vidimus **08** apograph, knock-off, likeness, manifold, simulate, specimen **09** archetype, borrowing, duplicate, facsimile, imitation, photocopy, Photostat®, polygraph, replicate, reproduce, semblance
10 carbon copy, mimeograph, plagiarism, plagiarize, transcribe, transcript, triplicate **11** counterfeit, counterpart, engrossment, impersonate, replication
12 reproduction **13** transcription
14 representation **15** exemplification

coquettish
06 flirty **07** amorous, flighty, teasing, vampish **08** dallying, inviting
09 seductive **10** come-hither
11 flirtatious, provocative

cord
03 guy, tie **04** bond, flex, lace, line, link, rope **05** cable, match, twine, twist
06 bobbin, myelon, ribbon, strand, string, tendon, thread **07** funicle, service **08** bell pull, chenille
09 funiculus **10** connection, draw-string **11** navel-string **12** spinal marrow

cordial
04 warm **05** shrub **06** genial, hearty
07 affable, cardiac, earnest, persico, ratafia, rosolio, sincere **08** amicable, anisette, cheerful, friendly, persicot, pleasant, rosoglio, sociable
09 agreeable, heartfelt, hippocras, rosa-solis, welcoming **10** pousse-café
11 Benedictine, stimulating, warm-hearted **12** affectionate, invigorating, wholehearted **13** aqua caelestis, aurum potabile

cordiality
05 heart **06** warmth **07** earnest, welcome **09** affection, geniality, sincerity **10** affability, heartiness
11 sociability **12** cheerfulness, friendliness **13** agreeableness

cordially
06 warmly **07** affably **08** amicably, genially, sociably **10** cheerfully, pleasantly **13** warm-heartedly
14 wholeheartedly

cordon
04 line, ring **05** chain, fence, plant
06 column, ribbon **07** barrier

• **cordon off**
07 enclose, isolate, seal off **08** close off, encircle, fence off, separate, surround

core
03 key, nub **04** crux, gang, gist, lead, main, nife, runt **05** basic, heart, shift, vital **06** centre, innate, kernel, middle
07 campana, central, company, corncob, crucial, essence, nucleus, typical **08** inherent, interior
09 essential, intrinsic, principal, substance **10** barysphere, definitive, underlying **11** constituent, fundamental, nitty-gritty **12** axis cylinder, quintessence
14 characteristic

cork
03 lid **04** bung, plug, seal, stop
05 cover, shive, suber **07** phellem, stopper

corm *see* **bulb**

cormorant
04 shag **05** scart, skart **06** duiker, duyker, scarth, skarth **07** sea crow

corn
03 mow, rye, Zea **04** oats **05** grain, maize, wheat **06** barley, cereal, farina, kernel, pinole **10** arable crop, cereal crop, intoxicate

corner
03 cor, fix, hog, jam **04** bend, fork, hole, nook, trap, tree **05** angle, catch, crook, curve, joint, niche **06** bail up, cantle, cavity, cranny, cut off, dièdre, pickle, plight, recess, scrape
07 confine, control, crevice, hideout, retreat, straits, turning **08** block off, dominate, hardship, hideaway, hunt down, junction **09** ingleneuk, inglenook, situation, tight spot
10 monopolize, run to earth
11 predicament **12** intersection
13 nowhere to turn **15** force into a place

• **around the corner**
04 near **05** close, local **06** at hand, coming, nearby **07** close by, looming
08 imminent, in the air **09** impending
10 accessible, convenient
11 approaching, within range, within reach **12** a stone's throw, neighbouring
13 about to happen

• **cut corners**
05 skimp

cornerstone
03 key **04** base, coin, core **05** basis, heart, quoin **06** thrust **07** bedrock, essence, keyhole, skew-put, support
08 keystone, mainstay **09** essential, principle, skew-table **10** essentials, groundwork, skew-corbel
11 fundamental **12** fundamentals
13 alpha and omega, starting-point
14 basic principle, main ingredient
15 first principles

Cornwall
02 SW

corny
04 dull **05** banal, horny, stale, trite **06** feeble, spammy **07** buckeye, cliché'd, maudlin, mawkish **08** clichéed, overused **09** hackneyed **11** commonplace, Mickey Mouse, sentimental, stereotyped **12** old-fashioned **13** platitudinous

corollary
05 rider **06** porism, result, upshot **08** function, illation **09** deduction, induction, inference **10** conclusion, consectary, consequent **11** consequence **13** supplementary

coronation
08 crowning **12** enthronement

coronet
05 crown, tiara **06** cornet, diadem, wreath **07** circlet, crownet, garland

corporal
03 Cpl, NCO, Nym **04** corp, naik, pall **06** actual, bodily, carnal **07** fleshly, somatic **08** concrete, material, physical, tangible **09** brigadier, corporeal **10** anatomical **11** substantial **13** lance sergeant

corporate
05 joint **06** allied, common, merged, pooled, shared, united **08** combined, communal **09** concerted **10** collective, collegiate **11** amalgamated **13** collaborative

corporation
04 firm, gild **05** belly, guild, house, trust **06** cartel, paunch **07** commune, company, concern, council, guildry **08** business, industry, pot-belly, township **09** authority, beer belly, syndicate **10** consortium **11** association, authorities, City Company, partnership **12** conglomerate, organization **13** burgh of barony, establishment, governing body, multinational **14** holding company
See also **paunch**; **stomach**

corporeal
05 human, hylic **06** actual, bodily, carnal, mortal **07** fleshly **08** concrete, corporal, material, physical, tangible **11** substantial

corps
01 C **02** CD **03** RAC **04** band, body, crew, team, unit **05** squad **07** brigade, company **08** division, regiment, squadron **10** contingent, detachment

corpse
04 body, like, mort **05** corse, mummy, relic, stiff, zombi **06** deader, relics, zombie **07** cadaver, carcase, carcass, remains **08** dead body, skeleton **09** flatliner

corpulent
03 fat **05** beefy, bulky, burly, large, obese, plump, poddy, podgy, stout, tubby **06** fleshy, portly, rotund **07** adipose, fattish **08** roly-poly **10** overweight, pot-bellied, well-padded **11** Falstaffian

corpus
04 body **05** whole **08** entirety **10** collection **11** aggregation, compilation

corral
03 sty **04** coop, fold **05** kraal, pound, stall **09** enclosure

correct
◇ *anagram indicator*
02 OK **03** fix **04** cure, edit, jake, just, mend, okay, real, sort, true **05** amend, debug, emend, exact, right, scold, tweak **06** actual, adjust, bang on, proper, punish, rebuke, reform, remedy, revise, seemly, spot-on, strict **07** fitting, improve, precise, rectify, redress, regular, reprove, right-on, sort out **08** accepted, accurate, admonish, disabuse, faithful, flawless, put right, regulate, set right, standard, suitable, truthful, unerring **09** faultless, reprimand **10** acceptable, ameliorate, blue-pencil, discipline **11** appropriate, comme il faut, put straight, put to rights, set to rights, word-perfect **12** conventional, rehabilitate **14** counterbalance

correction
◇ *anagram indicator*
05 tweak **06** rebuke, reform **07** reproof **08** equation, grafting, scolding **09** amendment, reduction, remedying, reprimand **10** adjustment, admonition, alteration, diorthosis, discipline, emendation, punishment **11** improvement, reformation **12** amelioration, chastisement, compensation, modification **13** rectification **14** rehabilitation

corrective
05 penal **08** curative, punitive, remedial **09** corrigent, medicinal **10** amendatory, emendatory, palliative **11** reformatory, restorative, therapeutic **12** disciplinary **14** rehabilitative

correctly
◇ *anagram indicator*
02 OK **04** okay **05** right **07** exactly, rightly **08** actually, properly, suitably **09** about east, fittingly, precisely **10** acceptably, accurately, flawlessly, unerringly **11** faultlessly **13** appropriately **14** conventionally

correlate
04 link **05** agree, tally, tie in **06** equate, relate **07** compare, connect **08** analogue, interact, parallel **09** associate **10** co-ordinate, correspond **15** show a connection

correlation
03 fit **04** link **10** connection **11** association, equivalence, interaction, interchange, reciprocity **12** relationship **14** correspondence **15** interdependence

correspond
03 fit, pen **05** agree, match, rhyme, tally, write **06** accord, answer, concur, square **07** balance, conform, match up **08** assonate, coincide, dovetail, register **09** be similar, correlate, harmonize, represent **10** complement, sympathize **11** be analogous, communicate, fit together, keep in touch **12** be consistent, be equivalent **13** be in agreement **15** exchange letters

correspondence
03 fit **04** mail, post **05** e-mail, match **07** analogy, harmony, letters, writing **08** relation **09** agreement, assonance, congruity **10** comparison, conformity, consonance, similarity **11** coincidence, concurrence, correlation, equivalence, resemblance, suitability **13** communication, comparability
See also **letter**

correspondent
06 keypal, pen pal, writer **08** agreeing, reporter, suitable **09** answering, columnist, pen friend **10** journalist, responsive **11** contributor, responsible **12** letter-writer

corresponding
04 like **07** similar, suiting **08** agreeing, matching, parallel, relative **09** accordant, analogous, answering, congruent, facsimile, identical **10** collateral, comparable, equivalent, reciprocal **12** commensurate, interrelated **13** complementary

corridor
04 hall **05** aisle, lobby **07** gallery, gangway, hallway, passage **08** alleyway **09** penthouse **10** passageway

corroborate
05 prove **06** attest, back up, ratify, uphold, verify **07** bear out, certify, confirm, endorse, support, sustain **08** document, evidence, underpin, validate **09** confirmed **12** authenticate, substantiate

corroboration
10 validation **11** attestation, endorsement **12** confirmation, ratification, verification **14** authentication, substantiation

corroborative
09 endorsing, verifying **10** confirming, evidential, supporting, supportive, validating **11** evidentiary **12** confirmative, confirmatory, verificatory **14** substantiating

corrode
03 eat, rot **04** burn, etch, fret, rust **05** eat in, erode, waste **06** abrade, impair **07** consume, crumble, destroy, eat away, eat into, oxidize, tarnish **08** wear away **11** deteriorate **12** disintegrate

corrosion
03 rot **04** rust **07** burning, erosion, rotting, rusting, wasting **08** abrasion **09** prerosion **10** tarnishing **13** deterioration **14** disintegration

corrosive
04 acid **07** caustic, cutting, erosive, wasting, wearing **08** abrasive
09 consuming, corroding
11 destructive

corrugated
06 fluted, folded, ridged **07** creased, grooved, rumpled, striate **08** crinkled, furrowed, wrinkled **10** channelled

corrupt
◇ *anagram indicator*
03 buy, mar, rot **04** bent, evil, lure, warp **05** bribe, decay, shady, spoil, taint, venal **06** blight, bribed, buy off, canker, debase, defile, doctor, impure, infect, poison, putrid, rotten, seduce, sleazy, suborn, wicked **07** abusive, crooked, debauch, defiled, deprave, falsify, immoral, obscene, pervert, pollute, putrefy, subvert, tainted, vitiate **08** bribable, depraved, empoison
09 barbarize, barbarous, debauched, dishonest, dissolute, inquinate, unethical **10** adulterate, bastardize, degenerate, demoralize, fraudulent, lead astray, tamper with
11 contaminate **12** contaminated, unprincipled, unscrupulous
13 untrustworthy **15** be a bad influence

corruption
03 rot **04** evil, vice **05** abuse, bobol, fraud, graft **06** sleaze **07** bribery, leprosy **08** impurity, iniquity, villainy
09 depravity, extortion, pollution, shadiness **10** adaptation, alteration, debauchery, dishonesty, distortion, immorality, perversion, rottenness, subversion, wickedness **11** criminality, crookedness, degradation, subornation **12** degeneration, modification **13** contamination, sharp practice

corset
04 belt, busk **05** stays **06** bodice, girdle, roll-on, shaper, waspie
08 corselet **11** panty girdle

cortège
05 suite, train **06** column, parade
07 retinue **09** cavalcade, entourage
10 procession

cosh *see* **weapon**

cosily
06 safely, snugly, warmly **08** securely
10 intimately **11** comfortably

cosmetic
04 fard **05** minor **06** beauty, make-up, slight **07** shallow, surface, trivial
08 external, skin-deep **10** maquillage, peripheral **11** beautifying, superficial

Cosmetics include:

05 rouge, toner
07 blusher, bronzer, mascara, perfume
08 cleanser, eyeliner, face mask, face pack, lip gloss, lip liner, lipstick, panstick
09 concealer, eye shadow, face cream
10 face powder, foundation, kohl pencil, nail polish
11 greasepaint, moisturizer, nail varnish
13 eyebrow pencil, pressed powder

cosmic
04 huge, mega, vast **05** large
07 immense, in space, massive, mundane, orderly, seismic **08** colossal, enormous, infinite **09** from space, grandiose, limitless, universal, worldwide **11** measureless, significant
12 immeasurable

cosmonaut
08 lunanaut, spaceman **09** astronaut, lunarnaut, taikonaut **10** spacewoman
14 space traveller

cosmopolitan
06 urbane **07** worldly **08** cultured
09 universal **11** broad-minded, multiracial, worldly-wise
12 unprejudiced **13** international, multicultural, sophisticated, well-travelled

cosmos
06 galaxy, nature, system, worlds
08 creation, universe

cosset
03 pet **04** baby **05** spoil **06** coddle, cuddle, fondle, pamper **07** cherish, indulge **11** mollycoddle, overindulge

cost
03 fee, pay, tab **04** exes, harm, hurt, levy, loss, rate, take, toll **05** coast, fetch, go for, price, quote, value, worth
06 amount, ask for, budget, buy for, charge, come to, damage, figure, injure, injury, outlay, tariff **07** be worth, cost out, deprive, destroy, expense, payment, penalty, sell for, set back, stand in, work out **08** amount to, estimate, expenses, retail at, spending
09 calculate, cause harm, detriment, knock back, outgoings, overheads, quotation, sacrifice, suffering, valuation **10** be priced at, be valued at
11 asking price, cause injury, deprivation, expenditure
12 disbursement, selling price
13 disbursements **14** cause the loss of

Costa Rica
02 CR **03** CRI

costly
04 dear, posh, rich, salt **05** steep
06 lavish, pricey **07** harmful, premium, ruinous, sky-high **08** damaging, high-cost, precious, splendid, valuable
09 big-ticket, chargeful, excessive, expensive, priceless, sumptuous
10 disastrous, exorbitant, high-priced, loss-making, overpriced
11 deleterious, destructive, detrimental
12 catastrophic, costing a bomb, extortionate **15** costing the earth, daylight robbery

costume
02 gi **03** gie, tog **04** garb, suit **05** dress, get-up, habit, robes **06** attire, bather, bikini, cossie, judogi, livery, outfit, rig-out, toilet **07** apparel, clobber, clothes, fashion, threads, uniform
08 clothing, ensemble, garments
09 gala-dress, vestments **10** diving suit, fancy dress **11** diving dress
12 style of dress
See also **clothes, clothing**

cosy
04 cosh, safe, snug, warm **05** comfy
06 homely, intime, secure **08** intimate
09 congenial, gemütlich, sheltered
11 comfortable

Côte d'Ivoire
02 CI **03** CIV

coterie
03 set **04** camp, club, gang **05** cabal, group **06** caucus, circle, clique
07 cenacle, faction **09** camarilla, community **11** association

cottage
03 cot, hut **04** crib, gite **05** bothy, cabin, dacha, lodge, shack, villa
06 bothie, chalet, shanty
08 bungalow **09** home-croft

cotton
04 lint **05** ceiba

Cotton fabrics include:

04 aida, duck, jean
05 chino, denim, dhoti, drill, jaspé, jeans, kanga, piqué, surat, toile
06 Bengal, calico, canvas, chintz, coutil, dhooti, diaper, dimity, humhum, jersey, khanga, madras, moreen, muslin, nankin, Oxford, pongee, sateen, T-cloth
07 batiste, buckram, challis, duvetyn, fustian, galatea, gingham, jaconet, kitenge, Mexican, nankeen, percale, printer, silesia
08 chambray, corduroy, coutille, cretonne, drilling, frocking, lambskin, marcella, nainsook, organdie, osnaburg, shantung, thickset
09 cottonade, huckaback, longcloth, percaline, sailcloth, satin jean, swans-down, velveteen
10 Balbriggan, candlewick, monk's cloth, seersucker, winceyette
11 cheesecloth, flannelette, mutton cloth, nettle-cloth, Oxford cloth, sponge cloth
13 casement cloth

• **foreign particle in cotton**
04 moit, mote

couch
03 bed, set **04** bear, sofa, word
05 divan, frame, quick, utter **06** cradle, day bed, litter, pallet, phrase, quitch, scutch, settee, twitch **07** express, lounger, ottoman, quicken, sofa bed, support, vis-à-vis **08** dog-grass, dog-wheat **10** quack grass, quick grass, triclinium **11** quitch grass, scutch grass, twitch grass **12** chaise-longue, chesterfield

cough
03 hem, ugh **04** ahem, bark, hack, hawk, kink, rasp **05** croak, hoast

06 tisick, tussis **07** hawking **08** kink-host **09** chincough, kink-cough, pertussis **15** clear your throat

• cough up

03 pay **04** give **05** pay up **06** ante up, pay out **07** fork out, stump up **08** hand over, shell out

could

• could be, could become

◇ *anagram indicator*

council

04 body, diet, duma, jury **05** board, boule, cabal, crowd, divan, douma, flock, forum, group, jirga, junta, panel, rally, shura, synod, witan **06** senate, soviet, throng **07** cabinet, chamber, company, conseil, consult, meeting **08** advisers, assembly, congress, ministry, trustees **09** committee, directors, executive, gathering, governors, Landsting, Loya Jirga, multitude, panchayat, Sanhedrim, Sanhedrin, syndicate **10** commission, conference, convention, focus group, government, Landsthing, management, parliament, presidency **11** city fathers, convocation, corporation, directorate, witenagemot **12** advisory body, ayuntamiento, body of people, congregation, working party **13** advisory group, governing body **14** administration, local authority

Council areas of Scotland:

04 Fife
05 Angus, Moray
07 Falkirk
08 Highland, Stirling
10 Dundee City, Eilean Siar, Inverclyde, Midlothian
11 East Lothian, Glasgow City, West Lothian
12 Aberdeen City, East Ayrshire, Renfrewshire
13 Aberdeenshire, Argyll and Bute, North Ayrshire, Orkney Islands, South Ayrshire
15 City of Edinburgh, Perth and Kinross, Scottish Borders, Shetland Islands
16 Clackmannanshire, East Renfrewshire, North Lanarkshire, South Lanarkshire
18 East Dunbartonshire, West Dunbartonshire
19 Dumfries and Galloway

Council areas of Wales:

05 Conwy, Powys
07 Cardiff, Gwynedd, Newport, Swansea, Torfaen, Wrexham
08 Bridgend
10 Caerphilly, Ceredigion, Flintshire
12 Blaenau Gwent, Denbighshire
13 Merthyr Tydfil, Monmouthshire, Pembrokeshire
14 Isle of Anglesey
15 Carmarthenshire, Neath Port Talbot, Vale of Glamorgan
16 Rhondda Cynon Taff

councillor

02 CC, Cr, PC **04** Cllr **05** vezir, vizir **06** induna, visier, vizier, wizier **07** burgess, provost **08** decurion

counsel

02 KC, QC **04** read, rede, silk, urge, warn **05** aread, arede, guide, teach **06** advice, advise, direct, exhort, lawyer **07** arreede, caution, opinion, suggest **08** admonish, advising, advocate, attorney, guidance, instruct, moralism **09** barrister, direction, recommend, solicitor, viewpoint **10** admonition, advisement, conference, conferring, suggestion **11** exhortation, forethought, information **12** amicus curiae, consultation, deliberation, give guidance **13** consideration **14** recommendation **15** give your opinion

counsellor

04 guru **05** coach, guide, tutor **06** mentor, Nestor **07** teacher **08** director **09** authority, barrister, confidant, directrix, therapist **10** Achitophel, Ahithophel, confidante, consultant, directress, instructor

count

03 add, Ory, sum **04** deem, feel, Graf, hold, list, poll, tell **05** add up, check, compt, Fosco, grave, judge, score, sum up, tally, think, total, tot up, whole **06** census, county, esteem, matter, number, reckon, regard **07** account, compute, Dracula, include, qualify, signify **08** allow for, consider, look upon **09** calculate, enumerate, landgrave, numbering, palsgrave, reckoning, totting-up **10** cut some ice, full amount, Rhinegrave **11** be important, calculation, carry weight, computation, enumeration **13** mean something, take account of **15** make a difference, take into account

See also **nobility**

• count in

05 put in **06** rope in **07** include, involve, let in on **08** allow for **09** introduce

• count on

05 trust **06** bank on, expect, lean on, rely on **07** bargain, believe, swear by **08** depend on, reckon on **10** bargain for

• count out

04 omit, tell **06** ignore **07** exclude **08** leave out, pass over **09** disregard, eliminate **10** include out

countenance

04 back, face, look, mien **05** agree, allow, brook **06** endure, favour, permit, uphold, visage **07** approve, condone, endorse **08** features, sanction, semblant, stand for, tolerate **09** patronage, put up with **10** appearance, expression **11** approbation, physiognomy **12** acquiescence

counter

03 bar **04** buck, chip, coin, desk, disc, dump, fish, meet **05** merel, meril, parry, piece, stand, table, token **06** answer, buffet, combat, marker, merell, offset, oppose, resist, retort, return **07** adverse, against, dispute, opposed, respond, surface, worktop **08** contrary, opposing, opposite **09** hit back at, retaliate, shopboard **10** contradict, conversely **11** conflicting, contrasting, work surface **12** in opposition **13** contradictory

counteract

04 foil, undo **05** annul, check **06** defeat, hinder, negate, offset, oppose, remedy, resist, thwart **07** prevent **09** frustrate **10** act against, invalidate, neutralize **11** countervail **14** counterbalance

counterbalance

04 undo **05** poise **06** cancel, offset, set-off **07** balance, correct, requite **08** equalize **09** make up for **10** compensate, neutralize **11** countervail **12** counterpoise **13** compensate for

counterfeit

03 dud **04** base, copy, fake, sham **05** bogus, dummy, faked, false, feign, forge, fraud, phony, pseud, queer, snide **06** copied, forged, phoney, pirate, pseudo **07** falsify, feigned, forgery, imitate, pretend, simular **08** borrowed, disguise, phantasm, postiche, simulate, spurious **09** brummagem, fabricate, imitation, pretended, reproduce, simulated **10** artificial, camouflage, fraudulent **11** impersonate **12** reproduction

See also **counterfeit coin** *under* **coin**

countermand

05 annul, quash **06** cancel, repeal, revoke **07** rescind, reverse, unorder **08** abrogate, override, overturn **10** revocation

counterpart

04 copy, mate, peer, twin **05** equal, match, moral, tally **06** double, fellow **07** obverse **08** parallel **09** duplicate **10** complement, equivalent, supplement **14** opposite number

counterpoint

04 foil **06** relief, set off, set-off **07** descant, enhance **08** contrast, faburden, heighten, opposite **09** intensify **10** complement **11** counterpane **13** differentiate **15** differentiation, throw into relief

countless

06 legion, myriad, untold **07** endless, umpteen **08** infinite **09** boundless, limitless **10** numberless, unnumbered, without end **11** innumerable, measureless **12** immeasurable, incalculable **13** inexhaustible

countrified

04 hick **05** rural **06** rustic **07** bucolic,

idyllic, outback **08** agrarian, pastoral **10** provincial **12** agricultural

country

04 area, bush, land, pays, soil
05 power, realm, rural, state, wilds
06 landed, nation, people, public, region, rustic, sticks, voters **07** bucolic, idyllic, kingdom, outback, terrain
08 agrarian, citizens, district, electors, farmland, locality, moorland, pastoral, populace, republic **09** backwater, backwoods, community, green belt, provinces, residents, rural area, territory **10** population, provincial
11 countryside, inhabitants
12 agricultural, back of beyond, principality **13** neighbourhood
15 middle of nowhere

Countries:

02 UK
03 PRC, UAE, USA
04 Chad, Cuba, Fiji, Iran, Iraq, Laos, Mali, Oman, Peru, Togo
05 Benin, Burma, Chile, China, Congo, Egypt, Gabon, Ghana, Haiti, India, Italy, Japan, Kenya, Libya, Malta, Nauru, Nepal, Niger, Palau, Qatar, Samoa, Spain, Sudan, Syria, Tonga, Yemen
06 Angola, Belize, Bhutan, Brazil, Canada, Cyprus, España, France, Greece, Guinea, Guyana, Israel, Italia, Jordan, Kuwait, Latvia, Malawi, Mexico, Monaco, Norway, Panama, Poland, Russia, Rwanda, Sweden, Taiwan, Turkey, Tuvalu, Uganda, Zambia
07 Albania, Algeria, Andorra, Armenia, Austria, Bahrain, Belarus, Belgium, Bolivia, Burundi, Comoros, Croatia, Denmark, Ecuador, Eritrea, Estonia, Finland, Georgia, Germany, Grenada, Holland, Hungary, Iceland, Ireland, Jamaica, Lebanon, Lesotho, Liberia, Moldova, Morocco, Myanmar, Namibia, Nigeria, Romania, Senegal, Somalia, St Lucia, Tunisia, Ukraine, Uruguay, Vanuatu, Vatican, Vietnam
08 Barbados, Botswana, Bulgaria, Cambodia, Cameroon, Colombia, Djibouti, Dominica, Ethiopia, Honduras, Kiribati, Malaysia, Maldives, Mongolia, Pakistan, Paraguay, Portugal, Slovakia, Slovenia, Sri Lanka, Suriname, Tanzania, Thailand, Zimbabwe
09 Argentina, Australia, Cape Verde, Costa Rica, East Timor, Guatemala, Indonesia, Lithuania, Macedonia, Mauritius, Nicaragua, San Marino, Singapore, Swaziland, The Gambia, Venezuela
10 Azerbaijan, Bangladesh, El Salvador, Kazakhstan, Kyrgyzstan, Luxembourg, Madagascar, Mauritania, Mozambique, New Zealand, North Korea, Seychelles, South Korea, Tajikistan, The Bahamas, Uzbekistan
11 Afghanistan, Burkina Faso, Côte d'Ivoire, Deutschland, Philippines, Saudi Arabia, Sierra Leone, South Africa, Switzerland
12 Guinea-Bissau, Turkmenistan
13 Czech Republic, Liechtenstein, United Kingdom, Western Sahara
14 Papua New Guinea, Solomon Islands, The Netherlands
15 Marshall Islands, St Kitts and Nevis
16 Brunei Darussalam, Equatorial Guinea
17 Antigua and Barbuda, Dominican Republic, Trinidad and Tobago
18 São Tomé and Príncipe, United Arab Emirates
19 Serbia and Montenegro
20 Bosnia and Herzegovina
21 United States of America
22 Central African Republic
25 St Vincent and the Grenadines
27 Federated States of Micronesia
28 Democratic Republic of the Congo

Country codes include:

03 ABW, AFG, AGO, AIA, ALB, AND, ANT, ARE, ARG, ARM, ASM, ATA, ATF, ATG, AUS, AUT, AZE, BDI, BEL, BEN, BFA, BGD, BGR, BHR, BHS, BIH, BLR, BLZ, BMU, BOL, BRA, BRB, BRN, BTN, BVT, BWA, CAF, CAN, CCK, CHE, CHL, CHN, CIV, CMR, COD, COG, COK, COL, COM, CPV, CRI, CUB, CXR, CYM, CYP, CZE, DEU, DJI, DMA, DNK, DOM, DZA, ECU, EGY, ERI, ESH, ESP, EST, ETH, FIN, FJI, FLK, FRA, FRO, FSM, GAB, GBR, GEO, GHA, GIB, GIN, GLP, GMB, GNB, GNQ, GRC, GRD, GRL, GTM, GUF, GUM, GUY, HGK, HMD, HND, HRV, HTI, HUN, IDN, IMN, IND, IOT, IRL, IRN, IRQ, ISL, ISR, ITA, JAM, JOR, JPN, KAZ, KEN, KGZ, KHM, KIR, KNA, KOR, KWT, LAO, LBN, LBR, LBY, LCA, LIE, LKA, LSO, LTU, LUX, LVA, MAC, MAR, MCO, MDA, MDG, MDV, MEX, MHL, MKD, MLI, MLT, MMR, MNG, MNP, MOZ, MRT, MSR, MTQ, MUS, MWI, MYS, MYT, NAM, NCL, NER, NFK, NGA, NIC, NIU, NLD, NOR, NPL, NRU, NZL, OMN, PAK, PAN, PCN, PER, PHL, PLW, PNG, POL, PRI, PRK, PRT, PRY, PYF, QAT, REU, ROU, RUS, RWA, SAU, SDN, SEN, SGP, SHN, SJM, SLB, SLE, SLV, SMR, SOM, SPM, STP, SUR, SVK, SVN, SWE, SWZ, SYC, SYR, TCA, TCD, TGO, THA, TJK, TKL, TKM, TLS, TON, TTO, TUN, TUR, TUV, TWN, TZA, UGA, UKR, URY, USA, UZB, VAT, VCT, VEN, VGB, VIR, VNM, VUT, WLF, WSM, YEM, YUG, ZAF, ZMB, ZWE

Former country names include:

04 Siam, USSR
05 Burma, Zaire
06 Bengal, Ceylon, Persia, Urundi
07 Dahomey, Formosa
08 Rhodesia
09 Abyssinia, Indochina, Kampuchea, Nyasaland
10 Basutoland, Ivory Coast, Senegambia, Tanganyika, Upper Volta, Yugoslavia
11 Dutch Guiana, French Sudan, New Hebrides, Ubangi Shari
12 Bechuanaland, French Guinea, Ruanda-Urundi
13 British Guiana, Ellice Islands, Khmer Republic, Spanish Guinea, Spanish Sahara, Trucial States
14 Czechoslovakia, French Togoland, Gilbert Islands
15 British Honduras, British Togoland, Dutch East Indies, South West Africa

See also **Africa**; **America**; **Arab**; **Asia**; **commonwealth**; **Europe**; **Middle East**

• open country

03 lay, lea, lee, ley **04** moor, veld, wold
05 field, heath, plain, range, veldt, weald

countryman, countrywoman

03 hob **04** boor, hick, hind **05** Hodge, yokel **06** farmer, rustic, yeoman
07 bumpkin, hayseed, landman, peasant **09** hillbilly **10** clodhopper, compatriot, provincial **11** bushwhacker
12 backwoodsman **13** fellow citizen
14 fellow national

countryside

06 nature **07** country, scenery
08 farmland, moorland, outdoors
09 green belt, landscape, rural area

countrywoman *see* **countryman, countrywoman**

county

02 Co **04** area **05** count, shire, state
06 parish, region **08** district, province
09 comitatus, territory **10** department

Counties and administrative areas of England:

04 Kent, York
05 Derby, Devon, Essex, Luton, Poole
06 Dorset, Durham, Halton, London, Medway, Slough, Surrey, Torbay
07 Cumbria, Norfolk, Reading, Rutland, Suffolk, Swindon
08 Cheshire, Plymouth, Somerset, Thurrock
09 Blackpool, Hampshire, Leicester, Wiltshire, Wokingham
10 Darlington, Derbyshire, East Sussex, Hartlepool, Lancashire, Merseyside, Nottingham, Portsmouth, Shropshire, Warrington, West Sussex
11 Bournemouth, Isle of Wight, Oxfordshire, Southampton, Tyne and Wear
12 Bedfordshire, Lincolnshire, Milton Keynes, Peterborough, Stoke-on-Trent, Warwickshire, West Midlands
13 City of Bristol, Herefordshire, Hertfordshire, Middlesbrough, North Somerset, Southend-on-Sea, Staffordshire, West Berkshire, West Yorkshire
14 Cambridgeshire, Leicestershire, Northumberland, North Yorkshire,

South Yorkshire, Stockton-on-Tees, Worcestershire
15 Bracknell Forest, Brighton and Hove, Buckinghamshire, Gloucestershire, Nottinghamshire
16 Northamptonshire, Telford and Wrekin
17 Greater Manchester, North Lincolnshire
18 Redcar and Cleveland
19 Blackburn with Darwen
20 South Gloucestershire, Windsor and Maidenhead
21 East Riding of Yorkshire, North East Lincolnshire
22 City of Kingston upon Hull
24 Bath and North East Somerset, Cornwall and Isles of Scilly

County abbreviations include:

02 Mx
03 Dev, Dur, Ess, Mon, Som, Sur, War
04 Beds, Camb, Ches, Corn, Cumb, Dors, Glos, Mont, Oxon, Suff
05 Berks, Bucks, Cambs, Cards, Derby, E Suss, Hants, Herts, Lancs, Leics, Lincs, Middx, Notts, Wilts, Worcs, Yorks
06 Caerns, Shrops, Staffs
08 Northumb
09 Northants

Counties of Ireland:

04 Cork, Leix, Mayo
05 Cavan, Clare, Kerry, Laois, Louth, Meath, Sligo
06 Carlow, Dublin, Galway, Offaly
07 Donegal, Kildare, Leitrim, Wexford, Wicklow
08 Kilkenny, Laoighis, Limerick, Longford, Monaghan
09 Roscommon, Tipperary, Waterford, Westmeath

See also **district**

• home counties
02 SE

• county town *see* **town**

coup

04 blow, deed, feat **05** stunt, upset **06** action, barter, putsch, revolt, stroke **07** exploit, success, triumph **08** exchange, overturn, takeover, uprising **09** coup d'état, manoeuvre, overthrow, rebellion **10** revolution **11** tour de force **12** insurrection, masterstroke **14** accomplishment

coup de grâce

04 kill **06** kibosh **07** quietus **08** clincher **09** death blow **11** kiss of death **13** finishing blow

coup d'état

04 coup **06** putsch, revolt **08** takeover, uprising **09** overthrow, rebellion **10** revolution **12** insurrection

couple

◇ *repetition indicator*

03 duo, two, wed **04** ally, bind, join, link, mate, meng, ming, pair, tway, yoke **05** brace, clasp, hitch, marry, match, menge, twain, unite **06** attach, buckle, fasten, lovers, marrow **07** combine, conjoin, connect, diarchy, shackle, twosome **08** double up, partners **09** accompany, associate, integrate, newlyweds **12** Darby and Joan **14** husband and wife

coupon

04 form, slip, stub **05** check, token **06** billet, docket, ticket **07** voucher **11** certificate, counterfoil

courage

04 grit, guts **05** balls, heart, metal, moxie, nerve, pluck, spunk, valor **06** bottle, daring, mettle, spirit, valour **07** bravery, cojones, heroism, stomach **08** audacity, backbone, boldness, coraggio, gumption **09** fortitude, gallantry **10** resolution **11** intrepidity **12** fearlessness **13** dauntlessness, determination

courageous

04 bold, game **05** brave, gutsy, hardy, wight **06** ballsy, daring, feisty, heroic, manful, plucky, spunky **07** gallant, valiant **08** fearless, generous, intrepid, resolute, valorous **09** audacious, dauntless **10** determined, stomachous **11** adventurous, full-hearted, high-hearted, indomitable, lion-hearted **12** stout-hearted

• courageous person
04 hero, lion

courageously

06 boldly **07** bravely **09** gallantly, valiantly **10** fearlessly, heroically, intrepidly, resolutely **11** audaciously, dauntlessly, indomitably **13** adventurously

courier

03 rep **05** envoy, guide **06** bearer, escort, herald, legate, nuncio, runner **07** carrier, postman **08** emissary **09** estafette, messenger, tour guide **10** pursuivant **11** travel guide **13** dispatch rider **14** representative

course

03 ren, rin, run, way **04** beat, dash, dish, flow, gush, hunt, lane, line, mess, mode, move, part, path, plan, pour, race, rise, road, rota, span, tack, term, time **05** ambit, chase, lapse, march, orbit, order, route, spell, stage, surge, sweet, track, trail **06** entrée, follow, ground, manner, method, period, policy, pursue, remove, series, stream, system, voyage **07** advance, channel, circuit, classes, current, dessert, lessons, passage, passing, process, pudding, regimen, starter, studies **08** approach, duration, lectures, movement, progress, run after, schedule, sequence, syllabus **09** appetizer, direction, entremets, procedure, programme, racetrack, unfolding **10** curriculum, flight path, golf course, main course, racecourse, succession, trajectory **11** development, furtherance, hors d'oeuvre, progression

See also **compass**; **golf**; **race**; **racecourse**

• alter course
04 gybe, jibe, tack, wear

• deviate from course
03 bag, yaw

• direct course
03 aim **04** head

• fixed course
03 rut **04** race

• in due course
02 so **06** in time **07** finally **09** in due time **10** eventually **13** all in good time, sooner or later

• of course
02 ay **03** aye **04** sure **05** natch **06** surely **07** no doubt **08** to be sure **09** certainly, naturally **10** by all means, definitely **11** bien entendu, doubtlessly, indubitably, undoubtedly **12** indisputably **13** needless to say, without a doubt **14** not unnaturally

• part of course
03 leg

court

02 ct **03** bar, Hof, see, sew, sue, woo, wow **04** date, quad, ring, risk, seek, yard **05** alley, arena, bench, chase, green, patio, plaza, suite, track, train **06** castle, go with, ground, incite, invite, palace, piazza, prompt, pursue, square **07** attract, cortège, flatter, provoke, retinue, solicit **08** cloister, game area, go steady, pander to, try to win **09** courtyard, cultivate, curtilage, enclosure, entourage, esplanade, forecourt, go out with, household, judiciary, peristyle **10** attendants, cozy up with, judicatory, judicature, praetorium, quadrangle **11** conservancy, go round with, playing area **12** go around with **13** spheristerion **14** royal residence **15** curry favour with

Courts include:

03 law
04 eyre, Fehm, high, Lyon, moot, open, Vehm
05 burgh, civil, crown, prize, trial, World, youth
06 appeal, Arches, church, claims, county, family, Honour, police, record
07 appeals, assizes, borough, circuit, Diplock, divorce, federal, justice, Probate, Session, sheriff, Supreme
08 chancery, coroner's, criminal, district, juvenile, kangaroo, Requests, superior, tribunal
09 children's, Exchequer, Faculties, municipal, Old Bailey, Piepowder, Sanhedrim, Sanhedrin, the Arches
10 Commercial, commissary, consistory, Divisional, Piepowders, Protection
11 Arbitration, Common Bench, Common Pleas, High Justice, magistrates', police-court, Prerogative, small claims
12 Aulic Council, court-martial, House of Lords, Privy Council
13 first instance

14 Criminal Appeal, High Commission, High Justiciary
15 Central Criminal, European Justice, Lord Chancellor's

• **bring to court**
04 file
• **court case**
04 suit 05 trial 06 action 07 lawsuit
• **court house**
02 ch
• **in court**
02 up 08 at the bar
• **right to hold court**
03 sac, soc
• **take to court**
03 law, sue

courteous
04 hend, kind 05 civil 06 polite, urbane 07 affable, courtly, gallant, refined, tactful 08 debonair, gracious, ladylike, mannerly, obliging, polished, well-bred 09 attentive 10 chivalrous, debonnaire, diplomatic, respectful, well-spoken 11 considerate, deferential, gentlemanly 12 well-mannered

courteously
06 kindly 07 civilly 08 politely, urbanely 09 gallantly, refinedly, tactfully 10 graciously, obligingly 11 attentively 12 chivalrously, respectfully 13 considerately, deferentially 14 diplomatically

courtesy
04 tact 06 comity, curtsy, devoir, favour, gentry 07 manners, respect 08 breeding, chivalry, civility, kindness, urbanity 09 attention, deference, etiquette, gallantry, gentility 10 generosity, gentilesse, politeness, refinement 11 good manners 12 good breeding, graciousness 13 consideration

courtier
04 lady, lord, page 05 noble, toady 07 steward, subject 08 follower, liegeman, nobleman 09 attendant, cup-bearer, flatterer, sycophant 11 train-bearer 13 lady-in-waiting

courtly
05 aulic, civil 06 formal, lordly, polite 07 elegant, gallant, refined, stately 08 decorous, gracious, high-bred, obliging, polished 09 dignified 10 chivalrous, flattering 11 ceremonious 12 aristocratic

courtship
04 suit 05 spoon 06 affair, dating, wooing 07 chasing, pursuit, romance 08 courting, going-out, love-suit 10 attentions, lovemaking 11 going steady

courtyard
04 area, quad, ward, yard 05 court, garth, marae, patio, plaza 06 atrium, square 07 cortile 08 cloister 09 enclosure, esplanade, forecourt 10 quadrangle

cove
03 bay, man 04 chap 05 bight, creek, fiord, firth, inlet 06 cavern 07 estuary

covenant
03 vow 04 bond, deed, pact 05 agree, trust 06 engage, pledge, treaty 07 compact, promise 08 contract, warranty 09 agreement, concordat, indenture, stipulate, testament, undertake 10 commitment, convention, engagement 11 arrangement, stipulation, undertaking 12 dispensation

cover
◇ *containment indicator*
◇ *hidden indicator*
02 do, go 03 cap, cup, hap, hat, lay, lep, lid, set, top 04 bury, cake, case, coat, cour, cowl, daub, deck, film, heal, heel, hele, hide, hood, leap, mask, pall, skin, tell, tilt, veil, vele, wrap 05 apron, brood, cloak, cloke, coure, cross, dress, duvet, front, guard, layer, paten, quoit, throw, treat 06 attire, be over, canopy, carpet, clothe, defend, embody, encase, extend, façade, incase, insure, jacket, mantle, pay for, refuge, report, review, screen, shield, shroud, sleeve, spread, survey, take in, toilet, travel 07 analyse, bedding, binding, blanket, coating, conceal, contain, cover-up, defence, embrace, envelop, examine, garment, include, involve, journey, measure, narrate, obscure, overlay, package, plaster, present, pretext, protect, put over, relieve, replace, shelter, stretch, swaddle, wrapper, wreathe 08 accoutre, bedcover, bespread, blankets, clothing, comprise, consider, continue, covering, deal with, deputize, describe, disguise, enshroud, envelope, go across, overveil, pretence, security, traverse 09 assurance, bedspread, encompass, fill in for, indemnify, indemnity, insurance, make up for, place over, safeguard, sanctuary, talk about, whitewash 10 balance out, bedclothes, camouflage, complicity, conspiracy, extend over, overspread, protection, provide for, recompense, stand in for, travel over, underwrite, write about 11 be enough for, concealment, confederate, hiding-place, incorporate, investigate, pinch-hit for, smokescreen 12 compensation, take over from 13 compensate for, give details of 14 counterbalance 15 give an account of, indemnification
• **cover up**
◇ *hidden indicator*
03 hap 04 hide 05 blank, fudge 06 hush up 07 conceal, repress 08 enshroud, hoodwink, keep dark, suppress 09 dissemble, gloss over, whitewash 10 keep secret
• **original cover**
02 OC

coverage
04 item 05 story 06 report 07 account, blanket, reports 08 analysis 09 reportage, reporting 11 description 13 investigation

covering
03 cap, lag, rug, top 04 aril, cape, case, coat, cope, film, hood, husk, mask, pall, roof, skin 05 armor, cloak, cloke, cover, crust, layer, shell 06 armour, awning, carpet, casing, sheath, tegmen, veneer 07 blanket, coating, housing, overlay, roofing, shelter 08 clothing, pavilion, sheeting, wrapping 09 tarpaulin 10 encasement, incasement, integument, overlaying, protection 11 descriptive, explanatory 12 accompanying, introductory

covert
06 hidden, secret, sneaky, veiled 07 furtive, private, shelter 08 sidelong, stealthy, ulterior 09 concealed, disguised, underhand 10 dissembled 11 clandestine, unsuspected 13 subreptitious, surreptitious, under the table

covertly
08 secretly 09 furtively, privately 15 surreptitiously

cover-up
05 front 06 façade, screen 08 pretence 09 deception, whitewash 10 complicity, conspiracy 11 concealment, smokescreen

covet
04 envy, want 05 crave, fancy 06 desire 07 long for 08 begrudge, yearn for 09 hanker for, hunger for, lust after, thirst for

covetous
06 greedy 07 craving, envious, jealous, longing, wanting 08 desirous, grasping, yearning 09 hankering, hungering, rapacious, thirsting 10 avaricious, insatiable 11 acquisitive, close-fisted, close-handed

covey
03 nid, set 04 band, bevy 05 brood, flock, group, hatch, party, skein 06 flight 07 cluster, company

cow
02 ox 03 mog 04 boss, mart, neat, quey, runt 05 besom, bossy, bully, daunt, doddy, moggy, mooly, muley, scare, stirk 06 crummy, dismay, hawkey, hawkie, heifer, humlie, Jersey, milker, moggie, mulley, rattle, rother, subdue 07 kouprey, overawe, unnerve 08 Alderney, browbeat, domineer, Friesian, frighten, springer 09 terrorize 10 discourage, dishearten, intimidate

coward
03 cat 04 Noel, sook, wimp, wuss 05 dingo, sissy 06 craven 07 chicken, cowherd, crybaby, dastard, hilding, nithing, viliaco, viliago 08 cowheard, deserter, poltroon, recreant, renegade, villagio, villiaco, villiago, weakling 10 faint-heart, poultroone,

Scaramouch, scaredy-cat
11 Scaramouche, yellow-belly

cowardice
08 timidity **11** fearfulness
12 cowardliness, timorousness
13 pusillanimity, spinelessness
14 spiritlessness

cowardly
04 nesh, soft, weak **05** faint, mangy, timid **06** coward, cowish, craven, mangey, maungy, scared, yellow
07 chicken, dastard, fearful, gutless, hilding, jittery, meacock, nithing, unmanly, wimpish **08** timorous, unheroic **09** dastardly, spineless, weak-kneed **10** spiritless **11** lily-livered, milk-livered **12** faint-hearted, weak-spirited, white-livered **13** pusillanimous, yellow bellied **14** chicken-hearted, chicken-livered

cowboy
05 cheat, rogue, waddy **06** drover, gaucho, herder, rascal, waddie
07 bungler, cowhand, cowpoke, herdboy, rancher, vaquero
08 buckaroo, buckayro, buckeroo, herdsman, ranchero, stockman, swindler, wrangler **09** cattleman, fraudster, scoundrel **10** cowpuncher
11 incompetent **12** bronco-buster, cattleherder

cower
04 ruck **05** quail, quake, shake, skulk, wince **06** cringe, crouch, flinch, grovel, recoil, shiver, shrink **07** croodle, tremble **08** draw back

cowhouse
04 byre **07** shippen, shippon

co-worker
04 aide, ally **06** helper **07** comrade, partner **08** confrère, teammate, workmate **09** assistant, associate, auxiliary, colleague, companion
11 confederate **12** collaborator, fellow worker

cows
02 ky **03** kye **04** kine, neat

coxcomb
03 fop **04** head, prig **07** princox
08 popinjay, princock

coy
03 shy **04** arch, nice, prim **05** squab, timid **06** caress, demure, modest, skeigh **07** bashful, disdain, evasive, prudish **08** backward, reserved, retiring, skittish **09** diffident, kittenish, reticence, shrinking, squeamish, withdrawn **10** coquettish **11** flirtatious
12 self-effacing

coyly
06 primly **07** timidly **08** demurely, modestly **09** bashfully, evasively, prudishly **11** diffidently **12** coquettishly
13 flirtatiously **14** self-effacingly

crab
04 claw, cock **05** decry, scrog, wreck
06 Cancer, hermit, partan, scrawl
07 fiddler, limulus, pagurid, souring, wilding **08** horseman, obstruct, ochidore, pagurian **09** criticize, frustrate, scrog-bush, scrog-buss, soft-shell **12** saucepan-fish

crabbed, crabby
04 sour, tart **05** acrid, cross, harsh, surly, testy, tough **06** cranky, morose, snappy **07** awkward, cankery, fretful, grouchy, iracund, prickly **08** cankered, captious, churlish, perverse, petulant, snappish **09** crotchety, difficult, fractious, irascible, irritable, splenetic
10 ill-natured **11** acrimonious, bad-tempered, ill-tempered
12 cantankerous, iracundulous, misanthropic

crack
◇ *anagram indicator*
02 go **03** ace, dig, gag, gap, hit, pop, try **04** bang, bash, beat, blow, boom, bump, chap, chat, chip, chop, clap, dope, dunt, fent, flaw, gibe, jest, joke, leak, line, quip, rent, rift, rima, rock, shot, slap, snap, stab, star **05** boast, break, burst, check, chink, cleft, clout, craic, crash, craze, joint, shake, slash, smack, solve, split, whack, whirl
06 breach, cave in, cavity, choice, cleave, cranny, decode, effort, expert, go bang, gossip, report, spring, strike, wallop **07** attempt, crackle, crevice, decrypt, dope out, explode, fissure, resolve, rupture, shatter, skilful, skilled, unravel, work out **08** collapse, crevasse, decipher, detonate, fracture, fragment, one-liner, repartee, splinter, superior, top-notch **09** break down, brilliant, excellent, explosion, figure out, first-rate, ready-wash, wisecrack, witticism **10** detonation, first-class, go to pieces, hand-picked **11** lose control, outstanding **15** find the answer to

• **crack down on**
03 end **04** stop **05** check, crush, limit
07 confine, control, repress **08** restrict, suppress **10** act against, get tough on, put a stop to **11** clamp down on

• **crack up**
◇ *anagram indicator*
05 go mad, laugh **06** praise **07** go crazy **08** collapse **09** break down, fall about, fall apart **10** go to pieces
11 go ballistic, lose control **14** split your sides

crackdown
03 end **04** stop **05** check **08** crushing
09 clampdown **10** repression
11 suppression

cracked
◇ *anagram indicator*
03 mad **04** bats, daft, nuts, torn
05 barmy, batty, crazy, harsh, loony, nutty, split **06** broken, crazed, faulty, flawed, insane **07** chapped, chipped, damaged, foolish, idiotic, starred
08 crackpot, deranged, dingbats, fissured **09** defective, imperfect
12 crackbrained, round the bend
13 off your rocker, out of your tree

crackers
◇ *anagram indicator*
03 mad **04** daft, nuts **05** batty, crazy, loony, matza, matzo, nutty **06** matzah, matzoh **07** cracked, foolish, idiotic
08 crackpot **10** unbalanced
12 crackbrained, round the bend

crackle
04 snap **05** crack, money **06** rustle, sizzle **08** crepitus **09** banknotes, crepitate **10** paper money
11 crepitation, decrepitate
13 decrepitation

crackpot
◇ *anagram indicator*
04 fool **05** freak, idiot, loony
06 nutter, weirdo **07** nutcase, oddball
10 basket case

cradle
03 bed, cot **04** base, crib, hold, lull, prop, rest, rock, tend **05** fount, frame, mount, nurse, stand **06** holder, nestle, origin, rocker, source, spring
07 berceau, infancy, nurture, shelter, support **08** bassinet, carry-cot, cunabula, mounting **09** beginning, framework, travel-cot **10** birthplace, gold-washer, incunabula, wellspring
11 Moses basket **12** fountain-head
13 starting-point

craft
◇ *anagram indicator*
03 art, job **04** boat, line, ship, work
05 flair, guile, knack, skill, trade, wiles
06 deceit, talent, vessel **07** ability, calling, cunning, finesse, foxship, mastery, pursuit, sleight, slyness
08 activity, aircraft, aptitude, artistry, business, deftness, subtlety, trickery, vocation **09** dexterity, expertise, handiwork, ingenuity, sharpness, spaceship, technique **10** adroitness, artfulness, astuteness, cleverness, craftiness, employment, expertness, handicraft, occupation, shrewdness, spacecraft **11** cunningness, deviousness, skilfulness, workmanship
12 fiendishness, landing craft
13 deceitfulness, inventiveness
15 imaginativeness, resourcefulness

See also **art**; **ship**

craftily
◇ *anagram indicator*
05 slyly **08** artfully, astutely, shrewdly
09 cunningly, deviously **10** guilefully
11 deceitfully **12** fraudulently

craftsman, craftswoman
05 maker, smith **06** artist, expert, master, wright **07** artisan, artsman, workman **08** mechanic **09** artificer, tradesman **10** technician
11 tradeswoman **12** craftsperson, tradesperson **13** skilled worker

See also **artist**

craftsmanship
05 skill **07** mastery **08** artistry
09 dexterity, expertise, technique
11 skilfulness, workmanship

craftswoman *see* **craftsman, craftswoman**

crafty
◇ *anagram indicator*
03 sly **04** foxy, slim, wily **05** canny, loopy, sharp **06** artful, astute, knacky, shrewd, subtle **07** crooked, cunning, devious, tricksy, versute **08** guileful, knackish, scheming **09** conniving, deceitful, designing, subdolous **10** fraudulent **11** calculating, duplicitous **12** disingenuous **13** Machiavellian

crag
03 tor **04** neck, noup, peak, rock **05** bluff, cliff, craig, heuch, heugh, ridge, scarp, stoss **06** throat **08** pinnacle **10** escarpment

craggy
05 rocky, rough, stony **06** cliffy, jagged, marked, rugged, uneven **07** cliffed, cragged **09** rough-hewn **11** precipitous **13** weather-beaten

cram
03 bag, jam, lie, ram **04** crap, fill, glut, pack, pang, stap, stop, swot, tuck **05** crowd, crush, farce, force, frank, gorge, grind, mug up, press, prime, stuff **06** fill up, revise, stodge **07** compact, squeeze **08** bone up on, compress, overfeed, overfill **09** overcrowd, study hard

cramp
03 tie **04** ache, pain, pang, rein **05** check, crick, limit, spasm **06** arrest, bridle, hamper, hinder, impede, narrow, stitch, stymie, thwart, twinge **07** confine, cramped, inhibit, shackle **08** handicap, obstruct, restrain, restrict **09** constrain, constrict, frustrate, hamstring, restraint, stiffness **10** convulsion **11** contraction **14** pins and needles **15** overuse syndrome, scrivener's palsy

cramped
04 full, poky **05** small, tight **06** narrow, packed **07** bounded, crabbed, crowded, squeezy **08** closed in, confined, hemmed in, niggling, overfull, squashed, squeezed **09** congested, jam-packed **10** compressed, restricted **11** constricted, overcrowded **12** incommodious **13** uncomfortable

crane
05 davit, hoist, Jenny, sarus, winch **06** brolga, hooper, jigger, tackle **07** cranium, derrick, whooper **08** adjutant **10** demoiselle **12** adjutant bird, cherry picker **14** block and tackle **15** native companion

crank
04 kook, whim **05** freak, idiot, loony, wince, winch **06** madman, nutter, weirdo **07** oddball **08** crackpot **09** character, eccentric **11** amphetamine
• **crank up**
05 add to **06** hike up, step up **07** build up, further **08** increase **09** intensify **10** strengthen

cranky
◇ *anagram indicator*
03 fey, odd **04** tart **05** cross, dotty, harsh, queer, shaky, surly, testy, wacky **06** crabby, Fifish, screwy, snappy **07** awkward, bizarre, crabbed, grouchy, prickly, strange **08** freakish, peculiar, unsteady **09** crotchety, difficult, eccentric, irritable **11** bad-tempered, ill-tempered **12** cantankerous **13** idiosyncratic **14** unconventional

cranny
03 gap **04** hole, nook, rent, slit **05** chink, cleft, crack **07** crevice, fissure, opening **08** cleavage **10** interstice

crash
◇ *anagram indicator*
03 din, hit, ram **04** bang, bash, boom, bump, clap, dash, fail, fall, fold, rack, ruin, thud, wham **05** break, clang, clank, clash, ditch, frush, knock, pitch, pound, prang, rapid, shunt, smash, thump, wreck **06** batter, bingle, cut out, fold up, fragor, go bust, go into, go phut, pack up, pile-up, plunge, racket, shiver, topple, urgent **07** clatter, collide, failure, founder, go kaput, go under, run into, shatter, smash-up, thunder **08** accident, collapse, downfall, fracture, fragment, meltdown, splinter **09** break down, collision, drive into, emergency, explosion, immediate, intensive, smash into **10** bankruptcy, depression, plough into, telescoped **11** accelerated, black Monday, come a gutser, go to the wall, malfunction, stop working, thunderclap **12** concentrated, disintegrate, go on the blink **13** round-the-clock

crass
04 naff, rude **05** crude, dense, gross, ocker **06** clumsy, coarse, oafish, obtuse, stupid **07** boorish, witless **08** tactless, unsubtle **09** tasteless, unrefined **10** blundering, indelicate **11** insensitive **15** unsophisticated

crassly
06 rudely **07** crudely **08** clumsily, coarsely, stupidly **10** tactlessly **11** tastelessly **12** indelicately **13** insensitively

crate
03 box, car **04** case, kist **05** chest, plane, seron **06** seroon **08** tea chest **09** container **10** packing-box **11** packing-case

crater
03 dip, pit **04** bowl, hole, maar **05** abyss, basin, chasm **06** cavity, hollow **07** caldera **09** shell-hole **10** depression

cravat
05 scarf, stock **06** o'erlay **07** overlay, owrelay, soubise **09** neckcloth, steenkirk, steinkirk

crave
03 beg **04** need, want, wish **05** claim, covet, fancy **06** desire, hunger **07** dream of, long for, longing, pant for, pine for, require, sigh for **08** yearn for **09** hunger for, lust after, thirst for **10** be dying for **11** hanker after

craven
04 soft, weak **05** timid **06** afraid, coward, scared, yellow **07** chicken, fearful, gutless **08** cowardly, poltroon, recreant, timorous, unheroic **09** spineless, weak-kneed **10** spiritless **11** lily-livered **12** faint-hearted, mean-spirited, weak-spirited, white-livered **13** pusillanimous **14** chicken-hearted, chicken-livered

craving
04 lust, need, pica, urge, wish **06** desire, greedy, hunger, pining, thirst **07** longing, malacia, panting, sighing **08** appetent, appetite, yearning **09** hankering **10** dipsomania, hydromania, methomania **11** toxicomania **13** morphinomania

crawl
04 drag, edge, fawn, inch, knee, swim, teem **05** creep, snail, swarm, toady **06** cringe, grovel, kowtow, seethe, squirm, suck up, writhe **07** bristle, flatter, slither, wriggle **08** be full of **09** be all over, freestyle **10** move slowly **11** curry favour **12** bow and scrape, go on all fours **13** advance slowly **14** be obsequious to
• **crawler**
06 insect

crayfish
05 yabby **06** gilgie, jilgie, marron, yabbie

craze
03 bug, fad **04** buzz, flaw, mode, rage, ramp, whim **05** crack, mania, thing, trend, vogue **06** frenzy, furore, impair, weaken **07** fashion, novelty, passion **08** insanity **09** melomania, obsession, the latest, typomania **10** anglomania, anthomania, enthusiasm **11** acronymania, infatuation, tulipomania **12** orchidomania, potichomania, theatromania **13** preoccupation

crazed
◇ *anagram indicator*
03 mad **04** nuts, wild **05** berko, crazy, loony **06** insane **07** berserk, lunatic **08** demented, deranged, unhinged **09** up the pole **10** moonstruck, unbalanced **12** moon-stricken, round the bend **13** off your rocker, out of your mind, round the twist

crazily
◇ *anagram indicator*
05 madly **06** wildly **08** insanely **09** manically **11** frantically **12** frenetically

crazy
◇ *anagram indicator*
03 mad, odd, wet **04** avid, bats, daft,

fond, gaga, gyte, keen, loco, nuts, wild, zany **05** barmy, batty, buggy, daffy, dippy, dotty, flaky, gonzo, loony, loopy, manic, nutty, potty, silly, wacko, wacky, wiggy **06** absurd, ardent, crazed, cuckoo, dottle, fruity, insane, maniac, mental, raving, screwy, stupid, unwise **07** bananas, barking, berserk, bonkers, cracked, devoted, dottled, foolish, frantic, haywire, idiotic, lunatic, meshuga, rickety, smitten, strange, zealous **08** crackers, crackpot, demented, deranged, dingbats, doolally, frenetic, peculiar, unhinged **09** disturbed, enamoured, fanatical, foolhardy, half-baked, imprudent, infuriate, ludicrous, lymphatic, pixilated, senseless, up the wall **10** bestraught, distracted, distraught, frantic mad, infatuated, off the wall, off your nut, outrageous, out to lunch, passionate, pixillated, ridiculous, unbalanced **11** hare-brained, impractical, nonsensical, not all there, off the rails, off your head, unrealistic **12** crackbrained, enthusiastic, mad as a hatter, off your chump, preposterous, round the bend **13** impracticable, irresponsible, off your rocker, out of your head, out of your mind, out of your tree, round the twist **14** off your trolley, wrong in the head

• **go crazy**

◇ *anagram indicator*

04 flip **05** go ape, go mad **06** blow up, wig out **09** go bananas **11** flip your lid, go ballistic **15** lose your marbles

creak

04 rasp **05** grate, grind, groan **06** scrape, screak, squeak, squeal **07** scratch, screech

creaky

05 rusty **07** grating, rasping, squeaky, unoiled **08** grinding, groaning, scraping **09** squeaking, squealing **10** scratching, screeching

cream

03 oil **04** best, pale, pick, ream, skim **05** creme, élite, ivory, milky, paste, pasty, prime, salve, sweet **06** finest, flower, lotion, thrash **07** unguent **08** cleanser, cosmetic, emulsion, liniment, off-white, ointment **09** emollient **10** choice part, select part **11** application, preparation **13** whitish-yellow **14** crème de la crème, pick of the bunch, yellowish-white

creamy

04 oily, pale, rich **05** ivory, milky, pasty, reamy, thick **06** smooth **07** buttery, velvety **08** off-white **13** cream-coloured, whitish-yellow **14** yellowish-white

crease

04 fold, kris, line, ruck, tuck **05** crimp, pleat, ridge **06** creese, furrow, groove, kreese, pucker, ruckle, rumple, runkle **07** crinkle, crumple, wreathe, wrinkle **09** corrugate **10** line of life **11** corrugation

• **crease up**

05 amuse **09** make laugh

create

04 coin, form, make **05** build, cause, erect, found, frame, hatch, mould, set up, shape **06** design, devise, invent, invest, lead to, ordain **07** appoint, compose, concoct, develop, install, produce **08** engender, generate, initiate, occasion, result in **09** construct, establish, fabricate, formulate, institute, originate **10** bring about, give rise to, inaugurate **13** cause to happen **14** bring into being

creation

◇ *anagram indicator*

04 life, work **05** birth, world **06** cosmos, design, making, nature, origin **07** concept, genesis, product **08** universe **09** formation, handiwork, handywork, invention, work of art **10** biopoiesis, brainchild, conception, concoction, everything, foundation, generation, initiation, innovation, production **11** achievement, chef d'oeuvre, composition, development, fabrication, institution, masterpiece, origination, procreation **12** constitution, construction **13** establishment

creative

06 clever, gifted **07** fertile **08** artistic, inspired, naturing, original, talented **09** forgetive, ingenious, intuitive, inventive, visionary **10** innovative, productive **11** full of ideas, imaginative, resourceful

creativity

04 gift **06** talent, vision **08** artistry **09** fertility, ingenuity **10** cleverness **11** imagination, inspiration, originality **13** inventiveness **14** productiveness **15** imaginativeness, resourcefulness

creator

03 God **05** maker **06** author, Brahma, father, mother, Ormazd, Ormuzd **07** builder, founder **08** composer, demiurge, designer, inventor, producer **09** architect, Artificer, demiurgus, initiator **10** Ahura Mazda, first cause, originator, prime mover

creature

03 man **04** bird, body, fish, soul, zoon **05** beast, being, human, thing, wight, woman **06** animal, cratur, insect, mortal, person, wretch **07** crathur, critter, crittur **08** organism **10** human being, individual **11** living thing

See also **animal**; **mythical**; **poison**

credence

05 faith, trust **06** belief, credit **07** support **08** reliance **09** sideboard **10** acceptance, confidence, dependence **11** credibility

credentials

04 deed **05** title **06** papers, permit **07** diploma, licence, warrant **08** passport **09** documents, reference **11** certificate, testimonial **12** identity card **13** accreditation, authorization **14** recommendation **15** proof of identity

credibility

04 cred **09** integrity **10** likelihood **11** probability, reliability **12** plausibility **14** reasonableness **15** trustworthiness

credible

06 honest, likely **07** credent, sincere, tenable **08** possible, probable, reliable **09** plausible, thinkable **10** believable, convincing, dependable, imaginable, persuasive, reasonable **11** conceivable, trustworthy

credibly

08 honestly, possibly, reliably **09** plausibly, sincerely, thinkably **10** believably, dependably, imaginably, reasonably **11** conceivably **12** convincingly, persuasively **13** trustworthily

credit

02 cr, HP **03** buy **04** fame, tick **05** asset, boast, faith, glory, kudos, mense, pride, strap, tally, trust **06** accept, assign, belief, charge, esteem, honour, impute, praise, rely on, thanks **07** acclaim, ascribe, believe, put down, swallow, tribute **08** accredit, approval, credence, plaudits, prestige **09** attribute, have faith, laudation **10** confidence, estimation, reputation **11** distinction, pride and joy, recognition, subscribe to **12** commendation **15** acknowledgement

• **in credit**

07 solvent **10** beforehand, in the black

• **on credit**

06 on tick **07** on lay-by, on trust **08** on the tab **09** on account **10** on the slate **12** on the knocker **13** by instalments **14** on hire purchase **15** on the never-never

creditable

04 good **06** worthy **08** laudable **09** admirable, deserving, estimable, excellent, exemplary, reputable **10** honourable **11** commendable, meritorious, respectable, trustworthy **12** praiseworthy

creditably

04 well **09** admirably **10** honourably **11** commendably, excellently, respectably

creditor

02 cr **06** debtee, lender **07** Shylock **08** apprizer **09** loan shark **11** moneylender

credulity

07 naivety **09** silliness, stupidity **10** dupability, simplicity **11** gullibility **13** credulousness **14** uncriticalness

credulous

04 fond **05** naive **06** simple **07** credent, dupable **08** gullable,

gullible, trusting, wide-eyed
10 uncritical **12** overtrusting, unsuspecting

creed
05 canon, credo, dogma, faith
06 belief, Ophism, symbol, tenets
08 articles, doctrine, ideology, standard, teaching **09** catechism, the belief **10** persuasion, principles

creek
03 bay, geo, gio, goe, pow, voe
04 cove, wick **05** bight, brook, crick, fiord, firth, fjord, fleet, inlet **06** slough, stream **07** estuary

creep
04 edge, fawn, fear, geek, grew, grue, inch, worm **05** alarm, crawl, slink, snake, sneak, steal, toady **06** cringe, fawner, grovel, horror, squirm, terror, tiptoe, unease, writhe, yes-man
07 shudder, slither, wriggle **08** disquiet
09 revulsion, sycophant **10** bootlicker
13 move unnoticed

creeper
04 vine **05** liana, plant **06** runner
07 climber, rambler, trailer **08** trailing, woodbind, woodbine **09** Boston ivy
10 ampelopsis, monkey rope, tropaeolum **13** climbing plant, trailing plant
See also **snake**

creepy
05 eerie, scary, weird **06** crawly, spooky **07** macabre, ominous
08 gruesome, horrible, horrific, menacing, sinister **10** disturbing, horrifying, mysterious, terrifying, unpleasant **11** frightening, hair-raising, nightmarish, threatening
13 bloodcurdling, spine-chilling

crescent
04 Cres **06** waxing **07** growing
09 croissant **10** increasing

crescent-shaped
05 moony **06** lunate **07** falcate, lunated, lunular **08** falcated **09** bow-shaped, falciform **12** sickle-shaped

crest
03 mon, top **04** apex, comb, edge, head, knap, mane, peak, tuft **05** badge, chine, crown, plume, ridge **06** cimier, copple, crista, device, emblem, summit, symbol, tassel **07** cornice, feather, panache, regalia, topknot
08 aigrette, caruncle, insignia, pinnacle, surmount **09** cockscomb
10 coat of arms

crestfallen
03 sad **08** dejected, downcast
09 depressed **10** cheesed off, despondent, dispirited
11 discouraged, downhearted
12 disappointed, disconsolate, disheartened **13** in the doldrums
14 down in the dumps

cretin
03 ass, mug, nit **04** clot, dolt, dope, dork, fool, geek, jerk, prat, twit
05 chump, dumbo, dunce, idiot, moron, ninny, schmo, twerp, wally
06 dimwit, nitwit, sucker **07** fathead, halfwit, jughead, pillock, plonker, schmuck **08** imbecile **09** birdbrain, blockhead, ignoramus, simpleton
10 bufflehead, nincompoop

crevasse
03 gap **05** abyss, chasm, cleft, crack, split **07** fissure **11** bergschrund

crevice
03 gap **04** hole, rift, slit **05** break, chink, cleft, crack, split **06** cranny
07 fissure, opening **10** interstice

crew
03 lot, man, mob, set **04** band, crue, gang, pack, ship, team, unit **05** bunch, corps, crowd, eight, force, group, party, squad, troop **06** torpid **07** company
09 lower deck **10** complement

crew member *see* **sailor**; **ship**

crib
03 bed, cot, key **04** copy, lift, pony, putz, trot **05** cheat, horse, pinch, stall, steal **06** cratch, pirate **07** brothel, purloin **08** bassinet, carry-cot, cribbage **09** reproduce, travel-cot
10 plagiarize **11** Moses basket

crick
04 kink, pain, rick **05** cramp, creek, spasm **06** twinge **09** stiffness
10 convulsion

cricket
04 grig **05** stool **09** churr-worm

Cricket teams include:

04 Kent
05 Essex
06 Durham, Surrey, Sussex
08 Somerset, Victoria
09 Glamorgan, Hampshire, Middlesex, Yorkshire
10 Derbyshire, Lancashire, Queensland
12 Warwickshire
13 New South Wales
14 Leicestershire, South Australia, Worcestershire
15 Gloucestershire, Nottinghamshire

Cricket terms include:

01 b, c, M, w
02 by, CC, in, lb, nb, no, on, ro
03 bat, box, bye, CCC, cut, ECB, ICC, lbw, leg, MCC, net, ODI, off, pad, peg, run, six, ton
04 bail, ball, blob, bowl, deep, draw, duck, edge, four, go in, grub, hook, Oval, over, pair, poke, pull, slip, tail, test, tice, walk, wide
05 Ashes, break, c and b, catch, cover, dolly, drive, extra, glide, gully, knock, Lords, mid-on, pitch, plumb, point, silly, skyer, snick, stump
06 appeal, beamer, bowled, bowler, caught, crease, doosra, eleven, glance, googly, ground, howzat, leg bye, long on, maiden, middle, mid-off, no-ball, not out, opener, play on, run out, single, square, stumps, the leg, umpire, whites, wicket, yorker
07 batsman, batting, bouncer, century, declare, dismiss, fielder, grubber, infield, innings, last man, leg side, leg slip, leg spin, long hop, long leg, long off, off spin, on the up, spinner, striker, stumped, wrong'un
08 bodyline, boundary, chinaman, delivery, fielding, flannels, follow on, full toss, how's that, leg guard, long slip, long stop, misfield, off break, off drive, off guard, one-dayer, outfield, pavilion, short leg, sledging, the Ashes, third man
09 batswoman, deep field, fieldsman, hit wicket, inswinger, leg before, leg theory, long field, mid-wicket, overpitch, short slip, square leg, test match, tip and run
10 all-rounder, cover drive, draw stumps, fast bowler, golden duck, leg spinner, maiden over, pace bowler, right guard, scoreboard, seam bowler, silly mid-on, skittle out, spin bowler, twelfth man
11 clean bowled, daisy-cutter, diamond duck, fast bowling, fieldswoman, grass-cutter, ground staff, half-century, limited-over, net practice, one-day match, pace bowling, seam bowling, sight screen, silly mid-off, spin bowling
12 carry your bat, wicketkeeper
13 break your duck, county cricket, keep your end up, maiden century, night-watchman, popping crease
14 off the back foot
15 bowl a maiden over, caught and bowled, leather on willow, leg before wicket, square leg umpire

See also **delivery**

Cricketers, commentators and umpires include:

03 **Fry** (Charles Burgess)
04 **Ames** (Leslie), **Bedi** (Bishen), **Bird** (Dicky), **Hall** (Wesley), **Hick** (Graeme), **Khan** (Imran), **Lara** (Brian), **Lock** (Tony), **Lord** (Thomas)
05 **Abbas** (Zaheer), **Akram** (Wasim), **Allen** (Sir Gubby), **Amiss** (Dennis), **Crowe** (Martin), **Evans** (Godfrey), **Gibbs** (Lance), **Gooch** (Graham), **Gough** (Darren), **Gower** (David), **Grace** (W G), **Greig** (Tony), **Healy** (Ian), **Hobbs** (Sir Jack), **Knott** (Alan), **Laker** (Jim), **Lawry** (William), **Lloyd** (Clive), **Marsh** (Rodney), **Pilch** (Fuller), **Walsh** (Courtney), **Warne** (Shane), **Waugh** (Mark), **Waugh** (Steve)
06 **Arlott** (John), **Bailey** (Trevor), **Benaud** (Richie), **Border** (Allan), **Botham** (Ian), **Cronje** (Hansie), **Dexter** (Ted), **Donald** (Allan), **Dravid** (Rahul), **Edrich** (Bill), **Edrich** (John), **Garner** (Joel), **Hadlee** (Sir Richard), **Haynes** (Desmond), **Hutton** (Len), **Jessop** (Gilbert), **Lillee** (Dennis), **Miller** (Keith), **Rhodes** (Wilfred),

Sobers (Sir Garfield), Thorpe (Graham), Titmus (Fred), Turner (Glenn), Warner (Sir Pelham 'Plum')
07 **Ambrose** (Curtley), **Boycott** (Geoffrey), **Bradman** (Sir Donald), **Compton** (Denis), **Cowdrey** (Colin, Lord), **Denness** (Michael), **De Silva** (Aravinda), **Gatting** (Mike), **Holding** (Michael), **Hussain** (Nasser), **Jardine** (Douglas), **Larwood** (Harold), **Miandad** (Javed), **Pollock** (Graeme), **Simpson** (Robert), **Stewart** (Alec), **Thomson** (Jeff), **Trueman** (Fred)
08 **Atherton** (Michael), **Chappell** (Greg), **Chappell** (Ian), **Chappell** (Trevor), **Flintoff** (Andrew), **Gavaskar** (Sunil), **Kapil Dev** (Nikhanj), **Richards** (Barry), **Richards** (Vivian), **Sheppard** (David)
09 **D'Oliveira** (Basil), **Greenidge** (Gordon), **Ranatunga** (Arjuna)
10 **Azharuddin** (Mohammad), **Barrington** (Ken), **Lillywhite** (William)
11 **Heyhoe Flint** (Rachel), **Illingworth** (Raymond), **Trescothick** (Marcus)

crier

06 beadle, herald **07** bellman **09** announcer, messenger, outrooper, town crier **10** proclaimer **15** bearer of tidings

crime

03 rap, sin **04** evil, fact, vice **06** crimen, felony **07** misdeed, offence, offense, outrage, villany **08** atrocity, enormity, iniquity, thievery, villainy **09** violation **10** illegal act, misconduct, wickedness, wrongdoing **11** delinquency, lawbreaking, lawlessness, malefaction, malfeasance, unlawful act **12** misdemeanour **13** transgression

Crimes include:

03 ABH, GBH
04 rape
05 arson, fraud, theft
06 hijack, murder, piracy
07 assault, battery, bribery, forgery, larceny, mugging, perjury, robbery, treason
08 burglary, filicide, homicide, poaching, sabotage, stalking
09 blackmail, extortion, hate crime, joy-riding, matricide, parricide, patricide, pilfering, terrorism, uxoricide, vandalism
10 corruption, cybercrime, fratricide, kidnapping
11 drug dealing, hooliganism, infanticide, shoplifting, sororicide, trespassing
12 drink-driving, embezzlement, manslaughter
13 assassination, drug smuggling, housebreaking
14 counterfeiting, insider dealing, insider trading
15 computer hacking

criminal

◇ *anagram indicator*

03 con **04** bent, crim, evil **05** felon, tough, wrong **06** chummy, guilty, outlaw, wicked **07** convict, corrupt, crooked, culprit, illegal, illicit, lawless, obscene, villain **08** crimeful, culpable, infamous, offender, prisoner, shameful, unlawful **09** dishonest, felonious, miscreant, nefarious, wrongdoer **10** delinquent, deplorable, disgusting, indictable, iniquitous, lawbreaker, malefactor, outrageous, scandalous, villainous **11** disgraceful, lawbreaking **12** preposterous **13** reprehensible

Criminal types include:

03 dip, lag
04 hood, thug, yegg
05 crook, thief
06 bandit, forger, gunman, killer, mugger, pirate, rapist, robber, vandal
07 abactor, brigand, burglar, filcher, hoodlum, mobster, poacher, prigger, rustler, stalker, tea leaf, yeggman
08 arsonist, assassin, batterer, bigamist, car-thief, gangster, hijacker, jailbird, joyrider, murderer, pederast, perjurer, receiver, saboteur, smuggler, swindler
09 buccaneer, cracksman, embezzler, kidnapper, larcenist, racketeer, ram-raider, strangler, terrorist
10 bootlegger, cat burglar, dope pusher, drug dealer, fire-raiser, highwayman, paedophile, pickpocket, shoplifter, trespasser
11 armed robber, blackmailer, bogus caller, drink-driver, kerb-crawler, safecracker, war criminal
12 drug smuggler, extortionist, housebreaker, sexual abuser
13 counterfeiter

Criminals include:

03 **Ray** (James Earl)
04 **Aram** (Eugene), **Hare** (William), **Hood** (Robin), **Kray** (Reginald), **Kray** (Ronnie), **Rais** (Gilles de), **Todd** (Sweeney), **West** (Frederick), **West** (Rosemary)
05 **Biggs** (Ronald), **Blood** (Thomas), **Booth** (John Wilkes), **Brady** (Ian), **Burke** (William), **Ellis** (Ruth), **James** (Jesse), **Kelly** (Ned), **Lucan** (Richard John Bingham, Lord)
06 **Barrow** (Clyde), **Bonney** (William H), **Borden** (Lizzie), **Capone** (Al), **Corday** (Charlotte), **Meehan** (Patrick), **Nilsen** (Dennis), **Oswald** (Lee Harvey), **Parker** (Bonnie), **Rob Roy**, **Sirhan** (Sirhan), **Turpin** (Dick)
07 **Bathori** (Elizabeth), **Chapman** (Mark), **Crippen** (Hawley), **Hindley** (Myra), **Huntley** (Ian), **Ireland** (William), **Luciano** (Charles 'Lucky'), **Shipman** (Harold), **Winters** (Larry)
08 **Barabbas**, **Christie** (John), **Hanratty** (James), **Sheppard** (Jack), **Son of Sam**
09 **Berkowitz** (David), **Dillinger** (John), **Sutcliffe** (Peter)
11 **Billy the Kid**
13 **Jack the Ripper**
14 **Moors Murderers**
15 **Yorkshire Ripper**

See also **highwayman**; **pirate**

crimp

04 bend, curl, fold, pote, tuck, wave **05** flute, pleat, quill, ridge **06** crease, furrow, gather, goffer, groove, hinder, pucker, rumple, thwart **07** crinkle, crumple, gauffer, wrinkle **09** corrugate

cringe

03 bow, shy **04** bend, duck, fawn **05** cower, crawl, creep, quail, sneak, start, stoop, toady, wince **06** blench, crouch, flinch, grovel, kowtow, quiver, recoil, shrink, suck up **07** flatter, tremble **08** draw back **09** be all over **11** curry favour **12** bow and scrape **14** tug the forelock

crinkle

04 curl, fold, line, ruck, tuck, wave **05** crimp, money, pleat, ridge, twist **06** crease, furrow, groove, pucker, ruffle, rumple **07** crumple, wrinkle **09** corrugate **10** paper money **11** corrugation

crinkly

05 curly, kinky, money **06** fluted, folded, frizzy, ridged, tucked **07** creased, crimped, grooved, pleated, rumpled, wrinkly **08** crinkled, crumpled, furrowed, gathered, puckered, wrinkled **10** corrugated, paper money

cripple

04 lame, maim, ruin **05** spoil **06** damage, hamper, impair, impede, injure, weaken **07** destroy, disable, lameter, lamiger, lamiter, vitiate **08** handicap, lammiger, mutilate, paralyse, sabotage **09** hamstring, undermine **10** debilitate, immobilize **12** incapacitate

crippled

04 halt, lame, maim **08** deformed, disabled **09** paralysed **11** handicapped **13** incapacitated

crisis

03 fit, fix, jam **04** acme, hole, mess, stew, turn **05** brunt, crise **06** crunch, pickle, scrape **07** dilemma, problem, trouble **08** calamity, disaster, exigency, hot water, quandary, solution **09** emergency, extremity **10** crossroads, difficulty **11** catastrophe, predicament **12** turning-point

crisp

04 chip, cool, firm, hard, neat **05** brief, brisk, clear, crump, fresh, pithy, short, terse **06** chilly, crispy, crumpy, snappy **07** bracing, brittle, chippie, concise, crackly, crumbly, crunchy, friable **08** decisive, incisive, succinct **09** breakable **10** refreshing **12** invigorating **13** authoritative

criterion
03 law **04** norm, rule, test **05** basis, canon, gauge, model, scale **06** square **07** measure **08** exemplar, standard **09** benchmark, principle, yardstick **10** shibboleth, touchstone

critic
05 judge **06** carper, censor, expert, pundit **07** analyst, knocker, monitor, Zoilist **08** attacker, censurer, observer, overseer, reviewer **09** Aristarch, authority, backbiter, find-fault, nit-picker **11** commentator, fault-finder
See also **literary**

critical
04 crit, nice **05** fatal, grave, major, vital **06** severe, urgent **07** carping, crucial, exigent, fateful, gingery, pivotal, probing, serious **08** captious, deciding, decisive, historic, niggling, perilous, pressing, scathing, venomous **09** cavilling, dangerous, essential, important, momentous, quibbling, vitriolic **10** analytical, censorious, compelling, derogatory, diagnostic, discerning, evaluative, expository, nit-picking, perceptive, precarious **11** climacteric, disparaging, explanatory, judgemental, penetrating, significant **12** all-important, condemnatory, disapproving, fault-finding, hypercorrect, life-and-death, sharp-tongued, vituperative **13** hypercritical **14** disapprobative, interpretative **15** uncomplimentary

- **critical position**
04 pass

critically
07 acutely, gravely, vitally **08** urgently **09** crucially, seriously **10** captiously, decisively, perilously **11** dangerously **12** analytically **13** disparagingly, significantly **14** diagnostically, disapprovingly **15** hypercritically

criticism
04 flak **05** blame, snipe, stick, strop **06** attack, niggle, review **07** censure, comment, reproof, ripping, slating, write-up, Zoilism **08** analysis, bad press, brickbat, critique, knocking, niggling, slamming **09** appraisal, judgement, stricture **10** assessment, commentary, evaluation, exposition, nit-picking, textualism **11** disapproval, explanation, explication **12** appreciation, condemnation, fault-finding **13** animadversion, disparagement **14** interpretation

criticize
03 bag, nag, pan, rip **04** carp, crab, flay, slag, slam, zing **05** blame, cut up, decry, judge, knock, roast, score, slash, slate, snipe, trash **06** assess, attack, hammer, impugn, niggle, peck at, review, tilt at **07** analyse, canvass, censure, condemn, dissect, explain, nit-pick, rip into, rubbish, run down, scarify, slag off, snipe at **08** appraise, badmouth, denounce, evaluate, wade into **09** castigate, denigrate, disparage, excoriate, have a go at, interpret, pull apart, slaughter, take apart, tear apart **10** animadvert, come down on, go to town on, have a pop at, speak ill of, take a pop at, vituperate **11** have a shot at, pick holes in **12** disapprove of, pick to pieces, pull to pieces, put the boot in, tear to shreds **13** find fault with, tear a strip off **14** cast aspersions, ultracrepidate **15** do a hatchet job on, pass judgement on

critique
05 essay **06** review **07** write-up **08** analysis **09** appraisal, criticism, judgement **10** assessment, commentary, evaluation, exposition **11** explanation, explication **12** appreciation **14** interpretation

croak
03 caw, die **04** crow, gasp, kill, rasp **05** crake, croup, grunt **06** squawk, wheeze **07** grumble **12** speak harshly

Croatia
02 HR **03** HRV

crock
03 jar, pig, pot, urn **04** dirt, smut **06** vessel **07** disable **08** potsherd **09** break down

crocked
◇ *anagram indicator*
See **drunk**

crockery
05 china **06** dishes **07** pottery **08** brockage **09** porcelain, stoneware, tableware **11** earthenware **12** breakfast-set

crocodile
04 croc **06** caiman, cayman, garial, gavial, mugger **07** gharial **09** leviathan, teleosaur **11** river-dragon, Teleosaurus

croft
04 farm, plot **07** pightle **08** farmland **12** smallholding

Cronus
06 Saturn

crony
03 pal **04** ally, chum, mate **05** buddy **06** friend **07** comrade **08** familiar, follower, intimate, sidekick **09** associate, colleague, companion, confidant **10** accomplice, confidante

crook
◇ *anagram indicator*
03 bow, ill **04** bend, flex, hook, kink, sick, tilt, warp **05** angle, angry, cheat, cromb, crome, cross, curve, fraud, nasty, rogue, shark, slant, thief, twist, wrong **06** con man, deform, gibbet, kebbie, robber, unfair, unwell **07** crosier, crozier, distort, dubious, villain **08** criminal, crummack, crummock, inferior, offender, operator, swindler **09** card sharp, dishonest, sheep-hook **10** distortion, lawbreaker, unpleasant **13** pastoral staff

crooked
◇ *anagram indicator*
04 awry, bent **05** askew, bowed, shady, wrong **06** angled, camsho, curved, hooked, shifty, thrawn, tilted, uneven, warped, zigzag **07** buckled, corrupt, illegal, illicit, sinuous, twisted, winding **08** camshoch, criminal, deformed, lopsided, slanting, thraward, thrawart, tortuous, unlawful **09** camsheugh, contorted, deceitful, dishonest, distorted, irregular, misshapen, nefarious, off-centre, skew-whiff, underhand, unethical **10** asymmetric, fraudulent **11** anfractuous, treacherous **12** unprincipled, unscrupulous

crookedly
04 agee, ajee, awry **05** askew **08** unevenly **09** off-centre **10** lopsidedly **14** asymmetrically

croon
03 hum **04** lilt, sing **06** warble **08** vocalize

- **crooner**
04 Bing
See also **singer**

crop
03 cut, lop, lot, mow, rod, set **04** clip, crap, craw, pare, poll, reap, snip, stow, trim **05** batch, gorge, group, prune, shear, stand, yield **06** finial, fruits, gather, growth, reduce **07** curtail, harvest, produce, reaping, shorten, vintage **08** gleaning, wool clip **09** gathering, ingluvies **10** collection

Arable crops include:

03 pea, rye, yam
04 bean, corn, flax, hemp, kale, milo, oats, rape, rice
05 colza, maize, swede, wheat
06 barley, kharif, millet, potato, turnip
07 alfalfa, cassava, linseed, lucerne, oilseed, popcorn, sorghum, soy bean
08 mung bean, soya bean, teosinte
09 milo maize, sugar beet, sugar cane, sunflower, sweetcorn, triticale
11 oilseed rape, sweet potato
12 mangel wurzel

- **crop up**
05 arise, occur **06** appear, arrive, come up, emerge, happen, turn up **09** take place **10** come to pass **13** present itself

cross
◇ *anagram indicator*
01 X **03** cut, ill, irk, mix, woe, wry **04** arch, crux, defy, edgy, foil, ford, join, lace, load, meet, pain, sign, sore, span, vext, wade **05** angry, annoy, blend, block, check, grief, harsh, irate, short, surly, thraw, trial, vexed, worry **06** bridge, burden, crabby, franzy, grumpy, hamper, hinder, hybrid, impede, misery, oppose, peeved, put out, resist, shirty, snappy, sullen, thwart **07** adverse, amalgam, annoyed, awkward, fretful, grouchy, mixture,

mongrel, oblique, peevish, prickly, trouble **08** bestride, confront, converge, diagonal, disaster, go across, obstruct, opposite, pass over, snappish, traverse, walk over **09** adversity, balancing, crosswise, crotchety, decussate, difficult, dishonest, fractious, frustrate, hybridize, impatient, intersect, irascible, irritable, splenetic, suffering **10** affliction, criss-cross, crossbreed, displeased, interbreed, intertwine, interweave, misfortune, mixed breed, mongrelize, overthwart, reciprocal, transverse **11** bad-tempered, catastrophe, combination, ill-tempered, tribulation **12** cantankerous, disagreeable, interchanged, intersecting, neutralizing, travel across **14** cross-fertilize, cross-pollinate

See also **hybrid**

Crosses include:

01 T
03 Red, tau
04 ankh, high, Iron, ring, rood, rose, rosy
05 fiery, Greek, Latin, papal, Rouen
06 ansate, botoné, Celtic, fleury, fylfot, Geneva, George, market, moline, potent, Y-cross
07 Avelian, Calvary, capital, Cornish, Maltese, Russian, saltire, Weeping
08 Buddhist, capuchin, cardinal, crosslet, crucifix, holy-rood, Lorraine, military, pectoral, quadrate, rood-tree, Southern, St Peter's, swastika, Victoria
09 encolpion, encolpium, Jerusalem, preaching, St Andrew's, St George's
10 St Anthony's
11 patriarchal
13 Constantinian, crux decussata
14 archiepiscopal

• **cross out**
06 cancel, cut out, delete, remove, rub out **07** edit out **09** strike out **10** blue-pencil, obliterate

• **make cross**
04 vote

• **make sign of cross over**
04 sain

cross-examination
04 quiz **08** grilling, quizzing **11** examination, questioning **13** interrogation **14** the third degree

cross-examine
04 pump, quiz **05** grill, targe **07** examine **08** question **11** interrogate **13** cross-question

crossing
◇ *containment indicator*
04 ford, trip **06** voyage **07** journey, passage, traject **08** junction, traverse **09** crosswalk, overgoing **10** crossroads, trajection **12** intersection **13** zebra crossing **14** Toucan crossing **15** grade separation, pelican crossing

crossover value
03 COV

crosswise
04 awry, over **06** across, aslant, thwart **07** athwart **08** sideways **09** crossways, obliquely **10** crisscross, diagonally, overthwart, transverse **11** catercorner **12** transversely **13** catercornered

crossword

Crosswords and crossword setters include:

03 Phi
04 Apex, Azed, Duck, Mass, Monk, Paul, Shed
05 Afrit, Owzat, Rufus, Wynne (Arthur)
06 Aelred, Crispa, Custos, Gemini, Merlin, Portia
07 Columba, Cyclops, Fidelio, Quixote, Spurius, Ximenes
08 Everyman, Giovanni, Mephisto, Pasquale
09 Araucaria, Beelzebub, Bunthorne, Cinephile, Virgilius
10 Enigmatist, Torquemada

crotch
04 fork **05** groin **06** crutch **08** genitals **11** bifurcation

crotchet
03 toy **04** whim **11** quarter note

crotchety
05 cross, surly, testy **06** crabby, crusty, grumpy **07** awkward, crabbed, grouchy, iracund, maggoty, peevish, prickly **08** contrary, petulant **09** difficult, fractious, irascible, irritable, whimsical **11** bad-tempered, ill-tempered **12** cantankerous, disagreeable, iracundulous, obstreperous **13** short-tempered

crouch
03 bow **04** bend, dare, duck, fawn, ruck **05** cower, hunch, kneel, squat, stoop **06** cringe

crow
03 daw, jay **04** brag, rook **05** boast, crake, exult, gloat, raven, vaunt **06** chough, corbie, corvid, hoodie **07** bluster, jackdaw, rejoice, show off, talk big, triumph **08** flourish **09** flute-bird **10** nutcracker, saddleback **12** cry roast-meat **13** Cornish chough **14** cock-a-doodle-doo **15** blow your own horn

crowd
03 jam, lot, mob, set **04** army, band, cram, gate, herd, host, mass, mong, pack, pile, push, raft, rout **05** bunch, crush, crwth, drove, elbow, flock, group, horde, house, meiny, press, shove, stuff, surge, swarm, three **06** bundle, circle, clique, gather, huddle, hustle, jostle, masses, meiney, meinie, menyie, muster, people, public, rabble, roll-up, squash, stream, throng, thrust **07** cluster, company, congest, scrooge, scrouge, squeeze, the many, turnout, viewers **08** assembly, audience, caboodle, compress, converge, frequent, overflow, populace, riff-raff, scrowdge, varletry, watchers **09** frequence, gathering, listeners, multitude, revel-rout **10** attendance, collection, congregate, fraternity, spectators **12** grex venalium

crowded
04 busy, full, pang **05** close, thick **06** filled, jammed, mobbed, packed, throng **07** chocker, crammed, cramped, crushed, teeming **08** frequent, overfull, swarming, thronged **09** congested, jam-packed **11** chock-a-block, overcrowded, overflowing **13** overpopulated **14** full to bursting

crown
02 cr **03** cap, taj, tip, top **04** acme, apex, bays, king, noll, pate, peak, tiar **05** adorn, award, crest, glory, kudos, prize, queen, ruler, tiara, title **06** anoint, cantle, climax, corona, diadem, empire, fulfil, height, honour, induct, invest, krantz, reward, sconce, summit, trophy, vertex, wreath **07** aureola, aureole, circlet, coronal, coronet, dignify, emperor, empress, festoon, foretop, garland, install, laurels, monarch, perfect, pschent, royalty, thick'un **08** complete, enthrone, finalize, kingship, laureate, monarchy, pinnacle, round off **09** sovereign **10** consummate **11** culmination, distinction, sovereignty **13** ultimus haeres

crowning
03 top **05** final **07** highest, perfect, supreme **08** greatest, ultimate **09** climactic, paramount, sovereign, unmatched **10** consummate, coronation **11** culminating, investiture, unsurpassed **12** enthronement, inauguration, incoronation, installation

crucial
03 key **05** major, vital **06** trying, urgent **07** central, pivotal, testing **08** critical, deciding, decisive, historic, pressing **09** essential, important, momentous, searching **10** compelling **12** all-important

crucially
07 vitally **09** centrally **10** critically, decisively **11** essentially, importantly, momentously

crucify
04 mock, rack, slam **05** knock, slate **06** punish **07** execute, rubbish, run down, torment, torture **08** ridicule **09** criticize, denigrate, excoriate, persecute **10** put to death **12** pull to pieces, tear to pieces, tear to shreds **14** kill on the cross

crude
◇ *anagram indicator*
03 hot, raw **04** blue, lewd, rude **05** basic, bawdy, brash, brute, dirty, gross, juicy, rough **06** coarse, earthy, risqué, simple, smutty, vulgar

07 natural, obscene, raunchy, uncouth 08 immature, indecent 09 half-baked, makeshift, offensive, primitive, unrefined, untreated 10 inartistic, undigested, unfinished, unpolished, unprepared 11 barrelhouse, rudimentary, unconcocted, undeveloped, unprocessed 12 down-and-dirty 13 rough and ready

crudely
◇ *anagram indicator*
06 rudely, simply 07 roughly
08 coarsely 09 basically, obscenely
10 indecently 11 offensively, primitively

cruel
◇ *anagram indicator*
03 raw 04 evil, fell, grim, mean
05 felon, nasty 06 bitter, bloody, brutal, fierce, flinty, immane, savage, severe, unkind, wanton, wicked
07 callous, cutting, hellish, inhuman, painful, vicious 08 barbaric, diabolic, felonous, fiendish, indurate, inhumane, Neronian, pitiless, ruthless, sadistic, spiteful, vengeful 09 atrocious, barbarous, butcherly, ferocious, heartless, malicious, merciless, murderous, truculent, unfeeling
10 blistering, heathenish, implacable, inexorable, iron-headed, malevolent
11 cold-blooded, hard-hearted, remorseless, unrelenting
12 bloodthirsty, bloody-minded, excruciating, stony-hearted
13 marble-hearted 14 marble-breasted

cruelly
08 brutally, fiercely, immanely, savagely, unkindly 09 callously, inhumanly, painfully, viciously 10 implacably, inhumanely, pitilessly, ruthlessly, spitefully 11 ferociously, heartlessly, maliciously, mercilessly, truculently
13 cold-bloodedly, hard-heartedly, remorselessly

cruelty
05 abuse, spite, venom 06 malice, sadism 07 tyranny 08 bullying, ferocity, immanity, meanness, savagery, severity, violence 09 barbarity, brutality, harshness 10 bestiality, inhumanity, unkindness 11 callousness, viciousness 12 ruthlessness
13 heartlessness, mercilessness, murderousness 15 hard-heartedness

cruise
04 busk, sail, taxi, trip 05 coast, drift, glide, slide 06 travel, voyage
07 holiday, journey 09 freewheel

crumb
03 bit, jot 04 atom, iota, mite, nirl
05 flake, grain, piece, scrap, shred, speck 06 morsel, sliver, titbit
07 granule, snippet, soupçon
08 fragment, particle

crumble
◇ *anagram indicator*
03 rot 04 fail, mull, murl 05 crush, decay, grind, pound 06 powder
07 break up, moulder 08 collapse, come away, fragment 09 break down, decompose, fall apart, pulverize
10 degenerate 11 deteriorate
12 disintegrate, fall to pieces

crumbly
◇ *anagram indicator*
04 nesh 05 frush, short 07 brittle, friable, powdery 11 pulverulent

crummy
04 poor, weak 05 cheap 06 grotty, rotten, shoddy, trashy 07 useless
08 inferior, pathetic, rubbishy 09 half-baked, miserable, third-rate, worthless
10 second-rate, unpleasant
11 substandard 12 contemptible

crumpet
04 head 05 woman, women
06 muffin 07 pikelet

crumple
04 fall, fold 05 crush 06 crease, pucker, raffle, rumple 07 crinkle, wrinkle 08 collapse, scrumple

crunch
04 bite, chew, crux, test 05 champ, chomp, crush, grind, munch, pinch, sit-up, smash 06 crisis 07 graunch, scranch, scrunch 09 emergency, masticate 13 critical point, moment of truth

crusade
03 war 04 push, work 05 cause, drive, fight, jihad 06 attack, battle, strive
07 holy war, promote 08 advocate, campaign, movement, strategy, struggle 09 offensive 10 expedition
11 undertaking

crusader
06 zealot 07 battler, fighter 08 activist, advocate, champion, promoter, reformer 10 campaigner, enthusiast, missionary

crush
◇ *anagram indicator*
03 jam 04 cram, love, mash, mill, mush, pack, pash, pulp, ruin 05 abash, break, chack, champ, check, crowd, grind, horde, pinch, pound, press, quash, quell, shame, smash, stamp, tread, upset 06 bruise, crease, crunch, defeat, liking, mangle, rumple, squash, squish, step on, subdue, throng
07 break up, conquer, contuse, crinkle, crumble, crumple, mortify, oppress, passion, put down, screw up, scrunch, shatter, squeeze, squelch, thrutch, wrinkle 08 compress, demolish, overcome, scrumple, squabash, suppress, vanquish 09 break down, comminute, devastate, humiliate, obsession, overpower, overwhelm, pulverize, telescope, triturate
10 annihilate 11 infatuation, steam-roller

• crush down
03 bow

crust
03 fur, reh 04 coat, film, husk, rind, scab, skin 05 argol, layer, shell, skull
06 caking, casing, gratin, pastry
07 caliche, capping, clinker, coating, outside, salband, surface, topping
08 beeswing, covering, exterior
09 wine-stone 10 concretion, livelihood 11 lithosphere
12 encrustation, impertinence, incrustation 13 efflorescence

Parts of the earth's crust include:

03 sal
04 sial, sima
06 craton, mantle

crustacean

Crustaceans include:

04 crab
05 krill, prawn, yabby
06 gilgie, hermit, jilgie, marron, partan, scampi, scrawl, shrimp, squill, yabbie
07 camaron, copepod, daphnia, dog-crab, fiddler, limulus, lobster, pagurid, pea-crab, pill bug
08 barnacle, crawfish, crayfish, crevette, king crab, land crab, ochidore, pagurian
09 centipede, devil-crab, fish louse, king prawn, langouste, millipede, phyllopod, schizopod, sea slater, shore crab, soft-shell, water flea, woodlouse
10 acorn-shell, edible crab, hermit crab, mitten-crab, robber crab, sandhopper, seed shrimp, spider crab, stomatopod, tiger prawn, velvet-crab, velvet worm, whale louse
11 brine shrimp, calling-crab, coconut crab, common prawn, Dublin prawn, fairy shrimp, fiddler crab, langoustine, rock lobster, soldier crab, spectre crab, tiger shrimp
12 common shrimp, mantis shrimp, mussel shrimp, saucepan-fish, sentinel crab, spiny lobster, squat lobster
13 acorn-barnacle, common lobster, goose barnacle, horseshoe crab, noble crayfish, Norway lobster, opossum shrimp, spectre shrimp, tadpole shrimp, velvet-fiddler
14 Dublin Bay prawn, skeleton shrimp, woolly-hand crab

See also **animal**

crusty
04 firm, hard 05 baked, cross, gruff, surly, testy 06 crabby, crispy, grumpy, snappy, touchy 07 awkward, brittle, brusque, crabbed, crumbly, crunchy, friable, grouchy, peevish, prickly
08 contrary, petulant, well-done
09 breakable, difficult, fractious, irascible, irritable, splenetic, well-baked 11 bad-tempered
12 cantankerous, disagreeable, obstreperous 13 short-tempered

crux
03 nub 04 core 05 cross, heart
06 centre, kernel, puzzle 07 essence, nucleus 13 the bottom line

See also **cross**

cry
03 caw, mew, sab, sob **04** bawl, blub, call, gowl, hoop, hoot, howl, keen, mewl, pipe, plea, rivo, roar, wail, weep, word, yawp, yell, yelp, yowl **05** bleat, chevy, chivy, clock, greet, havoc, mouth, neigh, pewit, shout, skirl, tears, whine, whoop **06** bellow, bubble, chivvy, lament, peewee, peewit, prayer, report, rumour, scream, shriek, slogan, snivel, squawk, squeal, yoicks **07** bawling, blubber, call out, clamour, exclaim, screech, tantivy, vagitus, whimper **08** peesweep, proclaim **09** alalagmos, be in tears, peaseweep, shed tears, watchword **11** ejaculation, exclamation, lamentation **14** burst into tears, cry your eyes out
See also **shout**; **war cry** *under* **war**

• cry off
06 cancel **07** back out **08** withdraw **13** decide against **14** change your mind, excuse yourself

• cry out for
04 need, want **06** demand **07** call for, require **11** necessitate

• cry up
04 sell **06** praise

crypt
04 tomb **05** vault **08** catacomb **09** mausoleum **10** undercroft **13** burial chamber

cryptic
04 dark **06** hidden, occult, secret, unseen, veiled **07** bizarre, obscure, strange **08** abstruse, esoteric, puzzling **09** ambiguous, enigmatic, equivocal **10** mysterious, perplexing

cryptically
08 secretly **09** bizarrely, obscurely, strangely **11** ambiguously **12** mysteriously **13** enigmatically

crystal
04 spar **05** macle, table **06** needle, raphis **07** cocaine, raphide, rhaphis, spicule **08** cut glass, rhaphide **09** microlite **10** watchglass **11** amphetamine, seeing stone

crystallize
04 form **05** candy, shoot **06** appear, emerge, harden **07** clarify **08** solidify **09** make clear **11** become clear, materialize **12** make definite **13** become clearer **14** become definite

cub
03 pup **04** baby, tiro **05** chest, puppy, whelp, young, youth **06** newbie, novice, rookie **07** fresher, learner, recruit, starter, student, trainee **08** beginner, freshman, initiate, neophyte **09** fledgling, greenhorn, offspring, youngster **10** apprentice, raw recruit, tenderfoot **11** probationer

Cuba
01 C **02** CU **03** CUB

cubbyhole
03 den **04** hole, slot **05** booth, niche **06** recess **07** cubicle **08** hideaway, tiny room **10** pigeonhole **11** compartment

cube
03 die **04** dice **05** block, solid **06** cuboid **10** hexahedron, triplicate

cuckoo
◇ *anagram indicator*
03 ani, mad **04** daft, gouk, gowk, koel, loco, nuts **05** batty, crazy, loony, nutty, silly **07** cracked, foolish, idiotic **08** crackpot, rainbird **12** crackbrained, round the bend **13** chaparral cock **14** brain-fever bird
See also **fool**; **foolish**

cucumber
05 choko, wolly **07** gherkin **10** dill pickle **11** bitter-apple

cuddle
03 hug, pet **04** hold, neck, snog **05** clasp, nurse **06** caress, enfold, fondle, nestle, smooch **07** embrace, smuggle, snuggle **08** canoodle

cuddly
04 cosy, soft, warm **05** plump **07** lovable **08** huggable, loveable **10** cuddlesome

cudgel
03 bat, hit **04** bash, beat, club, cosh, mace, patu, rung **05** clout, plant, pound, shrub, stick, towel **06** alpeen, ballow, batter, souple, strike, thwack, waster **07** clobber **08** bludgeon **09** bastinado, crabstick, fustigate, truncheon **10** shillelagh **12** an oaken towel

cue
01 Q **03** nod, rod **04** hint, mace, sign **06** prompt, signal **08** feed-line, half-butt, reminder, stimulus **09** catchword, incentive **10** indication, intimation, suggestion

cuff
03 box, hit **04** beat, belt, biff, clip, gowf, slap **05** clout, knock, scuff, smack, thump, whack **06** buffet, scruff, strike **07** armband, clobber, manacle **08** bracelet, gauntlet, handcuff, snitcher, wristlet **09** muffettee

• off the cuff
05 ad lib **09** extempore, impromptu **10** improvised, off the wall, unprepared, unscripted **11** unrehearsed **13** spontaneously

cuisine
07 cookery, cooking **10** cordon bleu **12** haute cuisine **15** nouvelle cuisine

cul-de-sac
04 loke **05** close **07** dead end **10** blind alley **13** no through road

cull
04 dupe, kill, pick, sift, thin **05** amass, glean, pluck **06** choose, gather, select **07** collect, destroy, pick out, thin out **09** slaughter

culminate
03 end **04** peak **05** close, crest, end up **06** climax, finish, wind up **08** conclude **09** terminate **10** consummate **11** come to a head **13** come to a climax

culmination
03 sum, top **04** acme, apex, head, peak, roof, turn **05** crown, point **06** apogee, climax, finale, height, heyday, summit, zenith **08** meridian, pinnacle **09** high point **10** completion, conclusion, perfection, perihelion **12** consummation

culpability
05 blame, fault, guilt **09** liability **13** answerability **14** accountability, responsibility **15** blameworthiness

culpable
05 wrong **06** faulty, guilty, liable, sinful **07** at fault, peccant, to blame **08** blamable, criminal **09** blameable, offending **10** answerable, censurable, in the wrong **11** blameworthy, responsible **13** reprehensible

culprit
05 felon **07** convict, villain **08** criminal, offender **09** miscreant, wrongdoer **10** delinquent, lawbreaker **11** guilty party

cult
03 fad **04** sect **05** craze, faith, mania, party, trend, vogue, Wicca **06** belief, cultus, school, Shinto **07** faction, fashion, in-thing, macumba **08** fixation, movement, navalism, religion **09** obsession **11** affiliation **12** denomination, macrobiotics

cultivate
◇ *anagram indicator*
03 aid, dig, sow, woo **04** back, farm, grow, help, tend, till, work **05** court, fancy, groom, plant, raise, train **06** assist, enrich, foster, garden, labour, manure, plough, polish, pursue, refine, work on **07** advance, bring on, cherish, culture, develop, enhance, forward, further, harvest, husband, improve, nurture, prepare, produce, promote, support **08** civilize **09** encourage, enlighten, fertilize

cultivated
04 tame **06** polite, sative, urbane **07** genteel, refined **08** advanced, cultured, educated, highbrow, polished, well-read **09** civilized, scholarly **10** discerning **11** enlightened **12** well-informed **13** sophisticated **14** discriminating

cultivation
05 tilth **06** sowing **07** backing, culture, farming, growing, nurture, support, tilling, working **08** planting **09** advancing, fostering, manurance, nurturing **10** assistance, cherishing, forwarding, furthering, harvesting, refinement **11** agriculture, development, improvement, preparation **12** civilization **13** encouragement

cultural
04 folk **06** ethnic, tribal **07** liberal **08** artistic, communal, edifying, national, societal **09** aesthetic, educative, elevating, enriching,

improving **10** broadening, civilizing, humanizing **11** educational, traditional **12** enlightening **13** developmental **15** anthropological

culture
04 arts, crop **05** mores, music **06** growth, habits **07** customs, history, society, the arts **08** heritage, learning, painting **09** behaviour, cultivate, education, lifestyle, nurturing, tendering, way of life **10** humanities, literature, philosophy, production, refinement, traditions **11** cultivation **12** civilization

cultured
04 arty **06** polite, urbane **07** erudite, genteel, learned, refined **08** advanced, artistic, educated, highbrow, polished, tasteful, well-bred, well-read **09** arty-farty, civilized, scholarly **10** cultivated **11** enlightened **12** intellectual, well-educated, well-informed **13** sophisticated

culvert
04 duct **05** drain, sewer **06** gutter **07** channel, conduit, ponceau **11** watercourse

cumbersome
04 slow **05** bulky, heavy **07** awkward, complex, onerous, weighty **08** cumbrous, involved, unwieldy, wasteful **09** difficult **10** burdensome **11** complicated, inefficient **12** incommodious, inconvenient, unmanageable **14** badly organized

Cumbrian
◇ *dialect indicator*

cumulative
07 growing **08** mounting **09** enlarging **10** collective, increasing **11** multiplying, progressive, snowballing

cunning
03 art, fly, sly **04** arch, deep, deft, foxy, rusé, slee, wily **05** canny, carny, craft, guile, guyle, leery, sharp, skill, wiles **06** artful, astute, carney, cautel, clever, crafty, dainty, deceit, knacky, policy, quaint, shifty, shrewd, slight, sneaky, subtle, tricky **07** crabbit, devious, finesse, knowing, practic, skilful, sleekit, sleight, slyness, varment, varmint, vulpine **08** artifice, deftness, fiendish, guileful, knackish, slippery, subtlety, trickery **09** deceitful, dexterous, ingenious, ingenuity, insidious, inventive, knowledge, sharpness **10** adroitness, artfulness, astuteness, cleverness, craftiness, shrewdness **11** cunningness, deviousness, imaginative, resourceful **12** fiendishness, manipulative **13** cunning as a fox, deceitfulness, inventiveness **15** imaginativeness, resourcefulness

cup
03 mug, nut, pot, tig, tot **04** bowl, tass, wine **05** award, bidon, calix, cruse, medal, plate, prize, punch **06** beaker, bumper, cotyle, goblet, hollow, noggin, quaich, quaigh, reward, rhyton, tassie, trophy **07** chalice, cyathus, scyphus, tankard, tumbler **08** pannikin **09** cantharus, gripe's egg **11** doch-an-doris **12** deuch-an-doris, doch-an-dorach **13** deoch-an-doruis

See also **drinking**

cupbearer
04 Hebe **08** Ganymede

cupboard
05 ambry, awmry, chest, press, store **06** almery, aumbry, awmrie, closet, locker, pantry **07** almirah, armoire, cabinet, dresser, tallboy **08** cellaret, hot press, meat safe, wardrobe **09** sideboard **12** clothes-press, Welsh dresser **14** Coolgardie safe

Cupid
04 Eros

cupidity
05 greed **06** hunger **07** avarice, avidity, itching, longing **08** rapacity, voracity, yearning **09** eagerness, hankering **10** greediness **12** covetousness, graspingness **13** rapaciousness **14** avariciousness **15** acquisitiveness

curable
08 operable **09** medicable, reparable, treatable **10** reformable, remediable **11** rectifiable

curative
05 tonic **07** healing **08** medcinal, remedial, salutary **09** healthful, medicinal, vulnerary **10** corrective, febrifugal **11** alleviative, restorative, therapeutic **12** health-giving

curator
06 keeper, warden, warder **07** steward **08** guardian **09** attendant, caretaker, custodian **11** conservator

curb
03 bit **04** bend, bent, rein **05** brake, check, corbe, courb **06** bridle, damper, hamper, hinder, impede, muzzle, rebuff, reduce, retard, subdue **07** contain, control, inhibit, refrain, repress **08** hold back, keep back, moderate, restrain, restrict, suppress **09** constrain, deterrent, hindrance, kerbstone, restraint, retardant **10** constraint, impediment, limitation, repression, unofficial **11** holding-back, keep in check, restriction, suppression

curdle
03 run **04** clot, earn, grew, grue, sour, turn, whig **05** yearn **06** lapper, lopper, posset **07** congeal, cruddle, ferment, thicken **08** solidify, turn sour **09** coagulate

curd, curds
04 skyr **06** junket
• **bean curd**
04 tofu

cure
◇ *anagram indicator*
03 dry, dun, fix **04** ease, heal, help, mend, salt **05** amend, break, reast, reest, reist, smoke, treat **06** elixir, hobday, kipper, pickle, remedy, repair **07** correct, cure-all, dry-salt, healing, panacea, recover, rectify, relieve, restore, therapy **08** antidote, barbecue, make well, medicine, preserve, recovery, smoke-dry, solution, specific, unpoison **09** alleviate, treatment **10** corrective, make better **11** alleviation, restorative **12** fever therapy

cure-all
06 elixir **07** nostrum, panacea **10** catholicon **12** panpharmacon **13** diacatholicon **15** universal remedy

curfew
04 gate

curie
02 Ci

curio
06 bygone **07** antique, bibelot, trinket **09** curiosity, objet d'art **10** knick-knack **12** objet de vertu **13** object of virtu **14** article of virtu

curiosity
05 curio, freak **06** bygone, gabion, marvel, oddity, prying, rarity, search, wonder **07** antique, exotica, inquiry, novelty, trinket **08** interest, nosiness, querying, snooping **09** objet d'art, spectacle **10** knick-knack, phenomenon **11** peculiarity, questioning **12** interference **15** inquisitiveness

curious
◇ *anagram indicator*
03 odd **04** agog, nosy, rare **05** funny, nosey, novel, queer, weird **06** exotic, prying, quaint, unique **07** bizarre, strange, unusual **08** freakish, meddling, peculiar, puzzling, querying, singular, snooping **09** inquiring, intrigued, searching **10** fascinated, interested, keen to know, meddlesome, mysterious, remarkable, unorthodox **11** inquisitive, interfering, questioning **13** extraordinary **14** unconventional, wanting to learn
• **be curious**
03 pry

curiously
◇ *anagram indicator*
05 oddly **08** quaintly **09** bizarrely, strangely, unusually **10** peculiarly, remarkably **11** inquiringly **12** meddlesomely, mysteriously **13** inquisitively, interferingly, questioningly

curium
02 Cm

curl
04 bend, coil, eddy, friz, kink, loop, purl, ring, roll, tong, turn, wave, wind **05** crimp, curve, dildo, frizz, helix, pinch, snake, swirl, twine, twirl, twist, whorl **06** becurl, ripple, scroll, spiral,

wreath, writhe **07** crimple, crinkle, earlock, frizzle, frounce, meander, ringlet, wreathe **08** curlicue, kiss-curl, lovelock **09** corkscrew, favourite **12** heartbreaker **13** permanent wave

curly
04 wavy **05** fuzzy, kinky **06** curled, frizzy, permed **07** coiling, crimped, curling, looping, turning, winding **08** twirling, twisting **09** corkscrew, spiralled, wreathing **10** spiralling

currant
05 Ribes **06** rizard, rizzar, rizzer **07** rizzart

currency
03 tin **04** cash **05** bills, brass, coins, money, notes, vogue **07** coinage **08** exposure **09** publicity **10** acceptance, popularity, prevalence **11** circulation, legal tender **13** dissemination

Currencies include:

02 nu
03 ecu, kip, lat, lei, lek, leu, lev, som, sum, won, yen
04 baht, birr, cedi, dong, dram, euro, kina, kuna, kyat, lari, lats, lira, loti, mark, peso, pula, punt, rand, real, rial, riel, taka, tala, vatu, yuan
05 colón, denar, dinar, dobra, franc, frank, krona, krone, kroon, kunar, leone, litas, manat, marka, naira, nakfa, pence, pound, riyal, rupee, sucre, tenge, tolar, zaïre, zloty
06 ariary, balboa, dalasi, dirham, dollar, escudo, forint, gourde, gulden, hryvna, koruna, kwacha, kwanza, maloti, markka, new sol, pa'anga, pataca, peseta, rouble, rupiah, shekel, somoni, tugrik, tugrug
07 afghani, bolivar, cordoba, drachma, guarani, guilder, hyrvnia, lempira, metical, new peso, ouguiya, quetzal, ringgit, rufiyaa
08 new dinar, ngultrum, nuevo sol, renminbi, shilling, sterling, US dollar
09 boliviano, lilangeni, new dollar, schilling
10 emalangeni, Swiss franc
11 Deutschmark, French franc, karbovanets, Turkish lira
12 Belgian franc, Deutsche mark, renminbi yuan
14 Canadian dollar

See also **coin**

Former currencies include:

01 m
02 DM
03 pie
04 inti, lira, mark, pice, punt, reis
05 belga, franc, krone, sucre, zaïre
06 décime, ekuele, escudo, gilder, lepton, markka, peseta
07 austral, cruzado, drachma, guilder, milreis
08 cruzeiro, groschen
09 schilling
11 Deutschmark

current
01 I **02** AC, DC, in **03** amp, cur, ebb, jet, now **04** curt, eddy, flow, live, mood, race, rife, rill, soom, swim, tide **05** drift, going, juice, swirl, tenor, trend, valid **06** abroad, common, course, extant, modern, outset, stream, trendy **07** backset, bombora, draught, exhaust, feeling, flowing, general, indraft, instant, in vogue, ongoing, outflow, popular, present, running, thermal, topical **08** accepted, backwash, existing, movement, progress, reigning, tendency, tide race, up-to-date **09** direction, indraught, in fashion, prevalent **10** mainstream, present-day, prevailing, widespread **11** back-draught, fashionable, going around, present-time **12** contemporary, undercurrent **13** in circulation, up-to-the-minute

currently
03 now **05** today **07** just now **08** right now **09** at present, presently, these days **10** at this time **11** at the moment **15** for the time being

curriculum
06 course, module **07** program **08** subjects, syllabus **09** programme, timetable **10** discipline **13** course of study **14** core curriculum **15** course of studies

curry
04 beat **06** madras, quarry **07** cuittle, scratch **08** vindaloo

curse
02 wo **03** ban, eff, hex, moz, pox, woe **04** bane, blow, cuss, damn, evil, harm, jinx, mozz, oath, ruin **05** beset, blast, blind, shrew, spell, swear, weary, winze **06** berate, blight, maugre, ordeal, plague **07** accurse, afflict, beshrew, condemn, malison, scourge, torment, trouble **08** anathema, calamity, cussword, denounce, disaster, execrate, maledict **09** blaspheme, blasphemy, curse-word, expletive, fulminate, imprecate, obscenity, profanity, swear-word, vengeance **10** affliction, execration, Indian sign, misfortune, put a jinx on **11** bad language, eff and blind, imprecation, malediction, tribulation **12** anathematize, damn and blast **13** excommunicate **14** four-letter word, use bad language

cursed
04 vile **05** curst **06** bloody, cussed, damned, darned, dashed, odious **07** blasted, flaming, hateful, unlucky **08** annoying, blinking, blooming, dratting, fiendish, flipping, infamous, infernal **09** execrable, loathsome **10** abominable, confounded, detestable, pernicious, unpleasant

cursory
05 brief, hasty, quick, rapid **06** casual, slight **07** hurried, offhand, passing, summary **08** careless, fleeting, slapdash **09** desultory **10** dismissive **11** perfunctory, superficial

curt
04 rude, tart **05** blunt, brief, gruff, pithy, sharp, short, squab, terse **06** abrupt **07** brittle, brusque, concise, laconic, offhand, summary, uncivil **08** snappish, succinct **10** ungracious **11** short-spoken **13** short and sweet, unceremonious

curtail
◇ *tail deletion indicator*
03 cut **04** clip, dock, pare, slim, trim **05** abate, limit, prune **06** hamper, lessen, reduce, shrink **07** abridge, cut back, cut down, shorten **08** cut short, decrease, pare back, pare down, restrict, truncate **09** cut back on **10** abbreviate, guillotine **12** circumscribe

curtailment
◇ *tail deletion indicator*
03 cut **06** paring **07** cutback, docking, pruning **08** decrease, slimming, trimming **09** lessening, reduction, shrinkage **10** abridgment, guillotine, limitation, shortening, truncation **11** abridgement, contraction, restriction **12** abbreviation, retrenchment

curtain
04 pall, swag, vail, veil **05** blind, cover, drape, scene **06** purdah, screen **07** drapery, hanging, shutter, vitrage **08** backdrop, portière, tapestry, traverse **10** net curtain **13** window hanging
• **theatre curtain**
03 tab **04** drop, iron **05** cloth

curtly
05 short **06** rudely **07** bluntly, briefly, gruffly, pithily, sharply, shortly, tersely **08** abruptly **09** brusquely, concisely, uncivilly **10** succinctly **11** laconically **12** ungraciously **15** unceremoniously

curtsy
03 bob, bow, dop **06** kowtow, salaam **08** courtesy **09** genuflect

curvaceous
05 buxom, curvy **06** bosomy, comely **07** shapely **09** curvesome **10** voluptuous **11** well-rounded, well-stacked

curve
03 arc, bow **04** arch, bend, coil, hook, kink, loop, ogee, turn, wind **05** bulge, crook, graph, helix, rhumb, round, swell, twist **06** bought, camber, circle, record, spiral, spiric, swerve **07** caustic, cissoid, compass, flexure, incurve, quadric, quartic, winding **08** apophyge, catenary, conchoid, crescent, envelope, liquidus, parabola, sinusoid, trochoid **09** curvature, loxodrome **10** epicycloid, isoseismal, meandering, trajectory **11** catacaustic, harmonogram **12** hypotrochoid **15** brachistochrone, Lissajous figure

curved
04 bent 05 bowed, wrong 06 arched, convex, cupped, humped, warped 07 arcuate, bending, bulging, concave, crooked, rounded, scooped, sinuous, twisted 08 sweeping, swelling, tortuous 09 curviform, incurvate 10 incurvated, serpentine

cushion
03 cod, mat, pad 04 bank, tyre 05 squab 06 absorb, buffer, dampen, deaden, lessen, muffle, pillow, prop up, reduce, soften, stifle 07 beanbag, bolster, bum roll, hassock, kneeler, padding, pillion, protect, sandbag, support 08 buttress, diminish, headrest, mitigate, pulvinus, suppress 09 pulvillus, upholster 10 lace-pillow, protection 11 booster seat 13 shock absorber 14 vegetable sheep

cushy
04 easy, plum, soft 05 jammy 11 comfortable, undemanding

cusp
04 horn 05 point 07 spinode

custard
04 flam 05 flamm, flawn 06 flaune 07 sabayon 08 zabaione 10 zabaglione

custodian
05 guard 06 custos, keeper, warden, warder 07 curator 08 claviger, guardian, overseer, watchdog, watchman 09 caretaker, castellan, protector 11 conservator 12 conservatrix 14 superintendent

custody
◇ *containment indicator*
04 bail, care, hand, hold, ward 05 hands 06 arrest, charge, prison 07 keeping 08 guarding, guidance, handfast, security, wardship, watching 09 captivity, detention, retention 10 possession, protection 11 confinement, safekeeping, supervision, trusteeship 12 guardianship, imprisonment, preservation 13 custodianship, incarceration 14 responsibility

custom
03 use, way, won 04 form, rite, thew 05 ethos, habit, mores, style, trade, usage 06 manner, policy, ritual 07 fashion, routine 08 business, ceremony, practice 09 etiquette, formality, patronage, procedure, rusticism, sacred cow, tradition 10 consuetude, convention, observance 11 institution 13 way of behaving

customarily
07 as a rule, usually 08 commonly, normally 09 generally, popularly, regularly, routinely 10 habitually, ordinarily 11 fashionably 13 traditionally 14 conventionally

customary
03 set 04 used 05 nomic, usual 06 common, normal, vulgar, wonted 07 general, popular, regular, routine 08 accepted, everyday, familiar, habitual, ordinary 10 obligatory, prevailing 11 established, fashionable, traditional 12 conventional, prescriptive 14 consuetudinary

customer
05 buyer, trick 06 client, patron, punter 07 regular, shopper 08 consumer, prospect 09 purchaser, shillaber

customize
03 fit 04 suit 05 adapt, alter, tweak 06 adjust, modify, tailor 07 convert 08 fine-tune 09 transform 11 personalize

customs
04 dues 05 mores, taxes 06 duties, excise, impost, levies 07 tariffs 08 protocol

cut
◇ *anagram indicator*
◇ *deletion indicator*
◇ *insertion indicator*
◇ *tail deletion indicator*
02 ax 03 axe, bit, end, hew, lop, mow, rip, saw 04 blow, burn, chop, clip, crop, curb, dash, dice, dock, edit, form, gash, hack, halt, kerf, make, nick, omit, pare, part, race, rase, raze, reap, sawn, shun, skip, slit, sned, snee, snip, snub, stab, stop, tape, trim 05 avoid, blank, block, break, carve, cross, fault, grate, joint, knife, lance, lower, mince, notch, piece, prune, quota, scalp, score, scorn, sever, shape, share, shave, shear, shred, slash, slice, slish, sneck, snick, split, spurn, style, whack, wound 06 chisel, chop up, cleave, delete, design, dilute, divide, excise, ignore, incise, insult, lessen, pierce, précis, ration, rebuff, record, reduce, saving, slight, stroke, trench 07 abridge, curtail, cutback, cut dead, diluted, dissect, economy, engrave, failure, fashion, incised, portion, profile, rake-off, scratch, section, shorten, suspend 08 break off, castrate, cleaving, condense, decrease, diminish, dividing, excision, incision, lacerate, lowering, obstruct, renounce, stoppage 09 breakdown, expurgate, intercept, interrupt, intersect, lessening, reduction, summarize, videotape 10 abbreviate, adulterate, allocation, cutting-out, diminution, disconnect, laceration, proportion, tape-record 11 adulterated, discontinue, make shorter 12 breaking-down, bring to an end, cold-shoulder, retrenchment 14 malfunctioning, send to Coventry, slice of the cake 15 pretend not to see

See also **hairstyle**; **meat**

• cut across
08 go beyond, surmount 09 intersect, rise above, transcend 11 leave behind

• cut and dried
05 clear, fixed 06 sewn up 07 certain, decided, settled 08 definite 09 automatic, organized 11 prearranged 13 predetermined

• cut back
03 lop 04 crop, curb, trim 05 check, lower, prune, slash 06 lessen, reduce 07 coppice, curtail 08 decrease, downsize, retrench 09 economize, scale down

• cut down
02 ax 03 axe, hew, lop, mow, saw 04 curb, fell, kill, maim, raze, reap 05 level, lower, prune, slash 06 lessen, reduce 07 curtail 08 chop down, decrease, diminish

• cut in
05 nip in 06 butt in 07 barge in, break in, intrude 09 interject, interpose, interrupt, intervene

• cut off
03 end 04 clip, halt, nick, stop 05 block, sever, shred 06 detach, excide, remove, unhook 07 abscind, chop off, exscind, handsel, isolate, seclude, shelter, suspend, take off, tear off 08 amputate, break off, insulate, obstruct, prescind, retrench, separate, smite off 09 intercept, interrupt, keep apart 10 disconnect, interclude, stormbound 11 discontinue 12 bring to an end

• cut out
04 clip, drop, edit, fail, omit, quit, stop 05 block, cease, debar, shape, sneck, snick 06 delete, desist, excise, exsect, go phut, lay off, pack in, pack up, remove 07 conk out, eclipse, exclude, extract, go kaput, go wrong, refrain, ride out, take out, tear out 08 carve out, contrive, knock off, leave off, leave out, separate, supplant 09 break down 11 discontinue, malfunction, stop working 12 go on the blink

• cut out for
04 good, made 05 right 06 suited 08 suitable 09 qualified 11 appropriate

• cut short
◇ *tail deletion indicator*
04 crop, dock, snub 05 roach 07 abridge, bobtail, chapped, concise, curtail 08 prescind, truncate 10 detruncate

• cut slantwise
04 bias

• cut square across
03 bob 04 bang

• cut up
04 chop, dice, hurt 05 break, carve, het up, mince, slash, slice, upset 06 chop up, divide, put out 07 annoyed, dissect, slice up, unhappy 08 bothered, saddened, tomahawk, troubled, worked up 09 dismember 10 distressed

cutback
◇ *reversal indicator*
03 cut 06 saving 07 economy 08 decrease, lowering, slashing 09 lessening, reduction 11 curtailment 12 retrenchment

cute
04 twee 05 ankle, sweet 06 astute, clever, lovely, pretty 07 lovable

08 adorable, charming, loveable
09 appealing, endearing **10** attractive, delightful

cutlery
06 silver **07** canteen **08** flatware

Cutlery items include:

04 fork
05 knife, ladle, spoon
08 fish fork, teaspoon
09 fish knife, fish slice, salt spoon, soupspoon
10 bread knife, caddy spoon, cake server, chopsticks, pickle fork, steak knife, sugar tongs, tablespoon
11 butter knife, carving fork, cheese knife, corn holders
12 apostle spoon, carving knife, dessertspoon, salad servers
14 vegetable knife

cutlet
04 chop **09** côtelette, schnitzel
15 Wiener schnitzel

cut-price
04 sale **05** cheap **07** bargain, cut-rate, reduced **08** discount **09** low-priced
10 marked-down

cutpurse
03 nip **04** bung **06** nipper
10 pickpocket

cutter
04 pone **05** axman **06** axeman
08 lapidary

Cutters include:

03 axe, fox, saw, sax
04 adze, bill, celt
05 bilbo, blade, brand, knife, mower, plane, razor, saber, sabre, sword
06 chisel, colter, culter, dagger, ice axe, jigsaw, labrys, lopper, meat-ax, piolet, poleax, rapier, scythe, shears, sickle, sparth
07 chopper, cleaver, coulter, cutlass, fretsaw, gisarme, hacksaw, halberd, hatchet, meat-axe, poleaxe, poll-axe, sparthe, twibill
08 battle-ax, billhook, chainsaw, claymore, clippers, palstaff, palstave, partisan, scimitar, scissors, shredder, stone axe, Strimmer®, tomahawk
09 battle-axe, double-axe, Excalibur, holing-axe, lawnmower, secateurs
10 broadsword, coal-cutter, cork-cutter, guillotine, putty-knife, spokeshave
11 chaff-cutter, coup de poing, glass-cutter, grass-cutter, Lochaber axe, paper-cutter, straw-cutter
12 cookie-cutter, hedgetrimmer, Jeddart staff, marble-cutter
13 mowing machine, pinking shears

See also **dagger**; **knife**; **saw**; **weapon**

cut-throat
04 keen, thug **05** cruel, razor
06 brutal, cutter, fierce **07** ruffian, sworder **08** assassin, pitiless, ruthless
09 dog-eat-dog, merciless, murderous
10 relentless **15** keenly contested

cutting
◇ *insertion indicator*
03 raw **04** acid, clip, keen, sect, sien, slip, syen **05** chill, piece, plant, scion, scrap, sharp, snide **06** bitchy, biting, bitter, secant **07** caustic, coupure, excerpt, extract, gingery, hurtful, mordant, pointed **08** clipping, incision, incisive, piercing, quickset, scathing, scission, scissure, stinging, wounding **09** malicious, sarcastic, trenchand, trenchant **11** penetrating

cuttle-bone
03 pen **06** pounce, sepium

cycle
03 age, eon, era, orb **04** aeon, bike, rota **05** epoch, order, phase, round, trike **06** circle, period, rhythm, series
07 pattern **08** go-around, rotation, sequence **09** biorhythm, body clock
10 revolution, succession **11** oscillation

cyclical
06 cyclic **07** regular **08** repeated
09 recurrent, recurring **10** repetitive

cyclist

Cyclists include:

03 Hoy (Chris)
04 Gaul (Charly)
05 Binda (Alfredo), Bobet (Louison), Coppi (Fausto), Kelly (Sean), Moser (Francesco), Zabel (Erik)
06 Burton (Beryl), Fignon (Laurent), Harris (Reg), LeMond (Greg), Merckx (Eddy)
07 Bartali (Gino), Hinault (Bernard), Museeuw (Johan), Pantani (Marco), Queally (Jason), Simpson (Tom), Ullrich (Jan), Van Looy (Rik)
08 Anquetil (Jacques), Boardman (Chris), Indurain (Miguel), Maertens (Freddy), Opperman (Sir Hubert), Poulidor (Raymond), Virenque (Richard)
09 Armstrong (Lance), Zoetemelk (Joop)
10 Bahamontes (Federico), van Moorsel (Leontien Ziljaard-)
11 De Vlaeminck (Roger)
13 Longo-Ciprelli (Jeannie)

cyclone
05 storm **07** monsoon, tempest, tornado, typhoon **09** hurricane, whirlwind, windstorm **10** cockeye bob, depression, willy-willy
11 cockeyed bob **13** tropical storm

cylinder
04 drum, reel, roll **05** spool **06** barrel, bobbin, column, roller **07** spindle

cymbal
03 zel **07** symbole

cynic
05 surly **07** doubter, killjoy, knocker, sceptic, scoffer **08** Diogenes, snarling
09 pessimist **10** spoilsport
11 misanthrope

cynical
05 surly **06** bitter, ironic **07** mocking
08 critical, derisive, Diogenic, doubtful, doubting, negative, sardonic, scoffing, scornful, snarling, sneering
09 hardnosed, sarcastic, sceptical
10 embittered, hard-boiled, streetwise, suspicious **11** distrustful, pessimistic, worldly-wise
12 contemptuous, disenchanted
13 disillusioned, unsentimental
14 Mephistophelic
15 Mephistophelean, Mephistophelian

cynically
08 bitterly **09** mockingly **10** critically, derisively, negatively, scornfully
11 sceptically **12** suspiciously
13 distrustfully **14** contemptuously
15 pessimistically

cynicism
05 doubt, irony, scorn **07** mocking, sarcasm **08** contempt, distrust, scoffing, sneering **09** disbelief, pessimism, surliness, suspicion
10 scepticism **11** misanthropy
13 heartlessness **14** disenchantment
15 disillusionment

Cyprus
02 CY **03** CYP

cyst
03 sac, wen **04** bleb **06** growth, ranula
07 abscess, bladder, blister, capelet, dermoid, hydatid, utricle, vesicle
08 atheroma, capellet, steatoma
09 chalazion

Czech Republic
02 CZ **03** CZE

D

D
03 dee **05** delta

dab
03 bit, mop, pat, tad, tap **04** blot, dash, daub, drop, peck, spot, swab, wipe **05** fleck, press, smear, speck, tinge, touch, trace **06** dollop, smudge, splash, stroke **07** smidgen, trickle **08** sprinkle **09** lemon sole **10** sandsucker

• dab hand
03 ace, dip, toy, wet **04** play **05** adept, dally **06** dampen, expert, paddle, potter, splash, tinker, trifle, wizard **07** amateur, dallier, moisten, trifler **08** splatter, sprinkle, tinkerer **09** lay person **10** dilettante, past master

dabble
03 dip, toy, wet **04** play **05** dally, flirt, plash **06** clatch, dampen, fiddle, guddle, muddle, paddle, potter, putter, splash, tinker, trifle **07** immerse, moisten, plotter, plouter, plowter, smatter **08** splatter, sprinkle

dabbler
07 amateur, dallier, trifler **08** tinkerer **09** lay person, literator **10** dilettante

dad *see* **father**

daemon
04 deva **05** demon, devil, force, geist **06** animus, genius, spirit **09** cacodemon **10** evil spirit, genius loci, good spirit

daft
◇ *anagram indicator*
03 dim, mad, odd **04** avid, dull, dumb, fond, keen, nuts, slow, wild **05** barmy, batty, crazy, daffy, dense, dopey, dotty, inane, loony, loopy, nutty, potty, silly, sweet, thick, wacky **06** absurd, ardent, crazed, insane, mental, simple, stupid, unwise **07** berserk, bonkers, devoted, fatuous, foolish, glaiket, glaikit, idiotic, lunatic, smitten, touched, zealous **08** crackpot, demented, deranged, dingbats, farcical, gormless, obsessed, peculiar, unhinged **09** dim-witted, disturbed, enamoured, fanatical, foolhardy, half-baked, imprudent, laughable, ludicrous, senseless **10** infatuated, irrational, outrageous, passionate, ridiculous, slow-witted, unbalanced **11** hare-brained, nonsensical, unrealistic **12** addle-brained, crackbrained, enthusiastic, preposterous, round the bend, simple-minded **13** impracticable, irresponsible, off your rocker, out of your mind, round the twist, thick as a plank

dagger
05 blade, knife **06** obelus

Daggers include:

04 dirk, kris
05 kukri, skean, skene
06 anlace, bodkin, crease, creese, hanjar, kirpan, kreese
07 anelace, dudgeon, handjar, jambiya, khanjar, poniard, yatagan
08 baselard, jambiyah, puncheon, skean-dhu, skene-dhu, stiletto, yataghan
10 bowie knife, misericord, skene-occle
11 misericorde

See also **knife**; **sword**

Dáil member
02 TD

daily
04 char **05** adays **06** common **07** cleaner, diurnal, journal, per diem, regular, routine **08** constant, day by day, day-to-day, everyday, habitual, ordinary **09** circadian, customary, quotidian, regularly **10** constantly **11** commonplace, day after day

See also **newspaper**

dainty
04 cate, fine, neat, nice, trim **05** dinky, faddy, fancy, fussy, genty, juicy, small, tasty **06** bonbon, choice, choosy, friand, little, luxury, mignon, morsel, petite, pretty, sunket, titbit **07** cunning, elegant, finicky, friande, genteel, minikin, refined, savoury **08** charming, delicacy, delicate, graceful, luscious, mignonne, tasteful **09** delicious, enjoyable, exquisite, lickerish, liquorish, succulent, sweetmeat **10** appetizing, delectable, delightful, fastidious, particular, scrupulous **11** bonne-bouche **12** hard to please **14** discriminating

dairy

Dairy produce includes:

04 ghee, milk, whey
05 cream, curds, quark
06 beurre, butter, cheese, yogurt
07 UHT milk, yoghurt
08 ice cream, yoghourt
09 butter oil, goat's milk, milk shake, sour cream, whole milk
10 buttermilk, milk powder
11 double cream, semi-skimmed, single cream, skimmed milk, soured cream
12 clotted cream, crème fraîche, fromage frais, long-life milk, powdered milk
13 condensed milk, full cream milk, low-fat yoghurt, whipping cream
14 evaporated milk, sterilized milk, unsalted butter
15 clarified butter, homogenized milk, semi-skimmed milk

dairymaid
03 dey **08** dey-woman

dais
05 stage, stand **06** estate, podium **07** haut pas, rostrum, staging **08** footpace, platform

daisy
05 gowan, ox-eye **07** felicia, guayule **08** feverfew, ox-tongue **10** cupid's dart, horse-gowan, marguerite, moonflower **14** hen-and-chickens

dale
03 cwm, den, ria **04** dean, dell, dene, gill, glen, vale **05** coomb, griff, grike, gulch, heuch, slade **06** dingle, strath, valley

dalliance
04 play **05** delay, sport **06** toying **07** playing **08** dawdling, flirting, sporting, tarrying, trifling **09** loitering, pottering

dally
03 toy **04** play **05** delay, flirt, tarry **06** coquet, dawdle, frivol, linger, loiter, pingle, trifle **07** carry on **08** coquette **10** tick and toy **12** take your time **13** procrastinate

dam
03 pen **04** bund, stem, sudd, wall, wear, weir **05** block, cauld, check, stank **06** anicut, mother **07** annicut, barrage, barrier, confine, staunch **08** blockage, obstruct, restrict **09** barricade, decametre, hindrance, restraint **10** draughtman, embankment, millstream **11** obstruction

Dams include:

04 Guri, Hume, Kiev, Mica
05 Aswan, Ertan, Nurek, Rogun
06 Beaver, Bratsk, Hoover, Inguri, Itaipu, Kariba, Vaiont
07 Benmore, Boulder, Tarbela
08 Akosombo, Chapetón, Gezhouba
09 Aswan High, Mauvoisin, Owen Falls
10 Glen Canyon

11 Afsluitdijk, Grand Coulee, La Esmeralda, Three Gorges
13 Alberto Lleras, Alvaro Obregon, Grande Dixence, Manuel M Torres
14 Afsluitdijk Sea
15 Sayano-Shushensk

damage
◇ *anagram indicator*
03 mar, rip **04** cost, dent, fine, harm, hurt, loss, ruin **05** abuse, havoc, price, spoil, wreck, wrong **06** charge, deface, impair, injure, injury, weaken **07** blemish, destroy, empeach, expense, impeach, vitiate **08** decimate, mischief, mutilate, sabotage **09** desecrate, detriment, disprofit, indemnity, suffering, vandalism, vandalize **10** defacement, defilement, impairment, mutilation, recompense, reparation, tamper with **11** depredation, desecration, destruction, devastation, restitution **12** compensation, disadvantage, incapacitate, satisfaction **13** play havoc with, reimbursement, vandalization **14** wreak havoc with **15** indemnification

damaged
◇ *anagram indicator*
04 mard **07** cracked, unsound **08** impaired

damaging
03 bad **07** harmful, hurtful, ruinous **09** injurious **10** pernicious **11** deleterious, destructive, detrimental, prejudicial **12** unfavourable **15** disadvantageous

dame
03 DBE, DCB **04** Edna, lady **05** broad, woman **06** female, matron, mother **07** dowager, peeress **08** baroness **10** aristocrat, noblewoman

damn
01 d **03** dee, jot, pan **04** dang, darn, dash, doom, hang, hoot, iota, sink, slag, slam, toss **05** blank, blast, curse, decry, knock, slate, swear **06** attack, berate, jigger, revile **07** accurse, censure, condemn, inveigh, monkey's, run down, slag off **08** denounce, execrate, maledict, two hoots **09** blaspheme, castigate, criticize, denigrate, excoriate, fulminate, imprecate **10** come down on, denunciate **11** pick holes in, tinker's cuss **12** anathematize, pull to pieces, tear to shreds **13** brass farthing **14** use bad language

damnable
06 cursed, damned, wicked **07** hateful, hellish **08** horrible, infernal **09** atrocious, execrable, offensive **10** abominable, despicable, detestable, diabolical, iniquitous, pernicious, unpleasant **12** disagreeable **13** objectionable

damnation
04 doom, hell **08** anathema, hell-fire **09** perdition **12** condemnation, denunciation, proscription **15** excommunication

damned
04 lost, very, vile **05** pocky **06** blamed, bloody, cursed, darned, dashed, deuced, doomed, effing, odious **07** blasted, flaming, hateful **08** accursed, annoying, blinking, blooming, complete, dratting, fiendish, flipping, infernal, jiggered, thorough **09** condemned, execrable, execrated, loathsome, reprobate **10** abominable, confounded, despicable, detestable, pernicious, unpleasant **11** exceedingly **13** anathematized, blankety-blank **14** blankety-blanky

damning
09 damnatory **10** condemning **11** implicating, implicative, inculpatory **12** accusatorial, condemnatory **13** incriminating

damp
03 dew, fog, wet **04** dank, dewy, dull, mist, rain **05** check, foggy, gloom, humid, misty, mochy, moist, muggy, rainy, soggy **06** clammy, fousty, mochie, moisty, rheumy, vapour **07** drizzle, drizzly, wetness, wettish **08** dampness, dankness, humidity, moisture, vaporous **09** moistened **10** clamminess, discourage **14** discouragement, unenthusiastic

• damp down
04 calm, dull **05** check **06** deaden, lessen, quench, reduce **08** decrease, diminish, moderate, restrain

dampen
03 wet **04** damp, dash, dull **05** check, deter, spray **06** deaden, dismay, lessen, muffle, reduce, stifle **07** depress, inhibit, moisten, smother **08** damp down, decrease, diminish, moderate, restrain **10** discourage, dishearten **12** put a damper on

damper
04 mute **07** sordino **10** wet blanket **13** register-plate

• put a damper on
04 dash, dull **05** check, deter **06** deaden, dismay, lessen, muffle, reduce, stifle, subdue **07** depress, inhibit, smother **08** damp down, decrease, diminish, moderate, restrain **10** discourage, dishearten

dampness
03 dew, fog, wet **04** damp, mist, rain **06** vapour **07** drizzle, wetness **08** dankness, humidity, moisture **09** mugginess **10** clamminess

damsel
04 girl, lass **06** lassie, maiden **09** young lady **10** young woman

dance
◇ *anagram indicator*
04 juke, jump, leap, play, rock, skip, spin, sway **05** caper, flash, frisk, swing, twirl, waver, whirl **06** bounce, cavort, frolic, gambol, gyrate, hoof it, prance, ripple, spring **07** flicker, shimmer, sparkle, twinkle **09** pirouette, shake a leg **11** move lightly, move to music **13** tread a measure

See also **ballet**

Dances include:

03 bop, hay, hey, jig, war
04 dump, fado, giga, haka, hula, jive, jota, juba, kolo, nach, polo, reel, shag
05 conga, gigue, mambo, natch, polka, rumba, salsa, samba, skank, stomp, sword, tango, twist, waltz
06 Balboa, bolero, can-can, cha-cha, hustle, minuet, morris, valeta, veleta
07 beguine, csárdás, foxtrot, gavotte, hoe-down, Lancers, mazurka, morrice, musette, one-step, tordion
08 boogaloo, cakewalk, excuse-me, fandango, flamenco, galliard, hay-de-guy, hey-de-guy, hornpipe, hula-hula, kantikoy, lindy hop, Playford, the twist
09 bossanova, cha-cha-cha, clogdance, écossaise, jitterbug, paso doble, passepied, Paul Jones, quadrille, quickstep, rock 'n' roll, roundelay
10 Charleston, corroboree, hokey-cokey, slow rhythm, turkey-trot
11 black bottom, Lambeth Walk, morris-dance, schottische, varsovienne
12 boogie-woogie, mashed potato
13 Highland fling, Viennese waltz
15 military two-step

Dance types include:

03 tap
04 clog, folk, jazz, line
05 belly, break, disco, Irish, limbo, salsa, swing
06 ballet, hip-hop, modern, morris, square
07 bogling, country, morrice, old-time
08 ballroom, flamenco, Highland, robotics, skanking
10 bellydance, breakdance
12 contemporary
13 Latin-American

Dance functions include:

02 ba'
03 hop
04 ball, prom, rave
05 disco
06 social
07 ceilidh, knees-up, shindig
08 hunt ball, tea dance
09 barn dance
10 thé dansant
11 charity ball, dinner dance
14 fancy dress ball

Dance steps include:

03 dig, dip, fan, pas, set
04 buck, chop, chug, clip, comb, dame, drag, draw, drop, ocho, riff, spin, turn, vine, whip
05 abajo, brush, catch, corté, cramp, flare, galop, glide, grind, hitch, pivot, scuff, seven, spike, stamp,

stomp, strut, Suzi-Q, three, twist, whisk
06 aerial, breaks, bronco, chassé, circle, jockey, paddle, riffle, shimmy, uprock
07 box step, fan kick, feather, jig step, locking, lollies, popping, pop turn, rocking, scuffle, shuffle, six-step, swivels, toprock, twinkle
08 back step, crab walk, flat step, four-step, hair comb, headspin, heel pull, heel turn, hook turn, neck wrap, pas-de-bas, push spin, rock step, shedding, spot turn, swingout, throwout, time step, windmill
09 allemagne, applejack, crazy legs, cross over, cross turn, dile que no, grapevine, lindy turn, pas de deux, poussette, promenade, quick stop, sugarfoot, sugarpush
10 ball-change, chainé turn, change step, charleston, chassé turn, come-around, Cuban walks, cucarachas, inside turn, jackhammer, rubber legs, spiral turn, texas tommy, triple step
11 alemana turn, impetus turn, natural turn, outside turn, pas de basque, quarter turn, reverse turn, setting step
12 last shedding, shake and turn, under-arm turn
13 double-shuffle, fall off the log, first shedding
14 change of places, kick-ball-change, transition step, travelling step

• **dance company**
03 set

Dance companies include:

10 Ballet West
11 Kirov Ballet, Royal Ballet
12 Sadler's Wells, Kirov Ballet, Royal Ballet
13 Ballet Rambert, Ballets Russes, Bolshoi Ballet, Joffrey Ballet
14 National Ballet

dancer
04 alma, alme **05** almah, almeh **06** bopper, exotic, hoofer **07** baladin, danseur, kachina, morisco, skipper, slammer, waltzer **08** coryphee, danseuse, figurant, joncanoe, junkanoo, matachin, première, showgirl **09** ballerina, figurante, John Canoe, John Kanoo, tap-dancer **10** pyrrhicist **11** belly-dancer, comprimario **12** ballet dancer **13** terpsichorean **14** Jack-in-the-green

Dancers include:

03 **Lee** (Gypsy Rose)
04 **Bull** (Deborah), **Edur** (Thomas), **Oaks** (Agnes)
05 **Ailey** (Alvin, Jnr), **Baker** (Josephine), **Cohan** (Robert), **Dolin** (Anton), **Kelly** (Gene), **Laban** (Rudolf von), **Lifar** (Serge), **Perón** (Isabelita), **Sleep** (Wayne), **Tharp** (Twyla)
06 **Ashton** (Sir Frederick), **Béjart** (Maurice), **Blasis** (Carlo), **Childs** (Lucinda), **Clarke** (Michael), **Cooper** (Adam), **Davies** (Siobhan), **Dowell** (Anthony), **Duncan** (Isadora), **Fokine** (Michel), **Graham** (Martha), **Paxton** (Steve), **Petipa** (Marius), **Rogers** (Ginger), **Sibley** (Antoinette), **Wigman** (Mary)
07 **Astaire** (Fred), **Bussell** (Darcey), **Durante** (Viviana), **Edwards** (Leslie), **Fonteyn** (Dame Margot), **Guillem** (Sylvie), **Markova** (Dame Alicia), **Massine** (Léonide), **Nureyev** (Rudolf), **Pavlova** (Anna), **Rambert** (Dame Marie), **Seymour** (Lynn), **Ulanova** (Galina)
08 **Danilova** (Alexandra), **De Valois** (Dame Ninette), **Hayworth** (Rita), **Helpmann** (Sir Robert), **Humphrey** (Doris), **Nijinska** (Bronislava), **Nijinsky** (Vaslav)
09 **Diaghilev** (Sergei), **Macmillan** (Sir Kenneth)
10 **Balanchine** (George), **Cunningham** (Merce), **Mukhamedov** (Irek)
11 **Baryshnikov** (Mikhail), **Mistinguett**

See also **ballet**

dandelion
09 kok-saghyz, taraxacum

dandle
03 pet **04** toss **05** dance **06** bounce, cradle, cuddle, doodle, fondle, jiggle

dandy
03 fop **04** beau, buck, dude, fine, lair, posh, toff **05** blade, blood, great, smart, swell **06** Adonis, masher **07** capital, coxcomb, jessamy, musk-cat, peacock, princox **08** macaroni, muscadin, popinjay, splendid **09** excellent, exquisite, fantastic, first-rate **10** beau garçon, dapperling, fantastico **12** man about town **13** puss-gentleman

Dandies include:

04 **Nash** (Richard 'Beau')
05 **Crisp** (Quentin), **Wilde** (Oscar)
06 **Coward** (Noel)
08 **Beerbohm** (Max), **Brummell** (George 'Beau')
12 **Yankee Doodle**

danger
04 risk **05** nasty, peril, power **06** hazard, menace, risque, threat **07** pitfall **08** jeopardy **09** liability **10** insecurity **11** imperilment **12** endangerment, perilousness **13** vulnerability **14** precariousness **15** snake in the grass

• **danger signal**
03 red **08** red light

• **hidden danger**
04 trap **07** pitfall

dangerous
03 hot **05** dicey, dodgy, grave, hairy, nasty, risky, tight **06** chancy, daring, severe, unsafe **07** exposed, no'canny, ominous, serious **08** alarming, arrogant, critical, high-risk, insecure, menacing, perilous, reckless, unchancy **09** breakneck, hazardous, minacious, mischancy **10** jeopardous, periculous, precarious, vulnerable **11** defenceless, stand-offish, susceptible, threatening, treacherous

dangerously
07 acutely, gravely **08** severely **09** seriously **10** alarmingly, critically, menacingly, perilously **12** precariously **13** threateningly

dangle
03 sag **04** fall, flap, hang, loll, lure, sway, wave **05** droop, offer, swing, tempt, trail **06** entice, flaunt, seduce **07** hold out **08** flourish **09** tantalize

dank
03 wet **04** damp, dewy **05** madid, moist, musty, slimy, soggy **06** chilly, clammy, sticky

Daphne
08 lacebark, mezereon, mezereum **09** eaglewood, widow wail **12** spurge laurel

dapper
04 chic, neat, spry, tidy, trim **05** brisk, natty, smart **06** active, dainty, nimble, spruce **07** stylish **08** debonair, spruncy **11** well-dressed, well-groomed **13** well-turned-out

dappled
04 pied **06** dotted **07** blotchy, flecked, mottled, piebald, spotted **08** blotched, freckled, speckled, stippled, streaked **09** chequered **10** bespeckled, variegated

dare
04 dace, dart, daze, defy, doze, face, goad, lurk, risk **05** brave, flout, stake, stare, stump, taunt **06** crouch, gamble, hazard, invite, resist, shrink **07** daunton, presume, provoke, venture **08** boldness, confront, endanger, frighten, gauntlet **09** adventure, challenge, go so far as, stand up to, ultimatum **11** provocation **12** be bold enough, go out on a limb **13** be brave enough **14** have the courage

daredevil
04 bold, rash **05** brave, hasty **06** daring, madcap, plucky **07** hothead, valiant **08** fearless, intrepid, reckless, stuntman **09** audacious, dauntless, desperado, hotheaded, impetuous, impulsive **10** adventurer **11** adventurous **12** swashbuckler

daring
04 bold, gall, grit, guts, rash, wild **05** brave, hardy, moxie, nerve, pluck, spunk **06** bottle, plucky, spirit, valour **07** bravery, courage, gallows, prowess, valiant **08** audacity, boldness, defiance, fearless, intrepid, rashness, reckless, shocking, ventrous, wildness **09** audacious, dauntless, foolhardy, impulsive, undaunted, venturous **10** courageous, jeopardous **11** adventurous, intrepidity, venturesome **12** fearlessness,

high-spirited, recklessness
13 foolhardiness **15** adventurousness

daringly
06 boldly **07** bravely **10** fearlessly
11 audaciously **12** courageously
13 adventurously

dark
02 dk **03** bad, dim, fog, sad, wan
04 base, drab, dusk, evil, foul, grim, mirk, mist, murk, vile **05** awful, black, bleak, blind, brown, dingy, dirty, dusky, foggy, gloom, misty, moody, murky, night, olive, sable, shade, shady, tawny, unlit, wrong **06** arcane, auburn, cloudy, dismal, gloomy, hidden, morose, opaque, secret, sombre, tanned, tragic, veiled, wicked
07 bronzed, crooked, cryptic, dimness, evening, immoral, joyless, mystery, obscure, ominous, pit-mirk, privacy, secrecy, shadows, shadowy, sunless, swarthy **08** abstruse, badly lit, brunette, chestnut, darkness, dejected, dimly lit, esoteric, hopeless, horrible, menacing, mournful, overcast, puzzling, sinister, twilight, worrying
09 blackness, cheerless, concealed, enigmatic, half-light, ignorance, intricate, murkiness, nightfall, night-time, obscurity, poorly lit, recondite, shadiness, suntanned, tenebrity, tenebrose, tenebrous **10** caliginous, cloudiness, dark-haired, despicable, disastrous, forbidding, gloominess, iniquitous, mysterious, tenebrious, unpleasant **11** concealment, crepuscular, dark-skinned, distressing, frightening, inscrutable, sunlessness, tenebrosity **12** crepusculous
13 unenlightened, unilluminated
14 unintelligible

darken
03 dim, fog **04** fade **05** blind, cloud, colly, frown, sable, shade, sully
06 deject, sadden, shadow
07 benight, blacken, depress, eclipse, embrown, imbrown, obscure **08** cast down **09** cloud over, grow angry, look angry, obfuscate, overshade, weigh down **10** grow darker, make gloomy, obnubilate, overshadow, sclerotize
11 become angry **12** become darker
13 disilluminate

darkly
05 dimly **06** glumly **07** at night, blackly, by night **08** dismally, gloomily, sullenly **09** obscurely **11** cryptically, inscrutably **12** in the shadows, mysteriously **13** enigmatically

darkness *see* **dark**

darling
03 hon, luv, pet **04** dear, duck, hero, idol, love, peat **05** angel, honey, loved, sugar, sweet **06** adored, dautie, dawtie, minion, poppet, prized
07 acushla, asthore, beloved, dearest, dilling, minikin, sweetie **08** dearling, precious, sweeting, treasure
09 celebrity, cherished, favourite, treasured **10** delightful, mavourneen, sweetheart **11** blue-eyed boy, teacher's pet, white-haired **13** fair-haired boy **14** apple of your eye

darmstadtium
02 Ds

darn
03 sew **04** drat, mend **05** patch, sew up **06** cobble, repair, stitch

dart
03 fly, run **04** barb, bolt, cast, cook, dace, dare, dash, flit, hurl, leap, plan, race, rush, send, skit, tear, toss
05 arrow, bound, flash, fling, lance, lanch, scoot, shaft, shoot, sling, start, throw **06** endart, flight, glance, launch, pounce, propel, scheme, scurry, spring, sprint, strike, wheech
07 feather, harpoon, project
08 spiculum **09** fléchette, love-arrow, love-shaft **10** banderilla

dash
◇ *anagram indicator*
03 bit, cut, dad, dah, fly, hie, jaw, nip, pop, run, tad, zip **04** bang, beat, bolt, brio, dart, daud, ding, dive, drop, élan, hint, hurl, lash, life, pash, race, ramp, rash, ruin, rule, rush, slam, spot, tear, toss **05** blank, blash, bound, break, bribe, crash, crush, fling, force, grain, gusto, hurry, pinch, plash, pound, scart, shine, smash, souse, spang, speck, speed, spoil, spurt, swash, swill, throw, tinge, touch, trace, verve, wreck
06 blight, dampen, energy, hurtle, jabble, little, relish, sadden, sluice, spirit, splash, sprint, streak, strike, stroke, thwart, vigour, wheech
07 depress, destroy, fervour, flavour, let down, passion, pizzazz, scuttle, shatter, smidgen, soupçon, sparkle, viretot **08** confound, gratuity, scramble, vitality, vivacity
09 animation, devastate, frustrate
10 disappoint, discourage, dishearten, enthusiasm, liveliness, suggestion
• **dash off**
06 scrawl **07** jot down **08** scribble

dashing
◇ *anagram indicator*
04 bold **05** doggy, showy, smart
06 dapper, daring, lively, plucky, rakish
07 elegant, gallant, go-ahead, raffish, stylish, varment, varmint **08** animated, debonair, slap-bang, slashing, smashing, spirited, vigorous
09 energetic, exuberant **10** attractive, flamboyant **11** fashionable

dastard
06 coward **07** hilding

dastardly
03 low **04** base, evil, mean, vile
06 craven, wicked **07** nithing
08 cowardly, fiendish **09** underhand
10 despicable, diabolical, iniquitous
11 lily-livered **12** contemptible, faint-hearted

data
04 info **05** facts, input **07** details, figures **08** features, material, research
09 documents **10** statistics
11 information, particulars
• **collection of data**
04 file

date
01 d **03** age, day, era **04** ides, time, week, year **05** court, epoch, go out, month, stage, tryst **06** belong, decade, epocha, escort, friend, go back, go with, period, steady **07** century, meeting, partner, take out **08** come from, young man **09** boyfriend, exist from, go out with, man friend, obsolesce, originate, young lady **10** be together, engagement, girlfriend, go out of use, lady friend, millennium, rendezvous, show its age
11 appointment, assignation, woman friend **12** go steady with **14** become obsolete, be involved with
• **to date**
03 yet **05** as yet, so far **07** up to now
08 until now **14** up to the present
• **without date**
02 sa, sd

dated
05 passé **06** old hat, square **07** archaic
08 obsolete, outdated, outmoded
09 out-of-date, unstylish
10 antiquated, superseded
11 obsolescent **12** old-fashioned
13 unfashionable

daub
03 dab **04** blot, coat, gaum, gorm, spot, teer **05** cover, paint, slake, smalm, smarm, smear, stain, sully
06 bedaub, blotch, clatch, smirch, smudge, splash **07** plaster, slubber, spatter, splodge, splotch **08** splatter
09 beplaster, bespatter **10** blottesque

daughter
01 d **03** dau **04** girl, lass **05** child, fille
06 lassie **08** disciple **09** offspring
10 descendant, inhabitant

Daughters include:

04 Anne (Princess), Hero, Kate, Page (Anne)
05 Freud (Anna), Lloyd (Emily), Mills (Hayley), O'Neal (Tatum), Regan
06 Bhutto (Benazir), Bianca, Fatima, Fisher (Carrie), Forbes (Emma), Gandhi (Indira), Imogen, Juliet, Marina
07 Electra, Forsyte (Fleur), Goneril, Jessica, Lavinia, Miranda, Ophelia, Perdita, Presley (Lisa Marie)
08 Cordelia, Lovelace (Ada), Minnelli (Liza), Williams (Shirley)
09 Cassandra, du Maurier (Daphne), Katharina, McCartney (Stella), Pankhurst (Christabel)
10 Beckinsale (Kate), Richardson (Joely), Richardson (Natasha), Rossellini (Isabella)
13 Princess Royal

daunt
03 cow **04** adaw, faze, pall **05** abash, alarm, amate, deter, quail, scare, shake
06 dismay, put off, rattle, ruffle, subdue

07 overawe, unnerve **08** dispirit, frighten **09** take aback **10** demoralize, disconcert, discourage, dishearten, intimidate **11** disillusion

daunted
04 mate **05** quayd

daunting
05 scary **08** alarming **09** unnerving
11 dispiriting, frightening
12 demoralizing, discouraging, intimidating **13** disconcerting, disheartening

dauntingly
07 scarily **10** alarmingly
11 unnervingly **13** dispiritingly, frighteningly **14** demoralizingly, discouragingly, intimidatingly
15 disconcertingly, dishearteningly

dauntless
04 bold **05** brave, stout **06** daring, plucky **07** doughty, valiant **08** fearless, intrepid, resolute **09** undaunted
10 courageous, determined
11 indomitable

dawdle
03 lag **05** dally, delay, drawl, tarry, trail
06 diddle, linger, loiter, potter, putter
07 saunter **08** go slowly **09** faff about, hang about **10** dilly-dally **11** take too long **12** drag your feet, take your time

dawn
04 open, rise **05** begin, birth, break, gleam, onset, start, sun-up **06** advent, appear, arrive, Aurora, be born, emerge, origin, spring **07** arrival, day-peep, develop, genesis, glimmer, lighten, morning, sunrise **08** brighten, cock-crow, commence, daybreak, daylight **09** beginning, dayspring, emergence, grow light, inception, originate **10** break of day, first light
11 become light, crack of dawn
12 commencement **13** come into being

• **dawn on**
03 hit **05** click **06** sink in, strike
07 occur to, realize **12** register with

day
01 d **03** age, era **04** date, dies, Ides, jour, peak, time **05** bloom, epoch, flush, Nones, prime **06** heyday, period
07 calends, daytime, kalends
08 daylight **09** golden age
10 generation **13** daylight hours

Days of the week:

03 Fri, Mon, Sat, Sun, Thu, Tue, Wed
04 Thur, Tues, Weds
05 Thurs
06 Friday, Monday, Sunday
07 Tuesday
08 Saturday, Thursday
09 Wednesday

French day names:

05 jeudi, lundi, mardi
06 samedi
08 dimanche, mercredi, vendredi

German day names:

06 Montag
07 Freitag, Samstag, Sonntag
08 Dienstag, Mittwoch
10 Donnerstag

Italian day names:

06 lunedì, sabato
07 giovedì, martedì, venerdì
08 domenica
09 mercoledì

Latin day names:

09 Jovis dies, Lunae dies, Solis dies
10 Martis dies
11 Saturni dies, Veneris dies
12 Mercurii dies

Spanish day names:

05 lunes
06 jueves, martes, sàbado
07 domingo, viernes
09 miércoles

Named days include:

02 VE, VJ
09 Fig Sunday, Low Sunday, Red Friday, Red Letter
10 Good Friday, Holy Friday, Palm Sunday, Whit Sunday
11 Bible Sunday, Black Friday, Black Monday, Egg Saturday, Fat Thursday
12 Advent Sunday, Ash Wednesday, Black Tuesday, Bloody Monday, Bloody Sunday, Easter Monday, Easter Sunday, Golden Friday, Stir-up Sunday
13 Passion Sunday, Shrove Tuesday, Trinity Sunday
14 Easter Saturday, Maundy Thursday, Pancake Tuesday, Rogation Sunday
15 Mothering Sunday

See also **Christmas**

• **day after day**
09 endlessly, regularly **10** repeatedly
11 continually, perpetually
12 monotonously, persistently, relentlessly, time and again **13** again and again

• **day by day**
08 steadily **09** gradually
13 progressively **15** slowly but surely

• **day in, day out**
08 every day **09** endlessly, regularly
10 repeatedly **11** continually
12 monotonously, persistently, time and again **13** again and again

• **day's end**
03 e'en, ene, eve **04** even **07** evening

• **have had its day**
08 be past it **11** be out of date

• **number of days**
04 week, year **05** month **07** weekend
09 fortnight

• **these days**
02 AD

• **three times a day**
03 tid

• **time of day**
04 seal, seel, seil, sele

daybreak
04 dawn, morn **05** sun-up **06** Aurora
07 morning, sunrise **08** cock-crow, daylight **10** break of day, first light
11 crack of dawn **12** skreigh of day

daydream
04 muse, wish **05** dream, fancy
06 musing, trance, vision **07** fantasy, figment, imagine, reverie **09** fantasize, imagining, pipe dream, switch off
11 inattention **13** be lost in space, woolgathering **14** stare into space
15 be in a brown study, castles in the air, not pay attention

daydreamer
06 rêveur **07** dreamer, rêveuse
08 idealist, romantic **09** fantasist, visionary **10** Don Quixote, fantasizer
11 Walter Mitty

daylight
03 day **04** dawn **05** light, sun-up
07 daytime, high day, morning, sunrise
08 broad day, cock-crow, daybreak, sunlight **10** break of day, first light
11 crack of dawn **12** natural light

daze
04 dare, numb, spin, stun **05** amaze, blind, gally, knock, shock, whirl
06 baffle, dazzle, stupor, trance
07 astound, confuse, perplex, stagger, startle, stupefy **08** astonish, bewilder, blow away, bowl over, knock out, numbness, paralyse, surprise
09 confusion, dumbfound, take aback
11 distraction, flabbergast, knock for six **12** bewilderment

dazed
◇ *anagram indicator*
03 out **05** muzzy, silly, totty, woozy
06 amazed, groggy, numbed, punchy
07 baffled, dazzled, shocked, stunned
08 confused, startled **09** astounded, blown away, paralysed, perplexed, staggered, stupefied, surprised
10 astonished, bewildered, bowled over, punch-drunk, speechless, taken aback **11** dumbfounded, unconscious
13 flabbergasted

dazzle
03 awe, wow **04** blur, daze **05** amaze, blaze, blend, blind, flare, flash, glare, gleam **06** bedaze, strike **07** bewitch, confuse, glitter, impress, overawe, sparkle, stupefy **08** astonish, bedazzle, bowl over, knock out
09 dumbfound, fascinate, hypnotize, overpower, overwhelm, splendour
10 brightness, brilliance, razzmatazz
11 scintillate **12** magnificence
13 scintillation

dazzling
05 glaik, grand **06** bright, superb
07 glaring, radiant, shining
08 blinding, glorious, splendid, stunning **09** brilliant, ravishing, sparkling **10** foudroyant, glittering, impressive **11** psychedelic, sensational, spectacular **12** awe-inspiring, breathtaking **13** scintillating

dazzlingly
08 brightly, superbly **09** glaringly, radiantly **10** blindingly, gloriously **11** brilliantly **12** impressively **13** sensationally, spectacularly **14** breathtakingly

deactivate
04 stop **07** disable **08** paralyse **10** immobilize **14** put out of action

dead
01 d **03** dec **04** bang, bung, bust, cold, dull, flat, gone, late, numb, very **05** dated, exact, inert, kaput, napoo, passé, quiet, quite, smack, stiff, tired, total, utter, waned **06** asleep, barren, benumb, boring, broken, deaden, entire, frigid, no more, old hat, really, sleepy, torpid **07** awfully, defunct, disused, exactly, expired, extinct, humdrum, perfect, tedious, utterly, worn out **08** absolute, ad patres, benumbed, complete, dead beat, deceased, departed, directly, inactive, lifeless, lukewarm, obsolete, outright, passed on, perished, straight, terribly, thorough, tired out, unerring **09** apathetic, bloodless, conked out, deathlike, downright, exanimate, exhausted, extremely, inanimate, inelastic, insensate, knackered, out of date, paralysed, thanatoid, unfeeling **10** absolutely, breathless, broken-down, brown bread, completely, insentient, not working, on the blink, on the fritz, out of order, passed away, spiritless, unexciting **11** dead as a dodo, emotionless, gone to sleep, immediately, indifferent, ineffective, insensitive, off the hooks, ready to drop, unemotional, unqualified **12** discontinued, six feet under, unresponsive **13** exceptionally, uninteresting, unsympathetic **14** no longer spoken **15** dead as a doornail

deaden
04 dull, hush, mute, numb **05** abate, allay, blunt, check, slake **06** benumb, dampen, harden, lessen, muffle, obtund, reduce, soothe, stifle, subdue, weaken **07** assuage, mortify, quieten, smother **08** diminish, mitigate, moderate, paralyse, suppress **09** alleviate **11** desensitize **12** anaesthetize **14** take the edge off **15** make insensitive

deadline
04 term, time **06** time up **08** timeline **09** time limit **10** target date

deadlock
04 halt **05** stale **06** log jam **07** dead end, impasse **08** stand-off, stoppage **09** checkmate, stalemate **10** standstill

deadly
04 dull, fell, grim, sure, true **05** fatal, feral, great, hated, quite, toxic **06** bitter, boring, fierce, funest, lethal, marked, mortal, savage **07** deathly, extreme, humdrum, intense, killing, noxious, perfect, precise, serious, tedious, totally, utterly **08** accurate, deathful, entirely, flawless, mortific, unerring, venomous **09** dangerous, deathlike, effective, extremely, malignant, murderous, perfectly, pestilent, thanatoid, unfailing **10** absolutely, completely, dreadfully, implacable, monotonous, pernicious, thoroughly, unexciting **11** destructive, internecine, internecive **12** death-dealing **13** uninteresting **14** irreconcilable **15** life-threatening

deadpan
05 blank, empty **09** impassive **10** poker-faced **11** emotionless, inscrutable **12** inexpressive, unexpressive **13** dispassionate, straight-faced **14** expressionless

deaf
04 surd **05** dunny **07** unmoved **08** heedless **09** oblivious, stone-deaf, unmindful, untouched **10** cloth-eared, impervious, unaffected **11** deaf as a post, inattentive, indifferent, unconcerned **13** hard of hearing **15** hearing-impaired

deafening
07 booming, ringing, roaring **08** piercing, very loud **09** very noisy **10** resounding, thundering, thunderous **11** ear-piercing **12** ear-splitting, overwhelming **13** reverberating

deal
02 go **03** act, buy, lot **04** flog, hand, load, mart, mete, pact, push, vend **05** allot, reach, round, serve, share, stock, trade, treat **06** amount, assign, bestow, degree, direct, divide, export, extent, handle, market, strike **07** bargain, deliver, dish out, dole out, give out, inflict, mete out, operate, portion, traffic **08** contract, covenant, dispense, quantity **09** agreement, apportion, negotiate, treatment **10** administer, buy and sell, distribute, do business **11** arrangement, transaction **12** distribution **13** understanding

• **deal out**
04 dole, help **06** divide **08** dispense **10** distribute

• **deal with**
04 cope, sort **05** cover, see to, touch, treat **06** handle, manage, tackle **07** be about, concern, process, sort out **08** attend to, consider, cope with **09** look after **10** take care of **12** have to do with **14** get to grips with

• **good deal**
07 bargain

• **great deal**
03 lot **04** heap, mort, much, some **05** heaps, power, sight, world

dealer
03 dlr **04** tout **05** agent, coper **06** broker, couper, hawker, monger, pedlar, pusher, seller, totter, trader, vendor **07** chapman, fripper **08** marketer, merchant, retailer, salesman, supplier **09** brinjarry, fripperer **10** saleswoman, trafficker, wholesaler **11** distributor, salesperson **12** merchandizer

dealing, dealings
05 trade, truck **07** trading, traffic **08** business, commerce **09** marketing, operation, relations **10** chevisance, operations **11** association, connections, intercourse, merchandise, trafficking, transaction **12** negotiations, transactions **13** communication

dean
03 den **04** dell, dene, head **05** doyen, slade, Swift **08** director **09** principal, rural dean **11** chapter head, vicar-forane **12** Very Reverend **13** head of faculty **14** cardinal-bishop

• **rural dean**
02 RD **10** arch-priest **11** vicar-forane

dear
03 joy, pet **04** cher, chou, high, lamb, leve, lief, love, posh, salt **05** angel, chère, close, honey, lieve, loved, steep, sugar, sweet **06** adored, costly, pricey, scarce, valued **07** beloved, darling, earnest, machree, sky-high, sweetie **08** esteemed, familiar, favoured, grievous, high-cost, intimate, loved one, not cheap, precious, treasure **09** big-ticket, chargeful, cherished, endearing, excessive, expensive, favourite, respected, treasured **10** exorbitant, high-priced, mavourneen, overpriced, sweetheart **11** well-beloved **12** au poids de l'or, costing a bomb, extortionate **15** costing the earth, daylight robbery

dearer
04 loor

dearly
06 deeply, fondly **07** greatly **08** lovingly, tenderly, very much **09** adoringly, devotedly, earnestly, extremely **10** a great deal, intimately, profoundly, with favour **11** with respect **12** at a great cost, at a high price **13** with affection, with great loss **14** affectionately

dearth
04 lack, need, want **06** famine **07** absence, paucity, poverty **08** dearness, scarcity, shortage, sparsity **10** barrenness, deficiency, inadequacy, meagreness, scantiness **12** exiguousness **13** insufficiency

death
03 end **04** loss, ruin **06** finish **07** decease, undoing **08** curtains, downfall, the grave **09** cessation, departure, mortality, perishing **10** defunction, expiration, extinction **11** destruction, dissolution, eradication, extirpation, termination **12** annihilation, obliteration **13** extermination

Death-related terms include:

03 DOA, RIP, urn
04 bier, cist, mort, obit, pall, pyre, sati, soul, toll, tomb, wake, will
05 ashes, bardo, cairn, dirge, elegy, éloge, elogy, grave, mourn, shiva, tangi, vigil, widow
06 Azrael, bedral, burial, chadar, coffin, corpse, demise, entomb, eulogy, exequy, fossor, grieve, hearse, lament, lethal, martyr, monody, mortal, orphan, rosary, shibah, shivah, shroud, suttee, wreath
07 autopsy, bederal, bereave, coroner, cortège, cremate, crucify, elogium, epitaph, funeral, inquest, karoshi, keening, mastaba, mourner, passing, quietus, requiem, widower
08 casualty, cemetery, cenotaph, deathbed, death row, deceased, disinter, dispatch, eulogium, fatality, grieving, hara-kiri, interred, last post, long home, mortbell, mortuary, mourning, necropsy, necrosis, obituary, yahrzeit
09 committal, cremation, dead march, death mask, graveside, graveyard, headstone, interment, last rites, mass grave, mausoleum, mortician, obsequies, passing on, sacrifice, sepulchre, testament, tombstone, year's mind
10 death knell, euthanasia, grim reaper, necropolis, obituarist, pall-bearer, posthumous, predecease, strae death, undertaker
11 bereavement, crematorium, eternal rest, funeral home, grave-digger, last honours, passing away, passing bell, requiem mass, rest in peace, rigor mortis, sarcophagus, suicide pact
12 burial ground, debt of nature, disinterment, last farewell, mercy killing, resting place, the other side
13 burial society, natural causes
14 extreme unction, funeral parlour
15 funeral director, resurrectionist

• **after death**
02 PM **10** posthumous, post-mortem
• **approach of death**
03 fit
• **by reason of death**
02 cm
• **put to death**
03 gas **04** do in, hang, kill **05** lynch, press, shoot, waste **06** behead, martyr, rub out **07** bump off, crucify, execute, take out **08** blow away, despatch, dispatch, knock off **09** transport **10** decapitate, guillotine **11** electrocute, exterminate
• **repose of death**
04 rest

deathless
07 eternal, undying **08** immortal, timeless **09** memorable **10** ever-living **11** everlasting, never-ending **12** imperishable **13** incorruptible, unforgettable

deathly
03 wan **04** grim, pale **05** ashen, fatal, white **06** deadly, mortal, pallid, utmost **07** extreme, ghastly, ghostly, haggard, harmful, intense **08** terrible **09** deathlike, ghost-like, thanatoid **10** cadaverous, colourless

debacle
04 hash, rout, ruin **05** farce, havoc **06** cock-up, defeat, fiasco, foul-up **07** failure, screw-up, turmoil, washout **08** collapse, disaster, downfall, reversal, stampede **09** cataclysm, overthrow, ruination **11** catastrophe, devastation **14** disintegration

debar
03 ban, bar **04** deny, stop **05** eject, expel **06** cut out, forbid, hamper, hinder **07** exclude, keep out, prevent, shut out, suspend **08** conclude, obstruct, preclude, prohibit, restrain **09** blackball, proscribe, segregate **10** disqualify

debarred
03 out

debase
05 abase, allay, alloy, lower, shame, taint **06** bemean, defile, demean, dilute, embace, embase, humble, imbase, reduce **07** cheapen, corrupt, degrade, devalue, pollute, vitiate **08** disgrace **09** discredit, dishonour, humiliate **10** adulterate, bastardize, sensualize **11** contaminate

debased
03 low **04** base, vile **05** hedge **06** abased, fallen, impure, shamed, sinful, sordid, vulgar **07** corrupt, defiled, humbled, immoral, tainted **08** degraded, devalued, polluted, reversed **09** cheapened, debauched, disgraced, perverted **10** degenerate, humiliated, prostitute **11** adulterated, discredited, dishonoured **12** contaminated

debasement
05 shame **08** disgrace **09** abasement, dishonour, pollution **10** cheapening, corruption, defilement, perversion **11** degradation, depravation, devaluation, humiliation **12** adulteration, degeneration **13** contamination

debatable
04 moot **06** unsure **07** dubious, unclear **08** arguable, doubtful **09** uncertain, undecided, unsettled **10** disputable **11** contentious, contestable **12** questionable **13** controversial, problematical **14** open to question

debate
05 argue, fight, flyte, forum, weigh **06** combat, ponder, powwow, reason **07** contend, contest, discept, discuss, dispute, flyting, polemic, reflect, teach-in, wrangle, wrestle **08** argument, cogitate, consider, mull over, polemics, talk over **09** altercate, forensics, kick about, talk about, talkathon, think over, thrash out **10** contention, deliberate, discussion, kick around, knock about, meditate on, reflection **11** altercation, controversy, disputation, knock around, talk through **12** cut and thrust, deliberation **13** consideration **15** exchange of views

debauch
03 wet **04** ruin **05** whore **06** debosh, ravish, seduce **07** corrupt, deprave, pervert, pollute, subvert, violate, vitiate **10** lead astray **11** over-indulge

debauched
04 lewd **06** wanton **07** corrupt, debased, immoral, riotous **08** decadent, degraded, depraved, rakehell **09** abandoned, carousing, corrupted, dissolute, excessive, perverted **10** degenerate, dissipated, licentious, profligate **11** intemperate, promiscuous **13** overindulgent

debauchery
04 lust, orgy, riot **05** revel **06** excess **07** licence, license **08** carousal, lewdness **09** decadence, depravity **10** corruption, degeneracy, immorality, rakishness, wantonness **11** degradation, dissipation, libertinage, libertinism **12** intemperance **13** dissoluteness **14** licentiousness, overindulgence
• **place of debauchery**
03 sty

debenture
04 bond

debilitate
03 sap **04** tire **05** drain **06** impair, weaken **07** cripple, exhaust, fatigue, wear out **08** enervate, enfeeble **09** undermine **10** devitalize **12** incapacitate

debilitating
06 tiring **09** crippling, fatiguing, impairing, weakening **10** enervating, enervative, enfeebling, exhausting, wearing out **11** undermining **14** incapacitating

debility
05 atony **07** fatigue, frailty, languor, malaise **08** asthenia, weakness **09** atonicity, faintness, infirmity, tiredness, weariness **10** enervation, exhaustion, feebleness, incapacity, myasthenia **11** decrepitude **12** enfeeblement, lack of energy, neurasthenia **14** lack of vitality

debit
• **direct debit**
02 DD

debonair
05 suave **06** breezy, jaunty, smooth, urbane **07** affable, buoyant, dashing, elegant, refined, stylish **08** carefree, charming, cheerful, cultured, well-bred **09** courteous, dignified **12** light-hearted **13** sophisticated

debrief
05 grill **07** examine **08** question **09** interview **11** interrogate **12** cross-examine **13** cross-question

debris
◇ *anagram indicator*
04 bits, muck **05** drift, dross, ruins, scrap, trash, waste, wreck **06** bahada, bajada, litter, pieces, refuse, rubble, tephra **07** eluvium, remains, rubbish **08** detritus, wreckage **09** fragments, sweepings **12** pyroclastics
• **pile of debris**
03 tel **04** tell

debt
03 dew, due, IOU, sin **04** bill, duty, hock **05** claim, debit, score **06** charge **07** account, arrears **08** money due **09** amount due, liability, overdraft **10** aes alienum, commitment, money owing, obligation **11** amount owing **12** indebtedness
• **in debt**
06 in hock **08** in the red **09** gone under, in arrears, insolvent **10** owing money **11** in overdraft **13** gone to the wall, in Queer Street
• **indication of debt**
03 red
• **in someone's debt**
07 obliged **08** beholden, indebted, thankful **11** honour-bound **12** appreciative

debtor
02 Dr **07** debitor **08** bankrupt, borrower, deadbeat **09** defaulter, insolvent, mortgagor **10** abbey-laird, fly-by-night

debunk
04 mock **05** quash **06** expose, show up **07** deflate, explode, lampoon **08** disprove, puncture, ridicule **13** cut down to size

debut, début
05 start **06** launch **08** entrance, première **09** beginning, coming-out, first time, launching **10** first night, initiation **12** inauguration, introduction, presentation **14** first recording **15** first appearance

debutante, débutante
03 bud, deb **05** debby

decadence
04 fall **05** decay **07** decline **09** depravity **10** corruption, debasement, debauchery, degeneracy, immorality, perversion **11** dissipation, dissolution **12** degeneration **13** deterioration, retrogression **14** degenerateness, licentiousness, self-indulgence

decadent
06 effete **07** corrupt, debased, immoral **08** decaying, degraded, depraved **09** debauched, declining, dissolute, symbolist **10** Babylonian, degenerate, dissipated, licentious **12** degenerating, unprincipled **13** deteriorating, self-indulgent

decamp
03 fly, guy **04** bolt, flee, flit **05** lam it, scrap, slide, slope, split **06** desert, escape, hook it, levant, mizzle, run off **07** abscond, do a bunk, make off, run away, scamper, scarper, take off, vamoose **08** light out, slope off, up sticks **09** do a runner, skedaddle **10** hightail it, make tracks **12** absquatulate **14** take in on the lam

decant
03 tap **05** drain **07** draw off, pour out **08** transfer **09** siphon off

decapitate
◇ *head deletion indicator*
06 behead, unhead **07** execute **10** guillotine

decay
03 rot **04** blet, doat, dote, fail, ruin, rust, sink **05** faint, go bad, go off, mould, spoil, waste **06** blight, canker, caries, dry rot, empare, fading, fester, fungus, impair, mildew, perish, weaken, wet rot, wither **07** atrophy, corrode, crumble, decline, dwindle, empaire, empayre, failing, failure, forfair, go to pot, putrefy, rotting, shrivel, wasting **08** collapse, downfall, foxiness, going bad, wear away **09** crumbling, decadence, decadency, decompose, perishing, putridity, waste away, weakening, withering **10** debasement, declension, decompound, degenerate, go downhill **11** deteriorate, go to the dogs, labefaction, putrescence **12** degeneration, disintegrate, putrefaction **13** consenescence, consenescency, decomposition, deterioration, labefactation **14** disintegration

decayed
03 bad, off **04** rank, sour **05** druxy, stale **06** addled, failed, mouldy, putrid, rotten, sleepy, wasted **07** carious, carrion, doddard, rotting, ruinous, spoiled **08** corroded, doddered, mildewed, perished, withered **09** putrefied **10** decomposed, dirt-rotten, putrescent **12** impoverished

decease
03 die, end **04** rest **05** death, dying **06** demise **07** passing **09** departure, passing on **10** expiration **11** dissolution, passing away

deceased
03 dec **04** dead, gone, late, lost **06** asleep, former, no more **07** defunct, expired, extinct **08** departed, finished **12** six feet under **15** dead as a doornail

deceit
03 con **04** fake, game, ruse, sham, wile **05** abuse, dodge, feint, fraud, guile, guyle **06** barrat **07** cunning, forgery, glozing, slenter, slinter, slyness, swindle **08** artifice, cheating, coquetry, cozenage, pretence, trickery, wiliness **09** chicanery, deception, duplicity, falseness, gold brick, hypocrisy, invention, malengine, phenakism, stratagem, treachery **10** craftiness, imposition, subterfuge **11** fraudulence **13** double-dealing **14** monkey business **15** underhandedness

deceitful
03 sly **04** foxy, jive, rusé **05** false, lying, Punic, sharp **06** braide, crafty, double, forked, sneaky, tricky **07** crooked, cunning, devious, elusory, knavish **08** coloured, guileful, illusory, two-faced **09** deceiving, deceptive, designing, dishonest, insincere, underhand **10** deceptious, fraudulent, Janus-faced, mendacious, perfidious, untruthful **11** counterfeit, dissembling, duplicitous, prestigious, treacherous **12** false-hearted, hypocritical **13** double-dealing, double-tongued, untrustworthy

deceitfully
05 slyly **06** double **07** falsely **08** craftily, sneakily **09** cunningly **11** deceivingly, deceptively, dishonestly, insincerely **12** fraudulently, mendaciously, perfidiously, untruthfully **13** duplicitously, treacherously, underhandedly **14** hypocritically

deceive
02 do **03** cog, con, gag, kid, lie **04** bite, do in, dupe, flam, fool, gull, hoax, mock **05** abuse, blind, bluff, cheat, false, put on, trick, trump **06** befool, betray, delude, entrap, have on, humbug, lead on, misuse, outwit, seduce, slip up **07** beguile, cheat on, chicane, defraud, ensnare, mislead, swindle, two-time **08** hoodwink, misguide, outsmart **09** bamboozle, dissemble, mislippen **10** camouflage, disappoint, impose upon **11** double-cross, hornswoggle, set a trap for, string along **12** put one over on, take for a ride **13** put a cheat upon **14** pull a fast one on

deceiver
04 fake **05** cheat, crook, fraud **06** abuser, con man, falser, guiler, guyler, hoaxer **07** deluder, diddler, seducer **08** betrayer, impostor, swindler, treacher **09** charlatan, hypocrite, inveigler, treachour, tregetour, trickster **10** dissembler, mountebank **11** treachetour **12** double-dealer

decelerate
04 slow **05** brake **06** retard **08** slow down **11** reduce speed **12** go more slowly **14** put the brakes on

December
03 Dec

decency
07 decorum, fitness, modesty **08** civility, courtesy, fairness **09** etiquette, good taste, integrity, propriety **10** politeness, seemliness **11** correctness, helpfulness, uprightness **14** respectability

decent
02 OK **03** fit **04** fair, kind, nice, pure **05** civil **06** chaste, honest, modest, polite, proper, seemly, worthy **07** correct, ethical, fitting, gradely, helpful, upright **08** adequate, becoming, decorous, generous, gracious, graithly, moderate, obliging, passable, pleasant, suitable, tasteful, virtuous, wise-like **09** befitting, competent, courteous, dignified, tolerable **10** acceptable, dependable, reasonable, salubrious, sufficient, thoughtful **11** appropriate, presentable, respectable, trustworthy **12** satisfactory **13** accommodating

decently
06 fairly, nicely **08** honestly, politely, properly, suitably **09** correctly, ethically, helpfully, tolerably **10** acceptably, adequately, becomingly, decorously, generously, graciously, obligingly, reasonably **11** courteously, presentably, respectably **12** sufficiently, thoughtfully **13** appropriately **14** satisfactorily

decentralize
07 devolve **08** delegate, localize **11** regionalize **13** deconcentrate **14** spread outwards **15** spread downwards

deception
03 cog, con, fib, kid, lie **04** hoax, hype, ruse, scam, sell, sham, wile **05** bluff, cheat, fraud, glaik, guile, kiddy, moody, set-up, snare, sting, trick **06** deceit, have-on, humbug, take-in **07** abusion, cunning, eyewash, fallacy, fubbery, gullery, leg-pull, swindle **08** artifice, cheating, flim-flam, illusion, nonsense, pretence, put-up job, trickery **09** chicanery, chicaning, duplicity, hypocrisy, imposture, stratagem, treachery **10** craftiness, hocus-pocus, maskirovka, pious fraud, subterfuge **11** dissembling, fraudulence, insincerity, supercherie **13** deceptiveness, double-dealing, funny business, jiggery-pokery **14** false pretences **15** smoke and mirrors, underhandedness

deceptive
03 sly **04** fake, foxy, mock, sham **05** bogus, false, sharp **06** bubble, catchy, crafty, hollow **07** amusive, crooked, cunning, elusive **08** cheating, delusive, delusory, fraudful, illusive, illusory, imposing, specious, spurious **09** ambiguous, dishonest, faithless, underhand **10** fallacious, fraudulent, misleading, unreliable **11** dissembling, duplicitous

deceptively
07 falsely **10** illusively, speciously, spuriously **11** ambiguously, dishonestly **12** fraudulently, misleadingly

decibel
02 dB

decide
03 end, fix, opt **04** pick, rule, seal **05** aread, arede, go for, judge, opt in **06** choose, clinch, define, make up, opt for, select, settle, wrap up **07** adjudge, arreede, darrain, darrayn, deraign, discuss, resolve, work out **08** conclude, darraign, darraine, plump for **09** arbitrate, darraigne, determine, establish **10** adjudicate, dijudicate **11** give a ruling **12** turn the scale **13** make a decision **14** commit yourself, give a judgement, make up your mind, reach a decision **15** come to a decision

decided
04 ared, firm **05** clear **06** marked **07** certain, express, obvious **08** absolute, clear-cut, decisive, definite, distinct, emphatic, positive, resolute **10** deliberate, determined, forthright, pronounced, purposeful, undeniable, undisputed, unswerving, unwavering, well-marked **11** categorical, unambiguous, unequivocal **12** indisputable, unhesitating, unmistakable **14** unquestionable

decidedly
04 very **05** quite **07** clearly **08** markedly **09** certainly, downright, obviously **10** absolutely, decisively, definitely, distinctly, noticeably, positively **12** unmistakably **13** unequivocally **14** unquestionably

decider
08 clincher **10** determiner **11** coup de grâce

deciding
03 key **05** chief, final, prime **06** crunch **07** crucial, supreme **08** critical, decisive **09** principal **10** conclusive **11** determining, influential, significant

decimate
05 tithe, tythe **07** destroy, flatten **09** devastate, eliminate, eradicate **10** annihilate, obliterate

decipher
04 dope **05** break, crack, solve **06** decode, detect, reveal **07** dope out, make out, suss out, unravel, work out **08** construe **09** figure out, interpret, translate **10** descramble, understand, unscramble **11** make sense of **13** transliterate

decision
05 arrêt, award, parti **06** decree, firman, result, ruling **07** finding, opinion, outcome, purpose, resolve, verdict **08** firmness, last word, sentence **09** judgement **10** conclusion, resolution, settlement **11** arbitration **12** adjudication, decisiveness, forcefulness **13** determination, pronouncement **14** recommendation

decisive
03 key **04** firm **05** crisp, fatal, final, prime **06** strong **07** crucial, decided, fateful **08** absolute, critical, deciding, definite, forceful, positive, resolute **09** effectual, momentous, principal **10** conclusive, definitive, determined, forthright, purposeful, unswerving, unwavering **11** determinate, determining, influential, significant **12** single-minded, strong-minded

decisively
06 firmly **08** strongly **09** crucially, fatefully **10** absolutely, critically, forcefully, positively, resolutely **11** momentously **12** conclusively, definitively, determinedly, forthrightly, purposefully, unswervingly, unwaveringly **13** influentially, significantly **14** single-mindedly

deck
02 dk **03** rig, tog **04** pack, prim, trap, trim **05** adorn, array, cover, grace **06** bedeck, betrim, clothe, enrich, ground, tart up **07** festoon, garland, garnish, trick up **08** beautify, covering, decorate, ornament, platform, prettify, trick out **09** embellish

• **deck out**
03 rig, tog **04** do up, garb, robe **05** adorn, array, dress, get up, prick **06** clothe, doll up, tart up **07** dress up **08** decorate

declaim
04 rant **05** mouth, orate, spiel, spout **06** recite **07** bespout, elocute, lecture **08** disclaim, harangue, perorate, proclaim, sound off **09** hold forth, pronounce, sermonize **11** expostulate, speak boldly

declamation
04 rant **06** sermon, speech, tirade **07** address, lecture, oration **08** harangue **10** recitation **12** speechifying

declamatory
04 bold **05** stagy **07** fustian, orotund, pompous, stilted **08** dramatic, inflated, parlando **09** bombastic, grandiose, high-flown, overblown **10** discursive, oratorical, rhetorical, theatrical **12** magniloquent **13** grandiloquent

declaration
03 dec **04** call, dick, word **05** edict **06** avowal, decree **08** averment **09** affidavit, assertion, assurance, broadcast, manifesto, outgiving, statement, testimony **10** confession, deposition, disclosure, profession, revelation **11** affirmation, attestation, certificate, enunciation **12** announcement, asseveration, confirmation, denunciation, notification, proclamation, promulgation, protestation **13** communication, pronouncement **15** acknowledgement

declare
02 go **03** say, vie **04** aver, avow, read, show **05** aread, arede, claim, speak, state, swear **06** affirm, assert, attest, decree, notify, reveal **07** arreede,

certify, confess, confirm, discuss, express, profess, protest, publish, signify, testify, witness **08** announce, disclose, maintain, manifest, proclaim, set forth, validate **09** broadcast, make known, pronounce **10** asseverate, promulgate **11** communicate

declared
04 ared **06** avowed, stated **07** confest **09** confessed, professed

decline
03 dip, ebb, rot, sag, set **04** balk, deny, drop, fade, fail, fall, flag, hill, nill, sink, slip, wane, welk **05** abate, avoid, baulk, decay, droop, forgo, lapse, quail, slant, slide, slope, slump, stoop, traik
06 devall, forego, go down, lessen, plunge, recede, reduce, refuse, reject, sunset, waning, weaken, wither, worsen **07** descend, descent, deviate, drop-off, dwindle, evening, failing, failure, fall off, get less, go to pot, incline, plummet, regress, say no to, subside, tail off **08** come down, decrease, diminish, downturn, fall away, lowering, nosedive, peter out, turn down **09** abatement, catabasis, decadence, decadency, declivity, deviation, downswing, dwindling, lessening, recession, reduction, repudiate, weakening, worsening
10 become less, condescend, de-escalate, degenerate, diminution, divergence, falling-off, go downhill, go to pieces, sunsetting **11** declination, dégringoler, deteriorate **12** de-escalation, degeneration
13 deterioration, retrogression

decode
04 dope **05** clear, crack **07** decrypt, dope out, make out, unravel, work out
08 construe, decipher, uncipher
09 figure out, interpret, translate
10 understand, unscramble
13 transliterate

decomposable
10 degradable **12** destructible
13 biodegradable
14 decompoundable

decompose
◇ *anagram indicator*
03 rot **05** decay, go bad, go off, spoil
06 fester **07** break up, crumble, degrade, putrefy **08** dissolve, fragment, pyrolyse, separate **09** break down **10** decompound
12 depolymerize, disintegrate

decomposition
03 rot **05** decay **07** rotting **08** going bad, going off **09** perishing, putridity, pyrolysis **10** corruption, hydrolysis, photolysis, radiolysis **11** degradation, dissolution, putrescence
12 electrolysis, fermentation, putrefaction **14** disintegration

decontaminate
05 clean, purge **06** purify **07** cleanse
08 fumigate, sanitize **09** disinfect, sterilize

décor
07 scenery **10** decoration
11 furnishings **12** colour scheme
13 ornamentation

decorate
03 ice **04** cite, deck, do up, hang, pink, trim **05** adorn, array, chase, crown, grace, paint, paper **06** bedaub, colour, daiker, enrich, fangle, honour, parget, reward, tart up **07** bedizen, bemedal, deck out, embrave, festoon, furbish, garland, garnish, smarten, trick up
08 beautify, damaskin, ornament, prettify, renovate, spruce up, trick out
09 damascene, damaskeen, damasquin, embellish, guilloche, refurbish, scrimshaw, wallpaper
10 damasceene **12** give a medal to
13 give an award to **14** give an honour to

decoration
04 paua, star **05** award, badge, cross, crown, décor, frill, honor, medal, mural, order, title **06** bauble, doodad, doodah, emblem, honour, laurel, parget, ribbon, scroll, wreath
07 bunting, colours, garland, garnish, trinket **08** diamanté, flourish, frou-frou, insignia, ornament, parament, trimming **09** adornment
10 enrichment, Japanesery, knick-knack **11** elaboration, enhancement, furnishings **12** colour scheme
13 embellishment, ornamentation
14 beautification

See also **honour**; **military**

decorative
05 fancy **06** flashy, ornate, pretty, rococo **08** adorning **09** elaborate, enhancing **10** ornamental
11 beautifying, prettifying
12 embellishing **13** non-functional

decorous
03 fit **05** staid **06** comely, decent, modest, polite, proper, sedate, seemly
07 correct, courtly, refined
08 becoming, mannerly, menseful, suitable **09** befitting, dignified
11 appropriate, comme il faut, well-behaved **13** parliamentary

decorum
05 grace **07** decency, dignity, honesty, modesty **08** breeding, courtesy, good form, protocol **09** behaviour, etiquette, propriety, restraint
10 conformity, deportment, politeness, seemliness **11** good manners **14** respectability

decoy
04 bait, draw, lead, lure, tice, tole, toll, trap **05** dummy, piper, roper, shill, snare, stale, stall, tempt **06** allure, bonnet, button, entice, entrap, seduce, trepan **07** attract, deceive, ensnare, pitfall, roper-in **08** inveigle, pretence
09 diversion **10** allurement, attraction, enticement, inducement, red herring, temptation **11** ensnarement, stool pigeon, tame cheater

decrease
03 ebb **04** drop, ease, fall, loss, slim, trim, wane **05** abate, decay, let up, lower, slide, taper, wanze **06** decrew, go down, lessen, plunge, reduce, shrink
07 curtail, cut back, cutback, cut down, decline, dwindle, fall off, plummet, slacken, subside **08** come down, contract, diminish, downturn, lowering, make less, peter out, rollback, slim down, step-down, taper off **09** abatement, decrement, dwindling, lessening, reduction, scale down, shrinkage
10 become less, de-escalate, degression, diminution, falling-off, subsidence
11 contraction **12** de-escalation

decree
03 act, law, saw **04** fiat, rule, will
05 edict, enact, grace, irade, novel, order, ukase, write **06** decern, decide, direct, enjoin, firman, modify, ordain, ruling **07** command, dictate, lay down, mandate, novelle, precept, statute
08 proclaim, psephism, rescript
09 determine, directive, enactment, indiction, interdict, judgement, manifesto, ordinance, prescribe, pronounce, testament **10** regulation
11 hatti-sherif **12** interlocutor, proclamation, promulgation
13 interlocution **14** senatus consult

decrepit
03 old **04** aged, weak **05** frail, warby
06 feeble, infirm, past it **07** elderly, rickety, run-down, worn-out
08 battered, spavined **09** crumbling, doddering, enfeebled, getting on, senescent, tottering **10** broken-down, clapped-out, in bad shape, ramshackle, tumbledown
11 dilapidated, over the hill **12** falling apart **13** falling to bits **14** in bad condition **15** falling to pieces

decrepitude
04 ruin **05** decay **06** dotage, old age
08 debility, senility, weakness
09 infirmity **10** disability, feebleness, incapacity, senescence **11** ricketiness
12 degeneration, dilapidation
13 deterioration **14** incapacitation

decriminalize
05 allow **06** permit, ratify **07** approve, license, warrant **08** legalize, sanction, validate **09** authorize **10** legitimize

decry
03 pan **04** carp, crab, slam **05** blame, knock, slate, snipe **06** attack
07 censure, condemn, devalue, nit-pick, run down, traduce **08** belittle, denounce, derogate **09** criticize, denigrate, disparage, excoriate, underrate **10** animadvert, come down on, depreciate, preach down, undervalue **12** disapprove of, pull to pieces, tear to shreds **13** find fault with, tear a strip off **14** declaim against, inveigh against **15** do a hatchet job on

dedicate
04 bind, give, name, open **05** bless, offer **06** assign, commit, devote,

hallow, pledge **07** address, devoted, present **08** inscribe, make holy, sanctify, set apart **09** sacrifice, surrender **10** consecrate, give over to, inaugurate

dedicated
06 oblate **07** bespoke, devoted, sold out, staunch, zealous **08** diligent **09** committed, sold out on **10** customized, purposeful **11** custom-built, given over to, hard working, industrious **12** card-carrying, enthusiastic, single-minded, wholehearted **13** dyed-in-the-wool, single-hearted

dedication
04 wake, zeal **07** address, loyalty **08** blessing, devotion **09** adherence, hallowing **10** allegiance, attachment, commitment, enthusiasm **11** benediction, inscription **12** consecration, faithfulness, presentation **13** self-sacrifice **14** sanctification

deduce
04 dope, draw, suss **05** glean, infer **06** derive, gather, reason **07** dope out, surmise, work out **08** conclude **09** figure out, syllogize **10** understand

deduct
04 dock **06** deduce, reduce, remove, weaken **07** take off **08** knock off, reduce by, separate, subtract, take away, take from, withdraw **09** strike off **10** decrease by

deduction
04 dock **06** result **07** finding, removal, reprise **08** decrease, discount **09** abatement, allowance, corollary, inference, reasoning, reduction, surmising, taking off **10** assumption, conclusion, consectary, diminution, hypothesis, taking away, withdrawal **11** consequence, presumption, subtraction **12** off-reckoning

• **clear of deductions**
03 net **04** nett

deed
03 act **04** fact, feat, work **05** issue, starr, title, truth **06** action, escrow, factum, record **07** charter, exploit, reality **08** activity, contract, document, mortgage, valiance, valiancy **09** actuality, agreement, endeavour, indenture, quitclaim, specialty **10** attainment, backletter, bill of sale **11** achievement, disposition, enfeoffment, infeudation, performance, transaction, undertaking **14** accomplishment

deem
03 see **04** hold **05** judge, think **06** esteem, reckon, regard **07** account, adjudge, believe, imagine, opinion, suppose **08** conceive, consider, estimate

deep
03 far, low, sea **04** bass, dark, full, lost, main, rapt, rich, warm, wise **05** briny, grave, ocean, quiet, sound, thick, vivid **06** arcane, ardent, astute, clever, gaping, intent, severe, strong **07** abysmal, abyssal, booming, cunning, earnest, extreme, faraway, fervent, glowing, intense, learned, obscure, serious, yawning **08** absorbed, abstruse, a long way, esoteric, high seas, immersed, powerful, profound, reserved, resonant, sonorous, the drink, vigorous **09** brilliant, cavernous, difficult, engrossed, excessive, full-toned, heart-felt, intensely, recondite, sagacious, unplumbed, very great **10** bottomless, discerning, fathomless, low-pitched, mysterious, passionate, perceptive, profoundly, resounding, unfathomed **11** deep as a well, impassioned, preoccupied, uncrossable **12** immeasurable, intellectual, wholehearted **13** knowledgeable, perspicacious **14** a great distance

deepen
04 grow **06** bump up, dig out, extend, hike up, hollow, step up, worsen **07** build up, magnify **08** excavate, get worse, heighten, increase, mushroom, scoop out **09** intensify, reinforce, scrape out **10** strengthen **11** deteriorate

deeply
04 upsy **05** sadly, upsee, upsey **06** keenly **07** acutely, gravely, greatly, sharply **08** ardently, movingly, severely, strongly, very much **09** earnestly, extremely, feelingly, fervently, intensely, seriously **10** completely, mournfully, profoundly, thoroughly, to the quick, vigorously **12** passionately **13** distressingly

deep-seated
04 deep **05** fixed **07** chronic, settled **08** intimate, Plutonic, profound **09** confirmed, ingrained **10** deep-rooted, entrenched **11** fundamental

deer
03 doe **04** buck, fawn, hart, hind, spay, stag **05** Bambi, spade, spayd **06** cervid, rascal, spayad **07** pricket, spitter **08** staggard

Deer include:

03 elk, hog, red, roe
04 axis, mule, musk, pudu, rusa, sika
05 moose, water
06 chital, fallow, forest, sambar, sambur, tufted, wapiti
07 barking, brocket, caribou, jumping, muntjac, muntjak
08 cariacou, carjacou, Irish elk, reindeer, Virginia
09 barasinga
10 barasingha, chevrotain, Père David's
11 black-tailed, white-tailed
12 Chinese water, Indian sambar
13 Indian muntjac

deface
◇ *head deletion indicator*
03 mar **04** ruin **05** spoil, sully **06** damage, defame, deform, impair, injure **07** blemish, destroy, tarnish **08** mutilate **09** disfigure, vandalize **10** disfeature, obliterate

de facto
04 real **06** actual, in fact, really **08** actually, existing, in effect **10** in practice

defamation
04 slur **05** libel, smear **07** calumny, obloquy, scandal, slander **08** innuendo, slamming **09** aspersion **10** backbiting, derogation, opprobrium **11** badmouthing, denigration, malediction, mud-slinging, slagging-off, traducement **12** vilification **13** disparagement, smear campaign

defamatory
09 aspersory, injurious, insulting, libellous, vilifying **10** calumnious, derogatory, pejorative, scandalous, scurrilous, slanderous **11** denigrating, disparaging, maledictory, mud-slinging **12** contumelious

defame
04 slag, slam **05** cloud, libel, smear **06** deface, infame, infamy, malign, vilify **07** asperse, blacken, blemish, detract, run down, scandal, slag off, slander, traduce **08** badmouth, besmirch, disgrace, infamize **09** bespatter, denigrate, discredit, dishonour, disparage **10** calumniate, sling mud at, stigmatize, throw mud at, vituperate **11** speak evil of **14** cast aspersions

default
04 fail, lack, loss, want **05** dodge, evade, fault, lapse **06** defect **07** absence, defraud, failing, failure, neglect, offence, swindle **08** omission **09** backslide **10** deficiency, negligence, non-payment **11** dereliction

defaulter
04 duck **08** absentee, lame duck, non-payer, offender **11** non-appearer

defeat
03 gub, lam, war **04** balk, beat, best, drub, foil, kill, lick, loss, rout, ruin, tank, tonk, undo, whip **05** annul, block, crush, excel, paste, quell, repel, smash, stump, throw, thump, worst **06** baffle, granny, hammer, outwit, puzzle, reject, subdue, thrash, thwart **07** beating, clobber, conquer, debacle, eclipse, failure, inch out, outplay, pasting, perplex, reverse, setback, surpass, tanking, trounce **08** confound, conquest, crushing, downfall, drubbing, obstruct, outmatch, outscore, outsmart, overcome, squabash, throw out, vanquish, Waterloo, whipping, whupping **09** breakdown, checkmate, defeature,

devastate, discomfit, disfigure, frustrate, marmelize, overmatch, overpower, overthrow, overwhelm, pulverize, rejection, repulsion, shoot down, slaughter, subjugate, thrashing, thwarting, trouncing **10** annihilate, defeasance, disappoint, disconcert, overcoming **11** frustration, subjugation **12** annihilation, pip at the post, vanquishment **13** have the edge on, put to the worse, run rings round **14** disappointment, get the better of **15** make mincemeat of

defeatist

06 gloomy **07** quitter, yielder **08** helpless, hopeless, negative, resigned **09** doomsayer, pessimist **10** despairing, despondent, fatalistic **11** doomwatcher, pessimistic **13** prophet of doom

defecate

03 poo **04** crap, mute, plop, poop **05** egest **07** excrete, scumber, skummer **08** evacuate **11** do number two, pass a motion **12** cover the feet, ease yourself **13** void excrement **14** do your business, move your bowels **15** empty your bowels, relieve yourself

defect

03 bug **04** flaw, lack, snag, spot, want **05** craze, error, fault, rebel, taint **06** desert, hiatus, renege, revolt, wreath **07** abandon, abscond, absence, blemish, default, demerit, failing, frailty, mistake **08** hamartia, omission, psellism, weakness, weak spot **09** deformity, shortfall **10** apostatize, break faith, deficience, deficiency, inadequacy **11** change sides, jump the dyke, loup the dyke, shortcoming, turn traitor **12** imperfection, tergiversate

defection

06 mutiny, revolt **07** perfidy, treason **08** apostasy, betrayal **09** breakaway, desertion, rebellion **10** absconding, disloyalty, renegation **11** abandonment, backsliding, defalcation, dereliction **14** tergiversation

defective

◇ *anagram indicator*

04 bust, duff **05** kaput, trick, wrong **06** broken, faulty, flawed **08** abnormal **09** deficient, imperfect **10** on the blink, on the fritz, out of order **11** in disrepair **12** insufficient **14** malfunctioning

defector

03 rat **05** Judas, rebel **07** traitor **08** apostate, betrayer, deserter, mutineer, quisling, recreant, renegade, turncoat **10** backslider **13** tergiversator

defence

04 army, case, keep, navy, plea, wall **05** alibi, cover, guard **06** excuse, screen, shield, troops **07** apology, bastion, bulwark, outpost, rampart, shelter, weapons **08** advocacy, air force, apologia, argument, buttress, fortress, garrison, immunity, military, munition, pleading, security, soldiers, weaponry **09** armaments, barricade, deterrent, safeguard, testimony **10** apologetic, deterrence, munifience, protection, resistance, stronghold **11** armed forces, exoneration, explanation, explication, extenuation, vindication **12** propugnation **13** fortification, justification

• **air defence**

02 AD

See also **fortification**

defenceless

04 weak **05** naked, silly **07** exposed, unarmed **08** helpless, impotent **09** guardless, powerless, unguarded **10** undefended, vulnerable **11** susceptible, unprotected **12** open to attack

defend

04 back, fend, hold **05** cover, deter, guard, plead **06** assert, forbid, oppose, resist, screen, secure, shield, uphold **07** bolster, bulwark, contest, endorse, enguard, explain, fortify, justify, protect, shelter, stand by, support, warrant **08** argue for, bestride, buttress, champion, garrison, maintain, preserve, prohibit **09** barricade, exonerate, safeguard, vindicate, watch over, withstand **10** go to bat for, speak up for, stand up for, stick up for **12** keep from harm, make a case for **15** fight your corner, stand your corner

defendant

03 def, dft **07** accused **08** litigant, offender, prisoner **09** appellant **10** respondent

defender

04 back **05** guard **06** backer, keeper, patron **07** bastion, counsel, sponsor, warrant **08** advocate, asserter, assertor, champion, endorser, guardian, upholder **09** apologist, bodyguard, defendant, preserver, promachos, protector, supporter **10** vindicator

defensible

04 safe **05** valid **06** secure **07** tenable **08** arguable **09** plausible **10** pardonable, vindicable **11** impregnable, justifiable, permissible **12** maintainable, unassailable

defensive

04 wary **08** cautious, opposing, watchful **09** defending **10** apologetic, protecting, protective **12** safeguarding **13** Maginot-minded, oversensitive, self-defensive **14** self-justifying

• **defensive ring**

04 laer **06** corral, laager

defer

03 bow **05** delay, waive, yield **06** accede, comply, give in, put off, shelve, submit **07** adjourn, give way, put back, rejourn, respect, suspend **08** hold over, postpone, prorogue, protract, put on ice, roll over **09** acquiesce, surrender **10** capitulate **13** procrastinate

deference

04 duty **06** esteem, honour, regard **07** respect **08** civility, courtesy, yielding **09** obedience, reverence, servility **10** compliance, politeness, submission **12** acquiescence **13** attentiveness, consideration **14** respectfulness, submissiveness, thoughtfulness

deferential

05 civil **06** humble, polite **07** dutiful **08** obeisant, reverent **09** attentive, courteous, regardful **10** morigerous, obsequious, respectful **11** complaisant, reverential **12** ingratiating

deferment

04 stay **05** delay **07** waiving **08** deferral, shelving **10** moratorium, putting-off, suspension **11** adjournment, holding-over, prorogation **12** postponement **15** procrastination

defiance

08 contempt **09** challenge, contumacy, disregard, insolence **10** opposition, resistance, truculence **12** disobedience **13** confrontation, recalcitrance **14** rebelliousness **15** insubordination

• **expression of defiance**

03 yah **04** nuts **05** ya-boo **06** yah-boo **10** ya-boo sucks **11** yah-boo sucks

defiant

04 bold **08** insolent, militant, roisting, roysting, scornful **09** obstinate, resistant, truculent **10** aggressive, rebellious, refractory **11** challenging, disobedient, provocative **12** antagonistic, contemptuous, contumacious, intransigent, recalcitrant **13** insubordinate, unco-operative

defiantly

05 acock **06** boldly **10** insolently, militantly, scornfully **11** obstinately, truculently **12** aggressively, rebelliously **13** disobediently, provocatively **14** contemptuously, contumaciously, intransigently, recalcitrantly **15** insubordinately, unco-operatively

deficiency

04 flaw, lack, want **05** fault, minus **06** dearth, defect, shorts **07** absence, deficit, failing, frailty, poverty, wantage **08** scarcity, shortage, weakness **10** inadequacy, scantiness **11** shortcoming **12** imperfection **13** insufficiency

Deficiencies include:

07 acapnia, amentia, hypoxia

09 cytopenia, hypinosis, hypoxemia, oligaemia, spanaemia

10 hypoxaemia
11 hypospadias, sideropenia
14 leucocytopenia, oligocythaemia

deficient
◇ *anagram indicator*
03 low **04** poor, weak **05** minus, scant, short **06** meagre, scanty, scarce, skimpy **07** lacking, wanting
08 bankrupt, exiguous, inferior
09 imperfect **10** defectible, inadequate, incomplete **12** insufficient
14 unsatisfactory

deficit
04 lack, loss **07** arrears, default
08 shortage **09** shortfall **10** deficiency

defile
◇ *anagram indicator*
03 col, ray **04** file, gate, moil, pass, soil
05 dirty, gorge, gully, halse, hause, hawse, spoil, stain, sully, taint
06 debase, defame, defoul, enseam, infect, ravine, valley **07** blacken, corrupt, degrade, passage, pollute, profane, tarnish, violate, vitiate
08 disgrace, maculate **09** denigrate, desecrate, dishonour, inquinate
10 make impure **11** contaminate, make unclean

defilement
04 moil **08** foulness, impurity, staining, sullying, tainting, tainture **09** pollution, profanity, violation **10** debasement, defamation, tarnishing **11** degradation, denigration, desecration
13 conspurcation, contamination

definable
05 exact, fixed **07** precise
08 definite, specific **10** explicable
11 describable, perceptible
12 determinable, identifiable
13 ascertainable

define
03 fix **05** bound, limit **06** decide, detail **07** clarify, delimit, explain, expound, mark out, pin down, specify
08 describe, pinpoint, spell out
09 delineate, demarcate, designate, determine, elucidate, establish, interpret **12** characterize, circumscribe

definite
04 firm, hard, sure **05** clear, exact, fixed **06** marked **07** assured, certain, decided, obvious, precise, settled
08 clear-cut, distinct, explicit, positive, specific **10** determined, guaranteed, noticeable, particular
12 unmistakable

definitely
06 easily, indeed, surely **07** clearly, for sure, plainly **09** certainly, doubtless, expressly, no denying, obviously, out-and-out **10** absolutely, distinctly, in terminis, positively, undeniably
11 indubitably, undoubtedly
12 unmistakably, without doubt
13 categorically, determinately, unmistakeably **14** unquestionably
15 without question

definition
03 def **05** focus, sense **07** clarity, diorism, meaning **08** contrast
09 clearness, precision, sharpness
10 denotation, exposition, visibility
11 description, elucidation, explanation **12** distinctness, significance **13** clarification, determination **14** interpretation

definitive
05 exact, final **07** classic, correct, perfect **08** absolute, complete, decisive, positive, reliable, standard, ultimate **09** classical **10** conclusive, exhaustive **11** categorical, terminative
13 authoritative

definitively
07 finally **10** absolutely, completely, decisively **12** conclusively
13 categorically **15** authoritatively

deflate
04 dash, slow, void **05** empty, lower
06 debunk, humble, lessen, reduce, shrink, squash, subdue **07** chasten, depress, devalue, exhaust, flatten, let down, mortify, put down, squeeze
08 collapse, contract, decrease, diminish, dispirit, puncture, slow down
09 humiliate **10** depreciate, disappoint, disconcert

deflect
04 bend, draw, turn, veer, wind
05 avert, drift, snick, twist **06** glance, swerve **07** deviate, diverge, head off, refract **08** ricochet, withdraw
09 glance off, sidetrack, turn aside
12 change course

deflection
04 bend, veer **05** drift, snick, throw
06 swerve **07** turning **08** ricochet, twisting **09** deviation, diversion
10 aberration, divergence, refraction
11 glancing-off **12** sidetracking, turning aside **14** changing course

deflower
03 mar **04** harm, rape, ruin **05** force, spoil **06** defile, molest, ravish, seduce
07 assault, despoil, violate
09 deflorate, desecrate

deform
◇ *anagram indicator*
03 mar **04** maim, ruin, warp **05** spoil, twist **06** buckle, damage, deface
07 contort, distort, hideous, malform, pervert **08** misshape, mutilate
09 disfigure, unshapely

deformation
04 bend, warp **05** curve, twist
06 buckle **08** twisting **10** cataclasis, contortion, defacement, distortion, mutilation **11** compression
12 diastrophism, malformation
13 disfiguration, misshapenness

deformed
◇ *anagram indicator*
04 bent **06** camsho, inform, maimed, marred, ruined, warped **07** buckled, crooked, defaced, dismayd, gnarled, mangled, misborn, mishapt, twisted
08 camshoch, crippled
09 camsheugh, contorted, corrupted, distorted, malformed, miscreate, misshaped, misshapen, mutilated, perverted **10** disfigured, miscreated, out of shape

deformity
06 defect **08** claw-foot, misshape, ugliness, vileness **09** grossness
10 corruption, defacement, distortion, misfeature, perversion **11** abnormality, contracture, crookedness, monstrosity
12 imperfection, irregularity, malformation **13** disfigurement, misproportion, misshapenness

defraud
02 do **03** con, rob **04** dupe, fool, nick, rook, rush, swiz **05** cheat, cozen, lurch, screw, sting, trick, wrong **06** delude, diddle, fiddle, fleece, outwit, rip off
07 beguile, deceive, mislead, swindle, swizzle **08** embezzle, hoodwink

defray
03 pay **04** meet **05** cover, repay
06 refund, settle, square **07** appease, satisfy **09** discharge, reimburse
10 recompense

defrost
04 melt, thaw **08** defreeze

deft
04 able, feat, neat **05** adept, agile, handy, natty, nifty **06** adroit, clever, expert, nimble **07** skilful **09** dexterous
10 proficient

deftly
04 ably **05** slick **06** neatly, nimbly
07 adeptly **08** cleverly, expertly
09 skilfully **12** proficiently

defunct
04 dead, gone **05** passé **06** bygone, unused **07** disused, expired, extinct, invalid **08** deceased, departed, finished, obsolete, outmoded
11 inoperative

defuse
◇ *anagram indicator*
04 calm, cool **06** disarm **07** disable, quieten, relieve **08** calm down, cool down, disorder **09** alleviate
10 deactivate, immobilize **11** clear the air

defy
04 dare, face, foil, mock **05** avoid, beard, brave, elude, flout, repel, scorn, spurn **06** baffle, defeat, ignore, resist, slight, thwart **07** despise, discard, dislike, disobey, outdare, provoke
08 confront **09** challenge, disregard, frustrate, stand up to, withstand
10 disrespect **12** rebel against **14** fly in the face of

degeneracy
08 vileness **09** decadence
10 corruption, debasement, debauchery, effeteness, fallenness, immorality, perversion, sinfulness, wickedness **11** degradation,

depravation **12** degeneration **13** deterioration, dissoluteness

degenerate
03 low, rot **04** base, fail, mean, rake, roué, sink, slip, vile **05** decay, knave, lapse, rogue, scamp **06** effete, fallen, rascal, recoil, sinful, sinner, wicked, worsen, wretch **07** corrupt, dastard, debased, decline, fall off, go to pot, ignoble, immoral, regress, villain **08** criminal, decadent, decrease, degender, degraded, depraved, derogate, evildoer, vagabond **09** abandoned, debauched, dissolute, miscreant, perverted, reprobate, scallywag, scoundrel, wrongdoer **10** bastardize, go downhill, ne'er-do-well, profligate **11** degenerated, deteriorate, off the rails **12** deteriorated, troublemaker **13** mischief-maker **14** go down the tubes

degeneration
03 rot **04** drop, slip **05** decay, lapse, slide **06** dry rot **07** atrophy, decline, failure, sinking **08** decrease **09** caseation, steatosis, worsening **10** debasement, falling-off, involution, regression, retrogress **11** degradation **13** deterioration

degradation
05 shame **07** decline **08** comedown, demotion, disgrace, ignominy, vileness **09** abasement, decadence, demission, dishonour **10** corruption, culvertage, debasement, debauchery, degeneracy, fallenness, immorality, perversion, sinfulness, wickedness **11** depravation, downgrading, humiliation **12** degeneration, immiseration **13** decomposition, deterioration, dissoluteness, mortification **14** immiserization

degrade
04 sink **05** abase, erode, lower, shame, sully **06** debase, defile, demean, demote, depose, embace, embase, humble, imbase, impair, reduce, unseat, weaken **07** cashier, cheapen, corrupt, declass, deprive, devalue, drum out, embrute, imbrute, mortify, pervert, put down **08** belittle, diminish, disgrace, dishonor, relegate **09** brutalize, decompose, discredit, dishonour, downgrade, humiliate **10** adulterate, disennoble, prostitute **11** deteriorate, lower in rank **12** reduce in rank

degrading
04 base **07** ignoble **08** debasing, lowering, shameful, unworthy **09** demeaning **10** belittling, cheapening, mortifying **11** disgraceful, humiliating, undignified **12** contemptible, discrediting **13** dishonourable

degree
01 d **02** BA, MA **03** deg, pin **04** mark, rank, rate, rung, step, unit **05** class, first, grade, level, limit, order, point, range, stage, third **06** amount, extent, second, status **07** Desmond, measure **08** position, standard, standing, strength **09** intensity **11** double first **13** baccalaureate

See also **qualification**

• **in a high degree**
02 so **03** far **04** much, very **05** great

• **in a lower degree**
04 less

• **in whatever degree**
02 as

dehydrate
03 dry **05** drain, dry up, parch **06** dry out **09** desiccate, evaporate, exsiccate, lose water **10** effloresce

dehydration
06 drying **08** parching **11** desiccation, evaporation **13** dehumidifying

• **treatment for dehydration**
03 ORT

deification
07 worship **08** revering **09** elevation, extolling, reverence **10** apotheosis, exaltation, veneration **11** ennoblement, idolization **12** divinization, idealization **13** glorification **14** divinification **15** immortalization

deify
03 god **05** exalt, extol **06** revere **07** elevate, ennoble, glorify, idolize, worship **08** idealize, venerate **10** aggrandize **11** immortalize

deign
05 daine, stoop **07** consent **10** condescend **13** lower yourself **14** demean yourself

deity
03 god **04** idol **05** numen, power **06** avatar, heaven, spirit **07** demigod, eternal, goddess, godhead, godhood **08** divinity, immortal, numinous **10** genius loci **11** divine being **12** supreme being

See also **God**; **god, goddess**

dejected
03 low, sad **04** blue, down, flat, glum **05** amort **06** abattu, dismal, gloomy, morose **07** alamort, crushed, doleful, subdued **08** cast down, downcast, wretched **09** depressed, jaw-fallen, miserable, sorrowful **10** chopfallen, despondent, dispirited, melancholy, spiritless **11** crestfallen, demoralized, discouraged, downhearted, melancholic **12** disconsolate, disheartened **14** down in the dumps

dejectedly
05 sadly **06** glumly **08** dismally, gloomily, morosely **09** miserably **10** wretchedly **12** despondently **14** disconsolately

dejection
04 crab **05** blues, dumps, gloom **06** misery, sorrow **07** despair, sadness **09** faintness **10** depression, gloominess, low spirits, melancholy, moroseness **11** despondence, despondency, dolefulness, melancholia, unhappiness **12** wretchedness **14** disconsolation, discouragement, dispiritedness **15** downheartedness

de jure
05 legal **07** legally **08** rightful **10** rightfully

Delaware
02 DE **03** Del

delay
03 lag, let **04** halt, keep, lull, mora, slow, stay, stop, wait **05** check, dally, defer, frist, sit on, stall, stave, tarry **06** dawdle, detain, dilute, dither, hamper, hang on, hinder, hold up, hold-up, impede, linger, loiter, put off, retard, shelve, temper, weaken **07** adjourn, forsloe, forslow, put back, respite, set back, setback, suspend, waiving **08** dawdling, foreslow, hang fire, hesitate, hold back, hold over, interval, obstruct, postpone, put on ice, reprieve, restrain, shelving, stalling, stoppage, tarrying **09** dalliance, deferment, demurrage, detaining, detention, faff about, hesitance, hesitancy, hindrance, lag behind, lingering, loitering, stonewall, tarriance **10** cunctation, dilly-dally, filibuster, hesitation, impediment, moratorium, putting-off, suspension **11** adjournment, holding-over, obstruction, retardation **12** interruption, postponement **13** dilly-dallying, procrastinate **15** procrastination

delayed
04 late **08** retarded

delectable
05 tasty, yummy **06** dainty, lovely **07** savoury **08** adorable, charming, engaging, exciting, luscious, pleasant, pleasing **09** agreeable, beautiful, delicious, palatable, succulent **10** appetizing, attractive, delightful, enchanting **11** flavoursome, scrumptious **13** mouthwatering

delectation
06 relish **07** comfort, delight **08** pleasure **09** amusement, diversion, enjoyment, happiness **11** contentment, refreshment **12** satisfaction **13** entertainment, gratification

delegate
03 del **04** give, name **05** agent, envoy, leave, proxy, vicar **06** assign, charge, commit, depute, deputy, legate, ordain, pass on, second, syndic **07** appoint, consign, deputed, devolve, empower, entrust **08** emissary, hand over, nominate, pass over **09** authorize, designate, messenger, secondary, spokesman **10** ambassador, amphictyon, commission, substitute **11** spokeswoman **12** commissioner, spokesperson **14** representative

delegation
07 embassy, mission **08** legation **09** committal, passing on **10** assignment, commission, contingent, deputation, devolution, entrusting **11** consignment, empowerment, passing over **12** substitution, transference **15** representatives

delete
01 d **03** cut **04** dele, edit **05** erase **06** cancel, cut out, efface, excise, remove, rub out, strike **07** blot out, destroy, edit out, expunge, scratch, take out **08** cross out, white out **09** strike out **10** blue-pencil, obliterate

deleterious
03 bad **07** harmful, hurtful, noxious, ruinous **08** damaging **09** injurious, poisonous, predatory **10** pernicious **11** destructive, detrimental, prejudicial

deliberate
03 set **04** muse, slow **05** think, voulu, weigh **06** advise, debate, ponder, steady, wilful, willed **07** advised, careful, consult, discuss, heedful, knowing, planned, prudent, reflect, studied, weigh up, willful, witting **08** cautious, cogitate, consider, designed, evaluate, measured, meditate, mull over, propense, resolute, ruminate, studious, volitive **09** conscious, leisurely, ponderous, think over, unhurried **10** calculated, considered, excogitate, methodical, preplanned, think about, thoughtful, unwavering **11** circumspect, considerate, intentional, prearranged **12** preconceived, premeditated, professional, unhesitating

deliberately
06 slowly **08** by design, steadily, wilfully **09** carefully, knowingly, on purpose, pointedly, prudently, wittingly **10** cautiously, studiously **11** consciously, in cold blood, ponderously, unhurriedly **12** methodically, thoughtfully **13** calculatingly, circumspectly, coldbloodedly, intentionally

deliberation
04 care **05** study **06** debate, musing **07** caution, counsel, mulling, thought **08** brooding, calmness, coolness, prudence, slowness **09** pondering **10** advisement, cogitation, conferring, discussion, evaluation, excogitate, meditation, reflection, rumination, steadiness, weighing-up **11** calculation, carefulness, forethought **12** consultation **13** consideration, unhurriedness **14** circumspection, thoughtfulness

delicacy
04 care, cate, tact **05** goody, taste, treat **06** dainty, delice, junket, luxury, nicety, relish, sunket, tidbit, titbit **07** finesse, savoury, trinket **08** elegance, fineness, kickshaw, niceness, subtlety, weakness **09** diplomacy, fragility, kickshaws, lightness, precision, sweetmeat **10** daintiness, discretion, morbidezza, refinement, speciality, tenderness **11** bonne-bouche, sensitivity **12** niminy-piminy **13** consideration, exquisiteness, luxuriousness **14** discrimination

delicate
04 fine, mild, nesh, nice, pale, soft, weak **05** bland, dorty, exact, faint, fairy, frail, light, muted **06** ailing, dainty, flimsy, friand, gentle, incony, infirm, luxury, pastel, polite, sickly, slight, subtle, tender, touchy, tricky, unwell **07** awkward, band-box, brittle, careful, elegant, fragile, friande, inconie, precise, subdued, tactful **08** accurate, critical, delicacy, discreet, graceful, hothouse, kid-glove, ladylike **09** airy-fairy, breakable, difficult, exquisite, fairylike, fingertip, luxurious, precision, sensitive **10** diaphanous, diplomatic, fastidious **11** considerate, debilitated, problematic **12** easily broken, in poor health, niminy-piminy, softly-softly **13** controversial, easily damaged, insubstantial

delicately
06 finely, gently, mildly, palely, softly, subtly **07** blandly, faintly **08** daintily **09** carefully, elegantly, tactfully **10** critically, gracefully **11** exquisitely, sensitively **14** diplomatically

delicious
04 good **05** juicy, tasty, yummy **06** choice, delish, morish **07** moreish, savoury, scrummy **08** charming, pleasant, pleasing, tempting **09** agreeable, ambrosial, enjoyable, exquisite, palatable, succulent, toothsome **10** appetizing, delectable, delightful, enchanting, goloptious, goluptious, gratifying, nectareous **11** captivating, fascinating, lip-smacking, pleasurable, scrumptious **12** entertaining **13** mouth-watering

delight
03 joy **04** fain, glee, like, love, rape **05** amuse, bliss, charm, cheer, enjoy, feast, mirth **06** delice, excite, please, ravish, relish, savour, thrill, tickle **07** boast of, ecstasy, elation, enchant, gladden, glory in, gratify, rapture, revel in **08** bowl over, entrance, euphoria, felicity, gladness, pleasure, wallow in **09** amusement, captivate, enjoyment, enrapture, entertain, happiness, transport **10** appreciate, exultation, jubilation, tickle pink **11** contentment, delectation, take pride in **13** entertainment, gratification **14** take pleasure in **15** give enjoyment to

delighted
04 glad **05** happy **06** elated, joyful, joyous, made up, stoked **07** charmed, excited, gleeful, pleased **08** ecstatic, euphoric, jubilant, thrilled **09** enchanted, entranced, gratified, overjoyed **10** captivated, enraptured **11** over the moon, tickled pink **12** happy as Larry **14** pleased as Punch **15** happy as a sandboy

delightful
03 ace **04** nice **05** great, magic, super, sweet **06** divine, groovy, lovely, wizard **07** amusing, darling, the tops **08** charming, engaging, exciting, glorious, luscious, pleasant, pleasing **09** agreeable, appealing, beautiful, diverting, enjoyable, ravishing, thrilling **10** attractive, delectable, enchanting, entrancing, felicitous, gratifying **11** captivating, fascinating, pleasurable, scrumptious **12** entertaining **14** out of this world

• **something delightful**
03 gas

delimit
03 fix, set **04** mark **05** bound **06** define **09** demarcate, determine, establish

delineate
03 fix **04** draw, line, mark **05** bound, chart, stell, trace **06** define, depict, design, render, sketch **07** outline, portray **08** describe, set forth **09** determine, establish, represent

delineation
06 sketch **07** tracing **09** depiction, portrayal, rendering **11** description, presentment **14** representation

delinquency
05 crime, fault **07** misdeed, offence **10** misconduct, wrongdoing **11** criminality, lawbreaking **12** misbehaviour, misdemeanour **13** transgression

delinquent
03 ned, ted **06** bodgie, guilty, remiss, vandal, widgie **07** culprit, lawless, ruffian **08** criminal, culpable, hooligan, offender **09** miscreant, negligent, offending, wrongdoer **10** lawbreaker, malefactor **11** Halbstarker, lawbreaking **13** young offender

delirious
◇ *anagram indicator*
03 mad **04** gone, wild **05** crazy, light **06** elated, insane, raving **07** frantic **08** babbling, demented, deranged, ecstatic, euphoric, frenetic, frenzied, jubilant, rambling, unhinged **09** overjoyed, phrenetic, rapturous, spaced out, wandering **10** hysterical, incoherent, irrational **11** carried away, light-headed, over the moon **13** out of your mind **14** beside yourself

deliriously
◇ *anagram indicator*
10 jubilantly **11** rapturously **12** ecstatically, hysterically

delirium
03 joy **05** fever **06** frenzy, lunacy, raving **07** ecstasy, elation, jimjams, madness, passion, rapture **08** dementia, euphoria, hysteria, insanity, wildness **09** craziness,

phrenesis **10** excitement, jubilation **11** derangement, incoherence **13** hallucination, irrationality

• delirium tremens
03 DTs **05** jumps **07** jimjams **09** Joe Blakes **10** the horrors **11** the dingbats

deliver
02 do **03** aim, rid **04** bowl, cede, deal, free, give, hand, make, save, send, take **05** bring, carry, grant, serve, speak, utter, voice, yield **06** commit, convey, direct, fulfil, launch, nimble, ransom, redeem, render, rescue, strike, supply **07** declare, entrust, express, give out, inflict, manumit, present, provide, release, set free **08** announce, carry out, dispatch, hand over, liberate, live up to, proclaim, transfer, turn over **09** enunciate, implement, pronounce, surrender **10** administer, distribute, emancipate, relinquish **11** give voice to **15** help give birth to

deliverance
06 escape, ransom, rescue **07** freedom, release **08** riddance **09** salvation **10** liberation, redemption **11** extrication **12** emancipation

deliveries
04 over

delivery
04 ball, dlvy, load **05** batch, birth **06** labour, speech, supply **07** travail **08** carriage, dispatch, shipment, transfer **09** elocution, transport, utterance **10** childbirth, conveyance, intonation **11** confinement, consignment, enunciation, parturition **12** accouchement, articulation, distribution, transmission **13** pronunciation **14** transportation

Cricket deliveries include:

06 doosra, googly, teesra, yorker
07 bouncer, swinger
08 Chinaman, fastball, leg break, off break
09 inswinger, leg-cutter, off-cutter
10 outswinger
11 daisy-cutter

• deliveries
04 over

dell
04 dale, dean, hole, vale **05** slade, trull **06** dargle, dimble, dingle, hollow, valley **10** prostitute

delta
01 D

delude
03 kid **04** dupe, fool, hoax **05** blend, cheat, elude, kiddy, trick **06** cajole, have on, lead on, take in **07** beguile, deceive, mislead, two-time **08** hoodwink, misguide **09** bamboozle, misinform **11** double-cross **12** take for a ride **14** pull a fast one on, put the change on

deluge
04 rush, soak, wave **05** drown, flood, spate, swamp **06** drench, engulf **07** barrage, torrent **08** downpour, inundate, submerge **09** avalanche, overwhelm, snow under **10** inundation **11** overflowing

delusion
05 error, fancy **07** fallacy **08** illusion, tricking **09** deception, misbelief **11** false belief **13** hallucination, misconception **14** misinformation **15** false impression, misapprehension

de luxe, deluxe
04 fine, rich **05** grand, plush, swish **06** choice, costly, lavish, luxury, select **07** elegant, opulent, quality, special **08** palatial, splendid, superior **09** exclusive, expensive, luxurious, sumptuous

delve
04 cave, hole, poke, root **05** probe **06** burrow, go into, hollow, hunt in, search **07** dig into, examine, explore, ransack, rummage **08** look into, research, scrabble **10** depression **11** hunt through, investigate

demagogue
06 orator **07** speaker **08** agitator **09** firebrand, haranguer **10** tub-thumper **12** rabble-rouser **13** public speaker

demand
03 ask, run **04** call, need, plea, sale, take, tell, urge, want **05** claim, draft, exact, order **06** ask for, desire, market **07** call for, clamour, command, dictate, inquire, inquiry, involve, request, require, solicit **08** exaction, exigency, insist on, petition, press for, pressure, question **09** cry out for, necessity, stipulate, ultimatum **10** hold out for, insistence **11** interrogate, necessitate, requirement **13** interrogation

• in demand
02 in **03** big **06** trendy **07** desired, popular **08** asked for **09** requested **11** fashionable, of the moment, sought after

demanding
04 hard **05** tough **06** taxing, trying, urgent **07** exigent, nagging, testing, wearing **08** exacting, pressing **09** difficult, harassing, insistent **10** a tall order, exhausting **11** challenging **12** back-breaking

demarcate
03 fix **04** mark **05** bound, limit **06** define, divide **07** delimit, mark off, mark out **08** separate **09** determine, establish

demarcation
04 line **05** bound, limit **06** fixing, margin **08** boundary, division **09** enclosure **10** definition, marking off, marking out, separation **11** distinction **12** delimitation **13** determination, establishment **15** differentiation

demean
03 air **04** bear **05** abase, lower, stoop, treat **06** behave, debase, demote, humble **07** bearing, conduct, degrade, descend **08** belittle, ill-treat **09** deprecate, humiliate, treatment **10** condescend

demeaning
04 base **07** ignoble **08** debasing, shameful, unworthy **09** degrading **10** belittling, cheapening, mortifying **11** disgraceful, humiliating, undignified **12** contemptible, discrediting **13** dishonourable

demeanour
03 air **04** mien, port **06** manner **07** bearing, conduct **08** carriage, semblant **09** behaviour **10** deportment **11** comportment, countenance

demented
◇ *anagram indicator*
03 ape, mad **04** bats, gyte, loco, nuts, wild **05** barmy, batty, buggy, crazy, daffy, dippy, dotty, flaky, gonzo, loony, loopy, nutty, potty, wacko, wacky, wiggy **06** crazed, cuckoo, fruity, insane, maniac, mental, raving, screwy **07** bananas, barking, berserk, bonkers, cracked, frantic, lunatic, meshuga **08** crackers, deranged, dingbats, doolally, frenetic, unhinged **09** disturbed, infuriate, lymphatic, up the wall **10** bestraught, distracted, distraught, frantic-mad, off the wall, off your nut, out to lunch, unbalanced **11** not all there, off the rails, off your head **12** mad as a hatter, off your chump, round the bend **13** off your rocker, out of your head, out of your mind, out of your tree, round the twist **14** off your trolley, wrong in the head

Demeter
05 Ceres

demigod
04 aitu, hero **05** pagod **06** garuda, pagoda

demise
03 end **04** fall, ruin **05** death, dying **07** decease, failure, passing **08** collapse, downfall **09** cessation, departure **10** expiration **11** termination **14** disintegration

demobilize
05 demob **07** break up, disband, dismiss **08** disperse

democracy
08 autonomy, republic **12** commonwealth **14** self-government

democratic
01 D **04** left **07** elected, popular **08** populist **10** autonomous, republican **11** egalitarian **12** Jeffersonian **13** self-governing **14** representative

Democratic Republic of the Congo
03 COD, ZRE

demolish
◇ *anagram indicator*
04 beat, lick, rase, raze, rout, ruin, undo **05** abate, crush, excel, level, quash, quell, repel, wreck **06** hammer, subdue, thrash **07** break up, conquer, destroy, flatten, ruinate, surpass, unbuild **08** bulldoze, knock out, lay waste, massacre, overcome, overturn, pull down, take down, tear down, vanquish **09** break down, devastate, dismantle, knock down, overpower, overthrow, overwhelm, pulverize, slaughter, subjugate, throw down **10** annihilate **14** get the better of

demolition
04 rout, ruin **06** razing **07** beating, licking **08** massacre **09** hammering, levelling, overthrow, slaughter, thrashing **10** breaking-up, clobbering, flattening, surpassing **11** destruction, dismantling, pulling-down, tearing-down **12** annihilation, knocking-down, overpowering, overwhelming

demon
03 ace, imp **04** atua, buff, ogre, Rahu **05** afrit, beast, brute, devil, fiend, freak, ghoul, rogue, satyr **06** addict, afreet, daemon, duende, nicker, savage, wizard **07** dab hand, fanatic, incubus, monster, rakshas, villain, warlock **08** familiar, succubus **09** blue devil, cacodemon **10** evil spirit **11** fallen angel

demonic
03 mad **05** manic **06** crazed **07** frantic, furious, hellish, satanic **08** devilish, fiendish, frenetic, frenzied, infernal, maniacal **09** possessed **10** diabolical

demonstrable
05 clear **07** certain, evident, obvious **08** arguable, positive, provable **09** evincible **10** attestable, verifiable **11** self-evident

demonstrate
04 show **05** march, prove, rally, sit in, teach **06** betray, evince, parade, picket, verify **07** approve, bespeak, betoken, display, exhibit, explain, expound, express, protest **08** describe, indicate, manifest, register, validate **09** determine, establish, make clear, testify to **10** illustrate **11** communicate, remonstrate **12** substantiate **13** bear witness to

demonstration
04 demo, show, test **05** march, proof, rally, sit-in, trial **06** morcha, muster, parade, picket **07** display, protest **08** evidence **09** événement, mass rally, testimony **10** evincement, exhibition, exposition, expression, indication, validation **11** affirmation, description, elucidation, explanation, hunger march **12** confirmation, illustration, presentation, verification **13** communication, manifestation **14** substantiation

demonstrative
04 open, warm **06** loving **07** gushing **08** effusive **09** emotional, expansive, extrovert **10** expressive, scientific, unreserved **12** affectionate

demonstratively
06 openly, warmly **08** lovingly **11** emotionally **12** expressively **14** affectionately

demonstrator
06 shower

demoralize
05 crush, daunt, lower **06** debase, defile, deject, weaken **07** corrupt, deprave, depress, pervert **08** cast down, dispirit **09** undermine **10** disconcert, discourage, dishearten **11** contaminate **14** make despondent

demoralizing
08 daunting **09** weakening **10** depressing **11** dispiriting **12** discouraging **13** disconcerting, disheartening

demote
04 bust **05** break **06** humble **07** cashier, degrade **08** relegate **09** downgrade **12** reduce in rank

demotic
06 vulgar **07** popular **08** enchoric **09** enchorial **10** colloquial, vernacular

demotion
09 degrading **10** relegation **11** downgrading

demur
04 balk, stop **05** cavil, doubt, pause, qualm **06** boggle, object, refuse **07** dispute, dissent, protest, scruple **08** demurral, disagree, hesitate, question **09** misgiving, objection **10** hesitation **11** be unwilling, compunction, reservation **12** disagreement, make question **13** express doubts, take exception

demure
03 coy, mim, shy **04** prim **05** grave, mimsy, quiet, sober, staid, timid **06** chaste, mimsey, modest, prissy **07** primsie, prudish, serious **08** reserved, reticent, retiring **10** unassuming **11** strait-laced

demurely
05 coyly, shyly **06** primly **07** quietly, staidly, timidly **08** modestly **09** seriously **10** reticently **12** unassumingly

den
04 dive, Hell, hole, home, lair, lare, nest **05** haunt, joint, patch, pitch, study **06** bothan, hollow, hotbed, studio **07** hideout, retreat, shelter, spieler **08** hideaway **09** Domdaniel, rock house, sanctuary **12** meeting-place

denial
02 no **03** nay **04** veto **05** denay **06** rebuff **07** démenti, dissent, gainsay, refusal **08** negation, rebuttal, traverse **09** disavowal, dismissal, disowning, forsaking, rejection **10** abjuration, denegation, disclaimer, opposition, refutation **11** prohibition, repudiation **12** disagreement, renunciation **13** contradiction **14** disaffirmation

denigrate
03 bag **05** abuse, decry **06** assail, defame, impugn, malign, revile, vilify **07** blacken, run down, slander **08** belittle, besmirch, fling mud, sling mud, talk down, throw mud, vilipend **09** blackened, criticize, deprecate, disparage **10** calumniate **11** pick holes in

denigration
05 abuse **07** calumny, slander **10** belittling **11** degradation, deprecation **12** vilification **13** disparagement

denizen
07 citizen, dweller, habitué, inhabit **08** habitant, occupant, resident, townsman **10** inhabitant, townswoman

Denmark
02 DK **03** DNK

denomination
04 cult, kind, sect, sort, unit **05** class, creed, faith, grade, order, value, worth **06** belief, Church, parish, school **08** religion **09** communion, face value, tradition **10** persuasion **11** designation **12** constituency **13** religious body **14** religious group

denote
04 mark, mean, note, show **05** imply **06** typify **07** betoken, express, refer to, signify, suggest **08** indicate, stand for **09** be a sign of, designate, represent, symbolize

dénouement
05 close, event **06** climax, finale, finish, pay-off, upshot **07** last act, outcome **08** solution **10** conclusion, resolution **11** culmination, unravelling **13** clarification

denounce
04 post, slag **05** decry, knock, slate **06** accuse, attack, betray, impugn, indict, revile, vilify **07** arraign, censure, condemn, declaim, deplore, rubbish, run down, slag off, thunder, trumpet **08** announce, badmouth, execrate, proclaim **09** castigate, criticize, fulminate, inculpate, pronounce, proscribe **10** denunciate, stigmatize **11** pick holes in **12** pull to pieces, put the boot in, tear to pieces **13** inform against

dense
03 dim **04** dull, dumb, rank, slow **05** close, dopey, heavy, solid, stiff, thick **06** obtuse, opaque, packed, stupid **07** compact, crammed, crowded, intense **08** gormless **09** close-knit, condensed, dim-witted **10** compressed, slow-witted **11** close-packed **12** concentrated,

impenetrable **13** tightly packed **14** jammed together

densely
05 close **06** firmly **07** closely, heavily, solidly, thickly, tightly **09** compactly

density
01 d **04** body, bulk, mass **08** solidity **09** closeness, denseness, solidness, thickness, tightness **10** spissitude **11** compactness, consistency **15** impenetrability

• of little density
04 thin

dent
03 cut, dip, pit **04** bash, dint, drop, fall **05** gouge **06** crater, damage, dimple, hollow, indent, lessen, push in, reduce, weaken **07** depress **08** diminish **09** concavity, deduction, lessening, reduction **10** depression **11** indentation

dentist
03 BDS, DDS, LDS, MDS **06** doctor **08** odontist **09** gum-digger **13** dental surgeon

denude
04 bare **05** clear, strip **06** divest, expose **07** uncover **08** deforest **09** defoliate

denunciation
03 ban **06** attack, threat **07** censure, decrial, obloquy, thunder **09** criticism, invective **10** accusation **11** castigation, commination, fulmination **12** condemnation, counterblast, denouncement **13** incrimination

deny
03 nay **04** nick, reny, veto **05** denay, rebut, renay, reney, renig, unget **06** abjure, disown, forbid, naysay, negate, oppose, rebuff, recant, refuse, refute, reject, renege **07** decline, disavow, dismiss, gainsay, nullify, renague, renegue, sublate **08** abnegate, disallow, disclaim, disprove, forswear, prohibit, renounce, traverse, turn down, withhold **09** disaffirm, repudiate **10** contradict **12** disagree with **14** turn your back on

deodorant
05 scent **06** roll-on **08** fumigant **09** fumigator **10** deodorizer **12** air-freshener, disinfectant **14** anti-perspirant

deodorize
06 aerate, purify **07** freshen, refresh, sweeten **08** fumigate **09** disinfect, ventilate

depart
02 go **03** dep, die, off **04** blow, exit, fork, part, quit, scat, vade, vary, veer, walk, wend **05** go off, lam it, leave, quite, quyte, scoot, scram, skive, split **06** avaunt, decamp, differ, divide, egress, escape, go away, quight, remove, retire, set off, set out, swerve, vamose, vanish **07** bunk off, deviate, digress, diverge, do a bunk, drop off, make off, migrate, pull out, push off, retreat, scarper, swan off, take off, tear off, vamoose, walk off **08** check out, clear off, drop away, get going, make wing, separate, shove off, start out, take wing, turn away, up sticks, withdraw **09** branch off, disappear, do a runner, evaporate, push along, skedaddle, turn aside **10** hightail it, hit the road, make tracks **11** hit the trail, take the road **12** shoot through **13** sling your hook, take your leave **14** absent yourself, make a bolt for it, rattle your dags, take it on the lam **15** make a break for it, take to your heels

departed
04 dead, gone, late, lost, went **07** expired **08** deceased **10** passed away

department
01 D **03** Dep, dpt **04** area, Dept, line, nome, part, unit, wing **05** field, realm **06** agency, branch, bureau, domain, office, region, sector, sphere **07** concern, section, station **08** district, division, function, interest, province **10** cost centre, speciality **11** subdivision **12** organization **14** responsibility

Départements of France:

03 Ain, Lot, Var
04 Aube, Aude, Cher, Eure, Gard, Gers, Jura, Nord, Oise, Orne, Tarn
05 Aisne, Doubs, Drôme, Indre, Isère, Loire, Marne, Meuse, Paris, Rhône, Somme, Yonne
06 Allier, Ariège, Cantal, Creuse, Landes, Loiret, Lozère, Manche, Nièvre, Sarthe, Savoie, Vendée, Vienne, Vosges
07 Ardèche, Aveyron, Bas-Rhin, Corrèze, Côte-d'Or, Essonne, Gironde, Hérault, Mayenne, Moselle
08 Ardennes, Calvados, Charente, Dordogne, Haut-Rhin, Morbihan, Val-d'Oise, Vaucluse, Yvelines
09 Finistère, Puy-de-Dôme
10 Corse-du-Sud, Deux-Sèvres, Haute-Corse, Haute-Loire, Haute-Marne, Haute-Saône, Loir-et-Cher, Val-de-Marne
11 Côtes-d'Armor, Eure-et-Loire, Hautes-Alpes, Haute-Savoie, Haute-Vienne, Pas-de-Calais
12 Haute-Garonne, Hauts-de-Seine, Indre-et-Loire, Lot-et-Garonne, Maine-et-Loire, Saône-et-Loire, Seine-et-Marne, Ville de Paris
13 Ille-et-Vilaine, Seine-Maritime, Tarn-et-Garonne
14 Alpes-Maritimes, Bouches-du-Rhône, Hautes-Pyrénées
15 Loire-Atlantique, Seine-Saint-Denis
16 Charente-Maritime, Meurthe-et-Moselle
18 Pyrénées-Orientales
19 Pyrénées-Atlantiques, Territoire de Belfort
20 Alpes-de-Haute-Provence

departs
01 d **03** dep

departure
03 dep **04** exit **05** going, lucky, shift **06** change, egress, escape, exodus **07** forking, leaving, removal, retreat, veering **08** farewell, going off **09** branching, decession, deviation, egression, going away, variation **10** difference, digression, divergence, innovation, retirement, setting-off, setting-out, withdrawal **11** leave-taking **12** branching out

depend
03 lie **04** need, rely, turn **06** bank on, expect, hang on, lean on, lippen, rely on, rest on, ride on, turn on **07** cling to, count on, hinge on, trust in **08** reckon on **09** be based on, build upon **11** be decided by, be subject to, calculate on **13** be dependent on, revolve around **14** be contingent on, be determined by

dependable
04 sure **06** honest, stable, steady, trusty **07** certain **08** faithful, reliable **09** rock-solid, steadfast, unfailing **11** responsible, trustworthy **13** conscientious **14** tried and tested

dependant
04 ward **05** child, minor **06** charge, client, feeder, minion, vassal **07** protégé, relying **08** creature, hanger-on, henchman, parasite, relative, retainer **09** pensioner **10** contingent **11** subordinate

dependence
04 need **05** abuse, faith, trust **08** reliance **09** addiction, vassalage **10** attachment, confidence, dependency **11** expectation **12** helplessness, subservience **13** subordination

dependency
05 abuse, habit **06** colony **07** support **08** dominion, pendicle, province, reliance, weakness **09** addiction, satellite, territory **10** attachment, immaturity **12** helplessness, protectorate, subservience **13** subordination **14** submissiveness

dependent
04 weak **05** based **07** decided, leaning, reliant, relying, subject **08** dictated, helpless, immature, relative **09** adjective, supported, sustained **10** contingent, controlled, determined, influenced, vulnerable **11** conditional, subordinate

depict
04 draw, show **05** paint, trace **06** detail, devise, record, render, sketch **07** depaint, impaint, outline, picture, portray, present, recount **08** describe, resemble **09** delineate, represent, reproduce **10** illustrate **12** characterize

depiction
05 image **06** sketch **07** drawing, outline, picture **08** likeness

09 detailing, portrayal, rendering 10 caricature 11 delineation, description 12 illustration 14 representation

deplete
05 drain, empty, erode, spend, use up 06 expend, lessen, reduce, weaken 07 consume, eat into, exhaust, run down 08 bankrupt, decrease, diminish, evacuate 09 attenuate 10 impoverish 11 whittle away

depletion
07 using-up 08 decrease, lowering 09 dwindling, lessening, reduction, shrinkage, weakening 10 deficiency, diminution, evacuation, exhaustion 11 attenuation, consumption, expenditure 14 impoverishment

deplorable
◇ *anagram indicator*
03 sad 04 dire 05 woful 06 rueful, woeful 07 chronic, ghastly 08 criminal, grievous, pitiable, shameful, wretched 09 appalling, miserable 10 abominable, despicable, disastrous, lamentable, melancholy, outrageous, scandalous 11 blameworthy, disgraceful, distressing, regrettable, unfortunate 12 disreputable 13 dishonourable, heartbreaking, reprehensible

deplorably
08 shocking 09 miserably 10 abominably, despicably, lamentably, shamefully 11 appallingly 12 outrageously, scandalously 13 disgracefully, unfortunately

deplore
03 cry, rue 04 pine, slam, weep 05 blame, mourn, slate 06 bemoan, berate, bewail, lament, regret, revile 07 censure, condemn, reprove, upbraid 08 denounce, reproach 09 castigate, criticize, deprecate, disparage, grieve for, reprehend, shed tears 12 disapprove of

deploy
◇ *anagram indicator*
03 use 04 open 06 extend, unfold 07 arrange, dispose, scatter, station, utilize 08 position 09 make use of, spread out 10 distribute

depopulate
05 empty 08 unpeople 09 dispeople

deport
03 act 04 bear, hold, oust 05 carry, exile, expel 06 acquit, banish, behave, manage 07 comport, conduct, perform 09 extradite, ostracize, transport 10 repatriate

deportation
05 exile 07 ousting 09 expulsion, ostracism 10 banishment 11 extradition 12 repatriation 14 transportation

deportment
03 air 04 gait, mien, port, pose 06 aspect, manner, stance 07 address, bearing, conduct, manners, posture 08 behavior, carriage 09 behaviour, demeanour, etiquette 10 appearance 11 comportment

depose
04 fire, oust, sack 05 swear 06 attest, demote, remove, topple, unseat 07 degrade, dismiss, unfrock 08 dethrone, displace, down with 09 discharge, downgrade, overthrow 12 disestablish

deposit
◇ *hidden indicator*
03 bed, dep, dew, fan, lay, put, set, sit 04 bank, bung, drop, dump, file, gage, land, lees, park, save, silt, soot, stow, ware, warp 05 amass, dregs, hoard, lay-by, lodge, pay in, place, plant, put by, stake, store 06 depone, locate, margin, pledge, settle, tophus 07 consign, earnest, entrust, fall-out, lay down, put away, put down, reposit, saburra, set down, sublime 08 alluvium, oviposit, retainer, security, sediment, stratify 10 deposition, hypostasis, instalment 11 down payment, part payment, precipitate 12 accumulation

deposition
07 ousting, removal 08 evidence, sediment, toppling 09 affidavit, dismissal, overthrow, statement, testimony, unseating 11 attestation, declaration, illuviation, information 12 dethronement, displacement 13 sedimentation

depository
05 cache, depot, store 07 arsenal 09 warehouse 10 repository, storehouse 15 bonded warehouse

depot
04 camp 05 cache, store 06 garage 07 arsenal, station 08 terminal, terminus 09 barracoon, warehouse 10 depository, repository, storehouse 14 receiving-house

deprave
04 warp 06 debase, defile, infect, seduce 07 corrupt, debauch, degrade, pervert, pollute, subvert, viciate, vitiate 10 demoralize, lead astray 11 contaminate

depraved
04 base, evil, vile 06 sinful, warped, wicked 07 bestial, corrupt, debased, immoral, obscene, vicious 08 criminal 09 debauched, dissolute, felonious, graceless, perverted, reprobate, shameless 10 degenerate, iniquitous, licentious

depravity
04 evil, vice 08 baseness, iniquity, vileness 09 reprobacy, turpitude 10 corruption, debasement, debauchery, degeneracy, immorality, perversion, sinfulness, wickedness 13 dissoluteness

deprecate
04 slam 05 blame, knock, slate 06 berate, reject, revile 07 censure, condemn, deplore, reprove, rubbish, run down, upbraid 08 denounce, object to, reproach 09 castigate, criticize, disparage, protest at, reprehend 12 disapprove of

deprecatory
09 regretful 10 apologetic, censorious, dismissive, protesting 11 reproachful 12 condemnatory, disapproving

depreciate
04 drop, fall 05 lower, slump 06 defame, lessen, malign, reduce, revile, slight 07 decline, deflate, devalue, disable, run down 08 belittle 09 denigrate, disparage, downgrade, underrate 10 undervalue 11 fall in value, make light of 13 go down in value, underestimate 15 decrease in value

depreciation
04 fall 05 slump 08 mark-down, ridicule 09 deflation 10 cheapening, depression, derogation, detraction 11 denigration, devaluation 12 belittlement 13 disparagement 15 underestimation

depredation
04 prey 05 theft 06 damage 07 looting, pillage, plunder, raiding, robbery 08 hardship, harrying, ravaging 09 marauding 10 denudation, desolation, despoiling, plundering, ransacking 11 destruction, devastation, laying waste

depress
03 cut, sap 04 down, push, tire 05 daunt, drain, level, lower, press, slash, upset, weary 06 burden, deject, hammer, humble, impair, lessen, reduce, sadden, weaken 07 cheapen, devalue, exhaust, get down, make sad, oppress 08 cast down, enervate, hold down, push down 09 bring down, press down, undermine, weigh down 10 debilitate, depreciate, discourage, dishearten, overburden

depressant
06 downer 07 calmant 08 relaxant, sedative 09 calmative 13 tranquillizer

depressed
03 low, sad 04 blue, down, glum, poor 05 cowed, doomy, fed up, moody, needy 06 dented, gloomy, hollow, moping, morose, sunken 07 accablé, concave, dumpish, humbled, lowered, run-down, unhappy 08 cast down, dejected, deprived, downbeat, downcast, indented, pushed in, recessed 09 destitute, exanimate, flattened, heartsick, jaw-fallen, miserable 10 a peg too low, despondent, dispirited, distressed, emarginate, melancholy 11 crestfallen, discouraged, downhearted, low-spirited, pessimistic 12 disheartened, low in spirits, out of spirits, under hatches 13 broken-hearted,

disadvantaged **14** down in the dumps **15** poverty-stricken

depressing
03 sad **04** grey, grim **05** black, bleak, doomy, grave **06** dismal, dreary, gloomy, leaden, sombre **07** unhappy **08** daunting, downbeat, hopeless **09** cheerless, dejecting, saddening, upsetting **10** melancholy **11** dispiriting, distressing **12** discouraging **13** disheartening, heartbreaking

depressingly
05 sadly **07** bleakly **08** drearily, gloomily **09** unhappily **10** dauntingly **11** cheerlessly **13** dispiritingly, distressingly **14** discouragingly **15** dishearteningly, heartbreakingly

depression
03 col, dip, pit, PND **04** bowl, dent, dint, dish, glen, hole, sink, slot, swag **05** basin, blues, crash, delve, dumps, fossa, gloom, slump **06** cafard, cavity, dimple, downer, hollow, recess, trough, valley **07** cyclone, decline, despair, foveola, foveole, megrims, sadness, sinkage, sinking **08** black dog, doldrums, glumness, lowering, slowdown **09** baby blues, concavity, dejection, demission, hard times, pessimism, recession, umbilicus **10** desolation, excavation, gloominess, impression, inactivity, low spirits, melancholy, scrobicule, stagnation, standstill, the horrors **11** despondency, indentation, melancholia, unhappiness **12** hopelessness **14** discouragement **15** downheartedness

deprivation
04 lack, loss, need, want **06** denial, penury **07** poverty, removal **08** hardship **09** privation **10** withdrawal **11** bereavement, destitution, withholding **12** disadvantage **13** dispossession **14** impoverishment

deprive
03 rob **04** deny, geld, twin **05** spoil, strip, twine **06** amerce, denude, divest, refuse **07** bereave **08** take away, withhold **09** destitute **10** confiscate, dispossess **11** expropriate

deprived
04 gelt, poor **05** needy **06** bereft, in need **07** lacking **09** destitute **12** impoverished **13** disadvantaged **15** underprivileged

• **be deprived of**
04 lose

depth
01 d **03** bed **04** deep, drop, glow, gulf **05** abyss, floor, midst, range, scope **06** acumen, amount, bottom, extent, middle, vigour, warmth, wisdom **07** fervour, gravity, insight, measure, passion **08** darkness, deepness, richness, severity, strength **09** awareness, intensity, intuition, vividness **10** astuteness, brilliance, cleverness, perception, profundity, shrewdness **11** discernment, earnestness, penetration, seriousness **12** profoundness, remotest area, thoroughness **13** extensiveness **14** third dimension

• **depth charge**
03 can

• **in depth**
08 in detail, thorough **09** extensive **10** thoroughly **11** extensively **12** exhaustively **13** comprehensive **15** comprehensively

deputation
07 embassy, mission **08** legation **09** committee **10** commission, delegation **15** representatives

depute
06 charge, second **07** appoint, consign, empower, entrust, mandate **08** accredit, delegate, hand over, nominate **09** authorize, designate **10** commission

deputize
05 cover **06** act for, double, sub for **07** relieve, replace **08** take over **09** fill in for, represent **10** stand in for, substitute, understudy **11** pinch-hit for **14** take the place of

deputy
02 TD **03** Dep **04** Dept, mate, vice- **05** agent, envoy, locum, nawab, prior, proxy, vicar **06** commis, -depute, legate, second, vidame **07** stand-in **08** delegate, official, prioress, sidekick, sidesman, Tanaiste, vicaress, viscount **09** alternate, assistant, secondary, surrogate **10** ambassador, commissary, lieutenant, subchanter, substitute, vice-consul, vice-regent **11** locum tenens, subordinate **12** commissioner, spokesperson, under-sheriff, vice-chairman, vice-governor **13** pro-chancellor, sheriff depute, vice-president **14** representative **15** second-in-command, vice-chairperson, vice-chamberlain

derail
05 ditch, upset **06** impede **07** disrupt, disturb, prevent **08** displace, hold back, obstruct **14** throw off course

deranged
◇ *anagram indicator*
03 ape, fey, mad **04** bats, loco, nuts, wild **05** barmy, batty, buggy, crazy, daffy, dippy, dotty, flaky, gonzo, loony, loopy, manic, nutty, potty, wacko, wacky, wiggy **06** crazed, cuckoo, fruity, insane, maniac, mental, raving, screwy, skivie **07** bananas, barking, berserk, bonkers, cracked, frantic, lunatic, meshuga **08** confused, crackers, demented, dingbats, doolally, frenetic, frenzied, maniacal, unhinged, unstable **09** brainsick, delirious, disturbed, lymphatic, psychotic, unsettled, up the wall **10** bestraught, disordered, distracted, distraught, frantic-mad, irrational, off the wall, off your nut, out to lunch, unbalanced **11** not all there, off the rails, off your head **12** mad as a hatter, off your chump, round the bend **13** off your rocker, of unsound mind, out of your head, out of your mind, out of your tree, round the twist **14** off your trolley, wrong in the head **15** non compos mentis, out of your senses

derangement
05 mania **06** frenzy, lunacy **07** madness **08** delirium, dementia, disarray, disorder, insanity, neurosis **09** agitation, confusion **10** aberration **11** dislocation, distraction, disturbance **13** hallucination

Derek
02 Bo **03** Del

derelict
04 hobo **05** jakey, tramp **06** beggar, dosser, no-good, ruined, wretch **07** drifter, no-hoper, outcast, run-down, swagman, vagrant **08** deserted, desolate, forsaken, vagabond **09** abandoned, discarded, neglected **10** down-and-out, ne'er-do-well, ramshackle, tumbledown **11** dilapidated, in disrepair **12** down-and-outer **14** good-for-nothing **15** falling to pieces

dereliction
04 ruin **05** ruins **07** evasion, failure, neglect **08** apostasy, betrayal **09** desertion, disrepair, forsaking **10** abdication, desolation, negligence, remissness, renegation **11** abandonment **12** dilapidation, renunciation **13** faithlessness **14** relinquishment

deride
03 rag **04** gibe, jeer, mock, slag **05** knock, laugh, scorn, taunt, tease **06** bemock, chiack, chyack, insult, jeer at **07** disdain, laugh at, scoff at, slag off, sneer at **08** belittle, pooh-pooh, ridicule, satirize **09** disparage, make fun of

de rigueur
04 done **05** right **06** decent, proper **07** correct, fitting **08** decorous, expected, required **09** necessary **10** compulsory **11** fashionable **12** conventional, the done thing

derision
05 scorn **06** insult, satire **07** disdain, hissing, mockery, ragging, teasing **08** contempt, ridicule, scoffing, sneering, taunting **10** disrespect **13** disparagement

• **expression of derision**
02 ho **03** gup, hoa, hoh, mew, yah **05** sucks!, te-hee, ya-boo **06** tee-hee, yah-boo **07** so there **10** get knotted!, sucks to you!, ya-boo sucks **11** yah-boo sucks

derisive
06 ribald **07** jeering, mocking **08** irrisory, scoffing, scornful, taunting **09** insulting **10** disdainful, irreverent **12** contemptuous **13** disrespectful

derisively
10 scornfully **12** disdainfully, irreverently **14** contemptuously
15 disrespectfully

derisory
04 tiny **05** small **06** absurd, paltry
07 risible **08** pathetic, scoffing
09 insulting, laughable, ludicrous
10 inadequate, outrageous, ridiculous
12 contemptible, insufficient, preposterous

derivation
03 der **04** root **05** basis, deriv
06 origin, source **07** descent
08 ancestry, pedigree **09** beginning, deduction, etymology, genealogy, inference **10** extraction, foundation
13 parasynthesis

derivative
03 der **05** deriv, trite **06** branch, copied **07** cribbed, derived, product, spin-off **08** acquired, borrowed, obtained, offshoot, rehashed **09** by-product, formative, hackneyed, imitative, outgrowth, secondary
10 derivation, descendant, second-hand, unoriginal **11** development, plagiarized

derive
03 get **04** draw, flow, gain, reap, stem, take **05** arise, fetch, infer, issue
06 borrow, deduce, evolve, follow, obtain, spring **07** acquire, descend, develop, emanate, extract, proceed, procure, receive **09** originate **14** have its roots in **15** have as the source, have its origin in

• **derived from**
02 of

derogatory
05 snide **06** snidey **08** critical
09 injurious, insulting, offensive, slighting, vilifying **10** belittling, defamatory, detracting, detractive, detractory, pejorative **11** denigratory, disparaging **12** depreciative, disapproving, unfavourable
15 uncomplimentary

descend
03 dip **04** dive, drop, fall, sink, stem
05 deign, issue, pitch, slope, stoop, storm, swoop **06** alight, arrive, derive, go down, invade, plunge, spring, tumble **07** decline, emanate, go to pot, incline, pancake, plummet, proceed, subside **08** come down, dismount, move down, take over **09** originate, parachute **10** condescend, degenerate, go downhill **11** dégringoler, deteriorate, go to the dogs **13** lower yourself
14 arrive suddenly

descendant
03 son **04** cion, sien, slip, syen
05 child, niece, scion **06** nephew, sprout **08** daughter

• **descendant of**
01 O'

descendants
04 line, race, seed **05** heirs, issue
06 family, scions **07** descent, lineage, progeny **08** children, mokopuna
09 offspring, posterior, posterity
10 generation, posteriors, successors

descended
04 alit

descent
03 dip **04** dive, down, drop, fall, line, raid **05** blood, pitch, slant, slope, stock, stoop **06** origin, plunge
07 decline, incline, lineage, sinking
08 ancestry, comedown, gradient, heredity, invasion, pedigree
09 decadence, declivity, genealogy, going-down, parentage, subsiding
10 debasement, declension, degeneracy, extraction, family tree
11 degradation **12** degeneration, dégringolade **13** deterioration

describe
◇ *containment indicator*
04 call, draw, hail, talk, tell **05** brand, label, style, sweep, think, trace, write
06 define, depict, detail, relate, report, scrive, sketch, strike **07** explain, express, mark out, narrate, outline, portray, present, recount, scrieve, specify **08** consider, descrive
09 character, delineate, designate, elucidate, represent **10** illustrate
12 characterize **13** give details of

description
04 kind, make, sort, type **05** brand, breed, class, order, style **06** report, sketch **07** account, outline, picture, profile, variety **08** category, portrait
09 chronicle, depiction, narration, portrayal, statement **10** commentary, definement, exposition **11** delineation, designation, elucidation, explanation, portraiture **12** presentation
13 particularism, specification
14 representation

descriptive
05 vivid **07** graphic **08** detailed, striking **09** colourful, pictorial
10 blottesque, expressive
11 elucidatory, explanatory
12 illustrative

descry
03 get, see **04** espy, mark, spot
06 detect, notice, reveal **07** discern, glimpse, make out, observe
08 discover, perceive **09** discovery, recognize **11** distinguish **12** catch sight of

desecrate
◇ *anagram indicator*
05 abuse **06** damage, debase, defile, insult **07** pervert, pollute, profane, violate **09** blaspheme, dishallow, dishonour, vandalize **10** unsanctify
11 contaminate

desecration
06 damage, insult **07** impiety
09 blasphemy, pollution, sacrilege, violation **10** debasement, defilement
11 profanation **12** dishonouring

desegregate
04 join **05** blend, merge **08** intermix
09 harmonize, integrate **10** assimilate
11 incorporate

desert
03 dry, due, fly, rat **04** arid, bare, deny, fail, flee, jilt, quit, void, wild **05** empty, leave, merit, rat on, right, waste, wilds, worth **06** barren, betray, bug out, decamp, defect, forhow, give up, go AWOL, lonely, maroon, recant, return, reward, strand, virtue **07** abandon, abscond, cast off, demerit, deserts, dried up, forsake, parched, payment, run away, sterile **08** desolate, dust bowl, renounce, run out on, solitary, solitude **09** infertile, throw over, walk out on, wasteland **10** apostasize, barrenness, chicken out, recompense, relinquish, wilderness **11** change sides, comeuppance, retribution, uninhabited **12** moistureless, remuneration, tergiversate, uncultivated, unproductive **14** turn your back on, what you deserve
15 leave high and dry, leave in the lurch

Deserts include:

04 Gobi, Thar
05 Kavir, Namib, Ordos, Sturt
06 Gibson, Mojave, Nubian, Sahara, Syrian, Ust'-Urt
07 Alashan, Arabian, Atacama, Kara Kum, Simpson, Sonoran
08 Kalahari, Kyzyl Kum
09 Dzungaria
10 Bet-Pak-Dala, Chihuahuan, Great Basin, Great Sandy, Patagonian, Takla Makan
13 Great Victoria
14 Bolson de Mapimi

deserted
01 d **04** left, lorn, void **05** empty
06 bereft, lonely, vacant **08** betrayed, derelict, desolate, forsaken, isolated, solitary, stranded **09** abandoned, neglected **10** unoccupied **11** god-forsaken, uninhabited
14 underpopulated

deserter
03 rat **06** bug-out, truant **07** escapee, runaway, traitor **08** apostate, betrayer, defector, fugitive, renegade, turncoat
09 absconder **10** backslider, delinquent

desertion
06 bug-out, denial, flight, give up
07 jilting, leaving, truancy **08** apostasy, betrayal, giving-up, quitting
09 decamping, defection, forsaking, going AWOL **10** absconding, casting-off, renegation **11** abandonment, dereliction, running-away
12 renunciation **14** relinquishment, tergiversation

deserve
03 win **04** earn, rate **05** incur, merit
07 justify, warrant **10** be worthy of
12 be entitled to, have a right to, have it coming

deserved
03 apt, due **04** fair, just, meet **05** right **06** earned, proper **07** condign, fitting, merited **08** apposite, rightful, suitable **09** justified, warranted **10** legitimate, well-earned **11** appropriate, justifiable

deservedly
04 duly **06** fairly, justly **07** rightly **08** by rights, properly, suitably **09** fittingly **10** rightfully **11** justifiably **13** appropriately

deserving
05 worth **06** worthy **07** upright **08** laudable, virtuous **09** admirable, estimable, exemplary, righteous **11** commendable, meritorious **12** praiseworthy

desiccated
03 dry **04** arid, dead **05** dried **07** drained, dried up, parched, sterile **08** lifeless, powdered **10** dehydrated, exsiccated

desiccation
07 aridity, dryness **08** parching, xeransis **09** sterility **11** dehydration, exsiccation

desideratum
04 must, need, want **09** essential, necessity, requisite **10** sine qua non **11** requirement **12** prerequisite

design
◇ *anagram indicator*
03 aim, end, lay, map **04** draw, etch, form, gear, goal, hope, logo, make, mean, plan, plot, seal, tatu, tool, wish **05** draft, dream, guide, hatch, model, motif, point, shape, style, think **06** cipher, create, desire, device, devise, draw up, emblem, figure, format, intend, intent, invent, make-up, object, scheme, sketch, slight, tailor, target, tattoo **07** destine, develop, diagram, drawing, fashion, meaning, outline, pattern, project, propose, purpose, sleight, think up, thought **08** conceive, contrive, indicate, monogram **09** blueprint, construct, delineate, fabricate, intention, objective, originate, prototype, structure **10** assignment, compassing, enterprise **11** arrangement, composition, delineation, destination, undertaking **12** construction, contrivement, organization

• **by design**
08 wilfully **09** knowingly, on purpose, pointedly, wittingly **11** consciously **12** deliberately **13** calculatingly, intentionally

designate
03 dub **04** call, name, show, term **05** class, elect, style, title **06** assign, choose, define, denote, select **07** appoint, earmark, entitle, express, specify **08** christen, classify, describe, indicate, nominate, set aside **09** stipulate

designation
03 tag **04** name, term, type **05** label, style, title **07** epithet, marking **08** category, denoting, election, nickname **09** selection, sobriquet **10** definition, indication, nomination **11** appellation, appellative, appointment, description, stipulation **12** denomination **13** specification **14** classification

designer
05 maker **06** author, deccie **07** creator, deviser, planner, plotter, stylist **08** inventor, producer **09** architect, contriver, couturier, fashioner **10** originator **11** draughtsman
See also **fashion**

designing
03 sly **04** wily **05** sharp **06** artful, crafty, shrewd, tricky **07** couture, cunning, devious **08** guileful, plotting, scheming **09** deceitful, underhand **10** conspiring, intriguing **11** calculating

desirability
05 merit, worth **06** allure, appeal, profit **07** benefit **08** sexiness **09** advantage **10** attraction, excellence, popularity, preference, usefulness **12** advisability **13** seductiveness **14** attractiveness

desirable
03 fit, hot **04** good, sexy **06** plummy **07** popular, wishful **08** alluring, beddable, eligible, fetching, in demand, pleasant, pleasing, sensible, tempting **09** advisable, agreeable, appetible, expedient, seductive **10** attractive, beneficial, preferable, profitable, worthwhile **11** appropriate, sought-after, tantalizing **12** advantageous

desire
03 ask, yen **04** Cama, earn, envy, erne, fain, itch, Kama, lech, like, list, lust, need, salt, urge, vote, want, will, wish **05** bosom, covet, crave, fancy, greed, mania, yearn **06** ardour, besoin, demand, libido, take to **07** avidity, burn for, craving, erotism, gasp for, long for, longing, passion, wish for **08** appetite, covetise, feel like, sex drive, yearn for, yearning **09** cacoëthes, hankering, hunger for, lust after, sexuality **10** aphrodisia, aspiration, be dying for, desiderate, preference, proclivity, sensuality **11** hanker after **12** be crazy about, ephebophilia, have a crush on, predilection, take a shine to **13** concupiscence, have designs on **14** have the hots for, have your eyes on, lasciviousness, predisposition, set your heart on **15** give the world for

desired
05 exact, right **06** proper, wanted **07** correct, fitting **08** accurate, expected, in demand, required **09** necessary **10** particular **11** appropriate **13** in great demand

desirous
04 avid, keen **05** eager, ready **06** fervid, hoping, hungry **07** anxious, burning, craving, fervent, hopeful, itching, longing, wanting, willing, wishful, wishing **08** aspiring, yearning **09** ambitious, desirable **10** cupidinous **12** enthusiastic

desist
03 end **04** halt, stay, stop **05** cease, leave, pause, remit, stash **06** give up **07** abstain, forbear, refrain, suspend **08** break off, have done, leave off, peter out **09** supersede **11** discontinue

desk
04 ambo **05** desse, table **06** bureau, carrel, pulpit **07** carrell, lectern, lecturn, lettern, rolltop **08** prie-dieu, vargueño **09** davenport, écritoire, faldstool, secretary **10** secretaire **11** litany-stool, reading-desk **12** writing-table **13** bonheur-du-jour

desolate
03 sad **04** arid, bare, wild **05** bleak, floor, gaunt, upset, waste **06** barren, bereft, desert, dismal, dreary, gloomy, gousty, lonely **07** forlorn, get down, nonplus, shatter, unhappy **08** confound, dejected, deserted, downcast, forsaken, isolated, solitary, unpeeled, wasteful, wretched **09** abandoned, depressed, devastate, discomfit, miserable, overwhelm, take aback, wasteland **10** depressing, despondent, disconcert, distressed, drearisome, melancholy, unoccupied **11** comfortless, god-forsaken, heartbroken, uninhabited **12** disheartened, god-forgotten, unfrequented **13** broken-hearted

desolation
04 ruin **05** gloom, grief, waste **06** misery, sorrow **07** anguish, despair, ravages, sadness **08** distress, solitude, wildness **09** bleakness, dejection, emptiness, isolation **10** barrenness, depression, loneliness, melancholy, remoteness, wilderness **11** despondency, destruction, devastation, forlornness, laying waste, unhappiness **12** wretchedness

despair
05 gloom **06** give in, give up, misery **07** anguish, wanhope **08** collapse, distress, lose hope **09** dejection, dysthymia, lose heart, pessimism, surrender **10** depression, melancholy **11** desperation, despondency **12** be despondent, hopelessness, wretchedness **13** be discouraged, hit rock bottom **15** throw in the towel

despairing
08 dejected, desolate, dismayed, downcast, hopeless, suicidal, wretched **09** anguished, depressed, desperate, miserable, sorrowful **10** despondent, distraught **11** au désespoir, desperation, discouraged, heartbroken, pessimistic **12** disconsolate, disheartened, inconsolable **13** grief-stricken

despatch *see* **dispatch, despatch**

desperado
04 thug **06** badman, bandit, gunman, mugger, outlaw **07** brigand, hoodlum, ruffian **08** criminal, gangster **09** cut-throat, terrorist **10** lawbreaker

desperate
◇ *anagram indicator*
04 bold, dire, rash, wild **05** acute, dying, grave, great, hasty, risky
06 daring, severe, urgent **07** acharné, crucial, do-or-die, extreme, frantic, furious, lawless, serious, violent
08 critical, dejected, desolate, dismayed, downcast, frenzied, hairless, hopeless, pressing, reckless, suicidal, wretched **09** abandoned, anguished, audacious, dangerous, depressed, foolhardy, hazardous, impetuous, miserable, sorrowful
10 compelling, despondent, determined, distraught, incautious, on the ropes **11** discouraged, heartbroken, in great need, pessimistic, precipitate **12** at rock-bottom, crying out for, disconsolate, disheartened, inconsolable **13** grief-stricken **15** needing very much, wanting very much

desperately
◇ *anagram indicator*
05 badly **07** acutely, gravely, greatly
08 severely, urgently **09** extremely, fearfully, seriously **10** critically, dreadfully, hopelessly **11** à corps perdu, dangerously, frightfully

desperation
04 fury, pain **05** agony, gloom, worry
06 misery, sorrow **07** anguish, anxiety, despair, trouble **08** distress
10 depression, despairing
11 despondency **12** hopelessness, recklessness, wretchedness

despicable
03 bum, low **04** base, mean, vile
05 dirty, spewy **07** caitiff, lowdown, pitiful **08** dwarfish, shameful, wretched **09** dastardly, degrading, loathsome, reprobate, worthless
10 abominable, detestable, disgusting
11 disgraceful **12** contemptible, disreputable **13** reprehensible
15 beneath contempt

despise
04 hate, mock, shun **05** abhor, scorn, sneer, spurn **06** deride, detest, forhow, loathe, revile, slight **07** condemn, conspue, contemn, deplore, disdain, dislike **08** vilipend **10** look down on, undervalue **11** set at naught, set at nought **14** hold in contempt

despite
07 against, defying **09** in spite of **11** in the face of **12** regardless of, undeterred by **15** notwithstanding

despoil
03 rob **04** loot, rape **05** pluck, rifle, spoil, strip, wreck **06** bezzle, denude, divest, maraud, ravage **07** bereave, deprive, destroy, pillage, plunder, ransack **08** spoliate **09** depredate, devastate, vandalize **10** disgarnish, dispossess, untreasure

despondency
04 hump **05** blues, gloom, grief
06 misery, sorrow **07** despair, sadness
08 distress, glumness **09** dejection, heartache, pessimism **10** depression, melancholy **11** desperation, melancholia **12** hopelessness, wretchedness **14** discouragement, dispiritedness **15** downheartedness, inconsolability

despondent
03 low, sad **04** blue, down, glum
06 gloomy **07** doleful **08** dejected, downcast, mournful, wretched
09 depressed, heartsick, miserable, sorrowful **10** despairing, distressed, melancholy **11** discouraged, heartbroken **12** disheartened, inconsolable **14** down in the dumps

despot
04 boss, czar, tsar, tzar **06** sultan, tyrant **08** autocrat, dictator
09 oppressor **10** absolutist
13 absolute ruler

Despots include:

03 Idi
04 Amin (Idi)
05 Timur
06 Caesar (Julius), Führer, Hitler (Adolf), Stalin (Joseph)
07 Papa Doc
08 Duvalier (François)
09 Ceausescu (Nicolae), Mao Zedong, Tamerlane
10 Mao Tse-tung
11 Robespierre (Maximilien de), Tamburlaine
15 Ivan the Terrible

despotic
08 absolute, arrogant **09** arbitrary, imperious, tyrannous **10** autocratic, high-handed, oppressive, tyrannical
11 dictatorial, domineering, overbearing **13** authoritarian

despotism
07 tyranny **09** autocracy
10 absolutism, oppression, repression
11 stratocracy **12** dictatorship
15 totalitarianism

dessert
03 pud **05** sweet **06** afters **07** pudding
09 sweet dish **11** aftersupper, sweet course

Desserts and puddings include:

03 ice, pie
04 flan, fool, sago, tart
05 bombe, jelly, kulfi
06 mousse, mud pie, sorbet, sundae, trifle, yogurt
07 baklava, cobbler, compote, crumble, parfait, pavlova, soufflé, tapioca, tartufo, yoghurt
08 Eton mess, ice cream, pandowdy, plum-duff, syllabub, tiramisu, vacherin, yoghourt
09 clafoutis, cranachan
10 blancmange, Brown Betty, cheesecake, egg custard, frangipane, fruit salad, panna cotta, peach Melba, zabaglione
11 baked Alaska, banana split, banoffee pie, crème brûlée, Eve's pudding, milk pudding, plum pudding, rice pudding, spotted dick
12 crème caramel, crêpe suzette, fruit crumble, profiteroles
13 fruit cocktail, millefeuilles, summer pudding
14 charlotte russe
15 clootie dumpling, queen of puddings, roly-poly pudding

See also **cake**

destabilize
◇ *anagram indicator*
05 upset **08** unsettle

destination
03 aim, end **04** fate, goal, gole, list, stop **06** design, object, target
07 purpose, station **08** ambition, terminus **09** intention, objective
10 aspiration **11** journey's end **12** end of the line, landing place **15** final port of call, jumping-off place

destined
04 born **05** bound, fatal, fated, meant
06 booked, doomed, headed, marked, routed **07** certain, en route, heading
08 assigned, designed, directed, intended, ordained, set apart
09 appointed, scheduled **10** inevitable
11 inescapable, preordained, unavoidable **12** foreordained
13 predetermined

destiny
03 lot **04** doom, fate, luck **05** karma, Moera, Moira **06** future, kismet
07 fortune, portion **09** necessity
10 predestiny **14** predestination

destitute
04 poor **05** broke, needy, skint
06 bereft, hard up, rooked **07** lacking, wanting **08** badly off, bankrupt, depleted, deprived, devoid of, dirt-poor, forsaken, helpless, indigent
09 deficient, penniless, penurious
10 cleaned out, distressed, down-and-out, friendless, innocent of, stony-broke **11** impecunious, necessitous, on the street **12** impoverished **14** on the breadline, on your beam-ends
15 poverty-stricken, strapped for cash

destitution
06 penury **07** beggary, poverty, straits
08 distress **09** indigence, pauperdom
10 bankruptcy, starvation
13 pennilessness **14** impoverishment
15 impecuniousness

destroy
◇ *anagram indicator*
03 eat, end, gut, zap **04** kill, raze, ruin, slay, undo **05** break, crush, erase, fordo, harry, level, smash, spoil, waste, wreck **06** banjax, canker, defeat, delete, finish, perish, quench, ravage,

subdue, thwart, wither **07** attrite, deep-six, flatten, handbag, kill off, nullify, put down, ransack, ruinate, scuttle, shatter, stonker, torpedo, unshape, vitiate **08** decimate, demolish, dispatch, knock out, lay waste, overturn, pull down, sabotage, stamp out, tear down **09** devastate, dismantle, eliminate, eradicate, extirpate, knock down, marmelize, overthrow, pulverize, slaughter, undermine **10** annihilate, do away with, extinguish, obliterate, put to sleep, spiflicate **11** spifflicate

destroyer

06 locust, vandal **07** flivver, ravager, stew-can, wrecker **08** Apollyon **09** desolater, despoiler, ransacker **10** demolisher, destructor **11** annihilator, kiss of death

destruction

◇ *anagram indicator*

03 end **04** bane, loss, rack, ruin **05** death, havoc, stroy, waste, wrack, wreck **06** defeat, murder, razing **07** killing, undoing, wastage **08** crushing, downfall, massacre, smashing, wreckage **09** levelling, overthrow, ruination, shipwreck, slaughter, vandalism **10** demolition, desolation, extinction, killing-off, ravagement, shattering **11** depredation, devastation, dismantling, elimination, eradication, extirpation, liquidation, pulling-down, tearing-down **12** annihilation, depopulation, knocking-down, obliteration **13** extermination, nullification

destructive

05 fatal **06** deadly, lethal **07** adverse, baneful, harmful, hostile, hurtful, killing, noxious, ruinous, vicious **08** contrary, damaging, deathful, negative **09** injurious, malignant, withering **10** derogatory, disastrous, disruptive, nullifying, pernicious, subversive, unfriendly **11** deleterious, denigrating, detrimental, devastating, disparaging, mischievous, undermining **12** antagonistic, catastrophic, discouraging, pestilential, slaughterous, unfavourable

destructively

08 lethally **09** harmfully, hurtfully **12** disastrously **13** detrimentally

desultorily

07 loosely **08** casually, fitfully **09** aimlessly **11** erratically **13** half-heartedly

desultory

◇ *anagram indicator*

05 hasty, loose **06** casual, fitful, random **07** aimless, chaotic, erratic **08** rambling **09** haphazard, irregular, spasmodic **10** capricious, discursive, disorderly, undirected **11** half-hearted **12** disconnected, inconsistent, unmethodical, unsystematic **13** uncoordinated

detach

04 free, undo **05** calve, draft, sever, split, unfix **06** cut off, divide, loosen, remove, unglue **07** disjoin, divorce, isolate, take off, tear off, unhitch, unloose, unrivet **08** break off, disunite, estrange, separate, take away, uncouple, unfasten, unloosen, withdraw **09** disengage, segregate **10** disconnect, dissociate **11** disentangle

detachable

07 movable **08** moveable **09** removable, separable **10** eradicable, removeable **12** transferable

detached

04 cold, free **05** aloof, loose **06** remote **07** divided, neutral, severed **08** clinical, discreet, discrete, outlying, separate **09** impartial, objective, uncoupled, withdrawn **10** disengaged, impersonal, unattached, undivested, unfastened **11** dissociated, independent, indifferent, unconcerned, unconnected, unemotional **12** disconnected **13** disinterested, dispassionate

detachment

04 unit **05** corps, force, party, squad **06** detail, patrol **07** brigade, removal, reserve, undoing **08** coolness, disunion, fairness, squadron **09** aloofness, isolation, loosening, severance, task force, unconcern **10** dispassion, lack of bias, neutrality, remoteness, separation, uncoupling, withdrawal **11** impassivity, objectivity, unfastening **12** impartiality, indifference, provost guard **13** disconnection, disengagement, disentangling, lack of emotion

detail

◇ *tail deletion indicator*

04 fact, item, list, unit **05** corps, force, point, squad **06** aspect, assign, charge, choose, depict, factor, nicety, patrol, relate, set out **07** appoint, brigade, element, feature, itemize, portray, present, recount, respect, specify **08** allocate, delegate, describe, minutiae, point out, rehearse, specific, spell out, tabulate **09** attribute, catalogue, component, delineate, enumerate, intricacy, precision, task force **10** commission, complexity, ingredient, ins and outs, particular, refinement, triviality **11** elaboration, nitty-gritty **12** circumstance, complication, nuts and bolts, technicality, thoroughness **13** particularity, specification **14** characteristic, meticulousness

• in detail

05 fully **07** in depth **08** at length **09** carefully, piecemeal **10** item by item, thoroughly **12** exhaustively, in particular, particularly, point by point **15** comprehensively

detailed

◇ *tail deletion indicator*

04 full **05** close, exact **06** minute, narrow **07** complex, in-depth, precise, special **08** complete, itemized, specific, thorough **09** elaborate, intricate **10** blow-by-blow, convoluted, exhaustive, meticulous, particular **11** complicated, descriptive **13** comprehensive

detain

04 hold, keep, slow, stay, stop **05** check, delay **06** arrest, hinder, hold up, impede, intern, lock up, retard **07** confine, inhibit **08** hold back, imprison, keep back, make late, restrain, withhold **09** detention **11** incarcerate, put in prison **13** hold in custody, keep in custody **15** take into custody

detainee

03 POW

detect

03 spy **04** find, nose, note, spot, take **05** catch, sense, sight, trace **06** accuse, expose, notice, reveal, turn up, unmask **07** discern, find out, make out, nose out, observe, uncover, unearth **08** decipher, disclose, discover, identify, perceive **09** ascertain, deprehend, recognize, track down **11** distinguish **12** bring to light **13** become aware of

detectable

◇ *containment indicator*

05 clear **07** visible **08** apparent, distinct **10** noticeable **11** discernible, perceivable, perceptible **12** discoverable, identifiable, recognizable **14** before your eyes

detection

04 note **06** exposé **08** exposure, noticing, sighting **09** discovery, unmasking **10** disclosure, perception, revelation, uncovering, unearthing **11** discernment, observation, recognition, smelling-out, sniffing-out **12** ascertaining, tracking-down **14** distinguishing, identification

detective

02 DC, DI, DS, PI **03** Det, eye, 'tec **04** busy, dick, jack, tail **05** plant **06** shadow, shamus, sleuth **07** gumshoe **08** prodnose, sherlock **09** operative **10** bloodhound, private eye, thief-taker **11** sleuth-hound **12** investigator, thief-catcher **13** police officer

Detectives include:

03 Zen (Aurelio)
04 **Bony** (Napoleon Bonaparte), **Chan** (Charlie), **Cuff** (Richard), **Dean** (Sam), **Gray** (Cordelia), **Vane** (Harriet)
05 **Brown** (Father), **Drake** (Paul), **Duffy** (Nicholas), **Dupin** (C Auguste), **Ghote** (Inspector Ganesh), **Grant** (Alan), **Lewis** (Sergeant), **Mason** (Perry), **Morse** (Inspector

Endeavour), **Queen** (Ellery), **Rebus** (John), **Spade** (Sam), **Vance** (Philo), **Wolfe** (Nero)
06 **Alleyn** (Roderick), **Archer** (Lew), **Essrog** (Lionel), **Hanaud** (Inspector), **Holmes** (Sherlock), **Marple** (Miss Jane), **Pascoe** (Peter), **Poirot** (Hercule), **Silver** (Miss Maude), **Vidocq** (Eugène Françoise), **Watson** (Dr John), **Wimsey** (Lord Peter)
07 **Appleby** (John), **Cadfael** (Brother), **Campion** (Albert), **Charles** (Nick), **Columbo** (Lieutenant), **Dalziel** (Andy), **Fansler** (Kate), **Laidlaw** (Jack), **Maigret** (Inspector), **Marlowe** (Philip), **Milhone** (Kinsey), **Moseley** (Hoke), **Wexford** (Reginald)
08 **Bergerac** (Jim), **Lestrade** (Inspector), **Ramotswe** (Precious)
09 **Bonaparte** (Napoleon), **Dalgliesh** (Adam), **Hawksmoor** (Nicholas), **Pinkerton** (Allan), **Scarpetta** (Kay)
10 **Van Der Valk** (Piet), **Warshawski** (V I)
13 **Continental Op**

• detectives
03 CID, FBI

detention
05 delay **07** custody, jankers
09 captivity, hindrance, restraint, slowing-up **10** constraint, detainment, internment, punishment, quarantine
11 confinement, holding-back
12 imprisonment **13** incarceration

deter
04 stop, warn **05** check, daunt
06 hinder, put off **07** caution, inhibit, prevent, turn off **08** dissuade, frighten, prohibit, restrain, scare off **09** talk out of **10** discourage, disincline, intimidate

detergent
04 soap **07** cleaner **08** cleanser
09 cetrimide, detersive **10** abstergent, surfactant **13** washing powder
15 washing-up liquid

deteriorate
03 ebb **04** drop, fade, fail, slip, wane
05 decay, go bad, go off, lapse, slide, spoil **06** go down, starve, weaken, worsen **07** break up, decline, degrade, fall off, go to pot, relapse, tail off **08** get worse, go to seed, tail away
09 decompose, fall apart, grow worse, run to seed **10** degenerate, depreciate, go downhill, retrograde, retrogress
11 become worse **12** disintegrate, fall to pieces **13** go down the tube

deterioration
◇ *anagram indicator*
03 ebb **04** drop **05** decay, lapse, slide
06 waning **07** atrophy, decline, failure, relapse **08** downturn, senility, slipping
09 corrosion, worsening
10 debasement, falling-off, pejoration
11 degradation, dégringoler
12 degeneration, exacerbation
13 retrogression **14** disintegration

determinate
05 fixed **07** certain, decided, defined, express, limited, precise, settled
08 absolute, clear-cut, decisive, definite, distinct, explicit, positive, specific **09** specified **10** conclusive, definitive, quantified **11** established

determination
◇ *ends selection indicator*
03 end **04** grit, guts, push, will
05 assay, drive, value **06** decree, ruling, thrust **07** opinion, purpose, resolve, stamina, verdict **08** backbone, decision, firmness, sentence, tenacity
09 fortitude, judgement, willpower
10 conclusion, conviction, dedication, insistence, resolution, settlement
11 arbitrament, arbitrement, persistence **12** perseverance, resoluteness **13** steadfastness

determine
03 fix, set **04** rule **05** check, elect, fix on, guide, hight, impel, learn, limit, point, shape **06** affect, assign, choose, clinch, decide, define, detect, direct, finish, govern, ordain, prompt, settle, verify **07** agree on, control, dictate, find out, purpose, resolve
08 conclude, discover, identify, regulate **09** ascertain, condition, establish, influence **12** turn the scale
14 make up your mind

determined
03 out, set **04** bent, dour, firm **05** fixed
06 dogged, gritty, intent, single, strong
07 certain, dead set, decided **08** hell-bent, resolute, resolved, stubborn
09 convinced, dedicated, insistent, steadfast, tenacious **10** iron-willed, persistent, purposeful, unwavering
11 ascertained, persevering, tough-minded, unflinching, well-defined
12 single-minded, strong-minded, strong-willed **14** uncompromising

determinedly
06 firmly **08** strongly **09** decidedly
10 resolutely, stubbornly **11** insistently, steadfastly, tenaciously **12** persistently, purposefully **13** unflinchingly
14 single-mindedly, strong-mindedly

deterrence
09 avoidance, hindrance, obviation
10 dissuasion, heading-off, prevention, warding-off **11** elimination

deterrent
03 bar **04** curb **05** block, check
07 barrier **08** obstacle **09** hindrance, repellent, restraint **10** difficulty, impediment **11** obstruction
12 disincentive **14** discouragement

detest
04 hate **05** abhor **06** loathe
07 deplore, despise, dislike
08 execrate **09** abominate, can't stand
10 recoil from

detestable
04 vile **06** horrid, odious, sordid
07 hateful, heinous **08** accursed, horrible, shocking **09** abhorrent, execrable, loathsome, obnoxious, offensive, repellent, repugnant, repulsive, revolting, villanous
10 abominable, despicable, disgusting, villainous **11** abhominable, distasteful **12** contemptible, insufferable, pestilential
13 reprehensible

detestation
04 hate **05** odium **06** hatred
07 dislike **08** anathema, aversion, loathing **09** animosity, antipathy, hostility, revulsion **10** abhorrence, execration, repugnance
11 abomination

dethrone
04 oust **06** depose, topple, unseat
07 uncrown **08** unthrone

detonate
04 pink **05** blast, go off, knock, shoot
06 blow up, ignite, kindle, let off, set off
07 explode **08** spark off **09** discharge, fulminate

detonation
04 bang, boom **05** blast, burst
06 blow-up, report **08** igniting, ignition **09** blowing-up, discharge, explosion **11** fulmination

detour
◇ *anagram indicator*
05 byway **06** bypass, bypath, byroad
09 deviation, diversion **10** digression
11 scenic route **13** indirect route
15 circuitous route, roundabout route

detract
03 mar **04** take **05** abate, lower, spoil
06 defame, lessen, reduce **08** belittle, derogate, diminish, distract, take away
09 devaluate, disparage **10** depreciate
12 subtract from, take away from

detractor
05 enemy **06** critic **07** defamer, reviler
08 traducer, vilifier **09** backbiter, belittler, muck-raker, slanderer
10 denigrator, disparager
11 substractor **13** scandalmonger

detriment
03 ill **04** evil, harm, hurt, loss
05 wrong **06** damage, injury
07 empeach, impeach **08** mischief
09 prejudice **10** diminution, disservice, impairment
12 disadvantage

detrimental
07 adverse, harmful, hurtful
08 damaging, inimical, scathing
09 injurious **10** pernicious
11 deleterious, destructive, mischievous, prejudicial
15 disadvantageous

detritus
04 junk, scum **05** waste **06** debris, litter, rubble **07** garbage, remains, rubbish **08** wreckage **09** fragments

devalue
04 slag, slam **05** knock, lower, slate
06 demean, reduce **07** deflate,

dismiss, run down, slag off
08 decrease, minimize, play down
09 devaluate, disparage, underrate
10 devalorize, undervalue **11** make light of **12** pull to pieces, tear to pieces

devastate

◇ *anagram indicator*
04 raze, ruin, sack **05** floor, level, shock, spoil, waste, wreck **06** ravage **07** despoil, destroy, flatten, nonplus, perturb, pillage, plunder, ransack, shatter **08** confound, demolish, desolate, lay waste, overcome, populate **09** discomfit, overwhelm, take aback **10** discompose, disconcert, traumatize

devastated

◇ *anagram indicator*
05 upset, waste **06** gutted **07** crushed, shocked, stunned **08** appalled, desolate, overcome **09** horrified, in anguish **10** distressed, taken aback
11 heartbroken, overwhelmed, traumatized **13** knocked for six

devastating

05 great **06** lovely **07** harmful, ruinous, wasting **08** crushing, damaging, dazzling, fabulous, gorgeous, incisive, ravaging, shocking, smashing, striking, stunning **09** brilliant, effective, wonderful **10** disastrous, impressive, marvellous, remarkable, shattering, staggering **11** destructive, magnificent, spectacular
12 catastrophic, overwhelming, traumatizing **13** extraordinary

devastation

04 ruin, sack **05** havoc, ruins, waste, wrack **06** damage, ravage **07** pillage, plunder, ravages **08** wreckage
09 wasteness **10** demolition, desolation, spoliation **11** destruction
12 annihilation, fire and sword

develop

◇ *anagram indicator*
03 get **04** grow **05** arise, begin, catch, educe, ensue, found, hatch, ripen, shape, start **06** create, evolve, expand, follow, foster, happen, invent, mature, pick up, result, set off, spread, unfold
07 acquire, advance, amplify, enhance, enlarge, improve, nurture, open out, produce, prosper, shape up, work out
08 argument, commence, contract, dilate on, disclose, expand on, fetch out, flourish, generate, initiate, progress, set about **09** branch out, come about, elaborate, establish, institute, originate, succumb to **10** go down with **11** fall ill with, materialize, set in motion **13** become ill with

development

◇ *anagram indicator*
04 area, land **05** block, event, issue
06 centre, change, estate, growth, result, spread **07** advance, complex, outcome **08** genetics, incident, increase, maturing, maturity, progress, upgrowth **09** evolution, expansion, extension, happening, promotion, situation, unfolding **10** blossoming, occurrence, phenomenon, prosperity, refinement, upbuilding **11** elaboration, enlargement, flourishing, furtherance, improvement, progression
12 circumstance, turn of events

- **stage of development**

04 pupa

deviance

07 anomaly **08** variance **09** disparity
10 aberration, divergence, perversion
11 abnormality **12** eccentricity, irregularity

deviant

◇ *anagram indicator*
04 bent, geek, goof, kook **05** crank, freak, kinky **06** misfit, oddity, quirky, weirdo **07** bizarre, dropout, oddball, odd sort, pervert, twisted, variant, wayward **08** aberrant, abnormal, freakish, perverse **09** anomalous, disparate, divergent, eccentric, irregular, perverted **13** nonconformist
15 with a screw loose

deviate

◇ *anagram indicator*
03 bag, err, yaw **04** part, seam, turn, vary, veer **05** drift, sheer, sport, stray
06 change, depart, differ, swerve, wander **07** decline, deflect, digress, diverge, incline, oblique, turn off
08 aberrate, go astray, turn away
09 turn aside **11** prevaricate **13** go off the rails

deviation

◇ *anagram indicator*
03 yaw **05** break, drift, error, freak, quirk, sheer, shift **06** change, detour, swerve **07** anomaly, decline, turning
08 variance **09** deflexion, deflexure, departure, disparity, excursion, inflexion, variation **10** aberration, alteration, deflection, difference, digression, divergence, inflection
11 abnormality, declination, discrepancy, fluctuation, inclination
12 eccentricity, inordination, irregularity, turning-aside
13 inconsistency, prevarication

device

04 bomb, logo, plan, plot, ploy, ruse, seal, sign, tool, wile **05** badge, crest, dodge, gizmo, motif, motto, stunt, token, trick, waldo **06** design, emblem, gadget, gambit, masque, scheme, shield, symbol, tactic **07** conceit, machine, slinter, utensil **08** artifice, colophon, insignia, strategy
09 apparatus, appliance, implement, manoeuvre, mechanism, stratagem
10 coat of arms, instrument
11 contraption, contrivance, machination

Devices include:

04 iPod®, Xbox®
05 clock, phone, razor, torch, watch
06 juicer, scales, shaver
07 Game Boy®, lighter, stapler, Walkman
08 CD player, egg timer, Gamecube®, nail file, scissors, tweezers
09 can opener, cell phone, corkscrew, hairdryer, hole punch, magnifier, pedometer, staple gun, stopwatch, telephone, tin opener
10 calculator, coin sorter, fax machine, ice scraper, wine cooler
11 answerphone, baby monitor, electric fan, manicure set, mobile phone, PlayStation®, thermometer
12 bottle opener, curling tongs, games console, kitchen timer, nail clippers
13 remote control, smoke detector, staple remover
14 personal stereo, Swiss army knife

See also **electrical**; **optical**; **rhetorical**

devil

03 div, imp, Pug **04** bogy, fend, Nick, ogre **05** beast, bogey, brute, demon, deuce, fiend, fient, rogue, Satan, sorra, worry **06** Belial, Cloots, daemon, daimon, drudge, Hornie, Mahoun, Old One, pester, ragman, rascal, savage, sorrow, terror, wretch **07** bogyman, Clootie, dickens, Evil One, goodman, incubus, Lucifer, Mahound, monster, Old Nick, Scratch, succuba, the deil
08 Apollyon, bogeyman, firework, goodyear, man of sin, Mephisto, mischief, Old Harry, Old Poker, succubus, the enemy, wirricow, worricow, worrycow **09** Adversary, arch-fiend, Beelzebub, cacodemon, Davy Jones, goodyears, Nickie-ben, yoke-devil **10** cacodaemon, evil spirit, Old Scratch, Ragamuffin, the evil one, the Tempter **11** arch-traitor, the old enemy **12** the wicked one
14 Mephistopheles, Mephistophilis, Mephostophilus

devilish

◇ *anagram indicator*
04 evil, very, vile **05** cruel, jolly
06 highly, knotty, really, thorny, tricky, wicked **07** awfully, awkward, demonic, greatly, hellish, satanic
08 accursed, damnable, delicate, diabolic, dreadful, fiendish, infernal, severely, shocking, terribly, ticklish
09 atrocious, difficult, execrable, extremely, intensely, malignant, nefarious, sensitive, unusually
10 diabolical, disastrous, dreadfully, outrageous, remarkably, thoroughly, uncommonly **11** complicated, exceedingly, excessively, frightfully, problematic **12** excruciating, immoderately, unreasonably
13 exceptionally **15** extraordinarily

devil-may-care

04 rash **06** casual **08** careless, cavalier, flippant, heedless, reckless
09 audacious, easy-going, frivolous, unworried **10** insouciant, nonchalant, swaggering **11** unconcerned
12 happy-go-lucky **13** swashbuckling

devilry

03 sin **04** evil **07** impiety **08** atrocity, enormity, foulness, iniquity, vileness

09 amorality, depravity, diabolism, reprobacy **10** corruption, immorality, sinfulness, wickedness **11** abomination, corruptness, heinousness **12** fiendishness, shamefulness **13** dissoluteness **15** unrighteousness

devious
◇ *anagram indicator*
03 sly **04** wily **06** artful, crafty, erring, subtle, tricky **07** crooked, cunning, erratic, evasive, winding **08** indirect, rambling, scheming, slippery, tortuous **09** deceitful, designing, deviating, dishonest, insidious, insincere, underhand, wandering **10** circuitous, misleading, roundabout **11** calculating, treacherous **12** disingenuous, unscrupulous **13** double-dealing, surreptitious

devise
02 do **04** cast, form, plan, plot, talk, will **05** forge, frame, guess, hatch, hit on, shape, study **06** cook up, create, decoct, depict, design, invent, scheme **07** arrange, compose, concoct, dream up, hit upon, imagine, project, purpose, suppose, think up, work out **08** bequeath, conceive, consider, conspire, contrive, describe, meditate **09** construct, fabricate, formulate, originate **10** come up with **11** put together

devoid
04 bare, free, vain, void **05** empty **06** barren, bereft, vacant **07** lacking, wanting, without **08** deprived **09** deficient, destitute

devolution
09 dispersal **12** distribution

devolve
06 convey, depute, fall to, pass on **07** consign, deliver, entrust, succeed **08** delegate, hand down, pass down, rest with, transfer **10** commission

Devon
02 SW

devote
04 doom, give **05** allot, apply, offer, put in **06** assign, commit, pledge **07** appoint, consign, reserve **08** allocate, dedicate, enshrine, set apart, set aside **09** sacrifice, surrender **10** consecrate **11** appropriate **12** give yourself

devoted
04 fond, true **05** loyal **06** ardent, caring, devout, doomed, loving, sacred **07** staunch, zealous **08** constant, dedicate, faithful, tireless **09** attentive, committed, concerned, dedicated, steadfast **10** unswerving

devotedly
06 fondly **07** loyally **08** ardently, caringly, devoutly, lovingly **09** staunchly **10** faithfully, tirelessly **11** attentively, committedly, dedicatedly, steadfastly **12** unswervingly

devotee
03 bum, fan **04** buff **05** fiend, freak, hound, lover **06** addict, votary, voteen, zealot **07** admirer, fanatic **08** adherent, disciple, follower, merchant **09** supporter **10** aficionado, enthusiast

devotion
04 alms, love, zeal **05** faith, piety **06** ardour, prayer, regard **07** fervour, loyalty, passion, support, worship **08** fidelity, fondness, holiness, sanctity, trueness, warmness **09** adherence, adoration, affection, closeness, constancy, godliness, reverence **10** admiration, allegiance, attachment, commitment, dedication, devoutness, observance, solidarity **11** earnestness, schwärmerei, staunchness **12** consecration, faithfulness, heart-service, spirituality **13** religiousness, steadfastness

• object of devotion
03 god **09** Jugannath **10** Juggernaut

devotional
04 holy **05** pious **06** devout, sacred, solemn **07** dutiful **09** pietistic, religious, spiritual **11** reverential

devour
◇ *insertion indicator*
03 eat **04** bolt, cram, gulp **05** eat up, enjoy, gorge, raven, scarf, scoff, skoff, snarf, stuff, worry **06** absorb, engulf, gobble, guzzle, ravage, relish, take in **07** consume, destroy, drink in, engorge, envelop, feast on, put away, revel in, swallow **08** dispatch, lay waste, tuck into, wolf down **09** depredate, devastate, finish off, knock back, polish off **10** appreciate, gormandize **13** be engrossed in, gourmandize

devout
04 deep, holy **05** godly, pious **06** ardent, solemn **07** devoted, earnest, fervent, genuine, intense, saintly, serious, sincere, staunch, zealous **08** constant, faithful, orthodox, profound, reverent, vehement **09** committed, dedicated, heartfelt, prayerful, religious, steadfast **10** passionate, practising, unswerving **11** church-going **12** wholehearted

devoutly
06 deeply **07** piously **08** ardently **09** earnestly, fervently, sincerely, staunchly, zealously **10** faithfully, reverently **11** prayerfully, religiously, steadfastly **12** passionately **14** wholeheartedly

dewy
05 roral, roric, rorid **06** roscid **07** bedewed **08** blooming, innocent, youthful **10** starry-eyed

dexterity
03 art **05** craft, knack, skill **06** slight **07** ability, address, agility, finesse, mastery, sleight **08** aptitude, artistry, deftness, facility **09** adeptness, expertise, handiness, ingenuity, readiness **10** adroitness, expertness, nimbleness **11** legerdemain, proficiency, skilfulness **14** effortlessness **15** right-handedness

dexterous
04 able, deft **05** adept, agile, handy, nifty, nippy, ready **06** adroit, artful, clever, expert, facile, habile, nimble, subtle, wieldy **07** featous, skilful **08** feateous, featuous **10** neat-handed, proficient **11** right-handed **12** accomplished **14** nimble-fingered

diabolical
◇ *anagram indicator*
04 evil, vile **05** nasty **06** sinful, wicked **07** demonic, hellish, satanic **08** absolute, complete, damnable, devilish, dreadful, fiendish, infernal, shocking **09** appalling, atrocious, execrable, monstrous **10** disastrous, outrageous **12** excruciating

diacritic
05 acute, breve, grave, haček, tilde **06** accent, macron, umlaut **07** cedilla **08** dieresis, modifier

diadem
05 crown, mitre, round, tiara **07** circlet, circuit, coronet **08** headband

diagnose
06 detect **07** analyse, explain, isolate **08** identify, pinpoint **09** determine, interpret, recognize **11** distinguish, investigate

diagnosis
06 answer **07** opinion, verdict **08** analysis, scrutiny **09** detection, judgement **10** conclusion **11** diagnostics, examination, explanation, recognition **13** investigation **14** identification, interpretation

diagnostic
10 analytical, indicative **11** symptomatic **12** interpretive, recognizable **13** demonstrative **14** distinguishing, interpretative **15** differentiating

diagonal
05 cater, cross **06** angled **07** crooked, oblique, sloping **08** crossing, slanting **09** crosswise **10** cornerways **11** catercorner, catty-corner **13** catercornered, catty-cornered, kitty-cornered

diagonally
05 cater **06** aslant **08** bendwise **09** at an angle, crossways, crosswise, obliquely, on the bias, slantwise **10** cornerways, cornerwise, on the cross, on the slant **11** catercorner, catty-corner **13** catercornered, catty-cornered, kitty-cornered

diagram
03 key **04** abac, plan, plat, tree **05** chart, draft, graph, table **06** figure, layout, schema, scheme, sketch **07** cutaway, drawing, outline,

picture **08** bar chart, isopleth, nomogram, pie chart, run chart **09** floor plan, flow chart, indicator, nomograph, schematic **10** family tree, stereogram **11** delineation **12** exploded view, illustration **14** alignment chart, representation

diagrammatic
07 graphic, tabular **09** schematic **12** illustrative **14** diagrammatical

dial
03 map, pan **04** bass, call, disc, face, mush, ring **05** clock, phone, tuner, watch **06** call up, circle, treble **07** control **09** give a bell, give a buzz, hourplate, telephone

• compass dial
04 card

dialect
03 Twi **04** Norn **05** argot, idiom, lingo **06** accent, jargon, patois, speech **07** diction, variety **08** language, localism **10** vernacular **11** regionalism **13** provincialism

• dialect society
03 EDS

dialectic
05 logic **06** debate **07** logical **08** analysis, logistic, polemics, rational **09** deduction, deductive, induction, inductive, polemical, rationale, reasoning **10** analytical, contention, dialectics, discussion **11** dialectical, disputation **12** disputatious **13** argumentation, argumentative, ratiocination, rationalistic

dialogue
04 chat, talk **05** lazzo, lines **06** debate, gossip, script **08** colloquy, converse, exchange **09** discourse, tête-à-tête **10** conference, discussion **11** interchange, pastourelle **12** conversation, stichomythia **13** communication, interlocution

diameter
01 d **03** dia **04** diam

diametrically
07 utterly **08** directly **10** absolutely, completely **14** antithetically

diamond
04 bort, pick, rock **05** boart, spark **06** carbon, lasque **07** adamant, paragon, rhombus **08** sparkler **09** brilliant, solitaire **10** Rhinestone

Diamonds include:

04 Hope
05 Orlov, Sancy
06 Orloff, Regent
07 Tiffany
08 Blue Hope, Cullinan, Idol's Eye, Koh-I-Noor
09 Centenary, Excelsior, Hortensia
10 Florentine, Great Mogul
12 Star of Africa, Taylor-Burton

• diamonds
01 D **03** ice

Diana
02 Di **07** Artemis

diaphanous
04 fine, thin **05** clear, filmy, gauzy, light, sheer, veily **08** chiffony, cobwebby, delicate, gossamer, pellucid **09** gossamery **10** see-through **11** translucent, transparent

diarrhoea
05 scour **06** scours **07** the runs **08** lientery, the trots, wood-evil **09** dysentery, looseness **10** Delhi belly, gippy tummy, gyppy tummy **12** Aztec two-step, holiday tummy, Spanish tummy, weaning brash

diary
03 log **06** memoir **07** day-book, diurnal, Filofax®, journal, logbook **08** year-book **09** chronicle **13** journal intime **14** engagement book **15** appointment book

Diarists include:

03 **Lee** (Lorelei)
04 **Byrd** (William), **Gide** (André), **Mole** (Adrian), **Ooka** (Shohei)
05 **Birde** (William), **Frank** (Anne), **Grant** (Elizabeth), **Jones** (Bridget), **Pasek** (Jan Chryzostom), **Pepys** (Samuel), **Reyes** (Alfonso), **Scott** (Robert Falcon), **Torga** (Miguel)
06 **Burney** (Fanny), **Evelyn** (John), **Pooter** (Charles)
07 **Andrews** (Pamela), **Carlyle** (Jane Welsh), **Chesnut** (Mary), **Creevey** (Thomas), **Kilvert** (Francis), **Régnier** (Paule)
08 **Greville** (Charles Cavendish Fulke), **Melville** (James), **Robinson** (Henry Crabb)
09 **Schreiber**, **Slaveykov** (Petko)
10 **Ooka Shohei**
11 **Lichtenberg** (Georg Christoph), **Thermopolis** (Mia)
12 **Bashkirtseva** (Marya)

diatribe
05 abuse **06** attack, insult, rebuke, tirade **07** reproof, slating **08** harangue, knocking, reviling, slamming **09** criticism, invective, onslaught, philippic, reprimand **10** upbraiding **11** running-down **12** denunciation, vituperation

dice
04 bale **05** bones **09** astragals **11** devil's bones

• spot on dice
03 pip **04** peep **05** peepe

dicey
04 iffy **05** dodgy, hairy, risky **06** chancy, tricky **07** dubious **09** dangerous, difficult, uncertain **11** problematic **13** unpredictable

dichotomy
08 conflict, division, variance **09** deviation, disparity, variation **10** difference, divergence, opposition **11** discrepancy **13** dissimilarity **15** differentiation

dicky
◇ *anagram indicator*
03 ass **04** weak **05** frail, shaky **06** ailing, infirm **07** unsound **08** unsteady

dictate
03 law, say **04** dite, read, rule, word **05** edict, order, speak, utter **06** behest, charge, decree, demand, direct, impose, indite, insist, ruling **07** bidding, command, lay down, mandate, precept, read out, set down, statute **08** announce, instruct, transmit **09** direction, ordinance, prescribe, principle, pronounce, read aloud, ultimatum **10** injunction, promulgate **11** requirement **12** give orders to, promulgation

dictator
04 dict, duce **06** despot, tyrant **07** supremo **08** autocrat **09** oppressor **10** autarchist, Big Brother **12** little Hitler **13** absolute ruler
See also **despot**

dictatorial
05 bossy **08** absolute, despotic, dogmatic **09** arbitrary, autarchic, imperious, unlimited **10** autocratic, omnipotent, oppressive, peremptory, repressive, tyrannical **11** all powerful, domineering, magisterial, overbearing **12** totalitarian, unrestricted **13** authoritarian, authoritative

dictatorship
07 fascism, tyranny **09** autocracy, despotism, Hitlerism **11** police state **12** absolute rule **13** reign of terror **15** totalitarianism

diction
05 lexis, style **06** saying, speech **07** fluency **08** delivery, language, locution, phrasing, speaking **09** elocution **10** expression, inflection, intonation **11** enunciation **12** articulation **13** pronunciation

dictionary
03 DNB, OED, TCD **04** dict **06** gradus **07** alveary, lexicon **08** Chambers, glossary, wordbook **09** gazetteer, thesaurus **10** vocabulary **11** concordance, onomasticon, synonymicon **12** encyclopedia, etymologicon, etymologicum

dictum
04 fiat **05** axiom, edict, maxim, order **06** decree, ruling, saying **07** command, dictate, precept, proverb **08** aphorism **09** direction, ipse dixit, utterance **12** proclamation **13** pronouncement

did
01 'd

didactic
05 moral **08** pedantic **09** educative, pedagogic **10** didascalic, moralizing, preceptive, protreptic **11** educational, informative, instructive **12** prescriptive

die
02 go **03** dee, ebb, end, pip **04** ache, cark, exit, fade, fail, kark, long, pass, pine, sink, stop, wane, wilt **05** be mad, choke, croak, decay, drown, go off, lapse, merge, punch, quell, swelt, yearn **06** be nuts, be wild, cut out, depart, desire, expire, famish, finish, go bung, go west, pass on, peg out, perish, pip out, pop off, starve, sterve, vanish, wither **07** be crazy, conk out, decease, decline, dwindle, kick off, kiss off, long for, pass out, pine for, snuff it, subside, succumb **08** be raring, decrease, dissolve, flatline, intaglio, melt away, pass away, pass over, peter out, spark out **09** break down, disappear, go belly up, have had it, lose power **10** hop the twig **11** be desperate, bite the dust, come to an end **12** lose your life, pop your clogs, slip the cable **13** close your eyes, kick the bucket, meet your maker, push up daisies **14** depart this life, give up the ghost, turn up your toes **15** breathe your last, cash in your chips, join the majority

• **die away**
04 fade, fall **07** evanish, fall off **09** disappear **10** become weak **11** become faint

• **die down**
04 drop, stop **05** abate, slake **06** quench **07** decline, quieten, subside **08** blow over, decrease

• **die out**
06 vanish **08** peter out **09** disappear **10** extinguish **11** become rarer

• **soon to die**
03 fay, fey, fie **05** fated

died
01 d **02** ob **05** obiit

diehard
05 blimp **06** zealot **07** fanatic **08** hardline, old fogey, rightist **09** fanatical, hardliner **11** reactionary **12** conservative, intransigent **13** dyed-in-the-wool, stick-in-the-mud **14** traditionalist

diet
04 bant, fare, fast, food, slim, VLCD **06** reduce, regime, viands **07** abstain, cut down, Landtag, rations, regimen **08** fishmeal, victuals **09** nutrition **10** abstinence, conference, foodstuffs, lose weight, provisions, sustenance **11** comestibles, subsistence, weight-watch

differ
04 vary **05** argue, clash **06** debate, oppose **07** contend, deviate, dispute, dissent, diverge, fall out, quarrel **08** be unlike, conflict, contrast, disagree **09** altercate, take issue **10** contradict, depart from, disconsent **11** deviate from **12** be at odds with, be at variance, be dissimilar **14** not see eye to eye

difference
03 row **04** rest, spat, tiff **05** clash, set-to **07** balance, dispute, quarrel, residue, variety **08** argument, conflict, contrast, variance **09** deviation, dichotomy, disparity, diversity, exception, remainder, variation **10** antithesis, contention, divergence, inequality, unlikeness **11** altercation, controversy, discrepancy, disputation, distinction, incongruity, singularity **12** disagreement, distinctness **13** dissimilarity, dissimilitude **14** discrimination **15** differentiation

different
◇ *anagram indicator*
03 new, odd **04** allo-, many, rare **05** novel, other **06** at odds, sundry, unique, unlike, varied **07** a far cry, another, awkward, bizarre, diverse, opposed, several, special, strange, unusual, variant, various, varying **08** assorted, clashing, discrete, distinct, ill-timed, mixed bag, numerous, original, peculiar, separate, untimely **09** anomalous, deviating, disparate, divergent, otherwise **10** at variance, dissimilar, individual, poles apart, remarkable, unsuitable **11** contrasting, distinctive, inopportune, worlds apart **12** heterologous, inconsistent, inconvenient, poles asunder, streets apart, unfavourable, unmanageable **13** extraordinary, miscellaneous **14** unconventional

differential
03 gap **08** contrast, separate, variance **09** different, disparate, disparity, divergent **10** difference, divergence **11** contrasting, discrepancy, distinctive **14** discriminating

differentiate
06 modify **07** mark off **08** contrast, separate **09** diversify, tell apart **10** specialize **11** distinguish **12** discriminate **13** individualize, particularize

differentiation
08 contrast **10** separation **11** demarcation, distinction **12** modification **14** discrimination, distinguishing

differently
◇ *anagram indicator*
06 at odds **07** a far cry **09** diversely **10** at variance, poles apart **11** worlds apart **12** dissimilarly, incompatibly **13** contrastingly **14** inconsistently

difficult
03 ill **04** dark, hard, high **05** rough, steep, stiff, tough **06** arcane, Augean, badass, gnarly, knotty, thorny, tiring, tricky, trying, uneath, uphill **07** arduous, awkward, complex, Gordian, obscure, onerous, testing **08** abstract, abstruse, badassed, baffling, esoteric, exacting, involved, perverse, puzzling, stubborn, ticklish, tiresome **09** demanding, difficile, gruelling, intricate, laborious, obstinate, recondite, strenuous, wearisome **10** burdensome, exhausting, formidable, perplexing, refractory **11** complicated, intractable, troublesome **12** back-breaking, hard to please, recalcitrant, unmanageable **13** problematical, unco-operative

difficulty
03 ado, fix, ill, jam, net, rub **04** hole, knot, mess, node, snag, spot, stew **05** bitch, block, devil, nodus, trial **06** aporia, bother, hang-up, hassle, hiccup, hobble, hurdle, labour, pickle, plight, strain **07** barrier, dilemma, nonplus, perplex, pitfall, problem, quarrel, scruple, straits, trouble **08** distress, exigency, hardship, hot water, obstacle, quandary, struggle **09** deep water, hindrance, how-d'you-do, Lob's pound, nineholes, objection, tall order, tight spot **10** cleft stick, disability, impediment, opposition, perplexity, pretty pass, struggling **11** arduousness, awkwardness, dire straits, obstruction, painfulness, predicament, tribulation **12** complication **13** embarrassment, laboriousness, strenuousness **14** stumbling-block

• **get through difficulty**
04 pass

• **in difficulties**
06 in a fix, in a jam **07** in a hole, in a mess, in a stew, stumped, up a tree **08** bunkered **09** in a scrape, in the soup, in trouble **10** hard-pushed, in hot water, up the creek **11** hard-pressed, in deep water, up against it **12** in a tight spot **13** in dire straits **14** having problems, out of your depth

• **with difficulty**
03 ill **04** hard **06** hardly, scarce, uneath **10** at a stretch

diffidence
07 modesty, reserve, shyness **08** humility, meekness, timidity **09** hesitancy, self-doubt **10** inhibition, insecurity, reluctance **11** bashfulness **12** backwardness, self-distrust **14** self-effacement **15** unassertiveness

diffident
03 shy **04** meek **05** timid **06** modest, unsure **07** abashed, bashful, nervous **08** hesitant, insecure, reserved, sheepish **09** inhibited, reluctant, shrinking, tentative, unassured, withdrawn **10** shamefaced **11** distrusting, unassertive **12** self-effacing **13** self-conscious

diffuse
03 ren, rin, run **05** large, vague, wordy **06** prolix, spread, winnow **07** profuse, publish, scatter, send out, verbose **08** diffused, dispense, disperse, permeate, rambling, waffling **09** circulate, dispersed, dissipate, imprecise, propagate, scattered **10** discursive, distribute, long-winded, loquacious, promulgate **11** disseminate **12** disconnected, periphrastic **14** circumlocutory, unconcentrated

diffusion
07 osmosis **08** bleeding **09** dispersal, extension, spreading **10** permeation, scattering **11** circulation, dissipation, propagation **12** distribution, promulgation **13** dissemination

dig
03 get, jab **04** cast, fork, gibe, gird, grub, howk, jeer, mine, poke, prod, spit, spud, till, twig, work **05** click, crack, delve, ditch, gouge, graft, grasp, grave, lodge, probe, punch, scoop, sneer, spade, taunt **06** burrow, follow, go into, grub up, harrow, hollow, insult, pierce, plough, quarry, search, take in, thrust, trench, tunnel **07** approve, break up, channel, fossick, grub out, realize, scratch, unearth **08** disinter, entrench, excavate, research, turn over **09** cultivate, figure out, make a hole, penetrate, undermine, wisecrack **10** appreciate, compliment, excavation, understand **11** insinuation, investigate **12** get the hang of

• dig up
04 find **06** exhume, expose **07** root out, uncover, unearth **08** discover, disinter, excavate, retrieve **09** extricate, track down **12** bring to light

• digging implement
02 ko **04** spud **05** spade

digest
◇ *anagram indicator*
04 code **05** endew, endue, grasp, indew, indue, study **06** absorb, codify, ponder, précis, reduce, résumé, take in **07** abridge, process, shorten, stomach, summary **08** abstract, canon law, compress, condense, consider, dissolve, macerate, meditate, mull over, synopsis **09** break down, reduction, summarize **10** assimilate, compendium, comprehend, understand **11** abridgement, compression, contemplate, incorporate **12** abbreviation

digestion
08 eupepsia **09** ingestion **10** absorption, maceration **12** assimilation, breaking-down **14** transformation

digit
03 toe **05** index, thumb **06** dactyl, figure, finger, hallux, number **07** integer, numeral **10** forefinger, ring finger **12** little finger, middle finger

dignified
04 high **05** grand, grave, lofty, manly, noble **06** august, formal, lordly, sedate, solemn **07** courtly, exalted, stately **08** decorous, handsome, imposing, majestic, reserved **10** honourable, impressive **11** ceremonious **13** distinguished

dignify
05 adorn, crown, exalt, grace, raise **06** honour **07** advance, elevate, enhance, ennoble, glorify, promote **10** aggrandize **11** apotheosize, distinguish

dignitary
03 VIP **04** dean, name **05** canon **06** big gun, bigwig, high-up, worthy **07** big name, big shot, grandee, notable, provost **08** alderman, luminary, somebody, top brass **09** personage **10** archdeacon

dignity
05 poise, pride, state **06** honour, status **07** decorum, majesty, worship **08** cathedra, eminence, grandeur, nobility, standing **09** elevation, greatness, loftiness, nobleness, propriety, solemnity **10** excellence, importance, preferment, self-esteem **11** courtliness, self-respect, stateliness **13** honourability **14** respectability, self-importance, self-possession

digress
05 drift, stray **06** depart, ramble, wander **07** deviate, diverge, excurse **08** divagate **09** turn aside **13** be sidetracked **15** go off at a tangent, go off the subject

digression
05 aside **06** ecbole, flight, vagary **08** excursus, footnote, straying **09** departure, deviation, diversion, evagation, excursion, wandering **10** apostrophe, divagation, divergence **11** parenthesis **12** extravagance, obiter dictum

digs
03 pad **05** place, rooms **06** billet **08** lodgings, quarters **13** accommodation, boarding-house

dilapidated
◇ *anagram indicator*
05 shaky **06** beat-up, ruined, shabby **07** decayed, in ruins, rickety, run-down, worn-out **08** decaying, decrepit **09** crumbling, neglected **10** broken-down, ramshackle, tumbledown, uncared-for **12** falling apart

dilapidation
04 ruin **05** decay, waste **08** collapse **09** disrepair **10** demolition **11** destruction **13** deterioration **14** disintegration

dilate
04 tent **05** bloat, swell, widen **06** expand, extend, spread **07** broaden, distend, enlarge, inflate, stretch **08** increase **09** spread out

dilatory
04 lazy, slow **05** slack, tardy **08** dawdling, delaying, sluggish, stalling, tarrying **09** lingering, loitering, snail-like **10** postponing, prolixious **11** time-wasting **13** lackadaisical **15** procrastinating

dilemma
03 fix **04** mess, spot **06** plight, puzzle, why-not **07** problem **08** conflict, quandary **10** cleft stick, difficulty, double bind, perplexity **11** predicament, tight corner **13** embarrassment, vicious circle **14** no-win situation

dilettante
07 amateur, dabbler, trifler **08** aesthete, potterer, sciolist **15** non-professional

diligence
04 care **08** industry **09** assiduity, attention, constancy **10** conscience, dedication, intentness **11** application, earnestness, painstaking, pertinacity **12** perseverance, sedulousness, thoroughness **13** assiduousness, attentiveness, laboriousness

diligent
04 busy **06** eident **07** careful, earnest **08** constant, sedulous, studious, thorough, tireless **09** assiduous, attentive, dedicated **10** meticulous, persistent **11** hard-working, industrious, painstaking, persevering **13** conscientious

dilly-dally
05 dally, delay, hover, tarry, waver **06** dawdle, dither, falter, linger, loiter, potter, trifle **08** hesitate **09** faff about, vacillate, waste time **12** shilly-shally, take your time **13** procrastinate

dilute
03 cut, dil **04** kill, thin **05** allay, delay, lower, small, water **06** lessen, reduce, temper, weaken **07** diffuse, thin out **08** decrease, diminish, mitigate, moderate, tone down, waterish **09** attenuate, water down **10** adulterate, attenuated, make weaker **11** make thinner

diluted
03 cut **04** weak **06** watery **07** thinned **10** thinned out, wishy-washy **11** watered down

dim
04 blur, dark, dull, dumb, dusk, fade, grey, hazy, pale, paly, slow, weak **05** appal, bedim, blear, cloud, dense, dingy, dopey, dusky, faint, foggy, fuzzy, misty, shade, thick, unlit, vague **06** bleary, cloudy, darken, feeble, gloomy, leaden, obtuse, simple, sombre, stupid **07** adverse, becloud, blurred, doltish, obscure, shadowy, tarnish, unclear **08** clouding, confused, gormless, overcast **09** dim-witted, imperfect, make faint, tenebrous **10** caliginous, ill-defined, indistinct, lacklustre, obfuscated, slow-witted **11** become faint, crepuscular, make blurred, unpromising **12** crepusculous, discouraging, inauspicious, simple-minded, unfavourable **13** become blurred

dimension
01 D **03** dim **04** area, bulk, mass, side, size **05** depth, facet, range, scale, scope, width **06** aspect, extent, factor, height, length, volume **07** breadth, element, feature, measure **08** capacity

09 greatness, largeness, magnitude
10 importance 11 measurement, proportions

diminish
03 cut, ebb 04 bate, damp, drop, fade, pare, sink, wane 05 abate, lower, mince 06 defame, die out, impair, lessen, minify, minish, rebate, recede, reduce, shrink, vilify, weaken
07 assuage, attrite, decline, deflate, degrade, detract, devalue, die away, drop off, dwindle, slacken, subside, whittle 08 belittle, contract, decrease, derogate, grow less, minimize, pare down, peter out, retrench, taper off, wear down 09 denigrate, deprecate, disparage 10 become less, deactivate, grow weaker 11 whittle away, whittle down 12 become weaker 14 take the edge off

diminuendo
03 dim 04 fade 11 decrescendo

diminution
03 cut, ebb 04 loss 05 decay, taper
07 atrophy, cutback, decline
08 decrease, drawdown
09 abatement, deduction, detriment, lessening, reduction, shrinkage, weakening 10 shortening, subsidence
11 contraction, curtailment, defalcation 12 retrenchment

diminutive
03 dim, wee 04 mini, tiny 05 dinky, elfin, pigmy, pygmy, small, teeny
06 little, midget, minute, petite, pocket, tottie 07 compact, minikin
08 dwarfish, pint-size 09 miniature, pint-sized 10 contracted, homuncular, hypocorism, small-scale, teeny-weeny, undersized 11 hypocorisma, Lilliputian, microscopic, pocket-sized
13 infinitesimal

dimly
05 dully 06 darkly, feebly, hazily, weakly 07 dingily, faintly, mistily
08 gloomily, sombrely 09 obscurely, unclearly 12 indistinctly

dimness
04 dusk, mist 06 caligo 08 darkness, dullness, greyness, twilight
09 dinginess, half-light 10 cloudiness, crepuscule 12 caliginosity

dimple
04 dint 05 fovea 06 hollow
09 concavity, umbilicus 10 depression
11 indentation

dimwit
03 git 04 berk, clot, dope, dork, fool, geek, prat, twit 05 dumbo, dunce, dweeb, idiot 06 nitwit 07 dullard, halfwit, plonker 08 bonehead, numskull 09 blockhead, ignoramus
10 dunderhead 11 knuckle-head

See also **fool**

din
03 row 04 deen, reel, utis 05 alarm, chirm, clash, crash, noise, noyes, raird, reird, shout 06 babble, hubbub, outcry, racket, randan, stound, stownd, tumult, uproar 07 clamour, clatter, yelling 08 brouhaha, clangour, shouting 09 charivari, commotion, loud noise 10 hullabaloo
11 pandemonium

dine
03 eat, sup 04 feed, mess 05 feast, lunch 06 dinner 07 banquet 10 have dinner

dingy
03 dim, dun 04 dark, drab, dull, fusc, worn 05 dirty, dusky, faded, grimy, murky, oorie, ourie, owrie, seedy
06 dismal, dreary, gloomy, isabel, shabby, soiled, sombre 07 fuscous, obscure, run-down, squalid
08 isabella 09 cheerless
10 colourless, isabelline
11 discoloured 12 disreputable

dinky
04 fine, mini, neat, trim 05 natty, small
06 dainty, little, petite 07 trivial
09 miniature 13 insignificant

dinner
03 tea 04 dine, hall, kail, kale, meal
05 feast 06 repast, spread, supper
07 banquet, blow-out 08 main meal
09 beanfeast, refection, wasegoose, wayzgoose 11 evening meal
• **dinner time**
07 evening

dinosaur

Dinosaurs include:

04 T Rex
06 Raptor
08 Coelurus, Sauropod, Theropod
09 Hadrosaur, Iguanodon, Oviraptor
10 Allosaurus, Anatotitan, Barosaurus, Diplodocus, Megalosaur, Ophiacodon, Torosaurus, Utahraptor
11 Apatosaurus, Ceteosaurus, Coelophysis, Coelurosaur, Deinonychus, Dromaeosaur, Polacanthus, Prosauropod, Saurischian, Stegosaurus, Triceratops, Tyrannosaur
12 Ankylosaurus, Brontosaurus, Camptosaurus, Ceratosaurus, Megalosaurus, Ornithischia, Ornithomimus, Plateosaurus, Titanosaurus, Velociraptor
13 Atlantosaurus, Brachiosaurus, Compsognathus, Corythosaurus, Dwarf Allosaur, Edmontosaurus, Herrerasaurus, Ornitholestes, Styracosaurus, Tyrannosaurus
14 Leaellynasaura
15 Cryolophosaurus, Parasaurolophus

dint
04 blow, dent 05 force 06 hollow, indent, stroke 09 concavity
10 depression, impression
11 indentation
• **by dint of**
09 by means of 10 by virtue of 13 by the agency of

diocese
03 see 04 Ebor, Exon, Oxon
06 Cantab, Dunelm 07 Cantuar, eparchy 09 bishopric, eparchate

Dioceses and archdioceses of the UK:

03 Ely
04 York
05 Derby, Derry, Leeds, Truro
06 Armagh, Bangor, Connor, Durham, Exeter, Hallam, London, Oxford
07 Brechin, Bristol, Cardiff, Chester, Clifton, Clogher, Dromore, Dunkeld, Glasgow, Kilmore, Lincoln, Menevia, Norwich, Paisley, Salford, St Asaph, Wrexham
08 Aberdeen, Bradford, Carlisle, Coventry, Galloway, Hereford, Llandaff, Monmouth, Plymouth, St Albans, St Davids
09 Blackburn, Brentwood, Edinburgh, Guildford, Lancaster, Leicester, Lichfield, Liverpool, Newcastle, Rochester, Salisbury, Sheffield, Southwark, Southwell, Wakefield, Worcester
10 Birmingham, Canterbury, Chelmsford, Chichester, East Anglia, Gloucester, Manchester, Motherwell, Nottingham, Portsmouth, Shrewsbury, Winchester
11 Northampton, Sodor and Man, Westminster
12 Bath and Wells, Peterborough
13 Down and Connor, Middlesbrough, Ripon and Leeds
14 Derry and Raphoe, Down and Dromore
16 Swansea and Brecon
17 Aberdeen and Orkney, Argyll and the Isles
18 Arundel and Brighton, Glasgow and Galloway, Hexham and Newcastle
21 Moray, Ross and Caithness, St Andrews and Edinburgh
23 St Edmundsbury and Ipswich
27 St Andrews, Dunkeld and Dunblane

Dionysus
07 Bacchus 10 Liber Pater

dip
03 dap, dib, dim, dop, nod, sag
04 bath, dent, dive, drop, duck, dunk, fall, hole, pawn, plot, sink, soak, swim
05 basin, bathe, cream, delve, douse, lower, merge, ploat, sauce, slope, slump, souse 06 dibble, go down, hollow, plunge, relish 07 baptize, decline, descend, descent, ducking, immerge, immerse, incline, moisten, sloping, soaking, subside, suffuse
08 decrease, dressing, infusion, lowering, mortgage, submerge
09 concavity, drenching, immersion, lessening, reduction 10 depression, pickpocket 11 indentation
• **dip into**
03 use 04 skim 05 spend 06 browse, draw on, look at 10 run through 11 leaf through, look through 12 flick through, thumb through

diplomacy
04 tact 05 craft, skill 07 finesse 08 delicacy, politics, prudence, subtlety 10 cleverness, discretion, statecraft 11 manoeuvring, negotiation, savoir-faire, sensitivity, tactfulness 12 negotiations 13 judiciousness, statesmanship

diplomat
02 CD, HE 05 envoy 06 consul, legate 07 attaché 08 emissary, mediator 09 go-between, moderator, statesman 10 ambassador, arbitrator, negotiator, peacemaker, politician 11 conciliator 12 ambassadress 15 plenipotentiary

diplomatic
06 clever, subtle 07 politic, prudent, skilful, tactful 08 consular, discreet 09 judicious, sensitive 13 ambassadorial
• **diplomatic corps**
02 CD
• **period of diplomatic service**
04 tour

diplomatically
09 prudently, skilfully, tactfully 10 discreetly 11 judiciously, politically, sensitively 13 by negotiation, with diplomacy 14 conciliatorily

dipsomaniac
03 sot 04 lush, soak, wino 05 alkie, bloat, dipso, drunk, souse, toper 06 boozer, sponge 07 Bacchus, drinker, tippler, tosspot 08 drunkard, habitual 09 alcoholic, inebriate 10 wine-bibber 11 hard drinker 12 heavy drinker

dire
> *anagram indicator*
04 fell 05 awful, grave, vital 06 urgent 07 crucial, drastic, extreme, ominous 08 alarming, dreadful, horrible, pressing, shocking, terrible 09 appalling, atrocious, desperate, frightful 10 calamitous, disastrous, portentous 11 distressing 12 catastrophic

direct
> *anagram indicator*
03 aim, con, run, set 04 airt, conn, bold, lead, mean, near, show, tell, turn 05 apply, bluff, blunt, focus, frank, guide, level, order, point, ready, right, shape, steer, teach, usher 06 adjure, candid, charge, escort, govern, handle, honest, intend, manage, market, target 07 address, command, conduct, control, incline, non-stop, oversee, primary, sincere, through, up-front 08 directly, explicit, instruct, organize, personal, regulate, straight, unbroken 09 first-hand, immediate, outspoken, supervise 10 administer, face-to-face, forthright, give orders, mastermind, point-blank, show the way, unswerving 11 be the boss of, plainspoken, point the way, preside over, superintend, unambiguous, undeviating, unequivocal 12 be in charge of, call the shots 13 be in control of, uninterrupted 15 straightforward, uninterruptedly
• **directed towards**
02 on
• **direct from**
02 ex

direction
03 set, way 04 airt, goal, lead, line, path, plan, road 05 brief, drift, route, rules, tenor, track, trend 06 course, orders 07 bearing, command, control, running 08 briefing, guidance, handling, tendency 10 current aim, government, guidelines, indication, leadership, management, overseeing, regulation 11 inclination, information, orientation, regulations, supervision 12 instructions 14 administration 15 recommendations, superintendency
See also **compass**
• **directions**
06 recipe
• **general direction**
03 ren, rin, run
• **in the direction of**
02 on, to 03 for 07 towards
• **in the wrong direction**
03 wry
• **sharp change in direction**
03 zig
• **take a different direction**
07 diverge
• **take a direction**
02 go 04 chop 06 strike

directive
04 fiat 05 edict, order 06 charge, decree, notice, ruling 07 bidding, command, concern, dictate, mandate 09 direction, ordinance, speech act 10 imperative, injunction, regulation 11 instruction

directly
03 due 04 bang, dead, full, just, slap, soon 05 plumb, right, smack 06 at once, pronto, square 07 bluntly, clearly, exactly, frankly, plainly, quickly 08 candidly, honestly, outright, promptly, slap-bang, speedily, squarely, straight 09 forthwith, instantly, precisely, presently, right away, sincerely 10 explicitly, point-blank, straightly 11 immediately, straight out, straightway 12 straightaway, straightways, unswervingly, without delay 13 unambiguously, unequivocally 15 instantaneously

directness
07 honesty 09 bluntness, frankness, immediacy 10 candidness 13 immediateness, outspokenness 14 forthrightness 15 plainspokenness

director
01 D 03 Dir 04 boss, head 05 chair, chief 06 auteur, leader, top dog 07 manager 08 chairman, governor, overseer, Pole Star, producer 09 conductor, corrector, executive, film-maker, intendant, organizer, president, principal, régisseur, top banana 10 chairwoman, controller, counsellor, supervisor 11 agonothetes, chairperson, choirmaster, symposiarch 12 chapel master, chorus master, contributory, manufacturer 13 administrator, kapellmeister 14 chief executive, superintendent 15 Astronomer Royal

Film and theatre directors and producers include:

03 **Cox** (Brian), **Lee** (Spike), **May** (Elaine), **Ozu** (Yasujiro), **Ray** (Satyajit), **Woo** (John)
04 **Alda** (Alan), **Axel** (Gabriel), **Bond** (Edward), **Coen** (Ethan), **Coen** (Joel), **Eyre** (Sir Richard), **Ford** (John), **Gray** (Simon), **Hall** (Sir Peter), **Hare** (David), **Hart** (Moss), **Hill** (George Roy), **Lang** (Fritz), **Lean** (Sir David), **Nunn** (Trevor), **Reed** (Sir Carol), **Roeg** (Nicolas), **Tati** (Jacques), **Todd** (Mike), **Weir** (Peter), **Wise** (Robert)
05 **Allen** (Woody), **Barba** (Eugenio), **Boyle** (Danny), **Brook** (Peter), **Capra** (Frank), **Carné** (Marcel), **Clair** (René), **Craig** (Gordon), **Cukor** (George Dewey), **Dante** (Joe), **Demme** (Jonathan), **Fosse** (Bob), **Gance** (Abel), **Hands** (Terry), **Hawks** (Howard), **Ivory** (James), **Kazan** (Elia), **Kelly** (Gene), **Korda** (Sir Alexander), **Leigh** (Mike), **Leone** (Sergio), **Losey** (Joseph), **Lucas** (George), **Lumet** (Sidney), **Lynch** (David), **Malle** (Louis), **Mamet** (David), **Marsh** (Dame Ngaio), **Mayer** (Louis B), **Miles** (Bernard, Lord), **Noble** (Adrian), **Pabst** (Georg Wilhelm), **Perry** (Antoinette), **Roach** (Hal), **Scott** (Ridley), **Stein** (Peter), **Stone** (Oliver), **Vadim** (Roger), **Varda** (Agnès), **Verdy** (Violette), **Vidor** (King), **Wajda** (Andrzej), **Wells** (John), **Wolfe** (George C), **Wyler** (William)
06 **Abbott** (George), **Altman** (Robert), **Ang Lee**, **Artaud** (Antonin), **Arzner** (Dorothy), **August** (Bille), **Badham** (John), **Barton** (John), **Beatty** (Warren), **Besson** (Luc), **Brecht** (Bertolt), **Brooks** (Mel), **Bryden** (Bill), **Buñuel** (Luis), **Burton** (Tim), **Callow** (Simon), **Cooney** (Ray), **Copeau** (Jacques), **Corman** (Roger), **Curtiz** (Michael), **Cusack** (Cyril), **Daldry** (Stephen), **Davies** (Howard), **Davies** (Terence), **De Sica** (Vittorio), **Devine** (George), **Dexter** (John), **Disney** (Walt), **Donner** (Richard), **Dunlop** (Frank), **Dybwad** (Johanne), **Ephron** (Nora), **Forbes** (Bryan), **Forman** (Milos), **Frears** (Stephen), **Fugard** (Athol), **Gibson** (Mel), **Godard** (Jean-Luc), **Godber** (John), **Haydee** (Marcia), **Herzog** (Werner), **Hopper** (Dennis), **Hughes** (Howard), **Huston** (John), **Jarman** (Derek), **Jordan** (Neil), **Jouvet** (Louis), **Kantor** (Tadeusz), **Kasdan** (Lawrence), **Landis** (John), **Lupino**

(Ida), **Mendes** (Sam), **Miller** (George), **Miller** (Jonathan), **Moreau** (Jeanne), **Murnau** (F W), **Ophuls** (Max), **Parker** (Alan), **Powell** (Michael), **Prince** (Hal), **Prowse** (Philip), **Quayle** (Sir Anthony), **Reiner** (Carl), **Renoir** (Jean), **Siegal** (Don), **Tairov** (Aleksandr), **Usigli** (Rodolfo), **Warhol** (Andy), **Warner** (Deborah), **Warner** (Jack), **Welles** (Orson), **Wilder** (Billy), **Wilson** (Robert), **Zanuck** (Darryl)

07 **Akerman** (Chantal), **Aldrich** (Robert), **Asquith** (Anthony), **Belasco** (David), **Benigni** (Roberto), **Bennett** (Alan), **Bennett** (Michael), **Bergman** (Ingmar), **Berkoff** (Steven), **Bigelow** (Kathryn), **Boorman** (John), **Branagh** (Kenneth), **Bresson** (Robert), **Cameron** (James), **Campion** (Jane), **Chabrol** (Claude), **Chaikin** (Joseph), **Chaplin** (Charlie), **Clavell** (James), **Clooney** (George), **Clurman** (Harold), **Cocteau** (Jean), **Coppola** (Francis Ford), **Costner** (Kevin), **De Mille** (Cecil Blount), **De Palma** (Brian), **Douglas** (Bill), **Douglas** (Michael), **Fellini** (Federico), **Fleming** (Tom), **Fleming** (Victor), **Forsyth** (Bill), **Gaumont** (Léon), **Gilliam** (Terry), **Goldwyn** (Samuel), **Guthrie** (Sir Tyrone), **Hartley** (Hal), **Heiberg** (Gunnar), **Holland** (Agnieszka), **Jackson** (Peter), **Joffrey** (Robert), **Kaufman** (George S), **Kaufman** (Philip), **Kubrick** (Stanley), **McBride** (Jim), **McGrath** (John), **Nichols** (Mike), **Olivier** (Sir Laurence), **Poitier** (Sidney), **Pollack** (Sydney), **Redford** (Robert), **Resnais** (Alain), **Robbins** (Tim), **Russell** (Ken), **Sellars** (Peter), **Sennett** (Mack), **Stiller** (Mauritz), **Sturges** (Preston), **Webster** (Margaret), **Wenders** (Wim)

08 **Anderson** (Lindsay), **Barrault** (Jean-Louis), **Berkeley** (Busby), **Björnson** (Björnstjerne), **Bogdanov** (Michael), **Brustein** (Robert), **Carrière** (Jean-Claude), **Clements** (Sir John), **Crawford** (Cheryl), **Eastwood** (Clint), **Friedkin** (William), **Griffith** (David Wark), **Houseman** (John), **Jarmusch** (Jim), **Kurosawa** (Akira), **Levinson** (Barry), **Lubitsch** (Ernst), **Luhrmann** (Baz), **Lyubimov** (Yuri), **Marshall** (Penny), **Merchant** (Ismail), **Minnelli** (Vincente), **Mitchell** (Arthur), **Miyazaki** (Hayao), **Ninagawa** (Yukio), **Pasolini** (Pier Paulo), **Piscator** (Erwin), **Polanski** (Roman), **Pudovkin** (Vsevolod), **Schepisi** (Fred), **Scorsese** (Martin), **Selznick** (David Oliver), **Sjöström** (Victor), **Stroheim** (Erich von), **Truffaut** (François), **Visconti** (Luchino), **von Trier** (Lars), **Zemeckis** (Robert)

09 **Alexander** (Bill), **Almodóvar** (Pedro), **Antonioni** (Michelangelo), **Armstrong** (Gillian), **Carpenter** (John), **Chen Kaige**, **Fernández** (Emilio), **Greenaway** (Peter), **Grotowski** (Jerzy), **Hitchcock** (Sir Alfred), **Malkovich** (John), **Meyerhold** (Vsevolod), **Minghella** (Anthony), **Mizoguchi** (Kenji), **Mountford** (Charles P), **Peckinpah** (Sam), **Plowright** (Joan), **Preminger** (Otto), **Spielberg** (Steven), **Stevenson** (Robert), **Strasberg** (Lee), **Streisand** (Barbra), **Tarantino** (Quentin), **Tavernier** (Bertrand), **Von Trotta** (Margarethe), **Wanamaker** (Sam), **Zinnemann** (Fred)

10 **Bertolucci** (Bernardo), **Cronenberg** (David), **Eisenstein** (Sergei), **Fassbinder** (Rainer Werner), **Kaurismäki** (Aki), **Kiarostami** (Abbas), **Kieslowski** (Krzystof), **Littlewood** (Joan), **Makhmalbaf** (Mohsen), **Mankiewicz** (Joseph L), **Mnouchkine** (Ariane), **Rossellini** (Roberto), **Saint-Denis** (Michel), **Sucksdorff** (Arne E), **Vakhtangov** (Evgeny), **Wertmuller** (Lina), **Zeffirelli** (Franco), **Zetterling** (Mai), **Zhang Yimou**

11 **Bogdanovich** (Peter), **Dingelstedt** (Franz von), **Mackendrick** (Alexander), **Pressburger** (Emeric), **Riefenstahl** (Leni), **Roddenberry** (Gene), **Schlesinger** (John)

12 **Attenborough** (Sir Richard), **Espert Romero** (Nuria), **Stanislavsky**, **Von Sternberg** (Josef)

13 **Aguilera Malta** (Demetrio), **Gutiérrez Alea** (Tomás), **Stafford-Clark** (Max)

• directors

05 board

• managing director

02 MD **06** Man Dir

directory

04 list **05** guide, index **06** folder **07** listing, red book, who's who **09** catalogue, inventory **10** court guide **11** Yellow Pages®

dirge

05 elegy **06** dirige, lament, monody **07** requiem **08** coronach, threnody **09** dead-march **11** funeral song

dirk

07 whinger **08** skean-dhu, skene-dhu, whiniard, whinyard **10** skene-occle

dirt

03 mud **04** clay, crap, crud, dust, grot, gunk, loam, mess, mire, muck, pick, smut, soil, soot, yuck **05** bilge, clart, crock, earth, filth, grime, gunge, scuzz, slime, stain **06** clarts, grunge, ordure, scunge, sleaze, sludge, smudge **07** gutters, rubbish, tarnish **08** impurity, lewdness **09** excrement, indecency, obscenity, pollution **10** sordidness **11** pornography **13** salaciousness

dirty

03 bad, mud, ray **04** blue, dark, dull, foul, lewd, mean, mess, miry, poxy, soil, soss **05** bawdy, black, clart, dusty, grimy, manky, messy, mucky, muddy, nasty, slimy, smear, sooty, spoil, stain, sully, yucky **06** assoil, chatty, clarty, cloudy, coarse, cruddy, defile, filthy, greasy, grotty, grubby, grungy, mess up, mingin', muck up, ribald, risqué, scungy, shabby, skanky, sleazy, smirch, smudge, smutty, soiled, sordid, splash, stormy, unfair, vulgar, X-rated **07** begrime, blacken, clouded, corrupt, defiled, draggle, grufted, immoral, minging, obscene, piggish, pollute, raunchy, scruffy, squalid, stained, sullied, tarnish, unclean **08** bedaggle, besmirch, discolor, enormous, improper, indecent, polluted, unwashed **09** bedraggle, deceitful, discolour, dishonest, salacious, tarnished **10** adulterate, despicable, flea-bitten, insanitary, suggestive, unhygienic, unpleasant **11** contaminate, treacherous, undesirable **12** contaminated, contemptible, pornographic, unscrupulous

disability

04 maim **06** defect, malady **07** ailment, illness **08** disorder, handicap, weakness **09** complaint, inability, infirmity, unfitness **10** affliction, difficulty, impairment, incapacity **11** disablement **12** incapability

disable

04 lame, maim, stop **05** crock, wreck **06** damage, defuse, impair, weaken **07** cripple, invalid **08** enfeeble, handicap, knock out, paralyse **09** disparage, hamstring, make unfit, prostrate **10** deactivate, debilitate, depreciate, disqualify, immobilize, invalidate, undervalue **12** incapacitate **14** put out of action

disabled

04 lame, weak **05** unfit **06** infirm, maimed **07** invalid, wrecked **08** crippled, impaired, weakened **09** bed-ridden, enfeebled, paralysed **10** indisposed **11** debilitated, handicapped, immobilized, out of action **12** hors de combat **13** incapacitated

disabuse

09 enlighten, undeceive **10** disappoint, disenchant **11** disillusion

disadvantage

03 out **04** flaw, harm, hurt, lack, loss, snag **05** catch, minus **06** damage, defect, hang-up, injury **07** own goal, penalty, trouble **08** downside, drawback, handicap, hardship, nuisance, weakness **09** detriment, hindrance, liability, prejudice, privation, weak point **10** disamenity, disbenefit, disservice, disutility, impediment, limitation **11** disinterest **12** Achilles heel **13** inconvenience

disadvantaged

04 poor **06** in need, in want **08** deprived **10** in distress, struggling

11 handicapped **12** impoverished
15 poverty-stricken, underprivileged

disadvantageous
07 adverse, hapless, harmful, hurtful, unlucky **08** damaging, ill-timed
09 injurious **11** deleterious, detrimental, inexpedient, inopportune, prejudicial, unfortunate
12 inconvenient, unfavourable

disaffected
07 hostile **08** disloyal, mutinous
09 alienated, estranged, malignant, seditious **10** rebellious, unfriendly
11 disgruntled, ill-disposed
12 antagonistic, discontented, dissatisfied

disaffection
07 discord, dislike, ill-will **08** aversion, coolness **09** animosity, hostility
10 alienation, antagonism, disharmony, disloyalty, resentment
12 disagreement, estrangement
14 discontentment, disgruntlement, unfriendliness **15** dissatisfaction

disagree
04 vary **05** argue, clash, fight, upset
06 bicker, differ, object, oppose, sicken **07** contend, contest, discord, dispute, dissent, diverge, fall out, quarrel, wrangle **08** conflict, nauseate, squabble **09** be against, disaccord, take issue **10** contradict, make unwell, think wrong **11** beg to differ **12** argue against, be at odds with, cause illness, disapprove of **13** agree to differ, take issue with

disagreeable
03 bad **04** evil, rude, sour **05** cross, nasty, surly **07** awkward, beastly, brusque, grouchy, peevish **08** churlish, contrary, dreadful, horrible, impolite
09 difficult, irritable, obnoxious, offensive, repellent, repugnant, repulsive, unhelpful, unsavoury
10 abominable, disgusting, ill-natured, unfriendly, ungrateful, unpleasant
11 bad-tempered, disobliging, displeasing, distasteful, ill-humoured, unpalatable **13** objectionable

disagreeably
07 nastily **08** horribly **10** dreadfully
11 obnoxiously, offensively, repulsively
12 disgustingly, unpleasantly
13 objectionably

disagreement
03 row **04** flak, tiff **05** clash, fight
06 bust-up, strife **07** discord, dispute, dissent, quarrel, wrangle **08** argument, clashing, conflict, disunion, friction, squabble, variance **09** deviation, disparity, dissensus, diversity
10 conformity, contention, difference, disharmony, dissension, dissidence, dissonance, divergence, falling-out, unlikeness **11** altercation, contretemps, discrepancy, disputation, incongruity
13 dissimilarity, dissimilitude, inconsistency **14** unpleasantness, unsuitableness **15** incompatibility

• **expression of disagreement**
02 ah, h'm **03** boo, gup, hmm, hum, nah, naw, rot **04** booh, quep, uh-uh
05 arrah **06** hardly **08** nonsense
09 do you mind?

disallow
03 ban **04** veto **05** debar **06** abjure, cancel, disown, forbid, rebuff, refuse, reject **07** disavow, dismiss, embargo, exclude, say no to **08** disclaim, overrule, prohibit **09** disaffirm, dispraise, interdict, proscribe, repudiate, surcharge

disappear
◇ *deletion indicator*
02 go **03** ebb, end, fly **04** exit, fade, flee, hide, melt, pass, walk, wane
05 cease, ghost, slope **06** depart, die out, escape, expire, go cold, perish, recede, retire, vanish **07** die away, drop off, drop out, get lost, pass off, scarper, vamoose **08** dissolve, drop away, evanesce, melt away, peter out, withdraw **09** dissipate, evaporate, go missing **10** make tracks, take flight
12 go out of sight **13** become extinct, dematerialize, pass from sight **14** go like hot cakes **15** take French leave

disappearance
◇ *deletion indicator*
03 end **04** exit, loss **05** going
06 expiry, fading, flight **07** passing
08 dying-out, fade-away
09 departure, desertion, immersion, vanishing **10** extinction, karyolysis, resolution, withdrawal
11 evanescence, evaporation, melting away

disappoint
03 vex **04** fail, foil, mock **06** baffle, betray, defeat, delude, dismay, hamper, hinder, sadden, slip up, thwart
07 deceive, depress, let down
08 dispirit, mistryst **09** devastate, frustrate, mislippen **10** disconcert, discourage, disenchant, disgruntle, dishearten, dissatisfy **11** disillusion, make a fool of

disappointed
04 sick **05** upset, vexed **06** balked, choked, gutted, miffed **07** let-down
08 betrayed, cast down, deflated, saddened, thwarted **09** depressed
10 despondent, devastated, dischuffed, distressed, frustrated, unequipped **11** discouraged, disgruntled, downhearted, ill-equipped **12** disconsolate, disenchanted, disheartened, dissatisfied **13** disillusioned, sick as a parrot

disappointing
03 sad **05** bogus, sorry **07** unhappy
08 inferior, pathetic, unworthy
10 depressing, inadequate
12 disagreeable, discouraging, insufficient **13** anticlimactic, disconcerting, underwhelming
14 unsatisfactory

disappointment
04 balk, blow, sell, swiz **05** baulk, frost, lemon **06** bummer, fiasco, fizzer, regret, suck-in, take-in **07** chagrin, failure, let-down, sadness, setback, swizzle, washout, wipeout
08 calamity, comedown, disaster, distress, non-event **09** damp squib
10 anticlimax, bitter pill, discontent, misfortune **11** cold comfort, despondency, displeasure, frustration
14 discouragement, disenchantment, dispiritedness **15** disillusionment, dissatisfaction

• **expression of disappointment**
02 aw **04** nuts, pity **05** shoot
06 shucks

disapprobation
05 blame **07** censure, dislike, mislike, reproof **08** reproach **09** criticism, disfavour, exception, objection
11 disapproval, displeasure
12 condemnation, denunciation
13 disparagement, remonstration
14 discountenance **15** dissatisfaction

disapproval
04 veto **05** blame **06** rebuke
07 censure, disgust, dislike, reproof
08 reproach **09** criticism, exception, misliking, objection, rejection
11 displeasure **12** condemnation, denunciation, disallowance
13 disparagement, remonstration, the thumbs-down **14** disapprobation
15 dissatisfaction

• **expression of disapproval**
01 O **02** oh **03** boo, fie, tut **04** booh, toot, tuts, umph, what **05** humph, toots **06** tut-tut **07** fie upon **10** hoity-toity

• **indication of disapproval**
03 boo **04** booh, hiss **05** frown
07 catcall, walk out **09** dirty look, raspberry **10** Bronx cheer, thumbs down **12** slow handclap **13** shake your head

disapprove
04 veto **05** blame, spurn **06** reject
07 censure, condemn, deplore, dislike, frown on, mislike **08** denounce, disallow, disfavor, disprove, harrumph, object to **09** be against, deprecate, disesteem, disfavour, disparage, disproove, reprobate **10** animadvert, look down on **11** not hold with **12** think badly of **13** think little of
14 discountenance, hold in contempt, take a dim view of **15** take exception to

disapproving
04 prim **07** killjoy **08** critical, frowning
09 reproving **10** censorious, derogatory, pejorative **11** deprecatory, disparaging, improbative, improbatory, reproachful **12** condemnatory
14 disapprobative, disapprobatory

disarm
05 charm, unarm **07** appease, disable, disband, mollify, placate, unsteel, win over **08** persuade, unweapon
10 conciliate, deactivate, demobilize,

immobilize **11** lay down arms **12** demilitarize **13** make powerless **14** lay down weapons, put out of action

disarmament
11 arms control **12** deactivation **13** arms reduction **14** arms limitation, demobilization

disarming
07 winning **08** charming, likeable **10** mollifying, persuasive **12** conciliatory, irresistible

disarmingly
10 charmingly, pleasantly **12** irresistibly, persuasively

disarrange
◇ *anagram indicator*
04 mess, muss **05** musse **06** jumble, tousle, touzle, untidy **07** confuse, derange, disturb, shuffle **08** dishevel, disorder, displace, unsettle **09** dislocate **10** discompose **11** disorganize **13** put out of place

disarray
◇ *anagram indicator*
04 mess, tash **05** chaos, rifle, upset **06** jumble, muddle, tangle **07** clutter, undress **08** disorder, shambles **09** confusion **10** unruliness, untidiness **11** derangement **12** dishevelment, indiscipline **13** unsettledness **15** disorganization

disassemble
08 separate **09** dismantle, pull apart, take apart **12** pull to pieces, take to pieces

disassociate
05 break **06** cut off, remove **08** separate, withdraw **10** disconnect, dissociate

disaster
04 blow, flop, ruin **06** fiasco, mishap, mucker, stroke **07** debacle, failure, reverse, screw-up, setback, tragedy, trouble, washout, wipeout **08** accident, act of God, calamity, reversal **09** adversity, cataclysm, holocaust, mischance, ruination, shipwreck, sticky end **10** misfortune, providence **11** catastrophe, horror story **12** misadventure

disastrous
◇ *anagram indicator*
04 dire **05** fatal **06** gloomy, tragic **07** adverse, harmful, ruinous, unlucky **08** dreadful, ill-fated, ravaging, shocking, terrible, tragical **09** appalling, injurious, miserable **10** calamitous, ill-starred **11** cataclysmic, destructive, devastating, unfortunate **12** catastrophic

disavow
04 deny **06** abjure, disown, reject **08** disvouch, renounce **09** disaffirm, disavouch, repudiate **10** contradict **15** wash your hands of

disavowal
06 denial **07** dissent **09** rejection **10** abjuration, disclaimer **11** repudiation **12** disclamation, renunciation **13** contradiction **14** disaffirmation

disband
◇ *anagram indicator*
05 demob **06** disarm, reduce, reform **07** break up, dismiss, scatter **08** disperse, dissolve, separate **10** demobilize **11** part company **14** go separate ways

disbelief
05 doubt **07** atheism, dubiety, scruple **08** acosmism, distrust, mistrust, unbelief **09** discredit, rejection, suspicion **10** infidelity, scepticism **11** incredulity, questioning

• **expression of disbelief**
03 huh, tut **04** as if!, hoot **05** hoots **06** heaven, indeed, phooey, Walker **07** get away, says you **08** honestly, hoot-toot **09** away you go! **11** away with you, Betty Martin **12** Hookey Walker **13** what do you know?

disbelieve
05 doubt **06** reject **07** suspect **08** discount, distrust, mistrust, question **09** discredit, miscredit, repudiate **13** be unconvinced

disbeliever
07 atheist, doubter, sceptic, scoffer **08** agnostic **10** questioner, unbeliever **11** non-believer, nullifidian **14** doubting Thomas

disbelieving
07 cynical, infidel **08** doubtful, doubting **09** sceptical, uncertain **10** suspicious **11** distrustful, incredulous, unbelieving, unconvinced

disburse
05 spend **06** expend, lay out, pay out **07** cough up, dish out, fork out **08** shell out

disbursement
06 outlay **07** payment **08** disposal, spending **09** disbursal, outgiving **11** expenditure

disc
01 O **02** CD, EP, LP **03** DVD **04** disk, face, gong, ring **05** album, CD-ROM, elpee, paten, plate, round, vinyl, wheel **06** button, circle, discus, record, saucer **07** counter, rosette, roundel **08** diskette, hard disk, roundlet **10** floppy disk **11** compact disk, microfloppy

discard
03 bin **04** cast, defy, drop, dump, jilt, junk, kill, shed **05** ditch, scrap, trash **06** reject, remove **07** abandon, cashier, cast off, dismiss, forsake, lay away, toss out **08** chuck out, get rid of, jettison, lay aside, throw out **09** cast aside, chuck away, discharge, dismissal, dispose of, repudiate, supersede, throw away, throw over **10** pension off, relinquish **11** abandonment **12** dispense with

discards
04 crib

discern
03 get, see, wit **04** spot, tell **05** judge **06** descry, detect, notice, scerne **07** make out, observe, pick out **08** discover, perceive, tell from **09** ascertain, determine, recognize **11** distinguish **12** discriminate **13** differentiate

discernible
05 clear, plain **06** patent **07** obvious, visible **08** apparent, distinct, manifest **10** detectable, noticeable, observable **11** appreciable, conspicuous, perceptible **12** discoverable, recognizable **15** distinguishable

discerning
04 wise **05** acute, quick, sharp, sound **06** astute, clever, seeing, shrewd, subtle **07** prudent, sapient, trained **08** critical, piercing, tasteful **09** clear-eyed, eagle-eyed, ingenious, judicious, sagacious, selective, sensitive **10** perceptive, percipient **11** intelligent, penetrating **12** clear-sighted, eagle-sighted **13** perspicacious, understanding **14** discriminating

discernment
05 flair, sense, taste **06** acumen, wisdom **07** insight **08** keenness, sagacity, sapience **09** acuteness, awareness, good taste, ingenuity, judgement, sharpness **10** cleverness, perception, shrewdness **11** penetration, percipience **12** intelligence, perspicacity **13** ascertainment, understanding **14** discrimination, perceptiveness

discharge
02 do **03** arc, axe, pay, pus, ren, rin, ru[n] **04** emit, fire, flow, free, gush, leak, meet, ooze, oust, pass, pour, sack, vent, void **05** clear, congé, doing, drain, egest, eject, empty, expel, exude, issue, let go, loose, rheum, salvo, shoot, spout **06** acquit, congee, firing, forbid, fulfil, honour, let fly, let off, let out, pardon, remove, sanies, set off, settle, unload **07** absolve, boot out, discard, dismiss, excrete, explode, exuding, fire off, fluxion, give off, ousting, outflow, payment, perform, release, relieve, removal, sacking, satisfy, send out, set free, the boot, the sack, turf out **08** carry out, detonate, disgorge, dispense, displode, ejection, emission, evacuate, get rid of, liberate, settling, the elbow, turn away **09** acquittal, bowler-hat, broadside, clearance, colluvies, disburden, dismissal, excretion, exculpate, execution, exonerate, expulsion, honouring, quitclaim, repayment, secretion, unfraught, unloading **10** absolution, cashiering, disburthen,

disembogue, fulfilment, liberation, the heave-ho **11** achievement, carrying-out, exculpation, exoneration, performance, suppuration **12** give the elbow **13** give the boot to **14** accomplishment

disciple
03 son **05** chela, child, pupil **06** votary **07** apostle, convert, devotee, learner, scholar, student **08** adherent, believer, follower, upholder **09** proselyte, supporter
See also **apostle**

disciplinarian
06 despot, ramrod, tyrant **08** autocrat, martinet, stickler **10** taskmaster **13** authoritarian **14** hard taskmaster

discipline
04 bull, curb, judo **05** check, drill, inure, limit, order, teach, train, tutor **06** branch, disple, govern, ground, moguls, punish, rebuke, school **07** break in, chasten, control, correct, educate, regimen, reprove, routine, subject **08** chastise, dressage, exercise, feng shui, instruct, mathesis, penalize, practice, regulate, restrain, restrict, training **09** castigate, direction, inculcate, reprimand, restraint, schooling **10** correction, punishment, regulation, speciality, strictness **11** area of study, castigation, keep in check, orderliness, self-control **12** chastisement, field of study **13** course of study, mortification, self-restraint **14** self-discipline **15** make an example of

disclaim
04 deny **06** abjure, disown, refuse, reject **07** abandon, declaim, decline, disavow **08** renounce **09** repudiate **15** wash your hands of

disclaimer
06 denial **09** disavowal, rejection **10** abjuration, abnegation, disownment, retraction **11** repudiation **12** renunciation **13** contradiction **14** disaffirmation

disclose
04 blab, leak, open, show, tell **05** hatch, let on, unrip **06** betray, evolve, expose, impart, open up, relate, reveal, squeal, unfold, unheal, unhele, unlock, unveil **07** confess, develop, divulge, exhibit, lay bare, let drop, let slip, open out, propale, publish, unclose, uncover **08** blurt out, develope, discover **09** broadcast, make known, tell a tale **10** disclosure, make public **11** blow the gaff, communicate **12** bring to light **13** spill the beans **14** blow the whistle **15** give the game away, take the wraps off

disclosure
04 leak **06** exposé **08** exposure, overture **09** admission, broadcast, discovery **10** apocalypse, confession, divulgence, laying bare, revelation, uncovering **11** declaration, publication **12** announcement **15** acknowledgement, bringing to light

discoloration
04 blot, mark, spot **05** patch, stain **06** blotch, foxing, streak **07** blemish, blue-rot, pink-eye, splotch, tarnish **08** cyanosis, dyschroa, foxiness **09** dyschroia, melanosis **10** ecchymosis **12** acrocyanosis, weather stain **13** xanthochromia

discolour
03 fox, mar **04** fade, mark, rust, soil **05** dirty, stain, tinge **06** bruise, streak **07** tarnish, weather **09** disfigure

discomfit
◇ *anagram indicator*
04 balk, faze, rout **05** abash, shend, throw **06** baffle, defeat, outwit, rattle, ruffle, thwart **07** confuse, fluster, perplex, perturb **08** confound, unsettle **09** embarrass, frustrate **10** demoralize, discompose, disconcert

discomfiture
05 lurch **06** unease **07** chagrin **09** abashment, confusion **10** uneasiness **11** frustration, humiliation **12** discomposure **13** embarrassment **14** demoralization, disappointment

discomfort
04 ache, hell, hurt, pain, pang **05** worry **06** bother, hassle, jet lag, misery, twinge, unease **07** malaise, trouble **08** disquiet, distress, drawback, hardship, nuisance, soreness, vexation **09** annoyance, purgatory **10** cardialgia, difficulty, irritation, tenderness, uneasiness **12** apprehension, disadvantage, restlessness, unpleasantry **13** embarrassment, inconvenience

discompose
◇ *anagram indicator*
06 ruffle **07** agitate, disturb **08** disorder **10** disarrange

discomposure
05 upset **06** unease **07** anxiety, fluster **09** agitation, annoyance **10** inquietude, irritation, uneasiness **11** disquietude, disturbance **12** perturbation, restlessness

disconcert
◇ *anagram indicator*
04 faze **05** abash, alarm, blank, quell, shake, tease, throw, upset **06** baffle, defeat, dismay, put off, put out, rattle, ruffle **07** break up, confuse, disturb, fluster, nonplus, perplex, perturb, startle, stumble, unnerve **08** bewilder, disunion, surprise, throw off, throw out, unsettle **09** discomfit, embarrass, frustrate, knock back, take aback **14** discomboberate, discombobulate **15** throw off balance

disconcerting
◇ *anagram indicator*
07 awkward **08** alarming, baffling, daunting **09** confusing, dismaying, unnerving, upsetting **10** bothersome, disturbing, off-putting, perplexing, perturbing, unsettling **11** bewildering, distracting **12** embarrassing

disconnect
04 part, undo **05** loose, sever, split **06** cut off, detach, divide, ungear, unhook, unplug **07** disjoin, unhitch **08** disjoint, separate, uncouple **09** disengage **10** de-energize

disconnected
05 loose **06** abrupt **07** garbled, jumbled, mixed-up, scrappy **08** confused, rambling, staccato **09** illogical, separated, wandering **10** disjointed, incoherent, irrational **12** inconsequent **13** unco-ordinated **14** unintelligible

disconnection
07 undoing **08** division **09** severance **10** detachment, separation, uncoupling, unplugging **13** disengagement

disconsolate
03 low, sad **04** down **06** gloomy **07** crushed, forlorn, unhappy **08** dejected, desolate, downcast, hopeless, wretched **09** depressed, miserable **10** despondent, dispirited, melancholy **11** heartbroken, low-spirited **12** heavy-hearted, inconsolable **13** grief-stricken **14** down in the dumps

disconsolately
05 sadly **09** miserably, unhappily **10** dejectedly, desolately, wretchedly **12** despondently, inconsolably **14** heavy-heartedly

discontent
06 misery, regret, unrest **08** disquiet, vexation **09** fed-upness **10** impatience, uneasiness **11** displeasure, fretfulness, unhappiness **12** disaffection, dissatisfied, heartburning, restlessness, wretchedness **15** dissatisfaction

discontented
05 fed up **07** unhappy **08** restless, wretched **09** impatient, miserable, pissed off **10** browned off, cheesed off, displeased, malcontent **11** complaining, disaffected, disgruntled, exasperated **12** dissatisfied

discontinue
03 end **04** drop, halt, quit, stop **05** cease, scrap **06** cancel, finish **07** abandon, abolish, refrain, suspend **08** break off, knock off, withdraw **09** interrupt, terminate **10** do away with **11** come to an end, come to a stop

discontinued
03 dis, off **07** at an end

discontinuity
05 break, comma **06** breach **07** rupture **08** disunion **09** nickpoint **10** disruption, knickpoint

11 incoherence 12 interruption
13 disconnection 14 disjointedness

discontinuous
06 broken, fitful 08 discrete, periodic, sporadic 09 irregular, separated, spasmodic 10 punctuated
11 interrupted 12 disconnected, intermittent

discord
◇ *anagram indicator*
03 row 05 split 06 jangle, strife
07 dispute, dissent, jarring
08 argument, clashing, conflict, disagree, disunity, division, friction, jangling 09 cacophony, disaccord, harshness, wrangling 10 contention, difference, disharmony, dissension, dissonance, opposition, suspension
11 discordance 12 disagreement
13 inharmonicity 15 discord of sounds, incompatibility

discordant
◇ *anagram indicator*
04 flat 05 harsh, sharp 06 at odds, atonal, hoarse, off-key 07 grating, hostile, jarring 08 absonant, clashing, jangling, opposing, strident
09 differing, dissonant 10 at variance, dissenting 11 cacophonous, conflicting, disagreeing, disharmonic, incongruous, unagreeable
12 incompatible, inconsistent, inharmonious 13 contradictory

discount
03 cut 04 agio 05 slash 06 deduct, ignore, rebate, reduce 07 dismiss, take off 08 cut price, knock off, mark down, mark-down, overlook, pass over, pooh-pooh 09 allowance, deduction, disregard, gloss over, reduction
10 concession, disbelieve, rebatement

discourage
04 damp 05 chill, daunt, deter
06 dampen, deject, dismay, hinder, put off 07 depress, prevent, unnerve
08 cast down, choke off, dispirit, dissuade, hold back, restrain 09 talk out of 10 demoralize, disappoint, dishearten 12 put a damper on
13 advise against 14 discountenance
15 pour cold water on

discouraged
04 glum 06 dashed 07 daunted, let down 08 deflated, dejected, dismayed, downcast 09 depressed
10 dispirited 11 crestfallen, demoralized, pessimistic
12 disheartened 14 down in the dumps

discouragement
04 curb, damp 05 gloom 06 damper, dismay, rebuff 07 barrier, despair, setback 08 obstacle 09 dejection, deterrent, hindrance, pessimism, restraint 10 depression, impediment, opposition 11 despondency
12 disincentive, hopelessness
14 disappointment
15 downheartedness

discouraging
08 daunting 09 dampening
10 depressing, dissuasive, dissuasory, off-putting 11 dehortatory, dispiriting
12 demoralizing, inauspicious, unfavourable, unpropitious
13 disappointing, disheartening

discourse
04 chat, tale, talk 05 essay, speak, spell
06 confer, debate, homily, preach, reason, sermon, speech, tongue
07 address, discuss, lecture, oration
08 chit-chat, colloquy, converse, dialogue, exercise, treatise
09 discursus, hold forth, rigmarole
10 discussion, exposition, meditation, preachment 11 exhortation, highfalutin 12 conversation, disquisition, dissertation, exercitation, highfaluting 13 communication, confabulation

discourteous
04 curt, rude 05 gruff, short 06 abrupt
07 boorish, brusque, ill-bred, offhand, uncivil, uncouth 08 ignorant, impolite, impudent, insolent 09 offensive, truculent 10 ungracious, unmannerly, unpleasant 11 bad-mannered, ill-mannered, impertinent
13 disrespectful, unceremonious

discourteously
06 curtly, rudely 07 gruffly
08 abruptly 09 brusquely, uncivilly
10 impolitely, impudently, insolently
11 offensively, offhandedly
12 ungraciously, unpleasantly
13 impertinently 15 disrespectfully, unceremoniously

discourtesy
04 snub 06 insult, rebuff, slight
07 affront 08 curtness, rudeness
09 indecorum, insolence 10 bad manners, disrespect, incivility
11 brusqueness, ill-breeding
12 impertinence, impoliteness
14 indecorousness, ungraciousness, unmannerliness

discover
◇ *anagram indicator*
◇ *hidden indicator*
03 see, spy, sus 04 espy, find, spot, suss, twig 05 dig up, hit on, learn, trace
06 create, descry, detect, devise, fathom, invent, locate, notice, reveal, rumble, sus out, turn up, unmask
07 analyse, compose, discern, discure, exhibit, find out, get onto, hit upon, light on, make out, pioneer, realize, suss out, uncover, unearth, work out
08 disclose, discoure, perceive, smoke out, sound out 09 ascertain, determine, establish, fathom out, ferret out, get wind of, get wise to, originate, recognize, stumble on 10 come across, come to know, excogitate
11 come to light 12 find out about
13 stumble across

discoverer
05 scout 06 author, finder 07 creator, deviser, founder, pioneer 08 explorer, informer, inventor 09 initiator
10 originator

discovery
04 find 06 descry, eureka 07 finding, heureka 08 devising, findings, learning, location, research
09 detection, invention 10 disclosure, innovation, pioneering, revelation
11 discernment, exploration, origination, realization, recognition
12 breakthrough, introduction
13 determination
• **expression of discovery**
05 bingo, hallo, hello, hullo 06 eureka
07 heureka

discredit
04 deny, slag, slur 05 blame, doubt, shame, slate, smear 06 damage, debunk, defame, infamy, refute, reject, stigma, vilify 07 censure, degrade, discard, explode, rubbish, run down, scandal, slag off, slander, tarnish
08 badmouth, belittle, disgrace, disprove, distrust, ignominy, mistrust, question, reproach 09 aspersion, challenge, dishonour, disparage, disrepute, ill-repute, reflect on
10 disbelieve, invalidate, opprobrium
11 humiliation 14 put in a bad light, reflect badly on

discreditable
06 shabby 08 improper, infamous, shameful, unworthy 09 degrading
10 scandalous 11 blameworthy, disgraceful 12 disreputable
13 dishonourable, reprehensible

discreet
04 wary, wise 05 witty 06 modest
07 careful, guarded, politic, prudent, tactful 08 cautious, delicate, detached, reserved, sensible, separate
09 judicious 10 diplomatic
11 circumspect, considerate
13 unpretentious

discreetly
06 wisely 08 sensibly 09 carefully, prudently, tactfully 10 cautiously, delicately 11 judiciously
13 circumspectly, considerately
14 diplomatically

discrepancy
08 conflict, variance 09 deviation, disparity, variation 10 difference, divergence, inequality 11 discordance, incongruity 12 disagreement
13 contradiction, dissimilarity, inconsistency

discrete
08 abstract, detached, disjunct, distinct, separate 09 disjoined
10 individual, unattached
12 disconnected 13 discontinuous

discretion
04 care, tact, will, wish 06 choice, desire, wisdom 07 caution, freedom, reserve 08 prudence, volition, wariness 09 diplomacy, good sense, judgement 10 preference
11 carefulness, discernment,

guardedness, inclination
12 predilection **13** consideration, judiciousness **14** circumspection

discretionary
04 open **08** elective, optional
09 voluntary **12** unrestricted

discriminate
06 secern **07** discern **08** be biased, separate **09** segregate, tell apart, victimize **11** distinguish **12** be intolerant, be prejudiced
13 differentiate, show prejudice, treat unfairly

discriminating
04 keen **05** acute **06** astute, nasute, shrewd **08** critical, delicate, tasteful
09 invidious, selective, sensitive
10 cultivated, discerning, fastidious, particular, perceptive, respective
12 differential, preferential

discrimination
04 bias **05** skill, taste **06** acumen, ageism, racism, sexism, sizism
07 ableism, bigotry, fattism, insight, Jim Crow, lookism, sizeism **08** classism, inequity, judgment, keenness, subtlety
09 acuteness, colour bar, judgement, prejudice **10** astuteness, difference, differency, homophobia, perception, refinement, shrewdness, unfairness
11 discernment, distinction, favouritism, intolerance, penetration, segregation, sensitivity
12 heterosexism, perspicacity **14** male chauvinism

discriminatory
06 biased, loaded, unfair, unjust
07 partial **08** one-sided, partisan, weighted **09** favouring **10** prejudiced
11 inequitable, prejudicial
12 preferential **14** discriminative

discursive
05 wordy **06** prolix **07** diffuse, verbose **08** rambling **09** wandering
10 circuitous, digressing, long-winded, meandering **11** wide-ranging

discuss
03 vex **04** sift, toss **05** argue, study, treat **06** confer, debate, decide, dispel, go into, handle, parley, reason, review, settle, take up **07** agitate, analyse, belabor, beprose, canvass, consult, declare, examine, speak to, weigh up
08 belabour, consider, converse, critique, deal with, question, talk over
09 discourse, kick about, pro and con, talk about, thrash out **10** deliberate, interplead, kick around, knock about, politicize **11** confabulate, expostulate, knock around **12** go into detail
15 exchange views on

discussion
03 rap **04** chat, conf, moot, talk
05 forum, study, talks **06** debate, korero, parley, powwow, review, talk-in
07 gabfest, palaver, seminar
08 analysis, argument, dialogue, exchange, question, scrutiny, speaking, talkfest **09** discourse, symposium, talkathon **10** colloquium, conference, rap session **11** examination
12 consultation, conversation, deliberation, negotiations
13 consideration

disdain
03 coy **04** snub **05** scorn, sdayn, sdein, spurn **06** deride, ignore, rebuff, reject, sdaine, sdeign, slight
07 contemn, despise, disavow, dislike, sdeigne, sneer at **08** belittle, contempt, derision, pooh-pooh, sneering, turn down **09** arrogance, contumely, disregard **10** look down on, sour grapes, undervalue
11 deprecation, haughtiness **12** cold shoulder, snobbishness, think scorn of
13 disparagement

• **expression of disdain**
04 pooh, tush **06** powwaw

• **show disdain**
04 geck

disdainful
05 aloof, proud, saucy **07** haughty, pompous **08** arrogant, derisive, insolent, scornful, sneering, superior
09 slighting **11** disparaging
12 contemptuous, supercilious

disease
03 bug, pox **05** virus **06** malady
07 ailment, illness **08** disorder, epidemic, sickness **09** complaint, condition, contagion, ill-health, infection, infirmity **10** affliction, disability, uneasiness **13** indisposition, unhealthiness

Diseases and medical conditions include:

02 CF, ME, MS, TB
03 CFS, CJD, DVT, flu, FMS, IBS, PID, PKU, PVS, tic, TSS
04 AIDS, clap, cold, coma, gout, kuru, Lyme, mono, rash, SARS
05 colic, croup, favus, lupus, mumps, polio, Weil's
06 angina, apnoea, asthma, autism, cancer, chorea, Crohn's, dropsy, eczema, emesis, goitre, Grave's, hernia, herpes, oedema, otitis, Paget's, quinsy, rabies, scurvy, stroke, thrush, tumour, typhus
07 abscess, allergy, anaemia, anthrax, anxiety, atrophy, Batten's, bird flu, Bright's, bulimia, cholera, coeliac, kissing, leprosy, lockjaw, malaria, Marburg, measles, myalgia, mycosis, rickets, rubella, sarcoma, scabies, tetanus, typhoid, vertigo
08 Addison's, alopecia, aneurism, anorexia, avian flu, beriberi, botulism, bursitis, cachexia, coxalgia, Cushing's, cynanche, cystitis, dementia, diabetes, embolism, epilepsy, fibroids, gangrene, glaucoma, Hodgkin's, impetigo, jaundice, kala-azar, listeria, lymphoma, melanoma, Ménière's, migraine, necrosis, orchitis, pyelitis, Raynaud's, rhinitis, ringworm, sciatica, shingles, smallpox, stenosis, syphilis, tapeworm, Tay-Sachs, tinnitus, trachoma, venereal, viraemia
09 arthritis, arthrosis, bilharzia, chlamydia, chlorosis, cirrhosis, cri du chat, distemper, dysentery, eclampsia, emphysema, enteritis, hepatitis, influenza, ketonuria, leukaemia, neoplasia, nephritis, nephrosis, neuralgia, paralysis, parotitis, pertussis, pneumonia, psoriasis, pyorrhoea, silicosis, sinusitis, sunstroke, Sydenham's, toothache, urticaria, varicella
10 acromegaly, Alzheimer's, amoebiasis, asbestosis, Bell's Palsy, Black Death, bronchitis, chickenpox, common cold, depression, diphtheria, gingivitis, gonorrhoea, laryngitis, Lassa fever, meningitis, Parkinson's, rhinorrhea, thrombosis
11 anaphylaxis, brucellosis, cholestasis, consumption, dehydration, dengue fever, farmer's lung, green monkey, haemophilia, haemorrhage, heart attack, Huntington's, hydrophobia, hyperplasia, hypertrophy, hypotension, listeriosis, mastoiditis, motor neuron, myocarditis, peritonitis, pharyngitis, pneumonitis, proteinuria, psittacosis, sarcoidosis, septicaemia, spina bifida, tonsillitis, trench fever, yellow fever
12 appendicitis, athlete's foot, cor pulmonale, encephalitis, endocarditis, foot-and-mouth, heart failure, Legionnaires', liver failure, osteoporosis, pericarditis, scarlet fever, tuberculosis
13 bronchiolitis, bubonic plague, cerebral palsy, coronary heart, Down's syndrome, elephantiasis, endometriosis, German measles, kidney failure, leishmaniasis, mononucleosis, osteomyelitis, poliomyelitis, Rett's syndrome, Reye's syndrome, schizophrenia, toxoplasmosis, varicose veins, West Nile virus, whooping cough
14 angina pectoris, break-bone fever, conjunctivitis, cystic fibrosis, glandular fever, osteoarthritis, pneumoconiosis, rheumatic fever, river blindness, sleepy sickness, thyrotoxicosis
15 anorexia nervosa, atherosclerosis, bipolar disorder, gastro-enteritis, Gulf War syndrome, manic depression, phenylketonuria, schistosomiasis

See also **skin**

Animal diseases include:

03 BSE, FMD, gid, orf
04 gape, gout, loco, roup, wind
05 bloat, braxy, farcy, frush, hoove, pearl, surra, vives
06 canker, Johne's, mad cow, Marek's,

nagana, rabies, spavie, spavin, sturdy
07 anthrax, blue ear, dourine, hard pad, measles, mooneye, moorill, murrain, roaring, rubbers, scrapie, yellows
08 bovine TB, fowl-pest, glanders, pullorum, scaly-leg, seedy-toe, sheep-pox, staggers, swayback, swine-pox, wildfire, wire-heel
09 Aujeszky's, blackhead, distemper, Newcastle, scratches, sheep scab, spauld-ill, St Hubert's, strangles
10 blue tongue, louping-ill, ornithosis, rinderpest, sallenders, swamp fever, swine fever, Texas fever, water-brain
11 blood-spavin, brucellosis, mad staggers, myxomatosis, parrot fever, psittacosis
12 black-quarter, bush sickness, cattle-plague, foot-and-mouth, furunculosis, gall-sickness
13 grass sickness, grass staggers, leptospirosis
14 sleepy staggers
15 Rift Valley fever, stomach staggers

Plant diseases include:

04 bunt, curl, rust, smut
05 ergot
06 blight, blotch, canker, mildew, mosaic, red rot
07 ferrugo, oak wilt, ring rot, rosette, soft rot, yellows
08 blackleg, black rot, clubroot, crown rot, Dutch elm, leaf curl, loose-cut, wheat eel
09 crown gall, potato rot, tulip root
10 fire-blight, leaf mosaic, silver leaf, sooty mould, vine-mildew
11 anthracnose, wheat mildew
12 finger-and-toe, peach-yellows, potato blight
13 powdery mildew
14 psyllid yellows

Disease symptoms include:

04 pain, rash
05 cramp, fever, hives, sniff
06 aching, lesion, tremor
07 anxiety, fatigue, fitting, itching
08 bruising, coughing, deafness, fainting, headache, insomnia, numbness, sickness, sneezing, swelling, tingling, vomiting, weakness
09 blindness, diarrhoea, dizziness, heartburn, impotence, lassitude, nosebleed, paralysis, stiffness, twitching
10 congestion, depression, flatulence, irritation, sore throat, tenderness
11 convulsions, indigestion, loss of voice, trapped wind
12 constipation, incontinence, inflammation, irritability, loss of libido, muscle cramps
13 loss of hearing, stomach cramps, swollen glands
14 loss of appetite, pins and needles
15 high temperature, loss of sensation

• **abatement of disease**
05 lysis
• **infectious diseases**
02 ID

diseased
◇ *anagram indicator*
03 ill **04** poxy, sick **06** ailing, infirm, unwell **07** unsound **08** blighted, infected, soul-sick **09** unhealthy **12** contaminated, distemperate

disembark
04 land **05** leave **06** alight, arrive, debark, get off **07** deplane, detrain, disbark, step off **08** dismount

disembarkation
07 arrival, landing **09** alighting

disembodied
07 ghostly, phantom **08** bodiless, spectral **09** spiritual **10** discarnate, immaterial, intangible **11** incorporeal **12** discorporate

disembowel
◇ *middle deletion indicator*
03 gut **04** draw **06** paunch **07** embowel **08** disbowel, gralloch **09** viscerate **10** eviscerate, exenterate

disenchanted
05 blasé, fed up **06** soured **07** cynical, let down **09** jaundiced **11** discouraged, indifferent **12** disappointed, dissatisfied **13** disillusioned

disenchantment
08 cynicism **09** fed-upness, revulsion **11** disillusion **14** disappointment **15** disillusionment, dissatisfaction

disengage
04 free, slip, undo **05** untie **06** detach, loosen, remove, unhook **07** release, unhitch **08** disunite, liberate, separate, throw off, uncouple, unfasten, withdraw **09** extricate **10** disconnect **11** disentangle

disengaged
04 free **05** clear, freed, loose **08** detached, released, separate **09** liberated, separated, unhitched **10** unattached, unoccupied **11** unconnected **12** disentangled

disengagement
07 release, removal, retreat **09** loosening, releasing **10** detachment, retirement, separating, taking away, withdrawal **13** disconnection **15** disentanglement

disentangle
03 red **04** free, redd, undo **05** loose, ravel **06** detach, unfold, unknot, unwind **07** clarify, release, resolve, unravel, unsnarl, untwist **08** distance, ravel out, separate, simplify, unfasten, untangle **09** debarrass, disengage, extricate **10** disconnect, disinvolve, straighten **11** distinguish **13** straighten out

disfavour
06 oppose **07** disgust, dislike **08** distaste, ignominy **09** discredit, disesteem, disregard, disrepute, hostility **10** disapprove, low opinion, opprobrium **11** disapproval, displeasure **12** unpopularity **14** disapprobation **15** dissatisfaction

disfigure
◇ *anagram indicator*
03 mar **04** blad, blur, flaw, maim, ruin, scar, tash **05** blaud, spoil **06** agrise, agrize, agryze, beweep, damage, deface, defeat, deform, injure, mangle **07** blemish, distort **08** discolor, make ugly, mutilate **09** defeature, discolour

disfigurement
04 scar, spot, wart **05** stain **06** blotch, defect, injury **07** blemish **08** disgrace **09** defeature, deformity **10** defacement, distortion, impairment, mutilation **12** uglification

disgorge
04 hawk, spew **05** belch, eject, empty, expel, spout, vomit **06** effuse **07** pour out, throw up **09** discharge **11** regurgitate

disgrace
04 blot, slur **05** abase, atimy, blame, shame, shend, smear, stain, sully, taint **06** baffle, debase, defame, ignomy, infamy, stigma **07** attaint, degrade, obloquy, reproof, scandal, villany **08** belittle, contempt, dishonor, ignominy, reproach, ugliness, villainy **09** attainder, black mark, denigrate, discredit, disfavour, dishonour, disparage, disrepute, humiliate, indignify, indignity **10** debasement, defamation, disrespect, disworship, loss of face, opprobrium, put to shame, scandalize, stigmatize **11** degradation, humiliation **12** bring shame on **13** disfigurement **14** disapprobation **15** cause to lose face

disgraced
06 shamed **07** branded **08** degraded **10** humiliated **11** discredited, dishonoured, stigmatized, under a cloud **13** in the doghouse

disgraceful
05 awful **06** indign **08** culpable, dreadful, infamous, shameful, shocking, terrible, unworthy **09** appalling, degrading **10** despicable, inglorious, outrageous, scandalled, scandalous **11** blameworthy, ignominious, opprobrious, reproachful **12** contemptible, dishonorable, disreputable **13** discreditable, dishonourable, reprehensible

disgracefully
07 awfully **08** terribly **10** despicably, dreadfully, shamefully, shockingly **11** appallingly **12** contemptibly, disreputably, outrageously, scandalously **13** dishonourably, ignominiously, reprehensibly

disgruntled
◇ *anagram indicator*
05 fed up, sulky, testy, vexed

06 grumpy, peeved, put out, sullen 07 annoyed, chuffed, peevish 08 petulant 09 hacked off, irritated, resentful 10 brassed off, browned off, cheesed off, displeased, malcontent 11 exasperated 12 discontented, dissatisfied

disguise
◇ *anagram indicator*
04 face, fake, hide, mask, ring, veil 05 cloak, cloke, color, cover, feign, front, fudge, visor, vizor 06 colour, façade, immask, mantle, screen, shroud, veneer, vizard 07 conceal, costume, cover up, deceive, dress up, falsify, pretend, repress 08 palliate, pretence, suppress, travesty 09 coverture, deception, dissemble, gloss over, whitewash 10 camouflage, masquerade 11 concealment, dissimulate, impersonate 12 be under cover, cook the books, false picture, misrepresent 15 put on a brave face

disguised
◇ *anagram indicator*
04 fake 05 false 06 covert, hidden, made up, masked, veiled 07 cloaked, feigned 09 incognito 10 under cover 11 camouflaged 14 unrecognizable

disgust
03 irk, pip 04 cloy 05 repel, shock 06 hatred, nausea, offend, put off, revolt, sicken, turn up 07 outrage, scunner, turn off 08 aversion, distaste, gross out, loathing, nauseate, scomfish 09 disfavour, displease, disrelish, repulsion, revulsion 10 abhorrence, repugnance 11 detestation, disapproval, displeasure 15 turn your stomach

• **expression of disgust**
02 aw, fy 03 bah, fie, foh, huh, pah, paw, pho, sis, ugh, wow, yah, yuk 04 damn, phoh, pooh, tush, whow, yech, yuck 05 faugh, shoot, wowee 06 powwaw 07 brother 11 for God's sake 14 for heaven's sake

disgusted
04 sick 06 put off 08 appalled, offended, outraged, repelled, repulsed, revolted, sickened, up in arms 10 cheesed off

disgusting
03 bad 04 foul, vile 05 grody, gross, nasty, slimy, yucky, yukky 06 odious, putrid, ugsome 07 mawkish, noisome, obscene 08 nauseous, shocking 09 appalling, offensive, repellent, repugnant, repulsive, revolting, sickening 10 abominable, detestable, nauseating, off-putting, outrageous, unpleasant 11 disgraceful, distasteful, rebarbative, unpalatable 12 unappetizing 13 objectionable

dish
◇ *anagram indicator*
04 bowl, fare, food, ruin, tray 05 plate 06 course, recipe, tureen 07 platter 08 delicacy 10 speciality

See also **food**

• **dish out**
◇ *anagram indicator*
07 dole out, give out, hand out, inflict, mete out 08 allocate, dispense, share out 09 hand round, pass round 10 distribute

• **dish up**
05 ladle, offer, scoop, serve, spoon 07 present 08 dispense

disharmony
05 clash 06 strife 07 discord, dissent 08 conflict, friction 09 disaccord 10 dissonance 11 discordance, incongruity 12 disagreement 15 incompatibility

dishearten
04 dash 05 chill, crush, daunt, deter 06 dampen, deject, dismay 07 depress, unheart 08 cast down, dispirit 09 disparage, weigh down 10 demoralize, disappoint, discourage 12 put a damper on 13 make depressed

disheartened
◇ *middle deletion indicator*
04 down 07 crushed, daunted 08 dejected, dismayed, downcast 09 depressed 10 dispirited 11 crestfallen, demoralized, discouraged, downhearted 12 disappointed

dishevelled
◇ *anagram indicator*
04 wild 05 daggy, messy 06 blowsy, blowzy, untidy 07 in a mess, ruffled, rumpled, scruffy, tousled, unkempt 08 slovenly, uncombed 09 windswept 10 bedraggled, disordered 11 disarranged

dishonest
03 sly 04 bent, iffy 05 cross, dirty, dodgy, false, fishy, lying, shady, snide 06 crafty, shifty, untrue 07 corrupt, crooked, cunning, devious, knavish 08 cheating, unchaste 09 deceitful, deceptive, insincere, irregular, swindling 10 fraudulent, mendacious, perfidious, untruthful 11 duplicitous, treacherous 12 disreputable, unprincipled, unscrupulous 13 dishonourable, double-dealing, untrustworthy

dishonestly
05 false 07 falsely 09 corruptly, deviously 10 on the cross 11 deceitfully, deceptively 12 disreputably, fraudulently, perfidiously 13 dishonourably, treacherously 14 unscrupulously

dishonesty
05 fraud 06 deceit 07 falsity, knavery, perfidy 08 cheating, trickery 09 chicanery, duplicity, falsehood, improbity, shadiness, treachery 10 corruption, dirty trick 11 criminality, crookedness, fraudulence, insincerity 12 irregularity 13 double-dealing, sharp practice 14 untruthfulness

dishonour
04 slur 05 abuse, shame, stain, sully, wrong 06 debase, defame, defile, demean, ignomy, infamy, insult, offend, refuse, reject, seduce, slight, stigma 07 affront, debauch, degrade, offence, outrage, scandal 08 disgrace, ignominy, reproach, turn down 09 abasement, aspersion, discredit, disfavour, disparage, disrepute, humiliate, indignity 10 debasement, disworship, opprobrium 11 degradation, discourtesy, humiliation

dishonourable
05 shady 07 corrupt, disleal, ignoble, low-down 08 infamous, shameful, unhonest, unworthy 09 shameless, unethical 10 despicable, perfidious, scandalous 11 disgraceful, ignominious, treacherous 12 contemptible, disreputable, unprincipled, unscrupulous 13 discreditable, untrustworthy

dishy
04 sexy 05 hunky 08 charming, gorgeous, handsome 10 attractive 11 good-looking

disillusion
08 disabuse 09 undeceive 10 disappoint, disenchant 14 disappointment, disenchantment 15 disillusionment

disillusioned
07 let-down 09 disabused 10 undeceived 12 disappointed, disenchanted

disincentive
06 damper 07 barrier, turn-off 08 obstacle 09 determent, deterrent, hindrance, repellent 10 constraint, dissuasion, impediment 11 restriction 14 discouragement

disinclination
07 dislike 08 aversion 09 antipathy, loathness, objection 10 alienation, averseness, hesitation, opposition, reluctance, repugnance, resistance 13 indisposition, unwillingness

disinclined
05 loath 06 averse 07 opposed 08 hesitant 09 reluctant, resistant, unwilling 10 indisposed, undisposed 14 unenthusiastic

disinfect
05 clean, purge 06 bleach, purify 07 cleanse 08 fumigate, sanitize 09 sterilize 13 decontaminate

disinfectant
05 lysol 06 cineol, cresol, phenol 07 cineole 08 fumigant, sheep-dip, terebene 09 germicide, sanitizer 10 antiseptic, sterilizer 11 bactericide 12 methyl violet 13 decontaminant 14 glutaraldehyde

disingenuous
03 sly 04 wily 06 artful, crafty, shifty 07 cunning, devious, feigned

08 guileful, two-faced, uncandid
09 deceitful, designing, dishonest, insidious, insincere 11 duplicitous

disingenuously
05 slyly 08 artfully 09 cunningly, deviously 11 deceitfully, dishonestly, insidiously, insincerely

disinherit
06 cut off, reject 07 abandon
08 renounce 09 repudiate
10 dispossess, exheredate, impoverish
14 turn your back on

disintegrate
◇ *anagram indicator*
03 rot 05 decay, smash 06 reduce
07 break up, crumble, moulder, shatter
08 separate, splinter 09 decompose, fall apart 10 break apart 12 fall to pieces, self-destruct

disintegration
◇ *anagram indicator*
03 rot 05 decay 07 breakup
08 biolysis, decaying 09 breakdown, crumbling 10 karyolysis, separation, shattering 11 dissolution 12 falling-apart 13 decomposition, radioactivity, spondylolysis

disinter
05 dig up 06 exhume, expose, reveal, unbury 07 uncover, unearth
08 excavate, exhumate 09 disentomb, disinhume, resurrect 12 bring to light

disinterest
08 fairness 09 unconcern
10 detachment, neutrality
12 disadvantage, impartiality, unbiasedness

disinterested
04 cool, fair, just 07 neutral
08 detached, generous, unbiased
09 equitable, impartial, objective, unselfish 10 even-handed, open-minded, uninvolved 12 unprejudiced
13 dispassionate

disjointed
◇ *anagram indicator*
05 bitty, loose, split 06 abrupt, broken, fitful 07 aimless, divided
08 confused, rambling 09 displaced, disunited, separated, spasmodic, wandering 10 dislocated, disordered, incoherent 11 unconnected
12 disconnected 13 directionless
14 disarticulated

dislike
04 defy, down, hate, lump, mind, shun
05 abhor, derry, scorn, thing
06 animus, detest, enmity, hatred, loathe, needle 07 allergy, despise, disgust, mislike 08 aversion, disfavor, distaste, dyspathy, execrate, loathing, object to 09 abominate, animosity, antipathy, disesteem, disfavour, disrelish, hostility, objection
10 antagonism, disapprove, repugnance, resentment
11 detestation, disapproval, displeasure, take against 12 have a derry on 14 disapprobation, disinclination, take a scunner to

dislocate
◇ *anagram indicator*
04 do in, pull, slip 05 shift, twist
06 luxate, put out, sprain, strain
07 confuse, disrupt, disturb
08 disjoint, disorder, displace, disunite, misplace 09 disengage 10 disconnect
11 disorganize 13 put out of joint, put out of place

dislocation
◇ *anagram indicator*
04 slip 05 fault 08 disarray, disorder, luxation 10 disruption 11 disturbance
12 displacement 15 disorganization

dislodge
04 bump, move, oust, tuft 05 eject, shift 06 remove, uproot 08 displace, force out, untenant 09 extricate

disloyal
05 false 06 untrue 07 disleal
08 apostate, two-faced 09 deceitful, faithless 10 perfidious, traitorous, un-American, unfaithful 11 treacherous, unpatriotic 13 double-dealing

disloyalty
06 deceit 07 falsity, perfidy, treason
08 adultery, apostasy, betrayal, sedition 09 falseness, treachery
10 infidelity 11 inconstancy, waka-jumping 12 disaffection 13 breach of trust, double-dealing
14 perfidiousness, unfaithfulness

dismal
03 bad, sad 04 blue, dark, drab, dull, glum, gray, grey, grim, naff, poor, ropy
05 awful, black, bleak, dingy, dowie, lousy, morne, trist, wormy 06 crummy, dreary, dreich, gloomy, somber, sombre, sullen, triste 07 forlorn, useless 08 desolate, dolesome, dreadful, funereal, ghastful, hopeless, terrible 09 cheerless, frightful, ghastfull, long-faced, miserable, sorrowful 10 depressing, despondent, grimlooked, lugubrious, melancholy, sepulchral 11 low-spirited
12 discouraging, unsuccessful

dismally
05 badly, sadly 06 darkly, drably
08 drearily, gloomily, terribly
09 miserably 10 dreadfully
11 frightfully 12 despondently
14 unsuccessfully

dismantle
◇ *anagram indicator*
05 derig, strip 06 strike 08 demolish, pull down, separate, take down 09 pull apart, strip down, take apart
11 disassemble 12 take to pieces

dismay
04 fear 05 alarm, amate, appal, daunt, dread, scare, shake, shock, upset, worry 06 bother, fright, horror, put off, terror 07 concern, depress, disturb, horrify, perturb, unnerve 08 cast down, dispirit, distress, frighten, unsettle 09 agitation, take aback
10 disappoint, disconcert, discourage, dishearten 11 consternate, disillusion, heart-strike, trepidation
12 apprehension 13 consternation
14 disappointment, discouragement
• **expression of dismay**
02 ha 03 hah 04 argh, heck, hell, oops, whew 05 aargh 06 crumbs, dear me, heaven, oh dear!, wheugh
07 cravens, crivens, deary me, heavens
08 crivvens, dearie me 09 good grief
11 that's done it, that's torn it

dismember
04 limb 05 sever 06 divide 07 break up, disject, dislimb, dissect, quarter
08 amputate, disjoint, mutilate, separate 09 dislocate, piecemeal, pull apart

dismemberment
07 breakup 08 division 10 amputation, dissection, mutilation, separation

dismiss
◇ *deletion indicator*
04 boot, daff, drop, fire, free, sack
05 chuck, eject, expel, lay by, let go, spurn 06 banish, bounce, chassé, lay off, reject, remove, shelve 07 boot out, cashier, discord, fall out, kick out, kiss off, put away, release, send off, suspend, turn off 08 brush off, discount, dispatch, dissolve, relegate, send away, set aside 09 bowler-hat, discharge, disregard, repudiate
10 brush aside, give notice, give the air, pension off 11 send packing 13 give the bucket, make redundant 15 pour cold water on

dismissal
◇ *deletion indicator*
01 b, c 02 ax, hw, ro, st 03 axe, lbw
04 bird, boot, push, road, sack
05 chuck, congé, elbow 06 avaunt, bounce, bowled, caught, congee, firing, mitten, notice, papers, run-out
07 discard, heave-ho, kiss-off, removal, sacking, stumped 08 brush-off, bum's rush, despatch, dispatch, mittimus 09 discharge, expulsion, hit wicket, laying-off 10 cashiering, redundancy 11 cashierment 12 golden bowler 13 walking-orders, walking papers, walking-ticket 14 marching-orders 15 leg before wicket
• **expression of dismissal**
03 och, out, via 04 poof, pooh, tush
06 avaunt, begone, powwaw
07 voetsak

dismissed
03 out

dismissive
07 off-hand 08 scornful, sneering
10 disdainful, dismissory
12 contemptuous 13 disrespectful, inconsiderate

dismissively
10 scornfully, sneeringly 11 off-handedly 12 disdainfully
14 contemptuously

dismount
04 lite **05** light **06** alight, get off
07 descend, get down, unmount
09 disembark

disobedience
06 mutiny, revolt **08** defiance
09 contumacy, rebellion **10** infraction, unruliness, wilfulness **11** contumacity, waywardness **12** contrariness, indiscipline **13** recalcitrance
15 insubordination

disobedient
06 unruly, wilful **07** defiant, froward, naughty, wayward **08** contrary, recusant **10** disorderly, rebellious, refractory **11** intractable, mischievous
12 contumacious, obstreperous, recalcitrant **13** insubordinate

disobey
04 defy **05** flout, rebel **06** ignore, resist **07** violate **08** infringe, overstep
09 disregard **10** contravene, transgress
13 step out of line

disobliging
04 rude **06** unkind **07** awkward, uncivil **09** unhelpful, unwilling
11 inofficious **12** bloody-minded, disagreeable, discourteous **13** unco-operative **15** unaccommodating

disorder
◇ *anagram indicator*
03 ADD, OCD, SAD **04** ADHD, mess, muss, PMDD, PTSD, riot, rout **05** brawl, chaos, deray, fight, mêlée, musse
06 defuse, fracas, jumble, malady, muddle, ruffle, rumple, rumpus, tumble, tumult, unrest, uproar
07 ailment, anarchy, clamour, clutter, confuse, derange, disease, flutter, garboil, illness, misrule, overset, quarrel **08** brouhaha, confound, disarray, pell-mell, shambles, sickness
09 commotion, complaint, condition, confusion, mistemper **10** affliction, disability, disarrange, discompose, disruption, untidiness
11 derangement, disturbance
12 confusedness **14** disorderliness
15 disorganization

disordered
◇ *anagram indicator*
03 mad **04** wild **05** messy, mussy, oncus, onkus, upset **06** turbid, untidy
07 jumbled, muddled, unkempt
08 confused, deranged, madbrain, troubled **09** betumbled, cluttered, disturbed **10** madbrained, out of joint, unbalanced, upside-down
11 distempered, maladjusted
12 disorganized, disreputable

disorderly
◇ *anagram indicator*
04 wild **05** messy, rough, rowdy
06 ragtag, unruly, untidy **07** chaotic, jumbled, lawless **08** confused
09 cluttered, irregular, turbulent
10 boisterous, confusedly, in disarray, ragmatical, rebellious, refractory, tumultuous **11** disobedient
12 disorganized, hugger-mugger, obstreperous, unmanageable
13 undisciplined **14** uncontrollable

disorganization
◇ *anagram indicator*
05 chaos **06** muddle **08** disarray, disorder, shambles **09** confusion
10 disruption, untidiness
11 dislocation

disorganize
◇ *anagram indicator*
05 mix up, upset **06** jumble, mess up, muddle **07** break up, confuse, destroy, disrupt, disturb **08** disorder, unsettle, unstring **09** dislocate **10** disarrange, discompose **11** unmechanize **12** play hell with **13** play havoc with

disorganized
◇ *anagram indicator*
07 chaotic, jumbled, muddled
08 careless, confused, unsorted
09 haphazard, shambolic
10 disordered, topsy-turvy, untogether
11 unorganized **12** unmethodical, unstructured, unsystematic
13 undisciplined **14** unsystematized

disorientate
◇ *anagram indicator*
04 faze **05** upset **06** muddle, puzzle
07 confuse, mislead, perplex
09 disorient

disorientated
◇ *anagram indicator*
04 lost **05** at sea, upset **06** adrift, astray **07** mixed up, muddled, puzzled
08 all at sea, confused **09** perplexed, unsettled **10** bewildered, unbalanced
11 disoriented

disorientation
◇ *anagram indicator*
06 muddle **08** lostness **09** confusion
10 perplexity, puzzlement
12 bewilderment

disown
04 deny **05** unget **06** reject
07 abandon, cast off, disavow, forsake
08 abnegate, disallow, disclaim, renounce **09** reprobate, repudiate
14 disacknowledge, turn your back on

disparage
04 mock, slag, slam, slur **05** decry, knock, scorn, slate **06** defame, deride, lessen, malign, vilify **07** cry down, degrade, disable, disdain, dismiss, empeach, impeach, rubbish, run down, slag off, slander, traduce
08 belittle, derogate, disvalue, minimize, ridicule, vilipend
09 criticize, denigrate, deprecate, discredit, dishonour, sell short, underrate **10** calumniate, depreciate, dishearten, undervalue **11** detract from
13 underestimate

disparagement
04 slur **05** scorn **07** decrial, disdain, slander **08** contempt, decrying, derision, ridicule **09** aspersion, contumely, criticism, discredit
10 debasement, derogation, detraction **11** degradation, deprecation **12** belittlement, condemnation, denunciation, depreciation, vilification
15 underestimation

disparaging
05 snide **07** mocking **08** critical, derisive, knocking, scornful
09 insulting **10** derogatory, dismissive, pejorative **11** deprecating, deprecatory

disparate
06 unlike **07** diverse, unequal
08 contrary, distinct **09** different
10 discrepant, dissimilar **11** contrasting

disparity
03 gap **04** bias, gulf **08** contrast, inequity **09** imbalance **10** difference, inequality, unevenness, unfairness, unlikeness **11** discrepancy, distinction, incongruity **13** disproportion, dissimilarity, dissimilitude, inconsistency

dispassionate
04 calm, cool, fair **07** neutral
08 composed, detached, unbiased
09 equitable, impartial, objective, unexcited **10** impersonal
11 unemotional **12** unprejudiced
13 disinterested, self-possessed
14 self-controlled

dispassionately
06 coolly, fairly **09** equitably
11 impartially, objectively, unexcitedly
12 impersonally **13** unemotionally
15 disinterestedly

dispatch, despatch
04 do in, item, kill, mail, news, post, send, ship **05** haste, piece, remit, speed **06** convey, finish, letter, murder, report, settle **07** account, article, bump off, consign, dépêche, dismiss, execute, express, forward, mailing, message, perform, posting, sending, send off, special **08** alacrity, bulletin, celerity, conclude, deal with, expedite, knock off, rapidity, transmit
09 discharge, dismissal, dispose of, slaughter, swiftness **10** accelerate, communiqué, expedience, expedition, forwarding, promptness, put to death **11** assassinate, consignment, promptitude, transmittal
13 communication

dispel
◇ *anagram indicator*
03 rid **04** rout **05** allay, expel **06** assoil, banish **07** discuss, dismiss, scatter
08 disperse, get rid of, melt away
09 chase away, dissipate, drive away, eliminate **11** disseminate

dispensable
07 useless **08** needless **10** disposable, expendable, gratuitous, pardonable
11 inessential, replaceable, superfluous, unnecessary **12** non-essential

dispensation
04 plan **05** issue, order **06** relief, scheme, system **07** economy, licence, release **08** bestowal, covenant, immunity, reprieve **09** allotment, authority, direction, discharge, endowment, exception, exemption, provision, remission **10** allocation, handing out, permission, sharing out **11** application, arrangement **12** distribution, organization **13** apportionment **14** administration

dispense
05 allot, apply, issue, share **06** assign, bestow, confer **07** deal out, deliver, dole out, enforce, execute, expense, give out, hand out, mete out, operate **08** allocate, carry out, compound, share out, supplies **09** apportion, discharge, divide out, implement, pass round **10** administer, distribute, effectuate **11** expenditure **12** dispensation
• dispense with
02 ax **03** axe **04** omit, want **05** forgo, waive **06** cancel, forego, give up, ignore, revoke **07** abolish, discard, not need, rescind **08** get rid of, renounce **09** dispose of, disregard, do without **10** do away with, relinquish

dispersal
07 breakup **09** dismissal **10** breaking-up, disbanding, scattering, separation **11** segregation **12** distribution

disperse
◇ *anagram indicator*
04 melt, shed **05** break, scail, scale, skail **06** dispel, spread, vanish **07** break up, diffuse, disband, dismiss, resolve, scatter, split up, thin out **08** dissolve, melt away, separate, squander **09** dissipate **10** distribute **11** disseminate

dispersion
◇ *anagram indicator*
07 scatter **08** diaspora **09** broadcast, diffusion, dispersal, spreading **10** scattering **11** circulation, dissipation **12** distribution **13** dissemination

dispirit
04 damp, dash **05** deter **06** dampen, deject, sadden **07** depress **10** demoralize, discourage, dishearten **12** put a damper on

dispirited
03 low, sad **04** down, glum **05** fed up **06** feeble, gloomy, morose **08** cast down, dejected, downcast, sackless **09** depressed **10** brassed off, browned off, cheesed off, despondent, spiritless **11** crestfallen, demoralized, discouraged, pale-hearted **12** disheartened **14** down in the dumps

displace
04 move, oust **05** eject, evict, expel, heave, shift **06** depose, luxate, remove **07** boot out, dismiss, disturb, replace, succeed, turf out **08** dislodge, force out, misplace, relocate, supplant **09** discharge, dislocate, supersede **10** disarrange

displacement
03 jee **04** warp **05** heave, hitch, shift, throw **06** ectopy, moving, ptosis **07** ectopia, upthrow **08** shifting **09** proptosis **10** aberration, compliance, dislodging **11** dislocation, disturbance, heterotaxis, heterotopia, subluxation, superseding, supplanting **12** misplacement, retroversion **14** Chandler wobble, disarrangement **15** Chandler's wobble

display
03 air, HUD, LCD **04** expo, pomp, shaw, show, wear **05** array, boast, state **06** betray, blazon, evince, expose, flaunt, layout, muster, parade, reveal, set out, splash, unfold, unfurl, unveil **07** airshow, bravura, breathe, étalage, exhibit, pageant, parafle, present, promote, show off, splurge **08** disclose, evidence, flourish, manifest, paraffle, put forth, set forth, showcase **09** advertise, pageantry, publicize, put on show, spectacle, spread out, unfolding **10** disclosure, displaying, evincement, exhibition, exposition, revelation, tournament **11** demonstrate **12** presentation **13** demonstration, manifestation

displease
03 bug, irk, vex **05** anger, annoy, upset **06** offend, put out **07** dislike, disturb, incense, mislike, perturb, provoke **08** irritate **09** aggravate, infuriate, misplease **10** discompose, disgruntle, dissatisfy, exasperate **11** displeasure

displeased
05 angry, cross, upset, vexed **06** peeved, piqued, put out **07** annoyed, furious **08** offended **09** irritated **10** aggravated, dischuffed, infuriated **11** disgruntled, exasperated, out of humour

displeasure
03 ire **05** anger, pique, wrath **07** chagrin, disgust, offence, offense **08** distaste **09** annoyance, disfavour **10** irritation, resentment **11** disapproval, indignation **12** exasperation, perturbation **14** disapprobation, discontentment, disgruntlement **15** dissatisfaction

disport
◇ *anagram indicator*
04 play, romp **05** amuse, cheer, frisk, revel, sport **06** cavort, divert, frolic, gambol **07** delight, get down **09** entertain

disposable
09 throwaway **10** expendable **11** replaceable **13** biodegradable, non-returnable

disposal
05 order **07** command, control, liberty, removal, service **08** bestowal, grouping, ordering, riddance **09** clearance, direction, scrapping **10** deployment, discarding, management **11** arrangement, jettisoning, positioning **12** getting rid of, throwing-away
• at someone's disposal
05 on tap, ready **06** at hand, to hand **09** available **10** obtainable

dispose
◇ *anagram indicator*
03 put, set **04** do in, dump, kill, plot, shed, sort **05** align, group, order, place, posit, scrap, see to, sew up, tempt **06** battle, decide, finish, handle, line up, murder, settle, tackle, wrap up **07** arrange, bump off, destroy, discard, dismiss, dispone, incline, situate, sort out **08** attend to, chuck out, clear out, deal with, dispatch, get rid of, jettison, organize, position, throw out **09** clear away, determine, get shot of, look after, polish off, throw away **10** distribute, do away with, put to death, take care of **15** make short work of
• try to dispose of
04 hawk

disposed
◇ *anagram indicator*
03 apt **04** bent **05** dight, eager, prone, ready **06** liable, likely, minded **07** subject, willing **08** inclined, pregnant, prepared **11** affectioned, predisposed

disposition
◇ *anagram indicator*
03 lay, lie **04** bent, make, mood, trim **05** cheer, habit, humor, order **06** humour, kidney, layout, line-up, make-up, nature, spirit, system, talent, temper **07** leaning, pattern, placing, stomach **08** disposal, grouping, ordnance, position, sequence, tendency, transfer **09** affection, alignment, character, proneness **10** allocation, conveyance, deployment, giving-over, proclivity, propension, propensity **11** arrangement, inclination, personality, positioning, temperament **12** constitution, distribution, ministration, predilection, propenseness **14** predisposition

dispossess
03 rob **04** oust **05** eject, evict, expel, strip **06** divest **07** deprive **08** dislodge, take away **11** expropriate

disproportion
09 asymmetry, disparity, imbalance **10** inadequacy, inequality, unevenness **11** discrepancy **12** lopsidedness **13** insufficiency

disproportionate
06 uneven **07** unequal **09** excessive **10** inordinate, unbalanced **12** unreasonable **14** incommensurate **15** incommensurable, out of proportion

disproportionately
08 unevenly **11** excessively **12** inordinately, unreasonably

disprove
04 deny **05** rebut, refel **06** debunk, expose, negate, refute **07** confute, reprove **08** blow away **09** discredit **10** contradict, controvert, invalidate, prove false **12** give the lie to

disputable
04 moot **07** dubious **08** arguable, doubtful **09** debatable, litigious, uncertain **12** questionable **13** controversial

disputation
03 act **06** debate **07** dispute, schools **08** argument, diatribe, exercise, polemics **09** quodlibet **10** apposition, discussion, dissension **11** controversy **12** deliberation, kilfud-yoking **13** argumentation

disputatious
08 captious **09** litigious, polemical **10** pugnacious **11** contentious, quarrelsome **12** cantankerous **13** argumentative

dispute
03 row **04** deny, feud, moot, odds, plea, spar, spat, tilt **05** argue, clash, doubt **06** bicker, cangle, debate, differ, strife, threap **07** contend, contest, discept, discuss, gainsay, quarrel, wrangle, wrestle **08** argument, conflict, litigate, question, squabble, traverse, variance **09** altercate, challenge, have words, tug-of-love **10** contention, contradict, controvert, litigation **11** altercation, controverse, controversy, cross swords **12** disagreement, disceptation

disqualification
03 ban, bar **04** veto **10** disability, incapacity, preclusion **11** elimination, prohibition **13** ineligibility **14** disentitlement

disqualified
06 banned **08** debarred **09** incapable, precluded, struck off **10** eliminated, ineligible **11** disentitled

disqualify
03 ban, bar **05** debar, unfit **06** impair **07** disable, rule out, suspend **08** handicap, preclude, prohibit **09** eliminate, strike off **10** debilitate, disentitle, immobilize, invalidate **12** incapacitate **13** dishabilitate

disquiet
03 vex **04** faze, fear, fret **05** alarm, annoy, dread, shake, upset, worry **06** bother, harass, hassle, pester, plague, ruffle, unease, uneasy, unrest **07** agitate, anguish, anxiety, concern, disturb, perturb, trouble, turmoil, unnerve **08** distress, restless, unsettle **09** agitation, incommode **10** discompose, foreboding, inquietude, make uneasy, uneasiness **11** disquietude, disturbance, fretfulness, make anxious, nervousness **12** perturbation, restlessness

disquieting
04 ugly **06** trying **07** anxious **08** worrying **09** unnerving, upsetting **10** disturbing, nail-biting, perturbing, unsettling **11** distressing, troublesome

disquisition
05 essay, paper **06** sermon, thesis **07** descant **08** treatise **09** discourse, monograph **10** exposition **11** explanation **12** dissertation

disregard
◇ *deletion indicator*
04 bend, omit, pass, shun, snub **05** flout, waive **06** ignore, insult, offend, slight **07** affront, despise, disdain, disobey, neglect, oversee, smile at **08** brush-off, contempt, discount, laugh off, overlook, pass over, set aside **09** denigrate, disesteem, disoblige, disparage, gloss over, oversight, sacrilege **10** brush aside, disrespect, negligence **11** denigration, desperation, inattention, make light of, set at naught, walk all over **12** carelessness, cold shoulder, cold-shoulder, dispense with, indifference **13** give the go-by to, non-regardance, put out of court **14** rule out of court, take no notice of **15** close your eyes to, turn a blind eye to

disrepair
04 ruin **05** decay **08** collapse **10** shabbiness **11** rack and ruin **12** dilapidation **13** deterioration

disreputable
03 low **04** base, mean **05** dodgy, seamy, seedy, shady **06** louche, shabby, shifty, untidy **07** corrupt, dubious, scruffy, unkempt **08** infamous, shameful, shocking, slovenly, unworthy **09** notorious, unsavoury **10** outrageous, scandalous, suspicious **11** disgraceful, dishevelled, ignominious, opprobrious **12** contemptible, unprincipled **13** discreditable, dishonourable, unrespectable

disrepute
05 shame **06** infamy **07** ill fame, obloquy **08** disgrace, ignominy **09** discredit, disesteem, disfavour, dishonour **13** disreputation

disrespect
05 cheek, scorn **08** contempt, rudeness **09** dishonour, disregard, impudence, insolence, misesteem **10** incivility **11** discourtesy, irreverence **12** impertinence, impoliteness

disrespectful
04 rude **05** sassy **06** cheeky **07** uncivil **08** flippant, impolite, impudent, insolent **09** insulting **10** dismissive, irreverent, unmannerly **11** impertinent **12** contemptuous, discourteous **13** inconsiderate

disrespectfully
06 rudely **08** cheekily **09** uncivilly **10** impolitely, impudently, insolently **11** insultingly **12** irreverently **13** impertinently **14** contemptuously, discourteously

disrobe
04 bare, shed **05** strip **06** denude, divest, remove **07** take off, uncover, undress **08** unclothe **10** disapparel

disrupt
◇ *anagram indicator*
05 burst, split, upset **06** butt in, hamper, impede **07** blemish, break up, confuse, disturb, intrude, screw up **08** sabotage, unsettle **09** dislocate, interrupt **10** disarrange **11** disorganize **13** interfere with

disruption
◇ *anagram indicator*
05 upset **06** bust-up **07** burst-up, turmoil **08** disarray, disorder, stoppage, upheaval **09** cataclasm, confusion **11** disordering, disturbance **12** interference, interruption **14** disorderliness **15** disorganization

disruptive
05 noisy, rogue **06** unruly **09** turbulent, upsetting **10** boisterous, disorderly, disturbing, unsettling **11** distracting, troublesome **12** obstreperous **13** troublemaking, undisciplined

dissatisfaction
05 anger **06** regret **07** chagrin, dislike **08** vexation **09** annoyance **10** discomfort, discontent, irritation, resentment, uneasiness **11** disapproval, displeasure, frustration, unhappiness **12** disaffection, exasperation, restlessness **14** disappointment, disapprobation
• **expression of dissatisfaction**
02 oh **03** boo, huh, tut **04** booh, umph, whow **05** humph

dissatisfied
05 angry, fed up **07** annoyed, unhappy **09** irritated, pissed off **10** brassed off, browned off, cheesed off, discontent, displeased, frustrated, malcontent **11** disaffected, disgruntled, exasperated, unfulfilled, unsatisfied **12** disappointed, discontented, disenchanted, malcontented **13** disillusioned

dissatisfy
03 vex **05** anger, annoy **06** put out **07** let down **08** irritate **09** displease, frustrate **10** disappoint, discontent, disgruntle, exasperate

dissect
05 cut up, probe, study **07** analyse, examine, explore, inspect **08** pore over, vivisect **09** anatomize, break down, dismember **10** scrutinize **11** investigate

dissection
05 probe, study **07** anatomy, autopsy, zootomy **08** analysis, necropsy, scrutiny **09** breakdown, cutting up, necrotomy **10** inspection

11 cephalotomy, examination, exploration, vivisection
13 dismemberment, encephalotomy, investigation

dissemble
04 fain, fake, hide, mask, sham
05 cloak, faine, fayne, feign **06** affect
07 conceal, cover up, falsify, pretend
08 disguise, simulate **10** camouflage, play possum **11** counterfeit, dissimulate

dissembler
04 fake, liar **05** fraud **06** con man
07 feigner **08** deceiver, impostor
09 charlatan, hypocrite, pretender, trickster **12** dissimulator **15** whited sepulchre

disseminate
03 sow **05** scale **06** spread **07** diffuse, publish, scatter **08** disperse, proclaim
09 broadcast, circulate, propagate, publicize, scattered **10** distribute, promulgate

dissemination
06 spread **09** broadcast, diffusion, spreading **10** dispersion, publishing
11 circulation, propagation, publication **12** broadcasting, distribution, promulgation

dissension
04 flak **06** square, strife **07** discord, dispute, dissent, faction, quarrel
08 argument, conflict, dispeace, disunion, disunity, friction, variance
10 contention **12** disagreement

dissent
05 demur **06** differ, object, refuse
07 discord, dispute, protest, quibble
08 disagree, friction **09** objection
10 difference, disconsent, disharmony, dissension, opposition, resistance
11 controversy **12** disagreement

dissenter
05 rebel **07** heretic, sectary
08 objector, recusant **09** disputant, dissident, protester, Raskolnik
10 protestant, schismatic, separatist
11 dissentient, Old Believer
12 demonstrator **13** nonconformist, revolutionary

dissentient
08 opposing, recusant **09** differing, dissident, heretical **10** dissenting, protesting, rebellious **11** conflicting, disagreeing **13** nonconformist, revolutionary

dissertation
05 essay, paper **06** thesis **08** critique, excursus, treatise **09** discourse, monograph **10** exposition
11 prolegomena **12** disquisition, propaedeutic

disservice
04 harm, hurt **05** wrong **06** injury
07 bad turn **08** con trick, mischief
09 disfavour, injustice **10** dirty trick, unkindness **13** sharp practice **14** kick in the teeth

dissidence
04 feud **06** schism **07** dispute, dissent, rupture **08** variance **09** recusancy
11 discordance **12** disagreement

dissident
05 rebel **07** heretic **08** agitator, frondeur, objector, opposing, recusant, refusnik **09** differing, dissenter, heretical, heterodox, protester, refusenik **10** discordant, dissenting, protesting, rebellious, schismatic **11** conflicting, disagreeing
13 nonconformist, revolutionary

dissimilar
06 unlike **07** diverse, unalike, various, varying **08** bifacial, distinct
09 deviating, different, disparate, divergent, unrelated **10** mismatched
11 contrasting, hemimorphic
12 incompatible **13** heterogeneous

dissimilarity
07 variety **08** contrast **09** disparity, diversity **10** difference, differency, divergence, inequality, unlikeness
11 discrepancy, distinction
13 dissimilitude, heterogeneity, unrelatedness **15** incomparability, incompatibility

dissimulate
03 lie **04** fake, hide, mask **05** cloak, feign **06** affect **07** conceal, cover up, pretend **08** disguise **09** dissemble
10 camouflage

dissipate
◇ *anagram indicator*
04 blow **05** drain, spend, use up, waste
06 burn up, dispel, expend, lavish, vanish, wanton **07** break up, consume, deplete, diffuse, exhaust, resolve, scatter, splurge **08** disperse, dissolve, melt away, squander **09** disappear, drive away, evaporate **10** get through, run through **11** fritter away

dissipated
◇ *anagram indicator*
03 gay **04** wild **06** rakish, wasted
07 corrupt **08** depraved
09 abandoned, debauched, dissolute
10 degenerate, licentious, profligate
11 intemperate **13** self-indulgent

• be dissipated
04 melt **08** peter out

dissipation
06 excess, racket **07** licence
08 pleasure **09** depletion, depravity, diffusion, dispersal **10** corruption, debauchery, immorality
11 abandonment, consumption, evaporation, expenditure, prodigality, squandering **12** extravagance, intemperance **13** disappearance
14 licentiousness, self-indulgence

dissociate
04 quit **05** sever **06** cut off, detach, secede **07** break up, disband, disrupt, divorce, isolate **08** break off, distance, disunite, separate, set apart, withdraw
09 disengage, segregate, separated
10 disconnect **12** disassociate

dissociation
05 break, split **07** divorce **08** disunion, division, severing **09** isolation, severance **10** cutting-off, detachment, distancing, separation **11** dissevering, segregation **12** setting apart
13 disconnection, disengagement
14 disassociation

dissolute
◇ *anagram indicator*
04 fast, lewd, wild **05** loose **06** rakish, wanton **07** corrupt, immoral, outward
08 depraved **09** abandoned, debauched **10** Corinthian, degenerate, dissipated, licentious, profligate **11** Falstaffian, intemperate
12 unrestrained **13** self-indulgent

dissolution
06 ending, Repeal **07** break-up, divorce, melting **08** collapse, dialysis, disposal, division **09** annulment, cessation, loosening, overthrow
10 conclusion, karyolysis, separation, suspension **11** destruction, evaporation, termination, thermolysis
13 decomposition, disappearance
14 disintegration **15** discontinuation

dissolve
03 end **04** melt **05** annul, begin, break, burst, solve, start **06** digest, finish, revoke, vanish, wind up
07 break up, crumble, disband, dismiss, divorce, dwindle, liquefy, nullify, rescind, solvate, unmarry **08** collapse, discandy, disperse, evanesce, melt away, separate **09** disappear, discandie, dissipate, evaporate, terminate **10** deliquesce, invalidate
11 discontinue, lose control **12** bring to an end, disintegrate **14** be overcome with, go into solution

dissonance
03 jar **04** wolf **05** clash **06** jangle
07 discord, grating, jarring **08** variance
09 cacophony, disparity, harshness, stridency **10** difference, disharmony, dissension **11** discordance, discrepancy, incongruity
12 disagreement **13** inconsistency
15 incompatibility

dissonant
◇ *anagram indicator*
05 harsh **07** grating, jarring, raucous
08 clashing, jangling, strident, tuneless
09 anomalous, differing, irregular, unmusical **10** discordant
11 cacophonous, conflicting, disagreeing, incongruous, unmelodious **12** incompatible, inconsistent, inharmonious
13 contradictory **14** irreconcilable

dissuade
04 stop **05** deter **06** dehort, nobble, put off **07** prevent **09** talk out of
10 discounsel, discourage, disincline
13 persuade not to

dissuasion
07 caution **09** deterring **10** deterrence
11 dehortation **12** remonstrance

13 expostulation, remonstration
14 discouragement

distance
03 gap, way 04 span, step 05 break, depth, lunar, piece, range, reach, space, width 06 cut off, detach, extent, height, length, remove, secede
07 breadth, faraway, farness, reserve, stretch 08 coldness, coolness, interval, separate, throw out, withdraw
09 aloofness, formality, stiffness
10 detachment, dissociate, opposition, remoteness, separation
11 mountenance 12 disassociate, mountenaunce 13 codeclination
14 unfriendliness 15 inaccessibility, standoffishness
See also **measurement**

• at a distance
04 afar, wide 06 afield 12 at arm's length

• short distance
03 wee 06 bittie 11 stone's-throw

distant
03 far, icy 04 cold, cool, deep
05 aloof, blank, stiff 06 abroad, dreamy, far-off, formal, remote, slight, vacant 07 faraway, glacial
08 detached, far-flung, indirect, isolated, not close, outlying, reserved
09 dispersed, withdrawn
10 antisocial, distracted, indistinct, restrained, unfriendly 11 daydreaming, out-of-the-way, preoccupied, stand-offish, up the Boohai 12 absent-minded, back of beyond, unresponsive
14 unapproachable
15 uncommunicative

distantly
05 dimly, miles 06 coldly, coolly
07 faintly, far away, stiffly, vaguely
08 a long way, formally, remotely, slightly, vacantly 10 not closely
11 imprecisely 12 some distance
13 great distance, unemotionally
14 unresponsively

distaste
06 dégoût, horror, offend 07 disgust, dislike, offence 08 aversion, loathing
09 antipathy, disfavour, disrelish, revulsion 10 abhorrence, repugnance
11 displeasure

• expression of distaste
03 ugh, wow, yuk 04 whow, yech, yuck 05 wowee

distasteful
04 gory, icky 08 god-awful
09 abhorrent, loathsome, obnoxious, offensive, repellant, repellent, repugnant, repulsive, revolting, unsavoury 10 detestable, disgusting, uninviting, unpleasant 11 displeasing, undesirable, unpalatable
12 disagreeable 13 objectionable

distend
04 puff 05 bloat, bulge, swell, widen
06 dilate, expand 07 balloon, enlarge, fill out, inflate, stretch 09 intumesce
10 exaggerate

distended
05 puffy 06 astrut, puffed 07 bloated, dilated, distent, swollen 08 enlarged, expanded, inflated, varicose
09 puffed-out, stretched, tumescent
10 ventricose, ventricous
13 emphysematous

distension
05 swell 06 spread 07 breadth
08 bloating, dilation, swelling
09 emphysema, expansion, extension
10 flatulence, flatulency, tumescence, tympanites, wind dropsy
11 enlargement, turgescence
12 intumescence 14 hydronephrosis

distil
04 drip, flow, leak 05 still 06 derive, purify, refine 07 draw out, express, extract, rectify, trickle 08 condense, press out, vaporize 09 evaporate, sublimate

distillation
◇ *anagram indicator*
06 spirit 07 essence, extract
10 extraction 11 evaporation
12 condensation, purification

distinct
05 clear, plain, sharp 06 marked
07 defined, diverse, evident, obvious, several 08 apparent, clear-cut, definite, detached, discrete, manifest, separate 09 different, disparate, trenchant 10 dissimilar, individual, noticeable, variegated
11 unambiguous, unconnected, well-defined 12 recognizable, unassociated, unmistakable
13 distinguished 14 differentiated

distinction
04 fame, mark, note 05 éclat, honor, merit, siege, worth 06 credit, honour, luster, lustre, renown, repute
07 diorism, feature, quality
08 contrast, division, eminence, prestige 09 celebrity, greatness
10 difference, excellence, importance, prominence, reputation, separation
11 consequence, discernment, peculiarity, superiority 12 distinctness, significance 13 dissimilarity, dissimilitude, individuality
14 characteristic, discrimination
15 differentiation, distinguishment
See also **honour**

distinctive
06 unique 07 special, typical
08 original, peculiar, singular
09 different 10 individual, noteworthy, particular 13 extraordinary, idiosyncratic 14 characteristic, distinguishing

distinctiveness
10 uniqueness 11 originality, peculiarity, singularity 12 idiosyncrasy
13 individuality 14 noteworthiness

distinctly
05 plain 07 clearly, plainly
08 markedly 09 decidedly, evidently, obviously 10 definitely, manifestly, noticeably 12 unmistakably
13 unambiguously, unmistakeably

distinguish
03 see 04 dist, mark 05 excel, judge, stamp 06 descry, detect, divide, do well, notice, pick up, secern, typify
07 dignify, discern, ennoble, glorify, make out, mark off, pick out 08 classify, identify, perceive, set apart, tell from
09 ascertain, determine, recognize, signalize, single out, tell apart
10 categorize 11 bring fame to
12 characterize, discriminate 13 bring honour to, differentiate, particularize
14 bring acclaim to

distinguishable
05 clear, plain 07 evident, obvious
08 dividant, manifest 10 noticeable, observable 11 appreciable, conspicuous, discernible, perceptible, plainly seen 12 recognizable

distinguished
04 fine 05 famed, noble, noted
06 famous, marked, of note
07 eminent, notable, refined, shining
08 distinct, especial, esteemed, eximious, honoured, identify, renowned, striking 09 acclaimed, egregious, prominent, well-known
10 celebrated, nameworthy
11 conspicuous, illustrious, outstanding
12 aristocratic 13 extraordinary

distinguishing
06 marked, unique 07 typical
08 peculiar, singular 09 diacritic, different 10 diagnostic, episematic, individual 11 diacritical, distinctive
14 characteristic, discriminative, discriminatory 15 differentiating, differentiation, individualistic

distort
◇ *anagram indicator*
04 bend, bias, rack, skew, warp
05 color, fudge, slant, thraw, twist, wrest, wring 06 buckle, colour, deform, detort, garble, hamper, jumble, mangle, wrench, writhe
07 contort, falsify, pervert, screw up, torment, torture 08 misshape
09 disfigure, pull about 10 tamper with 12 cook the books, misrepresent

distorted
◇ *anagram indicator*
03 wry 04 awry, bent, skew 05 false, thraw 06 biased, skewed, thrawn, warped 07 twisted 08 deformed, tortured 09 falsified, misshapen, perverted 10 disfigured, out of shape
14 misrepresented

distortion
04 bend, bias, skew, warp 05 slant, twist 06 buckle 07 warping
08 cinching, garbling, twisting
09 colouring, deformity
10 contortion, perversion
11 crookedness 13 falsification

distract
◇ *anagram indicator*
05 amuse 06 divert, harass, madden,

occupy, put off, puzzle **07** confuse, deflect, detract, disturb, embroil, engross, fluster, perplex **08** bewilder, confound, draw away, forhaile, throw out, turn away **09** entertain, sidetrack, turn aside **10** discompose, disconcert **08** bothered, dismayed, in a state, perished, troubled, worked up **09** aggrieved, disturbed, heart-sore, on the rack, perturbed, strung out, unsettled **11** discomposed **12** impoverished

distracted
◇ *anagram indicator*
03 mad **04** wild **05** crazy, upset **06** éperdu, raving **07** anxious, éperdue, frantic, madding **08** agitated, confused, diverted, dreaming, frenetic, harassed, maddened, worked up **09** miles away, not with it, scattered, up the wall, wandering **10** abstracted, bestraught, bewildered, distraught, distressed, hysterical **11** inattentive, overwrought, preoccupied **12** absent-minded **13** grief-stricken **14** beside yourself

distracting
07 diverse **08** annoying **09** confusing **10** disturbing, irritating, off-putting, perturbing, unsettling **11** bewildering **13** disconcerting

distraction
04 game **05** hobby, sport **07** madness, pastime **09** agitation, amusement, avocation, confusion, diversion **10** perplexity, recreation, relaxation **11** derangement, disturbance, interrupted **12** interference **13** entertainment **14** divertissement

• drive to distraction
05 anger, annoy, upset **06** madden **10** drive crazy, exasperate

distraint
03 nam **04** naam **06** stress

distraught
◇ *anagram indicator*
03 mad **04** wild **05** crazy, elvan, elven, het up, upset **06** elfish, elvish, raving **07** anxious, frantic, worried **08** agitated, in a state, worked up, wretched **09** perplexed **10** distracted, distressed, hysterical **11** overwrought **14** beside yourself

distress
03 irk, vex, woe **04** hurt, need, pain, prey **05** agony, cut up, grief, peril, trial, upset, worry **06** danger, grieve, harass, harrow, misery, penury, sadden, sorrow, unease **07** afflict, agonize, anguish, anxiety, disturb, misease, oppress, perturb, poverty, put to it, sadness, torment, torture, trouble **08** aggrieve, calamity, distrain, exigence, exigency, hardship, straiten **09** adversity, extremity, heartache, indigence, privation, suffering **10** affliction, compulsion, desolation, difficulty, discomfort, exhaustion, misfortune **11** destitution, make anxious, tribulation **12** deforciation, difficulties, perturbation, wretchedness **13** make miserable

distressed
03 ill **04** hurt, sore **05** upset **06** pained, put out **07** uptight, worried

distressing
05 sorry **06** crying, tragic, trying, uneath **07** painful **08** alarming, tragical, worrying **09** harrowing, startling, upsetting **10** afflicting, disturbing, off-putting, perturbing, unsettling **11** frightening **13** disconcerting

distribute
◇ *anagram indicator*
04 deal, dish, part **05** allot, carve, issue, ladle, share **06** assort, digest, divide, spread, supply **07** deal out, deliver, diffuse, dish out, dispose, dole out, give out, hand out, mete out, pass out, prorate, scatter **08** allocate, dispense, disperse, ladle out, serve out, transmit **09** apportion, circulate, discharge, pass round **10** measure out, reticulate **11** disseminate

distribution
◇ *anagram indicator*
05 range **06** supply **07** dealing, sharing **08** delivery, division, grouping, handling, position **09** allotment, diffusion, dispersal, giving-out, placement, proration, spreading, transport **10** allocation, conveyance, handing-out, scattering **11** arrangement, circulation, disposition, repartition **12** organization **13** apportionment, dissemination **14** classification, transportation

district
03 gau, way **04** area, belt, hunt, land, leet, pale, ride, side, soke, walk, ward, zila, zone **05** block, patch, place, shire **06** barrio, bounds, circar, county, domain, locale, parish, region, riding, sector, sircar, sirkar, suburb **07** circuit, quarter, section **08** faubourg, highland, locality, precinct, province, quartier, stannary, vicinity **09** community, territory **12** constituency, municipality, neighborhood **13** neighbourhood **15** circumscription

Districts of Northern Ireland:

04 Ards, Down
05 Derry, Larne, Moyle, Omagh
06 Antrim, Armagh
07 Belfast, Lisburn
08 Limavady, Strabane
09 Ballymena, Banbridge, Coleraine, Cookstown, Craigavon, Dungannon, Fermanagh, North Down
10 Ballymoney
11 Castlereagh, Magherafelt
12 Newtownabbey
13 Carrickfergus
14 Newry and Mourne

See also **county**; **London**; **New York**; **Paris**

• District of Columbia
02 DC

• outer district
03 end

• squalid district
04 slum

distrust
05 doubt, qualm **07** suspect **08** be wary of, misfaith, mistrust, question, wariness **09** chariness, disbelief, discredit, misgiving, mislippen, suspicion **10** disbelieve, scepticism **11** questioning **12** doubtfulness **14** be suspicious of **15** have doubts about

distrustful
04 wary **05** chary **06** uneasy **07** cynical, dubious **08** doubtful, doubting **09** sceptical **10** suspicious, untrustful, untrusting **11** distrusting, mistrustful **12** disbelieving

disturb
◇ *anagram indicator*
03 jee, vex **04** fret, stir **05** annoy, rouse, shake, sturt, touch, upset, worry **06** affray, beat up, bother, dismay, hassle, infest, muddle, pester, put off, racket, ruffle, tumult, turn up **07** agitate, commove, concern, concuss, confuse, disrupt, fluster, inquiet, mismake, perturb, trouble **08** butt in on, disorder, disquiet, distract, distress, unsettle **09** discomfit, dislocate, interrupt **10** disarrange, discompose, disconcert, distrouble, perturbate **11** disorganize, make anxious

disturbance
◇ *anagram indicator*
03 row **04** dust, fray, muss, riot, rout **05** brawl, broil, musse, sturt, upset **06** bother, cangle, fracas, hassle, hoop-la, kick-up, muddle, racket, ruckus, rumble, rumpus, tumult, turn-up, unrest, uproar, upturn **07** illness, ruction, stashie, stishie, stushie, trouble, turmoil **08** disorder, neurosis, outbreak, sickness, stooshie, stramash, upheaval, williwaw **09** agitation, annoyance, commotion, complaint, confusion, hindrance, intrusion **10** convulsion, disruption, hullabaloo, inquietude, perplexity, rough-house **11** derangement, distraction, embroilment, molestation **12** interference, interruption **13** collieshangie **14** distemperature

• freedom from disturbance
04 ease

disturbed
◇ *anagram indicator*
04 vext **05** upset, vexed **06** hung-up, uneasy **07** anxious, inquiet, unquiet, worried **08** bothered, confused, neurotic, paranoid, troubled, unstable **09** concerned, flustered, psychotic, screwed-up, turbulent **10** mistrysted, unbalanced **11** discomposed, maladjusted, mentally ill **12** apprehensive **13** dysfunctional

disturbing
◇ *anagram indicator*
08 alarming, worrying **09** agitating, confusing, dismaying, startling, troubling, troublous, upsetting
10 disturbant, perturbing, unsettling
11 bewildering, disquieting, distressing, frightening, threatening
12 discouraging, disturbative
13 disconcerting

disunited
05 split **07** divided **09** alienated, disrupted, estranged, separated
10 dissevered

disunity
05 split **06** breach, schism, strife
07 discord, dissent, rupture
08 conflict, division **10** alienation, dissension **11** discordance
12 disagreement, estrangement

disuse
05 decay **07** neglect **09** desuetude
11 abandonment, inusitation
14 discontinuance

disused
04 idle **06** unused **07** decayed
08 obsolete **09** abandoned, neglected
12 discontinued

ditch
04 delf, dike, drop, dump, dyke, foss, grip, ha-ha, lode, moat, rean, reen, sike, syke **05** canal, chuck, delph, drain, fosse, graft, gripe, gully, level, rhine, rhyne, scrap, stank **06** derail, furrow, gulley, gutter, haw-haw, sheuch, sheugh, the sea, trench, trough
07 abandon, channel, discard, euripus
08 get rid of, jettison, throw out
09 dispose of, sunk fence, throw away
11 watercourse

dither
◇ *anagram indicator*
04 faff, flap, stew, tizz **05** delay, panic, quake, tizzy, waver **06** bother, dicker, falter, pother, shiver **07** agitate, confuse, fluster, flutter, perturb, tremble **08** hang back, hesitate **09** faff about, vacillate **10** dilly-dally, indecision **12** be in two minds, perturbation, shilly-shally, take your time

ditto
02 do

divan
04 sofa **05** couch, dewan **06** day bed, lounge, settee **07** council, lounger, ottoman, sofa bed **08** assembly
12 chaise-longue, chesterfield

dive
03 bar, dip, fly, ken, pub **04** bolt, club, dart, dash, drop, duck, dump, fall, hole, jump, leap, rush, tear **05** hurry, joint, lunge, pitch, sound, swoop **06** go down, header, plunge, refuge, saloon, spring, subway **07** descend, go under, plummet **08** nose-dive, submerge, tailspin **09** belly-flop, jackknife, nightclub **11** move quickly

diver
04 loom, loon **05** grebe **08** aquanaut, urinator **09** guillemot **10** pickpocket
See also **swimmer**

diverge
04 fork, part, vary **05** clash, drift, split, stray **06** branch, depart, differ, divide, spread, wander **07** deflect, deviate, digress, dissent, radiate **08** conflict, disagree, divagate, separate
09 bifurcate, branch off, spread out, subdivide **10** contradict, divaricate
12 be at variance

divergence
03 gap **05** clash, slant **07** parting
08 conflict **09** departure, deviation, dichotomy, disparity, variation
10 deflection, difference, digression, separation **12** branching-out, disagreement, divarication

divergent
07 diverse, variant, varying
08 separate **09** deviating, different, differing, diverging **10** dissimilar, divaricate, tangential **11** conflicting, disagreeing

divers
04 many, some **06** sundry, varied
07 several, various, varying
08 manifold, numerous **09** different
12 multifarious **13** miscellaneous

diverse
◇ *anagram indicator*
05 mixed **06** sundry, unlike, varied
07 several, various, varying
08 assorted, discrete, distinct, manifold, separate **09** different, differing, multiform **10** all means of, dissimilar **11** contrasting, distracting
13 heterogeneous, miscellaneous

diversification
09 extension, variation **10** alteration
11 variegation **12** branching-out, modification, spreading-out

diversify
03 mix **04** vary **05** alter, paint, spice
06 assort, change, expand, extend, modify **08** sprinkle **09** branch out, spread out, variegate **11** intersperse
13 differentiate **14** bring variety to

diversion
◇ *anagram indicator*
03 fun **04** game, play **05** hobby, sport
06 change, detour **07** pastime
09 amusement, avocation, deviation, switching **10** alteration, recreation, relaxation, rerouteing **11** distraction, redirection **13** divertisement, entertainment **14** divertissement

diversionary
09 divertive **10** deflecting
11 distracting

diversity
05 range **06** medley **07** mixture, variety **08** variance **09** pluralism
10 assortment, difference, embroidery, miscellany **11** variegation
12 biodiversity **13** dissimilarity, dissimilitude, heterogeneity
15 diversification

divert
◇ *anagram indicator*
04 sway **05** amuse, avert **06** absorb, baffle, occupy, put off, siphon, switch, syphon **07** deflect, delight, engross, hive off, pervert, reroute, turn off
08 call away, distract, draw away, estrange, interest, intrigue, redirect, turn away **09** entertain, sidetrack

diverting
◇ *anagram indicator*
03 fun **05** funny, witty **07** amusing
08 humorous, pleasant **09** enjoyable
11 pleasurable **12** entertaining

divest
04 doff **05** strip **06** denude, remove
07 deprive, despoil, disrobe, undress
08 unclothe **09** disentail
10 dispossess

divide
◇ *insertion indicator*
03 cut, div, gap **04** deal, divi, fork, gulf, part, rank, rift, sort **05** allot, break, cut up, grade, group, order, sever, share, split **06** bisect, branch, breach, cantle, cleave, depart, detach **07** arrange, break up, carve up, deal out, discide, dispart, diverge, dole out, fissure, hand out, opening, sort out, split up
08 alienate, allocate, classify, dispense, disunite, division, estrange, polarize, separate, share out **09** apportion, break down, segregate, watershed
10 categorize, disconnect, distribute, divergence, drive apart, measure out, separation **11** come between, distinguish

• **divide up**
05 allot, share **07** dole out **08** allocate, share out **09** apportion, dismember, parcel out **10** measure out

dividend
03 cut, div, FID **04** divi, gain, perk, plus
05 bonus, divvy, extra, share, whack
07 benefit, portion, surplus
09 advantage **10** percentage, perquisite

divination
05 -mancy **06** augury **07** presage
08 divining, prophecy **10** conjecture, prediction **11** foretelling, hariolation, second sight, soothsaying **14** fortune-telling **15** prognostication

Divination and fortune-telling techniques include:

04 dice
05 runes, tarot
06 I Ching, sortes
07 dowsing, scrying
08 geomancy, myomancy, taghairm, zoomancy
09 aeromancy, astrology, belomancy, ceromancy, gyromancy, oenomancy, palmistry, pyromancy, sortilege, tea leaves, theomancy
10 axinomancy, capnomancy, cartomancy, chiromancy,

cleromancy, dukkeripen, hieromancy, hydromancy, lithomancy, numerology, spodomancy
11 bibliomancy, botanomancy, crithomancy, gastromancy, hepatoscopy, oneiromancy, onychomancy, rhabdomancy, tephromancy
12 clairvoyance, coscinomancy, lampadomancy, omphalomancy, ornithomancy, radiesthesia, scapulomancy
13 Book of Changes, crystal gazing, dactyliomancy, fortune cookie, omoplatoscopy
14 crystallomancy

divine
04 holy, spae **05** godly, guess, infer **06** cleric, deduce, intuit, lovely, parson, pastor, priest, sacred **07** angelic, exalted, godlike, prelate, saintly, suppose, supreme, surmise, suspect **08** charming, foretell, glorious, heavenly, minister, mystical, perceive, reverend, seraphic, splendid **09** apprehend, beautiful, celestial, churchman, clergyman, excellent, prescient, religious, spiritual, wonderful **10** conjecture, delightful, sanctified, superhuman, theologian, understand **11** churchwoman, clergywoman, consecrated **12** ecclesiastic, supernatural, transcendent **13** prognosticate

See also **clergyman, clergywoman**; **religious**

divinely
08 heavenly **10** charmingly, gloriously, mystically **11** angelically, celestially, excellently, spiritually, wonderfully **12** delightfully **14** supernaturally

diviner
04 seer **05** augur, sibyl **06** dowser, oracle **07** prophet **08** haruspex **09** divinator, visionary **10** astrologer, soothsayer **11** clairvoyant, conjecturer, water-finder **12** crystal-gazer

diving *see* **swimming**

divinity
02 RE, RI **03** god **05** deity **06** spirit **07** goddess, godhead, godship **08** holiness, numinous, religion, sanctity, theology **09** godliness **10** divineness

See also **God**; **god, goddess**

division
03 arm, div **04** feud, part, rift, side **05** class, group, limit, share, split, tribe, tuath, world **06** border, branch, breach, divide, region, schism, sector **07** barrier, cutting, discord, parting, portion, rupture, scruple, section, segment, sharing **08** boundary, category, conflict, disunion, disunity, dividing, frontier, scission, scissure, townland **09** allotment, cutting up, detaching, partition, severance **10** alienation, allocation, department, digitation, dividing up, separation, sharing out, subsection **11** compartment, distinction **12** disagreement, distribution, dividing-line, estrangement **13** apportionment **15** demarcation line

divisive
08 damaging **09** injurious **10** alienating, discordant, disruptive, estranging, schismatic **11** troublesome **12** inharmonious **13** troublemaking

divorce
03 div **04** part **05** annul, sever, split, talak, talaq **06** breach, bust up, detach, divide **07** break up, break-up, isolate, put away, rupture, split up, split-up **08** dissolve, disunion, disunite, division, separate **09** annulment, partition, repudiate, severance **10** disconnect, dissociate, separation **11** dissolution, divorcement **13** diffarreation

divorced
03 div

divorcee
02 ex

divulge
04 leak, talk, tell **05** let on, split **06** babble, betray, bewray, expose, impart, repeat, reveal **07** confess, declare, let slip, publish, uncover **08** disclose, evulgate, proclaim **09** broadcast, make known, unconfine **10** promulgate **11** blow the gaff, communicate **12** break the news **13** spill the beans

dizziness
06 megrim **07** megrims, vertigo **09** faintness, giddiness, mirligoes, wooziness **10** scotodinia **15** light-headedness, vertiginousness

dizzy
◇ *anagram indicator*
04 mazy **05** dazed, ditsy, faint, giddy, shaky, silly, woozy **06** wobbly **07** confuse, extreme, foolish, muddled, reeling **08** confused, Disraeli **09** airheaded, confusing, Gillespie **10** bewildered, off-balance **11** addle-headed, bewildering, light-headed, vertiginous **13** irresponsible, rattle-brained **14** feather-brained, scatterbrained, weak at the knees

Djibouti
03 DJI

do
◇ *anagram indicator*
02 ut **03** act, con, dae, end, fix, put, rob **04** bash, char, comb, cook, dope, do up, dupe, fare, fuss, go at, have, hoax, make, raid, read, take, tidy, tour, wash, work **05** brush, cause, cheat, clean, crack, event, feast, get on, learn, mimic, offer, party, place, put on, reach, serve, solve, study, style, treat, trick, visit **06** adjust, affair, beat up, behave, bestow, come on, confer, create, finish, fleece, fulfil, manage, master, rave-up, render, rip off, soirée, supply, tackle, tart up, thrash, thrive, tidy up, work as, work at, work on **07** achieve, arrange, assault, clean up, deceive, defraud, develop, dope out, execute, exhaust, explore, furnish, go round, knees-up, major in, perform, prepare, present, proceed, produce, provide, resolve, satisfy, sort out, suffice, swindle, work out **08** activity, be enough, carry out, complete, conclude, deal with, decorate, function, get along, get ready, hoodwink, occasion, organize, progress, sightsee, travel at **09** come along, discharge, figure out, gathering, implement, look after, overreach, prosecute, puzzle out, reception, undertake **10** accomplish, be adequate, effectuate, fit the bill, have as a job, take care of, try to solve **11** celebration, impersonate, travel round **12** be employed as, be in charge of, be sufficient, take for a ride **13** earn a living as, make a bad job of **14** acquit yourself, be satisfactory, make a good job of **15** comport yourself, conduct yourself, find the answer to, put into practice

• **do away with**
04 do in, kill, slay **05** annul, scrap **06** murder, remove **07** abolish, bump off, destroy, discard, nullify **08** get rid of, knock off **09** dispose of, eliminate, finish off, liquidate, slaughter **10** put to death **11** assassinate, discontinue, exterminate

• **do down**
04 slag, slam **05** blame, cheat **06** dump on, subdue **07** censure, condemn, put down, rubbish, slag off **08** badmouth, belittle **09** criticize, disparage **13** find fault with

• **do in**
04 kill, ruin, slay **06** murder **07** bump off, deceive, exhaust **08** knock off **09** slaughter **10** put to death **11** assassinate, exterminate

• **do out of**
06 fleece **08** con out of **09** deprive of **10** cheat out of, trick out of **11** diddle out of **12** swindle out of

• **dos and don'ts**
04 code **05** rules **07** customs **09** etiquette, standards **11** regulations **12** instructions

• **do up**
03 tie **04** lace, pack **05** tie up, zip up **06** button, fasten, repair **07** arrange, restore **08** decorate, renovate **09** modernize, refurbish **10** redecorate **11** recondition

• **do without**
04 miss, want **05** forgo, spare **06** eschew, forego, give up **07** refrain **09** go without **10** relinquish **11** abstain from **12** deny yourself, dispense with **13** manage without

• **that will do**
02 so **03** sae

docile
07 dutiful, willing **08** amenable, flexible, obedient, obliging, yielding

09 childlike, compliant, tractable
10 controlled, manageable, submissive 11 co-operative
12 controllable

docilely
08 amenably 09 dutifully, willingly
10 obediently, obligingly
11 compliantly 13 co-operatively

docility
07 pliancy 08 meekness 09 ductility, obedience 10 compliance, pliability
11 amenability 12 biddableness, complaisance, tractability
13 manageability 14 submissiveness

dock
◇ *tail deletion indicator*
02 dk 03 bob, cut, pen 04 clip, crop, land, moor, pier, quay, rump 05 basin, berth, jetty, put in, Rumex, tie up, wharf
06 anchor, deduct, detail, lessen, marina, reduce, remove, sorrel
07 bistort, curtail, harbour, shorten
08 boat yard, canaigre, decrease, diminish, patience, quayside, subtract, truncate, withhold 09 grapetree, polygonum 10 drop anchor, tidal basin, waterfront 12 monk's rhubarb, submarine pen 15 fitting-out basin

• **docked**
02 in

• **in the dock**
07 on trial

docker
04 ship 06 lumper 08 labourer
09 stevedore 11 farmer's wife
12 longshoreman

docket
03 tab, tag 04 bill, chit, file, mark
05 index, label, tally 06 chitty, coupon, record, ticket 07 receipt, voucher
08 document, register 09 catalogue, paperwork 10 categorize
11 certificate, counterfoil
13 documentation

doctor
◇ *anagram indicator*
02 Dr 03 doc 04 cook, drug, fake, lace, load, pill, spay 05 alter, bones, medic, quack, spike 06 change, crocus, dilute, fiddle, mganga, neuter, repair, weaken 07 falsify, massage, pervert, sangoma 08 castrate, disguise, marabout, medicate, medicine, sawbones 09 body-curer, clinician, physician, sterilize 10 add drugs to, adulterate, manipulate, tamper with 11 add poison to, contaminate, witch-finder
12 misrepresent, sophisticate
13 interfere with

Doctor types include:

02 BM, GP, MB, MD, MO
03 vet
05 locum
06 intern
07 dentist, surgeon
08 houseman, resident
09 registrar
10 consultant
12 family doctor
14 hospital doctor, medical officer

See also **medical**

Doctors include:

03 Who
04 Bell (Sir Charles), Koch (Robert), Lind (James), Mayo (Charles), Razi (ar-), Reed (Walter), Ross (Sir Ronald)
05 Broca (Paul Pierre), Bruce (Sir David), Galen, Lower (Richard), Osler (Sir William), Paget (Sir James), Remak (Robert), Steno (Nicolaus)
06 Bichat (Marie), Bright (Richard), Carrel (Alexis), Celsus (Aulus), Cooper (Sir Astley), Fernel (Jean), Finsen (Niels), Garrod (Sir Archibald), Harvey (William), Hunter (John), Jekyll, Jenner (Edward), Lister (Joseph, Lord), Manson (Sir Patrick), Mesmer (Franz), Watson (John), Willis (Thomas)
07 Addison (Thomas), Barnard (Christiaan), Beddoes (Thomas), Burkitt (Denis), Cushing (Harvey), Eijkman (Christiaan), Gilbert (William), Hodgkin (Thomas), Laënnec (René), Laveran (Charles), Linacre (Thomas), MacEwen (Sir William), McIndoe (Sir Archibald), Nicolle (Charles), Winston (Robert, Lord)
08 Anderson (Elizabeth Garrett), Barnardo (Thomas), Beaumont (William), Billroth (Theodor), Charnley (Sir John), Duchenne (Guillaume), Magendie (François), Morgagni (Giovanni Battista), Sydenham (Thomas), Tournier (Paul)
09 Bartholin (Erasmus), Boerhaave (Hermann), Dutrochet (Henri), Fabricius (Johannes), Hahnemann (Samuel), Mackenzie (Sir James), Parkinson (James)
10 Fracastoro (Girolamo), Paracelsus, Sanctorius
11 Hippocrates, Ramón y Cajal (Santiago)
12 Erasistratus

See also **surgeon**

doctrinaire
05 rigid 06 biased 08 armchair, dogmatic, pedantic 09 fanatical, insistent 10 inflexible 11 impractical, opinionated, theoretical

doctrine
03 ism 04 lore 05 canon, credo, creed, dogma, tenet 06 belief
07 esotery, mystery, opinion, precept
08 teaching 09 principle 10 conviction

See also **philosophy**

document
04 chop, cite, deed, form, list, roll, writ
05 chart, paper, proof, prove 06 back up, billet, detail, patent, record, report, verify 07 charter, support, warning, write up 08 evidence, register, validate
09 affidavit, chronicle, write down
10 chirograph, commission, instrument 11 certificate, corroborate, instruction, put on record
12 command paper, commit to film, give weight to, keep on record, substantiate 13 commit to paper

documentary
07 charted, factual, written
08 detailed, recorded 09 reportage
10 chronicled, documented, featurette

documentation
06 papers, record 08 evidence
09 authority, paperwork
12 verification 14 qualifications

doddering
◇ *anagram indicator*
04 aged, weak 05 frail 06 feeble, infirm, senile 07 elderly 08 decrepit
09 tottering

doddery
◇ *anagram indicator*
04 aged, weak 05 shaky 06 feeble, infirm 07 tottery 08 unsteady
09 doddering, faltering, tottering
10 staggering

dodge
03 tip 04 bolt, dart, dash, dive, duck, fake, jink, jook, jouk, lurk, ploy, ruse, rush, shun, veer, wile 05 avoid, elude, evade, fudge, shift, shirk, trick
06 bypass, device, racket, scheme, swerve 07 evasion, fend off, quibble, shuffle, slinter, wrinkle 08 fakement, get out of, get round, gimcrack, jimcrack, jump away, side-step
09 deception, manoeuvre, stratagem
10 subterfuge 11 contrivance, machination 12 move suddenly, steer clear of 13 sharp practice

dodger
06 evader, skiver 07 avoider, dreamer, goof-off, shirker, slacker 08 layabout, slyboots 09 lazybones, trickster
11 goldbricker, lead-swinger

dodgy
◇ *anagram indicator*
04 iffy 05 crook, dicey, fishy, risky
06 artful, chancy, tricky, unsafe
07 dubious, fraught, suspect
08 doubtful, unstable 09 dangerous, dishonest, uncertain 10 unreliable
12 disreputable 13 problematical

doer
04 hand 05 agent 06 dynamo, factor, worker 07 bustler 08 achiever, activist, executor, go-getter, live wire
09 organizer 10 powerhouse
12 accomplisher 14 mover and shaker

doff
03 tip 04 lift, shed, vail 05 avail, avale, raise, strip, touch 06 availe, lay off, remove 07 discard, take off, undight
08 throw off

dog
03 cur, pup, tag 04 cock, Fido, mutt, stag, tail, tike, tyke 05 bitch, harry,

haunt, hound, piper, pooch, puppy, rogue, Rover, stalk, track, trail, worry **06** barker, bitser, canine, follow, infest, plague, pursue, rascal, shadow, touser, towser, wretch, yapper **07** andiron, mongrel, traitor, trouble, villain, whiffet, yapster **08** informer **09** scoundrel **10** tripehound **11** Montmorency, trendle-tail, trindle-tail, trundle-tail

See also **animal**

Dogs include:

03 gun, lab, Pom, pug
04 chow, kuri, Peke, tosa
05 akita, boxer, corgi, dhole, dingo, husky, hyena, laika, spitz
06 badger, bandog, beagle, bitser, borzoi, briard, collie, gun dog, moppet, poodle, saluki, Scotty, setter, vizsla, Westie
07 basenji, bouvier, bulldog, bush dog, coondog, griffon, lurcher, Maltese, mastiff, pitbull, pointer, Samoyed, Scottie, Shar-Pei, sheltie, shih tzu, sloughi, spaniel, terrier, volpino, whippet
08 Airedale, alsatian, chow-chow, coach dog, Doberman, elkhound, foxhound, keeshond, komondor, Labrador, malamute, papillon, Pekinese, Sealyham, sheepdog, warrigal
09 boar-hound, chihuahua, coonhound, dachshund, Dalmatian, Eskimo dog, Great Dane, greyhound, Kerry Blue, lhasa apso, Pekingese, red setter, retriever, schnauzer, St Bernard, wolfhound
10 bloodhound, fox terrier, Iceland-dog, Maltese dog, otter hound, Pomeranian, raccoon dog, Rottweiler, sausage-dog, spotted dog, St Bernard's
11 Afghan hound, basset-hound, bichon frise, bull-mastiff, bull terrier, carriage dog, Irish setter, Jack Russell, kangaroo dog, wishtonwish
12 Border collie, cairn terrier, Irish terrier, Japanese tosa, Newfoundland
13 affenpinscher, bearded collie, Boston terrier, cocker spaniel, Scotch terrier
14 English terrier, German Shepherd, Irish wolfhound, pit bull terrier
15 golden retriever, Scottish terrier, springer spaniel

See also **spaniel**; **terrier**

Dog types include:

02 pi
03 gun, hot, lap, pet, pie, pye, sea, top, toy, war
04 corn, rach, wild
05 guard, guide, house, pooch, rache, ratch, sheep, under, watch, water, zorro
06 kennet, pariah, police, ranger, ratter, sleeve, yellow
07 harrier, hearing, leading, mongrel, tracker, truffle
08 huntaway, turnspit
09 retriever
10 sheep-biter, shin-barker
11 sleuth-hound

Famous dogs include:

03 Lad
04 Lucy, Nana, Odie, Shep, Spot, Toby, Toto
05 Balto, Butch, Flush, Goofy, Laika, Petra, Pluto, Pongo, Sadie, Snowy, Timmy
06 Buster, Droopy, Gelert, Gromit, Hector, Lassie, Missis, Nipper, Sirius, Snoopy
07 Charley, Gnasher, Perdita, Roobarb
08 Bullseye, Cerberus, Dogmatix
09 Rin Tin Tin, Scooby Doo
10 Deputy Dawg, Fred Basset
12 Real Huntsman
13 Master McGrath, Mick the Miller
15 Greyfriars Bobby, The Littlest Hobo

• **dog's breakfast, dog's dinner**
04 mess

• **reproof to dog**
04 rate

dogged
04 firm **06** intent, steady, sullen **07** staunch **08** obdurate, resolute, stubborn, tireless **09** obstinate, steadfast, tenacious **10** determined, persistent, relentless, unflagging, unshakable, unyielding **11** indomitable, persevering, unfaltering, unshakeable **12** pertinacious, single-minded **13** indefatigable

doggedly
06 firmly **09** staunchly **10** resolutely, stubbornly, tirelessly, unshakably **11** obstinately, steadfastly, tenaciously, unshakeably **12** persistently, relentlessly **13** indefatigably **14** single-mindedly

doggedness
08 firmness, tenacity **09** endurance, obstinacy **10** resolution, steadiness **11** persistence, pertinacity **12** perseverance, stubbornness **13** determination, steadfastness, tenaciousness **14** indomitability, relentlessness

doggerel
03 jig **08** nonsense, rat-rhyme **11** cramboclink **12** crambo-jingle

dogma
04 code **05** credo, creed, maxim, tenet **06** belief **07** article, opinion, precept **08** doctrine, teaching **09** principle **10** conviction **12** code of belief **14** article of faith

dogmatic
08 arrogant, emphatic, pontific, positive **09** arbitrary, assertive, canonical, doctrinal, imperious, insistent **10** ex cathedra, intolerant, peremptory, pontifical **11** affirmative, categorical, dictatorial, doctrinaire, domineering, opinionated, overbearing, pragmatical **13** authoritarian, authoritative **14** unquestionable **15** unchallengeable

dogmatically
10 arrogantly **11** assertively, imperiously, insistently **12** emphatically, intolerantly **13** categorically, dictatorially, domineeringly **15** authoritatively

dogmatism
07 bigotry **11** presumption **12** positiveness **13** arbitrariness, assertiveness, imperiousness **14** peremptoriness **15** dictatorialness, opinionatedness

dogsbody
05 gofer, slave **06** drudge, lackey, menial, skivvy **07** doormat **08** factotum **11** galley-slave **12** bottle-washer, man-of-all-work **13** maid-of-all-work

doings
04 acts, work **05** deeds, feats **06** events **07** actions, affairs **08** concerns, dealings, exploits, goings-on **09** handiwork **10** activities, adventures, happenings **11** enterprises, proceedings **12** achievements, transactions

doldrums
05 blues, dumps, ennui, gloom **06** acedia, apathy, tedium, torpor **07** boredom, inertia, malaise, megrims **08** dullness **09** dejection, lassitude **10** depression, melancholy, stagnation **12** listlessness, sluggishness **15** downheartedness, low-spiritedness

dole
03 JSA **04** broo, pain, vail **05** grief, guile, share, vails, vales **06** credit, income **07** benefit, payment, support **08** pittance **09** allowance **12** state benefit **14** social security

• **dole out**
04 deal **05** allot, issue, share **06** assign, divide, ration **07** deal out, dish out, give out, hand out, mete out **08** allocate, dispense, divide up, share out **09** apportion **10** administer, distribute

doleful
03 sad **04** blue **06** dismal, dreary, gloomy, rueful, sombre, woeful **07** forlorn, painful, pitiful **08** dolorous, mournful, pathetic, wretched **09** cheerless, miserable, sorrowful, woebegone **10** depressing, lugubrious, melancholy **11** distressing **12** disconsolate **14** down in the dumps

dolefully
05 sadly **08** dismally, gloomily **09** forlornly, miserably, unhappily **10** mournfully, wretchedly **12** pathetically **14** disconsolately

doll
03 toy **04** babe **05** dolly **06** figure **08** figurine **09** plaything

Dolls include:

03 kid, rag, wax
04 baby
05 China, cloth, Dutch, metal, paper, Paris, Sindy®
06 artist, Barbie®, bisque, blow-up, ethnic, fabric, Hamble, kewpie, modern, moppet, poppet, puppet, voodoo, wooden
07 fashion, jointed, kachina, kokeshi, nesting, rag baby, Russian
08 golliwog, gollywog
09 miniature, porcelain, tachibina, Tiny Tears
10 marionette, matryoshka, Raggedy Ann, topsy-turvy
11 composition, papier-mâché, Polly Pocket
12 reproduction
15 Cabbage Patch Kid, frozen Charlotte

• doll up
05 preen, primp **06** tart up **07** deck out, dress up, trick up **08** titivate, trick out

dollar
03 cob, dol **04** buck, peso **05** scrip, wheel **06** loonie, single **07** iron man, Mexican, smacker **09** greenback
• eighth of a dollar
04 real
• five dollars
03 fin **04** spin **05** fiver

dollop
03 gob **04** ball, blob, glob, lump
05 bunch, clump **06** gobbet, slairg

dolly
05 peggy **06** maiden, Parton, Varden

dolorous
03 sad **06** rueful, sombre, woeful
07 doleful, painful **08** grievous, mournful, wretched **09** anguished, harrowing, miserable, sorrowful, woebegone **10** lugubrious, melancholy **11** distressing **12** heart-rending

dolour
04 pain **05** grief **06** misery, sorrow
07 anguish, sadness **08** distress, mourning **09** heartache, suffering
10 heartbreak **11** lamentation

dolphin
06 sea-pig **07** grampus **08** porpoise
09 coryphene, Delphinus, mere swine
10 bottle-nose

dolt
03 ass, git, oaf **04** clot, dope, dork, fool, geek, nerd, twit **05** chump, clunk, golem, idiot, ninny, twerp, wally
06 dimwit, nitwit **07** nutcase, plonker
08 dipstick, imbecile, mooncalf, numskull **09** blockhead, simpleton
10 clodhopper, nincompoop, sheep's-head **11** chuckle-head

domain
04 area **05** arena, bourn, field, lands, realm, reame, reign, world **06** bourne, empire, estate, region, sphere
07 concern, kingdom, section
08 dominion, province, seignory, universe **09** ownership, seigneury, seigniory, territory **10** department, discipline, seigneurie, speciality
12 jurisdiction

See also **classification**

dome
04 tope **05** igloo, mound, stupa, vault
06 bubble, cupola, dagaba, dagoba, tholus **07** rotunda **09** astrodome, macrodome **10** brachydome, hemisphere

domestic
03 dom, pet **04** char, cook, esne, help, home, maid, tame **05** daily, house, local, tamed **06** au pair, broken, family, homely, native **07** cleaner, private, servant **08** broken in, char lady, familiar, fireside, home-bred, home help, internal, national, personal
09 charwoman, daily help, household
10 home-loving, indigenous, stay-at-home **11** domiciliary **12** domesticated, domestic help, housekeeping, house-trained

Domestic appliances include:

03 Aga®, hob, Vax®
04 iron, oven, spit
05 grill, mixer, radio, stove
06 cooker, fridge, Hoover®, juicer, kettle, washer
07 blender, fan oven, freezer, griddle, ionizer, toaster
08 barbecue, gas stove, hotplate, wireless
09 deep fryer, Dutch oven, DVD player, steam iron
10 coffee mill, deep-freeze, dishwasher, humidifier, liquidizer, percolator, rotisserie, slow cooker, steam press, television, waffle iron
11 tumble-drier, washer-drier
12 kitchen range, refrigerator, stereo system, trouser press
13 carpet sweeper, electric grill, floor polisher, food processor, fridge-freezer, ice-cream maker, microwave oven, sandwich maker, vacuum cleaner, video recorder
14 electric cooker, juice extractor, upright cleaner, washing machine
15 carpet shampooer, cylinder cleaner

domestically
06 at home **07** locally **08** near home
09 in private **10** internally, nationally

domesticate
04 tame **05** break, train **07** break in
08 accustom **09** habituate
10 assimilate, house-train, naturalize
11 acclimatize, familiarize

domesticated
03 pet **04** tame **05** tamed **06** broken, homely **08** broken in, domestic
10 home-loving, house-proud
11 housewifely, naturalized **12** house-trained

domestication
06 taming **08** training **10** breaking-in
11 habituation **12** assimilation
13 house-training **14** naturalization

domesticity
09 homecraft **10** homemaking, housecraft **12** housekeeping
13 domestication, home economics
15 domestic science

domicile
04 home, live **05** abode, house
06 settle **07** lodging, mansion
08 dwelling, lodgings, quarters
09 establish, residence, residency
10 habitation, settlement **12** make your home, put down roots **15** take up residence

dominance
04 rule, sway **05** power **07** command, control, mastery **08** hegemony
09 authority, supremacy
10 ascendancy, centrality, domination, government, leadership
11 paramountcy, pre-eminence, superiority

dominant
03 key **04** main **05** chief, major, prime
06 ruling, strong **07** central, leading, primary, supreme **08** powerful
09 assertive, besetting, governing, important, paramount, presiding, prevalent, principal, prominent
10 commanding, overriding, pre-eminent, prevailing **11** all-powerful, controlling, influential, outstanding, predominant **13** authoritative, most important

dominate
04 lead, rule **05** dwarf **06** direct, govern, master, rule OK **07** command, control, eclipse, preside, prevail
08 domineer, overbear, overgang, overlook, overrule **09** mesmerize, tower over, tyrannize **10** intimidate, monopolize, overmaster, overshadow, run the show **11** have on toast, predominate **12** hold the floor **15** have over a barrel, wear the trousers

dominating
06 strong **08** dominant, powerful, superior **09** assertive, confident, directing **10** commanding, overruling
11 controlling **12** advantageous
13 authoritative

domination
04 rule, sway **05** power **07** bossism, command, control, mastery, tyranny
09 authority, despotism, influence, prelatism, supremacy **10** ascendancy, government, leadership, militarism, oppression, repression, subjection
11 pre-eminence, superiority, suppression **12** dictatorship, predominance **13** subordination

domineer
04 boss, ride **07** henpeck **08** jackboot

domineering
05 bossy, pushy **07** haughty, kick-ass

08 arrogant, coercive, despotic, forceful, managing 09 imperious, masterful, tyrannous 10 aggressive, autocratic, high-handed, iron-handed, oppressive, peremptory, tyrannical 11 dictatorial, overbearing 13 authoritarian

Dominica
02 WD 03 DJI, DMA

Dominican
03 Dom

Dominican Republic
03 DOM

Dominicans
02 OP

dominion
03 Dom 04 rule, sway 05 power, realm 06 colony, domain, empire 07 command, control, country, kingdom, mastery 08 lordship, province 09 authority, direction, supremacy, territory 10 ascendancy, dependency, domination, government 11 sovereignty 12 jurisdiction, protectorate 14 rangatiratanga

don
◇ *insertion indicator*
04 Juan 05 adept, put on, swell, tutor 06 assume, expert, fellow, reader 07 address, dress in, get into, scholar, teacher 08 academic, Giovanni, lecturer, slip into 09 professor

donate
03 gie 04 give 06 bestow, chip in, confer, pledge 07 cough up, fork out, present 08 bequeath, give away, shell out 09 make a gift, subscribe 10 contribute 12 club together 13 make a donation

donation
04 alms, gift, koha, wakf, waqf 05 grant 07 bequest, charity, largess, present 08 gratuity, largesse, memorial, offering 11 benefaction 12 contribution, presentation, subscription

done
◇ *anagram indicator*
02 OK 04 over 05 baked, crisp, ended, fried, ready, right 06 agreed, boiled, cooked, proper, seemly, stewed, tender 07 browned, correct, decided, fitting, roasted, settled 08 accepted, arranged, complete, decorous, executed, finished, prepared, realized, suitable, well-done 09 completed, concluded, fulfilled 10 absolutely, acceptable, terminated 11 appropriate, consummated 12 accomplished, conventional
• **done for**
04 lost 06 beaten, broken, dashed, doomed, foiled, ruined, undone 07 wrecked 08 defeated, finished, spitcher, washed-up 09 destroyed 10 vanquished 14 for the high jump
• **done in**
04 dead 05 all in, weary 06 bushed, pooped, zonked 07 whacked, worn out 08 dead beat, dog-tired, fatigued, tired out 09 exhausted, fagged out, fit to drop, flaked out, knackered, pooped out, shattered, stonkered 11 bushwhacked, tuckered out 14 on your last legs, worn to a frazzle
• **have done with**
04 stop 05 cease 06 desist, give up 08 over with 09 throw over 10 finish with, thrash with 12 finished with 13 be through with 15 over and done with, wash your hands of

Don Juan
04 rake 05 lover, romeo 06 gigolo 08 Casanova 09 ladies' man, philander, womanizer 10 lady-killer 11 philanderer

donkey
03 ass 04 moke, mule 05 burro, cuddy, genet, hinny, jenny, neddy 06 cuddie, gennet, jennet 07 jackass 11 cardophagus 13 Jerusalem pony

donnish
07 bookish, erudite, learned, serious 08 academic, pedantic, studious 09 pedagogic, scholarly 10 scholastic 11 formalistic 12 intellectual

donor
05 angel, giver 06 backer 07 donator 08 provider 09 supporter 10 benefactor 11 contributor 14 fairy godmother, philanthropist

doom
03 lot 04 damn, date, dome, fate, ruin 05 death, judge, weird 06 decree, devote 07 condemn, consign, destine, destiny, fortune, portion, verdict 08 disaster, downfall, judgment, sentence 09 destinate, judgement, pronounce, ruination 10 death-knell, predestine 11 catastrophe, destruction, rack and ruin 12 condemnation 13 pronouncement

doomed
03 fay, fey, fie 05 fated 06 cursed, damned, marked, ruined 07 accurst, devoted, unlucky 08 accursed, destined, hopeless, ill-fated, luckless 09 condemned, ill-omened 10 bedevilled, ill-starred 11 star-crossed

door
03 way 04 exit, haik, hake, heck, road, yett 05 entry, hatch, route, way in 06 access, portal 07 doorway, gateway, opening, postern 08 entrance, open door 11 opportunity
• **guard door**
04 tile

doorkeeper
05 tiler, tyler, usher 06 porter 07 doorman, janitor, ostiary 08 huissier 09 caretaker, concierge 10 gatekeeper 14 commissionaire

doorpost
04 dern, durn

dope
01 E 03 gen, git, LSD, oaf, pot, tea 04 acid, berk, clot, coke, dolt, dork, drug, fool, geek, hash, info, lace, prat, twit, weed 05 crack, drugs, dunce, facts, grass, idiot, ninny, opium, speed, spike, twerp 06 dimwit, doctor, heroin, inject, nitwit, opiate, sedate 07 buffoon, details, Ecstasy, halfwit, low-down, plonker, stupefy 08 cannabis, knock out, medicate, narcotic 09 absorbent, blockhead, marijuana, narcotize, simpleton, specifics 10 nincompoop 11 amphetamine, barbiturate, information, particulars 12 anaesthetize, hallucinogen
See also **fool**

dopey
04 daft, dozy 05 silly 06 drowsy, groggy, simple, sleepy, stupid, torpid 07 foolish, muddled, nodding 08 confused, narcotic 09 lethargic, somnolent, stupefied 12 addle-brained 14 not the full quid

dormancy
04 rest 05 sleep 07 latency, slumber 09 inertness 10 estivation, inactivity 11 aestivation, hibernation

dormant
05 inert, joist 06 asleep, fallow, latent, torpid 07 resting 08 comatose, inactive, latitant, sleeping, sluggish 09 crossbeam, lethargic, potential, quiescent 10 slumbering, unrealized 11 hibernating, undeveloped, undisclosed

dormouse
04 loir

dosage
04 dose 06 amount 07 measure, portion 08 quantity

dose
03 fix, hit 04 pill, shot 05 bolus, treat 06 amount, dosage, drench, potion, powder 07 booster, draught, measure, portion 08 dispense, medicate, quantity 09 prescribe 10 administer 11 horse-drench 12 prescription
• **lethal dose**
02 LD

dosh *see* **money**

dossier
04 case, data, file 05 brief, notes 06 folder, papers, report 09 documents, portfolio 11 information

dot
03 dab, dit, hit, jot, set 04 atom, iota, limp, mark, spot, stud, tick 05 fleck, point, prick, speck 06 bullet, circle, pepper, stigme, tittle 07 punctum, scatter, speckle, stipple 08 full stop, particle, pin-point, punctule, sprinkle 09 punctuate 11 bullet point 12 decimal point
• **on the dot**
05 sharp 06 on time 07 exactly

08 promptly **09** precisely
10 punctually **13** exactly on time

dotage
06 old age **07** anility **08** agedness, senility, weakness **09** infirmity
10 feebleness, imbecility
11 decrepitude, elderliness **12** autumn of life **13** evening of life **15** second childhood

dote
• **dote on**
04 love **05** adore, spoil **06** admire, pamper **07** idolize, indulge, worship
08 hold dear, treasure

doting
04 fond, soft **06** loving, tender
07 adoring, devoted **09** indulgent
12 affectionate

dotty
◇ *anagram indicator*
03 ape **04** bats, loco, nuts **05** barmy, batty, buggy, crazy, daffy, dippy, flaky, gonzo, loony, loopy, nutty, potty, wacko, wacky, weird, wiggy
06 cuckoo, fruity, mental, raving, screwy **07** bananas, barking, bonkers, cracked, meshuga, touched
08 crackers, demented, dingbats, doolally, peculiar, unsteady
09 eccentric, lymphatic, up the wall
10 bestraught, frantic-mad, off the wall, off your nut, out to lunch **11** not all there, off the rails, off your head
12 feeble-minded, mad as a hatter, off your chump, round the bend **13** off your rocker, out of your head, out of your tree, round the twist **14** off your trolley, wrong in the head

double
◇ *repetition indicator*
02 bi-, di- **03** dbl, twi-, twy- **04** copy, dual, fold, twin **05** clone, duple, image, match, trick, twice **06** binate, clench, do also, duplex, fill in, paired, repeat, ringer, two-ply **07** coupled, doubled, enlarge, magnify, replica, stand in, twofold **08** geminate, geminous, increase, turn down, two-edged
09 ambiguous, bifarious, deceitful, duplicate, equivocal, facsimile, insincere, lookalike **10** ambivalent, substitute, understudy **11** counterpart, deceitfully, double-edged, paradoxical, reduplicate
12 doppelgänger, hypocritical, impersonator **13** double-meaning, have a dual role, multiply by two, spitting image **14** be an understudy, have a second job **15** have a second role
• **at the double**
06 at once **07** quickly **09** right away
11 at full speed, immediately
12 straight away, without delay
• **double back**
04 loop **05** dodge, evade **06** circle, return **07** reverse **09** backtrack

double-cross
03 con **05** cheat, trick **06** betray
07 defraud, mislead, swindle, two-time **08** hoodwink **12** take for a ride **14** pull a fast one on

double-dealing
07 perfidy **08** betrayal, cheating, tricking **09** duplicity, mendacity, swindling, treachery, two-timing
10 defrauding, misleading
11 crookedness, dissembling, hoodwinking **12** ambidextrous, two-facedness

double entendre
03 pun **08** innuendo, wordplay
09 ambiguity **11** play on words
13 double meaning **14** suggestiveness

doubling
04 fold, loop **05** plait, trick
08 mantling **10** gemination
11 duplicature **12** diplogenesis
13 reduplication

doubly
03 bis **05** again, extra, twice
07 twofold **10** especially

doubt
04 fear **05** demur, qualm, query, waver
06 aporia, danger, mammer, wonder
07 dilemma, dubiety, impeach, problem, scepsis, scruple, skepsis, suspect **08** distrust, dubitate, hesitate, misdoubt, mistrust, quandary, question, wavering **09** ambiguity, be dubious, confusion, hesitance, hesitancy, misgiving, suspicion, vacillate **10** difficulty, disbelieve, hesitation, indecision, perplexity, scepticism, skepticism, uneasiness
11 be uncertain, be undecided, incredulity, reservation, uncertainty
12 apprehension, be suspicious, mixed feeling **14** call in question **15** have qualms about
• **expression of doubt**
02 ha, h'm, um **03** erm, hah, hmm, hum **05** humph
• **in doubt**
04 moot **08** doubtful **09** ambiguous, debatable, uncertain, undecided **10** in question, unreliable, unresolved, up in the air **12** open to debate, questionable **14** open to question
• **no doubt**
04 iwis, ywis **06** surely **08** of course, probably **09** certainly, doubtless, no denying **10** definitely, most likely, presumably, sure enough
11 undoubtedly **12** bang to rights, without doubt **13** in anyone's book
14 unquestionably

doubter
05 cynic **06** Thomas **07** sceptic, scoffer **08** agnostic **10** questioner, unbeliever **11** disbeliever, non-believer, questionist **14** doubting Thomas

doubtful
04 iffy **05** crook, fishy, shady, vague
06 uneasy, unsure **07** dubious, in doubt, obscure, suspect, unclear
08 hesitant, insecure, unlikely, wavering **09** ambiguous, debatable, sceptical, skeptical, tentative, uncertain, undecided
10 improbable, in two minds, irresolute, suspicious, touch and go
11 distrustful, vacillating
12 apprehensive, inconclusive, questionable **14** open to question

doubtfully
◇ *anagram indicator*
08 uneasily **10** hesitantly
11 sceptically, uncertainly
12 irresolutely **14** apprehensively

doubtless
04 sure **05** truly **06** surely **07** clearly, no doubt **08** of course, probably
09 assuredly, certainly, dreadless, precisely, seemingly **10** most likely, presumably, supposedly
11 indubitably, undoubtedly **12** bang to rights, indisputably, without doubt
13 in anyone's book
14 unquestionably

dough
04 cake, duff, masa **05** knish, money, pasta, paste **08** kreplach **09** hush puppy
See also **money**

doughnut
05 torus **06** sinker **07** olycook, olykoek **09** friedcake

doughty
04 able, bold, fell, tall **05** brave, gutsy
06 daring, gritty, heroic, plucky, spunky, strong **07** gallant, valiant
08 fearless, intrepid, unafraid, valorous
09 confident, dauntless, unabashed, undaunted **10** courageous, unblinking
11 indomitable, lion-hearted, unblenching, unflinching
14 unapprehensive

doughy
03 sad **04** soft **05** heavy, pasty
06 pallid, sodden

dour
04 grim, hard, sour **05** gruff, harsh, rigid, stern **06** dismal, dreary, gloomy, morose, severe, strict, sullen
07 austere **08** churlish, rigorous
09 obstinate, unsmiling
10 determined, forbidding, inflexible, unfriendly, unyielding

douse, dowse
03 dip, wet **04** duck, dunk, soak
05 flood, snuff, souse, steep
06 deluge, drench, plunge, put out, quench, splash, strike **07** blow out, immerge, immerse, smother
08 saturate, submerge **10** extinguish
13 pour water over

dove
03 doo **06** culver, pigeon, rocker, turtle **07** rockier **10** rock pigeon

dovetail
04 join, link **05** agree, match, tally
06 accord **07** conform **08** coincide
09 harmonize, interlock
10 correspond **11** fit together

dowdy
04 drab **05** dingy, mopsy, tacky, tatty
06 frowsy, frumpy, shabby
08 frumpish, slovenly **10** ill-dressed
12 old-fashioned **13** unfashionable

down
01 d **02** dn **03** ill, low, nap, sad **04** à bas, blue, bust, fell, flue, fuzz, gulp, oose, ooze, pile, shag, swig, wool
05 along, bloom, drink, floor, floss, fluff, kaput, swill, throw, wonky
06 pappus, topple **07** consume, crashed, depress, descent, floccus, put away, swallow, toss off, unhappy
08 dejected, downcast, feathers, fine hair, gulp down, wretched **09** bring down, conked out, depressed, knock back, knock down, miserable, overthrow, prostrate, southward
10 behindhand, dispirited, melancholy, not working, on the blink, on the fritz, out of order, to the floor
11 downhearted, inoperative, out of action, to the bottom, to the ground
12 soft feathers **13** to a lower level
14 down in the dumps, malfunctioning
• **down with**
03 hip **04** à bas **06** depose **07** abolish, put down, swallow **08** away with, get rid of **10** in tune with
• **set down**
03 lay **04** drop, dump, land, snub, take
05 judge, state **06** depose, esteem, record, regard **07** ascribe, deposit, detrain **09** attribute, discharge
10 disentrain

down-and-out
03 bum **04** hobo, wino **05** caird, jakey, loser, piker, rogue, tramp **06** dosser, ruined, toerag, truant, vagrom, walker
07 dingbat, floater, gangrel, tinkler, vagrant **08** clochard, cursitor, deadbeat, derelict, homeless, straggle, stroller, vagabond **09** destitute, landloper, penniless, sundowner
11 rinthereout, scatterling, Weary Willie **12** down-and-outer, hallan-shaker, impoverished, on your uppers
15 knight of the road

down-at-heel
04 drab, poor **05** dingy, dowdy, seedy, tacky, tatty **06** frayed, frowsy, ragged, shabby **07** run-down **08** slovenly, tattered **09** neglected **10** ill-dressed, ramshackle, tumbledown, uncared for
11 dilapidated, in disrepair

downbeat
03 low **04** calm **06** casual, gloomy
07 cynical, relaxed **08** downcast, informal, laid-back, negative
09 cheerless, depressed, easy-going, unhurried, unworried **10** despondent, insouciant, nonchalant **11** pessimistic
15 fearing the worst

downcast
03 low, sad **04** blue, down, dull, glum
05 fed up **06** gloomy **07** daunted, hanging, unhappy **08** dejected, dismayed, wretched **09** depressed, miserable **10** despondent, dispirited, downlooked **11** crestfallen, discouraged, downhearted, low-spirited **12** disappointed, disconsolate, disheartened

downfall
04 fall, ruin **05** decay **07** debacle, failure, undoing **08** collapse, disgrace
09 overthrow **10** debasement
11 degradation, destruction, humiliation

downgrade
05 decry, lower **06** defame, demote, depose, do down, humble **07** deflate, degrade, run down **08** belittle, minimize, relegate **09** denigrate, disparage, sell short, underrate
11 lower in rank, make light of
12 reduce in rank

downhearted
03 sad **04** glum **06** gloomy
07 daunted, unhappy **08** dejected, dismayed, downcast **09** depressed
10 browned off, despondent, dispirited **11** discouraged, low-spirited
12 disappointed, disconsolate, disheartened

down-market
04 poor, sale **05** cheap, tacky, tatty
06 budget, cheapo, common, shoddy, tawdry **07** bargain, economy, low-cost, reduced **08** cut-price, giveaway, inferior, low-price, no-frills
09 cheapjack, cheap-rate, knock-down, throwaway, worthless
10 affordable, discounted, economical, marked-down, ramshackle, rock-bottom, second-rate
11 inexpensive **15** bargain-basement

downpour
04 pelt, rain **05** flood, plash **06** deluge
07 torrent **09** rainstorm
10 cloudburst, inundation, waterspout

downright
04 flat **05** clear, plain, plump, sheer, total, utter **06** arrant, simply
07 brusque, clearly, plainly, totally, utterly **08** absolute, complete, even-down, outright, positive, straight, thorough **09** out-and-out, up-and-down, wholesale **10** absolutely, completely, forthright, positively, thoroughly **11** categorical, plain-spoken, unequivocal, unqualified
13 categorically

downside
04 flaw, snag **05** minus **06** defect
07 penalty, trouble **08** drawback, nuisance, weakness **09** liability, weak point **10** impediment, limitation
12 Achilles heel, disadvantage
13 inconvenience

downsize
04 slim **06** reduce, shrink **08** contract, diminish, minimize, moderate **11** make smaller

down-to-earth
04 sane **07** mundane **08** sensible
09 practical, realistic **10** hard-headed, no-nonsense **11** commonsense, plain-spoken **12** matter-of-fact **13** plain-speaking, unsentimental
14 commonsensical

downtrodden
06 abused **07** bullied **08** burdened, helpless **09** exploited, oppressed, powerless **10** subjugated, trampled on, tyrannized, victimized
11 overwhelmed, subservient, weighed-down

down under
02 Oz **09** Australia

downward
07 sliding **08** downhill, slipping
09 declining, going down
10 descending, moving down

downy
04 fine, soft **05** fuzzy, nappy **06** fleecy, fluffy, smooth, woolly **07** cottony, dowlney, knowing, pappose, pappous, velvety **08** feathery **09** plumulate
10 lanuginose, lanuginous

dowry
03 dot **04** gift **05** share **06** legacy, talent, tocher **07** faculty, portion
09 endowment, provision
11 inheritance **12** wedding-dower
15 marriage portion

dowse *see* **douse, dowse**

doxology
04 hymn, song **05** chant, psalm
06 anthem, gloria, praise **07** chorale
08 response **11** recessional **12** hymn of praise, song of praise **13** glorification

doze
03 kip, nap **04** dare, zizz **05** dover, go off, sleep **06** catnap, drowse, nod off, siesta, snooze **07** drop off, shut-eye **08** drift off, take a nap
10 forty winks
• **doze off**
06 catnap, nod off, snooze **08** drift off
10 fall asleep **14** have forty winks

dozen
02 dz **03** doz, XII **04** twal **06** twelve
07 stupefy

dozy
04 daft **05** dopey, silly, tired, weary
06 dreamy, drowsy, simple, sleepy, stupid, torpid **07** foolish, nodding, yawning **09** somnolent **10** half-asleep

drab
04 dull, flat, grey **05** dingy, whore
06 boring, dismal, dreary, gloomy, isabel, shabby, sombre **07** tedious
08 isabella, lifeless **09** cheerless
10 colourless, isabelline, lacklustre
11 featureless **12** Quaker-colour
13 uninteresting

drabness
05 gloom **08** dullness, greyness
09 dinginess **10** dreariness, shabbiness, sombreness
12 lifelessness **13** cheerlessness
14 colourlessness

Draconian
04 grim, hard **05** cruel, harsh, stern **06** brutal, savage, severe, strict **07** inhuman **08** abrasive, pitiless, ruthless **09** merciless, unfeeling **10** iron-fisted, iron-handed **13** unsympathetic

draft
03 dft **04** bill, draw, plan **05** essay, rough **06** cheque, design, detach, draw up, scroll, sketch **07** compose, drawing, ébauche, outline, paste-up **08** abstract, bank-bill, protocol **09** blueprint, delineate, formulate, treatment **10** money order **11** delineation, postal order, rough sketch **14** bill of exchange, letter of credit

drag
03 lag, lug, tow, tug **04** bind, bore, draw, hale, harl, haul, pain, pest, pull, rash, shoe, sled, snig, trek, tump, yank **05** crawl, creep, shlep, snake, sweep, trail, train **06** bother, drogue, schlep, wear on **07** schlepp, skidpan, trouble **08** go slowly, headache, nuisance **09** annoyance, go on and on, influence **11** go on for ever **12** become boring **13** become tedious, pain in the neck

• drag on
04 go on **05** run on **07** persist **08** continue **09** be lengthy **14** be long-drawn-out

• drag out
06 extend, hang on **07** draw out, persist, prolong, spin out **08** lengthen, protract

• drag up
05 raise **06** rake up, remind, revive **07** bring up, mention **09** introduce

dragon
04 worm **05** Draco, drake **08** lindworm **09** firedrake **12** flying lizard

dragonfly
05 naiad, nymph **07** Odonata **10** demoiselle

dragoon
05 bully, drive, force, impel **06** coerce, compel, harass **08** browbeat, pressure **09** constrain, press-gang, strongarm **10** intimidate, pressurize

drain
02 ea **03** dry, eau, pot, sap, sew, tap, tax **04** buzz, delf, duct, grip, leak, milk, nala, ooze, pipe, pour, sink, suck, tile, void **05** bleed, cundy, ditch, drink, empty, exude, fleet, gripe, gully, ladle, leach, leech, nalla, nulla, quaff, sewer, siver, sough, stank, syver, use up **06** condie, effuse, emulge, filter, gutter, nallah, nullah, outlet, remove, sheuch, sheugh, sluice, sponge, strain, trench **07** channel, conduit, consume, culvert, cunette, deplete, dewater, draw off, drink up, exhaust, extract, flow out, piscina, pump off, seep out, swallow, trickle, unwater **08** bleed dry, evacuate, withdraw **09** depletion, discharge, lickpenny **10** bleed white, exhaustion, underdrain **11** common-shore, consumption, watercourse **12** exsanguinate

• drained
05 tired

dram
02 dr **03** tot, wet **04** shot, suck, tiff, tift **06** chasse, drachm **07** caulker, morning, nobbler, snifter, tickler **08** chota peg, meridian **10** stirrup cup

See also **drink**

drama
02 no **03** noh **04** auto, play, show **05** opera, piece, scene **06** acting, azione, comedy, crisis, kabuki, thrill **07** dilemma, tension, theater, theatre, tragedy, turmoil **08** operetta **09** dramatics, melodrama, sensation, spectacle **10** dramaturgy, excitement, stagecraft **11** histrionics

See also **play**

• drama students
04 RADA

dramatic
05 stage, tense, vivid **06** abrupt, marked, sudden **07** drastic, graphic **08** distinct, exciting, stirring, striking, Thespian **09** effective, thrilling **10** artificial, expressive, flamboyant, histrionic, impressive, noticeable, theatrical, unexpected **11** exaggerated, personative, sensational, significant, spectacular, substantial **12** considerable, melodramatic

dramatically
07 vividly **08** abruptly, suddenly **10** noticeably, strikingly **12** considerably, expressively, impressively **13** significantly, spectacularly, substantially

dramatist
06 writer **08** comedian **09** tragedian **10** dramaturge, playwright, play-writer **12** dramaturgist, screen writer, scriptwriter

See also **playwright**

dramatization
07 staging **10** adaptation **11** arrangement **12** presentation

dramatize
03 act, ham **05** adapt, ham up, put on, stage **06** overdo **07** play-act **09** overstate **10** arrange for, exaggerate **12** lay it on thick **14** present as a film, present as a play **15** make a big thing of

drape
◇ *containment indicator*
04 drop, fold, hang, veil, vest, wrap **05** adorn, cloak, cover, droop **06** shroud **07** arrange, envelop, overlay, suspend **08** decorate

drapery
05 arras, blind, cloth **06** blinds **07** curtain, hanging, valance, valence **08** backdrop, covering, curtains, hangings, mantling, tapestry **09** coverings **10** jardinière, lambrequin

drastic
◇ *anagram indicator*
03 bad **04** dire **05** harsh **06** severe, strong **07** extreme, radical, serious, violent **08** dramatic, forceful, forcible, rigorous **09** desperate, Draconian, swingeing **10** unpleasant **11** far-reaching

drastically
07 greatly **08** severely, strongly **09** extremely, radically, seriously **10** forcefully, rigorously

draught
03 cup **04** flow, gulp, puff, pull, rush, swig **05** draft, drink, privy, quaff, swill **06** breath, drench, influx, potion, waucht, waught **07** current, drawing, pulling, swallow **08** cesspool, dragging, movement, potation, quantity, quencher, traction **10** attraction **12** williewaught

draw
02 go **03** get, lug, tap, tie, tow, tug **04** bait, come, drag, haul, limn, lure, milk, move, pick, pull, pump, suck, take, walk **05** chart, drain, drive, frame, go for, infer, paint, sweep, trace, trail **06** allure, appeal, be even, choose, come to, deduce, depict, design, doodle, elicit, entice, gather, infuse, inhale, map out, obtain, pencil, prompt, raffle, reason, remove, resort, select, siphon, sketch, travel **07** advance, attract, be equal, bring in, extract, inspire, lottery, portray, proceed, procure, produce, pull out, receive, respire, take out, tombola **08** approach, bring out, conclude, dead heat, decide on, describe, interest, lengthen, persuade, plump for, progress, scribble, withdraw **09** breathe in, delineate, influence, magnetism, represent, stalemate, unsheathe **10** attraction, enticement, eviscerate, sweepstake **11** be all square

• draw back
04 cock, funk **05** wince **06** boggle, flinch, recoil, retire, shrink **07** fall off, retract, retreat **08** withdraw **09** start back **10** disadvance

• draw in
◇ *containment indicator*
04 pull, suck **05** hunch, rough **06** absorb, inhale **07** involve, retract **08** contract

• draw near
04 come, nigh **08** approach

• draw on
03 use **05** apply, train **06** allure, call on, employ, induce, lead on, quarry, rely on **07** exploit, utilize **08** approach, put to use **09** make use of **14** have recourse to

• draw out
04 make, spin, tose, toze **05** educe, evoke, leave, start, toaze **06** depart, extend, set out **07** drag out, extract,

move out, prolong, pull out, spin out, stretch **08** continue, elongate, lengthen, protract **09** put at ease **12** induce to talk **13** induce to speak **15** encourage to talk

• draw together

04 knit **06** gather **07** close up **08** astringe, contract **10** constringe

• draw up

04 halt, stop **05** draft, frame, run in **06** pull up **07** compile, compose, make out, prepare **08** write out **09** formulate **12** put in writing

• goalless draw

02 0-0

drawback

03 out **04** flaw, snag **05** catch, fault, hitch **06** damper, defect, hurdle **07** barrier, problem, take-off, trouble **08** handicap, nuisance, obstacle, pullback, weak spot **09** hindrance, liability **10** deficiency, difficulty, disamenity, disbenefit, disutility, impediment, limitation **12** disadvantage, imperfection **14** discouragement, stumbling-block

drawer

02 dr **04** till **07** shottle, shuttle

• bottom drawer

08 glory box **09** hope chest

drawing

05 study **06** pencil, pin-man, sketch **07** cartoon, diagram, graphic, outline, picture **08** graffito, portrait, scribble **09** attrahent, depiction, pen-and-ink, portrayal **11** composition, delineation, scenography **12** illustration **14** representation

drawl

03 haw **05** drant, drone, twang **06** dawdle, draunt, haw-haw **08** protract **09** say slowly **11** speak slowly

drawn

◇ *anagram indicator*

04 taut, worn **05** gaunt, tense, tired **06** closed, sapped **07** fraught, haggard, hassled, pinched **08** fatigued, harassed, strained, stressed **09** etiolated, washed out **10** unsheathed **11** eviscerated

dread

03 awe, shy **04** dire, fear, funk, fury **05** alarm, awful, quail, qualm, worry **06** dismay, feared, flinch, fright, grisly, horror, terror **07** dreaded, ghastly, shudder, tremble **08** alarming, blue funk, cringe at, disquiet, dreadful, frighten, gastness, gruesome, horrible, terrible **09** cold sweat, frightful, gastnesse, ghastness, misgiving **10** be afraid of, be scared of, blind panic, shrink from, terrifying **11** fit of terror, frightening, trepidation **12** apprehension, awe-inspiring, perturbation **13** be terrified by **14** be anxious about, be frightened by, be worried about

See also **phobia**

dreadful

◇ *anagram indicator*

04 dern, dire, grim **05** awful, dearn, nasty **06** awsome, tragic **07** awesome, ghastly, heinous, hideous **08** alarming, grievous, horrible, horrific, shocking, terrible, terrific **09** appalling, frightful **10** abortional, calamitous, horrendous, outrageous, terrifying, tremendous, unpleasant **11** frightening

dreadfully

◇ *anagram indicator*

04 very **07** awfully **08** terribly **09** extremely **10** shockingly **11** appallingly, atrociously, exceedingly, frightfully **12** horrendously

dream

03 aim, joy **04** dwam, goal, hope, long, mare, muse, plan, wish **05** crave, dwalm, dwaum, fancy, ideal, mirth, model, music, sound, yearn **06** beauty, design, desire, marvel, superb, sweven, trance, vision **07** aisling, delight, fantasy, imagine, perfect, phantom, reverie, supreme **08** ambition, daydream, delusion, envisage, illusion, somniate, yearning **09** excellent, fantasize, nightmare, pipe dream, switch off, wonderful **10** aspiration, minstrelsy, perfection **11** expectation, hallucinate, imagination, inattention, speculation **12** want very much **13** be lost in space, hallucination **14** phantasmagoria, stare into space **15** castles in the air, not pay attention

• dream up

04 spin **05** hatch **06** create, devise, invent **07** concoct, imagine, think up **08** conceive, contrive **09** conjure up, fabricate

• not dream of

08 not think **10** not imagine **11** not conceive, not consider

dreamer

07 Utopian **08** idealist, romancer, romantic **09** fantasist, stargazer, theorizer, visionary **10** daydreamer, fantasizer

dreamily

06 gently, softly **08** absently **10** peacefully, pleasantly **12** romantically

dreamlike

06 unreal **07** phantom, surreal **08** ethereal, illusory **09** fantastic, visionary **10** chimerical, trance-like **13** hallucinatory, insubstantial, unsubstantial **14** phantasmagoric

dreamy

03 dim **04** hazy, soft **05** faint, misty, moony, spacy, vague **06** absent, gentle, lovely, musing, spacey, unreal **07** calming, faraway, lulling, pensive, shadowy, unclear **08** ethereal, fanciful, relaxing, romantic, soothing **09** fantastic, imaginary, visionary **10** abstracted, idealistic, indistinct, thoughtful **11** daydreaming, fantasizing, impractical, preoccupied **12** absent-minded **13** wool-gathering

drearily

08 boringly, dismally **09** routinely, tediously **11** monstrously **12** depressingly

dreary

03 sad **04** dark, drab, dull **05** bleak, oorie, ourie, owrie **06** boring, dismal, dreich, gloomy, gousty, sombre **07** humdrum, routine, tedious **08** desolate, ghastful, lifeless, mournful, overcast, unvaried **09** cheerless, ghastfull, wearisome **10** colourless, depressing, monotonous, uneventful **11** commonplace, featureless **12** run-of-the-mill **13** uninteresting

dredge

• dredge up

05 dig up, raise **06** drag up, draw up, fish up, rake up **07** scoop up, uncover, unearth **08** discover

dregs

04 lags, lees, scum **05** draff, dross, legge, trash, waste **06** bottom, dunder, faeces, fecula, graves, mother, rabble, tramps, ullage **07** bottoms, deposit, dossers, greaves, grounds, residue, taplash **08** detritus, outcasts, residuum, riff-raff, sediment, tailings, vagrants **09** excrement, scourings, sublimate **10** faex populi **11** down-and-outs, precipitate

drench

03 wet **04** duck, soak **05** douse, drook, drouk, drown, flood, imbue, souse, steep, swamp **06** embrue, imbrue, sluice **07** embrewe, immerse **08** inundate, permeate, saturate **09** milk shake **13** soak to the skin

dress

◇ *anagram indicator*

02 do **03** don, fig, fit, ray, rig, tog **04** boun, busk, comb, deck, doll, draw, garb, gear, gown, rail, robe, tend, tidy, tiff, tift, tire, togs, trim, wear **05** adorn, array, bowne, chide, clean, cover, drape, erect, frock, get-up, groom, guise, habit, preen, primp, put on, style, treat **06** adjust, attire, betrim, bind up, clothe, finish, fit out, graith, manure, outfit, smooth, swathe, thrash **07** apparel, arrange, bandage, bravery, clobber, clothes, costume, deck out, dispose, flatten, garment, garnish, get into, prepare, throw on, turn out **08** accoutre, clothing, decorate, ensemble, garments, get ready, slip into **10** habiliment, straighten **13** put a plaster on **14** wearing-apparel

See also **clothes, clothing**

Dresses include:

03 mob

04 ball, coat, maxi, sack, sari, tent

05 shift, shirt, smock, tasar

06 caftan, dirndl, jumper, kaftan, kimono, muu-muu, sheath, tusser

07 bathing, chemise, evening, gym slip, kitenge, matinee, matinée, tussore, wedding

08 ball-gown, cocktail, gym tunic, negligée, pinafore, princess, sundress
09 cheongsam, farandine, going-away, minidress, slammakin, trollopee
10 dinner-gown, farrandine, slammerkin, wraparound
11 d'écolletage, Dolly Varden, riding habit
12 shirtwaister

• dress down
05 chide, scold **06** berate, carpet, rebuke, thrash **07** reprove, rouse on, tell off, tick off, upbraid **09** castigate, reprimand **13** dress casually, give a rocket to, tear off a strip, tear strips off **15** dress informally

• dress up
◇ *anagram indicator*
04 deck, gild, perk **05** adorn, dizen, tog up **06** buck up, doll up, dude up, jazz up, tart up **07** dandify, improve **08** beautify, decorate, disguise, ornament **09** embellish **10** masquerade **12** dress smartly **13** dress formally

dresser

• showy dresser
03 cat **04** beau

• special dresser
03 Mod

dressing

◇ *anagram indicator*
03 jus, pad **04** lint **05** gauze, patch, sauce, spica **06** coulis, relish **07** bandage, Band-aid®, clothes, plaster **08** compress, ligature, poultice **09** condiment **10** tourniquet **11** Elastoplast®, vinaigrette

See also **salad**

dressmaker

06 tailor **07** modiste **09** couturier, midinette, tailoress **10** couturière, seamstress **11** mantua-maker, needlewoman, sewing woman **12** garment-maker

dressy

05 natty, ritzy, sharp, showy, smart, swish **06** classy, formal, ornate **07** elegant, stylish **09** elaborate

dribble

03 run **04** drib, drip, drop, foam, leak, ooze, seep, spit **05** drool, exude, froth, gloop **06** drivel, saliva, slaver **07** droplet, seepage, slobber, trickle **10** sprinkling

dried

04 arid, sear, sere **06** wilted **07** drained, parched, wizened **08** withered **09** mummified **10** dehydrated, desiccated, exsiccated, shrivelled

drier

04 oast **07** tumbler

drift

◇ *anagram indicator*
03 aim, sag **04** bank, core, crab, flow, ford, gist, heap, hull, mass, pile, rack, roam, rove, rush, vein, waft, wisp **05** amass, coast, drive, drove, float, mound, point, scope, shift, stray, sweep, tenor, trend **06** course, design, gather, heap up, import, leeway, pierce, pile up, stream, thrust, tunnel, wander, wreath **07** current, driving, essence, meaning, purport **08** movement, tendency **09** direction, freewheel, intention, substance, variation **10** accumulate, digression **11** implication **12** accumulation, significance **14** be carried along **15** go with the stream

drifter

04 hobo **05** nomad, rover, tramp **06** drover **07** swagger, swagman, vagrant **08** vagabond, wanderer **09** itinerant, sundowner, traveller **11** beachcomber **12** rolling stone

drill

02 PE, PT **03** awl, bit **04** bore **05** borer, coach, prick, punch, teach, train **06** gimlet, ground, jumper, manual, pierce, reamer, school, seeder **07** routine, tuition, wildcat **08** coaching, exercise, instruct, practice, practise, puncture, rehearse, training **09** exercises, grounding, inculcate, penetrate, perforate, procedure **10** discipline, jackhammer, repetition **11** counterbore, inculcation, instruction, make a hole in, preparation **13** square-bashing **14** indoctrination, manual exercise

drink

03 bib, cup, jar, lap, nip, one, peg, sea, sip, sup, tot **04** brew, down, dram, grog, gulp, have, lush, neck, pint, pull, shot, suck, swig, tass, tiff, tift, tope, toss **05** booze, drain, hooch, juice, plonk, quaff, revel, sauce, smoke, swill, tinct, toast **06** absorb, grog on, guzzle, hootch, imbibe, liquid, liquor, rotgut, salute, swally, tank up, tiddly, tipple **07** alcohol, carouse, draught, drink to, indulge, shicker, spirits, swallow **08** aperitif, beverage, get drunk, infusion **09** firewater, get pissed, hard stuff, knock back, overdrink, partake of, polish off, soft drink, stiffener, the bottle, throw back **10** amber fluid **11** have too much, jungle juice, refreshment, strong drink, the creature, tickle-brain **12** Dutch courage, go on the shout, hit the bottle **13** knock back a few **14** be a hard drinker, drink like a fish, have one too many, thirst-quencher **15** be a heavy drinker, propose a toast to

See also **glass**

Alcoholic drinks include:

02 it
03 ale, dop, gin, kir, mum, nog, rum, rye, tay
04 arak, beer, bull, fine, flip, grog, hock, mead, nipa, ouzo, pils, port, purl, sake, saki, sour, sura, vino, wine
05 cider, G and T, lager, perry, Pimm's®, plonk, stout, vodka
06 arrack, bishop, brandy, bubbly, Cognac, eggnog, grappa, porter, poteen, Scotch, shandy, sherry, whisky
07 alcopop, aquavit, Bacardi®, bourbon, Campari, Gordon's®, liqueur, Marsala, Martell®, martini, oloroso, pink gin, red wine, retsina, sangria, sloe gin, spirits, tequila, vin rosé, whiskey
08 advocaat, Armagnac, Calvados, cold duck, Guinness®, hot toddy, schnapps, Smirnoff®, vermouth, vin blanc, vin rouge
09 badminton, Beefeater®, champagne, cocktails, Laphroaig®, snakebite, white wine, Wincarnis®
10 ginger wine, Remy Martin®
11 black-and-tan, boilermaker, Courvoisier®, gin-and-tonic, Glenfiddich®, Irish coffee, Jack Daniel's®
12 Famous Grouse®, Glenmorangie®, malternative
13 peach schnapps, Scotch and soda
14 Bombay Sapphire®

See also **beer**; **cocktail**; **liqueur**; **spirits**; **wine**

Non-alcoholic drinks include:

03 cha, pop, tea
04 Coke®, cola, kola, milk, soda
05 assai, Assam, cocoa, float, julep, latte, mixer, Pepsi®, tonic, water
06 coffee, Indian, Irn-Bru®, Ribena®, squash, tisane
07 beef tea, cordial, limeade, Perrier®, seltzer
08 café noir, China tea, Coca-Cola®, Earl Grey, espresso, expresso, fruit tea, green tea, Horlicks®, lemonade, lemon tea, Lucozade®, Ovaltine®, root beer, smoothie
09 Aqua Libra®, ayahuasco, Canada Dry®, cherryade, cream soda, ginger ale, herbal tea, milk shake, mint-julep, orangeade, soda water
10 café au lait, café filtre, cappuccino, fizzy drink, fruit juice, ginger beer, rosehip tea, still water, tonic water, Vichy water
11 barley water, bitter lemon, camomile tea
12 hot chocolate, mineral water, sarsaparilla
13 peppermint tea, Turkish coffee
14 sparkling water
15 lapsang souchong

Drinks of the gods include:

06 amrita, nectar
08 ambrosia

Special drinks include:

03 ava
04 kava, soma
05 haoma
09 ayahuasco

• drink hard
04 bend, tank **06** bezzle

• **drink in**
05 grasp **06** absorb, digest, imbibe, take in **07** inhaust, realize **10** appreciate

drinkable
04 safe **05** clean **07** potable **10** fit to drink

drinker
03 sot **04** lush, soak, wino **05** alkie, dipso, drunk, toper **06** barfly, boozer, sponge, sucker **07** imbiber, pint-pot, tippler, tosspot **08** drunkard **09** fuddle-cap, inebriate **10** winebibber **11** dipsomaniac, froth-blower, hard drinker **12** heavy drinker **14** serious drinker
• **reformed drinkers**
02 AA

drinking
◇ *insertion indicator*
• **drinking cup**
03 nut, tig, tot **04** bowl, tass **05** cylix, kylix **06** cotyle, goblet, quaich, quaigh, rhyton **07** chalice, scyphus **09** cantharus **10** parting-cup
• **drinking session**
03 bat, bum **04** bend, bevy, bout, bust, lush, sesh **05** bevvy, binge, blind, booze, drunk, spree **06** beer-up, bender, bottle, fuddle, grog-on, grog-up, razzle, screed **07** blinder, booze-up, carouse, session, wassail
• **expressions relating to drinking**
04 evoe, rivo, skol **05** evhoe, evohe, skoal **06** cheers, prosit **07** slàinte **08** chin-chin **10** good health **12** mud in your eye
• **given to drinking**
03 wet

drip
02 IV **03** wet **04** bead, bore, drop, leak, ooze, plop, tear, weed, weep, wimp **05** gloop, ninny, pansy, sissy, softy **06** filter, splash **07** dewdrop, dribble, drizzle, trickle **08** sprinkle, weakling **09** percolate **10** stillicide
• **dripping**
03 fat

drive
02 ca', Dr, go **03** caa', dig, put, ram, ren, rin, run, tax, vim, zip **04** bear, come, dash, firk, goad, herd, hunt, hurl, lash, lead, move, need, prod, push, rack, rate, ride, road, send, sink, spin, spur, take, trip, turn, urge, will **05** carry, chase, drift, fight, force, guide, impel, jaunt, knock, motor, pilot, power, press, screw, steer, surge, thump, verve **06** action, appeal, avenue, battle, burden, coerce, compel, convey, desire, direct, effort, energy, hammer, handle, incite, manage, oblige, outing, pizazz, plunge, prompt, propel, spirit, strike, thrust, travel, vigour **07** actuate, control, crusade, dragoon, enforce, go by car, impulse, journey, operate, overtax, provoke, resolve, roadway, round up **08** ambition, appetite, approach, campaign, driveway, instinct, motivate, movement, overdo it, overwork, persuade, pressure, struggle, tenacity **09** chauffeur, come by car, constrain, excursion, transport **10** enterprise, get-up-and-go, initiative, motivation, overburden, pressurize, propulsion **11** give a lift to, travel by car, work too hard **12** be at the wheel, kill yourself, transmission **13** determination **14** propeller shaft **15** be at the controls
• **drive at**
04 hint, mean **05** aim at, get at, imply **06** intend **07** refer to, signify, suggest **08** allude to, indicate, intimate **09** insinuate **10** have in mind
• **drive away**
04 hunt, shoo **05** chase **06** banish, dispel **07** repulse **08** exorcize
• **drive down**
03 ram
• **drive fast**
04 race **05** speed
• **drive inconsiderately**
03 hog
• **drive out**
04 fire **05** expel, wreak **07** turn out **11** exterminate
• **prepare to drive**
03 tee

drivel
03 rot **04** blah, bull, crap, drip, guff **05** balls, bilge, drool, hooey, slush, tripe **06** bunkum, slaver, waffle **07** baloney, dribble, eyewash, garbage, hogwash, maunder, rhubarb, rubbish, slabber, twaddle **08** claptrap, malarkey, nonsense **09** gibberish, poppycock **10** balderdash, mumbo-jumbo **12** gobbledygook

driver
02 Dr **04** Jehu, whip **05** mizen, rider **06** cabbie, jarvey, jarvie, mizzen **07** locoman, taximan, trucker, truckie **08** bullocky, motorist, muleteer, roadsman, truckman **09** chauffeur **12** motorcyclist **15** knight of the road
See also **racing**
• **new driver**
01 L

drivers
02 AA **03** RAC

driving
05 heavy **07** dynamic, violent **08** forceful, sweeping, vigorous **09** energetic **10** compelling, forthright

drizzle
04 drip, drop, mist, pour, rain, smir, smur, spit, spot **05** smirr, spray **06** mizzle, shower **07** dribble, scowder, skiffle, trickle **08** fine rain, scouther, scowther, sprinkle **09** light rain **10** rain finely, Scotch mist **11** rain lightly

droll
03 odd, rum **04** jest, zany **05** comic, funny, queer, witty **06** jester **07** amusing, bizarre, comical, jocular, risible, waggish **08** clownish, farcical, humorous, peculiar **09** diverting, eccentric, laughable, ludicrous, whimsical **10** ridiculous **12** entertaining

drone
03 dor, hum **04** buzz, dorr, purr **05** chant, drant, drawl, idler, leech, thrum, whirr **06** bumble, bummle, dog-bee, doodle, draunt, intone, loafer **07** bourdon, dreamer, goof-off, slacker, sponger, vibrate **08** hanger-on, layabout, parasite, whirring **09** bombilate, bombinate, go on and on, lazybones, murmuring, scrounger, vibration **10** lazy person **11** goldbricker

drool
04 dote, gush **05** gloat **06** drivel, slaver **07** dribble, enthuse, slobber **08** salivate **11** slobber over **15** water at the mouth

droop
03 bow, lob, nod, sag **04** bend, drop, fade, flag, peak, sink, weep, wilt **05** faint, slink, slump, stoop **06** dangle, falter, nutate, slouch, wither **07** decline **08** fall down, hang down, languish, pendency **09** lose heart

droopy
03 lax **04** lank, limp, weak **05** loose, saggy, slack **06** feeble, floppy **07** falling, sagging **08** drooping, dropping

drop
◇ *deletion indicator*
02 gt **03** bit, can, dab, end, lay, nip, sip, tad, tot **04** bead, blob, cast, dash, dive, drib, drip, fall, fire, glob, gout, jilt, land, leak, omit, plop, quit, sack, shed, sink, spat, spot, stop, take, tear **05** abyss, bring, candy, carry, cease, chasm, chuck, cliff, ditch, droop, forgo, gutta, lapse, let go, lower, pinch, slope, slump, sweet, trace **06** bonbon, bubble, desert, disown, dragée, drappy, finish, forego, give up, goutte, humbug, lessen, little, plunge, put off, reject, splash, tumble, weaken **07** abandon, boot out, cutback, decline, deliver, descend, descent, dismiss, drappie, dribble, driblet, droplet, dwindle, exclude, fall off, forsake, globule, let fall, let go of, lozenge, miss out, modicum, pendant, plummet, smidgen, sweetie, trickle, turf out **08** decrease, diminish, downturn, dribblet, globulet, leave out, lowering, mouthful, pastille, renounce, run out on, spheroid, sprinkle **09** bespatter, declivity, discharge, precipice, reduction, repudiate, terminate, throw over, transport, walk out on **10** falling-off, finish with, relinquish, slacken off **11** devaluation, discontinue **12** depreciation, dispense with **13** deterioration, make redundant
• **drop back**
03 lag **07** retreat **08** fall back **09** lag behind **10** fall behind
• **drop in**
04 call **05** pop in, visit **06** call by, come

by, instil **07** instill **08** come over **09** call round, come round

• drop off

04 doze, sink **05** go off **06** catnap, depart, hand in, lessen, nod off, plunge, snooze, unload **07** decline, deliver, deposit, doze off, dwindle, fall off, plummet, set down **08** decrease, diminish, drift off **09** disappear **10** fall asleep, slacken off **14** have forty winks

• drop out

04 quit **05** leave **06** cry off, give up **07** abandon, back out, forsake **08** renounce, withdraw

• drop out of

04 quit **05** leave **06** opt out, renege **07** abandon, pull out **08** opt out of, renege on, renounce **09** back out of **10** cry off from **12** withdraw from

dropout

05 loner, rebel **06** hippie **07** beatnik, deviant **08** Bohemian, renegade **09** dissenter **10** malcontent **11** dissentient **13** nonconformist

droppings

04 dung, scat, skat **06** egesta, faeces, manure, ordure, stools **07** excreta, spraint **09** excrement

dross

04 junk, lees, rust, scum, slag **05** dregs, lucre, slack, trash, waste **06** debris, refuse, scoria **07** remains, rubbish **08** impurity **09** recrement

drought

04 want **06** drouth, thirst **07** aridity, dryness **08** shortage **11** dehydration, desiccation, parchedness

drove

03 mob **04** herd, host, pack **05** crowd, crush, drift, flock, horde, press, swarm **06** string, throng **07** company **09** gathering, multitude

drown

02 go **03** die **04** sink **05** flood, swamp **06** deluge, drench, engulf, perish **07** founder, go under, howl out, immerse, silence, wipe out **08** drown out, inundate, outvoice, overcome, submerge **09** overpower, overwhelm **10** extinguish **12** lose your life

drowsily

06 dopily, dozily **07** wearily **08** sleepily **10** sluggishly **13** lethargically

drowsiness

06 torpor **08** dopiness, doziness, lethargy, narcosis **09** oscitancy, tiredness, weariness **10** grogginess, sleepiness, somnolence, somnolency **12** sluggishness

drowsy

04 dozy, dull **05** dopey, dozed, heavy, tired, weary **06** bleary, dozing, dreamy, sleepy, torpid **07** nodding, slumbry, yawning **08** comatose, slumbery **09** lethargic, somnolent **10** half-asleep **11** heavy-headed

drubbing

06 defeat **07** beating, licking **08** flogging, pounding, whipping **09** hammering, thrashing, trouncing, walloping **10** clobbering, cudgelling, pummelling

drudge

04 drug, hack, moil, plod, toil, work **05** devil, droil, grind, grunt, scrub, slave, snake, sweat **06** beaver, labour, lackey, menial, skivvy, slavey, stooge, toiler, worker **07** servant **08** dogsbody, factotum, labourer, plug away, slog away, trauchle **09** packhorse **10** afterguard, Cinderella **11** galley-slave

drudgery

03 fag **04** slog, toil **05** chore, grind, sweat, yakka **06** labour, yacker, yakker **07** faggery, slavery **08** hackwork, trauchle **09** skivvying, slaistery, spadework, treadmill **10** collar-work, donkey-work, menial work **13** sweated labour

drug

04 cure, dose, numb **06** deaden, drudge, potion, remedy, sedate **07** stupefy **08** knock out, medicate, medicine, shanghai **09** stimulant **10** medication **12** anaesthetize, tranquillize **15** make unconscious

See also **medicine**

Medicinal drugs include:

03 AZT
04 Soma®
05 Intal®, NSAID, salep, Taxol®, Zyban®
06 opiate, Prozac®, statin, sulpha, Valium®, Viagra®, Zantac®
07 antacid, aspirin, codeine, heparin, insulin, Nurofen®, quinine, Relenza®, Ritalin®, Seroxat®, steroid
08 Antabuse®, diazepam, diuretic, hyoscine, methadon, morphine, narcotic, neomycin, orlistat, Rohypnol®, sedative, warfarin
09 aciclovir, acyclovir, analgesic, co-codamol, cortisone, digitalis, ibuprofen, methadone, oestrogen, stimulant, tamoxifen, temazepam
10 antibiotic, anxiolytic, chloroform, chloroquin, dimorphine, interferon, penicillin, ranitidine, salbutamol
11 allopurinol, amoxycillin, amyl nitrate, anaesthetic, beta-blocker, chloroquine, cyclosporin, haloperidol, ipecacuanha, neuroleptic, paracetamol, propranolol, vasodilator
12 ACE-inhibitor, chlorambucil, methotrexate, progesterone, sleeping pill, streptomycin, sulphonamide, tetracycline
13 antibacterial, anticoagulant, antihistamine, streptokinase, tranquillizer
14 anticonvulsant, antidepressant, azidothymidine, bronchodilator, corticosteroid, erythropoietin, hallucinogenic, hydrocortisone
15 chloramphenicol, vasoconstrictor

Recreational drugs include:

01 C, E, H
03 hop, ice, kef, kif, LSD, PCP, pot, tab
04 acid, bang, barb, blow, coca, coke, dope, dove, gage, hash, hemp, junk, kaif, pill, scag, skag, snow, weed
05 bhang, crack, crank, dagga, horse, jelly, opium, shmek, smack, speed, sugar, upper
06 basuco, charas, downer, heroin, mescal, peyote, pituri, popper
07 charlie, churrus, cocaine, crystal, ecstasy, fantasy, guaraná, pep pill, roofies, schmeck
08 cannabis, freebase, ketamine, laudanum, meconium, mescalin, methadon, moonrock, morphine, nepenthe, Rohypnol, snowball, Special K
09 angel dust, dance drug, marijuana, mescaline, methadone, nose candy, peace pill, ready-wash, speedball, temazepam
10 white stuff
11 amphetamine, barbiturate, purple heart
12 date-rape drug
13 phencyclidine

See also **cannabis**; **cocaine**; **heroin**

• drug dose

03 fix **05** bolus

• drug experience

04 trip

drug addict

04 head, hype, user **05** freak **06** junkie **07** druggie, hop-head, tripper **08** coke-head, snowbird **09** dope-fiend, mainliner

drugged

04 high **05** doped **06** ripped, stoned, wasted, zonked **07** on a trip **08** comatose, hopped-up, turned on **09** spaced out, stupefied **10** knocked out

drum

03 rap, tap **04** beat, dhol, reel, swag **05** bongo, conga, daiko, house, knock, naker, ridge, tabor, taiko, throb, thrum **06** atabal, barrel, bundle, cannon, kettle, rigger, tabour, tabret, tam-tam, tattoo, timbal, tom-tom, tum-tum, tymbal **07** bodhrán, drumlin, mridang, pulsate, tambour, timpano, tympano **08** mridanga, tympanum **09** mridamgam, mridangam **11** reverberate

• drum into

06 hammer, harp on, instil **07** din into **09** drive home, inculcate, reiterate

• drum out

05 expel **07** dismiss **08** throw out **09** discharge

• drum up

03 get **06** gather, obtain, summon **07** attract, canvass, collect, round up, solicit **08** petition

drumbeat

04 flam, roll, ruff, touk, tuck **05** hurry

06 rafale, rappel, rattan, tattoo
08 assembly 10 paradiddle

drummer
02 Dr 07 swagman 09 timpanist, tympanist

drunk
◇ *anagram indicator*
03 fap, fou, lit, sot, wat, wet 04 full, high, inky, lush, paid, soak, wino
05 alkie, dipso, foxed, happy, inked, lit up, merry, moppy, slued, tight, tipsy, toper, woozy 06 blotto, bombed, boozer, canned, corked, in wine, jagged, jarred, juiced, loaded, mashed, mellow, mortal, ratted, ripped, slewed, soused, sponge, stewed, stinko, stoned, tanked, tiddly, wasted
07 bevvied, bonkers, bottled, crocked, drinker, drunken, ebriose, fairish, half-cut, legless, maggoty, pickled, pie-eyed, shicker, sloshed, smashed, sozzled, squiffy, tiddled, tiddley, tippler, tosspot, trashed, wrecked
08 bibulous, drunkard, footless, hammered, in liquor, juiced up, liquored, moon-eyed, overseen, overshot, sow-drunk, stocious, stotious, tanked up, whiffled, whistled
09 alcoholic, blootered, crapulent, incapable, inebriate, inebrious, paralytic, plastered, saturated, shickered, stonkered, up the pole, well-oiled 10 blind drunk, capernoity, inebriated, obfuscated 11 capernoitie, cappernoity, dipsomaniac, hard drinker, high as a kite, intoxicated, on the tiddly, slaughtered 12 drunk as a lord, drunk as a newt, heavy drinker, roaring drunk 13 drunk as a piper, drunk as a skunk, having had a few, under the table 14 Brahms and Liszt
15 a sheet in the wind, one over the eight, the worse for wear, under the weather

• getting drunk
02 on 12 half-seas-over 13 mops and brooms

• make drunk
03 cup 05 sew up, souse 07 tipsify
09 inebriate 10 intoxicate

drunkard
03 sot 04 lush, soak, wino 05 alkie, bloat, dipso, drunk, souse, toper
06 boozer, sponge 07 bloater, drinker, fuddler, hophead, shicker, tippler, tosspot 08 bacchant, habitual
09 alcoholic, inebriate 10 wine-bibber 11 dipsomaniac, hard drinker
12 heavy drinker

drunken
◇ *anagram indicator*
03 wat 05 boozy, drunk, happy, lit up, merry, tight, tipsy 06 bombed, boozey, loaded, spongy, stoned, tiddly 07 Bacchic, drucken, riotous, sloshed 08 Bacchian, besotted
09 crapulent, debauched, inebriate, worthless 10 dissipated
11 baccanalian, intemperate, intoxicated

drunkenness
07 ebriety, ivresse 08 methysis
09 ebriosity, inebriety, temulence, tipsiness 10 alcoholism, crapulence, debauchery, dipsomania, insobriety
11 inebriation 12 bibulousness, hard drinking, intemperance, intoxication
13 St Martin's evil 15 serious drinking

dry
02 TT 03 air, sec, xer- 04 arid, brut, dull, fair, flat, kiln, sear, seco, sere, welt, wilt, wipe, xero- 05 baked, drain, droll, husky, parch, secco, witty, xeric
06 barren, boring, clever, dreary, formal, frigid, ironic, low-key, rizzar, rizzer, rizzor, scorch, subtle, torrid, wilted, wither 07 cutting, cynical, deadpan, drouthy, gasping, hirstie, laconic, make dry, parched, precise, shrivel, tedious, thirsty, trocken
08 droughty, rainless, scorched, teetotal, withered 09 abstinent, become dry, dehydrate, desiccate, dry as dust, sarcastic, temperate, unwatered, waterless, wearisome
10 abstemious, dehumidify, dehydrated, desiccated, dry as a bone, monotonous, on the wagon, shrivelled, unbuttered, unexciting 11 alcohol-free
12 moistureless 13 uninteresting
14 prohibitionist

• dry up
04 fade, fail, sear, stop, wane 05 arefy
06 die out, ensear, scorch, shut up
07 dwindle 09 desiccate, disappear, exsiccate 11 come to an end, stop talking 15 forget your lines

dryness
06 drouth, thirst 07 aridity, drought, siccity, xerasia, xerosis 08 aridness
09 xerostoma 10 barrenness, xerostomia 11 dehydration, thirstiness

dual
04 twin 06 binary, double, duplex, paired 07 coupled, matched, twofold
08 combined, two-piece 09 duplicate

duality
07 twoness 09 duplicity
10 doubleness, opposition, separation
11 combination, duplication
12 polarization

dub
03 tag 04 call, name, term, trim
05 label, style 06 bestow, confer, puddle 07 entitle 08 christen, nickname 09 designate

dubiety
05 doubt, qualm 08 mistrust
09 misgiving, suspicion 10 hesitation, indecision, scepticism 11 incertitude, uncertainty 12 doubtfulness

dubious
◇ *anagram indicator*
04 iffy 05 crook, fishy, shady 06 shifty, unsure 07 obscure, suspect
08 doubtful, elliptic, hesitant, wavering
09 ambiguous, debatable, sceptical, uncertain, undecided, unsettled
10 backhanded, elliptical, irresolute, left-handed, suspicious, unreliable
11 vacillating 12 questionable
13 untrustworthy

dubiously
09 debatably 10 hesitantly
11 ambiguously, uncertainly, undecidedly 12 questionably, suspiciously

dubnium
02 Db

duchy
07 dukedom

duck
01 O 03 bob, dip, wet 04 bend, dive, dook, drop, dunk, jook, jouk, shun, zero 05 avoid, dodge, douse, drake, elude, evade, lower, shirk, skive, souse, squat, stoop, yield 06 cringe, crouch, plunge 07 bow down, darling, immerse 08 bankrupt, sidestep, submerge 09 defaulter 10 sweetheart
12 steer clear of, wriggle out of
See also **animal**

Ducks include:
04 blue, musk, smee, smew, surf, teal, wood
05 eider, Pekin, ruddy, scaup
06 burrow, hareld, herald, magpie, Peking, runner, scoter, smeath, smeeth, spirit, tufted, velvet, wigeon
07 crested, gadwall, mallard, moulard, muscovy, old wife, pintail, pochard, steamer
08 garganey, hookbill, mandarin, old squaw, shelduck
09 Cuthbert's, goldeneye, goosander, harlequin, merganser, sheldrake, shielduck, shoveller
10 bufflehead, canvasback, long-tailed, ring-necked
11 ferruginous, St Cuthbert's, white-headed
12 common scoter, Indian runner, velvet scoter
13 ruddy shelduck

• string of ducks
04 sord, team

• two ducks
02 OO 04 pair

duct
03 vas 04 pipe, tube 05 canal
06 funnel, ureter, vessel 07 channel, conduit, fistula, passage, Venturi, wireway 08 deferent, diffuser
09 emunctory, excretory 11 Venturi tube

ductile
06 pliant 07 plastic, pliable
08 amenable, biddable, flexible, tractile, yielding 09 compliant, malleable, tractable 10 manageable
11 manipulable

dud
03 bum 04 bust, duff, flop 05 kaput
06 broken, failed, faulty, stumer
07 failure, let-down, washout 08 bum steer, nugatory 09 conked out,

valueless, worthless **11** counterfeit, inoperative **14** disappointment

dude
03 cat, fop, Roy **04** buck, lair **05** dandy

dudgeon
04 hilt **05** pique **10** resentment

due
03 fee, fit, lot **04** dead, just, levy, owed, toll **05** ample, owing, right **06** charge, direct, earned, enough, merits, proper, rights, unpaid **07** awaited, charges, correct, deserts, dewfull, exactly, fitting, merited, payable, tribute **08** adequate, deserved, directly, expected, plenty of, required, rightful, straight, suitable **09** appointed, in arrears, justified, precisely, privilege, repayable, requisite, scheduled **10** birthright, sufficient **11** anticipated, appropriate, comeuppance, just deserts, long-awaited, outstanding, prerogative **12** contribution, subscription **13** membership fee

• **due to**
07 owing to **08** caused by **09** because of **11** as a result of

duel
04 tilt **05** clash, fight **06** battle, combat, duello **07** contest, rivalry **08** struggle **09** encounter, monomachy **10** dependence, engagement, monomachia **11** competition **14** affair of honour **15** affaire d'honneur

duff
◇ *anagram indicator*
03 bad **04** naff, poor, poxy, ropy, rump, weak **05** awful, dough, lousy, pants **06** broken, bungle, crummy, faulty **07** botched, the pits, useless **08** buttocks, hopeless, inferior, mediocre, pathetic, terrible **09** defective, deficient, imperfect, third-rate **10** inadequate, mismanaged, second-rate **11** incompetent, ineffective, poor-quality, substandard **12** unacceptable **14** a load of garbage, a load of rubbish, unsatisfactory

duffer
03 git, oaf **04** clod, clot, dolt, dork, fool, geek, muff, prat **05** fogey, idiot **06** dimwit **07** bungler, halfwit, plonker, rustler **08** bonehead **09** blunderer, ignoramus **11** cattle-thief

dugong
06 sea cow, sea-pig **08** halicore, sirenian

duke
01 D **04** fist, lord

dulcet
04 soft **05** sweet **06** gentle, mellow **08** pleasant, soothing **09** agreeable, melodious **10** harmonious **11** mellifluous **13** sweet-sounding

dulcimer
06 santir, santur **07** cembalo, cymbalo, santoor, santour **08** cimbalom **09** pantaleon

dull
03 dim, dry, mat, sad **04** blah, damp, dark, dead, dowf, dozy, drab, drug, dumb, fade, flat, gray, grey, idle, logy, matt, mild, mull, numb, slow, soft, tame, weak **05** allay, bland, blunt, cloud, corny, dense, dingy, dopey, dowdy, dowie, dusty, faint, gross, heavy, ho-hum, inert, lower, matte, murky, muted, plain, prose, prosy, quiet, rusty, slack, thick, vapid **06** barren, boring, bovine, cloudy, dampen, darken, deaden, deject, dismal, dreary, drowsy, feeble, gloomy, leaden, lessen, mopish, obtund, obtuse, opaque, opiate, rebate, reduce, sadden, sleepy, soften, sombre, sopite, stodgy, stupid, subdue, sullen, torpid, wooden **07** assuage, blacken, depress, disedge, doltish, humdrum, insipid, insulse, lumpish, muffled, mumpish, obscure, prosaic, relieve, stupefy, tedious, wash out **08** blockish, Boeotian, decrease, diminish, downcast, edgeless, hebetate, inactive, lifeless, mitigate, moderate, overcast, paralyse, sluggish, tiresome, tone down, toneless, workaday **09** alleviate, cheerless, dead-alive, dimwitted, inanimate, lethargic, ponderous, prosaical, wearisome **10** discourage, dishearten, indistinct, insensible, lackluster, lacklustre, monochrome, monotonous, pedestrian, perstringe, uneventful, unexciting **11** birdbrained, blunt-witted, desensitize, distressing, heavy-headed, stereotyped, stultifying, thick-witted, troublesome, unsharpened **12** dead-and-alive, thick-skulled, tranquillize **13** uncomfortable, unimaginative, unintelligent, uninteresting **15** slow on the uptake

• **become dull**
04 rust **05** blunt **07** tarnish **08** hebetate

dullard
03 git, oaf, owl **04** clod, clot, dolt, dope, dork, prat **05** chump, dumbo, dunce, idiot, moron **06** dimwit, nitwit **07** plonker **08** bonehead, imbecile, numskull **09** blockhead, ignoramus, simpleton **10** bufflehead, dunderhead

See also **fool**

dullness
04 drab, yawn **05** cloud **06** fadeur, tedium, torpor **07** dryness, vacuity **08** flatness, monotony, slowness, vapidity **09** emptiness, plainness **10** dreariness, oppression **12** sluggishness

duly
05 fitly **08** properly, suitably **09** correctly, fittingly **10** decorously, deservedly, rightfully, sure enough **11** accordingly, befittingly **13** appropriately

dumb
03 mum **04** dozy, mute **05** dense, dopey, shtum, stumm, thick **06** shtoom, shtumm, silent, stupid **07** foolish, schtoom **08** gormless **09** brainless, dim-witted, soundless **10** speechless, tongue-tied **12** inarticulate, lost for words **13** unintelligent, without speech **15** at a loss for words

• **dumb down**
07 deskill **08** simplify

dumbfound
03 wow **04** daze, stun **05** amaze, floor, shock **07** astound, flummox, stagger, startle, stupefy **08** astonish, bewilder, bowl over, confound, gobsmack, surprise **09** take aback **11** flabbergast, knock for six **12** blow your mind **15** knock all of a heap

dumbfounded
04 dumb **06** amazed, thrown **07** baffled, floored, stunned, stupent **08** confused, overcome, startled **09** astounded, paralysed, staggered **10** astonished, bewildered, bowled over, confounded, gobsmacked, nonplussed, speechless, taken aback **11** overwhelmed **12** lost for words **13** flabbergasted, knocked for six

dumbly
06 mutely **08** silently **11** soundlessly **12** speechlessly **14** inarticulately

dumbo *see* **fool**

dumbstruck
03 mum **04** dumb, mute **06** aghast, amazed, silent **07** shocked **09** astounded **10** speechless, tongue-tied **11** dumbfounded, obmutescent **12** inarticulate **13** thunderstruck

dummy
03 git, oaf **04** clot, copy, dork, fake, fool, form, mock, prat, sham, teat **05** bogus, chump, false, idiot, model, trial **06** dimwit, figure, mock-up, nitwit, phoney, sample, silent **07** feigned, plonker, soother **08** imbecile, numskull, pacifier, practice **09** blockhead, comforter, duplicate, imitation, lay-figure, mannequin, simulated **10** artificial, bufflehead, substitute **11** counterfeit **12** reproduction **14** representation

See also **fool**

dump
03 tip **04** bung, drop, hole, jilt, mess, park, pool, slum **05** chuck, ditch, hovel, joint, leave, place, plonk, scrap, shack, shoot, store **06** desert, marble, midden, pigpen, pigsty, shanty, tip out, unload **07** abandon, counter, deposit, discard, forsake, lay down, let fall, offload, pour out, put down, set down **08** empty out, get rid of, jettison, junkyard, throw out **09** chuck away, discharge, dispose of, fling down, scrapyard, throw away, throw down, walk out on **10** rubbish tip **11** rubbish heap **14** give the elbow to

• **down in the dumps**
03 low, sad **04** blue **07** unhappy **08** dejected, downcast **09** depressed,

miserable **10** dispirited, melancholy **11** downhearted
• **dumps**
08 doldrums

dumpling
06 dim sum, perogi, pirogi, won ton **07** gnocchi, knaidel, kneidel, pierogi **08** doughboy, quenelle **09** doughball, matzo ball **10** corn dodger

dumpster
04 skip

dumpy
05 plump, podgy, pudgy, short, squab, squat, stout, tubby **06** chubby, chunky, stubby

dun
04 dull, hill **05** dingy, dusky **06** harass, pester, plague **11** mud-coloured **12** greyish-brown **13** mouse-coloured

dunce
01 d **03** git **04** dork, fool, nerd, prat, twit **05** idiot, ninny, twerp, wally **06** dimwit, nitwit **07** dullard, plonker **08** bonehead, dipstick, imbecile, numskull **09** blockhead **10** bufflehead, loggerhead, nincompoop

dune *see* **sand dune, sand dunes** *under* **sand**

dung
04 chip, cock, dirt, muck, soil, tath **05** argol, dreck, guano, mulch, shard, sharn, siege **06** cowpat, doo-doo, faeces, fumets, manure, ordure **07** buttons, fewmets, scumber, skummer, spraint **08** spraints **09** droppings, excrement, spawn cake **10** spawn brick **11** animal waste **12** album Graecum, buffalo chips
• **devil's dung**
04 hing
• **dog's dung**
04 pure
• **plaster with dung**
04 leep

dung-beetle
03 dor **04** dorr **06** scarab **11** coprophagan

dungeon
04 cage, cell, gaol, jail, keep **05** vault **06** lock-up, prison **09** oubliette

dupe
03 con, gum, mug **04** cony, cull, flat, fool, geck, gull, hoax, pawn **05** cheat, coney, cully, shaft, trick **06** chouse, delude, diddle, outwit, plover, puppet, rip off, sitter, stooge, sucker, take in, victim **07** deceive, defraud, dottrel, fall guy, swindle **08** dotterel, hoodwink, pushover, soft mark **09** bamboozle, goldbrick, simpleton **10** instrument **11** make a fool of

duplicate
03 dup, fax **04** copy, echo, fold, like, mate, twin **05** clone, ditto, match, model, Roneo®, spare, Xerox® **06** carbon, double, paired, repeat, ringer **07** do again, forgery, matched, replica, twofold **08** matching **09** facsimile, identical, imitation, lookalike, photocopy, Photostat®, replicate, reproduce **10** carbon copy, dead ringer, equivalent, transcript **11** alternative, counterpart **12** reproduction **13** corresponding, spitting image

duplication
04 copy **05** clone **07** cloning, copying **08** doubling **09** photocopy **10** gemination, repetition **11** dittography, replication **12** photocopying, reproduction

duplicity
05 fraud, guile **06** deceit **07** perfidy **08** artifice, betrayal **09** chicanery, deception, falsehood, hypocrisy, mendacity, treachery **10** dishonesty, doubleness **11** insincerity **13** deceitfulness, dissimulation, double-dealing

durability
04 wear **07** durance, wearing **08** strength **09** constancy, endurance, longevity, stability **10** permanence **11** durableness, lastingness, persistence **15** imperishability

durable
04 fast, firm **05** fixed, hardy, pakka, pucka, pukka, solid, sound, tough **06** robust, stable, strong, sturdy **07** abiding, lasting **08** constant, enduring, reliable, unfading **09** heavy-duty, permanent, resistant **10** dependable, persistent, persisting, reinforced, unchanging **11** hard-wearing, long-lasting, serviceable, substantial

duration
04 span, term, time **05** spell **06** extent, length, period **07** stretch **08** fullness, standing, time span **09** endurance, time scale **10** protension **11** continuance, persistence, persistency, running time **12** continuation, length of time, perpetuation, prolongation

duress
05 force **06** threat **08** coercion, exaction, pressure **09** restraint **10** compulsion, constraint **11** arm-twisting, enforcement **12** imprisonment

during
◇ *insertion indicator*
02 in, of **03** dia-, for **04** over **07** pending **10** throughout **11** all the while, at the time of, in the time of **12** for the time of **13** in the course of, in the middle of

dusk
03 dim, eve **04** dark **05** gloom, shade **06** sunset **07** darkish, evening, shadows, sundown **08** darkness, gloaming, owl-light, twilight **09** nightfall **10** crepuscule **11** candlelight

dusky
03 dim, dun, sad **04** dark, hazy **05** black, brown, foggy, misty, murky, swart, tawny **06** cloudy, gloomy, phaeic, swarth, twilit **07** shadowy, subfusc, subfusk, swarthy, umbrose **09** tenebrous **10** fuliginous **11** crepuscular, dark-skinned **12** dark-coloured

dust
03 ash, mop **04** bort, clay, coom, culm, dirt, duff, fuzz, grit, mote, seed, smut, soil, soot, wipe **05** ashes, boart, brawl, brush, clean, cover, earth, grime, lemel, money, smoke, spray, stour **06** bedust, ground, limail, polish, pother, powder, pudder, spread **07** burnish, fallout, scatter, smother, turmoil **08** bulldust, sprinkle, stardust **09** particles, pozzolana **10** cryoconite, haemoconia **11** disturbance **13** meteor streams **14** micro-meteorite
• **dust storm**
05 devil **06** calima **07** Shaitan

dust-up
05 brawl, brush, fight, scrap, set-to **06** barney, bust-up, fracas, tussle **07** punch-up, quarrel, scuffle **08** argument, conflict, skirmish **09** argy-bargy, commotion, encounter **11** disturbance **12** disagreement

dusty
03 bad **04** dull **05** dirty, grimy, sandy, sooty **06** chalky, filthy, grubby, stoury **07** crumbly, friable, powdery **08** granular, lifeless **09** pulverous **11** dust-covered **12** contemptible, old-fashioned

Dutch
01 D **02** Du
• **Cape Dutch**
04 Taal

dutiful
05 pious **06** filial **07** devoted **08** obedient **09** compliant, officious **10** obsequious, respectful, submissive, thoughtful **11** considerate, deferential, reverential **13** conscientious

duty
03 job, tax **04** debt, dues, levy, onus, part, role, task, toll, work **05** chore **06** burden, charge, excise, office, tariff **07** calling, customs, loyalty, mission, respect, service **08** business, fidelity, function **09** deference, obedience **10** allegiance, assignment, attendance, commission, obligation **11** requirement **12** faithfulness **14** responsibility
• **active duty**
02 AD
• **duty list**
04 rota
• **off duty**
03 off **04** free **07** off work, resting **08** inactive **09** at leisure, not at work, on holiday **10** not working
• **on duty**
04 busy **06** active, at work, on call,

tied up **07** engaged, working **08** occupied

dwarf
03 elf, toy **04** baby, Mime, mini, tiny, trow **05** check, gnome, pigmy, pygmy, small, stunt, troll **06** arrest, droich, durgan, goblin, little, midget, minute, petite, pocket, retard **07** atrophy, manikin, stunted **08** Alberich, dominate, homuncle, mannikin, Tom Thumb **09** homuncule, miniature, tower over **10** diminutive, homunculus, overshadow, undersized **11** Lilliputian

Snow White's dwarfs:

03 Doc
05 Dopey, Happy
06 Grumpy, Sleepy, Sneezy
07 Bashful

dwell
03 won **04** bide, home, live, rest, stay **05** abide, lodge, stall **06** people, remain, reside, settle, tenant **07** hang out, inhabit, sojourn **08** populate **11** be domiciled
• dwell on
06 harp on **07** brood on **08** mull over **09** elaborate, emphasize, expatiate, reflect on **10** linger over, meditate on, ruminate on, think about

dweller
07 denizen **08** occupant, occupier, resident **10** inhabitant

dwelling
03 cot, dug, hut, won **04** flat, home, roof, tent, tipi, weem, woon **05** abode, bothy, bower, donga, gundy, house, hovel, humpy, lodge, place, tepee **06** grange, gunyah, mia-mia, pondok, shanty, teepee, wurley **07** cottage, doghole, lodging **08** domicile, messuage, quarters, tenement **09** apartment, penthouse, residence, single-end **10** habitation, pied-à-terre **11** continuance **13** dwelling-house, establishment
See also **accommodation**; **house**

dwindle
03 ebb **04** fade, fail, fall, wane **06** die out, lessen, reduce, shrink, vanish, weaken, wither **07** decline, shrivel, subside, tail off **08** decrease, diminish, fall away, grow less, peter out, taper off **09** disappear, waste away **10** become less
• dwindle away
05 peter

dye
03 hew, hue **04** tint, wash **05** agent, imbue, shade, stain, tinct, tinge
06 colour, embrue, imbrue
07 embrewe, pigment **09** colouring
See also **colour**; **pigment**

Dyes include:

04 anil, Saxe, wald, weld, woad
05 chica, eosin, henna, mauve
06 anatto, archil, corkir, flavin, fustic, indigo, kamala, korkir, madder, mauvin, orcein, orchel, orchil
07 alkanet, annatto, azurine, cudbear, flavine, magenta, mauvein, mauvine, para-red, ponceau, saffron
08 amaranth, fuchsine, mauveine, orchella, orchilla, safranin, turnsole
09 cochineal, nigrosine, primuline, safranine, Saxon blue, Turkey red, Tyrian red
10 carthamine, Saxony blue, tartrazine
12 Tyrian purple

• dyeing technique
04 ikat
• source of dye
04 chay

dyed-in-the-wool
05 fixed **07** diehard, settled
08 complete, hard-core, hardened, thorough **09** confirmed **10** deep-rooted, entrenched, inflexible, inveterate, unshakable **11** established, unshakeable **12** card-carrying, long-standing, unchangeable
14 uncompromising

dying
04 last **05** final, going, waned
06 ebbing, ending, fading, mortal
07 closing, failing, passing
08 expiring, moribund **09** declining, finishing, perishing, vanishing
10 concluding **11** near to death **12** at death's door, close to death **14** on your deathbed, on your last legs

dynamic
◇ *anagram indicator*
05 vital **06** active, causal, lively, potent, strong **07** driving, go-ahead
08 forceful, powerful, spirited, vigorous **09** effective, energetic, go-getting **11** high-powered **12** full of energy, self-starting

dynamically
07 vitally **08** actively, strongly
10 forcefully, powerfully, vigorously
11 effectively **13** energetically

dynamism
02 go **03** pep, vim, zap, zip **04** push
05 drive **06** energy, spirit, vigour
07 pizzazz **10** enterprise, get-up-and-go, initiative, liveliness **12** forcefulness

dynasty
04 line, rule **05** house **06** empire, regime **07** lineage **08** dominion
09 authority **10** government, succession **11** sovereignty
12 jurisdiction

Dynasties include:

02 Yi
03 Jin, Qin, Sui
04 Asen, Avis, Chin, Lodi, Ming, Qing, Song, Sung, Tang, Vasa, Yuan, Zhou
05 Ch'ing, Piast, Qajar, Shang
06 Chakri, Sayyid, Valois, Wettin, Zangid
07 'Abbasid, Ayyubid, Chakkri, Fatimid, Romanov, Safavid, Tughlaq
08 Capetian, Habsburg, Ilkhanid
09 Jagiellon
10 Qarakhanid
11 Plantagenet
12 Hohenstaufen, Hohenzollern
14 Petrovic-Njegos

dyspepsia
07 acidity, pyrosis **08** dyspepsy
09 heartburn **10** cardialgia, water-brash

dyspeptic
04 edgy **05** humpy, ratty, testy
06 crabby, feisty, gloomy, shirty, touchy
07 crabbed, grouchy, in a huff, in a sulk, peevish, stroppy **08** snappish
09 crotchety, irritable **10** indigested
11 bad-tempered, cacogastric, indigestive **13** short-tempered

dysprosium
02 Dy

E
04 echo **07** epsilon

each
02 ea **03** ilk, per **05** every **06** apiece, singly **07** each one, per head **09** per capita, per person **10** separately **11** every single **12** individually, respectively **15** each and every one, every individual

• for each
03 per

eager
04 agog, avid, bore, fain, keen, rath, toey **05** antsy, dying, frack, hasty, prone, rathe, sharp **06** ardent, greedy, gung-ho, hungry, intent, raring, watery **07** anxious, earnest, fervent, longing, thirsty, up for it, willing, wishful, wishing, zealous **08** desirous, diligent, empressé, yearning **09** desperate, impatient, perfervid **12** affectionate, enthusiastic, wholehearted

eagerly
04 sore **06** avidly, keenly **08** ardently, greedily, intently **09** earnestly, fervently, zealously **11** impatiently **14** wholeheartedly

eagerness
03 yen **04** lust, zeal **05** ardor, greed **06** ardour, hunger, thirst **07** avidity, fervour, longing **08** fainness, fervency, keenness, yearning **09** fervidity **10** enthusiasm, greediness, impatience, intentness **11** earnestness, impetuosity

eagle
04 erne **05** harpy **06** Aquila **07** alerion, lectern **08** allerion, bateleur, berghaan **11** king of birds

ear
◇ *homophone indicator*
03 ere, lug **04** heed, till **05** skill, souse, taste **06** notice, plough, regard **07** ability, earhole, hearing, lughole **09** attention, shell-like **10** perception **11** sensitivity **12** appreciation **13** attentiveness **14** discrimination

Ear parts include:

04 drum, lobe
05 anvil, helix, incus, pinna, scala
06 concha, cupola, hammer, stapes, tragus
07 alveary, auricle, cochlea, eardrum, ear lobe, malleus, saccule, stirrup, utricle
08 pavilion, sacculus, tympanum
09 columella, endolymph, labyrinth, perilymph, vestibule
10 oval window
11 Corti's organ, round window
12 organ of Corti
13 auditory canal, auditory nerve
14 columella auris, Eustachian tube
15 vestibular nerve

• of the ear
04 otic

• play it by ear
05 ad-lib **06** busk it, wing it **09** improvise **11** extemporize **15** think on your feet

earlier
02 ex **06** before **07** already, prior to **08** formerly, previous **10** previously

early
02 am **04** auld, rare, rath, rear, soon **05** first **06** at dawn **07** advance, ancient, forward, initial, morning, opening, too soon **08** advanced, primeval, untimely **09** in advance, premature, primaeval, primitive **10** at daybreak, beforehand, in good time, precocious, primordial **11** ahead of time, prematurely, undeveloped **12** in the morning **13** autochthonous **15** ahead of schedule, with time to spare

earmark
03 tag **05** label **07** mark out, reserve **08** allocate, keep back, lay aside, put aside, set aside **09** designate

earn
03 ern, get, net, win **04** draw, gain, make, rate, reap **05** clear, gross, merit **06** attain, be owed, be paid, curdle, obtain, pocket, pull in, rake in, secure **07** achieve, acquire, bring in, collect, deserve, get paid, realize, receive, warrant **08** take home

earnest
03 sad **04** dear, firm, keen **05** arles, eager, fixed, grave, token, truth **06** ardent, devout, intent, pledge, solemn, steady, urgent **07** deposit, devoted, fervent, forward, intense, promise, serious, sincere, wistful, zealous **08** diligent, resolute, security **09** assiduous, assurance, committed, dedicated, guarantee, heartfelt, sincerity **10** persistent, press-money, resolution, thoughtful **11** down payment, impassioned, seriousness **12** earnest-penny, enthusiastic **13** conscientious, determination

• in earnest
07 genuine, serious, sincere, stand-up **08** ardently, intently, steadily **09** not joking, seriously, zealously **10** resolutely **12** passionately, purposefully **14** wholeheartedly **15** conscientiously

earnestly
04 hard **06** dearly, firmly, keenly, warmly, wistly **07** eagerly **08** intently **09** fervently, seriously, sincerely, zealously **10** resolutely

earnestness
04 zeal **06** ardour, warmth **07** fervour, gravity, passion **08** devotion, fervency, keenness **09** eagerness, sincerity, vehemence **10** enthusiasm, intentness, resolution **11** seriousness **13** determination **14** purposefulness

earnings
03 fee, pay **04** gain **05** wages **06** income, net pay, return, reward, salary **07** profits, revenue, stipend **08** gross pay, proceeds, receipts **09** emolument **10** honorarium **11** take home pay **12** remuneration

earring
04 drop, hoop, snap, stud **06** clip-on **07** pendant, pendent, sleeper

earshot
04 hail **05** sound **07** hearing

• beyond earshot
10 out of range

earth
01 E **02** Ge **03** orb, sod **04** clay, dirt, dust, eard, Gaea, Gaia, land, loam, mold, soil, turf, yerd, yird **05** globe, humus, mould, world **06** ground, planet, sphere **07** topsoil

• rammed earth
04 pisé

earthenware
03 pig, pot **04** delf, pots, waly **05** cloam, delft, delph, wally **07** faience, pottery **08** ceramics, crockery, figuline, maiolica, majolica **09** creamware, ironstone, porcelain, stoneware **10** Samian ware, terracotta **14** terra sigillata

earthly
04 vile **05** human **06** likely, mortal **07** fleshly, mundane, profane, secular, sensual, terrene, worldly **08** feasible, material, physical, possible, sublunar, telluric, temporal **09** slightest, sublunary, tellurian **10** imaginable **11** conceivable, terrestrial **13** materialistic

earthquake
05 quake, seism, shake, shock **06** tremor **07** temblor **08** trembler,

upheaval **10** aftershock, convulsion **11** earth-tremor

earthwork
04 berm, ring **06** cursus, sconce **07** parados **10** breastwork, embankment, roundabout **12** entrenchment, intrenchment, maiden castle

earthy
04 blue, rude **05** bawdy, crude, gross, rough **06** cloddy, coarse, direct, ribald, simple, vulgar **07** natural, raunchy, terrene **08** claylike, dirtlike, soil-like **09** earthlike, unrefined **10** indecorous **11** down to earth, uninhibited **15** unsophisticated

ease
04 calm, edge, inch, rest **05** abate, allay, guide, peace, quiet, relax, salve, slide, steer **06** lessen, reduce, relent, repose, smooth, soothe, wealth **07** assuage, comfort, leisure, lighten, quieten, relieve **08** deftness, diminish, facility, grow less, mitigate, moderate, opulence, otiosity, palliate **09** affluence, alleviate, dexterity, enjoyment, happiness, manoeuvre **10** adroitness, ameliorate, become less, bed of roses, cleverness, easy street, facilitate, otioseness, prosperity, relaxation **11** contentment, lap of luxury, life of Riley, naturalness, skilfulness **12** peacefulness **14** effortlessness

• at ease
04 calm **06** secure **07** natural, relaxed **08** composed, sans gêne **11** comfortable

• ease off
04 wane **05** abate **06** relent **07** die away, die down, slacken, subside **08** decrease, diminish, moderate, slack off **10** become less, slacken off

easily
◇ *anagram indicator*
04 eath, ethe, well **05** by far, eathe **06** simply, surely **07** clearly, readily **08** fluently, probably **09** certainly **10** definitely, far and away, undeniably **11** comfortably, doubtlessly, undoubtedly **12** effortlessly, indisputably, without doubt

• easily handled
04 yare

east
01 E **04** Asia **06** Levant, Orient **07** sunrise **08** Old World **09** sunrising **11** morning-land

• East End
◇ *dialect indicator*

• from the east, goes east
◇ *reversal indicator*

Easter
04 Pace **05** Pasch

eastern
01 E **06** exotic, Levant, Orient **08** Oriental

East German *see* German

East Timor
03 TLS

easy
◇ *anagram indicator*
04 calm, eath, ethe, glib, soft **05** cushy, eathe **06** a cinch, casual, dégagé, facile, simple, smooth **07** a doddle, natural, relaxed, running **08** carefree, homelike, informal, laid-back, painless, unforced **09** a cakewalk, a pushover, easy as ABC, easy as pie, easy-going, easy-peasy, foolproof, leisurely, unstudied **10** child's play, effortless, manageable, unlaboured **11** comfortable, undemanding **12** a piece of cake **13** uncomplicated **14** a walk in the park **15** straightforward

• easy thing
03 pie **08** pushover

• take it easy
04 loll **05** relax

easy-going
04 calm **06** placid, serene **07** equable, lenient, relaxed **08** amenable, carefree, indolent, laid-back, tolerant **10** insouciant, nonchalant **11** undemanding **12** even-tempered, happy-go-lucky **13** imperturbable

eat
◇ *containment indicator*
02 go **03** hog, pig, rot, sup **04** bite, chew, chop, cram, dine, feed, fret, grub, guts, mess, nosh, peck, pick, take **05** binge, decay, erode, feast, graze, hog it, lunch, munch, scoff, snack, snarf, taste, twist, upset, worry **06** begnaw, devour, gobble, guttle, ingest, pig out, slairg, tuck in **07** consume, corrode, crumble, predate, put away, swallow **08** bite into, bolt down, chow down, demolish, dissolve, gulp down, irritate, tuck into, wear away, wolf down **09** breakfast, have a bite, knock back, manducate, partake of, polish off, undermine **10** gormandize, have a snack

Eating places include:

04 hall, mess
06 frater, fratry
07 canteen
08 takeaway
09 refectory
10 commissary, dining-hall
11 frater-house

See also **restaurant**

• eat away
04 etch, gnaw **05** erode **06** begnaw **07** corrode

• eat quickly
04 bolt, cram, gulp

eatable
04 good **06** edible **08** esculent **09** palatable, wholesome **10** comestible, digestible

eavesdrop
03 bug, spy, tap **05** snoop **06** earwig **07** monitor **08** listen in, overhear **10** stillicide

eavesdropper
03 spy **05** snoop **07** monitor, snooper **08** listener

ebb
04 drop, fall, flag, sink, wane **05** abate, decay, go out **06** lessen, recede, reflow, reflux, shrink, waning, weaken **07** decline, dwindle, ebb tide, lagging, low tide, retreat, slacken, subside **08** decrease, diminish, fade away, fall back, flow back, going-out, low water, peter out, receding **09** abatement, dwindling, lessening, refluence, retrocede, subsiding, weakening **10** degenerate, slackening, subsidence **11** deteriorate, flowing-back **12** degeneration **13** deterioration

ebony
03 jet **04** dark, inky **05** black, heben, jetty, sable, sooty **08** jet-black **09** cocuswood **10** calamander, coromandel

ebullience
04 zest **07** elation **08** buoyancy, vivacity **10** breeziness, brightness, bubbliness, chirpiness, enthusiasm, excitement, exuberance **11** high spirits **12** effusiveness, exhilaration

ebullient
06 breezy, bright, bubbly, chirpy, elated **07** buoyant, excited, gushing, zestful **08** agitated, effusive **09** exuberant, vivacious **11** exhilarated **12** effervescent, enthusiastic **13** irrepressible

eccentric
◇ *anagram indicator*
03 cam, dag, fay, fey, fie, nut, odd, off **04** card, case, cure, ditz, geek, kook, loon, wack, zany **05** crank, ditsy, ditzy, dotty, flake, flaky, freak, geeky, kinky, kooky, loony, loopy, nutty, queer, spacy, wacko, wacky, weird **06** cranky, kookie, nutjob, nutter, oddity, quirky, screwy, spacey, way-out, weirdo, whacko **07** bizarre, cupcake, dingbat, erratic, nutcase, oddball, odd fish, off-beat, strange, weirdie **08** aberrant, abnormal, crackpot, freakish, peculiar, singular **09** character, ding-a-ling, screwball **10** loony tunes, off the wall, outlandish **13** idiosyncratic, nonconformist **14** fish out of water, unconventional

eccentricity
01 e **05** quirk **06** oddity **07** anomaly **09** weirdness **10** aberration, quirkiness, screwiness **11** abnormality, bizarreness, peculiarity, singularity, strangeness, unorthodoxy **12** freakishness, idiosyncrasy **13** nonconformity **14** capriciousness

ecclesiastic
04 abbé, dean **05** canon, padre, vicar **06** bishop, cleric, curate, deacon, father, lector, parson, pastor, priest, rector **08** chaplain, man of God, minister, preacher, reverend **09** churchman, clergyman, deaconess, presbyter **10** archbishop, woman of God **11** churchwoman, clergywoman

13 man of the cloth **15** woman of the cloth

See also **clergyman, clergywoman**

ecclesiastical
04 holy **06** church, divine **07** canonic **08** churchly, clerical, pastoral, priestly **09** canonical, religious, spiritual **10** sacerdotal **11** ministerial

echelon
04 rank, rung, tier **05** grade, level, place **06** degree, status **08** position

echinoderm
07 crinoid, cystoid, sea-lily, trepang **08** starfish **09** sea-urchin **10** bêche-de-mer **11** brittlestar, sea-cucumber

echo
01 E **04** copy, hint, ring **05** angel, clone, ditto, image, mimic, reply, trace **06** answer, memory, mirror, parrot, repeat, report **07** imitate, rebound, reflect, remains, resound, respeak, ringing, vestige **08** allusion, imitator, parallel, rebellow, reminder, resemble **09** duplicate, evocation, flashback, imitation, reiterate, repercuss, reproduce **10** reflection, repetition, resounding **11** mirror image, reiteration, remembrance, replication, reverberate **12** reproduction **13** reverberation

éclat
04 fame, show **05** glory, style **06** effect, lustre, renown **07** acclaim, display, success **08** applause, approval, plaudits **09** celebrity, splendour **10** brilliance **11** acclamation, distinction, flamboyance, ostentation, stylishness

eclectic
04 wide **05** broad **06** varied **07** diverse, general, liberal **08** catholic **09** many-sided, selective **11** diversified, wide-ranging **12** all-embracing, multifarious **13** comprehensive, heterogeneous

eclipse
03 dim, ebb **04** fall, loss, veil **05** block, cloud, cover, decay, dwarf, excel, outdo **06** darken, exceed, shroud **07** blot out, conceal, decline, dimming, failure, obscure, shading, surpass, veiling **08** covering, darkness, outshine **09** darkening, deliquium, transcend, weakening **10** concealing, overshadow **11** blotting-out, obscuration **13** overshadowing **14** run rings around **15** cast a shadow over, put into the shade

economic
05 cheap, trade **06** fiscal, viable **08** business, monetary **09** budgetary, financial, pecuniary, rewarding **10** commercial, industrial, productive, profitable **11** moneymaking **12** profit-making, remunerative **13** cost-effective

economical
05 cheap, tight **06** budget, frugal, modest, saving **07** careful, low-cost, prudent, sparing, thrifty **08** low-price, skimping **09** efficient, low-budget, low-priced, provident, scrimping **10** reasonable **11** inexpensive **12** parsimonious **13** cost-effective **15** bargain-basement

economics

Economics theories and schools include:

07 Marxian
09 Keynesian
10 game theory
11 physiocracy
12 mercantilism, neo-classical, neo-Keynesian, neo-Ricardian, new classical
13 Chicago school, post-Keynesian
14 Austrian school
15 classical school

Economic problems include:

08 scarcity
09 deflation, inflation, skills gap
10 depression
12 trade barrier, trade deficit, unemployment
13 budget deficit

economist
10 chrematist

Economists include:

03 **Say** (Jean-Baptiste), **Sen** (Amartya)
04 **Nash** (John), **Ward** (Dame Barbara), **Webb** (Sidney)
05 **Arrow** (Kenneth J), **Meade** (James Edward), **North** (Douglass C), **Petty** (Sir William), **Smith** (Adam), **Solow** (Robert Merton), **Stone** (Sir Richard), **Tobin** (James)
06 **Allais** (Maurice), **Cobden** (Richard), **Cripps** (Sir Stafford), **Debreu** (Gerard), **Erhard** (Ludwig), **Frisch** (Ragnar), **Horner** (Francis), **Keynes** (John Maynard), **Myrdal** (Gunnar), **Tawney** (Richard Henry)
07 **Bagehot** (Walter), **Kuznets** (Simon), **Malthus** (Thomas Robert), **Ricardo** (David), **Robbins** (Lionel, Lord), **Scholes** (Myron), **Stigler** (George Joseph), **Toynbee** (Arnold), **Vickrey** (William)
08 **Buchanan** (James McGill), **Friedman** (Milton), **Leontief** (Wassily), **Marshall** (Alfred), **Mirrlees** (James), **Robinson** (Joan Violet), **Schiller** (Karl), **Shatalin** (Stanislav), **Youngson** (Alexander John)
09 **Beveridge** (William, Lord), **Galbraith** (John Kenneth), **Greenspan** (Alan), **Tinbergen** (Jan)
10 **Modigliani** (Franco)
11 **Kantorovich** (Leonid)

economize
03 eke **04** save **06** budget **07** cut back, use less **08** cut costs, retrench **10** buy cheaply, cut corners **12** be economical **13** keep down costs, scrimp and save **14** cut expenditure, live on the cheap **15** tighten your belt

economy
04 care **06** saving, thrift, wealth **08** prudence, skimping **09** frugality, husbandry, parsimony, plutology, plutonomy, restraint, scrimping **10** providence **11** carefulness **12** catallactics, retrenchment **13** chrematistics **14** financial state, system of wealth **15** financial system

ecstasy
01 E **03** joy, tab **04** dove **05** bliss **06** frenzy **07** delight, elation, fervour, rapture **08** euphoria, pleasure **09** transport **10** exultation, jubilation **11** sublimation **12** disco biscuit

• **rouse to ecstasy**
04 send

ecstatic
04 rapt, sent **06** elated, joyful, Pythic **07** fervent **08** blissful, euphoric, frenzied, jubilant **09** delirious, overjoyed, rapturous, rhapsodic **10** blissed-out, enraptured, in raptures **11** high as a kite, on cloud nine, over the moon, tickled pink **13** jumping for joy **15** in seventh heaven

Ecuador
02 EC **03** ECU

ecumenical
07 general **08** catholic **09** universal **10** broad-based **12** all-embracing, nonsectarian

eddy
04 curl, pirl, purl, reel, roll, spin, turn, weal, weel, well **05** rotor, swirl, swish, twirl, twist, whirl **06** vortex **07** backset **08** swirling **09** maelstrom, whirlpool, whirlwind

edge
◇ *ends selection indicator*
◇ *head selection indicator*
03 hem, lip, rim **04** bite, brim, ease, head, inch, kerb, lead, line, side, worm, zest **05** brink, crawl, creep, elbow, force, limit, sidle, steal, sting, verge **06** border, fringe, margin **07** outline **08** acerbity, boundary, frontier, keenness, pungency, severity, whip-hand **09** acuteness, advantage, dominance, extremity, perimeter, periphery, sharpness, threshold, upper hand **10** ascendancy, causticity, outer limit, trenchancy **11** pick your way, superiority **12** incisiveness

• **on edge**
04 edgy, toey **05** jumpy, nervy, tense **06** touchy **07** anxious, keyed-up, nervous, twitchy, uptight **09** ill at ease, irritable **12** apprehensive, highly-strung

• **rough edge**
03 bur **04** burr

• **straight edge**
04 lute, rule

edgy
05 nervy, tense **06** on edge, touchy **07** anxious, brittle, keyed-up, nervous, uptight **09** ill at ease, irritable **12** highly-strung

edible
04 good **07** eatable **08** fit to eat, harmless **09** palatable, safe to eat, wholesome **10** comestible, digestible
• edible shoots
03 udo

edict
03 act, law **04** bull, fiat, rule **05** order, ukase **06** decree, ruling **07** command, mandate, process, statute **08** decretal, rescript **09** forbiddal, manifesto, pragmatic **10** golden bull, injunction, regulation **11** forbiddance
12 proclamation **13** pronouncement
14 pronunciamento

edification
07 tuition **08** coaching, guidance, teaching **09** education, elevation, uplifting **10** upbuilding
11 improvement, instruction
13 enlightenment

edifice
08 building, erection **09** structure
12 construction

edify
05 build, coach, guide, teach, tutor
06 inform, school, uplift **07** build up, educate, elevate, improve, nurture
08 instruct **09** enlighten, establish

edit
◇ *anagram indicator*
◇ *deletion indicator*
04 head **05** adapt, amend, check, emend **06** censor, choose, direct, garble, gather, head up, modify, polish, redact, revise, reword, select
07 arrange, collect, compile, correct, reorder, rewrite, subedit **08** annotate, assemble, copy-edit, organize, rephrase **09** proofread, rearrange
10 blue-pencil, bowdlerize **11** put together **12** be in charge of

edition
02 ed **04** Aufl, copy, edit **05** extra, issue, print **06** number, urtext, volume
07 hexapla, omnibus, reprint, version
08 printing, tetrapla, variorum
10 impression **11** publication **12** extra-special, reproduction
• limited edition
04 Aufl

editor
02 ed **04** hack **06** journo, writer
07 amender, checker, newsman, reviser
08 director, overseer, reporter, reviewer, rewriter **09** corrector, newswoman, publisher, subeditor **10** copy editor, desk editor, journalist, newscaster, undertaker **11** factchecker, proofreader
12 newspaperman **13** correspondent
14 newspaperwoman
See also **journalist**
• assistant editor
03 sub

editorial
06 column

educable
09 teachable, trainable **12** instructible

educate
05 coach, drill, edify, prime, teach, train, tutor **06** inform, school **07** bring up, develop, improve, nourish, nurture, prepare, train up, uptrain **08** hothouse, instruct **09** cultivate, enlighten, inculcate, institute **10** discipline, take in hand **12** indoctrinate

educated
02 ed **04** wise **06** brainy, taught
07 erudite, learned, refined, trained, tutored **08** all there, cultured, informed, lettered, literate, schooled, well-bred, well-read **09** civilized, sagacious **10** cultivated, instructed
11 enlightened **12** clever-clever
13 knowledgeable

education
02 ed **07** culture, letters, nurture, tuition **08** coaching, drilling, guidance, learning, teaching, training, tutoring **09** fostering, informing, knowledge, schooling **10** upbringing
11 cultivation, development, edification, improvement, inculcation, instruction, preparation, scholarship
13 enlightenment **14** indoctrination
• basic education
03 RRR
• education journal
03 TES
• further education
02 FE
• higher education
02 HE

educational
08 academic, cultural, didactic, edifying, learning, teaching
09 educative, improving, pedagogic
10 scholastic **11** informative, instructive, pedagogical
12 enlightening **13** instructional
14 institutionary

Educational establishments include:

03 CFE, CTC, uni
04 poly, tech
07 academy, college
08 seminary
10 high school, playschool, prep school, university
11 city academy, faith school, polytechnic, upper school
12 beacon school, infant school, junior school, kindergarten, middle school, public school, summer school, Sunday school
13 comprehensive, convent school, grammar school, nursery school, primary school, private school
14 boarding school, business school, combined school, flagship school
15 community school, finishing school, grant-maintained, secondary modern, secondary school, voluntary school

educative
08 didactic, edifying **09** improving
10 catechetic **11** catechismal, catechistic, educational, informative, instructive **12** enlightening
13 catechistical

educator
05 coach, tutor **06** master, mentor
07 teacher, trainer **08** academic, lecturer, mistress **09** pedagogue, professor, schoolman **10** instructor
11 headteacher **12** schoolmaster
13 schoolteacher **14** educationalist, schoolmistress

educe
05 infer **06** elicit **07** develop, draw out, extract

Edward
02 Ed **03** Ted

eel

Eels and similar fish include:

03 hag, sea
04 grig, lant, sand, snig, tuna
05 elver, lance, moray, murry, siren, snake, wheat
06 conger, gulper, gunnel, launce, murena, murray, murrey
07 hagfish, muraena
08 Anguilla, electric, sandling
09 sand lance, wheatworm
10 spitchcock

• bait for eel
03 bob

eerie
05 scary, unked, unket, unkid, weird
06 creepy, spooky **07** ghostly, scaring, strange, uncanny **08** sinister, timorous
09 unearthly, unnatural **10** mysterious
11 frightening **13** bloodcurdling, spine-chilling

eerily
07 weirdly **09** strangely, uncannily
11 unnaturally **12** mysteriously

efface
04 dele **05** erase **06** cancel, delete, excise, remove, rub out **07** blot out, destroy, dislimn, expunct, expunge, wipe out **08** blank out, cross out, wear away **09** eliminate, eradicate, extirpate, strike out **10** obliterate

effect
03 win **04** gear, make **05** carry, cause, drift, force, fruit, goods, issue, power, sense, stuff, tenor **06** action, create, fulfil, impact, import, result, things, thread, upshot **07** achieve, baggage, clobber, execute, luggage, meaning, outcome, perform, produce, purport
08 carry out, chattels, complete, contrive, efficacy, generate, initiate, movables, property, strength
09 aftermath, influence, moveables, repulsion, trappings **10** accomplish, belongings, bring about, conclusion, effectuate, give rise to, impression
11 consequence, possessions
12 significance **13** accoutrements, paraphernalia
• in effect
06 in fact, really **07** en effet, in truth
08 actually **09** in reality, virtually **10** in

practice **11** effectively, essentially **12** in actual fact **13** substantially **14** produce results

• produce an effect
03 act

• special effects
02 FX **03** SFX

• take effect
04 bite, take, talk, vest, work **05** begin
06 kick in **07** come off, succeed
08 function **09** become law
11 become valid, be effective **13** be implemented, come into force
14 produce results **15** become operative, come into service

effective
04 home, neat **05** legal, valid
06 active, actual, cogent, potent, superb, useful **07** capable, current, helpful, in force, operant, telling, virtual
08 adequate, exciting, forceful, fruitful, in effect, powerful, striking
09 efficient, energetic, essential, operative, practical **10** attractive, compelling, convincing, impressive, persuasive, prevailing, productive, successful, sufficient, worthwhile
11 devastating, efficacious, energetical, functioning, implemental, in operation, serviceable

effectively
04 home, well **06** in fact, really **07** in truth **08** actually, in effect **09** in reality, virtually **10** fruitfully, in practice
11 efficiently, essentially **12** in actual fact, productively, successfully

effectiveness
03 use **05** clout, force, power
06 vigour, weight **07** ability, cogency, potence, potency, success **08** efficacy, strength, validity **09** influence
10 capability, efficacity, efficiency, usefulness **12** fruitfulness
14 productiveness **15** efficaciousness

effectual
05 legal, sound, valid **06** lawful, proper, useful **07** binding, capable
08 decisive, forcible, powerful
09 authentic, effective, magistral, operative **10** perficient, productive, successful **11** influential, serviceable
13 authoritative

effeminate
04 soft **05** cissy, minty, pansy, sissy
06 prissy, queeny **07** epicene, meacock, unmanly, wimpish, womanly
08 delicate, feminine, womanish
11 limp-wristed

effervesce
04 boil, fizz, foam **05** froth **06** bubble
07 ferment, sparkle **08** be lively **10** be animated **11** be ebullient, be vivacious
13 be exhilarated

effervescence
03 gas, vim, zip **04** fizz, foam, zing
05 froth **07** bubbles, ferment, foaming, sparkle **08** bubbling, buoyancy, frothing, vitality, vivacity
09 animation, fizziness, gassiness
10 ebullience, enthusiasm, excitement, exuberance, liveliness
11 excitedness, high spirits
12 exhilaration, fermentation

effervescent
◇ *anagram indicator*
05 fizzy, gassy, vital **06** bubbly, frothy, lively **07** aerated, buoyant, excited, fizzing, foaming **08** animated, bubbling **09** ebullient, exuberant, sparkling, vivacious **10** carbonated, fermenting **11** exhilarated
12 enthusiastic **13** irrepressible

effete
04 weak **05** spent **06** barren, feeble, used up, wasted **07** corrupt, debased, decayed, drained, shotten, spoiled, sterile, worn out **08** decadent, decrepit, infecund, tired out
09 enervated, enfeebled, exhausted, fruitless, played out **10** degenerate, unfruitful, unprolific **11** debilitated, ineffectual **12** unproductive

efficacious
06 active, potent, strong, useful
07 capable **08** adequate, powerful
09 competent, effective, effectual, operative, potential, sovereign
10 productive, successful, sufficient

efficacy
03 use **04** feck **05** force, power, value
06 effect, energy, virtue **07** ability, potency, success **08** strength
09 influence **10** capability, competence, usefulness
13 effectiveness **14** successfulness

efficiency
05 order, skill **07** ability **09** expertise
10 capability, competence, competency **11** orderliness, proficiency, skilfulness
12 organization, productivity
13 effectiveness

efficient
04 able **05** smart **06** expert, strong
07 capable, skilful, well-run
08 powerful **09** competent, effective, organized, practical **10** methodical, productive, proficient, systematic
11 streamlined, well-ordered, workmanlike **12** businesslike, rationalized **13** well-conducted, well-organized

effigy
03 guy **04** icon, idol, sign **05** dummy, image **06** figure, statue **07** carving, picture **08** likeness, portrait **09** Jack-straw **14** representation

efflorescence
03 reh

effluent
05 waste **06** efflux, sewage
07 outflow **08** emission **09** discharge, effluence, effluvium, emanation, pollutant, pollution **10** exhalation
11 liquid waste

effort
02 go **03** try **04** bash, beef, deed, feat, opus, push, shot, stab, toil, work
05 crack, essay, force, nisus, pains, power, sweat, whirl **06** energy, labour, result, strain, stress **07** attempt, exploit, muscles, product, travail, trouble
08 creation, exertion, hard work, striving, struggle **09** endeavour
10 attainment, production
11 achievement, application, elbow-grease, muscle power
14 accomplishment **15** sweat of your brow

• calling for effort
02 yo

• sudden effort
03 fit

• utmost efforts
03 all

effortless
04 easy **06** facile, simple, smooth
07 passive **08** painless **10** unexacting
11 undemanding **13** uncomplicated
15 straightforward

effrontery
03 lip **04** face, gall, sass **05** brass, cheek, nerve **07** hutzpah **08** audacity, boldness, brazenry, chutzpah, temerity
09 arrogance, brashness, brass neck, impudence, insolence **10** brazenness, cheekiness, disrespect **11** presumption
12 impertinence **13** shamelessness

effulgent
07 glowing, radiant, shining
08 glorious, splendid **09** brilliant, refulgent **11** resplendent
12 incandescent

effusion
04 gush **06** efflux, stream **07** outflow
08 emission, outburst, shedding, voidance **09** discharge, effluence
10 outpouring

effusive
03 OTT **05** gabby, gassy, gushy
06 lavish **07** fulsome, gushing, lyrical, profuse, voluble **08** all mouth
09 ebullient, expansive, exuberant, rhapsodic, talkative **10** big-mouthed, over the top, unreserved
11 extravagant, overflowing
12 enthusiastic, unrestrained
13 demonstrative

eg
02 as, zB **03** say **06** such as **10** for example, par exemple **11** zum Beispiel
13 exempli gratia

egalitarian
04 fair, just **07** sharing **09** equitable
10 democratic **12** equalitarian

egg
01 O **03** nit **04** blow, bomb, mine, ovum **05** berry, ovule **06** oocyte
08 oosphere

• egg on
03 set, tar **04** abet, coax, edge, goad, prod, push, spur, urge **05** drive, prick
06 excite, exhort, incite, prompt, urge on **08** talk into **09** encourage, stimulate

• egg-supplier *see* **bird**

• lower half of egg
04 doup, dowp
• spot on egg
03 eye

egghead
03 don **05** brain **06** boffin, genius **07** know-all, scholar, thinker **08** academic, bookworm, brainbox, Einstein **09** intellect, know-it-all **12** intellectual

eggs
02 OO **03** ova, roe **06** clutch, graine **11** pullet-sperm

ego
01 I **03** sel **04** self, soul **07** egotism **08** identity **09** self-image, self-worth **10** self-esteem **14** self-confidence, self-importance **15** sense of identity

egocentric
07 selfish **09** egotistic **11** egotistical, self-centred, self-seeking, self-serving **12** narcissistic, self-absorbed **14** self-interested

egoism
07 egotism **08** egomania, self-love **10** narcissism, self-regard **11** amour-propre, selfishness, self-seeking **12** self-interest **13** egocentricity **14** self-absorption, self-importance **15** self-centredness

egoist
07 egotist **09** egomaniac **10** narcissist, self-seeker

egoistic
09 egotistic **10** egocentric, egoistical **11** egomaniacal, egotistical, self-centred, self-seeking **12** narcissistic, self-absorbed, self-involved, self-pleasing **13** self-important

egotism
03 ego **05** pride, swank **06** egoism, vanity **08** egomania, self-love, selfness, snobbery **10** narcissism, self-regard **11** braggadocio, self-conceit, selfishness, superiority **12** boastfulness **13** bigheadedness, conceitedness, egocentricity **14** self-admiration, self-importance **15** self-centredness

egotist
06 egoist **07** bighead, bluffer, boaster, show-off **08** big mouth, braggart **09** egomaniac, smart alec, swaggerer **10** clever dick **11** braggadocio, clever clogs, self-admirer

egotistic
04 vain **05** proud **07** selfish **08** boasting, bragging, egoistic, superior **09** bigheaded, conceited **10** egocentric **11** self-centred, swell-headed **12** narcissistic, self-admiring **13** self-important, swollen-headed

egregious
04 fine, rank **05** gross **06** arrant **07** glaring, heinous **08** flagrant, grievous, infamous, precious, shocking **09** appalling, monstrous, notorious, prominent **10** outrageous, scandalous **11** intolerable **12** insufferable **13** distinguished

egress
04 exit, vent **05** issue **06** depart, escape, exodus, outlet, way out **07** leaving **09** departure, emergence **11** escape route

Egypt
02 ET **03** EGY

Egyptian
07 Thebaic

Ancient Egyptian rulers include:

05 Khufu
06 Ahmose, Cheops
07 Ptolemy, Rameses
08 Berenice, Thutmose
09 Akhenaten, Amenhotep, Cleopatra, Nefertiti, Sesostris, Tuthmosis
10 Hatshepsut
11 Tut'ankhamun

See also **god, goddess**; **pharaoh**

eight
04 VIII **05** octad, octet **06** octave, octett, ogdoad **07** octette **08** octonary

eighteen
05 XVIII

eighty
04 LXXX

einsteinium
02 Es

ejaculate
03 cry **04** call, come, emit, yell **05** blurt, eject, expel, shout, spurt, utter **06** cry out, scream **07** call out, exclaim, release **08** blurt out, shout out **09** discharge

ejaculation
03 cry **04** call, yell **05** shout, spurt **06** climax, coming, scream **07** release **08** ejection, emission **09** discharge, expulsion, utterance **11** exclamation **12** interjection

eject
04 emit, fire, oust, sack, spew, spit **05** belch, degas, evict, exile, expel, exude, spout, vomit **06** banish, bounce, deport, get out, propel, remove **07** bail out, boot out, dismiss, exclude, excrete, expulse, kick out, release, turf out, turn out **08** chuck out, disgorge, drive out, evacuate, get rid of, splutter, throw out **09** discharge, ejaculate, thrust out **11** expectorate

ejection
05 exile **06** firing, ouster, outing **07** ousting, removal, sacking, the boot, the sack **08** eviction, vomiting **09** discharge, dismissal, exclusion, expulsion **10** banishment **11** deportation, ejaculation

eke
• eke out
03 ech, ich **04** eche, eech **05** add to, get by **06** scrape **07** fill out, help out, husband, scratch, spin out, stretch, survive **08** increase, piece out **10** go easy with, supplement **11** economize on **12** feel the pinch **13** scrimp and save

elaborate
◇ *anagram indicator*
05 exact, fancy, fussy, showy **06** devise, minute, ornate, polish, quaint, refine, rococo, work up **07** amplify, careful, complex, develop, enhance, explain, improve, precise, studied, work out **08** detailed, develope, expand on, flesh out, involved, laboured, thorough **09** decorated, enlarge on, expatiate, extensive, intricate, perfected, storiated **10** ornamental **11** complicated, extravagant, highwrought, historiated, overwrought, painstaking **12** ostentatious

élan
04 brio, dash, zest **05** flair, oomph, style, verve **06** esprit, pizazz, spirit, vigour **07** panache, pizzazz **08** flourish, vivacity **09** animation **10** confidence, liveliness **11** impetuosity, stylishness

elapse
02 go **03** ren, rin, run **04** go by, go on, pass **05** lapse **06** go past, slip by **07** passing **08** overpass, pass away, slip away

elastic
◇ *anagram indicator*
04 easy **05** buxom, fluid **06** bouncy, pliant, supple **07** buoyant, plastic, pliable, rubbery, springy **08** flexible, stretchy, tolerant, yielding **09** adaptable, compliant, resilient **10** adjustable **11** elasticated, stretchable **13** accommodating

elasticity
04 give, play **05** tonus **06** bounce, spring **07** stretch **08** buoyancy **09** tolerance **10** plasticity, pliability, resilience, suppleness **11** flexibility, springiness **12** adaptability, stretchiness **13** adjustability

elated
04 high **05** happy **06** joyful, joyous **07** excited **08** blissful, ecstatic, euphoric, exultant, glorious, jubilant, thrilled **09** delighted, overjoyed, rapturous, rhapsodic **11** exhilarated, on cloud nine, over the moon

elation
03 joy **04** glee, lift, ruff **05** bliss, ruffe **06** thrill **07** delight, ecstasy, rapture **08** euphoria **09** happiness **10** exaltation, exultation, joyfulness, joyousness, jubilation **11** high spirits **12** exhilaration, intoxication

elbow
04 bump, push **05** ancon, barge, crowd, force, knock, nudge, shove **06** jostle, justle **08** shoulder

elbow-grease
04 beef **06** effort, energy **07** muscles **08** exertion, hard work, strength **11** muscle power **15** sweat of your brow

elbow-room
04 play, room **05** scope, space **06** leeway **07** freedom **08** latitude **10** Lebensraum **14** breathing space

elder
03 OAP **04** aîné, sire **05** aînée, older, oldie **06** deacon, father, leader, senior **07** ancient, wise man **08** ancestor, boortree, bountree, bourtree, kaumatua **09** first-born, old person, pensioner, presbyter **11** older person

elderly
03 old **04** aged, OAPs **05** aging, hoary **06** ageing, mature, oldies, past it, senile **07** fossils **08** badgerly, has-beens **09** old people, senescent, wrinklies **10** grey-haired, pensioners **11** golden agers, older adults, over the hill **13** retired people **14** long in the tooth, senior citizens **15** older generation

eldest
05 first **06** oldest **09** first-born **13** first-begotten

elect
03 opt **04** pick, -to-be, vote **05** adopt, co-opt, élite, voice **06** choose, chosen, future, opt for, picked, prefer, return, select, vote in **07** appoint, vote for **08** decide on, nominate, plump for, selected **09** cast a vote, chosen few, designate, determine, preferred **10** hand-picked **11** prospective **12** go to the polls

elected
02 in

election
04 poll, vote **06** ballot, choice, return, voting **07** picking, primary **08** choosing, decision, free will, hustings **09** rectorial, selection **10** preference, referendum **11** appointment **13** determination

electioneering
08 fighting, hustings, lobbying
09 crusading, promotion
10 canvassing, struggling
11 campaigning, championing
13 mainstreeting

elector
05 voter **08** selector **10** electorate **11** constituent

electorate

Australian electorates:

04 Bass, Cook, Grey, Holt, Hume, Indi, Lowe, Lyne, Mayo, Page, Reid, Ryan, Swan
05 Aston, Banks, Blair, Brand, Bruce, Casey, Corio, Cowan, Forde, Groom, Lalor, Lyons, Makin, Moore, Oxley, Perth, Sturt, Wills
06 Barker, Barton, Batman, Bonner, Bowman, Calare, Cowper, Curtin, Dawson, Deakin, Dobell, Fadden, Farrer, Fisher, Fowler, Fraser, Gorton, Gwydir, Hotham, Hughes, Hunter, Isaacs, Lilley, Mallee, McEwan, Murray, Parkes, Pearce, Petrie, Rankin, Sydney, Wannon, Watson
07 Bendigo, Berowra, Boothby, Braddon, Calwell, Canning, Chifley, Denison, Dickson, Dunkley, Fairfax, Forrest, Gilmore, Hasluck, Herbert, Higgins, Hinkler, Kennedy, Kooyong, La Trobe, Lindsay, Longman, Maranoa, Menzies, Moreton, O'Conner, Scullin, Solomon, Tangney, Throsby, Werriwa, Wide Bay
08 Adelaide, Ballarat, Blaxland, Brisbane, Canberra, Charlton, Chisholm, Flinders, Franklin, Greenway, Griffith, Jagajaga, Kingston, Lingiari, McMillan, Mitchell, Paterson, Prospect, Richmond, Riverina, Stirling
09 Bennelong, Bradfield, Fremantle, Gippsland, Goldstein, Grayndler, Hindmarsh, Macarthur, Mackellar, Macquarie, McPherson, Melbourne, Moncrieff, Newcastle, Robertson, Shortland, Wakefield, Warringah, Wentworth
10 Cunningham, Eden-Monaro, Gellibrand, Kalgoorlie, Leichhardt, New England, Parramatta
11 Capricornia, Corangamite, Maribyrnong, North Sydney
12 Port Adelaide
14 Kingsford Smith, Melbourne Ports

New Zealand electorates:

04 Ilam, Mana
05 Epsom, Otago, Otaki, Piako, Taupo
06 Aoraki, Napier, Nelson, Rakaia, Rodney, Tainui, Tamaki, Wigram
07 Mangere, New Lynn, Rotorua, Te Atatu
08 Clevedon, Manurewa, Mt Albert, Rimutaka, Rongotai, Tauranga, Tukituki, Waiariki
09 East Coast, Hutt South, Mt Roskill, Northcote, Northland, Pakuranga, Wairarapa, Waitakere, Whanganui, Whangarei
10 Coromandel, North Shore, Rangitikei, Te Tai Tonga
11 Bay of Plenty, Helensville, Manukau East, New Plymouth, Port Waikato, Waimakariri
12 Dunedin North, Dunedin South, Hamilton East, Hamilton West, Invercargill, Maungakiekie, Te Tai Hauauru, Te Tai Tokerau
13 East Coast Bays, Ikaora-Rawhiti, Ohariu-Belmont
14 Banks Peninsula, Tamaki Makaurau
15 Auckland Central, Clutha-Southland, Palmerston North, West Coast-Tasman
16 Christchurch East
17 Wellington Central
19 Christchurch Central, Taranaki-King Country

electric
04 live **05** tense **07** charged, dynamic, powered, rousing **08** cordless, exciting, stirring **09** startling, thrilling **11** stimulating **12** electrifying, rechargeable **13** mains-operated **15** battery-operated, electric-powered

• **electric fluid**
04 vril

electrical

Electrical components and devices include:

04 fuse
05 cable
06 socket
07 adaptor, ammeter, battery, conduit, fusebox
08 armature, neon lamp, test lamp
09 light bulb
10 lampholder, multimeter, transducer, two-pin plug
11 ceiling rose, earthed plug, fuse carrier, transformer
12 dimmer switch, three-pin plug
13 extension lead
14 bayonet fitting, circuit breaker, dry-cell battery, insulating tape, three-core cable, voltage doubler
15 copper conductor, fluorescent tube

electrify
04 fire, jolt, stir **05** amaze, rouse, shock **06** charge, excite, thrill **07** animate, astound, stagger **08** astonish **09** electrize, galvanize, stimulate **10** invigorate

elegance
04 chic **05** grace, poise, style, taste **06** beauty, luxury, polish **07** dignity **08** grandeur **09** gentility, propriety, smartness **10** concinnity, politeness, refinement **11** discernment, distinction, stylishness **12** gracefulness, tastefulness **13** exquisiteness, sumptuousness **14** sophistication **15** fashionableness

elegant
04 chic, fine, jimp, neat **05** bijou, ritzy, smart **06** dainty, humane, la-di-da, lovely, modish, smooth, snazzy, swanky, urbane **07** genteel, refined, stylish **08** artistic, charming, cultured, debonair, delicate, graceful, gracious, handsome, lah-di-dah, polished, tasteful **09** beautiful, excellent, exquisite **10** concinnous, cultivated, debonnaire **11** fashionable **13** sophisticated

elegiac
03 sad **07** doleful, keening **08** funereal, mournful **09** epicedial, epicedian, lamenting, plaintive, threnetic, threnodic **10** threnodial **11** melancholic, threnetical, valedictory

elegy
05 dirge **06** lament, plaint **07** requiem **08** threnode, threnody **10** burial hymn **11** funeral poem, funeral song

element
03 set **04** hint, part **05** grain, group, haunt, niche, party, piece, touch, trace **06** basics, clique, factor, member, storms, strand **07** climate, faction, feature, habitat, soupçon, weather **08** filament, fragment **09** component, electrode, rudiments, suspicion, territory **10** essentials, individual, ingredient, principles **11** constituent, foundations, individuals, small amount, wind and rain **12** fundamentals **15** first principles

Elements and their symbols include:

01 B (boron), C (carbon), F (fluorine), H (hydrogen), I (iodine), K (potassium), N (nitrogen), O (oxygen), P (phosphorus), S (sulphur), U (uranium), V (vanadium), W (tungsten), Y (yttrium)
02 Ac (actinium), Ag (silver), Al (aluminium), Am (americium), Ar (argon), As (arsenic), At (astatine), Au (gold), Ba (barium), Be (beryllium), Bh (bohrium), Bi (bismuth), Bk (berkelium), Br (bromine), Ca (calcium), Cd (cadmium), Ce (cerium), Cf (californium), Cl (chlorine), Cm (curium), Co (cobalt), Cr (chromium), Cs (caesium), Cu (copper), Db (dubnium), Ds (darmstadtium), Dy (dysprosium), Er (erbium), Es (einsteinium), Eu (europium), Fe (iron), Fm (fermium), Fr (francium), Ga (gallium), Gd (gadolinium), Ge (germanium), Ha (hahnium), He (helium), Hf (hafnium), Hg (mercury), Ho (holmium), Hs (hassium), In (indium), Ir (iridium), Kr (krypton), La (lanthanum), Li (lithium), Lr (lawrencium), Lu (lutetium), Lw (lawrencium), Md (mendelevium), Mg (magnesium), Mn (manganese), Mo (molybdenum), Mt (meitnerium), Na (sodium), Nb (niobium), Nd (neodymium), Ne (neon), Ni (nickel), No (nobelium), Np (neptunium), Os (osmium), Pa (protactinium), Pb (lead), Pd (palladium), Pm (promethium), Po (polonium), Pr (praseodymium), Pt (platinum), Pu (plutonium), Ra (radium), Rb (rubidium), Re (rhenium), Rf (rutherfordium), Rg (roentgenium), Rh (rhodium), Rn (radon), Ru (ruthenium), Sb (antimony), Sc (scandium), Se (selenium), Sg (seaborgium), Si (silicon), Sm (samarium), Sn (tin), Sr (strontium), Ta (tantalum), Tb (terbium), Tc (technetium), Te (tellurium), Th (thorium), Ti (titanium), Tl (thallium), Tm (thulium), Xe (xenon), Yb (ytterbium), Zn (zinc), Zr (zirconium)
03 tin (Sn)
04 gold (Au), iron (Fe), lead (Pb), neon (Ne), zinc (Zn)
05 argon (Ar), boron (B), radon (Rn), xenon (Xe)
06 barium (Ba), carbon (C), cerium (Ce), cobalt (Co), copper (Cu), curium (Cm), erbium (Er), helium (He), indium (In), iodine (I), nickel (Ni), osmium (Os), oxygen (O), radium (Ra), silver (Ag), sodium (Na)
07 arsenic (As), bismuth (Bi), bohrium (Bh), bromine (Br), cadmium (Cd), caesium (Cs), calcium (Ca), dubnium (Db), fermium (Fm), gallium (Ga), hafnium (Hf), hahnium (Ha), hassium (Hs), holmium (Ho), iridium (Ir), krypton (Kr), lithium (Li), mercury (Hg), niobium (Nb), rhenium (Re), rhodium (Rh), silicon (Si), sulphur (S), terbium (Tb), thorium (Th), thulium (Tm), uranium (U), yttrium (Y)
08 actinium (Ac), antimony (Sb), astatine (At), chlorine (Cl), chromium (Cr), europium (Eu), fluorine (F), francium (Fr), hydrogen (H), lutetium (Lu), nitrogen (N), nobelium (No), platinum (Pt), polonium (Po), rubidium (Rb), samarium (Sm), scandium (Sc), selenium (Se), tantalum (Ta), thallium (Tl), titanium (Ti), tungsten (W), vanadium (V)
09 aluminium (Al), americium (Am), berkelium (Bk), beryllium (Be), germanium (Ge), lanthanum (La), magnesium (Mg), manganese (Mn), neodymium (Nd), neptunium (Np), palladium (Pd), plutonium (Pu), potassium (K), ruthenium (Ru), strontium (Sr), tellurium (Te), ytterbium (Yb), zirconium (Zr)
10 dysprosium (Dy), gadolinium (Gd), lawrencium (Lr, Lw), meitnerium (Mt), molybdenum (Mo), phosphorus (P), promethium (Pm), seaborgium (Sg), technetium (Tc)
11 californium (Cf), einsteinium (Es), mendelevium (Md), roentgenium (Rg)
12 darmstadtium (Ds), praseodymium (Pr), protactinium (Pa)
13 rutherfordium (Rf)

• old element
03 air **04** fire **05** earth, water

elemental
05 basic **07** immense, natural, primary, radical **08** forceful, powerful **09** primitive, principal **11** fundamental, rudimentary **12** uncontrolled

elementary
04 easy **05** basic, clear **06** simple **07** primary **09** principal **10** principial **11** fundamental, rudimentary **12** introductory, uncompounded **13** uncomplicated **15** straightforward

elephant
05 Babar, jumbo, rogue **07** mammoth **08** oliphant **09** pachyderm **13** megaherbivore **14** megavertebrate

• elephant carrier
03 roc, rok, ruc **04** rukh

elephantine
04 huge, vast **05** bulky, great, heavy, large **06** clumsy **07** awkward, hulking, immense, massive, weighty **08** enormous **09** lumbering

elevate
◇ *reversal down indicator*
04 lift **05** boost, cheer, exalt, hoist, raise, rouse **06** buoy up, hike up, refine, uplift **07** advance, ennoble, gladden, magnify, promote, upgrade **08** brighten, heighten **09** intensify, sublimate **10** aggrandize, exhilarate **11** give a lift to **12** kick upstairs **14** put on a pedestal **15** move up the ladder

elevated
◇ *anagram indicator*
◇ *reversal down indicator*
04 high **05** grand, great, lofty, moral, noble **06** aerial, lifted, raised, rising **07** exalted, hoisted, stilted, sublime, uplying **08** advanced, lifted up, towering, uplifted **09** dignified, high-flown, high-toned, important **10** high-raised, high-reared **11** exhilarated

elevation
04 back, face, hill, rise, side **05** agger, arsis, front, leg-up, mound, mount, ridge **06** aspect, façade, height, random, uplift **07** dignity, majesty, upright **08** altitude, eminence, foothill, grandeur, monticle, nobility, tallness, upheaval **09** go-getting, loftiness, monticule, promotion, sublimity, upgrading **10** exaltation, monticulus, preferment **11** advancement, sublimation **14** aggrandizement **15** step up the ladder

elevator
04 jack, lift

eleven
02 XI

elf
03 imp **04** peri, puck **05** dwarf, fairy, gnome, pigmy, pixie, pygmy, troll **06** goblin, sprite, urchin **07** banshee, brownie **08** entangle **09** hobgoblin **10** leprechaun

• elf's child
03 auf

elfin
03 fay, fey, fie **05** small **06** dainty, elfish, impish, petite **07** elflike, playful, puckish **08** charming, delicate **09** sprightly **10** frolicsome **11** mischievous

elicit
04 pump, tose, toze **05** cause, educe, evoke, exact, sweep, toaze, wrest **06** derive, extort, obtain **07** draw out, extract, mole out, worm out **08** bring out, outlearn **09** call forth

eligibility
09 allowance, condition **11** entitlement, suitability

12 desirability 13 acceptability, qualification

eligible
03 fit 06 proper, worthy 07 fitting 08 entitled, suitable 09 desirable, qualified 10 acceptable 11 appropriate

eliminate
03 ice, rid 04 beat, cure, do in, drop, kill, lick, omit, wipe 05 expel, whack 06 cancel, cut out, defeat, delete, hammer, murder, reject, remove, rub out, thrash 07 abolish, bump off, conquer, deep-six, exclude, take out, wipe out 08 get rid of, knock out, preclude, stamp out 09 cancel out, dispose of, disregard, eradicate, liquidate, overwhelm 10 annihilate, do away with, extinguish, put an end to, put a stop to 11 exterminate 12 dispense with

elimination
07 quietus, removal 08 deletion, disposal, omission 09 abolition, exclusion, expulsion, rejection 11 eradication

élite
04 best, pick 05 cream, elect, noble 06 choice, gentry, jet set 08 nobility, selected 09 exclusive 10 first-class, upper-class 11 aristocracy, high society 12 aristocratic, upper classes 13 establishment 14 crème de la crème, pick of the bunch

elixir
04 pith 05 daffy, syrup, tinct 06 potion, remedy 07 arcanum, cure-all, essence, extract, mixture, nostrum, panacea 08 solution, tincture 09 principle 11 concentrate 12 quintessence

elliptical
04 oval 05 ovoid, terse 07 concise, cryptic, dubious, laconic, oblique, obscure, oviform, ovoidal 08 abstruse, succinct 09 ambiguous, condensed, egg-shaped, recondite 12 concentrated, unfathomable 13 comprehensive

elocution
06 speech 07 diction, oratory 08 delivery, phrasing, rhetoric 09 eloquence, utterance 11 enunciation 12 articulation 13 pronunciation 15 voice production

elongate
06 extend 07 draw out, prolong, stretch 08 lengthen, protract 10 make longer, stretch out

elongated
04 long, shot 08 extended 09 prolonged, stretched 10 lengthened, protracted

elope
04 bolt, flee 05 leave 06 decamp, escape, run off 07 abscond, do a bunk, make off, run away, scarper, vamoose 08 slip away 09 disappear, do a runner, skedaddle, steal away 10 hightail it, hit the road 11 hit the trail 14 make a bolt for it 15 make a break for it

eloquence
07 blarney, diction, fluency, oratory 08 facility, rhetoric 09 elocution, facundity, gassiness 10 expression 11 flow of words 12 forcefulness, gift of the gab 14 articulateness, expressiveness, persuasiveness

eloquent
04 glib 05 vivid, vocal 06 fluent, moving 07 voluble 08 forceful, graceful, stirring 09 effective, Mercurial, plausible 10 articulate, Ciceronian, expressive, persuasive, well-spoken 11 Demosthenic 12 honey-tongued 13 silver-tongued, well-expressed

El Salvador
02 ES 03 SLV

elsewhere
06 abroad, absent 07 not here, removed 10 otherwhere 13 somewhere else 14 in another place, to another place

• and elsewhere
04 et al 07 et alibi

elucidate
06 fill in, unfold 07 clarify, clear up, explain, expound 08 simplify, spell out 09 exemplify, explicate, interpret, make clear 10 dilucidate, illuminate, illustrate 11 shed light on, state simply 12 throw light on 13 give an example

elucidation
05 gloss 07 comment 08 footnote 10 annotation, commentary, exposition, marginalia 11 explanation, explication 12 illumination, illustration 13 clarification 14 interpretation

elude
◇ *deletion indicator*
04 bilk, duck, flee, foil, jink, slip 05 avoid, dodge, evade, shirk, stump 06 baffle, delude, escape, puzzle, thwart 08 confound, shake off 09 frustrate 10 circumvent 11 get away from

elusive
05 dodgy 06 shifty, slippy, subtle, tricky 07 evasive 08 baffling, puzzling, slippery 09 deceptive, transient 10 intangible, misleading, transitory 11 hard to catch, indefinable 12 unanalysable 15 difficult to find

elusiveness
06 puzzle 08 subtlety 10 transience 11 evasiveness 13 intangibility 14 indefinability, transitoriness

emaciated
04 bony, lean, thin 05 drawn, gaunt 06 meagre, skinny, wasted 07 haggard, pinched, scrawny 08 anorexic, skeletal 10 attenuated, cadaverous, wanthriven 11 thin as a rake 14 all skin and bone

emaciation
07 atrophy 08 boniness, leanness, thinness 09 gauntness, symptosis 11 haggardness, scrawniness, tabefaction

emanate
04 come, emit, flow, stem 05 arise, exude, issue 06 derive, emerge, exhale, spring, vanish 07 give off, give out, proceed, radiate, send out 09 discharge, originate

emanation
04 aura, flow 06 efflux 08 effluent, effusion, emission 09 discharge, effluence, effluvium, effluxion, radiation 10 exhalation

emancipate
04 free 05 loose, untie 06 unyoke 07 deliver, manumit, release, set free, unchain 08 liberate, set loose, unfetter 09 discharge, unshackle 11 enfranchise 14 forisfamiliate

emancipation
07 freedom, freeing, liberty, release 09 discharge, unbinding 10 liberation, unchaining 11 deliverance, manumission, setting free, unfettering 15 enfranchisement

emasculate
04 geld, spay 06 neuter, soften, weaken 07 cripple 08 castrate, enervate 10 debilitate, impoverish

emasculation
09 abatement, lessening, reduction, weakening 10 moderation 12 debilitation, diminishment 14 impoverishment

embalm
04 balm 05 store 06 balsam, lay out 07 cherish, mummify 08 conserve, enshrine, preserve, treasure 10 consecrate

embankment
03 dam 04 bank, bund 05 levee, mound 06 staith 07 banking, rampart, remblai, seabank, staithe 08 causeway, stopbank 09 earthwork

embargo
03 ban, bar 04 stop, tapu 05 block, check, seize 06 impede 07 barrier, seizure 08 blockage, obstruct, prohibit, restrain, restrict, stoppage 09 hindrance, interdict, proscribe, restraint 10 impediment 11 obstruction, prohibition, restriction 12 interdiction, proscription

embark
04 ship 05 board 06 inship 08 go aboard, take ship 09 board ship

• embark on
05 begin, enter, start 06 engage 07 enter on 08 commence, initiate, set about 09 undertake 10 launch into 11 venture into

embarkation
06 vessel 08 boarding, entrance, mounting 09 embussing, emplaning, getting-on 11 entrainment

embarrass
◇ *anagram indicator*
05 shame, upset **06** show up
07 chagrin, confuse, fluster, mortify, perplex **08** distress, encumber, incumber **09** discomfit, humiliate
10 discompose, disconcert **11** make ashamed, make awkward
14 discountenance

embarrassed
◇ *anagram indicator*
03 red **05** upset **06** guilty, shamed, uneasy **07** abashed, ashamed, awkward, shown up **08** confused, sheepish **09** ill at ease, mortified, perplexed, unnatural **10** distressed, humiliated **11** constrained, discomfited
12 disconcerted **13** self-conscious, uncomfortable

embarrassing
06 touchy, tricky **07** awkward, painful, shaming **08** shameful **09** sensitive, upsetting **10** indelicate, mortifying
11 distressing, humiliating
12 compromising, cringe-making, cringeworthy, discomfiting
13 disconcerting, uncomfortable

embarrassment
03 fix, jam **04** gene, mess **05** guilt, shame **06** excess, pickle, plight, scrape, unease **07** chagrin, dilemma, surplus **08** distress, embarras
09 abundance, confusion, profusion
10 constraint, difficulty, perplexity, uneasiness **11** awkwardness, bashfulness, humiliation, predicament
12 difficulties, discomfiture, discomposure, sheepishness
13 mortification, overabundance
14 superabundance

embassy
07 mission **08** legation, ministry
09 consulate, embassade, embassage
10 commission, delegation, deputation

embed
03 bed, fix, lay, set **04** dock, nest, root, sink **05** drive, inlay, plant **06** hammer, insert **07** implant

embellish
03 pan **04** deck, gild, trim, vary
05 adorn, grace **06** bedeck, enrich
07 dress up, enhance, festoon, garnish
08 beautify, decorate, ornament
09 bespangle, elaborate, embroider
10 exaggerate

embellishment
07 garnish, gilding **08** ornament, trimming, vignette **09** adornment, agreement **10** decoration, embroidery, enrichment **11** elaboration, enhancement **13** ornamentation

• **musical embellishment**
04 turn **07** melisma, roulade
09 fioritura, grace note

embers
05 ashes, coals **06** gleeds **07** cinders, clinker, residue **08** charcoal **09** live coals

embezzle
03 nab, rob **04** nick **05** filch, pinch, steal **06** impair, pilfer, rip off
07 purloin, swindle **08** peculate, shoulder **09** defalcate **11** appropriate
14 misappropriate

embezzlement
05 fraud, theft **07** nabbing, nicking, swindle, swizzle **08** filching, stealing
09 pilfering **11** defalcation
13 appropriation

embezzler
05 cheat, crook, fraud, thief **06** con man, robber **07** diddler **08** swindler
09 peculator **10** defalcator

embittered
04 sour **05** angry **06** bitter, piqued, soured **07** rankled **08** enfested
09 rancorous, resentful **11** disaffected, discouraged, exasperated
12 disenchanted, disheartened
13 disillusioned

emblazon
04 laud **05** adorn, extol, paint
06 blazon, colour, depict, praise
07 display, glorify, publish, trumpet
08 decorate, ornament, proclaim
09 celebrate, embellish, publicize
10 illuminate

emblem
04 flag, logo, mark, sign, type
05 badge, crest, image, token, totem
06 device, figure, symbol
08 colophon, insignia **09** symbolize
11 service mark **14** representation

See also **emblem of authority** *under* **authority**

Floral and plant emblems include:

04 rose
06 wattle
07 thistle, waratah
08 daffodil, shamrock
09 maple leaf, maple tree
10 fleur-de-lis, fleur-de-lys, silver fern
11 common heath, kangaroo paw
12 golden wattle
13 royal bluebell
14 Cooktown orchid
15 Sturt's desert pea
16 Sturt's desert rose, Tasmanian blue gum

emblematic
07 typical **08** symbolic **10** figurative, symbolical **11** allegorical
12 emblematical, representing
14 representative

embodiment
04 soul, type **05** model **06** vessel
07 epitome, example **10** expression
11 incarnation, realization
12 quintessence **13** concentration, incorporation, manifestation
14 representation, representative
15 exemplification, personification

embody
◇ *containment indicator*
05 shape **06** take in, typify **07** collect, combine, contain, express, include
08 manifest, organize, stand for
09 corporify, exemplify, incarnate, integrate, personify, represent, symbolize **10** assimilate, synonymize
11 encarnalize, impersonate, incorporate **12** substantiate **13** bring together

embolden
04 fire, stir **05** cheer, nerve, rouse
07 animate, hearten, inflame, inspire
08 make bold, reassure, vitalize
09 encourage, make brave, stimulate
10 invigorate, strengthen **13** give courage to

embrace
◇ *containment indicator*
◇ *hidden indicator*
03 hug **04** bind, clip, coll, fold, hold, lock, neck, pash, snog, span, wrap
05 admit, adopt, bosom, brace, clasp, cover, grasp, halse, hause, hawse, inarm **06** abrazo, accept, clinch, cuddle, enfold, enlace, fasten, inclip, infold, inlace, smooch, strain, take in, take up **07** colling, contain, espouse, include, involve, necking, receive, squeeze, welcome **08** accolade, canoodle, complect, compress, comprise **09** embrasure, encompass
10 tangle with **11** incorporate, take on board **13** slap and tickle **14** receive eagerly

embrocation
03 rub **05** cream, salve **06** lotion
07 epithem **08** liniment, ointment

embroider
03 sew **04** darn, purl, work **05** sprig
06 colour, enrich, stitch **07** dress up, enhance, garnish, tambour
08 decorate **09** elaborate, embellish, hemstitch **10** exaggerate **11** cross-stitch

embroidery
04 work **05** braid **06** crewel, sewing
07 apparel, cutwork, orphrey, sampler, tambour, tatting **08** braiding, fagoting, tapestry **09** faggoting, fancywork, stump work **10** canvas-work, needlework **11** needlecraft, needlepoint **13** embellishment, ornamentation

Embroidery stitches include:

04 back, long, moss, stem, tent
05 chain, cross, queen, satin
07 blanket, bullion, chevron, feather, running
08 couching, fishbone, straight, wheat-ear
09 gros point, half-cross, honeycomb, lazy daisy
10 French knot, longstitch
11 herringbone
12 long-and-short, Swiss darning

embroil
◇ *anagram indicator*
05 mix up **06** enmesh **07** involve
08 distract, draw into, entangle
09 catch up in, implicate **11** incriminate

embryo
04 germ, root, seed **06** basics, foetus **07** nucleus **08** gastrula, plantule **09** beginning, rudiments **11** unborn child
• **embryo transfer**
02 ET

embryonic
05 early **07** primary **08** emerging, germinal, immature, inchoate, unformed **09** beginning, fledgling, incipient **10** elementary **11** rudimentary, undeveloped

emend
◇ *anagram indicator*
03 fix **04** edit **05** alter, amend **06** polish, redact, refine, repair, revise **07** correct, improve, rectify, rewrite **09** castigate

emendation
◇ *anagram indicator*
07 editing **08** revision **09** amendment, redaction, rewriting **10** alteration, correction, refinement **11** corrigendum, improvement **13** rectification

emerald
07 smaragd

emerge
◇ *anagram indicator*
◇ *hidden indicator*
03 out **04** rise **05** arise, issue **06** appear, cast up, crop up, turn up **07** come out, debouch, develop, emanate, outcrop, proceed, surface, turn out **09** come forth, transpire **10** be revealed **11** become known, come to light, materialize **12** come into view **14** become apparent

emergence
04 dawn, rise **05** issue **06** advent, coming **07** arrival, outcrop **08** disclose, eclosion **09** unfolding **10** appearance, disclosure **11** development, springing-up

emergency
03 fix **04** mess **05** extra, pinch, spare **06** back-up, crisis, crunch, danger, pickle, plight, scrape, strait, urgent **07** dilemma, reserve **08** accident, calamity, disaster, exigence, exigency, fall-back, hot water, quandary **09** extremity, immediate **10** difficulty, substitute **11** alternative, catastrophe, predicament, top-priority **13** extraordinary

emergent
06 coming, rising **07** budding **08** emerging **09** coming out, embryonic, fledgling **10** burgeoning, developing **11** independent

emetic
04 puke **05** puker, vomit **06** emetin, ipecac **07** emetine **08** emetical, vomitary, vomitive, vomitory **11** ipecacuanha, sanguinaria

emigrate
04 move **06** depart **07** migrate **08** relocate, resettle **10** move abroad **13** leave your home

emigration
06 exodus **07** journey, removal **09** departure, migration **10** relocation **12** expatriation, moving abroad

eminence
03 tor **04** berg, fame, hill, knob, note, rank **05** ridge **06** esteem, height, renown **07** dignity, stature **08** altitude, majority, prestige **09** advantage, celebrity, greatness, prelation **10** importance, notability, prominence, promontory, reputation, trochanter **11** distinction, pre-eminence, sovereignty, superiority **14** honourableness **15** illustriousness

eminent
04 high **05** first, grand, great, noted **06** famous **07** notable **08** elevated, esteemed, renowned, superior **09** important, prominent, respected, well-known **10** celebrated, noteworthy, pre-eminent **11** conspicuous, high-ranking, illustrious, outstanding, prestigious, superlative **13** distinguished

eminently
04 high, most, very, well **06** highly **07** greatly, notably **08** signally **09** extremely, obviously **10** remarkably, strikingly **11** exceedingly, prominently **12** surpassingly **13** conspicuously, exceptionally, outstandingly, par excellence

emissary
03 spy **05** agent, envoy, scout **06** deputy, herald **07** courier **08** delegate, diplomat, outgoing **09** go-between, messenger **10** ambassador **12** intermediary **14** representative

emission
04 vent **05** issue **06** escape **07** release **08** effusion, ejection **09** diffusion, discharge, emanation, exudation, giving-off, giving-out, radiation **10** exhalation, outpouring, production **11** ejaculation **12** transmission

emit
03 ren, rin, run, say **04** boak, bock, boke, leak, ooze, pass, shed, spew, vent, void **05** eject, eruct, exude, issue, sound, speak, throw, utter, voice **06** exhale, expire, let out **07** diffuse, emanate, excrete, express, give off, give out, pour out, produce, radiate, release, send out **08** eructate, throw out, vocalize **09** discharge, give forth, send forth, verbalize

emollient
03 oil **04** balm **05** cream, salve **06** lotion **07** calming, lenient, unguent **08** balsamic, lenitive, liniment, ointment, poultice, soap-ball, soothing **09** appeasing, assuaging, assuasive, demulcent, placatory, softening **10** mitigative, mollifying, palliative **11** moisturizer **12** conciliatory, moisturizing, propitiatory

emolument
03 fee, pay **04** gain, hire **05** wages **06** charge, profit, return, reward, salary **07** benefit, payment, profits, stipend **08** earnings **09** advantage, allowance **10** honorarium, recompense **12** compensation, remuneration

emotion
03 ire, joy **04** envy, fear, hate, pang, turn **05** anger, dread, grief, sense, shock, spasm, whirl **06** affect, ardour, motion, sorrow, spirit, thrill, warmth **07** anoesis, despair, ecstasy, feeling, fervour, passion, sadness, upsurge **08** movement, reaction, surprise **09** affection, happiness, reverence, sensation, sentiment, sublimity, transport, vehemence **10** excitement **11** sensibility
• **expression of emotion**
01 O **02** ha, oh **03** hah, hoo, wow **05** arrah, hoo-oo, wowee
• **sign of emotion**
04 tear

emotional
04 warm **05** fiery, moved, soppy **06** ardent, fervid, heated, loving, moving, red-hot, roused, tender **07** emotive, feeling, fervent, glowing, gushing, radiant, soulful, tearful, zealous **08** effusive, exciting, hysteric, pathetic, poignant, stirring, swelling, touching, white-hot **09** excitable, schmaltzy, sensitive, thrilling **10** hot-blooded, hysterical, passionate, responsive **11** full-hearted, impassioned, overcharged, sentimental, susceptible, tear-jerking, tempestuous **12** enthusiastic, gut-wrenching, heartwarming, soul-stirring **13** demonstrative, psychological, temperamental

emotionally
06 warmly **07** tensely **08** ardently, lovingly, tenderly **09** awkwardly, fervently, nervously, zealously **10** delicately, poignantly, touchingly **11** sensitively **12** passionately **13** sentimentally, under pressure **14** heartwarmingly **15** controversially, demonstratively, psychologically, temperamentally

emotionless
04 cold, cool **05** blank **06** frigid, remote **07** deadpan, distant, glacial, unmoved **08** clinical, cold-fish, detached, toneless **09** impassive, unfeeling **10** antiseptic, impassible, insensible, phlegmatic, unaffected, unblinking **11** cold-blooded, indifferent, unemotional **13** imperturbable **15** undemonstrative

emotive
06 touchy **07** awkward **08** delicate **09** emotional, sensitive **12** inflammatory **13** controversial

empathize
05 share **07** comfort, feel for, support **10** understand **12** have a rapport, identify with

emperor
03 Emp, Imp **04** czar, Inca, king, tsar **05** kesar, tenno **06** kaiser, keasar, mikado, purple, shogun **08** imperial, padishah **09** imperator, sovereign **12** kaisar-i-Hindi

Emperors include:

03 Leo
04 John, Nero, Otho, Otto, Paul, Pu Yi
05 Akbar (the Great), Babur, Basil, Boris, Galba, Henry, Louis, Murad, Nerva, Pedro, Peter, Selim, Titus
06 Caesar (Julius), Conrad, Joseph, Jovian, Julian, Justin, Mehmet, Philip (the Arab), Rudolf, Trajan
07 Agustín (de Itúrbide), Akihito, Alamgir, Alexius, Baldwin, Charles, Charles (the Bald), Charles (the Fat), Francis, Gordian, Hadrian, Leopold, Lothair, Marcian, Michael, Severus, William
08 Augustus, Aurelius, Caligula, Claudius, Commodus, Constans, Domitian, Galerius, Hirohito, Honorius, Jahangir, Licinius, Matthias, Maximian, Napoleon, Nicholas, Süleyman, Tiberius, Valerian
09 Alexander, Antoninus, Atahualpa, Aurangzeb, Caracalla, Carausius, Ferdinand, Frederick, Gallienus, Heraclius, Justinian, Maxentius, Montezuma, Mutsuhito, Shah Jahan, Sigismund, Vespasian, Vitellius, Yoshihito
10 Andronicus, Augustulus, Diocletian, Elagabalus, Kublai Khan, Maximilian, Meiji Tenno, Theodosius
11 Charlemagne, Constantine, Constantius, Jean Jacques, Valentinian
12 Chandragupta, Heliogabalus, John Comnenus, Samudragupta
13 Antoninus Pius, Francis Joseph, Haile Selassie
14 Marcus Aurelius
15 Alexius Comnenus

See also **Roman**

emphasis
04 birr, mark **05** focus, force, power **06** accent, moment, stress, weight **07** urgency **08** priority, strength **09** attention, intensity **10** importance, insistence, prominence **11** pre-eminence **12** accentuation, positiveness, significance, underscoring

• expression of emphasis
04 Jeez **05** Jeeze **07** you know

emphasize
06 accent, play up, stress, weight **07** dwell on, enforce, feature, point up **08** heighten, insist on **09** highlight, intensify, press home, punctuate, spotlight, underline **10** accentuate, foreground, strengthen **11** put stress on **14** bring to the fore **15** call attention to, draw attention to

emphatic
04 firm **05** vivid **06** direct, marked, strong **07** certain, decided, earnest, marcato, telling **08** absolute, decisive, definite, distinct, forceful, forcible, positive, powerful, striking, vehement, vigorous **09** energetic, important, insistent, momentous **10** conclusive, expressive, impressive, pronounced, punctuated **11** categorical, distinctive, significant, unequivocal **12** unmistakable **13** unmistakeable

emphatically
06 firmly **08** in spades, strongly **09** certainly **10** absolutely, definitely, forcefully, vehemently, vigorously **11** insistently **13** categorically, distinctively, unequivocally

empire
03 Emp **04** firm, rule, sway **05** power, realm **06** domain, empery **07** command, company, control, kingdom **08** business, dominion, province **09** authority, supremacy, territory **10** consortium, government **11** corporation, sovereignty **12** commonwealth, conglomerate, jurisdiction, organization **13** multinational

Empires and kingdoms include:

04 Cush, Kush, Moab
05 Akkad, Alban, Media, Mogul, Roman
06 Naples
07 Argolis, Assyria, Bohemia, British, Chinese, Galicia, Ottoman, Persian
08 Dalriada, Lombardy, Sardinia
09 Abyssinia, Byzantine, Holy Roman
10 New Kingdom, Old Kingdom
11 Northumbria
13 Middle Kingdom
15 Austro-Hungarian

See also **classification**

• part of empire
04 land

empirical
08 observed **09** practical, pragmatic **11** a posteriori **12** experiential, experimental

empirically
11 practically **13** pragmatically **14** experientially, experimentally

employ
03 ply, use **04** fill, hire **05** apply, exert, spend **06** bestow, draw on, engage, enlist, expend, occupy, retain, sign up, take on, take up **07** appoint, exploit, recruit, service, utilize **08** exercise, put to use **09** make use of **10** apprentice, commission **11** bring to bear **13** bring into play **15** put on the payroll, take advantage of

employed
04 busy, used **05** hired **06** active, in work **07** earning, engaged, working **08** occupied, with a job **11** preoccupied **12** in employment

employee
03 cog, man **04** hand, help **05** gofer, woman **06** casual, worker **08** labourer, munchkin **09** assistant, job-holder, operative, rainmaker **10** wage-earner, waterclerk, working man **12** working woman **13** member of staff, working person

employer
03 guv **04** boss, firm, head, user **05** malik, melik, owner **06** gaffer, master, old man **07** company, manager, padrone, skipper **08** business, director, governor, mistress **09** executive **10** management, proprietor, taskmaster, workmaster **12** entrepreneur, organization, taskmistress, workmistress **13** establishment

employment
03 job, use **04** hire, line, ploy, post, work **05** craft, place, trade **06** employ, hiring, métier **07** calling, pursuit, service **08** business, position, taking-on, vocation **09** signing-up, situation **10** engagement, enlistment, livelihood, occupation, profession **11** application, recruitment **12** exercitation **14** apprenticeship

emporium
04 fair, mart, shop **05** store **06** bazaar, market **08** boutique **11** market-place **13** establishment **15** department store

empower
05 equip **06** enable, permit **07** certify, entitle, license, qualify, set free, warrant **08** accredit, delegate, sanction **09** authorize **10** commission **11** give means to, give power to

empress
03 Emp, Imp **05** queen, ruler **07** czarina, tsarina **08** czaritsa, imperial, kaiserin, tsaritsa **09** imperator, sovereign

Empresses include:

02 Lü, Wu
03 Zoë
04 Anna, Cixi
05 Irene, Livia
06 Helena (St), Tz'u Hsi, Wu Chao, Wu Zhao
07 Eugénie, Wu Zhaov
08 Adelaide (St), Cunegund (St), Faustina, Nur Jahan, Theodora, Victoria
09 Agrippina (the Younger), Alexandra, Catherine, Catherine (the Great), Elizabeth, Joséphine, Kunigunde (St), Messalina, Old Buddha, Theophano
11 Marie Louise
12 Anna Ivanovna, Maria Theresa
13 Livia Drusilla

emptiness
04 void **05** blank **06** hiatus, hollow, hunger, vacuum **07** inanity, vacancy,

vacuity **08** bareness, futility, voidness **09** unreality **10** barrenness, desolation, flatulence, hollowness, vacantness **11** aimlessness, uselessness **13** senselessness, worthlessness **15** ineffectiveness, meaninglessness, purposelessness

empty
◇ *middle deletion indicator*
03 gut **04** bare, boss, free, idle, lade, pump, teem, toom, vain, void **05** addle, blank, clear, drain, go out, inane, issue, leave, strip, use up, waste **06** barren, devoid, frothy, futile, gousty, hollow, hot-air, hungry, unload, unpack, unreal, vacant, vacate **07** aimless, deadpan, deplete, exhaust, flow out, pour out, trivial, turn out, useless, vacuate, vacuous, viduous **08** clear out, deserted, desolate, evacuate, soulless, unfilled **09** available, discharge, fruitless, insincere, pointless, senseless, worthless **10** unoccupied **11** ineffective, ineffectual, meaningless, purposeless, unfurnished, uninhabited **13** insubstantial **14** expressionless, unsatisfactory **15** with nothing in it

empty-headed
04 daft, vain **05** batty, dippy, ditsy, ditzy, dopey, dotty, inane, silly **06** scatty, stupid **07** foolish, vacuous **09** frivolous **13** rattle-brained, unintelligent **14** feather-brained, scatter-brained

emulate
04 copy, echo **05** emule, match, mimic, rival **06** aemule, follow **07** imitate, vie with **09** ambitious, reproduce **11** compete with, contend with **15** model yourself on

emulation
06 strife **07** contest, copying, echoing, mimicry, paragon, rivalry **08** matching **09** challenge, following, imitation, rivalship **10** contention **11** competition **12** contestation

enable
03 fit, let **04** able, help **05** allow, endue, equip **06** permit **07** empower, entitle, further, license, prepare, qualify, warrant **08** accredit, sanction, validate **09** authorize **10** commission, facilitate, make easier **12** make possible **13** pave the way for **14** clear the way for

enact
04 pass, play, rule **05** order **06** act out, decree, depict, ordain, ratify **07** approve, command, make law, perform, portray **08** appear as, sanction **09** authorize, establish, legislate, represent

enactment
03 act, law **04** bill, play, rule **05** edict, order **06** acting, decree **07** command, measure, passing, playing, purview, staging, statute **08** approval, sanction **09** ordinance, portrayal **10** performing, regulation **11** commandment, institution, legislation, performance **12** ratification **13** authorization **14** representation

enamoured
03 mad **04** fond, keen, wild **05** taken **07** charmed, smitten **08** besotted **09** bewitched, enchanted, entranced **10** captivated, enthralled, fascinated, infatuated, in love with

en bloc
05 as one **07** en masse, in a body **08** as a group, as a whole, ensemble **09** all at once, wholesale **11** all together

encampment
04 base, camp, duar, laer **05** douar, dowar, tents **06** laager **07** bivouac, hutment, manyata **08** barracks, campsite, manyatta, quarters **13** camping-ground

encapsulate
◇ *containment indicator*
03 pot **05** sum up **06** digest, précis, take in, typify **07** abridge, capture, contain, include **08** compress, condense **09** epitomize, exemplify, represent, summarize

encapsulation
06 digest, précis **07** summary **10** expression **14** representation **15** exemplification

encase
04 line, wrap **05** bound, cover, frame **07** confine, enclose, envelop **08** surround

enchant
05 charm, spell **06** allure, appeal, thrill **07** attract, becharm, beguile, bewitch, delight, enamour, enthral, glamour **08** entrance, sirenize **09** captivate, enrapture, fascinate, hypnotize, mesmerize, spellbind

enchanter
05 magus, witch **06** wizard **07** warlock **08** conjurer, magician, sorcerer **09** archimage, mesmerist **10** reim-kennar **11** necromancer, spellbinder

enchanting
06 lovely **07** magical, winsome **08** alluring, charming, pleasant **09** appealing, endearing, ravishing, wonderful **10** attractive, bewitching, delightful, entrancing **11** captivating, fascinating, mesmerizing **12** irresistible

enchantment
05 bliss, charm, magic, spell **06** allure, appeal, glamor **07** delight, ecstasy, glamour, gramary, rapture, sorcery **08** gramarye, malefice, witching, wizardry **09** hypnotism, mesmerism **10** allurement, necromancy, witchcraft **11** conjuration, fascination, incantation **14** attractiveness

enchantress
04 vamp **05** Circe, fairy, lamia, siren, witch **07** charmer **08** conjurer, magician **09** sorceress **10** seductress **11** femme fatale, necromancer, spellbinder

encircle
◇ *containment indicator*
04 belt, clip, gird, hoop, pale, ring, wind **05** crowd, girth, hem in, inorb, orbit, twine, wheel **06** circle, embail, enfold, engird, enlace, enring, girdle, inlace, stemme **07** close in, compass, enclose, envelop, environ, enwheel **08** surround **09** encompass **12** circumscribe

enclose
◇ *containment indicator*
02 in **03** box, pen, pin **04** cage, case, coop, hold, ring, seal, tine, womb, wrap **05** bound, bower, clasp, cover, fence, frame, hedge, hem in, pound, put in **06** circle, cocoon, corral, embale, emboss, encase, enfold, enlock, girdle, immure, incase, infold, inhoop, insert, pocket, prison, shut in, take in **07** close in, compass, confine, contain, embound, embowel, embrace, enchase, envelop, include, seclude **08** conclude, encircle, send with, surround **09** encompass, ring-fence **10** comprehend, interclude **12** circumscribe

enclosed
03 enc **04** encl, pend, pent **07** bosomed, recluse **08** included

enclosure
03 box, enc, haw, pen, pit, ree, ren, rin, run, sty **04** area, bawn, boma, cage, camp, encl, fank, fold, hope, lair, pale, peel, pele, reed, ring, town, yard **05** arena, close, court, garth, kraal, pound, sekos, stell **06** corral, runway **07** enclave, fencing, haining, paddock, parrock, pightle, pinfold **08** addition, cloister, compound, enceinte, seraglio, stockade, townland **09** inclusion, insertion **10** encincture

encode
05 ravel **06** cipher, garble **07** encrypt, obscure **08** disguise, encipher, scramble **11** put into code **14** make mysterious

encompass
◇ *containment indicator*
04 gird, hold, ring, span **05** admit, bathe, brace, cover, hem in **06** begird, circle, embody, enfold, infold, shut in, sphere, take in **07** close in, confine, contain, embrace, enclose, envelop, include, involve, procure **08** cincture, comprise, encircle, surround **10** circumvent, comprehend **11** incorporate **12** circumscribe

encore
03 bis **06** ancora, repeat, replay **10** repetition

encounter
04 cope, face, meet, tilt **05** brush, clash, close, fight, joust, match, run-in,

set-to **06** action, battle, combat, engage, oppose, ruffle, strive, tackle, tussle **07** contact, contend, contest, dispute, meeting, run into **08** bump into, conflict, confront, cope with, deal with, happen on, skirmish, struggle **09** clash with, collision, rencontre, run across **10** chance upon, come across, engagement, experience, rencounter, rendezvous **11** be faced with, be up against, compete with, grapple with **12** do battle with **13** come up against, confrontation, passage of arms, stumble across **15** cross swords with

encourage
03 aid **04** abet, back, coax, fuel, help, lift, root, spur, stir, sway, urge **05** boost, cheer, egg on, gee up, jolly, pep up, rally, rouse **06** assist, buck up, buoy up, exhort, favour, foster, incite, induce, prompt, second, spirit, spur on, stroke **07** advance, animate, cheer on, cherish, comfort, console, forward, further, hearten, inspire, promote, support, sustain, upcheer, win over **08** accorage, advocate, convince, embolden, inspirit, motivate, persuade, reassure, talk into **09** accourage, enhearten, influence, stimulate **10** barrack for, strengthen **14** be supportive to

encouragement
03 aid **04** help **05** boost, cheer **06** come-on, urging **07** backing, coaxing, comfort, pep talk, succour, support **08** cheering, stimulus **09** incentive, promotion **10** assistance, heartening, incitement, motivation, persuasion **11** consolation, endorsement, exhortation, furtherance, inspiration, reassurance, stimulation **12** shot in the arm
• **expression of encouragement**
02 ha, on **03** hah, olé, via, yay **04** come, sa sa **05** heigh, hollo, there **06** giddap, now now **07** attaboy, come now **08** attagirl, come come **09** ups-a-daisy, upsy-daisy

encouraging
04 rosy **06** bright **07** hopeful **08** cheerful, cheering **09** hortative, hortatory, incentive, inspiring, promising, uplifting **10** auspicious, comforting, heartening, protreptic, reassuring, supportive **11** cohortative, stimulating **12** satisfactory **14** proceleusmatic

encroach
03 jet **05** pinch, usurp **06** invade, trench **07** impinge, intrude, overrun **08** entrench, infringe, intrench, overstep, trespass **10** infiltrate, muscle in on **11** make inroads

encroachment
06 inroad **08** invasion, trespass **09** incursion, intrusion **11** purpresture, trespassing **12** entrenchment, infiltration, infringement, intrenchment, overstepping

encrypt
05 ravel **06** cipher, encode, garble **07** obscure **08** disguise, encipher, scramble **11** put into code **14** make mysterious

encumber
03 jam **04** cram, load, pack **05** block, check, cramp, stuff **06** accloy, burden, hamper, hinder, impede, retard, saddle, strain, stress **07** bog down, burthen, congest, oppress, overlay, prevent **08** handicap, obstruct, overload, restrain, slow down **09** constrain, embarrass, weigh down **13** inconvenience

encumbrance
04 load **05** cross **06** burden, strain, stress, weight **08** handicap, obstacle **09** albatross, cumbrance, hindrance, liability, millstone, restraint **10** constraint, difficulty, impediment, obligation **11** obstruction **13** inconvenience **14** responsibility

encyclopedia
04 ency **05** encyc

encyclopedic
04 vast **05** broad **07** in-depth **08** complete, thorough **09** universal **10** exhaustive **11** compendious, wide-ranging **12** all-embracing, all-inclusive **13** comprehensive, thoroughgoing **15** all-encompassing

end
◇ *tail selection indicator*
01 Z **03** aim, tip **04** abut, area, butt, doom, edge, fine, goal, part, ruin, side, stop, stub, tail, term **05** cease, close, death, dying, field, issue, limit, omega, point, scrap **06** aspect, be over, border, branch, demise, design, die out, ending, expire, finale, finish, intent, margin, motive, object, period, reason, region, result, run out, target, upshot, wind up **07** abolish, destroy, outcome, purpose, remnant, section, vestige **08** boundary, break off, complete, conclude, dissolve, downfall, epilogue, fade away, fragment, round off **09** cessation, checkmate, culminate, extremity, intention, leftovers, objective, remainder, terminate **10** annihilate, completion, conclusion, dénouement, department, extinction, extinguish **11** come to an end, consequence, culmination, destruction, discontinue, dissolution, exterminate, termination **12** bring to an end **13** extermination
• **at an end**
02 up **03** oer **04** over
• **at the end of**
◇ *juxtaposition indicator*
◇ *tail selection indicator*
• **at the far end**
03 out
• **east end**
04 apse
• **ends**
◇ *ends selection indicator*
• **nearly at an end**
04 late
• **the end**
06 enough **07** too much **08** the limit, the worst **10** unbearable **11** intolerable, unendurable **12** insufferable, the final blow, the last straw **15** beyond endurance

endanger
04 risk **06** expose, hazard, risque **07** imperil **08** threaten **09** prejudice, put at risk **10** compromise, jeopardize **11** periclitate, put in danger **13** put in jeopardy

endearing
04 cute **05** sweet **07** lovable, winsome **08** adorable, charming, engaging, loveable **09** appealing **10** attractive, delightful, enchanting **11** captivating

endearment
04 love **07** pet-name **08** fondness **09** affection, sweet talk **10** attachment, diminutive, hypocorism **12** sweet nothing **15** term of affection
• **term of endearment**
03 bud, hon, luv, pet, pug **04** burd, cony, dear, dove, fool, love, peat **05** chick, chuck, coney, ducks, ducky, heart, hinny, honey, jarta, lovey, mopsy, mouse, popsy, puggy, sugar, yarta, yarto **06** flower, monkey, moppet, pigsny **07** alannah, chuckie, cupcake, pigsney, pigsnie, princox **08** honeybun, precious, princock, treasure **09** pillicock, sugarplum **10** honeybunch, honey-chile, sweetie-pie **11** chick-a-biddy **12** chick-a-diddle

endeavour
02 go **03** aim, try **04** bash, seek, shot, stab **05** assay, crack, Morse **06** aspire, effort, labour, strive **07** attempt, venture, working **08** striving, struggle **09** take pains, undertake **10** do your best, enterprise **11** undertaking **13** try your hand at

ended
02 up **04** over, past

ending
◇ *tail selection indicator*
03 end **04** last **05** close, death, dying **06** climax, finale, finish **07** closing, closure **08** epilogue, terminal **09** cessation, desinence, extremity, finishing **10** completing, completion, concluding, conclusion, dénouement, resolution **11** culmination, termination **12** consummation

endless
◇ *ends deletion indicator*
◇ *tail deletion indicator*
05 whole **06** boring, entire **07** eternal, undying **08** constant, fineless, infinite, termless, unbroken, unending **09** boundless, ceaseless, continual, incessant, limitless, perpetual, Sisyphean, unlimited **10** continuous, monotonous, objectless, without end

11 everlasting, measureless
12 interminable 13 inexhaustible, uninterrupted

endlessly
◇ *tail deletion indicator*
09 eternally 10 constantly, infinitely, unendingly, without end 11 ceaselessly, continually, day after day, day in day out, limitlessly, perpetually
12 continuously, interminably
15 uninterruptedly, without stopping

endmost
◇ *tail selection indicator*
04 last 07 extreme 08 farthest, hindmost

endorse
02 OK 04 back, okay, sign 05 adopt
06 affirm, endoss, favour, ratify, uphold
07 approve, confirm, initial, support, sustain, warrant 08 advocate, be behind, sanction, vouch for
09 authorize, get behind, recommend
11 countersign, subscribe to 15 sign on the back of

endorsement
02 OK 04 okay, visa, visé 07 backing, support, warrant 08 advocacy, approval, sanction, thumbs-up
09 signature 10 green light
11 affirmation, approbation, initialling, testimonial 12 commendation, confirmation, ratification, subscription
13 authorization 14 recommendation, seal of approval

endow
04 fund, gift, give, have, vest, will
05 award, boast, dower, endew, enjoy, found, grant, leave, state 06 bestow, confer, donate, pay for, supply
07 finance, furnish, possess, present, provide, support 08 bequeath, make over 12 be endued with 13 be blessed with

endowment
04 fund, gift, wakf, waqf 05 award, dower, dowry, flair, grant, power
06 genius, income, legacy, talent
07 ability, bequest, faculty, finance, funding, present, quality, revenue
08 aptitude, bestowal, capacity, donation, dotation 09 attribute, character, provision 10 capability, fellowship, settlement 11 benefaction, studentship 13 qualification

endurable
07 lasting 08 bearable, portable
09 tolerable 10 manageable, sufferable 11 supportable, sustainable
13 withstandable

endurance
04 guts, stay 05 spunk 06 bottle
07 lasting, stamina 08 backbone, duration, patience, stoicism, strength, tenacity 09 captivity, fortitude, stability, tolerance 10 durability, resolution, sufferance, toleration
11 continuance, persistence, resignation 12 perseverance, staying power, stickability 13 long-suffering

endure
03 aby 04 abye, bear, bide, dree, dure, face, have, hold, keep, last, live, lump, meet, stay, take, wear 05 abear, abide, allow, brave, brook, stand, stick, thole
06 harden, hold up, permit, remain, suffer 07 abrooke, hold out, perdure, persist, prevail, stick it, stomach, support, survive, sustain, swallow, undergo, weather 08 continue, cope with, outstand, stand for, submit to, tolerate 09 encounter, go through, put up with, withstand 10 experience, sweat it out, tough it out

enduring
04 firm 05 stout 06 stable, steady
07 abiding, chronic, durable, dureful, eternal, lasting 08 immortal, livelong, patience, tolerant 09 permanent, perpetual, remaining, steadfast, surviving 10 continuing, persistent, persisting, prevailing, undergoing, unwavering 11 long-lasting, substantial, unfaltering
12 imperishable, long-standing

enemy
03 foe 04 time 05 Devil, rival
06 foeman 07 anemone, hostile, opposer 08 opponent 09 adversary, other side 10 antagonist, competitor, philistine 13 the opposition 14 the competition

energetic
04 wick 05 brisk, pithy, vital, zappy, zippy 06 active, lively, potent, punchy, strong 07 dynamic, go-ahead, rackety, slammin', zestful 08 animated, bouncing, forceful, forcible, powerful, slamming, spirited, tireless, vigorous
09 effective, go-getting, strenuous
10 boisterous 11 full of beans, high-powered, throughgaun 12 through-going 13 indefatigable

energize
04 stir 05 liven, pep up 06 arouse, excite, fire up, vivify 07 animate, enliven, quicken 08 activate, motivate, vitalize 09 electrify, galvanize, stimulate 10 invigorate

energy
01 E 02 go 03 pep, vim, zip 04 brio, fire, fuel, gism, head, jism, life, push, zeal, zest, zing 05 drive, force, might, power, verve 06 ardour, spirit, vigour
07 pizzazz, potency, sparkle, stamina
08 activity, dynamism, exertion, strength, vitality, vivacity
09 animation, intensity 10 efficiency, enthusiasm, get-up-and-go, liveliness, propellant 11 motive power
12 forcefulness 13 effectiveness, effervescence, kinetic energy
15 potential energy
• **lacking energy**
04 nesh, poky 05 pokey 09 out of curl
• **lose energy**
04 flag, wilt
• **primitive energy**
02 id
• **renewable energy department**
04 ETSU

enervated
04 limp, weak 05 spent, tired
06 beaten, done in, effete, feeble, pooped, sapped 07 run-down, worn out 08 fatigued, unmanned, unnerved, weakened 09 enfeebled, exhausted, paralysed, pooped out, washed-out
10 undermined 11 debilitated, devitalized, tuckered out
13 incapacitated

enervating
04 hard 05 tough 06 taxing, tiring
07 arduous 08 draining, exacting, relaxing, wearying 09 demanding, difficult, fatiguing, laborious, strenuous, wearisome 10 exhausting

enfeeble
03 sap 04 geld 05 waste 06 reduce, weaken 07 deplete, exhaust, fatigue, unhinge, unnerve, wear out
08 diminish, enervate 09 undermine
10 debilitate, devitalize

enfold
◇ *containment indicator*
03 hug, lap 04 fold, hold, wind, wrap
05 clasp, imply 06 clutch, enwrap, inclip, inwrap, plight, shroud, swathe, wimple, wrap up 07 embrace, enclose, envelop, whimple 08 encircle
09 encompass, implicate

enforce
04 urge 05 apply, drive, exact, force
06 coerce, compel, fulfil, impose, lean on, oblige, strive 07 execute, impress, require 08 carry out, insist on, pressure
09 constrain, discharge, emphasize, implement, prosecute, reinforce
10 administer, pressurize
11 necessitate 14 put the screws on

enforced
06 forced 07 binding, imposed, obliged
08 dictated, ordained, required
09 compelled, mandatory, necessary
10 compulsory, obligatory, prescribed
11 constrained, involuntary, unavoidable

enforcement
08 coaction, coercion, pressure
09 discharge, execution
10 compulsion, constraint, fulfilment, imposition, insistence, obligation
11 application, prosecution, requirement 14 administration, implementation

enfranchise
04 free 07 manumit, release
08 liberate 10 emancipate 13 give the vote to 14 give suffrage to

enfranchisement
07 freedom, freeing, release
08 suffrage 10 liberating, liberation
11 manumission 12 emancipation, voting rights

engage
02 do 03 win 04 book, busy, draw, fill, gain, grip, hire, hold, join, lock, mesh,

take **05** catch, charm, enrol, fight, share, tie up **06** absorb, allure, assail, attach, attack, combat, employ, enlist, enmesh, fasten, occupy, pledge, sign on, sign up, take on, take up
07 appoint, attract, betroth, capture, engross, involve, recruit, reserve
08 contract, embark on, entangle, interact, intrigue, practise, take part
09 captivate, clash with, encounter, enter into, guarantee, interlock, partake of, preoccupy, undertake
10 battle with, commission **11** fit together, participate, wage war with
12 interconnect **15** put on the payroll

• **engage in**
◇ *insertion indicator*
04 play, wage **05** enter **07** enter on
08 voutsafe **09** enter upon, prosecute, undertake, vouchsafe

engaged
04 busy **05** in use, taken **06** active, in mesh, tied up **07** pledged
08 absorbed, employed, espoused, immersed, involved, occupied, plighted, promised **09** affianced, betrothed, committed, engrossed, intrigued, spoken for **11** preoccupied, unavailable **12** in conference

engagement
03 gig, vow, war **04** bond, date, snap
05 clash, fight, troth **06** action, attack, battle, combat, pledge, plight, strife
07 assault, booking, contest, fixture, meeting, promise, sharing **08** conflict, contract, espousal, struggle
09 agreement, assurance, betrothal, encounter, interview, offensive, partaking **10** commitment, employment, obligation, rendezvous, taking part **11** appointment, arrangement, assignation, betrothment, hand-promise, involvement, reservation, undertaking
13 confrontation, participation

engaging
05 sweet **07** likable, lovable, winning, winsome **08** adorable, charming, fetching, likeable, loveable, pleasant, pleasing **09** agreeable, appealing
10 attractive, delightful, enchanting
11 captivating, fascinating

engender
04 bear **05** beget, breed, cause
06 arouse, create, effect, excite, incite, induce, kindle, lead to **07** inspire, nurture, produce, provoke
08 generate, occasion **09** encourage, instigate, procreate, propagate
10 bring about, give rise to

engine
03 way **04** tool **05** agent, cause, means, motor, snare, trick **06** device, dynamo, factor, genius, medium, source **07** ability, channel, machine, vehicle **09** apparatus, appliance, generator, implement, ingenuity, machinery, mechanism **10** instrument, locomotive **11** contraption, contrivance

Engines include:

03 air, gas, ion, jet, oil
04 aero, beam, heat
05 motor, steam, water
06 diesel, donkey, petrol, Petter, radial, rocket, rotary, Wankel
07 orbital, turbine, V-engine
08 compound, Stirling, traction, turbojet
09 aerospike, turboprop
10 stationary
11 atmospheric, sleeve-valve
13 fuel-injection, reciprocating
15 linear aerospike

Engine parts include:

04 pump, sump
05 choke
06 con-rod, gasket, piston, tappet
07 fan belt, oil pump, oil seal, push-rod
08 camshaft, flywheel, radiator, rotor arm
09 air filter, drive belt, oil filter, rocker arm, spark plug
10 alternator, cooling fan, crankshaft, inlet valve, petrol pump, piston ring, thermostat, timing belt
11 carburettor, rocker cover
12 cylinder head, exhaust valve, fuel injector, ignition coil, starter motor, timing pulley, turbocharger
13 camshaft cover, connecting rod, cylinder block, inlet manifold, power-steering
15 exhaust manifold

engineer
◇ *anagram indicator*
02 BE, CE, ME **03** BAI, eng, rig **04** plan, plot **05** cause **06** create, devise, direct, driver, effect, manage, sapper, scheme **07** arrange, builder, control, deviser, greaser, handler, planner
08 contrive, designer, inventor, mechanic, operator **09** architect, machinist, manoeuvre, originate
10 bring about, controller, manipulate, mastermind, originator, technician
11 orchestrate, stage-manage
12 engine driver **13** civil engineer, sound engineer

Engineers include:

03 **Fox** (Sir Charles)
04 **Bell** (Alexander Graham), **Benz** (Karl), **Eads** (James Buchanan), **Ford** (Henry), **Otto** (Nikolaus August), **Page** (Sir Frederick Handley), **Watt** (James)
05 **Baird** (John Logie), **Baker** (Sir Benjamin), **Braun** (Wernher von), **Dodge** (Grenville), **Gooch** (Sir Daniel), **Grove** (Sir George), **Locke** (Joseph), **Maxim** (Sir Hiram Stevens), **Reber** (Grote), **Rolls** (Charles Stewart), **Royce** (Sir Henry), **Ruska** (Ernst August Friedrich), **Smith** (William), **Tesla** (Nikola)
06 **Brunel** (Isambard Kingdom), **Brunel** (Sir Marc Isambard), **Carnot** (Sadi), **Cayley** (Sir George), **Claude** (Georges), **Cugnot** (Nicolas Joseph), **Diesel** (Rudolf Christian Karl), **Donkin** (Bryan), **Eckert** (John Presper), **Edison** (Thomas Alva), **Eiffel** (Gustave), **Fokker** (Anthony Herman Gerard), **Fuller** (Buckminster), **Fulton** (Robert), **Jansky** (Karl Guthe), **Jessop** (William), **Lenoir** (Jean Joseph Étienne), **McAdam** (John Loudon), **Napier** (Robert), **Nipkow** (Paul), **Rennie** (John), **Savery** (Thomas), **Séguin** (Marc), **Sperry** (Elmer Ambrose), **Taylor** (Frederick Winslow), **Vauban** (Sebastien le Prestre de), **Wallis** (Sir Barnes Neville), **Wankel** (Felix), **Wright** (Orville), **Wright** (Wilbur)
07 **Balfour** (George), **Boulton** (Matthew), **Carlson** (Chester Floyd), **Citroën** (André Gustave), **Daimler** (Gottlieb), **Dornier** (Claude), **Eastman** (George), **Fleming** (Sir John Ambrose), **Giffard** (Henri), **Goddard** (Robert Hutchings), **Gresley** (Sir Nigel), **Heinkel** (Ernst), **Houston** (Edwin J), **Junkers** (Hugo), **Keldysh** (Mstislav), **Lesseps** (Ferdinand Marie, Vicomte de), **Nasmyth** (James), **Parsons** (Sir Charles Algernon), **Porsche** (Ferdinand), **Rankine** (William John Macquorn), **Siemens** (Sir William), **Siemens** (Werner von), **Smeaton** (John), **Sopwith** (Sir Thomas Octave Murdoch), **Telford** (Thomas), **Thomson** (Elihu), **Tupolev** (Andrei), **Whittle** (Sir Frank)
08 **Bertrand** (Henri Gratien, Comte), **Bessemer** (Sir Henry), **Brindley** (James), **De Forest** (Lee), **Ericsson** (John), **Ferranti** (Sebastian Ziani de), **Huntsman** (Benjamin), **Ilyushin** (Sergei), **Kennelly** (Arthur Edwin), **Korolyov** (Sergei), **Leonardo** (da Vinci), **Maudslay** (Henry), **Mitchell** (Reginald Joseph), **Poncelet** (Jean Victor), **Reynolds** (Osborne), **Roebling** (John Augustus), **Sikorsky** (Igor), **Sinclair** (Sir Clive), **Zeppelin** (Ferdinand, Graf von)
09 **Armstrong** (Edwin Howard), **Clapeyron** (Emile), **Cockerell** (Sir Christopher Sydney), **Fairbairn** (Sir William), **Fessenden** (Reginald Aubrey), **Issigonis** (Sir Alec), **Trésaguet** (Pierre Marie Jerome), **Whitworth** (Sir Joseph)
10 **Bazalgette** (Sir Joseph William), **Freyssinet** (Marie Eugène Léon), **Hounsfield** (Sir Godfrey Newbold), **Lilienthal** (Otto), **Stephenson** (George), **Stephenson** (Robert), **Trevithick** (Richard)
11 **De Havilland** (Sir Geoffrey), **Montgolfier** (Joseph Michel)
12 **Westinghouse** (George)
13 **Messerschmitt** (Willy)
15 **Leonardo da Vinci**

engineers
02 RE, SE **04** REME **07** sappers

England
03 Eng
See also **county**; **town**

English
01 E **03** Eng **04** side
See also **alphabet**; **monarch**

• **early English**
02 EE
• **English as a second language**
03 ESL
• **English language teaching**
03 ELT
• **in English**
03 Ang **07** Anglice

engorged
04 full **05** puffy **07** swollen **08** enlarged, expanded, inflated, overfull

engrave
03 cut, fix, set **04** etch, mark **05** brand, carve, chase, embed, inter, lodge, print, scalp, sculp, stamp, write **06** chisel, incise **07** enchase, engrain, impress, imprint, insculp **08** inscribe **09** character, mezzotint

engraving
03 cut, eng **04** mark **05** block, plate, print, steel **06** niello **07** carving, cutting, etching, imprint, woodcut **08** cerotype, dry-point, glyptics, intaglio **09** headpiece, mezzotint, sculpture, tailpiece **10** chiselling, heliograph, impression, lithoglyph, photoglyph, xylography **11** inscription, stylography, zincography **12** glyptography, heliogravure, photo-etching, photogravure **15** photoxylography

engross
04 grip, hold **05** rivet **06** absorb, arrest, engage, enwrap, inwrap, occupy, take up, wrap in **07** enthral, immerse, involve **08** interest, intrigue **09** captivate, fascinate, preoccupy **10** monopolize

engrossed
04 deep, lost, rapt **06** intent **07** engaged, fixated, gripped, riveted, taken up, wrapped **08** absorbed, caught up, immersed, occupied **09** intrigued **10** captivated, enthralled, fascinated, mesmerized **11** preoccupied **13** up to the elbows

engrossing
08 gripping, riveting **09** absorbing, consuming **10** compelling, intriguing **11** captivating, enthralling, fascinating, interesting, suspenseful **12** monopolizing **13** unputdownable

engulf
◇ *containment indicator*
04 bury **05** drown, flood, gulph, swamp **06** absorb, deluge, devour, plunge, suck in **07** consume, engross, envelop, immerse, overrun, swallow **08** inundate, overtake, submerge **09** overwhelm, swallow up

enhance
04 lift **05** add to, boost, exalt, raise, swell **06** enrich, stress **07** augment, elevate, improve, magnify, upgrade **08** heighten, increase **09** embellish, emphasize, intensify, reinforce **10** strengthen

enhancement
05 boost **06** stress **08** emphasis, increase **09** elevation **10** enrichment **11** heightening, improvement **12** augmentation **13** magnification, reinforcement **15** intensification

enigma
04 egma **05** poser **06** puzzle, riddle **07** dilemma, mystery, paradox, problem **08** quandary **09** conundrum **11** brain-teaser **12** brain-twister

enigmatic
◇ *anagram indicator*
06 arcane **07** cryptic, obscure, strange **08** baffling, esoteric, puzzling, riddling **09** recondite **10** mysterious, mystifying, perplexing, sphinxlike **11** inscrutable, paradoxical **12** inexplicable, unfathomable

enjoin
03 ban, bar **04** urge **05** order **06** advise, charge, decree, demand, direct, forbid, impose, ordain **07** command, require **08** disallow, encharge, instruct, prohibit **09** encourage, interdict, prescribe, proscribe

enjoy
03 joy **04** have, like, love **05** fancy, go for, taste, wield **06** relish, savour **07** possess, revel in, undergo **08** be fond of **09** delight in, partake of, rejoice in **10** appreciate **11** benefit from, go a bundle on **12** have the use of **13** be blessed with, be endowed with, get a buzz out of, get a kick out of **14** be favoured with, take pleasure in

• **enjoy yourself**
03 jol **04** ball, rage **05** party, sport **07** have fun, large it **08** live it up **09** have a ball, make merry **10** have a blast **11** have it large **12** get your kicks **13** have a good time **14** get your jollies **15** let your hair down, paint the town red

enjoyable
03 ace, bad, fab, fun **04** cool, fine, good, mega, neat, nice, wild **05** brill, rorty, super, triff **06** lekker, lovely, wicked, wizard **07** amusing, gustful, kicking, radical, triffic **08** fabulous, glorious, pleasant, pleasing, smashing, terrific **09** agreeable, beautiful, brilliant, delicious, fantastic **10** delectable, delightful, gratifying, satisfying **11** pleasurable **12** entertaining

enjoyment
03 fun, joy, use **04** glee, zest **05** gusto **06** favour, relish **07** benefit, comfort, delight **08** blessing, fruition, gladness, pleasant, pleasure **09** advantage, amusement, diversion, happiness, pleasance, privilege **10** indulgence, possession, recreation, suffisance **11** delectation **12** satisfaction **13** entertainment, gratification

enlarge
03 pan **04** ream, zoom **05** add to, piece, swell, widen **06** blow up, dilate, expand, extend, let out **07** amplify, augment, broaden, develop, distend, inflate, magnify, stretch **08** dilate on, elongate, expand on, heighten, increase, jumboize, lengthen, multiply **09** expatiate, intumesce **10** make bigger, make larger, supplement **11** elaborate on, expatiate on **12** become bigger, become larger **13** go into details

enlargement
05 swell, tumor **06** blow-up, bouton, goiter, goitre, growth, oedema, spavin, tumour **07** release **08** aneurism, aneurysm, dilation, increase, root-knot **09** exostosis, expansion, extension **10** ampliation, distension, stretching, varicocele **11** countersink, development **12** augmentation, cardiomegaly, hepatomegaly, intumescence, splenomegaly **13** amplification, magnification **14** multiplication

enlighten
05 edify, teach, tutor **06** advise, inform, notify **07** apprise, counsel, educate **08** civilize, instruct **09** cultivate, make aware **10** illuminate, illustrate **12** open your eyes

enlightened
03 lit **04** wise **05** aware **07** erudite, learned, liberal, refined **08** cultured, educated, informed, literate **09** civilized **10** conversant, cultivated, illuminate, Illuminati, open-minded, reasonable **11** broad-minded **12** intellectual **13** knowledgeable, sophisticated

enlightenment
05 light **06** satori, wisdom **07** insight **08** learning, literacy, sapience, teaching **09** awareness, education, erudition, eye-opener, knowledge **10** Aufklärung, refinement **11** cultivation, edification, information, instruction **12** civilization, illumination **13** comprehension, understanding **14** open-mindedness, sophistication **15** broad-mindedness

enlist
03 get, win **04** hire, join, list **05** enrol, enter, prest **06** employ, engage, enroll, gather, induct, join up, muster, obtain, rope in, secure, sign up, take on **07** procure, recruit **08** register **09** conscribe, conscript, volunteer **14** join the colours

enliven
◇ *anagram indicator*
04 fire, jazz **05** cheer, juice, liven, pep up, rouse, spark **06** buoy up, excite,

ginger, jazz up, kindle, perk up, soup up, vivify, wake up **07** animate, cheer up, gladden, hearten, inspire, juice up, liven up, quicken **08** brighten, ginger up **09** stimulate **10** brighten up, exhilarate, invigorate, revitalize **11** give a lift to

en masse
05 as one **06** en bloc, in sort **07** in a body **08** as a group, as a whole, as one man, ensemble, together **09** all at once, wholesale **10** in the quill **11** all together

enmeshed
07 mixed up **08** caught up, involved **09** concerned, entangled **10** associated

enmity
04 feud, hate **05** venom **06** hatred, malice, needle, rancor, strife **07** discord, ill-will, rancour **08** acrimony, aversion, bad blood, ill blood **09** animosity, antipathy, hostility **10** antagonism, bitterness, ill feeling **11** malevolence **14** unfriendliness

ennoble
05 exalt, raise **06** gentle, honour, uplift **07** dignify, elevate, enhance, glorify, magnify **10** aggrandize, nobilitate **11** distinguish

ennui
04 bore **05** weary **06** acedia, tedium **07** accidie, boredom, languor, malaise **09** lassitude, tiredness **11** the doldrums **12** listlessness **15** dissatisfaction

enormity
04 evil **05** crime **06** horror **07** outrage **08** atrocity, evilness, iniquity, vastness, vileness **09** depravity, violation **10** wickedness **11** abnormality, abomination, immenseness, monstrosity, viciousness **13** atrociousness **14** outrageousness

enormous
04 huge, mega, vast **05** dirty, giant, gross, jumbo **07** immense, mammoth, massive, monster, Titanic, whaling **08** colossal, gigantic, great big, plonking, whacking, whopping **09** abounding, atrocious, ginormous, humongous, humungous, monstrous, walloping **10** astronomic, gargantuan, hellacious, large-scale, monstruous, outrageous, prodigious, stupendous, tremendous **11** God-almighty **12** considerable, hulking great

enormously
04 dead, very, well **05** jolly **06** hugely **08** devilish, terribly **09** extremely, immensely, massively **10** especially **11** exceedingly, God-almighty **12** tremendously **13** exceptionally, to a huge extent, to a vast extent **15** extraordinarily

enormousness
07 expanse **08** hugeness, vastness **09** greatness, immensity, largeness, magnitude **11** immenseness, massiveness **13** extensiveness

enough
04 anow, enow, nuff **05** ample, amply, basta, belay **06** fairly, plenty **08** abundant, adequacy, adequate, passably **09** abundance, amplitude, tolerably **10** adequately, moderately, reasonably, satisfying, sufficient **11** ample supply, sufficience, sufficiency **12** sufficiently **14** satisfactorily

en passant
02 ep **08** by the way **09** cursorily, in passing **12** incidentally **15** parenthetically

enquire, enquirer, enquiring, enquiringly, enquiry *see* **inquire, enquire**; **inquirer, enquirer**; **inquiring, enquiring**; **inquiringly, enquiringly**; **inquiry, enquiry**

enrage
03 bug, irk, vex **04** rile **05** anger, annoy **06** incite, madden, needle, wind up **07** agitate, hack off, incense, inflame, provoke **08** irritate **09** enranckle, infuriate, make angry **10** exasperate, push too far

enraged
03 mad **04** wild **05** angry, irate, livid **06** fuming, raging **07** angered, annoyed, furious, horn-mad **08** incensed, inflamed, seething, storming **09** infuriate, irritated, pissed off **10** aggravated, infuriated **11** exasperated

enrapture
05 charm **06** ravish, thrill **07** beguile, bewitch, delight, enchant, enthral **08** enravish, entrance **09** captivate, fascinate, spellbind, translate, transport **10** emparadise, imparadise **13** please greatly

enrich
04 gild, lard **05** add to, adorn, endow, grace **06** fatten, manure, refine **07** augment, develop, enhance, fortify, garnish, improve **08** beautify, decorate, ornament, treasure **09** cultivate, embellish, fertilize **10** aggrandize, ameliorate, supplement

enrol
03 tax **04** list, note **05** admit, enter **06** attest, engage, enlist, enwrap, join up, muster, record, sign on, sign up **07** go in for, put down, recruit **08** inscribe, muster in, register **10** enregister **15** put your name down

enrolment
04 list **09** admission, enlisting, joining up, signing on, signing up **10** acceptance, enlistment **11** recruitment **12** conscription, registration

en route
05 march **08** on the way **09** in transit, on the move, on the road **12** on the journey

ensconce
03 put **05** lodge, niche, place **06** locate, nestle, screen, settle, shield **07** install, protect, shelter **08** entrench **09** establish

ensemble
03 set, sum **04** band, cast, suit, unit **05** get-up, group, total, whole **06** chorus, circle, entity, outfit, rig-out, troupe **07** company, costume **08** entirety **09** aggregate, orchestra **10** collection, whole shoot **11** co-ordinates **12** accumulation **13** corps de ballet, whole caboodle **14** whole bang shoot

enshrine
05 exalt, guard **06** embalm, hallow, revere, shield **07** cherish, enchase, idolize, lay down, protect, set down **08** dedicate, preserve, sanctify, treasure **10** consecrate **11** apotheosize, immortalize

enshroud
04 hide, pall, veil, wrap **05** cloak, cloud, cover **06** enfold, enwrap, shroud **07** conceal, enclose, envelop, obscure

ensign
03 Ens **04** flag, jack, mark, sign, waft **05** badge, color, crest **06** banner, colors, colour, pennon, shield **07** ancient, colours, pennant **08** gonfalon, pavilion, standard **10** coat of arms

enslave
04 bind, trap, yoke **05** thirl **06** thrall **07** enchain, subject **08** bethrall, dominate **09** subjugate **14** disenfranchise

enslavement
07 bondage, dulosis, serfdom, slavery **08** thraldom **09** captivity, servitude, vassalage **10** oppression, repression, subjection **11** enthralment, subjugation

ensnare
◇ *containment indicator*
03 net **04** hook, lime, trap **05** benet, catch, snare, snarl **06** enmesh, entoil, entrap, trepan **07** capture, embroil **08** entangle **09** mousetrap **10** illaqueate

ensue
04 flow, stem **05** arise, issue, occur **06** befall, derive, follow, happen, result **07** develop, proceed, succeed, turn out **08** come next **09** transpire

ensure
05 guard **06** effect, secure **07** betroth, certify, protect, warrant **08** make safe, make sure **09** guarantee, safeguard **11** make certain

entail
03 cut **04** need **05** carve, cause, infer **06** demand, lead to, tailye **07** call for, fashion, involve, produce, require, taillie, tailzie **08** occasion, result in **10** bring about, give rise to **11** necessitate

entangle
◇ *anagram indicator*
03 elf **04** ball, knot, wrap **05** catch, mix up, ravel, snare, twist **06** emmesh, engage, enlace, enmesh, enroot, entoil, entrap, fankle, immesh, inlace, inmesh, jumble, muddle, puzzle, taigle, tangle **07** confuse, embroil, ensnare, ensnarl, involve, perplex, trammel **08** quagmire **09** implicate, interlace **10** complicate, intertwine

entanglement
◇ *anagram indicator*
03 tie **04** knot, mesh, mess, trap **05** mix-up, snare, tie-up **06** affair, jumble, muddle, tangle **07** entrail, liaison, snarl-up **09** confusion **10** difficulty, entrapment, perplexity **11** ensnarement, involvement, predicament **12** complication, relationship **13** embarrassment

entente
04 deal, pact **06** treaty **07** compact **09** agreement **10** friendship **11** arrangement **13** understanding **15** entente cordiale

enter
◇ *insertion indicator*
03 log, ren, rin, run **04** come, go in, join, list, note **05** begin, board, enrol, get in, input, lodge, pop in, start **06** arrive, come in, enlist, go in to, insert, occupy, pierce, record, sign up, submit, take up **07** break in, burst in, get in to, go in for, put down, set down, sneak in **08** come in to, commence, embark on, engage in, inscribe, register, set about, take down, take part **09** introduce, penetrate, undertake, write down **10** embark upon, infiltrate, launch into **11** participate, put on record **12** gain access to **13** get involved in, worm your way in **15** become a member of

enterprise
03 SME **04** firm, plan, push, show, task **05** drive, oomph **06** design, effort, energy, scheme, spirit, voyage **07** company, concern, courage, emprise, project, venture **08** ambition, boldness, business, campaign, gumption, industry, vitality **09** adventure, endeavour, operation, programme, undertake **10** assignment, designment, enthusiasm, expedience, get-up-and-go, initiative **11** imagination, undertaking **13** establishment, strong feeling **15** adventurousness, resourcefulness

enterprising
04 bold, goey, keen **05** eager, pushy **06** active, daring **07** go-ahead, pushful, pushing, zealous **08** aspiring, spirited, vigorous **09** ambitious, energetic, ingenious **11** adventurous, imaginative, resourceful, self-reliant, undertaking, venturesome **12** enthusiastic **13** self-motivated **14** self-motivating **15** entrepreneurial

entertain
◇ *containment indicator*
04 fête, have, host, meet, wine **05** amuse, charm, cheer, put up, treat **06** divert, engage, foster, harbor, junket, occupy, please, regale **07** accourt, ask over, cherish, delight, engross, harbour, imagine, nurture, receive **08** ask round, conceive, consider, distract, interest, maintain **09** captivate, flirt with, have round **10** experience, have guests, invite over, play host to, think about **11** accommodate, contemplate, countenance, invite round

entertainer
04 host **06** diseur **07** diseuse, hostess **09** top banana **10** Amphitryon
See also **actor, actress**; **comedian**; **musician**; **singer**

Entertainers include:

02 DJ
04 bard, fool, Joey
05 actor, clown, comic, mimic
06 artist, august, busker, cowboy, dancer, jester, mummer, player, singer
07 acrobat, actress, artiste, auguste, juggler, Pierrot
08 comedian, conjuror, go-go girl, gracioso, jongleur, magician, minstrel, musician, showgirl, stripper
09 bunny girl, chanteuse, ecdysiast, fire-eater, harlequin, hypnotist, ice-skater, lap dancer, lion tamer, performer, pierrette, presenter, puppeteer, strong man
10 comedienne, disc jockey, go-go dancer, knockabout, mime artist, mind-reader, pole dancer, ring master, rope-walker, unicyclist, wire-dancer
12 chat-show host, escapologist, exotic dancer, game-show host, impersonator, snake charmer, stand-up comic, street singer, trick cyclist, vaudevillean, vaudevillian
13 contortionist, impressionist, thimblerigger, trapeze artist, ventriloquist
14 pavement artist, sword-swallower
15 jerry-come-tumble, song-and-dance act, tightrope walker

entertaining
◇ *containment indicator*
03 fun **05** funny, jolly, witty **07** amusing, amusive, comical **08** humorous, pleasant, pleasing **09** diverting, enjoyable **10** delightful **11** interesting, pleasurable **12** recreational

entertainment
03 fun **04** boff, olio, show **05** cheer, drama, hobby, sport, table **07** leisure, pastime, variety **08** activity, pleasure, semblant **09** amusement, diversion, enjoyment, honky-tonk, spectacle **10** confection, recreation **11** distraction, merrymaking, performance **12** extravaganza, presentation **14** divertissement

Entertainments include:

03 BBQ, DVD, gig
04 fête, film, play, show
05 dance, disco, opera, radio, revue, rodeo, video
06 circus
07 airshow, cabaret, concert, karaoke, musical, pageant, recital, showbiz
08 barbecue, carnival, festival, gymkhana, waxworks
09 burlesque, fireworks, floor show, magic show, music hall, nightclub, pantomime, video game
10 puppet show, television, vaudeville
11 discothèque, variety show
12 computer game, Punch-and-Judy, show business
13 firework party
14 laser-light show
15 greyhound racing

See also **television**; **theatrical**

Entertainment places include:

03 pub, zoo
04 club, dogs, fair, hall
05 arena, disco
06 big top, casino, cinema, circus, museum, nitery
07 cabaret, funfair, gallery, hot spot, ice rink, marquee, niterie, stadium, theatre
08 ballroom, carnival, dog track, flesh pot
09 bandstand, bingo hall, dance hall, music hall, nightclub, strip club
10 auditorium, fairground, opera house, restaurant, social club
11 boîte de nuit, concert hall, discothèque, public house, skating rink
12 amphitheatre, bowling alley, cattle market
13 leisure centre
15 amusement arcade

• **entertainment industry**
12 show business

• **undemanding entertainment**
03 pap

enthral
◇ *containment indicator*
04 grip **05** charm, rivet **06** absorb, thrill **07** beguile, bewitch, delight, enchant, engross **08** entrance, intrigue **09** captivate, enrapture, fascinate, hypnotize, mesmerize, spellbind

enthralling
◇ *containment indicator*
08 charming, gripping, mesmeric, riveting **09** beguiling, thrilling **10** compelling, compulsive, enchanting, entrancing, intriguing **11** captivating, fascinating, hypnotizing, mesmerizing **12** spellbinding

enthuse
04 fire, gush, rave **05** drool **06** excite, fire up, praise **07** inspire **08** motivate

10 bubble over, effervesce, wax lyrical 14 go into raptures

enthusiasm
04 brio, buzz, fire, hype, rage, zeal, zest 05 ardor, craze, estro, furor, hobby, mania, oomph, thing, verve 06 ardour, frenzy, furore, relish, spirit, warmth 07 ecstasy, fervour, passion, pastime 08 appetite, delirium, devotion, interest, keenness 09 eagerness, vehemence 10 commitment, ebullience, ebulliency, excitement, fanaticism 11 acclamation, earnestness, schwärmerei 12 entraînement 13 preoccupation

• **expression of enthusiasm**
03 boy, gee 04 Jeez 05 Jeeze, oh boy!, whack 06 whacko 10 hubba hubba

• **lose enthusiasm**
04 cool 08 languish

enthusiast
03 bug, fan, nut 04 buff, zeal 05 fiend, freak, lover 06 maniac, zealot 07 admirer, amateur, devotee, fanatic 08 follower 09 supporter 10 aficionado 11 eager beaver

See also **collector**

enthusiastic
03 mad 04 avid, daft, into, keen, nuts, rave, warm, wild 05 crazy, eager, potty 06 ardent, gung-ho, hearty, mad for 07 devoted, earnest, excited, fervent, intense, up for it, zealous 08 empressé, gaga over, mad about, spirited, vehement, vigorous 09 committed, ebullient, exuberant, fanatical, gaga about 10 passionate 11 rhapsodical 12 rootin'-tootin', wholehearted 13 keen as mustard, self-motivated

entice
04 coax, draw, lure, tice, tole 05 tempt 06 allure, cajole, induce, lead on, seduce 07 attempt, attract, beguile, wheedle 08 inveigle, persuade 09 sweet-talk, tantalize

enticement
04 bait, lure, tice 05 decoy 06 allure, carrot, come-on 07 coaxing 08 cajolery 09 seduction, sweet-talk 10 allurement, attraction, inducement, invitation, persuasion, temptation 11 beguilement 12 inveiglement 13 blandishments

enticing
08 alluring, charming, inviting, tempting 09 appealing, seductive 10 attractive 11 captivating 12 irresistible

entire
04 full, meer 05 round, sound, total, utter, whole 06 intact, within 07 genuine, plenary, untired 08 absolute, complete, integral, livelong, outright, stallion, thorough 09 sincerely, unmingled 10 unimpaired 11 unmitigated, unqualified 12 completeness

entirely
03 all 04 inly, only, tout 05 clean, fully, quite 06 in toto, merely, purely, quight, solely, wholly 07 all over, totally, utterly 08 every bit, properly 09 every inch, every whit, perfectly, tout à fait 10 absolutely, altogether, completely, in every way, thoroughly 11 exclusively 12 unreservedly 14 in every respect

entirety
03 all, sum 05 total, whole 08 fullness, totality 09 wholeness 12 completeness

entitle
03 dub 04 call, name, term 05 allow, label, style, title 06 enable, know as, permit 07 empower, ennoble, license, qualify, warrant 08 accredit, christen, sanction 09 authorize, designate 12 give the title, make eligible

• **to be entitled to**
04 bear 07 deserve

entitlement
03 due 05 claim, right, title 07 warrant 09 authority, privilege 11 opportunity, prerogative

entity
03 ens, Tao 04 body 05 being, thing 06 object, tensor 08 creature, organism 09 existence, substance 10 individual

entomb
04 bury, tomb 05 inter, inurn, plant 06 inhume, shroud, wall up 07 inearth 09 lay to rest, sepulcher, sepulchre, sepulture 15 put six feet under

entombment
06 burial 09 interment, sepulture 10 inhumation 12 laying to rest

entourage
04 gang 05 court, posse, staff, suite, train 06 escort 07 company, cortège, coterie, retinue 09 followers, following, hangers-on, retainers 10 associates, attendants, companions

entrails
04 guts 05 offal, tripe 06 bowels, haslet, inside, quarry, umbles 07 giblets, harslet, humbles, innards, insides, inwards, numbles, pudding, viscera 08 chawdron, gralloch, puddings 10 intestines 11 vital organs 14 internal organs

entrance
03 eye 04 adit, door, gate, hall, ingo, pend, pipe 05 charm, debut, drive, entry, foyer, gorge, inlet, lobby, mouth, porch, start, way in 06 access, atrium, avenue, dromos, entrée, income, infare, ingate, portal, ravish 07 arrival, Avernus, beguile, bewitch, delight, doorway, enchant, enthral, gateway, hallway, ingoing, ingress, jawhole, opening 08 anteroom, approach, driveway 09 admission, captivate, closehead, enrapture, fascinate, hypnotize, introitus, mesmerize, spellbind, threshold, transport, vestibule 10 admittance, appearance, initiation, passageway 12 introduction, porte-cochère, right of entry

• **narrow entrance**
04 jaws 06 throat

entranced
04 rapt 10 spellbound

entrancing
06 lovely 07 winsome 08 alluring, charming, pleasant 09 appealing, endearing, ravishing, wonderful 10 attractive, bewitching, delightful, enchanting 11 captivating, fascinating, mesmerizing 12 irresistible

entrant
05 entry, pupil, rival 06 novice, player 07 convert, fresher, learner, starter, student, trainee 08 beginner, freshman, initiate, newcomer, opponent 09 applicant, candidate, contender 10 apprentice, competitor, contestant, new arrival 11 participant, probationer

entrap
03 net 04 lure, trap 05 catch, decoy, snare, tempt, trick 06 allure, ambush, delude, enmesh, entice, seduce 07 beguile, capture, deceive, embroil, ensnare 08 entangle, inveigle 09 crossbite, implicate, underfong

entreat
03 ask, beg, sew, sue 04 pray, prig 05 crave 06 induce, invoke, objure 07 beseech, beseeke, implore, request, solicit 08 appeal to, petition 09 flagitate, importune, plead with 10 supplicate

entreaty
03 cry 04 plea, suit 06 appeal, prayer 07 beseech, request 08 petition, pleading 09 exoration 10 cri de coeur, invocation 11 conjuration 12 solicitation, supplication

entrée
05 entry 06 access 07 ingress, prelude, starter 08 main dish 09 admission, appetizer 10 admittance, main course 11 first course 12 introduction, right of entry

entrench
03 fix, set 04 root, seat 05 dig in, embed, lodge, plant, wound 06 anchor, sconce, settle 07 ingrain, install 08 ensconce, stop a gap 09 establish 14 take up position

entrenched
03 set 04 firm 05 fixed 06 inbred, rooted 07 diehard 09 implanted, indelible, ingrained 10 deep-rooted, deep-seated, inflexible, unshakable 11 established, unshakeable 12 ineradicable, intransigent 13 dyed-in-the-wool, stick-in-the-mud 15 well-established

entrepreneur
05 agent 06 broker, dealer, tycoon 07 magnate, manager 08 promoter 09 financier, middleman 10 contractor, impresario, moneymaker, speculator, undertaker

11 businessman, enterpriser
13 businesswoman, industrialist

entrepreneurial
05 trade 08 business, economic, monetary 09 budgetary, financial
10 commercial, industrial, managerial
11 contractual 12 professional

entrust
04 aret 05 arett, endow, trust
06 assign, charge, commit, depute, invest, resign 07 commend, confide, consign, deliver, deposit 08 delegate, encharge, hand over, turn over
09 authorize 11 put in charge

entry
04 door, gate, hall, item, note 05 annal, foyer, lobby, porch, rival, way in
06 access, entrée, minute, player, record 07 account, arrival, doorway, entrant, gateway, ingress, listing, opening, passage 08 anteroom, approach, entrance, opponent, register, registry 09 admission, applicant, candidate, contender, statement, threshold, vestibule
10 admittance, appearance, competitor, contestant, memorandum
11 description, participant
12 introduction, right of entry

entwine
◇ *anagram indicator*
04 coil, knit, knot, mesh, warp, wind
05 braid, plait, ravel, twine, twist, weave 06 enlace, inlace 07 embroil, entrail, intwine, wreathe 08 entangle
09 implicate, interlace, interlink
10 intertwine, intervolve, interweave

enumerate
04 cite, list, name, tell 05 count, quote, score 06 detail, number, recite, reckon, relate 07 compute, itemize, mention, recount, specify
08 rehearse, spell out 09 calculate, catalogue 13 particularize

enunciate
03 say 05 sound, speak, state, utter, voice 06 affirm 07 declare, enounce, express, propose 08 announce, proclaim, propound, vocalize
09 pronounce 10 articulate, promulgate, put forward

enunciation
05 sound 06 speech 07 diction
08 sounding 09 statement, utterance
10 expression 11 affirmation, declaration, proposition
12 announcement, articulation, proclamation, promulgation, vocalization 13 pronunciation

envelop
◇ *containment indicator*
04 hide, pack, veil, wrap 05 cloak, cover 06 encase, enfold, engulf, enwrap, muffle, shroud, swathe, wrap up 07 blanket, conceal, enclose, obscure, smother 08 encircle, enshroud, surround 09 encompass, enwreathe, inwreathe

envelope
03 sae 04 case, skin, wrap 05 cover, frank, shell 06 casing, entire, gasbag, holder, jacket, sachet, sheath, sleeve
07 coating, utricle, wrapper
08 covering, Jiffy bag®, wrapping
09 involucre

enviable
04 fine 05 lucky 07 blessed
08 favoured 09 desirable, excellent, fortunate, invidious 10 attractive, privileged 11 sought-after
12 advantageous

envious
05 green 07 jealous 08 covetous, grudging, spiteful 09 green-eyed, jaundiced, resentful 10 begrudging
12 dissatisfied 13 green with envy

enviously
08 with envy 09 jealously
10 covetously, desirously, grudgingly
11 resentfully 12 begrudgingly

environment
04 Gaia, mood 05 earth, scene, world
06 domain, locale, medium, milieu, nature 07 climate, context, element, habitat, setting 08 ambiance, ambience, creation 09 situation, territory 10 atmosphere, background, conditions, influences 11 mother earth
12 mother nature, natural world, surroundings 13 circumstances 15 the lie of the land

Environmental problems include:

06 litter
07 drought
08 acid rain, landfill, oil slick, oil spill
09 pollution
10 extinction, fossil fuel, toxic waste
11 soil erosion
12 air pollution, nuclear waste
13 climate change, deforestation, global dimming, global warming, water shortage
14 light pollution, ozone depletion, water pollution
15 desertification, greenhouse gases

environmentalist
05 green 06 econut 07 greenie
08 ecofreak 09 ecologist 10 tree-hugger 15 conservationist, preservationist
• **environmentalists**
03 FOE 10 Green Party

environs
07 suburbs 08 district, locality, purlieus, vicinage, vicinity
09 outskirts, precincts
12 surroundings 13 neighbourhood
15 circumjacencies, surrounding area

envisage
03 see 05 image 07 foresee, imagine, picture, predict, think of 08 envision
09 see coming, visualize 10 anticipate, conceive of 11 contemplate, preconceive

envision
03 see 07 imagine, picture, think of
08 envisage 09 see coming, visualize
11 contemplate

envoy
05 agent 06 consul, deputy, legate
07 attaché, courier, plenipo
08 delegate, diplomat, emissary, mediator, minister 09 go-between, messenger 10 ambassador
12 intermediary 14 representative
15 plenipotentiary

envy
05 covet, crave, spite 06 desire, grudge, malice, resent 07 ill-will
08 begrudge, jealousy 09 hostility
10 resentment 12 covetousness
13 resentfulness 15 dissatisfaction

enzyme

Enzymes include:

05 DNase, lyase, renin, RNase
06 cytase, kinase, ligase, lipase, papain, pepsin, rennin, zymase
07 amylase, emulsin, erepsin, inulase, lactase, maltase, oxidase, pepsine, plasmin, trypsin, uricase
08 bromelin, catalase, ceramide, elastase, esterase, lysozyme, nuclease, permease, protease, thrombin
09 amylopsin, bromelain, cellulase, coagulase, hydrolase, invertase, isomerase, peptidase, reductase, urokinase
10 insulinase, luciferase, peroxidase, polymerase, sulphatase, telomerase, tyrosinase
11 collagenase, glutaminase, histaminase, hydrogenase, lecithinase, nitrogenase, phosphatase, transferase
12 alpha amylase, asparaginase, chymotrypsin, endonuclease, fibrinolysin, ribonuclease, transaminase
13 decarboxylase, dehydrogenase, DNA polymerase, neuraminidase, penicillinase, phosphorylase, RNA polymerase, streptokinase, thrombokinase, transcriptase
14 cholinesterase, thromboplastin

Eos
06 Aurora

ephemeral
05 brief, short 07 fungous, passing
08 fleeting, flitting 09 fugacious, momentary, temporary, transient
10 evanescent, short-lived, transitory
11 impermanent

epic
04 epos, huge, long, myth, saga, vast
05 grand, great, Iliad, large, lofty
06 epopee, heroic, legend
07 Dunciad, exalted, history, Homeric, Odyssey, romance, sublime
08 colossal, elevated, epopoeia, imposing, Kalevala, long poem, majestic, Ramayana, rhapsody
09 ambitious, colubriad, long story, narrative 10 heroic poem, impressive, large-scale 13 grandiloquent

epicure
06 friand **07** friande, glutton, gourmet **08** gourmand, hedonist, Sybarite **09** bon vivant, bon viveur, epicurean **10** gastronome, sensualist, voluptuary **11** connoisseur, gastronomer

epicurean
04 lush **07** gourmet, sensual **08** luscious **09** libertine, luxurious, Sybaritic **10** gluttonous, hedonistic, sensualist, voluptuous **11** gastronomic **12** gormandizing, unrestrained **13** self-indulgent

epidemic
04 pest, rash, rife, rise, wave **05** spate **06** growth, plague, spread **07** endemic, rampant, scourge, upsurge **08** increase, outbreak, pandemia, pandemic, sweeping **09** extensive, pervasive, prevalent **10** prevailing, widespread **11** wide-ranging

epigram
03 pun **04** quip **05** gnome, maxim **06** bon mot, saying **07** proverb **08** aphorism **09** witticism **10** apophthegm **11** old chestnut, play on words

epigrammatic
05 brief, pithy, sharp, short, terse, witty **06** ironic **07** concise, laconic, piquant, pointed, pungent **08** incisive, succinct **10** aphoristic

epilepsy
08 eclampsy, grand mal, petit mal **09** eclampsia **15** falling sickness
• **sensation before epilepsy**
04 aura

epilogue
02 PS **04** coda **08** appendix, swan song **09** afterword **10** conclusion, postscript

episcopate
03 see

episode
03 fit **04** bout, part **05** event, scene, spasm, spell **06** affair, attack, matter, period **07** chapter, passage, section **08** business, incident, occasion **09** adventure, happening **10** experience, instalment, occurrence **12** circumstance

episodic
08 periodic, sporadic **09** anecdotal, irregular, spasmodic **10** digressive, disjointed, occasional, picaresque **12** disconnected, intermittent

epistle
02 Ep **04** Epis, line, note **06** letter **07** message, missive, preface **08** bulletin **10** encyclical **13** communication **14** correspondence

epitaph
03 RIP **05** elegy **08** obituary **11** inscription, rest in peace **13** commemoration **14** funeral oration

epithet
03 tag **04** name, term **05** title **06** by-name, to-name **08** cognomen, nickname **09** apathaton, sobriquet **10** expression **11** appellation, description, designation **12** denomination

epitome
04 type **05** model **06** digest, précis, résumé **07** essence, example, outline, summary **08** abstract, exemplar, synopsis **09** archetype, prototype **10** abridgment, embodiment **11** abridgement **12** quintessence **14** representation **15** personification

epitomize
03 cut, pot **05** sum up **06** embody, précis, reduce, typify **07** abridge, curtail, shorten **08** abstract, compress, condense, contract **09** exemplify, incarnate, personify, represent, summarize, symbolize **10** abbreviate, illustrate **11** encapsulate, incorporate

epoch
03 age, era **04** date, span, time **06** period
See also **geology**

equable
04 calm, even **05** equal **06** placid, serene, smooth, stable, steady **07** regular, unfazed, uniform **08** composed, constant, laid-back, moderate, tranquil **09** easy-going, temperate, unvarying **10** consistent, even-minded, unchanging **11** level-headed, unexcitable, unflappable **12** even-tempered **13** imperturbable

equably
06 calmly **08** placidly, serenely **10** tranquilly **11** unexcitably **13** level-headedly

equal
02 eq **03** fit, par **04** able, egal, even, fair, fear, feer, fere, just, like, maik, make, mate, peer, twin, view **05** alike, feare, fiere, level, match, reach, rival, total **06** fellow, pheere, strong, suited **07** add up to, balance, capable, coequal, compeer, contend, emulate, matched, neutral, peregal, regular, the same, uniform **08** adequate, amount to, balanced, come up to, constant, corrival, equalize, parallel, suitable, unbiased **09** competent, identical, impartial, match up to, semblable, tally with, unvarying **10** be as good as, comparable, equate with, equivalent, even-steven, fifty-fifty, keep up with, square with, sufficient, unchanging **11** be a match for, be level with, be the same as, compare with, counterpart, even-stevens, measure up to, neck and neck, non-partisan, symmetrical **12** be on a par with, coincide with, commensurate, correspond to, well balanced **13** corresponding, evenly matched **14** be equivalent to

equality
03 par, tie **05** match **06** owelty, parage, parity **07** balance, egality, justice **08** evenness, fairness, identity, likeness, rivality, sameness, symmetry **10** neutrality, proportion, similarity, uniformity **11** equal rights, equivalence, parallelism **12** impartiality, partisanship **13** comparability **14** correspondence, egalitarianism

equalization
08 matching **09** balancing, levelling **10** evening-out **12** compensation **15** standardization

equalize
05 equal, level, match **06** equate, even up, smooth, square **07** balance, even out **08** keep pace, make even **09** draw level **10** compensate, regularize **11** standardize

equally
02 as **05** alike **06** evenly, fairly, just as, justly **07** ex aequo **08** likewise **09** similarly, uniformly **11** as important **12** in like manner, in the same way, on equal terms **14** by the same token, proportionally **15** correspondingly, proportionately

equanimity
04 calm, ease **05** poise **06** aplomb **07** dignity **08** calmness, coolness, serenity **09** assurance, composure, placidity, sangfroid **10** confidence **11** impassivity, self-control **12** tranquillity **13** self-assurance **14** self-possession, unflappability **15** level-headedness

equate
06 offset **07** balance, be equal, compare, liken to **08** equalize, link with, pair with, parallel **09** agree with, compare to, match with, tally with **10** square with **11** compare with, connect with **12** correspond to, identify with **13** juxtapose with **14** correspond with **15** bracket together, regard as the same

equation
02 eq **05** cubic, match **07** pairing **08** equality, identity, likeness, matching, parallel **09** agreement, balancing, quadratic **10** comparison, similarity **11** calculation, equivalence **13** juxtaposition **14** correspondence, identification

equator
07 the line **11** aclinic line
• **near the equator**
03 low

Equatorial Guinea
03 GNQ

equestrian
05 rider **06** cowboy, equine, herder, hussar, jockey, knight, riding **07** courier, cowgirl, mounted, rancher, trooper **08** cavalier, horseman **10** cavalryman, horse-rider, horsewoman **11** horse-riding

Equestrians and showjumpers include:

03 Hoy (Andrew), Hoy (Bettina)
04 Anne (Princess), Leng (Virginia), Tait (Blyth), Todd (Mark)
05 Green (Lucinda), Meade (Richard), Smith (Harvey)
06 Astley (Philip), Broome (David), D'Inzeo (Raimondo), Klimke (Reiner), Smythe (Pat)
07 Winkler (Hans-Günther)
08 Phillips (Mark), Whitaker (John), Whitaker (Michael)

See also **horseman, horsewoman**

equilibrium
05 poise **06** aplomb, stasis **07** balance, dignity **08** calmness, coolness, evenness, serenity, symmetry **09** assurance, composure, equipoise, sangfroid, stability **10** confidence, equanimity, steadiness **11** self-control **12** counterpoise, tranquillity **13** self-assurance **14** self-possession, unflappability **15** level-headedness

equip
03 arm, fit, rig **04** tool **05** array, dight, dress, endow, fit up, issue, rig up, stock **06** aguise, aguize, clothe, fit out, kit out, outfit, supply **07** apparel, appoint, bedight, deck out, furnish, prepare, provide **08** accouter, accoutre, equipage **10** accomplish

equipment
03 kit, rig **04** gear **05** stock, stuff, tools **06** doings, graith, outfit, rig-out, tackle, things **07** baggage, battery, clobber, fixings, luggage **08** articles, hardware, material, materiel, supplies **09** apparatus, furniture, inventory **10** appliances **11** accessories, apparelment, furnishings **12** appointments **13** accoutrements, paraphernalia

See also **farm**; **gardening**; **laboratory**; **medical**; **office**; **photographic**; **plumbing**; **sport**

equipoise
05 poise **07** balance, ballast **08** evenness, symmetry **09** libration, stability **10** steadiness **11** equibalance, equilibrium **12** counterpoise **13** counter-weight **14** counterbalance, equiponderance

equitable
03 due **04** fair, just **05** equal, right **06** honest, proper, square **07** ethical **08** rightful, unbiased **09** impartial, objective **10** even-handed, legitimate, reasonable **12** unprejudiced **13** disinterested, dispassionate, fair-and-square

equitably
06 fairly, justly **07** ex aequo **08** honestly **09** ethically **10** reasonably, rightfully **11** impartially **12** even-handedly **15** disinterestedly, dispassionately

equity
05 right **06** square **07** honesty, justice **08** fairness, fair play, justness **09** integrity, rectitude **11** objectivity, uprightness **12** impartiality **13** equitableness, righteousness **14** even-handedness, fair-mindedness, reasonableness

equivalence
06 amount, parity **08** equality, identity, likeness, parallel, sameness **09** agreement **10** conformity, similarity **11** correlation **13** comparability, identicalness **14** correspondence

equivalent
02 eq **04** even, like, peer, same, twin **05** alike, equal, match, value **06** double, fellow **07** similar **08** parallel **09** homologue, identical **10** comparable, homologous, tantamount **11** alternative, correlative, counterpart, equipollent **12** commensurate **13** correspondent, corresponding, substitutable **14** opposite number **15** interchangeable

equivocal
05 fishy, vague **07** dubious, evasive, oblique, obscure **08** oracular **09** ambiguous, confusing, oraculous, uncertain **10** ambivalent, homonymous, indefinite, misleading, suspicious **12** questionable

equivocate
05 dodge, evade, fence, hedge, mudge **06** boggle, palter, waffle, weasel **07** mislead **09** pussyfoot, vacillate **11** prevaricate **12** shilly-shally, tergiversate **13** chop and change, hedge your bets **14** change your mind, change your tune

equivocation
06 waffle **07** evasion, flannel, hedging **08** shifting **09** quibbling, shuffling **10** double talk **11** weasel words **12** pussyfooting **13** prevarication **14** tergiversation **15** dodging the issue

era
03 age, day **04** aeon, date, days, time **05** cycle, epoch, stage, times **06** period, season **07** century **10** generation

See also **geology**

• **bygone era**
02 BC

• **common era**
02 CE

• **current era**
02 AD

eradicate
04 root, wipe **05** erase **06** efface, remove, uproot **07** abolish, destroy, expunge, root out, weed out, wipe out **08** get rid of, stamp out, suppress **09** eliminate, extirpate **10** annihilate, do away with, extinguish, obliterate **11** crack down on, exterminate

eradication
07 removal **08** riddance **09** abolition **10** effacement, expunction, extinction **11** destruction, elimination, extirpation, suppression **12** annihilation, deracination, obliteration **13** extermination

erasable
08 washable **09** removable **10** effaceable, eradicable

erase
03 rub, zap **04** race, rase, raze **06** cancel, delete, efface, excise, remove, rub off, rub out, scrape **07** blot out, destroy, expunge, rub away, scratch, wipe out **08** get rid of **09** eradicate **10** obliterate, scratch out

erasure
06 rasure, razure **07** removal **08** deletion **09** cleansing, erasement, wiping-out **10** effacement, expunction, rubbing-out **11** blotting-out, elimination, eradication **12** cancellation, obliteration

erbium
02 Er

erect
04 firm, form, hard, lift, rear **05** build, dress, found, mount, on end, pitch, prick, put up, raise, right, rigid, set up, stiff **06** create, raised **07** elevate, prick up, stand-up, upright **08** assemble, initiate, organize, standing, straight, vertical **09** construct, displayed, establish, institute, tumescent **10** upstanding **11** orthostatic, put together **13** perpendicular, straight-pight

erection
04 pile **07** edifice, raising **08** assembly, building, creation, priapism, rigidity **09** elevation, stiffness, structure **10** tumescence **11** fabrication, manufacture **12** construction **13** establishment

ergo
02 so **04** then, thus **05** argal, hence **09** therefore **11** accordingly **12** consequently **13** for this reason, in consequence

Erica
04 ling **07** heather

Eritrea
03 ERI

erode
05 spoil **06** abrade **07** consume, corrode, degrade, deplete, destroy, eat away, eat into **08** fragment, wear away, wear down **09** excoriate, grind down, undermine **11** deteriorate **12** disintegrate

Eros
05 Cupid

erosion
04 wash, wear **07** wash-out **08** abrasion, scouring, wash-away

09 attrition, corrosion 10 denudation 11 degradation, destruction, excoriation, undermining, wearing away 13 deterioration 14 disintegration

erotic
03 hot 04 blue, go-go, sexy 05 adult, dirty, horny 06 carnal, steamy 07 amatory, amorous, lustful, raunchy, sensual 08 erogenic, venereal 09 erogenous, seductive 10 lascivious, suggestive, voluptuous 11 Anacreontic, aphrodisiac, stimulating, titillating 12 pornographic

erotically
08 steamily 09 raunchily, sensually 10 explicitly 11 seductively 12 suggestively 15 anacreontically

err
◇ *anagram indicator*
03 sin 04 boob, flub, goof 05 fluff 06 cock up, duff it, goof up, mess up, offend, slip up, wander 07 be wrong, blunder, deviate, do wrong, louse up, mistake, screw up, stumble 08 go astray, misjudge 09 make a slip, misbehave 10 transgress 11 be incorrect, make a booboo, misconstrue 12 come a cropper, drop a clanger, make a mistake, miscalculate 13 fall from grace, misunderstand 15 put your foot in it

errand
03 job 04 duty, task 05 chore 06 charge 07 message, mission 10 assignment, commission 11 undertaking
- **person who runs errands**
03 cad 05 caddy, cadee, cadie 06 caddie 07 express, galopin 10 message-boy 11 message-girl 13 printer's devil

errant
◇ *anagram indicator*
05 loose, stray, wrong 06 erring, roving, sinful 07 deviant, lawless, nomadic, peccant, roaming, sinning, wayward 08 aberrant, criminal, quixotic, rambling, straying, thorough 09 itinerant, offending, wandering 10 journeying 11 disobedient, peripatetic

erratic
◇ *anagram indicator*
06 fitful 07 vagrant, varying 08 aberrant, abnormal, shifting, sporadic, unstable, unsteady, variable, volatile 09 desultory, eccentric, irregular, planetary, unsettled, wandering 10 capricious, changeable, inconstant, meandering, unbalanced, unreliable 11 fluctuating 12 inconsistent, intermittent 13 unpredictable

erratically
◇ *anagram indicator*
08 fitfully, variably 10 changeably, unreliably 11 irregularly 12 inconstantly, sporadically 13 unpredictably 14 inconsistently, intermittently

erring
◇ *anagram indicator*
05 loose, stray, wrong 06 errant, guilty, sinful 07 deviant, devious, lawless, peccant, sinning, wayward 08 criminal, culpable, straying 09 misguided, offending, wandering 11 disobedient

erroneous
◇ *anagram indicator*
05 false, wrong 06 erring, faulty, flawed, untrue 07 inexact, invalid 08 mistaken, specious, spurious, straying 09 illogical, incorrect, misguided, misplaced, unfounded, wandering 10 fallacious, inaccurate

error
◇ *anagram indicator*
04 boob, flaw, flub, goof, slip, typo 05 fault, fluff, gaffe, lapse, mix-up, wrong 06 booboo, cock-up, foul-up, glitch, hickey, howler, slip-up 07 blooper, blunder, clanger, erratum, fallacy, faux pas, jeofail, literal, miscopy, mistake, own goal 08 delusion, mesprize, misprint, omission, solecism 09 oversight 10 aberration, inaccuracy, misjudgment 12 misjudgement 13 misconception 14 miscalculation 15 misapprehension, slip of the tongue, spelling mistake
- **errors excepted**
02 EE
- **in error**
03 out 07 falsely, wrongly 08 unfairly, unjustly 09 by mistake 10 mistakenly 11 erroneously, incorrectly, misguidedly 12 fallaciously, inaccurately 15 inappropriately
- **sign of error**
01 X

ersatz
04 fake, sham 05 bogus 06 phoney 07 man-made 09 imitation, simulated, synthetic 10 artificial, substitute 11 counterfeit

erstwhile
02 ex 03 old 04 late, once, past 06 bygone, former 07 one-time 08 previous, sometime

erudite
04 wise 06 brainy 07 learned 08 academic, cultured, educated, highbrow, lettered, literate, profound, well-read 09 scholarly 12 intellectual, well-educated 13 knowledgeable

erudition
05 facts 06 wisdom 07 culture, letters 08 learning 09 education, knowledge 10 profundity 11 learnedness, scholarship 13 reconditeness, scholarliness

erupt
◇ *anagram indicator*
04 emit, gush, spew, vent 05 belch, burst, eject, expel, spout 06 blow up 07 come out, explode, flare up 08 break out, emit lava 09 burst open, discharge, pour forth 13 discharge lava, pour forth lava

eruption
◇ *anagram indicator*
04 rash, spot 06 blow-up, eczema, lichen, red gum, tetter 07 ecthyma, flare-up, morphew, prurigo, Purpura, venting 08 ejection, emission, empyesis, exanthem, malander, outbreak, outburst, rose drop 09 discharge, emphlysis, exanthema, explosion, mallander, mallender, pompholyx, salt rheum 12 inflammation

erysipelas
04 rose 10 sideration 14 St Anthony's fire

escalate
04 grow, rise, soar 05 climb, mount, raise 06 ascend, expand, extend, rocket, spiral, step up 07 amplify, develop, enlarge, magnify, shoot up 08 heighten, increase, mushroom 09 intensify 10 accelerate, hit the roof

escalation
04 rise 06 growth 07 soaring 08 increase 09 expansion, extension 11 development, heightening, mushrooming 12 acceleration 13 magnification 15 intensification

escalator
04 lift 08 elevator 10 travelator, travolator 13 moving walkway 15 moving staircase

escapable
08 eludible, evadable 09 avertible, avoidable

escapade
04 hoot, lark, ploy, romp 05 antic, caper, fling, prank, scape, spree, stunt, trick 06 escape, frolic, scheme, splore 07 exploit 08 escapado, fredaine 09 adventure, excursion 10 skylarking 11 monkey shine

escape
03 esc, fly, lam, out 04 bolt, bunk, duck, flee, flit, flow, go-by, gush, hole, leak, ooze, pass, scat, seep, shun, skip, slip, vent 05 avoid, break, ditch, dodge, drain, elope, elude, evade, issue, lam it, leg it, prank, sally, scape, scoot, scram, spurt 06 blower, decamp, efflux, flight, forget, get off, outlet 07 abscond, bail out, do a bunk, dodging, ducking, evasion, fantasy, get away, getaway, leakage, not know, outflow, outpour, overrun, pastime, pour out, run away, scarper, seepage, trickle, wilding 08 break out, breakout, dreaming, emission, escapism, loophole, not place, run for it, shake off, sidestep, slip away 09 avoidance, breakaway, break free, cut and run, discharge, diversion, do a runner, emanation, jailbreak, pour forth 10 absconding, break loose, circumvent, decampment, have it away, hop the twig, Houdini act, recreation, relaxation 11 distraction,

fantasizing, safety-valve **12** steer clear of **13** circumvention, extravasation, not be recalled, transgression **14** make a bolt for it, make your escape, run for your life, take it on the lam, take to the boats **15** make a break for it, make your getaway, not be remembered, take to your heels, wishful thinking

- **allow to escape**

03 let **04** vent

- **means of escape**

04 hole, loop **08** loophole

- **way of escape**

03 out **04** mews, muse **05** meuse **06** get-out **08** bolthole

escapee

06 truant **07** escaper, refugee, runaway **08** defector, deserter, fugitive **09** absconder **11** jailbreaker

escapism

07 fantasy, pastime **08** dreaming **09** diversion **10** recreation, relaxation **11** distraction, fantasizing, pie in the sky, safety-valve **15** castles in the air, wishful thinking

escapist

07 dreamer, ostrich **09** Billy Liar **10** daydreamer, Don Quixote, fantasizer, non-realist **11** Walter Mitty **14** wishful thinker

eschew

04 shun **05** avoid, forgo, spurn **06** abjure, forego, give up **07** abandon, disdain **08** forswear, renounce **09** repudiate **11** abstain from, keep clear of, refrain from

escort

03 see, set **04** aide, beau, date, hand, lead, take, tend, wait, walk **05** bring, guard, guide, suite, train, usher **06** convoy, defend, gigolo, squire **07** company, conduct, cortège, esquire, janizar, partner, protect, retinue, take out **08** attend on, chaperon, come with, defender, janizary, shepherd, take down **09** accompany, attendant, bodyguard, chaperone, companion, entourage, janissary, protector **10** attendance, attendants, javelin-man **13** come along with, guard of honour

esoteric

05 inner **06** arcane, hidden, inside, mystic, occult, Orphic, secret **07** cryptic, obscure, private **08** abstruse, mystical, rarefied **09** recondite **10** acroamatic, mysterious **11** inscrutable **12** acroamatical, confidential

esparto grass

04 alfa **05** halfa

especial

06 marked, signal, unique **07** express, notable, special, unusual **08** peculiar, singular, specific, striking, uncommon **09** exclusive, principal **10** noteworthy, particular, pre-eminent, remarkable **11** distinctive, exceptional, outstanding **13** distinguished, extraordinary

especially

03 esp **04** very **05** espec **06** mainly, mostly, namely **07** chiefly, largely, notably **08** above all, markedly, uniquely **09** expressly, in special, most of all, primarily, specially, supremely, unusually **10** remarkably, strikingly, uncommonly **11** exclusively, principally **12** in particular, particularly, pre-eminently **13** exceptionally, outstandingly **15** extraordinarily

espionage

05 scout **06** spying **07** bugging, probing **08** snooping **10** tradecraft **11** fifth column, penetration, wiretapping **12** infiltration, intelligence, intercepting, surveillance **13** investigation, secret service **14** reconnaissance, undercover work

espousal

06 choice **07** backing, defence, support, wedding **08** adoption, advocacy, taking-up **09** embracing, promotion **11** championing, maintenance **12** championship

espouse

04 back **05** adopt **06** choose, defend, opt for, take up **07** embrace, support **08** advocate, champion, maintain **09** patronize **10** stand up for

esprit de corps

10 team spirit **12** group loyalty, mutual respect, public spirit **13** mutual feeling

espy

03 see, spy **04** spot **05** sight, watch **06** behold, descry, detect, notice **07** discern, glimpse, make out, observe **08** discover, perceive **11** distinguish **12** catch sight of

essay

02 go **03** try **04** bash, push, shot, stab, test **05** assay, crack, go for, offer, paper, piece, study, theme, tract, trial **06** leader, review, sketch, strain, strive, tackle, take on, thesis **07** article, attempt, have a go, venture **08** causerie, critique, struggle, treatise **09** discourse, endeavour, have a bash, have a stab, prolusion, undertake **10** assignment, commentary, experiment, have a crack **11** composition **12** disquisition, dissertation

essayist

Essayists include:

04 **Greg** (William Rathbone), **Hunt** (Leigh), **Lamb** (Charles), **Lynd** (Robert), **Rodó** (José Enrique)
05 **Bacon** (Francis), **Gould** (Stephen Jay), **Lucas** (Edward Verrall), **Pater** (Walter Horatio), **Smith** (Sydney), **White** (E B)
06 **Borges** (Jorge Luis), **Breton** (André), **Orwell** (George), **Ruskin** (John), **Steele** (Sir Richard)
07 **Addison** (Joseph), **Calvino** (Italo), **Carlyle** (Thomas), **Chapone** (Hester), **Emerson** (Ralph Waldo), **Hayward** (Abraham), **Hazlitt** (William), **Lazarus** (Emma), **Meynell** (Alice Christiana Gertrude), **Montagu** (Lady Mary Wortley), **Thoreau** (Henry David)
08 **Beerbohm** (Sir Max), **Macaulay** (Thomas Babington, Lord)
09 **De Quincey** (Thomas), **Dickinson** (Goldsworthy Lowes), **Montaigne** (Michel Eyquem de)
10 **Chesterton** (G K), **Crèvecoeur** (Michel Guillaume Jean de)
12 **Quiller-Couch** (Sir Arthur)

essence

03 nub **04** alma, core, crux, esse, life, otto, pith, soul **05** being, heart, juice, point, stuff **06** centre, entity, kernel, marrow, nature, spirit **07** alcohol, extract, meaning, quality, quiddit, ratafia, reality, spirits **08** bergamot, quiddity, whatness **09** actuality, character, principle, substance **10** attributes, distillate, heart-blood, hypostasis, ylang-ylang **11** concentrate, heart's-blood **12** distillation, quintessence, significance **13** concentration, individuation, ylang-ylang oil **15** characteristics, sum and substance

- **in essence**

07 in grain **08** at bottom **09** basically **11** essentially **13** fundamentally, substantially

- **of the essence**

05 vital **06** needed **07** crucial **08** required **09** essential, important, necessary, requisite **13** indispensable

essential

03 key **04** gist, main, must, pure **05** basic, vital **06** formal, innate, needed **07** central, crucial, typical **08** inherent, key point, required, rudiment **09** important, intrinsic, key points, main point, necessary, necessity, principal, principle, requisite **10** definitive, main points, sine qua non, underlying **11** constituent, fundamental, requirement, substantial **12** all-important, constitutive, prerequisite **13** indispensable **14** characteristic

essentially

05 per se **07** at heart **08** deep down **09** basically, in essence, primarily **10** inherently **13** fundamentally, intrinsically

establish

03 fix **04** base, form, haft, make, open, seat, show **05** begin, build, edify, erect, found, lodge, pitch, plant, prove, raise, set up, start, state, stell **06** affirm, attest, create, ordain, ratify, secure, settle, verify **07** certify, confirm, install, start up **08** nail down, organize, validate **09** institute, introduce **10** constitute, inaugurate **11** corroborate, demonstrate **12** authenticate, substantiate **14** bring into being

established
03 est, set **05** fixed **06** proved, proven, rooted, secure, stable, stated
07 settled **08** accepted, radicate, ratified, standing **09** ensconced, radicated, respected, steadfast
10 entrenched **11** experienced, traditional **12** conventional **14** tried and tested
• to be established
04 root **06** obtain

establishment
03 fix **04** firm, shop, them **05** store
07 company, concern, forming
08 business, creation, founding
09 formation, inception, institute, setting up, the system **10** enterprise, foundation **11** corporation, down-sitting, institution, ruling class
12 inauguration, installation, organization **13** the government
14 the authorities **15** the powers that be

estate
03 pen **04** alod, area, land, odal, park, rank, site, udal **05** allod, class, goods, lands, manor, place, state, taluk, tract, trust **06** assets, centre, domain, entail, having, realty, region, status
07 demesne, effects, grounds, havings
08 allodium, executry, hacienda, holdings, position, property, standing
09 condition, patrimony, princedom, situation **10** belongings, latifundia, personalty, plantation, real estate
11 development, landholding, possessions **14** conditional fee

estate agent
07 realtor **09** land agent **13** property agent **15** real-estate agent

esteem
03 way **04** deem, have, hold, love, pass, rate, view **05** compt, count, favor, izzat, judge, prise, prize, set by, store, think, value **06** admire, credit, favour, honour, make of, reckon, regard, revere **07** account, adjudge, believe, cherish, respect, set down
08 consider, judgment, treasure, venerate **09** judgement, reckoning, reverence **10** admiration, estimation, veneration **11** approbation, good opinion **12** appreciation, regard highly
13 consideration, put a premium on

esteemed
06 prized, valued, worthy **07** admired, revered **08** favorite, honoured, precious **09** admirable, excellent, favourite, of warrant, reputable, respected, treasured, venerated
10 honourable **11** prestigious, respectable **13** distinguished, of good warrant, well-respected, well-thought-of **14** highly regarded

estimable
04 good **06** valued, worthy
07 notable **08** esteemed, laudable, valuable **09** admirable, excellent, reputable, respected **10** creditable, honourable, noteworthy, worthwhile
11 commendable, meritorious, respectable, warrantable
12 praiseworthy **13** distinguished

estimate
03 aim **04** cost, gage, rate, view
05 carat, gauge, guess, judge, level, value, weigh **06** assess, belief, carrat, reckon, strike **07** compute, opinion
08 appraise, evaluate, judgment, thinking **09** calculate, judgement, quotation, reckoning, valuation
10 appreciate, assessment, conclusion, conjecture, estimation, evaluation, reputation, rough guess
11 calculation, computation, guesstimate **13** approximation, consideration **14** ballpark figure
15 approximate cost

estimated
03 est

estimation
04 rate, view **05** guess, honor, sight, stock **06** belief, credit, esteem, honour, regard **07** account, feeling, opinion, respect **08** estimate, judgment, thinking **09** judgement, reckoning, valuation **10** assessment, conception, conclusion, conjecture, evaluation, importance, reputation, rough guess **11** calculation, computation **12** appreciation
13 consideration, way of thinking
15 approximate cost

Estonia
03 EST

estrange
04 part **05** alien, sever **06** cut off, divide, remove **07** break up, divorce, split up **08** alienate, disunite, separate, withdraw, withhold **09** disaffect
10 antagonize, drive apart, set against
13 set at variance

estranged
05 alien, apart, fraim, fremd **06** fremit
07 aliened, divided **08** alienate, divorced, separate **09** alienated, separated **11** antagonized, disaffected

estrangement
05 split **06** breach **07** break-up, parting **08** disunion, disunity, division
09 antipathy, hostility, severance
10 alienation, antagonism, separation, withdrawal **11** withholding
12 disaffection, dissociation
14 unfriendliness

estuary
03 arm, bay, Est **04** cove **05** creek, firth, fiord, fjord, inlet, mouth **07** sea-loch

et cetera
01 &c **03** etc **04** et al **07** and so on
10 and all that, and so forth, and the like, and the rest, or whatever **11** and suchlike, and whatever **14** and what have you

etch
03 cut, dig **04** bite, burn **05** carve, eat in, stamp **06** furrow, groove, incise
07 corrode, eat away, engrave, impress, imprint, ingrain **08** inscribe

etching
03 cut **05** print **06** sketch **07** carving, imprint **08** aquatint **09** aquatinta, engraving **10** aqua fortis, impression
11 inscription

eternal
07 abiding, aeonian, endless, lasting, non-stop, undying **08** constant, enduring, immortal, infinite, timeless, unending **09** ceaseless, deathless, eviternal, incessant, limitless, perennial, perpetual **10** continuous, persistent, relentless, unchanging
11 everlasting, never-ending, remorseless, unremitting
12 imperishable, interminable, unchangeable **14** indestructible

eternally
04 ever **06** always **07** for ever
09 endlessly, lastingly **10** constantly
11 ceaselessly, continually, incessantly, permanently, perpetually
12 interminably **13** everlastingly
14 indestructibly

eternity
03 age, eon **04** aeon, ages **05** yonks
06 heaven **07** forever **08** Ewigkeit, infinity, long time, paradise **09** after-life, hereafter, next world **10** perpetuity
11 ages and ages, endlessness, everlasting, immortality, world to come **12** donkey's years, immutability, timelessness **13** deathlessness
15 everlasting life, everlastingness, imperishability, world without end

ethereal
04 airy, fine **05** light **06** dainty, subtle
07 refined, tenuous **08** delicate, empyreal, empyrean, gossamer, heavenly, rarefied **09** airy-fairy, celestial, elemental, exquisite, spiritual, unearthly, unworldly **10** diaphanous, immaterial, impalpable, intangible
13 insubstantial

ethical
04 fair, good, just **05** moral, noble, right **06** decent, honest, proper, seemly **07** correct, fitting, upright
08 decorous, virtuous **09** righteous
10 high-minded, honourable, principled **11** commendable, responsible **13** above reproach

ethically
05 nobly **06** justly **07** morally, rightly
08 honestly **09** reputably
10 honourably, virtuously
11 responsibly **12** high-mindedly, respectfully **13** ideologically
14 moralistically

ethics
04 code **05** rules **06** equity, morals, values **07** beliefs **08** morality
09 moral code, propriety, standards
10 conscience, deontology, principles
11 moral values **13** descriptivism, moral theology **14** moral standards
15 moral philosophy, moral principles

Ethiopia
03 ETH

ethnic
04 folk **06** exotic, native, racial, tribal **07** foreign **08** cultural, national, societal **10** aboriginal, indigenous **11** traditional **12** ethnological **13** autochthonous **15** anthropological

ethnically
08 racially, socially, tribally **10** culturally, societally **13** traditionally **14** humanistically

ethos
04 code **05** tenor **06** ethics, spirit **07** beliefs, flavour, manners **08** attitude, morality **09** character, rationale, standards **10** atmosphere, principles **11** disposition

etiquette
04 code, form, kawa **05** rules **07** customs, decency, decorum, manners **08** ceremony, civility, courtesy, good form, protocol **09** propriety, standards **10** politeness **11** convenances, conventions, correctness, formalities, good manners **12** unwritten law **13** code of conduct **14** code of practice **15** code of behaviour

etymology
03 ety **06** origin, source **08** word-lore **09** philology, semantics **10** derivation, lexicology **11** linguistics, word history, word origins

eucalyptus
03 box, gum **05** karri, marri, sally, tuart **06** jarrah, mallee, red gum, sallee, tewart, tooart, wandoo **07** blue gum, gum tree **08** coolabah, coolibah, coolibar, ghost gum, ironbark, sugar gum **09** black butt, bloodwood, fever tree **10** tallow wood, woollybutt **11** mountain ash

eulogize
04 hype, laud, plug **05** exalt, extol **06** honour, praise **07** acclaim, applaud, approve, commend, glorify, magnify **09** celebrate, rave about **10** compliment, panegyrize, wax lyrical **12** congratulate

eulogy
04 laud **05** paean **06** praise **07** acclaim, plaudit, tribute **08** accolade, applause, encomion, encomium **09** laudation, laudative, laudatory, panegyric **10** compliment, exaltation **11** acclamation **12** commendation **13** glorification

euphemism
07 evasion **09** softening **10** genteelism, politeness, polite term, substitute **12** substitution **14** understatement **15** mild alternative

See also **oath**

euphemistic
04 mild **05** vague **06** polite **07** evasive, genteel, neutral **08** indirect **09** soft-toned **10** substitute **11** understated

euphonious
04 soft **05** clear, sweet **06** dulcet, mellow **07** melodic, musical, silvery, tuneful **08** canorous, euphonic, pleasant **09** consonant, melodious **10** harmonious, sweet-toned **11** dulcifluous, mellifluous, symphonious **12** dulciloquent **13** sweet-sounding

euphoria
03 joy **04** glee, high, rush **05** bliss **07** ecstasy, elation, rapture **08** buoyancy **09** happiness, transport, wellbeing **10** enthusiasm, exaltation, exultation, jubilation **11** high spirits **12** cheerfulness, exhilaration, intoxication

euphoric
04 high **05** happy **06** elated, joyful, joyous **07** buoyant, exulted, gleeful **08** blissful, cheerful, ecstatic, exultant, jubilant **09** rapturous **10** enraptured **11** exhilarated, intoxicated **12** enthusiastic

Europe

European countries include:

02 UK
05 Italy, Malta, Spain
06 Cyprus, France, Greece, Latvia, Monaco, Norway, Poland, Russia, Sweden, Turkey
07 Albania, Andorra, Austria, Belarus, Belgium, Croatia, Denmark, Estonia, Finland, Germany, Hungary, Iceland, Ireland, Moldova, Romania, Ukraine, Vatican
08 Bulgaria, Portugal, Slovakia, Slovenia
09 Lithuania, Macedonia, San Marino
10 Luxembourg
11 Switzerland, Vatican City
13 Czech Republic, Liechtenstein, United Kingdom
14 The Netherlands
19 Serbia and Montenegro
20 Bosnia and Herzegovina

European landmarks include:

02 Po
04 Alps, Arno, Como, Etna, Lido, Main, Oder
05 Delos, Eiger, Garda, Loire, Prado, Rhine, Rhône, Seine, Somme, Tiber, Urals, Volga
06 Azores, Dachau, Danube, Delphi, Fátima, Geysir, Liffey, Rhodes, Tatras, Tivoli
07 Algarve, Kremlin, Lapland, La Scala, Madeira, Moselle, Pompeii, Shannon, Siberia
08 Alhambra, Ardennes, Auvergne, Canaries, Caucasus, Dordogne, Jungfrau, Lake Como, Legoland, Oude Kerk, Pantheon, Provence, Pyrenees, St Peter's, Strokkur, Tenerife, Vesuvius
09 Acropolis, Balearics, Bantry Bay, Campanile, Colosseum, Connemara, Dolomites, Dublin Bay, Keukenhof, Lake Garda, Lanzarote, Menin Gate, Mont Blanc, Mount Etna, Notre Dame, Parc Güell, Parthenon, Red Square, Reichstag, Temple Bar, Zuider Zee
10 Bran Castle, Grand Canal, IJsselmeer, Interlaken, Julian Alps, Lake Geneva, Lenin's tomb, Matterhorn, Nieuwe Kerk, Pont du Gard, Rubenshuis, Schönbrunn, Versailles, Wienerwald
11 Afsluitdijk, Black Forest, Eiffel Tower, Königsplatz, Manneken Pis, Mount Elbrus, Rijksmuseum, Simplon Pass, Vatican City, Vienna Woods
12 Abbey Theatre, Bavarian Alps, Blarney Stone, Frauenkirche, Lake Maggiore, Leaning Tower, Mont St Michel, Mount Olympus, Mozart's House, Ponte Vecchio, Rialto Bridge, Rubens's House, Summer Palace, Tower of Belém, Winter Palace
13 Anne Frank Huis, Arc de Triomphe, Bridge of Sighs, Canary Islands, Ha'penny Bridge, Lake Constance, Little Mermaid, Massif Central, Millau Viaduct, Mount Vesuvius, Museo del Prado, Oresund Bridge, Sistine Chapel, St Mark's Square, Uffizi Gallery, Ural Mountains, Vatican Palace
14 Bolshoi Theatre, Mount Parnassus, O'Connell Street, Palazzo Vecchio, Piazza San Marco, Potsdamer Platz, Sagrada Familia, Trinity College
15 Anne Frank's house, Balearic Islands, Brandenburg Gate, Dingle Peninsula, Hermitage Museum, Rock of Gibraltar, Stedelijk Museum

European
◇ *foreign word indicator*
01 E **03** Eur **04** Euro

Europeans include:

04 Balt, Brit, Dane, Esth, Finn, Flem, Lapp, Pict, Pole, Scot, Serb, Slav, Turk
05 Angle, Czech, Croat, Greek, Latin, Vlach, Swede, Swiss
06 Almain, Basque, Briton, German, Nordic, Sabine, Salian, Teuton, Zyrian
07 Belgian, Bosnian, Cypriot, Fleming, Iberian, Italian, Latvian, Lombard, Maltese, Manxman, Monacan, Russian, Samnite, Serbian, Walloon
08 Albanian, Andorran, Austrian, Croatian, Dutchman, Estonian, Irishman, Moldovan, Romanian, Scotsman, Siberian, Silurian, Spaniard, Welshman
09 Britisher, Bulgarian, Englander, Englisher, Frenchman, Hungarian, Icelander, Manxwoman, Norwegian, Sardinian, Slovakian, Slovenian, Ukrainian
10 Anglo-Saxon, Belarusian, Dutchwoman, Englishman, Irishwoman, Lithuanian, Macedonian, Monégasque,

Portuguese, Welshwoman
11 Belarussian, Frenchwoman, Montenegrin, Sammarinese
12 Luxembourger, Scandinavian
13 Englishwoman, Herzegovinian
15 Liechtensteiner

• European Union
02 EU

European Union member countries include:

05 Italy, Malta, Spain
06 Cyprus, France, Greece, Latvia, Poland, Sweden
07 Austria, Belgium, Denmark, Estonia, Finland, Germany, Hungary, Ireland
08 Portugal, Slovakia, Slovenia
09 Lithuania
10 Luxembourg
13 Czech Republic, United Kingdom
14 The Netherlands

europium
02 Eu

euthanasia
07 quietus, release **12** happy release, mercy killing **15** assisted suicide, merciful release

evacuate
04 ease, quit, void **05** clear, eject, empty, expel, leave, purge, stool **06** decamp, depart, desert, getter, remove, vacate **07** abandon, excrete, forsake, nullify, relieve, retreat, vacuate **08** clear out, defecate, withdraw **09** discharge, eliminate, make empty, move out of, pull out of **10** go away from, relinquish, retire from, stercorate

evacuation
06 exodus, flight **07** Dunkirk, leaving, purging, removal, retreat **08** ejection, emptying, quitting, vacating **09** clearance, departure, desertion, discharge, expulsion, forsaking, gettering, urination, vacuation **10** defecation, retirement, withdrawal **11** abandonment, elimination **14** relinquishment

evade
04 balk, duck, shun **05** avoid, blink, burke, dodge, elude, fence, fudge, hedge, parry, sheer, shift, shirk, skive, waive **06** baffle, bludge, bypass, cop out, escape **07** fend off, quibble, shuffle, wriggle **08** get round, sidestep, skive off **09** back out of, duckshove, gold brick, weasel out **10** chicken out, circumvent, equivocate, scrimshank, skrimshank **11** prevaricate **12** steer clear of, wriggle out of

evaluate
04 rank, rate **05** gauge, judge, value, weigh **06** assess, reckon, size up **07** compute, measure **08** appraise, estimate **09** calculate, determine **15** get the measure of

evaluation
05 audit **06** rating **07** opinion **08** estimate, judgment **09** appraisal, judgement, reckoning, valuation **10** assessment, estimation **11** calculation, computation **13** determination

evanescent
05 brief **06** fading **07** passing **08** fleeting, unstable **09** ephemeral, momentary, temporary, transient, vanishing **10** perishable, short-lived, transitory **11** evaporating, impermanent **12** disappearing **13** insubstantial

evangelical
03 Sim **06** Marist **07** zealous **08** biblical, orthodox, Stundist **09** crusading, High-flier, High-flyer, Simeonite **10** converting, missionary, Morisonian, scriptural **11** campaigning **12** Bible-bashing, enthusiastic, evangelistic, propagandist **13** Bible-punching, Bible-thumping, proselytizing **14** Bible-believing, fundamentalist, propagandizing

• Evangelical Union
02 EU

evangelist
04 John, Luke, Mark **07** Matthew **08** crusader, preacher **09** gospeller, missioner **10** campaigner, missionary, revivalist **12** hot gospeller, proselytizer **13** televangelist

evangelize
06 preach **07** baptize, convert, crusade **08** campaign **09** gospelize **10** missionize **11** proselytize **12** missionarize, propagandize **13** spread the word

evaporate
03 dry, end **04** fade, melt **05** steme, vapor **06** depart, dispel, distil, exhale, vanish, vapour **08** boil away, disperse, dissolve, evanesce, melt away, vaporize **09** dehydrate, desiccate, disappear, dissipate **10** volatilize **13** dematerialize

evaporation
06 drying, fading **07** melting **09** vanishing **10** exhalation **11** dehydration, desiccation, dissolution **12** condensation, distillation, vaporization

evasion
04 go-by **05** dodge, fudge, quirk **06** cop-out, deceit, escape, excuse, put-off **07** dodging, ducking, elusion, fencing, fig leaf, fudging, hedging, quibble, shuffle, skiving **08** go-around, shirking, shunning, trickery **09** avoidance, deception, quibbling, shuffling **10** scrimshank, skrimshank, subterfuge **12** equivocation **13** circumvention, prevarication **14** tergiversation **15** steering clear of

evasive
03 coy **05** cagey, vague **06** shifty, slippy, tricky **07** cunning, devious, elusive, elusory, fudging, oblique **08** indirect, slippery, waffling **09** deceitful, deceptive, quibbling, secretive, shuffling **10** misleading **12** equivocating **13** prevaricating, unforthcoming

evasiveness
06 deceit **07** cunning, fudging, secrecy **08** caginess **09** quibbling, vagueness **12** equivocation, indirectness **13** deceptiveness, prevarication

eve
03 e'en **04** edge **05** brink, verge, vigil **09** day before, threshold **10** time before **12** period before

even
◇ *hidden alternately indicator*
03 all, e'en, too, yet **04** also, calm, cool, eevn, fair, flat, just, like, more, same, true **05** align, alike, at all, clean, drawn, eeven, equal, exact, flush, level, match, oddly, plain, plane, quits, still **06** as well, hardly, indeed, in fact, nearly, placid, serene, smooth, square, stable, steady **07** balance, compare, eevning, equable, exactly, flatten, neutral, regular, similar, uniform **08** actually, balanced, composed, constant, equalize, likewise, matching, parallel, scarcely, so much as, straight, tranquil **09** equitable, identical, impartial, make equal, stabilize, still more, unexcited, unruffled, unusually, unvarying **10** all the more, balance out, consistent, even-handed, fifty-fifty, horizontal, regularize, side by side, straighten, unchanging, unwavering **11** make uniform, more exactly, neck and neck, non-partisan, symmetrical, unexcitable, unflappable **12** even-tempered, surprisingly, unexpectedly **13** evenly matched, more precisely, unperturbable **14** strike a balance

• even so
03 but, yet **05** still **07** however **10** all the same **11** despite that, nonetheless **12** nevertheless **13** in spite of that

• get even
05 repay **06** avenge **07** pay back, requite **11** have revenge, reciprocate **12** settle a score **14** get your own back **15** revenge yourself, take your revenge

• not even
06 odd **06** uneven

even-handed
04 fair, just **06** square **07** neutral **08** balanced, unbiased **09** equitable, impartial **10** reasonable **12** unprejudiced **13** disinterested, dispassionate, fair and square

evening
03 e'en, ene, eve **04** dusk, eevn, even **05** eeven, night **06** sunset, vesper **07** eevning, sundown **08** eventide, twilight **09** forenight, nightfall **10** close of day

evenly
◇ *hidden alternately indicator*
04 flat **06** calmly, square, stably **07** equally **08** placidly, serenely, steadily **09** regularly, similarly, uniformly **10** constantly, tranquilly **12** consistently **13** evenly matched, symmetrically

event
03 end **04** case, fact, fate, gala, game, item, meet, pass, race **05** issue, match, round **06** affair, effect, matter, result, upshot **07** contest, episode, fixture, fortune, meeting, ongoing, outcome **08** business, incident, occasion **09** adventure, aftermath, happening, milestone **10** conclusion, engagement, experience, occurrence, proceeding, tournament **11** competition, consequence, eventuality, possibility, termination **12** circumstance

• **in any event**
06 anyhow, anyway **09** in any case **11** whether or no **12** no matter what, whether or not **15** whatever happens

even-tempered
04 calm, cool **06** placid, serene, stable, steady **07** equable, unfazed **08** composed, laid-back, peaceful, tranquil **09** peaceable **11** level-headed, unflappable **13** imperturbable

eventful
04 busy, full **06** active, lively **07** crucial, notable **08** critical, exciting, historic **09** checkered, chequered, important, memorable, momentous **10** noteworthy, remarkable **11** interesting, ripsnorting, significant **12** action-packed **13** unforgettable

eventual
04 last **05** final, later **06** future **07** closing, ensuing, planned **08** ultimate **09** impending, projected, resulting **10** concluding, subsequent **11** prospective

eventuality
04 case **05** event **06** chance, crisis, mishap **07** outcome **09** emergency, happening, incidence **10** likelihood, occurrence **11** contingency, possibility, probability **12** circumstance, happenstance

eventually
06 at last, in time **07** finally **08** after all, at length, in the end **10** ultimately **11** in due course **12** in the long run, subsequently **13** sooner or later

ever
02 ay **03** aye, e'er **05** at all **06** always **07** for ever **08** evermore **09** at any time, endlessly, eternally, in any case **10** at all times, constantly **11** continually, incessantly, permanently, perpetually **12** on any account, till doomsday **13** on any occasion

• **ever so**
04 very **05** jolly **06** really **07** awfully **08** terribly, very much **09** extremely, immensely **11** exceedingly, frightfully **12** tremendously **13** exceptionally

evergreen *see* **pine**; **tree**

everlasting
07 endless, eternal, non-stop, undying **08** cat's-foot, constant, immortal, infinite, timeless, unending **09** continual, deathless, incessant, permanent, perpetual, unceasing **10** continuous, immortelle, perdurable, persistent, relentless **11** Helichrysum, never-ending, remorseless, sempiternal, strawflower, unremitting, xeranthemum **12** imperishable, interminable **14** indestructible

evermore
04 ever **06** always **07** for ever **09** eternally, ever after, hereafter **10** henceforth **11** in perpetuum, unceasingly **12** in perpetuity, till doomsday **14** for ever and a day, for ever and ever, to the end of time

every
03 all, per **04** each, full, tout **05** total **06** entire **08** complete **11** all possible, every single **15** every individual

everybody
03 all **05** a'body **07** each one **08** everyman, everyone **09** one and all **10** each person **11** all the world, every person, tout le monde **12** all and sundry, every man Jack **13** the whole world

everyday
05 basic, daily, plain, stock, usual **06** common, folksy, modern, normal, simple **07** average, regular, routine **08** day-to-day, familiar, frequent, habitual, informal, ordinary, standard, workaday **09** customary, quotidian **10** accustomed, monotonous **11** commonplace **12** conventional, run-of-the-mill **13** unimaginative **14** common-or-garden

everyone
03 all **07** each one **08** universe **09** allcomers, everybody, one and all **10** each person **11** every person **12** all and sundry, every man Jack **13** the whole world

everything
03 all **04** lock **06** a'thing, the lot, the sum **08** the total, the works **09** all things, each thing **11** all the world, the entirety, the whole lot **12** the aggregate **14** stock and barrel **15** the whole shebang

everywhere
04 left **06** a'where, passim, ubique **07** all over **09** all around, eachwhere **10** every place, far and near, far and wide, high and low, near and far, throughout, ubiquitous **11** at every turn, in all places, in each place, to all places, to each place **12** the world over **14** right and centre

evict
04 oust **05** eject, expel **06** put out, remove **07** cast out, kick out, turf out, turn out **08** chuck out, dislodge, force out, throw out **10** dispossess **11** expropriate **12** force to leave

eviction
07 removal, the boot, the push **08** ejection, the elbow **09** clearance, expulsion **11** the bum's rush **12** dislodgement **13** dispossession, expropriation **14** defenestration

evidence
04 data, deed, hint, mark, show, sign, test **05** proof, prove, stamp, title, token, trace, vouch **06** affirm, assert, attest, avouch, betray, denote, evince, reveal **07** bespeak, confirm, display, exhibit, grounds, signify, support, symptom, witness **08** argument, document, indicate, instance, manifest, surrebut, warranty **09** adminicle, affidavit, establish, guarantee, testimony **10** indication, smoking gun, suggestion **11** affirmation, attestation, credentials, declaration, demonstrate **12** compurgation, confirmation, precognition, verification **13** corroboration, demonstration, documentation, manifestation **14** substantiation

• **in evidence**
05 clear, plain **06** patent **07** obvious, visible **08** apparent, clear-cut **10** noticeable **11** conspicuous **12** unmistakable

evident
05 clear, naked, overt, plain **06** patent **07** confest, obvious, visible **08** apparent, clear-cut, distinct, manifest, sensible, tangible **09** confessed, undoubted **10** noticeable **11** conspicuous, discernible, perceptible, transparent **12** indisputable, unmistakable **13** incontestable

evidently
07 clearly, plainly, visibly **08** patently **09** doubtless, obviously, outwardly, seemingly, so it seems **10** apparently, manifestly, ostensibly **11** doubtlessly, so it appears, undoubtedly **12** indisputably **13** as it would seem, on the face of it **15** as it would appear

evil
03 bad, ill, sin, woe **04** bale, base, blow, dire, eale, foul, harm, hurt, pain, ruin, vice, vile **05** amiss, black, cruel, curse, hydra, nasty, wrong **06** deadly, injury, misery, sinful, sorrow, wicked **07** adverse, badness, corrupt, demonic, disease, harmful, heinous, hurtful, illness, immoral, noisome, noxious, ruinous, unlucky, vicious **08** baseness, calamity, depraved, devilish, diabolic, disaster, distress, iniquity, mischief, sinister, stinking, vileness **09** adversity, depravity, injurious, malicious, malignant, malignity, nefarious, offensive, poisonous, suffering **10** affliction, calamitous, corruption, disastrous, immorality, iniquitous, malevolent, misconduct, misfortune, pernicious, sinfulness, wickedness, wrongdoing **11** catastrophe, deleterious, destructive, detrimental, heinousness,

mischievous, unfortunate, viciousness **12** catastrophic, devilishness, inauspicious, unfavourable, unpropitious **13** reprehensible

evildoer
05 rogue **06** sinner **07** badmash, budmash, villain **08** criminal, offender **09** bad person, miscreant, reprobate, scoundrel, wrongdoer **10** delinquent, malefactor **12** transgressor

evildoing
03 sin **07** badness, cruelty **08** iniquity, vileness **09** depravity, nastiness **10** corruption, immorality, sinfulness, wickedness **11** malefaction, malfeasance

evince
04 show **06** attest, betray, reveal **07** bespeak, betoken, confess, declare, display, exhibit, express, signify, witness **08** evidence, indicate, manifest, overcome **09** establish, make clear, overpower **11** demonstrate

eviscerate
03 gut **04** draw **06** paunch **08** gralloch **10** disembowel, exenterate

evocation
04 echo **06** recall **07** arousal, calling **08** inducing, kindling, stirring **10** activation, excitation, invocation, suggestion **11** elicitation, stimulation, summoning-up

evocative
05 vivid **07** graphic **08** redolent **09** memorable **10** expressive, indicative, suggestive **11** reminiscent

evoke
04 call, draw, stir **05** cause, raise, waken **06** arouse, awaken, call up, elicit, excite, induce, invoke, kindle, recall, summon **07** provoke **08** summon up **09** call forth, conjure up, stimulate **10** bring about, call to mind **11** bring to mind

evolution
◇ *anagram indicator*
06 growth **07** biogeny, descent **08** increase, progress, ripening **09** expansion, phytogeny, unfolding, unrolling **10** derivation, noogenesis, opening-out, working-out **11** development, progression, unravelling **12** cladogenesis, Neo-Darwinism, orthogenesis, phytogenesis, transformism

evolve
◇ *anagram indicator*
04 grow **06** derive, emerge, expand, mature, result, unfold, unroll **07** advance, descend, develop, enlarge, open out, unravel, work out **08** develope, disclose, generate, increase, progress **09** elaborate

ewe
03 keb, yow **04** yowe **05** crone, yowie **06** gimmer, lamber, theave

ex
01 X **03** old **04** dead, late **06** former **07** outside, without

exacerbate
03 vex **06** deepen, enrage, worsen **07** inflame, provoke, sharpen **08** embitter, heighten, increase, irritate **09** aggravate, infuriate, intensify, make worse **10** exaggerate, exasperate **12** fan the flames **15** make things worse

exacerbation
09 worsening **10** irritation **11** aggravation **12** embitterment, exaggeration, exasperation **15** intensification

exact
04 even, flat, just, milk, true **05** bleed, claim, close, force, right, wrest, wring **06** bang on, compel, dead on, demand, extort, impose, insist, minute, spot on, square, strict **07** call for, careful, command, correct, estreat, express, extract, factual, literal, orderly, perfect, precise, require, squeeze **08** accurate, definite, detailed, exacting, explicit, faithful, finished, flawless, insist on, punctual, rigorous, specific, thorough, unerring **09** faultless, identical, on the nail, religious, veracious **10** blow-by-blow, consummate, methodical, meticulous, on the money, particular, scrupulous **11** on the button, painstaking, point-device, point-devise, punctilious, word-perfect

exacting
04 firm, hard **05** harsh, stern, tough **06** severe, strict, taxing, tiring **07** arduous, exigent, onerous **08** exigeant, rigorous **09** demanding, difficult, exigeante, laborious, stringent, unsparing **10** fastidious, unyielding **11** challenging, painstaking

exactitude
04 care **05** print **06** detail, rigour **08** accuracy **09** exactness, precision **10** strictness **11** carefulness, correctness, orderliness **12** rigorousness, thoroughness **13** faultlessness, perfectionism **14** meticulousness, scrupulousness **15** painstakingness

exactly
02 on **03** due, e'en, yes **04** dead, even, flat, jump, just, to a T, true **05** plumb, quite, right, smash, spang, truly **06** agreed, bang on, dead on, indeed, just so, spot on, to a tee **07** quite so, to a hair **08** of course, on the dot, strictly, verbatim, you got it **09** carefully, certainly, correctly, expressly, literally, on the nail, precisely **10** absolutely, accurately, definitely, explicitly, faithfully, rigorously, that's right, unerringly **11** faultlessly, on the button, religiously, to the letter, veraciously **12** methodically, particularly, scrupulously, specifically, without error **13** point for point, unequivocally
• **exactly what's looked for**
02 it

exactness
04 care **06** rigour **08** accuracy, justness **09** precision **10** exactitude, strictness **11** carefulness, correctness, orderliness **12** rigorousness, thoroughness **13** faultlessness **14** meticulousness, scrupulousness

exaggerate
05 color **06** bounce, colour, overdo, stress **07** amplify, distend, enhance, enlarge, lay it on, magnify, stretch **08** overdo it, overdraw, overplay, oversell, pile it on **09** dramatize, embellish, embroider, emphasize, intensify, overstate **10** aggrandize, goliathize, shoot a line **11** overstretch **12** come it strong, lay it on thick, overdo things **13** make too much of, overdramatize, overemphasize, pile it on thick **15** stretch the truth

exaggerated
04 camp, tall **05** steep **07** exalted **08** inflated, overdone **09** amplified, bombastic, excessive, overblown **10** burlesqued, cartoonish, euphuistic, hyperbolic, overstated, theatrical **11** caricatured, embellished, extravagant, overcharged, pretentious **12** overstrained **13** overestimated **14** larger than life

exaggeration
06 excess, parody **07** stretch **08** emphasis **09** burlesque, hyperbole, stretcher **10** caricature **11** enlargement **12** extravagance, overemphasis **13** amplification, embellishment, magnification, overstatement **14** overestimation **15** pretentiousness

exalt
04 laud **05** adore, bless, deify, elate, erect, extol, honor, raise, set up **06** excite, honour, praise, prefer, refine, revere, throne, uplift **07** acclaim, advance, applaud, delight, dignify, elevate, enliven, glorify, magnify, overjoy, promote, sublime, upgrade, upraise, worship **08** enthrone, eulogize, venerate **09** reverence, subtilize, transport **10** aggrandize, enthronize, exhilarate

exaltation
03 joy **05** bliss, glory, larks **06** eulogy, honour, praise **07** acclaim, ecstasy, elation, raising, rapture, worship **08** erection **09** adoration, elevation, promotion, rejoicing, reverence **10** enthusiasm, excitement, jubilation, veneration **11** advancement, high spirits **12** exhilaration **13** glorification **14** aggrandizement

exalted
04 haut, high **05** elate, grand, happy, hault, lofty, moral, noble, regal **06** elated, haught, joyful, lordly **07** eminent, stately, sublime **08** blissful, ecstatic, elevated, exultant, jubilant, magnific, supernal, virtuous **09** dignified, rapturous **10** idealistic, magnifical **11** exaggerated **13** high and

mighty, in high spirits **15** in seventh heaven

exam, examination
02 ex **03** bac, CSE, GCE, MOT, mug **04** exam, GCSE, mods, oral, quiz, scan, test, viva **05** audit, check, final, paper, probe, study, trial **06** Abitur, A-level, biopsy, Greats, higher, O-level, prelim, review, search, survey **07** canvass, check-up, great go, inquiry, perusal **08** analysis, concours, critique, little go, necropsy, once-over, research, scrutiny, viva voce **09** appraisal, exercises, going-over, practical, questions **10** agrégation, assessment, inspection, post-mortem **11** exploration, inquisition, observation, preliminary, questioning **13** baccalaureate, interrogation, investigation

• reject at examination
04 fail, plow, spin **06** plough

examine
03 eye, pry, try, vet **04** case, jerk, palp, pump, quiz, scan, seek, sift, test, view, viva **05** assay, audit, check, grill, probe, quote, study **06** appose, assess, depose, go into, go over, jerque, look at, peruse, ponder, reason, review, revise, search, survey **07** analyse, canvass, check up, collate, discuss, dissect, explore, eyeball, inquire, inspect, observe, palpate, process, weigh up **08** appraise, check out, cognosce, consider, look into, look over, overhale, overhaul, pore over, question, research, traverse, viva voce, work over **09** catechize, check over, check up on, overhaile, speculate **10** go to town on, scrutinize **11** interrogate, investigate **12** cross-examine **13** cross-question **14** put the screws on

examinee
07 entrant **09** applicant, candidate **10** competitor, contestant **11** interviewee

examiner
05 judge, juror **06** censor, critic, marker, reader, tester **07** analyst, arbiter, assayer, auditor **08** assessor, external, reviewer **09** examinant, inspector, moderator, scrutator **10** questioner, scrutineer **11** adjudicator, interviewer, scrutinizer **12** interlocutor

example
02 ex **04** case, lead, type **05** guide, ideal, model, peach, pearl, piece, thing **06** corker, lesson, mirror, muster, sample **07** caution, epitome, exemple, pattern, warning **08** ensample, exemplar, exemplum, exponent, instance, monument, paradigm, specimen, standard **09** archetype, criterion, exemplify, footsteps, precedent, prototype, role model **10** admonition, apotheosis, assay-piece, peacherino, punishment **11** case in point, typical case **12** illustration **14** representative **15** exemplification

• for example
02 as, eg, zb **03** say **04** like **06** such as **10** par exemple **11** as an example, for instance, zum Beispiel **12** as an instance, to illustrate **13** exempli gratia

exasperate
03 bug, irk, vex **04** bait, gall, goad, rile **05** anger, annoy, get to, rouse **06** enrage, madden, needle, rankle, wind up **07** incense, provoke **08** irritate **09** aggravate, infuriate, irritated **14** drive up the wall

exasperated
05 angry, fed up, irked, riled, vexed **06** bugged, galled, goaded, peeved, piqued **07** angered, annoyed, needled, nettled **08** incensed, maddened, provoked **09** indignant, irritated **10** aggravated, infuriated

exasperating
06 vexing **07** galling, irksome **08** annoying, infernal **09** maddening, provoking, vexatious **10** bothersome, confounded, irritating, pernicious **11** aggravating, infuriating, troublesome **12** disagreeable

exasperation
04 fury, rage **05** anger **07** chagrin **09** annoyance **10** discontent, irritation **11** aggravation, indignation, stroppiness **12** exulceration **14** disgruntlement

excavate
03 cut, dig **04** mine, sink **05** delve, dig up, drive, gouge, navvy, scoop, stope **06** burrow, dig out, exhume, hollow, quarry, reveal, tunnel **07** uncover, unearth **08** disinter **09** hollow out

excavation
03 cut, dig, pit **04** delf, hole, mine **05** delph, ditch, drift, graft, heuch, heugh, shaft, stope **06** burrow, cavity, crater, dugout, hollow, mining, quarry, trench, trough **07** cutting, digging, sondage **08** catacomb, colliery, diggings, open-cast **09** burrowing, glory hole, hollowing **10** digging out, exhumation, tunnelling, unearthing **11** countermine, side cutting **12** hollowing out

exceed
03 cap, top **04** beat, pass **05** excel, outdo **06** better, go over, outrun, overdo, overgo **07** eclipse, o'ergang, outrace, overtop, surpass **08** go beyond, outreach, outshine, outstrip, outweigh, overgang, overpass, overstep, overtake **09** outnumber, overshoot, transcend **10** be more than, transgress **12** be larger than, be superior to **13** be greater than

exceedingly
04 main, very **05** amain, dooms **06** damned, highly, hugely, proper, vastly **07** greatly, not half, passing **08** almighty, devilish, heavenly, powerful, very much, wondrous **09** amazingly, extremely, immensely, monstrous, unusually, vengeance **10** consumedly, enormously, especially **11** excessively **12** inordinately, out of all nick, surpassingly **13** astonishingly, exceptionally, superlatively **14** with a vengeance **15** extraordinarily, unprecedentedly

excel
03 war **04** beat, ring **05** outdo, shine **06** better, exceed, outtop, overdo **07** eclipse, outpeer, outrank, succeed, surpass **08** outclass, outrival, overpeer, stand out **09** be skilful **10** outperform **11** be excellent, go one better, predominate **12** be better than, be pre-eminent, be superior to **13** be outstanding **15** go one better than

excellence
05 merit, skill, value, worth **06** purity, virtue, worthy **07** quality **08** eminence, fineness, goodness, nobility **09** greatness, supremacy **10** choiceness, perfection **11** distinction, high quality, pre-eminence, superiority **13** transcendence

excellent
02 A1, ME **03** ace, def, exc, fab, rad **04** best, boss, cool, fine, good, high, mean, mega, neat, pure, rare, tops **05** beaut, boffo, brave, bravo, brill, bully, crack, dicty, dilly, great, hunky, jammy, lummy, noble, noted, prime, socko, triff, wally **06** beauty, beezer, bonzer, castor, cushty, dickty, divine, famous, goodly, groovy, grouse, peachy, purler, ripper, select, spot-on, superb, way-out, whizzo, whizzy, wicked, worthy **07** capital, classic, corking, cracker, crucial, elegant, eminent, kicking, notable, perfect, radical, ripping, shining, stellar, supreme, tipping, topping, triffic, trimmer, Utopian **08** champion, clinking, cracking, eximious, fabulous, flawless, heavenly, inspired, jim-dandy, knockout, smashing, spiffing, splendid, sterling, stonking, stunning, superior, terrific, top-notch, very good, whizbang **09** admirable, brilliant, copacetic, copasetic, exemplary, fantastic, faultless, first-rate, hunky-dory, kopasetic, matchless, righteous, top-drawer, whizz-bang, wonderful **10** first-class, marvellous, noteworthy, not half bad, pre-eminent, remarkable, surpassing, unequalled **11** commendable, exceptional, high-quality, magnificent, outstanding, sensational, superlative **12** praiseworthy, second to none, the bee's knees, unparalleled **13** above reproach, distinguished **14** out of this world **15** unexceptionable

excellently
04 well **06** goodly **08** champion, divinely, superbly **09** admirably, capitally, eminently, first-rate, perfectly **10** remarkably, splendidly **11** brilliantly, commendably, wonderfully

12 marvellously, terrifically
13 exceptionally, fantastically, sensationally, superlatively

except
02 ex, sa' 03 bar, but, exc 04 less, omit, only, save, than 05 minus
06 bating, but for, nobbut, reject
07 barring, besides, exclude, outtake, rule out, short of, without 08 leave out, omitting, pass over 09 apart from, aside from, except for, excepting, excluding, other than, outside of
10 leaving out 11 not counting

exception
02 ex 03 exc 05 freak, quirk
06 oddity, rarity 07 anomaly, offence
09 departure, deviation, exclusion, objection 11 abnormality, peculiarity, special case 12 irregularity
13 inconsistency
• **take exception**
05 argue, demur, rebut 06 object, oppose, refuse, resist 07 protest
08 complain 09 challenge, repudiate, take issue, withstand 10 disapprove
11 beg to differ, expostulate, remonstrate
• **with the exception of**
03 bar, but 04 less, save 05 minus
07 barring, besides 08 omitting
09 apart from, except for, excepting, excluding, other than 10 leaving out
11 not counting

exceptionable
09 abhorrent, offensive, repugnant
10 deplorable, disgusting, unpleasant
12 disagreeable, unacceptable
13 objectionable

exceptional
03 odd 04 rare 06 way-out
07 notable, special, strange, unusual
08 aberrant, abnormal, atypical, peculiar, singular, superior, uncommon
09 anomalous, brilliant, excellent, irregular 10 marvellous, noteworthy, phenomenal, prodigious, remarkable, unequalled 11 outstanding
13 extraordinary, one in a million
14 one in a thousand

exceptionally
05 extra 06 rarely 07 notably
09 amazingly, extremely, unusually
10 abnormally, especially, remarkably, uncommonly 11 irregularly, wonderfully 13 outstandingly
15 extraordinarily

excerpt
04 clip, part 05 piece, quote, scrap
07 cutting, extract, passage, portion, section 08 citation, clipping, fragment, pericope 09 quotation, selection

excess
04 glut, rest 05 extra, spare 06 gutful, pilth 07 backlog, nimiety, o'ercome, residue, surfeit, surplus, too much
08 bellyful, left-over, overcome, overflow, overkill, owrecome, plethora, residual 09 leftovers, redundant, remainder, remaining
10 additional, debauchery, oversupply
11 dissipation, exorbitance, exorbitancy, prodigality, superfluity, superfluous, unrestraint
12 extravagance, immoderation, intemperance 13 dissoluteness, overabundance, supernumerary
14 immoderateness, more than enough, overindulgence, superabundance
• **in excess of**
04 over 05 above 08 more than

excessive
03 OTT 04 deep, over, rank 05 steep, stiff, undue 06 lavish 07 burning, extreme, fulsome, too much
08 needless, overdone, unneeded
09 exceeding, overblown
10 exorbitant, immoderate, inordinate, over the top 11 extravagant, superfluous, uncalled-for, unnecessary, unwarranted
12 overabundant, unreasonable
13 superabundant

excessively
06 overly, troppo, unduly 07 too much
08 overmuch, to a fault, woundily
09 extremely 10 needlessly 11 God-almighty 12 exorbitantly, immoderately, inordinately, out of all cess, unreasonably 13 beyond measure, exaggeratedly, extravagantly, intemperately, superfluously, unnecessarily

exchange
◇ *anagram indicator*
02 ex 04 chat, chop, cope, exch, swap, swop 05 bandy, bazar, swits, trade, trock, troke, truck 06 barter, bazaar, change, excamb, market, niffer, scorse, switch 07 bargain, commute, convert, dealing, replace, traffic 08 argument, commerce, dialogue, trade-off
09 transpose 10 discussion, stand in for, substitute 11 give and take, interchange, reciprocate, reciprocity, replacement 12 conversation, substitution

excise
03 cut, GST, tax, VAT 04 duty, levy, toll
05 erase 06 cut off, cut out, delete, impost, remove, tariff 07 customs, destroy, expunge, extract, rescind
09 eradicate, expurgate, extirpate, surcharge 11 exterminate

excision
◇ *deletion indicator*
03 cut 07 removal 08 deletion
10 expunction 11 destruction, eradication, expurgation, extirpation
13 extermination

excitable
04 edgy 05 fiery, hasty, nappy, nervy
06 feisty 07 nervous, rackety
08 choleric, volatile 09 emotional, hot-headed, irascible, mercurial, sensitive 10 passionate
11 combustible, hot-tempered, susceptible 12 highly-strung 13 quick-tempered, temperamental

excite
◇ *anagram indicator*
04 fire, move, stir, sway, urge, wake, warm, whet, yerk 05 evoke, flush, hop up, impel, rouse, steer, stire, styre, touch, upset, waken 06 accite, aerate, arouse, awaken, emmove, enmove, fire up, ignite, incite, induce, kindle, stir up, thrill, tickle, turn on, wind up, work up
07 agitate, animate, commove, disturb, enliven, ferment, impress, inflame, inspire, provoke, upraise 08 blow away, energize, engender, enkindle, generate, irritate, motivate
09 electrify, galvanize, instigate, sensitize, set on edge, stimulate, suscitate, titillate 10 bring about, intoxicate

excited
◇ *anagram indicator*
02 up 03 het, hot 04 high, warm, wild
05 antsy, astir, eager, hyper, moved, nervy, proud, radge, randy 06 elated, juiced, randie, roused 07 aroused, fevered, fired up, flushed, frantic, hyped up, sexed-up, stirred, uptight
08 agitated, animated, frenzied, hopped-up, restless, revved-up, thrilled, turned on, worked up
09 delirious, red-headed, wrought-up
10 corybantic, stimulated, up in the air
11 exhilarated, overwrought
12 enthusiastic 13 in high spirits, on tenterhooks 14 beside yourself, thrilled to bits

excitement
03 ado, rut, tew 04 fume, fuss, kick, ruff, spin, stir 05 fever, furor, kicks, pride, ruffe 06 action, didder, dither, flurry, furore, hoop-la, thrill, tumult, unrest 07 arousal, elation, emotion, ferment, passion 08 activity, brouhaha, delirium, erethism, flat spin, hilarity, pleasure 09 adventure, agitation, animation, commotion, eagerness, fleshment, rousement, sensation 10 enthusiasm, salutation
11 fun and games, stimulation
12 discomposure, exhilaration, Hobson-Jobson, intoxication, perturbation, restlessness
• **expression of excitement**
04 whee 05 yahoo 06 yippee 07 way to go! 08 hey-go-mad
• **seeking excitement**
04 fast
• **state of excitement**
10 fever pitch

exciting
03 hot 04 sexy 05 heady, magic
06 moving 07 rousing 08 dramatic, excitant, gripping, stirring, striking
09 inspiring, thrilling 10 nail-biting
11 aphrodisiac, enthralling, hair-raising, interesting, provocative, sensational, stimulating 12 action-packed, breathtaking, cliff-hanging, electrifying, exhilarating, intoxicating
13 swashbuckling
• **something exciting**
03 gas

exclaim
03 cry **04** call, roar, yell **05** blurt, shout, utter **06** bellow, cry out, outcry, shriek **07** declare **08** blurt out, proclaim **09** ejaculate, interject **10** vociferate **11** come out with, exclamation

exclamation
02 ho, wo **03** boo, cry, fen, hip, olé, pah, tut, ugh, woe, wow, yah, yay **04** call, go on, hech, I say!, oops, phew, pish, poof, pooh, push, roar, sa sa, shoo, skol, upsy, when, yell **05** bingo, fancy, house, hurra, my hat!, shout, skoal, upsee, upsey, yahoo **06** banzai, bellow, by Jove, hooray, hurrah, hurray, outcry, phooey, shriek, shucks, walker, whoops, zounds **07** bless me!, crivens, good egg, good-now, heigh-ho, hosanna, right on, whoopee **08** crivvens, hear hear!, here goes!, man alive, stroll on! **09** expletive, fancy that, good grief, unberufen, utterance **10** ecphonesis, epiphonema, Great Scott!, hoity-toity, how dare you!, upon my soul! **11** bless my soul!, bumpsadaisy, ejaculation, good heavens, marry come up **12** boomps-a-daisy, Hookey Walker, interjection, strike a light! **15** shiver my timbers
• **exclamation mark**
05 pling **06** shriek **08** screamer

exclude
03 ban, bar **04** drop, omit, skip, veto **05** debar, eject, evict, expel, hatch **06** delete, except, forbid, ice out, ignore, refuse, reject, remove **07** boot out, boycott, keep out, kick out, lock out, miss out, push out, rule out, shut off, shut out, turf out **08** count out, disallow, leave out, preclude, prohibit, throw out **09** blacklist, eliminate, freeze out, interdict, ostracize **10** include out **13** excommunicate **14** send to Coventry

excluding
◇ *deletion indicator*
06 except **07** barring **08** omitting **09** debarring, except for, excepting, ruling out **10** leaving out **11** exclusive of, not counting **12** not including

exclusion
03 ban, bar **04** veto **07** boycott, embargo, refusal, removal **08** ejection, eviction, omission **09** exception, expulsion, interdict, rejection, ruling out **10** preclusion **11** elimination, prohibition, repudiation **12** proscription

exclusive
03 few **04** chic, coup, only, posh, sole **05** plush, ritzy, scoop, swish, total, whole **06** choice, classy, cliquy, closed, clubby, exposé, narrow, select, single, snazzy, unique **07** cliquey, elegant, limited, private **08** boutique, cliquish, complete, peculiar, rarefied, snobbish, unshared, up-market **09** high-class, sectarian, sensation, undivided **10** individual, restricted, revelation, upper-crust **11** fashionable, inside story, restrictive **12** incompatible **14** discriminative
• **exclusive of**
06 except **07** barring **08** omitting **09** debarring, except for, excepting, excluding, ruling out **10** leaving out **11** not counting **12** not including

excommunicate
03 ban, bar **05** curse, debar, eject, expel **06** banish, outlaw, remove **07** exclude **08** denounce, execrate, unchurch **09** blacklist, proscribe, repudiate **12** anathematize **13** disfellowship

excommunication
07 banning, barring **08** ejection **09** exclusion, expulsion, outlawing **10** banishment **11** unchurching **12** denunciation **13** disfellowship

excoriate
03 nag **04** carp, slam **05** blame, decry, knock, slate, snipe **06** attack **07** censure, condemn, nit-pick, run down **08** denounce **09** denigrate, disparage **10** animadvert, come down on, vituperate **12** disapprove of **13** find fault with

excrement
03 poo **04** crap, crud, dung, flux, mess, poop **05** frass, guano, scats, stool **06** doo-doo, egesta, faeces, ordure **09** droppings, excretion **11** waste matter **12** rejectamenta, sir-reverence

excrescence
03 bur, pin **04** blot, boil, bump, burr, knob, lump, moss, nail, nurl, wart, wolf **05** knurl **06** cancer, growth, tumour, wattle **07** eyesore, rat-tail, sarcoma, twitter **08** rat's-tail, swelling **09** appendage, carnosity, misgrowth, outgrowth **10** projection, prominence, proud flesh **11** monstrosity, twitter-bone **12** intumescence, protuberance **13** disfigurement

excrete
03 poo **04** crap, pass, void **05** eject, expel, exude **07** secrete, urinate **08** defecate, evacuate **09** discharge

excretion
03 poo **04** crap, dung **05** stool **06** faeces, ordure **07** excreta **09** discharge, droppings, excrement, urination **10** defecation, evacuation **12** perspiration

excruciate
◇ *anagram indicator*
04 rack **07** torture **08** irritate

excruciating
05 acute, sharp **06** bitter, savage, severe **07** burning, extreme, intense, painful, racking **08** piercing **09** agonizing, atrocious, harrowing, torturing **10** tormenting, unbearable **11** intolerable **12** cringe-making, cringeworthy, insufferable

excruciatingly
07 acutely **08** severely **09** extremely, intensely, painfully **10** unbearably **11** atrociously, intolerably

exculpate
04 free **05** clear **06** acquit, excuse, let off, pardon **07** absolve, deliver, forgive, justify, release **09** discharge, exonerate, vindicate

excursion
02 ex **03** exc **04** raid, ride, tour, trip, walk **05** drive, jaunt, jolly, sally, visit **06** airing, detour, junket, outing, picnic, ramble, sashay, sortie, vagary **07** day trip, journey, outleap **08** breather, escapade, straying **09** departure, diversion, wandering **10** digression, expedition **11** mystery tour **12** pleasure trip

excusable
05 minor **06** slight, venial **09** allowable **10** defensible, forgivable, pardonable **11** explainable, justifiable, permissible **14** understandable

excuse
04 faik, free, hook, plea **05** alibi, front, salvo, scuse, shift, spare **06** acquit, cop-out, defend, essoin, exempt, get-out, ignore, let off, pardon, reason **07** absolve, apology, condone, cover-up, defence, essoyne, evasion, explain, forgive, grounds, indulge, justify, pretext, release, relieve **08** liberate, mitigate, occasion, overlook, palliate, pretence, tolerate **09** allowance, discharge, exculpate, exonerate, vindicate **10** indulgence, mitigation, substitute **11** exoneration, explanation, forgiveness, vindication **12** apologize for **13** justification **14** whittie-whattie

execrable
04 foul, vile **05** awful **06** odious **07** hateful, heinous **08** accursed, damnable, dreadful, horrible, nauseous, shocking **09** abhorrent, appalling, atrocious, loathsome, obnoxious, offensive, repulsive, revolting **10** abominable, deplorable, despicable, detestable, disgusting

execrate
04 damn, hate **05** abhor, blast, curse **06** detest, loathe, revile, vilify **07** condemn, deplore, despise **08** denounce **09** abominate, excoriate, fulminate, imprecate **10** denunciate **12** anathematize **14** inveigh against

execute
02 do **03** cut, fry, run **04** hang, kill, take **05** dance, enact, serve, shoot, stage, throw **06** behead, effect, finish, fulfil, render **07** achieve, crucify, deliver, enforce, garotte, garrote, perform, produce, realize **08** bring off, carry out, complete, despatch, dispatch, engineer, expedite, garrotte, validate **09** discharge, implement, liquidate **10** accomplish, administer, consummate, decapitate, guillotine,

perpetrate, put to death **11** electrocute **13** put into effect **15** put into practice

execution
03 run **04** mode **05** style **06** effect, manner **07** killing, staging **08** delivery, dispatch **09** discharge, effecting, enactment, operation, rendering, rendition, technique **10** completion, fulfilment **11** achievement, carrying-out, enforcement, performance, realization **12** consummation, death penalty, presentation **13** death sentence **14** accomplishment, administration, implementation, putting to death

Execution methods include:

06 noyade
07 burning, gassing, hanging, stoning
08 lynching, shooting
09 beheading
10 garrotting
11 crucifixion, firing squad, stringing up
12 decapitation, guillotining
13 electric chair, electrocution
15 lethal injection

executioner
06 axeman, hit man, killer, slayer
07 hangman **08** assassin, carnifex, headsman, murderer **09** deathsman, Jack Ketch, tormenter, tormentor
10 liquidator **11** firing squad
12 exterminator **15** Monsieur de Paris

executive
02 ex **04** exec, suit **06** leader **07** big guns, guiding, leading, manager **08** big shots, chairman, director, governor, official, superior, top brass
09 directing, governing, hierarchy, lawmaking, organizer **10** chairwoman, controller, government, leadership, management, managerial, organizing, regulating **11** chairperson, controlling, directorial, ministerial, supervisory
13 administrator **14** administration, administrative, decision-making, organizational, superintendent

exegesis
09 opening-up **10** exposition, expounding **11** explanation, explication **13** clarification
14 interpretation

exemplar
04 copy, type **05** ideal, model
07 epitome, example, paragon, pattern, sampler **08** instance, paradigm, specimen, standard
09 archetype, criterion, prototype, yardstick **10** embodiment
12 illustration **15** exemplification

exemplary
04 good **05** ideal, model **06** worthy
07 correct, perfect, warning
08 flawless, laudable **09** admirable, estimable, excellent, faultless
10 admonitory, cautionary, honourable **11** commendable, meritorious **12** praiseworthy

exemplify
03 sum **04** cite, show, type **06** depict, embody, typify **07** display, example, exhibit **08** instance, manifest
09 epitomize, personify, represent
10 illustrate, synonymize
11 demonstrate **12** characterize **13** be an example of

exempt
04 free **05** clear, exeem, exeme, spare, waive **06** excuse, immune, let off, spared **07** absolve, dismiss, exclude, excused, release, relieve **08** absolved, excluded, liberate, released
09 discharge, dismissed, exonerate, liberated, not liable **10** discharged, not subject **11** grandfather **15** grant immunity to, make an exception

exemption
07 freedom, release **08** immunity, variance **09** discharge, exception, exclusion, indemnity, privilege
10 absolution, indulgence, indulgency, overslaugh **11** exoneration
12 dispensation

exercise
◇ *anagram indicator*
02 PE, PT **03** gym, jog, try, use, vex
04 task, work **05** annoy, apply, drill, exert, sport, theme, train, upset, wield, worry **06** burden, effort, employ, labour, lesson, sports, warm up, warm-up **07** afflict, agitate, concern, disturb, exploit, perturb, problem, project, running, trouble, utilize, work out, workout **08** activity, ceremony, distress, exertion, movement, practice, practise, pump iron, training, warm down, warm-down **09** discharge, discourse, implement, make use of, operation, preoccupy, quodlibet
10 assignment, discipline, employment, fulfilment, gymnastics, isometrics **11** application, bring to bear, do exercises, piece of work, utilization **12** exercitation **13** bring into play, exert yourself
14 accomplishment, implementation

Exercises include:

04 yoga
05 Medau
06 qigong, t'ai chi
07 aquafit, chi kung, jogging, keep fit, Pilates, press-up
08 aerobics
09 boxercise, hatha yoga
10 aquarobics, daily dozen, dancercise
11 Callanetics, eurhythmics
12 body-building, calisthenics, step aerobics
13 callisthenics, cross-training, physical jerks
15 circuit training

exert
02 do **03** use **05** apply, spend, wield
06 employ, expend, extend, put out
07 utilize **08** exercise, put forth
11 bring to bear **13** bring into play
• **exert yourself**
04 hump, pull, toil, work **05** sweat
06 labour, pingle, strain, strive **07** try hard **08** go all out, slog away, struggle
09 endeavour, take pains **10** do your best **11** give your all **12** do your utmost **13** apply yourself **15** make every effort

exertion
03 use **04** toil, work **05** graft, pains, trial **06** action, effort, labour, pingle, strain, stress **07** attempt, travail, trouble
08 endeavor, exercise, industry, striving, struggle **09** diligence, endeavour, hard graft, operation
10 employment **11** application, utilization **12** perseverance
13 assiduousness

exhalation
04 mist **06** meteor, vapour
08 emission, fumosity, mephitis
09 discharge, effluvium, emanation, expulsion **10** expiration
11 evaporation, respiration
12 breathing-out

exhale
04 blow, emit, reek **05** expel, issue, smoke, steam **06** expire, vanish
07 blow out, breathe, emanate, give off, respire **08** perspire **09** discharge, evaporate, transpire **10** breathe out

exhaust
02 do **03** beg, dry, sap, tax **04** do in, jade, kill, poop, suck, tire, wear
05 drain, empty, fordo, fumes, smoke, spend, steam, use up, waste, weary, whack **06** expend, fag out, finish, strain, vapour, weaken **07** consume, deplete, fatigue, knacker, overrun, overtax, play out, tire out, wash out, wear out, work out **08** bankrupt, emission, enervate, forspend, forswink, knock out, overlive, override, overteem, overtire, overwork, squander, weary out **09** discharge, dissipate, emanation, forespend, overshoot, overspend, overweary, overwrite, tucker out **10** almost kill, exhalation, impoverish, nearly kill, run through **11** take it out of

exhausted
03 dry **04** done, mate, shot, void, weak, worn **05** all in, empty, jaded, spent, tired, weary **06** all out, beaten, bushed, done in, effete, pooped, used up, wabbit, wasted, zonked **07** at an end, drained, emptied, euchred, fainted, fordone, puggled, shagged, shotten, waygone, whacked, worn out
08 a cot case, burnt out, consumed, dead-beat, depleted, dog-tired, fatigued, finished, forfairn, half-dead, jiggered, tired out, wiped out
09 burned out, dead tired, enervated, enfeebled, fagged out, knackered, played-out, pooped out, prostrate, shattered, stonkered, washed-out, zonked out **10** clapped-out, euchred out, forfeuchen, forfoughen, shagged out **11** bush whacked, forfoughten, ready to drop, stressed-out, tuckered out

exhausting
04 hard **06** severe, taxing, tiring
07 arduous, killing, testing, wearing
08 draining, grueling, wearying
09 depletion, gruelling, laborious, punishing, strenuous **10** enervating, formidable **12** backbreaking, debilitating

exhaustion
06 jet-lag **07** fatigue **08** distress, lethargy, weakness **09** tiredness, weariness **10** enervation, feebleness

exhaustive
04 full **05** total **06** all-out **07** in-depth
08 complete, detailed, sweeping, thorough **09** extensive, full-scale, intensive **10** definitive **11** far-reaching
12 all-embracing, all-inclusive, encyclopedic **13** comprehensive

exhaustively
05 fully **07** totally **10** completely, thoroughly **11** extensively, intensively
12 definitively **14** all-inclusively
15 comprehensively

exhibit
03 air **04** hang, shew, show, wear
05 array, exude, model, offer, sport
06 expose, flaunt, parade, reveal, set out, unveil **07** display, express, present, propose, showing **08** disclose, discover, indicate, manifest, set forth, showcase **09** make clear, make plain, showpiece **10** exhibition
11 demonstrate **12** illustration, presentation, put on display
13 demonstration

exhibition
04 demo, expo, fair, gift, show
05 grant, rodeo, Salon, simul **06** airing
07 academy, diorama, display, exhibit, ice show, preview, showing
08 aquacade, pavilion, showcase, sideshow, waxworks **09** allowance, spectacle **10** cattle show, disclosure, exposition, expression, flower show, indication, panopticon, puppet show, revelation **11** performance
12 presentation, simultaneous
13 cinematograph, demonstration, manifestation, retrospective
14 representation

exhibitionism
09 dramatics, flaunting, staginess
10 overacting, showing-off
11 flamboyance, histrionics, self-display **12** boastfulness

exhibitionist
05 poser **06** poseur **07** show-off
09 extrovert **14** self-advertiser

exhilarate
04 lift **05** cheer, elate **06** excite, perk up, thrill **07** animate, cheer up, delight, elevate, enliven, gladden **08** brighten, vitalize **09** inebriate, make happy, stimulate **10** intoxicate, invigorate, revitalize **11** make excited

exhilarating
05 heady, sapid **06** breezy
08 cheerful, cheering, exciting
09 heartsome, thrilling **10** delightful, enlivening, gladdening **11** mind-blowing, stimulating **12** breathtaking, intoxicating, invigorating, revitalizing
13 heart-stirring

exhilaration
03 joy **04** dash, élan, glee, zeal
05 gusto, mirth **06** ardour, gaiety, thrill
07 delight, elation **08** euphoria, gladness, hilarity, vivacity
09 animation, happiness
10 enthusiasm, exaltation, excitement, joyfulness, joyousness, liveliness
11 high spirits, stimulation
12 cheerfulness, invigoration
14 revitalization

exhort
03 bid **04** goad, spur, urge, warn
05 press **06** advise, call on, enjoin, incite, prompt **07** beseech, caution, counsel, entreat, implore, inflame, inspire **08** admonish, call upon, persuade **09** encourage, instigate

exhortation
04 call **06** advice, appeal, sermon, urging **07** bidding, caution, counsel, goading, lecture, warning **08** entreaty
09 enjoinder, parenesis
10 admonition, allocution, beseeching, incitement, injunction, invitation, paraenesis, persuasion, protreptic **13** encouragement

exhumation
10 excavation, unearthing
12 disinterment **13** disentombment

exhume
05 dig up **06** unbury **07** unearth
08 disinter, excavate **09** disentomb, disinhume, resurrect

exigency
04 need, turn **06** crisis, demand, plight, stress **07** urgency **08** distress, pressure, quandary **09** emergency, necessity **10** difficulty **11** predicament, requirement **12** criticalness
14 imperativeness

exigent
06 urgent **07** crucial **08** critical, exacting, pressing **09** demanding, extremity, insistent, necessary, stringent

exiguous
04 bare, slim **05** scant **06** meagre, scanty, slight, sparse **07** slender
10 inadequate, negligible
12 insufficient

exile
03 ban, bar **04** exul, oust **05** eject, expat, expel, Galut **06** banish, deport, émigré, Galuth, outlaw, pariah, uproot, wretch **07** Babylon, cast out, outcast, refugee **08** deportee, Diaspora, drive out, fugitive, separate **09** expulsion, extradite, ostracism, ostracize, uprooting **10** banishment, expatriate, repatriate, separating, separation
11 deportation **12** expatriation
13 excommunicate **14** transportation
15 displaced person

exist
02 be **04** last, live **05** abide, occur, stand **06** endure, happen, remain
07 be alive, be found, breathe, consist, persist, prevail, subsist, survive
08 continue, have life **09** be present, have being **10** have breath **11** be available **13** eke out a living, have existence

existence
03 ens **04** esse, fact, life **05** being, thing **06** breath, entity, living
07 inbeing, reality **08** creation, creature, survival, the world
09 actuality, endurance, lifestyle, way of life **11** continuance, subsistence, way of living **12** continuation, mode of living **13** individuation
• **loss of independent existence**
03 LIE

existent
04 real **05** alive **06** actual, around, extant, living **07** abiding, current, present **08** enduring, existing, standing **09** obtaining, remaining, surviving **10** prevailing **11** in existence

exit
02 go **03** die **04** door, gate, vent
05 death, going, go out, issue, leave
06 depart, egress, exodus, flight, log off, log out, outlet, retire, way out
07 doorway, leaving, off-ramp, outgate, retreat **08** farewell, withdraw
09 departure **10** going forth, retirement, withdrawal **11** leave-taking
13 take your leave

exodus
02 Ex **04** exit, Exod **06** escape, flight, hegira **07** fleeing, leaving, retreat
09 departure, long march, migration
10 evacuation, retirement, withdrawal
13 mass departure **14** mass evacuation

exonerate
04 free **05** clear, spare **06** acquit, excuse, exempt, let off, pardon
07 absolve, justify, release, relieve
08 liberate **09** discharge, exculpate, vindicate **15** declare innocent

exoneration
06 pardon, relief **07** amnesty, freeing, release **08** clearing, excusing, immunity **09** acquittal, discharge, dismissal, exemption, indemnity
10 absolution, liberation
11 exculpation, vindication
13 justification

exorbitant
05 steep, undue **07** a rip-off
08 enormous **09** excessive, monstrous
10 immoderate, inordinate
11 extravagant, unwarranted
12 extortionate, preposterous, unreasonable **15** daylight robbery

exorbitantly
06 unduly **11** excessively
12 immoderately, inordinately,

unreasonably **13** extravagantly
14 extortionately, through the nose

exorcism
07 freeing **09** expulsion **10** adjuration, casting out **11** deliverance
12 exsufflation, insufflation, purification

exorcize
03 lay **04** free **05** expel **06** adjure, purify **07** cast out **08** drive out
10 exsufflate, insufflate

exotic
◇ *anagram indicator*
05 alien **06** ethnic, way-out
07 bizarre, curious, foreign, strange, unusual **08** external, imported, peculiar, striking, tropical
09 colourful, different, glamorous, non-native, recherché **10** impressive, introduced, outlandish, outrageous, remarkable, unfamiliar **11** extravagant, fascinating, sensational
13 extraordinary

exotically
09 curiously, strangely, unusually
10 remarkably, strikingly, tropically
12 impressively, outlandishly
13 sensationally **15** extraordinarily

expand
03 pad **04** grow **05** swell, widen
06 blow up, dilate, extend, fatten, intend, put out, spread, unfold, unfurl, work up **07** amplify, broaden, develop, distend, enlarge, fill out, inflate, magnify, open out, puff out, stretch, thicken **08** dispread, enlargen, escalate, increase, lengthen, multiply, mushroom **09** branch out, diversify, intensify, intumesce **10** decompress, make bigger, make larger **12** become bigger, become larger

• **expand on**
08 dilate on, flesh out **09** embroider, enlarge on **11** elaborate on, expatiate on **13** go into details

expanse
03 sea **04** area, main, mass, moor, muir, vast **05** field, ocean, plain, range, sheet, space, sweep, tract, vague, waste **06** extent, region, spread **07** breadth, stretch
08 vastness **09** champaign, immensity, outspread **11** immenseness
13 extensiveness

expansion
04 boom **06** growth, spread
07 expanse **08** dilation, increase, swelling **09** diffusion, explosion, extension, inflation, unfolding, unfurling **10** broadening, dilatation, distension, thickening
11 development, enlargement, lengthening **12** augmentation
13 amplification, decompression, magnification **14** multiplication
15 diversification

expansive
04 open, warm, wide **05** broad
06 genial **07** affable, growing
08 effusive, friendly, outgoing, sociable, sweeping, thorough
09 diffusive, enlarging, expanding, extensive, talkative **10** developing, increasing, loquacious, magnifying, widespread **11** expatiative, expatiatory, forthcoming, multiplying, uninhibited, wide-ranging **12** all-embracing, diversifying **13** communicative, comprehensive

expatiate
06 dilate, expand **07** amplify, develop, dwell on, enlarge, expound
08 enlargen **09** elaborate, embellish, give forth **11** hold forth on

expatriate
04 oust **05** exile, expat, expel
06 banish, deport, émigré, exiled, uproot **07** outcast, refugee
08 banished, deported, drive out, emigrant, expelled, uprooted
09 extradite, ostracize, proscribe
10 repatriate **15** displaced person

expect
04 hope, look, wait, want, ween, wish
05 await, guess, think, trust **06** ask for, assume, bank on, demand, lippen, look to, reckon, rely on **07** believe, call for, count on, foresee, hope for, imagine, look for, predict, presume, project, require, suppose, surmise
08 envisage, figure on, forecast, insist on, think for, watch for **09** bargain on, look after **10** anticipate, bargain for, conjecture **11** contemplate **13** look forward to

expectancy
04 hope **07** waiting **08** suspense
09 curiosity, eagerness **10** conjecture
11 expectation **12** anticipation

expectant
05 eager, great, quick, ready **06** gravid
07 anxious, curious, excited, hopeful
08 awaiting, carrying, enceinte, preggers, pregnant, watchful
09 expecting, in the club, in trouble, with child **10** big-bellied, in suspense
11 open-mouthed **12** anticipating, apprehensive **13** on tenterhooks
14 in the family way, looking forward
15 with bated breath

expectantly
07 eagerly **09** hopefully **10** in suspense **11** expectingly
14 apprehensively, in anticipation, optimistically

expectation
04 hope, view, want, wish **05** trust
06 belief, demand **07** outlook, promise, suppose, surmise
08 forecast, optimism, prospect, reliance, suspense, tendance
09 assurance, eagerness
10 assumption, confidence, conjecture, insistence, looking-for, prediction, projection **11** calculation, possibility, presumption, probability, requirement, supposition
12 anticipation

expecting
05 great, quick **06** gravid **08** carrying, enceinte, preggers, pregnant
09 expectant, in the club, in trouble, with child **10** big-bellied **14** in the family way

expedience
05 haste **07** aptness, benefit, fitness, utility **08** despatch, dispatch, prudence **09** advantage, propriety
10 enterprise, expediency, pragmatism, properness, usefulness
11 convenience, helpfulness, suitability
12 advisability, desirability, practicality
13 effectiveness, judiciousness, profitability **14** profitableness, utilitarianism **15** appropriateness

expedient
04 plan, ploy **05** dodge, means, salvo, shift, trick **06** device, method, scheme, tactic, useful **07** fitting, measure, politic, prudent, stopgap
08 artifice, resource, sensible, suitable, tactical **09** advisable, manoeuvre, opportune, practical, pragmatic, stratagem **10** beneficial, convenient, profitable **11** appropriate, contrivance, expeditious **12** advantageous

expedite
05 hurry, press, quick **06** assist, hasten, prompt, step up **07** further, promote, quicken, speed up **08** despatch, dispatch **09** discharge **10** accelerate, facilitate **11** precipitate **12** hurry through, unencumbered

expedition
03 dig **04** crew, hike, raid, sail, team, tour, trek, trip **05** group, haste, party, quest, shoot, speed **06** outing, ramble, safari, voyage **07** company, crusade, hosting, journey, mission, project, warpath **08** alacrity, campaign
09 adventure, excursion, field trip, swiftness **10** enterprise, pilgrimage, promptness **11** exploration, undertaking

expeditious
04 fast **05** alert, brisk, hasty, quick, rapid, ready, swift **06** active, prompt, speedy **07** express, instant **08** diligent, meteoric **09** efficient, expedient, immediate

expel
03 ban, bar, rid **04** hoof, oust, void
05 belch, eject, evict, exile **06** banish, deport, let out, outlaw, put out, reject
07 boot out, cast out, dismiss, drum out, expulse, extrude, fire out, kick out, read out, spew out, turn out **08** chuck out, drive out, evacuate, send down, sideline, throw out **09** discharge, eliminate, proscribe, turn forth
10 expatriate

expend
03 buy, pay, sap, use **04** blow **05** drain, empty, spend, use up, waste **06** afford, employ, lay out, outlay, pay out
07 consume, deplete, dispend, exhaust, fork out, fritter, procure, utilize

08 disburse, purchase, shell out, squander **09** dissipate, go through, overspend, splash out **10** get through

expendable
09 throwaway **10** disposable
11 dispensable, inessential, replaceable, unimportant, unnecessary **12** non-essential

expenditure
03 use **04** mise **05** costs, outgo, waste
06 outlay, output **07** expense, payment, sapping **08** dispense, draining, expenses, outgoing, spending **09** goings-out, outgoings
10 employment **11** application, consumption, dissipation, squandering, utilization
12 disbursement
• **reduction of expenditure**
02 ax **03** axe **06** saving
11 economizing

expense, expenses
03 fee **04** cost, harm, loss, rate
05 costs, price **06** charge, outlay
07 payment **08** spending
09 detriment, outgoings, overheads, paying-out, sacrifice **11** expenditure, incidentals **12** disadvantage, disbursement
• **share of expense**
03 law

expensive
04 dear, posh, salt **05** fancy, pricy, steep **06** costly, lavish, pricey **07** sky-high **08** high-cost, splendid **09** big-ticket, chargeful, excessive, executive
10 exorbitant, high-priced, overpriced
11 costing a lot, extravagant **12** costing a bomb, extortionate **15** costing the earth, daylight robbery

experience
03 see, try **04** case, face, feel, find, have, know, meet, pass, spin **05** event, skill, taste **06** affair, endure, expert, ordeal, suffer **07** contact, episode, knowhow, receive, sustain, undergo
08 exposure, incident, learning, perceive, practice, training
09 adventure, encounter, go through, happening, knowledge **10** occurrence
11 familiarity, involvement, live through, observation, pass through
12 circumstance **13** participate in, participation, understanding
• **cause to experience**
04 lead
• **irritating experience**
03 rub **06** rubber
• **lacking experience**
05 green, naive
• **painful experience**
03 fit

experienced
03 old **04** wise **05** adept, suave, tried
06 around, au fait, expert, mature
07 capable, skilful, skilled, trained, veteran, weighed **08** familiar, schooled, seasoned, traveled **09** au courant, competent, practised, qualified, travailed, travelled
10 proficient, streetwise, well-versed
11 worldly wise **12** accomplished, experimented, professional
13 knowledgeable, sophisticated

experiment
03 exp, try **04** test **05** assay, essay, proof, trial **06** dry run, sample, try out, try-out, verify **07** attempt, examine, explore, inquiry, observe, testing, venture **08** analysis, dummy run, piloting, research, trial run
09 procedure **10** conclusion, experience, pilot study **11** examination, investigate, observation **13** carry out tests, demonstration, investigation, trial and error **15** experimentation

experimental
03 exp **04** test **05** pilot, trial
09 empirical, peirastic, tentative
10 scientific **11** exploratory, preliminary, provisional, speculative
13 investigative, observational, trial-and-error **15** at the trial stage

experimentally
11 empirically, tentatively
12 innovatively, provisonally **13** by rule of thumb, speculatively
14 scientifically **15** by trial and error, investigatively

experimentation
07 zoopery **08** research
10 empiricism, pragmatism
11 exploration, rule of thumb
12 verification **13** inventiveness, investigation

expert
03 ace, dab, don, gun, pro, sly **04** able, buff, nark, oner, up on **05** adept, crack, fundi, maven, mavin, one-er, whizz
06 boffin, master, pundit, wunner
07 dab hand, egghead, hotshot, maestro, old hand, skilful, skilled, wise guy **08** dextrous, masterly, top-notch, virtuoso, well up on **09** authority, brilliant, dexterous, excellent, old master, practised, qualified
10 experience, past master, proficient, specialist **11** cognoscente, connoisseur, experienced
12 accomplished, practitioner, professional **13** knowledgeable

expertise
05 knack, skill **07** ability, command, finesse, knowhow, mastery
08 deftness, facility **09** dexterity, knowledge **10** cleverness, expertness, tradecraft, virtuosity **11** proficiency, savoir-faire, skilfulness
13 understanding **15** professionalism

expertly
04 ably **07** capably **08** masterly
09 skilfully **11** competently, efficiently, excellently **12** proficiently
14 professionally

expiate
05 atone, purge **06** attone, pay for
07 redress, work out **08** atone for
09 make up for **12** do penance for
13 make amends for

expiation
06 amends, ransom, shrift
07 penance, redress **09** atonement
10 recompense, redemption, reparation

expire
03 die, end **04** emit, stop **05** cease, close, lapse **06** depart, finish, pass on, peg out, perish, pop off, run out
07 decease, snuff it **08** conclude, pass away, pass over **09** have had it, terminate **11** bite the dust, come to an end, discontinue **12** lose your life, pop your clogs **13** kick the bucket, meet your maker **14** depart this life, give up the ghost **15** be no longer valid, breathe your last, cash in your chips

expiry
03 end, exp, ish **05** close, lapse
06 finish **09** cessation **10** conclusion, expiration **11** termination
15 discontinuation

explain
04 tell **05** gloze, solve, teach
06 decode, defend, define, excuse, open up, set out, unfold **07** clarify, expound, justify, resolve, unravel
08 decipher, describe, disclose, simplify, spell out, untangle
09 delineate, elaborate, elucidate, enucleate, explicate, interpret, lie behind, make clear, translate, vindicate
10 account for, illustrate
11 demonstrate, explain away, rationalize, shed light on **12** throw light on **14** give a reason for

explanation
04 note **05** alibi, gloss **06** answer, excuse, motive, reason, report
07 account, comment, defence, meaning, warrant **08** apologia, decoding, exegesis, footnote, solution
09 unfolding **10** annotation, commentary, definition, exposition, expounding **11** deciphering, delineation, description, elucidation, explication, vindication **12** illustration
13 clarification, demonstration, justification **14** interpretation, reconciliation, simplification
15 éclaircissement, rationalization

explanatory
08 exegetic **10** exegetical, expositive, expository, justifying **11** declaratory, descriptive, elucidative, elucidatory, explicative **12** illustrative, interpretive
13 demonstrative **14** interpretative

expletive
04 cuss, oath **05** curse **08** anathema, cussword **09** blasphemy, obscenity, profanity, swear-word **10** execration
11 bad language, imprecation **14** four-letter word

explicable
08 solvable **09** definable, exponible
10 resolvable **11** accountable, explainable, justifiable
12 determinable, intelligible
13 interpretable **14** understandable

explicate
06 define, unfold **07** clarify, develop, explain, expound, unravel, work out **08** describe, set forth, spell out, untangle **09** elucidate, interpret, make clear **10** illustrate **11** demonstrate

explication
10 exposition **11** description, elucidation, explanation **12** illustration **13** clarification **14** interpretation

explicit
04 open **05** adult, bawdy, clear, dirty, exact, frank, plain **06** candid, direct, filthy, full-on, smutty, stated, X-rated **07** certain, express, obscene, pointed, precise **08** absolute, declared, definite, detailed, distinct, hard-core, positive, shocking, specific **09** offensive, outspoken **10** forthright, uncensored, unreserved **11** categorical, near the bone, plain-spoken, unambiguous, unequivocal, uninhibited **12** pornographic, unrestrained **14** near the knuckle **15** straightforward

explicitly
06 barely **07** clearly, in terms, overtly, plainly **08** directly **09** expressly **10** definitely **12** specifically **13** in so many words, unambiguously, unequivocally

explode
◇ *anagram indicator*
04 blow, boom, go up, leap **05** blast, burst, erupt, go off, rebut, surge **06** blow up, debunk, go bang, refute, rocket, see red, set off, spring **07** flare up **08** boil over, burst out, detonate, displode, disprove, escalate, mushroom **09** blow a fuse, discharge, discredit, do your nut, fulminate, repudiate **10** accelerate, hit the roof, invalidate **11** blow your top, go up the wall, grow rapidly, lose your rag **12** blow your cool, fly into a rage, give the lie to, lose your cool **13** hit the ceiling **14** lose your temper **15** fly off the handle, go off the deep end

• **cause to explode**
04 fire **06** spring **08** detonate **09** fulminate

exploit
03 act, tap, use **04** deed, feat, gest, milk, mine **05** abuse, apply, bleed, geste, stunt **06** action, draw on, employ, fleece, misuse, rip off **07** oppress, utilize **08** activity, cash in on, ill-treat, impose on, profit by **09** adventure, make use of, profiteer **10** attainment, manipulate **11** achievement, walk all over **12** capitalize on, put to good use, take for a ride **13** take liberties, turn to account **14** accomplishment, play off against, pull a fast one on **15** take advantage of

exploitation
03 use **05** abuse **06** misuse, rip-off **07** milking **08** bleeding, fleecing **10** employment, oppression **11** application, cashing in on, making use of, utilization **12** manipulation **14** taking for a ride **15** taking advantage

exploration
04 tour, trip **05** probe, study **06** safari, search, survey, travel, voyage **07** inquiry **08** analysis, research, scrutiny **10** expedition, inspection **11** examination, observation **13** investigation **14** reconnaissance

exploratory
05 pilot, trial **07** probing, wildcat **08** analytic **09** searching, tentative **11** fact-finding **12** experimental **13** investigative

explore
02 do **04** feel, palp, tour **05** probe, scout, study **06** review, search, survey, travel **07** analyse, examine, inspect **08** consider, look into, prospect, research, traverse **10** scrutinize **11** inquire into, investigate, reconnoitre, see the world

explorer
05 scout **06** tourer **08** surveyor **09** navigator, traveller **10** discoverer, prospector **11** bandeirante **12** reconnoitrer

Explorers and pioneers include:

03 **Cam**, **Caõ**, **Rae** (John)
04 **Byrd** (Richard Evelyn), **Cano** (Juan Sebastian del), **Cook** (James), **Diaz** (Bartolomeu), **Eyre** (Edward John), **Gama** (Vasco da), **Park** (Mungo), **Polo** (Marco), **Ross** (Sir James Clark), **Soto** (Fernando de), **Soto** (Hernando de)
05 **Barth** (Heinrich), **Beebe** (Charles William), **Boone** (Daniel), **Bruce** (James), **Cabot** (John), **Clark** (William), **Drake** (Francis), **Fuchs** (Sir Vivian Ernest), **Hanno**, **Lewis** (Meriwether), **Newby** (Eric), **Oates** (Lawrence), **Peary** (Robert Edwin), **Scott** (Robert Falcon), **Speke** (John Hanning)
06 **Baffin** (William), **Balboa** (Vasco Núñez de), **Bering** (Vitus), **Burton** (Sir Richard), **Cabral** (Pedro Alvares), **Carson** (Kit), **Nansen** (Fridtjof), **Tasman** (Abel Janszoon), **Torres** (Luis de)
07 **Andrews** (Roy Chapman), **Fiennes** (Sir Ranulph), **Fleming** (Peter), **Hillary** (Sir Edmund), **La Salle** (Robert Cavelier, Sieur de), **Pytheas**, **Raleigh** (Sir Walter), **Stanley** (Sir Henry Morton)
08 **Amundsen** (Roald), **Columbus** (Christopher), **Cousteau** (Jacques), **Flinders** (Matthew), **Franklin** (Sir John), **Linnaeus** (Carolus), **Magellan** (Ferdinand), **Standish** (Myles), **Thesiger** (Sir Wilfred), **Vespucci** (Amerigo), **Williams** (Roger)
09 **Emin Pasha**, **Frobisher** (Sir Martin), **Heyerdahl** (Thor), **Rasmussen** (Knud), **Vancouver** (George)
10 **Erik the Red**, **Oglethorpe** (James Edward), **Shackleton** (Sir Ernest Henry), **Van der Post** (Sir Laurens)
11 **Livingstone** (David)
12 **Leif Eriksson**, **Younghusband** (Sir Francis)
14 **Bellingshausen** (Fabian Gottlieb von), **Blashford-Snell** (Colonel John), **Hanbury-Tenison** (Robin Airling)

explosion
03 fit, pop **04** bang, boom, chug, clap, leap, rage, roll **05** blast, burst, crack, pluff, surge **06** blow-up, report, rumble **07** Big Bang, flare-up, tantrum, thunder **08** airburst, eruption, outbreak, outburst, paroxysm **09** discharge **10** detonation, displosion **14** dramatic growth, sudden increase

explosive
◇ *anagram indicator*
02 HE **04** bomb, mine, wild **05** angry, fiery, jelly, rapid, tense **06** abrupt, raging, stormy, sudden, touchy **07** charged, fraught, violent **08** critical, dramatic, meteoric, perilous, powerful, unstable, volatile, volcanic, worked-up **09** dangerous, fulminant, hazardous, initiator, plastique, rocketing, sensitive **10** burgeoning, propellant, unexpected **11** exponential, mushrooming, overwrought **12** nerve-racking, unrestrained

Explosives include:

03 RDX, TNT
04 ANFO
06 amatol, dualin, Semtex®, tonite
07 ammonal, cordite, dunnite, lyddite, plastic
08 cheddite, dynamite, melinite, roburite, xyloidin
09 cyclonite, gelignite, guncotton, gunpowder, xyloidine
11 nitrocotton
14 nitrocellulose, nitroglycerine, trinitrotoluol
15 trinitrotoluene

explosively
06 wildly **07** angrily, fierily, rapidly, tensely **08** suddenly, unstably **09** violently **10** critically, powerfully **11** dangerously, hazardously **12** dramatically, unexpectedly, volcanically **13** destructively, exponentially

exponent
05 adept, index, power **06** backer, expert, master, player **08** adherent, advocate, champion, defender, promoter, upholder **09** performer, proponent, spokesman, supporter **10** specialist **11** spokeswoman **12** practitioner, spokesperson

export
02 ex **03** exp **05** trade **08** deal with, Klondike, Klondyke, re-export, transfer **09** traffic in, transport **10** sell abroad

12 foreign trade, sell overseas
13 exported goods 15 exported product

expose
03 ope 04 open, risk, show 05 flash, strip 06 betray, detect, hazard, reveal, show up, unmask, unveil 07 display, divulge, exhibit, imperil, lay bare, lay open, present, uncover, unearth
08 denounce, disclose, endanger, manifest 09 lay open to, make known, put at risk, subject to 10 jeopardize
11 introduce to, present with
12 acquaint with, bring to light 13 put in jeopardy, take the lid off 14 blow the whistle, make vulnerable 15 familiarize with

exposé
07 account, article 08 exposure
10 disclosure, divulgence, revelation, uncovering

exposed
03 out 04 bare, open 05 naked, shown 06 object, on show, on view
07 subject 08 laid bare, revealed
09 exhibited, in the open, on display
10 vulnerable 11 susceptible, unprotected

exposition
04 expo, fair, show 05 moral, paper, study 06 aperçu, exposé, theory, thesis 07 account, display, exposal, Midrash, working 08 analysis, critique, exegesis 09 discourse, monograph, unfolding 10 commentary, enarration, exhibition 11 description, elucidation, explanation, explication
12 illumination, illustration, presentation 13 clarification, demonstration 14 interpretation

expository
08 exegetic 11 declaratory, descriptive, elucidative, explanatory, explicatory, hermeneutic
12 illustrative, interpretive
14 interpretative

expostulate
05 argue, claim, plead 06 reason
07 protest 08 disagree, dissuade
11 remonstrate

exposure
03 air 04 hype, plug, risk 05 flash
06 airing, danger, exposé, hazard
07 contact, display, exposal, showing
08 jeopardy 09 awareness, detection, discovery, exposture, knowledge, notoriety, promotion, publicity, unmasking, unveiling 10 disclosure, divulgence, exhibition, experience, revelation, uncovering 11 advertising, familiarity 12 acquaintance, denunciation, presentation
13 manifestation, vulnerability
14 susceptibility 15 public attention

expound
04 open, read, rede 06 open up, preach, set out, unbolt, unfold
07 analyse, clarify, dissect, explain, unravel 08 describe, prophesy, set forth, spell out, untangle 09 comment on, elucidate, explicate, interpret, sermonize 10 illuminate, illustrate
11 demonstrate

express
02 ex 03 air, exp, put, say 04 emit, fast, have, show, sole, tell, vent, word
05 brisk, clear, couch, exact, plain, quick, rapid, speak, state, swift, utter, voice 06 assert, convey, denote, depict, embody, intend, report, reveal, speedy, stated, strain 07 certain, declare, divulge, exhibit, get over, non-stop, precise, put over, signify, special, testify 08 announce, clear-cut, conceive, definite, disclose, distinct, explicit, indicate, intimate, manifest, point out, positive, register, specific, stand for 09 designate, enunciate, estafette, formulate, high-speed, pronounce, put across, represent, specially, symbolize, ventilate, verbalize 10 articulate, particular
11 categorical, communicate, demonstrate, expeditious, give voice to, unambiguous, unequivocal, well-defined 12 put into words

expression
◇ *homophone indicator*
03 air 04 look, mien, show, sign, term, tone, word 05 adage, axiom, depth, force, idiom, maxim, power, scowl, style, voice 06 aspect, phrase, saying, speech, symbol, vigour 07 diction, emotion, feeling, gesture, grimace, passion, proverb, voicing, wording
08 aphorism, artistry, delivery, language, locution, phrasing
09 assertion, intensity, set phrase, statement, utterance, verbalism, vividness 10 appearance, creativity, embodiment, exhibition, indication, intimation, intonation, modulation
11 countenance, declaration, enunciation, imagination
12 announcement, articulation, illustration, proclamation, turn of phrase, vocalization
13 communication, demonstration, manifestation, pronouncement, verbalization 14 representation
• **prevent free expression**
03 gag

expressionless
04 dull 05 blank, empty 06 glassy, glazed 07 deadpan, vacuous
08 toneless 09 impassive, unmeaning
10 poker-faced 11 emotionless, inscrutable, meaningless 13 straight-faced

expressive
05 vivid 06 lively, moving 07 showing, telling 08 animated, eloquent, emphatic, forceful, poignant, striking
09 evocative, revealing, speechful
10 articulate, indicative, meaningful, suggesting, suggestive, thoughtful
11 informative, significant, sympathetic
13 communicative, demonstrating, demonstrative

expressively
07 vividly 09 meaningly
10 eloquently, espressivo
11 evocatively 12 emphatically, meaningfully, suggestively
13 informatively 15 demonstratively

expressiveness
09 poignancy, vividness 10 articulacy
13 evocativeness 14 articulateness, meaningfulness

expressly
◇ *homophone indicator*
06 solely 07 clearly, exactly, plainly
09 decidedly, on purpose, pointedly, precisely, purposely, specially
10 absolutely, definitely, distinctly, especially, explicitly, manifestly
12 particularly, specifically
13 categorically, intentionally, unambiguously, unequivocally

expropriate
04 take 05 annex, seize, usurp
06 assume 07 impound, unhouse
08 arrogate, disseise, take away
09 sequester 10 commandeer, confiscate, dispossess 11 appropriate, requisition

expropriation
07 seizure 10 arrogation, impounding, taking-away 12 confiscation
13 appropriation, dispossession, sequestration

expulsion
05 exile, purge 07 removal, sacking, the boot, the sack, voiding
08 belching, ejection, eviction
09 discharge, dismissal, ejectment, exclusion, excretion, extrusion, ostracism, rejection 10 banishment, evacuation 11 throwing out

expunge
04 raze 05 annul, erase 06 cancel, delete, efface, remove, rub out
07 abolish, blot out, destroy, wipe out
08 cross out, get rid of 09 eradicate, extirpate 10 annihilate, extinguish, obliterate 11 exterminate

expurgate
03 cut 04 geld 05 emend, purge
06 censor, purify 07 clean up
08 sanitize 10 blue-pencil, bowdlerize

exquisite
04 fine, keen, pink, rare 05 acute, sharp 06 choice, dainty, lovely, picked, pretty, too-too 07 elegant, fragile, intense, perfect, refined 08 abstruse, charming, cultured, delicate, flawless, piercing, pleasing, poignant, precious
09 beautiful, delicious, excellent, sensitive 10 attractive, cultivated, delightful, discerning, far-fetched, fastidious, impeccable, meticulous
11 outstanding 14 discriminating

exquisitely
06 finely 08 daintily 09 elegantly
10 charmingly, delicately, pleasingly
11 beautifully 12 attractively, delightfully

ex-serviceman
03 vet **07** veteran

extant
05 alive **06** living **08** existent, existing **09** remaining, surviving **10** subsistent, subsisting **11** in existence **13** still existing

extempore
05 ad-lib **07** offhand **08** suddenly **09** ad libitum, impromptu, unplanned **10** improvised, off the cuff, unprepared, unscripted **11** spontaneous, unrehearsed **13** spontaneously **14** extemporaneous

extemporize
04 pong **05** ad-lib **06** make up, wing it **09** improvise **11** play it by ear **15** speak off the cuff, think on your feet

extend
02 go **03** lap, run **04** draw, give, grow, last, pass, span **05** cover, grant, offer, range, reach, renew, seize, value, widen **06** assess, bestow, come to, confer, deploy, expand, go up to, impart, intend, put out, spread, step up, take in, unfold, unwind **07** amplify, augment, broaden, carry on, develop, drag out, draw out, embrace, enlarge, hold out, include, involve, present, produce, proffer, prolong, spin out, stretch **08** come up to, continue, elongate, go down to, increase, lengthen, protract, put forth, reach out **09** go as far as, intensify **10** come down to, comprehend

extendable
07 elastic **08** stretchy **09** dilatable, extensive **10** expandable **11** enlargeable, magnifiable, stretchable

extended
04 long, wide **06** spread **07** distent, lengthy **08** at length, enlarged, expanded **09** amplified, continued, developed, expansive, increased, prolonged **10** diastaltic, lengthened

extension
03 ext **04** wing **05** add-on, delay **06** annexe **07** adjunct, stretch **08** addendum, addition, appendix, deferral, increase, more time, protense, quantity, widening **09** diffusion, expansion **10** broadening, elongation, production, stretching, supplement **11** development, enhancement, enlargement, lengthening, protraction **12** continuation, postponement, prolongation **13** proliferation **14** additional time

extensive
04 huge, long, main, vast, wide **05** broad, large, roomy **07** general, in depth, lengthy **08** complete, extended, far-flung, sizeable, spacious, thorough **09** boundless, capacious, fair-sized, pervasive, prevalent, universal, unlimited, wholesale **10** commodious, large-scale, voluminous, widespread **11** far-reaching, substantial, wide-ranging **12** all-inclusive **13** comprehensive

extensively
06 widely **07** greatly, largely **09** generally, wholesale **10** completely, thoroughly **11** boundlessly **13** substantially **15** comprehensively

extent
04 area, bulk, play, size, span, term, time **05** level, limit, range, reach, scope, sweep, width **06** amount, attack, bounds, degree, length, sphere, spread, volume **07** breadth, compass, expanse, lengths, measure, seizure, stretch **08** coverage, duration, quantity **09** dimension, magnitude **10** dimensions

- **to full extent**

04 hard, much

- **to some extent**

◇ *hidden indicator*

- **to that extent**

02 as

- **to the extent of**

02 by **03** for

extenuate
06 excuse, lessen, modify, soften **07** qualify **08** diminish, minimize, mitigate, palliate

extenuating
08 excusing **09** lessening, modifying, softening **10** justifying, minimizing, mitigating, moderating, palliating, palliative, qualifying **11** diminishing, exculpatory, extenuative, extenuatory

exterior
03 ext **04** face, skin **05** glaze, outer, shell **06** façade, finish **07** coating, foreign, outside, outward, surface **08** covering, external **09** externals, extrinsic, objective, outermost **10** appearance, peripheral **11** superficial, surrounding **12** outer surface **15** external surface

exterminate
04 do in, kill **06** kill up **07** abolish, bump off, destroy, kill off, wipe out **08** knock off, massacre **09** eliminate, eradicate, extirpate, liquidate, slaughter **10** annihilate, do away with

extermination
07 killing **08** genocide, massacre **09** ethnocide **11** destruction, elimination, eradication, extirpation **12** annihilation

external
03 ext, out **05** outer **07** foreign, outside, outward, surface, visible **08** apparent, cortical, exterior, visiting **09** extrinsic, outermost **10** accidental, extramural, extraneous, peripheral **11** independent, non-resident, superficial

externally
03 ext **07** visibly **09** outwardly **10** apparently **12** extraneously, peripherally **13** superficially

extinct
03 ext, old, out **04** dead, gone, lost **05** ended, passé **06** bygone, former **07** defunct, died out, expired, invalid **08** burnt out, inactive, obsolete, outmoded, quenched, squashed, vanished, wiped out **09** abolished **10** antiquated, terminated **11** non-existent **12** exterminated, extinguished

extinction
05 death **07** quietus **08** dying-out, excision **09** abolition, vanishing **11** destruction, eradication, termination **12** annihilation, obliteration **13** disappearance, extermination

extinguish
03 end **04** dout, kill **05** choke, douse, dowse, drown, erase, quash, quell, slake **06** die out, put out, quench, remove, rub out, sloken, stifle **07** abolish, blow out, destroy, expunge, slocken, smother, stub out **08** snuff out, suppress **09** eliminate, eradicate, extirpate **10** annihilate, dampen down **11** exterminate

extirpate
04 root **05** erase **06** cut out, remove, uproot **07** abolish, destroy, expunge, root out, weed out, wipe out **08** stamp out **09** eliminate, eradicate **10** annihilate, deracinate, extinguish **11** exterminate

extol
04 laud, puff **05** exalt, raise **06** lift up, praise **07** acclaim, advance, applaud, commend, glorify, magnify **08** eulogize **09** celebrate **10** rhapsodize, wax lyrical

extort
04 milk, rack **05** bleed, bully, exact, force, screw, wrest, wring **06** coerce **07** extract, squeeze **08** get out of, outwrest **09** blackmail, shake down

extortion
05 chout, force **06** demand **07** milking **08** chantage, coercion, exaction **09** blackmail **10** oppression **12** malversation, racketeering

extortionate
04 hard **05** harsh **06** severe **08** exacting, grasping, grinding **09** excessive, rapacious **10** exorbitant, immoderate, inordinate, oppressive, outrageous **12** preposterous, unreasonable

extortionist
05 screw, shark **06** yakuza **07** bleeder, exacter, exactor, menacer **09** exactress, exploiter, profiteer, racketeer **11** blackmailer, bloodsucker, extortioner

extra
01 w **02** ex, lb, nb **03** bye, ext, new, odd, too **04** also, gash, more, over, wide **05** added, bonus, fresh, other, spare, super- **06** as well, excess, leg bye, no ball, unused, walk-on

07 adjunct, and so on, another, besides, further, reserve, surplus **08** addendum, addition, additive, buckshee, left-over, let alone, unneeded **09** accessory, along with, ancillary, appendage, auxiliary, bit player, excessive, extension, extremely, minor role, redundant, unusually **10** additional, attachment, complement, especially, in addition, remarkably, subsidiary, supplement, uncommonly, walk-on part **11** superfluous, unnecessary **12** additionally, not to mention, particularly, spear-carrier, together with **13** exceptionally, extraordinary, not forgetting, supernumerary, supplementary **14** above and beyond, into the bargain **15** extraordinarily

extract
◇ *anagram indicator*
◇ *hidden indicator*
03 ext, get, gut, try **04** cite, clip, copy, cull, draw, grog, milk, pick, pull, suck, worm **05** educe, exact, glean, juice, pluck, prise, quote, wrest, wring **06** choose, cut out, decoct, derive, distil, elicit, extort, gather, get out, gobbet, obtain, quarry, remove, render, select, uproot, wrench **07** cutting, derived, draw out, essence, estreat, excerpt, extrait, logwood, passage, pull out, recover, spirits, take out **08** abstract, boil down, citation, clipping, euonymin, pericope, withdraw **09** decoction, enucleate, quotation, reproduce, selection **10** deracinate, distillate **11** concentrate **12** distillation

extraction
04 race **05** birth, blood, brood, stock **06** family, origin **07** descent, drawing, extreat, lineage, pulling, removal **08** ancestry, pedigree **09** obtaining, parentage, retrieval, taking-out, uprooting **10** derivation, drawing-out, separation, withdrawal

extradite
05 exile, expel **06** banish, deport **08** hand over, send back, send home **10** repatriate

extradition
05 exile **08** handover **09** expulsion **10** banishment **11** deportation, sending back **12** repatriation

extraneous
05 alien, extra, inapt **07** foreign, strange **08** exterior, external, needless, unneeded **09** extrinsic, redundant, unrelated **10** additional, immaterial, inapposite, incidental, irrelevant, peripheral, tangential **11** inessential, superfluous, unconnected, unessential, unnecessary **12** inapplicable, non-essential **13** inappropriate, supplementary

extraordinarily
◇ *anagram indicator*
05 oddly **07** notably **08** uniquely **09** amazingly, bizarrely, curiously, specially, strangely, unusually **10** remarkably, uncommonly **12** astoundingly, particularly, unexpectedly **13** exceptionally, significantly

extraordinary
◇ *anagram indicator*
03 odd **04** rare **06** unique **07** amazing, bizarre, curious, notable, special, strange, unusual **08** peculiar, singular, uncommon **09** by-ordinar, emergency, fantastic, wonderful **10** astounding, marvellous, noteworthy, particular, portentous, remarkable, surprising, tremendous, unexpected **11** astonishing, exceptional, outstanding, significant **13** unprecedented **14** out of this world, unconventional

extrapolate
04 plan **05** gauge **06** expect, reckon, sample **07** project **08** estimate **09** calculate **11** approximate

extraterrestrial
02 ET **05** alien

extravagance
05 extra, folly, treat, waste **06** excess, luxury, vanity **07** riotise, splurge **08** wildness **09** profusion **10** digression, enthusiasm, imprudence, lavishness, ornateness, profligacy **11** dissipation, ostentation, prodigality, squandering **12** exaggeration, immoderation, improvidence, overspending, recklessness, wastefulness **13** excessiveness **14** outrageousness, thriftlessness **15** pretentiousness

extravagant
◇ *anagram indicator*
03 OTT **04** dear, wild **05** outré, steep **06** costly, flashy, lavish, ornate, pricey, rococo **07** baroque, bizarre, profuse, sky-high **08** fanciful, prodigal, reckless, romantic, wasteful **09** excessive, expensive, fanatical, fantastic, high-flown, imprudent, irregular, wasterful **10** exorbitant, extra modum, flamboyant, high-flying, immoderate, outrageous, overpriced, over the top, profligate, thriftless **11** exaggerated, improvident, pretentious, spendthrift, squandering **12** costing a bomb, extortionate, ostentatious, preposterous, unrestrained **15** churrigueresque, costing the earth, daylight robbery

extravaganza
04 show **06** féerie **07** display, pageant **09** spectacle **11** spectacular

extreme
◇ *head selection indicator*
◇ *tail selection indicator*
◇ *ends selection indicator*
03 end, top **04** acme, apex, dire, edge, last, line, mark, peak, pink, pole, wack **05** acute, depth, final, great, gross, harsh, limit, rigid, stern, ultra, utter **06** climax, excess, far-off, height, red-hot, severe, strict, utmost, zenith **07** distant, drastic, endmost, faraway, highest, intense, maximum, outside, radical, serious, supreme, zealous **08** farthest, greatest, hardline, outlying, pinnacle, remotest, terminal, ultimate **09** desperate, downright, Draconian, excessive, extremist, extremity, fanatical, out-and-out, outermost, stringent, uttermost **10** immoderate, inordinate, iron-fisted, iron-handed, most remote, pre-eminent, remarkable, unyielding **11** exceptional, termination, unrelenting **12** unreasonable **13** extraordinary **14** uncompromising

• **in the extreme**
04 very **06** highly **07** awfully, greatly, utterly **08** terribly **09** intensely **10** dreadfully, remarkably, uncommonly **11** exceedingly, excessively, frightfully **12** immoderately, inordinately, terrifically **13** exceptionally **15** extraordinarily

• **opposite extreme**
04 pole

extremely
◇ *ends selection indicator*
03 too **04** high, mega, very **05** jolly **06** deuced, highly, mighty, mortal, pretty, really **07** acutely, awfully, greatly, majorly, only too, parlous, utterly **08** deucedly, severely, terribly **09** decidedly, intensely, seriously, unusually **10** dreadfully, remarkably, thoroughly, uncommonly **11** exceedingly, excessively, frightfully **12** immoderately, inordinately, terrifically, tremendously, unreasonably **13** exceptionally **15** extraordinarily

extremism
04 zeal **08** zealotry **09** terrorism **10** fanaticism, radicalism **13** excessiveness

extremist
05 ultra **06** zealot **07** diehard, fanatic, Jacobin, radical **08** militant **09** hardliner, terrorist **11** merveilleux **12** merveilleuse **14** fundamentalist

extremity
03 arm, end, fix, jam, leg, tip, toe, top **04** acme, apex, edge, foot, hand, hole, limb, mess, peak, pole, spot, tail **05** bound, brink, depth, limit, point, verge **06** apogee, border, crisis, danger, ending, excess, finger, height, margin, pickle, plight, zenith **07** exigent, extreme, maximum, minimum, trouble **08** boundary, exigency, frontier, hardship, outrance, pinnacle, terminal, terminus, ultimate **09** adversity, emergency, indigence, periphery, tight spot, utterance **10** misfortune **11** dire straits, termination

extricate
04 free **05** clear **06** detach, get out, remove, rescue **07** deliver, extract,

outwind, release, relieve, set free
08 let loose, liberate, withdraw
09 disengage **11** disentangle

extrinsic
05 alien **06** exotic **07** foreign, outside
08 exterior, external, imported
10 extraneous, forinsecal

extrovert
03 lad **05** mixer **06** joiner **07** mingler
08 outgoing **10** socializer **14** outgoing person, sociable person

extroverted
06 hearty **07** amiable **08** amicable, friendly, outgoing, sociable
09 exuberant **13** demonstrative
14 outward-looking

extrude
05 expel, mould **08** force out, press out, protrude, put forth **09** thrust out
10 squeeze out

exuberance
04 life, zest **05** pride **06** energy, vigour
07 elation, pizzazz **08** buoyancy, lushness, outburst, rankness, richness, vitality, vivacity **09** abundance, animation, eagerness, plenitude, profusion **10** ebullience, enthusiasm, excitement, lavishness, liveliness, luxuriance, luxuriancy, redundancy
11 copiousness, fulsomeness, high spirits, joie de vivre, prodigality
12 cheerfulness, effusiveness, exaggeration, exhilaration
13 effervescence, excessiveness
14 superabundance

exuberant
03 mad **04** lush, rank, rich **06** elated, lavish, lively, skippy **07** buoyant, excited, fulsome, profuse, zestful
08 abundant, animated, cheerful, effusive, spirited, thriving, vigorous
09 ebullient, energetic, luxuriant, luxurious, plenteous, plentiful, sparkling, vivacious **10** boisterous, full of life **11** exaggerated, exhilarated, overflowing **12** effervescent, enthusiastic, high-spirited, rambunctious, unrestrained
13 irrepressible **15** on top of the world

exude
03 gum **04** emit, leak, ooze, seep, show, weep, well **05** bleed, issue, still, sweat, swelt **07** display, emanate, excrete, exhibit, flow out, give off, give out, guttate, radiate, secrete, swelter, trickle **08** manifest, perspire
09 discharge

exult
03 joy **04** crow **05** gloat, glory, revel
06 relish **07** delight, rejoice, triumph
08 be joyful, jubilate **09** celebrate
10 tripudiate **11** be delighted **13** be over the moon

exultant
06 elated, joyful, joyous **07** gleeful
08 exulting, jubilant, thrilled **09** cock-a-hoop, delighted, overjoyed, rejoicing, revelling **10** enraptured, triumphant **11** on cloud nine, over the moon **12** transporting **15** in seventh heaven

exultation
03 joy **04** glee, pean **05** glory, paean
06 eulogy **07** crowing, delight, elation, triumph **08** gloating, glorying
09 jubilance, jubilancy, merriness, rejoicing, revelling, transport
10 joyfulness, joyousness, jubilation
11 celebration

eye
02 ee **03** aim, orb, see **04** glim, glom, lamp, mind, ogle, peep, scan, view
05 brood, light, optic, sight, study, taste, watch **06** appear, assess, belief, gaze at, keeker, look at, notice, ocular, peeper, peruse, regard, survey, vision, winker **07** blinker, examine, goggler, inspect, lookout, observe, ocellus, opinion, pigsney, stare at **08** eyesight, glance at, ommateum **09** attention, awareness, judgement, viewpoint, vigilance, water pump **10** estimation, perception, scrutinize **11** contemplate, discernment, observation, point of view, recognition, sensitivity
12 appreciation, surveillance, watchfulness **13** look up and down, power of seeing, way of thinking
14 discrimination, faculty of sight

Eye parts include:

03 rod
04 cone, irid, iris, lens, uvea
05 fovea, pupil, white
06 areola, cornea, eyelid, retina, sclera
07 choroid, eyeball, eyelash, papilla, vitreum
08 chorioid, tear duct
09 blind spot, optic disc
10 optic nerve
11 ciliary body, conjunctiva, lower eyelid, upper eyelid
12 chorioid coat, lacrimal duct, ocular muscle
13 aqueous humour, lachrymal duct, sclerotic coat
14 lachrymal gland, vitreous humour
15 anterior chamber, crystalline lens, hyaloid membrane

• black eye
05 mouse **06** keeker, shiner

• keep an eye on
04 mind **07** monitor **08** attend to
09 look after **10** keep tabs on, take care of **12** watch closely

• reflection in eye
04 baby

• see eye to eye
05 agree **06** concur, go with **07** be at one **11** be of one mind, go along with

• set eyes on
03 see **04** meet **06** behold, notice
07 observe **08** come upon
09 encounter, lay eyes on **10** clap eyes on, come across

• up to your eyes
04 busy **06** tied up **08** involved, occupied **09** engrossed, inundated
11 overwhelmed, snowed under
13 overstretched **14** fully stretched

eyebrow
04 bree

eye-catching
05 showy **08** gorgeous, imposing, striking, stunning **09** arresting, beautiful, prominent **10** attractive, impressive, noticeable **11** captivating, conspicuous, spectacular

eye-opener
06 wonder **10** disclosure, revelation
14 quite something, surprising fact
15 surprising thing

eyes
03 een **04** eine, eyne

eyeshadow
04 kohl

eyesight
04 view **05** sight **06** vision
10 perception **11** observation
13 power of seeing **14** faculty of sight

eyesore
03 sty **04** blot, mess, scar, stye
06 blight, horror **07** blemish
08 atrocity, disgrace, ugliness
09 carbuncle **10** defacement
11 monstrosity **13** disfigurement

eyewitness
06 viewer **07** watcher, witness
08 looker-on, observer, onlooker, passer-by **09** bystander, spectator

F

02 ef **07** foxtrot

fable

03 lie **04** epic, myth, saga, tale, yarn
05 feign, story **06** invent, legend
07 fiction, Märchen, parable, untruth
08 allegory, apologue **09** falsehood, invention, moral tale, tall story
11 fabrication **12** old wives' tale

Fable writers include:

03 **Ade** (George), **Fay** (András), **Gay** (John)
04 **Esop**, **Ruiz** (Juan)
05 **Aesop**, **Boner** (Ulrich), **Torga** (Miguel)
06 **Bidpai**, **Dryden** (John), **Halévy** (Lon), **Krylov** (Ivan), **Ramsay** (Allan), **Tessin** (Carl-Gustaf)
07 **Arreola** (Juan José), **Babrius**, **Fénelon** (François de Salignac de la Mothe), **Gellert** (Christian Fürchtegott), **Iriarte** (Tomás de), **Kipling** (Rudyard), **Sologub** (Fyodor)
08 **Andersen** (Hans Christian), **de France** (Marie), **Phaedrus**, **Saltykov** (Michail)
09 **Furetière** (Antoine)
10 **La Fontaine** (Jean de)
15 **Iriarte y Oropesa** (Tomás de)

fabled

05 famed **06** famous **07** feigned
08 mythical, renowned **09** legendary
10 celebrated, remarkable

fabric

03 web **05** cloth, frame, stuff
06 make-up **07** textile, texture
08 material **09** construct, framework, structure **10** contexture
11 foundations **12** constitution, construction, organization
14 infrastructure

Fabrics include:

03 aba, abb, kid, net, rep, rug, say, tat
04 abba, aida, baft, buff, ciré, cord, drab, duck, ecru, felt, harn, ikat, jean, kelt, lace, lamé, lawn, leno, line, lyne, mull, nude, pall, piña, puke, repp, reps, roan, silk, wool
05 abaya, baize, batik, beige, braid, camel, chino, crape, crash, crêpe, denim, dhoti, doily, doyly, drill, duroy, foulé, gauze, gazar, gunny, jaspé, kente, khaki, linen, lisle, llama, loden, Lurex®, Lycra®, moire, ninon, nylon, Orlon®, panne, piqué, plaid, plush, rayon, satin, scrim, serge, suede, surah, tabby, tamin, tammy, terry, Tibet, toile, tulle, tweed, twill, voile, wigan
06 alpaca, angora, armure, barège, Bengal, bouclé, broché, burlap, burnet, burrel, byssus, calico, camlet, canvas, chintz, cloqué, coburg, cotton, coutil, cubica, Dacron®, damask, dévoré, dowlas, doyley, Dralon®, duffel, durant, durrie, faille, fleece, frieze, gloria, harden, jersey, kersey, kincob, linsey, madras, merino, mohair, moreen, muslin, Oxford, plissé, poplin, rateen, ratine, russet, samite, satara, sateen, saxony, sendal, shoddy, sindon, Tactel®, tamine, tartan, Thibet, tissue, tricot, tusser, velour, velvet, vicuña, wadmal, wincey, winsey
07 alepine, baracan, batiste, brocade, buckram, bunting, cambric, camelot, caracul, challis, chamois, Cheviot, chiffon, cramesy, cypress, doeskin, dornick, drabbet, droguet, drugget, duvetyn, façonné, fake fur, flannel, foulard, fustian, gingham, Gore-Tex®, grogram, hessian, holland, hopsack, jaconet, karakul, khaddar, kidskin, leather, lockram, Mexican, mockado, morocco, nacarat, nankeen, oil silk, organza, orleans, paisley, percale, rabanna, raschel, raw silk, sagathy, scarlet, schappe, seating, silesia, Spandex®, stammel, suiting, tabaret, taffeta, ticking, veiling, Viyella®, webbing, woolsey, worsted
08 barathea, barracan, bayadère, box-cloth, buckskin, cashmere, casimere, chambray, chenille, corduroy, coutille, cramoisy, cretonne, diamanté, drilling, frocking, gambroon, gossamer, homespun, jacquard, lambskin, marcella, mazarine, moleskin, oilcloth, organdie, osnaburg, pashmina, plaiding, pleather, quilting, sarsenet, shagreen, shalloon, shantung, sheeting, shirting, spun silk, suedette, swanskin, Terylene®, toilinet, waxcloth, whipcord
09 astrakhan, baldachin, bombasine, calamanco, carmelite, cassimere, Chantilly, Crimplene®, crinoline, farandine, folk-weave, fur fabric, gaberdine, georgette, grenadine, grosgrain, haircloth, horsehair, huckaback, interlock, kalamkari, macintosh, matelassé, Moygashel®, open-weave, organzine, paramatta, petersham, pinstripe, polyester, raven-duck, sackcloth, sailcloth, satinette, sharkskin, sheepskin, stockinet, swans-down, tarpaulin, velveteen
10 Balbriggan, broadcloth, brocatelle, candlewick, farrandine, florentine, grass cloth, habit-cloth, hop-sacking, kerseymere, mackintosh, microfibre, monk's cloth, mousseline, mummy-cloth, needlecord, paper-cloth, peau-de-soie, pilot cloth, polycotton, seersucker, sicilienne, Tattersall, toilinette, winceyette
11 cheesecloth, flannelette, Harris tweed®, interfacing, Kendal green, marquisette, mutton cloth, nettle-cloth, sempiternum, stockinette
12 bolting cloth, Brussels lace, butter-muslin, cavalry twill, crêpe de chine, leather-cloth, Lincoln green, Shetland wool
13 boulting cloth, casement cloth, foundation-net, linsey-woolsey
14 heather mixture, terry towelling

See also **cotton**

fabricate

◇ *anagram indicator*
04 coin, fake, form, make **05** build, erect, forge, frame, hatch, shape, weave **06** cook up, create, devise, invent, make up **07** concoct, falsify, fashion, produce, trump up
08 assemble **09** construct
11 counterfeit, manufacture, put together

fabrication

03 fib, lie, web **04** fake, myth **05** fable, story **06** mock-up **07** coinage, fiction, figment, forgery, untruth **08** assembly, building, erection **09** falsehood, invention **10** assemblage, concoction, fairy story, production **11** manufacture
12 construction

fabulous

03 def, fab, rad **04** cool, mean, mega, neat **05** false, great, magic, super, triff
06 divine, fabled, grouse, made-up, mythic, superb, unreal, way-out, wicked **07** amazing, cracker, crucial, feigned, immense, radical **08** heavenly, invented, mythical, stonking, top-notch **09** excellent, fantastic, fictional, imaginary, legendary, wonderful
10 apocryphal, astounding, fictitious, incredible, marvellous, mythologic, not half bad, phenomenal, remarkable,

tremendous **11** astonishing, sensational, spectacular **12** breathtaking, mythological, unbelievable, unimaginable **13** inconceivable **14** out of this world

façade
04 face, mask, show, veil **05** cloak, cover, front, guise **06** veneer **07** frontal **08** disguise, exterior, frontage, pretence **09** semblance **10** appearance, storefront

face
◇ *head selection indicator*
03 air, jib, mug, pan **04** clad, coat, dare, defy, dial, form, head, line, look, meet, mien, moue, name, phiz, pout, puss, side, trim **05** anger, brave, clock, cover, dress, flank, front, frown, looks, pitch, scowl **06** aspect, esteem, façade, favour, honour, kisser, nature, oppose, polish, resist, smooth, tackle, veneer, visage **07** affront, grimace, outside, overlay, profile, respect, surface **08** boldness, confront, cope with, deal with, exterior, face up to, features, frontage, give on to, look onto, overlook, presence, prestige, standing **09** demeanour, encounter, look out on, withstand **10** admiration, appearance, be opposite, effrontery, experience, expression, reputation **11** countenance, look towards, physiognomy **13** come up against

Face parts include:

03 ear, eye, gum, jaw, lip
04 brow, chin, hair, iris, jowl, lips, neck, nose, skin
05 beard, cheek, mouth, pupil, teeth
06 eyelid, sclera, septum, temple, tongue
07 earlobe, eyeball, eyebrow, eyelash, freckle, jawbone, nostril, wrinkle
08 philtrum
09 cheekbone, moustache
10 complexion, double chin

See also **hair**

• **face to face**
06 facing **07** vis-à-vis **08** eye to eye, in person, opposite **09** confronté, tête-à-tête **11** confronting **12** a quattr'occhi **14** across-the-table **15** in confrontation

• **face up to**
04 nose **06** accept **08** confront, cope with, deal with **09** recognize, stand up to **10** meet head-on **11** acknowledge **15** come to terms with

• **flat face**
04 pane

• **fly in the face of**
04 defy **05** clash **06** insult, oppose **08** be at odds, conflict, contrast, disagree **09** go against **10** contradict **12** be at variance, be in conflict

• **on the face of it**
07 clearly, plainly **08** patently **09** obviously, outwardly, reputedly, seemingly **10** apparently, manifestly, ostensibly **12** on the surface **13** superficially

• **pull a face**
03 moe, mow **04** girn, gurn, lour, pout, sulk **05** fleer, frown, scowl **06** glower **07** grimace **13** knit your brows

• **tilted face**
04 cant

facelift
05 refit **08** makeover **10** renovation **11** restoration **12** redecoration, rhytidectomy **13** refurbishment **14** plastic surgery, transformation **15** cosmetic surgery

facet
04 face, side **05** angle, plane, point, slant **06** aspect, factor **07** element, feature, surface **10** ommatidium **14** characteristic

facetious
04 glib **05** comic, droll, funny, witty **06** jocose, joking **07** amusing, comical, jesting, jocular, playful, waggish **08** flippant, humorous **09** frivolous **12** light-hearted **13** tongue-in-cheek

facile
04 easy, glib **05** hasty, light, quick, ready, slick **06** fluent, simple, smooth **07** affable, shallow **08** yielding **09** plausible **10** simplistic **11** superficial **13** uncomplicated

facilitate
04 ease, help **06** assist, grease, smooth **07** advance, forward, further, promote, speed up **08** expedite **09** encourage, lubricate **10** accelerate, make easier **12** smooth the way

facilitation
07 helping **09** promotion **10** assistance, expediting, forwarding, furthering **12** acceleration **13** encouragement

facility
03 aid **04** ease, gift **05** knack, means, skill **06** mod con, talent **07** ability, amenity, feature, fluency, pliancy, service, utility **08** aptitude, resource **09** advantage, appliance, dexterity, eloquence, equipment, provision, quickness, readiness **10** affability **11** convenience, opportunity, proficiency, skilfulness **12** prerequisite **14** articulateness, effortlessness

facing
06 façade, lining, veneer **07** coating, overlay, surface **08** cladding, covering, dressing, trimming **09** revetment **10** false front **13** reinforcement

facsimile
03 fax **04** copy **05** image, print, repro, Xerox® **06** carbon **07** replica, telefax **09** duplicate, imitation, photocopy, Photostat®, reproduce **10** carbon copy, mimeograph, transcript **11** electrotype **12** reproduction **13** telefacsimile

fact
03 act, gen **04** deed, info, item, poop **05** datum, event, point, score, thing, truth **06** detail, factor **07** element, feature, low-down, reality **08** incident, specific **09** actuality, certainty, component, happening **10** factuality, ins and outs, occurrence, particular **11** information **12** circumstance, fait accompli

• **in fact**
03 e'en, nay, yes **04** even **05** truly **06** indeed, really **07** de facto, en effet, in truth **08** actually **09** in reality **10** come to that, in practice **12** in actual fact **13** in point of fact **15** as a matter of fact

faction
03 set **04** band, camp, ring, side **05** cabal, group, junta, junto, lobby, party **06** caucus, clique, sector, strife **07** coterie, discord, section, trouble **08** argument, conflict, division, fraction, friction, grouplet, minority, quarrels, tendency **10** contention, contingent, disharmony, dissension, infighting **11** ginger group **12** disagreement **13** pressure group, splinter group

factious
05 rival, split **06** at odds **07** divided, warring **08** clashing, divisive, mutinous, partisan **09** dissident, sectarian, seditious, turbulent **10** discordant, rebellious, refractory, tumultuous **11** conflicting, contentious, quarrelling, quarrelsome **12** disputatious **13** at loggerheads, troublemaking **15** insurrectionary

factitious
04 made, sham **05** bogus, false **09** contrived, imitation, pretended, unnatural **10** artificial, fabricated **11** counterfeit

factor
04 fact, gene, item, part **05** cause, facet, point **06** aspect, detail **07** divisor, element, feature **09** component, influence **10** ingredient **11** constituent, contingency, determinant, submultiple **12** circumstance **13** consideration **14** characteristic

• **unknown factor**
01 x, y, z

factory
04 mill, yard **05** plant, works **07** foundry **08** workshop **09** shop floor **11** manufactory **12** assembly line, assembly shop

factotum
05 do-all **06** circar, sircar, sirkar **07** famulus **08** handyman **09** Man Friday, odd-jobman **10** Girl Friday **12** bottle-washer **13** maid-of-all-work **15** jack-of-all-trades

facts
04 data, poop **05** truth **09** bare bones

factual
04 real, true **05** close, exact **06** actual, strict **07** correct, genuine, literal, precise **08** accurate, detailed, faithful,

truthful, unbiased **09** authentic, objective, realistic **10** historical, true-to-life **12** unprejudiced

factually
05 truly **06** really **08** actually
09 genuinely, in reality **10** truthfully
12 historically

faculties
04 wits **06** powers, reason, senses
12 capabilities, intelligence

faculty
03 ear, wit **04** bent, bump, gift, nose
05 flair, knack, power, sight, skill, taste
06 school, talent **07** ability, licence, section **08** aptitude, capacity, division, facility, function **10** capability, department **11** proficiency
12 organization

fad
04 buzz, cult, mode, rage, whim
05 craze, fancy, mania, trend, vogue
06 maggot **07** fashion **10** enthusiasm
11 affectation **14** passing fashion

faddy
05 exact, fussy, picky **06** choosy
07 finicky **10** fastidious, nit-picking, particular, pernickety **11** persnickety
12 hard-to-please

fade
03 die, dim, ebb **04** dull, fail, fall, flag, melt, miff, pale, vade, wane, weak, wilt
05 appal, droop, faint **06** blanch, bleach, blench, die out, perish, recede, vanish, wallow, weaken, whiten, wither
07 decline, die away, dwindle, ebb away, shrivel, wash out **08** diminish, dissolve, etiolate, evanesce, grow pale, melt away, peter out, tone down, wear away **09** disappear, discolour, fizzle out, waste away **10** become pale, lose colour **11** become paler **12** become weaker

faeces
04 crap, crud, dung, flux, mute, poop, pure **05** frass, guano, scats, stool
06 doo-doo, egesta, ordure, stools
07 excreta, motions **09** body waste, droppings, excrement, number two
11 waste matter **12** rejectamenta, sir-reverence

fag
03 cig, tab **04** bind, bore, drag, pest, slog **05** chore, ciggy, grind, joint, smoke, weary, whiff **06** bother, ciggie, dog end, fag end, gasper, low-tar, roll-up **07** high-tar **08** drudgery, king-size, nuisance **09** cigarette, filter-tip
10 coffin-nail, irritation **11** cancer-stick, roll-your-own **13** inconvenience

fagged
04 beat, done **05** all in, jaded, weary
06 beaten, bushed, done in, pooped, wasted, zonked **07** euchred, whacked, worn out **08** burnt out, dead-beat, dog-tired, fatigued, jiggered
09 exhausted, knackered, pooped out
10 euchred out **11** ready to drop, tuckered out **14** on your last legs

fail
02 go **03** die, ebb, mis, sod **04** bomb, fade, feal, flag, flop, fold, lose, miss, omit, plow, sink, stop, turf, wane
05 abort, crash, decay, droop, flunk, fudge, leave, smash **06** blow it, cut out, desert, falter, forget, go bung, go bust, go phut, pack up, play up, plough, weaken **07** abandon, conk out, crap out, deceive, decline, dwindle, forsake, founder, go broke, go kaput, go under, go wrong, let down, misluck, neglect, not work **08** bottle it, collapse, diminish, fall down, fall flat, miscarry, not start **09** break down, come short, fall apart, fizzle out, go belly-up, not make it **10** come undone, disappoint, draw a blank, get nowhere, go bankrupt, not come off **11** bite the dust, come a gutser, come to grief, come unglued, come unstuck, dégringoler, deteriorate, fall through, go to the wall, malfunction **12** come a cropper, come to naught, go into the red, go on the blink, go on the fritz, underachieve **13** come to nothing
14 be unsuccessful, not do something, score an own goal **15** become insolvent, blow your chances

• **without fail**
08 reliably **09** regularly **10** constantly, dependably, faithfully, punctually
11 predictably, religiously, unfailingly
13 like clockwork **15** conscientiously

failing
03 sin **04** flat, flaw **05** error, fault, lapse
06 defect, foible **07** blemish, default, failure, lacking, wanting, without
08 drawback, on the ebb, weakness, weak spot **10** deficiency **11** in default of, shortcoming **12** imperfection **14** in the absence of

failure
03 dud **04** flop, hash, mess, miss, no go, no-no, ruin **05** botch, crash, decay, flunk, loser **06** cock-up, defeat, demise, ebbing, fading, fiasco, misfit, reject, slip-up, victim, waning **07** also-ran, burst-up, debacle, decline, default, dropout, flivver, folding, has-been, let-down, neglect, no-hoper, screw-up, sinking, washout, wipeout
08 abortion, calamity, collapse, dead loss, disaster, downfall, flagging, meltdown, omission, shambles, shutdown, stalling, stopping, write-off
09 born loser, breakdown, disregard, oversight, packing-up, unsuccess, weakening **10** bankruptcy, conking-out, cutting-out, foundering, going under, ill success, insolvency, misfortune, negligence, non-starter, remissness **11** dereliction, frustration, malfunction, miscarriage **12** waste of space **13** deterioration, forgetfulness, lack of success **14** disappointment, going to the wall, malfunctioning
15 coming to nothing

faint
03 dim, low, wan **04** drop, dull, fade, gone, hazy, mild, pale, soft, weak
05 decay, dizzy, droop, faded, giddy, light, muted, queer, quiet, sound, swarf, swelt, swerf, swoon, swoun, vague, woozy **06** feeble, hushed, slight, stanck, swarve, swerve, swound, vanish **07** blurred, ghostly, languid, muffled, obscure, pass out, subdued, syncope, unclear **08** black out, blackout, bleached, collapse, flake out, keel over, unsteady **09** exhausted
10 indistinct, oppressive **11** half-hearted, lightheaded
14 unenthusiastic **15** unconsciousness

faint-hearted
04 soft, weak **05** timid, wussy
06 craven, scared, yellow **07** chicken, fearful, gutless, jittery, wimpish
08 cowardly, timorous **09** diffident, spineless, weak-kneed **10** hen-hearted, irresolute, spiritless **11** half-hearted, lily-livered **12** weak-spirited, white-livered **13** pusillanimous, yellow-bellied **14** chicken-hearted, chicken-livered

faintly
04 a bit **06** feebly, softly, weakly **07** a little, vaguely **08** slightly, somewhat

fair
02 OK **03** dry **04** even, expo, fete, fine, full, gaff, gala, good, just, mela, open, pale, pure, show, so-so, warm
05 blond, civil, clean, clear, cream, ivory, legit, light, quite, right, sunny, tryst, white, woman **06** bazaar, beauty, blonde, bright, decent, flaxen, golden, honest, kosher, lawful, likely, market, modest, not bad, proper, square, yellow **07** upright **08** adequate, all right, carnival, detached, directly, exchange, festival, handsome, mediocre, middling, moderate, passable, pleasing, specious, sporting, unbiased **09** beautiful, cloudless, craft fair, equitable, impartial, objective, out-and-out, plausible, tolerable, trade fair, unclouded, veritable **10** above board, acceptable, even-handed, exhibition, exposition, fair-haired, fair-headed, favourable, honourable, legitimate, on the level, prosperous, reasonable, straight up, sufficient
11 light-haired, respectable, trustworthy **12** satisfactory, unobstructed, unprejudiced
13 disinterested, dispassionate, done by the book **14** going by the book
15 played by the book

fairground
• **fairground attraction**
04 ride

Fairground attractions include:

06 hoop-la
07 Dodgems®
08 carousel, waltzers
10 bumper cars, coconut shy, ghost train, swing boats
11 Ferris wheel, wall of death
12 bouncy castle, chair-o-planes, merry-go-round, tunnel of love
13 helter-skelter, rollercoaster

fairly
03 gay, gey **05** fully, quite **06** enough, gently, justly, neatly, pretty, quight, rather, really, square **07** legally, plainly **08** honestly, lawfully, middling, passably, properly, somewhat **09** equitably, neutrally, tolerably, veritably **10** absolutely, adequately, moderately, positively, reasonably, unbiasedly **11** beautifully, impartially, objectively

fair-minded
04 fair, just **05** right **06** honest, proper, square **07** upright **08** detached, unbiased **09** equitable, impartial, objective **10** even-handed, honourable, on the level, straight up **11** trustworthy **12** unprejudiced **13** disinterested, dispassionate

fairness
06 equity, square **07** decency, justice **09** rightness **10** legitimacy **11** uprightness **12** impartiality, rightfulness, unbiasedness **13** equitableness **14** even-handedness, honourableness, legitimateness

fairy
03 elf, fay, fée, hob, imp, Mab **04** peri, pixy, Puck **05** faery, nymph, pisky, pixie, pouke **06** faerie, sprite **07** brownie, rusalka, sandman **08** delicate, fanciful **09** hobgoblin, Puck-hairy, whimsical **10** leprechaun **11** enchantress **15** Robin Goodfellow

fairy tale
03 fib, lie **04** myth **07** fantasy, fiction, romance, untruth **08** folk-tale **09** invention, tall story **10** fairy story **11** fabrication

Fairy tales include:

07 Aladdin, Ali Baba, The Bell
08 Momo Taro, Peter Pan, Rapunzel, Snowdrop, The Angel, The Daisy, The Raven, Tom Thumb
09 Ashputtel, Bluebeard, Briar Rose, Pinocchio, Snow White, The Shadow, The Storks
10 Cinderella, Clever Hans, Goldilocks, Hans in Luck, The Fir Tree, The Rose-Elf, Thumbelina
11 Clever Elsie, Hop o' my Thumb, Little Thumb, Mother Elder, Mother Goose, Puss in Boots, The Old House, The Red Shoes
12 Holger Danske, Little Red-Cap, The Elderbush, The Goose Girl, The Pied Piper, The Snow Queen, The Tinderbox, The Wild Swans, Urashima Taro
13 Chicken Licken, Red Riding Hood, The Frog Prince, The Golden Bird, The Neighbours, The Tin Soldier, The White Snake, The Wizard of Oz
14 Babes in the Wood, Sleeping Beauty, The Flying Trunk, The Golden Goose, The Juniper Tree, The Nightingale, The Seven Ravens, The Water of Life
15 Dick Whittington, Hansel and Gretel, Rumpelstiltskin, The Elfin Hillock, The Little Lovers, Three Little Pigs, The Ugly Duckling

Fairy tale characters include:

03 Cat, Dog
04 Duck, Jack, John, Liza, Nana, Nibs
05 Beast, Curly, Wendy
06 Beauty, Conrad, Donkey, Falada, Gretel, Hansel
07 Michael, Rooster, Rose Red, The King, The Ogre, The Wolf, Tootles
08 Baby Bear, Foxy Loxy, Geppetto, Peter Pan, Rapunzel, Slightly, The Elves, The Giant, The Queen, The Troll, The Twins, Tom Thumb
09 Briar Rose, Daddy Bear, Good Fairy, Mummy Bear, Pinocchio, Snow White, The Miller, The Mirror, The Prince
10 Cinderella, Ducky Lucky, Goldilocks, Henny Penny, Stepmother, The Emperor, Thumbelina, Tinker Bell
11 Captain Hook, Grandmother, Pedlar Woman, Puss in Boots, The Huntsman, The Lost Boys, The Princess, Ugly Sisters, Wicked Fairy, Wicked Witch
12 Goosey Loosey, The Goose Girl, The Shoemaker
13 Band of Robbers, Chicken Licken, Red Riding Hood
14 Fairy Godmother, The Golden Goose, The Seven Dwarfs
15 Alice Fitzwarren, Billy Goats Gruff, Dick Whittington, Fairy Godmothers, Mr and Mrs Darling, Rumpelstiltskin, The Little Red Hen, The Rich Merchant, The Ugly Duckling, Three Little Pigs

faith
03 fay, lay **04** faix, sect **05** creed, dogma, fides, troth, trust **06** belief, church, credit, fealty, honour, indeed **07** believe, honesty, loyalty **08** credence, devotion, doctrine, fidelity, reliance, religion, teaching **09** assurance, obedience, sincerity **10** allegiance, commitment, confidence, conviction, dedication, dependence, persuasion **12** denomination, faithfulness, truthfulness

• **in faith**
04 fegs

faithful
04 feal, leal, true **05** afald, close, exact, loyal **06** aefald, afawld, strict, trusty **07** aefauld, devoted, precise, staunch **08** accurate, brethren, constant, obedient, reliable, soothful, truthful **09** adherents, believers, believing, committed, dedicated, followers, soothfast, steadfast **10** dependable, supporters, unflagging, unswerving, unwavering **11** true-hearted, trustworthy **12** communicants, congregation

faithfully
04 true **05** truly **06** firmly **07** closely, exactly, loyally **08** reliably, solemnly, strictly **09** devotedly, precisely, staunchly **10** accurately, constantly, dependably **11** steadfastly

faithfulness
05 truth **06** fealty **07** loyalty **08** accuracy, devotion, fidelity **09** closeness, constancy, exactness **10** allegiance, commitment, dedication, strictness **11** reliability, staunchness **13** dependability, steadfastness **14** scrupulousness **15** trustworthiness

faithless
05 false **06** fickle, untrue **08** agnostic, disloyal, doubting **09** atheistic, deceptive **10** adulterous, inconstant, perfidious, traitorous, unfaithful, unreliable, untruthful **11** nullifidian, treacherous, unbelieving **12** disbelieving, false-hearted **13** untrustworthy

faithlessness
06 deceit **07** perfidy **08** adultery, apostasy, betrayal **09** treachery **10** disloyalty, fickleness, infidelity **11** inconstancy **14** unfaithfulness

fake
◇ *anagram indicator*
03 rob **04** coil, cook, copy, faux, fold, hoax, mock, sham **05** bogus, dodge, false, feign, filch, flake, forge, fraud, fudge, phony, pseud, put on, quack **06** affect, assume, attack, bodgie, doctor, ersatz, forged, phoney, pirate, pseudo **07** assumed, forgery, hyped-up, imitate, pretend, replica, swindle **08** affected, impostor, simulate, spurious **09** charlatan, fabricate, imitation, simulated **10** artificial, fraudulent, mountebank, simulation **11** counterfeit **12** reproduction

falcon

Falcons include:

05 hobby, saker
06 gentle, lanner, merlin
07 Iceland, kestrel
08 duck-hawk
09 gerfalcon, gyrfalcon, jerfalcon, peregrine, stone hawk
11 tassell-gent
12 falcon-gentil, falcon-gentle, tassel-gentle, tercel-gentle, tercel-jerkin

Falkland Islands
03 FLK

fall
◇ *anagram indicator*
◇ *reversal indicator*
02 fa **03** cut, die, ebb, get, lot, sin **04** dive, drip, drop, grow, hang, purl, rain, ruin, rush, sink, slip, soss, trap, trip, turn **05** abate, chute, crash, falls, lapse, occur, onset, pitch, slant, slide, slope, slump, souse, spill, yield **06** alight, autumn, become, be lost, chance, dangle, defeat, demise, give in, go down, gutzer, happen, lessen, perish, plunge, recede, revert, shower, submit, topple, tumble **07** be slain, be taken,

cadence, capture, cascade, decline, descend, descent, dwindle, failure, fall off, fall-off, fortune, impinge, incline, offence, plummet, stumble, subside, torrent **08** be killed, cataract, collapse, come down, come to be, conquest, decrease, diminish, down-come, downfall, fall down, giving-in, grow into, keel over, nose-dive, yielding **09** come about, declivity, dwindling, lessening, overthrow, reduction, surrender, take place, terminate, waterfall **10** be defeated, capitulate, plummeting, submission, topple over, wrongdoing **11** be conquered, come a gutser, destruction, keeling-over, lose control, original sin, precipitate, resignation **12** be vanquished, capitulation, come a cropper, disobedience, lose your life, pitch forward, precipitance, precipitancy **13** loss of control, transgression

• **fall apart**
03 rot **04** fail **05** break, decay **06** divide **07** break up, crack up, crumble, shatter **08** collapse, come away, dissolve, disunite, go to bits **09** break down, decompose **10** fall to bits, go to pieces **11** lose control **12** come to pieces, disintegrate, fall to pieces **15** break into pieces

• **fall asleep**
04 doze **06** get off, nod off, pop off **07** doze off, drop off **08** crash out, drift off, flake out, spark out **13** pass into sleep **15** go out like a light

• **fall away**
04 drop, fail **05** lapse **06** go down, revolt **07** decline, drop off, dwindle, relapse **08** drop away, languish **09** slope away, slope down

• **fall back**
06 depart, recoil, recule, revert **07** back off, give way, recoyle, recuile, relapse, retreat **08** draw back, pull back, withdraw **09** disengage **10** give ground, lose ground

• **fall back on**
03 use **06** call on, employ, look to, turn to **08** resort to **09** make use of **12** call into play **14** have recourse to

• **fall behind**
03 lag **05** trail **08** drop back, straggle **09** lag behind, not keep up

• **fall down**
04 fail, flop **07** founder **08** collapse **09** break down **11** come unglued, come unstuck **12** come a cropper **13** come to nothing **14** be unsuccessful

• **fall for**
03 buy **05** fancy **06** accept, desire, take to **07** swallow **10** be fooled by **11** be taken in by **12** be attached to, be crazy about, be deceived by, have a crush on **14** fall in love with

• **fall in**
04 sink **05** array, crash **06** cave in, line up, revert **07** give way, subside **08** collapse, come down **11** stand in line **14** get in formation

• **fall in with**
06 accept **07** support **08** assent to, hang with **09** agree with **10** comply with **11** go along with, hang out with **12** go around with **13** co-operate with, hang about with **14** hang around with **15** get involved with

• **fall off**
04 drop, shed, slow **05** crash, slump **06** lessen, perish, worsen **07** decline, die away, drop off, slacken, slip off **08** decrease, draw back **11** deteriorate

• **fall on**
04 meet **06** assail, attack, snatch **07** assault, lay into, set upon **08** pounce on **09** descend on

• **fall out**
05 argue, clash, fight **06** bicker, differ, happen **07** dismiss, quarrel **08** disagree, squabble

• **fall slightly**
04 ease

• **fall through**
04 fail **05** abort **07** founder, go wrong **08** collapse, miscarry **11** come to grief **13** come to nothing

• **fall to**
05 begin, set to, start **07** stand to **08** commence, set about **10** get stuck in **11** be the duty of, be the task of **13** apply yourself

fallacious
05 false, wrong **06** untrue **07** inexact **08** delusive, delusory, illusory, mistaken, spurious **09** deceptive, erroneous, illogical, incorrect, sophistic **10** fictitious, inaccurate, misleading **11** casuistical, sophistical

fallacy
04 flaw, myth **05** error **06** idolon, idolum **07** idolism, mistake, sophism **08** delusion, illusion **09** deception, falsehood, false idea, sophistry **12** equivocation, misjudgement **13** deceitfulness, inconsistency, misconception **14** miscalculation, mistaken belief **15** misapprehension

fallen
04 dead, died, lost **05** loose, slain **06** killed, ruined, shamed **07** immoral, seduced **08** murdered, perished **09** disgraced **10** degenerate, overthrown **11** promiscuous, slaughtered

fallibility
07 failing **08** weakness **09** mortality **10** inaccuracy **12** imperfection **13** unreliability

fallible
04 weak **05** frail, human **06** errant, erring, flawed, mortal **08** ignorant **09** imperfect, uncertain **10** unreliable

fallow
03 lay, lea, ley **04** idle **06** barren, unsown, unused **07** dormant, resting **08** inactive **09** unplanted **10** unploughed **11** undeveloped **12** uncultivated, unproductive

false
◇ *anagram indicator*
03 bum **04** fake, faux, mock, sham **05** bogus, lying, pseud, wrong **06** faulty, forged, phoney, pseudo, untrue **07** assumed, bastard, feigned, inexact, invalid, pretend **08** disloyal, fabulous, illusive, illusory, invented, mistaken, postiche, pseudish, recreant, spurious, strumpet, two-faced **09** deceitful, dishonest, erroneous, faithless, imitation, incorrect, insincere, pretended, simulated, synthetic, trumped-up **10** artificial, fabricated, fallacious, fictitious, fraudulent, inaccurate, misleading, perfidious, traitorous, unfaithful, ungrounded, unreliable **11** counterfeit, double-faced, duplicitous, treacherous **12** hypocritical **13** double-dealing, untrustworthy

falsehood
03 fib, lie **04** flam **05** fable, porky, story **06** deceit **07** fiction, leasing, perfidy, perjury, untruth, whopper **09** deception, duplicity, hypocrisy, invention, mendacity, tall story, treachery **10** dishonesty, fairy story **11** fabrication, insincerity **12** two-facedness **13** deceitfulness, double dealing **14** untruthfulness

falsely
07 in error, untruly, wrongly **09** by mistake, deviously **10** mistakenly, wrongfully **11** deceitfully, dishonestly, erroneously, incorrectly, insincerely **12** artificially, fallaciously, fraudulently **13** counterfeitly, treacherously **14** hypocritically

falsetto
04 alto **08** high note **09** high pitch, high voice **10** shrillness **12** head register

falsification
06 change, deceit **07** forgery **08** adultery **09** tampering **10** alteration, distortion, perversion **12** adulteration **13** dissimulation

falsify
◇ *anagram indicator*
03 lie, rig **04** cook, fake, rort **05** alter, belie, false, feign, forge, twist **06** diddle, doctor, fiddle, garble, wangle **07** distort, massage, pervert **08** misstate **10** adulterate, manipulate, tamper with **11** counterfeit **12** misrepresent, sophisticate

falter
04 fail, flag **05** delay, quail, shake, waver **06** flinch, hiccup, totter **07** be shaky, stammer, stoiter, stumble, stutter, tremble **08** hesitate, hiccough **09** vacillate **10** be unsteady, dilly-dally **12** be in two minds, drag your feet, shilly-shally, take your time, unsteadiness **13** sit on the fence **14** fluff your lines

faltering
◇ *anagram indicator*
04 weak **05** timid **06** broken **07** failing **08** flagging, hesitant, unsteady **09** stumbling, tentative, uncertain **10** irresolute, stammering

fame
04 name, note **05** glory, kudos **06** esteem, honour, renown, report, repute, rumour **07** stardom **08** eminence **09** celebrity, greatness **10** importance, notability, prominence, reputation **11** distinction **15** illustriousness

famed
05 noted **06** famous **08** esteemed, renowned **09** acclaimed, prominent, well-known **10** celebrated, recognized **11** widely known

familiar
03 fam, old **04** bold, dear, easy, free, maty, near, open **05** aware, close, known, matey, pally, privy, usual **06** au fait, casual, chummy, common, homely, smarmy, versed, well up **07** abreast, clued up, forward, natural, relaxed, routine **08** everyday, fireside, frequent, friendly, genned up, habitual, homelike, informal, intimate, ordinary, repeated, sociable **09** au courant, customary, household, up to speed, well-known **10** accustomed, acquainted, conversant, recognized, unreserved **11** comfortable, commonplace, free-and-easy, impertinent **12** confidential, conventional, over-familiar, over-friendly, presumptuous, recognizable, run-of-the-mill, unmistakable **13** disrespectful, knowledgeable, unceremonious

familiarity
04 ease **05** grasp, habit, skill **07** liberty, mastery **08** boldness, intimacy, nearness, openness **09** awareness, closeness, impudence, knowledge, liberties, palliness, pushiness **10** casualness, chumminess, consuetude, disrespect, experience, inwardness **11** conversance, conversancy, forwardness, informality, naturalness, presumption, sociability **12** acquaintance, friendliness, impertinence **13** comprehension, intrusiveness, understanding **15** over-familiarity

familiarize
05 brief, coach, gen up, prime, teach, train **06** clue up, school **08** accustom, acquaint, instruct **09** habituate, make aware **11** acclimatize **12** get up to speed, indoctrinate, make familiar **13** keep up to speed **14** make acquainted

family
03 fam, kin **04** clan, folk, gens, kids, kind, line, name, race, stem, type **05** birth, blood, brood, class, flesh, genus, group, house, issue, order, stock, tribe **06** kinred, people, scions, stirps, strain, whanau **07** descent, dynasty, kiddies, kindred, kinsmen, lineage, parents, progeny, species **08** ancestry, children, pedigree, subclass **09** ancestors, forebears, household, next of kin, offspring, parentage, relations, relatives **10** extraction, generation, little ones **11** descendants, you and yours **13** nuclear family **14** classification, extended family **15** one-parent family

• **member of family**
08 relation, relative

See also **relative**

• **family tree**
04 line **06** stemma **07** descent, lineage **08** ancestry, pedigree **09** genealogy, whakapapa **10** background, extraction

famine
04 lack, want **05** death **06** dearth, hunger **08** scarcity **10** starvation **11** deprivation, destitution **12** exiguousness, malnutrition **14** shortage of food

famished
06 hungry **07** starved **08** ravenous, starving **09** famishing, voracious **14** undernourished

famous
04 name **05** famed, great, noted **06** legend, signal **07** eminent, notable, popular **08** esteemed, glorious, honoured, infamous, renowned **09** acclaimed, celebrity, excellent, legendary, notorious, prominent, respected, venerable, well-famed, well-known **10** celebrated, remarkable **11** illustrious, world-famous **13** distinguished

famously
04 well **07** greatly, happily, notably **08** superbly **09** eminently, popularly **10** infamously, splendidly, swimmingly **11** brilliantly, notoriously, prominently, wonderfully **13** conspicuously

fan
◇ *anagram indicator*
03 air, nut **04** blow, buff, cone, cool, vane, wing **05** fiend, freak, lover, punka, rouse **06** addict, aerate, arouse, backer, blower, Colmar, cooler, excite, groupy, ignite, incite, kindle, punkah, stir up, whip up, winnow, work up **07** admirer, agitate, air-cool, devotee, flutter, freshen, groupie, provoke, refresh **08** adherent, follower, increase **09** air cooler, extractor, flabellum, instigate, intensify, propeller, rhipidion, stimulate, supporter, ventilate **10** aficionado, enthusiast, ventilator **11** afficionado **12** air-condition, extractor fan **14** air-conditioner

• **fan out**
04 open **06** spread, unfold, unfurl **07** move out, open out **09** spread out

fanatic
03 nut **05** bigot, fiend, freak **06** addict, maniac, zealot **07** devotee, radical **08** activist, militant **09** extremist, visionary **10** enthusiast **14** fundamentalist

fanatical
03 mad **04** wild **05** rabid **07** bigoted, burning, extreme, fervent, radical, zealous **08** activist, dogmatic, frenzied, militant **09** extremist, obsessive **10** immoderate, passionate **11** extravagant **12** narrow-minded, single-minded **14** fundamentalist

fanaticism
04 zeal **06** frenzy **07** bigotry, fervour, madness **08** activism, wildness, zealotry **09** dogmatism, extremism, militancy, monomania **10** dedication, enthusiasm **11** infatuation, schwärmerei **13** obsessiveness **14** fundamentalism

fancier
03 fan **05** fiend, freak **06** keeper **07** breeder, devotee **08** follower **10** enthusiast

fanciful
◇ *anagram indicator*
04 wild **05** fairy **06** exotic, ornate, quaint, unreal **07** curious, flighty **08** chimeric, creative, fabulous, illusory, mythical, notional, romantic, vaporous **09** airy-fairy, decorated, elaborate, fairytale, fantastic, imaginary, legendary, visionary, whimsical **10** chimerical **11** extravagant, fantastical, imaginative, make-believe, unrealistic **12** metaphysical

fancy
◇ *anagram indicator*
03 yen **04** flam, idea, itch, like, love, urge, want, ween, whim, wish **05** covet, dream, go for, guess, humor, showy, taste, think **06** desire, fangle, favour, humour, lavish, liking, notion, ornate, prefer, raving, reckon, rococo, take to, vision **07** adorned, baroque, believe, caprice, chimera, dream of, elegant, fantasy, imagine, impulse, long for, longing, not mind, opinion, picture, suppose, surmise, thought, wish for **08** chimaera, conceive, crotchet, delusion, fanciful, fantasia, feel like, fondness, illusion, penchant, phantasy, superior, yearn for, yearning **09** decorated, elaborate, expensive, fantastic, lust after **10** be mad about, conception, conjecture, creativity, far-fetched, have in mind, impression, not say no to, ornamented, preference **11** be wild about, embellished, extravagant, have eyes for, imagination, inclination **12** be crazy about, have a crush on, ostentatious, predilection, take a shine to **13** be attracted to, particoloured, take a liking to **14** be interested in, find attractive, have the hots for **15** think the world of

fanfare
04 fuss, show **05** trump **06** parade, sennet, tucket **07** display **08** flourish **09** fanfarade, pageantry, publicity, tarantara **11** flamboyance, ostentation, taratantara, trumpet call

fang
04 claw, grip, tang, tusk **05** catch, prong, talon, tooth **10** venom-tooth

fantasize
05 dream **06** invent **07** imagine, romance **08** daydream **11** hallucinate **12** live in a dream

fantastic
◇ *anagram indicator*
03 ace, odd **04** cool, mega, neat, wild **05** antic, brill, fancy, great, magic, outré, super, weird **06** absurd, antick, exotic, superb, unreal, wicked **07** amazing, anticke, antique, bizarre, extreme, foppish, radical, strange **08** enormous, fabulous, fanciful, illusory, romantic, smashing, terrific, top-notch **09** brilliant, eccentric, excellent, first-rate, grotesque, imaginary, storybook, visionary, whimsical, wonderful **10** capricious, impressive, incredible, marvellous, outlandish, phenomenal, remarkable, tremendous **11** extravagant, imaginative, sensational **12** overwhelming, transcendent, unbelievable **14** out of this world

fantastically
09 amazingly, extremely **10** incredibly **12** phenomenally, terrifically, tremendously, unbelievably

fantasy
03 GBH, GHB **04** idol, love, myth **05** dream, fancy **06** mirage, vision, whimsy **07** caprice, reverie, whimsey **08** daydream, delusion, fantasia, illusion **09** fantasque, invention, moonshine, nightmare, pipe dream, unreality **10** apparition, creativity **11** imagination, inspiration, originality, pie in the sky, speculation **12** fancifulness **13** flight of fancy, hallucination, inventiveness, misconception **15** cloud-cuckoo-land, imaginativeness, resourcefulness

far
03 way **04** away, much **05** miles, other **06** far-off, remote **07** distant, faraway, further, greatly, removed **08** a good way, a long way, far-flung, markedly, opposite, outlying, secluded, very much **09** decidedly, distantly, extremely **10** far-removed **11** back o' Bourke, godforsaken, nowhere near, out-of-the-way, up the Boohai **12** considerably, immeasurably, inaccessible, incomparably, in the boonies, in the wop-wops, some distance **13** great distance, significantly, the black stump **14** in the boondocks

• **as far as**
02 to, up **04** up to

• **far and wide**
06 widely **07** broadly **08** all about **09** worldwide **10** everywhere, far and near **11** extensively, in all places **13** from all places

• **far end, far side**
◇ *tail selection indicator*

• **far out**
05 weird **06** exotic, way out **07** bizarre, extreme, radical, strange, unusual **10** outlandish, unorthodox **14** unconventional

• **go far**
05 get on **06** arrive **07** succeed **08** go places **12** be successful, make your mark **14** achieve success **15** get on in the world

• **not far**
02 nl

• **so far**
02 as **03** als **06** to date **07** thus far, till now, up to now **08** hitherto **12** to some extent, within limits **13** up to this point

faraway
03 far **04** lost **06** absent, dreamy, far-off, remote **07** distant **08** far-flung, outlying **10** abstracted **11** preoccupied **12** absent-minded

farce
03 jig **04** cram, joke, mime, sham **05** exode, lazzo, stuff **06** comedy, parody, satire **07** mockery **08** burletta, nonsense, shambles, stuffing, travesty **09** absurdity, burlesque, forcemeat, pantomime, slapstick **10** buffoonery **11** opera bouffe **14** ridiculousness

farcical
05 comic, silly **06** absurd, stupid **08** derisory **09** diverting, laughable, ludicrous **10** ridiculous **11** nonsensical **12** preposterous

fare
02 be, do, go **03** fee **04** cost, diet, eats, food, go on, menu, nosh, tack, what **05** board, cheer, get on, meals, price, speed, table **06** charge, course, happen, manage, ticket, travel, viands **07** make out, passage, proceed, prosper, rations, succeed, turn out **08** eatables, get along, progress, victuals **09** nutriment, passenger **10** provisions, sustenance **11** nourishment **12** passage-money

farewell
02 BV **03** bye **04** ciao, ta-ta, vale **05** adieu, adios, aloha, later, leave **06** bye-bye, cheers, see you, so long, valete **07** cheerio, goodbye **08** au revoir, take care **10** all the best **11** arrivederci, be seeing you, leave-taking, see you later, valediction, valedictory **12** have a nice day, mind how you go, see you around **14** auf Wiedersehen

• **expression of farewell**
03 bye **04** ciao, ta-ta, vale **05** addio, adieu, adiós, aloha, later **06** hooray, hooroo, see you, shalom, sheers, so long **07** cheerio, goodbye **08** au revoir, chin-chin, sayonara, toodle-oo **11** arrivederci, be seeing you, see you later **14** auf Wiedersehen, shalom aleichem

far-fetched
05 crazy **06** forced **07** dubious **08** fanciful, unlikely **09** exquisite, fantastic, recherché, unnatural **10** improbable, incredible **11** implausible, unrealistic **12** preposterous, unbelievable, unconvincing

farm
03 mas **04** ferm, land, sted, till **05** acres, mains, plant, ranch **06** bowery, grange, plough, shamba **07** acreage, holding, mailing, operate, station **08** farmland, hacienda, property **09** cultivate, farmstead, homestead **11** co-operative, work the land

Farms and farming types include:

03 dry, ley, pig
04 deer, fish, hill, stud, wind
05 croft, dairy, mixed, store, trash, trout
06 arable, estate, salmon, turkey
07 factory, organic, ostrich, poultry
09 extensive, free-range, intensive
10 collective, plantation
11 cattle ranch, monoculture, subsistence
12 sheep station, smallholding, stock station

Farm animals include:

02 ox
03 ass, cow, ewe, hen, pig, ram, sow
04 bull, calf, cock, duck, foal, goat, lamb, mare, mule
05 goose, horse, sheep
06 cattle, donkey, piglet, rabbit, turkey
07 chicken, rooster
08 cockerel, stallion
09 billy goat

Farming equipment includes:

03 ard, ATV, axe, hoe, saw
04 fork, plow, rake, wain
05 baler, drill, flail, gambo, mower, share, spade
06 harrow, plough, ricker, ripple, scythe, shovel, sickle, tanker, tedder
07 combine, draw hoe, grubber, hayfork, hayrake, mattock, scuffle, sprayer, tractor, trailer
08 buckrake, chainsaw, hay knife, haymaker, scuffler, spreader
09 corn drill, drop-drill, harvester, irrigator, pitchfork, power lift, rotary hoe, Rotavator®, Rotovator®, scarifier, seed drill, whetstone
10 cropduster, cultivator, disc harrow, disc plough, earth-board, flail mower, seed-harrow
11 bale wrapper, broadcaster, chaff-cutter, chaff-engine, drill-harrow, hedgecutter, mole drainer, reaping hook, wheelbarrow, wheel plough
12 muckspreader, slurry tanker
13 fork-lift truck, potato planter, slurry sprayer
14 field sprinkler, front end loader, milking machine

• **farm out**
08 delegate **09** outsource **11** contract out, subcontract **12** give to others, pass to others

• **farm worker**
03 dey **04** peon **06** sheepo **07** orra man **08** farmhand

• **healthy farm animal**
04 doer

farmer
04 Boer, ryot **05** cocky, colon, gebur **06** cockie, mailer, raiyat, yeoman **07** crofter, grazier, métayer, rancher **08** cockatoo **09** campesino, cow-cockie, sodbuster **10** agronomist, estanciero, husbandman **11** flock-master, share-milker, smallholder, stock-farmer, store farmer **12** sharecropper **13** agriculturist **15** agriculturalist

farming
06 arable **07** tilling **08** agronomy, crofting **09** geoponics, husbandry **11** agriculture, agroscience, cultivation **12** agribusiness, share-milking

Faroe Islands
02 FO **03** FRO

far-off
03 far **06** remote **07** distant, faraway **08** far-flung, outlying

farrago
04 hash **06** jumble, medley **07** mélange, mixture **08** mishmash **09** pot-pourri **10** dog's dinner, hodgepodge, hotchpotch, miscellany, salmagundi **11** gallimaufry **13** dog's breakfast

far-reaching
04 wide **05** broad **06** global **08** profound, sweeping, thorough **09** extensive, important, momentous **10** widespread **11** significant, wide-ranging **13** comprehensive

far-sighted
04 wise **05** acute, canny **06** shrewd **07** politic, prudent **08** cautious **09** far-seeing, judicious, prescient, provident **10** discerning **11** circumspect **14** forward-looking

farther
07 further, remoter **11** more distant, more extreme

farthest
08 furthest, remotest **11** most distant, most extreme

farthing
01 f **03** rag **06** farden **07** farding

fascia
04 band, sign **05** board, front, panel **06** fillet **07** console **08** platband **09** dashboard **15** instrument panel

fascinate
04 draw, lure **05** charm, rivet, witch **06** absorb, allure, entice **07** attract, beguile, bewitch, delight, enchant, engross, enthral **08** intrigue, transfix **09** captivate, enrapture, hypnotize, mesmerize, spellbind

fascinated
06 hooked **07** charmed, curious, enticed, smitten **08** absorbed, beguiled **09** bewitched, delighted, engrossed, entranced, intrigued **10** captivated, enthralled, hypnotized, infatuated, mesmerized, spellbound

fascinating
04 sexy **07** killing **08** alluring, charming, engaging, enticing, exciting, fetching, gripping, riveting, tempting, witching **09** absorbing, seductive **10** bewitching, compelling, compulsive, delightful, enchanting, engrossing, intriguing **11** captivating, interesting, mesmerizing, stimulating **12** irresistible

fascination
04 draw, lure, pull **05** charm, magic, spell **06** allure, appeal **07** delight, sorcery **08** interest, witchery **09** magnetism **10** attraction, compulsion **11** captivation, enchantment **13** preoccupation

fascism
09 autocracy, Falangism, Hitlerism **10** absolutism, Sinarchism **12** dictatorship **15** totalitarianism

fascist
04 duce, Nazi **08** autocrat **09** Falangist, Hitlerist, Hitlerite **10** absolutist, autocratic, Blackshirt, Brownshirt, sinarchist **12** totalitarian **13** authoritarian

fashion
◇ *anagram indicator*
03 cut, fad, fit, ton, way **04** fain, feat, form, kind, line, look, make, mode, rage, sort, suit, turn, twig, type, wear, work **05** adapt, alter, build, craze, faine, fayne, feign, model, mould, shape, smith, style, trend, vogue **06** adjust, aguise, aguize, create, custom, design, entail, latest, manner, method, system, tailor **07** clothes, couture, entayle, in thing, pattern **08** approach, practice, rag trade, tendency **09** construct **10** appearance, convention **11** high fashion, manufacture **12** haute couture **13** designer label **15** clothes industry, fashion business

Fashion designers include:

04 **Choo** (Jimmy), **Dior** (Christian), **Erté**, **Lang** (Helmut), **Muir** (Jean)
05 **Amies** (Sir Hardy), **Dolce** (Domenico), **Farhi** (Nicole), **Karan** (Donna), **Kenzo** (Takada), **Klein** (Calvin), **Ozbek** (Rifat), **Patou** (Jean), **Pucci** (Emilio), **Quant** (Mary), **Ricci** (Nina), **Smith** (Sir Paul)
06 **Armani** (Giorgio), **Ashley** (Laura), **Cardin** (Pierre), **Chanel** (Coco), **Conran** (Jasper), **Davies** (Betty), **Lauren** (Ralph), **Miyake** (Issey), **Rhodes** (Zandra), **Ungaro** (Emanuel)
07 **Balmain** (Pierre), **Fassett** (Kaffe), **Gabbana** (Stefano), **Hamnett** (Katharine), **Lacroix** (Christian), **Laroche** (Guy), **McQueen** (Alexander), **Missoni** (Tai Otavio), **Versace** (Gianni)
08 **Galliano** (John), **Gaultier** (Jean-Paul), **Givenchy** (Hubert James Marcel Taffin de), **Hartnell** (Sir Norman), **Hilfiger** (Tommy), **Molyneux** (Edward), **Oldfield** (Bruce), **Richmond** (John), **Westwood** (Dame Vivienne), **Yamamoto** (Yohji)
09 **Claiborne** (Liz), **Courrèges** (André), **Lagerfeld** (Karl), **McCartney** (Stella), **Valentino**
10 **Balenciaga** (Cristobal), **Mainbocher**, **Vanderbilt** (Gloria)
12 **Saint Laurent** (Yves), **Schiaparelli** (Elsa)

• **after a fashion**
08 in a sense **11** not very well **12** to some extent

• **current fashion**
02 go

• **out of fashion**
03 out **05** dated, passé **06** démodé, old hat, square **08** dismoded, obsolete, outmoded **09** out of date, unpopular **10** antiquated **12** old-fashioned **13** unfashionable

fashionable
02 in **03** fly, hip, hot **04** chic, cool, tony **05** culty, flash, funky, natty, ritzy, smart, toney, vogue **06** chichi, glitzy, latest, modern, modish, snappy, snazzy, swanky, trendy, with it **07** à la mode, cultish, current, elegant, genteel, in vogue, mondain, popular, stylish, swagger **08** all the go, designer, fantoosh, mondaine, swinging, up-to-date **09** exclusive, happening, high-toned **10** all the rage, prevailing **11** in the groove **12** contemporary **13** up-to-the-minute

fast
03 pdq **04** diet, firm, pacy, rash, shut, slim, wild **05** apace, brisk, faced, fiery, fixed, fleet, fully, hasty, nippy, pacey, quick, rapid, sound, swift, thick, tight **06** closed, deeply, firmly, flying, presto, secure, speedy, starve **07** abstain, express, fasting, fixedly, hastily, hurried, immoral, like mad, quickly, rapidly, refrain, riotous, swiftly, tightly **08** cracking, doggedly, exciting, fastened, go hungry, immobile, in a hurry, securely, speedily **09** breakneck, dissolute, fortified, high-speed, hurriedly, immovable, immovably, indelible, like a shot, like crazy, permanent, shameless, thrilling, turbulent **10** abstinence, blistering, boisterous, dissipated, like a flash, resolutely, starvation, stubbornly **11** accelerated, double-quick, lickety-spit, like the wind, ripsnorting **12** action-packed, deny yourself, dissipatedly, exhilarating, hunger strike, like the devil **13** extravagantly, like lightning, self-indulgent, unflinchingly **14** at a rate of knots, hell for leather **15** like the clappers

Fast-days and fasting periods include:

04 Lent
06 Ashura
07 Ramadan
08 Moharram, Muharram, Muharrem, Ramadhan, Tisha Bov

09 Ember-days, Tisha Baav, Tisha be'Ab, Tisha Be'Av, Tishah b'Ab, Tishah B'Av, Yom Kippur
10 Holy Friday
12 Golden Friday

fasten
03 aim, bar, fix, pin, tag, tie **04** bind, bolt, clip, do up, grip, join, lace, link, lock, moor, nail, seal, shut, spar, tack, zero **05** affix, chain, clamp, close, focus, hitch, latch, point, rivet, steek, unite, zip up **06** anchor, attach, buckle, button, direct, secure, take up, tether **07** connect **09** interlock **11** concentrate

fastened
02 to **05** bound

fastener, fastening

Fasteners include:

03 bar, fly, pin, tie, zip
04 bond, clip, frog, hasp, hook, knot, lace, link, lock, loop, nail, stud, tach, tack
05 catch, clasp, hinge, latch, morse, rivet, screw, tache
06 buckle, button, clinch, cotter, eyelet, holder, staple, stitch, tassel, toggle, Velcro®, zipper
07 padlock, tacking
08 cufflink, shoelace, split pin
09 paperclip, press stud, strapping
10 collar stud, hook-and-eye
11 bulldog clip, Chelsea clip, treasury tag
12 espagnolette
13 alligator clip, crocodile clip

fast food *see* **food**; **restaurant**

fastidious
04 nice **05** chary, faddy, fussy, picky **06** choosy, dainty, quaint, queasy, queazy, spruce **07** choosey, finicky, precise **08** delicate, overnice, precious **09** difficult, exquisite, niff-naffy, squeamish, superfine **10** meticulous, niffy-naffy, particular, pernickety, scrupulous **11** persnickety, punctilious **12** hard-to-please **13** hypercritical **14** discriminating

fat
02 OS **03** big, ghi, oil, pot, wax **04** bard, bulk, flab, fozy, ghee, lard, oily, rich, spek, suet, wide **05** beefy, broad, buxom, cream, dumpy, fatty, gross, heavy, keech, large, money, obese, plump, podgy, porky, pursy, round, solid, sonsy, speck, squab, stout, thick, tubby **06** butter, cheese, chubby, creesh, degras, flabby, fleshy, grease, greasy, lipoid, paunch, portly, rotund, tallow **07** adipose, blubber, fatness, fleshed, fulsome, in flesh, lanolin, obesity, paunchy, pinguid, sizable, tubbish **08** dripping, fruitful, generous, handsome, palmitin, pot belly, sizeable **09** animal fat, corpulent, fat as a pig, margarine, plumpness, sebaceous, solidness, spare tyre, stoutness **10** chubbiness, corpulence, deutoplasm, gor-bellied, kitchen-fee, oleaginous, overweight, pot-bellied, profitable **11** chylomicron, lipomatosis, substantial, well-endowed **12** considerable, saturated fat, steatopygous, vegetable fat **15** well-upholstered

fatal
05 final, vital **06** deadly, lethal, mortal **07** fateful, killing **08** critical, decisive, destined, terminal **09** incurable, malignant **10** calamitous, disastrous **11** destructive, mortiferous, unavoidable **12** catastrophic

fatalism
08 stoicism **09** endurance, passivity **10** acceptance **11** resignation

fatalistic
07 passive, patient, stoical **08** resigned, yielding **09** defeatist **10** reconciled, submissive **11** acquiescent **13** long-suffering, philosophical

fatality
04 dead, loss **05** death **08** casualty, disaster **09** lethality, mortality **10** deadliness **11** catastrophe

fate
03 end, lot **04** doom, joss, luck, Norn, ruin **05** cavel, death, event, issue, karma, Moera, Moira, Norna, stars, weird **06** chance, defeat, future, kismet **07** destiny, fortune, outcome **08** disaster, God's will **09** horoscope **10** ill-fortune, predestiny, providence **11** catastrophe, destruction **14** predestination

The Greek Fates:

06 Clotho
07 Atropos
08 Lachesis

The Norse Fates:

03 Urd
05 Skuld
08 Verdande

fated
03 fay, fey, fie **04** sure **06** doomed **07** certain **08** destined **09** enchanted **10** inevitable **11** ineluctable, inescapable, predestined, preordained, unavoidable **12** foreordained, predestinate

fateful
05 fatal **07** crucial, pivotal **08** critical, decisive **09** important, momentous, prophetic **10** portentous **11** significant

fatefully
09 crucially **10** critically, decisively **11** importantly, momentously **13** significantly

father
02 da, Fr, pa **03** dad, gov, guv, pop **04** abba, abbé, bapu, curé, male, papa, père, pops, sire **05** adopt, beget, daddy, elder, maker, padre, pappy, pater **06** author, invent, leader, old man, parent, parson, pastor, patron, priest **07** creator, founder, genitor, produce **08** ancestor, beau-pere, begetter, engender, forebear, governor, inventor, minister **09** architect, clergyman, initiator, originate, patriarch, procreate **10** forefather, give life to, originator, prime mover, procreator, progenitor **11** birth father, predecessor **12** guiding light **13** paterfamilias

Father Christmas
05 Santa **06** St Nick **10** Santa Claus **11** Kris Kringle **12** Kriss Kringle
See also **reindeer**

fatherland
04 home **08** homeland **10** motherland, native land, old country **13** mother-country **15** land of your birth

fatherly
04 kind **06** benign, kindly, tender **08** paternal **09** avuncular, indulgent **10** benevolent, forbearing, protective, supportive **11** patriarchal **12** affectionate

fathom
01 f **02** fm **03** fth, get, see **04** fthm, twig **05** gauge, grasp, plumb, probe, sound **06** rumble **07** measure, plummet, suss out, work out **08** estimate, perceive **09** interpret, latch onto, penetrate, search out **10** comprehend, understand **12** get the hang of

fathomless
04 deep **07** complex, endless **08** infinite **09** enigmatic, intricate **10** bottomless, mysterious **11** complicated **12** immeasurable, impenetrable

fatigue
02 ME **03** CFS, sap, tax **04** do up, PVFS, tire, toil **05** drain, weary **06** overdo, weaken **07** exhaust, wear out **08** debility, enervate, lethargy, overwork, weakness **09** lassitude, tiredness, weariness, yuppie flu **10** debilitate, enervation, exhaustion **11** take it out of **12** listlessness **13** wearisomeness

fatigued
04 beat **05** all in, jaded, tired, weary **06** beaten, bushed, done in, fagged, pooped, swink't, wasted, zonked **07** euchred, swinked, wappend, whacked **08** dead-beat, jiggered, tired out **09** exhausted, fagged out, knackered, overspent, overtired, pooped out **10** euchred out **11** tuckered out

fatness
04 bulk, flab **06** grease **07** obesity **08** richness **09** bulkiness, fertility, grossness, heaviness, largeness, plumpness, podginess, rotundity, stoutness, tubbiness **10** corpulence, corpulency, overweight, pinguidity, pinguitude, portliness

fatten
04 cram, feed, lard, soil **05** bloat, flesh, frank, stuff, swell, widen **06** batten, battle, enrich, expand, feed up, spread **07** broaden, build up, engross, fill out, nourish, nurture, thicken **08** overfeed, pinguefy, saginate **09** stall-feed

fatty
03 fat **04** oily, waxy **05** oleic, suety **06** creamy, fleshy, greasy, lipoid, suetty **07** adipose, buttery, pinguid **08** unctuous **09** aliphatic, sebaceous **10** oleaginous

fatuous
04 daft, gaga **05** dense, inane, moony, silly **06** absurd, stupid **07** asinine, foolish, idiotic, lunatic, moronic, puerile, vacuous, witless **08** imbecile, mindless **09** brainless, ludicrous **10** ridiculous, weak-minded

fault
◇ *anagram indicator*
03 bug, nag, sin **04** beam, boob, carp, flaw, flub, gall, goof, slam, slip, trap, vice **05** blame, error, fluff, hitch, judge, knock, lapse, pinch, scold, slate, wrong **06** booboo, defect, foible, glitch, impugn, nibble, slip-up **07** blemish, blunder, censure, default, demerit, failing, impeach, misdeed, mistake, offence, quarrel **08** omission, weakness **09** criticize, inculpate, liability, oversight, reprehend, weak point **10** culpa levis, deficiency, negligence, peccadillo, wrongdoing **11** culpability, delinquency, pick holes in, shortcoming **12** imperfection, indiscretion, misdemeanour, pull to pieces **13** answerability, call to account, find fault with **14** accountability, responsibility **15** blameworthiness

• at fault
◇ *anagram indicator*
03 out **05** wrong **06** guilty **07** at a loss, to blame **08** culpable **10** in the wrong **11** accountable, blameworthy, responsible

• to a fault
06 unduly **07** too much **09** extremely **10** over the top, to extremes **11** excessively **12** immoderately, inordinately, in the extreme **13** unnecessarily

fault-finding
04 crab **07** carping, nagging **08** captious, critical, niggling **09** cavilling, complaint, criticism, grumbling, querulous, quibbling **10** censorious, nit-picking **11** complaining **12** captiousness, pettifogging **13** hair-splitting, hypercritical **14** finger-pointing, hypercriticism

faultless
04 pure **05** model **07** correct, perfect **08** accurate, flawless, spotless **09** blameless, exemplary, lily-white, unsullied **10** immaculate, impeccable **11** unblemished **13** unimpeachable **14** irreproachable, without blemish

faulty
◇ *anagram indicator*
03 bad **04** bust, duff, weak **05** kaput, wonky, wrong **06** broken, flawed **07** damaged, invalid, vicious **08** culpable **09** casuistic, conked out, defective, erroneous, illogical, imperfect, incorrect, playing up **10** fallacious, inaccurate, not working, on the blink, out of order **11** inoperative, out of action **14** malfunctioning

Faunas
03 Pan

faux pas
04 boob, goof **05** error, gaffe **06** booboo, howler, slip-up **07** blunder, clanger, mistake **08** solecism **11** impropriety **12** indiscretion

favour
03 aid **04** back, boon, gree, help, like, pick **05** go for, grace, spoil **06** assist, choose, esteem, opt for, pamper, prefer, select **07** aggrace, approve, backing, benefit, endorse, indulge, make for, promote, service, succour, support **08** advocate, approval, befriend, champion, courtesy, good deed, good turn, goodwill, kindness, plump for, resemble, sanction, sympathy **09** advantage, encourage, patronage, recommend **10** acceptance, act of grace, assistance, attraction, indulgence, obligation, partiality, preference **11** approbation, countenance, favouritism **12** commendation, friendliness, take kindly to **13** act of kindness

• in favour of
03 for, pro **06** all for, behind **07** backing **10** supporting **11** on the side of

• obtain favour
03 win

favourable
04 fair, good, kind **05** white **06** benign, toward **08** amicable, Favonian, friendly, pleasing, positive, suitable, towardly **09** agreeable, approving, benignant, effective, opportune, promising **10** auspicious, beneficial, convenient, heartening, propitious, reassuring **11** appropriate, encouraging, meliorative, sympathetic **12** advantageous, enthusiastic, well-disposed **13** complimentary, understanding

favourably
04 well **09** agreeably, helpfully **10** in good part, positively, profitably **11** approvingly, fortunately, opportunely **12** auspiciously, conveniently, propitiously **14** advantageously **15** sympathetically

favoured
05 élite, fa'ard, faurd **06** chosen, graced **07** blessed, fancied **08** selected **09** favourite, predilect, preferred **10** advantaged, privileged **11** predilected, recommended

favourite
03 nap, pet **04** fave, idol, peat, pick **05** great **06** choice, chosen, minion, winger **07** beloved, best boy, darling, dearest, nostrum, special **08** Benjamin, best girl, esteemed, favoured, gracioso, white boy **09** best-loved, boyfriend, certainty, form horse, golden boy, most-liked, number one, preferred, treasured **10** girlfriend, particular, preference **11** blue-eyed boy, first choice, teacher's pet **12** likely winner **13** fair-haired boy **14** apple of your eye, white-headed boy **15** odds-on favourite

favouritism
04 bias **08** inequity, nepotism **09** injustice, prejudice **10** inequality, partiality, preference, unfairness **12** one-sidedness, partisanship

fawn
04 buff, claw **05** beige, court, crawl, creep, khaki, kotow, sandy, smalm, smarm, toady **06** cosy up, cozy up, cringe, crouch, grovel, kowtow **07** adulate, cervine, flatter, spaniel **08** bootlick, butter up, cosy up to, pay court, soft-soap, suck up to **09** pale brown **10** cozy up with **11** curry favour **12** bow and scrape, sand-coloured **14** be obsequious to, yellowish-brown

fawning
06 abject, supple **07** servile, spaniel **08** crawling, cringing, toadying, toadyish, unctuous **10** flattering, grovelling, obsequious, oleaginous **11** bootlicking, deferential, sycophantic **12** ingratiating, knee-crooking

fay *see* **fairy**

faze
03 rub **04** beat, rush, stun **05** drive, shake, shock, worry **06** dismay, put off, put out, puzzle, rattle **07** disturb, fluster, perturb, startle, unnerve **08** disquiet, drive off, surprise, unsettle **09** dumbfound, take aback **10** disconcert **12** perturbation

FBI member
03 Fed **04** G-man

fear
03 awe **04** risk **05** alarm, doubt, dread, panic, scope, worry **06** adread, affray, chance, dismay, expect, fright, honour, horror, phobia, qualms, regret, revere, terror, unease, wonder **07** anxiety, concern, foresee, phobism, redoubt, respect, shaking, suspect, terrify **08** aversion, be afraid, disquiet, distress, freak out, prospect, venerate, wonder at **09** agitation, bête noire, fear of God, nightmare, quivering, reverence, shudder at, suspicion, tremble at, trembling **10** anticipate, be afraid of, be scared of, foreboding, heart-quake, likelihood, likeliness, misgivings, shrink from, solicitude,

tremble for, uneasiness, veneration **11** expectation, fearfulness, pantophobia, possibility, probability, trepidation **12** affrightment, apprehension, get the wind up, stand in awe of, take fright at **13** be in a blue funk, be uneasy about, consternation, have a horror of, lose your nerve **14** be anxious about, be in a cold sweat, lose your bottle, your heart melts **15** have qualms about, hold in reverence

• for fear that
04 lest

fearful
04 dire, grim **05** adred, afear, awful, ferly, nervy, tense, timid **06** afraid, aghast, hunted, scared, uneasy, yellow **07** alarmed, anxious, ghastly, hideous, in dread, nervous, panicky, shaking **08** affrayed, agitated, dreadful, effraide, fearsome, gruesome, hesitant, horrible, horrific, shocking, terrible, timorous **09** appalling, atrocious, frightful, harrowing, monstrous, petrified, quivering, spineless, trembling, tremulous **10** frightened **11** distressing, in a blue funk **12** apprehensive, faint-hearted, in a cold sweat **13** having kittens, scared to death

fearfully
04 most, very, well **05** jolly **06** highly **07** awfully, timidly **08** terribly, uneasily **09** anxiously, extremely, intensely, nervously, unusually **10** dreadfully, hesitantly, incredibly **11** exceedingly, frightfully **12** terrifically, unbelievably **13** exceptionally **14** apprehensively

fearless
04 bold, game **05** brave, gutsy, proud **06** ballsy, daring, feisty, gritty, heroic, plucky, spunky **07** aweless, doughty, gallant, impavid, valiant **08** intrepid, unafraid, valorous **09** confident, dauntless, unabashed, undaunted **10** courageous, unblinking **11** indomitable, lion-hearted, unblenching, unflinching **14** unapprehensive

fearsome
04 unco **05** awful **07** awesome, dreaded **08** alarming, daunting, horrible, horrific, menacing, terrible **09** appalling, dismaying, frightful, unnerving **10** formidable, horrendous, horrifying, terrifying **11** frightening, hair-raising **12** awe-inspiring

feasibility
09 viability **10** expedience **11** possibility, workability **12** practicality **13** achievability **14** practicability, reasonableness

feasible
02 on **06** doable, likely, viable **08** possible, probable, workable **09** expedient, practical, realistic **10** achievable, attainable, realizable, reasonable **11** practicable **14** accomplishable

feast
02 do **03** ale, pig **04** fest, fete, gala, luau, wake, Yule **05** agape, beano, binge, gaudy, gorge, hangi, Purim, revel, treat **06** bridal, dinner, double, Isodia, junket, kaikai, Lammas, pig out, regale, repast, revels, spread, Sukkot, wealth **07** banquet, blow-out, convive, holiday, holy day, lamb-ale, name day, potlach, Rood Day, Shavuot, Sukkoth **08** carnival, carousal, feast day, festival, Id al-Adha, Id al-Fitr, Passover, potlatch, Shabuoth, Shavuoth, Shevuoth **09** abundance, Eid al-Adha, Eid al-Fitr, entertain, epulation, Hallowmas, indulge in, junketing, love-feast, Martinmas, Martlemas, partake of, Pentecost, profusion, saint's day **10** cornucopia, jour de fête, Roodmas Day, slap-up meal **11** celebration, eat your fill, festivities, Holy-rood Day, wine and dine **13** All-hallowmass

feat
03 act, art **04** deed **05** point, skill **06** action, henner, splits, stroke **07** exploit **08** hat trick, shanghai **09** keepy-uppy **10** attainment, Houdini act **11** achievement, performance, tour de force, undertaking **14** accomplishment

feather
03 pen **04** down, tuft **05** crest, egret, penna, pinna, plume, quill, wedge **06** covert, fletch, hackle, manual, pinion, sickle **07** plumage, plumula, plumule, primary, rectrix, tectrix **08** aigrette, standard, tertiary, vibrissa **09** condition, filoplume, secondary, semiplume

• coil of feathers
03 boa

• part of feather
04 harl, herl

feathery
04 soft **05** downy, light, plumy, wispy **06** fledgy, fleecy, flimsy, fluffy, plumed **07** plumate, plumose, plumous **08** delicate **09** feathered, penniform **10** pennaceous **11** featherlike

feature
03 act, mug, pan **04** chin, dial, face, form, item, mark, nose, phiz, show, side, star **05** clock, facet, focus, looks, piece, point, shape, story, trait **06** appear, aspect, beauty, column, factor, figure, kisser, phizog, play up, report, visage **07** article, comment, perform, phantom, present, promote, quality **08** hallmark, property **09** attribute, character, emphasize, highlight, lineament, spotlight **10** accentuate, attraction, focal point, lineaments, speciality **11** centrepiece, countenance, participate, peculiarity, physiognomy **14** characteristic **15** call attention to, draw attention to

featureless
04 dull **05** bland, blank, plain, vague **07** anaemic, insipid, vanilla **08** ordinary **11** commonplace, nondescript, uninspiring **12** cookie cutter, run of the mill, unattractive, unclassified, unremarkable **13** indeterminate, undistinctive, unexceptional, uninteresting **14** common or garden **15** undistinguished

febrile
03 hot **05** fiery **07** burning, fevered, flushed, pyretic **08** feverish, inflamed **09** delirious

February
03 Feb

feckless
03 wet **04** weak **06** feeble, futile, no-good **07** aimless, useless, wimpish **08** helpless, hopeless **09** shiftless, worthless **11** incompetent, ineffectual **13** irresponsible

fecund
07 fertile, teeming **08** fruitful, prolific **09** feracious, fructuous **10** productive **12** fructiferous

fecundity
08 feracity **09** fertility **12** fruitfulness **14** productiveness

federal
03 Fed **06** allied, united **07** unified **08** combined, in league **10** associated, integrated **11** amalgamated **12** confederated

federate
04 ally **05** unify, unite **06** league **07** combine **09** associate, integrate, syndicate **10** amalgamate **11** confederate **12** confederated, join together

federation
05 union **06** league **08** alliance, federacy **09** coalition, syndicate **11** association, combination, confederacy **12** amalgamation **13** confederation, copartnership

fed up
03 ate **04** blue, down, glum, jack **05** bored, jaded, sated, tired, weary **06** dismal, gloomy **07** annoyed, chocker, pig sick **09** depressed, hacked off, pissed off **10** brassed off, browned off, cheesed off **11** disgruntled **12** discontented, dissatisfied, sick and tired **13** have had enough

fee
03 due, pay, sub **04** bill, cost, fine, hire, rent, toll, wage **05** money, price, terms, tithe, tythe **06** cattle, charge, hirage, mouter, reward, salary, towage **07** account, faldage, footing, hireage, moorage, multure, payment, premium, service, tuition **08** chummage, pilotage, property, retainer **09** emolument, livestock, obvention, ownership, refresher, vassalage **10** bell-siller, honorarium, possession, recompense **11** inheritance **12** remuneration, subscription **15** appearance money

feeble
03 wet 04 lame, poor, puny, tame, thin, weak 05 faint, frail, silly, sober, washy, wersh, wussy 06 ailing, debile, effete, flabby, flimsy, futile, infirm, sickly, slight, weakly 07 failing, rickety, wastrel, wearish, wimpish 08 daidling, decrepit, delicate, feckless, helpless, lustless, pathetic, sackless
09 enervated, exhausted, graspless, powerless, weak-kneed 10 dispirited, fizzenless, foisonless, impuissant, inadequate, indecisive, namby-pamby, spiritless, wishy-washy 11 debilitated, fushionless, incompetent, ineffective, ineffectual, vacillating
12 unconvincing, unsuccessful

feeble-minded
04 dumb 05 dotty, silly 06 simple, stupid 07 idiotic, moronic
08 imbecile, retarded 09 deficient, dim-witted, imbecilic 10 half-witted, indecisive, slow-witted, weak-minded
11 not all there 13 soft in the head
14 mouth breathing, not the full quid
15 slow on the uptake

feebly
06 lamely, sickly, weakly 07 faintly
08 slightly 10 helplessly
11 powerlessly 12 dispiritedly, indecisively, pathetically
13 ineffectively

feed
◇ *insertion indicator*
03 eat, put 04 crop, dine, food, fuel, give, paid, slip, soil, tire 05 graze, slide
06 battle, browse, dine on, fodder, forage, foster, insert, repast, silage, stooge, suckle, supply, take in, tuck-in
07 consume, deliver, fortify, gratify, nourish, nurture, pasture, provide, support, victual 08 cater for, ruminate
09 encourage, foodstuff, introduce, partake of, provender 10 give food to, provide for, strengthen

feedback
05 reply 06 answer 08 comeback, response 11 respondence

feel
02 be 03 air, paw, rub 04 aura, bear, bent, deem, gift, hand, hold, know, look, maul, mood, palp, poke, seem
05 enjoy, flair, grasp, grope, judge, knack, nurse, sense, skill, think, touch, vibes 06 appear, caress, clutch, detect, endure, finger, finish, fondle, fumble, handle, notice, reckon, stroke, suffer, talent 07 ability, believe, contact, discern, faculty, feeling, harbour, massage, observe, quality, realize, surface, texture, undergo
08 ambience, aptitude, consider, instinct, perceive 09 be aware of, give way to, go through 10 atmosphere, experience, impression, manipulate, understand 11 consistency, live through 12 be overcome by 15 feel in your bones

• **feel for**
04 pity 07 weep for 09 be moved by, grieve for 10 be sorry for, sympathize
11 commiserate 13 empathize with
14 sympathize with 15 commiserate with

• **feel like**
04 want, wish 05 fancy 06 desire
09 would like

feeler
04 horn, palp 05 probe 06 palpus
07 advance, antenna 08 approach, overture, tentacle 09 overtures
10 sense organ 12 ballon d'essai, trial balloon

feeling
03 air, ego 04 aura, bent, care, feel, gift, idea, love, mood, pity, view
05 flair, hunch, knack, sense, skill, touch, vibes 06 ardour, belief, motion, notion, spirit, talent, theory, warmth
07 ability, concern, emotion, fervour, inkling, opinion, passion, pitying, quality, thought 08 aptitude, emotions, esthesia, fondness, instinct, passions, sympathy 09 aesthesia, aesthesis, affection, intensity, intuition, sensation, sentience, sentiment, suspicion 10 affections, atmosphere, compassion, Empfindung, impression, perception, self-esteem, tenderness
11 point of view, sensibility, sensitivity, sympathetic 12 appreciation
13 compassionate, sensibilities, sensitivities, understanding, way of thinking 14 natural ability, sentimentality, susceptibility

• **show feeling**
05 emote

• **with no feeling**
04 numb

feign
03 act 04 fain, fake, sham 05 fable, faine, false, fayne, forge, put on, shape
06 affect, assume, gammon, invent, make up 07 falsify, fashion, imagine, imitate, pretend, put it on 08 misfeign, simulate 09 dissemble, fabricate
11 counterfeit, dissimulate, make a show of, make believe

feint
04 play, ruse, sham, wile 05 blind, bluff, dodge, dummy 06 gambit 08 artifice, pretence 09 deception, expedient, manoeuvre, stratagem 10 subterfuge
11 distraction, make-believe, mock-assault 12 dissemblance

feisty
04 bold 05 brave, gutsy, tough
06 gritty, lively, plucky, spunky, touchy
08 spirited 09 excitable, irritable
10 courageous, determined

feldspar, felspar
06 albite 08 adularia, andesine, sanidine, sunstone 09 anorthite, moonstone 10 hyalophane, oligoclase, orthoclase 11 anorthosite, labradorite, peristerite, plagioclase

felicitous
03 apt 05 happy 06 timely
07 apropos, fitting 08 apposite, inspired, suitable 09 fortunate, opportune, well-timed 10 delightful, propitious, prosperous, well-chosen, well-turned 11 appropriate
12 advantageous

felicity
03 joy 05 bliss 07 aptness, delight, ecstasy, rapture 08 blessing, euphoria
09 eloquence, happiness, propriety
11 delectation, suitability
12 suitableness 13 applicability
15 appropriateness

feline
03 cat, tom 04 eyra, puss 05 catty, felid, manul, moggy, ounce, pussy, queen, quoll, rumpy, sleek, tabby
06 kitten, malkin, mouser, ocelot, serval, slinky, smooth, Tibert, tomcat
07 catlike, cattish, leonine, sensual, sinuous, wildcat 08 alleycat, baudrons, graceful, stealthy 09 grimalkin, sealpoint, seductive 10 jaguarundi

See also **cat**

fell
02 ax, KO 03 axe, hew, lit, log 04 alit, dire, gall, hide, hill, keen, moor, pelt, raze, skin, very 05 cruel, felon, floor, great, level 06 deadly, fierce, lay low, mighty, poleax 07 cut down, doughty, flatten, poleaxe, pungent 08 chop down, demolish, felonous, membrane, ruthless 09 knock down, overthrow, prostrate 10 bitterness, strike down
15 raze to the ground

fellow
01 F, m 02 bo, co-, he 03 boy, bud, cat, cod, don, guy, Joe, lad, man, pal, sod, wag 04 bozo, chap, chum, cove, dean, dude, gent, like, male, mate, oppo, peer, twin 05 bloke, buddy, crony, devil, equal, match 06 buffer, callan, double, friend, person, rascal, sister
07 callant, compeer, comrade, partner, related, similar 08 confrère, co-worker
09 associate, boyfriend, character, colleague, companion, semblable
10 associated, compatriot, individual
11 counterpart 12 contemporary

See also **boy**

• **little fellow**
03 elf, imp

fellow feeling
04 care 07 empathy, feeling
08 sympathy 10 compassion
13 commiseration, understanding

fellowship
04 club 05 guild, order, union
06 league 07 society 08 intimacy, matiness, sodality, sorority
09 communion, palliness 10 affability, amiability, chumminess, consortium, fraternity, friendship, sisterhood
11 affiliation, association, brotherhood, camaraderie, comradeship, familiarity, sociability
13 companionship, compatibility

felon *see* **criminal**

felspar *see* **feldspar, felspar**

felt
03 bat **04** batt

female
01 f **03** doe, -ess, gal, hen, her, pen, rib, she **04** bird, girl, hind, miss **05** woman
06 maiden **07** girlish, womanly
08 feminine, ladylike, womanish
09 petticoat **10** carpellate, pistillate
See also **animal**; **girl**

feminine
01 f **03** fem **04** weak **05** cissy, girly
06 female, gentle, pretty, tender
07 girlish, unmanly, wimpish, womanly
08 delicate, graceful, ladylike, womanish **09** petticoat **10** effeminate

femininity
08 delicacy **09** sissiness, womanhood
10 effeminacy, gentleness, muliebrity, prettiness, tenderness **11** girlishness, womanliness **12** feminineness, gracefulness, womanishness

feminism
09 women's lib **12** women's rights
14 women's movement

Feminists include:

04 **Daly** (Mary), **Hite** (Shere), **Mott** (Lucretia), **Shaw** (Anna Howard), **Wolf** (Naomi)
05 **Abzug** (Bella), **Astor** (Nancy), **Beale** (Dorothea), **Greer** (Germaine), **Stone** (Lucy)
06 **Callil** (Carmen), **Cixous** (Hélène), **Faludi** (Susan), **Friday** (Nancy), **Fuller** (Margaret), **Gilman** (Charlotte Perkins), **Grimké** (Sarah Moore), **Orbach** (Susie), **Rankin** (Jeannette), **Stopes** (Marie), **Weldon** (Fay)
07 **Anthony** (Susan B), **Davison** (Emily), **Dworkin** (Andrea), **Egerton** (Sarah), **Fawcett** (Dame Millicent), **Friedan** (Betty), **Goldman** (Emma), **Kennedy** (Helena, Baroness), **Lenclos** (Ninon de), **Steinem** (Gloria), **Tennant** (Emma)
08 **Beauvoir** (Simone de), **Brittain** (Vera), **MacPhail** (Agnes), **Rathbone** (Eleanor)
09 **Blackwell** (Elizabeth), **Pankhurst** (Adela), **Pankhurst** (Christabel), **Pankhurst** (Emmeline), **Pankhurst** (Sylvia)
11 **Burgos Seguí** (Carmen de)
14 **Wollstonecraft** (Mary)

femme fatale
04 vamp **05** Circe, siren **06** Sirens
07 charmer, Delilah, Lorelei **08** Mata Hari **09** temptress **10** seductress
11 enchantress

fen
03 bog **04** moss, quag, wash
05 marsh, swamp **06** morass, slough
08 quagmire

fence
◇ *containment indicator*
03 hay, pen **04** coop, oxer, pale, rail, wall, wear, weir, wire **05** bound, dodge, evade, guard, hedge, parry
06 defend, fraise, paling, pusher, rasper, rustic, secure, shield, shut in
07 barrier, confine, defence, enclose, fortify, inclose, protect, quibble, railing, rampart **08** encircle, palisade, palisado, restrict, separate, sepiment, stockade, surround **09** barricade, enclosure, pussyfoot, stonewall, vacillate, windbreak **10** digladiate, equivocate, trafficker **11** prevaricate
12 circumscribe, shilly-shally, tergiversate
• **sit on the fence**
06 dither **08** be unsure **09** vacillate
11 be uncertain, be undecided **12** be irresolute, shilly-shally **13** be uncommitted **14** blow hot and cold

fencing
07 railing **08** guarding **09** defending, swordplay

Fencing terms include:

03 bib, cut, hit
04 bout, épée, foil, pass, pink, volt, ward
05 allez, appel, carte, feint, forte, lunge, parry, piste, prime, punto, sabre, sixte, touch, volte
06 attack, button, come in, doigté, faible, flèche, foible, octave, parade, puncto, quarte, quinte, remise, thrust, tierce, touché
07 barrage, counter, en garde, on guard, passado, reprise, riposte, seconde, septime, stop hit
08 back edge, balestra, coquille, plastron, tac-au-tac, traverse
09 disengage, repechage
10 flanconade, imbroccata, time-thrust
11 corps à corps, punto dritto
12 colichemarde, counter-parry, punto reverso
14 counter-riposte

fend
05 avert, parry, repel **06** defend, divert, resist **07** beat off, deflect, head off, keep off, provide, repulse, shut out, support, sustain, ward off **08** maintain, stave off **09** hold at bay, look after, turn aside **10** take care of

feral
04 wild **06** animal, brutal, deadly, fierce, savage **07** bestial, brutish, untamed, vicious **08** funereal, unbroken **09** ferocious
12 uncultivated **14** undomesticated

ferment
◇ *anagram indicator*
04 boil, brew, foam, fret, fuss, heat, rise, stew, stir, work, zyme **05** cause, fever, froth, mould, rouse, yeast
06 arouse, bubble, enzyme, excite, fester, foment, frenzy, furore, hubbub, incite, leaven, seethe, stir up, tumult, unrest, uproar, work up **07** agitate, inflame, provoke, ptyalin, turmoil
08 bacteria, brouhaha, smoulder
09 agitation, commotion, confusion
10 disruption, effervesce, excitement, turbulence

fermium
02 Fm

fern

Ferns include:

03 oak
04 hard, lady, male, tree
05 beech, brake, chain, crown, holly, marsh, royal, sword, water
06 Boston, ribbon, shield, silver, tongue
07 bladder, bracken, buckler, Dickie's, elkhorn, Goldie's, leather, ostrich, parsley, rockcap, wall rue, woodsia
08 aspidium, cinnamon, climbing, hairy lip, licorice, moonwort, pillwort, polypody, staghorn
09 asparagus, asplenium, bird's nest, hare's foot, rusty-back, sensitive
10 Asian chain, Korean rock, maidenhair, soft shield, spleenwort
11 hart's tongue, rabbit's foot
12 broad buckler, elephant's ear, resurrection
13 crested ribbon, Japanese holly, scolopendrium, squirrel's foot
14 brittle bladder
15 Japanese painted

ferocious
04 deep, grim, wild **05** cruel, feral
06 bitter, brutal, fierce, savage, severe, strong **07** extreme, inhuman, intense, salvage, untamed, vicious, violent
08 barbaric, pitiless, ruthless, sadistic, Tartarly, vigorous **09** barbarous, merciless, murderous **12** bloodthirsty, catamountain, cat o' mountain

ferocity
06 sadism **07** cruelty **08** savagery, severity, violence, wildness
09 barbarity, brutality, extremity, intensity **10** fierceness, inhumanity
11 viciousness **12** ruthlessness

ferret
03 hob **04** gill, hunt, jill **05** rifle, scour
06 forage, search **07** rummage **09** go through
• **ferret out**
04 find **05** dig up, trace **06** elicit
07 extract, nose out, root out, suss out, unearth, worm out **08** discover, hunt down **09** search out, track down
10 fossick out, run to earth

ferry
03 ply, run **04** boat, move, pont, ro-ro, ship, take, taxi **05** carry, drive, shift
06 convey, packet, ponton, vessel
07 passage, pontoon, shuttle, traject, tranect **08** car ferry **09** ferry-boat, transport **10** packet boat **12** flying bridge **13** Interislander®, roll-on roll-off

fertile
04 rich **06** battle, broody, fecund, potent, virile **08** abundant, creative, fruitful, inspired, pregnant, prolific
09 ingenious, inventive, luxuriant, visionary **10** generative, productive
11 imaginative, resourceful
12 reproductive

fertility
07 fatness, potency **08** richness, virility **09** abundance, fecundity **10** luxuriance **12** fruitfulness, prolificness **14** generativeness, productiveness

fertilization
03 IVF **04** ICSI **07** selfing **10** conception **11** fecundation, pollination, procreation, propagation, siphonogamy **12** implantation, impregnation, insemination **13** palmification, superfetation

fertilize
04 dung, feed, self **05** dress, mulch **06** enrich, manure **07** compost **08** fructify, top-dress **09** fecundate, pollinate, procreate **10** impregnate, inseminate **12** make fruitful, make pregnant

fertilizer
04 dung, marl **05** guano, humus, mulch **06** manure **07** compost, humogen, kainite, nitrate, tankage **08** bone meal, dressing **09** cyanamide, plant food, soda nitre **10** fish-manure **11** top-dressing **13** sodium nitrate **14** superphosphate **15** ammonium nitrate

fervent
03 hot **04** warm **05** eager, fiery **06** ardent, devout **07** earnest, excited, intense, sincere, zealous **08** spirited, vehement, vigorous **09** emotional, energetic, heartfelt **10** passionate **11** full-blooded, impassioned **12** enthusiastic, wholehearted

fervently
07 eagerly **08** ardently **09** earnestly, excitedly, intensely, sincerely **10** vigorously **11** emotionally **12** passionately **13** energetically **14** wholeheartedly

fervour
04 fire, heat, hwyl, zeal **05** verve **06** ardour, energy, spirit, vigour, warmth **07** emotion, passion **09** animation, eagerness, intensity, sincerity, vehemence **10** enthusiasm, excitement **11** earnestness

fester
03 irk, rot **04** brew, gall **05** anger, annoy, chafe, decay, go bad **06** gather, infect, perish, rankle **07** moulder, putrefy **08** maturate, smoulder, ulcerate **09** decompose, discharge, suppurate

festival
03 ale **04** fair, fete, gala, play, tide, wake **05** feast, festa, party, revel **06** double, fiesta, pardon **07** gala day, high day, holiday, jubilee **08** carnival, high tide, panegyry **10** merry-night, semi-double **11** anniversary, celebration, festivities, merrymaking **13** commemoration, entertainment

See also **celebration**; **service**

Ancient festivals and celebrations include:

03 Bon, Mod
04 feis, Lots, Yule
05 Purim, Saman, Weeks, Wesak
06 Advent, Diwali, Easter, Floria, Lammas, May Day, Oimelc, Opalia, Pesach, Plebii
07 Beltane, Equiria, Feralia, Fugalia, holy-ale, Imbolic, Lady Day, Lemuria, Mop Fair, Navrati, Palilia, Parilia, Ramadan, Samhain, Sukkoth, Sullani, Theseia, Vinalia
08 Agonalia, Cerealia, Fasching, Faunalia, Floralia, Hanukkah, Hogmanay, Homstrom, Hull Fair, Id ul-Adha, Id ul-Fitr, Lucia Day, Lugnasad, Mahayana, Matralia, Nit de toc, Passover, Samhuinn, Setsubun, Shabuoth, Stow Fair, Tanabata, Vestalia
09 Baishakhi, Boxing Day, Christmas, church-ale, Floralies, Goose Fair, Hallowe'en, Hallowmas, Ides of Mar, Liberalia, Ludi Magni, Lugnasadh, Magalesia, Magha-puja, Mardi Gras, Martinmas, Nemoralia, Paganalia, Pentecost, Puanepsia, Robigalia, Thargelia, Ullambana, Up-Helly-Aa, Wakes Week, Yom Kippur
10 Allhallows, Ambarvalia, Barnet Fair, Fordicidia, Fornicalia, Good Friday, Larentalia, La Tomatina, Lee Gap Fair, Ludi Romani, Lupercalia, Matronalia, Mother's Day, Neptunalia, Palm Sunday, Pancake Day, Parentalia, Portunalia, Quirinalia, Regifugium, Saturnalia, Swan Upping, Terminalia, Volcanalia
11 Acension Day, All Fools' Day, All Souls' Day, Bacchanalia, Carmentalia, Epulum Jovis, Hina Matsuri, Lady Luck Day, Oktoberfest, Oskhophoria, Panathenaea, Quinquatrus, Semo Sanctus, St David's Day, Tabernacles
12 All Saints' Day, Annunciation, Armilustrium, Ash Wednesday, Barranquilla, Day of the Dead, Doll Festival, Holy Wells Day, Kanda Matsuri, Ludi Merceruy, Mahashivrati, Meditrinalia, Moon Festival, Nutters Dance, Rosh Hashanah, St Andrew's Day, St George's Day, Thanksgiving, Tubilustrium, Twelfth Night, Well-dressing
13 April Fool's Day, Haxey Hood Game, Ludi Consualia, Ludi Martiales, Midsummer's Eve, Raksha Bandhan, Shrove Tuesday, St Patrick's Day, The Furry Dance, Water Festival, Widecombe Fair
14 Chinese New Year, Maundy Thursday, St Nicholas's Day, Vinalia Rustica, Walpurgis Night
15 Festival of Light, Harvest Festival, Lares Praestites, Ludi Apollinares, Mahavira Jayanti, Mothering Sunday, Priddy Sheep Fair, St Valentine's Day

Modern festivals and celebrations include:

05 VE Day, VJ Day, WOMAD
08 Anzac Day, Earth Day, Labor Day
09 Canada Day, Labour Day
10 Burns Night, Eisteddfod
11 Bastille Day, Cinco de Mayo, Glastonbury, Republic Day, Waitangi Day
12 Armistice Day, Australia Day, Bonfire Night, Glyndebourne, Groundhog Day
13 New Zealand Day
14 Guy Fawkes' Night, Remembrance Day
15 Edinburgh Fringe, Edinburgh Tattoo, Independence Day

Religious festivals include:

02 Id
03 Eid
04 Holi, Lent, Lots, mela, Obon, Oram, puja, Yule
05 Litha, Pesah, Purim
06 Advent, Bakrid, Basant, Dhamma, Divali, Diwali, Easter, Lammas, Pesach, Sukkot
07 Baisaki, Beltane, holy day, matsuri, New Year, Ramadan, Samhain, Shavuot, Sukkoth
08 All Souls, Baisakhi, Dipavali, Dusserah, Epiphany, feast day, Hanukkah, Id-al-Adha, Id al-Fitr, Id-ul-Zuha, Muharram, Passover
09 All Saints, Ascension, Candlemas, Christmas, Deepavali, Dolayatra, Durga-puja, Easter Day, Eid-al-Adha, Eid al-Fitr, Mardi Gras, Navaratri, Oshogatsu, Pentecost, Up-Helly-Aa, Yom Kippur
10 All Hallows, Assumption, Good Friday, Lughnasadh, Lupercalia, Michaelmas, Palm Sunday, Ramanavami, Rathayatra, Saturnalia, Vulcanalia, Whit Sunday
11 All Souls' Day, Bacchanalia, Lakshmi-puja, Milad-un-Nabi, Panathenaea, Rosh Hashana
12 All Saints' Day, Annunciation, Ascension Day, Ash Wednesday, Christmas Day, Easter Sunday, Holy Saturday, Holy Thursday, Night of Power, Ohinamatsuri, Prakash Utsav, Rosh Hashanah, Simchat Torah, Star Festival, Tango no Sekku
13 Buddha Purnima, Corpus Christi, Holy Innocents, Night of Ascent, Passion Sunday, spring equinox, Trinity Sunday, vernal equinox
14 Chinese New Year, Day of Atonement, Easter Saturday, Maundy Thursday, summer solstice, winter solstice
15 autumnal equinox, Lantern Festival, Tanabata Matsuri, Transfiguration

• **day before a festival**
03 eve
• **octave of a festival**
04 utas

festive
04 gala **05** happy, jolly, merry

06 cheery, festal, hearty, jovial, joyful, joyous **07** cordial, holiday **08** carnival, cheerful, feastful, jubilant **09** convivial **11** celebratory **12** light-hearted

festivity
03 fun, rag **04** gala, gaud **05** party, revel, sport **06** fiesta, gaiety, let-off **07** jollity, joyance, revelry, triumph **08** carousal, feasting, festival, pleasure **09** amusement, enjoyment, joviality, junketing, merriment **10** banqueting, cheeriness, joyfulness, jubilation **11** celebration, fun and games, merrymaking **12** cheerfulness, conviviality **13** entertainment, glorification, jollification

festoon
04 deck, hang, swag **05** adorn, array, drape **06** bedeck, swathe, wreath **07** bedizen, chaplet, garland, garnish, wreathe **08** decorate, encarpus, ornament

fetch
03 fet, get **04** earn, fett, make, take **05** bring, carry, ghost, go for, reach, yield **06** arrive, attain, convey, derive, double, escort **07** bring in, collect, conduct, deliver, realize, sell for **08** go and get **09** stratagem, transport **10** apparition
- **fetch up**
05 end up, vomit **06** arrive, show up, turn up, wind up **07** recover **08** finish up **11** materialize

fetching
04 cute **05** sweet **06** pretty **07** winsome **08** adorable, alluring, charming **09** appealing **10** attractive, enchanting **11** captivating, fascinating

fête, fete
04 fair, gala **05** treat **06** bazaar, honour, regale **07** holiday, lionize, welcome **08** carnival, festival **09** entertain **10** sale of work **11** garden party

fetid, foetid
04 foul, rank **05** pongy **06** filthy, rancid, sickly, smelly, whiffy **07** humming, noisome, noxious, odorous, reeking **08** mephitic, stinking **09** offensive **10** disgusting, graveolent, malodorous, nauseating

fetish
03 obi **04** idol, ju-ju, obia **05** charm, image, mania, obeah, thing, totem **06** amulet **08** fixation, idée fixe, talisman **09** obsession **10** cult object

fetter
03 tie **04** bind, curb, gyve, iron **05** chain, tie up, truss **06** hamper, hinder, hobble, impede **07** confine, hopples, leg-iron, manacle, shackle **08** encumber, obstruct, restrain, restrict **09** constrain, entrammel, hamstring **10** hamshackle

fetters
05 bands, bonds, curbs, irons **06** chains, checks, slangs **07** bondage **08** manacles, shackles **09** bracelets, captivity, handcuffs **10** hindrances, restraints **11** constraints, inhibitions **12** obstructions, restrictions

fettle
◇ *anagram indicator*
- **in fine fettle**
03 fit **04** trim **05** sound **06** on form, strong **07** healthy, in shape **09** shipshape **10** in fine form, in good nick **11** in good shape **12** in good health **13** hale and hearty **15** in good condition

feud
03 row, war **04** duel, food **05** argue, brawl, clash, fight **06** bicker, enmity, strife **07** contend, discord, dispute, ill will, quarrel, rivalry, wrangle **08** argument, bad blood, be at odds, conflict, squabble, vendetta **09** altercate, animosity, bickering, hostility **10** antagonism, bitterness **12** disagreement

fever
04 heat **06** frenzy, unrest **07** ecstasy, ferment, passion, pyrexia, turmoil **08** delirium **09** agitation, calenture **10** excitement **11** temperature **12** feverishness, restlessness **15** high temperature

Fevers include:

01 Q
03 hay, tap
04 ague, camp, gaol, gold, jail, Rock, ship, tick, worm
05 brain, cabin, dandy, Lassa, Malta, marsh, stage, swamp, swine, Texas
06 dengue, dumdum, hectic, jungle, parrot, plague, rabbit, spring, trench, typhus, valley, yellow
07 biliary, enteric, gastric, malaria, measles, ratbite, sandfly, scarlet, splenic, spotted, typhoid, verruga
08 childbed, kala-azar, undulant
09 breakbone, calenture, East Coast, glandular, phrenitis, puerperal, relapsing, remittent, rheumatic
10 blackwater, Rift Valley, scarlatina, yellow Jack
12 African coast
13 cerebrospinal, leptospirosis, Mediterranean
14 kissing disease
15 acute rheumatism

fevered
03 hot, red **07** burning, excited, febrile, flushed, frantic, nervous **08** feverish, frenzied, restless, worked up **09** impatient **10** passionate

feverish
◇ *anagram indicator*
03 hot, red **05** hasty **06** hectic, rushed **07** burning, excited, febrile, flushed, frantic, hurried, in a tizz, nervous **08** agitated, bothered, febrific, frenzied, in a tizzy, restless, troubled, worked up **09** delirious, flustered, impatient, in a dither **10** passionate **11** overwrought **12** in a kerfuffle **14** hot and bothered

few
04 rare, some, thin **05** scant, wheen **06** meagre, scanty, scarce, sparse **07** a couple, handful, not many, several **08** one or two, sporadic, uncommon **09** a minority, exclusive, hardly any **10** inadequate, infrequent, negligible, scattering, sprinkling, two or three **11** scarcely any **12** insufficient **13** in short supply **14** a small number of, inconsiderable **15** thin on the ground

fey
03 fay, fie, odd, shy **05** dotty, droll, elfin, funny, weird **06** doomed, quaint, quirky **07** curious, playful, unusual **08** childish, fanciful, peculiar **09** eccentric, impulsive, whimsical **10** capricious **11** mischievous **12** supernatural **13** unpredictable

fiancé, fiancée
08 intended, wife-to-be **09** betrothed, bride-to-be **10** future wife **11** husband-to-be **13** future husband **14** bridegroom-to-be **15** prospective wife

fiasco
04 bomb, flop, mess, rout, ruin **05** flask **06** bottle, fizzer, lash-up **07** cropper, debacle, failure, screw-up, washout **08** calamity, collapse, disaster **09** damp squib **11** catastrophe

fiat
02 OK **05** edict, order **06** decree, dictum, diktat **07** command, dictate, mandate, precept, warrant **08** sanction **09** directive, ordinance **10** injunction, permission **12** proclamation **13** authorization

fib
03 gag, lie **04** tale, yarn **05** evade, fable, porky, punch, story **06** invent, pummel **07** evasion, falsify, fantasy, fiction, untruth, whopper **08** sidestep, white lie **09** dissemble, fabricate, falsehood, fantasize, invention **10** concoction, taradiddle **11** prevaricate, tarradiddle **13** prevarication

fibre
04 coir, hair, pile, pita, silk **05** cloth, nerve, sinew, stuff, viver **06** fibril, make-up, nature, strand, thread **07** calibre, courage, funicle, resolve, stamina, tendril, texture **08** backbone, filament, firmness, material, roughage, strength **09** character, substance, toughness, willpower **10** resolution **11** disposition, temperament **12** resoluteness **13** determination

fibres
03 tow **04** pons

fickle
◇ *anagram indicator*
06 kittle, labile, volage **07** flighty, mutable **08** disloyal, unstable, unsteady, variable, volatile **09** choiceful, faithless, mercurial, volageous **10** capricious, changeable, inconstant, irresolute, unfaithful, unreliable **11** treacherous,

vacillating **12** inconsistent, wind-changing **13** unpredictable

- **be fickle**

04 turn

fickleness

06 change, levity **09** treachery **10** disloyalty, fitfulness, mutability, volatility **11** flightiness, inconstancy, instability **12** unsteadiness **13** changeability, faithlessness, unreliability **14** capriciousness, changeableness, unfaithfulness

fiction

03 fib, lie **04** myth, pulp, tale, yarn **05** fable, story **06** legend, novels **07** fantasy, parable, romance, stories, untruth **08** chick lit, noveldom, pretence **09** falsehood, invention, tall story **10** concoction **11** fabrication **12** splatterpunk, storytelling **15** creative writing

See also **literature**; **non-fiction**

- **science fiction**

02 SF **05** sci-fi **09** cyberpunk

fictional

06 made-up, unreal **08** fabulous, invented, literary, mythical **09** imaginary, legendary **11** make-believe, non-existent **12** mythological

See also **literary**; **novel**

Fictional places include:

02 Ix, Oz
04 Alph, Rhun
05 Arnor, Holby, Moria, Rohan
06 Canley, Dibley, Gondor, Laputa, Leonia, Lorien, Mordor, Narnia, Titipu, Utopia, Vulcan, Wessex, Xanadu
07 Avonlea, Bedrock, Camelot, Erewhon, Eriador, Eurasia, Midwich, Mole End, Prydain, Sun Hill, Toyland, Walford
08 Ambridge, Blefuscu, Borduria, Calormen, Earthsea, Flatland, Hobbiton, Islandia, Lilliput, Llaregyb, Meccania, Mirkwood, New Crete, Polyglot, Ragnarok, Stepford, Syldavia, Sylvania, Tartarus, The Shire, Toad Hall
09 Barataria, Brigadoon, Discworld, Emmerdale, Freedonia, Hollyoaks, Llareggub, Ringworld, Rivendell, River Alph, Ruritania, Shangri-La, Summer Bay, Venusberg, Westworld
10 Archenland, Barchester, Borchester, Moominland, Shieldinch, Vanity Fair, Wonderland
11 Airstrip One, Ankh-Morpork, Barsetshire, Borsetshire, Brobdingnag, Diagon Alley, Emerald City, Gormenghast, Middle-Earth, Orbitsville, Skull Island, The Wild Wood
12 Albert Square, Celesteville, Erinsborough, Glubbdubdrib, Jurassic Park, Ramsay Street, Sleepy Hollow, Tralfamadore, Weatherfield
13 Celestial City, Christminster, Montego Street
14 Brookside Close, Doubting-Castle, Hogwarts School, Never-Never Land, Nightmare Abbey, Treasure Island
15 Baskerville Hall

fictitious

04 fake, sham **05** bogus, false **06** made-up, mythic, untrue **07** assumed, feigned, fictive **08** invented, mythical, romantic, spurious, supposed **09** concocted, imaginary **10** apocryphal, artificial, fabricated, improvised **11** counterfeit, non-existent

Fictitious places include:

07 Speewah
08 Woop Woop
10 Snake Gully
11 Bandywallop
12 Bullamakanka, Oodnagalahbi, Waikikamukau
13 the black stump

fiddle

02 do, gu **03** con, fix, gju, gue, kit, toy **04** fuss, play, rasp, rote, scam **05** cheat, fraud, graft, viola **06** diddle, fidget, juggle, meddle, racket, rip-off, scrape, tamper, tinker, trifle, violin **07** falsify, sultana, swindle **09** gold brick, interfere, manoeuvre, racketeer **10** fool around, mess around **12** cook the books **13** sharp practice

fiddling

05 petty **06** fiddly, paltry **07** trivial **08** trifling **10** negligible **13** insignificant

fidelity

05 faith, fides, troth, trust **07** honesty, loyalty **08** accuracy, devotion **09** adherence, closeness, constancy, exactness, precision **10** allegiance, strictness **11** devotedness, reliability **12** authenticity, faithfulness **13** dependability **15** trustworthiness

fidget

03 toy **04** fike, fret, fuss, jerk, jump **05** hotch **06** bustle, fiddle, footer, hirsle, jiggle, niggle, squirm, tamper, tinker, trifle, twitch, writhe **07** shuffle, twiddle, wriggle **09** mess about **10** play around **11** toss and turn **12** restlessness

fidgety

05 jumpy **06** on edge, uneasy **07** excited, jittery, nervous, restive, twitchy, uptight **08** agitated, restless **09** impatient

field

03 lea, ley **04** area, lawn, line, mead, play, slip, stop **05** catch, champ, close, forte, glebe, green, parry, pitch, put up, range, sawah, scene, scope, sward **06** answer, bounds, domain, ground, handle, lea-rig, limits, meadow, padang, pick up, regime, return, select, sphere **07** deflect, paddock, pasture, present, runners, send out, stubble **08** ball park, confines, cope with, deal with, entrants, province, retrieve **09** grassland, opponents, possibles, territory **10** applicants, candidates, contenders, department, discipline, opposition, speciality **11** competition, competitors, contestants, environment **12** choose to play, participants, playing-field

See also **athletics**; **cricket**

- **stubble field**

05 arish **06** arrish

Field Marshal

02 FM **13** velt-mareschal

Field Marshals include:

04 **Haig** (Douglas, Earl)
05 **Lucan** (George Bingham, Earl of), **Monty**
06 **French** (Sir John), **Raglan** (Fitzroy Somerset, Lord)
07 **Allenby** (Edmund Hynman, Viscount), **Roberts** (Frederick, Earl)
08 **Ironside** (William, Lord), **Wolseley** (Garnet Joseph, Viscount)
09 **Robertson** (Sir William)
10 **Alanbrooke** (Alan Francis Brooke, Viscount), **Auchinleck** (Sir Claude John Eyre), **Kesselring** (Albert), **Montgomery** (Bernard, Viscount)

fiend

03 fan, nut **04** buff, ogre **05** beast, brute, demon, devil, fient, freak, ghoul **06** addict, savage **07** devotee, fanatic, monster **10** aficionado, enthusiast, evil spirit

fiendish

05 cruel **06** brutal, clever, savage, wicked **07** complex, cunning, inhuman, obscure, vicious **08** barbaric, devilish, infernal, involved, ruthless **09** difficult, ferocious, ingenious, intricate, monstrous **10** aggressive, diabolical, horrendous, malevolent **11** challenging, complicated, imaginative, resourceful, unspeakable **12** bloodthirsty **14** Mephistophelic **15** Mephistophelean, Mephistophelian

fierce

03 hot, wud **04** fell, grim, keen, wild, wood **05** angry, breem, breme, cruel, felon, grave, stern, stout **06** brutal, raging, savage, severe, strong, wrathy **07** furious, intense, rampant, vicious, violent **08** menacing, powerful, ruthless, terrible, walleyed **09** cut-throat, dangerous, ferocious, merciless, murderous, truculent **10** aggressive, passionate, relentless **11** frightening, tempestuous, threatening **12** bloodthirsty, uncontrolled

fiercely

06 keenly, wildly **07** cruelly, sternly **08** bitterly, brutally, savagely, severely, strongly, terribly **09** furiously, intensely, viciously, violently **10** implacably, menacingly, powerfully, ruthlessly **11** dangerously, fanatically, ferociously, mercilessly, murderously

12 aggressively, passionately, relentlessly, tooth and nail
13 tempestuously, threateningly

fiery
03 hot 05 afire, aglow, sharp, spicy
06 ablaze, aflame, ardent, fierce, heated, red-hot, spiced, spunky, sultry, torrid 07 blazing, burning, fervent, flaming, flushed, frampal, glowing, piquant, pungent, violent
08 frampold, inflamed, seasoned
09 excitable, hot-headed, impatient, impetuous, impulsive, irritable
10 passionate, phlogistic, sulphurous
11 empassioned, high-mettled, impassioned

fiesta
04 gala 05 feast, party 07 holiday, jubilee 08 carnival, festival 09 festivity
11 celebration, merrymaking

fifteen
02 XV

fifty
01 L
• **fifty per cent**
02 so

fight
03 box, hit, row, wap, war 04 blue, bout, camp, curb, defy, duel, feud, fray, grit, guts, mill, riot, rout, ruck, spar, stem, yike 05 aggro, argue, bandy, brawl, brush, clash, drive, fence, joust, mêlée, mix-in, pluck, punch, rammy, scrap, set-to, spunk, yikes 06 action, attack, barney, battle, bicker, bottle, bovver, bundle, combat, debate, dust-up, engage, fracas, meddle, medley, oppose, repugn, resist, ruckus, ruffle, rumble, scrape, shindy, spirit, stifle, stoush, strike, strive, take on, thwart, tussle 07 bashing, be at war, contend, contest, crusade, discord, dispute, fall out, grapple, lay into, make war, pasting, punch-up, quarrel, repress, resolve, ruction, scuffle, smother, tuilyie, tuilzie, wage war, warfare, wrangle, wrestle 08 argument, be at odds, bottle up, campaign, champion, conflict, ding-dong, do battle, dogfight, exchange, firmness, gunfight, have a row, hold back, keep back, militate, movement, object to, pell-mell, restrain, set about, skirmish, squabble, struggle, suppress, tenacity
09 altercate, bloodshed, cockfight, duke it out, encounter, force back, monomachy, skiamachy, stand up to, weigh into, willpower, withstand
10 aggression, bandy words, digladiate, dissension, Donnybrook, engagement, fisticuffs, free-for-all, graplement, will to live 11 altercation, come to blows, cross swords, disturbance, hostilities, snickersnee, work against 12 disagreement, resoluteness 13 confrontation, determination, measure swords, take issue with 14 hold out against
15 campaign against, do battle against, struggle against

• **fight back**
04 curb 05 check, reply 06 resist, retort 07 contain, control, repress
08 bottle up, hold back, restrain, suppress 09 force back, retaliate
11 put up a fight 13 counter-attack
14 defend yourself, hold out against
• **fight off**
04 rout 05 repel 06 rebuff, resist
07 beat off, hold off, ward off 08 stave off 09 hold at bay, keep at bay 11 put to flight
• **incite to fight**
03 tar 05 tarre

fighter
01 F 03 EFA, MiG 05 rival 07 bruiser, chetnik, fechter, jump jet, soldier, trouper, warrior 08 attacker, hired gun, opponent 09 adversary, combatant, contender, disputant, man-at-arms, mercenary 10 antagonist, contestant
11 bushwhacker 13 Messerschmitt
15 sparring partner

Fighters include:

05 boxer, pugil
06 fencer, hitman, knight
07 matador, picador, sworder
08 pugilist, toreador, wrestler
09 gladiator, kick boxer, spadassin, swordsman
10 rejoneador
11 bullfighter, digladiator
12 banderillero, prizefighter

See also **aeroplane**

figment
• **figment of your imagination**
05 fable, fancy 07 fiction 08 delusion, illusion 09 deception, falsehood, invention 10 concoction 11 fabrication
13 improvisation

figurative
03 fig 07 typical 08 symbolic, tropical
09 parabolic, pictorial 10 emblematic
11 allegorical, descriptive
12 metaphorical, naturalistic
14 representative

figure
03 fig, sum 04 body, form, icon, idol, ikon, sign, sums 05 build, digit, frame, guess, image, judge, maths, price, shape, think, torso, total, value
06 amount, appear, crop up, design, emblem, leader, number, person, reckon, sketch, symbol, worthy
07 believe, diagram, drawing, feature, integer, notable, numeral, outline, passage, pattern, picture, suppose
08 conclude, consider, estimate, foreshow, physique 09 authority, celebrity, character, dignitary, horoscope, personage, symbolize
10 appearance, silhouette, statistics
11 mathematics, personality 12 be included in, calculations, illustration
13 be mentioned in 14 representation

Figures include:

04 cone, cube, kite, oval
05 prism
06 circle, cuboid, oblong, sector, sphere, square
07 decagon, diamond, ellipse, hexagon, nonagon, octagon, polygon, pyramid, rhombus
08 crescent, cylinder, heptagon, pentagon, quadrant, tetragon, triangle
09 chiliagon, dodecagon, rectangle, trapezium, undecagon
10 hemisphere, hendecagon, octahedron, polyhedron, quadrangle, semicircle
11 pentahedron, tetrahedron
13 parallelogram, quadrilateral
15 scalene triangle

See also **circle**; **triangle**

• **figure of speech**
05 image, trope 06 flower, simile, zeugma 07 imagery, meiosis
08 diallage, metaphor, oxymoron
09 prolepsis 10 abscission, antithesis, hyperbaton, synecdoche
11 parenthesis 12 antimetabole, turn of phrase
• **figure on**
04 plan 06 expect 07 plan for
08 depend on, reckon on 10 bargain for 13 be prepared for 15 take into account
• **figure out**
03 see 04 dope, make, twig 05 count
06 fathom, reason, reckon
07 compute, dope out, make out, resolve, work out 08 decipher, estimate, tumble to 09 calculate, latch onto, puzzle out 10 understand 13 get the picture

figurehead
04 bust, name 05 dummy, image, token 06 figure, puppet 07 carving
08 front man 10 man of straw, mouthpiece 11 nominal head, titular head

Fiji
03 FJI

filament
04 cord, hair, pile, wire 05 cable, fiber, fibre, seton 06 cirrus, elater, sleave, strand, string, thread 07 fimbria, tendril, whisker 08 fibrilla, tentacle
09 microwire, protonema
10 paraphysis 11 gonimoblast

filch
03 nab, rob 04 crib, drib, fake, lift, nick, palm, prig, take 05 lurch, pinch, steal, swipe 06 nobble, pilfer, rip off, smouch, snitch, thieve 07 purloin, snaffle 08 embezzle, knock off, peculate 09 knock down
14 misappropriate

file
03 ask, box, row, rub 04 case, data, hone, line, list, make, note, rake, rasp, risp, roll, sand, text, whet 05 apply, enter, grate, march, plane, put in, queue, scour, shape, shave, store, trail, train, troop 06 abrade, binder, column, folder, format, papers, parade, polish, record, scrape, smooth, stream, string,

submit, thread **07** box file, cortège, data set, details, dossier, pollute, process, program, Rolodex®, rub down **08** classify, document, organize, register **09** catalogue, crocodile, lever arch, portfolio **10** categorize, pickpocket, pigeonhole, procession, put in place, walk in line **11** information, particulars

filial

04 fond **05** loyal **06** loving
07 devoted, dutiful **10** daughterly, respectful **12** affectionate

filibuster

05 delay, stall **06** hinder, impede, pirate, put off **07** prevent **08** obstruct, perorate **09** buccaneer, hindrance, speechify, waste time **10** impediment, peroration **11** obstruction
12 postponement, speechifying
13 procrastinate **15** delaying tactics, procrastination

filigree

04 lace **07** lattice, tracery **08** fretwork, lacework, wirework **09** interlace
10 scrollwork **11** latticework

fill

◇ *insertion indicator*
04 brim, bung, clog, cork, cram, glut, hold, line, pack, plug, seal, soak, stop **05** ample, block, close, crowd, imbue, prime, stack, stock, stuff **06** bishop, charge, englut, enough, fulfil, occupy, plenty, riddle, stop up, supply, take up
07 congest, furnish, implete, perform, pervade, provide, satisfy, suffuse
08 complete, make full, permeate, saturate **09** abundance, replenish
10 all you want, impregnate, sufficient
11 sufficiency **13** all you can take
14 more than enough

• **fill in**

05 brief, write **06** act for, advise, answer, inform **07** cover in, fill out, replace, stand in **08** acquaint, complete, deputize **09** represent
10 substitute, understudy **11** pinch-hit for **13** bring up to date

• **fill out**

06 answer, fill in **08** complete **10** gain weight, grow fatter **11** put on weight
12 become fatter **13** become plumper
14 become chubbier

fillet

04 list **05** label **06** anadem, fascia, reglet, regula **07** annulet, cloison
09 sphendone, tournedos

filling

◇ *insertion indicator*
03 big **04** full, rich **05** ample, heavy, large, solid **06** filler, hearty, inside, square, stodgy **07** padding, wadding
08 contents, generous, stuffing
09 impletion, substance **10** nutritious, satisfying **11** substantial

fillip

04 goad, prod, push, spur **05** boost, flick, shove **06** incite, snitch
07 impetus **08** stimulus **09** incentive, stimulant, stimulate **10** inducement, motivation **11** stimulation
13 encouragement

film

03 cel, ISO, pic, web **04** cell, cine-, coat, epic, haze, kell, mist, reel, skin, veil, weft **05** cloud, cover, flick, glaze, layer, movie, sheet, shoot, short, spool, video **06** cinema, deepie, screen, silent, tissue **07** blanket, coating, dusting, feature, footage, picture
08 cassette, covering, membrane, pellicle, televise **09** blue movie, cartridge, mistiness, skinflick, videogram, videotape **10** featurette, horse opera, photograph, screenplay, video nasty **11** documentary, feature film **12** record on film **13** motion picture, video cassette

See also **director**

Films include:

02 ET, If...
03 Big, JFK, Kes, Ran
04 Antz, Babe, Dr No, Gigi, Heat, Jaws, MASH, Reds
05 Alfie, Alien, Bambi, Bugsy, Crash, Dumbo, Fargo, Ghost, Giant, Rocky, Shrek
06 Aliens, Amélie, Batman, Ben-Hur, Blow-Up, Casino, Gandhi, Grease, Heimat, Lolita, Mad Max, Misery, Psycho, The Fly, Top Gun, Top Hat
07 Amadeus, Big Fish, Cabaret, Das Boot, Die Hard, Dracula, Rain Man, Rebecca, Robocop, Titanic, Tootsie, Traffic, Vertigo
08 Apollo 13, Body Heat, Born Free, Cape Fear, Chocolat, Duck Soup, Fantasia, High Noon, Insomnia, Key Largo, Kill Bill, King Kong, Scarface, Star Wars, The Birds, The Piano, The Sting, The Thing, The Tramp, Toy Story
09 12 Monkeys, A Bug's Life, Annie Hall, Betty Blue, Cat Ballou, Chinatown, City of God, Easy Rider, Excalibur, Funny Girl, Get Shorty, Gladiator, GoldenEye, Home Alone, Local Hero, Manhattan, Moonraker, Nosferatu, Octopussy, Pinocchio, Rio Grande, Spartacus, Spider-Man, Stand by Me, Vera Drake
10 Blue Velvet, Braveheart, Casablanca, Chicken Run, Cry Freedom, Dirty Harry, East of Eden, Goldfinger, GoodFellas, Grand Hotel, High Sierra, Men in Black, Metropolis, My Fair Lady, My Left Foot, Now Voyager, Paris Texas, Raging Bull, Rear Window, Stagecoach, Taxi Driver, The Big Easy, The Hustler, The Postman, The Shining, The Wild One, Unforgiven, Wall Street
11 A Few Good Men, All About Eve, American Pie, Beetlejuice, Blade Runner, Citizen Kane, Deliverance, Don't Look Now, Finding Nemo, Forrest Gump, Gosford Park, Heaven's Gate, La Dolce Vita, Mary Poppins, Mean Streets, Monsters, Inc, Mystic River, Notting Hill, Out of Africa, Pretty Woman, Public Enemy, Pulp Fiction, The 400 Blows, The Big Sleep, The Evil Dead, The Exorcist, The Fugitive, The Gold Rush, The Graduate, The Lion King, The Red Shoes, The Third Man, Thunderball, Wayne's World, Wild at Heart
12 A View to a Kill, Brighton Rock, Casino Royale, Cool Hand Luke, Eyes Wide Shut, Frankenstein, Ghostbusters, Gregory's Girl, Groundhog Day, Jurassic Park, Lethal Weapon, Philadelphia, Prizzi's Honor, Roman Holiday, Rome, Open City, Salaam Bombay!, Seven Samurai, Sleepy Hollow, The Apartment, The Godfather, The Searchers, The Wicker Man, The Wild Bunch, Whisky Galore!, Withnail and I
13 Apocalypse Now, Basic Instinct, Batman Forever, Batman Returns, Burnt by the Sun, Death in Venice, Die Another Day, Doctor Zhivago, Educating Rita, Eight and a Half, His Girl Friday, Licence to Kill, Live and Let Die, Mildred Pierce, Raining Stones, Reservoir Dogs, Scent of a Woman, Some Like It Hot, The Crying Game, The Dam Busters, The Deer Hunter, The Dirty Dozen, The Fisher King, The Jazz Singer, The Jungle Book, The Right Stuff, The Terminator, To Catch a Thief, Trainspotting, West Side Story, Wings of Desire, Zorba the Greek
14 A Day at the Races, American Beauty, American Psycho, As Good as it Gets, Blazing Saddles, Bonnie and Clyde, Brief Encounter, Bringing Up Baby, Central Station, Chariots of Fire, Cinema Paradiso, Dial M for Murder, Empire of the Sun, Enter the Dragon, Erin Brockovich, Five Easy Pieces, Gangs of New York, Goodbye Mr Chips, Jean de Florette, LA Confidential, Midnight Cowboy, Minority Report, Muriel's Wedding, Schindler's List, Secrets and Lies, The Big Lebowski, The Commitments, The Elephant Man, The Great Escape, The Ladykillers, The Last Emperor, The Life of Brian, The Lost Weekend, The Mask of Zorro, The Music Lovers, The Seventh Seal, Un Chien Andalou
15 Annie Get Your Gun, A Passage to India, Back to the Future, Crocodile Dundee, Dog Day Afternoon, Do the Right Thing, Fatal Attraction, For Your Eyes Only, Full Metal Jacket, Gone With the Wind, Good Will Hunting, Heart of Darkness, Independence Day, Life Is Beautiful, Manon des Sources, Meet Me in St Louis, On the Waterfront, Return of the Jedi, Road to Perdition, Singin' in the Rain, Sunset Boulevard, Tarzan the Ape Man, The African Queen,

The Bicycle Thief, Thelma and Louise, The Piano Teacher, The Seven Samurai, The Sound of Music, Thirty-nine Steps

Film types include:

03 spy, war
04 blue, cult, epic, noir
05 adult, anime, buddy, crime, farce, heist, short, spoof, vogue, weepy
06 action, auteur, biopic, B-movie, comedy, Disney, erotic, family, horror, murder, police, re-make, rom-com, silent, weepie
07 Carry-on, cartoon, classic, diorama, fantasy, musical, neo-noir, new wave, passion, realist, robbery, slasher, tragedy, war hero, western
08 animated, disaster, escapist, film noir, gangster, newsreel, romantic, space-age, thriller
09 adventure, Bollywood, burlesque, chopsocky, detective, film à clef, flashback, Hitchcock, Hollywood, James Bond, love story, low-budget, melodrama, political, road movie, satirical, skin flick, Spielberg, whodunnit
10 avant-garde, bonkbuster, gay-lesbian, neo-realist, period epic, snuff movie, surrealist, tear-jerker, travelogue
11 black comedy, blockbuster, cliff-hanger, documentary, kitchen sink, period drama, tragicomedy, underground
12 cinéma-vérité, Ealing comedy, ethnographic, fly-on-the-wall, mockumentary, pornographic, rockumentary, social comedy
13 comic-book hero, expressionist, multiple-story, murder mystery, nouvelle vague, sexploitation, sexual fantasy, social problem
14 blaxploitation, Charlie Chaplin, comedy thriller, police thriller, rites of passage, romantic comedy, science fiction
15 animated cartoon, cowboy and Indian, romantic tragedy, screwball comedy

• **film classification**
01 A, U, X **02** AA, PG
• **film company**
05 indie **06** studio
• **film over**
03 fog **04** blur, dull **05** glaze **08** mist over **09** cloud over **13** become blurred
• **horror film** *see* **horror**
• **part of film**
04 reel

filmy
04 fine, thin **05** gauzy, light, sheer **06** flimsy, floaty **07** clouded, fragile **08** chiffony, cobwebby, delicate, gossamer **09** gossamery **10** diaphanous, see-through, shimmering **11** translucent, transparent **13** insubstantial

filter
04 leak, mesh, ooze, seep, sift **05** drain, gauze, leach, sieve **06** purify, refine, riddle, screen, sifter, strain **07** clarify, dribble, netting, trickle **08** colander, filtrate, membrane, strainer **09** percolate

filth
03 mud **04** crap, crud, dirt, dung, gore, grot, gunk, mire, muck, porn, smut, soil, yuck **05** addle, bilge, dreck, dross, grime, gunge, slime, trash **06** faeces, grunge, manure, refuse, sewage, sleaze, sludge, wallow **07** garbage, rubbish, squalor, sullage **08** effluent, foulness, hard porn, impurity **09** blue films, colluvies, excrement, indecency, obscenity, pollution, vulgarity **10** coarseness, corruption, defilement, dirty books, sordidness **11** pornography, putrescence, raunchiness, uncleanness **12** putrefaction **13** contamination, sexploitation

filthy
03 bad, low, wet **04** base, blue, foul, lewd, mean, vile, wild **05** adult, angry, bawdy, black, cross, dirty, grimy, gross, manky, mucky, muddy, nasty, rainy, ratty, rough, slimy, sooty, yucky **06** Augean, coarse, crabby, cruddy, faecal, grubby, impure, putrid, rotten, shirty, smutty, soiled, sordid, stormy, vulgar, X-rated **07** corrupt, obscene, raunchy, squalid, stroppy, swinish, unclean **08** decaying, depraved, explicit, indecent, polluted, unwashed, wretched **09** irritable, offensive, worthless **10** despicable, putrefying, suggestive **11** bad-tempered, foul-mouthed **12** contaminated, contemptible, disagreeable, pornographic

fin
03 arm **04** hand, skeg, tail, vane **05** fiver, pinna, skegg **06** dorsal **07** Finland, ventral **08** pectoral

final
◇ *tail selection indicator*
03 end, net **04** last, nett **05** dying **06** latest **07** closing, settled, supreme **08** decisive, definite, eventual, farewell, terminal, ultimate **09** finishing **10** concluding, conclusive, conclusory, definitive, last-minute, peremptory **11** determinate, irrefutable, irrevocable, terminating, unalterable **12** indisputable
• **final word**
04 amen

finale
◇ *tail selection indicator*
03 end **05** close **06** climax, ending **07** curtain **08** epilogue, final act **10** conclusion, dénouement **11** culmination **13** crowning glory

finality
08 firmness, ultimacy **09** certitude **10** conviction, resolution **11** decidedness **12** decisiveness, definiteness **13** inevitability **14** conclusiveness, inevitableness, irrevocability, unavoidability **15** irreversibility

finalize
03 end **05** agree, close, sew up **06** clinch, decide, finish, settle, wrap up **07** resolve, work out **08** complete, conclude, round off

finally
◇ *tail selection indicator*
04 last **06** at last, in fine, lastly **07** for ever, for good **08** at length, in the end **10** decisively, definitely, eventually, to conclude, ultimately **11** irrevocably, permanently **12** conclusively, in conclusion, irreversibly **13** for good and all, once and for all

finance
04 back, cash, fund **05** float, funds, means, money, set up, trade **06** assets, budget, income, pay for, wealth **07** affairs, banking, capital, funding, revenue, savings, sponsor, subsidy, support **08** accounts, bankroll, business, commerce **09** economics, guarantee, liquidity, resources, subsidize **10** accounting, capitalize, habilitate, investment, underwrite **11** bank account, sponsorship, stock market, wherewithal **15** money management

financial
05 money **06** fiscal **08** economic, monetary **09** budgetary, pecuniary **10** commercial **15** entrepreneurial
• **financial expert**
09 economist **10** monetarist

financier
05 bania, gnome **06** banian, banker, banyan, trader **07** swindle **08** investor **10** moneymaker, speculator **11** stockbroker, white knight **12** financialist, Wall-Streeter **13** industrialist

finch
05 spink, twite **06** canary, linnet, siskin, towhee, whidah, whydah **07** bunting, chewink, manikin, redbird, waxbill **08** grosbeak, mannikin, snowbird, wheatear **09** brambling, crossbill, grassquit **10** fallow-chat, indigo bird, marsh-robin, weaver bird, whidah bird, whydah bird **11** green linnet, tree sparrow **12** cardinal-bird **13** indigo bunting

find
02 be **03** get, try, win **04** boon, coup, deem, earn, gain, meet, rate, rule, spot **05** asset, catch, exist, gauge, judge, learn, occur, reach, think, trace **06** attain, come by, decree, detect, dig out, expose, locate, notice, obtain, regain, reveal, review, secure, turn up, umpire **07** achieve, acquire, adjudge, bargain, believe, declare, examine, get back, godsend, good buy, mediate, observe, procure, realize, recover, referee, uncover, unearth **08** come upon, consider, discover, perceive, retrieve, sentence **09** arbitrate, be

present, discovery, encounter, recognize, stumble on, track down **10** adjudicate, chance upon, come across, experience, happen upon, lay hands on, run to earth, trouvaille **11** acquisition **12** bring to light, pass sentence **13** give a sentence, stumble across **14** sit in judgement **15** deliver a verdict

• **find in**

◇ *anagram indicator*
◇ *hidden indicator*
◇ *insertion indicator*

• **find out**

03 see, sus **04** note, suss, take, twig **05** catch, get at, learn **06** detect, expose, gather, reveal, rumble, show up, unmask **07** extract, lay bare, observe, realize, suss out, uncover **08** disclose, discover, identify, perceive, pinpoint, tumble to **09** ascertain, establish, expiscate, get wind of **10** cotton on to, understand **11** make certain **12** bring to light **13** make certain of

finding

04 find **05** award, order **06** decree **07** verdict **08** decision, judgment **09** discovery, judgement **10** conclusion, innovation **12** breakthrough **13** pronouncement **14** recommendation

fine

01 F **02** A1, OK **03** A-OK, dry, end, fit, log, oke, yes **04** braw, eric, fair, good, jake, keen, mooi, nice, pawn, phat, pure, safe, slim, thin, well **05** beaut, bonny, clear, dandy, exact, gauzy, great, light, mulct, nifty, right, sharp, sheer, showy, smart, sound, sting, sunny, unlaw **06** agreed, amerce, assess, bonnie, bright, choice, dainty, flimsy, goodly, ground, incony, lovely, minute, narrow, on form, pledge, punish, purify, refine, sconce, select, slight, strong, subtle **07** clement, crushed, damages, elegant, forfeit, fragile, gradely, healthy, immense, inconie, in shape, penalty, powdery, precise, radical, refined, slender, stylish **08** accurate, all right, critical, delicate, gossamer, graithly, handsome, jim-dandy, narrowly, penalize, precious, properly, splendid, striking, superior, very good, very well, vigorous **09** admirable, agreeable, beautiful, brilliant, cloudless, correctly, egregious, excellent, expensive, exquisite, first-rate, sensitive, shipshape, temperate **10** acceptable, acceptably, amercement, attractive, diaphonous, discerning, first-class, forfeiture, punishment, remarkable, tickety-boo **11** amerciament, exceptional, fashionable, fine-grained, flourishing, in good shape, lightweight, magnificent, outstanding, pretentious, tickettyboo, up to scratch **12** in good health, satisfactory, successfully **13** distinguished, hair-splitting, hale and hearty **14** satisfactorily **15** in good condition

fine-looking

04 waly **05** wally

finely

05 wally **06** nicely, subtly, thinly **07** exactly, lightly, sharply **08** minutely **09** admirably, precisely **10** critically, delicately, splendidly **11** brilliantly, excellently **12** attractively **13** magnificently

finery

07 bravery, gaudery, regalia, wallies **08** frippery, glad rags **09** jewellery, ornaments, showiness, splendour, trappings **10** rattletrap, Sunday best **11** bedizenment, best clothes, decorations

finesse

◇ *anagram indicator*

04 tact **05** bluff, evade, flair, skill, trick **06** polish **07** knowhow **08** deftness, delicacy, elegance, neatness, strategy, subtlety **09** adeptness, diplomacy, expertise, manoeuvre, quickness **10** adroitness, cleverness, discretion, manipulate, refinement **11** savoir-faire, tactfulness **12** gracefulness **14** sophistication

finger

03 paw **04** feel, name **05** pinky, share, talon, touch **06** agency, caress, fondle, handle, medius, paddle, pilfer, pinkie, stroke **07** annular, toy with **08** interest, virginal **09** prepollex **10** fiddle with, manipulate, meddle with **13** play about with

• **put your finger on**

05 place **06** locate, recall **07** find out, hit upon, isolate, pin down **08** discover, identify, indicate, pinpoint, remember

fingerhole

04 lill, lilt, stop **07** ventage, ventige

finial

03 tee **04** crop **06** pommel **09** pineapple, poppy-head

finicky

◇ *anagram indicator*

05 faddy, fussy, picky **06** choosy, fiddly, tricky **08** critical, delicate **09** difficult, finickety, intricate, selective **10** fastidious, meticulous, nit-picking, particular, pernickety, scrupulous **11** persnickety **13** hypercritical **14** discriminating

finish

◇ *tail selection indicator*

02 do **03** eat, end, use **04** coat, coda, down, rout, ruin, stop **05** apply, cease, close, crush, drain, drink, empty, glaze, gloss, grain, scoff, sew up, shine, use up **06** attain, be over, defeat, devour, ending, expend, finale, fulfil, guzzle, lustre, pack in, polish, settle, topple, veneer, wind up, wind-up, wrap up **07** absolve, achieve, coating, conquer, consume, deplete, destroy, exhaust, lacquer, outwork, perfect, surface, texture, varnish, wipe out **08** carry out, complete, conclude, curtains, deal with, get rid of, overcome, round off, run out of **09** be through, bring down, cessation, culminate, discharge, get shot of, overpower, overthrow, overwhelm, polish off, put paid to, terminate, winding-up **10** accomplish, annihilate, appearance, be done with, call it a day, completion, conclusion, consummate, do away with, fulfilment, get through, lamination, perfection, smoothness **11** achievement, come to an end, culmination, destruction, discontinue, exterminate, termination **12** bring to an end **14** accomplishment, get the better of

• **finish off**

03 end, ice, top **04** do in, slay **05** drain, mop-up, quash, quell, still, use up **06** defeat, murder **07** bump off, destroy, execute, put down, wipe out **08** despatch, dispatch, knock off **09** dispose of, eliminate, eradicate, liquidate, polish off, slaughter **10** annihilate, do away with, extinguish, put an end to, put to death, put to sleep **11** assassinate, exterminate

finished

02 up **04** arch, dead, done, lost, neat, over, past, ripe **05** empty, exact, spent **06** doomed, expert, made up, ruined, sewn up, undone, urbane, zonked **07** all done, at an end, defunct, done for, drained, perfect, refined, rounded, through, useless **08** complete, defeated, flawless, masterly, polished, unwanted, virtuoso **09** completed, concluded, dealt with, exhausted, faultless, played out, unpopular, wrapped up **10** consummate, impeccable, proficient **11** all over with, consummated **12** accomplished, professional **13** sophisticated **15** over and done with

• **before it is finished**

03 yet

finite

05 fixed **07** bounded, limited **08** numbered **09** countable, definable **10** calculable, demarcated, measurable, restricted, terminable

Finland

03 FIN

fire

03 axe, can, fan **04** bake, flak, heat, hurl, kiln, life, sack, stir, whet, zeal **05** blame, blaze, eject, let go, light, rouse, salvo, shoot, start, stick, torch, verve **06** ardour, arouse, attack, energy, excite, firing, flames, heater, ignite, incite, kindle, launch, let off, set off, spirit, stir up, vigour **07** animate, barrage, bombing, bonfire, boot out, burning, censure, dismiss, enliven, explode, feeling, fervour, gunfire, inferno, inflame, inspire, kick out, passion, reproof, slating, sniping, sparkle, trigger **08** brickbat, detonate, dynamism, get rid of, knocking, motivate, radiance, radiator, shelling, slamming, spark off, vivacity **09** animation, cannonade, cauterize,

convector, criticism, discharge, eagerness, electrify, fusillade, galvanize, holocaust, intensity, lightning, set ablaze, set alight, set fire to, set on fire, stimulate **10** combustion, creativity, enthusiasm, excitement, liveliness, trigger off **11** bombardment, disapproval, put a match to
12 condemnation, fault-finding
13 conflagration, disparagement, inventiveness

• fire up
06 arouse

• on fire
03 lit **05** eager, fiery **06** ablaze, aflame, alight, ardent **07** blazing, burning, excited, flaming, ignited
08 creative, in flames, inspired
09 energetic, inventive, sparkling
10 passionate **12** enthusiastic

firearm
03 gun **04** heat **05** rifle **06** musket, pistol, weapon **07** handgun, shotgun
08 revolver **09** automatic **10** self-cocker **12** breech-loader, muzzle-loader, shooting iron, single-action
13 semi-automatic
See also **gun**; **weapon**

firebrand
05 rebel **07** fanatic, radical
08 agitator, militant **09** extremist, insurgent **10** incendiary **12** rabble-rouser, troublemaker **13** revolutionary
15 insurrectionist

fireplace

Fireplaces include:

04 kiln, oven
05 forge, grate, ingle, range, stove
06 boiler, hearth
07 bonfire, brazier, firebox, furnace, gas fire
08 campfire, open fire
09 wood stove
10 backboiler
11 incinerator
12 electric fire
13 paraffin stove

firepower
04 ammo

fireproof
10 flameproof **12** non-flammable
13 fire-resistant, incombustible
14 flame-resistant, non-inflammable

fireside *see* **fireplace**

firewater *see* **drink**

fireworks
03 fit **04** rage, rows **05** storm
06 frenzy, sparks, temper, uproar
07 trouble **08** outburst **09** hysterics
10 explosions **12** pyrotechnics **13** feux d'artifice, illuminations

Fireworks include:

04 cake, mine, pioy
05 devil, flare, gerbe, peeoy, pioye, shell, squib, wheel
06 banger, fisgig, fizgig, maroon, petard, rocket
07 cracker, serpent, volcano
08 flip-flop, fountain, pinwheel, slap-bang, sparkler, whizbang
09 firedrake, girandola, girandole, sky-rocket, throw-down, waterfall, whizz-bang
10 golden rain, Indian fire, tourbillon
11 firecracker, firewriting, jumping-jack, roman candle, tourbillion
14 Catherine wheel, Chinese cracker, indoor firework
15 Pharaoh's serpent, Waterloo cracker

firm
02 Co, OK **03** Cie, oke, set **04** boon, fast, good, hard, oaky, sure, true
05 close, crisp, dense, fixed, house, rigid, solid, stiff, tight **06** dogged, secure, siccar, sicker, stable, stanch, steady, steeve, stieve, strict, strong, sturdy, trusty **07** adamant, compact, company, concern, decided, riveted, secured, settled, staunch, unmoved
08 anchored, business, constant, definite, embedded, fastened, forceful, hardened, obdurate, resolute, resolved, stubborn, unshaken, vigorous **09** committed, immovable, inelastic, obstinate, rock-solid, sclerotic, steadfast, syndicate, tenacious **10** compressed, dependable, determined, enterprise, inflexible, motionless, solidified, stationary, unchanging, unshakable, unswerving, unwavering, unyielding
11 association, corporation, established, institution, long-lasting, partnership, substantial, substantive, unalterable, unfaltering, unflinching, unshakeable **12** close-grained, concentrated, conglomerate, long-standing, organization, unchangeable
13 establishment

firmament
03 sky **05** ether, skies, space
06 heaven, welkin **07** expanse, heavens, the blue **08** empyrean
10 atmosphere

firmly
04 fast **06** fastly, stably, steeve, stieve, surely **07** tightly **08** doggedly, robustly, securely, steadily, strictly, strongly, sturdily **09** immovably, staunchly
10 decisively, definitely, enduringly, inflexibly, resolutely, unshakably
11 steadfastly, unalterably
12 determinedly, unchangeably, unwaveringly **13** unflinchingly

firmness
06 fixity, fixure **07** density, resolve, tension **08** fixation, hardness, obduracy, rigidity, solidity, strength, sureness, tautness **09** constancy, stability, stiffness, tightness, willpower
10 conviction, doggedness, resistance, resolution, steadiness, strictness
11 compactness, reliability, staunchness **12** immovability, inelasticity **13** dependability, determination, inflexibility, steadfastness **14** changelessness, indomitability, strength of will

• body firmness
04 tone

first
◇ *head selection indicator*
◇ *juxtaposition indicator*
01 A **03** 1st, key, one, top **04** arch-, best, head, main **05** basic, chief, prima, prime, primo, prior, proto-, start
06 eldest, oldest, origin, outset, primal, rather, ruling, senior, sooner **07** at first, earlier, firstly, highest, initial, leading, opening, origins, premier, primary, supreme **08** cardinal, champion, earliest, foremost, greatest, original, paravant, première, primeval
09 beginning, inaugural, inception, initially, paramount, paravaunt, primaeval, primitive, principal, prototype, sovereign, square one, the word go, unveiling, uppermost
10 beforehand, elementary, first of all, originally, pre-eminent, primordial
11 at the outset, fundamental, predominant, preliminary, rudimentary, to begin with, to start with **12** commencement, in preference, introduction, introductory
14 at the beginning **15** in the first place

• at first
◇ *head selection indicator*
04 erst **07** at first **09** initially **10** first of all **11** at the outset, to begin with, to start with **15** in the first place

• come first
◇ *juxtaposition indicator*
04 lead **05** outdo **07** precede

• first lady
03 Eve

first-born
04 aîné **05** aînée, eigne, elder, older
06 eldest, oldest, senior **10** primogenit
12 primogenital **13** primogenitary, primogenitive

first-class
01 A **02** A1 **03** ace, top **04** cool, fine, mean, mega **05** crack, prime, super
06 slap-up, superb, way-out, wicked
07 crucial, leading, premier, radical, supreme, top-hole **08** fabulous, peerless, splendid, superior, top-notch
09 admirable, excellent, first-rate, matchless, top-flight **11** exceptional, outstanding, superlative **12** second-to-none **14** out of this world

firsthand
06 direct **07** hands-on, primary
08 directly, on the job, personal
09 immediate, in service **10** personally
11 immediately

firstly
04 once **07** at first **09** initially **10** first of all **11** at the outset, to begin with, to start with **15** in the first place

first name
08 forename **09** given name
13 baptismal name, Christian name

first-rate
01 A **02** A1 **03** ace, top **04** cool, fine, jake, mean, mega **05** crack, prime, super **06** superb, way-out, wicked **07** crucial, leading, premier, radical, supreme **08** fabulous, peerless, splendid, superior, top-notch **09** admirable, excellent, matchless, top-flight **10** first-class **11** excellently, exceptional, outstanding, superlative **12** second-to-none **14** out of this world

firth

Firths include:

03 Tay
04 Lorn, Wide
05 Clyde, Forth, Lorne, Moray
06 Beauly, Solway, Thames
07 Dornoch, Westray
08 Cromarty, Pentland, Stronsay, Szczecin
09 Inverness
14 North Ronaldsay

fiscal
03 tax **05** money **06** bursal **07** capital **08** economic, monetary, treasury **09** budgetary, financial, pecuniary, treasurer

• **procurator fiscal**
02 PF

fiscally
09 moneywise **11** financially, pecuniarily **12** economically

fish
03 ask, bob, dap, dib, dip, fry, jig, net **04** harl, hunt, look, sean, seek, spin, trot **05** angle, catch, delve, grope, otter, seine, spoon, trawl, troll, whiff **06** guddle, ledger, search **07** counter, ransack, skitter, snigger, sniggle **08** hand line, try to get **09** go fishing **11** try to obtain

See also **animal**

Fish, crustaceans and shellfish include:

02 ai, id
03 aua, ayu, bar, bib, cod, dab, eel, gar, ged, hag, ide, lax, par, ray, sar, sei, tai
04 barb, bass, blay, bley, brit, carp, chad, char, chub, chum, clam, coho, crab, cray, cusk, dace, dare, dart, dory, fugu, gade, goby, hake, hoki, huso, huss, kelt, keta, kina, lant, ling, luce, lump, moki, opah, orfe, parr, paua, pawa, peal, peel, pike, pipi, pope, pout, pupu, rudd, scad, scar, scat, scup, seer, shad, sild, slip, snig, sole, spot, tang, tope, tuna, tusk
05 ablet, allis, basse, bleak, bream, brill, bully, cohoe, coley, danio, flake, guppy, koura, lance, loach, molly, perch, platy, porgy, prawn, roach, shark, skate, smelt, sprat, squid, tench, tetra, torsk, trout, tunny, whelk, yabby, zebra
06 allice, angler, barbel, blenny, braise, braize, cockle, doctor, dorado, gadoid, groper, hapuku, jilgie, kipper, kokopu, launce, marlin, marron, minnow, mullet, mussel, oyster, piraña, plaice, porgie, puffer, red cod, red-eye, salmon, saurel, shrimp, tailor, turbot, wrasse
07 abalone, anchovy, bloater, blue cod, catfish, cavalla, cavally, cichlid, cobbler, codfish, cowfish, dhufish, dogfish, garfish, gourami, grouper, gurnard, haddock, halibut, herring, kahawai, lamprey, lobster, morwong, mudfish, octopus, piranha, sardine, scallop, sea bass, snapper, toheroa, warehou, whiting
08 blowfish, bluefish, bluenose, brisling, calamari, characid, crawfish, crayfish, dragonet, flathead, flounder, goldfish, grayling, ichthyic, John Dory, kingfish, luderick, mackerel, monkfish, Moray eel, pilchard, pipefish, rockfish, sailfish, scuppaug, sea bream, seahorse, skipjack, stingray, sturgeon, tarakihi, toadfish, trevally, tuna fish
09 allis shad, angel-fish, barracuda, conger eel, Dover sole, greenling, grenadier, king prawn, lemonfish, lemon sole, Murray cod, neon tetra, red mullet, sea urchin, stonefish, swordfish, trumpeter, tunnyfish, whitebait, wobbegong, zebrafish
10 angler fish, Balmain bug, barracouta, barramundi, bluebottle, Bombay duck, brown trout, butterfish, cuttlefish, damsel fish, flying fish, grey mullet, gummy shark, jellied eel, mossbunker, parrot-fish, puffer fish, red snapper, rock salmon, tommy rough
11 electric eel, rock lobster, stickleback
12 jellyblubber, orange roughy, rainbow trout, scorpion fish, skipjack tuna
13 butterfly fish, horse mackerel, leatherjacket, Moreton Bay bug, sergeant-major
14 Arbroath smokie

See also **crustacean**; **mollusc**; **shark**; **seafood**

• **fish out**
04 find **07** extract, haul out, produce, pull out, take out **08** dredge up, retrieve **10** come up with

• **fish tank**
04 stew **08** aquarium

• **queer fish**
04 cure

fisherman
03 rod **05** liner **06** angler, banker, codder, fisher, rodman, Walton **07** crabber, drag-man, drifter, rodsman, rodster **08** peter-man, piscator, shareman **09** cockleman, rodfisher, sharesman, Waltonian, trawlerman **11** piscatorian

fishing
07 angling **08** trawling **09** piscatory **11** piscatorial **12** catching fish

Fishing- and angling-related terms include:

03 fly, net, rod, tag, tie
04 bait, barb, bite, cast, drag, gimp, hook, lead, line, lure, reel, sean, weel, weir, whip
05 angle, baker, catch, clean, creel, seine, snell, troll
06 angler, bob-fly, coarse, dry-fly, fly-rod, leader, sagene, sinker, tackle, waders, wet-fly
07 angling, bycatch, drifter, dropper, flyline, fly reel, harpoon, keepnet, piscary, setline, spinner
08 backcast, drift net, roll cast, trotline
09 brandling, drabbling, false cast, hairy Mary, halieutic, indicator, leger line, night-line, piscatory
10 bait bucket, casting arc, casting-net, fly casting, fly fishing, halieutics, landing net, ledger bait, ledger line, net-fishing, sea-fishing, weigh sling
11 forward cast, game fishing, line-fishing, paternoster
12 drift fishing, night crawler, night-fishery, shooting line
13 bottom-fishing, coarse fishing
15 catch-and-release

See also **fly**

fishy
◇ *anagram indicator*
03 odd **05** funny, queer, shady **06** unsafe **07** dubious, piscine, suspect **08** doubtful, fish-like **09** equivocal, irregular, piscatory **10** improbable, suspicious **11** implausible, piscatorial **12** questionable

fission
06 schism **07** parting, rending, rupture **08** breaking, cleavage, cleaving, division, scission **09** severance, splitting

fissure
03 gap **04** chop, gape, gash, hole, rent, rift, rime, slit, vein **05** break, chasm, chink, cleft, crack, fault, grike, gryke, porta, shake, split, zygon **06** breach, cleave, cranny, divide, groove, sulcus **07** crevice, foramen, opening, rupture **08** cleavage, crevasse, fracture, scissure, sink hole **10** interstice **11** swallow hole

fist
03 paw, pud **04** dook, duke, hand, mitt, neif, nief, palm **05** index, neafe, neive, nieve, puddy **06** neaffe **08** knuckles **11** handwriting **12** bunch of fives, clenched hand

fit
◇ *anagram indicator*
02 A1, go **03** apt, arm, cry, due, fix, gee, jag, pet, rig, sit **04** able, ague, bout, hard, huff, join, lune, mate, meet, song, sort, suit, well **05** adapt, agree, alter, burst, canto, coach, equal, equip, exies, flaky, gapes, groom, hardy, ictus, match, place, prime, put in, queme, ready, right, shape, sharp, sound,

spasm, spell, surge, tally, train **06** access, adjust, attach, attack, belong, change, concur, crisis, didder, dither, dueful, follow, habile, insert, in trim, modify, passus, proper, robust, seemly, square, strong, sturdy, tailor, worthy **07** arrange, be right, capable, chipper, conform, connect, correct, debauch, dewfull, fashion, fitting, get into, gradely, healthy, in shape, install, prepare, provide, qualify, seizure, tantrum, trained **08** decorous, dovetail, eligible, equipped, eruption, graithly, outbreak, outburst, paroxysm, position, prepared, regulate, suitable, vigorous **09** agreement, befitting, competent, condition, explosion, harmonize, interlock, make ready, pertinent, qualified **10** able-bodied, be a good fit, be suitable, conformity, conniption, convenient, convulsion, correspond, good enough, in good form, put in place, the shivers **11** accommodate, appropriate, be consonant, concurrence, correlation, equivalence, flourishing, in good shape, put together **12** be consistent, in good health, make suitable, relationship **13** be appropriate, fit like a glove, hale and hearty, put in position **14** correspondence **15** in good condition

• fit for use
04 ripe

• fit in
◇ *insertion indicator*
04 slot **05** agree, match **06** accord, belong, concur, square **07** conform, squeeze **10** correspond

• fit out, fit up
03 arm, rig **04** trim **05** equip, frame **06** kit out, outfit, rig out, supply **07** furnish, prepare, provide **08** accoutre

• fit together
04 nest

• in fits and starts
08 brokenly, fitfully, off and on, unevenly **11** erratically, irregularly **12** occasionally, sporadically **13** spasmodically **14** intermittently

fitful
06 broken, catchy, patchy, uneven **07** erratic **08** sporadic **09** disturbed, haphazard, irregular, spasmodic **10** occasional **12** disconnected, intermittent

fitfully
08 unevenly **11** erratically, haphazardly, irregularly **12** occasionally, sporadically **13** spasmodically **14** intermittently **15** by fits and starts, in fits and starts

fitness
04 trim **05** shape **06** health, vigour **07** aptness **08** adequacy, aptitude, haleness, property, strength **09** condition, edibility, readiness **10** capability, competence, competency, edibleness, good health, pertinence, robustness **11** eligibility, healthiness, opportunity, suitability **12** preparedness **13** applicability **14** qualifications **15** appropriateness

• condition of fitness
04 form

fitted
03 fit **05** armed, fixed, right **06** cut out, shaped, suited **07** built-in **08** equipped, integral, prepared, provided, suitable, tailored **09** appointed, furnished, permanent, qualified, rigged out **10** integrated

fitting
03 apt, fit **04** meet, part, unit **05** piece, right **06** extras, liable, proper, seemly, square **07** condign, correct, fitment, fixture **08** decorous, deserved, fitments, fixtures, suitable, wise-like **09** accessory, component, desirable, equipment, furniture **10** attachment, connection, convenable **11** accessories, appropriate, furnishings **12** appointments **13** accoutrements, installations

fittings
04 trim **09** trimmings **11** furnishings

five
01 V **06** pentad **07** quinary, quintet **08** quintett **09** quintette **10** quintuplet

• one of five
04 quin

five hundred
01 D

fix
◇ *anagram indicator*
02 do **03** aim, hit, jam, pin, rig, set, tie **04** bang, bind, comb, cook, dose, draw, fake, glue, hang, hold, hole, join, link, make, mend, mess, nail, name, root, scam, seal, shoo, shot, slug, sort, spay, spot, tidy, turn **05** affix, clamp, dress, embed, emend, focus, groom, level, lodge, order, plant, point, rivet, score, screw, see to, set up, set-up, stell, stick **06** adjust, anchor, answer, assign, attach, cement, corner, couple, decide, define, direct, fasten, fiddle, freeze, harden, locate, muddle, neaten, pickle, plight, remedy, repair, scrape, secure, settle, strike, way out **07** agree on, appoint, arrange, attract, connect, correct, destine, dilemma, falsify, implant, install, knock up, patch up, prepare, rectify, resolve, restore, rigging, situate, specify, station, stiffen, the soup **08** arrive at, castrate, chastise, finalize, get ready, position, put right, quandary, solidify, solution, valorize **09** destinate, determine, establish, injection, manoeuvre, stabilize, tight spot **10** difficulty, manipulate, put in order, resolution, straighten, tamper with **11** concentrate, predicament, put together **12** manipulation **13** throw together

• fix up
04 clew, clue, plan **05** equip, lay on, plant **06** settle, supply **07** agree on, arrange, furnish, produce, provide, sort out **08** organize **10** bring about

fixated
03 set **06** phobic **07** gripped **08** hung up on, neurotic, obsessed **09** dominated **10** compulsive, infatuated **11** preoccupied **12** pathological

fixation
05 mania, thing **06** fetich, fetish, hang-up, phobia **07** complex, fetiche, setting **08** firmness, idée fixe, neurosis **09** obsession **10** compulsion, steadiness **11** infatuation **13** preoccupation

fixed
◇ *anagram indicator*
03 set **04** fake, fast, firm **05** false, rigid, tight **06** phoney, rooted, secure, steady **07** decided, lasting, planned, pretend, settled, well-set **08** arranged, constant, definite, immobile, standing **09** appointed, insincere, permanent, pretended **10** determined, entrenched, inflexible, persistent, set in stone, stationary **11** cast in stone, determinate, established

fixedly
04 hard **07** closely **08** intently, steadily **09** staringly **10** watchfully **11** attentively, searchingly

fixity
09 constancy, fixedness, stability **10** permanence, steadiness **11** persistence **12** immutability

fixture
04 game, race, unit **05** event, match, round **06** fixing **07** contest, fitting, meeting **09** equipment, furniture **11** competition, furnishings **13** installations

fizz
03 gas, vim, zip **04** foam, hiss, zing **05** froth **06** bubble, fizzle **07** bubbles, ferment, foaming, sparkle **08** bubbling, buoyancy, frothing, vitality, vivacity **09** animation, champagne, fizziness, gassiness **10** effervesce, enthusiasm, excitement, exuberance, liveliness **11** excitedness, high spirits **12** exhilaration, fermentation **13** effervescence

fizzle

• fizzle out
04 fail, flop, fold, stop **07** die away, die down, subside **08** collapse, peter out, taper off **09** disappear, dissipate, evaporate **11** come to grief, fall through **13** come to nothing

fizzy
05 gassy **06** bubbly, frothy **07** aerated, foaming **08** bubbling **09** sparkling **10** carbonated **12** effervescent

flab
03 fat, pot **04** bulk **06** paunch **07** blubber, fatness, obesity **08** pot belly **09** plumpness, solidness, spare tyre, stoutness **10** chubbiness, corpulence, overweight

flabbergasted
◇ *anagram indicator*
05 dazed **06** amazed **07** stunned **08** overcome **09** astounded, blown away, staggered **10** astonished, bowled over, confounded, gobsmacked, nonplussed, speechless **11** dumbfounded, overwhelmed **13** knocked for six

flabby
03 fat, lax **04** limp, soft **05** loose, plump, slack **06** feeble, flaggy, fleshy, floppy, sloppy **07** flaccid, hanging, sagging **08** drooping, wasteful, yielding **09** lymphatic, nerveless **10** overweight **11** inefficient **12** disorganized, uneconomical

flaccid
03 lax **04** lank, limp, soft, weak **05** loose, slack **06** clammy, droopy, flabby, floppy **07** relaxed, sagging **08** drooping, toneless **09** nerveless

flag
03 die, ebb, rag, sag, tag **04** fade, fail, fall, flop, hail, iris, jade, mark, note, sink, slow, tire, waft, wane, wave, wilt **05** abate, color, droop, faint, label, slump, weary **06** Acorus, colors, colour, falter, lessen, marker, motion, salute, weaken **07** calamus, decline, dwindle, fall off, slacken, subside **08** diminish, hang down, indicate, languish, peter out, taper off, wave down **09** grow tired, reed-grass **12** signal to stop

Flags include:

05 Union
07 Saltier, Saltire
08 Crescent, Old Glory, Red Cross
09 Blue Peter, dannebrog, Red Dragon, Red Duster, Red Ensign, Rising Sun, Tricolour, Union Jack
10 Blue Ensign, Jolly Roger, Yellow Jack
11 Olympic Flag, Red Crescent, White Ensign
12 Stars and Bars
15 Cross of St George, Hammer and Sickle, Stars and Stripes

Flag types include:

03 red
04 blue, fane, jack, sick
05 black, house, peter, pilot, union, whiff, whift, white
06 banner, burgee, cornet, ensign, fanion, pennon, prayer, signal, yellow
07 ancient, bunting, colours, pennant
08 banderol, gonfalon, pavilion, penoncel, standard, streamer, tricolor, vexillum
09 blackjack, chequered, oriflamme, pennoncel, pilot jack, tricolour
10 penoncelle, quarantine
11 pennoncelle, swallow tail
13 defaced ensign

• flags
07 bunting

flagellation
07 beating, flaying, lashing, whaling **08** flogging, whipping **09** scourging, thrashing **10** vapulation **11** castigation, verberation, vice anglais **12** chastisement

flagging
06 ebbing, fading, tiring, waning **07** abating, failing, languid, sagging, sinking, slowing, wilting **08** drooping, pavement **09** declining, dwindling, faltering, lessening, subsiding, weakening **10** decreasing **11** diminishing

flagon
03 jug **04** ewer **05** flask, half-g, peter **06** bottle, carafe, vessel **07** pitcher **08** decanter **09** container

flagrant
04 bold, open, rank **05** gross, naked, overt **06** arrant, brazen, raging **07** blatant, burning, glaring, heinous **08** blattant, dreadful, enormous, infamous **09** atrocious, audacious, barefaced, egregious, notorious, shameless, unashamed **10** outrageous, scandalous **11** conspicuous, disgraceful, undisguised **12** ostentatious

flagstaff
03 pin

flail
◇ *anagram indicator*
04 beat, whip **06** batter, strike, thrash, thresh **08** threshel, thresher **11** swing wildly

flair
04 bent, feel, gift, nose **05** knack, skill, style, taste **06** acumen, genius, talent **07** ability, faculty, mastery, panache **08** aptitude, elegance, facility **11** discernment, stylishness **14** natural ability

flak
02 AA **05** abuse, blame, stick **07** censure, panning **08** bad press, knocking **09** brickbats, criticism, hostility, invective **10** aspersions, complaints, opposition **11** disapproval **12** condemnation, fault-finding **13** disparagement **14** animadversions, disapprobation

flake
◇ *anagram indicator*
03 bit **04** chip, flaw, peel, smut **05** flash, scale, scurf, shark, spark, wafer **06** furfur, paring, shiver, sliver, squama **07** blister, flaught, peeling, shaving, spangle **08** fragment, particle, splinter **09** eccentric, exfoliate, flocculus **10** desquamate **11** exfoliation **12** desquamation

• flake out
04 drop **05** faint **07** pass out **08** collapse, keel over **10** fall asleep **15** relax completely

flaky
◇ *anagram indicator*
03 dry **05** crazy, inept, scaly **06** scurfy, stupid **07** laminar, layered **08** scabrous, squamate, squamose, squamous **09** eccentric **10** flocculent **11** exfoliative, incompetent **12** desquamative, desquamatory, furfuraceous

flamboyance
04 dash, élan **05** style **06** colour **07** glamour, panache, pizzazz **09** showiness **10** brilliance **11** ostentation **12** extravagance **13** theatricality

flamboyant
04 rich **05** gaudy, showy **06** bright, flashy, florid, ornate, rococo **07** baroque, dashing **08** dazzling, exciting, striking **09** brilliant, colourful, elaborate, glamorous **10** theatrical **11** extravagant **12** ostentatious

flame
03 low **04** beam, burn, fire, glow, heat, lowe, lunt, rage, zeal **05** blaze, flake, flare, flash, flush, glare, gleam, go red, light, lover, shine **06** ardour, redden, warmth **07** fervour, partner, passion, radiate, sparkle, turn red **08** fervency, flammule, keenness, radiance **09** become red, boyfriend, catch fire, eagerness, intensity **10** brightness, enthusiasm, excitement, girlfriend, sweetheart **13** conflagration **15** burst into flames

• in flames
06 ablaze, aflame, alight, on fire **07** blazing, burning, flaming, ignited

• old flame
02 ex

flameproof
09 fireproof **12** non-flammable **13** fire-resistant, incombustible **14** flame-resistant, non-inflammable

flaming
03 mad **04** vile **05** angry, fiery, gaudy, vivid **06** aflame, alight, bloody, bright, cursed, damned, darned, dashed, odious, on fire, raging, red-hot **07** blasted, blazing, burning, enraged, furious, glowing, hateful, intense, violent **08** annoying, blinking, blooming, dratting, fiendish, flipping, incensed, infamous, infernal, in flames, wretched **09** brilliant, execrable, loathsome **10** abominable, confounded, detestable, infuriated, pernicious, unpleasant **11** smouldering **13** scintillating

flammable
08 burnable **09** ignitable **11** combustible, inflammable

flank
◇ *containment indicator*
03 hip **04** edge, line, lisk, loin, side, wall, wing **05** bound, skirt, thigh **06** border, fringe, haunch, screen **07** confine, quarter

flannel
03 rot **05** spiel **06** waffle **07** blarney, flatter, rubbish, washrag **08** flattery, nonsense, soft soap **09** facecloth, sweet talk, washcloth **10** smooth talk **13** blandishments

flap
◇ *anagram indicator*
03 fly, lap, lug, tab, tag, wag, wap
04 beat, fall, flag, flip, fold, fuss, loma, slat, stew, sway, tail, waff, wave
05 apron, flaff, lapel, panic, shake, skirt, state, swing, swish, tizzy, tuner, visor
06 dither, elevon, lappet, thrash, thresh, tiswas, tizwas, tongue, waggle, wallop, winnow **07** agitate, aileron, flacker, fluster, flutter, overlap, tent-fly, vibrate **08** aventail, barn-door, covering, epiploon, overhang
09 agitation, aventaile, commotion
10 clack valve, epiglottis, fluttering
12 great omentum **13** move up and down

flare
04 beam, burn, glow, Very **05** blaze, burst, erupt, flame, flash, glare, gleam, light, splay, torch, widen **06** beacon, dazzle, flanch, rocket, signal, spread
07 broaden, explode, flaunch, flicker, glimmer, glitter, sparkle **08** flare out, widening **09** spread out, Very light
10 broadening, Verey light **13** warning signal **14** distress signal
- **flare out**
04 bell
- **flare up**
05 blaze, erupt, go ape, go mad
06 blow up **07** explode **08** boil over, break out, burst out, freak out **09** blow a fuse, do your nut, go berserk **10** go to market, hit the roof **11** blow your top, do your block, flip your lid, go ballistic, go up the wall, lose control, lose your rag **12** fly into a rage, lose your cool, throw a wobbly **14** foam at the mouth, lose your temper **15** fly off the handle, go off the deep end

flare-up
04 rash **07** venting **08** ejection, emission, eruption, outbreak, outburst
09 discharge, explosion
12 inflammation

flash
◇ *anagram indicator*
02 mo **03** fly, ray **04** beam, bolt, dart, dash, fork, pond, pool, race, rush, show, tear, zoom **05** blaze, blink, bound, burst, dance, flake, flare, gaudy, glaik, glare, gleam, glint, quick, shaft, shine, shoot, showy, smart, spark, speed **06** career, flaunt, glaiks, glance, kitsch, moment, streak, strobe, sudden, vulgar **07** bluette, display, flaught, flicker, glimmer, glisten, glitter, instant, lighten, light up, shimmer, show off, sparkle, twinkle **08** brandish, concetto, fire-flag, flourish, green ray, outbreak, outburst **09** coruscate, expensive, fulgurate, fulminate, glamorous, lightning **10** exhibition
11 coruscation, fashionable, fire-flaught, fulguration, pretentious, scintillate **12** ostentatious
13 scintillation **14** expose yourself
- **in a flash**
03 pdq **06** pronto **08** in a jiffy, in a trice, in no time **09** in a moment, instantly **11** in an instant **12** in a twinkling **13** in no time at all **14** in a split second

flashy
04 bold, loud **05** brash, cheap, flash, gaudy, jazzy, lairy, showy, tacky, vapid
06 garish, glitzy, kitsch, snazzy, tawdry, vulgar **07** buckeye, raffish, tigrish
08 tigerish **09** glamorous, tasteless
10 bling-bling, flamboyant
11 pretentious **12** meretricious, ostentatious
- **flashy person**
04 lair, raff

flask
04 cask, mick **05** dewar, micky
06 bottle, carafe, coffin, fiasco, flagon, mickey, retort, vessel **07** ampulla, balloon, canteen, costrel, flacket, matrass, Thermos® **08** decanter, lekythos **09** aryballos, container, livery pot **10** powder horn **12** pocket-pistol

flat
03 low, OYO, pad, set **04** bust, dead, down, duff, dull, even, firm, flew, flue, fool, slow, tame, true, unit, weak
05 banal, bland, burst, empty, exact, final, fixed, haugh, kaput, level, plain, plane, prone, quiet, rigid, rooms, sheer, slack, stale, still, stock, suite, total, utter, vapid **06** bedsit, boring, callow, direct, evenly, planar, sleepy, smooth, supine, used up, watery **07** exactly, flatlet, insipid, not deep, not tall, plainly, planned, regular, shallow, tedious, totally, uniform, utterly **08** absolute, arranged, blown-out, complete, defeated, definite, deflated, dejected, directly, downcast, entirely, explicit, finished, home unit, inactive, levelled, lifeless, not thick, outright, positive, ruptured, sluggish, stagnant, standard, straight, tenement, toneless, unbroken **09** apartment, bedsitter, collapsed, depressed, downright, miserable, out-and-out, penthouse, pointless, precisely, prostrate, punctured, reclining, recumbent, unvarying
10 absolutely, completely, despondent, homaloidal, horizontal, lacklustre, maisonette, monotonous, point-blank, spiritless, unexciting
11 categorical, discouraged, maisonnette, unequivocal, unqualified
12 outstretched, spread-eagled
13 categorically, no longer fizzy, unconditional, uninteresting **14** flat as a pancake
- **flat out**
04 hard **06** all out **10** at top speed **11** at full speed
- **flat place**
04 plat

flatly
10 absolutely, completely, point-blank, positively **12** peremptorily
13 categorically **14** unhesitatingly
15 unconditionally

flatness
06 tedium **07** boredom, languor
08 dullness, evenness, monotony, vapidity **09** emptiness, levelness, platitude, staleness **10** insipidity, smoothness, uniformity
13 horizontality, tastelessness

flatten
02 KO **04** fell, iron, raze, roll
05 amaze, crush, dress, floor, level, plane, press **06** defeat, smooth, squash, subdue **07** even out, planish
08 compress, demolish, knock out, make even, make flat, tear down
09 knock down, overwhelm, prostrate

flatter
04 claw, coax, fawn, soap, suit, word
05 befit, court, creep, gloze, grace, toady **06** become, butter, cozy up, cringe, fleech, humour, kowtow, phrase, praise, sawder, smooth, soothe, stroke **07** adulate, enhance, flannel, gratify, lay it on, palaver, show off, soother, wheedle **08** beslaver, blandish, butter up, collogue, eulogize, inveigle, make up to, play up to, smooth it, soft-soap, suck up to **09** beslobber, embellish, sweet-talk **10** bear in hand, compliment, cozy up with, look good on, overpraise, pay court to, soft sawder, soft sowder **12** sycophantize
14 tickle the ear of **15** curry favour with, make fair weather, show to advantage

flatterer
05 carny, creep, toady **06** carney, earwig, fawner, lackey, minion, yes-man **07** crawler, creeper, proneur
08 adulator, incenser, incensor, smoother **09** encomiast, eulogizer, groveller, sycophant **10** bootlicker, foot-licker **11** lickspittle **12** court-dresser **13** back-scratcher

flattering
04 kind **06** honied, sugary
07 candied, fawning, fulsome, honeyed, servile, sugared
08 becoming, effusive, unctuous
09 adulatory, enhancing, gnathonic, laudatory **10** favourable, gratifying, obsequious **11** gnathonical, soft-soaping, sycophantic **12** honey-tongued, ingratiating, smooth-spoken, sweet-talking **13** complimentary, smooth-talking, smooth-tongued

flattery
04 fawn, soap **05** carny, sugar, taffy
06 butter, carney, eulogy, praise, sawder **07** blarney, fawning, flannel, glozing, mamaguy **08** cajolery, soft soap, toadyism **09** adulation, fair words, fleeching, laudation, servility, sweet talk **10** cajolement, flapdoodle, fleechment, soft sawder, soft sowder, sycophancy **11** compliments, fulsomeness **12** blandishment, ingratiation **13** blandishments **14** back scratching, court holy water

flatulence
03 gas **04** wind **06** flatus **07** farting
09 gassiness, ventosity, windiness
10 eructation **11** borborygmus

flatulent
05 gassy, windy **07** ventose

flaunt
03 air **05** boast, flash, skyre, sport, strut, vaunt, wield **06** dangle, parade, strout **07** display, disport, exhibit, show off **08** brandish, flourish

flavour
03 hop **04** feel, gust, hint, lace, race, soul, tack, tang, tone, zest, zing **05** aroma, flava, imbue, lemon, odour, sapor, savor, smack, spice, style, taste, tinge, touch, twang **06** aspect, infuse, nature, palate, pepper, relish, savour, season, spirit **07** essence, feeling, liqueur, quality, spice up **08** ginger up, piquancy, property **09** character **10** atmosphere, impression, indication, suggestion

flavouring
04 hops, miso, sage, tang, zest, zing **05** caper, shoyu, spice **06** borage, Bovril®, cassis, cloves, relish, savory **07** bay leaf, bitters, caramel, essence, extract, flavour, ratafia, saffron, vanilla **08** additive, costmary, piquancy, rosemary, tarragon **09** coriander, fenugreek, pistachio, seasoning, spearmint **10** peach-water **11** citronellal, malt-extract, wintergreen **12** bouquet garni, butterscotch
See also **herb**

flaw
04 chip, gall, mark, rent, rift, slip, spot, tear **05** brack, break, cleft, crack, craze, error, fault, flake, lapse, speck, split, thief **06** defect, foible, uproar **07** blemish, crevice, failing, fallacy, fissure, mistake **08** fracture, fragment, hamartia, splinter, weakness, weak spot **09** windshake **11** shortcoming **12** Achilles' heel, imperfection

flawed
◊ *anagram indicator*
06 broken, faulty, marked, marred, spoilt **07** chipped, cracked, damaged, unsound **09** blemished, defective, erroneous, imperfect **10** fallacious

flawless
05 sound, whole **06** intact **07** perfect **08** spotless, unbroken **09** faultless, stainless, undamaged **10** immaculate, impeccable, unimpaired **11** unblemished **12** indefectible **14** without blemish

flax
03 tow **04** harl, herl, line, lint **05** hards, hurds **06** byssus **07** allseed **08** Phormium **12** mill-mountain

flay
03 pan **04** flog, skin, slam **05** knock, slate **06** attack, flench, flense, flinch, revile, uncase **07** condemn, lambast, run down, scourge, upbraid **08** denounce, execrate, frighten **09** castigate, criticize, excoriate, pull apart, skin alive, tear apart **12** pull to pieces **13** find fault with, tear a strip off

flea
05 Pulex **06** chigoe, chigre, jigger **07** chigger, Daphnia, daphnid **09** turnip fly **11** Aphaniptera **12** Siphonaptera

fleck
03 dot **04** dust, mark, spot **05** point, speck, stain **06** dapple, mottle, streak **07** freckle, spatter, speckle, stipple **08** sprinkle

fledgling
03 new **04** tiro **05** squab **06** coming, novice, rising, rookie **07** budding, learner, nascent, recruit, trainee **08** beginner, emergent, emerging, neophyte, newcomer **09** coming out, embryonic, greenhorn, novitiate **10** apprentice, burgeoning, developing, tenderfoot **11** independent

flee
03 fly, lam, ren, rin, run **04** bolt, bunk, loup, quit, rush, scat **05** lam it, leave, scoot, scram, skive, split **06** decamp, depart, escape, get out, vanish **07** abscond, bunk off, do a bunk, get away, make off, push off, retreat, run away, scarper, take off, vamoose **08** clear off, shove off, up sticks, withdraw **09** cut and run, disappear, do a runner, push along, skedaddle **10** hightail it, hit the road, make tracks, take flight **11** hit the trail **13** sling your hook **14** make a bolt for it **15** make a break for it, take to your heels

fleece
02 do **03** con, jib, rob, teg **04** bilk, coat, down, gull, plot, rook, skin, tegg, wool **05** bleed, cheat, mulct, ploat, pluck, shave, shear, steal, sting **06** diddle, fiddle, rip off, toison **07** defraud, plunder, squeeze, swindle **08** fetch off **09** shearling, toison d'or **10** overcharge **11** string along **12** pull a fast one, put one over on, take for a ride **13** have someone on

fleecy
04 soft **05** downy, hairy, nappy **06** fluffy, pilose, shaggy, woolly **07** velvety **08** floccose **10** flocculate, lanuginose **11** eriophorous

fleet
02 RN **04** fast, flit, flow, navy **05** agile, flitt, float, flota, quick, rapid, swift **06** armada, flying, marine, nimble, speedy, winged **07** caravan **08** flotilla, meteoric, navarchy, squadron **09** mercurial, task force, transient **10** naval force **11** expeditious, light-footed

fleeting
04 flit **05** brief, flitt, quick, short **06** bubble, flying, hollow, rushed, sudden **07** passing **08** fugitive, volatile **09** ephemeral, fugacious, momentary, temporary, transient **10** evanescent, short-lived, transitory

fleetingly
07 briefly, quickly **08** casually **10** for a moment, for a second **11** momentarily **12** for an instant

flesh
03 fat **04** boar, body, meat, pith, pulp, skin **05** brawn, braxy, stuff **06** matter, muscle, tissue, weight **08** solidity **09** carnality, sexuality, substance **10** sensuality **11** human nature, physicality **12** carnal nature, corporeality, significance, sinful nature **14** physical nature

• **flesh and blood**
03 kin **04** rels **05** folks **06** family **07** kindred, rellies **08** relative **09** relations

• **flesh out**
08 expand on **09** elaborate **10** add details **11** elaborate on, give details **12** make complete

• **flesh round jaw**
04 gill

• **in the flesh**
05 alive **06** bodily **08** in person **09** incarnate **10** in real life **12** in actual life

fleshly
05 human **06** animal, bodily, carnal, earthy, erotic, sexual **07** bestial, brutish, earthly, lustful, sensual, worldly **08** corporal, material, physical **09** corporeal

fleshy
03 fat **05** ample, beefy, hefty, meaty, obese, plump, podgy, pulpy, stout, tubby **06** brawny, chubby, chunky, flabby, portly, rotund **07** carnose, paunchy **08** carneous **09** corpulent, succulent **10** overweight, well-padded

flex
03 bow, ply **04** bend, cord, lead, wire **05** angle, cable, crook, curve **07** stretch, tighten **08** contract, double up

flexibility
04 give **06** spring **07** flexion, pliancy **09** tensility **10** elasticity, pliability, resilience, suppleness **11** amenability, bendability, springiness **12** adaptability, agreeability, complaisance **13** adjustability

flexible
◊ *anagram indicator*
04 open **05** agile, bendy, lithe, withy **06** docile, floppy, limber, lissom, mobile, pliant, supple **07** elastic, flexile, lissome, plastic, pliable, springy, willowy **08** amenable, bendable, stretchy, variable, yielding **09** adaptable, compliant, complying, malleable, mouldable, open-ended, tractable **10** adjustable, changeable, manageable **13** accommodating, double-jointed

flick
03 dab, hit, rap, tap **04** flip, jerk, lash, lick, snap, whip **05** click, flirt, swish, touch **06** fillip, strike

• **flick through**
04 scan, skim, skip **08** glance at

10 glance over, run through 11 flip through, leaf through 12 thumb through 13 browse through

flicker
03 bat 04 atom, drop, iota, jump, lick, play, wink 05 blink, flare, flash, gleam, glint, spark, trace, waver 06 gutter, quiver, yucker 07 flaught, flutter, glimmer, glitter, shimmer, sparkle, twinkle, vibrate 08 lambency 09 flaughter 10 indication

flier
02 FO, PO 07 handout, leaflet 08 brochure, bulletin, circular, pamphlet 09 statement 10 literature 12 press release

See also **bird**

• expert flier
03 ace

• non-flier *see* **flightless birds** *under* **bird**

fliers
03 RAF

flight
03 fly, guy, lam, set 04 exit, pair, rout, rush, trap, trip, wing 05 steps 06 escape, exodus, flying, roding, stairs, voyage 07 fleeing, getaway, journey, retreat, roading, runaway, shuttle, soaring 08 aviation, stairway 09 air travel, breakaway, departure, skedaddle, staircase 10 absconding, exaltation, running off, volitation, withdrawal 11 aeronautics, running away 12 air transport 13 globetrotting

• take flight
03 fly, run 04 bolt, flee, quit, rush, scat 05 lam it, leave, leg it, scoot, scram, skive, split 06 decamp, depart, escape, vanish 07 abscond, bunk off, do a bunk, get away, make off, push off, retreat, run away, scarper, take off, vamoose 08 clear off, shove off, up sticks, withdraw 09 cut and run, disappear, do a runner, push along, skedaddle 10 hightail it, hit the road, make tracks 11 hit the trail 13 sling your hook 14 make a bolt for it, take it on the lam 15 make a break for it, take to your heels

flighty
◇ *anagram indicator*
04 wild 05 giddy, silly, swift 06 fickle, volage 07 erratic, flyaway 08 fanciful, hellicat, skipping, skittish, unstable, unsteady, volatile 09 butterfly, frivolous, impetuous, impulsive, mercurial, volageous 10 bird-witted, capricious, changeable, inconstant, unbalanced 11 birdbrained, flirtatious, hare-brained, lightheaded, loup-the-dyke, thoughtless, unballasted 12 bubble-headed, rattle-headed, whisky-frisky 13 irresponsible, rattle-brained, weather-headed 14 scatterbrained

• flighty type
04 bird

flimsy
04 fine, poor, thin, weak 05 filmy, light, shaky, sheer, wispy 06 feeble, meagre, slight, slimsy 07 band-box, fragile, rickety, shallow, trivial 08 banknote, delicate, ethereal, gossamer, trifling, vaporous 09 airy-fairy, cardboard, gossamery, makeshift, paper-thin 10 inadequate, jerry-built, ramshackle 11 implausible, lightweight, superficial 12 unconvincing 13 insubstantial

flinch
04 balk, duck, flay, flee, funk 05 avoid, cower, dodge, quail, quake, shake, shirk, start, wince 06 blench, cringe, crouch, falter, recoil, shiver, shrink 07 retreat, shudder, shy away, tremble 08 draw back, pull back, withdraw 10 shrink back

fling
02 go 03 lob, shy, try 04 cast, dart, dash, hurl, jerk, jibe, rush, send, shot, toss, turn 05 amour, binge, chuck, crack, heave, lance, lanch, pitch, sling, spang, spree, taunt, throw, trial, whirl 06 affair, gamble, launce, launch, let fly, propel 07 affaire, attempt, carry-on, flounce, liaison, romance, venture 08 catapult, good time, intrigue, spanghew, throw out 10 indulgence, love affair, send flying 12 relationship 13 affaire d'amour, grande passion

flinty
03 icy 04 cold, hard 05 blank, cruel, stern, stony 06 chilly, frigid, frosty, severe, steely 07 adamant, callous, deadpan, hostile 08 obdurate, pitiless 09 heartless, merciless, unfeeling 10 inexorable, poker-faced 11 emotionless, indifferent, unforgiving 12 unresponsive 14 expressionless

flip
◇ *reversal indicator*
04 cast, flap, jerk, pert, snap, spin, toss, turn 05 click, flick, pitch, throw, twirl, twist 09 pitch-pole, pitch-poll

• flip through
04 scan, skim, skip 08 glance at 10 glance over 11 leaf through 12 flick through, thumb through 13 browse through

flippancy
05 cheek 06 levity 08 glibness, pertness 09 frivolity, sauciness 10 cheekiness, disrespect, persiflage 11 irreverence, shallowness 12 impertinence 13 facetiousness 14 superficiality 15 thoughtlessness

flippant
04 flip, glib, pert, rude 05 saucy 06 cheeky, nimble 07 offhand, playful, shallow 08 impudent 09 facetious, frivolous 10 insouciant, irreverent 11 impertinent, superficial, thoughtless 12 light-hearted 13 disrespectful, irresponsible

flippantly
06 glibly, rudely 11 facetiously, frivolously 12 irreverently 13 impertinently, irresponsibly, superficially, thoughtlessly 14 light-heartedly 15 disrespectfully

flipping
06 cursed, damned, darned, dashed 07 blasted 08 annoying, blinking, blooming, dratting, fiendish, infernal, wretched 10 confounded, unpleasant

flirt
03 rap, toy 04 jerk, mash, ogle, vamp 05 dally, eye up, flick, hussy, tease 06 chat up, chippy, coquet, gillet, lead on, masher, wanton 07 carry on, pickeer, trifler 08 coquette, make up to 09 gillflirt, philander 10 make eyes at 11 make a pass at, philanderer 12 heart-breaker

• flirt with
03 try 04 mash 05 hit on 06 coquet 07 carry on, hit upon, toy with 08 consider, coquette, dabble in, play with 09 entertain 10 trifle with

flirtation
05 amour, sport 06 affair, come-on, lumber, toying 07 teasing 08 coquetry, dallying, intrigue, trifling 09 dalliance 10 chatting up 12 philandering

flirtatious
05 loose 06 come-on, flirty, wanton 07 amorous, flighty, teasing 08 flirtish, sportive 10 come-hither, coquettish 11 promiscuous, provocative

flit
◇ *anagram indicator*
03 bob, fly 04 dart, dash, pass, rush, skim, skip, slip, wing 05 dance, flash, fleet, light, speed, whisk 07 flitter, flutter 08 fleeting

float
03 bob 04 cart, cork, hang, hull, pram, sail, swim, waft 05 balsa, camel, drift, fleet, glide, hover, quill, set up, slide, table 06 bobber, launch, smooth, submit, wander 07 oropesa, pontoon, present, promote, propose, suggest, suspend 08 get going, initiate, levitate, lifebuoy 09 be buoyant, establish, recommend 10 come up with, put forward, stay afloat 13 pneumatophore 15 get off the ground

floating
◇ *anagram indicator*
04 free 06 afloat, natant 07 bobbing, buoyant, movable, sailing, wafting 08 drifting, hovering, swimming, variable 09 migratory, unsettled, wandering 10 indecisive, transitory, unattached, unsinkable 11 fluctuating, uncommitted

flock
03 mob 04 band, bevy, fold, game, herd, host, mass, mill, pack, rout, sord, trip, tuft, walk, wing, wisp, wool 05 bunch, charm, chirm, covey, crowd, drove, flush, group, shoal, skein, swarm, troop, watch 06 flight, gaggle, gather, huddle, school, spring, throng

07 cluster, collect, company, dopping 08 assemble, assembly, converge, paddling 09 flocculus, gathering, multitude 10 collection, congregate, unkindness 11 murmuration 12 come together, congregation

flog
◇ *anagram indicator*
03 tan, tat, taw 04 beat, belt, cane, drub, flay, hawk, hide, lash, sell, whip 05 birch, knout, strap, swish, trade, whack, whang 06 breech, deal in, handle, larrup, peddle, punish, strike, thrash, wallop 07 scourge, sjambok 08 chastise, urticate, vapulate 09 horsewhip 10 flagellate 12 offer for sale, put up for sale

flogging
06 caning, hiding 07 beating, belting, flaying, lashing 08 birching, whacking, whipping 09 scourging, strapping, thrashing, walloping 10 vapulation 12 flagellation 13 horsewhipping, whipping-cheer

flood
04 bore, eger, fill, flow, glut, gush, pour, rage, rush, soak, tide 05 drown, eager, eagre, spate, speat, surge, swamp, swell 06 deluge, drench, engulf, excess, series, stream 07 debacle, freshet, immerse, smother, torrent 08 alluvion, brim over, diluvion, diluvium, downpour, inundate, overflow, plethora, saturate, submerge 09 abundance, cataclysm, overwhelm, profusion 10 flash flood, inundation, outpouring, spring tide, succession, transgress 11 superfluity 13 Ogygian deluge

floor
02 fl, KO 04 area, base, beat, dais, deck, fell, loft, tier 05 attic, basis, étage, level, stage, stump, throw 06 baffle, defeat, ground, planch, puzzle, storey 07 flummox, landing, nonplus, perplex 08 basement, bel étage, bewilder, confound, entresol, flooring, platform 09 discomfit, dumbfound, frustrate, knock down, overwhelm, prostrate 10 disconcert, downstairs, strike down 11 piano nobile

• first floor
11 ground level

• floor material
04 lino, pisé, rung

floozy *see* **tart**

flop
◇ *anagram indicator*
03 sag 04 bomb, drop, fail, fall, fold, hang, sink, swap, swop 05 crash, droop, flump, slump 06 dangle, fiasco, go bust, pack up, slip-up, topple, tumble 07 also-ran, debacle, failure, founder, go broke, has-been, misfire, no-hoper, washout 08 collapse, disaster, fall flat, lay an egg, shambles 10 non-starter 11 go to the wall 12 come a cropper, go into the red 14 be unsuccessful

• flop down
03 wop 04 whap, whop 05 plump

floppy
◇ *anagram indicator*
04 limp, soft 05 baggy, loose 06 droopy, flabby 07 flaccid, hanging, sagging 08 dangling, diskette, flexible 12 flexible disk

flora
06 botany, Cybele, plants 07 herbage 08 plantage 09 plant life 10 vegetation

floral emblem *see* **emblem**

florid
03 red 04 high 05 Asian, fussy, ruddy 06 ornate, purple, rococo 07 baroque, flowery, flushed, pompous, reddish, taffeta, verbose 08 beetroot, blushing, figurate, red-faced, rubicund, sanguine, taffetas 09 bombastic, elaborate, high-flown 10 coloratura, flamboyant, melismatic 11 embellished, extravagant 12 high-sounding 13 grandiloquent, overelaborate

Florida
02 FL 03 Fla

flotsam
04 junk 05 dreck 06 debris, jetsam 07 flotage, rubbish 08 detritus, floatage, oddments, wreckage 11 odds and ends

flounce
03 bob 04 jerk, toss 05 fling, frill, stamp, storm, throw, twist 06 bounce, fringe, ruffle, spring 07 falbala, valance 08 furbelow, trimming

flounder
◇ *anagram indicator*
05 fluke, grope, slosh 06 dither, falter, fumble, jumble, tolter, wallop, wallow 07 blunder, go under, stagger, stumble 08 struggle 10 be confused, flail about 11 thresh about 12 lose the place

flour
04 meal 06 red-dog 07 cribble, pollard 08 tailings 09 wheatmeal 11 strong wheat

flourish
◇ *anagram indicator*
03 wag, wax 04 boom, élan, grow, lick, mort, show, wave 05 bloom, get on, serif, shake, swash, sweep, swing, swirl, swish, twirl, twist, vaunt, wield 06 do well, flaunt, flower, parade, paraph, rubric, swinge, thrive, tucket 07 blossom, burgeon, cadenza, develop, display, exhibit, fanfare, gesture, panache, pizzazz, prosper, show off, succeed, wampish 08 be strong, brandish, curlicue, increase, ornament, progress 09 bear fruit 10 decoration

flourished
◇ *anagram indicator*
02 fl 04 flor

flourishing
◇ *anagram indicator*
04 pert 05 green, palmy 06 bloomy 07 booming 08 blooming, thriving 10 blossoming, burgeoning, prosperous, successful 11 going strong

flout
04 defy, gibe, jibe, lout, lowt, mock 05 break, scorn, scout, spurn 06 jeer at, reject 07 disdain, disobey, laugh at, scoff at, sneer at, violate 08 ridicule 09 disregard, go against 11 set at nought 15 show contempt for

flow
◇ *anagram indicator*
02 go 03 jet, ren, rin, run 04 drip, flux, gush, leak, make, melt, move, ooze, pour, rail, roll, rush, seep, slip, spew, stem, teem, tide, well, wend 05 arise, drift, flood, glide, issue, raile, rayle, slide, spate, spill, spout, spurt, surge, sweep, swirl, whirl 06 babble, bubble, course, deluge, derive, emerge, gurgle, morass, plenty, result, ripple, spring, squirt, stream 07 cascade, current, emanate, passage, proceed, trickle 08 effusion, movement, overflow, plethora, recourse 09 abundance, circulate, originate, quicksand 10 outpouring

flower
03 bud 04 acme, best, grow, open, peak, pick 05 bloom, cream, élite, prime 06 choice, finest, floret, height, heyday, mature, select, sprout, thrive, zenith 07 blossom, burgeon, come out, develop, prosper, succeed 08 best part, flourish, floweret, maturity, pinnacle 10 perfection 11 culmination, florescence 13 efflorescence, inflorescence 14 crème de la crème

See also **birth**; **river**

Flower parts include:

05 calyx, ovary, ovule, petal, sepal, spike, stalk, style, torus, umbel
06 anther, carpel, corymb, pistil, raceme, spadix, stamen, stigma
07 corolla, nectary, panicle, pedicel
08 filament, thalamus
09 capitulum, dichasium, gynoecium
10 receptacle
11 monochasium

Garden flowers include:

04 lis
04 aloe, daff, flag, glad, iris, lily, pink, rose, sego
05 aster, daisy, lotus, lupin, pansy, phlox, poppy, stock, tulip, viola
06 allium, azalea, crocus, dahlia, orchid, salvia, squill, violet, zinnia
07 alyssum, anemone, begonia, campion, day-lily, freesia, fuchsia, lobelia, nemesia, nigella, petunia, primula, verbena
08 arum lily, asphodel, bluebell, cyclamen, daffodil, dianthus, foxglove, gardenia, geranium, gladioli, hyacinth, marigold, pond lily, primrose, snowdrop, sweet pea
09 amaryllis, aubrietia, calendula, candytuft, carnation, digitalis, gladiolus, hollyhock, narcissus,

nicotiana, regal lily, sunflower, tiger lily, torch lily
10 agapanthus, busy lizzie, cornflower, delphinium, Easter lily, fleur-de-lis, fleur-de-lys, fritillary, nasturtium, poinsettia, polyanthus, ragged-lady, snake's head, snapdragon, wallflower
11 African lily, antirrhinum, forget-me-not, gillyflower, love-in-a-mist, Madonna-lily, naked ladies, red-hot poker, tiger flower
12 devil-in-a-bush, flower of Jove, rose geranium, Solomon's seal, sweet william, wild hyacinth, Zantedeschia
13 African violet, butcher's broom, chrysanthemum, grape hyacinth, lily of the Nile, winter aconite
14 belladonna lily, glory of the snow, Ithuriel's spear
15 dog's tooth violet, lily of the valley, star of Bethlehem

See also **lily**

Wild flowers include:

03 kex, meu
04 daff, geum, ling, nard, woad
05 clary, daisy, gowan, laser, poppy
06 clover, oxslip, teasel, violet, yarrow
07 ale hoof, bistort, campion, comfrey, cowslip, dog rose, goldcup, heather, spignel
08 bluebell, crowfoot, dog daisy, foxglove, harebell, lungwort, primrose, rock rose, self-heal, spicknel, toadflax, wild iris
09 Aaron's rod, baldmoney, birthwort, broomrape, buttercup, celandine, columbine, edelweiss, goldenrod, horsetail, moneywort, stonecrop, water lily, wild pansy
10 crane's bill, goatsbeard, heartsease, lady's smock, marguerite, masterwort, oxeye daisy, pennyroyal, wild endive, wild orchid
11 ragged robin, wild chicory, wood anemone
12 common mallow, cuckoo flower, great mullein, lady's slipper, solomon's seal, white campion, yellow rocket
13 butter-and-eggs, field cow-wheat, shepherd's club, wild gladiolus
14 black-eyed susan, bladder campion, common toadflax, multiflora rose
15 New England aster

• **garland of flowers**
03 lei **05** toran **06** torana
• **mass of flowers**
04 head

flowery
05 fancy **06** bloomy, floral, florid, ornate **07** baroque, chintzy, pompous, verbose **08** blossomy **09** bombastic, elaborate, high-flown **10** euphuistic, rhetorical **13** grandiloquent

flowing
04 easy, flux **05** loose **06** floppy, fluent, liquid, moving, oozing, smooth **07** current, cursive, falling, flaccid, gushing, hanging, natural, pouring, rolling, running, rushing, seeping, surging, welling **08** bubbling, sweeping, unbroken **09** cascading, streaming **10** continuous, effortless **11** loose-bodied, overflowing **12** hanging loose **13** hanging freely, uninterrupted

fluctuate
◇ *anagram indicator*
04 sway, trim, vary, yo-yo **05** alter, float, range, shift, swing, waver **06** change, differ, seesaw **07** balance **08** hesitate, undulate **09** alternate, come and go, oscillate, vacillate **10** ebb and flow **11** go up and down, rise and fall **13** chop and change

fluctuation
05 range, shift, swing **06** change, seiche **08** floating, nutation, wavering **09** variation **10** fickleness **11** alternation, ambivalence, inconstancy, instability, oscillation, vacillation, variability **12** irresolution, unsteadiness **14** capriciousness

flue
03 fur **04** duct, flat, pipe, vent **05** shaft, tewel **06** flared, tunnel, uptake **07** channel, chimney, passage, shallow, splayed **08** fluework **09** influenza

fluency
04 ease, flow **07** command, control **08** facility, glibness **09** assurance, eloquence, facundity, flippancy, readiness, slickness **10** outpouring, smoothness, volubility **12** flippantness **13** copia verborum **14** articulateness

fluent
04 easy, glib **05** fluid, ready, slick **06** facile, smooth **07** elegant, flowing, natural, voluble **08** eloquent, graceful **10** articulate, effortless **11** free-flowing, mellifluous **13** silver-tongued

fluently
03 pat **05** patly **06** easily, glibly **08** smoothly **09** elegantly, naturally **10** eloquently, gracefully **12** articulately, effortlessly

fluff
◇ *anagram indicator*
03 fug, nap **04** blow, boob, dowl, down, dust, flue, fuzz, lint, muff, oose, ooze, pile **05** botch, dowle, flosh, floss, spoil **06** bungle, cock up, foul up, fumble, mess up, muck up, muddle **07** do badly, screw up **09** dust bunny, mismanage **11** make a mess of **13** make a bad job of **15** put your foot in it

fluffy
04 soft **05** downy, furry, fuzzy, hairy, silky **06** fleecy, pluffy, shaggy, woolly **07** velvety **08** feathery

fluid
◇ *anagram indicator*
02 fl **03** gas **04** easy, open **05** chyle, grume, juice, runny **06** liquid, liquor, melted, mobile, molten, smooth, vapour, watery **07** aqueous, elegant, flowing, natural, protean, running **08** atrament, flexible, graceful, shifting, solution, unstable, unsteady, variable **09** adaptable, diffluent, liquefied, unsettled **10** adjustable, changeable, effortless, inconstant, karyolymph **11** fluctuating, free-flowing **12** unsolidified

fluke
03 fan **04** barb, worm **05** break, freak, quirk **06** chance, stroke, upcast **07** killick, killock, scratch **08** accident, blessing, flounder, fortuity, windfall **09** trematode **10** lucky break **11** coincidence, serendipity **12** stroke of luck

fluky
05 jammy, lucky **06** chance **08** freakish **09** fortunate, uncertain **10** accidental, fortuitous **12** coincidental, incalculable **13** serendipitous

flummox
03 fox **04** faze **05** floor, stump **06** baffle, defeat, puzzle, stymie **07** confuse, mystify, nonplus, perplex **08** bewilder, confound **09** bamboozle

flummoxed
05 at sea, fazed, foxed **07** at a loss, baffled, floored, puzzled, stumped, stymied **08** confused **09** mystified, perplexed **10** bamboozled, bewildered, confounded, nonplussed

flunk
04 bomb, fail, flop, fold **06** blow it **07** failure, founder **08** fall flat **09** not make it **10** come undone, not come off **11** bite the dust, come to grief, come unglued, come unstuck **12** come a cropper **14** be unsuccessful **15** blow your chances

flunkey
05 slave, toady, valet **06** drudge, Jeames, lackey, menial, minion, yes-man **07** cringer, footman, servant, steward **08** hanger-on **09** assistant, underling **10** bootlicker, manservant

fluorine
01 F

flurried
◇ *anagram indicator*
05 fazed, upset **07** in a flap, in a tizz, rattled **08** in a tizzy, unnerved **09** disturbed, flustered, perturbed, unsettled **12** all of a lather **13** having kittens

flurry
◇ *anagram indicator*
04 bout, flap, fuss, gust, stir, to-do **05** blast, burst, hurry, spell, spurt, swirl, upset, whirl **06** bother, bustle, hassle, hubbub, hustle, rattle, ruffle, scurry, shower, squall, tumult **07** agitate, confuse, disturb, fluster, flutter, perturb, swither **08** bewilder, outbreak, unsettle **09** agitation, commotion

10 disconcert, excitement
11 disturbance 12 perturbation
14 discountenance

flush
03 rud 04 burn, even, flat, full, gild, glow, hose, rich, swab, true, wash
05 bloom, blush, clear, eject, elate, empty, expel, flame, go red, level, plane, rinse, rouse, scour, start
06 colour, hectic, heyday, lavish, puddle, redden, sluice, smooth, square, vigour 07 cleanse, crimson, disturb, moneyed, redness, replete, suffuse, turn red, uncover, wealthy, well-off 08 abundant, colour up, discover, drive out, evacuate, force out, generous, rosiness, well-to-do
09 abounding, abundance, freshness, reddening, ruddiness 10 prosperous, run to earth, well-heeled
11 overflowing

flushed
03 hot, red 04 pink, rosy 05 aglow, rosed, ruddy 06 ablaze, aflame, blowsy, blowzy, elated, florid, hectic
07 aroused, burning, crimson, excited, glowing, scarlet 08 animated, blushing, enthused, exultant, inspired, rubicund, sanguine, thrilled
11 embarrassed, exhilarated, intoxicated

fluster
◇ *anagram indicator*
04 faze, flap, heat, tizz 05 panic, state, tizzy, upset 06 bother, bustle, dither, flurry, pother, pudder, put off, rattle, ruffle 07 agitate, confuse, disturb, perturb, turmoil, unnerve
08 confound, distract, hurrying, unsettle 09 agitation, commotion, confusion, embarrass, flustrate
10 discompose, disconcert
11 disturbance, flustration, make nervous 12 perturbation
13 embarrassment

flute
04 fife 05 quena, tibia 06 poogye, zufolo 07 chamfer, piccolo, poogyee, zuffolo 08 recorder 09 flageolet
10 shakuhachi

fluted
06 ribbed, ridged 07 grooved
08 furrowed 10 channelled, corrugated

flutter
◇ *anagram indicator*
03 bat, bet, fan, fly 04 beat, flap, play, punt, risk, toss, waff, wave 05 dance, flaff, hover, shake, wager, waver
06 gamble, quiver, ripple, ruffle, shiver, tremor, twitch, winnow 07 agitate, flacker, flaffer, flicker, flitter, pulsate, shudder, tremble, twitter, vibrate
08 flapping, flichter, volitate
09 agitation, confusion, flaughter, fluctuate, palpitate, vibration
11 palpitation, speculation

flux
04 flow, fuse, melt 05 issue
06 change, motion, unrest 08 fluidity, movement, mutation 10 alteration, transition 11 development, fluctuation, instability 12 modification
13 changeability
• **electric flux displacement**
01 D
• **magnetic flux density**
01 B

fly
◇ *anagram indicator*
03 jet, run, sly 04 bolt, dart, dash, flap, flee, flit, quit, race, rise, rush, scat, show, soar, tear, wave, wily, wing, zoom
05 alert, canny, float, glide, guide, hover, hurry, leave, mount, pilot, scoot, scram, sharp, shoot, skive, smart, speed, split, steer 06 artful, ascend, astute, career, decamp, depart, escape, flight, get out, hasten, reveal, shrewd, slip by, sprint, stream, vanish, winnow 07 abscond, careful, control, cunning, display, do a bunk, exhibit, flutter, get away, go by air, make off, operate, present, prudent, push off, retreat, run away, scarper, stylish, take off, vamoose 08 clear off, shove off, volitate, withdraw 09 cut and run, disappear, do a runner, golden-eye, go quickly, manoeuvre, on the ball, push along, sagacious, skedaddle 10 hit the road, make tracks, take flight
11 fashionable, hit the trail, nobody's fool, pass quickly, travel by air 14 make a bolt for it 15 make a break for it, take to your heels

Flies include:

03 bee, bot, day, dor, gad, hop, ked, may, med
04 beet, blow, boat, bulb, bush, cleg, corn, deer, dung, fire, frit, gnat, gout, kade, lamp, meat, pium, sand
05 alder, birch, black, crane, drone, flesh, froth, fruit, horse, house, hover, march, midge, onion, sedge, snake, snipe, water, wheat
06 blowie, caddis, carrot, cuckoo, forest, motuca, muscid, mutuca, pomace, robber, stable, tipula, tsetse, turnip, tzetse, tzetze, warble
07 blister, brommer, cabbage, cluster, diptera, dolphin, harvest, Hessian, lantern, sciarid, smother, Spanish, vinegar
08 glossina, ruby-tail, scorpion, sheep ked, simulium, tachinid
09 cantharis, ichneumon, screw-worm
10 bluebottle, Cecidomyia, drosophila, spittle bug
11 biting midge, buffalo gnat, cabbage-root, greenbottle
12 cheesehopper
13 cheese skipper, spittle insect

Fishing flies include:

03 bob
04 harl, herl, tail
05 sedge
06 doctor, hackle, palmer, salmon
07 watchet
09 hairy Mary, Jock Scott
10 cock-a-bondy

• **fly at**
03 hit 05 go for 06 attack, charge, let fly, strike 07 assault, lay into 08 fall upon 09 have a go at, lash out at
• **fly open**
◇ *anagram indicator*
05 burst 15 burst at the seams

fly-by-night
05 shady 06 cowboy 07 dubious
09 ephemeral 10 short-lived, unreliable 12 disreputable, questionable, undependable
13 discreditable, irresponsible, untrustworthy

flyer *see* **flier**

flying
04 fast 05 brief, hasty, rapid
06 mobile, rushed, speedy, volant, winged 07 gliding, hurried, soaring, winging 08 airborne, flapping, fleeting, flighted, floating, hovering, volitant 09 on the wing, wind-borne
10 fluttering, volitation 11 upon the wing, whistle-stop

foam
03 fry 04 boil, fizz, head, scum, suds, surf 05 froth, spume, yeast
06 befoam, bubble, lather, mousse, seethe 07 aerogel, bubbles 08 sea froth 10 effervesce 13 effervescence

foamy
05 spumy, sudsy 06 bubbly, frothy, yeasty 07 foaming, lathery
10 spumescent

fob
• **fob off**
04 dump 05 foist 06 impose, put off, unload 07 deceive, inflict, palm off, pass off 08 get rid of

focus
03 aim, fix, hub 04 axis, core, crux, join, meet, turn 05 heart, hinge, pivot
06 accent, center, centre, direct, home in, kernel, stress, target, weight, zero in, zoom in 07 nucleus 08 converge, emphasis, linchpin, pinpoint, priority
09 attention, spotlight 10 focal point, importance, metropolis, prominence
11 concentrate, pre-eminence
12 accentuation, significance, underscoring 13 concentration
14 bring into focus
• **in focus**
05 clear, crisp, sharp 08 distinct
11 well-defined
• **out of focus**
04 hazy 05 fuzzy, muzzy 06 blurry
07 blurred 10 ill-defined, indistinct

fodder
02 ti 03 hay 04 feed, food, milo
05 grass, vetch 06 eatage, forage, fother, lucern, luzern, silage, stover
07 alfalfa, lucerne, pabulum, provand, provend, rations, soilage, timothy
08 browsing, goat's-rue, oat grass, proviant, rye grass, sainfoin, teosinte

09 foodstuff, milk vetch, milo maize, provender, sago grass, saintfoin 10 cow parsnip, serradella, serradilla, Sudan grass 11 nourishment, white clover 12 meadow fescue, timothy grass 13 kangaroo grass

foe
05 enemy, rival 08 opponent, wrangler 09 adversary, combatant, ill-wisher 10 antagonist

foetid *see* **fetid, foetid**

foetus
06 embryo 10 unborn baby 11 unborn child

fog
◇ *anagram indicator*
03 dim 04 blur, daze, dull, haar, haze, mist, moss, smog 05 befog, brume, cloud, gloom, smoke 06 baffle, darken, muddle, stupor, trance 07 aerosol, confuse, obscure, pea-soup, perplex, sea fret, steam up 08 bewilder, haziness 09 confusion, mistiness, murkiness, obfuscate, obscurity, pease-soup, pea-souper, vagueness 10 bafflement, perplexity, puzzlement 12 bewilderment 14 disorientation

foggy
03 dim 04 damp, dark, grey, hazy 05 misty, muggy, murky, thick, vague 06 cloudy, gloomy, smoggy, stupid 07 brumous, clouded, muddled, obscure, shadowy, unclear 08 overcast 10 indistinct

foible
05 fault, habit, quirk 06 defect, faible, oddity 07 failing, oddness 08 penchant, weakness 09 weak point 11 peculiarity, shortcoming, strangeness 12 eccentricity, idiosyncrasy, imperfection

foil
03 pip 04 balk, stop 05 baulk, block, chaff, check, elude, foyle, stump 06 baffle, defeat, hamper, hinder, outwit, relief, set-off, thwart, window 07 balance, counter, fleuret, nullify, paillon, prevent, repulse, scupper, scuttle, setting 08 contrast, obstruct 09 frustrate 10 antithesis, background, beauty spot, circumvent, complement 11 frustration, silver paper

foist
03 fob 05 force 06 fob off, impose, saddle, thrust, unload, wish on 07 palm off, pass off 08 get rid of 09 introduce

fold
03 hug, lap, pen, ply 04 bend, cuff, dart, fail, fake, flop, hood, line, lirk, purl, ring, ruck, tuck, turn, wrap, yard 05 clasp, close, court, crash, crimp, flock, kraal, layer, paper, pleat, plica, pouch, pound, prank, quill, quire 06 church, crease, crista, diapir, dog-ear, double, enfold, furrow, gather, go bust, mantle, middle, pack up, pleach, plight, pranck, pucker, ruffle, rumple, wimple, wrap up 07 company, crinkle, crumple, dog's-ear, embrace, enclose, entwine, envelop, flexion, folding, go broke, go under, omentum, overlap, paddock, prancke, squeeze, whimple, wrinkle 08 assembly, collapse, compound, doubling, patagium, shut down, stockade, syncline, turn down, turn over 09 community, duplicate, enclosure, gathering, gill cover, inflexure, knife-edge, mesentery, monocline, plication, plicature, replicate, turn under 10 epicanthus, fellowship, go bankrupt, intertwine 11 convolution, corrugation, duplicature, go to the wall 12 congregation, parishioners 14 hospital corner 15 go out of business

folder
04 file 05 folio 06 binder, holder, jacket, pocket, wallet 08 envelope 09 directory, matchbook, portfolio 13 lever arch file

foliage
06 canopy, leaves 07 boscage, boskage, leafage, verdure 08 greenery 09 foliation, foliature, vernation 10 vegetation 12 frondescence

folio
01 f 02 fo 03 fol

folios
02 ff

folk
03 kin, men 04 clan, race 05 tribe 06 ethnic, family, humans, nation, native, people, public, tribal, tupuna 07 kindred, parents, persons, popular, society 08 kinsfolk, national 09 ancestral, relations, relatives 10 indigenous, population 11 ethnic group, traditional
See also **singer**

folklore
04 lore 05 myths, tales 06 fables 07 beliefs, customs, legends, stories 09 folktales, mythology, tradition 13 superstitions

folksy
04 fond, kind, maty, warm 05 basic, close, crude, matey, pally, plain, thick, tight 06 chummy, genial, kindly, rustic, simple 07 affable, amiable, cordial, helpful, natural 08 amicable, everyday, familiar, friendly, intimate, ordinary, outgoing, sociable 09 comradely, convivial, receptive 10 hospitable 11 good-natured, inseparable, neighbourly, sympathetic, traditional 12 affectionate, approachable, time-honoured 13 companionable 15 unsophisticated

follow
◇ *juxtaposition indicator*
03 ape, dog, ren, rin, run, sew, sue, use 04 copy, flow, heed, heel, hunt, mind, note, obey, stag, suss, tail, twig 05 arise, catch, chase, ensue, grasp, hound, issue, mimic, stalk, track, trail, watch 06 accept, attend, escort, fathom, go with, pursue, repeat, result, second, shadow, spring, take in 07 develop, emanate, emulate, go after, imitate, observe, proceed, replace, stick to, succeed, support, suss out, yield to 08 adhere to, be a fan of, carry out, come next, go behind, practise, run after, supplant, tag along 09 accompany, come after, conform to, give chase, latch onto, supersede 10 appreciate, come behind, comply with, comprehend, keep up with, understand, walk behind 11 be devoted to, go along with, tread behind 14 be a supporter of, be interested in, take the place of 15 take your cue from

- **follow slavishly**
04 echo

- **follow through**
06 finish, fulfil, pursue 08 complete, conclude, continue 09 implement 10 see through

- **follow up**
06 pursue 07 succeed 08 check out, continue, look into, research 09 prosecute, reinforce 11 consolidate, investigate

follower
03 fan, man 04 buff 05 freak, pupil 06 backer, cohort, escort, helper, lackey, voteen 07 acolyte, acolyth, admirer, Anthony, apostle, convert, devotee, janizar, lacquey, sectary 08 adherent, believer, disciple, emulator, hanger-on, imitator, janizary, retainer, sidekick 09 attendant, companion, janissary, poodle-dog, satellite, supporter 10 aficionado, enthusiast, pursuivant, running dog 11 afficionado

following
◇ *juxtaposition indicator*
01 f 03 fol 04 fans, next 05 later, suite 06 circle, public 07 backers, backing, coterie, ensuing, patrons, retinue, sequent, support 08 admirers, audience, secundum 09 adherents, clientèle, entourage, favorable, followers, hereunder, patronage, resulting 10 consequent, favourable, subsequent, succeeding, succession, successive, supporters 13 body of support

- **following pages**
02 ff

folly
03 sin 04 whim 05 folie, moria, tower 06 gazebo, idiocy, lunacy, vanity 07 foolery, foppery, idiotcy, inanity, madness 08 insanity, monument, nonsense, rashness 09 absurdity, belvedere, craziness, silliness, stupidity 10 imbecility, imprudence 11 fatuousness, foolishness 12 illogicality, indiscretion, recklessness 13 foolhardiness, ludicrousness, senselessness 14 ridiculousness

foment
04 brew, goad, spur **05** raise, rouse
06 arouse, excite, foster, incite, kindle, prompt, stir up, whip up, work up
07 agitate, promote, provoke, quicken
08 activate, incubate **09** encourage, instigate, stimulate

fond
03 hot, try **04** daft, dote, vain, warm
05 basis, naive **06** absurd, caring, doting, keen on, liking, loving, nuts on, spoony, tender **07** adoring, amatory, amorous, attempt, deluded, devoted, foolish, proceed **08** hooked on, mad about **09** credulous, daft about, indulgent, nuts about, partial to
10 addicted to, attached to, background, crazy about, dotty about, foundation **11** enamoured of, impractical **12** affectionate **14** over-optimistic

fondle
03 hug, pat, pet **05** grope **06** caress, cocker, cosset, cuddle, dandle, stroke
07 smuggle, touch up

fondly
06 warmly **08** lovingly, tenderly
09 amorously **14** affectionately

• speak fondly
03 coo **04** bill

fondness
04 love **05** fancy, taste **06** dotage, liking, tender, tendre **07** leaning
08 devotion, kindness, penchant, soft spot, weakness **09** affection, engoûment, tendresse **10** attachment, engouement, enthusiasm, partiality, preference, tenderness, well-liking
11 inclination **12** predilection
14 susceptibility

font
08 bénitier, delubrum

food
03 kai **04** chow, diet, dish, eats, fare, feed, feud, grub, meal, menu, nosh, tack, tuck **05** board, meals, scoff, scran, table **06** fodder, kaikai, staple, stores, tucker, viands **07** aliment, cooking, cuisine, pabulum, pasture, rations **08** delicacy, eatables, victuals
09 nutriment, nutrition, provender, repasture **10** foodstuffs, provisions, speciality, sustenance **11** comestibles, nourishment, subsistence
12 refreshments

Foods include:

03 dal, dip, ham, pie, poi
04 dhal, eddo, flan, fool, hash, luau, mash, olio, olla, pâté, rice, soss, soup, stew, taco, tart, tofu, wrap
05 balti, bhaji, boxty, brose, broth, champ, chips, crêpe, curry, daube, dolma, grits, gumbo, jelly, kebab, kofta, laksa, latke, pasta, pasty, pesto, pilau, pizza, Quorn®, roast, salad, salmi, salsa, satay, sauce, sushi, tapas, tikka, toast
06 bhajee, borsch, burger, canapé, caviar, cheese, cookie, faggot, fajita, fondue, fu yung, gratin, haggis, hotpot, hummus, kipper, mousse, paella, pakora, panini, pastry, pilaff, quiche, ragout, samosa, scampi, sorbet, tahina, tamale, trifle, waffle
07 biryani, biscuit, borscht, burrito, chowder, chutney, cobbler, compote, cracker, crowdie, crumble, fajitas, falafel, felafel, fritter, friture, galette, gnocchi, goulash, gravlax, lasagne, oatcake, pancake, pavlova, polenta, pudding, rarebit, risotto, rissole, sashimi, sausage, seafood, soufflé, stir fry, stovies, tempura, terrine, timbale, tostada
08 barbecue, biriyani, calamari, chop suey, chow mein, cocktail, coleslaw, consommé, coq au vin, couscous, dolmades, dumpling, fishcake, fricasee, gado-gado, gazpacho, ice cream, kedgeree, meringue, moussaka, nut roast, omelette, porridge, pot-roast, raclette, sandwich, souvlaki, syllabub, tandoori, teriyaki, tortilla, turnover, tzatziki, vindaloo, yakitori
09 casserole, cassoulet, charlotte, colcannon, croquette, enchilada, fricassée, galantine, gravadlax, guacamole, Irish stew, jambalaya, macedoine, meatballs, nut cutlet, souvlakia, succotash, tabbouleh
10 blancmange, cannelloni, cheesecake, corned beef, cottage pie, enchiladas, fish-finger, fruit salad, Greek salad, green salad, minestrone, mixed grill, peperonata, quesadilla, salmagundi, salmagundy, sauerkraut, spring roll, stroganoff
11 baba ganoush, caesar salad, cockaleekie, French fries, fritto misto, gefilte fish, potato salad, ratatouille, rumblethump, smorgasbord, vichyssoise, winter salad
12 eggs Benedict, fish and chips, mulligatawny, pease pudding, rumblethumps, Russian salad, shepherd's pie, taramasalata, Waldorf salad, welsh rarebit
13 bouillabaisse, fisherman's pie, prawn cocktail, salade niçoise, toad-in-the-hole
14 chilli con carne, macaroni cheese, pickled herring
15 bubble-and-squeak, Wiener schnitzel

See also **bean**; **biscuit**; **bread**; **cake**; **cheese**; **fruit**; **herb**; **meat**; **mushroom**; **nut**; **pasta**; **pastry**; **sauce**; **sausage**; **sweet**; **vegetable**

Fast food includes:

03 KFC®
04 taco, wrap
05 bagel, chips, donut, fries, kebab, pizza
06 Big Mac®, burger, hot dog, nachos
07 burrito, chalupa, falafel, noodles, shwarma, Whopper®
08 doughnut, sandwich
09 bacon roll, chip butty, hamburger, Happy Meal®, milkshake
10 beanburger, beefburger, doner kebab, fish 'n' chips, fish supper, onion rings, shish kebab
11 bacon burger, baked potato, French fries, sausage roll
12 cheeseburger, chicken wings, club sandwich, fish and chips, tortilla wrap, veggie burger
13 chicken burger, sausage supper
14 chicken nuggets, quarter pounder

See also **restaurant**

• provide food
05 cater

fool
04 goof, hoax, jest, joke **05** bluff, cheat, feign, tease, trick **06** delude, diddle, have on, play up, take in, trifle
07 beguile, carry on, deceive, mislead, pretend, swindle **08** hoodwink
09 bamboozle, lark about, mess about, play about **10** mess around, play around, play tricks **11** horse around, monkey about, string along **12** monkey around, put one over on

Fools include:

02 bf
03 ass, auf, con, fon, git, kid, mug, nit, nut, oik, sap, sot, yap
04 berk, bête, bozo, burk, butt, cake, calf, clot, cony, coof, coot, cuif, dill, dope, dork, dupe, geek, goat, goof, goon, goop, gouk, gowk, gull, gump, hash, jerk, kook, loon, lump, lunk, muck, mutt, nana, nerd, nerk, nong, ouph, poop, prat, punk, putz, sham, shmo, simp, soft, tony, twit, yo-yo
05 chump, clown, cluck, comic, coney, divvy, droll, dumbo, dunce, dweeb, eejit, galah, idiot, moron, neddy, nelly, ninny, patch, patsy, prick, purée, schmo, snipe, softy, twerp, wally
06 bampot, bauble, cretin, dimwit, donkey, doofus, dottle, drongo, dum-dum, jester, josser, madcap, monkey, motley, muppet, nitwit, nutter, sawney, schmoe, stooge, sucker, turkey, wallie, wigeon, Yorick
07 airhead, barmpot, bourder, buffoon, Charley, Charlie, dingbat, fat-head, God's ape, gubbins, halfwit, haverel, jackass, jughead, lemming, muggins, pillock, plonker, saphead, tomfool, want-wit, wazzock, widgeon
08 boofhead, dipstick, flathead, fondling, Fred Nerk, imbecile, Jack-fool, lunkhead, merryman, mooncalf, omadhaun, shlemiel, Tom-noddy, Trinculo
09 April fool, birdbrain, blockhead, capocchia, chipochia, cloth head, court fool, dumb-cluck, ignoramus, joculator, lack-brain, lamebrain,

mumchance, philander, schlemiel, schlemihl, simpleton
10 head-banger, nincompoop, silly-billy, Touchstone
11 chowderhead, knuckle-head,
13 laughing-stock, poisson d'avril, proper Charlie

• play the fool
03 fon **04** daff **07** act dido **09** fool about, mess about, muck about **10** act the fool, fool around, mess around, muck around **11** clown around, horse around **12** monkey around

foolery
05 farce, folly, larks **06** antics, capers, pranks **07** carry-on, daffing, fooling, waggery, zanyism **08** clowning, drollery, mischief, nonsense, trumpery **09** high jinks, horseplay, silliness **10** buffoonery, tomfoolery **11** shenanigans **12** childishness, monkey tricks **14** practical jokes

foolhardiness
08 boldness, rashness **10** imprudence **12** recklessness **13** impulsiveness

foolhardy
04 bold, rash **06** daring **08** kamikaze, reckless **09** daredevil, imprudent, impulsive **10** ill-advised, incautious **11** temerarious **13** irresponsible

foolish
◇ *anagram indicator*
03 mad, twp **04** daft, dumb, fond, fool **05** barmy, batty, crazy, dilly, divvy, doilt, dotty, glaik, goofy, inane, inept, nutty, potty, seely, silly, wacky **06** absurd, doiled, dottle, insane, paltry, simple, stupid, unwise **07** dottled, étourdi, fatuous, glaiket, glaikit, goatish, gudgeon, idiotic, moronic, peevish, risible, sottish, tomfool, unwitty, vacuous **08** étourdie, gormless, ignorant, imbecile, overfond **09** half-baked, idiotical, ill-judged, ludicrous, pointless, senseless **10** half-witted, idle-headed, ill-advised, pea-brained, ridiculous **11** hare-brained, injudicious, nonsensical **12** crack-brained, short-sighted, simple-minded, unreasonable **13** cockle-brained, ill-considered, out of your mind, rattle-brained, unintelligent

foolishly
◇ *anagram indicator*
05 fonly, madly **06** daftly **07** crazily, ineptly, wackily **08** absurdly, stupidly, unwisely **09** fatuously, shallowly **10** mistakenly **11** idiotically, imprudently, senselessly **12** ill-advisedly, incautiously, indiscreetly, ridiculously **13** injudiciously **14** short-sightedly

foolishness
03 rot **04** bunk, crap **05** balls, bilge, folly **06** bunkum, lunacy, piffle **07** baloney, foolery, hogwash, inanity, madness, rubbish **08** claptrap, cobblers, daftness, nonsense, unreason, unwisdom, weakness **09** absurdity, craziness, incaution, meshugaas, mishegaas, niaiserie, poppycock, silliness, stupidity **10** imprudence, ineptitude **12** indiscretion **13** senselessness

foolproof
04 safe, sure **07** certain **08** fail-safe, sure-fire **09** unfailing **10** dependable, guaranteed, idiot-proof, infallible **11** trustworthy

foot
01 f **02** ft **03** end, leg, pad, paw, pes, toe **04** base, heel, hoof, kick, sole **05** dance, limit, paeon **06** border, bottom, dactyl, far end, iambus, tarsus **07** anapest, paeonic, pyrrhic, spondee, tootsie, trochee, trotter **08** anapaest, bacchius, choriamb, dochmius, molossus, tribrach **09** extremity **10** amphibrach, amphimacer, choriambus, foundation **12** antibacchius, tootsy-wootsy

• discomfort of foot
04 corn

• division of foot
04 inch

• model of foot
04 last

• part of foot
03 toe **04** arch, vola **06** instep

football
02 RL, RU **04** camp **06** soccer

See also **American football**; **Australian football**

English league football teams:

03 QPR
04 Bury
06 Barnet, Fulham, Yeovil
07 Arsenal, Burnley, Chelsea, Everton, Reading, Walsall, Watford, Wrexham
08 Barnsley, Hull City, Millwall, Port Vale, Rochdale
09 Blackpool, Brentford, Liverpool, Luton Town, Stoke City
10 Aston Villa, Darlington, Gillingham, Portsmouth, Sunderland
11 Bournemouth, Bristol City, Cardiff City, Chester City, Derby County, Grimsby Town, Ipswich Town, Leeds United, Lincoln City, Norwich City, Notts County, Southampton, Swansea City, Swindon Town
12 Boston United, Bradford City, Chesterfield, Coventry City, Leyton Orient
13 Bristol Rovers, Crystal Palace, Leicester City, Mansfield Town, Middlesbrough, Torquay United, West Ham United, Wigan Athletic
14 Birmingham City, Carlisle United, Cheltenham Town, Crewe Alexandra, Hereford United, Manchester City, Oldham Athletic, Plymouth Argyle, Shrewsbury Town, Southend United, Tranmere Rovers
15 Blackburn Rovers, Bolton Wanderers, Doncaster Rovers, Newcastle United, Northampton Town, Preston North End, Rotherham United, Sheffield United, Stockport County
16 Charlton Athletic, Colchester United, Hartlepool United, Huddersfield Town, Macclesfield Town, Manchester United, Milton Keynes Dons, Nottingham Forest, Scunthorpe United, Tottenham Hotspur, Wycombe Wanderers
17 Accrington Stanley, Queen's Park Rangers
18 Peterborough United, Sheffield Wednesday, West Bromwich Albion
21 Brighton and Hove Albion
22 Wolverhampton Wanderers

Scottish league football teams:

04 Hibs
05 Clyde
06 Celtic, Dundee, Gretna, Hearts
07 Falkirk, Rangers
08 Aberdeen, Arbroath, East Fife, Montrose, St Mirren
09 Ayr United, Dumbarton, Elgin City, Hibernian, Peterhead, Stranraer
10 Kilmarnock, Livingston, Motherwell, Queen's Park, Ross County
11 Brechin City, Cowdenbeath, Raith Rovers, St Johnstone
12 Albion Rovers, Dundee United
13 Airdrie United, Alloa Athletic, Stenhousemuir
14 Berwick Rangers, Forfar Athletic, Greenock Morton, Partick Thistle, Stirling Albion
15 Queen of the South
17 East Stirlingshire, Heart of Midlothian
18 Hamilton Academical
19 Dunfermline Athletic
26 Inverness Caledonian Thistle

European football teams include:

04 Ajax
05 Lazio, Malmö, Parma, Porto
06 Alaves, AS Roma, Bastia, Monaco, Napoli, Torino
07 AC Milan, Antwerp, Benfica, Cologne, Español, FC Porto, Hamburg, Schalke
08 Bordeaux, Juventus, Mallorca, Mechelen, Salzburg, Valencia
09 Barcelona, Feyenoord, FK Austria, Marseille, Sampdoria, St Etienne, Stuttgart, SV Hamburg, TSV Munich
10 Anderlecht, Club Bruges, Club Brugge, Dynamo Kiev, Fiorentina, Inter Milan, Real Madrid
11 FC Magdeburg, Ferencvaros, Galatasaray, MTK Budapest, Rapid Vienna, Ujpest Dozsa
12 Bayern Munich, Dinamo Zagreb, Gornik Zabrze, Moscow Dynamo, PSV Eindhoven, Real Zaragoza, Stade de Reims, Werder Bremen
13 Carl Zeiss Jena, Dynamo Tbilisi, IFK Gothenburg, Panathinaikos, Standard Liège
14 Athletic Bilbao, Atletico Madrid, Paris St Germain, Sporting Lisbon, Twente Enschede

15 Bayer Leverkusen, Red Star Belgrade, Steaua Bucharest

Football club nicknames include:

02 O's, R's, U's
03 Ton
04 Bees, Boro, City, Dale, Dons, Gers, Jags, Owls, Pars, Pool, Posh, Rams, Reds, Sons, Well
05 Arabs, Bhoys, Binos, Blues, Foxes, Gills, Gulls, Hoops, Irons, Lions, Loons, Shire, Spurs, Stags, Swans, Villa, Wasps
06 Accies, Albion, Bairns, Blades, County, Eagles, Fifers, Hibees, Jambos, Killie, Latics, Pompey, Robins, Rovers, Royals, Saints, Tigers, United, Whites, Wolves
07 Addicks, Baggies, Bantams, Buddies, Clarets, Glovers, Gunners, Hammers, Hatters, Hornets, Magpies, Pirates, Potters, Quakers, Red Imps, Shakers, Silkmen, Spiders, Terrors, Toffees, Villans
08 Blue Toon, Bully Wee, Canaries, Cherries, Citizens, Cobblers, Diamonds, Filberts, Harriers, Jam Tarts, Mariners, Pilgrims, Saddlers, Seagulls, Sky Blues, Terriers, Trotters, Valiants, Villains, Warriors
09 Black Cats, Bluebirds, Borderers, Chairboys, Cottagers, Cumbrians, Dark Blues, Honest Men, Red Devils, Seasiders, Shrimpers, Spireites, Throstles, Toffeemen, Wee Rovers
10 Blue Brazil, Doonhamers, Light Blues, Lilywhites, Livvy Lions, Minstermen, Railwaymen, Tangerines, Teddy Bears
11 Gable Endies, Red Lichties, Tractor Boys
12 Caley Thistle, Merry Millers
13 Blue and Whites
14 Black and Whites

Football-related terms include:

03 box, cap, lob, net
04 back, dive, foul, goal, half, head, hole, loan, mark, pass, post, save, shot, trap, wall, wing
05 bench, chest, pitch
06 assist, corner, double, futsal, goalie, handle, header, keeper, libero, nutmeg, one-two, soccer, tackle, treble, volley, winger
07 booking, caution, dribble, far post, forward, kick-off, offside, own goal, penalty, red card, referee, stopper, sweeper, throw-in, whistle
08 back heel, crossbar, dead ball, defender, free kick, friendly, full back, goal kick, goal line, half time, hand ball, hat-trick, left back, linesman, midfield, near post, outfield, play-offs, set piece, transfer, wall pass, wingback
09 extra time, five-a-side, formation, give-and-go, goalmouth, promotion, right back, touchline
10 centre back, centre half, centre spot, corner flag, corner kick, goalkeeper, golden goal, half volley, injury time, man marking, midfielder, off-the-ball, penalty box, possession, relegation, sending off, silver goal, substitute, suspension
11 bicycle kick, half-way line, keepie-uppie, obstruction, offside trap, penalty area, penalty kick, penalty spot, six-yard area, straight red, time wasting
12 back-pass rule, Bosman ruling, centre circle, overhead kick, stoppage time
13 centre forward, dangerous play, technical area
14 fourth official, goal difference, relegation zone
15 eighteen-yard box

footballer

Footballers and associated figures include:

03 **Fry** (Charles Burgess), **Law** (Denis)
04 **Best** (George), **Dean** (Dixie), **Didi**, **Figo** (Luis), **Hall** (Sir John), **Owen** (Michael), **Pelé**, **Rush** (Ian), **Zico**, **Zoff** (Dino)
05 **Adams** (Tony), **Banks** (Gordon), **Busby** (Sir Matt), **Carey** (Johnny), **Giggs** (Ryan), **Greig** (John), **Henry** (Thierry), **Hurst** (Sir Geoff), **James** (Alex), **Moore** (Bobby), **Revie** (Don), **Rimet** (Jules), **Rossi** (Paolo), **Stein** (Jock), **Young** (George)
06 **Baggio** (Roberto), **Baresi** (Franco), **Barnes** (John), **Baxter** (Jim), **Bosman** (Jean-Marc), **Clough** (Brian), **Cruyff** (Johann), **Finney** (Sir Tom), **Ginola** (David), **Graham** (George), **Gullit** (Ruud), **Haynes** (Johnny), **Hoddle** (Glenn), **Keegan** (Kevin), **Lawton** (Tommy), **McColl** (Robert Smyth), **McStay** (Paul), **Mercer** (Joe), **Morton** (Alan Lauder), **Müller** (Gerd), **Puskas** (Ferenc), **Ramsey** (Sir Alf), **Robson** (Sir Bobby), **Robson** (Bryan), **Rooney** (Wayne), **Seaman** (David), **Stiles** (Nobby), **St John** (Ian), **Walker** (Tommy), **Wenger** (Arsene), **Wright** (Billy), **Wright** (Ian), **Yashin** (Lev), **Zidane** (Zinedine)
07 **Ardiles** (Osvaldo), **Beckham** (David), **Bremner** (Billy), **Butcher** (Terry), **Cantona** (Eric), **Charles** (John), **DiCanio** (Paolo), **Eastham** (George), **Edwards** (Duncan), **Eusebio** (Silva), **Greaves** (Jimmy), **Lineker** (Gary), **Macleod** (Ally), **Mannion** (Wilfred), **McCoist** (Ally), **McNeill** (Billy), **Paisley** (Bob), **Platini** (Michel), **Rivaldo**, **Ronaldo**, **Shankly** (Bill), **Shearer** (Alan), **Shilton** (Peter), **Souness** (Graeme), **Toshack** (John), **Waddell** (Willie)
08 **Bergkamp** (Dennis), **Charlton** (Sir Bobby), **Charlton** (Jack), **Dalglish** (Kenny), **Docherty** (Tommy), **Ferguson** (Sir Alex), **Fontaine** (Just), **Harkness** (Jack), **Jennings** (Pat), **Johnston** (Maurice), **Maradona** (Diego), **Matthaus** (Lothar), **Matthews** (Sir Stanley), **Mourinho** (José), **Nicholls** (Sir Douglas Ralph), **Rivelino** (Roberto)
09 **Batistuta** (Gabriel), **Collymore** (Stan), **DiStefano** (Alfredo), **Garrincha**, **Gascoigne** (Paul 'Gazza'), **Greenwood** (Ron), **Johnstone** (Jimmy), **Klinsmann** (Jurgen), **Lofthouse** (Nat), **Van Basten** (Marco)
10 **Schmeichel** (Peter)
11 **Beckenbauer** (Franz)
12 **Blanchflower** (Danny)

• **footballers**
02 FA **03** SFA

footing

04 base, cost, grip, rank, trod **05** basis, coast, coste, dance, grade, state, terms, track, tread, troad, trode **06** ground, status, troade **07** balance, support, surface **08** foothold, position, roothold, standing **09** relations **10** conditions, foundation **12** relationship

footling

05 minor, petty **06** paltry **07** trivial **08** piffling, trifling **10** irrelevant **13** insignificant

footloose

04 free **09** available, fancy-free **10** unattached, uninvolved **11** uncommitted

footnote

04 note **05** gloss **07** comment, subtext **08** scholium **10** annotation, commentary, marginalia **12** marginal note

footnotes

04 note **05** gloss **07** scholia **10** annotation, commentary, marginalia **12** marginal note

footprint

03 pad, pug **04** mark, seal, step **05** prick, spoor, trace, track, trail, tread **07** ichnite, vestige **08** footmark, footstep **09** ichnolite **13** ornithichnite

footprints

04 slot

footstep

04 plod, step **05** track, tramp, tread **06** trudge **08** footfall, footmark

footwear

Footwear includes:

03 dap, tie
04 boot, clog, geta, mule, pump, shoe, vibs
05 jelly, sabot, tacky, thong, wader, welly
06 bootee, brogue, casual, galosh, lace-up, loafer, Oxford, patten, sandal, slip-on
07 gumboot, slipper, sneaker, tap shoe, trainer
08 boat shoe, deck shoe, flip-flop, jazz shoe, Mary Jane, moccasin,

overshoe, pantofle, plimsoll, snow-shoe
09 court shoe, Derry boot, rugby boot, slingback, wedge heel
10 ballet shoe, combat boot, Doc Martens®, espadrille, hiking-boot, kitten-heel, riding boot, tennis shoe
11 bowling shoe, Chelsea boot, Hush Puppies®, walking boot
12 climbing boot, football boot, platform heel, stiletto heel
13 beetle-crusher
14 beetle-crushers, brothel creeper, wellington boot
15 brothel-creepers

See also **boot**; **clothes, clothing**

fop
04 beau, dude, toff **05** dandy, swell **07** coxcomb, peacock **08** muscadin, popinjay, skipjack **09** exquisite, fantastic **10** Jack-a-dandy **11** petit maître **12** barber-monger

foppish
04 vain **05** apish, natty **06** dainty, dapper, dressy, fallal, la-di-da, spruce **07** fangled, finical **08** affected, dandyish, preening, swellish **09** coxcombic, dandified, fantastic **10** coxcomical **11** coxcombical, fantastical, overdressed

for
03 pro

forage
04 feed, food, guar, hunt, loot, prog, raid, seek **05** étape, foray, scour **06** fodder, invade, ladino, ravage, search **07** assault, pickeer, plunder, ransack, rummage, scratch **08** mung bean, scavenge **09** cast about, gama grass, pasturage, provender **10** foodstuffs, provisions

foray
04 raid **05** sally, swoop **06** attack, creach, creagh, forray, inroad, ravage, sortie **07** assault, attempt, journey, spreagh, venture **08** invasion **09** incursion, offensive **14** reconnaissance

forbear
04 hold, omit, stay, stop **05** avoid, cease, pause **06** desist, eschew **07** abstain, decline, refrain **08** ancestor, hesitate, hold back, keep from, withhold

forbearance
05 mercy **06** pardon **08** clemency, leniency, mildness, patience **09** avoidance, endurance, restraint, tolerance **10** abstinence, indulgence, indulgency, moderation, refraining, self-denial, sufferance, temperance, toleration **11** longanimity, resignation, self-control **13** long-suffering

forbearing
04 easy, mild **07** clement, lenient, patient **08** merciful, moderate, tolerant **09** forgiving, indulgent **10** restrained **13** long-suffering **14** self-controlled

forbid
03 ban, bar **04** deny, tabu, veto, warn **05** block, debar, taboo **06** defend, enjoin, forsay, hinder, not let, outlaw, refuse **07** exclude, foresay, forwarn, inhibit, prevent, rule out **08** disallow, forewarn, forspeak, not allow, preclude, prohibit, restrain **09** blacklist, discharge, forespeak, interdict, proscribe **13** excommunicate **14** contraindicate

forbidden
02 nl **04** tabu, tapu, tref **05** not on, taboo, trefa, treif **06** banned, vetoed **07** illicit, profane **08** debarred, defended, excluded, outlawed, unlawful, verboten **10** contraband, prohibited, proscribed, restrained **11** out of bounds

forbidding
04 grim **05** harsh, stern **06** severe **07** awesome, hostile, ominous **08** daunting, menacing, sinister **09** repulsive **10** Acherontic, foreboding, formidable, off-putting, unfriendly, uninviting **11** frightening, hard-grained, prohibitory, threatening **15** unprepossessing

force
◇ *anagram indicator*
01 F **02** od **03** put, vis, zap **04** army, body, care, cops, dint, gist, make, odyl, pull, push, sway, unit, urge **05** blast, bully, corps, crack, drive, exact, group, impel, might, odyle, power, press, prise, sense, squad, stuff, troop, wrest, wring **06** coerce, compel, duress, dynamo, effort, energy, extort, impose, lean on, muscle, oblige, patrol, propel, ravish, stress, strive, thrust, vigour, wrench **07** cogency, essence, extract, impetus, impulse, inflict, meaning, passion, platoon, stamina **08** armament, bulldoze, coercion, division, dynamism, emphasis, exertion, momentum, pressure, railroad, regiment, squadron, strength, validity, vehement, violence, vitality **09** battalion, break open, constrain, force open, influence, intensity, necessity, pressgang, substance, the screws, vehemence, waterfall **10** aggression, compulsion, constraint, detachment, pressurize **11** arm-twisting, enforcement **12** significance **13** determination, effectiveness, put pressure on **14** persuasiveness, put the screws on, the third degree

See also **army**; **police**

• **in force**
05 valid **07** binding, current, working **08** in crowds, in droves, in flocks **09** effective, operative **10** in strength **11** functioning, in operation **14** in great numbers, in large numbers

forced
◇ *anagram indicator*
02 sf **03** sfz **05** false, stiff **06** wooden **07** binding, feigned, stilted **08** affected, enforced, laboured, overdone, sforzato, strained **09** compelled, contrived, excessive, insincere, mandatory, sforzando, unnatural **10** artificial, compulsory, far-fetched, non-natural, obligatory **11** constrained, involuntary

forceful
05 gutty, valid **06** cogent, mighty, potent, strong, urgent **07** dynamic, telling, weighty **08** emphatic, forcible, powerful, vehement, vigorous **09** assertive, effective, energetic **10** compelling, convincing, impressive, persuasive **11** high-powered **12** high-pressure

forcefully
07 con brio **08** strongly **10** powerfully, vehemently, vigorously **11** assertively, effectively **12** convincingly, emphatically, persuasively **13** energetically

forcible
04 vive **05** pithy **06** cogent, forced, mighty, potent, strong **07** by force, drastic, marrowy, telling, violent, weighty **08** coercive, forceful, powerful, vehement **09** effective, energetic **10** aggressive, compelling, compulsory, impressive, using force **11** energetical

forcibly
03 out **04** hard **07** by force **09** vi et armis, violently **10** using force, vehemently, vigorously, willy-nilly **11** under duress **12** compulsorily, emphatically, obligatorily **15** against your will, under compulsion

ford
04 rack, wade **05** drift **06** Model T **08** causeway, crossing **09** tin lizzie **11** Irish bridge **13** crossing place

forebear
06 father, tupuna **08** ancestor **10** antecedent, forefather, forerunner, progenitor **11** predecessor **12** primogenitor

foreboding
04 fear, omen, sign **05** dread, token, worry **06** hoodoo **07** anxiety, feeling, presage, warning **09** abodement, intuition, misgiving, suspicion **10** prediction, sixth sense **11** premonition **12** apprehension, presentiment **15** prognostication

forecast
03 tip **04** omen, perm **05** augur, guess **06** augury, divine, expect, tip off **07** foresee, metcast, outlook, portend, predict, presage, project **08** estimate, foretell, forewarn, prophecy, prophesy **09** calculate, prognosis **10** anticipate, conjecture, prediction, projection **11** calculation, expectation, extrapolate, forewarning, guesstimate, permutation, second-guess, speculation **13** extrapolation, prognosticate, weather report **15** prognostication

See also **shipping**

forefather
06 father **08** ancestor, forebear
10 ancestress, antecedent, forerunner, progenitor **11** predecessor
12 primogenitor

forefront
03 van **04** fore, head, lead **05** front
06 vaward **08** vanguard **09** front line, spearhead **10** avant-garde, firing line
11 leading edge **15** leading position

forego, forgo
05 leave, waive, yield **06** abjure, eschew, give up, pass up, resign
07 abandon, forfeit, precede
08 renounce **09** do without, go without, sacrifice, surrender
10 relinquish **11** abstain from, refrain from

foregoing
05 above, prior **06** former **07** earlier
08 previous **09** aforesaid, precedent, preceding **10** antecedent
14 aforementioned

foregone
- **foregone conclusion**

04 fact **09** certainty, sure thing
10 inevitable **13** inevitability

foreground
04 fore **05** front **06** centre
09 forefront, limelight **10** prominence
15 leading position

forehead
04 brow **05** front **06** metope, temple
07 temples **08** audacity
10 confidence

foreign
◇ *anagram indicator*
◇ *foreign word indicator*
03 odd **05** alien, fraim, fremd
06 ethnic, exotic, forane, forren, fremit
07 distant, faraway, migrant, outside, strange, unknown **08** borrowed, étranger, exterior, external, imported, overseas, peculiar **09** barbarian, étrangère, extrinsic, immigrant
10 extraneous, forinsecal, outlandish, tramontane, unfamiliar
11 unconnected **12** adventitious
13 international
See also **nationality**

foreigner
05 alien **06** gaijin, taipan **07** incomer, visitor **08** étranger, newcomer, outsider, stranger **09** Ausländer, barbarian, étrangère, immigrant, outlander, uitlander **10** tramontane

foreknowledge
09 foresight, prevision **10** prescience
11 forewarning, premonition, second sight **12** clairvoyance, precognition
15 prognostication

foreleg
04 gamb

foreman
04 bo's'n, boss **05** bosun **06** gaffer, ganger, honcho, induna, leader
07 manager, overman, steward, topsman **08** gangsman, overseer
09 boatswain, straw boss
10 chancellor, charge hand, supervisor
14 superintendent

foremost
◇ *head selection indicator*
03 top, van **04** main **05** chief, first, front, prime **07** central, highest, leading, premier, primary, supreme, up front **08** advanced, cardinal, vanguard **09** paramount, principal, uppermost **10** pre-eminent **13** most important

foreordained
05 fated **08** destined **09** appointed, predevote **10** foredoomed
11 prearranged, predestined, preordained **12** predestinate
13 predetermined

forerunner
04 omen, sign **05** envoy, token
06 herald **08** ancestor **09** harbinger, messenger, precurrer, precursor
10 antecedent, forefather
11 forewarning, predecessor **12** vaunt-courier
- **be a forerunner**

04 lead, pace

foresee
06 divine, expect, prevue **07** predict, preview, previse **08** envisage, forebode, forecast, foreknow, foretell, prophesy **10** anticipate
13 prognosticate

foreshadow
04 bode, mean, type **05** augur
06 signal **07** portend, predict, presage, promise, signify, suggest **08** indicate, prophesy **09** adumbrate, forepoint, prefigure **13** prognosticate

foreshore
04 hard

foresight
04 care **06** vision **07** caution
08 forecast, planning, prudence
09 prevision, provision, readiness
10 precaution, prescience, providence
11 discernment, forethought, prospection **12** anticipation, perspicacity, preparedness
13 judiciousness **14** circumspection, discrimination, far-sightedness
15 forward planning

forest
04 bosk, wood **05** Arden, trees, woods **06** rustic, sylvan, timber
07 boscage **08** Sherwood, tree farm, woodland **09** backwoods

Forests and woods include:

04 bush, gapó
05 brush, igapò, monte, selva, taiga, urman
06 boreal, jungle, mallee, maquis, pinery
07 coastal, garigue, lowland, macchie, wetland
08 caatinga, garrigue, littoral, mangrove
09 broadleaf, chaparral, deciduous, evergreen, greenwood, temperate
10 coniferous, equatorial, peat forest, plantation, rainforest
11 cloud forest, heath forest, lignum-scrub, lignum-swamp, mallee scrub, moist forest
12 vàrzea forest
13 ancient forest, gallery forest, mangrove swamp, savanna forest
14 moist evergreen

forestall
03 bar **04** balk, beat, stop **05** avert, lurch, parry **06** hinder, impede, thwart
07 head off, obviate, pre-empt, prevent, ward off **08** obstruct, preclude, stave off **09** frustrate, intercept **10** anticipate, get ahead of
11 second-guess

forested
05 bosky **06** wooded **12** reafforested

forester
06 foster, walker **08** woodsman

forestry
09 woodcraft **10** dendrology
11 forestation, woodmanship
12 silviculture, sylviculture
13 afforestation, arboriculture

foretaste
05 whiff **06** prevue, sample, taster
07 earnest, example, pre-echo, preview, trailer, warning **08** antepast, specimen **09** appetizer, avant-goût, foretoken **10** anticipate, indication
11 forewarning, prelibation, premonition **12** anticipation, pregustation

foretell
04 bode, spae **05** augur, write
06 divine **07** bespeak, foresay, foresee, predict, presage, signify
08 forebode, forecast, foreread, forewarn, indicate, prophesy, soothsay
10 foreshadow **13** prognosticate

forethought
07 caution **08** planning, prudence
09 foresight, provision **10** precaution
11 discernment, preparation
12 anticipation, perspicacity
13 judiciousness **14** circumspection, far-sightedness **15** forward planning

forever
02 ay **03** aye **04** ever **06** always **07** à jamais, for good **08** evermore
09 endlessly, eternally **10** all the time, constantly, for all time **11** continually, incessantly, permanently, perpetually
12 interminably, persistently, till doomsday **13** everlastingly **15** till kingdom come

forewarn
04 warn **05** alert, weird **06** advise, forbid, tip off **07** apprise, caution, previse **08** admonish, dissuade **10** give notice, precaution **11** preadmonish

forewarning
06 tip-off **10** forerunner
11 premonition **12** early warning

13 advance notice 14 advance warning

foreword
07 preface, prelims 08 prologue
11 frontmatter 12 introduction, prolegomenon

forfeit
04 fine, lose, loss 05 cheat, forgo
06 forego, give up, pass up, sconce
07 abandon, damages, penalty
08 hand over, renounce 09 sacrifice, surrender 10 amercement, confiscate, relinquish, rue-bargain
12 confiscation 13 sequestration
14 relinquishment

forfeiture
04 loss 07 escheat 08 forgoing, giving up 09 attainder, déchéance, foregoing, sacrifice, surrender
12 confiscation 13 sequestration
14 relinquishment

forge
◇ *anagram indicator*
04 cast, copy, fake, form, make, tilt, work 05 build, feign, found, frame, mould, shape, smith 06 create, devise, invent, smithy, stithy 07 beat out, falsify, fashion, imitate, stiddie
08 simulate 09 construct, hammer out
11 counterfeit, put together, rivet hearth 13 beat into shape
• **forge ahead**
07 advance 08 progress 09 go forward 11 make headway, move forward, push forward 12 make progress, move steadily

forged
◇ *anagram indicator*
04 fake, sham 05 bogus, faked, false, pseud, snide 06 copied, phoney, pirate, pseudo 07 feigned, simular
08 borrowed, spurious 09 imitation, pretended, simulated 10 artificial, fraudulent 11 counterfect, counterfeit

forger
05 faker 06 coiner, framer
09 contriver, falsifier 10 fabricator
13 counterfeiter

forgery
03 dud 04 copy, fake, sham 05 fraud
06 deceit, faking, phoney 07 replica
09 imitation 11 counterfeit, falsi crimen 12 reproduction
13 falsification 14 counterfeiting
15 counterfeisance, counterfesaunce

forget
04 fail, omit, wipe 05 dry up
06 corpse, ignore 07 dismiss, let slip, neglect, unlearn 08 not place, overlook, put aside 09 disregard
11 disremember, leave behind, lose sight of, misremember 12 put behind you, slip your mind 13 think no more of
14 fail to remember
• **forget yourself**
09 be naughty, misbehave 11 behave badly

forgetful
03 lax 06 dreamy, remiss 08 careless, heedless 09 negligent, oblivious, unheeding 10 abstracted, distracted, neglectful 11 inattentive, not all there, preoccupied 12 absent-minded
14 scatterbrained

forgetfulness
05 lapse 07 amnesia, laxness, neglect
08 oblivion 10 dreaminess
11 abstraction, inattention
12 carelessness, heedlessness, obliviscence 13 obliviousness, wool-gathering

forgivable
05 minor, petty 06 slight, venial
08 innocent, trifling 09 excusable
10 condonable, pardonable

forgive
05 clear, remit, spare 06 acquit, excuse, let off, pardon 07 absolve, condone, let it go 08 overlook 09 exculpate, exonerate, shake on it 10 shake hands
13 think no more of 14 bury the hatchet

forgiveness
05 mercy 06 excuse, pardon
07 amnesty 08 clemency, leniency, oblivion 09 acquittal, remission
10 absolution, misericord
11 condonation, exoneration, misericorde

forgiving
04 kind, mild 06 humane 07 clement, lenient, pitying 08 merciful, placable, tolerant 09 indulgent, remissive
10 forbearing 11 magnanimous, soft-hearted 13 compassionate

forgo *see* **forego, forgo**

forgotten
04 gone, lost, past 06 buried, bygone
07 ignored, omitted 09 neglected, oblivious, out of mind 10 blotted out, in the shade, left behind, overlooked, past recall, unrecalled 11 disregarded, obliterated, unretrieved
12 unremembered 13 irrecoverable, irretrievable 15 in the wilderness

fork
01 Y 04 part 05 grain, graip, prong, spear, split, twist 06 branch, crotch, divide 07 diverge, furcate, toaster
08 division, junction, separate
09 bifurcate, branching, branch off, furcation, tormenter, tormentor
10 divaricate, divergence, separation
11 bifurcation 12 divarication, intersection, toasting iron 14 go separate ways
• **fork out**
03 pay 04 give 05 pay up 06 pony up
07 cough up, stump up 08 shell out

forked
05 split, tined 06 furcal 07 divided, furcate, pronged, Y-shaped
08 biramous, branched, furcated, furcular 09 bifurcate, branching, deceitful, forficate, insincere, separated 10 trifurcate 11 divaricated

forlorn
◇ *anagram indicator*
03 sad 04 lost 06 bereft, lonely
07 unhappy 08 deserted, desolate, forsaken, helpless, homeless, hopeless, pathetic, pitiable, wretched
09 abandoned, cheerless, desperate, destitute, forgotten, miserable, neglected 10 despairing, drearisome, friendless, uncared-for
12 disconsolate

forlornly
05 sadly 06 in vain 09 miserably, to no avail, unhappily 10 hopelessly
11 desperately, pointlessly
12 despondently 14 unsuccessfully

form
◇ *anagram indicator*
03 cut, set 04 cast, face, grow, kind, make, mode, rite, sort, trim, turn, type, year 05 bench, build, class, forge, found, frame, genre, genus, grade, guise, model, mould, order, paper, set up, shape, sheet, style, usage
06 appear, beauty, create, custom, design, devise, draw up, fettle, figure, format, health, line up, make up, manner, nature, ritual, show up, stream, system 07 acquire, arrange, compose, develop, fashion, fitness, manners, outline, pattern, produce, serve as, species, spirits, variety 08 assemble, ceremony, comprise, conceive, contrive, document, organize, planning, protocol 09 be a part of, behaviour, character, condition, construct, establish, etiquette, formation, formulate, framework, structure, take shape 10 appearance, constitute, convention, regularity, silhouette 11 application, arrangement, crystallize, description, disposition, manufacture, materialize, put together 12 construction, organization, the done thing
13 become visible, configuration, manifestation, questionnaire
15 application form, correct practice, polite behaviour

formal
03 dry, set 04 prim, sane 05 aloof, exact, fixed, rigid, stiff 06 proper, pusser, remote, ritual, solemn, starch, strict 07 correct, ordered, orderly, outward, precise, regular, starchy, stately, stilted 08 academic, approved, arranged, black tie, literary, methodic, official, orthodox, reserved, standard
09 customary, essential, organized, unbending 10 ceremonial, controlled, inflexible, methodical, prescribed
11 ceremonious, established, perfunctory, punctilious, ritualistic, strait-laced, symmetrical, traditional
12 conventional

formality
03 ice 04 form, rite, rule 06 custom, ritual, starch 07 decorum, red tape, wiggery 08 ceremony, pedantry, protocol 09 etiquette, procedure, propriety, punctilio, sociality, stiffness

10 convention, politeness
11 bureaucracy, correctness 12 matter of form 13 spit and polish
15 ceremoniousness, conventionality

formalization
08 ordering 09 arranging
11 arrangement, structuring
12 arrangements, confirmation, organization 15 standardization, systematization

formalize
03 fix, set 05 order 06 affirm, ordain, ratify 07 arrange, confirm, stylize
08 organize 09 ritualize, structure
10 make formal, regularize
11 standardize, systematize 12 make official

formally
06 primly 07 exactly, rigidly
08 properly, ritually, solemnly
09 correctly, precisely 10 formaliter, inflexibly, officially 12 ceremonially, methodically 13 punctiliously
14 conventionally

format
03 GIF, PDF, PNG, RTF, ZIP 04 form, JPEG, look, plan, TIFF, type 05 order, shape, style 06 design, layout, make-up 07 pattern, tabloid 08 portrait
09 landscape, letterbox, structure
10 appearance, dimensions, widescreen 11 arrangement
12 construction, presentation
13 configuration

formation
04 make 05 order 06 design, figure, format, layout, make-up, making, series 07 pattern, phalanx, shaping
08 building, creation, founding, grouping, starting 09 emergence, structure 10 appearance, generation, production 11 arrangement, composition, development, disposition, institution, manufacture
12 constitution, construction, inauguration, organization
13 configuration, establishment

formative
06 creant, pliant 07 growing, guiding, plastic, shaping 08 dominant, moulding 09 malleable, mouldable, sensitive, teachable 11 controlling, determining, influential, susceptible
13 determinative, developmental
14 impressionable

former
02 ex- 03 old 04 auld, fore, late, once, onst, past 05 above, first, olden, prior
06 bygone, of yore, whilom
07 ancient, earlier, long ago, old-time, one-time, quondam 08 ci-devant, departed, long-gone, previous, pristine, sometime 09 erstwhile, foregoing, preceding 10 antecedent, historical 14 first-mentioned

formerly
04 erst, once, onst 05 as was, earst, of old 06 before 07 earlier, whilere
08 ci-devant, erewhile, hitherto, sometime, while-ere 09 at one time, erstwhile, in the past, yesterday
10 heretofore, previously
12 historically 15 at an earlier time

formidable
04 huge 05 great, scary, stiff, stoor, stour, sture 06 gorgon, no mean, shrewd, spooky, stowre 07 awesome, fearful, mammoth, onerous
08 alarming, colossal, daunting, dreadful, horrific, menacing, powerful, terrific 09 frightful, leviathan
10 horrifying, impressive, prodigious, staggering, terrifying, tremendous
11 challenging, frightening, mind-blowing, redoubtable, threatening
12 intimidating, overwhelming

formidably
07 awfully 09 fearfully 10 dreadfully, menacingly, shockingly 11 frightfully
12 horrifically, tremendously
14 overwhelmingly

formless
05 vague 06 inform 07 chaotic
08 confused, inchoate, indigest, nebulous, unformed, unshaped
09 amorphous, shapeless
10 incoherent, indefinite
12 disorganized, invertebrate
13 indeterminate

formula
03 mix, way 04 code, form, rule
05 spell 06 method, recipe, rubric
07 precept, wording 08 equation, exorcism, fog index, proposal, protocol 09 blueprint, principle, procedure, technique 10 convention
12 prescription 13 set expression
15 fixed expression
• **Formula One** *see* **racing**

formulate
04 cast, form, plan 05 found, frame, state 06 create, define, design, detail, devise, draw up, evolve, invent, map out 07 compose, develop, express, formate, itemize, lay down, prepare, propose, put down, set down, specify, think up, work out 08 conceive
09 originate, symbolize 10 articulate

formulation
07 formula, framing, product
08 creating, devising 10 conception, definition, expression, production
11 composition, development, preparation 13 specification

fornication
06 affair 07 avoutry, liaison
08 adultery, cheating, idolatry 09 two-timing 10 flirtation, infidelity, unchastity 12 entanglement 13 a bit on the side, playing around
14 unfaithfulness 15 extramarital sex, playing the field

forsake
04 jilt, quit 05 chuck, ditch, forgo, leave, waive 06 desert, disown, forego, give up, reject 07 abandon, cast off, discard, forlese 08 jettison, renounce, set aside 09 destitute, repudiate, surrender, throw over 10 relinquish
12 have done with 14 turn your back on 15 leave in the lurch

forsaken
04 lorn 06 dreary, jilted, lonely, remote
07 cast off, forlorn, ignored, outcast, shunned 08 derelict, deserted, desolate, disowned, isolated, lasslorn, lovelorn, marooned, rejected, solitary
09 abandoned, destitute, discarded, neglected 10 friendless
11 godforsaken 14 left in the lurch

forswear
03 lie 04 deny, drop, reny 05 forgo, renay, reney 06 abjure, cut out, disown, forego, give up, jack in, pack in, recant, reject, renege 07 abandon, disavow, forsake, retract 08 disclaim, renounce 09 do without, repudiate
15 perjure yourself

fort
02 Ft, pa 03 pah 04 camp, keep, rath
05 tower 06 castle, donjon, turret
07 citadel, parapet, redoubt, station
08 fortress, garrison, martello, pentagon 09 castellum
10 blockhouse, stronghold, watchtower 11 battlements
13 fortification, martello tower

forte
01 f 04 bent, gift, loud 05 skill
06 métier, talent 08 aptitude, strength
10 speciality 11 strong point

forth
02 on 03 off, out 04 away 05 furth
06 abroad, onward 07 forward, onwards, outside 08 forwards, into view 13 into existence

forthcoming
04 open 05 frank, on tap, ready
06 chatty, coming, direct, future
07 voluble 08 expected, friendly, imminent, sociable, upcoming
09 available, expansive, impending, projected, talkative 10 accessible, loquacious, obtainable, up for grabs 11 approaching, informative, in the offing, prospective
13 communicative 14 at your disposal, conversational

forthright
04 bold, open 05 blunt, frank, plain
06 at once, candid, direct, honest
07 up-front 09 outspoken, trenchand, trenchant 10 four-square 11 plain-spoken 15 straightforward

forthwith
03 eft 04 asap, away 06 at once, pronto 07 quickly 08 directly, eftsoons 09 instantly, right away
11 immediately 12 straightaway, there and then, without delay

fortification
08 munition 09 munitions
10 munifience, protection, stronghold 12 embattlement, entrenchment 13 reinforcement, strengthening

Fortifications include:

02 pa
03 pah
04 bawn, fort, gate, keep, laer, moat, wall
05 ditch, fence, hedge, limes, tower
06 abatis, castle, glacis, laager, sconce, trench, Vauban
07 barrier, bastion, bulwark, citadel, defence, flanker, moineau, outwork, parapet, pillbox, rampart, redoubt, sandbag
08 buttress, cavalier, fortress, outworks, palisade, stockade
09 barricade, earthwork, fieldwork, fortalice, gabionade, gatehouse, razor wire
10 barbed wire, bridgehead, fieldworks, trou de loup
11 battlements, buttressing, crémaillère
13 cheval-de-frise, Martello tower
14 motte-and-bailey
15 circumvallation, contravallation

fortify
04 fort, load, wall **05** boost, brace, cheer, cover, fence, guard, mound **06** buoy up, castle, defend, munify, munite, revive, secure **07** bulwark, hearten, protect, rampart, shore up, support, sustain **08** buttress, embattle, energize, entrench, garrison, intrench, reassure **09** encourage, reinforce **10** invigorate, strengthen

fortitude
04 grit, guts **05** nerve, pluck, spine **06** mettle, valour **07** bravery, courage **08** backbone, firmness, patience, stoicism, strength, tenacity **09** endurance, hardihood, willpower **10** resolution **11** forbearance **12** perseverance **13** determination **14** strength of mind

fortress
04 burg, fort, keep **05** guard, place, tower **06** casbah, castle, kasbah **07** alcázar, citadel, defence **08** bastille, fastness, garrison **09** fortalice **10** stronghold **11** battlements **13** fortification

fortuitous
05 fluky, lucky **06** casual, chance, random **09** arbitrary, fortunate, haphazard, unplanned **10** accidental, incidental, unexpected, unforeseen **12** providential **13** unintentional

fortuitously
07 luckily **08** at random, by chance, casually, randomly **11** arbitrarily, fortunately, haphazardly **12** accidentally, incidentally, unexpectedly **13** inadvertently **15** unintentionally

Fortuna
05 Tyche

fortunate
04 rich, well **05** canny, happy, lucky, seely **06** timely **07** blessed, well-off **08** favoured **09** fairytale, opportune, promising, well-timed **10** auspicious, convenient, favourable, felicitous, fortuitous, profitable, propitious, prosperous, successful **11** encouraging, flourishing **12** advantageous, providential

fortunately
07 happily, luckily **10** thankfully **12** conveniently **13** encouragingly **14** providentially

fortune
03 cup, hap, lot **04** bomb, doom, fall, fate, life, luck, mint, pile, seal, seel, seil, sele **05** means, speed **06** assets, befall, bundle, chance, estate, future, income, packet, riches, wealth **07** destiny, heiress, history, portion, success **08** accident, big bucks, opulence, position, property, treasure **09** affluence, condition, megabucks, situation, substance **10** experience, prosperity, providence **11** coincidence, possessions, serendipity **13** circumstances **14** state of affairs

- **loss of fortune**

04 ruin **05** decay

- **sudden good fortune**

08 windfall

fortune-teller
04 seer **05** augur, sibyl **06** oracle **07** diviner, prophet, psychic **08** telepath **09** visionary **10** prophetess, soothsayer **11** clairvoyant

fortune-telling *see* divination

forty
02 XL

- **forty winks**

03 nap **04** rest **05** sleep

forum
03 BBS **05** arena, stage **06** debate **07** meeting, rostrum **08** assembly **09** gathering, symposium **10** conference, discussion **12** meeting-place

forward
02 on, to **03** aid, out **04** back, bold, fore, head, help, mail, post, send, ship **05** ahead, brash, cocky, early, first, forth, fresh, front, hurry, pushy, ready, speed **06** assist, avanti, brazen, cheeky, favour, foster, future, hasten, onward, pass on, send on, step up **07** advance, deliver, earnest, frontal, further, go-ahead, leading, onwards, promote, speed up, support **08** advanced, dispatch, expedite, familiar, foremost, forwards, impudent, into view, long-term, redirect **09** advancing, assertive, audacious, barefaced, confident, encourage, long-range, officious, premature, presuming, readdress, thrusting, transport **10** accelerate, aggressive, facilitate, medium-term, precocious **11** impertinent, into the open, medium-range, progressing, progressive, prospective **12** enterprising, overfamiliar, presumptuous, well-advanced **13** over-assertive, over-confident, progressively, well-developed **14** forward-looking

forward-looking
04 goey **06** modern **07** dynamic, go-ahead, liberal **09** go-getting, reforming **10** avant-garde, far-sighted, innovative **11** enlightened, progressive **12** enterprising

forwardness
04 neck **05** cheek **08** audacity, boldness, pertness **09** brashness, brass neck, impudence, pushiness **10** brazenness, cheekiness, confidence **11** presumption **12** forth-putting, impertinence **14** aggressiveness, over-confidence

forwards
02 on **03** out **04** pack **05** ahead, forth **06** onward **07** forward, onwards **13** progressively

fossil
05 relic **07** remains, remnant **09** reliquiae **10** antiquated

Fossils include:

04 bone, cast
05 amber, shell
06 burrow
07 bivalve, crinoid
08 ammonite, baculite, dinosaur, echinoid, nautilus, skeleton
09 belemnite, coccolith, coprolite, fish teeth, steinkern, trilobite
10 cast fossil, gastrolith, graptolite, snakestone
11 ichnofossil, microfossil, mould fossil, resin fossil, sharks' teeth, trace fossil
12 Burgess shale, stromatolite

fossilized
04 dead **05** passé, stony **07** archaic, extinct **08** hardened, obsolete, ossified, outmoded **09** out of date, petrified **10** antiquated **11** prehistoric **12** antediluvian, old-fashioned **13** anachronistic

foster
03 aid **04** back, feed, help, hold, rear **05** boost, nurse, raise **06** assist, foment, mother, nousle, nuzzle, uphold **07** advance, bring up, care for, cherish, further, harbour, nourish, noursle, nousell, nurture, promote, support, sustain **08** forester, incubate **09** cultivate, encourage, entertain, look after, stimulate **10** make much of, take care of

foster-child
04 dalt **05** dault

foul
◇ *anagram indicator*
03 bad, jam, low, paw, wet **04** base, blue, clog, edgy, lewd, mean, rank, soil, ugly, vile, wild **05** angry, black, block, catch, choke, cross, dirty, fetid, gross, humpy, mucky, muddy, narky, nasty,

putid, rainy, ratty, reeky, rough, snarl, stain, sully, taint, testy, twist **06** coarse, crabby, defile, dreggy, feisty, filthy, foetid, foul up, grumpy, impure, odious, pawpaw, putrid, reekie, ribald, rotten, shirty, smelly, smutty, snappy, soiled, stingy, stormy, tangle, tetchy, unfair, untidy, virose, vulgar, wicked
07 abusive, bilious, blacken, collide, crabbed, decayed, defiled, ensnare, gnarled, grouchy, heinous, obscene, peppery, pollute, prickly, profane, rotting, squalid, squally, stroppy, tainted, unclean, vicious **08** blustery, choleric, entangle, feculent, harlotry, horrible, indecent, infected, obstruct, polluted, shameful, stagnant, stinking
09 abhorrent, crotchety, dyspeptic, entangled, execrable, fractious, impatient, inclement, irritable, loathsome, nefarious, off-colour, offensive, repellent, repulsive, revolting, sickening, splenetic, technical **10** abominable, capernoity, despicable, detestable, disfigured, disgusting, indelicate, iniquitous, nauseating, putrescent, unpleasant
11 bad-tempered, blasphemous, carnaptious, contaminate, disgraceful
12 contaminated, contemptible, disagreeable, foul-smelling, putrefactive, unfavourable **13** quick-tempered

• **foul play**
05 crime **06** murder **08** violence
09 deception, dirty work **13** double-dealing, funny business, sharp practice
15 unfair behaviour

foul-mouthed
06 coarse, ribald, ribaud **07** abusive, obscene, profane, rybauld
09 offensive **10** foul-spoken
11 blasphemous

foul-smelling stuff
04 hing **10** asafoetida

found
03 fix, met, set **04** base, cast, rest, root
05 build, endow, erect, merit, plant, raise, set up, start **06** bottom, create, ground, locate, settle **07** develop
08 initiate, organize, position
09 construct, establish, institute, originate **10** constitute, inaugurate
14 bring into being

• **found in**
◇ *anagram indicator*
◇ *containment indicator*
◇ *hidden indicator*

foundation
◇ *tail selection indicator*
03 key **04** base, call, core, crib, fond, foot, fund, rock, root **05** basis, cause, heart, score **06** bottom, excuse, ground, motive, reason, rip-rap, thrust
07 account, bedrock, charity, essence, footing, grounds, keynote, premise, reasons, roadbed, support
08 argument, creation, cribwork, founding, grillage, occasion, pitching
09 endowment, essential, grounding, institute, principle, rationale, setting-up, substance **10** essentials, grass-roots, groundwork, hypostasis, inducement, initiation, stereobate, substratum **11** fundamental, institution, vindication **12** constitution, fundamentals, inauguration, organization, quintessence, substructure, underpinning **13** alpha and omega, establishment, justification, starting-point **14** main ingredient, understructure **15** first principles

founder
◇ *anagram indicator*
04 fail, fall, sink **05** abort, maker
06 author, father, go down, mother, oecist, oikist **07** builder, capsize, creator, endower, go wrong, misfire, stumble, subside **08** belleter, collapse, designer, inventor, miscarry, submerge
09 architect, break down, developer, initiator, organizer, patriarch
10 benefactor, discoverer, institutor, originator, prime mover, progenitor
11 come to grief, constructor, establisher, fall through **13** come to nothing, go to the bottom **14** be unsuccessful

foundling
04 waif **05** stray **06** orphan, urchin
07 outcast **12** enfant trouvé
15 abandoned infant

fount
04 font, rise, well **05** birth, cause
06 origin, source, spring **08** wellhead
09 beginning, inception
10 mainspring **12** commencement, fountainhead

fountain
03 jet **04** fons, font, pant, rise, well
05 birth, cause, fount, gerbe, laver, spout, spray, spurt **06** origin, source, spring **07** bubbler, conduit, jet d'eau
08 Aganippe, wellhead **09** beginning, Castalian, inception, reservoir
10 Hippocrene, mainspring, waterworks, wellspring **11** Aonian fount, scuttlebutt, scuttle cask
12 commencement, fountainhead

four
02 IV **04** IIII, mess **06** tetrad
07 quartet **08** quartett **09** quartette
10 quaternary, quaternion, quaternity

• **one of four**
04 quad

four-square
05 frank **06** firmly, honest **07** frankly, solidly **08** honestly, squarely
10 forthright, resolutely

fourteen
03 XIV

fowl
03 hen **04** bird, cock, coot, duck
05 chook, goose, poult **06** bantam, boiler, Brahma, houdan, rumkin, sultan, turkey **07** chicken, Hamburg, leghorn, pintado, poultry **08** Hamburgh, pheasant, rose comb, wildfowl
09 wyandotte **10** chittagong, spatchcock **11** brissel-cock **14** Rhode Island red

fox
03 pug, tod **05** cheat, puggy, vixen, zerda, zorro **06** baffle, corsac, fennec, Lowrie **07** Charley, Charlie, deceive, Reynard **09** Lowrie-tod, Tod-lowrie
10 Basil Brush

foxglove
09 digitalis **13** dead-men's bells
14 witches' thimble

foxtrot
01 F

foxy
03 fly, sly **04** wily **05** canny, sharp
06 artful, astute, crafty, shrewd, tricky
07 cunning, devious, knowing, vulpine
08 guileful

foyer
04 hall **05** lobby **07** hallway
08 anteroom **09** reception, vestibule
11 antechamber **12** entrance hall

fracas
03 row **04** riot, rout, spat **05** aggro, brawl, fight, mêlée, scrap, set-to
06 affray, barney, bust-up, ruckus, ruffle, rumpus, shindy, uproar
07 quarrel, ruction, scuffle, trouble
10 Donnybrook, free-for-all
11 disturbance

fraction
03 bit **04** half, part **05** ratio, third
06 amount **07** decimal, ligroin, quarter
08 repeater, tailings **10** proportion, sexagenary **11** sexagesimal, subdivision

fractional
04 tiny **05** small **06** little, minute, slight, subtle **07** partial **10** negligible
13 imperceptible, insignificant, insubstantial

fractious
05 cross, testy **06** crabby, grumpy, touchy, unruly **07** awkward, fretful, grouchy, peevish **08** captious, choleric, petulant **09** crotchety, irritable, querulous **10** refractory
11 bad-tempered, quarrelsome
12 recalcitrant

fracture
◇ *anagram indicator*
03 gap **04** chip, rent, rift, slit, snap
05 break, cleft, crack, fault, split
06 breach, schism **07** fissure, opening, rupture **08** aperture, breakage, breaking, splinter **09** splitting
10 microcrack

fragile
04 fine, weak **05** frail **06** dainty, feeble, flimsy, infirm, slight, tender
07 brittle **08** delicate, unstable
09 breakable, frangible **13** insubstantial

fragility
07 frailty **08** delicacy, weakness
09 infirmity **10** feebleness
11 brittleness **12** frangibility
13 breakableness

fragment
◇ *hidden indicator*
02 fr **03** bit, end, ort **04** blad, chip, flaw, mite, part, rift, snip, spar **05** blaud, break, chink, crumb, frust, patch, piece, scrap, shard, shred, split **06** cinder, divide, morsel, sheave, shiver, sliver, snatch **07** break up, cantlet, crumble, flinder, flitter, fritter, morceau, portion, remains, remnant, shatter, snippet, split up **08** disunite, fraction, particle, potshard, potshare, potsherd, quantity, splinter, xenolith **09** come apart, remainder **10** sequestrum, smithereen **11** smithereens **12** come to pieces, disintegrate **13** smash to pieces

fragmentary
05 bitty **06** broken, snippy, uneven **07** partial, scrappy, sketchy **08** separate, snippety **09** piecemeal, scattered **10** disjointed, incoherent, incomplete **11** fractionary **12** disconnected **13** discontinuous

fragmentation
07 break-up **08** division **09** crumbling, splitting **10** separation, shattering **11** atomization, splitting-up **13** decomposition **14** disintegration

fragmented
06 broken, in bits **07** divided **08** in pieces, separate **09** disunited **10** disjointed, incomplete **13** disintegrated

fragrance
04 balm, otto **05** aroma, attar, odour, scent, smell **07** bouquet, perfume **09** redolence **10** sweet smell

fragrant
04 nosy **05** balmy, nosey, spicy, sweet **07** balsamy, odorous, savoury, scented **08** aromatic, perfumed, redolent **09** ambrosial **10** suaveolent **11** odoriferous **12** sweet-scented **13** sweet-smelling

frail
04 puny, rush, weak **05** shaky **06** feeble, flimsy, infirm, slight, slimsy, unwell **07** brittle, fragile, unsound **08** delicate **09** breakable, frangible **10** vulnerable **11** susceptible **12** easily broken **13** insubstantial

frailty
04 flaw **05** fault **06** defect, foible **07** blemish, failing **08** delicacy, weakness **09** fragility, infirmity, weak point **10** deficiency **11** brittleness, fallibility, shortcoming **12** imperfection **13** vulnerability **14** susceptibility

frame
◇ *containment indicator*
◇ *ends selection indicator*
03 set **04** body, case, draw, edge, form, husk, loom, make, plan, plot, sash, size, tent, trap **05** adapt, box in, build, draft, erect, fit up, forge, model, mould, mount, pin on, plant, set up, shape, shell **06** adjust, border, casing, cook up, create, devise, draw up, encase, fabric, figure, map out, redact, sketch **07** carcase, chassis, compose, concoct, enclose, fashion, monture, pretend, setting, support, taboret **08** assemble, bodywork, conceive, contrive, mounting, physique, skeleton, stitch up, surround, tabouret **09** construct, establish, fabricate, formulate, framework, structure **10** articulate, foundation **11** incriminate, manufacture, put together, scaffolding **12** construction, substructure **13** cook up a charge

• **frame of mind**
04 mood, tune **05** state **06** humour, spirit, temper **07** outlook **08** attitude **09** condition **11** disposition, state of mind

frame-up
03 fix **04** plot, trap **05** fit-up **08** put-up job **10** conspiracy **11** fabrication **15** trumped-up charge

framework
◇ *containment indicator*
04 grid, plan, rack **05** frame, shell **06** casing, cradle, fabric, scheme **07** lattice, outline, tressel, trestle **08** scaffold, skeleton **09** bare bones, structure **10** foundation, groundwork, parameters **11** constraints, trestlework **12** substructure

France
01 F **02** Fr **03** FRA **04** Gaul
See also **department**

• **in France**
◇ *foreign word indicator*

• **South of France**
04 Midi **07** Riviera **09** Côte d'Azur

franchise
05 right **07** candour, charter, consent, freedom, liberty, licence, warrant **08** immunity, suffrage **09** exemption, frankness, privilege **10** concession, permission **11** prerogative **13** authorization **15** enfranchisement

francium
02 Fr

frank
04 free, mark, open **05** bluff, blunt, plain, stamp **06** cancel, candid, direct, honest, pigsty **07** genuine, liberal, sincere, up-front **08** explicit, postmark, straight, truthful **09** downright, ingenuous, outspoken, Ripuarian **10** forthright, four-square **11** hard-hitting, open-hearted, plain-spoken, transparent, undisguised **12** unrestrained **13** simple-hearted **15** straightforward

frankincense
04 thus **08** olibanum

frankly
06 freely, openly **07** bluntly, in truth, plainly **08** candidly, directly, eye to eye, honestly, straight **09** to be blunt, to be frank **10** explicitly, to be honest, truthfully **11** straight out **14** without reserve

frankness
06 candor **07** candour, freedom, honesty **08** openness **09** bluntness, franchise, sincerity **10** directness **12** truthfulness **13** ingenuousness, outspokenness, plain speaking **14** forthrightness

frantic
◇ *anagram indicator*
03 mad **04** wild **06** hectic, raging, raving **07** berserk, fraught, furious **08** agitated, frenetic, frenzied **09** desperate **10** distracted, distraught, distressed **11** overwrought **12** out of control **13** at your wits' end, panic-stricken **14** beside yourself

frantically
◇ *anagram indicator*
05 madly **06** wildly **09** furiously **11** desperately **12** hysterically, out of control **13** at your wits' end **14** beside yourself

fraternity
03 set **04** clan, club **05** guild, order, union **06** circle, fratry, league **07** company, fratery, kinship, society **08** sodality **10** fellowship **11** association, brotherhood, camaraderie, comradeship **13** companionship

fraternize
03 mix **04** move **05** unite **06** hobnob, mingle **07** consort **08** go around **09** affiliate, associate, forgather, hang about, pal up with, socialize **10** cordialize, foregather, gang up with, sympathize **11** keep company **12** rub shoulders

fraud
03 con, fix **04** fake, hoax, scam, sham, swiz **05** cheat, guile, phony, quack, snare, trick **06** con man, deceit, diddle, hoaxer, humbug, hustle, phoney, racket, riddle, rip-off, take-in **07** bluffer, forgery, roguery, swindle, swizzle **08** cheating, fraus pia, impostor, pia fraus, swindler, trickery **09** charlatan, chicanery, deception, duplicity, embezzler, fraudster, gold brick, imposture, pretender, swindling, trickster **10** mountebank **11** counterfeit, fraudulence, stellionate, supercherie **12** double-dealer, embezzlement **13** double-dealing, sharp practice **15** salami technique

fraudulent
04 sham **05** bogus, cronk, false, quack, shady **06** phoney **07** crooked, knavish **08** cheating, covinous, criminal **09** deceitful, deceptive, dishonest, shameless, swindling **11** counterfeit, duplicitous **12** exploitative, unscrupulous **13** double-dealing, surreptitious

fraudulently
07 falsely **09** corruptly, illegally **11** deceitfully, dishonestly, shamelessly **14** unscrupulously

fraught
04 full, load **05** cargo, laden, tense **06** filled **07** anxious, charged, freight, replete, uptight, worried **08** agitated, attended **09** abounding, bristling, freighted **10** distraught, distressed **11** accompanied, overwrought, stressed out, under stress

fray
03 rag, row, tax, vex **04** riot, wear **05** aggro, brawl, clash, fight, scrap, set-to **06** affray, battle, bovver, combat, dust-up, fridge, rumpus, scrape, strain, stress **07** bashing, frazzle, overtax, pasting, punch-up, quarrel, scuffle, unravel, wear out **08** conflict, frighten, irritate, wear thin **09** challenge, make tense, put on edge **10** excitement, free-for-all, push too far **11** disturbance, make nervous **12** become ragged **14** wigs on the green

frayed
04 thin, worn **06** ragged **08** tattered, worn thin **10** threadbare, unravelled

freak
◇ *anagram indicator*
03 fan, nut, odd **04** buff, geek, turn, whim **05** fiend, fluky, queer, quirk, twist **06** addict, chance, mutant, oddity, vagary, weirdo **07** anomaly, bizarre, caprice, devotee, erratic, fanatic, monster, oddball, unusual **08** aberrant, abnormal, atypical, mutation, surprise **09** curiosity, deformity, eccentric **10** aberration, aficionado, capricious, enthusiast, fortuitous, unexpected **11** abnormality, exceptional, monstrosity **12** irregularity, lusus naturae, malformation **13** freak of nature, unpredictable

• freak out
◇ *anagram indicator*
06 go wild, wig out **07** explode, go crazy **09** go bananas, go berserk **11** lose control **12** throw a wobbly **15** go off the deep end, go out of your mind

freakish
03 odd **05** weird **06** fitful, freaky **07** erratic, strange, unusual **08** aberrant, abnormal, fanciful, peculiar **09** arbitrary, fantastic, grotesque, malformed, monstrous, whimsical **10** capricious, changeable, outlandish **13** unpredictable **14** unconventional

freckle
04 spot **07** ephelis, lentigo **08** heatspot **09** fernticle **10** fernitickle, ferntickle, fernyticle **11** fairniticle, fairnyticle, fernitickle, fernytickle **12** fairnitickle, fairnytickle

free
◇ *anagram indicator*
03 ope, out, rid **04** bold, easy, idle, open, quit, save **05** broad, clear, empty, fluid, let go, loose, rough, spare, unmew, untie, vague **06** acquit, casual, except, excuse, exempt, freely, giving, gratis, lavish, let out, ransom, redeem, rescue, smooth, solute, svelte, unbind, vacant **07** absolve, acquite, at large, clear of, deliver, for free, for love, general, inexact, lacking, liberal, natural, off duty, relaxed, release, relieve, set free, unbowed, unchain, unleash, untaken, without **08** acquight, at no cost, buckshee, devoid of, generous, immune to, indecent, laid-back, lavishly, liberate, safe from, set loose, unburden **09** at liberty, autarchic, available, copiously, debarrass, disburden, discharge, disengage, easy-going, extricate, imprecise, liberally, liberated, sovereign, turn loose, unblocked, unimpeded, unsecured, voluntary **10** abundantly, autonomous, charitable, democratic, disburthen, emancipate, exempt from, for nothing, generously, hospitable, munificent, on the house, on the loose, open-handed, self-ruling, unattached, unconfined, unemployed, unfastened, unhampered, unoccupied, unstinting **11** Anacreontic, disentangle, emancipated, free as a bird, independent, requiteless, spontaneous, uninhibited **12** free of charge, unaffected by, unobstructed, unrestrained, unrestricted **13** at no extra cost, complimentary, extravagantly, make available, self-governing, without charge **15** with compliments

• free and easy
06 casual **07** relaxed **08** carefree, informal, laid-back, tolerant **09** easy-going **11** spontaneous **12** happy-go-lucky **13** unconstrained

• free hand
05 power, scope **07** freedom, liberty, licence **08** free rein, latitude **09** authority **10** discretion, permission **12** carte blanche

• setting free
03 lib **07** release **09** unbinding **10** liberation

freebooter
07 cateran, pindari **08** pindaree **09** snaphance **10** snaphaunce, snaphaunch

freedom
04 ease, play **05** power, range, right, scope **06** leeway, margin **07** liberty, licence, release **08** autarchy, autonomy, free hand, free rein, home rule, immunity, impunity, latitude **09** democracy, exemption, frankness, privilege **10** separation **11** deliverance, flexibility, open slather, opportunity, prerogative, sovereignty **12** emancipation, independence **13** outspokenness **14** self-government

free-for-all
03 row **04** fray **05** brawl, broil, clash, fight, mêlée, rammy, scrap **06** affray, bust-up, dust-up, fracas, fratch, ruckus, rumpus, stoush **07** bagarre, brabble, brangle, dispute, punch-up, quarrel, scuffle, tuilyie **08** argument, disorder, skirmish, squabble **10** Donnybrook, fisticuffs **11** altercation, open slather

freely
◇ *anagram indicator*
05 ad-lib, amply **06** easily, openly **07** bluntly, frankly, loosely, plainly, readily **08** candidly, lavishly, smoothly **09** liberally, naturally, willingly **10** abundantly, generously **11** voluntarily **12** unreservedly **13** extravagantly, spontaneously **14** frictionlessly, without jerking **15** in all directions

freeman
05 ceorl, thete **07** burgess, burgher, citizen **09** liveryman

freethinker
05 deist **07** doubter, infidel, sceptic **08** agnostic **09** libertine **10** esprit fort, unbeliever **11** independent, rationalist **13** nonconformist

freethinking
07 liberal **08** agnostic **09** sceptical **10** open-minded **11** broad-minded, independent, rationalist **13** nonconformist **14** unconventional

free will
07 autarky, freedom, liberty **08** autonomy, election, volition **11** spontaneity **12** independence **15** self-sufficiency

• of your own free will
06 freely **08** by choice **09** purposely, willingly **11** consciously, voluntarily **12** deliberately **13** intentionally, spontaneously **15** of your own accord

freeze
03 fix, ice, peg, set **04** cool, halt, hold, stay, stop, take **05** chill, frost, ice up **06** fixing, harden, quiver, shiver **07** congeal, embargo, get cold, ice over, stiffen, suspend **08** cold snap, enfreeze, freeze-up, glaciate, preserve, shutdown, solidify, stoppage **09** freeze-dry, stabilize **10** deep-freeze, immobilize, moratorium, stand still, standstill, suspension **11** catch a chill, refrigerate **12** anaesthetize, interruption, postponement **15** become paralysed

• freeze out
03 cut **04** snub **05** eject, evict, expel **06** ice out, ignore, remove **07** boot out, boycott, exclude, kick out, lock out, turf out **08** brush off, throw out **09** ostracize **13** excommunicate **14** send to Coventry

freezing
03 icy, raw **04** cold, numb **05** polar **06** arctic, baltic, biting, bitter, chilly, frosty, wintry **07** cutting, glacial, numbing **08** piercing, Siberian, stinging **09** perishing **10** frigorific **11** penetrating **12** bitterly cold, brass monkeys

freight
04 hire, load **05** cargo, goods **06** lading, let out **07** fraught, haulage,

payload, portage **08** carriage, contents, shipment **10** conveyance, freightage **11** consignment, merchandise **14** transportation

French
◇ *foreign word indicator*
02 Fr
See also **day**; **month**; **number**; **shop**
• **Old French**
02 OF

French Guiana
03 GUF

Frenchman
01 M

French first names include:

03 Luc
04 Jean, Léon, Rémi, Rémy, René, Yves,
05 Alain, André, Denis, Émile, Henri, Jules, Louis, Serge
06 Claude, Didier, Gaston, Gérard, Honoré, Jérôme, Marcel, Michel, Pascal, Pierre, Xavier
07 Antoine, Édouard, Étienne, Georges, Gustave, Jacques, Laurent, Olivier, Patrice, Thibaut, Thierry, Vincent
08 Frédéric, Matthieu, Philippe, Stéphane, Thibault
09 Guillaume

French Revolutionary Calendar
see **month**

frenetic
◇ *anagram indicator*
03 mad **04** wild **05** manic **06** hectic, insane, madman **07** berserk, excited, frantic **08** demented, frenzied, maniacal **09** delirious, obsessive **10** distracted, distraught, hysterical, unbalanced **11** hyperactive, overwrought

frenetically
◇ *anagram indicator*
05 madly **06** wildly **09** excitedly, intensely, manically **10** hectically **11** frantically **12** hysterically

frenzied
03 mad **04** amok, wild **05** manic **06** crazed, hectic, raving **07** berserk, frantic, furious **08** demented, feverish, frenetic **09** desperate, obsessive, phrenetic, raving mad **10** distracted, distraught, hysterical **11** overwrought **12** out of control, uncontrolled **13** at your wits' end, panic-stricken **14** beside yourself

frenzy
◇ *anagram indicator*
03 fit **04** bout, fury, must, rage **05** burst, fever, mania, musth, spasm **06** lunacy **07** madness, oestrum, oestrus, passion, seizure, turmoil **08** delirium, hysteria, insanity, outburst, paroxysm, tailspin, wildness **09** agitation, phrenesis, transport **10** convulsion **11** derangement, distraction, nympholepsy **13** furor poeticus
• **expression of frenzy**
04 euoi, evoe **05** evhoe, evohe, yahoo

frequency
01 f **06** resort **09** constancy, incidence, oftenness **10** commonness, prevalence, recurrence, repetition **11** commonality, periodicity **12** frequentness

frequent
05 daily, haunt, lobby, often, thick, usual, visit **06** attend, common, hourly, normal, weekly **07** crowded, regular **08** addicted, constant, everyday, familiar, habitual, numerous, practise, repeated **09** continual, countless, customary, habituate, hang out at, incessant, patronize, prevalent, recurrent, recurring **10** accustomed, persistent, prevailing, visit often **11** commonplace, hang about at, predominant **13** associate with, go to regularly **14** go to frequently, happening often

frequenter
06 client, patron **07** habitué, haunter, regular **08** customer, resorter **14** regular visitor

frequently
02 fr **03** oft **04** much **05** daily, often, thick **06** hourly, weekly **08** commonly **09** many a time, many times, regularly **10** habitually, oftentimes, repeatedly **11** continually, customarily, half the time, over and over **12** persistently

fresh
◇ *anagram indicator*
03 hot, new, raw **04** bold, cool, fair, firm, just, keen, more, pert, pink, pure, rosy, span, warm **05** alert, brisk, clean, clear, cocky, crisp, crude, extra, green, newly, novel, other, right, sassy, saucy, spick, sweet, vital, windy **06** afresh, brazen, bright, caller, cheeky, chilly, direct, latest, lively, maiden, modern, recent, rested **07** bracing, forward, freshly, further, glowing, healthy, natural, renewed, revived, span new, uncured, undried, unfaded, unusual, vibrant **08** blooming, bouncing, brand-new, dewy-eyed, exciting, familiar, impudent, insolent, original, pristine, restored, straight, up-to-date, vigorous, youthful **09** different, energetic, refreshed, virescent **10** additional, a new person, innovative, new-fangled, raring to go, refreshing, stimulated, unpolluted **11** impertinent, invigorated, unpreserved, unprocessed **12** enthusiastic, invigorating, overfamiliar, presumptuous, ready for more **13** disrespectful, fresh as a daisy, inexperienced, revolutionary, supplementary, yourself again **14** healthy-looking, unconventional
• **remain fresh**
04 keep, last

freshen
◇ *anagram indicator*
03 air **05** clean, clear, liven, rouse **06** purify, refill, revive, tart up **07** enliven, liven up, refresh, restore **09** deodorize, stimulate, ventilate, vernalize **10** revitalize **12** reinvigorate
• **freshen up**
09 get washed, have a wash **12** get spruced up, wash yourself **14** tidy yourself up

freshly
◇ *anagram indicator*
04 anew, just **05** newly **06** barely, lately, of late **08** recently **10** not long ago **13** a short time ago

freshman
05 bajan, frosh **06** bejant, pennal **07** fresher **08** newcomer **09** first-year **13** underclassman

freshness
04 glow **05** bloom, flush, shine **06** vigour, youths **07** May-morn, newness, novelty, sparkle, verdure **09** cleanness, clearness, fraîcheur, immediacy, vernality **10** brightness, May-morning **11** originality **13** wholesomeness
• **early freshness**
03 dew

fret
03 rub, vex **04** mope, pine, rile, stop **05** anger, annoy, brood, chafe, grate, worry **06** bother, nettle, ripple **07** agonize, anguish, be upset, concern, corrode, disturb, torment, trouble, whittle **08** irritate **09** be anxious, infuriate, make a fuss, variegate **10** exasperate **12** be distressed **15** concern yourself

fretful
04 edgy **05** tense, upset **06** uneasy **07** anxious, fearful, peevish, unhappy, uptight, worried **08** restless, troubled **09** disturbed, impatient **10** distressed

fretfully
06 edgily **07** tensely **08** uneasily **09** anxiously, fearfully, worriedly **10** restlessly

friable
05 crisp, crump **07** brittle, crumbly, powdery **12** pulverizable

friar
02 Fr **03** fra **04** monk **05** abbot, frate, frier, minim, prior **06** frater **07** brother, limiter **08** Capuchin, récollet **09** Carmelite, Cordelier, Dominican, mendicant, Observant, predicant, recollect, religieux, religious **10** Franciscan, religioner **12** Observantine **13** Redemptionist

friction
06 strife **07** arguing, chafing, discord, dispute, erosion, gnawing, grating, jarring, rasping, rivalry, rubbing **08** abrading, abrasion, bad blood, clashing, conflict, disunity, scraping, traction **09** animosity, attrition, hostility **10** antagonism, bad feeling, disharmony, dissension, ill feeling, irritation, opposition, resentment, resistance **11** disputation, excoriation,

quarrelling, wearing away, xerotripsis **12** disagreement

Friday
02 Fr **03** Fri

fridge
03 rub **04** fray, frig **06** cooler, icebox **07** minibar **12** refrigerator **13** refrigeratory

friend
03 ami, bud, pal **04** ally, amie, chum, ehoa, mate, tosh **05** amigo, buddy, crony, ingle, lover **06** backer, belamy, bon ami, cobber, co-mate, gossib, gossip, inward, mucker, patron **07** best boy, comrade, goombah, paisano, partner, privado, sponsor **08** alter ego, best girl, compadre, familiar, intimate, playmate, sidekick, soul mate **09** associate, belle amie, bonne amie, boyfriend, companion, confidant, confident, paranymph, pen friend, supporter **10** back-friend, benefactor, best friend, better half, buddy-buddy, confidante, girlfriend, good friend, subscriber, well-wisher **11** bosom friend, cater-cousin, close friend, condisciple **12** acquaintance, fidus Achates, schoolfriend **15** sparring partner

• **mans' best friend**
03 dog

friendless
05 alone **06** lonely **07** forlorn, shunned, unloved **08** deserted, forsaken, isolated, lonesome, solitary **09** abandoned, destitute, unbeloved, unpopular **10** by yourself, ostracized, unattached **11** lonely-heart **12** unbefriended **13** companionless **14** cold-shouldered

friendliness
06 warmth **08** bonhomie, kindness, matiness **09** geniality, palliness **10** affability, amiability, chumminess, kindliness **11** sociability **12** congeniality, conviviality **13** Gemütlichkeit **15** approachability, neighbourliness

friendly
04 fond, kind, maty, nice, tosh, warm **05** close, matey, pally, thick, tight **06** chummy, couthy, folksy, genial, kindly **07** affable, amiable, cordial, couthie, helpful **08** amicable, down-home, familiar, informal, intimate, outgoing, pleasant, sociable **09** agreeable, comradely, congenial, convivial, favorable, peaceable, receptive, welcoming **10** favourable, hospitable **11** forthcoming, good-natured, inseparable, neighbourly, sympathetic **12** affectionate, approachable, well-disposed **13** companionable

friendship
04 love **05** amity, amour **06** warmth **07** company, concord, harmony, rapport **08** affinity, alliance, fondness, goodwill, intimacy, mateship **09** affection, closeness **10** amiability, attachment, fellowship, kindliness **11** camaraderie, comradeship, familiarity **12** friendliness **13** companionship, confraternity, understanding

fright
04 fear, fleg, funk **05** alarm, dread, gliff, glift, panic, scare, shock, skrik **06** creeps, dismay, horror, terror, tirrit **07** jitters, shivers, willies **08** affright, blue funk, disquiet **09** bombshell, cold sweat **10** blind panic **11** fearfulness, trepidation **12** affrightment, apprehension, perturbation **13** consternation, heebie-jeebies, knocking knees **15** bolt from the blue

• **expression of fright**
03 eek **04** yike **05** yikes

frighten
03 awe **04** dare, flay, fleg, fley, fray, gast, shoo **05** afear, alarm, appal, daunt, dread, ghast, panic, scare, shock, spook, unman **06** affear, affray, boggle, dismay, gallow, rattle **07** affeare, horrify, petrify, scarify, startle, terrify, unnerve **08** affright **09** terrorize **10** affrighten, intimidate, scare silly, scare stiff **12** put the wind up

frightened
04 frit **05** cowed, feart, windy **06** afraid, frozen, scared **07** alarmed, chicken, panicky, quivery, trembly **08** dismayed, startled, unnerved **09** petrified, terrified **10** terrorized **11** in a blue funk, scared stiff **13** having kittens, panic-stricken, scared to death **14** terror-stricken

frightening
04 eery, grim **05** eerie, hairy, scary **06** creepy, scarey, spooky **08** alarming, daunting, fearsome, terrific **09** traumatic **10** forbidding, formidable, petrifying, terrifying **11** hair-raising **12** white-knuckle **13** bloodcurdling, spine-chilling

frightful
◇ *anagram indicator*
04 dire, grim, huge, ugly **05** awful, great, nasty **06** grisly, horrid, odious **07** fearful, ghastly, hideous, macabre, very bad **08** alarming, dreadful, fearsome, gruesome, horrible, horrific, shocking, terrible **09** abhorrent, appalling, harrowing, loathsome, repulsive, revolting **10** frightsome, horrendous, unbearable, unpleasant **11** affrightful, schrecklich, unspeakable **12** disagreeable

frightfully
◇ *anagram indicator*
04 much, very **07** awfully, beastly, greatly **08** terribly **09** decidedly, extremely **10** dreadfully, ghastfully, thoroughly **11** desperately, exceedingly

frigid
03 dry, icy **04** cold, cool **05** aloof, chill, polar, stiff, stony **06** arctic, bitter, chilly, formal, frosty, frozen, remote, wintry **07** distant, glacial, passive, unmoved **08** clinical, freezing, lifeless, reserved, Siberian, unloving, very cold **09** unfeeling **10** impersonal, unanimated **11** indifferent, passionless, standoffish, unemotional, unexcitable **12** unresponsive **13** unsympathetic

frigidity
05 chill **07** iciness **08** coldness **09** aloofness, passivity, stiffness **10** chilliness, frostiness **11** impassivity **12** lifelessness **15** cold-heartedness

frill
04 fold, ruff, tuck **05** extra, jabot, ruche **06** finery, fringe, purfle, ruffle **07** armilla, flounce, orphrey, ruching, valance **08** addition, frippery, furbelow, trimming **09** accessory, fanciness, fandangle, gathering, trimmings **10** decoration, frilliness **11** chitterling, ostentation, superfluity **13** embellishment, ornamentation

frilly
◇ *anagram indicator*
04 lacy **05** fancy **06** ornate **07** crimped, frilled, ruffled, trimmed **08** flounced, gathered

fringe
◇ *ends selection indicator*
03 hem, rim **04** bang, edge, fall, loma, purl, trim **05** bangs, frill, limit, skirt, thrum, verge **06** border, edging, margin, pelmet, tassel **07** bullion, enclose, fimbria, macramé, macrami, off-beat, valance **08** frisette, surround, trimming **09** left-field, outskirts, perimeter, periphery, peristome **10** avant-garde, borderline, unofficial, unorthodox **11** alternative **12** experimental **14** unconventional

fringed
05 edged **06** fringy, hemmed **07** trimmed **08** bordered, tasselly **09** fimbriate, tasselled **10** fimbriated

frippery
05 froth **06** finery, frills, trivia **07** baubles, foppery, gewgaws, trifles, useless **08** glad rags, nonsense, trifling, trinkets **09** fanciness, fussiness, gaudiness, nick-nacks, ornaments, showiness **10** adornments, fandangles, flashiness, frilliness, tawdriness, triviality **11** decorations, knick-knacks, ostentation **15** pretentiousness

frisk
03 hop **04** fisk, jump, leap, play, romp, skip, trip **05** caper, check, dance, sport **06** bounce, cavort, curvet, frolic, gambol, prance, search **07** inspect **09** shake down **10** body-search

friskily
08 actively **09** playfully **10** spiritedly **11** exuberantly

frisky
◇ *anagram indicator*
04 high **05** hyper **06** active, bouncy,

lively, wanton **07** buckish, coltish, dashing, playful, romping **08** skittish, spirited **09** exuberant **10** frolicsome, rollicking **11** full of beans **12** high-spirited **13** in high spirits **15** alive and kicking

fritter
04 blow, idle **05** waste **06** misuse **07** beignet, friture **08** fragment, misspend, squander **09** dissipate, go through, overspend **10** get through **14** spend like water

frivolity
03 fun **04** jest **05** folly, froth **06** gaiety, levity **07** inanity **08** nonsense
09 flippancy, pettiness, silliness
10 triviality **11** foolishness
13 facetiousness, senselessness
14 superficiality

frivolous
04 idle, vain **05** inane, light, petty, silly **06** futile **07** étourdi, foolish, jocular, puerile, shallow, trivial **08** étourdie, flippant, juvenile, skittish, trifling
09 airheaded, facetious, pointless, senseless **11** empty-headed, giddy-headed, light-minded, superficial, unimportant **12** bubble-headed, light-hearted **13** irresponsible
14 featherbrained
• **frivolous person**
09 butterfly

frivolously
04 idly **06** vainly **09** foolishly, jocularly
11 pointlessly, senselessly, whimsically
13 irresponsibly **14** light-heartedly

frizzle
03 fry **04** bend, coil, curl, hiss, kink, loop, purl, roll, spit, tong, turn, wave, wind **05** crimp, curve, frizz, twine, twirl, twist **06** becurl, scorch, scroll, sizzle, spiral **07** crackle, crimple, crinkle, sputter, wreathe

frizzy
04 wiry **05** crisp, curly **06** curled
07 crimped, frizzed **10** corrugated

frock
04 gown, robe **05** dress
See also **dress**

frog
04 hyla, Rana **05** frush **06** peeper
07 paddock, puddock **08** platanna, tree toad **12** spring peeper **15** Cape nightingale

frolic
◇ *anagram indicator*
03 fun, hop, rig **04** game, lark, leap, play, rant, romp, skip **05** caper, dance, frisk, merry, mirth, prank, revel, sport, spree **06** antics, bounce, buster, cavort, curvet, gaiety, gambol, prance, pranky, razzle, splore, wanton
07 disport, gambado, gammock, jollity, May-game, rollick, skylark, stashie, stishie, stushie **08** escapade, stooshie **09** amusement, galravage, gilravage, high jinks, make merry, merriment **10** galravitch, gillravage, gilravitch, lark around **11** fun and games, gillravitch, merrymaking
12 razzle-dazzle **13** barnsbreaking

frolicsome
◇ *anagram indicator*
03 gay **05** ludic, merry **06** frisky, lively, skippy **07** coltish, kitteny, playful
08 skittish, sportive **09** kittenish, sprightly **10** rollicking

from
◇ *anagram indicator*
◇ *hidden indicator*
01 à **02** ab-, ex, of, on **03** fro, off, out
04 frae **05** out of, since

front
◇ *head selection indicator*
03 air, bow, top, van **04** face, fore, head, lead, look, mask, meet, prow, show **05** blind, cover, first **06** aspect, façade, facing, manner, oppose, vaward **07** cover-up, leading, obverse, outside, pretext **08** confront, disguise, exterior, foremost, forepart, frontage, look over, overlook, pretence, vanguard **09** forefront, front line, look out on **10** appearance, battle zone, expression, firing line, foreground
11 countenance
• **in front**
◇ *juxtaposition indicator*
04 fore **05** ahead, first **06** before, en face **07** leading **08** anterior, paravant
09 in advance, paravaunt, preceding, to the fore
• **in front of**
◇ *juxtaposition indicator*
06 before, facing **07** ahead of **11** in advance of **14** under the nose of **15** in the presence of

frontier
04 edge **05** limit, verge **06** border, bounds **07** marches **08** boundary, confines **09** bordering, partition, perimeter **10** borderline

front-runner
03 nap **07** top seed **08** finalist
09 certainty, favourite, form horse
12 likely winner **15** odds-on favourite

frost
03 ice, mat **04** rime **06** freeze
08 coldness, freeze-up **09** hoar-frost, Jack Frost

frostily
06 coldly, coolly **07** stiffly

frosty
03 icy **04** cold, cool, rimy **05** aloof, chill, frore, frorn, nippy, parky, polar, stiff **06** arctic, chilly, frigid, froren, frorne, frozen, wintry **07** glacial, hostile **08** freezing, Siberian
10 unfriendly **11** standoffish, unwelcoming **12** bitterly cold, discouraging

froth
03 pap **04** barm, fizz, foam, head, mill, ream, scum, suds **05** spume, yeast
06 bubble, lather, mantle, trivia
07 bubbles, chatter, ferment, sea foam, trifles **10** cuckoo-spit, effervesce
12 trivialities **13** cuckoo-spittle, effervescence, irrelevancies

frothy
04 vain **05** barmy, empty, fizzy, foamy, light, nappy, reamy, spumy, sudsy
06 bubbly, slight, yeasty **07** foaming, spumous, trivial **08** bubbling, trifling
09 frivolous **10** spumescent
11 lightweight **13** insubstantial

frown
03 mow **04** lour, moue, pout **05** glare, scowl **06** glower **07** frounce, grimace
09 dirty look **13** look daggers at, raised eyebrow
• **frown on**
05 glare, scowl **06** glower **07** dislike, grimace **08** object to **10** discourage
12 disapprove of, think badly of
14 take a dim view of **15** not take kindly to

frowsty
05 fuggy, fusty, musty **06** stuffy
07 airless **12** unventilated

frowsy
05 dirty, fusty, messy **06** frumpy, sloppy, stuffy, untidy **07** scruffy, unkempt **08** frumpish, slovenly, sluttish, unwashed **09** offensive, ungroomed **10** slatternly
11 dishevelled

frozen
03 icy, raw **04** hard, iced, numb
05 fixed, frore, frorn, glacé, polar, rigid, stiff **06** arctic, frigid, froren, frorne, frosty **07** chilled, frosted, glacial, ice-cold **08** freezing, icebound, Siberian
10 ice-covered, solidified **11** frozen-stiff **12** bitterly cold

frugal
05 spare **06** meagre, paltry, saving, scanty, stingy **07** careful, miserly, prudent, sparing, spartan, thrifty
09 husbandly, niggardly, penny-wise, provident **10** economical, inadequate
12 parsimonious **13** penny-pinching

frugality
06 saving, thrift **07** economy
08 prudence **09** husbandry, parsimony **11** carefulness
12 conservation

frugally
05 spare **08** meagrely, scantily
09 carefully, prudently, thriftily
12 economically, inadequately
14 parsimoniously

fruit
03 haw, hep, hip, nut, pod **04** crop
05 acorn, berry, yield **06** effect, profit, result, return, reward **07** benefit, harvest, outcome, produce, product, rosehip **08** fruitage **09** advantage
11 consequence

Fruits include:

03 bel, Cox, fig
04 bael, bhel, Cox's, date, gage, kaki, lime, pear, plum, sloe, Ugli®

05 apple, carob, galia, grape, guava, Jaffa, lemon, mango, melon, olive, peach, prune
06 banana, cherry, damson, loquat, litchi, lychee, medlar, orange, papaya, pawpaw, pippin, pomelo, quince, raisin, russet, tomato, wampee
07 acerola, apricot, avocado, bramble, Bramley, chayote, kumquat, mineola, rhubarb, satsuma, Seville, soursop, tangelo, William
08 bilberry, Braeburn, date plum, goosegog, honeydew, kalumpit, mandarin, minneola, mulberry, muscatel, physalis, Pink Lady, rambutan, sebesten, sunberry, tamarind
09 beach plum, blueberry, cantaloup, carambola, cherimoya, crab apple, cranberry, greengage, Juneberry, kiwi fruit, nectarine, persimmon, pineapple, raspberry, rose apple, sapodilla, saskatoon, shadberry, star-apple, star fruit, tangerine, ugli®fruit
10 blackberry, breadfruit, cantaloupe, clementine, Conference, damask plum, elderberry, gooseberry, granadilla, grapefruit, loganberry, mangosteen, redcurrant, salal berry, sour cherry, spiceberry, strawberry, watermelon
11 blood orange, boysenberry, eating apple, Granny Smith, Jaffa orange, navel orange, pomegranate, sallal berry, sharon fruit, sweet cherry
12 blackcurrant, buffalo-berry, cooking apple, costard apple, custard apple, passion fruit, Red Delicious, serviceberry, victoria plum, whitecurrant, winter cherry
13 kangaroo-apple, morello cherry, sapodilla plum, Seville orange
14 Cape gooseberry, pink grapefruit
15 Golden Delicious

- **fruit juice**

03 oil **05** mobby **06** mobbie

- **fruit refuse**

04 marc

- **fruit stone**

03 pip, pit **06** pyrene **07** putamen

- **fruit syrup**

03 rob

fruitful

03 fat **04** rich **06** fecund, useful
07 fertile, teeming **08** abundant, fructive, pregnant, prolific **09** effective, effectual, feracious, fructuous, plenteous, plentiful, rewarding, well-spent **10** beneficial, productive, profitable, successful, worthwhile
11 conceptious, efficacious, increaseful
12 advantageous, fruit-bearing

fruitfully

08 usefully **10** profitably **11** effectively
12 beneficially, productively, successfully **14** advantageously

fruitfulness

06 uberty **08** feracity **09** fecundity, fertility **10** usefulness **11** fecundation
13 profitability **14** productiveness

fruition

07 success **08** maturity, ripeness
09 enjoyment **10** attainment, completion, fulfilment, maturation, perfection **11** achievement, realization
12 consummation **13** actualization

fruitless

04 idle, vain **06** barren, futile
07 sterile, useless **08** abortive, hopeless **09** pointless, worthless
11 ineffectual, infructuous
12 unproductive, unsuccessful

fruitlessly

06 in vain, vainly **09** uselessly
10 hopelessly **11** pointlessly
14 unproductively, unsuccessfully

fruity

03 low **04** blue, deep, full, racy, rich, sexy **05** bawdy, crazy, juicy, saucy, spicy **06** mellow, risqué, smutty, vulgar
07 naughty **08** indecent, resonant
09 salacious **10** indelicate, suggestive
11 titillating

frumpy

04 drab **05** dated, dingy, dowdy
06 dreary **08** frumpish **09** out of date
10 ill-dressed **12** badly dressed

frustrate

03 bug **04** balk, beat, crab, dash, foil, miff, nark, rile, stop **05** anger, annoy, baulk, block, check, get at, spike, stimy
06 baffle, balked, blight, defeat, hamper, hinder, hogtie, impede, needle, nobble, scotch, stimie, stymie, thwart, wind up **07** counter, depress, inhibit, nullify, scupper, useless
08 drive mad, embitter, irritate, obstruct **09** aggravate, forestall, infuriate **10** disappoint, disconcert, discourage, dishearten, dissatisfy, drive crazy, exasperate, neutralize
11 ineffectual

frustrated

05 angry **06** dished **07** annoyed
08 blighted, thwarted **09** repressed, resentful **10** embittered
11 discouraged **12** disappointed, discontented, disheartened, dissatisfied

frustrating

08 annoying **09** maddening
10 irritating **11** infuriating
12 discouraging, exasperating
13 disappointing, disheartening

frustration

04 balk, foil **05** anger, baulk **06** defeat, thwart **07** balking, curbing, failure, foiling **08** blocking, vexation
09 annoyance, thwarting **10** irritation, resentment **11** obstruction
12 exasperation **13** circumvention, contravention, non-fulfilment
14 disappointment, discouragement
15 dissatisfaction

- **expression of frustration**

11 for God's sake **12** for pete's sake
14 for Christ's sake, for heaven's sake
15 for goodness sake

fry

04 burn, foam **05** sauté, spawn
06 scorch, sizzle **07** frizzle, skegger
09 whitebait

frying-pan

03 wok **06** spider **07** skillet

fuddled

◇ *anagram indicator*
03 fap **04** hazy **05** drunk, mused, muzzy, tipsy, woozy **06** addled, groggy, swipey, tavert **07** bemused, muddled, sozzled, taivert **08** confused
09 overtaken, stupefied **10** inebriated, tossicated, tosticated **11** intoxicated

fuddy-duddy

04 prim **06** fossil, square, stuffy
07 carping **08** old fogey **10** back number, censorious, conformist
11 museum piece, old-fogeyish
12 buttoned-down, conservative, old-fashioned, stuffed shirt **13** stick-in-the-mud **14** traditionalist

fudge

◇ *anagram indicator*
03 fix **04** cook, fail, fake **05** avoid, cheat, dodge, evade, hedge, stall, stuff
06 fiddle, humbug **07** distort, evasion, falsify, shuffle **08** nonsense
10 distortion, equivocate
12 misrepresent

fuel

03 fan **04** feed, fire **05** boost **06** incite
07 goading, inflame, nourish, stoke up, sustain **08** material, stimulus
09 encourage, incentive, stimulate
10 ammunition, incitement, propellant
11 combustible, motive power, provocation **13** encouragement

Fuels include:

03 gas, LNG, LPG, MOX, oil, RDF
04 coal, coke, derv, logs, peat, slug, SURF, wood
05 argol, eldin, fagot, vraic
06 benzol, billet, borane, butane, diesel, elding, faggot, gas oil, hydyne, petrol, smudge, Sterno®
07 astatki, benzine, benzole, biofuel, Coalite®, eilding, gasahol, gasohol, mesquit, methane, propane, uranium
08 calor gas®, charcoal, firewood, gasoline, kerosene, kerosine, kindling, mesquite, paraffin, tan balls, triptane
09 acetylene, biodiesel, Campingaz®, cane-trash, diesel oil, hydrazine, plutonium, red diesel
10 anthracite, atomic fuel, fossil fuel, natural gas, Orimulsion®
11 electricity, North Sea gas, nuclear fuel
12 buffalo chips, nitromethane, nuclear power, vegetable oil
13 smokeless fuel
14 aviation spirit

See also **petrol**

fug
04 reek **05** stink **09** fetidness, fustiness, staleness **10** foetidness, stuffiness **11** frowstiness

fuggy
04 foul **05** close, fetid, fusty, stale **06** foetid, stuffy **07** airless, frowsty, noisome, noxious **11** suffocating **12** unventilated

fugitive
04 AWOL **05** brief, exile, short **06** flying, maroon, runner **07** elusive, escapee, fleeing, passing, refugee, runaway **08** deserter, fleeting, hideaway, runagate **09** ephemeral, fugacious, momentary, temporary, transient **10** evanescent, short-lived, transitory

fulfil
04 fill, keep, meet, obey **05** honor **06** answer, effect, finish, honour **07** achieve, act up to, execute, live out, observe, perfect, perform, qualify, realize, satisfy **08** carry out, complete, conclude, live up to, make good **09** conform to, discharge, implement, stand up to **10** accomplish, comply with, consummate **15** come up to scratch

fulfilled
05 happy **07** content, pleased **09** gratified, satisfied

fulfilling
08 pleasing **10** comforting, completion, completory, gratifying, satisfying **12** satisfactory **14** accomplishment

fulfilment
04 pass **07** success **08** enacture, fruition **09** discharge, execution, impletion **10** completion, observance, perfection **11** achievement, performance, realization **12** consummation, satisfaction **14** accomplishment, implementation

full
◇ *anagram indicator*
03 fat, fed, top **04** bang, busy, deep, loud, rich, vast, walk, warm, wauk, wide **05** ample, baggy, broad, buxom, clear, drunk, flush, laden, large, loose, obese, plump, quite, right, round, sated, smack, stout, total, truly, waulk, whole **06** active, chubby, entire, filled, fruity, gorged, hectic, intact, jammed, lively, loaded, packed, rotund, strong, tiring, utmost **07** bulging, chocker, copious, crammed, crowded, exactly, filling, frantic, highest, intense, maximum, perfect, profuse, replete, rounded, shapely, stuffed, swelled, vibrant, well fed **08** abundant, bursting, chockers, chockful, complete, detailed, directly, distinct, eventful, exciting, generous, greatest, resonant, satiated, sonorous, squarely, straight, thorough **09** abounding, chock-full, corpulent, extensive, packed out, plentiful, satisfied **10** exhaustive, full-bodied, overweight, sufficient, thoroughly, unabridged, voluminous **11** chock-a-block, overflowing, protuberant, well-rounded, well-stocked **12** all-inclusive, loose-fitting, unexpurgated **13** comprehensive, full to the brim

• **be full**
04 teem

• **in full**
05 fully, uncut **06** wholly **07** at large, in pleno, in total **08** at length, in detail **10** completely **13** in its entirety

• **to the full**
05 fully **07** utterly **08** entirely **10** completely, thoroughly **11** to the utmost

full-blooded
06 hearty **07** devoted **08** thorough, vigorous **09** committed, dedicated, out-and-out **11** sanguineous **12** enthusiastic, wholehearted

full-blown
04 full **05** major, total **06** all-out **07** intense **08** complete, thorough **09** full-scale, out-and-out **11** full-fledged

full-bodied
03 fat **04** deep, full, rich **06** fruity, strong **07** amoroso, intense

full-frontal
05 total **06** direct, strong **08** absolute, complete, forceful, thorough **09** out-and-out **12** unexpurgated, unrestrained

full-grown
04 ripe **05** adult, of age **06** mature, seeded **07** grown-up **09** developed, full-blown, full-scale **10** fully grown **12** fully fledged **14** fully developed

fullness
04 body, fill, glut **05** depth, force, power, width **06** growth, plenty, wealth **07** breadth, fatness, pleroma, satiety **08** dilation, loudness, plethora, richness, solidity, strength, swelling, totality, vastness **09** abundance, ampleness, greatness, impletion, intensity, largeness, plenitude, plumpness, profusion, repletion, resonance, satedness, satiation, wholeness **10** complement, congestion, tumescence **11** enlargement, repleteness, shapeliness **12** completeness, inflammation, satisfaction, thoroughness **13** extensiveness **14** curvaceousness, voluptuousness

• **in the fullness of time**
06 in time **07** finally **08** in the end **10** eventually, ultimately **11** in due course

full-scale
05 major **06** all-out **07** in-depth **08** complete, sweeping, thorough **09** extensive, intensive **10** exhaustive **11** wide-ranging **13** comprehensive, thoroughgoing **15** all-encompassing

fully
02 up **05** quite **06** fairly, wholly **07** totally, utterly **08** entirely **09** perfectly **10** altogether, completely, positively, thoroughly, to the nines **12** sufficiently, unreservedly **13** in all respects **14** satisfactorily, without reserve

fully fledged
06 mature, senior **07** trained **08** graduate **09** full-blown, qualified **10** proficient **11** experienced **12** professional **14** fully developed

fulminate
04 fume, rage, rail, slam **05** curse, decry, flash, slate **07** condemn, declaim, inveigh, protest, thunder **08** denounce, detonate **09** criticize **10** animadvert, vituperate

fulmination
06 tirade **07** decrial, obloquy, slating **08** brickbat, diatribe **09** criticism, invective, philippic **10** detonation, thundering **11** thunderbolt **12** condemnation, denunciation

fulsome
03 fat, OTT **05** gross, slimy **06** smarmy **07** buttery, cloying, fawning **08** effusive, luscious, nauseous, overdone, unctuous **09** adulatory, excessive, insincere, offensive, sickening **10** immoderate, inordinate, nauseating, obsequious, over the top, saccharine **11** extravagant, sycophantic, well-rounded **12** enthusiastic, ingratiating **13** well-developed

fulsomely
10 effusively, over the top **11** excessively, insincerely, sickeningly **12** immoderately, inordinately, nauseatingly **13** extravagantly

fumble
◇ *anagram indicator*
04 faff, feel **05** botch, grope, spoil **06** bobble, bungle, huddle, mumble **07** blunder **08** flounder, scrabble **09** faff about, feel about, mishandle, mismanage

fume
04 boil, rage, rant, rave, reek, stum **05** go mad, nidor, smoke, steam, storm, vapor **06** blow up, seethe, vapour **07** be livid, explode **08** boil over, smoulder **09** be furious **10** hit the roof **11** blow your top, lose your rag, rant and rave **12** blow your cool, fly into a rage, lose your cool **15** fly off the handle, go off the deep end

fumes
03 fog, gas **04** haze, reek, smog **05** gases, smell, smoke, stink **06** stench, vapour **07** exhaust, vapours **09** pollution **10** exhalation

fumigate
05 smoke **06** purify, smudge **07** cleanse, incense, perfume **08** sanitize **09** deodorize, disinfect, sterilize

fumigation
09 cleansing, purifying
12 disinfecting, purification, sanitization **13** sterilization

fuming
03 mad **05** angry, livid **06** raging
07 boiling, enraged, furious, smoking, uptight **08** incensed, seething, up in arms **09** in a lather, raving mad, seeing red, steamed up, ticked off **10** hopping mad **11** disgruntled

fun
03 gig, joy **04** game, hoax, jest, joke, lark, play, romp **05** bourd, crack, craic, mirth, music, sport, trick, witty
06 joking, laughs, lekker, lively
07 amusing, foolery, gammock, jesting, jollity **08** gladness, hilarity, laughter, pleasure **09** amusement, diversion, diverting, enjoyable, enjoyment, frivolity, horseplay, merriment **10** buffoonery, delightful, jocularity, recreation, relaxation, skylarking, tomfoolery **11** celebration, distraction, merrymaking, pleasurable
12 cheerfulness, entertaining, recreational **13** entertainment

• **for fun**
08 for kicks **09** for a laugh **12** for enjoyment **14** for the hell of it

• **in fun**
06 in jest **07** as a joke, playful, to tease
08 jokingly **09** for a laugh, playfully, teasingly **11** mischievous
13 mischievously, tongue in cheek

• **make fun of**
03 cod, guy, rib **04** goof, jeer, joke, mock **05** get at, jolly, sport, taunt, tease **06** banter, deride, jeer at, send up **07** laugh at, scoff at, sneer at
08 ridicule **09** humiliate, poke fun at
11 have a shot at, poke borak at **13** take the mickey **15** pull someone's leg

function
02 do, go **03** act, cos, cot, job, log, run, sec, sin, tan, use **04** cosh, coth, duty, part, post, role, sech, sine, sinh, tanh, task, work **05** chore, cosec, party, serve **06** affair, behave, charge, cosech, cosine, dinner, office, result, upshot **07** concern, mission, operate, perform, purpose, tangent **08** activity, business, capacity, luncheon
09 corollary, deduction, gathering, induction, inference, reception, situation **10** conclusion, employment, occupation **11** concomitant, consequence, social event **12** have the job of **13** play the part of
14 responsibility

See also **dance**

functional
05 plain **06** useful **07** running, utility, working **08** clinical **09** operative, practical **11** hard-wearing, operational, serviceable, utilitarian

functionally
08 usefully **11** efficiently, practically
13 operationally

functionary
07 officer **08** employee, official
09 dignitary **10** bureaucrat **12** office-bearer, office-holder

fund
03 box, IMF **04** back, bank, cash, dosh, gelt, loot, mine, pool, well
05 brass, bread, cache, dough, endow, float, fonds, grant, gravy, hoard, kitty, lolly, means, money, rhino, stack, stock, store **06** assets, greens, moolah, pay for, source, supply, wealth **07** backing, capital, finance, jackpot, promote, readies, reserve, savings, shekels, sponsor, support, tracker **08** treasury
09 endowment, megabucks, reservoir, resources, slate club, subsidize
10 capitalize, collection, foundation, investment, repository, storehouse, underwrite **11** spondulicks
12 accumulation, the necessary
14 community chest

• **reserve fund**
04 rest

• **transfer funds**
04 vire

fundamental
03 key **04** main, root **05** basal, basic, chief, first, prime, vital **06** bottom, primal **07** bedrock, central, crucial, initial, organic, primary, radical
08 cardinal, integral, original, profound, ultimate **09** elemental, essential, important, necessary, primitive, principal **10** elementary, underlying **11** rudimentary
12 foundational **13** indispensable

fundamentalist
05 fundy, rigid, Talib **06** fundie, strict
08 orthodox, rigorous
14 uncompromising

fundamentally
05 à fond **06** deeply **07** acutely, at heart **08** at bottom, deep down
09 basically, crucially, in essence, primarily, radically **10** cardinally, critically, inherently, profoundly
11 essentially **13** intrinsically, substantially

fundamentals
04 laws **05** facts, rules **06** basics
09 rudiments **10** brass tacks, essentials
11 necessaries, nitty-gritty **12** nuts and bolts **14** practicalities **15** first principles

fundraising *see* **charity**

funeral
04 obit, wake **05** tangi **06** burial
08 exequies **09** cremation, interment, obsequies **10** entombment, inhumation

funereal
03 sad **04** dark **05** feral, grave
06 dismal, dreary, gloomy, solemn, sombre, woeful **07** serious
08 exequial, funebral, mournful
09 deathlike, funebrial, lamenting
10 depressing, lugubrious, sepulchral

fungus
11 thallophyte

Fungi include:

04 rust, scab, smut
05 ergot, yeast
06 blight
07 candida
08 botritis, brown rot, mushroom
09 black spot, grey mould, toadstool
10 saprophyte, slime mould, sooty mould
11 downy mildew, penicillium, slime fungus
12 brewer's yeast, potato blight
13 powdery mildew

See also **mushroom**

funk
04 fear, flap, fuss, stew **05** alarm, dodge, panic, spark, state, tizzy
06 balk at, blench, cop out, dither, flinch, frenzy, fright, terror, tiswas, tizwas **07** fluster **08** blue funk
09 agitation, cold sweat, commotion, duck out of, shirk from, touchwood
10 flinch from, recoil from **12** chicken out of

funnel
02 go **04** flue, horn, move, pass, pipe, pour, tube, vent **05** guide, shaft, stack
06 choana, convey, direct, drogue, filter, siphon **07** channel, chimney, tundish **08** sink hole, transfer, windsail
10 smokestack **11** swallow hole
12 infundibulum

funnily
◇ *anagram indicator*
09 amazingly **10** incredibly, remarkably **12** surprisingly
13 astonishingly

funny
◇ *anagram indicator*
03 odd, rum **04** rich **05** a hoot, comic, corny, droll, queer, shady, silly, wacky, weird, witty **06** absurd, way-out
07 amusing, a scream, bizarre, comical, curious, dubious, killing, oddball, off-beat, riotous, risible, strange, unusual **08** farcical, humorous, peculiar, puzzling
09 diverting, facetious, hilarious, laughable **10** hysterical, mysterious, perplexing, remarkable, ridiculous, suspicious, uproarious **12** entertaining, knee-slapping **13** side-splitting

• **something funny**
04 hoot, yell

fur
03 boa **04** coat, down, fell, flue, hair, hide, mane, muff, pane, pean, pelt, skin, wool **06** fleece, pelage
07 necklet

Furs include:

03 fox
04 flix, gris, mink, vair
05 budge, civet, fitch, genet, grise, otter, sable, skunk
06 beaver, ermine, marten, nutria, ocelot, rabbit, racoon, zorino

07 blue fox, caracal, caracul, crimmer, fitchet, fitchew, genette, karakul, krimmer, minever, miniver, muskrat, opossum, raccoon
08 cony-wool, kolinsky, moleskin, musquash, ponyskin, sealskin, sea otter, zibeline
09 broadtail, silver fox, wolverene, wolverine, zibelline
10 chinchilla
11 beech marten, Persian lamb, stone marten

furbish
04 do up **05** refit, renew **06** polish, purify, reform, repair, revamp
07 improve, remodel, restore
08 overhaul, renovate **09** modernize, refurbish **10** redecorate
11 recondition **12** rehabilitate
15 give a facelift to

furious
◇ *anagram indicator*
03 mad, wud **04** wild, wood, yond
05 angry, irate, livid **06** fierce, fuming, raging, savage, stormy **07** acharné, boiling, enraged, flaming, frantic, in a huff, in a stew, intense, salvage, violent
08 brainish, frenzied, in a paddy, incensed, inflamed, maenadic, seething, sizzling, up in arms, vehement, vigorous **09** desperate, in a lather, indignant **10** boisterous, hopping mad, infuriated, outrageous
11 tempestuous **12** incandescent
14 purple with rage

furiously
05 madly **06** wildly **07** angrily, crossly, in anger, irately, like mad **08** fiercely, in a paddy, stormily, up in arms
09 intensely, seeing red, violently
10 like blazes, vehemently, vigorously
11 indignantly **12** passionately
13 infuriatingly, tempestuously **15** avec acharnement

furnace *see* **oven**

furnish
03 fit, rig **04** gird, give, suit **05** besee, endue, equip, grant, offer, plant, stock, stuff, yield **06** afford, bestow, fit out, kit out, purvey, supply **07** appoint, bedight, garnish, present, provide
08 decorate, minister

furniture
06 things **07** effects **08** fitments, fittings, movables **09** equipment, moveables **10** appliances
11 accessories, furnishings, possessions **12** appointments
14 household goods

Furniture items include:

03 bed, cot
04 bunk, desk, sofa
05 chair, chest, couch, divan, stool, suite, table, trunk, wagon
06 buffet, bureau, carver, coffer, cradle, daybed, fender, lowboy, mirror, pouffe, settee, waggon
07 armoire, beanbag, bunkbed, cabinet, camp-bed, commode, dresser, ottoman, sofa bed, tallboy, whatnot
08 armchair, bar chair, bedstead, bookcase, cupboard, end table, hatstand, recliner, toy chest, tub chair, wall unit, wardrobe, water bed
09 bed-settee, card table, coatstand, easy chair, fireplace, footstool, hallstand, high-chair, lamp table, sideboard, side table, step-stool, washstand, wine table
10 blanket box, chiffonier, dumb-waiter, encoignure, escritoire, firescreen, four-poster, secretaire, truckle bed, vanity unit
11 coffee table, dining chair, dining table, mantelpiece, room-divider, swivel chair
12 bedside table, chaise-longue, chesterfield, china cabinet, computer desk, folding table, gateleg table, kitchen chair, kitchen table, magazine rack, nest of tables, rocking chair, Welsh dresser
13 dressing table, four-poster bed, umbrella stand
14 chest of drawers, display cabinet, extending table, refectory table
15 bathroom cabinet, butcher's trolley, occasional chair, occasional table

See also **office**

Furniture styles include:

04 Adam, buhl
06 boulle, Empire, Gothic, rococo, Shaker
07 Art Deco, Baroque, Regency, Windsor
08 Colonial, Georgian, Sheraton
09 Charles II, Edwardian, Queen Anne, Shibayama, Victorian, William IV
10 Art Nouveau, Mackintosh, provincial
11 Anglo-Indian, Biedermeier, Chippendale, Cromwellian, Hepplewhite, Louis-Quinze, Restoration
12 Gainsborough, Transitional, Vernis Martin
13 Anglo-Colonial, Arts and Crafts, Dutch Colonial, Louis Philippe, Louis-Quatorze
14 William and Mary

furore
04 flap, fury, fuss, rage, stir, to-do
05 craze, stink, storm **06** frenzy, outcry, tumult, uproar **08** outburst
09 commotion **10** excitement, hullabaloo **11** disturbance

furrow
03 fur, rut **04** furr, knit, line, list, mill, plow, rill, seam **05** flute, gouge, stria, track **06** crease, feerin, groove, gutter, hollow, plough, sulcus, trench, trough
07 chamfer, channel, crinkle, feering, wrinkle **08** engroove, ingroove
09 corrugate, crow's foot, vallecula
11 canaliculus, lister ridge **12** draw together
• **draw first furrow**
04 feer

furry
04 soft **05** downy, fuzzy, hairy
06 fleecy, fluffy, woolly

further
03 aid, als, new, too **04** agen, also, ease, help, more, push **05** again, extra, fresh, other, speed **06** assist, as well, foster, hasten **07** advance, besides, develop, farther, forward, promote, remoter, speed up **08** champion, expedite, moreover **09** encourage, what's more **10** accelerate, additional, facilitate, in addition
11 furthermore, more distant, more extreme **12** additionally
13 supplementary

furtherance
04 help **07** backing, pursuit
08 advocacy, boosting, speeding
09 advancing, promoting, promotion **10** preferment
11 advancement, carrying-out, championing **12** facilitation
13 encouragement

furthermore
03 too **04** also **06** as well **07** besides, further **08** moreover **09** what's more
10 in addition **12** additionally **14** into the bargain

furthermost
06 utmost **07** extreme, outmost
08 farthest, furthest, remotest, ultimate **09** outermost, uttermost

furthest
06 utmost **07** extreme, outmost
08 farthest, remotest, ultimate
09 outermost, uttermost
11 furthermost

furtive
03 sly **06** covert, hidden, secret, shifty, sneaky, veiled **07** cloaked **08** stealthy, thievish, weaselly **09** secretive, underhand **11** clandestine
13 surreptitious

furtively
05 slyly **08** covertly, secretly
11 secretively **15** surreptitiously

fury
03 ire **04** rage **05** anger, dread, force, furor, power, wrath **06** Erinys, frenzy
07 madness, passion **08** ferocity, severity, violence, wildness
09 Eumenides, intensity, vehemence
10 fierceness, turbulence
11 desperation

The Furies:

06 Alecto, Megara
07 Megaera
09 Tisiphone

furze
04 whin **05** gorse

fuse
03 ren, rin, run **04** flux, join, meld, melt, weld **05** blend, fusee, fuzee, merge, smelt, unite **06** mingle, solder
07 combine **08** ankylose, coalesce, conflate, intermix **09** anchylose,

commingle, integrate, interfuse
10 amalgamate, colliquate, synthesize
11 agglutinate, intermingle, put together

fusillade
04 fire, hail **05** burst, salvo **06** volley
07 barrage **08** outburst **09** broadside, discharge

fusion
05 blend, union **06** merger
07 melting, running, welding
08 blending, smelting **09** ankylosis, synthesis **10** anchylosis, conflation, federation **11** coalescence, integration **12** amalgamation, colliquation

fuss
02 do **03** ado, row **04** coil, faff, flap, fret, rout, song, stir, to-do, work
05 hoo-ha, hurry, panic, tizzy, upset, worry **06** bother, bustle, chichi, create, fidget, fikery, flurry, furore, hassle, hoo-hah, pother, pudder, racket **07** agitate, carry-on, fluster, grumble, palaver, parafle, stashie, stishie, stushie, tamasha, trouble **08** ballyhoo, brouhaha, complain, paraffle, squabble, stooshie **09** agitation, be all over, commotion, confusion, kerfuffle, pantomime, take pains **10** be in a tizzy, excitement, make a thing **11** piece of work **13** a song and dance **14** storm in a teacup

fussiness
08 busyness, niceness, niggling
09 finicking **10** choosiness, finicality
11 finicalness **13** particularity, perfectionism **14** meticulousness, pernicketiness

fusspot
06 fantod, fidget **07** old maid, worrier
08 old woman, stickler **09** nit-picker
10 fussbudget **11** hyper-critic
13 perfectionist

fussy
◇ *anagram indicator*
04 busy **05** faddy, fancy, picky, tatty
06 chichi, choosy, ornate, prissy, rococo, spoffy **07** baroque, finical, finicky **08** niggling, pedantic, spoffish
09 cluttered, demanding, difficult, elaborate, quibbling, selective
10 fastidious, nit-picking, old-maidish, particular, pernickety, scrupulous
11 old-womanish, persnickety
12 fiddle-faddle, hard to please, pettifogging **13** grandmotherly, overdecorated **14** discriminating

fusty
04 damp, dank, rank **05** fuggy, musty, passé, stale **06** fousty, frowsy, frowzy, mouldy, stuffy **07** airless, archaic, frowsty **08** outdated **09** out-of-date
10 antiquated, malodorous, mouldering **11** ill-smelling, old-fogeyish **12** old-fashioned, unventilated

futile
04 idle, no go, vain **05** empty, inept
06 barren, hollow, in vain, no good, otiose, wasted **07** forlorn, useless
08 abortive, feckless, nugatory, tattling, trifling **09** fruitless, pointless, to no avail, worthless **10** profitless, sleeveless, unavailing **11** ineffective, ineffectual, meaningless
12 unproductive, unprofitable, unsuccessful

futility
05 waste **06** vanity **07** mockery
08 vainesse **09** emptiness
10 barrenness, hollowness
11 aimlessness, uselessness
12 nugatoriness **13** fruitlessness, pointlessness, worthlessness
15 ineffectiveness, meaninglessness

future
03 fut **04** next, to be **05** fated, later
06 avenir, coming, to come, unborn
07 by-and-by, outlook, planned
08 destined, eventual, expected, imminent, tomorrow **09** designate, hereafter, impending, prospects
10 subsequent, time to come
11 approaching, coming times, forthcoming, in the offing, prospective
12 expectations

• in future
04 once **05** hence **09** after this, from now on, hereafter **10** henceforth
11 hereinafter **12** henceforward
13 from this day on **14** from this time on

fuzz
03 fug, nap **04** blur, down, hair, lint, pile **05** fibre, flock, floss, fluff
06 police

fuzzy
◇ *anagram indicator*
04 hazy **05** downy, faint, foggy, furry, linty, muzzy, vague **06** fleecy, fluffy, frizzy, napped, woolly **07** blurred, fuddled, muffled, shadowy, unclear, velvety **08** confused **09** distorted, unfocused **10** ill-defined, indefinite, indistinct

G

G
03 gee **04** golf

gab
03 jaw, yak **04** blab, brag, buzz, chat, jest, talk **05** boast, prate, vaunt
06 babble, drivel, gossip, jabber, tattle
07 blabber, blarney, blather, blether, chatter, mockery, prattle **08** chitchat
09 loquacity, prattling, small talk
10 blethering, yackety-yak
12 conversation, tittle-tattle
13 tongue-wagging

gabble
04 blab **05** spout **06** babble, cackle, drivel, gaggle, gibber, jabber, patter, rabble, rattle, waffle **07** blabber, blether, chatter, prattle, sputter, twaddle **08** cackling, nonsense, splutter **09** gibberish **10** blethering
12 gibble-gabble, ribble-rabble

Gabon
01 G **03** GAB

gad
- **gad about**

04 fisk, roam, rove **05** jaunt, range, stray **06** ramble, travel, wander
07 traipse **08** dot about **09** flit about, gallivant, run around

gadabout
05 rover **07** rambler **08** runabout, wanderer **10** stravaiger **11** gallivanter
14 pleasure-seeker

gadget
03 toy **04** tool **05** gismo, gizmo, thing, waldo **06** device, doodad, doodah, hickey, jimjam, widget **07** gimmick, gubbins, novelty, whatnot, whatsit
08 thingamy **09** apparatus, appliance, doohickey, implement, invention, jigamaree, jiggumbob, mechanism, thingummy
10 instrument **11** contraption, contrivance, thingamybob
12 executive toy, thingummyjig
14 what-d'you-call-it

gadolinium
02 Gd

Gaelic
04 Erse

gaffe
◇ *anagram indicator*
04 boob, flub, goof, slip **05** brick, error
06 boo-boo, howler, slip-up
07 bloomer, blunder, clanger, faux pas, mistake **08** solecism **09** gaucherie
12 indiscretion

gaffer
03 gov, guv **04** boss **06** bigwig, ganger, honcho **07** foreman, manager, overman **08** overseer **09** big cheese
10 supervisor **14** superintendent

gag
03 pun **04** clog, curb, hoax, jest, joke, plug, pong, quip **05** block, check, choke, crack, funny, heave, quiet, retch, still **06** muffle, muzzle, stifle, wheeze
07 deceive, silence, smother **08** one-liner, restrain, suppress, throttle **09** put a gag on, wisecrack, witticism **11** nearly vomit

gaga
03 mad **04** nuts **05** barmy, batty, crazy, dotty, loony, loopy, potty
06 cuckoo, insane, raving **07** fatuous
08 demented, deranged, doolally, unhinged **09** disturbed
10 distracted, unbalanced **11** not all there, off the rails **12** mad as a hatter **13** off your rocker **14** wrong in the head

Gaia
05 Terra

gaiety
03 fun, joy **04** glee, show **05** mirth
06 colour, frolic, racket **07** daffing, delight, frolics, gayness, glitter, jollity, joyance, revelry, sparkle **08** buoyancy, gladness, hilarity, pleasure, vivacity
09 festivity, happiness, joviality, merriment, showiness **10** blitheness, brightness, brilliance, exuberance, good humour, liveliness **11** celebration, galliardise, high spirits, joie de vivre, merrymaking **12** cheerfulness
13 colourfulness

gaily
07 happily, merrily **08** blithely, brightly, joyfully **10** cheerfully **11** brilliantly, colourfully **12** flamboyantly **14** light-heartedly

gain
03 add, ern, get, nab, net, win **04** earn, make, near, nett, reap, rise **05** bunce, carry, clear, get to, gross, put on, reach, yield **06** attain, collar, come to, gather, growth, income, obtain, pick up, profit, rake in, return, reward, secure
07 achieve, acquire, advance, benefit, bring in, capture, collect, harvest, headway, improve, procure, produce, realize, revenue, takings **08** addition, arrive at, dividend, earnings, increase, interest, pickings, proceeds, progress, straight, winnings **09** accretion, advantage, emolument, increment
10 attainment, chevisance, convenient
11 achievement, acquisition, advancement, improvement
12 augmentation
- **gain on**

07 catch up **08** approach, overtake
09 catch up on, close in on, close with, level with **11** catch up with, get closer to, get nearer to, outdistance
12 narrow the gap
- **gain time**

05 delay, stall **09** temporize **10** dilly-dally **11** play for time **12** drag your feet
13 procrastinate
- **seek to gain**

03 woo **09** cultivate

gainful
04 paid **06** paying, useful **08** fruitful
09 fructuous, lucrative, rewarding
10 beneficial, productive, profitable, worthwhile **11** moneymaking
12 advantageous, remunerative

gainfully
08 usefully **10** profitably **11** lucratively
12 beneficially, productively
14 advantageously

gainsay
04 deny **06** oppose **07** dispute
09 challenge, disaffirm **10** contradict, contravene, controvert **12** disagree with

gait
03 get **04** brat, gyte, pace, step, walk
05 child, going, tread **06** allure, manner, stride **07** bearing **08** carriage
10 deportment

gaiter
04 spat **06** hogger **07** cutikin, spattee
08 cootikin, cuitikin **11** spatterdash

gala
04 fair, fete **05** party **07** jubilee, pageant **08** carnival, festival, jamboree
09 festivity **10** procession
11 celebration

galaxy
04 host, mass **05** array, stars **06** blazar, nebula **07** cluster **09** gathering, multitude **10** collection, star system
11 solar system **13** constellation, group assembly

Galaxies include:

03 Leo
04 Arp's, Lost, Mice
05 Bode's, Helix, Malin
06 Baade's, Carafe, Hydra A, Maffei, Spider, Virgo A, Zwicky

07 Cannon's, Cygnus A, Pancake, Sextans, Spindle, The Eyes
08 Antennae, Barnard's, Bear's Paw, Black Eye, Milky Way, Papillon, Perseus A, Pinwheel, Seashell, Sombrero
09 Andromeda, Bear's Claw, Cartwheel, Centaurus, Hercules A, Sunflower, Whirlpool
10 Draco Dwarf, Silver Coin, The Garland, Triangulum
11 Carina Dwarf, Hardcastle's, Pisces Cloud, Pisces Dwarf, The Ringtail
12 Atom For Peace, Integral Sign, Pegasus Dwarf, Siamese Twins, Virgo Cluster
13 Aquarius Dwarf, Sculptor Dwarf, Serpens Sextet, Virgo Pinwheel
14 Capricorn Dwarf, Copeland Septet, Reticulum Dwarf, Ursa Minor Dwarf
15 Exclamation Mark, Horologium Dwarf, Magellanic Cloud, Miniature Spiral

gale
03 fit **04** wind **05** blast, burst, storm **06** Myrica, squall, wester **07** cyclone, norther, sea turn, snorter, souther, tornado, typhoon **08** eruption, outbreak, outburst **09** bog myrtle, explosion, hurricane, sou'wester **10** ripsnorter **11** equinoctial, sweet willow

gall
03 irk, nag, vex **04** bile, dyke, fell, flaw, neck, rile **05** annoy, brass, cheek, fault, get to, nerve, peeve, scoff, spite, venom **06** animus, bother, enmity, harass, malice, nettle, oak-nut, pester, plague, rankle, ruffle **07** ill-will, provoke, rancour **08** acrimony, bedeguar, chutzpah, irritate, oak apple, sourness, tacahout **09** aggravate, animosity, antipathy, assurance, brass neck, hostility, impudence, insolence, sage apple, sauciness, virulence **10** bitterness, brazenness, effrontery, exasperate **11** malevolence, presumption **12** impertinence, mycodomatium **13** get on your wick, get up your nose, get your back up, put your back up

gallant
03 fop, gay **04** beau, bold **05** brave, dandy, lover, manly, noble **06** daring, heroic, plucky, polite **07** amorous, courtly, dashing, valiant **08** cavalier, cicisbeo, fearless, gracious, intrepid, splendid **09** attentive, audacious, chamberer, chevalier, chivalric, courteous, dauntless **10** chivalrous, courageous, honourable, thoughtful **11** considerate, gentlemanly, magnificent

gallantly
05 nobly **07** bravely **08** politely **09** valiantly **10** fearlessly, graciously, heroically, honourably, intrepidly **11** audaciously, courteously, dauntlessly **12** chivalrously, courageously, thoughtfully **13** considerately

gallantry
04 game **05** pluck **06** daring, honour, spirit, valour **07** bravery, courage, heroism **08** audacity, boldness, chivalry, courtesy, nobility, valiance **09** manliness **10** politeness **11** courtliness, intrepidity **12** fearlessness, graciousness **13** attentiveness, consideration, courteousness, dauntlessness **14** courageousness, thoughtfulness **15** gentlemanliness

gallery
04 brow, gods, loft, mine, pawn, walk **05** alure, level **06** arcade, circle, dedans, museum **07** balcony, passage, terrace, veranda **08** bartisan, bartizan, brattice, brattish, brettice, casemate, rood loft, traverse, verandah **09** choir loft, triforium **10** art gallery, earth-house, hall of fame, pinakothek, scaffolage, spectators **11** display room, dress circle, pinacotheca, scaffoldage **14** exhibition area

See also **museum**

galley *see* **ship**

galling
06 bitter, vexing **07** irksome **08** annoying, nettling, plaguing, rankling **09** harassing, provoking, vexatious **10** bothersome, irritating **11** aggravating, embittering, humiliating, infuriating **12** exasperating

gallium
02 Ga

gallivant
04 roam, rove **05** range, stray **06** ramble, travel, wander **07** traipse **08** dot about, gad about, stravaig **09** flit about, run around

gallon
01 g **03** gal **04** cong, gall **07** congius

gallop
03 fly, run **04** bolt, dart, dash, race, rush, tear, zoom **05** burst, hurry, shoot, speed **06** canter, career, hasten, scurry, sprint, wallop **07** cariere

gallows
03 nub **04** tree, wild **05** bough, cheat, perky, saucy **06** daring, gallus, gibbet, plucky, woodie **07** stifler, the rope **08** damnably, dule-tree, impudent, scaffold, spirited, tiresome **09** sprightly **10** Tyburn-tree, villainous **11** mischievous **12** confoundedly, nubbing-cheat, unmanageable

galore
06 lots of, plenty, tons of **07** aplenty, heaps of, to spare **08** stacks of **09** in numbers **10** everywhere, millions of **11** in abundance, in profusion

galvanize
04 fire, jolt, move, prod, spur, stir, urge, zinc **05** rouse, shock **06** arouse, awaken, excite **07** animate, enliven, inspire, provoke, quicken, startle **08** energize, vitalize **09** electrify, stimulate **10** invigorate

Gambia
03 GMB, WAG

gambit
04 move, play, ploy, ruse, wile **05** trick **06** device, tactic **07** tactics **08** artifice **09** manoeuvre, stratagem **11** machination

gamble
03 bet **04** back, dice, gaff, game, jeff, play, punt, risk, spec **05** stake, wager **06** chance, hazard, plunge, toss-up **07** flutter, lottery, pot luck, venture **08** chance it **09** speculate, take a risk **10** put money on **11** speculation, take a chance, try your luck **12** have a flutter, play for money **13** leap in the dark, play the horses

gambler
06 better, punter **07** plunger, tinhorn, tipster **08** gamester **09** bookmaker, daredevil, desperado, risk-taker, thrower **14** turf accountant

gambling
04 play **07** betting **10** risk-taking **11** speculation **15** playing for money

Gambling-related terms include:

03 hit, lay, pot
04 back, bust, dice, hold, odds, punt, shoe, tout
05 bingo, cards, craps, jeton, lotto, motza, poker, pools, stake, stick, wager, welsh
06 bookie, casino, chip in, fan-tan, fulham, gaming, jetton, lay off, motser, punter
07 flutter, lottery, tipster
08 levanter, long shot, outsider, roulette, teetotum
09 blackjack, bookmaker, card shark, dog racing, favourite, place a bet, vingt-et-un
10 put-and-take, put money on, sweepstake
11 card-sharper, find the lady, go one better, horse racing, numbers game, rouge-et-noir, slot machine
12 break the bank, card counting, debt of honour, pitch-and-toss, scoop the pool
13 hedge your bets, shoot the works, spread betting
14 shove-halfpenny, three-card trick, wheel of fortune
15 cash in your chips, disorderly house, greyhound racing, make a clean sweep

See also **bet**

• **gambling place**
04 hell **06** arcade, casino

gambol
◇ *anagram indicator*
03 hop **04** jump, leap, romp, skip **05** bound, caper, dance, frisk **06** bounce, cavort, frolic, prance,

spring **07** disport **09** cut a caper, cut capers **15** kick up your heels

game

03 bag, fun, jeu, pit, tie **04** ball, bold, bout, jest, joke, lame, meat, meet, play, prey, romp **05** brave, eager, event, flesh, match, prank, ready, round, sport, trick, up for **06** daring, frolic, gamble, plucky, quarry, spoils **07** contest, gallant, meeting, pastime, valiant, willing **08** activity, business, desirous, fearless, inclined, intrepid, prepared, resolute, spirited, wild fowl **09** amusement, diversion, gallantry, merriment, operation **10** courageous, interested, recreation, tournament **11** competition, distraction, lion-hearted, unflinching **12** enthusiastic **13** entertainment, practical joke

Game animals and birds include:

03 elk, fox
04 bear, boar, coot, deer, duck, guan, hare, lion, stag, teal, wolf
05 bison, goose, hyena, moose, quail, scaup, snipe, tiger, zebra
06 curlew, grouse, plover, rabbit, wigeon
07 buffalo, caribou, giraffe, mallard, moorhen, muntjac, pintail, pochard, red deer, roe deer, widgeon
08 antelope, elephant, kangaroo, pheasant, sika deer, squirrel, wild boar, woodcock
09 blackcock, blackgame, crocodile, partridge, ptarmigan, waterfowl
10 fallow deer, guinea fowl, tufted duck, wild turkey, wood grouse, woodpigeon
11 Canada goose
12 capercaillie, capercailzie, hippopotamus, mountain lion

See also **poultry**

Games include:

03 loo, nap
04 brag, crib, dice, faro, I-spy, ludo, pool, snap
05 bowls, chess, clubs, craps, darts, halma, jacks, Jenga®, poker, rummy, whist
06 bridge, Cluedo®, quinze
07 bezique, bowling, canasta, hangman, mah-jong, marbles, old maid, picquet, pinball, pontoon, snooker
08 baccarat, card game, charades, checkers, cribbage, dominoes, draughts, forfeits, gin rummy, Kim's game, Monopoly®, napoleon, patience, ping pong, reversis, roulette, sardines, Scrabble®
09 bagatelle, billiards, blackjack, board game, draw poker, hopscotch, newmarket, Pelmanism, Simon says, solitaire, solo whist, stud poker, tic-tac-toe, twenty-one, vingt-et-un
10 backgammon, Balderdash®, fivestones, jackstraws, Pictionary®, spillikins
11 battleships, beetle drive, chemin de fer, hide-and-seek, table tennis, tiddlywinks
12 consequences, partner whist, shove ha'penny
13 blind man's buff, clock patience, happy families, musical chairs, pass the parcel, postman's knock, spin the bottle, table football, ten-pin bowling
14 contract bridge, follow-my-leader, hunt-the-thimble, nine men's morris, Trivial Pursuit®
15 Chinese checkers, Chinese whispers, duplicate bridge

Board games include:

02 go
04 ludo, Risk®, siga
05 chess, darts, goose, halma, lurch, marls, nyout, senet, shogi, Sorry®
06 Boggle®, Cluedo®, gobang, gomuku, merels, merils, morals, morris, tables, tabula, uckers
07 Cranium®, mah-jong, mancala, marrels, merells, pachisi, petteia, reverse, reversi, Yahtzee
08 checkers, chequers, cribbage, Dingbats®, draughts, miracles, Monopoly®, parchesi, Rummikub®, Scrabble®
09 bagatelle, Buccaneer®, Operation®, Parcheesi®, solitaire, tic-tac-toe
10 backgammon, Go for Broke®, latrunculi, Mastermind®, Pictionary®
11 Battleships®, fox and geese, Frustration®
12 pente grammai
13 Concentration®, table skittles, The Game of Life®
14 nine men's morris, Trivial Pursuit®
15 Chinese checkers, Chinese chequers, duodecim scripta, fivepenny morris, ninepenny morris, three men's morris

See also **sport**

Card games include:

03 don, nap, pig, war
04 brag, bust, faro, fish, golf, king, loba, may I?, phat, pits, push, rook, scat, skat, snap, solo, spit, tunk, tute, ugly
05 blitz, cheat, cinch, crash, flush, knack, nerts, pairs, pedro, pitch, poker, ronda, rummy, samba, shoot, speed, tarok, tarot, whist
06 big two, boodle, bridge, casino, church, crates, cuckoo, dakota, deuces, écarté, euchre, fan tan, five up, go fish, hearts, henway, kaiser, knaves, oh hell!, palace, pepper, piquet, pounce, red dog, sevens, spades, spoons, squeal, stitch, switch, tarock, taroky, trumps, turtle, valets
07 auction, authors, bezique, bone ace, canasta, clabber, last one, mah jong, old maid, pontoon, quartet, setback, spitzer, whipsaw
08 ace-deuce, all fives, all fours, anaconda, baccarat, bid whist, blackout, carousel, cribbage, drunkard, elevator, gin rummy, high five, Michigan, napoleon, patience, pinochle, Pope Joan, sequence, shanghai, Welsh don
09 abyssinia, bid euchre, blackjack, catch five, golden ten, king pedro, king rummy, let it ride, newmarket, Pelmanism, poker bull, president, quadrille, racehorse, solitaire, solo whist, stud poker, tic-tac-toe, tile rummy, vingt-et-un
10 black maria, buck euchre, capitalism, chinese ten, cincinnati, crazy nines, dirty clubs, German solo, parliament, preference, ride the bus, sheepshead, strip poker, three in one, Wall Street
11 cat and mouse, chase the ace, chemin de fer, chicken foot, crazy eights, English stud, find the lady, French tarot, French whist, German whist, high-low-jack, Indian poker, Mexican stud, nine-card don, Oklahoma gin, racing demon, Russian bank, six-card brag, speculation, Texas hold 'em
12 Chinese poker, devil's bridge, draw dominoes, five-card brag, five-card draw, four-card brag, high-card pool, kings corners, Mexican sweat, Mexican train, nine-card brag, one and thirty, pick a partner, ruff and trump, Russian poker, shoot pontoon
13 concentration, contract rummy, contract whist, happy families, knockout whist, lame-brain Pete, Michigan rummy, Romanian whist, sergeant major, seven-card brag, Shanghai rummy, three-card brag
14 Caribbean poker, contract bridge, five hundred rum, fives and threes, follow the queen, good, better, best, jack the shifter, Liverpool rummy, Minnesota whist, rich man, poor man, ruff and honours, second hand high, spite and malice, spit in the ocean, three-card monte, trust–don't trust
15 back alley bridge, cut-throat euchre, double solitaire, nomination whist, railroad canasta, stealing bundles

• **end to game**
04 draw, mate **09** checkmate, stalemate

• **point out game**
03 set

• **preliminary to game**
04 toss

• **right to begin game**
04 pose

gamekeeper

06 keeper, warden **07** venerer

gamely

06 boldly **07** bravely **09** valiantly **10** fearlessly, intrepidly, resolutely **12** courageously **13** unflinchingly

gamut
04 area **05** field, gamme, range, scale, scope, sweep **06** series
07 compass, variety **08** sequence, spectrum

gang
02 go **03** lot, mob, set **04** band, club, core, crew, crue, ging, herd, nest, pack, push, ring, team **05** coven, crowd, group, horde, party, posse, shift, squad
06 circle, clique, coffle, outfit, troupe
07 company, coterie, massive, ratpack
09 gathering **11** tribulation
• **gang up on, gang up against**
12 unite against **13** team up against
15 conspire against

gangling
04 bony, tall **05** gawky, lanky, rangy
06 gangly, gauche, skinny **07** angular, awkward, spindly **08** raw-boned, ungainly **12** loose-jointed

gangrene
07 mortify **08** necrosis **09** phagedena
10 phagedaena, thanatosis

gangster
02 Al **04** hood, thug **05** crook, heavy, rough, tough **06** bandit, Capone, robber, yakuza, Yardie **07** brigand, gangsta, goombah, greaser, hoodlum, mobster, ruffian, steamer, tumbler, wise guy **08** criminal, enforcer
09 desperado, goodfella, racketeer, terrorist

gangway
04 brow **05** aisle **07** passage, walkway
08 corridor **10** passageway

gannet
04 guga **05** booby, solan **10** solan goose

gaol, gaoler *see* **jail, gaol**; **jailer, gaoler**

gap
04 gulf, hole, lack, leap, lull, rent, rift, rima, slap, void **05** blank, break, chasm, chink, cleft, crack, gorge, musit, notch, pause, shard, sherd, space **06** breach, bunker, cavity, cranny, divide, hiatus, lacuna, recess, spread, street, window **07** crevice, opening, orifice, passage, saw gate, saw kerf, vacancy, vacuity **08** aperture, distance, fontanel, fracture, interval, sliprail **09** disparity, interlude
10 difference, divergence, fontanelle, interstice, separation **12** intermission, interruption **13** discontinuity, node of Ranvier **14** expansion joint

gape
04 bawl, gaup, gawk, gawp, gaze, open, part, yawn **05** crack, gerne, split, stare **06** goggle, rictus, wonder
07 dehisce **10** rubberneck

gaper
03 Mya **06** comber

gaping
04 open, vast, wide **05** broad, hiant
06 rictus **07** ringent, yawning
09 cavernous, fatiscent, interrupt
11 open-mouthed **12** fissirostral

garage
04 barn **06** lock-up **07** car port **10** gas station **11** muffler shop **13** petrol station **14** service station

garb
03 rig **04** form, gear, look, robe, togs, vest, wear **05** array, cover, dress, get-up, guise, robes, style **06** aspect, attire, clothe, livery, outfit, rig out, rig-out
07 apparel, clobber, clothes, costume, fashion, garment, raiment, regalia, uniform, vesture **08** clothing
09 semblance, vestiment, vestments
10 appearance, habiliment, habilitate

garbage
03 rot **04** blah, bosh, bull, bunk, cock, crap, guff, junk, muck **05** balls, bilge, dross, filth, hooey, slops, swill, trash, tripe, waste **06** bunkum, debris, drivel, hot air, litter, piffle, refuse, scraps
07 baloney, eyewash, hogwash, remains, rhubarb, rubbish, twaddle
08 claptrap, cobblers, detritus, malarkey, nonsense, tommyrot **09** gibberish, leftovers, moonshine, poppycock, scourings, sweepings **10** codswallop
11 odds and ends **13** bits and pieces

garble
◇ *anagram indicator*
04 edit, sift, warp **05** mix up, slant, twist **06** doctor, jumble, mangle, muddle **07** cleanse, confuse, corrupt, distort, falsify, pervert **08** mutilate, scramble **10** tamper with
12 misinterpret, misrepresent

garbled
◇ *anagram indicator*
07 jumbled, mixed-up, muddled
08 confused **09** scrambled
14 undecipherable, unintelligible

garden
03 erf **04** bagh, park, plot, yard
05 garth **06** herbar **08** backyard, paradise **09** curtilage

Gardens include:

03 Kew
04 Eden, Ness
05 Stowe
06 Het Loo, Monet's, Suzhou, Tivoli, Wisley
07 Alnwick, Bodnant, Boxwood, Giverny, Heligan, Kane'ohe, Motsuji, Urakuen
08 Alhambra, Biltmore, Blenheim, Claymont, Ermitage, Hopewood, Hyde Hall, Longwood, Mt Vernon, Nanzenji, Pleasure, Rikugien, Rosedown, Rosemoor, Sankeien
09 Bagatelle, Claremont, Lingering, Lion Grove, Stourhead, Tuileries
10 Capel Manor, Chatsworth, Harlow Carr, Kensington, Levens Hall, Schönbrunn, Versailles
11 Chanticleer, Eden Project, Ji Chang Yuan
12 Castle Howard, Hampton Court, Hidcote Manor, Jingshan Park, Katsura Rikyu, Royal Botanic, Sissinghurst, Studley Royal
13 Dumbarton Oaks, Harewood House, Orange Botanic, Vaux le Vicomte
14 Biddulph Grange, Drummond Castle, Hua Ching Palace, Stone Lion Grove
15 Arnold Arboretum

Garden types include:

03 tea
04 beer, herb, knot, lawn, rock, roof, rose
05 arbor, fruit, water
06 alpine, arbour, border, flower, herbar, indoor, market, physic, rosary, rosery, sunken, walled, winter
07 cottage, hanging, Italian, kitchen, olitory, orchard, rockery, rose bed
08 chinampa, Japanese, kailyard, rosarium
09 allotment, arboretum, botanical, cole-garth, flower bed, kailyaird, raised bed, shrubbery, terrarium, truck-farm, window box
10 ornamental, rose arbour
13 plantie-cruive, vegetable plot

gardener
03 Eve **04** Adam, mali **06** mallee
07 trucker

Gardeners include:

03 **Don** (Monty)
04 **Kent** (William), **Page** (Russell)
05 **Brown** (Lancelot 'Capability'), **Gavin** (Diarmuid), **Lloyd** (Christopher), **Monet** (Claude), **Wilde** (Kim)
06 **Gilpin** (William Sawrey), **Ingram** (Collingwood 'Cherry'), **Jekyll** (Gertrude), **Paxton** (Sir Joseph), **Repton** (Humphry)
07 **Clusius** (Carolus), **Dimmock** (Charlie), **Le Nôtre** (André), **Thrower** (Percy)
08 **Hamilton** (Geoff), **Jellicoe** (Sir Geoffrey), **Robinson** (William)
10 **Titchmarsh** (Alan), **Tradescant** (John, the Elder), **Tradescant** (John, the Younger)
13 **Sackville-West** (Vita)

garden flower *see* **flower**

gardening

Gardening tools include:

03 axe, hoe
04 fork, pots, rake
05 Flymo®, spade
06 cloche, gloves, scythe, shears, trowel
07 fan rake, hatchet, kneeler, loppers, netting, pruners, trellis, wellies
08 chainsaw, clippers, hosepipe, shredder, strimmer
09 cold frame, fruit cage, garden saw, lawn edger, lawnmower, lawn raker, secateurs, sprinkler, water butt
10 compost bin, cultivator, fertilizer, garden cart, greenhouse, lawn

roller, soil tester, weedkiller
11 incinerator, watering can, wheelbarrow
12 hedge trimmer, potting table
13 garden sprayer, lawn scarifier
14 rotary spreader

Gardening-related terms include:

03 bed
04 bulb, clay, loam, plot, seed, soil, tree, weed
05 bower, graft, hedge, mulch, plant, shrub
06 annual, hoeing, hybrid, manure, raking
07 climber, compost, cutting, digging, growing, organic, produce, pruning, staking, topiary, topsoil, weeding
08 gardener, layering, planting, thinning, watering
09 deciduous, germinate, leaf-mould, perennial, pesticide
10 coniferous, fertilizer, hardy plant
11 cultivation, green manure, ground cover, hydroponics, potting shed, propagation
12 bedding plant, conservatory, horticulture, hybrid vigour
13 double digging, growing season, transplanting
15 window gardening

Gardner
03 Ava

gargantuan
03 big **04** huge, vast **05** giant, large **07** immense, mammoth, massive, titanic **08** colossal, enormous, gigantic, towering **09** ginormous, humongous, humungous, leviathan, monstrous **10** monumental, prodigious, tremendous
11 elephantine **14** Brobdingnagian

garish
04 heal, loud, rory **05** cheap, flash, gaudy, jazzy, lurid, roary, rorie, showy **06** criant, flashy, glitzy, roarie, tawdry, vulgar **07** glaring, raffish **08** luminous, tinselly **09** flaunting, tasteless
10 glittering **12** meretricious

garishly
06 loudly **07** gaudily, jazzily, luridly
08 glitzily **09** glaringly **11** tastelessly

garland
03 lei **04** bays, deck **05** adorn, crown, glory, toran **06** crants, stemma, torana, wreath **07** chaplet, coronal, coronet, festoon, flowers, girlond, honours, laurels, wreathe **08** decorate, headband, ornament **09** engarland
10 decoration, naval crown

garments
04 garb, gear, togs, wear **05** dress, get-up **06** attire, outfit **07** apparel, clothes, costume, uniform **08** clothing, menswear
See also **clothes, clothing**

garner
04 cull, heap, save **05** amass, hoard, lay up, put by, store **06** gather, pile up
07 collect, deposit, granary, husband, reserve, stack up **08** assemble, stow away, treasure **09** stockpile
10 accumulate

garnet
06 pyrope **08** melanite **09** almandine, andradite, carbuncle, demantoid, grossular, pyreneite, rhodolite, uvarovite **10** alabandine, topazolite
11 schorlomite, spessartine, spessartite **12** grossularite
13 cinnamon stone **14** Uralian emerald

garnish
04 deck, lard, trim **05** adorn, grace
06 kit out, relish, set off, supply
07 deck out, enhance, festoon, furnish
08 beautify, decorate, ornament, trimming **09** adornment, embellish, gremolata **10** decoration
11 enhancement **13** embellishment, ornamentation

garret
04 loft **05** attic, roost, solar **06** turret
07 mansard **09** roof space
10 watchtower

garrison
03 man **04** base, camp, fort, post, unit
05 guard, mount, place, stuff
06 assign, casern, defend, occupy, troops, zareba **07** command, furnish, protect, station **08** barracks, fortress, position **10** armed force, detachment, encampment, engarrison, stronghold
13 fortification

garrulous
04 glib **05** gabby, gassy, windy, wordy
06 chatty, mouthy, prolix **07** gushing, prating, verbose, voluble, wordish
08 babbling, effusive, gaggling
09 gossiping, prattling, talkative, yabbering **10** chattering, long-winded, loquacious

garrulousness
09 loquacity, prolixity, verbosity
10 mouthiness, volubility
11 verboseness, wordishness
13 talkativeness **14** long-windedness, loquaciousness

gas

Gases include:

02 CS
03 air, LNG, LPG
04 neon, tear, town
05 ether, marsh, nerve, niton, ozone, radon, xenon
06 butane, helium, ketene
07 ammonia, krypton, methane, mustard, natural, propane
08 cyanogen, ethylene, firedamp, laughing
09 acetylene, black damp, chokedamp
10 chloroform
12 nitrous oxide
13 carbon dioxide, dimethylamine
14 carbon monoxide

See also **talk**

gash
03 cut **04** hack, nick, rend, rent, slit, tear **05** extra, gouge, score, slash, spare, split, wound **06** incise, scotch, tattle **07** ghastly, hideous **08** incision, lacerate **09** talkative **10** laceration

gasp
04 blow, gulp, kink, pant, puff
05 chink, choke, heave **06** breath, wheeze **07** breathe **11** exclamation
15 catch your breath

gassy
06 bubbly, frothy **07** aerated, foaming, gaseous, verbose **08** bubbling
09 sparkling **10** carbonated
12 effervescent

gastric
07 coeliac, enteric, stomach
09 abdominal, stomachic **10** intestinal

gastropod *see* **mollusc**

gate
03 way **04** door, exit, goat, path, port, yate, yett **05** hatch, koker **06** access, portal, street, vimana, wicket
07 barrier, caisson, channel, doorway, gateway, opening, passage, pontoon, postern, shutter **08** aboideau, aboiteau, entrance, sliprail
See also **circuit**

gatecrash
04 sorn

gateway
04 arch, port **05** pylon, toran, torii
06 torana **08** propylon **09** sallyport
10 propylaeum

gather
◇ *containment indicator*
02 in **03** add **04** camp, club, crop, cull, draw, fold, gain, grow, heap, hear, mass, meet, pick, pull, rake, reap, tuck
05 amass, build, crowd, flock, get in, glean, group, hoard, infer, learn, pleat, pluck, rally, shirr **06** assume, deduce, garner, muster, pick up, pile up, pucker, pull in, rake in, ruffle, select, summon, throng **07** accrete, advance, attract, believe, build up, cluster, collect, convene, develop, harvest, hoard up, improve, marshal, round up, surmise
08 assemble, conclude, converge, increase, progress **09** stash away, stockpile, suppurate **10** accumulate, congregate, understand **12** come together **13** bring together

gathering
◇ *containment indicator*
03 bee, hui, lek, mob **04** band, feis, fest, mass, meet, rave, rout, ruck, shir
05 coven, crowd, flock, group, hangi, horde, party, rally, salon, shirr, spree
06 huddle, love-in, muster, rabble, social, throng **07** company, gabfest, husking, Kommers, meeting, reunion, round-up, turnout **08** assembly, conclave, function, jamboree, musicale, singsong, tea party
09 wapenshaw, wapinshaw
10 assemblage, collective, convention,

corroboree, logrolling, wapenschaw, wapinschaw, wappenshaw
11 convocation, gallimaufry, get-together, wappenschaw
12 congregation **14** belle assemblée

gauche
03 shy **05** gawky, inept **06** clumsy
07 awkward, ill-bred **08** farouche, ignorant, tactless, ungainly
09 graceless, inelegant, maladroit
10 uncultured, ungraceful, unpolished
11 ill-mannered, insensitive
15 unsophisticated

gaudiness
08 loudness **09** harshness, showiness
10 brightness, brilliance, flashiness, garishness, tawdriness **11** raffishness
13 tastelessness

gaudy
03 gay **04** loud **05** flash, harsh, merry, showy, stark, tacky **06** bright, flashy, garish, glitzy, kitsch, snazzy, tawdry, tinsel, vulgar **07** flaming, glaring, raffish **08** tinselly **09** brilliant, colourful, flaunting, shrieking, tasteless, too bright **12** meretricious, ostentatious **13** multicoloured

gauge
04 area, bore, norm, rate, rule, size, span, test **05** basic, check, count, depth, guess, guide, judge, meter, model, scale, scope, sizer, value, weigh, width **06** assess, degree, extent, figure, height, reckon, sample
07 apprise, calibre, compute, example, measure, pattern, scantle **08** capacity, estimate, evaluate, exemplar, standard
09 ascertain, benchmark, calculate, criterion, determine, guideline, indicator, magnitude, marijuana, scantling, thickness, yardstick
11 guesstimate

Gauges include:

03 oil
04 rain, ring, snap, tide, tyre, wind
05 drill, paper, steam, taper, water
06 feeler, radius, strain, vacuum
07 Bourdon, cutting, loading, marking, mortise
08 gauge rod, pressure, udometer
09 Nilometer
10 anemometer, gauge glass, gauge wheel, hyetograph, hyetometer, micrometer, ombrometer, planometer, touchstone
11 pluviometer
15 hyetometrograph

gaunt
04 bare, bony, grim, lank, lean, thin, yawn **05** bleak, harsh, stark **06** barren, dismal, dreary, skinny, wasted
07 angular, forlorn, haggard, rawbone, scraggy, scrawny, spindly **08** desolate, rawboned, skeletal **09** emaciated
10 cadaverous, forbidding, hollow-eyed **12** skin and bones

Gauss
01 G **02** gs

gauze
04 film **07** tiffany **08** illusion
11 cheesecloth

gauzy
04 thin **05** filmy, light, sheer **06** flimsy
08 delicate, gossamer **10** diaphanous, see-through **11** transparent
13 insubstantial, unsubstantial

gawk
04 gape, gawp, gaze, look, ogle
05 stare **06** goggle

gawky
05 inept, lanky **06** clumsy, gauche, oafish **07** awkward, loutish
08 gangling, ungainly **09** graceless, lumbering, maladroit **13** unco-ordinated

gawp
04 gape, gawk, gaze, look, ogle
05 stare **06** goggle

gay
04 camp, pink, rich **05** gaudy, happy, jolly, merry, nitid, riant, showy, sunny, vivid **06** blithe, bright, flashy, garish, joyful, lively, wanton **07** festive, gallant, lesbian, playful, sapphic, spotted
08 animated, bisexual, carefree, cheerful, debonair, speckled
09 brilliant, colourful, exuberant, fun-loving, homophile, sparkling, sprightly, vivacious **10** dissipated, flamboyant, homosexual **12** light-hearted **13** in good spirits, in high spirits **15** pleasure-seeking

gaze
03 eye **04** gape, gawk, look, moon, muse, pore, view **05** stare, watch
06 goggle, regard, wonder
08 aftereye, gazement, outstare, wait upon **09** fixed look, moon about
10 moon around **11** contemplate
12 look vacantly, stare fixedly **13** stare intently

gazebo
03 hut **07** shelter **08** pavilion
09 belvedere **11** summerhouse

gazelle
03 goa **04** mohr **05** ariel, mhorr
07 chikara **08** chinkara

gazette
03 gaz **05** organ, paper **06** notice
07 journal, tabloid **08** despatch, dispatch, magazine **09** newspaper, news-sheet **10** broadsheet, periodical

gear
03 cog, fit, kit, low, top **04** garb, togs
05 adapt, dress, drugs, first, get-up, shift, stuff, third, tools, works **06** affair, armour, attire, design, devise, doings, matter, outfit, second, tackle, tailor, things **07** apparel, baggage, clobber, clothes, effects, gearing, harness, luggage, prepare, ratchet, reverse, threads **08** business, clothing, cogwheel, garments, organize, supplies, utensils **09** apparatus, engrenage, equipment, gearwheel, machinery, mechanism **10** appliances, belongings, implements, link-motion, tooth-wheel, underdrive
11 accessories, instruments, possessions, synchromesh
12 contrivances, toothed wheel
13 accoutrements, paraphernalia
See also **clothes, clothing**; **garments**

geegee
02 GG
See also **horse**

geezer
03 man **04** chap, cove **05** bloke
06 fellow

gel, jell
03 set **04** form **06** harden **07** congeal, stiffen, thicken **08** finalize, solidify
09 coagulate, take shape **11** crystallize, materialize **12** come together

gelatinous
05 gluey, gooey, gummy **06** sticky, viscid **07** jellied, rubbery, viscous
09 congealed, glutinous, jelly-like
12 mucilaginous

geld
03 cut, lib, tax **04** sort, spay
05 unman, unsex **06** neuter
07 deprive **08** castrate, enfeeble
09 expurgate **10** emasculate

gem
03 bud **04** rose **05** cameo, jewel, prize, stone **06** scarab **08** gemstone, marquise, sparkler, treasure
09 bespangle, brilliant, scaraboid
11 masterpiece, pride and joy **12** the bee's knees **13** precious stone
14 crème de la crème

Gemstones include:

03 jet
04 jade, onyx, opal, ruby
05 agate, amber, beryl, coral, pearl, topaz
06 garnet, jasper, zircon
07 cat's eye, citrine, crystal, diamond, emerald, peridot
08 amethyst, fire opal, sapphire, sunstone
09 cairngorm, carbuncle, carnelian, cornelian, demantoid, malachite, marcasite, moonstone, morganite, soapstone, tiger's eye, turquoise, uvarovite
10 aquamarine, bloodstone, chalcedony, chrysolite, rhinestone, rose quartz, serpentine, spinel ruby, tourmaline
11 alexandrite, chrysoberyl, chrysoprase, lapis lazuli, spessartite
13 cubic zirconia, mother-of-pearl, white sapphire

gen
04 data, dope, info **05** facts **07** details, low-down **09** knowledge
10 background **11** information
• **gen up on**
05 study **08** bone up on, read up on, research, swot up on **09** brush up on
12 find out about

gene *see* **genetics**

genealogy
04 line **05** birth **06** family **07** dynasty **08** breeding **09** parentage, whakapapa **10** derivation, extraction **11** generations **13** family history

Genealogy-related terms include:

03 DSP, IGI, née
04 AGRA, clan, deed, heir, late, race, will
05 issue, trace, widow
06 census, degree, estate, legacy, relict
07 archive, bastard, bequest, consort, descent, divorce, epitaph, kinship, lineage, peerage, probate, progeny, removed, surname, testate, trustee, widower, witness
08 ancestor, ancestry, bachelor, bequeath, canon law, deceased, decedent, emigrant, forebear, maternal, paternal, pedigree, relation, spinster
09 ascendant, given name, immigrant, indenture, intestate, necrology, offspring, sine prole, testament
10 ahnentafal, descendant, family name, family tree, forefather, generation, maiden name, onomastics, progenitor, succession
11 beneficiary, genealogist, record agent
12 burial record, census record, cousin-german, Domesday Book, illegitimate, primogenitor, vital records
13 Christian name, consanguinity, pedigree chart, primogeniture
14 cemetery record, common ancestor, marriage record
15 vital statistics

general
05 broad, loose, mixed, rough, total, usual, vague **06** common, global, normal, public, varied **07** blanket, diverse, inexact, overall, popular, regular, typical **08** accepted, all-round, assorted, everyday, habitual, ordinary, standard, sweeping **09** customary, extensive, imprecise, panoramic, prevalent, universal **10** ill-defined, indefinite, prevailing, unspecific, variegated, widespread **11** approximate, wide-ranging **12** all-inclusive, conventional **13** comprehensive, heterogeneous, miscellaneous **14** across-the-board

Generals include:

03 **Doe** (Samuel K), **Ike**, **Lee** (Robert E), **Ney** (Michel)
04 **Alba** (Ferdinand Alvarez de Toledo, Duke of), **Alva** (Ferdinand Alvarez de Toledo, Duke of), **Asad** (Hafez al-), **Dyer** (Reginald), **Haig** (Alexander), **Prem** (Tinsulanonda)
05 **Assad** (Hafez al-), **Booth** (William), **Clive** (Robert, Lord), **Gates** (Horatio), **Grant** (Ulysses S), **Scott** (Winfield), **Soult** (Nicolas Jean de Dieu), **Wolfe** (James)
06 **Anders** (Wladyslaw), **Caesar** (Julius), **Custer** (George Armstrong), **Franco** (Francisco), **Moreau** (Jean Victor), **Napier** (Sir Charles), **Powell** (Colin), **Rommel** (Erwin), **Scipio** (the Younger), **Sharon** (Ariel), **Zhukov** (Georgi)
07 **Agrippa** (Marcus Vipsanius), **Atatürk** (Mustapha Kemal), **Fairfax** (Thomas, Lord), **Masséna** (André), **Spínola** (António de)
08 **Agricola** (Gnaeus Julius), **Badoglio** (Pietro), **Brisbane** (Sir Thomas Makdougall), **Camillus** (Marcus Furius), **Cardigan** (James Thomas Brudenell, Earl of), **de Gaulle** (Charles), **Hamilton** (Sir Ian Standish Monteith), **Hannibal**, **Montrose** (James Graham, Marquis of)
09 **Antigonus**, **Aristides**, **Boulanger** (Georges), **MacArthur** (Douglas), **Omar Pasha**, **Santander** (Francisco de Paula), **Townshend** (George, Viscount and Marquess), **Townshend** (Sir Charles Vere Ferrers)
10 **Abercromby** (Sir Ralph), **Eisenhower** (Dwight D 'Ike'), **Oglethorpe** (James Edward), **Timoshenko** (Semyon)
11 **Baden-Powell** (Robert, Lord), **Jiang Jieshi**, **Schwarzkopf** (H Norman)
12 **Clive of India**
13 **Chiang Kai-shek**
14 **Osman Nuri Pasha**

General Electric
02 GE **03** GEC

generality
03 run **04** bulk, many, most **07** breadth, the many **08** majority **09** broadness, looseness, nearly all, vagueness **10** commonness, larger part, popularity, prevalence **11** catholicity, ecumenicity, greater part, inexactness **12** more than half, universality **13** extensiveness, impreciseness, miscellaneity **14** generalization, indefiniteness **15** approximateness

generalization
09 looseness, vagueness **11** inexactness **12** axioma medium, inexactitude **13** impreciseness **14** indefiniteness **15** approximateness

generalize
05 infer **06** assume, deduce **08** conclude, theorize **11** standardize

generally
06 mainly, mostly **07** as a rule, at large, broadly, chiefly, largely, overall, usually **08** commonly, normally **09** in general **10** by and large, habitually, more or less, on the whole, ordinarily **11** customarily, in most cases, universally **13** predominantly **14** for the most part

generate
◇ *anagram indicator*
04 form, make **05** breed, cause, spawn **06** arouse, create, evolve, gender, whip up **07** produce **08** engender, initiate, occasion **09** originate, procreate, propagate **10** bring about, give rise to **11** give birth to **14** bring into being

generation
03 age, era **04** days, kind, race, time **05** class, epoch **06** family, period **07** descent, genesis, progeny **08** age group, breeding, creation **09** engendure, formation, offspring **10** engendrure, production **11** engendering, origination, procreation, propagation **12** reproduction

generic
04 wide **06** common **07** blanket, general **08** superior, sweeping **09** inclusive, unbranded, universal **10** collective **12** all-inclusive **13** comprehensive, non-registered, untrademarked **14** non-proprietary, non-trademarked **15** all-encompassing

generically
08 commonly **09** generally **11** inclusively, universally **14** all-inclusively **15** comprehensively

generosity
06 bounty **07** charity, largess **08** goodness, kindness, largesse **10** lavishness, liberality **11** benevolence, magnanimity, munificence **12** philanthropy, selflessness **13** unselfishness **14** big-heartedness, open-handedness

generous
03 big **04** free, full, good, kind, rich **05** ample, large, lofty, noble, plump, roomy **06** giving, lavish **07** copious, liberal **08** abundant, handsome, menseful, selfless, sporting **09** bounteous, bountiful, plentiful, unselfish, unsparing **10** altruistic, beneficent, benevolent, big-hearted, charitable, courageous, free-handed, high-minded, munificent, open-handed, unstinting **11** gentlemanly, magnanimous, open-hearted, overflowing, soft-hearted, warm-hearted **12** large-hearted, wholehearted **13** disinterested, philanthropic **14** public-spirited

generously
05 amply, fully, nobly **06** freely, richly **08** lavishly **09** copiously, liberally **10** abundantly, charitably, handsomely, selflessly **11** bountifully, plentifully, unselfishly **12** open-handedly **13** magnanimously

genesis
03 Gen **04** dawn, root **05** birth, start **06** origin, outset, source **08** creation, founding **09** beginning, formation, inception **10** foundation, generation, initiation, production **11** development, engendering, propagation **12** commencement

genetic
07 genomic **09** inherited **10** biological, hereditary **11** chromosomal

genetics
06 origin **11** development

Geneticists include:

05 **Brown** (Michael S), **Jones** (Steve), **Leder** (Philip), **Ochoa** (Severo), **Sager** (Ruth), **Snell** (George Davis)
06 **Beadle** (George Wells), **Biffen** (Sir Rowland Harry), **Bodmer** (Sir Walter), **Boveri** (Theodor Heinrich), **Cantor** (Charles), **Fisher** (Sir Ronald Aylmer), **Galton** (Sir Francis), **Gurdon** (Sir John), **Morgan** (Thomas Hunt), **Müller** (Hermann Joseph), **Zinder** (Norton David)
07 **Bateson** (William), **Correns** (Carl), **De Vries** (Hugo Marie), **Gehring** (Walter), **Hopwood** (Sir David), **Lysenko** (Trofim)
08 **Auerbach** (Charlotte), **Lewontin** (Richard), **Yanofsky** (Charles)
09 **Baltimore** (David), **Goldstein** (Joseph), **Lederberg** (Joshua)
10 **Darlington** (Cyril Dean), **Dobzhansky** (Theodosius), **Kettlewell** (Henry Bernard David), **McClintock** (Barbara), **Sturtevant** (Alfred Henry), **Waddington** (C H), **Weatherall** (Sir David)
12 **Maynard Smith** (John)

Genetics-related terms include:

02 GM
03 DNA, PCR, RNA
04 base, gene
05 allel, clone, codon, helix, sperm
06 allele, gamete, genome, hybrid, intron, vector, zygote
07 diploid, meiosis, mitosis
08 autosome, dominant, heredity, mutation, promoter, sequence
09 amino acid, homologue, inversion, karyotype, offspring, recessive, repressor, variation
10 adaptation, chromosome, generation, geneticist, homozygous, nucleosome, nucleotide, polymerase, speciation
11 double helix, epigenetics, genetic code, inheritance, nucleic acid, polypeptide, X-chromosome, Y-chromosome
12 cell division, heterozygous, reproduction
13 DNA sequencing, fertilization, recombination, transcription, translocation

genial
04 kind, maty, mild, warm **05** happy, human, jolly, matey, pally, sunny
06 chummy, hearty, jovial, kindly, mellow **07** affable, amiable, cordial
08 amicable, cheerful, cheering, friendly, pleasant, sociable, sunshiny
09 agreeable, convivial, easy-going, healthful **11** good-natured, sympathetic, warm-hearted **12** good-humoured

geniality
06 warmth **07** jollity **08** bonhomie, gladness, kindness, sunshine
09 happiness, joviality **10** affability, amiability, cheeriness, cordiality, good nature, kindliness **12** cheerfulness, conviviality, friendliness, pleasantness
13 agreeableness, congenialness
15 warm-heartedness

genially
06 warmly **07** affably, amiably
08 amicably, heartily **09** cordially
10 cheerfully, pleasantly **13** warm-heartedly

genie
04 jann **05** demon, fairy, jinni
06 djinni, jinnee, spirit

genitals
08 privates **09** genitalia **12** private parts, sexual organs

genius
04 bent, gift, nous, sage **05** adept, brain, demon, flair, knack **06** boffin, brains, daemon, daimon, engine, expert, ingine, master, talent, wisdom, wizard **07** ability, egghead, faculty, maestro, prodigy **08** aptitude, capacity, fine mind, ingenium, virtuoso
09 bel esprit, intellect **10** brightness, brilliance, cleverness, grey matter, mastermind, past master, propensity, time spirit **11** inclination
12 intellectual, intelligence **15** little grey cells

genocide
08 massacre **09** ethnocide, slaughter
13 extermination **15** ethnic cleansing

genre
04 epic, form, kind, sort, type
05 brand, class, conte, genus, group, novel, sci-fi, style **06** comedy, satire, school, strain **07** fantasy, fashion, romance, variety **08** category, intimism, pastoral, prog rock
09 character, chopsocky, cyberpunk, reality TV **10** rare groove, whodunitry
11 fête galante, pastourelle, tragicomedy, whodunnitry
12 splatterpunk **13** fête champêtre
14 science fiction **15** progressive rock

gent *see* **gentleman**

genteel
05 civil **06** dainty, formal, polite, urbane **07** courtly, elegant, refined, stylish **08** cultured, graceful, ladylike, mannerly, polished, well-bred
09 courteous **10** cultivated **11** comme il faut, fashionable, gentlemanly, respectable **12** aristocratic, well-mannered

gentile
03 goy **06** ethnic **13** uncircumcised

gentility
04 rank **05** élite **06** gentry, nobles
07 culture, decorum, manners
08 breeding, civility, courtesy, elegance, nobility, poshness, urbanity
09 blue blood, etiquette, formality, high birth, propriety **10** good family, politeness, refinement, upper class
11 aristocracy, courtliness, gentle birth
12 mannerliness **14** respectability

gentle
04 calm, easy, gent, kind, meek, mild, slow, soft, tame **05** balmy, bland, canny, light, milky, quiet, sweet
06 benign, humane, kindly, placid, serene, slight, smooth, tender
07 amiable, clement, ennoble, gradual, lenient **08** delicate, lamb-like, maidenly, mansuete, merciful, moderate, peaceful, pleasant, soothing, tranquil, well-born
10 charitable, low-pitched **11** soft-hearted, sympathetic
13 compassionate, imperceptible, tender-hearted

gentleman
02 Mr **03** rye, sir **04** gent **05** Señor
06 gemman, knight, Signor, squire, stalko, yeoman **07** esquire, hidalgo, Signior, Signore, younker **08** cavalier
09 caballero, Signorino **10** duniwassal, pukka sahib **11** duniewassal, gentilhomme **12** dunniewassal
13 grand seigneur

gentlemanly
04 gent **05** civil, janty, noble, suave
06 jantee, jaunty, polite, urbane
07 gallant, genteel, jauntee, refined
08 generous, mannerly, obliging, polished, well-bred **09** civilized, courteous, reputable **10** chivalrous, cultivated, honourable **12** well-mannered **13** gentlemanlike

gentleness
05 mercy **06** warmth **08** calmness, kindness, meekness, mildness, softness, sympathy **09** sweetness
10 compassion, humaneness, tenderness

gently
01 p **04** soft **05** small **06** calmly, fairly, mildly, slowly, stilly, warmly **07** lightly
08 serenely, slightly, tenderly
09 gradually **10** charitably, moderately, pleasantly, sordamente, tranquilly
14 hooly and fairly
15 compassionately, sympathetically

gentry
05 élite **06** nobles **08** nobility, squirage **09** gentility, squireage, top drawer **10** upper class, upper crust
11 aristocracy

gents *see* **toilet**

genuflect
03 bow **05** kneel **11** bend the knee
12 pay obeisance **13** make obeisance
14 humble yourself **15** pay your respects

genuine
04 echt, good, open, pure, real, true
05 frank, legal, pakka, pucka, pukka, right, sound **06** actual, candid, dinkum, entire, honest, kosher, lawful, native, pusser **07** dinky-di, earnest,

factual, natural, sincere **08** bona fide, dinky-die, original, sterling, truthful, unartful **09** authentic, intrinsic, real McCoy, simon-pure, undoubted, veritable **10** fair dinkum, legitimate, ridgy-didge, sure-enough **11** honest-to-God, intrinsical **12** unadulterate **13** unadulterated, with integrity **14** unsophisticate **15** unsophisticated

genuinely
04 echt **06** dinkum, really **07** dinky-di **08** actually, dinky-die, honestly **09** earnestly, sincerely

genus
03 set **04** kind, race, sort, type **05** breed, class, genre, group, order, taxon **07** species **08** category, division **11** subdivision

geography

Geographical regions include:

04 veld
05 basin, coast, heath, plain, polar, veldt
06 Arctic, desert, forest, jungle, orient, pampas, steppe, tundra
07 outback, prairie, riviera, savanna, seaside, tropics
08 lowlands, midlands, occident, savannah, woodland
09 Antarctic, grassland, green belt, marshland, scrubland, wasteland
10 Third World, wilderness
11 countryside
13 Mediterranean, rural district, urban district
14 developed world
15 developing world

Geography terms include:

03 bay, col, cwm
04 arid, crag, mesa, tail, veld, wadi, wady
05 butte, delta, shott, taiga, veldt
06 canyon, cirque, corrie, tundra, valley
07 aggrade, caldera, equator, glacial, hachure, isthmus, tropics, volcano
08 alluvium, altitude, landmass, landslip, latitude, meridian, prograde
09 accretion, antipodes, base level, billabong, deviation, ethnology, landslide, longitude, metroplex, relief map
10 co-ordinate, demography, glaciation, landlocked, topography
11 archipelago, cartography, chorography, conurbation, demographic, hydrography, triangulate, vulcanology
13 hanging valley, Ordnance Datum, shield volcano
14 plate tectonics, roche moutonnée

Geographers include:

03 **Dee** (John)
04 **Cary** (John), **Mela** (Pomponius)
05 **Barth** (Heinrich), **Cabot** (Sebastian), **Darby** (Clifford), **Guyot** (Arnold), **Hedin** (Sven), **Penck** (Albrecht), **Sauer** (Carl), **Stamp** (Sir Lawrence Dudley)
06 **Batuta**, **Behaim** (Martin), **Bowman** (Isaiah), **Clüver** (Phillip), **Gmelin** (Johann Georg), **Harvey** (David), **Idrisi**, **Ritter** (Karl), **Strabo**
07 **Haggett** (Peter), **Hakluyt** (Richard), **Markham** (Sir Clements), **Ogilvie** (Alan), **Ptolemy**
08 **Büsching** (Anton Friedrich), **Filchner** (Wilhelm), **Humboldt** (Alexander, Baron von), **Mercator** (Gerhardus), **Ortelius** (Abraham Ortel), **Robinson** (Arthur)
09 **Kropotkin** (Pyotr), **Mackinder** (Sir Halford John), **Muqaddasi**, **Pausanias**
10 **Hartshorne** (Richard), **Huntington** (Ellsworth), **Richthofen** (Ferdinand Baron von), **Wooldridge** (Sydney)
11 **Christaller** (Walter), **Hägerstrand** (Torsten), **Kingdon-Ward** (Frank)
12 **Eratosthenes**, **Leo Africanus**
15 **Eudoxus of Cnidus**, **Vidal de la Blache** (Paul)

geology

Geological time periods include:

06 Eocene (Epoch)
07 Miocene (Epoch), Permian (Period)
08 Cambrian (Period), Cenozoic (Era), Devonian (Period), Holocene (Epoch), Jurassic (Period), Mesozoic (Era), Pliocene (Epoch), Silurian (Period), Tertiary (Period), Triassic (Period)
09 Oligocene (Epoch)
10 Cretaceous (Period), Ordovician (Period), Palaeocene (Epoch), Palaeozoic (Era), Quaternary (Period)
11 Phanerozoic (Eon), Pleistocene (Epoch), Precambrian (Era), Proterozoic (Eon)
13 Carboniferous (Period), Mississippian (Epoch), Pennsylvanian (Epoch)

Geology-related terms include:

02 aa
03 bar, cwm, mya, ore
04 clay, dome, dune, fold, lava, limb, lode, Moho, Riss, till, trap, tuff, vein, wadi
05 agate, atoll, basin, butte, chert, delta, epoch, esker, fault, fiord, fjord, focus, gorge, gully, guyot, horst, joint, Karst, lahar, levee, magma, plain, P-wave, ridge, S-wave, talus
06 albite, arkose, arroyo, basalt, bolson, canyon, cirque, corrie, debris, gabbro, geyser, gneiss, graben, mantle, oolite, quartz, runoff, schist, scoria, stress, tephra, trench, uplift
07 aquifer, barchan, bauxite, bed-load, blowout, breccia, caldera, drumlin, glacier, granite, hogback, igneous, isograd, lapilli, meander, mineral, moraine, orogeny, outwash, plateau, pothole, vesicle, volcano
08 A-horizon, alluvium, backwash, basement, B-horizon, C-horizon, feldspar, fumarole, isostasy, leaching, lopolith, monolith, mountain, obsidian, oilfield, oil shale, pahoehoe, pediment, regolith, rhyolite, syncline, xenolith
09 alabaster, batholith, carbonate, deflation, epicentre, flood tide, hot spring, intrusion, laccolith, landslide, limestone, Mohs scale, monadnock, monocline, oxidation, peneplain, rock cycle, rockslide, sandstone, slip fault, striation, tableland, viscosity, volcanism
10 anthracite, astrobleme, block fault, cinder cone, deposition, depression, earthquake, flood plain, kettle hole, mineralogy, rift valley, subsidence, topography, travertine, water table, weathering
11 alluvial fan, central vent, exfoliation, geosyncline, groundwater, maar volcano, metamorphic, normal fault, sublimation, swallow hole, thrust fault, volcanic ash
12 artesian well, coastal plain, fringing reef, magma chamber, pyroclastics, stratigraphy, unconformity, volcanic bomb, volcanic cone, volcanic dome, volcanic pipe
13 angle of repose, barrier island, drainage basin, geomorphology, hanging valley, recumbent fold, shield volcano, stratovolcano, U-shaped valley, V-shaped valley
14 bituminous coal, eustatic change, lateral moraine, longshore drift, stratification, subduction zone, transform fault, wave-cut terrace
15 million years ago, sedimentary rock, strike-slip fault, terminal moraine

Georgia
02 GA, GE **03** GEO

germ
03 bud, bug, wog **04** root, seed, zyme **05** cause, shoot, spark, start, virus **06** embryo, origin, source, sprout **07** microbe, nucleus **08** bacillus, fountain, rudiment **09** bacterium, beginning, inception, swarm-cell **10** seminality, swarm-spore **12** commencement **13** micro-organism

German
◇ *foreign word indicator*
01 G **03** Ger, Hun **04** Jute, Ossi **05** boche, Gerry, Jerry, Wessi **06** Almain, bosche, Teuton

German first names include:

03 Jan, Max, Uwe
04 Dirk, Eric, Erik, Jens, Jörg, Ralf, Sven, Swen
05 Bernd, Erich, Fritz, Jonas, Klaus, Lukas, Ralph
06 Dieter, Jürgen, Markus, Niklas, Stefan, Tobias, Ulrich
07 Andreas, Dominik, Mathias, Steffen, Stephan, Torsten

08 Kristian, Matthias, Thorsten, Wolfgang

See also **day**; **month**; **number**

• East German

03 Ost

germane

03 apt **04** akin **06** allied, proper **07** apropos, fitting, related **08** apposite, material, relevant, suitable **09** connected, pertinent **10** applicable **11** appropriate

germanium

02 Ge

Germany

01 D **03** DDR, DEU, FDR, FRG, GDR, Ger **05** Reich **06** Almany **07** Almaine **08** Alemaine

• in Germany

◇ *foreign word indicator*

germinal

07 seminal **09** embryonic **10** developing, generative **11** preliminary, rudimentary, undeveloped

germinate

03 bud **04** grow **05** shoot, swell **06** sprout **07** burgeon, develop **08** spring up, take root **09** originate

gestation

08 drafting, planning, ripening **09** evolution, pregnancy **10** conception, incubation, maturation **11** development

gesticulate

04 sign, wave **06** motion, signal **07** gesture **08** indicate **09** make a sign

gesticulation

04 sign, wave **06** motion, signal **07** gesture **08** movement **09** chironomy **10** indication **12** body language

gesture

03 act **04** geck, gest, mint, sign, wave **05** geste, point, snook **06** action, beckon, motion, signal **08** dumbshow, indicate, movement **09** beau geste, behaviour, chirology, reverence **10** indication **11** gesticulate **13** gesticulation

get

◇ *juxtaposition indicator*

02 go **03** bug, buy, cop, fix, hit, nab, see, vex, wax, win **04** brat, bust, coax, come, cook, earn, gain, grab, grow, have, hear, kill, land, make, move, nick, rile, suss, sway, take, trap, turn, twig, urge **05** annoy, bring, catch, child, clear, fetch, get it, go for, grasp, learn, reach, seize, snare **06** answer, arrest, arrive, attain, baffle, become, bother, collar, come by, descry, fathom, follow, induce, manage, obtain, pick up, secure, take in, travel, wangle, wind up, work it **07** achieve, acquire, arrange, be given, bring in, capture, collect, develop, discern, make out, prepare, procure, provoke, realize, receive, succeed, suss out, win over, work out **08** come to be, contract, convince, find a way, get ready, hunt down, irritate, organize, persuade, purchase, rustle up, talk into **09** aggravate, apprehend, figure out, influence, infuriate, lay hold of, recognize, succumb to **10** comprehend, drive crazy, exasperate, go down with, understand **11** get the point, prevail upon, put together **12** come down with, get the hang of **13** be afflicted by

• get about

02 go **06** travel **08** go widely **09** move about **10** move around **12** travel widely

• get across

06 convey, impart **07** express, get over, put over **08** transmit **09** make clear, put across **11** bring home to, communicate

• get ahead

05 get on **06** do well, make it, thrive **07** advance, prosper, succeed **08** flourish, get there, go places, make good, progress **11** go great guns **12** get somewhere, make your mark **14** go up in the world, make the big time

• get along

04 cope, fare **05** agree, get by, get on **06** giddap, giddup, manage, relate **07** develop, giddy-up, make out, survive **08** hit it off, progress, rub along **09** harmonize

• get around

◇ *containment indicator*

04 coax, move, sway **05** avoid, evade **06** bypass, cajole, induce, travel **07** win over **08** persuade **09** talk round **10** circumvent **11** prevail upon

• get at

04 find, hint, mean, slam **05** begin, bribe, imply, knock, reach, slate, touch **06** areach, attack, attain, intend, nobble, obtain, pick on, suborn **07** corrupt, suggest **08** discover **09** criticize, influence, insinuate, make fun of **11** pick holes in **12** gain access to **13** find fault with

• get away

04 flee, scat **05** be off, leave, never!, scoot, scram **06** begone, depart, escape, get out **07** do a bunk, run away, scarper **08** break out, run for it **09** break away, break free, do a runner **13** sling your hook **14** make a bolt for it, run for your life **15** make a break for it, take to your heels

• get back

06 go back, go home, recoup, recure, redeem, regain, return **07** pay back, recover **08** come back, come home, retrieve **09** repossess, retaliate **11** get even with **13** take revenge on **15** take vengeance on

• get by

04 cope, fare **05** exist **06** hang on, manage **07** subsist, survive **08** get along **12** make ends meet, see it through **13** scrape through **15** weather the storm

• get down

06 alight, get off, sadden **07** depress, descend, make sad **08** dismount, dispirit **09** disembark **10** dishearten

• get in

◇ *insertion indicator*

04 come, land **05** enter **06** arrive, embark **09** penetrate **10** infiltrate

• get into

◇ *insertion indicator*

05 enjoy, enter, put on **06** arrive **09** penetrate **10** infiltrate

• get off

04 shed **05** learn, leave **06** alight, detach, escape, get out, remove **07** descend, get down **08** climb off, dismount, get out of, memorize, separate **09** disembark **10** alight from

• get on

03 age **04** cope, fare **05** agree, board, get in, mount, shift **06** ascend, embark, manage, relate, thrive **07** advance, climb on, get into, make out, press on, proceed, prosper, succeed **08** continue, get along, hit it off, progress **09** harmonize **12** hit it off with

• get on well

03 gee

• get out

04 away, flee, quit, scat **05** leave, scoot, scram **06** depart, escape, spread, vacate **07** come out, do a bunk, extract, leak out, produce, scarper, take out **08** be leaked, break out, clear off, clear out, evacuate, run for it, withdraw **09** circulate, do a runner **11** become known **12** become public, free yourself **14** make a bolt for it, run for your life **15** make a break for it, take to your heels

• get out of

05 avoid, dodge, evade, shirk, skive **06** escape, outwin **07** goof off **09** gold-brick

• get over

06 convey, defeat, impart, master **07** explain, get well, put over, survive **08** complete, deal with, get round, overcome, shake off, surmount **09** get across, get better, make clear **10** be restored **11** communicate, pull through, recover from **14** recuperate from

• get ready

04 boun **05** bowne, fix up, ready **06** set out **07** arrange, prepare **08** rehearse

• get round

◇ *containment indicator*

04 coax, move, sway **05** avoid, evade **06** bypass, cajole, induce, travel **07** win over **08** persuade **09** talk round **10** circumvent **11** prevail upon

• get there

06 arrive, make it **07** advance, prosper, succeed **08** go places, make good

• get through

04 pass

• get together

04 join, meet **05** rally, unite **06** finish, gather **07** collect **08** assemble, organize **10** congregate **11** collaborate

• get up
03 fig **04** rise, stir **05** arise, climb, mount, scale, stand **06** ascend, huddup **07** stand up **08** show a leg **11** get out of bed

getaway
05 break, start **06** escape, flight **08** breakout **10** absconding, decampment

get-together
02 do **04** bash **05** party, rally **06** social, soirée **07** meeting, reunion **08** assembly, function, sing-sing **09** gathering, reception

get-up
03 kit, set **04** gear, togs **06** make-up, outfit, rig-out **07** clobber, clothes, threads, turnout **08** clothing, garments **09** equipment

Ghana
02 GH **03** GHA

ghastliness
08 grimness **09** awfulness, nastiness **11** hideousness **12** dreadfulness, gruesomeness **13** frightfulness

ghastly
03 bad, ill **04** gash, grim, ropy, sick **05** awful, grave, lousy, lurid, nasty, ropey **06** grisly, horrid, poorly, rotten, unwell **07** greisly, griesly, hideous, macabre, serious **08** critical, dreadful, gruesome, horrible, shocking, terrible **09** appalling, dangerous, deathlike, frightful, loathsome, off colour, repellent **10** deplorable, horrendous, terrifying **11** frightening **12** unrepeatable **15** under the weather

ghost
04 hint, soul, waff **05** duppy, fetch, haunt, jumby, larva, lemur, shade, spook, trace, umbra **06** duende, jumbie, shadow, spirit, wraith **07** gytrash, phantom, specter, spectre **08** manifest, presence, revenant, visitant **09** semblance **10** apparition, astral body, impression, suggestion **11** poltergeist

ghostly
05 eerie, faint, spook, weird **06** creepy, spooky **07** phantom, shadowy **08** chthonic, illusory, spectral **09** chthonian, ghostlike, religious, spiritual, sprightly, unearthly **10** wraith-like **12** supernatural

ghoulish
04 sick **06** grisly, morbid **07** macabre **08** gruesome **09** revolting, unhealthy **11** unwholesome

giant
04 eten, huge, ogre, vast **05** ettin, jotun, jumbo, large, titan, troll **06** jötunn, ogress **07** immense, mammoth, massive, monster, titanic **08** behemoth, Briarean, colossal, colossus, cyclopic, enormous, gigantic, great big, king-size, titaness, whopping **09** cyclopean, cyclopian, ginormous, humongous, humungous, leviathan, rounceval **10** gargantuan, monumental, Patagonian, prodigious, tremendous **11** gigantesque **14** Brobdingnagian

Giants include:

03 Gog
04 Gaia, Gerd, Grid, Loki, Rhea, Ymir
05 Aegir, Arges, Argus, Atlas, Grawp, Hymir, Jotun, Magog, Orion, Pan Gu, Skadi, Theia, Thrym
06 Albion, Bestla, Cronus, Hagrid, Phoebe, Tethys, Themis, Thiazi, Titans
07 Cyclops, Geirrod, Goliath, Iapetus, Oceanus, Suttung
08 Angrboda, Cyclopes, Gigantes, Gogmagog, Hrungnir, Hyperion, Jarnsaxa, Morgante, Nephilim, Panoptes, Steropes
09 Angerboda, Bergelmir, Enceladus, Gandareva, Gargantua, Mnemosyne, Olentzero
10 Angerbotha, Epimetheus, Paul Bunyan, Prometheus
11 Finn MacCool, Galligantus, Gog and Magog, Utgardaloki
12 Giant Despair, Vafthruthnir
15 Cerne Abbas Giant, Fionn MacCumhail

gibber
04 blab, cant **05** stone **06** babble, cackle, gabble, jabber **07** blabber, blather, boulder, chatter, prattle

gibberish
04 blah, bosh, guff **05** hooey **06** bunkum, drivel, jargon, linsey, yammer **07** baloney, eyewash, hogwash, prattle, ravings, rhubarb, rubbish, twaddle **08** cobblers, malarkey, nonsense, tommyrot **09** moonshine, poppycock **10** balderdash, codswallop, jabberwock, mumbo-jumbo **11** abracadabra, jabberwocky **12** gobbledygook **13** linsey-woolsey

gibbet
05 crook, cross **07** gallows, potence

gibbon
06 wou-wou, wow-wow **07** hoolock, siamang **08** hylobate

gibe, jibe
03 bob, dig, shy **04** gird, goof, jeer, mock, poke, quip, wipe, yerk **05** crack, fleer, fling, flout, gleek, scoff, slant, sneer, taunt, tease **06** deride **07** brocard, mockery, sarcasm, teasing **08** derision, outfling, ridicule **09** make fun of, wisecrack, witticism

Gibraltar
03 GBZ, GIB

giddily
◇ *anagram indicator*
06 wildly **07** dizzily, woozily **09** excitedly **10** restlessly, unsteadily **11** frantically **12** euphorically **13** lightheadedly

giddiness
06 frenzy, nausea, thrill **07** vertigo **08** staggers **09** animation, dizziness, faintness, wooziness **10** excitement, wobbliness **11** glaikitness **12** exhilaration **15** lightheadedness

giddy
◇ *anagram indicator*
04 high, wild **05** dizzy, faint, light, queer, silly, woozy **06** elated, sturdy, volage **07** excited, flighty, glaiket, glaikit, reeling, stirred **08** frenzied, hellicat, skipping, thrilled, unsteady **09** volageous **10** capernoity, hoity-toity, stimulated **11** capernoitie, cappernoity, exhilarated, hair-brained, hare-brained, lightheaded, vertiginous

gift
03 foy, tip **04** bent, boon, give, koha, turn **05** bonus, bribe, flair, grant, knack, offer, power, skill **06** befana, bestow, bounty, confer, donate, genius, hansel, legacy, talent **07** ability, aptness, beffana, bequest, cumshaw, étrenne, faculty, fairing, freebie, handsel, minding, present, pressie, prezzie, propine **08** aptitude, capacity, donation, donative, facility, gratuity, largesse, offering, thankyou **09** attribute, book token, endowment **10** capability, contribute, exhibition **11** beneficence, inheritance, proficiency **12** Christmas box, contribution

See also **Christmas**

gifted
04 able **05** adept, sharp, smart **06** bright, clever, expert **07** capable, endowed, skilful, skilled **08** masterly, talented **09** brilliant **10** proficient **11** intelligent **12** accomplished

gig
03 fun **04** moze **05** buggy, sport **06** dennet, whisky **07** whiskey **11** hurly-hacket

gigantic
04 huge, mega, vast **05** giant, jumbo **07** immense, mammoth, massive, monster, titanic **08** colossal, enormous, great big, king-size, whopping **09** Atlantean, ginormous, Herculean, humongous, humungous, leviathan, rounceval **10** Babylonian, gargantuan, monumental, Patagonian **14** Brobdingnagian

giggle
05 laugh **06** titter **07** chortle, chuckle, snicker, snigger

gilbert
02 Gb

• Gilbert and Sullivan
05 G and S

gild
04 coat, deck, trim **05** adorn, array, grace, paint **06** bedeck, enrich, golden **07** dress up, enhance, festoon, garnish **08** beautify, brighten, ornament **09** elaborate, embellish, embroider

gilded
04 gilt, gold **06** golden **07** aureate **08** inaurate **10** gold-plated **11** gold-layered

gill
04 glen **05** brook **06** noggin, ravine **08** branchia **09** ctenidium

gilt
03 elt

gimcrack
05 cheap, dodge, tacky, trick **06** fisgig, fizgig, shoddy, tawdry, trashy **08** rubbishy, trumpery **10** jerry-built

gimmick
04 hype, ploy, ruse **05** dodge, stunt, trick **06** device, gadget, scheme **07** novelty **09** publicity, stratagem **10** attraction **11** contrivance

gimmickry
07 novelty **09** modernity **10** innovation

gin
02 by, if **03** max **04** ruin, trap **05** snare **06** geneva, Old Tom, scheme, spring **07** schnaps, springe, twankay **08** artifice, blue ruin, Hollands, schiedam, schnapps **10** square-face **11** contrivance, mother's ruin

• **gin and tonic**
02 gt **05** g and t

ginger
◇ *anagram indicator*
03 pop **04** race, rase, raze **05** bluey, sandy **06** amomum, asarum, mettle **07** curcuma, enliven, reddish **08** cardamom, cardamon, cardamum, turmeric, zingiber **09** galingale **10** cassumunar **11** stimulation

gingerbread
05 parly **06** parkin, parley, perkin **10** parliament, pepper-cake **14** parliament-cake

gingerly
06 warily **07** charily **09** carefully, prudently **10** cautiously, delicately, hesitantly, watchfully **11** attentively, judiciously, tentatively, with caution

Gipsy *see* **Gypsy, Gipsy**

gird
03 pen **04** belt, bind, girr, hoop, ring **05** brace, hem in, ready, steel, taunt **06** enfold, fasten, girdle **07** accinge, enclose, fortify, prepare **08** cincture, encircle, get ready, surround **09** encompass

girder
04 beam, spar **05** H-beam, I-beam **06** rafter **07** box beam

girdle
03 hem **04** band, belt, bind, gird, ring, sash, zona, zone **05** bound, mitre, waist **06** cestos, cestus, circle, corset **07** enclose, go round, griddle, zonulet **08** ceinture, cincture, cingulum, encircle, surround **09** encompass, surcingle, waistband **10** cummerbund, encincture **15** cingulum Veneris

girl
03 bit, cub, gal, gel, gig, hen, her, kid, mor, tit **04** babe, baby, bint, bird, chit, dell, gill, jill, Judy, lass, maid, mawr, minx, miss, peat, puss, romp, tart **05** belle, chick, child, cutie, cutty, dolly, fille, filly, flirt, gerle, gilpy, hussy, madam, peach, popsy, quean, randy, tabby, wench **06** au pair, blowze, chokri, cummer, damsel, female, fizgig, gamine, geisha, giglet, kimmer, lassie, maiden, moppet, mousmé, nipper, number, pigeon, sheila, shiksa, tawpie, tomboy, tottie **07** blushet, chapess, chicken, colleen, flapper, mauther, mawther, mousmee, nymphet **08** chappess, daughter, grisette, jail-bait, princess, teenager **09** backfisch, dolly bird, maid-child, young lady, youngster **10** adolescent, bit of fluff, bit of skirt, bit of stuff, bobbysoxer, Cinderella, girlfriend, jeune fille, schoolgirl, sweetheart, young woman **11** beauty queen, kinchin-mort, maidservant, teeny-bopper **12** bachelorette, bobby-dazzler

Girls' names include:

02 Di, Jo, Mo, Vi
03 Ada, Ali, Amy, Ann, Ava, Bab, Bea, Bee, Bel, Bet, Cis, Con, Deb, Dee, Die, Dot, Edy, Emm, Ena, Eva, Eve, Fay, Flo, Gay, Ida, Ina, Isa, Ivy, Jan, Jay, Jen, Joe, Joy, Kay, Kim, Kit, Lea, Lee, Liv, Liz, Lou, Mae, Mag, Mat, May, Meg, Mia, Nan, Pam, Pat, Peg, Pen, Pia, Pru, Rae, Ray, Ria, Ros, Roz, Sal, Sue, Una, Val, Viv, Win, Zoë
04 Abby, Addy, Afra, Aggy, Alex, Ally, Alma, Alme, Angy, Anna, Anne, Asma, Babs, Bell, Bess, Beth, Cara, Caro, Cass, Ceri, Cher, Cleo, Cora, Dana, Dawn, Dian, Dora, Edel, Edie, Edna, Ella, Elma, Elsa, Elva, Emma, Emmy, Enid, Erin, Evie, Faye, Floy, Fred, Gabi, Gaea, Gaia, Gail, Gale, Gaye, Gene, Gert, Gill, Gina, Gita, Gwen, Hope, Ibby, Ines, Inez, Inga, Inge, Iona, Iris, Irma, Isla, Jade, Jane, Jean, Jess, Jill, Joan, Jodi, Jody, Joey, Joni, Joss, Jozy, Jude, Judy, June, Kate, Kath, Katy, Kaye, Lara, Leah, Lena, Lian, Lily, Lina, Lisa, Lise, Livy, Liza, Lois, Lola, Lucy, Lynn, Maev, Mary, Maud, Meta, Mina, Moll, Mona, Myra, Nell, Nina, Nita, Noel, Nola, Nona, Nora, Olga, Page, Phyl, Poll, Prue, Rana, Rene, Rita, Rona, Rosa, Rose, Ruby, Ruth, Sara, Sian, Sìne, Siri, Suke, Suky, Susy, Suzy, Tess, Thea, Tina, Toni, Trix, Vera, Vita, Zara, Zena, Zola
05 Addie, Adela, Adèle, Aggie, Agnes, Ailie, Ailsa, Aisha, Alexa, Alice, Allie, Amber, Amina, Anaïs, Angel, Angie, Anila, Anita, Annie, Annis, Annot, Aphra, April, Areta, Aruna, Avril, Aysha, Becky, Bella, Belle, Beryl, Bessy, Betsy, Betty, Biddy, Bride, Brona, Bunny, Bunty, Candy, Carla, Carly, Carol, Carys, Cathy, Celia, Cerys, Chère, Chloe, Chris, Ciara, Cindy, Cissy, Clara, Clare, Coral, Daisy, Debby, Debra, Delia, Della, Diana, Diane, Dilys, Dinah, Dolly, Donna, Doris, Edith, Effie, Eliza, Ellen, Ellie, Elsie, Emily, Emmie, Erica, Essie, Ethel, Ethna, Ethne, Faith, Fanny, Farah, Ffion, Fiona, Fleur, Flora, Freda, Freya, Gabby, Gauri, Gayle, Geeta, Gemma, Gerda, Ginny, Golda, Golde, Grace, Greta, Haley, Hatty, Hazel, Heidi, Helen, Helga, Hetty, Hilda, Holly, Honor, Ilana, Ilona, Irena, Irene, Isbel, Isold, Ivana, Jaime, Jamie, Janet, Janis, Jemma, Jenna, Jenny, Jessy, Jinny, Jodie, Joely, Josie, Joyce, Judie, Julia, Julie, Kanta, Karen, Karin, Karla, Kathy, Katie, Katya, Kelly, Kenna, Kerry, Kiera, Kitty, Kylie, Lalla, Lally, Laura, Leigh, Leila, Leona, Letty, Liana, Libby, Linda, Lindy, Lorna, Lorne, Louie, Lubna, Lucia, Lydia, Lynda, Lynne, Mabel, Madge, Maeve, Magda, Máire, Màiri, Mamie, Mandy, Margo, Maria, Marie, Matty, Maude, Maura, Mavis, Meena, Megan, Mercy, Meryl, Moira, Molly, Morag, Morna, Moyra, Myrna, Nabby, Nadia, Nance, Nancy, Nelly, Nerys, Nessa, Nesta, Netta, Netty, Ngaio, Niamh, Nicky, Noele, Norah, Norma, Nuala, Olive, Olwen, Olwin, Olwyn, Onora, Oprah, Paddy, Padma, Paige, Pansy, Patsy, Patty, Paula, Pearl, Peggy, Penny, Petra, Pippa, Polly, Priya, Raine, Rajni, Renée, Rhian, Rhoda, Rhona, Robin, Robyn, Rosie, Sacha, Sadie, Sally, Sarah, Sasha, Senga, Shona, Shula, Sibyl, Sindy, Sonia, Sonya, Sophy, Stacy, Sukie, Susan, Susie, Sybil, Tamar, Tammy, Tania, Tanya, Terry, Tessa, Thora, Tibby, Tilda, Tilly, Tracy, Trina, Trish, Trixy, Trudy, Unity, Viola, Wanda, Wendy, Wilma, Zahra, Zelda, Zowie
06 Adella, Agatha, Aileen, Alexia, Alexis, Alicia, Alison, Althea, Amabel, Amanda, Amelia, Andrea, Angela, Anneka, Annika, Anthea, Aphrah, Aretha, Ashley, Astrid, Audrey, Auriel, Auriol, Aurora, Aurore, Averil, Ayesha, Babbie, Barbie, Beatty, Bertha, Bertie, Bessie, Bianca, Biddie, Blanch, Bonnie, Brenda, Bridie, Brigid, Brigit, Briony, Bryony, Bunnie, Caddie, Candia, Carina, Carlie, Carmel, Carmen, Carola, Carole, Carrie, Cassie, Cathie, Cecily, Celina, Cherie, Cherry, Cheryl, Cicely, Cissie, Claire, Connie, Daphne, Davina, Deanna, Deanne, Debbie, Delyth, Denise, Dervla, Dianne, Dionne, Dolina, Doreen, Dorrie, Dottie, Dulcie, Dympna, Eartha, Edwina, Eileen, Eilidh, Eirian, Eirlys, Eithna, Eithne, Elaine, Elinor, Eloisa, Eloise, Elspet, Eluned, Elvira, Esther, Eunice, Evadne, Evelyn, Evonne, Fatima, Fedora, Felice, Finola, Flavia, Freddy, Frieda, Gaynor, Gertie,

Gladys, Glenda, Glenys, Gloria, Glynis, Goldie, Gracie, Grania, Granya, Gudrun, Gwenda, Hannah, Hattie, Hayley, Helena, Hermia, Hester, Hilary, Honora, Honour, Imelda, Imogen, Indira, Ingrid, Isabel, Iseult, Ishbel, Isobel, Isolda, Isolde, Jamila, Jancis, Janice, Janina, Janine, Jeanie, Jemima, Jennie, Jessie, Joanie, Joanna, Joanne, Joelle, Joleen, Jolene, Judith, Juliet, Kamala, Karena, Karina, Kathie, Kirsty, Kittie, Kumari, Lalage, Lalita, Lallie, Laurel, Lauren, Laurie, Leanne, Leonie, Lesley, Lettie, Lianna, Lianne, Lilian, Lilias, Linnet, Lisbet, Lizzie, Lolita, Lottie, Louisa, Louise, Lynsey, Madhur, Maggie, Maisie, Marcia, Marian, Marina, Marion, Marsha, Martha, Mattie, Maxine, Melody, Meriel, Millie, Minnie, Miriam, Monica, Morven, Muriel, Myriam, Myrtle, Nabila, Nadine, Nellie, Nessie, Nettie, Nicola, Nicole, Noelle, Noreen, Odette, Olivia, Olwyne, Paloma, Pamela, Pattie, Petula, Phemie, Phoebe, Rachel, Rajani, Raquel, Regina, Renata, Rhonda, Robina, Rodney, Roisin, Roshan, Rosina, Rowena, Roxana, Roxane, Rubina, Sabina, Sabine, Salome, Sandra, Saskia, Selina, Seonag, Serena, Sharon, Shashi, Sheela, Sheena, Sheila, Sherry, Sheryl, Silvia, Simone, Sinéad, Sophia, Sophie, Stacey, Stella, Suhair, Sydney, Sylvia, Tamara, Tammie, Tamsin, Teenie, Teresa, Thelma, Tibbie, Tracey, Tricia, Trisha, Trixie, Ulrica, Ursula, Vanora, Verity, Vijaya, Vinaya, Violet, Vivian, Vivien, Vyvian, Vyvyan, Winnie, Winona, Wynona, Xanthe, Yasmin, Yvette, Yvonne, Zainab, Zaynab

07 Abigail, Aisling, Allegra, Allison, Andrina, Annabel, Annette, Antonia, Anushka, Ariadne, Augusta, Barbara, Beatrix, Belinda, Bernice, Bethany, Bettina, Bharati, Blanche, Bridget, Bronach, Bronagh, Bronwen, Caitlín, Camilla, Candace, Candice, Candida, Carolyn, Cecilia, Chandra, Chantal, Charity, Charley, Chelsea, Christy, Clarice, Claudia, Colette, Colleen, Corinna, Corinne, Crystal, Cynthia, Daniela, Deborah, Deirdre, Désirée, Dolores, Dorothy, Eleanor, Elspeth, Emerald, Estella, Estelle, Eugenia, Eugénie, Felicia, Fenella, Floella, Florrie, Flossie, Frances, Francie, Frankie, Freddie, Georgia, Georgie, Gillian, Giselle, Gwennie, Gwenyth, Gwyneth, Harriet, Heather, Heloise, Isadora, Isidora, Jacinta, Jacinth, Janetta, Janette, Jasmine, Jeannie, Jessica, Jillian, Jocasta, Jocelin, Jocelyn, Johanna, Jonquil, Josette, Juliana, Justina, Justine, Kathryn, Katrina, Katrine, Kirstie, Kirstin, Lakshmi, Lavinia, Leonora, Letitia, Lettice, Lillian, Lillias, Lindsay, Lindsey, Linette, Lisbeth, Lisette, Lizbeth, Loretta, Lucilla, Lucille, Lucinda, Lynette, Madonna, Margery, Marilyn, Marjory, Marlene, Martina, Martine, Matilda, Maureen, Melanie, Melissa, Mildred, Miranda, Myfanwy, Nanette, Natalia, Natalie, Natasha, Nichola, Nigella, Ninette, Ophelia, Pandora, Parvati, Pascale, Paulina, Pauline, Phyllis, Queenie, Rachael, Rebecca, Roberta, Rosabel, Rosalie, Rosanna, Rosetta, Roxanne, Sabrina, Saffron, Sharifa, Shelagh, Shelley, Shirley, Sidonie, Silvana, Siobhán, Surayya, Susanna, Sybilla, Tabitha, Theresa, Tiffany, Valerie, Vanessa, Venetia, Yolanda, Zuleika

08 Adelaide, Adrianne, Adrienne, Angelica, Angelina, Angharad, Arabella, Ashleigh, Beatrice, Berenice, Beverley, Caroline, Catriona, Charlene, Charmian, Chrissie, Clarinda, Clarissa, Claudine, Cordelia, Cornelia, Courtney, Cressida, Daniella, Danielle, Dorothea, Eleanore, Emmeline, Euphemia, Felicity, Florence, Francine, Georgina, Germaine, Gertrude, Griselda, Grizelda, Gurinder, Hermione, Isabella, Jacintha, Jacinthe, Jeanette, Jennifer, Joceline, Joscelin, Katerina, Kathleen, Kimberly, Kirsteen, Lauretta, Lorraine, Madeline, Magdalen, Margaret, Marigold, Marjorie, Mathilda, Meredith, Michaela, Michelle, Morwenna, Ottoline, Patience, Patricia, Paulette, Penelope, Philippa, Primrose, Prudence, Prunella, Rhiannon, Rosalind, Rosamond, Rosamund, Roseanna, Roseanne, Rosemary, Samantha, Scarlett, Susannah, Theodora, Tomasina, Veronica, Victoria, Virginia, Winifred

09 Albertina, Alexandra, Anastasia, Annabella, Annabelle, Cassandra, Catharine, Catherina, Catherine, Charlotte, Charmaine, Christina, Christine, Claudette, Cleopatra, Constance, Elisabeth, Elizabeth, Frederica, Gabrielle, Genevieve, Georgette, Georgiana, Geraldine, Ghislaine, Guinevere, Gwendolen, Henrietta, Jaqueline, Jeannette, Josephine, Katharine, Katherine, Kimberley, Madeleine, Magdalene, Mélisande, Millicent, Nicolette, Parminder, Priscilla, Rosemarie, Sigourney, Silvestra, Stephanie, Sylvestra, Thomasina, Valentine

10 Antoinette, Bernadette, Christabel, Clementina, Clementine, Jacqueline, Shakuntula, Wilhelmina

---

• society girl
03 deb **09** débutante

girlfriend
03 mot **04** babe, baby, bint, bird, date, girl, lady, lass, moll **05** chick, lover, woman **06** steady **07** fiancée, partner, squeeze **08** best girl, mistress, old flame **09** cohabitee, young lady **10** sweetheart **11** live-in lover **15** common-law spouse

girlish
08 childish, immature, innocent, youthful **09** childlike **10** adolescent **11** unmasculine

girth
04 band, bulk, size **05** strap **06** asylum **07** compass, measure **08** encircle **09** perimeter, sanctuary, surcingle **13** circumference

gist
03 nub **04** core, crux, idea, pith **05** drift, point, sense **06** import, marrow, matter, thrust **07** essence, keynote, meaning, nucleus, purport **09** direction, substance **12** quintessence, significance **15** sum and substance

give
◇ *juxtaposition indicator*
02 do **03** aim, gie **04** bend, cede, fall, gift, have, lead, lend, make, move, play, show, sink, slip, tell, turn, will, yeve **05** admit, allow, award, break, cause, endow, focus, grant, lay on, leave, offer, put on, slack, throw, utter, yield **06** accord, afford, bestow, buckle, commit, confer, convey, create, devote, direct, donate, fetter, give up, impart, induce, permit, prompt, render, reveal, supply **07** arrange, concede, declare, deliver, display, dispose, entrust, exhibit, furnish, give way, incline, perform, present, produce, proffer, provide, publish, shackle, stretch **08** announce, bequeath, carry out, collapse, estimate, hand over, indicate, make over, manifest, occasion, organize, set forth, transfer, transmit, turn over, yielding **09** break down, fall apart, pronounce, surrender **10** administer, contribute, distribute, elasticity, give rise to **11** cause to have, communicate, concentrate, springiness **12** stretchiness, take charge of **14** cause to undergo, let someone have

• give away
04 leak, shed, tell **06** betray, expose, let out, reveal **07** concede, divulge, let slip, uncover **08** disclose, inform on

• give in
04 quit **05** yield **06** give up, jack in, submit **07** chuck up, concede, give way, succumb **08** pack it in **09** chuck it in, surrender **10** call it a day, capitulate, knock under **11** admit defeat **13** concede defeat **15** throw in the cards, throw in the towel, throw up the cards

• give off
04 emit, fume, vent **05** exude **06** evolve, exhale **07** give out, pour out, produce, release, send out **08** liberate, throw out **09** discharge

• give on to
06 lead to **08** open on to, overlook

• give out
04 deal, emit, vent **05** allot, exude,

yield **06** exhale, impart, notify, pack up, report, run out **07** conk out, declare, dish out, dole out, give off, hand out, mete out, pour out, produce, publish, release, send out
08 announce, depleted, disperse, share out, throw out, transmit
09 advertise, be mixed up, break down, broadcast, circulate, discharge, make known **10** be depleted, distribute, pass around, relinquish
11 be exhausted, come to an end, communicate, disseminate, stop working **12** be all mixed up

• give over
03 lin **07** chuck it **08** transfer

• give up
03 cut **04** cede, quit, stop **05** cease, forgo, remit, waive **06** cut out, forego, give in, render, resign, turn in
07 abandon, chuck in, chuck up, concede, crap out, deliver, forbear, forgive, lay down, put down, respite, throw up **08** abdicate, forswear, leave off, renounce **09** sacrifice, surrender
10 capitulate, relinquish **11** admit defeat, discontinue **13** concede defeat
14 drop your bundle **15** throw in the towel

give-and-take
08 goodwill **10** compliance, compromise **11** co-operation, flexibility, negotiation, willingness
12 adaptability

given
05 prone **06** liable, likely, stated
08 assuming, definite, disposed, distinct, inclined, in view of, specific
09 specified **10** individual, particular
11 considering **12** in the light of
13 bearing in mind

giver
05 angel, donor **06** backer, friend, helper, patron **07** sponsor
08 promoter, provider **09** supporter
10 benefactor, subscriber, subsidizer, well-wisher **11** contributor **14** fairy godmother, philanthropist

glacial
03 icy, raw **04** cold **05** chill, gelid, polar, stiff **06** arctic, biting, bitter, chilly, frigid, frosty, frozen, wintry
07 brumous, distant, hostile
08 freezing, inimical, piercing, Siberian **10** unfriendly **12** antagonistic

glaciation stage
04 Günz, Riss, Würm **06** Mindel

glad
04 fain, keen **05** eager, happy, merry, ready **06** bright, cheery, elated, joyful
07 chuffed, gleeful, pleased, welcome, willing **08** cheerful, disposed, gladsome, inclined, prepared, thrilled
09 contented, delighted, gratified, overjoyed, satisfied **11** over the moon, tickled pink

gladden
05 cheer, elate **06** buck up, please
07 delight, enliven, gratify, hearten, rejoice **08** brighten **09** encourage
10 exhilarate

glade
03 gap **04** dell, land **05** laund, space
07 opening **08** clearing **09** cock-shoot

gladiator
07 Samnite, sworder **09** retiarius, Spartacus

gladly
04 fain **06** fainly, freely **07** happily, readily **09** willingly **10** cheerfully, gladsomely **12** with pleasure **13** with good grace

gladness
03 joy **04** glee **05** mirth **06** gaiety
07 delight, jollity **08** felicity, hilarity, pleasure **09** happiness **10** brightness, joyousness **11** high spirits
12 cheerfulness

glamorous
04 glam **05** ritzy, smart **06** exotic, flashy, glammy, glitzy, glossy, lovely
07 elegant **08** alluring, charming, dazzling, exciting, gorgeous
09 appealing, beautiful, colourful, thrilling **10** attractive, bewitching, enchanting, glittering **11** captivating, fascinating, well-dressed

glamour
02 it, SA **04** gilt, Ritz **05** charm, magic
06 allure, appeal, beauty, thrill
07 glitter **08** elegance, prestige, witchery **09** magnetism **10** attraction, excitement **11** captivation, enchantment, fascination
14 attractiveness

• sentimental glamour
04 halo

glance
03 dip, ray **04** flip, leaf, leer, look, ogle, peek, peep, scan, skim, view **05** blink, dekko, eliad, flash, flick, glide, slant, squiz, thumb, tweer, twire **06** amoret, aspect, browse, eyliad, gander, gledge, illiad, shufti, shufty, skelly, squint, vision
07 deflect, eye-beam, eyeliad, eyeshot, eye-wink, glimpse, skellie
08 butcher's, oeillade, ricochet
09 brief look, quick look **10** redruthite
13 look briefly at, look quickly at
15 catch a glimpse of

• at first glance
09 outwardly, seemingly
10 apparently, ostensibly, prima facie
12 at first sight, on the surface **13** on the face of it, superficially

• glance off
07 rebound **08** ricochet **09** bounce off **10** spring back

gland

Glands include:

05 lymph, ovary
06 cortex, pineal, thymus
07 adrenal, eccrine, mammary, medulla, parotid, thyroid
08 apocrine, exocrine, pancreas, prostate, testicle
09 endocrine, holocrine, lachrymal, lymph node, merocrine, pituitary, sebaceous
11 parathyroid

glare
04 beam, glow, look, lour **05** blaze, flame, flare, frown, lower, scowl, shine, stare **06** dazzle, glassy, glower
07 daggers, reflect **08** iceblink
09 black look, dirty look, limelight, look frown, spotlight **10** brightness, brilliance

glaring
04 open **05** glary, gross, lurid, overt
06 garish, patent **07** blatant, obvious
08 flagrant, manifest, walleyed
10 outrageous **11** conspicuous

glaringly
06 openly **07** overtly **08** patently
09 blatantly, obviously **10** flagrantly, manifestly **13** conspicuously

glass
04 lens, opal, pony **05** loupe, poney, specs **06** beaker, copita, cullet, goblet, mirror, psyche, rummer **07** brimmer, crystal, monocle, opaline, sleever, tumbler, vitrail, vitrics **08** pince-nez
09 barometer, glassware, lorgnette
10 avanturine, aventurine, dildo-glass, eyeglasses, spectacles **12** opera-glasses, supernaculum **13** contact lenses

Glass sizes include:

03 pot, six, ten
04 pint
05 bobby, middy, seven
06 handle
07 butcher, sleever
08 half pint, schooner

• flaw in glass
04 tear

• substitute for glass
04 mica

glassy
03 icy **04** cold, dull **05** blank, clear, dazed, empty, fixed, glare, shiny
06 glazed, glazen, glossy, smooth, vacant **07** deadpan, hyaline, vacuous
08 lifeless, polished, slippery, unmoving, vitreous **09** glasslike
10 mirrorlike **11** transparent **12** crystal clear **14** expressionless

glaze
04 ciré, coat **05** aspic, cover, glass, gloss, shine, smear **06** enamel, finish, luster, lustre, polish, sancai **07** burnish, celadon, coating, eggwash, lacquer, varnish **08** tiger eye **09** peach-blow, tiger's eye

gleam
03 ray **04** beam, glow, leam, leme
05 blink, flame, flare, flash, glint, gloss, light, shaft, sheen, shine **06** glance, lustre **07** flicker, glimmer, glimpse, glisten, glitter, radiate, shimmer, sparkle
08 sun-blink **10** brightness, shimmering **11** scintillate

glean
04 cull, pick, reap **05** amass, learn, lease **06** garner, gather, pick up, select **07** collect, find out, harvest **10** accumulate

glee
03 fun, joy **04** gley **05** mirth, verve **06** gaiety, squint **07** delight, elation, jollity, triumph **08** gladness, hilarity, pleasure **09** joviality, merriment **10** exuberance, exultation, jocularity, joyfulness, joyousness, liveliness **12** cheerfulness, exhilaration **13** gratification

gleeful
05 happy, merry **06** elated, jovial, joyful, joyous **07** pleased **08** cheerful, exultant, jubilant, mirthful **09** cock-a-hoop, delighted, exuberant, gratified, overjoyed **10** triumphant **11** over the moon **14** beside yourself

gleefully
07 happily, merrily **08** joyfully, joyously **10** cheerfully, jubilantly **11** exuberantly **12** triumphantly

glen
03 cwm **04** gill **05** ghyll **10** depression

glib
04 easy **05** gabby, gassy, quick, ready, slick, suave **06** facile, fluent, smooth **07** voluble **08** castrate **09** insincere, plausible, talkative **10** loquacious **13** silver-tongued, smooth-talking, smooth-tongued

glibly
05 patly, slick **06** easily **07** quickly, slickly **08** fluently, smoothly **11** insincerely

glide
03 fly, run **04** cost, flow, pass, roll, sail, skim, slip, slur, soar, swan, swim **05** coast, coste, drift, float, lapse, skate, sleek, slide **06** vanish **07** scrieve **08** volplane **10** portamento **12** move smoothly

glimmer
03 ray **04** glow, hint, wink **05** blink, flash, gleam, glint, grain, shine, stime, styme, trace **07** flicker, glimpse, glisten, glitter, inkling, shimmer, sparkle, twinkle **10** suggestion

glimmering
04 clue, hint, idea, sign **06** notion **07** inkling, pointer, whisper **08** allusion, faintest, foggiest, innuendo **09** suspicion **10** indication, intimation, suggestion **11** insinuation

glimpse
03 spy **04** espy, glim, look, peek, peep, spot, view, waff **05** blink, flash, gliff, glift, glisk, sight, stime, styme, whiff **06** aperçu, glance, gledge, squint **08** sighting **09** brief look, foregleam, quick look **12** catch sight of

glint
05 flash, gleam, shine **07** glimmer, glisten, glitter, reflect, shimmer, sparkle, twinkle **10** glistening, reflection **11** scintillate

glisten
05 flash, gleam, glint, shine **07** flicker, glimmer, glitter, shimmer, sparkle, twinkle **09** coruscate

glitch
04 snag **05** block, catch, check, delay **06** hiccup, hold-up, mishap **07** barrier, problem, setback, trouble **08** drawback, obstacle **09** hindrance **10** difficulty, impediment **11** obstruction

glitter
04 gilt, glee **05** flare, flash, gleam, glint, glitz, sheen, shine **06** bicker, dazzle, lustre, tinsel **07** flicker, glamour, glimmer, glisten, glister, shimmer, spangle, sparkle, twinkle **08** radiance **09** coruscate, showiness, splendour **10** brightness, brilliance, flashiness, razzmatazz **11** coruscation, scintillate **12** razzle-dazzle **13** scintillation

glitz
05 swank **07** glitter, pizzazz **09** gaudiness, showiness **10** flashiness, garishness, razzmatazz **11** flamboyance, ostentation **12** razzle-dazzle **13** tastelessness **14** attractiveness **15** pretentiousness

glitzy
04 loud, posh **05** cheap, fancy, flash, gaudy, ritzy, showy, vivid **06** flashy, garish, ornate, swanky, tawdry **07** pompous **09** brilliant, tasteless **10** flamboyant, glittering **11** pretentious **12** ostentatious

gloat
04 crow **05** boast, exult, glory, vaunt **06** relish **07** rejoice, revel in, rub it in, triumph **09** delight in

global
05 total **07** general **08** thorough **09** spherical, universal, worldwide **10** exhaustive **11** wide-ranging **12** all-inclusive, encyclopedic **13** comprehensive, encyclopaedic, international **15** all-encompassing

globally
09 generally, worldwide **10** everywhere **11** in every land, under the sun, universally **12** in every place **14** in every country **15** internationally

globe
03 orb **04** ball, pome **05** earth, round, world **06** planet, sphere **08** roundure

globular
05 round **07** globate **08** spheroid **09** orbicular, spherical **10** ball-shaped

globule
04 ball, bead, blob, drop, pill **05** pearl **06** bubble, pellet **07** droplet, vesicle **08** globulet, particle, vesicula

gloom
03 woe **04** damp, dark, dusk, mirk, mood, murk **05** cloud, drere, grief, scowl, shade **06** dreare, misery, shadow, sorrow **07** despair, dimness, sadness **08** darkness, dullness, glumness, the blues, twilight **09** blackness, dejection, murkiness, obscurity, pessimism **10** cloudiness, depression, desolation, low spirits, melancholy, sullenness **11** despondency, unhappiness **12** hopelessness **14** discouragement

gloomily
05 sadly **06** glumly **08** dismally, drearily, morosely **09** miserably **11** cheerlessly **12** depressingly, despondently **13** downheartedly **15** pessimistically

gloomy
03 dim, low, sad, wan **04** dark, down, dull, glum, grim, mirk, murk **05** dingy, drear, dusky, heavy, morne, murky, sable, unlit **06** cloudy, dismal, dreary, drumly, morose, somber, sombre **07** obscure, shadowy, Stygian **08** darksome, dejected, desolate, downbeat, downcast, frowning, overcast **09** cheerless, Cimmerian, depressed, dyspeptic, miserable, saturnine, sorrowful, tenebrose, tenebrous **10** Acherontic, depressing, despondent, disastrous, dispirited, downlooked, melancholy, sepulchral, tenebrious **11** crepuscular, downhearted, dyspeptical, pessimistic **12** disconsolate, in low spirits **14** down in the dumps

• **gloomy appearance**
04 lour

glorification
06 avatar, praise **07** lauding, worship **08** doxology, thanking **09** adoration, extolling, gratitude, honouring, reverence **10** apotheosis, veneration **11** celebration, idolization, lionization **13** magnification **15** romanticization, transfiguration

glorify
04 hail, laud **05** adore, bless, exalt, extol, thank **06** honour, praise, revere **07** elevate, heroize, idolize, lionize, magnify, worship **08** emblazon, enshrine, eulogize, sanctify, venerate **09** celebrate **10** panegyrize **11** immortalize, romanticize, transfigure

glorious
04 fine **05** famed, grand, great, noble, noted, super, tipsy **06** bright, elated, famous, superb **07** eminent, perfect, radiant, shining, supreme **08** boastful, dazzling, gorgeous, heavenly, honoured, majestic, renowned, splendid, terrific **09** beautiful, brilliant, excellent, wonderful **10** celebrated, delightful, marvellous, triumphant, victorious **11** illustrious, magnificent **13** distinguished

glory
03 sun **04** crow, fame, halo, pomp **05** boast, crown, exult, gloat, kudos, revel, strut **06** beauty, diadem, gloire,

gloria, homage, honour, praise, relish, renown **07** acclaim, aureola, delight, dignity, garland, majesty, preface, rejoice, tribute, triumph, worship **08** accolade, blessing, doxology, eminence, gloriole, grandeur, prestige, radiance **09** adoration, celebrity, gratitude, greatness, splendour **10** brightness, brilliance, exaltation, veneration **11** distinction, recognition **12** magnificence, resplendence, thanksgiving **13** pride yourself **14** impressiveness **15** illustriousness

gloss
04 mask, note, show, veil **05** front, gleam, sheen, shine **06** define, façade, luster, lustre, polish, postil, veneer **07** comment, explain, shimmer, sparkle, surface, varnish **08** annotate, construe, disguise, footnote, scholion **09** elucidate, interpret, semblance, translate **10** annotation, appearance, brightness, brilliance, camouflage, commentary, definition **11** elucidation, explanation, explication, translation **12** add glosses to **14** interpretation, window-dressing

• **gloss over**
04 fard, gild, hide, mask, veil **05** avoid, evade **06** ignore, soothe **07** conceal, cover up **08** disguise **09** whitewash **10** camouflage, double-gild, smooth over **11** explain away **13** draw a veil over **15** deal with quickly

glossary
05 index **06** clavis **07** lexicon **08** wordbook, word list **09** thesaurus **10** dictionary **11** concordance

glossy
05 glacé, shiny, silky, sleek, slick **06** bright, glassy, glazed, polite, sheeny, silken, smooth **07** shining, wet-look **08** gleaming, lustrous, polished **09** brilliant, burnished, enamelled, sparkling **10** shimmering

glove
03 kid **04** gage, left, mitt **05** right **06** beaver, cestus, mitten, muffle **07** caestus, chevron **08** cheveron, gauntlet **09** oven glove

glow
04 burn, leam, leme, rose **05** bloom, blush, flush, gleam, glory, light, shine **06** ardour, colour, redden, warmth **07** burning, fervour, glimmer, passion, radiate, redness, sunglow **08** grow pink, look pink, outflush, pinkness, radiance, richness, rosiness, smoulder **09** afterglow, corposant, happiness, intensity, reddening, splendour, vividness **10** brightness, brilliance, enthusiasm, excitement, luminosity **11** gegenschein, St Elmo's fire **12** satisfaction **13** incandescence **15** phosphorescence

glower
04 look **05** frown, glare, scowl, stare **09** black look, dirty look **11** look daggers

glowing
03 red **04** rave, rich, warm **05** ruddy, vivid **06** bright, fervid **07** candent, flaming, flushed, lambent, radiant, vibrant **08** ecstatic, luminous, rutilant **09** laudatory, rhapsodic **10** candescent, eulogistic, favourable **11** noctilucent, noctilucous, panegyrical, smouldering **12** enthusiastic, incandescent **13** complimentary **14** phosphorescent

glue
03 fix, gum **04** bond, grip, seal, size **05** affix, epoxy, paste, rivet, stick **06** absorb, cement, compel, engage, mortar **07** engross, gelatin **08** adhesive, Araldite®, fixative, gelatine, propolis **09** hypnotize, mesmerize **11** agglutinate **12** conglutinate, ichthyocolla **14** impact adhesive

gluey
05 gummy **06** sticky, viscid **07** viscous **08** adhesive **09** glutinous

glum
03 low, sad **04** down, sour **05** gruff, moody, sulky, surly **06** gloomy, grumpy, morose, solemn, sullen **07** crabbed, doleful, forlorn, unhappy **08** churlish, dejected **09** depressed, miserable **10** despondent **11** crestfallen, ill-humoured, pessimistic **14** down in the dumps

glumly
05 sadly **06** sourly **08** gloomily, gruffily, grumpily, morosely, sullenly **09** forlornly, miserably, unhappily **10** dejectedly **12** despondently

glut
04 clog, cram, fill, sate **05** choke, flood, gorge, stuff **06** deluge, excess **07** engorge, satiate, surfeit, surplus **08** inundate, overfeed, overflow, overload, saturate **10** oversupply, saturation **11** superfluity **13** overabundance **14** superabundance

glutinous
04 limy, ropy **05** gluey, gummy, ropey **06** mucous, sticky, viscid **07** viscous **08** adhesive, cohesive **09** emplastic **12** mucilaginous

• **glutinous formation**
04 rope

glutton
03 pig **06** gorger, gutser, gutzer **07** gobbler, guzzler, lurcher **08** belly-god, carcajou, gourmand **09** cormorant, free-liver, wolverine **10** greedy guts **11** gormandizer

gluttonous
05 gutsy **06** greedy **07** hoggish, piggish **08** edacious, esurient, gourmand, ravenous **09** rapacious, voracious **10** gluttonish, insatiable, omnivorous **12** gormandizing

gluttony
05 greed **07** edacity, surfeit **08** gulosity, voracity **09** esurience **10** gormandize, greediness **11** gourmandism, piggishness **13** insatiability

G-man
03 fed

gnarled
◇ *anagram indicator*
05 bumpy, lumpy, rough **06** gnarly, knotty, knurly, rugged **07** gnarred, knarred, knotted, twisted **08** leathery, wrinkled **09** contorted, distorted **13** weather-beaten

gnash
04 grit **05** grate, grind **06** scrape

gnaw
03 eat, nag **04** bite, chew, fret, prey, wear **05** erode, harry, haunt, munch, worry **06** crunch, devour, harass, nibble, niggle, plague **07** consume, eat away, torment, trouble **09** masticate

gnome
03 saw **05** adage, dwarf, maxim, motto **06** goblin, kobold, saying **07** proverb **08** aphorism **09** financier

go
03 act, bet, bid, die, fit, gae, gee, get, pep, run, try, zip **04** bash, bout, cark, deal, emit, fail, fare, gang, go by, grow, hark, head, kark, lead, life, move, pass, push, quit, scat, shot, span, stab, suit, turn, walk, work, yead, yede, yeed, zing **05** begin, blend, crack, croak, drive, drown, end up, fit in, force, lapse, leave, match, occur, oomph, reach, ready, scoot, scram, sound, spell, stake, start, whirl **06** accord, affair, beat it, be axed, become, be kept, belong, cark it, depart, effort, elapse, energy, expire, extend, go away, kark it, manage, matter, pan out, pass by, pass on, peg out, perish, pop off, repair, result, roll on, set off, set out, slip by, spirit, spread, starve, travel, unfold, vanish, vigour **07** advance, attempt, bargain, be fired, be found, be given, be spent, carry on, decease, develop, give off, journey, make for, operate, perform, pizzazz, proceed, release, retreat, send out, snuff it, stretch, success, turn out, urinate, work out **08** activity, be sacked, be used up, clear off, come to be, continue, dynamism, function, get rid of, melt away, pass away, progress, slip away, tick away, vitality, withdraw **09** animation, be donated, be given to, be located, be pledged, be spent on, disappear, endeavour, eventuate, harmonize **10** be consumed, be finished, be situated, complement, co-ordinate, correspond, get-up-and-go, go together, make a sound, make tracks **11** be awarded to, be discarded, be dismissed, be exhausted, be presented, bite the dust **12** be allotted to, be assigned to, be thrown away, lose your life, pop your clogs, shoot through **13** be changed into, close your eyes, kick the bucket, push up daisies, take your leave **14** be given the push, be given the sack, be shown the door,

depart this life, give up the ghost **15** be made redundant, breathe your last, cash in your chips, go with each other

• **go about**

◇ *containment indicator*

02 do **04** stir **05** begin **06** tackle **07** address, perform **08** approach, attend to, embark on, engage in, set about **09** undertake

• **go ahead**

04 move **05** begin **07** advance, carry on, precede, proceed **08** continue, fire away, progress **12** make progress

• **go along with**

04 obey **06** accept, follow **07** abide by, support **09** accompany, agree with **10** comply with, concur with, fall in with

• **go and get**

03 fet **05** fetch

• **go around, go round**

◇ *anagram indicator*

◇ *containment indicator*

◇ *reversal indicator*

04 reel, spin, turn **05** swirl, twirl, twist, wheel, whirl, whirr **06** bypass, circle, gyrate, rotate, swivel **07** go about, revolve **09** circulate, pirouette, turn round **13** be passed round, be talked about **14** be spread around

• **go at**

05 argue, blame **06** attack, tackle **08** set about **09** criticize

• **go away**

04 scat **05** choof, hence, imshi, imshy, leave, scoot, scram, swith **06** begone, depart, vanish **07** abscond, do a bunk, gertcha, nick off, rack off, retreat **08** choof off, run for it, withdraw **09** disappear, do a runner **10** get knotted **13** sling your hook **14** make a bolt for it, run for your life **15** make a break for it, take to your heels

• **go back**

◇ *reversal indicator*

06 return, revert **07** regress, retreat **09** backslide

• **go back on**

◇ *reversal indicator*

04 deny **05** break **08** renege on **09** default on

• **go by**

04 flow, heed, obey, pass **05** lapse **06** elapse, follow **07** observe **10** comply with

• **go down**

03 dip, set **04** drop, fail, fall, fold, lose, sink **07** decline, descend, founder, go under, sustain **08** be beaten, collapse, decrease, fall down **09** be met with, be reduced **10** be defeated, be honoured, be received, be recorded, degenerate **11** be reacted to, be submerged, deteriorate **12** be recognized, be remembered, come a cropper, suffer defeat **15** have as a response

• **go down with**

05 catch **06** pick up **07** develop **08** contract **09** succumb to **12** come down with **13** be afflicted by

• **go for**

04 like **05** enjoy **06** admire, aim for, assail, attack, choose, favour, prefer, rush at, select **07** assault, lunge at **08** set about

• **go forward**

03 rip

• **go freely**

03 run

• **go in for**

05 adopt, enter **06** follow, go into, pursue, take up **07** embrace, espouse **08** engage in, practise **09** undertake **10** take part in **13** participate in

• **go into**

◇ *insertion indicator*

05 probe, study **06** review **07** analyse, discuss, dissect, examine **08** check out, consider, look into, research **09** delve into **10** scrutinize **11** inquire into, investigate

• **go off**

◇ *anagram indicator*

03 rot **04** quit, sour, turn **05** blast, burst, go bad, leave **06** blow up, depart, go bang, set out, vanish **07** abscond, be fired, explode, go stale **08** detonate **09** disappear **11** deteriorate **12** be discharged

• **go on**

03 gab, gas, hup **04** last, stay **05** occur **06** endure, happen, natter, rabbit, remain, witter **07** carry on, chatter, persist, proceed **08** continue, ramble on **09** take place

• **go out**

03 ebb **04** date, exit **05** court, leave **06** depart, go with **07** go round **08** go around, go steady, withdraw **11** be turned off **12** see each other **13** be switched off **14** be extinguished

• **go over**

04 list, read, scan **05** check, study **06** peruse, repeat, review, revise **07** discuss, examine, inspect **08** look over, rehearse **10** think about

• **go quickly**

03 cut, run, zap **04** hare, race, spin

• **go round**

04 ring, turn **06** rotate

• **go slow**

04 lose

• **go through**

04 bear, face, hunt **05** check, spend, stand, use up **06** endure, search, suffer **07** consume, examine, exhaust, explore, undergo **08** be passed, be signed, rehearse, squander, tolerate **09** be adopted, be carried, withstand **10** be accepted, be approved, experience, get through **11** be confirmed, investigate, look through **12** be authorized **13** be subjected to

• **go together**

◇ *juxtaposition indicator*

03 fit **04** suit **05** blend, match **06** accord **09** harmonize **10** complement, co-ordinate

• **go under**

◇ *juxtaposition down indicator*

03 die **04** fail, flop, fold, sink **05** drown **06** go bust, go down **07** default, founder, succumb **08** collapse, submerge **09** close down **10** go bankrupt **11** go to the wall **15** go out of business

• **go with**

03 fit **04** suit, take **05** blend, match, usher **06** escort **09** accompany, harmonize **10** complement, co-ordinate, correspond

• **go without**

04 lack, want **05** forgo **06** forego **07** abstain **09** do without **12** deny yourself **13** manage without

• **tell to go**

04 send

goad

03 gad, nag, vex **04** brod, jolt, prod, push, spur, urge **05** ankus, annoy, drive, hound, impel, prick, sound, sting, taunt **06** arouse, harass, incite, induce, needle, prompt **07** inspire, provoke **08** irritate, motivate **09** instigate, stimulate **10** cattle prod, pressurize

go-ahead

02 OK **05** pushy **06** assent **07** consent, dashing, dynamic, forward **08** approval, sanction, thumbs-up, vigorous, warranty **09** agreement, ambitious, clearance, energetic, go-getting **10** aggressive, green light, permission, pioneering **11** opportunist, progressive, resourceful, up-and-coming **12** confirmation, enterprising **13** authorization **14** forward-looking

goal

03 aim, end **04** cage, dool, dule, hail, home, mark, race **05** bourn, grail, ideal, limit **06** bourne, design, object, target **07** purpose **08** ambition, boundary, terminus **09** direction, equalizer, intention, objective **10** aspiration **11** competition, destination

• **prevent goal**

04 save

goat

03 bok, kid **04** gate, ibex, tahr, tehr, thar **05** nanny **06** Angora, butter, caprid, lecher, Saanen **07** bucardo, markhor **09** Capricorn

goat-antelope

05 goral, serow **07** chamois

goatsucker

06 evejar **07** bullbat, dorhawk, fern-owl **08** churn-owl, nightjar, poorwill **09** nighthawk **10** moth-hunter, night-churr **11** screech-hawk **12** mosquito hawk, whippoorwill **15** chuck-will's-widow

gobble

◇ *containment indicator*

04 bolt, cram, gulp, wolf **05** gorge, scoff, snarf, stuff **06** devour, guzzle **07** consume, put away, slabber, slubber, swallow **10** eat quickly

gobbledygook

06 drivel, jargon **07** prattle, rubbish, twaddle **08** nonsense **09** buzz words, gibberish **10** balderdash, journalese

11 computerese, officialese
12 psychobabble

go-between
05 agent **06** broker, dealer, factor, medium **07** contact, liaison **08** mediator **09** messenger, middleman **10** love-broker **11** ring-carrier **12** intermediary

goblet
03 cup **05** glass, hanap **06** beaker
07 chalice, stem cup, tumbler

goblin
03 elf, imp, nis, pug **04** bogy, puck **05** bogey, bogle, demon, fiend, gnome, nisse, nixie, pooka, pouke, troll **06** bodach, duende, Empusa, kelpie, kobold, redcap, spirit, sprite **07** bargest, brownie, gremlin, knocker, red-cowl **08** barghest **09** barghaist, gobbeline, hobgoblin **10** leprechaun, shellycoat **11** lubber fiend **12** esprit follet

gobsmacked
04 dumb **06** amazed, thrown
07 baffled, floored, shocked, stunned
08 confused, overcome, startled
09 astounded, paralysed, staggered
10 astonished, bewildered, bowled over, confounded, nonplussed, speechless, taken aback
11 dumbfounded, overwhelmed
12 lost for words **13** flabbergasted, knocked for six

God
01 D **02** od **03** dod, dog, gad, Gog, gum, Jah, odd **04** Dieu, gosh, King, Lord, Zeus **05** Allah, Deity, Judge, Maker, monad **06** Brahma, Elohim, Father, Yahweh **07** all-seer, Bhagwan, Creator, Eternal, Godhead, Holy One, Jehovah, Saviour **08** all-giver, Almighty, gracious, infinite **09** All-father **10** first cause, prime mover, Providence **11** Divine Being, Everlasting, king of kings **12** Supreme Being

• **God willing**
02 DV **09** inshallah **10** Deo volente, volente Deo

god, goddess
02 as **04** aitu, cock, deus, deva, Fate, faun, icon, idol, kami, Muse, Norn **05** deify, deity, Grace, Norna, power **06** spirit, sylvan **08** divinity **09** promachos **11** divine being, graven image

Babylonian gods include:

02 Ea
03 Anu, Bel, Sin
04 Adad, Apsu, Baal, Enki, Nabu
05 Ellil, Enlil, Hadad, Mummu
06 Anshar, Dumuzi, Marduk, Nergal, Tammuz
07 Ninurta, Shamash, Thammuz

Babylonian goddesses include:

03 Aja
04 Antu
05 Antum, Belit, Nintu
06 Ishtar, Kishar, Ningal, Ninlil, Nintur, Tiamat
07 Anunitu, Damkina
10 Ereshkigal

Central and South American gods include:

04 Chac, Inti
06 Tlaloc
07 Huang-ti, Hunab Ku, Itzamma
08 Catequil, Kukulkan
09 the Bacabs, Viracocha, Xipe Totec
10 Apu Punchau, Manco Capac, Pachacamac, Xochipilli
12 Quetzalcoatl, Tezcatlipoca, Xiuhtecuhtli
15 Huitzilopochtil

Central and South American goddesses include:

05 Aknah
06 Ixchel
09 Coatlicue, Ixazaluoh, Mama Oella, Pachamama
10 Mama Quilla
11 Tlazolteotl
12 Xochiquetzal
15 Chalchiuhtlicue

Egyptian gods include:

02 Ra, Re
03 Bes, Geb, Nut
04 Apis, Aten, Atum, Ptah, Seth
05 Horus, Thoth
06 Amun-Re, Anubis, Osiris
07 Khonsou, Sarapis, Serapis

Egyptian goddesses include:

03 Nut
04 Isis, Maat
05 Khnum
06 Hathor, Sakmet, Sekmet
07 Nepthys, Sakhmet, Sekhmet
08 Nephthys

Greek gods include:

03 Pan
04 Ares, Atys, Eros, Zeus
05 Atlas, Attis, Hades
06 Adonis, Aeolus, Apollo, Boreas, Cronus, Helios, Hermes, Hypnos, Nereus
07 Oceanus
08 Dionysus, Ganymede, Morpheus, Poseidon, Thanatos
09 Asclepius
10 Hephaestus
11 Aesculapius

Greek goddesses include:

03 Eos, Nyx
04 Gaea, Gaia, Hebe, Hera, Iris, Nike, Rhea
05 Tyche
06 Athene, Cybele, Hecate, Hestia, Hygeia, Selene, Themis, Thetis
07 Alphito, Artemis, Demeter, Erinyes, Nemesis
08 Arethusa, the Fates, the Horae, the Muses
09 Aphrodite, the Furies, the Graces
10 Persephone

Hindu gods include:

04 Agni, Kama, Rama, Siva, Soma, Yama
05 Indra, Kurma, Radha, Rudra, Shani, Shiva, Surya
06 Brahma, Ganesa, Ganesh, Garuda, Iswara, Narada, Pushan, Ravana, Skanda, Varuna, Vishnu
07 Ganesha, Hanuman, Krishna, Savitri
08 Ganapati, Nataraja
09 Kartikeya, Lakshmana, Narasimha, Prajapati
10 Jagannatha

Hindu goddesses include:

03 Uma
04 Devi, Kali, Maya, Sita
05 Aditi, Durga, Gauri, Radha, Sakti
06 Shakti
07 Lakshmi, Parvati
09 Sarasvati

Maori gods include:

02 Tu
03 Uru
04 Maui, Tane
05 Rangi, Rongo
06 Haumia
07 Tawhiri
08 Ranginui, Ruaumoko, Tangaroa
10 Tane Mahuta
11 Rongomatane, Tumatauenga
12 Tawhiri Matea

Maori goddesses include:

04 Papa
10 Hinetitama
11 Hinenuitepo, Papatuanuku

Norse gods include:

03 Bor, Otr, Tyr, Ull
04 Frey, Logi, Loki, Odin, Thor
05 Aegir, Aesir, Alcis, Bragi, Donar, Freyr, Hoder, Mimir, Njord, Vanir, Vidar, Woden, Wotan
06 Balder, Fafnir, Hermod, Hoenir, Kvasir, Weland
07 Volundr, Wayland, Weiland
08 Heimdall

Norse goddesses include:

03 Hel, Ran, Sif
04 Hela
05 Frigg, Idunn, Nanna, Norns, Sigyn
06 Freyja, Gefion
07 Nerthus
08 Fjorgynn
09 Valkyries
10 Nehallenia

Roman gods include:

04 Mars
05 Cupid, Fides, Janus, Lares, Orcus, Picus, Pluto
06 Apollo, Consus, Faunus, Genius, Mithra, Saturn, Vulcan
07 Bacchus, Jupiter, Mercury, Mithras, Neptune, Penates
08 Portunus, Silvanus
09 Vertumnus
10 Liber Pater

Roman goddesses include:

03 Ops
04 Juno, Luna, Maia
05 Ceres, Diana, Epona, Fauna, Flora, Pales, Venus, Vesta
06 Pomona, Rumina
07 Bellona, Egreria, Feronia, Fortuna, Minerva
08 Libitina, Victoria
10 Proserpina

Gods and goddesses of other regions and cultures include:

03 Rod, Wak
04 Amma, Kane, Tane
05 Epona, Pan Gu, Perun
06 Guan Di, Inanna, Kuan Ti, Mithra, Modimo, Moloch, Shango, Svarog, Tengri, Teshub, Vahagn
07 Anahita, Astarte, Kumarbi, Taranis, Triglav, Zanhary
08 Rosmerta, Skyamsen, Sucellus, Teutates
09 Amaterasu, Sventovit
10 Ahura Mazda
11 Thunderbird
15 Izanagi no Mikoto, Izanami no Mikoto

god-forsaken
05 bleak **06** dismal, dreary, gloomy, lonely, remote **07** forlorn **08** deserted, desolate, isolated, wretched
09 abandoned, miserable **10** depressing

godless
03 bad **04** evil **05** pagan **06** sinful, unholy, wicked **07** atheous, heathen, immoral, impious, profane, ungodly
08 agnostic **09** atheistic, faithless
10 irreverent **11** irreligious, nullifidian, unrighteous **12** sacrilegious

godlessness
07 atheism, impiety **08** paganism
10 irreligion, wickedness
11 agnosticism, irreverence, ungodliness **13** faithlessness
14 unfaithfulness

godlike
04 holy **06** divine, sacred **07** deiform, exalted, perfect, saintly, sublime
08 heavenly, Olympian **09** celestial
10 superhuman **11** theomorphic
12 transcendent

godliness
05 piety **06** belief, purity **08** holiness, morality, religion, sanctity
10 devoutness **13** righteousness

godly
04 good, holy, pure, wise **05** moral, pious **06** devout **07** saintly
08 innocent, virtuous **09** believing, religious, righteous **10** God-fearing

godsend
04 boon **07** bonanza, miracle
08 blessing, windfall **11** benediction
12 stroke of luck

goggle
04 gawk, gawp, gaze, ogle **05** stare
06 wonder **08** protrude

going-over
03 row **05** check, study **06** attack, rebuke, review, survey **07** beating, check-up, chiding, pasting **08** analysis, scolding, scrutiny, whipping
09 criticism, reprimand, thrashing, trouncing **10** inspection
11 castigation, examination
12 chastisement, dressing-down
13 investigation

goings-on
06 events, scenes **07** affairs
08 business, mischief **09** behaviour
10 activities, happenings
11 occurrences **12** misbehaviour
13 funny business

gold
02 Au, or **03** bar, Sol **04** gool, gule, leaf
05 goold, ingot **06** nugget, riches, yellow **07** bullion **12** king of metals
13 precious metal

• **yield gold**
03 pan

golden
03 red **04** fair, gilt, gold, rosy **05** blond, happy, sunny **06** blonde, bright, flaxen, gilded, gilden, gylden, joyful, yellow
07 aureate, goldish, luteous, shining
08 aurelian, dazzling, gleaming, glorious, inaurate, lustrous, precious
09 brilliant, excellent, promising, rewarding, Saturnian, treasured
10 auspicious, delightful, favourable, millennial, propitious, prosperous, successful **11** flourishing, hyacinthine, resplendent **12** gold-coloured

goldfinch
06 redcap **09** goldspink, gowdspink
10 yellowbird

golf
01 G **04** gowf

Golf courses include:

04 Deal, Eden
05 Troon
06 Manito, Merion, Skokie
07 Balgove, Buffalo, Hoylake, Jubilee, Medinah, Newport, Oak Hill, Oakmont, Oak Tree, Prince's, Sahalee
08 Bethesda, Birkdale, Blue Hill, Glen View, Portland, Sandwich, Valhalla
09 Aronimink, Baltimore, Baltusrol, Bellerive, Brookline, Englewood, Hazeltine, Inverness, Minikahda, Muirfield, New Course, Old Course, Onwentsia, Pinehurst, Prestwick, St Andrews, The Belfry, Turnberry
10 Canterbury, Carnoustie, Garden City, Royal Troon, Shoal Creek, Tanglewood, Winged Foot
11 Cherry Hills, Kemper Lakes, Miami Valley, Musselburgh, Olympic Club, Pebble Beach, Strathtyrum
12 Crooked Stick, Laurel Valley, Oakland Hills
13 Northwood Club, Olympia Fields, Royal Birkdale, Royal Portrush, Southern Hills
14 Keller Golf Club, Myopia Hunt Club, NCR Country Club, Pelham Golf Club
15 Augusta National, Chicago Golf Club, Shinnecock Hills

golf club

Golf clubs include:

04 iron, wood
05 baffy, blade, cleek, mashy, spoon, wedge
06 brassy, bulger, driver, jigger, mashie, putter
07 blaster, brassie, midiron, niblick
08 long iron
09 midmashie, sand wedge, short iron
10 mashie iron
11 belly putter, driving iron, fairway wood, spade mashie
12 putting-cleek
13 mashie-niblick, pitching wedge, two-ball putter
15 pitching niblick

golfer
06 gowfer, yipper

Golfers include:

03 **Els** (Ernie)
04 **Lyle** (Sandy), **Webb** (Karrie)
05 **Braid** (James), **Brown** (Ken), **Duval** (David), **Faldo** (Nick), **Floyd** (Raymond), **Hagen** (Walter), **Hogan** (Ben), **Jones** (Bobby), **Locke** (Bobby), **Lopez** (Nancy), **Singh** (Vijay), **Snead** (Sam Jackson), **Woods** (Tiger)
06 **Alliss** (Peter), **Cotton** (Sir Henry), **Davies** (Laura), **Garcia** (Sergio), **Langer** (Bernhard), **Nelson** (Byron), **Norman** (Greg), **O'Meara** (Mark), **Palmer** (Arnold), **Player** (Gary), **Taylor** (John), **Vardon** (Harry), **Watson** (Tom)
07 **Charles** (Bob), **Couples** (Fred), **Jacklin** (Tony), **Sarazen** (Gene), **Stewart** (Payne), **Strange** (Curtis), **Thomson** (Peter), **Trevino** (Lee Buck), **Woosnam** (Ian), **Zoeller** (Fuzzy)
08 **Crenshaw** (Ben), **Nicklaus** (Jack), **Olazábal** (Jose Maria), **Torrance** (Sam), **Westwood** (Lee), **Zaharias** (Babe)
09 **Mickelson** (Phil), **Sorenstam** (Annika), **Whitworth** (Kathy)
11 **Ballesteros** (Severiano), **Montgomerie** (Colin)

gone
◇ *anagram indicator*
03 ago, ygo **04** away, dead, done, gane, lost, over, past, used, ygoe
05 agone, spent **06** absent, astray
07 defunct, elapsed, extinct, missing, worn-out **08** departed, finished, vanished **11** disappeared **15** over and done with

goo
03 mud **04** crud, grot, gunk, mire, muck, ooze, scum, slop, yuck

05 gloop, grime, gunge, slime, slush **06** grease, grunge, matter, sludge **10** stickiness **14** sentimentality

good
01 g **02** OK **03** bad, bon, fab, fit, rum, top, use **04** able, best, dear, fair, fine, gain, kind, mega, neat, nice, safe, sake, true, well **05** adept, avail, beaut, bewdy, bonne, bosom, brill, bully, close, great, large, lucky, merit, moral, nasty, noble, pakka, pious, pucka, pukka, right, sound, super, valid, whole, worth **06** agreed, behalf, bonzer, bosker, castor, clever, corker, cushty, ethics, expert, gifted, honest, honour, indeed, just so, loving, morals, polite, profit, ripper, strong, superb, useful, virtue, wicked, worthy **07** awesome, benefit, capable, ethical, fitting, genuine, healthy, helpful, honesty, perfect, purpose, service, sizable, skilful, skilled, upright, welfare **08** adequate, all right, budgeree, cheerful, complete, cracking, fabulous, faithful, friendly, goodness, gracious, interest, intimate, morality, obedient, passable, pleasant, pleasing, reliable, sensible, sizeable, smashing, suitable, superior, talented, terrific, thorough, very well, vigorous, virtuous **09** admirable, advantage, agreeable, bodacious, brilliant, competent, compliant, desirable, dexterous, efficient, enjoyable, excellent, exemplary, fantastic, first-rate, fortunate, integrity, in the pink, rectitude, righteous, tolerable, wellbeing, wonderful **10** acceptable, altruistic, auspicious, beneficial, benevolent, charitable, convenient, convincing, dependable, favourable, first-class, good as gold, honourable, marvellous, persuasive, proficient, profitable, propitious, prosperity, reasonable, respectful, satisfying, sufficient, thoughtful, usefulness, worthwhile **11** appropriate, commendable, considerate, convenience, exceptional, kind-hearted, pleasurable, serviceable, substantial, sympathetic, trustworthy, uprightness, well-behaved **12** accomplished, advantageous, bewdy bottler, considerable, fit as a fiddle, professional, satisfactory, under control, well-disposed, well-mannered **13** hale and hearty, philanthropic, righteousness **14** salt of the earth

• **for good**
04 ever **06** always **07** for ever **08** evermore, for keeps **09** eternally **10** for all time **11** irrevocably, permanently **15** till kingdom come

• **make good**
02 do **04** abet **05** go far **06** arrive, effect, fulfil, make it, recoup, repair, supply **07** justify, perform, restore, succeed, support **08** carry out, get ahead, live up to, progress, put right, retrieve **09** establish **10** compensate **12** be successful **13** compensate for, make amends for, put into action **15** get on in the world

• **neither good nor bad**
04 so-so **14** comme çi comme ça

• **no good**
02 ng **03** bad, bum **04** duff **06** futile, no chop **07** useless **09** worthless

• **pretty good**
04 fair, tidy **06** decent, not bad **08** middling **09** tolerable **14** fair to middling

• **unusually good**
04 gear **10** incredible

• **very good**
02 OK, so, vg **03** sae, top **04** keen, mega **05** bonza, grand **06** bangin', beezer, bonzer, boshta, bosker, grouse, peachy **07** banging, boshter, crucial, immense, ripping **08** all right, cracking, terrific **09** brilliant **10** marvellous, tremendous

goodbye
03 bye **04** ciao, ta-ta **05** addio, adieu, adiós, later **06** bye-bye, cheers, hooray, hooroo, kia ora, haere ra, see you, so long, valete **07** bonsoir, cheerio, good-day, good-den, good-e'en, parting **08** au revoir, chin-chin, farewell, good-even, sayonara, swan song, take care, toodle-oo **09** bon voyage, good night, toodle-pip **10** all the best, a rivederci, good morrow **11** arrivederci, be seeing you, good evening, good morning, leave-taking, see you later, valediction, valedictory **12** have a nice day, mind how you go, see you around **13** good afternoon **14** auf Wiedersehen

See also **farewell**

good-for-nothing
03 bum **04** idle, lazy **05** idler, lorel, losel, stiff **06** donnat, donnot, loafer, lozell, no-good, skiver, waster **07** bludger, lorrell, sculpin, slacker, useless, vaurien, wastrel **08** feckless, indolent, layabout, scalawag **09** lazybones, reprobate, scallawag, scallywag, worthless **10** black sheep, ne'er-do-weel, ne'er-do-well, profligate **11** scant-o'-grace **13** irresponsible

good-humoured
05 happy **06** genial, jovial **07** affable, amiable **08** cheerful, friendly, pleasant **09** congenial **12** approachable, good-tempered

good-looking
04 fair **05** dishy **06** comely, goodly, lovely, pretty **08** handsome, weel-far'd, weel-far't **09** beautiful, weel-faird, weel-faur'd, weel-faurt **10** attractive, personable **11** presentable **12** well-favoured

goodly
04 fine, good, tidy **05** ample, large **06** comely, proper **07** sizable **08** sizeable **09** excellent **10** sufficient **11** good-looking, significant, substantial **12** considerable

good-natured
04 kind, nice **05** sonsy **06** clever, gentle, kindly, sonsie **07** helpful, patient **08** friendly, generous, tolerant **10** benevolent **11** kind-hearted, neighbourly, sympathetic, warm-hearted **12** approachable, good-tempered

goodness
02 my **03** boy, law, wow **05** mercy, value **06** virtue **07** benefit, honesty, probity **08** altruism, goodwill, kindness **09** integrity, rectitude **10** compassion, excellence, generosity **11** beneficence, benevolence, helpfulness, uprightness **12** friendliness, graciousness **13** righteousness, unselfishness, wholesomeness

goods
04 bona, gear **05** lines, stock, stuff, wares **06** taonga, things **07** effects, freight **08** chattels, products, property **10** belongings **11** commodities, merchandise, possessions **13** accoutrements, appurtenances, paraphernalia

• **package of goods**
04 bale, wrap

good-tempered
04 kind **06** gentle, kindly **07** helpful, patient **08** friendly, generous, tolerant **10** benevolent **11** good-natured, kind-hearted, neighbourly, sympathetic, warm-hearted **12** approachable

goodwill
04 gree, zeal **05** amity, favor **06** favour **08** kindness **10** compassion, friendship, generosity **11** benevolence, well-wishing **12** friendliness

goody-goody
05 pious **08** priggish, unctuous **13** sanctimonious, self-righteous, ultra-virtuous

gooey
04 soft **05** gluey, gucky, gungy, gunky, tacky, thick **06** gloopy, sickly, sloppy, slushy, sticky, syrupy, viscid **07** cloying, maudlin, mawkish, squidgy, viscous **09** glutinous **10** nauseating **11** sentimental **12** mucilaginous

goose
04 nene, wavy **05** roger, wavey **06** gander, goslet **07** gosling, grey-lag **08** barnacle **09** whitehead **10** saddleback **13** brent barnacle

See also **fool**

• **goose's lungs**
04 soul

gooseberry
06 groser, groset **07** grosert **08** goosegob, goosegog, grossart **09** honey-blob **14** worcesterberry

goosefoot
04 beet **05** blite, orach **06** fat hen, kochia, orache, quinoa, saxaul **07** pigweed, saksaul **08** saltbush, saltwort, seablite **10** greasewood, Mexican tea **13** good-King-Henry

gore
02 Al **04** cloy, gair, horn, stab **05** blood, cruor, filth, grume, skirt, spear, stick, wound **06** engore, impale, pierce **07** carnage **08** butchery **09** bloodshed, penetrate, slaughter **10** bloodiness

gorge
03 gap **04** bolt, cram, feed, fill, glut, gulp, pass, rift, sate, wolf **05** abyss, cañon, chasm, cleft, gully, stuff **06** canyon, defile, devour, gobble, guzzle, ravine, stodge **07** crevice, fissure, overeat, surfeit, swallow **08** barranca

See also **ravine**

gorgeous
04 fine, good, rich, sexy **05** grand, showy, sweet **06** lovely, pretty, superb **07** opulent **08** dazzling, glorious, handsome, pleasing, splendid, stunning **09** beautiful, brilliant, enjoyable, glamorous, luxurious, ravishing, splendent, sumptuous, wonderful **10** attractive, delightful, impressive, marvellous **11** good-looking, magnificent, resplendent **15** pulchritudinous

gorgeously
06 richly **08** superbly **10** gloriously, splendidly **11** brilliantly, luxuriously, sumptuously, wonderfully **12** delightfully, impressively, marvellously **13** magnificently

gorilla
04 thug **05** pongo **08** King Kong **10** silverback

gorse
04 ulex, whin **05** furze, gosse

gory
05 goary **06** bloody, brutal, grisly, savage **07** violent **09** murderous **10** sanguinary **11** blood-soaked, distasteful **12** bloodstained

gospel
04 fact, John, Luke, Mark **05** credo, creed, truth **06** verity **07** evangel, kerygma, Matthew **08** doctrine, good news, teaching **09** certainty **12** life of Christ, New Testament **14** Protevangelium **15** message of Christ

See also **Bible**

gossamer
04 airy, fine, thin **05** gauzy, light, sheer, silky **06** flimsy **08** cobwebby, delicate **10** diaphanous, see-through, shimmering **11** translucent, transparent **13** insubstantial

gossip
03 ana, gab, gas, gup, jaw **04** aunt, buzz, chat, dirt, goss, talk **05** clash, crack, rumor, yenta **06** babble, claver, cummer, gabble, jabber, kimmer, natter, rabbit, report, rumour, tatler, tattle, tittle, waffle **07** babbler, blather, blether, chatter, chinwag, clatter, hearsay, prattle, scandal, shmoose, shmooze, tattler, whisper **08** busybody, causerie, chitchat, clatters, idle talk, prattler, rabbit on, schmooze, tell-tale **09** reportage, tell tales, whisperer **10** chatterbox, chew the fat, chew the rag, clish-clash, newsmonger, talebearer **11** mud-slinging, Nosey Parker, scuttlebutt, sweetie-wife **12** gossip-monger, spread gossip, tittle-tattle **13** bush telegraph, clishmaclaver, scandal-bearer, scandalmonger, smear campaign, spread a rumour **14** clash-ma-clavers

gouge
03 cut, dig **04** claw, gash, hack **05** scoop, score, slash, wench **06** chisel, groove, hollow, incise **07** extract, scratch, swindle

gourd
05 guiro, loofa, luffa **06** bryony, cacoon, loofah **07** pumpkin **08** calabash **11** white bryony **12** Hercules' club

Gourde
01 G **03** Gde

gourmand
03 hog, pig **06** gorger **07** glutton, guzzler **08** omnivore **09** voracious **10** gluttonous **11** gormandizer

gourmet
06 foodie **07** epicure **09** bon vivant, epicurean **10** gastronome **11** connoisseur

gout
04 drop, spot **05** taste **06** relish **07** podagra **08** chiragra **09** arthritis **10** cephalagra **12** hamarthritis

govern
03 run **04** curb, head, lead, rein, rule, sway, tame **05** check, guide, order, pilot, quell, reign, steer **06** bridle, direct, manage, master, rein in, subdue **07** command, conduct, contain, control, oversee, preside **08** dominate, hold back, keep back, regulate, restrain **09** be in power, constrain, determine, influence, supervise **10** administer, discipline, hold office **11** keep in check, superintend **12** be in charge of

governess
05 guide **06** duenna, mentor **07** teacher, tutress **08** fräulein, tutoress **09** companion **11** gouvernante **12** instructress, mademoiselle

governing
06 ruling **07** guiding, leading, supreme **08** dominant, reigning **09** kingcraft, uppermost **10** commanding, dominative, overriding, prevailing, regulatory **11** controlling, predominant **12** transcendent

government
01 g **03** Gov, HMG, raj **04** Govt, rule, sway **05** power, state **06** charge, circar, papacy, policy, régime, sircar, sirkar **07** cabinet, command, conduct, control, council, regence, regency, regimen, serkali **08** congress, dominion, guidance, ministry, politics, steerage **09** archology, authority, direction, executive, restraint **10** domination, governance, leadership, management, parliament, regulation **11** authorities, sovereignty, supervision **12** powers that be, surveillance **13** Establishment **14** administration **15** superintendence

Government systems include:

05 junta
06 empire
07 kingdom
08 monarchy, republic
09 autocracy, communism, democracy, despotism, theocracy
10 absolutism, federation, hierocracy, plutocracy
11 triumvirate
12 commonwealth, dictatorship

• member of government
02 in

governor
02 Pa **03** Ban, beg, bey, Dad, dey, gov, guv **04** boss, head, khan, naik, vali, wali **05** chief, guide, hakim, mudir, pilot, ruler, tutor **06** eparch, exarch, grieve, leader, legate, master, Pilate, rector, satrap, tuchun, warden **07** alcaide, alcayde, catapan, harmost, manager, nomarch, podestà, rectrix, subadar, vaivode, viceroy, voivode **08** alderman, burgrave, director, ethnarch, gospodar, hospodar, kaimakam, overseer, pentarch, provedor, providor, resident, subahdar **09** beglerbeg, castellan, commander, corrector, directrix, dominator, executive, governess, intendant, president, proconsul, provedore, regulator **10** adelantado, controller, directress, gubernator, Lord Warden, proveditor, stadholder, supervisor **11** proveditore, stadtholder **12** commissioner **13** administrator **14** chief executive, superintendent

Colonial governors of New South Wales:

04 **King** (Captain Philip Gidley)
05 **Bligh** (Captain William), **Gipps** (Sir George)
06 **Bourke** (Major-General Richard), **Hunter** (Captain John)
07 **Darling** (Lieutenant-General Ralph), **Denison** (Sir William), **FitzRoy** (Sir Charles), **Phillip** (Captain Arthur)
08 **Brisbane** (Sir Thomas)
09 **Macquarie** (Colonel Lachlan)

Governors-general of Australia:

04 **Kerr** (Sir John), **Slim** (Field-Marshal Sir William)
05 **Casey** (Richard Gardiner, Baron), **Cowen** (Sir Zelman), **Deane** (Sir William)
06 **Denman** (Thomas, Baron), **Dudley** (William Humble Ward, Earl of), **Gowrie** (Alexander Hore-Ruthven,

Baron), **Hayden** (William), **Isaacs** (Sir Isaac), **McKell** (Sir William)
07 **De L'Isle** (William, Viscount), **Forster** (Henry William, Baron), **Hasluck** (Sir Paul), **Stephen** (Sir Ninian)
08 **Hopetoun** (John Adrian Louis Hope, Earl of), **Tennyson** (Hallam, Baron)
09 **Dunrossil** (William, Viscount), **Northcote** (Henry, Baron)
10 **Gloucester** (Prince Henry, Duke of), **Stonehaven** (Sir John Lawrence Baird, Baron)
12 **Hollingworth** (Dr Peter)
13 **Munro-Ferguson** (Sir Ronald)

Governors-general of New Zealand:

06 **Cobham** (Charles George Lyttleton), **Galway** (Earl of), **Newall** (Cyril Louis Norton), **Norrie** (Lord), **Reeves** (Paul Alfred), **Tizard** (Catherine)
07 **Beattie** (David Stuart), **Porritt** (Arthur Espie)
08 **Blundell** (Edward Denis), **Freyberg** (Bernard Cyril), **Holyoake** (Keith Jacka), **Jellicoe** (John Henry Rushworth)
09 **Bledisloe** (Charles Bathurst), **Fergusson** (Bernard), **Fergusson** (Charles), **Liverpool** (Earl of)
10 **Hardie Boys** (Michael)

Governors of New Zealand:

04 **Grey** (George), **Weld** (Frederick Aloysius)
05 **Bowen** (Charles Ferguson)
06 **Browne** (Thomas Robert Gore), **Gordon** (Arthur Hamilton), **Hobson** (William), **Onslow** (Earl of), **Onslow** (William Hillier)
07 **FitzRoy** (Robert), **Glasgow** (Earl of), **Jervois** (William Francis Drummond), **Plunket** (Lord)
08 **Normanby** (Marquess of), **Ranfurly** (Earl of), **Robinson** (Hercules George Robert)
09 **Fergusson** (James), **Islington** (Lord), **Liverpool** (Earl of)

gown
04 garb, robe, sack, silk **05** bania, dress, frock, habit, manto, shift, stole **06** banian, banyan, kirtle, mantua, sacque **07** costume, garment, manteau, negligé **08** mazarine, negligee, peignoir **09** sack dress, slammakin **10** slammerkin **12** bearing cloth, dressing-gown **13** Mother Hubbard

grab
◇ *containment indicator*
03 bag, nab, rap **04** grip, nail, take **05** annex, catch, grasp, pluck, seize, swipe, usurp **06** arrest, clutch, collar, nobble, snap up, snatch **07** capture, impress **08** interest **09** lay hold of **10** commandeer, take hold of **11** appropriate, catch hold of
See also **steal**

• **up for grabs**
06 at hand **07** to be had **09** available **10** obtainable **12** for the asking

grace
04 ease, trim **05** adorn, charm, honor, mense, mercy, poise, Venus **06** beauty, become, enrich, favour, honour, pardon, polish, prayer, set off, virtue **07** aggrace, charity, decency, decorum, dignify, enhance, finesse, fluency, garnish, manners, quarter, unction **08** beautify, blessing, breeding, clemency, courtesy, decorate, elegance, goodness, goodwill, kindness, leniency, ornament, reprieve **09** bethankit, embellish, etiquette, good taste, propriety **10** benedicite, comeliness, compassion, generosity, indulgence, kindliness, loveliness, refinement, smoothness **11** benediction, beneficence, benevolence, cultivation, distinguish, forgiveness, shapeliness **12** gracefulness, mercifulness, tastefulness, thanksgiving **13** consideration **14** attractiveness, prayer of thanks

The Three Graces:

06 Aglaia, Thalia
10 Euphrosyne

graceful
04 deft, easy, fine, kind **05** agile, fluid, genty, suave **06** comely, fluent, gainly, nimble, polite, smooth, supple, svelte **07** elegant, flowing, genteel, natural, refined, slender, tactful, willowy **08** charming, cheerful, cultured, generous, gracious, grazioso, pleasant, polished, sylphine, sylphish, tasteful **09** agreeable, appealing, beautiful, courteous, sylphlike **10** attractive, cultivated, diplomatic, respectful

gracefully
06 deftly, nimbly **08** grazioso, politely, smoothly **09** agreeably, elegantly, naturally, tactfully **10** cheerfully, generously, graciously, pleasantly, tastefully **11** beautifully, courteously **12** attractively, respectfully **14** diplomatically

graceless
04 rude **05** crude, gawky, rough **06** clumsy, coarse, forced, gauche, vulgar **07** awkward, uncouth **08** impolite, improper, ungainly **09** barbarous, inelegant, menseless, shameless **10** indecorous, ungraceful, unmannerly **11** ill-mannered **12** unattractive **15** unsophisticated

gracelessly
06 rudely **07** roughly **08** clumsily **09** awkwardly **10** impolitely **11** inelegantly **12** ungracefully

gracious
04 hend, kind, mild **05** sweet **06** benign, kindly, polite **07** affable, clement, elegant, lenient, refined **08** friendly, generous, handsome, menseful, merciful, obliging, pleasant, tasteful **09** benignant, courteous, forgiving, indulgent, luxurious, sumptuous **10** acceptable, beneficent, benevolent, charitable, favourable, hospitable **11** comfortable, considerate, kind-hearted, magnanimous **12** well-mannered **13** accommodating, compassionate, condescending

graciously
06 goodly, kindly **07** civilly **08** politely **09** tactfully **10** handsomely, pleasantly **11** courteously **12** respectfully **14** diplomatically

gradation
04 mark, rank, step **05** array, cline, level, stage **06** ablaut, change, degree, series **07** grading, shading, sorting **08** ordering, progress, sequence **10** succession **11** arrangement, progression

grade
03 gon **04** mark, rank, rate, rung, size, sort, step, type **05** brand, class, group, label, level, notch, order, place, range, stage, value **06** assess, degree, rating, status **07** arrange, echelon, quality, station **08** category, classify, evaluate, position, standard, standing **09** condition **10** categorize, pigeonhole **14** classification

• **equivalent grade**
02 EG

• **first grade**
05 alpha

• **fourth grade**
05 delta

• **make the grade**
04 pass **07** succeed **10** win through **11** come through **13** cut the mustard **15** come up to scratch

• **second grade**
04 beta

• **third grade**
05 gamma

gradient
04 bank, hill, rise **05** grade, lapse, slope **07** incline **09** acclivity, declivity

gradual
04 easy, even, slow **05** grail **06** gentle, steady **07** regular **08** measured, moderate **09** leisurely, unhurried **10** continuous, step-by-step **11** progressive

gradually
06 evenly, gently, slowly **08** bit by bit, gingerly, steadily **09** by degrees, piecemeal, regularly **10** cautiously, inch by inch, moderately, step by step **11** unhurriedly **12** continuously, successively **13** imperceptibly, progressively **14** little by little

graduate
02 BA, MA **04** grad, pass, rank, sort **05** grade, group, order, ovate, range **06** alumna, doctor, expert, fellow, master, member, move up **07** advance, alumnus, arrange, go ahead, mark off, qualify **08** bachelor, classify, graduand, progress, whizz kid **09** calibrate **10** be promoted, categorize, consultant, forge ahead, licentiate, measure out,

proportion, specialist **11** make headway, move forward
12 professional **13** skilled person, valedictorian **15** complete studies, qualified person
See also **qualification**

graft
03 bud, dig, imp **04** join, scam, slog, take, toil **05** affix, ditch, graff, plant, scion, shoot, sting **06** branch, effort, growth, inarch, insert, labour, rip-off, sleaze, splice, sprout, sucker
07 bribery, cuckold, engraft, implant
08 exertion, hard work **09** allograft, autograft, con tricks, extortion, homograft, inoculate, xenograft
10 corruption, dishonesty, excavation, transplant **11** dirty tricks, heterograft
12 implantation **13** dirty dealings, shady business **14** sharp practices
15 sweat of your brow

grain
02 gr **03** bit, jot, nap, rye **04** atom, corn, curn, fork, hint, iota, mite, oats, ragi, rice, seed **05** berry, crumb, emmer, fibre, grits, maize, minim, piece, prong, scrap, speck, trace, weave, wheat **06** barley, branch, fabric, groats, kernel, maslin, morsel
07 cereals, graddan, granule, marking, mashlam, mashlim, mashlin, mashlum, modicum, pattern, soupçon, surface, texture **08** fragment, mashloch, molecule, particle **09** scintilla
10 suggestion
• **soften grain**
04 cree

gram
01 g **02** gm, gr **03** urd **05** anger, grief, pulse **07** trouble **08** chickpea

grammar
05 Donat, Donet, style, usage
06 syntax **11** good English **14** correct English **15** linguistic rules
See also **speech**

grammatical
07 correct **09** syntactic **10** acceptable, linguistic, structural, well-formed
11 appropriate, syntactical **14** well-structured
See also **tense**

grand
01 G **03** fab **04** arch, cool, fine, head, main, mega **05** chief, final, great, large, lofty, noble, regal, showy, super **06** in full, lavish, lordly, pretty, senior, superb, wicked **07** exalted, highest, leading, opulent, pompous, stately, sublime, supreme **08** complete, exalting, glorious, imposing, majestic, palatial, precious, smashing, splendid, striking, terrific, thousand **09** ambitious, dignified, enjoyable, excellent, fantastic, first-rate, grandiose, inclusive, luxurious, mausolean, principal, sumptuous, wonderful
10 delightful, impressive, marvellous, monumental, pre-eminent
11 illustrious, magnificent, outstanding, pretentious **12** all-inclusive, ostentatious
13 comprehensive

grandchild
02 oe, oy **03** oye

grandeur
04 fame, pomp **05** state **06** renown
07 dignity, majesty **08** eminence, nobility, opulence, vastness
09 greatness, splendour
10 importance, lavishness, prominence **11** stateliness
12 magnificence **13** luxuriousness
14 impressiveness **15** illustriousness, pretentiousness

grandfather
04 oupa, papa **06** gramps, granda
07 grandad, grandpa, granfer, gutcher
08 goodsire, granddad, gudesire
09 grandaddy, grandpapa, grandsire, luckie-dad **10** granddaddy
11 grandparent

grandiloquent
06 rotund, turgid **07** flowery, fustian, orotund, pompous, swollen
08 inflated **09** bombastic, high-flown, ororotund **10** euphuistic, rhetorical
11 exaggerated, pretentious **12** high-sounding, magniloquent
13 grandiloquous

grandiose
04 long **05** grand, lofty, showy
07 pompous, stately **08** imposing, majestic, splendid, striking
09 ambitious, bombastic, high-flown, mausolean **10** flamboyant, impressive, monumental, over-the-top
11 extravagant, magnificent, pretentious **12** high-sounding, magniloquent, ostentatious

grandly
07 regally **09** pompously
10 gloriously, strikingly **11** excellently
12 impressively, majestically
13 magnificently, pretentiously

grandmother
03 nan **04** gran, nana, ouma **05** nanna, nanny **06** beldam, granny
07 beldame, grandam, grandma, grannam, grannie **08** babushka, good-dame, gude-dame
09 grandmama **10** grandmamma
11 grandparent

grandparental
04 aval **06** avital

granite
07 greisen **08** resolute **09** pegmatite, protogine **10** china stone, unyielding
11 luxulianite, luxulyanite
12 luxullianite

grant
03 aid, fee, feu, let **04** Cary, gift, give, lend, send **05** admit, allot, allow, award, feoff, yield **06** accept, accord, assign, bestow, beteem, confer, donate, impart, permit, supply **07** agree to, annuity, appoint, bequest, beteeme, bursary, charter, concede, consent, furnish, licence, license, pension, present, provide, subsidy **08** accede to, allocate, dispense, donation, granting, transmit **09** allowance, apportion, consent to, endowment, vouchsafe **10** concession, condescend, contribute, exhibition, honorarium, subvention
11 acknowledge, benefaction, expectative, scholarship
12 contribution
• **granted**
06 agreed

granular
04 corn **05** curny, lumpy, rough, sandy
06 curney, grainy, gritty **07** crumbly, friable **10** granulated

granule
03 jot **04** atom, bead, iota, seed
05 crumb, grain, pearl, piece, scrap, speck **06** pellet **07** plastid **08** bioblast, fragment, molecule, particle
09 chondrule, microsome

grape
03 uva
See also **wine**

grapefruit
06 pomelo **07** pompelo
10 pompelmous, pumple-nose
11 pampelmoose, pampelmouse, pompelmoose, pompelmouse

grapeskins
04 marc

graph
04 grid, plot **05** chart, curve, ogive, table **07** diagram, profile **08** bar chart, bar graph, nomogram, pie chart, waveform **09** histogram, nomograph, waveshape **10** carpet plot **11** demand curve, supply curve **13** learning curve
14 scatter diagram

graphic
05 clear, drawn, lucid, vivid
06 cogent, lively, visual **07** telling
08 detailed, explicit, specific, striking, symbolic **09** effective, pictorial, realistic **10** blow-by-blow, expressive **11** delineative, descriptive, well-defined **12** diagrammatic, illustrative

graphically
07 clearly, vividly **10** explicitly, strikingly **12** expressively
13 descriptively, realistically

graphite
04 kish, lead **08** plumbago
09 blacklead, pencil-ore **10** pencil-lead

grapple
04 face, grab, grip, hold, lock **05** clash, clasp, close, fight, grasp, seize
06 battle, clinch, clutch, combat, craple, engage, snatch, tackle, tussle
07 address, contend, wrestle
08 confront, cope with, deal with, struggle **09** encounter, lay hold of
14 get to grips with

grasp
◇ *containment indicator*
03 get, see **04** clat, grab, grip, have, hend, hent, hold, holt, rule **05** catch, clamp, clasp, claut, gripe, power, seize, sense **06** clench, clutch, follow, graple, griple, master, rumble, snatch, strain, take in **07** catch on, command, compass, control, embrace, grapple, gripple, mastery, prehend, realize, squeeze **08** clutches, conceive, dominion, handgrip, perceive
09 apprehend, awareness, knowledge, latch onto, lay hold of
10 comprehend, perception, possession, understand **11** familiarity
12 apprehension, get a handle on, get the hang of **13** comprehension, understanding

grasping
◇ *containment indicator*
04 mean **06** grabby, greedy, griple, stingy **07** griping, gripple, miserly, seizing, selfish **08** covetous
09 mercenary, niggardly, rapacious
10 avaricious **11** acquisitive, close-fisted, large-handed, tight-fisted
12 parsimonious **13** money-grubbing

grass
03 fog, hay, lea, pot, rat, rip **04** blab, lawn, mead, nark, shop, tell, turf, veld **05** dob in, downs, field, green, rough, split, sward, veldt **06** betray, common, inform, snitch, squeal, steppe, tell on **07** foggage, pasture, prairie, savanna, stool on **08** denounce, informer, stitch up **09** asparagus, grassland
11 incriminate

See also **cannabis**

Grasses include:

03 nit, nut, oat, poa, rye, sea, seg, tef
04 alfa, bent, cane, cord, corn, crab, dari, diss, doob, dura, gama, holy, kans, knot, lyme, moor, nard, oats, ragi, reed, rice, rusa, sago, sand, star, tape, tath, teff
05 alang, arrow, beard, brome, bunch, canna, chess, China, couch, doura, float, grama, halfa, lemon, maize, melic, paddy, panic, plume, quack, quick, ragee, raggy, roosa, spear, spike, starr, stipa, Sudan, wheat
06 bamboo, barley, canary, cotton, darnel, dhurra, fescue, finger, fiorin, guinea, kikuyu, lalang, marram, marrum, meadow, melick, millet, pampas, panick, quitch, raggee, rattan, redtop, rescue, scutch, sesame, switch, twitch, vernal
07 Bermuda, bristle, buffalo, cannach, esparto, feather, pannick, papyrus, quaking, sacaton, sorghum, timothy, wild oat
08 cat's-tail, cockspur, dog's-tail, Flinders, kangaroo, moss-crop, ryegrass, spinifex, teosinte
09 bluegrass, buckwheat, cocksfoot, danthonia, hare's-tail, marijuana, porcupine, sugar cane
10 citronella
12 creeping bent, Kentucky blue, squirrel-tail
13 meadow foxtail
15 English ryegrass, Italian ryegrass

• **grass after hay**
03 fog **07** foggage
• **handful of grass**
03 rip **04** ripp
• **stem of grass**
04 cane, culm

grasshopper
04 grig, weta **09** wart-biter

grate
03 irk, jar, rub, vex **04** bray, cage, gall, grid, grit, rasp, risp **05** annoy, chirk, creak, gride, grind, gryde, mince, peeve, shred, stove **06** rankle, scrape, squeak **07** scratch, screech **08** irritate
09 aggravate, pulverize, triturate
10 exasperate **12** kitchen-range **15** get on your nerves

grateful
07 obliged, pleased **08** beholden, indebted, thankful **09** obligated
12 appreciative

gratefully
10 thankfully **13** with gratitude
14 appreciatively

gratification
03 joy, tip **04** glee, gust **05** bribe, feast, kicks **06** relish, thrill **07** delight, elation
08 easement, pleasure **09** enjoyment
10 indulgence, indulgency, recompense **11** contentment
12 satisfaction

gratify
03 pay **05** charm, cheer, flesh, humor, spoil **06** arride, cosset, favour, fulfil, humour, pamper, please, thrill
07 aggrate, delight, flatter, gladden, indulge, placate, satiate, satisfy
08 pander to, recreate **09** make happy

grating
04 grid, hack, haik, hake, heck, iron, rack **05** frame, grate, grill, harsh, siver, syver **06** grille **07** braying, galling, grizzly, irksome, jarring, lattice, rasping, raucous, squeaky, trellis
08 annoying, cancelli, creaking, grinding, gritting, mort-safe, scrannel, scraping, scratchy, strident **09** fire-grate, graticule, offensive
10 discordant, irritating, portcullis, scratching, screeching, unpleasant
12 disagreeable, exasperating

gratis
04 free **08** at no cost, buckshee **10** for nothing, on the house **12** free of charge **13** complimentary, without charge

gratitude
06 thanks **10** obligation **11** recognition
12 appreciation, gratefulness, indebtedness, thankfulness
15 acknowledgement
• **expression of gratitude**
02 ta **06** thanks **07** thankee
08 bless you!, gramercy, thank you
09 God-a-mercy **10** grand merci
11 God bless you!

gratuitous
04 free **06** gratis, unpaid, wanton
08 buckshee, needless **09** unfounded, unmerited, voluntary **10** for nothing, groundless, unasked-for, undeserved, unprovoked, unrewarded
11 superfluous, uncalled-for, unjustified, unnecessary, unsolicited, unwarranted **12** free of charge
13 complimentary, without reason

gratuitously
10 needlessly **12** undeservedly
13 unjustifiably, unnecessarily

gratuity
03 tip **04** boon, dash, gift, mags, perk
05 bonus, maggs **06** bounty, reward
07 bansela, cumshaw, present, primage **08** bonsella, donation, donative, lagnappe, largesse
09 backshish, bakhshish, baksheesh, beer-money, lagniappe, pourboire
10 backsheesh, drink-money, glove-money, gratillity, perquisite, recompense

grave
03 dig, pit, sad **04** bass, bury, dust, grim, high, lair, loss, tomb **05** acute, cairn, count, crypt, death, graff, heavy, mouls, quiet, sober, staid, vault, vital
06 barrow, demise, gloomy, moulds, sedate, severe, solemn, sombre, urgent
07 austere, crucial, decease, earnest, exigent, passing, pensive, prefect, serious, subdued, tumulus, weighty
08 Catonian, critical, curtains, fatality, long home, matronal, menacing, perilous, pressing, reserved
09 dangerous, departure, dignified, hazardous, important, long-faced, mausoleum, momentous, plague-pit, saturnine, sepulchre **10** burial site, expiration, loss of life, restrained, thoughtful **11** bed of honour, burial mound, burial place, destruction, passing away, significant, threatening
12 last farewell

gravel
04 grit **05** grail **06** chesil, chisel, graile, grayle, hoggin, murram, stones
07 channel, channer, hogging, pebbles, shingle
• **layer of gravel**
04 hard

gravelly
05 gruff, harsh, rough, thick **06** grainy, gritty, hoarse, pebbly **07** grating, shingly, throaty **08** glareous, granular, guttural, sabulose, sabulous

gravely
07 acutely, quietly **08** gloomily, severely, solemnly, urgently **09** crucially, earnestly, pensively, seriously
10 critically **11** dangerously, importantly
12 thoughtfully **13** significantly

gravestone
05 stone, table **08** memorial
09 headstone, tombstone

graveyard
08 cemetery, God's acre **10** burial site, churchyard, necropolis **11** burial place **12** burial ground, charnel house **13** burying ground

gravitas
06 weight **07** gravity **09** solemnity **10** importance **11** earnestness, seriousness

gravitate
04 drop, fall, lean, move, sink, tend **05** drift **06** settle **07** descend, head for, incline **09** be drawn to **11** precipitate **12** be attached to

gravity
01 g **04** pull **05** peril, state **06** danger, hazard, weight **07** dignity, reserve, urgency **08** exigency, grimness, severity, sobriety **09** acuteness, graveness, heaviness, restraint, soberness, solemnity **10** attraction, gloominess, importance, sombreness **11** consequence, earnestness, gravitation, seriousness, weightiness **12** significance **13** momentousness **14** thoughtfulness

gray
02 Gy
See also **grey**

graze
03 rub **04** crop, feed, kiss, rake, rase, raze, skim, skin **05** brush, chafe, gride, gryde, scuff, shave, touch **06** abrade, browse, bruise, crease, fodder, scrape **07** pasture, scratch **08** abrasion, ruminate **09** depasture, glance off

grease
03 fat, oil **04** dope, lard, seam **05** bribe, seame, smear **06** creesh, dubbin, enlard, enseam, tallow **07** dubbing **08** dripping **09** lubricate **10** facilitate **11** lubrication

greasy
04 oily, waxy **05** fatty, lardy, oleic, slimy **06** smeary, smooth **07** adipose, buttery, obscene, shearer **08** slippery, unctuous **09** sebaceous **10** oleaginous **12** ingratiating
• **greasy substance**
04 glit

great
02 gt **03** ace, big, fit, gay, gey **04** able, bulk, cool, fell, fine, gran, huge, main, mass, mega, neat, tall, unco, up on, vast, well **05** adept, brill, chief, crack, eager, famed, grand, jumbo, large, major, noted, stoor, stour, sture, super, titan, vital, whole **06** august, awsome, bangin', cushty, expert, famous, grouse, lively, mickle, muckle, stowre, superb, wicked **07** awesome, banging, crucial, eminent, extreme, healthy, immense, leading, mammoth, massive, notable, primary, rousing, salient, serious, sizable, skilful, skilled, sublime, tearing, teeming, weighty **08** colossal, cracking, critical, dextrous, enormous, fabulous, gigantic, glorious, great big, habitual, imposing, masterly, powerful, pregnant, renowned, sizeable, smashing, spacious, splendid, terrific, top-notch, virtuoso, well up on, whopping **09** admirable, boundless, brilliant, dexterous, energetic, essential, excellent, excessive, extensive, fantastic, favourite, first-rate, ginormous, humongous, humungous, important, momentous, paramount, practised, principal, prominent, qualified, swingeing, wholesale, wonderful **10** celebrated, impressive, inordinate, marvellous, noteworthy, proficient, pronounced, remarkable, specialist, successful, tremendous **11** experienced, illustrious, magnificent, outstanding, significant, substantial **12** accomplished, considerable, enthusiastic, professional **13** distinguished, knowledgeable

Great Britain
02 GB, UK **03** GBR

greatly
04 much **06** highly, hugely, sorely, vastly **07** big-time, majorly, notably **08** markedly, mightily, very much **09** extremely, immensely **10** abundantly, enormously, noticeably, powerfully, remarkably **11** exceedingly **12** considerably, impressively, tremendously **13** significantly, substantially

greatness
04 fame, note **05** glory, power **06** genius, renown, weight **07** heroism, success **08** eminence, grandeur, muchness **09** intensity, magnitude **10** excellence, excellency, importance, mightiness **11** distinction, seriousness **12** significance **13** momentousness **14** successfulness **15** illustriousness

Greece
02 GR **03** GRC

greed
06 desire, hunger **07** avarice, avidity, craving, edacity, longing **08** bingeing, cupidity, gluttony, rapacity, voracity **09** eagerness, esurience, pleonexia **10** impatience **11** gourmandise, gourmandism, hoggishness, itching palm, piggishness, selfishness **12** covetousness, ravenousness **13** insatiability **15** acquisitiveness

greedily
06 avidly **07** eagerly **09** selfishly **10** esuriently, ravenously **11** impatiently, rapaciously **12** avariciously

greedy
04 avid, gare **05** eager **06** grabby, griple, having, hungry **07** craving, gripple, hoggish, piggish, selfish **08** covetous, desirous, edacious, esurient, grabbing, grasping, ravenous, starving **09** impatient, on the make, rapacious, voracious **10** avaricious, cupidinous, gluttonous, insatiable, omnivorous, pleonectic **11** acquisitive, itchy-palmed, open-mouthed **12** gormandizing **13** money-grubbing

Greek
02 Gk, Gr

Greeks include:

04 Esop
05 Aesop, Galen, Homer, Plato
06 Euclid, Lucian, Pindar, Sappho, Thales
07 Hypatia, Pytheas (of Marseilles)
08 Damocles, Epicurus, Plotinus, Plutarch, Polybius, Socrates, Xenophon
09 Aeschylus, Aristotle, Euripides, Herodotus, Sophocles
10 Archimedes, Democritus, Empedocles, Heraclitus, Hipparchos, Hipparchus, Praxiteles, Protagoras, Pythagoras, Theocritus, Thucydides, Xenophanes
11 Hippocrates
12 Aristophanes, Theophrastus

See also **alphabet**; **god, goddess**; **muse**; **mythology**; **seven**

green
03 eco, lea, new, raw **04** lawn, long, lush, pine, sage, turf **05** field, fresh, grass, leafy, naive, sward, virid, yearn, young **06** common, grassy, meadow, recent, simple, tender, unripe, virent **07** budding, envious, growing, healthy, jealous, pasture, undried, verdant **08** blooming, covetous, glaucous, grudging, gullible, ignorant, immature, inexpert, unversed, vigorous **09** grassland, resentful, untrained, verdurous, virescent **10** ecological, olivaceous, porraceous, smaragdine, unseasoned **11** eco-friendly, flourishing, unqualified, viridescent **13** environmental, inexperienced **15** conservationist, preservationist, unsophisticated

Greens include:

04 jade, lime, teal, vert
05 lovat, olive
06 reseda, sludge
07 avocado, celadon, corbeau, emerald
08 eau de Nil, pea-green, sap-green, sea green
09 moss green, Nile green, pistachio, sage green, turquoise
10 apple-green, aquamarine, chartreuse, rifle green
11 bottle green
12 Lincoln green
14 turquoise-green

greenery
04 vert **07** foliage, verdure **08** verdancy, viridity **09** greenness **10** vegetation, virescence **12** viridescence

greenhorn
03 put **04** putt, tiro **06** newbie, novice, rookie **07** learner, recruit **08** beginner,

initiate, neophyte, newcomer
09 fledgling, Johnny-raw
10 apprentice, tenderfoot

greenhouse
06 vinery **08** hothouse, orangery, pavilion **09** coldhouse, coolhouse **10** glasshouse **12** conservatory

Greenland
03 GRL

greet
03 bid, bow **04** hail, kiss, meet, weep, wish **05** halse, hongi, nod to
06 accost, salute, wave to **07** address, receive, regreet, weeping, welcome
08 congreet, remember **10** say hello to, shake hands, tip your hat
11 acknowledge, doff your hat
14 shake hands with **15** give someone five

greeting
03 bow, nod **04** kiss, wave **05** hongi
06 abrazo, accost, salute **07** accoast, address, air kiss, namaste **08** glad hand, high five, namaskar
09 handshake, reception, time of day
10 how-do-you-do, salutation **12** the time of day **15** acknowledgement
• **expression of greeting**
02 hi, yo **03** ave, how **04** ciao, g'day, hail, heil!, hiya **05** aloha, chimo, hallo, hello, holla, howdy, hullo, jambo, salve, skoal **06** salaam, shalom, wotcha
07 all-hail, bonjour, bonsoir, good-day, good-den, good-e'en, salaams, salvete, save you, welcome, well met, wotcher **08** chin-chin, good-even, haeremai **09** how are you?, son of a gun, what cheer? **10** benedicite, good-morrow, how do you do? **11** good-evening, good-morning **13** good afternoon **14** shalom aleichem

greetings
04 love **05** salve **07** regards, regreet, salaams **08** regreets, respects **10** best wishes, good wishes **11** compliments, kind regards, salutations, warm regards
12 remembrances **15** congratulations

gregarious
04 warm **06** social **07** affable, cordial
08 friendly, outgoing, sociable
09 convivial, extrovert **10** hospitable
13 companionable

Grenada
02 WG **03** GRD

grenade
09 Mills bomb, pineapple **15** Molotov cocktail

grey
02 gr **03** dim, old, wan **04** dark, dull, gris, pale **05** ashen, bleak, foggy, grise, grisy, misty, murky **06** cloudy, dismal, dreary, gloomy, gryesy, leaden, mature, pallid **07** griesie, neutral, unclear
08 bloncket, doubtful, griseous, grizzled, overcast **09** ambiguous, anonymous, canescent, cheerless, cinereous, debatable, uncertain
10 colourless, depressing, dove-colour **13** uninteresting **14** open to question

Greys include:

03 ash
04 drab
05 liard, liart, lyart, perse, stone, taupe
06 isabel, pewter, silver
07 grizzle
08 charcoal, dove grey, feldgrau, graphite, gridelin, platinum
09 field grey, pearl-grey, slate-grey, steel-grey
10 dapple-grey, dove-colour

• **greyish-brown**
03 dun **04** ecru **05** mousy **06** mousey
07 chamois
• **greyish-white**
04 hoar, hore

greyhound
04 grew **07** lurcher, sapling, whippet
08 long-tail **09** deerhound, grewhound

grid
05 frame, grate, grill **06** grille
07 grating, lattice, network, trellis
08 gridiron **09** framework, graticule

grief
02 wo **03** vex, woe **04** dole, dool, gram, pain, sore, teen, tene **05** agony, dolor, doole, grame, teene **06** bother, dolour, misery, regret, sorrow, tsuris
07 anguish, despair, remorse, sadness, thought, trouble, tsouris, wayment
08 distress, mourning **09** bemoaning, dejection, grievance, heartache, suffering, tristesse **10** affliction, depression, desiderium, desolation, heartbreak **11** bereavement, despondency, lamentation, tribulation, unhappiness **12** dolorousness
• **come to grief**
04 bomb, flop, fold **05** crash, spill
06 mucker **07** founder, go wrong, miswend **08** collapse, fall down, fall flat **09** break down **10** not come off
11 bite the dust, come unglued, come unstuck, fall through **12** come a cropper **13** come to nothing **14** be unsuccessful
• **emblem of grief**
03 yew
• **expression of grief**
02 io, oh **03** wow **04** alas **05** ohone, waugh, wowee **06** dear me, ochone, oh dear! **07** deary me **08** dearie me
• **feel grief**
04 earn **05** yearn

grief-stricken
03 sad **06** broken **07** crushed, unhappy **08** dejected, desolate, grieving, mourning, overcome, troubled, wretched **09** afflicted, anguished, depressed, sorrowful, sorrowing, woebegone **10** despairing, despondent, devastated, distressed
11 heartbroken, overwhelmed
12 disconsolate, inconsolable
13 broken-hearted

grievance
04 beef, moan **05** grief, gripe, peeve, score, trial, wrong **06** charge, damage, grouse, injury **07** grumble, offence, protest, trouble **08** distress, gravamen, hardship **09** complaint, injustice, objection **10** affliction, bone to pick, resentment, unfairness **11** tribulation

grieve
03 cry, rue, sob, vex **04** ache, hone, hurt, mope, pain, wail, weep **05** brood, crush, mourn, shock, upset, wound
06 bemoan, dismay, lament, offend, sadden, sorrow, suffer **07** afflict, condole, horrify, sheriff, wayment
08 distress, engrieve, governor, pine away

grievous
04 dear, sore **05** deare, deere, grave, heavy **06** noyous, severe, strong, tragic **07** careful, glaring, harmful, hurtful, painful **08** damaging, dolorous, dreadful, flagrant, shameful, shocking, wounding **09** appalling, atrocious, dolorific, injurious, monstrous, plightful, sorrowful
10 afflicting, burdensome, calamitous, deplorable, outrageous, unbearable
11 devastating, distressing, intolerable
12 doloriferous, overwhelming

grievously
04 sore **06** dernly **07** dearnly
08 severely **10** dolorously, dreadfully, shockingly, tragically, unbearably
11 appallingly, intolerably
12 outrageously

grill
04 cook, grid, heat, pump **05** bar-b-q, broil, frame, roast, toast **06** grille, wicket **07** grating, lattice, scallop
08 barbecue, barbeque, gridiron
09 charbroil **10** flame-grill

grim
◇ *anagram indicator*
03 ill **04** dire, dour **05** awful, grisy, gurly, harsh, stern, surly **06** dismal, dogged, fierce, gloomy, griesy, grisly, grysie, horrid, morose, severe, sullen
07 ghastly **08** dreadful, fearsome, gruesome, horrible, menacing, obdurate, resolute, shocking, sinister, stubborn, terrible **09** appalling, ferocious, harrowing, repellent, tenacious **10** depressing, determined, forbidding, formidable, horrendous, inexorable, persistent, unpleasant, unshakable, unyielding **11** frightening, threatening, unappealing, unshakeable, unspeakable **12** unattractive

grimace
03 moe, mop, mou, mow, mug
04 face, girn, moue, mump, pout
05 frown, mouth, scowl, smirk, sneer
07 murgeon **09** make a face, pull a face **12** fit of the face

grime
03 mud **04** coom, crud, dirt, dust, grot, muck, soot, yuck **05** filth, gunge
06 grunge, smutch

grimly
07 harshly, sternly **08** fiercely, gloomily, morosely, sullenly

grimy
05 dirty, dusty, mucky, muddy, sooty
06 filthy, grubby, rechie, reechy, smudgy, smutty, soiled **07** reechie, stained **10** besmirched

grin
04 beam, girn, gren, leer, trap
05 gerne, laugh, risus, smile, smirk, snare, sneer **06** giggle, titter
07 chuckle, snigger

grind
03 pug, rub **04** bray, chew, file, grit, meal, mill, rasp, sand, task, toil, whet
05 chore, crush, gnash, grate, pound, round, slime, stamp, sweat **06** abrade, crunch, kibble, labour, polish, powder, scrape, smooth **07** chamfer, crumble, graunch, routine, sharpen, slavery
08 drudgery, exertion, levigate
09 comminute, granulate, masticate, pulverize, triturate

• grind down
05 crush, harry, hound **06** harass, plague **07** afflict, oppress, torment, trouble **08** wear down **09** persecute, tyrannize

grip
◇ *containment indicator*
03 bag, get, hug **04** bite, case, fang, grab, hold, vice, vise **05** catch, clasp, cling, ditch, drain, grasp, power, rivet, sally, seize **06** absorb, clench, clutch, compel, engage, graple, griple, kitbag, strain, thrill, trench, valise
07 command, control, embrace, engross, enthral, fingers, grapple, gripple, holdall, involve, mastery
08 clutches, entrance, foothold, handfast, suitcase, traction
09 fascinate, get hold of, hypnotize, influence, latch onto, mesmerize, spellbind **10** domination, grab hold of
11 catch hold of, shoulder bag
12 overnight bag **13** travelling bag

• come to grips with, get to grips with
◇ *containment indicator*
05 grasp **06** handle, tackle, take on
08 confront, cope with, deal with, face up to **09** encounter, look after **10** take care of

gripe
03 nag **04** beef, carp, moan **05** bitch, ditch, drain, groan, whine **06** grouch, grouse, trench, whinge **07** griffin, griping, grumble, protest, vulture
08 complain **09** bellyache, complaint, grievance, objection **15** have a bone to pick

gripping
◇ *containment indicator*
06 griple **07** gripple **08** exciting, riveting **09** absorbing, thrilling
10 compelling, compulsive, enchanting, engrossing, entrancing
11 enthralling, fascinating, suspenseful
12 spellbinding **13** unputdownable

• gripping instrument
04 grip, vice, vise **05** clamp
08 tweezers

grisly
04 gory, grim **05** awful, grisy **06** griesy, grysie, horrid **07** ghastly, hideous, macabre **08** dreadful, gruesome, horrible, shocking, terrible
09 abhorrent, appalling, frightful, loathsome, repulsive, revolting
10 abominable, disgusting, horrifying

gristly
04 hard **05** chewy, tough **06** sinewy
07 fibrous, rubbery, stringy
08 leathery **13** cartilaginous

grit
04 dust, guts, rasp, sand **05** gnash, grate, great, grind, swarf **06** clench, gravel, mettle, scrape **07** bravery, courage, pebbles, resolve, shingle
08 backbone, hardness, strength, tenacity **09** endurance, toughness
10 doggedness, resolution
12 perseverance **13** determination, steadfastness

gritty
05 brave, dusty, gutsy, gutty, hardy, rough, sandy, tough **06** dogged, feisty, grainy, pebbly, plucky, spunky
07 powdery, shingly **08** abrasive, granular, gravelly, resolute, sabuline, sabulose, sabulous, spirited
09 steadfast, tenacious
10 courageous, determined, mettlesome **14** uncompromising

grizzle
03 cry **04** fret, moan **05** whine
06 snivel, whinge **07** grumble, sniffle, snuffle, whimper **08** complain

grizzled
04 grey, hoar **05** hoary **07** greying
08 griseous **09** canescent **10** grey-haired, grey-headed **13** pepper-and-salt

groan
03 cry **04** beef, moan, sigh, wail
05 whine **06** grouch, grouse, lament, object, outcry, whinge **07** griping, grumble, protest, whimper
08 complain **09** bellyache, complaint, grievance, objection

grocer
06 dealer **07** épicier **08** pepperer, purveyor, supplier **10** victualler
11 greengrocer, storekeeper, supermarket

groggy
◇ *anagram indicator*
04 weak **05** dazed, dizzy, dopey, faint, muzzy, shaky, woozy **06** wobbly
07 reeling, stunned **08** confused, unsteady **09** befuddled, stupefied
10 bewildered, punch-drunk, staggering

groin
04 lisk **05** growl, grunt **06** crotch, crutch **07** grumble **08** genitals

groom
◇ *anagram indicator*
02 do **03** fix **04** sice, syce, tidy
05 brush, clean, coach, curry, dress, drill, preen, prime, prink, saice, teach, train, tutor **06** adjust, neaten, school, smooth, spouse, tidy up **07** arrange, educate, husband, prepare, smarten, turn out **08** coistrel, coistril, instruct, newly-wed, spruce up, strapper
09 make ready, stableboy, stable lad, stableman **10** bridegroom, palfrenier, put in order, stable hand, stable lass
11 honeymooner, husband-to-be
15 marriage partner

groove
03 cut, pod, rut **04** kerf, mark, oche, race, sipe, slot **05** canal, chase, croze, ditch, flute, gouge, quirk, ridge, rigol, score, slide, track **06** cullis, furrow, gutter, hollow, keyway, rabbet, raggle, rebate, riffle, scrobe, sulcus, throat, trench, trough **07** chamfer, channel, diglyph, fissure, fossula, key-seat **09** cannelure, vallecula
11 indentation

grooved
06 fluted, rutted, scored, sulcal
07 exarate, sulcate **08** furrowed, rabbeted, sulcated **09** chamfered
10 channelled **12** canaliculate, scrobiculate **13** canaliculated

grope
04 feel, fish, hunt, pick, poke, ripe
05 abuse, probe, touch **06** feel up, fondle, fumble, molest, search
07 grabble, touch up **08** flounder, scrabble **09** cast about **13** abuse sexually, interfere with

gross
◇ *anagram indicator*
02 gr **03** big, fat **04** blue, dull, earn, foul, huge, lewd, make, rank, rude, slow, take **05** bawdy, bulky, crass, crude, dirty, heavy, large, nasty, obese, plain, sheer, solid, thick, total, utter, whole, yucky **06** coarse, earthy, entire, filthy, odious, pull in, rake in, ribald, risqué, smutty, strong, stupid, vulgar
07 blatant, boorish, bring in, extreme, glaring, hulking, immense, lumpish, massive, obscene, obvious, sensual, serious **08** colossal, complete, enormous, flagrant, grievous, improper, indecent, manifest, material, nauseous, outright, palpable, shameful, shocking
09 aggregate, before tax, corpulent, egregious, inclusive, offensive, repugnant, repulsive, revolting, sickening, tasteless, unrefined
10 accumulate, disgusting, earthbound, nauseating, off-putting, outrageous, overweight, salt-butter, uncultured, unpleasant **11** disgraceful, distasteful, insensitive, unpalatable
12 all-inclusive, pornographic, unappetizing, unrepeatable
13 coarse-grained, comprehensive
15 unsophisticated

grossly
04 very **05** fatly **06** highly, really
07 acutely, awfully, greatly, utterly
08 severely, terribly **09** decidedly, extremely, intensely, unusually
10 dreadfully, remarkably, thoroughly, uncommonly **11** exceedingly, excessively, frightfully
12 immoderately, inordinately, terrifically, unreasonably
13 exceptionally **15** extraordinarily

grotesque
◇ *anagram indicator*
03 odd **04** ugly **05** antic, black, weird
06 absurd, antick, Gothic, rococo
07 anticke, antique, bizarre, hideous, macabre, strange, surreal, twisted
08 deformed, fanciful, freakish, peculiar **09** distorted, fantastic, ludicrous, malformed, misshapen, monstrous, unnatural, unsightly, whimsical **10** outlandish, ridiculous
11 extravagant

grotesquely
09 bizarrely, hideously, strangely
11 unnaturally **12** outlandishly, unpleasantly

grotto
04 cave, grot **05** speos **06** cavern
07 chamber **08** catacomb, Lupercal
09 Mithraeum, nymphaeum
10 subterrane

grotty
03 ill **04** sick, ugly **05** dirty, grody, mangy, rough, seedy, tatty **06** ailing, crummy, groggy, poorly, shabby, sleazy, untidy, unwell **07** run-down, scruffy, squalid **08** decaying **09** off-colour
10 out of sorts **11** dilapidated **15** under the weather

grouch
04 moan **05** gripe, grump, sulks
06 griper, grouse, kvetch, moaner, sulker, whiner, whinge **07** grouser, grumble, whinger **08** grumbler, kvetcher, murmurer, mutterer, sourpuss **09** complaint, grievance, objection **10** bellyacher, complainer, crosspatch, malcontent **11** fault-finder

grouchy
05 cross, sulky, surly, testy **06** grumpy
07 peevish **08** captious, churlish, petulant **09** crotchety, grumbling, irascible, irritable, querulous, truculent
11 bad-tempered, complaining, ill-tempered **12** cantankerous, discontented, dissatisfied

ground
◇ *anagram indicator*
03 fix, set, sod **04** base, call, clay, dirt, dust, eard, land, lees, loam, marl, park, plot, soil, yerd, yird **05** acres, arena, basis, cause, coach, dregs, drill, earth, field, found, lawns, pitch, score, teach, terra, train, tutor, yeard **06** bottom, campus, domain, estate, excuse, fields, inform, motive, reason, settle
07 account, deposit, dry land, educate, gardens, holding, prepare, residue, stadium, surface, terrain
08 argument, initiate, instruct, occasion, position, property, sediment
09 advantage, background, establish, introduce, principle, scourings, territory **10** foundation, inducement, terra firma **11** precipitate, vindication
12 acquaint with, surroundings
13 justification **15** familiarize with
See also **stadium**

- **leave the ground**

04 yump

- **patch of ground**

03 lot, tee **04** area

- **run along ground**

04 taxi

groundbait
04 chum **06** berley, burley

groundless
05 empty, false **08** baseless, illusory
09 imaginary, unfounded
10 unprovoked **11** uncalled-for, unjustified, unsupported, unwarranted
13 without reason **15** unsubstantiated

grounds
04 lees **05** dregs

groundwork
04 base **05** basis **06** bottom
07 footing **08** homework, research
09 spadework **10** essentials, foundation, metaphysic
11 cornerstone, preparation
12 fundamentals **13** preliminaries, underpinnings

group
03 lot, mob, set **04** band, body, club, crew, gang, knot, link, mass, pack, pool, rank, sort, team, unit **05** batch, bunch, class, clump, crowd, flock, genus, grade, guild, order, party, range, squad, troop, unite **06** circle, clique, cohort, family, gather, huddle, league, line up, school **07** arrange, bracket, cluster, collect, company, coterie, element, faction, marshal, society, species **08** assemble, assembly, category, classify, grouping, organize
09 associate, formation, gathering
10 categorize, collection, congregate, contingent, detachment
11 association, combination
12 congregation, organization
14 classification, conglomeration
See also **singer**

- **group of women**

02 WI **05** coven

- **unit group**

04 cell

grouse
04 beef, carp, good, moan, neat
05 bitch, gripe, groan, peeve, whine
06 grouch, whinge **07** grumble, protest **08** complain **09** bellyache, complaint, excellent, find fault, grievance, objection

Grouse include:

03 red
04 sage, sand
05 black, hazel
06 ruffed, willow
07 gorcock, greyhen, pintail, prairie, red game
08 hazel hen, heath-hen, moorcock, moorfowl, moor-poot, moor-pout, muir-poot, muir-pout, pheasant, sage cock
09 blackcock, blackgame, heathbird, heathcock, heath-fowl, partridge, ptarmigan
10 heath-poult, prairie hen
11 prairie fowl, sharp-tailed
12 capercaillie, capercailzie
14 prairie chicken

See also **game**

- **grouse-shooters' lair**

04 butt

grove
03 Gro **04** tope, wood **05** copse, hurst
06 arbour, avenue, covert, lyceum
07 coppice, spinney, thicket
08 woodland **10** plantation

grovel
04 fawn **05** cower, crawl, creep, defer, kneel, kotow, stoop, toady **06** cheese, cringe, crouch, kowtow, lie low, suck up **07** bow down, flatter, lie down
08 kiss up to **12** bow and scrape
14 demean yourself **15** butter someone up, fall on your knees

grow
02 go **03** bud, get, sow, wax **04** farm, rise, stem, turn **05** arise, breed, issue, plant, raise, shoot, swell, widen
06 become, change, deepen, expand, extend, flower, mature, spread, spring, sprout, thrive **07** advance, broaden, burgeon, develop, enlarge, fill out, harvest, improve, produce, prosper, stretch, succeed, thicken
08 bourgeon, come to be, elongate, escalate, flourish, increase, lengthen, multiply, mushroom, progress
09 cultivate, germinate, get bigger, get taller, originate, propagate **11** make headway, proliferate **12** become bigger, become larger, become taller
14 increase in size

- **grow up**

03 age **06** mature

growl
03 yap **04** bark, gnar, gurl, howl, roar, roin, snap, snar, yelp **05** groin, royne, snarl **06** rumble **07** grumble

grown-up
03 big, man **05** adult, of age, woman
06 mature **09** full-grown **10** fully grown **12** fully fledged **14** fully developed

growth
04 crop, gall, lump, rise **05** plant
06 antler, flower, spread, tumour
07 advance, budding, flowers, headway, success **08** greenery, increase, progress, shooting, swelling
09 deepening, evolution, expansion, extension, flowering, outgrowth, springing, sprouting **10** burgeoning,

maturation, prosperity
11 development, enlargement, excrescence, germination, improvement **12** augmentation, intumescence, protuberance
13 amplification, magnification, proliferation **14** aggrandizement, multiplication
• **halt growth**
03 nip

grub
03 dig, eat, wog **04** eats, food, hunt, nosh, pupa, root, rout, stub, tuck, worm **05** delve, grout, larva, meals, probe, scour, wroot **06** burrow, ferret, forage, gru-gru, maggot, muddle, rootle, search, tucker **07** explore, rummage, snuzzle, uncover, unearth **08** bookworm, excavate, flag-worm, groo-groo, muck-worm **09** chrysalis, nutrition, provision, witchetty **10** gru-gru worm, sustenance **11** caterpillar, refreshment **12** refreshments
13 leatherjacket

grubby
05 dirty, grimy, messy, mucky, seedy
06 filthy, shabby, soiled, thumby
07 scruffy, squalid **08** unwashed

grudge
04 envy, hate, mind **05** covet, pique, score, spite, venom **06** animus, enmity, grutch, hatred, malice, malign, murmur, repine, resent **07** dislike, ill-will, rancour **08** aversion, begrudge, jealousy, object to **09** animosity, antipathy, grievance **10** antagonism, bitterness, resentment **11** be jealous of, malevolence **12** hard feelings **15** take exception to

grudging
07 envious, jealous **08** hesitant
09 reluctant, resentful, unwilling
11 half-hearted **12** heartburning
14 unenthusiastic

gruel
05 kasha **06** congee, conjee, skilly
07 brochan **08** loblolly **10** punishment
11 skilligalee, skilligolee

gruelling
04 hard **05** harsh, tough **06** severe, taxing, tiring, trying **07** arduous
08 crushing, draining, grinding
09 demanding, difficult, laborious, punishing, strenuous **10** exhausting
12 backbreaking

gruesome
04 grim, sick **05** awful **06** grisly, grooly, horrid **07** ghastly, hideous, macabre **08** dreadful, horrible, horrific, shocking, terrible
09 abhorrent, appalling, frightful, loathsome, monstrous, repellent, repugnant, repulsive, revolting, sickening **10** abominable, disgusting

gruesomely
06 grimly **08** horribly, terribly
09 hideously **10** dreadfully
11 frightfully, monstrously, repulsively

gruff
04 curt, rude, sour **05** blunt, harsh, husky, rough, surly, testy, thick
06 abrupt, grumpy, hoarse, sullen, tetchy **07** brusque, crabbed, rasping, throaty **08** churlish, croaking, guttural, impolite **09** crotchety
10 unfriendly **11** bad-tempered
12 discourteous

gruffly
06 curtly, rudely **07** harshly, huskily, roughly **08** abruptly, hoarsely
09 brusquely **10** gutturally, impolitely
14 discourteously

grumble
04 beef, carp, moan, mump, nark, roar
05 bitch, bleat, croak, gripe, groin, growl, grump, whine **06** grouch, grouse, gurgle, mumble, murmur, mutter, object, rumble, whinge
07 chunder, chunner, chunter, grizzle, maunder, protest **08** chounter, complain **09** bellyache, complaint, find fault, grievance, muttering, objection

grumbler
04 moan **06** grouch, moaner, whiner
07 croaker, fusspot, grouser, niggler, whinger **09** nit-picker **10** bellyacher, complainer, fussbudget **11** fault-finder

grumpily
07 crossly, in a huff, in a sulk, sulkily
08 sullenly **09** grouchily **10** churlishly

grumpy
05 crabby, cross, moany, ratty, sulky, surly **06** snappy, sullen, tetchy
07 crabbed, grouchy, in a huff, in a sulk
08 churlish, grumpish, petulant
09 crotchety, irritable **11** bad-tempered, ill-tempered
12 cantankerous, discontented

grunt
03 ugh **04** oink, rasp **05** cough, croak, grate, groin, power, snore, snort
06 drudge, grumph **07** pig-fish, soldier
08 labourer

Guadeloupe
03 GLP

Guam
03 GUM

guarantee
04 back, bond, gage, oath **05** swear, token **06** assure, avouch, engage, ensure, insure, pledge, secure, surety
07 certify, earnest, endorse, promise, protect, sponsor, support, warrant
08 contract, covenant, guaranty, make sure, security, vouch for, warranty
09 answer for, assurance, insurance, stipulate, undertake, vouchsafe
10 collateral, underwrite, warrandice, warrantise **11** endorsement, make certain, testimonial **12** word of honour
15 give an assurance

guarantor
05 angel **06** backer, surety **07** referee, sponsor, voucher **08** bailsman, bondsman **09** guarantee, supporter, warrantor **10** covenantor
11 underwriter

guard
◇ *containment indicator*
03 pad **04** care, keep, mind, rail, save, wait, wall, ward, wear, weir **05** check, cover, fence, garda, hedge, scout, watch **06** beware, buffer, bumper, captor, charge, defend, escort, fender, keeper, minder, patrol, picket, police, screen, secure, sentry, shield, warden, warder **07** barrier, be alert, control, cushion, defence, enguard, look out, lookout, oversee, protect, shelter, watcher **08** bostangi, defender, fortress, guardian, preserve, savegard, scrutiny, security, sentinel, splasher, take care, watchman **09** bodyguard, conductor, custodian, direction, keep watch, protector, safeguard, supervise, vigilance **10** inspection, monitoring, protection, regulation **11** observation, stewardship, supervision
12 guardianship, surveillance
15 superintendence
• **officer of the Guard**
04 exon
• **off your guard**
06 unwary **07** napping, unaware, unready **08** careless, unawares
09 red-handed, surprised
10 unprepared **11** inattentive
12 unsuspecting
• **on your guard**
04 wary **05** alert, ready **07** careful
08 cautious, excubant, prepared, vigilant, watchful **09** attentive, wide awake **10** on the alert **11** circumspect
12 on the lookout

guarded
04 wary **05** cagey, chary **07** careful, striped, trimmed **08** cautious, defended, discreet, reserved, reticent, watchful **09** reluctant, secretive
10 restrained **11** circumspect **12** non-committal

guardedly
06 warily **07** charily **09** carefully
10 cautiously **11** reluctantly, secretively
13 circumspectly **14** non-committally

guardian
05 angel, guard, Janus, tutor **06** custos, escort, gryfon, keeper, patron, warden, warder **07** curator, Granthi, griffin, griffon, gryphon, steward, trustee, tutelar **08** Cerberus, champion, curatrix, defender, tutelary
09 attendant, caretaker, custodian, preserver, protector **10** depositary, depository, protecting **11** conservator
12 conservatrix
• **guardian of women**
04 Juno

guardianship
04 care, ward **05** aegis, guard, hands, trust **07** custody, defence, keeping, tuition **08** guidance, tutelage, wardenry, wardship **09** patronage
10 attendance, protection, wardenship
11 curatorship, safekeeping,

stewardship, trusteeship
12 preservation, protectorate
13 custodianship

Guatemala
03 GCA, GTM

Guernsey
03 GBG

guerrilla
03 Che **06** haiduk, maquis, sniper
07 chetnik, fedayee, heyduck
08 komitaji, partisan, Viet Cong
09 irregular, terrorist, Zapatista
10 Tamil tiger **11** bushwhacker, franc-tireur, guerrillero **14** freedom fighter

guess
03 aim, bet **04** feel, idea, shot
05 aread, arede, augur, fancy, hunch, judge, level, think **06** assume, belief, devise, divine, notion, reckon, theory
07 arreede, believe, feeling, imagine, opinion, predict, suppose, surmise, suspect, work out **08** consider, estimate **09** guesswork, intuition, judgement, postulate, reckoning, speculate, suspicion **10** assumption, conjecture, hypothesis, make a guess, prediction **11** guesstimate, hypothesize, speculation, supposition
13 shot in the dark **14** a shot in the dark, a stab in the dark, ballpark figure, put something at

guessing-game
04 mora **05** morra

guesstimate
05 guess **09** judgement, quotation, reckoning, valuation **10** assessment, estimation, evaluation, rough guess
11 computation **13** approximation
14 ballpark figure **15** approximate cost

guesswork
06 theory **07** surmise **09** intuition, reckoning **10** assumption, conjecture, estimation, hypothesis, prediction
11 guesstimate, speculation, supposition

guest
02 PG **05** umbra **06** caller, lodger, patron **07** boarder, invitee, regular, visitor **08** manuhiri, resident, symphile, visitant **09** synoecete, synoekete

guesthouse
03 inn **05** hotel **06** hostel **07** Gasthof, hospice, pension, taverna
08 Gasthaus, hostelry, minshuku
11 xenodochium **12** rooming-house
13 boarding-house **15** bed-and-breakfast

guff
03 rot **04** blah, bosh, bull, bunk, cock, crap **05** balls, bilge, hooey, smell, stink, trash, tripe **06** bunkum, drivel, hot air, humbug, piffle **07** baloney, eyewash, hogwash, rhubarb, rubbish, twaddle
08 claptrap, cobblers, malarkey, nonsense, tommyrot **09** gibberish, moonshine, poppycock
10 codswallop

guffaw
04 hoot, roar **05** laugh, whoop
06 bellow, cackle, haw-haw, shriek
09 loud laugh **11** laugh loudly

guidance
03 tip **04** help, hint, lead, rule, tips
05 hints **06** advice, charge
07 conduct, control, counsel, leading, pointer **08** pointers, teaching
09 direction **10** assistance, directions, guidelines, indication, leadership, management, suggestion
11 counselling, indications, information, instruction, suggestions
12 instructions **14** recommendation
15 recommendations
• **Parental Guidance**
02 PG

guide
03 ABC, key **04** guru, lead, mark, norm, rule, show, sign, wise **05** abcee, absey, gauge, maxim, model, pilot, point, steer, teach, train, tutor, usher, weise, weize **06** advise, attend, beacon, direct, escort, govern, leader, manage, manual, marker, mentor, ranger, signal **07** adviser, command, conduct, control, counsel, courier, educate, example, inspire, labarum, measure, oversee, pattern, pointer, red book, shikari, teacher, waymark
08 Bradshaw, chaperon, cicerone, cynosure, director, engineer, exemplar, Good Food, handbook, helmsman, instruct, landmark, navigate, Pole Star, regulate, road book, shikaree, signpost, standard **09** accompany, archetype, attendant, benchmark, catalogue, chaperone, companion, conductor, criterion, directory, guidebook, guideline, influence, manoeuvre, navigator, sightsman, steersman, supervise, tombstone, yardstick **10** counsellor, indication, instructor, show the way **11** preside over, superintend **12** be in charge of, valet de place **14** Tyrian cynosure
• **weaver's guide**
04 card

guidebook
03 ABC **04** A to Z® **05** guide
06 manual **08** Baedeker, handbook
09 companion **10** prospectus
15 instruction book

guideline
04 rule **05** terms **06** advice
07 measure, road map **08** standard
09 benchmark, criterion, direction, framework, parameter, principle, procedure, yardstick **10** constraint, indication, regulation, suggestion, touchstone **11** information, instruction
14 recommendation

guild
03 WAG **04** club, tong **05** artel, lodge, order, union **06** chapel, league
07 basoche, company, mistery, mystery, society **08** alliance, sorority
10 federation, fellowship, fraternity
11 association, brotherhood, corporation **12** organization
13 incorporation

guile
04 dole, ruse **05** craft, fraud, trick
06 deceit **07** cunning, knavery, slyness
08 artifice, trickery, wiliness
09 deception, duplicity, stratagem, treachery **10** artfulness, cleverness, craftiness, trickiness **11** deviousness
12 gamesmanship **13** double-dealing

guileless
04 open **05** frank, naive **06** candid, direct, honest, simple **07** artless, genuine, natural, sincere **08** innocent, sackless, straight, trusting, truthful
09 ingenuous, unworldly
10 unreserved **11** transparent
13 simple-hearted **15** straightforward, unsophisticated

guilt
03 sin **05** blame, shame, wrong
06 regret **07** remorse **08** disgrace
09 dishonour, guilt trip, penitence
10 blood-guilt, conscience, contrition, misconduct, repentance, sinfulness, wrongdoing **11** compunction, criminality, culpability **12** self-reproach, unlawfulness
14 responsibility, self-accusation
15 blameworthiness

guiltily
07 at fault, to blame, wrongly
09 illegally, illicitly **10** contritely, shamefully, unlawfully, with sorrow
11 regretfully, responsibly
12 remorsefully, unforgivably
13 penitentially, reprehensibly, without excuse **14** caught in the act **15** caught red-handed

guiltless
04 free, pure **05** clean, clear **07** sinless
08 innocent, spotless **09** blameless, faultless, stainless, undefiled, unspotted, unsullied, untainted **10** immaculate, impeccable, inculpable, unblamable
11 untarnished **13** above reproach, unimpeachable **14** irreproachable

guilty
03 bad **04** evil **05** sorry, wrong
06 faulty, nocent, sinful, wicked
07 ashamed, at fault, illegal, illicit, to blame **08** blamable, contrite, criminal, culpable, infamous, penitent, sheepish, unlawful **09** condemned, convicted, offending, regretful, repentant
10 delinquent, flagitious, remorseful, shamefaced **11** blameworthy, guilt-ridden, responsible **12** bloodstained, compunctious

guinea
02 Ls, RG **03** GIN **04** quid **06** canary, George **07** Geordie
• **guineas**
02 gs

Guinea-Bissau
03 GNB, RGB

guinea pig
04 cavy, paca **05** aguti **06** agouti,

agouty **08** capybara **09** do-nothing, triallist

Guinness
04 Alec

guise
03 air **04** face, form, mask, show **05** dress, front, shape **06** aspect, custom, façade, manner **07** purport **08** disguise, features, likeness, pretence **09** behaviour, demeanour, semblance **10** appearance

guitar
02 ax **03** axe, uke **04** bass **05** Dobro®, sanko **06** sancho **07** gittern, samisen, ukulele **08** shamisen **09** humbucker

• **play guitar**
05 strum

gulf
03 bay, gap, maw **04** cove, hole, rift, void **05** abyss, basin, bight, chasm, cleft, gorge, inlet, split **06** breach, canyon, divide, hollow, ravine, vorago **07** crevice, fissure, opening **08** division **09** whirlpool **10** separation

Gulfs include:

04 Aden, Huon, Lion, Moro, Oman, Riga, Siam, Suez
05 Ancud, Aqaba, Càdiz, Davao, Dulce, Gabes, Gaeta, Genoa, Kutch, Lions, Maine, Panay, Papua, Penas, Ragay, Saros, Sidra, Sirte, Tunis
06 Aegina, Alaska, Cambay, Chania, Darien, Gdansk, Guinea, Kavala, Mannar, Mexico, Naples, Nicoya, Orosei, Panama, Parita, Patras, St Malo, Tonkin, Triste, Venice
07 Almeria, Arabian, Asinara, Boothia, Bothnia, Cazones, Corinth, Edremit, Exmouth, Finland, Fonseca, Hauraki, Kachchh, Lepanto, Obskaya, Persian, Salerno, San Blas, Saronic, Spencer, Taranto, The Gulf, Trieste, Udskaya
08 Amundsen, Batabano, Cagliari, Campeche, Chiriqui, Honduras, Khambhat, Liaotung, Lingayen, Martaban, Mosquito, Oristano, Papagayo, San Jorge, Taganrog, Thailand, Valencia
09 Buor-Khaya, Corcovado, Dvinskaya, Guayaquil, Queen Maud, San Matias, San Miguel, St Florent, St Vincent, Van Diemen, Venezuela
10 California, Chaunskaya, Cheshskaya, Coronation, Kyparissia, Policastro, St Lawrence, Tazovskaya, Thermaikos
11 Carpentaria, Guacanayabo, Manfredonia, Pechorskaya, Strymonikos, Tehuantepec
12 los Mosquitos, Penzhinskaya
13 Baydaratskaya, Santa Catalina
15 Joseph Bonaparte

gull
04 dupe, fool, hoax **05** cheat **07** deceive

See also **bird**; **fool**

gullet
03 maw **04** craw, crop, gula **06** throat **07** Red Lane, weasand **09** esophagus **10** oesophagus

gullibility
07 naivety **09** credulity, innocence **10** simplicity **11** foolishness **12** trustfulness

gullible
05 green, naive **07** foolish, verdant **08** innocent, trustful, trusting **09** credulous, ingenuous **11** suggestible **12** overtrusting, unsuspecting **13** inexperienced **14** easily deceived, impressionable **15** unsophisticated

gully
03 geo, gio, goe **05** ditch, donga, gorge, gulch **06** canyon, grough, gutter, ravine, valley **07** channel, couloir **11** watercourse

See also **ravine**

gulp
◇ *containment indicator*
04 bolt, slug, swig, wolf **05** gulch, quaff, stuff, swill, swipe **06** devour, gobble, gollop, guzzle **07** draught, swallow **08** mouthful, tuck into **09** knock back

gum
03 fix, God, jaw **04** clog, dupe, glue, guar, seal **05** affix, cheat, myrrh, paste, resin, stick **06** acajou, angico, balata, cement, chewie, chicle, chuddy, humbug, mastic **07** benzoin, deceive, dextrin, gamboge, mastich **08** adhesive, bdellium, benjamin, dextrine, fixative, galbanum, mucilage, nonsense, olibanum, opopanax, scammony **09** courbaril, insolence, sagapenum, tacamahac, tacmahack **10** ammoniacum, asafoetida, caoutchouc, euphorbium, sarcocolla, tragacanth

• **gum tree**
04 arar **05** karri **06** tupelo **08** sandarac **10** eucalyptus

• **gum up**
04 clog **05** choke **06** hinder, impede **08** obstruct

gummy
05 gluey, gooey, tacky **06** sticky, viscid **07** viscous **08** adhesive **09** toothless

gumption
03 wit **04** nous **05** savvy, sense **06** acumen **07** ability, courage **08** sagacity **09** acuteness **10** astuteness, cleverness, enterprise, initiative, shrewdness **11** common sense, discernment **15** resourcefulness

gumshoe *see* **detective**

gun
03 rod **05** piece, shoot **06** expert, heater, weapon **07** firearm, shooter **10** pre-eminent **12** shooting iron

Guns include:

02 MG
03 air, dag, gas, gat, ray, six, Uzi
04 AK-47, Bren, burp, Colt®, hand, pump, punt, shot, sten, stun
05 baton, field, fusil, Lewis, Maxim, rifle, siege, spear, tommy
06 airgun, Archie, Bofors, cannon, mortar, musket, needle, pistol, pom-pom, Purdey®, Quaker, turret
07 bazooka, carbine, chopper, gatling, Long Tom, machine, pounder, scatter
08 air rifle, arquebus, elephant, falconet, firelock, howitzer, pederero, revolver, starting, Sterling
09 Archibald, Big Bertha, flintlock, harquebus
10 black Maria, demi-cannon, six-shooter, submachine, Winchester®
11 blunderbuss, four-pounder, half-pounder, Kalashnikov
12 fowling-piece, mitrailleuse, three-pounder

• **gun's catch**
04 sear

• **row of guns**
04 tier

gunfire
04 flak **05** salvo **06** firing **08** gunshots, pounding, shelling, shooting **09** cannonade **11** bombardment

gunman
04 thug **05** bravo **06** bandit, gunsel, hit man, killer, sniper **07** mobster **08** assassin, gangster, murderer, shootist **09** desperado, terrorist **10** gunslinger, hatchet man **11** armed robber

gurgle
03 lap **04** crow **05** brawl, clunk, plash **06** babble, bubble, buller, burble, guggle, murmur, ripple, ruckle, splash **08** bubbling

guru
04 sage **05** swami, tutor **06** expert, gooroo, leader, master, mentor, pundit **07** Bhagwan, teacher, tohunga **08** luminary, Svengali **09** authority, maharishi **10** instructor **12** guiding light

gush
03 goo, jet, run **04** boak, bock, boke, emit, flow, fuss, go on, pour, rail, rave, rush, tide, well **05** burst, flood, issue, raile, rayle, slush, spate, spout, spurt, surge **06** babble, drivel, effuse, jabber, stream **07** blather, cascade, chatter, enthuse, outflow, regorge, torrent **08** fountain, outburst **10** bubble over, effervesce, outpouring **11** regurgitate **12** effusiveness **14** sentimentality

gushing
05 gushy **06** sickly, too-too **07** cloying, fulsome, mawkish **08** effusive **09** emotional, excessive **10** saccharine, scaturient **11** sentimental

gust
03 fit **04** blow, flaw, gale, puff, rush, scud, wind **05** blast, blore, burst,

erupt, storm, surge **06** breeze, flurry, relish, squall **07** bluster, flaught, flavour **08** burst out, eruption, outbreak, outburst, williwaw **13** gratification

gustily
06 wildly **07** windily **08** breezily, stormily **13** tempestuously

gusto
04 élan, zeal, zest **05** verve **06** energy, relish **07** delight, fervour, unction
08 pleasure **09** enjoyment
10 enthusiasm, exuberance
12 appreciation, exhilaration

gusty
05 blowy, windy **06** breezy, stormy
07 savoury, squally **08** blustery
10 blustering **11** tempestuous

gut
◇ *middle deletion indicator*
03 rob **04** draw, gill, grit, lane, loot, sack **05** balls, basic, belly, clean, clear, dress, empty, nerve, pluck, rifle, spunk, strip **06** bottle, bowels, innate, mettle, paunch, ravage, strong **07** bravery, courage, destroy, enteron, innards, insides, natural, plunder, ransack, stomach, viscera **08** audacity, backbone, boldness, clean out, clear out, entrails, tenacity **09** devastate, emotional, fortitude, heartfelt, intuitive **10** deep-seated, disembowel, eviscerate, exenterate, intestines, mesenteron, unthinking
11 archenteron, instinctive, involuntary, spontaneous, vital organs **14** internal organs

gutless
◇ *middle deletion indicator*
04 nesh, weak **05** timid **06** abject, craven, feeble **07** chicken
08 cowardly **09** spineless
10 irresolute **11** lily-livered **12** faint-hearted **14** chicken-hearted, chicken-livered

gutsily
06 boldly **07** bravely **08** spunkily
10 resolutely, staunchily
11 indomitably **12** courageously, passionately

gutsy
04 bold, game **05** brave, gutty, lusty
06 ballsy, plucky, spunky **07** gallant, staunch **08** resolute, spirited
10 courageous, determined, gluttonous, mettlesome, passionate
11 indomitable

gutter
04 duct, grip, pipe, roan, rone, tube
05 ditch, drain, gripe, gully, rhone, rigol, sewer, swale, swayl, sweal, sweel
06 cullis, gulley, kennel, rigoll, runnel, sluice, strand, trench, trough
07 channel, conduit, culvert, passage
08 downpipe, roanpipe, ronepipe
09 guttering

guttersnipe
04 waif **05** gamin **06** urchin
07 mudlark **10** ragamuffin
14 tatterdemalion

guttural
03 low **04** deep **05** gruff, harsh, husky, rough, thick **06** hoarse **07** grating, rasping, throaty **08** croaking, gravelly

guy
02 bo **03** boy, lad, man, sod **04** boyo, chap, cove, dude, joke, lark, stay, vang
05 bloke, bucko, fella, youth
06 decamp, Fawkes, fellow, flight, geezer, person **09** character, decamping **10** individual

Guyana
03 GUY

guzzle
04 bolt, cram, gulp, soak, swig, wolf
05 quaff, scoff, stuff, swill **06** devour, gobble **07** put away, swallow **08** tuck into **09** knock back, polish off
10 gormandize

gymnastics
02 PE, PT **03** gym

Gymnastics disciplines include:

04 ball, beam, hoop
05 clubs, floor, rings, vault
06 ribbon
07 high bar
08 tumbling
10 horse vault, uneven bars
11 balance beam, pommel horse
12 parallel bars, trampolining
13 horizontal bar
14 asymmetric bars, floor exercises, side horse vault, sports aerobics

Gymnastics-related terms include:

04 beam, pike, tuck
05 cross, floor, giant, rings, salto, stick, twist, vault
06 aerial, bridge, layout
07 element, flyaway, Gaylord
08 dismount, flic-flac, rotation, round-off, straddle, walkover, whip back
09 all-around, apparatus, cartwheel, execution, handstand, Yurchenko
10 double back, handspring, somersault, uneven bars
11 balance beam, double twist, pommel horse, Swedish fall
12 compulsories, parallel bars
13 horizontal bar, inverted cross
14 asymmetric bars

Gymnasts include:

03 Kim (Nellie), Ono (Takashi)
06 Korbut (Olga Valentinovna), Miller (Shannon), Retton (Mary Lou)
07 Scherbo (Vitaly), Tweddle (Beth)
08 Comaneci (Nadia), Ditiatin (Aleksandr), Latynina (Larissa Semyonovna), Shakhlin (Boris Anfiyanovich)
09 Andrianov (Nikolai Yefimovich), Cáslavská (Vera)
10 Boginskaya (Svetlana), Turischeva (Lyudmila Ivanovna)

gym shoe
03 dap **08** plimsole, plimsoll, sandshoe

Gypsy, Gipsy
03 chi, faw, rom, rye **04** chai, chal, Roma **05** caird, nomad, rover
06 gipsen, gitana, gitano, hawker, roamer, Romani, Romany, tinker
07 rambler, Rommany, tinkler, tsigane, tzigany, Zincala, Zincalo, Zingana, Zingano, Zingara, Zingaro
08 Bohemian, diddicoy, Egyptian, huckster, wanderer, Zigeuner
09 out-of-door, traveller
14 unconventional

gyrate
04 gyre, spin, turn **05** swirl, twirl, wheel, whirl **06** circle, rotate, spiral, swivel **07** revolve **09** pirouette

gyration
04 spin, turn **05** swirl, twirl, twist, whirl, whorl **06** circle, spiral, swivel
08 rotation, spinning, wheeling, whirling **09** pirouette **10** revolution
11 convolution

H
05 aitch, hotel **07** hydrant

habit
03 way, won **04** bent, cowl, gear, mode, robe, rule, togs, ways, wont **05** dress, ethos, get-up, knack, quirk, trick, usage **06** custom, manner, monkey, outfit, policy **07** costume, garment, leaning, routine, uniform **08** clothing, fixation, practice, tendency, vestment, weakness **09** addiction, assuetude, mannerism, obsession, procedure **10** dependence, proclivity, propensity **11** familiarity, inclination **12** second nature **14** accustomedness, matter of course
See also **clothes, clothing**

• bad habit
04 vice **09** cacoethes

habitable
07 livable **08** liveable **09** livable in **10** liveable in **11** fit to live in, inhabitable

habitat
04 home **05** abode, niche **06** domain **07** element, station, terrain **08** dwelling, locality **09** territory **10** metropolis **11** environment **12** surroundings

habitation
03 hut, pad **04** digs, flat, gaff, home **05** abode, house, joint **06** biding **07** cottage, housing, lodging, mansion, tenancy **08** domicile, dwelling, quarters, tenement **09** apartment, occupancy, residence, residency **10** occupation **11** inhabitance, inhabitancy **12** inhabitation **13** accommodation, dwelling-place **14** living quarters

habitual
03 set **05** fixed, great, usual **06** common, normal, wonted **07** chronic, natural, regular, routine **08** addicted, constant, familiar, hardened, ordinary, standard **09** confirmed, customary, dependent, obsessive, recurrent **10** accustomed, inveterate, persistent, systematic **11** established, intemperate, traditional **12** pathological, systematical

habitually
06 mainly, mostly **07** as a rule, chiefly, usually **08** commonly, normally **09** generally, in the main, on average, regularly, routinely, typically **10** by and large, on the whole, ordinarily **13** traditionally **14** for the most part

habituate
03 use **04** tame **05** adapt, break, enure, inure, train **06** harden, school, season, settle **07** break in **08** accustom, make used, settle in **09** condition **10** discipline **11** acclimatize, familiarize

habitué
06 patron **07** denizen, regular **10** frequenter **15** frequent visitor, regular customer

hack
03 cut, hag, hew, saw **04** chop, fell, gash, hash, kick, pick, rack **05** clear, cough, hired, notch, slash, slave **06** drudge, mangle, writer **07** grating, hackney, mattock **08** lacerate, mediocre, mutilate, reporter, tomahawk **09** hackneyed, mercenary, scribbler **10** journalist **11** hedge-writer, penny-a-liner
See also **horse**

• hack it
04 cope **05** get by, get on **06** manage **07** carry on, make out **08** get along **10** get through **13** muddle through

hackle
• make someone's hackles rise
03 bug, irk, vex **04** gall, miff, nark, rile **05** anger, annoy, get at **06** bother, enrage, hassle, heckle, madden, needle, nettle, offend, ruffle, wind up **07** affront, hatchel, incense, outrage, provoke **08** flax-comb, irritate **09** aggravate, infuriate, make angry **10** antagonize, exasperate **13** make sparks fly **15** get on your nerves

hackneyed
03 old **04** hack, worn **05** banal, corny, hoary, stale, stock, tired, trite **06** common **07** cliché'd, percoct, worn-out **08** clichéed, overused, time-worn **09** twice-told **10** overworked, pedestrian, prostitute, threadbare, uninspired, unoriginal, yawn-making **11** commonplace, stereotyped, wearing thin **12** cliché-ridden, run-of-the-mill **13** platitudinous, unimaginative

had
01 'd

haddock
05 capon, scrod, smoky **06** finnan, rizzar, rizzer, rizzor, smokie **07** findram, speldin **08** spelding, speldrin **09** speldring **14** Arbroath smokie

Hades
05 Pluto

hafnium
02 Hf

haft
04 grip, hilt, knob **05** shaft, stock **06** handle **07** dudgeon **08** handgrip

hag
03 hew **04** fury, hack **05** crone, harpy, rudas, shrew, vixen, witch **06** beldam, gorgon, virago **07** beldame, hellcat **08** harridan **09** battle-axe, termagant

haggard
03 wan **04** lean, pale, thin **05** drawn, gaunt, Rider **06** pallid, wasted **07** drained, ghastly, pinched, untamed **08** careworn, shrunken **10** cadaverous **11** intractable **13** hollow-cheeked

haggle
04 prig **05** cavil **06** barter, bicker, dicker, higgle, mangle, niffer, palter **07** bargain, chaffer, dispute, quarrel, quibble, wrangle **08** beat down, huckster, squabble **09** negotiate

hahnium
02 Ha

hail
03 ave **04** ahoy, beat, come, goal, hale, heil, laud, pelt, rain, skol **05** cheer, exalt, greet, nod to, salve, score, skoal, sleet, sound, speak, storm **06** accost, assail, attack, batter, health, honour, praise, salute, shower, volley, wave to, what ho **07** acclaim, address, applaud, barrage, bombard, earshot, torrent, welcome **08** be born in, flag down, greeting, signal to, wave down, whoa-ho-ho **09** call out to, frozen ice, hail-storm, originate, whoa-ho-hoa **10** frozen rain, hailstones, say hello to **11** acknowledge, bombardment, communicate **13** precipitation **14** have your home in **15** have your roots in

hail-fellow-well-met
05 jolly, merry **06** genial, hearty, jovial, lively **07** affable, cordial, festive **08** cheerful, friendly, sociable **09** convivial, fun-loving

hair
03 fur, mop **04** coat, hide, pelt, pile, type, wool **05** fibre, locks, pilus, shock **06** fibril, fleece, lanugo, thatch, villus **07** bristle, tresses **08** strammel, strummel **09** character

Hair-related terms include:

03 bob, cue, cut, dod, dye, gel, wax, wig
04 bald, body, clip, coif, comb, crop, curl, down, fine, grip, hank, kesh, lank, lice, lock, mane, perm, pouf, tête, tint, tong, trim, tuft, wavy, wiry
05 bangs, black, blond, bluey, braid, brown, brush, crimp, curly, frizz, henna, layer, moult, mousy, queue, quiff, rinse, roots, sandy, serum, shade, shaft, shine, short, slick, slide, snood, tease, thick, tress
06 auburn, barber, barnet, blonde, bobble, brunet, coarse, colour, crinal, fillet, flaxen, fringe, frizzy, ginger, greasy, hairdo, kangha, mousey, mousse, peruke, pomade, pompom, pompon, pouffe, ribbon, roller, silver, tangle, titian
07 balding, bandeau, blow-dry, cowlick, crinate, flyaway, frizzle, greying, haircut, hair gel, hair net, hair oil, hirsute, keratin, lacquer, parting, periwig, pin curl, rat-tail, redhead, ringlet, shampoo, streaks, stylist, tonsure, topknot, tow-head, tressed, wet-look, xerasia
08 alopecia, ash-blond, back-comb, baldpate, barrette, bar slide, bouffant, brunette, canities, chestnut, clippers, coiffeur, coiffure, combover, cow's lick, crinated, dandruff, diffuser, elflocks, fixature, follicle, forelock, grizzled, hair band, hairless, hairline, headring, kisscurl, lovelock, peroxide, rat's-tail, receding, roulette, scrunchy, side comb, sidelock, split end, straight
09 Alice band, ash-blonde, bandoline, blue rinse, Brylcreem®, capillary, chevelure, coiffeuse, colourant, curlpaper, finger-dry, fright wig, hairbrush, hairdryer, hairpiece, hair slide, hairspray, hairstyle, headdress, Kirbigrip®, lowlights, madarosis, mop-headed, papillote, redheaded, scalp lock, scrunchie, tow-headed, trichosis, water wave
10 bad hair day, bald-headed, detangling, extensions, fair-haired, fair-headed, finger wave, hair-powder, highlights, leiotrichy, long-haired, perruquier, piliferous, pocket-comb, scrunch-dry, trichology, widow's peak
11 conditioner, flame-haired, hairdresser, hairstylist, side-parting, tow-coloured, white-haired, white-headed
12 bottle-blonde, brilliantine, Cain-coloured, close-cropped, curling tongs, cymotrichous, hair restorer, leiotrichous, straightener, trichologist
13 centre-parting, corkscrew curl, Judas-coloured, lissotrichous, pepper-and-salt, permanent wave, platinum-blond
14 shoulder-length
15 strawberry blond, styling products

Facial hair-related terms include:

05 beard, pluck, razor
06 goatee, tweeze, waxing
07 epilate, eyelash, goateed, shaving, stubble
08 bumfluff, depilate, stubbled, sugaring, tweezers
09 depilator, moustache, sideburns
10 aftershave, depilation, depilatory, face-fungus, pogonotomy, shaving gel
11 clean-shaven, shaving foam, shaving-soap
12 electrolysis, shaving-brush, shaving-stick, side whiskers
13 eyebrow pencil, eyelash curler
15 designer stubble

• let your hair down
05 relax **08** chill out, loosen up
09 hang loose **13** have a good time, let yourself go **15** let it all hang out

• make someone's hair stand on end
03 jar **04** daze, jolt, numb, stun
05 amaze, appal, repel, shake, shock, upset **06** dismay, revolt **07** agitate, astound, disgust, horrify, outrage, perturb, stagger, startle, stupefy, terrify, unnerve **08** bewilder, confound, disquiet, distress, frighten, paralyse, unsettle **09** dumbfound, take aback
10 scandalize, traumatize

• not turn a hair
04 calm **08** stay cool **10** remain calm
11 see it coming **12** keep your cool
14 not bat an eyelid, remain composed

• piece of hair
03 cue **04** lock **05** tress

• split hairs
05 cavil **07** nit-pick, quibble
08 pettifog **09** find fault **10** over-refine

haircut, hairdo *see* **hairstyle**

hairdresser
06 barber **07** crimper, friseur, stylist
08 coiffeur **09** coiffeuse **11** hairstylist
12 trichologist

Hairdressers include:

06 Clarke (Nicky), Sorbie (Trevor)
07 Grateau (Marcel), Sassoon (Vidal)
08 Collinge (Andrew), Mitchell (Paul)
10 Teazy Weazy, Toni and Guy
11 Worthington (Charles)

hairless
04 bald **05** shorn **06** shaven, smooth
08 glabrate, glabrous, tonsured
09 beardless, desperate **10** bald-headed **11** clean-shaven

hairpiece
03 jiz, rug, tie, wig **04** gizz, jasy, jazy
05 caxon, jasey, major, syrup
06 bagwig, bobwig, Brutus, merkin, peruke, tie-wig, toupee, toupet
07 buzz-wig, periwig, Ramilie, scratch, spencer **08** postiche, Ramilies, Ramillie **09** fright wig, Ramillies
10 full-bottom, scratch-wig
12 Gregorian wig **14** transformation

hair-raising
05 eerie, scary **06** creepy
08 alarming, exciting, shocking
09 startling, thrilling **10** horrifying, petrifying, terrifying **11** frightening
13 bloodcurdling, spine-chilling

hair's-breadth
03 jot **04** hair, inch **07** whisker
08 fraction

hairstyle
03 cut, set **05** style **06** barnet, hairdo
07 haircut **08** coiffure

Hairstyles include:

02 DA
03 bob, bun, wig
04 Afro, crop, perm, shed
05 bangs, braid, plait, quiff, weave
06 curled, dreads, fringe, mullet, pouffe, toupee
07 beehive, bunches, chignon, cowlick, crewcut, crimped, mohican, pageboy, pigtail, shingle, tonsure, topknot
08 bouffant, combover, corn rows, Eton crop, frizette, ponytail, ringlets, skinhead, undercut
09 duck's arse, hair-piece, Hoxton fin, number one, pompadour, sideburns
10 backcombed, dreadlocks, extensions, marcel wave, sideboards
11 French pleat
13 hair extension

hairy
◇ *anagram indicator*
05 bushy, dicey, dodgy, furry, fuzzy, grave, nasty, risky **06** chancy, daring, fleecy, pilose, pilous, severe, shaggy, unsafe, woolly **07** bearded, crinite, crinose, exposed, hirsute, ominous, serious **08** alarming, critical, high-risk, insecure, menacing, perilous, reckless, unshaven **09** breakneck, dangerous, hazardous **10** precarious, vulnerable
11 crinigerous, frightening, susceptible, threatening, treacherous

• hairy person
04 Esau

Haiti
02 RH **03** HTI

halcyon
04 calm, mild **05** balmy, happy, quiet, still **06** gentle, golden, placid, serene
07 pacific **08** carefree, peaceful, tranquil **10** kingfisher, prosperous
11 flourishing, undisturbed

hale
03 fit **04** drag, hail, well **05** sound
06 hearty, raucle, robust, strong
07 healthy **08** athletic, blooming, vigorous, youthful **09** in the pink
10 able-bodied **11** flourishing **12** in fine fettle

half
◇ *deletion indicator*
◇ *insertion indicator*
02 hf **04** demi-, hemi-, part, semi-
05 share **06** barely, halved, moiety,

partly, slight **07** à moitié, divided, limited, partial, portion, section, segment **08** bisected, fraction, moderate, slightly **09** bisection, equal part, partially **10** equal share, fractional, hemisphere, incomplete, moderately, semicircle **11** imperfectly **12** divided in two, fifty per cent, inadequately, incompletely **13** hemispherical **14** insufficiently

• by half
03 too **04** very **11** excessively **12** considerably

• by halves
05 à demi **07** à moitié **11** imperfectly **12** inadequately, incompletely **14** insufficiently

• not half
04 very **06** indeed, really **08** not at all, very much **09** not nearly **11** exceedingly

• other half
04 wife **06** spouse **07** husband, partner **08** alter ego

• too ... by half
03 too **04** over **06** unduly **11** excessively **12** immoderately, inordinately, unreasonably **13** unjustifiably, unnecessarily

half-baked
05 crazy, crude, silly **06** stupid **07** foolish **08** crackpot, immature **09** ill-judged, senseless, underdone, unplanned **10** half-witted, incomplete **11** harebrained, impractical, undeveloped **12** ill-conceived, short-sighted

half-caste
05 griff, metif, Métis, sambo **06** Creole, griffe, mestee **07** mestiza, mestizo, Métisse, mongrel, mulatta, mulatto **08** miscegen, quadroon **09** miscegene, miscegine, quintroon **10** mulattress, quarteroon **12** quarter-blood

half-cough
03 hem

half-hearted
◇ *middle deletion indicator*
04 cool, weak **05** tepid **06** feeble **07** neutral, passive **08** listless, lukewarm **09** apathetic, Laodicean **10** lacklustre **11** indifferent, unconcerned **12** uninterested **14** unenthusiastic

half-heartedly
◇ *middle deletion indicator*
06 feebly **09** neutrally **10** listlessly **13** apathetically

half-moon
04 lune **08** demilune

halfpenny
03 mag, meg, rap **04** maik, mail, make, posh **05** maile **06** bawbee, magpie, obolus **07** patrick **10** portcullis

halfway
03 mid **04** mean **06** barely, median, middle, midway **07** central **08** slightly **09** centrally **11** equidistant, imperfectly, in the middle, to the middle **12** intermediate

• meet someone halfway
09 make a deal, negotiate **10** compromise **11** give and take **15** make concessions

halfwit
03 ass, git, mug, nit **04** berk, butt, clot, dill, dope, dork, dupe, fool, geek, nerk, nong, prat, twit **05** chump, clown, comic, dumbo, dunce, eejit, galah, idiot, moron, ninny, prick, twerp, wally **06** cretin, dimwit, doofus, jester, nitwit, numpty, stooge, sucker **07** airhead, buffoon, fat-head, pillock, plonker **08** imbecile **09** birdbrain, blockhead, ignoramus, simpleton **10** nincompoop **13** laughing-stock

half-witted
04 dull, dumb **05** barmy, batty, crazy, dotty, nutty, potty, silly, wacky **06** simple, stupid **07** foolish, idiotic, moronic **08** crackpot **09** dim-witted **12** crack-brained, feeble-minded, simple-minded **14** not the full quid

hall
02 ha' **04** aula, gild **05** foyer, guild, lobby, odeon, salle **06** atrium, exedra **07** apadana, chamber, citadel, commons, exhedra, hallway, megaron, passage **08** basilica, corridor **09** concourse, Domdaniel, longhouse, vestibule **10** auditorium, passageway **11** concert hall **12** assembly hall, assembly room, entrance-hall **14** conference hall

See also **college**

hallmark
04 mark, sign **05** badge, stamp **06** device, emblem, symbol **09** brand-name, indicator, platemark, trademark **10** indication **12** official mark **13** official stamp **14** typical quality

hallo
02 hi **04** g'day **05** chimo, hello, hillo, hullo **06** holloa **07** welcome **09** greetings **11** good evening, good morning **13** good afternoon

hallowed
04 holy, tapu **06** age-old, sacred **07** blessed, revered **08** honoured **09** dedicated, venerable **10** inviolable, sacrosanct, sanctified **11** consecrated, established

hallucinate
04 trip **05** dream **07** imagine **08** daydream, freak out **09** fantasize, see things **10** see visions **13** imagine things

hallucination
04 trip **05** dream **06** mirage, vision **07** fantasy, figment **08** daydream, delirium, delusion, freak-out, illusion **09** autoscopy **10** apparition **14** phantasmagoria **15** hypnagogic image, hypnogogic image

halo
01 O **04** aura, ring **05** crown, glory **06** corona, gloria, nimbus **07** aureola, aureole **08** gloriole, halation, radiance **12** vesica piscis **13** circle of light

halt
03 alt, end **04** curb, lame, limp, quit, rest, stem, stop, wait **05** block, break, cease, check, close, crush, pause **06** arrest, desist, draw up, finish, impede, pull up **07** limping, respite **08** break off, crippled, deadlock, full stop, hold back, interval, obstruct, stoppage **09** cessation, stalemate, terminate, vacillate **10** call it a day, come to rest, desistance, put an end to, standstill **11** come to a rest, come to a stop, discontinue, termination **12** bring to a stop, draw to a close, interruption **13** bring to a close **14** breathing space, discontinuance **15** discontinuation

halting
06 broken **07** awkward **08** hesitant, laboured, unsteady **09** faltering, imperfect, stumbling, uncertain **10** stammering, stuttering

halve
◇ *insertion indicator*
05 sever, share, split **06** bisect, divide, lessen, reduce **07** cut down **09** cut in half **10** split in two **11** dichotomize **13** divide equally

halved
03 cut **05** split **06** shared **07** divided **08** bisected **09** dimidiate

ham
◇ *anagram indicator*
04 hock **05** hough **06** clumsy, coarse **07** amateur, overact, pigmeat **08** inexpert **10** prosciutto

ham-fisted
03 ham **05** gawky, inept **06** clumsy, thumby **07** awkward, unhandy **08** bungling **09** all thumbs, lumbering, maladroit, two-fisted, unskilful **10** blundering, cack-handed **11** heavy-handed **13** accident-prone, unco-ordinated

hamlet
05 aldea, thorp **06** thorpe

hammer
◇ *anagram indicator*
02 ax **03** axe, din, hit **04** bang, bash, beat, drum, form, lick, make, mall, maul, pane, pean, peen, pein, pene, pick, plug, rout, slam, slap, slog **05** blame, bully, decry, dolly, drive, force, forge, gavel, grind, knock, madge, mould, pound, rivet, shape, slate **06** attack, batter, beetle, defeat, drudge, instil, keep on, labour, mallet, martel, monkey, oliver, plexor, sledge, strike, thrash **07** censure, clobber, condemn, dog-head, fashion, malleus, Mjölnir, outplay, persist, plessor, run down, trounce **08** malleate, Mjöllnir, overcome, trouncer, work away **09** criticize, denigrate, drive home, overwhelm, percussor, persevere, reiterate, slaughter **10** annihilate, claw hammer, sheep's-foot, tack hammer,

tilt-hammer, trip hammer **11** about-sledge, steam hammer, stone hammer, walk all over, water hammer
12 sledgehammer **13** run rings round, tear a strip off **14** knapping-hammer
15 make mincemeat of

• hammer out
◇ *anagram indicator*
06 finish, settle **07** produce, resolve, sort out, work out **08** complete
09 negotiate, thrash out
10 accomplish, bring about **12** carry through

hammered
◇ *anagram indicator*
06 incuse **07** excudit

hammerhead
04 pane, pean, peen, pein, pene
05 umbre **07** Zygaena **08** umbrette
09 umber-bird

hammock support
04 clew, clue

hamper
◇ *anagram indicator*
◇ *containment indicator*
03 box, pad, ped **04** curb, foil, stop, tuck **05** baulk, block, bribe, cabin, check, cramp, creel, pinch, seron
06 basket, bridle, fetter, hinder, hobble, hold up, impede, retard, seroon, stymie, tangle, thwart **07** curtail, distort, inhibit, pannier, prevent, shackle **08** encumber, handicap, incumber, obstruct, restrain, restrict, slow down **09** container, frustrate, hamstring

hamstring
03 hox **04** foil, hock, stop **05** baulk, block, check, cramp, hough
06 hinder, hold up, impede, stymie, thwart **07** cripple, disable
08 encumber, handicap, paralyse, restrain, restrict **09** frustrate
12 incapacitate

hand
03 aid, fin, paw, pud **04** care, doer, fist, give, help, hond, mitt, palm, part, pass, side **05** arrow, manus, offer, power, skill, style, touch, yield **06** author, charge, convey, marker, needle, pledge, script, stroke, submit, worker
07 acclaim, command, conduct, control, custody, deliver, ovation, pointer, present, quarter, succour, support, workman, writing
08 applause, cheering, clapping, clutches, employee, farm-hand, handclap, hand over, hireling, labourer, producer, transmit **09** authority, direction, handiwork, indicator, influence, operative, performer, signature, workwoman **10** assistance, management, penmanship, possession
11 calligraphy, handwriting, helping hand, supervision **12** manual worker
13 participation **14** responsibility
15 instrumentality, round of applause

• at hand
04 near, nigh **05** close, handy, ready
06 to hand, toward **08** imminent
09 available, to the fore **10** accessible
11 forthcoming, in the offing **13** about to happen

• by hand
07 à la main **08** manually **13** with your hands **14** using your hands

• from hand to mouth
09 in poverty **10** insecurely
11 dangerously, uncertainly **12** au jour le jour, from day to day, precariously
14 on the breadline

• hand down
04 give, will **05** grant, leave **06** pass on
07 devolve **08** bequeath, pass down, transfer

• hand in glove
09 in cahoots **11** very closely

• hand in hand
12 holding hands **13** with hands held
14 closely related **15** closely together, with hands joined

• hand on
04 give **06** pass on, supply **08** transfer, transmit **09** surrender **14** let someone have

• hand out
04 dole **07** deal out, dish out, give out, mete out, pass out **08** dispense, share out **10** distribute **11** disseminate

• hand over
04 give, pass, turn **05** yield **06** donate, give up, render **07** consign, deliver, present, release **08** transfer, turn over
09 surrender **10** relinquish

• hollow of hand
04 vola

• in hand
05 put by, ready, spare **07** à la main
08 under way **09** available, in reserve
10 attended to, considered **12** under control **14** being dealt with

• on the other hand
03 but **04** then **05** again
12 contrariwise

• out of hand
◇ *anagram indicator*
06 at once **11** immediately **12** out of control

• to hand
04 near **05** close, handy, ready **06** at hand, nearby **07** ad manum
08 imminent **09** available
10 accessible **13** about to happen

• try your hand
03 try **04** seek **06** strive **07** attempt, have a go **09** have a shot, have a stab
10 have a crack **13** see if you can do

• win hands down
09 win easily **15** win effortlessly

• winning hand
04 post

handbag
04 caba, grip **05** cabas, purse
07 holdall **08** handgrip, reticule
09 clutch bag, flight bag, vanity bag
10 pocketbook **11** shoulder bag

handbill
05 flier **06** letter, notice **07** leaflet
08 circular, flysheet, pamphlet
09 throwaway **12** announcement
13 advertisement

handbook
03 ABC **05** guide **06** manual
08 Baedeker **09** companion, guidebook, vade-mecum
10 prospectus **11** enchiridion
12 encheiridion **15** instruction book

handcuff
03 tie **04** cuff **06** fasten, fetter, secure
07 manacle, shackle **08** bracelet, snitcher, wristlet

handcuffs
05 cuffs, snaps **07** darbies, fetters, mittens, nippers **08** manacles, shackles, snippers **09** bracelets, snitchers, wristlets

handful
03 few, rip **04** hank, pain, pest, ripp
05 bunch, pugil **06** bother, little
07 fistful, loofful **08** nieveful, nuisance
10 scattering, smattering, sprinkling
11 small amount, small number
13 pain in the neck **15** thorn in the flesh

handgun
03 gat, gun, rod **04** iron **05** piece
06 pistol **07** sidearm **08** culverin, revolver **09** derringer **10** six-shooter
11 blunderbuss

See also **gun**

handicap
03 hcp **04** curb **05** block, check, limit
06 bridle, burden, defect, hamper, hinder, impair, impede, retard
07 barrier, disable, half-one, penalty
08 drawback, encumber, hold back, obstacle, obstruct, restrict
09 hindrance **10** constraint, disability, impairment, impediment, limitation
11 abnormality, encumbrance, obstruction, restriction, shortcoming
12 disadvantage **14** stumbling-block

• concede as handicap
03 owe

• with adverse handicap
04 plus

• with a handicap of
03 off

handicapped
08 disabled **10** challenged
13 disadvantaged, incapacitated

handicraft
03 art **05** craft, skill **08** artifice, handwork **09** craftwork, handiwork, scrimshaw **11** scrimshandy, workmanship **12** scrimshander
13 craftsmanship

handily
06 at hand, nearly, to hand **07** adeptly, readily **08** adroitly, cleverly, usefully
09 helpfully, skilfully **10** accessibly
11 practically, within reach
12 conveniently

handiwork
03 art **04** hand, work **05** craft, doing, skill **06** action, design, result
07 product **08** creation **09** craftwork, invention **10** handicraft, production
11 achievement, artisanship,

workmanship **13** craftsmanship **14** responsibility

handkerchief
03 rag **04** wipe **05** blind, fogle, hanky, romal, rumal **06** hankie, napkin, tissue **07** bandana, foulard, Kleenex®, nose-rag, orarium, snotrag **08** kerchief, monteith, mouchoir **09** muckender
• **keep in a handkerchief**
04 mail

handle
03 bow, lug, paw **04** bail, feel, grip, haft, hilt, hold, knob, name, work **05** brake, drive, grasp, shaft, staff, stale, steal, steel, steer, steil, stele, stock, sweep, touch, treat, wield **06** behave, deal in, finger, fondle, manage, market, pick up, steale, tackle **07** control, discuss, operate, trade in, traffic **08** cope with, deal with, handgrip **09** handstaff, supervise **10** plough-tree, take care of **11** plough-stilt **12** be in charge of, do business in

handling
07 conduct, running **08** approach, managing **09** direction, operation, treatment **10** discussion, management **11** transaction **12** manipulation **14** administration

handout
04 alms, dole **05** gifts, issue, share **07** charity, freebie, leaflet **08** brochure, bulletin, circular, largesse, pamphlet **09** statement **10** free sample, literature **12** press release

handover
04 move **05** shift **06** change **07** removal **08** transfer **10** assignment, changeover, conveyance, relocation **12** displacement, transference, transmission **13** transposition

hand-picked
05 elect, élite **06** choice, chosen, picked, select **08** screened, selected **09** recherché

hands
02 hh

handsome
04 fair, fine **05** ample, brave, dishy, hunky, large, noble **06** comely, lavish, seemly **07** elegant, featous, liberal, sizable, stately **08** abundant, becoming, feateous, featuous, generous, gorgeous, gracious, sizeable, suitable **09** bountiful, dignified, featurely, goodfaced, plentiful, unsparing **10** attractive, convenient, personable, unstinting **11** good-looking, magnanimous **12** considerable

handsomely
05 amply **06** richly **08** lavishly **09** carefully, liberally **10** abundantly, generously, graciously **11** bountifully, plentifully, unsparingly **12** munificently, unstintingly **13** magnanimously

handwriting
03 paw **04** fist, hand **05** Neski **06** Naskhi, Neskhi, niggle, scrawl, script **07** writing **08** half-text, join-hand, printing, scribble **09** autograph, character, court hand, scripture **10** penmanship **11** calligraphy, chirography, copperplate, running hand **13** secretary hand **15** Lombardic script

handy
04 deft, near **05** adept, gemmy, jemmy, ready **06** adroit, at hand, clever, expert, nearly, nimble, to hand, useful **07** helpful, skilful, skilled **08** handsome **09** available, dexterous, practical **10** accessible, convenient, functional, proficient **11** practicable, within reach

handyman
05 DIYer **08** factotum **09** odd-jobber, odd-jobman **10** bluejacket **15** Jack-of-all-trades

hang
03 fix, nub, sag **04** bend, damn, drop, flit, flop, glue, kill, kilt, lean, loll, pend **05** affix, cling, drape, drift, droop, float, hover, lynch, paste, put up, run up, scrag, stick, strap, swing, trail, truss **06** append, attach, cement, dangle, fasten, impend, linger, remain, string **07** execute, flutter, justify, meaning, stretch, suspend, turn off **08** hang down, string up **09** declivity **10** put to death **11** be suspended **13** supercollate **15** send to the gibbet
• **get the hang of**
04 twig **05** grasp, learn **06** fathom, master **10** comprehend, understand **13** get the knack of
• **hang about**
04 lime, mike, stay **05** haunt **06** dawdle, linger, loiter, remain **07** hang out, persist **08** frequent **09** waste time **10** hang around **13** associate with **15** keep company with
• **hang back**
05 demur, stall **06** recoil **07** shy away **08** hesitate, hold back **10** shrink back, stay behind **11** be reluctant
• **hang down loosely**
03 lop
• **hang fire**
04 stop, wait **05** delay, stall, stick **06** hold on **08** hang back, hesitate, hold back **09** vacillate **13** procrastinate
• **hang on**
04 grip, wait **05** cling, grasp **06** append, clutch, endure, hold on, remain, rest on, turn on **07** carry on, hinge on, hold out, persist **08** continue, depend on, hold fast **09** persevere **14** be contingent on, be determined by **15** be conditional on
• **hang over**
04 loom **06** impend, menace **08** approach, threaten **10** be imminent, overshadow

hangdog
05 cowed **06** abject, guilty **07** furtive **08** cringing, defeated, downcast, sneaking, wretched **09** miserable **10** browbeaten, shamefaced

hanger-on
05 toady **06** client, lackey, minion, sponge **07** flunkey, sponger **08** follower, henchman, parasite **09** courtling, dependant, dependent, sycophant **10** freeloader

hanging
04 drop **05** drape, loose, tapis **06** dossal, dossel, floppy **07** curtain, drapery, draping, frontal, pendant, pendent, pending, pensile **08** dangling, downcast, drooping, flapping, flopping, parament, swinging **09** drop-scene, pendulous, suspended **10** suspending, unattached **11** antependium, unsupported

hangman
07 lockman, topsman **08** rascally **09** Jack Ketch **11** nubbing-cove

hang-out
03 den **04** dive, home **05** haunt, joint, local, patch **12** meeting-place, watering-hole **14** stamping-ground

hangover
08 survival **10** crapulence **12** after-effects, katzenjammer, morning after

hang-up
05 block, thing **06** phobia **07** problem **08** fixation, idée fixe, neurosis **09** obsession **10** difficulty, inhibition **11** mental block **13** preoccupation

hank
04 coil, fank, loop, roll, tuft **05** catch, piece, skein, twist **06** length **07** handful **08** selvagee

hanker
06 linger
• **hanker after, hanker for**
04 want **05** covet, crave **06** desire **07** itch for, long for, pine for, wish for **08** yearn for **09** hunger for, thirst for **10** be dying for **14** set your heart on

hankering
04 ache, itch, urge, wish **06** desire, hunger, pining, thirst **07** craving, longing **08** yearning

hankie, hanky *see* **handkerchief**

hanky-panky
05 fling **06** affair, tricks **07** carry-on, devilry **08** adultery, cheating, mischief, nonsense, trickery **09** chicanery, deception **10** dishonesty, subterfuge **11** shenanigans **12** bit on the side, machinations **13** fooling around, funny business, jiggery-pokery, slap and tickle **14** how's-your-father, monkey business

haphazard
◇ *anagram indicator*
04 wild **06** casual, chance, random, randon **07** aimless, wildcat **08** careless, slapdash, slipshod **09** arbitrary, hit-or-miss, irregular, orderless, unplanned **10** disorderly, hitty-missy, tumultuary, willy-nilly

11 promiscuous **12** disorganized, unmethodical, unsystematic
14 indiscriminate, rough-and-tumble

haphazardly
◇ *anagram indicator*
06 wildly **08** by chance, randomly
10 carelessly, willy-nilly **11** arbitrarily, irregularly **14** unmethodically

hapless
06 cursed, jinxed **07** unhappy, unlucky
08 ill-fated, luckless, wretched
09 miserable **10** ill-starred **11** star-crossed, unfortunate

happen
02 be **03** hap **04** come, fall, find, go on, pass, tide **05** arise, ensue, hit on, occur, worth **06** appear, arrive, befall, chance, crop up, follow, result, turn up
07 develop, light on, perhaps, turn out
08 become of, bump into, chance on, come true, discover **09** come about, eventuate, run across, stumble on, supervene, take place, transpire
10 come across, come to pass **11** be the fate of, eventualize, materialize
13 come into being, present itself

happening
04 case **05** event, scene, thing, weird
06 action, affair, chance **07** episode
08 accident, business, incident, occasion **09** adventure, événement, occurrent **10** experience, occurrence, phenomenon **11** eventuality, fashionable, proceedings
12 circumstance

happily
06 gladly **07** luckily, merrily, perhaps
08 by chance, heartily, joyfully, joyously **09** agreeably, feliciter, fittingly, gleefully, willingly
10 cheerfully **11** contentedly, delightedly, fortunately, opportunely
12 auspiciously, propitiously
14 providentially

happiness
03 joy **04** glee, life, seal, seel, seil, sele
05 bliss **06** gaiety, heaven **07** delight, ecstasy, elation **08** delirium, euphoria, felicity, gladness, pleasure
09 beatitude, enjoyment, eudaemony, hog heaven, merriment, merriness
10 blitheness, cheeriness, eudaemonia, exuberance, joyfulness
11 contentment, good spirits, high spirits **12** cheerfulness

happy
◇ *anagram indicator*
03 apt, gay **04** glad **05** blest, jolly, lucky, merry, seely **06** blithe, elated, golden, jovial, joyful, joyous, proper
07 blessed, chuffed, content, exalted, fitting, gleeful, halcyon, helpful, pleased, radiant, smiling **08** apposite, carefree, cheerful, ecstatic, euphoric, gruntled, thrilled **09** cock-a-hoop, confident, contented, delighted, delirious, exuberant, fortunate, gratified, high-blest, opportune, overjoyed, rapturous, satisfied, unworried **10** auspicious, beneficial, convenient, favourable, felicitous, propitious, starry-eyed, untroubled
11 appropriate, in a good mood, on cloud nine, over the moon, tickled pink, unconcerned **12** advantageous, happy as a clam, happy as Larry, light-hearted, walking on air **13** floating on air, in good spirits, in high spirits
15 happy as a sandboy, in seventh heaven, on top of the world

• be happy
03 ave

happy-go-lucky
06 blithe, casual **08** carefree, cheerful, heedless, reckless **09** easy-going, unworried **10** insouciant, nonchalant, untroubled **11** improvident, unconcerned **12** devil-may-care, light-hearted **13** irresponsible

harangue
05 orate, spout **06** lay off, preach, sermon, speech, spruik, tirade
07 address, declaim, lecture, oration
08 diatribe, perorate **09** hold forth, speechify **10** peroration, talky-talky
11 exhortation, paternoster **12** talkee-talkee

harass
◇ *anagram indicator*
03 dun, nag, vex **04** bait, cark, fret, tire
05 annoy, chevy, chivy, grind, harry, hound, pinch, press, trash, weary, worry **06** argufy, badger, bother, chivvy, harrow, hassle, infest, overdo, pester, pingle, plague, pursue, stress
07 afflict, disturb, dragoon, exhaust, fatigue, provoke, torment, trouble, trounce, turmoil, wear out **08** distract, distress, irritate **09** importune, persecute **10** antagonize, exasperate
11 have it in for **12** put the wind up

harassed
◇ *anagram indicator*
05 vexed **06** hunted **07** harried, hassled, hounded, plagued, uptight, worried **08** careworn, pestered, strained, stressed, troubled
09 pressured, tormented
10 distracted, distraught, distressed
11 pressurized, stressed-out, under stress **13** under pressure

harassment
05 grief **06** bother, hassle, molest
07 mobbing, torment, trouble
08 distress, nuisance, vexation
09 annoyance, badgering, pestering
10 irritation, pressuring **11** aggravation, bedevilment, molestation, persecution

harbinger
04 host, omen, sign **06** herald
07 pioneer, portent, warning
09 foretoken, messenger, precursor
10 forerunner, indication **12** avant-courier

harbour
◇ *containment indicator*
04 bear, dock, herd, hide, hold, keep, mole, port, quay **05** basin, haven, house, lodge, nurse, reset, wharf
06 foster, marina, refuge, retain, shield, take in **07** believe, cherish, cling to, conceal, imagine, lodging, mooring, nurture, protect, receive, shelter
08 maintain **09** anchorage, entertain

hard
01 H **03** bad, raw, set **04** bony, busy, cold, firm, grim, keen, live, near, real, sore, true **05** badly, close, cruel, dense, flint, harsh, heavy, horny, irony, rigid, sharp, solid, stern, stiff, stony, tough
06 actual, bitter, busily, crusty, deeply, flinty, keenly, knotty, marble, potent, severe, stingy, strict, strong, tiring, wooden **07** acutely, arduous, austere, callous, certain, closely, compact, complex, eagerly, harmful, harshly, heavily, hornish, intense, onerous, painful, sharply, violent, zealous
08 baffling, definite, diligent, exacting, forceful, forcibly, freezing, intently, involved, narcotic, obdurate, pitiless, powerful, puzzling, reliable, rigorous, ruthless, scleroid, sedulous, severely, steadily, strongly, toilsome, uneasily, verified, vigorous **09** addictive, arduously, assiduous, carefully, compacted, condensed, difficult, earnestly, energetic, intensely, intricate, laborious, merciless, niggardly, resistant, strenuous, unfeeling, unpliable, unsparing, violently
10 compressed, critically, diligently, exhausting, forcefully, hard as iron, hard as rock, implacable, inflexible, oppressive, perplexing, powerfully, tyrannical, undeniable, unpleasant, unyielding, vigorously **11** assiduously, attentively, bewildering, cold-hearted, complicated, constrained, distressing, hard as flint, hard as stone, hard-hearted, hard-working, industrious, insensitive, intractable, laboriously, strenuously, troublesome, unrelenting
12 backbreaking, disagreeable, enthusiastic, habit-forming, impenetrable, indisputable
13 conscientious, energetically, industriously, reverberating, uncomfortable, unsympathetic
14 after a struggle, unquestionable, with difficulty **15** conscientiously

• hard and fast
03 set **05** fixed, rigid **06** strict
07 binding **08** definite **09** immutable, stringent **10** inflexible, invariable, unchanging **11** unalterable
12 unchangeable **14** uncompromising

• hard black
02 HB

• hard up
04 bust, poor, puir **05** broke, short, skint **07** boracic, lacking **08** bankrupt, dirt-poor, in the red, strapped
09 penniless **10** cleaned out, stony broke **11** impecunious, near the bone
12 impoverished, on your uppers
14 on your beam ends **15** strapped for cash

• very hard
02 HH

hard-bitten
05 tough **06** inured, shrewd **07** callous, cynical **08** ruthless **09** hard-nosed, practical, realistic, toughened **10** hard-boiled, hard-headed **11** down-to-earth **12** case-hardened, matter-of-fact **13** unsentimental

hard-boiled
05 tough **06** brazen **07** callous, cynical **09** practical **10** hard-headed **11** down-to-earth **13** unsentimental

hard-core
05 rigid **07** blatant, diehard, extreme, staunch **08** explicit **09** dedicated, obstinate, steadfast **12** intransigent **13** dyed-in-the-wool

harden
03 set **04** bake, cake, geal, gird **05** brace, chill, enure, flesh, inure, nerve, steel, train **06** anneal, bronze, deaden, endure, freeze, season, temper **07** calcify, congeal, fortify, petrify, stiffen, toughen **08** accustom, buttress, concrete, indurate, sclerose, solidify **09** habituate, reinforce, vulcanize **10** case-harden, sclerotize, strengthen, work-harden

hardened
03 set **06** inured **07** bronzed, callous, chilled, chronic, coctile, steeled **08** habitual, obdurate, scleroid, seasoned **09** reprobate, shameless, toughened, unfeeling **10** accustomed, habituated, inveterate **12** incorrigible, irredeemable

hard-headed
05 sharp, tough **06** astute, shrewd **08** pitiless, rational, sensible **09** hard nosed, practical, pragmatic, realistic **10** cool-headed, hard-bitten, hard-boiled **11** down-to-earth, level-headed, tough-minded **12** businesslike **13** clear-thinking, unsentimental

hard-hearted
04 cold, hard **05** cruel, stony **06** unkind **07** callous, inhuman **08** pitiless, uncaring **09** heartless, merciless, unfeeling **10** flint-heart **11** cold-blooded, unconcerned **12** stony-hearted **13** unsympathetic **14** marble-breasted

hard-hitting
04 bold **05** blunt, frank, tough **06** direct **08** critical, forceful, straight, vigorous **09** unsparing **10** forthright **12** condemnatory **13** no-holds-barred **14** uncompromising

hardihood
04 grit, guts, risk **05** pluck **06** bottle, daring, valour **07** bravery, courage **08** audacity, boldness, rashness **10** enterprise, robustness **11** intrepidity **12** fearlessness, recklessness **13** dauntlessness **15** adventurousness

hardiness
06 valour **07** courage **08** boldness **09** fortitude, toughness **10** resilience, resolution, robustness, ruggedness, sturdiness **11** intrepidity

hardline
05 tough **06** strict **07** extreme **08** militant **10** immoderate, inflexible, unyielding **11** undeviating **12** intransigent **14** uncompromising

hardly
04 jimp, just **06** barely, jimply, uneath **07** harshly, none too **08** not at all, not quite, only just, scarcely, severely **09** almost not, by no means **14** with difficulty

hardness
06 rigour **07** granite **08** coldness, firmness, rigidity, severity **09** harshness, sternness, toughness **10** difficulty, inhumanity **12** pitilessness **13** insensitivity, laboriousness

hard-nosed
05 tough **08** ruthless **09** practical, realistic **10** hard-bitten, hard-boiled, hard-headed, no-nonsense **13** unsentimental

hard-pressed
06 pushed, strait **07** hard put, harried **08** harassed **09** in a corner, overtaxed **10** hard-pushed **11** under stress, up against it **12** in a tight spot, overburdened **13** under pressure

hardship
04 need, pain, want **05** trial **06** misery, murder, rigour, strait, stress **07** burdens, penance, poverty, trouble **08** distress **09** adversity, austerity, grievance, privation, suffering **10** affliction, difficulty, misfortune **11** depredation, deprivation, destitution, tribulation **12** depredations

hardware
03 kit **04** gear **05** stuff, tools **06** outfit, rig-out, tackle, things **08** articles, supplies **09** apparatus, equipment, furniture **10** appliances **11** accessories, apparelment, ironmongery **13** accoutrements, paraphernalia

hard-wearing
05 stout, tough **06** rugged, strong, sturdy **07** durable, lasting **08** well-made **09** resilient **10** made to last **11** built to last

hard-working
04 busy, keen **07** zealous **08** diligent, sedulous **09** assiduous, energetic **11** industrious **12** enthusiastic **13** conscientious

hardy
03 fit **04** bold, Olly **05** brave, sound, stout, tough **06** daring, heroic, plucky, robust, strong, sturdy, trusty **07** durable, healthy, spartan, stoical **08** fearless, impudent, indurate, intrepid, resolute, stalwart, vigorous **09** confident, heavy-duty, indurated, iron-sided, undaunted **10** courageous **11** indomitable **12** stout-hearted

hare
03 doe, wat **04** baud, bawd, buck, mara, pika, puss, scut **06** hasten, malkin, mawkin **07** leveret **08** baudrons **10** Dolichotis, jack rabbit, sage rabbit, springhaas **14** snowshoe rabbit
See also **rabbit**

hare-brained
04 daft, rash, wild **05** giddy, inane, silly **06** scatty, stupid **07** foolish **08** careless, crackpot, headlong, heedless, reckless **09** half-baked **12** ill-conceived **14** scatterbrained

harem
05 serai **06** zenana **08** seraglio
- **room in a harem**
03 oda

hark
04 hear, mark, note **06** listen, notice **07** give ear, hearken, pay heed, whisper **12** pay attention
- **hark back**
06 go back, hoicks, recall, revert **07** regress, try back **08** remember, turn back **09** recollect

harlequin
04 fool, zany **05** clown, comic, joker **06** jester **07** buffoon **10** variegated

harlot
03 pro **04** base, lewd, loon, lown, slag, tart **05** hussy, lowne, tramp, whore **06** hooker **07** slapper, trollop, wagtail **08** callgirl, scrubber, strumpet **10** loose woman, prostitute **11** fallen woman, working girl **12** streetwalker

harm
◇ *anagram indicator*
03 ill, mar **04** bane, evil, hurt, loss, pain, ruin **05** abuse, annoy, scath, spoil, touch, wound, wreak, wrong **06** damage, impair, injure, injury, misuse, molest, scathe **07** blemish, destroy **08** ill-treat, maltreat **09** adversity, detriment, prejudice, suffering, vengeance **10** disservice, impairment, misfortune **11** destruction, work against **12** do violence to **15** be detrimental to

harmful
03 bad, ill **04** evil **05** toxic **06** wicked **07** hurtful, noxious **08** damaging, wounding **09** dangerous, hazardous, injurious, poisonous, unhealthy **10** pernicious **11** deleterious, destructive, detrimental, unwholesome

harmless
04 mild, safe **05** silly **06** gentle **07** anodyne **08** -friendly, hurtless, innocent, non-toxic **09** blameless, innocuous, woundless **11** inoffensive

harmonious
06 dulcet, in sync, mellow **07** amiable, cordial, in synch, musical, tuneful **08** amicable, balanced, friendly, matching, peaceful, pleasant, rhythmic **09** according, agreeable, congruous,

consonant, consonous, melodious, peaceable **10** Apollonian, compatible, concinnous, concordant, concordial, consistent, euphonious, like-minded **11** co-ordinated, harmonizing, mellifluous, sympathetic, symphonious **13** sweet-sounding

harmoniously
08 amicably **09** agreeably, cordially **10** compatibly, peacefully **11** congruously **12** consistently **13** symmetrically **14** in a balanced way **15** sympathetically

harmonization
08 matching **09** agreement, balancing **10** adaptation **11** arrangement **12** co-ordination **13** accommodation **14** correspondence, reconciliation

harmonize
02 go **03** mix **04** mesh, rime, suit, tone **05** adapt, agree, atone, blend, fit in, match, rhyme, salve **06** accord, attone **07** arrange, balance, compose, concord **08** coincide **09** get on with, reconcile **10** co-ordinate, correspond, go together **11** accommodate, be congruent, be congruous

harmony
04 tone, tune **05** amity, chime, music, peace, unity **06** accord, assent, melody, unison **07** balance, chiming, concent, concert, concord, euphony, keeping, oneness, rapport **08** blending, diapason, eurythmy, faburden, goodwill, symmetry, sympathy, symphony **09** agreement, concentus, eurhythmy, unanimity **10** concinnity, conformity, consonance, consonancy **11** amicability, concurrence, consistence, consistency, co-operation, tunefulness **12** co-ordination, friendliness, thorough bass **13** compatibility, melodiousness, understanding **14** correspondence, correspondency, like-mindedness **15** mellifluousness

• in harmony
08 together **15** never a cross word

• out of harmony
04 ajar

harness
03 use **04** gear, tack, team **05** apply, hitch, put to, trace **06** employ, straps, tackle **07** channel, control, exploit, gearing, hitch up, utilize **08** mobilize, tackling **09** equipment, make use of **10** baby-jumper **11** baby-bouncer **13** accoutrements

• in harness
04 busy **06** active, at work **07** working **08** employed, together **11** co-operating **13** collaborating, in co-operation

harp
04 kora, lyre **05** nebel **06** trigon **07** sambuca **08** clarsach **09** harmonica **10** mouth organ

• harp on
03 nag **05** grind, press, renew **06** labour, repeat **07** dwell on **09** go on about, reiterate **11** flog to death, keep on about **14** go on and on about

harpoon
03 peg **04** barb, dart **05** arrow, spear **06** fisgig, fizgig, grains **07** fishgig, trident **10** toggle iron

harpsichord
06 spinet **07** cembalo, spinnet **08** clavecin, spinette, virginal **09** virginals **12** clavicembalo **15** pair of virginals

harridan
03 hag, nag **04** fury **05** harpy, scold, shrew, vixen, witch **06** dragon, gorgon, tartar, virago **07** hell-cat **09** battle-axe, termagant, Xanthippe

harried
05 beset **07** anxious, hassled, plagued, ravaged, worried **08** agitated, bothered, harassed, troubled **09** pressured, tormented **10** distressed **11** hard-pressed, pressurized

harrow
04 drag, haro **05** brake, herse, wring **09** pitch-pole, pitch-poll

• point of harrow
04 tine

harrowing
05 rough **08** alarming, daunting, lacerant **09** agonizing, traumatic, upsetting **10** disturbing, perturbing, terrifying, tormenting **11** distressing, frightening **12** excruciating, heart-rending, nerve-racking

harry
03 nag, vex **05** annoy, hound, worry **06** badger, bother, chivvy, harass, hassle, molest, pester, plague, ravage **07** destroy, disturb, oppress, plunder, torment, trouble **09** persecute **10** pressurize

harsh
03 raw **04** bold, grim, hard, iron, rude, wild **05** asper, bleak, cruel, gaudy, gruff, lurid, rough, sharp, showy, stark, stern, stoor, stour, sture **06** barren, bitter, bright, brutal, coarse, flashy, garish, hoarse, savage, severe, shrill, stowre, strict, unkind **07** acerbic, austere, cracked, glaring, grating, hostile, inhuman, jarring, rasping, raucous, spartan **08** abrasive, croaking, dazzling, desolate, gravelly, grinding, guttural, jangling, metallic, pitiless, rigorous, ruthless, scabrous, strident **09** barbarian, barbarous, dissonant, Draconian, inclement, merciless, unfeeling, untunable **10** discordant, unpleasant, untuneable **11** comfortless, ear-piercing **12** inhospitable **13** unsympathetic

harshly
04 hard **06** grimly, hardly **07** cruelly, gruffly, roughly, sharply, sternly **08** brutally, hoarsely, severely, unkindly **10** pitilessly, ruthlessly, stridently **11** mercilessly **12** discordantly, unpleasantly

harshness
06 rigour **07** tyranny **08** acerbity, acrimony, asperity, hardness, severity, sourness **09** austerity, brutality, ill-temper, roughness, starkness, sternness **10** bitterness, coarseness, strictness **12** abrasiveness

harum-scarum
04 rash, wild **05** hasty **06** scatty **07** erratic **08** careless, reckless **09** haphazard, impetuous, imprudent **11** hare-brained, precipitate **12** disorganized **13** ill-considered, irresponsible **14** scatterbrained

harvest
02 in **03** mow **04** crop, gain, kirn, pick, rabi, reap **05** amass, glean, horde, pluck, stock, store, yield **06** autumn, effect, fruits, garner, gather, hairst, hockey, obtain, result, return, secure, silage, supply **07** acquire, collect, hopping, produce, product, reaping, returns **08** gather in, ingather, Spätlese, vendange **10** accumulate, collection, harvesting **11** consequence, harvest-home, harvest-time, ingathering **12** accumulation **13** tattie-howking, tattie-lifting

has
◇ *juxtaposition indicator*
01 's **04** hath

• has not, hasn't
03 an't

hash
◇ *anagram indicator*
04 hack, mash, mess, stew **05** botch, mince, mix-up **06** bungle, hachis, hotpot, jumble, muddle, scouse **07** goulash, hashish **08** mishmash **09** confusion, lobscouse, pound sign **10** hotchpotch, lob's course **11** olla-podrida **13** mismanagement

hashish
03 pot **04** dope, hash, hemp, weed **05** bhang, ganja, grass **08** cannabis **09** marijuana **12** electric puha

hassium
02 Hs

hassle
03 bug **04** fuss **05** aggro, annoy, fight, harry, hound, trial, upset **06** badger, bother, chivvy, harass, mither, moider, pester, strife **07** dispute, moither, problem, quarrel, trouble, wrangle **08** argument, nuisance, squabble, struggle **09** bickering **10** difficulty **11** altercation **12** disagreement **13** inconvenience

hassled
05 vexed **07** harried, hounded, plagued, uptight, worried **08** careworn, harassed, pestered, strained, stressed, troubled **09** pressured, tormented **10** distraught, distressed **11** pressurized, stressed-out, under stress **13** under pressure

hassock
04 pouf **06** pouffe **07** kneeler
09 footstool

haste
03 hie **04** post, rush **05** hurry, speed
06 bustle, hasten, hustle, scurry
07 urgency **08** alacrity, celerity, despatch, dispatch, fastness, rapidity, rashness, velocity **09** briskness, quickness, swiftness **10** expedience
11 impetuosity **12** carelessness, precipitance, precipitancy, recklessness **13** foolhardiness, impulsiveness, precipitation
15 expeditiousness

• in haste
04 fast, rash **05** apace **06** subito
07 hotfoot, quickly, rapidly **08** in a hurry, promptly, speedily
12 straightaway

hasten
03 aid, fly, hie, ren, rin, run **04** bolt, dash, help, race, rush, spur, tear, urge
05 boost, hurry, press, speed **06** assist, bustle, go fast, hustle, sprint, step up
07 advance, be quick, forward, hurry up, quicken, speed up **08** despatch, dispatch, expedite, step on it **09** go quickly, hotfoot it, make haste
10 accelerate, get a move on
11 precipitate, push forward **12** step on the gas **15** put your foot down

hastily
04 fast **05** apace **06** rashly **07** quickly, rapidly **08** chop-chop, promptly, speedily **09** hurriedly **10** heedlessly, recklessly **11** double-quick, impetuously, impulsively
12 straightaway **13** precipitately

hasty
04 fast, rash **05** brief, brisk, eager, quick, rapid, short, swift **06** prompt, rushed, speedy, sudden **07** cursory, hurried, running **08** careless, fleeting, headlong, heedless, reckless
09 desultory, festinate, hotheaded, impatient, impetuous, impulsive, irritable **10** transitory **11** expeditious, perfunctory, precipitant, precipitate, subitaneous, thoughtless

hat
03 lid, nab **04** tile **06** titfer
09 headpiece **10** upper crust

Hats include:

03 cap, fez, sun, taj, tam, tin, top, toy
04 doek, hard, hood, kepi, poke, tall
05 beret, Bronx, busby, derby, mitre, mutch, opera, shako, snood, straw, tammy, toque, tuque
06 beanie, beaver, biggin, boater, bobble, bonnet, bowler, chapka, cloche, fedora, helmet, kalpak, mob-cap, panama, pileus, sailor, trilby, turban
07 bicorne, biretta, bycoket, Cossack, flat-cap, Homburg, leghorn, montero, picture, pill-box, pork-pie, stetson, tricorn
08 balmoral, bearskin, chaperon, fool's cap, nightcap, skullcap, sombrero, tricorne, yarmulka
09 Balaclava, cock's-comb, dunce's cap, forage cap, glengarry, jockey cap, muffin-cap, peaked cap, school cap, sou'wester, stovepipe, sun bonnet, ten-gallon
10 cockernony, college cap, hunting-cap, Kilmarnock, pith helmet, poke-bonnet
11 baseball cap, crash helmet, deerstalker, mortar-board, tam-o'-shanter, trencher cap
12 cheesecutter, hummle bonnet, Scotch bonnet

See also **straw hat** *under* **straw**

• shade attached to hat
04 ugly

hatch
◇ *anagram indicator*
04 plan, plot **05** breed, brood, cleck, covey, sit on **06** clutch, design, devise, invent, scheme **07** concoct, develop, dream up, exclude, guichet, project, think up **08** conceive, contrive, disclose, incubate **09** formulate, originate

hatchet
03 axe **07** chopper, cleaver, machete, mattock, pickaxe **08** tomahawk
09 battle-axe, hedgebill **11** hedging-bill

hate
02 ug **04** whit **05** abhor, spite
06 detest, enmity, grudge, hatred, loathe, regret **07** be loath, be sorry, despise, dislike, ill-will, rancour
08 aversion, execrate, loathing, not stand **09** abominate, animosity, apologize, hostility **10** abhorrence, antagonism, bitterness, recoil from, resentment **11** abomination, be reluctant, be unwilling **15** feel revulsion at

• pet hate
04 bane, bogy **05** bogle, dread, fiend, poker **06** horror **07** bugbear, rawhead
08 anathema **09** bête noire, nightmare

hateful
04 evil, foul, loth, vile **05** loath, nasty
06 cursed, damned, goddam, horrid, odious **07** goddamn, heinous
08 damnable, horrible **09** abhorrent, execrable, goddamned, loathsome, obnoxious, offensive, repellent, repugnant, repulsive, revolting
10 abominable, despicable, detestable, disgusting, unpleasant
11 abhominable **12** contemptible, disagreeable

hating
04 miso-

hatred
04 hate **05** odium, spite **06** animus, enmity, grudge, phobia **07** despite, disgust, dislike, ill-will, phobism, rancour **08** aversion, haterent, loathing
09 animosity, antipathy, hostility, malignity, revulsion **10** abhorrence, antagonism, bitterness, execration, repugnance, resentment
11 abomination, detestation

haughtily
07 proudly **08** snootily **10** arrogantly, cavalierly, scornfully **11** imperiously
12 disdainfully **14** contemptuously, superciliously

haughtiness
04 airs **05** pride **06** hubris, morgue
07 conceit, disdain, hauteur
08 contempt **09** aloofness, arrogance, insolence, loftiness, pomposity
10 hogen-mogen, snootiness
12 snobbishness

haughty
04 bold, haut, high, vain **05** hault, lofty, proud, surly **06** haught, lordly, snooty, superb **07** paughty, stuck-up
08 arrogant, assuming, cavalier, fastuous, orgulous, scornful, snobbish, stomachy, superior, toplofty
09 conceited, imperious, orgillous
10 disdainful, hoity-toity, stomachful, stomachous **11** cavalierish, egotistical, overbearing, patronizing, stiff-necked, toploftical **12** contemptuous, supercilious **13** condescending, high and mighty, self-important, swollen-headed **14** proud-stomached **15** on your high horse

haul
03 lug, rug, tow, tug **04** cart, drag, draw, find, gain, harl, hump, loot, mess, move, pull, push, ship, swag, wind
05 booty, bouse, bowse, brail, carry, catch, heave, scoop, slack, touse, touze, towse, towze, trail, trice, wince, winch, yield **06** convey, convoy, spoils
07 plunder, takings **09** transport

haunches
04 hips, rump **05** hucks, nates
06 thighs **07** huckles, hunkers, rear end **08** buttocks

haunt
03 den **04** houf, howf, walk **05** beset, curse, ghost, harry, houff, howff, local, recur, spook, visit, worry **06** burden, obsess, plague, prey on, resort, show up **07** disturb, hangout, inhabit, oppress, possess, spright, torment, trouble **08** frequent **09** honky-tonk, patronize **10** rendezvous **11** hang about in, materialize, spend time in
12 hang around in, meeting-place
13 appear often in, favourite spot
14 stamping-ground, visit regularly

haunted
05 eerie **06** cursed, jinxed, spooky
07 ghostly, plagued, worried
08 infested, obsessed, troubled
09 hag-ridden, possessed, tormented
10 frequented **11** preoccupied

haunting
08 poignant **09** evocative, memorable, nostalgic, recurrent
10 persistent **11** atmospheric
13 unforgettable

hauteur
04 airs **05** pride **06** hubris **07** conceit, disdain **08** contempt **09** aloofness, arrogance, insolence, loftiness, pomposity **10** snootiness
11 haughtiness **12** snobbishness

have
02 ha', 've **03** ask, bid, con, eat, get, hae, han, own, put, use **04** bear, down, dupe, feel, find, fool, gain, gulp, hold, keep, know, make, meet, must, show, take, tell **05** abide, allow, beget, brook, cheat, drink, enjoy, force, order, ought, stand, trick **06** accept, assert, coerce, compel, devour, diddle, embody, endure, enjoin, esteem, guzzle, oblige, obtain, permit, secure, should, suffer, take in **07** acquire, arrange, be given, cause to, command, consume, contain, deceive, develop, display, embrace, exhibit, express, include, possess, procure, put away, receive, request, require, swallow, swindle, undergo
08 be forced, comprise, contract, manifest, organize, persuade, submit to, talk into, tolerate, tuck into, wolf down **09** be obliged, consist of, encounter, go through, knock back, partake of, put up with, succumb to
10 be required, bring forth, comprehend, experience, suffer from, take part in **11** be compelled, demonstrate, give birth to, incorporate, prevail upon **13** be delivered of, be subjected to, participate in
• **have had it**
06 be lost **10** be defeated, have no hope **11** be exhausted, be in trouble, bite the dust
• **have on**
03 kid, rag **04** hoax, wear **05** chaff, tease, trick **11** be clothed in, be dressed in, have planned, play a joke on
12 have arranged, take for a ride
13 wind someone up **15** pull someone's leg

haven
03 bay **04** dock, port **05** basin, hithe, oasis **06** asylum, harbor, refuge
07 harbour, retreat, shelter
09 anchorage, sanctuary

haversack
06 kitbag **08** backpack, knapsack, rucksack

havoc
◇ *anagram indicator*
04 Hell, ruin **05** chaos, waste, wreck
06 damage, mayhem **08** disorder, ravaging, shambles, wreckage
09 confusion, ruination **10** desolation, disruption **11** destruction, devastation, rack and ruin **12** depopulation, despoliation

Hawaii
02 HI

hawk
03 cry **04** bark, eyas, kite, nyas, sell, soar, sore, tout, vend **05** offer, soare, trant **06** falcon, keelie, market, peddle, tarcel, tarsal, tarsel, tassel, tercel
07 buzzard, goshawk, haggard, harrier, tassell, tiercel **08** brancher, huckster
10 eyas-musket **11** sparrowhawk
12 honey buzzard, offer for sale
• **accustom hawk to handling**
03 man

hawker
04 spiv **05** crier **06** auceps, cadger, coster, dealer, mugger, pedlar, seller, sutler, trader, vendor **07** camelot, chapman, slanger, tranter **08** huckster
09 barrow-boy, cheap-jack, cheap John **10** colporteur **11** speech-crier
12 costermonger
• **hawker's round**
04 walk

hawseholes
04 eyes

hawthorn
05 quick, thorn **07** may tree
08 cockspur **09** albespine, albespyne, mayflower, thornbush, thorntree
10 quickthorn, whitethorn

hay
• **bundle of hay**
03 wad, wap **04** wise, wisp **06** bottle
• **pile of hay**
03 mow **04** cock, rick **05** stack
07 haycock **08** haystack

haywire
◇ *anagram indicator*
03 mad **04** wild **05** crazy, wrong
07 chaotic, tangled **08** confused
10 disordered, topsy-turvy
12 disorganized, out of control

hazard
04 jump, luck, risk, wage **05** offer, peril, stake, wager **06** bunker, chance, danger, gamble, menace, niffer, risque, submit, threat **07** pitfall, suggest, venture **08** accident, endanger, jeopardy **09** deathtrap, hazardize, put at risk, speculate **10** jeopardize, put forward **12** endangerment **13** put in jeopardy **14** expose to danger

hazardous
04 nice **05** hairy, risky **06** chancy, queasy, queazy, tricky, unsafe
07 chancey **08** insecure, menacing, perilous **09** dangerous, difficult, uncertain **10** jeopardous, precarious
11 threatening **13** unpredictable

hazardously
07 riskily **10** insecurely, perilously
11 dangerously, uncertainly
12 jeopardously, precariously
13 unpredictably

haze
03 fog, rag **04** blur, daze, film, mist, smog **05** bully, cloud, steam
06 muddle, vapour **07** dimness
09 confusion, fogginess, mistiness, obscurity, smokiness, vagueness
10 cloudiness **11** uncertainty
12 bewilderment **14** indistinctness

hazelnut
03 cob **06** cobnut **07** filberd, filbert
12 Barcelona nut

hazy
◇ *anagram indicator*
03 dim **05** faint, foggy, fuzzy, milky, misty, muzzy, smoky, vague **06** cloudy, veiled, woolly **07** blurred, clouded, misting, obscure, unclear
08 confused, nebulous, overcast
09 uncertain **10** ill-defined, indefinite, indistinct

head
◇ *head selection indicator*
03 cop, nab, nob, nut, pow, ras, ren, rin, run, tip, top, van, wit **04** apex, bean, bent, boss, cape, conk, face, fizz, foam, fore, gift, lead, loaf, main, mind, ness, pash, pate, peak, poll, rise, rule, suds, tête, wits **05** bonce, brain, caput, chair, chief, crest, crown, first, flair, fount, front, froth, guide, knack, onion, power, prime, ruler, sense, skill, skull, steer, title **06** bigwig, brains, charge, climax, crisis, crunch, direct, genius, govern, height, lather, leader, manage, mazard, napper, noddle, noggin, noodle, origin, source, spring, summit, talent, vertex, wisdom **07** ability, aptness, bubbles, captain, command, control, cranium, crumpet, dilemma, faculty, go first, heading, headway, highest, leading, manager, obverse, oversee, premier, supreme, thought, topknot, topmost **08** aptitude, calamity, capacity, chairman, controls, director, dominant, facility, foremost, governor, headland, pressure, strength, vanguard, wellhead **09** attribute, be first in, big cheese, capitulum, commander, emergency, endowment, forefront, intellect, mentality, president, principal, reasoning, supervise, top banana **10** administer, capability, chairwoman, controller, grey matter, headmaster, leadership, management, pre-eminent, supervisor, upper crust, upperworks, wellspring **11** catastrophe, chairperson, common sense, head teacher, proficiency, superintend, supervision, upper storey **12** be in charge of, directorship, headmistress, intelligence **13** administrator, be in control of, critical point, understanding
14 be at the front of, superintendent
15 little grey cells, mental abilities

See also **toilet**

• **fox's head**
04 mask
• **go to your head**
06 puff up **08** befuddle **09** inebriate, make dizzy, make drunk, make proud, make woozy **10** intoxicate **12** make arrogant **13** make conceited
• **head for**
06 aim for **07** make for, point to, turn for **08** steer for **09** go towards
11 move towards **13** direct towards, travel towards
• **head off**
◇ *head deletion indicator*
04 stop **05** avert **06** cut off, divert
07 deflect, fend off, prevent, ward off

09 forestall, intercept, interpose, intervene, turn aside

• head over heels

◇ *reversal down indicator*

06 wildly 07 utterly 08 headlong 09 intensely 10 completely, recklessly, thoroughly 14 uncontrollably, wholeheartedly

• head up

04 lead 06 direct, manage 12 be in charge of, take charge of

• keep your head

08 keep calm 12 keep your cool

• lose your head

◇ *head deletion indicator*

04 flap 05 panic 08 freak out 12 lose your cool

• muffle head

03 mob

• top of head

04 nole, noll, noul, nowl 05 noule

headache

04 bane, head, pest 05 worry 06 bother, hassle 07 problem, trouble 08 migraine, nuisance, splitter, vexation 09 neuralgia 10 hemicrania 11 cephalalgia 13 inconvenience, pain in the neck

headdress

Headdresses include:

03 cap, taj
04 coif, head, kell, tête, tire
05 mitre, tower
06 cornet, modius, pinner, turban
07 commode, coronet, kufiyah
08 coiffure, fontange, fool's cap, head-tire, joncanoe, junkanoo, kaffiyeh, keffiyeh, ship-tire, stephane
09 John Canoe, John Kanoo, porrenger, porringer, war bonnet
10 lappet-head
11 tire-valiant
13 feather-bonnet

See also **hat**; **helmet**; **scarf**

headgear

03 hat, jiz, lid, wig 04 call, caul, gizz, hood, tiar 05 crown, tiara 07 coronet 08 silly-how

See also **hat**; **helmet**; **scarf**

heading

◇ *head selection indicator*

04 head, name, text 05 class, point, title 06 header, rubric 07 bearing, caption, section, subject 08 category, division, headline 09 direction 10 capitulary, descriptor, letterhead 14 classification

See also **compass**

headland

03 ras 04 cape, head, naze, ness, noup, scaw, skaw 05 morro, point 07 headrig 08 foreland 10 promontory

headless

◇ *head deletion indicator*

07 trunked 10 acephalous, leaderless 11 decapitated

headlong

04 rash 05 ahead, hasty, steep 06 rashly, wildly 07 hastily, ramstam, tantivy 08 careless, full tilt, pell-mell, proclive, reckless 09 breakneck, dangerous, head first, hurriedly, impetuous, impulsive 10 carelessly, heedlessly, recklessly 11 hair-brained, hare-brained, impetuously, impulsively, precipitate, prematurely 12 hand over head 13 precipitately, thoughtlessly 15 without thinking

headman

05 chief, ruler 06 ataman, leader, sachem 07 captain 08 caboceer, mocuddum, mokaddam, muqaddam, starosta 09 chieftain

head-on

06 direct 08 straight 10 straight-on 11 full-frontal

headquarters

02 HQ 04 base, hall 05 depot, SHAPE 06 armory, Temple 07 station 08 base camp, Pentagon 10 head office, main office, officialty, praetorium 11 command post, nerve centre, officiality

headstone

06 plaque 08 memorial 09 tombstone 10 gravestone 11 cornerstone

headstrong

06 unruly, wilful 07 wayward, willful 08 contrary, obdurate, perverse, stubborn 09 obstinate, pigheaded 10 refractory, self-willed 11 intractable 12 intransigent, recalcitrant, ungovernable

headway

03 way 06 ground 07 advance 08 distance, movement, progress 11 development, improvement

headwear *see* **headgear**

heady

04 rash 05 nappy 06 potent, strong 07 huff-cap, rousing, violent 08 ecstatic, euphoric, exciting, inflamed 09 thrilling 11 stimulating 12 exhilarating, intoxicating, invigorating, overpowering

heal

04 cure, hide, mend, sain 05 cover, salve, treat 06 balsam, garish, physic, recure, remedy, settle, soothe 07 assuage, comfort, conceal, guarish, improve, patch up, restore 08 make good, make well, palliate, put right, set right 09 cicatrize, incarnate, reconcile 10 make better 12 conglutinate

healer

03 Asa

See also **doctor**

health

04 form, heal, tone, trim 05 shape, state, toast 06 fettle, sanity, vigour 07 fitness, welfare 08 strength 09 condition, good shape, soundness, wellbeing 10 robustness 11 healthiness 12 constitution 13 good condition

• good health

04 tope 06 cheers, kia-ora 07 cheerio, slàinte, wassail 08 chin-chin, waes hail 09 bene vobis, drink hail 10 Gesundheit 12 mud in your eye

healthily

04 well 07 soundly 08 robustly, strongly 10 vigorously 11 in condition, in good shape 12 in fine fettle

healthy

03 fit 04 fine, good, hale, well, wise 05 hardy, jolly, lusty, sound 06 robust, strong, sturdy 07 bracing, lustick, prudent 08 blooming, lustique, sensible, thriving, vigorous 09 healthful, in the pink, judicious, wholesome 10 able-bodied, beneficial, hartie-hale, healthsome, nourishing, nutritious, refreshing, salubrious, successful 11 flourishing, in condition, in good shape, right as rain, stimulating 12 considerable, fit as a fiddle, in fine fettle, invigorating, well-disposed 13 hale and hearty

heap

03 lot, mow, pit, pot 04 a lot, bank, bing, bulk, cock, load, lots, mass, pile, pots, raff, raft, rick, ruck, ruin, tass, tons 05 amass, build, cairn, clamp, drift, hoard, loads, mound, stack, store 06 bestow, bundle, burden, confer, gather, lavish, lumber, midden, oodles, pile up, plenty, quarry, rickle, scores, shower, stacks, supply, toorie 07 collect, company, congest, cumulus, store up, uphoard 08 assemble, cumulate, dunghill, lashings, millions, molehill, mountain 09 abundance, congeries, embroglio, great deal, imbroglio, stockpile 10 accumulate, acervation, assemblage, coacervate, collection, quantities 12 accumulation 13 agglomeration, kitchen midden 14 clearance cairn

hear

◇ *homophone indicator*

03 get, try 04 heed 05 catch, judge, learn 06 be told, gather, listen, pick up, take in 07 examine, find out, inquire, make out 08 consider, discover, overhear, perceive 09 ascertain, eavesdrop, latch onto 10 adjudicate, be informed, understand 11 investigate 12 pay attention 13 be in touch with, pass judgement

• hearer

03 ear

hearing

◇ *homophone indicator*

03 ear 04 case, news, oyer 05 audit, range, reach, sound, trial 06 review 07 earshot, inquest, inquiry 08 audience, audition, scolding 09 interview, judgement 10 perception 11 examination, inquisition 12 adjudication 13 chance

to speak, investigation **15** hearing distance

hearsay
◇ *homophone indicator*
04 buzz, talk **05** on-dit, rumor, say-so **06** gossip, report, rumour **10** common talk **11** word of mouth **12** tittle-tattle **15** common knowledge

heart
◇ *middle selection indicator*
03 hub, nub **04** core, crux, guts, love, mind, pith, pity, soul **05** bosom, pluck, spunk **06** bottle, centre, kernel, marrow, middle, nature, spirit, vigour, warmth **07** bravery, concern, courage, emotion, essence, feeling, heroism, nucleus, passion, stomach **08** boldness, keenness, kindness, sympathy **09** affection, character, eagerness, fortitude, sentiment, substance **10** compassion, cordiality, enthusiasm, resolution, tenderness **11** disposition, intrepidity, temperament **12** fearlessness, quintessence **13** determination, essential part **14** responsiveness

Heart parts include:

04 vein
05 aorta, valve
06 artery, atrium, AV node, muscle, SA node
07 auricle
08 vena cava
09 sinus node, ventricle
10 epicardium, left atrium, myocardium
11 aortic valve, endocardium, mitral valve, pericardium, right atrium
13 bicuspid valve, carotid artery, left ventricle
14 ascending aorta, pulmonary valve, Purkinje fibres, right ventricle, sino-atrial node, tricuspid valve
15 papillary muscle

• **at heart**
◇ *insertion indicator*
◇ *middle selection indicator*
06 really **08** at bottom **09** basically, in essence **11** essentially **13** fundamentally
• **by heart**
03 pat **06** by rote, off pat **08** verbatim **09** memoriter **10** from memory **11** word for word **13** parrot-fashion
• **change of heart**
07 rethink **12** change of mind **14** second thoughts
• **from the bottom of your heart**
06 deeply **08** devoutly **09** earnestly, fervently, sincerely **10** profoundly **12** passionately
• **heart and soul**
06 gladly **07** eagerly **08** entirely, heartily **09** devotedly **10** absolutely, completely **12** unreservedly **14** wholeheartedly
• **hearts**
01 H **10** black Maria
• **lose heart**
◇ *middle deletion indicator*
08 collapse **13** be discouraged
• **set your heart on**
05 crave, yearn **06** desire **07** long for, wish for
• **take heart**
05 rally **06** buck up, perk up, revive **07** cheer up **10** brighten up **12** be encouraged
• **take to heart**
09 be moved by, be upset by **12** be affected by **13** be disturbed by

heartache
04 pain **05** agony, grief, worry **06** sorrow **07** anguish, anxiety, despair, remorse, torment, torture **08** distress **09** dejection, suffering **10** affliction, bitterness, heartbreak **11** despondency

heartbreak
04 pain **05** agony, grief **06** misery, sorrow **07** anguish, despair, sadness **08** distress **09** dejection, suffering **10** crève-coeur, desolation

heartbreaking
03 sad **05** cruel, harsh **06** bitter, crying, tragic **07** painful, pitiful **08** grievous, poignant **09** agonizing, harrowing **11** distressing **12** excruciating, heart-rending **13** disappointing

heartbroken
03 sad **07** crushed, grieved **08** dejected, desolate, downcast **09** anguished, miserable, sorrowful, suffering **10** despondent, dispirited **11** crestfallen **12** disappointed, disheartened, in low spirits **13** broken-hearted

heartburn
05 brash **07** pyrosis **09** cardialgy, dyspepsia **10** cardialgia **11** indigestion

hearten
05 boost, cheer, pep up, rouse **06** buck up **07** animate, cheer up, comfort, console, inspire **08** energize, reassure **09** encourage, stimulate **10** invigorate, revitalize

heartening
06 moving **08** cheering, pleasing, touching **09** affecting, rewarding, uplifting **10** gladdening, gratifying, satisfying **11** encouraging **12** heartwarming

heartfelt
04 deep, warm **06** ardent, devout, honest **07** earnest, fervent, genuine, sincere **08** profound **09** unfeigned **12** wholehearted **13** compassionate

heartily
◇ *middle selection indicator*
04 upsy, very **05** agood, upsee, upsey **06** deeply, gladly, warmly **07** cheerly, eagerly, hartely, lustily, totally **08** con amore, entirely **09** cordially, earnestly, extremely, feelingly, genuinely, sincerely, staunchly, zealously **10** absolutely, completely, profoundly, resolutely, thoroughly, upsey Dutch, vigorously **11** unfeignedly, upsey Friese **12** upsey English **13** warm-heartedly

heartless
◇ *middle deletion indicator*
04 cold, hard **05** cruel, harsh **06** brutal, unkind **07** callous, inhuman, unmoved **08** pitiless, ruthless, sardonic, uncaring **09** merciless, unfeeling **11** cold-blooded, cold-hearted, hard-hearted **13** inconsiderate, unsympathetic

heartlessly
◇ *middle deletion indicator*
06 coldly **07** cruelly, harshly **08** brutally **09** callously **10** pitilessly **11** mercilessly **13** cold-heartedly, hard-heartedly

heart-rending
03 sad **06** moving, tragic **07** piteous, pitiful **08** pathetic, poignant **09** affecting, agonizing, harrowing **11** distressing **13** heartbreaking

heartsick
03 sad **04** glum **08** dejected, downcast **09** depressed **10** despondent, melancholy **12** disappointed, heavy-hearted

heart-throb
04 hunk, idol, star **05** pin-up **09** dreamboat

heart-to-heart
08 cosy chat **09** tête-à-tête **10** honest talk **12** friendly talk

heartwarming
06 moving **08** cheering, pleasing, touching **09** affecting, rewarding, uplifting **10** gladdening, gratifying, heartening, satisfying **11** encouraging

hearty
04 maty, warm **05** ample, bluff, eager, hardy, large, lusty, matey, solid, sound **06** blokey, jovial, robust, stanch, strong **07** affable, cordial, filling, genuine, healthy, sincere, sizable, staunch **08** abundant, blokeish, bouncing, cheerful, effusive, friendly, generous, sizeable, stalwart, vigorous **09** ebullient, energetic, exuberant, heartfelt, unfeigned **10** boisterous, nourishing, nutritious, unreserved **11** substantial, warm-hearted **12** enthusiastic, unrestrained, wholehearted

heat
◇ *anagram indicator*
03 hot **04** bake, boil, cook, fire, fury, glow, race, rost, stir, warm, zeal **05** anger, annoy, beath, fever, flush, roast, rouse, toast **06** ardour, arouse, calefy, enrage, excite, fervor, reheat, sizzle, warmth, warm up **07** agitate, animate, fervour, firearm, hotness, inflame, passion, swelter, trouble **08** fervency **09** closeness, eagerness, fieriness, heaviness, intensity, microwave, stimulate, vehemence

10 enthusiasm, excitement, sultriness, torridness 11 calefaction, earnestness, impetuosity 12 feverishness 15 high temperature

• **dead heat**

03 tie 04 draw

heated

05 angry, fiery, fired 06 bitter, fierce, raging, roused, stormy 07 enraged, excited, furious, intense, stirred, violent 08 animated, frenzied, inflamed, vehement, worked-up 10 passionate, stimulated 11 impassioned, tempestuous

heatedly

07 angrily 08 bitterly, fiercely
09 excitedly, furiously, intensely, violently 10 vehemently
12 passionately

heater

03 gun 04 fire 06 boiler, pistol
08 Califont®, radiator 09 convector, fan heater, gas heater, immersion
11 solar heater 12 electric fire
13 storage heater 14 central heating, electric heater 15 immersion heater

heath

03 Ted 04 bent, fell, ling, moor, muir
05 briar, brier, erica 06 kalmia, manoao, upland 07 arbutus, heather
08 moorland 09 andromeda, bearberry 10 gaultheria

heathen

05 pagan 06 ethnic, paynim, savage
07 Gentile, godless, infidel, nations
08 barbaric, idolater 09 barbarian
10 idolatress, idolatrous, philistine, unbeliever 11 irreligious, nullifidian, unbelieving, uncivilized
13 unenlightened

heather

04 ling 05 erica 07 calluna
08 foxberry 11 Labrador tea

heave

◇ *deletion indicator*

03 cat, gag, tug 04 barf, boke, cast, drag, give, haul, honk, hump, hurl, lift, puke, pull, rise, send, sigh, spew, toss
05 chuck, fling, heeze, hitch, hoist, lever, pitch, raise, retch, sling, surge, swell, throw, utter, vomit 06 be sick, let fly, let out, popple, sick up, wallow
07 breathe, bring up, chuck up, chunder, cough up, express, fetch up, throw up, upchuck 08 disgorge, parbreak, swelling 10 egurgitate

heaven

03 joy, sky 04 Zion 05 bliss, ether, glory, skies 06 Asgard, on high, Svarga, Swarga, Swerga, utopia, welkin
07 delight, ecstasy, Elysium, nirvana, Olympus, rapture, the blue, up there
08 empyrean, holy city, paradise, Valhalla 09 afterlife, firmament, happiness, hereafter, home of God, next world, Shangri-La 10 abode of God, life to come 12 Land o' the Leal, New Jerusalem, promised land, upper regions 13 elysian fields, fiddler's green, seventh heaven, vault of heaven

• **the heavens**

03 sky 04 pole 06 region
08 empyrean 12 upper regions

heavenly

04 holy, pure 06 cosmic, divine, lovely
07 angelic, blessed, godlike, perfect, sublime, Uranian 08 beatific, blissful, cherubic, empyreal, empyrean, ethereal, etherial, glorious, immortal, seraphic 09 ambrosial, beautiful, celestial, enjoyable, excellent, exquisite, rapturous, spiritual, unearthly, wonderful 10 delightful, enchanting, marvellous 12 other-worldly, supernatural 14 out of this world

heaven-sent

05 happy 06 bright, timely
09 fortunate, opportune
10 auspicious, favourable

heavily

04 hard, upsy 05 thick, upsee, upsey
06 slowly 07 closely, densely, roundly, solidly, soundly, thickly, too much, utterly 08 clumsily, to excess, woodenly 09 awkwardly, compactly, copiously, painfully, weightily
10 abundantly, completely, decisively, sluggishly, thoroughly, upsey Dutch
11 excessively, laboriously, ponderously, upsey Friese
12 immoderately, upsey English
14 with difficulty

heaviness

04 bulk 05 depth, gloom 06 weight
07 density, languor, sadness
08 deadness, severity, solidity
09 dejection, greatness, heftiness, intensity, lassitude, thickness
10 depression, drowsiness, gloominess, melancholy, oppression, sleepiness, somnolence
11 despondency, onerousness, seriousness, weightiness
12 sluggishness 13 ponderousness
14 burdensomeness, oppressiveness

heavy

03 big, dry, sad 04 dark, deep, dowf, dull, full, grey, hard, rich, sour, thug
05 bulky, close, dense, Dutch, grave, great, harsh, hefty, humid, laden, large, muggy, sharp, solid, tense, thick, tough
06 clammy, cloudy, clumpy, doughy, drowsy, gloomy, hearty, leaden, loaded, severe, sombre, steamy, sticky, stodgy, strong, sultry, taxing, trying, wooden 07 arduous, awkward, crushed, extreme, filling, hulking, intense, irksome, lumping, lumpish, massive, onerous, pesante, pompous, serious, starchy, tedious, violent, weighty 08 burdened, crushing, downcast, exacting, forceful, grievous, groaning, highbrow, overcast, pedantic, powerful, profound, strained
09 abounding, burdenous, demanding, depressed, difficult, emotional, excessive, important, laborious, miserable, ponderous, sorrowful, squabbish, strenuous, wearisome 10 burdensome, cumbersome, despondent, encumbered, immoderate, inordinate, oppressive, unbearable
11 discouraged, heavy as lead, intemperate, intolerable, substantial, troublesome, weighed down
12 considerable, indigestible, sodden-witted, weighing a ton
13 overindulgent, uninteresting

heavy-duty

02 HD 05 solid, sound, tough
06 robust, strong, sturdy 07 abiding, durable, lasting 08 enduring
09 resistant 10 reinforced 11 hard-wearing, long-lasting, substantial

heavy-handed

05 harsh, inept, stern 06 clumsy, severe 07 awkward 08 bungling, despotic, forceful, tactless, unsubtle
09 ham-fisted, maladroit
10 autocratic, blundering, cack-handed, oppressive 11 domineering, insensitive, overbearing, thoughtless

heavy-hearted

03 sad 04 glum 06 gloomy, morose
07 crushed, forlorn 08 downcast, mournful 09 depressed, heartsick, miserable, sorrowful 10 despondent, melancholy 11 discouraged, downhearted 12 disappointed, disheartened

Hebe

08 Juventas

Hebrew

03 Heb, Jew

See also **alphabet**

Hebrew alphabet *see* **alphabet**

Hecate

06 Trivia

heckle

04 bait, gibe, jeer 05 taunt 06 needle, pester 07 barrack, catcall, disrupt
09 interrupt, shout down

hectare

02 ha

hectic

◇ *anagram indicator*

04 busy, fast, wild 06 heated, rushed
07 chaotic, excited, flushed, frantic, furious 08 agitated, bustling, feverish, frenetic, frenzied 09 turbulent
10 tumultuous 11 consumptive

hector

03 nag 04 huff 05 annoy, bully, worry
06 badger, chivvy, harass, menace
07 bluster, provoke 08 browbeat, bulldoze, bullyrag, threaten
09 blusterer 10 intimidate

hedge

◇ *containment indicator*

03 haw, hay, low 04 duck, dyke, edge
05 cover, dodge, evade, fence, guard, hem in, limit, mound, stall 06 insure, lay off, raddle, screen, shield, waffle,

zareba, zariba, zereba, zeriba
07 barrier, confine, debased, enclose, fortify, ox-fence, protect, quibble, shuffle, wayside, zareeba
08 boundary, encircle, hedgerow, obstruct, quickset, restrict, sepiment, sidestep, surround **09** safeguard, temporize, windbreak **10** equivocate, protection **11** prevaricate **13** sit on the fence
• escape through hedge
04 mews, muse **05** meuse

hedgehog
06 urchin **08** herisson **11** tiggywinkle

hedonism
09 dolce vita, epicurism
10 sensualism, sensuality, sybaritism
12 Epicureanism **13** gratification, luxuriousness **14** self-indulgence, voluptuousness **15** pleasure-seeking

hedonist
07 epicure **08** sybarite **09** bon vivant, bon viveur, epicurean **10** sensualist, voluptuary **14** pleasure-seeker

hedonistic
09 epicurean, luxurious, sybaritic
10 voluptuous **13** self-indulgent
15 pleasure-seeking

heed
03 ear **04** care, gaum, gorm, mark, mind, note, obey, reak, reck, tent
06 follow, listen, notice, regard
07 caution, hearken, observe, respect, thought **08** attend to, consider
09 attention **10** bear in mind, observance, take note of
11 heedfulness **12** take notice of, watchfulness **13** animadversion, consideration **14** pay attention to
15 take into account

heedful
04 wary **05** chary **07** careful, jealous, mindful, prudent **08** cautious, vigilant, watchful **09** advertent, attentive, observant, regardful **10** respective
11 circumspect

heedless
04 rash **06** blithe, remiss, unwary
08 careless, reckless, tactless, uncaring
09 foolhardy, forgetful, negligent, oblivious, unguarded, unmindful
10 incautious, indiscreet, insouciant, regardless, unthinking **11** hair-brained, hare-brained, inattentive, inobservant, precipitate, thoughtless, unconcerned, unobservant **12** absent-minded
13 inconsiderate, irresponsible

heedlessly
06 rashly **09** blindfold **10** carelessly, recklessly **11** negligently
12 neglectingly, unthinkingly
13 inattentively, thoughtlessly

heel
03 cad, cow, rat, tip **04** bank, hele, hide, knob, lean, list, puke, seel, spur, sway, tilt **05** angle, cover, slant, slope
06 ratbag, toerag, wretch **07** conceal, incline, ratfink **08** lean over, stiletto

hefty
03 big **04** hard, huge, very **05** ample, beefy, bulky, burly, heavy, large, solid, stout **06** brawny, robust, strong
07 awkward, hulking, immense, massive, sizable, violent, weighty
08 abundant, colossal, forceful, generous, muscular, powerful, sizeable, unwieldy, vigorous
09 strapping **11** substantial
12 considerable

Hegira
• in the year of Hegira
02 AH

heifer
04 quey

height
01 H **02** ht **03** alp, sum, top, tor
04 apex, hill, peak, torr **05** crest, crown, level, limit, pitch **06** apogee, climax, summit, vertex, zenith
07 ceiling, hill top, maximum, stature
08 altitude, eminence, highness, pinnacle, tallness, ultimate
09 elevation, extremity, loftiness, uttermost **10** perfection
11 culmination, mountain top, sublimation

heighten
04 lift **05** add to, boost, elate, exalt, raise **07** amplify, augment, build up, elevate, enhance, improve, magnify, sharpen **08** increase **09** intensify
10 strengthen

heinous
04 evil **05** awful, grave **06** odious, wicked **07** hateful, hideous, vicious
08 flagrant, infamous, shocking
09 abhorrent, atrocious, execrable, loathsome, monstrous, nefarious, revolting, unnatural **10** abominable, despicable, detestable, facinorous, iniquitous, outrageous, villainous
11 unspeakable **12** contemptible

heir, heiress
03 her **05** scion **06** co-heir, tanist
07 fortune, legatee **08** apparent, atheling, parcener **09** inheritor, successor **10** cesarevich, cesarewich, coparcener, fellow-heir, inheritrix, next in line, substitute **11** beneficiary, cesarevitch, cesarewitch, coinheritor, crown prince, inheritress, tsesarevich, tsesarewich **12** tsesarevitch, tsesarewitch **13** crown princess

heist *see* **robbery**

held
• held by, held in
◇ *insertion indicator*
◇ *hidden indicator*

helicopter
05 hover **06** copter **07** chopper, medevac **08** sikorsky **09** egg beater
10 rotorcraft, rotor plane, whirlybird
12 air ambulance

Helios
03 Sol

helium
02 He

helix
04 coil, curl, loop **05** screw, twist, whorl **06** spiral, volute **07** wreathe
08 curlicue **09** corkscrew

hell
03 Dis, pit **04** Ades, fire, heck, hele, ruin **05** abyss, agony, below, Hades, havoc, Sheol **06** Erebus, misery, ordeal, Tophet, uproar **07** Abaddon, Acheron, anguish, Gehenna, inferno, the heck, torment, torture **08** Tartarus, the deuce **09** commotion, down there, Malebolge, nightmare, perdition, suffering, the blazes
10 other place, the dickens, underworld **11** nether world, tribulation **12** lower regions, wretchedness **13** bottomless pit, nether regions **15** abode of the devil, infernal regions
• give someone hell
03 vex **04** beat, flog **05** annoy, scold
06 harass, pester, punish **07** tell off, torment, trouble **08** chastise
09 criticize **13** tear off a strip
• hell for leather
06 rashly, wildly **07** quickly, rapidly, swiftly **08** very fast **09** hurriedly, like crazy, post-haste **10** recklessly **11** very quickly **13** precipitately **15** like the clappers
• raise hell
07 run riot **09** be furious **10** hit the roof
11 be very angry, make trouble
13 object noisily, protest loudly
15 cause a commotion

hell-bent
03 set **04** bent **05** fixed **06** dogged, intent **07** settled **08** obdurate, resolved **09** tenacious **10** determined, inflexible, unwavering **12** intransigent, unhesitating

hellish
◇ *anagram indicator*
04 very **05** cruel, nasty **06** savage, wicked **07** awfully, demonic, satanic, Stygian **08** accursed, barbaric, damnable, devilish, dreadful, fiendish, infernal **09** atrocious, execrable, extremely, immensely, intensely, monstrous, nefarious **10** abominable, diabolical, dreadfully, unpleasant
12 disagreeable, unpleasantly
13 exceptionally

hello
02 hi, yo **04** g'day **05** hallo, hillo, howdy, hullo **06** holloa **07** bonjour, welcome **08** chin-chin **09** greetings
10 buon giorno **11** good evening, good morning **13** good afternoon

helm
05 steer, stern, timon, wheel **06** direct, helmet, rudder, tiller
• at the helm
07 leading **08** in charge **09** directing, in command, in control **11** in the saddle
15 holding the reins

helmet
03 pot, top **04** topi **05** armet, salet, topee **06** basnet, casque, heaume, morion, murren, murrin, sallet, tin hat **07** basinet, hard hat, morrion, murrion, pith hat, skid lid, sola hat **08** burganet, burgonet, knapscal, sola topi **09** Balaclava, headpiece, knapscull, knapskull, sola topee **11** pickelhaube

helmsman
03 cox **08** coxswain, timoneer **09** cockswain, steersman **10** steersmate

help
03 aid, use **04** back, balm, cure, ease, heal **05** avail, boost, guide, nurse, salve, serve, stead **06** advice, assist, backup, helper, Mrs Mop, oblige, relief, remedy, soothe, worker **07** assuage, backing, benefit, be of use, bestead, charity, cleaner, further, healing, improve, promote, relieve, service, stand by, succour, support, utility **08** adjuvant, employee, guidance, home help, mitigate **09** advantage, alleviate, charwoman, co-operate, do your bit, encourage, lend a hand, moderator **10** ameliorate, assistance, contribute, facilitate, mitigation, rally round **11** alleviation, collaborate, co-operation, helping hand, improvement, restorative **12** amelioration, contribute to, give a boost to, shot in the arm **13** collaboration, encouragement **14** be of assistance, do something for **15** tower of strength
• **call for help**
03 SOS **06** mayday **09** au secours **14** distress signal
• **cannot help**
14 be unable to stop

helper
02 PA **03** aid **04** aide, ally, maid, mate **06** deputy, second, worker **07** partner, servant **08** adjutant, co-worker, employee, helpmate, treasure **09** assistant, associate, attendant, auxiliary, colleague, man Friday, paraclete, supporter **10** accomplice, girl Friday, subsidiary **11** subordinate **12** collaborator, right-hand man **14** right-hand woman **15** second-in-command

helpful
04 kind **05** of use **06** caring, second, useful **08** friendly, obliging, valuable **09** of service, practical **10** beneficial, benevolent, charitable, profitable, supportive, worthwhile **11** considerate, co-operative, furthersome, neighbourly, sympathetic **12** advantageous, constructive, instrumental **13** accommodating

helpfully
06 kindly **08** usefully **10** obligingly **12** conveniently, reassuringly **13** considerately **15** sympathetically

helping
05 order, piece, share **06** aidant, amount, dollop, ration **07** bowlful, portion, serving **08** adjuvant, plateful, spoonful **09** assistant, auxiliary **12** contributive

helpless
04 weak **06** feeble, infirm **07** exposed, forlorn **08** clueless, desolate, disabled, feckless, impotent **09** abandoned, dependent, destitute, incapable, paralysed, powerless **10** friendless, high and dry, vulnerable **11** debilitated, defenceless, incompetent, unprotected

helplessly
06 feebly, weakly **10** desolately, impotently, vulnerably **11** powerlessly **13** defencelessly

helpmate
04 wife **06** helper, spouse **07** consort, husband, partner, support **08** helpmeet **09** assistant, associate, companion, other half **10** better half

helter-skelter
◇ *anagram indicator*
06 random, rashly, wildly **07** hastily, jumbled, muddled **08** confused, headlong, pell-mell **09** haphazard, hit-or-miss, hurriedly **10** carelessly, confusedly, disordered, recklessly, topsy-turvy **11** impulsively **12** disorganized, like hey-go-mad, tumultuously, unsystematic

hem
04 bind, edge, fold, trim **05** frill, skirt **06** border, edging, fringe, margin **07** fimbria, flounce, valance **08** trimming **09** fimbriate
• **hem in**
04 trap **05** box in, limit, pen in **06** pocket, shut in **07** close in, confine, enclose, hedge in **08** restrict, surround **09** constrain

hemispherical
04 domy **07** rose-cut

hemlock
05 Tsuga **07** cowbane **10** insane root **13** water dropwort

hemp
03 tow **04** pita, sida, sunn **05** abaca, bhang, dagga, ganja, hards, hurds, murva **06** fimble, moorva **07** boneset, hashish **08** agrimony, cannabis, hasheesh, henequen, henequin, heniquin, love-drug, neckweed **09** marihuana, marijuana, true dagga **10** crotalaria **13** Pantagruelion
See also **cannabis**

hen
04 balk **05** biddy, chook, layer, poule **06** Cochin, eirack, female, pullet **07** chookie, clocker, Partlet, poulard **08** Langshan **09** incubator **10** Australorp **11** Cochin-China, Spanish fowl
See also **chicken**

hence
04 away!, ergo, thus **06** begone! **09** therefore **11** accordingly **12** consequently **13** for this reason **14** as a consequence

henceforth
05 hence **09** from now on, hereafter **11** hereinafter, in the future **12** henceforward **14** from this time on

henchman, henchwoman
04 aide, page **05** crony, heavy **06** hit man, lackey, minder, minion **07** servant **08** follower, sidekick **09** associate, attendant, bodyguard, supporter, underling **10** hatchet man, led captain **11** subordinate **12** right-hand man **14** right-hand woman

henna
08 camphire

henpecked
04 meek **05** timid **07** bullied **08** badgered, harassed, pestered **09** dominated, hag-ridden, tormented **10** browbeaten, criticized, subjugated, woman-tired **11** intimidated

Henry
01 H, O **03** Hal

Hephaestus
06 Vulcan

her
04 elle

Hera
04 Juno

herald
04 Lyon, omen, show, sign **05** augur, crier, token, usher **06** augury, Hermes, signal **07** courier, fanfare, portend, portent, precede, presage, promise, trumpet, usher in **08** announce, blazoner, indicate, Lord Lyon, proclaim **09** advertise, announcer, broadcast, harbinger, make known, messenger, precursor, publicize **10** forerunner, foreshadow, indication, king-at-arms, king-of-arms, Lyon-at-arms, make public, pave the way, proclaimer, promulgate **14** Lyon King of arms

heraldry

Heraldry terms include:

02 or
04 arms, fess, lion, orle, pall, pile, semé, urdé, vert
05 azure, badge, crest, eagle, eisen, fesse, field, gules, motto, sable, tawny, tenné, undee
06 argent, bezant, blazon, canton, centre, charge, dexter, emblem, ensign, helmet, impale, mullet, murrey, sejant, shield, volant, wivern
07 annulet, bordure, cendreé, chevron, dormant, griffin, gyronny, lozenge, martlet, passant, phoenix, quarter, rampant, regalia, roundel, saltire, statant, tierced, unicorn, urinant

08 addorsed, antelope, caboched, couchant, insignia, mantling, sanguine, sinister, tincture
09 carnation, displayed, hatchment
10 camelopard, cinquefoil, coat of arms, cockatrice, emblazonry, escutcheon, fleur-de-lis, quatrefoil, supporters
11 bleu celeste, compartment
15 regaliamantling

herb
04 forb, weed, wort 07 olitory

Herbs and spices include:

03 bay, nep, nip
04 balm, dill, mace, mint, sage
05 anise, basil, cumin, curry, thyme
06 borage, cassia, chilli, chives, cloves, fennel, garlic, ginger, hyssop, lovage, nutmeg, pepper, savory, sesame, sorrel
07 catmint, chervil, comfrey, mustard, oregano, paprika, parsley, pimento, saffron, vanilla
08 allspice, angelica, bergamot, camomile, cardamom, cardamum, cinnamon, lavender, marjoram, rosemary, tarragon, turmeric
09 chamomile, coriander, fenugreek, hypericum, lemon balm
10 gaillardia
12 caraway seeds
13 cayenne pepper

• magic herb
04 moly 13 Pantagruelion

herbal tea *see* **tea**

herbicide
06 diquat 08 paraquat, simazine 10 glyphosate 11 glufosinate, graminicide

herculean
04 hard, huge 05 great, heavy, large, tough 06 strong 07 arduous, mammoth, massive, onerous
08 colossal, daunting, enormous, exacting, gigantic, powerful, toilsome
09 demanding, difficult, gruelling, laborious, strenuous 10 exhausting, formidable, tremendous

herd
03 mob 04 band, goad, host, lead, mass, pack, race, rout, tail, urge
05 crowd, crush, drive, drove, flock, force, guide, horde, meiny, plebs, press, rally, swarm, troop 06 gather, huddle, meiney, meinie, menyie, muster, proles, rabble, throng 07 collect, round up, sounder, wrangle
08 assemble, riff-raff, shepherd
09 look after, multitude, the masses
10 congregate, take care of 11 get together

herdsman
06 cowman, drover 07 cowherd, grazier, vaquero 08 shepherd, stockman, wrangler 10 stock rider

here
02 in 03 ici, now 05 adsum 06 around 07 present 10 at this time 11 at this place, at this point, at this stage, in this place, to this place

• here is
04 ecco

hereabouts
04 here 08 near here 10 around here 11 in this place 12 in these parts

hereafter
05 hence, later 06 beyond, heaven
08 paradise 09 afterlife, from now on, next world 10 eventually, henceforth, life to come 11 in the future
12 henceforward 13 elysian fields
14 life after death

here and there
05 about, among 06 thinly 08 to and fro 11 irregularly 12 sporadically 15 in various places

hereditary
04 left 06 family, inborn, inbred, innate, willed 07 genetic, natural
08 inherent 09 ancestral, inherited
10 bequeathed, congenital, handed down 11 transferred 13 transmissible

• hereditary factor
02 id 04 gene

heredity
03 DNA 04 gene 05 genes
08 genetics 11 chromosomes, inheritance 13 genetic make-up

herein
◇ *containment indicator*
06 within 11 contained in 13 in this respect

heresy
05 error 06 schism 07 atheism, dissent 08 apostasy, Docetism, unbelief 09 blasphemy, Montanism, recusance 10 dissension, dissidence, heterodoxy, scepticism, separatism
11 agnosticism, revisionism, unorthodoxy 12 free-thinking, sectarianism 13 nonconformity

heretic
06 zendik 07 atheist, sceptic
08 agnostic, apostate, recusant, renegade 09 dissenter, dissident, miscreant, sectarian 10 schismatic, separatist, unbeliever 11 free-thinker, revisionist 13 nonconformist

heretical
07 impious 08 agnostic, recusant, renegade 09 atheistic, dissident, heterodox, sceptical, sectarian
10 dissenting, irreverent, schismatic, separatist, unorthodox
11 blasphemous, revisionist, unbelieving 12 free-thinking, iconoclastic 13 rationalistic

heritage
03 due, lot 04 past 05 share 06 estate, family, legacy 07 bequest, culture, descent, dynasty, history, lineage, portion 08 ancestry, cultural
09 endowment, tradition
10 background, birthright, extraction, traditions 11 inheritance
See also **world**

hermaphrodite
08 bisexual 09 androgyne, polygamic
10 monoecious 11 androgynous, monoclinous, protogynous
12 heterogamous 13 gynodioecious, male and female 14 androdioecious

Hermes
07 Mercury

hermetic
04 shut 06 sealed 07 magical, obscure 08 abstruse, airtight
10 hermetical, watertight

hermit
04 monk 05 loner, Peter 07 ancress, ascetic, eremite, pagurid, recluse, stylite 08 beadsman, marabout, pagurian, sannyasi, solitary
09 anchoress, anchorite, pillarist
10 robber crab, solitarian
11 Hieronymite, pillar-saint, soldier crab

hermitage
05 haven 06 ashram, asylum, refuge
07 hideout, retreat, shelter 08 cloister, hideaway 09 sanctuary 11 hiding-place

hero
03 cid, god 04 idol, lead, lion, star
05 ideal, pin-up, sheik 06 eponym, sheikh, victor 07 demigod, good guy, paragon 08 cavalier, champion, male lead 09 celebrity, conqueror, lead actor, superstar 10 heart-throb
11 brave person, demigoddess, protagonist 12 leading actor
15 leading male part, leading male role, person of courage

Heroes include:

04 **Ajax**, **Bond** (James), **Dare** (Dan), **Hood** (Robin)
05 **Bruce** (Robert), **El Cid**, **Jason**, **Jones** (Indiana), **Kelly** (Ned), **Zorro**
06 **Arthur**, **Barton** (Dick), **Batman**, **Brutus** (Lucius Junius), **Rogers** (Buck), **Sharpe** (Richard),**Tarzan**
07 **Beowulf**, **Biggles**, **Glyn Dwr** (Owain), **Ivanhoe**, **Perseus**, **Theseus**, **Wallace** (William)
08 **Achilles**, **Heracles**, **Hercules**, **Lancelot**, **Odysseus**, **Superman**
09 **Churchill** (Sir Winston), **D'Artagnan**, **Glendower** (Owain), **MacGregor** (Rob Roy), **Schindler** (Oskar), **Spiderman**
10 **Coriolanus**, **Cú Chulainn**, **Hornblower** (Horatio), **Little John**, **Lone Ranger**, **Richthofen** (Manfred von 'the Red Baron')
11 **Bellerophon**, **Finn MacCool**, **Wilberforce** (William)
14 **Finn MacCumhail**, **Robert the Bruce**
15 **Three Musketeers**

heroic
04 bold, epic 05 brave, noble
06 daring 07 doughty, gallant, Homeric, valiant 08 fearless, intrepid, selfless, valorous 09 dauntless, undaunted 10 chivalrous, courageous,

determined **11** adventurous, lion-hearted **12** stout-hearted

heroically
05 nobly **06** boldly **07** bravely **09** valiantly **10** fearlessly, selflessly **11** dauntlessly **12** courageously

heroin
01 H **04** junk, scag, skag, snow **05** horse, shmek, smack, sugar **07** schmeck **10** white stuff **11** diamorphine

heroine
04 diva, idol, lead, star **05** ideal, pin-up **06** Amazon, victor **07** goddess, paragon **08** champion **09** celebrity, conqueror, lead actor, superstar **10** brave woman, female lead, prima donna **11** leading lady, protagonist **14** leading actress, prima ballerina, woman of courage

Heroines include:

04 Lane (Lois)
05 Croft (Lara), Szabo (Violette)
06 Cavell (Edith), Judith, Ripley (Ellen)
07 Ariadne, Darling (Grace), Deirdre
08 Antigone, Atalanta, Boadicea, Boudicca, Penelope
09 Cassandra, Joan of Arc, Macdonald (Flora), Snow White
10 Cinderella
11 Helen of Troy, Nightingale (Florence), Wonderwoman

heroism
06 daring, valour **07** bravery, courage, prowess **08** boldness, chivalry **09** fortitude, gallantry **11** doughtiness, intrepidity **12** fearlessness, selflessness **13** dauntlessness, determination **14** courageousness **15** lion-heartedness

heron
04 hern **05** Ardea, egret **07** bittern, squacco **08** boatbill, hernshaw, heronsew **09** heronshaw

hero-worship
07 worship **09** adoration, adulation **10** admiration, exaltation, veneration **11** deification, idolization **12** idealization **13** glorification

herring
04 brit, sild **05** capon **06** kipper, matjes, mattie **07** anchovy, bloater, clupeid, maatjes, rollmop, soldier **08** buckling, clupeoid, menhaden, sea stick **09** gaspereau **10** mossbunker **12** Norfolk capon
• **measure of herring**
04 cran, maze, warp **05** maise, maize, mease

hesitancy
05 delay, demur, doubt, qualm **08** scruples, wavering **09** misgiving **10** indecision, reluctance, stammering **11** reservation, uncertainty **12** doubtfulness, irresolution **13** unwillingness **14** disinclination

hesitant
03 shy **04** wary **05** timid **06** unsure **07** dubious, halting **08** delaying, doubtful, stalling, wavering **09** demurring, reluctant, sceptical, tentative, uncertain, unwilling **10** hesitating, indecisive, irresolute, stammering, stuttering **11** disinclined, half-hearted, vacillating

hesitate
04 halt, wait **05** delay, demur, doubt, pause, stall, waver **06** boggle, dicker, dither, falter, mammer, tarrow, teeter **07** balance, scruple, stammer, stumble, stutter, swither, um and ah **08** dubitate, hang back, hang fire, hold back **09** hum and haw, vacillate **10** dilly-dally, shrink from, think twice **11** be reluctant, be uncertain, be unwilling **12** shilly-shally **13** be disinclined

hesitation
05 delay, demur, doubt, dwell, pause, qualm **06** demure, qualms **07** scruple, waiting **08** misdoubt, scruples, stalling, wavering **09** faltering, hesitance, stumbling **10** cunctation, indecision, misgivings, reluctance, scepticism, stammering, stuttering, unsureness **11** hanging-back, holding-back, uncertainty, vacillation **12** doubtfulness, irresolution **13** dilly-dallying, unwillingness **14** disinclination, second thoughts **15** shilly-shallying
• **expression of hesitation**
02 er, ha, um, ur **03** erm, hah **04** well

Hestia
05 Vesta

heterodox
07 unsound **09** dissident, heretical **10** dissenting, schismatic, unorthodox **11** revisionist **12** free-thinking, iconoclastic

heterogeneous
05 mixed **06** motley, unlike, varied **07** diverse, opposed, piebald, pyebald **08** assorted, catholic, contrary **09** different, disparate, divergent, multiform, unrelated **10** contrasted, discrepant, dissimilar **11** diversified, incongruous, polymorphic **13** miscellaneous

heterogeneously
09 diversely **10** contrarily **11** differently, disparately, divergently **12** dissimilarly **13** incongruously

heterosexual
03 het **06** hetero **07** breeder **08** straight

het up
05 angry, tense, upset **07** anxious, in a rage, uptight, worried, wound up **08** agitated, offended, stressed, worked up **09** indignant, pissed off, resentful **11** stressed-out **14** beside yourself

hew
03 axe, cut, dye, hag, hue, lop, saw **04** chip, chop, fell, form, hack, make, tint, trim **05** carve, model, prune, sever, shape, split **06** chisel, colour, hammer, sculpt **07** fashion, whittle **09** sculpture **10** appearance

heyday
04 peak **05** bloom, flush, prime **06** summer **08** boom time, pinnacle **09** flowering, golden age **11** culmination

hiatus
03 gap **04** lull, rest, rift, void **05** blank, break, chasm, lapse, pause, space **06** breach, defect, lacuna **07** opening **08** aperture, interval **10** suspension **12** interruption **13** discontinuity **14** discontinuance

hibernate
06 winter

hibernating
06 torpid **07** dormant **08** latitant

hibiscus
04 okra **07** roselle, rozelle **10** cotton tree, rose mallow **12** rose of Sharon

hiccup
03 hic, yex **04** snag, yesk **05** block, catch, check, delay, hitch **06** glitch, hold-up, mishap **07** barrier, problem, setback, trouble **08** drawback, obstacle **09** hindrance **10** difficulty, impediment **11** obstruction

hick *see* **bumpkin**

hickory
05 pecan **08** shagbark **09** scaly-bark, shellbark

hidden
◇ *hidden indicator*
04 dark, dern **05** close, dearn **06** arcane, covert, latent, masked, occult, secret, unseen, veiled **07** covered, cryptic, obscure, unknown **08** abstruse, mystical, shrouded, ulterior **09** concealed, disguised, invisible, recondite **10** indistinct, mysterious, out of sight, under wraps **11** camouflaged, clandestine **12** subterranean, under hatches

hide
◇ *containment indicator*
◇ *hidden indicator*
03 fur **04** buff, bury, coat, fell, flog, heal, heel, hele, hell, lurk, mask, pell, pelt, robe, skin, stow, veil, whip, wrap **05** cache, cloak, cloud, cover, earth, slink, store **06** darken, encave, fleece, hole up, incave, lie low, screen, shadow, shroud, spetch **07** abscond, conceal, eclipse, envelop, flaught, leather, obscure, secrete, shelter, tappice **08** bottle up, disguise, keep dark, lie doggo, lock away, obstruct, suppress, withhold **09** dissemble, stash away, take cover **10** camouflage, go to ground, keep secret **12** go into hiding **13** draw a veil over, put out of sight **14** keep out of sight, keep under wraps, lay a false scent **15** conceal yourself, cover your tracks, keep a low profile

hideaway
03 den **04** hole, lair, nest **05** haven **06** refuge **07** hideout, retreat, shelter **08** cloister, fugitive **09** hermitage, sanctuary **11** hiding-place

hidebound
03 set **05** fixed, rigid **06** narrow **07** bigoted **08** stubborn **09** obstinate **10** entrenched, intolerant **11** Biedermeier, intractable, reactionary, strait-laced **12** conventional, narrow-minded **14** uncompromising

hideous
◇ *anagram indicator*
04 gash, grim, huge, ugly **05** awful **06** deform, horrid, ugsome **07** ghastly, loathly, macabre **08** dreadful, gruesome, horrible, shocking, terrible **09** appalling, frightful, grotesque, monstrous, repellent, repulsive, revolting, unsightly **10** abominable, disgusting, horrendous, horrifying, monstruous, outrageous, terrifying

hideously
08 horribly, horridly, terribly **10** abominably, dreadfully, gruesomely, shockingly **11** frightfully, grotesquely, repulsively **12** disgustingly, horrendously, outrageously, terrifyingly

hideout
03 den **04** hole, lair, nest **05** haven **06** refuge **07** retreat, shelter **08** cloister, hideaway **09** hermitage, sanctuary **11** hiding-place

hiding
◇ *containment indicator*
04 dern, mask, veil **05** cover, dearn **06** caning, shroud **07** beating, belting, licking, tanning, veiling **08** disguise, drubbing, flogging, spanking, whacking, whipping **09** battering, screening, thrashing, walloping **10** camouflage **11** concealment

hiding-place
03 den, mew **04** hide, hole, lair, nest **05** cache, cover, haven, stash **06** refuge **07** hideout, hidling, hidlins, retreat, shelter **08** cloister, hideaway, hidlings, hidy-hole **09** glory hole, hidey-hole, sanctuary

hierarchy
05 scale **06** ladder, series, strata, system **07** grading, ranking **08** echelons **09** structure **12** pecking order

hieroglyphics
04 code **05** runes, signs **06** cipher **07** scratch, symbols **08** scrabble, scribble, squiggle **10** bad writing, cacography, pictograms **13** secret symbols **14** picture writing

higgledy-piggledy
◇ *anagram indicator*
06 anyhow, untidy **07** jumbled, muddled **08** confused, pell-mell, untidily **09** any old how, haphazard **10** confusedly, disorderly, topsy-turvy **11** haphazardly **12** disorganized, through-other **14** indiscriminate

high
◇ *anagram indicator*
03 bad, off, top **04** dear, fine, gamy, good, haut, loud, peak, tall, trip **05** acute, aloft, angry, chief, doped, drunk, great, gusty, lofty, moral, nervy, noble, sharp, steep, tinny, wired **06** bombed, choice, classy, costly, de luxe, elated, height, loaded, piping, putrid, rancid, record, select, senior, severe, shrill, smelly, stoned, stormy, strong, summit, tiptop, treble, turn-on, wasted, worthy, zenith, zonked **07** blasted, blitzed, complex, decayed, eminent, ethical, exalted, extreme, haughty, intense, leading, notable, on a trip, out of it, perfect, quality, rotting, shrilly, soaring, soprano, squally, upright, violent **08** abstruse, admiring, advanced, arrogant, blue-chip, blustery, elevated, falsetto, forceful, freak-out, high-tech, inflated, piercing, positive, powerful, smelling, superior, top-class, towering, turned on, vigorous, virtuous **09** admirable, agreeable, approving, difficult, dignified, elaborate, eminently, excellent, excessive, exemplary, expensive, extremely, first-rate, gilt-edged, high-level, important, luxurious, principal, prominent, spaced out **10** arrogantly, exorbitant, favourable, first-class, freaked out, honourable, inebriated, noteworthy, powerfully, surpassing, unequalled **11** anticyclone, commendable, high-pitched, high-ranking, inebriation, influential, intoxicated, luxuriously, outstanding, penetrating, progressive, superlative, tempestuous, ultra-modern **12** altitudinous, appreciative, extortionate, intoxication, unparalleled, unreasonable, well-disposed **13** complimentary, distinguished, hallucinating, hallucination, high-frequency

• **high and dry**
06 bereft, dumped **07** ditched **08** helpless, marooned, stranded **09** abandoned, destitute

• **high and low**
07 all over **09** all around **10** every place, everywhere, far and near, throughout **11** in all places, in each place **12** in every place

• **high and mighty**
05 proud **06** swanky **07** exalted, haughty, stuck-up **08** arrogant, cavalier, snobbish, superior, toplofty **09** conceited, egotistic, imperious **10** disdainful, hogen-mogen **11** overbearing, overweening, patronizing, toploftical **13** condescending, self-important

• **hit high**
03 lob, sky

• **on high**
02 up **05** ahigh, aloft **07** aheight **08** supernal **10** in excelsis

high-born
05 noble **08** well-born **09** patrician **11** blue-blooded **12** aristocratic, thoroughbred

highbrow
04 deep **05** heavy **06** boffin, brains, brainy, genius **07** bookish, egghead, scholar, serious **08** academic, brainbox, cultured, long-hair, profound **09** classical, know-it-all, scholarly **10** cultivated, long-haired, mastermind **11** clever clogs **12** intellectual **13** sophisticated **14** third-programme

high-class
01 U **04** posh **05** dicty, élite, pakka, pucka, pukka, super **06** choice, classy, de luxe, dickty, select **07** elegant, quality **08** superior, top-class **09** excellent, exclusive, first-rate, luxurious, top-flight **10** upper-class **11** high-quality

highest
03 top **04** best **05** chief **07** supreme, topmost **08** crowning **09** uppermost

highfalutin, highfaluting
05 lofty **06** la-di-da, swanky **07** pompous **08** affected **09** bombastic, grandiose, high-flown **11** pretentious **12** high-sounding, magniloquent, supercilious

high-flown
05 lofty **06** florid, la-di-da, ornate, turgid **07** pompous, stilted **08** affected, elevated **09** bombastic, elaborate, grandiose **10** artificial, flamboyant **11** exaggerated, extravagant, highfalutin, pretentious **12** high-sounding, ostentatious, supercilious **13** grandiloquent, grand-sounding

high-handed
05 bossy **07** haughty **08** arrogant, despotic **09** arbitrary, imperious **10** autocratic, oppressive, peremptory, tyrannical **11** dictatorial, domineering, overbearing

high-handedness
09 arrogance, bossiness **13** arbitrariness, imperiousness, inflexibility **14** peremptoriness

high jinks
06 antics, capers, pranks **07** foolery, fooling, jollity **08** clowning **09** horseplay **10** buffoonery, skylarking, tomfoolery **11** fun and games **13** fooling around **14** monkey business, practical jokes, rough-and-tumble

highland
04 hill, rise **05** mound, mount, ridge **06** height, upland **07** plateau **08** mountain **09** elevation

Highlander
04 Gael **06** Gadhel, Goidel **07** nainsel' **08** nainsell, plaidman, teuchter **09** Irish Scot

highlight
04 best, peak **05** cream, focus **06** accent, climax, play up, set off, show up, stress **07** feature, focus on, point up **08** high spot **09** emphasize, high point, spotlight, underline **10** accentuate, illuminate **11** main feature **13** put emphasis on **15** call attention to

highly
04 most, very, well **06** hugely, really, thrice, vastly, warmly **07** greatly **08** very much **09** certainly, decidedly, extremely, immensely **10** favourably, thoroughly **11** approvingly **12** considerably, tremendously **13** exceptionally **14** appreciatively **15** extraordinarily

highly-strung
04 edgy **05** jumpy, nervy, tense **06** on edge **07** nervous, uptight, wound up **08** neurotic, restless, stressed **09** excitable, sensitive **11** easily upset, overwrought **13** temperamental

high-minded
04 fair, good, pure **05** lofty, moral, noble **06** worthy **07** ethical, upright **08** elevated, virtuous **09** righteous **10** honourable, idealistic, principled **14** high-principled

high-pitched
05 acute, sharp, steep, tinny **06** piping, shrill, treble **07** orthian, soprano **08** falsetto, piercing **11** penetrating

high-powered
05 pushy, valid **06** mighty, potent, strong, urgent **07** dynamic, go-ahead, telling, weighty **08** emphatic, forceful, forcible, powerful, vehement, vigorous **09** assertive, effective, energetic **10** compelling, convincing, impressive, persuasive

high-priced
04 dear, high **05** steep, stiff **06** costly, pricey **09** excessive, expensive **10** exorbitant **12** extortionate, unreasonable

high-sounding
06 florid **07** orotund, pompous, stilted **08** affected, imposing, strained **09** bombastic, grandiose, high-flown, overblown, ponderous **10** altisonant, artificial, flamboyant **11** extravagant, pretentious **12** magniloquent, ostentatious **13** grandiloquent

high-speed
05 brisk, fleet, hasty, quick, rapid, swift **06** flying, speedy **07** express, hurried **11** accelerated

high-spirited
04 bold **05** proud **06** active, bouncy, daring, lively **07** dashing, dynamic, mettled, playful, rampant, vibrant **08** animated, cheerful, spirited, vigorous **09** ebullient, energetic, exuberant, sparkling, vivacious **10** boisterous, frolicsome, hot-blooded, mettlesome **11** full of beans, high-mettled **12** effervescent, great-hearted, thoroughbred

high spirits
06 bounce, capers, energy, heyday, spirit **07** elation, sparkle **08** boldness, buoyancy, hilarity, vivacity **09** animation, good cheer **10** ebullience, exuberance, liveliness **11** high feather, joie de vivre **12** exhilaration **14** boisterousness

highway
04 road, rode **05** grove, route **06** avenue, bypass **07** flyover, freeway, roadway, tollway **08** Autobahn, broadway, clearway, main road, motorway, ring road, toll road, turnpike **09** autoroute, boulevard, trunk road **10** autostrada, camino real, expressway, high street, interstate **11** carriageway **12** arterial road, primary route, thoroughfare **15** dual carriageway

highwayman
03 pad **05** scamp **06** bandit, hold-up, robber **07** footpad **08** hijacker **09** bandolero, rank-rider, road agent **10** bushranger, highjacker, land-pirate **15** knight of the road

Highwaymen include:

04 King (Tom)
05 Duval (Claude)
06 Turpin (Dick)
07 Brennan (Willie), Nevison (John), Nevison (William)
08 MacHeath
09 Abershawe (Jerry), Swift Nick
12 Mack the Knife

hijack
05 seize **07** carjack, skyjack **08** take over **10** commandeer **11** expropriate

hike
03 tug **04** jack, jerk, lift, plod, pull, ramp, trek, walk, yank **05** hitch, hoist, march, put up, raise, tramp **06** jack up, pull up, push up, ramble, trudge, wander **08** bushwalk, increase

hilarious
05 funny, jolly, merry, noisy **06** jovial **07** amusing, a scream, comical, killing, riotous, risible **08** farcical, humorous **09** laughable **10** boisterous, hysterical, rollicking, uproarious **12** entertaining **13** side-splitting

hilariously
09 comically, laughably **10** farcically, humorously **12** boisterously, hysterically, uproariously

hilarity
03 fun **05** mirth **06** comedy, gaiety, levity **07** jollity **08** laughter **09** amusement, frivolity, merriment **10** exuberance **11** high spirits **12** conviviality, exhilaration **14** boisterousness

hill
03 dod, dun, how, kip, kop, law, low, man, pap, tel, tor **04** berg, cone, down, drop, dune, fell, holt, howe, knot, loma, mesa, pike, ramp, rise, tell, toot, torr **05** butte, coast, jebel, knoll, kopje, morro, mound, mount, slope **06** ascent, barrow, cuesta, djebel, height, koppie, pimple, rising **07** descent, hillock, hilltop, hummock, incline, mamelon **08** eminence, foothill, gradient, mountain **09** acclivity, declivity, elevation, monadnock, monticule, sugarloaf **10** prominence, saddleback **12** rising ground

Rome's seven hills:

07 Caelian, Viminal
08 Aventine, Palatine, Quirinal
09 Esquiline
10 Capitoline

• **over the hill**
03 old **04** gone **06** past it **09** getting on **13** past your prime

hillbilly
03 oaf **04** boor, hick, lout **06** rustic **07** bumpkin, hawbuck, hayseed, hoedown, peasant **08** clodpoll **10** clodhopper, provincial **11** bushwhacker **12** country yokel **14** country bumpkin

hill fort
04 rath

hillock
04 dune, knap, knob, toft, tump **05** knoll, knowe, mound **06** barrow **07** hommock, hummock **08** monticle **10** monticulus

hill-slope
04 brae

hilltop
03 dod, nab **05** crest

hilt
04 grip, haft, heft **05** helve, shaft **06** basket, handle **08** coquille, handgrip

• **to the hilt**
05 fully **06** wholly **07** utterly **08** entirely, to the end **09** all the way, to the full **10** completely, thoroughly **14** in every respect **15** from first to last

him
02 un

hind
04 back, rear, rump, tail **05** after, stern **06** caudal, hinder **09** posterior

hinder
03 bar, let **04** balk, curb, foil, halt, hind, last, rear, stay, stop **05** block, check, crimp, debar, delay, deter, dwarf, embar, estop, imbar, stunt **06** arrest, cumber, hamper, hold up, impede, oppose, resist, retard, stymie, taigle, thwart **07** empeach, forelay, impeach, inhibit, keep off, porlock, prevent, set back, trammel **08** encumber, handicap, hold back, obstruct, preclude, slow down **09** forestall, frustrate, hamstring, interrupt, throw back, withstand **10** overslaugh **13** interfere with

hindmost
03 lag **04** last, tail **05** final **07** aftmost, endmost **08** furthest, rearmost, remotest, terminal, trailing, ultimate **09** aftermost **10** concluding **12** furthest back **14** farthest behind

hindrance
03 bar, let **04** curb, drag, foil, snag, stop **05** block, check, delay, hitch **06** hold-up, thwart **07** barrier, empeach, impeach, shackle **08** drawback, handicap, obstacle, pullback, stoppage **09** cumbrance, deterrent, impedance, restraint, thwarting **10** difficulty, impediment, limitation, prevention **11** encumbrance, obstruction, obstructive, restriction **12** disadvantage, interference, interruption **13** inconvenience **14** stumbling-block

hindsight
06 review, survey **10** reflection, retrospect **11** remembrance **12** afterthought, recollection, thinking back **13** re-examination

Hindu *see* **god, goddess; month**

Hindustani
04 Hind, Urdu **05** Hindi

hinge
◇ *reversal indicator*
04 hang, rest, turn **05** gemel, pivot **06** centre, depend, garnet **07** revolve **09** ginglymus **11** cross-garnet **12** be contingent

hint
03 cue, tip **04** clue, dash, help, mint, note, sign, tang, wind, wink, word **05** hunch, imply, light, point, savor, speck, taste, tinge, touch, trace, whiff **06** advice, allude, moment, nuance, office, prevue, prompt, savour, signal, squint, tip off, tip-off **07** glimmer, inkling, let fall, mention, pointer, preview, soupçon, suggest, thought, whisper, wrinkle **08** allusion, indicate, innuendo, intimate, reminder **09** insinuate, scintilla, suspicion **10** indication, intimation, sprinkling, suggestion **11** implication, insinuation, opportunity, subindicate

hinterland
08 backveld, interior **10** back-blocks, hinderland **11** back-country

hip
02 in **03** hep **04** cool, huck, loin, rump **05** croup, funky, thigh **06** dog-hep, dog-hip, groovy, haunch, huckle, modish, pelvis, trendy, with it **07** stylish, voguish **08** buttocks **09** happening, posterior **10** all the rage **11** fashionable **12** hindquarters, hypochondria **13** up to the minute

• **hip bone**
04 coxa **10** huckle-bone **14** innominate bone

hippie, hippy
05 loner, rebel **07** beatnik, deviant, dropout **08** bohemian **10** long-haired **11** flower child

hire
03 fee, job, let, pay **04** book, cost, lend, rent, wage **05** lease, price **06** charge, employ, engage, enlist, rental, retain, salary, sign on, sign up, take on **07** appoint, charter, freight, reserve **10** commission

hire-purchase
02 HP **09** easy terms **10** never-never **14** instalment plan

hirsute
05 hairy, rough **06** crinal, hispid, shaggy **07** bearded, bristly, crinate, crinite, crinose **08** unshaven **11** bewhiskered, crinigerous

hiss
03 boo **04** buzz, hish, hizz, hoot, jeer, mock **05** goose, scorn, taunt, whiss, whizz **06** deride, fizzle, shrill, siffle, sizzle **07** catcall, hissing, mockery, scoff at, the bird, whistle **08** contempt, derision, ridicule, scoffing, sibilant, sibilate, taunting **09** raspberry, shout down, sibilance **10** assibilate, effervesce, sibilation **15** blow raspberries

historian
07 diarist **08** annalist, narrator, recorder **09** archivist **10** chronicler **11** chronologer **15** historiographer

Historians include:

04 **Bede** (St, 'The Venerable'), **Bois** (William Edward Burghardt du), **Livy**, **Read** (Sir Herbert Edward), **Webb** (Sidney)
05 **Barth** (Heinrich), **Blunt** (Anthony Frederick), **Clark** (Kenneth, Lord), **Ensor** (Sir Robert), **Gates** (Henry Louis, Jnr), **Henry** (of Huntingdon), **Lodge** (Henry Cabot), **Nepos** (Cornelius), **Paris** (Matthew), **Ranke** (Leopold von), **Renan** (Ernest), **Stone** (Norman)
06 **Arrian**, **Berlin** (Sir Isaiah), **Bolton** (Geoffrey), **Briggs** (Lord Asa), **Eliade** (Mircea), **Froude** (James Anthony), **Gibbon** (Edward), **Guizot** (François), **Irving** (David), **Namier** (Sir Lewis), **O'Brien** (Conor Cruise), **Schama** (Simon), **Strabo**, **Strong** (Sir Roy), **Tabari** (Abu Jafar Mohammed Ben Jarir al-), **Tawney** (Richard Henry), **Taylor** (Alan John Percivale), **Terkel** (Studs), **Thiers** (Adolphe), **Vasari** (Giorgio)
07 **Barbour** (John), **Bullock** (Alan, Lord), **Carlyle** (Thomas), **Comines** (Philippe de), **Mommsen** (Theodor), **Pevsner** (Sir Nikolaus Bernhard), **Sallust**, **Severin** (Timothy), **Starkey** (David), **Tacitus**, **Toynbee** (Arnold), **William** (of Malmesbury), **William** (of Tyre)
08 **Foucault** (Michel), **Geoffrey** (of Monmouth), **Gombrich** (Sir Ernst Hans Josef), **Josephus** (Flavius), **Las Casas** (Emmanuel), **Macaulay** (Thomas Babington, Lord), **Michelet** (Jules), **Palgrave** (Sir Francis), **Panofsky** (Erwin), **Plutarch**, **Polybius**, **Wedgwood** (Dame Cicely), **Xenophon**
09 **Dionysius** (of Halicarnassus), **Froissart** (Jean), **Herodotus**, **Holinshed** (Raphael), **Pausanias**, **Plekhanov** (Giorgiy), **Procopius**, **Rowbotham** (Sheila), **Suetonius**, **Trevelyan** (George Macaulay)
10 **Baldinucci** (Filippo), **Burckhardt** (Jacob Christopher), **Dio Cassius**, **Thucydides**
11 **Schlesinger** (Arthur Meier), **Tocqueville** (Alexis de), **Trevor-Roper** (Hugh Redwald)
12 **Guicciardini** (Francesco)
15 **Diodorus Siculus**

historic
05 famed **06** famous **07** notable **08** renowned **09** important, memorable, momentous, red-letter **10** celebrated, remarkable **11** epoch-making, outstanding, significant **13** consequential, extraordinary

historical
03 old **04** past, real **05** prior **06** actual, bygone, former, of yore **07** ancient, factual **08** attested, recorded, verified **09** authentic, confirmed **10** chronicled, documented, verifiable

Historical periods include:

05 Bruce, Tudor
06 Norman, Stuart
07 Angevin, Cold War, Post-War, Regency, Stewart, Yorkist
08 Civil War, Dark Ages, Medieval
09 Edwardian, Mediaeval, Modern Age, Victorian
10 Anglo-Saxon, Hanoverian, Middle Ages
11 Interbellum, Interregnum, Lancastrian, Plantagenet, Reformation, Renaissance, Restoration, Roman Empire, Romanticism
13 British Empire, Enlightenment, Ottoman Empire
15 Byzantine Empire

historically
04 once **07** long ago **08** formerly **09** in the past, yesterday **10** originally **11** some time ago **13** in former times, in years gone by

history
04 life, saga, tale **05** story, study **06** annals, family, record, report **07** account, memoirs, records, reports, the past **08** archives **09** antiquity, biography, chronicle, days of old, education, narrative, olden days, yesterday **10** background, bygone days, chronology, days of yore, experience, the old days, yesteryear **11** credentials, former times **13** autobiography, circumstances **14** qualifications, the good old days

histrionic
03 ham **05** bogus, stagy **06** forced **08** affected, dramatic, operatic

09 insincere, unnatural 10 artificial, theatrical 11 exaggerated, sensational 12 hypocritical, melodramatic

histrionics
05 scene 08 tantrums 09 dramatics, melodrama, staginess, theatrics 10 overacting 11 affectation, insincerity, performance 13 artificiality, theatricality, unnaturalness 14 sensationalism

hit
◇ *anagram indicator*
03 bat, bop, box, cue, dod, dot, fit, get, hay, pat, tap, tip, wow, zap 04 bang, bash, beat, belt, biff, blow, boff, bonk, bump, clip, club, cuff, daud, dawd, harm, hurt, move, polt, shot, skit, slap, slew, slog, sock, suit, swap, swat, tonk 05 catch, clonk, clout, crash, knock, pound, prang, punch, smack, smash, smite, thump, touch, upset, whack 06 affect, batter, buffet, come to, damage, dawn on, impact, strike, stroke, thrash, wallop, winner 07 beating, clobber, disturb, occur to, perturb, run into, success, triumph, trouble 08 knockout 09 collision, crash into, devastate, overwhelm, smash into, thrashing 10 clobbering, come to mind, meet head-on, plough into 11 be thought of, blockbuster, collide with, knock for six 12 be remembered 13 enter your mind 14 have an effect on
See also **kill**

• **hit back**
06 return 07 respond 09 retaliate 10 strike back 11 reciprocate 13 counter-attack

• **hit it off**
05 agree, click, fadge 06 warm to 09 get on with 10 grow to like 12 get along with 13 become friends, get on well with 14 be friendly with

• **hit on**
05 guess 06 invent 07 light on, realize, think of, uncover 08 arrive at, chance on, discover 09 stumble on

• **hit out**
04 rail 05 flail 06 assail, attack, strike, vilify 07 condemn, inveigh, lash out 08 denounce 09 criticize, strike out

hitch
03 rub, tie, tug 04 bind, hike, hook, jerk, join, limp, pull, snag, yank, yoke 05 block, catch, check, delay, heave, hoist, hotch, stick, unite 06 attach, couple, fasten, glitch, hiccup, hike up, hobble, hold-up, mishap, tether 07 barrier, cat's-paw, connect, harness, problem, setback, trouble 08 drawback, obstacle 09 hindrance 10 difficulty, impediment 11 contretemps, obstruction

hitherto
03 yet 05 so far 07 thus far, till now, up to now 08 formerly, until now 10 beforehand, heretofore, previously

hitman
03 gun 06 ice man 08 assassin

hit-or-miss
06 casual, hobnob, random, uneven 07 aimless, cursory, offhand 08 careless 09 apathetic, haphazard, unplanned 10 undirected 11 perfunctory 12 disorganized 13 lackadaisical, trial-and-error 14 indiscriminate

hive
03 gum 04 skep 07 alveary, bee-skep

hoard
04 fund, heap, keep, mass, pile, pose, save 05 amass, buy up, cache, hoord, hutch, lay in, lay up, plant, put by, spare, stash, store, uplay 06 coffer, gather, heap up, mucker, pile up, supply 07 collect, put away, reserve, stack up, stock up, uphoard 08 hoarding, salt away, set aside, squirrel, treasure 09 reservoir, stash away, stockpile 10 accumulate, collection 11 aggregation 12 accumulation, squirrel away 13 treasure-trove 14 conglomeration

hoarder
05 miser, saver 06 magpie 07 niggard 08 gatherer, squirrel 09 collector

hoarse
05 gruff, harsh, husky, raspy, roopy, rough 06 croaky, roopit 07 grating, rasping, raucous, throaty 08 croaking, gravelly, growling, guttural 10 discordant

hoarsely
07 gruffly, harshly, huskily, roughly 08 croakily 09 raucously 10 gutturally

hoarseness
04 roop, roup

hoary
03 old 04 aged, grey 05 banal, trite, white 06 old-hat 07 ancient, antique, archaic, cliché'd, silvery 08 clichéed, familiar, grizzled 09 canescent, senescent, venerable 10 antiquated, grey-haired 11 predictable, white-haired 12 overfamiliar

hoax
02 do 03 bam, cod, con, fun, gag, hum, kid 04 dupe, fake, fool, gull, jest, joke, josh, quiz, ruse, scam, sham, skit 05 bluff, cheat, fraud, kiddy, prank, put-on, spoof, stuff, trick 06 canard, delude, gammon, have on, humbug, pigeon, string, take in 07 deceive, fast one, frame-up, leg-pull, mystify, swindle, two-time 08 hoodwink, put-up job 09 April-fish, April fool, bamboozle, deception, gold brick 10 huntiegowk 11 double-cross, hunt-the-gowk, supercherie 12 take for a ride 13 practical joke 14 pull a fast one on

hoaxer
05 joker 06 humbug 07 sharper, spoofer 09 mystifier, prankster, trickster 10 bamboozler, hoodwinker 14 practical joker

hobble
04 clog, limp, reel 05 hilch, hitch 06 dodder, falter, fetter, hamper, scrape, totter 07 pastern, perplex, shackle, shuffle, spancel, stagger, stumble, trammel 10 walk lamely 13 walk awkwardly, walk with a limp

hobbling
04 game, lame 06 lamish

hobby
03 fad 04 game 05 sport 07 pastime, pursuit 08 interest, play-mare, sideline 09 amusement, avocation, diversion 10 recreation, relaxation 13 entertainment 14 divertissement, leisure pursuit 15 leisure activity

Hobbies and pastimes include:

05 batik, chess
06 acting, baking, bonsai, hiking, poetry, raffia
07 camping, CB radio, collage, cookery, crochet, dancing, drawing, macramé, mosaics, origami, pottery, quizzes, reading, singing, tatting, topiary, weaving, writing
08 basketry, cat shows, dog shows, draughts, feng shui, knitting, knotting, lacework, lapidary, marbling, painting, quilling, quilting, spinning, tapestry
09 astrology, astronomy, decoupage, gardening, genealogy, marquetry, millinary, model cars, philately, rug-making, sketching, strawwork, toy-making, train sets
10 beekeeping, board games, crosswords, doll-making, embroidery, kite-flying, lace-making, pub quizzes, pyrography, renovating, upholstery, wine-making
11 archaeology, beadworking, bell-ringing, book-binding, calligraphy, card playing, cat breeding, cross-stitch, dog breeding, dressmaking, home brewing, model-making, model trains, needlepoint, numismatics, ornithology, paper crafts, papier-mâché, photography, wine-tasting, woodcarving, woodworking
12 amateur radio, basketmaking, candle-making, games playing, phillumenism
13 bungee jumping, egg decorating, toy collecting
14 book collecting, coin collecting, cruciverbalism, doll collecting, flower pressing, herpetoculture, metal detecting
15 aquarium keeping, ballroom dancing, flower arranging, jewellery making, model aeroplanes, stamp collecting

hobgoblin
03 elf, imp 05 bogey, dwarf, gnome 06 buggan, buggin, goblin, spirit, sprite 07 bugaboo, bugbear, buggane,

spectre **08** wirricow, worricow, worrycow **10** apparition, bull-beggar, evil spirit

hobnob
03 mix **06** mingle **07** consort **08** go around **09** associate, hang about, hit-or-miss, pal around, socialize **10** fraternize **11** keep company

hock
03 ham, hox **04** pawn **07** gambrel, Rhenish **09** Rhine wine **11** Rhenish wine

See also **pawn**

hockey

Hockey-related terms include:

01 D
03 hit
04 ball, feet, goal, push
05 flick, scoop
06 aerial, tackle
07 dribble, free hit, red card, striker, sweeper
08 back line, bully-off, left back, left half, left wing
09 corner hit, drag flick, field goal, green card, right back, right half, right wing
10 centre half, centre pass, goal circle, goalkeeper, inside left, long corner, yellow card
11 field player, hockey stick, inside right, obstruction, short corner
12 penalty flick, reverse stick
13 centre forward, penalty corner, penalty stroke
14 shooting circle, striking circle

hocus-pocus
04 cant, hoax **05** cheat, spell **06** deceit, humbug, jargon, juggle **07** juggler, swindle **08** artifice, delusion, hoky-poky, nonsense, trickery **09** chicanery, conjuring, deception, gibberish, imposture, rigmarole **10** hokey-pokey, magic words, mumbo-jumbo **11** abracadabra, legerdemain, trompe-l'oeil **12** gobbledygook **13** sleight of hand

hodgepodge
03 mix **04** mess **06** jumble, medley **07** melange, mixture **08** mishmash **09** confusion **10** collection, hotchpotch, miscellany

hoe
04 clat **05** claut **06** pecker **07** scuffle **10** promontory

hog
03 pig **04** boar **05** swine **06** corner, porker **07** control, grunter **08** babirusa, dominate, shilling, take over, wild boar **09** babirussa **10** babiroussa, monopolize **14** keep to yourself

hogshead
04 muid

• **two hogsheads**
04 pipe

hogwash
03 rot **04** blah, bosh, bunk, crap, guff, tosh **05** balls, bilge, hooey, swill, trash, tripe **06** bunkum, drivel, hot air, piffle **07** baloney, eyewash, rubbish, twaddle **08** claptrap, cobblers, malarkey, nonsense, tommyrot **09** gibberish, moonshine, poppycock **10** balderdash

hoi polloi
07 the herd **08** riff-raff, the plebs, varletry **09** the masses, the proles, the rabble **11** the peasants, the populace **14** the proletariat, the third estate **15** the common people

hoist
04 jack, lift, rear, sway, wind **05** crane, erect, heave, hoise, raise, steal, wince, winch **06** jack up, pulley, tackle, teagle, uplift, wind up **07** capstan, elevate, winch up **08** elevator, windlass

hoity-toity
05 giddy, huffy, lofty, noisy, proud **06** snooty, uppity **07** haughty, pompous, stuck-up **08** arrogant, scornful, snobbish **09** conceited **10** disdainful **11** overweening, toffee-nosed **12** supercilious **13** high and mighty

hold
◇ *containment indicator*
02 ho **03** aim, bet, hoa, hoh, hug, own, ren, rin, run **04** bear, bind, bulk, call, curb, deem, fill, go on, grip, have, holt, hook, keep, last, soft, stay, stop, sway, take, view **05** apply, belay, brace, carry, catch, check, clasp, cling, clout, grasp, gripe, judge, power, rivet, seize, stick, think, treat **06** absorb, adhere, arrest, assume, clutch, detain, direct, endure, enfold, engage, esteem, fulfil, hold up, keep up, lock up, nelson, occupy, prop up, reckon, regard, remain, retain, summon, suplex, take up **07** adjudge, armlock, bear hug, believe, carry on, claucht, claught, cling to, conduct, confine, contain, control, convene, custody, embrace, enclose, engross, enthral, holding, impound, mastery, observe, persist, possess, presume, reserve, soft you, support, suppose, sustain, toehold **08** assemble, buttress, consider, continue, dominion, headlock, hold down, imprison, leverage, maintain, organize, purchase, restrain, scissors, tenacity **09** authority, be in force, captivate, celebrate, dominance, fascinate, influence **10** Boston crab, compromise, full nelson, half nelson, hammerlock, monopolize, remain true, stronghold **11** accommodate, backbreaker, have room for, incarcerate, preside over, remain valid, scissor hold **12** have space for, stranglehold **13** be in operation, hold in custody, remain in force **14** have in your hand **15** have a capacity of, have in your hands

See also **wrestling**

• **get hold of**
◇ *containment indicator*
03 get **05** reach **06** obtain **07** acquire, contact, speak to **12** get through to **14** get in touch with, get your hands on **15** communicate with

• **hold back**
03 bar **04** curb, hang, pull, stop **05** check, delay, pause **06** desist, impede, refuse, retain, retard, shrink, stifle **07** contain, control, forbear, inhibit, prevent, refrain, repress **08** hesitate, keep back, obstruct, restrain, strangle, suppress, withhold

• **hold down**
03 pin **04** have, keep **06** occupy **07** oppress **08** dominate, keep down, restrain, suppress **09** tyrannize **10** continue in

• **hold fast**
03 pin **04** clip, nail **05** avast, stick **07** enchain, pin down

• **hold forth**
04 show, talk **05** orate, speak, spout **06** preach **07** declaim, lecture **08** harangue **09** discourse **12** talk at length **13** speak at length

• **hold off**
04 wait **05** avoid, defer, delay, repel **06** put off, rebuff, resist **07** fend off, hang off, keep off, ward off **08** fight off, postpone, stave off **09** keep at bay

• **hold on**
04 grip, stop, wait **05** clasp, cling, grasp, seize **06** clutch, endure, hang on, remain **07** carry on, cling to, survive **08** continue **09** keep going, persevere

• **hold out**
04 give, last, stay **05** offer, reach **06** endure, extend, hang on, resist **07** carry on, last out, persist, present, proffer, protend, subsist **08** continue **09** persevere, stand fast, stand firm, withstand

• **hold over**
05 defer, delay **06** put off, shelve **07** adjourn, put back, suspend **08** postpone

• **hold up**
◇ *reversal down indicator*
03 mug, rob **04** bear, lift, rear, show, slow, stay **05** apply, brace, carry, delay, raise **06** burgle, detain, endure, hinder, impede, nobble, prop up, remain, retard, upbear, uphold **07** bolster, display, exhibit, present, put back, set back, shore up, stick up, support, sustain **08** hold high, knock off, obstruct **09** be in force, break into, knock over, steal from **10** burglarize, remain true **11** remain valid **13** be in operation, remain in force

• **hold with**
06 accept **07** support **09** agree with, approve of **11** countenance, go along with, subscribe to

• **hold your own**
06 resist **07** survive **09** stand fast, stand firm, withstand **15** stand your ground

• put on hold
05 defer, delay **06** put off **07** hold off **08** postpone

holder
04 case, rest **05** cover, haver, owner, stand **06** bearer, casing, keeper, sheath **07** housing **08** occupant **09** container, custodian, incumbent, possessor, purchaser **10** proprietor, receptacle

holdings
04 land **05** bonds **06** assets, estate, shares, stocks, tenure **08** property **09** resources **10** real estate, securities **11** investments, possessions

hold-up
03 jam **04** raid, snag, wait **05** delay, heist, hitch, theft **07** break-in, mugging, problem, robbery, setback, stick-up, trouble **08** burglary, stoppage **10** bottleneck, difficulty, stick-up job, traffic jam **11** obstruction

hole
03 cup, den, eye, fix, gap, jam, pit, set, tip **04** bind, bore, cave, dent, drop, dump, flaw, gash, geat, lair, mess, mine, nest, pore, rent, rift, slit, slot, slum, snag, spot, stab, stew, tear, vent **05** break, chasm, crack, delve, error, fault, hovel, notch, scoop, shack, shaft, space, spike, split, thirl, whole **06** breach, burrow, cavern, cavity, corner, covert, crater, defect, dimple, eyelet, hollow, outlet, pickle, pierce, pigpen, pigsty, plight, pocket, recess, scrape **07** chamber, fissure, mistake, opening, orifice, pothole **08** aperture, hot water, loophole, puncture, quandary, weakness **09** deep water, perforate **10** depression, difficulty, excavation, pretty pass, subterfuge **11** discrepancy, perforation, predicament **13** inconsistency

See also **fingerhole**

• hole in one
03 ace

• hole up
04 hide **06** lie low **09** take cover **10** go to ground **12** go into hiding **15** conceal yourself

• pick holes in
04 slag **05** slate **07** nit-pick, run down, slag off **09** criticize **12** pull to pieces **13** find fault with

hole-and-corner
06 covert, secret, sneaky **07** furtive **08** back-door, hush-hush, stealthy **09** secretive, underhand **10** backstairs **11** clandestine **13** surreptitious **15** under-the-counter

holiday
03 vac **04** fete, play, rest, trip, wake **05** break, festa, leave, wakes **06** day off, fiesta, recess **07** half-day, high day, holy day, play-day, time off **08** feast day, festival, fly-drive, furlough, half-term, leisure, vacation **09** honeymoon, minibreak, saint's day **11** anniversary, bank holiday, celebration, package tour **12** legal holiday, long vacation **13** public holiday **14** leave of absence

National holidays include:

05 UN Day
07 Flag Day
08 Anzac Day, Unity Day
09 Labour Day, Women's Day
10 Culture Day, Freedom Day, Martyrs' Day, Mothers' Day, Victory Day
11 Bastille Day, National Day, Republic Day
12 Armistice Day, Australia Day, Children's Day, Discovery Day, Thanksgiving
13 King's Birthday, Liberation Day, Revolution Day
14 Armed Forces Day, Queen's Birthday, Remembrance Day, Unification Day
15 Constitution Day, Emancipation Day, Independence Day

holier-than-thou
04 smug **05** pious **08** priggish, unctuous **09** pietistic, religiose **10** complacent, goody-goody **13** sanctimonious, self-approving, self-righteous, self-satisfied

holiness
05 piety **06** purity **07** halidom **08** divinity, goodness, sanctity **09** godliness **10** dedication, devoutness, perfection, sacredness, sanctimony **11** blessedness, saintliness, sinlessness **12** consecration, spirituality, virtuousness **13** religiousness, righteousness

holler
03 cry **04** bawl, call, howl, roar, yell, yelp, yowl **05** cheer, shout, whoop **06** bellow, shriek **07** clamour

hollow
03 cup, dig, dip, how, lap, low, pan, pit **04** boss, bowl, cave, comb, dale, deaf, deep, dell, dent, dish, dull, flat, glen, hole, howe, khud, nook, sham, vain, vale, void, vola, well **05** basin, chasm, clean, combe, coomb, delve, empty, false, gorge, gouge, niche, scoop, womby **06** burrow, cavern, cavity, cirque, coombe, cranny, crater, dimple, dingle, furrow, futile, groove, indent, ravine, recess, sunken, trough, tunnel, unreal, vacant, valley **07** caved-in, channel, concave, deep-set, dishing, echoing, muffled, Pyrrhic, unsound, useless, vacuity **08** coreless, excavate, fleeting, fossette, indented, inflated, rumbling, unfilled **09** cavernous, concavity, deceitful, deceptive, depressed, emptiness, fruitless, incurvate, insincere, of no avail, pointless, pretended, valueless, worthless **10** artificial, completely, depression, excavation, profitless, semicirque, unavailing **11** indentation, meaningless, reverberant **12** hypocritical

• beat someone hollow
04 lick, rout **05** crash **06** hammer, thrash **07** clobber, trounce **09** devastate, overwhelm, slaughter **10** annihilate **13** defeat soundly

holly
04 holm, ilex, mate **06** yaupon **13** Aquifoliaceae

holmium
02 Ho

holocaust
05 Shoah **06** flames, pogrom **07** carnage, inferno **08** disaster, genocide, hecatomb, massacre **09** cataclysm, sacrifice, slaughter **10** extinction, immolation, mass murder **11** catastrophe, destruction, devastation **12** annihilation **13** conflagration, extermination **15** ethnic cleansing

holy
02 pi **04** good, pure **05** godly, moral, pious, saint **06** devout, divine, sacred **07** blessed, perfect, revered, saintly, sinless **08** faithful, hallowed, virtuous **09** dedicated, pietistic, religious, righteous, spiritual, venerated **10** God-fearing, sacrosanct, sanctified **11** consecrated **13** sanctimonious

• holy book *see* **Bible**

holy of holies
05 altar **06** shrine **07** sanctum **12** inner sanctum **13** most holy place

homage
03 awe **06** esteem, honour, manred, praise, regard **07** incense, manrent, respect, service, tribute, worship **08** devotion **09** adoration, adulation, deference, reverence **10** admiration, veneration **11** knee-tribute, recognition **15** acknowledgement

home
02 in **03** den, pad **04** base, digs, flat, goal, nest, semi **05** abode, fount, house, local, place, roots, villa **06** asylum, centre, cradle, family, hostel, inland, libken, native, refuge, source **07** address, blighty, cottage, element, habitat, retreat **08** bungalow, domestic, domicile, dwelling, fireside, homeland, home town, interior, internal, national **09** apartment, effective, household, residence, safe place, searching **10** birthplace, fatherland, habitation, motherland, native town **11** effectively, institution, nursing home **13** children's home, dwelling-place, mother country, native country, place of origin **14** old people's home, retirement home **15** country of origin, residential home, somewhere to live

See also **animal**

• at home
02 in **06** at ease, well up, within **07** relaxed, skilled **08** familiar **09** competent, confident **10** conversant **11** comfortable, experienced **13** knowledgeable

• at home of
04 chez

• bring home
05 prove **06** instil **07** impress **08** convince **09** emphasize, inculcate

• home improvements
03 DIY

• home in on
03 aim **05** focus **06** direct **08** pinpoint, zero in on, zoom in on **11** concentrate

• not at home
03 out **04** away

• nothing to write home about
02 OK **04** drab, dull **06** boring **08** inferior, mediocre, ordinary **11** not exciting, predictable **13** no great shakes **14** not interesting

homecoming
06 return **07** arrival **10** coming-back, return home **13** arrival at home

homeland
04 home **10** fatherland, motherland, native land **13** mother country, native country **15** country of origin

homeless
06 exiled, tramps **07** dossers, dossing, evicted, nomadic, outcast, vagrant **08** forsaken, rootless, vagrants **09** abandoned, derelicts, destitute, displaced, itinerant, squatters, unsettled, vagabonds, wandering **10** down-and-out, travellers, travelling **11** down-and-outs, on the street **12** dispossessed, on the streets **13** on the pavement, sleeping rough **14** of no fixed abode

• homeless person
04 hobo, waif **05** skell

homelessness
07 dossing **08** vagrancy **11** abandonment, destitution **12** displacement, no fixed abode, rootlessness **13** sleeping rough

homely
04 cosy, homy, snug, ugly **05** homey, mumsy, plain **06** folksy, modest, russet, simple **07** natural, relaxed **08** cheerful, domestic, everyday, familiar, friendly, homelike, homespun, informal, intimate, ordinary, unlovely **09** welcoming **10** hospitable, unassuming **11** comfortable **12** unattractive **13** unpretentious **15** not much to look at, unprepossessing, unsophisticated

homer
03 cor **09** Maeonides

homespun
04 rude **05** crude, plain, rough **06** coarse, folksy, homely, russet, rustic, simple **07** artless, raploch **08** home-made **09** inelegant, unadorned, unrefined **10** amateurish, unpolished **13** uncomplicated **15** unsophisticated

homestead
04 toft

homework
04 prep **09** spadework **10** groundwork **11** preparation

homey
04 cosy, snug **07** relaxed **08** cheerful, familiar, friendly, homelike, informal, intimate **09** welcoming **10** hospitable **11** comfortable

homicidal
06 bloody, deadly, lethal, mortal **07** violent **08** maniacal **09** murderous **10** sanguinary **12** bloodthirsty, death-dealing

homicide
06 murder **07** killing, slaying **09** bloodshed, slaughter **12** chance-medley, manslaughter **13** assassination

homily
04 talk **05** prone, spiel **06** postil, sermon, speech **07** address, lecture, oration **08** harangue **09** discourse, preaching

homogeneity
07 oneness **08** likeness, sameness **09** agreement **10** consonancy, similarity, similitude, uniformity **11** consistency, resemblance **13** analogousness, comparability, identicalness **14** correspondence

homogeneous
04 akin **05** alike **07** cognate, kindred, similar, the same, uniform **08** of a piece, unvaried **09** analogous, identical, unvarying **10** all the same, comparable, compatible, consistent, harmonious, indiscrete **11** all of a piece, correlative **13** corresponding, of the same kind

homogeneously
07 the same **09** similarly, uniformly **10** all the same **11** all of a piece, identically **12** consistently **13** of the same kind **15** correspondingly

homogenize
04 fuse **05** blend, merge, unite **07** combine **08** coalesce **10** amalgamate **11** make similar, make uniform

homologous
04 like **07** related, similar **08** matching, parallel **09** analogous **10** comparable, equivalent **13** correspondent, corresponding

homosexual
03 gay **04** pink **07** lesbian, same-sex **08** bisexual
See also **gay**

Honduras
02 HN **03** HND

hone
04 edge, file, whet **05** grind, point **06** polish **07** develop, sharpen

honest
04 fair, jake, just, open, real, true **05** afald, blunt, clean, frank, legal, moral, plain, round, white **06** aefald, afawld, candid, chaste, dinkum, direct, lawful, seemly, simple, single, square, trusty **07** aefauld, dinky-di, ethical, genuine, sincere, up-front, upright **08** bona fide, dinky-die, even-down, outright, reliable, soothful, straight, truthful, virtuous, yeomanly **09** equitable, impartial, ingenuous, objective, outspoken, reputable, righteous, soothfast **10** above-board, dependable, fair dinkum, forthright, four-square, high-minded, honourable, law-abiding, legitimate, on the level, principled, scrupulous, upstanding **11** respectable, right-minded, trustworthy **12** on the up and up, plain-hearted **13** fair and square, incorruptible, plain-speaking, unpretentious **14** straight as a die **15** straightforward

honestly
04 true **05** truly **06** dinkum, direct, fairly, justly, really, simply, square **07** dinky-di, frankly, legally, morally, plainly, up-front, upright **08** dinky-die, directly, lawfully, straight **09** equitably, ethically, no messing, sincerely, uprightly **10** above board, honourably, on the level, straight up, to be honest, truthfully **11** impartially, in good faith, objectively, on the square **12** legitimately **13** fair and square

honesty
05 faith **06** equity, ethics, honour, lunary, morals, square, virtue **07** balance, candour, decorum, probity, realtie **08** chastity, fairness, fidelity, justness, legality, moonwort, morality, openness, veracity **09** bluntness, frankness, integrity, rectitude, sincerity **10** legitimacy, principles **11** genuineness, objectivity, uprightness **12** explicitness, impartiality, truthfulness **13** outspokenness, plain-speaking, righteousness **14** even-handedness, forthrightness, scrupulousness **15** trustworthiness

honey
03 hon, mel, sis **04** babe **05** sweet **06** nectar **07** sweeten

• honey buzzard
04 pern **07** bee-kite

• honey guide
03 tui

• honey possum
04 tait **08** Tarsipes

honeyed
04 cute, dear, kind **05** sweet **06** lovely, pretty, tender **07** winning **08** charming, engaging, pleasant, pleasing, precious, unctuous **09** agreeable, appealing, beautiful, seductive **10** attractive, delightful, flattering **11** mellifluous **12** affectionate

honeysuckle
06 abelia **08** Lonicera, rewarewa, suckling, woodbind, woodbine **09** anthemion, caprifoil, caprifole, eglantine, snowberry, wolfberry **14** Caprifoliaceae

Hong Kong
02 HK **03** HGK

honorarium
03 fee, pay **06** reward, salary **07** payment **09** emolument **10** recompense **12** remuneration

honorary
03 Hon **06** formal, unpaid **07** nominal, titular **09** ex officio, honorific **10** in name only, unofficial

honour
01 A, J, K, Q **03** pay **04** fame, keep, take **05** adorn, award, clear, crown, exalt, glory, izzat, pride, prize, title, value **06** accept, admire, credit, esteem, ethics, favour, fulfil, homage, laurel, morals, praise, purity, regard, renown, repute, revere, reward, trophy, virtue, worthy **07** acclaim, applaud, commend, decency, dignity, execute, glorify, honesty, modesty, observe, perform, probity, respect, tribute, worship **08** accolade, applause, be true to, carry out, celibacy, chastity, decorate, good name, goodness, morality, remember, venerate **09** adoration, celebrate, discharge, innocence, integrity, privilege, recognize, rectitude, reverence, virginity **10** abstinence, admiration, compliment, continence, continency, decoration, estimation, maidenhood, principles, reputation, singleness, veneration **11** acclamation, acknowledge, commemorate, distinction, pay homage to, recognition, self-respect, uprightness **12** commendation, pay tribute to, truthfulness **13** righteousness, temperateness **14** immaculateness, unmarried state **15** acknowledgement, trustworthiness

Honours include:

02 GC, KG, OM, VC
03 CBE, DBE, DSC, DSO, GBE, KBE, MBE, OBE
09 Iron Cross
10 Bronze Star, Grand Cross, knighthood, Silver Star
11 George Cross, Purple Heart
12 Order of Merit
13 Croix de Guerre, Legion of Merit, Medal for Merit, Victoria Cross, Victoria Medal
14 Légion d'Honneur

• in honour of
02 to **05** after **11** celebrating

honourable
03 Hon **04** fair, good, just, true **05** great, moral, noble, noted, right, white **06** decent, family, famous, honest, trusty, worthy **07** eminent, ethical, notable, sincere, upright **08** reliable, renowned, straight, truthful, virtuous, worthful **09** admirable, ingenuous, reputable, respected, righteous **10** dependable, high-minded, principled, upstanding **11** illustrious, prestigious, respectable, trustworthy **13** distinguished **14** high-principled

honourably
04 well **05** nobly, truly **07** morally **08** decently, honestly, worthily **09** ethically, reputably, sincerely **10** virtuously **11** respectably

hood
02 Al **04** cowl **05** amice, blind, Robin, scarf, snood, visor, vizor **06** almuce, biggin, bonnet, calash, domino, mantle **07** bashlik, capouch, capuche, hoodlum, surtout **08** calyptra, capeline, capuccio, chaperon, trot-cozy **09** calyptera, capelline, chaperone, condition, Nithsdale, trot-cosey

hoodlum
03 yob **04** hood, lout, thug **05** brute, felon, rowdy, tough **06** gunman, mugger, vandal **07** mobster, ruffian **08** criminal, gangster, hooligan, offender **09** bovver boy **10** lawbreaker **11** armed robber

hoodoo
04 jinx **05** magic, spell **06** voodoo **07** bewitch, sorcery **08** wizardry **09** occultism, the occult **10** black magic, divination, necromancy, witchcraft **11** conjuration, enchantment, incantation, the black art

hoodwink
03 con **04** dupe, fool, gull, hide, hoax, rook, seel **05** blear, cheat, trick **06** baffle, delude, have on, outwit, take in **07** deceive, defraud, mislead, swindle **09** bamboozle, blindfold **12** take for a ride **14** get the better of, pull a fast one on

hoof
04 foot, kick **05** cloot, expel **06** ungula **07** trotter **10** cloven hoof

hoofed
08 ungulate **10** horn-footed **11** unguligrade **12** cloven-footed, cloven-hoofed

hook
03 arc, bag, bow, box, dog, fix, hit, peg, rap **04** barb, bend, blow, clip, cuff, curl, gaff, grab, hasp, loop, snig, trap **05** angle, catch, chape, clasp, cleek, clout, crome, crook, curve, elbow, hinge, hitch, knock, punch, snare, thump, uncus **06** attach, becket, enmesh, entrap, excuse, fasten, griple, scythe, secure, sickle, strike, stroke, tenter, wallop **07** attract, cantdog, capture, ensnare, gripple, hamulus, pretext, sniggle **08** crotchet, crummock, entangle, fastener **09** goose-neck, tenaculum **10** tenterhook **13** grappling-iron

• by hook or by crook
07 somehow **10** by any means **11** by some means, come what may **15** one way or another

• hook, line and sinker
05 fully, quite **06** in full, wholly **07** solidly, totally, utterly **08** entirely **09** every inch, perfectly **10** absolutely, altogether, completely, thoroughly **12** heart and soul **13** root and branch **14** in every respect **15** from first to last

• off the hook
07 cleared **08** scot free **09** acquitted, ready-made **10** exonerated, in the clear, vindicated

hookah
06 kalian **07** chillum, nargile, nargily **08** narghile, narghily, nargileh, nargilly **09** narghilly, water pipe **12** hubble-bubble

hooked
04 bent **05** adunc, beaky **06** barbed, beaked, curled, curved, hamate, hamose, hamous, uncate **07** devoted, falcate, hamular **08** addicted, aduncate, aduncous, aquiline, hamulate, obsessed, unciform, uncinate **09** aduncated, dependent, enamoured **10** enthralled **12** sickle-shaped

hooligan
03 ned, yob **04** hoon, lout, thug **05** droog, rough, rowdy, tough **06** apache, mugger, skolly, tsotsi, vandal **07** hoodlum, mobster, ruffian, skollie **08** larrikin, tough guy **09** bovver boy, roughneck **10** delinquent

hoop
04 bail, band, gird, girr, loop, ring, tire **05** round, wheel **06** basket, circle, girdle **07** circlet, sleeper, stirrup, trochus, trundle **08** encircle, hula-hoop **10** laggen-gird

hoot
03 boo, cry, jot, wit **04** beep, call, care, hiss, hoop, howl, jeer, mock, riot, toot, yell **05** blare, comic, joker, laugh, shout, sneer, taunt, whoop **06** scream, shriek **07** screech, ululate, whistle **08** howl down, ridicule **09** character **12** tu-whit tu-whoo **13** amusing person

• not give a hoot
12 not care a toss, not give a damn **13** not be bothered **15** not give a monkey's

hooter
03 owl **04** horn, nose **05** siren

• little hooter
05 owlet

hop
03 fly, nip, pop **04** jump, leap, limp, skip, step, trip **05** bound, dance, disco, frisk, jaunt, opium, party, vault **06** bounce, flight, hobble, prance, social, spring **07** journey, knees-up, shindig **09** excursion **10** fly quickly **11** quick flight

• caught on the hop
07 unready **11** ill-equipped **14** caught in the act, caught unawares

• stem of hop
04 bind, bine

hope
03 aim **04** fear, long, pray, rely, wish **05** await, combe, crave, dream, faith,

inlet, trust, yearn **06** aspire, assume, belief, desire, expect **07** believe, craving, foresee, longing, promise **08** ambition, optimism, prospect, reckon on, yearning **09** assurance, be hopeful, enclosure, esperance, pipe dream **10** anticipate, aspiration, assumption, confidence, conviction, expectance, expectancy **11** be ambitious, contemplate, expectation, hopefulness **12** anticipation **13** look forward to **14** have confidence, pin your hopes on **15** hope against hope

hopeful
04 rosy **06** bright **07** assured, bullish, buoyant **08** aspirant, aspiring, cheerful, pleasant, positive, sanguine **09** confident, expectant, promising **10** auspicious, favourable, gladdening, heartening, optimistic, propitious, reassuring **11** encouraging

hopefully
05 I hope **07** eagerly **08** probably, with hope, with luck **09** bullishly **10** expectedly, sanguinely **11** conceivably, confidently, expectantly **12** all being well **13** if all goes well **14** optimistically

hopefulness
04 wish **05** faith, trust **06** belief, desire **07** craving, longing **08** ambition, optimism, prospect, yearning **09** assurance **10** aspiration, assumption, confidence, conviction **11** expectation **12** anticipation

hopeless
◇ *anagram indicator*
03 bad **04** lost, poor, vain, weak **05** all up, awful, bleak, grave, lousy **06** futile, gloomy, no-hope **07** foolish, forlorn, useless **08** dejected, downcast, helpless, negative, pathetic, wretched **09** all up with, defeatist, desperate, incurable, pointless, worthless **10** despairing, despondent, impossible **11** demoralized, downhearted, incompetent, irreparable, pessimistic **12** beyond remedy, beyond repair, irremediable, irreversible, unachievable, unattainable **13** impracticable **14** past praying for

hopelessly
◇ *anagram indicator*
05 badly **06** weakly **07** awfully **08** gloomily **09** unhappily, uselessly **10** dejectedly, negatively **11** desperately **12** despairingly, despondently, pathetically **13** incompetently, inefficiently **15** pessimistically

hopelessness
05 blues, dumps, gloom **06** misery **07** despair, wanhope **09** dejection, pessimism **10** gloominess **11** despondency, forlorn hope **12** wretchedness **14** discouragement

hophead *see* **addict**

horde
03 mob **04** army, band, crew, gang, herd, host, mass, pack **05** crowd, drove, flock, swarm, troop **06** throng **09** multitude

horizon
05 range, scope, verge, vista **07** compass, outlook, skyline **08** prospect **10** experience, perception **11** perspective **13** range of vision

• **on the horizon**
04 near **05** close **06** at hand, coming **07** brewing, looming **08** imminent, in the air, menacing, on the way **09** impending **11** approaching, forthcoming, in the offing, threatening **13** about to happen, almost upon you **15** fast approaching

horizontal
04 flat **05** level, plane **06** smooth, supine **08** levelled, straight **09** on its side

hormone

Hormones include:

05 kinin
07 gastrin, insulin, relaxin
08 abscisin, androgen, autacoid, estrogen, florigen, glucagon, oxytocin, secretin, thyroxin
09 adrenalin, cortisone, melatonin, oestrogen, pituitrin, prolactin, thyroxine
10 adrenaline, calcitonin
11 thyrotropin, vasopressin
12 androsterone, melanotropin, noradrenalin, progesterone, somatostatin, somatotropin, testosterone, thyrotrophin
14 erythropoietin, glucocorticoid

horn
04 butt, cusp, gore, push **05** bugle, corno, cornu **06** klaxon **07** keratin **08** cornicle, oliphant **09** telephone **10** corniculum **15** corno di bassetto

• **horn band**
04 frog

• **horn sound**
03 mot **04** beep, honk, hoot, parp **05** blast

• **part of horn**
03 bay, bez **04** tray, trey, trez **07** bay-tine, bez-tine **08** brow-tine, trey-tine **09** bay-antler, bez-antler **10** brow-antler, trey-antler

hornless
05 mooly, muley, poley **06** dodded, humble, hummel, mulley, polled

horny
04 hard, sexy **05** corny, randy **06** ardent **07** aroused, callous, lustful, ruttish **08** ceratoid, corneous **09** lecherous **10** keratinous, lascivious, libidinous **12** concupiscent

horrendous
08 dreadful, horrible, horrific, shocking, terrible **09** appalling, frightful **10** horrifying, terrifying **11** frightening

horrible
◇ *anagram indicator*
04 foul, grim, ugly **05** awful, black, grisy, nasty, scary **06** griesy, grisly, grysie, horrid, unkind **07** ghastly, hideous **08** dreadful, gruesome, horrific, shocking, terrible **09** appalling, frightful, harrowing, loathsome, monstrous, obnoxious, offensive, repulsive, revolting **10** abominable, detestable, disgusting, horrendous, horrifying, monstruous, terrifying, unpleasant **11** frightening, hair-raising **12** disagreeable **13** bloodcurdling

horribly
◇ *anagram indicator*
03 ill **06** grimly **07** awfully **08** terribly **09** hideously **10** dreadfully, gruesomely **11** appallingly, frightfully, repulsively **12** disagreeably, horrifically, unpleasantly

horrid
◇ *anagram indicator*
04 grim, mean **05** awful, cruel, nasty, rough **06** shaggy, unkind **07** beastly, ghastly, hateful, hideous **08** dreadful, gruesome, horrific, shocking, terrible **09** appalling, bristling, frightful, harrowing, obnoxious, repellent, repulsive, revolting **10** abominable, detestable, horrifying, terrifying **11** frightening, hair-raising **13** bloodcurdling

horrific
◇ *anagram indicator*
05 awful, scary **07** ghastly **08** dreadful, gruesome, shocking, terrible **09** appalling, frightful, harrowing **10** horrifying, terrifying **11** frightening **13** bloodcurdling

horrifically
07 awfully **08** terribly **10** dreadfully, shockingly **11** appallingly, frightfully, repulsively **12** disagreeably

horrify
05 abhor, alarm, appal, panic, repel, scare, shock, spook **06** agrise, agrize, agryze, dismay, offend, revolt, sicken **07** disgust, outrage, startle, terrify **08** frighten, nauseate **09** terrorize **10** intimidate, scandalize **12** put the wind up, scare to death

horror
04 fear, hate **05** alarm, dread, panic, shock **06** dismay, fright, terror **07** disgust, outrage **08** distaste, loathing **09** awfulness, revulsion **10** abhorrence, raggedness, repugnance, shagginess, shuddering **11** abomination, detestation, ghastliness, hideousness, trepidation **12** apprehension **13** consternation, frightfulness **14** unpleasantness

• **horror film**
07 chiller **10** hair raiser

horror-struck
06 aghast **07** shocked, stunned **08** appalled **09** horrified, petrified,

terrified **10** frightened **11** scared stiff **14** horror-stricken

hors d'oeuvre
04 meze **05** mezze **06** hummus, matjes **07** ceviche, maatjes, zakuska **08** crudités **09** antipasto, carpaccio **11** smörgåsbord

horse
01 H **02** GG **03** pad **04** crib, hack, hoss, moke, pony, prad, yaud **05** filly, mount, neddy **06** dobbin, gee-gee, heroin, keffel, sorrel **07** broncho, cavalry, centaur, charger, trotter **08** yarraman

See also **animal**; **heroin**; **pony**

Horses and ponies include:

03 Don
04 Arab, Barb, Fell
05 Dales, Iomud, Lokai, Pinto, Shire, Toric, Waler, Welsh
06 Auxois, Breton, Brumby, Exmoor, Morgan, Nonius, Tersky
07 Comtois, Criollo, Finnish, Furioso, Hackney, Hispano, Jutland, Masuren, Muraköz, Murgese, Mustang, Salerno
08 Budyonny, Danubian, Dartmoor, Friesian, Highland, Holstein, Kabardin, Karabair, Karabakh, Lusitano, Palomino, Paso Fino, Poitevin, Shetland, Welsh Cob
09 Akhal-Teké, Alter-Réal, Anglo-Arab, Appaloosa, Ardennias, Brabançon, Calabrese, Connemara, Falabella, Groningen, Kladruber, Knabstrup, Kustanair, Maremmana, New Forest, New Kirgiz, Oldenburg, Percheron, Sardinian, Tchenaran, Trakehner, Welsh Pony
10 Andalusian, Boulonnais, Clydesdale, Einsiedler, Freiberger, Gelderland, Hanoverian, Lipizzaner, Mangalarga, Shagya Arab
11 Anglo-Norman, Døle Trotter, Irish Hunter, Mecklenburg, Przewalski's, Trait du Nord, Württemberg
12 Cleveland Bay, Dutch Draught, East Friesian, French Saddle, Irish Draught, Metis Trotter, North Swedish, Orlov Trotter, Suffolk Punch, Thoroughbred
13 East Bulgarian, Frederiksborg, French Trotter, German Trotter, Welsh Mountain
14 American Saddle, Latvian Harness, Plateau Persian
15 American Quarter, American Trotter, Swedish Halfbred

Points of a horse include:

03 ear, eye, hip
04 back, chin, dock, face, head, heel, hock, hoof, knee, lips, mane, neck, nose, poll, ribs, rump, shin, tail
05 atlas, belly, canon, cheek, chest, crest, croup, elbow, ergot, flank, girth, loins, mouth, thigh
06 breast, cannon, gaskin, haunch, muzzle, sheath, stifle, temple, throat
07 abdomen, brisket, buttock, coronet, crupper, fetlock, forearm, hind leg, pastern, quarter, shannon, tendons, withers
08 chestnut, forefoot, forehead, forelock, lower jaw, lower lip, nostrils, shoulder, under lip, upper lip, windpipe
09 hamstring, hock joint, nasal peak
10 chin groove, point of hip, wall of foot
11 back tendons, point of hock, stifle joint
12 fetlock joint, hindquarters, hollow of heel, point of elbow
13 dock of the tail, flexor tendons, jugular groove, root of the tail
14 Achilles tendon, crest of the neck
15 point of shoulder

Horses' tack includes:

03 bit
05 arson, cinch, girth, hames, reins
06 bridle, cantle, collar, halter, numnah, pommel, saddle, traces
07 alforja, crupper, housing, stirrup
08 backband, blinders, blinkers, noseband, shabrack
09 bellyband, breeching, hackamore, headstall, saddlebag, saddlebow, saddlepad, surcingle
10 martingale, saddletree, shabracque, throatlash
11 bearing rein, saddlecloth, saddle-girth, throatlatch
13 saddle blanket

See also **bridle**

Horse-related terms include:

03 bay, cob, dun, hie, hup, nag, shy
04 bolt, buck, colt, foal, gait, grey, mare, roan, stud, trot, walk
05 break, forge, gee up, groom, hands, lunge, mount, nappy, pinto, steed
06 bronco, brumby, canter, equine, gallop, hippic, livery, manège, riding, stable
07 astride, blanket, gelding, giddy-up, hacking, nosebag, paddock, passade, piebald
08 chestnut, dismount, horse box, skewbald, stallion
09 horseshoe, roughshod
10 blood horse, draft horse, en cavalier, equestrian, heavy horse, side-saddle
11 riding habit
12 broken-winded, pony-trekking, thoroughbred
13 champ at the bit, mounting block, put out to grass
14 strawberry roan

Racehorses include:

05 Arkle, Cigar, Pinza
06 Nearco, Red Rum, Sir Ken
07 Alleged, Dawn Run, Eclipse, Phar Lap, Sceptre, Shergar, Sir Ivor
08 Aldaniti, Best Mate, Corbiere, Esha Ness, Hyperion, Istabraq, Mill Reef, Nijinsky
09 John Henry, L'Escargot, Oh So Sharp
10 Night Nurse, Persian War, Seabiscuit, See You Then, Sun Chariot
11 Cottage Rake, Never Say Die, Pretty Polly
12 Dancing Brave, Desert Orchid, Golden Miller, Hatton's Grace

See also **racecourse**; **racing**

• **call to horse**
03 hie, hup **04** high, proo, pruh

• **inferior horse**
03 nag, rip **04** moke

• **pair of horses**
04 span

• **shying horse**
03 jib **06** jibber

• **thin horse**
04 rake

• **working horse**
03 cut

• **worn-out horse**
03 tit **04** jade, plug **07** knacker

horsefly
04 cleg

horseman, horsewoman
05 rider **06** hussar, jockey, knight **07** dragoon, hobbler, pricker **08** stradiot, wrangler **09** caballero **10** cavalryman, equestrian **12** horse soldier

Horseriders, jockeys and trainers include:

04 Anne (Princess), **Hern** (Major Dick), **Leng** (Virginia), **Pipe** (Martin), **Tait** (Blyth), **Todd** (Mark)
05 **Cecil** (Henry), **Green** (Lucinda), **Krone** (Julie), **Lukas** (D Wayne), **McCoy** (Tony), **Meade** (Richard), **Smith** (Harvey), **Smith** (Robyn)
06 **Arcaro** (Eddie), **Archer** (Fred), **Carson** (Willie), **Eddery** (Pat), **Fallon** (Keiren), **O'Brien** (Vincent), **O'Neill** (Jonjo), **Pitman** (Jenny)
07 **Dettori** (Frankie), **Francis** (Dick), **Gifford** (Josh), **Piggott** (Lester), **Winkler** (Hans Günter)
08 **Champion** (Bob), **Donoghue** (Steve), **Dunwoody** (Richard), **Phillips** (Captain Mark), **Richards** (Sir Gordon)
09 **Scudamore** (Peter), **Shoemaker** (Willie)

See also **equestrian**

horseplay
03 rag **06** antics, capers, pranks **07** foolery, fooling **08** clowning **09** high jinks **10** buffoonery, skylarking, tomfoolery **11** fun and games **13** fooling around **14** monkey business, practical jokes, rough-and-tumble

horsepower
02 CV, hp, PS

horseradish tree
03 ben

horsewoman *see* **horseman, horsewoman**

hortatory
03 pep **08** didactic, edifying, inciting **09** homiletic, hortative, practical **10** heartening, preceptive **11** encouraging, exhortative, exhortatory, inspiriting, instructive, stimulating

horticulture
09 gardening **11** agriculture, cultivation **12** floriculture **13** arboriculture

hosanna
06 praise, save us **07** worship **08** alleluia **09** laudation

hose
03 sox **04** duct, pipe, tube **05** socks **06** piping, trunks, tubing **07** airline, channel, conduit **08** chausses **09** stockings **12** galligaskins

hosiery
04 hose **05** socks **06** tights **07** hold-ups, stay-ups **08** leggings **09** stockings **12** leg-coverings

hospitable
04 kind, warm **05** cadgy **06** genial, kidgie **07** cordial, helpful, liberal **08** amicable, friendly, generous, gracious, sociable **09** bountiful, congenial, convivial, receptive, welcoming **10** open-handed **11** kind-hearted, neighbourly

hospital
01 H **03** CHE, san **04** GOSH, Guy's, home, lock, MASH **05** Bart's **06** clinic, spital **07** hospice, spittle **08** clinique, nuthouse, snake-pit **09** ambulance, funny farm, hôtel-Dieu, infirmary, institute, leprosery **10** booby hatch, leproserie, polyclinic, sanatorium **11** nursing home **12** health centre **13** lunatic asylum, medical centre

• **hospital department**
03 ENT **04** gyny **05** A and E **08** casualty

hospitality
05 cheer **06** warmth **07** welcome **08** kindness **09** open house **10** generosity, liberality, philoxenia **11** helpfulness, sociability **12** congeniality, conviviality, friendliness, housekeeping **13** accommodation, entertainment **14** open-handedness, tea and sympathy **15** neighbourliness

host
◇ *containment indicator*
02 MC **03** mob **04** army, band, give, herd, mass, pack **05** array, crowd, crush, emcee, horde, swarm, troop **06** anchor, myriad, throng **07** compère, linkman, present **08** landlady, landlord, publican **09** anchorman, announcer, harbinger, innkeeper, introduce, multitude, presenter **10** party-giver, proprietor **11** anchorwoman, entertainer **12** proprietress

hostage
04 pawn **06** pledge, surety **07** captive **08** detainee, prisoner, security

hostel
01 Y **03** inn **04** hall, YMCA, YWCA **05** entry, hotel, motel **07** hospice, pension **08** hospital **09** dormitory, dosshouse, flophouse, residence **10** guesthouse **11** youth hostel **13** boarding-house **15** bed-and-breakfast

hostelry
03 bar, inn, pub **05** hotel, motel **06** tavern **07** canteen, pension **09** public bar **10** guesthouse **11** public house **13** boarding-house

hostile
03 icy **05** enemy **06** averse, infest, wintry **07** adverse, glacial, opposed, warlike, wintery **08** contrary, inimical, opposite **09** bellicose, oppugnant **10** aggressive, inveterate, malevolent, unfriendly **11** adversarial, belligerent, disinclined, ill-disposed **12** antagonistic, antipathetic, disapproving, inauspicious, inhospitable, unfavourable **13** unsympathetic **14** at daggers drawn

• **become hostile**
04 rise

hostilities
03 war **04** arms **06** action, battle, strife **07** warfare **08** conflict, fighting **09** bloodshed

hostility
03 war **04** envy, hate **05** anger **06** animus, enmity, hatred, malice **07** cruelty, dislike, ill-will **08** aversion, disfavor **09** animosity, antipathy, disfavour, militancy, prejudice **10** abhorrence, aggression, antagonism, bitterness, opposition, resentment **11** bellicosity, malevolence **12** belligerence, estrangement, hard feelings **14** unfriendliness, unpleasantness

hot
01 h **02** in **03** het, hip, new, red **04** chic, cool, keen, warm **05** angry, balmy, eager, fiery, fresh, funky, livid, quick, ritzy, sharp, spicy **06** ardent, baking, fervid, fierce, fuming, glitzy, heated, latest, modern, piping, raging, recent, red hot, snazzy, spiced, stolen, strong, sultry, swanky, torrid, trendy, uncool, with it **07** boiling, burning, candent, current, devoted, earnest, enraged, flushed, furious, illicit, intense, in vogue, lustful, peppery, piquant, popular, pungent, searing, stylish, summery, violent, zealous **08** animated, diligent, exciting, feverish, incensed, inflamed, parching, pilfered, powerful, roasting, scalding, seething, sizzling, steaming, swinging, toasting, tropical, up-to-date, vehement **09** cut-throat, dangerous, delirious, dog-eat-dog, ill-gotten, indignant, scorching **10** all the rage, blistering, candescent, contraband, passionate, prevailing, sweltering **11** fashionable **12** contemporary, enthusiastic, incandescent **13** up-to-the-minute

See also **warm**

• **be hot**
04 boil

• **blow hot and cold**
04 sway **05** haver, waver **08** hesitate, hum and ha **09** fluctuate, hum and haw, oscillate, temporize, vacillate **10** dilly-dally **12** shilly-shally

• **feel hot**
04 burn

• **hot air**
03 gas **04** bosh, bunk, crap, foam **05** bilge, froth **06** bunkum, piffle, vapour **07** baloney, blather, blether, bluster, bombast, eyewash, vapours **08** blethers, claptrap, cobblers, nonsense, verbiage **09** bullswool, emptiness, empty talk, mere words **10** balderdash, codswallop

hotbed
03 den **04** hive, nest **06** cradle, school **07** nursery, seedbed **08** seed plot **12** forcing-house **14** breeding-ground

hot-blooded
04 bold, rash, wild **05** eager, fiery, lusty **06** ardent, heated **07** fervent, lustful, sensual **08** spirited **09** excitable, impetuous, impulsive, irritable, perfervid **10** passionate **11** precipitate **12** high-spirited, homothermous **13** temperamental

hotchpotch
◇ *anagram indicator*
03 mix, pie **04** mess **06** jumble, medley **07** melange, mixture **08** mishmash **09** confusion, potpourri **10** collection, hodgepodge, miscellany

hotel
01 H **03** inn, pub **04** Ritz **05** botel, hydro, motel **06** boatel, hostel, tavern **07** Gasthof, pension **08** Gasthaus, hostelry **09** flophouse **10** aparthotel, guesthouse, trust house **11** hydropathic, public house **13** boarding-house, sporting house **15** bed and breakfast

• **hotel employee**
04 chef, page **05** boots **06** porter **07** bell boy, bell hop **11** chambermaid

hotfoot
07 flat out, hastily, in haste, quickly, rapidly, swiftly **08** pell-mell, speedily **09** hurriedly, posthaste **10** at top speed **11** at the double **12** lickety-split, without delay **13** helter-skelter **14** at a rate of knots, hell for leather **15** like the clappers

• **hotfoot it**
04 belt, dash, pelt, race, rush, tear, zoom **05** hurry, speed **06** career, gallop, hurtle, sprint **07** quicken **08** step on it **09** bowl along **10** accelerate **15** put your foot down

hothead
06 madcap, madman, terror
07 hotspur **08** cacafogo, tearaway
09 cacafuego, daredevil, desperado

hotheaded
04 rash, wild **05** fiery, hasty
08 reckless, volatile, volcanic
09 excitable, explosive, foolhardy, impetuous, impulsive, irascible
10 headstrong **11** hot-tempered
13 quick-tempered, short-tempered

hothouse
05 stove **06** vinery **07** brothel
08 orangery **10** glasshouse, greenhouse **12** conservatory, forcing-house

hotly
04 near, nigh **06** keenly, nearly
07 closely, tightly **08** ardently, fiercely, narrowly, strongly **09** fervently, intensely **10** forcefully, vehemently, vigorously **12** at close range, passionately **15** at close quarters

hot-tempered
05 fiery, hasty, ratty, testy **07** crabbit, stroppy, violent **08** choleric, petulant, volcanic **09** explosive, irascible, irritable **10** splenative **13** quick-tempered, short-tempered

hound
03 dog, nag **04** goad, hunt, lime, lyam, lyme, prod, urge **05** brach, bully, chase, drive, force, harry, stalk, track, trail
06 badger, basset, beagle, chivvy, follow, harass, jowler, pester, pursue, talbot, tufter **07** coondog, disturb, provoke **08** hunt down **09** persecute
• **pack of hounds**
03 cry **04** hunt **06** kennel

hour
01 h **02** hr

Hours include:

04 rush
05 flexi, happy, lunch, small
06 dinner, golden, office, waking
07 trading, working
08 business, eleventh, midnight, unsocial, visiting, witching

See also **canonical**
• **early hours**
02 am
• **outside hours**
04 kerb

house
◇ *containment indicator*
02 ho **03** Hse, inn, ken, mas, pad
04 body, casa, clan, door, firm, gaff, hame, hold, home, keep, line, race
05 bingo, blood, board, cover, crowd, guard, lodge, place, put up, store, tribe
06 billet, family, ménage, reside, strain, take in **07** chamber, company, contain, convent, dynasty, harbour, kindred, lineage, protect, quarter, sheathe, shelter, turnout, viewers **08** ancestry, assembly, audience, building, business, congress, domestic, domicile, dwelling
09 gathering, household, listeners, onlookers, residence **10** auditorium, enterprise, habitation, parliament, spectators **11** accommodate, corporation, have room for, legislature
12 family circle, have space for, organization **13** establishment

Houses include:

03 hut
04 flat, hall, semi, weem
05 croft, igloo, lodge, manor, manse, shack, villa, whare
06 bedsit, chalet, duplex, grange, mia-mia, pondok, prefab, shanty, studio, wurley
07 cottage, mansion, rectory
08 bungalow, detached, hacienda, log cabin, terraced, vicarage
09 apartment, but and ben, farmhouse, homestead, parsonage, penthouse, single-end, town house, treehouse, villa home, villa unit
10 granny flat, maisonette, pied-à-terre, ranch house, state house
11 condominium
12 council house, semi-detached
14 chalet bungalow
15 thatched cottage

See also **accommodation**; **building**; **zodiac**
• **House of Commons**
02 HC
• **House of Lords**
02 HL
• **on the house**
04 free **06** gratis **08** at no cost **10** for nothing **11** without cost **12** free of charge **13** at no extra cost, without charge **14** without payment

household
04 home **05** house, plain, set-up
06 common, family, famous, ménage, people **08** domestic, everyday, familiar, ordinary **09** well-known
11 established **12** family circle
13 establishment

Household items include:

03 bin, mop
04 comb, hook, pram, vase
05 broom, brush, diary, match, potty, range, towel
06 basket, candle, duster, pet bed, sponge
07 ashtray, coaster, dustpan, flannel, key rack, key ring, wash bag
08 aquarium, bassinet, birdcage, calendar, coat hook, dish rack, fish tank, flatiron, hat stand, hip flask, ornament, place mat, shoe rack, soap dish, suitcase, tea towel, waste bin, wine rack
09 cat basket, dishcloth, dog basket, door wedge, fireguard, hairbrush, hearth rug, highchair, memo board, phone book, pushchair, sponge bag, stair gate, stepstool, towel rail, washboard, washcloth
10 baby bottle, baby walker, coathanger, laundry bag, letter rack, oven gloves, photo album, photo frame, stepladder, storage box, toothbrush
11 address book, candlestick, changing mat, first aid kit, paperweight, toilet brush
12 clothes airer, clothes-brush, clothes horse, ironing board, magazine rack, perambulator, picnic basket, thermos flask
13 feather duster, laundry basket, satellite dish, soap dispenser, umbrella stand, washing-up bowl
14 hot water bottle, phone directory
15 draught excluder, photograph album, photograph frame

householder
05 owner **06** tenant **07** goodman, gude-man **08** landlady, landlord, occupant, occupier, resident
09 home-owner **10** freeholder, proprietor **11** leaseholder **13** owner-occupier

housekeeping
08 domestic **10** homemaking
11 hospitality, housewifery
12 domestic work, running a home
13 home economics **15** domestic matters, domestic science

houseman
05 valet **06** butler, doctor, intern
07 interne, servant **08** resident, retainer **10** manservant **12** house-surgeon, junior doctor **14** house-physician

house-trained
04 tame **05** tamed **11** house-broken
12 domesticated, well-mannered

housing
◇ *containment indicator*
04 case **05** cover, guard, homes
06 casing, holder, houses, jacket, sheath **07** shelter **08** covering, shabrack **09** container, dwellings
10 habitation, protection, shabracque
13 accommodation

hovel
03 hut **04** dump, hole, shed, slum
05 cabin, shack, whare **06** kennel, shanty **07** shelter

hover
03 fly **04** flap, hang, hove, wave
05 drift, float, hoove, pause, poise, waver **06** linger, loiter, seesaw
07 flutter **08** hesitate **09** alternate, fluctuate, hang about, oscillate, vacillate **10** helicopter **11** be suspended

however
03 but, yet **05** howbe, still **06** anyhow, even so, though **07** howbeit
08 actually **09** as it comes, howsoever, in any case, leastways, leastwise **10** howsomever, leastaways, regardless
11 howsomdever, just the same, nonetheless **12** nevertheless
13 at the same time
15 notwithstanding

howl
03 bay, cry, wow **04** bawl, gowl, hoot, moan, roar, wail, yawl, yell, yelp, yowl **05** groan, laugh, shout **06** bellow, scream, shriek

howler
04 boob, flub, goof **05** boner, error, fluff, gaffe **07** bloomer, blunder, clanger, mistake, Mycetes **08** solecism **11** malapropism

HQ *see* **headquarters**

hub
03 hob **04** axis, boss, core, nave **05** focus, heart, pivot **06** centre, middle **08** linchpin **10** focal point **11** nerve centre

hubbub
03 din, row **04** coil, riot **05** chaos, noise **06** racket, rumpus, tumult, uproar **07** clamour, whoobub **08** disorder, hubbuboo, rowdedow, rowdydow **09** commotion, confusion, level-coil **10** hullabaloo, hurly-burly **11** disturbance, pandemonium

hubris
05 nerve, pride, scorn **06** vanity **07** conceit, disdain, egotism, hauteur **08** boasting, contempt **09** arrogance, contumely, insolence, lordiness, pomposity **11** haughtiness, overweening, presumption, superiority **12** snobbishness **13** condescension, imperiousness **14** high-handedness, self-importance

huckster
04 hawk **06** barker, dealer, hawker, kidder, peddle, pedlar, tinker, trader, vendor **07** haggler, kiddier, packman, pitcher **11** salesperson

huddle
04 cram, heap, herd, knot, mass, meet, pack, ruck **05** clump, crowd, flock, hunch, press **06** bundle, crouch, cuddle, curl up, fumble, gather, hustle, jumble, muddle, nestle, pester, powwow, throng **07** cluster, meeting, snuggle, squeeze **08** conclave, converge **09** confusion, gravitate **10** conference, congregate, discussion **12** consultation

hue
03 dye, hew **04** tint, tone **05** color, light, shade, tinge **06** aspect, chroma, colour, nuance **07** clamour **08** shouting **10** appearance, complexion

hue and cry
03 ado **04** fuss, to-do **05** chase, hoo-ha, tizzy **06** furore, outcry, rumpus, uproar **07** carry-on, clamour, ruction **08** ballyhoo, brouhaha **09** commotion, kerfuffle **10** hullabaloo **13** a song and dance

huff
03 pet **04** mood, rage, stew, tiff **05** anger, bully, paddy, pique, snuff, sulks **06** hector, strunt **07** bad mood, bluster, passion **09** blusterer

huffily
07 angrily, crossly, in a huff **08** in a paddy, in a strop, morosely, snappily **09** in a temper, irritably, peevishly **11** resentfully

huffy
05 angry, cross, moody, short, sulky, surly, testy **06** crusty, grumpy, miffed, moping, morose, shirty, snappy, snuffy, touchy **07** crabbed, peevish, stroppy, waspish **08** offended, petulant **09** crotchety, irritable, querulous, resentful **10** hoity-toity **11** disgruntled

hug
◇ *containment indicator*
01 O **04** coll, grip, hold **05** clasp, press **06** clinch, clutch, cuddle, enfold **07** cherish, cling to, embrace, enclose, snuggle, squeeze **08** stay near **09** hold close **11** keep close to, stay close to **13** follow closely

huge
02 OS **03** big **04** mega, vast **05** bulky, enorm, giant, great, heavy, jumbo, large **06** immane **07** hideous, hugeous, immense, mammoth, massive, socking, titanic **08** colossal, enormous, gigantic, unwieldy **09** cavernous, extensive, frightful, gigantean, ginormous, Herculean, humongous, humungous, monstrous, swingeing **10** Babylonian, gargantuan, monumental, prodigious, stupendous, tremendous **11** mountainous, stupendious

hugely
04 very **06** highly, really, vastly **07** awfully, greatly, largely **08** terribly, very much **09** extremely, immensely, massively **10** enormously, thoroughly **11** frightfully **12** terrifically, tremendously **15** extraordinarily

hugger-mugger
03 sly **06** closet, covert, hidden, secret, sneaky, untidy **07** chaotic, furtive, jumbled, mixed-up, muddled, private, secrecy **08** backroom, confused, stealthy **09** concealed, confusion, underhand **10** behind-door, disordered, disorderly, fraudulent, out of order, undercover **11** clandestine, disarranged, underground **12** disorganized **13** surreptitious **14** cloak-and-dagger **15** under-the-counter

Hughes
03 Ted

hulk
03 oaf **04** clod, hull, lout, lump **05** frame, shell, wreck **06** lubber **07** remains **08** derelict **09** shipwreck **10** clodhopper

hulking
03 big **05** bulky, heavy, large **06** clumsy **07** awkward, massive, weighty **08** ungainly, unwieldy **09** lumbering **10** cumbersome

hull
03 pod **04** body, bulk, husk, pare, peel, rind, skin, trim **05** frame, shell, shuck, strip **06** casing, legume **07** capsule, epicarp **08** covering, skeleton **09** framework, monocoque, structure

hullabaloo
03 din, hue **04** fuss, to-do **05** hoo-ha, noise, tizzy **06** furore, hubbub, outcry, racket, rumpus, tumult, uproar **07** carry-on, palaver, ruction, turmoil **08** ballyhoo, brouhaha, razmataz **09** commotion, hue and cry, kerfuffle **10** razzmatazz **11** disturbance, pandemonium, razzamatazz **13** a song and dance

hum
03 bum **04** buzz, hoax, lilt, purr, sing **05** chirm, croon, drone, pulse, sough, throb, thrum, whirr **06** be busy, mumble, murmur **07** applaud, buzzing, purring, vibrate **08** whirring **09** bombilate, bombinate, pulsation, throbbing, vibration **10** imposition

• **hum and haw**
04 sway **05** waver **06** dither **08** hesitate **09** fluctuate, oscillate, vacillate **10** dilly-dally **12** be indecisive, shilly-shally **14** blow hot and cold

human
03 man **04** body, kind, soul, weak **05** child, woman **06** genial, humane, mortal, person **07** fleshly **08** fallible, physical, rational, tolerant **09** anthropic **10** anthropoid, human being, individual, reasonable, vulnerable **11** anthropical, considerate, Homo sapiens, susceptible, sympathetic **13** compassionate, flesh and blood, understanding

• **human affairs**
04 life

humane
04 good, kind, mild **06** benign, gentle, kindly, loving, polite, tender **07** elegant, lenient **08** generous, merciful **09** classical, forgiving **10** benevolent, charitable, forbearing, humanizing, thoughtful **11** considerate, good-natured, kind-hearted, sympathetic **12** humanitarian **13** compassionate, understanding

humanely
06 gently, kindly, mildly **08** lovingly, tenderly **10** generously, mercifully **12** thoughtfully **13** kind-heartedly **15** compassionately, sympathetically

humanitarian
04 kind **06** humane **07** welfare **08** altruist, do-gooder, generous **09** unselfish **10** altruistic, benefactor, benevolent, charitable **11** considerate, sympathetic **13** compassionate, good Samaritan, philanthropic, understanding **14** philanthropist, public-spirited

humanitarianism
07 charity **08** goodwill, humanism **10** generosity **11** beneficence, benevolence **12** philanthropy **14** charitableness, loving-kindness

humanities
04 arts **08** classics **10** literature, philosophy **11** liberal arts

humanity
03 man **04** pity **05** mercy **06** mandom, people, ubuntu **07** mankind, mortals **08** goodness, goodwill, kindness, sympathy **09** humankind, human race, mortality, tolerance, womankind **10** compassion, generosity, gentleness, humaneness, tenderness **11** benevolence, Homo sapiens **13** brotherly love, fellow-feeling, understanding **14** thoughtfulness **15** kind-heartedness

humanize
04 tame **05** edify **06** better, polish, refine **07** educate, improve **08** civilize **09** cultivate, enlighten **11** domesticate

humankind
03 man **06** people **07** mankind, mortals **08** humanity **09** human race, mortality, womankind **11** Homo sapiens

humanness
08 goodness, goodwill, humanity, kindness, sympathy **09** tolerance **10** compassion, generosity, gentleness, tenderness **11** benevolence, human nature **13** understanding **14** thoughtfulness **15** kind-heartedness

humble
03 low **04** base, mean, meek, poor, sink **05** abase, crush, lower, lowly, plain, pluck, shame, silly, small **06** abased, common, demean, demiss, hummel, modest, polite, simple, subdue **07** afflict, awnless, chasten, deflate, degrade, depress, mortify, servile **08** belittle, bring low, disgrace, hornless, inferior, ordinary, yeomanly **09** afflicted, bring down, demissive, discredit, disparage, humiliate, prideless, unrefined **10** low-ranking, obsequious, put to shame, respectful, submissive, unassuming **11** commonplace, deferential, subservient, sycophantic, unassertive, unimportant **12** self-effacing, supplicatory **13** cut down to size, insignificant, unpretentious **14** unostentatious **15** undistinguished

humbleness
07 modesty **08** humility, meekness **09** deference, lowliness, servility **10** diffidence **13** self-abasement **14** self-effacement, submissiveness, unassumingness **15** unassertiveness

humbly
03 low **06** meekly, simply **08** docilely, modestly **09** cap in hand, servilely **10** sheepishly **11** diffidently **12** obsequiously, respectfully, submissively, unassumingly **13** deferentially, subserviently **15** unpretentiously

humbug
03 con, gum, rot **04** bunk, cant, fake, gaff, guff, hoax, sham **05** actor, balls, bluff, cheat, fraud, fudge, poser, rogue, trick **06** barney, berley, blague, bunkum, burley, cajole, con man, deceit, gammon, string **07** baloney, bluffer, deceive, eyewash, rubbish, swindle **08** buncombe, cheating, claptrap, cobblers, flummery, impostor, nonsense, pretence, swindler, trickery **09** charlatan, deception, gold brick, hypocrisy, kidstakes, poppycock, trickster **10** balderdash, hollowness

humdrum
04 dull **05** banal, prosy **06** boring, dreary **07** droning, mundane, routine, tedious **08** everyday, monotony, ordinary, tiresome, unvaried **09** bourgeois **10** monotonous, uneventful **11** commonplace, repetitious **12** run-of-the-mill **13** uninteresting

humid
03 wet **04** damp, dank **05** close, heavy, mochy, moist, muggy **06** clammy, mochie, steamy, sticky, sultry **10** oppressive

humidity
03 dew **04** damp, mist **07** wetness **08** dampness, dankness, moisture **09** closeness, heaviness, humidness, moistness, mugginess, sogginess **10** clamminess, steaminess, stickiness, sultriness, vaporosity **12** vaporousness

humiliate
05 abase, abash, break, crush, shame **06** demean, humble, wither **07** chasten, deflate, degrade, mortify, put down **08** bring low, confound, disgrace, take down **09** discomfit, discredit, embarrass **11** make a fool of **12** bring shame on, take down a peg

humiliating
07 shaming **08** crushing, humbling, snubbing **09** deflating, degrading, humiliant, withering **10** chastening, disgracing, inglorious, mortifying **11** disgraceful, humiliative, humiliatory, ignominious **12** discomfiting, embarrassing

humiliation
04 snub **05** shame **06** ignomy, rebuff **07** affront, put-down **08** crushing, disgrace, downfall, humbling, ignominy, take-down **09** abasement, deflation, discredit, dishonour, humble pie, indignity **10** chastening, loss of face **11** confounding, degradation **12** discomfiture **13** embarrassment, mortification

humility
07 modesty **08** meekness **09** deference, lowlihead, lowliness, servility **10** diffidence, humbleness **13** self-abasement **14** self-effacement, submissiveness, unassumingness **15** unassertiveness

humming *see* **smelly**

hummingbird
05 sylph, topaz **06** hermit, hummer **07** colibri, jacobin, rainbow **08** coquette **09** sabrewing, swordbill, trochilus **10** racket-tail, rubythroat, sicklebill **11** whitethroat **12** sapphire-wing

hummock
04 hump **05** knoll, mound **06** barrow **07** hillock **09** elevation **10** prominence

humorist
03 wag, wit **05** clown, comic, joker **06** gagman, jester **08** comedian, satirist **10** cartoonist **12** caricaturist

humorous
04 zany **05** comic, droll, funny, pawky, witty **06** absurd **07** amusing, comical, giocoso, jocular, playful, risible, waggish **08** farcical **09** facetious, funny ha-ha, hilarious, irregular, laughable, ludicrous, satirical, whimsical **10** capricious, Gilbertian, humoristic, ridiculous **11** Falstaffian, Rabelaisian **12** entertaining, knee-slapping **13** side-splitting

humour
03 fun, wit **04** coax, gags, mood, vein **05** jokes, jolly, spoil **06** comedy, cosset, favour, kidney, pamper, pecker, permit, please, temper **07** flatter, gratify, indulge, jesting, mollify, observe, satisfy, spirits **08** badinage, drollery, hilarity, pander to, repartee, tolerate **09** absurdity, amusement, wittiness **10** comply with, jocularity, wisecracks **11** accommodate, acquiesce in, disposition, frame of mind, go along with, state of mind, temperament **13** facetiousness **14** ridiculousness

The four bodily humours include:

05 blood
06 choler, phlegm
09 black bile
10 melancholy, yellow bile

Humour includes:

03 dry
04 blue, sick
05 black
07 gallows, surreal
08 farcical
09 satirical, slapstick
10 lavatorial
11 barrack-room, Pythonesque
12 Chaplinesque

humourless
02 po **03** dry **04** dour, dull, glum, grim **05** grave **06** boring, morose, solemn, sombre **07** earnest, po-faced, serious, tedious **09** long-faced, unsmiling **10** unlaughing

hump
03 hog, lug, pip, vex 04 arch, bend, bump, haul, knob, lift, lump, mass, ramp 05 annoy, bulge, bunch, carry, crook, curve, heave, hoist, humph, hunch, hurry, mound, ridge 08 shoulder, swelling 09 outgrowth, speed bump 10 projection, prominence, protrusion 11 excrescence 12 intumescence, protuberance
• **get the hump**
04 mope, sulk 09 be annoyed, get the pip 11 be irritated 13 be exasperated
• **give someone the hump**
03 bug, irk, nag, vex 04 gall, rile 05 anger, annoy, tease 06 bother, harass, hassle, madden, pester, plague, ruffle, wind up 07 disturb, hack off, provoke, tick off, trouble 08 brass off, irritate 09 aggravate, cheese off 10 exasperate 13 make sparks fly 14 drive up the wall 15 get someone's goat
• **over the hump**
12 over the worst 13 past the crisis

hump-backed
06 humped 07 crooked, gibbose, gibbous, hunched, stooped 08 deformed, kyphotic 09 misshapen 11 bunch-backed, crookbacked, hunchbacked

humped
04 bent 06 arched, curved 07 bunched, crooked, gibbose, gibbous, hunched

humus
03 mor 04 mull 05 moder

hunch
04 arch, bend, bump, hint, hump, idea, knob, lump, mass, ramp 05 bulge, curve, guess, mound, squat, stoop 06 crouch, curl up, draw in, huddle 07 feeling, inkling 08 swelling 09 intuition, outgrowth, suspicion 10 impression, projection, prominence, protrusion, sixth sense 11 premonition 12 presentiment, protuberance

hundred
01 C 04 cent 05 centi- 06 centum 07 cantred, cantref 09 centenary

hundredweight
03 cwt 07 quintal

Hungary
01 H 03 HUN 04 Hung

hunger
03 yen 04 ache, itch, long, need, pine, want, wish 05 crave, greed, raven, yearn 06 desire, famine, hanker, pining, starve, thirst 07 bulimia, craving, longing 08 appetite, voracity, yearning 09 emptiness, esurience, esuriency, hankering 10 famishment, greediness, hungriness, starvation 12 malnutrition, ravenousness 15 have a craving for, have a longing for

hungrily
06 avidly 07 eagerly 08 greedily 09 longingly 10 covetously, insatiably, ravenously

hungry
04 avid, lean, mean, poor, yaup 05 eager, empty, sharp 06 aching, greedy, hollow, pining, stingy 07 craving, itching, longing, needing, peckish, thirsty 08 covetous, desirous, esurient, famished, hungerly, ravenous, sharp-set, starving, underfed, yearning 09 ahungered, hankering, hungerful, voracious 10 insatiable 12 malnourished 14 could eat a horse, undernourished

hunk
04 base, clod, dish, goal, lump, mass, safe, slab, stud 05 block, chunk, he-man, piece, wedge 06 dollop, gobbet, secure 08 beefcake, macho man 09 dreamboat, strong man 10 studmuffin

hunt
03 cub, dog, rat, ren, rin, run 04 fish, hawk, meet, seal, seek, slug 05 chase, chevy, chivy, drive, hound, mouse, quest, scour, stalk, track, trail 06 battue, beagle, chivvy, course, ferret, follow, forage, halloo, prey on, pursue, rabbit, search, shadow, turtle 07 dismiss, look for, predate, pursuit, ransack, rummage, scare up 08 scouring, scrounge, stalking, tire down, tracking, venation 09 persecute, rummaging, still-hunt, try to find 11 investigate, run to ground 12 ride to hounds 13 investigation

hunter
05 hound, jäger 06 chaser, hawker, jaeger, Nimrod, ratter, shikar, wolfer 07 Actaeon, beagler, montero, shikari, turtler, venator, venerer, woodman 08 chasseur, free-shot, huntsman, rabbiter, shikaree, woodsman 10 lion-hunter, seal-fisher 11 still-hunter 13 rabbit trapper

hunting
05 chase 06 shikar, venery 07 birding, cubbing, ducking, lamping, ratting, wolfing, wolving 08 beagling, coursing, falconry, stalking, trapping, turtling, venation 11 field sports
• **expressions relating to hunting**
04 alew, so-ho 05 chevy, chivy 06 chivvy, halloa, halloo, hoicks, yoicks 07 tally-ho, tantivy
• **hunting-coat**
04 pink
• **hunting-cry**
04 alew 05 chevy, chivy 06 chivvy, halloa, halloo
• **hunting ground**
04 walk
• **hunting group**
04 meet

huntsman
04 Peel 05 jäger, yager 06 jaeger 07 montero, skirter, venator, woodman 08 chasseur, woodsman

hurdle
03 bar 04 doll, jump, snag, wall 05 fence, flake, hedge 06 raddle, wattle 07 barrier, problem, railing 08 handicap, obstacle 09 barricade, hindrance 10 difficulty, impediment 11 obstruction 12 complication 14 stumbling-block

hurl
◇ *anagram indicator*
03 bum, put 04 cast, dart, dash, fire, pelt, putt, send, toss 05 chuck, fling, heave, lanch, pitch, sling, swing, throw, wheel 06 hurtle, launch, let fly, propel 07 project 08 catapult 11 precipitate

hurly-burly
05 chaos 06 bedlam, bustle, frenzy, furore, hassle, hubbub, hustle, racket, tumult, unrest, uproar 07 trouble, turmoil 08 brouhaha, disorder, upheaval 09 agitation, commotion, confusion 10 disruption, turbulence 11 distraction, pandemonium

hurricane
04 gale, rout 05 storm 06 baguio, squall, tumult 07 cyclone, tempest, tornado, typhoon 09 commotion, whirlwind

hurried
03 ran 04 fast 05 brief, hasty, quick, rapid, short, swift 06 hectic, rushed, speedy 07 cursory, offhand, passing, rush job, shallow 08 careless, fleeting, slapdash 09 breakneck, festinate, transient 10 transitory 11 perfunctory, precipitate, superficial

hurriedly
07 flat out, hastily, hotfoot, in haste, quickly, rapidly, swiftly 08 pell-mell, speedily 09 posthaste 10 at top speed 11 at the double 12 lickety-split, without delay 13 helter-skelter 14 at a rate of knots, hell for leather 15 like the clappers

hurry
03 fly, hie, ren, rin, run 04 belt, dash, hare, hump, push, race, rush, tear 05 chase, drive, haste, mosey, press, pronto, speed 06 buck up, bustle, flurry, giddap, hasten, hubbub, hustle, scurry 07 press on, quicken, speed up, urgency, vamoose 08 celerity, chop-chop, despatch, dispatch, expedite, fastness, go all out, jump to it!, rapidity, step on it 09 beetle off, commotion, confusion, cut and run, festinate, hastiness, look alive, look smart, make haste, quickness, swiftness 10 accelerate, expedition, hightail it, look slippy, look snappy 11 run like hell 12 get a wiggle on, make it snappy, step on the gas 13 precipitation

hurt
◇ *anagram indicator*
03 ake, cut, hit, mar, noy, sad 04 ache, burn, gall, harm, maim, pain, sore 05 abuse, annoy, grief, smart, spoil, sting, throb, upset, wound, wring 06 aching, be sore, blight, bruise,

damage, grazed, grieve, impair, injure, injury, lesion, maimed, misery, offend, sadden, sorrow, tingle **07** afflict, annoyed, blemish, bruised, burning, disable, injured, painful, sadness, scarred, scratch, torture, wounded **08** distress, ill-treat, lacerate, maltreat, mischief, nuisance, offended, saddened, smarting, soreness, tingling **09** affronted, aggrieved, be painful, in anguish, lacerated, miserable, sorrowful, suffering, throbbing **10** affliction, debilitate, discomfort, distressed **12** cause sadness **13** grief-stricken

hurtful
03 bad, ill **04** mean **05** catty, cruel, nasty **06** naught, nocent, shrewd, unkind **07** baleful, cutting, harmful, nocuous, noysome, ruinous, vicious **08** damaging, grievous, scathing, spiteful, wounding **09** injurious, malicious, obnoxious, offensive, pestilent, scatheful, upsetting **10** derogatory, maleficent, maleficial, pernicious **11** deleterious, destructive, detrimental, distressing, malefactory

hurtle
03 fly **04** belt, dash, dive, hurl, pelt, race, rush, spin, tear **05** clash, crash, shoot, speed **06** career, charge, plunge, rattle **08** brandish, step on it **12** step on the gas **14** step on the juice **15** put your foot down

husband
01 h **03** man **04** lord, mate, save **05** baron, groom, hoard, hubby, put by, store **06** budget, eke out, manage, master, old boy, old man, ration, save up, spouse **07** consort, goodman, manager, partner, reserve **08** conserve, preserve, put aside **09** cultivate, economize, other half **10** better half, hoddy-doddy, married man **12** gander-mooner, use carefully, use sparingly **15** mari complaisant

• husband and wife
04 pair **06** couple

• without husband or wife
04 sole

husbandry
06 saving, thrift **07** economy, farming, tillage **08** agronomy **09** frugality **10** agronomics, management **11** agriculture, cultivation, thriftiness **12** agribusiness, conservation **14** farm management, land management

hush
04 calm **05** peace, quiet, still **06** repose, settle, silent, soothe, subdue **07** be quiet, bestill, compose, mollify, quieten, silence **08** calmness, serenity **09** quietness, stillness **12** peacefulness, tranquillity

• hush up
03 gag **04** smug **06** huddle, stifle **07** conceal, cover up, smother **08** keep dark, suppress **10** keep secret

hush-hush
06 secret **09** top-secret **10** classified, restricted, under wraps **12** confidential

husk
03 pod **04** bran, case, coir, hull, peel, pill, rind, skin **05** chaff, shale, sheal, sheel, shell, shiel, shill, shuck, strip **06** legume **07** capsule, epicarp **08** covering **09** corn shuck

huskily
06 deeply **07** gruffly, harshly **08** croakily, gravelly, hoarsely **10** gutturally

husky
03 dry, low **04** deep **05** beefy, burly, gruff, harsh, hefty, Inuit, rough, thick **06** brawny, coarse, croaky, hoarse, strong **07** rasping, throaty **08** croaking, gravelly, guttural, muscular **09** strapping, well-built

hussy
04 minx, slag, slut, tart, vamp **05** huzzy, tramp **06** hussif, limmer **07** floozie **08** scrubber **09** housewife, temptress **10** loose woman

hustle
03 fly, tew **04** dash, fuss, push, rush, sell, stir **05** crowd, elbow, force, fraud, hurry, nudge, shove **06** bounce, bundle, bustle, hasten, huddle, jostle, justle, rustle, thrust, tumult **07** swindle **08** activity **09** agitation, commotion, manhandle **10** hurly-burly, pressurize

hut
03 den **04** shed, skeo, skio, tilt **05** banda, booth, bothy, cabin, hogan, humpy, shack, sheal, shiel, whare **06** bothan, bothie, chalet, gunyah, lean-to, mia-mia, pondok, rancho, saeter, shanty, succah, sukkah, wiltja, wurley **07** caboose, shelter, wickiup **08** log cabin, rondavel, shealing, shieling **09** pondokkie, rancheria

hybrid
◇ *anagram indicator*
05 cross, mixed **06** mosaic **07** amalgam, bigener, mixture, mongrel **08** combined, compound **09** composite, crossbred, half-blood, half-breed **10** crossbreed **11** combination, single-cross **13** heterogeneous **14** conglomeration

Hybrids include:

02 zo
03 dso, dzo, zho
04 dzho, mule, OEIC, Ugli®
05 oxlip, topaz
06 oxslip
07 beefalo, Bourbon, cattabu, cattalo, Jersian, lurcher, plumcot, tangelo, tea rose
08 citrange, noisette, sunberry, tayberry
09 perpetual, tiger tail, triticale
10 clementine, loganberry, polyanthus
11 boysenberry, bull-mastiff, Jacqueminot, marionberry, miracle rice
13 polecat-ferret

hybridize
05 cross **10** bastardize, crossbreed, interbreed

hydrant
01 H **02** FP **08** fireplug

hydrocarbon

Hydrocarbons include:

03 wax
05 halon
06 aldrin, alkane, alkene, alkyne, butane, cetane, decane, ethane, hexane, indene, nonane, octane, olefin, picene, pyrene, retene
07 benzene, heptane, methane, olefine, pentane, propane, styrene, terpene
08 camphane, camphene, diphenyl, isoprene, pristane, stilbene
09 butadiene
10 benzpyrene, mesitylene
11 hatchettite, naphthalane
12 cyclopropane

hydrogen
01 H

hyena
09 tiger wolf **10** strandwolf

hygiene
06 purity **09** sterility **10** sanitation **11** cleanliness **12** disinfection, sanitariness **13** wholesomeness

hygienic
04 pure **05** clean **07** aseptic, healthy, sterile **08** germ-free, sanitary **09** wholesome **10** salubrious, sterilized **11** disinfected

hymn
03 air **04** song **05** carol, chant, dirge, motet, paean, psalm **06** anthem, choral, chorus, mantra, Te Deum **07** cantata, chorale, introit, mantram, Sanctus **08** canticle, cathisma, dies irae, doxology, hymeneal, sequence **09** dithyramb, offertory, spiritual, sticheron, trisagion, troparion **10** paraphrase, procession, Tantum ergo **11** recessional, Stabat Mater **12** Marseillaise, processional, song of praise

hype
04 fuss, plug, puff **06** racket, talk up **07** build up, build-up, promote, puffery **08** ballyhoo, plugging **09** advertise, deception, promotion, publicity, publicize **10** razzmatazz **11** advertising **13** advertisement

hyped up
04 fake, high, wild **05** eager, hyper, moved **06** elated **07** anxious, excited, fired up, frantic, stirred, uptight **08** agitated, animated, frenzied, restless, thrilled, worked up **09** wrought-up **10** artificial, stimulated **11** exhilarated, overwrought **12** enthusiastic **13** in high spirits, on tenterhooks **14** beside yourself, thrilled to bits

hyperbole
06 excess **07** auxesis **08** overkill **12** exaggeration, extravagance **13** magnification, overstatement

hypercritical
05 fussy, picky **06** choosy, strict **07** carping, finicky **08** captious, niggling, pedantic **09** cavilling, quibbling **10** censorious, nit-picking, pernickety **11** persnickety **12** fault-finding **13** hair-splitting **14** over-particular

Hypnos
06 Somnus

hypnotic
07 numbing **08** magnetic, sedative **09** soporific **10** compelling, magnetical **11** fascinating, mesmerizing, somniferous **12** irresistible, spellbinding, stupefactive **13** sleep-inducing

hypnotism
08 Braidism, hypnosis **09** mesmerism **10** suggestion **12** neurypnology **14** auto-suggestion, electrobiology, neurohypnology **15** animal magnetism

hypnotize
06 dazzle **07** beguile, bewitch, enchant **08** entrance **09** captivate, fascinate, magnetize, mesmerize, spellbind **10** put to sleep

hypochondria
03 hip, hyp **08** neurosis **15** hypochondriasis

hypochondriac
08 neurotic **10** melancholy, phrenesiac **11** atrabilious **14** hypochondriast, valetudinarian **15** hypochondriacal

hypocrisy
04 cant **06** deceit **07** falsity **08** pretence **09** deception, duplicity **10** dishonesty, double-talk, lip service, pharisaism, phoneyness **11** dissembling, insincerity **12** two-facedness, wearing a mask **13** deceitfulness, dissimulation, double-dealing

hypocrite
05 fraud, Janus, pseud **06** canter, mucker, phoney, pseudo **08** deceiver, impostor, Pharisee, Tartuffe **09** charlatan, Pecksniff, pretender **10** dissembler, Holy Willie, mountebank **15** whited sepulchre

hypocritical
05 false, lying **06** double, hollow, phoney **08** specious, spurious, two-faced **09** deceitful, deceptive, dishonest, insincere, pharisaic, self-pious, Tartufian, Tartufish **10** false-faced, fraudulent, histrionic, Janus-faced, perfidious, Tartuffian, Tartuffish **11** dissembling, double-faced, duplicitous, Janian-faced, pharisaical **12** histrionical, Pecksniffian **13** double-dealing, sanctimonious, self-righteous

hypothesis
03 hyp **05** axiom **06** notion, theory, thesis **07** premise, theorem **09** postulate **10** assumption, conjecture **11** presumption, proposition, speculation, supposition

hypothetical
03 hyp **07** assumed **08** imagined, notional, presumed, proposed, supposed **09** imaginary **11** conjectural, speculative, theoretical **13** suppositional

hypothetically
07 ideally **08** in theory **10** supposedly **13** conjecturally, speculatively, theoretically

hysteria
05 mania, panic **06** frenzy, mother **07** habdabs, madness **08** delirium, neurosis **09** agitation, hysterics **15** fits of the mother

hysterical
03 mad **04** rich **06** crazed, raving **07** berserk, frantic **08** demented, farcical, frenzied, in a panic, neurotic **09** delirious, hilarious, ludicrous, priceless **10** ridiculous, uproarious **11** overwrought **12** out of control **13** side-splitting **14** beside yourself, extremely funny, uncontrollable

hysterically
05 madly **08** absurdly, in a panic **10** farcically **11** frantically, hilariously, ludicrously, screamingly **12** neurotically, out of control, ridiculously, uproariously **13** out of your mind **14** beside yourself, uncontrollably

hysterics
05 mania, panic **06** frenzy **07** habdabs, madness **08** delirium, hysteria, neurosis **09** agitation **12** crise de nerfs

I

I
02 ch, me **03** aye, che, ego, ich, one, yes **05** India **06** indeed, iodine

• I am
02 I'm **03** sum

ice
04 cool, kill **05** chill, frost, glaze **06** freeze, harden **07** diamond, iciness, reserve **08** coldness, coolness, diamonds, distance, enfreeze **09** formality **10** freeze over, frostiness **11** frozen water, refrigerate

Ice types include:

03 dry, pan, sea
04 floe, grew, grue, hail, pack, rime, slob, snow
05 black, brash, crust, drift, field, shelf, shell, sleet, virga
06 anchor, frazil, ground, icicle, stream
07 glacier, hummock, pancake, verglas
10 silver thaw
13 tickly-benders

• ice cream
04 cone **05** bombe, kulfi **06** bucket, cornet, gelato, ripple, slider, sorbet, sundae **07** cassata, choc-bar, granita, sherbet, spumone, spumoni, tortoni **08** hoky-poky, macallum **10** hokey-pokey, Neapolitan **11** tutti-frutti

• put on ice
05 defer, delay **06** put off, shelve **07** suspend **08** postpone **14** hold in abeyance **15** leave in abeyance

iceberg
04 berg, calf **07** growler

ice-cold
03 icy, raw **04** hard, iced, numb **05** algid, fixed, gelid, polar, rigid, stiff **06** arctic, baltic, frigid, frosty, frozen **07** chilled, frosted, glacial **08** freezing, icebound, Siberian **10** solidified **11** frozen-stiff **12** bitterly cold

ice hockey

Ice hockey-related terms include:

04 cage, goal, puck
05 bully, check, icing, stick, zones
06 assist, boards, period, sin-bin
07 face-off, forward, offside, penalty, red line, shut-out, Zamboni
08 blue line, boarding, defender, five-hole, linesman, one-timer, overtime, slap shot, slashing, spearing
09 blueliner, bodycheck, centreman, netminder, power play
10 centre line, cross-check, defenceman, goaltender, penalty box
11 penalty shot, short-handed, sudden-death
12 icing the puck, penalty bench
13 defending zone

Iceland
02 IS **03** ISL

ice skating

Ice skaters include:

04 **Dean** (Christopher), **Koss** (Johann Olav), **Kwan** (Michelle), **Witt** (Katarina), **Yang** (Yang 'A')
05 **Baiul** (Oksana), **Blair** (Bonnie), **Curry** (John), **Heiss** (Carol), **Henie** (Sonja), **Kania** (Karin), **Syers** (Madge)
06 **Button** (Dick), **Hamill** (Dorothy)
07 **Boitano** (Brian), **Cousins** (Robin), **Fleming** (Peggy), **Grinkov** (Sergei), **Harding** (Tonya), **Rodnina** (Irina), **Salchow** (Ulrich), **Torvill** (Jayne), **Yagudin** (Alexei)
08 **Browning** (Kurt), **Dijkstra** (Sjoukje), **Dmitriev** (Artur), **Eldredge** (Todd), **Gordeeva** (Ekaterina), **Hamilton** (Scott), **Kazakova** (Oksana), **Kerrigan** (Nancy), **Lipinski** (Tara), **Petrenko** (Viktor)
09 **Yamaguchi** (Kristi)
10 **Ballangrud** (Ivar)

Ice skating-related terms include:

04 Axel, edge, flip, loop, Lutz
05 blade, pairs, skate, waltz
06 figure, Mohawk, rocker, walley
07 bracket, Choctaw, Salchow, sit spin, toe jump, toe loop, toe pick
08 ice dance, Ina Bauer, stag leap
09 camel spin, crossover, free dance
10 inside edge
11 death spiral, flying camel, layback spin, outside edge, spread eagle, upright spin
12 headless spin, speed skating
13 Biellmann spin, figure skating, flying sit spin, free programme
14 short programme
15 compulsory dance, set pattern dance

icily
06 coldly, coolly, rudely **07** stiffly
08 formally, morosely **12** forbiddingly

icon
04 idol **05** image **06** figure, smiley, sprite, symbol **08** likeness, portrait **09** portrayal **14** representation

iconoclast
05 rebel **06** critic **07** heretic, radical, sceptic **08** opponent **09** denouncer, dissenter, dissident **10** questioner, unbeliever **11** denunciator **12** image-breaker

iconoclastic
07 impious, radical **08** critical
09 dissident, heretical, sceptical
10 innovative, irreverent, rebellious, subversive **11** dissentient, questioning
12 denunciatory

icy
03 raw **04** cold, cool, rimy, rude
05 aloof, chill, gelid, polar, stiff, stony
06 arctic, biting, bitter, chilly, formal, frigid, frosty, frozen, glassy, morose, slippy **07** distant, glacial, hostile, ice-cold **08** chilling, freezing, icebound, reserved, Siberian, slippery
10 forbidding, frostbound, restrained, unfriendly **11** indifferent

id
04 orfe

Idaho
02 ID

idea
03 aim, end **04** clou, clue, goal, idée, plan, view **05** fancy, guess, image, point **06** belief, design, notion, object, reason, scheme, target, theory, vision **07** conceit, concept, feeling, inkling, opinion, purpose, thought, wrinkle **08** proposal **09** brainwave, intention, judgement, objective, obsession, suspicion, viewpoint **10** conception, conjecture, hypothesis, impression, perception, suggestion **11** abstraction, connotation, inspiration, proposition **13** understanding **14** interpretation, recommendation

ideal
04 acme, best, type **05** cause, dream, image, model **06** ethics, morals, unreal, Utopia **07** eidolon, epitome, example, highest, optimal, optimum, paragon, pattern, perfect, supreme, utopian **08** absolute, abstract, complete, exemplar, fanciful, notional, romantic, standard **09** archetype, benchmark, criterion, imaginary, nonpareil, principle, prototype, visionary, yardstick **10** archetypal, conceptual, consummate, idealistic, perfection **11** impractical, moral values, theoretical **12** hypothetical, unattainable **13** ethical values, philosophical **14** moral standards, quintessential

• ideal state
06 Utopia **07** nirvana

idealism
09 mentalism **10** utopianism
11 romanticism **13** perfectionism
14 impracticality

idealist
07 dreamer **08** optimist, romantic
09 visionary **11** romanticist
13 perfectionist

idealistic
07 utopian **08** quixotic, romantic
09 visionary **10** optimistic, starry-eyed
11 impractical, unrealistic
13 impracticable, perfectionist

idealization
07 worship **10** apotheosis, exaltation
11 ennoblement, idolization
13 glamorization, glorification, romanticizing **15** romanticization

idealize
05 exalt **07** glorify, idolize, worship
09 glamorize **10** utopianize
11 romanticize

ideally
06 at best **08** in theory, mentally
09 perfectly **13** theoretically
14 hypothetically, in an ideal world
15 in a perfect world

idée fixe
06 hang-up **07** complex **08** fixation
09 fixed idea, leitmotiv, monomania, obsession

identical
04 like, same, self, twin **05** alike, equal, right **06** cloned **07** identic, numeric, precise, similar **08** matching, self-same **09** analogous, congruent, duplicate, syngeneic **10** coincident, consistent, equivalent **11** a dead ringer
12 doppelgänger **13** corresponding, one and the same, spitting image
15 interchangeable

identically
05 alike **07** equally **09** similarly
11 analogously, congruently, just the same **12** consistently, equivalently, in the same way **15** correspondingly, interchangeably

identifiable
05 known **10** detectable, noticeable
11 discernible, perceptible
12 recognizable, unmistakable
13 ascertainable **15** distinguishable

identification
02 ID **03** tie **04** bond, link **05** badge, label **06** naming, papers **07** empathy, rapport **08** passbook, passport, relation, spotting, sympathy
09 biometric, detection, diagnosis, documents, labelling **10** connection
11 association, correlation, credentials, involvement, pointing-out, recognition **12** dactyloscopy, identity card, relationship **13** fellow feeling, interrelation **14** classification, driving licence, fingerprinting

identify
03 tag **04** know, name, spot **05** label, place **06** couple, detect, finger, notice, relate **07** connect, discern, feel for, find out, involve, make out, pick out, pin down, specify **08** classify, diagnose, discover, perceive, pinpoint, point out, relate to **09** ascertain, associate, catalogue, establish, recognize, respond to, single out **11** distinguish
13 associate with, empathize with
14 put the finger on, sympathize with
15 think of together

identity
02 ID **03** ego **04** face, name, self
05 image, roots, seity, unity
07 oneness, profile **08** equality, likeness, property, sameness, selfhood
09 character, closeness, existence
10 appearance, background, impression, personhood, public face, similarity, uniqueness **11** equivalence, personality, resemblance, singularity
12 selfsameness **13** individuality, particularity, public persona
14 correspondence **15** distinctiveness

ideologist
07 teacher, thinker **08** theorist
09 ideologue, visionary **11** doctrinaire, philosopher

ideology
05 credo, creed, dogma, faith, ideas
06 belief, tenets, theory, thesis
07 beliefs, opinion **08** doctrine, opinions, teaching **09** doctrines, world-view **10** philosophy, principles
11 convictions, metaphysics
See also **political**

idiocy
05 folly **06** lunacy **07** inanity
08 daftness, insanity **09** absurdity, craziness, silliness, stupidity
10 imbecility **11** fatuousness
13 foolhardiness, senselessness

idiom
04 talk **05** style, usage **06** jargon, phrase, speech, Syrism **07** Arabism, dialect, Grecism, Pahlavi, Pehlevi, Persism, Slavism, Syriasm
08 Aramaism, Graecism, Hebraism, idiotism, Irishism, language, Latinism, locution, parlance, polonism, prosaism, Saxonism, Semitism, Sinicism **09** anglicism, Celticism, Chaldaism, Gallicism, Germanism, Gothicism, Hellenism, Italicism, Scoticism, Syriacism, Syrianism
10 classicism, cockneyism, Englishism, expression, femininism, Italianism, Johnsonese, Scotticism, vernacular, Yiddishism
11 Americanism, Hibernicism, phraseology **12** classicalism, Hibernianism, turn of phrase
13 Australianism, colloquialism, vernacularism

idiomatic
06 native **07** correct, natural
08 everyday **09** dialectal
10 colloquial, idiolectal, vernacular
11 dialectical, grammatical

idiosyncrasy
03 way **05** freak, habit, quirk, trait
06 oddity **07** feature, quality
09 mannerism **10** speciality
11 peculiarity, singularity
12 eccentricity **13** individuality
14 characteristic

idiosyncratic
03 odd **06** quirky **08** peculiar, personal, singular **09** eccentric
10 individual **11** distinctive
14 characteristic

idiot
03 ass, mug, nit, nut, oaf **04** berk, clod, clot, dill, dope, dork, fool, geek, jerk, nana, nerd, nerk, nong, prat, putz, twit
05 chump, clown, divvy, dumbo, dunce, eejit, galah, klutz, moron, nelly, ninny, prick, schmo, twerp, wally
06 bammer, bampot, cretin, dimwit, doofus, drongo, dum-dum, muppet, nidget, nitwit, numpty, sucker
07 airhead, barmpot, dumb-ass, fat-head, halfwit, jughead, natural, pillock, plonker, schmuck, wazzock
08 boofhead, dipstick, flathead, imbecile, innocent, numskull, pea-brain **09** birdbrain, blockhead, cloth head, ignoramus, lame brain, malt-horse, simpleton, thickhead
10 bufflehead, nincompoop
11 chowderhead, knuckle-head
See also **fool**

idiotic
◇ *anagram indicator*
03 mad, twp **04** daft, dozy, dumb
05 barmy, batty, crazy, dorky, dotty, goofy, inane, inept, nutty, potty, silly, wacky **06** absurd, insane, oafish, simple, stupid, unwise **07** asinine, dumb-ass, fatuous, foolish, moronic, risible **08** gormless, ignorant **09** dim-witted, half-baked, ludicrous, pointless, senseless **10** half-witted, ill-advised, ridiculous **11** hare-brained, injudicious, nonsensical, thick-headed
12 crack-brained, short-sighted, simple-minded, unreasonable **13** ill-considered, knuckle-headed, unintelligent

idle
03 lig **04** dead, doss, laze, lazy, loaf, mike, move, vain **05** dally, empty, light, petty, relax, shirk, skive, slack, waste, while **06** bludge, casual, daidle, dawdle, fester, fiddle, futile, loiter, lollop, lounge, potter, putter, unused, wanton **07** dormant, dronish, foolish, fritter, goof off, jobless, loafish, shallow, sit back, trivial, useless, work-shy
08 baseless, bone-idle, inactive, indolent, kill time, lallygag, lollygag, slothful, sluggish, sod about, tick over, trifling **09** bum around, do nothing, fruitless, gold-brick, lethargic, on the dole, pointless, redundant, while away, worthless **10** mothballed, not working, take it easy, unedifying, unemployed, unoccupied, whip the cat **11** fiddle about, horse around,

ineffective, ineffectual, inoperative, unimportant **12** be ready to run, fiddle around, fiddle-faddle, unproductive, unsuccessful **13** be operational, be ready to work, insignificant, lackadaisical

idleness
04 ease **05** sloth **06** lazing, torpor **07** idlesse, inertia, leisure, loafing, skiving, vacancy, vacuity **08** inaction, laziness, otiosity **09** indolence, pottering **10** inactivity, otioseness, vegetating **12** slothfulness, sluggishness, unemployment **13** shiftlessness **14** dolce far niente

idler
04 slob, spiv **05** drone, sloth **06** bumble, bummle, dodger, donnat, donnot, dosser, loafer, skiver, truant, waster **07** bludger, dawdler, goof-off, laggard, Lollard, lounger, shirker, slacker, wastrel **08** do-naught, fine lady, layabout, sluggard **09** do-nothing, gold brick, lazybones **10** malingerer **11** couch potato **12** carpet-knight, clock-watcher **13** fine gentleman **14** good-for-nothing

idol
03 god, pet **04** hero, icon, joss, sham, star, wood **05** deity, image, pagod, pin-up, swami **06** effigy, fetish, figure, mammet, maumet, mawmet, mommet, pagoda **07** beloved, darling, fantasy, goddess, heroine, phantom **08** Baphomet, impostor, likeness **09** favourite, semblance, superstar **11** blue-eyed boy, graven image

idolater
06 adorer, votary **07** admirer, devotee, idolist **10** iconolater, idolatress, worshipper **14** idol-worshipper

idolatrous
05 pagan **07** adoring **09** adulatory, heretical, idolizing, lionizing **10** glorifying, uncritical **11** reverential, worshipping **15** idol-worshipping

idolatry
07 idolism **08** mammetry, maumetry, mawmetry, paganism, whoredom **09** adoration, adulation, fetishism, idolizing, reverence **10** admiration, exaltation, heathenism, iconolatry **11** deification, fornication, hero-worship, icon worship, worshipping **13** glorification

idolize
04 love **05** adore, deify, exalt **06** admire, dote on, revere **07** adulate, glorify, lionize, worship **08** venerate **09** reverence **11** hero-worship **14** put on a pedestal

idyllic
05 happy **06** rustic **07** perfect **08** blissful, charming, heavenly, pastoral, peaceful, romantic **09** idealized, unspoiled, wonderful **10** delightful **11** picturesque, Theocritean

ie
02 so

if
02 an **03** and, gin **06** though **07** suppose, whether **08** as long as, assuming, in case of, provided, so long as, whenever **09** condition, providing, supposing **11** supposition, uncertainty **12** assuming that, in the event of **13** supposing that **15** on condition that

- **even if**

03 and, tho **04** albe **05** albee, all-be **06** albeit, though **07** suppose

- **if it**

03 an't

iffy
04 suss **05** dodgy, risky **07** dubious **08** doubtful, low-grade **09** defective, imperfect, tentative, uncertain, undecided, unsettled **10** second-rate **11** substandard **13** disappointing **14** not up to scratch, unsatisfactory

ignite
04 burn, fire **05** light, torch **06** kindle **07** flare up, inflame **08** spark off, touch off **09** catch fire, set alight, set fire to, set on fire **11** conflagrate, put a match to **15** burst into flames

ignoble
03 low **04** base, mean, vile **05** petty, small **06** vulgar **07** heinous **08** infamous, shameful, unworthy, wretched **09** worthless **10** despicable **11** disgraceful **12** contemptible **13** dishonourable

ignobly
06 meanly, vilely **07** pettily **10** despicably, infamously, shamefully, wretchedly **12** contemptibly **13** disgracefully, dishonourably, without honour

ignominious
04 base **05** sorry **06** abject **08** infamous, shameful **09** degrading **10** despicable, mortifying, scandalous **11** disgraceful, humiliating, undignified **12** contemptible, disreputable, embarrassing **13** discreditable, dishonourable

ignominiously
10 despicably, shamefully **12** disreputably, scandalously **13** disgracefully, dishonourably

ignominy
05 odium, shame **06** infamy, stigma **07** obloquy, scandal **08** contempt, disgrace, reproach **09** discredit, dishonour, disrepute, indignity **10** opprobrium **11** degradation, humiliation **13** mortification

ignoramus
03 ass **04** dolt, fool **05** dunce **06** dimwit, duffer, ignaro **07** dullard, halfwit **08** bonehead, ignorant, imbecile, numskull **09** blockhead, simpleton **10** illiterate **11** know-nothing

ignorance
05 night **07** naivety **08** oblivion **09** greenness, innocence, nescience, stupidity, thickness **10** illiteracy **11** unawareness **12** inexperience **13** obliviousness, unfamiliarity **14** unintelligence **15** unconsciousness

ignorant
04 dumb, lewd, rude **05** blind, dense, naive, thick **06** ingram, ingrum, stupid, unread **07** ill-bred, redneck, unaware, unknown **08** backward, clueless, innocent, inscient, nescient, untaught **09** benighted, in the dark, lack-Latin, oblivious, unknowing, unlearned, untrained, unwitting **10** analphabet, illiterate, innumerate, uneducated, unfamiliar, uninformed, unschooled **11** analphabete, ill-educated, ill-informed, know-nothing, unconfirmed, unconscious, uninitiated **12** discourteous, having no idea, unacquainted **13** inexperienced, unenlightened

ignore
◇ *deletion indicator*
03 cut **04** balk, omit, snub **05** baulk, blank, blink, spurn, waive **06** bypass, pass by, reject, slight **07** cut dead, high-hat, neglect, tune out **08** brush off, discount, overlook, pass over, set aside, shrug off **09** disregard **10** brush aside, scrub round, slight over **11** not listen to, run away from **12** cold-shoulder **13** be oblivious to, keep in the dark **14** shut your eyes to, take for granted, take no notice of, turn a deaf ear to, turn your back on **15** close your eyes to, look the other way, turn a blind eye to

ilk
04 each, kind, make, same, sort, type, ylke **05** brand, breed, class, stamp, style **07** variety **09** character **11** description

ill
◇ *anagram indicator*
03 bad **04** down, evil, harm, hurt, pain, sick, weak **05** amiss, badly, cronk, crook, dicky, frail, harsh, rough, seedy, trial **06** ailing, barely, crummy, feeble, groggy, grotty, hardly, infirm, injury, laid up, naught, poorly, queasy, severe, sorrow, trials, unkind, unweal, unwell, wicked **07** adverse, ailment, cruelty, grieved, harmful, hostile, hurtful, ominous, peevish, problem, ruinous, run down, trouble, unlucky **08** critical, damaging, disaster, diseased, scantily, scarcely, sinister, unkindly **09** adversely, afflicted, bedridden, by no means, difficult, in a bad way, incorrect, injurious, off-colour, resentful, suffering, unhealthy, unluckily **10** affliction, broken-down, distressed, indisposed, misfortune, out of sorts, unfriendly, unpleasant, wickedness, wrongfully **11** belligerent, deleterious, destruction, destructive, detrimental, incompetent, peelie-wally, threatening, tribulation,

unfortunate, unpromising
12 antagonistic, inadequately, inauspicious, infelicitous, unfavourable, unfavourably, unpropitious **13** reprehensible, unfortunately **14** disapprovingly, inauspiciously, insufficiently, unpleasantness, unsuccessfully, valetudinarian **15** under the weather

- **ill at ease**

◇ *anagram indicator*
04 edgy **05** tense **06** on edge, uneasy, unsure **07** anxious, awkward, fidgety, nervous, strange, worried **08** farouche, hesitant, restless **09** disturbed, unrelaxed, unsettled **10** disquieted **11** embarrassed **13** on tenterhooks, self-conscious, uncomfortable

- **speak ill of**

03 nag, pan **04** carp, slag, slam **05** blame, cut up, decry, knock, roast, score, slash, slate, trash **06** attack, hammer, impugn, niggle, peck at, tilt at **07** censure, condemn, nit-pick, rubbish, run down, scarify, slag off, snipe at **08** backbite, badmouth, denounce, wade into **09** castigate, criticize, denigrate, disparage, excoriate, have a go at, misreport, pull apart, take apart, tear apart **10** animadvert, come down on, go to town on, vituperate **11** pick holes in **12** disapprove of, pull to pieces, put the boot in, tear to shreds **13** find fault with, tear a strip off **15** do a hatchet job on, pass judgement on

ill-advised

04 rash **05** hasty **06** unwise **07** foolish **08** careless, overseen, reckless **09** ill-judged, imprudent, misguided **11** injudicious, thoughtless **12** short-sighted **13** ill-considered, inappropriate

ill-assorted

◇ *anagram indicator*
08 unsuited **09** misallied **10** discordant, mismatched **11** incongruous, uncongenial **12** incompatible, inharmonious

ill-bred

◇ *anagram indicator*
04 rude **05** crass, crude, ocker **06** coarse, vulgar **07** boorish, loutish, uncivil, uncouth **08** ignorant, impolite, unseemly **10** indelicate, misbehaved, unmannerly, unnurtured **11** bad-mannered, ill-mannered, uncivilized **12** discourteous

ill-considered

04 rash **05** hasty **06** unwise **07** foolish **08** careless, heedless **09** ill-judged, imprudent, overhasty **10** ill-advised **11** improvident, injudicious, precipitate **12** misconceived

ill-defined

03 dim **04** hazy **05** fuzzy, vague **06** blurry, woolly **07** blurred, mongrel, shadowy, unclear **08** nebulous **09** imprecise, shapeless **10** indefinite, indistinct

ill-disposed

04 anti **06** averse **07** against, hostile, opposed **08** inimical **10** malevolent, unfriendly **11** disaffected, unwelcoming **12** antagonistic **13** unco-operative, unsympathetic

illegal

05 wrong **06** banned, barred **07** bootleg, crooked, illicit **08** criminal, outlawed, unlawful, wrongful, wrongous **09** felonious, forbidden **10** adulterine, fraudulent, prohibited, proscribed **11** black-market, interdicted **12** criminalized, illegitimate, unauthorized **15** under-the-counter

illegality

05 crime, wrong **06** felony **09** wrongness **11** criminality, illicitness, lawlessness, malfeasance **12** illegitimacy, unlawfulness, wrongfulness

illegally

07 wrongly **08** guiltily **09** illicitly **10** criminally, unlawfully, wrongfully **13** against the law, disobediently **14** illegitimately

illegible

05 faint **07** obscure **08** scrawled **10** hard to read, indistinct, unreadable **12** hieroglyphic **14** indecipherable, unintelligible

illegitimacy

08 bastardy **10** bastardism **12** bend-sinister **13** baton-sinister **14** fatherlessness

illegitimate

04 base, love **07** bastard, illegal, illicit, invalid, lawless, natural, unsound **08** base-born, improper, misbegot, nameless, spurious, unlawful **09** illogical, incorrect **10** adulterine, fatherless, unfathered, unlicensed **11** misbegotten, unwarranted **12** inadmissible, unauthorized

ill-equipped

07 exposed **10** unprovided, unsupplied **11** ill-supplied, underfunded, undermanned, unprotected **12** disappointed, understaffed **13** underfinanced, under strength, unprovided for **14** under-resourced

ill-fated

06 doomed **07** hapless, unhappy, unlucky **08** blighted, luckless **09** ill-omened, star-crost **10** ill-starred **11** star-crossed, unfortunate

ill-favoured

04 ugly **05** plain **06** homely **07** hideous **08** unlovely **09** repulsive, unsightly **12** unattractive **15** unprepossessing

ill-feeling

05 anger, odium, pique, spite, wrath **06** animus, enmity, grudge, malice **07** dudgeon, ill-will, offence, rancour **08** bad blood, sourness **09** animosity, hostility **10** antagonism, bitterness, resentment, unkindness **11** frustration, indignation **12** hard feelings **14** disgruntlement **15** dissatisfaction

ill-founded

07 unsound **08** baseless **10** groundless **11** unconfirmed, unjustified, unsupported **15** unsubstantiated

ill-gotten

03 hot **04** bent **05** dodgy, taken **06** nicked, stolen, swiped **07** nobbled **08** pilfered **09** purloined, ripped off **10** knocked off

ill-humour

03 dod **04** bile, dump **05** dumps, rheum **06** spleen **09** distemper

ill-humoured

04 tart **05** cross, huffy, moody, ratty, sharp, sulky, testy **06** crabby, grumpy, morose, shirty, snappy, sullen **07** crabbed, grouchy, peevish, stroppy, waspish **08** petulant, snappish **09** crotchety, impatient, irascible, irritable **11** acrimonious, bad-tempered, distempered **12** cantankerous, disagreeable **13** quick-tempered

illiberal

04 mean **05** petty, tight **06** stingy **07** bigoted, miserly **08** verkramp **09** hidebound, niggardly **10** intolerant, prejudiced, ungenerous **11** close-fisted, reactionary, small-minded, tight-fisted **12** narrow-minded, parsimonious, uncharitable **13** unenlightened

illicit

03 sly **05** black, wrong **06** banned, barred, shonky **07** bootleg, furtive, illegal **08** criminal, improper, stealthy, unlawful **09** forbidden, ill-gotten, secretive **10** contraband, prohibited, unlicensed **11** black-market, clandestine **12** illegitimate, unauthorized **13** surreptitious, under-the-table **15** under-the-counter

illicitly

07 wrongly **08** guiltily **09** illegally **10** criminally, unlawfully, wrongfully **13** against the law, disobediently **14** illegitimately

Illinois

02 IL **03** Ill

illiteracy

09 ignorance **15** inability to read, lack of education, lack of schooling

illiterate

08 ignorant, untaught **09** benighted, unlearned, untutored **10** letterless, uncultured, uneducated, unlettered, unschooled **12** analphabetic

ill-judged

04 daft, rash **05** hasty **06** unwise **07** foolish **08** mistaken, reckless **09** foolhardy, impolitic, imprudent, misguided, overhasty, unadvised

10 ill-advised, incautious, indiscreet
11 injudicious, wrong-headed
12 short-sighted 13 ill-considered

ill-mannered
04 rude 05 crude 06 coarse
07 boorish, cubbish, ill-bred, loutish, uncivil, uncouth 08 churlish, impolite, insolent 10 ill-behaved, unmannerly
11 bad-mannered, insensitive 12 badly behaved, discourteous

ill-natured
03 wry 04 acid, mean, ugly 05 cross, nasty, sulky, surly 06 crabby, gnarly, shrewd, sullen, unkind 07 crabbed, vicious 08 churlish, perverse, petulant, shrewish, spiteful 09 malicious, malignant 10 malevolent, unfriendly, unpleasant, vindictive 11 bad-tempered 12 disagreeable

illness
03 wog 04 bout, evil, tout, towt, weed, weid 05 touch 06 attack, malady 07 ailment, disease
08 disorder, sickness 09 complaint, condition, ill health, infirmity
10 affliction, disability, poor health
13 indisposition
See also **disease**

illogical
05 crazy, wrong 06 absurd, faulty
07 invalid, unsound 08 fallible, specious, spurious 09 casuistic, incorrect, senseless, untenable
10 fallacious, irrational 11 meaningless, sophistical 12 inconsequent, inconsistent, unreasonable, unscientific, woolly minded

illogicality
07 fallacy 08 unreason 09 absurdity
10 invalidity 11 unsoundness
12 speciousness 13 inconsistency, irrationality, senselessness
14 fallaciousness

ill-starred
06 doomed 07 hapless, unhappy, unlucky 08 blighted, ill-fated 09 star-crost 11 star-crossed, unfortunate
12 inauspicious

ill-tempered
04 curt 05 cross, curst, ratty, sharp, testy 06 crabby, cranky, girnie, grumpy, morose, shirty, tetchy, touchy
07 crabbed, grouchy, stroppy, vicious
08 choleric, spiteful 09 crotchety, impatient, irascible, irritable 10 ill-natured 11 acrimonious, bad-tempered, ill-humoured 12 cantankerous

ill-timed
05 crass, inept 07 awkward
08 mistimed, tactless, untimely
09 unwelcome 10 wrong-timed
11 inopportune, unfortunate
12 inconvenient, unseasonable
13 inappropriate

ill-treat
◇ *anagram indicator*
04 harm 05 abuse, wrong 06 damage, demean, injure, misuse 07 neglect, oppress 08 maltreat, misguide, mistreat 09 mishandle

ill-treatment
04 harm 05 abuse 06 damage, ill-use, injury, misuse 07 neglect
11 manhandling, mishandling
12 maltreatment, mistreatment

illuminate
04 limn 05 adorn, edify, light
07 clarify, clear up, explain, lighten, light up, miniate, shine on 08 brighten, decorate, illumine, instruct, ornament, twilight 09 back-light, elucidate, embellish, enlighten, limelight, overshine 10 floodlight, illustrate
12 throw light on

illuminating
07 helpful 08 edifying 09 revealing
10 revelatory 11 explanatory, informative, instructive
12 enlightening

illumination
03 ray 04 beam 05 flash, light
06 lights 07 insight 08 learning, lighting, radiance 09 adornment, awareness, education, miniature, theosophy 10 brightness, decoration, perception, revelation 11 candlelight, elucidation, instruction, irradiation
12 illustration 13 clarification, embellishment, enlightenment, ornamentation, understanding, zodiacal light

illusion
04 maya 05 error, fancy 06 déjà vu, mirage 07 chimera, fallacy, fantasy, mocking, phantom, spectre
08 delusion, phantasm, prestige
09 deception, phantosme
10 apparition, fata Morgana
12 misjudgement, will-o'-the-wisp
13 hallucination, misconception
15 false impression, misapprehension

illusory
04 sham 05 false 06 unreal, untrue
07 fancied, phantom, seeming
08 apparent, deluding, delusive, delusory, illusive, imagined, mistaken, specious 09 deceptive, erroneous, imaginary 10 chimerical, fallacious, misleading 11 illusionary
13 unsubstantial

illustrate
04 draw, show 05 adorn 06 depict, sketch 07 clarify, exhibit, explain, miniate, picture 08 decorate, instance, ornament, renowned 09 elucidate, embellish, enlighten, exemplify, interpret 10 illuminate 11 demonstrate

illustrated
08 miniated 09 decorated, pictorial
11 embellished, illuminated 12 with drawings, with pictures

illustration
04 case, note 05 bleed, chart, gloss, plate, quote 06 blow-up, design, figure, remark, sample, sketch
07 analogy, artwork, comment, diagram, drawing, example, graphic, picture 08 exemplar, exponent, half-tone, instance, specimen, vignette
09 adornment, hors texte, quotation, sidelight 10 decoration, photograph
11 case in point, elucidation, explanation, observation
12 frontispiece 13 clarification, demonstration, embellishment, ornamentation 14 interpretation, representation 15 exemplification

illustrative
06 sample 07 graphic, typical
08 specimen 09 pictorial
10 expository 11 delineative, descriptive, explanatory, explicatory
12 diagrammatic, exemplifying, illustratory 14 illustrational, interpretative, representative

illustrious
04 dull 05 famed, great, noble, noted
06 bright, famous 07 eminent, exalted, notable 08 esteemed, glorious, honoured, luminous, renowned, splendid 09 acclaimed, brilliant, excellent, prominent, well-known 10 celebrated, honourable, pre-eminent, remarkable
11 magnificent, outstanding
13 distinguished

ill-will
04 envy, gall 05 anger, odium, spite, wrath 06 animus, enmity, grudge, hatred, malice, maugre 07 dislike, envying, maulgre, rancour 08 aversion, bad blood 09 animosity, antipathy, hostility, maltalent 10 antagonism, ill-feeling, resentment 11 indignation, malevolence 12 disaffection, hard feelings 14 unfriendliness

image
03 pic 04 bust, copy, doll, face, icon, idea, idol, tiki, twin 05 clone, fancy, match 06 double, effigy, figure, idolon, idolum, mirror, notion, reflex, ringer, shadow, simile, statue, typify, vision
07 concept, eidolon, fantasy, imagery, imagine, persona, picture, portray, profile, replica, thought 08 figurine, identity, likeness, metaphor, phantasy, portrait 09 depiction, duplicate, facsimile, lookalike, portrayal, statuette
10 appearance, conception, dead ringer, impression, perception, photograph, projection, public face, reflection 11 graven image, resemblance 12 doppelgänger, reproduction, turn of phrase 13 public persona, spitting image 14 figure of speech, representation

imaginable
06 likely 08 credible, feasible, possible, probable 09 plausible, thinkable 10 believable, supposable
11 conceivable

imaginary
06 dreamy, made-up, unreal
07 assumed, fancied, fictive, ghostly, phantom, pretend, shadowy
08 fabulous, fanciful, illusory,

imagined, invented, mythical, notional, spectral, supposed **09** fantastic, fictional, legendary, visionary **10** chimerical, fictitious **11** fantastical, make-believe, non-existent **12** hypothetical, mythological **13** hallucinatory, insubstantial

imagination
03 wit **05** dream, fancy **06** schema, vision **07** chimera, fantasy, imagery, insight, project **08** illusion, mind's eye, phantasy **09** dreamland, ingenuity **10** creativity, enterprise, mental view **11** inspiration, originality **12** fancifulness **13** contemplation, flight of fancy, ingeniousness, inventiveness **15** imaginativeness, resourcefulness

imaginative
05 vivid **06** clever, poetic **07** lyrical **08** creative, fanciful, inspired, original, poetical **09** fantastic, ingenious, inventive, visionary, whimsical **10** innovative **11** full of ideas, resourceful **12** enterprising

imagine
03 see **04** deem, plan, ween **05** dream, fancy, feign, guess, image, judge, think **06** assume, create, devise, figure, gather, ideate, invent, reckon, scheme, take it, vision **07** believe, conceit, dream up, picture, presume, pretend, project, propose, suppose, surmise, think up **08** conceive, contrive, daydream, envisage **09** conjure up, fantasize, visualize **10** conjecture **11** make believe **14** form a picture of

imbalance
04 bias **08** inequity, variance **09** disparity **10** inequality, partiality, unevenness, unfairness **13** disproportion

imbecile
◇ *anagram indicator*
03 ass, mug, nit **04** berk, clot, daft, dope, dork, dumb, fool, geek, jerk, nana, nerd, nerk, nong, prat, putz, twit **05** anile, barmy, batty, chump, crazy, dorky, dotty, dumbo, dunce, eejit, goofy, idiot, inane, klutz, moron, ninny, nutty, potty, silly, twerp, wacky, wally **06** absurd, bammer, bampot, cretin, dimwit, doofus, dum-dum, nitwit, numpty, stupid, sucker **07** asinine, bungler, fatuous, foolish, halfwit, idiotic, jughead, moronic, pillock, plonker, wazzock, witless **08** flathead, innocent, numskull **09** birdbrain, blockhead, cloth head, lame brain, ludicrous, simpleton, thickhead **10** nincompoop **11** chowderhead, knuckle-head, thick-headed **12** crack-brained **13** knuckle-headed

imbecility
06 idiocy **07** amentia, fatuity, idiotcy, inanity **08** daftness **09** asininity, craziness, cretinism, stupidity **11** foolishness **12** childishness, incompetence

imbibe
◇ *containment indicator*
03 sip **04** gain, gulp, suck, swig **05** drink, lap up, quaff **06** absorb, gather, ingest, soak up, take in **07** acquire, consume, drink in, receive, swallow **09** knock back **10** assimilate

imbroglio
04 mess **06** muddle, scrape, tangle **07** dilemma **08** quandary **09** confusion **10** difficulty **11** embroilment, involvement **12** complication, entanglement

imbue
04 fill, tint **05** embay, steep, taint, tinct, tinge **06** charge, infuse, inject, instil, season **07** breathe, ingrain, inspire, moisten, pervade, possess, suffuse **08** permeate, saturate, tincture **09** inbreathe, inculcate, inoculate, transfuse **10** impregnate **12** indoctrinate

imitate
03 act, ape, hit **04** copy, echo, fake, mock **05** feign, forge, mimic, spoof **06** follow, hit off, mirror, parody, parrot, repeat, send up **07** copycat, emulate, take off **08** simulate **09** duplicate, replicate, reproduce **10** caricature, do likewise, follow suit **11** counterfeit, impersonate **12** take as a model

imitation
04 copy, echo, -ette, fake, faux, mock, sham **05** apery, aping, dummy, spoof **06** ersatz, parody, phoney, pseudo, send-up **07** forgery, man-made, mimesis, mimicry, mockery, mocking, replica, take-off **08** knock-off, likeness, parrotry, travesty **09** burlesque, duplicate, emulation, simulated, synthetic **10** artificial, caricature, impression, reflection, simulation **11** counterfeit, resemblance **12** reproduction **13** impersonation

imitative
04 mock **05** apish, me-too, mimic **07** copying, mimetic, servile **09** emulating, mimetical, mimicking, simulated **10** derivative, parrot-like, second-hand, unoriginal **11** plagiarized **12** onomatopoeic

imitator
03 ape **04** echo **05** mimic **06** copier, epigon, parrot **07** copycat, copyist, epigone **08** emulator, follower, parodist **10** plagiarist **12** impersonator **13** impressionist

immaculate
04 pure **05** clean **07** perfect, sinless **08** flawless, innocent, pristine, spotless, unsoiled **09** blameless, faultless, guiltless, incorrupt, stainless, undefiled, unstained, unsullied, untainted **10** impeccable **11** unblemished **12** spick and span, squeaky clean

immaculately
06 purely **09** perfectly, sinlessly **10** flawlessly, impeccably, innocently, spotlessly, without sin **11** blamelessly, faultlessly, guiltlessly, incorruptly **12** to perfection, without blame, without guilt

immanent
06 innate **08** inherent **09** ingrained, intrinsic, pervading **10** permeating, ubiquitous **11** omnipresent **12** all-pervading

immaterial
05 minor, petty **07** trivial **08** trifling **10** irrelevant **11** incorporeal, inessential, of no account, unessential, unimportant **13** insignificant **15** inconsequential

immature
◇ *tail deletion indicator*
03 raw **05** crude, green, naive, vealy, young **06** callow, jejune, unripe **07** babyish, budding, puerile, unbaked, unready **08** childish, juvenile, under-age, unformed, untimely **09** beardless, embryonic, fledgling, half-baked, infantile, ingenuous, unfledged, unsizable **10** adolescent, incomplete, unmellowed, unprepared, unsizeable **11** undeveloped **13** inexperienced

immaturity
05 youth **07** crudity, rawness **09** crudeness, greenness, puerility **10** callowness, juvenility, unripeness **11** adolescence, babyishness **12** childishness, immatureness, imperfection, inexperience **14** unpreparedness

immeasurable
04 vast **07** endless, immense **08** infinite **09** boundless, limitless, unbounded, unlimited **10** bottomless, fathomless **11** illimitable, inestimable, never ending **12** immensurable, incalculable, interminable, unfathomable **13** inexhaustible

immeasurably
06 vastly **09** endlessly, immensely **10** infinitely **11** boundlessly, illimitably, inestimably, limitlessly **12** incalculably, interminably **13** beyond measure, inexhaustibly

immediacy
07 urgency **08** instancy **09** freshness, imminence, swiftness **10** directness, importance, promptness **11** spontaneity **12** criticalness, simultaneity **13** instantaneity

immediate
04 main, near, next **05** basic, chief, close, swift, vital **06** direct, prompt, recent, speedy, sudden, urgent **07** closest, crucial, current, instant, nearest, present, primary, soonest **08** abutting, adjacent, critical, existing, next-door, pressing **09** adjoining, first-time, important, posthaste, principal, proximate **11** fundamental, top-priority **12** high-priority, without delay **13** instantaneous

immediately
03 now, pdq **04** anon, ASAP, next, stat, then, tite **06** at once, belive, pronto, statim, subito **07** bang off, quickly **08** as soon as, directly, promptly, right now, speedily, straight, urgently **09** at a glance, forthwith, instantly, like a shot, on the spot, out of hand, presently, right away, thereupon, yesterday **10** this minute **11** incessantly, incontinent, in the wake of, on the morrow, straightway, therewithal, this instant, tout de suite **12** lickety-split, no sooner than, on the instant, on the knocker, straight away, straightways, there and then, without delay **13** incontinently, straightforth **14** unhesitatingly, without more ado **15** before you know it, instantaneously, without question

immemorial
05 fixed, hoary **06** age-old, of yore **07** ancient, archaic **08** timeless **09** ancestral **11** traditional **12** long-standing, time-honoured

immense
04 fine, huge, mega, vast **05** enorm, giant, great, jumbo **06** bumper, cosmic, myriad **07** mammoth, massive, titanic **08** colossal, cyclopic, enormous, fabulous, gigantic, whopping **09** cyclopean, cyclopian, extensive, ginormous, herculean, humungous, limitless **10** monumental, tremendous **11** Brobdingnag, elephantine **14** Brobdingnagian, extremely large

immensely
04 very **05** jolly **06** highly, really, vastly **07** acutely, awfully, greatly, utterly **08** severely, terribly **09** decidedly, extremely, intensely, massively, unusually **10** dreadfully, enormously, remarkably, uncommonly **11** exceedingly, excessively, frightfully **12** immoderately, inordinately, terrifically, unreasonably **13** exceptionally **15** extraordinarily

immensity
04 bulk **07** expanse **08** hugeness, infinity, vastness **09** expansion, greatness, magnitude **11** massiveness **12** enormousness, giganticness **13** extensiveness, limitlessness

immerse
◇ *hidden indicator*
03 dip **04** bury, duck, dunk, sink, soak **05** bathe, douse, souse **06** absorb, blanch, drench, engage, engulf, occupy, plunge, wallow **07** baptize, demerge, demerse, embathe, engross, imbathe, immerge, involve **08** saturate, submerge, submerse, wrap up in **09** preoccupy

immersed
◇ *hidden indicator*
04 busy, deep, rapt, sunk **06** buried **07** taken up **08** absorbed, consumed, involved, occupied **09** engrossed, wrapped up **11** preoccupied

immersion
03 dip **05** bathe **07** baptism, dipping, dousing, ducking, dunking, sinking, soaking **08** plunging **09** drenching **10** absorption, engagement, engrossing, saturation, submersion **11** involvement **13** concentration, preoccupation

immigrant
03 pom **04** Balt **05** alien, issei, pommy **06** merino **07** greener, incomer, migrant, new chum, settler, wetback **08** newcomer, outsider **09** foreigner, Pakistani **10** Aussiedler, new arrival, overstayer **13** new Australian

immigrate
06 come in, move in, remove, settle **07** migrate **08** resettle

imminence
06 menace, threat **08** approach, instancy, nearness **09** closeness, immediacy **11** propinquity

imminent
04 near **05** close **06** at hand, coming **07** brewing, in store, jutting, looming **08** in the air, menacing, on the way, upcoming **09** impending **11** approaching, forthcoming, in the offing, overhanging, threatening **12** on the horizon **13** about to happen, almost upon you **14** round the corner **15** fast approaching

immobile
05 fixed, rigid, stiff, still **06** at rest, frozen, rooted, static **07** riveted **08** moveless, unmoving **09** immovable **10** motionless, stationary, stock-still **11** immobilized

immobility
06 fixity **08** catatony, firmness **09** catatonia, fixedness, inertness, stability, stillness **10** disability, steadiness **12** immovability **14** motionlessness

immobilize
04 halt, stop **05** Taser® **06** freeze **07** cripple, disable **08** paralyse, transfix **10** deactivate, inactivate **14** put out of action

immoderate
03 OTT **05** steep, undue **06** lavish, wanton **07** extreme, fulsome **08** enormous, uncurbed **09** egregious, excessive, hubristic, unbridled, unlimited **10** exorbitant, inordinate, outrageous, over the top, profligate **11** exaggerated, extravagant, intemperate, overweening, uncalled-for, unjustified, unwarranted **12** distemperate, uncontrolled, unreasonable, unrestrained, unrestricted **13** self-indulgent **14** unconscionable

immoderately
06 unduly **08** to excess, wantonly **09** extremely **11** excessively **12** exorbitantly, inordinately, out of all cess, unreasonably **13** exaggeratedly, extravagantly, unjustifiably **14** unrestrainedly, without measure

immoderation
06 excess **08** unreason **10** inordinacy, lavishness **11** dissipation, exorbitance, prodigality, unrestraint **12** extravagance, intemperance **13** excessiveness **14** immoderateness, overindulgence

immodest
04 bold, lewd **05** cocky, fresh, saucy **06** brazen, cheeky, coarse, risqué **07** forward, immoral, obscene **08** boastful, improper, impudent, indecent **09** revealing, shameless **10** indecorous, indelicate

immodesty
04 gall **05** brass **08** audacity, boldness, impurity, lewdness, temerity **09** bawdiness, impudence, indecorum, obscenity **10** coarseness, impudicity, indelicacy **11** forwardness **13** shamelessness **14** indecorousness

immolate
04 burn, kill **05** offer **07** offer up **09** sacrifice

immoral
03 bad **04** base, blue, evil, lewd, vile **05** juicy, loose, wrong **06** impure, naught, sinful, wanton, wicked **07** corrupt, godless, obscene, raunchy, vicious **08** depraved, indecent, unhonest **09** debauched, dishonest, dissolute, nefarious, reprobate, unethical **10** degenerate, iniquitous, licentious **11** promiscuous **12** pornographic, questionable, unprincipled, unscrupulous **13** against nature

• **immoral act**
03 sin

immorality
03 sin **04** evil, vice **05** wrong **07** badness **08** impurity, iniquity, lewdness, vileness **09** depravity, indecency, obscenity, turpitude **10** corruption, debauchery, dishonesty, profligacy, sinfulness, wickedness, wrongdoing **11** pornography **12** indiscretion **13** dissoluteness **14** licentiousness

immortal
03 god **04** hero **05** deity, great **06** famous, genius **07** abiding, ageless, endless, eternal, goddess, lasting, undying **08** constant, divinity, enduring, fadeless, honoured, Olympian, timeless, unfading **09** amarantin, ambrosial, ceaseless, deathless, memorable, perennial, perpetual, well-known **10** celebrated, ever-living **11** divine being, everlasting, sempiternal **12** imperishable **13** distinguished, unforgettable **14** indestructible

immortality
04 fame **05** glory **06** honour, renown **08** eternity **09** celebrity, greatness **10** amritattva, perpetuity

11 distinction, endlessness, eternal life 12 gloriousness, timelessness 13 deathlessness, glorification 15 everlasting life, imperishability

immortalize
04 laud 07 glorify 08 enshrine, eternize 09 celebrate 10 eternalize, perpetuate 11 commemorate, memorialize

immovable
03 set 04 fast, firm, real 05 fixed, stuck 06 dogged, jammed, moored, rooted, secure, stable 07 adamant, riveted 08 anchored, constant, immobile, resolute, stubborn 09 impassive, obstinate, steadfast 10 determined, inflexible, motionless, unshakable, unswerving, unwavering, unyielding 11 unalterable, unshakeable 12 intransigent 14 marble-constant, uncompromising

immune
04 free, safe 05 clear, proof 06 exempt, secure, spared 07 excused 08 absolved, released, relieved 09 protected, resistant 12 invulnerable 13 unsusceptible

immunity
05 right 06 safety 07 freedom, liberty, licence, release 08 impunity 09 exception, exemption, franchise, indemnity, privilege 10 permission, protection, resistance 11 exoneration, inoculation, vaccination 12 immunization, mithridatism

immunization
03 jab 09 injection 10 protection 11 inoculation, vaccination

immunize
04 salt 06 inject, shield 07 protect 09 inoculate, safeguard, vaccinate

immure
04 cage, jail 06 enwall, shut up, wall in 07 confine, enclose 08 cloister, imprison 11 incarcerate 13 put behind bars

immutability
09 constancy, fixedness, stability 10 durability, permanence 13 immutableness, invariability 14 changelessness 15 unalterableness

immutable
05 fixed 06 stable 07 abiding, lasting 08 constant, enduring 09 permanent, perpetual, steadfast 10 changeless, inflexible, invariable, sacrosanct 11 unalterable 12 unchangeable

imp
03 elf 04 brat, limb, minx, puck, ympe 05 demon, devil, gamin, gnome, graft, Ralph, rogue, scamp, scion, shoot 06 goblin, rascal, sprite, urchin 09 hobgoblin, prankster, trickster 12 troublemaker 13 mischief-maker 15 flibbertigibbet

impact
03 act, fix, hit 04 bang, belt, blow, bump, dush, jolt, work 05 brunt, clash, crash, crush, force, knock, poise, power, shock, smash, souse 06 affect, effect, glance, strike 07 apply to, collide, contact, impinge, meaning, results 09 collision, influence 10 impression, percussion 12 consequences, significance 13 press together, repercussions 14 have an effect on, reverberations

impair
◇ *anagram indicator*
03 mar 04 harm, rust 05 alloy, blunt, craze, decay, spoil, wrong 06 damage, hinder, injure, lessen, reduce, weaken, worsen 07 cripple, disable, empeach, impeach, tarnish, vitiate, wear out 08 decrease, diminish, embezzle, emperish, enervate, enfeeble, wear away, wear down 09 undermine 10 debilitate 11 deteriorate

impaired
◇ *anagram indicator*
04 poor, weak 05 rusty, stale 06 faulty, flawed, spoilt 07 damaged, unsound, vicious 08 disabled, vitiated, weakened 09 defective, imperfect 10 challenged 11 handicapped

impairment
04 flaw, harm, hurt, ruin, wear 05 allay, fault, spoil 06 damage, injury 07 empeach, impeach 08 handicap, weakness 09 paralogia, reduction, vitiation 10 disability 11 disablement, dysfunction 13 deterioration
See also **sight**

impale
04 spit, stab 05 ganch, lance, prick, spear, spike, stick 06 gaunch, pierce, skewer 08 puncture, transfix 09 perforate 10 disembowel, run through

impalpable
04 airy, fine, thin 06 subtle 07 elusive, shadowy, tenuous 08 delicate 10 indistinct, intangible 11 incorporeal, indefinable 13 imperceptible, insubstantial, unsubstantial 15 inapprehensible

impart
04 give, lend, shed, tell 05 break, grant, offer 06 accord, assign, bestow, confer, convey, pass on, relate, report, reveal 07 divulge 08 disclose, transmit 09 make known 10 contribute 11 communicate

impartial
04 fair, just 05 equal 06 candid 07 neutral 08 detached, judicial, unbiased 09 equitable, objective 10 crossbench, even-handed, fair-minded, open-minded 11 non-partisan, uncommitted, unconcerned 12 unprejudiced 13 disinterested, dispassionate

impartiality
06 candor, equity 07 candour, justice 08 equality, fairness 10 detachment, dispassion, neutrality 11 disinterest, objectivity 12 unbiasedness 14 even-handedness, open-mindedness 15 non-partisanship

impassable
06 closed 07 blocked, invious 08 pathless 09 trackless 10 invincible, obstructed, unpassable 11 insuperable, unnavigable 12 impenetrable, unassailable, unvoyageable 13 untraversable 14 insurmountable

impasse
04 halt 06 log jam 07 dead end 08 cul-de-sac, deadlock 09 checkmate, stalemate 10 blind alley, standstill 15 Mexican standoff

impassioned
05 eager, fiery 06 ardent, fervid, heated 07 blazing, earnest, excited, fervent, furious, glowing, intense, rousing, violent 08 animated, forceful, inflamed, inspired, spirited, stirring, vehement, vigorous 09 emotional, heartfelt 10 passionate 12 enthusiastic

impassive
04 calm, cool 05 bland 06 stolid 07 stoical, unmoved 08 composed, laid-back 09 apathetic, immovable, unfeeling, unruffled 10 impassible, phlegmatic 11 emotionless, indifferent, unconcerned, unemotional, unemotioned, unexcitable, unflappable 13 dispassionate, imperturbable 14 expressionless

impassively
06 calmly, coolly 11 unfeelingly 13 apathetically, emotionlessly, imperturbably, unemotionally 14 phlegmatically 15 dispassionately

impatience
05 haste 07 anxiety 08 curtness, edginess, keenness, rashness 09 agitation, dysphoria, eagerness, shortness, tenseness 10 abruptness, indignance, uneasiness 11 brusqueness, impetuosity, intolerance, nervousness 12 excitability, irritability, restlessness
• **expression of impatience**
03 ach, dam, och, poh, tut 04 chut, damn, phew, pish, push, toot, tush, tuts, when 05 damme, devil, pshaw, toots 06 dammit, tut-tut 07 crimine, crimini 10 tilly-fally, tilly-vally 12 Donnerwetter, tilley-valley

impatient
04 curt, edgy, keen 05 angry, eager, hasty, narky, ratty, short, tense, testy 06 abrupt, snappy 07 anxious, brusque, fidgety, fretful, jittery, nervous 08 restless 09 excitable, impetuous, irritable, querulous 10 intolerant 11 hot-tempered 13 on tenterhooks, quick-tempered

impeach
05 blame 06 accuse, attack, charge, damage, hinder, impair, impede, impugn, indict, revile 07 arraign, censure, prevent 08 denounce 09 criticize, detriment, disparage, hindrance 10 impairment, prevention

impeachment
06 appeal, charge **10** accusation, indictment **11** arraignment **13** disparagement

impeccable
04 pure **05** exact **06** just so **07** correct, perfect, precise, upright **08** flawless, innocent **09** blameless, exemplary, faultless, stainless **10** immaculate **11** unblemished **12** squeaky clean **14** irreproachable

impecunious
04 poor **05** broke, needy, skint **07** boracic **08** dirt-poor, indigent, strapped **09** destitute, insolvent, penniless, penurious **10** cleaned out, stony-broke **12** impoverished, on your uppers **15** poverty-stricken

impedance
01 Z **09** hindrance
• measure of impedance
03 ohm

impede
03 bar, rub **04** clog, curb, slow, stop **05** block, check, delay **06** hamper, hinder, hogtie, hold up, retard, thwart **07** disrupt, empeach, impeach, trammel **08** encumber, handicap, hold back, incumber, obstruct, restrain, slow down, strangle

impediment
03 bar, bur, log, rub **04** burr, clog, curb, halt, snag **05** block, check **06** burden, defect, rubber **07** barrier, setback, stammer, stutter **08** handicap, obstacle **09** hindrance, restraint **10** difficulty **11** encumbrance, obstruction, restriction **14** stumbling-block

impedimenta
04 gear **05** stuff **06** things **07** baggage, effects, luggage **09** equipment **10** belongings **12** encumbrances **13** accoutrements, bits and pieces, paraphernalia

impel
03 put **04** goad, move, prod, push, spur, urge **05** drive, force, press **06** compel, excite, incite, oblige, prompt, propel, strike **07** inspire **08** get going, motivate, pressure **09** constrain, instigate, stimulate **10** pressurize

impending
04 near **05** close **06** at hand, coming, toward **07** brewing, looming **08** imminent, in the air, menacing, on the way, upcoming **11** approaching, forthcoming, in the offing, threatening **12** on the horizon **13** about to happen

impenetrable
04 dark **05** dense, solid, thick **07** cryptic, obscure **08** abstruse, airtight, baffling, puzzling **09** enigmatic, overgrown, recondite **10** adamantine, impassable, impervious, mysterious, soundproof **11** inscrutable **12** unfathomable **13** indiscernible **14** unintelligible

impenitence
08 defiance, obduracy **11** impenitency **12** stubbornness **15** hard-heartedness, incorrigibility

impenitent
07 defiant **08** hardened, obdurate **09** unabashed, unashamed **10** uncontrite, unreformed **11** remorseless, unrepentant **12** incorrigible, unregenerate, unremorseful **13** without regret **14** without remorse

imperative
05 vital **06** urgent **07** crucial **08** critical, pressing **09** essential, necessary **10** compulsory, obligatory, peremptory **13** authoritative, indispensable

imperceptible
04 fine, tiny **05** faint, small, vague **06** minute, slight, subtle **07** gradual, muffled, obscure, unclear **09** inaudible, minuscule **10** impalpable, indefinite, indistinct, negligible, unapparent **11** microscopic **12** undetectable, unnoticeable **13** inappreciable, indiscernible, infinitesimal

imperceptibly
06 slowly, subtly, unseen **08** bit by bit **09** gradually **10** insensibly **12** unnoticeably **13** inappreciably, indiscernibly, unobtrusively **14** little by little

imperfect
◇ *anagram indicator*
04 lame **06** broken, faulty, flawed **07** chipped, damaged, sketchy **08** impaired **09** blemished, defective, deficient, embryonic, unperfect **10** inadequate, incomplete **12** insufficient

imperfection
03 cut **04** blot, dent, flaw, kink, spot, tear **05** break, crack, fault, stain, taint **06** blotch, defect, foible, hickey, mackle **07** blemish, failing, scratch **08** weakness **09** deformity **10** deficiency, impairment, inadequacy **11** shortcoming **13** insufficiency **15** malconformation

imperial
03 Imp **05** grand, great, lofty, noble, regal, royal **06** august, kingly **07** queenly, stately, supreme **08** absolute, glorious, majestic, splendid **09** sovereign **10** commanding **11** magnificent, monarchical

imperialism
10 flag-waving **11** adventurism, colonialism, flag-wagging **12** expansionism **14** empire-building **15** acquisitiveness

imperil
04 harm, risk **06** expose, hazard, injure **08** endanger, threaten **10** compromise, jeopardize **11** put in danger, take a chance **12** expose to risk **13** put in jeopardy

imperious
06 lordly **07** haughty **08** arrogant, despotic **09** assertive, masterful **10** autocratic, commanding, high-handed, peremptory, tyrannical **11** dictatorial, domineering, overbearing, overweening

imperishable
07 abiding, eternal, undying **08** enduring, immortal, unfading **09** deathless, perennial, permanent, perpetual **11** everlasting **13** immarcescible, incorruptible, unforgettable **14** indestructible

impermanence
09 briefness **10** transience, transiency **11** elusiveness, inconstancy **12** ephemerality **13** temporariness **14** transitoriness

impermanent
05 brief **06** flying, mortal **07** elusive, passing, unfixed **08** fleeting, fugitive, unstable **09** ephemeral, fugacious, momentary, temporary, transient, unsettled **10** evanescent, fly-by-night, inconstant, perishable, short-lived, transitory

impermeable
05 proof **06** sealed **08** airtight, hermetic **09** damp-proof, non-porous, resistant **10** impassable, impervious, waterproof, watertight **11** greaseproof **12** impenetrable **14** water-repellent, water-resistant

impersonal
04 cold, cool **05** aloof, stiff **06** formal, frigid, remote, stuffy **07** distant, neutral **08** clinical, detached, official, unbiased **09** objective, unfeeling **11** unemotional **12** businesslike, unprejudiced **13** dispassionate

impersonally
06 fairly, justly **09** equitably, neutrally **11** objectively, without bias **12** open-mindedly **14** with an open mind **15** dispassionately

impersonate
02 do **03** act, ape **04** mock **05** mimic **06** embody, parody, pose as, send up **07** imitate, portray, present, take off **09** incarnate, pass off as **10** caricature **12** masquerade as

impersonation
05 apery, aping, fraud, spoof **06** parody, send-up **07** mimicry, take-off **09** burlesque, imitation **10** caricature, impression

impertinence
03 lip **04** face, gall, sass **05** brass, cheek, crust, mouth, nerve, sauce, snash **08** attitude, audacity, backchat, boldness, chutzpah, rudeness **09** brass neck, flippancy, impudence, insolence, intrusion **10** brazenness, disrespect, effrontery **11** discourtesy, forwardness, presumption

12 flippantness, impoliteness
13 shamelessness

impertinent
04 bold, pert, rude 05 brash, fresh, sassy, saucy 06 brazen, cheeky 07 forward 08 impolite, impudent, insolent 09 audacious, intrusive, shameless 10 unmannerly 11 ill-mannered 12 discourteous, presumptuous 13 disrespectful

imperturbability
04 cool 08 calmness, coolness 09 composure, sangfroid 10 equanimity 11 complacency 12 tranquillity 14 self-possession

imperturbable
04 calm, cool 06 serene 07 unfazed, unmoved 08 composed, laid-back, tranquil 09 collected, impassive, supercool, unruffled 10 complacent, unruffable, untroubled 11 unexcitable, unflappable 12 even-tempered 13 self-possessed 15 cool as a cucumber

impervious
05 proof, tight 06 closed, immune, opaque, sealed 07 unmoved 08 gas-tight, hermetic 09 damp-proof, dustproof, non-porous, rainproof, resistant, star-proof, untouched 10 light-proof, smokeproof, smoketight, steamtight, unaffected, waterproof, watertight 11 adiathermic, impermeable, showerproof 12 impenetrable, invulnerable

impetuosity
04 birr, dash, élan, rush 05 haste 08 rashness 09 hastiness, vehemence 10 impatience 11 spontaneity 12 recklessness 13 foolhardiness, impetuousness, impulsiveness 15 precipitateness, thoughtlessness

impetuous
04 rash 05 brash, fiery, hasty 06 sturdy 07 violent 08 headlong, reckless, tearaway 09 foolhardy, hot-headed, impatient, impulsive, unplanned 10 bull-headed, unreasoned, unthinking 11 precipitate, spontaneous, thoughtless 12 ill-conceived, uncontrolled 14 unpremeditated 15 spur-of-the-moment

impetuously
06 rashly 10 recklessly, vehemently 11 impulsively 12 passionately, unthinkingly 13 precipitately, spontaneously

impetus
04 birr, goad, push, send, spur 05 boost, drive, force, power, sweep, swing 06 energy, travel, urging 07 impulse 08 momentum, stimulus 09 actuation, incentive, influence 10 motivation 11 inspiration 13 encouragement

impiety
06 hubris 08 iniquity 09 blasphemy, profanity, sacrilege 10 irreligion, sinfulness, unholiness, wickedness 11 godlessness, irreverence, profaneness, ungodliness 15 unrighteousness

impinge
03 hit 04 beat, fall 05 souse, touch 06 affect, invade, strike 07 intrude, touch on 08 encroach, infringe, trespass 09 influence

impious
06 sinful, unholy, wicked 07 godless, profane, ungodly 09 hubristic 10 iniquitous, irreverent 11 blasphemous, irreligious, unrighteous 12 sacrilegious

impish
05 elfin, gamin 07 naughty, puckish, roguish, tricksy, waggish 08 devilish, rascally, sportive 09 pranksome, tricksome 10 frolicsome 11 mischievous

implacability
12 pitilessness, ruthlessness, vengefulness 13 inexorability, inflexibility, intransigence, mercilessness, rancorousness 14 implacableness, intractability, relentlessness 15 remorselessness, unforgivingness

implacable
05 cruel 06 deadly, mortal 07 adamant 08 pitiless, ruthless, vengeful 09 heartless, impacable, merciless, rancorous 10 inexorable, inflexible, relentless, unyielding 11 intractable, remorseless, unforgiving, unrelenting 12 intransigent, unappeasable 14 irreconcilable, uncompromising

implant
03 fix, put, sow 04 root 05 embed, graft, inset, place, plant 06 enrace, enroot, insert, instil 07 embosom, engraft, imbosom 09 inculcate, introduce 10 inseminate, transplant

implausible
04 lame, thin, weak 06 flimsy 07 dubious, suspect 08 doubtful, unlikely 10 far-fetched, improbable, incredible 11 transparent 12 questionable, unbelievable, unconvincing 13 hard to believe, inconceivable

implausibly
10 doubtfully, improbably, incredibly 12 questionably, unbelievably 13 inconceivably

implement
02 do 04 celt, comb, loom, rake, tool 05 apply, brush, dolly, flail, raker, razor, steel, whisk 06 anchor, device, effect, eolith, fulfil, gadget, pusher, ricker, ripple, sickle, taster, tedder 07 enforce, execute, grubber, perform, realize, utensil 08 carry out, complete, fly whisk, scuffler, shoehorn, spreader, squeegee, squilgee, tint tool 09 apparatus, appliance, discharge, fire-stick, fish slice, microlith, poop scoop, requisite, scarifier 10 accomplish, bring about, cultivator, extirpator, fish-carver, fish-trowel, gold-washer, instrument, loggerhead, snowplough, sucket fork, wheel brace 11 contrivance, road scraper, sucket spoon, turfing iron 13 pooper-scooper, put into action, put into effect 14 rostrocarinate

implementation
06 action 09 discharge, effecting, execution, operation 10 completion, fulfilling, fulfilment, performing 11 application, carrying-out, enforcement, performance, realization 14 accomplishment

implicate
◇ *anagram indicator*
05 imply 06 enfold 07 concern, connect, embroil, include, involve 08 entangle 09 associate, be a part of, be party to, inculpate 10 be a party to, compromise 11 incriminate

implicated
◇ *anagram indicator*
07 party to 08 included, involved 09 concerned, connected, embroiled, entangled, suspected 10 associated, inculpated 11 compromised, responsible 12 incriminated

implication
06 effect 07 meaning 08 overtone 09 deduction, inference, undertone 10 conclusion, connection, suggestion 11 association, consequence, embroilment, inculpation, insinuation, involvement 12 entanglement, ramification, repercussion, significance 13 incrimination 15 subintelligitur

implicit
04 full 05 sheer, tacit, total, utter 06 entire, hidden, hinted, latent, unsaid 07 implied, perfect 08 absolute, complete, indirect, inferred, inherent, positive, unspoken, unstated 09 deducible, entangled, steadfast, suggested 10 insinuated, understood, unreserved 11 intertwined, unexpressed, unqualified 12 unhesitating, wholehearted 13 unconditional, unquestioning

implicitly
06 firmly 07 totally, utterly 10 absolutely, completely 11 steadfastly 12 unreservedly 14 unhesitatingly, wholeheartedly 15 unconditionally, unquestioningly

implied
05 tacit 06 hinted 07 assumed 08 implicit, indirect, inherent, unspoken, unstated 09 suggested 10 insinuated, undeclared, understood 11 unexpressed

implore
03 ask, beg 04 pray 05 crave, plead, press 06 appeal, invoke 07 beseech, beseeke, conjure, entreat, request,

solicit **09** importune, obsecrate **10** supplicate

imply
04 hint, mean **05** infer, state **06** denote, enfold, entail, signal **07** connote, involve, point to, require, signify, suggest, suppose **08** indicate, intimate **09** implicate, insinuate, predicate **10** presuppose, understand **13** say indirectly

impolite
04 rude **05** crude, rough **06** abrupt, cheeky, coarse, vulgar **07** boorish, ill-bred, loutish, uncivil **08** insolent **09** unrefined **10** indecorous, ungracious, unladylike, unmannerly **11** bad-mannered, ill-mannered, impertinent, uncivilized **12** discourteous **13** disrespectful, inconsiderate, ungentlemanly

impolitely
06 rudely **07** crudely **09** uncivilly **10** insolently **12** indecorously, ungraciously **13** impertinently **14** discourteously **15** disrespectfully, inconsiderately

impoliteness
08 rudeness **09** crassness, gaucherie, indecorum, insolence, roughness **10** abruptness, bad manners, coarseness, disrespect, incivility, indelicacy **11** boorishness, discourtesy **12** churlishness, impertinence **14** indecorousness, unmannerliness

impolitic
04 daft, rash **06** unwise **07** foolish **09** ill-judged, imprudent, maladroit, misguided **10** ill-advised, indiscreet, unpoliced **11** inexpedient, injudicious **12** short-sighted, undiplomatic **13** ill-considered

import
03 nub **04** gist **05** buy in, drift, sense, state **06** amount, behove, convey, moment, ship in, thrust, weight **07** bring in, content, essence, meaning, message, portend, purport, signify **08** reimport, tendency **09** importing, intention, introduce, substance **10** importance **11** consequence, implication, seriousness **12** foreign goods, foreign trade, significance **13** buy from abroad, imported goods **14** foreign product **15** imported product

importance
04 mark, note, pith **05** power, state, value, worth **06** esteem, import, matter, status, weight **07** concern, urgency **08** eminence, gravitas, interest, prestige, standing **09** graveness, influence, magnitude, substance **10** prominence, usefulness **11** consequence, distinction **12** criticalness, significance **13** consideration, momentousness, signification **14** noteworthiness

• **anything of importance**
04 much

• **anything of minor importance**
02 by **03** bye

• **be of importance**
04 mean **06** matter

important
03 big, key, top **04** main **05** chief, grave, heavy, major, noted, vital **06** mighty, urgent, valued **07** big-time, capital, central, crucial, eminent, fateful, leading, notable, pivotal, pompous, primary, salient, seminal, serious, weighty **08** critical, esteemed, foremost, historic, material, powerful, priority, relevant, ultimate, valuable **09** essential, front-page, high-level, momentous, number one, of warrant, paramount, principal, prominent **10** meaningful, noteworthy, pre-eminent **11** epoch-making, far-reaching, fundamental, high-ranking, influential, outstanding, prestigious, significant, substantial **12** world-shaking **13** consequential, distinguished, of good warrant **15** world-shattering

importunate
06 dogged, urgent **08** annoying, pressing **09** impatient, insistent, tenacious **10** burdensome, persistent **11** inopportune, troublesome **12** pertinacious

importune
03 beg, dun, ply **04** prig, urge **05** annoy, beset, hound, press **06** appeal, badger, cajole, harass, import, pester, plague, urgent **07** besiege, request, signify, solicit **08** untimely **09** flagitate, plead with **10** burdensome, lay siege to, resistless, supplicate **11** inopportune

importunity
06 urging **07** urgency **08** cajolery, hounding, pressing **09** harassing, pestering **10** entreaties, harassment, importance, insistence **11** persistence **12** solicitation

impose
03 fix, lay, put, set **04** levy, palm **05** abuse, apply, clamp, exact, foist, force, lay on, place, put on **06** burden, butt in, charge, decree, enjoin, impone, saddle, thrust **07** break in, command, enforce, exploit, inflict, intrude, mislead, obtrude, place on, presume, put over, put upon **08** encroach, encumber, trespass **09** establish, institute, introduce **13** force yourself, take liberties **14** thrust yourself **15** take advantage of

imposing
05 grand, lofty **06** august **07** stately **08** majestic, matronly, specious, splendid, striking **09** deceptive, dignified, grandiose, mausolean **10** commanding, impressive, statuesque **12** high-sounding

imposition
03 hum, tax **04** bite, duty, levy, load, task, toll **05** impot **06** burden, charge, decree, fixing, hassle, pensum, tariff **07** levying, setting **08** exaction, pressure, trickery **09** intrusion **10** constraint, infliction, punishment **11** application, encumbrance, enforcement, institution, trespassing **12** encroachment, introduction **13** establishment

See also **tax**

impossibility
04 no-no **09** absurdity, inability **10** non-starter **11** unviability **12** hopelessness, untenability **13** ludicrousness **14** ridiculousness **15** unacceptability

impossible
03 out **06** absurd **08** hopeless **09** beyond you, insoluble, ludicrous **10** incredible, outlandish, ridiculous, unbearable, unworkable **11** intolerable, prohibitive, unthinkable **12** pigs might fly, preposterous, unacceptable, unachievable, unattainable, unbelievable, unimaginable, unobtainable, unrealizable, unreasonable **13** anybody's guess, impracticable, inconceivable **15** and pigs might fly

impostor
04 fake, idol, sham **05** cheat, fraud, quack, rogue **06** bunyip, con man, faitor, phoney, ringer **07** deluder, faitour **08** deceiver, phantasm, swindler **09** charlatan, defrauder, pretender, trickster **10** hoodwinker, mountebank **12** impersonator

imposture
03 con **04** hoax, sham **05** cheat, fraud, trick **07** swindle **08** artifice, con trick, pretence, quackery **09** deception **10** imposition **11** counterfeit **13** impersonation

impotence
07 frailty **08** ligature, weakness **09** inability, infirmity, paralysis **10** disability, enervation, feebleness, inadequacy, incapacity, inefficacy **11** impuissance, uselessness **12** helplessness, incompetence **13** powerlessness **15** ineffectiveness

impotent
04 weak **05** frail **06** feeble, futile, infirm, unable **07** useless, worn out **08** crippled, disabled, helpless **09** enervated, exhausted, incapable, paralysed, powerless, worthless **10** impuissant, inadequate **11** debilitated, incompetent, ineffective **12** unrestrained **13** incapacitated

impound
04 cage **05** hem in, pen in, poind, seize **06** coop up, immure, keep in, lock up, remove, shut up **07** confine, pinfold **08** take away **10** commandeer, confiscate **11** appropriate, expropriate, incarcerate

impoverish
04 ruin **05** break, drain, waste **06** beggar, denude, reduce, weaken **07** deplete, exhaust **08** bankrupt, diminish, distress, make poor **09** pauperize **11** depauperate

impoverished
04 bare, bust, dead, poor **05** broke, empty, needy, skint, waste **06** barren, ruined **07** boracic, decayed, drained, reduced **08** bankrupt, desolate, dirt-poor, indigent, weakened **09** destitute, exhausted, penniless, penurious **10** cleaned out, distressed, down-and-out, stony-broke **11** depauperate, impecunious **12** on your uppers, without a bean **14** on your beam ends **15** poverty-stricken

impracticability
08 futility **11** unviability, uselessness **12** hopelessness **13** impossibility, infeasibility, unworkability **14** unsuitableness

impracticable
04 wild **07** useless **08** unviable, wild-eyed **09** non-viable, visionary **10** impossible, inoperable, unfeasible, unworkable **11** unrealistic **12** unachievable, unattainable, unmanageable **13** unpracticable, unserviceable

impractical
05 crazy **07** awkward **08** academic, romantic **09** visionary **10** idealistic, impossible, ivory-tower, starry-eyed, unworkable **11** doctrinaire, unrealistic **12** inconvenient **13** impracticable, unserviceable

impracticality
08 idealism **11** romanticism **12** hopelessness **13** impossibility, infeasibility, unworkability **14** unworkableness

imprecation
04 oath, pize **05** abuse, curse **08** anathema, goodyear **09** blasphemy, goodyears, profanity **10** execration **11** malediction **12** denunciation, vilification, vituperation

imprecise
04 hazy **05** loose, rough, vague **06** sloppy, woolly **07** blurred, inexact **09** ambiguous, equivocal, estimated **10** ill-defined, inaccurate, indefinite, inexplicit **11** approximate

imprecision
04 haze **08** estimate **09** ambiguity, vagueness **10** inaccuracy, sloppiness **11** inexactness **12** inexactitude **13** approximation

impregnable
04 safe **05** solid **06** secure, strong **09** fortified **10** adamantine, invincible, inviolable, unbeatable **11** irrefutable **12** impenetrable, inexpugnable, invulnerable, unassailable **13** unconquerable **14** indestructible, unquestionable

impregnate
03 pad **04** fill, melt, milt, soak **05** imbue, stain, steep **06** drench, infuse **07** pervade, suffuse **08** permeate, saturate **09** fecundate, fertilize, penetrate **10** inseminate **12** make pregnant

impregnation
07 imbuing **10** saturation **11** fecundation, fertilizing, fructifying **12** insemination **13** fertilization **14** fructification

impresario
07 manager, showman **08** director, producer, promoter **09** exhibitor, organizer

impress
03 gas, wow **04** drum, grab, mark, move, slay, stir, sway **05** knock, press, prest, print, rouse, stamp, touch **06** affect, deboss, emboss, excite, incuse, indent, instil, stress, strike **07** enforce, engrave, impresa, imprint, inspire, possess **08** astonish, bowl over, knock out **09** beglamour, bring home, emphasize, fix deeply, go over big, highlight, inculcate, influence, overwhelm, pressgang, underline, watermark **10** bear in upon, hammer home, prepossess **11** knock for six **13** go over big with

impressed
05 moved, taken, wowed **06** marked, struck **07** excited, grabbed, stamped, stirred, touched **08** affected, overawed **10** bowled over, influenced, knocked out **13** knocked for six

impression
04 dent, feel, idea, mark, note, ring, seal, sway **05** fancy, hunch, power, print, sense, sound, spoof, stamp, vibes **06** belief, effect, impact, memory, notion, parody, repute, send-up **07** control, feeling, imprint, mimicry, opinion, outline, tableau, take-off, thought **08** illusion, pressure, printing **09** awareness, burlesque, imitation, influence, sensation, suspicion **10** caricature, conviction, gut feeling **11** indentation **12** funny feeling, recollection **13** consciousness, impersonation

- **confused impression**

04 blur

- **give false impression**

03 lie

- **make an impression**

03 let **08** register **10** come across

impressionability
07 naivety **09** greenness **11** gullibility, receptivity, sensitivity **13** ingenuousness, receptiveness, vulnerability **14** suggestibility, susceptibility

impressionable
04 open, waxy **05** naive **07** pliable **08** gullible **09** ingenuous, mouldable, receptive, sensitive **10** responsive, vulnerable **11** persuadable, susceptible

impressive
04 epic **05** grand, noble **06** awsome, killer, moving, rotund, solemn, superb, whizzo, whizzy **07** awesome, rousing, stately **08** dazzling, dramatic, emphatic, exciting, imposing, lapidary, powerful, stirring, stonking, striking, touching **09** affecting, effective, inspiring **10** commanding, emphatical, monumental, portentous **11** magnificent, spectacular **12** awe-inspiring, breathtaking **13** scintillating

impressively
07 grandly **09** awesomely **10** powerfully, strikingly **11** effectively **12** emphatically **13** magnificently, spectacularly

imprint
03 fix **04** etch, logo, mark, sign, tool **05** badge, brand, power, press, print, stamp **06** burn in, effect, emblem, emboss **07** engrave, impress, meaning, results **08** colophon **09** character, establish, influence **10** impression **11** indentation, rubber-stamp **12** consequences, significance **13** repercussions **14** reverberations

See also **publisher**

imprison
◇ *containment indicator*
03 jug, lag, pen **04** cage, gaol, jail, quad, quod, shop **06** bang up, cage in, detain, immure, intern, lock up, lumber, shut in, shut up **07** confine, put away **08** restrain, send down **11** incarcerate, put in prison **12** send to prison

imprisoned
◇ *insertion indicator*
05 caged **06** inside, jailed **07** captive, immured, put away **08** banged up, confined, locked up, sent down **09** doing bird, doing time **10** behind bars **12** incarcerated **13** doing porridge **15** under lock and key

imprisonment
04 bird, life **05** bonds **06** duress **07** custody, durance, duresse **08** porridge **09** captivity, committal, detention **10** commitment, internment **11** confinement **13** incarceration

improbability
05 doubt **07** dubiety **11** dubiousness, uncertainty **12** doubtfulness, unlikelihood, unlikeliness **14** far-fetchedness, implausibility, ridiculousness

improbable
06 farfet **07** dubious **08** doubtful, unlikely **09** uncertain **10** far-fetched, incredible, marvellous, ridiculous **11** implausible **12** preposterous, questionable, unbelievable, unconvincing

impromptu
05 ad-lib **07** offhand **09** ad libitum, extempore, makeshift **10** improvised,

off the cuff, unprepared, unscripted
11 spontaneous, unrehearsed
13 spontaneously **14** extemporaneous

improper
◇ *anagram indicator*
04 rude **05** false, unfit, wrong
06 risqué, vulgar **07** immoral
08 immodest, indecent, shocking, unlawful, unseemly **09** erroneous, incorrect, irregular, unfitting
10 inadequate, indecorous, indelicate, indiscreet, out of place, unbecoming, unsuitable **11** incongruous, inopportune **12** illegitimate
13 inappropriate

improperly
◇ *anagram indicator*
05 amiss, wrong **06** rudely **07** falsely, wrongly **09** immorally **10** immodestly, indecently, unlawfully, unsuitably
11 erroneously, incorrectly, irregularly, unfittingly **12** indecorously, indiscreetly **13** incongruously
15 inappropriately

impropriety
04 slip **05** gaffe, lapse **07** blunder, faux pas, mistake **08** bad taste, solecism
09 gaucherie, immodesty, indecency, indecorum, vulgarity **11** incongruity
12 unseemliness **13** unsuitability
14 indecorousness

improve
04 beet, bete, do up, file, grow, help, mend, rise **05** amend, do for, emend, fix up, rally **06** better, buck up, enrich, look up, occupy, perk up, pick up, polish, reform, revamp, revise, uplift, work on **07** advance, correct, develop, enhance, perfect, recover, rectify, touch up, upgrade **08** increase, progress, put right, set right, work upon **09** get better, meliorate, modernize **10** ameliorate, convalesce, make better, recuperate, streamline
11 make headway **12** gain strength, mend your ways, rehabilitate
14 be on the up and up **15** give a facelift to

improvement
04 gain, rise **05** rally **06** growth, pick-up, profit, reform **07** advance, headway, upswing **08** increase, progress, recovery, revision
09 amendment, bettering, upgrading
10 betterment, correction, rectifying, refinement **11** development, enhancement, furtherance, modernizing, reformation
12 amelioration **13** rectification
14 rehabilitation

improvident
06 wastry **07** wastery **08** careless, heedless, prodigal, reckless, wasteful
09 imprudent, negligent, shiftless, unthrifty **10** profligate, thriftless, unprepared **11** extravagant, inattentive, Micawberish, spendthrift, thoughtless **12** uneconomical
13 underprepared

improvisation
04 vamp **05** ad-lib **06** improv, lash-up
08 ad hocery **09** ad-libbing, expedient, impromptu, invention, makeshift **11** spontaneity
13 autoschediasm, extemporizing
15 extemporization

improvise
03 jam **04** vamp, wing **05** ad-lib, rig up, run up **06** busk it, devise, invent, make do, noodle, wing it **07** concoct, knock up **08** contrive **09** play by ear
11 extemporize, play it by ear **13** throw together **14** cobble together, have a brainwave **15** speak off the cuff
• **improvise on**
04 ride

improvised
◇ *anagram indicator*
05 ad-lib, scrub **06** sudden **07** scratch
08 drumhead, on the fly
09 extempore, impromptu, makeshift
10 off-the-cuff, unprepared, unscripted **11** spontaneous, unrehearsed **12** extemporized
14 extemporaneous

imprudence
05 folly, haste **08** rashness
12 carelessness, heedlessness, recklessness **13** foolhardiness
15 thoughtlessness

imprudent
04 rash **05** hasty **06** unwise **07** foolish
08 careless, heedless, reckless
09 foolhardy, ill-judged, impolitic
10 ill-advised, incautious, indiscreet, unthinking **11** improvident, injudicious, thoughtless **12** short-sighted **13** ill-considered, inconsiderate, irresponsible

impudence
03 lip **04** face, gall, neck, sass
05 cheek, front, mouth, nerve, snash
06 bronze **07** hutzpah **08** attitude, boldness, chutzpah, pertness, rudeness **09** brass neck, insolence, sauciness **10** brazenness, effrontery
11 presumption **12** impertinence, impertinency

impudent
04 bold, calm, cool, pert, rude
05 bardy, cocky, fresh, hardy, nervy, sassy, saucy **06** brazen, cheeky, gallus
07 forward, gallows **08** immodest, impolite, insolent, malapert, petulant
09 audacious, barefaced, boldfaced, out of line, shameless **10** brass-faced, unblushing **11** impertinent
12 presumptuous **13** disrespectful

impugn
06 assail, attack, berate, oppose, resist, revile, vilify **07** censure, dispute, traduce **08** question, vilipend
09 challenge, criticize **10** vituperate
14 call in question

impulse
04 push, send, urge, whim, wish
05 drive, force, nisus, pulse, spike, surge **06** desire, impact, motion, motive, notion, signal, thrust
07 caprice, conatus, feeling, impetus, passion **08** instinct, momentum, movement, pressure, stimulus
09 brainwave, impulsion, incentive, premotion **10** compulsion, incitement, inducement, motivation, propulsion
11 inclination, stimulation, thought-wave
• **on impulse**
06 rashly **07** hastily **08** suddenly
10 recklessly **11** impatiently, impetuously, impulsively, intuitively
13 automatically, instinctively, irresponsibly, spontaneously, thoughtlessly **15** without thinking

impulsive
04 rash **05** hasty, quick **06** madcap, sudden **08** reckless **09** automatic, emotional, foolhardy, ill-judged, impatient, impetuous, intuitive
10 headstrong, passionate, unthinking
11 instinctive, precipitate, spontaneous, thoughtless **13** ill-considered

impulsively
06 rashly **07** hastily **08** suddenly
09 on impulse **10** recklessly
11 impatiently, impetuously, intuitively
13 automatically, instinctively, irresponsibly, spontaneously, thoughtlessly **15** without thinking

impulsiveness
05 haste **07** emotion, passion
08 instinct, rashness **09** hastiness, quickness **10** impatience, suddenness
11 impetuosity, spontaneity
12 recklessness **13** foolhardiness, impetuousness, intuitiveness, precipitation **15** precipitateness, thoughtlessness

impunity
07 amnesty, excusal, freedom, liberty, licence **08** immunity, security
09 exemption **10** permission
12 dispensation
• **with impunity**
06 freely, safely **08** in safety **11** without risk

impure
04 foul, lewd, sexy **05** bawdy, crude, dirty, mixed **06** coarse, drossy, erotic, filthy, ribald, risqué, smutty, vulgar
07 alloyed, blended, corrupt, debased, defiled, diluted, immoral, lustful, obscene, sullied, tainted, unclean, vicious **08** combined, depraved, immodest, improper, indecent, infected, polluted, unchaste
09 lecherous, offensive, shameless, unrefined **10** licentious, suggestive
11 adulterated, promiscuous
12 contaminated, pornographic

impurity
04 dirt, mark, smut, spot **05** blend, donor, dross, filth, grime, taint
07 crudity, mixture **08** dilution, foulness, lewdness **09** dirtiness, eroticism, immodesty, indecency, infection, looseness, obscenity,

pollutant, pollution, vulgarity **10** coarseness, corruption, debasement, immorality, unchastity **11** contaminant, foreign body, impropriety, lustfulness, pornography, promiscuity **12** adulteration **13** contamination, offensiveness, shamelessness **14** licentiousness

impute
03 lay, put **05** refer **06** assign, charge, credit, object **07** ascribe **08** accredit **09** attribute, put down to

in
◇ *hidden indicator*
◇ *insertion indicator*
01 i' **02** at, by, of, on **03** hip, per **04** cool, each, into, with **05** abode, among, every, funky, smart **06** alight, during, inside, modish, trendy, within **07** current, enclose, in vogue, popular, stylish, through **10** all the rage, enclosed by, throughout **11** fashionable **12** surrounded by **15** during the time of
• **in for**
12 due to receive **13** going to suffer
• **in itself**
04 in se **05** per se **13** intrinsically
• **in on**
07 aware of **09** clued up on **10** involved in **14** acquainted with
• **in with**
07 liked by **12** friendly with **15** on good terms with

inability
08 handicap, weakness **09** impotence **10** disability, inadequacy, incapacity, ineptitude **11** uselessness **12** incapability, incompetence **13** powerlessness **15** ineffectiveness

inaccessibility
08 distance **09** isolation **10** remoteness, separation **15** unattainability

inaccessible
06 remote **08** isolated **10** out of reach **11** beyond reach, god-forsaken, out of the way, unavailable, uncomatable, unget-at-able, unreachable **12** impenetrable, unattainable, uncomeatable, unfrequented **14** inapproachable, unapproachable

inaccuracy
04 flub, goof, slip **05** error, fault, gaffe **06** boo-boo, defect, howler, slip-up **07** blunder, clanger, erratum, mistake **11** corrigendum, imprecision, inexactness **12** mistakenness **13** erroneousness, unreliability **14** fallaciousness, miscalculation

inaccurate
◇ *anagram indicator*
03 out **05** false, loose, wrong **06** adrift, faulty, flawed, untrue **07** inexact, unsound **08** mistaken **09** defective, erroneous, imperfect, imprecise, incorrect **10** fallacious, unfaithful, unreliable
• **be inaccurate**
03 err

inaccurately
06 wildly **07** falsely, loosely, wrongly **08** clumsily **09** inexactly **10** carelessly, unreliably **11** defectively, erroneously, imperfectly, imprecisely, incorrectly **12** unfaithfully

inaction
04 rest **06** torpor **07** inertia **08** idleness, lethargy, slowness **09** passivity **10** immobility, inactivity, stagnation **12** lifelessness, sluggishness **14** motionlessness

inactivate
04 stop **07** cripple, disable, scupper **08** mothball, paralyse **09** stabilize **10** deactivate, immobilize

inactive
04 dead, idle, lazy, slow **05** inert, still **06** shadow, sleepy, torpid, unused **07** dormant, passive **08** immobile, indolent, lifeless, slothful, sluggish, stagnant, unactive **09** dead-alive, lethargic, quiescent, sedentary **10** motionless, stationary, unemployed, vegetating **11** hibernating, inoperative **12** dead-and-alive

inactivity
04 rest **05** sloth **06** stasis, torpor **07** inertia, languor, vacancy **08** abeyance, dormancy, dullness, idleness, inaction, laziness, lethargy **09** heaviness, indolence, inertness, lassitude, passivity **10** immobility, quiescence, quiescency, stagnation, vegetation **11** hibernation **12** dilatoriness, lifelessness, sluggishness, unemployment

inadequacy
04 flaw, lack, want **05** fault **06** dearth, defect, foible **07** deficit, failing, paucity, poverty **08** scarcity, shortage, weakness **09** inability **10** deficiency, inefficacy, inequality, meagreness, scantiness **11** shortcoming **12** imperfection, incapability, incompetence **13** defectiveness, insufficiency **15** ineffectiveness

inadequate
03 bad **04** poor **05** scant, short, unfit **06** faulty, meagre, scanty, scarce, skimpy, sparse, too few **07** sketchy, unequal, wanting **08** careless, derisory, inexpert, pathetic **09** defective, deficient, imperfect, incapable, niggardly, too little **11** incompetent, ineffective, ineffectual, substandard, unqualified **12** insufficient, unproficient **13** disappointing, inefficacious, not good enough **14** incommensurate, not up to scratch, unsatisfactory **15** thin on the ground

inadequately
05 badly **06** poorly, thinly **08** meagrely, scantily, skimpily, sparsely **09** sketchily **10** carelessly **11** imperfectly **14** insufficiently

inadmissible
08 improper **09** precluded **10** disallowed, immaterial, inapposite, irrelevant, prohibited **11** unallowable **12** unacceptable **13** inappropriate

inadvertent
06 chance **08** careless **09** negligent, unadvised, unguarded, unplanned, unwitting **10** accidental, unintended **11** inattentive, involuntary, thoughtless, unconscious **12** uncalculated **13** unintentional **14** unpremeditated

inadvertently
08 by chance, remissly **09** by mistake **10** by accident, carelessly, heedlessly, mistakenly **11** negligently, unwittingly **12** accidentally, unthinkingly **13** involuntarily, thoughtlessly, unconsciously **15** unintentionally

inadvisable
05 silly **06** unwise **07** foolish **09** ill-judged, imprudent, misguided **10** ill-advised, indiscreet **11** inexpedient, injudicious **13** ill-considered

inalienable
08 absolute, inherent **09** permanent **10** inviolable, sacrosanct **11** unremovable **12** unassailable **13** non-negotiable **14** untransferable **15** imprescriptible, non-transferable

inane
04 vain, void **05** empty, silly, vapid **06** absurd, drippy, futile, stupid, vacant **07** fatuous, foolish, idiotic, puerile, vacuous **08** mindless, trifling **09** frivolous, ludicrous, senseless, worthless **10** ridiculous **11** nonsensical **13** characterless, unintelligent

inanely
08 absurdly, futilely, stupidly **09** fatuously, foolishly, vacuously **11** idiotically, ludicrously **12** ridiculously **13** nonsensically

inanimate
04 dead, dull, lazy **05** inert **06** torpid, wooden **07** abiotic, defunct, dormant, extinct **08** immobile, inactive, lifeless, stagnant **09** apathetic, insensate, lethargic **10** insentient, spiritless **11** unconscious

inanity
05 folly **06** waffle **07** fatuity, vacancy, vacuity **08** daftness, vapidity **09** absurdity, asininity, emptiness, frivolity, puerility, silliness, stupidity **10** imbecility **11** foolishness **13** ludicrousness, senselessness **14** ridiculousness

inapplicable
05 inapt **08** unsuited **09** unrelated **10** immaterial, inapposite, irrelevant, unsuitable **11** unconnected **12** inconsequent **13** inappropriate

inapposite
10 immaterial, irrelevant, out of place, unsuitable **13** inappropriate

inappreciable
04 fine, tiny **05** faint, small, vague **06** minute, slight, subtle **07** gradual, muffled, obscure, unclear **09** inaudible, minuscule, priceless **10** impalpable, indefinite, indistinct, negligible, unapparent **11** microscopic **12** undetectable, unnoticeable **13** imperceptible, indiscernible, infinitesimal

inappropriate
05 inapt, undue **08** ill-timed, improper, tactless, unseemly, untimely **09** facetious, ill-fitted, ill-suited, tasteless, unfitting **10** inapposite, indecorous, irrelevant, malapropos, out of place, unbecoming, unsuitable **11** incongruous, inopportune **12** infelicitous **13** unappropriate

inappropriately
07 unfitly **08** off topic **10** malapropos, out of place, tactlessly, unsuitably **11** off the point, tastelessly **12** irrelevantly **13** incongruously, inopportunely **14** beside the point, infelicitously

inapt
05 unfit **07** unhappy **08** ill-timed, unsuited **09** ill-fitted, ill-suited **10** inapposite, irrelevant, malapropos, out of place, unsuitable **11** inopportune, unfortunate, unqualified **12** infelicitous **13** inappropriate

inarticulacy
08 mumbling **09** hesitancy, stumbling **10** stammering, stuttering **11** incoherence **14** indistinctness, speechlessness, tongue-tiedness

inarticulate
04 dumb, mute **07** blurred, halting, muffled, mumbled, quavery, shaking, unclear **08** hesitant **09** faltering, gibbering, soundless, stumbling, trembling, voiceless **10** disjointed, hesitating, incoherent, indistinct, speechless, stammering, stuttering, tongue-tied **14** unintelligible

inattention
07 absence **09** disregard, misregard **10** dreaminess, negligence **11** daydreaming, distraction **12** carelessness, heedlessness, unobservance **13** forgetfulness, preoccupation, unmindfulness **15** inattentiveness, thoughtlessness

inattentive
04 deaf **05** loose, slack **06** absent, asleep, dreamy, remiss **08** careless, distrait, heedless **09** forgetful, incurious, miles away, negligent, unmindful **10** distracted, neglectful, regardless **11** daydreaming, inadvertent, preoccupied, thoughtless **12** absent-minded, disregarding, unrespective **13** somewhere else, wool-gathering

inaudible
03 low **04** dull, soft **05** faint, muted **06** silent **07** muffled, mumbled, stifled **08** murmured, muttered **09** noiseless, whispered **10** indistinct **13** imperceptible

inaugural
05 first **06** maiden **07** initial, opening **08** exordial, original **09** launching **12** introductory

inaugurate
04 open **05** begin, set up, start **06** hansel, induct, invest, launch, ordain **07** handsel, install, instate, swear in, usher in **08** commence, dedicate, enthrone, get going, initiate **09** auspicate, institute, introduce, originate **10** commission, consecrate **11** set in motion **13** admit to office **14** open officially

inauguration
06 launch **07** opening **08** starting **09** induction, launching, setting up **10** initiation, installing, ordination, swearing-in **11** institution, investiture **12** commencement, consecration, enthronement, installation

inauspicious
03 bad **05** black **07** ominous, unlucky **08** ill-fated, sinister, untimely **09** ill-boding, ill-omened **10** ill-starred, sinistrous **11** threatening, unfortunate, unpromising **12** discouraging, infelicitous, unfavourable, unpropitious

inborn
06 inbred, innate, native **07** connate, natural **08** inherent, untaught **09** ingrained, inherited, intuitive **10** congenital, hereditary, ingenerate **11** instinctive, in the family

inbred
03 sib **06** innate, native **07** connate, natural **08** inherent **09** incrossed, ingrained **10** ingenerate **14** constitutional

inbuilt
05 basic **07** built-in **08** inherent, integral **09** elemental, essential **11** constituent, fundamental

incalculable
04 vast **06** untold **07** endless, immense, sumless **08** enormous, infinite **09** boundless, countless, limitless, unlimited **10** numberless **11** inestimable, innumerable, measureless **12** immeasurable **13** unpredictable, without number

incandescence
04 fire, glow, leam **05** gleam, glory **07** glimmer, sunglow **08** outflush, radiance, richness **09** afterglow, splendour, vividness **10** brightness, brilliance, luminosity **15** phosphorescence

incandescent
03 mad **05** aglow, angry, irate, livid **06** bright, fuming, raging **07** boiling, enraged, furious, glowing, shining **08** dazzling, frenzied, gleaming, incensed, inflamed, seething, sizzling, up in arms, white-hot **09** brilliant, in a lather, indignant **10** hopping mad, infuriated **14** purple with rage

incantation
03 hex **04** rune **05** chant, charm, spell **06** mantra **07** formula, karakia, mantram **10** invocation **11** abracadabra, conjuration **12** magic formula

incapable
◇ *anagram indicator*
04 weak **05** drunk, inept, unfit **06** feeble, unable **07** useless **08** helpless, impotent, unfitted, unsuited **09** powerless **10** inadequate **11** incompetent, ineffective, ineffectual, unqualified **12** disqualified, not hacking it **14** not up to scratch **15** out of your league

incapacitate
05 lay up **07** cripple, disable, scupper **08** paralyse **10** debilitate, disqualify, immobilize **14** put out of action

incapacitated
05 drunk, tipsy, unfit **06** laid up, unwell **08** crippled, disabled **09** hamstrung, paralysed, prostrate, scuppered **10** indisposed **11** immobilized, out of action **12** disqualified

incapacity
08 weakness **09** impotence, inability, unfitness **10** disability, feebleness, inadequacy, ineptitude, non-ability **11** uselessness **12** incapability, incompetence, incompetency **13** powerlessness **14** ineffectuality **15** ineffectiveness

incarcerate
04 cage, gaol, jail **06** bang up, commit, coop up, detain, encage, immure, intern, lock up, wall in **07** confine, impound, put away **08** imprison, restrain, restrict, send down **09** put in jail, put inside **11** put in prison

incarceration
04 jail **07** bondage, custody **09** captivity, detention, restraint **10** internment **11** confinement, restriction **12** imprisonment

incarnate
04 heal **05** human **07** fleshly **08** embodied, typified **09** corporeal, made flesh, personify **10** in the flesh **11** impersonate, incardinate, in human form, personified

incarnation
06 avatar **09** human form **10** embodiment **13** impersonation, manifestation **15** personification

Incarnations include:

04 Rama
07 Krishna
09 Jugannath
10 Juggernaut

incautious
04 rash **05** hasty **06** unwary **07** foolish **08** careless, cavalier,

reckless, wareless **09** foolhardy, ill-judged, imprudent, impulsive, unguarded **10** ill-advised, unthinking, unwatchful **11** inattentive, injudicious, precipitate, thoughtless, unobservant **13** ill-considered, inconsiderate, uncircumspect

incendiary
04 bomb, mine **06** charge **07** carcase, carcass, firebug, grenade **08** agitator, arsonist, fireball, firebomb, inciting, stirring **09** demagogue, explosive, firebrand, flammable, insurgent, pétroleur, seditious **10** fire-raiser, petrol bomb, pétroleuse, pyromaniac, rick-burner, subversive **11** combustible, dissentious, fire-raising, provocative **12** inflammatory, rabble-rouser **13** rabble-rousing, revolutionary **14** proceleusmatic **15** Molatov cocktail

incense
03 irk, vex **04** balm, rile, thus, urge **05** anger, aroma, myrrh, scent **06** enrage, excite, hassle, homage, incite, kindle, madden, nettle, stacte **07** agitate, benzoin, bouquet, inflame, perfume, provoke **08** irritate, pastille **09** adulation, aggravate, fragrance, infuriate, joss-stick **10** exasperate **12** frankincense **14** drive up the wall

incensed
03 mad **04** waxy **05** angry, cross, irate, ratty, spewy **06** choked, fuming, ireful **07** crooked, enraged, furious, ropable, stroppy, uptight **08** burned up, furibund, hairless, in a paddy, in a strop, maddened, up in arms, wrathful **09** in a lather, indignant, pissed off, raving mad, seeing red, steamed up, ticked off **10** aggravated, hopping mad, infuriated **11** disgruntled, exasperated, fit to be tied **12** on the warpath

incentive
04 bait, goad, lure, spur **06** carrot, motive, reason, reward **07** impetus **08** igniting, inciting, stimulus **09** stimulant, sweetener **10** enticement, incitation, incitement, inducement, motivation **11** encouraging **13** encouragement

inception
04 dawn, rise **05** birth, start **06** origin, outset **07** kick-off, opening **09** beginning **10** initiation **12** commencement, inauguration, installation **13** establishment

incessant
07 endless, eternal, non-stop **08** constant, unbroken, unending **09** ceaseless, continual, perpetual, recurrent, unceasing, weariless **10** continuous, persistent **11** everlasting, never-ending, unremitting **12** interminable **13** uninterrupted

incessantly
07 for ever **09** endlessly, eternally **10** constantly, unendingly **11** at every turn, ceaselessly, immediately, unceasingly **12** continuously, interminably **13** everlastingly, unremittingly **14** for ever and ever **15** twenty-four seven, uninterruptedly

incidence
04 rate **05** range **06** amount, degree, extent, to-fall **09** frequency **10** commonness, occurrence, prevalence

incident
03 bar, row **04** baur, bawr, page **05** brush, clash, event, fight, scene, upset **06** affair, comedy, fracas, matter, mishap, period **07** affaire, episode, falling, passage, subject **08** conflict, instance, occasion, skirmish **09** adventure, commotion, happening **10** consequent, experience, occurrence, proceeding **11** disturbance **12** circumstance **13** confrontation **14** unpleasantness

incidental
05 minor, petty, small **06** casual, chance, random **07** passing, related, trivial **08** by chance, striking **09** ancillary, attendant, impinging, occurrent, secondary **10** accidental, background, fortuitous, occasional, peripheral, subsidiary **11** concomitant, contingency, facultative, subordinate **12** accompanying, contributory, non-essential **13** supplementary

incidentally
07 apropos, by the by **08** by chance, by the way, casually **09** as an aside, en passant, in passing **10** by accident **11** secondarily **12** accidentally, digressively, episodically, fortuitously, unexpectedly **13** as a digression **14** coincidentally **15** parenthetically

incinerate
04 burn **07** cremate **09** carbonize **13** reduce to ashes

incineration
07 burning **09** cremation **13** carbonization **14** turning to ashes

incipient
07 nascent, newborn **08** inchoate, starting **09** beginning, embryonic, impending, inaugural, inceptive **10** commencing, developing **11** originating, rudimentary

incise
03 cut **04** etch, gash, nick, slit **05** carve, notch, slash **06** chisel, scribe, sculpt **07** cut into, engrave **09** sculpture

incision
03 cut **04** gash, nick, slit **05** notch, slash, wound **07** coupure, cutting, opening **08** colotomy, incisure, lobotomy, oncotomy **09** cystotomy, insection, iridotomy **10** craniotomy, discission, enterotomy, episiotomy, nephrotomy, phlebotomy, pleurotomy, sclerotomy, trenchancy **11** hysterotomy, myringotomy, thoracotomy, tracheotomy, venesection, venisection **12** pharyngotomy, tonsillotomy

incisive
04 acid, keen **05** acute, sharp **06** astute, biting, shrewd **07** caustic, cutting, mordant, pungent **08** piercing, stinging, surgical **09** sarcastic, trenchant **10** perceptive **11** penetrating **13** perspicacious

incisively
06 keenly, tartly **07** acutely, sharply **08** astutely **09** mordantly, pungently **10** piercingly **11** caustically, trenchantly **13** penetratingly, sarcastically

incisiveness
04 bite, edge **07** acidity, sarcasm **08** astucity, keenness, pungency, tartness **09** acuteness, sharpness **10** astuteness, trenchancy **11** penetration **12** perspicacity

incite
03 egg, hoi, hoy, put, set, sic, tar **04** abet, fuel, goad, poke, prod, sick, spur, urge, whet **05** drive, egg on, impel, prick, put on, rouse, tarre **06** arouse, excite, fillip, foment, induce, kindle, prompt, stir up, whip up, work up **07** actuate, agitate, animate, incense, inflame, premove, provoke, solicit **09** encourage, instigate, stimulate **13** stir the possum

incitement
04 goad, prod, spur, whet **05** drive, sting **06** motive, urging **07** impetus, rousing **08** stimulus **09** agitation, animation, incentive, onsetting, prompting **10** inducement, motivation, suggestion **11** instigation, provocation, stimulation **13** encouragement

inciting
08 stirring **09** hortative, hortatory, incentive, seditious **10** incendiary, subversive **11** provocative **12** inflammatory **13** rabble-rousing **14** proceleusmatic

incivility
08 rudeness **09** indignity, roughness, vulgarity **10** bad manners, coarseness, disrespect, inurbanity **11** boorishness, discourtesy, ill-breeding **12** impoliteness **14** unmannerliness

inclemency
07 rawness **08** foulness, severity **09** harshness, roughness **10** bitterness, storminess **15** tempestuousness

inclement
03 raw, wet **04** cold, foul **05** harsh, nasty, rough **06** bitter, severe, stormy **07** squally **08** blustery **11** intemperate, tempestuous

inclination
03 bow, maw, nod, set **04** bank, bend, bent, bias, cant, kant, lift, list, mind, rake, ramp, tilt **05** angle, pitch, slant, slope, study, taste, trend **06** ascent, liking, notion **07** incline, leaning

08 affinity, fondness, gradient, penchant, tendency **09** acclivity, affection, declivity, deviation, steepness **10** attraction, partiality, preference, proclivity, propension, propensity **11** disposition
12 predilection, propenseness
14 predisposition

• with inclination towards
02 on

incline
03 bow, dip, kip, nod, tip **04** bank, bend, bias, hade, heel, hill, lean, list, peck, rake, ramp, rise, slip, stay, sway, tend, tilt, veer **05** curve, offer, slant, slope, stoop, swell, swing, tempt, verge **06** affect, ascent, direct, prefer, shelve, steeve **07** descent, deviate, dispose, diverge, propend, recline **08** gradient, persuade **09** acclivity, declivity, influence, prejudice

inclined
03 apt **04** bent, wont **05** given, ready
06 liable, likely, minded **07** oblique, of a mind, sloping, tending, willing
08 disposed, proclive, propense
10 well-minded **11** predisposed

• be inclined
04 care

• inclined to
01 -y

include
◇ *containment indicator*
◇ *hidden indicator*
03 add **04** hold, span **05** add in, admit, carry, cover, enter, put in **06** embody, insert, reckon, rope in, take in
07 connote, contain, count in, embrace, enclose, involve, let in on, subsume, throw in **08** allow for, classify, comprise, conclude
09 encompass, introduce
10 comprehend **11** incorporate
15 take into account

including
◇ *containment indicator*
03 inc **04** incl, with **08** as well as, counting, included **11** inclusive of
12 together with

inclusion
08 addition **09** insertion
10 embodiment **11** involvement, subsumption **12** encompassing
13 comprehension, incorporation

inclusive
03 inc **04** full, incl **05** all-in **07** blanket, general, overall **08** catch-all, included, sweeping **09** enclosing **12** all-embracing, all-inclusive
13 comprehensive **14** across-the-board

incognito
06 masked, veiled **07** unknown
08 nameless, unmarked **09** disguised
10 in disguise **11** camouflaged
12 unidentified **14** unidentifiable, unrecognizable **15** under a false name

incognizant
07 unaware **08** ignorant
09 unknowing **10** uninformed
11 inattentive, unconscious, unobservant **12** unacquainted
13 unenlightened

incoherence
05 mix-up **06** jumble, muddle, mumble, mutter **07** stammer, stutter
08 wildness **09** confusion
10 brokenness **11** garbledness
12 illogicality **13** inconsistency
14 disjointedness

incoherent
05 loose **06** broken **07** garbled, jumbled, mixed-up, muddled, mumbled, unclear **08** confused, muttered, rambling, wandered
09 illogical, rigmarole, scrambled, unjointed, wandering **10** disjointed, disordered, stammering, stuttering
11 unconnected **12** disconnected, inarticulate, inconsistent **14** skimble-skamble, unintelligible

incombustible
09 fireproof **10** flameproof, unburnable **12** non-flammable **13** fire-resistant **14** flame-resistant, flame-retardant, non-inflammable

income
03 pay **05** gains, means, rente, wages
06 inflow, profit, salary **07** arrival, profits, returns, revenue, takings
08 benefice, earnings, entrance, interest, proceeds, receipts, rent roll
09 allowance, comings-in, penny-rent
10 emoluments **12** independency, remuneration

incoming
03 new **04** next **06** coming
07 ensuing, revenue **08** accruing, arriving, entering, homeward
09 returning **10** succeeding
11 approaching

incommensurate
07 extreme, unequal **09** excessive
10 inadequate, inordinate
11 extravagant, inequitable
12 insufficient **15** incommensurable

incommunicable
09 ineffable **11** unspeakable, unutterable **12** unimpartable
13 indescribable, inexpressible

incomparable
06 superb **07** supreme **08** peerless
09 brilliant, matchless, nonpareil, paramount, unmatched **10** inimitable, unequalled, unrivalled **11** superlative, unsurpassed **12** second to none, unparalleled, without equal **13** beyond compare **15** without parallel

incomparably
05 by far **06** easily **08** superbly
09 eminently, supremely **10** far and away, infinitely **11** brilliantly
12 immeasurably **13** beyond compare, superlatively

incompatibility
05 clash **08** conflict, mismatch, variance **09** antipathy, disparity
10 antagonism, difference
11 discrepancy, incongruity
12 disagreement **13** contradiction, disparateness, inconsistency
14 uncongeniality

incompatible
05 alien, wrong **06** at odds
08 clashing, unsuited **09** disparate, dissonant, exclusive, repugnant **10** at variance, discordant, ill-matched, in conflict, insociable, mismatched
11 conflicting, disagreeing, ill-assorted, incongruous, uncongenial
12 antagonistic, inconsistent
13 contradictory **14** irreconcilable

incompetence
08 bungling **09** inability, ineptness, stupidity, unfitness **10** inadequacy, ineptitude, inequality **11** uselessness
12 incapability, inefficiency
13 insufficiency, unsuitability
14 ineffectuality **15** ineffectiveness, ineffectualness

incompetent
03 ill **04** naff, poxy, ropy **05** awful, flaky, lousy, pants, ropey, unfit
06 clumsy, crummy, stupid, unable
07 awkward, botched, the pits, useless
08 bungling, fumbling, handless, hopeless, inexpert, pathetic, schleppy, terrible **09** deficient, incapable, unskilful **10** amateurish, inadequate, unsuitable **11** a load of crap, ineffective, inefficient, unqualified **12** insufficient
14 a load of garbage, a load of rubbish

incomplete
◇ *tail deletion indicator*
04 half, part **05** short **06** broken, patchy **07** lacking, partial, pendant, pendent, scrappy, sketchy, wanting
08 abridged **09** defective, deficient, embryonic, half-baked, imperfect, piecemeal, shortened **10** catalectic, unfinished **11** fragmentary, rudimentary, undeveloped
14 unaccomplished

incomprehensible
04 deep **06** opaque **07** complex, obscure, unaware **08** abstruse, baffling, involved, profound, puzzling
09 enigmatic, limitless, recondite
10 mysterious, perplexing, unfamiliar, unreadable **11** complicated, double Dutch, inscrutable **12** impenetrable, mind-boggling, over your head, unfathomable **13** above your head, all Greek to you, inconceivable
14 unintelligible

incomprehension
09 ignorance, obscurity
10 complexity, profundity
11 unawareness **12** incognizance
13 unfamiliarity **14** inscrutability, mysteriousness **15** impenetrability

inconceivable
06 absurd **08** shocking **09** ludicrous, unheard-of **10** impossible, incredible, outrageous, ridiculous, staggering
11 implausible, unthinkable **12** mind-boggling, unbelievable, unimaginable

inconclusive
04 open, weak **05** vague
09 ambiguous, uncertain, undecided, unsettled **10** indecisive, indefinite, up in the air **11** left hanging
12 unconvincing, unsatisfying
13 indeterminate **14** open to question

incongruity
05 clash **08** conflict **09** disparity, inaptness **10** disharmony
11 discrepancy **13** contradiction, inconsistency, unsuitability
14 dissociability **15** dissociableness, incompatibility

incongruous
03 odd **06** absurd, at odds, patchy
07 jarring, strange **08** clashing, contrary, out of key **09** dissonant
10 out of place, unsuitable
11 conflicting, disharmonic, dissociable **12** incompatible, inconsistent, out of keeping
13 contradictory, inappropriate
14 irreconcilable

incongruously
08 off topic **10** out of place, unsuitably
11 off the point **12** irrelevantly
13 inopportunely **14** beside the point, infelicitously **15** inappropriately

inconsequential
05 minor, petty **07** trivial **08** trifling
09 small beer **10** immaterial, negligible
11 unimportant **13** inappreciable, insignificant **14** of no importance

inconsiderable
04 mean, weak **05** minor, petty, small
06 slight **07** nominal, trivial **08** trifling
10 negligible **11** unimportant
13 insignificant

inconsiderate
04 rash, rude **06** unkind **07** selfish
08 careless, heedless, tactless, uncaring **09** egotistic, imprudent
10 dismissive, intolerant, regardless, unthinking, unweighing **11** insensitive, light-minded, self-centred, thoughtless, unconcerned **12** light-hearted, uncharitable, undiscerning

inconsiderateness
08 rudeness **09** unconcern
10 unkindness **11** intolerance, selfishness **12** carelessness, tactlessness **13** insensitivity **15** self-centredness, thoughtlessness

inconsistency
04 odds **07** paradox **08** conflict, variance **09** disparity **10** divergence, fickleness, repugnance **11** contrariety, discrepancy, gallimaufry, incongruity, inconstancy, instability
12 disagreement, unsteadiness
13 contradiction, unreliability
14 changeableness **15** incompatibility

inconsistent
05 alien **06** at odds, fickle, spotty
07 erratic, jarring, varying **08** contrary, in and out, unstable, unsteady, variable
09 differing, irregular, mercurial, repugnant **10** at variance, capricious, changeable, discordant, dissimilar, inconstant, out of place **11** conflicting, incongruent, incongruous, unagreeable **12** incompatible, in opposition, out of keeping
13 contradictory, self-repugnant, unpredictable **14** disconformable, irreconcilable

inconsolable
08 desolate, wretched **09** miserable
10 despairing, devastated
11 heartbroken **12** disconsolate
13 broken-hearted, grief-stricken

inconspicuous
05 plain, quiet **06** hidden, low-key, modest **07** obscure **08** discreet, ordinary, retiring **09** concealed
10 indistinct, unassuming
11 camouflaged, unobtrusive
12 unremarkable **13** insignificant **15** in the background, undistinguished

inconspicuously
07 faintly, quietly **08** modestly
12 unassumingly **13** unobtrusively
15 insignificantly, in the background

inconstancy
05 range, shift, swing **06** change
08 wavering **09** variation **10** fickleness
11 alternation, ambivalence, fluctuation, instability, oscillation, vacillation, variability **12** irresolution, unsteadiness, variableness

inconstant
06 fickle, giglet, giglot **07** erratic, moonish, mutable, Protean, vagrant, varying, wayward **08** strumpet, unstable, unsteady, variable, volatile, wavering **09** changeful, faithless, fluxional, mercurial, uncertain, unsettled **10** capricious, changeable, fluxionary, irresolute, unfaithful, unreliable **11** fluctuating, vacillating
12 inconsistent, undependable

incontestable
04 sure **05** clear **07** certain, evident, obvious **08** cast-iron **10** undeniable
11 indubitable, irrefutable, self-evident
12 indisputable **14** unquestionable

incontinent
04 lewd **05** loose **06** wanton
07 lustful **08** unchaste **09** debauched, dissolute, lecherous, unbridled, unchecked **10** dissipated, lascivious, licentious, ungoverned, unstanched
11 immediately, promiscuous, unstaunched **12** uncontrolled, ungovernable, unrestrained
14 uncontrollable

incontrovertible
05 clear **07** certain **10** undeniable
11 beyond doubt, indubitable, irrefutable, self-evident
12 indisputable **13** incontestable
14 beyond question, unquestionable

incontrovertibly
07 clearly **09** certainly **10** undeniably
11 beyond doubt, indubitably, irrefutably **12** indisputably **14** beyond question, unquestionably

inconvenience
03 irk **04** bind, bore, burr, drag, fuss, pain **05** annoy, upset, worry
06 bother, burden, hassle, put out
07 disrupt, disturb, problem, trouble, turn-off **08** drawback, flea-bite, headache, nuisance, vexation
09 annoyance, disoblige, hindrance, incommode **10** difficulty, discommode, disruption, disutility, impose upon **11** awkwardness, disturbance, incommodity
12 disadvantage, discommodity

inconvenient
06 ungain **07** awkward **08** annoying, ill-timed, untimely, untoward, unwieldy
09 difficult **10** bothersome, cumbersome, unhandsome, unsuitable
11 inexpedient, inopportune, troublesome **12** embarrassing, incommodious, unmanageable, unseasonable **13** inappropriate

incorporate
◇ *containment indicator*
03 mix **04** fuse **05** blend, merge, unify, unite **06** absorb, embody, imbody, take in **07** build in, combine, contain, embrace, include, piece up, subsume
08 coalesce, incorpse **09** integrate, multiplex **10** amalgamate, assimilate
11 consolidate

incorporated
03 inc

incorporation
05 blend, union **06** fusion, merger
07 company, society **08** unifying
09 inclusion, subsuming
10 absorption, assumption, embodiment, federation
11 association, coalescence, combination, integration, unification
12 amalgamation, assimilation

incorporeal
04 aery **05** aerie **06** unreal **07** ghostly
08 bodiless, ethereal, illusory, spectral, unfleshy **09** spiritual, unfleshly
10 immaterial, intangible, phantasmal, phantasmic

incorrect
◇ *anagram indicator*
03 bad, ill **05** false, wrong **06** faulty, untrue **07** inexact, off beam
08 improper, mistaken, not right
09 erroneous, imprecise **10** fallacious, inaccurate, unsuitable, way off beam
12 illegitimate **13** inappropriate, ungrammatical

incorrectly
05 false, wrong **07** falsely, in error, wrongly **08** unfairly, unjustly **09** by mistake **10** mistakenly **11** erroneously, misguidedly **12** fallaciously, inaccurately **15** inappropriately

incorrectness
05 error **07** fallacy **09** falseness, wrongness **10** faultiness, inaccuracy

11 imprecision, inexactness, unsoundness 12 inexactitude, mistakenness, speciousness 13 erroneousness, impreciseness, unsuitability

incorrigible
08 hardened, hopeless 09 incurable 10 beyond hope, inveterate 12 irredeemable 13 dyed-in-the-wool, irreclaimable

incorruptibility
06 honour, virtue 07 honesty, probity 08 justness, morality, nobility 09 integrity 11 uprightness 15 trustworthiness

incorruptible
04 just 05 moral 06 honest 07 ethical, upright 08 straight, virtuous 10 honourable, unbribable 11 trustworthy 14 high-principled

increase
02 up 03 add, ech, eik, eke, ich, wax 04 eche, eech, gain, go up, grow, hike, rise, soar, wave 05 add to, boost, breed, bulge, climb, mount, raise, surge, swell, widen 06 bump up, deepen, expand, extend, flow-on, gather, growth, hike up, mark-up, profit, pump up, rocket, spiral, spread, step up, step-up, uplift, upturn 07 advance, augment, broaden, build up, build-up, develop, enhance, enlarge, further, improve, inflate, magnify, produce, progeny, prolong, scale up, upsurge 08 addition, escalate, heighten, interest, maximize, multiply, mushroom, progress, redouble, snowball 09 expansion, extension, increment, intensify, propagate, rocketing, skyrocket 10 accumulate, escalation, strengthen 11 development, enlargement, heightening, mushrooming, proliferate, snowballing 12 augmentation, bring to a head 13 become greater, proliferation 14 bring to the boil 15 be on the increase, intensification

increasingly
06 more so 10 all the more 11 more and more 12 cumulatively 13 exponentially, on the increase, progressively

incredible
04 tall 05 great, steep 06 absurd, unreal 07 amazing 08 smashing, terrific 09 fantastic, wonderful 10 astounding, cockamamie, far-fetched, formidable, impossible, improbable, marvellous, past belief, remarkable, surprising, tremendous 11 astonishing, cock-and-bull, exceptional, implausible, jaw-dropping, magnificent, unthinkable 12 beyond belief, mind-boggling, preposterous, unbelievable, unimaginable 13 extraordinary, inconceivable 14 out of this world

incredibly
04 very 06 highly 07 greatly 09 amazingly, extremely 10 impossibly, remarkably 11 unspeakably, wonderfully 12 marvellously, surprisingly, terrifically, tremendously, unbelievably, unimaginably 13 exceptionally, fantastically, inconceivably, inexpressibly 15 extraordinarily

incredulity
05 doubt 08 cynicism, distrust, mistrust, unbelief 09 amazement, disbelief, suspicion 10 scepticism

incredulous
07 cynical, dubious 08 doubtful, doubting 09 sceptical, uncertain 10 suspicious 11 distrustful, distrusting, unbelieving, unconvinced 12 disbelieving, unbelievable

increment
04 gain 06 growth, step-up 07 accrual 08 addendum, addition, increase 09 accretion, accrument, expansion, extension 10 growth ring, supplement 11 advancement, enlargement 12 augmentation

incriminate
05 blame, set up 06 accuse, charge, indict 07 arraign, impeach, involve 08 stitch up 09 implicate, inculpate 13 put the blame on

inculcate
03 fix 05 teach 06 infuse, instil, preach 07 din into, engrain, implant, impress, imprint 08 drum into 09 drill into 10 hammer into 12 indoctrinate

inculpate
05 blame 06 accuse, charge, indict 07 arraign, censure, impeach, involve 09 implicate 11 incriminate, recriminate 13 put the blame on

incumbent
04 up to 05 right 06 bearer, holder, member, parson 07 binding, officer 08 official 09 mandatory, necessary, overlying 10 compulsory, obligatory, prescribed 11 functionary, overhanging 12 office-bearer, office-holder 15 perpetual curate

incur
03 ren, rin, run 04 earn, gain, risk 05 run up 06 arouse, suffer 07 provoke, sustain 08 contract, meet with 10 experience

incurable
05 fatal 08 hardened, hopeless, terminal 10 beyond hope, inoperable, inveterate, remediless, unhealable, unrecuring 11 immedicable, untreatable 12 incorrigible 13 dyed-in-the-wool, unmedicinable

incurably
07 fatally 10 beyond hope, hopelessly, inoperably, terminally 12 incorrigibly, inveterately

incursion
04 raid, road, rode 05 foray, sally 06 attack, inroad, razzia, sortie 07 assault, inroads 08 invasion 09 intrusion, irruption, onslaught 11 penetration 12 infiltration

indebted
05 owing 07 obliged 08 beholden, grateful, thankful 09 obligated 12 appreciative

• be indebted
03 owe

indebtedness
09 gratitude 10 obligation 12 appreciation 15 debt of gratitude

indecency
07 crudity 08 foulness, impurity, lewdness 09 grossness, immodesty, indecorum, obscenity, vulgarity 10 coarseness 11 pornography 13 offensiveness 14 licentiousness

indecent
◇ *anagram indicator*
04 blue, foul, free, lewd, ripe 05 bawdy, crude, dirty, gross, nasty 06 coarse, filthy, fruity, impure, ribald, risqué, sleazy, smutty, sultry, vulgar 07 corrupt, immoral, obscene, raunchy 08 depraved, immodest, improper, scabrous, shocking, uncomely, unhonest, unseemly 09 off colour, offensive, perverted 10 degenerate, indecorous, indelicate, licentious, outrageous, suggestive, unbecoming, unsuitable 11 near the bone, Rabelaisian 12 pornographic, unrepeatable 13 inappropriate 14 close to the bone, near the knuckle

indecipherable
04 tiny 07 crabbed, cramped, unclear 09 illegible 10 indistinct, unreadable 14 unintelligible

indecision
05 doubt 07 swither 08 suspense, wavering 09 hesitancy 10 hesitation 11 ambivalence, fluctuation, uncertainty, vacillation 12 irresolution 13 tentativeness 14 indecisiveness 15 shilly-shallying

indecisive
04 open 06 unsure 07 unclear 08 doubtful, hesitant, wavering 09 faltering, tentative, uncertain, undecided, unsettled 10 ambivalent, hesitating, indefinite, in two minds, irresolute, undecisive, up in the air, weak-willed, wishy-washy 11 fluctuating, vacillating 12 feeble-minded, inconclusive, pussyfooting, undetermined 13 indeterminate 15 shilly-shallying

indecorous
04 rude 05 crude, rough 06 coarse, vulgar 07 boorish, ill-bred, naughty, uncivil, uncouth 08 churlish, immodest, impolite, improper, indecent, seemless, unseemly, untoward 09 graceless, tasteless, unfitting 10 high-kilted, in bad taste,

seemelesse, unladylike, unmannerly, unsuitable **11** ill-mannered, undignified **13** inappropriate, ungentlemanly

indecorum
07 crudity **08** bad taste, rudeness **09** immodesty, indecency, roughness, vulgarity **10** coarseness, uncivility **11** impropriety **12** impoliteness, unseemliness **13** tastelessness

indeed
01 I **02** ay, la **03** aye, e'en, nay, yah, yea, yes **04** deed, even, faix, just **05** faith, haith, marry, quite, sooth, truly **06** atweel, in fact, quotha, rather, really **07** for sure, insooth, in truth, quite so, soothly **08** actually, forsooth, to be sure **09** certainly, soothlich **10** absolutely, definitely, in good time, positively, undeniably **11** doubtlessly, undoubtedly **12** without doubt **13** for that matter, in anyone's book, in point of fact

indefatigable
06 dogged **07** patient, undying **08** diligent, tireless, untiring **09** unfailing, unresting, unwearied **10** relentless, unflagging, untireable, unwearying **11** indomitable, persevering, unremitting, unweariable **13** inexhaustible

indefatigably
08 doggedly **09** patiently **10** diligently, tirelessly **11** indomitably, unfailingly, unrestingly **12** relentlessly, unflaggingly **13** unremittingly

indefensible
05 wrong **06** faulty, flawed **07** exposed, unarmed **08** disarmed, specious **09** unguarded, untenable **10** unshielded, vulnerable **11** defenceless, ill-equipped, inexcusable, unfortified, unprotected **12** undefendable, unforgivable, unpardonable **13** insupportable, unjustifiable

indefinable
03 dim **04** hazy **05** vague **06** subtle **07** obscure, unclear **08** nameless **10** impalpable, indistinct, unrealized **13** indescribable, inexpressible

indefinite
04 hazy **05** fuzzy, loose, vague **07** blurred, general, inexact, obscure, unclear, unfixed, unknown **08** confused, doubtful, twilight **09** ambiguous, equivocal, imprecise, uncertain, undecided, undefined, unlimited, unsettled **10** ambivalent, ill-defined, indistinct, unresolved **11** nondescript, unspecified **12** inconclusive, undetermined **13** indeterminate

indefinitely
06 always **07** for ever **09** endlessly, eternally **11** ad infinitum, continually, permanently **12** without limit

indelible
04 fast **07** lasting **08** enduring, unfading **09** ingrained, permanent **12** imperishable, ineffaceable, ineradicable **14** indestructible

indelibly
10 enduringly **11** permanently **12** ineradicably **14** indestructibly

indelicacy
07 crudity **08** bad taste, rudeness **09** grossness, immodesty, indecency, obscenity, vulgarity **10** coarseness, smuttiness **11** impropriety **13** offensiveness, tastelessness **14** suggestiveness

indelicate
03 low **04** blue, rude, warm **05** crude, gross **06** coarse, risqué, sultry, vulgar **07** obscene **08** immodest, improper, indecent, tactless, unseemly, untoward **09** off-colour, offensive, tasteless **10** in bad taste, indecorous, suggestive, unbecoming **12** embarrassing

indemnify
03 pay **04** free **05** repay **06** exempt, insure, recoup, repair, secure **07** endorse, protect, requite, satisfy **09** guarantee, reimburse **10** compensate, remunerate, underwrite

indemnity
07 amnesty, redress **08** immunity, requital, security **09** assurance, exemption, guarantee, insurance, repayment, safeguard **10** protection, reparation **11** restitution **12** compensation, remuneration **13** reimbursement

indent
03 cut **04** dent, dint, mark, nick, pink **05** notch, order **06** ask for, crenel, demand, recess **07** bargain, impress, request, scallop, serrate **08** apply for, crenelle **09** penetrate **10** apprentice **11** requisition

indentation
03 cut, dip, pit **04** dent, nick **05** gouge, notch, sinus **06** crenel, dimple, furrow, groove, hollow, recess **08** crenelle **09** serration **10** depression **11** engrailment

indenture
04 bond, deal, deed **08** contract, covenant **09** agreement **10** commitment, settlement **11** certificate

independence
01 I **05** uhuru **06** swaraj **07** autarky, freedom, liberty **08** autonomy, home rule, self-rule **10** competency, separation **11** nationalism, sovereignty **12** independency, self-reliance **13** individualism **14** decolonization, self-government **15** self-sufficiency

independent
01 I **03** Ind **04** fair, free, just **07** neutral, private, unaided **08** absolute, autarkic, discrete, distinct, separate, unbiased **09** autarchic, freelance, impartial, liberated, objective, sovereign, unrelated **10** autogenous, autonomous, crossbench, individual, non-aligned, self-ruling, unattacked **11** self-reliant, unconnected **12** free-standing, free-thinking, self-standing, unprejudiced, unrestrained **13** autocephalous, disinterested, dispassionate, individualist, self-contained, self-governing, unconstrained **14** self-sufficient, self-supporting, unconventional **15** going your own way, individualistic, self-determining, self-legislating

independently
04 solo **05** alone **07** unaided **09** on your own, on your tod **10** by yourself, separately **12** autonomously, individually

indescribable
07 amazing **08** nameless **09** ineffable **10** incredible **11** exceptional, indefinable, inenarrable, undefinable, unspeakable, unutterable **13** extraordinary, inexpressible

indescribably
04 very **06** highly **07** greatly **09** amazingly, extremely **10** incredibly **11** unspeakably, unutterably **13** exceptionally, inexpressibly **15** extraordinarily

indestructible
05 tough **06** strong **07** abiding, durable, endless, eternal, lasting **08** enduring, immortal **09** permanent **10** undecaying **11** everlasting, infrangible, unbreakable **12** imperishable **15** tough as old boots

indeterminate
04 hazy **05** vague **07** inexact, unclear, unfixed, unknown **08** unstated, variable **09** ambiguous, equivocal, imprecise, open-ended, uncertain, undecided, undefined **10** ambivalent, ill-defined, indefinite **11** unspecified **12** inconclusive, undetermined **13** unpredictable

index
03 BMI, key, RPI **04** clue, dial, hand, hint, list, mark, nose, rate, sign **05** guide, power, ratio, scale, style, table, token **06** alidad, gnomon, needle, number **07** average, formula, pointer, preface, symptom **08** card file, exponent, fraction, prologue **09** catalogue, directory, indicator **10** difference, forefinger, indication, percentage, proportion **11** concordance **12** introduction **13** card catalogue **14** correspondence

India
01 I **03** IND
See also **state**

Indian *see* **American**; **Asian**

Indiana
02 IN **03** Ind

indicate
03 put, say, tip **04** mark, mean, note, read, shew, show, sign, tell **05** argue, arrow, imply, point, spell, state, utter, voice **06** affirm, assert, denote, evince, record, report, reveal, set out **07** declare, display, divulge, express, point to, present, signify, specify, suggest **08** announce, disclose, evidence, manifest, point out, register **09** designate, formulate, make known, represent **10** articulate **11** communicate **15** be symptomatic of

indicated
06 marked, needed **08** required **09** advisable, called-for, desirable, necessary, suggested **11** recommended

indication
03 nod **04** clue, hint, lead, mark, note, omen, shew, show, sign **05** token, trace **06** augury, oracle, record, signal **07** glimpse, pointer, portent, symptom, warning **08** endeixis, evidence, monument, register, signpost **10** denotement, expression, intimation, suggestion **11** explanation **13** demonstration, manifestation

indicative
07 typical **08** indicant, symbolic, telltale **10** denotative, exhibitive, indicatory, suggestive **11** significant, symptomatic **13** demonstrative, significative **14** characteristic

indicatively
07 as a sign **09** as a symbol, typically **10** as evidence **12** symbolically **13** significantly **14** as an expression **15** symptomatically

indicator
04 dial, hand, mark, sign **05** bezel, gauge, guide, index, meter, token **06** gnomon, marker, needle, signal, symbol **07** display, flasher, pointer **08** signpost **09** barometer **10** litmus test, turn signal

indict
04 dite **06** accuse, charge, summon **07** arraign, article, impeach, summons, trounce **09** inculpate, prosecute **10** put on trial **11** incriminate

indictment
06 charge, dittay **07** summons **10** accusation, allegation **11** arraignment, impeachment, inculpation, prosecution **13** incrimination, recrimination

indifference
06 apathy, phlegm, slight **08** coldness, coolness **09** disregard, unconcern **10** negligence, neutrality **11** impassivity, inattention, nonchalance **12** heedlessness **13** lack of concern, lack of feeling **14** lack of interest

indifferent
02 OK **03** bad **04** cold, cool, easy, fair, so-so **05** aloof, blasé **06** medium **07** average, callous, distant, easy-osy, neutral, not good, unmoved **08** adequate, careless, detached, heedless, inferior, jack easy, mediocre, middling, moderate, ordinary, passable, uncaring **09** apathetic, impassive, incurious, unexcited, unfeeling **10** insouciant, nonchalant, uninvolved **11** cold-hearted, pococurante, unconcerned, unemotional **12** could be worse, run of the mill, uninterested, unresponsive **13** could be better, disinterested, dispassionate, uninteresting, unsympathetic **14** unenthusiastic **15** all the same to you, undistinguished

indigence
04 need, want **06** penury **07** poverty **08** distress **09** necessity, privation **11** deprivation, destitution

indigenous
05 local **06** native **08** original **09** home-grown **10** aboriginal, vernacular **13** autochthonous

indigent
04 bust, poor **05** broke, needy, skint **06** in need, in want **08** dirt-poor **09** destitute, penniless, penurious **10** cleaned out, down and out, stony-broke **11** impecunious, necessitous, up against it **12** impoverished, on your uppers **13** in dire straits **14** on your beam ends **15** poverty-stricken

indigestion
07 acidity, apepsia, pyrosis **08** dyspepsy **09** dyspepsia, heartburn **10** cardialgia, water-brash **13** grass staggers **15** stomach staggers

indignant
03 mad **05** angry, cross, irate, livid, riled **06** bitter, fuming, heated, miffed, narked, peeved **07** annoyed, enraged, furious, in a huff **08** in a strop, incensed, outraged, up in arms, wrathful **09** aggrieved, resentful, steamed up **10** got the hump, infuriated **11** acrimonious, disgruntled, exasperated

indignantly
07 angrily, crossly, in a huff, irately **08** bitterly, up in arms **09** furiously, steamed up **11** resentfully **13** acrimoniously, reproachfully

indignation
03 ire **04** fury, rage **05** anger, pique, scorn, wrath **06** furore **07** dudgeon, outrage **08** contempt **09** annoyance **10** resentment **12** exasperation **15** saeva indignatio

indignity
04 snub **05** abuse, shame **06** injury, insult, slight **07** affront, obloquy, offence, outrage, putdown **08** contempt, disgrace, reproach **09** contumely, dishonour **10** disrespect, incivility, opprobrium **11** humiliation **12** cold shoulder, mistreatment, unworthiness **13** slap in the face **14** kick in the teeth

indigo
04 anil

indirect
02 by **03** bye **06** remote, squint, ungain, zigzag **07** curving, devious, mediate, oblique, winding **08** allusive, rambling, tortuous **09** ancillary, divergent, secondary, wandering **10** back-handed, circuitous, discursive, incidental, meandering, roundabout, subsidiary, unintended **11** subordinate **12** periphrastic **14** circumlocutory

indirectly
05 round **09** deviously, hintingly, obliquely **10** allusively, second-hand **12** at second hand, incidentally, roundaboutly

indiscernible
04 tiny **06** hidden, minute **07** obscure, unclear **09** invisible, minuscule **10** impalpable, indistinct, unapparent **11** microscopic **12** undetectable, unnoticeable **13** imperceptible, undiscernible

indiscreet
04 rash **05** hasty **06** unwary, unwise **07** foolish **08** careless, heedless, immodest, reckless, tactless **09** foolhardy, ill-judged, impolitic, imprudent, shameless **10** ill-advised, indelicate, unthinking **11** injudicious, insensitive **12** undiplomatic **13** ill-considered

indiscreetly
06 rashly **08** unwisely **09** foolishly **10** carelessly, heedlessly, immodestly, recklessly, tactlessly **11** shamelessly **12** indelicately **13** insensitively

indiscretion
04 boob, flub, slip **05** error, folly, gaffe, lapse **06** slip-up **07** blunder, faux pas, mistake **08** rashness **09** immodesty **10** imprudence, indelicacy **11** foolishness **12** carelessness, recklessness, tactlessness **13** shamelessness

indiscriminate
◇ *anagram indicator*
05 mixed **06** motley, random, varied **07** aimless, chaotic, diverse, general **08** careless, confused, pell-mell, sweeping **09** haphazard, hit or miss, wholesale **10** hit and miss **11** promiscuous, scattershot, unselective **12** unmethodical, unrespective, unsystematic **13** miscellaneous

indiscriminately
08 randomly **09** aimlessly, generally, in the mass, wholesale **10** carelessly **11** haphazardly **13** unselectively **14** unmethodically **15** indistinctively

indispensable
03 key **05** basic, vital **06** needed **07** crucial, needful **08** required **09** essential, important, necessary, requisite **10** absolutely, imperative **11** fundamental

indisposed
03 ill **04** sick **05** crook, loath **06** ailing, averse, groggy, laid up, poorly, unwell **09** reluctant, unwilling **10** not of a mind, not willing, out of sorts **11** disinclined **12** not of a mind to **13** confined to bed, incapacitated **15** under the weather

indisposition
03 ail **06** malady **07** ailment, disease, dislike, illness **08** aversion, disorder, distaste, sickness **09** bad health, complaint, hesitancy, ill health **10** reluctance **13** unwillingness **14** disinclination, distemperature

indisputable
04 sure **06** liquid **07** certain, dead set **08** absolute, definite, positive **10** inarguable, unarguable, undeniable, undisputed **11** indubitable, irrefutable **13** incontestable **14** beyond question, uncontrollable, unquestionable

indissoluble
05 fixed, solid **07** abiding, binding, eternal, lasting **08** enduring **09** permanent **10** inviolable **11** inseparable, sempiternal, unbreakable **12** imperishable **13** incorruptible **14** indestructible

indistinct
03 dim, low **04** hazy, pale **05** blear, faded, faint, fuzzy, misty, muted, vague **06** grainy, woolly **07** blurred, clouded, distant, muffled, obscure, shadowy, unclear **08** confused, muttered **09** ambiguous, undefined **10** ill-defined, indefinite, out of focus **14** indecipherable, unintelligible
• **indistinct appearance**
04 blur, loom

indistinctly
05 dimly **06** hazily **07** fuzzily, vaguely **09** obscurely, unclearly **10** out of focus **14** unintelligibly

indistinguishable
04 same, twin **05** alike **06** cloned **09** identical **10** tantamount **13** indiscernible **15** interchangeable

indium
02 In

individual
03 one, own **04** body, idio-, lone, poll, sole, sort, soul, type, unit **05** being, party **06** fellow, mortal, person, proper, single, unique, versal **07** private, several, special, typical **08** creature, distinct, isolated, original, peculiar, personal, separate, singular, solitary, specific **09** character, exclusive **10** human being, particular, respective, subjective **11** distinctive, inseparable **12** personalized **13** idiosyncratic **14** characteristic

individualism
06 egoism **09** anarchism **11** freethought, originality **12** eccentricity, freethinking, independence, self-interest, self-reliance **13** egocentricity, self-direction **14** libertarianism

individualist
05 loner **06** egoist **08** bohemian, lone wolf, maverick, original **09** anarchist, eccentric **10** egocentric, free spirit **11** freethinker, independent, libertarian **13** nonconformist

individualistic
06 unique **07** special, typical **08** bohemian, egoistic, original **09** eccentric **10** egocentric, individual, particular, unorthodox **11** anarchistic, independent, libertarian, self-reliant **13** idiosyncratic, nonconformist **14** unconventional

individuality
07 oneness **08** identity, property **09** character, propriety **10** uniqueness **11** distinction, originality, peculiarity, personality, singularity **12** separateness **15** distinctiveness

individually
06 singly **08** one by one **09** in several, severally **10** one at a time, personally, separately **12** in particular, particularly **13** independently

indivisible
10 impartible **11** inseparable, intrenchant, undividable **12** indissoluble **14** indiscerptible

indoctrinate
05 drill, teach, train **06** ground, instil, school **07** impress **08** instruct **09** brainwash, inculcate **12** propagandize

indoctrination
08 drilling, teaching, training **09** grounding, schooling **10** catechesis, instilling **11** catechetics, inculcation, instruction **12** brainwashing

Indo-European
02 IE
See also **European**

indolence
05 sloth **06** apathy, torpor **07** inertia, languor **08** idleness, laziness, lethargy, shirking, slacking **09** heaviness, inertness, torpidity, torpitude **10** inactivity, torpidness **11** languidness **12** do-nothingism, listlessness, sluggishness

indolent
04 idle, lazy, slow **05** inert, slack **06** otiose, supine, torpid **07** languid, lumpish **08** bone-idle, fainéant, inactive, listless, slothful, sluggard, sluggish **09** apathetic, do-nothing, easy-going, lethargic, shiftless **13** lackadaisical

indomitable
04 bold, firm **05** brave **07** staunch, valiant **08** fearless, intrepid, resolute, stalwart **09** steadfast, undaunted **10** courageous, determined, invincible, unbeatable, unyielding **11** impregnable, lion-hearted, unflinching **12** intransigent, unassailable, undefeatable **13** unconquerable

Indonesia
02 RI **03** IDN

indubitable
04 sure **07** certain, evident, obvious **08** absolute **09** undoubted **10** unarguable, undeniable **11** beyond doubt, irrefutable, undoubtable **12** indisputable, irrebuttable, irrefragable, unanswerable **13** beyond dispute, incontestable **14** unquestionable

indubitably
05 truly **06** surely **07** clearly, no doubt **08** of course, probably **09** assuredly, certainly, doubtless, precisely **10** most likely, presumably **11** undoubtedly **12** indisputably, without doubt **14** unquestionably

induce
03 get **04** coax, draw, lead, move, urge **05** cause, force, impel, press, tempt **06** effect, incite, lead to, prompt, seduce **07** actuate, bring on, entreat, inspire, intreat, procure, produce, provoke **08** generate, motivate, occasion, persuade, talk into **09** encourage, influence, instigate, originate **10** bring about, give rise to **11** prevail upon, set in motion

inducement
04 bait, goad, lure, spur **05** bribe, cause, drink **06** carrot, motive, reason, reward **07** impetus **08** stimulus **09** incentive, influence, sweetener **10** attraction, back-hander, enticement, incitement, persuasion **11** seditionary **13** encouragement

induct
05 admit, place, stall **06** enlist, invest, ordain **07** install, swear in **08** enthrone, initiate **09** conscript, introduce **10** consecrate, inaugurate

inductance
01 L
• **measure of inductance**
01 H **05** henry

induction
07 epagoge, prelude **09** deduction, inference **10** conclusion, initiation, ordination **11** institution, investiture **12** consecration, enthronement, inauguration, installation, introduction **14** generalization

indulge
03 pet **05** allow, spoil, treat **06** cocker, cosset, cuiter, favour, humour, pamper, pettle, regale **07** cater to, gratify, revel in, satisfy, yield to **08** give in to, pander to, wallow in **09** give way to, make merry **11** go along with, luxuriate in, mollycoddle **14** give free rein to

indulgence
03 law **04** luxe, riot **05** favor, swing, treat **06** excess, excuse, favour, luxury,

pardon **08** lenience, spoiling **09** pampering, remission, tolerance **10** fulfilment, generosity, sensualism, sensuality **11** dissipation, forbearance **12** extravagance, immoderation, intemperance, satisfaction **13** dissoluteness, gratification, mollycoddling

indulgent
04 fond, kind **06** humane, tender **07** lenient, liberal, patient **08** generous, merciful, spoiling, tolerant **09** compliant, cosseting, easy-going, forgiving, humouring, pampering **10** forbearing, permissive **11** sympathetic **13** compassionate, mollycoddling, understanding

indulgently
06 fondly, kindly **08** humanely, tenderly **09** leniently, liberally, patiently, with mercy **10** generously, mercifully, tolerantly **12** with sympathy **14** with compassion **15** compassionately, sympathetically

industrial
05 trade **08** business **09** technical **10** commercial **13** manufacturing

industrialist
05 baron **06** tycoon **07** magnate **08** producer **09** financier **10** capitalist **12** manufacturer

industrious
04 busy, hard **05** deedy **06** active, dogged, steady **07** notable, on the go, skilful, workful, zealous **08** diligent, sedulous, studious, tireless, vigorous, worksome **09** assiduous, dedicated, energetic, laborious **10** busy as a bee, determined, persistent, productive **11** hard-working, persevering **13** conscientious, indefatigable

industriously
04 hard **08** doggedly, steadily **10** diligently, sedulously **11** assiduously **13** perseveringly **15** conscientiously

industry
04 line, toil, zeal **05** field, trade **06** effort, energy, labour, vigour **07** service **08** activity, business, commerce, hard work, sedulity **09** assiduity, diligence **10** enterprise, intentness, production, steadiness **11** application, persistence **12** perseverance, sedulousness, stickability, tirelessness **13** assiduousness, concentration, determination, laboriousness, manufacturing **14** productiveness **15** industriousness

inebriated
◇ *anagram indicator*
04 full, high, inky **05** drunk, happy, inked, lit up, merry, moppy, tight, tipsy, woozy **06** blotto, bombed, canned, corked, jarred, juiced, loaded, mortal, pished, ripped, rotten, soused, stewed, stinko, stoned, tiddly, wasted **07** bevvied, bonkers, bottled, crocked, drunken, half-cut, legless, maggoty, pickled, pie-eyed, sloshed, smashed, sozzled, squiffy, tiddled, wrecked **08** bibulous, footless, hammered, in liquor, juiced up, liquored, moon-eyed, ossified, sow-drunk, steaming, stocious, tanked up, whiffled, whistled **09** bladdered, crapulent, paralytic, plastered, shickered, up the pole, well-oiled **10** blind drunk, obfuscated **11** intoxicated, off your face **12** drunk as a lord, drunk as a newt, roaring drunk **13** drunk as a piper, drunk as a skunk, having had a few, under the table **14** Brahms and Liszt **15** one over the eight, the worse for wear, under the weather

inedible
03 bad, off **05** stale **06** deadly, rancid, rotten **07** harmful, noxious **09** poisonous, uneatable **10** inesculent **11** not fit to eat, unpalatable **12** indigestible, unconsumable

ineducable
08 indocile **11** unteachable **12** incorrigible

ineffable
07 fearful **10** remarkable **11** beyond words, unspeakable, unutterable **12** unimpartible **13** indescribable, inexpressible **14** incommunicable

ineffably
09 fearfully **10** absolutely, remarkably **11** beyond words, unspeakably, unutterably **13** indescribably, inexpressibly

ineffective
03 dud **04** idle, lame, vain, weak **05** inept **06** feeble, futile **07** useless **08** abortive, impotent **09** burned out, fruitless, powerless, to no avail, toothless, worthless **10** inadequate, profitless, unavailing, unpregnant **11** incompetent, ineffectual **12** unproductive, unsuccessful

ineffectiveness
08 futility, weakness **10** feebleness, inadequacy **11** uselessness **13** fruitlessness, worthlessness

ineffectual
03 wet **04** lame, vain, void, weak **05** inept, resty, wimpy **06** feeble, futile, unable **07** useless **08** abortive, chinless, feckless, impotent **09** fruitless, frustrate, powerless, worthless **10** inadequate, unavailing **11** incompetent **12** unproductive **13** inefficacious, lackadaisical

ineffectually
06 feebly, in vain, lamely, weakly **09** to no avail, uselessly **11** fruitlessly, to no purpose **14** unproductively, unsuccessfully

inefficacy
08 futility **10** inadequacy **11** uselessness **14** ineffectuality **15** ineffectiveness, ineffectualness

inefficiency
05 waste **06** laxity, muddle **09** slackness **10** ineptitude, negligence, sloppiness **12** carelessness, incompetence, wastefulness **15** disorganization

inefficient
03 lax **05** inept, slack **06** flabby, sloppy **08** careless, inexpert, slipshod, wasteful **09** negligent, shiftless **10** uneconomic **11** incompetent, ineffective, time-wasting, unorganized **12** disorganized, money-wasting **13** unworkmanlike

inelegant
04 ugly **05** crude, rough **06** clumsy, gauche, vulgar **07** awkward, ill-bred, uncouth **08** homespun, laboured, ungainly, unpolite **09** graceless, unrefined **10** uncultured, unfinished, ungraceful, unpolished **12** uncultivated **15** unsophisticated

ineligible
05 unfit **08** ruled out, unfitted, unworthy **10** unequipped, unsuitable **11** incompetent, undesirable, unqualified **12** disqualified, unacceptable

ineluctable
04 sure **05** fated **07** assured, certain **08** destined **10** ineludible, inevitable, inexorable **11** inescapable, irrevocable, unalterable, unavoidable

inept
◇ *anagram indicator*
04 void **05** flaky, lousy, silly **06** clumsy, stupid **07** awkward, foolish, useless **08** bungling, inexpert, pathetic **09** appalling, ham-fisted, incapable, maladroit, unskilful **10** cack-handed, inadequate, unsuitable **11** heavy-handed, incompetent **12** unsuccessful

ineptitude
07 fatuity **08** bungling **09** crassness, gaucherie, ineptness, stupidity, unfitness **10** clumsiness, gaucheness, incapacity **11** awkwardness, glaikitness, unhandiness, uselessness **12** incapability, incompetence, inexpertness **13** unskilfulness

inequality
03 rub **04** bias, odds, wave **05** whelk **08** contrast, imparity **09** disparity, diversity, imbalance, prejudice, roughness, variation **10** difference, inadequacy, unevenness **11** discrepancy, unequalness **12** incompetence, irregularity **13** disproportion, dissimilarity, nonconformity **14** discrimination

inequitable
06 biased, unfair, unjust **07** bigoted, partial, unequal **08** one-sided, partisan, wrongful **10** intolerant, prejudiced **12** preferential **14** discriminatory

inequity
04 bias **05** abuse **09** injustice, prejudice **10** inequality, partiality, unfairness, unjustness

12 maltreatment, mistreatment, one-sidedness, wrongfulness
14 discrimination

inert
04 cold, dead, dull, idle, lazy **05** slack, still **06** leaden, sleepy, static, supine, torpid **07** dormant, languid, passive, restive **08** comatose, immobile, inactive, indolent, lifeless, listless, sluggish, stagnant, thowless, unmoving **09** apathetic, inanimate, lethargic, nerveless **10** motionless, stationary, stock-still **12** unresponsive

inertia
05 sloth **06** apathy, torpor **07** languor **08** idleness, inaction, laziness, lethargy **09** indolence, inertness, passivity, stillness **10** immobility, inactivity, Oblomovism, stagnation
12 listlessness, slothfulness
14 motionlessness

inescapable
04 sure **05** fated **07** assured, certain **08** destined **10** ineludible, inevitable, inexorable **11** ineluctable, irrevocable, unalterable, unavoidable

inescapably
06 surely **09** assuredly, certainly
10 definitely, inevitably, inexorably
11 irrevocably, necessarily, unavoidably
13 automatically

inessential
05 extra, spare **06** luxury **07** surplus
08 needless, optional, trimming
09 accessory, appendage, extrinsic, redundant, secondary **10** accidental, expendable, extraneous, immaterial, irrelevant, unasked-for **11** dispensable, superfluity, superfluous, uncalled-for, unessential, unimportant, unnecessary
12 extravagance, non-essential

inestimable
04 vast **06** untold **07** immense
08 infinite, precious **09** priceless, unlimited **10** invaluable, prodigious
11 measureless, uncountable
12 immeasurable, incalculable, incomputable, mind-boggling, unfathomable **13** worth a fortune

inevitability
04 fact **05** truth **07** reality, safe bet
08 dead cert, validity **09** certainty, sure thing **14** matter of course

inevitable
04 sure **05** fated, fixed **07** assured, certain, decreed, fateful, settled, unshun'd **08** definite, destined, ordained **09** automatic, necessary, unavoided, unshunned **10** inexorable, infallible **11** ineluctable, inescapable, irrevocable, predestined, unalterable, unavoidable **13** unpreventable

inevitably
06 surely **09** assuredly, certainly, fatefully, presently **10** definitely, inexorably, infallibly, willy-nilly
11 inescapably, irrevocably, necessarily, unavoidably **13** automatically

inexact
03 lax **05** fuzzy, loose **06** untrue, woolly **07** muddled, of a sort, of sorts
09 erroneous, imprecise, incorrect
10 fallacious, inaccurate, indefinite, indistinct **11** approximate
13 indeterminate

inexactitude
05 error **07** blunder, mistake
09 looseness **10** inaccuracy, woolliness **11** imprecision, inexactness
13 approximation, impreciseness, incorrectness **14** indefiniteness, miscalculation

inexcusable
08 shameful **10** outrageous
11 blameworthy, intolerable
12 indefensible, unacceptable, unforgivable, unpardonable
13 reprehensible, unjustifiable

inexcusably
10 shamefully **12** indefensibly, outrageously, unacceptably
13 reprehensibly, unjustifiably

inexhaustible
07 endless **08** abundant, infinite, tireless, untiring **09** boundless, limitless, unbounded, unfailing, unlimited, unwearied, weariless
10 unflagging, unwearying
11 illimitable, measureless, never-ending **12** unrestricted
13 indefatigable

inexorable
04 sure **05** fated **07** certain
08 definite, destined, ordained
09 immovable, incessant, unceasing
10 implacable, inevitable, relentless, unyielding **11** ineluctable, inescapable, irrevocable, remorseless, unalterable, unavertable, unfaltering, unrelenting, unstoppable **12** intransigent, irresistible **13** unpreventable

inexorably
06 surely **09** certainly **10** definitely, implacably, inevitably, pitilessly
11 ineluctably, inescapably, irrevocably, mercilessly **12** irresistibly, relentlessly, resistlessly **13** remorselessly

inexpedient
05 wrong **06** unwise **07** foolish
09 ill-chosen, ill-judged, impolitic, imprudent, misguided, senseless
10 ill-advised, indiscreet, unsuitable
11 detrimental, impolitical, impractical, inadvisable, injudicious, unadvisable, undesirable
12 inconvenient, undiplomatic, unfavourable **13** inappropriate
15 disadvantageous

inexpensive
05 a snip, cheap **06** a steal, budget, modest **07** bargain, cut-rate, low-cost, reduced **08** dog-cheap, low-price, uncostly **09** dirt-cheap, low-priced, ten a penny **10** discounted, economical, reasonable **13** going for a song, on a shoestring

inexperience
07 newness, rawness **09** freshness, ignorance, innocence, naiveness
10 immaturity **11** strangeness
12 inexpertness **13** unfamiliarity

inexperienced
03 new, raw **04** puny **05** fresh, green, naive, young **06** callow, rookie, unseen **07** amateur **08** farouche, ignorant, immature, inexpert, innocent, unsifted, wide-eyed
09 fledgling, unfledged, unskilled, untrained, untutored **10** apprentice, fledgeling, unfamiliar, uninformed, unseasoned **11** new to the job, unexperient, unpractised, unqualified
12 probationary, unaccustomed, unacquainted **14** out of your depth, unsophisticate **15** unsophisticated
• **inexperienced person**
03 cub **04** baby **09** fledgling
10 fledgeling

inexpert
03 ham **05** inept **06** clumsy
07 amateur, awkward, unhandy
08 bungling, untaught **09** ham-fisted, maladroit, unskilful, unskilled, untrained, untutored **10** amateurish, blundering, cack-handed **11** incompetent, unpractised, unqualified
13 unworkmanlike **14** unprofessional

inexplicable
05 weird **07** strange **08** abstruse, baffling, puzzling **09** enigmatic, insoluble **10** incredible, miraculous, mysterious, mystifying, perplexing
11 bewildering, inscrutable
12 inextricable, unbelievable, unfathomable **13** inexplainable, unaccountable, unexplainable
14 unintelligible

inexplicably
09 strangely **10** bafflingly, incredibly, puzzlingly **12** miraculously, mysteriously, mystifyingly
13 unaccountably, unexplainably

inexpressible
08 nameless, termless **09** ineffable, unsayable **10** untellable **11** indefinable, unspeakable, unutterable
12 inexpressive **13** indescribable, undescribable **14** incommunicable

inexpressibly
09 ineffably **11** beyond words, unspeakably, unutterably
13 indescribably

inexpressive
04 cold, dead **05** blank, empty
06 vacant **07** deadpan **08** lifeless
09 impassive **10** poker-faced
11 emotionless, inscrutable
12 unexpressive **14** expressionless

inextinguishable
07 eternal, lasting, undying
08 enduring, immortal **09** deathless
11 everlasting, unquellable
12 imperishable, unquenchable
13 irrepressible, unconquerable
14 indestructible, unsuppressible

inextricable
08 confused **09** intricate **11** indivisible, inescapable, inseparable
12 indissoluble, inexplicable, irreversible **13** irretrievable

inextricably
11 indivisibly, inescapably, inseparably, intricately, irresolubly
12 indissolubly, irreversibly
13 irretrievably

infallibility
06 safety **08** accuracy, sureness
09 inerrancy, supremacy
10 perfection **11** omniscience, reliability **12** inerrability, unerringness
13 dependability, faultlessness, impeccability **14** irrefutability
15 trustworthiness

infallible
04 sure **05** sound **07** certain, perfect
08 accurate, fail-safe, flawless, reliable, sure-fire, unerring **09** faultless, foolproof, inerrable, unfailing
10 dependable, impeccable, inevitable **11** trustworthy

infamous
03 bad **04** base, evil, vile **06** wicked
07 hateful **08** ill-famed, shameful, shocking **09** dastardly, egregious, nefarious, notorious **10** abominable, detestable, iniquitous, outrageous, scandalous **11** disgraceful, ignominious, opprobrious
12 disreputable **13** discreditable, dishonourable

infamy
04 evil **05** shame **06** defame, ignomy
08 baseness, disgrace, ignominy, vileness, villainy **09** depravity, discredit, dishonour, disrepute, notoriety, turpitude **10** opprobrium, wickedness

infancy
04 dawn, rise **05** birth, roots, seeds, start, youth **06** cradle, nonage, origin, outset **07** genesis, origins, silence
08 babyhood **09** beginning, childhood, emergence, inception
11 early stages **12** commencement
14 speechlessness

infant
03 new, tot **04** babe, baby **05** bairn, child, early, sprog, young **07** dawning, growing, initial, nascent, newborn, toddler **08** emergent, immature, juvenile, nursling, youthful
09 beginning, fledgling, little one, nurseling **10** babe in arms, burgeoning, developing
11 rudimentary

infantile
05 young **07** babyish, puerile
08 childish, immature, juvenile, youthful **10** adolescent
11 undeveloped

infantry
02 LI **03** inf **06** pultan, pulton, pultun, tercio, tertia **07** phalanx, pultoon

infantryman
04 kern, naik, peon **05** grunt, kerne, Turco **06** ensign, evzone, Zouave
07 dragoon, footman, hoplite, pandoor, pandour **08** chasseur, doughboy **10** voetganger **11** foot soldier, landsknecht **13** beetle-crusher

infatuated
03 mad **06** assott, entêté, in love, sold on **07** entêtée, far gone, smitten, sweet on, wild for **08** assotted, besotted, mad about, obsessed, ravished
09 bewitched, daft about, enamoured, nuts about, wild about **10** bowled over, captivated, crazy about, enraptured, fascinated, lovestruck, mesmerized, potty about, spellbound
11 carried away **12** having a crush, having a thing, love-stricken

infatuation
04 love, mash, pash, rave **05** craze, crush, mania, shine, thing **07** passion
08 fixation, fondness **09** engoûment, obsession **10** engouement
11 fascination **12** besottedness

infect
03 mar, pox **04** clap, move, smit
05 spoil, taint, touch **06** affect, blight, canker, defile, excite, measle, pass on, poison **07** animate, corrupt, inspire, overrun, pervert, pollute, tainted
08 spread to, ulcerate **09** influence, stimulate, syphilize **10** parasitize
11 contaminate, tuberculize

infection
03 bug, wog **04** cold, germ, smit
05 taint, virus **06** blight, poison, sepsis
07 disease, fouling, illness **08** bacteria, epidemic, spoiling, tainting
09 complaint, condition, contagion, influence, pollution **10** corruption, defilement, pestilence
13 contamination

See also **disease**

infectious
05 toxic **06** deadly, septic, taking
07 noxious, smittle **08** catching, defiling, epidemic, virulent
09 infective, polluting, spreading
10 compelling, contagious, corrupting
12 communicable, irresistible
13 contaminating, transmissible, transmittable

infelicitous
03 sad **05** inapt **07** unhappy, unlucky
08 untimely, wretched **09** miserable, sorrowful, unfitting **10** despairing, unsuitable **11** incongruous, inopportune, unfortunate
13 inappropriate **15** disadvantageous

infer
05 educe, imply **06** allude, assume, deduce, derive, gather, induce, reason, render **07** conster, presume, surmise
08 conclude, construe **09** figure out
10 conjecture, generalize, understand
11 extrapolate

inference
07 reading, surmise **08** illation
09 corollary, deduction, reasoning
10 assumption, conclusion, conjecture
11 consequence, presumption
12 construction **13** extrapolation
14 contraposition, interpretation

inferior
03 bad, dog, inf, low **04** less, naff, poor, ropy, weak **05** awful, cheap, crook, grody, lousy, lower, lowly, minor, ropey
06 coarse, crummy, faulty, grotty, humble, impair, junior, lesser, menial, minion, ornery, second, shoddy, vassal
07 low-rent, of a sort, of sorts, provant, rubbish, shilpit, tinhorn, useless
08 hopeless, mediocre, paravail, pathetic, slipshod, underman
09 ancillary, cheap-jack, defective, deficient, imperfect, secondary, underling, underrate **10** fourth-rate, inadequate, low-quality, second-best, second-rate, subsidiary
11 incompetent, indifferent, second-class, subordinate, subservient, substandard, under-sawyer
12 unacceptable **14** unsatisfactory

inferiority
08 meanness, ropiness **09** lowliness
10 bad quality, crumminess, faultiness, grottiness, humbleness, inadequacy, low quality, mediocrity, shoddiness
11 poor quality **12** imperfection, incompetence, slovenliness, subservience **13** defectiveness, subordination **14** insignificance

infernal
04 evil, vile **06** cursed, damned, darned, dashed, Hadean, wicked
07 blasted, demonic, fecking, flaming, hellish, satanic, Stygian **08** accursed, all-fired, blinking, blooming, devilish, fiendish, flipping, wretched
09 atrocious, execrable
10 confounded, diabolical, malevolent, outrageous, sulphurous

infertile
04 arid **06** barren, effete **07** dried-up, parched, sterile **08** infecund
09 childless **10** unfruitful
11 unfructuous **12** unproductive
13 non-productive

infertility
07 aridity **08** aridness **09** sterility
10 barrenness, effeteness
11 infecundity **14** unfruitfulness

infest
03 dog **04** teem **05** beset, crawl, flood, swarm **06** harass, invade, pester, plague, ravage, throng **07** bristle, disturb, overrun, pervade
08 permeate, take over **09** penetrate
10 infiltrate, overspread, parasitize, trichinize **13** spread through

infestation
04 pest **05** crabs **06** blight, plague
07 scourge **09** pervasion, taeniasis
10 affliction, ascariasis, giardiasis, pestilence, visitation **11** molestation, overrunning, parasitosis, phthiriasis, shigellosis **12** infiltration, strongylosis,

uncinariasis **13** cysticercosis, helminthiasis, verminousness **14** trichinization

infested
04 mity **05** alive, batty, beset, buggy, lousy, midgy, mousy, ratty **06** chatty, grubby, mousey, ridden **07** haunted, overrun, plagued, rattish, ravaged, teeming, verminy, weevily **08** crawling, pervaded, swarming, thievish, vermined, weeviled, weevilly **09** bristling, permeated, verminous, weevilled **10** overspread, stylopized **11** helminthous, infiltrated **12** pestilential

infidel
05 pagan **06** giaour **07** atheist, heathen, heretic, sceptic **09** miscreant, sceptical **10** unbeliever **11** disbeliever, freethinker, nullifidian, unbelieving **13** irreligionist

infidelity
05 amour **06** affair **07** liaison, perfidy, romance **08** adultery, betrayal, cheating, intrigue **09** duplicity, falseness, treachery **10** disloyalty **12** relationship **13** faithlessness, fooling around, playing around **14** unfaithfulness

infiltrate
04 seep, slip, soak **05** enter **06** filter, invade **07** intrude, pervade **08** permeate **09** creep into, insinuate, penetrate, percolate

infiltration
07 entrism **08** entryism, invasion **09** intrusion, pervasion **10** permeation **11** insinuation, penetration, percolation

infiltrator
03 spy **07** entrist **08** entryist, intruder **09** subverter **10** insinuator, penetrator, subversive **11** seditionary **14** fifth columnist

infinite
03 all **04** huge, vast **05** total **06** untold **07** endless, immense **08** absolute, enormous **09** boundless, countless, extensive, limitless, unbounded, unlimited **10** bottomless, fathomless, numberless **11** illimitable, inestimable, innumerable, never-ending, uncountable **12** immeasurable, incalculable, interminable, unfathomable **13** inexhaustible, unconditioned, without number **14** indeterminable

infinitely
03 all **09** endlessly, immensely **10** absolutely, enormously, without end **11** ad infinitum, boundlessly, inestimably, limitlessly **12** interminably, without limit **13** inexhaustibly

infinitesimal
03 wee **04** tiny **05** teeny **06** minute **08** trifling **09** minuscule **10** negligible **11** microscopic **13** imperceptible, inappreciable, insignificant **14** inconsiderable

infinitesimally
06 tinily **08** minutely **10** negligibly **13** imperceptibly, inappreciably **15** insignificantly, microscopically

infinity
07 allness **08** eternity, vastness **09** immensity **10** perpetuity **11** endlessness **12** enormousness **13** boundlessness, countlessness, extensiveness, limitlessness

infirm
03 ill, old **04** lame, weak **05** frail, shaky **06** ailing, feeble, poorly, sickly, unwell, wobbly **07** doddery, failing **08** decrepit, disabled, unstable, unsteady **09** faltering **11** debilitated

infirmity
06 malady **07** ailment, disease, failing, frailty, illness **08** debility, disorder, frailtee, senility, sickness, weakness **09** complaint, frailness, ill health **10** feebleness, sickliness **11** decrepitude, dodderiness, instability **13** vulnerability

inflame
03 fan **04** fire, fuel, heat, rile, stir **05** anger, rouse **06** arouse, enrage, excite, foment, ignite, incite, kindle, madden, stir up, whip up, work up, worsen **07** agitate, incense, provoke **08** enkindle, increase **09** aggravate, impassion, infuriate, intensify, make worse, stimulate **10** exacerbate, exasperate

inflamed
03 het, hot, raw, red **04** sore **05** angry, heady **06** heated, septic **07** fevered, flushed, glowing, swollen **08** festered, feverish, infected, poisoned, reddened **11** carbuncular

inflammable
06 ardent **07** piceous **08** burnable **09** flammable, ignitable **10** tinder-like **11** combustible, combustious

inflammation
04 fire, heat, rash **07** burning, hotness, redness **08** eruption, soreness, swelling **09** festering, infection **10** irritation, tenderness **11** painfulness

Inflammations include:

03 RSI, sty
04 acne, boil, bubo, sore, stye
05 croup, felon, mange
06 ancome, angina, bunion, canker, otitis, quinsy, sepsis, thrush, ulitis
07 abscess, colitis, empyema, pink-eye, sycosis, tylosis, whitlow
08 bursitis, carditis, cynanche, cystitis, erythema, mastitis, myelitis, neuritis, orchitis, prunella, rhinitis, windburn
09 arthritis, carbuncle, enteritis, fasciitis, frostbite, gastritis, glossitis, hepatitis, keratitis, laminitis, nephritis, phlebitis, retinitis, septicity, sinusitis, vaginitis
10 bronchitis, cellulitis, dermatitis, erysipelas, gingivitis, intertrigo, laryngitis, meningitis, sore throat, tendinitis, tonsilitis, tracheitis, vasculitis
11 mad staggers, myocarditis, peritonitis, pharyngitis, pneumonitis, prickly heat, shin splints, spondylitis, tennis elbow, thyroiditis, tonsillitis
12 appendicitis, encephalitis, endocarditis, pancreatitis, pericarditis, vestibulitis
13 jogger's nipple, labyrinthitis
14 conjunctivitis, diverticulitis, housemaid's knee, sleepy staggers
15 gastroenteritis

inflammatory
04 sore **05** fiery, rabid **06** septic, tender **07** painful, riotous, swollen **08** allergic, anarchic, inciting, infected **09** demagogic, explosive, festering, inflaming, insurgent, seditious **10** incendiary, incitative, phlogistic **11** instigative, intemperate, provocative **13** rabble-rousing

inflate
05 blast, bloat, boost, elate, raise, swell **06** aerate, blow up, dilate, expand, extend, hike up, puff up, pump up, push up, step up **07** amplify, augment, balloon, bombast, distend, enlarge, magnify, puff out **08** escalate, increase, overrate, sufflate **09** intensify, overstate **10** aggrandize, daisy-chain, exaggerate **11** fill with air **12** overestimate

inflated
04 tall **05** tumid **06** puffed, raised, turgid **07** bloated, blown up, bombast, bullate, dilated, pompous, swollen, upblown **08** extended, puffed up, rhetoric, tumefied **09** ballooned, bombastic, distended, escalated, high-blown, increased, overblown, puffed out **10** euphuistic, rhetorical **11** exaggerated, intensified, overweening **12** magniloquent, ostentatious **13** grandiloquent

inflation
04 rise **08** afflatus, cost push, increase **09** expansion, turgidity **10** escalation **11** inspiration **14** hyperinflation
• **measure of inflation**
03 RPI

inflection
04 tone **05** pitch **06** ending, rhythm, stress **07** bending, cadence **08** emphasis **09** deviation **10** comparison, modulation **11** conjugation **12** change of tone

inflexibility
06 fixity **08** hardness, obduracy, rigidity **09** obstinacy, stiffness **10** stringency **12** immovability, immutability, incompliance, inelasticity, stubbornness, unsuppleness **13** immutableness, intransigence **14** intractability

inflexible
03 set **04** fast, firm, hard, iron, taut **05** fixed, rigid, solid, stern, stiff **06** ramrod, steely, strict **07** adamant, uniform **08** obdurate, pitiless, resolute, rigorous, standard, stubborn, unsupple **09** calcified, immovable, immutable, merciless, obstinate, stringent, tramlined, unbending, unelastic, unvarying **10** entrenched, implacable, intolerant, relentless, unbendable, unyielding **11** hard and fast, intractable **12** intransigent, standardized, unchangeable **13** dyed-in-the-wool **14** uncompromising **15** unaccommodating

inflict
03 hit, lay **04** deal, levy **05** apply, exact, lay on, wreak **06** burden, impose, strike, thrust **07** deal out, deliver, enforce, mete out **10** administer, perpetrate

infliction
05 worry **06** burden **07** penalty, trouble **08** delivery, exaction, wreaking **10** affliction, imposition, punishment **11** application, castigation, enforcement, retribution **12** chastisement, perpetration **14** administration

influence
03 say **04** bias, drag, hand, hold, mark, move, pull, rule, stir, sway, toll **05** alter, clout, force, guide, impel, mould, power, reign, rouse, shape **06** affect, arouse, change, colour, direct, effect, impact, incite, induce, inflow, modify, prompt, weight **07** control, dispose, holding, impress, incline, mastery **08** ambiance, ambience, dominate, guidance, impact on, interest, motivate, persuade, pressure, prestige, standing **09** authority, condition, determine, direction, dominance, have clout, instigate, manoeuvre, operation, prejudice, pull wires, restraint, supremacy, transform **10** domination, importance, manipulate **11** carry weight, pull strings **12** wheel and deal **14** have an effect on **15** hold over a barrel

• **easily influenced**
09 malleable

• **unlucky influence**
04 jinx

influential
06 moving, potent, strong **07** guiding, leading, telling, weighty **08** dominant, powerful **09** effective, important, inspiring, momentous **10** compelling, convincing, meaningful, persuasive **11** charismatic, controlling, far-reaching, heavyweight, prestigious, significant, substantial **12** instrumental **13** authoritative

influx
04 flow, rush, salt **05** flood **06** inflow, inrush, stream **07** arrival, ingress **08** invasion **09** accession, avalanche, incursion, influence, intrusion **10** inundation, visitation **11** instreaming

inform
◇ *homophone indicator*
03 rat **04** blab, blow, fink, leak, mark, nark, shop, sing, tell **05** avail, brand, brief, cue in, dob in, grass, peach, split, stamp **06** advise, betray, clue in, clue up, direct, fill in, impart, notify, relate, rumble, snitch, squeak, squeal, tell on, tip off, typify, wise up **07** animate, apprise, certify, educate, inspire, let know, partake, possess, put wise, resolve, sing out, stool on **08** acquaint, announce, deformed, denounce, formless, identify, instruct, permeate, unformed **09** advertise, advertize, enlighten, misshapen, recommend **10** give notice, illuminate, keep posted **11** blow the gaff, communicate, distinguish, incriminate **12** characterize **13** spill the beans **15** put in the picture, sing like a canary

informal
03 inf **04** easy, free **06** candid, casual, simple **07** invalid, natural, relaxed **08** everyday, familiar, friendly, unsolemn **09** easy-going, officious **10** colloquial, unofficial, vernacular **12** off the record **13** go-as-you-please, unceremonious, unpretentious

informality
04 ease **07** freedom **08** cosiness **10** casualness, homeliness, relaxation, simplicity **11** familiarity, naturalness **12** congeniality **15** approachability

informally
06 easily, freely, simply **08** casually **09** privately **10** familiarly, on the quiet **12** colloquially, off the record, unofficially **13** sans cérémonie **14** confidentially **15** unceremoniously, without ceremony

information
02 SP **03** gen, inf, wit **04** bumf, data, dope, file, info, news, poop, word **05** clues, facts, input, score **06** advice, notice, record, report **07** counsel, details, dossier, good oil, low-down, message, tidings, witting **08** briefing, bulletin, databank, database, evidence, izvestia **09** hard stuff, izvestiya, knowledge **10** communiqué, propaganda **11** instruction, particulars **12** intelligence **13** enlightenment

• **measure of information**
03 bit, nit **05** field, nepit, qubit **08** location **11** binary digit

informative
05 newsy **06** chatty, useful **07** gossipy, helpful **08** edifying **09** revealing **11** educational, forthcoming, instructive **12** constructive, enlightening, illuminating **13** communicative

informed
02 up **03** hep, hip **05** aware **06** au fait, expert, posted, primed, sussed, versed **07** abreast, briefed, clued-up, erudite, knowing, learned **08** educated, familiar, up to date, well-read **09** au courant, in the know, in the loop, up to speed **10** acquainted, conversant, well-versed **11** enlightened, intelligent, well-briefed **12** well-informed **13** authoritative, knowledgeable **14** well-researched

informer
03 dog, rat, spy **04** fink, mole, nark, nose, stag **05** grass, Judas, shelf, sneak, snout **06** dobber, canary, finger, fizgig, moiser, singer, snitch **07** fizzgig, grasser, peacher, pentito, stoolie, traitor **08** animator, approver, betrayer, inspirer, promoter, snitcher, squeaker, squealer, tell-tale **09** informant, sycophant, whisperer **10** discoverer, supergrass **11** stool pigeon **13** whistle-blower

infraction
06 breach **08** breaking **09** violation **12** encroachment, infringement **13** contravention, transgression

infrared
02 ir

infrequent
04 rare **06** scanty, seldom, sparse **07** unusual **08** sporadic, uncommon **09** spasmodic **10** occasional **11** exceptional **12** intermittent, like gold dust

infringe
04 defy **05** break, flout **06** ignore, invade **07** disobey, impinge, infract, intrude, violate **08** encroach, overstep, trespass **10** contravene, transgress

infringement
06 breach, piracy **07** evasion **08** breaking, defiance, invasion, trespass **09** intrusion, violation **10** infraction **12** disobedience, encroachment **13** contravention, non-compliance, non-observance, transgression

infuriate
03 bug, vex **04** miff, nark, rile **05** anger, annoy, get at, rouse **06** enrage, madden, needle, nettle, wind up **07** incense, inflame, provoke **08** drive mad, irritate **09** aggravate **10** antagonize, drive crazy, exasperate **12** drive bananas **13** make sparks fly **14** drive up the wall

infuriated
03 mad **04** wild **05** angry, cross, irate, radge, ratty, spewy, vexed **06** choked, heated, miffed, narked, peeved, roused **07** crooked, enraged, flaming, furious, ropable, stroppy, uptight, violent **08** agitated, burned up, hairless, in a paddy, incensed, maddened, provoked, up in arms **09** in a lather, irritated, pissed off, raving mad, seeing red, ticked off **10** aggravated, apoplectic, hopping mad **11** disgruntled, exasperated, fit to be tied **12** on the warpath **14** beside yourself

infuriating
05 pesky **07** galling **08** annoying **09** maddening, provoking, thwarting, vexatious **10** irritating, unbearable **11** aggravating, frustrating, intolerable **12** exasperating

infuse
◇ *insertion indicator*
04 brew, draw, fill, mash, mask, pour, shed, soak **05** imbue, immit, steep **06** inject, instil **07** implant, inspire, pervade **08** impart to, saturate **09** inculcate, introduce **11** breathe into

infusion
03 tea **04** brew, mate **06** saloop, tisane **07** malt tea, sage tea, soaking, uva-ursi **08** infusing, senna tea, steeping, tar water **09** sassafras **10** capillaire **11** inculcation, inspiration **12** implantation, instillation

ingenious
03 sly **04** neat, wily **05** adept, natty, nifty, sharp, slick, smart, witty **06** adroit, astute, bright, clever, crafty, gifted, patent, pretty, quaint, shrewd **07** cunning, skilful **08** creative, masterly, original, talented **09** brilliant, inventive **10** artificial, innovative **11** imaginative, resourceful

ingeniously
07 niftily **08** cleverly **09** cunningly, skilfully **10** originally **11** brilliantly **13** imaginatively

ingenuity
03 wit **04** gift **05** flair, knack, skill **06** engine, genius, ingine **07** cunning, faculty, slyness **08** deftness **09** invention, nattiness, niftiness, sharpness, slickness **10** adroitness, astuteness, cleverness, shrewdness **11** originality, skilfulness **12** creativeness **13** ingeniousness, ingenuousness, inventiveness **14** innovativeness **15** resourcefulness

ingenuous
04 open **05** frank, naive, plain **06** candid, direct, honest, simple **07** artless, genuine, sincere **08** freeborn, innocent, trustful, trusting **09** guileless **10** forthright, honourable **11** transparent **12** single-minded **13** undissembling **14** unsophisticate **15** unsophisticated

ingenuously
06 openly, simply **07** naively, plainly **08** directly, honestly **09** artlessly, genuinely, sincerely **10** innocently, trustingly **11** guilelessly **12** without guile

ingenuousness
07 candour, honesty, naiveté, naivety **08** openness **09** frankness, innocence, unreserve **10** directness **11** artlessness, genuineness **12** trustfulness **13** guilelessness **14** forthrightness

inglorious
06 unsung **07** ignoble, obscure, unknown **08** infamous, shameful, unheroic **10** irrenowned, mortifying, unhonoured **11** blameworthy, disgraceful, humiliating, ignominious **12** disreputable, unsuccessful **13** discreditable, dishonourable

ingrain
03 dye, fix **04** root **05** embed, imbue, infix **06** instil **07** build in, engrain, implant, impress, imprint **08** entrench **09** establish, ingrained

ingrained
05 fixed **06** inborn, inbred, rooted **07** built-in, inbuilt **08** embedded, inherent **09** immovable, implanted, permanent **10** deep-rooted, deep-seated, entrenched **11** established **12** ineradicable **13** thorough-going

ingratiate
04 fawn, sook **05** crawl, creep, toady **06** cozy up, grovel **07** flatter **08** play up to, soft-soap, suck up to **09** get in with **10** cozy up with **11** curry favour **12** bow and scrape **15** butter someone up

ingratiating
05 suave, sweet **06** greasy, silken **07** fawning, servile **08** crawling, toadying, unctuous **10** flattering, obsequious **11** bootlicking, sycophantic, time-serving **13** smooth-tongued

ingratitude
13 thanklessness **14** ungraciousness, ungratefulness, unthankfulness

ingredient
◇ *anagram indicator*
04 base, item, part, unit **05** basis **06** bottom, factor **07** amalgam, element, feature **09** component **11** constituent

See also **salad**

- **little boy ingredients**
05 frogs, snips **06** snails **14** puppy dogs' tails
- **little girl ingredients**
05 sugar, spice **13** all things nice **14** everything nice

ingress
05 entry **06** access **08** entrance **09** admission **10** admittance **12** means of entry, right of entry **15** means of approach

inhabit
05 dwell, haunt **06** live in, occupy, people, settle, stay in **07** denizen, dwell in, possess **08** colonize, populate, reside in **14** make your home in

inhabitable
09 habitable **11** fit to live in

inhabitant
03 son **05** child, towny **06** inmate, lodger, native, tenant **07** citizen, denizen, dweller, settler **08** habitant, occupant, occupier, resident **09** indweller **10** residenter **12** residentiary

inhabited
04 held **07** lived-in, peopled, settled **08** occupied, populate, populous, tenanted **09** colonized, developed, populated, possessed

inhalation
05 whiff **06** breath **07** suction **08** inhaling **09** breathing, spiration **11** inspiration, respiration

inhale
04 draw, take, toot, tout **05** whiff **06** draw in, suck in **07** inspire, respire **09** breathe in, inbreathe

inharmonious
03 out **04** sour **05** harsh **06** atonal, patchy **07** grating, jarring, raucous **08** clashing, jangling, perverse, strident, tuneless **09** dissonant, unmusical, untuneful **10** discordant, out of place, unfriendly **11** cacophonous, conflicting, disagreeing, inconsonant, quarrelsome, unmelodious **12** antipathetic, incompatible, unharmonious **13** contradictory, unsympathetic **14** irreconcilable

inherent
05 basic **06** inborn, inbred, innate, native, natura **07** built-in, inbuilt, natural, radical **08** immanent, resident **09** essential, ingrained, inherited, intrinsic **10** hereditary, inexistant, inexistent, in the blood, subsistent **11** fundamental, intrinsical

inherently
08 inwardly **09** basically, centrally **10** integrally **11** essentially **13** constituently, fundamentally, intrinsically

inherit
04 heir **06** assume, be left **07** receive, succeed **08** accede to, be heir to, come into, take over **09** succeed to **10** fall heir to **12** be bequeathed

inheritance
03 fee **06** legacy **07** bequest, descent **08** heredity, heritage **09** accession, endowment, patrimony **10** birthright, proportion, succession **13** primogeniture **15** secundogeniture

inheritor
04 heir **05** scion **06** co-heir, tanist **07** devisee, heiress, heritor, legatee **08** heritrix, legatary **09** heritress, recipient, successor **10** fellow-heir, inheritrix, next in line, substitute **11** beneficiary, inheritress **12** reversionary

inhibit
04 balk, curb, stem, stop **05** baulk, check **06** bridle, hamper, hinder, hold in, impede, rein in, stanch, thwart **07** prevent, repress, staunch **08** hold back, obstruct, restrain, restrict, slow down, suppress **09** constrain, frustrate **10** discourage **12** put a damper on, straitjacket **13** interfere with

inhibited
03 shy **06** wooden **07** guarded, subdued, uptight **08** reserved, reticent **09** repressed, withdrawn **10** frustrated, restrained **11** constrained, embarrassed, introverted **13** self-conscious **14** self-restrained

inhibition
03 bar **04** curb **05** check **06** hang-up **07** coyness, reserve, shyness **09** hampering, hindrance, restraint, reticence, thwarting **10** impediment, repression **11** frustration, obstruction, restriction **12** interference **13** embarrassment

inhospitable
04 bare, cold, cool, wild **05** aloof, bleak, empty **06** barren, lonely, unkind **07** hostile, uncivil **08** desolate, inimical **09** hostlesse **10** antisocial, forbidding, unfriendly, ungenerous, uninviting, unsociable, xenophobic **11** uncongenial, unreceptive, unwelcoming **12** unfavourable **13** uninhabitable, unneighbourly

inhuman
03 odd **05** cruel, harsh **06** animal, brutal, savage **07** bestial, strange, vicious **08** barbaric, fiendish, non-human, ruthless, sadistic **09** barbarous, merciless **10** diabolical **11** cold-blooded

inhumane
05 cruel, harsh **06** brutal, unkind **07** callous **08** pitiless, uncaring **09** heartless, unfeeling **11** cold-hearted, dehumanized, hard-hearted, insensitive **13** inconsiderate, unsympathetic

inhumanity
06 sadism **07** cruelty **08** atrocity **09** barbarism, barbarity, brutality **10** savageness, unkindness **11** brutishness, callousness, viciousness **12** pitilessness, ruthlessness **13** heartlessness **15** cold-bloodedness, cold-heartedness, hard-heartedness

inimical
07 adverse, harmful, hostile, hurtful, noxious, opposed **08** contrary **09** injurious, repugnant **10** intolerant, pernicious, unfriendly **11** destructive, disaffected, ill-disposed, unwelcoming **12** antagonistic, antipathetic, inhospitable, unfavourable

inimitable
06 unique **07** sublime, supreme **08** peerless **09** matchless, nonpareil, unmatched **10** consummate, unequalled, unexampled, unrivalled **11** distinctive, exceptional, superlative, unsurpassed **12** incomparable, unparalleled **13** unsurpassable

iniquitous
04 base, evil **05** awful **06** sinful, unjust, wicked **07** heinous, immoral, vicious **08** accursed, criminal, dreadful, infamous **09** atrocious, nefarious, reprobate **10** abominable, facinorous, flagitious, outrageous **11** unrighteous **13** reprehensible

iniquity
03 sin **04** evil, vice **05** crime, wrong **06** infamy **07** misdeed, offence **08** baseness, enormity **09** evil-doing, injustice **10** sinfulness, wickedness, wrongdoing **11** abomination, heinousness, lawlessness, ungodliness, viciousness **13** transgression **15** unrighteousness

initial
◇ *head selection indicator*
04 sign **05** basic, early, first, prime **07** bloomer, endorse, opening, primary **08** inchoate, original, starting **09** autograph, beginning, formative, inaugural, inceptive, incipient **10** commencing, elementary **11** countersign **12** foundational, introductory

initially
◇ *head selection indicator*
05 first **07** at first, firstly **08** first off **10** at the start, first of all, originally **11** at the outset, to begin with, to start with **14** at the beginning

initiate
04 open, tiro **05** admit, begin, blood, cause, crash, drill, enrol, enter, lanch, let in, set up, start, teach, train, tutor **06** accept, induce, induct, instil, invest, launch, novice, ordain, prompt, rookie, sign up **07** convert, entrant, install, kick off, learner, pioneer, receive, recruit, start up, trigger, welcome **08** activate, beginner, bejesuit, commence, instruct, neophyte, newcomer **09** auspicate, establish, greenhorn, inculcate, instigate, institute, introduce, new member, novitiate, originate, proselyte, stimulate **10** bring about, catechumen, inaugurate, tenderfoot **11** get under way, probationer, set in motion **13** sow the seeds of **15** get off the ground, get things moving

initiation
05 debut, entry, start **07** baptism, opening **08** entrance **09** admission, beginning, enrolment, inception, induction, launching, reception, setting-up **10** admittance, enlistment, ordination **11** investiture, origination **12** inauguration, installation, introduction **13** rite of passage

• **initiation rite**
04 bora

initiative
02 go **04** lead, plan, push **05** drive **06** action, energy, scheme **07** lead-off **08** ambition, démarche, dynamism, gumption, proposal **09** first move, first step **10** creativity, enterprise, get-up-and-go, suggestion **11** opening move, originality **12** introductory **13** inventiveness **14** innovativeness, recommendation **15** resourcefulness

inject
03 add, hit, jab **04** bang, hype **05** bring, immit, shoot, spike **06** hype up, infuse, insert, instil **07** bring in, crank up, hit it up, inspire, shoot up, skin-pop, syringe **08** immunize, mainline **09** inoculate, introduce, vaccinate

injection
03 fix, jab, jag **04** bang, dose, shot **06** needle **07** skin-pop **08** addition, infusion **09** insertion **10** hypodermic, instilling **11** inoculation, vaccination **12** immunization, introduction **13** a shot in the arm

injudicious
04 rash **05** hasty **06** stupid, unwise **07** foolish **08** ill-timed **09** ill-judged, impolitic, imprudent, misguided **10** ill-advised, incautious, indiscreet, unthinking **11** inadvisable, inexpedient, wrong-headed **13** inconsiderate

injunction
05 order **06** dictum, ruling **07** command, dictate, mandate, precept **09** direction, directive **10** admonition **11** conjunction, exhortation, instruction

injure
◇ *anagram indicator*
03 cut, get, mar **04** bomb, burn, dere, harm, hurt, kill, lame, maim, maul, ruin, skin **05** abuse, annoy, break, chill, choke, deare, misdo, rifle, scald, scath, shend, spoil, touch, upset, waste, wound, wring, wrong **06** accloy, blight, damage, deface, deform, impair, mangle, nobble, offend, poison, put out, scaith, scathe, skaith, strain, weaken **07** blemish, carve up, cripple, disable, outrage, shoot up **08** aggrieve, fracture, ill-treat, maltreat, mutilate, override **09** disfigure, disoblige, humiliate, overshoot, prejudice, undermine **10** vitriolize **11** hospitalize **13** stab in the back

injured
◇ *anagram indicator*
03 bad **04** hurt, lame, sore **05** upset **06** abused, harmed, pained, put out, tender **07** bruised, damaged, defamed, grieved, misused, unhappy, unsound, wounded, wronged **08** crippled, disabled, insulted, maligned, offended, weakened **09** aggrieved **10** displeased, ill-treated, maltreated, vulnerable **11** disgruntled, wither-wrung **13** cut to the quick

• **easily injured**
04 nice

injurious
03 bad **06** malign, noyous, unjust **07** adverse, baneful, harmful, hurtful, noxious, ruinous **08** damaging, wrongful **09** insulting, libellous, unhealthy **10** calumnious, corrupting, defamatory, derogatory, iniquitous,

offenceful, pernicious, slanderous **11** deleterious, destructive, detrimental, mischievous, prejudicial, unconducive **15** disadvantageous

injury
03 cut, ill, RSI **04** bale, dere, gash, harm, hurt, maim, ruin, sore, teen, tene, tort **05** abuse, deare, teene, wound, wrong **06** bruise, damage, insult, lesion, scathe, trauma **07** offence, offense, outrage **08** abrasion, fracture, mischief, violence **09** annoyance, contusion, grievance, injustice, prejudice **10** affliction, contrecoup, disservice, impairment, laceration, mutilation, traumatism
12 endamagement, ill-treatment
13 disfigurement
• **after injury**
◇ *anagram indicator*

injustice
04 bias **05** abuse, wrong **06** injury
07 offence, unright **08** inequity, iniquity, unreason **09** disparity, prejudice **10** inequality, oppression, partiality, unfairness, unjustness
11 favouritism **12** ill-treatment, one-sidedness, partisanship
14 discrimination

inkling
04 clue, hint, idea, sign **06** notion
07 glimmer, pointer, umbrage, whisper
08 allusion, faintest, foggiest, innuendo **09** suspicion
10 glimmering, indication, intimation, suggestion **11** insinuation

inky
◇ *anagram indicator*
03 jet **05** black, drunk, sooty **08** dark-blue, jet-black **09** coal-black **10** pitch-black
• **inky blotch**
04 monk

inlaid
03 set **05** inset, lined, tiled **06** mosaic
07 studded **08** enchased
09 empaestic, enamelled
10 damascened **11** tessellated

inland
05 inner **06** upland **07** central, midland, refined **08** domestic, interior, internal, landward **09** up-country
10 within land **13** sophisticated

inlay
05 embed, inset **06** enamel, insert, lining, mosaic, tiling **07** emblema, setting **08** damaskin, studding
09 damascene, damaskeen, damasquin
10 damasceene **12** tessellation

inlet
03 arm, bay **04** cove, hope **05** bight, creek, fiord, firth, fjord, haven, sound
06 infall, ingate **07** opening, passage
08 entrance

inmate
03 zek **04** case **06** client, intern
07 convict, patient **08** detainee, prisoner **09** collegian **10** collegiate

inmost
04 deep **05** basic **06** buried, hidden, secret **07** central, closest, dearest, deepest, private **08** esoteric, intimate, personal **09** essential, innermost
12 confidential

inn
03 bar, pub **04** khan **05** abode, hotel, house, howff, local, lodge, put up
06 boozer, hostel, imaret, posada, public, ryokan, shanty, tavern
07 albergo, auberge, canteen, potshop
08 bona fide, groggery, hostelry
09 free house, gin palace, lush-house, posthouse, roadhouse **11** caravansary, change-house, public house
12 caravansarai, caravanserai, halfway house **13** watering-house

innards
◇ *middle selection indicator*
04 guts **05** works **06** entera, organs, umbles, vitals **07** giblets, insides, viscera **08** entrails, interior
09 mechanism **10** intestines **13** inner workings **14** internal organs

innate
06 inborn, inbred, native **07** connate, natural **08** inherent, original
09 inherited, intrinsic, intuitive
10 congenital, hereditary, indigenous, ingenerate **11** instinctive

innately
08 inwardly **09** basically, centrally
10 inherently, integrally **11** essentially
13 constituently, fundamentally, intrinsically

inner
04 deep **06** entire, hidden, inside, inward, mental, middle, secret
07 central, obscure, private
08 esoteric, interior, internal, intimate, personal, profound **09** concealed, emotional, innermost, spiritual
10 restricted **13** psychological

innermost
04 deep **05** basic **06** buried, hidden, inmost, secret **07** central, closest, dearest, deepest, private **08** esoteric, intimate, personal **09** essential
12 confidential

innkeeper
04 host **07** hostess, manager, padrone
08 boniface, hotelier, landlady, landlord, mine host, publican
09 barkeeper, innholder
10 aubergiste, proprietor **11** hotel-keeper **12** restaurateur

innocence
06 purity, safety, virtue **07** honesty, naivety **08** chastity, openness
09 credulity, frankness, ignorance, integrity, naiveness, virginity
10 simplicity **11** artlessness, gullibility, naturalness, playfulness, sinlessness **12** harmlessness, inexperience, spotlessness, trustfulness **13** blamelessness, childlikeness, faultlessness, guilelessness, guiltlessness, impeccability, inculpability, ingenuousness, innocuousness, righteousness, stainlessness, unworldliness **14** immaculateness
15 inoffensiveness

innocent
04 babe, lamb, naif, open, pure, safe
05 bland, canny, child, clear, frank, fresh, green, idiot, naive, seely, white
06 benign, chaste, gentle, honest, infant, novice, simple **07** angelic, anodyne, artless, ingénue, natural, playful, sinless, upright **08** Arcadian, beginner, dewy-eyed, dovelike, gullible, harmless, imbecile, lamblike, neophyte, sackless, spotless, trustful, trusting, virginal, virtuous
09 blameless, childlike, credulous, crimeless, faultless, greenhorn, guileless, guiltless, incorrupt, ingenuous, innocuous, righteous, stainless, unsullied, untainted, unworldly **10** babe in arms, immaculate, impeccable, inculpable, tenderfoot **11** inoffensive, offenceless, unblemished, uncorrupted
12 prelapsarian, simple-minded, unsuspecting, unsuspicious
13 inexperienced, unblameworthy, unimpeachable **14** above suspicion, irreproachable, uncontaminated
15 unsophisticated

innocently
06 simply **07** naively **09** artlessly
10 harmlessly, trustfully, trustingly
11 blamelessly, credulously, ingenuously, innocuously
13 inoffensively, unoffendingly
14 unsuspiciously

innocuous
04 mild, safe **05** bland **07** anodyne, playful **08** harmless, innocent
11 inoffensive, unobtrusive
15 unobjectionable

innovation
06 change, novity, reform **07** newness, novelty **08** novation, novelism, progress **09** departure, neologism, new method, variation **10** alteration, new product **12** introduction
13 modernization

innovative
03 new **04** bold **05** fresh **06** daring
07 go-ahead **08** creative, original
09 inventive, reforming **10** avant-garde, Promethean **11** adventurous, imaginative, progressive, resourceful
12 enterprising, trail-blazing
14 groundbreaking

innovator
06 source **07** creator, deviser, pioneer
08 novelist, reformer **09** developer
10 modernizer, originator
11 progressive, trailblazer **12** fresh thinker

innuendo
04 hint, slur **07** whisper **08** allusion, overtone **09** aspersion **10** intimation, suggestion **11** implication, insinuation

innumerable
04 many, tons **05** heaps, loads, piles **06** dozens, masses, oodles, stacks, untold **07** umpteen **08** hundreds, infinite, millions, numerous **09** countless, thousands **10** numberless, unnumbered **11** uncountable **12** incalculable

inoculate
05 graft, imbue **06** inject **07** protect **08** immunize **09** safeguard, syphilize, vaccinate, variolate **10** give a jab to **11** give a shot to

inoculation
03 jab, jag **04** shot **09** injection **10** protection **11** vaccination, variolation **12** immunization

inoffensive
04 mild, safe **05** bland, quiet **07** anodyne **08** harmless, innocent, pleasant, retiring **09** innocuous, peaceable **11** unassertive, unobtrusive **15** unexceptionable, unobjectionable

inoperable
05 fatal **06** deadly **08** hopeless, terminal **09** incurable **10** unhealable **11** intractable, irremovable, unremovable, untreatable

inoperative
04 bust, duff, idle **05** kaput, resty **06** broken, futile, kaputt, silent, unused **07** invalid, useless **08** nugatory **09** defective, worthless **10** broken-down, inadequate, not working, on the blink, on the fritz, out of order, unworkable **11** ineffective, ineffectual, inefficient, inofficious, out of action **12** not operative, out of service **13** inefficacious, unserviceable **14** non-functioning **15** out of commission

inopportune
06 clumsy **08** ill-timed, mistimed, tactless, untimely **09** ill-chosen, importune **10** unsuitable, wrong-timed **11** importunate, out of season, unfortunate **12** inauspicious, inconvenient, infelicitous, intempestive, unpropitious, unseasonable **13** inappropriate

inordinate
◇ *anagram indicator*
03 OTT **05** great, undue **07** extreme **08** vaulting **09** excessive **10** exorbitant, immoderate, outrageous, over the top **11** God-almighty, unwarranted **12** preposterous, unmeasurable, unreasonable, unrestrained, unrestricted **14** unconscionable

inorganic
04 dead **07** mineral **08** lifeless **09** inanimate **10** artificial, non-natural

input
04 code, data, load **05** enter, facts, key in, put in, store **06** feed in, insert **07** capture, details, figures, process **08** material **09** resources **10** statistics **11** information, particulars **12** contribution

inquest
07 hearing, inquiry **10** inspection, post-mortem **11** examination **13** investigation

inquietude
05 worry **06** unease **07** anxiety **08** disquiet **09** agitation, jumpiness **10** solicitude, uneasiness **11** disquietude, disturbance, nervousness **12** apprehension, discomposure, perturbation, restlessness

inquire, enquire
03 ask, see **04** call, quiz, scan, seek **05** probe, query, snoop, speer, speir, study **06** quaere, search **07** examine, explore, inquere, inspect **08** look into, question, research **10** scrutinize **11** interrogate, investigate

inquirer, enquirer
06 seeker **07** querist, student **08** explorer, searcher **10** inquisitor, questioner, researcher **12** interrogator, investigator

inquiring, enquiring
04 nosy **05** eager, nosey **06** prying **07** curious, probing, zetetic **08** doubtful **09** sceptical, searching, wondering **10** analytical, interested **11** inquisitive, questioning **13** interrogatory, investigative, investigatory **14** outward-looking

inquiringly, enquiringly
06 keenly **07** eagerly **09** curiously **11** wonderingly **12** analytically **13** inquisitively, questioningly

inquiry, enquiry
04 poll **05** probe, query, quest, study **06** demand, quaere, search, survey **07** hearing, inquest, inquire **08** etiology, question, scrutiny, sounding **09** aetiology **10** inspection **11** examination, exploration, inquisition, star chamber **12** perquisition **13** interrogation, interrogatory, investigation **14** reconnaissance

inquisition
07 inquest, inquiry **08** grilling, quizzing **09** witch hunt **10** Holy Office **11** examination, questioning **13** interrogation, investigation **14** the third degree

inquisitive
04 nosy **05** nosey **06** prying, snoopy, spying **07** curious, peeping, peering, probing **08** snooping **09** inquiring, intrusive, searching **10** meddlesome **11** interfering, questioning **12** scrutinizing

inquisitively
06 keenly **07** eagerly **09** curiously **11** inquiringly, searchingly **12** meddlesomely **13** interferingly, questioningly

inquisitor
04 Deza **07** Ximenes **10** Torquemada

inroad
04 raid **05** foray, sally **06** attack, charge, infall, sortie **07** advance, assault **08** invasion, progress, trespass **09** incursion, intrusion, irruption, offensive, onslaught, sea breach **11** impingement, trespassing **12** encroachment

insane
◇ *anagram indicator*
03 ape, fey, mad **04** bats, daft, gyte, loco, nuts, wild, wood, yond **05** barmy, batty, buggy, crazy, daffy, dippy, dotty, flaky, gonzo, loony, loopy, manic, nutty, potty, queer, wacko, wacky, wiggy **06** absurd, crazed, cuckoo, dement, fruity, maniac, mental, raving, red-mad, screwy, stupid **07** bananas, barking, berserk, bonkers, cracked, foolish, frantic, horn-mad, idiotic, lunatic, meshuga **08** bughouse, crackers, crackpot, demented, deranged, dingbats, doolally, frenetic, frenzied, maniacal, unhinged, unstable **09** delirious, disturbed, half-baked, lymphatic, psychotic, senseless, up the wall **10** bestraught, distracted, distraught, frantic-mad, off the wall, off your nut, out to lunch, ridiculous, stone-crazy, unbalanced **11** hare-brained, impractical, nonsensical, not all there, off the rails, off your head **12** crackbrained, mad as a hatter, off your chump, round the bend **13** off your rocker, of unsound mind, out of your head, out of your mind, out of your tree, round the twist **14** off your trolley, wrong in the head **15** non compos mentis, out of your senses

insanely
◇ *anagram indicator*
05 madly **08** absurdly **09** foolishly **11** ludicrously, senselessly **12** outrageously, ridiculously

insanitary
04 foul **05** dirty **06** filthy, impure **07** dirtied, noisome, noxious, unclean **08** feculent, infected, infested, polluted **09** unhealthy **10** unhygienic, unsanitary **11** unhealthful, unsanitized **12** contaminated, insalubrious **13** disease-ridden

insanity
◇ *anagram indicator*
05 craze, folie, folly, mania **06** frenzy, lunacy **07** madness **08** daftness, delirium, dementia, neurosis **09** absurdity, craziness, psychosis, stupidity **10** insaneness **11** derangement, foolishness, hebephrenia, psychopathy **13** mental illness, senselessness **14** ridiculousness

See also **lunacy**

insatiable
04 avid **06** greedy, hungry **07** craving **08** ravenous, sateless **09** rapacious,

voracious **10** gluttonous, immoderate, inordinate **12** unappeasable, unquenchable **13** unsatisfiable

inscribe

03 cut **04** etch, mark, sign **05** brand, carve, enrol, enter, print, stamp, write **06** endoss, enlist, incise, record, scrive **07** address, engrave, impress, imprint, scrieve **08** dedicate, register **09** autograph

inscription

04 ogam **05** ogham, title, words **06** legend **07** caption, epitaph, etching, message, trigram, wording, writing **08** colophon, epigraph, kakemono **09** autograph, engraving, lettering, signature, tetragram **10** chronogram, dedication **11** insculpture **15** circumscription

inscrutable

04 deep **06** arcane, hidden, invis'd **07** cryptic **08** baffling, puzzling **09** enigmatic **10** mysterious, unreadable **12** impenetrable, inexplicable, unfathomable, unsearchable **13** unexplainable **14** unintelligible

insect

Insects include:

03 ant, bee, bug, fly, ked, nit
04 cleg, flea, frit, gnat, kade, moth, tick, wasp
05 aphid, aphis, cimex, emmet, louse, midge, ox-bot, roach, sedge
06 bedbug, beetle, bembex, capsid, cicada, cootie, drongo, earwig, gadfly, gru-gru, hornet, jigger, locust, maggot, mantis, may bug, mayfly, muscid, red ant, sawfly, thrips, tipula, tsetse, tzetse, tzetze, weevil
07 antlion, blowfly, buzzard, chigger, cornfly, cricket, deer fly, fire ant, gallfly, gold-bug, hive bee, June bug, katydid, lace bug, lady bug, lamp fly, pill bug, rose bug, soldier, termite, wood ant
08 berry bug, birch fly, blackfly, bookworm, cornworm, crane fly, fruit fly, gall wasp, glowworm, greenfly, honey bee, horse fly, house fly, hoverfly, lacewing, ladybird, mealy bug, mosquito, onion fly, sand wasp, sedge fly, snake fly, stink bug, white ant, whitefly, woodworm
09 amazon ant, ant weaver, bumblebee, butterfly, caddis fly, carpet bug, cochineal, cockroach, coffee bug, damselfly, doodlebug, dragonfly, golden-eye, humble-bee, leaf miner, mason wasp, mining bee, mud dauber, paper wasp, shield bug, squash bug, stable fly, tsetse fly, tzetse fly, tzetze fly, velvet ant, wax insect, woodlouse
10 blister fly, bluebottle, boll weevil, bulldog ant, cabbage-fly, cockchafer, dolphin-fly, drosophila, froghopper, grapelouse, kissing bug, leaf-cutter, leaf insect, Pharaoh ant, pondskater, silverfish, vinegar-fly, web spinner
11 backswimmer, biting louse, biting midge, bristletail, bush cricket, caterpillar, froth-hopper, grasshopper, greenbottle, harvest mite, harvest tick, honeypot ant, stick insect, umbrella-ant, vine-fretter, walking leaf, walking twig
12 house cricket, lightning bug, walking stick, water boatman
13 daddy longlegs, diamond-beetle, leatherjacket, praying insect, praying mantis, water measurer, water scorpion

See also **animal**; **beetle**; **butterfly**; **invertebrate**; **moth**

Insect parts include:

03 eye, jaw, leg
04 head, vein, wing
06 cercus, feeler, scutum, thorax
07 abdomen, antenna, cuticle, maxilla, ocellus, pedicel, segment
08 antennae, forewing, hindwing, mandible, peduncle, spiracle, tympanum
09 mouthpart, proboscis
10 epicuticle, integument, ovipositor
11 compound eye

• **study of insects**

03 ent **10** entomology

insecticide

Insecticides include:

02 Bt
03 BHC, DDT
05 timbó, zineb
06 aldrin, derris
07 cinerin, safrole
08 camphene, carbaryl, chlordan, chromene, diazinon, dieldrin, flyspray, rotenone
09 chlordane, Gammexane®, Malathion®, parathion, toxaphene
10 carbofuran, dimethoate, Paris green, piperazine
15 organophosphate

insectivore

04 mole, tody **05** shrew **06** agouta, desman, tanrec, tenrec, Tupaia **08** hedgehog, serotine **09** solenodon, tree shrew **10** golden mole, otter shrew **11** diamond bird, gnatcatcher **13** elephant shrew

• **insectivorous plant**

06 sundew **07** Dionaea, drosera **10** butterwort, sarracenia **11** gobe-mouches **12** pitcher plant, Venus flytrap **13** Venus's flytrap

insecure

◇ *anagram indicator*

04 weak **05** frail, loose, shaky **06** afraid, flimsy, tickle, unsafe, unsure **07** anxious, exposed, fearful, nervous, worried **08** doubtful, hesitant, perilous, unstable, unsteady **09** dangerous, hazardous, unassured, uncertain, unguarded **10** precarious, vulnerable **11** defenceless, unprotected **12** apprehensive, open to attack

insecurity

04 fear **05** peril, worry **06** danger, hazard **07** anxiety **08** unsafety, weakness **09** frailness, shakiness **10** flimsiness, uneasiness, unsafeness, unsureness **11** instability, nervousness, uncertainty **12** apprehension, unsteadiness **13** vulnerability **14** precariousness **15** defencelessness

insensate

04 deaf, numb **05** blind **07** unaware **08** comatose, ignorant **09** inanimate, oblivious, senseless, unfeeling, unmindful **10** insensible, insentient **11** unconscious **12** unresponsive **13** anaesthetized

insensible

03 out **04** cold, deaf, dull, hard, numb **05** aloof, blind, faint **06** marble, slight, stupid, wooden, zonked **07** callous, distant, unaware, unmoved **08** comatose, detached, ignorant **09** oblivious, senseless, unfeeling, unmindful, untouched **10** insentient, iron-witted, knocked out, unaffected, unapparent **11** emotionless, hard-hearted, insensitive, unconscious **12** undetectable, unresponsive **13** anaesthetized, imperceptible, indiscernible **14** dead to the world, out for the count

insensitive

04 dead, hard, iron **05** crass, tough **06** immune, obtuse **07** callous, unmoved **08** hardened, tactless, uncaring **09** anomalous, heartless, impassive, oblivious, resistant, unfeeling, untouched **10** hypalgesic, impervious, unaffected **11** hard-hearted, indifferent, thoughtless, unconcerned **12** case-hardened, impenetrable, thick-skinned, unresponsive **13** unsusceptible, unsympathetic **14** pachydermatous

insensitivity

08 hardness, hypalgia, immunity **09** bluntness, crassness, toughness, unconcern **10** crassitude, hypalgesia, obtuseness, resistance **11** callousness **12** indifference, tactlessness **14** hard-headedness, imperviousness **15** hard-heartedness, impenetrability

inseparable

05 bosom, close **07** devoted **08** constant, intimate **10** individual **11** individuate, indivisible, undividable **12** indissoluble, inextricable

inseparably

05 as one **06** firmly **07** closely **08** arm in arm, together **10** hand in hand, intimately **11** indivisibly **12** indissolubly, inextricably

insert

03 cue, put, set **04** sink **05** embed, enter, immit, infix, inlay, inset, let in, place, plant, press, put in, stick **06** notice, push in, slip in **07** enchase, enclose, engraft, implant, ingraft, slide in, stick in **08** addition, circular, intromit, thrust in **09** enclosure, insertion, interject, interpose, introduce **10** interleave, supplement **11** intercalate, interpolate **13** advertisement

insertion
05 entry, inset, miter, mitre **06** insert **07** implant **08** addition **09** inclusion, intrusion **10** supplement **12** introduction, intromission **13** intercalation, interpolation

inside
◇ *hidden indicator*
◇ *insertion indicator*
04 core, guts **05** belly, heart, inner **06** centre, indoor, inward, middle, secret, within **07** content, indoors, private **08** contents, hush-hush, implicit, inherent, interior, internal, intromit, inwardly, reserved, secretly **09** innermost, intrinsic, privately **10** classified, internally, restricted **12** confidential

insider
06 member **07** one of us **08** co-worker **11** participant, staff member **15** one of the in-crowd

insides
04 guts **05** belly, tummy **06** bowels, organs **07** abdomen, giblets, innards, stomach, viscera **08** entrails **10** intestines **14** internal organs

insidious
03 sly **04** wily **06** artful, crafty, sneaky, subtle, tricky **07** cunning, devious, furtive **08** sneaking, stealthy **09** cautelous, deceitful, deceptive, dishonest, insincere **10** perfidious **11** duplicitous, treacherous **13** Machiavellian, surreptitious

insidiously
05 slyly **06** subtly **09** cunningly

insight
05 grasp, sight **06** acumen, aperçu, vision, wisdom **08** epiphany **09** awareness, furniture, intuition, judgement, knowledge, sharpness **10** perception, shrewdness **11** discernment, observation, penetration, realization, sensitivity **12** apprehension, intelligence, perspicacity **13** comprehension, enlightenment, understanding

insightful
04 wise **05** acute, sharp **06** astute, seeing, shrewd **07** prudent **08** inscient **09** observant, sagacious **10** discerning, perceptive, percipient **11** intelligent, penetrating **13** knowledgeable, perspicacious, understanding

insignia
03 tab **04** arms, logo, mark, sign, type **05** armor, badge, brand, clasp, crest, eagle, order, signs **06** armour, emblem, ensign, ribbon, symbol **07** regalia **08** hallmark **09** hallmarks, medallion, trademark **10** coat of arms, decoration **11** cap and bells

insignificance
08 meanness, tininess **09** pettiness, smallness **10** paltriness, triviality **11** irrelevance, nothingness **12** nugatoriness, unimportance **13** immateriality, inconsequence, negligibility, worthlessness **15** meaninglessness

insignificant
04 tiny **05** C-list, dinky, minor, petit, petty, scrub, small **06** insect, meagre, paltry, puisne, puisny, scanty, slight **07** minimal, nebbich, scrubby, trivial **08** marginal, nugatory, piddling, trifling **09** jerkwater, no-account, small beer, small-time **10** fractional, immaterial, irrelevant, negligible, peripheral **11** meaningless, Mickey Mouse, unimportant **12** cutting no ice, non-essential **13** hole-in-the-wall, insubstantial, no great shakes **14** inconsiderable **15** inconsequential

insincere
04 jive **05** false, lying **06** double, forked, hollow, phoney, untrue **07** devious, feigned, lip-deep **08** disloyal, rhetoric, two-faced **09** deceitful, dishonest, faithless, mouth-made, pretended, underhand, unnatural **10** backhanded, mendacious, perfidious, rhetorical, unfaithful, untruthful **11** dissembling, duplicitous, pretentious, treacherous **12** disingenuous, hypocritical, meretricious **13** double-dealing

insincerely
07 falsely **09** deviously **10** disloyally **11** deceitfully, dishonestly **12** perfidiously, unfaithfully, untruthfully **13** duplicitously, pretentiously, treacherously **14** hypocritically

insincerity
04 cant **06** humbug **07** falsity, perfidy **08** bad faith, pretence **09** duplicity, falseness, hypocrisy, mendacity, phoniness **10** dishonesty, hollowness, lip service **11** deviousness, dissembling, evasiveness **13** artificiality, deceitfulness, dissimulation, faithlessness **14** untruthfulness **15** pretentiousness

insinuate
04 hint, wind **05** get at, imply **06** allude **07** mention, suggest, whisper **08** indicate, innuendo, intimate, work into **10** serpentine

• insinuate yourself
04 work, worm **05** crawl, sidle **07** wriggle **09** get in with **10** ingratiate **11** curry favour

insinuation
04 hint, slur **05** slant **08** allusion, innuendo **09** aspersion, inference **10** insinuendo, intimation, suggestion **11** implication **12** introduction

insipid
03 dry **04** blah, drab, dull, fade, flat, lash, tame, thin, weak **05** banal, bland, trite, vapid, wersh **06** boring, pallid, watery **07** anaemic, insulse, mawkish, missish, shilpit, tedious, wearish **08** lifeless, waterish **09** inanimate, sapidless, tasteless, unsavoury, wearisome **10** albuminous, colourless, monotonous, spiritless, wishy-washy **11** flavourless **12** milk-and-water, unappetizing **13** characterless, unimaginative, uninteresting

insist
03 vow **04** aver, hold, urge **05** claim, press, swear **06** assert, demand, harp on, repeat, strain, stress, threap **07** contend, declare, dwell on, entreat, persist, require, stand on **08** maintain **09** emphasize, reiterate, stand firm, stipulate **10** hang out for **11** state firmly, stick out for **12** ask for firmly **15** put your foot down, stand your ground, stick to your guns

insistence
05 claim **06** demand, stress, urging **08** emphasis, entreaty, firmness **09** assertion **10** contention, repetition, resolution **11** declaration, exhortation, maintenance, persistence, reiteration, requirement **13** assertiveness, determination

insistent
06 dogged, urgent **07** adamant, exigent **08** constant, emphatic, forceful, pressing, repeated, resolute **09** assertive, demanding, incessant, tenacious **10** determined, inexorable, persistent, relentless, unyielding **11** importunate, persevering, unrelenting, unremitting

insobriety
09 inebriety, tipsiness **10** crapulence **11** drunkenness, inebriation **12** hard drinking, intemperance, intoxication

insolence
03 gum, lip **04** gall, sass **05** abuse, cheek, mouth, nerve, sauce, snash **06** hubris, hybris **07** insults **08** attitude, audacity, boldness, chutzpah, defiance, pertness, rudeness **09** arrogance, contumely, impudence, sauciness **10** cheekiness, disrespect, effrontery, incivility **11** forwardness, presumption **12** impertinence **13** offensiveness **15** insubordination

insolent
04 bold, rude **05** bardy, brash, fresh, lairy, lippy, sassy, saucy **06** brazen, cheeky, mouthy, wanton **07** abusive, defiant, forward **08** arrogant, impudent **09** audacious, insulting **10** purse-proud **11** ill-mannered, impertinent **12** contemptuous, contumelious, presumptuous **13** disrespectful, insubordinate

insoluble
07 complex, obscure **08** baffling, involved, puzzling **09** enigmatic, intricate **10** mysterious, mystifying, perplexing, unsolvable **11** inscrutable **12** impenetrable, inexplicable, unfathomable **13** unexplainable **14** indecipherable

insolvency
04 ruin **07** default, failure **10** bankruptcy **11** destitution, liquidation, queer street **12** indebtedness **13** impecuniosity, pennilessness **14** impoverishment

insolvent
04 bust **05** broke, skint **06** failed, in debt, ruined **07** boracic **08** bankrupt, in the red, strapped **09** destitute, gone under, penniless **10** liquidated, on the rocks **11** impecunious **12** impoverished **13** gone to the wall, in queer street **14** on your beam ends **15** strapped for cash

insomnia
11 wakefulness **12** insomnolence, restlessness **13** sleeplessness
• **insomnia drug**
06 Ativan® **07** Mogadon® **08** Rohypnol® **09** lorazepam, Temazepam **10** nitrazepam

insouciance
04 ease **08** airiness **09** flippancy, unconcern **10** breeziness, jauntiness **11** nonchalance **12** carefreeness, heedlessness, indifference

insouciant
04 airy **06** breezy, casual, jaunty **07** buoyant **08** carefree, flippant, heedless **09** apathetic, easy-going, unworried **10** nonchalant, untroubled **11** free and easy, indifferent, unconcerned **12** happy-go-lucky, light-hearted

inspect
03 vet **04** case, scan, tour, view **05** audit, check, study, visit **06** assess, go over, review, search, survey **07** examine, oversee, see over **08** appraise, check out, look into, look over, pore over **09** supervise **10** scrutinize **11** investigate, perlustrate, reconnoitre, superintend

inspection
04 scan, tour, view **05** audit, check, dekko, recce, study, visit **06** alnage, muster, review, search, survey **07** autopsy, check-up, inspect, rag-fair, vetting, vidimus **08** analysis, autopsia, look-over, once-over, overview, scrutiny **09** appraisal, Cook's tour, look-round **10** assessment **11** examination, perspective, supervision **12** tracheoscopy **13** investigation

inspector
06 conner, critic, exarch, keeker, tester, viewer **07** alnager, auditor, checker, officer, scanner, visitor **08** assessor, examiner, overseer, provedor, providor, reviewer, searcher, surveyor **09** appraiser, provedore **10** controller, proveditor, scrutineer, supervisor **11** proveditore **12** investigator **14** superintendent

inspiration
04 goad, hoop, hwyl, idea, muse, spur **05** estro, whoop **06** breath, duende, fillip, genius **07** insight **08** afflatus, Aganippe, arousing, inflatus, infusion, stimulus, stirring, taghairm **09** afflation, awakening, brainwave, inflation, influence, theosophy **10** brainstorm, bright idea, creativity, enthusiasm, incitement, motivation, revelation **11** imagination, originality, stimulation, theopneusty **12** illumination **13** encouragement, enlightenment, inventiveness **14** stroke of genius

inspirational
09 emotional, inspiring, spiritual **10** devotional, heartening, motivating, suggestive **11** encouraging, influential, instinctive **13** psychological

inspire
04 fire, goad, spur, stir **05** guide, imbue, rouse **06** arouse, enamor, excite, inform, infuse, inject, kindle, prompt, thrill **07** animate, breathe, embrave, enamour, enliven, enthral, enthuse, hearten, impress, inflame, produce, provoke, quicken, trigger **08** energize, instruct, motivate, spark off, touch off **09** encourage, galvanize, infatuate, influence, instigate, stimulate **10** bring about, exhilarate

inspired
05 vatic **08** afflated, creative, daemonic, daimonic, dazzling, exciting, splendid, talented, visioned **09** brilliant, memorable, thrilling, wonderful **10** impressive, marvellous, remarkable, theopneust **11** enthralling, exceptional, imaginative, outstanding, superlative **12** theopneustic

inspiring
06 moving **07** rousing **08** exciting, stirring **09** affecting, memorable, thrilling, uplifting **10** heartening, impressive **11** encouraging, enthralling, interesting, stimulating **12** enthusiastic, exhilarating, invigorating **13** inspirational

inspirit
04 fire, move **05** cheer, nerve, rouse **06** incite **07** animate, enliven, gladden, hearten, inspire, quicken, refresh **08** embolden **09** encourage, galvanize, stimulate **10** exhilarate, invigorate **12** reinvigorate

instability
07 frailty **08** wavering **09** lubricity, shakiness **10** fickleness, fitfulness, flimsiness, insecurity, transience, unsafeness, volatility **11** flightiness, fluctuation, inconstancy, oscillation, temperament, uncertainty, unsoundness, vacillation, variability **12** impermanence, irresolution, unsteadiness **13** unreliability **14** capriciousness, changeableness, precariousness

install
03 fit, fix, lay, put **04** site **05** lodge, place, plant, put in, set up, state **06** induct, insert, invest, locate, nestle, ordain, settle **07** instate, plumb in, situate, station, swear in **08** ensconce, enthrone, entrench, position **09** establish, institute, introduce **10** consecrate, inaugurate

installation
02 HQ **04** base, camp, post, site **05** plant **06** centre, siting, system **07** artwork, fitting, placing, station **08** location **09** apparatus, equipment, induction, insertion, machinery **10** ordination, settlement, swearing-in **11** instatement, investiture, positioning **12** consecration, headquarters, inauguration **13** establishment

instalment
02 HP **04** call, heft, part **06** lesson **07** chapter, episode, payment, portion, section, segment, tranche **08** division, rhapsody **09** repayment **11** part payment **12** continuation, hire purchase **13** the never-never

instance
04 case, cite, give, name, suit **05** cause, proof, quote **06** adduce, behest, demand, motive, sample, urging **07** example, mention, point to, process, refer to, request, specify **08** citation, entreaty, evidence, occasion, pressure **09** exemplify, prompting **10** incitement, initiative, insistence, occurrence, particular **11** case in point, exhortation, importunity, instigation **12** illustration, solicitation **15** exemplification
• **for instance**
02 as, eg, zB **10** for example **13** exempli gratia

instant
02 mo **03** sec **04** fast, jiff, tick, time, whip **05** flash, jiffy, quick, rapid, swift, trice **06** direct, minute, moment, prompt, second, urgent **07** current, present **08** juncture, occasion **09** immediate, on-the-spot, twinkling **10** ready mixed **11** convenience, pre-prepared, split second **12** unhesitating **13** instantaneous **14** easily prepared **15** quickly prepared

instantaneous
05 rapid **06** direct, prompt, snappy, sudden **07** instant **09** immediate, momentary, on-the-spot **12** momentaneous, unhesitating

instantaneously
03 pdq **04** anon, ASAP **06** at once, pronto **07** quickly, rapidly **08** directly, in a jiffy, promptly, speedily **09** forthwith, instantly, on the spot, right away **11** immediately **12** straight away, there and then, without delay **14** unhesitatingly

instantly
03 now, pdq **04** ASAP **06** at once, pronto **08** directly, in a jiffy, on the dot **09** forthwith, like a shot, on the spot, right away, zealously **11** immediately **12** straight away, there and then, without delay **13** importunately **15** instantaneously

instead
04 else **06** rather **10** by contrast, in contrast, preferably, substitute **11** replacement **13** alternatively **15** as an alternative

• **instead of**
04 vice **07** against **08** in lieu of **09** in place of **10** in favour of, on behalf of, rather than **11** as opposed to **12** in contrast to **14** in preference to

instigate
04 goad, move, prod, spur, urge **05** begin, cause, impel, press, rouse, set on, spark, start **06** excite, foment, incite, induce, kindle, prompt, stir up, whip up **07** inspire, provoke **08** generate, initiate, persuade **09** encourage, influence, stimulate **10** bring about

instigation
06 behest, motion, urging **07** bidding **09** incentive, prompting, prompture **10** incitement, inducement, initiation, initiative, insistence **11** fomentation **13** encouragement

instigator
04 goad, spur **06** leader **07** inciter **08** agitator, fomenter, incensor, provoker, putter-on **09** firebrand, initiator, motivator **10** incendiary, prime mover, ringleader **12** troublemaker **13** mischief-maker

instil
05 drill, imbue, plant, teach **06** infuse, inject **07** breathe, din into, implant, impress, ingrain **09** inculcate, insinuate, introduce, transfuse

instinct
04 bent, feel, gift, urge **05** drive, flair, hunch, knack, moved **06** imbued, nature, talent **07** ability, charged, faculty, feeling, impulse, incited **08** animated, aptitude, tendency **09** intuition, principle **10** gut feeling, instigated, sixth sense **11** gut reaction **14** inbred response, predisposition **15** natural response

instinctive
03 gut **06** inborn, innate, native, reflex **07** natural **08** inherent, knee-jerk, primeval, untaught, visceral **09** automatic, immediate, impulsive, intuitive, primaeval, unlearned **10** mechanical, unthinking **11** involuntary, spontaneous **13** unintentional **14** seat-of-the-pants, unpremeditated

instinctively
09 naturally **11** intuitively **12** mechanically, unthinkingly **13** automatically, involuntarily, spontaneously **15** without thinking

institute
01 I **03** law **04** Inst, open, rule **05** begin, enact, found, order, raise, set up, start **06** create, custom, decree, induct, invest, launch, ordain, school **07** academy, appoint, college, develop, educate, install, precept **08** commence, initiate, organize, seminary **09** establish, introduce, originate, principle **10** foundation, inaugurate, regulation **11** institution, put in motion, set in motion **12** conservatory, organization

Institutes include:

02 IA, IM, WI
03 BFI, CGI, CIB, CMI, EMI, ICA, MIT
04 NICE, RIBA, RNIB, RNID, RTPI
05 C and G, UMIST, UWIST
07 Caltech

institution
03 law **04** club, home, rule **05** guild, usage **06** center, centre, custom, league, ritual, system **07** college, concern, society **08** creation, founding, hospital, practice, starting **09** enactment, formation, inception, institute, setting-up, tradition **10** convention, foundation, initiation **11** association, corporation **12** commencement, installation, introduction, organization **13** establishment

institutional
03 set **04** cold, drab, dull **06** dreary, formal **07** orderly, routine, uniform **08** accepted, clinical, orthodox **09** cheerless, customary, organized **10** forbidding, impersonal, methodical, monotonous, regimented, systematic **11** established, ritualistic, uninspiring, unwelcoming **12** bureaucratic, conventional **13** establishment

instruct
03 bid **04** shew, show, tell, warn **05** brief, coach, drill, guide, order, prime, study, teach, train, tutor **06** advise, charge, demand, direct, enjoin, gospel, ground, inform, lesson, notify, school, taught **07** call out, command, counsel, educate, inspire, lecture, mandate, prepare, require **09** catechize, enlighten, make known **10** discipline **12** indoctrinate

instruction
03 key **05** brief, order, rules **06** advice, charge, legend, lesson, manual, orders, ruling **07** classes, command, lecture, lessons, mandate, priming, telling, tuition **08** briefing, coaching, drilling, guidance, handbook, lectures, pedagogy, teaching, training, tutelage, tutoring **09** direction, directive, education, grounding, knowledge, schooling **10** directions, discipline, guidelines, injunction **11** book of words, edification, information, inspiration, preparation, requirement **13** enlightenment **14** indoctrination, recommendation **15** recommendations

instructive
06 useful **07** helpful **08** didactic, edifying, teaching **09** doctrinal, educative, improving, uplifting **10** didactical **11** educational, informative, informatory **12** enlightening, illuminating

instructor
04 guru **05** coach, guide, swami, tutor **06** master, mentor, sensei **07** adviser, teacher, trainer **08** educator, exponent, lecturer, mistress **09** maharishi, pedagogue, preceptor **10** counsellor, instituter, institutor **11** preceptress **12** demonstrator

instrument
03 act, way **04** mean, rule, tool **05** agent, cause, gauge, gismo, means, meter, organ **06** agency, device, factor, gadget, medium **07** channel, measure, utensil, vehicle **09** apparatus, appliance, guideline, implement, indicator, mechanism, yardstick **11** contraption, contrivance

See also **measurement**; **optical**; **scientific**; **torture**; **writing**

Musical instruments include:

02 gu
03 gju, gue, lur, oud, sax, saz, uke, zel
04 alto, bass, bell, drum, erhu, fife, gong, harp, horn, kora, koto, lure, lute, lyre, Moog®, oboe, pipe, rote, sang, tuba, vibe, vina, viol, zeze
05 Amati, banjo, bells, bongo, bugle, cello, chime, crwth, flute, gusla, gusle, gusli, hi-hat, kazoo, mbira, organ, piano, pipes, rebec, shalm, shawm, sitar, strad, tabla, tabor, vibes, viola, zanze, zirna, zurna
06 carnyx, cither, citole, cornet, cymbal, Fender, fiddle, guitar, rattle, spinet, tom-tom, tympan, vielle, violin, zither
07 alphorn, bagpipe, bandore, bandura, baryton, bassoon, bazouki, bodhran, buccina, celeste, cembalo, cithara, cithern, cittern, clarion, clavier, cowbell, hautboy, lyricon, maracas, marimba, ocarina, pandora, Pianola®, piccolo, sackbut, sambuca, sarangi, saxhorn, serpent, sistrum, tambura, theorbo, timpani, trumpet, ukulele, vihuela, whistle, zithern
08 angklung, bagpipes, barytone, bass drum, bass viol, bouzouki, calliope, carillon, charango, cimbalom, clappers, clarinet, clarsach, cornpipe, crumhorn, dulcimer, handbell, hornpipe, humstrum, jew's harp, keyboard, mandolin, manzello, melodeon, Pan-pipes, polyphon, psaltery, recorder, side-drum, spinette, Steinway, surbahar, tamboura, theramin, theremin, timbales, triangle, trombone,

virginal, vocalion, zambomba
09 accordion, alpenhorn, balalaika, banjolele, bugle-horn, castanets, chime bars, decachord, euphonium, flageolet, harmonica, harmonium, Mellotron®, polyphone, saxophone, snare-drum, tenor-drum, wood block, Wurlitzer®, xylophone
10 arpeggione, bass guitar, bird-scarer, bongo-drums, bullroarer, clavichord, concertina, cor anglais, didgeridoo, double bass, eolian harp, flugelhorn, French horn, grand piano, hurdy-gurdy, kettle-drum, mouth organ, oboe d'amore, pentachord, pianoforte, sousaphone, squeeze-box, tambourine, thumb piano, tin whistle, vibraphone
11 aeolian harp, barrel organ, harpsichord, phonofiddle, player-piano, sleigh bells, synthesizer, violoncello
12 glockenspiel, harmonichord, penny whistle, stock and horn, Stradivarius, tubular bells, viola da gamba
13 contra-bassoon, Ondes Martenot, panharmonicon, slide trombone, Swanee whistle
14 acoustic guitar, electric guitar, jingling Johnny
15 Moog synthesizer®, wind synthesizer

instrumental
06 active, useful **07** helpful, organic **08** involved **09** auxiliary, conducive, important **10** subsidiary
11 implemental, influential, ministerial, significant, subservient
12 contributory

insubordinate
04 rude **06** unruly **07** defiant, riotous **08** impudent, mutinous **09** insurgent, seditious, turbulent **10** disorderly, rebellious, refractory **11** disobedient, impertinent **12** contumacious, recalcitrant, ungovernable
13 undisciplined

insubordination
06 mutiny, revolt **08** defiance, rudeness, sedition **09** impudence, rebellion **11** riotousness
12 disobedience, impertinence, indiscipline, insurrection, mutinousness **13** recalcitrance
15 ungovernability

insubstantial
04 idle, poor, thin, weak **05** false, frail, wispy **06** bubble, feeble, flimsy, frothy, meagre, slight, unreal, yeasty
07 tenuous **08** fanciful, illusory, tenuious, vaporous **09** airy-fairy, cardboard, ephemeral, imaginary, moonshine **10** chimerical, immaterial, intangible **11** incorporeal

insufferable
08 dreadful, shocking **09** loathsome, repugnant, revolting **10** detestable, impossible, outrageous, unbearable
11 intolerable, unendurable
13 insupportable, too much to bear

insufferably
10 impossibly, shockingly, unbearably
11 intolerably, repugnantly
12 outrageously

insufficiency
04 lack, need, want **06** dearth
07 paucity, poverty **08** scarcity, shortage **10** deficiency, inadequacy
11 short supply **14** inadequateness

insufficient
05 scant, short **06** meagre, scanty, scarce, sparse **07** lacking, wanting
09 defective, deficient, not enough
10 inadequate **13** in short supply

insular
05 aloof, petty **06** biased, closed, cut off, narrow, remote **07** bigoted, limited
08 detached, isolated, separate, solitary **09** blinkered, insulated, parochial, withdrawn **10** prejudiced, provincial, restricted, xenophobic
12 narrow-minded, short-sighted
13 inward-looking

insularity
04 bias **07** bigotry **09** isolation, pettiness, prejudice **10** detachment, xenophobia **12** parochiality, solitariness **13** parochialness

insulate
03 lag, pad **04** wrap **05** cover
06 cocoon, cut off, detach, encase, shield **07** cushion, envelop, exclude, isolate, protect, shelter **08** separate
09 segregate, sequester

insulation
05 cover **06** shield **07** lagging, padding, shelter **08** asbestos, cladding, covering, sleeving, stuffing, wrapping **09** cocooning, corkboard, exclusion, fibrefill, foam glass, isolation
10 cushioning, detachment, fiberglass, fibreglass, protection, separation, Thermalite® **11** segregation **12** foam plastics **13** building paper, double-glazing, triple glazing **14** foamed plastics, Willesden paper **15** contour feathers, vulcanized fibre

insulator

Insulators include:

03 lag
04 mica
07 bushing, tea cosy
08 rock wool
09 pink batts®
10 dielectric
11 vermiculite
12 friction tape
14 insulating tape, Willesden paper

insult
04 bait, barb, gibe, hurt, slur, snub
05 abuse, libel, taunt, wound
06 damage, impugn, injure, injury, malign, mud pie, offend, rebuff, revile, slight, verbal **07** affront, mortify, offence, outrage, put-down, slander, traduce, trample, triumph
08 derogate, repriefe, ridicule, rudeness **09** call names, contumely, disparage, indignity, insolence
10 aspersions, calumniate, defamation, fling mud at, insultment, revilement, sling mud at, throw mud at
11 triumph over **13** disparagement, slap in the face **14** fly in the face of, kick in the teeth

insulting
04 rude **07** abusive, hurtful
08 insolent, reviling **09** degrading, injurious, libellous, offensive, slighting
10 affronting, derogatory, outrageous, scurrilous, slanderous **11** disparaging, opprobrious **12** contemptuous, contumelious

insuperable
10 formidable, impassable, invincible
12 overwhelming, unassailable
13 unconquerable **14** insurmountable

insupportable
07 hateful **08** dreadful **09** loathsome, untenable **10** detestable, unbearable
11 intolerable, unendurable
12 indefensible, insufferable, irresistible, unacceptable
13 unjustifiable

insuppressible
06 lively, unruly **09** energetic, go-getting **11** unstoppable, unsubduable
12 incorrigible, obstreperous, ungovernable **13** irrepressible
14 uncontrollable

insurance
02 NI **03** ins **05** cover **06** policy, surety **07** premium **08** security, warranty **09** assurance, guarantee, indemnity, provision, safeguard
10 protection **15** indemnification

insure
05 cover **06** assure, ensure **07** protect, warrant **08** reinsure **09** guarantee, indemnify **10** overinsure, underwrite

insurer
07 assurer **09** abandonee, guarantor, protector, warrantor **11** indemnifier, underwriter

insurgence
04 coup, riot **06** mutiny, putsch, revolt, rising **08** sedition, uprising **09** coup d'état, rebellion **10** revolution
12 insurrection

insurgent
05 pandy, rebel **06** rioter, rising
07 riotous **08** Camisard, mutineer, mutinous, partisan, resister, revolted, revolter **09** revolting, seditious
10 rebellious **11** disobedient, seditionist **13** insubordinate, revolutionary, revolutionist
15 insurrectionary, insurrectionist

insurmountable
08 hopeless **10** impossible, invincible
11 insuperable **12** overwhelming, unassailable **13** unconquerable

insurrection
04 coup, riot **06** mutiny, putsch, revolt, rising, uproar **08** sedition, uprising **09** coup d'état, rebellion **10** insurgence, insurgency, revolution

intact
05 sound, whole **06** entire, unhurt **07** perfect **08** complete, flawless, integral, unbroken, unharmed **09** faultless, undamaged, uninjured, unscathed, untouched **10** in one piece, unimpaired **12** undiminished **13** all in one piece

intangible
04 airy **05** vague **06** subtle, unfelt, unreal **07** elusive, obscure, shadowy, unclear **08** abstract, fleeting **09** invisible, touchless **10** impalpable, indefinite **11** incorporeal, indefinable, undefinable **12** immeasurable, imponderable **13** indescribable, insubstantial

integer
04 unit **05** digit, whole **06** figure, number **07** numeral **11** whole number

integral
04 full **05** basic, total, whole **06** entire, intact **07** built-in, inbuilt, unitary **08** complete, inherent **09** component, elemental, essential, intrinsic, necessary, requisite, undivided **10** integrated, unimpaired **11** constituent, fundamental **13** indispensable

integrate
03 mix **04** fuse, join, knit, mesh **05** blend, merge, unite, whole **06** mingle **07** combine **08** coalesce, complete, intermix **09** harmonize **10** amalgamate, assimilate, co-ordinate, homogenize, mainstream **11** consolidate, desegregate, incorporate

integrated
05 fused, mixed **06** hybrid, joined, merged, meshed, united **07** blended, mingled, mongrel, unified **08** cohesive, combined, joined-up **09** coalesced, connected, one-nation, tight-knit **10** harmonious, harmonized **11** amalgamated, assimilated, tightly knit, unseparated **12** consolidated, desegregated, incorporated, interrelated **13** part and parcel

integration
03 mix **05** blend, unity **06** fusion, merger **07** harmony **11** combination, unification **12** amalgamation, assimilation **13** consolidation, desegregation, incorporation **14** homogenization

integrity
05 honor, unity **06** honour, purity, virtue **07** decency, honesty, justice, probity **08** cohesion, entirety, fairness, goodness, morality, totality **09** coherence, principle, rectitude, sincerity, wholeness **10** entireness **11** unification, uprightness **12** completeness, impartiality, truthfulness **13** righteousness

intellect
04 mind, nous **05** brain, sense **06** brains, genius, noesis, reason, wisdom **07** egghead, noology, thinker, thought **08** academic, brainbox, highbrow **09** judgement **10** brainpower, brilliance, mastermind **12** intellectual, intelligence **13** comprehension, understanding

intellectual
04 blue **05** titan **06** boffin, brainy, far-out, genius, mental, noetic **07** bookish, egghead, erudite, learned, logical, thinker **08** academic, brainbox, cerebral, cultural, good mind, highbrow, studious, well-read **09** intellect, scholarly **10** mastermind, noematical, thoughtful **11** intelligent **12** bluestocking, pointy-headed, well-educated **15** rocket scientist

intellectually
08 mentally **10** cerebrally, culturally, studiously **12** academically, conceptually, noematically

intelligence
01 G **02** IQ **03** gen, wit **04** data, dope, news, nous, wits **05** brain, facts **06** acumen, advice, brains, notice, reason, report, rumour, spying, tip-off **07** account, low-down, thought, warning **08** aptitude, findings **09** alertness, espionage, intellect, knowledge, quickness, sharpness **10** brainpower, brightness, brilliance, cleverness, grey matter, perception **11** discernment, information, observation **12** notification, surveillance **13** comprehension, understanding **15** little grey cells

• intelligence service
02 MI **03** CIA, KGB, SIS **05** Stasi **06** Mossad

intelligent
05 acute, alert, quick, sharp, smart **06** brainy, bright, clever **07** knowing **08** all there, educated, informed, rational, sensible, thinking **09** brilliant, sagacious **10** discerning, perceptive **11** quick-witted **12** apprehensive, knowledgable, pointy-headed, well-informed **13** communicative, knowledgeable, perspicacious, understanding, using your loaf

intelligently
07 quickly **08** all there, cleverly, sensibly **09** knowingly **10** rationally **11** sagaciously **12** discerningly, perceptively **13** using your loaf **15** perspicaciously

intelligentsia
06 brains **08** eggheads, literati **09** academics, highbrows **10** illuminati **11** cognoscenti **13** intellectuals

intelligibility
07 clarity **08** lucidity **09** clearness, lucidness, plainness, precision **10** legibility, simplicity **11** exotericism **12** distinctness, explicitness

intelligible
04 open **05** clear, lucid, plain **07** legible **08** distinct, exoteric, explicit **10** exoterical, fathomable, penetrable **12** decipherable **14** comprehensible, understandable

intemperance
06 excess **07** licence **10** crapulence, debauchery, insobriety **11** drunkenness, inebriation, unrestraint **12** extravagance, immoderation, intoxication **14** overindulgence, self-indulgence

intemperate
03 OTT **04** wild **06** severe, strong **07** drunken, extreme, violent **08** prodigal **09** dissolute, excessive, unbridled **10** immoderate, inebriated, inordinate, licentious, over the top, passionate, profligate **11** dissipation, distempered, extravagant, incontinent, intoxicated, tempestuous **12** uncontrolled, ungovernable, unreasonable, unrestrained **13** self-indulgent **14** irrestrainable, uncontrollable

intend
03 aim **04** mean, plan, plot, turn **05** ettle, hight, think **06** choose, design, devise, direct, expand, expect, extend, scheme, strain **07** be going, destine, earmark, express, mark out, project, propose, purport, purpose, resolve **08** foremean, meditate, set apart **09** be looking, calculate, destinate, determine, have a mind, intensify **10** have in mind **11** contemplate **12** be determined

intended
06 fiancé, future **07** fiancée, planned **08** destined, proposed, purposed, wife-to-be **09** betrothed, designate **10** deliberate, designated, future wife **11** husband-to-be, intentional, prospective **13** future husband

• as intended
15 according to plan

intense
04 deep, full, keen **05** acute, dense, eager, great, harsh, heavy, sharp, tense, vivid **06** ardent, fervid, fierce, opaque, potent, severe, strong **07** burning, earnest, excited, extreme, fervent, nervous, serious, violent, zealous **08** blinding, electric, forceful, powerful, profound, strained, vehement, vigorous **09** consuming, emotional, energetic, exquisite, intensive **10** heightened, passionate, thoughtful **11** impassioned **12** concentrated, enthusiastic

intensely
04 deep, very **06** deeply **07** greatly **08** ardently, fiercely, strongly **09** extremely, fervently, like stink **10** profoundly **12** passionately **14** with a vengeance

intensification
05 boost **07** build-up **08** emphasis, increase **09** deepening, intension, worsening **10** building-up, escalation, stepping-up **11** aggravation, enhancement, heightening **12** acceleration, augmentation, exacerbation **13** concentration, magnification, reinforcement, strengthening **14** exacerbescence

intensify
03 fan **04** fire, fuel, whet **05** add to, boost, hot up, raise, widen **06** bump up, deepen, fester, hike up, intend, step up, worsen **07** augment, broaden, build up, enhance, magnify, quicken, sharpen **08** compound, escalate, heighten, increase, maximize **09** aggravate, emphasize, reinforce **10** exacerbate, exaggerate, strengthen **11** concentrate **12** bring to a head

intensity
04 fire, zeal **05** depth, force, power **06** accent, ardour, energy, strain, vigour **07** emotion, fervour, passion, potency, tension **08** fervency, fullness, keenness, severity, strength **09** acuteness, eagerness, extremity, greatness, intension, vehemence **10** enthusiasm, fanaticism, fierceness, profundity **11** earnestness, intenseness **13** concentration

intensive
04 full **05** total **06** all-out **07** in-depth, intense **08** detailed, rigorous, strained, thorough **10** exhaustive **11** unremitting **12** concentrated **13** comprehensive, thoroughgoing

intensively
05 fully **07** closely, totally **09** intensely **10** completely, rigorously, thoroughly **11** extensively **12** exhaustively **15** comprehensively

intent
03 aim, end, set **04** bent, firm, goal, hard, idea, keen, plan, rapt, view **05** alert, close, eager, ettle, fixed, point **06** design, enrapt, object, steady, target **07** earnest, focused, meaning, purpose, wistful **08** absorbed, occupied, resolved, watchful **09** attentive, committed, engrossed, intention, objective, searching, wrapped up **10** determined **11** connotation, preoccupied **13** concentrating

• **to all intents and purposes**
06 almost, nearly **07** morally **08** as good as, in effect **09** in essence, just about, virtually **10** more or less, pretty much, pretty well **11** effectively, practically

intention
03 aim, end **04** goal, hent, idea, plan, view, wish **05** point **06** animus, design, intent, object, target **07** concept, meaning, purpose, thought **08** ambition **09** objective **10** aspiration, attendment, designment **11** attendement

intentional
03 set **05** meant **06** wilful **07** planned, studied, willful, willing **08** designed, intended, prepense, purposed **09** conscious, on purpose, voluntary, weighed-up **10** calculated, considered, deliberate, purposeful, systematic **11** prearranged **12** preconceived, premeditated, systematical

intentionally
08 by design, wilfully **09** advisedly, knowingly, meaningly, on purpose, purposely, willingly **10** designedly, prepensely **11** in cold blood **12** deliberately

intently
04 hard **06** keenly **07** closely, fixedly **08** steadily **09** carefully, earnestly, staringly **10** diligently, watchfully **11** attentively, searchingly

inter
04 bury **05** earth, inurn **06** entomb, inhume **07** inearth **08** inhumate **09** lay to rest, sepulchre

interbreed
03 mix **05** cross **09** hybridize **10** crossbreed, mongrelize **11** miscegenate **14** cross-fertilize

interbreeding
07 syngamy **08** crossing **13** cross-breeding, hybridization, miscegenation

intercede
05 plead, speak **07** beseech, entreat, mediate **08** moderate, petition **09** arbitrate, interpose, intervene, negotiate

intercept
◇ *insertion indicator*
04 stop, take **05** block, catch, check, cut in, delay, seize **06** ambush, arrest, cut off, impede, thwart, waylay **07** deflect, head off **08** obstruct **09** frustrate, interrupt **10** commandeer

interception
◇ *insertion indicator*
06 ambush **07** seizure **08** blocking, checking, stopping **10** cutting-off, deflection, heading-off **11** obstruction

intercession
04 plea **06** agency, prayer **08** advocacy, entreaty, pleading **09** mediation **10** beseeching **11** arbitration, good offices, negotiation **12** intervention, solicitation, supplication **13** interposition **14** interpellation

intercessor
04 mean **05** agent **06** broker, prayer **08** advocate, mediator **09** go-between, middleman, moderator, paraclete **10** arbitrator, negotiator **12** intermediary

interchange
04 swap **05** trade **06** barter, switch **07** permute, replace, reverse, trading **08** crossing, exchange, junction **09** alternate, crossfire, crossroad, interplay, permutate, transpose **10** alternance, crossroads, substitute **11** alternation, give-and-take, reciprocate **12** intersection **13** reciprocation

interchangeability
04 swap **06** barter **08** exchange, synonymy **10** congruence, similarity **11** equivalence, interaction, parallelism, reciprocity **13** comparability, reciprocation **14** correspondence **15** exchangeability, transposability

interchangeable
07 similar, the same **08** fungible, standard **09** identical **10** comparable, equivalent, permutable, reciprocal, synonymous **11** commutative **12** exchangeable, transposable **13** corresponding

interconnect
04 join, link **06** join up **07** network **09** interlink, interlock **10** interweave **11** communicate, interrelate

intercourse
05 trade, trock, troke, truck **07** contact, traffic **08** commerce, congress, converse, dealings **10** connection **11** association **12** conversation **13** communication **14** correspondence

interdependent
06 mutual, two-way **10** correlated, reciprocal **11** interlinked **12** interlocking, interrelated **13** complementary **14** interconnected

interdict
03 ban, bar **04** tabu, veto **05** debar, taboo **06** forbid, outlaw **07** embargo, prevent, rule out **08** disallow, preclude, prohibit **09** proscribe **10** injunction, preclusion **11** prohibition **12** disallowance, interdiction, proscription

interest
03 fad, int **04** care, gain, good, grip, heed, move, note, part, side **05** amuse, bonus, charm, claim, hobby, rivet, share, stake, stock, touch, value **06** absorb, allure, appeal, divert, engage, equity, moment, notice, occupy, profit, regard, return, weight **07** attract, benefit, concern, credits, engross, gravity, involve, pastime, portion, premium, pursuit, revenue, urgency **08** activity, appeal to, business, dividend, intrigue, priority, proceeds, receipts **09** advantage, amusement, attention, captivate, curiosity, diversion, fascinate, magnitude, relevance **10** attraction, engagement, importance, investment, percentage, prominence, recreation **11** consequence, fascination, involvement, seriousness **12** partisanship, significance

13 attentiveness, consideration, participation 15 inquisitiveness

• in the interests of

10 on behalf of 12 for the sake of 15 for the benefit of

• lack of interest

06 apathy 07 boredom

• object of interest

04 lion

interested

04 into, keen 05 hot on 06 intent 07 curious, devoted, engaged, gripped, riveted 08 absorbed, affected, involved 09 attentive, attracted, concerned, engrossed, intrigued 10 captivated, enthralled, fascinated, implicated 12 enthusiastic, having the bug

interesting

05 tasty 07 amusing, amusive, curious, unusual 08 engaging, exciting, gripping, readable, riveting, viewable 09 absorbing, appealing 10 attractive, compelling, compulsive, engrossing, intriguing 11 captivating, fascinating, stimulating 12 entertaining 13 unputdownable

interestingly

09 curiously 10 poignantly 11 ingeniously 12 intriguingly

interfere

03 jam, mar, pry 04 balk, rape 05 abuse, block, check, choke, clash, cramp, grope, upset 06 attack, butt in, feel up, hamper, hinder, impede, meddle, molest, tamper, thwart 07 assault, barge in, inhibit, intrude, touch up, trammel 08 conflict, handicap, intromit, mess with, obstruct, trespass 09 interpose, interrupt, intervene, mess about 10 mess around, muscle in on 11 intermeddle 12 put your bib in, put your oar in 13 get in the way of, poke your bib in, touch sexually 14 poke your nose in, stick your bib in, stick your oar in 15 sexually assault, stick your nose in

interference

03 EMI 05 noise, shash 06 prying, static 07 clutter, trammel 08 blocking, checking, clashing, conflict, handicap, meddling, trammels 09 cross-talk, hampering, hindrance, intrusion, thwarting 10 antagonism, impediment, inhibiting, opposition 11 disturbance, obstruction 12 interruption, intervention, intromission 13 interposition 14 meddlesomeness 15 intermodulation

interfering

04 nosy 05 nosey 06 prying 08 meddling 09 intruding, intrusive 10 meddlesome

interim

06 acting, pro tem 07 stand-in, stopgap 08 interval, meantime 09 caretaker, makeshift, meanwhile, temporary 10 improvised 11 interregnum, provisional

interior

03 int 04 core, home 05 heart, inner, local 06 centre, depths, hidden, inland, innate, inside, inward, mental, middle, remote, secret 07 central, innards, nucleus, private 08 domestic, internal, intimate, personal 09 emotional, impulsive, innermost, intrinsic, intuitive, spiritual, up-country 10 inside part 11 instinctive, involuntary, spontaneous 13 psychological

interject

03 cry 04 call 05 shout, utter 06 insert, pipe up 07 exclaim, throw in 09 ejaculate, interpose, interrupt, introduce 11 interpolate

interjection

03 cry 04 call 05 shout 09 utterance 11 ejaculation, exclamation 12 interruption 13 interpolation, interposition

interlace

04 knit 05 braid, cross, plait, twine, weave 06 enlace, inlace 07 entrail, entwine, intwine 08 intermix 09 interlock 10 intertwine, interweave, reticulate 11 intersperse 12 interwreathe

interlink

04 knit, link, mesh 07 network 09 intergrow, interlock 10 intertwine, interweave 12 interconnect, link together, lock together 13 clasp together

interlock

04 link, mesh 05 pitch, tooth 06 engage 10 intertwine 12 interconnect, link together, lock together 13 clasp together, interdigitate

interloper

07 invader 08 intruder 10 encroacher, trespasser 11 gatecrasher 14 uninvited guest

interlude

03 jig 04 halt, rest, stop, wait 05 break, delay, let-up, pause, spell 06 hiatus, kyogen, recess, verset 07 respite 08 antimask, breather, entr'acte, interact, interval, stoppage 09 interrupt 10 antimasque 11 parenthesis 12 intermission 14 breathing space, divertissement

intermediary

05 agent 06 broker 08 linguist, mediator 09 comprador, go-between, in-between, middleman 10 arbitrator, compradore, contact man, negotiator

intermediate

03 mid 04 mean 05 mesne 06 medial, median, medium, middle, midway 07 halfway 09 in-between 11 intervening 12 intermediary, transitional

interment

06 burial 07 burying, funeral, obsequy 08 exequies 09 obsequies, sepulture 10 inhumation

interminable

04 dull, long 06 boring, prolix 07 endless, eternal, tedious 08 dragging, infinite 09 boundless, ceaseless, limitless, perpetual, unlimited, wearisome 10 long-winded, loquacious, monotonous, without end 11 everlasting, never-ending 12 long-drawn-out

intermingle

03 mix 04 fuse, lace 05 blend, merge, mix up 06 commix 07 combine 08 intermix 09 commingle, interlace 10 amalgamate, interweave 11 mix together

intermission

04 halt, lull, rest, stop 05 break, let-up, pause 06 recess 07 respite 08 apyrexia, breather, interval, stoppage, suspense, vacation 09 cessation, interlude, remission 10 suspension 12 interruption 14 breathing space

intermittent

06 broken, cyclic, fitful 07 erratic 08 off and on, on and off, periodic, sporadic 09 irregular, spasmodic 10 occasional 11 spasmodical 13 discontinuous

intermittently

08 off and on, on and off 09 sometimes 11 erratically, irregularly 12 occasionally, periodically, sporadically 13 spasmodically 14 from time to time 15 by fits and starts, discontinuously, in fits and starts

intern

04 hold, jail, tiro 05 cadet, pupil 06 detain, inmate, novice 07 confine, learner, recruit, starter, student, trainee 08 beginner, graduate, imprison, newcomer, prentice 10 apprentice 11 probationer 13 hold in custody

internal

03 int 04 home 05 civil, inner, local 06 inside, inward, mental 07 in-house, private 08 domestic, interior, intimate, personal 09 emotional, intrinsic, spiritual 10 subjective 13 psychological

internally

06 inside, within 07 at heart, locally 08 deep down, inwardly, secretly 09 privately 10 to yourself 12 domestically, subjectively 13 deep inside you

international

01 I 03 cap, int 06 global, public 07 general 09 test match, universal, worldwide 12 cosmopolitan

internecine

05 civil, fatal 06 bloody, deadly, family, fierce, mortal 07 ruinous, violent 08 internal 09 murderous 11 destructive 13 exterminating

Internet *see* **computer**

interplay
08 exchange **11** alternation, give-and-take, interaction, interchange **13** reciprocation, transposition

interpolate
03 add **05** put in **06** insert **09** interject, interpose, intersert, introduce **10** spatchcock **11** intercalate

interpolation
03 gag **05** aside **06** insert **08** addition **09** insertion **12** interjection, introduction **13** intercalation

interpose
03 add **05** cut in, put in **06** butt in, chip in, horn in, insert, step in, strike **07** barge in, intrude, mediate, stickle **08** interlay, intermit, muscle in, strike in, thrust in **09** arbitrate, intercede, interfere, interject, interpone, interrupt, intervene, introduce **10** put between **11** come between, interpolate **12** place between, put your oar in **14** poke your nose in

interpret
04 read, scan, take **05** aread, arede, solve **06** decode, define, open up, render, unfold **07** arreede, clarify, conster, explain, expound **08** construe, decipher **09** elucidate, explicate, make clear, translate **10** paraphrase, understand **11** make sense of, rationalize, shed light on **12** interpretate, throw light on

interpretation
04 read, rede, spin, take **05** sense **07** anagoge, anagogy, meaning, opinion, reading, version **08** analysis, construe, decoding, exegesis **09** rendering **10** exposition, expounding, paraphrase **11** deciphering, elucidation, explanation, explication, performance, translation **12** construction **13** clarification, understanding

interpretative
08 exegetic **10** expository **11** explanatory, explicatory, hermeneutic **12** interpretive **13** clarificatory

interpreter
06 lawyer, munshi **07** dobhash, exegete, Latiner **08** dragoman, exponent, lingster, linguist, linkster, moonshee, truchman **09** annotator, expositor, expounder **10** elucidator, linguister, textualist, translator **11** commentator, expositress **12** hermeneutist, oneirocritic **13** interpretress, oneiroscopist

interrelate
04 link **09** interlink, interlock **10** interweave **11** communicate **12** interconnect

interrogate
04 pump, quiz **05** grill **07** debrief, examine **08** question **12** cross-examine **13** cross-question, give a roasting **14** give a going-over

interrogation
04 quiz **07** inquest, inquiry, pumping **08** grilling, question, quizzing **09** going-over **11** examination, inquisition, questioning, third degree **14** the third degree

interrogative
07 curious, probing **08** erotetic **09** inquiring, quizzical **11** inquisitive, questioning **12** catechetical **13** inquisitional, inquisitorial, interrogatory

interrupt
◇ *insertion indicator*
03 cut, end **04** halt, stop **05** block, break, cut in, delay **06** butt in, cancel, chip in, chop in, cut off, heckle, hold up, snap up, take up **07** barge in, barrack, break in, chequer, disrupt, disturb, intrude, suspend **08** cut short, obstruct, postpone **09** intercept, interject, interlude, interpose, intervene, punctuate, take short **10** disconnect **11** interpolate, take up short **12** put your oar in **13** interfere with, interjaculate

interruption
◇ *insertion indicator*
03 cut **04** halt, stop **05** break, delay, hitch, let-up, pause **06** cesure, hiatus, recess, remark **07** wipeout **08** blocking, breather, interval, obstacle, power cut, question **09** abatement, barging-in, butting-in, cessation, cutting-in, hindrance, interlude, intrusion **10** disruption, impediment, suspension **11** breaking-off, disturbance, obstruction **12** interference, interjection, intermission, solarization **13** disconnection, interpolation **14** discontinuance, interpellation

intersect
03 cut **04** meet **05** cross **06** bisect, divide **07** overlap **08** converge **09** cut across, decussate, intervein **10** criss-cross

intersection
04 edge, meet **06** carfax, carfox, chiasm, vertex **07** chiasma, meeting **08** crossing, junction **10** crossroads, roundabout **11** box junction, interchange **13** traffic circle **15** railway crossing

intersperse
03 dot **06** pepper, spread **07** scatter **08** dispense, intermix, sprinkle **09** diversify, interlard, interpose, punctuate **10** distribute

interstice
03 gap **04** gulf, hole, pore, rent, rift, void **05** blank, chink, cleft, crack, space **06** areola, breach, cavity, cranny, divide, lacuna **07** crevice, opening, orifice **08** aperture, fracture

intertwine
03 mix **04** coil, knit, lace **05** blend, braid, cross, plait, pleat, twine, twirl, twist, weave **06** pleach, writhe **07** connect, entwine **08** empleach, impleach **09** interlace, interlink, interwind **10** interweave **12** link together

interval
03 gap **04** leap, lull, rest, time, wait **05** break, comma, delay, pause, space, spell **06** period, recess, season **07** interim, opening **08** breather, distance, meantime **09** in-between, interlude, meanwhile **10** interspace **11** intervallum, parenthesis **12** intermission **14** breathing space

intervene
04 pass **05** arise, occur **06** befall, elapse, happen, step in **07** intrude, mediate **08** separate **09** arbitrate, intercede, interfere, interrupt, negotiate **10** come to pass

• **intervene boldly**
02 up

intervening
06 middle **07** between, mediate **09** in-between **11** interjacent, interposing **12** intercurrent, intermediate, intervenient

intervention
06 agency **09** intrusion, mediation **10** stepping-in **11** arbitration, involvement, negotiation **12** intercession, interference, interruption **13** interposition

interview
03 vet **04** talk, viva **05** grill **06** assess, talk to **07** examine, meeting **08** audience, dialogue, evaluate, one-to-one, question, sound out **09** appraisal, encounter, tête-à-tête **10** assessment, conference, discussion, evaluation **11** interrogate **12** consultation, cross-examine **13** cross-question **15** oral examination, press conference

interviewer
08 assessor, examiner, reporter **09** appraiser, evaluator **10** inquisitor, questioner **11** interrogant **12** interlocutor, interrogator, investigator **13** correspondent

interweave
03 mat, mix **04** coil, knit **05** blend, braid, cross, plash, twine, twist, weave **06** raddle, splice, tissue **07** connect, entwine, perplex **08** complect **09** interlace, interlink, interlock, interwind, interwork **10** criss-cross, intertwine, intertwist, reticulate **11** intermingle, intertangle **12** interconnect, interwreathe, link together

intestinal
05 ileac **07** coeliac, enteric, gastric **08** duodenal, internal, visceral **09** abdominal, stomachic **10** splanchnic

intestines
04 guts **05** colon, offal **06** bowels, casing, vitals **07** innards, insides, viscera **08** entrails **09** chidlings, chitlings **11** chitterling **12** chitterlings

intimacy
06 warmth **07** privacy **09** affection, closeness, connexion, knowledge **10** confidence, connection, friendship, inwardness **11** camaraderie, familiarity **13** understanding

intimate
03 pal **04** boon, chum, cosy, cozy, dear, deep, hint, mate, maty, near, pack, snug, tell, tosh, warm **05** bosom, buddy, chief, china, close, crony, imply, matey, pally, palsy, privy, state, thick, tight **06** allude, belamy, chummy, friend, impart, intime, inward, secret, signal, strict, throng **07** Achates, comrade, declare, gremial, in-depth, private, special, suggest **08** alter ego, announce, detailed, familiar, friendly, indicate, informal, internal, personal, profound, thorough **09** associate, cherished, confidant, gemütlich, innermost, insinuate, make known, welcoming **10** best friend, better half, confidante, deep-seated, exhaustive, give notice, palsy-walsy **11** bosom friend, cater-cousin, close friend, communicate, penetrating **12** affectionate, confidential, fidus Achates, heart-to-heart, let it be known **13** boon companion **14** well-acquainted

See also **friend**

intimately
04 well **05** fully **06** deeply, nearly, warmly **07** closely **08** commonly, in detail, tenderly **09** inside out, privately **10** familiarly, personally, thoroughly **11** confidingly, hand in glove **12** exhaustively, hand and glove, particularly **14** affectionately, confidentially

intimation
04 hint, note **05** sniff **06** notice, signal **07** inkling, warning **08** allusion, innuendo, reminder **09** reference, statement **10** indication, suggestion **11** declaration, implication, insinuation **12** announcement **13** communication

intimidate
03 cow **05** alarm, appal, bully, daunt, get at, scare **06** coerce, compel, dismay, extort, lean on, menace, subdue **07** overawe, terrify, warn off **08** ballyrag, browbeat, bulldoze, bullyrag, domineer, frighten, pressure, psych out, threaten **09** blackmail, terrorize, tyrannize **10** pressurize **13** turn the heat on **14** put the screws on

intimidation
04 fear **06** screws, terror **07** menaces, threats **08** big stick, bullying, coercion, pressure **10** compulsion, terrifying **11** arm-twisting, browbeating, domineering, frighteners, frightening, terrorizing, threatening **12** scare tactics **13** sabre-rattling, terrorization, tyrannization

intolerable
05 awful **06** the end, too bad **08** dreadful, the limit **09** loathsome **10** detestable, impossible, unbearable **11** unendurable **12** insufferable, the last straw, unacceptable **13** beyond the pale, insupportable

intolerably
10 impossibly, shockingly, unbearably **11** repugnantly **12** insufferably, outrageously

intolerance
06 ageism, racism, sexism **07** bigotry **08** jingoism **09** dogmatism, extremism, prejudice, racialism **10** chauvinism, fanaticism, impatience, insularity, narrowness, xenophobia **12** anti-Semitism, illiberality **14** discrimination **15** small-mindedness

intolerant
06 ageist, biased, narrow, racist, sexist **07** bigoted, insular, redneck **08** dogmatic, one-sided, partisan **09** extremist, fanatical, illiberal, impatient, parochial, racialist **10** jingoistic, prejudiced, provincial, xenophobic **11** anti-Semitic, opinionated, persecuting, small-minded **12** chauvinistic, incompatible, narrow-minded, uncharitable **14** discriminating

intonation
02 Om **04** lilt, tone **05** pitch, twang **06** stress, timbre **07** cadence **08** emphasis **10** expression, inflection, modulation **12** accentuation

intone
03 say **04** sing **05** chant, croon, speak, utter, voice **06** chaunt, incant, recite **07** declaim **08** intonate, monotone **09** enunciate, pronounce **10** cantillate

intoxicate
◇ *anagram indicator*
04 corn **05** elate **06** excite, fuddle, poison, sozzle, thrill **07** animate, enthuse, inflame, inspire, stupefy **08** befuddle, disguise **09** inebriate, make drunk, stimulate **10** exhilarate

intoxicated
◇ *anagram indicator*
04 full, high, inky, winy **05** drunk, happy, inked, lit up, merry, moppy, moved, tight, tipsy, winey, woozy **06** blotto, bombed, canned, corked, elated, groggy, in wine, jarred, juiced, loaded, mortal, ripped, soused, stewed, stinko, stoned, tiddly, wasted, zonked **07** bevvied, blasted, blitzed, bonkers, bottled, coked-up, crocked, drunken, ebriate, ebriose, excited, half-cut, in drink, legless, maggoty, pickled, pie-eyed, sloshed, smashed, sozzled, squiffy, stirred, tiddled, wrecked **08** besotted, bibulous, ebriated, footless, hammered, in liquor, juiced up, liquored, moon-eyed, sow-drunk, steaming, stocious, tanked up, thrilled, whiffled, whistled, worked up **09** crapulent, inebriate, paralytic, pixilated, plastered, shickered, up the pole, well-oiled, zonked out **10** blind drunk, inebriated, obfuscated, pixillated, stimulated, whiskified **11** carried away, exhilarated, whiskeyfied **12** drunk as a lord, drunk as a newt, enthusiastic, roaring drunk **13** drunk as a piper, having had a few, in high spirits, under the table **14** Brahms and Liszt **15** one over the eight, the worse for wear, under the weather

See also **drunk**

intoxicating
05 heady **06** moving, strong **07** rousing **08** dramatic, exciting, stirring **09** alcoholic, inebriant, inspiring, methystic, stimulant, thrilling **11** enthralling, stimulating **12** exhilarating **15** going to your head

intoxication
06 fuddle, thrill **07** elation, rapture **08** euphoria, methysis, pleasure **09** animation, inebriety, poisoning, temulence, temulency, tipsiness **10** alcoholism, crapulence, debauchery, dipsomania, enthusiasm, excitement, insobriety **11** drunkenness, inebriation, stimulation **12** bibulousness, exhilaration, hard drinking, intemperance **15** serious drinking

intractability
08 obduracy **09** obstinacy **10** perversity **11** awkwardness, waywardness **12** contrariness, indiscipline, perverseness, stubbornness **13** pig-headedness, unamenability **15** incorrigibility, ungovernability

intractable
04 hard, wild **05** tough **06** kittle, unruly, wilful **07** awkward, frampal, haggard, problem, unwayed, wayward **08** contrary, frampold, obdurate, perverse, stubborn **09** difficult, fractious, obstinate, pig-headed, unbending **10** headstrong, monolithic, refractory, self-willed, unamenable, unyielding **11** disobedient, untreatable **12** cantankerous, cross-grained, intransigent, ungovernable, unmanageable **13** unco-operative, undisciplined **14** uncontrollable

intransigence
08 obduracy, tenacity **09** toughness **10** obstinancy **12** stubbornness **13** determination, implacability, inflexibility, pig-headedness **14** intractability, relentlessness

intransigent
05 rigid, tough **06** uppity **08** hardline, obdurate, stubborn **09** immovable, obstinate, pig-headed, tenacious, unbending **10** determined,

implacable, inexorable, inflexible, relentless, unamenable, unyielding **11** intractable, unbudgeable, unrelenting **12** bloody-minded **13** unpersuadable **14** irreconcilable, uncompromising

intrepid
04 bold **05** brave, gutsy **06** daring, gritty, heroic, plucky, spunky **07** doughty, gallant, valiant **08** fearless, spirited, stalwart, unafraid, valorous **09** audacious, dauntless, undaunted **10** courageous, undismayed **11** lion-hearted, unflinching **12** stout-hearted

intrepidness
04 grit, guts **05** nerve, pluck **06** daring, spirit, valour **07** bravery, courage, heroism, prowess **08** audacity, boldness **09** fortitude, gallantry **11** doughtiness, intrepidity **12** fearlessness **13** dauntlessness, undauntedness **15** lion-heartedness

intricacy
06 enigma **09** obscurity **10** complexity, involution, knottiness, perplexity **11** complexness, convolution, involvement **12** complication, convolutions, entanglement **13** complexedness, elaborateness, intricateness **14** sophistication

intricate
◇ *anagram indicator*
05 dedal, fancy **06** daedal, knotty, ornate, rococo, twisty **07** complex, finicky, Gordian, tangled **08** baffling, intrince, involved, puzzling, ravelled, tortuous **09** Byzantine, contrived, difficult, elaborate, enigmatic, entangled **10** convoluted, perplexing **11** complicated **12** intrinsicate, tirlie-wirlie **13** sophisticated

intrigue
03 web **04** draw, pack, plot, pull, ruse, wile **05** amour, cabal, charm, dodge, junta, rivet **06** absorb, affair, brigue, puzzle, scheme **07** affaire, attract, connive, consult, liaison, romance, traffic **08** artifice, collogue, conspire, interest, intimacy, trickery **09** captivate, collusion, conniving, fascinate, gallantry, machinate, manoeuvre, stratagem, tantalize, undermine **10** conspiracy, courtcraft, dirty trick, love affair, manipulate **11** beguilement, machination **12** machinations **13** double-dealing, sharp practice, work the oracle **15** practise against

intriguer
06 Jesuit **07** plotter, schemer, wangler **08** conniver **09** intrigant, trinketer **10** intrigante, machinator, politician, wire-puller **11** conspirator **12** collaborator **13** Machiavellian, wheeler-dealer

intriguing
07 politic **08** charming, exciting, puzzling, riveting **09** absorbing, appealing, beguiling, diverting, stairwork **10** attractive, compelling **11** captivating, fascinating, interesting, tantalizing, titillating

intrinsic
05 basic **06** inborn, inbred, inward, native **07** built-in, central, genuine, in-built, natural, radical **08** inherent, integral, interior, internal **09** elemental, essential **10** congenital, indigenous, underlying **11** fundamental **14** constitutional

intrinsically
08 in itself, inwardly **09** basically, centrally **10** inherently, integrally **11** essentially **12** by definition **13** constituently, fundamentally

introduce
◇ *containment indicator*
03 add **04** open **05** begin, float, found, immit, offer, plant, put in, start **06** induct, inject, insert, launch, lead in, prolog, submit **07** advance, bring in, develop, precede, preface, present, propose, suggest, usher in **08** acquaint, announce, commence, initiate, intromit, lead into, organize, prologue **09** establish, instigate, institute, originate **10** inaugurate, put forward **11** familiarize, put in motion, set in motion
- **be introduced to**
04 meet

introduction
◇ *head selection indicator*
05 debut, intro, proem, start **06** basics, entrée, launch, lead-in **07** baptism, opening, preface, prelude **08** exordium, foreword, overture, preamble, prologue **09** beginning, knock-down, rudiments **10** essentials, initiation **11** acquainting, development, front matter, institution, origination, prolegomena **12** announcement, commencement, fundamentals, inauguration, intromission, organization, presentation, prolegomenon **13** establishment, preliminaries **15** familiarization, first principles

introductory
05 basic, early, first **07** initial, opening **08** exordial, isagogic, starting **09** beginning, essential, inaugural, prefatory, prelusory **10** elementary, initiative, initiatory, precursory **11** fundamental, preliminary, preparatory, rudimentary

introspection
08 brooding **11** navel-gazing, pensiveness **12** introversion, self-analysis **13** contemplation, soul-searching **14** heart-searching, thoughtfulness **15** self-centredness, self-examination, self-observation

introspective
06 musing **07** pensive **08** brooding, reserved **09** withdrawn **10** meditative, subjective, thoughtful **11** introverted, self-centred **12** self-absorbed **13** contemplative, inward-looking, self-analysing, self-examining, self-observing

introverted
03 shy **05** quiet **08** reserved **09** withdrawn **11** self-centred **12** self-absorbed **13** introspective, inward-looking, self-examining

intrude
04 sorn **05** abate **06** butt in, chip in, invade, meddle, thrust **07** aggress, barge in, impinge, obtrude, violate **08** encroach, infringe, trespass **09** gatecrash, interfere, interject, interlope, interrupt

intruder
05 thief **06** raider, robber **07** burglar, invader, prowler **08** Derby dog, pilferer **10** interloper, trespasser **11** gatecrasher, infiltrator **12** housebreaker **14** unwelcome guest

intrusion
04 vein **08** invasion, lopolith, meddling, trespass **09** incursion, obtrusion, phacolith, violation **12** encroachment, gatecrashing, impertinence, impertinency, infringement, interference, interruption

intrusive
04 nosy **05** nosey, pushy **06** prying **07** forward **08** annoying, intruded, invasive, snooping, unwanted **09** go-getting, obtrusive, officious, uninvited, unwelcome **10** disturbing, irritating, meddlesome **11** impertinent, importunate, interfering, trespassing, troublesome, uncalled-for **12** interrupting, presumptuous

intuition
03 ESP **05** hunch **06** belief **07** feeling, insight **08** instinct **10** gut feeling, perception, sixth sense **11** discernment, premonition **12** anticipation, presentiment **13** light of nature

intuitive
06 inborn, innate **08** untaught, visceral **09** automatic, unlearned **11** instinctive, intuitional, involuntary, spontaneous

intuitively
08 innately **10** by instinct **13** automatically, instinctively, spontaneously

inundate
04 bury, soak **05** drown, flood, swamp **06** deluge, engulf **07** immerse, overrun **08** overflow, saturate, submerge **09** overwhelm **10** overburden

inundation
04 glut **05** flood, spate, swamp **06** deluge, excess **07** surplus, torrent **08** diluvion, diluvium, overflow **09** land-flood, tidal wave **10** water flood

inure
03 use **05** flesh, train **06** commit, harden, season, temper **07** toughen **08** accustom, practise **09** habituate **10** strengthen **11** acclimatize, desensitize, familiarize

invade
◇ *insertion indicator*
04 raid **05** enter, seize, storm **06** attack, infest, maraud, occupy **07** assault, burst in, conquer, intrude, obtrude, overrun, pervade, pillage, plunder, violate **08** encroach, infringe, take over, trespass **09** descend on, interrupt, march into, penetrate, swarm over **10** infiltrate **12** enter by force

invader
04 Dane **06** raider **08** attacker, intruder, marauder, pillager **09** aggressor, assailant, infringer, plunderer **10** trespasser

invalid
◇ *anagram indicator*
03 ill **04** null, sick, void, weak **05** false, frail, wrong **06** ailing, feeble, infirm, poorly, sickly, unwell **07** chronic, expired, illegal, patient, quashed, revoked, unsound **08** baseless, disabled, informal, mistaken, sufferer **09** abolished, bedridden, cancelled, erroneous, illogical, incorrect, nullified, rescinded, unfounded, untenable, worthless **10** fallacious, groundless, ill-founded, irrational, overturned **11** debilitated, inoperative, null and void, unjustified, unwarranted **12** convalescent, unacceptable, unscientific **14** valetudinarian **15** unsubstantiated

invalidate
04 undo, veto, void **05** annul, avoid, quash **06** cancel, negate, revoke, weaken **07** nullify, rescind, vitiate **08** abrogate, overrule **09** discredit, overthrow, terminate, undermine

invalidity
07 fallacy, falsity, sophism **08** voidness **11** unsoundness **12** illogicality, speciousness **13** inconsistency, incorrectness, irrationality **14** fallaciousness

invaluable
06 costly, useful **07** crucial **08** critical, precious, valuable **09** priceless **11** inestimable **12** incalculable **13** indispensable

invariable
03 set **05** fixed, rigid **06** stable, steady **07** regular, uniform **08** constant, habitual **09** immutable, invariant, permanent, unvarying **10** changeless, consistent, inflexible, unchanging, unwavering **11** unalterable **12** unchangeable

invariably
06 always **09** regularly **10** constantly, habitually, inevitably, repeatedly **11** unfailingly, without fail **12** consistently

invasion
04 raid **05** foray **06** attack, breach, sepsis **07** descent **08** Overlord, storming **09** incursion, intrusion, irruption, offensive, onslaught, violation **10** occupation **11** penetration **12** encroachment, infiltration, infringement, interference, interruption

invective
05 abuse **06** rebuke, satire, tirade, verbal **07** censure, obloquy, sarcasm **08** berating, diatribe, reproach, scolding **09** contumely, philippic, reprimand **10** revilement **11** castigation, fulmination **12** denunciation, vilification, vituperation **13** recrimination, tongue-lashing

inveigh
04 rail **05** blame, scold **06** berate, revile **07** censure, condemn, lambast, thunder, upbraid **08** denounce, reproach, sound off **09** castigate, criticize, fulminate **10** tongue-lash, vituperate **11** expostulate, recriminate

inveigle
03 con **04** coax, lure, wile **05** decoy **06** allure, cajole, entice, entrap, lead on, seduce **07** beguile, ensnare, wheedle **08** persuade **09** bamboozle, manoeuvre, sweet-talk **10** manipulate

invent
04 coin, fain, find, mint, plan **05** fable, faine, fayne, feign, frame **06** cook up, create, design, devise, father, make up **07** concoct, dream up, hit upon, imagine, pioneer, think up, trump up **08** conceive, contrive, discover, innovate **09** fabricate, formulate, improvise, originate **10** come up with **11** confabulate, manufacture **12** swing the lead

invented
03 inv **06** made up **09** trumped-up **10** fictitious

invention
◇ *anagram indicator*
03 fib, lie, wit **04** baby, fake, gift, idea, myth **05** skill **06** deceit, design, device, gadget, genius, system, talent **07** coinage, coining, concept, fantasy, fiction, figment, forgery, machine, untruth **08** artistry, creation **09** discovery, falsehood, ingenuity, tall story **10** brainchild, concoction, contriving, creativity, innovation **11** contrivance, development, fabrication, imagination, inspiration, originality, origination **12** construction, contrivement, excogitation **13** falsification, inventiveness **15** resourcefulness

inventive
06 clever, devise, gifted **07** fertile, skilful **08** artistic, contrive, creative, inspired, original, pregnant, talented **09** ingenious **10** innovative **11** imaginative, resourceful

inventiveness
04 gift **05** power, skill **06** talent **10** creativity, enterprise, innovation **11** imagination, inspiration, originality **13** ingeniousness **14** innovativeness **15** imaginativeness, resourcefulness

inventor
05 maker **06** author, coiner, father, framer, mother **07** creator, deviser **08** designer, engineer, producer **09** architect, developer, innovator, scientist, sloganeer **10** discoverer, mint master, originator **11** emblematist **12** palindromist

Inventors include:

03 **Sax** (Antoine Joseph)

04 **Abel** (Sir Frederick), **Bell** (Alexander Graham), **Benz** (Karl), **Biro** (Laszlo), **Colt** (Samuel), **Davy** (Sir Humphry), **Hood** (Thomas), **Jobs** (Steve), **Land** (Edwin Herbert), **Moon** (William), **Otis** (Elisha Graves), **Swan** (Sir Joseph Wilson), **Tull** (Jethro), **Watt** (James), **Yale** (Linus)

05 **Baird** (John Logie), **Boehm** (Theobald), **Boyle** (Robert), **Cyril** (St), **Dyson** (James), **Hertz** (Heinrich), **Kilby** (Jack S), **Maxim** (Sir Hiram Stevens), **Monge** (Gaspard), **Morse** (Samuel), **Nobel** (Alfred), **Rubik** (Ernö), **Sousa** (John Philip), **Tesla** (Nikola), **Volta** (Alessandro, Count), **Zeiss** (Carl)

06 **Ampère** (André Marie), **Brunel** (Isambard Kingdom), **Brunel** (Sir Marc Isambard), **Bunsen** (Robert Wilhelm), **Diesel** (Rudolf), **Dunlop** (John Boyd), **Eckert** (J Presper), **Edison** (Thomas Alva), **Frisch** (Otto), **Hansom** (Joseph Aloysius), **Hornby** (Frank), **Hubble** (Edwin Powell), **Lenoir** (Jean Joseph Étienne), **Lister** (Samuel, Lord), **McAdam** (John Loudon), **Napier** (John), **Newton** (Sir Isaac), **Pascal** (Blaise), **Pitman** (Sir Isaac), **Schick** (Jacob), **Singer** (Isaac Merritt), **Sperry** (Elmer Ambrose), **Talbot** (William Henry Fox), **Wallis** (Sir Barnes), **Wright** (Orville), **Wright** (Wilbur)

07 **Babbage** (Charles), **Blériot** (Louis), **Carlson** (Chester Floyd), **Daimler** (Gottlieb), **Drebbel** (Cornelis), **Eastman** (George), **Faraday** (Michael), **Gaumont** (Léon), **Giffard** (Henri), **Goddard** (Robert Hutchings), **Huygens** (Christiaan), **Jacuzzi** (Candido), **Janssen** (Zacharias), **Lumière** (Auguste), **Lumière** (Louis Jean), **Marconi** (Guglielmo), **Mauchly** (John W), **Maxwell** (James Clerk), **Pasteur** (Louis), **Pullman** (George Mortimer), **Thomson** (Elihu), **Whitney** (Eli), **Whittle** (Sir Frank)

08 **Bessemer** (Sir Henry), **Birdseye** (Clarence), **Daguerre** (Louis Jacques Mandé), **De Forest** (Lee), **Ericsson** (John), **Ferranti** (Sebastian Ziani de), **Franklin** (Benjamin), **Gillette** (King Camp), **Goodyear**

(Charles), **Huntsman** (Benjamin), **Newcomen** (Thomas), **Sandwich** (John Montagu, Earl), **Sinclair** (Sir Clive), **Zamenhof** (Lazarus Ludwig), **Zeppelin** (Ferdinand von, Count)
09 **Arkwright** (Sir Richard), **Armstrong** (Edwin Howard), **Butterick** (Ebenezer), **Cockerell** (Sir Christopher Sydney), **Ctesibius**, **Fessenden** (Reginald Aubrey), **Gutenberg** (Johannes), **Hollerith** (Herman), **Macmillan** (Kirkpatrick), **McCormick** (Cyrus Hall), **Pinchbeck** (Christopher), **Remington** (Philo), **Whitworth** (Sir Joseph)
10 **Archimedes**, **Berners-Lee** (Tim), **Cristofori** (Bartolommeo), **Fahrenheit** (Gabriel), **Lilienthal** (Otto), **Pilkington** (Sir Alastair), **Senefelder** (Aloys), **Stephenson** (George), **Torricelli** (Evangelista), **Trevithick** (Richard)
11 **Montgolfier** (Jacques), **Montgolfier** (Joseph)
12 **Friese-Greene** (William)

inventory
04 file, list, roll **05** stock, sum up, tally **06** record, roster, scroll, supply **07** account, listing, terrier **08** register, schedule **09** catalogue, checklist, equipment **11** description, stocktaking

inverse
05 other **07** counter, obverse, reverse **08** contrary, converse, inverted, opposite, reversed **10** reciprocal, retrograde, transposed, upside down **12** antistrophic

inversion
◇ *reversal indicator*
07 reverse **08** contrary, converse, opposite, reversal **09** entropion, entropium **10** anastrophe, antithesis, transposal **11** contrariety **13** transposition **14** antimetathesis, contraposition

invert
◇ *reversal indicator*
05 upset **06** turn up, upturn **07** capsize, reverse **08** overturn, turn down **09** transpose **10** homosexual, turn around, turn turtle **11** transsexual **13** turn inside out **14** turn upside down **15** turn back to front

invertebrate

Invertebrates include:

05 coral, fluke, hydra, leech
06 chiton, insect, spider, sponge
07 bivalve, crinoid, mollusc, sea lily, sea wasp
08 arachnid, flatworm, nematode, sea pansy, starfish, tapeworm
09 arthropod, centipede, earthworm, gastropod, jellyfish, millipede, planarian, roundworm, sea spider, sea urchin, spoonworm, trilobite, water bear
10 cephalopod, crustacean, echinoderm, sand dollar, sea anemone, tardigrade
11 annelid worm, brittle star, chaetognath, feather star, sea cucumber
12 box jellyfish, coelenterate, Venus's girdle
13 crown-of-thorns, horseshoe crab, sea gooseberry
15 dead-men's fingers

See also **animal**; **butterfly**; **crustacean**; **insect**; **mollusc**; **moth**; **spider**; **worm**

invest
◇ *hidden indicator*
◇ *insertion indicator*
03 put **04** belt, fund, give, gown, robe, sink, vest **05** admit, adorn, cover, crown, endow, endue, frock, grant, imbue, place, put in, spend, tie up **06** bestow, clothe, confer, create, devote, enrobe, induct, lay out, lock up, ordain, supply **07** besiege, dignify, empower, entrust, install, mandate, provide, swear in **08** dedicate, sanction, surround **09** authorize, beglamour, subsidize **10** contribute, inaugurate

investigate
03 spy, sus **04** case, comb, feel, sift, suss **05** probe, study, trawl **06** go into, muzzle, nuzzle, pry out, search **07** analyse, check up, examine, explore, inspect, suss out **08** check out, consider, look into, research **09** delve into **10** scrutinize **11** inquire into **15** give the once-over

investigation
05 probe, quest, study **06** review, search, survey **07** enquiry, hearing, inquest, inquiry, sifting, zetetic **08** analysis, research, scrutiny **10** inspection **11** examination, exploration, inquisition **13** consideration
- **bear investigation**

04 wash

investigative
07 zetetic **08** research **09** heuristic **10** analytical, inspecting **11** exploratory, fact-finding, researching **13** investigating

investigator
02 PI **04** dick **06** ferret, prober, sleuth **07** analyst **08** analyser, examiner, explorer, inquirer, quaestor, reviewer, searcher **09** detective, inspector **10** private eye, questioner, researcher, scrutineer **11** scrutinizer

investiture
09 admission, induction, investing **10** coronation, investment, ordination, swearing-in **11** instatement **12** enthronement, inauguration, installation

investment
04 cash, gilt, risk, spec **05** asset, funds, money, stake, stock **06** outlay, wealth **07** capital, finance, reserve, savings, venture **08** blockade, property **09** principal, resources **11** expenditure, investiture, speculation, transaction **12** contribution **14** venture capital

inveterate
05 sworn **06** inured **07** chronic, diehard **08** addicted, habitual, hard-core, hardened, stubborn **09** confirmed, incurable, obstinate **10** double-dyed, entrenched **11** established **12** incorrigible, irreformable, long-standing **13** dyed-in-the-wool

invidious
06 odious **07** awkward, hateful **08** enviable **09** difficult, obnoxious, offensive, repugnant, slighting **10** unpleasant **11** undesirable **13** objectionable **14** discriminating, discriminatory

invigilate
05 watch **06** direct **07** inspect, monitor, oversee **09** look after, supervise, watch over **11** keep an eye on, superintend **12** be in charge of **13** be in control of

invigilation
04 care **06** charge **07** control, running **08** guidance **09** direction, oversight **10** inspection **11** supervision **12** surveillance **15** superintendence

invigilator
07 monitor, proctor **08** director, examiner, overseer **09** inspector **10** supervisor **14** superintendent

invigorate
04 buck **05** brace, pep up, renew, rouse **06** buck up, excite, perk up, soup up **07** animate, enliven, fortify, freshen, inspire, liven up, quicken, refresh **08** energize, motivate, vitalize **09** stimulate **10** exhilarate, rejuvenate, revitalize, strengthen

invigorating
05 brisk, fresh, tonic, vital **07** bracing **08** generous **09** animating, healthful, uplifting, vivifying **10** energizing, fortifying, life-giving, quickening, refreshing, salubrious **11** inspiriting, restorative, stimulating **12** exhilarating, rejuvenating

invincibility
05 force, power **08** strength **13** inviolability **14** impregnability, insuperability **15** impenetrability, invulnerability, unassailability

invincible
08 almighty **10** unbeatable, unshakable, unyielding **11** all-powerful, impregnable, indomitable, insuperable, unshakeable **12** impenetrable, invulnerable, unassailable, undefeatable **13** unconquerable **14** indestructible, unsurmountable

inviolability
08 holiness, sanctity **09** inviolacy **10** sacredness **14** inalienability, inviolableness, sacrosanctness **15** invulnerability

inviolable
04 holy **06** sacred **08** hallowed **10** intemerate, sacrosanct **11** inalienable, unalterable, untouchable

inviolate
04 pure **05** whole **06** entire, intact, sacred, unhurt, virgin **08** complete, unbroken, unharmed **09** stainless, undamaged, undefiled, uninjured, unspoiled, unstained, unsullied, untouched **10** intemerate, unpolluted, unprofaned **11** undisturbed

invisible
05 blind **06** hidden, unseen **08** viewless **09** concealed, disguised, imaginary, occulting, sightless, unnoticed, unseeable **10** evaporated, out of sight, unobserved **11** microscopic, non-existent **12** undetectable **13** imperceivable, imperceptible, inconspicuous, indiscernible, infinitesimal, microscopical **14** dematerialized

invitation
04 bait, call, draw, lure **06** appeal, come-on, invite **07** bidding, request, summons, welcome **08** overture, petition **09** challenge **10** allurement, attraction, come-hither, enticement, incitement, inducement, temptation **11** proposition, provocation **12** solicitation **13** encouragement

invite
03 ask, bid, woo **04** call, draw, lead, seek, will **05** press, tempt **06** allure, appeal, ask for, entice, summon **07** attract, bring on, look for, provoke, request, solicit, welcome **08** have over, petition **09** encourage, entertain, have round **15** give the come-on to

inviting
07 winning **08** alluring, engaging, enticing, pleasant, pleasing, tempting **09** agreeable, appealing, beguiling, seductive, welcoming **10** attractive, bewitching, come-hither, delightful, enchanting, entrancing, intriguing **11** captivating, fascinating, tantalizing **12** irresistible

invocation
04 call **05** curse **06** appeal, prayer **07** request, summons **08** entreaty, petition **09** epiclesis **10** beseeching **11** benediction, conjuration, imploration **12** solicitation, supplication
• **expression of invocation**
02 io

invoice
03 inv **04** bill **07** account, charges **08** manifest, pro forma **09** reckoning

invoke
03 beg **04** cite, wish **05** curse, swear **06** call on, pray to, rabbit, turn to **07** beseech, conjure, entreat, implore, refer to, request, solicit, swear by **08** appeal to, call down, call upon, petition, resort to **09** deprecate, imprecate, make use of **10** supplicate **14** have recourse to

involuntary
05 blind **06** forced, reflex **07** coerced **08** knee-jerk, unwilled **09** automatic, compelled, impulsive, mandatory, reluctant, unwilling **10** compulsory, mechanical, obligatory, unthinking **11** conditioned, instinctive, spontaneous, unconscious **12** uncontrolled **13** unintentional

involve
◇ *anagram indicator*
◇ *insertion indicator*
03 mix **04** cost, grip, hold, mean, wind, wrap **05** cover, imply, infer, mix up, rivet **06** absorb, affect, assume, commit, denote, draw in, engage, entail, mess in, occupy, take in **07** concern, connect, connote, count in, dip into, embrace, embroil, engross, immerse, include, require **08** entangle, interest, mess with, walk into **09** associate, embarrass, encompass, implicate, inculpate, preoccupy **10** complicate, comprehend, compromise, presuppose **11** incorporate, incriminate, necessitate **15** cause to take part

involved
◇ *anagram indicator*
04 deep, held, in on **06** implex, knotty **07** complex, engaged, gripped, jumbled, mixed up, riveted, tangled **08** absorbed, caught up, confused, immersed, intorted, involute, occupied, plighted, tortuous **09** concerned, confusing, difficult, elaborate, engrossed, intricate **10** associated, convoluted, implicated, inculpated, interested, taking part **11** anfractuous, complicated, preoccupied **12** incriminated, inextricable **13** participating
• **involved with**
◇ *insertion indicator*
02 in

involvement
04 part **05** share **06** action **07** concern **08** interest **09** immersion **10** attachment, connection **11** association, implication **12** contribution, entanglement **13** participation **14** responsibility

invulnerability
05 proof **06** safety **08** security, strength **13** invincibility, inviolability **14** impregnability **15** impenetrability, unassailability

invulnerable
04 safe **05** proof **06** secure **09** woundless **10** impervious, invincible **12** impenetrable, unassailable **14** indestructible

inward
02 in **05** inner **06** entire, hidden, infelt, inmost, inside, secret, toward **07** private **08** entering, homefelt, incoming, interior, internal, intimate, introrse, involute, personal, turned-in **09** heartfelt, incurrent, innermost, intrinsic **11** intrinsical **12** confidential

inwardly
04 inly **06** inside, within **07** at heart **08** deep down, secretly **09** privately **10** to yourself **13** deep inside you

inwards
06 inside, inward, within **07** indoors **08** inwardly

iodine
01 I

iota
03 bit, jot, tad **04** atom, hint, mite, whit **05** grain, scrap, speck, trace **06** morsel **08** fraction, particle

Iowa
02 IA

Iran
02 IR **03** IRN

Iraq
03 IRQ

irascibility
06 choler **08** edginess **09** bad temper, crossness, fieriness, ill-temper, petulance, shortness, testiness **10** crabbiness, impatience, irritation, touchiness **12** irritability, snappishness

irascible
05 cross, hasty, narky, ratty, testy **06** crabby, touchy **07** crabbed, iracund, prickly, toustie **08** choleric, petulant **09** irritable, querulous **10** ill-natured **11** bad-tempered, hot-tempered, ill-tempered **12** cantankerous, iracundulous **13** quick-tempered, short-tempered

irate
03 mad **04** waxy **05** angry, livid, vexed **06** fuming, raging **07** annoyed, enraged, furious, ranting **08** incensed, up in arms, worked up **09** indignant, irritated, pissed off, steamed up **10** hopping mad, infuriated **11** exasperated

irately
07 angrily, crossly, in a huff **08** bitterly **09** furiously **11** indignantly, resentfully **13** acrimoniously, reproachfully

ire
04 fury, rage **05** anger, wrath **06** choler **07** passion **09** annoyance **11** displeasure, indignation **12** exasperation

Ireland
03 IRL **04** Éire, Erin **08** Hibernia **09** Green Isle **11** blarney-land, Emerald Isle

Irish cities and notable towns include:

04 Cork
05 Sligo
06 Dublin, Galway
07 Dundalk
08 Drogheda, Limerick
09 Waterford

See also **county**; **province**

iridescent
04 shot **06** flambé, pearly **07** rainbow **08** dazzling **09** chatoyant, prismatic, sparkling **10** glittering, opalescent, shimmering, variegated **11** rainbow-like **13** multicoloured, polychromatic **15** rainbow-coloured

iridium
02 Ir

iris
03 lis, seg **04** flag, irid, ixia **05** orris, sedge **07** gladdon **09** water flag **10** fleur-de-lis, fleur-de-lys **12** flower-delice, flower-deluce **13** flower-de-leuce **14** roast-beef plant

Irish
02 Ir **04** Erse **08** Milesian **09** Hibernian

See also **Ireland**

Irish first names include:

03 Ena, Kit, Pat, Una
04 Aine, Cait, Colm, Edel, Elva, Eoin, Erin, Euan, Ewan, Ewen, Finn, Kath, Kyra, Liam, Maev, Maud, Mona, Neal, Neil, Nola, Nora, Nora, Owen, Rory, Ryan, Sean, Sine, Tara
05 Aidan, Aiden, Barry, Brona, Cahal, Ciara, Colum, Conor, Duane, Dwane, Elvis, Ethna, Ethne, Fionn, Kelly, Kerry, Kevan, Kevin, Kiera, Maeve, Maire, Maude, Maura, Moira, Moyra, Neale, Niall, Niamh, Norah, Norah, Nuala, Oscar, Paddy, Ronan, Rowan, Shane, Shaun, Shawn, Ultan
06 Aileen, Ailish, Arthur, Cathal, Ciaran, Connor, Declan, Dervla, Dympna, Eamonn, Eamunn, Eileen, Eithna, Eithne, Finbar, Fingal, Finola, Finola, Fintan, Garret, Grania, Granya, Kieran, Kieron, Kilian, Lorcan, Noreen, Noreen, Roisin, Seamas, Seamus, Shamus, Sheila, Sinead, Sorcha, Tyrone
07 Aisling, Brendan, Bronach, Bronagh, Caitlin, Christy, Clodagh, Colleen, Deirdre, Desmond, Dymphna, Feargal, Finbarr, Grainne, Killian, Mairead, Maureen, Padraic, Padraig, Patrick, Shannon, Shelagh, Siobhan
08 Kathleen, Ruaidhri
09 Fionnuala, Fionnuala

irk
03 bug, get, vex **04** gall, miff, rile **05** anger, annoy, get at, get to, weary **06** needle, nettle, put out, ruffle, wind up **07** disgust, incense, provoke **08** distress, drive mad, irritate **09** aggravate, infuriate **10** drive crazy, exasperate **12** drive bananas **13** make sparks fly **14** drive up the wall, piss someone off

irksome
06 boring, trying, vexing **07** painful, tedious **08** annoying, infernal, tiresome **09** vexatious, wearisome **10** bothersome, burdensome, confounded, irritating, ungrateful **11** aggravating, infuriating, troublesome **12** disagreeable, exasperating

iron
02 Fe **04** airn, firm, hard, Mars **05** harsh, press, rigid, stern, tough **06** fetter, pistol, robust, smooth, steely, strong **07** adamant, flatten, grating, stirrup **08** decrease, revolver, strength **10** determined, inflexible **11** insensitive **14** uncompromising

• iron out
06 settle **07** clear up, resolve, sort out **08** deal with, get rid of, put right **09** eliminate, eradicate, harmonize, reconcile **13** straighten out

ironic, ironical
03 wry **04** rich **05** bland **07** mocking **08** derisive, sardonic, scoffing, scornful, sneering **09** sarcastic, satirical **10** ridiculing, ridiculous **11** paradoxical **12** antiphrastic, contemptuous **14** antiphrastical

irons
05 bonds **06** chains **07** fetters **08** manacles, shackles, trammels

irony
04 hard **05** scorn **06** satire **07** asteism, mockery, paradox, sarcasm **08** ridicule **10** enantiosis **11** antiphrasis, incongruity **12** contrariness **14** sting in the tail

irradiate
06 expose, illume **07** lighten, light up, radiate, shine on **08** brighten, illumine **09** enlighten **10** illuminate

irrational
04 surd, wild **05** brute, crazy, silly **06** absurd, phobic, unwise **07** brutish, foolish, invalid, unsound **08** paranoid **09** arbitrary, beastlike, illogical, senseless **10** groundless, ridiculous **11** implausible, nonsensical, unreasoning **12** inconsistent, unreasonable **14** beside yourself

irrationality
06 lunacy **07** madness **08** insanity, unreason **09** absurdity **11** unsoundness **12** illogicality **13** senselessness **14** groundlessness, ridiculousness

irreconcilable
05 alien **06** at odds **07** opposed **08** clashing, contrary, frondeur, hardline, opposite **10** implacable, in conflict, inexorable, inflexible, unatonable **11** conflicting, incongruous **12** incompatible, inconsistent, intransigent **13** contradictory, intransigeant **14** uncompromising

irrecoverable
04 lost **09** unsavable **11** irreparable **12** irredeemable, irremediable **13** irreclaimable, irretrievable, unrecoverable, unsalvageable

irredeemable
08 past hope **09** incurable **10** beyond hope **11** irreparable, irrevocable **12** incorrigible **13** irretrievable

irrefutable
04 sure **07** certain **08** decisive, definite, positive **10** unarguable, undeniable **11** beyond doubt, indubitable **12** indisputable, unanswerable **13** incontestable **14** beyond question, unquestionable

irregular
◇ *anagram indicator*
03 odd **04** bent, iffy **05** bumpy, false, fishy, freak, lumpy, rough, shady, shaky **06** fitful, haiduk, jagged, patchy, pitted, ragged, random, rugged, shifty, sniper, uneven **07** corrupt, crooked, devious, erratic, lawless, scraggy, snatchy, strange, unusual, wayward **08** aberrant, abnormal, cheating, improper, indecent, lopsided, partisan, peculiar, scraggly, sporadic, unsteady, variable, wavering **09** anomalous, deceitful, dishonest, guerrilla, haphazard, incondite, maquisard, spasmodic, terrorist **10** asymmetric, asyntactic, disorderly, fraudulent, immoderate, mendacious, occasional, out of order, perfidious, scraggling, unofficial, unorthodox **11** anomalistic, bushwhacker, duplicitous, exceptional, extravagant, fluctuating, fragmentary, franc-tireur, guerrillero, heteroclite **12** disorganized, disreputable, immethodical, inconsistent, intermittent, unmethodical, unprincipled, unscrupulous, unsystematic **13** against the law, anomalistical, dishonourable, extraordinary, unsymmetrical **14** freedom fighter, unconventional **15** against the rules

irregularity
05 fraud, freak, spasm **06** breach, deceit, oddity **07** anomaly, falsity, perfidy **08** cheating, trickery, wavering **09** arhythmia, asymmetry, bumpiness, chicanery, deviation, duplicity, falsehood, improbity, lumpiness, obliquity, roughness, shadiness, treachery **10** aberration, arrhythmia, corruption, dirty trick, dishonesty, fitfulness, jaggedness, misconduct, patchiness, raggedness, randomness, unevenness **11** abnormality, criminality, crookedness, fluctuation, fraudulence, impropriety, inconstancy, insincerity, lawlessness, malpractice, obliqueness, peculiarity, singularity, uncertainty, unorthodoxy, unusualness, variability **12** eccentricity, inordination, lopsidedness, perturbation, unsteadiness **13** double-dealing, haphazardness, inconsistency, intermittence, sharp practice, unpunctuality **14** disorderliness, occasionalness, untruthfulness **15** disorganization

irregularly
06 anyhow **07** jerkily **08** fitfully, off and on, unevenly **11** erratically,

haphazardly, now and again **12** here and there, occasionally **13** eccentrically, interruptedly, spasmodically **14** disconnectedly, intermittently, unmethodically **15** by fits and starts, in fits and starts

irrelevance
07 tangent **09** inaptness **10** digression, red herring **11** irrelevancy **12** unimportance **13** inconsequence, unrelatedness **14** extraneousness, inappositeness **15** inapplicability

irrelevant
05 inapt, inept **09** not matter, ungermane, unrelated **10** extraneous, immaterial, inapposite, irrelative, out of place, peripheral, tangential **11** off the point, unconnected, unimportant **12** inapplicable, inconsequent **13** beside the mark, inappropriate **14** beside the point **15** having no bearing, not coming into it

irreligious
05 pagan **06** sinful, unholy, wicked **07** godless, heathen, impious, profane, ungodly **08** agnostic, undevout **09** atheistic, heretical, sceptical **10** heathenish, irreverent **11** blasphemous, nullifidian, unbelieving, unreligious, unrighteous **12** free-thinking, iconoclastic, sacrilegious **13** rationalistic

irremediable
05 fatal, final **06** deadly, mortal **08** hopeless, terminal **09** incurable **10** inoperable, remediless **11** irreparable **12** incorrigible, irredeemable, irreversible **13** irrecoverable, irretrievable, unmedicinable

irremovable
03 set **04** fast **05** fixed, stuck **06** rooted **07** durable **08** obdurate **09** immovable, ingrained, obstinate, permanent **10** inoperable, persistent **12** ineradicable **14** indestructible

irreparable
09 incurable **12** irremediable, irreversible, unrepairable **13** irreclaimable, irrecoverable, irretrievable

irreplaceable
05 vital **06** unique **07** special **08** peerless, precious **09** essential, matchless, priceless, unmatched **13** indispensable

irrepressible
06 bubbly, lively **07** buoyant **08** animated **09** ebullient, energetic, resilient, vivacious **10** boisterous **11** uninhibited, unstoppable **12** effervescent, ungovernable **13** uncontainable **14** insuppressible, uncontrollable, unrestrainable

irreproachable
04 pure **07** perfect, sinless **08** flawless, innocent, spotless **09** blameless, faultless, guiltless, stainless **10** immaculate, impeccable, unblamable **11** unblemished **13** unimpeachable **14** beyond reproach **15** irreprehensible

irresistible
06 potent, urgent **07** killing **08** alluring, almighty, charming, enticing, forceful, pressing, tempting **09** ravishing, seductive **10** compelling, compulsive, enchanting, imperative, importable, inevitable, inexorable, opposeless, resistless **11** captivating, fascinating, inescapable, tantalizing, unavoidable **12** overpowering, overwhelming **13** insupportable, irrepressible, overmastering, unpreventable **14** uncontrollable

irresolute
04 weak **06** fickle, unsure **07** dubious **08** doubtful, hesitant, shifting, unstable, unsteady, variable, wavering **09** dithering, tentative, uncertain, undecided, unsettled **10** ambivalent, hesitating, indecisive, in two minds, on the fence, unresolved, weak-willed, wishy-washy **11** fluctuating, half-hearted, vacillating **12** faint-hearted, invertebrate, pussyfooting, undetermined **15** shilly-shallying

irrespective
• irrespective of
07 however, whoever **08** ignoring, no matter, whatever **09** never mind, whichever **12** disregarding, not affecting, regardless of **15** notwithstanding

irresponsible
04 rash, wild **06** unwise **07** erratic, flighty **08** carefree, careless, heedless, immature, reckless **09** negligent **10** fly-by-night, unreliable **11** injudicious, thoughtless **12** light-hearted **13** ill-considered, untrustworthy **14** scatterbrained

irretrievable
04 lost **06** damned **08** hopeless **11** irreparable, irrevocable **12** irredeemable, irremediable, irreversible, unrecallable **13** irrecoverable, unrecoverable, unsalvageable

irretrievably
10 hopelessly **11** irreparably, irrevocably **12** irredeemably, irreversibly **13** irrecoverably

irreverence
05 cheek, sauce **06** heresy, levity **07** impiety, mockery **08** rudeness **09** blasphemy, flippancy, impudence, insolence, profanity, sacrilege **10** cheekiness, disrespect, irreligion **11** discourtesy, godlessness, ungodliness **12** impertinence, impoliteness

irreverent
04 rude **05** saucy **06** cheeky **07** godless, impious, mocking, profane, ungodly **08** flippant, impolite, impudent, insolent **09** heretical **10** unreverend **11** blasphemous, impertinent, irreligious **12** discourteous, sacrilegious **13** disrespectful

irreversible
05 final **07** lasting **08** hopeless **09** incurable, permanent **11** irreparable, irrevocable, unalterable **12** irremediable **13** irretrievable, unrectifiable

irrevocable
05 final, fixed **07** settled **09** immutable **10** changeless, invariable **11** unalterable **12** irreversible, unchangeable **13** irretrievable, predetermined

irrevocably
07 for good **10** hopelessly, inevitably **11** inescapably, insuperably, irreparably, unavoidably **13** for good and all

irrigate
03 wet **04** soak **05** drink, flood, spray, water **06** dampen, deluge **07** moisten **08** inundate, sprinkle

irritability
04 bile, edge **08** edginess, erethism **09** bad temper, crossness, hastiness, ill-temper, petulance, rattiness, testiness **10** crabbiness, grumpiness, impatience, tetchiness, touchiness **11** fretfulness, peevishness, prickliness, stroppiness **12** irascibility **13** fractiousness

irritable
04 edgy, sore **05** cross, fiery, gusty, hasty, humpy, narky, ratty, riley, short, spiky, techy, testy **06** chippy, crabby, crusty, feisty, grumpy, livery, on edge, shirty, snappy, tetchy, touchy **07** bilious, crabbit, fretful, gustful, peckish, peevish, peppery, prickly, stroppy **08** liverish, scratchy, snappish **09** crotchety, fractious, impatient, irascible, splenetic **10** capernoity, hot-blooded, nettlesome **11** bad-tempered, capernoitie, cappernoity, ill-tempered, out of temper, thin-skinned **12** cantankerous **13** quick-tempered, short-tempered **14** hypersensitive

irritant
04 gall, goad, pain **05** CS gas, savin **06** bother, menace, savine **07** trouble **08** nuisance, urushiol, vexation **09** annoyance **11** provocation **15** thorn in the flesh

irritate
03 bug, eat, get, irk, jar, rub, try, vex **04** fret, gall, goad, grig, hurt, itch, miff, nark, rile **05** anger, annoy, chafe, get at, grate, peeve, rouse, tease **06** bother, emboil, enrage, excite, gravel, harass, jangle, needle, nettle, niggle, put out, rattle, ruffle, tickle, wind up **07** enchafe, incense, inflame, provoke **08** acerbate, drive mad **09** aggravate, displease, drive nuts, infuriate, stimulate **10** drive crazy, exasperate, excruciate **12** drive bananas **13** get

your back up, make sparks fly **14** drive up the wall, piss someone off, rub the wrong way **15** get on your nerves, give the needle to

irritated

◇ *anagram indicator*

03 mad **04** edgy, sore **05** angry, cross, irked, raggy, ratty, riled, spewy, vexed **06** choked, miffed, narked, peeved, piqued, put out, roused **07** annoyed, crooked, in a huff, nettled, ropable, ruffled, stroppy, uptight **08** bothered, harassed, in a paddy, in a strop, up in arms **09** flappable, flustered, impatient, in a lather, irritable, pissed off, raving mad, seeing red, splenetic, ticked off **10** aggravated, displeased, exasperate, hopping mad **11** discomposed, disgruntled, exacerbated, exasperated, fit to be tied **12** on the warpath

irritating

04 sore **05** itchy, pesky **06** thorny, trying, vexing **07** chafing, galling, grating, irksome, nagging, rubbing **08** abrasive, annoying, infernal, ticklish, tiresome, urticant **09** maddening, provoking, upsetting, vexatious, worrisome **10** bothersome, confounded, disturbing **11** aggravating, displeasing, infuriating, troublesome **12** excruciating

irritation

03 rub **04** bind, drag, fret, fury, pain, pest **05** anger, pique **06** bother **07** scunner, trouble **08** nuisance, pinprick, vexation **09** annoyance, crossness, testiness **10** impatience, snappiness **11** aggravation, displeasure, disturbance, indignation, provocation, running sore, stimulation **12** exasperation, excruciation, heeby-jeebies, irritability **13** heebie-jeebies, pain in the neck **15** dissatisfaction, thorn in the flesh

See also **itch**

• display of irritation

04 tiff, tift

is

01 's **03** est

Islamic *see* **month**

island

01 I **02** Is **03** ait, cay, île, Isl, key **04** eyot, holm, inch, isle **05** atoll, islet **06** skerry **07** isolate **11** archipelago

Islands and island groups include:

03 Cos, Ely, Fyn, Hoy, IOM, Ios, IOW, Man, Rab, Rum

04 Bali, Coll, Cook, Corn, Cuba, Eigg, Elba, Fiji, Gozo, Guam, Holy, Iona, Java, Jura, Line, Long, Mahe, Maui, Muck, Mull, Nias, Niue, Oahu, Rota, Sado, Sark, Skye, Uist, Wake

05 Arran, Barra, Bioko, Bonin, Capri, Chios, Cocos, Coney, Corfu, Crete, Delos, Éfaté, Ellis, Farne, Faroe, Handa, Hondo, Hydra, Ibiza, Islay, Kauai, Kuril, Lanai, Lundy, Luzon, Malta, Melos, Nauru, Naxos, North, Öland, Orust, Palau, Paros, Pearl, Pemba, Samoa, Samos, South, Sunda, Timor, Tiree, Tonga, Wight

06 Aegean, Aegina, Andros, Azores, Baffin, Bikini, Borneo, Caicos, Canary, Chagos, Comino, Cyprus, Devil's, Easter, Euboea, Flores, Flotta, Hainan, Harris, Hawaii, Honshu, Icaria, Ionian, Jersey, Kodiak, Komodo, Kosrae, Kyushu, Lemnos, Lesbos, Midway, Orkney, Patmos, Penghu, Rhodes, Scilly, Sicily, Skiros, Staffa, Staten, Tahiti, Taiwan, Tinian, Tobago, Tubuai, Tuvalu, Virgin

07 Anjouan, Anthony, Antigua, Bahamas, Bahrain, Bermuda, Bonaire, Cabrera, Celebes, Channel, Chatham, Comoros, Corsica, Curaçao, Frisian, Gilbert, Gotland, Grenada, Iceland, Ireland, Iwo Jima, Jamaica, La Digue, Leeward, Lofoten, Loyalty, Madeira, Majorca, Mayotte, Menorca, Mikonos, Mindoro, Minorca, Molokai, Nicobar, Norfolk, Oceania, Okinawa, Palawan, Phoenix, Praslin, Rathlin, Réunion, Siberut, Society, Solomon, Stewart, St Kilda, St Lucia, Sumatra, Surtsey, Tokelau, Vanuatu, Visayan, Westman, Wrangel, Zealand

08 Aleutian, Anglesey, Anguilla, Balearic, Bornholm, Colonsay, Coral Sea, Cyclades, Dominica, Falkland, Guernsey, Hawaiian, Hebrides, Hokkaido, Hong Kong, Jan Mayen, Johnston, Kiribati, Lord Howe, Maldives, Marshall, Mindanao, Moluccas, Pitcairn, Sakhalin, Sandwich, São Tiago, Sardinia, Shetland, Skiathos, Sri Lanka, Sulawesi, Svalbard, Tenerife, Trinidad, Victoria, Viti Levu, Windward, Zanzibar

09 Admiralty, Ascension, Australia, Benbecula, Cape Verde, Christmas, Ellesmere, Galápagos, Greenland, Halmahera, Indonesia, Irian Jaya, Isle of Man, Kárpathos, Lanzarote, Las Palmas, Macquarie, Manhattan, Marquesas, Mascarene, Mauritius, Melanesia, Nantucket, New Guinea, North Uist, Rodrigues, Santorini, Singapore, South Seas, South Uist, Stromboli, Vanua Levu, Zacynthus

10 Ahvenanmaa, Basse-Terre, Cape Breton, Cephalonia, Cook Strait, Dodecanese, Formentera, Heligoland, Hispaniola, Ile d'Oléron, Kalimantan, Kiritimati, Madagascar, Martinique, Micronesia, Montserrat, New Britain, New Ireland, Puerto Rico, Samothrace, Seychelles, Vesterålen, West Indies

11 Gran Canaria, Grand Bahama, Grand Cayman, Grande-Terre, Guadalcanal, Iles d'Hyères, Iles du Salut, Isla Cozumel, Isle of Wight, North Island, Philippines, Saint Helena, Scilly Isles, South Island, South Orkney

12 Bougainville, Grande Comore, Great Britain, Isla de Pascua, Newfoundland, Novaya Zemlya, Prince Edward, Prince Rupert, South Georgia

13 American Samoa, British Virgin, Inner Hebrides, Isla Contadora, Isles of Scilly, New Providence, Outer Hebrides, South Shetland

14 Oki Archipelago, Papua New Guinea, The Philippines, Tierra del Fuego, Tristan da Cunha, Turks and Caicos

15 French Polynesia, Lewis with Harris, Martha's Vineyard, Wallis and Futuna

See also **Channel Islands** *under* **channel**

• reef island

04 motu

Isle of Man

03 GBM, IMN **11** Ellan Vannin

isn't

03 nis, nys **04** ain't

isolate

06 cut off, detach, enisle, inisle, island, maroon, remove, strand **07** divorce, exclude, seclude, shut out **08** abstract, alienate, insulate, separate, set apart, shut away **09** keep apart, ostracize, segregate, sequester **10** disconnect, quarantine **11** marginalize **12** cold-shoulder **14** send to Coventry

isolated

04 lone **05** alone, apart, freak, stray **06** cut off, lonely, remote, single, unique **07** insular, special, unusual **08** abnormal, atypical, deserted, detached, outlying, secluded, solitary, uncommon **09** anomalous, separated, unrelated, untypical **10** segregated **11** exceptional, god-forsaken, in the sticks, out-of-the-way **12** unfrequented

isolation

05 exile **08** solitude **09** aloneness, seclusion **10** alienation, detachment, insulation, loneliness, quarantine, remoteness, retirement, separation, withdrawal **11** abstraction, segregation **12** dissociation, separateness, solitariness **13** disconnection, sequestration **15** marginalization

Israel

02 IL **03** ISR

See also **tribe**

issue

03 ish, jet, son **04** come, copy, emit, fall, fine, flow, flux, gush, mark, ooze, rise, rush, seed, seep, stem, turn **05** ensue, equip, exude, fit up, heirs, point, proof, spurt, topic, young **06** affair, debate, derive, effect, embryo, emerge, escape, family, finale, fit out, follow, kit out, matter, number, outlet, pay-off, put out, result, rig out, scions, spread, spring, stream, supply, upshot **07** concern, deal out, debouch, deliver, develop, dispute, edition, emanate, give out, handout, outcome, outflow, problem, proceed, produce, profits, progeny, provide, publish, release, send out, subject, version **08** announce, argument, children, daughter, delivery, effusion, emission, printing, proclaim, question **09** broadcast, discharge, effluence, offspring, originate, supplying, terminate **10** break forth, burst forth, conclusion, dénouement, distribute, impression, instalment, promulgate, successors **11** circulation, consequence, controversy, descendants, disseminate, publication **12** announcement, distribution, promulgation **13** dissemination

• at issue
10 in question **12** being debated **14** being discussed **15** under discussion

• final issue
04 fate

• side issue
02 by **03** bye

• take issue
05 argue, fight **06** object **07** contest, dispute, protest, quarrel **08** be at odds, disagree **09** challenge **12** be at odds with **13** take exception

• violent issue
04 gush

• without issue
02 sp **03** dsp, osp **09** sine prole

it
01 a, 't **02** SA **05** oomph **08** vermouth **09** sex appeal

• it is not
05 'taint, 'tisn't **06** aikona

• it's
03 'tis

• on it
03 an't

Italian
◇ *foreign word indicator*
01 I **02** It **03** Sig **04** Ital, trat **05** Roman, tratt **08** Ausonian, Sicilian, Venetian **09** trattoria **10** Neapolitan

See also **day**; **month**; **number**

• Italian family
06 Medici

Italy
01 I **03** ITA **04** Ital

itch
03 die, euk, ewk **04** ache, burn, long, pine, yeuk, youk, yuck, yuke **05** crave, crawl, psora, yearn **06** desire, hanker, hunger, thirst, tickle, tingle **07** burning, craving, longing, passion, prickle, scabies **08** irritate, keenness, pruritus, tingling, yearning **09** cacoethes, eagerness, hankering, itchiness, prickling **10** irritation

itching
03 euk, ewk **04** avid, yeuk, youk, yuck, yuke **05** dying, eager **06** aching, greedy, raring **07** burning, longing **08** prurient, pruritus **09** hankering, impatient **11** inquisitive

item
03 job **04** also **05** entry, issue, piece, point, story, thing **06** aspect, detail, factor, matter, notice, number, object, report **07** account, article, element, feature **08** bulletin, likewise **09** component, paragraph **10** accidental, ingredient, particular **12** circumstance **13** consideration

itemize
04 list **05** count **06** detail, number, record **07** mention, specify **08** document, instance, overname, tabulate **09** catalogue, enumerate **13** particularize **15** make an inventory

itinerant
◇ *anagram indicator*
03 faw **04** hobo, Roma **05** caird, Gypsy, nomad, rover **06** gitano, hawker, pedlar, roamer, Romani, Romany, roving, tinker **07** chapman, didakai, didakei, didicoi, didicoy, nomadic, rambler, roadman, roaming, running, swagman, tzigany, vagrant, Zincalo, Zingaro **08** Bohemian, diddicoy, drifting, huckster, minstrel, preacher, rambling, rootless, stroller, vagabond, wanderer, Zigeuner **09** itinerary, migratory, muffin man, piepowder, strolling, sundowner, traveller, unsettled, wandering, wayfaring **10** evangelist, journeying, revivalist, travelling **11** gandy dancer, peripatetic, Scotch cuddy **12** on the wallaby, Scotch draper **15** New-Age Traveller, strolling player

itinerary
03 way **04** plan, tour **05** route **06** course **07** circuit, journey **08** schedule **09** itinerant, programme, timetable **10** travelling **12** arrangements

itself

• of itself
03 sui

ivory
07 dentine **08** eburnean **09** eburneous **10** whale's bone

IVR code *see* **vehicle**

ivy
03 tod, udo **04** gill **06** aralia, fatsia, Hedera **07** ale-hoof **08** cat's-foot

Ivy League *see* **university**

izzard
01 Z **03** zed

J

J
03 jay **06** Juliet

jab
03 box, dig, tap **04** poke, prod, push, shot, stab **05** elbow, lunge, nudge, punch **06** thrust **09** injection

jabber
03 gab, jaw, yap **05** prate **06** babble, gabble, mumble, rabbit, ramble, rattle, tattle, witter, yabber, yatter **07** blather, blether, chatter, prattle, sputter

jack
01 J **02** AB **03** Dee, jak, nob, pam, pur, tar **04** Jock, John, mark **05** bower, fed up, kitty, knave, makar, money, noddy, tired, winch **06** hopper, runner, sailor **07** pantine, sticker **08** mistress, saw-horse, turnspit **09** detective, hand-screw

• **jack up**
04 hike, lift **05** hoist, put up, raise **06** hike up, push up, refuse, resist **07** elevate, inflate **08** increase

jackal
04 dieb **13** lion's provider

jackass
04 fool **09** blockhead **10** kookaburra

jackdaw
02 ka **03** daw, kae **04** jack **07** dawcock

jacket
02 DJ **03** tux **04** baju, beat, case, skin, wrap **05** acton, bania, cover, duvet, gilet, grego, jupon, polka, sayon, shell, tunic **06** anorak, banian, banyan, Basque, blazer, bolero, casing, dolman, folder, jerkin, railly, sheath, tuxedo, Zouave **07** Barbour®, Mae West, spencer, vareuse, wrapper **08** camisole, covering, envelope, water box, wrapping **09** night-rail, shortgown, slip cover **10** body-warmer, bumfreezer, duffel coat, sports coat, windjammer **11** Barbour® coat, windcheater

jackpot
03 pot **04** mess, pool **05** award, kitty, prize **06** reward, stakes **07** big time, bonanza **08** winnings **10** first prize

• **hit the jackpot**
05 score **06** arrive, make it **07** clean up, get rich, succeed **08** rake it in **09** make a pile **11** make a bundle, make a packet **13** hit the big time

jade
02 yu **03** nag **06** limmer **08** axe-stone, nephrite **11** spleenstone

jaded
04 done **05** all in, bored, fed up, spent, tired, weary **06** bushed, done in, dulled, fagged, pooped **07** wearied, whacked, worn out **08** fatigued, jiggered, tired out **09** disjaskit, exhausted, knackered, played-out, pooped out, shattered **10** cheesed off **11** ready to drop, tuckered out **14** unenthusiastic

jag
03 dag, fit **04** barb, cart, load, snag, spur **05** cleft, notch, point, prick, slash, spell, spree, tooth **06** bundle, dentil, Jaguar, pierce **08** denticle, division, quantity **09** injection, saddlebag **10** projection, protrusion **11** inoculation

jagged
◇ *anagram indicator*
04 rag'd **05** drunk, ragde, rough **06** barbed, broken, craggy, hackly, nicked, ragged, ridged, snaggy, spiked, uneven **07** notched, pointed, snagged, toothed **08** indented, saw-edged, serrated **09** irregular **11** denticulate

jaggedness
09 roughness, serration, serrature **10** brokenness, raggedness, unevenness **12** irregularity

jaguar
03 Jag **05** ounce, tiger **07** leopard, tigress **10** leopardess **13** American tiger

jail, gaol
03 bin, can, jug, pen **04** nick, poky, quad, quod, stir **05** choky, clink, kitty, pokey **06** cooler, detain, immure, inside, intern, lock up, lock-up, prison **07** confine, custody, hoosgow, impound, put away, slammer **08** big house, hoosegow, imprison, porridge, send down **09** bridewell, jailhouse **10** guardhouse **11** incarcerate **12** penitentiary, send to prison **15** detention centre

See also **prison**

jailbird *see* **prisoner**

jailer, gaoler
04 Adam **05** guard, screw **06** captor, keeper, warden, warder **07** alcaide, alcayde, turnkey **09** dungeoner **12** under-turnkey **13** prison officer

jake
02 OK **04** fine, okay **05** yokel **06** honest **07** correct **09** first-rate

jam
03 fix, mob, ram **04** bind, clog, cram, herd, hole, lock, pack, push, spot, stew **05** block, close, crowd, crush, force, horde, jeely, jelly, press, seize, stall, stick, stuff, swarm, wedge **06** hold-up, insert, jeelie, konfyt, pickle, plight, scrape, spread, squash, throng, thrust **07** confine, congest, seize up, squeeze, straits, the soup, trouble **08** close off, conserve, gridlock, obstruct, preserve, quandary **09** confiture, interfere, marmalade, multitude, tight spot **10** bottleneck, congestion **11** obstruction, predicament **12** damson cheese

Jamaica
02 JA **03** JAM

jamb
04 dern, durn, pole, post, prop **05** frame, shaft **06** greave, pillar **07** support, upright **08** doorpost, side post **09** stanchion **10** ingle-cheek

jamboree
04 fête **05** party, rally, spree **06** frolic, junket **07** carouse, jubilee, revelry, shindig **08** carnival, festival, field day **09** festivity, gathering, merriment **10** convention **11** celebration, get-together

jammy
05 lucky **06** timely **07** charmed **08** favoured **09** excellent, expedient, fortunate, opportune **10** auspicious, fortuitous, propitious, prosperous, successful **12** providential

jangle
◇ *anagram indicator*
03 din, jar **05** chime, clang, clank, clash, clink, upset **06** bother, jingle, racket, rattle **07** clatter, discord, disturb, jarring, quarrel, stridor, trouble, vibrate, wrangle **08** clangour, irritate **09** cacophony **10** contention, dissonance **11** make anxious **13** reverberation

janitor
06 porter **07** doorman, ostiary **08** servitor **09** attendant, caretaker, concierge, custodian **10** doorkeeper, servitress

January
03 Jan

japan
01 J **03** JPN **07** lacquer

Japanese
03 eta **07** Japonic **09** Nipponese

See also **Asian**

Japanese art forms include:

02 no
03 noh
04 raku
05 haiku, Hizen, Imari, kendo
06 gagaku, kabuki, nogaku, saikei, ukiyo-e
07 bunraku, chanoyu, ikebana, nihonga, origami
08 kakemono, kakiemon, tsutsumu
11 linked verse, tea ceremony

• Japanese title
03 san **04** sama

jar
◇ *anagram indicator*
03 irk, jug, mug, pot, urn **04** jerk, jolt, olla, pint, rasp, turn, vase **05** annoy, caddy, clash, crock, cruet, flask, grate, grind, shake, stave, upset **06** bicker, carafe, dolium, flagon, jampot, jangle, jostle, justle, kalpis, nettle, offend, pithos, rattle, tinaja, tureen, vessel **07** agitate, amphora, disturb, pitcher, quarrel, stamnos, terrine, trouble, vibrate **08** be at odds, canister, conflict, disagree, irritate **09** albarello, bell-glass, container, greybeard **10** receptacle **11** water monkey **12** be at variance, be in conflict

jargon
04 cant, jive **05** argot, Greek, idiom, lingo, slang, usage **06** patois, patter, pidgin **07** chatter, Kennick, twitter **08** legalese, nonsense, parlance, pig Latin **09** baragouin, buzz words, Eurospeak, gibberish **10** Eurobabble, greenspeak, journalese, mumbo-jumbo, twittering, vernacular **11** computerese, diplomatese, lingoa geral, officialese, sociologese, technospeak **12** gobbledegook, gobbledygook, lingua franca, psychobabble, technobabble, telegraphese **13** commercialese, computerspeak, pidgin English

jarring
04 ajar **05** harsh, shock **06** off-key **07** grating, jolting, rasping **08** backlash, clashing, friction, jangling, strident **09** dissonant, troubling, upsetting **10** discordant, disturbing, irritating **11** cacophonous

jasmine
07 jessamy **09** gelsemium, gessamine, jessamine **10** frangipani

jaundiced
05 jaded **06** biased, bitter **07** bigoted, cynical, envious, hostile, jealous **09** distorted, resentful, sceptical **10** prejudiced, suspicious **11** distrustful, icteritious, pessimistic **12** disbelieving, misanthropic, preconceived **14** unenthusiastic

jaunt
04 ride, spin, tour, trip **05** drive, sally **06** outing, ramble, stroll **07** holiday **09** excursion

jauntily
06 airily **07** perkily, smartly **08** brightly, cheekily **10** cheerfully **13** energetically **15** self-confidently

jaunty
◇ *anagram indicator*
04 airy, pert, trim **05** perky, showy, smart **06** bouncy, breezy, cheeky, dapper, flashy, lively, rakish, spruce **07** buoyant, stylish **08** carefree, cheerful, debonair, sparkish **09** energetic, sprightly **11** gentlemanly, Micawberish **12** high-spirited **13** self-confident

javelin
04 dart, pile **05** jerid, pilum, spear **06** jereed **07** harpoon **08** gavelock **09** handstaff

jaw
03 gum, rap **04** chap, chat, chaw, chop, dash, jole, joll, jowl, talk, trap **05** chaft, chops, claws, grasp, mouth, power, scold, visit, wongi **06** babble, chafts, confab, gabble, gossip, jabber, muzzle, natter, rabbit **07** chatter, chinwag, control, lecture, maxilla **08** clutches, mandible, rabbit on, schmooze **09** threshold **10** discussion, masticator **12** conversation **13** talkativeness

• front of jaw
04 chin

jay
01 J **10** whisky jack, whisky john

jazz
◇ *anagram indicator*

Jazz types include:

03 bop, hot, rag
04 acid, Afro, cool, jive, soul, trad
05 bebop, blues, funky, kwela, modal, spiel, swing
06 fusion, groove, modern
07 classic, hard bop, New Wave, post-bop, ragtime
08 free-form, high life
09 Afro-Cuban, bossa nova, Dixieland, gutbucket, West Coast
10 avant-garde, improvised, mainstream, neo-classic, New Orleans
11 barrelhouse, third stream, traditional
12 boogie-woogie

See also **singer**

• jazz fan
03 cat

• jazz up
07 enliven, liven up **08** ginger up **09** smarten up **10** brighten up

jazzy
04 bold, wild **05** fancy, gaudy, smart **06** bright, flashy, lively, snazzy **07** stylish, zestful **08** spirited, swinging **09** vivacious

jealous
04 wary **05** green **07** anxious, careful, envious, gealous, mindful **08** covetous, desirous, doubting, grudging, insecure, vigilant, watchful **09** defensive, green-eyed, jaundiced, resentful **10** begrudging, possessive, protective, solicitous, suspicious **11** distrustful

jealously
08 with envy **09** enviously **10** covetously, desirously **11** resentfully **12** possessively **13** distrustfully

jealousy
04 envy **05** doubt, spite **06** gelosy, grudge **07** envying, ill-will **08** distrust, gealousy, mistrust, wariness **09** emulation, suspicion, vigilance, zelotypia **10** bitterness, insecurity, resentment, yellowness **11** carefulness, mindfulness **12** covetousness, grudgingness, watchfulness **13** defensiveness **14** possessiveness, protectiveness

jeans
05 Levis®

jeer
03 boo, dig **04** gibe, gird, goof, hiss, hoot, jest, jibe, mock, razz, twit **05** abuse, chaff, fleer, flout, frump, geare, knock, scoff, scorn, sneer, taunt, tease **06** banter, chiack, deride, heckle **07** barrack, catcall, mockery, teasing **08** derision, ridicule **09** make fun of, shout down **10** sling off at **11** have a shot at, poke borak at **12** laugh to scorn

jejune
03 dry **04** arid, dull **05** banal, empty, naive, silly, trite, vapid **06** barren, boring, callow, meagre, simple **07** insipid, prosaic, puerile **08** childish, immature, juvenile **09** senseless **10** colourless, spiritless, unoriginal, wishy-washy **13** uninteresting **15** unsophisticated

jell *see* **gel, jell**

jelly
03 gel **04** agar, jeel **05** aspic, jeely, shape **06** jeelie, kanten, napalm, Sterno® **07** congeal **08** agar-agar, quiddany, Vaseline® **09** calf's-foot, gelignite **10** petrolatum **14** liquid paraffin

jellyfish
05 jelly **06** medusa **07** acaleph, aurelia, blubber, sea wasp **08** acalephe, sea jelly **09** sea nettle **10** nettle-fish, scyphozoan, sea blubber

jeopardize
04 risk **05** stake **06** chance, expose, gamble, hazard, menace **07** imperil, venture **08** endanger, threaten **09** put at risk **11** take a chance **13** put in jeopardy **14** expose to danger

jeopardy
04 risk **05** peril **06** danger, hazard, menace, threat **07** venture **08** exposure **09** liability **10** insecurity **12** endangerment **13** vulnerability **14** precariousness

jerk
◇ *anagram indicator*
03 ass, bob, git, jar, jig, jog, mug, nit, sap, tug **04** berk, cant, clot, coot, dope, dork, fool, geek, goat, goof, goop, hoik, jolt, jump, kick, kook, nerd, nerk, peck, prat, pull, toss, twit, yank **05** braid, chump, dumbo, dweeb, flirt, hitch, hoick, idiot, lurch, neddy, ninny, pluck, prick, quirk, shrug, surge, throw, twerp, wally **06** bounce, dum-dum, fillip, jiggle, josser, nitwit, sawney, sucker, switch, thrust, turkey, twitch, wrench **07** Charlie, charqui, gubbins, pillock, plonker, saphead, tosspot, wazzock **08** dipstick **09** birdbrain, cloth head, schlemiel **10** headbanger, nincompoop, silly-billy **11** kangaroo hop **13** proper Charlie

jerkily
07 bumpily, jumpily, roughly **08** fitfully, unevenly **13** spasmodically

jerky
◇ *anagram indicator*
05 bumpy, jumpy, rough, shaky
06 bouncy, fitful, uneven **07** charqui, jolting, shaking, twitchy **08** lurching, saccadic **09** spasmodic **10** convulsive, incoherent **12** disconnected, uncontrolled **13** unco-ordinated

jerry-built
04 Lego® **05** cheap **06** faulty, flimsy, shoddy **07** rickety **08** slipshod, unstable **09** cheapjack, defective, slop-built **10** ramshackle **12** quickly built **13** insubstantial, unsubstantial
14 thrown together **15** built on the cheap

jersey
03 GBJ, top **04** polo **05** frock
06 gansey, jumper, woolly, zephyr
07 maillot, sweater **08** guernsey, polo neck, pullover **10** sweatshirt

Jerusalem
04 Zion

jest
03 cod, fun, gab, gag, jig, kid, toy
04 fool, game, hoax, jape, jeer, joke, mock, quip **05** bourd, crack, droll, gleek, prank, taunt, tease, trick
06 banter **07** fooling, kidding, leg-pull
08 drollery **09** Joe Miller, tell jokes, wisecrack, witticism **13** practical joke
• **in jest**
05 in fun **07** as a joke, to tease
08 jokingly **09** playfully
13 mischievously

jester
03 wag, wit **04** fool, scop, zany
05 clown, comic, droll, joker, patch
06 gagman, motley, mummer
07 bourder, buffoon, juggler
08 comedian, humorist, merryman, quipster **09** court-fool, harlequin, joculator, pantaloon, prankster **11** Jack-pudding, merry-andrew

Jesuits
02 SJ **09** Ignatians

jet
03 fly, jut **04** flow, gush, inky, jeat, rush, zoom **05** black, ebony, jumbo, raven, sable, shoot, sooty, spirt, spout, spray, spurt, strut **06** Airbus®, candle, career, douche, spring, squirt, stream
07 sprayer **08** encroach, fountain
09 delta wing, sprinkler **10** pitch-black, tankbuster
See also **aircraft**

jettison
04 drop, dump **05** chuck, ditch, eject, expel, heave, scrap **06** jetsam, unload
07 abandon, discard, offload **08** get rid of **09** throw away

jetty
04 dock, mole, pier, quay **05** jutty, wharf **06** groyne **07** harbour
10 breakwater **12** landing-place, landing-stage

jewel
03 gem **04** find, rock **05** bijou, pearl, prize **06** rarity **07** navette, paragon
08 gemstone, ornament, sparkler, treasure **09** jewellery, showpiece
10 ferronière **11** ferronnière, masterpiece, pride and joy
13 precious stone **14** crème de la crème

jewellery
03 tom **04** gems **05** gauds **06** bijoux, finery, jewels **07** gemmery, regalia
08 treasure, trinkets **09** ornaments
10 bijouterie, tomfoolery
13 paraphernalia

Jewellery types include:

04 prop, ring, stud
05 beads, bindi, cameo, chain, tiara
06 amulet, anklet, bangle, brooch, choker, corals, diadem, hatpin, locket, pearls, tiepin, torque
07 armilla, coronet, earring, necklet, pendant, rivière, sautoir, toe ring
08 bracelet, cufflink, necklace, negligee, nose ring, wristlet
09 medallion, navel ring
10 signet ring
11 mangalsutra
12 eternity ring
13 charm bracelet, solitaire ring
15 belly-button ring

Jewish calendar *see* **month**

Jezebel
04 jade, tart, vamp **05** hussy, whore, witch **06** harlot, wanton **07** Delilah
08 man-eater, scrubber **09** temptress
10 loose woman, seductress **11** femme fatale **12** scarlet woman

jib
03 shy **04** balk, face, stop **05** baulk, genoa, stall, strip **06** boggle, fleece, recoil, refuse, shrink **07** back off, retreat **09** stop short **10** standstill

jibe *see* **gibe**

jiffy
02 mo **03** bit, sec **04** tick **05** flash, trice, whiff **06** minute, moment, no time, second **07** instant **08** two ticks
09 twinkling **11** split second

jig
◇ *anagram indicator*
03 bob, hop **04** jerk, jest, jump, leap, skip **05** caper, prank, shake
06 bounce, jingle, prance, twitch, wiggle, wobble

jigger
04 damn, jerk, ruin **05** blast, break, shake, spoil, wreck **06** chigoe, chigre, jolley, kibosh **07** botch up, chigger, destroy, louse up, scupper, vitiate
08 sand flea **09** undermine **14** make a pig's ear of

jiggery-pokery
05 fraud **06** deceit **08** mischief, trickery **09** chicanery, deception
10 dishonesty, hanky-panky, subterfuge **13** funny business
14 monkey business

jiggle
◇ *anagram indicator*
03 jig, jog **04** jerk, jump **05** shake, shift
06 bounce, fidget, joggle, twitch, waggle, wiggle, wobble **07** agitate

jilt
04 drop, dump **05** chuck, ditch, leave, spurn **06** begunk, betray, desert, pack in, reject **07** abandon, discard
08 brush off **09** cast aside, throw over, walk out on

jingle
03 jig **04** ding, poem, ring, song, tune
05 carol, chant, chime, chink, clang, clink, ditty, rhyme, verse **06** chorus, jangle, melody, rattle, slogan, tinkle
07 clatter, refrain, ringing **08** clangour, doggerel, limerick **14** tintinnabulate

jingoism
10 chauvinism, flag-waving, insularity, patriotism **11** imperialism, nationalism
13 sabre-rattling

jinx
03 hex, moz **04** doom, mozz
05 charm, curse, spell **06** hoodoo, plague, voodoo **07** bad luck, bedevil, bewitch, evil eye, gremlin **10** affliction, black magic, Indian sign **11** malediction
12 cast a spell on

jitters
◇ *anagram indicator*
06 nerves **07** anxiety, fidgets, habdabs, jimjams **08** edginess
09 agitation, tenseness, the creeps, the shakes, trembling **10** the shivers, the willies, uneasiness **11** nervousness
12 collywobbles **13** heebie-jeebies

jittery
◇ *anagram indicator*
04 edgy **05** het up, jumpy, nervy, shaky
06 on edge, uneasy **07** anxious, fidgety, in a stew, keyed up, nervous, panicky, quaking, shivery, twitchy, uptight, wound up **08** agitated, in a sweat, in a tizzy **09** flustered, perturbed, quivering, screwed-up, trembling

job
04 char, darg, duty, part, peck, post, prod, role, spot, task, work **05** berth, chore, place, punch, share, stint, trade **06** affair, career, charge, errand, métier, office, thrust **07** calling, concern, mission, project, pursuit, venture **08** activity, business, capacity, function, position, province, sinecure, vocation **09** situation, soft thing **10** assignment, commission, employment, enterprise, line of work, livelihood, occupation, proceeding, profession **11** appointment, consignment, piece of work, undertaking **12** contribution **14** line of business, responsibility
See also **burglary**; **occupation**

• **have a job doing something**
14 find it a problem

• **just the job**
12 just the thing **13** just the ticket

jobless
04 idle **07** laid off **08** inactive, workless **09** on the dole, out of work, redundant **10** unemployed **11** without work

jock
02 DJ **03** Mac **04** jack **06** deejay **08** Scotsman **10** disc jockey

jockey
◇ *anagram indicator*
04 coax, ease, edge **05** rider **06** cajole, induce, manage **07** wheedle **08** engineer, horseman, inveigle, jockette **09** manoeuvre, negotiate **10** equestrian, horsewoman, jump-jockey, manipulate
See also **equestrian**; **horseman, horsewoman**

jocose
05 droll, funny, lepid, merry, witty **06** jovial, joyous **07** comical, jesting, playful, teasing, waggish **08** humorous, mirthful, pleasant, sportive **09** facetious **11** mischievous

jocular
05 comic, droll, funny, witty **06** jocose, joking, jovial **07** amusing, comical, jesting, playful, roguish, scurril, teasing, waggish **08** humorous, scurrile **09** facetious, hilarious, whimsical **12** entertaining

jocularity
03 wit **05** sport **06** gaiety, humour **07** fooling, jesting, teasing **08** drollery, hilarity, jocosity, laughter **09** amusement, funniness, jolliness, joviality, merriment **10** comicality, desipience, jocoseness, pleasantry **11** playfulness, roguishness, waggishness **12** sportiveness, whimsicality **13** entertainment, facetiousness

jog
◇ *anagram indicator*
03 hod, jar, run **04** bump, jerk, jolt, poke, prod, push, rock, shog, stir, trot, whig **05** dunch, dunsh, elbow, hotch, mosey, nudge, shake, shove **06** arouse, bounce, canter, jig-jog, joggle, jostle, prompt, remind **08** activate **09** stimulate

john
02 WC **03** bog, can, lat, lav, loo **04** jack, rear **08** lavatory
See also **toilet**

joie de vivre
03 joy **04** zest **05** gusto, mirth **06** bounce, esprit, gaiety, relish **08** buoyancy, pleasure **09** enjoyment, merriment **10** blitheness, ebullience, enthusiasm, exuberance, get-up-and-go, joyfulness **12** cheerfulness

join
◇ *juxtaposition indicator*
03 add, mix, oop, oup, sew, tie, wed **04** abut, ally, bind, fuse, glue, knit, link, meet, weld, yoke **05** annex, enrol, enter, marry, merge, touch, unify, unite **06** adhere, adjoin, attach, border, cement, couple, enlist, fasten, sign up, solder, splice **07** combine, conjoin, connect, injoint, verge on **08** border on, coincide, converge, splinter **09** accompany, affiliate, associate, co-operate, interjoin, march with **10** amalgamate, team up with **11** collaborate, compaginate **15** become a member of

• **join in**
04 help **06** chip in, muck in **07** chime in, get in on, partake, pitch in **08** take part **09** co-operate, lend a hand **10** contribute, take part in **11** participate

• **join up**
04 link **05** enrol, enter **06** accede, enlist, sign up

joint
01 J **03** bar, fit, pub **04** club, dive, join, knot, lith, seam, weld **05** carve, cut up, haunt, hinge, nexus, place, roach, sever, stick, union, unite **06** common, couple, divide, fasten, joined, mutual, reefer, shared, spliff, united **07** connect, dissect, joining, segment **08** combined, communal, conjunct, coupling, junction, juncture **09** cigarette, concerted, dismember, ginglymus, nightclub **10** articulate, collective, commissure, connection, cup-and-ball **11** amalgamated, co-operative, co-ordinated, enarthrosis **12** articulation, consolidated, intersection
See also **bone**

jointly
08 together, unitedly **09** in cahoots, in harmony **11** in agreement **13** co-operatively, in co-operation, in partnership **15** in collaboration

joke
03 bar, cod, fun, gag, guy, kid, one, pun, rot **04** baur, bawr, fool, hoax, hoot, jape, jest, josh, lark, mock, play, quip, yarn **05** chaff, clown, crack, farce, funny, kiddy, laugh, prank, spoof, sport, stunt, tease, trick **06** banter, frolic, gambol, parody, wheeze, whimsy **07** leg-pull, mockery **08** chestnut, nonsense, one-liner, repartee, shambles, travesty **09** absurdity, booby trap, fool about, tell jokes, throwaway, wisecrack, witticism **10** break a jest, crack a joke, fool around, funny story, rib-tickler, running gag, whip the cat **11** apple-pie bed, old chestnut **12** take for a ride **13** have someone on, practical joke **14** pull a fast one on, ridiculousness

joker
03 wag, wit **04** card **05** clown, comic, droll, laugh, sport **06** gagman, hoaxer, jester, kidder **07** buffoon, farceur, funster **08** comedian, farceuse, humorist, quipster **09** character, prankster, trickster **11** wisecracker **14** practical joker

jollity
05 mirth **08** gladness **09** happiness, high jinks, merriment **11** high spirits, merrymaking **12** cheerfulness

jolly
02 RM **03** gay **04** coax, dead, glad, spur, trip, urge, very, well **05** buxom, egg on, gaucy, gawcy, gawsy, happy, merry, party, plump **06** bootee, cheery, ever so, gaucie, hearty, highly, jovial, joyful, lively, outing, prompt, titupy **07** awfully, festive, gleeful, greatly, healthy, playful, tittupy **08** cheerful, mirthful, persuade, splendid, terribly **09** certainly, convivial, encourage, enjoyable, extremely, exuberant, influence, intensely **10** delightful **11** celebration, pleasurable, royal marine **12** entertaining **13** exceptionally **15** extraordinarily

jolt
◇ *anagram indicator*
03 hit, jar, jog **04** bang, blow, bump, jerk, push, stun **05** amaze, floor, knock, lurch, nudge, shake, shock, shove, start, upset **06** bounce, hotter, impact, jostle, jounce, jumble **07** astound, disturb, perturb, setback, shake up, startle **08** astonish, reversal, surprise **09** bombshell **10** discompose, disconcert **11** knock for six, thunderbolt **15** bolt from the blue

Jordan
03 HKJ, JOR

jostle
◇ *anagram indicator*
03 jog, vie **04** bang, bump, jolt, push, tilt **05** crowd, elbow, fight, joust, shake, shove **06** battle, hustle, jockey, joggle, throng **07** collide, compete, contend, squeeze **08** shoulder, struggle **11** hog-shouther

jot
03 ace, bit, dot, fig **04** atom, hint, hoot, iota, mite, whit **05** aught, gleam, grain, scrap, speck, stime, styme, trace

06 detail, morsel, tittle, trifle
07 glimmer, smidgen 08 fraction, particle 09 scintilla

• jot down

04 list, note 05 enter 06 record 07 put down 08 note down, register, scribble, take down 09 write down

jotting

04 line, memo, note 05 lines, notes
07 comment, message 08 reminder, scribble 10 memorandum

journal

01 J 03 log 04 blog 05 diary, e-zine, paper 06 record, review, weekly
07 account, daybook, diurnal, fanzine, gazette, logbook, monthly
08 magazine, register 09 chronicle, ephemeris, newspaper, waste book
10 periodical, trade paper
11 publication

See also **newspaper**

journalism

05 press 09 reportage, reporting
11 copy-writing, e-journalism, gutter press 12 broadcasting, fourth estate, news coverage 13 sportswriting, web journalism 14 correspondence, feature-writing, telejournalism

Journalism-related terms include:

03 cub, cut, NPA, run, tip
04 blat, bump, copy, deck, desk, kill, leak, news, op-ed
05 angle, blatt, blurb, break, extra, local, media, pitch, quote, radio, scoop, squib, story, tie in
06 anchor, Balaam, byline, column, editor, impact, kicker, leader, leg-man, rookie, source
07 advance, article, caption, compact, editing, feature, journal, kill fee, spoiler, subhead, tabloid, topical, writing
08 causerie, follow-up, headline, magazine, masthead, national, newshawk, news item, reporter, revision, stringer
09 broadcast, columnist, editorial, exclusive, freelance, freesheet, front-page, interview, newshound, newspaper, paragraph, pull quote, reportage, scare-head, scare-line, soundbite, statement, stop-press, strapline
10 broadsheet, centrefold, credit line, daily paper, journalist, leaderette, multimedia, newsreader, periodical, publishing, retraction, standfirst, television
11 Fleet Street, Sunday paper
12 breaking news, centre spread, press council, press release, scare-heading
13 correspondent, human interest, middle article
14 banner headline, blind interview, current affairs, leading article
15 photojournalism, press conference

journalist

02 Ed 03 man, sub 04 hack 06 editor, journo, scribe 07 diarist, wireman
08 hackette, pressman, reporter, reviewer, stringer 09 columnist, freelance, gazetteer, ink-jerker, newshound, paparazzo, sob sister, subeditor, thunderer 10 diurnalist, hatchet man, ink-slinger, news-writer, presswoman 11 broadcaster, commentator, contributor, e-journalist
12 gossip-writer, newspaperman, sportswriter 13 correspondent, feature-writer, web journalist
14 newspaperwoman, telejournalist

Journalists and editors include:

03 **Day** (Sir Robin), **Mee** (Arthur)
04 **Adie** (Kate), **Bell** (Martin), **Birt** (John, Lord), **Ford** (Anna), **Gall** (Sandy), **Hogg** (Sarah, Baroness), **Jane** (Frederick), **Marr** (Andrew), **Neil** (Andrew), **Rook** (Jean), **Self** (Will), **Snow** (Jon), **Snow** (Peter), **Wade** (Rebekah), **Wark** (Kirsty)
05 **Brown** (Helen Gurley), **Buerk** (Michael), **Cooke** (Alistair), **Dacre** (Paul), **Ensor** (Sir Robert), **Evans** (Sir Harold), **Frost** (Sir David), **Green** (Charlotte), **Hardy** (Bert), **James** (Clive), **Junor** (Sir John), **Laski** (Marghanita), **Levin** (Bernard), **Lewis** (Martyn), **Reith** (John, Lord), **Scott** (C P), **Waugh** (Auberon), **Wolfe** (Tom), **Young** (Toby)
06 **Bailey** (Trevor), **Barron** (Brian), **Bierce** (Ambrose), **Burnet** (Sir Alastair), **Deedes** (Bill, Lord), **Fisher** (Archie), **Forman** (Sir Denis), **Gallup** (George), **Gordon** (John), **Greene** (Sir Hugh), **Hislop** (Ian), **Hulton** (Sir Edward), **Hutton** (Will), **Isaacs** (Sir Jeremy), **Martin** (Kingsley), **Morgan** (Charles), **Morgan** (Piers), **Murrow** (Edward R), **O'Brien** (Conor Cruise), **Paxman** (Jeremy), **Pilger** (John), **Proops** (Marjorie), **Reuter** (Paul Julius von, Lord), **Rippon** (Angela), **Stuart** (Moira), **Wilkes** (John)
07 **Alagiah** (George), **Barclay** (William), **Boycott** (Rosie), **Bradlee** (Ben), **Brunson** (Michael), **Buckley** (William F, Jnr), **Cameron** (James), **Camrose** (William Berry, Viscount), **Cobbett** (William), **Dunnett** (Sir Alastair), **Edwards** (Huw), **Fairfax** (John), **Fleming** (Peter), **Gardner** (Frank), **Hellyer** (Arthur George Lee), **Ingrams** (Richard), **Jackson** (Dame Barbara), **Johnson** (Boris), **Kennedy** (Helena, Baroness), **Kennedy** (Sir Ludovic), **Leeming** (Jan), **Malcolm** (Derek), **Mencken** (H L), **Perkins** (Brian), **Rowland** (Tiny), **Simpson** (John), **Sissons** (Peter), **Stanley** (Sir Henry Morton), **Thomson** (Robert)
08 **Burchill** (Julie), **Cronkite** (Walter), **Dimbleby** (David), **Dimbleby** (Jonathan), **Dimbleby** (Richard), **Douglass** (Frederick), **Drawbell** (James Wedgwood), **Gellhorn** (Martha), **Hanrahan** (Brian), **Hobhouse** (Leonard), **Horrocks** (Sir Brian), **Humphrys** (John), **Lippmann** (Walter), **McCarthy** (John), **McDonald** (Sir Trevor), **Naughtie** (James), **Nevinson** (Henry Wood), **Rees-Mogg** (William, Lord), **Robinson** (Henry Crabb), **Thompson** (Hunter S), **Woodward** (Bob)
09 **Bernstein** (Carl), **Bosanquet** (Reginald), **Hopkinson** (Sir Tom), **Macdonald** (Gus, Lord), **MacGregor** (Sue), **Mackenzie** (Kelvin), **Magnusson** (Magnus), **Plekhanov** (Georgi), **Streicher** (Julius), **Trethowan** (Sir Ian)
10 **Greenslade** (Roy), **Guru-Murthy** (Krishnan), **Muggeridge** (Malcolm), **Rusbridger** (Alan), **Waterhouse** (Keith), **Worsthorne** (Sir Peregrine)
12 **Street-Porter** (Janet)

See also **newspaper**

journey

02 go, OE 03 fly, ren, rin, run, way
04 eyre, hike, mush, raik, rake, ride, roam, rove, sail, step, tour, trek, trip, went 05 drive, foray, jaunt, range, route, shlep, tramp 06 bummel, cruise, flight, outing, ramble, roving, safari, schlep, travel, voyage, wander
07 milk run, odyssey, passage, proceed, sailing, schlepp, stretch, travels
08 campaign, crossing, progress
09 excursion, gallivant, walkabout
10 expedition, pilgrimage, wanderings
11 peregrinate 13 globetrotting, peregrination

• good journey, safe journey

08 godspeed 09 bon voyage

• journey regularly

03 ply 07 commute

journeyer

07 pilgrim, rambler, tourist, trekker, tripper, voyager 08 wanderer, wayfarer
09 traveller 12 peregrinator

joust

03 vie 04 just, spar, tilt 05 fight, giust, trial 06 jostle, justle 07 compete, contest, quarrel, tourney, wrangle
08 skirmish 09 encounter, pas d'armes
10 engagement, tournament

jovial

03 gay 04 boon, glad 05 happy, jolly, merry 06 cheery, genial, joyous, lively, wanton 07 affable, Bacchic, buoyant, cordial, gleeful 08 animated, Bacchian, cheerful, mirthful, sociable
09 convivial 11 Falstaffian 13 in good spirits

joviality

03 fun 04 glee 05 mirth 06 gaiety
07 jollity 08 buoyancy, gladness, hilarity 09 happiness, merriment
10 affability, cheeriness, ebullience
12 cheerfulness

joy

03 gem 04 dear, glee, list, nuts
05 bliss, cheer, dream, exult, prize, treat 06 thrill 07 delight, ecstasy, elation, rapture, rejoice, success, victory 08 felicity, gladness, pleasure,

treasure **09** cloud nine, enjoyment, happiness, rejoicing, transport **10** exultation, joyfulness, jubilation **11** achievement **12** entrancement, satisfaction **13** gratification, seventh heaven **14** accomplishment, positive result

• expression of joy
02 ah, ha, ho, io **03** aha, hah, hey, hoa, hoh, ooh, rah, say, wow, yay **04** I say!, whee **05** heigh, hurra, huzza, oh boy!, tra-la, wowee, yahoo, yummy, zowie **06** banzai, gotcha, heyday, hooray, hurrah, hurray, yippee, yum-yum **07** whoopee

joyful
04 fain, glad **05** happy, merry **06** elated **07** festive, gleeful, pleased **08** cheerful, ecstatic, euphoric, feastful, gleesome, jubilant, pleasing, thrilled **09** delighted, gratified, overjoyed **10** exhilarant, triumphant **11** on cloud nine, over the moon, tickled pink **15** in seventh heaven, on top of the world

joyfully
06 gladly **07** happily **09** gleefully **10** cheerfully, jubilantly **12** ecstatically, euphorically, triumphantly

joyless
03 sad **04** dour, glum, grim **05** bleak, sober **06** dismal, dreary, gloomy, sombre **07** doleful, forlorn, serious, unhappy **08** dejected, downcast **09** cheerless, miserable **10** depressing, despondent, dispirited **12** discouraging

joyous
04 glad **05** happy, merry **06** festal, jovial, joyful **07** festive, gleeful **08** cheerful, ecstatic, frabjous, gladsome, jubilant **09** rapturous **10** blithesome, rollicking

joyously
06 gladly **07** happily, merrily **08** joyfully **10** cheerfully, jubilantly **11** rapturously **12** ecstatically

jubilant
06 elated, joyful **07** excited **08** ecstatic, euphoric, exultant, thrilled **09** delighted, exuberant, overjoyed, rejoicing, rhapsodic **10** triumphant **11** on cloud nine, over the moon, tickled pink **15** in seventh heaven, on top of the world

jubilation
03 joy **07** ecstasy, elation, jubilee, triumph **08** euphoria, jamboree **09** festivity, rejoicing **10** excitement, exultation **11** celebration **13** jollification

jubilee
04 fete, gala **07** holiday **08** carnival, feast day, festival **09** festivity **11** anniversary, celebration **13** commemoration **14** semi-centennial

Judas
07 traitor **08** betrayer, deceiver, quisling, renegade, turncoat **11** backstabber **13** tergiversator

judder
◇ *anagram indicator*
05 quake, shake **06** quiver **07** shudder, tremble, vibrate

judge
01 J **03** lud, ref, see, try, ump, wig **04** beak, damn, deem, doom, find, lord, rate, rule, scan **05** award, gauge, hakim, think, value, weigh **06** assess, critic, decern, decide, decree, expert, puisne, puisny, reckon, review, syndic, umpire **07** account, adjudge, arbiter, believe, censure, condemn, convict, coroner, discern, examine, her nibs, his nibs, justice, Law Lord, mediate, referee, set down, sheriff, weigh up **08** appraise, assessor, conclude, consider, doomsman, estimate, evaluate, mediator, recorder, reviewer, sentence **09** arbitrate, ascertain, authority, criticize, determine, evaluator, judiciary, justiciar, moderator, ombudsman, seneschal, syndicate **10** adjudicate, arbitrator, dijudicate, magistrate **11** adjudicator, connoisseur, distinguish **12** pass sentence **13** form an opinion, give a sentence **14** sit in judgement **15** deliver a verdict

Judges include:

04 Coke (Sir Edward)
05 Allen (Florence Ellinwood), Burgh (Hubert de), Draco, Minos, Solon
06 Aeacus, Burger (Warren Earl), Gideon, Holmes (Oliver Wendell), Irvine (Alexander, Lord), Mackay (James, Lord), Warren (Earl)
07 Brennan (William J), Denning (Alfred, Lord), Erskine (Thomas, Lord), O'Connor (Sandra Day), Scarman (Leslie, Lord)
08 Gardiner (Gerald, Lord), Ginsburg (Ruth Bader), Hailsham (Quintin McGarel Hogg, Viscount), Jeffreys (George, Lord), Marshall (John), Marshall (Thurgood)
09 Rehnquist (William), Vyshinsky (Andrei)
10 Elwyn-Jones (Frederick, Lord)
11 Butler-Sloss (Dame Elizabeth), Montesquieu (Charles-Louis de Secondat, Baron de)
12 Rhadamanthus

judgement
04 doom, fate, mind, view **05** award, order, sense, sight, taste **06** acumen, belief, decree, result, ruling, wisdom **07** decreet, finding, opinion, verdict **08** decision, estimate, prudence, sagacity, sapience, sentence, thinking **09** appraisal, criticism, damnation, diagnosis, good sense, mediation, reckoning, sentiment **10** assessment, conclusion, conviction, evaluation, judication, misfortune, perception, punishment, shrewdness **11** arbitration, common sense, discernment, penetration, retribution **12** adjudication, condemnation, intelligence, perspicacity **13** enlightenment, judiciousness, understanding **14** discrimination

judgemental
07 carping **08** critical, scathing **10** censorious, derogatory **11** disparaging **12** condemnatory, disapproving, fault-finding **13** hypercritical

judicial
05 legal **08** critical, forensic, official **09** decretory, impartial, judiciary, magistral **14** discriminating

judicially
07 legally **10** officially **11** impartially **12** forensically

judiciary
06 judges, the law **07** justice **08** the bench **10** magistracy **11** court system, legal system

judicious
04 wise **05** smart, sound **06** astute, clever, shrewd **07** careful, prudent **08** cautious, discreet, informed, rational, sensible, wise-like **09** sagacious, well-timed **10** considered, discerning, reasonable, thoughtful, well-judged **11** circumspect, common-sense, intelligent, well-advised **14** discriminating

judiciously
06 wisely **08** astutely, sensibly, shrewdly **09** carefully, prudently **10** cautiously **11** sagaciously **12** discerningly, thoughtfully **13** circumspectly

judo *see* **martial art**

jug
03 jar, urn **04** ewer, olpe, Toby **05** crock **06** carafe, flagon, pourie, prison, vessel **07** bombard, creamer, growler, pitcher, Toby jug **08** decanter, imprison **09** blackjack, container **10** aquamanale, aquamanile, bellarmine, receptacle **11** Enghalskrug

See also **prison**

juggle
◇ *anagram indicator*
03 rig **04** cook, fake **05** alter **06** adjust, change, doctor, fiddle, tamper **07** balance, conjure, falsify, massage **08** disguise, equalize **09** rearrange **10** hocus-pocus, manipulate, tamper with **12** misrepresent

juice
03 jus, oil, sap **04** must **05** fluid, serum **06** cremor, liquid, liquor, nectar, succus, walnut **07** enliven, essence, extract **08** piquancy, vitality **09** secretion **10** pancreatin

juicy
03 hot, wet **04** lush, racy **05** lurid, moist, sappy, spicy, vivid **06** risqué,

watery **07** flowing **08** exciting **09** colourful, succulent, thrilling **10** profitable, scandalous, suggestive **11** interesting, sensational

jujube
04 jube **05** lotus **08** zizyphus **12** Christ's-thorn

Juliet
01 J

July
02 Jy **03** Jul

jumble
◇ *anagram indicator*
02 pi **03** mix, pie, pye **04** jolt, junk, mess **05** chaos, mix up, mix-up **06** garble, huddle, jabble, jumbal, medley, mingle, muddle, raffle, tangle, tumble, wuzzle **07** clutter, confuse, jolting, mixture, rummage, shuffle **08** cast-offs, disarray, disorder, hotchpot, mishmash, mixy-maxy, oddments, pastiche, shambles **09** bric-à-brac, confusion, pasticcio, potpourri, praiseach **10** disarrange, hodgepodge, hotchpotch, miscellany, mixty-maxty **11** disorganize, printer's pie **12** mingle-mangle, mixter-maxter, mixtie-maxtie **14** conglomeration

jumbled
◇ *anagram indicator*
06 untidy **07** chaotic, garbled, huddled, mixed-up, muddled, tangled, tumbled **08** confused, shuffled, unsorted **10** disarrayed, disordered **11** farraginous **12** disorganized, mingle-mangle **13** miscellaneous

jumbo
02 OS **04** huge, mega, vast **05** giant **07** immense, mammoth, massive, outsize, Titanic **08** colossal, elephant, enormous, gigantic, whopping **09** ginormous, walloping **10** extra-large

jump
◇ *anagram indicator*
03 gap, hop, jar, lep, mug **04** axel, gain, gate, go up, hike, jerk, jolt, leap, lutz, miss, omit, rail, rise, risk, romp, skip **05** avoid, boost, bound, break, caper, clear, fence, frisk, halma, hedge, lapse, lurch, mount, ollie, quail, shake, shock, shoot, space, spasm, sport, start, surge, throb, vault, wince **06** ascend, attack, beat up, bounce, breach, bypass, cavort, cut out, do over, flinch, frolic, gambol, go over, hazard, hiatus, hurdle, ignore, lacuna, leap up, pounce, prance, quiver, recoil, shiver, spiral, spring, switch, twitch, upturn **07** advance, assault, barrier, digress, exactly, flicker, salchow, set upon, shoot up, swoop on, toe loop, upsurge, venture **08** batterie, bunny hop, escalate, go across, increase, interval, leave out, mounting, obstacle, omission, overlook, pass over, pounce on, spring on **09** barricade, disregard, elevation, increment, stage-dive **10** appreciate, escalation, quersprung, trampoline **12** Becher's Brook, interruption

• **jump at**
04 grab **05** seize **06** accept, leap at, snatch **07** agree to, fall for, seize on, swallow **08** pounce on **13** accept eagerly, accept quickly

• **jump on**
05 blame, chide, fly at, scold **06** berate, rebuke, revile **07** censure, reprove, tick off, upbraid **08** reproach **09** castigate, criticize, reprimand

• **jump the gun**
10 act hastily, act too soon, anticipate **13** start too early **14** act prematurely

jumper
03 roo **04** euro, flea **05** lammy **06** jersey, lammie, woolly **07** sweater **08** kangaroo, pullover, wallaroo **10** churn-drill, sweatshirt

jumpy
04 edgy **05** bumpy, het up, jerky, nappy, nervy, rough, shaky, tense **06** bouncy, fitful, on edge, uneasy **07** anxious, fidgety, in a stew, jittery, jolting, keyed up, nervous, panicky, restive, shaking, twitchy, uptight, wound up **08** agitated, in a sweat, in a tizzy, lurching **09** spasmodic, squirrely **10** convulsive, incoherent, squirrelly **12** apprehensive, disconnected, uncontrolled **13** uncoordinated

junction
01 T **04** bond, cove, join, link, node, seam, toll **05** close, crown, graft, joint, raphe, union **06** circus, collar, infall, suture **07** cornice, joining, linking, meeting, welding **08** abutment, coupling, crossing, juncture, knitting **09** interface, symphysis, T-junction **10** confluence, connection, crossroads, match-joint **11** box junction, combination, interchange **12** intersection, meeting-point

juncture
04 crux, time **05** point, stage, union **06** crisis, minute, moment, period **07** article, joining **08** occasion **09** emergency, situation **11** predicament

June
03 Jun

jungle
03 web **04** bush, heap, mass, maze **05** chaos, shola, snarl **06** growth, medley, tangle **07** clutter **08** disarray, disorder, mishmash **09** confusion, labyrinth **10** hotchpotch, miscellany, rainforest **14** tropical forest

junior
02 Jr **03** Jnr, Jun, lad **04** fils, Junr **05** chota, lower, minor, young **06** lesser, minion, puisne, puisny, rating **07** servant, younger **08** dogsbody, inferior, under-boy **09** assistant, associate, secondary, underling **10** subsidiary **11** subordinate

junk
◇ *anagram indicator*
◇ *deletion indicator*
04 dump, spam **05** chuck, chunk, ditch, dregs, scrap, trash, waste **06** debris, litter, refuse **07** clutter, discard, garbage, rubbish, rummage **08** cast-offs, get rid of, jettison, leavings, narcotic, nonsense, oddments, throw out, wreckage **09** bric-à-brac, dispose of, leftovers, throw away, worthless

junket
02 do **04** bash, trip **05** beano, feast, spree, visit **06** outing, picnic, regale **07** banquet, journey **09** entertain **11** celebration

Juno
04 Hera

junta
03 set **04** gang, ring **05** cabal, group, party **06** cartel, clique, league **07** coterie, council, faction, meeting **08** conclave **09** camarilla **11** confederacy

Jupiter
04 Zeus

jurisdiction
04 area, bail, rule, soke, sway, zone **05** field, orbit, power, range, reach, right, scope, soken, verge **06** bounds, region, sphere **07** command, control, mastery **08** capacity, district, dominion, province **09** authority, influence, territory **10** cognizance, competence, domination, judicature, leadership **11** prerogative, sovereignty **14** administration

jury
04 pais **05** panel, quest **06** assize, jurors **07** jurymen **09** grand jury, jurywomen, party-jury, petit jury, petty jury

just
03 all, apt, due **04** egal, even, fair, good, only, to a T **05** equal, exact, joust, legal, moral, quite, right, sound, valid **06** bang on, barely, earned, hardly, honest, indeed, lately, lawful, merely, normal, proper, purely, simply, spot-on **07** ethical, exactly, fitting, merited, neutral, sincere, upright **08** deserved, recently, rightful, scarcely, suitable, truthful, unbiased, virtuous **09** equitable, impartial, justified, objective, perfectly, precisely, righteous **10** absolutely, a moment ago, completely, even-handed, fair-minded, honourable, legitimate, nothing but, principled, reasonable, upstanding **11** appropriate, well-founded **12** unprejudiced, well-deserved, well-grounded **13** a short time ago, disinterested, incorruptible, true-disposing **14** irreproachable

• **just about**
06 all but, almost, nearly **08** as good as, well-nigh **09** virtually **10** more or less **11** practically

• just after
02 on

justice
01 J **02** CJ, JP, LJ **03** law **05** judge, right **06** amends, equity, ethics, honour, morals **07** honesty, nemesis, penalty, redress, sheriff **08** fairness, fair play, justness, legality, validity **09** integrity, propriety, rectitude, rightness, soundness **10** lawfulness, legitimacy, magistrate, neutrality, punishment, recompense, reparation **11** objectivity, uprightness **12** compensation, impartiality, rightfulness, satisfaction **13** equitableness, righteousness **14** even-handedness, fair-mindedness, reasonableness **15** justifiableness

justifiable
03 fit **05** legal, right, sound, valid **06** lawful, proper **07** tenable **08** sensible **09** excusable, justified, plausible, warranted **10** acceptable, defensible, explicable, forgivable, legitimate, pardonable, reasonable **11** explainable, supportable, sustainable, warrantable, well-founded **12** within reason **14** understandable

justifiably
07 legally, rightly, validly **08** lawfully, properly **09** excusably, plausibly **10** acceptably, defensibly, reasonably **12** legitimately, within reason **14** understandably

justification
04 plea **05** basis **06** excuse, reason **07** apology, defence, defense, grounds, warrant **08** warranty **10** absolution, mitigation **11** explanation, vindication **12** confirmation, verification **15** rationalization

justify
04 aver, avow **05** clear, prove **06** acquit, defend, excuse, pardon, punish, uphold, verify **07** absolve, bear out, confirm, darrain, darrayn, deraign, deserve, explain, forgive, support, sustain, warrant **08** darraign, darraine, maintain, make good, validate **09** authorize, darraigne, establish, exculpate, exonerate, vindicate **10** stand up for **11** rationalize **12** substantiate **13** show to be right **14** give grounds for, give reasons for

justly
04 duly **05** right **06** fairly **07** equally, rightly **08** honestly, lawfully, properly **09** equitably **10** rightfully, with reason **11** deservingly, impartially, justifiably, objectively **12** even-handedly, legitimately

jut, jut out
03 jet **04** butt **05** jetty, jutty, stick **06** beetle, extend **07** extrude, project **08** overhang, protrude, stick out **10** projection

jute
03 tow **05** gunny, kenaf, urena **06** burlap **07** Hessian, hopsack **09** Corchorus **10** hop-sacking, Jews' mallow

juvenile
03 boy, juv, kid **04** girl **05** child, green, minor, young, youth **06** callow, infant, junior **07** babyish, puerile, teenage **08** childish, immature, teenager, youthful **09** infantile, youngster **10** adolescent **11** young person **13** inexperienced **15** unsophisticated

Juventus
04 Hebe

juxtapose
06 empale, impale **11** put together **13** place together, put side by side **15** place side by side

juxtaposition
07 contact **08** nearness, vicinity **09** closeness, immediacy, proximity **10** apposition, contiguity, impalement

K

K
03 Kay **04** kara, kesh, kilo **06** kaccha, kangha, kirpan

kaleidoscopic
05 fluid **06** motley **08** manifold **10** changeable, poikilitic, polychrome, variegated **11** fluctuating **12** ever-changing, many-coloured, multifarious **13** multicoloured, parti-coloured, polychromatic **15** many-splendoured

kame
02 ås **05** eskar, esker

kangaroo
03 roo **04** euro, joey **06** boomer, old man **07** steamer, wallaby **08** forester, wallaroo

Kansas
02 KS **04** Kans

kaput
04 bust, phut **06** broken, ruined, undone **07** defunct, extinct, smashed, wrecked **08** finished **09** conked out, destroyed

karate
08 Shotokan

Shotokan belts include:

03 red
05 black, brown, green, white
06 orange, purple, yellow
20 brown with white stripe
21 purple with white stripe
24 brown with two white stripes

See also **martial art**

• **karate costume**
02 gi **03** gie

kay
01 K

Kazakhstan
02 KZ **03** KAZ

keel
04 back, base, cool, ship, skeg **05** barge, skegg **06** bottom, carina, ruddle **07** keelson **08** backbone **10** stabilizer **11** centreboard **12** cheesecutter

• **keel over**
◇ *reversal down indicator*
04 drop, fall **05** faint, swoon, upset **07** capsize, founder, pass out, stagger **08** black out, collapse, overturn **10** topple over, turn turtle **14** turn upside down

keen
03 cry, mad, sob **04** acid, avid, cold, deep, fell, fine, gleg, howl, moan, nuts, wail, weep, wild, wise, yowl **05** acute, breem, breme, crazy, eager, groan, mourn, potty, quick, razor, sharp, smart, snell **06** argute, astute, biting, caring, clever, fierce, fond of, grieve, intent, lament, liking, loving, narrow, severe, shrewd, shrill, strong **07** anxious, devoted, earnest, fervent, hawking, hawkish, intense, mordant, nipping, pointed, pungent, sharpen, ululate **08** diligent, incisive, piercing, ruthless, stinging **09** assiduous, cut-throat, devoted to, dog-eat-dog, enamoured, impatient, quick-eyed, razor-like, sagacious, sensitive, trenchant, wide awake, wonderful **10** attached to, discerning, double-eyed, perceptive, razor-sharp **11** heavily into, industrious, lamentation, penetrating, quick-witted, sharp-witted **12** enthusiastic **13** conscientious, keen as mustard, perspicacious **14** discriminating

keenly
06 deeply, shrewd **07** acutely, eagerly, quickly, sharply **08** astutely, cleverly, fiercely, shrewdly, strongly **09** earnestly, fervently, intensely **10** diligently, incisively **11** assiduously, sensitively **12** perceptively **13** penetratingly

keenness
03 eye **04** edge **06** wisdom **08** industry, sagacity, sapience, sedulity **09** diligence, eagerness, sharpness **10** astuteness, cleverness, enthusiasm, shrewdness, trenchancy **11** discernment, earnestness, penetration, sensitivity **12** incisiveness **15** industriousness

keep
◇ *containment indicator*
◇ *hidden indicator*
03 own, run **04** curb, feed, food, fort, have, heap, hold, last, mark, mind, obey, pile, rear, save, stay, tend **05** amass, block, board, breed, carry, check, delay, deter, guard, hoard, limit, means, place, raise, stack, stock, store, tower, watch **06** arrest, castle, deal in, defend, detain, donjon, endure, foster, fulfil, hamper, hinder, hold up, honour, impede, keep at, keep on, keep up, living, manage, pile up, remain, retain, retard, shield, upkeep **07** abide by, care for, carry on, citadel, collect, conduct, confine, control, deposit, dungeon, furnish, inhibit, nurture, observe, perform, persist, possess, prevent, protect, refrain, reserve, respect, shelter, store up, support, sustain **08** adhere to, carry out, conserve, continue, fortress, hang on to, hold back, hold on to, keep back, maintain, obstruct, preserve, restrain, withhold **09** celebrate, constrain, look after, persevere, recognize, safeguard, solemnize, subsidize, watch over **10** accumulate, comply with, effectuate, livelihood, perpetuate, provide for, stronghold, sustenance, take care of **11** commemorate, keep waiting, maintenance, not part with, nourishment, subsistence, superintend **12** be in charge of, have charge of **13** have custody of, interfere with, keep faith with **15** keep in good order

• **for keeps**
06 always **07** for ever, for good **10** for all time

• **keep at**
03 nag **04** last, stay, toil **05** grind **06** badger, drudge, endure, finish, labour, remain, slog at **07** carry on, persist, stick at **08** complete, continue, fight off, maintain **09** persevere **10** plug away at **11** be steadfast **12** beaver away at

• **keep back**
◇ *reversal indicator*
04 curb, hide, save, stop **05** check, delay, hoard, limit, store **06** censor, hinder, hold up, hush up, impede, retain, retard, stifle **07** conceal, control, inhibit, repress, reserve **08** hold back, keep down, lay aside, prohibit, restrain, restrict, set aside, suppress, withhold **09** constrain, stockpile **10** accumulate, keep secret

• **keep from**
04 halt, help, stop **06** desist, resist **07** forbear, prevent, refrain **08** restrain

• **keep in**
04 hide **05** quell **06** coop up, detain, shut in, stifle, stop up **07** conceal, confine, control, inhibit, repress **08** bottle up, keep back, restrain, suppress

• **keep off**
05 avoid, expel, fence, parry **07** stay off **08** hands off, keep away **09** not go near **10** body-swerve **12** stay away from, steer clear of **14** avoid going near

• **keep on**
04 go on, last, stay **06** endure, hold on, remain, retain **07** carry on, persist **08** continue, keep at it, maintain **09** persevere, soldier on, stick at it **13** stay the course **14** continue to hire

• **keep on at**
03 nag **05** harry **06** badger, chivvy, go

on at, harass, pester, plague, pursue **09** importune

- **keep secret**

04 hide **07** conceal **08** keep back, keep dark, suppress **09** dissemble **14** keep under wraps

- **keep to**

04 obey **06** fulfil **07** observe, respect, stick to **08** adhere to **10** comply with

- **keep up**

03 vie **05** equal, match, rival **06** retain **07** compete, contend, emulate, persist, support, sustain **08** continue, keep pace, maintain, preserve **09** entertain, persevere **10** keep tabs on **11** go along with **13** keep abreast of **15** keep in touch with

keeper

03 nab **05** guard **06** custos, escort, gaoler, jailer, mahout, minder, parker, parkie, warden, warder **07** curator, granger, marshal, steward **08** defender, governor, guardian, overseer, surveyor, vesturer **09** archivist, attendant, bodyguard, caretaker, castellan, constable, custodian, guard ring, inspector **10** austringer, châtelaine, proprietor, supervisor **11** conservator, park-officer **13** administrator **14** superintendent

keep fit

02 PE, PT

keeping

04 care, cure, hand, ward **05** aegis, hands, store, trust **06** accord, charge **07** balance, custody, harmony, support **08** auspices, tutelage **09** agreement, congruity, patronage, retention **10** compliance, conformity, observance, proportion, protection **11** consistency, maintenance, reservation, safe-keeping, supervision **12** guardianship, preservation, surveillance **14** correspondence

keepsake

05 relic, token **06** emblem, pledge **07** memento **08** reminder, souvenir **11** remembrance

keg

02 kg **03** tun, vat **04** butt, cask, drum **06** barrel, firkin **08** hogshead

kelvin

01 K

ken

04 know **05** field, grasp, range, reach, scope **06** notice **07** compass **09** awareness, knowledge **10** cognizance, perception **11** realization **12** acquaintance, appreciation **13** comprehension, understanding

Kent

02 SE

Kentucky

02 KY

Kenya

03 EAK, KEN

kerfuffle

03 ado **04** flap, fuss, to-do **05** hoo-ha, tizzy **06** bother, bustle, flurry, furore **07** agitate, carry-on, fluster, palaver **08** ballyhoo, brouhaha, disorder **09** agitation, commotion

kernel

03 nub, nut **04** core, corn, crux, germ, gist, seed **05** copra, gland, grain, heart, stone **06** almond, centre, marrow, nutmeg **07** essence, innards, nucleus **08** pichurim **09** pistachio, substance **11** nitty-gritty, quandong-nut **12** nuts and bolts, quintessence

kestrel

06 keelie **07** staniel, stannel, stanyel **08** stallion **09** windhover

key

01 A, B, C, D, E, F, G, H **03** cue **04** clue, code, crib, kaie, main, mood, note, sign, tone **05** basic, chief, gloss, guide, index, major, means, pitch, style, table, vital, wedge **06** answer, clavis, legend, secret, timbre, winder **07** central, crucial, leading, pointer, spanner **08** decisive, glossary, solution **09** character, essential, important, indicator, necessary, principal **11** explanation, explication, fundamental, translation **12** passe-partout **14** interpretation

See also **island**

Keys on a computer keyboard include:

03 alt, del, end, esc, ins, tab
04 ctrl, home, pg dn, pg up
05 alt gr, enter
06 delete, insert, page up
07 num lock
08 caps lock, page down

- **key stem**

03 pin

keynote

01 C **04** core, gist, mese, pith **05** final, heart, point, theme, tonic **06** accent, centre, marrow, stress **07** essence **08** emphasis **09** substance

keystone

04 base, core, crux, root **05** basis, quoin **06** ground, motive, source, spring **07** sagitta **08** linchpin **09** principle **10** foundation, mainspring **11** cornerstone

kick

◇ *anagram indicator*

03 fun, hit, pep, toe, zip **04** bite, blow, boot, buzz, chip, foot, hack, heel, high, hoof, jolt, knee, lark, lift, punt, quit, shin, spur, stop, tang, yerk, zing **05** break, fling, pause, power, punce, punch, react, shoot, spurn, wince **06** effect, falter, give up, jack in, let out, pack in, recoil, strike, thrill **07** abandon, dropout, fly-kick, grubber, lash out, misfire, penalty, potency, project, rebound, spurn at, tap-kick **08** back-heel, drop-kick, free kick, goal kick, grub kick, high kick, jump back, leave off, move back, pleasure, pungency, set piece, sixpence, spot kick, stimulus, strength, striking **09** boomerang, cross-kick, garryowen, place kick **10** desist from, excitement, pile-driver, point after, resilience, resistance, spring back **11** stimulation **12** recalcitrate, spurn against

- **kick against**

04 defy **05** rebel, spurn **06** oppose, resist **07** protest **09** withstand **14** hold out against

- **kick around**

03 use **05** abuse **07** discuss, exploit, toy with **08** ill-treat, maltreat, play with **09** mess about, push about, talk about, trample on **10** mess around, push around **15** take advantage of

- **kick off**

03 die **04** open **05** begin, start **08** commence, initiate **09** introduce **10** inaugurate **11** get under way

- **kick out**

04 oust, sack, spur **05** eject, evict, expel **06** reject, remove **07** boot out, dismiss, turf out **08** chuck out, get rid of, throw out **09** discharge **13** give the boot to, give the push to, give the sack to **14** give the elbow to

kickback

05 bribe **06** pay-off, recoil **07** rebound **08** backlash, reaction **09** incentive, sweetener **10** back-hander, inducement

kick-off

02 KO **05** start **06** outset, word go **07** opening **09** beginning, inception **12** commencement, introduction

kid

03 boy, con, imp, lad, rib, tot **04** brat, dupe, fool, girl, gull, hoax, jest, joke, wean **05** bairn, child, kiddy, sprog, tease, trick, youth **06** delude, faggot, have on, humbug, infant, nipper, rug rat, wind up **07** deceive, littlin, littl 'un, pretend, tiny tot, toddler, young 'un **08** cheverel, cheveril, hoodwink, juvenile, littling, teenager, yeanling, young one **09** bamboozle, deception, kiddywink, littleane, little boy, little one, youngster **10** adolescent, ankle-biter, little girl **11** young person

kidnap

05 seize, steal **06** abduct, hijack, snatch **07** capture **08** carry off **12** hold to ransom **13** hold as hostage, take as hostage

kill

03 axe, bag, end, ice, pip, sap, top, use, zap **04** ache, do in, dull, ease, fill, hang, hurt, pass, prey, ruin, slay **05** death, drain, mop-up, napoo, pound, quash, quell, shoot, smart, smite, spend, spoil, still, sting, throb, total, use up, waste, weary, whack **06** behead, be sore, climax, deaden, defeat, dilute, fag out, finish, lay low, muffle, murder, occupy, reject, rub out, settle, soothe, stifle, strain, suffer, twinge, weaken

07 abolish, bump off, butcher, cut down, destroy, discard, execute, exhaust, fatigue, kiss off, knacker, nullify, put down, relieve, scupper, smother, stonker, take out, tire out, wipe out **08** blow away, decimate, despatch, dispatch, knock off, massacre, moderate, ring-bark, shoot-out, suppress **09** alleviate, be painful, cause pain, death-blow, devastate, dispose of, do to death, eliminate, eradicate, finish off, liquidate, overexert, polish off, shoot dead, slaughter, while away **10** annihilate, conclusion, decapitate, dénouement, do away with, extinguish, guillotine, neutralize, put an end to, put to death, put to sleep **11** assassinate, coup de grâce, electrocute, exterminate, stab to death, take it out of

killer

03 gun, orc **04** orca **06** gunman, hit-man, ice man, slayer **07** butcher, matador, shooter **08** assassin, hired gun, homicide, murderer **09** cut-throat, destroyer **10** hatchet man, liquidator, man-queller, stupendous **11** axe murderer, executioner, slaughterer **12** exterminator, mass murderer, serial killer, woman-queller

• natural killer

02 NK

killing

03 hit **04** coup, gain, hard **05** booty, death, funny **06** absurd, big hit, deadly, murder, profit, taxing, tiring
07 amusing, arduous, a scream, bonanza, carnage, clean-up, comical, fortune, slaying, success, wearing
08 butchery, draining, fatality, genocide, homicide, massacre, windfall **09** bloodshed, execution, fatiguing, gruelling, hilarious, ludicrous, mactation, matricide, patricide, predation, slaughter, uxoricide **10** enervating, exhausting, fratricide, hysterical, lucky break, sororicide, uproarious **11** destruction, destructive, elimination, fascinating, infanticide, liquidation, rib-tickling
12 back-breaking, debilitating, irresistible, manslaughter, stroke of luck
13 assassination, extermination, side-splitting

killjoy

05 cynic **06** damper, grouch, misery, moaner, whiner **07** sceptic
08 buzzkill, dampener **09** pessimist
10 complainer, spoilsport, wet blanket
11 Weary Willie **12** trouble-mirth
13 prophet of doom

kiln

04 oast **05** stove **06** muffle

kilo

01 K

kilt

07 filabeg, filibeg **08** fillibeg, philabeg, philibeg **09** phillabeg, phillibeg **10** fustanella

kilter

• out of kilter

04 awry **05** askew **08** confused, lopsided **09** skew-whiff
10 misaligned, unbalanced **12** out of balance

kin

04 clan **05** blood, catty, stock, tribe
06 family, people **07** cousins, kindred, lineage, related **08** affinity
09 relations, relatives **10** extraction
12 relationship **13** consanguinity, flesh and blood

kina

01 K

kind

03 ilk, set **04** form, good, mild, nice, race, sort, type, warm **05** beget, brand, breed, class, genre, genus, stamp, style **06** benign, family, genial, gentle, giving, humane, kindly, loving, manner, nature, strain **07** amiable, cordial, helpful, lenient, patient, pitying, species, tactful, variety
08 amicable, category, friendly, generous, gracious, merciful, obliging, selfless, tolerant **09** agreeable, bounteous, character, congenial, courteous, indulgent, unselfish
10 altruistic, benevolent, big-hearted, charitable, forbearing, persuasion, thoughtful **11** considerate, description, good-hearted, good-natured, kind-hearted, magnanimous, neighbourly, soft-hearted, sympathetic, temperament, warm-hearted
12 affectionate, humanitarian
13 compassionate, philanthropic, tender-hearted, understanding

• in kind

08 in return, in specie **09** similarly, tit for tat **10** in exchange **12** in like manner

• kind of

◇ *anagram indicator*

04 a bit **05** kinda, quite **06** fairly, pretty, rather, sort of **07** a little
08 slightly, somewhat **10** moderately, relatively **12** to some degree, to some extent

kind-hearted

04 kind, warm **06** benign, humane, kindly **07** helpful **08** amicable, generous, gracious, obliging
10 altruistic, big-hearted
11 considerate, good-hearted, good-natured, sympathetic, warm-hearted
12 humanitarian **13** compassionate, philanthropic, tender-hearted

kindle

03 fan **04** blow, fire, lunt, stir, tind, tine, tynd **05** brood, light, rouse, spark, teend, tynde **06** accend, arouse, awaken, excite, ignite, incite, induce, litter, thrill **07** enlight, incense, inflame, inspire, provoke **09** set alight, set fire to, set on fire, stimulate

kindliness

06 nature, warmth **07** charity
08 kindness, sympathy **09** benignity
10 amiability, compassion, generosity
11 beneficence, benevolence
12 friendliness **14** loving-kindness

kindly

04 fond, good, kind, mild, nice, warm
06 benign, couthy, genial, gentle, gently, giving, goodly, humane, native, please, polite, tender, warmly
07 benefic, cordial, couthie, helpful, natural, patient **08** amicable, benignly, friendly, generous, humanely, lovingly, pleasant **09** agreeable, avuncular, helpfully, indulgent, patiently, tactfully
10 benevolent, big-hearted, charitable, charitably, favourable, generously, mercifully, selflessly, thoughtful, tolerantly **11** considerate, courteously, good-natured, kind-hearted, magnanimous, neighbourly, sympathetic, unselfishly
12 benevolently, thoughtfully
13 compassionate, considerately, grandfatherly, kind-heartedly, magnanimously, understanding
14 affectionately, altruistically
15 compassionately, sympathetically

kindness

03 aid **04** help, love **05** grace
06 favour, warmth **07** aggrace, benefit, candour, charity, service **08** altruism, courtesy, good deed, goodness, good turn, goodwill, humanity, leniency, mildness, niceness, patience, sympathy
09 affection, benignity, tolerance
10 assistance, benignancy, compassion, generosity, gentleness, humaneness, indulgence, kindliness **11** beneficence, benevolence, helpfulness, hospitality, magnanimity **12** friendliness, philanthropy, pleasantness
13 consideration, fellow feeling, Gemütlichkeit, understanding
14 loving-kindness, thoughtfulness
15 considerateness, humanitarianism, warm-heartedness

kindred

03 kin, sib **04** akin, clan, folk, hapu, like
05 flesh, house, stock **06** allied, common, family, people **07** cognate, lineage, related, similar **08** affinity, kinsfolk, matching **09** congenial, connected, relations, relatives
10 affiliated, similarity **11** connections
12 relationship **13** consanguinity, corresponding, flesh and blood

king

01 K, R **02** HM **03** Rex, Roi **04** Inca, lord, shah, star **05** chief, ruler
06 bigwig, kaiser, leader, master, prince, top dog **07** big shot, emperor, kingpin, majesty, monarch, supremo
08 big noise **09** big cheese, chieftain, sovereign **11** head of state, the greatest
12 leading light

Kings include:

03 Ban, Ida, Ine, Lot, Zog
04 Ahab, Cnut, Cole, Edwy, Erik, Fahd, Ivan, Ivan (the Terrible), John, John (the Blind), Karl, Knut, Lear, Offa, Olaf, Olav, Otto, Paul, Quin, Saud, Saul, Zeus

05 Boris, Brian, Bruce (Robert), Capet (Hugo or Hugh), Carol, Creon, David, Edgar, Edred, Edwin (St), Henri, Henry, Henry (the Fowler), Herod (the Great), Hiero, Ixion, James, Louis, Midas, Murat (Joachim), Penda, Pepin (the Short), Priam, Svein, Sweyn
06 Alaric, Albert, Alboin, Alfred, Alonso, Arthur, Attila, Baliol (Edward de), Canute, Cheops, Clovis, Darius, Donald, Duncan, Edmund, Edmund (Ironside), Edward, Edward (the Confessor), Edward (the Elder), Edward (the Martyr), Egbert, Faisal, Farouk, George, Gustav, Haakon, Harald, Harold, Harold (Harefoot), Hassan, Khalid, Magnus, Oberon, Oswald (St), Philip, Ramses, Robert, Robert (the Bruce), Rudolf, Sargon, Xerxes
07 Alfonso, Aragorn, Balliol (John de), Cepheus, Charles, Croesus, Emanuel, Francis, Fredrik, Humbert, Hussein, Ibn Saud, Kenneth, Leopold, Macbeth, Malcolm, Michael, Odoacer, Perseus, Ptolemy, Pyrrhus, Rameses, Richard, Romulus, Solomon, Stephen, Tarquin, Umberto, Wilhelm, William, William (the Conqueror), William (the Silent)
08 Baudouin, Birendra, Ethelred, Ethelred (the Unready), Frederik, Gaiseric, Gustavus, Jeroboam, Leonidas, Matthias, Ramesses, Sihanouk (Norodom), Thutmose
09 Aethelred, Akhenaten, Alexander, Alexander (the Great), Amenhotep, Antigonus, Antiochus, Athelstan, Christian, Cuchulain, Cymbeline, Ethelbert, Ethelwulf, Ferdinand, Frederick, Hammurabi, Hardaknut, Nadir Shah, Sigismund, Stanislaw, Taufa'ahau, Theodoric, Tuthmosis, Vortigern, Wenceslas, Wladyslaw, Zahir Shah (Mohammed)
10 Aethelbert, Aethelstan, Aethelwulf, Artaxerxes, Carl Gustaf, Esarhaddon, Fisher King, Juan Carlos, Moshoeshoe, Ozymandias, Tarquinius, Wenceslaus
11 Charlemagne, Constantine, Franz Joseph, Hardacanute, Hardicanute, Mithridates, Old King Cole, Sennacherib, Shalmaneser, Tut'ankhamun
12 Assurbanipal, Boris Godunov, Herod Agrippa
13 Chulalongkorn, Louis-Philippe
14 Nebuchadnezzar, Philip Augustus, Victor Emmanuel
15 Artaxerxes Ochus, Norodom Sihanouk

• **Three Kings** *see* **wise man** *under* **wise**

See also **Roman**

kingdom
04 land **05** realm, reign, state **06** domain, empire, nation, sphere **07** country, dynasty **08** division, dominion, grouping, monarchy, province **09** territory **11** sovereignty **12** commonwealth, principality

See also **classification**; **empire**

kingfisher
07 halcyon **10** kookaburra

kingly
05 grand, noble, regal, royal **06** august, lordly **07** stately, sublime, supreme **08** glorious, imperial, imposing, majestic, splendid **09** dignified, grandiose, imperious, sovereign **11** monarchical

Kingsley
03 Ben **04** Amis

kink
◇ *anagram indicator*
03 bug **04** bend, coil, curl, dent, flaw, gasp, knot, loop, null, whim **05** chink, cough, crick, crimp, curve, hitch, quirk, twirl, twist **06** defect, fetish, foible, glitch, tangle **07** blemish, caprice, crinkle, failing, wrinkle **08** weakness **09** deviation, weak point **10** deficiency, perversion **11** indentation, peculiarity, shortcoming **12** eccentricity, entanglement, idiosyncrasy, imperfection

kinkajou
05 potto **09** honey bear

kinky
◇ *anagram indicator*
03 odd **04** wavy **05** crazy, curly, funky, queer, weird **06** coiled, curled, frizzy, quirky, warped **07** bizarre, crimped, deviant, strange, tangled, twisted, unusual **08** abnormal, crumpled, depraved, freakish, peculiar, wrinkled **09** eccentric, perverted, unnatural, whimsical **10** capricious, degenerate, licentious, outlandish **13** idiosyncratic **14** unconventional

kinsfolk
03 kin **04** clan, hapu **06** family **07** cousins, kindred **09** relations, relatives **11** connections

kinship
03 kin, sib, tie **04** ties **05** blood **06** family **07** kindred, lineage **08** affinity, alliance, ancestry, likeness, relation **09** community **10** conformity, connection, similarity **11** association, equivalence **12** relationship **13** consanguinity **14** correspondence

kinsman
03 sib **04** ally **06** cousin **07** brother

kiosk
03 box **05** booth, cabin, stall, stand **07** counter **09** bandstand, bookstall, news-stand

Kiribati
03 KIR

Kirkpatrick
01 K

kismet
03 lot **04** doom, fate **05** karma **07** destiny, fortune, portion **10** predestiny, providence

kiss
01 X **03** fan, lip, pax **04** buss, lick, neck, pash, peck, snog **05** brush, cross, graze, mouth, smack, touch **06** caress, scrape, smooch, smouch **07** plonker, smacker **08** canoodle, deep kiss, osculate, suck face **09** baisemain, glance off **10** bill and coo, contrecoup, French kiss, osculation **11** touch gently **12** touch lightly **13** butterfly kiss

kit
03 rig, set **04** gear, togs **05** get-up, strip, stuff, tools **06** kitten, outfit, rig-out, tackle, things **07** baggage, clobber, clothes, colours, effects, luggage **08** clothing, supplies, utensils **09** apparatus, equipment, trappings **10** implements, provisions **11** instruments **13** accoutrements, appurtenances, paraphernalia

• **kit out**
03 arm **05** dress, equip, fix up **06** fit out, outfit, rig out, supply **07** deck out, furnish, garnish, prepare, provide

kitchen
03 but **06** galley **07** caboose, cookery, cuisine **08** scullery **10** percussion

See also **utensil**

kite
04 gled **05** belly, glede **06** dragon, elanet, Milvus, paunch **07** puttock, rokkaku **08** aircraft

kittenish
04 cute **05** ludic **06** frisky **07** playful **08** skittish, sportive **09** fun-loving **10** coquettish, frolicsome **11** flirtatious

kittiwake
06 haglet **07** hacklet

kitty
04 fund

knack
03 art, toy **04** bent, feel, gift, hang, turn **05** flair, forte, habit, quirk, skill, trick **06** genius, talent **07** ability, faculty **08** aptitude, capacity, facility, ornament **09** dexterity, expertise, handiness, quickness, technique **10** adroitness, capability, competence, propensity **11** proficiency, skilfulness

knapsack
03 bag **04** pack **06** kitbag **07** holdall, musette **08** backpack, rucksack **09** duffel bag, haversack

knave
01 J **03** boy, cad, nob, pam, pur **04** jack **05** cheat, drôle, rogue, scamp, swine **06** fripon, rascal, rotter, varlet **07** bounder, custrel, dastard, villain **08** blighter, coistrel, coistril, swindler **09** reprobate, scallywag, scoundrel

knavery
05 fraud **06** deceit, ropery **07** devilry, roguery **08** mischief, patchery,

trickery, villainy **09** chicanery, deception, duplicity, imposture **10** corruption, dishonesty, hanky-panky **11** caddishness, friponnerie, knavishness **13** double-dealing **14** monkey business

knavish

06 rascal, wicked **07** caddish, corrupt, roguish **08** devilish, fiendish, rascally **09** dastardly, deceitful, deceptive, dishonest, reprobate **10** fraudulent, villainous **11** mischievous, scoundrelly **12** contemptible, unprincipled, unscrupulous **13** dishonourable

knead

◇ *anagram indicator*

03 ply, rub **04** form, mold, work
05 malax, mould, pound, press, shape
06 conche, puddle, pummel
07 knuckle, massage, squeeze
08 malaxate **09** masticate
10 manipulate

kneel

03 bow **04** bend **05** stoop **06** curtsy, kowtow, revere **07** bow down, defer to **09** genuflect **13** make obeisance **15** fall to your knees

knees

03 lap

knell

03 end **04** peal, ring, toll **05** chime, knoll, sound **07** ringing

knickers

05 pants, thong **06** briefs, smalls
07 drawers, g-string, panties
08 bloomers, frillies, lingerie, scanties
09 underwear **10** underpants **12** bikini briefs, camiknickers
14 knickerbockers

knick-knack

04 quip **05** knack **06** bauble, gewgaw, jimjam, pretty, trifle **07** bibelot, trangam, trinket **08** gimcrack, jimcrack, nick-nack, ornament **09** bagatelle, bric-à-brac, plaything **11** whigmaleery **12** pretty-pretty, whigmaleerie

knife

03 cut, rip **04** stab **05** blade, slash, wound **06** cutter, pierce **08** lacerate

Knives include:

02 da
03 dah, hay, pen
04 bolo, case, chiv, dirk, fish, jack, moon, shiv, simi
05 bowie, bread, clasp, craft, cutto, flick, fruit, gully, kukri, panga, paper, putty, skean, skene, spade, steak, table
06 barong, butter, carver, chakra, cradle, cuttle, cuttoe, dagger, gulley, oyster, parang, pocket, sheath, trench
07 bayonet, carving, catling, drawing, dudgeon, hunting, leather, machete, palette, pruning, scalpel, Stanley®, whittle
08 bistoury, chopping, scalping, skean-dhu, skene-dhu, tranchet
09 butterfly, jockteleg, Swiss army, toothpick
10 skene-occle
11 snickersnee, switchblade
13 Kitchen Devils®, pusser's dagger

See also **dagger**; **sword**

• knife stand

03 nef **05** block

knight

01 K, N **02** AK, Kt **03** dub, Sir
07 gallant, soldier, warrior, younker
08 champion, horseman **09** freelance, man-at-arms **10** cavalryman, equestrian **12** carpet-knight, knight-errant

Knights include:

04 grey
05 black, white
06 Bayard, carpet, errant, kemper, ritter
07 paladin
08 bachelor, banneret, cavalier, douzeper, vavasour
09 chevalier, doucepere, valvassor
10 kempery-man
14 knight-bachelor, preux chevalier

Knights of the Round Table in Arthurian legend include:

03 Kay
05 Lucan, Safer
06 Degore, Gareth
07 Alymere, Dagonet, Galahad, Gawaine, Lamorak, Lionell, Mordred, Pelleas, Tristan
08 Bedivere, Tristram
09 Bleoberis, Palomedes, Percivale
10 King Arthur
11 Bors de Ganis
12 Brunor le Noir, Ector de Maris
13 Lancelot Du Lac
15 La Cote Male Taile

knightly

04 bold **05** noble **06** heroic
07 courtly, gallant, valiant **08** gracious, intrepid, valorous **09** dauntless, soldierly **10** chivalrous, courageous, honourable

knit

03 set, tie **04** ally, bind, join, knot, link, loop, mend **05** unite, weave
06 crease, fasten, furrow, gather, secure **07** connect, tighten, wrinkle **08** contract, crotchet
09 interlace **10** intertwine **12** draw together

Knitting-related terms include:

03 rib, row
04 aran, purl, wool
05 chart, pearl, plain
06 cast on, marker, needle, stitch
07 cast off, chevron, four-ply, tension, twin rib
08 ball band, fair isle, intarsia
09 box stitch, double rib, fingering, garter rib, single rib
10 double knit, French heel, moss stitch, rice stitch, row counter, seed stitch, tricoteuse
11 basketweave, cable needle, cable stitch, drop a stitch, plain stitch, thumb method
12 basket-stitch, garter-stitch, stitch holder
13 fisherman's rib, stocking frame
14 circular needle, double knitting, knitting needle, stocking stitch
15 knitting machine, knitting pattern

knob

03 bur, nub **04** ball, boll, boss, bump, burr, heel, knop, knot, knub, lump, node, noop, snub, stop, stud, umbo
05 berry, gnarl, knurl, mouse, offer, plook, plouk, rowel, swell, tuber, tuner
06 button, croche, handle, pommel, snubbe, switch, toorie, tourie, tumour
07 chesnut **08** chestnut, doorstop, eminence, pulvinar, register, swelling, tubercle **10** doorhandle, projection, protrusion, push-button
12 protuberance

knock

◇ *anagram indicator*

02 ca' **03** box, caa', con, dod, hit, pan, rap, tap **04** bang, bash, belt, blow, bump, chap, clip, cuff, dash, daud, dawd, daze, ding, jole, joll, jolt, jowl, pink, punt, slag, slam, slap, stun
05 clock, clour, clout, crash, joule, pound, punch, shock, slate, smack, stamp, swipe, thump, whack
06 attack, batter, defeat, nubble, rebuff, strike, wallop, whammy **07** bad luck, banging, censure, collide, condemn, failure, innings, knobble, knubble, rubbish, run down, setback, slag off **08** bump into, confound, pounding, reversal **09** criticism, criticize, deprecate, disparage, hammering, pull apart, rejection
10 misfortune **11** collide with, pick holes in **12** pull to pieces, tear to pieces **13** bad experience, find fault with

See also **beat**

• knock about

03 gad, hit **04** bash, hurt, roam, rove
05 abuse, punch, range, wound
06 bang up, batter, beat up, bruise, buffet, damage, injure, ramble, strike, travel, wander **07** consort, saunter, traipse **08** go around, maltreat, mistreat **09** associate, gallivant, hang about, manhandle **10** hang around

• knock back

◇ *reversal indicator*

04 cost, down, gulp, swig **05** drink, scoff, shock **06** devour, guzzle, rebuff, reject **07** swallow **08** gulp down
10 disconcert

• knock down

03 hit **04** fell, prop, raze **05** clout, floor, level, lower, pound, smash, wreck **06** batter, reduce, wallop
07 destroy, run down, run over, skittle

08 bowl over, decrease, demolish, pull down, take down 09 bring down, knock over

• **knocked down**

02 KD

• **knock off**

03 rob 04 do in, kill, lift, nick, slay, stop, whip 05 cease, filch, pinch, steal, swipe, waste 06 deduct, finish, murder, pack in, pilfer, pirate, rip off, snitch 07 bump off, snaffle 08 clock off, clock out, get rid of, pack it in, stop work, take away 09 polish off, terminate 10 do away with, finish work 11 assassinate, discontinue

• **knock out**

02 KO 04 beat, fell, kayo, rout, stun 05 amaze, crush, floor, level, shock 06 defeat, hammer, thrash 07 astound, destroy, disable, flatten, impress, startle 08 astonish, bowl over, demolish, overcome, surprise 09 eliminate, overwhelm, prostrate 10 strike down 11 knock for six 13 run rings round 14 get the better of 15 make unconscious

• **knock over**

◇ *anagram indicator*

04 fell 05 floor, level 07 run down, run over

• **knock up**

04 call, stir 05 awake, rouse, waken 06 awaken, wake up 07 wear out 09 improvise 10 impregnate, jerry-build 11 make quickly 12 build quickly, make pregnant, put in the club

knockout

02 KO 03 hit 04 coup, kayo 05 smash, socko 06 winner 07 king-hit, stunner, success, triumph 08 smash-hit 09 sensation 10 attraction

knoll

04 hill, rise 05 knell, knowe, mound 06 barrow, koppie 07 hillock, hummock 09 elevation

knot

◇ *anagram indicator*

02 kn, kt 03 bud, nur 04 band, bind, bond, boss, gnar, hill, knag, knar, knit, knob, knub, knur, lash, lump, node, nurr, ring, tags 05 bunch, clump, crowd, gnarl, group, joint, knurl, knurr, leash, mouse, ravel, snarl, twist, weave 06 circle, gaggle, nodule, secure, splice, tangle, tether 07 chignon, cluster, entwine 08 entangle, ligature, swelling 09 fastening, gathering 10 concretion, difficulty 14 marriage-favour

Knots include:

03 bow, tie
04 bend, flat, loop, love, reef, wale, wall
05 blood, chain, hitch, plait, thief, thumb, turle
06 Domhof, granny, lover's, prusik, square
07 bowline, Gordian, running, seizing, weaver's, Windsor
08 overhand, slipknot, spade-end, surgeon's, true-love
09 half hitch, lark's head, sheet bend, swab hitch, Turk's head
10 clove hitch, common bend, fisherman's, Flemish eye, sheepshank, true-lover's
11 carrick bend, donkey hitch, double blood, Englishman's, Hunter's bend, timber hitch
12 marling hitch, rolling hitch, simple sennit, weaver's hitch
13 drummer's chain, figure of eight, slippery hitch
14 Blackwall hitch, common whipping, double Cairnton, double-overhand, double-overhang, Englishman's tie, fisherman's bend, Matthew Walker's, running bowline

knotty

◇ *anagram indicator*

04 hard 05 bumpy, nirly, rough 06 knaggy, knobby, nirlie, nodose, nodous, rugged, thorny, tricky 07 complex, gnarled, gnarred, knarred, knobbly, knotted, nodular 08 baffling, puzzling 09 Byzantine, difficult, intricate 10 mystifying, perplexing 11 anfractuous, complicated, troublesome 13 problematical

know

03 con, ken, kon, see, wis, wit, wot 04 have, tell, weet, wish, wist 05 conne, savey, savvy, sense, weete 06 fathom, notice, savvey, weeten 07 approve, be aware, discern, make out, realize, undergo 08 identify, perceive 09 apprehend, be clued up, go through, have taped, recognize, tell apart 10 comprehend, experience, understand 11 distinguish, know by sight 12 be au fait with, discriminate 13 associate with, be cognizant of, be conscious of, be friends with, differentiate 14 be familiar with, be well-versed in

• **I don't know**

04 pass

know-all

06 Jowett 07 wise guy 08 polymath, wiseacre 09 know-it-all, smart alec 10 clever dick 11 clever clogs, smartypants

know-how

04 bent 05 flair, knack, savey, savvy, skill 06 savvey, talent 07 ability, faculty 08 aptitude, cum-savvy, gumption 09 adeptness, dexterity, expertise, ingenuity, knowledge 10 adroitness, capability, competence, experience 11 proficiency, savoir-faire

knowing

03 fly, hep, hip 05 aware, canny, downy 06 astute, shrewd, sussed 07 cunning, gnostic, skilful 08 informed 09 conscious, up to snuff 10 deliberate, discerning, expressive, meaningful, perceptive 11 intelligent, significant, worldly-wise

knowingly

08 by design, scienter, wilfully 09 on purpose, purposely, studiedly, willingly, wittingly 10 designedly 11 consciously 12 calculatedly, deliberately 13 intentionally

knowledge

03 art, gen, sus 04 data, suss 05 facts, grasp, jnana, light, skill, truth 06 gnosis, wisdom 07 ability, cunning, insight, knowhow, letters, tuition, witting 08 intimacy, learning, pansophy 09 awareness, cognition, education, erudition, expertise, judgement, schooling 10 cognizance 11 conversance, discernment, familiarity, information, instruction, proficiency, recognition, savoir-faire, scholarship 12 acquaintance, apprehension, intelligence 13 comprehension, consciousness, encyclopedism, enlightenment, understanding

• **full knowledge**

11 omniscience

• **range of knowledge**

03 ken

knowledgeable

02 up 05 aware, savey, savvy 06 au fait, expert, savvey 07 clued-up, erudite, learned 08 educated, familiar, genned up, informed, lettered, well-read, well up in 09 conscious, in the know, scholarly, up to speed 10 acquainted, conversant, well-versed 11 enlightened, experienced, intelligent 12 well-informed

known

04 kent 05 couth, noted, plain 06 avowed, famous, patent 07 obvious 08 admitted, familiar, revealed 09 confessed, published, well-known 10 celebrated, proclaimed, recognized 11 commonplace 12 acknowledged

• **also known as**

03 aka 05 alias

knuckle

• **knuckle down**

10 buckle down 12 begin to study 15 start to work hard

• **knuckle under**

05 defer, yield 06 accede, give in, submit 07 give way, succumb 09 acquiesce, surrender 10 capitulate 11 buckle under

Koran

05 Qoran, Quran 07 Alcoran

• **chapter of the Koran**

04 sura 05 surah

Korea
02 KP, KR **03** KOR, PRK, ROK

kosher
• not kosher
04 tref **05** trefa, treif

kowtow
04 fawn **05** defer, kneel, toady **06** cringe, grovel, pander, suck up **07** flatter **08** pay court **11** curry favour **12** bow and scrape

krypton
02 Kr

kudos
04 fame, mana **05** glory **06** cachet, credit, esteem, honour, praise, regard, renown, repute **07** acclaim, laurels **08** applause, plaudits, prestige **09** laudation **10** reputation **11** distinction

Kuwait
03 KWT

Kyrgyzstan
02 KS **03** KGZ

L

L
02 el **04** Lima

label
03 dub, tab, tag **04** call, logo, make, mark, name, seal, term **05** badge, brand, class, flash, stamp, tally, title **06** define, docket, marker, number, sticky, ticket **07** address, crowner, epithet, sticker **08** classify, describe, identify, nickname **09** bookplate, brand name, designate, dripstone, trademark **10** categorize, identifier, pigeonhole **11** description, designation **12** characterize **13** bumper sticker **14** attach a label to, categorization, classification, identification **15** proprietary name

laboratory

Laboratory apparatus includes:

05 clamp, flask, slide, stand, still, U-tube
06 beaker, Bunsen, funnel, Gilson®, mortar, pestle, retort, tripod, trough
07 bell jar, burette, cuvette, dropper, pipette, spatula, stirrer
08 crucible, cylinder, fume hood, glove box, test tube
09 autoclave, condenser, Petri dish, power pack, steam bath, stop clock
10 centrifuge, desiccator, ice machine, microscope, PCR machine, Petri plate, watchglass
11 boiling tube, filter flask, filter paper, fume chamber, thermometer
12 Bunsen burner, cloud chamber, conical flask, fume cupboard, heating block, test tube rack, Woulfe bottle
13 bubble chamber, Büchner funnel, top-pan balance
14 Kipp's apparatus
15 Erlenmeyer flask, evaporating dish, laminar flow hood, Liebig condenser, volumetric flask

laborious
04 hard **05** heavy, tough **06** tiring, uphill **07** arduous, careful, onerous, operose, painful, slavish, tedious **08** diligent, tiresome, toilsome, wearying **09** assiduous, difficult, fatiguing, Sisyphean, strenuous, wearisome **10** laboursome, working-day **11** hard-working, industrious, painstaking **12** backbreaking **13** indefatigable

laboriously
09 arduously, operosely, slavishly **10** drudgingly, tiresomely, toilsomely **11** strenuously, wearisomely **14** with difficulty

labour
◇ *anagram indicator*
03 job, Lab **04** hard, moil, plod, roll, slog, task, toil, toss, turn, work **05** begar, birth, chore, grind, hands, pains, pangs, pitch, slave, sweat, yakka **06** drudge, duties, effort, overdo, strain, strive, suffer, throes **07** dwell on, katorga, travail, try hard, workers, workmen **08** belabour, be misled, delivery, drudgery, drudgism, exertion, go all out, hard work, struggle, work hard **09** be blinded, diligence, do to death, elaborate, employees, endeavour, hard yakka, labourers, reiterate, servitude, workforce **10** be deceived, childbirth, do your best, employment, overstress **11** flog to death, give your all, harp on about, labour pains, parturition **12** contractions, kill yourself **13** exert yourself, labor improbus, overemphasize **14** go on and on about **15** industriousness

laboured
◇ *anagram indicator*
05 heavy, stiff **06** forced, leaden, worked **07** awkward, stilted, studied **08** affected, overdone, strained **09** contrived, difficult, effortful, ponderous, unnatural **10** cultivated **11** complicated, overwrought

labourer
03 boy **04** hand, jack, peon **05** churl, cooly, grunt, navvy **06** bohunk, coolie, docker, drudge, hodman, Kanaka, menial, worker **07** culchie, Grecian, hobbler, pioneer, redneck, seagull, wharfie, workman **08** cottager, dataller, daytaler, farm hand, hireling **09** field hand, operative **10** hod carrier, roustabout **11** gandy dancer **12** manual worker **15** unskilled worker

labyrinth
03 web **04** maze **06** enigma, jungle, puzzle, riddle, tangle, warren **07** mizmaze, network, winding **09** confusion, intricacy **10** complexity, perplexity **12** complication, entanglement

labyrinthine
◇ *anagram indicator*
04 mazy **06** knotty **07** complex, tangled, winding **08** confused, involved, mazelike, puzzling, tortuous **09** Byzantine, intricate **10** convoluted, perplexing **11** complicated

lace
◇ *anagram indicator*
03 net, tat, tie **04** bind, cord, do up **05** add to, blend, close, mix in, point, spike, thong, twine **06** attach, fasten, lacing, secure, string, tawdry, thrash, thread **07** crochet, flavour, fortify, latchet, netting **08** bobbinet, bootlace, filigree, mesh-work, open work, shoelace, stay tape **09** bobbin net **10** intertwine, interweave, strengthen **11** intermingle

Lace types include:

04 bone, gold
05 blond, filet, jabot, orris, point
06 blonde, bobbin, pillow, thread, trolly
07 footing, galloon, guipure, Honiton, Mechlin, pearlin, tatting, torchon, trolley
08 Brussels, dentelle, duchesse, net orris, pearling
09 Chantilly, reticella
10 Colbertine, mignonette
12 Valenciennes

lacerate
03 cut, rip **04** claw, gash, hurt, maim, rend, rent, tear, torn **05** ganch, slash, wound **06** gaunch, harrow, injure, mangle **07** afflict, cut open, scarify, torment, torture **08** distress, mutilate **09** lancinate

laceration
03 cut, rip **04** gash, maim, rent, tear **05** slash, wound **06** injury **10** mutilation

lachrymose
03 sad **05** teary, weepy **06** crying, woeful **07** maudlin, sobbing, tearful, weeping **08** dolorous, mournful **10** lugubrious, melancholy

lack
◇ *deletion indicator*
03 gap **04** miss, need, void, want **06** dearth, defect, penury **07** absence, not have, paucity, require, vacancy **08** scarcity, shortage **09** emptiness, privation **10** deficiency, have need of, scantiness **11** deprivation, destitution **12** be clean out of, be fresh out of **13** be deficient in, insufficiency **15** not have enough of

lackadaisical
04 dull, idle, lazy, limp **05** inert **06** dreamy **07** languid **08** careless, indolent, listless, lukewarm **09** apathetic, enervated, lethargic **10** abstracted, languorous, spiritless **11** half-hearted, indifferent

lackey
04 page, pawn, tool **05** gofer, guide, toady, valet **06** fawner, menial, minion, monkey, poodle, vassal, yes-man **07** doormat, equerry, footman, servant, steward **08** hanger-on, parasite, retainer **09** attendant, flatterer, sycophant **10** instrument, manservant, skip-kennel

lacking
◇ *deletion indicator*
03 shy **04** poor **05** minus **06** absent, flawed, to seek, wanted **07** missing, needing, short of, wanting, without **09** defective, deficient **10** inadequate

lacklustre
03 dim, dry **04** drab, dull, flat **05** vapid **06** boring, leaden **07** insipid, tedious **08** lifeless **10** spiritless, uninspired **11** commonplace **12** run-of-the-mill **13** unimaginative, uninteresting

laconic
04 curt **05** blunt, brief, crisp, pithy, short, terse **06** abrupt **07** concise, spartan **08** incisive, succinct, taciturn **10** economical, to the point **12** monosyllabic

laconically
07 bluntly, briefly, in a word, in brief, pithily, tersely **08** abruptly **09** concisely **10** incisively, succinctly, to the point

lacquer
05 japan **07** varnish **09** hairspray **12** vernis martin **14** Coromandel work

lacuna
03 gap **04** void **05** blank, break, space **06** cavity, hiatus **08** omission

lad
03 boy, guy, kid, son, tad **04** boyo, chap, sort, type **05** bloke, bucko, chiel, whelp, youth **06** callan, chield, fellow, nipper **07** callant, gossoon **08** juvenile, spalpeen **09** character, schoolboy, stripling, youngster **10** individual **13** gillie-wetfoot **14** whippersnapper **15** gillie-white-foot

ladder
03 run, sty **04** rank, rung, trap **05** level, point, rungs, scala, scale, steps **06** étrier, series, stairs **07** fish-way, grading, potence, ranking **08** echelons **09** companion, hierarchy **10** set of steps **12** pecking order

laden
04 full **05** heavy, taxed **06** jammed, loaded, packed **07** charged, fraught, gestant, stuffed **08** burdened, hampered, pregnant, weighted **09** chock-full, oppressed **10** encumbered **11** weighed down

la-di-da
04 posh **05** put-on **06** snooty **07** foppish, stuck-up **08** affected, mannered, snobbish **09** conceited **11** highfalutin, over-refined, pretentious, toffee-nosed

ladies *see* **toilet**

ladle
03 dip **04** bail, bale, dish, lade **05** scoop, shank, spoon **06** dipper, shovel **07** divider
• **ladle out**
07 bail out, bale out, dish out, dole out, hand out **08** disburse **10** distribute

lady
01 L **04** burd, dame, miss **05** begum, lakin, siren, woman **06** damsel, duenna, female, khanum, matron, Señora **07** hidalga, ladykin, old dear, sheikha, Signora **08** countess, Señorita **09** Signorina **10** demoiselle, grande dame, noblewoman, young woman **11** gentlewoman
See also **girl**; **woman**
• **lady's fingers**
04 okra **05** gumbo
• **lot of ladies**
04 bevy
• **organized ladies**
02 WI **15** Women's Institute

ladylike
04 soft **06** modest, polite, proper **07** courtly, elegant, genteel, queenly, refined **08** cultured, decorous, delicate, matronly, polished, well-bred **09** courteous **11** respectable **12** well-mannered

lag
04 drag, idle, late **05** dally, delay, steal, tardy, tarry, trail **06** arrest, dawdle, linger, loiter, lounge, retard **07** convict, saunter, shuffle **08** hang back, hindmost, imprison, straggle **10** behindhand, fall behind, retardment **11** retardation **12** drag your feet, shilly-shally **13** kick your heels **14** bring up the rear
See also **prisoner**

lager *see* **beer**

laggard
05 idler, snail **06** loafer **07** dawdler, lounger **08** lingerer, loiterer, sluggard **09** saunterer, slowcoach, straggler

lagoon
03 bog, fen **04** haff, lake, pond, pool **05** bayou, marsh, swamp **06** lagune, salina **08** shallows

laid-back
04 calm, cool **06** at ease, casual **07** relaxed **09** easy-going, leisurely, unhurried, unworried **10** untroubled **11** free and easy, unflappable **13** imperturbable

laid up
03 ill **04** sick **05** crook **07** injured **08** disabled **09** bedridden **10** housebound **11** immobilized, out of action **12** hors de combat **13** confined to bed, incapacitated, on the sick list

lair
03 den, lie **04** mire **05** couch **07** retreat
See also **animal**

laissez-faire
09 free-trade **10** free-market, permissive **14** free-enterprise, live and let live, non-interfering

laity
03 lay **06** people **08** amateurs **09** lay people, outsiders **10** temporalty, unordained **12** parishioners **14** the non-ordained

lake
01 L **03** dam, lac, sea **04** loch, meer, mere, pond, pool, tarn **05** basin, bayou, cowal, lough, playa, shott, water **06** lagoon, lagune, nyanza, salina **07** carmine **09** everglade, reservoir, saltchuck

The Great Lakes:

04 Erie
05 Huron
07 Ontario
08 Michigan, Superior

Lakes, lochs and loughs include:

03 Awe, Van
04 Abbé, Bala, Biwa, Bled, Chad, Como, Derg, Earn, Erie, Eyre, Kivu, Ness, Tana
05 Foyle, Garda, Great, Huron, Leven, Morar, Neagh, Nyasa, Ohrid, Onega, Patos, Poopó, Tahoe, Taupo, Volta
06 Albert, Baikal, Corrib, Crater, Finger, Geneva, Ladoga, Lomond, Louise, Malawi, Nasser, Saimaa, Taimyr, Taymyr, Vänern, Zurich
07 Aral Sea, Balaton, Chapala, Dead Sea, Katrine, Lucerne, Ontario, Rannoch, Scutari, Torrens, Turkana
08 Balkhash, Bodensee, Chiemsee, Issyk Kul, Lac Léman, Loch Earn, Loch Ness, Lough Awe, Maggiore, Michigan, Superior, Tiberias, Titicaca, Tonlé Sap, Victoria, Winnipeg
09 Constance, Great Bear, Great Salt, Kammer See, Loch Leven, Loch Morar, Lough Derg, Maracaibo, Neuchâtel, Nicaragua, Ullswater, Willandra, Zeller See
10 Caspian Sea, Great Slave, Loch Lomond, Lough Foyle, Lough Neagh, Okeechobee, Tanganyika, Windermere, Wörther See
11 Great Bitter, Loch Katrine, Lough Corrib
12 Derwent Water, Kielder Water
13 Bassenthwaite, Coniston Water

lam
03 hit **04** bash, beat, belt, pelt **05** clout, knock, pound, thump, whack **06** batter, escape, pummel, strike, thrash, wallop **07** leather

lamb
04 cade, Elia, yean **08** yeanling

lambast, lambaste
03 tan **04** beat, belt, drub, flay, flog, slag, whip **05** clout, roast, scold, thump, whack **06** batter, berate, rebuke, strike, thrash, wallop

07 censure, clobber, leather, reprove, rubbish, slag off, upbraid **08** badmouth **09** castigate, criticize, reprimand

lambert
01 L

lame
04 game, halt, hurt, maim, main, poor, tame, thin, weak **05** gammy **06** feeble, flimsy, maimed, mained, poorly **07** cripple, halting, injured, limping **08** crippled, disabled, hobbling, spavined **09** defective, hamstring, hamstrung **10** inadequate **11** handicapped **12** unconvincing **13** incapacitated **14** unsatisfactory

• **lame person**
04 gimp

lamely
06 feebly, tamely, weakly **07** shakily **09** with a limp **10** hobblingly, unsteadily **12** inadequately **14** unconvincingly

lament
03 cry, sob **04** howl, keen, mean, mein, mene, moan, wail, weep **05** dirge, dumka, elegy, groan, meane, mourn, plain, tears **06** bemoan, bewail, beweep, crying, grieve, regret, repine, sorrow, yammer **07** deplore, requiem, sobbing, ululate, wayment, weeping **08** complain, grieving, threnody **09** complaint **11** lamentation

lamentable
◇ *anagram indicator*
03 low, sad **04** mean, poor **05** lousy **06** crying, funest, grotty, meagre, measly, tragic, woeful **07** moanful, pitiful **08** grievous, mournful, terrible, wretched **09** miserable, niggardly, sorrowful, worthless **10** deplorable, inadequate **11** distressing, regrettable, unfortunate **12** insufficient **13** disappointing **14** unsatisfactory

lamentably
08 woefully **09** miserably, pitifully **10** deplorably, tragically **11** regrettably **12** inadequately **14** insufficiently **15** disappointingly

lamentation
03 cry **04** keen, moan **05** dirge, elegy, grief **06** lament, plaint, sorrow **07** keening, sobbing, wailing, wayment, weeping **08** grieving, jeremiad, mourning, threnody **09** ululation **11** deploration

laminate
04 coat, face **05** cover, flake, layer, plate, split **06** veneer **07** foliate, overlay **08** separate, stratify **09** exfoliate

lamp
03 eye **04** bulb, Davy **05** crusy, light, torch **06** argand, crusie, Leerie, sconce **07** cruisie, Geordie, lantern, lucigen, pendant, pendent, scamper **08** arc-light, fog light, torchier **09** light bulb, moderator, spotlight, torchière, veilleuse **10** Anglepoise®, Kleig light, Klieg light, night-light, photoflood **11** searchlight

lampoon
04 mock, skit **05** spoof, squib **06** parody, satire, send up, send-up **07** Pasquil, Pasquin, take off, take-off **08** ridicule, satirize, travesty **09** burlesque, make fun of **10** caricature, pasquinade

lampooner
07 Pasquil, Pasquin **08** parodist, satirist **09** pasquiler **10** pasquilant **11** pasquinader **12** caricaturist

lance
03 cut **04** pike, slit **05** lanch, prick, rejón, shaft, spear **06** incise, lancet, launch, pierce **07** bayonet, cut open, harpoon, javelin **08** puncture, white arm

land
03 bag, get, hit, nab, net, tax, win **04** area, deal, dock, drop, gain, give, loam, lord, moor, soil **05** acres, berth, catch, earth, end up, fetch, manor, reach, realm, state, tract **06** alight, anchor, arrive, burden, direct, domain, estate, fields, ground, lumber, nation, obtain, people, region, saddle, secure, settle, turn up, unload, whenua, wind up **07** achieve, acquire, acreage, capture, country, deliver, deplane, deposit, dry land, grounds, inflict, oppress, procure, terrain, trouble **08** dismount, district, encumber, farmland, finish up, go ashore, property, province, take down **09** bring down, disembark, get hold of, open space, rural area, territory, touch down, weigh down **10** administer, come to rest, fatherland, motherland, real estate, terra firma **11** countryside, terrestrial **12** come in to land, find yourself **13** bring in to land, native country

See also **country**; **continent**

• **amount of land**
03 are, lot, rod, ure **04** acre, shot **07** hectare

• **arable land**
03 lay, lea, ley

landing
04 dock, pier, quay **05** jetty, wharf **07** arrival, greaser, harbour **08** coming in **09** alighting, belly flop, deplaning, touchdown **12** landing-place, landing-stage, three-pricker **13** putting ashore **14** coming in to land, coming to ground, disembarkation

landing-stair
04 ghat **05** ghaut

landlady, landlord
04 host **05** owner **06** lessor **07** hostess, Rachman **08** hotelier, mine host, publican, slumlord **09** innkeeper, landowner **10** freeholder, proprietor **11** hotel-keeper **12** proprietress, restaurateur

landmark
05 cairn, meith **06** beacon, crisis **07** feature **08** boundary, milepost, monument, signpost **09** milestone, watershed **12** turning-point

See also **Africa**; **Asia**; **Australia**; **Canada**; **Europe**; **London**; **Middle East**; **New York**; **New Zealand**; **United Kingdom**; **United States of America**

landscape
04 view **05** scene, vista **06** aspect, saikei **07** outlook, paysage, scenery **08** panorama, prospect **11** countryside, perspective

landslide
04 slip **07** runaway **08** decisive, emphatic, landslip, rockfall **09** avalanche, earthfall **10** éboulement **12** overwhelming

lane
02 La **03** gut, way **04** loan, loke, lone, path, wynd **05** alley, byway, entry, track **06** avenue, boreen, byroad, ruelle, vennel **07** bikeway, channel, footway, loaning, passage, pathway, sea road, towpath, twitten **08** alleyway, driveway, footpath, twitting **10** backstreet, passageway

language
03 bat **04** cant, talk **05** argot, lingo, style **06** jargon, speech, tongue **07** diction, wording **08** converse, parlance, phrasing, rhetoric, speaking, swearing, uttering **09** discourse, utterance **10** expression, vocabulary, vocalizing **11** phraseology, terminology, verbalizing **12** conversation **13** communication

Languages include:

02 Wu
03 ASL, BSL, Edo, Gan, Giz, Ibo, Kru, Lao, Mam, Mon, Twi, Yue
04 Chad, Cree, Crow, Dari, Erse, Fang, Gaul, Inca, Lapp, Manx, Maya, Moto, Nupe, Pali, Susu, Thai, Tshi, Urdu, Xosa, Zulu
05 Attic, Aztec, Bantu, Cajun, Carib, Creek, Croat, Czech, Doric, Dutch, Farsi, Greek, Hindi, Inuit, Ionic, Iraqi, Irish, Karen, Kazak, Khmer, Latin, Malay, Maori, Masai, Norse, Osean, Punic, Saxon, Scots, Shona, Sioux, Tamil, Uzbek, Welsh, Xhosa, Yakut
06 Arabic, Bangla, Basque, Berber, Bokmål, Celtic, Coptic, Creole, Dakota, Danish, French, Gaelic, German, Gothic, Hebrew, Lydian, Magyar, Micmac, Mohawk, Mongol, Polish, Romany, Sherpa, Slovak, Tartar
07 Afghani, Amharic, Aramaic, Ayamará, Bengali, Bosnian, Catalan, Chinese, Chinook, Cornish, English, Euskera, Finnish, Flemish, Frisian, Guaraní, Italian, Kalmuck, Lappish, Latvian, Maltese, Mohican, Nynorsk, Punjabi, Quechua, Russian, Semitic, Siamese, Slovene, Spanish, Swahili, Swedish, Tagálog,

Turkish, Umbrian, Volapük, Walloon, Yiddish, Zapotec
08 Albanian, Armenian, Cherokee, Croatian, Demotiki, Estonian, Etruscan, Georgian, Japanese, Malagasy, Mandarin, Moldovan, Phrygian, Pilipino, Romanian, Romansch, Sanskrit, Setswana
09 Aborigine, Afrikaans, Algonquin, Bulgarian, Cantonese, Castilian, Dalmatian, Ethiopian, Hungarian, Icelandic, Kiswahili, Malayalam, Norwegian, Provençal, Sardinian, Ukrainian
10 Anglo-Saxon, Babylonian, Belarusian, Hindustani, Lithuanian, Macedonian, Malayaalam, Phoenician, Portuguese, Serbo-Croat, Vietnamese
12 ancient Greek, Katharevousa, Sign Language
13 Middle English
14 Lëtzebuergesch

Invented languages include:

03 Ido, Neo
06 Novial
07 Volapük
08 Newspeak
09 Esperanto
10 Occidental
11 Interglossa, Interlingua
12 Idiom Neutral

Computer programming languages include:

01 C
03 ADA, AWK, C++, XML
04 HTML, Java, Perl
05 BASIC, COBOL
06 Delphi, Pascal, Python
07 FORTRAN
10 Postscript

Language terms include:

02 RP
03 ASR, NLP
04 cant
05 argot, idiom, lingo, slang, usage
06 accent, brogue, creole, jargon, patois, patter, pidgin, syntax, tongue
07 dialect, grammar
08 buzz word, localism, Newspeak, standard
09 etymology, phonetics, semantics
10 journalese, vernacular, vocabulary
11 doublespeak, linguistics, non-standard, orthography, regionalism
12 gobbledygook, lexicography, lingua franca, vulgar tongue
13 colloquialism

• **bad language**
04 cuss, oath **05** curse **07** cussing **08** swearing **09** expletive, swearword

• **language unit**
04 word **07** phoneme

languid
04 dull, lazy, limp, slow, weak **05** faint, heavy, inert, slack, weary **06** feeble, pining, sickly, torpid **07** relaxed **08** drooping, flagging, inactive, listless, sluggish **09** enervated, lethargic **10** languorous, spiritless **11** debilitated, indifferent **12** uninterested **13** lackadaisical **14** unenthusiastic

languidly
05 dully **06** feebly, lazily, slowly, weakly **07** heavily, inertly **08** torpidly **10** inactively, listlessly **13** lethargically

languish
03 die, rot **04** fade, fail, flag, long, mope, pine, sigh, sink, want, wilt **05** brood, droop, faint, quail, waste, yearn **06** desire, grieve, hanker, hunger, sicken, sorrow, weaken, wither **07** decline **08** fall away **09** waste away **11** deteriorate

languor
04 calm, lull **05** ennui, sloth **06** pining, torpor **07** fatigue, frailty, inertia, silence **08** debility, laziness, lethargy, weakness **09** faintness, heaviness, indolence, lassitude, stillness, weariness **10** affliction, dreaminess, drowsiness, enervation, feebleness, relaxation, sleepiness **12** listlessness **14** oppressiveness

languorous
04 lazy, weak **05** weary **06** dreamy, feeble, sleepy, torpid **07** relaxed **08** listless **09** lethargic

lank
04 lean, limp, long, slim, tall, thin **05** gaunt, lanky **06** skinny **07** flaccid, scraggy, scrawny, slender **08** drooping, lifeless, rawboned **09** emaciated, slab-sided **10** lustreless, straggling

lanky
04 lean, slim, tall, thin **05** gaunt, rangy, weedy **06** gangly **07** scraggy, scrawny, slender **08** gangling

lantern
04 buat, glim, lamp **05** bowat, bowet, crown, darky **06** cupola, darkey, sconce **08** bull's-eye **09** Aldis lamp, belvedere **12** stereopticon

lanthanum
02 La

Laos
03 LAO

lap
03 leg, lip, rag, sip, sup **04** beat, dash, flap, flow, fold, lick, loop, roll, rush, slop, tour, wash, wind, wrap **05** ambit, break, cover, drink, knees, orbit, round, slosh, stage, swish, twine **06** circle, course, encase, enfold, hollow, lappet, splash, swathe, thighs **07** circuit, compass, envelop, overlap, scoop up, section, stretch, swaddle **08** distance, surround

• **lap up**
06 absorb, relish, savour **08** listen in **09** delight in **13** accept eagerly

lapse
03 end, gap **04** drop, fail, fall, go by, go on, lull, pass, sink, slip, stop, trip **05** blank, break, cease, drift, error, fault, glide, pause, slide **06** course, elapse, expire, hiatus, run out, slip by, worsen **07** blunder, decline, descent, failing, go to pot, mistake, passage, relapse, resolve, stumble **08** downturn, interval, omission, slip away, slipping **09** backslide, oversight, prescribe, terminate, worsening **10** aberration, become void, degenerate, go downhill, negligence **11** backsliding, dereliction, deteriorate, go to the dogs **12** degeneration, indiscretion, intermission, interruption **13** become invalid, deterioration, fall from grace **14** go down the tubes **15** go to rack and ruin

lapsed
04 once, void **05** ended **06** former, run out **07** expired, invalid **08** finished, obsolete, outdated **09** out of date, unrenewed **11** backslidden **12** discontinued **13** non-practising

lapwing
05 pewit, tewit **06** peewit, tewhit **07** teuchat **08** teru-tero

larceny
05 heist, theft **06** piracy **07** robbery **08** burglary, stealing **09** pilfering **10** purloining **13** expropriation

lard
04 load, saim, seam **05** enarm, seame, strew, stuff **06** fatten **07** garnish **14** interpenetrate

larder
06 pantry, spence **08** scullery **09** storeroom **11** springhouse, storage room

large
02 lg, OS **03** big, lge **04** full, high, huge, mega, tall, vast **05** ample, broad, bulky, giant, grand, great, heavy, jumbo, roomy **06** bumper **07** copious, diffuse, immense, liberal, mammoth, massive, monster, outsize, sizable **08** abundant, colossal, enormous, generous, gigantic, sizeable, spacious, spanking, sweeping, whopping **09** extensive, ginormous, good-sized, grandiose, humungous, king-sized, monstrous, plentiful **10** commodious, dirty great, exhaustive, monumental, prodigious, stupendous, voluminous **11** far-reaching, importantly, magnanimous, prominently, substantial, wide-ranging **12** considerable **13** comprehensive, wide-stretched **14** Brobdingnagian, ostentatiously

• **at large**
03 out **04** free **06** abroad, mainly **07** chiefly **08** on the run **09** at liberty, generally, in general, in the main **10** by and large, on the loose, on the whole, unconfined **11** independent

• **by and large**
06 mainly, mostly **07** as a rule **09** generally **10** on the whole **14** for the most part

largely
06 mainly, mostly, widely **07** chiefly, greatly **09** generally, in the main, primarily **10** by and large, especially **11** extensively, principally **12** considerably **13** predominantly **14** for the most part, to a large extent

largeness
04 bulk, size **08** vastness, wideness **09** ampleness, amplitude, broadness, grandness, greatness, heaviness, immensity **11** sizableness **12** enormousness, macrocephaly, sizeableness **13** expansiveness **14** stupendousness, voluminousness

large-scale
04 epic, mega, vast, wide **05** broad **06** global **08** sweeping **09** expansive, extensive, universal, wholesale **10** nationwide **11** country-wide, far-reaching, wide-ranging **12** wide-reaching

largesse
03 aid **04** alms, gift **05** grant **06** bounty **07** bequest, charity, handout, present **08** donation, kindness **09** allowance, endowment **10** generosity, liberality **11** benefaction, munificence **12** philanthropy **14** open-handedness

lark
◇ *anagram indicator*
03 guy, job **04** game, play, romp, task **05** antic, caper, chore, fling, prank, revel, sport, thing **06** cavort, frolic, gambol **07** fooling, gammock, have fun, rollick, skylark **08** activity, business, escapade, mischief **09** cavorting, fool about, horseplay, mess about **10** fool around, play tricks

larva
04 grub, moth, spat **05** ghost, naiad, ox-bot **06** caddis, chigoe, chigre, measle **07** budworm, chigger, hydatid, planula, pluteus, spectre, tadpole, veliger **08** army worm, bookworm, coenurus, cornworm, mealworm, wireworm, woodworm **09** auger-worm, bloodworm, doodlebug, glass-crab, joint-worm, screw-worm, sporocyst, strawworm, xylophage **10** bipinnaria, caddis-worm, cankerworm, miracidium, woolly bear **11** cabbage-worm, caterpillar, corn earworm, hellgramite **12** hellgrammite **13** leptocephalus, spruce budworm

• **larval stage**
04 zoea **08** cercaria

lascivious
04 blue, lewd **05** bawdy, crude, dirty, horny, randy, saucy **06** coarse, ribald, smutty, vulgar, wanton **07** lustful, obscene, Paphian, sensual, Sotadic **08** indecent, petulant, prurient, Sotadean, unchaste **09** lecherous, offensive, salacious **10** libidinous, licentious, scurrilous, suggestive **12** pornographic

lash
03 cat, hit, tie, wag **04** beat, belt, bind, blow, dash, flog, join, rope, rush, slow, soft, stop, welt, whip, wire **05** affix, break, flail, flick, horse, pound, scold, seize, slack, slash, smash, strap, swipe, swish, thong, whack **06** attack, batter, berate, buffet, fasten, gammon, lavish, rebuke, secure, strike, stripe, stroke, swinge, switch, tether, thrash, wallop **07** bawl out, censure, insipid, lay into, reprove, scourge **08** bullwhip, make fast, squander **09** bullwhack, criticize, fulminate, horsewhip **12** tear to shreds **13** tear a strip off

• **lash out**
04 yerk **06** thrash **07** lay into, run down **08** hit out at **09** have a go at **11** splash out on **12** tear to pieces, tear to shreds **13** tear a strip off, tear strips off **14** attack strongly **15** speak out against, spend a fortune on

lashings
04 lots, tons **05** heaps, loads, piles **06** masses, oodles, stacks **11** large amount **13** great quantity

lass
03 hen **04** bird, girl, miss **05** chick, filly, Jenny, popsy **06** damsel, lassie, maiden **10** schoolgirl, sweetheart, young woman **11** maid-servant

See also **girl**

lassitude
06 apathy, torpor **07** fatigue, languor **08** dullness, lethargy, weakness **09** faintness, heaviness, tiredness, weariness **10** drowsiness, enervation, exhaustion **11** spring fever **12** listlessness, sluggishness

lasso
04 lazo, rope **05** noose, reata, riata **06** lariat

last
◇ *tail selection indicator*
03 end, ult **04** back, dure, go on, hind, keep, live, load, stay, take, wear **05** abide, after, cargo, close, dying, exist, final **06** behind, ending, endure, finish, hold on, keep on, latest, live on, remain, utmost, yester **07** carry on, closing, dernier, endmost, extreme, finally, hold out, persist, stand up, subsist, survive, tail-end **08** at the end, continue, farthest, furthest, hindmost, previous, rearmost, remotest, terminal, ultimate **09** at the back, at the rear, finishing **10** completion, concluding, conclusion, get through, lattermost, most recent, stick it out, ultimately **11** least likely **12** most unlikely **13** least suitable **14** coming at the end, most improbable, most unsuitable

• **at last**
◇ *tail selection indicator*
07 finally **08** at length, in the end **10** eventually, ultimately **11** in due course **12** in conclusion

• **last word**
04 amen, best, pick, rage **05** cream, vogue **06** latest **08** final say, ultimate **09** ultimatum **10** dernier cri, perfection **11** ne plus ultra **12** quintessence **13** final decision **14** crème de la crème, final statement **15** definite comment

last-ditch
04 wild **05** final **06** all-out, heroic **07** frantic **08** frenzied, last-gasp **09** desperate, straining **10** last-chance, struggling **12** eleventh-hour

lasting
05 fixed **07** abiding, durable, dureful, undying **08** enduring, external, lifelong, long-term, unending **09** ceaseless, endurable, long-lived, permanent, perpetual, surviving, unceasing **10** continuing, monumental, persisting, unchanging **11** everlasting, never-ending **12** interminable, long-standing

lastly
◇ *tail selection indicator*
07 finally, to sum up **08** in the end **10** ultimately **12** in conclusion

last-minute
04 late **05** hasty **06** forced, rushed **07** overdue **11** superficial **12** eleventh-hour

latch
03 bar **04** bolt, hasp, hook, lock, mire **05** catch, clink, sneck **06** fasten **07** clicket **09** fastening **10** make secure

• **latch on to**
04 twig **05** grasp, learn **06** follow **07** realize **09** apprehend **10** comprehend, understand **14** not want to leave

late
03 lag, new, old **04** dead, past, slow **05** fresh, tardy **06** behind, former, latest, recent, slowly, whilom **07** current, defunct, delayed, overdue, tardily **08** backward, deceased, departed, formerly, overtime, previous, recently, sometime, umquhile, up-to-date **09** belatedly, in arrears, preceding **10** after hours, behindhand, behind time, dilatorily, last-minute, unpunctual **12** unpunctually **13** up-to-the-minute **14** behind schedule

• **of late**
05 newly **06** lately **08** latterly, recently **10** not long ago

lately
05 alate, newly **06** of late **08** latterly, recently **09** now of late **10** not long ago

lateness
05 delay **09** tardiness **11** belatedness, retardation **12** dilatoriness **13** unpunctuality

latent
06 hidden, secret, unseen, veiled **07** dormant, lurking, passive **08** inactive, possible **09** concealed, invisible, potential, quiescent **10** underlying, unrealized, unrevealed

11 delitescent, undeveloped, unexpressed 12 undiscovered

later

04 next, syne **05** after **06** latter **07** goodbye, later on **08** in a while **09** following, posterior **10** afterwards, eventually, subsequent, succeeding **11** in due course, in the future **12** at a later time, subsequently, successively **13** at a future date, at a future time, some other time **15** in the near future

lateral

03 lat **04** side **05** fresh **06** clever **07** oblique **08** creative, edgeways, flanking, indirect, inspired, marginal, original, sideward, sideways, slanting **09** brilliant, illogical, ingenious **10** unorthodox **11** alternative, imaginative **13** outside the box **14** unconventional

laterally

08 edgeways, sideways **09** obliquely **10** creatively, originally **11** illogically, ingeniously **13** imaginatively, outside the box

latest

02 in **03** hip, now **04** last **05** funky **06** modern, newest, trendy, with it **07** current **08** ultimate, up-to-date **10** most recent **11** fashionable **13** up-to-the-minute

lather

03 rub **04** flap, foam, fuss, soap, stew, suds **05** fever, froth, panic, state, sweat, tizzy **06** dither, whip up **07** anxiety, bubbles, fluster, flutter, shampoo **08** soapsuds **09** agitation

Latin

◇ *foreign word indicator*

01 L **03** Lat

Latin words and expressions include:

03 sic
04 idem, pace
05 ad hoc, circa
06 gratis, ibidem, passim
07 alumnus, a priori, de facto, erratum, floruit, in vitro, sub rosa
08 addendum, emeritus, ex gratia, gravitas, infra dig, mea culpa, nota bene, subpoena
09 ad nauseam, alma mater, carpe diem, et tu, Brute, ex officio, inter alia, ipso facto, per capita, status quo, sub judice, vox populi
10 anno Domini, ante-bellum, ex cathedra, in absentia, in extremis, magnum opus, post mortem, prima facie, quid pro quo, sine qua non, tabula rasa
11 ad infinitum, memento mori, non sequitur, tempus fugit
12 ante meridiem, caveat emptor, compos mentis, habeas corpus, post meridiem
13 camera obscura, deus ex machina, modus operandi
14 annus mirabilis, in loco parentis, pro bono publico, terra incognita
15 annus horribilis, curriculum vitae, delirium tremens, persona non grata

See also **day**; **month**; **number**

latitude

01 l **03** lat **04** play, room, span **05** field, range, reach, scope, space, sweep, width **06** extent, laxity, leeway, spread **07** breadth, freedom, liberty, licence **09** allowance, clearance **10** indulgence **11** flexibility **12** carte blanche

latter

03 end **04** last **05** final, later **06** modern, recent, second **07** closing, ensuing **10** concluding, succeeding, successive **13** last-mentioned

latter-day

06 modern, recent **07** current **10** present-day **12** contemporary

latterly

06 lately, of late **08** hitherto, recently **12** most recently

lattice

03 web **04** grid, mesh **05** grate, grill **06** grille, jacket **07** grating, network, tracery, trellis **08** espalier, fretwork, openwork **10** portcullis **11** latticework **12** reticulation

Latvia

02 LV **03** LVA

laud

04 hail **05** extol **06** admire, honour, praise **07** acclaim, applaud, approve, glorify, magnify **09** celebrate

laudable

06 of note, worthy **08** sterling **09** admirable, estimable, excellent, exemplary **10** creditable **11** commendable, meritorious **12** praiseworthy

laudation

05 glory, kudos, paean **06** eulogy, homage, praise **07** acclaim, tribute **08** accolade, blessing, devotion, encomion, encomium **09** adulation, celebrity, extolment, panegyric, reverence **10** veneration **11** acclamation **12** commendation **13** glorification

laudatory

06 eulogy **09** adulatory, approving **10** eulogistic, glorifying **11** acclamatory, approbatory, celebratory, encomiastic, panegyrical **12** commendatory **13** complimentary, encomiastical **14** congratulatory

laugh

03 fun, wag, wit, yok **04** boff, card, ha-ha, he-he, hoax, hoot, howl, jest, joke, lark, peal, peel, play, roar, yock **05** clown, comic, joker, lauch, prank, risus, snirt, sport, te-hee, trick **06** cackle, giggle, guffaw, haw-haw, hoaxer, jester, nicher, nicker, scream, tee-hee, titter **07** break up, buffoon, chortle, chuckle, snicker, snigger, snirtle **08** comedian, crease up, humorist, irrision, quipster **09** character, fall about, prankster, trickster **10** belly-laugh, cachinnate, horse laugh **11** wisecracker **12** be in stitches, cachinnation **14** practical joker, shake your sides, split your sides **15** laugh like a drain

• laugh at

04 jeer, mock **05** scorn, taunt **06** deride **07** scoff at **08** ridicule **09** make fun of, poke fun at **11** make a fool of **14** make jokes about

• laugh off

06 ignore **07** dismiss **08** belittle, minimize, pooh-pooh, shrug off **09** disregard **10** brush aside **12** make little of

laughable

05 comic, droll, funny **06** absurd **07** amusing, comical **08** derisive, derisory, farcical, humorous **09** diverting, hilarious, ludicrous **10** ridiculous, uproarious **11** nonsensical **12** entertaining, preposterous **13** side-splitting

laughably

08 absurdly **10** farcically **11** ludicrously **12** ridiculously **14** preposterously

laughing-stock

04 butt, dupe **05** sport **06** stooge, target, victim **08** derision, fair game **09** Aunt Sally **10** outspeckle **11** figure of fun

laughter

03 haw **04** glee, ha-ha **05** mirth **06** cackle, haw-haw, tee-hee **07** fou rire, hooting **08** cackling, giggling, hilarity, irrision, laughing, paroxysm **09** amusement, chortling, chuckling, guffawing, happiness, hysterics, merriment, tittering **10** risibility, sniggering **11** convulsions **12** cachinnation, cheerfulness

launch

04 dart, fire, hurl, open, shot **05** begin, float, found, lance, set up, shoot, start, throw **06** attack, propel **07** lancing, project, rollout, send off, unstock **08** commence, dispatch, embark on, initiate, organize **09** discharge, establish, instigate, institute, introduce, set afloat **10** inaugurate **11** set in motion **12** presentation

launder

◇ *anagram indicator*

04 wash **05** clean **06** trough **07** cleanse **09** washerman **11** washerwoman

laundry

04 wash **07** bagwash, clothes, steamie, washing **08** lavatory **10** Laundromat® **11** dry cleaner's, launderette **12** dirty clothes, dirty washing

laurel

03 bay **04** Stan **06** aucuba, daphne, kalmia, Laurus **08** pichurim, sweet bay

09 sassafras, spicebush 10 greenheart, mock orange

lava

04 bomb, slag 05 lahar 06 cinder, coulée, pumice, scoria 07 clinker, lapilli 08 pahoehoe 09 toadstone 10 palagonite 12 volcanic bomb 13 volcanic glass

lavatory

02 WC 03 bog, can, lav, loo 04 dike, dyke, john, kazi, rear, toot 05 dunny, Elsan®, gents', heads, karsy, karzy, khazi, lavvy, privy, rears 06 carsey, karsey, ladies', lavabo, lotion, office, throne, toilet, urinal 07 cludgie, cottage, crapper, latrine 08 bathroom, dunnakin, Portaloo®, rest room, superloo, washroom 09 cloakroom, necessary 10 facilities, powder room, reredorter, thunderbox 11 convenience, earth-closet, water closet 12 smallest room 14 comfort station, little boys' room

lavish

04 free, heap, lash, lush, pour, rich, wild 05 grand, spend, waste 06 bestow, deluge, expend, lordly, shower, slap-up 07 copious, fulsome, liberal, profuse 08 abundant, generous, gorgeous, princely, prodigal, prolific, splendid, squander, wasteful 09 bountiful, dissipate, excessive, expensive, exuberant, luxuriant, plentiful, profusion, sumptuous, unlimited, unsparing 10 give freely, immoderate, open-handed, profligate, thriftless, unstinting 11 extravagant, intemperate, spendthrift 12 unrestrained 13 unwithdrawing

lavishly

06 freely, lushly, richly, wildly 07 grandly 09 liberally, profusely 10 abundantly, generously, splendidly 11 excessively, luxuriously, sumptuously, unsparingly 13 extravagantly, intemperately

law

03 act, lay, lex 04 code, cops, pigs, rule 05 axiom, canon, edict, maxim, order, tenet 06 decree 07 charter, command, coppers, formula, lawsuit, precept, rozzers, statute, the Bill, the fuzz 08 standard, the force 09 criterion, determine, direction, directive, enactment, guideline, ordinance, principle, the police 10 boys in blue, expeditate, indulgence, litigation, regulation 11 commandment, instruction, legal action, legislation 12 constitution 13 jurisprudence, pronouncement 14 police officers, the police force

Laws and Acts include:

04 DORA
07 Riot Act, Test Act
08 Corn Laws, Poor Laws, Stamp Act, Sugar Act
10 Act of Union, Magna Carta, Patriot Act, Reform Acts
11 Abortion Act, Equal Pay Act
12 Bill of Rights, Homestead Act
13 Act of Congress, Enclosure Acts, Parliament Act
14 Act of Supremacy, Cat and Mouse Act, Civil Rights Act, Corporation Act, Declaratory Act, Native Title Act, Taft–Hartley Act
15 Act of Parliament, Act of Settlement, Act of Succession, Habeas Corpus Act

Scientific and other laws include:

04 Ohm's, Oral, Sod's
05 lemon, Roman, Salic
06 Boyle's, Hooke's, Mosaic, Snell's, Stoke's
07 Dalton's, Hubble's, Kepler's, Murphy's, natural
08 Charles's
09 Avogadro's
10 Parkinson's
13 inverse square

• by law

04 iure, jure

law-abiding

04 good 06 decent, honest, lawful 07 dutiful, orderly, upright 08 obedient, virtuous 09 complying, righteous 10 honourable, upstanding 15 whiter than white

lawbreaker

05 crook, felon 06 outlaw, sinner 07 convict, culprit 08 criminal, offender 09 infractor, miscreant, wrongdoer 10 delinquent, trespasser 11 perpetrator 12 transgressor

lawcourt

03 bar 05 bench, court, trial 07 assizes, session 08 tribunal 09 judiciary 10 court of law

lawful

04 just 05 legal, legit, licit, valid 06 proper 08 rightful 09 allowable, legalized, warranted 10 authorized, legitimate, recognized, sanctioned 11 permissible 14 constitutional

lawfully

05 by law 07 legally, validly 08 by rights, properly 10 rightfully 11 permissibly 12 legitimately

lawless

◇ *anagram indicator*

04 wild 05 rowdy 06 unruly 07 chaotic, illegal, riotous, rulesse 08 anarchic, criminal, mutinous, reckless, ruleless 09 insurgent, seditious, unsettled 10 anarchical, disorderly, rebellious, ungoverned, wrongdoing 11 lawbreaking 12 unrestrained 13 revolutionary, wild and woolly 15 insurrectionary

lawlessness

05 chaos 06 mob law, piracy 07 anarchy, mob rule 08 disorder, rent-a-mob, lynch-law, sedition 09 mobocracy, rebellion 10 insurgency, ochlocracy, revolution 12 insurrection, racketeering

lawman

03 Ohm 05 Boyle, Hooke, Mufti 09 Parkinson

Lawrence

02 DH, TE

lawrencium

02 Lr, Lw

lawsuit

04 case, plea, suit 05 cause, trial 06 action 07 contest, dispute, process 08 argument 10 indictment, litigation 11 legal action, proceedings, prosecution

lawyer

02 Av, BL 03 Att 04 Atty, silk 05 brief 06 jurist 07 counsel, mukhtar, shyster, templar 08 advocate, attorney, green-bag, Man of Law 09 lawmonger 10 legal eagle 12 legal adviser

See also **barrister**

Lawyer types include:

02 DA, KC, QC
05 avoué, judge
06 avocet
07 bencher, coroner, counsel, justice, sheriff
08 Recorder
09 barrister, solicitor
11 conveyancer, crown lawyer
12 circuit judge, jurisconsult, Lord Advocate
13 attorney at law, Crown attorney, district judge, Queen's Counsel, sheriff depute
14 criminal lawyer, deputy recorder, High Court judge, Lord Chancellor, public defender, Vice-Chancellor
15 ambulance-chaser, Attorney-General

Lawyers include:

04 **Hill** (Anita), **John** (Otto), **Reno** (Janet)
05 **Booth** (Cherie), **Finch** (Atticus), **Mason** (Perry), **Mills** (Dame Barbara Jean Lyon), **Nader** (Ralph), **Slovo** (Joe), **Vance** (Cyrus R)
06 **Bailey** (F Lee), **Butler** (Benjamin Franklin), **Carton** (Sydney), **Darrow** (Clarence), **Devlin** (Patrick, Lord), **Holmes** (Oliver Wendell), **Martin** (Richard)
07 **Acheson** (Dean), **Clinton** (Hillary Rodham), **Haldane** (Richard, Viscount), **Kennedy** (Helena, Baroness), **Mondale** (Walter), **O'Connor** (Sandra Day)
08 **Kunstler** (William), **Marshall** (Thurgood), **Mortimer** (Sir John)
09 **La Guardia** (Fiorello H), **Shawcross** (Hartley William, Baron)
10 **Birkenhead** (Frederick Edwin Smith, Earl of), **Dershowitz** (Alan)
11 **Hore-Belisha** (Leslie, Lord)
12 **Guicciardini** (Francesco)
14 **Brillat-Savarin** (Anthelme)

• lawyers

03 bar

lax
◇ *anagram indicator*
04 wide **05** broad, loose, slack, vague **06** casual, remiss, salmon, sloppy **07** flaccid, general, inexact, lenient **08** careless, heedless, laid-back, slipshod, tolerant, wide-open **09** easy-going, imprecise, indulgent, negligent **10** inaccurate, indefinite, neglectful, permissive **11** inattentive **14** latitudinarian

laxative
05 purge, salts, senna **06** ipecac, saline **07** cascara, Gregory **08** aperient, evacuant, lenitive, loosener, relaxant, solutive **09** aperitive, cathartic, purgative, taraxacum **10** eccoprotic, Epsom salts **11** health salts, ipecacuanha **14** cascara sagrada, Gregory's powder, liquid paraffin, Seidlitz powder **15** Gregory's mixture

laxity
07 freedom, neglect **08** latitude, leniency, softness **09** looseness, slackness, tolerance **10** indulgence, negligence, sloppiness **11** imprecision, inexactness, nonchalance **12** carelessness, heedlessness, indifference, laissez-faire, slovenliness **14** indefiniteness, permissiveness

lay
03 bet, ode, put, set **04** bear, bung, drop, laic, make, plan, poem, risk, song **05** allot, apply, beset, breed, civil, cover, embed, imbed, leave, lodge, lyric, offer, place, plant, plonk, posit, stick, wager **06** arable, assign, ballad, burden, chance, charge, design, devise, gamble, hazard, impose, impute, locate, meadow, saddle, set out, settle, submit, thrust, waylay **07** amateur, arrange, ascribe, deposit, dispose, inflict, oppress, pasture, prepare, present, produce, secular, set down, station, work out **08** encumber, engender, exorcize, madrigal, oviposit, position **09** attribute, establish, weigh down **10** make it with, put forward **11** give birth to, **12** non-qualified **13** non-specialist **15** non-professional

• **lay aside**
04 keep, save, void **05** defer, store **06** put off, reject, shelve **07** abandon, discard, dismiss **08** postpone, put aside, set aside **09** cast aside

• **lay bare**
04 show **05** scale, strip, unrip **06** expose, reveal, uncase, unveil **07** divulge, exhibit, explain, uncover **08** disclose, manifest

• **lay down**
04 drop, give **05** couch, plant, plonk, state, store, yield **06** affirm, assert, depone, give up, ordain, record, submit **07** deposit, discard **09** establish, formulate, postulate, prescribe, stipulate, surrender **10** relinquish

• **lay down the law**
07 dictate **09** crack down, dogmatize, emphasize **11** pontificate **12** rule the roost **14** read the riot act

• **lay hands on**
03 get **04** find, grab, grip **05** bless, catch, clasp, grasp, seize, set on **06** attack, beat up, clutch, locate, obtain, ordain **07** acquire, assault, confirm, lay into, unearth **08** discover **09** get hold of, lay hold of **10** consecrate **12** bring to light

• **lay in**
05 amass, glean, hoard, store **06** gather **07** build up, collect, stock up, store up **09** stockpile **10** accumulate

• **lay into**
06 assail, attack **08** hit out at, let fly at, set about, tear into **09** have a go at, lash out at, pitch into

• **lay it on**
07 flatter **08** butter up, overdo it, soft-soap **09** sweet-talk **10** exaggerate, overpraise

• **lay off**
04 doff, drop, quit, sack, stop **05** cease, hedge, let go, let up **06** desist, give up, pay off **07** dismiss, refrain **08** leave off **09** discharge **10** leave alone **11** discontinue **13** make redundant

• **lay on**
04 give **05** cater, pound, set up **06** impose, supply **07** furnish, inflict, provide **08** organize

• **lay out**
03 pay **04** fell, give, plan **05** floor, spend **06** design, expend, invest, put out, set out, streek **07** arrange, display, exhibit, flatten, fork out, stretch **08** demolish, disburse, knock out, shell out, straucht, straught **09** spread out **10** contribute

• **lay up**
04 hive, keep, save **05** amass, hoard, set by, store **07** deposit, put away, store up **08** mothball **10** accumulate

• **lay waste**
04 rape, raze, ruin, sack **05** havoc, spoil **06** locust, ravage **07** despoil, destroy, estrepe, pillage **08** demolish, desolate **09** depredate, devastate, vandalize

layabout
05 idler **06** loafer, skiver, waster **07** goof-off, laggard, lounger, shirker, wastrel **09** corner-boy, corner-man, lazybones, sundowner **10** ne'er-do-well **14** good-for-nothing

layer
01 E **03** bed, hen, lie, ply, row **04** band, coat, film, seam, skin, tier, vein **05** cover, flake, plate, sheet, table **06** course, lamina, mantle, scrape **07** blanket, coating, deposit, lamella, stratum **08** covering **09** mesoblast, thickness **10** lamination **11** superficies

See also **atmosphere**

• **layers**
06 strata

layman, layperson, laywoman
04 laic **07** amateur, secular **08** exhorter, outsider, tertiary **11** parabolanus, parishioner, terrestrial **12** impropriator **13** local preacher, unordained man **15** non-professional, unordained woman

lay-off
05 cards **06** firing, papers **07** jotters, sacking, the boot, the push, the sack **08** the elbow **09** discharge, dismissal **10** redundancy **12** unemployment

layout
◇ *anagram indicator*
03 map, set **04** plan, unit **05** draft **06** design, format, outfit, sketch **07** display, outline **09** blueprint, geography **11** arrangement **12** organization **13** comprehensive

layperson *see* **layman, layperson, laywoman**

laze
03 veg **04** idle, loaf, loll, lusk **05** chill, relax **06** bludge, lounge, unwind, veg out **08** chill out **09** bum around, lie around, sit around

lazily
◇ *anagram indicator*
04 idly **06** slowly **07** slackly **10** sluggishly **13** lethargically

laziness
05 sloth **07** languor **08** idleness, lethargy, slowness **09** fainéance, indolence, slackness, tardiness **10** inactivity, Oblomovism **12** dilatoriness, slothfulness, sluggishness

lazy
04 idle, lusk, slow **05** inert, slack, tardy **06** laesie, lither, torpid **07** dronish, languid, luskish, work-shy **08** bone-idle, fainéant, inactive, indolent, slothful, sluggish **09** lethargic **10** languorous, slow-moving **14** good-for-nothing

lazybones
04 lusk, slob, slug **05** drone, idler **06** loafer, lubber, skiver, slouch **07** goof-off, laggard, lounger, lubbard, mollusc, shirker **08** do-nought, fainéant, layabout, slowback, sluggard **09** do-nothing, sundowner **10** bedpresser, ne'er-do-well, sleepyhead **14** good-for-nothing

leach
04 seep **05** drain **06** filter, osmose, strain **07** extract **08** filtrate **09** lixiviate, percolate

lead
◇ *head selection indicator*
02 Pb **03** gap, tip, top, van **04** clue, cord, edge, hand, have, head, hint, hold, line, live, main, move, pass, rein, rule, shot, show, slip, star, sway **05** balls, cause, chain, chief, excel, first, guide, leash, model, outdo, pilot, plumb, prime, slugs, spend, start, steer, usher **06** convey, direct, escort, exceed, govern, induce, manage, margin, minium, outrun, prompt, sinker, string, tether, tip-off, weight **07** bring on, bullets, command,

conduct, dispose, eclipse, example, incline, leading, officer, pattern, pellets, plummet, pointer, precede, premier, primary, produce, provoke, running, surpass, undergo **08** foremost, guidance, interval, outstrip, persuade, priority, regulate, result in, star role, vanguard **09** advantage, be in front, call forth, come first, direction, extension, forefront, indicator, influence, precedent, principal, supervise, supremacy, title role, transcend **10** ammunition, bring about, experience, first place, indication, initiative, leadership, leading man, precedence, suggestion **11** be in the lead, heavy weight, leading lady, leading role, outdistance, pre-eminence, preside over, tend towards **12** be in charge of, call the shots, contribute to, starring part **13** be at the head of, principal part **15** advance position, leading position

• **lead gradually**
04 drib

• **lead off**
04 open **05** begin, start **07** kick off **08** commence, get going, initiate, start off **10** inaugurate

• **lead on**
04 dupe, lure **05** tempt, trail, trick **06** draw on, entice, seduce **07** beguile, deceive, mislead **08** persuade **11** string along **12** put one over on, take for a ride **14** pull a fast one on

• **lead the way**
04 show **05** guide **07** go first, pioneer **09** go in front, set a trend **10** be a pioneer, pave the way, show the way **11** blaze a trail **14** break new ground

• **lead up to**
05 usher **07** prepare **08** approach **09** introduce **10** open the way, pave the way, prepare for **13** make overtures

leaden

04 dull, grey, lead **05** ashen, dingy, heavy, inert, stiff **06** boring, cloudy, dismal, dreary, gloomy, sombre, wooden **07** greyish, humdrum, languid, onerous, stilted **08** laboured, lifeless, listless, overcast, plodding, sluggish **09** plumbeous **10** burdensome, cumbersome, depressing, lacklustre, oppressive, spiritless

leader

◇ *head selection indicator*
02 PM **03** dux, gov, guv **04** boss, cock, head, imam **05** ariki, chief, guide, ruler, sheik, usher **06** bigwig, escort, expert, honcho, sachem, sheikh, top dog, zaddik **07** big shot, captain, coryphe, courier, founder, general, khalifa, kingpin, mahatma, manager, pioneer, skipper, tsaddik, tsaddiq, tzaddik, tzaddiq **08** big noise, caudillo, director, governor, inventor, khalifah, mocuddum, mokaddam, muqaddam, overseer, superior **09** architect, authority, big cheese, chieftain, commander, conductor, developer, editorial, innovator, liturgist, principal **10** coryphaeus, discoverer, figurehead, head honcho, pathfinder, ringleader, supervisor **11** front-runner, trailblazer **12** guiding light, leading light **13** groundbreaker **14** mover and shaker, superintendent

See also **governor**; **emperor**; **empress**; **king**; **leader**; **Maori**; **president**; **queen**; **Roman**; **ruler**

leaderless

◇ *head deletion indicator*
08 headless **10** acephalous

leadership

◇ *head selection indicator*
04 lead, rule, sway **07** command, control **08** guidance, headship, hegemony **09** authority, captaincy, direction **10** apostolate, domination, management **11** generalship, pre-eminence, premiership, supervision **12** directorship, governorship **14** administration, rangatiratanga **15** superintendency

lead-in

05 debut, intro, proem, start **06** launch **07** opening, preface, prelude **08** exordium, foreword, overture, preamble, prologue **09** beginning **11** front matter **12** inauguration, introduction, presentation, prolegomenon **13** preliminaries

leading

◇ *head selection indicator*
03 top **04** main, star **05** chief, first, front **06** ruling, staple **07** guiding, highest, premier, primary, supreme, top-rank **08** dominant, foremost, greatest, guidance, mistress, superior **09** directing, governing, number one, paramount, preceding, principal **10** pre-eminent **11** outstanding

leaf

01 f, p **03** pad **04** flip, page, skim **05** bract, calyx, folio, frond, sepal, sheet, thumb **06** browse, folium, glance, needle, troely **07** foliole, leaflet, troelie, troolie **09** cataphyll, clinquant, cotyledon, marijuana **11** sclerophyll **12** thumb through

Leaf parts include:

03 tip
04 back, lobe, vein
05 blade, lobus, stoma, thorn
06 margin, midrib, sheath, stipel
07 petiole, stipule, stomata
08 leaf axil
09 epidermis, leaf cells
11 axillary bud, chloroplast

Leaf shapes include:

04 oval
05 acute, lobed, ovate
06 cusped, entire, linear, lyrate
07 acerose, ciliate, cordate, crenate, dentate, falcate, hastate, obovate, palmate, peltate, pinnate, ternate
08 digitate, elliptic, reniform, subulate
09 orbicular, runcinate, sagittate
10 lanceolate, pinnatifid, spathulate, trifoliate
13 doubly dentate
15 abruptly pinnate

• **turn over a new leaf**
05 amend, begin **06** change, reform **07** improve **10** begin again, start again **11** start afresh **12** mend your ways **14** better yourself, change your ways **15** improve yourself, make a fresh start, pull your socks up

leaflet

04 bill **05** flier, flyer, pinna, tract **06** dodger, mailer **07** booklet, foliole, handout **08** brochure, circular, handbill, pamphlet

leafy

05 bosky, green, shady, woody **06** bowery, leafed, leaved, shaded, wooded **07** foliose, verdant **08** frondent, frondose **11** frondescent **12** dasyphyllous

league

01 l **03** cup **04** ally, band, bond, Bund, link **05** class, group, guild, Hansa, Hanse, level, union, unite **06** cartel **07** combine, compact, consort, contest **08** alliance, category, conspire, division **09** associate, coalition, co-operate, syndicate **10** amalgamate, consortium, federation, fellowship, join forces, tournament **11** affiliation, amphictyony, association, collaborate, combination, competition, confederacy, confederate, co-operative, corporation, partnership **12** band together, championship, conglomerate, Holy Alliance **13** confederation

See also **Australian football**; **baseball**; **football**; **rugby**

• **in league**
06 allied, linked **08** in tandem **09** in cahoots **10** conspiring, in alliance **11** co-operating, hand in glove, in collusion **13** collaborating, in co-operation, in partnership

leak

03 cut, ren, rin, run **04** blab, drip, hole, ooze, seep, tell, weep **05** break, chink, crack, exude, let in, let on, spill **06** escape, exposé, impart, let out, oozing, pass on, relate, reveal, run out, squeal **07** crevice, divulge, fissure, leakage, leaking, let slip, opening, seepage, seeping, trickle, urinate **08** disclose, exposure, give away, overflow, puncture, spillage **09** discharge, make known, make water, percolate **10** disclosure, divulgence, make public, revelation, uncovering **11** percolation **12** blow the gaffe **13** spill the beans **15** bringing to light

leaky

05 holey, split **06** gizzen, porous **07** cracked, leaking **08** dripping

09 permeable, punctured
10 perforated, unstanched
11 unstaunched

lean
03 lie **04** abut, arid, bank, bare, bend, bony, hard, heel, lank, list, poor, prop, rest, slim, tend, thin, tilt **05** gaunt, lanky, slant, slink, slope, spare, tough **06** barren, favour, hungry, meagre, prefer, repose, scanty, skinny, slinky, sparse **07** angular, austere, haggard, incline, minceur, recline, scraggy, scrawny, slender **09** difficult, emaciated, fleshless, gravitate, rigwiddie, rigwoodie **10** inadequate, unfruitful, unpleasant **11** be at an angle **12** insufficient, unproductive, unprofitable, unsuccessful **13** uncomfortable **15** all skin and bones

• lean on
04 rest **05** force **06** bank on, coerce, rely on **07** trust in **08** depend on, persuade **10** intimidate, pressurize **13** put pressure on **14** put the screws on

leaning
04 bent, bias **06** liking **08** aptitude, fondness, penchant, tendency **10** attraction, partiality, preference, proclivity, propensity **11** disposition, inclination **12** predilection

leanness
08 boniness, lankness, slimness, thinness **09** gauntness, lankiness **11** scragginess, scrawniness, slenderness

lean-to
03 hut **04** pent, shed **05** shack **06** garage, lock-up **08** outhouse, skilling, skillion **09** penthouse

leap
◇ *anagram indicator*
03 hop, lep **04** jeté, jump, lope, loup, over, rise, romp, salt, skip, soar, volt **05** bound, caper, clear, dance, fence, flier, flyer, frisk, mount, pronk, salto, sault, spang, surge, vault, volte **06** basket, bounce, breach, cavort, curvet, frolic, gambol, rocket, spring **07** échappé, falcade, soaring, upsurge, upswing **08** assemblé, cabriole, capriole, croupade, escalate, fish-dive, increase, jump over, overskip, somerset **09** elevation, entrechat, pas de chat, skyrocket **10** escalation, pigeon-wing, somersault **11** summersault

• by leaps and bounds, in leaps and bounds
07 quickly, rapidly, swiftly **08** in no time **13** in no time at all

• leap at
04 grab **05** seize **06** jump at, snatch **07** agree to, fall for, swallow **08** pounce on **13** accept eagerly

learn
03 con, get, kon, see **04** cram, hear, larn, lear, leir, lere, read **05** conne, glean, grasp, leare, study, train **06** absorb, detect, digest, gather, get off, master, pick up, take in **07** acquire, discern, find out, gen up on, prepare, realize, receive, suss out **08** discover, memorize, remember **09** ascertain, determine, get wind of **10** assimilate, comprehend, have off pat, understand **12** get the hang of, learn by heart **13** become aware of **14** acquire skill in, commit to memory **15** gain knowledge of

learned
04 cond, read, wise **06** savant, versed **07** erudite, savante **08** academic, cultured, lettered, literary, literate, pedantic, scienced, studious, well-read **09** scholarly **10** widely read **11** literatured **12** intellectual, well-educated, well-informed **13** knowledgeable

learner
01 L **04** tiro, tyro **05** pupil **06** conner, intern, novice, rookie **07** scholar, student, trainee **08** beginner, neophyte **09** greenhorn **10** apprentice **11** abecedarian

See also **beginner**

learning
04 lear, leir, lere, lore **05** leare, study **06** wisdom **07** conning, culture, letters, tuition **08** pedantry, research **09** education, erudition, intellect, knowledge, schooling **11** edification, information, scholarship, schoolcraft

• basic learning
03 RRR

lease
03 let, set **04** farm, hire, loan, rent, tack **05** glean **06** let out, rental, sublet **07** chapter, charter, hire out, pasture, rent out, tenancy **08** contract **09** agreement

leash
03 lym **04** bind, cord, curb, hold, lead, lime, lyam, lyme, rein, slip **05** check, trash **06** string, tether **07** control **09** restraint **10** discipline

See also **three**

• strain at the leash
07 be dying, be eager **09** be anxious, be itching, be longing **11** be impatient

least
06 fewest, lowest **07** minimum, poorest **08** smallest **09** slightest

• at least
06 anyhow **07** however **09** at any rate, in any case **10** as a minimum, at the least, for all that, in any event, no less than **12** nevertheless, no matter what **14** at the very least, nothing short of **15** nothing less than, whatever happens

• to say the least
13 to put it mildly **14** at the very least

leather
03 taw **04** beat, butt **06** levant, spetch, thrash **08** studwork

Leathers include:

03 kid
04 buff, calf, napa, roan, shoe, wash, yuft
05 grain, Mocha, nappa, neat's, plate, split, suede, waxed, white
06 chrome, Nubuck, patent, Rexine®, Russia, shammy, skiver, spruce
07 chamois, cowhide, dogskin, hogskin, kidskin, kipskin, morocco, pigskin, saffian
08 buckskin, cabretta, calfskin, capeskin, cheverel, cheveril, cordovan, cordwain, deerskin, goatskin, lambskin, maroquin, shagreen
09 crocodile, lacquered, sheepskin, slinkskin, snakeskin
10 artificial
11 aqualeather, cuir-bouilli, whitleather

leathery
04 hard **05** rough, tough **06** rugged **07** corious, durable, wizened **08** hardened, leathern, wrinkled **10** coriaceous

leave
◇ *deletion indicator*
02 go, OK **03** let, vac **04** drop, dump, exit, jilt, levy, lose, miss, move, park, part, quit, will **05** allot, avoid, break, cause, cease, chuck, congé, ditch, endow, go off, raise, say-so, scoot, split **06** assign, commit, congee, create, day off, decamp, depart, desert, desist, devise, forget, give up, go away, hook it, lead to, mislay, resign, retire, set out, vamose **07** abandon, consent, consign, deliver, do a bunk, entrust, forsake, freedom, holiday, liberty, licence, license, produce, pull out, push off, retreat, take off, time off, vamoose, walk off, warrant **08** bequeath, choof off, clear off, come away, emigrate, farewell, furlough, generate, give over, hand down, hand over, holidays, make over, misplace, occasion, renounce, result in, run along, run out on, sanction, shove off, transmit, up sticks, vacation, withdraw **09** allowance, disappear, push along, sick leave, surrender **10** bring about, concession, give rise to, green light, hit the road, indulgence, make tracks, permission, relinquish, sabbatical **11** leave behind **12** dispensation, shoot through **13** authorization, sling your hook, take your leave **14** leave of absence, turn your back on **15** leave high and dry, take French leave

• leave off
03 end **04** halt, omit, quit, stop **05** cease **06** desist, lay off **07** abstain, refrain **08** break off, give over, knock off **09** terminate **11** discontinue

• leave out
03 bar, cut **04** miss, omit **06** bypass, cut out, except, ignore, reject **07** exclude, miss out, neglect **08** count out, overlook, pass over, suppress **09** cast aside, disregard, eliminate

• leave quickly
08 light out

leaven
04 barm, work, zyme **05** imbue, raise, swell, yeast **06** expand, puff up
07 enliven, ferment, inspire, lighten, pervade, quicken, suffuse
08 permeate **09** sourdough, stimulate **11** cause to rise **12** raising agent

leaves
03 tea **04** atap **05** attap

leavings
04 bits **05** dregs, dross, spoil, waste
06 debris, pieces, refuse, relics, scraps
07 remains, residue, rubbish
08 detritus, oddments, remnants
09 alms-drink, fragments, leftovers, remainder, sweepings **11** broken meats

Lebanon
02 RL **03** LBN

lecher
04 gate, goat, lech, perv, rake, roué, wolf **05** Romeo, satyr **06** wanton
07 Don Juan, flasher, seducer
08 Casanova, Lothario, Lovelace
09 adulterer, debauchee, libertine, womanizer **10** fornicator, libidinist, profligate, sensualist **11** dirty old man, whoremonger

lecherous
04 lewd **05** horny, pervy, randy
06 carnal, wanton **07** codding, leering, lustful, rammish, raunchy
08 prurient, unchaste **09** debauched, dissolute, lickerish, liquorish, salacious
10 degenerate, dissipated, lascivious, libidinous, licentious, womanizing
11 promiscuous **12** concupiscent

lechery
04 lust **08** lewdness, salacity
09 carnality, prurience, randiness
10 debauchery, rakishness, sensuality, wantonness, womanizing
11 libertinism, lustfulness, raunchiness
13 concupiscence, lickerishness, salaciousness **14** lasciviousness, libidinousness, licentiousness

lectern
04 ambo, desk **05** eagle, stand, table
07 lettern, oratory **11** reading-desk

lecture
03 act, jaw **04** read, talk **05** chide, class, scold, speak, teach **06** berate, homily, lesson, rebuke, rocket, sermon, speech **07** address, censure, chiding, expound, jawbone, prelect, reproof, reprove, tell off **08** admonish, berating, extender, harangue, instruct, reproach, scolding, travelog **09** chalk talk, discourse, give a talk, hold forth, reprimand, talking-to **10** conférence, prelection, rollicking, telling-off, travelogue, upbraiding **11** instruction, make a speech, pick holes in
12 disquisition, dressing-down, pull to pieces, tear to pieces **13** give lessons in
14 curtain lecture

lecturer
01 L **03** don **04** lect **05** tutor
06 docent, lector, orator, reader, talker
07 scholar, speaker, teacher
08 academic, preacher **09** declaimer, expounder, haranguer, pedagogue, preceptor, prelector, professor
10 instructor, sermonizer, theologian
11 speechifier, speechmaker
12 conférencier, extensionist, instructress

ledge
04 berm, lode, sill, step, vein **05** altar, bench, linch, ridge, shelf, stock
06 gradin, mantel, offset, settle, shelve
07 gradine, linchet, lynchet **08** fire-step, overhang **10** buttery-bar, firing-step, projection, scarcement
11 mantelpiece, mantelshelf

ledger
05 books **07** journal **08** accounts, register **09** inventory **10** record book
11 account book

lee
05 cover, river **06** arable, meadow, refuge **07** pasture, shelter
09 sanctuary **10** protection

leech
05 drain, toady **06** usurer **07** clinger, sponger **08** hanger-on, parasite
09 physician, scrounger, sycophant
10 freeloader **11** bloodsucker, extortioner

leer
03 eye **04** grin, ogle, perv, wink
05 gloat, smirk, sneer, stare, tweer, twire **06** colour, goggle, squint
07 glad eye **10** complexion
13 lecherous look

leery
04 wary **05** chary **06** unsure
07 careful, dubious, guarded
08 cautious, doubting **09** sceptical, uncertain **10** suspicious **11** distrustful, on your guard

lees
05 draff, dregs, grout **06** dunder, refuse **07** deposit, grounds, residue
08 sediment **09** settlings
11 precipitate

leeway
04 play, room **05** drift, scope, slack, space **06** margin **07** freedom
08 latitude **09** elbow-room
11 flexibility

left
◇ *deletion indicator*
01 L **03** red **04** gone, lorn, near, over, port, quit, went **06** Maoist **07** liberal, Marxist, radical **08** larboard, left-hand, left-wing, Leninist
09 communist, sinistral, socialist, Stalinist **10** Bolshevist, Spartakist, Trotskyist, Trotskyite **11** progressive, revisionist **12** collectivist
13 revolutionary

• turn left
03 hie **04** high

left-handed
06 clumsy, gauche **07** awkward, dubious, unlucky **08** southpaw
09 ambiguous, equivocal, insincere, sinistral **10** backhanded, cack-handed, kack-handed **12** corrie-fisted, hypocritical

left-hander
05 lefty **06** leftie **08** southpaw
09 sinistral **11** cackyhander, molly-dooker

left-over
04 orra **06** excess, unused
07 oddment, settled, surplus, uneaten
09 remaining **11** superfluous

leftovers
05 dregs **06** excess, refuse, scraps
07 remains, residue, surplus
08 leavings, remnants **09** remainder, sweepings

left-wing
04 left **06** Maoist **07** liberal, Marxist, radical **08** Leninist **09** communist, socialist, Stalinist **10** Bolshevist, Spartakist, Trotskyist, Trotskyite
11 progressive, revisionist
12 collectivist **13** revolutionary

• left-winger
04 trot

leg
02 on **03** bit, gam, lap, peg, pin
04 crus, gamb, limb, part, prop
05 brace, shank, stage, stump
06 member, timber **07** pleopod, portion, section, segment, stretch, support, upright **08** swindler
10 sheepshank **12** underpinning

• leg it
03 run **04** walk **05** hurry **06** hoof it
07 scarper **08** go by foot

• not have a leg to stand on
10 be unproved **11** lack support
12 lack an excuse **13** be unjustified

• on its last legs
04 weak **06** ailing **07** failing **10** fading fast, near to ruin **11** about to fail, near to death **12** at death's door **15** about to collapse, nearing collapse

• pull someone's leg
03 kid, rib **04** fool, joke **05** tease, trick
06 have on, wind up **07** deceive
09 make fun of **11** play a joke on
12 take for a ride **14** pull a fast one on

legacy
04 gift **06** estate **07** bequest
08 heirloom, heritage **09** endowment, heritance, patrimony **10** bequeathal, birthright **11** inheritance

legal
03 leg **05** legit, licit, right, sound, valid
06 lawful, proper **07** allowed
08 forensic, judicial, licensed, rightful
09 allowable, judiciary, legalized, permitted, statutory, warranted
10 above-board, acceptable, admissible, authorized, legitimate, sanctioned **11** permissible **12** within the law **14** constitutional

See also **court**; **crime**

Legal terms include:

02 JP, QC
03 bar, DPP, sue
04 ASBO, bail, deed, dock, fine, jury, oath, plea, will, writ
05 alibi, asset, bench, brief, by-law, claim, felon, grant, judge, juror, lease, party, proof, proxy, title, trial
06 appeal, arrest, bigamy, charge, client, demand, equity, estate, guilty, lawyer, legacy, pardon, parole, patent, remand, repeal, the bar, waiver
07 accused, alimony, amnesty, caution, charter, codicil, convict, coroner, custody, damages, defence, divorce, hearing, inquest, inquiry, Law Lord, lawsuit, mandate, penalty, probate, sheriff, statute, summons, tenancy, verdict, warrant, witness
08 act of God, adultery, advocate, civil law, contract, covenant, criminal, easement, eviction, evidence, executor, freehold, hung jury, innocent, judgment, juvenile, legal aid, mortgage, offender, prisoner, receiver, reprieve, sanction, sentence, subpoena, tribunal
09 accessory, acquittal, affidavit, agreement, annulment, barrister, common law, copyright, court case, defendant, endowment, fee simple, indemnity, intestacy, judgement, judiciary, leasehold, liability, plaintiff, precedent, probation, solicitor, testimony, trademark
10 accomplice, allegation, confession, conveyance, decree nisi, indictment, injunction, liquidator, magistrate, settlement
11 adjournment, arbitration, extradition, foreclosure, inheritance, local search, maintenance, plea bargain, plead guilty, proceedings, ward of court
12 age of consent, Bill of Rights, constitution, court martial, cross-examine, Lord Advocate, misadventure, notary public
13 King's evidence, public inquiry, Queen's Counsel, young offender
14 decree absolute, Lord Chancellor, plead not guilty, Queen's evidence
15 Act of Parliament, Attorney General, clerk of the court, contempt of court, power of attorney

• **legal document**
04 deed, writ

legality
08 validity **09** rightness, soundness **10** lawfulness, legitimacy **12** rightfulness **14** admissibleness, permissibility

legalize
05 admit, allow **06** accept, permit, ratify **07** approve, license, warrant **08** sanction, validate **09** authorize, make legal **10** legitimize **13** decriminalize

legally
05 by law **07** validly **08** by rights, lawfully, properly **10** rightfully **11** permissibly **12** legitimately

legate
03 leg **05** agent, envoy **06** deputy, exarch, nuncio **08** delegate, emissary **09** messenger **10** ambassador **12** commissioner **14** representative

legatee
04 heir **06** co-heir **07** devisee **08** legatary, receiver **09** co-heiress, inheritor, recipient **10** inheritrix **11** beneficiary

legation
07 embassy, mission **08** ministry **09** consulate **10** commission, delegation, deputation **14** representation

legend
03 key, VIP **04** myth, name, saga, star, tale **05** celeb, fable, motto, story **06** bigwig, cipher, legion, worthy **07** big name, big shot, caption, fiction, notable, romance **08** folk tale, luminary **09** celebrity, dignitary, narrative, personage, superstar, underline **11** explanation, inscription, personality **12** famous person, living legend **13** household name

See also **mythology**

Arthurian legend-related terms and locations include:

03 Usk
04 Bath, York
06 Avalon, Camlan, Logres
07 Camelot, Camlann, Carleon, Chester
08 Caerleon, Caliburn, Lyonesse, Tintagel
09 Badon Hill, Boscastle, Camelford, Excalibur, Holy Grail, Llyn Dinas, loadstone, Red Dragon, Roche Rock
10 Cader Idris, Grail Table, Llyn Barfog, Round Table, Stonehenge, Tintagalon, Winchester
11 Arthur's Seat, Cadbury Hill, Chalice Well, Craig y Dinas, Glastonbury, Merlin's Cave
12 Alderley Edge, Arthur's Cross, Dozemary Pool, Isle of Avalon, Perilous Seat, Vale of Avalon
13 Cadbury Castle, Questing Beast, Ship of Fairies, Siège Perilous, The Waste Lands
14 Bamburgh Castle, Caerleon Castle, Carleon upon Usk, Dolorous Stroke, Glastonbury Tor, Island of Avalon, St Govan's Chapel, Tintagel Castle
15 Slaughterbridge, St Michael's Mount, Sword in the Stone, The Tristan Stone, Valley of Delight

Characters from Arthurian legend include:

03 Ban, Kay, Lot
04 Bors
05 Nimue, Uther
06 Arthur, Elaine, Gareth (of Orkney), Gawain, Merlin, Modred
07 Caradoc, Galahad, Gawayne, Igraine, Launfal, Mordred, Tristan
08 Bedivere, Ironside, Lancelot, Palmerin, Parsifal, Perceval, Tristram
09 Arondight, Guinevere
10 Fisher King, King Arthur
11 Morgan le Fay
13 Lady of Shallot, Lady of the Lake
14 Launcelot du Lac, Uther Pendragon

See also **knight**

Characters from the Robin Hood legend include:

07 Sheriff (of Nottingham)
08 Merry Men, Prioress (of Kirklees)
09 Friar Tuck, Robin Hood
10 Allan-A-Dale, Little John, Maid Marian, Prince John
11 King Richard (the Lionheart), Will Scarlet
13 Guy of Gisborne, Much the Miller

legendary
06 fabled, famous **07** popular **08** fabulous, fanciful, glorious, honoured, immortal, mythical, renowned **09** acclaimed, fictional, storybook, well-known **10** celebrated, fictitious, remembered **11** illustrious, traditional

legerdemain
05 feint **06** tricky **07** cunning **08** artifice, jugglery, juggling, trickery **09** chicanery, deception, sophistry **10** artfulness, craftiness, hocus-pocus, subterfuge **11** contrivance, logodaedaly, manoeuvring **12** manipulation **13** sleight of hand, thaumaturgics

legibility
07 clarity **08** lucidity **09** clearness, lucidness, plainness, precision **10** simplicity **11** readability **12** distinctness, explicitness, readableness **15** intelligibility

legible
04 neat **05** clear, lucid, plain **06** simple **07** precise **08** distinct, explicit, readable **10** easy to read **12** decipherable, intelligible **14** comprehensible

legibly
06 simply **07** clearly, lucidly, plainly **08** readably **09** precisely **10** easily read, explicitly **12** intelligibly **14** comprehensibly

legion
04 army, host, mass, unit **05** drove, force, horde, swarm, troop **06** cohort, legend, myriad, number, throng **07** brigade, company **08** division, numerous, regiment **09** battalion, countless, multitude **10** numberless **11** illimitable, innumerable **13** multitudinous

• **British Legion**
03 BL

legislate
05 enact, order **06** codify, decree, ordain **08** make laws, pass laws **09** authorize, establish, formulate, prescribe

legislation
03 act, law, leg **04** bill, code **05** legis, rules **06** ruling **07** charter, measure, statute **09** enactment, lawmaking, ordinance **10** regulation **11** formulation **12** codification, prescription **13** authorization

legislative
03 leg **05** legis **08** judicial **09** lawgiving, lawmaking **10** senatorial **12** jurisdictive **13** congressional, parliamentary

legislator
02 MP **06** deputy **07** senator **08** lawgiver, lawmaker **09** nomothete **10** nomothetes **11** congressman **13** congresswoman **15** parliamentarian

legislature
03 leg **05** house, legis **06** senate, states **07** chamber **08** assembly, congress **10** parliament

See also **parliament**

legitimacy
08 fairness, legality, validity **09** rightness, soundness **10** lawfulness **11** credibility, rationality **12** plausibility, rightfulness, sensibleness **13** acceptability, admissibility **14** admissibleness, justifiability, permissibility, reasonableness

legitimate
04 fair, real, true **05** legal, legit, licit, loyal, sound, valid **06** kosher, lawful, proper **07** correct, genuine, logical, natural **08** credible, rational, rightful, sensible, true-born **09** competent, justified, plausible, statutory, warranted **10** acceptable, admissible, authorized, reasonable, sanctioned **11** justifiable, well-founded **12** acknowledged

legitimize
05 allow **06** permit **07** charter, entitle, license, warrant **08** legalize, sanction, validate **09** authorize **10** legitimate **13** decriminalize

leisure
04 ease, rest, time **05** break, R and R, space **06** by-time **07** freedom, holiday, leasure, liberty, respite, time off, time out, vacancy **08** free time, off-hours, vacation **09** spare time **10** recreation, relaxation, retirement

• at your leisure
11 unhurriedly **13** in your own time, when you want to **14** when it suits you **15** in your spare time

leisurely
04 easy, lazy, slow **05** loose **06** gentle **07** relaxed, restful, unhasty **08** carefree, laid-back, tranquil **09** easy-going, unhurried **10** leisurable **11** comfortable

lemur
05 indri, loris **06** aye-aye, colugo, galago, indris, macaco, sifaka **07** half-ape, meercat, meerkat, nagapie **08** mongoose, mungoose **09** babacoote, mangouste **10** angwantibo **12** Cynocephalus **13** Galeopithecus

lend
03 add, sub **04** give, loan, spot **05** grant, prest **06** bestow, confer, credit, donate, impart, on-lend, supply **07** advance, furnish, provide **08** overlend, put forth **10** allow to use, contribute **11** allow to have **13** let someone use

• lend a hand
03 aid **04** help **06** assist **07** help out, pitch in **09** do your bit **14** give assistance

• lend an ear
04 heed **06** listen **07** give ear, hearken **10** take notice **12** pay attention

• lend itself to
13 be suitable for **15** be easily used for

length
01 l **04** span, term **05** piece, reach, space **06** extent, period **07** measure, portion, section, segment, stretch **08** distance, duration **09** prolixity

• at length
05 fully **06** at last, in full **07** finally **10** eventually, thoroughly **11** in due course **12** exhaustively, for a long time **13** in great detail **14** after a long time **15** comprehensively

• go to any lengths
10 do anything **11** try very hard **12** go to extremes

lengthen
03 eik, eke **04** draw **06** eke out, expand, extend, pad out **07** draw out, prolong, spin out, stretch **08** continue, elongate, increase, protract **10** grow longer, prolongate

lengthwise
05 along **07** endlong, endways, endwise **10** fore-and-aft, lengthways, vertically **12** horizontally

lengthy
04 long **05** wordy **06** prolix **07** diffuse, tedious, verbose **08** drawn-out, extended, overlong, rambling **09** prolonged **10** lengthened, long-winded, protracted **12** interminable, long-drawn-out

leniency
05 mercy **08** clemency, kindness, lenience, mildness, softness **09** tolerance **10** compassion, generosity, gentleness, humaneness, indulgence, moderation, tenderness **11** forbearance, forgiveness, magnanimity **14** permissiveness **15** soft-heartedness

lenient
04 kind, mild **06** gentle, humane, tender **07** liberal, sparing **08** generous, merciful, moderate, soothing, tolerant **09** emollient, forgiving, indulgent, softening **10** forbearing, permissive **11** magnanimous, soft-hearted **13** compassionate

lenitive
06 easing **07** calming **08** laxative, soothing **09** assuaging, relieving **10** mitigating, mollifying, palliative **11** alleviating

lens
03 eye **05** glass, optic, power **06** finder, lentil, pebble, peeper **07** aplanat, contact **08** achromat, bull's-eye, eyeglass, eyepiece, meniscus **09** amplifier, condenser, magnifier, telephoto **10** anastigmat, apochromat, pantoscope **11** object-glass **12** burning-glass

Lent
04 fast **06** carême, spring

leopard
04 pard **05** ounce, tiger **06** pardal **07** libbard, panther, pardale **08** pardalis **12** catamountain, cat o' mountain

leper
05 lazar, mesel **06** meazel, pariah **07** leprosy, outcast **11** undesirable, untouchable **13** social outcast

leprechaun
03 elf, imp **04** puck **05** bogey, demon, fiend, gnome, nixie, pooka, troll **06** goblin, kelpie, kobold, red-cap, spirit, sprite **07** brownie, gremlin **09** hobgoblin

lesbian
03 gay **07** Sapphic **08** sapphist **10** homosexual

lesion
03 cut **04** gash, hurt, sore **05** wound **06** bruise, injury, scrape, trauma **07** scratch **08** abrasion **09** contusion **10** impairment, laceration

Lesotho
02 LS **03** LSO

less
03 bar **04** meno, save **05** fewer, minor, minus **06** except **07** short of, smaller, wanting, without, younger **08** inferior **09** excepting, excluding, not as many, not as much, not so many, not so much **13** smaller amount **15** to a lesser degree, to a lesser extent

lessen
03 cut, dip, ebb **04** alay, bate, dull, ease, fail, flag, wane **05** abate, aleye, allay, erode, let up, lower, slack **06** absorb, deaden, go down, impair, narrow, plunge, reduce, shrink, weaken **07** abridge, curtail, decline, die down, dwindle, ease off, lighten, plummet, relieve, slacken, subside, tail off **08** belittle, come down, contract, decrease, derogate, diminish, minimize, mitigate, moderate,

nosedive, peter out, slow down, tail away **09** disparage, extenuate **10** de-escalate

lessening
03 dip **05** allay, let-up **06** easing, ebbing, waning **07** cutting, decline, erosion, failure **08** batement, decrease, flagging **09** abatement, deadening, dwindling, reduction, shrinkage, weakening **10** derogation, diminution, imminution, mitigation, moderation, slackening **11** contraction, curtailment, extenuation, petering out **12** de-escalation, minimization

lesser
05 lower, minor **07** smaller **08** inferior, slighter **09** secondary **11** subordinate **13** less important

lesson
04 lear, leir, lere, task, text **05** class, drill, leare, model, moral, train **06** course, period, rebuke, sermon **07** example, lection, lecture, reading, seminar, warning **08** coaching, exercise, homework, instruct, liripipe, liripoop, practice, teaching, tutorial, workshop **09** deterrent, practical, scripture **10** assignment, recitation, schoolwork **11** application, instruction, master-class **12** Bible reading **13** demonstration

lest
06 in case, listen **07** for fear **11** for fear that **14** in order to avoid

let
02 OK **03** net **04** hire, make, rent **05** allow, cause, check, grant, lease **06** enable, hinder, let out, permit **07** agree to, hire out, prevent, rent out **08** assent to, obstacle, sanction, tolerate **09** authorize, consent to, give leave, give the OK, hindrance, restraint **10** constraint, give the nod, impediment, obstructed **11** obstruction, prohibition, restriction **12** interference **14** give permission, give the go-ahead **15** say the magic word

• **let alone**
04 also **08** as well as **09** apart from, never mind **12** not to mention **13** not forgetting

• **let down**
04 fail, vail **05** lower **06** betray, desert **07** abandon, depress **09** fall short **10** disappoint, disenchant, dissatisfy **11** disillusion **14** disappointment **15** leave in the lurch

• **let fly**
03 hit **05** fling, fly at, go for, shoot **06** attack, charge, strike **07** assault, lay into **08** fall upon **09** discharge, have a go at, lash out at

• **let go**
04 drop, free, omit, quit, sack **06** give up, unhand **07** dismiss, hang off, manumit, release, set free, slacken, unleash **08** liberate, released **10** relinquish **11** stop holding **13** make redundant

• **let in**
04 sink **05** admit, greet **06** accept, insert, take in **07** enchase, include, receive, welcome **11** incorporate **12** allow to enter

• **let in on**
04 tell **06** inform **07** include, let know **11** allow to know **14** allow to share in

• **let off**
04 emit, fire **05** spare **06** acquit, excuse, exempt, ignore, pardon **07** absolve, explode, forgive, give off, release **08** detonate, liberate, reprieve **09** discharge, exonerate

• **let on**
04 blab, tell **06** impart, pass on, relate, reveal, squeal **07** divulge, let slip **08** disclose, give away **09** make known **10** make public **13** spill the beans **15** give the game away

• **let out**
03 job **04** blab, emit, free, leak **05** let go, utter, widen **06** betray, reveal, squeal **07** enlarge, freight, let slip, release, slacken **08** disclose **09** discharge, make known **13** spill the beans

• **let up**
03 end **04** ease, halt, stop **05** abate, cease **06** lessen **07** die down, ease off, slacken, subside **08** decrease, diminish, moderate

let-down
04 sell **07** setback, washout **08** betrayal **09** desertion **10** anticlimax **14** disappointment **15** disillusionment

lethal
05 fatal, toxic **06** deadly, mortal **07** deathly, noxious, ruinous, vicious **08** venomous **09** dangerous, murderous, poisonous **10** disastrous **11** destructive, devastating **12** death-dealing

lethally
07 fatally **08** mortally **09** noxiously, toxically **11** dangerously **12** disastrously **13** destructively, devastatingly

lethargic
04 dull, idle, lazy, logy, slow **05** heavy, inert, weary **06** drowsy, sleepy, torpid **07** dormant, languid, passive **08** hebetant, inactive, lifeless, listless, slothful, sluggish **09** apathetic, enervated, somnolent **11** debilitated

lethargically
04 idly **05** dully **06** lazily, slowly **07** heavily, inertly, wearily **08** drowsily, sleepily, torpidly **09** languidly **10** inactively, lifelessly, listlessly, slothfully, sluggishly **11** somnolently **13** apathetically

lethargy
05 sloth **06** apathy, stupor, torpor **07** inertia, languor **08** dullness, idleness, inaction, laziness, slowness **09** lassitude, weariness **10** drowsiness, inactivity, sleepiness, somnolence **12** indifference, lifelessness, listlessness, sluggishness

let-out
04 cure **06** escape, excuse, get-out, remedy, way out **08** loophole **09** legal flaw **11** safety valve, way of escape **12** escape clause, technicality **13** error in the law, means of escape

letter
02 Ep **03** dak **04** chit, dawk, Epis, line, note, sign, sort, type **05** books, hirer, reply **06** device, figure, italic, lettre, scrawl, symbol, uncial **07** bloomer, capital, culture, epistle, message, missive, notelet, screeve, writing **08** academia, circular, dispatch, grapheme, learning, pastoral **09** character, education, epistolet, erudition, rune-stave **10** aerogramme, billet-doux, humanities, literature, round robin, semi-uncial **11** scholarship **13** belles-lettres, communication **14** correspondence **15** acknowledgement

Letters include:
03 ash, edh, eth, wen, wyn
04 aesc, ogam, wynn, yogh
05 thorn

See also **alphabet**; **typeface**

• **to the letter**
07 exactly **08** strictly **09** by the book, literally, precisely **10** accurately **11** religiously, word for word **13** in every detail, punctiliously

lettered
06 versed **07** erudite, learned, studied **08** academic, cultured, educated, highbrow, informed, literary, literate, well-read **09** scholarly **10** cultivated, widely read **12** accomplished, well-educated **13** knowledgeable

letter-opener
04 Dear

letters
04 mail, post

lettuce
07 Lactuca

Lettuce varieties include:
03 cos
04 flat
05 lamb's, round
06 frisée
07 cabbage, Chinese, iceberg, romaine
08 Batavian
09 little gem
10 butterhead, lollo rosso

let-up
03 end **04** lull **05** break, pause **06** recess, relief **07** ceasing, respite **08** breather, interval **09** abatement, cessation, lessening, remission **10** slackening

level
03 aim **04** avow, calm, even, flat, mark, rank, rase, raze, size, tell, tier, zone

05 admit, class, drawn, equal, flush, focus, grade, guess, layer, plain, plane, plumb, point, range, stage, train
06 amount, degree, direct, even up, extent, height, on a par, open up, smooth, stable, status, steady, storey, volume **07** abreast, aligned, be frank, confess, destroy, divulge, echelon, even out, flatten, gallery, horizon, measure, regular, station, stratum, tell all, uniform **08** altitude, balanced, bulldoze, composed, constant, demolish, equalize, estimate, highness, lay waste, make flat, matching, position, pull down, quantity, standard, standing, tear down, zero in on **09** be upfront, champaign, come clean, devastate, elevation, knock down, magnitude, make level, stabilize
10 horizontal, unchanging
11 concentrate, neck and neck, unemotional, unflappable **12** level pegging, speak plainly, well-balanced
13 self-possessed **14** tell it like it is
15 keep nothing back, raze to the ground

• **on the level**
04 fair, open **06** candid, honest
07 jannock, up-front **08** straight
10 above board, fair dinkum, straight-up **12** on the up and up **13** fair and square

level-headed
04 calm, cool, sane **06** steady
07 prudent **08** balanced, composed, rational, sensible **09** practical **10** cool-headed, dependable, reasonable
11 circumspect, unflappable **12** even-tempered **13** imperturbable, self-possessed

lever
03 bar, key, pry **04** lift, move, pull
05 brake, crank, force, heave, hoist, jemmy, peavy, pedal, pinch, prise, raise, shift **06** handle, peavey, switch, tiller
07 control, crowbar, treadle, treddle, trigger **08** backfall, crossbar, dislodge, joystick, knee-stop, throttle, tommy bar, water key **09** bell crank, handspike, knee-swell, rocker arm, whipstaff **10** pump-handle, tremolo arm **11** walking-beam

leverage
04 grip, hold, pull, rank **05** clout, force, grasp, power, prise, prize **06** weight
08 purchase, strength **09** advantage, authority, influence **10** ascendancy

leviathan
04 hulk **05** giant, Satan, Titan, whale
07 mammoth, monster **08** behemoth, colossus, gigantic **10** formidable, sea monster

levitate
03 fly **04** hang, waft **05** drift, float, glide, hover **07** suspend

levitation
06 flying **07** gliding, hanging, wafting
08 drifting, floating, hovering
10 suspension **11** yogic flying

levity
03 fun **08** hilarity **09** flippancy, frivolity, silliness, whifflery
10 fickleness, triviality **11** glaikitness, irreverence **12** carefreeness, flippantness **13** facetiousness **15** light-mindedness, thoughtlessness

levy
03 due, fee, tax **04** duty, rate, toll
05 exact, leave, raise, stent, tithe, tythe
06 charge, demand, duties, excise, gather, impose, impost, tariff
07 collect, customs, estreat, militia, precept, tallage **10** assessment, collection **12** contribution, subscription

lewd
03 bad **04** bare, blue **05** bawdy, randy **06** carnal, harlot, impure, smutty, vulgar, wanton **07** Cyprian, lustful, obscene, raunchy, sensual, unclean **08** ignorant, indecent, unchaste **09** debauched, dissolute, lecherous, lubricous, salacious
10 degenerate, lascivious, libidinous, licentious, lubricious, suggestive
11 promiscuous **12** concupiscent, pornographic

lewdly
07 randily **08** impurely, smuttily, vulgarly **09** lustfully, obscenely, raunchily **10** indecently **11** dissolutely, lecherously **12** degenerately
13 promiscuously

lewdness
04 smut **07** crudity, lechery
08 impurity, priapism **09** bawdiness, carnality, depravity, indecency, lubricity, obscenity, randiness, vulgarity
10 debauchery, smuttiness, unchastity, wantonness **11** lustfulness, pornography **13** concupiscence, salaciousness **14** lasciviousness, licentiousness

lexicographer
10 vocabulist

Lexicographers and philologists include:

04 **Bopp** (Franz)
05 **Pliny** (Gaius 'the Elder'), **Sapir** (Edward), **Skeat** (Walter William)
06 **Bierce** (Ambrose), **Brewer** (Ebenezer Cobham), **Fowler** (Henry Watson), **Freund** (Wilhelm), **Hornby** (A S), **Murray** (Sir James Augustus Henry), **Onions** (Charles Talbut), **Trench** (Richard Chenevix)
07 **Chomsky** (Noam), **Craigie** (Sir William Alexander), **Diderot** (Denis), **Johnson** (Samuel, 'Dr'), **Mencken** (H L), **Tolkien** (J R R), **Ventris** (Michael George Francis), **Webster** (Noah)
08 **Chambers** (Ephraim), **Chambers** (Robert), **Chambers** (William), **Larousse** (Pierre Athanase), **Saussure** (Ferdinand de)
09 **Furnivall** (Frederick James), **Jespersen** (Otto Harry), **Partridge** (Eric)
10 **Amarasimha**, **Burchfield** (Robert)

lexicon
03 lex, OED, TCD **08** glossary, wordbook, word-list **10** dictionary, phrase book, vocabulary
12 encyclopedia

Leytonstone
03 E11

liability
04 drag, dues, duty, onus **05** debit
06 burden, charge **07** arrears
08 drawback, nuisance **09** hindrance
10 impediment, obligation
11 culpability, encumbrance
12 disadvantage, indebtedness
13 answerability, inconvenience
14 accountability, responsibility
15 blameworthiness

liable
03 apt **04** open **05** prone **06** likely
07 at fault, exposed, fitting, subject, tending, to blame **08** amenable, disposed, inclined, suitable
10 answerable, changeable, vulnerable **11** accountable, predisposed, responsible, susceptible

liaise
07 contact, network **08** relate to
09 co-operate, interface
11 collaborate, communicate **12** work together

liaison
04 link **05** agent, amour, fling, union
06 affair, broker **07** affaire, carry-on, contact, romance **08** intrigue, mediator **09** go-between, middleman, two-timing **10** arbitrator, connection, flirtation, love affair, negotiator **11** co-operation, interchange **12** bit on the side, entanglement, intermediary, relationship **13** collaboration, communication **15** working together

liar
05 leear **06** falser, fibber **07** Ananias, bouncer **08** deceiver, fabulist, perjurer
09 falsifier **11** pseudologue, storyteller
12 false witness, prevaricator

libation
08 oblation **09** sacrifice **13** drink offering

libel
04 slur **05** abuse, smear **06** defame, malign, revile, vilify **07** calumny, slander, traduce **08** badmouth
09 aspersion, denigrate, disparage
10 calumniate, defamation, muck-raking, throw mud at **11** denigration, false report, mudslinging **12** vilification
13 disparagement **15** untrue statement

libellous
05 false **06** untrue **07** abusive
09 injurious, maligning, traducing, vilifying **10** defamatory, derogatory, scurrilous, slanderous **11** denigratory, disparaging **12** calumniatory

liberal
◇ *anagram indicator*
01 L **03** Lib **04** free, left, whig **05** ample, broad, frank **06** candid, giving, lavish, verlig **07** copious, leftish, lenient, profuse, radical **08** abundant, advanced, catholic, flexible, generous, handsome, left-wing, moderate, tolerant, unbiased **09** bountiful, impartial, plentiful, reformist, unsparing **10** altruistic, big-hearted, broad-based, free-handed, munificent, open-handed, open-minded **11** broad-minded, enlightened, free-hearted, libertarian, magnanimous, open-hearted, progressive, wide-ranging **12** large-hearted, unprejudiced **13** philanthropic, unwithdrawing **14** forward-looking, latitudinarian

liberalism
07 leftism **10** radicalism **12** free-thinking **13** progressivism **14** libertarianism **15** humanitarianism

liberality
06 bounty **07** breadth, candour, charity **08** altruism, kindness, largesse **09** tolerance **10** generosity, liberalism, toleration **11** beneficence, benevolence, catholicity, flexibility, magnanimity, munificence, prodigality **12** generousness, impartiality, magnificence, philanthropy **13** progressivism **14** free-handedness, libertarianism, open-handedness, open-mindedness, permissiveness **15** broad-mindedness, open-heartedness

liberalize
04 ease **05** relax **06** loosen, reduce, soften **07** ease off, slacken **08** moderate **10** deregulate **14** lift controls on

liberate
04 free **05** let go, steal **06** let out, ransom, redeem, rescue, uncage **07** deliver, manumit, release, set free, unchain **08** let loose, set loose, unfetter **09** discharge, disimmure, unshackle **10** emancipate **11** appropriate

liberation
03 lib **07** freedom, freeing, liberty, loosing, release **08** uncaging **09** discharge, ransoming, releasing, unpenning **10** liberating, redemption, unchaining **11** deliverance, manumission, unfettering, unshackling **12** emancipation, risorgimento **13** franchisement **15** enfranchisement

liberator
05 freer **07** rescuer, saviour **08** ransomer, redeemer **09** deliverer **10** manumitter **11** emancipator

Liberia
02 LB **03** LBR

Liber Pater
07 Bacchus

libertine
04 rake, roué **05** Romeo **06** lecher **07** Don Juan, lustful, seducer **08** Casanova, freedman, Lothario, Lovelace, palliard **09** debauched, debauchee, dissolute, lecherous, reprobate, salacious, womanizer **10** degenerate, licentious, profligate, sensualist, voluptuary, womanizing **11** gay deceiver, promiscuous
See also **womanizer**

liberty
03 ish **05** leave, right **07** freedom, leisure, licence, release **08** autonomy, boldness, disposal, sanction, self-rule **09** franchise, impudence, insolence, privilege **10** discretion, disrespect, indulgence, liberation, permission **11** deliverance, entitlement, familiarity, impropriety, manumission, prerogative, presumption, sovereignty **12** dispensation, emancipation, impertinence, independence **13** authorization **14** self-government **15** overfamiliarity

• **at liberty**
04 free **05** loose **07** allowed, at large **08** entitled **09** available, permitted **10** disengaged, unhindered, unoccupied **11** not confined **12** unrestrained, unrestricted **13** unconstrained

• **take the liberty**
08 make bold **10** be impudent **12** be so bold as to **13** be impertinent **14** show disrespect

libidinous
04 lewd **05** horny, loose, randy **06** carnal, impure, wanton, wicked **07** lustful, ruttish, sensual **08** prurient, unchaste **09** debauched, lecherous, salacious **10** cupidinous, lascivious **11** promiscuous **12** concupiscent **13** whoremasterly

libido
04 lust **06** ardour **07** passion, the hots **08** sex drive **09** eroticism, randiness **10** sexual urge **12** erotic desire, sexual desire **14** sexual appetite

libra
01 l **02** lb

librarian
03 ALA, lib

library
02 BL, PL, RL **03** lib

libretto
04 book, text **05** lines, words **06** lyrics, script

Librettists include:

04 Hart (Lorenz), Jouy (Étienne), Rice (Sir Tim), Stow (Randolph)
05 Swann (Donald)
06 Berlin (Irving), Lerner (Alan Jay), Malouf (David), Porter (Cole)
07 Gilbert (Sir W S), Harwood (Gwen)
08 Gershwin (Ira), Sondheim (Stephen)
11 Hammerstein (Oscar, II)

See also **composer**

Libya
03 LAR, LBY

licence
04 gale, pass **05** grant, leave, right, slang **06** excess, indult, permit, ticket **07** abandon, anarchy, charter, consent, faculty, freedom, liberty, warrant **08** approval, disorder, document, sanction, warranty **09** authority, decadence, deviation, exemption, franchise, privilege **10** creativity, debauchery, immorality, imprimatur, indulgence, permission, unruliness **11** certificate, dissipation, entitlement, impropriety, inspiration, lawlessness, libertinage, miner's right, originality, prerogative **12** carte blanche, dispensation, exaggeration, fancifulness, immoderation, independence, intemperance **13** accreditation, authorization, certification, dissoluteness, ticket of leave **14** letter-of-marque, licentiousness, self-indulgence **15** imaginativeness, letters-of-marque

license
03 let **05** allow **06** permit **07** certify, consent, dismiss, empower, entitle, warrant **08** accredit, sanction **09** authorize, franchise, privilege **10** commission **14** give permission

licentious
03 lax **04** lewd, wild **05** large, loose, randy **06** impure, ribald, ribaud, wanton **07** Cyprian, immoral, liberal, lustful, raunchy, rybauld **08** decadent, depraved, unchaste **09** abandoned, debauched, dissolute, lecherous, libertine **10** disorderly, dissipated, lascivious, profligate **11** promiscuous

licentiousness
04 lust **07** abandon, lechery, licence, license **08** impurity, lewdness, priapism, salacity **09** prurience, randiness **10** debauchery, immorality, wantonness **11** dissipation, libertinism, lustfulness, promiscuity, raunchiness **13** dissoluteness, salaciousness **14** cupidinousness

lichen
10 consortium
See also **alga, algae**

licit
04 real **05** legal, legit **06** lawful, proper **07** correct, genuine **08** rightful **09** allowable, statutory, warranted **10** authorized, legitimate, sanctioned **12** acknowledged

lick
03 bit, dab, lap, tad, wag, wet **04** beat, blow, dart, fawn, hint, spot, wash **05** brush, clean, flick, slake, smear, speck, taste, touch **06** defeat, hammer, little, ripple, sample, stroke, thrash, tongue **07** conquer, flicker, moisten, trounce **08** demolish, play over, smidgeon, vanquish **09** slaughter **13** run rings round **15** make mincemeat of

• lick your lips
05 enjoy **06** relish, savour **09** drool over **10** anticipate

licking
06 defeat, hiding **07** beating, lambent, tanning **08** drubbing, flogging, smacking, spanking, whipping **09** thrashing

lid
03 cap, hat, top **05** cover, slide **07** scuttle, stopper **08** covering, screw cap **09** operculum

lie
02 be **04** cram, keep, lair, laze, lean, rest, stay **05** abide, couch, dwell, exist, lodge, press, reach, stand **06** belong, bounce, deceit, depend, extend, invent, lounge, remain, repose **07** be found, consist, falsify, perjure, perjury, recline, romance, stretch **08** be placed, continue, tell a lie, white lie **09** be located, dissemble, fabricate, sprawl out **10** equivocate, stretch out **11** dissimulate, prevaricate **12** be positioned, make up a story, misrepresent

Lies include:

03 bam, fib, gag
04 cram, crap, flam, oner, whid
05 fable, one-er, porky, story
06 deceit, unfact, wunner, yanker
07 cretism, falsity, fiction, leasing, swinger, thumper, untruth, whacker, whopper
08 porkypie, strapper, white lie
09 fairy tale, falsehood, half-truth, invention, mendacity, tall story
10 concoction, fairy story, taradiddle
11 fabrication, made-up story, out-and-outer, pseudologia, tarradiddle
13 dissimulation, falsification, prevarication

• give the lie to
05 rebut **08** disprove **10** contradict, invalidate, prove false
• lie about
03 lig
• lie in sun
04 bask
• lie in wait for
04 lurk, trap **06** ambush, attack, waylay **08** surprise **09** ambuscade **10** lie at lurch **11** lay a trap for
• lie low
04 hide, lurk **05** skulk **06** hole up **07** hide out, tappice **08** hide away, lie doggo **09** go to earth, take cover **12** go into hiding **15** conceal yourself, keep a low profile

Liechtenstein
02 FL **03** LIE

liege
04 king, lord **05** chief **06** master, vassal **07** subject **08** nobleman, overlord, superior **09** liege-lord **10** feudal lord

lieutenant
02 DL, LL, Lt **04** loot **05** Lieut **06** deputy, guider, legate **09** assistant, number one, scavenger **11** subordinate **12** right-hand man **14** right-hand woman **15** second-in-command

life
03 bio, man, pep, zip **04** élan, soul, span, time, vita, zest, zing **05** being, child, diary, fauna, flora, oomph, plant, verve, woman **06** breath, career, course, energy, entity, person, spirit, vigour **07** diaries, journal, memoirs, pizzazz, sparkle **08** activity, duration, lifespan, lifetime, vitality, vivacity **09** aliveness, animation, biography, existence, human life, life story, viability **10** animal life, enthusiasm, excitement, experience, exuberance, human being, individual, liveliness, travelling **11** continuance, high spirits **12** cheerfulness, living things **13** autobiography, effervescence, fauna and flora, meeting people **14** life expectancy, wide experience
• come to life
04 rise **06** wake up **09** come alive **12** become active, become lively **14** become exciting
• enjoy life
04 live
• give your life
06 die for **14** give up your life **15** offer up your life
• in present life
04 here
• term of life
04 date

life-and-death
05 vital **07** crucial, serious **08** critical **09** important **12** all-important

lifeblood
04 core, soul **05** heart **06** centre, lethee, spirit **09** life-force **11** inspiration **13** essential part **15** essential factor

lifeless
04 arid, bare, cold, dead, dull, flat, gone, lank, slow **05** dusty, empty, stark, stiff **06** barren, wooden **07** defunct, insipid, key-cold, passive, sterile **08** clay-cold, deceased, desolate, listless, sluggish, soulless **09** apathetic, bloodless, cauldrife, exanimate, inanimate, lethargic, stone-dead **10** colourless, insensible, lacklustre, uninspired **11** unconscious, unemotional, uninhabited, uninspiring **12** unproductive

lifelike
04 real, true **05** exact, vivid **06** lively **07** ad vivum, graphic, natural **08** faithful, speaking **09** authentic, breathing, realistic **10** true-to-life

lifelong
07 abiding, lasting **08** constant, enduring, lifetime **09** permanent **10** persistent **11** long-lasting **12** long-standing **14** for all your life

lifestyle
04 life **08** position **09** situation, way of life **11** way of living **14** manner of living

lifetime
03 day **04** days, life, span, time **06** career, course, period **08** anthesis, duration, lifespan **09** existence **10** pilgrimage

lift
02 up **03** air, end, fly, run, sky **04** copy, crib, jack, move, nick, pick, ride, rise, spur, stop **05** annul, arsis, boost, clear, dig up, drive, elate, exalt, hitch, hoist, mount, press, raise, relax, shift, spout, steal **06** arrest, borrow, buoy up, cancel, convey, fillip, hold up, pick up, pull up, remove, revoke, snatch, teagle, uplift, vanish **07** airlift, elevate, heavens, relieve, rescind, root out, scatter, support, thin out, unearth, upraise **08** disperse, dissolve, elevator, hold high, increase, pick-me-up, transfer, withdraw **09** disappear, encourage, escalator, terminate, transport **10** plagiarize **11** paternoster, reassurance **12** shot in the arm **13** encouragement

See also **steal**

• lift off
04 rear **05** climb **06** ascend, depart **07** take off **08** blast off

lift-off
05 climb **06** ascent **07** take-off **08** blast-off **09** departure

lift-shaft
04 well

ligament
03 ACL, tie **04** bond **06** frenum **07** fraenum, urachus

ligature
03 tie **04** aesc, band, bond, cord, link, rope, slur **05** strap, thong **06** string **07** bandage, binding, funicle **08** ligament **09** diphthong **10** connection, deligation, tourniquet

light
◇ *anagram indicator*
03 day, eye, gay, ray, way **04** airy, beam, bulb, clue, dawn, deft, easy, fair, fine, fire, flit, glow, hint, idle, lamp, lyte, mild, pale, rest, side, soft, thin, weak **05** agile, angle, blaze, blond, cheer, faded, faint, flash, funny, glare, gleam, glint, happy, loose, match, merry, petty, put on, quick, shaft, shine, slant, small, style, sunny, taper, torch, witty **06** active, aspect, beacon, blithe, blonde, bright, candle, cheery, facile, flimsy, floaty, gentle, ignite, kindle, lively, lustre, manner, modest, nimble, pastel, porous, scanty, settle, slight, turn on **07** amusing, animate, buoyant, cheer up, cresset,crumbly, daytime, friable, glowing, insight, lantern, lenient, lighten, lighter, light up, shining, sunrise, trivial, well-lit, whitish **08** approach, bleached, brighten, carefree, cheerful, cockcrow, daybreak, daylight, delicate, dismount, feathery, graceful, humorous, lambency, luminous, moderate, pleasing, portable, radiance, switch on,

trifling, unchaste, untaxing **09** brilliant, dimension, diverting, easily dug, frivolous, irradiate, knowledge, set alight, set fire to, unheeding, worthless **10** brightness, brilliance, digestible, effortless, effulgence, first light, flashlight, floodlight, illuminate, luminosity, set burning, unexacting, weightless **11** crack of dawn, easily moved, elucidation, explanation, illuminated, lightweight, point of view, superficial, undemanding, unimportant **12** easy to digest, entertaining, illumination, light-hearted, luminescence, make cheerful **13** comprehension, enlightenment, incandescence, insubstantial, understanding **14** inconsiderable **15** inconsequential

• **bring to light**
04 rout **06** exhume, expose, notice, reveal **07** uncover, unearth **08** disclose, discover, disinter, exhumate **09** make known

• **come to light**
09 be exposed, be noticed, transpire **11** be made known, be uncovered **12** be discovered **13** become obvious

• **in the light of**
08 in view of **09** because of **11** considering, remembering **13** bearing in mind, keeping in mind **14** being mindful of

• **light on, light upon**
04 find, spot **05** hit on **06** notice **08** chance on, discover **09** encounter, stumble on **10** come across, happen upon

• **shed light on, throw light on, cast light on**
07 clarify, enlight, explain **09** elucidate, make clear, make plain **10** illuminate

• **speck of light**
04 peep

lighten
04 calm, ease, glow, lift **05** allay, cheer, elate, shine **06** buoy up, lessen, perk up, reduce, revive, unload, uplift **07** assuage, cheer up, gladden, hearten, inspire, light up, relieve, restore **08** brighten, illumine, inspirit, levigate, mitigate **09** alleviate, encourage **10** illuminate **11** make lighter **12** make brighter

• **lighten up**
04 cool **05** chill, relax **06** unwind **08** calm down, chill out **09** hang loose **10** take it easy **13** let yourself go, put your feet up

lighter
04 pram **05** barge, praam, Zippo **07** gondola, pontoon

light-fingered
03 sly **06** crafty, shifty **07** crooked, furtive **08** filching, stealing, thieving, thievish **09** dishonest, pilfering **11** shoplifting

light-footed
04 deft, spry **05** agile, lithe, swift **06** active, nimble **08** graceful **09** sprightly

light-headed
04 airy **05** dizzy, faint, giddy, silly, woozy **07** flighty, foolish, shallow, vacuous **08** flippant, trifling, unsteady **09** airheaded, delirious, frivolous **11** empty-headed, superficial, thoughtless, vertiginous **14** feather-brained, scatter-brained

light-hearted
03 gay **04** glad, high **05** happy, jolly, merry, sunny **06** blithe, bouncy, bright, chirpy, elated, jovial, joyful **07** amusing, playful **08** carefree, cheerful **10** frolicsome, untroubled **12** entertaining, happy-go-lucky **13** inconsiderate, in good spirits, in high spirits, irresponsible

• **light-heartedness**
06 levity

lighthouse
05 fanal, phare, tower **06** beacon, pharos **12** danger signal **13** warning signal

lightly
05 gaily **06** airily, easily, gently, mildly, softly, thinly **07** faintly, readily **08** breezily, casually, facilely, gingerly, slightly, sparsely **09** leniently, sparingly **10** carelessly, delicately, flippantly, heedlessly **11** frivolously, slightingly **12** effortlessly **13** thoughtlessly

lightness
05 grace **06** gaiety, levity **07** agility **08** airiness, buoyancy, deftness, delicacy, mildness, porosity, thinness **09** animation, frivolity, litheness, sandiness **10** blitheness, cheeriness, fickleness, flimsiness, gentleness, liveliness, nimbleness, porousness, slightness, triviality **11** crumbliness **12** cheerfulness, delicateness, gracefulness **14** weightlessness

lightning
04 fire **05** levin **08** fireball, wildfire **11** fulguration, thunderbolt, thunderclap, thunderdart **12** thunderstorm **13** ball lightning, clap of thunder, electric storm **14** chain lightning, sheet lightning **15** forked lightning, lightning strike, summer lightning, zigzag lightning

• **like lightning**
07 a rocket, hastily, quickly, rapidly **08** speedily, wildfire **11** immediately

lightweight
02 oz **04** thin **05** light, petty **06** flimsy, paltry, slight **07** trivial **08** delicate, feathery, nugatory, trifling **09** worthless **10** negligible, weightless **11** unimportant **13** insignificant, insubstantial **15** inconsequential

likable, likeable
04 nice **06** genial **07** amiable, lovable, winning, winsome **08** charming, engaging, friendly, loveable, pleasant, pleasing **09** agreeable, appealing, congenial **10** attractive, personable **11** sympathetic

like
02 as **03** à la, dig **04** akin, love, mate, peer, same, true, twin, want, wish **05** adore, alike, enjoy, equal, fancy, go for, match, prize, usual **06** admire, allied, choose, desire, esteem, fellow, normal, prefer, relish, select, such as, take to **07** approve, care for, cherish, of a kind, related, revel in, similar, suiting, typical, welcome **08** appeal to, be fond of, be keen on, decide on, hold dear, parallel, relating **09** analogous, befitting, delight in, identical, similar to **10** appreciate, comparable, equivalent, for example, resembling **11** counterpart, for instance, go a bundle on, much the same, would rather, would sooner **12** feel inclined, find pleasant, on the lines of, take a shine to, take kindly to **13** approximating, corresponding, find enjoyable **14** by way of example, characteristic, find attractive, in the same way as, opposite number, take pleasure in **15** along the lines of, find interesting

likeable *see* **likable**

likelihood
06 chance **08** prospect **09** liability **10** likeliness **11** possibility, probability

likely
03 apt, fit **04** fair **05** prone, right **06** liable, odds-on, proper **07** fitting, hopeful, in order, no doubt, tending **08** credible, expected, feasible, inclined, pleasing, possible, probable, probably **09** in the wind, plausible, promising **10** acceptable, believable, calculated, on the cards, presumably, reasonable **11** anticipated, appropriate, doubtlessly, foreseeable, likely as not, predictable **12** to be expected **13** as likely as not

like-minded
08 agreeing, in accord **09** in harmony, in rapport, of one mind, unanimous **10** compatible, harmonious **11** in agreement **13** of the same mind

liken
04 like, link **05** match **06** equate, relate **07** compare **08** parallel, similize **09** analogize, associate, correlate, juxtapose, set beside

likeness
04 bust, copy, form, icon **05** guise, image, shape, study **06** effigy, sketch, statue **07** analogy, drawing, picture, replica **08** affinity, painting, portrait **09** depiction, facsimile, sculpture, semblance **10** appearance, caricature, comparison, expression, photograph, similarity, similitude, simulacrum **11** counterpart, parallelism, personation, portraiture, resemblance **12** reproduction **14** correspondence, representation

likewise
02 do, so **03** als, eke, too **04** also, item **05** ditto **06** as also, to boot **07** besides,

further **08** moreover, same here
09 similarly **10** in addition
11 furthermore **12** in like manner, in the same way **14** by the same token **15** in the same manner

liking
04 bent, bias, broo, brow, love
05 fancy, taste, thing **06** desire, notion, palate **07** leaning **08** affinity, fondness, penchant, soft spot, tendency, weakness **09** affection, proneness
10 attraction, partiality, preference, proclivity, propensity **11** inclination
12 appreciation, predilection, satisfaction

lilac
07 laylock, syringa **08** pipe-tree

lilt
03 air, hum **04** beat, lill, song, sway
05 swing **06** rhythm **07** cadence, measure **10** fingerhole **11** rise and fall

lily

Lilies include:

03 day, may
04 aloe, arum, pond, sego
05 calla, camas, lotus, regal, tiger, torch, yucca
06 camash, camass, Canada, crinum, Easter, Nuphar, scilla, smilax
07 candock, day-lily, Madonna, may-lily, quamash, Tritoma
08 asphodel, galtonia, gloriosa, hyacinth, martagon, nenuphar, Phormium, trillium, Turk's cap, victoria
09 amaryllis, grass tree, herb-Paris, kniphofia, Richardia
10 agapanthus, aspidistra, belladonna, fritillary
11 cabbage-tree, Convallaria, Madonna-lily, red-hot poker, spatterdock
12 Annunciation, Hemerocallis, Solomon's seal, zantedeschia
13 butcher's broom, lily of the Nile
15 lily of the valley, star of Bethlehem

• **lily leaf**
03 pad

lily-white
04 pure **06** chaste, virgin **08** innocent, spotless, virtuous **09** blameless, faultless, incorrupt, milk-white, uncorrupt, unsullied, untainted
11 uncorrupted, untarnished
14 irreproachable

Lima
01 L

limb
03 arm, leg **04** edge, fork, part, spur, wing **05** bough, spald, spall, spaul
06 border, branch, member, spalle, spauld **07** flipper, quarter, section
08 offshoot **09** appendage, extension, extremity, pterygium **10** projection

• **out on a limb**
07 exposed **08** isolated **10** vulnerable
15 in a weak position

limber
05 agile, lithe **06** lissom, pliant, supple
07 elastic, plastic, pliable **08** flexible, graceful **11** loose-limbed **12** loose-jointed

• **limber up**
06 warm up **07** prepare, work out
08 exercise, loosen up

limbo

• **in limbo**
10 in abeyance, up in the air **11** left hanging **12** left in the air **14** awaiting action **15** on the back burner

lime
04 bass, bast, lind, line, teil, trap
05 leash, Tilia **06** linden, loiter, temper, viscum **07** ensnare **08** basswood

limelight
04 fame **06** notice, renown
07 stardom **08** eminence
09 attention, celebrity, public eye, publicity, spotlight **10** notability, prominence **11** recognition

limestone
03 cam **04** calm, calp, caum
06 kunkar, kunkur, oolite **07** coquina, scaglia **08** Coral Rag, dolomite
09 caen-stone, coral-rock, cornbrash, cornstone **10** Kentish rag, stinkstone, travertine **11** cement-stone, rottenstone, sarcophagus **12** Forest Marble, Purbeck stone **13** Purbeck marble **15** coralline oolite, Kentish ragstone, landscape-marble

limit
◇ *containment indicator*
◇ *tail deletion indicator*
◇ *ends selection indicator*
03 cap, end, lid, rim, tie **04** brim, curb, edge, goal, gole, line, mete, pale, rein, roof, term **05** bound, brink, check, hem in, stint, Thule, verge **06** border, bounds, bridle, hinder, impede, margin, ration, reduce, region, tropic, utmost **07** appoint, ceiling, compass, confine, contain, control, delimit, extreme, margent, maximum, outside, specify **08** boundary, confines, deadline, division, frontier, outgoing, restrain, restrict, terminus, ultimate
09 condition, constrain, demarcate, determine, extremity, perimeter, prescribe, restraint, threshold
10 constraint, limitation, parameters
11 cut-off point, demarcation, demarkation, hold in check, keep in check, restriction, termination, ultima Thule **12** circumscribe **14** greatest amount, greatest extent **15** saturation point

• **extend beyond limit**
03 lap

• **the limit**
06 enough, the end, utmost **07** too much **08** the worst **11** intolerable, the final bow **12** the final blow, the last straw

limitation
04 curb, snag, tail **05** block, check
06 burden, defect **07** control, reserve
08 drawback, tail male, weakness
09 condition, hindrance, inability, restraint, weak point **10** constraint, impediment, inadequacy
11 demarcation, reservation, restriction, shortcoming
12 delimitation, disadvantage, imperfection, incapability
13 qualification **15** circumscription

limited
◇ *ends deletion indicator*
03 Ltd **04** tail, tyde **05** basic, borné, fixed, small **06** finite, narrow, scanty
07 checked, defined, minimal
08 confined **09** imperfect, qualified
10 controlled, inadequate, incomplete, restricted **11** constrained, determinate **12** insufficient
13 circumscribed

limitless
◇ *ends deletion indicator*
◇ *head deletion indicator*
◇ *tail deletion indicator*
04 vast **06** untold **07** endless, immense **08** infinite, unending
09 boundless, countless, illimited, unbounded, undefined, unlimited
10 bottomless **11** measureless, never-ending, unspecified **12** immeasurable, incalculable, interminable
13 inexhaustible

limp
03 dot, hop, lax **04** flop, gimp, halt, lank, soft, weak **05** frail, hilch, hitch, loose, slack, spent, tired, weary
06 falter, feeble, flabby, flaggy, floppy, hamble, hobble, limber, totter
07 flaccid, pliable, relaxed, shamble, shuffle, stagger, stumble, worn out
08 drooping, fatigued, flexible, lameness **09** enervated, exhausted, lethargic, out of curl **10** uneven walk
11 debilitated, out of energy
12 claudication, walk unevenly
13 walk with a limp

limpid
04 pure **05** clear, lucid, plain, still
06 bright, glassy **07** flowing
08 coherent, pellucid **09** unruffled
10 untroubled **11** translucent, transparent **12** crystal-clear, intelligible
14 comprehensible

limply
06 softly **07** loosely, slackly
08 flabbily, flexibly **09** flaccidly

limpness
06 laxity **09** looseness, slackness
10 flabbiness, flaccidity **11** flaccidness, flexibility **12** claudication

Lincoln
03 Abe

line
01 l **03** bar, job, ley, pad, rew, rim, row, way **04** area, axis, back, band, bank, belt, book, card, ceil, ciel, cord, dash, draw, edge, face, file, fill, firm, flax, kind, lind, make, mark, memo, note, oche, part, path, race, rank, role, rope, rule, seam,

side, sort, talk, text, tier, type, wire, word, work **05** bound, brand, breed, cable, canon, chain, cover, e-mail, field, forte, front, hatch, inlay, limit, panel, pitch, queue, route, score, shape, skirt, slash, spiel, stock, story, strip, stuff, style, track, trade, trail, twine, verge, words **06** avenue, belief, border, career, column, course, crease, encase, family, figure, fringe, furrow, groove, letter, margin, method, parade, patter, policy, report, scheme, script, series, strain, strand, streak, string, stripe, stroke, system, thread **07** calling, channel, company, contour, descent, lineage, message, outline, pattern, profile, pursuit, scratch, variety, wrinkle **08** activity, ancestry, approach, attitude, boundary, business, defences, filament, frontier, heritage, ideology, inscribe, interest, libretto, pedigree, position, postcard, practice, province, sequence, vocation **09** crow's feet, direction, formation, front line, parentage, perimeter, periphery, procedure, reinforce, sales talk, specialty, technique, underline **10** appearance, battle zone, borderline, department, employment, extraction, firing-line, line of work, memorandum, occupation, procession, profession, silhouette, specialism, speciality, strengthen, succession, trajectory, underscore **11** battlefield, corrugation, delineation, demarcation, information **12** battleground **13** configuration, modus operandi **14** course of action, line of business, specialization **15** draughtsmanship

See also **poetry**; **railway**

• curved line
03 tie

• draw the line
05 limit **06** refuse, reject **07** exclude, rule out, say no to **08** say not to **09** stand firm **11** stop short of **15** put your foot down

• fishing line
04 gimp, gymp **05** guimp

• in line
03 due **06** in a row, in step, likely **08** in accord, in a queue, in series **09** in a column, in harmony **10** on the cards **11** in agreement **12** in the running **15** being considered

• lay on the line, put on the line
04 risk **07** imperil **08** endanger **10** jeopardize **13** put in jeopardy

• line up
05 align, array, group, lay on, order, queue, range **06** fall in, obtain, secure **07** arrange, marshal, prepare, procure, produce, queue up **08** assemble, organize, regiment **09** form ranks **10** form a queue, straighten, wait in line **11** stand in line

• new line
03 zag

• toe the line
07 conform **12** keep the rules **14** be conventional, follow the rules

lineage
04 line, race **05** birth, breed, house, stock **06** family, parage **07** descent, lignage, progeny **08** ancestry, heredity, pedigree **09** ancestors, forebears, genealogy, offspring, whakapapa **10** descending, extraction, succession **11** descendants

lineaments
04 face **05** lines **06** aspect, traits, visage **07** outline, profile **08** features, outlines **10** appearance **11** countenance, physiognomy **13** configuration

lined
04 worn **05** feint, ruled **07** creased, wizened **08** furrowed, wrinkled

linen
04 duck, ecru, harn, lawn, line, lint, snow **05** crash, drill, toile **06** byssus, damask, dowlas, napery, sendal, sheets, sindon, whites **07** byssine, cambric, dornick, drabbet, holland, lockram, napkins, silesia **08** bed linen, drilling, gambroon, marcella, osnaburg **09** huckaback, Moygashel®, tea towels **10** seersucker, table linen, white goods **11** pillowcases, tablecloths

• measure of linen
03 lay, lea, ley

• strip of linen
04 amis **05** amice

liner
04 boat, ship **07** steamer **10** cruise ship

linesman
04 poet **06** author, writer

line-up
03 row **04** bill, cast, line, list, team **05** array, queue **09** selection **11** arrangement

linger
03 lag **04** hang, hove, idle, last, lurk, stay, stop, wait **05** dally, delay, hoove, hover, tarry **06** dawdle, endure, hang on, hanker, loiter, remain, taigle **07** hold out, persist, survive **08** continue, smoulder, straggle **10** dilly-dally, hang around **11** stick around **12** take your time **13** procrastinate

• linger on scent
03 tie

lingerie
03 bra **04** slip **05** teddy **06** smalls, undies **07** panties **08** camisole, frillies, half-slip, knickers, scanties **09** brassiere, underwear **11** panty girdle **12** body stocking, camiknickers, underclothes **13** suspender belt, underclothing, undergarments **14** inexpressibles, unmentionables

lingering
04 slow **08** dragging **09** prolonged, remaining, surviving **10** persistent, persisting, protracted **11** languishing **12** long-drawn-out

lingo
03 bat **04** cant, talk **05** argot, idiom **06** jargon, patois, patter, speech, tongue **07** dialect **08** language, parlance **10** mumbo-jumbo, vernacular, vocabulary **11** terminology

liniment
04 balm, wash **05** cream, salve **06** balsam, lotion **07** unguent **08** ointment **09** carron oil, emollient, opodeldoc **11** embrocation **14** camphorated oil

lining
◇ *insertion indicator*
03 lag **04** cush **05** inlay, stean, steen, stein **06** casing, facing, fettle **07** backing, cushion, furring, padding, sarking, tubbing **08** brattice, brattish, brettice, doublure, steaning, steening, steining, wainscot **09** alignment, panelling **10** encasement, incasement, stiffening **11** interfacing **13** reinforcement

link
03 map, tie **04** ally, bind, bond, join, knot, loop, part, ring, yoke **05** cleek, joint, merge, piece, tie-up, torch, union, unite **06** attach, bridge, couple, fasten, hook up, liaise, member, relate, swivel, team up **07** bracket, connect, element, enchain, hot line, liaison, network, shackle **08** division, identify, osculate **09** air-bridge, associate, carabiner, component, interlink, karabiner **10** amalgamate, attachment, connection, join forces **11** association, concatenate, constituent, partnership **12** relationship **13** communication, concatenation

• link up
04 ally, dock, join **05** merge, unify **06** bridge, hook up, join up, meet up, team up **07** connect, network **10** amalgamate, join forces

linkage
03 tie **04** bond, knot **05** joint, tie-in, tie-up, union **06** merger **07** liaison **08** alliance **09** valve gear **10** attachment, connection **11** association, partnership **12** amalgamation, relationship **13** communication

link-up
05 tie-in, union **06** merger **08** alliance **10** connection **11** association, partnership **12** amalgamation, relationship

lion
03 Leo **05** Aslan **12** king of beasts

• lion's share
04 bulk, mass, most **08** main part, majority **09** almost all, nearly all **11** largest part **12** greatest part **13** preponderance

lion-hearted
04 bold **05** brave **06** daring, heroic **07** gallant, valiant **08** fearless, intrepid, resolute, stalwart, valorous

09 dauntless, dreadless
10 courageous 12 stout-hearted

lionize
04 fête 05 exalt 06 honour, praise
07 acclaim, adulate, glorify, idolize, magnify 08 eulogize 09 celebrate
10 aggrandize 11 hero-worship
12 treat as a hero 14 put on a pedestal

lip
03 jib, lap, rim 04 brim, edge, flew, kiss, lave 05 brink, cheek, mouth, sauce, spout, verge 06 border, fipple, helmet, labium, labrum, ligula, margin, muffle
07 corolla, hare-lip 08 attitude, backchat, labellum, rudeness, underlip 09 impudence, insolence, submentum 10 effrontery
12 impertinence

lippy
04 pert 05 fresh, sassy, saucy
06 brazen, cheeky, lippie, mouthy
07 forward 08 impudent, insolent
09 audacious 11 impertinent
12 overfamiliar 13 disrespectful

liquefaction
06 fusion 07 melting, thawing
08 solation, syntexis 10 dissolving, karyolysis, liquefying 11 dissolution
13 deliquescence

liquefy
03 run 04 flux, fuse, melt, thaw
05 smelt 08 dissolve, fluidize, liquesce
09 liquidize 10 deliquesce

liqueur

Liqueurs include:

04 ouzo
05 Aurum®, noyau
06 Glayva, Kahlúa®, kirsch, kümmel, Malibu®, Midori®, pastis, Pernod®
07 Baileys®, curaçao, ratafia, sambuca
08 absinthe, advocaat, amaretto, Drambuie®, Galliano®, Tia Maria®
09 Cointreau®, mirabelle, Triple sec
10 Chartreuse®, limoncello, maraschino
11 Benedictine
12 cherry brandy, crème de cacao, Grand Marnier®, kirschwasser, Parfait Amour
13 crème de cassis, crème de menthe, Cuarenta y Tres
15 Southern Comfort®

See also **cocktail**; **spirits**

liquid
02 aq 03 sap, wet 04 even, pure, thin
05 clear, drink, fluid, juice, moist, runny
06 liquor, lotion, mellow, melted, molten, sloppy, smooth, steady, thawed, watery 07 aqueous, flowing, hydrous, regular, running, unfixed
08 solution, unbroken 09 liquefied, melodious 12 indisputable
13 uninterrupted

• **coloured liquid**
03 dye, ink

• **liquid for washing**
03 lye

liquidate
03 pay 04 kill, sell 05 clear 06 cash in, murder, pay off, remove, rub out, wind up 07 abolish, break up, destroy, disband, sell off, wipe out 08 dispatch, dissolve, massacre 09 close down, discharge, eliminate, finish off, terminate 10 annihilate, do away with, put an end to 11 assassinate, exterminate 13 convert to cash

liquidize
03 mix 05 blend, cream, crush, purée
07 process 10 synthesize

liquor
03 liq 04 bree, broo, grog, malt, vino
05 boose, booze, bouse, broth, drink, gravy, hogan, hogen, hooch, juice, plonk, sauce, stock, tinct 06 hootch, liquid, porter, rotgut, strunt, tiddly, tipple 07 alcohol, essence, extract, hokonui, shicker, spirits 08 infusion, potation 09 firewater, hard stuff, stiffener, stimulant, the bottle
10 intoxicant 11 aguardiente, jungle juice, strong drink, the creature, tickle-brain 12 Dutch courage

See also **drink**

• **liquor house** *see* **public house**

liquorice
07 nail-rod, pomfret 09 jequirity, sugarally 10 sugarallie

lissom
05 agile, light, lithe 06 limber, nimble, pliant, supple 07 pliable, willowy
08 flexible, graceful 09 lithesome
11 loose-limbed 12 loose-jointed

list
◇ *homophone indicator*
03 lip 04 bill, book, cant, file, heel, lean, leet, menu, note, roll, roon, rota, tilt 05 enrol, enter, index, slant, slate, slope, strip, table, tally 06 agenda, border, fillet, litany, recipe, record, roster, scroll, series, stripe 07 compile, incline, invoice, itemize, listing, scedule, selvage, set down
08 boundary, calendar, classify, contents, heel over, lean over, register, schedule, syllabus, tabulate
09 catalogue, checklist, directory, enumerate, inventory, programme, write down 10 tabulation
11 alphabetize, enumeration

See also **lean**

listen
◇ *homophone indicator*
04 hark, hear, heed, lest, list, mind
05 lithe 06 attend, intend 07 give ear, hearken, monitor 09 eavesdrop, lend an ear 10 auscultate, get a load of, take notice 12 pay attention 15 prick up your ears

• **listen in**
◇ *homophone indicator*
03 bug, tap 07 monitor, wiretap
08 overhear 09 eavesdrop 15 pin back your ears, prick up your ears

listener
03 ear

listless
04 dull, limp, waff 05 bored, heavy, inert 06 mopish, torpid, vacant
07 languid, passive 08 inactive, indolent, lifeless, sluggish, thowless, toneless 09 apathetic, depressed, enervated, impassive, lethargic, upsitting 10 spiritless 11 indifferent, languishing 12 uninterested
13 lackadaisical

listlessly
05 dully 06 limply 07 inertly
09 passively 10 inactively, lifelessly, sluggishly 11 impassively 12 spiritlessly
13 apathetically, lacking energy, lethargically

listlessness
05 ennui, sloth 06 acedia, apathy, torpor 07 languor, vacuity 08 lethargy
09 indolence, torpidity, upsitting
10 enervation, supineness
11 inattention, languidness
12 indifference, lifelessness, sluggishness 14 spiritlessness

lit
◇ *anagram indicator*
02 in 05 drunk, light, merry, tight, tipsy
06 ablaze, blotto, rested, soused
07 drunken, legless, pickled, settled, sloshed, sozzled, squiffy 09 crapulent, paralytic, plastered 10 dismounted, inebriated 11 intoxicated

litany
04 list 06 prayer 07 account, recital, synapte 08 devotion, irenicon, petition 09 catalogue, eirenicon
10 invocation, procession, recitation, repetition 11 enumeration
12 supplication

literacy
07 culture 08 learning 09 education, erudition, knowledge 10 articulacy
11 cultivation, learnedness, proficiency, scholarship 12 intelligence 13 ability to read 14 ability to write, articulateness

literal
03 lit 04 dull, true, typo 05 clear, close, error, exact, plain 06 actual, boring, strict, verbal 07 erratum, factual, genuine, humdrum, mistake, precise, prosaic, tedious 08 accurate, faithful, misprint, verbatim
10 colourless, uninspired
11 corrigendum, down-to-earth, undistorted, unvarnished, word-for-word 12 matter-of-fact 13 printing error, unembellished, unexaggerated, unimaginative

literalism
06 letter 09 biblicism, verbalism
10 textualism 13 scripturalism
14 exact rendering, fundamentalism, letter of the law

literally
03 lit 05 truly 06 really 07 closely, exactly, plainly 08 actually, strictly, verbatim 09 certainly, precisely
10 faithfully 11 to the letter, word for word

literary

03 lit **06** formal, poetic **07** bookish, erudite, learned, refined, written **08** cultured, educated, lettered, literate, literose, well-read **09** scholarly **10** cultivated, epistolary, widely-read **12** old-fashioned

Literary characters include:

02 **Pi**
03 **Eva** (Little), **Fox** (Brer), **Jim** (Lord), **Kaa**, **Kim**, **Lee** (Lorelei), **Pan** (Peter), **Pip**, **Roo**, **Tom** (Uncle), **Una**
04 **Ahab** (Captain), **Bede** (Adam), **Bond** (James), **Budd** (Billy), **Dent** (Arthur), **Eyre** (Jane), **Finn** (Huckleberry), **Fogg** (Phileas), **Gamp** (Sarah), **Gray** (Charlotte), **Gray** (Dorian), **Gunn** (Ben), **Haze** (Dolores), **Heep** (Uriah), **Hood** (Robin), **Hook** (Captain), **Hyde** (Mister), **Jack**, **Mole**, **Mole** (Adrian), **Pooh**, **Pope** (Giant), **Ridd** (John), **Slop** (Doctor), **Tigg** (Montague), **Toad** (Mister), **Trim** (Corporal), **Troy** (Sergeant Francis), **Tuck** (Friar), **Wilt** (Henry)
05 **Akela**, **Aslan**, **Athos**, **Avery** (Shug), **Baloo**, **Bates** (Miss), **Bloom** (Leopold), **Bloom** (Molly), **Boxer**, **Brown** (Father), **Celie**, **Chips** (Mister), **Clare** (Angel), **Darcy** (Fitzwilliam), **Darcy** (Mark), **Doone** (Lorna), **Drood** (Edwin), **Flint** (Captain), **Geste** (Beau), **Jones** (Bridget), **Jones** (Tom), **Kanga**, **Kipps** (Arthur), **Loman** (Willy), **Lucky**, **March** (Amy), **Maria** (Mad), **Mitty** (Walter), **Moore** (Mrs), **Mosca**, **Nancy**, **O'Hara** (Kimball), **O'Hara** (Scarlett), **Parry** (Will), **Piggy**, **Polly** (Alfred), **Porgy**, **Pozzo**, **Price** (Fanny), **Quilp** (Daniel), **Ralph**, **Ratty**, **Rebus** (Inspector John), **Remus** (Uncle), **Rudge** (Barnaby), **Satan**, **Sharp** (Becky), **Sikes** (Bill), **Slope** (Reverend Obadiah), **Sloth**, **Smike**, **Smith** (Winston), **Spade** (Sam), **Stubb**, **Tarka** (the Otter), **Titus**, **Topsy**, **Trent** (Little Nell), **Twist** (Oliver), **Wonka** (Willy), **Yahoo**
06 **Aramis**, **Archer** (Isabel), **Arthur** (King), **Badger**, **Barkis**, **Belial**, **Bennet** (Elizabeth), **Bourgh** (Lady Catherine de), **Bovary** (Emma), **Brodie** (Miss Jean), **Brooke** (Dorothea), **Bucket** (Charlie), **Bumble** (Mister), **Bumppo** (Natty), **Bunter** (Billy), **Butler** (Rhett), **Carton** (Sydney), **Crusoe** (Robinson), **Dombey** (Paul), **Dorrit** (Amy), **Dorrit** (William), **Du Bois** (Blanche), **Eeyore**, **Friday** (Man), **Gamgee** (Sam), **Gatsby** (Jay), **Gawain**, **Gollum**, **Grimes**, **Hagrid** (Rubeus), **Hannay** (Richard), **Holmes** (Sherlock), **Jeeves** (Reginald), **Jekyll** (Doctor Henry), **Legree** (Simon), **Little** (Vernon Gregory), **Lolita**, **Marley** (Jacob), **Marner** (Silas), **Marple** (Jane), **Moreau** (Doctor), **Mowgli**, **Omnium** (Duke of), **Pickle** (Gamaliel), **Piglet**, **Pinkie**, **Pliant** (Dame), **Poirot** (Hercule), **Potter** (Harry), **Rabbit**, **Rabbit** (Brer), **Random** (Roderick), **Rob Roy**, **Salmon** (Susie), **Sawyer** (Bob), **Sawyer** (Tom), **Shandy** (Tristram), **Silver** (Long John), **Subtle**, **Tarzan**, **Tigger**, **Tybalt**, **Tyrone** (James), **Varden** (Dolly), **Wadman** (Widow), **Watson** (Doctor John), **Weller** (Samuel), **Wimsey** (Lord Peter), **Wopsle** (Mister), **Yahoos**
07 **Andrews** (Pamela), **Ayeesha**, **Baggins** (Bilbo), **Baggins** (Frodo), **Beowulf**, **Biggles**, **Bramble** (Matthew), **Brer Fox**, **Bromden** (Chief), **Clinker** (Humphry), **Corelli** (Captain Antonio), **Crackit** (Toby), **Danvers** (Mrs), **Dawkins** (Jack), **Dedalus** (Stephen), **Deronda** (Daniel), **Despair** (Giant), **Don Juan**, **Dorigen**, **Dorothy**, **Dracula** (Count), **Estella**, **Fairfax** (Jane), **Gandalf**, **Gargery** (Joe), **Granger** (Hermione), **Grendel**, **Harding** (Reverend Septimus), **Harlowe** (Clarissa), **Hawkins** (Jim), **Higgins** (Professor Henry), **Hopeful**, **Humbert** (Humbert), **Ishmael**, **Jaggers** (Mister), **Jellyby** (Mrs), **Le Fever** (Lieutenant), **Maigret** (Jules), **Marlowe** (Philip), **Mellors** (Oliver), **Newsome** (Chad), **Obadiah**, **Orlando**, **Peachum** (Thomas), **Pierrot**, **Porthos**, **Prefect** (Ford), **Proudie** (Doctor), **Raffles**, **Rebecca**, **Scarlet** (Will), **Scrooge** (Ebenezer), **Shalott** (Lady of), **Shipton** (Mother), **Slumkey** (Samuel), **Squeers** (Wackford), **Surface** (Charles), **Surface** (Joseph), **Tiny Tim**, **Weasley** (Ron), **Wemmick** (Mister), **Wickham** (George), **William**, **Witches** (The Three), **Wooster** (Bertie), **Would-be** (Sir Politic)
08 **Absolute** (Captain), **Anderson** (Pastor Anthony), **Backbite** (Sir Benjamin), **Bagheera**, **Bedivere** (Sir), **Belacqua** (Lyra), **Black Dog**, **Casaubon** (Reverend Edward), **Cratchit** (Bob), **Criseyde**, **Dalloway** (Mrs Clarissa), **Dashwood** (Elinor), **Dashwood** (Marianne), **de Winter** (Max), **de Winter** (Rebecca), **Everdene** (Bathsheba), **Faithful**, **Flanders** (Moll), **Flashman**, **Gloriana**, **Griselda** (Patient), **Gulliver** (Lemuel), **Havisham** (Miss), **Hrothgar**, **Jarndyce** (John), **Kowalski** (Stanley), **Kowalski** (Stella), **Ladislaw** (Will), **Lancelot** (Sir), **Lestrade** (Inspector), **MacHeath** (Captain), **Magwitch** (Abel), **Malaprop** (Mrs), **McMurphy** (Randle Patrick), **Micawber** (Wilkins), **Moriarty** (Dean), **Moriarty** (Professor James), **Napoleon**, **Nickleby** (Nicholas), **Paradise** (Sal), **Peggotty** (Clara), **Peterkin**, **Pickwick** (Samuel), **Queequeg**, **Ramotswe** (Precious), **Snowball**, **Starbuck**, **Svengali**, **Tashtego**, **Thatcher** (Becky), **The Clerk**, **The Friar**, **The Reeve**, **Trotwood** (Betsey), **Tulliver** (Maggie), **Twitcher** (Jemmy), **Vladimir**
09 **Archimago**, **Bounderby** (Josiah), **Britomart**, **Bulstrode** (Nicholas), **Caulfield** (Holden), **Cheeryble** (Charles), **Christian**, **Churchill** (Frank), **Constance**, **D'Artagnan**, **Doolittle** (Eliza), **Fezziwigg** (Mister), **Golightly** (Holly), **Gradgrind** (Thomas), **Grandison** (Sir Charles), **Harlequin**, **Knightley** (George), **Lismahago** (Obadiah), **Lochinvar**, **Minnehaha**, **Pecksniff** (Seth), **Pendennis** (Arthur), **Pollyanna**, **Robin Hood**, **Rochester** (Edward Fairfax), **Scudamour** (Sir), **Shere Khan**, **The Knight**, **The Miller**, **The Squire**, **The Walrus**, **Tiger Lily**, **Trelawney** (Squire), **Van Winkle** (Rip), **Voldemort** (Lord), **Woodhouse** (Emma), **Yossarian** (Captain John), **Zenocrate**
10 **Allan-a-Dale**, **Big Brother**, **Brer Rabbit**, **Challenger** (Professor), **Chatterley** (Lady Constance), **Chuzzlewit** (Martin), **Dumbledore** (Albus), **Evangelist**, **Fauntleroy** (Little Lord), **Great-heart** (Mister), **Heathcliff**, **Hornblower** (Horatio), **Houyhnhnms**, **Little John**, **Little Nell**, **Maid Marian**, **Quatermain** (Allan), **The Red King**, **The Tar Baby**, **Tinkerbell**, **Tweedledee**, **Tweedledum**
11 **Copperfield** (David), **D'Urberville** (Alec), **Durbeyfield** (Tess), **Mickey Mouse**, **Mutabilitie**, **Pumblechook** (Mister), **The Dormouse**, **The Franklin**, **The Man of Law**, **The Merchant**, **The Pardoner**, **The Prioress**, **The Red Queen**, **The Summoner**, **Tiggy-Winkle** (Mrs)
12 **Blatant Beast**, **Chaunticleer**, **Frankenstein** (Victor), **Humpty-Dumpty**, **Lilliputians**, **Osbaldistone** (Francis), **Rip Van Winkle**, **Silvertongue** (Lyra), **The Carpenter**, **The Mad Hatter**, **The March Hare**, **The Pied Piper** (of Hamelin), **The Red Knight**, **The Scarecrow**
13 **The Jabberwock**, **The Mock Turtle**, **The Tin Woodman**, **The Wife of Bath**, **Winnie-the-Pooh**
14 **Mephistopheles**, **Rikki-Tikki-Tavi**, **The White Rabbit**, **Worldly Wiseman** (Mister)
15 **The Artful Dodger**, **The Cowardly Lion**, **The Three Witches**, **Valiant-for-Truth**

See also **Shakespeare**

Literary critics include:

04 **Bell** (Clive), **Blum** (Léon), **Frye** (Northrop)
05 **Hicks** (Granville), **Lodge** (David), **Stead** (C K)
06 **Arnold** (Matthew), **Calder** (Angus), **Empson** (Sir William), **Leavis** (F R),

Leavis (Q D), Lukacs (Georg), Sontag (Susan), Wilson (Edmund)
07 Ackroyd (Peter), Alvarez (A), Barthes (Roland), Daiches (David), Derrida (Jacques), Hoggart (Richard), Kermode (Frank)
08 Bradbury (Sir Malcolm), Eagleton (Terry), Longinus, Nicolson (Sir Harold), Richards (I A), Trilling (Lionel), Williams (Raymond)
10 Saintsbury (George Edward Bateman)
11 Matthiessen (F O), Sainte-Beuve (Charles Augustin)

• literary work
04 book, poem **05** essay **07** article

literate
07 learned **08** cultured, educated **09** scholarly **10** able to read, proficient **11** able to write, intelligent **12** intellectual, well-educated **13** knowledgeable

• Literate in Arts
02 LA **03** LLA

literati
06 brains **08** eggheads **09** academics, highbrows **10** illuminati, the erudite, the learned **11** cognoscenti, the studious **12** men of letters, the scholarly **13** intellectuals **14** intelligentsia, women of letters **15** the well-informed

literature
03 lit **04** bumf, data, page **05** facts, paper **06** papers **07** hand-out, leaflet, letters **08** brochure, circular, hand-outs, leaflets, pamphlet, writings **09** brochures, circulars, pamphlets **11** information **12** printed works **13** printed matter **14** published works

Literature types include:

04 epic, play, saga
05 drama, essay, novel, prose, verse
06 comedy, parody, poetry, satire, thesis
07 aga-saga, epistle, fantasy, fiction, lampoon, novella, polemic, tragedy, trilogy
08 allegory, chick lit, libretto, pastiche, treatise
09 anti-novel, biography, children's, novelette
10 magnum opus, non-fiction, roman à clef, short story, travelogue
11 black comedy, Gothic novel, pulp fiction
12 bodice-ripper, crime fiction
13 autobiography, belles-lettres, Bildungsroman, penny dreadful, travel writing
14 science fiction
15 epistolary novel, historical novel, picaresque novel

lithe
05 agile **06** limber, lissom, listen, pliant, supple, svelte **07** lissome, pliable **08** flexible **09** lithesome **11** loose-limbed **12** loose-jointed **13** double-jointed

lithium
02 Li

Lithuania
02 LT **03** LTU **04** Lith

litigant
05 party **08** claimant, opponent **09** contender, disputant, litigator, plaintiff **10** contestant **11** complainant

litigate
03 sue

litigation
03 law **04** case, suit **06** action **07** dispute, lawsuit, process **09** legal case **10** contention **11** legal action, prosecution

litigious
10 disputable **11** belligerent, contentious, quarrelsome **12** disputatious **13** argumentative

litter
03 bed, hay **04** grot, junk, mess, muck, team, teme **05** brood, chaff, issue, sedan, straw, strew, trash, wagon, waste, young **06** debris, doolie, family, farrow, jumble, kindle, mahmal, mess up, refuse, shreds **07** bedding, bracken, cacolet, clutter, garbage, progeny, rubbish, scatter **08** brancard, detritus, disarray, disorder, shambles **09** confusion, fragments, offspring, palankeen, palanquin, stretcher **10** light couch, make untidy, untidiness **11** make a mess of, odds and ends

little
03 bit, dab, sma, wee **04** baby, curn, cute, dash, drop, hint, leet, lite, lyte, mini, nice, poco, some, spot, tine, tiny, tyne, whit **05** brief, chota, dwarf, minor, petty, pinch, scant, short, small, speck, sweet, taste, teeny, touch, trace, young **06** barely, hardly, junior, meagre, midget, minute, paltry, petite, rarely, seldom, skimpy, slight, sparse, trifle **07** faintly, modicum, nominal, not much, passing, peanuts, shortly, slender, soupçon, trickle, trivial, younger **08** exiguous, fleeting, fragment, nugatory, particle, pint-size, pleasant, scarcely, skerrick, slightly, trifling **09** ephemeral, miniature, momentary, pint-sized, transient **10** attractive, diminutive, negligible, short-lived, smattering, transitory **11** Lilliputian, microscopic, small amount, unimportant **12** infrequently, insufficient **13** infinitesimal, insignificant, next to nothing **14** inconsiderable **15** a drop in the ocean

See also **small**

• a little
03 tad **04** some

• little by little
04 Eric **06** slowly **08** bit by bit, inchmeal **09** by degrees, gradually, piecemeal, poco a poco **10** step by step **13** imperceptibly, progressively

• take a little
04 drib

liturgical
06 formal, ritual, solemn **08** hieratic **10** ceremonial, sacerdotal **11** eucharistic, sacramental

liturgy
04 form, rite **05** usage **06** office, ritual **07** formula, service, worship **08** ceremony **09** ordinance, sacrament **10** observance **11** celebration

livable, liveable
08 adequate, bearable **09** endurable, habitable, tolerable **10** acceptable, worthwhile **11** comfortable, inhabitable, supportable **12** satisfactory

• livable with, liveable with
08 bearable, passable, sociable **09** congenial, gemütlich, tolerable **10** compatible, harmonious **13** companionable

live
02 be **03** hot **04** hard, last, lead, pass, stay **05** abide, alert, alive, dwell, exist, lodge, spend, squat, vital, vivid **06** active, alight, behave, bodily, endure, lively, living, public, red hot, remain, reside, urgent **07** animate, be alive, blazing, breathe, burning, charged, comport, conduct, current, dynamic, flaming, glowing, have fun, ignited, inhabit, persist, see life, subsist, survive, topical, undergo **08** continue, existent, have life, in person, live it up, personal, pressing, real-time, relevant, stirring, unstable, vigorous, volatile **09** be settled, breathing, connected, energetic, enjoy life, explosive, important, pertinent, unwrought **10** applicable, draw breath, experience, having life, in the flesh, unexploded, unquarried **11** electrified, not recorded **12** have your home **13** controversial, enjoy yourself **14** earn your living, not prerecorded, with an audience **15** support yourself

• live it up
05 revel **09** celebrate, have a ball, make merry **10** go on a spree **11** make whoopee **14** push the boat out **15** paint the town red

• live on
04 feed, last **05** exist **06** rely on **07** live off, subsist **08** continue **09** subsist on

• live wire
06 dynamo **08** go-getter, whizz kid **10** ball of fire **11** eager beaver, self-starter

liveable *see* **livable**

livelihood
03 job **04** keep, work **05** bread, crust, means, trade **06** income, living, upkeep **07** livelod, support **08** livelood **09** existence **10** daily bread, employment, livelihead, occupation, profession, sustenance **11** maintenance, subsistence **13** means of living **14** bread-and-butter, means of support, source of income

liveliness
04 brio, life, salt **05** oomph **06** energy, esprit, spirit, vigour **07** entrain, pizzazz **08** activity, dynamism, vitality, vivacity **09** animation, briskness, quickness, smartness **10** livelihead **11** refreshment **13** animal spirits, sprightliness, vivaciousness **14** boisterousness

livelong
04 full, long **05** whole **06** entire, orpine **08** complete, enduring **10** protracted

lively
◇ *anagram indicator*
03 gay **04** busy, cant, go-go, keen, pacy, racy, spry, vive, vivo, warm, wick **05** agile, alert, alive, brisk, buxom, canty, cobby, kedge, kedgy, kidge, light, ludic, merry, pacey, peart, perky, piert, quick, rapid, vital, vivid, zappy, zippy **06** active, blithe, bouncy, breezy, bright, bubbly, chirpy, crouse, frisky, heated, hectic, jaunty, living, nimble, snappy, sporty, strong, titupy, vivace **07** buckish, buoyant, buzzing, crowded, dynamic, graphic, mettled, playful, slammin', teeming, tittupy, vibrant **08** animated, brushing, bustling, cheerful, eventful, exciting, friskful, galliard, lifesome, rattling, skittish, slamming, spirited, stirring, striking, swarming, vigorous **09** colourful, energetic, lightsome, sparkling, sprightly, vivacious **10** frolicsome, mettlesome, mouvementé, refreshing **11** imaginative, interesting, stimulating **12** effervescent, enthusiastic, high-spirited, invigorating

liven
04 stir **05** cheer, hot up, pep up, rouse, spice **06** buck up, jazz up, perk up, stir up **07** animate, cheer up, enliven, spice up **08** brighten, energize, vitalize **10** invigorate **11** put life into

liverish
05 testy **06** crabby, crusty, grumpy, snappy, tetchy **07** crabbed, peevish **09** crotchety, irascible, irritable, splenetic **11** ill-humoured **12** disagreeable **13** quick-tempered

livery
04 garb, gear, suit, togs **05** dress, get-up, habit **06** attire **07** apparel, clobber, clothes, costume, regalia, uniform **08** clothing, garments **09** irritable, vestments **11** habiliments

livid
03 mad, wan **04** blae, blue, pale, waxy **05** angry, ashen, irate, pasty, white **06** fuming, leaden, pallid, purple, raging **07** bruised, enraged, furious, ghastly, greyish **08** blanched, incensed, outraged, purplish, seething **09** bloodless, indignant **10** infuriated **11** deathly pale, discoloured, exasperated, Hippocratic **12** black-and-blue

living
03 job **04** life, live, true, work **05** alive, being, bread, close, crust, exact, in use, trade, vital **06** active, extant, income, lively, strong **07** animate, current, genuine, precise, support **08** animated, benefice, existing, faithful, property, vigorous **09** animation, breathing, existence, identical, lifestyle, operative, surviving, way of life **10** continuing, daily bread, livelihood, occupation, profession, sustenance **11** going strong, maintenance, subsistence **13** means of living **14** bread-and-butter, means of support, source of income

• **mode of living**
04 diet

living room
06 lounge **07** day room, parlour **09** front room **11** drawing room, sitting room **13** reception room

lizard

Lizards include:

03 eft
04 evet, gila, sand, seps, tegu, wall, worm
05 blind, Draco, fence, gecko, skink
06 agamid, dragon, flying, goanna, horned, iguana
07 bearded, frilled, monitor, perenty
08 basilisk, perentie, slowworm, teguexin
09 chameleon
10 blue-tongue, chamaeleon
11 gila monster
12 Komodo dragon

See also **animal**

llama
06 alpaca **07** guanaco, huanaco

load
03 arm, jag, put, tax, tod **04** a lot, cram, duty, fill, haul, heap, lade, lard, lots, onus, pack, pile, plug, seam, slot, tons **05** cargo, enter, equip, goods, heaps, miles, piles, prime, put in, scads, slide, stack, stuff, todde, worry **06** burden, charge, dozens, fill up, hordes, insert, lading, masses, oodles, scores, stacks, strain, weight **07** fraught, freight, oppress, prepare, put into, trouble **08** a million, contents, encumber, hundreds, incumber, lashings, millions, pressure, shipment **09** abundance, albatross, great deal, millstone, overwhelm, thousands, weigh down **10** commitment, obligation, oppression, overburden, saddle with **11** consignment, encumbrance, large amount, tribulation **13** prepare to fire **14** responsibility

loaded
◇ *anagram indicator*
03 fap, fou **04** full, high, inky, paid, rich **05** drunk, fixed, flush, foxed, happy, inked, laden, lit up, merry, moppy, piled, set up, tight, tipsy, woozy **06** biased, blotto, bombed, canned, corked, filled, heaped, jagged, juiced, mellow, mortal, packed, rigged, ripped, soused, stewed, stinko, stoned, tiddly, wasted **07** bevvied, bonkers, bottled, charged, crocked, drunken, ebriose, fairish, half-cut, legless, maggoty, pickled, pie-eyed, sloshed, smashed, sozzled, squiffy, stacked, tiddled, trashed, wealthy, well-off, wrecked **08** affluent, bibulous, burdened, footless, in liquor, juiced up, liquored, moon-eyed, overseen, overshot, pregnant, sow-drunk, stotious, tanked up, weighted, whiffled, whistled **09** blootered, crapulent, incapable, paralytic, plastered, shickered, up the pole, well-oiled **10** blind drunk, capernoity, inebriated, in the money, obfuscated, well-heeled **11** intoxicated, made of money, rolling in it, snowed under **12** drunk as a lord, drunk as a newt, on easy street, roaring drunk **13** drunk as a piper, having had a few, under the table **14** Brahms and Liszt **15** a sheet in the wind, one over the eight, the worse for wear, under the weather

loaf
03 bum, tin, veg **04** cake, cube, head, idle, laze, loll, lump, mass, mind, nous, pone, slab **05** block, brick, miche, mooch, relax, sense, slosh **06** bludge, brains, coburg, loiter, lounge, noddle, stotty, unwind, veg out **07** bloomer, brioche, challah, manchet, Panagia, stottie **08** baguette, corn pone, focaccia, gumption, Panhagia, scrapple **09** barmbrack, lie around, sit around **10** corn dodger, hang around, stand about, take it easy **11** common sense, French stick, spotted dick **12** lounge around

See also **bread**; **head**

• **loaf about**
04 laze **06** lounge

loafer
03 yob **04** slob **05** idler **06** bummer, skiver **07** goof-off, lounger, shirker, wastrel **08** layabout, sluggard **09** corner-boy, corner-man, lazybones, sundowner **10** ne'er-do-well **11** beachcomber

See also **footwear**

loam
04 clay, core, lome, malm, sand, soil **05** earth **09** brickclay, malmstone **10** brick-earth

loan
03 len', sub **04** lane, lend **05** allow, prest **06** credit, on-lend **07** advance, finance, imprest, lending **08** mortgage, overlend, put forth **09** allowance **12** floating debt, respondentia **13** accommodation

loath
04 ugly **05** laith **06** averse **07** against, hateful, opposed **08** grudging, hesitant **09** reluctant, repulsive,

resisting, unwilling **10** indisposed **11** disinclined

loathe
02 ug **04** hate **05** abhor **06** detest **07** despise, dislike **08** execrate, nauseate, not stand **09** abominate **10** recoil from **15** feel revulsion at

loathing
04 hate **05** odium **06** hatred, horror, nausea **07** disgust, dislike, ill-will **08** aversion **09** antipathy, repulsion, revulsion **10** abhorrence, execration, repugnance **11** abomination, detestation

loathsome
04 foul, vile **05** nasty **06** odious **07** hateful, mawkish, obscene **08** horrible, nauseous **09** abhorrent, execrable, lothefull, obnoxious, offensive, repellent, repugnant, repulsive, revolting **10** abominable, despicable, detestable, disgusting, nauseating **12** contemptible, disagreeable

lob
03 shy **04** hurl, lift, loft, lout, lump, puck, toss **05** chuck, droop, fling, heave, pitch, throw **06** launch **07** lobworm, pollack

lobby
04 hall, urge **05** entry, foyer, porch **06** demand **07** call for, faction, hallway, passage, promote, push for, solicit **08** anteroom, box-lobby, campaign, corridor, entrance, persuade, press for, pressure **09** influence, lobbyists, vestibule **10** passageway **11** campaign for, ginger group, waiting room **12** entrance hall **13** pressure group

lobster
04 cock **08** crawfish, crayfish **09** langouste **11** langoustine
• lobster cage
04 corf

local
◇ *foreign word indicator*
03 bar, inn, pub **04** city, town **05** place, urban **06** boozer, narrow, native, number, parish, saloon, tavern **07** citizen, limited, topical, vicinal, village **08** district, hostelry, regional, resident **09** community, municipal, parochial, small-town **10** inhabitant, parish-pump, provincial, restricted, vernacular **11** anaesthetic, examination, public house **12** watering-hole **13** neighbourhood
See also **public house**
• local worker
06 barman **09** bartender

locale
04 area, site, spot, zone **05** locus, place, scene, venue **07** setting **08** locality, location, position **11** environment **13** neighbourhood

locality
04 area, site, spot **05** locus, place, scene **06** locale, region **07** setting **08** district, position, vicinity **11** environment **12** neighborhood **13** neighbourhood **15** surrounding area

localize
05 limit **06** assign **07** ascribe, confine, contain, delimit, specify **08** identify, pinpoint, restrain, restrict, zero in on **10** delimitate, narrow down **11** concentrate **12** circumscribe

locate
03 fix, lay, put, set **04** find, seat, site, spot **05** build, place, plant **06** access, detect, finger, settle **07** hit upon, pick out, situate, station, uncover, unearth **08** allocate, discover, identify, pinpoint, position **09** establish, track down **10** come across, run to earth **14** lay your hands on
• be located
03 sit

location
04 farm, seat, site, spot **05** locus, place, point, scene, venue **06** locale, ubiety **07** setting **08** bearings, position **09** situation **11** whereabouts

loch
01 L **03** dam, sea **04** lake, mere, pond, pool, tarn **05** basin, lough, water **09** reservoir
See also **lake**

lock
03 bar, hug, jam, tag **04** curl, join, link, mesh, seal, shut, snap, trap, tuft **05** catch, clasp, grasp, latch, plait, sasse, stick, tress, unite **06** clench, clutch, engage, fasten, secure, strand **07** embrace, enclose, entwine, grapple, ringlet **08** encircle, entangle **09** certainty, fastening, interlock **12** scalping-tuft

Locks include:

03 rim
04 dead, Yale®
05 child, Chubb®, wagon
06 safety, spring
07 mortice, mortise, padlock
08 cylinder
10 night latch
11 combination

Lock parts include:

03 bit, key, pin
04 bolt, hasp, knob, post, rose, sash, ward
05 latch, talon
06 barrel, keyway, spring, staple
07 key card, keyhole, spindle, tumbler
08 cylinder, dead bolt, sash bolt
09 face plate, latch bolt
10 escutcheon, latch lever, push button
11 mortise bolt, spindle hole, strike plate
12 cylinder hole
13 latch follower

• lock out
03 bar **05** debar **07** exclude, keep out, shut out
• lock up
◇ *containment indicator*
◇ *hidden indicator*
03 pen **04** cage, jail **06** detain, secure, shut in, shut up, wall in **07** close up, confine, put away **08** imprison **11** incarcerate **13** put behind bars
• open lock
04 pick

locker
07 cabinet **08** cupboard **09** container **11** compartment

lock-up
03 can, jug **04** cell, gaol, jail, quod **05** choky, clink **06** chokey, cooler, garage, prison **07** slammer **09** storeroom, warehouse **10** depository, roundhouse, watch house **12** penitentiary, station house

locomotion
06 action, motion, moving, travel **07** headway, walking **08** movement, progress **10** ambulation, travelling **11** progression **13** perambulation

locus
04 site **05** place, point, polar, venue **06** locale, spiral **08** centrode, conchoid, envelope, locality, location, parabola, position, roulette **09** directrix, situation, wavefront **10** lemniscate **11** radical axis, whereabouts **14** director circle

locust
08 devourer **10** devastator, voetganger

locution
04 term **05** idiom, style **06** accent, cliché, phrase **07** diction, talking, wording **08** phrasing, speaking **10** expression, inflection, intonation **11** collocation **12** articulation, turn of phrase

lode
04 reef

lodge
03 box, cup, den, dig, fix, hut, inn, lay, lie, put **04** bank, club, file, host, keep, lair, live, make, nest, room, stay, stow, tent **05** board, bower, cabin, dwell, group, grove, haunt, house, imbed, infix, layer, place, put in, put up **06** billet, branch, chalet, grange, hand in, harbor, loggia, record, reside, show up, submit, teepee **07** barrack, chapter, cottage, deposit, hang out, harbour, implant, quarter, retreat, section, shelter, society, sojourn **08** campfire, get stuck, register **09** be settled, gatehouse, get caught, longhouse **10** habitation, put forward **11** accommodate, association **12** accumulation, have your home, hunting-lodge, meeting-place

lodger
02 PG **05** guest **06** inmate, roomer, tenant **07** boarder **08** resident **11** paying guest

lodgings
03 pad **04** digs, ferm **05** abode, board, place, rooms **06** bedsit, billet **07** flea-bag **08** dwelling, quarters
09 bedsitter, residence
13 accommodation, boarding house
14 bedsitting-room

loftily
07 proudly, stately **08** snootily
09 haughtily **10** arrogantly
12 disdainfully **14** superciliously

lofty
04 high, tall **05** brent, grand, noble, proud, steep, wingy **06** aerial, lordly, raised, skyish, snooty, winged
07 exalted, haughty, sky-high, soaring, stately, sublime **08** arrogant, elevated, esteemed, imperial, imposing, majestic, renowned, superior, towering **09** dignified **10** disdainful
11 illustrious, patronizing, toffee-nosed **12** supercilious
13 condescending, distinguished, high and mighty, high-stomached

log
04 book, clog, file, note **05** block, chart, chock, chunk, diary, piece, stock, tally, trunk **06** billet, loggat, record, timber **07** account, daybook, journal, logbook, set down, write up
08 register **09** logarithm

logbook
03 log **05** chart, diary, tally **06** record
07 account, daybook, journal
08 register

loggerheads
• at loggerheads
◇ *anagram indicator*
06 at odds **10** in conflict
11 disagreeing, quarrelling **12** in opposition **13** like cat and dog **14** at daggers drawn

logic
05 sense **06** reason **08** argument
09 coherence, deduction, judgement, rationale, reasoning, redecraft
10 dialectics **13** argumentation, ratiocination
See also **circuit**

logical
04 wise **05** clear, sound, valid
06 cogent **07** Boolean **08** coherent, rational, reasoned, relevant, sensible, thinking **09** deducible, deductive, dialectic, inductive, judicious
10 consistent, convergent, methodical, reasonable, sequacious
11 consecutive, dialectical, intelligent, syllogistic, well-founded **12** well-reasoned **13** well-organized **14** well-thought-out

logically
07 clearly, validly **08** sensibly
10 coherently, rationally, relevantly
11 deductively, inductively
12 consistently, methodically
13 consecutively, dialectically, intelligently

logistics
05 plans **07** tactics **08** planning, strategy **09** direction **10** management
11 arrangement, engineering **12** co-ordination, organization
13 masterminding, orchestration

logo
04 mark, sign **05** badge, image
06 device, emblem, figure, symbol
08 insignia **09** trademark
14 representation

loiter
03 lag **04** hove, idle, lime, loaf, lurk, mike **05** dally, delay, hoove, mooch, mouch, tarry **06** dawdle, linger, lounge, taigle **07** saunter **08** lallygag, lollygag **09** hang about, waste time
10 dilly-dally, hang around **12** take your time
• loitering with intent
03 sus **04** suss

loll
03 sag **04** drop, flap, flop, hang, lill, loaf
05 droop, relax, slump **06** dangle, lounge, slouch, sprawl **07** recline

lollop
03 run **04** idle, lope **05** bound
06 canter, gallop, lounge, spring, stride

lolly
05 money **06** sucker **07** lulibub **08** ice block, lollipop, Popsicle®
See also **money**

London
03 wen **08** great wen

London boroughs:

05 Brent
06 Barnet, Bexley, Camden, Ealing, Harrow, Merton, Newham, Sutton
07 Bromley, Croydon, Enfield, Hackney, Lambeth
08 Haringey, Havering, Hounslow, Lewisham
09 Greenwich, Islington, Redbridge, Southwark
10 Hillingdon, Wandsworth
12 Tower Hamlets
13 Waltham Forest
17 City of Westminster
18 Barking and Dagenham, Kingston upon Thames, Richmond upon Thames
20 Hammersmith and Fulham, Kensington and Chelsea

Other districts of London include:

02 EC
03 Bow, Kew, Lee
04 Bank, Oval, Soho
05 Acton, Angel, Erith, Hayes, Penge
06 Arkley, Balham, Barnes, Debden, Eltham, Epping, Euston, Fulham, Hendon, Heston, Hoxton, Ilford, Kenton, Leyton, Malden, Morden, Pinner, Poplar, Purley, Putney, Temple, Waddon
07 Aldgate, Archway, Barking, Beckton, Belmont, Borough, Brixton, Catford, Chelsea, Clapham, Cranham, Dalston, Dulwich, East End, East Ham, Edgware, Elm Park, Feltham, Hampton, Hanwell, Holborn, Hornsey, Kilburn, Mayfair, Mile End, Mitcham, Neasden, Norwood, Old Ford, Olympia, Peckham, Pimlico, Selsdon, Stepney, The City, Tooting, Wapping, Welling, Wembley, West End, West Ham, Yeading
08 Alperton, Bankside, Barbican, Brockley, Brompton, Chiswick, Coulsdon, Crayford, Dagenham, Deptford, Edmonton, Elmstead, Finchley, Finsbury, Grays Inn, Hanworth, Hatch End, Heathrow, Highbury, Highgate, Holloway, Homerton, Hyde Park, Ickenham, Kingston, Mill Hill, Mortlake, New Cross, Nine Elms, Northolt, Osterley, Perivale, Plaistow, Richmond, Shadwell, Southall, Stanmore, Surbiton, Sydenham, Tolworth, Uxbridge, Vauxhall, Victoria, Walworth, Wanstead, Waterloo, Woodford, Woolwich
09 Abbey Wood, Addington, Barnsbury, Battersea, Bayswater, Beckenham, Becontree, Belgravia, Blackwall, Brentford, Brimsdown, Canonbury, Chalk Farm, Chingford, Colindale, Crouch End, Docklands, Fitzrovia, Foots Cray, Gant's Hill, Gidea Park, Gipsy Hill, Goodmayes, Gospel Oak, Greenford, Green Park, Hampstead, Harefield, Harlesden, Harringay, Herne Hill, Isleworth, Kidbrooke, Kingsbury, Kingsland, Limehouse, Maida Vale, Mark's Gate, Newington, Northwood, Orpington, Park Royal, Petts Wood, Plumstead, South Bank, Southgate, Stockwell, St Pancras, Stratford, Streatham, Tottenham, Tower Hill, Tulse Hill, Upminster, Whetstone, White City, Whitehall, Willesden, Wimbledon, Wood Green
10 Addiscombe, Albany Park, Arnos Grove, Beddington, Bellingham, Bermondsey, Blackheath, Bloomsbury, Brent Cross, Camberwell, Chase Cross, Collier Row, Creekmouth, Dollis Hill, Earls Court, Earlsfield, Embankment, Farringdon, Forest Gate, Forest Hill, Goddington, Green Lanes, Haggerston, Harlington, Harold Hill, Harold Wood, Horse Ferry, Isle of Dogs, Kennington, Kensington, King's Cross, Manor House, Marylebone, Mottingham, Paddington, Piccadilly, Queensbury, Raynes Park, Seven Dials, Seven Kings, Shad Thames, Shoreditch, Silvertown, Smithfield, Teddington, Thamesmead, Totteridge, Twickenham, Wallington, Wealdstone
11 Bedford Park, Belsize Park, Bexleyheath, Blackfriars, Bounds Green, Brondesbury, Canada Water, Canary Wharf, Canning Town,

Chessington, Clerkenwell, Cockfosters, Cricklewood, East Dulwich, Fortis Green, Gunnersbury, Hammersmith, Highams Park, Holland Park, Kensal Green, Kentish Town, Leytonstone, Lincoln's Inn, Little Italy, Ludgate Hill, Muswell Hill, Notting Hill, Pentonville, Regent's Park, Rotherhithe, Snaresbrook, St John's Wood, Surrey Quays, Tufnell Park, Walthamstow, Westminster, Whitechapel

12 Bethnal Green, Billingsgate, Bromley-by-Bow, Charing Cross, City of London, Colliers Wood, Covent Garden, Crossharbour, Epping Forest, Finsbury Park, Golders Green, Hatton Garden, Havering Park, London Bridge, London Fields, Palmers Green, Parsons Green, Pool of London, Primrose Hill, Seven Sisters, Sloane Square, Stamford Hill, Swiss Cottage

13 Ardleigh Green, Chadwell Heath, Crystal Palace, Harmondsworth, Knightsbridge, Ladbroke Grove, Lancaster Gate, North Woolwich, Petticoat Lane, Shepherd's Bush, Thornton Heath, Tottenham Hale, Wanstead Flats, Winchmore Hill

14 Angel Islington, Becontree Heath, Hackney Marshes, Stoke Newington, Tottenham Green, Wormwood Scrubs

15 Alexandra Palace, Leicester Square, Westbourne Green

London streets include:

06 Strand

07 Aldgate, Aldwych, The Mall, Westway

08 Kingsway, Long Acre, Millbank, Minories, Pall Mall, Park Lane, York Road

09 Bow Street, Cheapside, Drury Lane, Haymarket, King's Road, Maida Vale, Queensway, Tower Hill, Whitehall

10 Bond Street, Dean Street, Eaton Place, Euston Road, Fetter Lane, Fulham Road, London Wall, Onslow Road, Piccadilly, Queen's Gate, Soho Square, Vine Street

11 Baker Street, Eaton Square, Edgware Road, Fleet Street, Goswell Road, Gower Street, High Holborn, Lambeth Road, Leather Lane, Ludgate Hill, Old Kent Road, Pimlico Road, Savoy Street, Warwick Road

12 Albany Street, Belgrave Road, Birdcage Walk, Brompton Road, Cannon Street, Chancery Lane, Cromwell Road, Gray's Inn Road, Hatton Garden, Jermyn Street, Oxford Street, Regent Street, Sloane Square, Sloane Street, Tooley Street

13 Bayswater Road, Bedford Square, Berwick Street, Carnaby Street, Downing Street, Garrick Street, Gerrard Street, Grosvenor Road, Knightsbridge, Lombard Street, Ludgate Circus, New Bond Street, New Fetter Lane, Newgate Street, Old Bond Street, Petticoat Lane, Portland Place, Portman Square, Russell Square, Wardour Street

14 Belgrave Square, Berkeley Square, Coventry Street, Earl's Court Road, Earnshaw Street, Exhibition Road, Gloucester Road, Holborn Viaduct, Horseferry Road, Hyde Park Square, Kensington Road, Marylebone Road, Mayfair Gardens, Portobello Road, Stamford Street

15 Albemarle Street, Blackfriars Road, Clerkenwell Road, Grosvenor Square, Horse Guards Road, Leicester Square, Liverpool Street, New Bridge Street, Pentonville Road, Southwark Street, St John's Wood Road, Trafalgar Square, Whitechapel Road

London landmarks include:

03 V&A

03 ICA, Kew

04 City, Eros, Oval, Soho

05 Barts, Lord's

06 Big Ben, Lloyds, Temple, Thames

07 Harrods, Mayfair, St Paul's, The City, The Mall

08 Bow bells, Cenotaph, Gray's Inn, Hyde Park, Liberty's, Monument, St Bride's

09 Chinatown, Cutty Sark, George Inn, Green Park, Guildhall, London Eye, London Zoo, Old Bailey, Rotten Row, Royal Mews, South Bank, Staple Inn, The Temple, Trocadero

10 Albert Hall, Camden Lock, Cock Tavern, Earl's Court, HMS Belfast, Jewel Tower, Kew Gardens, Marble Arch, Selfridge's, Serpentine, Tate Modern, the Gherkin

11 Apsley House, Canary Wharf, Golden Hinde, Lincoln's Inn, OXO building, Queen's House, Regent's Park, River Thames, St John's Gate, St Margaret's, St Mary-Le-Bow, Tate Britain, Tower Bridge

12 Charterhouse, Covent Garden, Design Museum, Dickens House, Festival Hall, Globe Theatre, Guards Museum, Hatton Garden, Hay's Galleria, London Bridge, Mansion House, Spencer House, statue of Eros, St James's Park, Telecom Tower, Temple Church, Traitors' Gate

13 Admiralty Arch, Bank of England, British Museum, Carnaby Street, Clarence House, Fortnum & Mason's, Gabriel's Wharf, Geffrye Museum, Greenwich Park, Lambeth Palace, London Dungeon, Madam Tussaud's, Nelson's Column, Petticoat Lane, Queen's Gallery, Royal Exchange, Science Museum, Somerset House, Tower of London, Wesley's Chapel

14 Albert Memorial, Barbican Centre, British Library, Hayward Gallery, Hermitage Rooms, Lancaster House, London Aquarium, Millennium Dome, Museum of London, Portobello Road, Speakers' Corner, St Clement Danes, St James's Palace, Waterloo Bridge, Wellington Arch

15 Bankside Gallery, Banqueting House, Brompton Oratory, Burlington House, Cabinet War Rooms, National Gallery, Royal Albert Hall, Royal Opera House, Temple of Mithras, Trafalgar Square, Westminster Hall

London Underground lines:

06 Circle

07 Central, Jubilee

08 Bakerloo, District, Northern, Victoria

10 East London, Piccadilly

12 Metropolitan

15 Waterloo and City

18 Hammersmith and City

21 Docklands Light Railway

London Underground stations include:

04 Bank, Oval

05 Angel

06 Balham, Cyprus, Epping, Euston, Leyton, Morden, Pinner, Poplar, Temple

07 Aldgate, Archway, Arsenal, Barking, Beckton, Borough, Bow Road, Brixton, Chesham, East Ham, Edgware, Holborn, Kilburn, Mile End, Neasden, Pimlico, Ruislip, St Paul's, Wapping, Watford, West Ham

08 Amersham, Barbican, Chigwell, Hainault, Heathrow, Highgate, Lewisham, Monument, Moorgate, Mudchute, New Cross, Northolt, Perivale, Plaistow, Richmond, Royal Oak, Shadwell, Stanmore, Uxbridge, Vauxhall, Victoria, Wanstead, Waterloo

09 Acton Town, All Saints, Bayswater, Blackwall, Bow Church, Chalk Farm, Cutty Sark, East Acton, East India, Greenford, Green Park, Greenwich, Hampstead, Harlesden, Limehouse, Maida Vale, Old Street, Park Royal, Queensway, South Quay, Southwark, Stockwell, Stratford, Tower Hill, Upton Park, West Acton, Westferry, White City, Wimbledon, Wood Green

10 Bermondsey, Bond Street, Brent Cross, Camden Town, Devons Road, Dollis Hill, Earl's Court, East Putney, Embankment, Farringdon, Grange Hill, Hanger Lane, Heron Quays, Hillingdon, Hornchurch, Kennington, Kew Gardens, Manor House, Marble Arch, Marylebone, North Acton, Paddington, Queen's Park, Shoreditch, Tooting Bec

11 Aldgate East, Baker Street, Barons Court, Beckton Park, Belsize Park, Blackfriars, Bounds Green, Canada

Water, Canary Wharf, Canning Town, Chorleywood, Cockfosters, Custom House, Edgware Road, Gunnersbury, Hammersmith, Holland Park, Kensal Green, Kentish Town, Kilburn Park, Latimer Road, Leytonstone, North Ealing, Northfields, Regent's Park, Rotherhithe, Royal Albert, South Ealing, Southfields, St John's Wood, Surrey Quays, Tufnell Park, Wembley Park, Westminster, Whitechapel

12 Bethnal Green, Bromley-by-Bow, Cannon Street, Chancery Lane, Charing Cross, Chiswick Park, Clapham North, Clapham South, Colliers Wood, Covent Garden, Dagenham East, Ealing Common, East Finchley, Elverson Road, Euston Square, Finchley Road, Finsbury Park, Golders Green, Goldhawk Road, Goodge Street, Holloway Road, Lambeth North, London Bridge, Mansion House, New Cross Gate, Oxford Circus, Parsons Green, Prince Regent, Putney Bridge, Seven Sisters, Sloane Square, Stepney Green, St James's Park, Swiss Cottage, Tower Gateway, Turnham Green, Turnpike Lane, Warren Street, West Brompton

13 Clapham Common, Gallions Reach, Hendon Central, Island Gardens, Knightsbridge, Ladbroke Grove, Lancaster Gate, Rickmansworth, Royal Victoria, Russell Square, Shepherd's Bush, Stamford Brook, Tottenham Hale, Warwick Avenue, West Hampstead, West India Quay, Wimbledon Park

14 Blackhorse Road, Caledonian Road, Deptford Bridge, Ealing Broadway, Fulham Broadway, Gloucester Road, Hyde Park Corner, North Greenwich, South Wimbledon, Westbourne Park, West Kensington, Willesden Green

15 Finchley Central, Harrow-on-the-Hill, Hounslow Central, Leicester Square, Liverpool Street, Notting Hill Gate, Pudding Mill Lane, Ravenscourt Park, South Kensington, Stonebridge Park, Tooting Broadway

---

lone

03 one **04** lane, only, sole **05** alone **06** barren, remote, single **07** widowed **08** deserted, desolate, divorced, forsaken, isolated, secluded, separate, solitary **09** abandoned, on your own, separated, unmarried **10** by yourself, unattached **11** out-of-the-way, uninhabited **12** unfrequented **15** without a partner

loneliness

08 solitude **09** aloneness, isolation, seclusion **10** desolation **12** lonesomeness, solitariness

lonely

03 sad **04** lone **05** alone, unked, unket, unkid **06** barren, remote **07** outcast, unhappy **08** deserted, desolate, forsaken, isolated, lonesome, rejected, secluded, solitary, wretched **09** abandoned, destitute, miserable, reclusive **10** friendless **11** god-forsaken, out-of-the-way, uninhabited **12** solitudinous, unfrequented **13** companionless, unaccompanied

loner

06 hermit **07** recluse **08** lone wolf, solitary **09** introvert **13** individualist **14** solitudinarian

lonesome

03 sad **04** lone **05** alone **06** barren, lonely, remote **07** outcast, unhappy **08** deserted, desolate, forsaken, isolated, rejected, secluded, solitary, wretched **09** abandoned, destitute, miserable, reclusive **10** friendless **11** out-of-the-way, uninhabited **12** unfrequented **13** companionless, unaccompanied

long

01 L **03** ake, die, far, yen **04** ache, hope, itch, lang, leng, lust, pant, pine, side, slow, tall, want, wish **05** covet, crave, dream, longa, tardy, yearn **06** desire, hanker, hunger, thirst **07** lengthy, spun out, tedious, verbose **08** expanded, extended, marathon, overlong **09** diuturnal, elongated, expansive, extensive, prolonged, spread out, stretched, sustained **10** protracted **11** far-reaching **12** interminable, long-drawn-out, stretched out

See also **want**

• before long

04 soon **07** by and by, shortly **09** in a moment, presently **12** in a short time **14** in a minute or two **15** in the near future

• long ago

03 eld **04** yore

• Long Island

02 LI

• long live

04 viva, vive **05** vivat **08** zindabad

long-drawn-out

06 prolix **07** lengthy, spun out, tedious **08** long-spun, marathon, overlong **09** long-drawn, prolonged **10** dragging on, long-winded, protracted **12** interminable, overextended

longer

04 more

• no longer

02 ex

longing

03 yen **04** avid, earn, erne, hope, itch, lust, urge, wish **05** brame, crave, dream, eager, greed, yearn **06** ardent, desire, hunger, hungry, pining, thirst **07** anxious, craving, wanting, wishful, wistful **08** ambition, appetent, coveting, desirous, yearning **09** breathing, cacoethes, hankering, hungering **10** aspiration, desiderium **11** languishing

longingly

06 avidly, wistly **07** eagerly **08** ardently **09** anxiously, wishfully, wistfully **10** yearningly

long-lasting

07 abiding, chronic **08** enduring, unfading **09** lingering, permanent, prolonged **10** continuing, protracted, unchanging **12** imperishable, long-standing

long-lived

07 durable, lasting **08** enduring **09** longevous, macrobian, vivacious **11** long-lasting, macrobiotic **12** long-standing

long-standing

07 abiding **08** enduring **09** long-lived **11** established, long-lasting, traditional **12** time-honoured **15** long-established, well-established

long-suffering

07 patient, stoical **08** resigned, tolerant **09** easy-going, forgiving, indulgent **10** forbearant, forbearing **13** uncomplaining

long-winded

05 wordy **06** prolix **07** diffuse, lengthy, tedious, verbose, voluble **08** overlong, rambling **09** garrulous, prolonged **10** discursive, protracted **11** repetitious **12** long-drawn-out

long-windedness

08 longueur **09** garrulity, macrology, prolixity, verbosity, wordiness **10** volubility **11** diffuseness, lengthiness, tediousness **14** discursiveness **15** repetitiousness

loo

02 WC **03** bog, lav **04** john, kazi, love, toot **05** dunny, Elsan®, gents', privy **06** ladies', throne, toilet, urinal **07** crapper, latrine **08** bathroom, lavatory, Portaloo®, rest room, superloo, washroom **09** cloakroom, lanterloo **10** facilities, powder room **11** convenience, water closet **12** smallest room **14** comfort station, little boys' room **15** little girls' room

See also **toilet**

look

02 hi, la, lo, oi **03** air, eye, ray, see, spy **04** deek, ecce, ecco, face, gape, gawp, gaze, geek, keek, leer, mien, peek, peep, peer, quiz, scan, seem, show, view, vise, vizy **05** check, decko, dekko, focus, front, frown, glout, guise, scowl, sight, squiz, stare, study, visie, watch **06** appear, aspect, behold, blench, effect, eyeful, façade, gander, give on, glance, gledge, manner, regard, review, shufti, shufty, squint, survey, take in, vision, vizzie **07** bearing, belgard, display, examine, exhibit, eyeball, front on, glimpse, inspect, observe **08** butcher's, consider, features, give on to, look onto, once-over, overlook, scrutiny **09** eye-glance, semblance, take a look **10** appearance, be opposite, complexion, expression, get a load of, impression, inspection, scrutinize **11** contemplate, countenance, examination, observation **12** butcher's hook, take a dekko at **13** contemplation, get an eyeful of, take a gander at, take a shufti at, take a squint at **14** give a going-over **15** give the once-over, run your eyes over

• look after
03 sit **04** heed, keep, mind, seek, tend **05** guard, nurse, see to, watch **06** expect **07** babysit, care for, protect **08** attend to, maintain **09** childmind, supervise, watch over **10** take care of **11** keep an eye on **12** take charge of

• look back
06 recall **08** remember **09** reminisce, think back **10** retrospect

• look down on
05 scorn, spurn **07** despise, disdain, sneer at **08** overpeer, pooh-pooh **09** disparage, patronize **10** talk down to **14** hold in contempt

• look for
04 seek **05** await, quest **06** expect **07** hunt for, hunt out **08** scavenge **09** forage for, search for, try to find **10** fossick out

• look forward to
05 await **06** expect **07** count on, hope for, long for, look for, wait for **08** envisage, envision **09** apprehend **10** anticipate

• look into
03 dig **05** delve, plumb, probe, study **06** fathom, go into **07** examine, explore, inspect **08** ask about, check out, look over, research **10** scrutinize, search into **11** investigate **12** inquire about

• look like
08 resemble **09** take after **11** be similar to, remind you of

• look on, look upon
03 eye **04** deem, hold, view **05** count, judge, think **06** regard **07** overeye **08** consider, spectate

• look out
04 mind **06** beware **07** Achtung, be alert **08** watch out **09** be careful **11** mind your eye **12** keep an eye out, pay attention **13** be on your guard, guard yourself **14** be on the qui vive

• look over
04 scan, view **05** check **07** examine, inspect, monitor, surview **08** check out **09** go through **11** look through, read through **13** cast an eye over, give a once-over **15** cast your eye over

• look to
05 await, besee, watch **06** expect, regard, rely on, turn to **07** count on, hope for, respect **08** consider, reckon on, resort to **10** anticipate, fall back on, think about **13** give thought to

• look up
04 find, seek **05** visit **06** call on, come on, drop by, perk up, pick up, stop by **07** advance, consult, develop, hunt for, improve **08** drop in on, look in on, progress, research **09** come along, get better, search for, track down **10** ameliorate **11** make headway, pay a visit to **12** make progress

• look up to
06 admire, esteem, honour, revere **07** respect **12** regard highly **13** think highly of

lookalike
04 spit, twin **05** clone, image **06** double, ringer **07** replica **10** dead ringer **11** living image **12** doppelgänger **13** exact likeness, spitting image

lookout
03 nit **04** huer, post, ward **05** guard, tower, watch, worry **06** affair, conder, conner, pigeon, sentry **07** concern, problem **08** business, cockatoo, prospect, sentinel, watchman, watch-out **10** speculator, watch-tower **14** responsibility **15** observation post

• keep a lookout
05 watch **09** keep guard **10** be vigilant **11** remain alert **14** be on the qui vive

loom
04 loon, rise, soar, tool **05** frame, mount, tower **06** appear, emerge, impend, menace **07** overtop **08** dominate, hang over, jacquard, overhang, threaten **09** implement, take shape **10** be imminent, overshadow, receptacle **13** become visible

loony
◇ *anagram indicator*
03 mad, nut **04** daft, hook, wild **05** barmy, crank, crazy, loopy, nutty, potty, silly **06** crazed, insane, madman, maniac, nutter, psycho, stupid **07** berserk, bonkers, foolish, frantic, idiotic, lunatic, nutcase, oddball, strange **08** crackpot, demented, deranged, headcase, imbecile, madwoman, unhinged **09** disturbed, eccentric, fruitcake, psychotic, screwball **10** basket case, distracted, distraught, psychopath, unbalanced

See also **madman, madwoman**

loop
01 O **03** eye, lug, tab, tie, tug **04** bend, coil, curl, fold, hank, hoop, join, kink, knop, knot, oval, purl, ring, roll, turn, wind **05** braid, curve, noose, pearl, picot, sling, snare, twirl, twist, whorl **06** becket, cannon, circle, eyelet, fasten, lasket, runner, spiral, stitch **07** connect, latchet **08** carriage, écraseur, encircle, loophole, surround **09** billabong, eye splice **10** curve round, rubber band **11** convolution, elastic band, jubilee clip

loophole
04 plea **06** escape, excuse, eyelet, get-out, let-out, wicket **07** evasion, mistake, pretext **08** omission, pretence **09** ambiguity **12** escape clause

loose
◇ *anagram indicator*
03 lax, off **04** ease, fast, free, lose, open, undo **05** baggy, broad, let go, losen, lowse, relax, shaky, shoot, slack, solve, unpen, untie, vague **06** detach, flabby, lessen, loosen, reduce, solute, unbind, undone, unhook, unknit, unlock, unmoor, untied, wanton, weaken, wobbly **07** at large, corrupt, escaped, flowing, general, hanging, immoral, inexact, movable, relaxed, release, sagging, set free, slacken, unbound, unclasp, unleash **08** diffused, diminish, insecure, liberate, moderate, rambling, released, unchaste, uncouple, unfasten, unlocked, unpicked, unsteady **09** abandoned, debauched, desultory, discharge, disengage, dissolute, imprecise, shapeless, uncoupled **10** degenerate, disconnect, ill-defined, inaccurate, incoherent, indefinite, indistinct, licentious, unattached, unconfined, unfastened, untethered **11** inattentive, light-heeled, promiscuous **12** disreputable, loose-fitting, unrestrained

• at a loose end
04 idle **05** bored, fed up **07** aimless, off duty **09** désoeuvré **11** out of action, purposeless **14** with time to kill **15** with nothing to do

• on the loose
04 free **07** at large, escaped **08** on the run **09** at liberty **10** unconfined

loosely
◇ *anagram indicator*
06 freely **07** baggily, broadly, movably, slackly, vaguely **09** generally, inexactly **10** insecurely, unsteadily **11** imprecisely, shapelessly **12** inaccurately

loosen
04 ease, free, undo **05** let go, loose, relax, untie **06** let out, unbind, unglue, weaken **07** deliver, release, set free, shake up, slacken, unscrew, work out **08** diminish, moderate, set loose, unfasten, unthread

• loosen up
05 let up, relax **06** cool it, ease up, go easy, lessen, unwind, warm up **07** prepare, work out **08** chill out, exercise, limber up, warm down **09** hang loose

loot
03 let, rob **04** haul, raid, sack, swag **05** booty, money, prize, rifle, steal **06** burgle, maraud, ravage, riches, spoils **07** despoil, pillage, plunder, ransack **08** pickings **09** steal from **10** lieutenant **11** stolen goods, stolen money

lop
03 cut **04** chop, clip, crop, dock, hack, sned, trim **05** prune, sever, shrub, trash **06** cut off, detach, reduce, remove,

shroud **07** curtail, shorten, take off **08** truncate **10** detruncate

lope
03 run **05** bound **06** canter, gallop, lollop, spring, stride

lopsided
05 askew **06** squint, uneven **07** crooked, slanted, sloping, tilting, unequal **08** one-sided **09** skew-whiff **10** off balance, unbalanced **12** asymmetrical

loquacious
05 gabby, gassy, wordy **06** chatty **07** gossipy, voluble **08** babbling **09** garrulous, speechful, talkative **10** blathering, chattering **12** multiloquent, multiloquous

loquacity
09 garrulity, gassiness **10** chattiness, multiloquy, volubility **12** effusiveness **13** multiloquence, talkativeness

lord
01 D **02** Ld **03** Dom, God, lud **04** duke, earl, Herr, kami, king, land, losh, peer, sire, tuan **05** baron, chief, count, Maker, noble, omrah, ruler **06** bishop, Christ, Father, leader, master, prince, Yahweh **07** captain, Creator, emperor, Eternal, Holy One, Jehovah, Messiah, monarch, Saviour, the Word **08** Almighty, governor, nobleman, overlord, Redeemer, seigneur, seignior, Son of God, Son of Man, superior, suzerain, viscount **09** commander, patrician, sovereign **10** aristocrat **11** Jesus Christ, King of kings **13** grand seigneur

See also **nobility**

• **lord it over**
06 act big **07** oppress, repress, swagger **08** domineer, pull rank **09** put on airs, tyrannize **10** boss around, overoffice **11** order around, queen it over **13** be overbearing

lordliness
05 pride **07** disdain, majesty **09** arrogance, grandness, nobleness **11** haughtiness, imperiality **12** magnificence, splendidness **13** big-headedness, condescension, imperiousness **14** high-handedness, impressiveness, overconfidence

lordly
05 grand, lofty, noble, proud **06** lavish, uppity **07** haughty, stately, stuck-up **08** arrogant, imperial, majestic, splendid **09** big-headed, dignified, grandiose, hubristic, imperious **10** disdainful, high-handed, hoity-toity, impressive, peremptory, tyrannical **11** dictatorial, domineering, magnificent, overbearing, patronizing, toffee-nosed **12** aristocratic, supercilious **13** condescending, high and mighty, overconfident

lore
04 lair, lare, lear, leir, lere **05** leare, myths, thong **06** cabala, kabala, wisdom **07** beliefs, cabbala, kabbala, legends, qabalah, sayings, stories **08** folklore, kabbalah, learning, teaching **09** erudition, knowledge, mythology **10** traditions **11** scholarship **13** superstitions

lorry
03 rig **04** drag **05** artic, float, truck, wagon **06** camion, pick-up, tipper **07** flatbed, trailer, vehicle **09** dump truck, Jugannath, semi-truck **10** juggernaut, removal van **11** dumper truck, semi-trailer **12** curtain-sider, double-bottom, flatbed truck, pantechnicon, trailer truck **13** drawbar outfit

lose
◇ *deletion indicator*
04 drop, fail, miss, tine, tyne **05** drain, elude, evade, leese, loose, losen, spend, use up, waste **06** expend, forget, go down, ignore, mislay, outrun **07** confuse, consume, deplete, exhaust, forfeit, fritter, get lost, neglect, not find **08** be beaten, bewilder, go astray, misplace, shake off, squander, throw off **09** disregard, dissipate, fall short, stray from **10** be defeated, depart from, escape from, stop having, wander from **11** be conquered, be taken away, come to grief, fail to grasp, leave behind **12** be bereaved of, be deprived of, be divested of, come a cropper, no longer have, suffer defeat **14** be unsuccessful **15** throw in the towel

• **lose out**
06 suffer **07** miss out **08** be beaten **14** be unsuccessful **15** be disadvantaged

• **lose yourself in something**
11 be riveted by **12** be absorbed in, be occupied in **13** be engrossed in, be taken up with **14** be captivated by, be enthralled by, be fascinated by **15** be preoccupied in

loser
04 flop **07** also-ran, failure, has-been, no-hoper, washout **08** dead loss, runner-up, write-off **10** non-starter **11** the defeated

loss
04 dead, debt, harm, hurt, miss **05** traik, waste **06** damage, defeat, tinsel **07** default, deficit, missing, undoing, wastage, wounded **08** casualty, decrease, deprival, dropping, fatality **09** death toll, detriment, disprofit, mislaying, privation **10** deficiency, diminution, forfeiture, forgetting, impairment **11** bereavement, deprivation, destruction **12** disadvantage, endamagement, misplacement **13** disappearance, dispossession

• **at a loss**
03 out **04** will, wull **07** at fault, baffled, puzzled **09** mystified, perplexed **10** bewildered, nonplussed

lost
◇ *anagram indicator*
04 dead, gone, lore, lorn, past, tint **05** stray, tyned **06** astray, bygone, cursed, damned, doomed, dreamy, fallen, former, missed, ruined, wasted, way-out **07** at a loss, baffled, defunct, extinct, forlorn, mislaid, missing, puzzled, riveted, strayed, wrecked **08** absorbed, amissing, confused, occupied, vanished **09** condemned, destroyed, engrossed, misplaced, neglected, off course, perplexed **10** bewildered, captivated, demolished, enthralled, fascinated, nonplussed, spellbound, squandered **11** disappeared, disoriented, out of the way, preoccupied, taken up with, untraceable **12** absent-minded, irredeemable **13** disorientated, frittered away, long-forgotten, unrecoverable **14** gone for a Burton

• **be lost**
04 tine, tyne

• **lost cause**
04 flop **07** also-ran, has-been, no-hoper, washout **08** dead loss, write-off **10** non-starter **12** hopeless case **14** hopeless person

lot, lots
03 cut, due, erf, set, tax **04** fall, fate, gobs, luck, many, part, plot, raft, scad, sort, tons **05** batch, bunch, cavel, crowd, group, heaps, loads, miles, piece, piles, quota, scads, share, weird **06** bundle, dozens, masses, oodles, parcel, ration, shower, stacks **07** destiny, fortune, portion **08** heritage, hundreds, jingbang, lashings, millions, quantity **09** a good deal, allotment, allowance, a quantity, gathering, shedloads, situation, sortilege, thousands **10** a great deal, assortment, collection, divination, percentage **11** bucketloads, consignment, great number, large amount, piece of land **13** circumstances, piece of ground

See also **fate**; **number**

• **a lot**
04 much, scad, slew, slue **05** loads, often **06** barrel **09** any amount **10** a great deal, frequently **12** for a long time **14** to a great degree, to a great extent

• **throw in your lot with**
06 muck in **07** pitch in **10** join forces, take part in, team up with **11** combine with **14** join forces with

lotion
04 balm, wash **05** cream, salve, scrub, toner **06** balsam, tanner **07** eyewash, washing **08** aftersun, cleanser, eye-water, lavatory, liniment, ointment **09** blackwash, collyrium, emollient, sunscreen **10** aftershave, astringent, witch-hazel, yellow wash **11** arquebusade, embrocation, fomentation **12** hairdressing, retinoic acid

lottery
04 draw, luck, risk **05** bingo, lotto, Tatts **06** chance, gamble, hazard, raffle

07 tombola, venture 08 art union
10 Golden Kiwi, sweepstake
11 speculation 12 gambling game

loud
01 f 02 ff 03 big 04 bold, high
05 brash, flash, forte, gaudy, lairy, noisy, rowdy, showy 06 brassy, brazen, flashy, garish, shrill, vulgar 07 blaring, booming, glaring, raucous, roaring
08 emphatic, gorblimy, piercing, plangent, resonant, strident, vehement
09 clamorous, deafening, gorblimey, insistent, obtrusive, tasteless
10 aggressive, flamboyant, fortissimo, resounding, stentorian, streperous, strepitant, thundering, vociferous
11 ear-piercing, full-mouthed, loud-mouthed, penetrating 12 ear-splitting, ostentatious 13 reverberating

• very loud
02 ff

loudly
01 f 02 ff 03 out 05 aloud, forte
07 lustily, noisily, shrilly 08 strongly
10 fortissimo, stridently, vehemently, vigorously 11 clamorously, deafeningly
12 resoundingly, streperously, strepitantly, uproariously, vociferously

• very loudly
02 ff

loudmouth
04 brag 06 gasbag 07 boaster, windbag 08 big mouth, blowhard, braggart 09 blusterer, swaggerer
11 braggadocio

loud-mouthed
04 bold 05 noisy 06 brazen, coarse, vulgar 08 boasting, bragging
10 aggressive, blustering

loudness

• unit of loudness
04 phon, sone

loudspeaker
06 woofer 07 tweeter 09 subwoofer

lough *see* **lake**

Louisiana
02 LA

lounge
04 hawm, idle, laze, loll 05 daker, relax, slump 06 dacker, daiker, lollop, repose, sprawl 07 day room, lie back, parlour, recline 08 kill time, lie about
09 front room, lie around, loll about, waste time 10 living room, take it easy
11 drawing room, sitting room
13 reception room

See also **laze**

lour, lower
04 loom 05 frown, glare, scowl
06 darken, glower, impend, menace
07 blacken 08 threaten 09 be brewing, cloud over 11 look daggers
14 give a dirty look

louring, lowering
04 dark, grey, grim 05 black, gurly, heavy 06 cloudy, gloomy 07 ominous
08 menacing, overcast 09 darkening, impending 10 forbidding, foreboding
11 threatening

louse
03 nit

See also **contemptible**

lousy
◇ *anagram indicator*
03 bad, ill, low 04 crap, poor, ropy, sick
05 awful, mingy, pants, ropey, rough, seedy 06 chatty, mouldy, no good, poorly, queasy, rotten, unwell
07 rubbish 08 below par, crawling, inferior, pathetic, terrible
09 miserable, off-colour, pedicular
10 inadequate, out of sorts, pediculous, second-rate
12 contemptible 14 unsatisfactory
15 under the weather

lout
03 bow, hob, lob, oaf, oik, yob
04 boor, calf, clod, coof, cuif, dolt, gawk, hick, hoon, jake, slob, swad
05 flout, loord, stoop, yahoo, yobbo
06 lubber 07 bumpkin, hallian, hallion, hallyon, lumpkin 08 bull-calf, loblolly
09 barbarian, roughneck
10 clodhopper 11 bushwhacker, chuckle-head, hobbledehoy

loutish
04 rude 05 crude, gawky, gruff, rough
06 coarse, oafish, rustic, vulgar
07 boorish, doltish, ill-bred, uncouth, yobbish 08 churlish, clownish, ignorant, impolite 09 unrefined
10 uneducated, unmannerly
11 clodhopping, ill-mannered, uncivilized

lovable, loveable
04 cute, dear 05 sweet 06 lovely, taking 07 amiable, likable, winsome
08 adorable, charming, engaging, fetching, likeable, pleasing
09 appealing, endearing 10 attractive, bewitching, delightful, enchanting
11 captivating

love
01 O 03 lo'e, loo, luv, nil, pet 04 amor, care, dear, doat, dote, Eros, lust, zeal, zero 05 adore, agape, amour, angel, Cupid, enjoy, fancy, honey, prize, sugar, taste 06 ardour, desire, dote on, liking, nought, poppet, regard, relish, savour, warmth 07 acushla, asthore, beloved, be mad on, care for, charity, cherish, concern, darling, dearest, dear one, delight, idolize, long for, machree, nothing, passion, rapture, sweetie, worship 08 amorance, be daft on, be fond of, be nuts on, be sold on, devotion, fondness, hold dear, intimacy, kindness, pleasure, precious, soft spot, sympathy, treasure, weakness 09 adoration, adulation, affection, be sweet on, delight in, enjoyment, favourite, Platonics, tendresse 10 appreciate, attachment, compassion, friendship, jeune amour, mavourneen, partiality, sweetheart, tenderness 11 amorousness, be devoted to, be partial to, brotherhood, inclination, infatuation, Platonicism
12 appreciation, belle passion, Frauendienst, have a crush on, like very much 13 amour courtois, be attracted to 14 have a liking for, have the hots for, take pleasure in 15 think the world of

• fall in love with
05 fancy 06 take to 07 fall for 09 have it bad 12 be crazy about, have a crush on, take a shine to 13 have a thing for
15 burn with passion, lose your heart to

• in love with
06 doting, hooked, soft on
07 charmed, smitten, stuck on, sweet on 08 besotted, mad about, mashed on 09 enamoured, nuts about, wild about 10 crazy about, infatuated, potty about 11 attracted to, enamoured of 12 have a crush on

• love affair
05 amour, fling 06 affair 07 carry-on, liaison, passion, romance 08 amour fou, intrigue 12 relationship 13 grande passion

• make love
09 philander, sleep with 11 go to bed with, have sex with 13 sleep together

loveable *see* **lovable**

loveless
03 icy 04 cold, hard 06 frigid
07 unloved 08 disliked, forsaken, unloving, unvalued 09 heartless, unfeeling 10 friendless, unfriendly
11 cold-hearted, insensitive, passionless, uncherished
12 unresponsive 13 unappreciated

lovelorn
06 pining 07 longing 08 desiring, lovesick, yearning 10 infatuated
11 languishing

lovely
04 fair 05 nasty, super, sweet
06 dreamy, pretty 07 amorous, winning 08 adorable, charming, handsome, pleasant, pleasing
09 agreeable, beautiful, enjoyable, exquisite, ravishing, wonderful
10 attractive, delightful, enchanting, marvellous 11 beautifully, good-looking 12 delightfully

lover
03 fan, lad 04 beau, bird, buff, date
05 fella, fiend, flame, freak, leman
06 fiancé, friend, suitor, toy boy
07 admirer, amorist, amoroso, beloved, devotee, fanatic, fiancée, partner, servant 08 amoretto, follower, lady love, loved one, mistress, other man, paramour, Platonic 09 boyfriend, man friend, philander, supporter
10 enthusiast, girlfriend, lady friend, other woman, sweetheart 11 woman friend 12 bit on the side 13 live-in partner

Lovers include:

04 Bess, Dido, Eros, Eyre (Jane), Hera, Hero, Ilsa, Joan, Lamb (Lady Caroline), Rick, Sand (George), Zeus

05 Byron (Lord), Cathy, Clyde, Dante, Darby, Darcy (Mr), Harry, Helen, Laura, O'Hara (Scarlett), Paris, Porgy, Pwyll, Romeo, Sally, Tracy (Spencer)
06 Aeneas, Antony, Bacall (Lauren), Bogart (Humphrey), Bonnie, Burton (Richard), Butler (Rhett), Caesar, Chopin, Isolde, Juliet, Marian (Maid), Nelson (Lord), Psyche, Samson, Taylor (Elizabeth), Thisbe
07 Abelard, Barrett (Elizabeth), Bennett (Elizabeth), Delilah, Don Juan, Héloïse, Hepburn (Katharine), Leander, Louis XV, Mellors, Orlando, Orpheus, Pyramus, Rimbaud, Simpson (Mrs), Tristan, Troilus, Vronsky (Count)
08 Beatrice, Benedick, Browning (Robert), Casanova (Giacomo Girolamo), Cressida, Eurydice, Hamilton (Lady Emma), Karenina (Anna), Lancelot, Lothario, Napoleon, Nell Gwyn, Odysseus, Penelope, Petrarch, Rhiannon, Rosalind, Verlaine
09 Charles II, Cleopatra, Guinevere, Joséphine, Launcelot, Pompadour (Madame de), Robin Hood, Rochester (Mr), Valentino (Rudolph)
10 Chatterley (Lady), Edward VIII, Heathcliff

lovesick
06 pining **07** longing **08** desiring, lovelorn, yearning **10** infatuated
11 languishing

love story
07 romance

loving
04 fond, kind, warm **06** ardent, caring, doting, lovely, tender **07** adoring, amorous, devoted **08** beloving, friendly **10** passionate **11** sympathetic, warmhearted **12** affectionate

lovingly
06 fondly, warmly **08** ardently, tenderly **12** passionately
14 affectionately **15** sympathetically

low
03 bad, law, moo, sad **04** base, bass, blue, deep, down, dull, evil, flat, glum, hill, late, mean, meek, mild, poor, rich, sale, slow, soft **05** a snip, blaze, cheap, early, fed up, flame, hedge, lowly, muted, nadir, nasty, plain, quiet, scant, short, small, squat **06** a steal, bellow, bottom, coarse, common, gentle, gloomy, humble, humbly, hushed, junior, little, meagre, modest, paltry, ribald, ribaud, scanty, scarce, shabby, simple, smutty, sparse, sunken, vulgar, wicked **07** adverse, debased, foolish, heinous, hostile, immoral, low-born, muffled, obscene, obscure, peasant, reduced, rybauld, shallow, slashed, stunted, subdued, tumulus, unhappy
08 degraded, dejected, depraved, dog-cheap, downcast, indecent, inferior, low-lying, low point, mediocre, moderate, negative, opposing, ordinary, plebeian, resonant, sea-level, sonorous, trifling
09 dastardly, deficient, depressed, dirt-cheap, knock-down, miserable, quietened, ten a penny, whispered
10 all-time low, cheesed off, despicable, despondent, inadequate, low-pitched, low-ranking, reasonable, rock-bottom, submissive
11 downhearted, ground-level, inexpensive, lowest point, low-spirited, subordinate, unimportant
12 antagonistic, contemptible, disconsolate, disheartened, insufficient, low-watermark, unfavourable **13** below standard, dishonourable, going for a song, insignificant, unintelligent **14** down in the dumps, unsatisfactory

low-born
04 poor **05** lowly **06** humble
07 obscure, peasant, plebean, villain
08 mean-born, plebeian **09** unexalted
10 low-ranking

lowbrow
04 rude **05** crude **07** tabloid
08 ignorant **09** unlearned, unrefined
10 downmarket, mass-market, uncultured, uneducated, unlettered
11 unscholarly **12** uncultivated

lowdown
03 gen **04** base, data, dope, info, mean, news, vile **05** facts **07** caitiff
08 shameful, wretched **09** dastardly, degrading, loathsome, reprobate, worthless **10** abominable, despicable, detestable, disgusting **11** disgraceful, information, inside story
12 contemptible, disreputable, intelligence **13** dishonourable, reprehensible

lower
03 cow, cut, dip **04** drop, hush, sink, vail **05** abase, abate, couch, demit, lowly, minor, slash, stoop, under
06 bottom, debase, demean, dilute, embace, embase, humble, imbase, junior, lessen, lesser, nether, reduce, settle, submit **07** beneath, cheapen, curtail, degrade, depress, descend, let down, let fall, quieten, set down
08 belittle, bring low, decrease, diminish, disgrace, inferior, look down, low-level, move down, take down
09 bring down, dishonour, disparage, secondary, undermost **10** nethermore, underneath **11** second-class, subordinate **12** speak quietly **13** move downwards

See also **lour, lower**

• lower in estimation
04 less

lowering
03 ebb **04** dark, drop, duck, grey, grim
05 black, gurly, heavy **06** cloudy, gloomy **07** ominous, sinking
08 menacing, overcast, reducing
09 darkening, degrading, demission, impending, reduction **10** depression, forbidding, foreboding
11 degradation, letting down, threatening

See also **louring, lowering**

lowest
03 net **04** nett

low-grade
03 bad **04** naff, poor, poxy, ropy
05 awful, lousy, pants, ropey
06 crummy **07** botched, the pits, useless **08** inferior, pathetic, terrible
09 cheap-jack, third-rate **10** second-rate **11** a load of crap, poor-quality, second-class, substandard **13** below standard **14** a load of garbage, a load of rubbish, not up to scratch

low-key
04 soft **05** muted, quiet **06** slight, subtle **07** relaxed, subdued **09** easy-going **10** restrained, undramatic
11 understated

lowliness
07 modesty, poverty **08** humility, meekness, mildness **09** obscurity
10 commonness, simplicity
11 inferiority **12** ordinariness, unimportance **14** submissiveness
15 subordinateness

lowly
04 base, mean, meek, mild, poor
05 plain **06** common, humble, junior, modest, simple **07** low-born, obscure, peasant **08** inferior, ordinary, plebeian
10 low-ranking, submissive
11 subordinate, unimportant

low-pitched
03 low **04** bass, deep, rich
08 resonant, sonorous

low-spirited
03 low, sad **04** down, glum **05** dowie, fed up, moody **06** gloomy
07 unhappy **08** dejected, downcast
09 depressed, miserable **10** cheesed off, despondent **11** discouraged, downhearted **12** heavy-hearted
14 down in the dumps

loyal
04 feal, firm, leal, true **06** stanch, trusty
07 devoted, sincere, staunch
08 constant, faithful, reliable
09 committed, dedicated, patriotic, steadfast **10** dependable, supportive, unchanging **11** true-hearted, trustworthy **12** well-affected

loyalty
06 fealty, lealty **08** devotion, fidelity
09 constancy, sincerity **10** allegiance, commitment, dedication, patriotism
11 reliability, staunchness
12 faithfulness **13** dependability, esprit de corps, steadfastness
15 trustworthiness

lozenge
05 rhomb **06** cachou, jujube, rustre, tablet, troche **07** gumdrop, rhombus
08 pastille, trochisk **09** cough drop
10 trochiscus

LSD
04 acid
• **LSD experience**
04 trip

lubber
03 oaf, yob **04** boor, clod, dolt, gawk, hick, lout, slob, swab **05** yahoo, yobbo **07** bumpkin **09** barbarian **10** clodhopper **11** hobbledehoy

lubberly
05 crude, dense, gawky **06** clumsy, coarse, oafish **07** awkward, doltish, loutish, lumpish, uncouth **08** bungling, churlish, clownish, ungainly **09** lumbering **10** blundering **11** clodhopping, heavy-handed

lubricant
03 fat, oil **04** lard, lube **06** ben-oil, grease **07** K-Y® jelly **08** oil of ben, ointment, Vaseline® **11** lubrication **14** petroleum jelly

lubricate
03 oil, wax **04** ease, help, lard, lube **05** bribe, smear **06** assist, grease, polish, smooth **07** advance, forward, further, promote, speed up **08** expedite **09** encourage **10** accelerate, facilitate, make easier, make smooth **12** smooth the way

luce
03 ged

lucid
04 pure, sane **05** clear, plain, sober, sound **06** bright, glassy, limpid **07** beaming, evident, obvious, radiant, shining **08** distinct, explicit, gleaming, luminous, pellucid, rational, sensible **09** brilliant, effulgent **10** diaphanous, reasonable **11** clear-headed, crystalline, of sound mind, perspicuous, resplendent, translucent, transparent **12** compos mentis, intelligible **14** comprehensible

lucidity
06 sanity **07** clarity **09** plainness, soundness **11** rationality **12** compos mentis **14** reasonableness **15** clear-headedness, intelligibility

lucidly
07 clearly, plainly **09** evidently, obviously **10** explicitly **12** intelligibly **14** comprehensibly

luck
03 hap **04** fate, joss, seal, seel, seil, sele **05** break, fluke **06** chance, hazard **07** destiny, fortune, godsend, success **08** accident, fortuity, good luck, the stars **10** prosperity, providence **11** good fortune, serendipity **14** predestination
• **bad luck**
06 hoodoo, mishap, mozzle **07** ambs-ace, ames-ace **08** deuce-ace **09** hard lines, mischance **10** hard cheese, ill fortune **12** misadventure
• **bring bad luck**
03 hex **04** jinx
• **good luck**
05 sonce, sonse **06** prosit **07** wassail **08** godspeed, waes hail **09** drink hail **11** bonne chance
• **in luck**
05 happy, jammy **06** timely **08** favoured **09** fortunate, opportune **10** advantaged, auspicious, successful
• **out of luck**
07 hapless, unlucky **08** luckless **11** unfortunate **12** inauspicious, unsuccessful **13** disadvantaged **14** down on your luck

luckily
07 happily **08** by chance **10** by accident, by good luck, mercifully **11** fortunately **12** fortuitously, propitiously **14** providentially

luckless
06 cursed, doomed, jinxed **07** hapless, unhappy, unlucky **08** hopeless, ill-fated **09** miserable **10** calamitous, disastrous, ill-starred **11** fortuneless, star-crossed, unfortunate **12** catastrophic, unpropitious, unsuccessful

lucky
05 canny, happy, jammy, tinny **06** chancy, in luck, spawny, timely **07** chancey, charmed **08** favoured **09** departure, expedient, fortunate, opportune, promising **10** auspicious, fortuitous, just as well, propitious, prosperous, successful **12** providential
• **lucky chance**
03 hit

lucrative
07 gainful **08** well-paid **10** high-paying, productive, profitable, worthwhile **11** moneymaking **12** advantageous, profit-making, remunerative

lucratively
09 gainfully **10** profitably **12** productively **14** advantageously, remuneratively

lucre
03 pay **04** cash, dosh, gain **05** brass, bread, dough, dross, gains, lolly, money, ready **06** income, mammon, profit, riches, spoils, wealth **07** profits, readies **08** greenies, proceeds, winnings **11** spondulicks **12** remuneration

ludicrous
◇ *anagram indicator*
03 odd **04** zany **05** comic, crazy, droll, funny, silly **06** absurd **07** amusing, comical, risible **08** farcical, humorous, sportive **09** burlesque, eccentric, grotesque, hilarious, laughable **10** outlandish, ridiculous **11** nonsensical **12** preposterous
• **something ludicrous**
04 jest

ludicrously
08 absurdly **09** laughably **11** grotesquely, hilariously **12** outlandishly, ridiculously **13** nonsensically **14** preposterously

lug
03 ear, tow, tug **04** bear, drag, haul, hump, lift, loop, pole, pull, tote **05** carry, heave, stick **06** handle

luggage
04 gear **05** stuff, traps **06** things **07** baggage, clobber **10** belongings **11** impedimenta **13** paraphernalia

Luggage includes:

03 bag, box
04 case, grip
05 chest, trunk
06 basket, hamper, kitbag, valise
07 holdall, satchel
08 backpack, knapsack, rucksack, suitcase
09 briefcase, flight bag, haversack, portfolio, travel bag
10 vanity-case
11 attaché case, hand-luggage, portmanteau
12 Gladstone bag, overnight bag

lugubrious
03 sad **04** glum **06** dismal, dreary, gloomy, morose, sombre, woeful **07** baleful, doleful, serious **08** funereal, mournful **09** sorrowful, woebegone **10** lachrymose, melancholy, sepulchral

lugworm
03 lob **07** lobworm

lukewarm
03 lew **04** cool **05** tepid **07** coolish, warmish **09** apathetic, impassive, Laodicean **11** half-hearted, indifferent, unconcerned **12** slightly warm, uninterested, unresponsive **14** unenthusiastic

lull
04 calm, ease, hush **05** abate, allay, let-up, pause, peace, quell, quiet, still **06** pacify, soothe, sopite, subdue **07** assuage, compose, silence, subside **08** calmness **09** stillness **11** quieten down **12** tranquillity

lullaby
05 baloo **07** hushaby **08** berceuse **10** cradle song

lumber
04 junk, land, load, pawn, plod, wood **05** clump, stamp, stump, trash **06** burden, charge, hamper, impose, jumble, prison, raffle, refuse, rumble, saddle, timber, trudge **07** clutter, rubbish, shamble, shuffle, stumble, trundle **08** encumber, imprison, pawnshop **10** flirtation **11** odds and ends **13** bits and pieces

lumbering
05 heavy **06** bovine, clumsy **07** awkward, hulking, lumpish, massive **08** bumbling, ungainly, unwieldy **09** ponderous **10** blundering **11** elephantine, heavy-footed

lumen
02 lm, lu

luminary
03 VIP **04** star **05** celeb **06** bigwig, candle, expert, leader, worthy **07** big name, notable **09** authority, celebrity, dignitary, personage, superstar
12 leading light

luminence
01 L
• **amount of luminence**
03 nit

luminescent
06 bright **07** glowing, radiant, shining
08 luminous **09** effulgent **10** luciferous
11 fluorescent **14** phosphorescent

luminosity
04 glow **05** light **06** lustre **08** radiance
10 brightness, brilliance
12 fluorescence, illumination

luminous
03 lit **05** clear, lucid **06** bright
07 glowing, lighted, radiant, shining
08 dazzling, lustrous **09** brilliant, effulgent **11** fluorescent, illuminated, illustrious, luminescent

lump
03 bur, cob, dab, dad, dod, gob, lob, nub, nut, pat, wad **04** ball, bear, bees, bump, burr, cake, clat, clod, core, daud, dawd, fuse, hunk, knob, knot, knub, loaf, mass, nirl, node, pool, rock, slub, slug, take **05** blend, block, bolus, brook, bulge, bunch, chuck, chump, chunk, claut, clump, crowd, gnarl, group, hunch, knarl, lunch, piece, plook, plouk, slump, stand, thole, tuber, unite, wedge, wodge **06** bruise, bunion, dallop, dollop, endure, gather, gobbet, growth, nodule, nubble, nugget, suffer, tumour **07** cluster, collect, combine, dislike, knubble, pustule, stomach, swallow **08** bear with, coalesce, swelling, tolerate
09 carbuncle, put up with
10 concretion, protrusion, tumescence
11 consolidate, mix together, put together **12** conglomerate, protuberance

lumpish
04 dull **05** gawky, gross, heavy
06 clumsy, oafish, obtuse, stolid, stupid, sullen **07** awkward, boorish, doltish, hulking **08** bungling, ungainly
09 lethargic, lumbering **10** dull-witted
11 elephantine

lumpy
04 slub **05** bumpy **06** cloggy, grainy, nodose, nodous **07** bunched, clotted, curdled, grumose, grumous, knobbly
08 granular **09** congealed
10 coagulated

Luna
06 Selene

lunacy
05 folly, mania **06** idiocy **07** inanity, madness **08** dementia, insanity, nonsense **09** absurdity, craziness, silliness, stupidity **10** aberration, imbecility **11** derangement, foolishness, moon-madness
12 dementedness, illogicality
13 irrationality, senselessness
14 outrageousness, ridiculousness
• **fit of lunacy**
04 lune

lunar *see* **Moon**

lunatic
◇ *anagram indicator*
03 mad **04** daft, nuts **05** barmy, crazy, inane, loony, loopy, nutty, potty, silly
06 absurd, insane, madman, maniac, nutter, psycho, stupid **07** bonkers, foolish, idiotic, nutcase, oddball
08 crackpot, demented, deranged, headcase, imbecile, madwoman, neurotic **09** disturbed, fruitcake, illogical, psychotic, senseless
10 irrational, moonstruck, psychopath, unbalanced **11** hare-brained, nonsensical **12** insane person, moon-stricken, round the bend **13** off your rocker, round the twist

lunch
04 tiff, tift **05** piece, snack **06** brunch, dinner, nacket, nocket, tiffin **07** tiffing
08 luncheon, nuncheon **10** light lunch, midday meal **11** packed lunch, Sunday lunch
• **out to lunch**
◇ *anagram indicator*
05 crazy

lunge
03 cut, hit, jab **04** dart, dash, dive, grab, leap, pass, poke, stab **05** bound, hit at **06** charge, grab at, plunge, pounce, spring, strike, thrust **08** fall upon, strike at **09** pitch into

lungs
• **goose lungs**
04 soul

lurch
04 list, reel, rock, roll, sway, swee, swey, veer, wait **05** filch, pitch, stoit
06 ambush, swerve, totter **07** defraud, stagger, stumble **09** forestall, overreach **11** weather roll
12 discomfiture
• **leave in the lurch**
04 fail **06** desert **07** abandon, let down **10** disappoint **13** leave stranded
15 leave high and dry

lure
03 jig **04** bait, draw, tole, toll **05** decoy, Devon, squid, stale, stool, tempt, train, troll **06** allure, carrot, entice, induce, lead on, seduce, trepan **07** attract, beguile, ensnare **08** inveigle
09 decoy-duck, honey-trap, seduction, spoonbait, spoonhook
10 allurement, attraction, enticement, inducement, temptation, trout-spoon
11 Devon minnow **12** trolling-bait
13 trolling-spoon **14** take a rise out of

lurid
04 gory, loud **05** showy, vivid
06 garish, Gothic, grisly, sultry
07 ghastly, glaring, graphic, intense, macabre **08** dazzling, explicit, gruesome, horrific, shocking
09 brilliant, brimstony, revolting, startling **11** exaggerated, sensational
12 melodramatic

luridly
07 vividly **08** garishly **09** intensely
10 explicitly, gruesomely, shockingly
11 brilliantly, graphically, revoltingly

lurk
04 dare, hide **05** dodge, prowl, skulk, slink, sneak, snoke, snook, snoop, snowk **06** crouch, lie low, loiter
07 swindle **09** lie in wait **15** conceal yourself

luscious
04 sexy **05** juicy, sweet, tasty, yummy
06 morish **07** cloying, fulsome, moreish, savoury **08** gorgeous, sensuous, smashing, stunning
09 beautiful, delicious, desirable, ravishing, succulent **10** appetizing, attractive, delectable, delightful, voluptuous **11** pleasurable, scrumptious **13** mouthwatering

lush
03 sot **04** posh, rich, soak, wino
05 alkie, dense, dipso, drink, drunk, grand, green, plush, ritzy, souse, toper
06 boozer, classy, glitzy, lavish, ornate, sponge, swanky **07** alcohol, bloater, drinker, fuddler, opulent, profuse, shicker, teeming, tippler, tosspot, verdant **08** abundant, drunkard, habitual, palatial, prolific **09** alcoholic, inebriate, luxuriant, luxurious, overgrown, sumptuous **10** wine-bibber **11** dipsomaniac, extravagant, flourishing, hard drinker **12** heavy drinker

lust
04 lech, will **05** greed **06** desire, hunger, libido, relish **07** avidity, craving, lechery, longing, passion, the hots **08** appetite, cupidity, lewdness, pleasure, yearning **09** horniness, prurience, randiness **10** greediness, sensuality **11** raunchiness, sexual drive
12 covetousness, sexual desire
13 concupiscence **14** lasciviousness, licentiousness
• **lust after**
04 need, want **05** covet, crave
06 desire, lecher, slaver **07** long for
08 yearn for **09** hunger for, thirst for

lustful
03 hot **04** lewd, rank **05** horny, radge, randy **06** carnal, randie, wanton
07 craving, goatish, rammish, raunchy, ruttish, sensual **08** prurient, unchaste
09 hankering, lecherous, lickerish, luxurious, salacious, venereous
10 cupidinous, lascivious, libidinous, licentious, passionate **12** concupiscent

lustily
04 hard **06** loudly **07** stoutly
08 heartily, robustly, strongly
10 forcefully, powerfully, vigorously

lustiness
05 power **06** energy, health, vigour **08** haleness, strength, virility **09** hardiness, stoutness, toughness **10** robustness, sturdiness **11** healthiness

lustre
04 fame, gaum, glow, gorm, silk **05** glare, gleam, glint, glory, gloss, merit, sheen, shine, water **06** credit, honour, renown **07** burnish, glitter, shimmer, sparkle, varnish **08** lambency, prestige, radiance, schiller **09** lovelight, splendour **10** brightness, brilliance, refulgence **11** distinction **12** resplendence **15** illustriousness

lustreless
03 mat **04** matt **05** matte

lustrous
05 glacé, shiny **06** bright, glossy, sheeny **07** glowing, lambent, radiant, shining **08** dazzling, gleaming, luminous **09** brilliant, burnished, sparkling, twinkling **10** glistening, glittering, shimmering

lusty
03 fit **04** hale, rank **05** beefy, bulky, frack, gutsy, stout, tough **06** hearty, lively, robust, rugged, strong, sturdy, virile **07** healthy, lustick **08** blooming, forceful, lustique, pleasant, pleasing, powerful, skelping, vigorous **09** energetic, strapping **13** hale and hearty

lute
03 oud **04** pipa **06** cither **07** bandura, cithern, cittern, dichord, pandora, pandore, theorbo **08** archlute, polyphon **09** orpharion, polyphone **10** chitarrone

lutetium
02 Lu

Luxembourg
01 L **03** LUX

luxuriance
06 excess **08** lushness, rankness, richness **09** abundance, denseness, fecundity, fertility, profusion **10** exuberance, exuberancy, lavishness, overgrowth **11** copiousness **13** sumptuousness

luxuriant
04 lush, rank, rich **05** ample, dense, fancy **06** fecund, florid, lavish, ornate, rococo **07** baroque, copious, fertile, flowery, opulent, profuse, riotous, teeming **08** abundant, prolific, thriving, tropical **09** elaborate, excessive, exuberant, plenteous, plentiful, sumptuous **10** flamboyant, productive **11** extravagant, overflowing **12** overabundant **13** superabundant

luxuriate
04 bask, grow **05** bloom, enjoy, revel **06** abound, frowst, relish, savour, thrive, wallow **07** burgeon, delight, indulge, prosper, relax in **08** flourish **09** have a ball **12** live in clover

luxurious
04 high, lush, posh, rich **05** cushy, grand, plush, ritzy **06** costly, de luxe, glitzy, lavish, plushy, silken, swanky **07** Apician, elegant, lustful, opulent **08** affluent, delicate, feastful, pampered, splendid **09** expensive, sumptuous **10** Babylonian, mollitious **11** comfortable, magnificent **13** self-indulgent, well-appointed

luxuriously
04 high **06** poshly **07** plushly **08** glitzily, lavishly, swankily **09** opulently **10** affluently **11** comfortably, deliciously, sumptuously **13** magnificently

luxury
03 pie **04** luxe, Ritz **05** extra, treat **06** dainty **07** comfort **08** delicacy, delicate, grandeur, hedonism, opulence, pleasure, richness **09** affluence, grand luxe, grandness, splendour **10** costliness, indulgence, wantonness **11** lap of luxury **12** extravagance, magnificence, milk and honey, satisfaction **13** expensiveness, gratification, sumptuousness **14** self-indulgence

lying
05 false **06** deceit **07** crooked, falsity, fibbing, leasing, perjury **08** two-faced **09** deceitful, dishonest, duplicity, falsehood, invention, white lies **10** dishonesty, mendacious, untruthful **11** crookedness, dissembling, fabrication, pseudologia **13** dissimulating, double-dealing, falsification **14** untruthfulness

lynch
04 hang, kill **06** dewitt **07** execute **08** string up **10** put to death **13** hang by the neck

lyre string
04 mese, nete **05** trite **06** hypate

lyric
03 lay, ode **04** lied, pean, song **05** melic, paean **06** poetic **07** melodic, musical **08** personal **09** emotional **10** passionate, subjective

lyrical
04 odic **06** poetic **07** musical **08** ecstatic, effusive, inspired, romantic **09** emotional, rapturous, rhapsodic **10** expressive, passionate **11** carried away, impassioned **12** enthusiastic

lyrically
09 musically **10** effusively, poetically **11** emotionally, rapturously **12** ecstatically, expressively, passionately, romantically

lyricist *see* **songwriter**

lyrics
04 book, text **05** words **08** libretto

M
02 em **04** Emma, Mike

macabre
◇ *anagram indicator*
04 gory, grim, sick **05** eerie, sicko **06** Gothic, grisly, morbid **07** ghastly, ghostly, hideous **08** chilling, dreadful, gruesome, horrible, horrific, shocking **09** frightful **10** terrifying **11** frightening

Macao
03 MAC

macaroni
04 zite, ziti **05** dandy **06** medley **10** rockhopper

mace
03 rod **04** club, maul **05** poker, staff, stick **06** cudgel

mace-bearer
05 bedel **06** beadle

Macedonia
02 MK **03** MKD

macerate
04 mash, pulp, soak **05** blend, steep **06** soften, squash **07** liquefy, mortify **08** marinade

Machiavellian
03 sly **04** foxy, wily **06** artful, astute, crafty, shrewd **07** cunning, devious **08** guileful, scheming **09** deceitful, designing, underhand **10** intriguing, perfidious **11** calculating, opportunist **12** unscrupulous **13** double-dealing

machination
04 plot, ploy, ruse, wile **05** cabal, dodge, trick **06** design, device, scheme, tactic **08** artifice, intrigue **09** manoeuvre, stratagem **10** conspiracy **11** shenanigans

machine
04 tool **05** motor, organ, robot **06** agency, device, engine, gadget, system, zombie **07** android, vehicle **08** catalyst, hardware, workings **09** apparatus, appliance, automaton, influence, mechanism, structure **10** instrument **11** contraption, contrivance **12** organization

machine-gun
02 MG **04** Bren **05** Maxim **07** Bren gun **08** Lewis gun, Maxim-gun **12** mitrailleuse

machinery
04 gear **05** tools **06** agency, system, tackle **07** channel **08** channels, gadgetry, workings **09** apparatus, equipment, mechanism, procedure, structure **11** instruments **12** organization

Machinery includes:

03 Cat®, JCB®
05 crane, dozer
06 digger, dumper, grader, jigger
07 dredger, grapple, gritter, skidder, tractor
08 dragline, dustcart, fork lift, jib crane
09 bulldozer, calfdozer, dump truck, excavator
10 angledozer, earthmover, pile-driver, road roller, snowplough, tower crane, tracklayer, truck crane, water crane
11 Caterpillar®, dumper truck, gantry crane, road-sweeper, wheel loader
12 cherry picker, crawler crane, luffing crane, pick-up loader
13 concrete mixer, floating crane, fork-lift truck, grabbing crane, platform hoist
14 container crane, crawler tractor, tractor-scraper
15 hydraulic shovel, luffing-jib crane, walking dragline

machinist
06 worker **08** mechanic, operator **09** operative **11** factory hand

machismo
08 maleness, strength, virility **09** manliness, toughness **11** masculinity

macrocosm
05 world **06** cosmos, entity, planet, system **07** culture, society **08** creation, humanity, totality, universe **09** community, structure **11** solar system **12** civilization, single entity

mad
◇ *anagram indicator*
03 ape, fay, fey, fie, wud **04** avid, bats, daft, fond, gyte, keen, loco, nuts, wild, wood, wowf, yond **05** angry, barmy, batty, berko, buggy, crazy, cross, daffy, dippy, dotty, flaky, gonzo, hasty, irate, livid, loony, loopy, manic, nutty, potty, queer, rabid, rapid, ratty, silly, spewy, wacko, wacky, wiggy **06** absurd, ardent, choked, crazed, cuckoo, fruity, fuming, insane, locoed, maniac, mental, raging, raving, red-mad, red-wud, screwy, stupid, troppo, whacko **07** bananas, barking, berserk, blazing, bonkers, cracked, crooked, devoted, enraged, excited, flipped, foolish, frantic, furious, hurried, idiotic, intense, lunatic, meshuga, red-wood, ropable, stroppy, uptight, violent, zealous **08** burned up, choleric, crackers, crackpot, demented, deranged, dingbats, doolally, frenetic, frenzied, hairless, in a paddy, in a strop, incensed, maniacal, meshugga, meshugge, reckless, unhinged, unstable, up in arms **09** abandoned, disturbed, energetic, fanatical, foolhardy, illogical, in a lather, infuriate, ludicrous, lymphatic, psychotic, raving mad, seeing red, ticked off, up the wall **10** aggravated, bestraught, distracted, distraught, frantic-mad, hopping mad, infatuated, infuriated, irrational, off the wall, off your nut, out to lunch, passionate, stone-crazy, unbalanced **11** disgruntled, fit to be tied, hare-brained, nonsensical, not all there, off the rails, off your head **12** crackbrained, enthusiastic, mad as a hatter, off your chump, on the warpath, preposterous, round the bend, uncontrolled, unreasonable, unrestrained **13** off your rocker, of unsound mind, out of your head, out of your mind, out of your tree, round the twist **14** off your trolley, wrong in the head **15** non compos mentis, out of your senses

• go mad
04 flip **05** go ape **06** blow up, wig out **07** go crazy **09** go bananas **11** flip your lid, go ballistic **15** lose your marbles

• like mad
06 avidly, wildly **07** quickly **09** furiously, hurriedly, zealously **11** fanatically, frantically **13** energetically

Madagascar
02 RM **03** MDG

madcap
04 cake, fury, rash, wild **05** crazy, silly **06** lively **07** flighty, hothead **08** crackpot, heedless, reckless, tearaway **09** daredevil, desperado, eccentric, firebrand, foolhardy, hotheaded, imprudent, impulsive **10** adventurer, ill-advised **11** birdbrained, hare-brained, thoughtless

madden
◇ *anagram indicator*
03 bug, irk, vex **05** anger, annoy, bemad, upset **06** enrage, hassle **07** agitate, incense, inflame, provoke **08** distract, irritate **09** aggravate, drive

nuts, infuriate **10** drive crazy, exasperate **13** get on your wick, get up your nose, get your back up **14** drive up the wall **15** get on your nerves, get your dander up

maddening
◇ *anagram indicator*
07 galling **08** annoying **09** upsetting, vexatious **10** disturbing, irritating **11** aggravating, infuriating, troublesome **12** exasperating

madder
04 chay **05** chaya, Rubia, shaya **07** alizari **08** gardenia **10** buttonbush

made
• **made it**
02 ff
• **recently made**
03 new

made-up
◇ *anagram indicator*
05 false **06** done up, unreal, untrue **07** painted **08** invented, mythical, powdered, specious **09** fairytale, fictional, imaginary, trumped-up **10** fabricated **11** make-believe **13** wearing make-up

madhouse
05 Babel, chaos **06** asylum, bedlam, mayhem, uproar **07** turmoil **08** disarray, disorder, loony bin, nuthouse **09** funny farm **11** pandemonium **13** lunatic asylum **14** mental hospital

madly
◇ *anagram indicator*
04 fast, very **06** wildly **07** crazily, hastily, rapidly, utterly **08** insanely **09** devotedly, excitedly, extremely, fervently, furiously, hurriedly, intensely, violently **10** completely, dementedly, frenziedly, recklessly **11** deliriously, exceedingly, frantically **12** distractedly, hysterically, irrationally, unreasonably **13** energetically, exceptionally

madman, madwoman
03 nut **04** gelt, kook **05** crank, loony **06** bedlam, maniac, nutter, psycho **07** cupcake, furioso, lunatic, nutcase, oddball **08** crackpot, frenetic, headcase, imbecile **09** bedlamite, fruitcake, psychotic, screwball **10** basket case, psychopath, Tom o' Bedlam

madness
◇ *anagram indicator*
03 ire **04** fury, rage, riot, zeal **05** anger, craze, folie, folly, mania, wrath **06** ardour, frenzy, lunacy, raving, uproar **07** abandon, inanity, passion **08** daftness, delusion, dementia, hysteria, insanity, keenness, nonsense, wildness **09** absurdity, agitation, craziness, furiosity, meshugaas, mishegaas, psychosis, silliness, stupidity, theomania **10** deliration, enthusiasm, excitement, fanaticism, insaneness **11** derangement, distraction, foolishness, infatuation, lycanthropy, unrestraint **12** exasperation, intoxication **13** foolhardiness, irrationality

madrigal
04 fa-la

madwoman *see* **madman, madwoman**

Mae
04 West

maelstrom
04 mess **05** chaos **06** bedlam, tumult, uproar, vortex **07** turmoil **08** disorder **09** Charybdis, confusion, whirlpool **10** turbulence **11** pandemonium

maestro
03 ace **06** expert, genius, master, wizard **07** prodigy **08** director, virtuoso **09** conductor

Mafia
06 the Mob **10** Cosa Nostra
• **Mafia boss**
03 don **04** capo **09** godfather
• **Mafia code**
06 omertà
• **Mafia member**
07 made man, pentito, soldier **09** goodfella

magazine
03 mag **04** pulp, zine **05** comic, depot, e-zine, paper, slick **06** glossy, lad mag, weekly **07** arsenal, fanzine, journal, monthly **08** carousel, ordnance **09** carrousel, quarterly **10** periodical, powder room, repository, storehouse, supplement **11** fortnightly, publication **12** contemporary **14** ammunition dump

See also **newspaper**

maggot
03 bot, fad **04** bott, mawk, whim, worm **06** gentle **09** fleshworm

Magi *see* **wise man** *under* **wise**

magic
03 ace, art **04** cool, mega, mojo, pull **05** brill, charm, curse, goety, great, spell, wicca **06** allure, hoodoo, occult, voodoo, wicked, wonder **07** conjury, demonic, glamour, gramary, mystery, sorcery **08** black art, charming, diablery, gramarye, hermetic, illusion, magnetic, prestige, romantic, smashing, spellful, stardust, terrific, trickery, wizardry **09** conjuring, deception, diablerie, excellent, magnetism, occultism, wonderful **10** allurement, bewitching, black magic, enchanting, enticement, entrancing, marvellous, mysterious, necromancy, tremendous, witchcraft **11** captivating, enchantment, fascinating, fascination, incantation, legerdemain, thaumaturgy **12** irresistible, metaphysical, spellbinding, supernatural **13** magical powers, sleight of hand, wonder-working

magical
05 magic **06** occult **07** demonic **08** charming, hermetic, spellful, stardust **09** wonderful **10** enchanting, hermetical, marvellous, mysterious **11** captivating, fascinating **12** spellbinding, supernatural

magician
03 ace **05** magus, pawaw, witch **06** expert, genius, master, powwow, wizard **07** juggler, maestro, warlock, wise man **08** conjurer, conjuror, sorcerer, virtuoso **09** archimage, enchanter **11** enchantress, illusionist, necromancer, spellbinder, spellworker, thaumaturge, witch doctor **12** wonder-worker **13** miracle-worker

magisterial
05 bossy **06** lordly **08** arrogant, despotic **09** assertive, imperious, masterful **10** commanding, high-handed, peremptory **11** dictatorial, domineering, overbearing **13** authoritarian, authoritative

magistrate
02 JP, RM **04** beak, cadi, doge, foud, kadi, qadi **05** amman, edile, judge, jurat, mayor, prior, reeve **06** aedile, amtman, avoyer, bailie, bailli, censor, cotwal, kotwal, pretor, sharif, sherif, syndic **07** alcalde, bailiff, baillie, burgess, justice, podestà, praetor, prefect, provost, shereef, tribune **08** dictator, landdros, mittimus, praefect, quaestor **09** landamman, landdrost, Lord Mayor, novus homo, portreeve, proconsul **10** corregidor, landammann, propraetor **11** baron bailie, burgomaster, field cornet, gonfalonier, stipendiary

magnanimity
05 mercy **07** charity **08** altruism, kindness, largesse, nobility **10** generosity, liberality **11** beneficence, benevolence, forgiveness, munificence **12** generousness, philanthropy, selflessness **13** bountifulness, unselfishness **14** big-heartedness, charitableness, high-mindedness, open-handedness

magnanimous
03 big **04** kind **05** large, noble **06** kindly **07** liberal **08** generous, merciful, selfless **09** bountiful, forgiving, unselfish **10** altruistic, beneficent, benevolent, big-hearted, charitable, munificent, open-handed, ungrudging **11** large-minded **12** great-hearted **13** philanthropic

magnate
05 baron, mogul, noble **06** bigwig, fat cat, leader, tycoon **07** big shot, notable **08** big noise, big timer **09** big cheese, executive, financier, moneybags, personage, plutocrat **12** entrepreneur **13** industrialist

See also **newspaper**

magnesium
02 Mg

magnet
04 bait, draw, lure **05** charm, focus **06** appeal, needle **08** solenoid **09** loadstone, lodestone **10** allurement, attraction, enticement, focal point

magnetic
03 mag **08** alluring, charming, engaging, gripping, hypnotic, tempting **09** absorbing, appealing, seductive **10** attractive, bewitching, enchanting, entrancing **11** captivating, charismatic, enthralling, fascinating, mesmerizing, tantalizing **12** irresistible

magnetism
02 it **03** mag **04** draw, grip, lure, pull **05** charm, magic, oomph, power, spell **06** allure, appeal, duende, glamor **07** glamour **08** charisma **09** hypnotism, mesmerism **10** attraction, temptation **11** captivation, enchantment, fascination **12** drawing power **13** seductiveness

magnification
05 boost **07** build-up **08** dilation, increase **09** deepening, expansion, extolling, extolment, hyperbole, inflation, overdoing **10** embroidery **11** enhancement, enlargement, heightening, lionization **12** augmentation, exaggeration, overemphasis **13** amplification, dramatization, embellishment, overstatement **14** aggrandizement **15** intensification

magnificence
04 pomp **05** glory, pride **06** luxury **07** majesty **08** grandeur, nobility, opulence, splendor **09** splendour, sublimity **10** brilliance, excellence, lavishness **11** stateliness **12** gorgeousness, resplendence **13** luxuriousness, sumptuousness **14** impressiveness

magnificent
04 fine, rich **05** grand, noble, royal, state **06** august, lavish, lordly, superb **07** elegant, exalted, gallant, opulent, stately, sublime **08** dazzling, glorious, gorgeous, imposing, majestic, princely, splendid, striking **09** brilliant, excellent, grandiose, luxurious, splendent, sumptuous, wonderful **10** impressive, marvellous **11** resplendent

magnify
05 boost **06** blow up, deepen, dilate, expand, extend, overdo **07** amplify, broaden, build up, enhance, enlarge, greaten, signify **08** heighten, increase, multiply, overplay **09** dramatize, embellish, embroider, intensify, overstate **10** exaggerate **13** overemphasize

magniloquence
07 bombast, fustian **08** euphuism, rhetoric **09** loftiness, pomposity, turgidity **10** orotundity **14** grandiloquence **15** pretentiousness

magniloquent
05 lofty **06** turgid **07** exalted, fustian, orotund, pompous, stilted **08** elevated, sonorous **09** bombastic, high-flown, overblown **10** euphuistic, rhetorical **11** declamatory, pretentious **12** high-sounding **13** grandiloquent

magnitude
03 mag **04** bulk, fame, mass, note, size **05** space **06** amount, extent, import, moment, volume, weight **07** expanse, measure **08** capacity, eminence, muchness, quantity, strength **09** amplitude, greatness, intensity, largeness **10** dimensions, importance **11** consequence, distinction, proportions **12** significance **13** absolute value

magnolia
03 bay **05** yulan **07** champac, champak **08** sweet bay **09** star anise, tulip tree **10** beaver-tree, beaver-wood **12** cucumber tree, umbrella tree

magnum opus
10 masterwork **11** chef d'oeuvre, masterpiece

magpie
03 mag, pie **04** Pica, piet, pyat, pyet, pyot **05** madge **06** maggie **09** organ-bird **10** piping crow

mahogany
04 toon **05** carap, khaya **06** acajou **07** Cedrela **10** chinaberry **14** chittagong wood

maid
03 may **04** ayah, girl, lass **05** bonne, daily, wench **06** au pair, maiden, Mrs Mop, skivvy, slavey, tweeny, virgin **07** abigail, dresser, Mrs Mopp, pucelle, servant **08** bonibell, charlady, domestic, home help, spinster, suivante, tabby cat, waitress **09** bonnibell, charwoman, housemaid, lady's maid, soubrette, tire-woman **10** bowerwoman, Cinderella, handmaiden **11** chambermaid, kitchenmaid, maidservant, serving-maid **12** cleaning lady, kitchen-wench **13** maid-of-all-work **14** femme de chambre

maiden
01 M **03** new **04** burd, girl, kore, lass, miss, pure, wili **05** first, nymph, popsy, unwed **06** chaste, damsel, decent, demure, female, gentle, lassie, modest, proper, seemly, vestal, virgin **07** girlish, initial **08** celibate, decorous, reserved, virginal, virtuous **09** inaugural, undefiled, unmarried, unsullied, young girl, young lady **10** initiatory, unbroached, young woman **12** bachelorette, introductory

maidenhood
06 honour, purity, virtue **08** chastity **10** chasteness, maidenhead

maidenly
04 pure **05** unwed **06** chaste, decent, demure, female, gentle, modest, proper, seemly, vestal, virgin **07** girlish **08** becoming, decorous, reserved, virginal, virtuous **09** undefiled, unmarried, unsullied **10** immaculate, unbroached

maidservant
03 may **04** amah, girl, maid **05** daily **06** au pair, maiden, skivvy, slavey **07** abigail, dresser, Mrs Mopp, pucelle, servant **08** charlady, domestic, suivante, waitress **09** bonnibell, charwoman, housemaid, lady's maid, soubrette **10** bowerwoman, handmaiden **11** chambermaid, kitchenmaid, parlour-maid, serving-maid **13** maid-of-all-work

mail
03 dak **04** dawk, post, rent, send, spam, spot **05** armor, e-mail **06** armour **07** airmail, fan mail, forward, junk fax, letters, packets, panoply, parcels, payment **08** delivery, dispatch, hate mail, junk mail, packages **09** chain mail, habergeon, halfpenny, snail mail **10** cataphract, direct mail, Post Office **11** chain armour, general post, surface mail **12** all-up service, iron-cladding, postal system, recorded mail **13** postal service **14** communications, correspondence, electronic mail, first-class mail, registered mail **15** second-class mail, special delivery

• **Royal Mail**
02 RM

mail-coach
04 drag

maim
03 mar **04** hurt, lame, main **05** wound **06** impair, injure, injury, scotch **07** cripple, cut down, disable **08** crippled, mutilate, truncate **09** disfigure **10** disability **12** incapacitate **14** put out of action

main
03 key, sea **04** duct, head, lame, lead, line, maim, pipe **05** cable, chief, first, grand, great, major, prime, sheer, vital **06** staple, strong **07** capital, central, channel, conduit, crucial, general, leading, pivotal, premier, primary, purpose, supreme **08** cardinal, critical, dominant, foremost, strength **09** essential, extensive, important, necessary, paramount, principal **10** pre-eminent **11** exceedingly, fundamental, outstanding, predominant **13** most important

• **in the main**
06 mostly **07** as a rule, chiefly, largely, usually **08** commonly **09** generally, in general **10** by and large, especially, on the whole **14** for the most part

Maine
02 ME

mainly
04 much **06** mostly **07** as a rule, chiefly, largely, overall, usually
08 above all, commonly **09** generally, in general, in the main, primarily **10** by and large, especially, on the whole
11 principally **13** predominantly **14** for the most part

mainspring
05 cause **06** motive, origin, reason, source **07** impulse **09** generator, incentive **10** motivation, prime mover, wellspring **11** inspiration **12** driving force, fountainhead

mainstay
04 base, prop **05** basis **06** anchor, pillar **07** bulwark, support
08 backbone, buttress, linchpin **09** key player **10** foundation **11** cornerstone
12 right-hand man **14** right-hand woman **15** tower of strength

mainstream
06 normal **07** average, central, general, regular, typical **08** accepted, mainline, orthodox, received, standard
11 established **12** conventional

maintain
04 aver, avow, feed, hold, keep
05 carry, claim, escot, state **06** affirm, assert, avouch, defend, insist, keep up, retain, supply, uphaud, uphold
07 believe, care for, carry on, contend, declare, finance, nourish, nurture, observe, possess, profess, stand by, support, sustain **08** announce, conserve, continue, fight for, practise, preserve **09** keep going, look after
10 asseverate, perpetuate, provide for, take care of

maintenance
04 care, keep **05** title **06** living, upkeep **07** aliment, alimony, defence, feeding, keeping, nurture, repairs, running, support **08** altarage, appanage **09** allowance, financing
10 carrying-on, livelihood, protection, sustenance **11** continuance, nourishment, subsistence, traineeship
12 conservation, continuation, perpetuation, preservation

maize
03 Zea **04** corn, maze, samp **05** maise, mealy, mease, stamp **06** hominy, mealie **07** mealies, popcorn **09** flint corn, sweetcorn **10** Indian corn, Indian meal, masa harina **12** corn on the cob

• **maize dough**
04 masa

• **maize loaf**
04 pone

• **styles of maize**
04 silk

majestic
05 grand, lofty, noble, regal, royal
06 august, kingly, lordly, superb
07 awesome, exalted, pompous, queenly, stately, sublime **08** elevated, glorious, imperial, imposing, princely, splendid **09** dignified **10** impressive, marvellous, monumental
11 magnificent, resplendent
13 distinguished

majestically
05 nobly **07** grandly, regally, royally, stately **08** maestoso, superbly
09 pompously, sublimely **10** gloriously, imperially, splendidly **12** impressively, marvellously **13** magnificently, resplendently

majesty
04 pomp **05** glory **06** beauty, Tuanku
07 dignity, royalty **08** grandeur, nobility, regality **09** grandness, loftiness, nobleness, splendour, sublimity **11** awesomeness, exaltedness, stateliness
12 magnificence, majesticness, resplendence **14** impressiveness, majesticalness

• **Her Majesty**
02 ER, HM **06** Brenda

• **His Majesty**
02 HM

major
03 key, Maj **04** best, main **05** chief, great, older, prime, vital **06** bigger, higher, larger, senior **07** crucial, greater, highest, keynote, largest, leading, notable, serious, supreme, weighty
08 greatest, superior **09** important, paramount, uppermost **10** pre-eminent **11** outstanding, significant

majority
04 bulk, many, mass, most **07** general, manhood, the many **08** legal age, maturity **09** adulthood, nearly all, plurality, womanhood **10** generality, larger part, lion's share **11** coming of age, greater part, pre-eminence **12** age of consent, larger number, more than half **13** greater number, preponderance **15** reaching full age

make
◇ *anagram indicator*
02 do **03** fix, get, mag, net, win
04 cook, earn, flow, form, gain, give, kind, maik, mark, mate, name, sort, tell, tend, turn, type, urge, vote **05** act as, add up, brand, build, cause, clear, drive, elect, equal, erect, force, frame, gross, impel, model, mould, offer, press, put up, reach, score, shape, start, state, style, total, write **06** become, coerce, come to, commit, compel, convey, create, devise, draw up, effect, impart, marque, matter, oblige, obtain, ordain, reckon, render, result, secure, select, settle, vote in, wrap up **07** achieve, acquire, add up to, appoint, arrange, attempt, bring in, chalk up, compose, compute, consort, convert, declare, deliver, dragoon, execute, fashion, install, notch up, perform, prepare, proceed, produce, promote, realize, require, serve as, shuffle, texture, think up, turn out, variety, work out
08 amount to, arrive at, assemble, bulldoze, carry out, comprise, conclude, contract, engender, estimate, generate, get ready, nominate, occasion, pressure, reckon up, set forth, take home **09** calculate, character, constrain, construct, designate, determine, discharge, establish, fabricate, formation, formulate, get down to, halfpenny, originate, pronounce, strongarm, structure, undertake **10** accomplish, bring about, constitute, contribute, function as, give rise to, perpetrate, pressurize **11** communicate, disposition, manufacture, mass-produce, prevail upon, put together
12 be to blame for **13** play the part of, play the role of **14** put the screws on
15 deliver the goods

See also **halfpenny**

• **make away with**
03 nab, rid **04** do in, kill, lift, nick
05 pinch, seize, steal, swipe **06** kidnap, murder, remove, snatch **07** bump off, destroy **08** carry off, fetch off, knock off
09 slaughter **10** do away with, run off with **11** assassinate, walk off with

• **make believe**
03 act **04** play **05** dream, enact, feign
07 imagine, play-act, pretend
09 fantasize

• **make do**
04 cope **05** get by **06** manage
07 make out, survive **08** get along, scrape by **09** improvise **13** muddle through

• **make for**
06 aim for, favour, lead to **07** forward, further, head for, produce, promote
09 go towards **10** facilitate **11** move towards **12** contribute to **13** be conducive to

• **make it**
05 get on, reach **06** arrive **07** prosper, succeed, survive **11** come through, pull through **12** be successful

• **make of**
04 rate **05** judge **06** assess, regard
07 think of, weigh up **08** consider, evaluate

• **make off**
03 fly **04** bolt **05** brush, leave, mosey, truss **06** beat it, decamp, depart, hook it, pop off, run off **07** run away, scarper
08 clear off, up sticks **09** cut and run, shemozzle, skedaddle **12** make a getaway **15** take to your heels

• **make off with**
03 nab **04** flog, nick, take **05** filch, pinch, steal, swipe **06** abduct, kidnap, pilfer **07** purloin **08** carry off, knock off
10 run off with **11** appropriate, walk off with

• **make out**
03 get, see, spy **04** aver, bang, bonk, cope, espy, fare, read, scan, shag
05 claim, get by, get on, grasp, imply, prove, screw, spell **06** affirm, assert, descry, detect, divine, draw up, fathom, fill in, follow, manage
07 achieve, declare, discern, fill out, succeed, work out **08** complete, decipher, describe, discover, get along, maintain, make love, perceive,

progress, write out **09** establish, recognize **10** bear in hand, comprehend, understand **11** demonstrate, distinguish, manage to see **12** manage to hear **13** sleep together **14** get your leg over

- **make over**

05 leave **06** assign, convey **07** dispone, dispose **08** bequeath, sign over, transfer

- **make the rounds of**

02 do

- **make up**

◇ *anagram indicator*
04 fill, form, meet **05** feign, frame, hatch, paint, rouge **06** create, decide, devise, doll up, invent, parcel, powder, render, repair, repent, settle, supply, tart up **07** arrange, collect, compose, concoct, dream up, perfume, provide, think up **08** complete, compound, comprise, round off **09** construct, fabricate, formulate, make peace, originate **10** constitute, shake hands, supplement **11** call it quits, put make-up on **12** be reconciled **13** Birminghamize, put on your face **14** bury the hatchet

- **make up for**

06 offset **07** redress **08** atone for **13** compensate for, make amends for

- **make up to**

03 eik, eke **05** court **06** chat up, cozy up, fawn on **07** toady to **08** butter up, suck up to **10** compensate, cozy up with **15** curry favour with, make overtures to

- **make way**

06 gather **07** advance, gangway **11** allow to pass, clear the way, make room for **12** make space for, stand back for **14** allow to succeed

make-believe
04 mock, sham **05** dream **06** made-up, unreal **07** charade, fantasy, feigned, pretend **08** dreaming, imagined, imitated, pretence, pretense, role-play **09** imaginary, pretended, simulated, unreality **10** fantasized, masquerade, play-acting **11** daydreaming, fabrication, imagination

maker
06 author, wright **07** builder, creator, deviser **08** director, producer, repairer **09** architect **10** fabricator **11** constructor **12** manufacturer

makeshift
06 cutcha, make-do **07** Band-aid®, fig leaf, stand-by, stopgap **08** pis aller **09** expedient, impromptu, temporary, timenoguy **10** improvised, substitute **11** provisional, rudimentary **13** rough and ready **14** thrown together **15** cobbled together

make-up
◇ *anagram indicator*
04 form, slap **05** get-up, paint, style **06** format, nature, powder, temper **07** pancake **08** assembly, panstick, war paint **09** blackface, character, cosmetics, formation, structure, whiteface **10** foundation, maquillage **11** arrangement, composition, disposition, greasepaint, personality, temperament **12** constitution, construction, organization **13** configuration

making
04 form **06** income **07** forging, profits, promise, returns, revenue, takings **08** assembly, building, capacity, creating, creation, earnings, moulding, proceeds **09** materials, modelling, potential, producing, qualities, structure **10** beginnings, capability, production **11** composition, fabrication, ingredients, manufacture **12** construction, potentiality **13** possibilities

- **in the making**

06 coming **07** budding, nascent **08** emergent **09** incipient, potential, promising **10** burgeoning, developing **11** up and coming

maladjusted
◇ *anagram indicator*
04 gaga **05** dotty **06** psycho, schizo **08** confused, neurotic, unstable **09** alienated, disturbed, estranged, screwed-up **10** disordered **12** round the bend

maladministration
07 misrule **08** bungling **09** stupidity **10** blundering, corruption, dishonesty, misconduct **11** malfeasance, malpractice, misfeasance, mishandling **12** incompetence, inefficiency, malversation **13** misgovernment, mismanagement

maladroit
05 inept **06** clumsy, gauche **07** awkward, unhandy **08** bungling, ill-timed, inexpert, tactless, untoward **09** graceless, ham-fisted, inelegant, unskilful **10** cack-handed **11** insensitive, thoughtless **12** undiplomatic **13** inconsiderate

maladroitness
10 clumsiness, inelegance, ineptitude **11** awkwardness **12** tactlessness **13** gracelessness, insensitivity, unskilfulness **15** thoughtlessness

malady
07 ailment, disease, illness, malaise **08** disorder, sickness **09** breakdown, complaint, infirmity **10** affliction **13** indisposition
See also **disease**

malaise
05 angst **06** unease **07** anguish, anxiety, disease, illness **08** disquiet, doldrums, sickness, weakness **09** lassitude, weariness **10** depression, discomfort, discontent, enervation, melancholy, uneasiness **11** unhappiness **12** restlessness **13** indisposition

malapropism
06 misuse **08** slipslop, solecism **09** wrong word **10** infelicity **11** Dogberryism **14** misapplication **15** slip of the tongue

malapropos
05 inapt **07** inaptly **08** ill-timed, tactless, unseemly, untimely **10** inapposite, misapplied, tactlessly, unsuitable, unsuitably **11** inopportune, uncalled-for **12** inappositely, unseasonably **13** inappropriate, inopportunely **15** inappropriately

malaria
04 ague

Malawi
02 MW **03** MWI

Malaysia
03 MAL, MYS

malcontent
05 fed up, rebel **06** grouch, moaner, morose **07** aginner, grouser, restive, unhappy, whinger **08** agitator, grumbler **09** nit-picker, resentful **10** bellyacher, cheesed off, complainer, rebellious **11** bellyaching, disaffected, disgruntled, dissentious, ill-disposed, unsatisfied **12** discontented, dissatisfied, fault-finding, troublemaker **13** mischief-maker

Maldives
03 MDV

male
01 m **02** he **03** dog, man, tom **04** bull, cock, mail, stag **05** macho, manly **06** armour, boyish, virile **07** laddish, manlike **09** masculine, staminate
See also **animal**

malediction
04 oath, wish **05** curse **07** cursing, damning, malison **08** anathema **09** damnation **10** execration **11** imprecation **12** denunciation

malefactor
05 crook, felon **06** outlaw **07** convict, culprit, villain **08** criminal, evildoer, offender **09** miscreant, misfeasor, wrongdoer **10** delinquent, lawbreaker **12** transgressor

malevolence
04 hate **05** spite, venom **06** hatred, malice **07** cruelty, ill-will, rancour **09** hostility, malignity **10** bitterness, fierceness, malignancy **11** viciousness **12** spitefulness, vengefulness **13** maliciousness **14** unfriendliness, vindictiveness

malevolent
05 cruel **06** bitter, fierce, malign **07** baleful, hostile, vicious **08** spiteful, vengeful, venomous **09** malicious, rancorous, resentful **10** evil-minded, ill-natured, maleficent, pernicious, unfriendly, vindictive

- **malevolent being**

04 peri

malevolently
07 cruelly **08** bitterly, fiercely **09** viciously **10** spitefully, vengefully,

venomously **11** maliciously, resentfully **13** vindicatively

malformation
04 warp **09** deformity **10** distortion **12** irregularity **13** disfigurement, misshapenness

malformed
◇ *anagram indicator*
04 bent **06** warped **07** crooked, twisted **08** deformed **09** distorted, irregular, misshapen **10** disfigured

malfunction
◇ *anagram indicator*
04 fail, flaw **05** crash, fault **06** defect, glitch, go phut, hiccup, pack up **07** conk out, failure, go kaput, go wrong **08** disorder, hiccough **09** break down, breakdown **11** stop working

Mali
03 MLI, RMM

malice
04 hate **05** spite, venom **06** animus, enmity, hatred, spleen **07** despite, ill-will, rancour **08** bad blood **09** animosity, hostility **10** bitchiness, bitterness, bone to pick, resentment **11** malevolence **13** maliciousness **14** vindictiveness

malicious
04 evil, mean **05** snide **06** bitchy, bitter, malign **07** baleful, hostile, vicious **08** narquois, spiteful, vengeful, venomous **09** poisonous, rancorous, resentful **10** dispiteous, evil-minded, ill-natured, malevolent, pernicious **11** mischievous

maliciously
08 bitterly **09** unhappily, viciously **10** spitefully, venomously **11** resentfully **12** malevolently, perniciously

malign
03 bad **04** bait, evil, harm, slur **05** abuse, libel, smear **06** defame, injure, insult, vilify **07** baleful, envenom, harmful, hostile, hurtful, run down, slander, traduce **08** badmouth, sinister **09** disparage, injurious, malignant, misintend, poor-mouth **10** calumniate, malevolent **11** destructive **13** stab in the back **14** kick in the teeth

malignancy
08 fatality **09** lethality, mortality, virulence **12** incurability

malignant
04 evil **05** black, fatal, swart **06** deadly, lethal, malign, sullen, swarth **07** baleful, harmful, hostile, hurtful, vicious **08** cankered, Cavalier, devilish, Royalist, spiteful, venomous, viperous, virulent **09** cancerous, dangerous, incurable, injurious, malicious, poisonous, rancorous **10** malevolent, pernicious, rebellious **11** destructive, disaffected **14** uncontrollable **15** life-threatening

malignity
04 gall, hate **05** spite, venom **06** animus, hatred, malice, taking **07** ill-will, rancour **08** bad blood **09** animosity, hostility, virulence **10** bitterness, deadliness, wickedness **11** balefulness, harmfulness, hurtfulness, malevolence, viciousness **12** vengefulness **13** maliciousness **14** perniciousness, vindictiveness **15** destructiveness

malinger
04 loaf **05** dodge, shirk, skive, skulk, slack **07** pretend, put it on **09** gold-brick **12** swing the lead **14** pretend to be ill

malingerer
06 dodger, loafer, skiver **07** shirker, slacker **11** lead-swinger

mall
04 beat, maul, mell, walk **05** plaza **06** arcade **08** galleria, precinct **13** outlet village **14** shopping centre **15** shopping complex

mallard
08 wild duck
- **mallard flock**

04 sord

malleability
07 pliancy **08** softness **10** compliance, plasticity, pliability, suppleness **11** ductileness, flexibility **12** adaptability **13** manageability, receptiveness, tractableness **14** susceptibility

malleable
◇ *anagram indicator*
04 soft **06** pliant, supple **07** ductile, plastic, pliable **08** biddable, flexible, tractile, workable, yielding **09** adaptable, compliant, receptive, tractable **10** governable, manageable **11** persuadable, susceptible **14** impressionable

mallow
04 sida

malnourished
06 hungry **07** starved **08** anorexic, underfed **09** anorectic **14** undernourished

malnutrition
06 hunger **08** anorexia **09** inanition **10** starvation **12** underfeeding **13** unhealthy diet **15** anorexia nervosa

malodorous
04 rank **05** fetid, niffy **06** foetid, putrid, smelly **07** miasmal, miasmic, noisome, reeking **08** mephitic, miasmous, stinking **09** miasmatic, offensive **10** infragrant, miasmatous, nauseating **12** evil-smelling, foul-smelling

malpractice
05 abuse **07** misdeed, offence **10** misconduct, negligence, wrongdoing **11** impropriety **12** carelessness **13** mismanagement

malt
04 wort

Malta
01 M **03** MLT

maltreat
◇ *anagram indicator*
04 harm, hurt, maul **05** abuse, bully, hound **06** damage, injure, misuse **07** torture **08** ill-treat, mistreat **09** mishandle, victimize **10** rough-house, treat badly **11** assassinate

maltreatment
04 harm, hurt **05** abuse **06** damage, ill-use, injury, misuse **07** torture **08** bullying, ill-usage **12** ill-treatment, mistreatment **13** victimization

mammal

Mammals include:

03 ape, ass, bat, cat, cow, dog, elk, fox, gnu, pig, rat, yak
04 bear, boar, cavy, deer, goat, hare, ibex, kudu, lion, lynx, mink, mole, paca, puma, seal, soor, tahr, vole, wolf, zebu
05 aguti, bison, camel, civet, coney, coypu, dingo, eland, genet, hippo, horse, human, hyena, hyrax, koala, lemur, llama, loris, moose, mouse, okapi, otter, ounce, panda, potto, rhino, sheep, shrew, skunk, sloth, stoat, takin, tapir, tiger, whale, zebra
06 aye-aye, baboon, badger, beaver, beluga, bobcat, cattle, colugo, cougar, coyote, cuscus, dassie, dugong, duiker, ermine, ferret, galago, gerbil, gibbon, gopher, hacker, impala, jackal, jaguar, jerboa, langur, marmot, marten, monkey, numbat, ocelot, possum, rabbit, racoon, reebok, rhebok, sea cow, serval, tenrec, vicuna, walrus, wapiti, weasel, wombat
07 ant-bear, bosvark, buffalo, caracal, caribou, chamois, cheetah, dolphin, echidna, fur seal, gazelle, gerenuk, giraffe, gorilla, grampus, grizzly, guanaco, guereza, gymnura, hamster, lemming, leopard, macaque, manatee, meercat, meerkat, mole rat, muntjac, muskrat, narwhal, opossum, pack rat, panther, peccary, polecat, primate, raccoon, red deer, roe deer, sea lion, sun bear, tamarin, tarsier, wallaby, warthog, wild ass, wildcat
08 aardvark, aardwolf, anteater, antelope, bushbaby, bushbuck, capybara, chipmunk, dormouse, duckbill, elephant, fruit bat, grey wolf, harp seal, hedgehog, house bat, kangaroo, mandrill, mangabey, marmoset, mongoose, musk deer, pacarana, pangolin, platypus, porpoise, reedbuck, reindeer, sea otter, sewer rat, squirrel, steenbok, steinbok, talapoin, wild goat
09 Arctic fox, armadillo, bamboo rat, bandicoot, black bear, blue sheep, blue whale, brown bear, dromedary, flying fox, grey whale, grindhval, guinea pig, jungle cat,

mouse-deer, orang utan, palm civet, phalanger, polar bear, porcupine, springbok, steinbuck, thylacine, waterbuck, wolverine
10 Barbary ape, chevrotain, chimpanzee, chinchilla, coatimundi, common seal, fallow deer, field mouse, giant panda, hartebeest, house mouse, human being, jack rabbit, kodiak bear, pilot whale, pine marten, prairie dog, rhinoceros, sperm whale, springbuck, springhare, vampire bat, white whale, wildebeest
11 beaked whale, flying lemur, green monkey, grizzly bear, honey badger, killer whale, muntjac deer, pipistrelle, rat kangaroo, red squirrel, snow leopard
12 Arabian camel, barbary sheep, elephant seal, grey squirrel, harvest mouse, hippopotamus, leaf-nosed bat, mountain goat, mountain lion, rhesus monkey, river dolphin, spider monkey, two-toed sloth, vervet monkey, water buffalo
13 American bison, Bactrian camel, colobus monkey, dwarf antelope, elephant shrew, European bison, hanuman monkey, howling monkey, humpback whale, marsupial mole, mouse-eared bat, spiny anteater, Tasmanian wolf
14 capuchin monkey, edible dormouse, flying squirrel, Indian elephant, marsupial mouse, mountain beaver, Patagonian hare, squirrel monkey, Tasmanian devil, three-toed sloth
15 African elephant, black rhinoceros, brushtail possum, hamadryas baboon, humpbacked whale, proboscis monkey, ring-tailed lemur, Thomson's gazelle, white rhinoceros

See also **animal**; **ape**; **cat**; **cattle**; **deer**; **dog**; **horse**; **marsupial**; **monkey**; **pig**; **rodent**; **sheep**; **whale**

mammoth

04 huge, vast **05** giant, jumbo **06** bumper, mighty **07** immense, massive **08** colossal, enormous, gigantic, whopping **09** ginormous, herculean, leviathan **10** gargantuan, monumental, prodigious, stupendous **14** Brobdingnagian

man

01 b, k, m, n, p, q, r **02** bo, he, Mr, ou **03** boy, guy, IOM, lad, mun, pin **04** chap, crew, gent, hand, homo, jack, king, male, page, pawn, rook, work **05** adult, bloke, cairn, human, lover, piece, queen, staff, valet **06** bishop, castle, fellow, fiancé, geezer, helper, knight, Mister, mortal, occupy, people, person, spouse, toy boy, vassal, worker **07** chequer, draught, husband, mankind, mortals, operate, partner, servant, soldier, workman **08** employee, factotum, follower, houseboy, houseman, humanity, labourer **09** attendant, boyfriend, gentleman, humankind, human race, odd-jobman **10** human being, individual, manservant, sweetheart **11** Homo sapiens, human beings **12** be in charge of, man-of-all-work, take charge of **15** jack-of-all-trades

See also **boy**; **chess**

• first man

04 Adam

• good man

01 S **02** St **04** sant **05** Saint

• old man *see* old man

• to a man

05 as one **07** bar none **09** one and all **11** unanimously **12** with one voice

• wise man

04 mage, sage **05** magus

manacle

03 tie **04** bind, curb **05** chain, check **06** fetter, hamper, secure **07** inhibit, shackle **08** handcuff, restrain **11** put in chains

manacles

05 bonds, cuffs, gyves, irons **06** chains **07** darbies, fetters, mittens, nippers **08** shackles **09** bracelets, handcuffs, snitchers, wristlets

manage

03 ren, rin, run, use **04** boss, cope, fare, head, keep, lead, play, rule, work **05** cut it, get by, get on, guide, shift, wield **06** direct, effect, govern, handle, head up, honcho, make do, manure, master **07** achieve, carry on, command, conduct, control, make out, operate, oversee, solicit, succeed, survive **08** be head of, bring off, contrive, deal with, engineer, get along, maneuver, navigate, organize **09** influence, manoeuvre, negotiate, supervise **10** accomplish, administer, bring about, manipulate **11** preside over, superintend **12** be in charge of

manageable

04 yare **05** handy **06** doable, docile, pliant, viable, wieldy **07** pliable **08** amenable, feasible, flexible, yielding **09** compliant, easy-to-use, tolerable, tractable **10** acceptable, attainable, functional, governable, reasonable, submissive **11** practicable **12** controllable **13** accommodating

management

04 care **05** admin, board **06** bosses, charge, owners, ruling **07** command, conduct, control, dispose, running **08** disposal, handling, managers, ordering **09** direction, directors, employers, executive, governall, governors, husbandry, stewardry, treatment **10** executives, government, intendance, intendancy, leadership, overseeing **11** directorate, proprietors, stewardship, supervision, supervisors **12** organization **14** administration **15** superintendence

manager

02 GM **03** guv, Mgr **04** boss, head, suit **05** agent, chair, chief **06** gaffer, honcho, serang **07** amildar, husband, planter, proctor **08** chairman, director, employer, governor, hotelier, landlady, landlord, motelier, overseer **09** conductor, contriver, directrix, executive, intendant, organizer, president, régisseur **10** chairwoman, controller, directress, head-bummer, head serang, impresario, manageress, procurator, supervisor **11** businessman, chairperson, comptroller, land-steward **12** commissioner, maître d'hôtel, manufacturer **13** administrator, businesswoman **14** chief executive, superintendent

managerial

09 executive **10** industrial **11** legislative, supervisory **12** departmental, governmental **14** administrative, organizational, superintendent **15** entrepreneurial

mandate

02 OK **03** law, let **04** okay **05** allow, edict, order **06** charge, decree, enable, permit, ratify, ruling **07** approve, bidding, command, confirm, dictate, empower, entitle, licence, precept, statute, warrant **08** legalize, sanction, validate **09** authority, authorize, consent to, direction, directive, make legal, ordinance **10** commission, injunction, king's brief **11** instruction **13** authorization **15** give authority to

mandatory

07 binding **08** required **09** essential, necessary, requisite **10** compulsory, imperative, obligatory

manful

04 bold **05** brave, hardy, manly, noble, stout **06** daring, heroic, strong **07** gallant, valiant **08** intrepid, powerful, resolute, stalwart, vigorous **09** steadfast **10** courageous, determined **11** indomitable, lion-hearted, noble-minded, unflinching **12** stout-hearted

manfully

04 hard **05** nobly **06** boldly **07** bravely, man-like, stoutly **08** pluckily, strongly **09** gallantly, valiantly **10** heroically, intrepidly, powerfully, resolutely, stalwartly, vigorously **11** desperately, steadfastly **12** courageously, determinedly **13** unflinchingly

manganese

02 Mn

• manganese ore

03 wad **04** wadd, wadt

manger

04 crib **06** cratch, feeder, trough **13** feeding trough

mangle

◇ *anagram indicator*

03 cut, mar **04** hack, maim, maul, rend, ruin, tear **05** botch, crush, mouth, spoil, twist, wreck **06** bungle, deform, garble, haggle, mess up **07** butcher, destroy, distort, mammock, screw up

08 calender, lacerate, mutilate
09 disfigure 11 make a hash of, make a mess of

mangy
04 mean, worn 05 dirty, seedy, tatty
06 filthy, scabby, shabby, shoddy
07 roynish, scruffy 08 cowardly
09 moth-eaten

manhandle
03 tug 04 haul, hump, maul, pull, push
05 abuse, heave, shove 06 jostle, misuse 07 rough up 08 maltreat, mistreat 10 knock about 13 handle roughly

manhood
08 machismo, maleness, maturity, virility 09 adulthood, manliness
10 manfulness 11 masculinity

mania
03 fad 04 rage, urge 05 craze, thing
06 desire, fetish, frenzy, lunacy, raving
07 craving, madness, passion
08 dementia, disorder, fixation, hysteria, insanity, wildness
09 craziness, gold-fever, obsession, psychosis, tarantism 10 aberration, compulsion, enthusiasm
11 derangement, fascination, infatuation 13 preoccupation

Manias include:

08 egomania
09 cynomania, demomania, ergomania, infomania, logomania, melomania, monomania, oenomania, opsomania, pyromania, theomania, tomomania, xenomania
10 anthomania, dipsomania, erotomania, hippomania, hydromania, methomania, metromania, mythomania, narcomania, necromania, nostomania
11 ablutomania, acronymania, ailuromania, bibliomania, cleptomania, demonomania, etheromania, graphomania, hedonomania, kleptomania, megalomania, nymphomania, technomania, toxicomania
12 arithmomania, balletomania, pteridomania, thanatomania, theatromania
13 flagellomania, morphinomania
14 eleutheromania

maniac
03 fan, nut 04 buff, kook 05 crank, fiend, freak, loony 06 madman, nutter, psycho 07 cupcake, fanatic, lunatic, nutcase, oddball 08 crackpot, headcase, madwoman 09 fruitcake, psychotic, screwball 10 enthusiast, psychopath 14 deranged person

manic
◇ *anagram indicator*
03 mad 04 amok, wild 05 barmy, batty, crazy, daffy, dippy, loopy 06 crazed, hectic, insane, raving 07 berserk, frantic, furious 08 demented, deranged, feverish, frenetic, frenzied
09 desperate, obsessive 10 distracted, distraught, hysterical 11 overwrought
12 uncontrolled 13 panic-stricken
14 beside yourself

manically
◇ *anagram indicator*
05 madly 06 wildly 09 excitedly, intensely 10 hectically 12 frenetically, hysterically

manifest
◇ *anagram indicator*
04 open, shew, show 05 clear, plain, prove 06 appear, attest, evince, expose, patent, reveal 07 blatant, confess, declare, display, evident, exhibit, express, glaring, obvious, present, visible 08 apparent, distinct, indicate, set forth 09 establish, extrovert, make clear, make plain, show forth 10 illustrate, noticeable
11 conspicuous, demonstrate, perceptible, transparent, unconcealed
12 be evidence of, unmistakable
13 unmistakeable

manifestation
◇ *anagram indicator*
04 mark, mode, show, sign 05 gleam, glory, token 06 avatar, reflex 07 display
08 Epiphany, evidence, exposure
09 theophany 10 appearance, disclosure, exhibition, exposition, expression, indication, revelation
11 angelophany, declaration, incarnation 12 illustration, presentation 13 demonstration
14 representation 15 exemplification

manifesto
08 platform, policies 09 programme, statement 11 declaration, publication
12 announcement, proclamation
14 pronunciamento

manifold
04 many 06 varied 07 copious, diverse, several, various
08 abundant, multiple, multiply, numerous 09 aggregate
12 multifarious 13 kaleidoscopic, multitudinous

manipulate
◇ *anagram indicator*
03 cog, ply, rig, use 04 cook, hand, milk, tong, work 05 fit up, frame, guide, knead, nurse, steer, wield
06 direct, doctor, employ, fiddle, handle, juggle, manage, wangle
07 control, exploit, falsify, finesse, massage, operate, process, shuffle, utilize 08 cash in on, engineer
09 influence, manoeuvre, negotiate
10 juggle with, tamper with, thimblerig
11 gerrymander, pull strings
12 capitalize on, wheel and deal
15 have over a barrel

manipulation
◇ *anagram indicator*
05 using 07 control, massage, milking, rigging, working 08 fiddling, guidance, handling, juggling, kneading, steering, wangling, wielding 09 directing, doctoring, influence, massaging, operation 11 manoeuvring, negotiation, utilization 12 exploitation, mobilization 13 falsification 14 pulling strings 15 cooking the books

manipulative
03 sly 04 foxy, wily 06 artful, crafty, tricky 07 cunning, devious
08 scheming, slippery 09 conniving, deceitful, designing, insidious, underhand 11 calculating, duplicitous
12 unscrupulous 13 Machiavellian

manipulator
04 user 05 slave 06 worker 07 handler, schemer, smoothy, wielder
08 director, engineer, operator, smart guy 09 exploiter 10 controller, influencer, manoeuvrer, negotiator, wirepuller 13 wheeler-dealer

Manitoba
02 MB

mankind
03 man 05 flesh 06 Bimana, people, public 07 mortals 08 humanity
09 humankind, human race 11 Homo sapiens, human beings

manliness
06 mettle, valour, vigour 07 bravery, courage, heroism, manhood
08 boldness, firmness, machismo, maleness, strength, virility
09 fortitude, hardihood
10 manfulness, resolution
11 intrepidity, masculinity
12 fearlessness, independence, resoluteness, stalwartness

manly
04 bold, firm, male 05 brave, macho, noble, tough 06 heroic, manful, robust, rugged, strong, sturdy, virile
08 fearless, intrepid, powerful, vigorous 09 dignified, masculine
10 courageous, determined

man-made
04 faux, mock 06 ersatz 09 imitation, simulated, synthetic 10 artificial
12 manufactured

manna
07 trehala 08 honeydew

manner
03 air, how, way 04 form, look, mien, mode 05 means, style 06 aspect, custom, mainor, method, stance
07 bearing, conduct, decorum, fashion, posture, process, p's and q's, routine, variety 08 approach, attitude, courtesy, good form, practice, protocol
09 behaviour, character, demeanour, etiquette, procedure, propriety, technique 10 appearance, deportment, politeness 11 formalities
12 social graces, the done thing 13 way of behaving

• **in the manner of**
02 as, of 03 à la, per

• **unconstrained manner**
04 ease

mannered
05 posed, put-on **06** pseudo, thewed **07** stilted **08** affected, precious **10** artificial, euphuistic **11** pretentious

See also **bad-mannered**

mannerism
05 habit, quirk, trait, trick **06** foible **07** feature **10** foreignism **11** peculiarity, stiltedness **12** idiosyncrasy **14** characteristic

mannerly
05 civil **06** formal, polite **07** civilly, genteel, refined **08** decorous, gracious, ladylike, polished, well-bred **09** civilized, courteous **10** respectful **11** deferential, gentlemanly, well-behaved **12** well-mannered

mannish
05 butch **07** laddish, mankind **09** Amazonian, masculine, tomboyish, unwomanly, viragoish **10** unfeminine, unladylike, viraginian, viraginous **11** virilescent

mannishness
08 virilism **09** butchness **11** masculinity **12** unfemininity, virilescence **13** unwomanliness **14** unladylikeness

manoeuvre
◇ *anagram indicator*
04 dock, ease, loop, move, pick, plan, plot, ploy, roll, ruse, turn **05** berth, cut in, dodge, drive, guide, pilot, stall, steer, trick **06** action, device, devise, direct, gambit, handle, jockey, manage, pesade, scheme, tactic, wangle **07** wheelie **08** alley-oop, artifice, contrive, engineer, exercise, intrigue, movement, navigate, snap roll, wingover **09** chandelle, checkmate, decursion, half board, negotiate, operation, stratagem **10** deployment, manipulate, subterfuge **11** machination, pull strings, skilful plan, victory roll **12** countermarch, manipulation, renversement **13** Immelmann turn

manor
03 Hof **04** hall, seat, vill **05** house, villa **06** barony **07** château, Schloss **12** country house

manpower
05 staff **07** workers **09** employees, personnel, workforce **14** human resources, skilled workers

manse
07 deanery, rectory **08** vicarage **09** parsonage **10** glebe-house

manservant
05 valet **06** butler, Jeeves **08** retainer **09** attendant

mansion
04 casa, hall, home, seat **05** abode, house, manor, place, villa **06** castle **07** château, Schloss **08** dwelling **09** residence **10** habitation, manor-house

manslaughter
06 murder **07** carnage, killing, slaying **08** butchery, fatality, genocide, homicide, massacre **09** bloodshed, execution, matricide, patricide, slaughter, uxoricide **10** fratricide, sororicide **11** destruction, elimination, infanticide, liquidation **13** assassination, extermination

mantle
04 cape, hide, hood, mask, pall, veil, wrap **05** blush, cloak, cloud, cover, froth, layer, palla, shawl, vakas **06** bubble, capote, dolman, rochet, screen, shroud **07** blanket, conceal, envelop, obscure, pallium, pelisse, pluvial **08** covering, disguise, envelope **13** asthenosphere

manual
03 ABC **05** bible, guide, human **06** by hand **07** cambist, positif **08** handbook, physical **09** companion, guidebook, portolano, vade-mecum **10** directions, mechanical, prospectus **11** book of words, enchiridion **12** encheiridion, hand-operated, instructions **13** with your hands **15** instruction book

manually
06 by hand **10** physically **13** with your hands

manufacture
◇ *anagram indicator*
04 form, make **05** build, forge, frame, model **06** create, devise, invent, make up, making **07** concoct, dream up, fashion, forming, process, produce, think up, turn out **08** assemble, assembly, building, creation **09** construct, fabricate, formation, modelling **10** fashioning, processing, production **11** fabrication, mass-produce, put together **12** construction **14** mass-production

manufacturer
05 maker **07** builder, chemist, creator **08** producer **09** fabricant **10** paper-maker, soap boiler **11** chocolatier, constructor, tobacconist **12** factory-owner **13** industrialist

See also **car**

manure
04 dung, hold, lime, muck, soil, tath **05** dress, guano, vraic **06** bedung, hen-pen, manage, occupy, ordure **07** compost **08** dressing **09** cultivate, droppings, fish-guano **10** composture, fertilizer **11** top-dressing **12** animal faeces, police-manure **15** animal excrement

manuscript
02 MS **04** text **05** codex, paper **06** scroll, uncial, vellum **07** papyrus **08** document **09** autograph, minuscule, parchment **10** Mabinogion, palimpsest, typescript **12** opisthograph

Manx
◇ *tail deletion indicator*
08 tailless

many
01 C, D, K, L, M **04** a lot, lots, tons, wads **05** a mass, heaps, loads, piles, scads **06** a lot of, a wheen, hantle, lots of, masses, oodles, plenty, scores, stacks, sundry, varied **07** copious, diverse, several, umpteen, various **08** billions, hundreds, manifold, millions, multiple, numerous, zillions **09** countless, hoi polloi, thousands **10** a multitude **11** any number of, innumerable **12** a large number **13** multitudinous **14** a large number of

Maori

Maori leaders include:

05 Ngata (Sir Apirana Turupa)
06 Cooper (Dame Whina), Mahuta (Sir Robert), O'Regan (Sir Tipene), Pomare (Sir Maui), Ratana (Tuhupotiki Wiremu)
07 Te Kooti (Arikirangi Te Turuki)
09 Heke Potai (Hone Wiremu), Hongi Hika, Rua Kenana (Hepetipa)
11 Te Rauparaha
14 Te Heuheu Tukino (Sir Hepi)

See also **god, goddess**; **mythology**

map
04 card, face, mark, plan, plot **05** atlas, chart, graph, inset **06** sketch **07** road-map **08** town plan **09** cartogram, delineate, gazetteer, horoscope, mappemond **10** projection, street plan **11** carte du pays, hypsography, planisphere, street guide **12** weather chart

• **map out**
04 draw **05** draft **06** draw up, sketch **07** outline, work out

maple
04 acer **05** mazer, plane **08** box elder, sycamore

mapmakers
02 OS

mar
◇ *anagram indicator*
04 harm, hurt, maim, ruin, scar **05** spoil, stain, sully, taint, wreck **06** damage, deface, deform, impair, injure, mangle, poison **07** blemish, tarnish **08** mutilate **09** disfigure, misguggle **10** mishguggle **11** contaminate, detract from

maraud
04 loot, raid, sack **05** foray, harry **06** forage, ravage **07** despoil, pillage, plunder, raiding, ransack **08** spoliate **09** depredate **10** plundering

marauder
05 rover **06** bandit, looter, mugger, outlaw, pirate, raider, robber **07** brigand, ravager, rustler **08** pillager, predator **09** buccaneer, plunderer **10** freebooter, highwayman

marble
03 taw **04** ally, bool, bowl, dump, marl, onyx **05** agate, alley, bonce, touch **06** nicker, Parian **07** cipolin, knicker, paragon, plonker, plunker

08 commoney, onychite 09 cipollino, pavonazzo, scagliola 10 nero-antico 11 ophicalcite

march
03 Mar 04 demo, file, gait, hike, Lide, pace, step, trek, walk, yomp 05 étape, hikoi, stalk, strut, tramp, tread, troop 06 border, defile, parade, stride 07 advance, debouch, en route, forward, headway, passage, swagger 08 boundary, footslog, progress 09 evolution, paso doble 10 procession, route-march, walk-around 11 development, make headway 12 countermarch 13 demonstration

• **March 15**
04 Ides

• **section of march**
04 trio

marches
06 border 08 boundary, frontier, protests 10 borderland 14 border district

mare
04 yaud

margarine
04 oleo

margin
03 rim 04 brim, curb, edge, kerb, marg, play, rand, room, side, tail 05 bound, brink, extra, limit, marge, scope, skirt, space, verge 06 border, leeway, limits, spread 07 confine, surplus, whisker 08 boundary, confines, frontier, latitude 09 allowance, perimeter, periphery 10 difference 12 differential 15 demarcation line

marginal
03 low 04 marg, tiny 05 minor, small 06 minute, slight 07 minimal 08 doubtful 09 on the edge 10 borderline, negligible, peripheral 11 subordinate 13 insignificant

• **marginal note**
03 k'ri

• **of marginal value**
04 lean

marginalization
05 exile 08 solitude 09 aloneness, isolation, seclusion 10 alienation, detachment, loneliness, remoteness, retirement, separation, withdrawal 11 abstraction, segregation 12 dissociation, separateness, solitariness 13 disconnection, sequestration

marginalize
06 cut off, detach, maroon, remove, strand 07 divorce, exclude, isolate, seclude, shut out 08 abstract, alienate, separate, set apart, shut away 09 keep apart, ostracize, segregate, sequester 10 disconnect 12 cold-shoulder

margosa
03 nim 04 neem, nimb 05 Melia, neemb

marijuana *see* **cannabis**

marina
04 dock, port 07 harbour, mooring 12 yacht station

marinade
04 soak 05 imbue, souse, steep 06 infuse 07 immerse 08 marinate, permeate, saturate 09 chermoula, escabeche

marine
02 RM 03 sea 05 jolly, naval 06 bootee 07 aquatic, oceanic, pelagic 08 maritime, nautical, seagoing, seascape, seawater 09 saltwater, seafaring, thalassic 10 ocean-going, thalassian 11 leatherneck

mariner
02 AB 03 tar 04 salt 05 limey, matlo 06 matlow, sailor, sea dog, seaman 07 Jack Tar, matelot 08 deckhand, seafarer 09 navigator

See also **sailor**

marital
06 wedded 07 married, nuptial, spousal, wedding 08 conjugal, marriage 09 connubial 11 matrimonial

maritally
09 by wedlock, in wedlock, nuptially 10 by marriage, conjugally, in marriage 11 connubially 13 matrimonially

maritime
03 sea 05 naval 06 marine 07 coastal, oceanic, pelagic, seaside 08 littoral, nautical, sea-coast, seagoing, sea-trade 09 seafaring

mark
01 m 02 DM, mk, NB 03 aim, cut, dot, end, see, tag, tee, zit 04 blot, butt, chip, clue, dash, dent, dool, dule, flag, goal, heed, hint, keep, line, ling, logo, mind, name, nick, norm, note, scar, seal, sign, spot, stop, tatu, tick, tika, type 05 badge, brand, gauge, grade, issue, label, level, limit, model, motto, notch, patch, point, print, proof, scale, score, smear, speck, stage, stain, stamp, tally, token, trace, track 06 accent, assess, blotch, bruise, caract, denote, device, emblem, honour, listen, notice, object, picket, pimple, piquet, record, regard, smudge, smutch, stigma, symbol, target, tattoo, tattow, tittle, tracks, typify 07 blemish, correct, discern, feature, freckle, imprint, jot down, measure, observe, picquet, purpose, quality, scratch, signify, specify, symptom 08 appraise, boundary, bull's-eye, evaluate, evidence, identify, indicate, monogram, note down, remember, standard 09 attribute, birthmark, celebrate, character, criterion, designate, discolour, footprint, idiograph, intention, objective, recognize, represent, trademark, write down, yardstick 10 assessment, bear in mind, evaluation, impression, indication, percentage, take heed of, take note of 11 acknowledge, commemorate, distinguish, fingerprint, take to heart 12 characterize, fingerprints, pay tribute to 13 put your name on 14 characteristic, noteworthiness, pay attention to

• **encircling mark**
03 rim 04 ring

• **make your mark**
05 get on 06 make it 07 prosper, succeed 12 be successful, make the grade 13 hit the big time 14 make the big time

• **mark down**
03 cut 05 lower, slash 06 reduce 08 decrease

• **mark out**
03 fix 04 line 07 delimit, destine, measure 08 set apart 09 delineate, demarcate, designate, draw lines, single out, tell apart 11 distinguish 12 discriminate 13 differentiate

• **mark up**
05 put up, raise 06 hike up, jack up 08 increase

• **mark well**
02 nb 08 nota bene

• **miss mark**
03 err

• **up to the mark**
02 OK 10 acceptable, good enough 11 up to scratch 12 satisfactory

• **wide of the mark**
04 gone, wild 06 abroad, far out 09 imprecise, incorrect, off target 10 inaccurate, irrelevant 14 beside the point

marked
05 clear, noted, thick 06 doomed, pimply, signal, spotty, strong 07 blatant, blotchy, bruised, decided, evident, glaring, marcato, obvious, scarred, spotted, stained, watched 08 apparent, blotched, distinct, emphatic, freckled, striking 09 blemished, condemned, indicated, prominent, scratched, suspected 10 noticeable, pronounced, remarkable 11 conspicuous 12 considerable, unmistakable

markedly
07 clearly 08 signally 09 blatantly, decidedly, evidently, glaringly, obviously 10 distinctly, noticeably, remarkably, strikingly 11 prominently 12 considerably, emphatically, unmistakably 13 conspicuously

marker
03 dan, tag 04 buck, flag, goal 07 counter 08 bookmark, gybe mark, milepost, tidemark 09 milestone, stake boat

market
03 AIM, mkt, USM 04 call, fair, hawk, kerb, mall, mart, need, sale, sell, shop, souk, vent, want 05 agora, trade, value 06 bazaar, buying, demand, desire, outlet, peddle, retail 07 bargain, promote, selling, trading 08 business, dealings, exchange, industry, occasion, shambles 09 advertize 10 Smithfield 11 market-place, requirement 12 Billingsgate, Covent Garden, offer for sale 14 shopping centre

• on the market
06 on sale **07** for sale **09** available, up for sale

marketable
06 wanted **08** in demand, saleable, sellable, vendible **11** sought after **12** merchantable

marketing
04 hype **05** sales **07** pushing **08** plugging **09** promotion, publicity **11** advertising **12** distribution **13** merchandizing

market-place
03 suk **04** sook, souk, sukh, tron

marksman, markswoman
04 shot **06** sniper **07** deadeye **08** dead shot, free-shot, shootist, wing shot **09** crack shot **12** sharpshooter

mark-up
04 hike, leap, rise **07** upsurge **08** increase **10** escalation **13** price increase

Marlowe
03 Kit

marmoset
04 mico **07** jacchus, wistiti

marmot
05 bobac, bobak **08** whistler **09** woodchuck

maroon
05 leave **06** desert, strand **07** abandon, forsake, isolate **08** cast away **09** put ashore **11** leave behind **14** turn your back on **15** leave high and dry, leave in the lurch

marriage
04 link **05** match, noose, union **06** fusion, merger **07** spousal, wedding, wedlock **08** alliance, coupling, nuptials, shidduch, spousage, spousals **09** espousals, matrimony **10** connection **11** affiliation, association, combination, handfasting, partnership, unification **12** amalgamation, married state **13** confederation

Marriage- and wedding-related terms include:

03 vow, wed
04 ring, veil, wife
05 aisle, altar, banns, bride, dowry, elope, groom, in-law, usher, vicar
06 beenah, bigamy, digamy, favour, fiancé, garter, huppah, prenup, priest, speech, spouse
07 best man, betroth, bouquet, chuppah, consort, divorce, espouse, exogamy, fiancée, husband, Ketubah, marital, merchet, Mr Right, nuptial, page boy, propose, punalua, trigamy, wedding
08 bedright, best maid, confetti, conjugal, endogamy, hen night, jointure, levirate, maritage, minister, monogamy, monogyny, polygamy
09 annulment, coemption, common-law, communion, connubial, honeymoon, hope chest, horseshoe, hypergamy, love match, matrimony, other half, reception, registrar, stag night, trousseau
10 better half, bridesmaid, buttonhole, consortium, consummate, engagement, first dance, first night, flower girl, her indoors, him indoors, honeymonth, invitation, Lucy Stoner, maiden name, matrilocal, morganatic, patrilocal, separation, settlement, uxorilocal, wedding day
11 deuterogamy, dissolution, Gretna Green, handfasting, misalliance, morning gift, mother in-law, outmarriage, wedding cake, wedding list
12 bottom drawer, bridal shower, concubitancy, mariage blanc, open marriage, prothalamion, something new, something old, wedding dress, wedding march, wedding night
13 church service, civil marriage, hedge-marriage, holy matrimony, marriage-lines, something blue
14 matron of honour, pop the question, steal a marriage
15 chief bridesmaid, going-away outfit, marriage-licence, plight one's troth

• promise of marriage
04 hand

married
01 m **03** wed **05** wived, yoked **06** joined, united, wedded, wifely **07** hitched, marital, nuptial, spliced, spousal **08** conjugal **09** connubial, husbandly **11** matrimonial

marrow
03 nub **04** core, gist, like, mate, pith, soul **05** equal, heart, match, quick, stuff **06** centre, couple, kernel, spirit **07** essence, medulla, nucleus **08** zucchini **09** companion, courgette, substance **11** nitty-gritty **12** nuts and bolts, quintessence

marry
03 wad, wed **04** ally, fuse, join, knit, link, mate, weld, wive **05** cleek, elope, match, merge, unite **06** couple, indeed!, spouse **07** combine, connect, hitch up **08** forsooth! **09** affiliate, associate **10** amalgamate, get hitched, get married, get spliced, intermarry, take to wife, tie the knot **12** go to the world, join together **13** take the plunge **14** become espoused, lead to the altar, lead up the aisle **15** join in matrimony

Mars
04 Ares

marsh
03 bog, fen **04** mire, salt, wash **05** bayou, swamp **06** marish, morass, muskeg, salina, slough **07** corcass **08** quagmire **09** everglade, marshland **10** Everglades

marshal
◇ *anagram indicator*
04 lead, rank, take **05** align, array, group, guide, order, usher **06** deploy, draw up, escort, gather, line up, muster, parade **07** arrange, collect, conduct, dispose, farrier **08** assemble, organize, shepherd **09** mareschal, marischal **10** put in order **13** velt-mareschal **14** gather together

Marshals include:

03 Ney (Michel)
04 Earp (Wyatt), Foch (Ferdinand), Saxe (Maurice, Comte de), Tito
06 Hickok (Wild Bill), Pétain (Philippe), Tedder (Arthur, Lord), Zhukov (Georgi)
08 MacMahon (Patrice de)

See also **Field Marshal**

Marshall Islands
03 MHL

marshy
03 wet **04** miry **05** boggy, fenny, moory, muddy **06** quaggy, slumpy, spongy, swampy **07** fennish, moorish, paludal **08** paludine, paludose, paludous, squelchy **09** paludinal **10** paludinous **11** waterlogged

marsupial

Marsupials include:

03 roo
04 euro, tuan
05 koala, quoll
06 boodie, cuscus, glider, numbat, possum, quokka, tammar, wombat
07 bettong, dasyure, dibbler, dunnart, opossum, potoroo, wallaby
08 kangaroo, macropod, tarsiped, wallaroo
09 bandicoot, boodie-rat, koala bear, native cat, pademelon, petaurist, phalanger, thylacine, wambenger
10 native bear, Notoryctes
11 diprotodont, honey possum, rat kangaroo, rock wallaby
12 marsupial rat, pouched mouse, tree kangaroo
13 brush kangaroo, marsupial mole, Tasmanian wolf
14 marsupial mouse, Tasmanian devil, vulpine opossum
15 flying phalanger

See also **animal**

mart
04 fair, mall, souk **06** bazaar, market, outlet, staple **08** emporium, exchange **10** repository **11** market-place **14** shopping centre

marten
05 pekan, sable **06** fisher **07** Mustela **09** woodshock

martial
04 army **05** brave **06** heroic **07** hawkish, warlike **08** militant, military **09** bellicose, combative, soldierly **10** aggressive, pugnacious **11** belligerent

martial art

Martial arts and forms of self-defence include:

04 judo
05 lai-do, sambo, wushu
06 aikido, karate, kung fu, t'ai chi
07 capuera, ju-jitsu
08 capoeira, jiu-jitsu, ninjitsu, ninjutsu, Shotokan
09 tae kwon do
10 kick boxing
11 self-defence, t'ai chi ch'uan

• martial art expert
03 dan

martinet
06 martin, tyrant 08 stickler
09 formalist 10 taskmaster 11 slave-driver 12 taskmistress 14 disciplinarian

Martinique
03 MTQ

martyr
05 stone 06 victim 07 crucify, torment, torture 09 persecute 10 put to death
12 give the works, put on the rack
13 make a martyr of 14 burn at the stake 15 throw to the lions

martyrdom
05 agony, death, stake 06 ordeal
07 anguish, passion, torment, torture, witness 09 suffering 11 persecution
12 excruciation 13 baptism of fire
14 baptism of blood

marvel
04 gape, gawp, gaze, marl 05 marle, stare 06 genius, goggle, wonder
07 miracle, portent, prodigy 08 be amazed, surprise 09 eye-opener, fairy tale, not expect, sensation, spectacle
10 fairy story, phenomenon
12 astonishment, be astonished
14 quite something 15 be flabbergasted

marvellous
03 ace, bad, def, fab, rad 04 cool, mean, mega, neat, phat 05 brill, great, magic, super 06 superb, wicked
07 amazing, awesome, crucial, épatant, mirific, radical, wondred
08 glorious, selcouth, splendid, terrific, wondered 09 bodacious, excellent, fantastic, mirifical, wonderful
10 astounding, improbable, incredible, miraculous, out of sight, remarkable, stupendous, super-duper, surprising
11 astonishing, fantabulous, magnificent, merveilleux, sensational, spectacular 12 merveilleuse, unbelievable 13 extraordinary

marvellously
04 very 06 highly, really 07 acutely, awfully, greatly, utterly 08 severely, terribly 09 decidedly, extremely, intensely, to a wonder, unusually
10 dreadfully, remarkably, thoroughly, uncommonly 11 exceedingly, excessively, frightfully 12 inordinately, terrifically 13 exceptionally
15 extraordinarily

Maryland
02 MD

masculine
01 m 02 he 03 mas 04 bold, male, masc 05 brave, butch, macho, manly
06 heroic, robust, rugged, strong, virile
07 gallant, manlike, mannish
08 fearless, muscular, powerful, resolute, vigorous 09 confident, strapping 10 determined, red-blooded
12 stout-hearted

masculinity
06 mettle, valour, vigour 07 bravery, courage, heroism, manhood
08 boldness, firmness, machismo, maleness, strength, virility
09 fortitude, hardihood, manliness
10 manfulness, resolution
11 intrepidity 12 fearlessness, independence, stalwartness

mash
◇ *anagram indicator*
03 pap 04 beat, hash, mush, pulp
05 champ, crush, grind, paste, pound, purée, smash 06 bungle, infuse, muddle, pummel, squash 09 pulverize

mask
04 hide, show, veil 05 blind, cloak, cover, front, guise, matte, steep, visor, vizor 06 domino, façade, immask, infuse, masque, screen, shield, veneer, vizard 07 conceal, cover up, cover-up, goggles, inhaler, obscure, persona
08 disguise, joncanoe, junkanoo, pretence 09 dissemble, false face, gas helmet, John Canoe, John Kanoo, semblance 10 camouflage, gorgoneion, masquerade, respirator
11 concealment

masquerade
◇ *anagram indicator*
03 mum 04 mask, mumm, play, pose
05 cloak, cover, front, guise
06 masque 07 cover-up, dress up, pretend, profess 08 disguise, pretence
09 deception 10 masked ball
11 costume ball, counterfeit, dissimulate, impersonate 14 fancy dress ball 15 fancy dress party, pass yourself off

mass
01 m 03 lot, mob, ped, sea, sum, wad
04 bags, ball, band, body, bulk, clod, hang, heap, herd, hunk, load, lots, lump, most, nest, pile, size, tons
05 amass, batch, block, bolus, bunch, chaos, chunk, crowd, group, heaps, horde, loads, piece, piles, plebs, rally, stack, swarm, total, troop, whole, wodge 06 dallop, dollop, gather, huddle, medley, muster, oodles, rabble, scores, tangle, throng, weight, welter
07 blanket, cluster, clutter, collect, general, popular 08 assemble, capacity, coagulum, entirety, indigest, majority, pandemic, quantity, riff-raff, sweeping, totality 09 abundance, aggregate, Communion, dimension, Eucharist, extensive, hoi polloi, immensity, magnitude, multitude, rotundity, universal, wholesale
10 accumulate, assemblage, collection, concretion, congregate, large-scale, Lord's Table, widespread
11 combination, greater part, large number, Lord's Supper, proletariat
12 accumulation, come together, common people, draw together, lower classes, working class 13 agglutination, bring together, comprehensive, Holy Communion, preponderance
14 across-the-board, conglomeration, indiscriminate, the rank and file, working classes

Massachusetts
02 MA 04 Mass

massacre
04 kill, slay 05 purge 06 murder, pogrom 07 butcher, carnage, killing, kill off, mow down, wipe out
08 butchery, decimate, genocide, homicide 09 bloodbath, holocaust, liquidate, slaughter 10 annihilate, blood purge, decimation
11 exterminate, liquidation
12 annihilation 13 extermination
15 ethnic cleansing

Massacres include:

04 Hama, Lari
05 Ambon, Katyn, My Lai, Paris, Sabra
06 Bezier, Boston, Cataví, Herrin, Kanpur, Lidice, Rishon
07 Amboyna, Babi Yar, Badajoz, Baghdad, Chatila, Glencoe, Halabja, Nanking, Tianjin
08 Amritsar, Cawnpore, Drogheda, El Mozote, Kishinev, Novgorod, Peterloo, Tientsin
09 Fetterman, Innocents, Jerusalem, Sand Creek, September, Trebizond
10 Addis Ababa, Fort Pillow, Myall Creek, Paxton Boys, Sack of Rome, Srebrenica, Tlatelolco
11 Janissaries, Sharpeville, Wounded Knee
12 Bloody Sunday, Sabra/Chatila
15 Oradour-sur-Glane, Sicilian Vespers, St Valentine's Day, Tiananmen Square

massage
◇ *anagram indicator*
03 rub 04 an mo, cook, do-in 05 alter, knead, reiki, tui na 06 doctor, fiddle, pummel 07 falsify, Jacuzzi®, rubbing, rub down, rub-down, shampoo, shiatsu, shiatzu, tripsis 08 aerotone, kneading 10 manipulate, osteopathy, percussion, petrissage, pummelling, tamper with 11 acupressure, reflexology 12 aromatherapy, manipulation, misrepresent
13 interfere with, physiotherapy
15 Reichian therapy, thalassotherapy

massive
03 big 04 bull, gang, huge, vast
05 beamy, bulky, great, heavy, hefty, jumbo, large, solid 06 mighty
07 hulking, immense, mammoth, popular, weighty 08 colossal, enormous, gigantic, timbered,

whopping **09** extensive, ginormous, ponderous **10** large-scale, monolithic, monumental, successful **11** substantial

massively
06 vastly **07** greatly, heavily **08** very much **09** immensely **10** enormously **11** extensively **12** monumentally **13** substantially

mast
03 bar, rod **04** boom, heel, nuts, pole, post, spar, yard **05** shaft, staff, stick **06** acorns, jigger **07** pannage, support, upright **10** topgallant

master
01 M **02** MA, PM, RM **03** ace, Dan, guv, Mas, Mes, pro **04** baas, beak, boss, buff, curb, guru, head, Herr, lord, main, Mass, Mess, rule, sire, tame, tuan **05** adept, bwana, check, chief, grand, grasp, great, guide, learn, maven, mavin, owner, prime, quell, ruler, tutor **06** bridle, defeat, expert, gaffer, genius, govern, honcho, leader, manage, mentor, pick up, pundit, season, subdue, temper **07** acquire, captain, conquer, control, dab hand, egghead, leading, maestro, manager, skilful, skilled, skipper, teacher, wise guy **08** director, employer, foremost, governor, masterly, overcome, overlord, overseer, suppress, vanquish, virtuoso **09** commander, dexterous, overpower, pedagogue, practised, preceptor, principal, Signorino, subjugate **10** controller, instructor, past master, proficient **11** controlling, experienced, grand master, predominant, symposiarch, triumph over **12** get the hang of, professional, schoolmaster **13** most important, schoolteacher **14** schoolmistress, superintendent

masterful
05 bossy, pithy **08** arrogant, despotic, powerful **09** imperious **10** autocratic, dominating, high-handed, peremptory, tyrannical **11** controlling, dictatorial, domineering, overbearing **13** authoritative

masterly
03 ace **05** adept, crack **06** adroit, artful, expert, superb **07** skilful, skilled, supreme **08** polished, superior, top-notch **09** dexterous, excellent, first-rate, magistral **10** consummate **11** overbearing **12** accomplished, professional

mastermind
04 mind, plan **05** forge, frame, hatch **06** brains, design, devise, direct, genius, manage **07** control, creator, dream up, inspire, manager, planner, think up **08** be behind, conceive, contrive, director, engineer, organize, virtuoso **09** architect, authority, initiator, intellect, organizer, originate **10** originator, prime mover

masterpiece
05 jewel **08** creation **09** work of art **10** magnum opus, masterwork **11** chef d'oeuvre

masterstroke
04 coup, feat **07** success, triumph, victory **10** attainment **11** achievement **12** coup de maître **14** accomplishment

mastery
04 grip, rule **05** grasp, skill **07** ability, command, control, knowhow, prowess, triumph, victory **08** dominion **09** authority, dexterity, direction, expertise, knowledge, supremacy, upper hand **10** ascendancy, capability, domination, virtuosity **11** familiarity, proficiency, sovereignty, superiority **13** comprehension, understanding

• **strive for mastery**
04 kemp

masticate
03 eat **04** chew **05** champ, chomp, knead, munch **06** crunch **08** ruminate **09** manducate **10** chew the cud

mastication
06 eating **07** chewing **08** champing, munching **10** rumination **11** manducation

mat
03 rug **04** dull, felt, knot, mass, matt, taut, tawt **05** frost, matte, tatty, twist **06** carpet, felter, paunch, tangle, tatami **07** cluster, coaster, doormat, drugget **08** place mat, table mat, underlay **09** underfelt **10** interweave, lustreless

match
03 fit, pit, tie, vie **04** ally, bout, copy, fuse, game, join, link, main, mate, meet, pair, peer, spar, suit, team, test, twin, yoke **05** adapt, agree, amate, blend, equal, event, fusee, fuzee, light, marry, rival, spill, tally, taper, trial, union, unite, vesta **06** accord, besort, couple, double, fellow, go with, marrow, merger, oppose, pair up, relate **07** combine, compact, compare, compete, connect, contend, contest, hitch up, Lucifer, pairing, paragon, pattern, replica **08** alliance, bonspiel, coupling, locofoco, marriage, parallel, tone with **09** accompany, companion, duplicate, encounter, harmonize, lookalike **10** competitor, complement, co-ordinate, correspond, dead ringer, equivalent, go together, keep up with, one of a pair, pit against, Promethean, tournament **11** affiliation, combination, competition, counterpart, measure up to, partnership, safety match **13** be in agreement

See also **game**; **sport**

• **match up to**
04 meet **05** reach **08** approach, come up to, live up to **11** compare with, measure up to **12** make the grade

• **start of match, start the match**
02 KO **05** break, bully **06** tee off **07** face-off, kick-off **13** break the balls

matching
04 like, same, twin **06** double, in sync, paired **07** coupled, in synch, similar **08** blending, parallel **09** analogous, duplicate, identical **10** comparable, equivalent **11** correlative, harmonizing **12** co-ordinating **13** complementary, complementing, corresponding

matchless
06 unique **07** perfect **08** makeless, peerless **09** nonpareil, unmatched **10** inimitable, unequalled, unexcelled, unrivalled **11** unsurpassed **12** incomparable, unparalleled, without equal **13** beyond compare

mate
03 fit, pal, wed, wus **04** chum, feer, fere, join, leap, line, maik, make, nick, oppo, pair, twin, wack, wife **05** breed, buddy, china, crony, cully, equal, feare, fiere, marry, match, rival **06** baffle, buffer, cobber, co-mate, couple, deputy, fellow, friend, gender, helper, hubbie, marrow, missis, missus, mucker, pheere, spouse, subdue **07** baffled, compeer, comrade, consort, daunted, husband, Mr Right, oldster, paragon, partner **08** confound, copulate, co-worker, sidekick, workmate **09** assistant, associate, boyfriend, checkmate, colleague, companion, exhausted, other half **10** accomplice, apprentice, better half, checkmated, china plate, confounded, equivalent, girlfriend **11** counterpart, subordinate **12** fellow worker **14** opposite number

material
03 gen, key **04** body, data, info, work **05** cloth, facts, gross, ideas, notes, stuff, vital **06** bodily, fabric, matter, medium **07** details, earthly, germane, low-down, numbers, serious, textile, weighty, worldly **08** apposite, concrete, evidence, palpable, physical, relevant, tangible **09** corporeal, essential, important, momentous, pertinent, substance **10** meaningful **11** information, particulars, significant, substantial **12** constituents **13** consequential, indispensable **15** facts and figures

See also **art**; **building**; **fabric**

• **set material in position**
03 lay

materialism
05 greed **06** hylism **08** hylicism, somatism **11** consumerism, worldliness **12** corporealism **15** acquisitiveness

materialistic
07 worldly **08** banausic **09** bourgeois, mammonist, mercenary **11** acquisitive, consumerist, mammonistic **13** money-grabbing **14** bread-and-butter

materialize
05 arise, occur, reify **06** appear, happen, turn up **09** take place, take shape **12** show yourself **13** become visible, come into being **14** reveal yourself

materially
04 much **07** gravely, greatly **09** basically, seriously **11** essentially **12** considerably **13** fundamentally, significantly, substantially

maternal
04 fond, kind, warm **05** mumsy **06** caring, doting, gentle, loving, tender **08** motherly, vigilant **09** nurturing **10** comforting, motherlike, nourishing, protective **12** affectionate **13** understanding

matey *see* **maty, matey**

mathematics

Branches of mathematics include:

06 conics
07 algebra, applied, fluxion
08 calculus, geometry
09 set theory
10 arithmetic, game theory, statistics
11 games theory, group theory
12 number theory, trigonometry
13 combinatorics
14 biomathematics
15 metamathematics, pure mathematics

Mathematics terms include:

02 pi
03 arc, set
04 apex, area, axes, axis, base, cube, edge, face, line, mean, mode, plus, root, side, sine, skew, unit, zero
05 angle, chaos, chord, curve, depth, equal, graph, group, helix, locus, minus, ogive, point, ratio, solid, speed, total, width
06 binary, chance, convex, cosine, degree, factor, height, length, linear, matrix, median, number, origin, radian, radius, sample, secant, sector, spiral, square, subset, vector, vertex, volume
07 algebra, average, bearing, bounded, breadth, chaotic, concave, decimal, divisor, formula, fractal, integer, mapping, maximum, measure, minimum, modulus, oblique, product, segment, tangent
08 addition, analysis, antipode, argument, bar chart, bar graph, binomial, calculus, capacity, constant, converse, cube root, diagonal, diameter, discrete, dividend, division, equation, exponent, fraction, function, geometry, gradient, identity, infinity, latitude, less than, multiple, parabola, pie chart, quadrant, quartile, quotient, rotation, symmetry, variable, variance, velocity, vertical
09 algorithm, Cartesian, congruent, factorial, frequency, histogram, hyperbola, iteration, logarithm, longitude, numerator, odd number, operation, parameter, perimeter, remainder
10 acute angle, arithmetic, complement, continuous, coordinate, covariance, derivative, even number, horizontal, hypotenuse, percentage, percentile, place value, proportion, protractor, Pythagoras, real number, reciprocal, reflection, regression, right-angle, square root, statistics, subtractor
11 approximate, coefficient, combination, coordinates, correlation, denominator, determinant, enlargement, equidistant, exponential, greater than, integration, magic square, mirror image, Möbius strip, obtuse angle, permutation, plane figure, prime number, probability, Pythagorean, real numbers, reflex angle, translation, Venn diagram, whole number
12 asymmetrical, cross section, distribution, random sample, straight line, trigonometry, universal set
13 circumference, complex number, Mandelbrot set, mixed fraction, natural number, ordinal number, parallel lines, perpendicular, quadrilateral, scalar segment, triangulation
14 axis of symmetry, cardinal number, common fraction, directed number, mirror symmetry, multiplication, negative number, parallel planes, positive number, rational number, transformation, vulgar fraction
15 conjugate angles, differentiation, imaginary number, scalene triangle

Mathematicians include:

03 **Dee** (John), **Lie** (Sophus)
04 **Abel** (Niels Henrik), **Hero** (of Alexandria), **Hopf** (Heinz), **Kerr** (Roy), **Pell** (John), **Tait** (Peter Guthrie), **Thom** (René), **Venn** (John), **Weil** (André), **Weyl** (Hermann)
05 **Bayes** (Thomas), **Boole** (George), **Dirac** (Paul), **Euler** (Leonhard), **Gauss** (Carl Friedrich), **Gödel** (Kurt), **Green** (George), **Hardy** (Godfrey), **Hoyle** (Sir Fred), **Klein** (Felix), **Monge** (Gaspard), **Peano** (Giuseppe), **Serre** (Jean-Pierre), **Snell** (Willebrod), **Vieta** (Franciscus)
06 **Ampère** (André), **Argand** (Jean-Robert), **Bessel** (Friedrich), **Briggs** (Henry), **Cantor** (Georg), **Cauchy** (Augustin Louis, Baron), **Cayley** (Arthur), **Euclid**, **Fermat** (Pierre de), **Fields** (J C), **Fisher** (Sir Ronald), **Galois** (Évariste), **Halley** (Edmond), **Jacobi** (Carl), **Jordan** (Camille), **Kelvin** (William Thomson, Lord), **Lorenz** (Edward), **Markov** (Andrei), **Möbius** (August Ferdinand), **Moivre** (Abraham de), **Napier** (John), **Newton** (Sir Isaac), **Pappus** (of Alexandria), **Pascal** (Blaise), **Picard** (Émile), **Stokes** (Sir George), **Turing** (Alan), **Wallis** (John), **Wiener** (Norbert)
07 **Alhazen**, **Babbage** (Charles), **Cardano** (Girolamo), **Carroll** (Lewis), **Eudoxus** (of Cnidus), **Fourier** (Joseph, Baron de), **Galileo**, **Germain** (Sophie), **Hilbert** (David), **Laplace** (Pierre, Marquis de), **Leibniz** (Gottfried), **Penrose** (Roger), **Poisson** (Siméon), **Riemann** (Bernhard), **Russell** (Bertrand, Earl), **Shannon** (Claude)
08 **Alembert** (Jean le Rond d'), **Birkhoff** (George David), **Dedekind** (Julius), **De Morgan** (Augustus), **Guldberg** (Cato), **Hamilton** (Sir William Rowan), **Lagrange** (Joseph de, Comte), **Legendre** (Adrien-Marie), **Lovelace** (Ada, Countess of), **Mercator** (Nicolaus), **Playfair** (John), **Poincaré** (Jules)
09 **Bernoulli** (Daniel), **Bernoulli** (Jacques), **Bronowski** (Jacob), **Descartes** (René), **Dirichlet** (Lejeune), **Fibonacci** (Leonardo), **Minkowski** (Hermann), **Whitehead** (Alfred)
10 **Apollonius** (of Perga), **Archimedes**, **Diophantus**, **Hipparchus**, **Maupertuis** (Pierre Louis de), **Pythagoras**, **Sierpinski** (Wactaw), **Torricelli** (Evangelista), **Zeno of Elea**
11 **al-Khwarizmi**
12 **Eratosthenes**

mating
06 fusing **07** coition, joining, pairing, uniting **08** breeding, coupling, matching, twinning **10** copulating, copulation

matriarch
04 nana

matrimonial
06 wedded **07** marital, married, nuptial, spousal, wedding **08** conjugal, marriage
• **matrimonial duties**
03 bed

matrimony
05 union **07** wedlock **08** marriage, nuptials, spousage **09** espousals **12** married state

matrix
03 gel, mat **04** cast, form, mold, womb **05** array, frame, mould, plasm, table **06** stroma **07** context, matrice **08** analysis, chondrin, Jacobian, template **09** composite, framework, transpose **11** arrangement

matron
04 dame

matted
05 taggy **06** tangly **07** knotted, tangled, tousled **08** uncombed **09** entangled **11** dishevelled **13** blood-boltered

matter
02 go **03** pus **04** body, case, hyle, note **05** count, event, issue, point, stuff, thing, topic, upset, value, worry

06 affair, bother, import, medium, weight 07 concern, content, episode, problem, subject, trouble 08 business, distress, incident, interest, material, nuisance, question, weakness
09 discharge, happening, make a stir, make waves, purulence, secretion, situation, substance 10 be relevant, difficulty, importance, occurrence, proceeding 11 be important, carry weight, consequence, shortcoming, suppuration 12 circumstance, cut a lot of ice, significance 13 have influence, inconvenience, mean something, momentousness
14 be of importance 15 make a difference

• **as a matter of fact**
05 truly 06 in fact, really 08 actually
11 as it happens 12 in actual fact

• **matter of no importance**
03 toy 10 triviality

• **no matter**
09 never mind 15 it does not matter, it is unimportant

matter-of-fact
03 dry 04 dull, flat 05 sober 06 thingy
07 deadpan, prosaic 08 lifeless, positive 09 practical, pragmatic, prosaical 10 pedestrian 11 down-to-earth, emotionless, pragmatical, unemotional 13 unimaginative, unsentimental 15 straightforward

matting
03 tat 04 bast

mattress
03 bed 04 Lilo® 05 futon 06 airbed, pallet 07 biscuit 08 crash-mat, water bed 09 paillasse, palliasse 10 feather bed

maturation
06 growth 08 fruition, ripening
09 seasoning 11 development

mature
03 age 04 bold, gray, grey, ripe, wise
05 adult, bloom, grown, of age, ready, ripen 06 evolve, grow up, mellow, nubile, season 07 concoct, develop, fall due, grown-up, perfect, prepare, ripened 08 balanced, complete, finished, joined-up, maturate, seasoned, sensible 09 come of age, finalized, full-grown, perfected
10 become ripe, precocious
11 become adult, draw to a head, experienced, responsible 12 become mellow, fully fledged 13 well-developed 14 become sensible, well-thought-out

maturity
03 age 06 summer, wisdom
07 manhood, puberty 08 majority, ripeness 09 adulthood, readiness, womanhood 10 experience, full growth, mellowness, perfection
11 coming of age 12 sensibleness
14 responsibility 15 age of discretion

matweed
04 nard

maty, matey
04 kind, warm 05 close, pally, thick, tight 06 blokey, chummy, folksy, genial
07 affable, cordial, helpful
08 amicable, blokeish, familiar, friendly, intimate, outgoing, sociable
09 agreeable, comradely, convivial, peaceable, receptive 10 favourable
11 good-natured, inseparable, neighbourly, sympathetic
12 affectionate, approachable, well-disposed 13 companionable

maudlin
05 drunk, gushy, mushy, soppy, tipsy, weepy 06 sickly, sloppy, slushy
07 fuddled, mawkish, tearful, weeping
09 emotional, half-drunk, schmaltzy
10 lachrymose 11 sentimental

maul
◇ *anagram indicator*
03 mug, paw 04 beat, belt, claw, mall, mell 05 abuse 06 attack, batter, beat up, do over, mangle, molest, thrash, wallop 07 assault, rough up 08 ill-treat, lacerate, maltreat, mutilate
09 manhandle 10 knock about

maunder
04 ease, inch, laze, roam, rove
05 amble, mooch, mosey, stray
06 babble, beggar, drivel, gabble, jabber, mutter, natter, rabbit, ramble, stroll, waffle, wander, witter 07 blather, chatter, grumble, meander, prattle, shuffle 08 rabbit on

Maureen
02 Mo

Mauritania
03 MRT, RIM

Mauritius
02 MS 03 MUS

mausoleum
04 mole, tomb 05 crypt, vault
08 catacomb, Taj Mahal 09 sepulchre
10 undercroft 13 burial chamber

maverick
05 rebel 08 agitator, outsider 09 odd one out 13 individualist, nonconformist 14 fish out of water

maw
04 gulf, jaws 05 abyss, chasm, mouth
06 gullet, throat 07 seagull, stomach
08 appetite 11 inclination

mawkish
04 flat, foul 05 gushy, mawky, mushy, soppy 06 feeble, gloopy, sickly, slushy
07 insipid, maggoty, maudlin
08 nauseous 09 emotional, loathsome, offensive, schmaltzy, squeamish 10 disgusting, nauseating
11 sentimental

mawkishly
06 feebly 07 mushily, soppily
11 emotionally, loathsomely
12 nauseatingly 13 sentimentally

maxim
03 saw 04 rule 05 adage, axiom, gnome, motto 06 byword, dictum, saying 07 epigram, precept, proverb
08 aphorism, apothegm, moralism, sentence 09 principle, sentiment, watchword 10 apophthegm, prudential

maximize
05 add to, boost, breed, raise, widen
06 bump up, deepen, expand, extend, hike up, spread, step up 07 advance, augment, broaden, build up, develop, enhance, enlarge, further, magnify, prolong, scale up 08 heighten, increase 09 intensify, propagate
10 accumulate, strengthen

maximum
03 max, top 04 acme, full, high, most, peak 06 apogee, height, summit, utmost, zenith 07 biggest, ceiling, highest, largest, supreme, topmost
08 greatest, pinnacle, top point, ultimate 09 extremity, uttermost
10 upper limit

may
04 mote 08 hawthorn

• **may it do**
04 dich

maybe
◇ *anagram indicator*
07 could be, perhaps 08 possibly
09 perchance 11 conceivably, possibility 12 peradventure 13 for all you know

mayfly
06 day-fly 08 ephemera 09 caddis fly, ephemerid 10 green-drake
11 Plectoptera, turkey brown

mayhem
◇ *anagram indicator*
04 mess, riot 05 chaos, havoc
06 bedlam, tumult, uproar 07 anarchy, maiming 08 disorder, madhouse
09 confusion 10 disruption
11 lawlessness 15 disorganization

mayor
02 LM 05 maire 07 alcalde

Mayotte
03 MYT

maze
◇ *anagram indicator*
03 web 04 mesh 05 maise, maize, mease 06 jungle, puzzle, tangle, warren 07 complex, meander, network 09 confusion, honeycomb, intricacy, labyrinth

me
02 mi, us 03 moi

meadow
03 ing, lay, lea, lee, ley 04 inch, mead
05 field, grass, green, haugh 06 leasow, saeter 07 paddock, pasture, salting
09 grassland 11 pastureland

meadow-grass
03 poa

meagre
03 bar 04 arid, bony, lean, poor, puny, thin, weak 05 gaunt, mingy, small,

spare **06** barren, frugal, jejune, Lenten, maigre, measly, paltry, scanty, skimpy, skinny, slight, sparse, stingy **07** scraggy, scrawny, slender **08** exiguous, roncador, scrannel **09** deficient, emaciated, niggardly **10** inadequate, negligible, threadbare **12** insufficient **13** insubstantial

meagreness
07 poverty **08** puniness **09** smallness **10** deficiency, inadequacy, measliness, scantiness, slightness, sparseness, stinginess **13** insufficiency

meal
03 kai **04** fare, feed, kail, kale, meat, mess, mush **05** grout, scoff, skoff **06** farina, repast **07** meltith, surfeit **08** freeload, racahout **09** collation, raccahout, refection, scambling **12** refreshments

Meals include:

03 BBQ, tea
04 bite
05 feast, lunch, snack
06 barbie, brunch, buffet, dinner, nosh-up, picnic, repast, spread, supper, tiffin
07 banquet, blow-out, high tea
08 barbecue, cream tea, luncheon, takeaway, tea break, tea party, TV dinner
09 breakfast, cold table, collation, elevenses
10 fork supper, midday meal, slap-up meal
11 dinner party, evening meal
12 afternoon tea, safari supper
13 harvest supper

• **before a meal**
02 ap

mealy-mouthed
04 glib, prim **07** mincing **08** indirect, reticent **09** equivocal, hestitant, plausible **10** flattering **11** euphemistic **12** overdelicate **13** over-squeamish, smooth-tongued

mean
03 ace, aim, low, rad **04** base, cool, fate, fine, mega, mein, mene, mode, neat, norm, plan, poor, rare, show, vile, wish, wont **05** boffo, brill, cause, crack, cross, cruel, dirty, footy, imply, lowly, mangy, meane, mingy, nasty, prime, scall, slink, snide, tight **06** abject, aspire, common, convey, crabby, denote, design, dismal, divine, effect, entail, humble, intend, lament, lead to, mangey, matter, maungy, median, medium, middle, normal, ordain, ornery, paltry, ribald, ribaud, shabby, simple, skimpy, snotty, sordid, stingy, superb, unkind, way-out **07** appoint, average, beastly, betoken, caitiff, chintzy, connote, crucial, destine, express, grouchy, halfway, involve, mesquin, miserly, niggard, obscure, perfect, piggish, produce, propose, purport, purpose, radical, roynish, rybauld, selfish, signify, skilful, spaniel, squalid, suggest, think of **08** beggarly, complain, fabulous, grasping, heavenly, indicate, intimate, mesquine, middling, mid-point, moderate, ordinary, result in, smashing, sneaking, spiteful, splendid, stand for, stunning, terrific, top-notch, very good, whoreson, wretched **09** admirable, brilliant, crotchety, cullionly, designate, earth-bred, excellent, fantastic, first-rate, malicious, matchless, middle way, miserable, niggardly, represent, symbolize, wonderful **10** base-minded, bring about, compromise, contracted, despicable, fast-handed, first-class, give rise to, golden mean, have in mind, ill-natured, marvellous, not half bad, predestine, remarkable, surpassing, threepenny, unequalled, unfriendly, ungenerous, unpleasant **11** bad-tempered, be important, carry weight, close-fisted, close-handed, exceptional, happy medium, high-quality, magnificent, near the bone, necessitate, outstanding, sensational, superlative, tight-fisted **12** cheese-paring, disagreeable, intermediate, middle course, parsimonious, second to none, unparalleled **13** have influence, penny-pinching, uncomfortable **14** inconsiderable, out of this world **15** make a difference

• **mean time**
02 MT

meander
04 bend, ease, inch, laze, maze, roam, rove, turn, wind **05** amble, curve, mooch, mosey, snake, stray, twist **06** ramble, stroll, wander, wimple, zigzag **07** shuffle, turning, whimple **09** sinuosity **10** perplexity

meandering
◇ *anagram indicator*
07 sinuous, snaking, turning, winding **08** indirect, rambling, tortuous, twisting **09** meandrous, wandering **10** circuitous, convoluted, roundabout, serpentine

meaning
03 aim **04** feck, gist, goal, hang, idea, plan, wish **05** drift, point, sense, trend, value, worth **06** import, letter, object, spirit, thrust **07** essence, message, purpose **08** sentence **09** intention, objective, substance **10** aspiration, definition, expression, usefulness **11** connotation, elucidation, explanation, explication, implication **12** construction, significance **13** signification **14** interpretation

meaningful
05 valid **06** useful **07** pointed, serious, telling, warning **08** eloquent, material, pregnant, relevant, speaking **09** effective, important **10** expressive, purposeful, suggestive, worthwhile **11** significant

meaningfully
08 usefully **09** pointedly **10** eloquently, relevantly **11** effectively, importantly **12** expressively, purposefully, suggestively **13** significantly

meaningless
04 vain **05** empty **06** absurd, futile, hollow **07** aimless, trivial, useless, vacuous **08** trifling, unsensed **09** gibberish, pointless, senseless, worthless **10** irrational, motiveless **11** nonsensical, purposeless **13** insignificant, insubstantial **14** expressionless, unintelligible

• **meaningless word, meaningless refrain**
05 nonny **07** ducdame, mirbane **08** falderal, fal de rol, folderol, rumbelow, rum-ti-tum **09** expletive **11** rumti-iddity **12** rumpti-iddity

meaninglessly
06 in vain, vainly **08** futilely **09** aimlessly, uselessly **11** pointlessly, senselessly **12** irrationally **13** purposelessly **14** unintelligibly

meanly
06 poorly, slight **07** cruelly, nastily **08** beggarly, commonly, scurvily, shabbily, unkindly **09** miserably, niggardly, selfishly **10** graspingly, spitefully **12** contemptibly, ungenerously, unpleasantly

meanness
09 parsimony **10** niggardise, niggardize, stinginess **11** mesquinerie, miserliness **12** illiberality **13** niggardliness, penuriousness **15** close-fistedness, close-handedness, tight-fistedness

means
03 way **04** mode **05** funds, money **06** agency, assets, avenue, course, income, manner, medium, method, riches, wealth **07** capital, channel, fortune, process, vehicle **08** property **09** affluence, resources, substance **10** instrument **11** wherewithal

• **by all means**
06 surely **08** of course **09** certainly, naturally **10** of all loves **11** à toute force **12** with pleasure

• **by means of**
03 per, via **04** with **05** using **07** through **08** by dint of **11** as a result of **12** with the aid of **13** with the help of

• **by no means**
04 none **05** never, no way **07** in no way **08** not at all **11** anything but **12** certainly not

• **having enough means**
04 able

meantime, meanwhile
05 among **06** for now **07** interim **12** concurrently, for the moment, in the interim **13** at the same time, in the interval, in the meantime **14** in the meanwhile, simultaneously **15** for the time being

measly
04 mean, poor, puny **05** mingy, petty **06** meagre, paltry, scanty, skimpy,

spotty, stingy **07** miserly, pitiful, trivial **08** beggarly, pathetic, piddling **09** miserable, niggardly **10** ungenerous **12** contemptible

measurable
08 material, mensural, moderate **09** gaugeable **10** assessable, computable, fathomable, mensurable, noticeable **11** appreciable, perceptible, significant **12** determinable, quantifiable, quantitative

measure
02 be **03** act, cut, lot, pit **04** area, bill, bulk, deed, gage, line, mass, mete, norm, pace, part, rate, read, rule, size, step, tape, test, time, unit **05** depth, gauge, judge, level, limit, means, meter, metre, piece, plumb, quota, range, ruler, scale, scope, share, sound, units, value, weigh, width **06** action, amount, assess, course, degree, extent, fathom, height, length, method, ration, record, rhythm, size up, strain, survey, system, volume, weight **07** compute, expanse, portion, rake-off, statute **08** acid test, appraise, capacity, division, estimate, evaluate, quantify, quantity, standard, traverse **09** allotment, barometer, benchmark, calculate, criterion, determine, dimension, enactment, expedient, magnitude, procedure, restraint, treatment, yardstick **10** allocation, dimensions, litmus test, measure off, measure out, moderation, proceeding, proportion, resolution, touchstone **11** proportions

See also **measurement**

• beyond measure
08 out of cry **09** endlessly, immensely **10** extra modum, infinitely **11** excessively, inestimably, limitlessly **12** beyond belief, incalculably

• for good measure
06 as well **07** besides **08** as a bonus **10** in addition **11** furthermore **12** over and above

• get the measure of, take the measure of
04 rate **05** gauge, judge, value **06** assess, handle, reckon, size up **08** appraise, estimate, evaluate **09** calculate, determine **12** get a handle on

• measure off
03 fix **05** limit **07** delimit, lay down, mark out, pace out **09** demarcate, determine **10** measure out **12** circumscribe

• measure out
05 allot, issue **06** assign, divide **07** deal out, dole out, hand out, mete out, pour out **08** dispense, share out **09** apportion, parcel out **10** distribute, proportion

• measure up
02 do **07** shape up, suffice **10** fit the bill, pass muster **11** fill the bill **12** make the grade **15** come up to scratch

• measure up to
04 meet **05** equal, match, rival, touch **07** satisfy **08** come up to, live up to **09** match up to **11** compare with **12** make the grade

measured
04 slow **06** steady **07** careful, planned, precise, regular, studied **08** reasoned **09** unhurried **10** calculated, considered, deliberate, mensurable, restrained, rhythmical **12** premeditated **14** well-thought-out

measureless
04 vast **07** endless, immense **08** infinite **09** boundless, limitless, unbounded **10** bottomless **11** inestimable, innumerable **12** immeasurable, incalculable

measurement
04 area, bulk, gage, mass, size, tare, unit **05** depth, range, width **06** amount, extent, height, length, sizing, survey, volume, weight **07** expanse, gauging, reading **08** capacity, quantity, weighing **09** amplitude, appraisal, dimension, judgement, magnitude **10** assessment, estimation, evaluation, proportion **11** calculation, calibration, computation, proportions **12** appreciation **14** quantification

Measurement units include:

01 f, g, k, l, m, t, y
02 as, cg, cm, ct, dg, em, en, ft, gm, gr, hg, kg, lb, li, mg, mm, oz, pt, st, yd
03 amp, are, bar, bel, bit, cab, cor, cup, cwt, day, ell, erg, gal, grt, hin, kat, kin, kip, kos, lay, lea, ley, log, lux, mho, mil, mna, nit, ohm, oke, pin, rem, rod, tod, ton, tun, wey
04 acre, aune, barn, bath, baud, boll, bolt, butt, cell, cord, coss, cran, demy, dyne, epha, foot, gill, gram, hand, hour, inch, kati, khat, knot, link, mile, mill, mina, mole, muid, nail, obol, omer, peck, pica, pint, pipe, pole, pood, ream, rood, rope, seer, sone, span, tael, thou, tola, torr, vara, volt, watt, week, yard, year
05 cable, caneh, catty, chain, cubit, ephah, farad, henry, hertz, joule, kaneh, katti, litre, lumen, metre, month, ounce, perch, point, pound, quart, stere, stone, tesla, therm, tonne, weber
06 ampere, barrel, bushel, decade, degree, fathom, firkin, gallon, gramme, kelvin, league, minute, newton, parsec, pascal, radian, second
07 calorie, candela, century, coulomb, decibel, fresnel, furlong, hectare, long ton, siemens, volt amp
08 angstrom, cord foot, hogshead, kilogram, millibar, short ton
09 becquerel, board foot, centigram, cubic foot, cubic inch, cubic yard, decimetre, foot-pound, kilolitre, kilometre, light year, metric ton, milligram, steradian
10 atmosphere, barleycorn, centilitre, centimetre, cubic metre, fluid ounce, hectolitre, hoppus foot, horsepower, kilogramme, micrometre, millennium, millilitre, millimetre, millistere, square foot, square inch, square mile, square yard
11 centigramme, milligramme, newton metre, square metre
12 cable's length, nautical mile
13 degree Celsius, hundredweight, volts per metre
14 cubic decimetre, farads per metre, henrys per metre
15 cubic centimetre, metres per second, newtons per metre, square decimetre, square kilometre

See also **measurement of pressure** *under* **pressure**; **timber**; **unit of weight** *under* **weight**; **wood**

• Old Measurement
02 OM

measuring instrument

Measuring instruments include:

04 rule
05 gauge, meter
06 octant
07 ammeter, balance, burette, pipette, sextant
08 luxmeter, odometer, ohmmeter, quadrant
09 altimeter, barometer, callipers, cryometer, dosimeter, flowmeter, focimeter, hodometer, hourglass, manometer, milometer, optometer, pedometer, plumb line, pyrometer, rheometer, steelyard, stopwatch, vinometer, voltmeter, volumeter, wattmeter, wavemeter
10 anemometer, audiometer, bathometer, clinometer, cyclometer, gravimeter, hydrometer, hyetometer, hygrometer, hypsometer, micrometer, mileometer, multimeter, ombrometer, photometer, planimeter, protractor, pulsimeter, radiosonde, tachometer, tachymeter, theodolite, vibrograph, vibrometer, viscometer
11 calorimeter, chronometer, colorimeter, dynamometer, pluviometer, pyranometer, salinometer, seismograph, seismometer, speedometer, spherometer, tape measure, tensiometer, thermometer, vaporimeter, velocimeter, weighbridge
12 Breathalyser®, densitometer, evaporimeter, galvanometer, inclinometer, magnetometer, psychrometer, respirometer, spectrometer, sphygmometer, trundle wheel, viscosimeter
13 accelerometer, decelerometer, Geiger counter, saccharometer
14 geothermometer, interferometer

See also **gauge**

meat
03 nub **04** core, crux, eats, fare, food, gist, grub, nosh, pith, tuck **05** flesh,

heart, point, scran **06** kernel, marrow, tucker, viands **07** essence, nucleus, rations **08** eatables, victuals **09** substance **10** provisions, sustenance **11** comestibles, nourishment, subsistence **12** fundamentals

Cold meats include:

03 ham
04 beef, game, pâté, pork, Spam®
06 salami, tongue, turkey
07 biltong, chicken, chorizo, kabanos, pork pie, sausage, terrine, venison
08 bresaola, Cervelat, cold cuts, cured ham, meat loaf, ox tongue, parma ham, pastrami, salt beef
09 Bierwurst, glazed ham, liver paté, Mettwurst, pepperoni, rillettes, saucisson, scotch egg
10 breaded ham, corned beef, crumbed ham, liverwurst, mortadella, prosciutto, Serrano ham
11 sausage roll
12 Ardennes pâté, Brunswick ham, Brussels pâté, jamón serrano, liver sausage, luncheon meat, peppered beef, Wiltshire ham
13 chicken breast, garlic sausage, honey roast ham, Schinkenwurst, smoked sausage
15 luncheon sausage

Meat cuts include:

03 leg, rib, sey
04 chop, clod, hand, hock, loin, neck, rack, rump, shin
05 baron, chine, chuck, flank, hough, round, scrag, shank
06 breast, collar, cutlet, fillet, saddle
07 best end, brisket, buttock, knuckle, sirloin, topside
08 escalope, forehock, noisette, popeseye, shoulder, spare rib
09 aitchbone, médaillon
10 silverside
11 filet mignon, porterhouse

Meats and meat products include:

03 ham, MRM, red
04 beef, bush, duck, hare, lamb, loaf, pâté, pork, Spam®, spek, veal
05 bacon, brawn, goose, heart, liver, mince, offal, quail, speck, steak, tripe, vifda, vivda, white
06 brains, burger, faggot, gammon, grouse, haggis, haslet, kidney, mutton, oxtail, pigeon, polony, rabbit, tongue, turkey
07 biltong, chicken, fatback, griskin, harslet, long pig, pemican, poultry, rissole, sausage, variety, venison
08 bushmeat, foie gras, fricadel, luncheon, meat loaf, pemmican, pheasant, scrapple, trotters
09 forcemeat, frikkadel, hamburger, partridge, rillettes
10 beefburger, horseflesh, minced beef, sweetbread
11 pig's knuckle, sausage meat
12 black pudding; luncheon meat
13 shield of brawn
14 mousse de canard

meaty
04 rich **05** beefy, burly, heavy, hunky, pithy, solid **06** brawny, fleshy, hearty, sturdy **08** muscular, profound **09** strapping **10** meaningful **11** interesting, significant, substantial

mechanic
07 artisan **08** engineer, operator **09** artificer, grauncher, groundman, machinist, operative, repairman, tradesman **10** groundsman, millwright, technician **11** card-sharper, mechanician, tradeswoman **12** grease monkey

mechanical
04 cold, dead, dull **06** manual, reflex **07** organic, routine **08** electric, habitual, lifeless, soulless **09** automated, automatic, dynamical, technical, unfeeling **10** impersonal, mechanized, unthinking **11** emotionless, instinctive, involuntary, machine-like, mechanistic, perfunctory, power-driven, unconscious, unemotional **12** matter-of-fact **14** machine-powered

mechanically
09 routinely **10** as a machine, by a machine, habitually **11** intuitively, on autopilot **12** unthinkingly **13** automatically, instinctively, involuntarily, unconsciously **14** electronically

mechanism
04 guts, tool **05** gears, means, motor, works **06** action, agency, device, engine, gadget, medium, method, system **07** channel, machine, process **08** gimcrack, jimcrack, movement, workings **09** apparatus, appliance, interlock, machinery, operation, procedure, propeller, structure, technique **10** components, instrument, propelment **11** contraption, contrivance, functioning, performance

mechanize
07 program **08** automate **11** computerize

medal
04 gold, gong **05** award, cross, model, prize **06** bronze, honour, reward, ribbon, silver, trophy **08** contorno, vernicle **09** gold medal, medallion **10** decoration, touch-piece **11** bronze medal, contorniate, silver medal
See also **military**

meddle
◇ *anagram indicator*
03 mix, pry **04** mell, mess **05** medle, snoop **06** butt in, fiddle, kibitz, tamper, temper, tinker **07** intrude **09** interfere, intervene **10** stickybeak **12** put your oar in **14** poke your nose in, stick your oar in **15** stick your nose in

meddlesome
04 nosy **05** nosey **06** prying **08** meddling, snooping **09** intruding, intrusive, pragmatic **11** interfering, mischievous, pragmatical

mediaeval *see* **medieval, mediaeval**

mediate
06 convey, middle, settle, step in, umpire **07** referee, resolve, stickle **08** indirect, moderate, transmit **09** arbitrate, intercede, interpose, intervene, negotiate, reconcile **10** conciliate **11** intervening **12** intermediate **13** act as mediator **15** act as peacemaker

mediation
11 arbitration, good offices, negotiation, peacemaking **12** conciliation, intercession, intervention **13** interposition **14** reconciliation

mediator
04 mean **05** judge **06** priest, umpire **07** arbiter, referee **08** stickler **09** go-between, middleman, moderator, Ombudsman, thirdsman **10** arbitrator, interceder, intervener, negotiator, peacemaker, reconciler **11** conciliator, intercessor, interventor **12** honest broker, intermediary

medical
03 med
See also **disease**

Medical and surgical equipment includes:

03 ECG, MRI
05 clamp, swabs
06 canula, scales
07 cannula, curette, dilator, forceps, inhaler, scalpel, scanner, syringe
08 catheter, iron lung, speculum, tweezers, X-ray unit
09 aspirator, auriscope, autoclave, CT scanner, endoscope, incubator, inhalator, nebulizer, retractor
10 audiometer, CAT scanner, ear syringe, hypodermic, kidney dish, microscope, MRI scanner, oxygen mask, rectoscope, respirator, rhinoscope, sterilizer, ultrasound
11 body scanner, first aid kit, laparoscope, stethoscope, stomach pump, thermometer
12 bronchoscope, isolator tent, laryngoscope, resuscitator, surgical mask, urethroscope
13 aural speculum, defibrillator, specimen glass
14 oesophagoscope, operating table, ophthalmoscope, oxygen cylinder
15 instrument table

Medical specialists include:

07 dentist
08 optician
09 dietician, homeopath
10 homoeopath, oncologist, orthoptist, pharmacist
11 audiologist, chiropodist, neurologist, optometrist, pathologist, radiologist

12 anaesthetist, cardiologist, chiropractor, embryologist, geriatrician, immunologist, obstetrician, orthodontist, orthopaedist, psychiatrist, psychologist, toxicologist
13 dermatologist, gerontologist, gynaecologist, haematologist, paediatrician, vaccinologist
14 bacteriologist, microbiologist, pharmacologist, rheumatologist
15 endocrinologist, ophthalmologist, physiotherapist

See also **doctor**; **nurse**

- **medical man** *see* **doctor**
- **medical records**

04 case

medicinal

06 physic 07 healing, medical 08 curative, physical, remedial 11 restorative, therapeutic 12 health-giving

medicinally

09 medically 10 curatively, remedially 13 restoratively 15 therapeutically

medicine

03 med 04 cure, drug 05 trade 06 remedy 07 panacea 09 analeptic, physician 10 medicament, medication 12 prescription 14 pharmaceutical

See also **drug**

Branches of medicine include:

05 ob-gyn
07 otology, urology
08 nosology, obs/gynae, oncology, pharmacy
09 andrology, audiology, chiropody, dentistry, neurology, optometry, pathology, radiology
10 cardiology, embryology, geriatrics, immunology, obstetrics, osteopathy, pediatrics, psychiatry, psychology, toxicology
11 dermatology, diagnostics, gerontology, gynaecology, haematology, paediatrics, physiatrics
12 anaesthetics, bacteriology, kinesiatrics, microbiology, orthodontics, orthopaedics, perinatology, pharmacology, radiotherapy, rheumatology
13 cytopathology, endocrinology, ophthalmology, physiotherapy, psychotherapy
14 electrotherapy, neuropathology, neuroradiology, sports medicine
15 neuropsychiatry

Branches of complementary medicine include:

04 yoga
05 reiki
07 massage, Pilates, Rolfing, shiatsu
08 Ayurveda
09 herbalism, iridology
10 art therapy, autogenics, homeopathy, meditation, osteopathy
11 acupressure, acupuncture, aura therapy, kinesiology, moxibustion, naturopathy, reflexology, t'ai chi ch'uan
12 aromatherapy, Bach remedies, chiropractic, hydrotherapy, hypnotherapy, macrobiotics
14 autosuggestion, crystal healing, herbal medicine
15 Chinese medicine, thalassotherapy

Medicine types include:

04 pill
05 tonic
06 arnica, emetic, gargle, tablet
07 antacid, capsule, inhaler, linctus, lozenge, pessary, steroid
08 diuretic, ear drops, eye drops, hypnotic, laxative, narcotic, ointment, pastille, sedative
09 analgesic, paregoric, stimulant
10 antibiotic, antiseptic, gripe-water, nasal spray, painkiller
11 anaesthetic, neuroleptic, suppository
13 antibacterial, anticoagulant, antihistamine, tranquillizer
14 anticonvulsant, antidepressant, bronchodilator, hallucinogenic

See also **antibiotic**; **drug**

- **medicine box**

04 inro

medieval, mediaeval

03 med, old 07 antique, archaic 08 historic, obsolete, old-world, outmoded 09 primitive 10 antiquated 12 antediluvian, old-fashioned 13 of the Dark Ages, unenlightened 15 of the Middle Ages

mediocre

04 hack, so-so 06 medium 07 average 08 adequate, inferior, middling, ordinary, passable 09 tolerable 10 not much cop, pedestrian, second-rate, uninspired 11 bog standard, commonplace, indifferent, not up to much, respectable 12 run-of-the-mill 13 insignificant, no great shakes, unexceptional 14 fair to middling 15 middle-of-the-road, undistinguished

mediocrity

06 nobody 07 no-hoper, nothing 08 adequacy, dead loss, poorness 09 nonentity 10 non-starter 11 averageness, inferiority 12 indifference, ordinariness, passableness, unimportance 14 insignificance

meditate

04 chew, muse, plan 05 brood, study, think 06 design, devise, intend, ponder, scheme 07 reflect 08 cogitate, consider, mull over, ruminate 09 speculate, think over 10 chew the cud, deliberate, have in mind 11 concentrate, contemplate

meditation

02 TM 05 study, zazen 06 musing 07 reverie, thought 08 brooding 09 pondering 10 brown study, cogitation, reflection, ruminating, rumination 11 cerebration, mulling over, speculation 12 deliberation, excogitation 13 concentration, contemplation

meditative

07 museful, pensive 08 ruminant, studious 09 prayerful 10 cogitative, reflective, ruminative, thoughtful 12 deliberative 13 contemplative

Mediterranean

03 Med

medium

01 m 03 med, way 04 fair, form, mean, mode, norm 05 ether, means, organ, stuff 06 agency, avenue, centre, medial, median, middle, midway, milieu 07 average, channel, element, habitat, midsize, psychic, setting, vehicle 08 ambience, material, middling, midpoint, moderate, standard 09 middle way, spiritist, substance 10 atmosphere, compromise, conditions, golden mean, influences, instrument 11 clairvoyant, environment, happy medium, necromancer 12 intermediate, middle ground, sound-carrier, spiritualist, surroundings 13 circumstances, fortune-teller 15 instrumentality, way of expressing

- **by the medium of**

02 in

medley

◇ *anagram indicator*

03 mix 04 mess, olio, olla 05 fight, mêlée 06 jumble, mingle 07 farrago, melange, mixture, variety 08 macaroni, mishmash, mixed bag, pastiche 09 confusion, macédoine, patchwork, potpourri, quodlibet 10 assortment, collection, hodgepodge, hotchpotch, miscellany, salmagundi, salmagundy 11 gallimaufry, smorgasbord 13 helter-skelter 14 conglomeration, omnium-gatherum

meek

04 mild, tame, weak 05 lowly, quiet, timid 06 docile, gentle, humble, modest 07 patient 08 peaceful, resigned, yielding 09 compliant, spineless 10 forbearing, spiritless, submissive, unassuming 11 deferential 13 long-suffering, unpretentious

meekly

06 gently, humbly, mildly 07 quietly 08 modestly 09 patiently 12 submissively 13 deferentially

meekness

07 modesty 08 docility, humility, mildness, patience, softness, tameness, timidity, weakness 09 deference, lowliness 10 compliance, gentleness, humbleness, submission 11 forbearance, resignation,

wimpishness **12** acquiescence, peacefulness **13** long-suffering, self-abasement, spinelessness **14** self-effacement, spiritlessness, submissiveness

meet
◇ *juxtaposition indicator*
03 get, pay, see **04** abut, bear, even, face, fill, game, give, hear, join, link, race, take **05** abide, cross, equal, event, greet, match, quits, rally, round, touch, unite **06** adjoin, answer, endure, fulfil, gather, handle, honour, hook up, link up, manage, muster, pay for, settle, suffer, tackle **07** balance, collect, connect, contest, convene, convoke, execute, fitting, fixture, meeting, perform, react to, receive, run into, satisfy, undergo **08** assemble, bump into, chance on, come upon, come up to, converge, cope with, deal with, listen to **09** discharge, encounter, fittingly, forgather, go through, intersect, look after, qualified, respond to, run across **10** come across, comply with, congregate, engagement, experience, foregather, happen upon, join up with, rencounter, rendezvous, tournament **11** competition, get together, measure up to **12** come together, intersection **14** get to grips with **15** make contact with
• **failure to meet**
04 gape

meeting
03 AGM, EGM, hui **04** date, meet, moot **05** rally, tryst, union, venue **07** cabinet, contact, gorsedd, session **08** abutment, assembly, camporee, concours, consulta, exercise, junction, wardmote **09** concourse, encounter, gathering, interface, interview **10** chautauqua, conference, confluence, convention, engagement, rencounter, rendezvous, watersmeet **11** appointment, assignation, conjunction, conventicle, convergence **12** intersection, introduction **13** confrontation **14** point of contact
See also **greeting**

meeting-place
04 gild, moot, Pnyx **05** guild, house, joint, lodge, marae, venue **06** baraza, centre **07** cenacle **10** confluence, rendezvous, vestry-room **11** senate-house **12** chapterhouse

megalomania
13 conceitedness **14** overestimation, self-importance **15** folie de grandeur

meitnerium
02 Mt

melancholy
03 low, sad **04** blue, down, glum **05** adust, blues, dumps, gloom, moody **06** dismal, gloomy, hipped, misery, rueful, somber, sombre, sorrow, spleen, woeful **07** doleful, pensive, sadness, unhappy **08** dejected, doldrums, downcast, mournful **09** allicholy, dejection, depressed, miserable, pessimism, sorrowful, splenetic, surliness, tristesse, woebegone **10** allycholly, deplorable, depression, despondent, dispirited, low spirits, lugubrious, pensieroso **11** atrabilious, despondency, downhearted, low-spirited, melancholia, melancholic, the black dog, unhappiness **12** disconsolate, heavy-hearted **13** hypochondriac, in the doldrums **14** down in the dumps
• **make melancholy**
03 hip, hyp

melange
◇ *anagram indicator*
03 mix **06** jumble, medley **07** farrago, mixture, variety **08** mishmash, mixed bag, pastiche **09** confusion, patchwork, potpourri **10** assortment, collection, hodgepodge, hotchpotch, miscellany, salmagundi **11** gallimaufry, smorgasbord **14** conglomeration, omnium-gatherum

mêlée
◇ *anagram indicator*
04 fray, mess **05** brawl, broil, chaos, fight, mix-up, rally, scrum, set-to **06** affray, fracas, jumble, medley, mellay, muddle, ruckus, rumpus, tangle, tussle **07** clutter, ruction, scuffle **08** disorder, dogfight, stramash **09** confusion, scrimmage, scrummage **10** free-for-all **11** battle royal **15** disorganization

Melia
03 nim **04** neem, nimb **05** neemb

mellifluous
04 soft **05** sweet **06** dulcet, mellow, smooth **07** honeyed, silvery, tuneful **08** canorous, soothing **10** euphonious, harmonious **13** sweet-sounding

mellow
04 full, kind, mild, rich, ripe, soft **05** happy, jolly, juicy, ripen, sweet **06** dulcet, fruity, genial, gentle, jovial, mature, placid, season, serene, smooth, soften, temper, tender **07** affable, amiable, cordial, improve, perfect, relaxed, rounded, sweeten, tuneful **08** amicable, cheerful, luscious, pleasant, resonant, tranquil **09** easy-going, melodious **10** euphonious, harmonious, pear-shaped **11** good-natured, kind-hearted **13** full-flavoured **15** make less extreme

melodic
05 sweet **06** dulcet **07** musical, silvery, tuneful **09** melodious **10** euphonious, harmonious **13** sweet-sounding

melodically
07 sweetly **09** musically, tunefully **11** melodiously **12** harmoniously

melodious
05 sweet **06** dulcet, pretty **07** melodic, musical, Orphean, silvery, songful, tuneful **09** cantabile **10** euphonious, harmonious **13** sweet-sounding

melodrama
07 tragedy **09** dramatics, high drama, staginess **10** overacting **11** histrionics, performance, tragicomedy **13** theatricality

melodramatic
03 OTT **05** hammy, stagy **06** stagey **08** overdone, theatric **10** histrionic, over-the-top, theatrical **11** exaggerated, extravagant, sensational **12** histrionical, overdramatic, overstrained, transpontine **13** overemotional **15** blood-and-thunder

melody
03 air **04** aria, ayre, part, song, tune **05** canto, chant, music, theme **06** cantus, rhythm, strain **07** euphony, harmony, melisma, musette, refrain **08** carillon, cavatina, part-song **09** cabaletta, cantilena, plainsong, sweetness **10** canto fermo, musicality **11** musicalness, tunefulness **12** augmentation, counterpoint **13** ranz-des-vaches **14** harmoniousness

melon
04 pepo **06** casaba **07** cassaba **09** cantaloup, musk melon, Ogen melon, rock melon **10** cantaloupe, Charentais, Galia melon **11** winter melon **13** honeydew melon

melt
◇ *anagram indicator*
03 ren, rin, run **04** blow, calm, flow, flux, fuse, move, thaw **05** smelt, touch **06** affect, relent, render, soften, spleen **07** defrost, liquate, liquefy, resolve **08** discandy, dissolve, moderate, unfreeze **09** discandie, uncongeal **10** colliquate, deliquesce, impregnate, make tender **12** become tender
• **melt away**
04 fade **06** dispel, vanish **08** disperse, dissolve, evanesce, fade away **09** disappear, evaporate

meltdown
06 defeat, fiasco **07** debacle, failure **08** abortion, calamity, collapse, disaster, downfall **09** breakdown **11** frustration, miscarriage **15** coming to nothing

member
01 M **02** MP **03** arm, leg, MBE, Mem **04** limb, part **05** organ **06** clause, fellow **07** comrade, dumaist, element **08** adherent **09** appendage, associate, extremity, stretcher **10** subscriber **12** incorporator **14** representative

membership
04 body, seat **07** fellows, members **08** comrades **09** adherence, adherents, enrolment **10** allegiance, associates, fellowship **11** affiliation, subscribers **13** participation **15** representatives

membrane
03 haw, rim **04** fell, film, kell, skin, veil **05** hymen, layer, sheet, velum

06 mucosa, septum, tissue
08 patagium 09 arachnoid, diaphragm, partition 10 integument

memento
03 mem 04 Goss 05 relic, token
06 record, trophy 07 vestige
08 keepsake, memorial, reminder, souvenir 11 remembrance

memo
03 fax 04 note 05 e-mail 06 letter
07 jotting, message 08 reminder
10 memorandum 11 aide-mémoire, remembrance 12 memory-jogger

memoir
04 life 05 essay 06 record, report
07 account, journal 08 register
09 biography, chronicle, monograph, narrative 13 autobiography

memoirs
05 diary 06 annals 07 diaries, records
08 journals, memories 09 life story
10 chronicles 11 confessions, experiences 13 autobiography, recollections, reminiscences

memorable
06 catchy, unique 07 notable, special
08 eventful, historic, striking
09 important, momentous
10 impressive, noteworthy, remarkable 11 distinctive, outstanding, significant 13 consequential, distinguished, extraordinary, unforgettable

memorandum
03 fax, mem 04 memo, note, slip 05 e-mail, jurat 06 letter 07 jotting, message
08 memorial, reminder 09 bordereau
11 aide-mémoire, remembrance
12 memory-jogger

memorial
03 mem 05 brass, relic, stone, stupa
06 dagaba, dagoba, marker, memory, plaque, record, shrine, statue, trophy, Yizkor 07 memento, relique
08 cenotaph, ebenezer, monument, Pantheon, souvenir 09 altar-tomb, mausoleum, tombstone
10 gravestone, memorandum, monumental, remembered
11 celebratory, Norman cross, remembrance, testimonial
13 commemorative
See also **monument**

memorize
05 learn 06 get off, record
08 remember 09 celebrate 11 learn by rote 12 learn by heart 14 commit to memory

memory
03 RAM, ROM 04 mind, rote
06 honour, recall 07 tribute
09 retention, sovenance
10 observance 11 recognition, remembrance 12 recollection, reminiscence 13 commemoration
14 powers of recall
• **memory block**
04 page

men
02 OR
See also **man**
• **excluding men**
03 hen

menace
04 loom, lour, pain, pest, risk 05 alarm, appal, bully, daunt, peril, press, scare, shore 06 bother, coerce, danger, dismay, hazard, screws, threat
07 terrify, warning 08 big stick, browbeat, bullying, coercion, frighten, jeopardy, nuisance, pressure, threaten
09 annoyance, terrorism, terrorize
10 intimidate, pressurize
11 browbeating, frighteners, ominousness, public enemy, terrorizing 12 intimidation, troublemaker 13 tyrannization
15 thorn in your side

menacing
04 grim 07 looming, louring, ominous, warning 08 alarming, minatory, sinister
09 Damoclean, dangerous, impending, minacious, threatful
10 portentous 11 frightening, threatening 12 intimidating, intimidatory

mend
03 fix, sew, toe 04 beet, bete, cure, darn, heal 05 amend, clout, emend, patch, plash, refit, renew, run up, stick
06 bushel, cobble, reform, remedy, repair, revise, solder 07 correct, improve, patch up, recover, rectify, restore 08 put right, renovate, solution
09 get better, make whole
10 ameliorate, put in order, recuperate, supplement 14 mend your fences
15 put back together
• **mend your ways**
06 reform 15 improve yourself, make a fresh start
• **on the mend**
07 healing 08 reviving 09 improving
10 recovering 12 convalescent, convalescing, recuperating

mendacious
05 false, lying 06 untrue 08 perjured
09 deceitful, deceptive, dishonest, insincere 10 fallacious, fictitious, fraudulent, perfidious, untruthful
11 duplicitous

mendacity
03 lie 05 lying 06 deceit 07 perfidy, perjury, untruth 09 duplicity, falsehood 10 dishonesty, distortion, inveracity 11 fraudulence, insincerity
13 deceitfulness, falsification
14 untruthfulness

mendelevium
02 Md

mendicant
03 bum 04 hobo 05 fakir, frate, friar, sadhu, tramp 06 beggar, cadger, canter, craver, pauper, saddhu, toerag
07 begging, bludger, cadging, jarkman, moocher, sponger, vagrant
08 besognio, blighter, calender, vagabond, whipjack 09 scrounger
10 down-and-out, freeloader, panhandler, scrounging, supplicant
11 beachcomber, petitionary

menial
03 eta, low 04 base, dull 05 lowly, slave
06 boring, drudge, humble, minion, ribald, skivvy 07 humdrum, routine, servant, servile, slavish, waister
08 dogsbody, domestic, labourer
09 attendant, degrading, demeaning, underling, unskilled 10 after-guard
11 ignominious, subservient

menstruation
04 flow 06 menses, period 07 courses
08 the curse, the usual 09 monthlies
10 menorrhoea 11 monthly flow
14 menstrual cycle, time of the month

mensuration
06 metage, survey 09 measuring, surveying, valuation 10 assessment, estimation, evaluation, planimetry
11 calculation, calibration, computation, measurement

mental
◇ *anagram indicator*
03 ape, fey, mad 04 bats, gyte, loco, nuts, wild 05 barmy, batty, buggy, crazy, daffy, dippy, dotty, flaky, gonzo, loony, loopy, manic, nutty, potty, queer, wacko, wacky, wiggy 06 crazed, cuckoo, fruity, insane, maniac, raving, red-mad, screwy, troppo 07 bananas, barking, berserk, bonkers, cracked, frantic, lunatic, meshuga 08 abstract, cerebral, crackers, demented, deranged, dingbats, doolally, frenetic, frenzied, maniacal, rational, unhinged, unstable 09 cognitive, disturbed, lymphatic, psychotic, up the wall
10 bestraught, conceptual, distracted, distraught, frantic-mad, off the wall, off your nut, out to lunch, ridiculous, stone-crazy, unbalanced 11 not all there, off the rails, off your head, theoretical, unconscious
12 intellectual, mad as a hatter, off your chump, round the bend 13 off your rocker, of unsound mind, out of your head, out of your mind, out of your tree, round the twist 14 off your trolley, wrong in the head 15 non compos mentis, out of your senses
• **mental health workers**
15 men in white coats

mentality
04 mind 06 brains, make-up
07 faculty, mindset, outlook
08 attitude, ingenium 09 character, intellect 10 grey matter, psychology
11 disposition, frame of mind, personality, rationality 12 intelligence
13 comprehension, understanding, way of thinking 14 mental attitude
15 little grey cells

mentally
07 ideally 08 inwardly 09 in the mind
10 rationally 11 emotionally
12 subjectively 14 intellectually
15 psychologically, temperamentally

mention
03 say **04** cite, hint, mind, name, note, talk **05** hight, mensh, quote, speak, state **06** bename, broach, cast up, drag up, exhume, hint at, impart, notice, remark, report, reveal, speech **07** bring up, declare, divulge, let fall, refer to, speak of, specify, touch on, tribute **08** allude to, allusion, citation, disclose, instance, intimate, nominate, point out, remember **09** introduce, make known, reference, statement **10** indication, particular **11** acknowledge, communicate, observation, recognition **12** announcement, notification **14** condescend upon **15** acknowledgement

• **don't mention it**
05 bitte **08** forget it, not at all **09** don't worry **12** it's a pleasure, it was nothing

• **not to mention**
05 let be **06** let-a-be **07** besides **08** as well as, let alone, much less **12** not including **13** not forgetting **14** to say nothing of

mentioned
05 cited **06** quoted, stated **08** foresaid, reported **09** aforesaid, fore-cited, forenamed **10** fore-quoted **13** forementioned **14** above-mentioned, aforementioned

mentor
03 rav **04** guru **05** coach, guide, swami, tutor **07** adviser, advisor, teacher, trainer **09** confidant, pedagogue, therapist **10** confidante, counsellor, instructor

menu
04 card, list **06** tariff **10** bill of fare **11** carte du jour

mercantile
05 trade **07** salable, trading **08** saleable **09** mercenary **10** commercial, marketable **12** merchantable

mercenary
04 hack, merc, paid **05** hired, venal **06** greedy, rutter, sordid **07** Hessian, pindari, Switzer **08** covetous, grasping, hired gun, hireling, huckster, pindaree **09** freelance, on the make, warmonger **10** avaricious, galloglass, lansquenet, mercantile, prostitute **11** acquisitive, condottiere, landsknecht, mammonistic **12** hired soldier, professional **13** free companion, materialistic, money-grubbing **15** money-orientated

merchandise
04 ware **05** cargo, goods, stock, trade, wares **07** dealing, freight, produce **08** products, shipment **09** vendibles **11** commodities

merchandize
04 hype, plug, push, sell, vend **05** carry, trade **06** deal in, market, peddle, retail, supply **07** promote **09** advertise, publicize, traffic in **10** buy and sell, distribute

merchant
05 agent, bunia, trade **06** broker, bunnia, dealer, factor, jobber, seller, trader, vendor **07** Antonio **08** hoastman, retailer, salesman **09** bourgeois, négociant **10** commercial, marcantant, saleswoman, shopkeeper, supercargo, trafficker, wholesaler **11** distributor, salesperson **14** sales executive

merciful
04 kind, mild **06** humane **07** clement, lenient, liberal, pitying, sparing **08** generous, gracious, tolerant **09** forgiving, merciable **10** forbearing **11** soft-hearted, sympathetic **12** humanitarian **13** compassionate, tender-hearted

mercifully
06 kindly **07** luckily **10** generously, graciously, thankfully, tolerantly **11** fortunately **15** compassionately, sympathetically, tender-heartedly

merciless
04 hard **05** cruel, harsh, rigid, stern **06** severe, wanton **07** callous, inhuman **08** inhumane, pitiless, ruthless **09** barbarous, heartless, unfeeling, unpitying, unsparing **10** implacable, inexorable, intolerant, relentless, unmerciful **11** hard-hearted, remorseless, unforgiving **13** unsympathetic

mercilessly
07 cruelly, harshly, sternly **08** severely **09** callously **10** implacably, inexorably, pitilessly, ruthlessly **11** heartlessly **12** relentlessly **13** hard-heartedly, remorselessly

mercurial
06 active, fickle, lively, mobile **07** erratic, flighty **08** spirited, unstable, variable, volatile **09** impetuous, impulsive, sprightly **10** capricious, changeable, inconstant **11** quicksilver **12** light-hearted **13** irrepressible, temperamental, unpredictable

mercury
02 Hg **06** Hermes

mercy
04 boon, pity **05** grace **06** favour, relief **07** godsend, quarter **08** blessing, clemency, good luck, kindness, leniency, mildness, sympathy **10** compassion, generosity, humaneness, misericord, tenderness **11** forbearance, forgiveness, misericorde **14** loving-kindness **15** humanitarianism

• **at the mercy of**
09 exposed to, prostrate **11** at the whim of **12** in the power of, vulnerable to **14** in the control of, unarmed against

mere
04 bare, lake, meer, meri, pool, poor, pure, very **05** bound, petty, plain, sheer, stark, utter **06** common, paltry, simple **07** unmixed **08** absolute, boundary, complete **10** absolutely, no more than **13** pure and simple, unadulterated

merely
03 but **04** just, only **06** barely, hardly, purely, simply **08** scarcely **10** nothing but

meretricious
04 bold, loud **05** cheap, flash, gaudy, jazzy, showy, tacky **06** flashy, garish, glitzy, kitsch, made up, tawdry, vulgar **09** glamorous, insincere, tasteless **10** flamboyant **11** pretentious **12** ostentatious

merganser
04 smew

merge
03 die, dip, mix **04** fuse, join, meet, meld, sink **05** blend, unite, verge **06** mingle, plunge, team up **07** collate, combine, run into **08** coalesce, converge, intermix, liquesce, melt into **10** amalgamate, be engulfed, join forces **11** consolidate, incorporate **12** become lost in, come together **13** bring together **15** be assimilated in, be swallowed up in

merger
05 blend, union **06** fusion **08** alliance **09** coalition **11** combination, convergence **12** amalgamation, assimilation **13** confederation, consolidation, incorporation

merit
03 due **04** earn, good, plus **05** asset, claim, found, value, worth **06** credit, desert, praise, reward, talent, virtue **07** be worth, deserts, deserve, justify, quality, warrant **08** goodness **09** advantage **10** be worthy of, excellence, excellency, recompense, worthiness **11** distinction, high quality, strong point **12** be entitled to, have a right to **13** justification

merited
03 due **04** just **06** earned, worthy **07** condign, fitting **08** deserved, entitled, rightful **09** justified, warranted **11** appropriate **12** well-deserved

meritorious
04 good **05** right **06** worthy **08** laudable, virtuous, worthful **09** admirable, deserving, estimable, excellent, exemplary, righteous **10** creditable, honourable **11** commendable **12** praiseworthy

mermaid
05 siren **06** undine **07** seamaid **08** sea nymph, seawoman **11** water-spirit, water sprite

merrily
06 gladly **07** happily **08** blithely, chirpily, jovially **10** cheerfully, pleasantly

merriment
03 fun **05** mirth **06** frolic, gaiety **07** jollity, revelry, waggery **08** buoyance, carnival, hilarity, laughter

09 amusement, festivity, jocundity, jolliment, joviality **10** blitheness, joyfulness, liveliness **11** high spirits **12** carefreeness, cheerfulness, conviviality, mirthfulness **13** jollification

merry

◇ *anagram indicator*

03 gay **04** cant, daft, gean, glad **05** gaudy, happy, jolly, nitid, riant, tipsy, vogie **06** blithe, cheery, chirpy, frolic, jocose, jocund, jovial, joyful, lively, tiddly **07** amusing, festive, gleeful, squiffy **08** carefree, cheerful, gleesome, mirthful, pleasant, sportful, sportive **09** convivial, heartsome, hilarious **10** frolicsome **11** saturnalian **12** high-spirited, light-hearted **13** in good spirits, slightly drunk **15** one over the eight

• make merry

04 gaud, rant, sing **05** dance, drink, revel **07** carouse, have fun, rejoice **09** celebrate **10** have a party **13** enjoy yourself

merry-andrew

05 clown **07** buffoon **11** Jack-pudding **13** pickle-herring

merry-go-round

08 carousel, galloper, joy-wheel **09** carrousel, gallopers, whirligig **10** roundabout

merrymaking

03 fun **05** party, revel **06** frolic, gaiety **07** revelry **08** carousal, merimake **09** carousing, festivity, galravage, gilravage, junketing, merriment **10** galravitch, gillravage, gilravitch, rejoicings **11** celebration, gillravitch **12** conviviality **13** jollification

mesh

03 net, web **04** trap **05** gauze, match, snare **06** engage, enmesh, inmesh, tangle **07** combine, connect, entwine, lattice, netting, network, tracery, trellis **08** dovetail, entangle **09** harmonize, interlock **10** co-ordinate, go together **11** fit together, latticework **12** come together, entanglement

mesmerize

04 grip **06** benumb **07** enthral, stupefy **08** entrance, transfix **09** captivate, fascinate, hypnotize, magnetize, spellbind **14** hold spellbound

mess

◇ *anagram indicator*

03 fix, jam, mix, mux, tip **04** dine, dirt, dump, hash, hole, meal, muck, muss, soss, spot, stew **05** botch, chaos, farce, filth, mix-up, musse, slosh **06** bungle, cock-up, course, guddle, hiccup, jumble, lash-up, litter, medley, midden, mucker, muddle, pickle, plight **07** balls-up, clutter, dilemma, failure, jackpot, pig's ear, screw-up, squalor, trouble, turmoil **08** disarray, disorder, hot water, quandary, shambles, slaister, whoopsie **09** confusion, deep water, dirtiness, praiseach, shemozzle, shimozzle, tight spot **10** difficulty, dog's dinner, filthiness, pretty pass, schemozzle, shlemozzle, untidiness **11** predicament **13** dog's breakfast, embarrassment, pig's breakfast **15** disorganization

• make a mess of

04 flub, goof

• mess about, mess around

04 goof, play **05** upset **06** piddle, puddle, putter **09** faff about, goof about, muck about, play about **10** faff around, fool around, goof around, play around **11** potter about **12** fiddle around

• mess about with, mess around with

05 upset **06** bother **07** trouble **08** play with **10** meddle with, tamper with, treat badly **13** fool about with, inconvenience, interfere with, play about with **14** fool around with, play around with

• mess up

04 foul, muff, ruin **05** bitch, bodge, botch, dirty, fluff, spoil **06** bungle, cock up, foul up, jumble, muck up, muddle, tangle, untidy **07** confuse, disrupt, louse up, screw up **08** dishevel **09** clutter up **10** disarrange **11** make a hash of, make a mess of

message

03 fax **04** gist, idea, memo, news, note, task, wire, word **05** cable, drift, e-mail, moral, point, sense, telex, theme **06** errand, import, letter, notice, report, thrust **07** dépêche, epistle, essence, express, meaning, missive, purport, tidings **08** aerogram, bulletin, dispatch, irenicon, mailgram, telegram, Teletype® **09** autoreply, eirenicon, telegraph, telepheme **10** communiqué, intimation, memorandum **11** implication, marconigram, Telemessage® **12** significance **13** communication

• end message

07 sign off

• get the message

03 see **04** twig **05** get it, grasp **06** follow, take in **07** catch on, latch on **08** cotton on, tumble to **09** latch onto **10** comprehend, cotton on to, get the hang, get the idea, understand **11** get the point **13** catch the drift, get the picture

messenger

04 page, peon, post, send **05** agent, angel, caddy, cadee, cadie, envoy **06** beadle, bearer, caddie, herald, Hermes, nuncio, runner **07** carrier, courier, express, Mercury, missive **08** dispatch, emissary, footpost **09** chaprassi, chaprassy, chuprassy, errand-boy, go-between, harbinger, woman post **10** ambassador, errand-girl, forerunner, pursuivant, shellycoat **11** internuncio **12** ambassadress, valet de place **13** gillie-wetfoot, secretary-bird **14** commissionaire **15** corbie messenger, gillie-white-foot

messy

◇ *anagram indicator*

05 dirty, gungy, yucky, yukky **06** filthy, grubby, grungy, sloppy, untidy **07** chaotic, muddled, unkempt **08** bungling, confused, littered, slobbish, slovenly **09** cluttered, shambolic **10** disordered, in disarray **11** dishevelled **12** disorganized

metal

Metals include:

01 K (potassium), U (uranium), V (vanadium), W (tungsten), Y (yttrium)

02 Ac (actinium), Ag (silver), Al (aluminium), Am (americium), Au (gold), Ba (barium), Be (beryllium), Bi (bismuth), Bk (berkelium), Ca (calcium), Cd (cadmium), Ce (cerium), Cf (californium), Cm (curium), Co (cobalt), Cr (chromium), Cs (caesium), Cu (copper), Dy (dysprosium), Er (erbium), Es (einsteinium), Eu (europium), Fe (iron), Fm (fermium), Fr (francium), Ga (gallium), Gd (gadolinium), Ge (germanium), Hf (hafnium), Hg (mercury), Ho (holmium), In (indium), Ir (iridium), La (lanthanum), Li (lithium), Lr (lawrencium), Lu (lutetium), Md (mendelevium), Mg (magnesium), Mn (manganese), Mo (molybdenum), Na (sodium), Nb (niobium), Nd (neodymium), Ni (nickel), No (nobelium), Np (neptunium), Os (osmium), Pa (protactinium), Pb (lead), Pd (palladium), Pm (promethium), Po (polonium), Pr (praseodymium), Pt (platinum), Pu (plutonium), Ra (radium), Rb (rubidium), Re (rhenium), Rh (rhodium), Ru (ruthenium), Sb (antimony), Sc (scandium), Sm (samarium), Sn (tin), Sr (strontium), Ta (tantalum), Tb (terbium), Tc (technetium), Th (thorium), Ti (titanium), Tl (thallium), Tm (thulium), Yb (ytterbium), Zn (zinc), Zr (zirconium)

03 tin (Sn)

04 gold (Au), iron (Fe), lead (Pb), zinc (Zn)

06 barium (Ba), cerium (Ce), cobalt (Co), copper (Cu), curium (Cm), erbium (Er), indium (In), nickel (Ni), osmium (Os), radium (Ra), silver (Ag), sodium (Na)

07 bismuth (Bi), cadmium (Cd), caesium (Cs), calcium (Ca), fermium (Fm), gallium (Ga), hafnium (Hf), holmium (Ho), iridium (Ir), lithium (Li), mercury (Hg), niobium (Nb), rhenium (Re), rhodium (Rh), terbium (Tb), thorium (Th), thulium (Tm), uranium (U), yttrium (Y)

08 actinium (Ac), antimony (Sb), chromium (Cr), europium (Eu),

francium (Fr), lutetium (Lu), nobelium (No), platinum (Pt), polonium (Po), rubidium (Rb), samarium (Sm), scandium (Sc), tantalum (Ta), thallium (Tl), titanium (Ti), tungsten (W), vanadium (V)
09 aluminium (Al), americium (Am), berkelium (Bk), beryllium (Be), germanium (Ge), lanthanum (La), magnesium (Mg), manganese (Mn), neodymium (Nd), neptunium (Np), palladium (Pd), plutonium (Pu), potassium (K), ruthenium (Ru), strontium (Sr), ytterbium (Yb), zirconium (Zr)
10 dysprosium (Dy), gadolinium (Gd), lawrencium (Lr), molybdenum (Mo), promethium (Pm), technetium (Tc)
11 californium (Cf), einsteinium (Es), mendelevium (Md)
12 praseodymium (Pr), protactinium (Pa)

Metal alloys include:

03 pot
04 type
05 brass, Dutch, Invar®, Muntz, potin, steel, terne, white
06 Alnico®, billon, bronze, latten, occamy, ormolu, oroide, pewter, solder, tambac, tombac, tombak, Y-alloy
07 amalgam, Babbit's, chromel, Nitinol, prince's, shakudo, similor, tutania, tutenag
08 Babbitt's, cast iron, gunmetal, Manganin®, Nichrome®, orichalc, speculum, zircaloy, Zircoloy®
09 Britannia, Duralumin®, Dutch gold, Dutch leaf, magnalium, pinchbeck, shibuichi, white gold
10 constantan, ferro-alloy, iridosmine, iridosmium, mischmetal, Monel metal®, mosaic gold, osmiridium, white brass
11 chrome steel, cupro-nickel, nicrosilial, white copper
12 German silver, nickel silver
14 high-speed steel, phosphor-bronze, stainless steel

• **design on metal**
04 etch
• **join metal**
04 weld
• **metal after heating**
04 calx
• **metal bar**
03 zed **05** ingot
• **piece of metal**
03 gib
• **precious metal**
03 ore
• **thin metal**
04 foil

metallic
03 tin **04** gold, iron, lead **05** harsh, rough, shiny, steel, tinny **06** copper, nickel, silver **07** grating, jarring **08** gleaming, jangling, polished **09** dissonant **10** unpleasant

metamorphose
◇ *anagram indicator*
05 alter **06** change, modify, mutate, remake **07** convert, remodel, reshape **09** transform, translate, transmute **11** transfigure **12** transmogrify

metamorphosis
◇ *anagram indicator*
06 change **07** rebirth **08** mutation **09** staminody **10** alteration, changeover, conversion, metabolism **12** modification, regeneration **13** transmutation **14** holometabolism, transformation **15** transfiguration

metaphor
03 met **05** image, trope **06** emblem, metaph, symbol, visual **07** analogy, picture **08** allegory **10** emblematic **12** transumption **14** figure of speech, representation

metaphorical
03 met **06** metaph, visual **08** symbolic **10** analogical, emblematic, figurative **11** allegorical

metaphysical
04 deep **05** basic, ideal **06** unreal **07** eternal, general **08** abstract, abstruse, esoteric, fanciful, profound **09** essential, high-flown, recondite, spiritual, universal **10** immaterial, impalpable, intangible, subjective **11** fundamental, incorporeal, speculative, theoretical **12** intellectual, supernatural **13** insubstantial, philosophical, unsubstantial **14** transcendental

mete
• **mete out**
05 allot **06** assign **07** deal out, dole out, hand out, portion **08** dispense, share out **09** apportion, divide out, ration out **10** administer, distribute, measure out

meteor
05 comet, drake **06** bolide **08** aerolite, aerolith, fireball **09** meteorite, meteoroid **10** exhalation **11** falling star **12** shooting star

Meteor showers include:

06 Lyrids, Ursids
07 Leonids, Taurids
08 Geminids, Orionids, Perseids
11 Quadrantids
12 Eta Aquariids
14 Alpha-Scorpiids, Delta Aquariids

meteoric
04 fast **05** brief, quick, rapid, swift **06** speedy, sudden **08** dazzling, flashing **09** brilliant, lightning, momentary, overnight, transient **11** spectacular **13** instantaneous

meteorologist
06 met man **10** weatherman **11** weathergirl, weatherlady **13** climatologist **14** weather prophet

meteorology

Meteorology-related terms include:

04 calm, eddy, flux, haar, haze, ITCZ, rime
05 flood, front, frost, Q-code, radar, ridge, SIGWX, solar, taiga, virga
06 arctic, el Niño, flurry, haboob, isobar, Kelvin, oxygen
07 Celsius, chinook, climate, cyclone, drizzle, drought, graupel, mistral, monsoon, rainbow, thunder, tornado, typhoon, weather
08 acid rain, blizzard, dewpoint, doldrums, forecast, humidity, isotherm, millibar, rainfall, windsock, wind vane
09 advection, aerograph, altimeter, barograph, barometer, cold front, hurricane, hyetology, jet stream, lightning, Met Office, nephology, radiation, rain gauge, satellite, sub-arctic, trade wind, warm front, wind chill, wind speed
10 aerography, air quality, anemometer, atmosphere, baroclinic, barotropic, cloud cover, conduction, convection, depression, Fahrenheit, Gulf stream, Hadley Cell, hemisphere, hyetograph, hyetometer, hygrometer, nephograph, nephoscope, nowcasting, ozone layer, rain shadow, rain shower, visibility, waterspout, wavelength
11 air pressure, anticyclone, climatology, evaporation, ground frost, hyetography, pollen count, temperature, thermograph, thermometer, thermopause, troposphere, ultra violet, water vapour, wave cyclone
12 cloud seeding, condensation, cyclogenesis, meteorograph, microclimate, pilot balloon, thunderstorm, weather chart, weather watch
13 ball lightning, Beaufort scale, boundary layer, climate change, fork lightning, frontogenesis, magnetosphere, occluded front, onshore breeze, precipitation
14 air temperature, continentality, horse latitudes, offshore breeze, prevailing wind, sheet lightning, transmissivity, weather station
15 hyetometrograph, stationary front, weather forecast, wind-chill factor

method
03 art, how, way **04** form, line, mode, plan, rule **05** means, order, route, style **06** course, design, manner, scheme, system **07** fashion, pattern, process, routine **08** approach, modality, planning, practice **09** procedure, programme, structure, technique **10** regularity **11** arrangement, orderliness **12** organization **13** modus operandi **14** classification

methodical
04 neat, tidy **06** formal **07** logical, ordered, orderly, planned, precise, regular **09** efficient, organized **10** deliberate, meticulous, scrupulous, structured, systematic **11** disciplined, painstaking, well-ordered **12** businesslike, systematical

methodically
06 neatly, tidily **07** in place, orderly **08** formally **09** as planned, by the book, logically, precisely, regularly, to the rule, uniformly **11** efficiently **12** meticulously, scrupulously **13** painstakingly **14** systematically

metical
02 Mt **03** MZM

meticulous
05 exact, fussy, timid **06** strict **07** careful, precise **08** accurate, detailed, rigorous, thorough **10** fastidious, particular, scrupulous **11** overcareful, painstaking, punctilious **13** conscientious

meticulously
07 exactly **08** strictly **09** carefully, precisely **10** accurately, rigorously, thoroughly **12** scrupulously **13** painstakingly, punctiliously **15** conscientiously

métier
03 job **04** line **05** craft, field, forte, trade **06** sphere **07** calling, pursuit **08** business, vocation **09** specialty **10** occupation, profession, speciality **14** line of business

metro *see* **underground**

metropolis
04 city **07** capital **08** main city **09** large city **10** cosmopolis **11** capital city, megalopolis **12** municipality **14** cultural centre
See also **city**

mettle
04 guts, pith **05** nerve, pluck, pride, spunk **06** daring, ginger, make-up, nature, spirit, valour, vigour **07** bravery, calibre, courage, resolve, smeddum **08** backbone, boldness **09** character, endurance, fortitude, gallantry **11** disposition, intrepidity, personality, temperament **12** fearlessness **13** determination, sprightliness **14** indomitability

mettlesome
04 bold **05** brave **06** ardent, daring, lively, plucky, spunky **07** gallant, valiant **08** fearless, intrepid, resolute, spirited **10** courageous **11** lion-hearted, unflinching **12** high-spirited, stout-hearted

mew
04 cast, coop, gull, meow, mewl, shed **05** miaow, miaul, moult, whine **07** confine, retreat **09** caterwaul

mewl
03 cry **05** whine **06** snivel, whinge **07** blubber, grizzle, whimper

Mexican
03 Mex

Mexico
03 MEX

miaow
03 mew **04** meow, mewl **05** miaul, whine **09** caterwaul

miasma
04 reek **05** fetor, odour, smell, stink **06** stench **07** malaria **08** mephitis **09** effluvium, pollution

miasmal
04 foul **05** fetid **06** foetid, putrid, smelly **07** miasmic, noisome, noxious, reeking **08** mephitic, miasmous, polluted, stinking **09** miasmatic **10** malodorous, miasmatous **11** unwholesome **12** foul-smelling

mica
03 mic **04** daze **07** biotite

Michigan
02 MI **04** Mich

microbe
03 bug **04** germ **05** virus **08** bacillus, pathogen **09** bacterium **13** micro-organism

Micronesia
03 FSM

microphone
03 bug

microscope
03 SEM, TEM

microscopic
04 tiny **06** minute **09** minuscule **10** negligible **13** imperceptible, indiscernible, infinitesimal **14** extremely small

microscopically
08 minutely **09** extremely **13** imperceptibly **15** infinitesimally

midday
01 m, n **04** noon **06** twelve **07** noonday **08** meridian, noontide, noontime **09** lunchtime **10** meridional, twelve noon **12** twelve o'clock

middle
◇ *middle selection indicator*
03 med, mid **04** core, mean, noon **05** belly, heart, inner, midst, tummy, waist **06** centre, inside, medial, median, medium, mesial, midway, paunch **07** central, halfway, mediate, midriff, stomach **08** bull's eye, midpoint **11** bread basket, equidistant, intervening **12** halfway point, intermediate

• **in the middle of**
05 among, while **06** during **08** busy with **09** engaged in **12** in the midst of, occupied with, surrounded by **14** in the process of

middle-class
08 suburban **09** bourgeois **10** gentrified **11** white-collar **12** conventional, professional

Middle East

Middle Eastern landmarks include:

05 Kabaa
06 Qumran, Red Sea, Tigris
07 Dead Sea, Ephesus
08 Bosporus
09 Bosphorus, Gallipoli
10 Persepolis
11 Grand Mosque, Hagia Sophia, River Jordan, Via Dolorosa, Wailing Wall, Western Wall
12 Sea of Galilee
13 Dome of the Rock
15 Elburz Mountains

middleman
05 fixer **06** broker **08** bummaree, regrater, regrator, retailer **09** go-between **10** negotiator **11** distributer, distributor **12** entrepreneur, intermediary

Middlesex
02 Mx

middling
02 OK **04** fair, so-so **06** fairly, medium, modest **07** average **08** adequate, mediocre, moderate, ordinary, passable **09** tolerable **10** not much cop **11** indifferent, not up to much **12** intermediate, run-of-the-mill, unremarkable **13** no great shakes, unexceptional **14** fair to middling

midget
03 toy **04** baby, tiny **05** dwarf, gnome, pygmy, small, teeny **06** little, minute, pocket **07** manikin **08** mannikin, Tom Thumb **09** itsy-bitsy, miniature **10** diminutive, homunculus, teeny-weeny **11** Lilliputian, pocket-sized, small person

midpoint
11 middle point **12** central point, halfway point

midshipman
03 mid **04** Easy **05** middy **06** reefer, snotty **07** oldster, snottie **11** midshipmate **12** brass-bounder

midst
03 hub **04** core **05** bosom, heart, thick **06** centre, depths, middle **07** nucleus **08** interior, midpoint

• **in the midst**
04 amid **05** among **06** during **12** in the thick of, surrounded by **13** in the middle of

midway
07 halfway **11** in the centre, in the middle **13** at the midpoint

midwife
05 howdy **06** granny, howdie, Lucina **07** grannie **09** wise woman **10** accoucheur **11** accoucheuse

mien
03 air **04** aura, look **06** allure, aspect, manner **07** bearing **08** carriage, presence **09** demeanour, semblance **10** appearance, complexion,

deportment, expression
11 countenance

miffed
04 hurt **05** irked, upset, vexed
06 narked, peeved, piqued, put out
07 annoyed, in a huff, nettled
08 offended **09** aggrieved, chagrined, irritated, resentful **10** cheesed off, displeased **11** disgruntled

might
04 sway **05** clout, force, power
06 energy, muscle, valour, vigour
07 ability, potency, prowess, stamina
08 capacity, efficacy, strength
09 heftiness, puissance **10** capability
11 muscularity **12** forcefulness, powerfulness

mightily
04 much, very **06** highly, hugely
07 greatly, lustily **08** manfully, strongly, very much **09** decidedly, extremely, intensely **10** forcefully, powerfully, vigorously **11** exceedingly, strenuously
13 energetically

mighty
04 fell, huge, vast, very **05** bulky, felon, grand, great, hardy, hefty, large, lusty, stout, tough **06** highly, manful, potent, really, robust, strong **07** awfully, doughty, greatly, immense, massive, titanic, utterly, valiant **08** almighty, colossal, dominant, enormous, forceful, gigantic, mightful, muscular, powerful, puissant, stalwart, terribly, towering, vigorous **09** extremely, important, intensely, strapping, unusually, wonderful **10** dreadfully, monumental, prodigious, remarkably, stupendous, thoroughly, tremendous
11 exceedingly, excessively, frightfully, indomitable, influential **12** terrifically, unreasonably **13** exceptionally
15 extraordinarily

mignonette
04 wald, weld **06** Reseda

migrant
05 Gypsy, nomad, rover **06** roving, tinker **07** drifter, nomadic, swagger, swagman, vagrant **08** drifting, emigrant, shifting, wanderer
09 immigrant, itinerant, migratory, transient, traveller, wandering
10 travelling **11** peripatetic
12 Gastarbeiter, globetrotter, transmigrant **13** globetrotting

migrate
04 hike, move, roam, rove, trek **05** drift
06 travel, voyage, wander **07** journey
08 emigrate, relocate, resettle

migration
03 ren, rin, run **04** trek **05** shift
06 roving, travel, voyage **07** journey, passage **08** diaspora, movement
09 walkabout, wandering
10 emigration **12** transhumance
15 Völkerwanderung

migratory
05 Gypsy **06** roving **07** migrant, nomadic, vagrant **08** drifting, shifting
09 immigrant, itinerant, transient, wandering **10** travelling **11** peripatetic
13 globetrotting

mike
01 M

mild
04 calm, fair, kind, meek, soft, warm, weak **05** balmy, bland, faint, vague
06 feeble, gentle, humane, mellow, modest, placid, slight, smooth, subtle, tender **07** amiable, clement, insipid, lenient, pacific **08** gall-less, mansuete, merciful, moderate, pleasant, soothing
09 easy-going, peaceable, sensitive, tasteless, temperate **10** forbearing
11 flavourless, good-natured, soft-hearted, sympathetic, warm-hearted
13 compassionate, imperceptible, tender-hearted

mildewy
05 fetid, fusty, mucid, musty **06** foetid, rotten **10** mucedinous

mildly
06 calmly, gently, meekly, softly, subtly, warmly, weakly **07** faintly, vaguely
08 slightly, tenderly **10** mercifully
11 sensitively **13** imperceptibly
15 compassionately

mildness
05 mercy **06** lenity, warmth
08 calmness, clemency, docility, kindness, leniency, meekness, softness, sympathy **09** blandness, milkiness, passivity, placidity **10** compassion, gentleness, indulgence, mellowness, moderation, smoothness, tenderness
11 forbearance, insipidness
12 tranquillity **13** tastelessness, temperateness

mile
01 m **02** mi, ml, nm **05** n mile

milieu
05 arena, scene **06** locale, medium, sphere **07** element, setting **08** location
10 background **11** environment
12 surroundings

militancy
08 activism **09** extremism
12 belligerence, vigorousness
13 assertiveness **14** aggressiveness, British disease

militant
07 fighter, soldier, warring, warrior
08 activist, fighting, partisan, vigorous
09 aggressor, assertive, combatant, combative, embattled, struggler
10 aggressive, pugnacious
11 belligerent, Black Muslim **12** Black Panther, militaristic

militantly
10 vigorously **11** assertively
12 aggressively **13** belligerently

military
03 mil **04** army, navy **05** armed, milit
06 forces **07** martial, militia, service, soldier, warlike **08** air force, services, soldiers, soldiery **09** soldierly
11 armed forces, disciplined

Military decorations include:

02 GC, GM, MC, MM, VC
03 AFC, AFM, BEM, CGM, CMH, DCM, DFC, DFM, DSC, DSM, DSO
09 Iron Cross
10 Bronze Star, Silver Star
11 George Cross, George Medal, Purple Heart
13 Air Force Cross, Air Force Medal, Croix de Guerre, Legion of Merit, Military Cross, Military Medal, Victoria Cross
14 Oak-leaf Cluster

Military units and groups include:

04 file, post, wing
05 corps, flank, fleet, group, squad, troop
06 cohort, convoy, flight, legion, patrol, picket
07 battery, brigade, company, echelon, militia, phalanx, platoon, section
08 division, flotilla, garrison, regiment, squadron
09 battalion, commandos, effective, task force
10 detachment, flying camp, rifle-corps
11 battle group, flying party
12 flying column, Royal Marines
13 guard of honour

• **military equipment**
05 train
• **military life**
04 camp
• **military men** *see* **soldiers** *under* **soldier**
• **military police**
02 MP

militate
• **militate against**
04 hurt **06** damage, oppose, resist
07 contend, counter **09** go against, prejudice **10** act against, counteract, discourage **11** be harmful to, tell against, work against **12** count against, weigh against **15** be detrimental to
• **militate for**
03 aid **04** back, help **07** advance, further, promote **08** speak for

militia
02 SA, TA **04** fyrd **06** Milice **07** reserve
08 yeomanry **09** fencibles, home guard, minutemen, trainband
10 reservists **13** National Guard
15 Territorial Army

milk
03 tap, use **04** draw, pump, skim, whig
05 bleed, drain, press, screw, wring
06 rip off, siphon, stroke **07** draw off, exploit, express, extract, oppress, squeeze **08** impose on, moo-juice
10 manipulate **11** semi-skimmed
15 take advantage of
• **milk producer**
03 cow **04** teat
• **not yielding milk**
04 eild, yeld, yell

milk-can
04 kirn 05 churn

milking
• **place for milking**
04 loan 07 loaning

milkman's cart
04 pram 05 float 09 milkfloat

milksop
04 wimp, wuss 05 cissy, molly, pansy 06 coward, jessie 07 meacock 08 weakling 09 mummy's boy 10 namby-pamby

milk-strainer
03 sye

milky
04 soft, weak 05 white 06 chalky, cloudy, gentle, opaque 07 clouded 08 lacteous 09 milk-white, snow-white, spineless

mill
◇ *anagram indicator*
03 box 04 nurl, roll, shop 05 crush, grate, grind, knurl, plant, pound, press, quern, works 06 crunch, powder, roller 07 crusher, factory, foundry, grinder 08 snuffbox, spinnery, workshop 09 comminute, pulverize 11 boxing match, molendinary 15 processing plant
• **mill around**
05 swarm 06 stream, throng 09 move about 11 crowd around, press around

millet
04 dari, dura, ragi 05 bajra, bajri, doura, durra, proso, ragee, raggy, whisk 06 bajree, dhurra, raggee 09 broom-corn 10 guinea corn

million
01 m

millstone
04 duty, load, onus 06 burden, ligger, runner, weight 07 trouble 09 buhrstone, burrstone 10 affliction, dead-weight, grindstone, obligation, quernstone 11 cross to bear, encumbrance
• **millstone support**
04 rind

millstream
04 lade

Milne
02 AA

mime
05 mimic 06 act out, signal 07 buffoon, charade, gesture, imitate, mimicry, mummery 08 dumb show, indicate, simulate 09 chironomy, pantomime, represent 11 impersonate

mimic
02 do 03 ape 04 copy, echo, mime, mina, mock, myna, play 05 mynah 06 mirror, monkey, parody, parrot, send up 07 copycat, copyist, emulate, imitate, mimetic, minnick, minnock, take off 08 imitator, look like, mimicker, resemble, simulate, starling 09 mimetical, personate 10 caricature 11 impersonate 12 caricaturist, impersonator 13 impressionist

mimicry
05 aping 06 parody 07 copying, mimesis, mockery, take-off 09 burlesque, imitating, imitation 10 caricature, impression, simulation 13 impersonation

minatory
04 grim 07 looming, ominous, warning 08 menacing, sinister 09 impending, minacious 10 cautionary, foreboding 11 threatening 12 inauspicious, intimidatory

mince
◇ *anagram indicator*
03 cut 04 chop, dice, hash, pose 05 grind, ponce 06 prance, simper 07 crumble, posture 11 strike a pose 12 attitudinize 14 walk affectedly
• **not mince your words**
11 talk plainly 13 speak directly

mincing
04 camp, nice 05 cissy, poncy 06 chi-chi, dainty, la-di-da 07 foppish, minikin 08 affected, chee-chee, precious 09 coxcombic 10 effeminate 11 coxcombical, pretentious 12 niminy-piminy

mind
03 wit 04 care, head, heed, mark, note, obey, soul, tend, urge, view, will, wish, wits 05 brain, fancy, guard, sense, watch 06 attend, belief, brains, desire, expert, follow, genius, memory, notion, object, psyche, reason, recall, record, resent, sanity, spirit 07 dislike, egghead, feeling, mention, observe, opinion, outlook, purpose, respect, scholar, thinker, thought 08 academic, attend to, attitude, brainbox, listen to, remember, take care, tendency, thinking, thoughts, watch out 09 attention, intellect, intention, judgement, look after, mentality, retention, sentiment, viewpoint 10 grey matter, mastermind 11 application, disposition, inclination, keep an eye on, personality, point of view, remembrance 12 intellectual, intelligence, pay attention, recollection, subconscious 13 commemoration, comprehension, concentration, consciousness, ratiocination, understanding, way of thinking 15 little grey cells
• **bear in mind, keep in mind**
04 note 06 retain 08 consider, remember 10 take note of 13 give thought to 15 take into account
• **be in two minds**
05 waver 06 dither 08 be unsure, hesitate 09 vacillate 10 be hesitant, dilly-dally 11 be uncertain, be undecided 12 shilly-shally 13 sit on the fence
• **cross your mind**
03 hit 06 come to, strike 07 occur to, think of 08 remember
• **have in mind**
03 aim 04 plan, talk, want 06 design, intend 07 think of 11 contemplate
• **make up your mind**
06 choose, decide, settle 07 resolve 09 determine 13 make a decision 14 reach a decision 15 come to a decision
• **mind out**
05 watch 06 beware 07 look out 08 take care, watch out 09 be careful 12 pay attention 13 be on your guard
• **mind's eye**
04 head 06 memory 11 imagination, remembrance 12 recollection 13 contemplation
• **never mind**
03 too 04 also 06 skip it! 08 as well as, forget it, let alone 09 apart from, don't worry 10 nix my dolly 12 not to mention 13 not forgetting 14 not bother about, take no notice of
• **out of your mind**
03 mad 04 nuts 05 barmy, batty, crazy, daffy, dippy, loony, loopy, manic, nutty, potty 06 crazed, cuckoo, insane, maniac, mental, raving, screwy 07 bananas, bonkers, flipped, lunatic 08 crackers, demented, deranged, doolally, frenzied, maniacal, unhinged, unstable 09 psychotic, up the wall 10 barking mad, distracted, distraught, off the wall, unbalanced 11 not all there, off the rails, off your head 12 mad as a hatter, off your chump, round the bend 13 off your rocker, of unsound mind, round the twist 14 off your trolley, wrong in the head 15 non compos mentis, out of your senses
• **put you in mind of**
06 prompt, remind 10 call to mind 11 bring to mind 14 make you think of
• **put your mind to**
09 persevere, take pains 10 buckle down 13 concentrate on, exert yourself
• **sharpness of mind**
04 edge
• **speak your mind**
11 talk plainly 14 tell it like it is
• **to my mind**
04 heed, mark, note, obey 05 guard, watch 06 ensure, follow, I think, object, regard, resent 07 dislike, observe, respect 08 as I see it, attend to, I believe, in my view, listen to, make sure, object to, remember, take care, watch out 09 be careful, care about, look after, not forget, pay heed to, watch over 10 comply with, disapprove, personally, take care of 11 be annoyed by, in my opinion, keep an eye on, make certain, take offence 12 be bothered by, be offended by, be troubled by, have charge of, pay attention 13 concentrate on, take offence at

mind-boggling
07 amazing 10 astounding, formidable, impossible, incredible, surprising 11 astonishing, exceptional, unthinkable 12 unbelievable, unimaginable 13 extraordinary, inconceivable

mindful
04 wary **05** alert, alive, aware, chary
07 alive to, careful, heedful
08 inclined, sensible, watchful
09 attentive, cognizant, conscious, observant

mindless
04 dull, dumb **05** dopey, thick
06 stupid **07** foolish, robotic, routine, tedious, witless **08** knee-jerk
09 automatic, illogical, negligent, senseless **10** gratuitous, irrational, mechanical **11** birdbrained, instinctive, involuntary, thoughtless
13 unintelligent

mindlessly
08 stupidly **09** foolishly, routinely
11 illogically, senselessly **12** irrationally, mechanically **13** automatically, instinctively, involuntarily, thoughtlessly

mine
02 my **03** dig, egg, pit, win **04** bomb, fund, lode, seam, vein, well **05** delve, dig up, hoard, shaft, stock, store, wheal
06 burrow, dig for, duffer, quarry, remove, search, source, supply, trench, tunnel, wealth **07** bonanza, coalpit, deposit, extract, reserve, unearth
08 claymore, colliery, excavate, landmine, treasury **09** coalfield, explosive, reservoir, undermine
10 excavation, repository, storehouse
11 depth charge
- **mine opening**
03 eye **04** adit
- **mine tunnel**
04 head
- **mining licence**
04 gale
- **surface over a mine**
03 day

mine-passage
04 road

miner
06 digger, hatter, pitman, tinner
07 collier, faceman **08** tributer
09 coalminer **10** faceworker, gold-digger, honeyeater, mineworker

mineral

Minerals include:

03 jet
04 alum, mica, ruby, salt, spar, talc
05 beryl, borax, emery, flint, fluor, topaz, umber
06 albite, blende, cerite, galena, gangue, garnet, glance, gypsum, halite, haüyne, humite, illite, jasper, kermes, lithia, maltha, natron, nosean, pyrite, quartz, rutile, silica, sphene, spinel, talcum, zircon
07 anatase, apatite, axinite, azurite, barytes, biotite, bornite, brucite, calcite, cassite, crystal, cuprite, desmine, diamond, dysodil, epidote, jacinth, jadeite, jargoon, kandite, leucite, nacrite, olivine, pennine, peridot, pyrites, realgar, syenite, thorite, uralite, uranite, zeolite, zincite, zoisite
08 allanite, ankerite, asbestos, autunite, blue john, boracite, brookite, calamine, calcspar, chlorite, chromite, cinnabar, corundum, crocoite, cryolite, diallage, diaspore, dolomite, dysodyle, epsomite, erionite, euxenite, feldspar, fluorite, goethite, graphite, gyrolite, hematite, hyacinth, idocrase, ilmenite, iodyrite, lazulite, lewisite, melilite, mimetite, nephrite, orpiment, plumbago, prehnite, pyroxene, rock salt, sanidine, sapphire, sardonyx, siderite, smaltite, sodalite, stannite, stibnite, stilbite, titanite, wurtzite
09 alabaster, amphibole, anhydrite, aragonite, atacamite, bentonite, blacklead, cairngorm, celestite, cobaltite, elaterite, evaporite, fibrolite, fluorspar, fool's gold, goslarite, grossular, haematite, kaolinite, lodestone, magnesite, magnetite, malachite, marcasite, margarite, microlite, muscovite, nepholine, niccolite, olivenite, pearl spar, quartzite, saltpetre, scheelite, soapstone, sylvanite, tantalite, turquoise, uraninite, vulpinite, wavellite
10 antimonite, aquamarine, aventurine, bloodstone, chalcedony, chrysolite, glauconite, hornblende, meerschaum, microcline, orthoclase, polyhalite, pyrolusite, samerskite, serpentine, sphalerite, tourmaline
11 alexandrite, amphibolite, chrysoberyl, French chalk, lapis lazuli, pitchblende, sal ammoniac, smithsonite, vesuvianite
12 chalcanthite, chalcopyrite, hemimorphite
13 arsenopyrites
14 hydroxyapatite, sodium chloride, yttro-columbite
15 gooseberry-stone

mineral water *see* **water**

Minerva
06 Athene

mingle
03 mix **04** fuse, join, mell **05** alloy, blend, go out, merge, unite
06 hobnob, medley **07** combine, mixture **08** coalesce, compound, intermix **09** associate, circulate, commingle, interfuse, socialize
10 amalgamate **11** intermingle, run together **12** rub shoulders

mingy
04 mean, poor, puny **05** close
06 meagre, measly, paltry, scanty, skimpy, stingy **07** miserly, pitiful, sparing, trivial **08** grudging, pathetic, piddling, ungiving **09** miserable, niggardly **10** hard-fisted, ungenerous
11 close-fisted, close-handed, tight-fisted **12** cheese-paring, parsimonious

miniature
03 toy, wee **04** baby, mini, tiny
05 cameo, dwarf, small, teeny, young
06 little, midget, minute **07** diorama, reduced **08** pint-size **09** microcosm, pint-sized **10** diminutive, scaled-down, small-scale **11** microcosmic, pocket-sized, rubrication

minimal
05 least, token **06** minute
07 minimum, nominal **08** littlest, smallest **09** slightest **10** negligible

minimize
03 cut **05** decry, slash **06** lessen, reduce, shrink **07** curtail **08** belittle, decrease, diminish, discount, laugh off, play down **09** deprecate, disparage, soft-pedal, underrate **10** trivialize
11 make light of **12** make little of
13 underestimate

minimum
◇ *head selection indicator*
03 min **05** least, nadir **06** bottom, lowest **07** minimal, tiniest **08** littlest, smallest **09** slightest **11** lowest point
12 lowest number

minion
05 leech **06** drudge, fawner, lackey, menial, stooge, yes-man **07** darling, flunkey, servant **08** follower, hanger-on, henchman, hireling, parasite
09 attendant, dependant, favourite, flatterer, sycophant, underling
10 bootlicker, henchwoman
11 henchperson

minister
02 PM **03** Min, Rev **04** aide, dean, tend
05 agent, dewan, diwan, elder, envoy, nurse, padre, serve, vezir, vicar, vizir
06 attend, cleric, consul, curate, deacon, divine, leader, legate, parson, pastor, priest, rector, supply, verger, visier, vizier, wait on, wizier **07** cater to, furnish, Mas-John, Mes-John, servant
08 chaplain, delegate, diplomat, emissary, Mass-John, Mess-John, official, preacher **09** churchman, clergyman, dignitary, executive, look after, presbyter **10** administer, ambassador, chancellor, politician, take care of **11** accommodate, clergywoman, Grand Vizier
12 ecclesiastic, office-holder, parish priest **13** administrator
14 representative **15** cabinet minister

See also **prime minister**

ministration
03 aid **04** care, help **06** favour, relief
07 backing, service, succour, support
09 patronage **10** assistance
11 disposition, supervision

ministry
03 Min, MOD, MOH **04** MAFF, METI
06 bureau, clergy, office **07** cabinet, service **08** the cloth **09** the church, the clergy **10** department, government, holy orders **13** the priesthood
14 administration

Minnesota
02 MN **04** Minn

minnow
04 pank, pink

minor
03 boy, kid, son, tot **04** baby, girl, less **05** child, light, lower, petty, small **06** infant, junior, lesser, nipper, slight **07** nominal, smaller, tiny tot, toddler, trivial, unknown, younger **08** daughter, inferior, juvenile, marginal, trifling, young one **09** little one, secondary, youngster **10** negligible, peripheral, subsidiary **11** little known, second-class, subordinate, unimportant, young person **12** unclassified **13** insignificant **14** inconsiderable

• **minor item**
02 by **03** bye

minstrel
04 bard, scop **05** rimer **06** rhymer, singer **07** gleeman **08** jongleur, musician **09** hamfatter, joculator **10** troubadour

mint
◇ *anagram indicator*
03 aim, nep, new, nip **04** bomb, cast, coin, fake, heap, hint, make, pile **05** as new, forge, fresh, hatch, punch, stack, stamp **06** bundle, catnep, catnip, devise, invent, make up, packet, riches, strike, unused, wealth **07** attempt, billion, concoct, falsify, fashion, fortune, million, mint-new, monarda, perfect, produce, purpose, trump up, venture **08** bergamot, billions, brand-new, millions **09** bugle-weed, construct, excellent, fabricate, megabucks, undamaged **10** first-class, immaculate, pennyroyal **11** king's ransom, loadsamoney, manufacture, unblemished

minus
03 bar **04** less, save **06** except **07** short of, without **08** negative **09** excepting, excluding **10** deficiency **11** subtraction

minuscule
04 fine, tiny **05** teeny **06** little, minute **09** itsy-bitsy, miniature, very small **10** diminutive, teeny-weeny **11** Lilliputian, microscopic **13** infinitesimal

minute
01 m **02** mo **03** min, sec **04** note, tick, tiny **05** close, exact, flash, jiffy, minim **06** moment, second, slight, strict **07** instant, precise, trivial **08** accurate, as soon as, critical, detailed, directly, no sooner, the point, trifling **09** miniature, minuscule, short time, the moment, very small **10** diminutive, exhaustive, meticulous, negligible, the instant **11** immediately, Lilliputian, microscopic, painstaking, punctilious **13** infinitesimal, insignificant, microscopical **14** circumstantial, inconsiderable

• **in a minute**
04 anon, soon **06** pronto **07** in a tick, shortly **08** in a flash, in a jiffy, very soon **09** in a moment **10** before long **15** in the near future

• **this minute**
03 now **04** next, then **06** at once, pronto **07** quickly **08** as soon as, directly, promptly, right now, speedily **09** forthwith, instantly, like a shot, right away, yesterday **11** immediately, this instant **12** no sooner than, straight away, there and then, without delay **14** unhesitatingly, without more ado **15** before you know it, instantaneously, without question

• **up to the minute**
02 in **03** now **06** latest, newest, with it **09** happening **10** all the rage, most modern, most recent **11** fashionable

minutely
07 closely, exactly **08** in detail **09** precisely **10** critically **12** exhaustively, meticulously, scrupulously **13** painstakingly **14** systematically

minutes
04 acta **05** notes, tapes **06** record **07** details, records **10** memorandum, transcript **11** proceedings **12** transactions

minutiae
07 details, trifles **08** niceties **10** small print, subtleties **11** fine details, finer points, intricacies, particulars **12** complexities, trivialities

miracle
04 sign **06** marvel, wonder **07** prodigy **10** phenomenon, wonderwork

miraculous
07 amazing **09** monstrous, unnatural, wonderful **10** astounding, incredible, marvellous, monstruous, phenomenal, remarkable, superhuman, surprising, unexpected **11** astonishing **12** inexplicable, supernatural, unbelievable **13** extraordinary, unaccountable

miraculously
09 amazingly **10** incredibly, remarkably **11** wonderfully **12** inexplicably, superhumanly, surprisingly, unbelievably, unexpectedly **13** unaccountably **14** supernaturally **15** extraordinarily

mirage
04 loom **07** fantasy **08** illusion, phantasm **11** fata Morgana **13** hallucination **14** phantasmagoria **15** optical illusion

mire
03 bog, fen, fix, jam, mud **04** dirt, hole, lair, mess, muck, ooze, quag, sink, spot, stew **05** glaur, latch, letch, marsh, slime, swamp **06** deluge, morass, pickle, slough, sludge **07** bog down, trouble **08** loblolly, quagmire **09** marshland, overwhelm **12** difficulties

mirror
03 ape **04** copy, echo, show, twin **05** clone, glass, image, mimic, stone **06** depict, double, follow, parrot **07** emulate, imitate, reflect **08** busybody, likeness, speculum **09** coelostat, condenser, hand-glass, pier-glass, reflector, represent **10** dead ringer, reflection, siderostat, wing mirror **11** cheval-glass, pocket-glass, tiring-glass, toilet glass **12** keeking-glass, laryngoscope, looking-glass **13** driving-mirror, exact likeness, spitting image **14** rear-view mirror

mirth
03 fun **04** glee **05** dream, sport **06** gaiety, spleen **07** delight, frolics, jollity, revelry **08** buoyancy, hilarity, laughter, pleasure **09** amusement, enjoyment, merriment, merriness **10** blitheness, jocularity **11** high spirits **12** cheerfulness

mirthful
03 gay **04** glad **05** funny, happy, jolly, ludic, merry **06** amused, blithe, cheery, jocund, jovial **07** amusing, buoyant, festive, playful **08** cheerful, gladsome, laughful, laughing, sportive **09** hilarious, laughable, vivacious **10** frolicsome, uproarious **11** pleasurable **12** light-hearted **13** light-spirited

mirthless
03 sad **04** glum, sour **05** gruff, moody, sulky, surly **06** gloomy, grumpy, morose, sullen **07** doleful, unhappy **08** churlish, dejected, unamused **09** depressed, miserable **10** despondent, humourless **11** crestfallen, ill-humoured, pessimistic

miry
04 oozy **05** boggy, dirty, fenny, mucky, muddy, slimy **06** glaury, marshy, sludgy, swampy

misadventure
06 mishap **07** bad luck, debacle, failure, ill luck, problem, reverse, setback, tragedy **08** accident, calamity, disaster, hard luck **09** cataclysm, misaunter, mischance **10** ill fortune, misfortune **11** catastrophe

misanthrope
05 cynic, loner, miser, Timon **06** hermit, meanie **07** recluse **08** solitary **14** unsocial person

misanthropic
05 surly **08** egoistic, inhumane **10** antisocial, malevolent, unfriendly, unsociable **13** unsympathetic

misanthropy
06 egoism **08** cynicism **10** inhumanity **11** malevolence **13** antisociality **14** unsociableness

misapply
05 abuse **06** misuse **07** exploit, pervert **09** misemploy **11** use unwisely **13** use unsuitably **14** misappropriate

misapprehend
07 misread, mistake **11** misconceive, misconstrue **12** misinterpret **13** miscomprehend, misunderstand **15** get the wrong idea

misapprehension
05 error, mix-up **07** fallacy, mistake **08** delusion **09** wrong idea **10** misreading **13** misconception **15** false impression

misappropriate
03 nab, rob **04** nick **05** abuse, filch, pinch, steal **06** misuse, pilfer, pocket, thieve **07** pervert, swindle **08** embezzle, misapply, misspend, peculate **09** defalcate, knock down

misappropriation
05 theft **06** misuse **07** robbing **08** stealing **09** pilfering, pocketing **10** peculation **11** defalcation **12** embezzlement **14** misapplication

misbegotten
05 shady **06** stolen **07** bastard, illicit, natural **08** abortive, unlawful **09** dishonest, ill-gotten, ill-judged, imprudent, monstrous, purloined, unadvised **10** ill-advised, monstruous **11** hare-brained **12** contemptible, disreputable, ill-conceived, illegitimate

misbehave
◇ *anagram indicator*
05 act up, lapse **06** be rude, offend, play up **07** carry on, disobey **08** trespass **09** be naughty, fool about, mess about, misdemean, muck about **10** fool around, transgress **11** behave badly **15** be beyond the pale, get up to mischief

misbehaviour
◇ *anagram indicator*
08 mischief, misguide **10** bad manners, carrying-on, misconduct **11** impropriety, naughtiness **12** bad behaviour, disobedience, misdemeanour, mucking about **15** insubordination

misbelief
05 error **06** heresy **07** fallacy, mistake **08** delusion, illusion **10** heterodoxy **11** unorthodoxy, wrong belief **13** misconception **15** misapprehension

miscalculate
03 err **04** boob **06** slip up **07** blunder, go wrong, miscast **08** get wrong, miscount, misjudge **09** misreckon **12** make a mistake, overestimate **13** underestimate

miscalculation
04 boob, slip **05** error, fault, gaffe, lapse **06** booboo, howler, slip-up **07** bloomer, blunder, clanger, mistake **08** miscount **09** oversight **10** aberration, inaccuracy **12** misjudgement, overestimate **13** underestimate **14** miscomputation **15** misapprehension

miscarriage
05 error **06** mishap **07** failure, misdeed **08** aborting, abortion **09** breakdown, ruination **10** misconduct, perversion **13** mismanagement **14** disappointment

miscarry
04 fail, flop, fold, warp **05** abort, slink **07** founder, go amiss, go wrong, misfire, miswend **10** not come off **11** bite the dust, come to grief, fall through, lose the baby **12** come a cropper **13** come to nothing

miscellaneous
04 chow **05** mixed **06** motley, sundry, varied **07** diverse, jumbled, mingled, various **08** assorted, eclectic **10** variegated **11** diversified, farraginous **12** multifarious **13** heterogeneous

• **miscellaneous lot**
04 raft

miscellany
03 mix **04** olio, olla **06** jumble, medley **07** farrago, mixture, variety **08** mishmash, mixed bag, pastiche **09** anthology, diversity, patchwork, potpourri **10** assortment, collection, hotchpotch, salmagundi, salmagundy **11** collectanea, gallimaufry, miscellanea, smorgasbord **14** conglomeration, omnium-gatherum

mischance
04 blow **06** mishap **07** ill luck, tragedy **08** accident, bad break, calamity, disaster **09** ill-chance **10** ill fortune, infelicity, misfortune **11** contretemps **12** misadventure

mischief
03 Ate, elf, hob, imp, wag **04** bale, bane, dido, evil, harm, hurt, lark, limb, pest, puck, tyke **05** cutty, devil, gamin, rogue, scamp **06** damage, gamine, injury, monkey, nickum, pranks, rascal, terror, tricks, urchin **07** carry-on, hellion, malicho, pliskie, stirrer, trouble, varmint, villain **08** diablery, escapade, makebate, nuisance, spalpeen **09** devilment, diablerie, scallywag, vengeance **10** cockatrice, disruption, disservice, hanky-panky, impishness, shenanigan, wrongdoing **11** limb of Satan, monkey shine, naughtiness, roguishness, shenanigans **12** bad behaviour, esprit follet, misbehaviour, monkey tricks **13** barnsbreaking, funny business, jiggery-pokery **14** monkey business **15** flibbertigibbet

mischievous
◇ *anagram indicator*
03 bad **04** arch, evil **05** elfin, elvan, elven, rogue **06** elfish, elvish, impish, shrewd, wicked **07** gallows, harmful, hurtful, naughty, playful, roguish, teasing, tricksy, unhappy, vicious, waggish **08** litherly, rascally, spiteful **09** ill-deedly, injurious, malicious, malignant, pestilent **10** frolicsome, pernicious, up to no good **11** destructive, detrimental, disobedient, misbehaving, troublesome **12** badly behaved

mischievously
◇ *anagram indicator*
08 impishly, wickedly **09** harmfully, naughtily, playfully, roguishly, teasingly, viciously, waggishly **10** spitefully **11** injuriously, maliciously **13** destructively, disobediently

misconceive
07 misread, mistake, suspect **08** misjudge **11** misconstrue **12** misapprehend, misinterpret **13** misunderstand

misconception
05 error **07** fallacy, mistake **08** delusion **09** wrong idea **10** misconceit, misreading **15** false impression, misapprehension

misconduct
◇ *anagram indicator*
08 adultery, misusage **10** wrongdoing **11** impropriety, malpractice, miscarriage **12** bad behaviour, misbehaviour, misdemeanour **13** mismanagement

misconstrue
◇ *anagram indicator*
07 misread, mistake, pervert **08** misjudge **09** misreckon **10** misconster **11** misconceive **12** misapprehend, misinterpret, mistranslate **13** misunderstand **15** take the wrong way

miscreant
05 knave, rogue, scamp **06** rascal, sinner, wicked, wretch **07** dastard, heretic, infidel, villain **08** criminal, evildoer, vagabond **09** reprobate, scallywag, scoundrel, wrongdoer **10** malefactor, profligate, villainous **11** misbeliever, scoundrelly, unbelieving **12** troublemaker **13** mischief-maker

misdeed
03 sin **05** amiss, crime, error, fault, wrong **06** felony **07** offence **08** trespass, villainy **10** misconduct, peccadillo, wrongdoing **11** delinquency, miscarriage, misdemeanor, mistreading **12** misdemeanour **13** transgression

misdemeanour
05 error, fault, lapse, wrong **07** misdeed, offence **08** trespass **10** misconduct, peccadillo, wrongdoing **11** malfeasance **12** indiscretion, infringement, misbehaviour **13** transgression

misdirect
◇ *anagram indicator*
05 avert **06** divert, misuse **07** mislead **08** misapply, misguide **09** misinform **10** misaddress **13** give a bum steer **14** misappropriate

miser
04 carl **05** hunks **06** meanie, wretch **07** niggard, save-all, Scrooge

08 muckworm, tightwad 09 skinflint 10 cheapskate, curmudgeon, scrapegood 11 cheeseparer, scrapepenny 12 money-grubber, penny-pincher

Misers include:

05 Burns (Montgomery)
06 Mammon, Marner (Silas)
07 Scrooge (Ebenezer)
08 Nickleby (Ralph), Trapbois
10 Fardorough, Van Swieten (Ghysbrecht)
11 Earlforward (Henry)

miserable
◇ *anagram indicator*
03 low, miz, sad 04 base, blue, down, glum, mean, mizz, poor, punk, vile 05 lousy, sorry, surly 06 dismal, dreary, gloomy, grumpy, meagre, measly, mouldy, paltry, rotten, scanty, shabby, sullen 07 crushed, forlorn, grouchy, joyless, pitiful, squalid, unhappy 08 dejected, desolate, downcast, pathetic, pitiable, shameful, wretched 09 cheerless, crotchety, depressed, irritable, niggardly, sorrowful, worthless 10 deplorable, depressing, despicable, despondent, detestable, distressed, unpleasant 11 bad-tempered, disgraceful, downhearted, god-forsaken, heartbroken, ignominious, ill-tempered, low-spirited, melancholic 12 contemptible, disagreeable, disconsolate, god-forgotten, impoverished 14 down in the dumps

miserably
◇ *anagram indicator*
05 sadly 06 glumly, poorly 07 greatly 08 gloomily, markedly, paltrily, scantily, stingily, very much 09 niggardly, pitifully, unhappily 10 desolately 11 dangerously, desperately, sorrowfully 12 despondently, pathetically 14 disconsolately

miserliness
07 avarice 08 meanness 09 frugality, minginess, parsimony, tightness 10 stinginess 12 cheeseparing, covetousness 13 niggardliness, penny-pinching, penuriousness 15 close-fistedness, tight-fistedness

miserly
04 gare, mean 05 close, mingy, tight 06 stingy 07 chintzy, sparing 08 beggarly 09 niggardly, penurious 11 close-fisted, close-handed, tight-fisted 12 candle-paring, cheeseparing, parsimonious 13 money-grubbing, penny-pinching

misery
02 wo 03 miz, woe 04 bale, hell, mizz, want 05 agony, gloom, grief 06 grouch, misère, moaner, penury, sorrow, whiner 07 anguish, avarice, despair, killjoy, poverty, sadness, whinger 08 buzzkill, distress, hardship, Jeremiah, sourpuss 09 adversity, indigence, perdition, pessimist, privation, suffering, the depths 10 affliction, complainer, depression, desolation, discomfort, melancholy, misfortune, oppression, spoilsport, wet blanket 11 deprivation, destitution, living death, melancholia, unhappiness 12 wretchedness 13 prophet of doom 14 dog in the manger

misfire
04 fail, flop 05 abort 06 go awry 07 founder, go amiss, go wrong 08 miscarry 09 fizzle out 10 not come off 11 bite the dust, come to grief, fall through 12 come a cropper

misfit
◇ *anagram indicator*
04 geek 05 freak, loner 06 weirdo 07 dropout, oddball, sad sack 08 lone wolf, maverick 09 eccentric, odd one out 13 individualist, nonconformist 14 fish out of water

misfortune
02 wo 03 ill, woe 04 blow, evil, ruth, woes 05 trial 06 mishap, sorrow, wroath 07 bad luck, failure, ill luck, misfare, misluck, reverse, setback, tragedy, trouble 08 accident, calamity, casualty, disaster, distress, hard luck, hardship, judgment 09 adversity, judgement, mischance, mishanter 10 affliction, infelicity, mischanter 11 catastrophe, tribulation 12 misadventure
• **expression of misfortune**
02 ah, ay, oh 03 out 04 alas, ay me, haro, waly 06 harrow 07 welaway 08 waesucks, welladay, wellaway 09 alack-a-day, wellanear 10 alas the day 12 alas the while

misgiving
04 fear 05 doubt, qualm, worry 06 niggle, unease 07 anxiety, scruple 08 distrust, misdoubt, mistrust 09 suspicion 10 hesitation 11 reservation, uncertainty 12 apprehension 14 second thoughts

misguided
◇ *anagram indicator*
04 rash 05 wrong 06 erring, misled 07 deluded, foolish, off-beam 08 mistaken 09 erroneous, ill-judged, imprudent, misplaced 10 fallacious, ill-advised 11 injudicious, misdirected, misinformed 12 misconceived 13 ill-considered

mishandle
◇ *anagram indicator*
04 muff 05 botch, fluff 06 bungle, fumble, mess up 07 balls up, screw up 08 maltreat, misjudge 09 mismanage 11 make a hash of, make a mess of 12 make a balls of 14 make a balls-up of, make a pig's ear of

mishap
◇ *anagram indicator*
04 blow 05 drere, shunt, trial 06 dreare, mucker 07 reverse, setback, trouble 08 accident, calamity, disaster, incident 09 adversity, misaunter, mischance 10 ill fortune, misfortune 11 catastrophe, disaventure, tribulation 12 disadventure, misadventure 15 stroke of bad luck

mishit
04 duff, thin 05 flier, flyer 06 sclaff

mishmash
04 hash, mess, olio, olla 05 salad 06 jumble, medley, muddle 07 farrago 08 pastiche 09 potpourri 10 hodgepodge, hotchpotch, salmagundi 11 gallimaufry 14 conglomeration

misinform
05 bluff 07 deceive, mislead 08 hoodwink, misguide 09 misdirect 12 take for a ride 13 give a bum steer

misinformation
04 dope, guff, hype, lies 05 bluff 07 baloney, eyewash 08 bum steer, nonsense 09 deception 10 misleading 12 misdirection 14 disinformation

misinterpret
◇ *anagram indicator*
04 warp 05 wrest 06 garble 07 distort, misread, mistake 08 misjudge 11 misconceive, misconstrue 12 misapprehend 13 misunderstand 15 take the wrong way

misinterpretation
10 misreading 12 misjudgement 13 misconception 14 misacceptation 15 false impression, misapprehension, misconstruction

misjudge
07 mistake 08 miscount 11 misconstrue 12 miscalculate, misinterpret, overestimate 13 misunderstand, underestimate

misjudgement
07 mistake 09 wrong idea 10 misdeeming 12 wrong opinion 14 miscalculation 15 wrong conclusion

mislay
04 lose, miss 07 misfile 08 misplace 11 lose sight of, lose track of 14 be unable to find

mislead
◇ *anagram indicator*
04 fool, snow 05 put on 06 delude 07 deceive 08 fool into, hoodwink, impose on, misguide 09 blindfold, misdirect, misinform 10 impose upon, lead astray 12 misrepresent, take for a ride 13 give a bum steer, lead into error 14 pull a fast one on, put off the scent

misleading
◇ *anagram indicator*
06 biased, loaded, tricky 07 evasive 08 delusive, illusive, illusory, sinister 09 ambiguous, confusing, deceiving, deceptive, equivocal 10 fallacious, unreliable

mismanage
◇ *anagram indicator*
03 mar 04 muff 05 botch, waste

06 bungle, foul up, mess up **07** balls up, blunder, misrule, screw up
08 misjudge, misspend **09** mishandle
11 make a hash of, make a mess of
12 make a balls of **14** make a balls-up of, make a pig's ear of

mismanagement
◇ *anagram indicator*
04 hash, mess **05** farce **06** bungle, cock-up, muddle **07** balls-up, failure, pig's ear **08** bungling, shambles
11 mishandling **12** misjudgement
13 pig's breakfast **14** misgovernaunce

mismatched
08 clashing, mismated, unsuited
09 disparate, irregular, misallied
10 discordant, unmatching **11** ill-assorted, incongruous **12** antipathetic, incompatible **14** unreconcilable

misogynist
03 MCP **06** sexist **10** woman-hater
12 anti-feminist **14** male chauvinist
15 male supremacist

misogyny
06 sexism **12** anti-feminism **13** male supremacy **14** male chauvinism

misplace
◇ *anagram indicator*
04 lose, miss **06** mislay **07** misfile
08 misapply **09** misassign **11** lose sight of, lose track of **14** be unable to find

misprint
◇ *anagram indicator*
04 typo **05** error **07** erratum, literal, mistake **11** corrigendum **12** literal error
13 printing error

misquote
05 twist **06** garble, muddle **07** distort, falsify, pervert **08** misstate
09 misreport **11** misremember
12 misrepresent

misread
◇ *anagram indicator*
06 garble **07** distort, mistake
08 misjudge **11** misconceive, misconstrue **12** misapprehend, misinterpret **13** misunderstand **15** take the wrong way

misrepresent
◇ *anagram indicator*
05 abuse, belie, color, slant, twist
06 colour, garble **07** distort, falsify, pervert **08** disguise, minimize, miscolor, misquote, misstate
09 miscolour, misreport
10 exaggerate, manipulate
11 misconstrue **12** misinterpret

misrepresentation
◇ *anagram indicator*
08 twisting **10** distortion, perversion
12 exaggeration, manipulation, misreporting **13** falsification
15 misconstruction

misrule
04 riot **05** chaos **06** tumult **07** anarchy, turmoil **08** disorder, unreason
09 confusion **10** turbulence
11 lawlessness **12** indiscipline
13 misgovernment, mismanagement
15 disorganization

miss
02 Ms **03** err **04** beat, blow, fail, flop, flub, girl, lack, lass, lose, maid, Mlle, muff, need, omit, skip, slip, trip, want, wish **05** avoid, dodge, error, evade, fault, forgo, let go, Mdlle, mourn
06 bypass, damsel, escape, fiasco, forego, kumari, lament, maiden, not see, pass up, regret **07** ache for, blunder, failure, let slip, long for, mistake, neglect, not go to, not spot, pine for **08** fräulein, leave out, miscarry, omission, overlook, pass over, Señorita, sidestep, teenager, yearn for **09** disregard, fail to get, fail to hit, grieve for, not notice, oversight, Signorina, sorrow for, young lady **10** be away from, circumvent, desiderate, not go to see, schoolgirl, young woman
11 fail to catch, fail to seize, not be part of **12** be absent from, be too late for, fail to attend, fail to notice, mademoiselle
13 feel the loss of, misunderstand, not take part in

See also **girl**; **woman**

• miss out
04 jump, omit, skip **06** bypass, ignore
07 exclude **08** leave out, pass over
09 disregard **12** dispense with

missal
08 breviary, mass-book, Triodion
09 formulary **10** office-book, prayerbook **11** euchologion, servicebook

misshapen
◇ *anagram indicator*
04 bent, ugly **06** inform, warped
07 crooked, dismayd, twisted
08 crippled, deformed **09** contorted, distorted, grotesque, malformed, monstrous **15** misproportioned

missile
04 bomb, dart, shot **05** arrow, shaft, shell **06** rocket, weapon **07** grenade, torpedo **10** flying bomb, projectile

Missiles include:

02 MX, V-2
03 AAM, ABM, AGM, ASM, ATM, SAM, SSM
04 ALCM, ASBM, ICBM, IRBM, MIRV, MRBM, Scud, SLBM, TASM
05 smart
06 AMRAAM, cruise, Exocet®, guided
07 Polaris, Trident
08 Maverick
09 ballistic, minuteman
10 sidewinder, wire-guided
11 heat-seeking
12 surface-to-air

• missile container
04 silo

missing
◇ *deletion indicator*
04 gone, lost **06** absent, astray
07 lacking, mislaid, strayed, wanting
08 awanting **09** misplaced **10** gone astray **11** disappeared **14** gone for a Burton, unaccounted-for

mission
02 op **03** aim, job **04** duty, goal, raid, task, work **05** chore, quest **06** action, charge, errand, office, sortie **07** calling, crusade, embassy, purpose, pursuit
08 business, campaign, exercise, legation, ministry, vocation
09 manoeuvre, operation, task force
10 assignment, commission, delegation, deputation **11** raison d'être, undertaking

missionary
05 envoy **07** apostle **08** champion, crusader, emissary, minister, preacher, promoter **09** converter
10 ambassador, campaigner, evangelist **12** propagandist, proselytizer

Missionaries include:

03 **Fox** (George), **Huc** (Evariste Régis)
04 **Luke** (St), **Mark** (St), **Paul** (St)
05 **Carey** (William), **David** (Père Armand), **Eliot** (John), **Ellis** (William), **Moody** (Dwight L), **Ricci** (Matteo), **Smith** (Eli)
06 **Damien** (Father Joseph), **Graham** (Billy), **Teresa** (Mother), **Wesley** (John)
07 **Aylward** (Gladys), **Columba** (St), **Liddell** (Eric), **ten Boom** (Corrie)
08 **Boniface** (St), **Crowther** (Samuel)
09 **McPherson** (Aimee Semple), **Southwell** (Robert)
10 **Huddleston** (Trevor), **Macpherson** (Annie), **Schweitzer** (Albert)
11 **Livingstone** (David)
13 **Francis Xavier** (St)

Mississippi
02 MS **04** Miss

missive
04 line, memo, note, sent **06** letter, report **07** epistle, message, missile
08 bulletin, dispatch **09** messenger
10 communiqué, memorandum
13 communication

Missouri
02 MO

misspell
◇ *anagram indicator*

misspent
04 idle **06** wasted **07** misused
08 prodigal **09** idled away
10 dissipated, misapplied, profitless, squandered, thrown away
12 unprofitable **13** frittered away

misstate
05 twist **06** garble **07** distort, falsify, pervert **08** misquote **09** misrelate, misreport **11** misremember
12 misrepresent

mist
03 dew, fog **04** drow, film, haar, haze, murk, rack, roke, smog, veil **05** cloud,

spray, steam **06** mizzle, nimbus, vapour **07** dimness, drizzle **10** exhalation **12** condensation

• **mist over, mist up**
03 dim, fog **04** blur, veil **05** fog up, glaze **07** obscure, steam up **09** cloud over **10** become hazy **12** become cloudy **13** become blurred

mistake
◇ *anagram indicator*
03 err **04** bish, blue, boob, boss, flaw, flub, goof, muff, slip, take, typo **05** error, fault, fluff, gaffe, lapse, mix up, mix-up **06** booboo, cock up, domino, duff it, foul up, foul-up, goof up, howler, mess up, miscue, muddle, ricket, slip up, slip-up, stumer **07** bad move, balls up, bloomer, blooper, blunder, botch-up, clanger, clinker, confuse, erratum, fallacy, faux pas, go wrong, louse up, misread, misstep, own goal, screw up, take for **08** confound, get wrong, mesprize, misfield, misjudge, misprint, misprise, misprize, muddle up, omission, solecism **09** make a slip, oversight **10** aberration, inaccuracy, misprision, misreading **11** corrigendum, make a booboo, misconceive, misconstrue, misspelling **12** come a cropper, drop a clanger, indiscretion, misapprehend, miscalculate, misjudgement **13** misunderstand **14** miscalculation **15** misapprehension, put your foot in it, slip of the tongue

mistaken
◇ *anagram indicator*
03 wet **05** false, wrong **06** faulty, misled, untrue **07** at fault, deluded, in error, inexact, off base, off-beam, vicious **08** deceived, overseen **09** erroneous, ill-judged, incorrect, misguided, misprised, unfounded **10** fallacious, inaccurate, up the booay **11** inauthentic, misinformed **13** inappropriate, wide of the mark **15** got the wrong idea

mistakenly
◇ *anagram indicator*
07 falsely, in error, wrongly **08** unfairly, unjustly **09** by mistake **11** erroneously, incorrectly, misguidedly **12** fallaciously, inaccurately **15** inappropriately

Mister
02 Mr

mistimed
08 ill-timed, tactless, untimely **10** malapropos **11** inopportune, unfortunate **12** inconvenient, infelicitous, unseasonable **14** unsynchronized

mistiness *see* **mist**

mistreat
◇ *anagram indicator*
04 harm, hurt, maul **05** abuse, bully **06** batter, beat up, ill-use, injure, misuse, molest **08** ill-treat, maltreat, walk over **09** mishandle **10** knock about, treat badly **11** walk all over

mistreatment
04 harm, hurt **05** abuse **06** ill-use, injury, misuse **07** cruelty, mauling **08** bullying, ill-usage **09** battering **10** unkindness **11** manhandling, mishandling, molestation **12** ill-treatment, maltreatment **13** brutalization

mistress
04 amie, dame, doxy, lady, miss, wife **05** lover, tutor, wench, woman **06** ruling **07** Aspasia, herself, hetaera, leading, partner, stepney, teacher **08** goodwife, lady-love, paramour **09** belle amie, concubine, courtesan, courtezan, governess, housewife, inamorata, kept woman, principal **10** canary-bird, châtelaine, fancy woman, girlfriend, school dame **11** live-in lover **12** bit on the side **13** schoolteacher

mistrust
04 fear **05** doubt, qualm **06** beware **07** caution, suspect **08** be wary of, distrust, wariness **09** chariness, hesitancy, misgiving, suspicion **10** scepticism **11** uncertainty **12** apprehension, reservations **13** have no faith in **14** be suspicious of, have misgivings **15** have doubts about

mistrustful
03 shy **04** wary **05** chary, leery **07** cynical, dubious, fearful **08** cautious, doubtful, hesitant **09** sceptical, uncertain **10** suspicious **11** distrustful **12** apprehensive

misty
03 dim **04** hazy **05** foggy, fuzzy, murky, smoky, vague **06** cloudy, opaque, veiled **07** blurred, clouded, obscure, tearful, unclear **08** nebulous **10** indistinct

misunderstand
07 mishear, misknow, misread, mistake **08** get wrong, misjudge **11** misconstrue, misperceive **12** misapprehend, misinterpret, miss the point **13** miscomprehend **15** get the wrong idea

misunderstanding
03 row **04** rift, tiff **05** clash, error, mix-up **06** breach **07** discord, dispute, mistake, quarrel **08** argument, conflict, squabble **09** wrong idea **10** difference, falling-out, malentendu, misreading **12** crossed wires, disagreement, misjudgement **13** misconception **15** false impression, misapprehension, misintelligence

misunderstood
07 misread **08** misheard, mistaken **09** ill-judged, misjudged **12** misconstrued, unrecognized **13** unappreciated **14** misappreciated, misinterpreted, misrepresented

misuse
◇ *anagram indicator*
04 harm, hurt **05** abuse, waste, wrong **06** ill-use, injure, injury **07** abusion, corrupt, deceive, distort, exploit, pervert **08** ill-treat, misapply, mistreat, squander, wrong use **09** dissipate, misemploy **10** corruption, perversion, treat badly **11** mishandling, squandering **12** exploitation, ill-treatment, maltreatment, mistreatment **13** misemployment **14** malappropriate, misapplication, misappropriate

mite
03 bit, jot, tad **04** atom, iota, whit, worm **05** grain, ounce, scrap, spark, touch, trace **06** acarus, lepton, morsel, varroa **07** modicum, smidgen **08** berry bug **09** red spider, Sarcoptes **11** trombiculid, tyroglyphid

mitigate
04 calm, dull, ease, help **05** abate, allay, blunt, check, mease, quiet, remit, slake, still **06** aslake, lenify, lessen, modify, pacify, reduce, soften, soothe, subdue, temper, weaken **07** appease, assuage, lighten, mollify, placate, qualify, relieve, sweeten **08** decrease, diminish, moderate, palliate, tone down **09** alleviate, extenuate

mitigating
08 lenitive, mitigant **09** assuasive, modifying, tempering **10** justifying, palliative, qualifying **11** extenuating, vindicating, vindicatory

mitigation
06 relief **07** remorse **08** allaying, decrease, easement **09** abatement, lessening, reduction, remission, tempering **10** diminution, moderation, palliation **11** alleviation, appeasement, assuagement, extenuation **13** mollification, qualification

mitre
04 tiar **05** tiara

mix
◇ *anagram indicator*
04 card, fuse, hash, join, mash, mell, meng, mess, ming, olio, stir, suit **05** agree, alloy, blend, cross, get on, menge, merge, union, unite, whisk **06** caudle, fold in, fusion, hobnob, jumble, meddle, medley, merger, mingle, muddle **07** amalgam, combine, consort, farrago, involve, mixture, shake up, swizzle **08** coalesce, compound, confound, emulsify, get along, intermix, mingling, mishmash, pastiche **09** associate, coalition, composite, harmonize, interfuse, introduce, potpourri, socialize, synthesis **10** amalgamate, assortment, complement, fraternize, go well with, hodgepodge, homogenize, hotchpotch, infiltrate, interbreed, meet others, salmagundi, synthesize **11** combination, gallimaufry, incorporate, intermingle, interpolate, olla-podrida, put together **12** amalgamation, be compatible, conglomerate

• **mix in**
◇ *anagram indicator*
05 add in, blend, merge **09** introduce **10** infiltrate **11** incorporate, interpolate

• **mix up**
◇ *anagram indicator*
05 upset **06** garble, jumble, muddle, puzzle **07** confuse, disturb, involve, mistake, perplex, snarl up **08** bewilder, confound, muddle up **09** implicate **10** complicate **12** get jumbled up

mixed
◇ *anagram indicator*
02 pi **03** pie, pye **04** chow, ment **05** fused, meint, meynt **06** hybrid, menged, minged, motley, united, unsure, varied **07** alloyed, blended, diverse, mingled, mongrel **08** assorted, combined, compound, confused **09** composite, crossbred, equivocal, half-caste, interbred, uncertain **10** ambivalent **11** amalgamated, conflicting, diversified, promiscuous **12** incorporated, through-other **13** contradicting, miscellaneous

• **mixed up**
◇ *anagram indicator*
04 in on **05** upset **06** hung up **07** chaotic, muddled, puzzled **08** caught up, confused, involved, messed up **09** disturbed, embroiled, entangled, perplexed, screwed up **10** bewildered, désorienté, disordered, distracted, distraught, implicated, inculpated **11** complicated, disoriented, maladjusted **12** incriminated

mixer
05 whisk **06** beater, joiner **07** blender, meddler, stirrer **08** busybody, makebate **09** disrupter, extrovert **10** interferer, liquidizer, socializer, subversive **12** troublemaker **13** food processor, mischief-maker

mixing
05 cross, union **06** fusion **08** blending, mingling **09** interflow, synthesis **10** commixtion, commixture, confection, minglement **11** association, coalescence, combination, socializing **12** amalgamation **13** hybridization, interbreeding, intermingling, miscegenation **14** fraternization

mixture
◇ *anagram indicator*
03 mix **04** brew, mong, olio, olla, wash **05** alloy, blend, cross, union **06** fusion, hybrid, jumble, medley, mingle **07** amalgam, compost, farrago, melange, variety **08** compound, mishmash, mixed bag, pastiche **09** composite, patchwork, potpourri, synthesis **10** assortment, composture, concoction, hodgepodge, hotchpotch, miscellany **11** coalescence, combination, olla-podrida, smorgasbord, temperature **12** amalgamation **14** conglomeration

mix-up
◇ *anagram indicator*
04 mess **05** chaos, snafu **06** foul-up, jumble, muddle, tangle **07** balls-up, mistake, snarl-up **08** disorder, nonsense **09** confusion **12** complication

moan
03 sob **04** beef, carp, hone, howl, mean, mein, mene, sigh, wail, weep **05** bleat, gripe, groan, meane, mourn, whine **06** bemoan, charge, grieve, grouse, lament, whinge **07** beefing, carping, censure, grumble, whimper **08** bleating, complain, grumbler **09** annoyance, bellyache, complaint, criticism, grievance, whingeing **10** accusation **11** bellyaching, kick up a fuss, lamentation **12** fault-finding **14** representation **15** dissatisfaction

moaner
06 whiner **07** fusspot, grouser, niggler, whinger **08** grumbler **09** nit-picker **10** bellyacher, complainer, fussbudget **11** fault-finder

mob
03 set **04** body, crew, fill, gang, herd, host, mass, pack **05** brood, crowd, drove, flock, group, horde, plebs, press, swarm, tribe, troop **06** attack, charge, jostle, masses, mobile, pester, proles, rabble, throng **07** besiege, company, king mob, overrun, set upon **08** canaille, fall upon, mobility, populace, riff-raff, surround **09** descend on, gathering, hoi polloi, multitude **10** assemblage, collection, common herd, crowd round, faex populi, rabble rout, swarm round **11** gather round, proletariat, rank and file **12** common people, ribble-rabble **13** great unwashed **15** many-headed beast

mobile
◇ *anagram indicator*
04 thin **05** agile, quick **06** active, lively, motile, moving, nimble, roving, supple **07** migrant, movable, roaming **08** changing, flexible, moveable, portable **09** adaptable, energetic, itinerant, revealing, wandering **10** able to move, adjustable, ambulatory, changeable, expressive, locomotive, suggesting, travelling **11** peripatetic **12** ever-changing **13** transportable

mobility
06 motion **07** agility **08** motility, motivity, vivacity **09** animation **10** locomotion, movability, suppleness **11** flexibility, movableness, portability **12** locomobility, locomotivity **14** expressiveness

mobilization
08 assembly **09** mustering, summoning **10** activation **11** marshalling, preparation **12** organization

mobilize
◇ *anagram indicator*
05 rally, ready **06** call up, enlist, muster, summon **07** animate, marshal, prepare **08** activate, assemble, get ready, organize **09** conscript, galvanize, make ready **14** call into action

mob rule
06 mob law **08** lynch law **09** mobocracy **10** ochlocracy **13** kangaroo court, Reign of Terror

mobster
04 thug **05** crook, heavy, rough, tough **06** bandit, robber **07** brigand, hoodlum, ruffian **08** criminal, gangster, hooligan, skinhead **09** bovver boy, desperado, racketeer, terrorist

mock
03 ape, cod, dor, kid, rag, rib **04** fake, geck, gibe, goof, jape, jeer, rail, sham, slag **05** bogus, chaff, dummy, faked, false, fleer, flout, knock, mimic, scoff, scorn, scout, sneer, taunt, tease **06** bemock, deride, ersatz, forged, insult, parody, phoney, pseudo, send up **07** emulate, feigned, imitate, lampoon, laugh at, murgeon, pretend, slag off, take off **08** ridicule, satirize, simulate, spurious **09** burlesque, disparage, imitation, imitative, make fun of, poke fun at, pretended, simulated, synthetic **10** artificial, caricature, fraudulent, substitute **11** counterfeit, poke borak at **13** poke mullock at
See also **imitation**

mocker
05 tease **06** critic, jeerer **07** clothes, derider, flouter, reviler, scoffer, scorner, sneerer **08** bellbird, satirist, vilifier **09** detractor, lampooner, ridiculer, tormentor **10** iconoclast, lampoonist **11** pasquinader

mockery
03 dor, gab **04** jeer, quiz, sham **05** farce, fleer, scoff, scorn, serve, sneer, spoof, sport **06** banter, parody, satire, send-up **07** apology, disdain, horning, jeering, kidding, lampoon, mimicry, ragging, ribbing, sarcasm, take-off, teasing **08** contempt, derision, raillery, ridicule, scoffing, sneering, taunting, travesty **09** burlesque, charivari, contumely, emulation, imitation **10** caricature, disrespect **12** mickey-taking **13** disparagement

mocking
03 wry **05** snide **07** cynical **08** derisive, derisory, illusion, impudent, irrisory, narquois, sardonic, scoffing, scornful, sneering, taunting **09** insulting, quizzical, sarcastic, satirical **10** disdainful, irreverent, wry-mouthed **12** contemptuous **13** disrespectful

mock-up
04 copy **05** dummy, image, model **07** replica **09** facsimile, imitation **11** fabrication **14** representation

mode
03 fad, way **04** form, kind, look, mood, plan, rage, rate **05** craze, modus, style, trend, vogue **06** custom, Dorian, lastic, Ionian, Lydian, manner, method, system **07** Aeolian, fashion, Locrian, process **08** approach, modality, Phrygian, practice **09** condition, procedure, technique **10** convention, dernier cri **11** latest thing **13** manifestation **15** fashionableness

model
◇ *anagram indicator*
01 T **03** sit, toy **04** base, cast, copy, form, kind, make, mark, mode, mold, plan, pose, sort, type, wear, work **05** carve, dummy, ideal, image, medal, mould, poser, shape, sport, style **06** byword, create, design, lovely, mirror, mock-up, module, sample, sculpt, sitter **07** cutaway, display, epitome, example, exemple, fashion, paragon, pattern, perfect, reduced, replica, show off, subject, typical, variety, version **08** bozzetto, exemplar, original, paradigm, specimen, standard, template **09** archetype, dress form, exemplary, facsimile, imitation, mannequin, miniature, prototype, superwaif **10** archetypal, embodiment, small-scale, stereotype **11** guiding star **12** artist's model, fashion model, guiding light, prototypical, reproduction **14** perfect example, representation

moderate
03 mod **04** calm, cool, curb, ease, fair, just, mean, mild, soft, so-so, tame **05** abate, allay, chair, check, slake, sober **06** decent, direct, gentle, lessen, medium, modest, modify, pacify, relent, soften, steady, subdue, temper **07** appease, assuage, average, chasten, control, die down, dwindle, fairish, liberal, qualify, repress, slacken, subside **08** adequate, attemper, centrist, chastise, decrease, diminish, don't know, mediocre, middling, mitigate, modulate, muscadin, ordinary, palliate, passable, play down, regulate, restrain, sensible, suppress, tone down **09** alleviate, attenuate, Menshevik, Octobrist, soft-pedal, soft-shell, supervise, temperate, tolerable, treatable **10** controlled, measurable, not much cop, reasonable, restrained **11** indifferent, keep in check, not up to much, preside over, soft-shelled **12** act as chair at, conservative, nonextremist **13** neutral person, no great shakes, well-regulated **14** fair to middling **15** act as chairman at, middle-of-the-road

moderately
05 mezzo, quite **06** fairly, rather **08** passably, slightly, somewhat **10** reasonably **12** to some extent, within reason **13** within measure **14** conservatively

moderation
02 ho **03** hoa, hoh **06** reason **07** caution, control, curbing, measure **08** chastity, decrease, sobriety **09** abatement, composure, lessening, reduction, restraint **10** golden mean, mitigation, regulation, relaxation, subsidence, temperance **11** alleviation, attenuation, self-control **13** self-restraint, temperateness **14** abstemiousness, reasonableness

• in moderation
10 moderately **12** within bounds, within limits, within reason **15** with self-control

modern
02 AD, in **03** hip, mod, new, now **04** cool, late **05** fresh, novel **06** latest, latter, modish, recent, trendy, with it **07** current, faddish, go-ahead, in style, in vogue, present, stylish, voguish **08** advanced, everyday, existing, neoteric, space-age, up-to-date **09** in fashion, inventive, latter-day, newfangle, the latest **10** all the rage, avant-garde, futuristic, innovative, neoterical, newfangled, present-day **11** commonplace, cutting edge, fashionable, modernistic, progressive, spanking new **12** contemporary **13** state-of-the-art, up-to-the-minute **14** forward-looking, hot off the press

modernity
07 newness, novelty **09** freshness **10** innovation, recentness **11** originality **14** innovativeness **15** contemporaneity, fashionableness

modernization
07 renewal **08** redesign, updating **09** revamping **10** renovation **11** improvement, remodelling **12** modification, regeneration **13** refurbishment **14** transformation

modernize
04 do up **05** fix up, renew **06** do over, modify, reform, remake, revamp, update **07** improve, refresh, remodel **08** progress, redesign, renovate **09** get with it, refurbish, transform **10** make modern, regenerate, rejuvenate, streamline **13** bring up-to-date

modest
03 coy, shy **04** fair, pure **05** lowly, plain, prude, pudic, quiet, small, timid **06** chaste, decent, demure, humble, proper, pudent, seemly, simple **07** bashful, limited, prudent **08** adequate, decorous, discreet, maidenly, moderate, ordinary, passable, reserved, retiring, verecund, virtuous **09** chastened, diffident, shamefast, tolerable **10** reasonable, shamefaced, unassuming **11** inexpensive, unobtrusive **12** satisfactory, self-effacing, unpretending **13** self-conscious, unexceptional, unpretentious **15** self-deprecating

modestly
05 coyly, shyly **06** humbly, purely **07** quietly, timidly **08** chastely, decently, demurely **09** bashfully **10** adequately, discreetly, moderately, reasonably, virtuously **11** diffidently **12** unassumingly **14** satisfactorily **15** self-consciously, unpretentiously

modesty
05 aidos, shame **07** coyness, decency, decorum, pudency, reserve, shyness **08** humility, pudicity, timidity **09** plainness, propriety, quietness, reticence **10** chasteness, demureness, humbleness, seemliness, simplicity **11** bashfulness **13** shamefastness **14** self-effacement, shamefacedness **15** inexpensiveness, self-deprecation

modicum
03 bit, tad **04** atom, dash, drop, hint, inch, iota, mite **05** crumb, grain, ounce, pinch, scrap, shred, speck, tinge, touch, trace, woman **06** degree, little **08** fragment, molecule, particle **09** little bit **10** suggestion **11** small amount

modification
◇ *anagram indicator*
05 tweak **06** change **08** mutation, revision **09** recasting, reworking, tempering, variation **10** adaptation, adjustment, alteration, limitation, moderation, modulation, refinement, remoulding **11** improvement, reformation, restriction **13** qualification **14** reorganization, transformation

modify
◇ *anagram indicator*
04 dash, dull, vary **05** abate, adapt, alter, limit, touch, tweak, vowel **06** adjust, change, invert, lessen, recast, reduce, reform, revise, rework, sculpt, soften, temper, umlaut **07** convert, improve, qualify, remould, reshape **08** attemper, decrease, diminish, mitigate, moderate, overrule, redesign, retrofit, tone down, vowelize **09** diversify, transform **10** assimilate, reorganize **11** explain away **13** differentiate, trim your sails

modish
02 in **03** hip, mod, now **04** chic, cool **05** jazzy, smart, vogue **06** latest, modern, tonish, trendy, with it **07** à la mode, current, stylish, tonnish, voguish **10** all the rage, avant-garde **11** fashionable, modernistic **12** contemporary **13** up-to-the-minute

modulate
04 tune, vary **05** alter, lower **06** adjust, change, modify, soften, temper **07** balance, inflect **08** moderate, regulate **09** harmonize

modulation
04 tone **05** shade, shift **06** accent, change, tuning **07** balance, cadence **08** lowering **09** inflexion, softening, variation **10** adjustment, alteration, inflection, intonation, moderation, regulation **12** modification **13** harmonization

module
02 LM 03 bug, LEM 04 item, part, SIMM, unit 05 image, model, piece 06 factor, plug-in 07 element, section 09 component

modus operandi
02 MO 03 way 04 plan, rule 06 manner, method, praxis, system 07 process 08 practice 09 operation, procedure, technique 11 rule of thumb

mogul
03 VIP 05 baron, Mr Big 06 big gun, big pot, bigwig, Mughal, top dog, tycoon 07 big shot, magnate, notable, supremo 08 big noise, big wheel, padishah 09 big cheese, personage, potentate

moist
03 wet 04 damp, dank, dewy 05 humid, juicy, muggy, rainy, soggy, washy 06 clammy, hydric, liquid, marshy, watery 07 drizzly, tearful, wettish 08 dripping 09 drizzling, humectant, hygrophil 12 hygrophilous

moisten
03 dew, dip, wet 04 damp, lick, soak, wash 05 bathe, bedew, bewet, imbue, latch, slake, water 06 dampen, embrue, humect, humefy, humify, imbrue, madefy, sloken, sparge 07 embrewe, make wet, slocken, spairge 08 humidify, irrigate 09 humectate 10 moisturize

moisture
03 dew, wet 04 damp, rain 05 humor, spray, steam, sweat, water 06 humour, liquid, vapour 07 drizzle, soaking, wetness 08 dampness, dankness, humidity 09 mugginess 10 wateriness 11 humectation, precipitate 12 condensation, perspiration 13 precipitation

molar
04 wang 08 jaw-tooth 09 mill-tooth

Moldova
02 MD 03 MDA

mole
03 mol, spy 04 dyke, mark, pier, spot, want 05 agent, jetty, Talpa 06 blotch, groyne 07 barrier, blemish, freckle, speckle 08 causeway 09 mouldwarp, mowdiwort 10 breakwater, embankment, moudiewart, moudiewort, mowdiewart, Notoryctes 11 double agent, infiltrator, secret agent

molest
03 bug, nag, vex 04 harm, hurt, rape 05 abuse, annoy, harry, hound, tease, upset, worry 06 accost, assail, attack, badger, bother, chivvy, harass, hassle, injure, needle, pester, plague, ravish 07 agitate, assault, disturb, fluster, provoke, torment, trouble 08 ill-treat, irritate, maltreat, mistreat 09 aggravate, persecute 10 exasperate 13 interfere with 15 sexually assault

molestation
04 harm, rape 05 abuse 06 attack, injury 07 assault 11 disturbance, infestation 12 interference

molester
06 abuser, rapist 08 attacker, ravisher 09 assaulter

mollify
04 calm, ease, lull 05 abate, allay, blunt, quell, quiet, relax 06 lessen, mellow, modify, pacify, soften, soothe, temper 07 appease, assuage, compose, cushion, placate, quieten, relieve, sweeten 08 mitigate, moderate 10 conciliate, propitiate

mollusc

Molluscs include:

03 Mya
04 clam, slug, Unio
05 conch, cowry, snail, spoot, squid, whelk
06 chiton, cockle, cowrie, cuttle, dodman, limpet, loligo, mussel, nerite, oyster, winkle
07 abalone, octopus, piddock, scallop, sea slug
08 escargot, nautilus, sea snail, shipworm, wallfish
09 cone shell, hodmandod, land snail, pond snail, razorclam, razorfish, tusk shell, wing shell, wing snail
10 cuttlefish, giant squid, nudibranch, periwinkle, razor shell, Roman snail
11 horse mussel, marine snail
12 sea butterfly
13 great grey slug, keyhole limpet, ramshorn snail, slipper limpet
15 freshwater snail

See also **animal**; **crustacean**

• **mollusc's tongue**
04 rasp

mollycoddle
03 pet 04 baby, ruin 05 spoil 06 coddle, cosset, mother, pamper 07 indulge 08 pander to 09 spoon-feed 11 overprotect

molten
05 fusil 06 fusile, melted 07 flowing 08 magmatic 09 liquefied 12 circumfusile

molybdenum
02 Mo

moment
02 mo 03 sec 04 hint, note, tick 05 flash, gliff, glift, jiffy, point, punto, trice, twink, value, worth 06 import, minute, puncto, second, stound, stownd, weight 07 concern, gravity, instant 08 as soon as, directly, gliffing, interest, occasion, the point, two ticks 09 short time, substance, the minute, twinkling 10 importance, the instant 11 consequence, immediately, little while, point in time, seriousness, split second, weightiness 12 significance 13 very short time 14 less than no time

• **a moment ago**
04 enow

momentarily
07 briefly 10 fleetingly, for a moment, for a second 11 temporarily 12 for an instant 13 for a short time 15 instantaneously

momentary
05 brief, hasty, quick, short 07 passing 08 fleeting 09 ephemeral, momentany, spasmodic, temporary, transient 10 evanescent, short-lived, transitory 12 momentaneous 13 instantaneous

momentous
05 grave, major, vital 07 crucial, fateful, pivotal, serious, weighty 08 critical, decisive, eventful, historic, pregnant 09 important 11 epoch-making, significant 12 earth-shaking, of importance 13 consequential 14 of significance 15 earth-shattering, world-shattering

momentum
04 push, urge 05 drive, force, poise, power, speed 06 energy, impact, thrust 07 impetus, impulse 08 stimulus, strength, velocity 09 incentive 10 propulsion 12 driving-power

• **angular momentum**
01 L

Monaco
02 MC 03 MCO

monarch
01 K, Q, R 02 ER, GR, HM, VR 03 rex, roi 04 Cole, czar, Inca, king, ksar, tsar, tzar 05 queen, ruler 06 Caesar, prince, regina 07 czarina, emperor, empress, tsarina 08 autocrat, czarevna, czaritsa, princess, the Crown, tsarevna, tsaritsa 09 cesarevna, czarevich, potentate, sovereign, tsarevich 10 cesarevich, cesarewich, czarevitch, tesarevna, tsarevitch 11 cesarevitch, cesarewitch, crowned head, king of kings, tsesarevich, tsesarewich 12 tsesarevitch, tsesarewitch

See also **king**; **prince**; **princess**; **queen**

Anglo-Saxon and English monarchs:

04 **Cnut** ('the Great'), **Edwy**, **Grey** (Lady Jane), **John** (Lackland), **Mary** (I, Tudor), **Offa**
05 **Edgar**, **Edred**, **Henry** (I, II, III, IV, V, VI, VII, VIII), **Svein** (I Haraldsson, 'Fork-Beard')
06 **Alfred** ('the Great'), **Canute**, **Edmund** (I, II 'Ironside'), **Edward** (I, II 'the Martyr', III 'the Confessor', IV, V, VI, 'the Elder'), **Egbert**, **Harold** (I Knutsson, 'Harefoot', II)
07 **Richard** (I 'the Lion Heart', II, III), **Stephen**, **William** (I 'the Conqueror', II 'Rufus')
08 **Ethelred** (I, II 'the Unready')
09 **Athelstan**, **Elizabeth** (I), **Ethelbald**, **Ethelbert**, **Ethelwulf**

11 Hardicanute
13 Edgar Atheling, Knut Sveinsson

Scottish monarchs:

03 Aed
04 Dubh, Duff
05 Bruce (Robert), Culen, David (I, II), Edgar, Giric, James (I, II, III, IV,V,VI)
06 Baliol (Edward de), Baliol (John de), Donald (I, II, III 'Bane'), Duncan (I, II), Indulf, Lulach, Robert (I 'the Bruce', II, III)
07 Balliol (Edward de), Balliol (John de), Kenneth (I, II, III), Macbeth, Malcolm (I, II, III 'Canmore', IV 'the Maiden'), William (I)
08 Margaret ('Maid of Norway')
09 Alexander (I, II, III)
11 Constantine (I, II)
16 Mary, Queen of Scots

British monarchs:

04 Anne, Mary (II)
05 James (VI and I), James (VII and II)
06 Edward (VII, VIII), George (I, II, III, IV, V,VI)
07 Charles (I, II), William (II and III of Orange, IV)
08 Victoria
09 Elizabeth (II)
14 William and Mary

monarchy
05 realm **06** domain, empire
07 kingdom, royalty, tyranny
08 dominion, kingship, royalism
09 autocracy, despotism, monocracy
10 absolutism **11** sovereignty
12 principality **14** sovereign state

monastery
03 wat **04** cell **05** abbey, gompa
06 friary, priory, vihara **07** convent, minster, nunnery **08** cloister, lamasery
09 coenobium, lamaserai
12 Charterhouse

Monasteries and convents include:

04 Iona
05 Cluny
07 Mt Athos, Shaolin
08 Hilandar, Sénanque
09 Melk Abbey, Tengboche
10 Chartreuse, Douai Abbey, El Escorial, Ettal Abbey, San Lorenzo, Santa Croce, Worth Abbey
11 Ealing Abbey, Glendalough, Lindisfarne, Parkminster, Simonopetra, Val-Duchesse, Whitby Abbey
12 Belmont Abbey, Colwich Abbey, Monte Cassino, Mont St Michel, St John's Abbey
13 Buckfast Abbey, Donglin Temple, Downside Abbey, Monasterboice, Rievaulx Abbey, Tyburn Convent
14 Fountains Abbey, Stanbrook Abbey
15 Ampleforth Abbey, Curzon Park Abbey, Portsmouth Abbey, St Cecilia's Abbey

See also **abbey**; **religious**

monastic
07 ascetic, austere, monkish, recluse
08 celibate, eremitic, secluded, solitary **09** canonical, reclusive, withdrawn **10** anchoritic, cloistered, coenobitic, meditative **11** sequestered
13 contemplative
See also **religious**

monasticism
07 monkery **08** monkhood
09 austerity, eremitism, monachism, reclusion, seclusion **10** asceticism
11 coenobitism, recluseness

Monday
03 Mon

monetary
04 cash **05** money **06** fiscal **07** capital
08 economic **09** budgetary, financial, pecuniary

money
01 L, M, P **03** fat, LSD, oof, tin, utu
04 cash, cent, coin, dibs, dosh, dust, gelt, gilt, hoot, jack, kail, kale, loot, pelf
05 blunt, brass, bread, bucks, chink, dough, dumps, funds, gravy, lolly, means, Oscar, purse, ready, rhino, smash, sugar, wonga **06** argent, assets, greens, moolah, riches, stumpy, wealth
07 capital, dingbat, ooftish, readies, savings, scratch, shekels **08** currency, finances, greenies **09** affluence, banknotes, megabucks, resources
10 big bikkies, prosperity **11** legal tender, spondulicks **12** the necessary
See also **coin**; **currency**

• **get money from**
03 tap

• **hand over money**
03 pay

• **in the money**
04 rich **05** flush **06** loaded **07** wealthy, well-off **08** affluent, well-to-do
10 prosperous, well-heeled **11** rolling in it **12** stinking rich

• **large amount of money**
03 wad **04** mint, pile, pots, scad

• **money collection**
03 cap **04** whip **09** whip-round

• **provide with money**
03 pay **04** fund

• **quantity of money**
03 sum

money-box
04 safe **05** chest **06** coffer **07** cash box, poor box **08** penny-pig **09** piggy-bank

money-changing
04 agio

moneyed
04 rich **05** flush **06** loaded **07** opulent, wealthy, well-off **08** affluent, well-to-do **10** prosperous, well-heeled
11 comfortable, rolling in it

money-grubbing
07 miserly **08** grasping
09 mammonish, mercenary
10 quaestuary **11** acquisitive, mammonistic

moneymaking
06 paying **09** lucrative **10** commercial, profitable, quaestuary, successful
12 profit-making, remunerative

Mongolia
03 MGL, MNG

mongoose
04 urva

mongrel
◇ *anagram indicator*
03 cur **04** kuri, mong, mutt **05** cross, mixed, pooch **06** bitser, hybrid
07 bastard **08** half-bred **09** crossbred, half-breed, yellow dog **10** crossbreed, ill-defined, mixed breed **12** of mixed breed

monicker
04 name **05** alias **07** pen name
08 nickname **09** false name, pseudonym, sobriquet, stage name
10 soubriquet **11** assumed name

monitor
03 VDU **04** CCTV, note, plot, scan
05 check, trace, track, varan, watch
06 detect, follow, goanna, iguana, leguan, marker, record, screen, survey, worral, worrel **07** adviser, advisor, display, head boy, leguaan, observe, oversee, perenty, prefect, scanner, Varanus **08** detector, head girl, observer, overseer, perentie, recorder, watchdog **09** supervise **10** supervisor
11 invigilator, keep an eye on, keep track of **12** dragon lizard, Komodo dragon, Komodo lizard **14** security camera

monk
03 Dan, Dom **04** lama **05** abbot, friar, prior **06** beguin, frater, hermit
07 brother **08** cenobite, monastic, talapoin **09** anchorite, bullfinch, coenobite, Dalai Lama, gyrovague, mendicant, religieux, religious
10 cloisterer, conventual, religioner
11 abbey-lubber, religionary
13 contemplative, possessionate

Monks and nuns include:

02 Fa (Hsien), Fa (Xian)
03 Orm
04 Gall (St), Hume (Basil), Rule (St), Sava (St)
05 Aidan (St), Barat (St Madeleine Sophie), Borde (Andrew), Jacob (Max), Ormin, Rancé (Armand Jean de), Sabas (St)
06 Arnulf, Boorde (Andrew), Colman (St), Eadmer, Ernulf, Gildas (St), Gyatso (Geshe Kelsang), Gyatso (Tenzin), Merton (Thomas), Teresa (Mother), Tetzel (Johann), Turgot
07 Adamnan (St), Adomnan (St), Arnauld (Angélique), Arnauld (Marie-Angélique), Beckett (Sister Wendy), Cabrini (St Francesca Xavier), Carpini (John of Plano), Cassian (St John), Gratian, Lydgate (John), Mortara (Edgar), Regulus (St), Schwarz (Berthold)
08 Alacoque (St Marguerite Marie),

Bonivard (François de), Duchesne (St Rose Philippine), Foucauld (Charles de), Houedard (Dom Sylvester), Pelagius, Rabelais (François), Rasputin (Grigori)
09 Bonnivard (François de), MacKillop (Mary), Skobtsova (Maria)
10 Bernadette (St), Fra Diavolo, Montfaucon (Bernard de), Torquemada (Tomás de), Walsingham (Thomas), Willibrord (St)
11 Bodhidharma, Ponce de León (Luis), Scholastica (St)
12 Guido d'Arezzo
13 The Singing Nun
14 Francis of Paola (St), Marianus Scotus, Peter the Hermit
15 Bernard of Morval

See also **religious**

monkey
03 imp, tup **04** brat, fool, mess, muck, play, tyke **05** anger, clown, mimic, rogue, scamp, sheep **06** fiddle, fidget, footle, lackey, meddle, potter, rascal, simian, tamper, tinker, trifle, urchin **07** primate **09** interfere, scallywag **10** jackanapes **13** mischief-maker

Monkeys include:

03 ape, pug, sai
04 douc, leaf, mico, mona, saki, titi, zati
05 Diana, drill, green, magot, night, sajou, Satan, toque
06 baboon, bandar, bonnet, coaita, grivet, guenon, howler, langur, malmag, rhesus, sagoin, saguin, spider, tee-tee, uakari, vervet, woolly
07 cacajou, colobus, guereza, hanuman, jacchus, macaque, sagouin, saimiri, sapajou, tamarin, tarsier, wistiti
08 capuchin, durukuli, entellus, mandrill, mangabey, marmoset, squirrel, talapoin, wanderoo
09 proboscis
10 Barbary ape, moustached
11 douroucouli, platyrrhine, white-eyelid
13 platyrrhinian

See also **animal**; **ape**

• **monkey business**
06 pranks **07** carry-on, foolery **08** clowning, mischief, trickery **09** chicanery **10** dishonesty, hanky-panky, tomfoolery **11** legerdemain, shenanigans, skulduggery **12** monkey tricks **13** funny business, jiggery-pokery, sleight-of-hand

• **monkey puzzle**
09 araucaria, Chile pine **11** Chilean pine

monochrome
05 sepia **08** monotone, unicolor **09** unicolour **10** monochroic, monotonous **11** unicolorate, unicolorous, unicoloured **13** black-and-white, monochromatic

monocle
04 quiz **05** glass **08** eyeglass **13** quizzing-glass

monogamous
09 monogamic **10** monandrous, monogynous

monogamy
08 monandry, monogyny

monolingual
08 monoglot **10** unilingual

monolith
05 shaft **06** menhir, sarsen **08** megalith **13** standing stone

monolithic
04 huge, vast **05** giant, rigid, solid **07** massive **08** colossal, faceless, gigantic, immobile, unmoving, unvaried **09** hidebound, immovable **10** fossilized, inflexible, monumental, unchanging **11** intractable

monologue
03 rap **05** spiel **06** homily, sermon, speech **07** address, lecture, oration **09** soliloquy

monomania
05 mania, thing **06** fetish **08** fixation, idée fixe, neurosis **09** fixed idea, obsession **10** fanaticism, hobby-horse **13** ruling passion **15** bee in your bonnet

monopolize
03 hog **05** tie up **06** corner, occupy, take up **07** control, engross **08** dominate, take over **09** preoccupy **11** appropriate **14** have sole rights, have to yourself, keep to yourself

monopoly
05 régie **06** corner **07** appalto, control **09** franchise, monopsony, privilege, sole right **10** ascendancy, domination, sole rights **14** exclusive right **15** exclusive rights

monotonous
04 drab, dull, flat **05** ho-hum, samey **06** boring, deadly **07** humdrum, routine, tedious, uniform **08** plodding, tiresome, toneless, unvaried **09** unvarying, wearisome **10** all the same, colourless, mechanical, monochrome, repetitive, unchanging, uneventful, unexciting **11** repetitious **12** run-of-the-mill **13** uninteresting **14** soul-destroying

monotony
06 tedium **07** boredom, humdrum, routine, taedium **08** ding-dong, dullness, flatness, sameness **10** repetition, uniformity **11** routineness **12** tiresomeness **13** wearisomeness **14** repetitiveness, uneventfulness

monster
04 huge, mega, vast **05** alien, beast, brute, devil, fiend, freak, giant, jumbo **06** mutant, savage **07** immense, mammoth, massive, villain **08** colossal, colossus, enormous, gigantic, teratism, whopping **09** barbarian, ginormous, monstrous **10** tremendous **11** miscreation, monstrosity **12** malformation **13** freak of nature **14** Brobdingnagian

Monster types include:

03 orc, roc
04 cete, gila, ogre
05 alien, gulon, harpy, lamia, phoca, troll, yowie, zombi
06 ajatar, bunyip, dragon, gorgon, kraken, nicker, ogress, sphinx, wivern, wyvern, zombie
07 cyclops, griffin, griffon, gryphon, prodigy, satyral, taniwha, triffid, wendigo, windigo, ziffius
08 basilisk, behemoth, bogeyman, dinosaur, lindworm, mooncalf, mushussu, seahorse
09 leviathan, manticore, marakihau, rosmarine, sea satyre, wasserman, whirlpool
10 chupacabra, cockatrice, crio-sphinx, salamander, sea monster
11 amphisbaena, hippocampus

Monsters include:

02 ET
05 Hydra, Smaug, snark
06 Balrog, Duessa, Empusa, Fafnir, Geryon, Medusa, Nazgul, Nessie, Python, Scylla, Shelob, Sphinx, Stheno, Typhon
07 Bathies, Caliban, Cecrops, Chimera, Cyclops, Dracula, Echidna, Euryale, Grendel
08 Cerberus, Chimaera, Godzilla, King Kong, Minotaur, Typhoeus
09 Charybdis
10 Black Annis, jabberwock, Jormangund, jubjub bird, Polyphemus
12 bandersnatch, Blatant Beast, Count Dracula, Frankenstein
13 Cookie Monster, Hecatonchires, Questing Beast
14 Incredible Hulk, Midgard serpent
15 Glatysaunt Beast, Loch Ness monster

See also **mythical**; **mythology**

monstrosity
04 evil **05** freak, teras **06** horror, mutant **07** eyesore, monster **08** atrocity, enormity, ugliness **09** carbuncle, obscenity **11** abnormality, heinousness, hellishness, hideousness, miscreation **12** dreadfulness **13** frightfulness, loathsomeness

monstrous
04 evil, foul, huge, vast, vile **05** cruel, nasty **06** grisly, savage, wicked **07** heinous, hideous, immense, inhuman, mammoth, massive, vicious **08** abnormal, colossal, criminal, deformed, dreadful, enormous, freakish, gigantic, gruesome, horrible, misbegot, shocking, teratoid, terrible **09** abhorrent, atrocious, frightful,

grotesque, malformed, misshapen, unnatural **10** abominable, horrifying, miraculous, outrageous, prodigious, scandalous, tremendous
11 disgraceful, misbegotten
12 preposterous

monstrously
06 hugely, vastly **08** terribly
09 immensely, massively **10** colossally, dreadfully, enormously, shockingly
11 atrociously, frightfully
12 gigantically, outrageously, scandalously, tremendously

Montana
02 MT **04** Mont

month
01 m **02** mo

Months:

02 Jy
03 Apr, Aug, Dec, Feb, Jan, Jul, Jun, Mar, May, Nov, Oct, Sep
04 July, June, Sept
05 April, March
06 August
07 January, October
08 December, February, November
09 September

French month names:

02 Av
03 mai
04 août, juin, mars
05 avril
07 février, janvier, juillet, octobre
08 décembre, novembre
09 septembre

French Revolutionary calendar month names:

06 Nivôse
07 Floréal, Ventôse
08 Brumaire, Frimaire, Germinal, Messidor, Pluviôse, Prairial
09 Fructidor, Thermidor
11 Vendémiaire

German month names:

03 Mai
04 Juli, Juni, März
05 April
06 August, Januar
07 Februar, Oktober
08 Dezember, November
09 September

Hindu calendar month names:

05 Magha, Pausa
06 Asadha, Asvina
07 Chaitra, Sravana
08 Jyaistha, Karttika, Phalguna, Vaisakha
10 Bhadrapada, Margasirsa
13 Dvitiya Asadha
14 Dvitiya Sravana

Islamic calendar month names:

05 Rabi I, Rajab, Safar
06 Rabi II, Shaban
07 Jumada I, Ramadan, Shawwal
08 Jumada II, Muharram
10 Dhu al-Qadah
11 Dhu al-Hijjah

Italian month names:

05 marzo
06 agosto, aprile, giugno, luglio, maggio
07 gennaio, ottobre
08 dicembre, febbraio, novembre
09 settembre

Jewish calendar month names:

02 Ab, Av
04 Abib, Adar, Elul, Iyar
05 Iyyar, Nisan, Sivan, Tebet, Tevet, Tisri
06 Hesvan, Kisleu, Kislev, Shebat, Shevat, Tammuz, Tebeth, Tishri, Veadar
07 Chislev, Heshvan
09 Adar Sheni

Latin month names:

05 Maius
06 Julius, Junius
07 Aprilis, Martius, October
08 Augustus, December, November, Sextilis
09 Januarius, Quintilis, September
10 Februarius

Spanish month names:

04 mayo
05 abril, enero, julio, junio, marzo
06 agosto
07 febrero, octubre
09 diciembre, noviembre
10 septiembre

• **in the last month**
03 ult **04** ulto **06** ultimo
• **the present month**
04 inst **07** instant

Montserrat
03 MSR

monument
04 tomb **05** cairn, cross, folly, relic, token, trace **06** barrow, column, heroon, marker, pillar, record, shrine, statue **07** hogback, martyry, memento, obelisk, prodigy, pyramid, talayot, trilith, witness **08** cenotaph, evidence, memorial, reminder, sacellum
09 headstone, mausoleum, testament, tombstone, trilithon **10** gravestone, immortelle, indication
11 remembrance, war memorial
13 commemoration

Monuments and memorials include:

04 Eros, Homo
05 Grant, Scott
06 Albert, Sphinx
07 Lincoln, Martyr's
08 Boadicea, Cenotaph, Daibutsu, Lion Gate, Taj Mahal, Victoria
09 Charminar, Menin Gate, Qutb Minar, Tsar's Bell
10 Berlin Wall, Broken Ring, Ishtar Gate, Kutab Minar, London Wall, Marble Arch, Mt Rushmore, Navigators', Stonehenge, Washington
11 Civil Rights, Eiffel Tower, Grande Arche, Great Sphinx, Machu Picchu, Madara Rider, Silbury Hill, Voortrekker
12 Antonine Wall, Eleanor Cross, Glass Pyramid, Great Pyramid, Hadrian's Wall, Spanish Steps, Statue of Zeus, Tower of Babel
13 Admiralty Arch, Arc de Triomphe, Great Zimbabwe, Mount Rushmore, Nelson's Column, People's Heroes, Trajan's Column, Trevi Fountain
14 Albert Memorial, Eleanor Crosses, Gateway of India, Glastonbury Tor, Hands of Victory, Hiroshima Peace, Lenin Mausoleum, Spasskaya Tower, Stone of Destiny, Tomb of Mausolus, Wayland's Smithy, Wright Brothers
15 Brandenburg Gate, Lincoln Memorial, Nubian monuments, Rollright Stones, Statue of Liberty, Thatta monuments

monumental
04 huge, vast **05** great **07** abiding, amazing, awesome, classic, immense, lasting, massive, notable **08** colossal, enduring, enormous, historic, immortal, imposing, majestic, memorial, striking
09 important, memorable, permanent
10 impressive, remarkable, tremendous
11 celebratory, epoch-making, exceptional, magnificent, outstanding, significant **12** awe-inspiring, overwhelming **13** commemorative, extraordinary, unforgettable

monumentally
06 hugely, vastly **09** immensely, massively **10** colossally, enormously
12 gigantically, tremendously

mood
03 fit, tid **04** feel, mode, sulk, tone, vein, whim **05** anger, blues, dumps, pique, tenor **06** humour, plight, spirit, temper **07** bad mood, climate, feeling, spirits **08** ambience, doldrums, optative, the sulks **09** bad temper, potential **10** atmosphere, depression, imperative, indicative, infinitive, low spirits, melancholy **11** conjunctive, disposition, frame of mind, state of mind, subjunctive
• **in the mood for**
06 keen on, keen to **07** eager to
08 ready for **09** willing to **10** disposed to, inclined to **11** feeling like, wanting to do **13** wanting to have

moody
04 glum, mopy **05** angry, faked, mopey, sulky, testy **06** broody, crabby, crusty, fickle, gloomy, morose, sullen, touchy **07** doleful, flighty, in a huff, in a mood **08** downcast, petulant, unstable, volatile **09** crotchety, impulsive, irascible, irritable, miserable, pretended **10** capricious, changeable, in a bad mood, melancholy **11** bad-tempered
12 cantankerous **13** short-tempered, temperamental, unpredictable

moon
04 idle, loaf, mope, pine 05 brood, dream, month, mooch 06 Lucina, Phoebe 08 daydream, languish 09 fantasize, satellite 13 Paddy's lantern 15 MacFarlane's buat

Lunar seas:

08 Bay of Dew
09 Moscow Sea, Sea of Cold, Smyth's Sea
10 Bay of Heats, Central Bay, Eastern Sea, Foaming Sea, Mare Nubium, Sea of Waves, Sinus Medii, Sinus Roris
11 Lacus Mortis, Lake of Death, Mare Crisium, Mare Humorum, Mare Imbrium, Mare Ingenii, Mare Smythii, Mare Spumans, Mare Undarum, Mare Vaporum, Marginal Sea, Palus Somnii, Sea of Clouds, Sea of Crises, Sea of Nectar, Sinus Iridum, Southern Sea
12 Humboldt's Sea, Lake of Dreams, Mare Australe, Mare Frigoris, Mare Marginis, Mare Nectaris, Marsh of Decay, Marsh of Mists, Marsh of Sleep, Sea of Showers, Sea of Vapours, Sinus Aestuum
13 Bay of Rainbows, Mare Orientale, Ocean of Storms, Sea of Geniuses, Sea of Moisture, Sea of Serenity
14 Lacus Somniorum, Palus Nebularum, Sea of Fertility
15 Mare Moscoviense, Mare Serenitatis, Palus Putredinis
16 Mare Fecunditatis, Marsh of Epidemics, Palus Epidemiarum
17 Mare Humboldtianum, Sea of Tranquillity
18 Oceanus Procellarum
19 Mare Tranquillitatis

Moons include:

02 Io
04 Moon, Rhea
05 Ariel, Dione, Mimas, Titan
06 Charon, Deimos, Europa, Nereid, Oberon, Phobos, Tethys, Triton
07 Iapetus, Miranda, Proteus, Titania, Umbriel
08 Callisto, Cruithne, Ganymede, Hyperion
09 Enceladus

Moon-related terms include:

05 lunar, phase
06 waning, waxing
07 far side, gibbous, new moon
08 blue moon, crescent, dark side, full moon, half-moon, lunation, near side
09 blood moon, moonlight, moonscape, moonshine
11 harvest moon, hunter's moon, last quarter, quarter moon
12 first quarter, man in the moon, synodic month, third quarter

• once in a blue moon
06 seldom 08 not often 10 hardly ever, very rarely 11 almost never

• over the moon
06 elated, joyful 07 fervent 08 blissful, ecstatic, euphoric, frenzied, jubilant 09 delighted, delirious, overjoyed, rapturous, rhapsodic 10 enraptured 11 high as a kite, on cloud nine, tickled pink 13 jumping for joy 15 in seventh heaven, on top of the world

moonlike
05 lunar, moony 06 lunate 07 lunular, selenic 08 crescent 09 meniscoid 10 crescentic, moon-shaped

moonshine
03 rot 04 bosh, bunk, crap, guff, tosh 05 hooch, month, stuff, tripe 06 bunkum, hootch, hot air, liquor, piffle, poteen 07 baloney, blather, blether, bootleg, eyewash, fantasy, hogwash, hokonui, potheen, rubbish, spirits, twaddle 08 blathers, blethers, bodiless, claptrap, nonsense, tommyrot 09 bull's wool

moor
03 fix 04 bind, dock, fell, lash, muir 05 berth, heath, hitch, tie up 06 anchor, fasten, secure, upland 07 Moresco, Morisco, mudéjar, Saracen 08 make fast, moorland 09 fix firmly 10 drop anchor

• tightly moored
04 girt

moot
04 open, pose, stir 05 argue, plead, raise, vexed 06 broach, debate, knotty, submit 07 advance, bring up, crucial, discuss, dispute, meeting, propose, suggest 08 academic, arguable, disputed, doubtful, propound 09 debatable, difficult, insoluble, introduce, undecided, unsettled 10 discussion, disputable, put forward, unresolved 11 contestable, problematic 12 open to debate, questionable, undetermined, unresolvable 13 controversial

mop
03 mat 04 mane, mass, soak, swab, wash, wipe 05 clean, dwile, shock, wiper 06 absorb, malkin, mawkin, sponge, tangle, thatch 07 grimace, swabber 08 squeegee 10 head of hair

• mop up
04 swab, wash 06 absorb, secure, soak up, sponge, tidy up, wipe up 07 clean up, round up 08 deal with 09 dispose of, eliminate, finish off 10 account for, neutralize, take care of

mope
04 fret, mump, peak, pine, sulk 05 boody, brood, droop, grump, moper 06 grieve, grouch, misery, moaner 07 despair, killjoy 08 languish 09 introvert, pessimist 10 depressive 11 be miserable, melancholic 12 melancholiac

• mope about
04 idle, loll, moon 05 mooch 06 lounge, wander 08 languish

moral
03 tag 04 good, just, pure 05 adage, maxim, noble, point, right 06 chaste, decent, dictum, honest, lesson, proper, saying, symbol 07 epigram, ethical, meaning, message, precept, proverb, upright 08 aphorism, straight, teaching, virtuous 09 blameless, certainty, emotional, righteous 10 high-minded, honourable, principled, upstanding 11 application, clean-living, encouraging 12 significance 13 incorruptible, psychological

morale
04 mood 05 heart 06 spirit 07 spirits 08 optimism 10 confidence, self-esteem 11 hopefulness, state of mind 13 esprit de corps 14 self-confidence

moralistic
04 smug 05 pious 08 priggish, superior 09 pietistic 10 complacent, goody-goody 11 pharisaical 12 hypocritical 13 sanctimonious, self-righteous 14 holier-than-thou

morality
04 good 06 ethics, ideals, morale, morals, purity, virtue 07 conduct, decency, honesty, justice, manners 08 chastity, goodness, moralism 09 integrity, principle, propriety, rectitude, standards 10 principles 11 moral values, uprightness 12 Sittlichkeit 13 righteousness

moralize
05 edify 06 preach 07 lecture 08 ethicize 09 discourse, preachify, sermonize 11 pontificate

morally
05 nobly 06 justly 08 properly, socially 09 ethically 10 honourably 11 practically 13 behaviourally

morals
06 ethics, habits, ideals 07 conduct, manners 08 morality, scruples 09 behaviour, integrity, moral code, standards 10 principles 11 moral values 12 Sittlichkeit 13 right and wrong

• lax in morals
04 wide

morass
03 bog, fen, jam 04 flow, mess, mire, moss, quag 05 chaos, marsh, mix-up, swamp 06 jumble, muddle, slough, tangle 07 clutter 08 quagmire 09 confusion, marshland, quicksand 10 can of worms

moratorium
03 ban 04 halt, stay 05 delay 06 freeze 07 embargo, respite 08 stoppage 10 standstill, suspension 12 postponement

morbid
04 down, grim, sick 06 ailing, gloomy, grisly, horrid, morose, sickly, sombre 07 ghastly, hideous, macabre, peccant, vicious 08 dejected, diseased, dreadful, ghoulish, gruesome, horrible 09 unhealthy 10 lugubrious, melancholy 11 pessimistic,

unwholesome **12** insalubrious **14** down in the dumps

morbidly

06 grimly **08** horribly, horridly **09** hideously **10** dreadfully, ghoulishly, gruesomely

mordant

04 acid, base **05** edged, harsh, sharp **06** biting, bitter **07** acerbic, caustic, cutting, mixtion, pungent, vicious, waspish **08** critical, incisive, scathing, stinging, venomous, wounding **09** sarcastic, trenchant **10** astringent, iron-liquor **11** acrimonious

more

02 mo **03** mae, moe, new, più **04** root **05** added, again, extra, fresh, other, plant, spare, stump **06** better, longer, rather **07** another, further **08** moreover, repeated **09** increased **10** additional **11** alternative **13** greater number, supplementary **15** greater quantity

• **more or less**

04 some **06** mainly, mostly **07** broadly **09** generally, in general, just about **10** by and large, on the whole, pretty much, pretty well **11** in most cases **13** predominantly **14** for the most part

• **more than**

04 plus

• **yet more**

03 nay

moreover

03 eft **04** also **06** as well, at that, either **07** besides, further **08** likewise **10** in addition, what is more **11** furthermore **12** additionally

mores

04 ways **06** custom, habits, usages **07** customs, manners **09** etiquette, practices **10** procedures, traditions, ways of life **11** conventions **14** ways of behaving

morgue

08 mortuary **09** arrogance, deadhouse **11** haughtiness **12** charnel house **14** funeral parlour

moribund

04 weak **05** dying **06** doomed, ebbing, fading, feeble, senile, waning **07** failing **08** comatose, expiring, lifeless, stagnant **09** crumbling, declining, dwindling **10** collapsing, in extremis, stagnating **11** obsolescent, on the way out, wasting away **14** on your last legs

morning

02 am **04** dawn, morn **05** matin **07** sunrise **08** cock-crow, daybreak, daylight, forenoon **10** before noon, break of day, first light **11** crack of dawn

• **morning star**

05 Venus **07** daystar, Lucifer **08** Phosphor **09** precursor **10** Phosphorus **11** morgenstern

Morocco

02 MA **03** MAR, Mor

moron

03 ass, git, mug, nit **04** berk, butt, clot, dolt, dope, dork, dupe, fool, geek, goof, jerk, kook, nerd, nerk, prat, twit **05** chump, clown, comic, dumbo, dunce, dweeb, idiot, neddy, ninny, prick, twerp, wally **06** cretin, dimwit, jester, muppet, nitwit, stooge, sucker **07** buffoon, Charlie, fat-head, halfwit, pillock, plonker, tosspot **08** dipstick, imbecile **09** birdbrain, blockhead, cloth head, ignoramus, simpleton **10** nincompoop, silly-billy **13** laughing-stock, proper Charlie

moronic

03 mad **04** daft, dumb **05** barmy, batty, crazy, dotty, inane, inept, nutty, potty, silly, wacky **06** absurd, insane, simple, stupid, unwise **07** foolish, idiotic **08** gormless, ignorant **09** half-baked, ludicrous, pointless, senseless **10** half-witted, ill-advised, ridiculous **11** hare-brained, nonsensical **12** crack-brained, shortsighted, simple-minded, unreasonable **13** ill-considered, out of your mind, unintelligent **14** with a tile loose **15** with a screw loose

morose

04 acid, glum, grim, grum, sour **05** gruff, moody, sulky, surly **06** crabby, gloomy, severe, sombre, sullen **07** grouchy **08** mournful, taciturn **09** depressed, saturnine **10** lugubrious **11** bad-tempered, ill-tempered, melancholic, pessimistic

morosely

06 sourly **07** gruffly, moodily **08** gloomily, sullenly **10** mournfully **12** lugubriously

morse

06 walrus **09** Endeavour, iddy-umpty

morsel

03 bit **04** atom, bite, part **05** crumb, grain, piece, scrap, slice, taste **06** dainty, nibble, sippet, titbit **07** modicum, morceau, segment, soupçon **08** fraction, fragment, mouthful, particle **11** bonne bouche

mortal

◇ *anagram indicator*

03 man **04** body, dire, Yama **05** awful, being, cruel, dying, fatal, grave, great, human, woman **06** bitter, bodily, deadly, lethal, person, severe **07** earthly, extreme, fleshly, intense, killing, worldly **08** creature, deathful, temporal, terrible, vengeful **09** corporeal, earthling, ephemeral, extremely, murderous, transient, worldling **10** human being, implacable, individual, perishable, relentless, thoroughly, unbearable **11** unrelenting **12** irremissible, unforgivable, unpardonable

• **first mortal**

04 Adam, Yama

mortality

05 death **07** carnage, killing **08** casualty, fatality, humanity **09** death rate, slaughter **10** loss of life, transience **11** earthliness, worldliness **12** ephemerality, impermanence **13** perishability

mortally

07 awfully, fatally, finally, gravely, greatly **08** lethally, severely, terribly **09** extremely, intensely **12** disastrously

mortgage

03 dip **04** bond, lien, loan **06** pledge, wadset **07** wadsett **08** home loan, security **09** debenture **11** hypothecate, impignorate

mortification

05 shame **06** denial **07** chagrin, control **08** disgrace, ignominy, vexation **09** abasement, annoyance, dishonour, sphacelus **10** asceticism, chastening, conquering, discipline, loss of face, punishment, self-denial **11** confounding, humiliation, self-control, subjugation **12** discomfiture **13** embarrassment

mortified

04 sick **06** shamed **07** ashamed, crushed, humbled **08** defeated **09** disgraced, horrified **10** confounded, gangrenous, humiliated **11** dishonoured, embarrassed

mortify

03 die **04** deny, kill **05** abash, annoy, crush, shame **06** humble, offend, subdue, wither **07** affront, chagrin, chasten, conquer, control, crucify, deflate, horrify **08** bring low, chastise, confound, disgrace, gangrene, macerate, restrain, suppress **09** discomfit, dishonour, embarrass, humiliate **10** disappoint, discipline, put to shame

mortifying

07 shaming **08** crushing, humbling, salutary **09** punishing, thwarting **10** chastening **11** humiliating, ignominious **12** discomfiting, embarrassing, overwhelming

mortuary

06 morgue **09** deadhouse **12** charnel house **14** funeral parlour

mosaic

06 musive, screen **08** terrazzo **10** pietra dura, pietre dure **11** opus musivum

moss

03 hag **04** hagg **05** Musci

Mosses include:

03 bog, bur, cup, fog
04 burr, club, long, peat, tree
05 fairy, usnea
06 hypnum
07 acrogen, foggage, lycopod
08 sphagnum, staghorn
09 wolf's claw, wolf's foot
10 fontinalis, ground pine

• **stalk of moss capsule**

04 seta

most
◇ *tail deletion indicator*
04 bulk, mass **08** majority **09** almost all, nearly all **10** lion's share **11** largest part **12** greatest part
13 preponderance

mostly
◇ *deletion indicator*
06 feckly, mainly **07** as a rule, chiefly, largely, overall, usually **08** above all
09 generally, in general, in the main
10 especially, on the whole
11 principally **13** predominantly **14** for the most part

moth

Moths include:

01 Y
02 Io
03 pug, wax
04 goat, hawk, luna, puss
05 ghost, gypsy, tiger
06 bogong, bugong, burnet, carpet, kitten, lackey, lappet, magpie, sphinx, turnip, winter
07 buff-tip, clothes, emerald, emperor, hook-tip, silver-Y, six-spot, tussock
08 cinnabar, peppered, silkworm
10 death's-head
11 garden tiger, pale tussock, swallowtail
12 Kentish glory, peach blossom, red underwing
13 processionary

See also **animal**; **butterfly**; **insect**

moth-eaten
03 old **04** worn **05** dated, mangy, musty, seedy, stale **06** mouldy, ragged, shabby **07** ancient, archaic, decayed, outworn, worn-out
08 decrepit, moribund, obsolete, outdated, tattered **10** antiquated, threadbare **11** dilapidated **12** old-fashioned

mother
02 ma **03** dam, mam, mom, mum
04 baby, base, bear, mama, rear, scum, tend **05** cause, dregs, fount, mamma, mammy, mater, mommy, mummy, mumsy, nanny, nurse, raise, roots, spoil
06 foster, matron, minnie, origin, pamper, parent, source, spring, venter
07 care for, cherish, indulge, nurture, old lady, produce **08** ancestor, fuss over, hysteria, old woman **09** look after, matriarch **10** bring forth, derivation, foundation, procreator, take care of, wellspring **11** birth mother, give birth to, overprotect **12** progenitress
13 materfamilias

See also **dregs**

motherly
04 fond, kind, warm **06** caring, gentle, loving, tender **08** maternal, matronal
09 nurturing **10** comforting, motherlike, protective **12** affectionate

motif
04 form, idea, logo **05** shape, theme, topic **06** design, device, emblem, figure **07** concept, pattern
08 ornament **10** decoration

motion
03 act, bid, nod **04** flow, plan, sign, wave **05** going, offer, usher **06** action, beckon, change, direct, moving, puppet, scheme, signal, travel
07 feeling, gesture, passage, passing, project, transit **08** activity, mobility, motility, movement, progress, proposal
09 agitation, manifesto, prompting
10 indication, locomotion, suggestion, travelling **11** gesticulate, inclination, instigation, proposition
12 presentation **13** changing place, gesticulation **14** changing places, recommendation

• **in motion**
◇ *anagram indicator*
03 off **05** about, astir, going **06** agoing, moving **07** on the go, running **08** under way **09** on the move, on the wing **10** in progress, travelling **11** functioning, operational, upon the wing

• **set in motion**
04 move, open, stir **05** begin, found, start, steer, stire, styre **06** set off, winnow **07** actuate, kick off, promote, start up **08** activate, commence, embark on, get going, initiate, set about
09 instigate, institute, introduce
10 launch into **11** get cracking **13** begin to happen, take the plunge

motionless
03 set **05** fixed, inert, rigid, still **06** at rest, frozen, halted, static **07** resting
08 becalmed, immobile, lifeless, moveless, sleeping, stagnant, standing, unmoving **09** immovable, inanimate, paralysed, unmovable
10 stationary, stock-still, transfixed
13 at a standstill

motivate
04 draw, goad, lead, move, push, spur, stir, urge **05** bring, cause, drive, impel
06 arouse, excite, incite, induce, kindle, prompt, propel **07** actuate, inspire, provoke, trigger **08** activate, initiate, persuade **09** encourage, kick-start, stimulate

motivation
04 push, spur, urge, wish **05** drive
06 desire, hunger, motive, reason
07 impulse **08** ambition, interest, momentum, stimulus **09** incentive, prompting **10** incitement, inducement, persuasion **11** inspiration, instigation, provocation

motive
03 aim **04** goad, lure, spur, urge
05 basis, cause, motif **06** design, desire, ground, moment, object, reason **07** grounds, impulse, pretext, purpose **08** instance, occasion, sanction, stimulus, thinking
09 incentive, influence, intention, rationale **10** attraction, incitement, inducement, mainspring, motivation, persuasion, propellent **11** inspiration
13 consideration, encouragement

motley
04 pied **05** mixed, tabby **06** jester, varied **07** dappled, diverse, mottled, piebald, pyebald, spotted, striped
08 assorted, brindled, many-hued, streaked **09** colourful, patchwork
10 variegated **11** diversified
12 multifarious **13** heterogeneous, miscellaneous, multicoloured, particoloured

motor club *see* **motoring organization**

motorcyclists *see* **racing**

motoring *see* **car**

motoring organization
02 AA **03** AAA, BSM, FIA, RAC

motor racing *see* **racing**

motor vehicle *see* **car**; **vehicle**

motorway
01 M **02** AB, M1 **07** freeway, thruway
08 Autobahn, turnpike **09** autopista, autoroute **10** autostrada, expressway, throughway **12** superhighway

mottled
04 marl **05** chiné, jaspe, pinto, tabby
06 dapple **07** blotchy, brinded, brindle, dappled, flecked, marbled, piebald, spotted **08** blotched, brindled, freckled, speckled, splotchy, stippled, streaked **10** poikilitic, variegated

motto
03 cry, mot, saw **04** posy, rule
05 adage, axiom, gnome, maxim, poesy **06** byword, device, dictum, legend, saying, slogan, truism
07 epigram, formula, ich dien, ichthys, impresa, imprese, precept, proverb
08 aphorism, epigraph **09** catchword, watchword **10** golden rule **13** e pluribus unum **15** per ardua ad astra

mould
◇ *anagram indicator*
03 cut, die, mix, rot **04** cast, form, fust, kind, line, make, must, sort, type, work
05 brand, build, carve, earth, forge, frame, knead, model, plasm, print, shape, stamp, style **06** affect, blight, create, design, direct, figure, format, fungus, matrix, mildew, nature, sculpt
07 calibre, casting, chessel, control, dariole, fashion, outline, pattern, quality, ramakin, ramekin
08 meringue, ramequin, template
09 character, construct, formation, framework, influence, mustiness, sculpture, structure **10** mouldiness
11 arrangement, blister pack
12 construction **13** configuration

moulder
03 rot **05** decay, waste **06** humify, perish **07** corrupt, crumble
09 decompose **10** turn to dust
12 disintegrate

moulding
◇ *anagram indicator*
04 ogee, tore **05** torus

mouldy
◇ *anagram indicator*
03 bad **04** fust, hoar **05** fusty, lousy, mochy, mucid, muggy, musty, stale
06 fousty, mochie, putrid, rotten
07 corrupt, foughty, spoiled, vinewed
08 blighted, decaying, mildewed
09 miserable **10** mucedinous

moult
03 mew **04** cast

mound
03 but, dun, hog, lot, orb, tel **04** bank, barp, butt, dike, dune, dyke, heap, hill, mote, pile, rise, tell, tump **05** agger, cairn, hoard, knoll, mogul, motte, mount, pingo, ridge, stack, store
06 barrow, bundle, kurgan, supply, tuffet **07** hillock, hummock, rampart, tumulus **08** mine dump, mountain
09 abundance, earthwork, elevation, monticule, stockpile, whaleback
10 collection, embankment
11 termitarium **12** accumulation

mound-bird
05 lowan **08** megapode **09** mallee-hen **10** junglefowl, mallee-bird, mallee-fowl **11** brush turkey

mount
◇ *reversal down indicator*
02 Mt **03** set, sty **04** back, base, go up, grow, lift, ride, rise, soar, stie, stye
05 build, climb, erect, frame, get on, get up, horse, put on, raise, scale, set up, stage, stand, steed, swell, tot up
06 accrue, ascend, jump on, launch, pile up, saddle, step up **07** arrange, backing, build up, climb on, climb up, display, exhibit, fixture, install, prepare, produce, support **08** escalade, escalate, increase, jump on to, mounting, multiply, organize, override, saddle up
09 clamber up, climb on to, inselberg, intensify, take horse **10** accumulate, get astride **12** passe-partout

mountain
03 alp, ben, lot, tor **04** berg, fell, heap, hill, mass, peak, pike, pile **05** guyot, jebel, mound, mount, stack **06** djebel, height, massif **07** backlog **08** pinnacle
09 abundance, elevation
12 accumulation

Mountains and mountain ranges include:

02 K2
03 Apo, Dom, Tai
04 Alai, Alps, Blue, Cook, Etna, Fuji, Jura, Meru, Ossa, Rila, Sion, Ural
05 Altai, Andes, Atlas, Coast, Downs, Eiger, Ghats, Halti, Huang, Kamet, Kékes, Kenya, Logan, Matra, Ozark, Qogir, Rocky, Sinai, Snowy, Table, Tatra
06 Ararat, Cho Oyu, Deccan, Denali, Egmont, Elbert, Elbrus, Haltia, Hoggar, Lhotse, Makalu, Mourne, Musala, Pindus, Taurus, Vosges, Zagros
07 Ahaggar, Belukha, Beskids, Everest, Fuji-san, Hua Shan, Lebanon, Manaslu, Nilgiri, Olympus, Rainier, Rhodope, Rockies, Roraima, Scafell, Skiddaw, Snowdon, Stanley, Tai Shan, Troödos
08 Ben Nevis, Cameroon, Catskill, Caucasus, Cévennes, Damavand, Five Holy, Fujiyama, Heng Shan, Jungfrau, Kinabalu, Mauna Kea, Mauna Loa, McKinley, Pennines, Pyrenees, Rushmore, song Shan, St Helens, Taranaki
09 Aconcagua, Allegheny, Altai Shan, Annapurna, Apennines, Blue Ridge, Broad Peak, Cotswolds, Dolomites, Grampians, Helvellyn, Himalayas, Hindu Kush, Inyangani, Karakoram, Kosciusko, Lenin Peak, Mont Blanc, Muz Tag Ata, Nanda Devi, Rakaposhi, Tirichmir, Tirol Alps, Zugspitze
10 Adirondack, Cader Idris, Cairngorms, Cantabrian, Carpathian, Chimborazo, Dhaulagiri, Gasherbrum, Gosainthan, Great Smoky, MacDonnell, Matterhorn, Pobedy Peak, Puncak Jaya, Sagarmatha
11 Appalachian, Arthur's Pass, Black Forest, Chomolungma, Drakensberg, Kilimanjaro, Mendip Hills, Mongo-Ma-Loba, Nanga Parbat, Pico Bolívar, Siula Grande
12 Bavarian Alps, Cascade Range, Cheviot Hills, Darling Range, Dufourspitze, Kanchenjunga, Popocatepetl, Sierra Nevada, Southern Alps, Tibet Plateau, Ulugh Muztagh, Victoria Peak, Vinson Massif
13 Carrantuohill, Chiltern Hills, Communism Peak, Great Dividing, Haltiatunturi, Kangchenjunga, Ojos del Salado, Stirling Range
14 Australian Alps, Bavarian Forest, Bohemian Forest, Fichtelgebirge, Flinders Ranges, Grand St Bernard, Hamersley Range, Mackenzie Range, Musgrave Ranges, Qomolangma Feng, Thadentsonyane, Trans-Antarctic
15 Guiana Highlands, Nevado de Illampu

See also **volcano**

• mountain pass
04 ghat

Mountain passes include:

04 Ofen
05 Haast, Lewis, South
06 Khyber, Lindis, Shipka
07 Arthur's, Brenner, Oberalp, Plöcken, Simplon, Wrynose
08 Hongshan, Yangguan
09 Khunjerab, St Bernard
10 St Gotthard
12 Roncesvalles
13 Cilician Gates, San Bernardino
14 Grand St Bernard
15 Little St Bernard

• mountain peak
03 ben

• mountain range
04 tier

mountaineering

Mountaineers include:

04 **Hunt** (John, Lord)
05 **Brown** (Joe), **Bruce** (C G), **Munro** (Sir Hugh), **Scott** (Doug), **Tabei** (Junko)
06 **Haston** (Dougal), **Herzog** (Maurice), **Irvine** (Andrew), **Smythe** (Frank), **Tilman** (Bill), **Uemura** (Naomi)
07 **Hillary** (Sir Edmund), **Mallory** (George), **Messner** (Reinhold), **Shipton** (Eric), **Simpson** (Myrtle), **Tazieff** (Haroun), **Tenzing** (Sherpa), **Whymper** (Edward)
08 **Coolidge** (W A B), **MacInnes** (Hamish), **Whillans** (Don)
09 **Bonington** (Sir Chris)
10 **Hargreaves** (Alison)
13 **Tenzing Norgay**

mountainous
04 high, huge, mega, vast **05** giant, hilly, jumbo, lofty, rocky, steep
06 alpine, craggy, upland **07** immense, mammoth, massive, soaring
08 colossal, enormous, gigantic, highland, towering **09** ginormous, humongous

mountebank
04 fake **05** antic, cheat, fraud, pseud, quack, rogue **06** antick, con man, phoney **07** anticke, antique, buffoon
08 impostor, jongleur, swindler
09 charlatan, pretender, trickster
11 saltimbanco

mourn
04 keen, miss, wail, weep **06** bemoan, bewail, grieve, lament, regret, sorrow
07 deplore

mourner
04 mute **06** keener, saulie, weeper
07 griever **08** bereaved, sorrower

mournful
03 sad **06** dismal, gloomy, rueful, sombre, tragic, woeful **07** dernful, doleful, elegiac, funèbre, unhappy
08 cast-down, dearnful, dejected, desolate, downcast, funereal
09 depressed, miserable, plaintive, sorrowful **10** lachrymose, lugubrious, melancholy **11** heartbroken, melancholic **12** disconsolate, heavy-hearted **13** broken-hearted, grief-stricken

mournfully
05 sadly **08** dismally, gloomily, ruefully, sombrely **09** con dolore, dolefully, miserably, unhappily **10** desolately
11 plaintively, sorrowfully **15** broken-heartedly

mourning
05 grief **06** sorrow **07** keening, sadness, wailing, weeping **08** grieving
09 sorrowing **10** desolation
11 bereavement, lamentation **13** sorry business

mouse
03 Mus **06** muscle, shiner **07** dunnart, Muridae, waltzer **08** black eye **09** Zapodidae

mousey, mousy
03 shy **04** drab, dull, meek **05** plain, quiet, timid **07** greyish **08** brownish, timorous **09** diffident, shrinking, withdrawn **10** colourless **11** unassertive **12** self-effacing **13** unforthcoming, uninteresting

moustache
04 tash **05** tache **06** walrus **07** Charley, Charlie **08** whiskers **09** excrement, mustachio **10** face fungus **15** zapata moustache

mousy *see* **mousey, mousy**

mouth
◇ *head selection indicator*
03 cry, gab, gam, gas, gob, gub, mou, mug, say **04** door, form, gall, jaws, kiss, rant, trap, vent **05** bazoo, bocca, cheek, chops, delta, hatch, inlet, nerve, sauce, stoma, utter, voice **06** babble, cavity, hot air, kisser, oscule, outlet, portal **07** debouch, declaim, doorway, estuary, gateway, grimace, opening, orifice, speaker, whisper **08** aperture, backchat, boasting, bragging, cakehole, entrance, idle talk, rudeness, traphole **09** brass neck, empty talk, enunciate, impudence, insolence, pronounce, utterance **10** articulate, blustering, disrespect, effrontery, embouchure, potato trap, rattletrap **12** impertinence, laughing gear

Mouth parts and features include:

03 gum, jaw, lip
04 lips
05 uvula
06 tongue, tonsil
07 hare lip
08 lower lip, upper lip
10 hard palate, soft palate
11 cleft palate
13 alveolar ridge
15 isthmus of fauces

See also **teeth**

• **keep your mouth shut**
06 clam up, shut up **07** cover up, keep mum **08** pipe down **09** keep quiet **10** say nothing **14** hold your tongue **15** not breathe a word

• **sew up mouth**
04 cope

mouthful
03 bit, gag, gob, sip, sup **04** bite, drop, gulp, slug **05** taste **06** gobbet, morsel, nibble, sample, titbit **07** forkful, swallow **08** spoonful **11** bonne-bouche

mouthpiece
04 horn **05** agent, organ, voice **07** journal **08** delegate **09** spokesman **10** periodical **11** publication, spokeswoman **12** propagandist, spokesperson **14** representative

movable
06 mobile **08** flexible, portable **09** alterable, portative **10** adjustable, changeable **12** transferable **13** transportable

movables
04 gear **05** goods, stuff **06** things **07** clobber, effects **08** chattels, property **09** furniture **10** belongings **11** impedimenta, plenishings, possessions

move
◇ *anagram indicator*
02 go **03** act, mix, wag **04** draw, lead, nose, pass, push, sell, step, stir, tack, take, urge, walk **05** bring, budge, carry, cause, drive, fetch, impel, leave, pal up, rouse, shift, shunt, swing, touch, upset **06** action, affect, arouse, change, decamp, depart, device, excite, gang up, go away, hobnob, incite, induce, mingle, motion, prompt, propel, remove, strike, submit, switch, travel **07** actuate, advance, agitate, consort, develop, disturb, gesture, hang out, impress, incline, inspire, measure, migrate, proceed, propose, provoke, quinche, removal, request, suggest **08** activity, advocate, go around, motivate, move away, movement, persuade, progress, relocate, transfer **09** associate, circulate, hang about, influence, instigate, manoeuvre, migration, move house, recommend, socialize, stimulate, stratagem, transport, transpose **10** fraternize, initiative, proceeding, put forward, relocation, take action **11** keep company, make strides, zwischenzug **12** rub shoulders **13** gesticulation, repositioning **15** change of address

• **get a move on**
07 hurry up, speed up **08** step on it **09** make haste, shake a leg **11** get cracking **12** step on the gas **15** put your foot down

• **make a move**
02 go **05** frame, leave, split **06** depart **07** push off **08** clear off, get going **10** make tracks **11** do something, get cracking **13** take the plunge, take your leave

• **move aimlessly**
04 mope

• **move around**
04 stir **05** steer, stire, styre

• **move gradually**
04 ease, edge

• **move in some direction**
04 tend

• **move lightly**
04 flit

• **move on**
03 gee, jee **06** avaunt

• **move quickly**
03 hop **04** tear, whid, whip, zoom

• **move round**
04 eddy, turn

• **move sideways**
04 crab

• **move silently**
06 tiptoe

• **move slowly**
03 lag **04** inch

• **move unsteadily**
03 yaw

• **move up and down**
03 bob **04** yo-yo

• **move violently**
04 tear

• **on the move**
05 astir **06** active, around, moving **07** on the go **08** under way **09** advancing, on the hoof, walkabout **10** journeying, travelling **11** progressing **13** moving forward **14** making progress

movement
◇ *anagram indicator*
03 act, bit **04** fall, flow, guts, move, pace, part, play, rise, stir, wing **05** drift, drive, group, party, piece, shift, swing, tempo, trend, works **06** action, change, moving, system **07** advance, crusade, current, emotion, faction, gesture, impulse, passage, portion, section **08** activity, campaign, division, progress, shifting, stirring, tendency, transfer, workings **09** agitation, coalition, evolution, machinery, mechanism, variation **10** relocation **11** development, improvement, progression **12** breakthrough, organization **13** gesticulation, repositioning **14** transportation

See also **art**, **poetry**

• **rapid eye movement**
03 REM

• **sudden movement**
04 dart, volt

movie
04 film **05** flick, video **06** cinema, talkie **07** fleapit, picture **09** multiplex **10** silent film **11** feature film, film theatre **12** movie theatre, picture-house **13** motion picture, picture-palace

See also **film**

moving
◇ *anagram indicator*
05 astir **06** active, mobile, motile, urging **07** driving, dynamic, emotive, flowing, kinetic, leading **08** arousing, exciting, in motion, pathetic, poignant, stirring, touching, worrying **09** affecting, emotional, inspiring, thrilling, upsetting **10** disturbing, impressive, motivating, persuasive **11** influential, stimulating **12** manoeuvrable **13** inspirational

movingly
10 poignantly, touchingly **11** with emotion, with feeling **12** expressively, pathetically **15** inspirationally

mow
03 cut, moe **04** barb, clip, crop, tass, trim **05** shear **06** scythe

• **mow down**
04 kill **07** butcher, cut down, gun down **08** decimate, massacre **09** shoot down, slaughter **11** cut to pieces

mowing
04 math

Mozambique
03 MOC, MOZ

much
04 a lot, lots, many 05 ample, great, heaps, loads, molto, often, piles, scads 06 masses, mickle, muckle, oodles, plenty, stacks 07 copious, greatly 08 abundant, lashings 09 extensive, plentiful 10 a great deal, frequently, widespread 11 substantial 12 considerable, considerably 14 a great number of, to a great degree, to a great extent

• **by so much**
03 the

• **how much**
03 the

• **not so much**
04 less

• **too much**
03 OTT 04 over

• **very much**
03 far 04 sore

muck
03 mud 04 crud, dirt, dung, gold, guck, mess, mire, scum, yuck 05 filth, grime, guano, gunge, slime 06 debris, faeces, grunge, manure, ordure, rubble, scunge, sewage, sludge 09 excrement

• **muck about, muck around**
05 upset 06 bother, meddle, mess up, potter, tamper, untidy 07 trouble 08 dishevel, disorder 09 fool about, goof about, interfere, lark about, mess about, play about 10 disarrange, fool around, goof around, lark around, mess around, play around 13 inconvenience 15 lead a merry dance, make life hell for

• **muck up**
04 ruin 05 botch, spoil, wreck 06 bungle, cock up, mess up 07 louse up, screw up 11 make a mess of

mucky
04 miry, oozy 05 dirty, grimy, gucky, messy, muddy, nasty, slimy 06 filthy, scungy, soiled, sticky 08 begrimed, mud-caked 11 bespattered

mucous
05 gummy, slimy 06 snotty, viscid 07 viscous 09 glutinous 10 gelatinous 12 mucilaginous

mud
03 dub 04 clay, dirt, dubs, mire, moya, ooze, silt, slab, soil 05 abuse, clart, slake, slush 06 clarts, sleech, sludge 07 clabber, slander 12 vilification

• **cover with mud**
04 lair

muddle
◇ *anagram indicator*
03 mix 04 daze, mash, mess, mull, muzz, stir 05 chaos, mix up, mix-up 06 bemuse, bungle, cock-up, fankle, guddle, jumble, mess up, pickle, puddle, puzzle, tangle 07 blunder, clutter, confuse, perplex 08 befuddle, bewilder, confound, disarray, disorder, jumble up, scramble, shambles 09 confusion 11 disorganize 12 bewilderment 15 disorganization

• **muddle through**
04 cope 05 get by 06 make do, manage 08 get along

muddled
◇ *anagram indicator*
05 addle, at sea, dazed, loose, messy, vague 06 tavert, woolly 07 chaotic, jumbled, mixed-up, taivert, tangled, unclear 08 confused 09 befuddled, perplexed, scrambled, stupefied 10 bewildered, disarrayed, disordered, incoherent 11 addle-headed, disoriented, muddy-headed 12 disorganized 13 disorientated

muddy
◇ *anagram indicator*
04 dull, foul, hazy, miry, oozy, soil 05 boggy, cloud, dingy, dirty, fuzzy, grimy, mix up, mucky, murky, slimy, smear, smoky 06 bedash, bedaub, cloudy, dreggy, drumly, filthy, grouty, grubby, jumble, limous, marshy, muddle, opaque, puddle, quaggy, slabby, sloppy, sludgy, slushy, smirch, stupid, swampy, tangle, turbid 07 begrime, blurred, confuse, obscure, splashy, trouble 08 confused, jumble up, scramble 09 befuddled, bespatter, make muddy 10 indistinct 11 disorganize, make unclear, waterlogged

muff
◇ *anagram indicator*
04 miss, mitt 05 botch, fluff, spoil 06 bungle, duffer, mess up, mishit 07 bungler 09 mishandle, mismanage

muffle
03 gag, mob 04 dull, hush, kill, mute, wrap 05 cloak, cover, moble 06 dampen, deaden, mobble, muzzle, soften, stifle, swathe, wrap up 07 cover up, envelop, quieten, silence, smother, swaddle 08 suppress 09 blindfold

mug
03 can, cup, pot, rob, sap 04 bash, bock, dupe, exam, face, fool, gull, jump, mush, phiz, swot, Toby 05 chump, clock, mouth, stein, tinny 06 attack, batter, beaker, beat up, do over, jump on, kisser, noggin, sconce, sucker, tinnie, visage, waylay 07 assault, muggins, rough up, set upon, tankard 08 features 09 simpleton, soft touch, steal from 10 knock about 11 countenance, physiognomy

See also **face**; **fool**

• **mug up**
03 con 04 cram, swot 05 get up, study 06 bone up

muggy
04 damp 05 close, foggy, humid, mochy, moist 06 clammy, mochie, sticky, stuffy, sultry 07 airless 10 oppressive, sweltering

mulberry
04 upas 05 Morus, mvule 06 murrey 07 cowtree 08 cecropia, sycamine 10 artocarpus 11 contrayerva, Osage orange

mule
04 moyl, muil 05 moyle 06 hybrid 07 slipper, sumpter 09 dziggetai

mulish
05 rigid 06 wilful 07 defiant 08 perverse, stubborn 09 difficult, obstinate, pig-headed 10 headstrong, inflexible, refractory, self-willed 11 intractable, stiff-necked, wrong-headed 12 intransigent, recalcitrant, unreasonable

mull

• **mull over**
05 study 06 muse on, ponder 07 examine, weigh up 08 chew over, consider, meditate, ruminate 09 reflect on, think over 10 deliberate, think about 11 contemplate

multicoloured
04 pied 06 motley 07 dappled, piebald, spotted, striped 08 brindled 09 colourful 10 variegated 11 psychedelic 13 kaleidoscopic, particoloured

multifarious
04 many 06 legion, sundry, varied 07 diverse 08 manifold, multiple, numerous 09 different, multiform 10 variegated 11 diversified 13 miscellaneous, multitudinous

multiple
04 many 06 sundry 07 several, various 08 compound, manifold, numerous, repeated 10 collective, multiplied

multiplicity
03 lot 04 host, lots, mass, tons 05 array, heaps, loads, piles 06 myriad, number, oodles, scores, stacks 07 variety 09 abundance, diversity, profusion 12 manifoldness, numerousness

multiplied with
01 x 02 by

multiply
04 grow 05 boost, breed 06 double, expand, extend, spread 07 augment, build up, decuple, octuple 08 centuple, increase, manifold, septuple, sextuple 09 intensify, propagate, quadruple, quintuple, reproduce 10 accumulate 11 proliferate

multipurpose
05 handy 08 all-round, flexible, variable 09 adaptable, many-sided, versatile 10 adjustable, all-purpose, functional 11 resourceful 12 multifaceted 14 general-purpose

multitude
03 lot, mob 04 army, herd, hive, host, lots, mass, ruck 05 crowd, horde, plebs, shoal, swarm 06 hirsel, legion, number, people, public, rabble, throng

07 king mob 08 assembly, canaille, populace, riff-raff 09 hoi polloi 10 common herd, the million 11 rank and file 12 common people, congregation 13 great unwashed

multitudinous
04 many 05 great 06 legion, myriad 07 copious, profuse, teeming, umpteen 08 abundant, infinite, manifold, numerous, swarming 09 abounding, countless 11 innumerable 12 considerable

mum
02 ma 04 dumb, ma'am, mama, marm, mute 05 mummy, quiet 06 mother, silent 07 silence 08 reticent 09 secretive 10 masquerade 11 close-lipped, tight-lipped 12 close-mouthed 13 chrysanthemum, unforthcoming 15 uncommunicative

mumble
04 moop, moup, mump, slur 06 fumble, murmur, mutter, rumble 07 grumble, stutter 08 splutter 11 speak softly 14 speak unclearly, talk to yourself

mumbo-jumbo
04 cant, rite 05 chant, charm, magic, spell 06 humbug, jargon, ritual 07 mummery 08 claptrap, nonsense 09 gibberish, rigmarole 10 double talk, hocus-pocus 11 abracadabra, conjuration, incantation 12 gobbledygook, superstition

mummer
05 actor 06 guiser, guizer 07 guisard, scudler, skudler 09 scuddaler 11 masquerader

munch
03 eat 04 chew, moop, moup, mump 05 champ, chomp 06 crunch 09 masticate

mundane
04 dull 05 banal, stale, trite, usual 06 boring, common, cosmic, normal 07 earthly, fleshly, humdrum, prosaic, regular, routine, secular, terrene, typical, worldly 08 everyday, ordinary, temporal, workaday 09 customary, hackneyed 11 commonplace, terrestrial

municipal
04 city, town 05 civic, civil, urban 06 public 07 borough 09 community 12 metropolitan

municipality
04 city, town 05 burgh 07 borough, council 08 district, precinct, township 10 department 11 département 15 local government

munificence
06 bounty 08 altruism, largesse 10 generosity, liberality 11 beneficence, benevolence, hospitality 12 generousness, philanthropy 13 bounteousness, bountifulness 14 charitableness, open-handedness 15 magnanimousness

munificent
04 rich 06 lavish 07 liberal 08 generous, princely 09 bounteous, bountiful 10 altruistic, beneficent, benevolent, big-hearted, charitable, free-handed, hospitable, open-handed, unstinting 11 magnanimous 15 philanthropical

munitions
03 kit 04 gear, guns 05 bombs, tools 06 shells, tackle 08 armament, materiel, ordnance, supplies 09 apparatus, equipment, materials 10 provisions

murder
03 hit, ice, rid 04 beat, do in, hell, kill, lick, rout, ruin, slay 05 agony, blood, botch, burke, spoil, stiff, waste, whack, wreck 06 fill in, hammer, mess up, misery, ordeal, outwit, rub out, rubout, thrash 07 anguish, bump off, butcher, clobber, destroy, execute, killing, murther, outplay, removal, slaying, take out, torment, torture, trounce, wipe out 08 blow away, butchery, dispatch, filicide, foul play, homicide, knock off, massacre, outsmart 09 bloodshed, do to death, eliminate, execution, liquidate, matricide, nightmare, overwhelm, parricide, patricide, slaughter, suffering, uxoricide 10 annihilate, fratricide, put to death, sororicide 11 assassinate, infanticide, liquidation, make a mess of 12 defeat easily, manslaughter, petty treason, wretchedness 13 assassination

See also **kill**

murderer
04 Cain 06 killer, slayer 07 butcher 08 assassin, filicide, homicide 09 bluebeard, cut-throat, matricide, murtherer, patricide 10 man-queller 11 slaughterer 12 serial killer

Murderers, alleged murderers and assassins include:

03 **Ray** (James Earl)
04 **Aram** (Eugene), **Cain**, **Edny** (Clithero), **Hare** (William), **Kray** (Reggie), **Kray** (Ronnie), **Retz** (Gilles de Laval, Baron), **Ruby** (Jack), **Todd** (Sweeney), **West** (Fred), **West** (Rosemary)
05 **Beane** (Sawney), **Booth** (John Wilkes), **Brady** (Ian), **Bundy** (Ted), **Burke** (William), **Craig** (Christopher), **Ellis** (Ruth), **Haigh** (John), **Havoc** (Jack), **Rudge**
06 **Barrow** (Clyde), **Borden** (Lizzie), **Corday** (Charlotte), **Dahmer** (Jeffrey), **Lecter** (Dr Hannibal), **Manson** (Charles), **Misfit** (the), **Nilsen** (Dennis), **Oswald** (Lee Harvey), **Parker** (Bonnie), **Sirhan** (Sirhan)
07 **Bathori** (Elizabeth), **Bentley** (Derek), **Bianchi** (Kenneth), **Chapman** (Mark), **Crippen** (Hawley Harvey), **Hindley** (Myra), **Macbeth**, **Manston** (Aeneas), **Neilson** (Donald), **Shipman** (Harold)
08 **Barabbas**, **Christie** (John Reginald Halliday), **Claudius**, **Dominici** (Gaston), **Hanratty** (James), **Son of Sam**, **Thompson** (Edith)
09 **Berkowitz** (David), **Bluebeard**, **Harmodius**, **McNaghten** (Daniel), **Sutcliffe** (Peter)
10 **McNaughten** (Daniel), **McNaughton** (Daniel), **Nirdlinger** (Phyllis)
11 **Anckarström** (Johan Jakob), **Quare Fellow** (the)
13 **Jack the Ripper**
14 **Moors Murderers**
15 **Yorkshire Ripper**

murderous
05 cruel, fatal 06 bloody, brutal, carnal, deadly, lethal, mortal, savage 07 arduous, killing 09 barbarous, butcherly, cut-throat, dangerous, difficult, ferocious, gruelling, homicidal, punishing, strenuous 10 exhausting, unpleasant 11 internecine, internecive 12 bloodthirsty, slaughterous

murderously
06 grimly 07 fatally 09 ominously 10 alarmingly, menacingly, sinisterly 11 dangerously, homicidally 12 portentously, unpleasantly 13 threateningly 14 bloodthirstily

murk
04 dark, dusk, mirk 05 gloom, night, shade 06 gloomy 07 dimness, obscure, shadows 08 darkness, twilight 09 blackness, half-light, murkiness, shadiness, tenebrity 10 cloudiness, gloominess 11 sunlessness, tenebrosity

murky
03 dim, sus 04 dark, dull, grey 05 dingy, dirty, fishy, foggy, misty, muddy, rooky, shady 06 cloudy, dismal, dreary, gloomy, secret, turbid, veiled 07 obscure 08 overcast 09 cheerless, tenebrose, tenebrous 10 mysterious, suspicious, tenebrious 12 questionable

murmur
◇ *homophone indicator*
03 bur, coo, hum 04 beef, burr, buzz, carp, fuss, moan, purl, purr 05 brawl, brool, bruit, drone, gripe, mourn, thrum, whine 06 babble, burble, grouse, grudge, intone, mumble, mutter, object, repine, rumble, rumour, rustle, whinge 07 beefing, carping, censure, croodle, grumble, humming, protest, purring, whisper 08 complain, rumbling, syllable 09 annoyance, bellyache, complaint, criticism, criticize, find fault, grievance, muttering, objection, undertone, whingeing 11 bellyaching 12 fault-finding 15 dissatisfaction

murmuring
04 buzz, purl, purr 05 drone 06 babble, mumble, mutter, rumble 07 buzzing, droning, humming,

purring, souffle, whisper
08 mumbling, rumbling, susurrus
09 murmurous, muttering
10 whispering **11** murmuration

Murphy

04 spud **05** praty, tater, tatie **06** potato, pratie, tattie

muscle

04 beef, thew **05** brawn, clout, force, might, power, sinew **06** mussel, tendon, weight **07** potency, stamina **08** ligament, strength **10** sturdiness **12** forcefulness

Muscles include:

02 ab
03 pec
04 delt
05 glute, psoas
06 biceps, rectus, soleus
07 cardiac, deltoid, gluteus, iliacus, omohyid, triceps
08 detrusor, masseter, platysma, pronator, risorius, scalenus, splenius
09 abdominal, complexus, eye-string, perforans, sartorius, stapedius, supinator, trapezius
10 buccinator, quadriceps
11 ciliary body, rhomboideus
13 gastrocnemius
14 xiphihumeralis
15 latissimus dorsi, pectoralis major, pectoralis minor, peroneal muscles

• muscle in

05 shove **06** butt in, jostle, push in **09** strongarm **13** interfere with **14** elbow your way in, force your way in, impose yourself

muscular

05 beefy, burly, hefty, husky, thewy **06** brawny, potent, robust, rugged, sinewy, strong, sturdy, thewed **07** fibrous **08** athletic, powerful, stalwart, vigorous **09** strapping **15** powerfully built

muse

04 mews **05** brood, dream, meuse, study, think, weigh **06** ponder, review **07** reflect **08** chew over, cogitate, consider, meditate, mull over, ruminate **09** speculate, think over **10** deliberate **11** contemplate **13** contemplation

The Greek Muses:

04 Clio
05 Erato
06 Thalia, Urania
07 Euterpe
08 Calliope, Polymnia
09 Melpomene
10 Polyhymnia
11 Terpsichore

• the Muses

07 the nine

museum

03 mus **07** palazzo **10** art gallery, collection, repository **14** heritage centre

Museums and galleries include:

02 BM, RA
03 ICA
04 MoMA, MOMI, Tate
05 Prado, Terme, V and A
06 Correr, London, Louvre, Uffizi
07 British, Fogg Art, Hofburg, Mankind, Pushkin, Russian, Science, Vatican
08 Bargello, Borghese, National, Pergamum
09 Accademia, Albertina, Arnolfini, Ashmolean, Belvedere, Cloisters, Deutsches, Hermitage, Holocaust, Modern Art, Sans Souci, Tretyakov
10 Guggenheim, Pinakothek, Pitt-Rivers, Serpentine, Tate Modern
11 Fitzwilliam, Imperial War, Mauritshuis, Musée d'Orsay, Pitti Palace, Rijksmuseum, Tate Britain
12 Royal Academy, Whitworth Art
13 Jean Paul Getty, Peace Memorial, Royal Pavilion
14 Barbican Centre, Natural History, State Hermitage
15 Centre Beaubourg, Frick Collection, South Bank Centre

mush

03 pap **04** corn, glop, mash, pulp **05** cream, dough, gloop, notch, paste, purée, slush, swill **07** rubbish, scallop, shmaltz **08** schmaltz, umbrella **11** mawkishness **14** sentimentality

mushroom

04 boom, grow **06** expand, spread, sprout **07** burgeon, shoot up, upstart **08** flourish, increase, spring up, umbrella **09** luxuriate, pixy-stool **11** proliferate

Mushrooms and toadstools include:

03 cep
04 base, ugly, wood
05 brain, field, gypsy, horse, magic, march, morel, naked
06 agaric, blewit, button, elf cup, ink cap, meadow, mower's, oyster, satan's, winter
07 amanita, blewits, blusher, boletus, Caesar's, griping, parasol, porcini, truffle
08 death cap, deceiver, hedgehog, penny bun, shiitake, sickener
09 cramp ball, earth ball, fairy ring, fly agaric, St George's, stinkhorn
10 champignon, false morel, lawyer's wig, liberty cap, panther cap, sweetbread, wood agaric
11 chanterelle, clean mycena, common morel, dingy agaric, honey fungus, stout agaric, sulphur tuft, velvet shank
12 common ink cap, dryad's saddle, false blusher, horn of plenty, larch boletus, lurid boletus, purple blewit, shaggy ink cap, slippery jack, white truffle, winter fungus, wood hedgehog
13 buckler agaric, clouded agaric, copper trumpet, devil's boletus, emetic russula, firwood agaric, honey mushroom, Jew's ear fungus, purple boletus, satan's boletus, shaggy milk cap, shaggy parasol, summer truffle, trumpet agaric, woolly milk cap, yellow stainer
14 common grisette, common laccaria, common puffball, fairies' bonnets, man on horseback, penny-bun fungus, saffron milk cap, yellow staining
15 beefsteak fungus, chestnut boletus, common earthball, common stinkhorn, destroying angel, garlic marosmius, périgord truffle, stinking parasol, stinking russula, verdigris agaric

See also **fungus**

mushy

◇ *anagram indicator*

03 wet **04** soft **05** pappy, pulpy, soppy, weepy **06** doughy, sloppy, slushy, sugary, syrupy **07** maudlin, mawkish, pulpous, squashy, squidgy **08** squelchy **09** schmaltzy **10** saccharine **11** sentimental

music

03 fun, mus **04** note, tune **05** dream **06** melody **07** harmony

Music types include:

03 AOR, MOR, pop, rai, rap, ska
04 folk, funk, jazz, jive, mood, raga, rock, Romo, soca, soul, zouk
05 bebop, blues, cajun, dance, disco, house, indie, muzak, R and B, salsa, samba, sokah, swing, world
06 atonal, ballet, choral, doo-wop, fusion, garage, gospel, grunge, hip-hop, jungle, lounge, reggae, sacred, techno, trance
07 ambient, baroque, bhangra, Big Beat, calypso, chamber, gamelan, gangsta, karaoke, nu-metal, ragtime, skiffle, trip-hop
08 acid jazz, ballroom, folk rock, glam rock, hardcore, hard rock, jazz-funk, jazz-rock, operatic, oratorio, punk rock, soft rock
09 acid house, bluegrass, classical, Dixieland, honky-tonk
10 electronic, gangsta rap, heavy metal, incidental, orchestral, twelve-tone
11 country rock, drum and bass, rock and roll, thrash metal
12 boogie-woogie, instrumental
13 easy listening
14 rhythm and blues
15 middle-of-the-road

See also **jazz**; **opera**

• compose music to

03 set

musical

03 mus **06** dulcet, mellow **07** lyrical, melodic, tuneful **09** melodious **10** euphonious, harmonious **11** mellifluous **13** sweet-sounding

See also **instrument**; **note**

Musicals include:

04 Cats, Fame, Hair, Rent
05 Annie, Blitz, Chess, Evita, Fosse, Zorba
06 Grease, Joseph, Kismet, Oliver!, The Wiz
07 Cabaret, Camelot, Chicago, Company, Follies
08 Carnival, Carousel, Fiorello!, Godspell, Mamma Mia!, Oklahoma!, Peter Pan, Show Boat
09 Brigadoon, Funny Girl, Girl Crazy, On the Town
10 Hello Dolly!, Kiss Me Kate, Miss Saigon, My Fair Lady
11 A Chorus Line, Babes in Arms, Billy Elliot, Bitter Sweet, Carmen Jones, Mary Poppins, Me and My Girl, Sweeney Todd, The King and I, The Lion King, The Music Man
12 Anything Goes, Bombay Dreams, Bye Bye Birdie, Guys and Dolls, Martin Guerre, South Pacific, The Boy Friend, The Producers
13 Aspects of Love, Blood Brothers, Les Miserables, Man of La Mancha, The Pajama Game, West Side Story
14 Babes in Toyland, Victor/Victoria
15 Annie Get Your Gun, La Cage aux Folles, Mister Wonderful, Sunset Boulevard, The Sound of Music, The Woman in White

Songs from musicals include:

03 One
04 Fame
05 Maria
06 Do-Re-Mi, Memory, People
07 America, Bali Ha'i, Cabaret, Camelot, Tonight
08 Aquarius, Day by Day, Oklahoma!, Time Warp, Tomorrow
09 Edelweiss, Evergreen, Footloose, Somewhere, Superstar, Tradition
10 42nd Street, Be Our Guest, Big Spender, Friendship, Hello, Dolly, I Am What I Am, I Got Rhythm, Matchmaker, Night Fever, Ol' Man River, Too Darn Hot, Willkommen
11 76 Trombones, All That Jazz, Luck, Be a Lady, Night and Day, Old Man River, Summer Lovin', Where is Love?, You're The Top
12 All I Ask of You, Broadway Baby, Circle of Life, Dancing Queen, Easter Parade, Hakuna Matata, Mack the Knife, Makin' Whoopee, Rich Man's Frug, Shall We Dance?, Sound of Music, Staying Alive, Summer Nights, There She Goes, We Go Together
13 Skimbleshanks, Sunrise, Sunset
14 Ain't Misbehavin', Any Dream Will Do, Chim Chim Cher-ee, Close Every Door, I Dreamed a Dream, I Know Him So Well, Lonely Goatherd, Mr Mistoffelees, New York, New York, So Long, Farewell, They All Laughed, We're in the Money
15 A Bushel and a Peck, Bells Are Ringing, Greased Lightnin', Honeysuckle Rose, I Am the Starlight, If I Were a Rich Man, Music of the Night, Put On a Happy Face, Send in the Clowns, Singin' in the Rain, Sunset Boulevard, Tell Me on a Sunday, The Lady is a Tramp, Till There Was You

People associated with musicals include:

04 **Bart** (Lionel), **Hart** (Lorenz), **Kaye** (Danny), **Kern** (Jerome), **Nunn** (Trevor), **Rice** (Tim)
05 **Black** (Don), **Donen** (Stanley), **Fosse** (Bob), **Kelly** (Gene), **Lenya** (Lotte), **Loewe** (Frederick)
06 **Berlin** (Irving), **Coward** (Sir Noel), **Gaynor** (Mitzi), **Jolson** (Al), **Lerner** (Alan Jay), **Merman** (Ethel), **Porter** (Cole), **Prince** (Hal), **Rogers** (Ginger), **Steele** (Tommy)
07 **Astaire** (Fred), **Burnett** (Carol), **Garland** (Judy), **Gilbert** (Sir W S), **Novello** (Ivor), **Rodgers** (Richard)
08 **Berkeley** (Busby), **Gershwin** (George), **Gershwin** (Ira), **Minnelli** (Liza), **Robinson** (Bill 'Bojangles'), **Sondheim** (Stephen), **Ziegfeld** (Florenz, Jnr)
09 **Bernstein** (Leonard), **Macintosh** (Cameron), **Offenbach** (Jacques)
10 **D'Oyly Carte** (Richard)
11 **Hammerstein** (Oscar, II), **Lloyd Webber** (Andrew, Lord)

Musical composition types include:

03 jig, lay, rag
04 aria, duet, hymn, lied, opus, raga, song, trio, tune
05 canon, carol, étude, fugue, gigue, march, opera, piece, polka, rondo, round, suite, tango, track, waltz
06 aubade, ballad, bolero, lieder, masque, minuet, number, pavane, shanty, sonata
07 ballade, bourrée, cantata, fanfare, gavotte, mazurka, partita, prelude, quartet, requiem, scherzo, toccata
08 berceuse, cavatina, chaconne, concerto, fandango, fantasia, galliard, hornpipe, madrigal, nocturne, operetta, overture, rhapsody, saraband, serenade, sonatina, symphony, zarzuela
09 allemande, arabesque, bagatelle, cabaletta, capriccio, écossaise, farandole, impromptu, invention, pastorale, polonaise, sarabande, spiritual, voluntary
10 barcarolle, bergamasca, concertino, humoresque, intermezzo, opera buffa, tarantella
11 bacchanalia, ballad opera, composition, pastourelle, sinfonietta
12 divertimento, extravaganza
13 missa solemnis
14 chorale fantasy, chorale prelude, concerto grosso

See also **song**

Musical compositions include:

04 Saul
05 Rodeo
06 Boléro, Elijah, Études, Façade, Images
07 Epitaph, Jephtha, Mazeppa, Messiah
08 Ballades, Caprices, Creation, Drum Mass, Ode to Joy, Peer Gynt
09 Capriccio, Fantaisie, Finlandia, Jerusalem, Nocturnes
10 Arabesques, Bacchanale, Bagatelles, Concertino, Nelson Mass, The Planets, The Seasons, Water Music
11 Curlew River, Gymnopédies, Harmony Mass, Minute Waltz, Requiem Mass, Stabat Mater, Winterreise
12 A Sea Symphony, Danse Macabre, Golden Sonata, Karelia Suite, Kinderscenen, Linz Symphony, Piano Fantasy, Schéhérazade, Trout Quintet
13 Alpensinfonie, Carmina Burana, Choral Fantasy, Ebony Concerto, Faust Symphony, Fêtes Galantes, German Requiem, Israel in Egypt, Metamorphoses, Missa Solemnis, On Wenlock Edge, The Art of Fugue
14 Canticum Sacrum, Choral Symphony, Colour Symphony, Eroica Symphony, Glagolitic Mass, Prague Symphony, Rhapsody in Blue, Slavonic Dances, The Four Seasons
15 A Child of our Time, Alexander's Feast, Children's Corner, Emperor Concerto, Haffner Symphony, Hungarian Dances, Italian Concerto, Judas Maccabaeus, Jupiter Symphony, Kossuth Overture, Manfred Symphony, Peter and the Wolf, Sicilian Vespers

See also **opera**; **oratorio**; **song**

Musical terms include:

03 bar, bis, cue, key, tie
04 a due, alto, arco, bass, beat, clef, coda, fine, flat, fret, hold, mode, mute, note, part, rest, root, slur, solo, tone, tune, turn
05 ad lib, breve, buffo, chord, dolce, drone, forte, grave, largo, lento, lyric, major, metre, minim, minor, molto, pause, piano, piece, pitch, scale, score, senza, shake, sharp, staff, stave, swell, tacet, tanto, tempo, tenor, theme, triad, trill, tutti
06 adagio, al fine, a tempo, da capo, duplet, encore, finale, legato, manual, medley, melody, octave, phrase, presto, quaver, rhythm, sempre, subito, tenuto, timbre, treble, tuning, unison, upbeat, vivace
07 agitato, allegro, al segno, amoroso, andante, animato, attacca, bar line, cadence, con brio, concert, con moto, descant, harmony, langsam, marcato, mediant, middle C, mordent, natural, recital,

refrain, soprano, tremolo, triplet, vibrato
08 acoustic, alto clef, arpeggio, baritone, bass clef, col canto, con fuoco, crotchet, diatonic, doloroso, dominant, downbeat, ensemble, interval, maestoso, moderato, movement, ostinato, perdendo, ritenuto, semitone, semplice, sequence, staccato, vigoroso, virtuoso
09 alla breve, cantabile, cantilena, chromatic, contralto, crescendo, glissando, harmonics, imitation, larghetto, mezza voce, microtone, non troppo, obbligato, orchestra, pizzicato, semibreve, sextuplet, sforzando, smorzando, sostenuto, sotto voce, spiritoso, tablature, tenor clef
10 accidental, affettuoso, allargando, allegretto, consonance, diminuendo, dissonance, dotted note, dotted rest, double flat, double stop, expression, fortissimo, intonation, ledger line, mezzo forte, modulation, pedal point, pentatonic, pianissimo, quadruplet, quintuplet, resolution, semiquaver, simple time, submediant, supertonic, tonic sol-fa, treble clef, two-two time
11 accelerando, arrangement, decrescendo, double sharp, double trill, fingerboard, leading note, quarter tone, rallentando, rinforzando, subdominant, syncopation
12 acciaccatura, alla cappella, appoggiatura, compound time, counterpoint, four-four time, key signature, six-eight time
13 accompaniment, double bar line, fifth interval, improvisation, major interval, minor interval, orchestration, sixth interval, sul ponticello, third interval, three-four time, time signature, transposition
14 cross-fingering, demisemiquaver, fourth interval, second interval
15 perfect interval, seventh interval

musician

Musician types include:

03 duo
04 band, bard, diva, duet, trio
05 choir, griot, group, nonet, octet, piper, waits
06 bugler, busker, folkie, jazzer, oboist, player, sextet, singer
07 cellist, drummer, fiddler, harpist, maestro, Orphean, pianist, quartet, quintet, soloist
08 clarsair, composer, ensemble, flautist, lutenist, minstrel, organist, virtuoso, vocalist
09 balladeer, conductor, guitarist, itinerant, orchestra, performer, trumpeter, violinist
10 one-man band, prima donna, trombonist
11 accompanist, saxophonist
12 backing group, clarinettist
13 percussionist, session singer
15 instrumentalist, session musician

See also **composer**; **conductor**; **libretto**; **pianist**; **singer**; **songwriter**

Classical musicians include:

02 **Ax** (Emmanuel), **Ma** (Yo-Yo)
03 **Mae** (Vanessa), **Pré** (Jacqueline du)
04 **Bell** (Joshua), **Hahn** (Hilary), **Hess** (Dame Myra), **Lupu** (Radu), **Mork** (Truls), **Wild** (Earl)
05 **Boehm** (Theobald), **Borge** (Victor), **Bream** (Julian), **Bülow** (Hans von), **Chung** (Kyung-Wha), **Dupré** (Marcel), **Elman** (Mischa), **Grove** (Sir George), **Isbin** (Sharon), **Ogdon** (John), **Sharp** (Cecil), **Stern** (Isaac)
06 **Casals** (Pablo), **Czerny** (Karl), **Galway** (James), **Gitlis** (Ivry), **Kissin** (Evgeny), **Köchel** (Ludwig von) **Rizzio** (David), **Schiff** (András)
07 **Blondel**, **Glennie** (Evelyn), **Heifetz** (Jascha), **Kennedy** (Nigel), **Menuhin** (Yehudi), **Mutter** (Anne-Sophie), **Perahia** (Murray), **Perlman** (Itzhak), **Pollini** (Maurizio), **Richter** (Sviatoslav), **Russell** (David), **Segovia** (Andrés), **Shankar** (Ravi), **Starker** (Janos)
08 **Argerich** (Martha), **Bronfman** (Yefim), **Browning** (John), **Goossens** (Léon), **Helfgott** (David), **Holliger** (Heinz), **Horowitz** (Vladimir), **Kreisler** (Fritz), **Paganini** (Niccolò), **Sarasate** (Pablo), **Steinway** (Henry), **Vengerov** (Maxim), **Williams** (John)
09 **Ashkenazy** (Vladimir), **Barenboim** (Daniel), **Benedetti** (Nicola), **Boulanger** (Nadia), **Broadwood** (John), **Dolmetsch** (Arnold), **Guarnieri**, **Tortelier** (Paul)
10 **Cristofori**, **de Larrocha** (Alicia), **Paderewski** (Ignacy), **Rubinstein** (Anton), **Rubinstein** (Artur), **Stradivari** (Antonio), **Villa-Lobos** (Heitor), **Williamson** (Malcolm)
11 **Theodorakis** (Mikis)
12 **Guido d'Arezzo**, **Rostropovich** (Mstislav)
14 **Jaques-Dalcroze** (Emile)

musing

05 study **07** reverie **08** dreaming, studying, thinking **10** brown study, cogitation, meditation, ponderment, reflection, rumination **11** abstraction, cerebration, daydreaming **13** contemplation, introspection, wool-gathering

musk

04 must **05** civet, moust, muist, scent **07** mimulus

musket

05 fusee, fusil **06** gingal, jezail, jingal **07** caliver, dragoon, gingall **08** Biscayan **09** brown Bess, queen's-arm **10** musquetoon

musketeer

12 mousquetaire

Musketeers include:

05 Athos
06 Aramis
07 Porthos
09 D'Artagnan

Muslim

Muslims include:

04 Shia
05 Shiah, Sunni
06 Senusi, Shiite
07 Alawite, dervish, Mevlevi , Senussi, Sonnite, Sunnite
08 Senoussi
10 Karmathian
11 Black Muslim
15 whirling dervish

muslin

04 leno, mull **05** sails **06** canvas, gurrah, mulmul **07** jamdani, mulmull, organdy **08** coteline, nainsook, organdie, tarlatan **09** persienne **10** mousseline

muss

◇ *anagram indicator*
03 row **04** mess **06** ruffle, tousle **08** dishevel, disorder, scramble **09** confusion **10** disarrange, make untidy **11** disturbance, make a mess of

mussel

04 Unio **06** muscle, muskle **07** Modiola, Mytilus **08** deer horn, Modiolus **09** clabby-doo, clappy-doo, date-shell

must

◇ *anagram indicator*
03 man, mun **04** amok, duty, maun, mote, musk, stum **05** amuck, basic, mould **06** frenzy, powder **09** essential, necessity, provision, requisite **10** imperative, obligation, sine qua non **11** fundamental, requirement, stipulation **12** fermentation, prerequisite

mustard

05 runch, senvy **08** charlock, flix-weed **09** praiseach **10** sauce-alone **14** jack-by-the-hedge

muster

04 mass, meet **05** enrol, group, rally **06** call up, gather, number, parade, review, summon, throng **07** collect, convene, convoke, display, example, hosting, marshal, meeting, round up, round-up, turnout **08** assemble, assembly, mobilize, register, summon up **09** concourse, gathering, march past **10** assemblage, collection, congregate, convention, inspection **11** convocation **12** call together, come together, congregation, mobilization **13** bring together, demonstration **14** gather together

• **pass muster**
07 shape up **09** measure up **10** be accepted, fit the bill **11** fill the bill **12** be

acceptable, be good enough, make the grade **15** come up to scratch

musty
◇ *anagram indicator*
04 amok, damp, dank **05** amuck, frowy, funky, fusty, mucid, stale **06** fousty, frowie, mochie, mouldy, smelly, stuffy **07** airless, decayed, foughty, froughy, mildewy, vinewed **08** decaying, mildewed

mutability
09 variation **11** variability **12** alterability **13** permutability **14** changeableness

mutable
06 fickle **08** changing, flexible, unstable, unsteady, variable, volatile, wavering **09** adaptable, alterable, uncertain, unsettled **10** changeable, inconstant, irresolute, permutable, unreliable **11** vacillating **12** inconsistent, undependable **15** interchangeable

mutate
◇ *anagram indicator*
05 alter, morph **06** change, evolve, modify, remake **07** convert, remodel, reshape **09** transform, translate, transmute **11** transfigure **12** metamorphose, transmogrify

mutation
◇ *anagram indicator*
06 change **07** anomaly **09** deviation, evolution, inversion, variation **10** adaptation, alteration, revolution **11** vicissitude **12** modification **13** metamorphosis **14** transformation

mute
03 mum **04** dull, dumb, stop **05** lower **06** dampen, damper, deaden, muffle, shtoom, silent, soften, stifle, subdue **07** aphasic, plosive, quieten, silence, smother, sordino **08** moderate, sourdine, suppress, taciturn, tone down, unspoken, wordless **09** noiseless, soft-pedal, voiceless **10** speechless **11** unexpressed **12** unpronounced **15** uncommunicative

muted
04 dull, soft **05** faint, quiet, sorda, sordo **06** low-key, subtle **07** muffled, stifled, subdued **08** dampened, discreet, softened **10** restrained, suppressed

mutely
06 dumbly **08** silently **09** in silence **10** taciturnly **11** noiselessly, voicelessly **12** speechlessly

mutilate
◇ *anagram indicator*
03 cut, mar **04** hack, lame, maim, ruin **05** cut up, spoil **06** censor, damage, garble, hack up, hamble, impair, injure, mangle **07** butcher, concise, cripple, disable, distort **08** lacerate **09** disfigure, dismember **10** bowdlerize, detruncate **11** cut to pieces

mutilation
◇ *anagram indicator*
06 damage **07** maiming **10** amputation **12** detruncation, dismembering **13** disfigurement

mutinous
◇ *anagram indicator*
06 unruly **07** bolshie, riotous **09** insurgent, seditious **10** disorderly, rebellious, refractory, subversive **11** anarchistic, disobedient **12** contumacious, ungovernable, unsubmissive **13** insubordinate, revolutionary **14** uncontrollable

mutiny
04 defy, riot **05** rebel **06** resist, revolt, rise up, rising, strife, strike, tumult **07** disobey, protest **08** defiance, uprising **09** rebellion **10** insurgence, resistance, revolution **12** disobedience, insurrection **15** insubordination

mutt
03 cur, dog **04** dolt, fool, kuri **05** bitch, hound, idiot, moron, pooch **07** mongrel **08** imbecile **09** blockhead, ignoramus, thickhead **10** dunderhead

mutter
◇ *homophone indicator*
04 beef, carp, fuss, mump, roin **05** gripe, royne, whine **06** grouse, mumble, murmur, object, rumble, whinge, witter **07** chunder, chunner, chunter, grumble, maunder, protest, stutter, whitter **08** chounter, complain, splutter **09** bellyache, criticize, find fault, murmuring, mussitate **14** talk to yourself, whittie-whattie

mutton
02 em **05** gigot, macon, sheep, traik **07** haricot **09** Irish stew, Southdown **10** Fanny Adams **13** colonial goose

mutual
05 joint **06** common, shared **09** commutual, exchanged **10** collective, commonable, reciprocal **12** interchanged **13** complementary **15** interchangeable

muzzle
03 gag **04** mute **05** check, choke, snout **06** censor, fetter, stifle **07** inhibit, silence **08** gunpoint, restrain, suppress

muzzy
04 hazy **05** dazed, faint, fuzzy, mused, tipsy **06** addled, groggy **07** blurred, muddled, unclear **08** confused **09** befuddled, unfocused **10** bewildered, indistinct

my
01 m' **02** ha **03** cor, gad, lor **04** gosh **08** well, well

Myanmar
03 BUR, MMR, MYA

myopic
06 narrow, unwise **08** purblind **09** half-blind, imprudent, localized, parochial, short-term **11** near-sighted, thoughtless **12** narrow-minded, short-sighted **13** ill-considered, unadventurous, uncircumspect, unimaginative

myriad
03 sea **04** army, host **05** flood, horde, swarm, toman **06** scores, throng, untold **08** millions, mountain, zillions **09** boundless, countless, limitless, multitude, thousands **10** numberless **11** innumerable **12** immeasurable, incalculable **13** multitudinous

mysterious
◇ *anagram indicator*
04 dark **05** shady, weird **06** arcane, creepy, hidden, mystic, occult, secret, veiled **07** cryptic, curious, furtive, obscure, shadowy, strange **08** abstruse, baffling, esoteric, mystical, puzzling, reticent, sinister **09** enigmatic, insoluble, recondite, secretive **10** mystifying, perplexing **11** as if by magic, inscrutable **12** inexplicable, unfathomable, unsearchable **13** surreptitious

mysteriously
◇ *anagram indicator*
08 arcanely, in secret, secretly **09** curiously, magically, obscurely, strangely **10** abstrusely, mystically, puzzlingly **11** cryptically, inscrutably **12** esoterically, inexplicably **13** engimatically **15** surreptitiously

mystery
06 enigma, puzzle, riddle, secret **07** arcanum, problem, secrecy **08** mystique, question **09** ambiguity, conundrum, curiosity, obscurity, reticence, sacrament, weirdness **10** closed book **11** concealment, furtiveness, miracle play, strangeness **12** question mark **14** inscrutability **15** inexplicability, unfathomability

mystic
04 Sofi, Sufi **05** swami **07** psychic **09** occultist, spiritist **11** allegorical, esotericist **12** spiritualist **13** metaphysicist **15** supernaturalist

mystical
05 weird **06** arcane, hidden, mystic, occult **07** obscure, strange **08** abstruse, baffling, esoteric **09** recondite, spiritual **10** mysterious, paranormal **12** inexplicable, metaphysical, other-worldly, supernatural, unfathomable **13** preternatural **14** transcendental

mysticism
05 deism **06** theism **07** mystery **09** occultism, spiritism **10** arcaneness **11** esotericism **12** spirituality **14** mysteriousness **15** inexplicability, supernaturalism

mystification
03 awe, fog **04** daze **06** muddle **08** surprise **09** confusion **10** perplexity, puzzlement

11 uncertainty 12 bewilderment, stupefaction 13 disconcertion 14 disorientation

mystify

04 hoax 06 baffle, puzzle 07 confuse, perplex 08 bewilder, confound 09 bamboozle 10 take to town 13 metagrabolize, metagrobolize

mystique

03 awe 05 charm, magic, spell 06 appeal 07 glamour, mystery, romance, secrecy 08 charisma 09 adventure 11 fascination

myth

03 fib, lie 04 saga, tale 05 fable, fancy, story 06 legend 07 fallacy, fantasy, fiction, parable, untruth 08 allegory, bestiary, delusion, folk tale, pretence 09 fairy tale, invention, tall story 10 fairy story 11 fabrication 13 misconception

• **book of myths**

04 Edda 09 Elder Edda, Prose Edda 11 Younger Edda

mythical

05 put-on 06 fabled, made-up, phoney, unreal, untrue 07 fantasy, pretend 08 fabulous, fanciful, invented 09 fairytale, fantastic, imaginary, legendary, pretended 10 chimerical, fabricated, fictitious 11 make-believe, non-existent 12 mythological

Mythical creatures and spirits include:

03 elf, hob, imp, orc, roc
04 faun, fury, jinn, ogre, peri, pixy, puck, yeti
05 afrit, demon, devil, djinn, dobby, dryad, dwarf, fairy, genie, ghost, ghoul, giant, gnome, golem, harpy, kelpy, lamia, naiad, nymph, oread, pixie, satyr, shade, Siren, sylph, troll, yowie
06 afreet, bunyip, dobbie, dragon, dybbuk, Fafnir, Furies, Geryon, goblin, Gorgon, kelpie, kobald, kraken, Lilith, Medusa, merman, nereid, ogress, Scylla, selkie, Sphinx, sprite, wivern, yaksha
07 banshee, Bigfoot, brownie, Cecrops, centaur, Chimera, Cyclops, Echidna, Erinyes, gremlin, Grendel, griffin, Harpies, incubus, lorelei, mermaid, Pegasus, phoenix, sandman, taniwha, unicorn, vampire, windigo
08 basilisk, Cerberus, Gigantes, lindworm, Minotaur, seahorse, succubus, werewolf
09 Charybdis, hamadryad, hobgoblin, mermaiden, sasquatch
10 cockatrice, hippogriff, leprechaun, salamander, sea serpent, tooth fairy
11 hippocampus
15 Loch Ness monster

See also **bird**; **monster**

Mythical places include:

03 Dis, Hel
04 Hell, Styx
05 Argos, Babel, Hades, Lethe, Pluto, Thule
06 Albion, Anghar, Asgard, Avalon, Heaven, Heorot, Nedyet, Utgard
07 Acheron, Agartha, Alfheim, Alpheus, Arcadia, Bifrost, Boeotia, Elysium, Lemuria, Nirvana, Pohjola, Tuonela
08 Amazonia, Archeron, Atlantis, El Dorado, Niflheim, Paradise, Tir-na-nOg, Tlalocan, Valhalla, Vanaheim
09 Cockaigne, Fairyland, Purgatory, River Styx, Yggdrasil
10 River Lethe, Stymphalos
11 Ultima Thule
12 River Acheron, River Alpheus
13 Jewel Mountain, River Archeron, The Underworld
14 Lake Stymphalos
15 Cloudcuckooland, The Garden of Eden, The Isle of Avalon, The Tower of Babel

See also **mythology**; **river**

mythological

06 fabled, mythic 08 fabulous, mythical 09 fairytale, folkloric, legendary 10 fictitious 11 traditional

mythology

04 lore 05 myths, tales 06 legend 07 stories 08 folklore, Pantheon 09 folk tales, tradition 10 traditions

See also **god, goddess**; **fate**; **fury**; **grace**; **muse**; **mythical**; **sage**

Characters from Celtic mythology include:

03 Anu, Lug
04 Badb, Bran, Danu, Lugh, Medb, Ogma
05 Balor, Boann, Dagda, Macha, Maeve, Neman, Nuada, Oisin, Pwyll
06 Brigit, Danaan, Deidre, Imbolc, Isolde, Ogmios, Ossian
07 banshee, Beltane, Branwen, Brighid, Deirdre, Samhain, Tristan
08 Manannan, Morrigan, Rhiannon, The Dagda, Tir nan-Og
09 Bean Sidhé, Cernunnos, Conchobar
10 Cú Chulainn, Lughnasadh
11 Finn mac Cool
13 Bendigeidfran, Finn mac Cumhal
14 Bran the Blessed, Finn mac Cumhail, Tuatha dé Danaan

Characters from Greek mythology include:

02 Io
04 Ajax, Dido, Echo, Eris, Hero, Leda, Leto, Rhea
05 Atlas, Chloe, Circe, Creon, Danae, Helen, Horae, Hydra, Irene, Ixion, Jason, Kreon, Laius, Lamia, Medea, Midas, Minos, Niobe, Orion, Paris, Priam, Rheia
06 Aeneas, Aeolus, Alecto, Amazon, Atreus, Cadmus, Castor, Charon, Chiron, Cronus, Danaoi, Daphne, Dryads, Europa, Europe, Furies, Graiae, Hecabe, Hector, Hecuba, Hellen, Icarus, Iolaus, Kronos, Latona, Medusa, Megara, Memnon, Naiads, Nessus, Nestor, Nymphs, Oreads, Peleus, Pelops, Phoebe, Pollux, Python, Satyrs, Scylla, Semele, Sileni, Sirens, Stheno, Syrinx, Titans, Triton, Typhon
07 Actaeon, Alcyone, Arachne, Ariadne, Calchas, Calypso, Cecrops, Cepheus, Chimera, Cyclops, Danaans, Daphnis, Diomede, Echidna, Electra, Epigoni, Erinyes, Euryale, Galatea, Gorgons, Griffin, Gryphon, Harpies, Iapetus, Jocasta, Kekrops, Laocoon, Lapiths, Leander, Maenads, Marsyas, Nereids, Oceanus, Oedipus, Orestes, Orpheus, Pandora, Pegasus, Perseus, Phaedra, Silenus, Theseus, Titania, Troilus, Ulysses
08 Achilles, Alcestis, Alcmaeon, Anchises, Antigone, Arethusa, Atalanta, Basilisk, Centaurs, Cerberus, Chimaera, Cressida, Cyclopes, Daedalus, Diomedes, Endymion, Eteocles, Eurydice, Ganymede, Gigantes, Halcyone, Heracles, Hyperion, Iphicles, Lycurgus, Meleager, Menelaus, Minotaur, Nausicaa, Oceanids, Odysseus, Pasiphae, Penelope, Pentheus, Phaethon, Pleiades, Sarpedon, Sisyphus, Tantalus, Thyestes, Tiresias, Typhoeus
09 Aegisthus, Agamemnon, Andromeda, Argonauts, Autolycus, Cassandra, Charybdis, Deucalion, Idomeneus, Lotophagi, Mnemosyne, Myrmidons, Narcissus, Patroclus, Polynices, Pygmalion, Semiramis, Tisiphone
10 Amphitryon, Andromache, Cassiopeia, Cockatrice, Erechtheus, Hamadryads, Hesperides, Hippolytus, Iphigeneia, Polyneices, Polyphemus, Procrustes, Prometheus, Telemachus
11 Bellerophon, Lotus-eaters, Neoptolemus, Philoctetes
12 Clytemnestra, Hyperboreans, Rhadamanthus, Rhadamanthys

Characters from Maori mythology include:

04 Kupe, Maui, Rona
05 Pania
07 Hinemoa, Mahuika
09 Tutanekai

Characters from Norse mythology include:

03 Lif
06 Gudrun, Sigurd
09 Berserker
10 Lifthrasir

Characters from Roman mythology include:

05 Lamia, Lares, Manes, Remus, Sibyl
07 Danaans, Latinus, Lemures, Lucrece, Penates, Romulus, Sibylla, Tarpeia
08 Anchises, Callisto, Hercules, Lucretia, Verginia

09 Androcles
10 Coriolanus, Rhea Silvia, Rhea Sylvia

Other mythological and legendary characters include:

03 Qat
04 Tell (William)
05 Adapa, El Cid, Faust, Frost (Jack)
06 Anansi, Arthur, Bunyan (Paul), Enkidu, George (St), Godiva (Lady), Kraken, Weland
07 Aladdin, Ali Baba, Beowulf, Grendel, Wayland, Weiland, Weyland
08 Baba Yaga, Brunhild, Hang Tuah, Hiawatha, Parsifal
09 Appleseed (Johnny), Bluebeard, Lohengrin
10 Yu the Great
11 Old King Cole
12 Lemminkainen, Rip Van Winkle, Scheherazade, Will-o'-the-Wisp
14 Flying Dutchman
15 Father Christmas

See also **fate**; **fury**; **god, goddess**; **grace**; **monster**; **muse**; **sage**

N

N
02 en **08** November

nab
03 hat **04** bone, grab, head, nail, nick **05** catch, run in, seize **06** arrest, collar, nobble, pull in, snatch **07** capture, hilltop **09** apprehend **10** projection, promontory

nabob
03 VIP **05** celeb, nawab **06** bigwig, tycoon **07** magnate **08** luminary **09** celebrity, financier, personage **11** billionaire, millionaire

nadir
04 zero **06** bottom, depths **07** minimum **08** low point **10** all-time low, rock bottom **11** lowest point **12** low-watermark

nag
03 bug, rip, tit, vex **04** carp, hack, jade, moan, moke, plug, yaff **05** annoy, harry, horse, scold, tease, worry **06** badger, berate, bother, grouse, harass, hassle, keep at, keffel, niggle, pester, pick on, plague, rouncy **07** earbash, henpeck, torment, trouble, upbraid **08** complain, ding-dong, irritate, keep on at **09** aggravate, Rosinante, Rozinante

nagging
06 aching **07** moaning, painful **08** critical, niggling, scolding, shrewish, worrying **09** upsetting **10** continuous, irritating, nit-picking, persistent, tormenting **11** distressing

nail
03 fix, nab, pin, toe **04** brad, brod, claw, grab, join, nick, stub, stud, tack, trap **05** catch, clout, rivet, screw, seize, spick, spike, sprig, talon **06** arrest, attach, collar, corner, detect, expose, fasten, hammer, nipper, nobble, pierce, pincer, reveal, secure, skewer, snatch, tingle, unguis, unmask **07** capture, clinker, pin down, toenail, uncover, unearth **08** fastener, holdfast, identify, panel pin, sparable **09** apprehend **10** fingernail, tenterhook

• hit the nail on the head
10 be accurate **14** be exactly right, score a bull's eye

naïve
04 naif, open **05** frank, green **06** candid, jejune, simple **07** artless, natural **08** gullible, immature, innocent, trusting, wide-eyed **09** childlike, credulous, guileless, ingenuous, primitive, simpliste, small-town, unworldly **10** simplistic, unaffected **11** unrealistic **12** having no idea, pollyannaish, unsuspecting, unsuspicious **13** born yesterday, inexperienced, unpretentious **14** bread-and-butter **15** unsophisticated

naively
06 simply **08** gullibly **09** artlessly, naturally **10** immaturely, innocently **11** guilelessly, ingenuously **14** simplistically, unsuspiciously

naivety
08 openness **09** credulity, frankness, innocence **10** candidness, immaturity, simplicity **11** artlessness, gullibility, naturalness **12** inexperience **13** childlikeness, guilelessness, ingenuousness

naked
03 raw **04** bald, bare, nude, open, weak **05** overt, plain, stark **06** Adamic, barren, patent, simple **07** artless, blatant, denuded, evident, exposed, glaring, skyclad, unarmed **08** Adamical, disrobed, flagrant, helpless, in the raw, starkers, stripped, treeless, undraped **09** au naturel, grassless, in the buff, in the scud, powerless, unadorned, unclothed, uncovered, undressed, unguarded **10** stark-naked, start-naked, unprovided, vulnerable **11** defenceless, mother-naked, unconcealed, undisguised, unprotected, unqualified, unvarnished **12** not a stitch on **13** with nothing on **15** in the altogether

nakedness
06 nature, nudity **07** the buff, undress **08** baldness, bareness, openness **09** plainness, starkness **10** barrenness, simplicity **13** the altogether

namby-pamby
03 wet **04** prim, weak **05** cissy, soppy, vapid, weedy, wussy **06** feeble, prissy **07** anaemic, insipid, maudlin, mawkish, wimpish **09** spineless, white-shoe **10** colourless, wishy-washy **11** sentimental **12** pretty-pretty

name
01 n **03** dub, nom, tag, VIP **04** call, cite, clan, fame, hero, nemn, note, noun, pick, star, term **05** celeb, label, state, style, title, utter **06** behalf, bigwig, choose, esteem, expert, family, famous, handle, honour, renown, repute, select **07** appoint, baptize, big name, entitle, epithet, mention, specify **08** big noise, christen, classify, cognomen, eminence, identify, luminary, monicker, nominate, prestige, somebody, standing **09** authority, celebrity, character, designate, dignitary, well-known **10** commission, denominate, give name to, popularity, prominence, reputation **11** appellation, designation, distinction **12** denomination, leading light

Names include:

03 pen, pet
04 code, full, last
05 alias, brand, false, first, given, place, stage
06 anonym, eponym, exonym, family, maiden, middle, proper, second
07 agnomen, allonym, assumed, autonym, surname, toponym
08 nickname
09 baptismal, Christian, cryptonym, pseudonym, sobriquet, trademark
10 diminutive, nom de plume, soubriquet
11 nom de guerre

See also **boy**; **cinema**; **French**; **German**; **girl**; **Irish**; **public house**; **Scottish**; **Welsh**

• in name only
07 titular

• list of names
04 roll

• name unknown
02 NU

named
03 dit, hot **04** hote **05** cited, nempt **06** called, chosen, dubbed, picked, styled, termed, titled **07** known as **08** baptized, entitled, labelled, selected **09** appointed, mentioned, nominated, specified **10** christened, classified, designated, identified, singled out **11** by the name of, denominated **12** commissioned

nameless
07 obscure, unknown, unnamed **08** untitled **09** anonymous, titleless, unheard-of **10** innominate, unlabelled **11** unspeakable, unspecified, unutterable **12** illegitimate, undesignated, unidentified **13** indescribable, inexpressible, unmentionable **15** undistinguished

namely
02 ie, sc **03** viz **04** scil, sciz **05** to wit **06** famous, that is **08** scilicet **09** videlicet **10** especially **11** that is to say **12** in other words, specifically

Namibia
03 NAM

nanny
03 nan, pet **04** amah, ayah, baby, nana **05** nanna, nurse, spoil **06** au pair, coddle, cosset, mother, pamper **07** indulge, she-goat **08** pander to, wet-nurse **09** governess, nursemaid, spoon-feed **11** childminder, grandmother, mollycoddle, mother's help, overprotect

nanosecond
02 ns

nap
03 kip, nod, ziz **04** down, doze, fuzz, oose, ooze, pile, rest, shag, zizz **05** fibre, grain, seize, sleep, steal, weave **06** catnap, nod off, siesta, snooze **07** bedding, bedroll, doze off, drop off, lie down, lie-down, surface, texture **08** meridian, napoleon **09** downiness **10** forty winks, light sleep **12** sleep lightly **14** get some shut-eye, have forty winks

napkin
05 doily, doyly, nappy **06** doyley **09** muckender, serviette **12** handkerchief

nappy
04 oosy, oozy **05** downy, heady, jumpy, terry, tipsy, towel **06** diaper, frothy, hippen, hippin, napkin, shaggy, strong **07** hipping, nervous **09** excitable, serviette **10** disposable

narcissism
06 vanity **07** conceit, egotism **08** egomania, self-love **10** self-regard **11** self-conceit **13** egocentricity, self-obsession **15** self-centredness

narcissistic
04 vain **09** conceited, egotistic **10** egocentric, self-loving **11** egomaniacal, self-centred **12** self-absorbed, self-obsessed

narcotic
03 hop **04** dopy, drug **05** dopey, upper **06** downer, opiate **07** anodyne, calming, dulling, numbing **08** hypnotic, sedative **09** analgesic, somnolent, soporific **10** painkiller, palliative, stupefying **11** anaesthetic, pain-dulling, painkilling **12** sleeping pill, stupefacient **13** sleep-inducing, tranquillizer **14** tranquillizing

Narcotics include:

03 ava
04 bang, benj, coca, dope, kava
05 bhang, dagga
06 charas, datura, pituri
07 churrus, narceen
08 narceine
10 belladonna
11 Indian berry, laurel-water
15 cocculus indicus

See also **drug**

• **packet of narcotic**
04 deck

narked
05 irked, riled, vexed **06** bugged, galled, miffed, peeved, piqued **07** annoyed, in a huff, nettled **08** bothered, in a paddy, provoked **09** irritated **10** brassed off, cheesed off, got the hump **11** exasperated

narrate
◇ *homophone indicator*
04 read, tell **05** state **06** detail, recite, record, relate, report, set out, unfold **07** explain, portray, recount **08** describe, rehearse, set forth **09** chronicle

narration
04 tale **05** story **06** detail, report, sketch **07** account, history, reading, recital, telling **09** chronicle, portrayal, recountal, rehearsal, statement, voice-over **11** description, explanation **12** storytelling

narrative
04 saga, tale **05** fable, novel, prose, récit, story **06** detail, report, sketch **07** account, history, process, reading, romance **08** allegory, anecdote, periplus, relation **09** chronicle, portrayal, statement **10** short story **11** description

narrator
06 author, writer **07** relater, relator, sagaman **08** annalist, reporter **09** describer, raconteur, recounter **10** anecdotist, chronicler, tale-teller **11** commentator, storyteller **12** mythographer

narrow
03 set **04** fine, keen, slim, thin, true **05** close, cramp, exact, limit, petty, rigid, scant, small, spare, taper, tight **06** biased, meagre, reduce, strait, strict **07** bigoted, confine, cramped, insular, limited, literal, precise, slender, tighten **08** confined, contract, detailed, diminish, dogmatic, exiguous, original, restrict, simplify, squeezed, straiten, tapering, thorough **09** attenuate, coarctate, constrict, hidebound, illiberal **10** attenuated, contracted, intolerant, prejudiced, restricted **11** close-minded, constricted, incapacious, reactionary, small-minded, strait-laced **12** circumscribe, conservative, incommodious, narrow-minded, parsimonious **13** circumscribed, dyed-in-the-wool

narrowing
06 intake **08** stenosis, tapering, thinning **09** gathering, reduction, reductive **10** emaciation, rebatement **11** attenuation, compression, contraction, curtailment **12** constipation, constriction

narrowly
04 fine, just, near **06** barely, strait **07** closely, exactly **08** only just, scarcely, straitly, strictly **09** carefully, precisely **10** by a whisker **11** attentively **12** by a short head **13** painstakingly **14** scrutinizingly

narrow-minded
03 set **05** borné, petty, rigid **06** biased, warped **07** bigoted, diehard, insular, redneck, twisted **08** blimpish, verkramp **09** claustral, exclusive, hidebound, illiberal, jaundiced, parochial **10** entrenched, inflexible, intolerant, prejudiced, provincial **11** close-minded, opinionated, petty-minded, reactionary, small-minded, strait-laced **12** conservative, unreasonable **13** dyed in the wool

narrow-mindedness
04 bias **07** bigotry **08** rigidity **09** prejudice **12** parochialism **13** exclusiveness, inflexibility **15** close-mindedness, petty-mindedness, small-mindedness

narrowness
04 bias **07** bigotry **08** nearness, rigidity, thinness **09** closeness, pettiness, prejudice, tightness **10** insularity, limitation, meagreness **11** attenuation, intolerance, slenderness **12** conservatism, constriction, parochialism **13** exclusiveness, provincialism **14** restrictedness **15** small-mindedness

narrows
05 sound **07** channel, passage, straits **08** waterway

nascent
05 young **06** rising **07** budding, growing **08** evolving, naissant **09** advancing, beginning, embryonic, incipient **10** burgeoning, developing

nastily
◇ *anagram indicator*
11 obnoxiously, offensively, repulsively **12** disagreeably, disgustingly, unpleasantly **13** objectionably

nastiness
04 porn **05** filth, spite **06** malice **07** squalor **08** foulness, impurity, meanness **09** dirtiness, indecency, obscenity, pollution **10** defilement, filthiness, smuttiness **11** malevolence, pornography, viciousness **12** horribleness, spitefulness **13** offensiveness, repulsiveness, uncleanliness, unsavouriness **14** unpleasantness

nasty
◇ *anagram indicator*
03 wet **04** blue, foul, good, mean, rank, sore, vile, wild **05** awful, crook, cruel, dirty, dodgy, foggy, grave, mucky, rainy, ribby, rough, yucky **06** filthy, grotty, horrid, lovely, odious, ribald, smutty, stormy, tricky, unkind **07** awkward, hateful, noisome, obscene, serious, squalid, vicious **08** alarming, annoying, critical, delicate, horrible, indecent, nauseous, polluted, spiteful, ticklish, worrying **09** dangerous, difficult, loathsome, malicious, obnoxious, offensive, repellent,

repugnant, repulsive, revolting, sickening **10** disgusting, ill-natured, malevolent, malodorous, unpleasant **11** bad-tempered, disquieting, distasteful, threatening **12** disagreeable, exasperating, pornographic **13** objectionable

nation
04 folk, land, race, volk **05** realm, state, tribe **06** people, public, vassal **07** country, kingdom, society **08** republic **09** community **10** population

See also **Africa**; **America**; **Asia**; **country**; **Europe**

national
01 N **03** Nat **05** civic, civil, state **06** native, public, social **07** citizen, federal, general, subject **08** domestic, internal, resident **10** inhabitant, nationwide, widespread **11** countrywide **12** governmental **13** comprehensive

See also **park**

nationalism
07 loyalty **08** jingoism **10** allegiance, chauvinism, patriotism, xenophobia

nationalist
01 N **03** Nat **07** patriot **08** jingoist, loyalist **09** flag-waver, xenophobe **10** chauvinist

nationalistic
05 loyal **09** patriotic **10** jingoistic, xenophobic **12** chauvinistic **13** ethnocentrist

nationality
04 clan, race **05** birth, tribe **06** nation **11** citizenship, ethnic group

Nationalities include:

03 Lao
04 Kiwi, Thai
05 Bajan, Congo, Cuban, Czech, Dutch, Greek, Iraqi, Irish, Omani, Saudi, Swazi, Swiss, Tajik, Uzbek, Welsh
06 Afghan, Danish, Fijian, French, German, Indian, Kenyan, Kyrgyz, Libyan, Malian, Polish, Qatari, Samoan, Somali, Syrian, Tongan, Yapese, Yemeni
07 Angolan, Basotho, Belgian, Bosnian, British, Burmese, Chadian, Chilean, Chinese, Comoran, Cypriot, Emirati, English, Finnish, Gambian, Guinean, Haitian, Iranian, Israeli, Italian, Ivorian, Kosraen, Kuwaiti, Laotian, Latvian, Maltese, Mexican, Monacan, Mosotho, Nauruan, Palauan, Russian, Rwandan, Sahrawi, Serbian, Spanish, Swedish, Tadzhik, Turkish, Turkmen, Ugandan, Zambian
08 Albanian, Algerian, American, Andorran, Antiguan, Armenian, Austrian, Bahamian, Bahraini, Barbudan, Batswana, Belizean, Beninese, Bolivian, Bruneian, Canadian, Chuukese, Croatian, Egyptian, Eritrean, Estonian, Filipina, Filipino, Gabonese, Georgian, Ghanaian, Grenadan, Guyanese, Honduran, Jamaican, Japanese, Lebanese, Liberian, Malagasy, Malawian, Moldovan, Moroccan, Motswana, Namibian, Nepalese, Nevisian, Nigerian, Nigerien, Peruvian, Romanian, Sahraoui, Scottish, St Lucian, Sudanese, Timorese, Togolese, Tunisian, Tuvaluan
09 Argentine, Barbadian, Bhutanese, Brazilian, Bulgarian, Burkinabé, Burundian, Cambodian, Colombian, Congolese, Dominican, Ethiopian, Grenadian, Hungarian, Icelandic, I-Kiribati, Jordanian, Kittitian, Malaysian, Maldivian, Mauritian, Mongolian, Ni-Vanuatu, Norwegian, Pakistani, Pohnpeian, Sahrawian, Santoméan, São Toméan, Singapore, Slovakian, Slovenian, Sri Lankan, Taiwanese, Tanzanian, Ukrainian, Uruguayan
10 Australian, Belarusian, Costa Rican, Djiboutian, Ecuadorean, Ecuadorian, Guatemalan, Indonesian, Lithuanian, Luxembourg, Macedonian, Monégasque, Mozambican, Myanmarese, New Zealand, Nicaraguan, Panamanian, Paraguayan, Philippine, Portuguese, Sahraouian, Salvadoran, Senegalese, Surinamese, Tobagonian, Venezuelan, Vietnamese, Vincentian, Zimbabwean
11 Argentinian, Azerbaijani, Bangladeshi, Cameroonian, Cape Verdean, Kazakhstani, Marshallese, Mauritanian, Micronesian, Montenegrin, North Korean, Sammarinese, Seychellois, Singaporean, South Korean, Tajikistani, Trinidadian
12 Luxembourger, Saudi Arabian, South African, St Vincentian
13 Equatoguinean, Herzegovinian, Liechtenstein, Sierra Leonean
14 Central African, Guinea-Bissauan
15 Liechtensteiner, Papua New Guinean, Solomon Islander

nationally
09 generally **10** nationwide **11** countrywide **15** comprehensively

National Trust
02 NT

nationwide
05 state **07** general, overall **08** national **09** extensive **10** widespread **11** countrywide **12** coast-to-coast **13** comprehensive

native
03 nat, son **04** home **05** local, natal **06** inborn, inbred, innate, mother, oyster **07** built-in, citizen, connate, dweller, genuine, natural **08** domestic, home-born, home-bred, indigene, inherent, national, original, resident **09** aborigine, home-grown, ingrained, inherited, intrinsic, intuitive **10** aboriginal, autochthon, congenital, hereditary, indigenous, inhabitant, vernacular **11** instinctive **13** autochthonous, tangata whenua **15** unsophisticated

See also **African**; **American**; **Asian**; **European**

nativity
04 putz **05** birth **06** jataka **08** delivery **09** horoscope **10** childbirth **11** parturition

NATO

NATO members:

02 UK
03 USA
05 Italy, Spain
06 Canada, France, Greece, Latvia, Norway, Poland, Turkey
07 Belgium, Denmark, Estonia, Germany, Hungary, Iceland, Romania
08 Bulgaria, Portugal, Slovakia, Slovenia
09 Lithuania
10 Luxembourg
13 Czech Republic, United Kingdom
14 The Netherlands
21 United States of America

• **NATO phonetic alphabet** *see* **alphabet**

natron
04 urao

natter
03 gab, jaw **04** chat, talk **06** confab, gabble, gossip, jabber, rabbit, witter **07** blather, blether, chatter, chinwag, prattle **08** chit-chat, rabbit on **10** chew the fat **11** confabulate **12** conversation **14** shoot the breeze

nattily
06 neatly **07** smartly **09** elegantly, stylishly **11** fashionably

natty
04 chic, deft, neat, trim **05** ritzy, smart **06** clever, dapper, snazzy, spruce, swanky **07** elegant, stylish, varment, varmint **09** ingenious **11** fashionable, well-dressed

natural
03 nat, raw **04** open, pure, real **05** frank, idiot, plain, usual, whole **06** candid, common, inborn, inbred, innate, kindly, native, normal, physic, simple, virgin **07** artless, built-in, connate, genuine, organic, regular, relaxed, routine, sincere, typical, unmixed **08** everyday, inherent, lifelike, ordinary, standard, unforced **09** authentic, certainty, guileless, ingenuous, ingrained, inherited, intuitive, unrefined, unstudied **10** congenital, indigenous, unaffected, unlaboured, unstrained **11** instinctive, spontaneous, unprocessed **12** additive-free, chemical-free, illegitimate, run-of-the-mill,

unregenerate **13** unpretentious **15** unsophisticated

See also **fool**

• natural order

02 NO

naturalist

08 botanist **09** biologist, Darwinist, ecologist, zoologist **11** creationist **12** evolutionist **13** life scientist **14** plant scientist

See also **biology**

naturalistic

07 factual, graphic, natural **08** lifelike, real-life **09** realistic **10** true-to-life **12** photographic

naturalize

05 adapt, adopt **06** accept **08** accustom **09** acclimate, endenizen, habituate, introduce **10** assimilate **11** acclimatize, acculturate, domesticate, enfranchise, familiarize, incorporate, nationalize

naturally

05 natch **06** simply **07** clearly, frankly **08** candidly, normally, of course **09** artlessly, certainly, genuinely, logically, obviously, sincerely, typically **10** absolutely **11** ingenuously, simpliciter **13** instinctively, spontaneously

naturalness

04 ease **06** purity **07** realism **08** openness, pureness **09** frankness, plainness, sincerity, wholeness **10** candidness, simpleness, simplicity **11** artlessness, genuineness, informality, spontaneity **13** ingenuousness **14** unaffectedness **15** spontaneousness

nature

04 Gaia, kind, mood, sort, type **05** being, class, earth, stamp, style, world **06** cosmos, humour, make-up, temper **07** country, essence, outlook, quality, scenery, species, variety **08** category, creation, features, identity, universe **09** character, chemistry, landscape, nakedness **10** attributes, complexion, kindliness **11** countryside, description, disposition, environment, mother earth, personality, temperament **12** constitution, mother nature **14** characteristic, natural history **15** characteristics

• according to nature

02 sn

• of nature

04 akin

naught

01 O **03** bad, ill, nil **04** evil, nowt, zero **05** zilch **06** cipher, cypher, foiled, nought, ruined **07** hurtful, immoral, nothing, sweet FA **09** worthless **10** wickedness **11** nothingness **15** sweet Fanny Adams

naughtily

06 lewdly **07** bawdily **08** coarsely, vulgarly **09** defiantly, obscenely, playfully, waywardly **10** indecently, perversely **12** badly behaved **13** disobediently, mischievously

naughtiness

08 defiance, lewdness, mischief **09** bawdiness, indecency, obscenity, vulgarity **10** coarseness, smuttiness **11** playfulness, waywardness **12** bad behaviour, disobedience, misbehaviour

naughty

◇ *anagram indicator*

03 bad **04** blue, bold, lewd **05** bawdy **06** coarse, ribald, risqué, smutty, unruly, vulgar, wicked **07** defiant, obscene, playful, roguish, wayward **08** indecent, perverse **09** off-colour, worthless **10** refractory **11** disobedient, misbehaving, mischievous, titillating **12** badly behaved, exasperating, incorrigible **13** undisciplined

Nauru

03 NAU, NRU

nausea

06 hatred, puking, wamble **07** disgust, gagging **08** aversion, distaste, loathing, retching, sickness, vomiting **09** revulsion **10** queasiness, repugnance, throwing up **11** airsickness, biliousness, carsickness, detestation, seasickness **12** sick headache **14** motion sickness, travel sickness **15** morning sickness

nauseate

04 turn **05** repel **06** loathe, offend, revolt, sicken **07** disgust, scunner, turn off **08** gross out, make sick **14** turn the stomach **15** turn your stomach

nauseating

06 odious **08** nauseous **09** abhorrent, loathsome, offensive, repellent, repugnant, repulsive, revolting, sickening **10** chunderous, detestable, disgusting **11** distasteful **14** stomach-turning **15** stomach-churning

nauseous

03 ill **04** puky, sick **05** nasty, pukey **06** queasy **07** airsick, carsick, seasick **09** loathsome, nauseated **10** disgusting, travel sick **14** about to throw up **15** under the weather

nautical

05 naval **07** boating, oceanic, sailing **08** maritime, seagoing, yachting **09** seafaring

naval

03 nav, sea **06** marine **08** maritime, nautical, seagoing **09** seafaring

navel

03 hub **06** centre, middle **07** nombril **08** omphalos **09** umbilicus **11** belly-button, tummy-button

navigable

03 nav **04** open **05** clear **08** passable, sailable **09** crossable, dirigible, unblocked **10** negotiable, voyageable **11** traversable **12** surmountable, unobstructed

navigate

04 helm, plan, plot, sail **05** cross, drive, guide, pilot, steer **06** cruise, direct, handle, voyage **07** journey, skipper **09** manoeuvre, negotiate **11** plan a course

navigation

03 nav **05** canal **06** voyage **07** guiding, nautics, sailing **08** cruising, guidance, pilotage, piloting, seacraft, steering, voyaging **09** directing, direction **10** seamanship **11** manoeuvring **12** helmsmanship **13** contact flight

Navigational aids and systems include:

03 gee, GPS, INS, log, Vor
05 chart, loran, pilot, radar
07 compass, navarho, sextant
08 bell buoy, dividers, VHF radio
09 lightship, omnirange
10 depth gauge, lighthouse, marker buoy
11 chronometer, conical buoy, echo-sounder, gyrocompass
13 nautical table, parallel ruler
15 astronavigation, flux-gate compass, magnetic compass

navigator

03 nav **05** navvy, pilot **06** master, sailor, seaman **07** mariner **08** helmsman **09** steersman

navvy

06 digger, ganger, worker **07** workman **08** labourer **09** navigator **12** manual worker **14** common labourer

navy

01 N **02** RN **03** RAN **05** fleet, ships **06** armada **08** flotilla, warships **10** naval fleet, naval force **12** merchant navy **15** merchant service

See also **rank**

nay

02 no **03** nae **06** denial, indeed, in fact **07** in truth **08** actually, not at all, or rather **09** not really **11** of course not **12** certainly not **13** absolutely not, in point of fact

near

02 by, nr, ny, to **03** nie, nye **04** akin, come, dear, inby, left, like, nigh **05** alike, close, ewest, forby, handy, inbye, local **06** almost, at hand, beside, come by, coming, nearby, nearly, next to, stingy **07** cling to, close by, closely, close to, looming, related, similar **08** adjacent, approach, familiar, imminent, intimate, left-hand, narrowly **09** adjoining, alongside, bordering, close in on, immediate, impending, proximate, thriftily **10** accessible, adjacent to, close-range, come closer, come nearer, comparable, contiguous, convenient, draw near to, not far away **11** approaching, bordering on, come towards, forthcoming, get closer to, in the offing, move towards, surrounding, within cooee, within range, within reach **12** contiguous to, draw nearer to, neighbouring, parsimonious

13 corresponding, within reach of 14 advance towards, closely related, parsimoniously 15 at close quarters

• draw near

04 come

• near thing

08 near miss 09 close call 10 close shave 11 nasty moment 12 narrow escape, narrow squeak

nearby

04 near 05 close, handy 06 beside 07 close by 08 adjacent 09 adjoining 10 accessible, convenient, not far away 11 close at hand, within cooee, within reach 12 neighbouring 13 in the vicinity 14 on your doorstep 15 at close quarters

nearly

◇ *deletion indicator*

◇ *tail deletion indicator*

02 ny 03 e'en, nie, nye 04 even, nigh 05 about, close 06 all but, almost, feckly, nigh on 07 closely, close on, close to, roughly 08 à peu près, as good as, nigh-hand, well-nigh 09 just about, verging on, virtually 10 intimately, more or less 11 practically 13 approximately 14 parsimoniously, scrutinizingly 15 close but no cigar

nearness

06 degree 08 affinity, dearness, intimacy, vicinity 09 closeness, handiness, immediacy, imminence, proximity 10 chumminess, contiguity 11 familiarity, propinquity 12 availability, neighborhood 13 accessibility, appropinquity, neighbourhood

near-sighted

06 myopic 08 purblind 09 half-blind 12 short-sighted

neat

02 ox 03 apt, cow, net 04 bull, cool, deft, dink, feat, good, mega, nett, nice, oxen, pure, smug, snod, tidy, tosh, trig, trim 05 clean, clear, crisp, dinky, genty, great, handy, jemmy, jimpy, natty, nifty, short, slick, smart, super, tight 06 adroit, cattle, clever, dainty, dapper, donsie, expert, nimble, pretty, simple, spruce, superb, wicked 07 band-box, cleanly, compact, elegant, featous, ordered, orderly, shining, skilful, unmixed 08 clean-cut, fabulous, feateous, featuous, finished, sensible, smashing, straight, terrific, well-made 09 admirable, dexterous, effective, efficient, excellent, fantastic, ingenious, organized, practised, shipshape, undiluted, wonderful 10 convenient, marvellous, tremendous 11 well-groomed, well-ordered 12 spick-and-span, undiminished, user-friendly, well-designed 13 unadulterated, well-organized 15 in apple-pie order

neaten

◇ *anagram indicator*

04 edge, prim, tidy, trim 05 clean, groom 06 tidy up 07 arrange, clean up, smarten 08 round off, spruce up 09 smarten up 10 square away, straighten 11 put to rights

neatly

04 jimp 05 aptly 06 deftly, fairly, featly, jimply, nicely, nimbly, tidily 07 adeptly, agilely, handily, smartly 08 adroitly, cleverly, daintily, expertly, prettily, sprucely 09 elegantly, precisely, skilfully, stylishly 10 accurately, feateously, gracefully 11 dexterously, efficiently 12 conveniently, effortlessly, methodically 14 systematically

neatness

05 grace, skill, style 06 nicety 07 agility, aptness 08 accuracy, deftness, elegance, niceness, tidiness, trimness 09 adeptness, dexterity, handiness, jemminess, precision, smartness 10 adroitness, cleverness, daintiness, efficiency, expertness, nimbleness, spruceness 11 orderliness, preciseness, skilfulness, stylishness 12 gracefulness, straightness 14 methodicalness

Nebraska

02 NE 04 Nebr

nebulous

03 dim 04 hazy 05 fuzzy, misty, vague 06 cloudy 07 obscure, shadowy, unclear 08 abstract, confused, formless, unformed 09 ambiguous, amorphous, imprecise, shapeless, uncertain 10 indefinite, indistinct 13 indeterminate

necessarily

04 thus 06 needly 08 no remedy, obligate, of course, perforce 09 certainly, naturally, therefore 10 inevitably, inexorably, willy-nilly 11 accordingly, ineluctably, inescapably, of necessity, unavoidably 12 by definition, compulsorily, consequently, nolens volens 13 automatically, axiomatically, indispensably

necessary

04 sure 05 money, needy, vital 06 needed, toilet 07 certain, crucial, needful 08 enforced, required 09 de rigueur, essential, mandatory, requisite 10 compulsory, imperative, inevitable, inexorable, obligatory 11 ineluctable, inescapable, predestined, unavoidable 13 indispensable

necessitate

04 mean, need, take 05 exact, force 06 compel, demand, entail, oblige 07 call for, involve, require 09 constrain 13 make necessary

necessity

04 fate, must, need, want 06 ananke, demand, mister, need-be, penury 07 destiny, poverty 08 exigence, exigency, extremes, hardship 09 certainty, emergency, essential, indigence, privation, requisite 10 compulsion, obligation, sine qua non 11 deprivation, desideratum, destitution, fundamental, needfulness, requirement 12 prerequisite 13 indispensable, inevitability, inexorability 14 inescapability

• of necessity

05 needs 08 no remedy, perforce 09 certainly 10 inevitably, inexorably 11 inescapably, unavoidably 12 by definition, compulsorily 13 automatically, indispensably

neck

03 col, pet 04 crag, kiss, nape, snog 05 drink, halse, hause, hawse, scrag 06 caress, cervix, scruff, smooch 08 audacity, canoodle 09 impudence

• neck and neck

04 even 05 drawn, equal, level 06 on a par 07 aligned, uniform 08 balanced, matching 10 nip and tuck, side by side 12 level pegging

necklace

04 band, torc 05 beads, chain 06 choker, corals, gorget, jewels, locket, pearls, string, torque 07 negligé, pendant, rivière, sautoir 08 carcanet, negligee 10 lavallière 11 mangalsutra

necromancer

05 witch 06 wizard 07 diviner, warlock 08 conjurer, magician, sorcerer 09 sorceress, spiritist 11 thaumaturge 12 spiritualist 13 thaumaturgist

necromancy

05 magic 06 hoodoo, voodoo 07 sorcery 08 black art, witchery, wizardry 09 spiritism 10 black magic, demonology, divination, nigromancy, witchcraft 11 conjuration, enchantment, thaumaturgy 12 spiritualism 13 magical powers, wonder-working

necropolis

08 cemetery, God's acre 09 graveyard 10 burial site, churchyard 11 burial place 12 burial ground, charnel house

need

04 call, lack, miss, must, want, wish 05 crave 06 besoin, demand, desire, egence, egency, have to, mister, rely on 07 call for, pine for, poverty, require 08 depend on, exigency, occasion, shortage, yearn for 09 cry out for, essential, necessity, neediness, requisite 10 have need of, inadequacy, obligation 11 be obliged to, be reliant on, desideratum, necessitate, requirement 12 prerequisite 13 be compelled to, be dependent on, insufficiency, justification 14 be desperate for 15 have occasion for

• in need

04 poor 05 needy 06 hard up 08 deprived, dirt-poor, indigent 09 destitute, penniless, penurious 11 impecunious 12 impoverished 13 disadvantaged 14 on the breadline 15 poverty-stricken, underprivileged

needed
06 wanted **07** desired, lacking **08** required **09** called for, essential, necessary, requisite **10** compulsory, obligatory

needful
05 needy, vital **06** needed **08** required **09** essential, necessary, requisite **10** stipulated **13** indispensable

needle
03 bug, irk, nag, nib, pin, sew **04** bait, barb, gall, goad, hand, hype, hypo, miff, nark, prod, rile, spud, spur **05** annoy, arrow, briar, get at, point, prick, quill, sharp, spike, spine, sting, taunt, thorn **06** bodkin, darner, enmity, harass, heckle, marker, nettle, niggle, pester, pierce, ruffle, stylus, thread, wind up **07** bramble, bristle, dislike, obelisk, pointer, prickle, provoke, spicule, syringe, torment **08** drive mad, dry-point, irritate, splinter **09** aggravate, indicator, penetrate **10** drive crazy **11** microneedle **12** drive bananas **13** darning-needle, make sparks fly, packing-needle **14** drive up the wall, knitting needle

needless
06 luxury **07** useless **08** unwanted **09** pointless, redundant, undesired **10** expendable, gratuitous **11** dispensable, purposeless, superfluous, uncalled-for, unnecessary

• **needless to say**
06 surely **07** no doubt **08** of course **09** certainly, naturally **10** by all means, definitely **11** doubtlessly, indubitably, undoubtedly **13** without a doubt

needlessly
09 uselessly **11** dispensably, pointlessly, redundantly **13** superfluously, unnecessarily

needlework
06 sewing **07** tatting **08** tapestry, woolwork **09** drawn work, fancywork, hemstitch, patchwork, piqué work, plainwork, stitching, white seam **10** crocheting, embroidery **11** cross-stitch, needlepoint, seamstressy, stitchcraft, worsted-work **12** saddle stitch

needy
04 poor **06** hard up, in need, strait **07** needful, wanting **08** deprived, dirt-poor, indigent **09** destitute, necessary, penniless, penurious **11** impecunious **12** impoverished **13** disadvantaged **14** on the breadline **15** poverty-stricken, underprivileged

ne'er-do-well
04 spiv **05** idler **06** dodger, dosser, loafer, skelum, skiver, waster **07** bludger, goof-off, lounger, shirker, skellum, slacker, wastrel **08** layabout, schellum **09** do-nothing **10** black sheep **14** good-for-nothing

nefarious
04 base, evil, foul, vile **06** odious, sinful, unholy, wicked **07** heinous, satanic, vicious **08** criminal, depraved, dreadful, horrible, infamous, infernal, shameful, terrible **09** atrocious, execrable, loathsome, monstrous **10** abominable, detestable, horrendous, iniquitous, outrageous, villainous **11** opprobrious

negate
04 deny, undo, void **05** annul, quash **06** cancel, oppose, refute, reject, repeal, revoke, squash **07** explode, gainsay, nullify, rescind, retract, reverse, wipe out **08** abrogate, disprove, renounce **09** discredit, repudiate **10** contradict, invalidate, neutralize **11** countermand

negation
04 veto **06** denial, repeal **07** inverse, reverse **08** contrary, converse, opposite **09** disavowal, rejection **10** abrogation, antithesis, disclaimer **12** cancellation, renunciation **13** contradiction, nullification **14** countermanding, neutralization

negative
03 bad, neg **04** acid, deny, veto, weak **05** minus **06** denial, gloomy **07** adverse, counter, cynical, denying, harmful, hostile, hurtful, opposed, refusal, unlucky **08** contrary, critical, opposing, opposite, refusing, saying no **09** annulling, defeatist, injurious, rejection, spineless, unhelpful, unwilling **10** censorious, dissension, dissenting, gainsaying, neutralize, nullifying, unfriendly **11** conflicting, destructive, detrimental, obstructive, pessimistic, subtractive, uncongenial, unfortunate **12** antagonistic, inauspicious, invalidating, neutralizing, unfavourable, uninterested, unpropitious **13** contradiction, laevorotatory, unco-operative **14** unconstructive, unenthusiastic **15** disadvantageous

negativity
08 cynicism **09** defeatism, pessimism **10** gloominess **12** criticalness **13** unhelpfulness, unwillingness **14** lack of interest

neglect
◇ *anagram indicator*
04 fail, omit **05** abuse, scorn, shirk, skimp, spurn **06** disuse, fail in, forget, ignore, laxity, pass by, pass up, pigeon, rebuff, slight **07** abandon, default, disdain, disobey, failure, forsake **08** ignoring, incivism, infringe, leave out, let slide, omission, overlook, spurning **09** desuetude, disregard, disrepair, mislippen, oversight, slackness **10** be lax about, culpa levis, disrespect, leave alone, misprision, negligence, remissness **11** inattention, rack and ruin, shortcoming **12** carelessness, heedlessness, indifference **13** forgetfulness **14** non-performance

neglected
◇ *anagram indicator*
04 waif **07** forlorn, run-down, squalid **08** derelict, deserted, forsaken, stranded, unheeded, untended, untilled, unweeded **09** abandoned, overgrown **10** uncared-for **11** dilapidated, disregarded, undervalued, unhusbanded **12** uncultivated, unmaintained **13** unappreciated

neglectful
03 lax **06** remiss, sloppy **08** careless, derelict, heedless, uncaring **09** forgetful, negligent, oblivious, slighting, unmindful **11** inattentive, indifferent, thoughtless **12** disregardful

négligé dress
03 mob

negligence
◇ *anagram indicator*
06 laches, laxity, slight **07** default, failure, neglect **08** omission **09** culpa lata, disregard, oversight, slackness **10** remissness, sloppiness **11** inattention, shortcoming **12** carelessness, heedlessness, inadvertence, inadvertency, indifference **13** forgetfulness **15** inattentiveness, thoughtlessness

negligent
◇ *anagram indicator*
03 lax **05** slack **06** casual, remiss, sloppy **07** cursory, offhand **08** careless, dilatory, heedless, uncaring **09** forgetful, unmindful **10** neglectful, neglecting, nonchalant **11** inattentive, indifferent, thoughtless

negligible
04 tiny **05** minor, petty, small **06** minute, paltry **07** minimal, trivial **08** trifling **09** off the map **11** neglectable, unimportant **13** imperceptible, inappreciable, insignificant

negotiable
03 neg **04** open **05** clear **08** arguable, passable **09** crossable, debatable, navigable, unblocked, undecided, unsettled **11** contestable, traversable **12** questionable, surmountable, unobstructed **14** open to question

negotiate
◇ *anagram indicator*
04 deal, pass, talk **05** agree, broke, clear, cross, float, treat **06** broker, confer, debate, fulfil, haggle, manage, parley, settle **07** arrange, bargain, consult, discuss, execute, mediate, pull off, resolve, traffic, work out **08** complete, conclude, contract, get round, pass over, surmount, transact, traverse **09** arbitrate, hammer out, intercede, intervene, thrash out **11** pass through **12** wheel and deal

negotiation
◇ *anagram indicator*
05 talks, treat **06** debate, parley, treaty **08** haggling, practice **09** diplomacy, mediation, parleying **10** bargaining,

conference, discussion, pulling-off
11 arbitration, transaction
12 hammering-out, thrashing-out

negotiator
06 broker **07** haggler **08** diplomat, mediator, parleyer **09** bargainer, go-between, moderator **10** ambassador, arbitrator **11** adjudicator, intercessor
12 intermediary **13** wheeler-dealer

neigh
04 bray **05** hinny **06** nicher, nicker, whinny **07** snicker, whicker

neighbour
03 bor **04** abut

neighbourhood
04 area, hood, part **06** locale, region
07 quarter **08** confines, district, environs, locality, precinct, presence, purlieus, vicinage, vicinity
09 community, proximity, voisinage
11 convicinity **12** surroundings

• **in the neighbourhood of**
04 near, up to **05** about, round
06 almost, around, nearby, next to
07 close to, roughly **13** approximately

neighbouring
04 near, next **05** local **06** nearby
07 nearest, vicinal **08** abutting, adjacent, next-door **09** adjoining, bordering, sistering **10** connecting, contiguous, near at hand **11** close at hand, surrounding

neighbourly
04 kind, warm **06** genial, social
07 affable, amiable, cordial, helpful
08 friendly, generous, obliging, sociable **10** hospitable **11** considerate
13 companionable

nemesis
04 fate, ruin **07** destiny **08** downfall
09 vengeance **10** punishment
11 destruction, retribution **14** just punishment

neodymium
02 Nd

neologism
07 coinage, new term, new word, novelty **09** new phrase, vogue word
10 innovation **13** new expression

neon
02 Ne

neophyte
01 L **04** tiro **06** newbie, novice, rookie
07 learner, recruit, trainee **08** beginner, newcomer **09** greenhorn, new member, noviciate, novitiate
10 apprentice, raw recruit
11 probationer

Nepal
03 NEP, NPL

nephrite
02 yu

nepotism
04 bias **10** partiality **11** favouritism
12 old school tie **13** Old Boy network
14 jobs for the boys

Neptune
08 Poseidon

neptunium
02 Np

nerd *see* **fool**

nerk *see* **fool**

nerve
03 lip **04** face, gall, grit, guts, neck, will
05 brace, cheek, force, mouth, pluck, sauce, sinew, spunk, steel **06** bottle, daring, mettle, spirit, valour, vigour
07 bolster, bravery, courage, fortify, hearten, prepare **08** audacity, boldness, chutzpah, embolden, firmness, strength, temerity
09 bowstring, brass neck, encourage, endurance, fortitude, hardihood, impudence, insolence **10** brazenness, effrontery, invigorate, resolution, strengthen **11** intrepidity, presumption
12 fearlessness, impertinence
13 determination, steadfastness
14 cool-headedness, self-confidence

Nerves include:
05 optic, ulnar, vagus
06 facial, lumbar, medial, median, radial, sacral, tibial
07 femoral, phrenic, plantar, sciatic
08 axillary, brachial, peroneal, thoracic
09 cutaneous, laryngeal, occipital, olfactory
10 splanchnic, trigeminal
11 intercostal
12 suboccipital
15 lesser occipital, spinal accessory

nerveless
04 calm, weak **05** inert, slack, timid
06 afraid, feeble, flabby **07** nervous
08 cowardly, unnerved **09** enervated, spineless **11** debilitated

nerve-racking
05 tense **06** trying **07** anxious
08 worrying **09** difficult, harrowing, maddening, stressful **10** nail-biting
11 disquieting, distressing, frightening

nerves
05 shock, worry **06** strain, stress, wobbly **07** anxiety, jitters, tension, twitter, willies **11** butterflies, fretfulness, nervousness
12 collywobbles, crise de nerfs
13 heebie-jeebies **14** nervous tension

• **get on someone's nerves**
03 bug, irk, nag, vex **04** fash, gall, rile
05 anger, annoy, tease **06** bother, harass, hassle, madden, molest, pester, plague, ruffle, wind up **07** disturb, hack off, provoke, tick off, trouble **08** brass off, irritate **09** aggravate, cheese off, displease, drive nuts **10** drive crazy, exasperate **12** drive bananas **13** make sparks fly **14** drive up the wall **15** get someone's goat, get your dander up

nervous
◇ *anagram indicator*
03 shy **04** edgy, toey **05** het up, jumpy, nappy, nervy, shaky, tense, timid **06** on edge, sinewy, strong, uneasy
07 anxious, fearful, fidgety, fretful, in a stew, jittery, keyed up, quaking, twitchy, uptight, worried, wound up
08 agitated, in a sweat, in a tizzy, neurotic, skittish, strained, timorous, vigorous **09** excitable, flustered, perturbed, screwed-up, squirrely, tremulous **10** disquieted, squirrelly
11 overwrought **12** all of a dither, apprehensive, highly-strung **13** having kittens, on tenterhooks

nervous breakdown
06 crisis **08** neurosis **10** cracking-up, depression **11** melancholia **15** mental breakdown, nervous disorder

nervously
◇ *anagram indicator*
06 edgily, on edge **07** in a stew, timidly
08 in a sweat, in a tizzy, uneasily
09 anxiously, fearfully, fretfully, twitchily **13** having kittens
14 apprehensively

nervousness
05 worry **06** strain, stress **07** anxiety, fluster, habdabs, tension, willies
08 disquiet, edginess, timidity
09 agitation **10** touchiness, uneasiness
11 stage fright **12** excitability, perturbation, restlessness, timorousness **13** heebie-jeebies, tremulousness

nervy
04 cool, edgy, high **05** het up, jumpy, shaky, tense **06** on edge, uneasy
07 anxious, fearful, fidgety, jittery, keyed up, twitchy, uptight, worried, wound up **08** agitated, impudent, neurotic, strained **09** audacious, excitable, flustered **12** apprehensive, highly-strung **13** having kittens

nescient
05 dense, thick **06** stupid, unread
07 unaware **08** backward, clueless, ignorant, untaught **09** unlearned, untrained, unwitting **10** illiterate, innumerate, uneducated, unfamiliar, uninformed, unschooled **11** ill-informed, uninitiated **12** unacquainted
13 inexperienced, unenlightened

ness
04 naze

See also **headland**

nest
03 den, mew, nid **04** aery, bike, bink, byke, cage, cote, dray, drey, eyry, lair, nide **05** aerie, ayrie, eyrie, haunt, lodge, nidus, perch, roost **06** refuge, settle, wurley **07** cabinet, hideout, retreat, shelter **08** hideaway, hive-nest, vespiary **09** bird-house, formicary, termitary **10** nesting-box
11 formicarium, hiding-place, termitarium **12** accumulation, nidification **14** breeding-ground

See also **animal**

nest egg
04 fund **05** cache, funds, store

07 deposit, reserve, savings
08 reserves 12 bottom drawer

nestle
06 cuddle, curl up, huddle, nuzzle
07 cherish, snuggle 08 cuddle up
09 snuggle up 14 huddle together

nestling
04 baby 05 chick 08 suckling, weanling 09 fledgling

net
◇ *containment indicator*
03 bag, end, get, let, nab, web 04 caul, drag, earn, gain, lace, leap, make, mesh, neat, nett, nick, pure, sean, take, toil, trap, trim 05 broad, catch, clean, clear, drift, final, raise, seine, snare, toils, total, trawl 06 bright, cobweb, collar, enmesh, lowest, obtain, pocket, pull in, rake in, sagene, tunnel 07 bring in, capture, dragnet, drop-net, ensnare, fishnet, general, lattice, netting, network, overall, realize, receive, tracery, trammel, unmixed, webbing
08 after tax, drift-net, entangle, filigree, meshwork, open work, seine net, take home, take-home, ultimate 09 inclusive, reticulum 10 accumulate, after taxes, conclusive, difficulty 11 latticework, take captive 15 after deductions

nether
03 low 05 basal, below, lower, under
06 bottom 07 beneath, hellish, Stygian
08 inferior, infernal 09 Plutonian
10 lower-level, underworld
11 underground

Netherlands
02 NL 03 NLD 04 Neth

Netherlands Antilles
02 NA 03 ANT

netherworld
03 pit 04 fire, hell 05 abyss, below, Hades, Sheol 06 Erebus, Tophet
07 Abaddon, Acheron, Gehenna, inferno 08 Tartarus 09 down there, Malebolge, perdition 10 other place, underworld 12 lower regions
13 bottomless pit 15 abode of the devil, infernal regions

nettle
03 bug, vex 04 fret, goad, miff, nark, rami, rile 05 annoy, chafe, get at, pique, ramee, ramie, sting, tease, upset
06 harass, hassle, hen-bit, needle, ruffle, urtica, wind up 07 incense, provoke, torment 08 drive mad, irritate
09 aggravate, archangel, pellitory
10 drive crazy, exasperate 12 drive bananas 13 make sparks fly
14 artillery-plant, discountenance, drive up the wall 15 yellow archangel

nettled
05 angry, cross, got at, huffy, riled, stung, vexed 06 bugged, galled, goaded, miffed, narked, peeved, piqued 07 annoyed, needled, rattled, ruffled, wound up 08 harassed, incensed, offended, provoked
09 aggrieved, driven mad, irritable, irritated 10 aggravated 11 driven crazy, exasperated 13 driven bananas
15 driven up the wall

network
03 CNN, LAN, MAN, net, PCN, WAN, web 04 fret, grid, ISDN, lace, maze, mesh, PSTN, rete 05 grill, nexus
06 matrix, plexus, sagene, system, tracks 07 complex, lattice, netting, tracery, webbing 08 channels, filigree, gridiron, meshwork, open work
09 circuitry, grapevine, labyrinth, reticulum, structure 10 Eurovision
11 arrangement, convolution, latticework 12 old school tie, organization, reticulation 13 bush telegraph, Old Boy network

neurosis
05 mania 06 phobia 08 disorder, fixation 09 deviation, obsession
10 affliction 11 abnormality, derangement, disturbance, instability
13 maladjustment 14 mental disorder

neurotic
05 manic 06 phobic 07 anxious, deviant, nervous 08 abnormal, deranged, paranoid, unstable
09 disturbed, obsessive, unhealthy
10 compulsive, hysterical, irrational
11 maladjusted, overanxious, overwrought 14 hypersensitive

neuter
01 n 03 fix, gib 04 geld, neut, spay
05 dress 06 agamic, clonal, doctor, gib-cat 07 agamous, asexual, neutral, sexless 08 caponize, castrate, conidial
09 castrated, sterilize 10 emasculate
11 monogenetic 12 intransitive

neutral
04 drab, dull, fawn, gray, grey, pale
05 beige, bland, white 06 neuter, pastel 07 anaemic, anodyne, insipid
08 detached, ordinary, unbiased
09 anonymous, impartial, objective, undecided 10 colourless, even-handed, indefinite, indistinct, non-aligned, open-minded, uninvolved
11 indifferent, inoffensive, nondescript, non-partisan, unassertive, uncommitted 12 non-combatant, non-committal, unprejudiced, unremarkable 13 disinterested, dispassionate, uninteresting
14 expressionless 15 unexceptionable

neutrality
10 detachment 11 disinterest
12 impartiality, non-alignment, unbiasedness 13 impartialness
14 non-involvement 15 non-intervention

neutralize
04 kill, undo 05 annul 06 cancel, negate, offset 07 balance, nullify
08 negative 09 cancel out, frustrate, make up for 10 counteract, invalidate
12 incapacitate 13 compensate for
14 counterbalance

Nevada
02 NV 03 Nev

never
03 not 04 nary, ne'er 05 no way 07 not ever, Tib's Eve 08 at no time, not at all, Tibb's Eve 09 St Tib's Eve 10 St Tibb's Eve 11 on no account, when pigs fly
13 not for a moment, not on your life
15 not on your nellie

never-ending
◇ *tail deletion indicator*
07 endless, eternal, non-stop
08 constant, infinite, unbroken, unending 09 boundless, incessant, limitless, permanent, perpetual, unceasing 10 continuous, persistent, relentless, unchanging, without end
11 everlasting, unremitting
12 interminable 13 uninterrupted

nevertheless
03 but, tho, yet 05 still 06 algate, anyhow, anyway, at that, even so, howe'er, though, withal 07 algates, however 08 after all 09 in any case, quand même 10 all the same, by any means, for all that, in any event, malgré tout, not but what, regardless, still and on, tout de même 11 by some means, just the same, none but what, nonetheless, still and all 13 at the same time 15 notwithstanding

new
◇ *anagram indicator*
01 N 04 mint, more, span 05 added, alien, extra, fresh, green, novel, young
06 latest, maiden, modern, modish, recent, trendy, unused, virgin, way out
07 altered, another, changed, current, further, newborn, nouveau, renewed, resumed, strange, topical, unknown, unusual 08 advanced, brand-new, creative, ignorant, improved, nouvelle, original, reformed, restored, unversed, up-to-date 09 a stranger, born-again, different, fledgling, ingenious, refreshed 10 additional, avant-garde, fledgeling, futuristic, innovative, modernized, newfangled, pioneering, present-day, redesigned, remodelled, unfamiliar 11 imaginative, regenerated, resourceful, spanking-new, ultra-modern 12 contemporary, experimental, unaccustomed, unacquainted 13 inexperienced, reinvigorated, revolutionary, state-of-the-art, supplementary, up-to-the-minute 14 ground-breaking, unconventional 15 newly discovered

New Brunswick
02 NB

newcomer
04 tiro 05 alien, pupil 06 blow-in, gryfon, newbie, novice, rookie 07 arrival, griffin, griffon, gryphon, incomer, learner, pilgrim, recruit, settler, trainee
08 beginner, colonist, freshman, intruder, jackaroo, jackeroo, jillaroo, neophyte, outsider, stranger 09 foreigner, greenhorn, immigrant 10 apprentice, new arrival, tenderfoot 11 probationer

newfangled
03 new 05 novel 06 modern, recent,

trendy **08** gimmicky **10** futuristic **11** fashionable, modernistic, ultra-modern **12** contemporary **13** state-of-the-art

Newfoundland and Labrador
02 NL

New Hampshire
02 NH

New Jersey
02 NJ

newly
◇ *anagram indicator*
04 anew, just **05** fresh **06** afresh, lately, of late **07** freshly **08** latterly, recently

New Mexico
02 NM **04** N Mex

newness
06 novity, oddity **07** novelty, recency **09** freshness **10** innovation, uniqueness **11** originality, strangeness, unusualness **13** unfamiliarity

news
03 gen, oil **04** data, dope, info, word **05** facts, story **06** advice, budget, exposé, gossip, latest, report, rumour **07** account, hearing, hearsay, lowdown, message, scandal, tidings **08** bulletin, dispatch, izvestia, newscast, news item **09** izvestiya, newsflash, speerings, speirings, statement **10** communiqué, disclosure, revelation **11** information **12** announcement, developments, intelligence, press release **13** advertisement, communication

News agencies include:

02 AP, PA
03 AAP, AFP, UPI
04 NZPA, Tass
07 Reuters
08 ITAR-Tass
15 Associated Press

• piece of news
04 item, unco

newspaper
03 rag **04** blat, post **05** blatt, daily, local, organ, paper, press, print, sheet **06** weekly **07** evening, gazette, journal, quality, tabloid, tribune **08** magazine, national, regional **09** telegraph **10** broadsheet, local paper, periodical, provincial **11** publication **12** evening paper, morning paper **13** national paper, regional paper **15** provincial paper

Newspapers and magazines include:

02 FT, GQ, Ms, OK!
03 FHM, NME, Red, She, Sun, TES, TLS, Viz
04 Best, Chat, Chic, Elle, Heat, Judy, Life, Mail, Mind, Mizz, Mojo, More!, Real, THES, Time
05 Bella, Bliss, Bunty, Hello!, Mandy, Maxim, Prima, Punch, Times, Vogue, Which?, Wired, Woman
06 Forbes, Granta, Lancet, Loaded, Mirror, Nature, The Sun, War Cry
07 Company, Esquire, Express, Fortune, Glamour, Hustler, Le Monde, Mayfair, Men Only, Newsday, Options, Playboy, Science, The Chap, The Face, The Lady, The Star, Time Out, Tribune, TV Times
08 Campaign, Die Woche, Gay Times, Guardian, Le Figaro, Newsweek, New Woman, Scotsman, The Beano, The Dandy, The Eagle, The Field, The Month, The Oldie, The Times, USA Today
09 Daily Mail, Daily Star, Ideal Home, Penthouse, Q Magazine, Red Pepper, Smash Hits, Telegraph, The Friend, The Grocer, The Herald, The Mirror, The People, The Tablet, The Tatler, Woman's Own
10 Asian Times, Daily Sport, Irish Times, Private Eye, Racing Post, Radio Times, Sunday Post, Take a Break, Vanity Fair
11 Church Times, Country Life, Daily Record, Marie Claire, Melody Maker, Morning Star, Sunday Sport, The Big Issue, The European, The Guardian, The Observer, The Universe, Woman's Realm
12 Angling Times, Cosmopolitan, Daily Express, Family Circle, Fortean Times, History Today, Mail on Sunday, New Scientist, New Statesman, Poetry Review, Sunday Mirror, The Economist, The Pink Paper, The Spectator, Time Magazine, Woman's Weekly
13 Catholic Times, Daltons Weekly, Farmers Weekly, Homes and Ideas, Horse and Hound, Just Seventeen, Mother and Baby, People's Friend, Reader's Digest, Sunday Express, The Bookseller, The Watchtower, Woman's Journal
14 Caribbean Times, Catholic Herald, Financial Times, House and Garden, Literary Review, News of the World, The Boston Globe, The Independent, The New York Post, The Sunday Times, The Times Higher, Washington Post
15 Evening Standard, Exchange and Mart, Harpers and Queen, Homes and Gardens, Sunday Telegraph, The Boston Herald, The Mail on Sunday, The New York Times

Newspaper proprietors and magnates include:

04 **King** (Cecil Harmsworth), **Ochs** (Adolph Simon), **Shah** (Eddy)
05 **Astor** (John Jacob, Lord), **Astor** (William Waldorf, Viscount), **Black** (Conrad, Lord)
06 **Aitken** (Sir Max), **Graham** (Katherine Meyer), **Hearst** (William Randolph), **Packer** (Sir Frank), **Ridder** (Bernard H, Jnr), **Walter** (John)
07 **Barclay** (Sir David), **Barclay** (Sir Frederick), **Camrose** (William Ewert Berry, Viscount), **Kemsley** (James Gomer Berry, Viscount), **Maxwell** (Robert), **Murdoch** (Rupert), **Pearson** (Sir Cyril Arthur), **Riddell** (George, Lord), **Scripps** (Edward Wyllis), **Thomson** (D C), **Thomson** (Roy, Lord)
08 **Pulitzer** (Joseph)
10 **Berlusconi** (Silvio), **Harmsworth** (Alfred, Viscount), **Harmsworth** (Harold, Viscount)
11 **Beaverbrook** (Max, Lord)

See also **journalist**

newspaperman *see* journalist

newsreader
06 anchor **07** newsman **08** reporter **09** anchorman, announcer, newswoman, presenter **10** journalist, newscaster **11** anchorwoman, commentator **13** correspondent

newsworthy
07 notable, topical, unusual **09** arresting, important **10** noteworthy, remarkable, reportable **11** interesting, significant, stimulating

newt
03 ask, eft **05** asker

New York
◇ *dialect indicator*
02 NY

New York boroughs include:

06 Queens
08 Brooklyn, The Bronx
09 Manhattan
12 Staten Island

Other districts of New York include:

04 Noho, Soho
06 Corona, Harlem, Hollis, Inwood, Nolita, Queens
07 Astoria, Chelsea, Clifton, Kips Bay, Midtown, Midwood, Tribeca
08 Brooklyn, Canarsie, East Side, El Barrio, Elmhurst, Flatbush, Flatiron, Flushing, Gramercy, Rego Park, Steinway, The Bronx, West Side
09 Briarwood, Chinatown, Flatlands, Manhattan, Ozone Park, Park Slope, Princeton, Ridgewood, The Bowery, Turtle Bay, Woodhaven, Yorkville
10 Cobble Hill, Douglaston, Greenpoint, Ground Zero, Kew Gardens, Marble Hill, Sunset Park
11 Borough Park, Central Park, Coney Island, East Village, Ellis Island, Forest Hills, Howard Beach, Little Italy, Little Korea, New Brighton, West Village
12 Alphabet City, Crown Heights, Cypress Hills, Hell's Kitchen, South Jamaica, Staten Island, Williamsburg
13 Brighton Beach, Lower East Side, Spanish Harlem, Upper East Side, Upper West Side
14 Jackson Heights, Long Island City, Lower Manhattan, Manhattan Beach, Stuyvesant Town
15 Brooklyn Heights, Garment District, Roosevelt Island

New York streets include:

06 Bowery
08 Broadway
10 14th Street, 34th Street, 42nd Street, Park Avenue, Wall Street
11 Canal Street, Fifth Avenue, Sixth Avenue, Union Square
13 Madison Square, Seventh Avenue
14 East 42nd Street, West 42nd Street
15 Central Park West, Lexington Avenue

New York landmarks include:

03 JFK, Met
04 CBGB, MoMA
05 Macy's
07 Barneys, Factory
08 Broadway, Bronx Zoo, Studio 54
09 East River, The Dakota
10 Bronx River, Cotton Club, FAO Schwarz, Ground Zero, Rose Center, Wall Street
11 Battery Park, Central Park, Coney Island, Ellis Island, Federal Hall, Harlem River, Hudson River, Penn Station, Shea Stadium, Times Square, Union Square
12 Carnegie Hall, Chelsea Hotel, Hotel Chelsea, Prospect Park, The Cloisters
13 Apollo Theater, Bloomingdale's, Lincoln Center, Lincoln Tunnel, Pan Am Building, St Paul's Church, Yankee Stadium
14 Brooklyn Bridge, Grand Army Plaza, Waldorf Astoria, Washington Arch
15 Flushing Meadows, Manhattan Bridge, Metlife Building, Saks Fifth Avenue, Seagram Building, Statue of Liberty, Trump World Tower

New Zealand
02 NZ **03** NZL

New Zealand cities and notable towns include:

06 Napier, Nelson, Timaru
07 Dunedin, Manukau, Rotorua
08 Auckland, Gisborne, Hamilton, Hastings, Tauranga, Wanganui
09 Whangarei
10 Wellington
11 New Plymouth
12 Christchurch, Invercargill
15 Palmerston North

New Zealand landmarks include:

05 Hawea
06 Mt Cook, Te Anau, Wanaka
07 Aorangi, Rotorua, Ruapehu, Waikato
08 Mt Egmont, Wakatipu, Wanganui
09 Fiordland, Lake Taupo
10 Mt Victoria
11 Rakaia Gorge
12 Milford Sound, Southern Alps
13 Stewart Island
14 Otago Peninsula
15 Mangere Mountain, Ninety Mile Beach, Whangaparaoa Bay

See also **electorate**; **governor**; **premier**; **prime minister**; **province**; **team**

next
04 syne, then **05** along, later **06** beside **07** closest, ensuing, nearest **08** adjacent **09** adjoining, alongside, bordering, following, immediate, proximate **10** afterwards, contiguous, subsequent, succeeding, successive, tangential, thereafter **11** approximate **12** neighbouring, subsequently **13** after that time

next-door
08 adjacent

nibble
03 bit, eat **04** bite, gnaw, knap, moop, moup, nosh, peck, pick **05** crumb, munch, piece, snack, taste **06** morsel, pick at, titbit **07** knapple

Nicaragua
03 NIC

nice
03 bad, coy **04** cute, fine, good, kind **05** canny, civil, close, exact, sweet **06** dainty, decent, genial, kindly, lovely, minute, polite, strict, subtle, tickle, wanton **07** amiable, amusing, careful, likable, precise, refined, welcome **08** accurate, careless, charming, critical, delicate, friendly, likeable, pleasant, ticklish **09** agreeable, appealing, courteous, endearing, enjoyable, hazardous **10** acceptable, attractive, delectable, delightful, fastidious, meticulous, particular, satisfying, scrupulous **11** good-natured, pleasurable, respectable, sympathetic **12** entertaining, good-humoured, satisfactory, well-mannered **13** understanding **14** discriminating

nicely
04 well **07** civilly **08** politely, properly **09** agreeably **10** pleasantly, pleasingly **11** courteously, pleasurably, respectably **12** attractively, delightfully **14** satisfactorily

niceness
05 charm **08** kindness **10** amiability, politeness **11** likableness **12** friendliness, likeableness, pleasantness **13** agreeableness **14** attractiveness, delightfulness, respectability

nicety
06 nuance **07** coyness, finesse, quiddit **08** accuracy, delicacy, quiddity, subtlety **09** exactness, fine point, precision, punctilio **10** choiceness, minuteness, perjinkity, refinement **11** distinction **14** fastidiousness, meticulousness, scrupulousness

niche
04 nook, slot **05** place **06** alcove, corner, cranny, exedra, hollow, métier, mihrab, recess, shrine **07** calling, exhedra, opening **08** position, vocation **09** cubbyhole **10** fenestella, pigeonhole, tabernacle **11** columbarium **14** specialist area **15** specialized area

nick
02 do **03** can, cut, jug, lag, nab, rob **04** bust, chip, dent, deny, form, jail, mark, nail, quod, scar, snip, take **05** catch, choky, clink, Devil, notch, pinch, run in, score, shape, sneck, snick, state, steal, swipe **06** arrest, collar, cooler, damage, fettle, groove, health, indent, inside, pick up, pilfer, pocket, prison, pull in, snitch **07** capture, defraud, scratch, slammer **08** knock off, porridge **09** apprehend, condition, jailhouse **11** indentation **13** police station

See also **prison**; **steal**

nickel
02 Ni

nickname
06 byname, to-name **07** epithet, moniker, pet name **08** cognomen, monicker **09** sobriquet **10** diminutive, soubriquet **12** familiar name

See also **Australian football**; **football**; **state**; **team**

nifty
03 apt **04** chic, deft, fine, neat **05** agile, nippy, quick, sharp, slick, smart **06** adroit, clever, spruce **07** skilful, stylish **08** pleasing **09** enjoyable, excellent

Niger
02 RN **03** NER

Nigeria
03 NGA, NGR, WAN

Nigerian
03 Ibo, Tiv **04** Efik, Igbo, Nupe **05** Hausa

niggardliness
08 meanness, scarcity **09** closeness, parsimony, smallness **10** inadequacy, meagreness, paltriness, scantiness, skimpiness, stinginess **11** miserliness **12** cheeseparing, grudgingness **13** insufficiency **14** ungenerousness **15** tight-fistedness

niggardly
04 hard, mean **05** close, mingy, nippy, nirly, small **06** meagre, measly, niding, nirlie, paltry, scanty, skimpy, stingy **07** miserly, nithing, sparing **08** grudging, near-gaun, nidering, ungiving **09** illiberal, miserable, niddering, niderling, penny-wise, penurious **10** hard-fisted, inadequate, near-begaun, nidderling, ungenerous **11** tight-fisted **12** cheeseparing, insufficient, parsimonious

niggle
03 bug, nag **04** carp, gnaw, moan **05** annoy, cavil, query, upset, worry **06** bother, hassle, pick on, potter, trifle **07** henpeck, nit-pick, protest, quibble, trouble **08** complain, irritate, keep on at **09** complaint, criticism, criticize, objection **10** nit-picking **12** equivocation, pettifogging **13** prevarication

night
04 dark, evil, nite **05** death **06** sorrow **07** evening **08** darkmans, darkness **09** ignorance, night-time, obscurity **10** affliction **11** dead of night **15** hours of darkness
• pass the night
03 lie

nightclub
04 club **05** disco **06** nitery **07** cabaret, hot spot, niterie **09** nightspot **11** boîte de nuit, discotheque

nightfall
04 dark, dusk **06** sunset **07** evening, sundown **08** gloaming, twilight **10** crepuscule

nightingale
04 Lind **06** bulbul, Progne **08** Philomel **09** Philomela, Philomene
• sound of nightingale
03 jug

nightly
07 at night **09** after dark, each night **10** every night **11** nocturnally **15** night after night

nightmare
05 agony, trial **06** horror, ordeal **07** anguish, incubus, torment, torture **08** bad dream, calamity **09** cacodemon, cauchemar, ephialtes **10** cacodaemon **11** oneirodynia **13** hallucination **15** awful experience

nightmarish
06 creepy, unreal **07** ghostly, scaring **08** alarming, dreadful, horrible, horrific **09** agonizing, harrowing **10** disturbing, terrifying **11** frightening

night-time
04 dark **05** night **08** darkness **11** dead of night **15** hours of darkness

nihilism
06 denial **07** anarchy, atheism, nullity **08** cynicism, disorder, negation, oblivion **09** disbelief, emptiness, pessimism, rejection, terrorism **10** abnegation, negativism, scepticism **11** agnosticism, lawlessness, nothingness, repudiation **12** non-existence, renunciation

nihilist
05 cynic **07** atheist, sceptic **08** agitator, agnostic **09** anarchist, extremist, pessimist, terrorist **10** antinomian, negativist **11** disbeliever, negationist **13** revolutionary

Nike
08 Victoria

nil
01 O **04** duck, love, none, nowt, zero **05** zilch **06** cipher, cypher, naught, nought **07** nothing

nimble
04 deft, spry, yald **05** agile, alert, brisk, fleet, light, lithe, nippy, quick, ready, smart, swack, swift, wanle, wight, yauld **06** active, clever, lissom, lively, prompt, quiver, volant, wandle, wannel, wimble **07** deliver, lissome, springe **08** flippant, graceful **09** fleet-foot, sharp-eyed, sprightly **10** sure-footed **11** light-footed, quick-moving, quick-witted, sharp-witted **13** quick-thinking

nimbleness
05 grace, skill **07** agility, finesse **08** alacrity, deftness, legerity, spryness **09** alertness, dexterity, lightness, niftiness, nippiness, smartness **10** adroitness **13** sprightliness

nimbly
04 fast **06** deftly, easily, spryly **07** agilely, alertly, briskly, lightly, quickly, readily, sharply, smartly, swiftly **08** actively, promptly, snappily, speedily **11** dexterously **12** proficiently **13** quick-wittedly

nincompoop
04 clot, dolt, fool, nerd, poop, twit **05** chump, dunce, idiot, twerp, wally **06** dimwit, nitwit **07** plonker **08** numskull **09** blockhead, ignoramus, simpleton

nine
02 IX **06** ennead **08** nonuplet, novenary, Pierides

nineteen
03 XIX

ninety
02 XC

ninny *see* **fool**

niobium
02 Nb

nip
02 go **03** fly, lop, nep, pop, ren, rin, run, sip **04** bite, clip, dart, dash, dock, dram, drop, grip, rush, shot, snip, tear **05** catch, chack, check, hurry, pinch, smart, sneap, steal, taste, tweak **06** arrest, nibble, snatch **07** catmint, draught, portion, squeeze, swallow **08** cutpurse, mouthful
• nip in the bud
04 curb, halt, stem, stop **05** block, check **06** arrest, impede **08** obstruct **09** frustrate

nipple
03 dug, pap, tit **04** teat **05** diddy, udder **06** breast **07** mamilla, papilla **08** mammilla

nippy
03 icy, raw **04** cold, fast, spry **05** agile, brisk, quick, sharp **06** active, biting, chilly, frosty, nimble, speedy **07** nipping, pungent **08** piercing, stinging, waitress **09** niggardly, sprightly

nirvana
03 joy **05** bliss, peace **06** heaven **07** ecstasy **08** paradise, serenity **10** exaltation **12** tranquillity **13** enlightenment

nit-picking
05 fussy **07** carping, finicky **08** captious, pedantic **09** cavilling, quibbling **12** pettifogging **13** hair-splitting, hypercritical

nitrogen
01 N **02** az- **03** azo-

nitty-gritty
06 basics **09** key points **10** bottom line, brass tacks, essentials, main points **12** fundamentals, nuts and bolts

nitwit
03 ass **04** clot, dope, fool, jerk, prat, twit **05** chump, dumbo, idiot, neddy, ninny, wally **06** dimwit, drongo **07** pillock, plonker **09** birdbrain, blockhead, simpleton **10** nincompoop, silly-billy

Niue
03 NIU

no
◇ *deletion indicator*
01 O **02** na **03** nae, nay, non, not **04** none, nope, uh-uh, zero **05** no way **06** aikona, denial, never a **07** refusal **08** not at all, no thanks **09** not really **11** of course not **12** certainly not, nothing doing **13** absolutely not, not on your life **14** not on your nelly, over my dead body

nob
03 VIP **04** head, toff **06** bigwig, fat cat **07** big shot **09** personage **10** aristocrat

nobble
◇ *anagram indicator*
02 do **03** buy, nab **04** bust, dope, drug, foil, grab, nail, nick, take **05** bribe, catch, check, get at, pinch, run in, seize, steal, swipe **06** arrest, buy off, collar, defeat, hinder, pick up, pilfer, pull in, snitch, thwart **07** disable, swindle, warn off **08** knock off, threaten **09** frustrate, hamstring, influence **10** intimidate **12** incapacitate **13** interfere with

nobelium
02 No

Nobel Prize

Nobel Prize winners include:

02 Fo (Dario), Oë (Kenzaburo)
03 Lee (Tsung-Dao), Orr (Lord Boyd), Paz (Octavio), Tum (Rigoberta Menchú)
04 Belo (Carlos), Bohr (Aage), Bohr (Niels), Böll (Heinrich), Born (Max), Buck (Pearl S), Cela (Camilo José), Duve (Christian de), Gide (André), Hume (John), Hunt (Tim), Katz (Sir Bernard), King (Martin Luther), Koch (Robert), Mann (Thomas), Mott (Sir Nevill F), Nash (John), Rabi (Isidor Isaac), Rous (Peyton), Shaw (George Bernard), Tutu (Desmond), Urey (Harold C)
05 Annan (Kofi), Bethe (Hans), Bloch (Felix), Bragg (Sir Lawrence), Bragg (Sir William), Bunin (Ivan), Camus (Albert), Chain (Sir Ernst), Crick (Francis), Curie (Marie), Curie

(Pierre), **Debye** (Peter), **Dirac** (Paul A M), **Ebadi** (Shirin), **Eliot** (T S), **Euler** (Ulf von), **Fermi** (Enrico), **Golgi** (Camillo), **Grass** (Günter), **Haber** (Fritz), **Hesse** (Hermann), **Jerne** (Niels), **Klerk** (F W de), **Krebs** (Sir Hans), **Kroto** (Sir Harold), **Lewis** (Sinclair), **Libby** (Willard F), **Lwoff** (André), **Monod** (Jacques), **Nurse** (Sir Paul), **Pauli** (Wolfgang), **Peres** (Shimon), **Rabin** (Yitzhak), **Sachs** (Nelly), **Salam** (Abdus), **Simon** (Claude), **Soddy** (Frederick), **Stern** (Otto), **Yeats** (W B)

06 **Arafat** (Yasser), **Baeyer** (Adolf von), **Bellow** (Saul), **Bordet** (Jules), **Calvin** (Melvin), **Carrel** (Alexis), **Cronin** (James Watson), **Debreu** (Gerard), **Enders** (John F), **Florey** (Howard, Lord), **France** (Anatole), **Frisch** (Ragnar), **Glaser** (Donald A), **Hamsun** (Knut), **Heaney** (Seamus), **Hevesy** (George von), **Hewish** (Antony), **Huxley** (Andrew F), **Lorenz** (Konrad), **Myrdal** (Gunnar), **Nernst** (Walther), **Neruda** (Pablo), **O'Neill** (Eugene), **Pavlov** (Ivan), **Perutz** (Max F), **Planck** (Max), **Porter** (George, Lord), **Sanger** (Frederick), **Sartre** (Jean-Paul), **Singer** (Isaac Bashevis), **Tagore** (Rabindranath), **Walesa** (Lech), **Watson** (James), **Wiesel** (Elie), **Wilson** (Robert)

07 **Akerlof** (George A), **Alferov** (Zhores I), **Alvarez** (Luis), **Axelrod** (Julius), **Banting** (Sir Frederick G), **Beckett** (Samuel), **Behring** (Emil von), **Brenner** (Sydney), **Brodsky** (Joseph), **Canetti** (Elias), **Coetzee** (JM), **Dae-jung** (Kim), **Ehrlich** (Paul), **Feynman** (Richard P), **Fleming** (Sir Alexander), **Glashow** (Sheldon), **Golding** (William), **Hershey** (Alfred), **Hodgkin** (Dorothy), **Hodgkin** (Sir Alan L), **Jelinek** (Elfriede), **Jiménez** (Juan Ramón), **Kendrew** (John), **Kertész** (Imre), **Khorana** (H Gobind), **Kipling** (Rudyard), **Laxness** (Halldór), **Maathai** (Wangari), **Mahfouz** (Naguib), **Mandela** (Nelson), **Marconi** (Guglielmo), **Márquez** (Gabriel García), **Mauriac** (François), **Medawar** (Sir Peter), **Mistral** (Frédéric), **Mommsen** (Theodor), **Naipaul** (VS), **Pauling** (Linus), **Penzias** (Arno), **Röntgen** (Wilhelm Konrad), **Rotblat** (Joseph), **Russell** (Bertrand, Earl), **Seaborg** (GlenT), **Seifert** (Jaroslav), **Soyinka** (Wole), **Thomson** (J J), **Trimble** (David), **Waksman** (Selman A), **Walcott** (Derek), **Whipple** (George H), **Wilkins** (Maurice)

08 **Appleton** (Sir Edward V), **Asturias** (Miguel Angel), **Chadwick** (Sir James), **Delbrück** (Max), **Einstein** (Albert), **Faulkner** (William), **Friedman** (Milton), **Gajdusek** (D Carleton), **Gell-Mann** (Murray), **Gordimer** (Nadine), **Hartwell** (Leland H), **Langmuir** (Irving), **Leontief** (Wassily), **Meyerhof** (Otto), **Millikan** (Robert A), **Milstein** (Cesar), **Morrison** (Toni), **Mulliken** (Robert S), **Northrop** (John H), **Sakharov** (Andrei), **Saramago** (José), **Shockley** (William B), **Tiselius** (Arne), **Tonegawa** (Susumu), **Weinberg** (Steven), **Xingjian** (Gao)

09 **Arrhenius** (Svante), **Becquerel** (Henri), **Cherenkov** (Pavel), **Churchill** (Sir Winston), **Dalai Lama**, **Gorbachev** (Mikhail), **Hemingway** (Ernest), **Kissinger** (Henry), **Markowitz** (Harry M), **Mechnikov** (Ilya), **Michelson** (Albert A), **Nirenberg** (Marshall W), **Pasternak** (Boris), **Prudhomme** (Sully), **Rainwater** (James), **Roosevelt** (Theodore), **Sholokhov** (Mikhail), **Steinbeck** (John), **Tinbergen** (Jan), **Tinbergen** (Nikolaas)

10 **Galsworthy** (John), **Heisenberg** (Werner), **Hofstadter** (Robert), **Lagerkvist** (Pär), **McClintock** (Barbara), **Modigliani** (Franco), **Pirandello** (Luigi), **Ramos-Horta** (José), **Rutherford** (Ernest, Lord), **Szymborska** (Wislawa)

11 **Joliot-Curie** (Frédéric), **Joliot-Curie** (Irène), **Kantorovich** (Leonid), **Landsteiner** (Karl), **Maeterlinck** (Maurice), **Ramón y Cajal** (Santiago), **Schrödinger** (Erwin), **van der Waals** (Johannes Diderik), **Zinkernagel** (Rolf M)

12 **Hammarskjöld** (Dag), **Mother Teresa**, **Solzhenitsyn** (Aleksandr), **Szent-Györgyi** (Albert)

13 **Aung San Suu Kyi**, **Chandrasekhar** (Subrahmanyan), **García Márquez** (Gabriel)

14 **Levi-Montalcini** (Rita)

nobility

04 nobs, rank **05** élite, glory, lords, peers, toffs **06** family, gentry, honour, nobles, virtue **07** dignity, majesty, peerage **08** eminence, grandeur, noblesse **09** grandness, integrity, nobilesse, nobleness, splendour **10** excellence, generosity, worthiness **11** aristocracy, high society, magnanimity, stateliness, superiority, uprightness **12** generousness, magnificence **14** impressiveness **15** illustriousness

The nobility includes:

01 d, E, P
02 Bt, Kt, Pr
03 Dom, Don, Duc
04 Bart, dame, duke, earl, jarl, lady, lord, Marq, peer
05 baron, count, laird, liege, nawab, noble, ruler, thane
06 daimio, Junker, knight, squire, vidame
07 baronet, dowager, duchess, marquis, peeress, vicomte
08 baroness, countess, governor, life peer, margrave, marquess, nobleman, seigneur, starosta, toiseach, vavasour, viscount
09 grand duke, liege lord, magnifico, patrician
10 aristocrat, noblewoman
11 marchioness, viscountess
12 grand duchess
13 grand seigneur

noble

04 fine, gent, high, lady, lord, peer **05** brave, grand, great, lofty, manly **06** gentle, landed, manful, titled, vidame, worthy **07** eminent, exalted, gallant, grandee, magnate, stately **08** atheling, douzeper, elevated, generous, glorious, handsome, high-born, honoured, imposing, majestic, nobleman, splendid, virtuous **09** dignified, doucepere, excellent, patrician, unselfish, venerated **10** aristocrat, honourable, impressive, noblewoman **11** blue-blooded, high-ranking, illustrious, magnanimous, magnificent, noble-minded **12** aristocratic, great-hearted **13** distinguished **15** self-sacrificing

See also **nobility**

nobly

07 bravely **08** manfully, worthily **09** gallantly **10** generously, honourably, virtuously **11** unselfishly

nobody

04 Nemo **05** no one **06** cipher, menial, Pooter **07** naebody, nothing **09** nonentity **10** mediocrity **11** lightweight

nocturnal

05 night **09** night-time **13** active at night

nod

03 bow, dip, nap **04** beck, doze, sign **05** agree, sleep **06** accept, assent, beckon, drowse, nid-nod, noddle, nutate, salute, signal **07** approve, doze off, drop off, gesture, incline, support **08** greeting, indicate, say yes to **10** fall asleep, indication **11** acknowledge **15** acknowledgement

• give the nod to

02 OK **03** buy **04** back, pass **05** adopt, allow, carry **06** accept, permit, ratify, second, uphold **07** agree to, approve, confirm, endorse, mandate, support **08** assent to, hold with, sanction, validate **09** authorize, consent to **11** rubber-stamp

• nod off

03 nap **04** doze **05** sleep **06** drowse **07** doze off, drop off, slumber **10** fall asleep

node

03 bud **04** bump, knob, knot, lump **05** joint, nodus **06** growth, nodule **08** junction, swelling **09** carbuncle **11** convergence **12** protuberance

noise

◇ *homophone indicator*

03 cry, din, pop, row **04** bang, boom, chug, clap, coil, roar, talk, wham, zoom

05 blare, clash, clunk, sound, whang 06 babble, bicker, clamor, hubbub, jangle, outcry, racket, report, rumble, rumour, tumult, uproar 07 brattle, clamour, clangor, clatter, discord, thunder 08 announce, clangour 09 circulate, commotion, publicize 11 pandemonium

• **amount of noise**

02 dB 03 bel, dBA 04 phon, PNdB 07 decibel

noiseless

04 mute, soft 05 mousy, quiet, still 06 hushed, mousey, silent 07 catlike 09 inaudible, soundless

noiselessly

06 softly 07 quietly 08 silently 09 inaudibly 11 soundlessly

noisily

06 loudly, wallop 07 rowdily 10 fortissimo 11 deafeningly 12 boisterously, resoundingly, tumultuously, vociferously

noisome

03 bad 04 foul 05 fetid 06 foetid, putrid, smelly 07 harmful, hurtful, noxious, reeking 08 mephitic, stinking 09 injurious, obnoxious, offensive, poisonous, repulsive, unhealthy 10 disgusting, malodorous, nauseating, pernicious 11 deleterious, pestiferous, unwholesome 12 disagreeable, pestilential

noisy

01 f 02 ff 04 loud 05 roary, rowdy, vocal 06 roarie 07 blaring, blatant, booming, rackety, roaring 08 blasting, blattant, boastful, piercing, plangent, strepent 09 clamorous, deafening, turbulent 10 blusterous, boisterous, hoity-toity, strepitant, strepitoso, thundering, tumultuous, vociferous 11 rumbustious 12 ear-splitting, obstreperous

• **not too noisy**

02 mf

nomad

03 San 04 Bedu 05 rover 06 Beduin, roamer, Tuareg 07 Bedouin, Bushman, migrant, rambler, Saracen, swagger, swagman, vagrant 08 Khoikhoi, vagabond, wanderer 09 Hottentot, itinerant, transient, traveller

nomadic

05 Gypsy 06 Beduin, roving, Tuareg 07 Bedouin, migrant, roaming, vagrant 08 drifting, Khoikhoi, Scythian 09 itinerant, migratory, unsettled, wandering 10 travelling 11 peripatetic 13 peregrinating

nom-de-plume

05 alias 07 pen-name 09 pseudonym 11 assumed name

nomenclature

06 naming 08 locution, taxonomy 10 vocabulary 11 phraseology, terminology 12 codification 14 classification

nominal

03 nom 04 tiny 05 nomin, small, token 06 formal, puppet 07 minimal, titular, trivial 08 so-called, supposed, symbolic, trifling 09 professed, purported 10 figurehead, in name only, ostensible, peppercorn, self-styled 11 theoretical 13 insignificant

nominally

08 formally 10 in name only, ostensibly 12 symbolically 13 theoretically

nominate

04 name, term 05 elect, put up, voice 06 assign, choose, select, submit 07 appoint, elevate, present, propose, suggest 09 designate, postulate, recommend 10 commission, substitute

nomination

06 choice, naming 08 election, proposal 09 selection 10 submission, suggestion 11 appointment, designation 14 recommendation

nominative

01 n 03 nom

nominee

06 runner 07 entrant 08 assignee 09 appointee, candidate 10 contestant

nomogram

04 abac

non-alcoholic drink *see* **drink**

non-aligned

07 neutral 09 impartial, undecided 10 uninvolved 11 independent, non-partisan, uncommitted 13 disinterested

nonchalance

04 calm, cool 06 aplomb 08 calmness, coolness 09 composure, sangfroid, unconcern 10 detachment, equanimity 11 insouciance 12 indifference 13 pococurantism 14 pococuranteism, self-possession

nonchalant

04 calm, cool 05 blasé 06 casual 07 offhand 08 careless, detached, laid-back 09 apathetic, collected, easy-going 10 insouciant 11 indifferent, pococurante, unconcerned 13 dispassionate, imperturbable 15 cool as a cucumber

non-combatant

06 dovish 07 conchie, neutral 08 civilian, pacifist 10 non-aligned, non-violent 11 non-fighting, peacemaking 12 conciliatory, unaggressive 14 non-belligerent 15 passive resister

non-committal

04 wary 05 vague 07 careful, evasive, guarded, neutral, politic, prudent, tactful 08 cautious, discreet, reserved 09 ambiguous, equivocal, tentative 10 diplomatic, indefinite 11 circumspect, unrevealing

non compos mentis

03 ape, fey, mad 04 bats, gyte, loco, nuts, wild 05 barmy, batty, buggy, crazy, daffy, dippy, dotty, flaky, gonzo, loony, loopy, manic, nutty, potty, queer, wacko, wacky, wiggy 06 crazed, cuckoo, fruity, insane, maniac, mental, raving, red-mad, screwy 07 bananas, barking, berserk, bonkers, cracked, frantic, lunatic, meshuga 08 crackers, demented, deranged, dingbats, doolally, frenetic, frenzied, maniacal, unhinged, unstable 09 disturbed, lymphatic, psychotic, up the wall 10 bestraught, distracted, distraught, frantic-mad, off the wall, off your nut, out to lunch, stone-crazy, unbalanced 11 not all there, off the rails, off your head 12 mad as a hatter, off your chump, round the bend 13 off your rocker, of unsound mind, out of your head, out of your mind, out of your tree, round the twist 14 off your trolley, wrong in the head 15 out of your senses

nonconformist

05 rebel 06 chapel 07 heretic, oddball, radical, seceder 08 maverick 09 dissenter, dissident, eccentric, heretical, protester 10 iconoclast 11 dissentient 12 secessionist 13 individualist, unco-operative 14 fish out of water

nonconformity

06 heresy 07 dissent 09 deviation, secession 10 heterodoxy 11 originality 12 eccentricity

nondescript

04 dull 05 bland, plain, vague 07 anaemic, insipid, vanilla 08 ordinary 11 commonplace, featureless, uninspiring 12 cookie-cutter, run of the mill, unattractive, unclassified, unremarkable 13 indeterminate, no great shakes, undistinctive, unexceptional, uninteresting 14 common or garden 15 undistinguished

non-drinking

02 TT 03 dry 10 on the wagon

none

01 O 02 no 03 nil 04 zero 05 no one, zilch 06 nobody, not any, not one 07 nothing 08 not a soul 10 not even one 13 not a single one

• **none the ...**

02 no 07 not a bit 08 not at all 10 to no extent

nonentity

06 cipher, cypher, menial, nobody 07 nothing 08 shlepper 09 non-person, schlepper 10 mediocrity 11 lightweight

non-essential

08 unneeded 09 accessory, excessive, redundant 10 expendable, extraneous, peripheral 11 dispensable, inessential, superfluous, unimportant, unnecessary 13 supplementary

nonetheless

03 but, yet 05 still 06 anyhow, anyway, even so, though 07 however 08 after all 09 in any case 10 all the same, by

any means, for all that, in any event, regardless **11** by some means, just the same **12** nevertheless **13** at the same time **15** notwithstanding

non-event
04 no-no **06** fiasco **07** let-down **08** comedown **09** damp squib **10** anticlimax **14** disappointment

non-existence
05 fancy **07** absence, chimera, unbeing **08** illusion **09** unreality **11** nothingness **12** illusiveness

non-existent
04 null **06** unborn, unreal **07** fancied, fantasy, missing, phantom, unbeing **08** fanciful, illusory, imagined, mythical **09** fictional, imaginary, legendary **10** chimerical, fictitious, immaterial **11** incorporeal **12** hypothetical **13** hallucinatory, insubstantial, suppositional

non-fiction

Non-fiction works include:

06 Walden
07 Capital, Who's Who
08 Self-Help
09 Kama Sutra, Leviathan, On Liberty, Table Talk, The Phaedo
10 Das Kapital, The Annales, The Gorgias, The Poetics, The Timaeus
11 Down the Mine, Mythologies, The Agricola, The Analects, The Germania, The Phaedrus, The Republic
12 Novum Organum, Silent Spring, The City of God, The Second Sex, The Symposium
13 The Story of Art
14 A Room of One's Own, Birds of America, Eudemian Ethics, Inside the Whale, Modern Painters, Past and Present, Sartor Resartus, The Age of Reason, The Golden Bough, The Life of Jesus, The Rights of Man, The Selfish Gene
15 Lives of the Poets, The Essays of Elia, The Female Eunuch, The Sleepwalkers

non-flammable
09 fireproof **10** flameproof **12** not flammable **13** fire-resistant, incombustible, uninflammable **14** flame-resistant

non-intervention
06 apathy **07** inertia **08** inaction **09** passivity **12** laissez-faire, non-alignment **14** hands-off policy, non-involvement **15** non-interference

non-Jew
03 goy **07** gentile

nonpareil
06 unique **09** matchless **10** inimitable, unequalled, unrivalled **12** incomparable, unparalleled, without equal **13** beyond compare

non-partisan
07 neutral **08** detached, unbiased **09** impartial, objective **10** even-handed **11** independent **12** unprejudiced **13** dispassionate

nonplus
04 faze, stun **05** sew up, stick, stump **06** baffle, dismay, puzzle **07** astound, confuse, flummox, mystify, perplex, stagger **08** astonish, bewilder, confound **09** discomfit, dumbfound, embarrass, take aback **10** disconcert, perplexity **11** flabbergast **14** discountenance

nonplussed
05 blank, fazed **07** at a loss, baffled, floored, puzzled, stumped, stunned **08** dismayed **09** astounded, flummoxed, perplexed **10** astonished, bewildered, confounded, taken aback **11** dumbfounded, embarrassed **12** disconcerted **13** flabbergasted **14** out of your depth

non-professional
03 lay **04** laic **07** amateur

nonsense
03 gum, rot **04** blah, bosh, bull, bunk, cack, cock, crap, gaff, guff, jazz, junk, kack, pulp, punk, tosh **05** balls, bilge, borak, borax, folly, fudge, haver, hooey, pants, squit, stuff, trash, tripe **06** blague, bunkum, drivel, faddle, footle, gammon, havers, hoop-la, humbug, kibosh, kybosh, piffle, waffle **07** baloney, blather, blether, boloney, doggrel, eyewash, flannel, garbage, hogwash, malarky, pisheog, rhubarb, rubbish, twaddle **08** all my eye, blah-blah, blathers, blethers, bumfluff, claptrap, cobblers, doggerel, flimflam, malarkey, pishogue, tommyrot, trifling, unreason **09** absurdity, bull's wool, fandangle, gibberish, kidstakes, moonshine, mouthwash, poppycock, silliness, stupidity **10** balderdash, clamjamfry, codswallop, flapdoodle, galimatias, jabberwock, mumbo-jumbo, taradiddle, tomfoolery **11** clanjamfray, double Dutch, fiddle-de-dee, fiddlestick, foolishness, jabberwocky, tarradiddle **12** blah-blah-blah, clamjamphrie, fiddle-faddle, fiddlesticks, gobbledegook, gobbledygook **13** gas and gaiters, horsefeathers, senselessness **14** how's your father, ridiculousness
See also **rubbish**

nonsensical
◇ *anagram indicator*
05 barmy, crazy, dotty, inane, nutty, potty, silly, wacky **06** absurd, stupid **07** fatuous, foolish **08** crackpot **09** gibberish, ludicrous, senseless **10** irrational, ridiculous **11** hare-brained, meaningless **12** preposterous **14** unintelligible

nonsmoker
02 ns

non-stop
07 endless, ongoing **08** constant, steadily, unbroken, unending **09** ceaseless, endlessly, incessant, unceasing **10** constantly, continuous, persistent, relentless, unbrokenly, unendingly **11** ceaselessly, incessantly, never-ending, unceasingly, unfaltering **12** continuously, interminable, interminably, relentlessly **13** round-the-clock, unfalteringly, uninterrupted, unrelentingly, unremittingly **15** uninterruptedly

non-violent
06 dovish, irenic **07** passive **08** pacifist, peaceful **09** peaceable

noodle
04 head, udon **05** moony, Sammy **09** blockhead, improvise, simpleton
See also **head**

nook
03 den **04** neuk **05** angle, niche **06** alcove, cavity, corner, cranny, recess, refuge **07** hideout, opening, retreat, shelter **08** hideaway **09** cubbyhole

noon
01 m, n **06** midday, middle **08** twelve pm **09** lunchtime **10** meridional, twelve noon **12** twelve o'clock

noose
04 fank **05** snare **06** twitch **07** necktie **08** marriage, rope's end **12** hempen caudle

norm
03 par **04** mean, rule, type **05** gauge, model, scale **07** average, measure, pattern **08** standard **09** benchmark, criterion, principle, reference, usual rule, yardstick **10** touchstone

normal
05 usual **06** common **07** average, general, natural, popular, regular, routine, typical **08** accepted, everyday, habitual, ordinary, rational, standard, straight **10** accustomed, mainstream, reasonable, regulation **11** bog standard, commonplace **12** conventional, run of the mill, twenty-twenty, well-adjusted **13** perpendicular

normality
06 reason **07** balance, routine **08** normalcy **09** usualness **10** adjustment, commonness, regularity, typicality **11** averageness, naturalness, rationality **12** ordinariness **14** reasonableness **15** conventionality

normally
07 as a rule, as usual, usually **08** commonly **09** generally, naturally, regularly, routinely, typically **10** ordinarily **14** conventionally

Norse
01 N
See also **god, goddess**

north
01 N

North Atlantic Treaty Organization *see* **NATO**

North America *see* **America**; **Canada**; **United States of America**

North Carolina
02 NC

North Dakota
02 ND **04** N Dak

north-east, north-eastern
02 NE

northern
01 N **05** north, polar **06** Arctic, boreal **09** northerly **11** hyperborean **13** septentrional

Northern Ireland *see* **district**; **town**

north-west, north-western
02 NW

Northwest Territories
02 NT

Norway
01 N **03** NOR

nose
03 neb, pry, pug **04** beak, bill, boko, conk, ease, edge, feel, inch, push, snub **05** aroma, flair, nudge, scent, sense, smell, snoot, snout **06** hooter, nozzle, nuzzle, schnoz, snitch **08** informer, instinct **09** proboscis, schnozzle **10** move slowly, perception, projection

• **get up your nose**
03 bug, irk, nag, vex **04** fash, gall, rile **05** anger, tease **06** bother, harass, hassle, madden, molest, pester, plague, ruffle, wind up **07** disturb, hack off, provoke, tick off, trouble **08** brass off, irritate **09** aggravate, cheese off, displease, drive nuts **10** drive crazy, exasperate **11** get your goat **12** drive bananas **13** get on your wick, get your back up, make sparks fly **14** drive up the wall, get your blood up, give you the hump **15** get on your nerves, get your dander up

• **nose around**
03 pry **05** snoop **06** search **10** poke around, rubberneck **14** poke your nose in

• **nose out**
06 detect, reveal **07** find out, inquire, uncover **08** discover, sniff out

• **poke your nose into**
03 pry **05** pry in, snoop **06** butt in, fiddle, tamper **07** intrude **08** meddle in **09** interfere, intervene **10** stickybeak, tamper with **11** interfere in **12** put your oar in **14** stick your oar in

• **under your nose**
07 clearly, plainly **09** obviously **10** plain to see **11** for all to see **12** in front of you

nosedive
04 dive, drop **05** swoop **06** go down, header, plunge, purler **07** decline, plummet **08** get worse, submerge

nosegay
04 posy **05** bunch, spray **07** bouquet

nosey, nosy
06 prying **07** curious, probing **08** fragrant, snooping **10** meddlesome **11** inquisitive, interfering **13** eavesdropping

• **Nosey Parker**
08 busybody

nosh
03 eat, kai **04** diet, dish, eats, fare, feed, food, grub, menu, tuck **05** board, meals, scran, table **06** fodder, nibble, stores, tucker, viands **07** cooking, cuisine, rations **08** delicacy, eatables, victuals **09** nutriment, nutrition **10** bush tucker, foodstuffs, provisions, speciality, sustenance **11** comestibles, nourishment, subsistence **12** refreshments

nosiness
06 prying **08** snooping **11** curiousness **12** interference **13** intrusiveness **14** meddlesomeness **15** inquisitiveness

nostalgia
06 pining, regret **07** longing, regrets **08** yearning **09** mal du pays **11** remembrance, wistfulness **12** homesickness, recollection, reminiscence **13** recollections, regretfulness, reminiscences

nostalgic
06 pining **07** longing, wistful **08** homesick, yearning **09** emotional, regretful **11** reminiscent, sentimental

nostril
04 nare

nostrum
04 cure, drug, pill **06** elixir, potion, remedy, secret **07** cure-all, panacea **08** medicine **13** universal cure **14** cure for all ills **15** universal remedy

nosy *see* **nosey, nosy**

not
◇ *anagram indicator*
◇ *deletion indicator*
02 na, ne, no, -n't **03** non **04** nary, ne'er **05** never **06** polled

• **and not**
03 nor

• **has not**
03 nas **04** ain't, ha'n't

• **is not**
03 nis, nys **04** ain't

• **not out**
02 in, no

notability
03 VIP **04** fame, note **05** celeb **06** bigwig, esteem, renown, worthy **07** big shot, magnate, notable, someone **08** big noise, eminence, luminary, somebody, top brass **09** big cheese, celebrity, dignitary, personage **10** importance **11** distinction, heavyweight **12** significance **14** impressiveness, noteworthiness, observableness

notable
03 VIP **04** rare, star **05** celeb, great **06** bigwig, clever, famous, marked, signal, worthy **07** big shot, capable, eminent, serious, someone, special, unusual **08** big noise, luminary, renowned, somebody, striking, terrible, top brass, uncommon **09** big cheese, celebrity, dignitary, important, memorable, momentous, notorious, personage, well-known **10** celebrated, impressive, notability, noteworthy, noticeable, observable, particular, pre-eminent, remarkable **11** heavyweight, illustrious, outstanding, significant **12** considerable **13** distinguished, extraordinary, unforgettable

notably
08 above all, markedly, signally **09** eminently **10** distinctly, especially, noticeably, remarkably, strikingly, uncommonly **12** impressively, in particular, particularly **13** conspicuously, outstandingly, significantly **15** extraordinarily

notation
04 code **05** Romic, signs **06** cipher, noting, record, script, system **07** symbols **08** alphabet **09** shorthand, tablature **10** characters **11** Laban system **13** hieroglyphics, orchesography

notch
01 V **03** cut, gap, jag, lip **04** dent, gash, gimp, hack, kerf, mark, mush, nick, nock, snip, step **05** cleft, crena, gouge, grade, level, score, sinus, stage, tally **06** degree, groove, indent, joggle, raffle **07** achieve, scratch, serrate, vandyke **08** incision, nail-hole, swan-mark, undercut **09** insection **11** indentation

• **notch up**
04 gain, make **05** score **06** attain, record **07** achieve, chalk up **08** register

notched
05 erose, jaggy **06** eroded, jagged, nicked, pinked **07** dentate, serrate **08** dentated, serrated **09** serrulate **10** crenellate, emarginate, serrulated **11** crenellated, denticulate **12** denticulated

note
01 A, B, C, D, E, F, G, H, n **02** NB **03** log, see **04** bill, care, chit, fame, heed, item, line, long, mark, memo, mese, nete, oner, show, tone, tune **05** breve, drone, e-mail, enter, entry, fiver, gloss, large, minim, music, one-er, token **06** chitty, denote, detect, letter, minute, notice, postil, quaver, record, regard, remark, renown, signal, single, sticky, stigma, symbol, tenner, twenty, wunner **07** account, apostil, comment, element, epistle, jot down, jotting, mention, message, middle c, missive, observe, put down, receipt, refer to, touch on, voucher, witness **08** allude to, annotate, Bradbury, crotchet, eminence, footnote, indicate, perceive, prestige, register, reminder, sforzato **09** apostille, attention, greatness, non placet, semibreve, sforzando, write down **10** annotation, cognizance, commentary, fortepiano, importance, impression, indication,

inflection, intimation, marginalia, memorandum, notability, reputation, semiquaver, stigmatize
11 consequence, distinction, explanation, explication, mindfulness, observation, pre-eminence
12 acciaccatura, put in writing, significance **13** attentiveness, become aware of, communication, consideration **14** characteristic, demisemiquaver **15** illustriousness

Musical notes of the sol-fa scale:

02 do (first), fa (fourth), la (sixth), me (third), mi (third), re (second), si (seventh), so (fifth), te (seventh), ti (seventh), ut (first)
03 doh (first), fah (fourth), lah (sixth), ray (second), soh (fifth), sol (fifth)

See also **strings of a lyre** *under* **string**

• highest note
03 e-la

• of note
04 some

• take note
02 NB **03** dig

notebook
03 log **05** diary **06** cahier, jotter, record **07** daybook, journal, logbook, notepad **09** field book, table-book
10 index rerum, pocket-book
11 address book **12** exercise book

noted
05 great **06** famous, marked, of note
07 eminent, notable **08** renowned
09 acclaimed, notorious, prominent, respected, well-known **10** celebrated, pre-eminent, recognized **11** illustrious
13 distinguished

notes
05 draft **06** record, report, sketch
07 minutes, outline **08** jottings, synopsis **10** adversaria, commentary, personalia, transcript **11** impressions

noteworthy
06 marked **07** notable, unusual
08 striking **09** important, memorable
10 impressive, particular, remarkable
11 exceptional, outstanding, significant
13 extraordinary

nothing
01 O **03** nil, nix, zip **04** love, nada, nowt, void, zero **05** nihil, squat, zilch, zippo **06** cipher, cypher, menial, naught, nix-nie, nobody, nought, sod all, trifle, vacuum **07** nullity, sweet FA
08 naething, oblivion **09** emptiness, nonentity, not an iota, not a thing, worthless **10** mediocrity **11** diddly-squat, lightweight, nothingness
12 non-existence **15** sweet Fanny Adams

• doing nothing
04 idle

• for nothing
04 free **06** gratis, in vain **08** at no cost, futilely **09** to no avail **10** as a freebie, needlessly, on the house **12** free of charge, with no result **13** complimentary, without charge **14** unsuccessfully

• nothing but
04 just, only **06** merely, simply, solely
11 exclusively

• nothing more
04 mere

nothingness
04 nada, void **06** vacuum **07** nullity, vacuity **08** nihilism, nihility, oblivion
09 emptiness **12** non-existence
13 worthlessness **14** insignificance

notice
02 ad **03** see **04** bill, crit, espy, gaum, gorm, heed, mark, mind, news, note, sign, spot, tent **05** order **06** advert, advice, behold, detect, poster, regard, remark, review, si quis **07** comment, discern, leaflet, make out, mention, observe, thought, warning, write-up
08 apprisal, bulletin, circular, civility, critique, handbill, interest, monition, pamphlet, perceive **09** attention, awareness, criticism **10** cognizance, intimation, take heed of, take note of
11 declaration, distinguish, information, instruction, observation
12 announcement, intelligence, notification, watchfulness
13 advertisement, become aware of, communication, consideration **14** pay attention to

• give in your notice
04 quit **05** leave **06** resign **07** walk out
08 step down **09** stand down **13** pack in your job **14** chuck in your job

• give someone notice
03 axe **04** fire, sack, warn **05** eject
07 boot out, dismiss, kick out **08** get rid of **09** discharge

noticeable
04 bold **05** clear, plain **06** marked, patent **07** evident, notable, obvious, visible **08** distinct, manifest, powerful, striking **10** detectable, impressive, measurable, observable, pronounced
11 appreciable, conspicuous, discernible, distinction, perceptible, significant **12** unmistakable
15 distinguishable

noticeably
07 clearly, notably, plainly, visibly
08 markedly, patently **09** evidently, obviously **10** distinctly, strikingly
11 discernibly, perceptibly
12 unmistakably **13** conspicuously, significantly

notification
05 aviso **06** advice, notice
07 message, telling, warning
09 informing, statement **10** disclosure, divulgence **11** declaration, information, publication **12** announcement, intelligence **13** communication
14 acknowledgment
15 acknowledgement

notify
04 tell, warn **05** alert **06** advise, inform, reveal **07** apprise, caution, declare, divulge, placard, publish **08** acquaint, announce, disclose **09** broadcast, make known **11** communicate

notion
04 idea, mind, view, whim, wish
05 fancy, vapor **06** belief, desire, liking, notice, revery, theory, vapour
07 caprice, concept, impulse, inkling, opinion, project, reverie, thought, wrinkle **08** crotchet, supposal, whim-wham **10** assumption, conception, conviction, hypothesis, impression
11 abstraction, inclination
12 anticipation, apprehension
13 understanding

notional
05 ideal **06** unreal **07** fancied
08 abstract, fanciful, illusory, thematic
09 imaginary, unfounded, visionary
10 conceptual, ideational
11 speculative, theoretical
12 hypothetical **14** classificatory

notionally
08 in theory **10** putatively
12 conceptually **13** conjecturally, theoretically **14** hypothetically

notoriety
06 infamy **07** obloquy, scandal
08 disgrace, ignominy **09** celebrity, dishonour, disrepute, esclandre, publicity **10** opprobrium

notorious
05 noted **06** arrant, notour **07** blatant, glaring **08** flagrant, ill-famed, infamous
09 egregious, well-known
10 proverbial, scandalous
11 disgraceful, ignominious, of ill repute, opprobrious **12** disreputable
13 dishonourable

notoriously
06 openly **07** notably, overtly
08 arrantly, patently **09** blatantly, glaringly, obviously **10** flagrantly, infamously **11** egregiously
12 disreputably, particularly, scandalously **13** disgracefully, dishonourably, ignominiously, opprobriously, spectacularly

notwithstanding
03 for, yet **05** howbe **06** even so, for all, maugre, though **07** despite, howbeit, however, maulgre **08** although, nathless, naythles **09** in spite of, natheless **10** for all that, nathelesse
11 nonetheless, non obstante
12 nevertheless, regardless of **13** at the same time

nought
01 O **03** nil, nix **04** nada, nowt, null, zero **05** zilch **06** cipher, cypher, naught
07 nothing **11** nothingness

See also **nothing**

noun
01 n **06** aptote, gerund **11** substantive

nourish
03 aid **04** feed, have, help, rear, tend
05 boost, nurse **06** assist, foster, suckle
07 advance, bring up, care for, cherish, educate, forward, further, nurture, promote, support, sustain **08** attend to, maintain **09** cultivate, encourage,

stimulate **10** provide for, strengthen, take care of

nourishing
04 good **06** battle **08** nutrient **09** healthful, nutritive, wholesome **10** beneficial, nutritious **11** substantial **12** alimentative, health-giving, invigorating **13** strengthening

nourishment
04 diet, eats, food, grub, nosh, tuck **05** juice, scran **07** aliment, ingesta, pabulum **08** goodness **09** nouriture, nutriment, nutrition **10** nourriture, sustenance **11** subsistence

nouveaux riches
08 parvenus, upstarts **10** arrivistes, the new rich

Nova Scotia
02 NS

novel
◇ *anagram indicator*
03 new **04** book, epic, rare, tale **05** fresh, roman, story **06** modern, unique **07** Aga saga, fiction, romance, strange, unusual **08** creative, hardback, original, uncommon **09** different, ingenious, inventive, narrative, paperback **10** innovative, pioneering, unfamiliar, unorthodox, yellowback **11** imaginative, resourceful, three-decker **12** bodice-ripper, double-decker, nouveau roman **13** Bildungsroman, unprecedented **14** ground-breaking, unconventional

Novels and fictional works include:

03 Kim, She, USA
04 Emma, Jazz, Nana, Voss
05 Kipps, Money, Porgy, Scoop, Sybil
06 Ben Hur, Carrie, Herzog, Lolita, Nausea, Pamela, Rob Roy, The Sea, Trilby, Utopia, Walden
07 Babbitt, Beloved, Candide, Catch-22, Cat's Eye, Dracula, Erewhon, Euphues, Ivanhoe, Justine, Lord Jim, Orlando, Rebecca, Shirley, The Bell, The Fall, Ulysses
08 Adam Bede, Birdsong, Clarissa, Cranford, Disgrace, Germinal, Jane Eyre, Lavengro, Lucky Jim, Moby Dick, Newcomes, Nostromo, Oroonoko, Peter Pan, Rasselas, The Idiot, The Trial, The Waves, The Years, Tom Jones, Tom Thumb, Villette, Waverley
09 About a Boy, Amsterdam, Beau Geste, Billy Budd, Billy Liar, Dead Souls, Dubliners, Gargantua, Hard Times, Kidnapped, L'Étranger, On the Road, Rogue Male, The Devils, The Egoist, The Hobbit, The Warden, Tom Sawyer, White Fang
10 A Man in Full, Animal Farm, Bleak House, Cancer Ward, Cannery Row, Clayhanger, Don Quixote, East of Eden, Edwin Drood, Fever Pitch, Goldfinger, Howards End, Kenilworth, Labyrinths, Lorna Doone, Persuasion, Rural Rides, The Leopard, The Rainbow, The Tin Drum, Titus Alone, Titus Groan, Uncle Remus, Vanity Fair, Westward Ho!, White Teeth
11 A Tale of a Tub, Black Beauty, Burmese Days, Cakes and Ale, Daisy Miller, Gormenghast, Greenmantle, Little Women, Middlemarch, Mrs Dalloway, Oliver Twist, Silas Marner, Steppenwolf, The Big Sleep, The Hireling, The Outsider, The Talisman, The Third Man, War and Peace, Women in Love
12 Anna Karenina, A Severed Head, A Suitable Boy, Barnaby Rudge, Brighton Rock, Casino Royale, Dombey and Son, Fear of Flying, Frankenstein, Little Dorrit, Madame Bovary, Moll Flanders, Of Mice and Men, Old Mortality, Rip Van Winkle, Room at the Top, The Go-Between, The Golden Ass, The Lost World, The Moonstone, The Old Devils, Volsungasaga
13 A Kind of Loving, Arabian Nights, Brave New World, Call of the Wild, Daniel Deronda, Doctor Zhivago, Finnegans Wake, Joseph Andrews, Just So Stories, Les Misérables, Mansfield Park, Metamorphosis, New Grub Street, North and South, Schindler's Ark, Sketches By Boz, Smiley's People, Sons and Lovers, Tarka the Otter, The Awkward Age, The Bostonians, The Golden Bowl, The Jungle Book, The Last Tycoon, The Mabinogion, The Naked Lunch, The Odessa File, Thérèse Raquin, The Virginians, Under Milk Wood, Winnie-the-Pooh, Zuleika Dobson
14 A Handful of Dust, A Room with a View, A Town Like Alice, Cider with Rosie, Death on the Nile, Decline and Fall, Fathers and Sons, Humphry Clinker, Jude the Obscure, Le Morte d'Arthur, Lord of the Flies, Lord of the Rings, Robinson Crusoe, Roderick Random, The Ambassadors, The Coral Island, The Da Vinci Code, The First Circle, The Forsyte Saga, The Great Gatsby, The Human Comedy, The Kraken Wakes, The Long Goodbye, The Lovely Bones, The Secret Agent, The Time Machine, The Water-Babies, The Woodlanders, Treasure Island, Tristram Shandy, Tropic of Cancer, Uncle Tom's Cabin, What Maisie Knew
15 A Christmas Carol, A Farewell to Arms, A Passage to India, Cold Comfort Farm, Daphnis and Chloe, Flaubert's Parrot, Gone with the Wind, Huckleberry Finn, Le Rouge et le Noir, Northanger Abbey, Our Mutual Friend, Peregrine Pickle, Tarzan of the Apes, The African Queen, The Invisible Man, The Little Prince, The Old Wives' Tale, The Secret Garden, The Woman in White, Three Men in a Boat, To the Lighthouse, Under the Volcano, Vernon God Little, Where Eagles Dare

novelist
06 author, fabler, writer **09** innovator **10** newsmonger, news-writer **11** storyteller **12** man of letters **13** fiction writer **14** creative writer, woman of letters
See also **author**

novelty
06 bauble, gadget, trifle **07** gimmick, memento, newness, primeur, trinket **08** gimcrack, rareness, souvenir **09** curiosity, freshness **10** creativity, difference, innovation, knick-knack, uniqueness **11** originality, strangeness, unusualness **13** unfamiliarity **15** imaginativeness

November
01 N **03** Nov

novice
01 L **03** cub, kyu **04** tiro, tyro **05** chela, pupil **06** gryfon, newbie, rookie **07** amateur, griffin, griffon, grommet, gryphon, learner, new chum, recruit, student, trainee **08** beginner, neophyte, newcomer **09** greenhorn, noviciate, novitiate **10** apprentice, raw recruit **11** probationer

noviciate
06 novice **08** training **09** novitiate, probation **10** initiation **11** trial period **13** trainee period **14** apprenticeship

now
02 AD **04** next, then **05** today **06** at once **07** just now, present **08** directly, nowadays, promptly, right now **09** at present, currently, instantly, presently, right away, these days **10** at this time **11** at the moment, immediately **12** straight away, without delay **15** for the time being

• **now and then**
07 at times **08** on and off **09** sometimes **10** on occasion **11** desultorily, now and again **12** infrequently, occasionally, once in a while, periodically, sporadically **13** spasmodically **14** from time to time, intermittently

nowadays
02 AD **03** now **05** today **09** at present, currently, presently, these days **10** at this time **11** at the moment **15** in this day and age

noxious
04 foul **05** toxic **06** deadly **07** harmful, nocuous, noisome, ruinous **08** damaging, menacing **09** injurious, malignant, obnoxious, poisonous, unhealthy **10** contagious, disgusting, pernicious **11** deleterious, destructive, detrimental, pestiferous, threatening, unwholesome

nozzle
03 jet **04** nose, rose **05** snout, spout,

tweer, twier, twire, twyer **06** stroup, tuyère, twyere **07** ajutage, sparger, sprayer **08** adjutage **09** nosepiece, sprinkler **10** projection **13** sprinkler head

nuance
04 hint **05** shade, tinge, touch, trace **06** degree, nicety **07** shading **08** overtone, subtlety **09** gradation, suspicion **10** refinement, suggestion **11** distinction **15** fine distinction

nub
04 core, crux, gist, hang, knob, lump, meat, pith **05** chunk, focus, heart, pivot, point **06** centre, kernel, marrow **07** essence, gallows, nucleus **12** central point, protuberance

nubile
04 sexy **05** adult **06** mature **09** desirable **10** attractive, voluptuous **12** marriageable

nuclear
01 N

nucleus
◇ *middle selection indicator*
03 nub **04** core, crux, meat **05** basis, focus, heart, pivot **06** centre, kernel, marrow **08** eucaryon, eukaryon, heartlet, nucellus **09** karyosome

nude
03 raw **04** bare **05** naked **06** Adamic **07** denuded, exposed, skyclad **08** disrobed, in the raw, starkers, stripped, undraped **09** butt-naked, in the buff, in the scud, unclothed, uncovered, undressed **10** start-naked **11** mother-naked **12** not a stitch on **13** with nothing on **15** in the altogether
See also **bare**; **naked**

nudge
03 dig, jab, jog **04** bump, knee, poke, prod, push **05** dunch, dunsh, elbow, shove **06** prompt

nudity
04 scud **06** nudism **07** undress **08** bareness **09** nakedness **10** déshabillé, dishabille **14** state of undress **15** in the altogether

nugatory
04 vain **06** futile **07** invalid, trivial, useless **08** trifling **09** valueless, worthless **10** inadequate, negligible, unavailing **11** ineffectual, inoperative, null and void **13** insignificant **15** inconsequential

nugget
03 wad **04** hunk, lump, mass **05** chunk, clump, piece, wodge

nuisance
04 bore, chiz, drag, hoha, hoop, hurt, pain, pest **05** chizz, trial **06** bother, burden, hoop-la, injury, plague, weight **07** problem, scunner, trouble **08** drawback, irritant, vexation **09** annoyance **10** affliction, difficulty, irritation **11** tribulation **13** inconvenience **15** thorn in your side

null
04 kink, vain, void, zero **05** annul, empty, knurl **06** cipher, cypher, nought **07** invalid, nullify, revoked, useless **08** annulled **09** abrogated, cancelled, nullified, powerless, worthless **11** ineffectual, inoperative, invalidated

nullify
04 kill, null, void **05** abate, annul, quash **06** cancel, negate, offset, repeal, revoke **07** abolish, rescind, reverse **08** abrogate, evacuate, renounce, set aside **10** counteract, invalidate, neutralize **11** countermand, discontinue **12** bring to an end

nullity
08 voidness **10** invalidity **11** uselessness **12** non-existence **13** immateriality, powerlessness, worthlessness **14** incorporeality **15** ineffectualness

numb
04 daze, dead, drug, dull, stun **05** dazed **06** benumb, deaden, freeze, frozen, torpid **07** drugged, in shock, stunned, stupefy, torpefy **08** benumbed, deadened, paralyse, sleeping **09** insensate, paralysed, stupefied, unfeeling **10** immobilize, insensible **11** immobilized, insensitive **12** anaesthetize **13** anaesthetized **14** without feeling

number
01 C, D, K, L, M, n **02** no **03** act, add, num, sum **04** copy, data, item, many, song, tale, turn, unit **05** count, crowd, dance, digit, group, horde, issue, limit, local, score, tally, total, track **06** amount, cipher, figure, reckon, sketch, throng, volume **07** add up to, company, compute, decimal, delimit, edition, imprint, include, integer, numeral, ordinal, routine, several, specify **08** cardinal, estimate, fraction, printing, quantity, restrain, restrict **09** aggregate, apportion, calculate, character, enumerate, multitude **10** collection, impression, statistics **11** anaesthetic, performance **12** anaesthetist, piece of music

Numbers include:

02 pi
03 one, six, ten, two
04 five, four, half, nine, zero
05 eight, fifty, forty, seven, sixty, three
06 eighty, eleven, googol, ninety, thirty, twelve, twenty
07 billion, chiliad, fifteen, hundred, million, seventy, sixteen
08 eighteen, fourteen, nineteen, thirteen, thousand, trillion
09 decillion, nonillion, octillion, seventeen
10 centillion, googolplex, one hundred, septillion, sextillion
11 quadrillion, quintillion

French numbers include:

02 un
03 dix, six
04 cent, cinq, deux, huit, neuf, onze, sept, zéro
05 douze, mille, seize, trois, vingt
06 quatre, quinze, treize, trente
07 dix-huit, dix-neuf, dix-sept
08 quarante, quatorze, soixante
09 cinquante, deux mille, un million
10 un milliard
11 soixante-dix
12 quatre-vingts

German numbers include:

03 elf
04 acht, drei, eins, fünf, neun, null, vier, zehn, zwei
05 sechs, zwölf
06 sieben
07 achtzig, Billion, fünfzig, hundert, Million, neunzig, sechzig, siebzig, tausend, vierzig, zwanzig
08 achtzehn, dreissig, dreizehn, fünfzehn, neunzehn, sechzehn, siebzehn, vierzehn
09 Milliarde
10 einhundert, eintausend

Italian numbers include:

03 due, sei, tre, uno
04 nove, otto
05 cento, dieci, sette, venti
06 cinque, dodici, sedici, trenta, undici
07 novanta, ottanta, quattro, tredici
08 diciotto, quaranta, quindici, sessanta, settanta
09 cinquanta
10 diciannove
11 diciassette, quattordici

Latin numbers include:

03 duo, mil, sex
04 octo, tres, unus
05 decem, mille, novem
06 centum, septem
07 quinque, sedecim, undecim, viginti
08 duodecim, quattuor, tredecim, trigenta
09 nonaginta, octoginta, sexaginta
11 quadraginta, septendecim, septuaginta, undeviginti
12 duodeviginti, quinquaginta, quinquedecim
13 quattuordecim

Spanish numbers include:

03 dos, mil, uno
04 diez, doce, ocho, once, seis, tres
05 cinco, nueve, siete, trece
06 ciento, cuatro, quince, veinte
07 catorce, noventa, ochenta, sesenta, setenta, treinta
08 cuarenta, un millón
09 cincuenta, dieciocho, dieciséis
10 diecinueve, diecisiete, quinientos
11 mil millones

• **any number**
01 n

• **large number**
01 n **03** lot, ten **04** army, host, raft, slew, slue
See also **many**

numberless
04 many **06** myriad, untold **07** endless **08** infinite, unsummed **09** countless, uncounted **10** unnumbered **11** innumerable **12** immeasurable **13** multitudinous, without number

numbness
06 stupor, torpor **08** deadness, dullness **09** paralysis **10** night-palsy **12** stupefaction **13** insensateness, insensibility, insensitivity, unfeelingness

numeral
03 num **04** unit **05** digit **06** cipher, figure, number **07** integer **09** character

Roman numerals include:

01 C (hundred), D (five hundred), I (one), L (fifty), M (thousand), V (five), X (ten)
02 II (two), IV (four), IX (nine), VI (six), XI (eleven), XV (fifteen), XX (twenty)
03 III (three), VII (seven), XII (twelve), XIV (fourteen), XIX (nineteen), XVI (sixteen)
04 VIII (eight), XIII (thirteen), XVII (seventeen)
05 XVIII (eighteen)

numerical
05 whole **06** graded, ranked, scalar **07** digital, figural **08** integral **09** identical **11** statistical **12** hierarchical **13** computational

numerically
07 in order **09** digitally **10** measurably **12** quantifiably **13** algebraically, exponentially **14** arithmetically, mathematically

numerous
04 many **05** great **06** a lot of, legion, strong, sundry, untold **07** copious, endless, profuse, several, various **08** abundant, a good few, manifold, populous **09** countless, plentiful, quite a few **10** rhythmical **11** innumerable **13** great in number, multitudinous

numerousness
06 number **08** multeity **09** abundance, plurality, profusion **10** numerosity **11** copiousness **12** manifoldness, multiplicity **13** countlessness, plentifulness

numinous
04 holy **05** deity, numen **06** divine, sacred **08** divinity, mystical **09** religious, spiritual **10** mysterious **12** supernatural, transcendent

numskull
03 ass, git, mug, nit, sap **04** berk, clot, coot, dill, dope, dork, fool, geek, goat, goof, goop, jerk, kook, nana, nerd, nerk, nong, prat, putz, twit, yo-yo **05** chump, dumbo, dunce, dweeb, galah, neddy, ninny, prick, schmo, twerp, wally **06** bampot, dimwit, doofus, dum-dum, josser, muppet, nig-nog, nitwit, sawney, sucker, turkey **07** Charlie, dingbat, gubbins, jughead, pillock, plonker, saphead, tosspot, wazzock **08** boofhead, dipstick, lunkhead **09** birdbrain, blockhead, cloth head, schlemiel, simpleton **10** headbanger, nincompoop, silly-billy **11** chowderhead **13** proper Charlie

nun
03 top **06** abbess, sister, vestal, vowess **07** ancress, blue tit, zelator **08** canoness, prioress, zelatrix **09** anchoress, deaconess, zelatrice **10** cloistress, conventual, religieuse **14** mother superior

See also **monk**

Nunavut
02 NU

nuncio
05 envoy **06** legate **09** messenger **10** ambassador **14** representative

nunnery
05 abbey **06** priory **07** convent, nunship **08** cloister

nuptial
06 bridal, wedded **07** marital, spousal, wedding **08** conjugal, hymeneal **09** connubial **11** epithalamic, matrimonial **12** epithalamial

nuptials
06 bridal **07** wedding **08** espousal, marriage, spousals **09** hymeneals, matrimony

nurse
◇ *containment indicator*
03 aid **04** feed, help, keep, tend **05** angel, boost, shark, treat **06** assist, cradle, foster, suckle **07** advance, care for, cherish, dogfish, further, harbour, nourice, nourish, nurture, promote, support, sustain **08** attend to, preserve **09** encourage, entertain, look after **10** breast-feed, take care of

Nurse types include:

02 EN, RN
03 aia, CNN, dry, pro, RGN, SEN, SRN, wet
04 amah, ayah, home, maid, sick
05 nanny, night, staff, tutor
06 charge, dental, matron, school, sister
07 midwife, nursery
08 district
09 auxiliary, children's, community, Macmillan
10 consultant, Iain Rennie, ward sister
11 night sister, psychiatric
12 practitioner
13 health visitor, State Enrolled, theatre sister
15 locality manager, State Registered

Nurses include:

05 Kenny (Elizabeth)
06 Barton (Clara), Cavell (Edith), Rayner (Claire), Sanger (Margaret)
07 Seacole (Mary)
08 Pattison (Dorothy Wyndlow)
10 Stephenson (Elsie)
11 Nightingale (Florence)
14 Queen Alexandra

See also **medical**

nurture
03 aid **04** care, diet, eats, feed, food, grub, help, nosh, rear, tend, tuck **05** boost, coach, nurse, scran, train, tutor **06** assist, cradle, foster, school **07** advance, bring up, care for, cherish, develop, educate, feeding, further, nourish, promote, rearing, support, sustain, tending **08** boosting, instruct, training **09** cultivate, education, fostering, nouriture, nutrition, promotion, schooling, stimulate **10** assistance, discipline, nourriture, sustenance, upbringing **11** cultivation, development, environment, furtherance, nourishment, stimulation, subsistence **13** encouragement

nut
02 en **03** fan, pip **04** buff, butt, head, seed **05** crank, fiend, freak, loony, stone **06** kernel, madman, maniac, nutter, psycho, zealot **07** admirer, devotee, fanatic, lunatic, nutcase, oddball **08** crackpot, follower, headcase, madwoman **09** fruitcake, screwball, supporter **10** aficionado, basket-case, enthusiast, psychopath **12** insane person

Nuts include:

03 ben, oak, pig
04 cola, horn, kola, pará, pili, pine, shea, wing
05 acorn, areca, arnut, beech, betel, cedar, cream, earth, ivory, lichi, pecan, tiger
06 almond, Brazil, cashew, castle, cobnut, cohune, corozo, ginger, hognut, illipe, lichee, litchi, lychee, monkey, oilnut, peanut, physic, poison, sleeve, souari, walnut
07 babassu, bladder, buffalo, chesnut, coconut, filberd, filbert, gallnut, hickory, leechee, locknut, marking, palmyra, pilinut, saouari
08 chestnut, clearing, cocoanut, cokernut, coquilla, hazelnut, quandong, sapucaia, thumbnut
09 Barcelona, beech mast, butterfly, butternut, groundnut, macadamia, mockernut, pistachio, sassafras, scaly-bark
10 locking-nut, Queensland, St Anthony's
11 Molucca bean
13 earth-chestnut, horse chestnut

See also **head**

• **do your nut**
05 go mad **06** blow up, see red **07** explode **08** boil over, freak out **09** blow a fuse, go berserk, raise hell **11** blow your top, flip your lid, go ballistic, go up the wall, have kittens, lose your rag **12** blow your cool, fly into a rage, lose your cool, throw a wobbly **13** hit the ceiling, throw a tantrum **14** foam at the mouth **15** fly off the handle, go off the deep end

nutriment
04 diet, eats, food, grub, nosh, tuck

05 scran **09** nutrition **10** sustenance **11** nourishment, subsistence

nutrition
04 diet, eats, food, grub, nosh, tuck **05** scran **08** eutrophy **09** nutriment **10** sustenance **11** nourishment, subsistence

nutritious
04 good **09** healthful, nutritive, wholesome **10** beneficial, nourishing, sustaining **11** substantial **12** body-building, health-giving, invigorating **13** strengthening

nuts
◇ *anagram indicator*
03 mad **04** avid, bats, daft, fond, keen, loco, mast, wild **05** barmy, batty, crazy, daffy, dippy, loony, loopy, nutty, potty **06** ardent, crazed, insane **07** berserk, bonkers, devoted, lunatic, smitten, zealous **08** demented, deranged, doolally, unhinged **09** disturbed, enamoured, fanatical **10** infatuated, out to lunch, passionate, unbalanced **12** enthusiastic, round the bend **13** off your rocker, out of your mind, round the twist **14** off your trolley

See also **mad**

nuts and bolts
06 basics **07** details **10** components, essentials **11** nitty-gritty **12** fundamentals **13** bits and pieces **14** practicalities

nutty
03 mad **04** nuts, wild **05** barmy, batty, crazy, daffy, dippy, loony, loopy, potty **06** crazed, insane **07** berserk, bonkers, lunatic **08** demented, deranged, doolally, unhinged **09** disturbed **10** out to lunch, unbalanced **12** round the bend **13** off your rocker, out of your mind, round the twist **14** off your trolley

nuzzle
03 pet, rub **04** nose, poke, root **05** nudge, press, sniff, train **06** burrow, caress, cuddle, fondle, foster, nestle **07** bring up, snoozle, snuggle, snuzzle

nymph
04 Echo, girl, lass, maid, pupa **05** dryad, houri, naiad, oread, sylph **06** damsel, maelid, maiden, nereid, sprite, Tethys, undine **07** mermaid, oceanid, rusalka **09** hamadryad

O

O
05 Oscar **06** nought **07** nothing, spangle

oaf
03 auf, oik **04** boor, clod, dolt, gawk, hick, hoon, lout, ouph, slob **05** idiot, ocker, ouphe, yahoo, yobbo **06** lubber **07** bumpkin **09** barbarian, roughneck **10** changeling, clodhopper **11** hobbledehoy

oafish
05 gawky, gross, ocker, rough **06** clumsy, coarse, lumpen, stolid **07** boorish, doltish, idiotic, ill-bred, loutish, lumpish, swinish, uncouth, yobbish **08** bungling, churlish, lubberly **10** unmannerly **11** clodhopping, ill-mannered

oak
04 holm, ilex **05** roble **06** cerris, kermes **07** durmast, Quercus **08** corktree, flittern, wainscot **10** quercitron **13** partridge-wood **15** king of the forest
• **oak bark**
03 tan

oar
03 row **05** blade, scull, spoon, sweep **06** bow-oar, paddle, stroke **09** stroke oar
• **oar blade**
04 peel

oasis
05 haven **06** island, refuge, spring **07** hideout, retreat, sanctum **08** hideaway **09** sanctuary **12** watering-hole

oath
03 vow **04** bond, cuss, word **05** curse **06** avowal, pledge **07** promise **08** cussword **09** assurance, blasphemy, curse-word, expletive, obscenity, profanity, sacrament, swear-word **11** affirmation, attestation, bad language, imprecation, malediction **12** word of honour **14** four-letter word
• **oaths and euphemisms**
02 od **03** dod, dog, gad, gee, Gog, odd **04** drat, ecod, egad, gosh, heck,hell, igad, life, odso, oons, rats, 'slid, 'zbud **05** bedad, begad, gadso, nouns, 'sfoot, 'slife, zooks **06** cricky, crikey, 'sblood, 'sdeath, 'sheart, 'snails **07** begorra, by Jingo, crickey, jabbers, odzooks, strewth **08** begorrah, bejabers, gadzooks **09** bismillah, 'sbodikins **10** sapperment, 'sbuddikins

obduracy
08 firmness, tenacity **09** obstinacy **10** doggedness, mulishness, perversity, wilfulness **11** frowardness, persistence, pertinacity **12** perseverance, resoluteness, stubbornness **13** inflexibility, intransigence, pigheadedness **14** relentlessness **15** hard-heartedness, wrongheadedness

obdurate
04 firm, hard, iron **05** stony **06** dogged, flinty, wilful **07** adamant **08** hardened, stubborn **09** immovable, obstinate, pigheaded, steadfast, tenacious, unbending, unfeeling **10** determined, headstrong, implacable, inflexible, persistent, self-willed, unyielding **11** hard-hearted, intractable, stiff-necked, unrelenting **12** bloody-minded, intransigent, strong-minded

obedience
04 duty **07** respect **08** docility **09** agreement, deference, obeisance, passivity, reverence **10** accordance, allegiance, compliance, observance, submission **11** amenability, dutifulness **12** acquiescence, amenableness, malleability, subservience, tractability **14** conformability, submissiveness

obedient
04 bent, obdt **06** docile **07** duteous, dutiful, pliable **08** amenable, biddable, yielding **09** compliant, malleable, observant, tractable **10** bridle-wise, conforming, law-abiding, obsequious, respectful, submissive **11** acquiescent, deferential, disciplined, subservient, well-trained

obeisance
03 bow **06** cringe, curtsy, homage, kowtow, salaam, salute **07** curtsey, respect **09** deference, obedience, reverence **10** salutation, submission, veneration **12** genuflection

obelisk
06 column, dagger, needle, obelus, pillar **08** memorial, monument

obese
03 big, fat **05** beefy, bulky, gross, heavy, hefty, large, plump, podgy, porky, round, stout, tubby **06** chubby, flabby, fleshy, portly, rotund **07** outsize, paunchy **08** roly-poly **09** corpulent, ponderous **10** overweight **11** Falstaffian, well-endowed **15** well-upholstered

obesity
04 bulk **07** fatness **09** grossness, plumpness, podginess, stoutness, tubbiness **10** chubbiness, corpulence, flabbiness, overweight, portliness, rotundness

obey
04 heed, keep, mind **05** bow to, defer, yield **06** comply, follow, fulfil, keep to, submit **07** abide by, act upon, conform, defer to, execute, give way, observe, perform, respect, respond **08** adhere to, carry out **09** be ruled by, consent to, discharge, surrender **10** come to heel, toe the line **11** acquiesce in, go by the book **14** do as you are told, take orders from **15** stick to the rules

obfuscate
◇ *anagram indicator*
04 blur, hide, mask, veil **05** cloak, cloud, cover, shade **06** darken, muddle, shadow, shroud **07** conceal, confuse, obscure **08** bewilder, disguise **10** complicate, overshadow

obfuscation
06 muddle **08** disguise **09** confusion, obscurity **11** concealment **12** complication

obituary
04 obit **06** eulogy **09** necrology **11** death notice

object
03 aim, end, jib **04** body, butt, goal, idea, item, sake **05** argue, cavil, demur, focus, point, rebut, thing **06** adduce, design, device, entity, gadget, impute, intent, motive, oddity, oppose, reason, recuse, refuse, resist, target, victim **07** article, exposed, opposed, present, protest, purpose **08** ambition, artefact, complain **09** challenge, intention, objective, recipient, repudiate, something, take issue, withstand **10** disapprove, interposed, phenomenon **11** beg to differ, expostulate, remonstrate **12** recalcitrate **13** interposition, take exception
• **provisional object**
02 it
• **with the object of**
02 to

objection
02 ob **03** but **05** cavil, demur **06** boggle **07** dislike, dissent, protest, quarrel, scruple **08** argument, demurrer, question **09** challenge, complaint, exception, grievance

10 difficulty, opposition, recusation **11** disapproval **13** expostulation, recalcitrance, remonstration, unwillingness **15** dissatisfaction

objectionable
04 pert **05** nasty **07** hateful **09** abhorrent, loathsome, obnoxious, offensive, repellent, repugnant, repulsive, revolting, sickening **10** deplorable, despicable, detestable, nauseating, unpleasant **11** distasteful, intolerable **12** contemptible, disagreeable, unacceptable **13** exceptionable, reprehensible

objective
03 aim, end, obj **04** fair, goal, idea, just, mark, real, true **05** point **06** actual, design, intent, object, target, thingy **07** factual, genuine, neutral, purpose **08** ambition, clinical, detached, unbiased **09** authentic, equitable, impartial, intention **10** even-handed, impersonal, open-minded, uninvolved **12** unprejudiced **13** disinterested, dispassionate

objectively
06 fairly, justly **09** equitably, neutrally **11** impartially **12** even-handedly **14** with an open mind **15** disinterestedly, dispassionately

objectivity
07 justice **08** fairness, justness, open mind **10** detachment, thinginess **11** disinterest, outwardness, thingliness **12** impartiality **13** equitableness **14** even-handedness, open-mindedness

objector
05 rebel **07** opposer, striker **08** agitator, opponent **09** dissenter, dissident, protester **10** complainer **12** demonstrator

obligate
04 bind, make **05** force, impel, press **06** coerce, compel, oblige **07** require **08** pressure **09** constrain **10** pressurize **11** necessitate

obligation
03 job, tie **04** bond, cess, debt, deed, duty, must, onus, task **05** trust **06** burden, charge, demand, duress, favour **07** astrict, burthen, command **08** contract, covenant, function, pressure **09** agreement, liability **10** assignment, commitment, compulsion, incumbency **11** obstriction, requirement **12** indebtedness **14** accountability, responsibility

obligatory
03 set **05** usual **06** normal **07** binding, bounden, regular, routine **08** accepted, enforced, familiar, habitual, ordinary, required **09** customary, essential, incumbent, mandatory, necessary, requisite, statutory **10** compulsory, imperative **11** established, fashionable, traditional, unavoidable **12** conventional

oblige
03 put, tie **04** bind, help, make **05** force, impel, press, serve **06** assist, coerce, compel, please **07** gratify, require **08** astringe, obligate, pressure **09** constrain **10** pressurize **11** accommodate, necessitate **15** be given no option

obliged
05 bound **06** debted, forced, in debt **08** beholden, grateful, having to, indebted, in debt to, required, thankful **09** compelled, duty-bound, gratified, obligated **11** constrained, having got to, honour-bound **12** appreciative **15** under compulsion

obliging
04 kind **05** civil **06** polite **07** helpful, willing **08** friendly, generous, pleasant **09** agreeable, courteous, indulgent, officious **11** complaisant, considerate, co-operative, good-natured **13** accommodating

obligingly
07 civilly **08** politely **09** agreeably, helpfully, willingly **10** generously **11** courteously **13** considerately

oblique
◇ *anagram indicator*
03 obl **04** skew **05** cross, slant, slash **06** angled, squint, stroke, tilted, zigzag **07** awkward, devious, sloping, solidus, virgule, winding **08** bevelled, diagonal, inclined, indirect, rambling, sidelong, sideways, slanting, tortuous, traverse **09** divergent, skew-whiff, underhand **10** circuitous, discursive, meandering, roundabout **12** forward slash, periphrastic **14** circumlocutory, slantendicular, slantindicular

obliquely
05 askew **06** askant, aslant, aslope, squint **07** askance, asquint **08** sidelong **09** at an angle, evasively, slantwise, slopewise **10** diagonally, indirectly **12** circuitously

obliterate
04 blot **05** erase **06** deface, delete, efface, rub out **07** blot out, destroy, expunge, wipe out **08** black out, vaporize, wash away **09** eliminate, eradicate, extirpate, overscore, strike out **10** annihilate

obliteration
04 blot **06** rasure, razure **07** erasure **08** deletion **10** effacement, expunction **11** blotting out, destruction, elimination, eradication, extirpation **12** annihilation

oblivion
04 void **05** Lethe, limbo **06** disuse, pardon, stupor **07** amnesty, silence **08** darkness, deafness **09** blankness, blindness, ignorance, obscurity **11** forgiveness, nothingness **12** carelessness, non-existence **13** forgetfulness, insensibility, unmindfulness **15** inattentiveness, unconsciousness

oblivious
04 deaf **05** blind **07** unaware **08** careless, heedless, ignorant **09** forgetful, forgotten, negligent, unheeding, unmindful **10** insensible **11** inattentive, preoccupied, unconcerned, unconscious **12** absent-minded

obliviousness
07 naivety **09** greenness, ignorance, innocence, stupidity, thickness **10** illiteracy **11** unawareness **12** inexperience **13** unfamiliarity **14** unintelligence **15** unconsciousness

obloquy
05 abuse, blame, odium, shame **06** attack, stigma **07** calumny, censure, slander **08** bad press, disgrace, ignominy, reproach **09** aspersion, contumely, criticism, discredit, disfavour, dishonour, invective **10** defamation, detraction, opprobrium **11** humiliation **12** vilification **13** animadversion

obnoxious
04 vile **05** nasty **06** horrid, odious **07** exposed, hateful, hurtful, noxious **08** horrible **09** abhorrent, loathsome, offensive, repellent, repugnant, repulsive, revolting, sickening **10** deplorable, detestable, disgusting, nauseating, unpleasant **11** intolerable **12** contemptible, disagreeable, unacceptable **13** objectionable

obscene
03 paw **04** blue, foul, lewd, rude, sexy, vile **05** bawdy, dirty, gross, nasty **06** carnal, coarse, filthy, fruity, greasy, impure, pawpaw, risqué, sleazy, smutty, vulgar, X-rated **07** immoral, raunchy **08** hard-core, immodest, improper, indecent, prurient, shocking, unchaste **09** loathsome, off-colour, offensive, repellent, shameless **10** disgusting, licentious, lubricious, outrageous, scandalous, scurrilous, suggestive **11** disgraceful, near the bone **12** pornographic **14** near the knuckle

obscenity
04 cuss, dirt, evil, smut **05** curse, filth **06** sleaze **07** offence, outrage **08** atrocity, cussword, foulness, impurity, lewdness, ribaldry, ribaudry, vileness **09** bawdiness, carnality, dirtiness, eroticism, expletive, grossness, immodesty, indecency, lubricity, profanity, prurience, rybaudrye, scatology, swear-word, vulgarity **10** balderdash, coarseness, filthiness, immorality, indelicacy, wickedness **11** bad language, heinousness, imprecation, impropriety, malediction, pornography, raunchiness **12** unchasteness **13** salaciousness, shamelessness **14** four-letter word, lasciviousness, licentiousness, scurrilousness, suggestiveness

obscure
◇ *anagram indicator*
03 dim, fog **04** blur, dark, deep, hazy,

hide, mask, mist, veil, wrap **05** cloak, cloud, cover, dusky, faint, fuzzy, lowly, minor, misty, murky, shade, shady, vague **06** arcane, cloudy, darken, fogged, gloomy, hidden, humble, muddle, occult, opaque, remote, screen, shadow, shroud, unsung **07** blurred, complex, conceal, confuse, cryptic, eclipse, shadowy, unclear, unknown **08** abstruse, block out, darkness, disguise, doubtful, esoteric, involved, nameless, oracular, puzzling, riddling, twilight **09** concealed, confusing, enigmatic, obfuscate, oraculous, recondite, uncertain, unheard-of **10** complicate, indefinite, indistinct, mysterious, overshadow, perplexing **11** god-forsaken, little-known, out-of-the-way, unexplained, unimportant **12** impenetrable, inexplicable, unfathomable, unrecognized **13** inconspicuous, insignificant **14** indistinctness **15** undistinguished

obscurity
03 fog **05** depth, night, shade **07** mystery **09** ambiguity, confusion, intricacy, lowliness, murkiness, mysticism **10** complexity, lack of fame **11** unclearness **12** abstruseness, namelessness, unimportance **13** reconditeness **14** insignificance **15** impenetrability

• **bring out of obscurity**
04 fish

obsequies
04 wake **06** burial **07** funeral **08** exequies **09** cremation, interment **10** entombment, inhumation

obsequious
04 oily **06** abject, creepy, menial, smarmy **07** dutiful, fawning, fulsome, kiss-ass, servile, slavish **08** crawling, cringing, obedient, toadying, toadyish, unctuous **10** flattering, grovelling, submissive **11** bootlicking, deferential, subservient, sycophantic **12** ingratiating, knee-crooking

observable
04 open **05** clear **06** patent **07** evident, notable, obvious, visible **08** apparent **09** scrutable **10** detectable, measurable, noticeable **11** appreciable, discernible, perceptible, significant **12** recognizable

observance
04 Lent, puja, rite **06** custom, maying, notice, ritual **07** heeding, keeping, service, trinket, triumph **08** ceremony, festival, practice **09** adherence, attention, discharge, execution, following, formality, honouring, obedience, punctilio, reverence, sabbatism, tradition **10** compliance, fulfilment **11** celebration, performance **13** lectisternium

observant
05 alert, sharp **06** seeing **07** devoted, dutiful, heedful, mindful, on guard **08** hawk-eyed, obedient, orthodox, vigilant, watchful **09** attentive, beady-eyed, committed, eagle-eyed, sharp-eyed, wide-awake **10** perceptive, percipient, practising **11** observative **12** card-carrying, on the lookout, on the qui vive

observation
04 data, note **05** study **06** espial, notice, regard, remark, result, review, seeing **07** comment, finding, opinion, thought, viewing **08** eyesight, noticing, scrutiny, watching **09** attention, criticism, statement, utterance **10** annotation, cognizance, inspection, monitoring, perception, reflection **11** declaration, description, discernment, examination, information **13** consideration, pronouncement

observatory
06 orrery **09** viewpoint **11** planetarium, planisphere

Observatories include:

04 Keck
05 Royal, Tower
06 Gemini
07 Arecibo, Palomar, Paranal
08 Kitt Peak, Mauna Kea
09 Greenwich
11 Jodrell Bank, Mount Wilson
12 Herstmonceux
13 Tower of London
14 Royal Greenwich

observe
02 la, lo **03** eye, say, see, spy, use **04** espy, heed, hold, keep, mark, note, obey, spot, take, twig, view **05** clock, smoke, state, study, utter, watch **06** behold, detect, follow, fulfil, honour, notice, regard, remark **07** abide by, comment, declare, discern, examine, execute, inspect, look you, mention, monitor, perform, respect **08** adhere to, maintain, perceive, remember, take note **09** celebrate, conform to, discharge, recognize, speculate, surveille **10** animadvert, comply with, keep tabs on, take notice **11** commemorate, contemplate, keep an eye on, keep watch on, miss nothing **12** catch sight of **14** watch like a hawk

observer
06 looker, viewer **07** watcher, witness **08** beholder, looker-on, onlooker, reporter **09** bystander, sightseer, spectator **10** eyewitness **11** commentator, speculation

obsess
04 grip, rule **05** beset, eat up, haunt, hound **06** plague, prey on **07** bedevil, besiege, consume, control, engross, possess, torment **08** dominate **09** preoccupy **10** monopolize **11** have a grip on, have a hold on

obsessed
05 beset **06** hipped **07** gripped, haunted, hounded, plagued **08** hung up on **09** dominated **10** bedevilled, immersed in, infatuated **11** in the grip of, preoccupied

obsession
03 bug **05** mania, siege, thing **06** fetish, hang-up, phobia **07** complex **08** fixation, idée fixe, neurosis **09** monomania **10** compulsion, enthusiasm, hobby-horse **11** fascination, infatuation **12** one-track mind **13** preoccupation, ruling passion **15** bee in your bonnet

obsessive
04 anal **05** fixed **08** gripping, haunting, neurotic **09** consuming, maddening **10** compulsive, tormenting **12** all-consuming, trainspotter

obsolescence
06 disuse **07** failure **09** rejection, scrapping **10** redundancy **12** obsoleteness **13** disappearance

obsolescent
05 aging, dated **06** ageing, fading, old hat, waning **08** dying out, moribund, outdated **09** declining, on the wane, out of date, redundant **10** on the shelf **11** on the way out, out of the ark **12** antediluvian, disappearing, old-fashioned, on the decline, past its prime

obsolete
03 obs, old **04** dead **05** dated, passé **06** bygone, old hat **07** ancient, antique, disused, expired, extinct, outworn **08** in disuse, outdated, outmoded **09** discarded, out of date **10** antiquated, on the shelf **11** on the way out, out of the ark **12** antediluvian, discontinued, old-fashioned, out of fashion, past its prime **13** superannuated **14** behind the times

obstacle
03 bar **04** boyg, curb, drag, gate, jump, oxer, rock, snag, stay, stop **05** catch, check, hitch, mogul **06** hazard, hiccup, hurdle, remora **07** barrier **08** blockade, blockage, drawback, handicap, stoppage, stubborn, tank trap **09** barricade, deterrent, hindrance **10** difficulty, hinderance, impediment **11** obstruction **12** Becher's Brook, entanglement, interference, interruption **14** stumbling-block

obstinacy
08 firmness, obduracy, self-will, tenacity **10** doggedness, mulishness, perversity, wilfulness **11** frowardness, persistence, persistency, pertinacity **12** perseverance, resoluteness, stubbornness **13** inflexibility, intransigence, pigheadedness **14** relentlessness **15** hard-heartedness, wrongheadedness

obstinate
04 dour, firm **05** rusty, stoor, stour, sture **06** cussed, dogged, kittle, mulish, stowre, sturdy, thrawn, wilful **07** adamant, bullish, diehard, hard-set,

restive, willful **08** camelish, stubborn, thraward, thrawart **09** hidebound, immovable, pigheaded, steadfast, unbending **10** bull-headed, determined, headstrong, inflexible, persistent, refractary, refractory, self-willed, stomachful, unyielding **11** hard-hearted, intractable, persevering, stiff-necked, unrelenting, wrongheaded **12** bloody-minded, contumacious, intransigent, pertinacious, pervicacious, recalcitrant, stiff-hearted, strong-minded **13** high-stomached, intransigeant

See also **stubborn**

• obstinate person
04 mule

obstreperous
◇ *anagram indicator*
04 loud, wild **05** noisy, radge, rough, rowdy **06** unruly **07** bolshie, raucous, restive, riotous, stroppy **09** clamorous, out of hand, turbulent **10** boisterous, disorderly, disruptive, refractory, rip-roaring, tumultuous, uproarious, vociferous **11** intractable, tempestuous **12** bloody-minded, uncontrolled, unmanageable **13** undisciplined

obstruct
◇ *containment indicator*
03 bar **04** clog, crab, curb, foul, halt, stap, stop **05** block, brake, check, choke, cross, delay, hedge, limit, stall, stimy, stuff **06** arrest, bridle, cut off, hamper, hinder, hold up, impede, retard, stimie, stymie, thwart, waylay **07** blanket, inhibit, obscure, prevent, sandbag, shut off **08** encumber, restrict, slow down **09** barricade, frustrate, hamstring, interfere, interrupt **10** portcullis **13** interfere with

obstruction
03 bar, let **04** clog, stop, veil **05** block, check, ileus, trump **07** barrier, embargo **08** blockade, blockage, obstacle, sanction, stoppage, traverse **09** barricade, body-check, deterrent, hindrance, roadblock **10** bottleneck, difficulty, filibuster, impediment, prevention **11** restriction **14** stumbling-block

obstructive
07 awkward **08** blocking, delaying, negative, stalling **09** difficult, hindering, hindrance, unhelpful **10** inhibiting **11** restrictive **12** interrupting **13** unco-operative

obtain
03 cop, get, pan **04** earn, gain, have, hold, make, rule, snag, take **05** exist, reach, reign, seize, stand **06** attain, come by, come to, derive, occupy, secure **07** achieve, acquire, be in use, compass, possess, prevail, procure, realize **08** hold sway **09** be in force, be the case, get hold of **11** be effective, be prevalent **14** get your hands on

obtainable
05 on tap, ready **06** at hand, on call **07** to be had **09** available **10** accessible, achievable, attainable, procurable, realizable

obtrude
04 sorn **05** abuse, foist **06** butt in, impose **07** break in, exploit, intrude, mislead, presume, put upon **08** encroach, protrude **13** force yourself **14** thrust yourself **15** take advantage of

obtrusive
04 bold, loud, nosy **05** nosey, pushy **06** prying **07** blatant, forward, obvious **08** flagrant, meddling **09** intrusive, prominent **10** noticeable, projecting, protruding **11** conspicuous, interfering

obtuse
03 dim **04** dozy, dull, dumb, slow **05** blunt, crass, dense, dopey, thick **06** stolid, stupid **09** dim-witted **10** dull-witted, slow-witted **11** insensitive **12** thick-skinned **13** unintelligent **15** slow on the uptake

obverse
05 cross, heads **07** inverse, reverse **08** contrary, converse, opposite **10** antithesis **12** complemental

obviate
04 save **05** avert **06** divert, remove **07** counter, prevent **08** preclude **09** forestall **10** anticipate, counteract

obvious
04 bald, open, rank **05** broad, clear, plain **06** patent **07** blatant, evident, glaring, visible **08** apparent, clear-cut, distinct, manifest, palpable, pregnant **09** prominent, writ large **10** detectable, noticeable, pronounced, undeniable, well-marked **11** conspicuous, open-and-shut, perceptible, self-evident, transparent, unconcealed **12** crystal clear, recognizable, unmistakable **14** self-explaining **15** self-explanatory, straightforward

obviously
03 duh **07** clearly, plainly **08** of course, patently **09** certainly, eminently, evidently **10** distinctly, manifestly, noticeably, undeniably **11** undoubtedly **12** unmistakably, without doubt

occasion
02 do **04** bash, call, case, gala, hour, make, need, rise, room, time, turn **05** breed, cause, event, evoke, party, point, throw **06** affair, chance, create, effect, elicit, excuse, ground, induce, lead to, prompt, reason **07** bring on, episode, grounds, inspire, pretext, produce, provoke **08** accustom, engender, function, generate, incident, instance, juncture, persuade **09** encheason, happening, influence, originate, situation **10** bring about, experience, give rise to, occurrence **11** celebration, get-together, opportunity, requirement, social event **12** circumstance **13** justification

See also **event**; **party**

occasional
03 odd **04** orra, rare **06** casual, daimen **08** fugitive, off and on, on and off, periodic, sometime, sporadic, uncommon **09** irregular **10** incidental, infrequent **12** intermittent

occasionally
07 at times **08** casually, off and on, on and off **09** sometimes **10** now and then, once in a way, on occasion **11** at intervals, irregularly, now and again **12** every so often, infrequently, once in a while, periodically, sporadically **14** from time to time, intermittently

occlude
◇ *containment indicator*
03 bar **04** clog, fill, halt, plug, seal, stop **05** block, check, choke, close, cover, dam up **06** absorb, arrest, bung up, clog up, hinder, impede, retain, stop up, thwart **08** obstruct

occlusion
03 jam **04** clot **05** block **06** log jam **08** blockage, blocking, stoppage **09** hindrance **10** congestion, impediment **11** obstruction

occult
03 art **04** arts **05** magic **06** arcane, hidden, secret, veiled **07** magical, obscure, unknown **08** abstruse, esoteric, mystical **09** black arts, concealed, mysticism, recondite **10** mysterious **12** metaphysical, supernatural **13** preternatural **14** transcendental **15** supernaturalism, the supernatural

Occult- and supernatural-related terms include:

03 ESP, obi
04 jinx, juju, omen, rune
05 charm, coven, curse, relic, spell, totem, witch
06 amulet, déjà vu, fetish, hoodoo, medium, séance, shaman, spirit, trance, vision, voodoo
07 cabbala, diviner, evil eye, palmist, psychic, satanic, sorcery, warlock
08 black cat, exorcism, exorcist, familiar, Satanism, Satanist, sorcerer, talisman
09 astrology, black mass, ectoplasm, Hallowe'en, horoscope, influence, palmistry, pentagram, tarot card
10 astrologer, black magic, broomstick, chiromancy, divination, evil spirit, hydromancy, necromancy, Ouija board®, paranormal, planchette, possession, sixth sense, white magic, witchcraft
11 chiromancer, clairvoyant, crystal ball, divining-rod, hydromancer, incantation, necromancer, oneiromancy, poltergeist, premonition, psychometer, psychometry, second sight, witch doctor
12 clairvoyance, oneiromancer, spiritualism, spiritualist,

supernatural, superstition, tarot reading
13 fortune-teller, witch's sabbath
14 Walpurgis Night

occupancy
03 use **04** term **06** tenure **07** holding, tenancy **09** ownership, residence **10** habitation, occupation, possession **11** inhabitancy **13** domiciliation **14** owner-occupancy

occupant
04 user **05** owner **06** holder, inmate, lessee, renter, tenant **08** occupier, resident, squatter **09** homeowner, incumbent **10** inhabitant **11** householder, leaseholder **13** owner-occupier

occupation
03 job, use **04** line, post, work **05** craft, field, trade **06** billet, career, employ, métier, tenure **07** calling, capture, control, holding, pursuit, seizure, tenancy **08** activity, business, conquest, interest, invasion, province, takeover, vocation **09** occupancy, overthrow, residence, residency **10** employment, habitation, possession, profession, walk of life **11** foreign rule, subjugation

Occupations include:

02 AM, DJ, GP, MD, MP, PA
03 MSP, nun, spy, vet
04 aide, chef, cook, dean, dyer, hack, maid, monk, page, poet
05 abbot, actor, agent, baker, boxer, buyer, caddy, clerk, coach, diver, envoy, friar, guide, judge, juror, mason, mayor, medic, miner, model, nanny, nurse, pilot, smith, tawer, tutor, usher, valet, vicar
06 abbess, artist, au pair, author, banker, barber, barman, bishop, bookie, bowyer, brewer, broker, butler, cabbie, cleric, cooper, copper, coster, cowboy, critic, curate, dancer, dealer, doctor, draper, driver, editor, eggler, factor, farmer, fitter, forger, gaffer, glazer, grocer, herald, hermit, hosier, hunter, jailer, jester, jockey, joiner, lawyer, mercer, miller, ostler, packer, parson, pastor, pig-man, pirate, player, porter, potter, priest, ragman, ranger, roofer, sailor, salter, server, singer, skater, sniper, sparks, spicer, tailor, tanner, teller, tinner, trader, tycoon, typist, vendor, verger, waiter, warden, warder, weaver, welder, writer
07 acrobat, actress, actuary, admiral, adviser, almoner, analyst, artisan, artiste, athlete, attaché, auditor, aviator, bailiff, barista, barmaid, bellboy, bellhop, bottle-o, breeder, builder, butcher, cashier, chemist, cleaner, climber, coalman, cobbler, collier, coroner, courier, cowherd, crofter, curator, cyclist, dentist, doorman, dresser, drummer, equerry, farrier, fiddler, fighter, fireman, florist, footman, foreman, frogman, general, glazier, gymnast, hangman, haulier, hostess, janitor, junkman, lace-man, lineman, lorimer, luthier, magnate, manager, marshal, masseur, midwife, milkman, oculist, officer, orderly, painter, partner, pianist, planner, plumber, poacher, popstar, postman, prefect, printer, rancher, referee, saddler, scholar, senator, servant, shearer, sheriff, showman, soldier, spinner, stapler, steward, student, surgeon, teacher, trainee, trainer, trapper, vintner, warrior, woolman, workman
08 advocate, animator, armourer, attorney, banksman, botanist, bottle-oh, brakeman, callgirl, cardinal, chairman, chandler, chaplain, comedian, compiler, composer, conjurer, conjuror, corporal, costumer, coxswain, croupier, dairyman, deckhand, designer, diplomat, director, druggist, educator, embalmer, engineer, engraver, essayist, executor, factotum, farmhand, ferryman, film star, fishwife, forester, gangster, gardener, goatherd, governor, gunsmith, handyman, henchman, herdsman, hireling, home help, hotelier, huntsman, inventor, jeweller, labourer, landlady, landlord, lecturer, linguist, lyricist, magician, maltster, mapmaker, masseuse, mechanic, merchant, milkmaid, milliner, minister, minstrel, muleteer, musician, novelist, operator, optician, organist, pardoner, perfumer, pig-woman, polisher, preacher, producer, promoter, publican, quarrier, recorder, reporter, retailer, reviewer, salesman, sales rep, satirist, scrap-man, sculptor, seedsman, sergeant, shepherd, showgirl, smuggler, sorcerer, spaceman, spurrier, stockman, stripper, stuntman, supplier, surveyor, thatcher, upholder, waitress, watchman, wet nurse, wig-maker, woodsman, wrangler
09 alchemist, anatomist, announcer, antiquary, architect, archivist, art critic, art dealer, assistant, associate, astronaut, attendant, barperson, barrister, biologist, bodyguard, bookmaker, brinjarry, buccaneer, bus driver, cab driver, caretaker, carpenter, charwoman, chauffeur, clergyman, coal miner, collector, columnist, commander, concierge, conductor, constable, cosmonaut, costumier, couturier, cricketer, decorator, detective, dietician, dramatist, ecologist, economist, executive, financier, fisherman, fruiterer, gas fitter, geologist, goldsmith, governess, guitarist, gutter-man, harvester, herbalist, historian, homeopath, horologer, housemaid, HR manager, hypnotist, innkeeper, inspector, ironsmith, jacksmith, landowner, launderer, laundress, librarian, lifeguard, locksmith, machinist, messenger, musketeer, navigator, newsagent, nursemaid, osteopath, outfitter, paralegal, paramedic, performer, physician, physicist, plasterer, ploughman, policeman, pop singer, poulterer, professor, publicist, publisher, puppeteer, registrar, robe maker, sailmaker, scientist, secretary, shoemaker, signaller, signalman, songsmith, spokesman, stagehand, stationer, staymaker, stevedore, subeditor, subtitler, swineherd, therapist, towncrier, tradesman, traveller, trumpeter, usherette, van driver, violinist, volunteer, whittawer, yachtsman, zookeeper, zoologist
10 accountant, advertiser, air hostess, air steward, amanuensis, apothecary, apprentice, archbishop, astrologer, astronomer, auctioneer, baby sitter, bank teller, beautician, bellringer, bill-broker, biochemist, biographer, blacksmith, bookbinder, bookkeeper, bookseller, bricklayer, bureaucrat, campaigner, cartoonist, cartwright, chairmaker, clockmaker, coastguard, compositor, consultant, controller, copywriter, corn-dealer, corn-factor, councillor, counsellor, disc jockey, dishwasher, dramaturge, dressmaker, dry cleaner, equestrian, fellmonger, fishmonger, footballer, forecaster, frame-maker, fundraiser, gamekeeper, game warden, gatekeeper, geneticist, geochemist, geographer, glassmaker, handmaiden, headhunter, headmaster, highwayman, horologist, instructor, ironmonger, journalist, junk-dealer, keyboarder, legislator, librettist, lumberjack, magistrate, manageress, manicurist, manservant, midshipman, millwright, missionary, naturalist, negotiator, newscaster, newsmonger, nurseryman, obituarist, pallbearer, park ranger, pawnbroker, peltmonger, perruquier, pharmacist, piano tuner, playwright, podiatrist, politician, postmaster, private eye, programmer, proprietor, prospector, railwayman, removal man, researcher, ringmaster, roadmender, sales clerk, saleswoman, sempstress, shipbroker, shipwright, shopfitter, shopkeeper, signwriter, songstress, stewardess, stock agent, stockinger, stonemason, supervisor, taxi driver, technician, translator, typesetter, undertaker, unguentary,

wainwright, wharfinger, whitesmith, wholesaler, woodcarver, woodcutter
11 accompanist, antiquarian, art director, astrologist, audio typist, bank manager, bingo caller, broadcaster, bullfighter, burn-the-wind, businessman, candlemaker, car salesman, chambermaid, cheerleader, chiropodist, clergywoman, commentator, coppersmith, delivery man, distributor, draughtsman, electrician, entertainer, estate agent, etymologist, executioner, firefighter, foot soldier, fund manager, glass blower, grave digger, greengrocer, haberdasher, hairdresser, hair stylist, head teacher, horse-dealer, illustrator, interpreter, interviewer, lifeboatman, linen-draper, lollipop man, lorry driver, metalworker, money broker, mountaineer, music-seller, neurologist, optometrist, panel beater, parlourmaid, pathologist, philatelist, philologist, philosopher, policewoman, proofreader, radiologist, relic-monger, secret agent, set designer, sociologist, sharebroker, ship builder, silversmith, steelworker, stockbroker, taxidermist, telephonist, ticket agent, tobacconist, travel agent, tree surgeon, truck driver, underwriter, upholsterer, vitraillist, wagonwright, wax-chandler, web designer, wheelwright, wool-stapler, youth worker
12 anaesthetist, broker-dealer, cabinet maker, calligrapher, cartographer, cheesemonger, chimney sweep, chiropractor, churchwarden, civil servant, coal merchant, corn-merchant, costermonger, demonstrator, dramaturgist, entomologist, entrepreneur, event manager, fent-merchant, film director, garret-master, hotel manager, immunologist, IT consultant, longshoreman, maitre d'hotel, make-up artist, media planner, metallurgist, mineralogist, nutritionist, obstetrician, orthodontist, photographer, physiologist, ploughwright, postal worker, practitioner, PR consultant, press officer, prison warder, psychologist, radiographer, receptionist, restaurateur, sales manager, schoolmaster, screenwriter, scriptwriter, ship chandler, slink butcher, social worker, spokesperson, stage manager, statistician, stenographer, toxicologist, urban planner, veterinarian, warehouseman, wine merchant, wood engraver
13 administrator, antique dealer, archaeologist, charity worker, choreographer, civil engineer, crane operator, criminologist, dental surgeon, food scientist, groundskeeper, gynaecologist, harbour master, health visitor, home economist, industrialist, lab technician, lexicographer, lollipop woman, mathematician, meteorologist, nightwatchman, oceanographer, old-clothesman, police officer, prison officer, rag-and-bone-man, rent collector, retail manager, scrap merchant, security guard, ship's chandler, shop assistant, sound engineer, streetcleaner, streetsweeper, support worker, traffic warden, window cleaner
14 anthropologist, camera operator, claims assessor, draughtsperson, market gardener, marriage-broker, merchant tailor, microbiologist, music therapist, naval architect, pharmacologist, pharmacopolist, store detective, superintendent, systems analyst, tallow chandler
15 biotechnologist, business analyst, commission agent, computer analyst, conservationist, costume designer, dental hygienist, fashion designer, flight attendant, funeral director, graphic designer, marine biologist, military officer, ophthalmologist, personal trainer, physiotherapist, police constable, refuse collector, speech therapist, stock controller, ticket collector

occupational

04 work **05** trade **06** career **08** business **10** employment, job-related, vocational **12** professional

occupied

04 busy, full **05** in use, taken **06** tied up **07** engaged, taken up, working **08** absorbed, employed, hard at it, immersed, tenanted **09** engrossed **11** preoccupied, unavailable

occupier

04 user **06** dealer, holder, inmate, lessee, renter, tenant **08** occupant, resident, squatter **09** homeowner, incumbent **10** inhabitant **11** householder, leaseholder **13** owner-occupier

occupy

◇ *insertion indicator*

03 own, use **04** busy, fill, have, hold, nest, rent, tire **05** amuse, beset, seize, trade, use up **06** absorb, divert, embusy, employ, engage, fill in, invade, live in, manure, move in, obsess, obtain, people, settle, stay in, take up, tenant **07** capture, cohabit, dwell in, engross, entreat, immerse, improve, inhabit, involve, overrun, possess **08** interest, occupate, overbusy, reside in, take over **09** entertain, preoccupy, stimulate **14** make your home in

occur

03 hit **04** fall, meet **05** arise, exist **06** appear, befall, chance, crop up, dawn on, happen, obtain, result, sink in, strike, turn up **07** be found, develop, turn out **09** be present, come about, come to you, eventuate, take place, transpire **10** come to mind, come to pass **11** materialize **12** have its being, spring to mind **13** cross your mind, enter your head, present itself, suggest itself **14** manifest itself

occurrence

04 case **05** event **06** action, affair **07** arising, episode **08** incident, instance **09** existence, happening, incidence **10** appearance **11** development, proceedings, springing-up **12** circumstance **13** manifestation

• trying occurrence

03 cow

ocean

03 sea **04** main **05** briny **07** the deep **08** high seas, millpond, profound, the drink **11** herring pond

Oceans include:

06 Arctic, Indian
07 Pacific
08 Atlantic, Southern
12 North Pacific, South Pacific
13 North Atlantic, South Atlantic

See also **sea**

Ocean trenches include:

03 Yap
04 Java
05 Japan, Kuril, Palau, Tonga
06 Cayman, Ryukyu
07 Atacama, Mariana
08 Aleutian, Izu Bonin, Kermadec, Marianas, Mindanao, Romanche
09 Peru-Chile
10 Philippine, Puerto Rico
11 Nansei Shoto
12 Bougainville, West Caroline
13 Middle America, South Sandwich

ocean-going

05 naval **06** marine **07** sailing **08** maritime, nautical, seagoing **09** seafaring

ochre

04 keel

octave

04 utas

October

03 Oct

octopus

05 polyp, poulp **06** polype, poulpe **07** octopod **08** Octopoda **09** devilfish

odd

◇ *anagram indicator*
◇ *hidden alternately indicator*

03 god, rum **04** fent, orra, rare, wild, zany **05** barmy, drôle, droll, extra, funny, kinky, queer, spare, wacky, weird **06** casual, far-out, freaky, quaint, quirky, random, single, sundry, way-out, whimsy **07** bizarre, curious, deviant, oddball, odd-like, strange, surplus, uncanny, unusual, various, whimsey **08** abnormal, atypical, crackers, freakful, freakish, left-over, original, part-time, peculiar, periodic, seasonal, singular, uncommon, unpaired **09** different, eccentric, haphazard, irregular, remaining, temporary, unmatched, whimsical **10** additional, fortuitous, incidental, mismatched, occasional, off the wall, outlandish, remarkable **11** exceptional, superfluous **13** extraordinary, idiosyncratic, miscellaneous **14** unconventional

• odd one out

04 case, cure **05** freak **06** odd bod, weirdo **07** oddball, odd fish **09** eccentric, odd man out, queer fish, tall poppy **11** odd woman out **13** nonconformist **14** fish out of water

oddball

◇ *anagram indicator*

03 dag, nut, rum **04** card, case, geek, kook, loon, wack **05** crank, flake, freak **06** nutter, oddity, weirdo **07** cupcake, dingbat, odd fish, strange **08** crackpot, peculiar **09** character, eccentric, queer fish **13** nonconformist **14** fish out of water

oddity

03 dag, nut, rum **04** card, case, geek, kook, loon, wack **05** flake, freak, quirk, twist **06** jimjam, misfit, nutter, object, rarity, weirdo **07** anomaly, cupcake, dingbat, oddball, odd fish **08** crackpot, queerity **09** character, curiosity, queer fish, queerness **10** phenomenon **11** abnormality, peculiarity, singularity, strangeness **12** eccentricity, idiosyncrasy **14** fish out of water

odd-looking person

04 quiz

oddly

◇ *anagram indicator*

◇ *hidden alternately indicator*

07 weirdly **09** curiously, strangely, unusually **10** abnormally, remarkably **11** irregularly

oddment

03 bit, end **04** fent **05** patch, piece, scrap, shred **06** offcut **07** remnant, snippet **08** fragment, leftover

odds

02 SP **04** edge, lead, line **05** price **06** scraps **07** chances, dispute, the line **09** advantage, supremacy **10** ascendancy, inequality, likelihood **11** probability, superiority **13** starting price

• at odds

06 at outs **07** arguing **08** clashing **09** differing, out of step **10** at variance, in conflict **11** disagreeing, quarrelling **13** at loggerheads **14** in disagreement

• ignore the odds

◇ *hidden alternately indicator*

• odds and ends

03 tat **04** bits, junk, tatt **06** debris, job-lot, litter, scraps **07** rubbish **08** cuttings, leavings, oddments, remnants, snippets **09** bric-à-brac **11** bits and bobs, odds and sods, this and that **13** bits and pieces, odd-come-shorts

ode

04 awdl **06** monody, threne **07** epicede, threnos **08** Pindaric, stasimon, threnode, threnody **09** epicedium, epinicion, epinikion **12** genethliacon

odious

04 foul, vile **06** horrid **07** hateful, heinous **08** horrible **09** abhorrent, execrable, loathsome, obnoxious, offensive, repugnant, repulsive, revolting **10** abominable, despicable, detestable, disgusting, unpleasant **12** contemptible, disagreeable **13** objectionable

odium

05 blame, shame **06** hatred, infamy **07** censure, dislike, obloquy **08** contempt, disgrace **09** animosity, antipathy, discredit, disfavour, dishonour, disrepute **10** abhorrence, execration, opprobrium **11** detestation, disapproval, reprobation **12** condemnation **13** offensiveness **14** disapprobation

odorous

05 balmy **07** pungent, scented **08** aromatic, fragrant, perfumed, redolent **11** odoriferous **13** sweet-smelling

odour

02 bo **04** niff, pong, sent, waff **05** aroma, savor, scent, smell, stink, whiff **06** repute, savour, stench **07** bouquet, perfume **09** fragrance, redolence

odourless

09 inodorous, unscented **10** deodorized **12** without smell **13** having no smell

odyssey

04 trek **06** voyage **07** journey, travels **09** adventure, wandering **13** peregrination

of

01 o' **02** de, du, on, to

off

◇ *anagram indicator*

03 bad, far, ill, out **04** away, from, gone, high, kill, sick, sour **05** apart, aside, right, rough, seedy, slack, wrong **06** absent, depart!, mouldy, poorly, queasy, rancid, rotten, spoilt, turned, unwell **07** dropped, off form, shelved **08** below par, scrapped **09** abandoned, called off, cancelled, elsewhere, incorrect, off-colour, postponed **10** decomposed, indisposed, out of sorts **11** at a distance, substandard, unavailable **12** unobtainable **13** disappointing **14** unsatisfactory **15** under the weather

offal

03 fry **05** gurry, heart, liver **06** kidney, refuse, tongue **07** garbage **08** entrails, lamb's fry **11** variety meat

offbeat

05 kooky, wacky, weird **06** far-out, freaky, way-out **07** bizarre, oddball, strange, unusual **08** abnormal **09** eccentric **10** unorthodox **13** untraditional **14** unconventional

off-colour

◇ *anagram indicator*

03 ill **04** blue, foul, lewd, rude, sexy, sick **05** crook, crude, dirty, gross, rough, seedy **06** coarse, crummy, filthy, impure, poorly, queasy, risqué, sleazy, smutty, unwell, vulgar **07** immoral, obscene, off form, run down **08** depraved, immodest, improper, indecent **09** offensive, perverted **10** degenerate, indelicate, indisposed, licentious, out of sorts, suggestive **11** peelie-wally **12** pornographic **15** under the weather

offence

03 ire, sin **04** hurt, snub **05** anger, crime, fault, pique, wrong **06** injury, insult, slight **07** affront, assault, misdeed, outrage, umbrage **08** atrocity, trespass **09** annoyance, antipathy, exception, indignity, stumbling, violation **10** illegal act, infraction, resentment, wrongdoing **11** disapproval, displeasure, indignation **12** exasperation, hard feelings, infringement, misdemeanour **13** transgression **14** breach of the law

See also **crime**

• take offence

04 huff, miff **06** be hurt, resent **07** be angry, be upset **08** be miffed, be put out, get huffy **09** be annoyed **10** be insulted, be offended, feel put out, get the hump **11** be indignant, go into a huff, take umbrage **13** be exasperated, take exception **14** take personally

offend

03 err, hip, hyp, sin **04** hurt, miff, snub **05** anger, annoy, repel, upset, wound, wrong **06** injure, insult, kittle, needle, put off, put out, revolt, sicken **07** affront, disgust, do wrong, incense, outrage, provoke, umbrage, violate **08** distaste, go astray, gross out, nauseate **09** disoblige, displease **10** exasperate, transgress **11** break the law, displeasure

offended

04 hurt **05** huffy, stung, upset **06** hipped, miffed, pained, piqued, put out **07** angered, annoyed, in a huff, wounded **08** incensed, outraged, smarting **09** affronted, disgusted, resentful **10** displeased **11** disgruntled, exasperated

offender

07 culprit **08** criminal **09** defaulter, miscreant, wrongdoer **10** delinquent, lawbreaker, malefactor **11** guilty party, probationer **12** transgressor

offensive

03 bad **04** foul, push, raid, rude, vile **05** alien, drive, grody, nasty **06** attack, charge, frowsy, frowzy, odious, sortie, thrust, wicked **07** abusive, assault, hostile, hurtful **08** annoying, impolite, indecent, insolent, invading, invasion, stinking, wounding **09** abhorrent, attacking, incursion, insulting, loathsome, obnoxious, onslaught, repellent, repugnant, revolting, sickening, unsavoury, upsetting **10** abominable, affronting, aggressive, detestable, disgusting, nauseating, outrageous, unpleasant **11** belligerent, displeasing, impertinent **12** antagonistic, disagreeable, discourteous, disrelishing, exasperating **13** disrespectful, objectionable

offensively

10 detestably **12** disagreeably, disgustingly, nauseatingly, unpleasantly **13** objectionably

offer

03 bid, try **04** bode, give, make, sell, show **05** essay, shore **06** afford, extend, prefer, submit, supply, tender **07** advance, attempt, bidding, express, hold out, offer up, present, proffer, propine, propose, provide, suggest, worship **08** approach, dedicate, overture, proposal, propound **09** celebrate, put in a bid, recommend, sacrifice, volunteer **10** consecrate, put forward, submission, suggestion **11** come forward, proposition, show willing **12** presentation **13** make available **14** put on the market

offering

03 IPO **04** gift **05** tithe **06** ex voto, xenium **07** handout, present **08** donation, oblation **09** sacrifice **10** dedication **11** celebration **12** consecration, contribution, subscription **13** heave-shoulder

offhand

04 airy, curt, rude, snap **05** ad lib, blasé, terse **06** abrupt, at once, casual **07** brusque, cursory **08** careless, cavalier, informal, laid-back **09** brevi manu, extempore, impromptu **10** cavalierly, nonchalant, off the cuff **11** free-and-easy, immediately, indifferent, perfunctory, unconcerned **12** at first blush, discourteous, happy-go-lucky, uninterested **13** unceremonious **14** currente calamo **15** at the first blush, take-it-or-leave-it, without checking

office

03 aid **04** base, duty, help, hint, part, post, role, wing, word, work **05** aegis, place **06** agency, back-up, branch, bureau, charge, favour, tenure **07** backing, cockpit, section, service, support **08** advocacy, auspices, business, division, function, lavatory, position, referral, workroom **09** affiliate, mediation, patronage, situation, workplace **10** assistance, commission, department, employment, obligation, occupation, subsection, subsidiary **11** appointment, local office, subdivision **12** intercession, intervention **14** recommendation, regional office, responsibility **15** place of business

See also **toilet**

Offices include:

02 CO, FO, PO, TO, WO
03 box, COI, CRO, DLO, EPO, FCO, GAO, GPO, IIP, IRO, Met, NAO, OFT, OME, ONS, OPW, ORR, OSS, OST, pay, PRO, RLO, SFO, War
04 back, BFPO, fire, HMSO, Holy, Home, land, loan, Pipe, Post
05 Assay, Crown, front, Ofcom, Offer, Ofgas, Ofgem, Oflot, Oftel, Ofwat, paper, press, stamp
06 Ofsted, Patent, Pat Off, police, Record, ticket
07 booking, Foreign, sorting
08 Chancery, Colonial, Eurostat, incident, printing, register, registry, Scottish
09 personnel, receiving, telegraph
10 dead-letter, employment, Quai d'Orsay, registered, Stationery
11 general post, left-luggage, victualling
12 Commonwealth, Serious Fraud
13 Inland Revenue, National Audit
14 European Patent, Meteorological, returned letter
15 Criminal Records

Office furniture includes:

04 desk, safe
07 lectern
08 desk lamp, fire safe
09 partition, plan chest, stepstool, work table
11 storage unit, swivel chair, workstation
12 computer desk, drawing-board, fire cupboard, printer stand, typist's chair
13 executive desk, filing cabinet, filing trolley
14 boardroom table, display cabinet, executive chair, filing cupboard, reception chair
15 conference table, secretarial desk

Office equipment includes:

03 OHP, VDU
05 mouse
06 inkpad, screen, tacker
07 cash box, monitor, planner, printer, scanner, stapler, trimmer
08 computer, intercom, keyboard, mouse mat, plan file, shredder
09 date-stamp, dust cover, laminator, telephone, textphone, time clock, wages book
10 calculator, comb binder, copy holder, Dictaphone®, duplicator, fax machine, guillotine, letter tray, monitor arm, paper punch, printwheel, typewriter
11 comb binding, hole puncher, noticeboard, photocopier, switchboard
12 acoustic hood, letter opener, letter scales, message board, parcel scales, screen filter, telex machine, visitors' book, wire bindings
13 data cartridge, desk organizer, microcassette, planning board, reference book, staple-remover, thermal binder, waste-paper bin, word processor
14 adhesive binder, diskette mailer, flip-chart easel, laptop computer, slide projector, telephone index

See also **stationery**

• **branch office**

02 bo

• **in office**

02 in

• **office of bishop**

03 see

• **office of cardinal**

03 hat

• **out of office**

04 late

officer

03 col, off **04** lead **05** agent, envoy, polis **06** deputy, fantad, fantod, non-com, pusser, schout, varlet **07** command **08** dog's-body, official **09** appointee, dignitary, executive, inspector, messenger, subaltern **10** bureaucrat **11** board member, functionary **12** office-bearer, office-holder **13** administrator, public servant **14** representative **15** committee member

See also **police officer**; **rank**; **religious**; **ship**

official

03 off **05** legal **06** Bumble, formal, kosher, lawful, proper, pusser, ritual, solemn **07** officer, stately **08** accepted, approved, bona fide, endorsed, licensed **09** authentic, certified, dignified, validated **10** accredited, authorized, ceremonial, legitimate, recognized, sanctioned **11** functionary **12** Jack-in-office, office-bearer, office-holder **13** authenticated, authoritative

Officials include:

02 JP, MP
05 agent, chief, clerk, druid, elder, envoy, hakim, mayor, reeve, usher
06 atabeg, atabek, consul, Euro-MP, notary, purser, pusser
07 bailiff, captain, coroner, equerry, manager, marshal, monitor, prefect, proctor, senator, sheriff, steward, vaivode, voivode
08 chairman, delegate, diplomat, director, Eurocrat, executor, governor, mandarin, mayoress, minister, mud-clerk, nipcheese, overseer, provedor, providor
09 commander, commissar, executive,

Gauleiter, inspector, ombudsman, president, principal, provedore, registrar
10 ambassador, bureaucrat, chairwoman, chancellor, councillor, magistrate, proprietor, proveditor, railroader, supervisor
11 chairperson, congressman, proveditore
12 baron-officer, borough-reeve, civil servant, commissioner
13 administrator, congresswoman, fonctionnaire
14 representative, superintendent

officialdom

04 them **08** ministry **09** mandarins, officials, the system **10** government **11** bureaucracy **12** civil service **13** administrator, civil servants **14** administration, the authorities **15** local government

officialese

06 jargon **07** rubbish **08** nonsense **09** buzz words, gibberish **10** journalese **11** computerese **12** gobbledygook, psychobabble

officially

08 formally, properly **09** correctly **11** on the record **12** managerially, procedurally **13** authentically **15** authoritatively

officiate

03 run **05** chair **06** manage **07** conduct, oversee, preside **10** be in charge, take charge **11** superintend **12** take the chair

officious

05 bossy, pushy **06** prying, spoffy **07** dutiful, forward **08** bustling, informal, meddling, obliging, overbusy, spoffish **09** diplomacy, intrusive, obtrusive **10** meddlesome **11** dictatorial, domineering, importunate, inquisitive, interfering, opinionated, over-zealous, pragmatical **13** self-important

officiously

07 bossily, pushily **13** dictatorially, over-zealously **15** self-importantly, with importunity

offing

• in the offing

04 near **06** at hand **07** in sight **08** coming up, imminent, on the way **10** coming soon, on the cards **11** close at hand **12** on the horizon **13** happening soon

offish

04 cool **05** aloof **07** haughty, stuck-up **10** unsociable **11** standoffish

off-key

07 jarring **09** dissonant, out of tune **10** discordant, unsuitable **11** conflicting **12** inharmonious, out of keeping **13** inappropriate

offload

04 drop, dump, palm **05** chuck, shift **06** unload **07** deposit **08** get rid of, jettison, unburden **09** disburden, discharge

off-putting

08 daunting **09** unnerving, upsetting **10** disturbing, formidable, unpleasant, unsettling **11** dispiriting, frightening, unappealing **12** demoralizing, discomfiting, discouraging, intimidating **13** disconcerting, disheartening

offset

06 cancel **07** balance **09** cancel out, make up for **10** balance out, counteract, neutralize **11** countervail **12** counterpoise **13** compensate for **14** counterbalance

offshoot

03 arm **04** limb, sien **05** bayou, plant, scion, swarm **06** branch, reform, result **07** outcome, product, spin-off **08** shoulder, sideslip **09** apophysis, appendage, billabong, by-product, outgrowth **11** consequence, development

offspring

03 get, kid, son **04** baby, burd, kids, seed, sons **05** breed, brood, child, heirs, issue, spawn, young **06** babies, family, infant, nipper, source **07** infants, nippers, product, progeny **08** ancestry, children, daughter, young one **09** daughters, little one, young ones, youngster **10** generation, little ones, successors, youngsters **11** descendants

often

03 oft **04** much **08** commonly, frequent, ofttimes **09** generally, many a time, many times, regularly **10** frequently, repeatedly **11** day in day out **12** time and again **13** again and again, time after time, week in week out **15** month in month out

ogle

03 eye **04** leer, look **05** eliad, eye up, stare **06** eyliad, illiad **07** eyeliad, glad eye **08** oeillade **10** make eyes at

ogre

03 orc **04** boyg **05** beast, bogey, brute, demon, devil, fiend, giant, troll **06** savage **07** monster, villain **08** bogeyman **09** barbarian

Ohio

02 OH

oik *see* **cad**

oil

03 fat **04** balm, news, oint **05** cream, salve, smear **06** anoint, grease, lotion **07** unguent **08** liniment, ointment **09** lubricant, lubricate **10** impregnate, make smooth **11** information

Oils include:

03 ben, gas, nim, nut, til
04 baby, cade, coal, corn, crab, derv, dika, fish, fuel, hair, neem, nimb, otto, palm, poon, rape, rock, rose, rusa, seed, tall, tung, wood, wool, zest
05 attar, carap, crude, grass, heavy, macaw, neemb, niger, olive, ottar, poppy, pulza, rosin, salad, savin, shale, shark, snake, sperm, spike, sweet, thyme, train, whale
06 ajowan, almond, canola, castor, chrism, cloves, cohune, diesel, illipe, jojoba, macoya, neroli, peanut, savine, Seneca, sesame
07 arachis, cajuput, camphor, coconut, gingili, jinjili, linseed, lumbang, mineral, mirbane, mustard, myrrhol, spindle, verbena, vitriol
08 ambrosia, bergamot, camphine, cinnamon, cod-liver, creosote, gingelly, kerosene, kerosine, lavender, macahuba, macassar, North Sea, paraffin, pristane, rapeseed, rosewood
09 black gold, candlenut, grapeseed, neat's-foot, patchouli, patchouly, safflower, sassafras, spikenard, sunflower, vanaspati, vegetable
10 citronella, eucalyptus, peppermint, petit grain, turpentine, ylang-ylang
11 camphorated, chaulmoogra, wintergreen
12 brilliantine
15 evening primrose

• oil platform

03 rig

• oil receptacle

04 sump

oily

03 fat **04** glib **05** fatty, slimy, suave **06** greasy, smarmy, smooth, urbane **07** buttery, servile **08** slippery, unctuous **10** flattering, obsequious, oleaginous **11** subservient **12** ingratiating **13** smooth-talking

ointment

03 gel **04** balm **05** cream, salve **06** balsam, cerate, lotion, pomade **07** pomatum, unction, unguent **08** eye-salve, liniment, lipsalve, Vaseline® **09** basilicon, cold cream, collyrium, emollient, inunction, lubricant, Tiger balm® **11** embrocation, preparation

• ointment base

07 lanolin

OK

03 A-OK, oke, yes **04** fair, fine, good, jake, okay, pass, so-so, sure, well **05** right **06** agreed, not bad, righto **07** agree to, approve, consent, correct, go-ahead, in order, up to par **08** accurate, adequate, all right, approval, okey-doke, passable, passably, sanction, say yes to, thumbs-up, very good, very well **09** agreement, authorize, certainly, consent to, no worries, okey-dokey, permitted, tolerable, tolerably **10** acceptable, all correct, convenient, good as gold, green light, no problems, permission, reasonable, reasonably **11** approbation, endorsement, rubber-stamp, up to scratch **12** satisfactory, she'll be right **13** authorization, Bob's your uncle, she'll be apples **14** satisfactorily

Oklahoma
02 OK **04** Okla

okra
05 gumbo **06** bhindi **11** lady's finger **12** lady's fingers

old
◇ *archaic word indicator*
01 O **02** ex- **03** eld, set **04** aged, auld, folk, gaga, gray, grey, oral, torn, wise, worn **05** aging, banal, corny, early, fixed, passé, stale, stock, tired, trite, usual **06** ageing, age-old, bygone, common, former, mature, past it, primal, senile, shabby **07** ancient, antique, archaic, cast-off, classic, cliché'd, decayed, earlier, elderly, lasting, one-time, quondam, routine, veteran, vintage, worn-out **08** clichéed, decaying, decrepit, earliest, enduring, habitual, historic, obsolete, original, outdated, overused, previous, primeval, pristine, sensible, sometime, time-worn **09** crumbling, customary, erstwhile, getting on, hackneyed, long-lived, out of date, primaeval, primitive, senescent, unwritten, worm-eaten **10** accustomed, antiquated, broken down, ceremonial, Dickensian, overworked, pedestrian, primordial, ramshackle, threadbare, tumbledown, uninspired, unoriginal, yawn-making **11** commonplace, established, on the way out, out of the ark, over the hill, prehistoric, stereotyped, traditional, wearing thin **12** antediluvian, cliché-ridden, conventional, long-standing, old-fashioned, run-of-the-mill, time-honoured **13** old as the hills, past your prime, platitudinous, unfashionable, unimaginative **14** behind the times, long in the tooth **15** advanced in years, long-established, no spring chicken

old age
03 age, eld **04** hoar, hore **05** years **06** dotage **07** oldness **08** agedness, senility **09** antiquity **10** senescence **11** elderliness, vale of years **14** advancing years, declining years **15** second childhood

old-fashioned
◇ *archaic word indicator*
03 old **04** dead, past **05** corny, dated, dusty, fusty, mumsy, passé, steam **06** antick, bygone, old hat, past it, Podunk, quaint, rococo, square, uncool **07** ancient, antique, archaic, arriéré, old-time **08** medieval, obsolete, outdated, outmoded, shmaltzy, vieux jeu **09** mediaeval, moth-eaten, out of date, primitive, rinky-dink, schmaltzy **10** antiquated, auld-farand, fuddy-duddy, oldfangled, written off **11** auld-farrant, Neanderthal, obsolescent, on the way out, out of the ark **12** antediluvian, out of fashion **13** unfashionable **14** behind the times

old maid
08 spinster

old man
02 pa **03** OAP **04** boss, koro **05** elder, oldie **06** bodach, father, gaffer, geezer, Nestor **07** grandad, husband, oldster **08** employer, granddad, old-timer, presbyte **09** greybeard, old codger, old stager, patriarch, pensioner **10** fuddy-duddy, golden ager, white-beard **11** grandfather **12** coffin-dodger **13** senior citizen **14** elder statesman **15** old-age pensioner
See also **father**; **old woman**

old-time
03 old **04** past **05** dated, passé **06** bygone **07** archaic **08** obsolete, outdated, outmoded **09** out of date **10** antiquated **12** old-fashioned, out of fashion **13** unfashionable **14** behind the times

old woman
03 bag, hag, OAP **04** aunt, kuia, trot, wife **05** biddy, crone, fagot, oldie **06** beldam, faggot, gammer, granny, grouch, mother **07** beldame, carline, fusspot, grandma, grannie, old dear **08** caillach, grumbler **09** cailleach, cailliach, grandmama, pensioner **10** complainer, golden ager, grandmamma **11** grandmother **12** coffin-dodger **13** senior citizen **15** old-age pensioner
See also **mother**; **old man**

old-world
04 past **06** bygone, quaint **07** archaic **09** auld-warld **10** antiquated, olde-worlde **11** picturesque, traditional **12** old-fashioned

olio
04 olla **06** medley **07** mixture **10** miscellany

olive
04 Olea **05** wolly **08** oleaster

Olympics

Olympians include:

03 Coe (Sebastian)
04 Clay (Cassius), Dean (Christopher), Ewry (Ray), Otto (Kristin), Papp (Laszlo), Todd (Mark), Witt (Katarina)
05 Blair (Bonnie), Bubka (Sergei), Chand (Dhyan), Cranz (Christl), Curry (John), Henie (Sonja), Killy (Jean-Claude), Lewis (Carl), Lewis (Denise), Longo (Jeannie), Meade (Richard), Nurmi (Paavo), Ottey (Merlene), Owens (Jesse), Popov (Aleksandr), Savon (Felix), Spitz (Mark), Tomba (Alberto)
06 Aamodt (Kjetil), Beamon (Bob), Bikila (Abebe), Biondi (Matt), Button (Dick), D'Inzeo (Raimondo), Fraser (Dawn), Heiden (Eric), Holmes (Dame Kelly), Korbut (Olga), Oerter (Al), Phelps (Michael), Ritola (Ville), Sailer (Toni), Thorpe (Ian), Thorpe (Jim)
07 Ainslie (Ben), Boitano (Brian), Cousins (Robin), Daehlie (Bjorn), Edwards (Jonathan), Fischer (Birgit), Johnson (Michael), Klammer (Franz), Mathias (Bob), Nykänen (Matti), Pinsent (Sir Matthew), Scherbo (Vitaly), Schmidt (Birgit), Torvill (Jayne), Voronin (Mikhail), Zatopek (Emil), Zelezny (Jan)
08 Christie (Linford), Comaneci (Nadia), Cuthbert (Betty), De Bruijn (Inge), Dityatin (Aleksandr), Elvstrøm (Paul), Gerevich (Aladár), Jernberg (Sixten), Latynina (Larissa), Louganis (Greg), Redgrave (Sir Steve), Stenmark (Ingemar), Thompson (Daley), Zijlaard (Leontien)
09 Andrianov (Nikolay), Babashoff (Shirley), Cáslavská (Vera), Egerszegi (Krisztina), Gräfström (Gillis), Schneider (Vreni), Seizinger (Katja), Stevenson (Teófilo)
10 Linsenhoff (Liselott), Moser-Proll (Annemarie), van Moorsel (Leontien)
11 Mangiarotti (Edouardo), Weissmuller (Johnny)
12 Blankers-Koen (Fanny), Gebrselassie (Haile), Germeshausen (Bernhard), Joyner-Kersee (Jackie), Suleymanoglu (Naim)
13 Longo-Ciprelli (Jeannie)
14 Griffith-Joyner (Florence)

Oman
03 OMN

omelette
08 frittata, tortilla

omen
04 sign **05** freet, freit, purse, token **06** augury, boding **07** auspice, portent, presage, warning **08** bodement, dead-fire, forecast, prodrome, soothsay **09** abodement, harbinger, night-crow, prodromus, prognosis **10** foreboding, forerunner, indication, night-raven, prediction, prognostic **11** premonition, presagement **12** corpse candle, presentiment

ominous
07 bodeful, fateful, unlucky **08** menacing, minatory, sinister **10** foreboding, portentous **11** threatening, unpromising **12** inauspicious, unfavourable, unpropitious

ominously
06 grimly **10** alarmingly **11** dangerously **13** frighteningly

omission
03 gap, out **04** balk, lack **05** baulk **06** lacuna **07** default, elision, erasure, failure, neglect **08** deletion **09** avoidance, disregard, exception, exclusion, haplology, oversight **10** expunction, leaving-out, lipography, negligence **11** dereliction

omit
03 let **04** drop, fail, miss, pass, skip

05 erase 06 delete, except, forget, rub out 07 edit out, exclude, expunge, miss out, neglect 08 cross out, leave out, overlook, overskip, pass over, white out 09 disregard, eliminate, pretermit 11 leave undone 13 fail to mention

omnibus
09 anthology, inclusive 10 collection, compendium 11 compendious, compilation, wide-ranging 12 all-embracing, encyclopedia, encyclopedic 13 comprehensive

omnipotence
07 mastery 09 supremacy 10 total power 11 divine right, sovereignty 12 almightiness, plenipotence 13 absolute power, invincibility 15 all-powerfulness

omnipotent
07 supreme 08 almighty 10 invincible 11 all-powerful, plenipotent

omnipresent
08 infinite 09 limitless, pervasive, universal 10 all-present, ubiquitary, ubiquitous 12 all-pervasive

omniscient
07 all-wise 09 all-seeing, pansophic 10 all-knowing

omnivorous
10 gluttonous 12 all-devouring, pantophagous 14 eating anything, indiscriminate

on
◇ *anagram indicator*
◇ *juxtaposition down indicator*
01 o 02 an, by, in, of, re, to 03 leg, sur 04 atop, over, side, upon 05 about, tipsy 06 beside, tiddly 07 against, forward!, proceed!, stuck to, towards 08 feasible, touching 09 apropos of, as regards, regarding, resting on 10 acceptable, attached to, concerning, relating to 11 dealing with, practicable, referring to 12 with regard to 13 concerned with, connected with, in contact with, in the matter of, with respect to 14 on the subject of 15 with reference to

• on and off
08 fitfully, off and on, sporadic 09 sometimes 10 now and then, occasional, on occasion 11 at intervals, irregularly, now and again 12 every so often, intermittent, occasionally, periodically, sporadically 13 spasmodically 14 from time to time, intermittently 15 discontinuously

• on and on
03 e'er 04 ever 06 always 07 forever, non-stop 09 endlessly, eternally, regularly 10 all the time, constantly, frequently, habitually, repeatedly 11 ceaselessly, continually, incessantly, perpetually, recurrently 12 interminably, persistently 13 everlastingly

once
◇ *archaic word indicator*
04 ance, onst, when 05 after 06 former 07 firstly, long ago, on a time, one time 08 as soon as, formerly 09 at one time, in the past, upon a time 10 at one point, previously 11 in times past 12 in the old days 13 in times gone by, once upon a time, on one occasion

• at once
03 now, tit 04 tite, tyte 05 alike, atone, ek dum, swith, tight 06 attone, presto, pronto, statim, titely 07 at a word, attonce, attones, offhand 08 directly, promptly, right now, together 09 forthwith, hey presto, instantly, like a shot, on the spot, right away, yesterday 10 forthright 11 immediately, tout de suite 12 straightaway, without delay 13 at the same time 14 simultaneously 15 at the same moment, before you know it

• more than once
04 anew, over 05 again 10 repeatedly

• once and for all
07 finally, for good 10 decisively, positively 11 permanently 12 conclusively, definitively 14 for the last time

• once in a while
07 at times 08 off and on, on and off 09 sometimes 10 now and then, on occasion 11 now and again 12 infrequently, occasionally, periodically, sporadically 14 from time to time, intermittently 15 once in a blue moon

once-over
04 gape, gaze, look, peek, peep, test 05 audit, check, dekko, probe, stare 06 eyeful, gander, glance, shufti, squint 07 checkup, glimpse, inquiry 08 analysis, butcher's, research, scrutiny 10 inspection, monitoring 11 examination 12 confirmation, verification 13 investigation

oncoming
07 looming, nearing 08 approach, upcoming 09 advancing, gathering, onrushing 11 approaching

one
01 a, I 02 ae, us 03 ace, ane, yin 04 lone, only, sole, tane, unit 05 alike, bound, equal, fused, monad, unity, whole 06 entire, joined, single, united, wedded 07 married 08 complete, solitary 09 identical, undivided 10 harmonious, individual, like-minded

• French one
02 un 03 une

• German one
03 ein 04 eine, eins

• Italian one, Spanish one
03 uno

oneness
05 unity 07 unicity 08 identity, sameness 09 wholeness 10 singleness, uniqueness 11 consistency, homogeneity, singularity 12 completeness 13 identicalness, individuality

onerous
04 hard 05 heavy 06 taxing, tiring 07 arduous, exigent, weighty 08 crushing, exacting, wearying 09 demanding, difficult, fatiguing, laborious, strenuous 10 burdensome, exhausting, oppressive 11 troublesome 12 back-breaking

oneself

• by oneself
04 solo 05 alone 06 lonely, singly 07 forlorn, unaided 08 deserted, desolate, forsaken, isolated, lonesome 09 abandoned, on your own, on your tod 10 by yourself, unassisted, unattended, unescorted 11 without help 12 single-handed 13 independently, unaccompanied 15 on your Pat Malone

one-sided
06 biased, one-way, uneven, unfair, unjust 07 bigoted, partial, unequal 08 lopsided, partisan, separate 09 separated 10 prejudiced, unbalanced, unilateral 11 independent, inequitable 12 disconnected, narrow-minded 14 discriminatory

one-time
02 ex- 03 old 04 late, past 06 former 07 quondam 08 previous, sometime 09 erstwhile

ongoing
05 event 07 current, growing, non-stop 08 constant, evolving, unbroken, unending 09 advancing, incessant, unfolding 10 continuing, continuous, developing, in progress, unfinished 11 progressing 13 uninterrupted

onion
04 head, moly, ramp, sybo 05 cibol, ingan, syboe, sybow 06 chibol, shalot 07 shallot 08 scallion
See also **head**

onlooker
06 gawper, viewer 07 watcher, witness 08 beholder, looker-on, observer 09 bystander, sightseer, spectator 10 eyewitness, rubberneck

only
03 but, one 04 just, lone, sole 05 alone 06 anerly, at most, barely, except, merely, nobbut, purely, simply, single, singly, solely, unique 07 onliest 08 solitary 09 allenarly, exclusive 10 individual, no more than, nothing but, one and only 11 exclusively, not more than

onrush
04 flow, push, rush 05 flood, onset, surge, sweep 06 career, charge, stream 07 cascade 08 stampede 09 onslaught

onset
04 dash, fall, push, raid, rush 05 break, start 06 access, affret, attack, charge, onding, onrush, outset 07 assault, kick-off 08 outbreak, storming 09 beginning, inception, onslaught 12 commencement

onslaught
04 push, raid 05 blitz, drive, foray,

onset, swoop **06** attack, charge, dismay, onfall, onrush, thrust **07** assault, dead-set **08** storming **09** offensive **11** bombardment

Ontario
02 ON

onus
04 duty, load, task **06** burden, charge, weight **09** albatross, liability, millstone **10** obligation **11** encumbrance **14** responsibility

onward
04 away

onwards
02 on **05** ahead, forth **06** beyond **07** forward, in front **08** forwards

oodles
04 bags, lots, tons **05** heaps, loads **06** masses **08** lashings **09** abundance

oomph
02 it, SA **03** pep **04** zing **06** bounce, energy, vigour **07** pizzazz, sparkle **08** sexiness, vitality, vivacity **09** animation, sex-appeal **10** enthusiasm, exuberance, get-up-and-go

ooze
03 mud, nap, sap, sew **04** drip, drop, emit, flow, leak, mire, muck, seep, silt, sipe, slob, spew, spue, sype, weep **05** bleed, drain, exude, fluff, slime **06** escape, exhale, filter, sludge **07** deposit, dribble, excrete, secrete, seepage, trickle **08** alluvium, filtrate, sediment **09** discharge, percolate, pour forth **12** overflow with

oozy
04 dewy, miry **05** moist, mucky, muddy, slimy, weepy **06** sloppy, sludgy, sweaty **07** weeping **08** dripping **09** uliginose, uliginous

opacity
04 body, onyx **06** nebula **07** density, leucoma **08** dullness **09** filminess, milkiness, murkiness, obscurity **10** cloudiness, opaqueness **11** obfuscation, unclearness **14** impermeability **15** impenetrability

opal
07 girasol, hyalite **08** girasole **09** cacholong **10** hydrophane

opalescence
05 prism **07** glitter, rainbow **08** dazzling **09** sparkling **10** glittering, shimmering **11** iridescence, multicolour **14** rainbow colours

opalescent
04 shot **06** pearly **07** rainbow **08** dazzling **09** prismatic, sparkling **10** glittering, iridescent, shimmering, variegated **11** cymophanous, rainbow-like **13** multicoloured, polychromatic **15** rainbow-coloured

opaque
03 dim **04** dark, dull, hazy **05** dense, dingy, misty, muddy, murky, shady, thick **06** cloudy, turbid **07** blurred, clouded, cryptic, doltish, intense, muddied, obscure, unclear **08** abstruse, baffling, esoteric, puzzling **09** confusing, difficult, enigmatic, recondite **12** as clear as mud, impenetrable, unfathomable **14** unintelligible

OPEC

OPEC members:

04 Iran, Iraq
05 Libya, Qatar
06 Kuwait
07 Algeria, Nigeria
09 Indonesia, Venezuela
11 Saudi Arabia
18 United Arab Emirates

open
03 dup **04** agee, airy, ajar, ajee, bare, fair, free, moot, undo, wide **05** apert, begin, blunt, broad, clear, crack, frank, holey, loose, overt, plain, split, start, unlid, unrip, untie **06** broach, candid, deploy, direct, expose, extend, flower, gaping, honest, launch, liable, ouvert, patent, porous, public, reveal, simple, spread, spring, unbolt, uncork, unfold, unfurl, unlock, unpack, unroll, unseal, unshut, vacant **07** blatant, divulge, evident, explain, exposed, general, kick off, lay bare, lidless, natural, obvious, ouverte, subject, topless, unblock, unclasp, unclose, uncover, unlatch, unscrew, upbreak, visible, yawning **08** apparent, arguable, cellular, commence, disclose, disposed, flagrant, initiate, manifest, openwork, passable, push open, separate, unbarred, unbolted, unclosed, unfasten, unfenced, unfolded, unfrozen, unhidden, unlocked, unripped, unsealed, wide open **09** available, break open, burst open, champaign, come apart, coverless, debatable, fenceless, force open, guileless, ingenuous, navigable, prise open, receptive, slide open, spread out, unblocked, uncovered, undecided, unlatched, unsettled, unstopped, well known **10** above-board, accessible, forthright, inaugurate, noticeable, obtainable, spongelike, unenclosed, unfastened, unoccupied, unreserved, unresolved, up in the air, vulnerable **11** conspicuous, get cracking, honeycombed, problematic, set in motion, susceptible, unconcealed, undisguised, unprotected, unsheltered, widely known **12** approachable, loosely woven, unobstructed, unrestricted **13** take the plunge **15** open to the risk of

• **opening words**
06 sesame

• **open onto**
04 face **06** lead to **08** give onto, overlook **14** command a view of

• **open up**
03 win

open-air
06 afield **07** outdoor, outside **08** alfresco, plein-air **10** out-of-doors

open-and-shut
05 clear **06** simple **07** obvious **12** easily solved **13** easily decided **15** straightforward

opener
◇ *head selection indicator*

open-handed
04 free **06** lavish **07** liberal **08** generous **09** bounteous, bountiful **10** munificent, unstinting **11** magnanimous **12** eleemosynary, large-hearted

opening
◇ *head selection indicator*
02 os **03** gap, gat, job **04** adit, anus, bole, cave, dawn, gape, gate, hole, pore, port, rent, scye, slit, slot, vent, yawn **05** birth, break, chasm, chink, cleft, crack, early, first, inlet, onset, place, space, split, start, stoma, thirl **06** breach, chance, hiatus, launch, outlet, outset, window **07** crevice, fissure, foramen, initial, kick-off, orifice, ostiole, portage, primary, rupture, undoing, vacancy **08** aperture, fenestra, occasion, position, starting **09** beginning, first base, inaugural, inception, mouse hole, square one, the word go **10** commencing, fenestella, interstice **11** opportunity, possibility **12** inauguration, introductory

openly
06 barely **07** bluntly, frankly, overtly, plainly, up front **08** brazenly, candidly, directly, honestly, in public, patently, publicly **09** blatantly, glaringly **10** above board, flagrantly, immodestly, in full view **11** on the square, shamelessly, unashamedly **12** forthrightly, unreservedly

open-minded
04 free **05** broad **07** liberal **08** catholic, tolerant, unbiased **09** impartial, objective, receptive **10** reasonable **11** broad-minded, enlightened **12** unprejudiced **13** dispassionate **14** latitudinarian

open-mindedness
06 equity **07** justice **08** equality, fairness **10** detachment, dispassion, neutrality **11** disinterest, objectivity **12** impartiality, unbiasedness **14** even-handedness **15** non-partisanship

open-mouthed
06 amazed, gaping, greedy **07** shocked **08** wide-eyed **09** astounded, clamorous, expectant, surprised **10** astonished, spellbound **11** dumbfounded, widechapped **13** flabbergasted, thunderstruck

openwork
04 mode

opera
03 ENO **05** works **08** burletta **09** pastorale **10** music drama

13 dramma giocoso 15 dramma per musica

See also **singer**

Operas and operettas include:

04 Aïda
05 Faust, Manon, Norma, Tosca
06 Carmen, Otello, Salome
07 Elektra, Fidelio, Macbeth, Nabucco, Thespis, The Ring, Werther, Wozzeck
08 Falstaff, Idomeneo, Iolanthe, La Bohème, Parsifal, Patience, Turandot
09 Billy Budd, Capriccio, Don Carlos, King Priam, Lohengrin, Rigoletto, Ruddigore, Siegfried, The Mikado, Véronique
10 Cinderella, Die Walküre, I Pagliacci, La Traviata, Oedipus Rex, Tannhäuser
11 Don Giovanni, Don Pasquale, HMS Pinafore, Il Trovatore, La Périchole, Peter Grimes, Princess Ida, The Sorceror, Trial by Jury, William Tell
12 Boris Godunov, Cosí Fan Tutte, Das Rheingold, Eugene Onegin, Manon Lescaut, Nixon in China, Porgy and Bess, The Grand Duke, The Huguenots, The Rhinegold, The Valkyries
13 Albert Herring, Der Freischütz, Dido and Aeneas, Die Fledermaus, La Belle Hélène, Moses and Aaron, Powder Her Face, The Fairy Queen, The Gondoliers, The Knot Garden, The Magic Flute, Utopia Limited
14 Le Grand Macabre, Samson et Dalila
15 Ariadne auf Naxos, Götterdämmerung, Hansel and Gretel, Le Nozze di Figaro, Madama Butterfly, Madame Butterfly, Orfeo ed Euridice, Simon Boccanegra, The Beggar's Opera, The Pearl Fishers

Opera houses include:

03 Met, ROH
05 Cairo, Lyric, Royal, State
06 De Munt, Sydney, the Met, Zurich
07 La Scala
08 La Fenice, San Carlo
09 La Monnaie
10 Mussorgsky, Semper Oper
11 Oper Leipzig, Teatro Liceo, Verona Arena
12 Glyndebourne, Komische Oper, Metropolitan, Opéra-Comique
13 Kennedy Center, Muziektheater, Opera Bastille, Teatro Massimo
14 Bolshoi Theatre, Estates Theatre, Hungarian State, Kungliga Operan, London Coliseum, Unter den Linden
15 Gothenburg Opera, Teatro alla Scala, Zheng Yici Peking

Opera characters include:

03 **Eva**, **Liu**
04 **Aïda**, **Bess**, **Budd** (Billy), **Erda**, **Froh**, **Iago**, **Il Re**, **Loge**, **Luna** (Il Conte di), **Mime**, **Mimì**, **Pang**, **Pike** (Florence), **Ping**, **Pong**, **Tito**, **Vere** (Captain)
05 **Caius** (Dr), **Calaf**, **Falke** (Dr), **Faust**, **Freia**, **Gilda**, **Herod**, **Jeník**, **Kecal**, **Porgy**, **Rocco**, **Sachs** (Hans), **Titus**, **Tosca**, **Vasek**, **Wotan**
06 **Alcina**, **Alzira**, **Carmen**, **Donner**, **Emilia**, **Fafner**, **Fasolt**, **Figaro**, **Fricka**, **Gretel**, **Grimes** (Peter), **Hänsel**, **Isolde**, **Lockit** (Lucy), **Mantua** (Duke of), **Onegin** (Eugene), **Otello**, **Pamina**, **Pogner** (Veit), **Rosina**, **Salome**, **Tamino**, **Valery** (Violetta), **Wagner**
07 **Bartolo** (Dr), **Bastien**, **Billows**, **Despina**, **Don José**, **Douphol** (Baron), **Germont** (Alfredo), **Godunov** (Boris), **Gunther**, **Gutrune**, **Herring** (Albert), **Hunding**, **Jocasta**, **Leonora**, **Manrico**, **Marenka**, **Micaëla**, **Musetta**, **Oedipus**, **Peachum** (Polly), **Pelléas**, **Quickly** (Mistress), **Radamès**, **Rodolfo**, **Scarpia** (Baron), **Susanna**, **Tristan**, **Wozzeck**
08 **Alberich**, **Almaviva** (Count), **Almaviva** (Countess), **Azeucena**, **Claggart** (John), **Falstaff** (Sir John), **Ferrando**, **Herodias**, **Hoffmann**, **Lucretia**, **Macheath**, **Marcello**, **Mercédès**, **Orlofsky** (Prince), **Papagena**, **Papageno**, **Parsifal**, **Roderigo**, **Sarastro**, **Siegmund**, **Turandot**, **Valentin**, **Woglinde**, **Yamadori** (Prince)
09 **Angelotti** (Cesare), **Bastienne**, **Butterfly** (Madame), **Cherubino**, **Cio-Cio-San**, **Desdemona**, **Donna Anna**, **Dorabella**, **Escamillo**, **Esmerelda**, **Florestan**, **Guglielmo**, **Leporello**, **Lohengrin**, **Maddalena**, **Mélisande**, **Narraboth**, **Pinkerton** (Lieutenant), **Rigoletto**, **Sharpless**, **Siegfried**, **Sieglunde**, **Vogelsang** (Kunz), **Waltraute**
10 **Beckmesser** (Sixtus), **Brünnhilde**, **Don Alfonso**, **Don Basilio**, **Don Ottavio**, **Eisenstein** (Gabriele von), **Eisenstein** (Rosalinde von), **Fiordiligi**, **Marcellina**, **Monostatos**, **Prince Igor**, **Tannhäuser**
11 **Cavaradossi** (Mario), **Don Giovanni**, **Donna Elvira**, **Marschallin**, **Sparafucile**, **The Dutchman**
14 **Henry the Fowler**, **John the Baptist**, **Mephistopheles**
15 **Queen of the Night**

operate

◇ *anagram indicator*

02 go **03** act, fly, ren, rin, run, set, use **04** play, trip, work **05** drive, pilot, serve **06** direct, employ, handle, make go, manage **07** actuate, conduct, control, perform, utilize **08** function, tick over **09** manoeuvre **12** be in charge of

operation

02 op **03** job, ure, use **04** deal, game, play, raid, task **05** using **06** action, affair, agency, attack, charge, effect, effort, motion **07** assault, control, process, running, surgery, working **08** activity, business, campaign, exercise, handling, movement **09** influence, manoeuvre, procedure **10** enterprise, management, proceeding **11** functioning, performance, transaction, undertaking, utilization **12** manipulation

• **combined operations**

02 CO

• **in operation**

02 on **04** live **05** going, valid **06** active, viable **07** in force, working **08** in action, in effect, prepared, workable **09** effective, efficient, in service **10** functional **11** functioning, operational, serviceable **12** taking effect

operational

05 going, in use, ready **06** usable, viable **07** running, working **08** in action, prepared, workable **09** in service **10** functional **11** functioning **12** up and running **14** in working order

operative

03 key, spy **04** dick, hand, mole **05** agent, valid, vital **06** active, shamus, sleuth, viable, worker **07** artisan, crucial, gumshoe, in force, operant, ouvrier, working, workman **08** employee, in action, in effect, labourer, mechanic, operator, ouvrière, relevant, workable **09** detective, effective, efficient, important, machinist **10** functional, private eye **11** double agent, efficacious, functioning, in operation, operational, secret agent, serviceable, significant **12** investigator

operator

02 op **05** mover **06** dealer, driver, punter, trader, worker **07** functor, handler, manager, operant, shyster **08** director, mechanic **09** machinist, operative **10** contractor, machinator, manoeuvrer, speculator, technician **11** manipulator **12** practitioner **13** administrator, wheeler-dealer

operetta *see* **opera**

opiate

04 drug, dull **06** downer **07** anodyne, bromide **08** narcotic, nepenthe, pacifier, sedative **09** soporific **10** depressant **12** stupefacient **13** tranquillizer

opine

03 say **05** guess, judge, think **07** believe, declare, presume, suggest, suppose, surmise, suspect, venture **08** conceive, conclude **09** volunteer **10** conjecture

opinion

03 bet **04** deem, doxy, idea, mind, view, vote **05** sense, tenet **06** belief, notion, stance, theory **07** feeling, thought **08** attitude, feelings, suffrage, thoughts **09** arrogance, judgement, sentiment, viewpoint **10** assessment, assumption, conception, conviction, estimation, impression, perception, persuasion, reputation, standpoint **11** point of view, supposition **13** way of thinking **15** school of thought

• in my opinion
03 IMO **06** I think **08** à mon avis, as I see it, I believe, in my book, in my view, me judice **10** for my money, if you ask me, personally

• opinion tester
04 kite

opinionated
06 biased, entêté **07** adamant, bigoted, entêtée, pompous
08 arrogant, cocksure, dogmatic, stubborn **09** obstinate, pigheaded, pragmatic **10** inflexible, pontifical, prejudiced **11** dictatorial, doctrinaire, pragmatical **12** single-minded **13** self-important **14** uncompromising

opium
03 hop

opossum
04 joey **05** yapok **06** yapock
07 marmose **09** phalanger
12 Didelphyidae

opponent
03 foe **04** anti **05** enemy, rival
07 opposer **08** objector, opposite
09 adversary, contender, dissenter, dissident, oppugnant **10** antagonist, challenger, competitor, contestant, opposition **11** dissentient

• opponents
02 NE, SW

opportune
03 apt, fit **04** good **05** happy, lucky
06 proper, timely **07** fitting, in place
08 suitable **09** fortunate, pertinent, well-timed **10** auspicious, convenient, favourable, felicitous, propitious, seasonable **11** appropriate
12 advantageous, providential

opportunism
07 realism **10** expediency, pragmatism
12 exploitation **15** taking advantage

opportunity
03 ren, rin, run **04** hour, pick, room, roum, turn **05** break, power, scope, space **06** chance, look-in, moment
07 fitness, opening, vantage
08 occasion, overture, prospect
09 privilege **11** possibility **14** crack of the whip

• alive to opportunity
04 go-go

oppose
03 bar, opp **04** defy, face **05** check, fight, match **06** attack, breast, combat, hinder, impugn, offset, oppugn, repugn, resist, thwart
07 balance, compare, contest, counter, dispute, play off, prevent **08** confront, contrary, contrast, disfavor, obstruct, traverse **09** be against, challenge, disfavour, encounter, juxtapose, stand up to, withstand **10** contradict, contravene, controvert, set against
11 take against **12** argue against, disagree with, disapprove of **13** take issue with **14** counterbalance, fly in the face of

opposed
03 opp **04** anti **06** averse, object
07 adverse, against, hostile
08 clashing, contrary, inimical, opposing, opposite **09** toto caelo
11 conflicting, disagreeing
12 antagonistic, incompatible, in opposition

• as opposed to
01 v **02** vs **06** versus **09** as against, instead of **10** rather than **12** in contrast to

opposing
05 enemy, rival **06** at odds **07** counter, hostile, opposed, warring **08** clashing, contrary, fighting, opponent, opposite
09 combatant, differing, oppugnant
10 at variance, contending
11 conflicting, contentious
12 antagonistic, antipathetic, disputatious, incompatible
14 irreconcilable

opposite
02 op **03** opp **06** at odds, en face, facing, unlike **07** adverse, counter, hostile, inverse, opposed, reverse
08 clashing, contrary, converse, flip side, fronting, opponent, opposing
09 different, differing, dissident
10 antipathic, antithesis, at variance, contrasted, face to face, overthwart, poles apart **11** conflicting, over against
12 antagonistic, antithetical, inconsistent **13** contradiction, contradictory, corresponding
14 irreconcilable

opposition
03 foe **05** enemy, rival **06** syzygy
07 dislike **08** clashing, contrast, distance, opponent **09** adversary, collision, hostility, other side
10 antagonism, antagonist, antithesis, reluctance, resistance **11** competition, contrariety, counter-time, counter-view, disapproval **12** colluctation, counter-stand, opposing side
13 confrontation **14** unfriendliness
15 obstructiveness

• set in opposition
04 play

oppress
03 vex **04** ride **05** abuse, bully, crush, grind, gripe, press, quash, quell, tread
06 burden, deject, hang on, harass, ravish, sadden, subdue, weight
07 afflict, depress, enslave, overset, repress, smother, torment, trample
08 desolate, dispirit, distress, hang over, maltreat, suppress **09** overpower, overpress, overwhelm, persecute, subjugate, suffocate, tyrannize, weigh down **10** discourage, dishearten, lie heavy on **11** walk all over **12** bear hard upon **13** treat like dirt, use as a doormat **15** bear heavily upon

oppressed
06 abused **07** crushed, misused, subject **08** burdened, enslaved, harassed, troubled **09** repressed
10 maltreated, persecuted, subjugated, tyrannized **11** downtrodden
13 disadvantaged **15** underprivileged

oppression
05 abuse **07** cruelty, tyranny
08 hardship **09** brutality, despotism, harshness, injustice **10** repression, subjection **11** persecution, subjugation, suppression
12 maltreatment, overpowering, overwhelming, ruthlessness

oppressive
05 close, cruel, faint, harsh, heavy, muggy **06** brutal, leaden, stuffy, sultry, unjust **07** airless, inhuman, onerous, sweltry **08** crushing, despotic, pitiless, ruthless, stifling **09** burdenous, Draconian, merciless, troubling, tyrannous **10** broodiness, burdensome, iron-fisted, repressive, tyrannical **11** domineering, heavy-handed, intolerable, overbearing, suffocating **12** extortionate, overpowering, overwhelming

oppressor
05 bully, tyran **06** despot, tyrant
08 autocrat, dictator, torturer
09 tormentor **10** persecutor, subjugator, taskmaster **11** intimidator, slave-driver **14** hard taskmaster

opprobrious
07 abusive **08** damaging, infamous, insolent, venomous **09** insulting, invective, offensive, vitriolic
10 calumnious, defamatory, derogatory, scandalous, scurrilous
11 disgraceful, dyslogistic, reproachful
12 calumniatory, contemptuous, contumelious, vituperative

opprobrium
04 slur **05** odium, shame **06** infamy, stigma **07** calumny, censure, obloquy
08 disgrace, ignominy, reproach
09 contumely, discredit, disfavour, dishonour, disrepute **10** debasement, scurrility **11** degradation

Ops
04 Rhea

opt
04 pick **05** elect, go for **06** choose, decide, prefer, select **08** decide on, plump for, settle on **09** single out

optical

Optical instruments and devices include:

05 laser
06 camera
07 sextant
08 spyglass
09 endoscope, periscope, telescope
10 binoculars, microscope, opera-glass, theodolite
12 field-glasses, stereocamera
13 film projector
14 slide projector
15 magnifying glass, photomicroscope, telescopic sight, telestereoscope

optimism
05 cheer **06** morale **08** buoyancy, idealism **10** brightness, confidence, expectancy **11** hopefulness
12 cheerfulness, sanguineness
13 Leibnizianism **14** feel-good factor, Leibnitzianism

optimistic
06 bright, upbeat **07** assured, bullish, buoyant, hopeful **08** cheerful, positive, sanguine **09** confident, expectant **10** idealistic, Panglossic
11 Panglossian, pollyannish **12** happy-go-lucky, pollyannaish

optimum
03 opt, top **04** best **05** ideal, model
06 choice **07** highest, optimal, perfect, supreme, utopian **08** flawless
11 superlative **14** most favourable

option
03 put **04** call, wish **06** choice
07 refusal **08** swaption **09** privilege, selection **10** preference **11** alternative, possibility

optional
03 opt **04** free **08** elective, unforced
09 voluntary **10** permissive
11 facultative **13** discretionary

options
04 menu

opulence
06 luxury, plenty, riches, wealth
07 fortune **08** fullness, richness
09 abundance, affluence, profusion
10 cornucopia, easy street, lavishness, luxuriance, prosperity **11** copiousness
13 sumptuousness
14 superabundance

opulent
04 posh, rich **05** plush, pluty **06** lavish
07 copious, moneyed, profuse, wealthy, well-off **08** abundant, affluent, prolific, well-to-do
09 luxuriant, luxurious, plentiful, sumptuous **10** prosperous, well-heeled **11** rolling in it
13 superabundant

opus
02 op **04** work **05** piece **06** oeuvre
08 creation **10** brainchild, production
11 composition

or
04 gold **05** ossia **06** before, yellow
10 conversely **13** alternatively **14** in preference to, on the other hand **15** as an alternative
See also **gold**

oracle
04 guru, sage, seer, Urim **05** augur, sibyl **06** answer, augury, expert, mentor, pundit, vision, wizard
07 adviser, prophet, Thummin
08 forecast, prophecy **09** authority
10 divination, forecaster, high priest, mastermind, prediction, prophetess, revelation, soothsayer, specialist
13 fortune teller **14** Urim and Thummim **15** prognostication

oracular
04 sage, wise **05** grave, vatic **06** arcane
07 cryptic, Delphic, obscure, ominous
08 abstruse, dogmatic, positive, two-edged **09** ambiguous, equivocal, prescient, prophetic, venerable
10 auspicious, haruspical, mysterious, portentous, predictive **11** dictatorial, significant **13** authoritative

oral
◇ *homophone indicator*
04 quiz, said, viva **05** vocal **06** buccal, lively, spoken, verbal **07** uttered
08 viva voce **09** unwritten
11 nuncupative

orally
◇ *homophone indicator*
07 by mouth, vocally **08** verbally, viva voce

orange
11 hesperidium

Oranges include:
04 gold
05 amber, chica, chico, coral, henna, tawny, tenné, tenny
06 anatta, anatto, aurora, chicha, kamala, kamela, kamila, roucou, salmon, tawney
07 annatta, annatto, apricot, arnotto, jacinth, nacarat, paprika, saffron
08 croceate, croceous, mandarin
09 bilirubin, tangerine
13 cadmium yellow, canthaxanthin

Orange varieties include:
04 mock, Ruta, sour
05 blood, Jaffa, navel, sweet, topaz
06 bitter
07 cumquat, kumquat, naartje, nartjie, satsuma, Seville
08 bergamot, bigarade, mandarin
09 clockwork, mandarine, tangerine
10 clementine

• segment of orange
03 pig

orate
04 talk **05** speak **07** declaim, lecture
08 harangue **09** discourse, hold forth, sermonize, speechify **11** pontificate

oration
05 éloge, elogy, spiel **06** eulogy, homily, korero, sermon, speech
07 address, elogium, lecture
08 eulogium, harangue **09** discourse, set speech **11** declamation

orator
06 Cicero, rhetor **07** speaker, spieler
08 lecturer **09** Boanerges, declaimer, demagogue, spokesman, thunderer
10 petitioner **11** Demosthenes, rhetorician, spellbinder
12 phrasemonger, prevaricator
13 public speaker

oratorical
08 eloquent, rhetoric, sonorous
09 bombastic, high-flown
10 Ciceronian, rhetorical
11 declamatory, Demosthenic
12 elocutionary, magniloquent
13 grandiloquent, silver-tongued, smooth-tongued

oratorio

Oratorios include:
04 Saul
06 Elijah, Esther, Joshua, Samson, Semele, St Paul
07 Athalia, Deborah, Jephtha, Messiah, Solomon, Susanna
08 Christus, Giuseppe, Hercules, Theodora
09 Christmas
10 Belshazzar, Oedipus Rex, The Seasons
11 The Creation
13 Israel in Egypt
14 Alexander Balus, La Resurrezione
15 Judas Maccabaeus

oratory
04 hwyl **06** chapel, speech **07** diction
08 rhetoric **09** elocution, eloquence, proseucha, proseuche **11** chapel royal, declamation **12** speechifying, speechmaking **14** grandiloquence, public speaking

orb
03 eye **04** ball, pome, ring **05** globe, mound, orbit, round, world **06** circle, sphere **07** eyeball, globule
08 bereaved, spherule

orbit
03 orb **04** path **05** ambit, cycle, range, reach, scope, sweep, track **06** circle, course, domain, sphere **07** circuit, compass, revolve **08** encircle, rotation
09 eye socket, influence **10** revolution, trajectory **14** circumgyration, circumnavigate

• point in orbit
04 apse **05** apsis **06** apogee
07 apolune, perigee **08** aphelion, perilune **10** perihelion
12 pericynthion, periselenium

orchestra

Orchestras include:
03 LPO, NSO, OAE, OSM, RPO
04 ASMF, CBSO, RLPO, RSNO
05 Hallé
06 Ulster
09 Minnesota
11 BBC Symphony, NBC Symphony
12 Milan La Scala, Philadelphia, San Francisco
13 Concertgebouw, Staatskapelle
14 Boston Symphony, English Chamber, LA Philharmonic, London Symphony, Sydney Symphony, Vienna Symphony
15 BBC Philharmonic, Chicago Symphony, Detroit Symphony, New York Symphony, Scottish Chamber, Seattle Symphony, The Philharmonia, Toronto Symphony

orchestrate
03 fix **05** score **07** arrange, compose, prepare, present **08** organize
09 integrate **10** co-ordinate,

mastermind **11** put together, stage-manage

orchestration

05 score **07** running, scoring, setting, version **08** planning **10** adaptation, management **11** arrangement, engineering, preparation **12** co-ordination, organization
13 harmonization, masterminding, stage-managing **14** interpretation
15 instrumentation

orchid

Orchids include:

03 bee, bog, bug, fen, fly, man, sun
04 blue, disa, frog, king, kite, lady, moth, musk, wasp
05 burnt, clown, comet, ghost, giant, pansy, queen, tiger, tulip
06 lizard, monkey, spider
07 leopard, slipper, vanilla
08 calanthe, cattleya, crucifix, fragrant, military, oncidium
09 bee-orchis, birds-nest, chocolate, Christmas, coralroot, cymbidium, false musk, fly orchis, pyramidal, twayblade
10 early marsh, epidendrum, late spider, small white
11 cockleshell, cypripedium, dancing lady, early purple, early spider, epidendrone, green-winged, helleborine
12 black vanilla, heath spotted, ladys' tresses, Lapland marsh, narrow-leaved, one-leaved bog, western marsh
13 Chinese ground, common spotted, dense-flowered, elder-flowered, ladies' tresses, loose-flowered, orange blossom, southern marsh
14 moccasin flower, violet birds-nest
15 lesser butterfly

ordain

03 fix, set **04** call, fate, rule, will
05 elect, frock, japan, order **06** anoint, assign, decree, invest, priest
07 appoint, arrange, destine, dictate, dispose, foresay, lay down, require
08 instruct, ordinate **09** destinate, establish, preordain, prescribe, pronounce **10** consecrate, foreordain, lay hands on, predestine
12 predetermine

ordeal

04 pain, test **05** agony, trial **07** anguish, torment, torture, trouble **08** distress, troubles **09** bier right, gruelling, nightmare, suffering **10** affliction
11 persecution, tribulation
12 tribulations **13** baptism of fire

order

◇ *anagram indicator*
02 OM **03** bid, law, OBE, ord **04** book, call, calm, chit, club, fiat, form, kind, line, nick, plan, rank, rota, rule, sect, sort, tell, type, writ **05** array, caste, class, cycle, edict, genus, grade, group, guild, level, lodge, peace, quiet, set-up, shape, state, union **06** codify, decree, degree, demand, direct, enjoin, family, fettle, kilter, lay out, layout, league, line-up, manage, method, ordain, system, tidy up **07** arrange, booking, call for, command, company, conduct, control, dictate, dispose, harmony, mandate, marshal, pattern, precept, request, require, reserve, society, sort out, species, station, summons, variety, warrant **08** apply for, classify, grouping, instruct, neatness, organize, position, practice, regulate, sequence, sorority, symmetry, tidiness **09** authorize, catalogue, community, condition, direction, directive, hierarchy, legislate, ordinance, prescribe, structure
10 commission, discipline, fellowship, fraternity, injunction, lawfulness, regularity, regulation, sisterhood, uniformity **11** application, arrangement, association, brotherhood, disposition, instruction, law and order, orderliness, requirement, requisition, reservation, send away for, stipulation, systematize, write off for **12** codification, denomination, notification, organization, pecking order, tranquillity, working order **13** secret society **14** categorization, classification

See also **command**; **honour**; **religious**

• in order

02 OK **04** done, neat, tidy **05** right
06 lawful, likely, mended, proper
07 allowed, correct, fitting, ordered, orderly, regular, working **08** all right, arranged, suitable **09** operative, organized, permitted, shipshape
10 acceptable, classified, good as gold, in sequence, methodical, systematic
11 appropriate, categorized, functioning **13** well-organized
15 secundum ordinem

• in order that

02 so

• in order to

02 to **05** for to **06** so that **11** intending to, with a view to **13** with the result
14 with the purpose

• order around

05 bully **07** lay down **08** browbeat, bulldoze, dominate, domineer **09** push about, tyrannize **10** boss around, order about, push around **13** lay down the law

• out of order

◇ *anagram indicator*
04 bust **05** amiss, kaput, messy, wrong
06 broken, untidy **07** haywire, muddled **08** confused, gone phut, improper, unlawful, unseemly
09 conked out, incorrect, irregular, off kilter **10** broken down, disordered, not working, on the blink, on the fritz, out of sorts, out of whack, unsuitable
11 inoperative, out of course, out of kilter, uncalled-for **12** disorganized, unacceptable **13** inappropriate, out of sequence **14** not functioning **15** out of commission

• set in order

02 do **03** red **04** redd, trim **05** dress, prank, right **06** betrim, fettle, pranck, snod up **07** dispone, prancke

• special order, standing order

02 SO

orderliness

08 neatness, tidiness, trimness
09 smartness **10** regularity, spruceness
12 organization, straightness
14 methodicalness

orderly

◇ *anagram indicator*
04 neat, ruly, tidy, trim **05** quiet
06 cosmic **07** in order, ordered, regular
09 chaprassi, chaprassy, chuprassy, efficient, regularly **10** controlled, law-abiding, methodical, restrained, systematic **11** disciplined, well-behaved **12** businesslike, methodically
13 well-organized, well-regulated
15 in apple-pie order

ordinance

03 law **04** fiat, rite, rule **05** canon, edict, order **06** bye-law, decree, dictum, ritual, ruling **07** command, statute **08** ceremony, planning, practice **09** directive, enactment, equipment, prescript, sacrament
10 dead-letter, injunction, observance, regulation **11** appointment, institution, preparation

ordinarily

07 as a rule, usually **08** commonly, normally **09** generally, in general
10 familiarly, habitually **11** customarily
14 conventionally

ordinary

01 O **03** ord **04** dull, fair **05** banal, bland, blunt, plain, usual **06** canton, common, cotise, modest, normal, simple **07** average, cottise, mundane, prosaic, quarter, regular, routine, typical, vanilla **08** everyday, familiar, habitual, mediocre, standard, workaday **09** customary, plain-Jane, quotidian **10** mainstream, pedestrian, working-day **11** bog standard, commonplace, indifferent, nondescript, unmemorable
12 conventional, run-of-the-mill, unremarkable **13** penny-farthing, unexceptional, uninteresting, unpretentious **14** bread-and-butter, common-or-garden
15 undistinguished

• out of the ordinary

04 rare **05** kinky **06** unique **07** unusual
09 different, left-field, memorable
10 noteworthy, remarkable, surprising, unexpected **11** exceptional, out of the way, outstanding
13 extraordinary

ordnance

03 ord **04** arms, guns **06** cannon
07 big guns, pelican, weapons
09 artillery, munitions **14** field artillery

ordure

03 poo **04** crap, dirt, dung, poop

05 filth, frass, guano, scats, stool 06 egesta, faeces 09 droppings, excrement, excretion 11 waste matter

ore

03 o'er 04 over 06 tangle 07 mineral, seaweed 09 sea tangle

Ores include:

03 wad
04 wadd, wadt
06 bog-ore, coltan, galena, rutile
07 bauxite, bog-iron, bornite, cuprite, iron ore, oligist, schlich, uranite, wood tin
08 beauxite, braunite, calamine, enargite, hematite, limonite, siderite, sinopite, stibnite, taconite, tenorite
09 anglesite, blackband, coffinite, haematite, hedyphane, ironstone, kidney ore, lodestone, magnetite, malachite, manganite, minestone, morass ore, proustite, tantalite
10 erubescite, melaconite, peacock-ore, pyrolusite, ruby silver, sphalerite, stephanite
11 cassiterite, chloanthite, pyrargyrite, tetradymite
12 babingtonite, chalcopyrite, pyromorphite, tetrahedrite
13 copper pyrites, horseflesh ore
15 stilpnosiderite

See also **seaweed**

• vein of ore

04 rake

Oregon

02 OR 04 Oreg

organ

04 part, tool, unit 05 forum, paper, pedal, regal, voice 06 agency, device, medium, member 07 element, journal, process, vehicle 08 magazine, melodeon, melodion 09 component, harmonium, implement, newspaper, structure 10 instrument, mouthpiece, periodical 11 apollonicon, constituent, publication 13 kist o' whistles

Organs include:

03 ear, eye
04 lung, nose, skin
05 bowel, brain, colon, liver, lungs, lymph, penis, vulva
06 cervix, rectum, spleen, testes, throat, thymus, ureter, uterus, vagina
07 bladder, kidneys, ovaries, oviduct, pharynx, scrotum, stomach, thyroid, tonsils, trachea, urethra
08 adenoids, appendix, bronchus, clitoris, pancreas, prostate, windpipe
09 diaphragm, pituitary, taste buds
10 epididymis, intestines, lymph nodes, oesophagus, spinal cord
11 gall bladder, parathyroid, vas deferens
12 hypothalamus, thymus glands, thyroid gland
13 adrenal glands, nervous system
14 fallopian tubes, large intestine, small intestine
15 ejaculatory duct, seminal vesicles

Organ stops include:

04 echo, oboe, sext, tuba
05 dolce, gamba, quint
06 cornet, nasard, octave, tierce
07 bombard, bourdon, clarino, clarion, fagotto, mixture, piccolo, salicet, trumpet
08 carillon, crumhorn, diapason, diaphone, dulciana, gemshorn, krumhorn, register, waldhorn
09 fifteenth, furniture, krummhorn, principal, pyramidon, vox humana, waldflute
10 clarabella, fourniture, salicional
11 superoctave, voix céleste
12 sesquialtera
15 corno di bassetto

organic

06 biotic, GM-free, living 07 animate, natural, ordered 08 coherent 09 organized 10 biological, harmonious, mechanical, structural, structured 11 non-chemical 12 additive-free, chemical-free, instrumental 13 not artificial, pesticide-free

organism

04 body, cell 05 being, biont, plant, set-up, unity, whole 06 animal, entity, system 08 creature 09 bacterium, structure 11 living thing 12 organization

See also **animal**; **cell**; **classification**

organization

◇ *anagram indicator*

04 body, club, firm, plan 05 group, order, set-up, union, unity, whole 06 design, layout, league, method, outfit, system 07 company, concern, council, pattern, running, society 08 grouping, planning 09 authority, formation, institute, operation, structure, syndicate 10 consortium, federation, management, regulation 11 arrangement, association, composition, corporation, development, institution, methodology 12 co-ordination 13 confederation, configuration, establishment 14 administration, classification, conglomeration

Organization of Petroleum Exporting Countries *see* **OPEC**

organize

◇ *anagram indicator*

03 ren, rin, run 04 form 05 begin, found, frame, group, mould, order, see to, set up, shape, start 06 create, embody, imbody, manage, obtain 07 arrange, develop, dispose, marshal, prepare, sort out 08 assemble, classify, regiment, tabulate 09 catalogue, construct, establish, institute, lemmatize, originate, structure 10 administer, co-ordinate, put in order 11 orchestrate, put together, rationalize, standardize, systematize 12 be in charge of

organized

◇ *anagram indicator*

04 neat, tidy 07 in order, ordered, orderly, organic, planned, regular 08 arranged 09 efficient 10 methodical, structured, systematic 11 well-ordered 12 businesslike 13 well-organized, well-regulated

orgiastic

04 wild 05 orgic 07 Bacchic 09 debauched, Dionysiac 12 bacchanalian

orgy

04 bout, riot 05 binge, party, revel, spree 06 excess, frenzy, revels 07 debauch, revelry, splurge 08 carousal, Dionysia 09 wild party 10 indulgence, Saturnalia 11 bacchanalia

orient

01 E 04 East 05 adapt, align 06 adjust, attune, rising 07 eastern, sunrise, the East 08 accustom 09 habituate, orientate 11 acclimatize, accommodate, familiarize 15 get your bearings

oriental

01 E 05 Asian 07 Asiatic, Eastern 10 Far Eastern

See also **Asian**

orientation

07 guiding, leading 08 attitude, bearings, location, position, training 09 alignment, direction, induction, placement, situation 10 adaptation, adjustment, initiation, settling-in 11 inclination, positioning 15 acclimatization, familiarization

orifice

03 gap 04 hole, pore, rent, rift, slit, slot, vent 05 break, cleft, crack, inlet, mouth, space, trema 06 breach, orifex 07 crevice, fissure, opening 08 aperture, spiracle 09 micropyle 10 blastopore 11 perforation

origin

04 base, dawn, germ, line, rise, root 05 basis, birth, cause, fount, roots, start, stock 06 family, launch, source, spring 07 dawning, descent, genesis, lineage 08 ancestry, creation, fountain, genetics, heritage, pedigree 09 beginning, emergence, etymology, inception, parentage, paternity, principle 10 conception, derivation, extraction, foundation, provenance, well-spring 12 commencement, fountainhead, inauguration 13 line of descent

original

◇ *anagram indicator*

02 ur- 03 new 04 real, true, type 05 early, first, fresh, model, novel, prime 06 actual, innate, master, primal, unique 07 genuine, initial, opening, pattern, primary, radical, unusual

08 creative, earliest, paradigm, primeval, pristine, standard, starting 09 archetype, authentic, embryonic, first-hand, ingenious, inventive, primaeval, primitial, primitive, prototype 10 archetypal, commencing, indigenous, innovative, pioneering, primordial, protoplast, unborrowed, unorthodox 11 imaginative, primigenial, resourceful, rudimentary 13 autochthonous 14 ground-breaking, unconventional

originality
06 daring 07 newness, novelty 08 boldness 09 freshness, ingenuity 10 cleverness, creativity, innovation 11 imagination, singularity, unorthodoxy 12 creativeness, eccentricity 13 individuality, inventiveness 14 creative spirit, innovativeness 15 imaginativeness, resourcefulness

• lacking originality
07 clichéd 08 clichéed 09 hackneyed

originally
05 first 07 at first, by birth 08 in origin 09 initially 10 at the start 11 at the outset, to begin with 12 by derivation 14 in the beginning 15 in the first place

originate
04 come, flow, form, head, rear, rise, seed, stem 05 arise, begin, found, hatch, issue, plant, set up, start 06 be born, create, derive, emerge, evolve, father, invent, launch, result, source, spring 07 develop, emanate, pioneer, proceed, produce 08 commence, conceive, discover, generate, take rise 09 establish, institute, introduce, set on foot 10 inaugurate, mastermind 11 give birth to, set in motion 13 be the father of, be the mother of

origination
07 forming 08 creation 09 invention, paternity 10 conception, generation, production 11 development

originator
06 author, father, mother 07 creator, founder, pioneer 08 designer, inventor 09 architect, developer, generator, initiator, innovator, the brains 10 discoverer, prime mover 11 establisher

ornament
04 deck, fall, gaud, gild, knob, ouch, spar, tiki, trim 05 adorn, crown, décor, frill, gnome, jewel, mense, spray, sprig, wally 06 almond, bauble, bedeck, fallal, gewgaw, gorget, griffe, labret, relish, set-off 07 dress up, emblema, figgery, fleuron, frigger, frounce, garland, garnish, hei-tiki, lunette, netsuke, pattern, pendant, pendent, rellish, trinket, twiddle 08 barrette, bar slide, beautify, brighten, carcanet, decorate, furbelow, rocaille, sunburst, trimming 09 accessory, adornment, arabesque, dog collar, embellish, fandangle, medallion, multifoil, scalework 10 decoration, escutcheon, Japanesery, knick-knack 11 garden gnome, garnishment 12 curliewurlie, jingle-jangle 13 embellishment

ornamental
05 fancy, showy 06 florid 08 adorning 10 attractive, decorative 12 embellishing, embroidering

ornamentation
04 fret, seam 06 frills 07 barbola, die-work 09 adornment, fallalery, garniture, strap work 10 decoration, embroidery, enrichment, figuration, ornateness 11 barbola work, elaboration, whigmaleery 12 whigmaleerie 13 embellishment

ornate
◇ *anagram indicator*
04 busy, fine 05 adorn, fancy, flash, fussy, showy 06 florid, rococo 07 baroque, elegant, flowery 08 barbaric, mandarin 09 barbarian, decorated, elaborate, grandiose, luxuriant, sumptuous 10 flamboyant, ornamented 11 embellished 12 ostentatious

orotund
04 deep, full, loud, rich 05 round 06 ornate, strong 07 booming, pompous 08 imposing, powerful, sonorous, strained 09 dignified 10 resonating 11 pretentious 12 magniloquent 13 grandiloquent

orthodox
04 true 05 sound, usual 06 devout, square, strict 07 canonic, correct, regular 08 accepted, catholic, faithful, official, received 09 canonical, customary, hardshell 10 conformist, recognized 11 bien pensant, established, traditional 12 conservative, conventional 13 authoritative 14 fundamentalist 15 well-established

orthodoxy
05 canon, credo, creed, dogma, tenet 06 belief 07 precept 08 devotion, doctrine, teaching, trueness 09 principle, soundness 10 conformism, conformity, conviction, devoutness, properness, strictness 11 correctness 12 conservatism, faithfulness 13 inflexibility 14 fundamentalism, received wisdom, traditionalism 15 conventionality

oscar
01 O

oscillate
03 wag 04 hunt, sway, vary, yo-yo 05 pitch, squeg, swing, waver 06 seesaw, wigwag 07 librate, vibrate 09 fluctuate, vacillate 12 move to and fro

oscillation
05 surge, swing 07 flutter 08 sine wave, swinging, wavering 09 seesawing, squegging, variation, vibration 10 swing-swang 11 fluctuation, instability, vacillation 15 shilly-shallying

osmium
02 Os

osprey
07 Pandion 08 fish-hawk 09 ossifrage

ossify
06 harden 07 petrify 08 indurate, make hard, rigidify, solidify 09 fossilize, make fixed 10 become hard 11 become fixed

ostensible
07 alleged, claimed, feigned, outward, seeming 08 apparent, presumed, so-called, specious, supposed 09 ostensive, pretended, professed, purported 11 superficial

ostensibly
09 allegedly, outwardly, reputedly, seemingly 10 apparently, supposedly 11 professedly, purportedly 12 on the surface 13 superficially

ostentation
03 dog 04 dash, fuss, pomp, puff, show 05 flash, pride, swank 06 ostent, parade, splash, tinsel, vanity 07 display 08 boasting, flourish, pretence, pretense, vaunting 09 flaunting, pageantry, showiness, trappings 10 flashiness, peacockery, phylactery, pretension, showing-off 11 affectation, fanfaronade, flamboyance 13 exhibitionism 14 window-dressing 15 pretentiousness

ostentatious
03 OTT 04 loud 05 flash, gaudy, showy 06 flashy, garish, glitzy, kitsch, vulgar 07 splashy 08 affected, barbaric, fastuous 09 barbarian, barbarous, flaunting, obtrusive 10 flamboyant, over the top 11 conspicuous, extravagant, pretentious 13 demonstrative

ostentatiously
03 OTT 05 large 06 loudly 07 showily 08 flashily, garishly 10 over the top 11 obtrusively 12 flamboyantly 13 conspicuously, extravagantly, pretentiously 15 demonstratively

ostracism
04 tabu 05 exile, taboo 07 barring, boycott 09 avoidance, exclusion, expulsion, isolation, rejection 10 banishment 12 cold-shoulder, proscription 13 disfellowship 15 excommunication

ostracize
03 bar, cut 04 shun, snub 05 avoid, exile, expel 06 banish, outlaw, reject 07 boycott, exclude, isolate 09 blackball, proscribe, segregate 12 cold-shoulder 13 excommunicate 14 send to Coventry

ostrich
04 rhea 05 nandu 06 nandoo, nhandu 07 estrich 08 estridge, oystrige, Struthio

OT *see* **Bible**

other
◇ *anagram indicator*
04 else, left, more **05** extra, spare **06** second, unlike **07** further, variant **08** distinct, separate **09** alternate, different, disparate, remaining **10** additional, dissimilar **11** alternative, contrasting **13** supplementary

• all others
04 rest

otherwise
◇ *anagram indicator*
02 or **03** aka **04** else **05** alias, if not **06** or else, unless **09** different **11** also known as, differently, failing that **12** in another way **15** in a different way, in other respects

otherworldly
03 fey **04** rapt **06** dreamy **07** bemused **08** ethereal **11** preoccupied **12** absent-minded

otiose
05 extra, spare **06** excess, futile **07** surplus, to spare **08** indolent, needless, unneeded, unwanted **09** excessive, redundant, remaining **10** gratuitous, unoccupied **11** superfluous, uncalled-for, unnecessary, unwarranted **12** functionless **13** supernumerary

ottoman
04 pouf **05** squab

ounce
02 oz **03** jot, tad **04** atom, drop, fl oz, iota, lynx, spot, tael, unce, whit **05** crumb, grain, liang, scrap, shred, speck, touch, trace **06** jaguar, morsel **07** cheetah, modicum **08** particle **11** snow leopard

oust
04 fire, sack **05** eject, evict, expel **06** depose, put out, topple, unseat **07** boot out, dismiss, kick out, replace, turn out **08** dislodge, displace, drive out, force out, get rid of, supplant, throw out **09** overthrow, thrust out **10** disinherit, dispossess **13** show the door to

out
◇ *anagram indicator*
◇ *deletion indicator*
02 to **03** KO'd, set **04** alas, away, bent, dead, gone **05** dated, forth, known, passé, ready **06** abroad, absent, démodé, doused, intent, old hat, public, remote, used up **07** evident, expired, exposed, in bloom, in print, out cold, outside, without **08** blooming, comatose, divulged, drawback, excluded, external, finished, forcibly, in flower, manifest, outlying, revealed, seawards **09** available, disclosed, dismissed, elsewhere, forbidden, insistent, in the open, not at home, out-of-date, published, unwelcome **10** antiquated, blossoming, completely, determined, disallowed, impossible, insensible, knocked out, not burning, not shining, obtainable, thoroughly, unsuitable **11** in full bloom, unconscious, undesirable **12** disadvantage, extinguished, inadmissible, old-fashioned, unacceptable, unreservedly **13** inappropriate, unfashionable

• not out
02 no

• out of
04 frae, from, hors

• out upon it
04 haro **06** harrow

out-and-out
04 fair, flat, rank **05** plumb, stark, total, utter **06** arrant, full-on, proper **07** perfect, regular **08** absolute, complete, outright, positive, teetotal, thorough, whole-hog **09** bald-faced, downright, right-down, up and down **10** consummate, definitely, heart-whole, inveterate **11** honest-to-God, straight-out, unmitigated, unqualified **12** unreservedly **13** dyed-in-the-wool, thoroughgoing **14** hundred-per-cent, uncompromising

outbreak
04 rash **05** burst, clash, flash, storm **06** putsch **07** flare-up, upbreak, upsurge **08** epidemic, eruption, hysteria, outburst **09** explosion **10** ebullition **11** disturbance, excrescence, sudden start **13** recrudescence

outburst
03 fit, rag **04** flaw, gale, gush, gust, song **05** blurt, burst, flaky, spasm, storm, surge **06** attack, escape, outcry, volley **07** boutade, flare-up, ovation, passion, seizure **08** eruption, mouthful, outbreak, paroxysm, sunburst **09** explosion **10** exuberance, exuberancy, outpouring, solar flare **11** fit of temper

outcast
05 cagot, exile, leper **06** abject, outlaw, pariah, reject, wretch **07** evacuee, quarrel, refugee **08** castaway, outsider, rejected **11** untouchable **15** persona non grata

outclass
03 top **04** beat **05** outdo **07** eclipse, outrank, surpass **08** outrival, outshine, outstrip **09** excel over, transcend **10** overshadow **11** outdistance **13** leave standing, put in the shade

outcome
05 issue, proof **06** answer, effect, pay-off, result, sequel, upcome, upshot, wash-up **07** proceed, product **08** proceeds **09** end result, outspring **10** conclusion, dénouement **11** after-effect, consequence

outcry
03 cry, row **04** fuss **05** noise **06** clamor, racket, rumour, steven, tumult, uproar, yammer **07** clamour, dissent, exclaim, protest **08** outburst **09** commotion, complaint, hue and cry, objection **10** hullabaloo, humdudgeon **11** exclamation, indignation **12** protestation, vociferation

outdated
03 obs **05** dated, mumsy, passé, steam **06** démodé, old hat, past it, square, uncool **07** antique, archaic **08** obsolete, outmoded **09** out of date **10** antiquated, fuddy-duddy, oldfangled, superseded **11** obsolescent, old-fogeyish, on the way out, out of the ark **12** antediluvian, old-fashioned, out of fashion **13** unfashionable **14** behind the times

outdistance
04 pass **06** outrun **07** outpace, surpass **08** outstrip, overhaul, overtake, shake off **11** leave behind, pull ahead of **13** leave standing

outdo
03 cap **04** beat, best, whip **05** excel, lurch **06** defeat, exceed **07** eclipse, surpass **08** outclass, out-Herod, outshine, outstrip, overcome, superate **09** come first, transcend **10** outperform **11** outdistance **12** walk away from **13** knock spots off, put in the shade, run rings round **14** get the better of **15** go one better than, run circles round

outdoors
03 out **06** abroad **07** outside **08** alfresco **10** en plein air, out-of-doors **12** in the open air

outer
06 fringe, remote **07** distant, faraway, further, outside, outward, surface **08** exterior, external, outlying **09** outermost **10** peripheral **11** superficial

outface
04 defy **05** beard, brave **08** confront, outbrave, outstare **09** brazen out, stand up to, stare down

outfit
03 kit, rig, set **04** crew, firm, gang, garb, gear, suit, team, togs, unit, weed **05** dress, equip, fit up, get-up, group, samfu, set-up, squad, stock, tools **06** attire, clique, fit out, fit-out, kit out, layout, rig-out, samfoo, setout, supply **07** apparel, appoint, bloomer, clothes, company, costume, coterie, furnish, provide, sunsuit, turn out, turnout **08** accoutre, business, ensemble **09** apparatus, equipment, provision, separates, trappings **10** sailor suit **11** bag of tricks, corporation **12** organization **13** accoutrements, paraphernalia, shalwar-kameez

outfitter
06 sartor, tailor **07** modiste **08** clothier, costumer **09** costumier, couturier **10** couturière, dressmaker **11** haberdasher

outflow
03 ebb, jet **04** gush, rush **05** spout **06** efflux, spring **07** outfall, outrush

08 drainage, effluent, effusion
09 discharge, effluence, effluvium, effluxion, emanation, emergence
10 outpouring 11 debouchment
14 disemboguement

outflowing
07 emanant, gushing, leaking, rushing
08 effluent, spurting 10 debouching
11 discharging

outfox
03 con, kid 04 beat, best, dupe
05 trick 06 have on, outwit 07 deceive
08 outsmart, out-think 10 outperform
12 outmanoeuvre, take for a ride 14 get the better of, pull a fast one on

outgoing
02 ex- 04 last, open, past, warm
06 former, genial 07 affable, amiable, cordial, leaving 08 emissary, friendly, retiring, sociable 09 departing, easy-going, expansive, extrovert, talkative
10 gregarious, unreserved
11 expenditure, sympathetic, uninhibited 12 affectionate, approachable 13 communicative, demonstrative

outgoings
04 exes 05 costs 06 outlay
08 expenses, spending 09 disbursal, overheads 11 expenditure
12 disbursement

outgrowth
03 ala 04 aril, hair, horn 05 shoot
06 air-sac, effect, sprout, stolon
07 enation, product, spin-off, verruca
08 caruncle, offshoot, root hair, swelling, trichome 09 apophysis, appendage, by-product, emanation, emergence, flocculus, propagule, rostellum 10 osteophyte, pollen tube, propagulum 11 consequence, excrescence 12 appressorium, effiguration, protuberance

outhouse
04 shed

outing
03 out 04 hike, romp, spin, tour, trip
05 jaunt, jolly, sally 06 junket, picnic
08 ejection 09 coach tour, excursion
10 expedition 11 mystery tour
12 pleasure trip

outlandish
◇ *anagram indicator*
03 odd 05 alien, wacky, weird
06 exotic, far-out, freaky, quaint, way-out 07 bizarre, curious, foreign, oddball, strange, unknown, unusual
08 peculiar 09 barbarous, eccentric, grotesque, peregrine, unheard-of, uplandish 10 unfamiliar
12 preposterous, unreasonable
13 extraordinary 14 unconventional

outlandishness
07 oddness 09 queerness, weirdness
10 exoticness, quaintness
11 bizarreness, peregrinity, strangeness, unusualness
12 eccentricity 13 grotesqueness

outlast
04 ride 07 outdure, outlive, outstay, survive, weather 11 come through

outlaw
03 ban, bar 04 horn, Tory 05 debar, exile 06 badman, bandit, banish, forbid, pirate, robber 07 brigand, condemn, embargo, exclude, outcast
08 criminal, disallow, fugitive, marauder, prohibit 09 broken man, desperado, interdict, proscribe, Robin Hood 10 bushranger, highwayman
12 put to the horn 13 excommunicate

outlay
04 cost, mise 05 price 06 charge, expend 07 expense, payment
08 expenses, spending 09 outgoings
11 expenditure 12 disbursement

outlet
04 duct, exit, port, shop, vent 05 issue, store, valve 06 egress, escape, let-off, market, nozzle, sluice, way out
07 channel, conduit, culvert, opening, outfall, release, sea gate 08 débouché, emissary, femerall, retailer, supplier
10 going forth 11 safety valve 12 retail outlet 14 means of release

outline
03 map 04 edge, form, plan, trim
05 braid, chart, draft, dress, shape, trace, trick 06 aperçu, design, figure, fringe, layout, précis, résumé, schema, sketch 07 balloon, contour, croquis, diagram, keyline, profile, skyline, summary, tracing 08 abstract, chalk out, contorno, esquisse, rough out, scenario, skeleton, synopsis
09 adumbrate, bare bones, bare facts, delineate, framework, lineament, programme, rough idea, sketch out, summarize, waterline 10 ground plan, main points, prospectus, silhouette
11 delineation 12 underdrawing
13 configuration 15 thumbnail sketch

outlive
07 outlast, outwear, survive, weather
08 overwear 11 come through, live through

outlook
04 view 05 angle, slant 06 aspect, future 07 mindset, opinion, picture
08 attitude, forecast, panorama, prospect 09 prognosis, prospects, viewpoint, world-view 10 standpoint
11 frame of mind, perspective, point of view 12 expectations
14 interpretation, Weltanschauung

outlying
03 out 05 outby, outer 06 far-off, forane, outbye, remote 07 distant, far-away, outland 08 detached, far-flung, isolated 10 provincial 11 out-of-the-way 12 inaccessible

outmanoeuvre
04 beat 05 outdo 06 outfox, outwit
07 sandbag 08 outflank, outsmart, outthink 10 circumvent, outgeneral
14 get the better of

outmoded
05 dated, passé, steam 06 démodé, old hat, past it, square, uncool
07 archaic 08 obsolete, outdated, shmaltzy 09 out of date, schmaltzy
10 antiquated, fuddy-duddy, oldfangled, superseded
11 obsolescent, old-fogeyish, on the way out, out of the ark 12 antediluvian, old-fashioned, out of fashion
13 unfashionable 14 behind the times

out of date
03 old 05 dated, passé, steam
06 démodé, old hat, passée, past it, square, uncool 07 archaic, belated, vintage 08 obsolete, outdated, outmoded, overworn 09 overdated
10 antiquated, behindhand, fuddy-duddy, oldfangled, superseded
11 obsolescent, old-fogeyish, on the way out, out of the ark, prehistoric
12 antediluvian, old-fashioned, out of fashion 13 horse-and-buggy, prehistorical, unfashionable 14 behind the times

See also **outdated**

out-of-the-way
03 odd 04 lost 05 outer 06 far-off, hidden, lonely, remote 07 distant, far-away, obscure, unusual 08 far-flung, isolated, outlying, secluded, singular, uncommon 10 outlandish, peripheral
11 god-forsaken, little-known
12 inaccessible, unfrequented

out of work
04 idle 07 jobless, laid off, resting
08 workless 09 on the dole, out of a job, redundant 10 unemployed
11 between jobs

outpace
04 beat, pass 05 outdo 06 outrun
07 surpass 08 outstrip, overhaul, overtake 11 outdistance

outpouring
04 flow, flux 05 blast, flood, spate, spurt 06 deluge, efflux, lavish, strain, stream 07 cascade, outflow, torrent, welling 08 effusion 09 effluence, emanation, word salad
11 debouchment 14 disemboguement

output
◇ *anagram indicator*
04 gain 05 yield 06 fruits, return
07 harvest, outturn, product, turnout
10 production, throughput
11 achievement, manufacture, performance 12 productivity
14 accomplishment

outrage
04 evil, fury, rage, rape 05 abuse, anger, appal, crime, shock, wrath
06 defile, enrage, horror, injure, injury, madden, offend, ravage, ravish
07 abusion, affront, assault, disgust, horrify, incense, offence, scandal, violate 08 atrocity, enormity, violence
09 barbarism, brutality, desecrate, infuriate, sacrilege, violation
10 scandalize 11 indignation

outrageous
◇ *anagram indicator*
04 foul, rich, vile, wild **05** enorm, gross **06** unholy **07** furious, ghastly, heinous, obscene, ungodly, violent **08** dreadful, enormous, flagrant, gruesome, horrible, infernal, shocking, terrible **09** atrocious, egregious, excessive, monstrous, offensive, turbulent **10** abominable, diabolical, exorbitant, immoderate, inordinate, monstruous, scandalous, unbearable **11** disgraceful, extravagant, intolerable, unchristian, unspeakable **12** extortionate, insufferable, preposterous, unacceptable, unreasonable **14** unconscionable

outrageously
08 horribly, terribly **09** obscenely **10** dreadfully, unbearably **11** intolerably, unspeakably **12** scandalously, unacceptably **13** disgracefully

outré
◇ *anagram indicator*
03 odd **05** weird **06** far-out, freaky, way-out **07** bizarre, oddball, strange, unusual **08** shocking **09** eccentric, fantastic **10** outrageous **11** extravagant **13** extraordinary **14** unconventional

outrider
05 guard **06** escort, herald **08** vanguard **09** attendant, bodyguard, precursor **12** advance guard

outright
04 pure **05** clear, total, utter **06** at once, direct, openly, wholly **07** perfect, totally, utterly **08** absolute, complete, definite, directly, entirely, thorough **09** downright, instantly, out-and-out **10** absolutely, completely, explicitly, positively, thoroughly, undeniable **11** categorical, immediately, unequivocal, unmitigated, unqualified **12** straight away, there and then, unmistakable, unreservedly **13** categorically, thoroughgoing, unconditional, undisguisedly **15** instantaneously, straightforward

outrun
04 beat, lose, pass **05** excel, outdo **06** exceed **07** outpace, surpass **08** outstrip, overhaul, overtake, shake off **11** leave behind, outdistance, spread-eagle **13** run faster than

outset
05 onset, start **07** kick-off, opening **09** beginning, inception, threshold **12** commencement, inauguration

outshine
03 top **04** beat, best **05** dwarf, excel, outdo **07** eclipse, outrank, put down, surpass, upstage **08** outclass, outstrip **09** outlustre, transcend **10** overshadow, put to shame **13** put in the shade

outside
◇ *anagram indicator*
◇ *containment indicator*
03 exo- **04** ecto-, face, hors, rind, rine, slim **05** cover, extra, faint, front, outer, small, vague **06** casual, façade, remote, slight **07** distant, extreme, furth of, neutral, outdoor, outward, slender, surface, without **08** exterior, external, marginal, unbiased, unlikely, visiting **09** impartial, objective, outermost, temporary **10** appearance, consulting, extramural, extraneous, improbable, negligible **11** independent, non-resident, peripatetic, superficial **12** outer surface, self-employed **13** subcontracted

outsider
05 alien **06** émigré, layman, misfit, ringer **07** outlier, roughie, visitor **08** emigrant, intruder, newcomer, stranger **09** foreigner, immigrant, non-member, odd one out, outlander **10** interloper **11** gatecrasher, non-resident

outsize
02 OS **04** huge, mega, vast **05** giant, great, jumbo **07** immense, mammoth, massive, titanic, very big **08** colossal, enormous, gigantic **09** extensive, frightful, ginormous, humongous, monstrous, very large **10** gargantuan, prodigious, stupendous, tremendous

outskirts
04 edge **05** edges, limit **06** margin **07** borders, fringes, suburbs **08** boundary, environs, frontier, purlieus, suburbia, vicinity **09** perimeter, periphery **13** neighbourhood

outsmart
03 con, kid **04** beat, best, dupe **05** trick **06** have on, outfox, outwit **07** deceive **08** out-think **10** outperform **12** outmanoeuvre, take for a ride **14** get the better of, pull a fast one on

outsource
07 farm out **08** delegate **11** contract out **12** give to others, pass to others

outspoken
04 free, rude **05** bluff, blunt, broad, frank, plain, vocal **06** candid, direct **07** brusque **08** explicit, straight **10** forthright, unreserved **11** plain-spoken, Rabelaisian, unequivocal **13** unceremonious **15** straightforward

outspokenness
07 freedom **08** rudeness **09** bluffness, bluntness, frankness, plainness **10** candidness, directness **11** brusqueness **14** forthrightness

outspread
04 open, wide **06** flared, opened **08** expanded, extended, unfolded, unfurled, wide-open **09** fanned out, spread out, stretched **12** outstretched

outstanding
03 ace, due **04** cool, some **05** brill, chief, famed, great, owing **06** famous, golden, superb, unpaid, wicked **07** eminent, notable, ongoing, payable, pending, radical, salient, special **08** left-over, renowned, smashing, striking, superior, to be done, top-notch **09** arresting, brilliant, excellent, important, memorable, prominent, remaining, unsettled, well-known **10** celebrated, impressive, noteworthy, pre-eminent, prosilient, remarkable, unfinished, unresolved **11** exceptional, superlative, uncollected **13** distinguished, extraordinary **14** extraordinaire, out of this world

outstandingly
07 greatly, notably **09** amazingly, extremely **10** especially, remarkably, strikingly **12** impressively **13** exceptionally **15** extraordinarily

outstrip
03 top **04** beat, cote, pass **05** outdo, outgo, strip **06** better, exceed, gain on, outrun **07** eclipse, outfoot, outpace, surpass **08** outshine, overtake **09** transcend **11** leave behind, outdistance **12** go faster than **13** leave standing

outward
05 outer **06** carnal, extern, formal, public **07** evident, externe, obvious, outside, seeming, surface, visible, worldly **08** apparent, exterior, external, supposed **09** dissolute, outermost, posticous, professed **10** accidental, additional, noticeable, observable, ostensible **11** discernible, perceptible, superficial, without-door **13** superficially

outwardly
07 visibly, without **09** seemingly **10** apparently, exteriorly, externally, supposedly **12** at first sight, on the outside, on the surface **13** on the face of it, superficially

outweigh
06 exceed **07** surpass **08** overcome, override **09** cancel out, make up for, overpoise **10** be more than, outbalance **11** predominate, prevail over **12** be superior to, preponderate **13** be greater than, compensate for

outwit
03 con, fox, kid **04** beat, best, dish, dupe **05** cheat, trick **06** better, euchre, have on, outfox **07** deceive, defraud, swindle **08** outsmart, outthink **09** crossbite, overreach **10** circumvent **12** outmanoeuvre, take for a ride **14** be cleverer than, get the better of, pull a fast one on

outwork
04 moon

outworn
05 stale **06** old hat, past it **07** ancient, archaic, defunct, disused **08** obsolete, outdated, outmoded, rejected

09 abandoned, exhausted, hackneyed, moth-eaten, out of date 10 antiquated 11 discredited, obsolescent 12 old-fashioned 14 behind the times

oval
05 ovate, ovoid 07 navette, obovate, oviform 08 elliptic 09 egg-shaped, vulviform 10 elliptical 11 ellipsoidal

ovation
06 bravos, cheers, praise 07 acclaim, bouquet, praises, tribute 08 accolade, applause, cheering, clapping, plaudits 09 laudation, rejoicing 11 acclamation 12 handclapping

oven
03 Aga, oon, umu 04 kiln, lear, leer, lehr, oast 05 hangi, micro, stove 06 calcar, cooker 07 furnace, tandoor 09 microwave 11 copper Maori 13 microwave oven

over
◇ *containment indicator*
◇ *juxtaposition down indicator*
◇ *reversal down indicator*
02 of, on, re, up 03 o'er, ore 04 gone, left, ower, owre, past, upon 05 about, above, aloft, along, ended, extra, upper 06 across, beyond, closed, during, excess, no more, on high, unused 07 at an end, on top of, settled, surplus 08 done with, finished, in excess, left over, more than, overhead, superior, unwanted 09 apropos of, as regards, completed, concluded, exceeding, excessive, forgotten, in the past, regarding, remaining, unclaimed 10 concerning, higher than, in addition, in charge of, in excess of, relating to, superior to, terminated, throughout 11 dealing with, in command of, referring to, superfluous 12 accomplished, with regard to 13 concerned with, connected with, in the matter of, with respect to 14 ancient history, on the subject of 15 over and done with, with reference to

• **over and above**
04 plus 06 beside 07 added to, besides, on top of 08 as well as, let alone 09 along with 12 in addition to, not to mention, together with

• **over and over**
05 often 09 ad nauseam, endlessly 10 frequently, repeatedly 11 ad infinitum, continually 12 time and again 13 again and again

overabundance
04 glut 06 excess 07 surfeit, surplus 08 plethora 09 profusion 10 oversupply 11 superfluity 14 superabundance 15 embarras de choix

overact
03 ham 04 hoke 06 overdo 07 lay it on 08 overplay, pile it on 10 exaggerate 12 lay it on thick 13 pile it on thick

overall
05 broad, pinny, total 06 global, pinnie 07 all-over, blanket, broadly, crawler, general, save-all, tablier 08 complete, dustcoat, out to out, pinafore, sweeping, umbrella 09 dungarees, inclusive, in general, siren suit, universal 10 altogether, boiler suit, by and large, everywhere, on the whole 12 all-embracing, all-inclusive 13 comprehensive 15 broadly speaking

overalls
06 jumper, pinnie 07 crawler, save-all, tablier 08 coverall, dust-coat, fatigues, pinafore, workwear 09 dungarees 10 boiler suit

overawe
03 awe, cow 05 abash, alarm, daunt, scare 06 dismay 07 buffalo, petrify, terrify, unnerve 08 browbeat, frighten 10 disconcert, intimidate

overbalance
04 slip, trip 05 upset 06 topple, tumble 07 capsize, tip over 08 fall over, keel over, overturn 10 somersault, topple over, turn turtle 15 lose your balance, lose your footing

overbearing
05 bossy, proud 06 la-di-da, lordly, snobby, snooty, snotty 07 haughty, stuck-up 08 arrogant, cavalier, despotic, dogmatic, masterly, smartass 09 imperious, officious, smartarse 10 autocratic, disdainful, dogmatical, high-handed, oppressive, tyrannical 11 dictatorial, domineering, toffee-nosed 12 contemptuous, presumptuous, supercilious

overblown
03 OTT 07 exalted 08 inflated, overdone 09 amplified, bombastic, excessive 10 burlesqued, overstated, over the top 11 caricatured, embellished, extravagant, overcharged, pretentious 13 overestimated, self-important

overcast
04 dark, dull, grey, hazy, whip 05 foggy, misty, shade 06 cloudy, dismal, dreary, gloomy, leaden, sombre 07 clouded, louring, recover, sunless 08 darkened 11 clouded over

overcharge
02 do, o/c 04 clip, rook, rush, soak 05 cheat, sting 06 diddle, extort, fleece, rip off 07 swindle 09 surcharge 11 short-change

overcoat *see* **coat**

overcome
04 beat, best, lick, rout 05 break, cover, force, fordo, moved, outdo, worst 06 broken, byword, defeat, evince, excess, expugn, hammer, master, mither, moider, outwit, subdue, thrash 07 beat off, clobber, conquer, consume, moither, outplay, overget, prevail, refrain, surplus, trounce 08 affected, choked up, convince, dead-beat, knock out, outsmart, superate, surmount, vanquish, wear down 09 exhausted, hit for six, overmatch, overpower, overthrow, overwhelm, rise above, slaughter, subjugate, underfong 10 bowled over, speechless, surmounted 11 knock for six, overpowered, overwhelmed, triumph over 12 lost for words, put on the foil 13 have the edge on 14 get the better of

over-confident
04 rash 05 brash, cocky 06 secure, uppish, uppity 08 arrogant, cocksure, sanguine 09 foolhardy, hubristic 10 blustering, incautious, swaggering 11 overweening, self-assured, temerarious 12 presumptuous 14 over-optimistic

overcook
04 burn, char 05 singe 07 blacken

overcritical
06 purist 07 carping, Zoilean 08 captious, over-nice, pedantic 09 cavilling 10 nit-picking, pernickety 11 persnickety 12 fault-finding, hard to please 13 hair-splitting, hypercritical 14 overparticular

overcrowded
06 packed 07 chocker, overrun, teeming 08 swarming 09 chock-full, congested, jam-packed, packed out 10 overloaded 11 chock-a-block, crammed full 13 overpopulated

overdo
05 excel 06 harass 07 fatigue, ham it up, lay it on, overact 08 camp it up, go too far, overplay, pile it on 09 overstate 10 exaggerate 11 cut it too fat, go overboard, overindulge 12 lay it on thick 13 carry to excess, pile it on thick, stretch a point

• **overdo it**
07 crack up 08 overwork 09 do too much 10 sweat blood 11 work too hard 14 strain yourself 15 burn yourself out

overdone
03 OTT 05 burnt, hokey, undue 07 charred, dried up, fulsome, gushing, percoct, spoiled 08 effusive, overshot 09 excessive, overbaked 10 histrionic, immoderate, inordinate, overcooked, overplayed, overstated, over the top 11 exaggerated, overwrought, unnecessary 13 overelaborate 14 burnt to a cinder 15 burnt to a frazzle

overdose
02 OD

overdraft
02 OD 04 debt 07 arrears, deficit 10 borrowings 11 liabilities 13 unpaid amounts

overdue
03 due 04 late, slow 05 owing, tardy 06 unpaid 07 belated, delayed, payable, pending 09 unsettled 10 behindhand, unpunctual 14 behind schedule

overeat
05 binge, gorge **06** guzzle, pig out **10** eat too much, go on a binge, gormandize **11** overindulge **13** stuff yourself

overeating
07 bulimia **08** bingeing, gluttony, guzzling **10** gormandise, gormandism **11** gourmandise, gourmandism, hyperphagia **14** overindulgence

overemphasize
06 labour **08** belabour **10** exaggerate, overstress **13** make too much of, overdramatize

overexert
• overexert yourself
07 fatigue **08** overdo it, overwork **11** work too hard **14** strain yourself **15** overtax yourself, wear yourself out

overfeed
04 cram, glut, sate

overflow
03 lip, ren, rin, run **04** ream, soak, teem **05** cover, flood, spill, surge, swamp, water **06** back-up, deluge, shower **07** overrun, redound, run over, surplus **08** brim over, flow over, inundate, outswell, pour over, spillage, submerge, surround, well over **09** discharge, overspill, spill over **10** bubble over, inundation **13** overabundance

overflowing
04 full, rife **05** flush **06** filled **07** brimful, copious, crowded, profuse, teeming **08** inundant, overfull, swarming, thronged **09** abounding, bountiful, exuberant, land-flood, plenteous, plentiful, redundant **13** superabundant

overgrown
04 rank

overgrowth
05 naeve, nevus **06** naevus **09** gigantism **10** escalation, luxuriance, luxuriancy, rhinophyma **11** gliomatosis, hyperplasia, hypertrophy **13** overabundance **14** superabundance **15** overdevelopment

overhang
03 jut **04** loom, poke **05** bulge **06** beetle, extend, impend, jut out **07** poke out, project **08** bulge out, protrude, stand out, stick out

overhanging
06 beetle, shelvy **07** bulging, jutting, pendant, pendent, pensile **08** beetling, imminent **09** incumbent, pendulous, prominent **10** bulging out, jutting out, projecting, protruding **11** standing out, sticking out **14** superincumbent

overhaul
03 fix **04** mend, pass **05** check **06** gain on, go over, repair, revamp, survey **07** check up, check-up, examine, inspect, outpace, rummage, service **08** outstrip, overtake, renovate **09** check over, going-over, re-examine **10** get ahead of, inspection, renovation **11** examination, investigate, outdistance, pull ahead of, recondition **14** reconditioning

overhead
03 air **05** above, aloft **06** aerial, on high, raised, upward **07** average, general, up above **08** all-round, elevated **11** overhanging

overheads
06 burden, oncost **07** oncosts **08** expenses **09** outgoings **10** fixed costs **11** expenditure **12** disbursement, regular costs, running costs **14** operating costs

overheated
05 angry, fiery **06** roused **07** excited, flaming **08** agitated, inflamed **10** passionate **11** impassioned, overexcited, overwrought
• overheated state
04 stew

overindulge
03 pet **04** lush, sate **05** binge, booze, gorge, spoil **06** cosset, guzzle, pamper, pander, pig out **07** debauch, satiate **09** spoon-feed **10** eat too much, gluttonize, gormandize **11** mollycoddle **12** drink too much

overindulgence
05 binge **06** excess **07** debauch, surfeit **10** overeating **12** immoderation, intemperance

overjoyed
04 rapt **06** elated, joyful **08** ecstatic, euphoric, jubilant, thrilled **09** delighted, rapturous **10** enraptured, in raptures **11** high as a kite, on cloud nine, over the moon, tickled pink **14** pleased as Punch **15** in seventh heaven, on top of the world

overlap
03 lap **04** ride **05** cover **07** overlay, overlie, shingle **08** coincide, flap over, override **09** imbricate

overlay
04 ceil, face, line, span, whip, wrap **05** adorn, belay, cover, inlay, patch **06** spread, veneer **07** blanket, envelop, surface, varnish **08** covering, decorate, encumber, laminate, ornament

overload
03 tax **04** glut **06** burden, excess, lumber, saddle, strain **07** oppress, overtax, surfeit, surplus **08** encumber, plethora **09** surcharge, weigh down **10** overburden, overcharge, oversupply **11** hypercharge, overfreight, superfluity **13** overabundance **14** superabundance

overlook
04 face, miss, omit **05** leave **06** excuse, forget, ignore, pardon, pass by, slight, wink at **07** condone, forgive, let pass, let ride, neglect, oversee **08** look onto, look over, open onto, overskip, pass over **09** disregard, front onto, mislippen **11** have a view of, superintend **14** command a view of, take no notice of **15** take no account of, turn a blind eye to

overlooked
07 unnoted **08** unheeded, unprized, unvalued **10** in the shade, unhonoured, unregarded, unremarked **12** unconsidered

overly
03 too **04** over **06** casual, unduly **08** casually, superior **11** exceedingly, excessively **12** immoderately, inordinately, supercilious, unreasonably **13** unnecessarily **14** superciliously

overmuch
06 unduly **07** too much **11** excessively **12** immoderately, inordinately, unreasonably **13** unnecessarily

overnice
07 finical **08** kid glove **10** nit-picking, oversubtle, pernickety **11** overprecise, persnickety **13** oversensitive **14** overfastidious, over-meticulous, overparticular, overscrupulous

overplay
06 colour, overdo, stress **07** amplify, enhance, enlarge, lay it on, magnify **08** oversell, pile it on **09** dramatize, embellish, embroider, emphasize, overstate **10** aggrandize, exaggerate, shoot a line **12** lay it on thick **13** make too much of, overdramatize, overemphasize, pile it on thick **15** stretch the truth

overpopulated
06 packed **07** overrun, teeming **08** swarming **09** chock-full, congested, jam-packed, packed out **10** overloaded **11** crammed full, overcrowded

overpower
04 beat, daze, move, rout **05** crush, floor, quash, quell, swelt, touch, whelm **06** dazzle, defeat, evince, master, overgo, subdew, subdue **07** confuse, conquer, perplex, stagger, swelter, trounce **08** bedazzle, bowl over, overbear, overcome, vanquish **09** dumbfound, hit for six, hypnotize, overthrow, overwhelm, subjugate, take aback **10** immobilize, overmaster **11** flabbergast, knock for six **12** affect deeply **14** affect strongly **15** gain mastery over, leave speechless

overpowering
06 strong **07** extreme **08** forceful, powerful, stifling **09** sickening, tyrannous **10** compelling, nauseating, oppressive, unbearable, undeniable **11** irrefutable, suffocating **12** irresistible, overwhelming **14** uncontrollable

over-productive
04 rank

overrate
06 blow up **07** magnify **09** overprize, overvalue **10** overpraise
12 overestimate **13** make too much of

overreach
• overreach yourself
08 go too far, overdo it **14** strain yourself, try to do too much **15** burn yourself out

override
05 annul, quash **06** cancel, exceed, ignore **07** nullify, overlap, rescind, reverse, surpass **08** abrogate, outweigh, overcome, overrule, overtake, set aside, vanquish
09 disregard, supersede
11 countermand, prevail over, trample over **12** be superior to **13** be greater than

overriding
05 final, first, major, prime, prior
06 ruling **07** pivotal, primary, supreme
08 cardinal, dominant, ultimate
09 essential, number one, paramount, principal **10** compelling, overruling, prevailing **11** determining, predominant **13** most important
15 most significant

overrule
05 annul **06** cancel, reject, revoke
07 nullify, outvote, prevail, rescind, reverse **08** abrogate, disallow, overbear, override, oversway, overturn, set aside, vote down **10** invalidate
11 countermand

overrun
03 lip **05** bleed, storm, swamp
06 attack, exceed, go over, infest, invade, occupy, ravage **07** besiege, run riot **08** inundate, overgrow, overstep, permeate **09** overreach, overshoot, overwhelm, penetrate, surge over, swarm over **10** depopulate, spread over

overseas
06 abroad, exotic, remote, widely
07 distant, faraway, foreign **08** external, outremer **10** far and wide
11 ultramarine **13** international **14** in foreign parts, to foreign parts **15** in foreign climes, out of the country, to foreign climes

oversee
03 ren, rin, run **05** guide, watch
06 direct, manage **07** conduct, control, inspect **09** disregard, look after, supervise, watch over
10 administer **11** keep an eye on, preside over, superintend **12** be in charge of **13** be in control of

overseer
03 guv **04** baas, boss **05** chief
06 bishop, critic, editor, gaffer, grieve, guv'nor, induna **07** captain, foreman, manager, overman, steward
08 banksman, decurion, oversman, surveyor **09** forewoman, woodreeve
10 foreperson, manageress, supervisor, workmaster **11** flock-master, mine-captain **12** workmistress
14 superintendent

overshadow
◇ *containment indicator*
03 dim, mar **04** veil **05** cloud, dwarf, excel, shade, spoil **06** blight, darken
07 eclipse, obscure, protect, shelter, surpass **08** bescreen, dominate, hang over, outshine **09** adumbrate, obumbrate, rise above **10** tower above
12 be superior to, put a damper on
13 put in the shade **14** take the edge off

oversight
04 boob, care, flub **05** error, fault, lapse
06 charge, howler, slip-up **07** blunder, control, custody, keeping, mistake, neglect **08** handling, omission
09 direction **10** management, parablepsy **11** dereliction, parablepsis, supervision **12** carelessness, inadvertence, inadvertency, surveillance **14** administration, responsibility **15** superintendence

oversize
04 huge, mega, vast **05** giant, great, jumbo **07** immense, mammoth, massive, titanic, very big **08** colossal, enormous, gigantic **09** extensive, frightful, ginormous, humongous, monstrous, very large **10** gargantuan, monumental, prodigious, stupendous, tremendous

overstate
06 colour, overdo, stress **07** amplify, enhance, enlarge, lay it on, magnify
08 oversell, pile it on **09** dramatize, embellish, embroider, emphasize
10 aggrandize, exaggerate, shoot a line
12 lay it on thick **13** make too much of, overdramatize, overemphasize, pile it on thick **15** stretch the truth

overstatement
06 excess, parody **08** emphasis
09 burlesque, hyperbole **10** caricature
11 enlargement **12** exaggeration, extravagance, overemphasis
13 amplification, embellishment, magnification **14** overestimation
15 pretentiousness

overt
04 open **05** plain **06** patent, public
07 evident, obvious, visible
08 apparent, manifest **09** professed
10 noticeable, observable
11 conspicuous, unconcealed, undisguised

overtake
03 lap **04** pass **05** catch **06** befall, engulf, gain on, go past, strike
07 forhent, run past **08** come upon, forehent, happen to, outstrip, overhaul, ride down **09** drive past, overcatch, overwhelm **10** come up with **11** catch up with, leave behind, outdistance, pull ahead of **13** catch unawares, draw level with **14** take by surprise

over the top *see* **over the top** *under* **top**

overthrow
◇ *anagram indicator*
03 end **04** beat, best, down, fall, oust, rout, ruin **05** crush, quash, quell, smite, spill, upset, whelm, worst **06** defeat, depose, invert, lay low, master, subdue, topple, tumble, unseat, upturn
07 abolish, conquer, ousting, put down, run down, run over, stonker, subvert, tip over, trounce, undoing, whemmle, whomble, whommle, whummle **08** bear down, confound, dethrone, displace, downfall, keel over, overcast, overcome, overturn, ride down, supplant, turn over, vanquish
09 bring down, confusion, knock over, overpower, overwhelm, prostrate, unseating, upsetting **10** deposition, subversion **11** destruction, humiliation, labefaction, overbalance, suppression, vanquishing **12** dethronement
13 labefactation **14** bouleversement

overtly
06 openly **07** clearly, plainly
08 patently **09** obviously **10** in full view, manifestly, noticeably **11** for all to see **13** conspicuously

overtone
04 hint **05** sense **06** nuance **07** feeling, flavour **08** harmonic, innuendo
10 intimation, suggestion
11 association, connotation, implication, insinuation
12 undercurrent **13** hidden meaning

overture
04 move **05** moves, offer **06** feeler, gambit, motion, signal **07** advance, feelers, opening, prelude, toccata
08 advances, aperture, approach, proposal **09** beginning **10** invitation, suggestion **11** opening move, opportunity, proposition
12 introduction **13** opening gambit

Overtures include:

05 Cuban, Herod, Wasps
06 Adonis, Choral, Comedy, Esther, French, Heroic, Solemn, Spring, Thalia, Tragic
07 Aladdin, Euterpe, Festive, Holiday, Idyllic, Jubilee, Leonora, Maytime, Othello
08 Carnival, Columbus, Coriolan, Hebrides, Hyperion, In Autumn, King Lear, Romantic, Waverley
09 Britannia, Children's, Fairy Land, In Bohemia, Pinocchio, The Naiads
10 Amid Nature, In the South, Salutatory
11 East and West, Fingal's Cave, Pickwickian, Shéhérazade, The Faithful, William Tell
12 Fair Melusina, In London Town, Rip van Winkle, Street Corner, The Rehearsal
13 In the Highland, Shadowy Waters, The Wood-Nymphs
14 Eighteen Twelve, Eighteen-Twelve, In Nature's Realm, In the Mountains, Romeo and Juliet
15 Comes Autumn Time, Portsmouth Point, The Fair Melusina

overturn
◇ *anagram indicator*
◇ *reversal down indicator*
03 tip **04** beat, coup, cowp, oust, veto **05** annul, crush, quash, spill, upset, whelm **06** cancel, defeat, depose, invert, repeal, revoke, topple, unseat, upturn **07** abolish, capsize, conquer, destroy, nullify, rescind, reverse, skittle, subvert, tip over, whemmle, whomble, whommle, whummle **08** abrogate, confound, dethrone, displace, keel over, overcome, override, overrule, set aside, turn over, vanquish **09** bring down, knock over, overpower, overthrow, overwhelm **11** overbalance

overused
04 worn **05** stale, tired, trite **07** cliché'd **08** bromidic, clichéed **09** hackneyed, played out **10** overworked, threadbare, unoriginal **11** commonplace, stereotyped **13** platitudinous

overview
05 study **06** review, survey **08** panorama, scrutiny **09** appraisal, valuation **10** assessment, inspection **11** examination, measurement **13** consideration

overweening
04 vain **05** cocky, proud **06** hubris, hybris, lordly **07** haughty, pompous, swollen **08** arrogant, cavalier, cocksure, inflated, insolent, vaulting **09** conceited, excessive, hubristic, overblown, upsetting **10** high-handed, immoderate **11** egotistical, extravagant, opinionated **12** presumptuous, supercilious, vainglorious **13** outrecuidance, over-confident, self-confident

overweight
03 fat **04** huge **05** ample, bulky, buxom, gross, heavy, hefty, obese, plump, podgy, stout, tubby **06** chubby, chunky, flabby, fleshy, portly **07** massive, outsize **09** corpulent **10** pot-bellied, voluptuous, well-padded **13** preponderance **15** well-upholstered

overwhelm
04 beat, best, bury, daze, kill, lick, move, rout **05** amaze, crush, floor, quash, quell, swamp, touch, worst **06** defeat, deluge, engulf, hammer, ingulf, outwit, subdue, thrash **07** clobber, confuse, destroy, engulph, ingulph, oppress, outplay, overrun, prevail, stagger, trounce **08** bowl over, inundate, knock out, outsmart, overbear, overcome, submerge, vanquish **09** devastate, hit for six, overpower, overthrow, slaughter, snow under, subjugate **10** overburden **11** knock for six **12** affect deeply **13** have the edge on, knock sideways **14** affect strongly, get the better of

overwhelming
04 huge, vast **05** great, large **06** strong **07** banging, extreme, immense, massive, runaway **08** crashing, enormous, forceful, powerful, stifling **09** sickening **10** compelling, formidable, foudroyant, nauseating, oppressive, unbearable, undeniable **11** irrefutable, suffocating **12** irresistible, overpowering **14** uncontrollable

overwork
05 weary **06** burden, strain **07** crack up, exhaust, exploit, oppress, overtax, overuse, wear out **08** overdo it, overload **09** do too much **10** overstrain, sweat blood **11** work too hard **14** strain yourself **15** burn yourself out

overworked
04 worn **05** stale, tired, trite **07** cliché'd, worn out **08** bromidic, clichéed, forswunk **09** exhausted, forswonck, hackneyed, overtaxed, played out **10** threadbare, unoriginal **11** commonplace, stereotyped, stressed out **12** overstrained **13** platitudinous

overwrought
04 edgy **05** nervy, tense **06** highly, on edge, strung **07** excited, frantic, keyed up, nervous, uptight, wound up **08** agitated, worked up **10** distraught **11** overcharged, overexcited **14** beside yourself

owe
10 be in debt to, be in the red, run up debts **11** be overdrawn, get into debt **12** be indebted to **13** be in arrears to

owing
03 dew, due **04** owed **06** unpaid **07** overdue, payable **09** imputable, in arrears, unsettled **11** outstanding
• **owing to**
02 of **05** due to **08** thanks to **09** because of **11** as a result of, on account of **15** in consequence of

owl
04 Bubo, ruru **05** madge **06** hooter, howlet, mopoke, strich **07** boobook, dullard, smuggle **08** longhorn, mopehawk, morepork, wiseacre **09** screecher **11** glimmer-gowk

own
03 ain, use **04** have, hold, keep, nain, nown **05** admit, enjoy **06** occupy, proper, retain **07** concede, confess, have got, possess, private **08** peculiar, personal **09** authentic, recognize **10** individual, monopolize, particular **11** acknowledge **12** be the owner of **13** idiosyncratic **14** have to yourself
• **on your own**
05 alone **06** singly **07** unaided **08** isolated **09** on your tod **10** by yourself, unassisted **13** independently, off your own bat, unaccompanied
• **own up**
05 admit **07** confess **09** come clean **11** acknowledge, plead guilty **12** tell the truth

owner
05 malik, melik **06** holder, keeper, master **08** landlady, landlord, mistress **09** homeowner, possessor **10** freeholder, proprietor **11** householder, proprietary **12** proprietress

ownership
04 uses **05** title **06** domain, rights **08** dominion, freehold, property **10** possession **11** proprietary **14** proprietorship

owning
02 of

ox
03 ure, yak **04** anoa, bull, gaur, gyal, mart, neat, urus, zebu **05** bison, bugle, gayal, steer, stirk **06** rother **07** aurochs, banteng, banting, buffalo, bullock **08** bull-beef, sapi-utan **09** sapi-outan
• **team of oxen**
04 span

Oxford University *see* **college**

oxygen
01 O

oyster
05 plant **06** native, Ostrea **07** spondyl **08** seedling
• **oyster bed**
04 stew

P

P
03 pee **04** papa

pace
04 gait, pass, rate, step, walk **05** amble, march, pound, speed, tempo, tramp, tread **06** flight, motion, patrol, stride **07** mark out, measure, passage, running **08** celerity, movement, progress, rapidity, velocity **09** quickness, swiftness **13** walk up and down **14** rate of progress

pacific
04 calm, mild **05** quiet, still **06** dovish, gentle, irenic, placid, serene, smooth **07** equable, halcyon **08** dovelike, friendly, irenical, pacifist, peaceful, tranquil **09** appeasing, peaceable, placatory, unruffled **10** diplomatic, non-violent **11** complaisant, peace-loving, peacemaking **12** conciliatory, pacificatory, propitiatory **14** nonbelligerent

pacification
07 calming **08** soothing **09** placating, silencing **10** moderating, moderation, quietening **11** appeasement, peacemaking **12** conciliation, propitiation **14** quietening down

pacifism
10 pacificism, satyagraha **11** non-violence, peacemaking

pacifist
02 CO **04** dove **06** conchy **08** peacenik **10** pacificist, peace-lover, peacemaker **11** peace-monger

pacify
04 calm, lull, tame **05** allay, crush, quell, quiet, still **06** defuse, soften, soothe, subdue **07** appease, assuage, compose, mollify, placate, put down, quieten, silence, sweeten **08** calm down, moderate **09** reconcile **10** conciliate, propitiate

pack
03 bag, box, jam, mob, ram, set, tin **04** bale, band, cram, crew, fill, gang, herd, load, plot, rout, stow, swag, wrap **05** bluey, bunch, cover, crate, crowd, drove, flock, group, press, put in, stock, store, stuff, tie up, troop, truss, wedge **06** bundle, burden, carton, charge, fardel, kitbag, packet, parcel, steeve, throng, wrap up **07** compact, company, dismiss, envelop, matilda, package, prepack, squeeze **08** backpack, canister, compress, intrigue, knapsack, rucksack **09** container, haversack **10** collection **11** blister card, canisterize

• pack in
03 end, jam, mob, ram **04** fill, load, stop **05** chuck, crowd, leave, press, stuff, wedge **06** charge, cram in, give up, jack in, resign, throng **07** squeeze, throw in

• pack off
04 send **07** dismiss **08** dispatch **09** bundle off

• pack round
04 tamp

• pack up
03 end **04** fail, stop **05** crash, truss **06** bundle, finish, give up, go phut, jack in, tidy up, wrap up **07** clear up, conk out, go kaput, put away, seize up, throw in **08** empacket, tidy away **09** break camp, break down **10** call it a day **11** malfunction, stop working **12** go on the fritz **13** put things away

package
03 box, lot, set **04** bale, pack, roll, unit, wrap **05** batch, group, whole **06** bundle, carton, entity, packet, pack up, parcel, wrap up **08** gift-wrap, parcel up **09** container **10** collection, shrink-wrap **11** consignment, package deal

packaging
03 box **06** packet **07** packing, wrapper **08** wrappers, wrapping **09** container, wrappings **12** presentation

• without packaging
03 net **04** nett

packed
04 full **05** thick **06** filled, jammed **07** brimful, chocker, crammed, crowded, serried **08** thronged **09** chockfull, congested, jam-packed **10** overloaded **11** chock-a-block, overflowing

packet
03 bag, box **04** a lot, bomb, case, deck, lots, mint, pack, pile, post, pots **06** bundle, carton, parcel, sachet **07** fortune, package, packing, tidy sum, wrapper **08** envelope, Jiffy bag®, wrapping **09** a bob or two, container, megabucks, padded bag **11** king's ransom, loadsamoney, pretty penny **12** small fortune **14** padded envelope

packhorse load
04 seam

packing-ring
04 lute

pact
04 bond, deal **06** cartel, treaty **07** bargain, compact, concord, entente **08** alliance, contract, covenant **09** agreement, concordat **10** convention, settlement **11** arrangement **13** understanding

pad
03 paw, ren, rin, run, wad **04** fill, flat, foot, home, line, lope, move, mute, pack, path, roll, room, sole, step, sunk, walk, wase, wrap **05** block, guard, inker, place, print, quilt, rooms, squab, stuff, tramp, tread **06** buffer, hamper, jotter, pillow, shield, tiptoe, trudge **07** blotter, bolster, bombast, bum roll, cushion, hang-out, memo pad, notepad, padding, pannier, pillion, protect, wadding **08** compress, dressing, leg-guard, notebook, quarters, stuffing **09** apartment, flip chart, footprint, penthouse **10** impregnate, protection, writing pad

• pad out
06 expand **07** amplify, augment, bolster, fill out, inflate, spin out, stretch **08** flesh out, increase, lengthen, protract **09** elaborate

padding
06 hot air, lining, waffle **07** bombast, filling, packing, wadding **08** crashpad, stuffing, verbiage **09** prolixity, verbosity, wordiness **10** cotton wool, cushioning, protection **11** verboseness

paddle
03 oar, row **04** pull, punt, slop, wade **05** canoe, scull, steer, sweep **06** dabble, finger, plunge, propel, splash, trifle **10** lumpsucker

paddock
03 pen **04** fold, frog, park, toad, yard **05** field, pound **06** corral **07** parrock **08** birdcage, compound, stockade **09** enclosure

paddy
03 pet **04** bate, fury, rage, tiff **05** sawah, strop **06** taking, temper **07** passion, tantrum **08** manrider **11** fit of temper **14** manriding train

padlock
03 bar **04** bolt, lock, seal, shut **05** catch, clasp, latch **06** fasten, secure **09** fastening **10** spring lock **11** mortise lock

padre
05 vicar **06** cleric, curate, deacon, father, parson, pastor, priest, rector **08** chaplain, minister, reverend **09** churchman, clergyman, deaconess

paean
04 hymn **05** psalm **06** anthem, eulogy

07 ovation **08** doxology, encomium, ode to joy **09** dithyramb, panegyric **10** exultation **12** song of praise

pagan
06 paynim **07** atheist, Gentile, godless, heathen, infidel, ungodly **08** idolater **09** atheistic **10** idolatrous, unbeliever **11** irreligious, nonbeliever, nullifidian, pantheistic

page
01 p **02** ro, vo **03** bid, era **04** call, leaf, side **05** epoch, event, folio, phase, recto, sheet, stage, title, verso **06** ask for, period, summon **07** bellboy, bellhop, chapter, episode, footman, pageboy, send for, servant **08** announce, henchman, incident, paginate **09** attendant, messenger, tearsheet **10** henchwoman **11** henchperson

• **pages**
02 pp

• **two pages**
04 leaf

pageant
04 play, show **05** antic, scene **06** antick, parade **07** anticke, antique, display, tableau, triumph **08** specious **09** cavalcade, spectacle **10** procession **12** extravaganza **14** representation

pageantry
04 pomp, show **05** drama **06** parade **07** display, glamour, glitter **08** ceremony, flourish, grandeur **09** melodrama, showiness, spectacle, splendour **12** extravagance, magnificence **13** theatricality

pageboy
04 page **07** bellboy, bellhop, footman, servant **09** attendant, messenger

paid-up
05 loyal **06** active, red-hot **07** devoted, fervent, zealous **08** involved **09** committed, dedicated **11** evangelical **12** card-carrying, enthusiastic

pail
03 can, kit, tub **04** bail, dixy **05** churn, dixie **06** bucket, leglan, leglen, leglin, piggin, vessel **07** pitcher, scuttle **10** slop bucket

pain
02 wo **03** ake, gip, gyp, mal, woe **04** ache, bore, dole, dool, drag, hurt, pang, pest, rack, stab, sten, teen, tene **05** agony, cramp, dolor, doole, grief, gripe, shoot, smart, spasm, stend, sting, teene, thraw, throb, throe, throw, upset, worry **06** aching, be sore, bother, bummer, burden, cramps, dolour, grieve, misery, sadden, sorrow, stitch, throwe, twinge **07** afflict, agonize, ailment, anguish, anxiety, penalty, torment, torture, trouble **08** be tender, distress, headache, irritate, nuisance, smarting, soreness, vexation **09** annoyance, causalgia, heartache, suffering, throbbing **10** affliction, desolation, discomfort, heartbreak, irritation, tenderness **11** indigestion, lancination, make anxious, tribulation **12** collywobbles, wretchedness **13** make miserable, pain in the neck

• **expression of pain**
01 O **02** oh, ow **04** argh, ouch **05** aargh

• **freedom from pain**
04 ease

pained
03 sad **04** hurt **05** stung, upset, vexed **06** piqued **07** grieved, injured, unhappy, worried, wounded **08** offended, saddened **09** aggrieved **10** distressed **11** reproachful

painful
03 bad **04** achy, hard, sore **05** tough **06** aching, bitter, guilty, tender, touchy, trying **07** arduous, awkward, baleful, hurting, irksome, panging, pungent, shaming, tedious **08** exacting, grievous, inflamed, poignant, rigorous, shameful, smarting, stabbing, tortured, wretched **09** agonizing, difficult, harrowing, laborious, miserable, saddening, sensitive, strenuous, throbbing, traumatic, upsetting **10** disturbing, irritating, mortifying, unpleasant **11** disquieting, distressing, humiliating **12** disagreeable, discomfiting, embarrassing, excruciating **13** disconcerting, uncomfortable

• **be painful**
04 tine, tyne, work

painfully
◇ *anagram indicator*
04 sore **05** sadly **07** clearly **08** markedly, pitiably, terribly, woefully **09** pitifully **10** alarmingly, deplorably, dreadfully, wretchedly **11** agonizingly, excessively **13** distressingly, unfortunately **14** excruciatingly

painkiller
04 bute, drug **06** remedy **07** anodyne, metopon, morphia, Nurofen® **08** lenitive, morphine, sedative **09** analgesia, analgesic **10** palliative **11** aminobutene, anaesthetic

See also **anaesthetic**; **analgesic**

painless
04 easy **05** cushy **06** simple **08** pain-free **10** child's play, effortless **11** comfortable, trouble-free, undemanding **12** a piece of cake, plain sailing

painlessly
06 easily, simply **11** comfortably **12** effortlessly **13** undemandingly

pains
04 care, fash, teen, tene **05** labor, teene **06** bother, effort, labour, rheums **07** trouble **09** diligence **10** rheumatics **13** assiduousness

• **be at pains**
06 bother **07** try hard **08** take care **09** be anxious **11** be concerned **14** put yourself out **15** make every effort

painstaking
07 careful, devoted **08** diligent, sedulous, studious, thorough **09** assiduous, attentive, dedicated, searching **10** meticulous, scrupulous **11** hardworking, industrious, persevering, punctilious **13** conscientious

paint
03 dye **04** bice, coat, daub, draw, fard, gaud, limn, tell, tint, wash **05** adorn, apply, brush, color, cover, evoke, smear, stain **06** bister, bistre, colour, depict, finish, sketch, tipple **07** narrate, picture, pigment, plaster, portray, priming, recount, respray, stipple, topcoat **08** colorant, decorate, depeinct, describe **09** colouring, delineate, depicture, diversify, oil colour, represent, vinyl wash **10** redecorate **11** boot-topping

Paints include:

03 oil
04 matt, oils
05 glaze, gloss, satin, spray
06 enamel, fabric, pastel, poster, primer
07 acrylic, gouache, lacquer, masonry, scumble, shellac, stencil, tempera, varnish
08 eggshell, emulsion
09 anti-climb, distemper, undercoat, whitewash
10 colourwash, egg tempera
11 watercolour

• **paint the town red**
04 rave **05** binge, go out **07** have fun, rejoice **08** live it up **09** celebrate, have a ball, whoop it up **10** have a party **11** throw a party **13** enjoy yourself, go on the razzle **14** go out on the town, push the boat out, put the flags out

painted
• **painted woman**
04 pict

painter
02 RA **06** artist, dauber, limner **07** Zeuxian **08** depicter **09** colourist, old master, paysagist, primitive, tactilist, vedutista **10** delineator, oil painter **11** landscapist, miniaturist, plein-airist **13** watercolorist **14** watercolourist

Painters, printmakers and other artists include:

03 **Arp** (Jean), **Dix** (Otto), **Ray** (Man)
04 **Bell** (Vanessa), **Dali** (Salvador), **Doré** (Gustave), **Dufy** (Raoul), **Eyck** (Jan van), **Goya** (Francisco de), **Gris** (Juan), **Hals** (Frans), **Hunt** (Holman), **John** (Augustus), **John** (Gwen), **Kent** (William), **Klee** (Paul), **Lely** (Sir Peter), **Long** (Richard), **Marc** (Franz), **Miró** (Joan), **Nash** (Paul)
05 **Bacon** (Francis), **Bakst** (Léon), **Blake** (Peter), **Blake** (William), **Bosch** (Hieronymus), **Brown** (Ford Madox), **Burra** (Edward), **Clark** (Kenneth, Lord), **Corot** (Camille),

David (Jacques Louis), **Degas** (Edgar), **Dürer** (Albrecht), **Ernst** (Max), **Freud** (Lucian), **Gorky** (Arshile), **Greco** (El), **Grosz** (George), **Hirst** (Damien), **Homer** (Winslow), **Hooch** (Pieter de), **Johns** (Jasper), **Kahlo** (Frida), **Kitaj** (R B), **Klimt** (Gustav), **Kline** (Franz), **Léger** (Fernand), **Lewis** (Wyndham), **Lippi** (Filippino), **Lippi** (Fra Filippo), **Lowry** (L S), **Lucas** (Sarah), **Manet** (Edouard), **Monet** (Claude), **Mucha** (Alphonse), **Munch** (Edvard), **Nolan** (Sir Sidney), **Peake** (Mervyn), **Piper** (John), **Riley** (Bridget), **Sarto** (Andrea del)

06 **Braque** (Georges), **Bratby** (John), **Cassat** (Mary), **Claude**, **Derain** (André Louis), **Escher** (Maurits Cornelis), **Fuseli** (Henri), **Giotto**, **Gordon** (Douglas), **Ingres** (Jean), **Jarman** (Derek), **Knight** (Dame Laura), **Mabuse**, **Marini** (Marino), **Martin** (John), **Massys** (Quentin), **Millet** (Jean François), **Morley** (Malcolm), **Moroni** (Giovanni Battista), **Morris** (William), **Newman** (Barnett), **O'Keefe** (Georgia), **Orozco** (José), **Palmer** (Samuel), **Peploe** (Samuel John), **Pisano** (Nicola), **Ramsay** (Allan), **Renoir** (Pierre Auguste), **Rivera** (Diego), **Rothko** (Mark), **Rubens** (Sir Peter Paul), **Scarfe** (Gerald), **Searle** (Ronald), **Seurat** (Georges), **Sisley** (Alfred), **Strong** (Sir Roy), **Stubbs** (George), **Tanguy** (Yves), **Tissot** (James), **Titian**, **Turner** (J M W), **Warhol** (Andy), **Wilkie** (Sir David), **Wright** (Joseph)

07 **Attwell** (Mabel Lucie), **Bellini** (Giovanni), **Bonnard** (Pierre), **Boucher** (François), **Cézanne** (Paul), **Chagall** (Marc), **Chirico** (Giorgio de), **Christo**, **Cimabué**, **Courbet** (Gustave), **Cranach** (Lucas, the Elder), **Daumier** (Honoré), **Delvaux** (Paul), **Duchamp** (Marcel), **El Greco**, **Gauguin** (Paul), **Hobbema** (Meindert), **Hockney** (David), **Hodgkin** (Sir Howard), **Hogarth** (William), **Hokusai** (Katsushika), **Holbein** (Hans), **Keating** (Tom), **Martini** (Simone), **Matisse** (Henri), **Millais** (Sir John Everett), **Morisot** (Berthe), **Pevsner** (Sir Nikolaus), **Picabia** (Francis), **Picasso** (Pablo), **Pollock** (Jackson), **Poussin** (Nicolas), **Rackham** (Arthur), **Raeburn** (Sir Henry), **Raphael**, **Sargent** (John Singer), **Schiele** (Egon), **Sickert** (Walter), **Spencer** (Sir Stanley), **Tenniel** (Sir John), **Thurber** (James), **Tiepolo** (Giovanni), **Uccello** (Paolo), **Utrillo** (Maurice), **Van Eyck** (Jan), **Van Gogh** (Vincent), **Vermeer** (Jan), **Watteau** (Antoine), **Wearing** (Gillian)

08 **Angelico** (Fra), **Annigoni** (Pietro), **Auerbach** (Frank), **Breughel** (Pieter), **Brueghel** (Pieter), **cummings** (e e), **Delaunay** (Robert), **Dubuffet** (Jean), **Goncourt** (Edmond de), **Gossaert** (Jan), **Hamilton** (Richard), **Hilliard** (Nicholas), **Landseer** (Sir Edwin), **Leonardo**, **Magritte** (René), **Malevich** (Kasimir), **Mantegna** (Andrea), **Masaccio**, **Mondrian** (Piet), **Munnings** (Sir Alfred), **Perugino**, **Piranesi** (Giambattista), **Pissarro** (Camille), **Reynolds** (Sir Joshua), **Rossetti** (Dante Gabriel), **Rousseau** (Henri, 'Le Douanier'), **Rousseau** (Théodore), **Ruisdael** (Jacob van), **Ruysdael** (Jacob van), **Topolski** (Feliks), **Vasarely** (Victor), **Veronese** (Paolo), **Vlaminck** (Maurice de), **Whistler** (James McNeill)

09 **Beardsley** (Aubrey), **Canaletto**, **Constable** (John), **Correggio**, **De Kooning** (Willem), **Delacroix** (Eugène), **Fergusson** (John Duncan), **Fragonard** (Jean), **Friedrich** (Caspar David), **Géricault** (Théodore), **Giorgione**, **Greenaway** (Kate), **Greenaway** (Peter), **Grünewald** (Matthias), **Kandinsky** (Wasily), **Kokoschka** (Oskar), **Lancaster** (Sir Osbert), **Nicholson** (Ben), **Nollekens** (Joseph), **Pisanello**, **Rembrandt**, **Rodchenko** (Alexander), **Velázquez** (Diego)

10 **Alma-Tadema** (Sir Lawrence), **Botticelli** (Sandro), **Burne-Jones** (Sir Edward), **Caravaggio** (Michelangelo), **Giacometti** (Alberto), **Modigliani** (Amedeo), **Motherwell** (Robert), **Parmigiano**, **Sutherland** (Graham), **Tintoretto**

12 **Bairnsfather** (Bruce), **Fantin-Latour** (Henri), **Gainsborough** (Thomas), **Lichtenstein** (Roy), **Michelangelo**

13 **Piero di Cosimo**

14 **Andrea del Sarto**, **Lucas van Leyden**

15 **Leonardo da Vinci**, **Toulouse-Lautrec** (Henri de)

painting

03 art, oil **04** daub, oils **08** likeness **09** cerograph, portrayal **11** delineation, scenography **13** belle peinture **14** representation

See also **art**

Painting terms include:

04 icon, tint, tone, wash

05 bloom, brush, easel, gesso, mural, paint, pieta, secco, tondo

06 canvas, fresco, frieze, primer, sketch

07 atelier, aureola, aureole, cartoon, collage, diptych, drawing, facture, gallery, gouache, impasto, limning, montage, palette, pastels, paysage, picture, pigment, scumble, sfumato, stipple, tempera

08 abstract, aquatint, bleeding, charcoal, esquisse, fixative, frottage, hard edge, hatching, paint-box, pastoral, portrait, seascape, skyscape, thinners, triptych, vignette

09 alla prima, aquarelle, brushwork, capriccio, encaustic, flat brush, grisaille, grotesque, landscape, mahlstick, maulstick, miniature, polyptych, scumbling, sgraffito, still life

10 art gallery, craquelure, dead colour, figurative, hair-pencil, monochrome, paint-brush, pentimento, pochade box, round brush, sable brush, silhouette, turpentine

11 canvas board, chiaroscuro, composition, fête galante, foreshorten, found object, illusionism, objet trouvé, oil painting, perspective, pointillism, trompe l'oeil, watercolour

12 anamorphosis, brush strokes, camera lucida, filbert brush, illustration, palette knife, pencil sketch

13 fête champêtre, genre painting, underpainting

14 foreshortening

Paintings and other artworks include:

04 Flag

05 Manga, Pietà, Trees

06 Spring

07 Bubbles, Erasmus, Gin Lane, Olympia, Targets, The Kiss

08 Guernica, L'Estaque, Maja Nude, Mona Lisa, The Dream

09 Bacchanal, Black Iris, Haystacks, Henry VIII, Jerusalem, L'Escargot, Night Café, Primavera, The Scream, The Tailor

10 Adam and Eve, Assumption, Beer Street, Blue Horses, Las Meninas, Sunflowers, The Angelus, The Hay Wain

11 100 Soup Cans, Arthur's Tomb, A Shrimp Girl, Crucifixion, Limp Watches, Maja Clothed, Starry Night, The Gleaners, View of Delft, Water Lilies

12 Beata Beatrix, Black on Black, Los Caprichos, Peasant Dance, The Nightmare, The Scapegoat, The Umbrellas

13 A Bigger Splash, Christ in Glory, Isenheim Altar, Man with a Glove, Sleeping Gypsy, The Last Supper, The Night Watch

14 A Rake's Progress, Disasters of War, Peasant Wedding, Random Sketches, Rouen Cathedral, Sistine Madonna, The Ambassadors, The Card Players, The Four Seasons, The Rokeby Venus, The Turkish Bath, View on the Stour

15 Absinthe Drinker, Commodore Keppel, Flight into Egypt, Madonna and Child, Madonna del Prato, Marriage à la Mode, The Annunciation, The Birth of Venus, The Charnel House, The Dance of Death, The Death of Marat, The Flagellation, The Potato Eaters, The Raft of Medusa, The Rape of Europa, Triumph of Caesar

pair
02 OO, pr 03 duo, set, twa, two, wed 04 duad, duet, join, link, mate, pack, team, twae, tway, twin, yoke 05 brace, marry, match, twain, twins, unite 06 couple, geminy, join up, link up, splice, team up 07 bracket, couplet, match up, partner, twosome 10 two of a kind 11 put together 14 arrange in pairs

paired
05 mated, yoked 06 double, in twos, joined, jugate, linked 07 coupled, matched, twinned 09 bracketed 10 associated

Pakistan
02 PK 03 PAK

pal
04 chum, mate 05 buddy, crony, cully 06 cobber, friend, winger 07 comrade, partner 08 intimate, sidekick, soul mate 09 companion, confidant 10 buddy-buddy, confidante

• **pal up**
06 chum up, gang up, join up 11 get together, make friends 13 become friends

palace
04 dome 05 court, hôtel 06 castle 07 alcázar, château, mansion, palazzo, schloss 08 basilica, seraglio 11 stately home

Palaces include:

05 Pitti, Royal, Savoy
06 Louvre, Mirror, Potala, Winter
07 Bishop's, Crystal, People's, Sultan's, Vatican
08 Alhambra, Blenheim, Borghese, Imperial, National, St James's, Valhalla, Walhalla
09 Episcopal, Maharaja's, Sans Souci, Tuileries, Whitehall
10 Buckingham, El Escorial, Fishbourne, Generalife, Kensington, Linlithgow, President's, Qusayr Amra, Quseir Amra, Schönbrunn, Versailles
11 Archbishop's, Westminster
13 Forbidden City, Holyrood House, Royal Pavilion, Tower of London, Windsor Castle
14 Charlottenburg
15 Palais de l'Elysée

paladin
04 peer

palaeontologist

Palaeontologists include:

04 Cope (Edward Drinker), Owen (Sir Richard)
05 Gould (Stephen Jay), Marsh (O C)
06 Dubois (Eugène), Forbes (Edward), Kurtén (Björn), Leakey (Louis), Leakey (Mary), Leakey (Richard), Osborn (Henry Fairfield), Zittel (Karl von)
07 Colbert (Ned), Mantell (Gideon), Simpson (George Gaylord)
08 Guettard (Jean Étienne), Johanson (Donald)

palanquin
04 kago 05 palki, sedan 06 doolie, litter, palkee 07 norimon

palatable
04 nice 05 tasty, yummy 06 delish, edible, morish 07 eatable, moreish, savoury, scrummy 08 pleasant, pleasing 09 agreeable, delicious, enjoyable, flavorous, succulent, toothsome 10 acceptable, appetizing, attractive, delectable 11 done to a turn, flavoursome, scrumptious 12 satisfactory 13 mouthwatering

palate
04 gout 05 heart, taste, velum 06 liking, relish 07 stomach 08 appetite 09 enjoyment, taste buds 10 enthusiasm 12 appreciation, sense of taste

palatial
04 posh 05 grand, plush, regal, ritzy 06 de luxe 07 opulent, stately 08 imposing, majestic, spacious, splendid 09 grandiose, luxurious, sumptuous 11 magnificent

Palau
03 PLW

palaver
04 flap, fuss, talk, to-do 05 hoo-ha 06 bother, bustle 07 carry-on, flatter, fluster 08 activity, business 09 commotion, kerfuffle, procedure, rigmarole 10 conference, discussion 12 song and dance

pale
03 dim, wan 04 ashy, fade, gray, grey, lily, melt, pall, pole, post, thin, waxy, weak 05 appal, ashen, blank, crown, faded, faint, fence, green, light, limit, livid, lurid, mealy, muted, pasty, peaky, shaft, stain, stake, vapid, verge, waxen, white 06 blanch, bleach, chalky, column, feeble, lessen, low-key, mealie, pallid, pastel, sallow, whiten 07 anaemic, drained, dwindle, high-key, insipid, upright, whitely, whitish 08 bleached, delicate, diminish, encircle, etiolate, grow pale, maid-pale 09 bloodless, enclosure, etiolated, grow white, washed-out, whey-faced 10 colourless, pallescent, pasty-faced, restrained, wishy-washy 11 peelie-wally 12 change colour 14 complexionless

• **beyond the pale**
08 improper, unseemly 10 unsuitable 11 intolerable 12 inadmissible, unacceptable, unreasonable 13 inappropriate

paleness
04 pale 06 pallor 07 anaemia, wanness 09 pastiness, whiteness 10 sallowness 11 pallescence 14 colourlessness

palindromic
07 Sotadic 08 cancrine, Sotadean

palisade
05 fence 06 fraise, paling 07 barrier, bulwark, defence, stacket 08 stockade 09 barricade, enclosure 13 fortification

pall
04 cloy, jade, pale, sate, tire, veil 05 cloak, cloud, daunt, gloom, weary 06 damper, mantle, shadow, shroud, sicken, weaken 07 curtain, frontal, pallium, satiate, wear off 08 corporal, covering 09 mortcloth 11 become bored, become tired, hearse-cloth

• **cast a pall over**
03 mar 04 harm, ruin 05 spoil, upset, wreck 06 impair 07 destroy

palladium
02 Pd

palliate
04 ease 05 abate, allay, cloak, cover 06 excuse, lenify, lessen, soften, soothe, temper 07 assuage, conceal, lighten, mollify, relieve 08 diminish, disguise, minimize, mitigate, moderate 09 alleviate, extenuate

palliative
07 anodyne, calming 08 lenitive, sedative, soothing 09 analgesic, assuasive, calmative, demulcent, paregoric 10 mitigating, mitigative, mitigatory, mollifying, painkiller 11 alleviating, alleviative, extenuative, extenuatory 13 tranquillizer

pallid
03 wan 04 ashy, dull, pale, tame, waxy, weak 05 ashen, bland, lurid, pasty, tired, vapid, waxen, white 06 boring, doughy, sallow, sickly 07 anaemic, insipid, sterile, whitish 08 lifeless 09 bloodless, etiolated, whey-faced 10 colourless, pallescent, pasty-faced, spiritless, unexciting, uninspired 11 peelie-wally 13 uninteresting 14 complexionless

pallor
07 anaemia, wanness 08 paleness 09 whiteness 10 chalkiness, etiolation, pallidness, sallowness 11 pallescence 13 bloodlessness

pally
04 warm 05 close, thick, tight 06 chummy, folksy 08 familiar, friendly, intimate 12 affectionate

palm
03 fob, paw 04 grab, hand, loof, mitt, take, vola 05 bribe 06 snatch, thenar 11 appropriate

Palms include:

03 dum, ita, oil, wax
04 atap, coco, date, doom, doum, hemp, nipa, sago
05 areca, assai, bussu, macaw, nikau, peach, royal, Sabal, sugar, toddy
06 buriti, cohune, corozo, Elaeis, gomuti, gru-gru, jupati, kentia, kittul, miriti, raffia, Raphia, rattan, troely
07 babassu, cabbage, calamus, coconut, coquito, Corypha, Euterpe, moriche, palmyra,

paxiuba, pupunha, talipat, talipot, troelie, troolie
08 carnauba, coco-tree, date-tree, groo-groo, palmetto
10 Chamaerops
12 chiquichiqui, Washingtonia
15 cabbage-palmetto

• have someone in the palm of your hand
13 have power over **15** have control over

• palm off
05 foist **06** fob off, impose, pass on, put off, thrust, unload **07** offload, pass off, work off **08** get rid of, pass upon

palmist
10 palm reader **11** clairvoyant
13 chirographist, fortune-teller

palmistry
10 chirognomy, chiromancy **11** palm reading **12** clairvoyancy **14** fortune-telling

palmy
05 happy **06** golden, joyous
07 halcyon **08** carefree, glorious, thriving **09** fortunate, luxurious
10 prosperous, successful, triumphant
11 flourishing

palpable
04 real **05** clear, gross, plain, solid
06 patent **07** blatant, evident, glaring, obvious, visible **08** apparent, concrete, manifest, material, tangible
09 touchable **11** conspicuous, perceptible, substantial
12 unmistakable **13** unmistakeable

palpably
07 clearly, plainly, visibly **08** patently
09 blatantly, evidently, glaringly, obviously **10** apparently, manifestly
12 unmistakably **13** conspicuously, unmistakeably

palpitate
04 beat, thud **05** pound, pulse, quake, shake, throb, thump **06** pit-pat, quiver, shiver **07** flutter, pitapat, pulsate, tremble, twitter, vibrate **08** pitty-pat

palpitation
05 shake, throb **06** quiver, shakes
07 flutter, shaking **08** pounding
09 quivering, throbbing, trembling, vibration **10** fluttering

paltry
03 low, tin **04** bald, bare, mean, poor, puny, vile, waff **05** cheap, minor, petty, scald, small, sorry, woful **06** jitney, meagre, measly, shabby, slight, tinpot, trashy, two-bit, vulgar, woeful
07 foolish, miserly, pelting, pimping, piteous, trivial **08** derisory, piddling, rubbishy, trifling, wretched
09 miserable, worthless **10** negligible, shoestring **11** unimportant
12 contemptible, pettifogging
13 insignificant **14** inconsiderable

pamper
03 pet **04** baby **05** spoil **06** cocker, coddle, cosher, cosset, cuiter, fondle, humour, pander, pompey **07** gratify, indulge **09** spoon-feed **10** featherbed
11 mollycoddle, overindulge

pampered
06 petted, spoilt **07** coddled, high-fed, overfed **08** cosseted, indulged, spoon-fed **10** lust-dieted **12** mollycoddled

pamphlet
03 pam **05** flyer, sheet, tract **06** folder, notice **07** booklet, handout, leaflet
08 brochure, chapbook, circular
10 mazarinade

pan
03 pit, pot, wok **04** bowl, cake, cave, face, flay, hole, lead, move, scan, slag, slam, turn, well **05** basin, betel, frier, fryer, knock, ladle, roast, scale, slate, sweep, swing, track, yield **06** cavern, cavity, circle, crater, Faunus, follow, hammer, hollow, obtain, spider, vessel
07 censure, channel, goat-god, rubbish, skillet, slag off **08** pancheon, panchion, pannikin, saucepan, traverse
09 bed-warmer, casserole, concavity, container, criticize, frying-pan, saltworks **10** corn popper, depression, excavation **11** calefactory **12** pull to pieces **13** find fault with

• pan out
05 yield **06** happen, result **07** turn out, work out **09** culminate, eventuate
11 be exhausted, come to an end

panacea
06 elixir, tutsan **07** allheal, cure-all, nostrum **10** catholicon, parkleaves
12 panpharmacon **13** diacatholicon
15 universal remedy

panache
04 brio, dash, élan, zest **05** flair, plume, style, verve **06** energy, pazazz, pizazz, spirit, vigour **07** pazzazz, pizzazz, swagger **08** flourish **10** enthusiasm
11 flamboyance, ostentation

Panama
02 PA **03** PAN

pancake
04 flam, taco **05** blini, crêpe, flamm, flawn, latke, rösti, wafer **06** blintz, flaune, fraise, froise, roesti, waffle
07 bannock, blintze, crumpet, pikelet
08 flapjack, omelette, tortilla **09** drop scone **10** battercake, spring roll
11 griddle-cake **12** crêpe suzette, dropped scone

pandemic
04 rife **06** common, global **07** general
09 extensive, pervasive, prevalent, universal **10** widespread **11** far-reaching

pandemonium
03 din **04** to-do **05** chaos **06** bedlam, hubbub, rumpus, tumult, uproar
07 turmoil **08** disorder **09** commotion, confusion, hue and cry, shemozzle
10 hullabaloo, turbulence

pander
04 bawd, pimp **06** broker **07** procure
08 procurer **11** whoremonger

• pander to
06 fulfil, humour, pamper, please
07 cater to, gratify, indulge, provide, satisfy

pane
04 pean, peen, pein, pene **05** glass, panel **06** window **07** quarrel
10 windowpane

panegyric
05 éloge, elogy, paean **06** eulogy, homage, praise **07** elogium, glowing, tribute **08** accolade, citation, encomium, eulogium, praising
09 laudation, laudatory, praiseful
10 eulogistic, favourable, flattering
11 encomiastic, panegyrical
12 commendation, commendatory
13 complimentary **14** speech of praise

panel
03 orb **04** beam, jury, mola, pane, sign, slab, team, unit **05** array, board, dials, knobs, plank, plate, sheet, table
06 coffer, levers, screen, tablet, timber
07 buttons, console, council, inn sign, lacunar, valance, valence **08** controls, mandorla, switches, trustees
09 cartouche, committee, dashboard, faceplate, headboard, medallion
10 commission, focus group, patchboard **11** compartment, directorate, instruments **13** advisory group **15** instrument panel

panelling
04 dado **06** coffer **07** lacunar, reredos
08 wainscot **09** panelwork, reredorse, reredosse **11** wainscoting
12 wainscotting

pang
04 ache, cram, pain, stab **05** agony, gripe, prick, qualm, spasm, sting, stuff, thraw, throe, throw, tight **06** shower, stitch, stound, stownd, throwe, twinge
07 anguish, crammed, crowded, scruple, stuffed **08** distress
09 misgiving **10** discomfort, uneasiness

pangolin
05 Manis **08** anteater **13** scaly anteater

panic
◇ *anagram indicator*
04 fear, flap, funk **05** alarm, amaze, scare **06** dismay, frenzy, fright, horror, panick, terror **07** pannick, unnerve
08 disquiet, flat spin, hysteria, tailspin
09 agitation, overreact, run scared
10 amazedness, go to pieces **11** have kittens, trepidation **12** get the shakes, lose your cool, lose your head, perturbation, sauve qui peut
13 consternation, get the jitters, get the willies, lose your nerve **14** lose your bottle

panic-stricken
06 aghast, scared **07** alarmed, frantic, panicky **08** frenzied, in a tizzy
09 horrified, perturbed, petrified, terrified **10** frightened, hysterical **11** in a blue funk, in a flat spin, scared stiff
12 in a cold sweat **14** terror-stricken

pannier
03 pad, ped **06** dosser **07** cacolet, kajawah **09** ambulance

panoply
04 garb, gear, show **05** array, dress, get-up, range **06** armour, attire **07** raiment, regalia, turn-out **08** insignia
09 equipment, trappings

panorama
04 view **05** scene, vista **06** survey
07 scenery **08** overview, prospect, wide view **09** broad view, cyclorama, landscape, spectacle **11** perspective
12 bird's-eye view

panoramic
04 wide **05** broad **06** scenic
07 general, overall **08** sweeping
09 extensive, universal **10** widespread
11 far-reaching, wide-ranging
13 comprehensive

pansy
05 pance, viola **06** kiss-me, paunce, pawnce **10** effeminate, heart's-ease, homosexual **11** herb-trinity, kiss-me-quick **14** love-in-idleness

pant
03 yen **04** ache, blow, gasp, huff, long, pech, pegh, pine, puff, sigh, want
05 covet, crave, flaff, heave, throb, yearn **06** desire, hanker, thirst, wheeze
07 breathe **09** palpitate **11** huff and puff

panting
05 eager **06** puffed, winded
07 anxious, craving, gasping, longing, puffing **09** hankering, impatient, puffed out **10** breathless **11** out of breath, short-winded

pantomime
04 mime, show **05** farce, panto
06 masque **07** charade **08** dumbshow
12 harlequinade

Pantomime characters include:

04 Jack, Jill
05 Giant, Wendy
06 Beauty, Gretel, Hansel
07 Buttons, Dandini, Emperor, King Rat
08 Abanazer, Idle Jack, Peter Pan, The Beast
09 Alan-a-dale, Columbine, Friar Tuck, Robin Hood
10 Billy Goose, Cinderella, Goldilocks, Little John, Maid Marian, Maid Marion, Prince John, Tinkerbell
11 Baron Hardup, Captain Hook, Daisy the Cow, Jack's Mother, King Richard, Mother Goose, Simple Simon, Will Scarlet
12 Pantomime Cow, Principal Boy, Sarah the Cook, Widow Twankey, Will Scarlett, Wishee Washee
13 Principal Girl
14 Baroness Hardup, Fairy Godmother, Genie of the Lamp, Pantomime Horse, Prince Charming, Princess Aurora, Slave of the Ring, The Ugly Sisters
15 Alice Fitzwarren, Princess Jasmine, Rumpelstiltskin

Pantomimes include:

07 Aladdin, Ali Baba, Cinders
08 Peter Pan, Rapunzel
09 Pinocchio, Robin Hood, Snow White
10 Cinderella, Goldilocks
11 Mother Goose, Old King Cole, Puss in Boots
12 The Pied Piper, The Snow Queen
13 Red Riding Hood
14 Babes in the Wood, Robinson Crusoe, Sleeping Beauty, Treasure Island
15 Dick Whittington, Hansel and Gretel, Rumpelstiltskin, Sinbad the Sailor, The Swan Princess

pantry
05 ambry, awmry **06** almery, aumbry, awmrie, larder, spence **07** butlery
08 scullery **09** stillroom, storeroom

pants
05 jeans, loons, teddy, thong **06** briefs, shorts, slacks, smalls, trunks, undies
07 drawers, joggers, panties, rubbish, Y-fronts **08** frillies, knickers, nonsense, trousers **10** underpants **11** boxer shorts, panty girdle **12** camiknickers

pap
03 goo, rot **04** crap, mash, mush, pulp
05 purée, trash **06** breast, drivel, hot air, nipple **07** rubbish, twaddle
08 claptrap, nonsense, soft food
09 gibberish, poppycock **14** semi-liquid food

papa
01 P
See also **father**

paper
03 rag **04** ream, work **05** daily, essay, organ, study **06** report, thesis, weekly
07 article, journal, tabloid **08** analysis, magazine, treatise **09** monograph, newspaper **10** broadsheet, periodical
11 composition, examination
12 dissertation
See also **newspaper**

Paper sizes and formats include:

02 A0, A1, A2, A3, A4, A5
03 pot
04 demy, post, pott
05 atlas, crown, folio, jésus, legal, royal
06 letter, medium, quarto
07 emperor, tabloid
08 Berliner, elephant, foolscap, imperial
09 antiquary, music-demy
10 super-royal

Paper types include:

03 art, rag
04 bank, bond, card, note, rice, wall
05 crêpe, graph, sugar
06 carbon, manila, silver, tissue, toilet, vellum
07 papyrus, tracing, writing
08 acid-free, blotting, handmade, recycled, wrapping
09 cardboard, cartridge, parchment
10 pasteboard
11 greaseproof

• on paper
07 ideally **08** in theory, recorded **09** in writing, seemingly **10** officially, supposedly **11** on the record, written down **13** theoretically
14 hypothetically, in your mind's eye
15 in black and white

• paper over
04 hide **07** conceal, cover up, obscure
08 disguise **10** camouflage **13** put out of sight

• paper size
03 pot **04** demy, pott

papers
02 ID **04** bumf **05** bumph, deeds, sheaf **07** records **08** document, evidence, passbook, passport
10 despatches, dispatches
11 credentials **12** certificates, identity card **13** authorization, documentation
14 driving licence, identification, qualifications

papery
04 thin **05** frail, light **06** flimsy
07 fragile **08** delicate **09** paper-thin
10 glumaceous, membranous
11 chartaceous, lightweight, membraneous, papyraceous, translucent **13** insubstantial, membranaceous

Papua New Guinea
03 PNG

par
04 mean, norm, parr **05** level, usual
06 median, parity **07** average, balance
08 equality, standard **09** paragraph
10 accordance, similarity
11 equilibrium, equivalence **12** equal footing **14** correspondence

• below par
05 lousy, rough, tired **06** unwell
08 inferior, under par **10** inadequate, not up to par, out of sorts **11** at a discount **12** below average **14** not up to scratch, unsatisfactory **15** under the weather

• deviation from par
04 agio

• on a par with
07 equal to **08** as good as
12 equivalent to

• par for the course
05 usual **06** normal **07** typical
08 standard **11** predictable

• up to par
02 OK **04** fine **08** adequate
10 acceptable **11** up to scratch
12 satisfactory

parable
05 fable, story **06** lesson **07** proverb
08 allegory **09** discourse, moral tale
10 comparison, similitude **15** story with a moral

parachute
04 pack **05** chute **06** drogue, pappus
08 parafoil, patagium **09** aeroshell, parabrake

parade
03 row 04 file, pass, shew, show 05 array, march, parry, train, vaunt 06 column, flaunt, line-up, prance, review 07 display, exhibit, pageant, process, show off, stand-to 08 brandish, ceremony, file past 09 cavalcade, decursion, motorcade, spectacle 10 appearance, exhibition, procession 11 ostentation, progression 13 demonstration

paradigm
05 ideal, model 07 example, pattern 08 exemplar, original 09 archetype, framework, prototype

paradise
03 joy 04 Eden 05 bliss 06 heaven, parvis, Svarga, Swarga, Swerga, utopia 07 delight, ecstasy, Elysium, rapture 08 felicity 09 afterlife, cloud nine, happiness, hereafter, home of God, next world, Shangri-La 10 life to come 12 Garden of Eden 13 Elysian Fields, seventh heaven

paradox
06 enigma, oddity, puzzle, riddle 07 anomaly, mystery 09 absurdity 11 incongruity 13 contradiction, inconsistency

paradoxical
06 absurd 08 baffling, puzzling 09 anomalous, enigmatic, illogical 10 impossible, improbable, mysterious 11 conflicting, incongruous 12 inconsistent 13 contradictory

paraffin
07 coal oil 08 earthwax, kerosene, kerosine, photogen 09 ozocerite, ozokerite, photogene 10 mineral wax 14 petroleum jelly

paragon
04 mate, rose 05 equal, ideal, match, model, pearl, rival 07 compare, epitome, paladin, pattern, phoenix, surpass 08 exemplar, standard 09 archetype, criterion, emulation, nonpareil, prototype 10 comparison 11 competition, masterpiece 12 quintessence, the bee's knees 14 crème de la crème, perfect example

paragraph
03 par 04 item, para, part 05 piece 06 clause 07 article, passage, portion, section, segment 08 causerie, te igitur 10 stand first, subsection 11 subdivision

Paraguay
02 PY 03 PRY

parallel
03 par 04 echo, like, twin 05 agree, equal, liken, match 06 be like 07 aligned, analogy, compare, conform, similar, uniform 08 analogue, likeness, matching, resemble 09 alongside, analogous, correlate, duplicate 10 co-existing, collateral, comparable, comparison, correspond, equivalent, homologous, resembling, side by side, similarity 11 be analogous, be similar to, coextensive, correlation, counterpart, equidistant, equivalence, resemblance 12 be equivalent 13 corresponding 14 correspondence

paralyse
04 dull, halt, lame, numb, stop 05 palsy, scram, shock 06 benumb, deaden, freeze 07 cripple, disable, terrify, torpefy 08 transfix 10 deactivate, debilitate, immobilize 12 anaesthetize, incapacitate

paralysed
04 lame, numb 08 crippled, disabled 09 paralytic 10 paraplegic 11 immobilized 12 quadriplegic 13 incapacitated

paralysis
04 halt 05 palsy, shock 07 paresis 08 deadness, diplegia, numbness, shutdown, stoppage 09 breakdown 10 Bell's palsy, hemiplegia, immobility, monoplegia, paraplegia, sideration, standstill 11 cycloplegia, paraparesis 12 debilitation, quadriplegia 13 cerebral palsy, powerlessness 15 ophthalmoplegia

paralytic
04 lame, numb 05 drunk 06 blotto, canned, soused, stewed, stoned, wasted 07 legless, palsied, pie-eyed, sloshed, smashed, sozzled, wrecked 08 crippled, disabled, immobile 09 incapable, paralysed, plastered 10 hemiplegic, inebriated, monoplegic 11 immobilized, intoxicated 12 quadriplegic 13 incapacitated 15 a sheet in the wind

parameter
05 limit 06 factor 08 boundary, variable 09 criterion, framework, guideline 10 indication, limitation 11 restriction 13 figure of merit, specification 14 limiting factor

paramilitaries
04 sena

paramount
04 main 05 chief, first, prime 07 highest, primary, supreme, topmost 08 cardinal, foremost, superior, suzerain 09 principal 10 pre-eminent 11 outstanding, predominant 13 most important

paramour
04 beau 05 leman, lover, woman 07 beloved, franion, hetaera, hetaira 08 copemate, fancy man, mistress 09 concubine, copes-mate, courtesan, inamorata, inamorato, kept woman 10 bit of fluff, fancy woman 12 bit on the side

paranoia
09 delusions, monomania, obsession, psychosis 11 megalomania

paranoid
05 fazed 06 afraid 07 fearful 08 confused 10 bewildered, suspicious 11 distrustful

paranormal
◇ *anagram indicator*
05 eerie, magic, weird 06 hidden, mystic, occult 07 ghostly, magical, phantom, psychic 08 abnormal, mystical 09 spiritual, unnatural 10 miraculous, mysterious 12 metaphysical, otherworldly, supernatural 13 preternatural

parapet
03 top 04 rail, wall 05 fence, guard 06 flèche, paling, parpen 07 barrier, bastion, bulwark, defence, parpane, parpend, parpent, perpend, perpent, railing, rampart 08 barbican, bartisan, bartizan, parpoint, traverse 09 barricade 10 balustrade, battlement, embankment 13 fortification

paraphernalia
04 gear 05 stuff, tools 06 tackle, things 07 baggage, effects 09 apparatus, equipment, materials, trappings 10 belongings, implements 11 accessories, odds and ends, possessions 13 accoutrements, bits and pieces

paraphrase
05 gloss 06 rehash, render, reword, Targum 07 restate, version 08 rephrase 09 interpret, rendering, rewording, translate 10 rephrasing 11 restatement, translation 14 interpretation 15 put in other words

parasite
03 bum, fly 05 drone, leech 06 cadger, ligger, sponge, sucker 07 bludger, epizoan, epizoon, moocher, sponger, vampire 08 endozoon, entozoon, epiphyte, hanger-on, quandang, quandong, quantong 09 endophyte, passenger, scrounger, sycophant 10 freeloader 11 bloodsucker 12 lick-trencher 14 trencher-friend, trencher-knight

Parasites include:

03 bot, ked, nit
04 bott, chat, crab, flea, kade, mite, tick
05 fluke, louse
06 chigoe, chigre, cootie, jigger
07 argulus, ascarid, ascaris, Babesia, bonamia, cestode, chalcid, chigger, Giardia, pinworm
08 hookworm, itch-mite, lungworm, nematode, sheep ked, strongyl, tapeworm, toxocara, whipworm
09 Bilharzia, bird louse, crab louse, fish louse, fluke-worm, head louse, pediculus, roundworm, sheep tick, sporozoan, strongyle, trematode
10 Guinea worm, Plasmodium, threadworm
11 biting louse, sarcocystis, scabies mite, trichomonad, trypanosome
12 echinococcus, ectoparasite, endoparasite, semiparasite
13 hyperparasite

parasitic
07 cadging, epizoan, epizoic

08 sponging **09** biogenous, leechlike **10** scrounging **11** freeloading, parasitical **12** bloodsucking

parasol

04 veil **05** shade **06** shield **07** shelter **08** marquise, sunshade, umbrella **09** en tout cas **10** protection

See also **umbrella**

parcel

03 box, dak, lot, mob, set **04** area, band, crew, dawk, deal, gang, herd, item, pack, plot, sort, wrap **05** bunch, crowd, flock, group, patch, piece, put up, tie up, tract, troop **06** bundle, carton, make up, packet, pack up, partly, wrap up **07** company, package, portion **08** bundle up, gift-wrap, quantity **09** allotment **10** collection **11** transaction

• **parcel out**

05 allot, whack **06** divide **07** carve up, deal out, dole out, hand out, mete out **08** allocate, dispense, share out **09** apportion, divide out **10** distribute

parch

03 dry **04** bake, burn, sear **05** dry up, toast **06** scorch, wither **07** blister, shrivel, torrefy **09** dehydrate, desiccate

parched

03 dry **04** arid, sear, sere **05** baked **06** burned, seared **07** dried up, gasping, thirsty **08** scorched, withered **09** blistered, waterless **10** dehydrated, desiccated, dry as a bone, shrivelled

parchment

04 pell, roll **05** forel, panel **06** mezuza, scroll, vellum **07** charter, diploma, mezuzah **08** document, membrane **09** sheepskin **10** palimpsest, phylactery **11** certificate

pardon

02 eh? **04** free, what? **05** bitte, grace, mercy, remit, sorry **06** acquit, excuse, let off **07** absolve, amnesty, condone, forgive, release, you what? **08** clemency, excuse me, lenience, liberate, oblivion, overlook, reprieve, say again?, tolerate **09** acquittal, come again?, discharge, exculpate, exonerate, remission, vindicate **10** absolution, act of grace, indulgence **11** condonation, cry you mercy, exculpation, exoneration, forbearance, forgiveness **13** let off the hook, what did you say? **14** I beg your pardon

pardonable

05 minor **06** slight, venial **09** allowable, excusable **10** condonable, forgivable **11** dispensable, justifiable, permissible, warrantable **14** understandable

pare

03 cut, lop **04** chip, clip, crop, dock, peel, skin, trim **05** prune, shave, shear, skive **06** reduce **07** cut back, whittle **08** clip coin, decrease

parent

02 ma, pa **03** dad, dam, mam, mom, mum, pop **04** papa, rear, root, sire **05** beget, cause, daddy, folks, mamma, mammy, mommy, mummy, mumsy, raise, teach, train **06** author, create, father, foster, mother, old man, origin, source **07** bring up, creator, educate, genitor, nurture **08** begetter, generant, genetrix, genitrix, guardian, old woman, relative **09** architect, bioparent, look after, procreate, prototype **10** forerunner, originator, procreator, progenitor, solo parent, step-parent, take care of **11** birth mother, birth parent, empty-nester, progenitrix **12** foster parent, progenitress, single parent **13** be the father of, be the mother of **14** adoptive parent **15** custodial parent

parentage

04 line, race **05** birth, brood, stock **06** family, origin, source, stirps **07** descent, lineage, origins **08** ancestry, pedigree **09** filiation, paternity, whakapapa **10** derivation, extraction **11** affiliation

parenthetical

08 inserted **09** as an aside, bracketed **10** extraneous, incidental, interposed, qualifying **11** elucidative, explanatory, intervening **13** in parenthesis

parenthetically

03 btw **08** by the way **09** as an aside **11** secondarily **12** incidentally **13** as a digression

par excellence

02 A1 **03** ace **04** best, cool, fine, mean, neat, rare **05** brill, great, noted, prime **06** divine, select, superb, wicked **07** eminent, notable, perfect, shining **08** fabulous, flawless, heavenly, smashing, splendid, stunning, superior, terrific, top-notch, very good **09** brilliant, excellent, exemplary, fantastic, faultless, first-rate, matchless, wonderful **10** first-class, marvellous, noteworthy, pre-eminent, remarkable, surpassing, unequalled **11** commendable, exceptional, high-quality, magnificent, outstanding, sensational, superlative **12** praiseworthy, second to none, unparalleled **13** distinguished **14** out of this world

pariah

05 exile, leper, pi-dog **06** outlaw, pie-dog, pye-dog **07** Ishmael, outcast **08** castaway, unperson **10** black sheep **11** undesirable, untouchable **15** persona non grata

paring

04 peel, rind, skin **05** flake, shave, shred, slice **06** sliver **07** cutting, flaught, peeling, shaving, snippet **08** clipping, fragment, trimming **09** flaughter

Paris

Paris districts include:

05 Bercy, Opéra
06 Étoile, Louvre, Marais
07 Pigalle
08 Bastille, Chaillot, Left Bank, Sorbonne
09 Chinatown, La Défense, Les Halles, Right Bank, Trocadero, Tuileries
10 Belleville, La Villette, Montmartre, Rive Droite, Rive Gauche, Tour Eiffel
11 Batignolles
12 Latin Quarter, Les Invalides, Montparnasse, Place d'Italie
13 Champs Élysées, Quartier Latin

Paris streets include:

07 Pigalle
09 Port Royal, Rue de Rome
10 Avenue Foch, Quai d'Orsay, Rue d'Alésia
11 Rue Dauphine, Rue de Clichy, Rue de Rennes, Rue de Rivoli, Rue de Sèvres, Rue Mazarine, Rue St-Honoré
12 périphérique, Place d'Italie, Place Vendôme, Quai du Louvre, Quai Voltaire, Rue St-Antoine
13 Avenue George V, Place du Tertre, Rue des Rosiers, Rue Mouffetard
14 Place des Vosges
15 Avenue Montaigne, Quai d'Austerlitz

Paris landmarks include:

05 Seine
06 Bourse, Louvre
07 Pyramid
08 Bastille, Panthéon, Pont Neuf, Sorbonne
09 Beaubourg, Bon Marché, Invalides, la Défense, Madeleine, Notre-Dame, Orangerie, St-Sulpice, Trocadero, Tuileries
10 Gare du Nord, Île St-Louis, Montmartre, Musée Rodin, Sacré Coeur
11 Champ de Mars, Eiffel Tower, Grande Arche, Grand Palais, Île de la Cité, Moulin Rouge, Musée d'Orsay, Palais Royal, Pont des Arts
12 Hôtel de Ville, Montparnasse, Opéra Garnier, Père Lachaise
13 Arc de Triomphe, Champs-Élysées, Les catacombes, Opéra Bastille
14 Bois de Boulogne, École Militaire, Forum des Halles, Palais du Louvre, Place de l'Étoile, Pompidou Centre, Sainte Chapelle
15 Bois de Vincennes, Cité des Sciences, Le stade de France, Palais de Justice

parish

03 par **04** fold, town **05** flock, title **06** church, county **07** village **08** district, parishen, parochin, peculiar, township **09** community, parischan, parochine **10** parischane **11** churchgoers **12** congregation, denomination, parishioners

Parisian

◇ *foreign word indicator*

parity

03 par **05** unity **07** analogy **08** affinity, equality, likeness, sameness

09 agreement, congruity, semblance
10 conformity, congruence, consonance, similarity, similitude, uniformity 11 consistency, equivalence, parallelism, resemblance
14 correspondence

park
01 P 02 Pk 03 put, set, zoo 04 bung, stop 05 field, leave, place, plonk, stand, walks 06 domain, draw up, pull up
07 deposit, grounds, reserve
08 paradise, position, woodland
09 grassland

Parks include:

04 Hyde, West
05 Green, Güell, Kings
06 Albert, Domain
07 Battery, Central, Phoenix, Regent's, Stanley
08 Gramercy, Richmond, St James's, Victoria
09 Battersea, Tuileries
10 Tiergarten
11 Champ de Mars, Vienna Woods
13 Madison Square, Tivoli Gardens
14 Bois de Boulogne
15 Bois de Vincennes

National parks in the UK:

06 Exmoor
08 Dartmoor
09 New Forest, Snowdonia, The Broads
10 Cairngorms
12 Lake District, Peak District
13 Brecon Beacons
14 Northumberland, North York Moors, Yorkshire Dales
18 Pembrokeshire Coast
25 Loch Lomond and the Trossachs

parking
01 P

parlance
04 cant, talk 05 argot, idiom, lingo
06 jargon, speech, tongue 07 diction
08 language, speaking 11 phraseology
12 conversation

parley
04 talk 05 parle, parly, speak, talks, treat 06 confab, confer, emparl, imparl, powwow 07 consult, council, discuss, meeting 08 colloquy, dialogue
09 negotiate, tête-à-tête
10 conference, deliberate, discussion, parliament 11 get together, get-together, negotiation 12 deliberation
14 parliament-cake

parliament
05 house, parly 06 parley 07 chamber
11 convocation, legislature

Parliament types include:

04 diet, duma, moot
05 boule, douma, gemot, jirga
06 majlis, senate
07 commons, council
08 assembly, congress
09 volksraad
10 consistory, lower house, upper house
12 lower chamber, upper chamber
14 Council of State
15 House of Assembly

Parliaments and political assemblies include:

02 EP, HK, HP
04 Dáil, Diet, Duma, Keys, Long, Pnyx, Rump, Sejm
05 boule, Forum, gemot, Lords, Porte
06 Cortes, kgotla, Majlis, Mejlis, Seanad, Senate, Senato, Soviet
07 Althing, comitia, Commons, Knesset, Lagting, Landtag, Rigsdag, Riksdag, Tynwald, zemstvo
08 Assembly, Congress, ecclesia, European, folkmoot, Imperial, Lagthing, Lok Sabha, Scottish, Sobranje, Sobranye, Stannary, Storting
09 Bundesrat, Bundestag, Directory, Eduskunta, Folketing, Landsting, Loya Jirga, Odelsting, Reichsrat, Reichstag, Skupstina, Ständerat, State Duma
10 Bundesrath, Convention, Landsthing, lower house, Odelsthing, Oireachtas, Rajya Sabha, Reichsrath, Skupshtina, St Stephen's, upper house
11 Dáil Eireann, Folketinget, House of Keys, Nationalrat, Star Chamber, Volkskammer, Westminster
12 House of Lords
13 House of States, Seanad Eireann, States General, Supreme Soviet, Welsh Assembly
14 Council of State, Estates General, House of Commons, Long Parliament, Rump Parliament, Staten-Generaal
15 Council of States, House of Assembly, People's Assembly, People's Congress

parliamentary
05 civil 07 elected, popular
08 decorous, official 09 lawgiving, lawmaking 10 democratic, republican, senatorial 11 legislative
12 governmental 13 congressional, legislatorial 14 representative

parlour
06 lounge, spence 09 front room
10 living room 11 drawing room, keeping-room, morning room, sitting room

parlous
04 dire 05 awful, grave 08 alarming, dreadful, horrible, perilous, shocking, terrible 09 appalling, atrocious, desperate, frightful 10 calamitous, disastrous 11 distressing
12 catastrophic

parochial
04 hick 05 petty 06 narrow 07 insular, limited 08 confined 09 blinkered, small-town 10 parish-pump, provincial, restricted 11 small-minded
12 narrow-minded 13 inward-looking
14 denominational

parochialism
09 pettiness 10 insularity, narrowness, parish pump 13 provincialism 15 small-mindedness

parody
03 ape 04 skit 05 mimic, spoof
06 satire, send up, send-up 07 imitate, lampoon, mimicry, take off, take-off
08 satirize, travesty 09 burlesque, imitation 10 caricature, corruption, distortion, pasquinade, perversion

paroxysm
03 fit 05 spasm, storm, thraw, throe, throw 06 attack, frenzy, throwe
07 flare-up, rapture, seizure
08 eruption, outbreak, outburst
09 explosion 10 convulsion

parrot
03 ape 04 copy, echo, Poll 05 mimic, Polly 06 repeat 07 copycat, imitate, phraser 08 imitator, popinjay, rehearse, repeater 09 reiterate

Parrots include:

03 fig, kea
04 grey, kaka, lory
05 galah, macaw, pygmy
06 Amazon, budgie, conure, kakapo, Nestor
07 corella, hanging, rosella
08 cockatoo, lorikeet, lovebird, parakeet, paroquet, Pesquet's, Strigops
09 cockateel, cockatiel, green leek, owl-parrot, paraquito, parrakeet, parroquet, parrotlet, Psittacus, Stringops
10 budgerigar, ring-necked
11 African grey, night-parrot, shell-parrot
13 Major Mitchell, zebra parakeet
14 shell parrakeet

parrot-fashion
06 by rote 10 mindlessly
12 mechanically, unthinkingly
13 automatically

parrot-wrasse
04 scar

parry
04 duck, shun, ward 05 avert, avoid, block, dodge, evade, field, put by, repel, sixte 06 parade, rebuff
07 counter, deflect, fend off, keep off, repulse, ward off 08 sidestep, stave off, tac-au-tac 09 hold at bay, keep at bay, turn aside 10 bodyswerve, circumvent
12 steer clear of

parsimonious
04 mean, near 05 close, mingy, tight
06 frugal, narrow, saving, scanty, stingy
07 miserly, scrimpy, sparing
08 grasping, stinting 09 niggardly, penurious 10 Aberdonian 11 close-fisted, close-handed, tight-fisted
12 candle-paring, cheeseparing
13 penny-pinching

parsimony
08 meanness 09 frugality, minginess, tightness 10 stinginess 11 miserliness

12 cheeseparing 13 niggardliness, penny-pinching 15 tight-fistedness

parson
03 Rev 05 padre, vicar 06 cleric, curate, deacon, pastor, priest, rector 07 holy Joe 08 minister, preacher, reverend 09 churchman, clergyman, soul-curer 10 Jack-priest

parson-bird
03 tui

part
◇ *hidden indicator*
◇ *hidden alternately indicator*
◇ *insertion indicator*
02 by, pt 03 bit, bye, job 04 area, book, duty, gift, half, hand, quit, role, shed, side, some, task, tear, twin, wing, work 05 break, chore, facet, leave, organ, party, piece, scene, scrap, sever, share, skill, slice, split, twine 06 aspect, branch, charge, cleave, depart, detach, divide, factor, genius, member, module, office, region, sector, talent, volume 07 ability, break up, calibre, chapter, concern, disband, disjoin, diverge, element, episode, excerpt, extract, faculty, limited, partial, passage, persona, portion, push off, quarter, scarper, scatter, section, segment, split up, take off 08 capacity, clear off, disperse, district, division, fraction, fragment, function, get going, interest, locality, particle, separate 09 attribute, character, come apart, component, dimension, direction, dismantle, endowment, expertise, imperfect, intellect, keep apart, portrayal, push along, take apart, territory 10 capability, depart from, department, disconnect, distribute, go away from, hit the road, ingredient, instalment, make tracks, percentage, proportion, restricted, say goodbye, unfinished 11 constituent, divorce from, fragmentary, hit the trail, involvement, not complete, split up from 12 intelligence, separate from, withdraw from 13 neighbourhood, participation, take your leave 14 accomplishment, representation, responsibility 15 get divorced from, part company with

• **act the part of**
04 come

• **assign part**
04 cast

• **even parts**
◇ *hidden alternately indicator*

• **for the most part**
06 mainly, mostly 07 as a rule, chiefly, largely, overall, usually 08 above all, commonly 09 generally, in general, in the main 10 by and large, especially, on the whole 11 principally 13 predominantly

• **in part**
◇ *hidden indicator*
04 half 06 parcel, partim, partly 08 slightly, somewhat 10 up to a point 12 to some degree, to some extent

• **in the part of**
02 as

• **odd parts**
◇ *hidden alternately indicator*

• **on the part of**
02 by 08 caused by 10 on behalf of 12 carried out by 13 from the side of

• **part of**
◇ *hidden indicator*

• **part with**
04 drop 05 forgo, yield 06 forego, give up 07 abandon, discard, let go of 08 jettison, renounce 09 surrender 10 relinquish

• **principal part**
04 lead, main, mass

• **take part in**
◇ *hidden indicator*
05 opt in 06 join in 07 go in for, partake, share in 08 assist in, engage in, help with 11 play a part in, play a role in 12 be involved in, contribute to 13 participate in

partake
05 enter, share 06 engage, inform 07 indulge 08 take part 10 be involved 11 participate

• **partake of**
03 eat 04 have, show, take 05 drink, evoke, share, taste 06 evince 07 consume, receive, suggest, undergo 08 manifest 11 demonstrate

partial
04 half, part 06 biased, in part, unfair, unjust 07 ex parte, limited 08 affected, coloured, one-sided, partisan, twilight 09 component, imperfect 10 incomplete, prejudiced, restricted, unfinished 11 fragmentary, inequitable, predisposed, subordinate 12 preferential 14 discriminatory

• **partial to**
06 fond of, keen on, liking, loving 08 mad about 09 taken with 10 crazy about

partiality
04 bias, love 05 favor 06 favour, liking 07 respect 08 fondness, inequity 09 injustice, prejudice 10 preference, proclivity, unfairness 11 inclination 12 partisanship, predilection 14 discrimination, predisposition 15 inequitableness

partially
05 slack 06 in part, partly 08 halflins, not fully, somewhat 09 halflings 12 fractionally, incompletely

participant
05 party 06 helper, member, sharer, worker 07 entrant, partner, sharing 09 associate 10 competitor, contestant, co-operator 11 contributor, shareholder 12 participator

participate
◇ *insertion indicator*
04 be in, help 05 enter, opt in, share 06 assist, be in it, engage, join in, muck in 07 partake 08 take part 09 co-operate, play a part, play a role 10 be involved, contribute 12 be associated

participation
04 part 07 sharing 09 mucking in, partaking 10 assistance 11 association, co-operation, involvement, partnership 12 contribution

particle
03 bit, jot, tad 04 atom, corn, curn, drop, iota, mite, spot, whit 05 crumb, grain, piece, scrap, shred, spark, speck, stime, styme, touch, trace 06 morsel, prefix, sliver, suffix, tittle 07 globule, granule, smidgen 08 fragment, molecule, ribosome 09 inclusion 11 conjunction 12 interjection

Particles include:

01 W, X, Z
03 ion, psi
04 kaon, muon, pion
05 anion, boson, gluon, meson, omega, quark, sigma
06 baryon, cation, hadron, kation, lambda, lepton, parton, photon, proton
07 neutron, nucleon, upsilon
08 electron, neutrino, positron, thermion
09 carbanion, gravitron, tau lepton
10 anti-proton, gauge boson, zwitterion
11 anti-neutron
12 anti-neutrino

parti-coloured
06 motley 07 piebald 10 variegated 11 polychromic 13 polychromatic, versicoloured

particular
04 fact, item 05 exact, faddy, fussy, picky, point 06 choosy, detail, marked 07 certain, feature, finicky, minutia, notable, precise, respect, several, special, unusual 08 accurate, definite, detailed, distinct, especial, exacting, faithful, peculiar, specific, thorough, uncommon 09 favourite, selective 10 fastidious, individual, meticulous, noteworthy, pernickety, remarkable 11 exceptional, outstanding, painstaking, persnickety 12 circumstance 14 discriminating

• **in particular**
07 exactly 08 in detail 09 in special, precisely, severally 10 especially, in especial 12 individually, particularly, specifically, to be specific

particularity
04 fact, item 05 point, quirk, trait 06 detail 07 feature 08 instance, property 10 uniqueness 11 peculiarity, singularity 12 circumstance, idiosyncrasy 13 individuality 14 characteristic 15 distinctiveness

particularize
06 detail 07 itemize, specify 09 enumerate, stipulate 11 individuate 13 individualize

particularly
07 notably 08 markedly 09 expressly, severally, unusually 10 distinctly, especially, explicitly, intimately, remarkably, uncommonly

12 individually, in particular, specifically, surprisingly **13** exceptionally **15** extraordinarily

parting
◇ *insertion indicator*
04 last, rift, shed **05** adieu, dying, final, going, leave, split **06** depart **07** closing, divorce, goodbye, leaving, rupture **08** breaking, division, farewell **09** departing, departure, partition, partitive **10** breaking-up, concluding, divergence, separation **11** leave-taking, valediction, valedictory **12** disseverance, disseverment **13** disseveration

See also **farewell**

partisan
03 fan **06** backer, biased, unfair, unjust, votary **07** devotee, partial **08** adherent, champion, disciple, follower, henchman, loyalist, one-sided, party man, queenite, sidesman, stalwart, upholder **09** factional, guerrilla, irregular, sectarian, supporter **10** henchwoman, prejudiced **11** henchperson, imperialist, inequitable, out-and-outer, predisposed **14** discriminatory, freedom fighter

partisanship
04 bias **08** interest, partyism **09** prejudice **10** partiality **12** factionalism, sectarianism

partition
03 bar **04** wall, with **05** panel, score, sever, share, shoji, withe **06** divide, hallan, parpen, replum, screen, septum, tabula, travis, trevis **07** barrier, break up, break-up, cloison, divider, eardrum, grating, parpane, parpend, parpent, parting, perpend, perpent, split up, treviss, wall off **08** brattice, brattish, brettice, divide up, division, fence off, parpoint, separate, traverse **09** dashboard, diaphragm, parcel out, screen off, segregate, separator, severance, splitting, subdivide **10** rood screen, separation **11** dissepiment, false bottom, room-divider, segregation, separate off, subdivision **12** dividing wall **14** dividing screen

partly
04 half, semi- **06** in part, parcel **07** a little **08** slightly, somewhat, to a point **09** partially **10** moderately, relatively, up to a point **12** fractionally, incompletely, to some degree, to some extent **13** in some measure

partner
03 man, pal, SOP **04** ally, lady, mate, oppo, pair, pard, wife **05** butty, catch, rival, woman **06** fiancé, friend, helper, lumber, sharer, spouse **07** comrade, consort, fiancée, husband, kept man, pardner **08** cavalier, copemate, co-worker, sidekick, teammate, yoke-mate **09** associate, boyfriend, cohabitee, colleague, companion, copesmate, kept woman, other half **10** accomplice, better half, co-operator, girlfriend, yoke-fellow **11** confederate, live-in lover **12** bit on the side, collaborator **13** common-law wife **14** opposite number

• **former partner**
02 ex

• **partners**
02 EW, NS

partnership
04 firm **05** stand, union **06** cahoot **07** company, consort, sharing, society **08** alliance **09** symbiosis, syndicate **10** fellowship, fraternity **11** affiliation, association, brotherhood, combination, co-operation, co-operative, corporation **12** conglomerate **13** collaboration, confederation, participation

partridge
05 quail **06** chikor, chukar, chukor **07** chikhor, flapper, tinamou **08** paitrick, percolin

part-song
04 glee

party
03 jol **04** band, body, camp, crew, fest, gang, rage, rort, rout, sect, side, team, unit **05** binge, cabal, go out, group, posse, quest, squad **06** league, parted, person, thrash **07** carouse, company, divided, faction, have fun, large it **08** alliance, function, grouping, litigant, live it up, party-goer **09** celebrate, defendant, festivity, gathering, have a ball, plaintiff, whoop it up **10** contingent, detachment, have a party, individual **11** affiliation, association, celebration, combination, get-together, have it large, throw a party **13** enjoy yourself, go on the razzle **14** go out on the town, push the boat out, put the flags out **15** paint the town red

Parties include:

02 do
03 hen, tea
04 bash, drum, foam, luau, orgy, rave, stag, toga, wine, wrap
05 beano, disco, hangi, house
06 at-home, beer-up, bottle, dinner, drinks, garden, grog-on, grog-up, hooley, Kneipe, picnic, pyjama, rave-up, shivoo, social, soirée, supper
07 blow-out, ceilidh, cookout, knees-up, leaving, new year, potluck, reunion, shindig, slumber
08 barbecue, birthday, bunfight, clambake, cocktail, farewell, tea fight, wingding
09 acid-house, beanfeast, Christmas, Hallowe'en, hootnanny, reception, sleepover, welcoming
10 baby shower, fancy dress, hootenanny, whist drive
11 cookie-shine, discotheque, flat-warming, muffin-fight, muffin-worry
12 bridal shower, house-warming
13 cheese and wine, coffee klatsch, fête champêtre, small-and-early

Political parties in the UK include:

01 L
03 BNP, Con, DUP, Lab, Lib, PUP, SNP
04 SDLP, Tory, Whig
05 Green
06 Labour
07 Liberal
08 Alliance, Sinn Féin
09 Communist
10 Democratic, Plaid Cymru, Republican, UK Unionist
11 Co-operative
12 Conservative
13 National Front, Parliamentary
14 UK Independence, Ulster Unionist
15 British National, Liberal Democrat

Political parties worldwide include:

02 AN, FN, PP
03 ALP, CDU, NDP, NPD, RPR
05 Green, Labor
06 Labour
07 Worker's
08 Batasuna, Democrat, Fine Gael, National, Sinn Féin
09 One Nation, Socialist
10 Fianna Fáil, Republican
12 Workers' Party
13 Bloc Québécois, Front National, National Front
14 Partido Popular

• **be a party to**
09 know about **12** be involved in

• **dancing party**
03 hop

party-goer
09 socialite

parvenu
07 climber, new rich, upstart **09** arriviste, pretender, vulgarian **12** nouveau riche **13** social climber

pascal
02 Pa

pasha
03 dey **06** bashaw

pass
02 go, OK **03** col, die, gap, hit, lap, nek, ren, rin, run, say, sit, tip, way **04** beat, chit, drag, emit, fill, flow, ghat, give, go by, hand, jark, kick, live, lose, make, move, okay, omit, pace, path, play, slap, turn, visa **05** adopt, allow, botte, cross, drive, enact, event, expel, ghaut, gorge, halse, hause, hawse, issue, lunge, notch, occur, outdo, poort, punto, reach, route, serve, sling, speak, spend, stand, state, swing, throw, use up, utter, voice **06** accept, assert, become, befall, be left, canyon, chalan, change, chitty, decree, defile, devote, elapse, employ, esteem, evolve, exceed, go over, go past, happen, let out, occupy, parade, permit, puncto, ratify, ravine, slip by, take up, thrust, ticket, travel **07** advance, agree to, approve, be given, challan, declare, deliver, develop, excrete, express, fade out, get over, licence, passage,

proceed, qualify, release, run past, succeed, surpass, undergo, vote for, warrant **08** advances, announce, approach, be willed, currency, go across, go beyond, graduate, outstrip, overhaul, overtake, overture, passport, proclaim, progress, sanction, slip away, transfer, transmit, traverse, validate **09** authorize, be endowed, be granted, circulate, come about, condition, disappear, discharge, disregard, drive past, get across, go through, pronounce, take place, transpire, while away **10** adjudicate, be made over, experience, fulfilment, get through, permission, protection, reputation, suggestion **11** be consigned, be inherited, go unnoticed, leave behind, make your way, outdistance, predicament, proposition, pull ahead of, sail through **12** be bequeathed, be handed down, consummation **13** authorization, be transferred, breeze through, draw level with, laissez-passer, scrape through **14** be successful in, identification, let someone have

See also **mountain pass** under **mountain**

• pass as, pass for
10 appear to be, be taken for **12** be regarded as **13** be mistaken for

• pass away
02 go **03** die **04** vade **05** forgo **06** elapse, expire, forego, pass on, peg out, pop off **07** decease **08** blow over **13** kick the bucket **14** depart this life, give up the ghost **15** breathe your last

• pass degree
04 poll

• pass off
04 fake **05** feign, go off, occur **06** happen, vanish **07** die down, palm off, put over, wear off **08** fade away, wear away **09** disappear, take place **11** counterfeit **12** misrepresent

• pass out
03 die **04** dole, drop **05** allot, faint, swoon **07** deal out, dole out, give out, hand out **08** allocate, black out, collapse, flake out, keel over, share out, spark out **10** distribute

• pass over
02 go **03** die **04** balk, miss, omit, skim **05** baulk, leave **06** forget, ignore, overgo, voyage **07** neglect **08** look over, overjump, overlook, overpass, override, overskip **09** disregard **14** take no notice of, turn a deaf ear to **15** turn a blind eye to

• pass quickly
03 fly, hie, ren, rin, run

• pass the ball to
04 feed

• pass up
04 miss **06** ignore, refuse, reject **07** let slip, neglect **08** renounce

passable
02 OK **04** fair, open, so-so **05** clear **06** decent **07** average **08** adequate, all right, mediocre, moderate, ordinary, pervious **09** allowable, navigable, tolerable, unblocked **10** acceptable, not much cop **11** practicable, presentable, respectable, traversable **12** run of the mill, satisfactory, unobstructed **13** no great shakes, unexceptional

passably
05 quite **06** fairly, rather **08** somewhat **09** tolerably **10** moderately, reasonably, relatively **13** after a fashion, indifferently

passage
03 cut, gap, gut, way **04** adit, coda, duct, exit, fare, flow, gate, hall, lane, lick, loan, main, neck, pace, pass, path, pend, pore, road, slap, text, tour, trek, trip **05** aisle, alley, alure, break, canal, chute, creep, cundy, entry, flume, fogou, gully, lapse, lento, lobby, locus, piano, piece, route, shaft, shoot, shute, sound, track, verse, vista **06** access, avenue, burrow, change, clause, condie, course, dromos, furrow, groove, gullet, gutter, legato, narrow, presto, screed, strait, street, throat, trance, transe, travel, trough, tunnel, voyage **07** advance, archway, cadenza, channel, conduit, doorway, episode, excerpt, extract, fistula, gallery, hallway, journey, offtake, opening, orifice, passing, prelude, running, sea lane, section, snicket, stretto, traffic, turning **08** adoption, alleyway, approval, citation, corridor, crossing, division, entrance, incident, longueur, movement, mutation, pericope, progress, ritenuto, sanction, southing, spiccato, staccato, straight, streight, thorough, transfer, waterway **09** admission, breezeway, enactment, migration, paragraph, quotation, ventiduct, vestibule **10** acceptance, occurrence, passageway, pianissimo, ritardando, scherzando, transition, tremolando, validation **11** development, safe conduct, watercourse **12** deambulatory, ratification, thoroughfare, transmission **13** authorization, metamorphosis

Passages include:

04 Mona
05 Drake, Gaspé, Umnak
06 Akutan, Amukta, Burias, Caicos, Colvos, Mompog, Seguam, Unimak
07 Oronsay, Palawan
08 Amchitka, Dominica, Fenimore, Mouchoir, Saratoga, Windward
09 Deception, Mayaguana, St Vincent
10 Backstairs, Guadeloupe, Martinique, Mira Por Vos, Silver Bank
11 Turks Island, Verde Island
13 Crooked Island
14 Jacques Cartier

passageway
03 way **04** exit, hall, lane, path, port **05** aisle, alley, lobby, track **06** arcade, runway **07** gangway, hallway, passage **08** corridor, entrance **11** back passage

passé
03 out **05** dated, faded **06** démodé, groovy, old hat, past it **07** outworn **08** obsolete, outdated, outmoded **09** out-of-date **10** antiquated **11** on the way out, past its best **12** old-fashioned **13** unfashionable

passenger
04 fare **05** drone, rider **07** outside, shirker, voyager **08** commuter, hanger-on **09** fare-payer, traveller **10** freeloader, hitchhiker **11** strap-hanger

• turn away passenger
04 bump

passer-by
06 gawper **07** witness **08** looker-on, observer, onlooker **09** bystander, spectator **10** eyewitness, rubberneck

passing
03 end **04** flow, loss, very **05** brief, death, hasty, march, quick, rapid, short **06** casual, course, demise, elapse, finish, slight **07** advance, cursory, decease, diadrom, passage, quietus, shallow **08** fleeting, movement **09** departure, ephemeral, momentary, perishing, temporary, transient **10** evanescent, expiration, incidental, short-lived **11** exceedingly, passing away, superficial, termination **12** transitional

• in passing
07 by the by **08** by the bye, by the way **09** en passant **12** incidentally **15** parenthetically

passion
03 fit, wax **04** fire, fury, heat, love, lust, pash, rage, zeal, zest **05** anger, brame, craze, mania, wrath **06** ardour, dander, desire, spirit, temper, warmth **07** avidity, craving, emotion, feeling, fervour, tantrum **08** fondness, keenness, outburst **09** adoration, affection, altitudes, eagerness, explosion, intensity, obsession, vehemence **10** enthusiasm, fanaticism **11** fascination, indignation, infatuation **12** sexual desire

• burst of passion
04 gust

passionate
03 hot, mad **04** avid, keen, nuts, sexy, warm, wild **05** crazy, eager, fiery, gutsy, horny, Latin, potty, randy **06** ardent, erotic, fervid, fierce, loving, stormy, strong, sultry, torrid, wilful **07** aroused, excited, fervent, intense, lustful, sensual, violent, zealous **08** choleric, frenzied, inflamed, turned on, vehement **09** emotional, excitable, fanatical, hotheaded, impetuous, impulsive, irritable, obstinate **10** headstrong, hot-blooded, self-willed **11** impassioned, tempestuous, warm-blooded **12** affectionate, enthusiastic **13** quick-tempered, waspish-headed

passionately
05 hotly **06** keenly **08** ardently, fiercely, lovingly, strongly **09** con

calore, fervently, intensely, lustfully, sensually, violently, zealously
10 erotically **11** fanatically
14 affectionately

passionless
03 icy **04** calm, cold **06** frigid, frosty **07** callous, neutral **08** detached, uncaring, unloving **09** apathetic, impartial, impassive, unfeeling, withdrawn **10** insensible, restrained, uninvolved **11** cold-blooded, cold-hearted, emotionless, indifferent, unemotional **12** unresponsive
13 dispassionate

passive
05 aloof, inert **06** docile, remote, supine **07** distant, patient, subdued, unmoved **08** detached, inactive, lifeless, resigned, yielding
09 apathetic, compliant, lethargic, receptive, suffering **10** effortless, non-violent, submissive, uninvolved
11 emotionless, indifferent, unassertive, unemotional, unresisting
13 dispassionate, long-suffering
14 unenterprising

passively
09 patiently **10** lifelessly
12 submissively **13** emotionlessly, unassertively

passport
02 ID **03** key, way **04** door, pass, path, visa **05** entry, route **06** avenue, papers, permit **07** doorway **09** admission
12 identity card **13** authorization, laissez-passer, means of access
15 travel documents

password
03 key **04** word **06** parole, signal
07 tessera **09** watchword **10** open sesame, shibboleth **11** countersign

past
02 by, pa, pt **03** ago, ygo **04** done, gone, last, late, life, near, over, ygoe, yore **05** after, agone, early, ended, forby, olden, round, since **06** behind, beside, beyond, bygone, by-past, former, gone by, latter, no more, recent, record **07** ancient, defunct, elapsed, extinct, history, long ago, one-time, worn-out **08** finished, foregone, overworn, preterit, previous, sometime **09** antiquity, completed, erstwhile, foregoing, forgotten, olden days, preceding, preterite, too old for, yesterday **10** background, bygone days, days gone by, days of yore, experience, olden times **11** bygone times, former times, good old days, track record **12** too mature for **15** over and done with

pasta

Pasta types include:

04 orza, ziti
05 penne, ruoti
06 anelli, ditali, noodle, trofie
07 fusilli, gnocchi, lasagna, lasagne, lumache, mafalde, maruzze, mezzani, noodles, pennine, ravioli
08 bucatini, farfalle, fedelini, linguini, macaroni, rigatoni, stelline
09 agnolotti, angel hair, casarecci, crescioni, fiochetti, manicotti, spaghetti
10 angel's hair, bombolotti, cannelloni, conchiglie, farfalline, fettuccine, strangozzi, tagliarini, taglierini, tortellini, vermicelli
11 cappelletti, pappardelle, tagliatelle
12 lasagne verde
13 elbow macaroni

paste
03 fix, gum, pap **04** glue, miso, mush, pack, pâté, pulp **05** blend, purée, putty, stick **06** cement, cerate, fasten, mastic, slurry, spread, thrash **07** mixture
08 adhesive

pastel
04 pale, soft, woad **05** chalk, faint, light, muted, quiet **06** crayon, low-key, sketch, subtle **07** drawing, subdued
08 delicate, discreet, pastille, soft-hued, vignette **11** sauce-crayon
13 light-coloured

pastiche
◇ *anagram indicator*
03 mix **04** olio **06** jumble, medley
07 farrago, melange, mixture, variety
08 mishmash, mixed bag **09** confusion, pasticcio, patchwork, potpourri
10 assortment, collection, hodgepodge, hotchpotch, miscellany, salmagundi
11 gallimaufry, olla-podrida, smorgasbord **14** conglomeration, omnium-gatherum

pastille
05 sweet **06** jujube, pastel, tablet, troche **07** lozenge **09** cough drop
10 confection, cough sweet

pastime
03 fun **04** game, play **05** hobby, sport
08 activity, pastance **09** amusement, avocation, diversion **10** abridgment, recreation, relaxation, suppliance
11 abridgement, distraction
12 Zeitvertreib **13** entertainment
14 leisure pursuit **15** leisure activity
See also **hobby**

past master
02 PM **03** ace **05** adept **06** artist, expert, wizard **07** dab hand, old hand
08 virtuoso **10** proficient

pastor
01 P **05** canon, vicar **06** cleric, deacon, divine, parson, priest, rector
08 minister, shepherd **09** churchman, clergyman **10** prebendary
12 ecclesiastic

pastoral
03 oat **04** idyl **05** idyll, rural **06** rustic, simple **07** bucolic, country, crosier, crozier, eclogue, idyllic **08** agrarian, Arcadian, clerical, priestly, serenata
09 bucolical, siciliano **11** ministerial, Theocritean **12** agricultural
14 ecclesiastical

pastry

Pastry types include:

04 filo, flan, puff
05 choux, flaky, plain, short, sweet
06 cheese, Danish
07 pork-pie
08 one-stage, piecrust
09 rough-puff, suetcrust
10 pâte brisée, pâte frolle, pâte sablée, pâte sucrée, shortcrust, wholewheat
12 biscuit-crumb, pâte à savarin
13 American crust, hot-water crust
14 rich shortcrust

See also **cake**

pasture
03 alp, lay, lea, lee, ley, tie, tye **04** feed, fell, food, gang, mead, raik, rake, soum, sowm, walk **05** downs, field, grass, graze, lease, leaze, range **06** leasow, meadow, saeter **07** feeding, grazing, leasowe, paddock **08** mountain, shealing, shieling **09** grassland, pasturage, sheepwalk **11** grazing land
• **pasture grass**
04 bent **05** grama **06** fescue
07 timothy **08** paspalum, rye grass
09 bent grass **10** grama grass
12 meadow fescue, sheep's fescue, timothy grass **13** dog's-tail grass, Flinders grass

pasty
03 wan **04** pale, waxy **06** doughy, pallid, sallow, sickly **07** anaemic
08 empanada **09** unhealthy **10** pasty-faced **11** oyster-patty

pat
03 dab, pet, pot, tap **04** ball, burp, clap, easy, glib, lump, mass, slap, tick
05 bepat, chunk, print, ready, slick, touch **06** caress, facile, fluent, fondle, patter, simple, smooth, stroke
07 exactly **08** coquille, fluently
09 perfectly, precisely **10** flawlessly, simplistic **11** faultlessly, word-for-word
• **pat someone on the back**
06 praise **10** compliment
12 congratulate **13** say well done to

patch
03 bed, fix, lot, sew **04** area, mend, plot, snip, spot, term, time, zona
05 botch, cloth, clout, cover, phase, piece, scrap, spell, tract **06** parcel, period, plaque, pocket, repair, shield, stitch **07** stretch **08** covering, dressing, fragment, material **09** reinforce
10 protection

patchwork
04 hash **06** jumble, medley, motley
07 farrago, mixture **08** mishmash, pastiche **10** assortment, hotchpotch
11 gallimaufry

patchy
◇ *anagram indicator*
05 bitty **06** fitful, random, spotty, uneven **07** blotchy, erratic, macular, sketchy, varying **08** variable

09 centonate, irregular 10 incomplete 11 incongruous 12 inconsistent, inharmonious

patent
03 pat 04 open 05 clear, overt, plain, right 07 blatant, charter, evident, glaring, licence, obvious, visible 08 apparent, flagrant, manifest, palpable 09 copyright, expanding, ingenious, invention, privilege, spreading 10 undeniable 11 certificate, conspicuous, self-evident, transparent, unequivocal 12 crystal clear, unmistakable 13 unmistakeable 15 clear as daylight

patently
06 openly 07 clearly, plainly, visibly 08 palpably 09 blatantly, glaringly, obviously 10 manifestly 12 unmistakably 13 conspicuously, unequivocally, unmistakeably

paternal
08 fatherly, vigilant 09 concerned 10 benevolent, fatherlike, protective

path
02 go 03 pad, sty, way 04 berm, gate, lane, road, trod, walk, went 05 allée, orbit, route, track, trail, troad, trode 06 avenue, course, troade 07 circuit, highway, passage, pathway, slidder, towpath, walkway 08 approach, cycleway, footpath 09 bridleway, direction, footsteps 10 bridle-road, forthright

pathetic
◇ *anagram indicator*
03 sad 04 poor 05 sorry 06 dismal, feeble, meagre, moving, tender, woeful 07 pitiful, useless 08 derisory, pitiable, poignant, touching, wretched 09 affecting, miserable, plaintive, worthless 10 deplorable, inadequate, lamentable 11 distressing 12 contemptible, heart-rending 13 heartbreaking 14 unsatisfactory

pathetically
05 sadly 08 dismally, pitiably, woefully 09 miserably, pitifully 10 deplorably, lamentably, wretchedly 12 contemptibly, inadequately

pathological
07 chronic 08 addicted, habitual, hardened 09 confirmed, dependent, obsessive 10 compulsive, inveterate, persistent

pathos
06 misery 07 sadness, tragedy 08 sob stuff 09 poignancy 10 inadequacy 11 pitifulness 12 pitiableness 13 plaintiveness

patience
04 cool 07 bistort 08 calmness, Klondike, Klondyke, serenity, stoicism, tenacity 09 composure, diligence, endurance, fortitude, restraint, solitaire, tolerance 10 doggedness, equanimity, submission, sufferance 11 forbearance, persistence, resignation, self-control 12 monk's rhubarb, perseverance, stickability, tranquillity 13 long-suffering 14 inexcitability, unflappability

patient
04 calm, case, cool, kind, mild 06 client, extern, serene, tender 07 externe, invalid, lenient, stoical, subject 08 ambulant, composed, enduring, laid-back, resigned, resolute, sufferer, tolerant 09 easy-going, forgiving, indulgent, leisurely, unhurried 10 forbearant, forbearing, out-patient, persistent, restrained, submissive 11 persevering, susceptible, unflappable 12 even-tempered, patient as Job 13 accommodating, imperturbable, long-suffering, philosophical, self-possessed, uncomplaining, understanding 14 hanging in there, self-controlled

• **be patient**
04 bear

• **hospital patients**
04 ward

patiently
06 calmly, kindly, mildly 08 tenderly 09 leisurely 10 enduringly, resolutely, tolerantly 11 unflappably, unhurriedly 12 persistently 13 considerately, perseveringly

patois
04 cant 05 argot, Gumbo, lingo, slang 06 Creole, jargon, patter 07 dialect 08 Guernsey 10 vernacular 11 local speech 12 lingua franca 13 local parlance

patriarch
04 pope, sire 05 abuna, elder 06 father 07 founder 09 greybeard 10 Catholicos 11 grandfather, grand old man 13 paterfamilias

Patriarchs include:

04 Levi, Noah
05 Aaron, Abram, Enoch, Isaac, Jacob
06 Joseph
07 Abraham, Ishmael
10 Methuselah, Theophilus

patrician
03 nob 04 peer 05 noble 06 gentle, lordly, patron 07 grandee 08 high-born, nobleman, well-born 09 gentleman, high-class 10 aristocrat, upper-crust 11 blue-blooded 12 aristocratic, thoroughbred

patrimony
05 share 06 estate, legacy 07 bequest, portion, revenue 08 heritage, property 10 birthright 11 inheritance, possessions

patriot
05 jingo 08 jingoist, loyalist 09 flag-waver 10 chauvinist 11 nationalist

patriotic
05 loyal 08 loyalist 10 flag-waving, jingoistic 11 nationalist 12 chauvinistic 13 nationalistic

patriotism
07 loyalty 08 jingoism 10 chauvinism, flag-waving 11 nationalism

patrol
04 beat, tour 05 guard, round, vigil, watch 06 defend, picket, piquet, police, sentry 07 defence, inspect, monitor, picquet, protect 08 defender, policing, sentinel, sentry-go, watchman 09 milk train, patrolman 10 patrolling, protection 11 be on the beat, do the rounds, go the rounds, keep guard on, keep watch on, patrolwoman, perambulate 12 surveillance 13 keep watch over, make the rounds, night-watchman, perambulation, police officer, security guard 14 make your rounds

patron
05 angel, buyer, stoop, stoup, Venus 06 Apollo, backer, client, fautor, friend, helper, Hermes 07 pattern, regular, shopper, sponsor 08 advocate, champion, customer, defender, guardian, Maecenas, promoter, upholder 09 protector, purchaser, supporter 10 benefactor, frequenter, subscriber 11 sympathizer 12 benefactress 13 guardian angel 14 fairy godmother, philanthropist

patronage
05 aegis, trade 06 buying, custom 07 backing, funding, support 08 auspices, business, commerce, shopping 09 promotion 10 protection, purchasing 11 countenance, sponsorship 12 financial aid, subscription 13 encouragement, financial help

patronize
03 aid 04 back, fund, help 05 scorn 06 assist, foster, shop at 07 buy from, despise, finance, promote, protect, sponsor, support 08 champion, deal with, empatron, frequent, maintain 09 disparage, encourage 10 look down on, talk down to 12 be a regular at

patronizing
05 lofty 06 snooty 07 haughty, stuck up 08 scornful, snobbish, stooping, superior 10 disdainful, high-handed 11 overbearing, toffee-nosed 12 contemptuous, supercilious 13 condescending, high-and-mighty 14 holier-than-thou 15 on your high horse

patter
03 pat, rap, tap, yak 04 beat, drum, line, pelt, trip 05 lingo, pitch, pound, spiel 06 bicker, gabble, gammon, jabber, jargon, pit-pat, scurry, verbal 07 beating, chatter, pitapat, scuttle, tapping, verbals 08 pitty-pat 09 monologue, pattering 12 pitter-patter

pattern
03 key 04 copy, form, mold, norm, plan, trim, type 05 guide, ideal, match, model, motif, mould, order, shape,

style, whirl **06** design, device, dicing, figure, follow, method, sample, stripe, swatch, system **07** emulate, example, fashion, Gestalt, grecque, imitate, stencil, tracery **08** decorate, Greek key, markings, original, ornament, parallel, standard, template **09** blueprint, criterion, influence, prototype, scantling **10** craquelure, decoration **11** arrangement, instruction **13** ornamentation

patterned
05 moiré **07** figured, printed, watered **09** decorated **10** ornamented

paucity
04 lack, want **06** dearth, rarity **07** fewness, poverty **08** scarcity, shortage, sparsity **09** smallness **10** deficiency, meagreness, paltriness, scantiness, slightness, sparseness **11** slenderness **12** exiguousness **13** insufficiency

paunch
03 gut, pod **04** kite, kyte **05** belly, rumen, tripe **07** abdomen, beer gut **08** pot-belly **09** beer belly **10** eviscerate, fat stomach **11** corporation

paunchy
03 fat **05** podgy, pudgy, tubby **06** portly, rotund **07** adipose **08** stomachy **09** corpulent **10** pot-bellied

pauper
06 beggar **07** have-not **08** bankrupt, indigent **09** insolvent, mendicant **10** down-and-out **11** church mouse

pause
03 gap **04** halt, hold, kick, lull, rest, stay, stop, wait **05** break, cease, close, delay, demur, dwell, let up, let-up, limma **06** cesura, desist **07** adjourn, breathe, caesura, fermata, respite, sit down, time out **08** break off, breather, dieresis, hesitate, hold back, interval, stoppage, take five **09** cessation, diaeresis, interlude, interrupt, take a rest **10** hesitation, take a break **11** discontinue, freeze-frame **12** intermission, interruption **13** take a breather **14** breathing space

pave
03 tar **04** flag, tile **05** cover, floor, pitch **06** cobble, tarmac **07** asphalt, surface **08** concrete **10** macadamize, tessellate **11** cobblestone
• **pave the way for**
08 lead up to **09** introduce, take steps **10** prepare for **11** get ready for **12** make ready for, take measures **14** clear the ground

pavement
03 bed, way **04** path **05** floor **07** footway, walkway **08** causeway, flagging, footpath, platform, sidewalk, trottoir **11** plainstanes, plainstones

pavilion
04 flag, tent **05** kiosk **06** canopy, ensign, houdah, howdah **09** belvedere **14** jingling Johnny

paving-block
03 set **04** sett

paw
03 pad, pah, pud **04** foot, foul, hand, maul, poke **05** mouse, puddy, touch **06** molest, stroke **07** obscene, touch up **08** forefoot **09** manhandle, mishandle

pawn
01 P **03** dip, pan, pop, toy **04** dupe, fine, hock, paan, pown, tool **05** betel, powin, spout, stake **06** impawn, lumber, pledge, puppet, stooge, wadset **07** cat's paw, deposit, gallery, peacock, wadsett **08** mortgage **09** pignerate, pignorate, plaything **10** instrument **11** impignorate, oppignerate, oppignorate **13** lay in lavender

pawnbroker
05 uncle **06** lender, sheeny, usurer **07** pop-shop **08** lumberer, pawnshop **10** gombeen-man **11** money-lender, mont-de-piété **12** monte di pietà

pay
02 do **03** fee **04** ante, bung, foot, give, make, pony, sold **05** atone, grant, offer, remit, repay, solde, spend, wages, yield **06** afford, answer, ante up, bestow, defray, expend, extend, income, invest, lay out, net pay, outlay, pay off, pay out, profit, rake in, refund, return, reward, salary, settle, square, suffer, supply **07** benefit, bring in, cough up, fork out, imburse, pay back, payment, produce, proffer, stipend, stump up **08** disburse, earnings, gross pay, hand over, settle up, shell out **09** discharge, indemnify, reimburse **10** be punished, commission, compensate, emoluments, honorarium, make amends, recompense, remunerate **11** foot the bill, take-home pay **12** compensation, pick up the tab, remuneration, satisfaction **13** meet the cost of, reimbursement **14** be beneficial to, be worthwhile to, let someone have
• **pay back**
05 repay **06** pay off, punish, refund, return, settle, square **08** give back **09** reimburse, retaliate **10** recompense **11** get even with, reciprocate, take revenge **13** counter-attack **14** get your own back
• **pay for**
04 take **05** atone, escot, prize, pryse **06** suffer **09** answer for **10** compensate, cost dearly, make amends **12** count the cost, face the music **13** be punished for **14** count the cost of, get your deserts, pay a penalty for, pay the price for
• **pay off**
03 fix **04** fire, meet, sack, work **05** bribe, clear, repay **06** buy off, grease, honour, lay off, settle, square, suborn **07** dismiss, requite, succeed **08** amortize **09** discharge, pay in full **10** extinguish, get results, take care of **12** be successful **13** make redundant
• **pay out**
04 veer **05** remit, spend **06** ante up, expend, lay out **07** cough up, dispend, fork out **08** disburse, hand over, part with, shell out

payable
03 due **04** owed **05** owing **06** mature, unpaid **08** to be paid **09** in arrears **10** profitable **11** outstanding **13** contributable

payload
04 haul, load **05** cargo, goods **06** lading **07** baggage, freight, tonnage **08** contents, shipment **11** consignment, merchandise

payment
03 fee, pay, sub **04** ante, dole, fare, farm, hire, mail, rent, scot, shot, toll, wage **05** arles, modus **06** amount, hansel, outlay, payola, reward **07** advance, annuity, deposit, expense, handsel, pension, premium, primage **08** danegeld, danegelt, donation, soul-scat, soul-scot, soul-shot **09** allowance, clearance, discharge **10** instalment, prestation, punishment, quarterage, recompense, remittance, settlement **12** compensation, contribution, remuneration, satisfaction **13** consideration
• **demand payment**
03 dun

pay-off
03 fee, pay **05** bribe, wages **06** crunch, income, net pay, result, reward, salary, upshot **07** benefit, outcome, payment, stipend **08** earnings, gross pay **09** advantage, hush money, punchline, slush fund, sweetener **10** allurement, back-hander, commission, dénouement, emoluments, enticement, honorarium, inducement, recompense, settlement **11** consequence, take-home pay **12** compensation, remuneration **13** moment of truth, reimbursement **15** protection money

PC *see* **police officer**

pea
03 dal **04** daal, dahl, dhal **05** dholl, pease **06** legume **08** kaka beak, kaka bill **09** chickling, mangetout, marrowfat, parrot-jaw, rounceval **10** parrot-beak, parrot-bill **14** chickling vetch

peace
03 pax **04** calm, ease, hush, pact, rest **05** amity, frith, olive, quiet, still, truce **06** accord, repose, shalom, treaty **07** concord, harmony, silence **08** calmness, goodwill, serenity **09** agreement, armistice, ceasefire, composure, placidity, quietness, stillness **10** friendship, relaxation **11** contentment, law and order, non-violence, peace treaty, restfulness

12 amicableness, conciliation, peacefulness, tranquillity 13 non-aggression

peaceable
04 mild 05 douce 06 dovish, gentle, irenic, placid 07 cordial, pacific 08 amicable, friendly 09 easy-going, unwarlike 10 harmonious, non-violent 11 good-natured, inoffensive, peace-loving 12 conciliatory, even-tempered 13 non-aggressive

peaceably
06 gently, mildly 08 amicably, placidly 09 cordially 11 pacifically 12 harmoniously 13 inoffensively

peaceful
04 calm 05 quiet, still 06 gentle, irenic, placid, serene, sleepy 07 halcyon, pacific, restful 08 amicable, friendly, in repose, relaxing, tranquil 09 peaceable, reposeful, unruffled 10 harmonious, untroubled 11 undisturbed

peacefully
06 calmly, gently 07 quietly 08 amicably, placidly, serenely, sleepily 09 restfully 12 harmoniously

peacemaker
04 dove 06 broker 08 appeaser, mediator, pacifier, pacifist, revolver 09 make-peace 10 arbitrator 11 conciliator, intercessor, pacificator, peace-monger

peacemaking
06 irenic 07 pacific 09 appeasing, mediating, mediative, mediatory 11 mediatorial 12 conciliatory, pacification

peach
03 dob 06 accuse, betray, inform 07 sing out, whittle 08 quandang, quandong, quantong 09 melocoton, nectarine, victorine 10 melicotton, melocotoon 11 malakatoone

peacock
03 pea 04 Pavo, pawn, pown 05 powin 06 paiock, pajock, pavone 07 paiocke, pajocke

peak
02 pk 03 ben, nib, pin, tip, top 04 apex, hill, mope, peag, rise 05 crest, crise, crown, droop, mount, pique, point, prick, spike, spire, visor, vizor 06 apogee, climax, height, summer, summit, zenith 07 maximum 08 aiguille, high noon, mountain, pinnacle 09 culminate, elevation, high point 11 come to a head, culmination

peaky
03 ill, wan 04 pale, sick 05 dicky, seedy 06 crummy, pallid, poorly, queasy, sickly, unwell 09 off-colour, washed-out 10 out of sorts 15 under the weather

peal
04 boom, clap, howl, ring, roar, roll, toll 05 chime, clang, crash, knell 06 firing, grilse, rumble, triple 07 resound, ringing, ring out 08 carillon, resonate 10 resounding 11 reverberate 13 reverberation

peanut
05 arnut 06 goober 07 arachis 08 earth-nut, earth-pea 09 goober pea, groundnut, monkey nut

pear
04 tuna 05 nashi, nelis, nopal 06 Colmar, comice, nelies, pepino, seckel, seckle, warden 07 avocado, poperin 08 aguacate, bergamot, blanquet, muscadel, muscatel 09 Indian fig, poppering 10 Conference, jargonelle 11 bon chrétien, queez-maddam 12 cuisse-madame

pearl
04 purl, Unio 05 nacre, union 06 barock, orient 07 barocco, baroque, granule, paragon 10 granulated

• **string of pearls**
04 rope

peasant
03 oaf 04 boor, hick, kern, lout, rude, ryot 05 churl, kerne, kisan, kulak, mujik, rural, swain, yokel 06 carlot, cottar, cotter, fellah, jungli, moujik, muzhik, raiyat, rustic 07 bumpkin, Cossack 09 campesino, contadina, contadino 10 blue-bonnet, clodhopper, provincial 13 country person 14 country bumpkin

pebble
04 chip, pelt, pumy, rock 05 agate, chuck, pumie, stone 06 gallet 07 chuckie 09 pumy stone 10 dreikanter, pumie stone 12 chuckie-stane, chuckie-stone

peccadillo
04 boob, slip 05 error, fault, lapse 06 slip-up 07 misdeed 10 infraction 11 delinquency 12 indiscretion, minor offence, misdemeanour

peck
02 pk 03 dab, hit, jab, job, nip, rap, tap 04 bite, food, jerk, kiss, pick 05 pitch, prick 06 pickle, strike

peculiar
◇ *anagram indicator*
03 ill, odd, own 04 sick 05 dizzy, droll, ferly, funny, queer, weird 06 exotic, poorly, proper, quaint, queasy, unique, unwell, way-out 07 bizarre, curious, oddball, offbeat, special, strange, unusual 08 abnormal, distinct, freakish, personal, singular, specific 09 eccentric, grotesque, preserved 10 individual, outlandish, out of sorts, particular, remarkable 11 distinctive, exceptional 12 appropriated 13 extraordinary, idiosyncratic 14 characteristic, distinguishing, unconventional 15 individualistic, under the weather

• **peculiar to**
04 like 08 unique to 09 typical of 11 belonging to 12 indicative of 13 in keeping with

peculiarity
04 mark 05 quirk, trait 06 foible, jimjam, oddity 07 feature, quality 08 hallmark, property 09 attribute, exception, mannerism, weirdness 10 shibboleth 11 abnormality, bizarreness, singularity 12 eccentricity, idiosyncrasy 13 individuality, particularity 14 characteristic 15 distinctiveness

peculiarly
◇ *anagram indicator*
05 oddly 08 quaintly, uniquely 09 bizarrely, curiously, strangely, unusually 10 distinctly, remarkably, singularly 12 particularly 13 distinctively, exceptionally 15 extraordinarily

pecuniary
06 fiscal 07 nummary 08 monetary 09 financial, nummulary 10 commercial

pedagogic
08 academic, didactic, teaching 09 tuitional 10 scholastic 11 educational 13 instructional

pedagogue
03 don 05 teach 06 master, pedant 07 dominie, teacher 08 educator, mistress 09 dogmatist, preceptor 10 instructor 12 educationist, schoolmaster 13 schoolteacher 14 educationalist, schoolmistress

pedagogy
07 tuition 08 teaching, training, tutelage 09 didactics 10 pedagogics 11 instruction

pedal
01 P

pedant
06 purist 07 academe, casuist, egghead 08 academic, highbrow, quibbler 09 dogmatist, Dryasdust, formalist, nit-picker, pedagogue, precisian 10 literalist, scholastic, schoolmarm 11 doctrinaire, pettifogger 12 hair-splitter, intellectual, precisionist, schoolmaster 13 perfectionist

pedantic
04 blue 05 exact, fussy, heavy 06 purist, stuffy 07 bookish, erudite, finical, inkhorn, pompous, precise, stilted 08 academic 09 formalist, quibbling 10 literalist, meticulous, nit-picking, particular, scholastic, scrupulous 11 pretentious, punctilious, sesquipedal 12 intellectual 13 hair-splitting, perfectionist, schoolmarmish 14 schoolmasterly, sesquipedalian

pedantry
09 cavilling, dogmatism, exactness, pedantism, pomposity, quibbling 10 finicality, nit-picking, pedagogism, stuffiness 11 bookishness 12 academicness 13 hair-splitting

14 meticulousness **15** intellectualism, pedagoguishness, pretentiousness, punctiliousness

peddle
◇ *anagram indicator*
04 flog, hawk, push, sell, tout, vend **05** trade **06** market, smouch, trifle **07** traffic **08** huckster **12** offer for sale **14** present for sale

pedestal
04 base, dado, foot **05** basis, stand, trunk **06** column, pillar, plinth, podium **07** acroter, support **08** mounting, platform **09** axle-guard, stylobate **10** acroterion, acroterium, foundation **11** pillow-block

• **put on a pedestal**
05 exalt **06** admire, revere **07** adulate, idolize **08** look up to **11** hero-worship

pedestrian
03 ped **04** dull, flat **05** banal, hiker **06** boring, hicker, stodgy, turgid, walker **07** humdrum, mundane, prosaic **08** mediocre, ordinary, plodding **09** jaywalker **10** unexciting, uninspired, voetganger **11** commonplace, indifferent, not up to much, peripatetic **12** matter-of-fact, run-of-the-mill **13** foot-traveller, no great shakes, unimaginative

pedigree
03 set **04** line, race, tree **05** blood, breed, stirp, stock **06** family, series, stemma, stirps, strain **07** descent, lineage **08** ancestry, breeding, pure-bred **09** genealogy, parentage, phylogeny **10** derivation, extraction, family tree, succession **11** full-blooded **12** aristocratic, phylogenesis, thoroughbred **13** line of descent

pediment
07 frontal, fronton **08** frontoon **09** fastigium **12** frontispiece

pedlar
06 bodger, cadger, hawker, jagger, pedder, pether, seller, smouch, smouse, vendor, walker, yagger **07** camelot, chapman, packman, smouser **08** huckster **09** boxwallah, cheap-jack, gutter-man, itinerant **10** colporteur **12** street-trader **14** gutter-merchant

pee
01 P
See also **urinate**

peek
03 spy **04** look, peep, peer **05** blink, dekko, squiz **06** gander, glance, shufti, squint **07** glimpse, look-see **11** have a gander **12** have a look-see

peel
◇ *ends deletion indicator*
04 bark, pale, pare, peal, pill, rind, skin, zest **05** flake, scale, shell, shuck, stake, strip **06** grilse, remove, shovel **07** epicarp, exocarp, peeling, pillage, plunder, take off, undress **08** flake off **10** desquamate, integument **11** decorticate

• **keep your eyes peeled**
07 be alert, monitor, observe **12** watch closely **15** keep a lookout for

peep
03 cry, eye, pip, pry, spy **04** cook, keek, kook, look, peek, peer, pink, pipe, slit, toot, word **05** blink, cheep, chirp, dekko, issue, noise, sound, speck, tweet **06** appear, emerge, gander, glance, shufti, squeak, squint, warble **07** chatter, chirrup, glimpse, look-see, twitter **09** quick look, utterance

peephole
04 hole, slit **05** chink, cleft, crack, slink **07** crevice, eyehole, fissure, keyhole, opening, pinhole, spyhole **08** aperture **09** Judas hole **10** interstice **11** Judas window

peer
03 pry, spy **04** dick, duke, earl, gaze, lady, like, look, lord, peep, pink, scan, toot **05** baron, count, equal, match, noble, snoop, stime, styme, trier, tweer, twire **06** appear, fellow, squint, squiny **07** compeer, examine, inspect, Law Lord, marquis, peeress, squinny **08** confrère, marquess, nobleman, protrude, viscount **09** patrician **10** antagonist, aristocrat, equivalent, scrutinize **11** counterpart **12** backwoodsman
See also **nobility**

peerage
07 Debrett, red book **08** nobility **09** top drawer **10** upper crust **11** aristocracy **14** lords and ladies

peeress
04 dame, lady **05** noble **07** duchess **08** baroness, countess **10** aristocrat, noblewoman **11** marchioness, viscountess

peerless
06 unique **07** supreme **09** excellent, matchless, nonpareil, paramount, unmatched **10** incompared, unbeatable, unequalled, unexcelled, unrivalled **11** outstanding, superlative, unsurpassed **12** incomparable, second to none, unparalleled, without equal **13** beyond compare

peeve
03 bug, irk, vex **04** gall, rile **05** annoy **06** grouse, hassle, wind up **07** hack off, tick off **08** brass off, irritate **09** aggravate, cheese off, drive nuts, grievance **10** drive crazy, exasperate **12** drive bananas **13** make sparks fly **14** drive up the wall

peeved
04 sore **05** irked, riled, upset, vexed **06** bugged, galled, miffed, narked, piqued, put out, shirty **07** annoyed, hassled, in a huff, nettled, stroppy **08** in a paddy **09** irritated, ticked off **10** brassed off, cheesed off, driven nuts, got the hump **11** driven crazy, exasperated

peevish
03 ill **04** sour **05** cross, moody, ratty, sulky, surly, testy **06** crusty, franzy, girnie, grumpy, hipped, snappy, sullen, tetchy, touchy **07** crabbed, foolish, frabbit, frampal, fretful, grouchy, nattery, pettish, wayward **08** captious, churlish, frampold, nattered, perverse, petulant **09** crotchety, fractious, irritable, querulous, splenetic, vexatious **10** capernoity, in a bad mood **11** capernoitie, cappernoity, complaining, ill-tempered, out of temper **12** cantankerous **13** short-tempered

peevishly
07 crossly **08** grumpily, sullenly **09** fretfully, irritably **10** churlishly, in a bad mood, petulantly **11** fractiously

peevishness
03 dod, pet **05** pique **08** acrimony, fretting **09** curstness, ill-temper, petulance, testiness **10** perversity, protervity **12** captiousness, irritability **13** querulousness

peg
03 fix, key, leg, nog, pin, set, tap **04** brad, hook, join, knag, knob, mark, nail, plug, poke, post, step **05** dowel, limit, perch, piton, score, screw, spike, stake, theme, thole, throw **06** attach, degree, fasten, freeze, hatpeg, marker, picket, piquet, secure, spigot, target, thrust **07** control, picquet, tent pin **08** cheville, hold down, thole pin **09** soft spile, stabilize, tuning pin

• **peg away**
06 hang in **07** persist **08** keep at it, plug away, work away, work hard **09** persevere, plod along, stick at it **10** beaver away **13** apply yourself

• **take down a peg or two, bring down a peg or two**
06 humble **09** humiliate **13** cut down to size **15** bring down to size

pejorative
03 bad **08** negative **09** slighting **10** belittling, derogatory, unpleasant **11** deprecatory, disparaging **12** depreciating, unflattering **15** uncomplimentary

pellet
04 ball, drop, pill, shot, slug **05** prill **06** bullet **07** capsule, granule, lozenge **08** pithball **09** coprolite, paintball

pell-mell
◇ *anagram indicator*
06 rashly **07** hastily **08** disorder, headlong **09** hurriedly, posthaste **10** at full tilt, confusedly, feverishly, heedlessly, recklessly, vehemently **11** hurry-scurry, impetuously **13** helter-skelter, precipitously **14** indiscriminate

pellucid
04 pure **05** clear **06** bright, glassy, limpid **10** diaphanous **11** translucent, transparent

pelt
03 fur, hit, ren, rin, run, zip **04** beat,

belt, blow, clod, coat, dash, fell, hide, hurl, pour, race, rush, skin, tear, teem **05** hurry, scoot, speed, stone, throw **06** assail, attack, batter, bucket, career, charge, fleece, pebble, pellet, pelter, pepper, shower, sprint, squail, strike **07** bombard **08** bearskin, bepepper, coonskin, downpour, lapidate, squirrel, wolfskin **10** bucket down **15** rain cats and dogs

pen
◇ *containment indicator*
03 Bic®, cub, dam, mew, nib, sty
04 Biro®, cage, coop, fold, J-pen, note, reed, shut, stie, stye, weir **05** crawl, cruve, draft, fence, hedge, hem in, hutch, kraal, penne, pound, quill, stall, write **06** author, corral, croove, cruive, estate, shut up **07** compose, confine, dash off, enclose, felt pen, felt-tip, gladius, jot down, rastrum, writing **08** compound, note down, scribble, take down **09** ballpoint, enclosure, marker pen, sheepfold, write down **10** felt-tip pen, plantation, Rollerball®, self-filler, stylograph **11** fountain pen, highlighter, Magic Marker® **12** ballpoint pen, penitentiary
See also **author**

penal
08 punitive **10** corrective, vindictive
11 retaliatory, retributive
12 disciplinary, penitentiary

penalize
04 fine **06** punish **07** correct, forfeit
08 chastise, handicap, sanction
09 castigate **10** discipline
12 disadvantage

penal servitude
03 lag **04** bird, time **07** katorga, stretch
08 porridge **10** hard labour

penalty
04 fine, pain, snag **05** minus, mulct
06 amende **07** forfeit **08** downside, drawback, handicap, sentence
09 weak point **10** punishment
11 castigation, retribution
12 chastisement, demerit point, disadvantage
• **pay penalty**
03 aby **04** abye

penance
06 shrift **07** penalty **08** hardship
09 atonement, expiation, penitence
10 punishment, reparation, repentance
13 mortification, self-abasement
14 self-punishment

penchant
04 bent, bias **05** taste **06** foible, liking
07 leaning **08** affinity, fondness, soft spot, tendency, weakness
09 proneness **10** partiality, preference, proclivity, propensity **11** disposition, inclination **12** predilection
14 predisposition

pencil
03 cam **04** calm, caum **05** stump
06 crayon **09** keelivine, keelyvine, tortillon **10** Chinagraph®

pendant
03 bob **04** drop, tika, tiki **05** cross
06 locket, luster, lustre **07** eardrop, earring, heitiki, necklet, pennant, sautoir **08** appendix, necklace, pear drop **09** girandola, girandole, lavaliere, medallion **10** lavallière, Rouen cross, stalactite

pendent
06 nutant **07** hanging, pensile
08 dangling, drooping, swinging
09 pendulous, suspended
11 overhanging

pending
02 to **04** near, till **05** until, while
06 before, coming, during, whilst
07 hanging, nearing **08** awaiting, imminent, so long as **09** impending, uncertain, undecided, unsettled
10 throughout, unresolved, up in the air **11** approaching, forthcoming, in the offing **12** in the balance

pendulous
06 droopy **07** hanging, pendent, sagging, swaying **08** dangling, drooping, swinging **09** suspended
11 overhanging

penetrable
04 open **05** clear **06** porous
08 passable, pervious **09** permeable
10 accessible, explicable, fathomable
12 intelligible **14** comprehensible, understandable

penetrate
◇ *insertion indicator*
03 cut, see **04** bite, bore, fill, seep, sink, stab, twig **05** crack, enter, grasp, imbue, prick, probe, sease, shear, spike
06 fathom, indent, invade, needle, pierce, rain in, sink in, strike **07** get into, make out, pervade, suffuse, suss out, work out **08** cotton on, permeate, perviate, puncture, register, saturate
09 perforate **10** comprehend, infiltrate, understand **11** make your way

penetrating
◇ *insertion indicator*
04 deep, hard, keen, loud, wise
05 acute, clear, sharp **06** biting, shrewd, shrill **07** cutting, in-depth, ingoing, intrant, probing **08** carrying, incisive, invasive, piercing, poignant, profound, stinging, strident
09 observant, searching **10** discerning, insightful, perceptive **14** discriminating

penetration
◇ *insertion indicator*
03 wit **05** entry **06** acumen, fathom, inroad **07** insight **08** entrance, incision, invasion, keenness, piercing, pricking, stabbing **09** acuteness, pervasion, sharpness **10** astuteness, perception, permeation, puncturing, shrewdness
11 discernment, perforation
12 infiltration, perspicacity

penguin
05 diver **06** gentoo, korora **07** pinguin
08 macaroni **10** rockhopper, Spheniscus **11** king penguin **12** fairy penguin **13** little penguin **14** emperor penguin

peninsula
03 Pen **04** cape, doab, mull **05** point
06 tongue **10** chersonese

Peninsulas include:

04 Ards, Cape, Eyre, Gyda, Huon, Kola
05 Gaspé, Gower, Italy, Lleyn, Malay, Otago, Qatar, Sinai
06 Alaska, Avalon, Azuero, Balkan, Carnac, Crimea, Iberia, Istria, Jaffna, Korean, Recife, Seward, Taymyr, Wirral
07 Alaskan, Arabian, Cape Cod, Chukchi, Florida, Furness, Iberian, Jiulong, Jutland, Kintyre, Kowloon, Olympic, Yucatàn
08 Apsheron, Cape York, Cotentin, Musandam, Pinellas, Sorrento, Yorktown
09 Cape Verde, Gallipoli, Kamchatka, Paraguana, Peary Land
10 Arnhem Land, Graham Land, Isle of Dogs, Nova Scotia
11 Peloponnese
12 Scandinavian
14 Baja California, Isle of Portland
15 Rinns of Galloway

See also **cape**

penitence
05 shame **06** regret, sorrow
07 remorse **10** contrition, repentance, ruefulness **11** compunction **12** self-reproach

penitent
05 sorry **06** humble, rueful
07 ashamed, mourner **08** contrite
09 regretful, repentant, sorrowful
10 apologetic, remorseful, shamefaced

pen-name
06 anonym **07** allonym **09** false name, pseudonym, stage-name **10** nom de plume **11** assumed name, nom de guerre

pennant
04 flag, jack **06** banner, burgee, ensign, guidon, pennon **07** colours, pendant, pendent **08** banderol, gonfalon, standard, streamer

penniless
04 bust, poor **05** broke, skint, stony
06 ruined **07** boracic **08** bankrupt, dirt-poor, indigent **09** destitute
10 cleaned out, down and out, on the rocks, stone-broke, stony-broke
11 impecunious **12** impoverished, on your uppers **14** on the breadline, on your beam-ends **15** poverty-stricken, strapped for cash

Pennsylvania
02 PA

penny
01 d, p **03** win **04** cent, wing, winn
08 denarius, sterling

penny-pincher
05 miser **06** meanie **07** niggard,

Scrooge **09** skinflint **10** cheapskate **11** cheeseparer **12** money-grubber

penny-pinching
04 mean **05** close, mingy, tight **06** frugal, stingy **07** miserly **09** niggardly, scrimping **10** ungenerous **11** tight-fisted **12** cheeseparing, parsimonious

pension
04 SIPP **05** board **06** corody, income **07** annuity, benefit, corrody, support, welfare **09** allowance **11** deferred pay **12** state pension **13** old-age pension **14** company pension, superannuation **15** personal pension

pensioner
03 OAP **07** boarder **09** dependant **12** out-pensioner **13** retired person, senior citizen **15** gentleman-at-arms, old-age pensioner

pensive
05 sober **06** dreamy, musing, solemn **07** serious, wistful **08** absorbed, thinking **09** pondering **10** cogitative, meditative, melancholy, reflective, ruminative, thoughtful **11** preoccupied **12** absent-minded **13** contemplative, lackadaisical

pensively
08 dreamily **09** seriously, wistfully **12** meditatively, thoughtfully **14** absent-mindedly **15** contemplatively

Pentateuch
05 Torah

penthouse
03 cat **04** pent

pent-up
06 curbed, held in **07** bridled, stifled **09** bottled-up, inhibited, repressed **10** restrained, suppressed

penurious
04 bust, mean, poor **05** close, mingy, tight **06** hard up, scanty, stingy **07** lacking, miserly **08** beggarly, grudging, indigent **09** destitute, flat broke, niggardly, penniless **10** inadequate, ungenerous **11** close-fisted, close-handed, impecunious, tight-fisted **12** cheeseparing, impoverished, on your uppers, parsimonious **14** on your beam-ends **15** poverty-stricken

penury
04 lack, need, want **06** dearth **07** beggary, poverty, straits **09** indigence, mendicity, pauperism **10** deficiency, insolvency **11** destitution **14** impoverishment

people
03 men, mob **04** clan, folk, gens, land, race **05** folks, laity, ngati, plebs, tribe, tuath **06** family, hordes, humans, masses, nation, occupy, proles, public, rabble, settle, voters **07** inhabit, mankind, mortals, parents, persons, punters, society **08** citizens, colonize, humanity, populace, populate, riff-raff, servants, subjects **09** community, employees, followers, hoi polloi, humankind, relations, relatives, retainers **10** attendants, electorate, kith and kin, population **11** ethnic group, human beings, individuals, inhabitants, rank and file **12** congregation, the human race **13** general public, great unwashed

Peoples include:

03 Han, Ibo, Jat, Kru, Mam, Mon, San, Tiv, Twi
04 Ainu, Cham, Efik, Goth, Hutu, Igbo, Jute, Kroo, Lett, Moor, Motu, Nair, Nupe, Roma, Saba, Shan, Sulu, Susu, Tshi, Zulu
05 Bajau, Bantu, Hausa, Iceni, Inuit, Karen, Khmer, Maori, Masai, Nayar, Nguni, Oriya, Saxon, Swazi, Taino, Tamil, Temne, Tonga, Tutsi, Vedda, Wolof, Yakut, Yupik
06 Angles, Aymara, Griqua, Gurkha, Herero, Innuit, Kabyle, Kalmyk, Kikuyu, Manchu, Nyanja, Ostiak, Ostyak, Sherpa, Tswana, Tungus, Yoruba, Zyrian
07 Barotse, Basotho, Calmuck, Cossack, Goorkha, Hittite, Kalmuck, Manchoo, Maratha, Pashtun, Quechua, Quichua, Samoyed, Swahili, Tagálog, Walloon
08 Khoikhoi, Mahratta, Polabian, Yanomami
09 Himyarite, Ostrogoth, Ruthenian, Sinhalese, Tocharian, Tokharian

pep
02 go **03** zip **04** life, zing **05** oomph, verve **06** energy, ginger, spirit, vigour **07** pizzazz, sparkle **08** dynamism, vitality **10** ebullience, exuberance, get-up-and-go, liveliness **11** high spirits **13** effervescence

• **pep up**
06 excite **07** animate, improve, inspire, liven up, quicken **08** energize, vitalize **09** stimulate **10** exhilarate, invigorate

pepper
03 dot **04** bomb, pelt, stud **05** blitz, Piper, strew **06** assail, attack, shower **07** bombard, scatter, spatter **08** sprinkle **09** bespatter

Pepper and peppercorns include:

03 ava, red
04 bird, kava, pink
05 black, chile, chili, green, sweet, white
06 cherry, chilli, yellow
07 cayenne, Jamaica, paprika, pimento
08 allspice, capsicum, habañero, jalapeño, pimiento, piquillo
12 Scotch bonnet

peppermint
06 humbug **07** pan drop **08** bull's-eye

peppery
03 hot **05** fiery, sharp, spicy, testy **06** biting, grumpy, touchy **07** caustic, piquant, pungent, waspish **08** choleric, incisive, seasoned, snappish, stinging **09** irascible, irritable, sarcastic, trenchant **10** astringent **11** hot-tempered **13** quick-tempered

peppy
04 spry **05** agile, alert, alive, brisk, quick **06** active, lively, nimble **07** dynamic **08** animated, spirited, vigorous **09** energetic, sprightly, vivacious **12** enthusiastic, high-spirited

per
01 a **02** by, pr **07** through

perceive
03 see **04** espy, feel, hear, know, note, spot, twig, view, wind **05** grasp, learn, sense, smell, taste **06** behold, deduce, detect, gather, notice, remark, survey **07** believe, discern, glimpse, make out, observe, realize, suppose **08** conclude, discover, subitize **09** apprehend, be aware of, get wind of, recognize, undertake **10** appreciate, comprehend, understand **11** distinguish **12** catch sight of **13** be cognizant of

perceptible
05 clear, plain **06** patent **07** evident, obvious, tactile, visible **08** apparent, distinct, manifest, palpable, sensible, tangible **10** detectable, noticeable, observable **11** appreciable, conspicuous, discernible, perceivable **15** distinguishable

perception
04 idea, view **05** grasp, sense, taste **06** vision **07** feeling, insight, percept **09** awareness, knowledge **10** cognizance, conception, experience, impression **11** discernment, observation, recognition, sensitivity **12** appreciation, apprehension **13** consciousness, light of nature, understanding **14** discrimination, interpretation, responsiveness

• **fine perception**
04 tact

perceptive
04 deep, keen **05** acute, alert, aware, quick, sharp **06** astute, shrewd **08** delicate **09** observant, sensitive, sharp-eyed **10** discerning, insightful, percipient, responsive **11** penetrating, quick-witted **13** perspicacious, understanding **14** discriminating

perceptively
06 keenly **07** sharply **08** astutely **11** observantly, sensitively **12** insightfully **15** perspicaciously

perch
03 bar, lug, rod, sit **04** bass, land, perk, pole, rest, rood, ruff **05** basse, gaper, Perca, roost, ruffe **06** alight, anabas, comber, darter, fogash, sander, sauger, settle, zander, zingel **07** balance, kahawai, walleye **09** blackfish, overperch, stone bass, wreckfish **12** walleyed pike

perchance
05 maybe **07** percase, perhaps **08** feasibly, possibly **11** conceivably

percipience
07 insight **08** sagacity **09** acuteness, alertness, awareness, intuition, judgement **10** astuteness, perception **11** discernment, penetration, sensitivity **12** perspicacity **13** understanding

percipient
05 alert, alive, aware, sharp **06** astute **07** knowing **09** judicious, observant, wide-awake **10** discerning, perceptive **11** intelligent, penetrating, quick-witted **13** perspicacious **14** discriminating

percolate
03 sop **04** drip, leak, ooze, perk, seep, sift **05** drain, leach, sieve **06** filter, strain **07** pervade **08** filtrate, permeate **09** penetrate **11** pass through **13** spread through **14** trickle through

perdition
04 doom, hell, loss, ruin **08** downfall, hellfire **09** confusion, damnation, ruination **11** destruction **12** annihilation, condemnation

peregrination
04 tour, trek, trip **06** roving, travel, voyage **07** journey, odyssey, roaming **08** trekking **09** excursion, wandering, wayfaring **10** expedition, pilgrimage, travelling **11** exploration **13** globetrotting

peremptory
04 curt **05** bossy, final, utter **06** abrupt, lordly **07** summary **08** absolute, dogmatic **09** arbitrary, assertive, imperious **10** autocratic, commanding, high-handed, imperative, tyrannical **11** dictatorial, domineering, irrefutable, overbearing **13** authoritative

perennial
07 abiding, endless, eternal, lasting, undying **08** constant, enduring, immortal, unending **09** ceaseless, continual, incessant, permanent, perpetual, unceasing, unfailing **10** persistent, unchanging **11** everlasting, never-ending **12** imperishable **13** uninterrupted

perfect
04 full, mint, perf, pure, true **05** exact, ideal, model, prize, right, sheer, total, utter **06** better, entire, expert, finish, fulfil, mature, polish, refine, superb, triple **07** certain, correct, improve, precise, sinless, skilful **08** absolute, accurate, complete, copybook, faithful, finished, flawless, peerless, spotless, textbook, thorough, ultimate, unmarred **09** blameless, completed, convinced, downright, elaborate, excellent, exemplary, faultless, matchless, out-and-out, wonderful **10** consummate, immaculate, impeccable, just the job, to the nines **11** experienced, superlative, unblemished **12** accomplished, incomparable

perfection
04 acme, best **05** bloom, crown, ideal, model, prime **06** flower **07** paragon **08** maturity, pinnacle, ripeness, ultimate **09** polishing **10** betterment, completion, excellence, refinement **11** improvement, ne plus ultra, point-device, point-devise, realization, roundedness, superiority **12** consummation, flawlessness **13** faultlessness, impeccability, one in a million **14** immaculateness

perfectionism
06 purism **08** idealism, pedantry **09** formalism **10** Utopianism

perfectionist
06 pedant, purist **08** idealist, stickler **09** formalist, Free-lover **12** precisionist

perfectly
04 very **05** fully, quite **06** à point, wholly **07** down pat, exactly, ideally, totally, utterly **08** entirely, superbly **09** correctly **10** absolutely, altogether, completely, flawlessly, impeccably, like a charm, thoroughly **11** faultlessly, wonderfully **12** consummately, immaculately, to perfection **14** without blemish

perfidious
05 false, Punic **07** corrupt **08** disloyal, two-faced **09** deceitful, dishonest, faithless **10** traitorous, treasonous, unfaithful **11** double-faced, duplicitous, treacherous **13** double-dealing, Machiavellian, untrustworthy

perfidy
06 deceit **07** falsity, treason **08** betrayal **09** duplicity, treachery **10** disloyalty, infidelity **13** double-dealing, faithlessness **14** perfidiousness, traitorousness

perforate
04 bore, gore, hole, stab, tear **05** burst, drill, prick, punch, spike, split **06** pierce **07** rupture **08** puncture, trephine **09** penetrate **11** make holes in

perforated
05 bored, holed **06** porous **07** drilled, ethmoid, pierced, punched **09** fenestral, punctured **10** cribriform, fenestrate, fenestrial, foraminous **11** fenestrated

perforation
04 bore, hole **05** prick **06** pierce **07** foramen **08** fenestra, puncture **10** dotted line **12** fenestration

perforce
10 inevitably, willy-nilly **11** necessarily, of necessity, unavoidably

perform
◇ *anagram indicator*
02 do, go **03** act, cut, run **04** make, play, sing, take, work **05** dance, enact, put on, stage, throw **06** behave, effect, fulfil, recite, render **07** achieve, conduct, execute, operate, portray, present, produce, pull off, satisfy **08** appear as, atchieve, bring off, carry out, complete, despatch, dispatch, function, make good, transact **09** discharge, implement, represent **10** accomplish, bring about **12** give effect to

performance
03 act **04** deed, duet, play, show, solo, spot, trio **05** doing, going, house **06** acting, action, acture, ballet, try-out **07** account, benefit, concert, conduct, recital, running, showing, working **08** hierurgy, première, set piece **09** behaviour, discharge, effecting, execution, happening, operation, portrayal, prolusion, rendering, rendition **10** appearance, completion, conducting, fulfilling, fulfilment, last hurrah, peroration, production **11** achievement, carrying-out, functioning, presentment, tour de force **12** presentation **14** accomplishment, implementation, interpretation, representation

performer
04 doer, hand, moke, star, turn **05** actor, clown, comic **06** artist, author, dancer, player, singer **07** actress, artiste, old hand, ripieno, trouper **08** achiever, comedian, executor, Fancy Dan, film star, musician, operator, star turn, Thespian, topliner **09** ecdysiast, executant **10** rope-walker **11** entertainer **12** improvisator, vaudevillean, vaudevillian **15** jerry-come-tumble

performers
04 cast

perfume
04 balm, musk, otto, sent **05** aroma, attar, odour, ottar, scent, smell **06** chypre **07** bouquet, cologne, essence, incense **08** fumigate, opopanax **09** aromatize, fragrance, redolence, sweetness **10** frangipane, frangipani, heliotrope, Jockey Club **11** millefleurs, toilet water **12** eau-de-cologne **13** eau-de-toilette, lavender water

perfunctorily
07 quickly **09** cursorily, hurriedly **10** carelessly **13** inattentively, superficially

perfunctory
05 brief, quick **06** wooden **07** cursory, hurried, offhand, routine **08** careless, heedless, slipshod, slovenly **09** automatic, desultory, negligent **10** mechanical **11** inattentive, indifferent, superficial

perhaps
◇ *anagram indicator*
03 say **05** haply, maybe **06** ablins, belike, happen, mayhap **07** aiblins, could be, happily, percase, yibbles **08** feasibly, possibly **09** perchance **11** conceivably **12** peradventure, you never know

peril
04 risk **06** danger, hazard, menace, threat **07** apperil **08** apperill, distress, jeopardy **10** insecurity **11** uncertainty **12** endangerment

perilous
04 dire **05** dicey, dodgy, hairy, risky **06** chancy, unsafe, unsure **07** exposed, parlous, perlous **08** high-risk, insecure, menacing **09** dangerous, hazardous **10** precarious, vulnerable **11** threatening

perimeter
04 edge **05** limit **06** border, bounds, fringe, limits, margin **07** circuit **08** boundary, confines, frontier **09** periphery **11** outer limits **13** circumference

period
03 age, end, eon, era, per **04** aeon, date, span, spin, stop, term, time, turn **05** class, cycle, epoch, phase, point, shift, space, spell, stage, stint, while, years **06** finish, lesson, menses, season **07** lecture, seminar, session, stretch **08** duration, full stop, interval, semester, the curse, tutorial **09** full point, monthlies **10** conclusion, end of story, generation **11** instruction **12** menstruation **13** menstrual flow **14** menstrual cycle, time of the month

See also **geological**; **historical**; **time**

periodic
05 round **06** cyclic **07** regular **08** cyclical, repeated, seasonal, sporadic **09** recurrent, recurring **10** infrequent, occasional, periodical **12** intermittent, once in a while

periodical
03 mag **05** organ **06** review, weekly **07** etesian, journal, monthly, regular **08** bi-weekly, bulletin, magazine **09** pictorial, quarterly, thunderer, tri-weekly **11** illustrated, publication, semi-monthly **12** trade journal

See also **newspaper**

periodically
07 at times **08** off and on, on and off **09** sometimes **10** now and then, on occasion **11** at intervals, irregularly, now and again **12** every so often, infrequently, occasionally, once in a while, sporadically **14** from time to time, intermittently **15** every now and then

peripatetic
06 mobile, roving **07** migrant, nomadic, roaming, vagrant **08** ambulant, vagabond **09** itinerant, migratory, traveling, wandering **10** ambulatory, journeying, pedestrian, travelling **12** Aristotelian

peripheral
05 add-on, input, minor, outer **06** lesser, output **07** storage, surface **08** computer, marginal, outlying **09** ancillary, auxiliary, disk drive, outermost, secondary, sidelined **10** additional, borderline, incidental, irrelevant, subsidiary, tangential **11** superficial, surrounding, unimportant, unnecessary **14** beside the point, graphics tablet

periphery
03 hem, rim **04** brim, edge **05** ambit, brink, skirt, verge **06** border, fringe, margin **07** circuit **08** boundary **09** outskirts, perimeter **12** outer regions **13** circumference

periphrastic
07 oblique **08** indirect, rambling, tortuous **09** wandering **10** circuitous, discursive, roundabout **12** long-drawn-out **14** circumlocutory

perish
02 go **03** die, rot **04** cark, exit, fail, fall, pass, ruin, tine, tyne, vade **05** choke, croak, decay, drown, go off, quell, swelt **06** depart, expire, famish, go bung, go west, pass on, peg out, pip out, pop off, starve, sterve, vanish **07** crumble, decease, destroy, die away, fall off, forfair, kick off, kiss off, snuff it, succumb **08** collapse, flatline, pass away, spark out **09** decompose, disappear, go belly up, have had it **10** hop the twig **11** bite the dust, come to an end **12** disintegrate, lose your life, pop your clogs, slip the cable **13** close your eyes, kick the bucket, meet your maker, push up daisies **14** depart this life, give up the ghost, turn up your toes **15** breathe your last, cash in your chips

perishable
10 short-lived **12** decomposable, destructible **13** biodegradable

periwinkle
05 vinca **06** winkle **08** Apocynum, dog-whelk **11** pennywinkle **12** strophanthus

perjure
• **perjure yourself**
03 lie **12** lie under oath **13** commit perjury

perjury
09 false oath, mendacity **11** crimen falsi, forswearing **12** false witness, hard swearing, oath-breaking **13** false evidence, false swearing, falsification **14** false statement, false testimony, lying under oath

perk
03 tip **04** plus **05** bonus, brisk, extra, perch **07** benefit, freebie **08** dividend, gratuity **09** advantage, baksheesh, percolate **10** percolator, perquisite **13** fringe benefit **15** golden handshake
• **perk up**
05 pep up, rally **06** buck up, cock up, look up, revive **07** cheer up, improve, liven up, recover **08** brighten **09** take heart **10** brighten up, make lively, revitalize **12** become lively

perky
03 gay **04** pert **05** cocky, peppy, sunny **06** bouncy, bright, bubbly, cheery, gallus, jaunty, lively **07** buoyant, gallows **08** animated, cheerful, spirited **09** ebullient, sprightly, vivacious **12** effervescent

permanence
09 constancy, endurance, fixedness, stability **10** durability, perpetuity **11** persistence **13** steadfastness **15** imperishability

permanent
04 firm **05** fixed, pakka, pucka, pukka, solid **06** stable **07** abiding, durable, eternal, lasting, regular, stative **08** constant, enduring, lifelong, standing, unfading **09** immutable, indelible, perennial, perpetual, steadfast **10** invariable, unchanging **11** established, everlasting, long-lasting **12** imperishable, unchangeable **14** indestructible

permanently
06 always **07** for ever, for good **08** ever more, for keeps **09** endlessly, eternally, indelibly **10** constantly, for all time, unendingly **11** ceaselessly, continually, incessantly, perpetually, unceasingly **12** in perpetuity, till doomsday **13** everlastingly, for good and all, once and for all, unremittingly **14** for ever and ever **15** till kingdom come

permeable
06 porous, spongy **08** passable, pervious **09** absorbent, poromeric **10** absorptive, penetrable

permeate
04 fill **05** imbue **06** leaven **07** diffuse, pervade, suffuse **08** saturate **09** penetrate, percolate **10** impregnate, infiltrate **11** impenetrate, pass through, seep through, soak through, transpierce **13** filter through, spread through

permissible
02 OK **05** legal, legit **06** kosher, lawful, proper, venial **07** allowed **08** all right **09** allowable, permitted, tolerable **10** acceptable, admissible, authorized, legitimate, sanctioned

permission
03 out **04** loan, pass **05** congé, exeat, leave, power **06** access, assent, congee, permit, placet, square **07** consent, freedom, go-ahead, liberty, licence, license, mandate, warrant **08** approval, pratique, sanction, thumbs-up, wayleave **09** admission, agreement, allowance, authority, clearance **10** green light, imprimatur **11** approbation, bill of sight, congé d'élire, permittance **12** dispensation **13** authorization **14** leave of absence, permis de séjour

permissive
03 lax **04** free **07** lenient, liberal **08** optional, tolerant **09** easy-going, indulgent, permitted **10** forbearing **11** broad-minded **13** overindulgent **14** latitudinarian

permit
03 let **04** give, pass, visa **05** admit, agree, allow, grant, smoke **06** carnet, docket, enable, suffer, ticket **07** consent, docquet, empower, indulge, licence, license, placard, warrant **08** intromit, passport, sanction, tolerate **09** authorize, green card **10** permission **11** safe-conduct **12** give the nod to **13** authorization, laissez-passer **14** permis de séjour

• it is not permitted
02 nl

permutation
04 perm **05** shift **06** barter, change **09** obversion, variation **10** alteration **11** commutation **13** configuration, transmutation, transposition **14** transformation

pernicious
03 bad **04** evil **05** fatal, ready, swift, toxic **06** deadly, prompt, wicked **07** baneful, harmful, hurtful, noisome, noxious, ruinous **08** damaging, damnable, venomous **09** dangerous, injurious, malicious, malignant, offensive, pestilent, poisonous, unhealthy **10** maleficent, malevolent **11** deleterious, destructive, detrimental, unwholesome

pernickety
04 fine, nice **05** fussy, picky **06** choosy, fiddly, tricky **07** careful, carping, finical, finicky **08** detailed, exacting **10** fastidious, nit-picking, particular **11** over-precise, painstaking, persnickety, punctilious **13** hair-splitting **14** over-particular

peroration
04 talk **06** korero, speech **07** address, lecture, oration, summary **08** diatribe, pirlicue, purlicue **09** recapping, summing-up **10** conclusion **11** declamation, reiteration **14** closing remarks, recapitulation

perpendicular
04 sine **05** atrip, erect, plumb, right, sheer, steep **06** abrupt, normal, offset **07** apothem, upright **08** cathetus, straight, vertical **09** downright, erectness **10** anticlinal **11** precipitous, verticality **13** at right angles

perpetrate
02 do **05** wreak **06** commit, effect **07** execute, inflict, perform **08** carry out **10** accomplish, effectuate **12** be to blame for

perpetration
05 doing **09** committal, execution **10** commitment **11** achievement, carrying-out, performance **14** accomplishment, implementation

perpetrator
04 doer, perp **05** agent **08** executor, offender **09** committer, executant

perpetual
07 abiding, endless, eternal, lasting, undying **08** constant, enduring, infinite, repeated, unbroken, unending **09** ceaseless, continual, incessant, perennial, permanent, recurrent, unceasing, unfailing, unvarying **10** continuous, persistent, persisting, unchanging **11** everlasting, never-ending, unremitting **12** interminable, intermittent **13** uninterrupted

perpetually
09 endlessly, eternally **10** constantly **11** ceaselessly, continually, incessantly, permanently, unceasingly **12** interminably, persistently **13** unremittingly

perpetuate
06 keep up **07** sustain **08** continue, maintain, preserve **09** keep alive, keep going **10** eternalize **11** commemorate, immortalize, memorialize

perpetuation
09 extension **10** sustaining **11** lengthening, maintenance, protraction **12** continuation, keeping alive, preservation, prolongation **13** commemoration

perpetuity
• in perpetuity
06 always **07** for ever **08** ever more **09** endlessly, eternally **10** for all time **11** perpetually **14** for ever and ever

perplex
◇ *anagram indicator*
04 pose **05** beset, stump, throw **06** baffle, bother, feague, fickle, gravel, hobble, muddle, pother, pudder, puzzle, tangle, tickle **07** bumbaze, confuse, flummox, mystify, nonplus **08** bewilder, confound, entangle, throw off **09** bamboozle, dumbfound, embarrass, embrangle, imbrangle **10** complicate, difficulty, distrouble, interweave

perplexed
05 spiny **07** at a loss, baffled, fuddled, muddled, puzzled, stumped, worried **08** confused **09** flummoxed, mystified, quizzical **10** bamboozled, bewildered, confounded, distraught, nonplussed, tosticated **11** embarrassed **12** disconcerted

perplexing
04 hard **05** weird **06** knotty, taxing, thorny **07** amazing, complex, strange **08** baffling, involved, puzzling **09** confusing, difficult, enigmatic, intricate **10** mysterious, mystifying **11** bewildering, complicated, paradoxical **12** inexplicable, labyrinthine

perplexity
05 doubt, tweak, worry **06** bother, enigma, puzzle, taking, tangle **07** dilemma, meander, mystery, nonplus, paradox **09** confusion, intricacy, labyrinth, obscurity **10** bafflement, complexity, difficulty, fickleness, puzzlement **11** distraction, disturbance, involvement, obfuscation, tostication **12** bewilderment, complication, entanglement **13** embarrassment, mystification **15** incomprehension

perquisite
03 tip **04** lock, perk, plus, vail **05** bonus, extra, vales **07** apanage, benefit, freebie **08** appanage, dividend, gratuity **09** advantage, baksheesh, royal fish **10** emoluments, kitchen-fee **13** fringe benefit

persecute
04 bait, hunt **05** abuse, annoy, hound, worry **06** badger, bother, harass, hassle, martyr, molest, pester, pursue **07** afflict, crucify, oppress, torment, torture **08** distress, hunt down, ill-treat, maltreat, mistreat **09** tyrannize, victimize

persecution
05 abuse **07** torture, tyranny **09** martyrdom **10** dragonnade, harassment, oppression, punishment **11** crucifixion, molestation, subjugation, suppression **12** ill-treatment, maltreatment, mistreatment **13** victimization **14** discrimination

Persephone
10 Proserpina

perseverance
07 purpose, resolve, stamina **08** tenacity **09** assiduity, constancy, diligence, endurance **10** commitment, dedication, doggedness, resolution **11** application, persistence, persistency, pertinacity **12** stickability **13** determination, intransigence, steadfastness **14** purposefulness

persevere
04 go on **05** truck **06** bash on, hang on, hold on, remain **07** carry on, persist, stick in **08** continue, plug away **09** keep going, prosecute, soldier on, stand fast, stand firm, stick at it **10** be resolute, hammer away, struggle on **11** hang in there **12** be determined, be persistent, mean business **15** stick to your guns

Persian
04 Babi, Mede **05** Babee, Farsi

persist
04 go on, hold, last **05** abide **06** endure, hang in, hang on, hold on, insist, keep on, linger, remain **07** carry on **08** continue, keep at it, plug away **09** hang about, keep going, persevere, soldier on, stand fast, stand firm, stick at it **10** be resolute, hang around **11** hang in there **12** be determined, be persistent

persistence
04 grit **07** stamina **08** sedulity, tenacity **09** assiduity, constancy, diligence, endurance, obstinacy **10** doggedness, resolution **11** pertinacity **12** continuation, perseverance, stickability, tirelessness

13 assiduousness, determination, steadfastness

persistent
05 fixed 06 dogged, steady, urgent 07 endless, lasting, zealous 08 constant, diligent, enduring, obdurate, repeated, resolute, stubborn, tireless 09 assiduous, ceaseless, continual, incessant, obstinate, perpetual, steadfast, tenacious, unceasing 10 continuous, determined, persisting, purposeful, relentless, unflagging 11 importunate, intractable, never-ending, persevering, unrelenting, unremitting 12 interminable, pertinacious, stick-to-it-ive 13 indefatigable

persistently
10 constantly, diligently, resolutely, stubbornly, tirelessly 11 assiduously, ceaselessly, continually, incessantly, obstinately, tenaciously, unceasingly 12 continuously, interminably, relentlessly

person
03 bod, chi, man, per 04 body, chai, chal, fish, pers, soul, type 05 being, human, woman 06 mortal 07 someone 08 somebody 09 character 10 human being, individual

- **good person**

01 S 02 St 04 sant 05 Saint

- **individual person**

03 one

- **in person**

06 bodily, myself 08 actually 10 face to face, in the flesh, personally 13 as large as life

persona
04 face, mask, part, role 05 front, image 06 façade 09 character 10 public face 11 personality

personable
04 nice, warm 07 affable, amiable, winning 08 charming, handsome, likeable, outgoing, pleasant, pleasing 09 agreeable 10 attractive 11 good-looking, presentable

personage
03 VIP 04 name 05 celeb 06 bigwig, figure, worthy 07 big shot, notable 08 big noise, luminary, somebody 09 big cheese, celebrity, dignitary, headliner 11 personality 12 public figure

personal
03 gut, own 04 live, pers, rude 05 privy 06 bodily, secret, unique 07 abusive, hurtful, private, special 08 critical, in person, intimate, peculiar, wounding 09 exclusive, insulting, offensive, upsetting 10 derogatory, individual, in the flesh, particular, subjective 11 distinctive 12 confidential 13 disrespectful, idiosyncratic 14 characteristic

personality
03 VIP 04 mind, self, star 05 charm 06 figure, make-up, nature, person, psyche, temper, traits, worthy 07 notable 08 charisma, identity, selfhood, selfness 09 celebrity, character, dignitary, magnetism, personage 10 the real you 11 beastly-head, disposition, temperament 12 public figure 13 individuality

personalize
03 fit 04 suit 05 adapt, alter 06 adjust, modify, tailor 07 convert 09 customize, personify, transform

personally
05 alone 06 I think, solely 08 as I see it, I believe, in my book, in my view, in person, uniquely 09 as a slight, ourselves, privately, specially 10 for my money, if you ask me 11 exclusively, in my opinion, insultingly, offensively 12 individually, particularly, subjectively, the way I see it 13 distinctively, independently 14 confidentially

personification
05 image 07 epitome, essence 08 likeness 09 portrayal, semblance 10 embodiment, recreation 11 delineation, incarnation 12 quintessence 13 manifestation 14 representation

personify
06 embody, imbody, mirror, typify 09 epitomize, exemplify, incarnate, personize, represent, symbolize 11 hypostatize, impersonate, personalize

personnel
04 crew 05 staff 06 people 07 members, service, workers 08 liveware, manpower 09 employees, workforce 11 labour force 14 human resources

perspective
04 take, view 05 angle, scene, slant, vista 06 aspect, optics 07 balance, optical, outlook 08 attitude, peepshow, prospect, relation 09 viewpoint 10 inspection, proportion, standpoint 11 equilibrium, frame of mind, point of view 12 vantage point

perspicacious
04 keen 05 alert, aware, quick, sharp 06 astute, shrewd 09 judicious, observant, sagacious, sensitive, sharp-eyed 10 discerning, perceptive, percipient, responsive 11 penetrating, quick-witted 13 understanding 14 discriminating

perspicacity
03 wit 06 acumen, brains 07 insight 08 keenness, sagacity 09 acuteness, sharpness 10 astuteness, cleverness, shrewdness 11 discernment, penetration, percipience, perspicuity 13 sagaciousness 14 discrimination, perceptiveness

perspicuity
07 clarity 08 lucidity 09 clearness, limpidity, plainness, precision 10 limpidness 12 distinctness, explicitness, transparency 13 penetrability 15 intelligibility

perspicuous
05 clear, lucid, plain 06 limpid 07 obvious 08 apparent, distinct, explicit, manifest 11 self-evident, transparent, unambiguous 12 crystal-clear, intelligible 14 comprehensible, understandable 15 straightforward

perspiration
04 foam 05 sudor, suint, sweat 07 wetness 08 hidrosis, moisture 09 exudation, secretion 11 diaphoresis

perspire
04 drip 05 exude, sweat 06 exhale, sudate 07 secrete, swelter

persuadable
07 pliable 08 amenable, flexible 09 agreeable, compliant, malleable, receptive 10 susceptive 11 acquiescent, persuasible 14 impressionable

persuade
03 con, win 04 coax, lure, move, snow, sway, urge 05 argue, lobby, moody, plead, tempt 06 cajole, coerce, incite, induce, lead on, lean on, nobble, prompt 07 convert, prevail, satisfy, swing it, wheedle, win over 08 convince, fast-talk, get round, inveigle, lamb down, perswade, soft-soap, talk into, talk over 09 argue into, influence, sweet-talk 10 bring round 11 prevail upon, pull strings 13 bring yourself 14 put the screws on

persuasion
04 camp, kind, pull, sect, side, sway, view 05 clout, creed, faith, party, power 06 belief, come-on, school, urging 07 coaxing, faction, opinion, suasion 08 cajolery, coercion, pressure, soft sell 09 influence, prompting, sweet talk, viewpoint, wheedling 10 conversion, conviction, enticement, incitement, inducement, philosophy, prevailing 11 affiliation, arm-twisting, point of view, talking into, winning over 12 denomination, sweet-talking 15 school of thought

persuasive
05 pushy, slick, sound, valid 06 cogent, moving, potent 07 telling, weighty, winning 08 eloquent, forceful, touching 09 effective, effectual, plausible 10 compelling, convincing 11 influential 12 high-pressure, honey-tongued, smooth-spoken 13 smooth-talking, smooth-tongued

persuasively
08 cogently 09 plausibly 10 forcefully, powerfully 11 effectively, effectually 12 compellingly, convincingly 13 influentially

pert
03 gay 04 bold, coxy, flip, open 05 brash, brisk, cocky, fresh, perky,

sassy, saucy, smart, tossy **06** adroit, cheeky, cocksy, daring, jaunty, lively **07** forward **08** flippant, impudent, insolent, spirited **09** sprightly **11** flourishing, impertinent, unconcealed **12** presumptuous **13** objectionable

pertain

04 long **05** apply, befit, refer **06** bear on, belong, regard, relate **07** concern **08** be part of **09** appertain, come under **10** be relevant **13** be appropriate **14** have a bearing on

pertinacious

05 stiff **06** dogged, mulish, wilful **08** obdurate, perverse, resolute, stubborn **09** obstinate, tenacious **10** determined, headstrong, inflexible, persistent, purposeful, relentless, self-willed, unyielding **11** intractable, persevering **12** strong-willed **13** inquisitorial **14** uncompromising

pertinent

03 apt **05** ad rem **07** apropos, fitting, germane, related **08** apposite, material, relating, relevant, suitable **10** applicable, to the point **11** appropriate

pertness

04 face, sass **05** brass, cheek **08** audacity, boldness, chutzpah, rudeness **09** brashness, cockiness, freshness, impudence, insolence, sassiness, sauciness **10** brazenness, cheekiness, effrontery **11** forwardness, presumption **12** impertinence

perturb

◇ *anagram indicator*

03 vex **04** faze **05** alarm, feese, feeze, phase, phese, upset, worry **06** aerate, bother, didder, dither, pheese, pheeze, rattle, ruffle **07** agitate, confuse, disturb, fluster, trouble **08** disquiet, unsettle **10** discompose, disconcert **11** make anxious **12** put the wind up

perturbation

04 faze, fear, flap **05** alarm, panic, scare, shock, worry **06** didder, dismay, dither, fright, horror, terror **07** anxiety **08** disquiet, distress **10** uneasiness **11** nervousness, trepidation **12** apprehension, irregularity **13** consternation

perturbed

◇ *anagram indicator*

05 upset **06** shaken, uneasy **07** alarmed, anxious, fearful, nervous, worried **08** agitated, flurried, harassed, restless, troubled **09** disturbed, flustered, unsettled **11** discomposed **12** disconcerted **13** uncomfortable

Peru

02 PE **03** PER

perusal

04 look, read, skim **05** check, sight, study **06** browse, glance **07** reading **08** scrutiny **10** inspection, run-through **11** examination

peruse

04 read, scan, skim **05** check, study **06** browse, revise **07** examine, inspect **08** pore over **10** run through, scrutinize **11** leaf through, look through **13** glance through

pervade

04 fill **05** imbue **06** affect, charge, infuse **07** diffuse, suffuse **08** permeate, saturate **09** penetrate, percolate **10** impregnate, infiltrate **11** pass through **13** spread through **14** interpenetrate

pervasive

04 rife **06** common **07** diffuse, general **08** immanent **09** extensive, prevalent, universal **10** ubiquitous, widespread **11** inescapable, omnipresent

perverse

◇ *anagram indicator*

03 wry **05** balky **06** cussed, donsie, thrawn, thwart, unruly, wilful **07** adverse, awkward, bolshie, crabbed, deviant, froward, peevish, stroppy, wayward **08** alarming, contrary, improper, obdurate, stubborn, worrying **09** camstairy, camsteary, difficult, incorrect, obstinate, pig-headed, senseless, unhelpful **10** camsteerie, headstrong, overthwart, rebellious, refractary, refractory, unyielding **11** disobedient, ill-tempered, intractable, obstructive, troublesome, wrong-headed **12** bloody-minded, cantankerous, cross-grained, intransigent, unmanageable, unreasonable **13** unco-operative **14** uncontrollable

perversely

◇ *anagram indicator*

04 awry **09** waywardly **10** alarmingly, stubbornly, worryingly **11** obstinately, thwartingly, unhelpfully **12** cross-grained **13** obstructively **15** unco-operatively

perversion

◇ *anagram indicator*

04 vice **06** misuse **08** deviance, travesty, twisting **09** depravity, deviation, kinkiness **10** aberration, corruption, debauchery, distortion, immorality, paraphilia, subversion, wickedness **11** abnormality **12** irregularity **13** exhibitionism, falsification **14** misapplication

perversity

◇ *anagram indicator*

03 gee **08** obduracy **09** adversity, contumacy, obstinacy **10** cussedness, protervity, unruliness, wilfulness **11** awkwardness, frowardness, gallowsness, waywardness **12** contrariness, disobedience, stubbornness **13** intransigence, senselessness **14** rebelliousness, refractoriness **15** troublesomeness, wrong-headedness

pervert

◇ *anagram indicator*

03 wry **04** perv, turn, vert, warp **05** abuse, avert, sicko, twist, wrest **06** debase, divert, garble, misuse, weirdo **07** corrupt, debauch, deflect, degrade, deprave, deviant, deviate, distort, falsify, oddball, subvert, vitiate **08** misapply **09** debauchee, misdirect, turn aside **10** degenerate, lead astray **11** misconstrue, prevaricate **12** misinterpret, misrepresent

perverted

◇ *anagram indicator*

04 evil **05** kinky, pervy, sicko **06** warped, wicked **07** corrupt, debased, deviant, immoral, twisted **08** abnormal, depraved, vitiated **09** corrupted, debauched, distorted, unhealthy, unnatural

pesky

06 thorny, trying, vexing **07** galling, grating, irksome, nagging **08** annoying, infernal, tiresome **09** maddening, provoking, upsetting, vexatious, worrisome **10** bothersome, confounded, disturbing, irritating **11** aggravating, displeasing, infuriating, troublesome

pessimism

05 gloom **07** despair **08** cynicism, distrust, fatalism, glumness **09** defeatism, dejection, doomwatch **10** depression, gloominess, melancholy **11** despondency, Weltschmerz **12** hopelessness

pessimist

05 cynic **07** doubter, killjoy, no-hoper, worrier **08** alarmist, doomsman, doomster, fatalist **09** defeatist, saturnist **10** wet blanket **11** crapehanger, crepehanger, dismal Jimmy, doomwatcher, gloom-monger, melancholic **12** doom merchant **13** prophet of doom **14** doubting Thomas

pessimistic

04 glum **05** bleak, doomy **06** dismal, gloomy, morose, negate **07** cynical **08** alarmist, dejected, doubting, hopeless, negative, resigned **09** defeatist, depressed **10** depressing, despairing, despondent, fatalistic, melancholy, off-putting, suspicious **11** distrustful, downhearted **12** discouraging

pest

03 bug, fly, nun **04** bane, frit, pain, pize **05** brize, curse, trial **06** blight, bother, breese, breeze, capsid, May bug, plague **07** blister, cane rat, fritfly, scourge **08** irritant, meal moth, mealy bug, nuisance, onion fly, vexation, viticide **09** annoyance, capsid bug, carrot fly, chinch bug, cornborer, May beetle, squash bug, stable fly **10** cicadellid, cockchafer, codlin moth, fowl-plague, house mouse, irritation, spider mite **11** codling moth, spermophile **13** jointed cactus, pain in the neck, red spider mite **14** American blight, Colorado beetle, Japanese beetle **15** thorn in the flesh

pester
03 bug, dun, irk, nag **04** clog, fret **05** annoy, chevy, chivy, devil, get at, hound, worry **06** badger, bother, chivvy, earwig, harass, hassle, huddle, infest, mither, moider, pick on, plague **07** besiege, disturb, moither, provoke, torment **08** doorstep, irritate **09** annoyance, beleaguer **12** rhyme to death **14** drive up the wall

pestilence
04 lues **06** plague **07** cholera, disease, murrain **08** epidemic, pandemic, sickness **09** contagion, infection **11** infestation

pestilent
06 deadly, vexing **07** harmful, irksome, ruinous **08** annoying, catching, diseased, infected, tiresome **09** poisonous, vexatious **10** bothersome, contagious, corrupting, infectious, irritating, pernicious **11** deleterious, destructive, detrimental, infuriating, mischievous, troublesome **12** communicable, contaminated, plague-ridden **13** disease-ridden

pestilential
06 vexing **07** baneful, harmful, irksome, ruinous **08** annoying, diseased, infected, tiresome **09** pestering, poisonous **10** bothersome, contagious, detestable, infectious, irritating, pernicious **11** destructive, infuriating, troublesome **12** contaminated, plague-ridden **13** disease-ridden

pet
04 cade, chou, coax, daut, dawt, dear, huff, hump, idol, kiss, neck, snog, stew, sulk, tame, tiff, tift, tout, towt **05** jewel, paddy, strop, sulks **06** caress, chosen, cosset, cuddle, dautie, dawtie, fondle, grumps, pamper, pettle, prized, smooch, stroke, temper **07** bad mood, darling, dearest, embrace, indulge, special, subdued, tantrum, the pits, trained **08** canoodle, favoured, fondling, indulged, personal, treasure **09** bad temper, cherished, favourite, preferred **10** manageable, particular **11** blue-eyed boy, teacher's pet **12** blue-eyed girl, domesticated, house-trained **14** apple of your eye

Pets include:

03 cat, cow, dog, pig, rat
04 bird, fish, goat, newt, pony
05 goose, horse, llama, mouse, sheep
06 alpaca, canary, donkey, ferret, gerbil, jerboa, lizard, parrot, rabbit, turtle
07 chicken, hamster
08 chipmunk, cyberpet, goldfish, parakeet, terrapin, tortoise
09 guinea pig, tarantula
10 budgerigar, chinchilla, salamander, virtual pet
11 stick insect

See also **cat**; **dog**; **fish**; **horse**; **rabbit**

peter
03 jar, jug **05** half-g **06** flagon

• peter out
03 ebb **04** fade, fail, stop, wane **05** cease **06** go cold **07** die away, dwindle **08** diminish, taper off **09** evaporate, fizzle out **11** come to an end **13** come to nothing

petite
05 bijou, dinky, small **06** dainty, little, slight **08** delicate

petition
03 ask, beg, bid, sue **04** boon, plea, pray, suit, urge **05** axiom, crave, plead, press **06** adjure, appeal, prayer **07** beseech, entreat, implore, protest, request, solicit **08** call upon, entreaty **09** postulate, supplicat **10** invocation, round robin, supplicate **11** application, deprecation, memorialize **12** solicitation, supplication **14** representation

pet name
03 mog, nan **04** nana **05** bunny, moggy, nanna, nanny **06** moggie **08** nickname **10** diminutive, endearment, hypocorism **11** hypocorisma

petrel
05 ariel, nelly, prion **06** fulmar **07** pintado, stinker **09** stormbird **10** Cape pigeon, sea swallow **11** Procellaria

petrified
04 numb **05** dazed **06** aghast, frozen **07** shocked, stunned **08** appalled, benumbed **09** horrified, stupefied, terrified **10** speechless, transfixed **11** dumbfounded, in a blue funk, scared stiff **13** having kittens, scared to death **14** horror-stricken, terror-stricken

petrify
04 numb, stun **05** alarm, appal, panic, spook **06** boggle, ossify, rattle **07** horrify, stupefy, terrify **08** frighten, paralyse **09** dumbfound, fossilize **11** turn to stone **12** put the wind up

petrol
03 gas, LRP **05** ethyl, juice, super **08** gasolene, gasoline

See also **fuel**

petticoat
04 coat, slip **05** jupon, woman **06** female, kirtle **07** placket **08** balmoral, basquine, feminine **09** crinoline, wyliecoat **10** underskirt

pettifogging
04 mean **05** petty **06** paltry, subtle **07** trivial **08** captious, niggling **09** casuistic, cavilling, quibbling **10** nit-picking **11** over-refined, sophistical **12** equivocating **13** hair-splitting

pettiness
08 meanness **09** quibbling **10** nit-picking **12** spitefulness **15** small-mindedness

pettish
05 cross, dorty, huffy, sulky **06** grumpy, tetchy, touchy **07** fretful, peevish, waspish **08** petulant, snappish **09** fractious, irritable, querulous, splenetic **11** bad-tempered, ill-humoured, thin-skinned

petty
04 mean **05** minor, petit, potty, small **06** grotty, lesser, little, measly, paltry, poking, puisne, puisny, slight **07** pimping, scantle, trivial **08** grudging, niggling, picayune, piddling, piffling, spiteful, trifling **09** parochial, quibbling, scantling, secondary, small-town **10** negligible, nit-picking, parish-pump, shoestring, ungenerous **11** in a small way, inessential, small-minded, unimportant **12** contemptible, narrow-minded **13** insignificant **14** inconsiderable **15** inconsequential

petulance
05 pique **06** spleen **09** bad temper, ill-humour, ill-temper, procacity, sulkiness **10** crabbiness, sullenness **11** crabbedness, peevishness, waspishness **12** irritability **13** querulousness

petulant
04 sour **05** cross, mardy, moody, ratty, sulky **06** crabby, sullen, touchy, toutie, wanton **07** crabbed, forward, fretful, in a stew, peevish **08** in a paddy, snappish **09** crotchety, impatient, irritable, querulous **10** browned off, humoursome, lascivious, ungracious **11** bad-tempered, complaining, ill-humoured

pew
03 box **04** seat **05** stall **08** horse box

phalanger
04 tait **06** cuscus, glider, possum **07** opossum **08** Tarsipes **09** petaurist **10** honey-mouse **11** honey possum **14** flying squirrel, vulpine opossum

phantasmagorical
06 unreal **07** surreal **08** ethereal, illusory **09** dreamlike, fantastic, visionary **10** chimerical, trance-like **13** hallucinatory, insubstantial, unsubstantial **14** phantasmagoric

phantom
04 idol **05** ghost, spook **06** fantom, spirit, unreal, vision, wraith **07** eidolon, feature, figment, specter, spectre **08** illusion, illusory, revenant, spectral **09** imaginary **10** apparition, Scotch mist **12** Pepper's ghost **13** hallucination

pharaoh
04 faro **11** river-dragon

Pharaohs include:

07 Rameses
08 Thutmose
09 Akhenaten
10 Hatshepsut
11 Tut'ankhamun

pharisaical
06 formal **07** preachy **09** insincere, pietistic **10** goody-goody, moralizing **12** hypocritical **13** sanctimonious, self-righteous **14** holier-than-thou

Pharisee
05 fraud **06** humbug, phoney **07** pietist **09** formalist, hypocrite **10** dissembler **12** dissimulator **15** whited sepulchre

phase
04 beat, faze, form, part, step, time **05** drive, morph, point, shape, spell, stage, state, worry **06** aspect, period, season **07** chapter, perturb **08** juncture, position, unsettle **09** condition **11** development

• **phase in**
05 start **06** ease in **07** bring in **08** initiate **09** introduce **10** start using

• **phase out**
04 stop **05** close **06** remove, wind up **07** ease off, run down **08** get rid of, taper off, wind down, withdraw **09** dispose of, eliminate, stop using, terminate

pheasant
05 argus, monal **06** coucal, monaul **08** fireback, lyrebird, tragopan **09** francolin

• **brood of pheasants**
03 eye, nid, nye **04** nide

phenomenal
06 unique **07** amazing, unusual **08** singular **09** fantastic, unheard of, wonderful **10** astounding, incredible, marvellous, remarkable, stupendous **11** astonishing, exceptional, mind-blowing, sensational **12** breathtaking, mind-boggling, unbelievable, unparalleled **13** extraordinary, unprecedented **15** too good to be true

phenomenally
09 amazingly **10** incredibly, remarkably **11** wonderfully **12** astoundingly, marvellously, unbelievably **13** astonishingly, exceptionally, sensationally **15** extraordinarily

phenomenon
04 fact **05** event, sight **06** marvel, phenom, rarity, wonder **07** episode, miracle, prodigy **08** incident **09** curiosity, happening, sensation, spectacle **10** appearance, experience, occurrence **12** circumstance

philander
05 dally, flirt, lover **08** womanize **10** fool around, play around **11** sleep around **12** have an affair, philandering, play the field

philanderer
04 rake, roué, stud, wolf **05** flirt **07** dallier, Don Juan, playboy **08** Casanova **09** ladies' man, libertine, womanizer **10** lady-killer

philanthropic
04 kind **06** humane **07** liberal **08** generous, selfless **09** bounteous, bountiful, unselfish **10** alms-giving, altruistic, benevolent, charitable, munificent, open-handed **11** kind-hearted **12** humanitarian **14** public-spirited

philanthropist
05 donor, giver **06** backer, helper, patron **07** sponsor **08** altruist **09** alms-giver **10** benefactor **11** contributor **12** humanitarian

philanthropy
04 help **06** giving **07** backing, charity **08** altruism, kindness **09** patronage **10** alms-giving, generosity, liberality **11** beneficence, benevolence, munificence, sponsorship **12** selflessness **13** bounteousness, bountifulness, social concern, unselfishness **14** open-handedness **15** humanitarianism, kind-heartedness, social awareness

Philip
04 Phil

philippic
05 abuse **06** attack, insult, rebuke, tirade **07** reproof **08** diatribe, harangue, reviling **09** criticism, invective, onslaught, reprimand **10** upbraiding **12** denunciation, vituperation

Philippines
02 RP **03** PHL

philistine
04 boor, lout **05** crass, enemy, yahoo **06** gigman, unread **07** bailiff, boorish, lowbrow **08** ignorant **09** barbarian, bourgeois, ignoramus, tasteless, unrefined, vulgarian **10** uncultured, uneducated, unlettered **12** uncultivated

Phillip
04 Phil

philologer *see* **lexicographer**

philosopher
04 guru, sage **06** expert **07** scholar, thinker **08** academic, analyser, logician, theorist **09** theorizer **12** dialectician **13** deipnosophist, metaphysicist, philosophizer **14** epistemologist

Philosophers include:

04 **Ayer** (Sir A J), **Hume** (David), **Joad** (C E M), **Kant** (Immanuel), **Mach** (Ernst), **Marx** (Karl), **Mill** (James), **Mill** (John Stuart), **More** (Henry), **Otto** (Rudolf), **Ryle** (Gilbert), **Vico** (Giambattista), **Weil** (Simone)

05 **Bacon** (Francis), **Bacon** (Roger), **Bayle** (Pierre), **Benda** (Julien), **Bodin** (Jean), **Broad** (Charlie Dunbar), **Bruno** (Giordano), **Buber** (Martin), **Burke** (Edmund), **Comte** (Auguste), **Croce** (Benedetto), **Dewey** (John), **Dunne** (John William), **Frege** (Gottlob), **Gödel** (Kurt), **Hegel** (Georg Wilhelm Friedrich), **Hulme** (T E), **James** (William), **Locke** (John), **Moore** (George Edward), **Occam** (William of), **Plato**, **Smith** (Adam), **Vivés** (Juan Luis)

06 **Adorno** (Theodor), **Anselm** (St), **Berlin** (Sir Isaiah), **Bonnet** (Charles), **Carnap** (Rudolf), **Celsus**, **Engels** (Friedrich), **Fichte** (Johann Gottlieb), **Goedel** (Kurt), **Herder** (Johann Gottfried von), **Hobbes** (Thomas), **Langer** (Suzanne Knauth), **Lukács** (Georg), **Ockham** (William of), **Palach** (Jan), **Popper** (Sir Karl), **Pyrrho**, **Sartre** (Jean-Paul), **Strato**, **Thales**

07 **Aquinas** (St Thomas), **Bentham** (Jeremy), **Buridan** (Jean), **Derrida** (Jacques), **Diderot** (Denis), **Dilthey** (Wilhelm), **Edwards** (Jonathan), **Erasmus** (Desiderius), **Gentile** (Giovanni), **Gorgias**, **Haldane** (Richard, Viscount), **Husserl** (Edmund), **Hypatia**, **Jaspers** (Karl), **Leibniz** (Gottfried Wilhelm), **Marcuse** (Herbert), **Mencius**, **Proclus**, **Russell** (Bertrand, Earl), **Sankara**, **Schlick** (Moritz), **Spencer** (Herbert), **Spinoza** (Baruch), **Steiner** (Rudolf), **Tillich** (Paul)

08 **Alcmaeon**, **Alembert** (Jean le Rond d'), **Averroës**, **Avicenna**, **Beauvoir** (Simone de), **Berkeley** (Bishop George), **Boethius** (Anicius Manlius Severinus), **Buchanan** (George), **Cassirer** (Ernst), **Cudworth** (Ralph), **Epicurus**, **Foucault** (Michel), **Habermas** (Jürgen), **Hamilton** (Sir William), **Hobhouse** (Leonard), **Longinus** (Dionysius), **Plotinus**, **Porphyry**, **Ram Singh**, **Rousseau** (Jean Jacques), **Sidgwick** (Henry), **Socrates**, **Spengler** (Oswald)

09 **Althusser** (Louis), **Aristotle**, **Avicebrón**, **Bronowski** (Jacob), **Condorcet** (Marie-Jean-Antoine-Nicolas de Caritat, Marquis de), **Confucius**, **Descartes** (René), **Feuerbach** (Ludwig), **Heidegger** (Martin), **Nietzsche** (Friedrich), **Plekhanov** (Giorgiy), **Santayana** (George), **Schelling** (Friedrich), **Whitehead** (Alfred North)

10 **Anaxagoras**, **Aristippus**, **Democritus**, **Duns Scotus** (John), **Empedocles**, **Heraclitus**, **Horkheimer** (Max), **Maimonides** (Moses), **Parmenides**, **Posidonius**, **Protagoras**, **Pythagoras**, **Schweitzer** (Albert), **Xenocrates**, **Xenophanes**, **Zeno of Elea**

11 **Anaximander**, **Kierkegaard** (Sören), **Montesquieu** (Charles-Louis, Baron de), **Reichenbach** (Hans), **Shaftesbury** (Anthony Ashley Cooper, Earl of), **Vivekananda**

12 **Merleau-Ponty** (Maurice), **Philo Judaeus**, **Schopenhauer** (Arthur), **Theophrastus**, **Wittgenstein** (Ludwig), **Zeno of Citium**

14 **Albertus Magnus** (St), **Schleiermacher** (Friedrich)

15 **William of Ockham**

philosophical
04 calm, cool, wise **05** stoic **06** placid, serene **07** erudite, learned, logical, patient, pensive, stoical **08** abstract, composed, rational, resigned **09** collected, impassive, realistic, unruffled **10** analytical, meditative, phlegmatic, reflective, thoughtful **11** theoretical, unemotional, unflappable **12** metaphysical **13** contemplative, dispassionate, imperturbable, self-possessed
See also **philosophy**

philosophically
06 calmly **08** placidly **09** logically, patiently, stoically **10** abstractly, resignedly **11** impassively, unflappably **12** analytically **13** theoretically, unemotionally **14** metaphysically

philosophy
04 view **06** reason, tenets, values, wisdom **07** beliefs, thought **08** attitude, doctrine, ideology, stoicism, thinking **09** knowledge, reasoning, viewpoint, world-view **10** principles **11** convictions, point of view

Branches of philosophy include:

03 est, law
04 mind, yoga
05 logic, moral
06 ethics
07 biology, eastern, history, Sankhya, science, Vedanta
08 axiology, language, medicine, ontology, politics, religion
09 bioethics, economics, education, semiotics
10 aesthetics, literature, psychology
11 informatics, mathematics, metaphysics
12 epistemology
13 applied ethics, jurisprudence, phenomenology

Philosophical schools, doctrines and theories include:

05 deism
06 egoism, monism, Taoism, theism
07 atheism, atomism, dualism, fideism, Marxism, realism, Thomism
08 altruism, ascetism, cynicism, fatalism, feminism, hedonism, humanism, idealism, nihilism, Stoicism
09 dogmatism, pantheism, Platonism, pluralism, solipsism
10 absolutism, Eleaticism, empiricism, gnosticism, Kantianism, naturalism, nominalism, positivism, pragmatism, Pyrrhonism, relativism, scepticism
11 agnosticism, determinism, Hegelianism, historicism, materialism, objectivism, rationalism, Sankhya-Yoga
12 behaviourism, Cartesianism, Confucianism, Epicureanism, essentialism, Neoplatonism, reductionism, subjectivism
13 antinomianism, conceptualism, descriptivism, immaterialism, neo-Kantianism, occasionalism, phenomenalism, scholasticism, structuralism
14 existentialism, interactionism, intuitionalism, libertarianism, Nyaya-Vaisesika, prescriptivism, Pythagoreanism, sensationalism, utilitarianism, Vedanta-Mimamsa
15 Aristotelianism, experimentalism, Frankfurt School, instrumentalism

Philosophy terms include:

05 deism, logic, moral
06 egoism, ethics, monism, theism
07 a priori, atheism, atomism, dualism, falsafa, Marxism, realism
08 altruism, ascetism, axiology, cynicism, fatalism, feminism, hedonism, humanism, idealism, identity, nihilism, ontology, stoicism
09 deduction, dogmatism, induction, intuition, pantheism, Platonism, pluralism, sense data, solipsism, substance, syllogism, teleology
10 absolutism, aesthetics, deontology, empiricism, entailment, gnosticism, Kantianism, naturalism, nominalism, positivism, pragmatism, relativism, scepticism
11 agnosticism, a posteriori, determinism, historicism, materialism, metaphysics, objectivism, rationalism
12 behaviourism, Confucianism, Epicureanism, epistemology, Neoplatonism, reductionism, subjectivism
13 antinomianism, conceptualism, immaterialism, jurisprudence, neo-Kantianism, phenomenalism, phenomenology, scholasticism, structuralism
14 existentialism, interactionism, intuitionalism, libertarianism, prescriptivism, sensationalism, utilitarianism
15 Aristotelianism, experimentalism, instrumentalism

phlegmatic
04 calm, cool **06** placid, stolid **07** stoical **08** tranquil **09** impassive, saturnine **11** indifferent, unconcerned, unemotional, unflappable **12** matter-of-fact **13** dispassionate, imperturbable **14** self-controlled

phobia
04 fear **05** dread, thing **06** hang-up, hatred, horror, terror **07** anxiety, dislike **08** aversion, loathing, neurosis **09** antipathy, obsession, repulsion, revulsion **11** detestation **14** irrational fear

Phobias include:

09 apiphobia, neophobia, panphobia, zoophobia
10 acrophobia, algophobia, aquaphobia, autophobia, canophobia, cynophobia, demophobia, hodophobia, musophobia, nosophobia, pyrophobia, toxiphobia, xenophobia
11 agoraphobia, astraphobia, cnidophobia, cyberphobia, gymnophobia, hippophobia, hydrophobia, hypnophobia, necrophobia, nyctophobia, ophiophobia, photophobia, scotophobia, tachophobia, taphephobia
12 achluophobia, ailurophobia, belonephobia, brontophobia, entomophobia, phasmophobia, technophobia
13 arachnophobia, arithmophobia, bacillophobia, herpetophobia
14 anthropophobia, bacteriophobia, claustrophobia, ereuthrophobia, thalassophobia

Phoebus
03 Sol, sun **05** Titan **06** Apollo, Helios

phoenix
03 fum **04** fung, huma **07** paragon **12** bird of wonder

phone
04 bell, buzz, call, dial, ring **06** blower, call up, mobile, ring up, tinkle **07** contact, handset **08** car phone, receiver **09** cell phone, give a bell, give a buzz, make a call, phone call, telephone **10** dog and bone, get in touch **11** give a tinkle, mobile phone **13** cordless phone

phonetic alphabet *see* **alphabet**

phoney
◇ *anagram indicator*
04 fake, mock, sham **05** bogus, faker, false, fraud, hokey, pseud, put-on, quack, trick **06** ersatz, forged, humbug, pseudo, unreal **07** assumed, feigned, forgery **08** affected, impostor, spurious **09** contrived, imitation, pretender, simulated **10** fraudulent, mountebank **11** counterfeit, pretentious

phosphorescent
06 bright **07** glowing, radiant **08** luminous **09** refulgent **11** luminescent, noctilucent, noctilucous

phosphorus
01 P

photocopy
04 copy **05** print, Xerox® **06** run off **09** duplicate, facsimile, Photostat®

photograph
03 pic, pin **04** film, shot, snap, take, X-ray **05** image, Kodak®, panel, photo, piccy, print, sepia, shoot, slide, still, video **06** blow up, blow-up, record, retake **07** close-up, enlarge, montage, mug shot, picture **08** abstract, exposure, headshot, hologram, likeness, microdot, portrait, seascape, skiagram, snapshot, sun print **09** angiogram, ferrotype, karyotype,

landscape, mammogram, microgram, nephogram, photogene, photogram, radiogram, rotograph, skiagraph, visual aid, wirephoto **10** centrefold, chromatype, ferro-print, micrograph, radiograph, sun picture
11 composition, enlargement, heliochrome, platinotype, spectrogram **12** cathodograph, röntgenogram, transparency
13 capture on film, chlorobromide, daguerreotype, encephalogram
14 pyrophotograph, take a picture of
15 microphotograph, take a snapshot of

photographer

07 snapper **09** cameraman, paparazzo
11 camerawoman **14** camera operator

Photographers include:

03 **Ray** (Man)
04 **Capa** (Robert), **Hill** (David Octavius), **Penn** (Irving)
05 **Adams** (Ansel), **Arbus** (Diane), **Hardy** (Bert), **Karsh** (Yousuf), **Lange** (Dorothea), **Ritts** (Herb), **Smith** (W Eugene)
06 **Arnold** (Eve), **Avedon** (Richard), **Bailey** (David), **Beaton** (Sir Cecil), **Brandt** (Bill), **Godwin** (Fay), **McBean** (Angus), **Miller** (Lee), **Newton** (Helmut), **Niepce** (Joseph Nicéphore), **Rankin**, **Talbot** (William Henry Fox), **Warhol** (Andy)
07 **Brassaï**, **Cameron** (Julia Margaret), **Carroll** (Lewis), **Dodgson** (Charles Lutwidge), **Eastman** (George), **Lumière** (Auguste), **McCurry** (Steve), **Salgado** (Sebastião), **Siskind** (Aaron), **Snowdon** (Antony Armstrong-Jones, Earl of), **Waddell** (Rankin)
08 **Daguerre** (Louis), **McCullin** (Don), **Sielmann** (Heinz), **Steichen** (Edward)
09 **Leibovitz** (Annie), **Lichfield** (Patrick, Earl of), **Muybridge** (Eadweard James), **Rodchenko** (Alexander), **Rosenblum** (Walter), **Stieglitz** (Alfred), **Winogrand** (Garry)
10 **Moholy-Nagy** (László)
11 **Bourke-White** (Margaret), **Wakabayashi** (Yasuhiro)
12 **Friese-Greene** (William)
13 **Ducos du Hauron** (Louis)
14 **Armstrong-Jones** (Antony), **Cartier-Bresson** (Henri)

photographic

05 exact, vivid **06** filmic, minute, visual
07 graphic, natural, precise
08 accurate, detailed, faithful, lifelike
09 cinematic, pictorial, realistic, retentive **12** naturalistic

Photographic equipment includes:

06 camera, tripod, viewer
08 enlarger, light-box, stop bath
09 camcorder, safelight
10 fixing bath, paper drier, Vertoscope®
11 print washer, slide viewer
13 developer bath, enlarger timer, film projector, flash umbrella
14 contact printer, developing tank, focus magnifier, slide projector
15 negative carrier, print-drying rack

Photographic accessories include:

04 film, lens
06 eye-cup, filter
07 battery, hot shoe, lens cap
08 diffuser, disc film, flashgun, lens hood, zoom lens
09 camera bag, flashbulb, flash card, flashcube, flash unit, macro lens, polarizer, spot meter
10 afocal lens, lens shield, light meter, memory card, slide mount, video light, video mixer, viewfinder
11 close-up lens, fish-eye lens, sepia filter, video editor
12 cable release, colour filter, memory reader
13 auxiliary lens, cartridge film, exposure meter, remote control, teleconverter, telephoto lens, wide-angle lens

Photostat®

04 copy **05** print, Xerox® **06** run off
09 duplicate, facsimile, photocopy

phrase

03 phr, put, say **04** cant, hook, riff, word **05** couch, frame, idiom, style, usage, utter **06** clause, cliché, mantra, remark, saying **07** comment, express, flatter, formula, mantram, present, wheedle **08** laconism, language, locution **09** catchword, formulate, pronounce, utterance
10 expression, laconicism, mondegreen **11** phraseology
12 construction, group of words, put into words **13** way of speaking **15** style of speaking

phraseology

04 cant **05** argot, idiom, style
06 patois, phrase, speech, syntax
07 diction, wording, writing
08 language, parlance, phrasing
10 expression **11** terminology

phrasing

05 idiom, style, words **07** diction, wordage, wording **08** language, verbiage **10** expression
11 phraseology, terminology **13** choice of words

physical

04 real **05** brute, solid **06** actual, bodily, carnal, fleshy, mortal **07** earthly, fleshly, medical, somatic, spatial, visible **08** concrete, material, palpable, tangible **09** corporeal, incarnate, medicinal, wholesome **11** substantial, unspiritual **13** materialistic

physically

06 bodily, really **07** visibly **08** actually, animally, tangibly **10** concretely, in your body, materially **13** substantially
15 physiologically

physician

02 GP **03** doc **05** hakim, leech, medic, Paean, quack **06** doctor, healer, intern, medico **08** external, houseman, medicine **09** internist, mediciner, registrar **10** consultant, medicaster, specialist **11** physicianer **12** school doctor

See also **doctor**

physics

Physics terms include:

03 gas, GUT, ion, law, QCD, QED, TOE
04 area, atom, barn, flux, gate, heat, lens, mass, node, rule, spin, wave, WIMP, work, X-ray
05 chaos, fermi, field, focus, force, laser, lever, light, phase, power, quark, ratio, sound, speed, SQUID, state
06 atomic, charge, couple, energy, engine, liquid, mirror, moment, motion, optics, phonon, photon, proton, scalar, SI unit, string, theory, volume, weight
07 circuit, density, digital, entropy, formula, gravity, inertia, neutron, nuclear, nucleus, orbital, process, statics, tension
08 alpha ray, dynamics, electron, equation, friction, gamma ray, half-life, harmonic, infrared, molecule, momentum, neutrino, particle, polarity, pressure, rest mass, spectrum, velocity
09 acoustics, amplitude, black body, cosmology, dimension, frequency, induction, magnetism, mechanics, Mohs scale, potential, principle, radiation, radio wave, resonance, sound wave, subatomic, substance, vibration, viscosity, white heat
10 efficiency, elasticity, flash point, gauge boson, heavy water, Higgs boson, hydraulics, latent heat, Mach number, microwaves, reflection, refraction, relativity, resistance, separation, shear force, ultrasound, wavelength
11 diffraction, electricity, equilibrium, evaporation, light source, oscillation, periodic law, sensitivity, temperature, ultraviolet
12 absolute zero, acceleration, boiling point, centre of mass, critical mass, hydrostatics, interference, Kelvin effect, laws of motion, luminescence, radioisotope, spectroscopy, speed of light, standing wave, string theory, time dilation, wave property
13 Appleton layer, beta particles, Big Bang theory, bubble-chamber, chain reaction, freezing point, hydrodynamics, incandescence, kinetic energy, kinetic theory, light emission, magnetic field, nuclear fusion, optical centre, quantum theory, radioactivity, semiconductor, supersymmetry, Thomson effect
14 alpha particles, analogue signal,

applied physics, circuit-breaker, Coriolis effect, light intensity, nuclear fission, nuclear physics, parallel motion, states of matter, superconductor, surface tension, thermodynamics, transverse wave
15 angular momentum, capillary action, centre of gravity, charged particle, electric current, electrodynamics, Fourier analysis, moment of inertia, perpetual motion, potential energy, specific gravity, visible spectrum

Physicists include:

02 **Wu** (Chien-Shiung)
03 **Lee** (Tsung-Dao), **Ohm** (Georg Simon)
04 **Abbe** (Ernst), **Biot** (Jean-Baptiste), **Bohr** (Niels), **Born** (Max), **Bose** (Satyendra Nath), **Dick** (Robert Henry), **Gray** (Stephen), **Haüy** (René Just), **Hess** (Victor Francis), **Katz** (Sir Bernard), **Kerr** (John), **Land** (Edwin Herbert), **Laue** (Max Theodor Felix von), **Lenz** (Heinrich Friedrich Emil), **Mach** (Ernst), **Mott** (Sir Nevill Francis), **Néel** (Louis Eugène Félix), **Rabi** (Isidor Isaac), **Saha** (Meghnad), **Ting** (Samuel Chao Chung), **Wien** (Wilhelm), **Yang** (Chen Ning)
05 **Aston** (Francis William), **Auger** (Pierre Victor), **Bethe** (Hans Albrecht), **Bloch** (Felix), **Bondi** (Sir Hermann), **Boyle** (Robert), **Bragg** (Sir Lawrence), **Bragg** (Sir William Henry), **Braun** (Ferdinand), **Curie** (Marie), **Curie** (Pierre), **Debye** (Peter), **Dewar** (Sir James), **Dirac** (P A M), **Dyson** (Freeman), **Esaki** (Leo), **Fermi** (Enrico), **Fuchs** (Klaus), **Gabor** (Dennis), **Gamow** (George), **Gauss** (Carl Friedrich), **Gibbs** (Josiah Willard), **Grove** (Sir William Robert), **Henry** (Joseph), **Hertz** (Heinrich Rudolf), **Higgs** (Peter), **Hooke** (Robert), **Jeans** (Sir James Hopwood), **Joule** (James Prescott), **Milne** (Edward Arthur), **Pauli** (Wolfgang), **Raman** (Sir Chandrasekhara Venkata), **Rossi** (Bruno), **Salam** (Abdus), **Segrè** (Emilio), **Stern** (Otto), **Tesla** (Nikola), **Vleck** (John Hasbrouck van), **Volta** (Alessandro Giuseppe Anastasio, Count), **Waals** (Johannes van der), **Young** (Thomas)
06 **Ampère** (André Marie), **Bunsen** (Robert Wilhelm), **Carnot** (Sadi), **Dalton** (John), **Edison** (Thomas Alva), **Frisch** (Otto Robert), **Geiger** (Hans Wilhelm), **Glaser** (Donald Arthur), **Huxley** (Hugh Esmor), **Kelvin** (William Thomson, Lord), **Lorenz** (Ludwig Valentin), **Newton** (Sir Isaac), **Pascal** (Blaise), **Planck** (Max), **Rohrer** (Heinrich), **Stokes** (Sir George Gabriel), **Taylor** (Sir Geoffrey Ingram), **Teller** (Edward), **Wigner** (Eugene Paul), **Wilson** (Robert), **Zwicky** (Fritz)
07 **Alferov** (Zhores I), **Alvarez** (Luis Walter), **Bednorz** (Georg), **Broglie** (Louis-Victor Pierre Raymond de), **Charles** (Jacques), **Compton** (Arthur Holly), **Coulomb** (Charles Augustin de), **Doppler** (Christian Johann), **Eastman** (George), **Faraday** (Michael), **Feynman** (Richard Phillips), **Fresnel** (Augustin Jean), **Galilei** (Galileo), **Galileo**, **Glashow** (Sheldon Lee), **Goddard** (Robert Hutchings), **Hawking** (Stephen), **Huygens** (Christiaan), **Langley** (Samuel Pierpont), **Lorentz** (Hendrik Antoon), **Marconi** (Guglielmo, Marchese), **Maxwell** (James Clerk), **Meitner** (Lise), **Oersted** (Hans Christian), **Peierls** (Sir Rudolf Ernst), **Penzias** (Arno Allan), **Poisson** (Siméon Denis), **Réaumur** (René Antoine Ferchault de), **Richter** (Burton), **Röntgen** (Wilhelm Konrad von), **Rotblat** (Sir Joseph), **Seaborg** (Glen Theodore), **Szilard** (Leo), **Thomson** (Sir J J), **Vernier** (Pierre)
08 **Ångström** (Anders Jonas), **Appleton** (Sir Edward Victor), **Avogadro** (Amedeo), **Beaufort** (Sir Francis), **Chadwick** (Sir James), **Clausius** (Rudolf), **De Forest** (Lee), **Delbrück** (Max), **Einstein** (Albert), **Foucault** (Jean Bernard Léon), **Gell-Mann** (Murray), **Langevin** (Paul), **Lemaître** (Georges Henri), **Millikan** (Robert Andrews), **Mulliken** (Robert Sanderson), **Oliphant** (Sir Mark), **Regnault** (Henri Victor), **Sakharov** (Andrei), **Shockley** (William Bradford), **Tomonaga** (Sin-Itiro), **Van Allen** (James Alfred), **Weinberg** (Steven)
09 **Aristotle**, **Bartholin** (Erasmus), **Becquerel** (Antoine Henri), **Birkeland** (Kristian Olaf Bernhard), **Boltzmann** (Ludwig), **Cavendish** (Henry), **Cherenkov** (Pavel), **Cockcroft** (Sir John Douglas), **Gay-Lussac** (Joseph Louis), **Heaviside** (Oliver), **Helmholtz** (Hermann von), **Michelson** (Albert Abraham)
10 **Anaximenes**, **Fahrenheit** (Daniel), **Heisenberg** (Werner Karl), **Rutherford** (Ernest, Lord), **Torricelli** (Evangelista), **Weizsäcker** (Carl Friedrich, Baron von), **Wheatstone** (Sir Charles), **Xenocrates**
11 **Chamberlain** (Owen), **Joliot-Curie** (Frédéric), **Joliot-Curie** (Irène), **Leeuwenhoek** (Antoni van), **Oppenheimer** (Robert), **Schrödinger** (Erwin), **Tsiolkovsky** (Konstantin), **Van de Graaff** (Robert Jemison)
13 **Chandrasekhar** (Subrahmanyan)

physiognomy

03 mug **04** dial, face, look, phiz **05** clock **06** aspect, kisser, phizog, visage **07** visnomy **08** features, fisnomie, phisnomy, visnomie **09** character **11** countenance, craniognomy

physiology

Physiologists include:

04 **Best** (Charles Herbert), **Dale** (Sir Henry Hallett), **Hess** (Walter Rudolf)
05 **Hubel** (David Hunter), **Kühne** (Wilhelm), **Lower** (Richard), **Marey** (Etienne-Jules), **Mayow** (John), **Prout** (William), **Yalow** (Rosalyn)
06 **Adrian** (Edgar Douglas, Lord), **Bordet** (Jules), **Cannon** (Walter Bradford), **Haller** (Albrecht von), **Huxley** (Sir Andrew), **Ludwig** (Karl), **Müller** (Johannes Peter), **Pavlov** (Ivan), **Pincus** (Gregory Goodwin)
07 **Banting** (Sir Frederick Grant), **Bayliss** (Sir William), **Beddoes** (Thomas Lovell), **Bernard** (Claude), **Borelli** (Giovanni Alfonso), **Diamond** (Jared Mason), **Galvani** (Luigi), **Haldane** (John Scott), **Helmont** (Johannes Baptista van), **Hodgkin** (Sir Alan Lloyd), **Schwann** (Theodor)
08 **Flourens** (Pierre Jean Marie), **Magendie** (François), **Mariotte** (Edmé), **Meyerhof** (Otto Fritz), **Purkinje** (Jan Evangelista), **Starling** (Ernest Henry)
09 **Blakemore** (Colin), **Dutrochet** (Henri), **Einthoven** (Willem), **Helmholtz** (Hermann von)
11 **Sherrington** (Sir Charles Scott)

physique

04 body, form **05** build, frame, set-up, shape **06** figure, make-up **09** structure **12** constitution

pi

03 pie, pye **05** pious **09** confusion, religious **13** sanctimonious

pianist

Pianists include:

02 **Ax** (Emmanuel)
04 **Bush** (Alan), **Cole** (Nat 'King'), **Hess** (Dame Myra), **John** (Sir Elton), **Lupu** (Radu), **Monk** (Thelonious Sphere), **Wild** (Earl)
05 **Alkan**, **Arrau** (Claudio), **Basie** (Count), **Beach** (Mrs H H A), **Blake** (Eubie), **Bolet** (Jorge), **Borge** (Victor), **Bülow** (Hans), **Corea** (Chick), **Evans** (Bill), **Evans** (Gil), **Field** (John), **Friml** (Rudolf), **Gould** (Glenn), **Hallé** (Sir Charles), **Harty** (Sir Hamilton), **Henri** (Florence), **Hines** (Earl), **Joyce** (Eileen), **Lewis** (Jerry Lee), **Liszt** (Franz), **Nyman** (Michael), **Ogdon** (John Andrew Howard), **Szell** (George), **Tatum** (Art), **Tovey** (Sir Donald), **Weber** (Carl Maria von)
06 **Albert** (Eugen d'), **Arnaud** (Yvonne), **Atwell** (Winifred), **Busoni** (Ferruccio), **Chopin** (Frédéric), **Cortot** (Alfred), **Cramer** (Johann), **Curzon** (Sir Clifford), **Czerny** (Karl), **Domino** (Fats), **Dussek** (Jan), **Garner** (Errol), **Hummel** (Johann), **Joplin** (Scott), **Kenton** (Stan), **Kissin**

(Evgeny), **Koppel** (Herman D), **Lamond** (Frederic), **Levine** (James), **Martin** (Frank), **Morton** (Jelly Roll), **Powell** (Bud), **Schiff** (András), **Serkin** (Rudolf), **Sitsky** (Larry), **Stoker** (Richard), **Taylor** (Cecil), **Tracey** (Stan), **Turina** (Joaquín), **Waller** (Fats), **Wilson** (Teddy)
07 **Albéniz** (Isaac), **Bennett** (Sir William), **Bentzon** (Niels), **Brendel** (Alfred), **Brubeck** (Dave), **Charles** (Ray), **Goodman** (Isador), **Hancock** (Herbie), **Ibrahim** (Abdullah), **Johnson** (James P), **Kentner** (Louis), **Lipatti** (Dinu), **Malcolm** (George), **Mathias** (William), **Matthay** (Tobias), **Medtner** (Nikolai), **Perahia** (Murray), **Richter** (Svyatoslav), **Solomon**, **Sorabji** (Kaikhosru), **Taneyev** (Sergei), **Vaughan** (Sarah)
08 **Argerich** (Martha), **Bronfman** (Yefim), **Browning** (John), **Clementi** (Muzio), **Dohnanyi** (Ernst), **Fou Ts'ong**, **Franklin** (Aretha), **Godowsky** (Leopold), **Grainger** (Percy), **Henschel** (Sir George), **Horowitz** (Vladimir), **Leighton** (Kenneth), **Lhévinne** (Josef), **Pachmann** (Vladimir de), **Peterson** (Oscar), **Richards** (Henry), **Schnabel** (Artur), **Schumann** (Clara), **Scriabin** (Aleksandr), **Skriabin** (Aleksandr), **Thalberg** (Sigismond), **Williams** (Mary Lou)
09 **Ashkenazy** (Vladimir), **Barenboim** (Daniel), **Bernstein** (Leonard), **Butterley** (Nigel), **Ellington** (Duke), **Gieseking** (Walter), **Henderson** (Fletcher), **Landowska** (Wanda), **MacDowell** (Edward), **Moscheles** (Ignaz), **Stevenson** (Ronald), **Westbrook** (Mike)
10 **de Larrocha** (Alicia), **Gottschalk** (Louis), **Moszkowski** (Moritz), **Paderewski** (Ignacy), **Rubinstein** (Anton), **Rubinstein** (Artur), **Scharwenka** (Xaver)
11 **Farren-Price** (Ronald), **Mitropoulos** (Dimitri), **Reizenstein** (Franz)
12 **Michelangeli** (Arturo), **Moiseiwitsch** (Benno), **Shostakovich** (Maxim)
13 **Little Richard**

piano

01 p **05** grand **06** flügel, joanna **07** upright **08** music box **09** baby grand, semi-grand **12** boudoir grand, concert grand

pick

04 best, bite, cull, hack, open, peck, pull, wale **05** begin, cause, crack, cream, elect, élite, fix on, go for, pique, pluck, prize, start **06** choice, choose, favour, flower, gather, lead to, nibble, opt for, option, pickle, pilfer, prefer, prompt, select, take in **07** collect, harvest, mandrel, mandril, produce, provoke **08** choicest, decide on, decision, plectrum, plump for, settle on **09** break open, force open, prise open, selection, single out **10** give rise to, preference **14** crème de la crème, make up your mind

• pick at

04 peck **06** nibble **07** toy with **08** play with

• pick off

03 hit **04** kill **05** shoot, snipe **06** detach, fire at, remove, strike **07** gun down, pull off, take out **08** take away

• pick on

03 nag **04** bait **05** blame, bully, get at **06** needle **07** torment **09** criticize, have a go at, persecute, victimize **13** find fault with

• pick out

04 cull, sort, spot **05** fix on, go for **06** choose, favour, notice, opt for, prefer, select, single **07** discern, make out **08** decide on, hand-pick, perceive, separate, settle on **09** recognize, single out, tell apart **11** distinguish **12** discriminate **14** make up your mind

• pick up

◇ *reversal down indicator*

03 buy, get, nab **04** bust, find, gain, go on, hear, lift, nick, peck, pull, tong **05** catch, fetch, glean, grasp, hoist, learn, pinch, raise, rally, run in **06** arrest, collar, detect, gather, master, obtain, perk up, resume, take in, take up **07** acquire, call for, carry on, collect, improve, receive, recover **08** continue, contract, discover, purchase **09** apprehend, get better, get to know, give a lift, give a ride **10** begin again, chance upon, come across, cop off with, get off with, go down with, start again **11** make headway **12** make progress **13** become ill with **15** take into custody

picket

03 peg **04** pale, pike, post **05** guard, rebel, spike, stake, watch **06** paling, patrol, piquet, sentry **07** boycott, enclose, lookout, outpost, picquet, protest, striker, upright **08** blockade, objector, picketer, surround **09** dissident, protester, stanchion **11** demonstrate **12** demonstrator **15** go on a picket line

pickings

04 loot, take **05** booty, gravy, yield **06** spoils **07** plunder, profits, returns, rewards **08** earnings, proceeds

pickle

◇ *anagram indicator*

03 fix, jam **04** bind, cure, mess, peck, pick, salt, spot **05** achar, pinch, sauce, souse, steep **06** crisis, muddle, pilfer, plight, relish, scrape **07** chutney, dilemma, put down, straits, vinegar **08** conserve, cucumber, exigency, hot water, marinade, preserve, quandary **09** condiment, seasoning, tight spot **10** difficulty, flavouring, piccalilli **11** predicament

pick-me-up

05 boost, tonic **06** fillip **07** cordial **08** roborant, stimulus **09** stimulant **11** refreshment, restorative **12** shot in the arm

pickpocket

03 dip **04** bung, file, wire **05** diver, thief **06** dipper, nipper **07** whizzer **08** cly-faker, cutpurse, snatcher **09** pick-purse **11** bagsnatcher

pick-up

02 PU **03** ute, van **04** gain, rise **05** float, lorry, rally, truck, wagon **06** bakkie, growth, reform **07** advance, headway, upswing, utility **08** increase, progress, recovery, revision **09** amendment, humbucker, reception, upgrading **10** betterment, correction, rectifying **11** development, enhancement, furtherance, improvement, modernizing, reformation **12** amelioration, utility truck **13** rectification **14** rehabilitation, utility vehicle

picky

05 faddy, fussy **06** choosy **07** finicky **08** exacting **09** selective **10** fastidious, particular, pernickety **11** persnickety **14** discriminating

picnic

05 cinch, gipsy, gypsy **06** doddle, junket, outing **08** clambake, pushover, tailgate, walkover, waygoose **09** excursion, wasegoose, wayzgoose **10** child's play **11** outdoor meal, piece of cake **13** a kettle of fish, fête champêtre

pictorial

05 vivid **06** scenic **07** graphic **08** striking **09** schematic **10** expressive, in pictures **11** illustrated, picturesque **12** diagrammatic **13** in photographs

picture

03 pic, see **04** draw, film, show, tale **05** flick, movie, paint, story **06** appear, cinema, depict, flicks, movies, report **07** account, epitome, essence, imagine, outlook, portray **08** conceive, describe, envisage, envision, exemplar **09** archetype, delineate, depiction, multiplex, narrative, portrayal, represent, reproduce, semblance, situation, visualize **10** call to mind, embodiment, illustrate, impression, similitude **11** delineation, description, film theatre **12** picture-house, quintessence **13** motion picture, picture-palace **15** personification

Pictures include:

04 E-fit®, icon, ikon, snap
05 cameo, image, mural, pin-up, plate, print, slide, still, study
06 bitmap, canvas, design, doodle, effigy, fresco, kit-cat, mosaic, sketch, veduta
07 cartoon, collage, diptych, drawing, etching, modello, montage, mugshot, tableau, tracing, vanitas
08 abstract, anaglyph, graffiti, graphics, kakemono, likeness,

monotype, negative, painting, panorama, Photofit®, portrait, snapshot, tapestry, transfer, triptych, vignette
09 bricolage, engraving, identikit, landscape, miniature, old master, oleograph, still life
10 altarpiece, caricature, photograph, silhouette
11 oil painting, trompe l'oeil, watercolour
12 illustration, photogravure, reproduction, self-portrait, transparency
13 passport photo
14 action painting, cabinet picture, representation

• get the picture
03 see **05** get it, grasp **06** follow, take in **07** catch on, latch on **08** cotton on, tumble to **10** comprehend, get the idea, understand **11** get the point **13** get the message
• put someone in the picture
04 tell **06** clue up, fill in, inform, notify, update **07** explain **10** keep posted **11** communicate

pictures
03 pix

picturesque
05 vivid **06** lovely, pretty, quaint, scenic, vulgar **07** graphic, idyllic **08** charming, pleasant, pleasing, romantic, striking **09** beautiful, colourful, depictive **10** attractive, delightful, impressive **11** descriptive

piddling
03 low **04** mean, poor, puny **05** minor, petty, small, sorry **06** meagre, measly, paltry, slight **07** trivial **08** derisory, piffling, trifling, wretched
09 miserable, worthless **10** negligible
11 unimportant **12** contemptible
13 inconsiderate, insignificant

pie
◇ *anagram indicator*
02 pi **03** mag, pye **04** flan, pâté, Pica, piet, pyat, pyet, pyot, tart **05** madge, pasty, patty, pirog **06** chewet, maggie, magpie, pastry **07** cobbler, floater
08 pandowdy **09** chatterer, confusion, coulibiac, croquante, vol-au-vent
10 Florentine, koulibiaca, tarte tatin
11 Banbury cake, oyster-patty
• pie in the sky
05 dream **06** hot air, mirage, notion
07 fantasy, reverie, romance
08 daydream, delusion **11** jam tomorrow **13** castle in Spain **14** castle in the air

piebald
04 pied **05** pinto **06** motley **07** dappled, flecked, mottled, spotted **08** brindled, skewbald, speckled **10** variegated
13 black and white, heterogeneous

piece
◇ *anagram indicator*
◇ *hidden indicator*
01 b, k, n, p, q, r **03** bar, bit, cut, die, dod, écu, end, gun, man, nip, pce
04 bite, chip, daud, dawd, dice, hunk, item, king, lump, opus, part, pawn, peso, rook, slab, snip, solo, unit, work, zack **05** block, cameo, chunk, crown, crumb, dumka, flake, fleck, patch, queen, quota, scrap, shard, share, sherd, shred, slice, small, speck, stick, story, strip, study, wedge **06** bishop, bittie, castle, dollop, jitney, knight, length, lesson, morsel, offcut, report, review, sample, scliff, skliff, sliver, tidbit, titbit **07** allegro, article, combine, element, example, intrada, mammock, mummock, peeling, portion, quarter, scaling, section, segment, snippet
08 creation, division, fraction, fragment, instance, louis-d'or, mouthful, nocturne, particle, picayune, quantity, specimen, splinter
09 allotment, component, dandiprat, dandyprat, interlude, truncheon
10 allegretto, allocation, comedietta, embodiment, percentage, production, smithereen **11** composition, constituent **12** illustration **14** morceau de salon **15** exemplification
• all in one piece
05 whole **06** entire, intact, unhurt
08 complete, integral, unbroken, unharmed **09** undamaged, uninjured
• go to pieces
05 break **06** blow up **07** break up, crack up, go to pot **08** collapse
09 break down, fall apart **10** be overcome **11** lose control **14** have a breakdown
• in pieces
◇ *anagram indicator*
05 kaput **06** broken, in bits, ruined
07 damaged, smashed **09** shattered
13 disintegrated, in smithereens
• piece together
03 fit, fix **04** join, mend **05** patch, unite
06 attach, repair **07** compose, restore
08 assemble **10** rhapsodize **11** put together
• pull to pieces, tear to pieces
03 nag, pan **04** slag, slam **05** blame, knock, slate, snipe **06** attack, tear up
07 censure, condemn, mammock, rubbish, run down, slag off
08 badmouth, denounce **09** criticize, dismember **10** come down on, go to town on **11** pick holes in **12** disapprove of, put the boot in, tear to shreds
13 find fault with, tear a strip off **15** do a hatchet job on

pièce de résistance
05 jewel, joint, prize **09** showpiece
10 magnum opus, masterwork **11** chef-d'oeuvre, masterpiece

piecemeal
06 patchy, slowly **07** partial **08** bit by bit, discrete, fitfully, in detail, sporadic
09 by degrees, dismember, partially, scattered **10** parcel-wise **11** at intervals, fragmentary, interrupted
12 intermittent, unsystematic
14 intermittently, little by little **15** in dribs and drabs

pied
04 piet, pyat, pyet, pyot **06** motley
07 brindle, dappled, flecked, mottled, piebald, spotted **08** brindled, skewbald, streaked **09** irregular
10 variegated **12** varicoloured
13 multicoloured, parti-coloured

pier
04 dock, mole, pile, post, quay **05** jetty, jutty, wharf **06** column, pillar
07 slipway, support, upright
08 buttress **09** Swiss roll **10** breakwater
12 landing-stage **15** clustered column

pierce
◇ *insertion indicator*
03 jag, peg, ren, rin, run, tap **04** barb, bore, fill, gore, hurt, move, nail, pain, pike, pink, pith, prog, rive, slap, stab
05 drift, drill, enter, gride, gryde, lance, perce, perse, prick, probe, punch, spear, spike, spile, stake, steek, stick, sting, thirl, touch **06** broach, cleave, engore, gimlet, impale, launce, launch, needle, pearce, percen, skewer, thrill, thrust **07** bayonet, emperce, light up
08 empierce, puncture, transfix
09 lancinate, penetrate, perforate, stick into **10** run through **11** pass through, perforation, transpierce **12** burst through **13** cut to the quick, thrill through

pierced
05 grypt, stung **06** pearst, pierst, pinked **07** impaled, pertuse
08 pertused **09** perforate, pertusate, punctured **10** fenestrate, foraminous, penetrated, perforated **11** fenestrated, foraminated

piercing
◇ *insertion indicator*
03 raw **04** cold, keen, loud **05** acute, alert, sharp **06** Arctic, astute, biting, bitter, fierce, frosty, severe, shrewd, shrill, wintry **07** extreme, intense, numbing, painful, probing **08** freezing, perceant, shooting, stabbing
09 agonizing, searching, thrillant
10 discerning, lacerating, perceptive
11 ear-piercing, high-pitched, penetrating, penetrative, sharp-witted
12 ear-splitting, excruciating

piercingly
06 keenly, loudly **07** alertly, sharply, shrilly **08** astutely, bitterly, fiercely, severely **09** extremely, intensely, numbingly, painfully **11** agonizingly
12 discerningly **13** penetratingly
14 excruciatingly

piety
04 fear, pity **05** faith **07** respect
08 devotion, holiness, religion, sanctity
09 deference, fear of God, godliness, piousness, reverence **10** devoutness
11 dutifulness, saintliness **12** spirituality
13 religiousness

piffle
03 rot **04** blah, bosh, bull, bunk, cock, guff, tosh **05** balls, hooey, trash, tripe
06 bunkum, drivel, trifle **07** baloney,

eyewash, hogwash, rhubarb, rubbish, twaddle **08** malarkey, nonsense, tommyrot **09** bull's wool, moonshine, poppycock **10** balderdash, codswallop **11** tarradiddle

piffling
04 idle **05** empty, minor, petty, silly, small **06** paltry, slight **07** foolish, shallow, trivial **08** trifling **09** frivolous, worthless **10** inadequate, negligible **11** superficial, unimportant **12** insufficient **13** insignificant **14** inconsiderable **15** inconsequential

pig
03 elt, hog, sow **04** boar, boor, cram, gilt, runt, slip, wolf, yelt **05** beast, brute, feast, gorge, piggy, scoff, shoat, shote, snarf, stuff, swine **06** animal, gobble, guffie, guzzle, piggie, piglet, porker, sucker, weaner **07** Anthony, glutton, grunter, guzzler, monster, pigling, roaster, tantony **08** gourmand, grumphie, porkling, potsherd, wild boar **09** policeman **10** greedy guts **11** earthenware, gormandizer **13** Captain Cooker

Pigs include:

05 Duroc
07 Old Spot
08 landrace, Pietrain, Tamworth, wild boar
09 Berkshire, Hampshire, Yorkshire
10 Large White, potbellied, saddleback
11 Middle White
15 Chinese Meishian

pigeon
03 nun, owl **04** barb, clay, dove, girl, gull, hoax, kuku, rock, ront, ruff, runt, spot **05** goura, homer, piper, quest, quist, ronte, squab, wonga **06** affair, culver, cushat, pouter, queest, quoist, roller, turbit, zoozoo **07** carrier, concern, cropper, fantail, jacinth, jacobin, laugher, manumea, pintado, tumbler **08** business, capuchin, horseman, ringdove, rock dove, squealer **09** archangel, solitaire, trumpeter **10** bronze-wing, Didunculus, wonga-wonga **12** mourning dove

pigeonhole
03 box, tag **04** file, slot, sort **05** class, defer, label, niche, place **06** locker, put off, shelve **07** cubicle, section **08** category, classify, postpone **09** catalogue, cubby-hole **10** categorize **11** alphabetize, compartment **14** classification

pigeon pea
03 dal **04** daal, dahl, dhal **05** dholl

pig-headed
06 mulish, stupid, wilful **07** froward **08** contrary, perverse, stubborn **09** obstinate **10** bull-headed, headstrong, inflexible, self-willed, unyielding **11** intractable, stiff-necked, wrong-headed **12** intransigent

piglet *see* **pig**

pigment
03 dye, hue **04** tint **05** paint, stain **06** colour, piment **08** tincture **09** colouring

Pigments include:

03 hem
04 haem, heme
05 henna, ochre, sepia, smalt, umber
06 bister, bistre, cobalt, cyanin, lutein, madder, sienna, zaffer, zaffre
07 carmine, etiolin, gamboge, melanin, sinopia, turacin
08 cinnabar, luteolin, orpiment, rose-pink, verditer, viridian
09 anthocyan, bilirubin, colcothar, Indian red, lamp-black, lithopone, phycocyan, quercetin, zinc white
10 Berlin blue, biliverdin, Chinese red, chlorophyl, green earth, lipochrome, madder-lake, Paris-green, pearl white, rhodophane, terre verte, vermillion
11 anthochlore, anthocyanin, chlorophyll, King's-yellow, phycocyanin, phycophaein, phytochrome, ultramarine, Venetian red
12 anthoxanthin, Cappagh-brown, Chinese white, chrome yellow, Naples-yellow, phaeomelanin, phycoxanthin, Prussian blue, turacoverdin, Tyrian purple, xanthopterin
13 cadmium yellow, phycoerythrin, Scheele's green, titanium white, xanthopterine
15 purple of Cassuis

See also **colour**; **dye**

pike
03 gar, ged **04** jack, luce, pick, toll **05** speed **06** renege **07** garfish, walleye **08** jackfish, pickerel, turnpike **11** Lepidosteus

Pikes include:

03 Esk, Red
04 Cold, High
05 Heron, Rispa
06 Causey, Kidsty, Ullock
07 Rossett, Scafell
08 Kentmere, Langdale
09 Angletarn, Grisedale, Sheffield
10 Dollywagon, Nethermost

pilaster
04 anta

pile
03 bar, fur, jam, nap **04** a lot, beam, bing, bomb, cock, down, fuzz, hair, heap, load, lots, mass, mint, pack, post, rush, shag, tons, wool **05** amass, crowd, crush, flock, flood, fluff, heaps, hoard, loads, mound, plush, stack, store **06** bundle, charge, column, fibres, gather, heap up, masses, oodles, packet, piling, riches, stacks, stream, wealth **07** build up, collect, edifice, fortune, mansion, rouleau, squeeze, stack up, support, surface, texture, threads, upright **08** assemble, big bucks, hundreds, lashings, millions, mountain **09** arrowhead, megabucks, stockpile, thousands **10** accumulate, a great deal, assemblage, assortment, collection, foundation, quantities **11** loadsamoney, soft surface **12** accumulation **13** large building, large quantity

• **pile it on**
06 overdo, stress **07** lay it on, magnify **08** overplay **09** dramatize, emphasize, overstate **10** exaggerate **12** lay it on thick **13** make too much of, overdramatize, overemphasize, pile it on thick

• **pile up**
03 big **04** deck, grow, soar **07** mount up **08** escalate, increase, multiply **10** accumulate

pile-up
04 bump **05** crash, prang, smash, wreck **07** smash-up **08** accident **09** collision

pilfer
03 bag, lag, mag, nim, rob **04** blag, lift, mill, nick, pick, pull, smug, whip **05** boost, filch, heist, hoist, miche, mooch, mouch, pinch, sneak, steal, swipe **06** finger, nobble, pickle, snitch, thieve **07** purloin, snaffle **08** knock off, peculate, shoplift **10** run off with **12** make away with

pilfering *see* **theft**

pilgrim
05 hadji **06** palmer **07** devotee **08** crusader, newcomer, wanderer, wayfarer **09** peregrine, traveller **10** worshipper

pilgrimage
03 haj **04** hadj, hajj, tour, trip **06** wander **07** crusade, journey, mission **08** lifetime **10** expedition **13** peregrination

pill
03 dex, tab **04** ball, husk, peel **05** bolus, upper **06** bomber, cachou, caplet, doctor, pellet, pilula, pilule, tablet **07** capsule, globule, lozenge, plunder **08** goofball, microdot, spansule **09** blackball **10** integument, number nine **12** multivitamin **13** pain in the neck

pillage
03 rob **04** loot, peel, raid, raze, sack **05** booty, rifle, spoil, strip **06** maraud, rapine, ravage, spoils **07** despoil, plunder, ransack, robbery, seizure **08** freeboot, harrying, spoliate **09** depredate, marauding, vandalize **10** spoliation **11** depredation, devastation

pillar
03 lat, man **04** goal, mast, pier, pile, pole, post, prop, rock **05** shaft, stack, stoop, stoup **06** cippus, column **07** bastion, obelisk, respond, support, telamon, trumeau, upright **08** baluster, caryatid, gendarme, lamppost, mainstay, monolith, pilaster, stalwart, standard **09** pillarbox, sandspout,

stanchion **12** lamp-standard **15** tower of strength

pillory
04 cang, lash, mock **05** brand **06** attack, cangue, show up **07** laugh at, tumbrel, tumbril **08** denounce, ridicule **09** criticize **10** little-ease, stigmatize **11** cast a slur on, pour scorn on **13** hold up to shame

pillow
03 bed, cod **04** rest **07** bolster, cushion **08** headrest, pulvinar

pillowcase
04 bear, beer, bere, slip

pilot
03 fly, run **04** crew, lead, test **05** drive, flier, flyer, guide, model, prune, steer, trial **06** airman, direct, George, handle, leader, manage, sample **07** aircrew, aviator, captain, conduct, control, hobbler, operate, shipman **08** airwoman, aviatrix, coxswain, director, governor, helmsman, lodesman, navigate **09** aviatress, commander, manoeuvre, navigator, rocketeer, steersman **10** cowcatcher, cropduster **12** experimental, first officer **14** flight engineer

pimp
04 bawd, hoon, mack **05** ponce **06** broker, pandar, pander **07** hustler, procure **08** fancy man, mackerel, panderer, procurer **09** solicitor **11** fleshmonger, whoremonger

pimpernel
06 burnet **09** brookweed, wincopipe, wink-a-peep **12** weather glass **14** shepherd's glass

pimple
03 zit **04** boil, quat, spot **05** botch, plook, plouk, whelk **06** button, milium, papula, papule, rum-bud **07** bubukle, pustule **08** swelling **09** blackhead, carbuncle, whitehead **10** rum-blossom

pin
03 fix, lay, leg, nog, peg, put **04** axle, bolt, clip, hold, join, nail, peak, stud, tack **05** affix, dowel, drift, pitch, pivot, place, preen, press, rivet, screw, spike, stage, stick, wrist **06** attach, brooch, cotter, degree, fasten, impute, pintle, secure, skewer, staple **07** ascribe, enclose, gudgeon, skittle, trenail **08** chessman, fastener, hold down, hold fast, restrain, treenail **09** attribute, constrain, thumbtack **10** immobilize

• pin down
03 peg **04** make, nail **05** force, press **06** compel, define **07** specify **08** hold down, hold fast, identify, nail down, pinpoint, restrain **09** constrain, determine **10** pressurize **15** put your finger on

pinafore
04 brat, tire **05** apron, pinny **06** jumper, pinner, pinnie **07** gym slip, overall, save-all **08** gym tunic

pincers
06 forfex **07** forceps, nippers **08** pinchers, tweezers **10** Jaws of Life®

pinch
◇ *containment indicator*
03 bag, bit, jot, nab, nip, tad **04** bite, book, bust, carp, dash, grip, hurt, lace, lift, mite, nail, nick, nirl, pook, pouk, save, shut, spot, tait, tate, whip **05** catch, chack, check, cramp, crush, filch, grasp, gripe, pleat, press, pugil, run in, seize, sneap, snuff, speck, steal, stint, swipe, taste, touch, trace, tweak, wring **06** arrest, budget, collar, crisis, detain, eke out, hamper, harass, narrow, pick up, pilfer, pincer, pull in, snatch, sneesh, stress, twinge, twitch **07** capture, confine, cut back, purloin, smidgen, soupçon, squeeze **08** compress, encroach, half-inch, hardship, knock off, peculate, pressure, restrict, sneeshan, sneeshin, souvenir **09** economize, emergency, sneeshing **10** difficulty **11** appropriate, predicament, walk off with **13** keep costs down, scrape a living, scrimp and save **14** live on the cheap **15** tighten your belt

• at a pinch
11 if necessary **13** in an emergency

• feel the pinch
06 be poor **12** hit a bad patch **13** have a hard time **14** be short of money, scratch a living **15** strike a bad patch, tighten your belt

pinched
04 pale, thin, worn **05** drawn, gaunt, peaky **07** haggard, starved **08** careworn, narrowed, strained **12** straightened

pine
04 ache, fade, fret, hone, long, sigh, wish **05** crave, dwine, mourn, yearn **06** desire, grieve, hanker, hunger, repine, thirst, weaken **08** languish **09** waste away

Pine trees include:

03 nut, red
04 blue, Huon, jack
05 Chile, kauri, pinon, Scots, stone, sugar, white
06 arolla, celery, cembra, Jersey, Korean, limber, Paraná, Scotch, spruce
07 Amboina, Chilean, cluster, Mexican, radiata
08 Japanese, Jeffrey's, knobcone, lacebark, loblolly, longleaf, mountain, Pandanus, pinaster, Scots fir, umbrella
09 lodgepole, Scotch fir
11 bristlecone
12 monkey puzzle
13 Norfolk Island

pineapple
04 bomb, piña, pine **05** anana **06** ananas **07** grenade **10** tillandsia

pining
04 sick

pinion
03 cog, tie **04** bind, wing **05** chain, penne, truss **06** fasten, fetter, hobble, pennon **07** confine, manacle, pin down, shackle **10** immobilize

pink
03 cut, top **04** acme, best, peak, peep, peer, penk, rosy, stab, wink **05** blink, knock, notch, pinky, prick, prime, punch, score, small **06** eyelet, flower, height, incise, minnow, pierce, pinkie, samlet, summit, tiptop **07** extreme, flushed, reddish, roseate, scallop, serrate **08** blinking, detonate **09** chaffinch, exquisite, perforate **10** crenellate, perfection, rose colour **12** rose-coloured

Pinks include:

04 puce, rose
05 coral, peach
06 oyster, salmon, shrimp
07 old rose
08 cyclamen
09 carnation, pompadour, shell pink
12 mushroom pink, shocking pink

• in the pink
03 fit **04** trim, well **07** healthy **08** very well **10** in good nick, in good trim, on good form **11** in good shape, right as rain **12** in fine fettle, in good health **15** in perfect health

pinnacle
03 cap, top **04** acme, apex, cone, peak **05** crest, crown, spire **06** apogee, height, hoodoo, needle, pinnet, summit, turret, vertex, zenith **07** minaret, obelisk, pyramid, steeple, sublime **08** eminence **11** culmination

pinpoint
04 spot **05** exact, place, right **06** define, locate **07** pin down, precise, specify **08** accurate, discover, home in on, identify, nail down, rigorous, zero in on **09** determine **10** meticulous, scrupulous **11** distinguish, punctilious **15** put your finger on

pint
02 pt

• nearly a pint
03 log

pint-size
03 wee **04** mini, tiny **05** dinky, dwarf, pygmy, small, teeny **06** little, midget, pocket **09** miniature, pint-sized **10** diminutive, teeny-weeny **11** pocket-sized

pioneer
05 begin, chips, found, set up, start **06** create, invent, launch, leader, open up **07** develop, founder, planter, settler **08** colonist, discover, explorer, initiate, inventor, labourer, way-maker **09** developer, establish, excavator, harbinger, innovator, instigate, institute, introduce, originate, spearhead **10** discoverer, lead the way, pathfinder, pave the way, sandgroper **11** bandeirante, blaze a trail, trailblazer,

voortrekker **12** First Fleeter, frontiersman **13** groundbreaker **14** break new ground, founding father, frontierswoman

See also **explorer**

pious
02 pi **03** pia **04** good, holy, wise **05** godly, moral **06** devout **07** devoted, dutiful, saintly **08** faithful, priggish, reverent, unctuous, virtuous **09** dedicated, insincere, religious, righteous, spiritual **10** goody-goody, sanctified **12** hypocritical **13** sanctimonious, self-righteous **14** holier-than-thou

piously
07 morally **08** devoutly **10** faithfully, priggishly, reverently, virtuously **11** insincerely, religiously, righteously, spiritually **14** hypocritically **15** sanctimoniously, self-righteously

pip
03 die **04** hump, kill, peep, roup, seed, spot, star **05** chirp, peepe, speck, wound **06** acinus, pippin, spleen **07** ailment, disgust, offence **08** fruitlet, syphilis **09** blackball, distemper **10** grapestone

pipe
03 ait, jet, oat, tap **04** clay, duct, fife, flue, hose, line, main, peep, play, pule, reed, sing, take, tube, vent, weep, worm **05** aulos, brier, bring, carry, cheep, chirp, crane, cutty, drone, flute, kelly, quill, riser, sound, tibia, trill, tweet **06** convey, dudeen, faucet, funnel, hookah, kalian, piping, shrike, shrill, siphon, supply, tubing, uptake, warble **07** calumet, channel, chanter, chibouk, chirrup, cob-pipe, conduct, conduit, dead-end, deliver, dip-pipe, nargile, nargily, passage, tweedle, twitter, whistle **08** aqueduct, bagpipes, blow pipe, claypipe, conveyor, cornpipe, cylinder, dry riser, feed-pipe, manifold, mirliton, narghile, narghily, nargileh, nargilly, overflow, pipeline, recorder, soil pipe, stopcock, tailpipe, transmit **09** blast-pipe, chibouque, drainpipe, goose-neck, narghilly, peace-pipe, pitch-pipe, standpipe, stovepipe, ventiduct, wastepipe, water pipe **10** chimney pot, gas-bracket, kill string, meerschaum **11** clyster-pipe, exhaust pipe, service pipe, tobacco-pipe **12** churchwarden, hubble-bubble, penny whistle, throttle-pipe **13** woodcock's-head **15** injection string

See also **tobacco**

• pipe down
06 shut up **07** be quiet **11** stop talking

pipeclay
03 cam **04** calm, caum

pipe dream
05 dream **06** mirage, notion, vagary **07** chimera, fantasy, reverie, romance **08** daydream, delusion **09** false hope **11** pie in the sky **13** castle in Spain **14** castle in the air

pipeline
04 duct, line, pipe, tube **07** channel, conduit, passage **08** conveyor

• in the pipeline
07 planned **08** on the way, under way **13** in preparation **14** already started

pipsqueak
05 creep, twerp **06** nobody, squirt **07** nothing, upstart **09** nonentity **11** hobbledehoy **14** whippersnapper

piquancy
03 pep, zip **04** bite, edge, kick, race, salt, tang, zest **05** juice, oomph, punch, spice **06** colour, ginger, relish, spirit, vigour **07** flavour, pizzazz **08** interest, pungency, raciness, vitality **09** sharpness, spiciness **10** excitement, liveliness **11** pepperiness **13** strong flavour

piquant
04 racy, tart **05** juicy, salty, sharp, spicy, tangy, zesty **06** biting, lively **07** peppery, pungent, savoury **08** poignant, seasoned, spirited, stinging **09** colourful, sparkling **10** appetizing, intriguing **11** fascinating, interesting, provocative, stimulating **14** highly seasoned

pique
03 bug, get, irk, vex **04** gall, goad, huff, miff, nark, peak, rile, spur, stir, whet **05** anger, annoy, get at, peeve, point, rouse, sting, wound **06** arouse, excite, grudge, kindle, needle, nettle, offend, put out, wind up **07** affront, dudgeon, incense, mortify, offence, provoke, umbrage **08** drive mad, irritate, vexation **09** aggravate, animosity, annoyance, displease, galvanize, punctilio, stimulate **10** drive crazy, ill-feeling, irritation, resentment **11** displeasure **12** drive bananas **13** make sparks fly **14** drive up the wall

piqued
03 mad **05** angry, cross, ratty, riled, vexed **06** choked, miffed, narked, peeved, put out **07** annoyed, stroppy, uptight **08** in a paddy, offended, up in arms **09** in a lather, irritated, raving mad, resentful, seeing red **10** aggravated, displeased, hopping mad **11** disgruntled, fit to be tied **12** on the warpath

piracy
05 theft **06** rapine **07** robbery **08** stealing **09** hijacking, sea-roving **10** plagiarism **11** bootlegging, freebooting **12** buccaneering, infringement

• practise piracy
04 rove

piranha
05 perai, pirai **06** caribe, piraña, piraya **08** characid, characin

pirate
04 copy, crib, lift, nick **05** pinch, poach, rover, steal **06** borrow, marque, raider, sea dog, sea rat, viking **07** brigand, corsair, sea wolf **08** algerine, knock off, marauder, picaroon, sea rover, water rat **09** buccaneer, infringer, sallee-man, sea robber **10** arch-pirate, filibuster, freebooter, plagiarist, plagiarize, water-thief **11** appropriate, plagiarizer

Pirates include:

03 Tew (Thomas)
04 Bart (Jean), Gunn (Ben), Hook (Captain), Kidd (William), Otto, Read (Mary), Smee
05 Barth (Jean), Bones (Billy), Bonny (Anne), Bunce (Jack), Drake (Sir Francis), Every (Henry), Ewart (Nanty), Flint (Captain), Tache (Edward), Teach (Edward)
06 Aubery (Jean-Benoit), Conrad, Jonsen (Captain), Morgan (Sir Henry), Silver (Long John), Thatch (Edward), Walker (William)
07 Dampier (William), Lafitte (Jean), O'Malley (Grace), Rackham (John), Roberts (Bartholomew), Sparrow (Captain Jack), Trumpet (Solomon)
08 Altamont (Frederick), Black Dog, Blackett (Nancy), Blackett (Peggy), Blind Pew, Redbeard, Ringrose (Basil)
09 Black Bart, Cleveland (Clement)
10 Barbarossa (Khair-ed-din), Blackbeard, Calico Jack
14 Long John Silver

pirouette
04 spin, turn **05** pivot, twirl, whirl **06** gyrate **08** gyration **15** turn on a sixpence

pistol
03 dag, gat, gun, pop, rod **04** Colt®, iron **05** Luger®, piece **06** barker, heater, puffer, zip gun **07** handgun, pistole, sidearm **08** revolver, water gun **09** derringer, squirt gun **10** six-shooter **11** barking iron

See also **gun**

piston
03 ram

pit
03 bed, den, put **04** dent, gulf, hole, khud, mark, mine, play, scar, silo, sump **05** abyss, chasm, ditch, fossa, fovea, notch, stone **06** cavity, crater, dimple, hollow, indent, quarry, trench **07** blemish, depress, measure, moss hag, pothole **08** alveolus, coalmine, diggings, moss hagg, pockmark, punctule, workings **10** depression, scrobicule **11** excavations, indentation

• pit against
05 match **06** oppose **07** compete **10** set against

• the pits
04 crap, naff **05** awful, lousy, pants, spewy **06** cruddy, crummy **07** abysmal **08** dreadful, inferior, pathetic, terrible, very poor **09** third-rate **10** inadequate, second-rate **14** a load of rubbish, unsatisfactory

Pitcairn Island
03 PCN

pitch
03 aim, fix, lob, pin, pop, set, tar, yak **04** bowl, cant, cast, dive, drop, face, fall, fire, hurl, keel, line, list, mark, nets, park, peck, reel, roll, stud, sway, talk, tilt, tone, toss **05** angle, arena, chuck, cover, erect, field, fling, grade, heave, level, lurch, place, plant, point, put up, set up, slant, sling, slope, sound, spiel, throw **06** alight, bounce, degree, direct, encamp, extent, gabble, ground, height, jargon, launch, maltha, patter, plunge, settle, timbre, topple, tumble, wallow, wicket **07** asphalt, bitumen, chatter, descent, incline, plummet, set down, stadium, station **08** flounder, gradient, position, tonality **09** determine, establish, frequency, intensity, interlock, steepness **10** modulation **11** inclination, sports field **12** fall headlong, playing-field **13** move up and down
• **make a pitch for**
05 offer, put up **06** bid for, submit, tender **07** advance, proffer, propose **08** put in for, try to get **09** try to sell **10** put forward **11** try to obtain
• **pitch in**
04 help **06** join in, muck in **07** help out **09** co-operate, do your bit, lend a hand **10** be involved **11** participate
• **too low in pitch, too high in pitch**
04 flat **05** sharp

pitch-black
04 dark, inky **05** black, unlit **08** jet-black **09** coal-black, pitch-dark **13** unilluminated

pitcher
03 can, jar, jug, urn **04** ewer, jack, sett **05** crock **06** bottle, closer, vessel **07** growler **09** container **11** screwballer **13** knuckleballer
• **pitcher plant**
08 nepenthe **09** Nepenthes **10** Sarracenia **12** Darlingtonia

piteous
03 sad **06** moving, paltry, rueful, woeful **07** pitiful, ruthful **08** mournful, pathetic, pitiable, poignant, touching, wretched **09** plaintive, sorrowful **10** lamentable **11** distressing **12** heart-rending **13** compassionate, heartbreaking

pitfall
04 risk, snag, trap **05** catch, peril, snare **06** danger, hazard **08** drawback, trapfall **10** difficulty **14** stumbling-block

pith
03 nub **04** core, crux, gist, meat **05** heart, point, value **06** import, kernel, marrow, matter, mettle, moment, vigour, weight **07** essence, medulla, papyrus **09** substance **10** importance **11** consequence **12** forcefulness, quintessence, salient point, significance **13** essential part

pithead
04 brow

pithily
07 in a word, in brief, tersely **09** compactly, concisely **10** succinctly, to the point **11** in a few words, in a nutshell **12** meaningfully

pithy
05 brief, meaty, short, terse **06** cogent, strong **07** compact, concise, marrowy, pointed, summary, telling **08** forceful, forcible, incisive, lapidary, material, pregnant, succinct **09** condensed, energetic, matterful, trenchant **10** expressive, meaningful

pitiable
03 sad **04** poor **05** silly, sorry **06** woeful **07** doleful, piteous, woesome **08** grievous, mournful, pathetic, wretched **09** miserable **10** distressed, lamentable **11** distressful, distressing **12** commiserable, contemptible **14** compassionable

pitiful
03 low, sad **04** base, mean, poor, vile **05** lousy, seely, sorry, waefu'
06 crummy, meagre, moving, paltry, shabby, waeful, woeful **07** doleful, piteous, ruthful, the pits, waesome **08** hopeless, mournful, pathetic, pitiable, terrible, wretched **09** affecting, miserable, worthless **10** deplorable, despicable, inadequate, lamentable **11** distressing **12** contemptible, heart-rending **13** compassionate, heartbreaking, insignificant

pitifully
05 sadly **08** terribly, woefully **09** miserably, piteously **10** deplorably, despicably, hopelessly, lamentably **12** contemptibly, pathetically **13** distressingly

pitiless
05 cruel, harsh, stony **06** brutal, severe **07** callous, inhuman **08** inhumane, ruthless, uncaring **09** heartless, merciless, unfeeling **10** dispiteous, hard-headed, inexorable, relentless **11** cold-blooded, cold-hearted, hard-hearted, unremitting **13** unsympathetic

pitilessly
07 cruelly, harshly **08** brutally **09** callously **10** ruthlessly **11** mercilessly **13** cold-bloodedly, cold-heartedly, hard-heartedly

pittance
04 dole, drop **05** crumb **06** trifle **07** modicum, peanuts **11** chickenfeed **14** drop in the ocean

pitted
05 holey, rough **06** dented, marked **07** foveate, notched, scarred **08** alveolar, indented, lacunose, potholed, punctate **09** alveolate, blemished, depressed, punctated **10** pockmarked

pity
03 rew, rue, sin **04** ruth **05** bleed, grace, mercy, piety, shame **06** bemoan, bepity, bowels, regret, sorrow **07** bad luck, emotion, feel for, feeling, mercify, remorse, sadness, weep for **08** distress, kindness, sympathy **09** grieve for **10** compassion, condolence, have a heart, misericord, misfortune, tenderness **11** crying shame, forbearance, forgiveness, misericorde **12** feel sorry for **13** commiseration, empathize with, fellow-feeling, understanding **14** disappointment, sympathize with **15** commiserate with
• **take pity on**
03 rue **05** spare **06** pardon **07** feel for **09** show mercy **11** have mercy on **12** feel sorry for **13** empathize with **14** emphathize with, sympathize with **15** commiserate with

pivot
03 hub, lie **04** axis, axle, hang, rely, spin, turn **05** focus, heart, hinge, swing **06** centre, depend, rotate, swivel **07** fulcrum, kingpin, revolve, spindle **08** cardinal, linchpin **10** focal point **12** be contingent, central point

pivotal
05 axial, focal, vital **07** central, crucial **08** critical, decisive **09** climactic, important **11** determining

pixie
03 elf, imp **04** pixy **05** fairy, pisky **06** goblin, sprite **07** brownie **10** leprechaun

pizzazz
04 brio, life **05** oomph **06** energy, esprit, spirit, vigour **07** entrain **08** activity, dynamism, vitality, vivacity **09** animation, briskness, quickness, smartness **10** liveliness **11** refreshment **13** sprightliness, vivaciousness **14** boisterousness

placard
02 ad **04** bill, sign **05** title **06** advert, notice, poster **07** affiche, placcat, placket, sticker **13** advertisement

placate
04 calm, lull **05** quiet **06** disarm, pacify, soothe **07** appease, assuage, mollify, win over **08** calm down **10** conciliate, propitiate

placatory
07 calming **08** soothing **09** appeasing **10** mollifying **11** peace-making **12** conciliatory, pacificatory, propitiative, propitiatory

place
01 P **02** do, Pl **03** fix, job, lay, pad, put, set **04** area, city, digs, duty, flat, home, know, lieu, park, part, pose, post, rank, rest, role, room, seat, site, sort, spot, sted, task, town **05** abode, class, grade, group, hotel, house, leave, locus, lodge, niche, order, plant, point, right, scene, space, stand, state, stead, stedd, stede, steed, topic, venue **06** assign, hamlet, induct, invest, locale, locate, region, settle, square,

status, stedde **07** appoint, arrange, concern, country, deposit, footing, install, lay down, put down, set down, setting, situate, station, village **08** allocate, building, business, classify, district, domicile, dwelling, fortress, function, identify, locality, location, pinpoint, position, property, remember, standing **09** apartment, establish, recognize, residence, situation **10** categorize, restaurant **11** appointment, battlefield, find a job for, institution, whereabouts **13** accommodation, establishment, neighbourhood **14** responsibility

See also **Bible**; **eating**; **entertainment**; **fictional**; **mythical**

• all over the place

◇ *anagram indicator*

04 awry **05** messy **07** muddled **08** confused **09** dispersed, scattered **12** disorganized

• at the right place

03 pat

• at that place

05 there

• at this place

04 here

• in place

05 set up **07** in order, working **08** arranged **10** in position

• in place of

04 lieu, vice **08** in lieu of **09** instead of **13** in exchange for

• in the same place

02 ib **04** ibid **06** ibidem

• no place

02 np

• out of place

◇ *anagram indicator*

04 away **08** improper, out of key, tactless, unseemly **09** unfitting **10** inapposite, malapropos, unbecoming, unsuitable **12** unseasonable **13** inappropriate

• put someone in their place

05 crush, shame **06** humble **07** deflate **08** bring low **09** humiliate

• take place

02 be **04** fall **05** occur **06** befall, be held, betide, happen **07** come off **09** come about, transpire **10** come to pass

• take the place of

06 act for **07** replace, serve as, succeed **09** supersede **10** stand in for **12** take over from **13** substitute for

placement

03 job **07** placing, ranking, setting **08** locating, location, ordering **10** assignment, deployment, employment, engagement, internship, stationing **11** appointment, arrangement, disposition, emplacement, positioning **12** distribution, installation **14** classification

placid

04 calm, cool, mild **05** quiet, still **06** gentle, serene **07** equable, pacific, restful, unmoved **08** composed, peaceful, tranquil **09** easy-going, peaceable, unruffled **10** untroubled **11** level-headed, undisturbed, unemotional, unexcitable, unflappable **12** even-tempered **13** imperturbable, self-possessed

placidly

06 calmly, gently, mildly **08** serenely **09** restfully **10** peacefully **11** unflappably **13** imperturbably

plagiarism

04 crib **05** theft **06** piracy **07** copying, lifting **08** cribbing **09** borrowing **12** infringement, reproduction **13** appropriation **14** counterfeiting

plagiarist

05 thief **06** copier, pirate, robber **08** imitator **09** Autolycus

plagiarize

04 copy, crib, lift, nick **05** poach, steal **06** borrow, pirate **07** imitate **09** reproduce **11** appropriate, counterfeit

plague

03 bug, dog, dun, pox, vex **04** bane, blow, pest **05** annoy, curse, death, haunt, hound, swarm, tease, trial, upset, worry, wound **06** bother, hamper, harass, hassle, hinder, influx, pester **07** afflict, bedevil, cholera, disease, disturb, murrain, scourge, torment, torture, trouble **08** calamity, distress, epidemic, goodyear, invasion, irritate, nuisance, pandemic, sickness, vexation **09** aggravate, annoyance, contagion, goodyears, infection, persecute **10** affliction, Black Death, huge number, pestilence **11** infestation **13** bubonic plague, pain in the neck **15** pneumonic plague, thorn in the flesh

The ten Biblical plagues:

04 lice
05 boils, flies, frogs
07 locusts
08 darkness
09 hailstorm
18 disease of livestock
19 death of the firstborn
21 Nile waters turn to blood

plain

04 even, flat, open, ugly **05** basic, blunt, clear, frank, level, lucid, muted, overt, prose, quite, secco, stark, utter **06** candid, direct, homely, honest, lament, modest, patent, rustic, simple, simply, **07** austere, clearly, evident, obvious, plateau, sincere, spartan, totally, unruled, utterly, visible **08** apparent, clinical, complain, flatland, home-bred, home-made, homespun, manifest, ordinary, truthful, uncurled, unlovely **09** downright, grassland, outspoken, plain-Jane, practical, tableland, unadorned **10** accessible, completely, distinctly, forthright, noticeable, restrained, thoroughly, unaffected, unassuming, uncoloured, undeniably **11** discernible, perceptible, plain-spoken, transparent, unambiguous, undecorated, unelaborate, unpatterned **12** intelligible, self-coloured, unattractive, unmistakable, unobstructed, unvariegated **13** uncomplicated, unembellished, unpretentious **14** understandable **15** clear as daylight, not much to look at, straightforward, undistinguished, unprepossessing, unsophisticated

Plains include:

04 vega
05 carse, lande, llano
06 maidan, pampas, sabkha, steppe, tundra
07 lowland, prairie, sabkhah, sabkhat
08 savannah

plain-spoken

04 open **05** blunt, frank, round **06** candid, direct, honest **08** explicit, outright, truthful **09** downright, outspoken **10** forthright **11** unequivocal **15** straightforward

plaintive

03 sad **06** woeful **07** doleful, piteous, pitiful, unhappy, wistful **08** mournful, wretched **09** lacrimoso, lagrimoso, querulous, sorrowful **10** melancholy **11** heartbroken, high-pitched **12** disconsolate, heart-rending **13** grief-stricken

plaintively

05 sadly **08** woefully **09** dolefully, lacrimoso, lagrimoso, pitifully, unhappily, wistfully **10** mournfully, wretchedly **14** disconsolately

plait

04 plat **05** braid, pedal, pleat, tress **06** plight **07** frounce, leghorn **08** doubling **09** Dunstable

plan

◇ *anagram indicator*

03 aim, lay, map, way **04** case, dart, hang, idea, mean, plat, plot, seek, want, wish **05** block, chart, draft, frame, means, model, shape, trace **06** design, device, devise, intend, invent, layout, map out, method, policy, schema, scheme, sketch, system **07** arrange, complot, concoct, develop, diagram, drawing, foresee, formula, outline, prepare, project, propose, purpose, resolve, think of, work out **08** conspire, contrive, envisage, organize, platform, proposal, scenario, schedule, strategy **09** architect, blueprint, formulate, intention, itinerary, procedure, programme, timetable **10** conception, mastermind, suggestion **11** arrangement, contemplate, contrivance, delineation, ichnography, premeditate, projectment, proposition **12** illustration, scale drawing **14** representation

plane

03 bus, fly, jet **04** even, flat, rank, rung, sail, skim, soar, VTOL, wing **05** class, flush, glide, jumbo, level, plain, skate, stage **06** bomber, degree, glider, planar, smooth, thrust **07** echelon, fighter, footing, jointer, regular, stratum, uniform **08** aircraft, airliner, airplane, jumbo jet, position, seaplane, sycomore, volplane **09** aeroplane, condition, fillister, swing-wing **10** buttonball, buttonwood, homaloidal, horizontal **11** flat surface **12** level surface

See also **aircraft**

planet

05 world

Planets:

04 Mars
05 Earth, Pluto, Venus
06 Saturn, Uranus
07 Jupiter, Mercury, Neptune

plank

04 beam, slab, slat **05** board, panel, sheet **06** planch, timber **08** stringer **09** washboard **12** weatherboard

planner

05 maker **06** author **07** creator, deviser, stylist **08** arranger, designer, inventor, producer **09** architect, contriver, developer, fashioner, organizer **10** mastermind, originator

planning

06 design **07** control, running **09** ordinance **10** management, projection, regulation **11** arrangement, development, preparation **12** co-ordination, organization **13** establishment **14** administration

plant

03 fix, put, set, sow **04** bury, gear, hide, land, mill, post, root, salt, seed, shop, slip, yard **05** found, imbed, inter, lodge, place, scion, stock, works **06** cudgel, insert, instil, locate, settle **07** conceal, cutting, factory, foundry, implant, scatter, secrete, situate, station **08** colonize, disguise, offshoot, position, workshop **09** apparatus, equipment, establish, introduce, machinery **10** transplant **11** put secretly **13** put out of sight

See also **flower**; **leaf**

Plant types include:

03 air, pot
04 bean, beet, bulb, bush, cane, corm, fern, herb, moss, tree, vine, weed
05 algae, grass, house, sedge, shrub, water
06 annual, cactus, cereal, flower, fungus, hybrid, lichen
07 bedding, climber, foliage, sapling
08 biennial, cultivar, epiphyte, seedling
09 aerophyte, evergreen, perennial, succulent, vegetable
10 herbaceous, wild flower
11 carnivorous
13 insectivorous

See also **alga, algae**; **bean**; **bulb**; **cactus**; **cereal**; **crop**; **disease**; **grass**; **herb**; **lily**; **orchid**; **palm**; **poison**; **seaweed**; **sedge**; **shrub**; **tree**; **vegetable**; **weed**

plantation

03 pen **04** tope **06** bosket **07** bosquet, fazenda, pinetum **08** vineyard **09** cornbrake, salicetum, shrubbery, tea garden, viticetum

plaque

04 sign, slab **05** badge, brass, medal, panel, plate **06** brooch, shield, tablet **07** plateau **09** cartouche, medallion, plaquette

plaster

03 mud **04** coat, daub, leep, teer **05** cover, gesso, grout, parge, patch, smarm, smear **06** bedaub, clatch, gypsum, laying, mortar, parget, peloid, render, screed, spread, stucco **07** bandage, Band-aid®, overlay, pugging **08** dressing, plaister, sinapism **09** beplaster, cataplasm, emplaster, Polyfilla®, rendering, roughcast **10** emplastron, emplastrum **11** Elastoplast®, plasterwork, scratchcoat **12** cover thickly, plasterboard **13** butterfly clip **14** plaster of Paris **15** sticking-plaster

plastered

◇ *anagram indicator*

See **drunk**

plastic

◇ *anagram indicator*

04 soft **05** false **06** phoney, pliant, supple **07** ductile, man-made, pliable, shaping **08** flexible, modeller, sculptor **09** compliant, formative, malleable, mouldable, receptive, shapeable, synthetic, tractable, unnatural **10** artificial, manageable, modifiable **14** impressionable

Plastics include:

03 PVC
04 PTFE, uPVC
05 vinyl
06 Biopol®, Teflon®
07 Perspex®
08 Bakelite®, laminate, silicone
09 celluloid®, Plexiglas®, polyester, polythene, Styrofoam®
10 epoxy resin, plexiglass
11 polystyrene
12 polyethylene, polyurethane
13 phenolic resin, polypropylene
14 polynorbornene

plasticity

07 pliancy **08** softness **10** pliability, suppleness **11** flexibility, pliableness **12** malleability, tractability

plate

01 L, T **03** seg, tin, web **04** bowl, coat, dish, foil, gild, pane, rove, sign, slab **05** ashet, cover, layer, ortho, panel, paten, print, sheet **06** baffle, lamina, latten, muffin, plaque, remark, salver, silver, tablet, veneer **07** anodize, gravure, helping, lamella, ossicle, overlay, picture, plateau, platter, portion, serving **08** laminate, mazarine, pattress, trencher **09** galvanize, osteoderm, platinize **10** lithograph, photograph, zincograph **11** photo-relief **12** electroplate, illustration, mazarine dish

See also **platter**

plateau

04 mesa, roof **05** grade, level, plane, stage, table **06** meseta, upland **08** highland, platform **09** Altiplano, stability, tableland

platform

03 pad, rig, top **04** aims, bema, dais, deck, kang, plan, site **05** basis, bench, crane, dolly, floor, ideas, stage, stand, stoep, stoop, stump **06** bridge, cradle, device, flotel, gantry, machan, oil rig, pallet, perron, podium, policy, pulpit, scheme, sketch, tenets **07** balcony, decking, estrade, floatel, foretop, maintop, plateau, rostrum, soapbox, sponson, terrace, tribune **08** barbette, flooring, labellum, predella, round top, scaffold, strategy **09** crow's-nest, drillship, footplate, gangboard, manifesto, party line, programme, traverser, turntable **10** dumb waiter, intentions, objectives, principles, roundabout **11** emplacement, entablement, monkey board, paint-bridge **12** landing stage, launching-pad

platinum

02 Pt

platitude

06 cliché, truism **07** bromide, inanity **08** banality, chestnut, flatness **10** generality, stereotype **11** commonplace **15** trite expression

platitudinous

03 set **04** dull, flat **05** banal, corny, inane, stale, stock, tired, trite, vapid **07** cliché'd **08** clichéed, truistic, well-worn **09** hackneyed **10** overworked **11** commonplace, stereotyped

platonic

05 ideal **09** non-sexual, spiritual **10** idealistic **11** incorporeal, non-physical, non-romantic **12** intellectual, transcendent

platoon

04 team, unit **05** group, squad, troop **06** outfit, patrol, volley **07** battery, company **08** squadron

platter

04 dish, lanx, tray **05** graal, grail, plate **06** grayle, salver **07** charger **08** trencher

See also **plate**

plaudits

04 hand **06** praise **07** acclaim, bouquet, hurrahs, ovation **08** accolade, applause, approval, clapping **09** good press **10** rave review **11** acclamation, approbation **12** commendation, pat on the back **15** congratulations, standing ovation

plausible

04 fair, glib **06** cogent, likely **07** logical,

proball **08** credible, possible, probable, specious **10** acceptable, believable, colourable, convincing, imaginable, persuasive, reasonable, soft-spoken **11** conceivable, smooth-faced **12** smooth-spoken **13** silver-tongued, smooth-talking, smooth-tongued

plausibly

08 possibly, probably **09** logically **10** imaginably, pleasantly, reasonably **11** commendably, conceivably **12** convincingly, persuasively

play

◇ *anagram indicator*

02 do, no **03** act, fun, noh, pit, ply, toy **04** game, give, jest, laik, lake, plot, romp, room, show, work **05** caper, dance, drama, farce, flash, frisk, gleam, hobby, kicks, laugh, range, revel, rival, scope, slack, space, sport, wield **06** action, cavort, comedy, frolic, gamble, gambol, glance, join in, joking, leeway, margin, nogaku, oppose, take on, trifle **07** compete, flicker, flutter, freedom, have fun, holiday, leisure, liberty, licence, operate, pastime, perform, portray, shimmer, teasing, tragedy, twinkle, vie with **08** activity, exercise, free rein, gambling, latitude, movement **09** amusement, challenge, dalliance, diversion, enjoyment, interplay, looseness, melodrama, operation, play games, represent **10** recreation, take part in **11** flexibility, impersonate, interaction, merrymaking, move lightly, performance, transaction **12** be involved in **13** amuse yourself, enjoy yourself, entertainment, participate in, play the part of **14** compete against, divert yourself, occupy yourself

Plays include:

03 RUR
04 Loot
05 Equus, Faust, Le Cid, Medea, Médée, Roots, Yerma
06 Becket, Phèdre, St Joan
07 Amadeus, Candida, Electra, Endgame, Galileo, La Ronde, Oedipus, Oleanna, Orestes, Volpone, Woyzeck
08 Antigone, Betrayal, Everyman, Hay Fever, Huis Clos, Oresteia, Peer Gynt, Tartuffe, The Birds, The Flies, The Frogs, The Miser, The Price, The Wasps
09 All My Sons, Happy Days, Miss Julie, Party Time, Pygmalion, Saint Joan, The Chairs, The Clouds, The Father, The Rivals, The Vortex
10 A Dream Play, All for Love, Andromache, Andromaque, Lysistrata, Misery Guts, No Man's Land, The Bacchae, The Robbers, The Seagull, Uncle Vanya
11 A Doll's House, Blood and Ice, Hedda Gabler, The Blue Bird, The Crucible, The Wild Duck, Trojan Women
12 Anna Christie, Blithe Spirit, Blood Wedding, Major Barbara, Private Lives, Punch and Judy, The Alchemist, The Caretaker, The Mousetrap
13 Arms and the Man, A Taste of Honey, Doctor Faustus, Educating Rita, Le Misanthrope, The Homecoming, The Jew of Malta, The White Devil, The Winslow Boy
14 Can't Pay? Won't Pay!, Krapp's Last Tape, Man and Superman, Orlando Furioso, Riders to the Sea, Separate Tables, The Country Wife, The Entertainer, The Silent Woman
15 Bartholomew Fair, Look Back in Anger, Prometheus Bound, The Beggar's Opera, The Iceman Cometh, The Three Sisters, Waiting for Godot

See also **Shakespeare**

• out of play

04 dead

• part of play

03 act

• play around with

◇ *anagram indicator*

07 toy with **08** fool with **09** dally with, flirt with **10** fiddle with, fidget with, meddle with, tamper with, trifle with **12** womanize with **13** interfere with, philander with **14** mess around with

• play at

06 affect **07** make out, pretend **10** put on an act **11** pretend to be

• play down

08 downplay, minimize **09** gloss over, underplay **10** understate, undervalue **11** make light of **13** underestimate

• play harshly

03 saw

• play on

07 exploit, trade on **08** profit by **12** capitalize on **13** turn to account **15** take advantage of

• play out

03 act **04** go on **05** enact **06** act out, unfold **07** carry on, exhaust, wear out **08** continue **10** be revealed

• play the fool

03 fon **04** daff, fool **07** act dido, tomfool

• play up

04 fool, hurt **05** annoy, boost **06** bother, stress **07** go wrong, not work, point up, trouble **09** be naughty, emphasize, highlight, misbehave, spotlight, underline **10** accentuate, exaggerate **11** give trouble, malfunction **12** be on the blink, go on the blink **13** be mischievous **15** call attention to

• play up to

04 fawn **05** toady **06** cozy up **07** flatter **08** blandish, bootlick, butter up, soft-soap, suck up to **15** curry favour with

• play with

◇ *anagram indicator*

play-act

03 act **04** fake, mime, sham **05** bluff, feign, put on **06** affect, assume **07** pretend **08** simulate **09** dissemble, fabricate **10** put on an act **11** counterfeit, impersonate **15** pass yourself off

playboy

04 rake, roué **09** debauchee, ladies' man, libertine, socialite, womanizer **10** lady-killer **11** philanderer **12** man about town

player

01 E, N, S, W **03** ace, ham, man **04** east, pone, star, west **05** actor, north, south **06** artist **07** actress, artiste, trifler, trouper **08** comedian, musician **09** performer, sportsman **10** all-rounder, competitor, contestant **11** accompanist, entertainer, participant, sportswoman **15** instrumentalist

See also **Australian football**; **baseball**; **basketball**; **chess**; **footballer**; **instrument**; **rugby**; **tennis**

• bit player

05 extra

• opposing player

02 it

players

04 band, cast, wind **05** brass **07** strings

See also **football**; **orchestra**

playful

03 gay, mad **05** funny, ludic **06** frisky, impish, joking, lively, toyish **07** jesting, kitteny, puckish, roguish, teasing, toysome, waggish **08** espiègle, flippant, friendly, gamesome, humorous, skittish, spirited, sportive **09** facetious, fun-loving, kittenish, piacevole **10** frolicsome, rollicking **11** mischievous **12** high-spirited, light-hearted **13** tongue-in-cheek

playfully

06 in jest **08** jokingly **09** piacevole **10** humorously **11** facetiously **14** light-heartedly

playground

04 park **08** play area **12** playing-field **13** amusement park **14** pleasure ground

playmate

03 pal **04** chum, mate **05** buddy **06** friend **07** comrade **09** companion, neighbour **10** playfellow

plaything

03 toy **04** game **05** sport **06** bauble, gewgaw, puppet, trifle **07** pastime, trinket **08** gimcrack **09** amusement

playwright

06 writer **09** dramatist, tragedian **10** dramaturge **12** dramaturgist, screen writer, scriptwriter

Playwrights and screenwriters include:

02 Fo (Dario)
03 **Fry** (Christopher), **Gay** (John), **Hay** (Ian), **Kyd** (Thomas), **May** (Elaine)
04 **Bolt** (Robert), **Bond** (Edward), **Coen** (Ethan), **Coen** (Joel), **Dane** (Clemence), **Ford** (John), **Hare**

(David), **Rowe** (Nicholas), **Shaw** (George Bernard), **Vega** (Lope de)
05 **Albee** (Edward), **Allen** (Woody), **Arden** (John), **Bates** (Herbert Ernest), **Behan** (Brendan), **Dumas** (Alexandre), **Eliot** (T S), **Frayn** (Michael), **Friel** (Brian), **Genet** (Jean), **Gogol** (Nikolai), **Havel** (Vaclav), **Ibsen** (Henrik), **Lodge** (Thomas), **Lorca** (Federico García), **Mamet** (David), **Nashe** (Thomas), **Odets** (Clifford), **Orton** (Joe), **Otway** (Thomas), **Sachs** (Hans), **Sachs** (Nelly), **Smith** (Dodie), **Stone** (Oliver), **Synge** (John Millington), **Udall** (Nicholas), **Wilde** (Oscar), **Yeats** (W B)
06 **Barrie** (Sir James Matthew), **Brecht** (Bertolt), **Bridie** (James), **Colman** (George), **Coward** (Sir Noël), **Dekker** (Thomas), **Dryden** (John), **Galdós** (Benito Pérez), **Goethe** (Johann Wolfgang von), **Greene** (Robert), **Herzog** (Werner), **Hilton** (James), **Huston** (John), **Jerome** (Jerome K), **Jonson** (Ben), **Kaiser** (Georg), **Lerner** (Alan Jay), **Mercer** (David), **Miller** (Arthur), **Miller** (Henry), **Musset** (Alfred de), **O'Casey** (Sean), **O'Neill** (Eugene), **Pinero** (Sir Arthur Wing), **Pinter** (Harold), **Powell** (Michael), **Racine** (Jean), **Sardou** (Victorien), **Sartre** (Jean-Paul), **Steele** (Sir Richard), **Storey** (David), **Tagore** (Rabindranath), **Wesker** (Arnold), **Wilder** (Thornton)
07 **Anouilh** (Jean), **Arrabal** (Fernando), **Beckett** (Samuel), **Bennett** (Alan), **Büchner** (Georg), **Chapman** (George), **Chekhov** (Anton), **Cocteau** (Jean), **Coppola** (Francis Ford), **Diderot** (Denis), **Garrick** (David), **Gregory** (Lady Isabella Augusta), **Holberg** (Ludvig, Baron), **Ionesco** (Eugène), **Klinger** (Friedrich Maximilian von), **Kubrick** (Stanley), **Labiche** (Eugène), **Lardner** (Ring), **Marlowe** (Christopher), **Marston** (John), **McGough** (Roger), **Mishima** (Yukio), **Molière**, **Novello** (Ivor), **Osborne** (John), **Plautus** (Titus Maccius), **Richler** (Mordecai), **Rostand** (Edmond), **Russell** (Willy), **Shaffer** (Peter), **Shepard** (Sam), **Terence**, **Ustinov** (Sir Peter), **Vicente** (Gil), **Walcott** (Derek), **Webster** (John)
08 **Andersen** (Hans Christian), **Banville** (Théodore de), **Beaumont** (Francis), **Björnson** (Björnstjerne), **Brentano** (Clemens), **Burgoyne** (John), **Congreve** (William), **Davenant** (Sir William), **Fielding** (Henry), **Fletcher** (John), **Hochhuth** (Rolf), **Lochhead** (Liz), **Menander**, **Mortimer** (Sir John), **Polanski** (Roman), **Rattigan** (Sir Terence), **Schiller** (Friedrich), **Shadwell** (Thomas), **Sheridan** (Richard Brinsley), **Stoppard** (Sir Tom), **Suckling** (Sir John), **Tourneur** (Cyril), **Vanbrugh** (Sir John), **Wedekind** (Frank), **Williams** (Emlyn), **Williams** (Tennessee)
09 **Aeschylus**, **Ayckbourn** (Sir Alan), **Corneille** (Pierre), **D'Annunzio** (Gabriele), **Euripides**, **Goldsmith** (Oliver), **Hauptmann** (Gerhart), **Isherwood** (Christopher), **Mankowitz** (Wolf), **Marinetti** (Filippo Tommaso), **Middleton** (Thomas), **Poliakoff** (Stephen), **Priestley** (J B), **Rosenthal** (Jack), **Sophocles**, **Wycherley** (William)
10 **Galsworthy** (John), **Pirandello** (Luigi), **Strindberg** (August)
11 **Maeterlinck** (Maurice), **Shakespeare** (William)
12 **Aristophanes**, **Beaumarchais** (Pierre-Augustin Caron de)

---

plea
05 alibi, claim, fains **06** appeal, excuse, fains I, placet, placit, prayer
07 defence, defense, lawsuit, pretext, request **08** demurrer, entreaty, fainites, petition, placitum, pleading
10 invocation **11** declinature, explanation, imploration, vindication
12 supplication **13** justification **14** nolo contendere

plead
03 ask, beg **04** moot, urge **05** argue, claim, state **06** adduce, allege, appeal, assert **07** beseech, entreat, implore, request, solicit **08** maintain, persuade, perswade, petition **09** intercede
10 put forward **12** intercede for
- **refusing to plead**

04 mute

pleasant
04 cute, fine, nice **05** amene, lepid, merry, tipsy **06** genial, groovy, jocund, lekker, lovely **07** affable, amiable, amusing, likable, welcome, winsome
08 all roses, charming, cheerful, friendly, gorgeous, likeable, pleasing, savorous, sunshiny **09** agreeable, congenial, enjoyable, piacevole, toothsome **10** acceptable, delightful, gratifying, refreshing, salubrious, satisfying **11** inoffensive
12 entertaining, good-humoured
14 roses all the way

pleasantly
07 nice and **09** enjoyably, piacevole, plausibly **10** pleasingly **12** delightfully, refreshingly **14** entertainingly

pleasantry
04 jest, joke, quip **05** sally **06** banter, bon mot **08** badinage **09** enjoyment, witticism **10** jocularity **12** casual remark, pleasantness **13** polite comment **14** friendly remark

please
04 like, list, suit, want, will, wish
05 agree, amuse, bitte, charm, cheer, queme **06** arride, choose, desire, divert, fulfil, humour, kindly, prefer, see fit, tickle **07** aggrate, attract, cheer up, content, delight, flatter, gladden, gratify, indulge, prithee, prythee, satisfy **08** appeal to, think fit
09 captivate, entertain, make happy
11 if you please **12** je vous en prie
14 give pleasure to
- **hard to please**

04 nice **09** difficult

pleased
04 glad, rapt **05** happy **06** elated
07 chuffed **08** cheerful, euphoric, grateful, gruntled, thrilled
09 contented, delighted, delirious, gratified, satisfied **10** complacent **11** on cloud nine, over the moon, tickled pink

pleasing
04 cute, fair, fine, good, nice **05** lusty
06 comely, liking, taking **07** amusing, savoury, winning **08** charming, engaging, pleasant **09** agreeable, desirable, enjoyable **10** acceptable, attractive, delectable, delightful, gratifying, satisfying **11** pleasurable
12 entertaining, heartwarming, honey-tongued **13** prepossessing

pleasurable
03 fun **04** good, nice **06** groovy, lovely
07 amusing, welcome **08** luscious, pleasant **09** agreeable, congenial, diverting, enjoyable **10** delightful, gratifying **12** entertaining

pleasure
03 fun, gem, joy **04** will, wish **05** glory, mirth, prize **06** choice, desire, heaven, solace, thrill **07** command, delight, elation, leisure, purpose **08** gladness, treasure **09** amusement, enjoyment, happiness, hog heaven, pleasance
10 preference, recreation, sensuality
11 complacence, complacency, contentment, dissipation, inclination
12 satisfaction **13** entertainment, gratification
- **expression of pleasure**

03 aha, boy, oho, ooh, wow **05** good-o, oh boy, tra-la, whack, wowee, zowie
06 good-oh, gotcha, whacko **07** way to go!, whoopee **10** hubba hubba
- **it's a pleasure**

07 any time **08** forget it, not at all **09** no problem **10** my pleasure **11** it's all right
12 it's no trouble, it was nothing, you're welcome **13** don't mention it, that's all right
- **with pleasure**

04 fain **06** gladly **07** happily, readily
08 of course **09** willingly **11** avec plaisir

pleasure-flight
04 flip

pleat
04 fold, kilt, purl, tuck **05** braid, crimp, flute, pinch, plait, prank **06** crease, gather, goffer, pranck, pucker
07 folding, gauffer, plicate, prancke
09 plication **10** intertwine

plebeian
03 low **04** base, boor, mean, non-U, pleb **05** prole **06** coarse, common, vulgar, worker **07** ignoble, low-born,

peasant, popular **08** commoner, roturier **09** unrefined, vulgarian **10** lower-class, uncultured **11** proletarian **12** common person, uncultivated, working-class **15** undistinguished

plebiscite
04 poll, vote **06** ballot **09** straw poll **10** referendum

pledge
03 vow, wad, wed **04** bail, band, bond, fine, gage, hand, oath, pass, pawn, wage, word **05** swear, vouch, wager **06** borrow, commit, engage, impawn, plight, secure, surety **07** betroth, deposit, earnest, hostage, promise, propine, warrant **08** contract, covenant, impledge, mortgage, security **09** assurance, committal, guarantee, pignorate, sacrament, undertake **10** collateral, commitment, take an oath **11** impignorate, undertaking **12** give your word, word of honour

plenary
04 full, open **05** whole **06** entire **07** general **08** absolute, complete, integral, sweeping, thorough **09** unlimited **11** unqualified **12** unrestricted **13** unconditional

plenipotentiary
05 envoy **06** legate, nuncio **08** absolute, diplomat, emissary, minister **09** dignitary **10** ambassador

plenitude
06 bounty, excess, plenty, wealth **08** fullness, plethora **09** abundance, amplitude, profusion, repletion **10** cornucopia, entireness **11** copiousness **12** completeness **13** plenteousness, plentifulness

plenteous
04 rich **05** ample **06** bumper, lavish **07** copious, fertile, liberal, profuse **08** abundant, fruitful, generous, infinite, prolific **09** abounding, bounteous, bountiful, luxuriant, plentiful **10** productive **11** overflowing **13** inexhaustible

plentiful
04 easy **05** ample, routh, rowth **06** bumper, lavish **07** copious, liberal, profuse, teeming **08** abundant, fruitful, generous, infinite **09** bounteous, bountiful **10** productive **11** overflowing **13** inexhaustible

plentifully
05 amply **08** lavishly **09** copiously, liberally, profusely **10** abundantly, fruitfully, generously **11** bountifully

plenty
04 bags, fund, mass, mine **05** store **06** enough, foison, riches, scouth, scowth, volume, wealth **07** fortune, fulness **08** fullness, plethora, quantity **09** abundance, affluence, profusion, substance **10** abundantly, cornucopia, prosperity **11** copiousness, sufficiency, wealthiness **12** milk and honey **13** plenteousness **14** stouth and routh

• **plenty of**
04 bags, lots, many **05** heaps, loads, piles **06** enough, masses, stacks **09** shedloads **11** large amount, large number **14** more than enough

plethora
04 glut **06** excess **07** surfeit, surplus **09** abundance, profusion, repletion **11** repleteness, superfluity **12** overfullness **13** overabundance **14** superabundance

pliability
08 docility **09** ductility **10** compliance, elasticity, plasticity **11** amenability, bendability, flexibility **12** adaptability, malleability **13** tractableness **14** suggestibility, susceptibility

pliable
05 bendy, lithe **06** docile, pliant, supple **07** elastic, plastic **08** bendable, biddable, cheverel, cheveril, flexible, yielding **09** adaptable, compliant, malleable, receptive, tractable **10** manageable, responsive **11** persuadable, susceptible **12** superplastic **13** accommodating **14** impressionable

pliant
05 bendy, lithe, swack, swank, wanle **06** docile, limber, supple, wandle, wannel, whippy **07** elastic, plastic, pliable **08** bendable, biddable, flexible, yielding **09** adaptable, compliant, malleable, receptive, tractable **10** manageable, responsive, sequacious **11** persuadable, susceptible **13** accommodating **14** impressionable

plight
03 fix, jam, vow **04** case, fold, hole, mood, risk, trim **05** array, plait, point, state, swear, vouch, weave **06** enfold, engage, liking, pickle, pledge, scrape, secure, taking **07** dilemma, pliskie, promise, propose, straits, trouble **08** affiance, contract, covenant, quandary **09** condition, extremity, guarantee, situation, tight spot **10** difficulty, engagement **11** dire straits, predicament **13** circumstances

plimsoll
03 dap **05** tacky **07** gym shoe **08** sandshoe

plod
04 plot, slog, thud, toil **05** clump, grind, stomp, stump, tramp **06** drudge, labour, lumber, stodge, trudge **07** peg away **08** plug away **09** persevere, policeman, soldier on **11** police force, walk heavily **13** plough through

plodder
03 mug, sap **06** drudge, toiler **07** dullard, slogger

plot
03 bed, erf, lay, lot, map, web **04** area, brew, burn, draw, mark, pack, plan, plod, ruse **05** cabal, chart, draft, frame, hatch, patch, piece, ploat, scald, story, theme, tract **06** action, cook up, design, devise, fleece, garden, locate, map out, parcel, scheme, scorch, sketch, thread **07** collude, concoct, connive, dispose, outline, project, subject **08** conspire, contrive, intrigue, scenario **09** allotment, calculate, machinate, narrative, storyline, stratagem **10** conspiracy **11** machination

plotter
06 dabble, potter **07** planner, schemer **08** dabbling, designer, paddling **09** intriguer **10** machinator **11** conspirator

plough
◇ *anagram indicator*
03 ard, dig, ear, ere, pip, rib **04** beam, fail, list, plow, rive, sill, till, work **05** break, ridge, spade **06** Dipper, fallow, furrow, lister, pleuch, pleugh, rafter, ridger, thwart, turn up **07** break up, scooter, tractor, triones, wrinkle **08** the Wagon **09** Big Dipper, cultivate, Great Bear, subsoiler, Ursa Major **10** Seven Stars **11** agriculture, drill-plough, swing-plough, wheel plough **12** Charles's Wain, septentrions **13** septentriones

• **plough into**
03 hit **06** go into **07** collide, run into **08** bump into **09** crash into, drive into, smash into

• **plough through**
11 plod through, wade through **13** trudge through

ploughshare
04 sock **05** share

plover
04 dupe **06** godwit **07** dottrel, killdee, lapwing **08** dotterel, killdeer, wire bird **09** thick knee **10** Charadrius, prostitute, stone snipe

• **flock of plovers**
04 wing

ploy
04 game, move, ruse, wile **05** dodge, trick **06** device, scheme, tactic **08** artifice **09** manoeuvre, stratagem **10** subterfuge **11** contrivance

pluck
03 pip, rob, tug **04** draw, fail, grit, guts, pick, plot, pook, pouk, pull, race, rase, yank **05** heart, nerve, ploat, plunk, spunk, strip, strum, thrum, twang **06** avulse, daring, evulse, finger, fleece, gather, humble, mettle, remove, rescue, snatch, spirit, take in, tweeze, twitch, valour **07** bravery, collect, courage, despoil, extract, harvest, pull off, swindle **08** audacity, backbone, boldness **09** fortitude **10** resolution **11** divellicate, intrepidity **12** fearlessness **13** determination

pluckily
06 boldly **07** bravely **08** daringly **09** valiantly **10** fearlessly, heroically,

intrepidly **11** audaciously, confidently **12** courageously **13** adventurously

plucky
04 bold, game, gamy **05** brave, gamey, gutsy, gutty **06** daring, feisty, gallus, gritty, heroic, spunky **07** gallows, valiant **08** fearless, intrepid, spirited **09** audacious **10** courageous, determined

plug
02 ad **03** DIN, wad **04** blow, bung, cake, chew, cork, dook, fill, hype, neck, pack, puff, push, seal, stem, stop, tent, tout **05** block, blurb, choke, close, promo, punch, SCART, shoot, spile, stuff, twist **06** dossil, dottle, fipple, market, spigot, stop up, tampon **07** go-devil, mention, pessary, promote, stopper, stopple, tampion, tompion **08** good word **09** access eye, advertise, promotion, publicity, publicize **10** commercial **11** suppository **13** advertisement **14** recommendation
• **plug away**
04 toil **06** plod on **07** peg away **08** preserve, slog away, toil away **09** persevere, soldier on **10** keep trying

plum
04 best, kaki **05** cushy, prize, prune **06** choice, damson, mussel **07** bullace, quetsch **08** damaskin, prunello, victoria **09** damascene, damaskeen, damasquin, excellent, greengage, mirabelle, myrobalan, naseberry, persimmon, sapodilla **10** damasceene, first-class

plumb
04 bang, dead, slap, true **05** gauge, level, probe, right, sheer, sound **06** bullet, fathom, search, spot-on **07** exactly, examine, explore, measure, plummet, utterly **08** sound out, vertical **09** delve into, out-and-out, penetrate, precisely, search out, up and down **10** straight up, vertically **11** investigate, verticality **12** straight down **13** thorough-going **15** perpendicularly
• **plumb in**
03 fit, fix, put **05** place, put in, set up **07** install **08** position
• **plumb the depths of**
13 reach the nadir **15** experience fully, reach rock bottom

plumbing

Plumbing fittings and equipment include:

02 WC
03 pan, tap, tee
04 bath, bend, bowl, flux, hose, pipe, plug, pump, sink, tank, trap
05 auger, basin, bidet, float, joint, P-trap, U-bend, union, valve
06 boiler, faucet, gasket, geyser, hopper, nipple, shower, solder, toilet, urinal, washer
07 cistern, coupler, plunger, reducer, stop end, Y-branch
08 ballcock, cylinder, drain rod, lavatory, lever tap, mixer tap, pedestal, pipe clip, radiator, soil vent, stopcock, sump pump, valve key
09 ball valve, blowtorch, draincock, gate valve, mains pipe, nipple key, waste pipe
10 back boiler, bottle trap, check valve, copper pipe, copper tube, elbow joint, flare joint, header tank, pipe bender, pipe cutter, pipe wrench, programmer, septic tank, shower head, Teflon® tape, thermostat, tube cutter
11 water closet
12 basin spanner, ceiling joint, monkey wrench, overflow bend, pipe coupling, siphon washer
13 deburring tool, expansion tank, lavatory chain
14 gas water heater, Stillson® wrench
15 immersion heater

plume
04 tuft **05** crest, preen, quill **06** osprey, pappus, pinion **07** feather, marabou, panache, plumule **08** aigrette, marabout, streamer
• **plume yourself on**
07 exult in **10** boast about **13** preen yourself, pride yourself

plummet
04 dive, drop, fall, lead **05** plumb, sound **06** fathom, hurtle, plunge, tumble **07** descend **08** nose-dive **09** plumb line **11** drop rapidly, fall rapidly **15** decrease quickly

plummy
01 U **04** posh **07** refined **08** affected **09** desirable, high-class **10** profitable, upper-class **12** aristocratic

plump
03 fat **04** blow, bold, drop, dump, fall, flop, full, plop, sink, soss, swap, swop, tidy **05** ample, beefy, blurt, bonny, buxom, clump, dumpy, gross, jolly, large, obese, plunk, podgy, round, shoot, slump, sonsy, souse, squab, stout, swell, tubby **06** bonnie, chubby, cuddly, flabby, fleshy, plunge, portly, rotund, sonsie, strike **07** cluster, deposit, descend, put down, set down, well-fed **08** chopping, collapse, generous, matronly **09** corpulent, downright **10** cuddlesome, embonpoint, roundabout, well-liking, well-padded **11** well-covered, well-rounded **15** well-upholstered
• **plump for**
04 back **06** choose, favour, opt for, prefer, select **07** support **08** side with

plumpness
03 fat **07** fatness, obesity **09** podginess, pudginess, rotundity, stoutness, tubbiness **10** chubbiness, corpulence, fleshiness, portliness

plunder
03 rob **04** loot, peel, pill, prey, raid, rape, reif, sack, swag **05** berob, booty, harry, prize, reave, reive, rifle, scoff, shave, skoff, spoil, steal, strip **06** fleece, forage, maraud, ravage, spoils, spulye **07** despoil, escheat, hership, pillage, ransack, spulyie, spulzie, stick up **08** lay waste, pickings, spoliate, spuilzie **09** depredate, devastate, herriment, herryment, sprechery **10** spreaghery **14** ill-gotten gains

plunge
03 dip, jab, ram **04** bull, dash, dive, drop, duck, enew, fall, jump, mire, push, rush, sink, stab, tank, tear **05** crash, douse, dowse, drive, lunge, merge, pitch, plump, raker, shove, souse, stick, swoop, throw, whelm **06** beduck, career, charge, go down, hurtle, launch, thrust, tumble **07** demerge, demerse, descend, descent, immerge, immerse, plummet **08** bull into, dive-bomb, emplonge, implunge, nose-dive, submerge **09** immersion **10** submersion **11** drop rapidly, fall rapidly **12** enew yourself **15** decrease quickly
• **take the plunge**
07 go for it **13** bite the bullet **14** commit yourself

plurality
04 bulk, mass, most **06** galaxy, number **07** variety **08** majority **09** diversity, profusion **12** multiplicity, numerousness **13** preponderance

plus
03 and **04** gain, perk, with **05** asset, bonus, extra **06** credit **07** added to, benefit, surplus **08** addition, as well as, increase, positive **09** advantage, good point **10** additional **12** advantageous, in addition to, not to mention, over and above, together with

plush
04 posh, rich **05** ritzy **06** costly, de luxe, glitzy, lavish, luxury, swanky **07** opulent, stylish **08** affluent, palatial **09** luxurious, sumptuous

Pluto
03 Dis **05** Hades

plutocrat
05 Dives **06** fat cat, tycoon **07** Croesus, gold-bug, magnate, rich man **09** moneybags **10** capitalist **11** billionaire, millionaire

plutonium
02 Pu

ply
◇ *anagram indicator*
02 go **03** ren, rin, run, set, use **04** bend, birl, feed, fold, leaf, lush, play **05** apply, beset, birle, ferry, layer, sheet, trade, wield **06** assail, employ, follow, handle, harass, lavish, pursue, strand, supply, travel, work at **07** bombard, carry on, furnish, provide, utilize **08** engage in, exercise, practise **09** condition, importune, thickness **10** manipulate **13** keep supplying

PM *see* **prime minister**

poach
04 copy, lift, nick, poke, take **05** potch, steal **06** borrow, pilfer, potche, thrust **07** intrude, trample **08** encroach, infringe, trespass **11** appropriate **13** hunt illegally **14** catch illegally

pocket
◇ *containment indicator*
03 bag, bin, fob, pot **04** gain, lift, mini, nick, poke, take, whip **05** filch, funds, means, money, patch, pinch, pouch, purse, small, steal, touch **06** assets, budget, cavity, hollow, little, pilfer, potted **07** capital, compact, concise, placket, purloin, trouser **08** abridged, envelope, finances, fob-watch, pint-size, portable, souvenir **09** miniature, plaid-neuk, resources, small area **10** receptacle, small group **11** appropriate, compartment, wherewithal, win unfairly **12** isolated area **14** help yourself to
See also **steal**

pockmark
03 pit **04** pock, scar **07** blemish, pockpit

pod
03 cod **04** case, hull, husk, pipi **05** chile, chili, shell, shuck **06** chilli, legume, loment, paunch, peacod, school **07** musk-bag, peascod, silicle, siliqua, silique **08** lomentum, peasecod, silicula, silicule, strombus, sugar pea, tamarind **09** green bean, mangetout **10** cotton boll **11** pudding-pipe **12** mangetout pea

podgy
03 fat **05** dumpy, plump, squat, stout, tubby **06** chubby, chunky, fleshy, rotund, spuddy, stubby, stumpy **07** paunchy **08** roly-poly **09** corpulent, roll-about

podium
04 dais, foot, hand **05** stage, stand **07** rostrum **08** platform **09** stylobate

poem

Poem types include:

03 dit, lay, ode
04 awdl, ditt, epic, epos, idyl, song, waka
05 ditty, elegy, epode, haiku, idyll, lyric, rhyme, tanka, verse
06 ballad, epopee, monody, sonnet
07 bucolic, couplet, eclogue, epigram, georgic, pantoum, rondeau, sestina, triolet, virelay
08 cinquain, clerihew, limerick, lipogram, madrigal, palinode, pastoral, thin poem, verselet, versicle
09 roundelay, shape poem
10 villanelle
12 concrete poem, epithalamium, nursery rhyme, prothalamion

Poems and poetry collections include:

02 If
04 A Red, Crow, Days, Edda, Hope, Howl, Maud, Odes
05 Comus, Lamia
06 Façade, Heaven, Hellas, Marina, The Fly, Villon
07 A Vision, Beowulf, Don Juan, Lycidas, Mariana, Marmion, Red Rose, Requiem, Rondeau, The Quip, Ulysses
08 Bermudas, Endymion, Georgics, Gunga Din, Hiawatha, Hudibras, Hysteria, Insomnia, Kalevala, Lupercal, Queen Mab, Ramayana, The Iliad, The Night, The Pearl, The Tyger, Tithonus, To Autumn
09 Decameron, Human Life, Jerusalem, Kubla Khan, The Aeneid, The Cantos
10 Cherry Ripe, Christabel, Dream Songs, In Memoriam, Lalla Rookh, On an Island, The Dunciad, The Odyssey, The Poetics, The Prelude, The Village, Up in the Air, Very Old Man, View of a Pig
11 Ars Amatoria, Empty Vessel, High Windows, Holy Sonnets, Humming-Bird, Jabberwocky, Mahabharata, Memorabilia, Remembrance, Song of my Cid, Sudden Light, Tall Nettles, Tam O'Shanter, The Eclogues, The Exstasie, The Peasants, The Retreate, The Sick Rose, The Sluggard, The Woodlark
12 A Glass of Beer, Ash Wednesday, A Song to Celia, A Song to David, Auld Lang Syne, Bhagavad Gita, Eugene Onegin, Faith Healing, Four Quartets, Goblin Market, Hawk Roosting, Homage to Clio, Jubilate Agno, Mercian Hymns, Morte d'Arthur, Ode to Evening, Paradise Lost, Piers Plowman, The Hill-Shade, The Lucy Poems, The Troop Ship, The Visionary, The Waste Land, The Windhover
13 Arms and the Boy, Behind the Line, Gilgamesh Epic, Leaves of Grass, Metamorphoses, Missing the Sea, Naming of Parts, Roman de la Rose, September Song, Song by Isbrand, The Book of Thel
14 A Shropshire Lad, Divina Commedia, Leda and the Swan, Les Fleurs du Mal, Love Songs in Age, Lyrical Ballads, Orlando Furioso, Song of Hiawatha, Strange Meeting, The Divine Image, The Feel of Hands, The Garden Party, The Lotus-Eaters, The Ship of Death, Venus and Adonis
15 Canterbury Tales, Cautionary Tales, Love without Hope, Magna est Veritas, Ode on Melancholy, Summoned by Bells, The Age of Anxiety, The Divine Comedy, The Eve of St Agnes, The Faerie Queene, The Garden of Love, The Grauballe Man, The Second Coming, The Sorrow of Love

See also **poetry**; **song**

poet
04 bard, scop **06** rhymer **07** elegist, rhymist **08** beat poet, idyllist, lyricist, minstrel **09** balladeer, poetaster, poeticule, rhymester, sonneteer, versifier **10** verse-maker **15** performance poet

Poets include:

03 **Gay** (John), **Lee** (Laurie), **Paz** (Octavio), **Poe** (Edgar Allan)
04 **Amis** (Kingsley), **Blok** (Alexander), **Cope** (Wendy), **Dunn** (Douglas), **Dyer** (Sir Edward), **Gray** (Thomas), **Gunn** (Thom), **Hill** (Geoffrey), **Hogg** (James), **Hood** (Thomas), **Hunt** (Leigh), **Lear** (Edward), **Maro** (Publius Vergilius), **Muir** (Edwin), **Nash** (Ogden), **Ovid**, **Owen** (Wilfred), **Pope** (Alexander), **Rich** (Adrienne), **Seth** (Vikram), **Vega** (Lope de)
05 **Auden** (W H), **Basho** (Matsuo), **Benét** (Stephen Vincent), **Blake** (William), **Burns** (Robert), **Byron** (George, Lord), **Clare** (John), **Crane** (Hart), **Dante**, **Donne** (John), **Duffy** (Carol Ann), **Eliot** (T S), **Frost** (Robert), **Hardy** (Thomas), **Harte** (Brett), **Heine** (Heinrich), **Henri** (Adrian), **Hesse** (Hermann), **Homer**, **Ibsen** (Henrik), **Iqbal** (Sir Muhammad), **Keats** (John), **Keble** (John), **Lodge** (Thomas), **Lorca** (Federico García), **Marot** (Clément), **Meung** (Jean de), **Moore** (Thomas), **Myers** (Frederic William Henry), **O'Hara** (Frank), **Opitz** (Martin), **Plath** (Sylvia), **Pound** (Ezra), **Prior** (Matthew), **Pulci** (Luigi), **Raine** (Craig), **Rilke** (Rainer Maria), **Sachs** (Hans), **Sachs** (Nelly), **Scott** (Sir Walter), **Smart** (Christopher), **Smith** (Stevie), **Spark** (Dame Muriel), **Tasso** (Torquato), **Wyatt** (Sir Thomas), **Yeats** (W B)
06 **Adcock** (Fleur), **Aragon** (Louis), **Arnold** (Matthew), **Artaud** (Antonin), **Atwood** (Margaret), **Barnes** (William), **Bellay** (Joachim du), **Belloc** (Hilaire), **Benoît**, **Binyon** (Laurence), **Bishop** (Elizabeth), **Brecht** (Bertolt), **Brontë** (Anne), **Brontë** (Emily), **Brooke** (Rupert), **Camões** (Luís de), **Carver** (Raymond), **Cowper** (William), **Crabbe** (George), **Dunbar** (William), **Eluard** (Paul), **Empson** (Sir William), **Ennius** (Quintus), **Fuller** (Roy), **Goethe** (Johann Wolfgang von), **Graves** (Robert), **Gurney** (Ivor), **Haller** (Albrecht von), **Heaney** (Seamus), **Herder** (Johann Gottfried von), **Hesiod**, **Horace**, **Hughes** (Langston), **Jensen** (Johannes Vilhelm), **Larkin** (Philip), **Lorris** (Guillaume de), **Lowell** (Amy), **Lowell** (Robert), **Millay** (Edna St Vincent), **Milosz** (Czeslaw), **Milton** (John), **Morris** (William), **Musset** (Alfred de), **Neruda** (Pablo), **Ossian**, **Patten** (Brian), **Pindar**, **Porter** (Peter), **Racine** (Jean), **Ramsay** (Allan), **Riding** (Laura), **Sappho**, **Sidney** (Sir Philip), **Surrey**

(Henry Howard, Earl of), **Tagore** (Rabindranath), **Thomas** (Dylan), **Thomas** (Edward), **Thomas** (R S), **Valéry** (Paul), **Villon** (François), **Virgil**, **Waller** (Edmund)
07 **Addison** (Joseph), **Akahito** (Yamabe no), **Alberti** (Leon Battista), **Aneurin**, **Angelou** (Maya), **Aretino** (Pietro), **Ariosto** (Ludovico), **Ashbery** (John), **Barbour** (John), **Beckett** (Samuel), **Beddoes** (Thomas Lovell), **Blunden** (Edmund Charles), **Boiardo** (Matteo Maria), **Brodsky** (Joseph), **Büchner** (Georg), **Caedmon**, **Campion** (Thomas), **Causley** (Charles), **Chapman** (George), **Chaucer** (Geoffrey), **Cocteau** (Jean), **Da Ponte** (Lorenzo), **Douglas** (Gawain), **Durrell** (Lawrence), **Emerson** (Ralph Waldo), **Flecker** (James Elroy), **Fröding** (Gustaf), **Gautier** (Théophile), **Herbert** (George), **Herrick** (Robert), **Holberg** (Ludvig, Baron), **Hopkins** (Gerard Manley), **Housman** (A E), **Jiménez** (Juan Ramón), **Johnson** (Samuel), **Kipling** (Rudyard), **Layamon**, **Lydgate** (John), **Macbeth** (George), **MacCaig** (Norman), **MacLean** (Sorley), **Manzoni** (Alessandro), **Martial**, **Marvell** (Andrew), **McGough** (Roger), **Mishima** (Yukio), **Mistral** (Frédéric), **Mistral** (Gabriela), **Montale** (Eugenio), **Novalis**, **Orléans** (Charles Duc d'), **Patmore** (Coventry), **Pushkin** (Alexander), **Quarles** (Francis), **Rimbaud** (Arthur), **Roethke** (Theodore), **Ronsard** (Pierre de), **Rostand** (Edmond), **Sassoon** (Siegfried), **Seferis**, **Seifert** (Jaroslav), **Shelley** (Percy Bysshe), **Sitwell** (Dame Edith), **Sitwell** (Sir Sacheverell), **Skelton** (John), **Spender** (Sir Stephen), **Spenser** (Edmund), **Stevens** (Wallace), **Terence**, **Thomson** (James), **Thoreau** (Henry David), **Vaughan** (Henry), **Vicente** (Gil), **Walcott** (Derek), **Whitman** (Walt), **Wieland** (Christoph Martin)
08 **Anacreon**, **Andersen** (Hans Christian), **Ausonius** (Decimus Magnus), **Banville** (Théodore de), **Berryman** (John), **Brentano** (Clemens), **Brittain** (Vera), **Browning** (Elizabeth Barrett), **Browning** (Robert), **Campbell** (Roy), **Carducci** (Giosuè), **Catullus** (Gaius Valerius), **Claudian**, **Congreve** (William), **cummings** (e e), **Cynewulf**, **Davenant** (Sir William), **De La Mare** (Walter), **Drummond** (William, of Hawthornden), **Firdausi**, **Ginsberg** (Allen), **Henryson** (Robert), **Laforgue** (Jules), **Langland** (William), **Lawrence** (D H), **Leopardi** (Giacomo), **Lovelace** (Richard), **Macaulay** (Dame Rose), **Macaulay** (Thomas), **MacLeish** (Archibald), **MacNeice** (Louis), **Malherbe** (François de), **Mallarmé** (Stéphane), **Menander**, **Milligan** (Spike), **Palgrave** (Francis Turner), **Paterson** (Andrew Barton), **Petrarch**, **Robinson** (Edwin Arlington), **Rossetti** (Christina), **Rossetti** (Dante Gabriel), **Sandburg** (Carl), **Schiller** (Friedrich), **Schlegel** (August Wilhelm von), **Suckling** (Sir John), **Taliesin**, **Tibullus**, **Traherne** (Thomas), **Verlaine** (Paul), **Whittier** (John Greenleaf)
09 **Aeschylus**, **Akhmatova** (Anna), **Bronowski** (Jacob), **Coleridge** (Samuel Taylor), **D'Annunzio** (Gabriele), **Dickinson** (Emily), **Froissart** (Jean), **Goldsmith** (Oliver), **Hölderlin** (Friedrich), **Lamartine** (Alphonse de), **Lucretius**, **Marinetti** (Filippo Tommaso), **Pasternak** (Boris), **Rochester** (John Wilmot, Earl of), **Rosenberg** (Isaac), **Santayana** (George), **Southwell** (Robert), **Swinburne** (Algernon Charles), **Ungaretti** (Giuseppe), **Zephaniah** (Benjamin)
10 **Baudelaire** (Charles), **Bradstreet** (Anne), **Chatterton** (Thomas), **Chesterton** (G K), **Empedocles**, **FitzGerald** (Edward), **La Fontaine** (Jean de), **Lagerkvist** (Pär), **Longfellow** (Henry Wadsworth), **MacDiarmid** (Hugh), **Mayakovsky** (Vladimir), **McGonagall** (William), **Propertius** (Sextus), **Theocritus**
11 **Apollinaire** (Guillaume), **Callimachus**, **Omar Khayyám**, **Shakespeare** (William), **Yevtushenko** (Yevegeny)
12 **Ferlinghetti** (Lawrence)
13 **Sackville-West** (Vita)
14 **Dante Alighieri**, **Saint-John Perse**
15 **Thomas the Rhymer**

• poet laureate

02 PL

Poets laureate:

03 **Pye** (Henry)
04 **Rowe** (Nicholas), **Tate** (Nahum)
06 **Austin** (Alfred), **Cibber** (Colley), **Dryden** (John), **Eusden** (Laurence), **Hughes** (Ted), **Jonson** (Ben), **Motion** (Andrew), **Warton** (Thomas)
07 **Bridges** (Robert), **Southey** (Robert)
08 **Betjeman** (Sir John), **Davenant** (Sir William), **Day-Lewis** (Cecil), **Shadwell** (Thomas), **Tennyson** (Alfred, Lord)
09 **Masefield** (John), **Whitehead** (William)
10 **Wordsworth** (William)

poetic

06 moving **07** flowing, lyrical, rhyming **08** artistic, creative, graceful, metrical, poetical, symbolic **09** beautiful, sensitive **10** expressive, figurative, rhythmical **11** imaginative

poetry

04 muse **05** poems, poesy, rhyme, verse **06** epopee, lyrics **07** doggrel, iambics, pennill, rhyming, versing **08** doggerel, epopoeia **09** free verse, macaronic, Parnassus, vers libre **10** macaronics **13** versification

Poetry movements include:

04 Beat
05 found, sound
07 Acmeism, digital, epitaph, erasure, imagism
08 concrete, medieval, pastoral, Trouvère
09 automatic, modernism, symbolism, Troubador, Victorian
10 Parnassian
11 Minnesinger, objectivist, performance, Romanticism, The Movement, traditional
12 metaphysical
13 Black Mountain, New York School, non-conformism, post-modernism
14 chanson de geste

See also **poem**

pogrom

06 murder **07** carnage, killing **08** butchery, genocide, homicide, massacre **09** bloodbath, holocaust, slaughter **10** decimation **11** liquidation **12** annihilation **13** extermination **15** ethnic cleansing

poignancy

04 pain **06** misery, pathos **07** emotion, feeling, sadness, tragedy **08** distress, keenness, piquancy, pungency **09** intensity, sentiment, sharpness **10** bitterness, tenderness **11** painfulness, piteousness **12** wretchedness **13** evocativeness

poignant

03 sad **05** sharp **06** moving, tender, tragic **07** painful, piquant, piteous, poynant, pungent, tearful **08** haunting, pathetic, pricking, stinging, touching, wretched **09** affecting, agonizing, emotional, heartfelt, miserable, sorrowful, upsetting **11** distressing, penetrating **12** heart-rending **13** heartbreaking

poignantly

05 sadly **08** movingly, tenderly **09** miserably, painfully, tearfully **10** tragically, wretchedly **11** emotionally, sorrowfully **12** pathetically

point

01 E, N, S, W **02** pt **03** ace, aim, dot, end, hit, neb, nib, nub, ord, tip, top, use **04** apex, area, cape, case, core, crag, crux, cusp, fang, feat, gist, goal, head, hint, item, lace, mark, meat, ness, node, peak, pike, pith, show, site, spot, stop, time, tine, vein, whit **05** drift, facet, heart, issue, level, place, score, sense, speck, spike, stage, state, sting, taper, tenor, theme, topic, total, train, trait, value, verge **06** aspect, burden, clause, denote, detail, direct, marrow, matter, moment, motive, object, period, plight, reason, signal, thrust **07** essence, feature, heading, instant, keynote, meaning, purpose, quality, sharpen, signify, subject, suggest **08** evidence, foreland, full stop, headland, indicate, juncture, locality, location, position, property, pungency, question, sharp end **09** attribute, condition, designate, extremity, full point, gesture at, intention, main point, north pole, objective, situation, south pole **10** conclusion, importance, particular, promontory, resolution **11** culmination **12** central point, decimal point, significance **14** characteristic, gesture towards

See also **compass**; **horse**

• beside the point
09 unrelated **10** immaterial, irrelevant, out of place, red herring **11** unconnected

• chief points
03 sum

• in point of fact
03 nay **06** indeed, in fact, really **08** actually **09** in reality **15** as a matter of fact

• lowest point
04 zero

• main point
04 clou, gist

• on the point of
07 about to, going to, ready to **10** in danger of **11** just about to, preparing to **12** on the brink of, on the verge of

• point of view
03 POV **04** view **05** angle, slant **06** aspect, belief, stance **07** feeling, opinion, outlook **08** approach, attitude, position **09** judgement, sentiment, viewpoint **10** Anschauung, standpoint **11** perspective

• point out
04 shew, show **05** judge **06** remind, reveal **07** bring up, mention, point to, presage, specify **08** allude to, identify, indicate **09** highlight **15** call attention to, draw attention to

• point up
06 stress **09** emphasize, highlight, underline **15** call attention to

• to the point
05 ad rem **07** germane, related **08** apposite, pregnant, relevant **09** connected, pertinent **10** applicable **11** appropriate

• up to a point
06 partly **08** slightly, somewhat **12** to some degree, to some extent

point-blank
04 flat, near, open **05** blunt, frank, level, plain, reach **06** candid, direct, openly, rudely **07** bluntly, closely, close to, frankly, plainly **08** abruptly, candidly, directly, explicit, outright, straight, touching **10** explicitly, forthright, unreserved **12** at close range, forthrightly **13** unequivocally **15** straightforward

pointed
04 keen, urdé, urdy **05** clear, edged, sharp, spicy, urdée **06** barbed, biting, Gothic, lancet **07** cutting, mordant, obvious, precise, telling **08** acicular, aculeate, explicit, forceful, incisive, striking, tapering **09** aculeated, cuspidate, mucronate, trenchant **10** cuspidated, fastigiate, lanceolate, mucronated **11** lanceolated, near the bone, penetrating **12** epigrammatic **14** epigrammatical

pointedly
07 bluntly, plainly **09** defiantly, on purpose **10** explicitly **13** intentionally, provocatively

pointer
03 rod, tip **04** cane, clue, hand, hint, pole, sign **05** arrow, guide, index, stick, style **06** advice, fescue, needle, tongue **07** caution, warning **09** guideline, hyperlink, indicator **10** indication, suggestion **11** trafficator **13** piece of advice **14** recommendation

pointless
◇ *tail deletion indicator*
04 vain **05** inane **06** absurd, futile **07** aimless, foolish, useless **08** muticous **09** a mug's game, fruitless, senseless, to no avail, valueless, worthless **10** ridiculous, unavailing **11** meaningless, nonsensical **12** a waste of time, unproductive, unprofitable **13** insignificant **14** a waste of effort

pointlessly
06 in vain **09** aimlessly **11** senselessly **12** unprofitably **13** meaninglessly **14** unproductively

poise
04 bias, cool, hang **05** grace, hover, pease, peaze, peise, peize, peyse, weigh **06** aplomb, impact, ponder, steady, weight **07** balance, dignity, librate, support, suspend **08** calmness, coolness, elegance, momentum, position, serenity, suspense **09** assurance, composure **10** equanimity **11** equilibrium, self-control **13** self-assurance **14** presence of mind, self-confidence, self-possession

poised
03 set **04** calm, cool **05** paysd, ready, suave **06** all set, serene, urbane **07** assured, waiting **08** balanced, composed, graceful, prepared **09** collected, dignified, expectant, unruffled **11** unflappable **13** self-confident, self-possessed **14** self-controlled

poison
03 mar **04** warp **05** spoil, taint **06** blight, cancer, canker, defile, infect, rankle **07** corrupt, deprave, envenom, pervert, pollute **08** embitter **09** contagion, pollution **10** adulterate, corruption, envenomate, malignancy **11** contaminate **13** contamination

Poisonous creatures include:

03 asp
04 fugu, gila, seps, weta
05 adder, cobra, viper
06 dugite, katipo, taipan
07 redback, sea wasp
08 blowfish, cerastes, jararaca, jararaka, mocassin, moccasin, ringhals, rinkhals, scorpion, sea snake
09 berg-adder, boomslang, funnel-web, globe fish, hamadryad, king cobra, puff adder, stonefish, tarantula
10 bandy-bandy, black snake, black widow, bushmaster, copperhead, coral snake, death adder, puffer fish
11 cottonmouth, gaboon viper, gila monster, rattlesnake
12 box jellyfish, scorpion fish, sea porcupine, violin spider
13 water moccasin
15 funnel-web spider

Poisonous plants include:

04 upas
05 dwale
06 antiar
07 aconite, amanita, anemone, cowbane, hemlock, lantana
08 banewort, foxglove, laburnum, mandrake, oleander, wild arum
09 digitalis, monkshood, naked boys, naked lady, poison ivy, stinkweed, wake-robin, wolfsbane
10 belladonna, cuckoo pint, jimson weed, stramonium, thorn apple, windflower
12 helmet flower
13 giant hockweed, meadow saffron
14 castor oil plant, lords-and-ladies
15 black nightshade

Poisons and toxic substances include:

03 BHC
04 bane, lead
05 abrin, conin, lysol, ozone, ricin, sarin, toxin, venin, venom, VX gas
06 arsine, curare, dioxin, G-agent, iodine, ketene, V-agent, wabain, war gas
07 arsenic, bromine, cacodyl, coniine, cyanide, digoxin, dioxane, mercury, mineral, neurine, ouabain, stibine, tanghin
08 antimony, atropine, chlordan, chlorine, cyanogen, cytisine, fluorine, gossypol, lobeline, melittin, nerve gas, Paraquat®, phosgene, ptomaine, ratsbane, rotenone, thebaine, urushiol
09 aflatoxin, amygdalin, chaconine, chlordane, muscarine, mycotoxin, nux vomica, saxitoxin, white damp
10 acrylamide, aqua Tofana, bufotenine, domoic acid, heptachlor, mustard gas, neurotoxin, oxalic acid, phosphorus, phytotoxin, picrotoxin, strychnine, tetrotoxin
11 enterotoxin, hyoscyamine, nitric oxide, prussic acid, sugar of lead
12 strophanthin, tetrodotoxin
13 Scheele's green, silver nitrate

14 carbon monoxide
15 hydrogen cyanide, nitrogen dioxide

poisoning
03 obi 04 obia 05 obeah

Poisoning types include:

04 food, lead
05 algae, blood
06 iodism
07 bromism, gassing, pyaemia, sausage, toxemia
08 botulism, ergotism, plumbism, ptomaine, toxaemia
09 brominism, crotalism, fluorosis, lead colic, mephitism, sapraemia, saturnism, zinc colic
10 alcoholism, molybdosis, salicylism, salmonella, stibialism, strychnism
11 phosphorism, septicaemia
12 hydrargyrism, intoxication, strychninism
13 mycotoxicosis

poisonous
05 fatal, toxic, venom 06 deadly, lethal, mortal, virose 07 baneful, harmful, noxious, vicious 08 spiteful, toxicant, venomous, virulent
09 cancerous, cankerous, malicious, malignant, offensive 10 corrupting, pernicious 11 deleterious
13 contaminating
See also **poison**

poke
03 bag, dig, hit, jab, peg 04 butt, pick, pock, pote, prod, prog, push, root, rout, stab 05 elbow, goose, grope, nudge, poach, prick, proke, punch, shove, stick, stoop, wroot 06 incite, nuzzle, pocket, potter, powter, stir up, thrust 07 scuffle, snuzzle 08 itchweed, protrude
• **poke around**
04 root, rout 07 look for 09 search for
11 grope around, rake through
13 rummage around 14 look all over for
• **poke fun at**
03 cod, rag, rib 04 jeer, joke, mock, quiz 05 get at, spoof, taunt, tease
06 parody, send up 08 ridicule
09 make fun of 11 poke borak at
13 poke mullock at, take the mickey
• **poke out**
06 beetle, extend, jut out 07 extrude, project 08 overhang, protrude, stick out

poker

Poker-related terms include:

03 pat, shy
04 ante, call, flop, pair, stay, stud
05 blind, bluff, check, flush
06 kicker, suited
08 hole card, showdown, stand pat, straight
09 four-flush, full house
10 royal flush
11 busted flush, pass the buck
13 community card, straight flush

poker-faced
05 blank, empty 06 glazed, vacant
07 deadpan, vacuous 08 lifeless
09 apathetic, impassive
11 emotionless, indifferent, inscrutable 12 uninterested
14 expressionless, without feeling
15 uncomprehending

poky
04 slow, tiny 05 small, tight 06 narrow, poking 07 cramped, crowded
08 confined, powerful 10 restricted
12 incommodious
See also **prison**

Poland
02 PL 03 POL

polar
03 icy 04 cold 05 axial 06 arctic, frozen 07 glacial 08 freezing, opposite, Siberian 09 Antarctic
10 ambivalent 11 conflicting, dichotomous 12 antithetical
13 contradictory

polarity
07 duality, paradox 09 dichotomy
10 antithesis, difference, opposition, separation 11 ambivalence, contrariety 12 oppositeness
13 contradiction

polarize
05 split 06 divide 07 break up, split up
08 alienate, disunite, estrange, separate 09 segregate 10 drive apart
11 come between

pole
01 N, S 02 po 03 bar, lug, nib, oar, rod
04 bail, boom, kent, mast, post, rood, spar 05 caber, limit, perch, quant, shaft, staff, stake, stang, stick, sting
06 janker, pillar, Polack, ripeck, rypeck
07 extreme, heavens, ryepeck, support, upright 08 Polander 09 cowl-staff, extremity, stanchion 10 river horse 11 clothes-prop 12 Venetian mast
• **poles apart**
11 worlds apart 12 incompatible
14 irreconcilable

polecat
05 fitch, skunk 06 ferret 07 fitchet, fitchew, foumart 08 foulmart
10 prostitute

polemic
06 debate 07 dispute, eristic
08 argument, diatribe 09 eristical, invective, polemical 11 contentious, controversy 12 disputatious
13 argumentative, controversial

polemicist
06 arguer 07 debater 08 disputer, polemist 09 contender, disputant
11 logomachist

polemics
06 debate 07 dispute 08 argument
09 logomachy 10 contention
11 controversy, disputation
13 argumentation

police
◇ *anagram indicator*
04 cops, fuzz, heat, pigs, plod
05 check, filth, guard, polis, watch
06 defend, patrol, the law 07 bizzies, control, coppers, monitor, observe, Old Bill, oversee, peelers, protect, rozzers, the Bill, the fuzz 08 regulate, the force 09 keep watch, supervise
10 boys in blue 11 police force
12 constabulary, keep the peace 13 the boys in blue 14 police officers

Police forces and branches include:

02 AP, KP, MP, PD, SS
03 CIB, CID, KGB, Met, MGB, RMP
04 Ogpu, PSNI, RCMP, SWAT
05 cheka, Garda, Stasi
07 Europol, Gestapo, sweeney, the Yard
08 Interpol
09 Air Police, bomb squad, drug squad, porn squad, riot squad, task force, vice squad
10 riot police, Securitate, water guard
11 flying squad, gendarmerie, strike force, sweeney todd, Yardie squad
12 mobile police, Scotland Yard, secret police, Texas Rangers
13 Garda Siochana, mounted police, Schutzstaffel, Special Branch, traffic police
14 military police
15 New Scotland Yard

Police-related terms include:

04 ACPO, beat, book, bust, cell, nick, raid, rank, shop, tana, tank
05 ACPOS, baton, cuffs, fit-up, force, frame, go off, grass, manor, plant, pound, set-up, snout, sting, tanna, thana, tunic
06 arrest, batoon, charge, cordon, curfew, fisgig, fizgig, helmet, line-up, rumble, search, tannah, thanah, thanna, wanted
07 caution, copshop, custody, dragnet, epaulet, jemadar, manhunt, mugshot, pentito, round-up, station, stinger, stoolie, thannah, uniform, warrant
08 evidence, mouchard, panda car, precinct, prowl car, speed gun, squad car
09 blue light, centenier, handcuffs, identikit, meat wagon, on the beat, police dog, radar trap, shakedown, speed trap, truncheon
10 body armour, police cell, police trap, supergrass, tenderloin, tracker dog, watch house
11 fingerprint, flying squad, jam sandwich, Judges' Rules, stool pigeon, utility belt, warrant card
12 bertillonage, incident room, police escort, police-manure, surveillance, walkie-talkie
13 police station, rogues' gallery, search warrant, stop-and-search
14 catch red-handed, criminal record, identity parade
15 bullet-proof vest, long arm of the law, scene of the crime

police officer

02 DI, PC, PS, PW, SC **03** cop, pig, 'tec, WPC **04** bogy, bull, flic, gill, nark, peon, plod, slop, SOCO, trap **05** beast, bizzy, bobby, bogey, Dixon, garda, jawan, polis, sepoy, sowar, traps, wolly **06** askari, copper, escort, lawman, Mounty, peeler, redcap, rozzer, sbirro, the law **07** captain, crusher, gumshoe, John Hop, marshal, Mountie, officer, trooper, zabtieh, zaptiah, zaptieh **08** flat-foot, gendarme, sergeant, serjeant, speed-cop, walloper **09** centenier, commander, constable, detective, inspector, patrolman, policeman, woodentop **10** bluebottle, carabinero, gangbuster, lieutenant, traffic cop **11** Black and Tan, carabiniere, patrolwoman, policewoman **12** master-at-arms, peace officer, state trooper **13** beetle-crusher, branch officer **14** police sergeant, superintendent, warrant officer

Police ranks in the UK:

08 Sergeant
09 Commander, Constable, Inspector
12 Commissioner
14 Chief Constable, Chief Inspector, Superintendent
18 Deputy Commissioner
19 Chief Superintendent
20 Deputy Chief Constable
21 Assistant Commissioner
23 Assistant Chief Constable
27 Deputy Assistant Commissioner

• police search

04 heat **07** dragnet, manhunt
09 shakedown

police station

04 nick, tana **05** tanna, thana
06 tannah, thanah, thanna **07** copshop, thannah **08** precinct **10** watch house
11 gendarmerie

policy

04 line, plan **05** rules **06** course, custom, method, scheme, stance, system **07** cunning **08** approach, position, practice, protocol, prudence, schedule, strategy **09** guideline, insurance, procedure, programme
10 guidelines, statecraft **12** constitution
14 code of practice, course of action

• the best policy

07 honesty

polish

03 lap, rub, wax **04** buff, bull, file, posh, sand **05** class, clean, glass, glaze, gloss, grace, poise, rub up, scour, sheen, shine, slick, style **06** finish, lustre, Polack, Poland, posh up, refine, smooth, veneer **07** beeswax, brush up, burnish, enhance, finesse, furbish, improve, perfect, planish, slicken, sparkle, touch up, varnish **08** breeding, brighten, elegance, glaciate
09 brilliant, cultivate **10** brightness, brilliance, refinement, smoothness
11 cultivation, rottenstone, satin finish
13 supercalender **14** sophistication

• polish off

03 zap **04** bolt, do in, down, kill, wolf
05 eat up, stuff, waste **06** devour, finish, gobble, murder, rub out **07** bump off, consume, destroy, put away, take out, wipe out **08** blow away, complete, dispatch, knock off **09** dispose of, eliminate, liquidate

polished

05 adept, filed, shiny, suave, waxed
06 expert, glassy, glossy, polite, sanded, smooth, snappy, urbane
07 elegant, genteel, perfect, refined, shining, skilful **08** cultured, flawless, gleaming, graceful, lapidary, lustrous, masterly, slippery, well-bred
09 burnished, civilized, excellent, faultless, perfected **10** consummate, cultivated, impeccable, proficient, remarkable **11** outstanding, superlative
12 accomplished, professional, well-mannered **13** sophisticated

polite

05 bland, civil, suave **06** glossy, humane, urbane **07** elegant, gallant, genteel, refined, tactful **08** cultured, delicate, gracious, ladylike, obliging, polished, well-bred **09** civilized, courteous, courtlike **10** chivalrous, cultivated, diplomatic, respectful, thoughtful **11** considerate, deferential, gentlemanly, well-behaved
12 Grandisonian, well-mannered
13 sophisticated

politely

09 gallantly, tactfully **10** graciously, obligingly **11** courteously
12 chivalrously, respectfully, thoughtfully **13** considerately
14 diplomatically

politeness

04 tact **05** grace **06** polish **07** culture, manners, respect **08** civility, courtesy, elegance **09** attention, deference, diplomacy, gentility, politesse
10 cordiality, discretion, refinement
11 courtliness, cultivation, good manners, savoir-vivre
12 complaisance, good breeding, graciousness, mannerliness
14 respectfulness, thoughtfulness
15 considerateness, gentlemanliness

politic

04 sage, wise **06** shrewd **07** prudent, tactful **08** discreet, sensible
09 advisable, expedient, judicious, opportune, political, sagacious
10 diplomatic **12** advantageous
14 constitutional

political

05 civil **06** public **08** judicial
09 executive **11** ministerial
12 bureaucratic, governmental
13 parliamentary **14** administrative, constitutional, party political

See also **parliament**; **party**

Political ideologies include:

06 holism, Maoism, Nazism
07 fascism, Marxism
08 third way, Whiggism
09 anarchism, communism, democracy, neo-nazism, pluralism, socialism, theocracy
10 absolutism, Bolshevism, federalism, liberalism, neo-fascism, Trotskyism
11 imperialism, nationalism, syndicalism, Thatcherism
12 collectivism, conservatism
13 individualism, republicanism, unilateralism
14 egalitarianism, neocolonialism
15 social democracy, totalitarianism

politician

02 MP **07** senator **08** minister
09 president **13** vice president

See also **president**; **prime minister**

Politicians include:

03 **Coe** (Sebastian, Lord), **Fox** (Charles James), **Fox** (Liam), **Fox** (Sir Marcus), **Jay** (Margaret, Lady), **Lee** (Jennie, Lady), **Lie** (Trygve), **May** (Theresa), **Pym** (John), **Wet** (Christian de), **Yeo** (Timothy)
04 **Amos** (Valerie, Baroness), **Aziz** (Tariq), **Bell** (Martin), **Benn** (Anthony Wedgwood 'Tony'), **Benn** (Hilary), **Cato** (Marcus Porcius), **Cook** (Robin), **Debs** (Eugene Victor), **Dole** (Robert), **Foot** (Michael), **Gore** (Albert), **Haig** (Alexander), **Hain** (Peter), **Hess** (Rudolf), **Hoon** (Geoff), **Howe** (Geoffrey, Lord), **Hume** (John), **Hurd** (Douglas, Lord), **Koch** (Ed), **Kohl** (Helmut), **More** (Sir Thomas), **Nagy** (Imre), **Opik** (Lembit), **Owen** (David, Lord), **Pitt** (William, the elder), **Reid** (John), **Reno** (Janet), **Rice** (Condoleezza), **Röhm** (Ernst), **Rusk** (Dean), **Vane** (Sir Henry)
05 **Adams** (Gerry), **Agnew** (Spiro), **Astor** (Nancy, Viscountess), **Bacon** (Francis), **Baker** (James Addison), **Baker** (Kenneth, Lord), **Bevan** (Aneurin), **Bevin** (Ernest), **Brown** (George), **Brown** (Gordon), **Burke** (Edmund), **Cecil** (William), **Cimon**, **Clark** (Alan), **Cleon**, **Davis** (David), **Dayan** (Moshe), **Dewar** (Donald), **Field** (Frank), **Freud** (Sir Clement), **Hague** (William), **Huhne** (Chris), **Kelly** (Ruth), **Kirov** (Sergey), **Krenz** (Egon), **Lenin** (Vladimir Ilyich), **Marat** (Jean Paul), **Maude** (Francis), **Nkomo** (Joshua), **Perón** (Eva), **Perón** (Isabelita), **Scott** (Sir Nicholas), **Scott** (Sir Richard), **Short** (Clare), **Smith** (Chris), **Smith** (Jacqui), **Smith** (John), **Solon**, **Steel** (David, Lord), **Straw** (Jack), **Sulla** (Lucius Cornelius), **Sully** (Maximilien de Béthune, Duc de), **Tambo** (Oliver), **Timms** (Stephen), **Vance** (Cyrus Roberts)
06 **Abacha** (Sanni), **Abbott** (Diane), **Antony** (Mark), **Archer** (Jeffrey), **Benton** (Thomas Hart), **Blears** (Hazel), **Boyson** (Sir Rhodes), **Brandt** (Willy), **Bright** (John), **Browne** (Des), **Butler** (Richard,

Lord), **Caesar** (Julius), **Castle** (Barbara, Lady), **Cicero** (Marcus Tullius), **Clarke** (Charles), **Clarke** (Kenneth), **Cobden** (Richard), **Cripps** (Sir Stafford), **Curzon** (George, Marquis), **Danton** (Georges), **Davies** (Denzil), **Djilas** (Milovan), **Dobson** (Frank), **Dubcek** (Alexander), **Dulles** (John Foster), **Erhard** (Ludwig), **Fowler** (Sir Norman), **Gummer** (John), **Hardie** (Keir), **Harman** (Harriet), **Healey** (Denis, Lord), **Hewitt** (Patricia), **Hitler** (Adolf), **Horthy** (Miklós), **Howard** (Michael), **Hughes** (Simon), **Hutton** (John), **Irvine** (Alexander, Lord), **Jinnah** (Muhammad Ali), **Joseph** (Keith, Lord), **Jowell** (Tessa), **Kaunda** (Kenneth), **Lamont** (Norman), **Lawson** (Nigel, Lord), **Letwin** (Oliver), **Lilley** (Peter), **Mallon** (Seamus), **Marius** (Gaius), **Mellon** (Andrew William), **Mellor** (David), **Merkel** (Angela), **Mornay** (Philippe de), **Morton** (John), **Mosley** (Sir Oswald), **Mowlam** (Doctor Marjorie 'Mo'), **Nansen** (Fridtjof), **Necker** (Jacques), **Norris** (Steven), **Pandit** (Vijaya Lakshmi), **Pompey**, **Powell** (Enoch), **Prasad** (Rajendra), **Quayle** (Dan), **Roland** (Jean Mari), **Sidney** (Algernon), **Somers** (John, Lord), **Steele** (Sir Richard), **Suslov** (Mikhail), **Tebbit** (Norman, Lord), **Thorpe** (Jeremy), **Waller** (Edmund), **Walter** (Hubert), **Warren** (Earl), **Wilkes** (John), **Wolsey** (Thomas)

07 **Acheson** (Dean), **Allende** (Salvador), **Arundel** (Thomas), **Ashdown** (Paddy), **Beckett** (Margaret), **Bedford** (John of Lancaster, Duke of), **Boateng** (Paul), **Bormann** (Martin), **Brittan** (Sir Leon), **Cameron** (David), **Canning** (George), **Cassius**, **Colbert** (Jean Baptiste), **Collins** (Michael), **Comines** (Philippe de), **Crassus** (Marcus Licinius), **Dalyell** (Tam), **Dandolo** (Enrico), **Darling** (Alistair), **De Klerk** (Frederik William), **Dorrell** (Stephen), **Fischer** (Joschka), **Fouquet** (Nicolas), **Gemayel** (Amin), **Gemayel** (Bashir), **Gemayel** (Sheikh Pierre), **Grattan** (Henry), **Grimond** (Jo, Lord), **Haldane** (Richard, Viscount), **Halifax** (Edward Frederick Lindley Wood, Earl of), **Halifax** (George Savile, Marquis of), **Harlech** (William David Ormsby Gore, Lord), **Hunyady** (János Corvinus), **Hussein** (Saddam), **Jackson** (Glenda), **Jackson** (Jesse), **Jameson** (Sir Leander Starr), **Jenkins** (Roy, Lord), **Johnson** (Alan), **Kalinin** (Mikhail), **Kaufman** (Gerald), **Kaunitz** (Wenzel Anton Fürst von), **Kennedy** (Charles), **Kennedy** (Edward M), **Kennedy** (Robert F), **Kinnock** (Neil), **Kossuth** (Lajos), **Lepidus** (Marcus Aemilius), **MacLeod** (Iain), **Malraux** (André), **Maxwell** (Robert), **Mazarin** (Jules, Cardinal), **Meacher** (Michael), **Mikoyan** (Anastas), **Milburn** (Alan), **Mondale** (Walter Frederick), **Osborne** (George), **Paisley** (Reverend Ian), **Profumo** (John), **Redmond** (John), **Redwood** (John), **Rifkind** (Sir Malcolm), **Russell** (William, Lord), **Salmond** (Alexander), **Schmidt** (Helmut), **Sithole** (Reverend Ndabaningi), **Skinner** (Dennis), **Tallien** (Jean Lambert), **Trimble** (David), **Warwick** (Richard Neville, Earl of), **William** (of Wykeham)

08 **Adenauer** (Konrad), **Albright** (Madeleine), **Antonius** (Marcus), **Blunkett** (David), **Campbell** (Sir Menzies), **Catiline**, **Constant** (Benjamin), **Cromwell** (Oliver), **Cromwell** (Thomas), **Crossman** (Richard), **Daladier** (Edouard), **Dimitrov** (Georgi), **Dollfuss** (Engelbert), **Falconer** (Charles, Lord), **Franklin** (Benjamin), **Genscher** (Hans-Dietrich), **Goebbels** (Joseph), **Hailsham** (Quintin McGarel Hogg, Viscount), **Hamilton** (Alexander), **Harriman** (William Averell), **Honecker** (Erich), **Humphrey** (Hubert Horatio), **Ibárruri** (Dolores), **Jumblatt** (Kemal), **Karadzic** (Radovan), **Khomeini** (Ayatollah Ruhollah), **Lansbury** (George), **Lucullus** (Lucius Licinius), **Malenkov** (Giorgiy), **Marshall** (George Catlett), **Maudling** (Reginald), **McCarthy** (Eugene Joseph), **McCarthy** (Joseph Raymond), **McGovern** (George Stanley), **McNamara** (Robert Strange), **Miliband** (David), **Mirabeau** (Honoré Gabriel Riqueti, Comte de), **Montfort** (Simon de), **Morrison** (Herbert, Lord), **Pericles**, **Polignac** (Auguste Jules Armand Marie, Prince de), **Portillo** (Michael), **Prescott** (John), **Rathenau** (Walther), **Sandwich** (John Montagu, Earl of), **Schröder** (Gerhard), **Schüssel** (Wolfgang), **Shephard** (Gillian), **Shinwell** (Manny, Lord), **Stanhope** (James, Earl), **Ulbricht** (Walter), **Whitelaw** (William 'Willie', Viscount), **Williams** (Shirley, Lady), **Zinoviev** (Grigoriy)

09 **Alexander** (Douglas), **Armstrong** (Hilary), **Boothroyd** (Betty), **Bottomley** (Virginia), **Buthelezi** (Chief Mangosuthu), **Ceausescu** (Nicolae), **Churchill** (Randolph, Lord), **Gaitskell** (Hugh), **Godolphin** (Sidney, Earl of), **Goldwater** (Barry Morris), **Heseltine** (Michael), **Kissinger** (Henry), **Kitchener** (Herbert, Earl), **Lafayette** (Marie Joseph, Marquis de), **La Guardia** (Fiorello Henry), **Luxemburg** (Rosa), **Mandelson** (Peter), **Miltiades**, **Parkinson** (Cecil, Lord), **Podgorniy** (Nikolay), **Ramaphosa** (Cyril), **Richelieu** (Armand Jean du Plessis, Cardinal and Duc de), **Robertson** (George, Lord), **Stevenson** (Adlai), **Strafford** (Thomas Wentworth, Earl of), **Streicher** (Julius), **Vyshinsky** (Andrei)

10 **Alcibiades**, **Carrington** (Peter, Lord), **Cunningham** (Doctor Jack), **Enver Pasha**, **Hattersley** (Roy, Lord), **McGuinness** (Martin), **Metternich** (Klemens Fürst von), **Ribbentrop** (Joachim von), **Stresemann** (Gustav), **Talleyrand** (Charles Maurice de), **Waldegrave** (William), **Walsingham** (Sir Francis), **Weinberger** (Caspar), **Widdecombe** (Ann)

11 **Beaverbrook** (Max Aitken, Lord), **Bolingbroke** (Henry St John, Viscount), **Castlereagh** (Robert Stewart, Viscount), **Chamberlain** (Joseph), **Chamberlain** (Sir Austen), **Cincinnatus** (Lucius Quinctius), **Demosthenes**, **George-Brown** (Lord), **Hore-Belisha** (Leslie, Lord), **Livingstone** (Ken), **Machiavelli** (Niccolò), **Mountbatten** (Louis, Earl), **Shaftesbury** (Anthony Ashley Cooper, Earl of), **Wilberforce** (William)

12 **Boutros-Ghali** (Boutros), **Hammarskjöld** (Dag), **Themistocles**

13 **Chateaubriand** (François Auguste René, Viscount of), **Fabius Maximus** (Quintus)

14 **Heathcoat-Amory** (David)

politics

05 state **06** civics **09** diplomacy, power game **10** government, statecraft **11** machination, manoeuvring, Weltpolitik **12** machinations, Machtpolitik, manipulation **13** party politics, power politics, power struggle, public affairs, statesmanship **14** affairs of state, haute politique, political views, wheeler-dealing **15** local government

poll

03 cut, dod, get, net, pow, win **04** clip, gain, head, trim, vote **05** count, shear, tally **06** ballot, census, obtain, parrot, return, sample, survey, voting **07** canvass, dishorn, pollard, receive, returns, solicit, sondage **08** campaign, question, register, sampling **09** ballot-box, head count, interview, straw poll, straw vote **10** Gallup poll, individual, plebiscite, referendum **11** electioneer, opinion poll, show of hands **14** market research

pollack

03 lob **05** coley, lythe **06** saithe **08** coalfish **09** sea salmon

polled

03 not **04** nott

pollen

06 farina **08** bee-bread **09** witchmeal

pollute
◇ *anagram indicator*
03 mar **04** file, foul, soil, warp
05 blend, dirty, spoil, stain, sully, taint
06 befoul, canker, debase, defile, infect, poison **07** besmear, blacken, corrupt, defiled, deprave, profane, tarnish, vitiate **09** make dirty
10 adulterate **11** contaminate

pollution
◇ *anagram indicator*
03 fug **04** smog **05** stain, taint
07 fouling, soilure **08** foulness, impurity, staining, sullying
09 depravity, dirtiness, infection, muckiness **10** blackening, corruption, debasement, defilement, filthiness, tarnishing **12** adulteration
13 contamination

polonium
02 Po

polychromatic
06 motley **07** mottled, rainbow
08 many-hued **10** polychrome, variegated **12** many-coloured, varicoloured **13** kaleidoscopic, multicoloured, parti-coloured

polyglot
08 linguist **11** multiracial, polyglottal, polyglottic **12** cosmopolitan, multilingual **13** international, multilinguist

polymath
06 oracle **07** know-all **10** all-rounder, pansophist, polyhistor

pomp
04 show **05** glory, state **06** parade, ritual, vanity **07** display, glitter, majesty, triumph **08** ceremony, flourish, grandeur **09** formality, pageantry, solemnity, spectacle, splendour
10 brilliance, ceremonial, procession
11 ostentation **12** magnificence **14** self-importance **15** ceremoniousness

pomposity
04 airs **05** pride **06** vanity **07** bombast, fustian **08** euphuism, rhetoric
09 arrogance, loftiness, turgidity
10 pretension, stuffiness **11** affectation, haughtiness, preachiness, presumption
13 condescension, imperiousness, magniloquence **14** grandiloquence, self-importance **15** pretentiousness

pompous
03 big **04** vain **05** budge, grant, heavy, lofty, proud, state, windy **06** la-di-da, snooty, solemn, stuffy, turgid
07 flowery, fustian, haughty, orotund, preachy, stately, stilted **08** affected, arrogant, inflated, magnific
09 bombastic, conceited, elaborate, grandiose, high-flown, imperious, important, ororotund, overblown
10 aldermanly, euphuistic, magnifical, portentous **11** highfalutin, magisterial, magnificent, overbearing, patronizing, pretentious **12** aldermanlike, highfaluting, high-sounding, magniloquent, ostentatious, presumptuous, supercilious
13 condescending, self-important

pond
04 lake, mere, pool, rink, stew, tank, tarn **05** flash, pound, viver **06** puddle
07 piscary, piscina, piscine **08** Atlantic, fish-stew, turlough **09** waterhole
10 oceanarium, seaquarium
12 watering-hole

ponder
04 mull, muse, pore **05** brood, poise, study, think, volve, weigh **06** muse on, reason **07** analyse, examine, reflect, revolve **08** cogitate, consider, incubate, meditate, mull over, pore over, turn over **09** cerebrate, ponderate **10** deliberate, excogitate, puzzle over **11** contemplate, ratiocinate **12** ruminate over **13** give thought to

ponderous
04 dull, huge **05** bulky, heavy, hefty
06 clumsy, dreary, prolix, stodgy, stolid
07 awkward, massive, serious, stilted, tedious, verbose, weighty
08 laboured, lifeless, pedantic, plodding, unwieldy **09** graceless, laborious, lumbering **10** cumbersome, flat-footed, humourless, long-winded, pedestrian, slow-moving
11 elephantine, heavy-footed, heavy-handed

ponderously
06 slowly **07** heavily **08** clumsily, stodgily **09** awkwardly, seriously, tediously, verbosely **11** gracelessly, laboriously **12** cumbersomely, pedantically

ponderousness
06 tedium **08** gravitas **09** heaviness, stolidity **10** stodginess **11** seriousness, weightiness **13** laboriousness
14 humourlessness

pong *see* **smell**

pontifical
05 papal **06** snooty **07** Aaronic, pompous, preachy **08** didactic, dogmatic, prelatic, splendid
09 Aaronical, apostolic, imperious
10 portentous **11** magisterial, overbearing, pretentious, sermonizing
13 condescending, self-important
14 ecclesiastical

pontificate
05 spiel **06** preach **07** declaim, expound, lecture **08** harangue, moralize, perorate, sound off
09 dogmatize, hold forth, pronounce, sermonize **13** lay down the law

pontoon
05 float **07** caisson, vingt-un
09 blackjack, twenty-one, vingt-et-un

pony *see* **horse**

pooh-pooh
04 pish **05** scoff, scorn, sneer, spurn
06 deride, reject, slight **07** disdain, dismiss, sniff at **08** belittle, minimize, play down, ridicule **09** disparage, disregard **10** brush aside **12** make little of **15** laugh out of court

pool
03 dub, hag, lin, pot, spa **04** ante, bank, bath, dump, flow, fund, hagg, lake, lido, linn, meer, mere, pond, ring, sump, tank, tarn, team **05** flash, group, kitty, merge, plash, plesh, purse, share, stank
06 cartel, chip in, lasher, muck in, puddle, supply **07** combine, jackpot, Jacuzzi®, piscina, piscine, reserve
08 Bethesda **09** backwater, composite, syndicate, waterhole
10 accumulate, amalgamate, collective, consortium, contribute, natatorium **11** put together
12 accumulation, paddling-pool, swimming-bath, swimming-pool, watering-hole **13** swimming-baths

poor
◇ *anagram indicator*
03 bad, low, sad **04** bare, duff, mean, mere, naff, puir, ropy, thin, weak
05 broke, cronk, crook, jerry, lowly, needy, pants, ropey, skint, sober, sorry, stony **06** barren, cruddy, crummy, faulty, feeble, hard-up, humble, hungry, ill off, in need, meagre, measly, ornery, paltry, rotten, scanty, shoddy, skimpy, sparse **07** hapless, lacking, low-rent, obolary, pitiful, reduced, rubbish, unhappy, unlucky, useless, wanting
08 badly off, bankrupt, beggared, beggarly, below par, depleted, deprived, dirt-poor, exiguous, ill-fated, indigent, inferior, low-grade, luckless, mediocre, one-horse, pathetic, pitiable, shameful, strapped, waterish, wretched **09** defective, deficient, destitute, exhausted, flat broke, fruitless, imperfect, miserable, penniless, penurious, third-rate, worthless **10** cleaned-out, distressed, ill-starred, inadequate, low-quality, second-rate, spiritless, stony-broke, straitened, threadbare
11 impecunious, near the bone, necessitous, substandard, unfortunate
12 impoverished, insufficient, on your uppers, unproductive, without means
13 below standard, disadvantaged, in Queer Street **14** on the breadline, on your beam ends, unsatisfactory
15 poverty-stricken, strapped for cash, underprivileged

poorly
◇ *anagram indicator*
03 ill **04** sick **05** badly, seedy **06** ailing, feebly, groggy, meanly, rotten, sickly, unwell **08** below par, faultily, rottenly, shabbily, shoddily **09** off colour
10 indisposed, inexpertly, inferiorly, out of sorts **12** inadequately
13 incompetently **14** insufficiently, unsuccessfully **15** under the weather

pop
◇ *anagram indicator*
03 nip, put **04** bang, boom, cola, dash, drop, papa, pawn, push, rush, shot, slip, snap, soda **05** burst, crack, go off,

hurry, poppa, shoot, shove, slide **06** insert, pistol, poppet, report, thrust **07** darling, explode, popular, propose **08** protrude, suddenly **09** explosion, go quickly **10** fizzy drink **12** leave quickly **13** fizzy lemonade **15** go for a short time

See also **father**; **pawn**; **singer**; **song**

• pop off
03 die **06** pass on, peg out **07** snuff it **08** flatline, pass away **09** have had it **13** kick the bucket

• pop up
05 occur **06** appear, crop up, show up, turn up **09** come along **11** materialize

pope
03 SSD **04** ruff **05** ruffe **06** Il Papa **07** pontiff **10** Holy Father **11** His Holiness **12** Bishop of Rome **13** Vicar of Christ

Popes:

03 Leo
04 Cono, Joan, John, Mark, Paul, Pius
05 Caius, Donus, Felix, Lando, Linus, Peter, Soter, Urban
06 Adrian, Agatho, Albert, Fabian, Julius, Lucius, Martin, Philip, Sixtus, Victor
07 Anterus, Clement, Damasus, Gregory, Hadrian, Hilarus, Hyginus, Marinus, Paschal, Pontian, Romanus, Sergius, Stephen, Ursinus, Zosimus
08 Agapetus, Anicetus, Benedict, Boniface, Calixtus, Eugenius, Eulalius, Eusebius, Formosus, Gelasius, Honorius, Innocent, John Paul, Liberius, Nicholas, Novatian, Pelagius, Siricius, Theodore, Vigilius, Vitalian
09 Adeodatus, Alexander, Anacletus, Callistus, Celestine, Cornelius, Deusdedit, Dionysius, Dioscorus, Evaristus, Hormisdas, Marcellus, Miltiades, Severinus, Silverius, Sisinnius, Sylvester, Symmachus, Theodoric, Valentine, Zacharias
10 Anastasius, Hippolytus, Laurentius, Sabinianus, Simplicius, Zephyrinus
11 Christopher, Constantine, Eleutherius, Eutychianus, Marcellinus, Telesphorus

popinjay
03 fop **04** beau, dude, toff **05** dandy, pansy, swell **06** parrot **07** coxcomb, peacock

poplar
03 asp **05** abele, aspen **06** aspine **09** tacamahac, tacmahack, tulip tree **10** cottonwood

poppy
07 Papaver, ponceau **08** argemone **09** bloodroot **10** coquelicot **12** eschscholzia **13** eschscholtzia

poppycock
03 rot **04** blah, bosh, bull, bunk, crap, guff, tosh **05** balls, bilge, folly, hooey, trash, tripe **06** drivel, humbug, piffle, waffle **07** baloney, blether, flannel, hogwash, rhubarb, rubbish, twaddle **08** blathers, claptrap, cobblers, nonsense, tommyrot **09** gibberish, silliness, stupidity **10** balderdash, codswallop **11** foolishness **12** gobbledygook

populace
03 mob **04** folk, herd **05** crowd, plebs **06** masses, people, proles, public, rabble **07** natives, punters, society **08** canaille, citizens, riff-raff **09** community, hoi polloi, multitude, occupants, residents **10** common herd, multitudes **11** inhabitants, proletariat, rank and file, third estate **12** common people **13** general public, great unwashed

popular
02 in **03** big, hip, lay, now, pop **04** cool, laic **05** famed, liked, noted, stock, usual **06** common, famous, modish, simple, trendy, vulgar, wanted **07** admired, amateur, current, demotic, desired, general, massive **08** accepted, approved, exoteric, favoured, idolized, in demand, in favour, ordinary, plebeian, renowned, standard **09** acclaimed, customary, favourite, household, prevalent, universal, well-known, well-liked **10** accessible, all the rage, celebrated, democratic, mass-market, prevailing, simplified, well-graced, widespread **11** fashionable, sought-after **12** conventional, non-technical **13** non-specialist **14** understandable

popularity
04 fame **05** glory, kudos, vogue **06** esteem, favour, regard, renown, repute **07** acclaim, worship **08** approval, currency **09** adoration, adulation **10** acceptance, mass appeal, reputation **11** approbation, idolization, lionization, recognition

popularize
06 spread **08** simplify **09** propagate, vulgarize **10** generalize **11** democratize, familiarize **12** universalize **14** give currency to, make accessible

popularly
03 pop **05** vulgo **06** widely **07** usually **08** commonly **09** generally, regularly **10** ordinarily **11** customarily, universally **13** traditionally **14** conventionally, non-technically

populate
05 dwell **06** live in, occupy, people, settle **07** inhabit, overrun, peopled **08** colonize **09** devastate, inhabited

population
03 pop **04** folk **06** people **07** natives, society **08** citizens, populace **09** community, occupants, residents, stabilate **11** inhabitants

populous
06 packed **07** crowded, teeming **08** crawling, numerous, swarming **11** overpeopled **13** overpopulated

porcelain

Porcelain makes include:

03 Bow
04 Ming, Noke, Wade
05 Arita, Delft, Derby, Spode
06 Minton, Sèvres, Vienna
07 Belleek, Bristol, Chelsea, Dresden, Limoges, Meissen, Nanking, Satsuma
08 Caughley, Coalport, Copeland, Wedgwood
09 Chantilly, Davenport, Worcester
10 Cookworthy, Crown Derby, Rockingham
12 Royal Doulton
14 Royal Worcester

Porcelain types include:

04 bisk, frit
05 Hizen, Imari, ivory, Kraak
06 bamboo, bisque, Canton, jasper, Parian, tender
07 biscuit, crackle, faience, nankeen
08 eggshell, Kakiemon, Yingqing
09 bone china, copper red, hard-paste, soft-paste
10 jasperware, saltglazed
11 Capodimonte, chinoiserie, clair de lune, famille rose
12 blanc-de-Chine, blue and white, famille jaune, famille verte
14 soapstone paste

See also **pottery**

porch
04 hall, stoa **05** foyer, lobby, stoep, stoop **07** galilee, hallway, portico, veranda **09** colonnade, vestibule **12** entrance-hall

porcupine
05 urson **10** porpentine

pore
04 hole, vent **05** stoma **06** outlet, stigma **07** foramen, opening, orifice **08** aperture, lenticel **09** micropore **11** perforation

• pore over
03 con, kon **04** read, scan **05** brood, conne, study **06** go over, peruse, ponder **07** dwell on, examine **10** scrutinize **11** contemplate **14** examine closely, study intensely

porgy
04 scup **06** braise, braize **08** scuppaug

porker *see* **pig**

pornographic
04 blue, lewd, pink, porn **05** adult, bawdy, dirty, gross, nasty, porno **06** coarse, erotic, filthy, risqué, X-rated **07** obscene **08** indecent, prurient **09** off-colour, salacious **11** titillating

pornography
04 dirt, porn, smut **05** filth, nasty, porno **07** curiosa, erotica **08** facetiae, peep-show **09** bawdiness, grossness, indecency, obscenity, skinflick, snuff film **10** snuff movie, snuff video, video nasty **13** sexploitation **15** girlie magazines

porous

04 airy, open **05** holey **06** spongy **07** foveate **08** cellular, pervious **09** absorbent, permeable **10** cancellate, cancellous, foraminous, penetrable, spongelike **11** cancellated, cavernulous, foraminated, honeycombed

porpoise

06 seahog, sea-pig **07** dolphin, pellach, pellack, pellock, porpess **08** Phocaena, porpesse, sea swine **09** mere swine, porcpisce

porridge

04 gaol, jail, samp, stir **05** kasha, sadza **06** hominy, supawn **07** brochan, polenta, pottage, suppawn **08** parritch, sentence **09** mealie pap, praiseach, stirabout **12** hasty pudding

port

01 L **02** pt **03** bag **04** dock, gate, left, ruby **05** carry, haven, hithe, jetty, roads **06** convey **07** bearing, borough, harbour, retinue, seaport **08** dockland, larboard, porthole, suitcase **09** anchorage, demeanour, docklands, roadstead **10** deportment, harbourage

Ports include:

03 Gao, Lae, Rio, Vac

04 Aden, Apia, Baku, Bari, Caen, Cebu, Ciba, Cork, Deal, Doha, Elat, Faro, Hull, Kiel, Kobe, Linz, Lomé, Lüda, Nice, Oban, Omsk, Oran, Oslo, Oulu, Pula, Riga, Safi, Sfax, Suez, Suva, Tyre, Vigo, Wick

05 Accra, Agana, Aqaba, Arica, Basle, Basra, Beira, Belém, Blyth, Brest, Busan, Colón, Dakar, Davao, Dover, Dubai, Emden, Galle, Gavle, Genoa, Ghent, Gijon, Haifa, Ibiza, Izmir, Kayes, Kazan, Koper, Lagos, Larne, Leith, Liège, Macao, Malmo, Masan, Miami, Nampo, Natal, Omaha, Osaka, Ostia, Palma, Paris, Poole, Praia, Pusan, Rouen, Sakai, Salem, Ségou, Sitra, Skien, Split, Surat, Tampa, Tanga, Tokyo, Tomsk, Torun, Tulsa, Tunis, Turku, Ulsan, Vaasa, Varna, Worms, Wuhan

06 Aarhus, Abadan, Agadir, Ancona, Annaba, Ashdod, Avarua, Aveira, Aviles, Balboa, Bamako, Banjul, Bastia, Batumi, Beirut, Bergen, Bissau, Bombay, Boston, Bremen, Bruges, Calais, Callao, Camden, Cannes, Cochin, Dalian, Dammam, Darwin, Denver, Dieppe, Douala, Dublin, Duluth, Dundee, Durban, Durres, El Paso, Galway, Gdansk, Gdynia, Grodno, Hamina, Havana, Hobart, Huelva, Inchon, Jarrow, Jeddah, Juneau, Kalgar, Kandla, Kaunas, Khulna, Lisbon, Lobito, London, Luanda, Lübeck, Madras, Malabo, Malaga, Manama, Manaus, Manila, Maputo, Matrah, Mersin, Mobile, Muscat, Nacala, Nagoya, Nantes, Napier, Naples, Narvik, Nassau, Nelson, Newark, Niamey, Ningbo, Nouméa, Nyborg, Odense, Odessa, Oporto, Ostend, Penang, Phuket, Quebec, Recife, Rijeka, Rimini, Samara, Samsun, Santos, Sasebo, Sittwe, Sousse, St John, St-Malo, St Paul, Sydney, Szeged, Tacoma, Thurso, Timaru, Toledo, Toulon, Toyama, Treves, Vannes, Velsen, Venice, Warsaw, Whitby, Xiamen, Yangon

07 Aalborg, Abidjan, Ajaccio, Alcudia, Algiers, Almeria, Antibes, Antwerp, Bangkok, Belfast, Berbera, Bizerta, Bourgas, Bristol, Buffalo, Cabinda, Calabar, Caldera, Calicut, Cardiff, Catania, Cayenne, Chicago, Cologne, Colombo, Conakry, Corinth, Corinto, Cotonou, Dampier, Detroit, Douglas, Dunedin, Dunkirk, Esbjerg, Fukuoka, Funchal, Geelong, Glasgow, Grimsby, Halifax, Hamburg, Harstad, Harwich, Hodeida, Honiara, Honiari, Houston, Ipswich, Iquique, Jakarta, Karachi, Kowloon, Kuching, Kushiro, La Plata, Larnaca, La Union, Le Havre, Livorno, Marsala, Melilla, Memphis, Messina, Mindelo, Mombasa, Newport, New Ross, Niigata, Niterói, Oakland, Okayama, Palermo, Papeete, Paradip, Pasajes, Piraeus, Portree, Rangoon, Ravenna, Rosaria, Rosario, Rostock, Salerno, San José, San Juan, San Remo, Santa Fe, Sao Tomé, Saratov, Seattle, Seville, Shimizu, Stanley, St John's, St Louis, Swansea, Tallinn, Tampico, Tangier, Taranto, Tel Aviv, Tianjin, Tilbury, Toronto, Trieste, Tripoli, Vitebsk, Vitoria, Wroclaw, Xingang, Zhdanov

08 Aberdeen, Abu Dhabi, Acajutla, Acapulco, Adelaide, Alicante, Arbroath, Asunción, Auckland, Benghazi, Bordeaux, Boulogne, Brindisi, Brisbane, Cagliari, Calcutta, Cape Town, Castries, Changsha, Chimbote, Djibouti, Dortmund, Duisburg, Dunleary, Falmouth, Flushing, Freeport, Freetown, Gisborne, Godthaab, Greenock, Guyaquil, Hakodate, Halmstad, Hamilton, Hay Point, Helsinki, Holyhead, Honolulu, Istanbul, Kawasaki, Keflavik, Kingston, Kinshasa, Kirkaldy, Kirkwall, Kismaayo, Klaipeda, La Coruna, La Guaira, La Spezia, Lattakia, Limassol, Limerick, Mandalay, Mannheim, Marbella, Matanzas, Mazatlan, Monrovia, Montreal, Montrose, Mormugao, Moulmein, Mulhouse, Murmansk, Nagasaki, New Haven, Newhaven, Pago Pago, Plymouth, Portland, Port Said, Port-Vila, Ramsgate, Richmond, Roskilde, Rosslare, Salonica, Salvador, San Diego, San Pedro, Santarém, Savannah, Semarang, Shanghai, Simbirsk, Smolensk, St Helier, Stockton, St-Tropez, Surabaya, Syracuse, Szczecin, Takoradi, Tauranga, Torshavn, Ullapool, Valencia, Valletta, Veracruz, Voronezh, Weymouth, Yokohama, Zanzibar

09 Algeciras, Amsterdam, Anchorage, Archangel, Astrakhan, Baltimore, Barcelona, Bujumbura, Cartagena, Cherbourg, Cleveland, Constance, Constanta, Dordrecht, Dubrovnik, Esztergom, Europoort, Famagusta, Fleetwood, Flensburg, Fortaleza, Frankfurt, Fremantle, Galveston, Gateshead, Gibraltar, Gravesend, Heraklion, Hiroshima, Immingham, Kagoshima, Kaohsiung, Karlsruhe, King's Lynn, Kingstown, Kozhikode, Langesund, Las Palmas, Launceton, Liverpool, Long Beach, Lowestoft, Magdeburg, Mahajanga, Maracaibo, Mariehamn, Melbourne, Milwaukee, Mizushima, Mogadishu, Nashville, Newcastle, Nuku'alofa, Palembang, Palm Beach, Paranagua, Peterhead, Phnom Penh, Port Limon, Port Louis, Port Natal, Port Sudan, Reykjavík, Rio Grande, Rochester, Rotterdam, Santander, Sassandra, Sheerness, Singapore, Stavanger, St-Nazaire, Stockholm, Stornoway, Stralsund, Stranraer, Sundsvall, Takamatsu, Tarragona, Toamasina, Trebizond, Trondheim, Tuticorin, Vancouver, Vicksburg, Vientiane, Volgograd, Walvis Bay, Yaroslavl, Zeebrugge, Zhenjiang, Zrenjanin

10 Alexandria, Basseterre, Baton Rouge, Belize City, Bratislava, Bridgeport, Bridgetown, Cap Haitian, Casablanca, Charleston, Chittagong, Cienfuegos, Copenhagen, East London, Felixstowe, Folkestone, Fray Bentos, Fredericia, George Town, Georgetown, Gothenburg, Hartlepool, Hildesheim, Iskenderun, Kansas City, Kitakyushu, Kompong Som, Kuwait City, Leeuwarden, Libreville, Little Rock, Los Angeles, Louisville, Manchester, Manzanillo, Marseilles, Mina Qaboos, Mina Sulman, Montego Bay, Montevideo, Mostaganem, New Orleans, Nouadhibou, Nouakchott, Oranjestad, Paramaribo, Pittsburgh, Port Gentil, Portishead, Portsmouth, Port Talbot, Providence, Sacramento, Salina Cruz, San Lorenzo, Santa Marta, Sebastopol, Sevastopol, Strasbourg, Sunderland, Talcahuano, Thunder Bay, Townsville, Valparaiso, Wellington, Willemstad, Wilmington, Workington, Zaporozhye

11 Antofagasta, Bahia Blanca, Bandar Abbas, Brazzaville, Bremerhaven, Bridlington, Brownsville, Buenos Aires, Charlestown, Chattanooga, Dar es Salaam, Fraserburgh, Grangemouth, Helsingborg,

Krasnoyarsk, Livingstone, Lossiemouth, Mar del Plata, Minneapolis, Narayanganj, New Plymouth, New York City, Novosibirsk, Panama Canal, Pasir Gudang, Point-a-Pitre, Pointe-Noire, Pondicherry, Port Cartier, Port Moresby, Porto Alegre, Port of Spain, Punta Arenas, Qinhuangdao, Richards Bay, Rostov-on-Don, Southampton, Three Rivers, Vladivostok

12 Barranquilla, Buenaventura, Fort de France, Frederikstad, Jacksonville, Kota Kinabalu, Kristiansand, Ludwigshafen, New Amsterdam, New Mangalore, Novorossiysk, Philadelphia, Ponta Delgada, Port Adelaide, Port-au-Prince, Port Harcourt, Port Victoria, Puerto Cortes, Rio de Janeiro, Saint George's, San Francisco, San Sebastian, Santo Domingo, St Petersburg, Tel Aviv-Jaffa, Ujung Pandang, Villahermosa

13 Ellesmere Port, Frederikshavn, Great Yarmouth, Ho Chi Minh City, Hook of Holland, Middlesbrough, Port Elizabeth, Semipalatinsk, Sihanoukville

14 Dnepropetrovsk, Port Georgetown, Santiago de Cuba

15 Barrow-in-Furness, Charlotte Amalie, Frankfurt am Main, Nizhniy Novgorod

---

• port authority
03 PLA

portability
09 handiness **10** movability **11** compactness, convenience **13** manageability

portable
05 handy **07** compact, movable **08** luggable **09** endurable, portatile **10** convenient, conveyable, manageable **11** lightweight **13** transportable

portal
04 door, gate **05** way in **06** access **07** doorway, gateway, opening **08** entrance

portend
04 bode, omen **05** augur **06** herald, import, warn of **07** bespeak, betoken, point to, predict, presage, promise, purport, signify **08** announce, forebode, forecast, foreshow, foretell, forewarn, indicate, threaten **09** adumbrate, be a sign of, foretoken, harbinger **10** foreshadow **13** prognosticate

portent
04 omen, sign **05** augur, token **06** augury, boding, marvel, ostent, threat **07** presage, prodigy, warning **08** forecast, prodrome **09** harbinger, precursor **10** foreboding, forerunner, indication, prognostic **11** forewarning, ominousness, premonition **12** presentiment **13** foreshadowing, prefiguration, signification **15** prognostication

portentous
04 dire, vain **05** proud **06** snooty, solemn **07** amazing, crucial, fateful, haughty, ominous, pompous **08** affected, arrogant, menacing, sinister **09** conceited, grandiose, imperious, important, momentous **10** astounding, foreboding, impressive, miraculous, prodigious, remarkable **11** epoch-making, magisterial, overbearing, patronizing, pretentious, significant, threatening **12** awe-inspiring, earth-shaking, ostentatious, presumptuous, supercilious **13** condescending, extraordinary, self-important

portentously
08 snootily **09** haughtily, pompously **10** arrogantly **11** conceitedly **13** patronizingly **14** superciliously **15** condescendingly, self-importantly

porter
04 page **05** caddy, cadee, cadie, hamal **06** bearer, caddie, entire, hammal, humper, redcap **07** bell-boy, bellhop, carrier, doorman, dvornik, janitor **08** bummaree, doorsman **09** caretaker, concierge, out-porter **10** door-keeper, gatekeeper **11** double-stout, night-porter **12** ticket-porter **13** door attendant **14** baggage-carrier, baggage-handler, commissionaire

portico
04 stoa **05** porch **06** exedra, parvis, xystus **07** distyle, exhedra, narthex, parvise, veranda **08** prostyle, verandah **09** colonnade, decastyle, hexastyle, octastyle, octostyle **10** pentastyle, tetrastyle **11** dodecastyle

portion
02 go **03** bit, cut, dot, lot, rag **04** deal, dole, dose, fate, luck, meed, mite, part, tait, tate, what **05** allot, dowry, grist, order, piece, quota, ratio, share, slice, small, space, taste, wedge, whack, wodge **06** assign, chance, divide, kismet, morsel, parcel, ration, region **07** carve up, destiny, dole out, fortune, helping, kenning, measure, rake-off, scantle, section, segment, serving, slice up, tranche **08** allocate, division, fraction, fragment, particle, pittance, quantity, share out **09** allotment, allowance, apportion, partition, scantling, something **10** allocation, distribute, percentage, proportion

portliness
07 fatness, obesity **08** fullness **09** ampleness, beefiness, dumpiness, heaviness, plumpness, rotundity, roundness, stoutness, tubbiness **10** chubbiness, corpulence, fleshiness **11** paunchiness

portly
03 fat **05** ample, gaucy, gawcy, gawsy, heavy, large, obese, plump, round, stout **06** gaucie, rotund, stocky **08** matronly **09** corpulent **10** aldermanly, overweight **12** aldermanlike

portrait
04 icon **05** image, pin-up, story, study **06** Kit-Cat, sketch **07** account, drawing, picture, profile, retrate **08** likeness, painting, pourtray, retraitt, vignette **09** composite, depiction, miniature, portrayal **10** caricature, full-length, half-length, photograph, pourtraict **11** description, whole-length **12** carte-de-viste, self-portrait **14** representation **15** thumbnail sketch

portray
03 act **04** draw, play, take **05** evoke, image, paint **06** depict, sketch **07** perform, picture, present **08** describe, portrait, pourtray **09** pantomime, personify, represent **10** illustrate **11** impersonate **12** act the part of, characterize **13** play the part of

portrayal
05 study **06** acting, sketch **07** drawing, picture **08** painting **09** depiction, evocation, rendering **11** delineation, description, performance **12** presentation **14** interpretation, representation

Portugal
01 P **02** Pg **03** PRT

Portuguese
02 Pg

pose
03 act, air, ask, put, set, sit **04** airs, role, sham **05** cause, claim, feign, front, model, posit **06** affect, assert, create, façade, lead to, puzzle, stance, submit **07** advance, arrange, bearing, posture, present, pretend, produce, propose, suggest **08** attitude, carriage, position, pretence, propound, result in **09** postulate, put on airs **10** constitute, deportment, give rise to, masquerade, put forward, put on an act **11** affectation, impersonate **12** attitudinize, contrapposto **15** pass yourself off

Poseidon
07 Neptune

poser
04 sham **05** pseud **06** enigma, phoney, poseur, puzzle, riddle, sitter **07** dilemma, mystery, poseuse, problem, show-off, sticker **08** impostor, posturer **09** charlatan, conundrum, play-actor **10** mind-bender **11** brainteaser **12** brain-twister **13** attitudinizer, exhibitionist, vexed question

poseur
04 sham **05** poser, pseud **06** phoney **07** poseuse, show-off **08** impostor, posturer **09** charlatan, play-actor **13** attitudinizer, exhibitionist

posh
01 U **04** rich, swag **05** dandy, fancy,

grand, money, plush, pluty, smart, swish **06** classy, de-luxe, la-di-da, lavish, luxury, select, snazzy, superb, swanky **07** elegant, opulent, stylish **08** top-class, up-market **09** exclusive, expensive, halfpenny, high-class, luxurious, sumptuous **10** upper-class **11** fashionable

posit
03 set **04** pose **05** state **06** assert, assume, submit **07** advance, dispose, presume **08** propound **09** postulate, predicate **10** put forward

position
03 fix, job, lie, pos, put, set **04** area, case, duty, pose, post, rank, role, site, spot, view **05** array, grade, level, place, point, pozzy, scene, stand, state **06** belief, deploy, factor, lay out, locate, office, orient, plight, possie, settle, stance, status **07** arrange, bearing, dispose, factors, install, opinion, outlook, posture, ranking, setting, situate, station **08** attitude, capacity, function, locality, location, prestige, standing **09** condition, establish, influence, postulate, situation, viewpoint **10** background, employment, occupation, standpoint **11** appointment, arrangement, disposition, point of view, predicament, whereabouts **13** circumstances **14** state of affairs

• in fixed position
02 to

positive
01 p **03** pos **04** firm, good, plus, rank, real, sure **05** basic, clear, sheer, utter **06** actual, direct, upbeat, useful **07** assured, certain, express, helpful, hopeful, perfect, positif, precise, reality **08** absolute, cheerful, clear-cut, complete, concrete, decisive, definite, emphatic, explicit, material, outright, thorough **09** assertive, categoric, confident, convinced, downright, out-and-out, practical, promising, veritable **10** conclusive, consummate, convincing, definitive, encouraged, favourable, optimistic, productive, undeniable **11** affirmative, categorical, encouraging, irrefutable, unequivocal, unmitigated **12** constructive, indisputable, matter-of-fact, unmistakable **13** incontestable **14** dextrorotatory

positively
06 firmly, surely **07** finally **09** assuredly, certainly, expressly **10** absolutely, decisively, definitely, undeniably **12** conclusively, emphatically, indisputably, unmistakably **13** categorically, incontestably, unequivocally **14** unquestionably

possess
◇ *containment indicator*
03 get, own **04** gain, have, hold, take **05** boast, enjoy, haunt, imbue, seize, wield **06** attain, inform, obsess, obtain, occupy **07** acquire, bedevil, bewitch, control, enchant, inhabit, inherit, overget **08** acquaint, demonize, dominate, maintain, take over **09** infatuate, influence **12** be gifted with **13** be blessed with, be endowed with, take control of

possessed
03 mad **06** crazed, cursed, raving **07** berserk, haunted **08** besotted, consumed, demented, frenzied, maddened, obsessed, spirited **09** bewitched, demonized, dominated, enchanted, hag-ridden **10** bedevilled, controlled, infatuated, mesmerized

possession
03 fee **04** grip, hand, hold **05** craze, thing, title **06** having, tenure **07** control, custody, holding, tenancy **08** haunting **09** obsession, occupance, occupancy, ownership **10** domination, occupation **11** infatuation **14** proprietorship

• in possession
◇ *containment indicator*

possessions
03 all, ana **04** aver, gear, good **05** goods, stuff, worth **06** assets, estate, riches, things, wealth **07** baggage, clobber, effects, luggage **08** chattels, movables, outsight, property **09** sprechery, territory **10** belongings, spreaghery **12** temporalties **13** accoutrements, paraphernalia, temporalities, worldly wealth **15** personal effects

possessive
06 greedy **07** jealous, selfish **08** clinging, covetous, genitive, grasping **10** dominating **11** acquisitive, controlling, domineering **14** overprotective

possessiveness
05 greed **08** jealousy **11** selfishness **12** covetousness **13** exclusiveness **15** acquisitiveness

possibility
04 fear, hope, odds, risk **05** maybe, posse **06** chance, choice, danger, hazard, option, talent **07** promise **08** prospect, recourse **09** off-chance, potential, prospects **10** advantages, likelihood, preference **11** alternative, contingency, feasibility, probability, proposition **12** capabilities, expectations, potentiality **13** attainability **14** conceivability, practicability

possible
◇ *anagram indicator*
06 doable, likely, odds-on, viable **07** tenable **08** credible, feasible, probable, workable **09** potential, promising **10** achievable, attainable, imaginable, on the cards, realizable **11** conceivable, practicable **13** that can be done **14** accomplishable

possibly
◇ *anagram indicator*
03 e'er **04** ever, well **05** at all, maybe **07** in posse, perhaps **09** hopefully **10** by any means **11** by any chance, conceivably **12** peradventure

possum
04 tait **07** opossum **08** Tarsipes **09** phalanger **10** honey-mouse **11** sugar glider

post
03 dak, job, leg, pin, put **04** beat, bitt, jamb, mail, move, pale, pole, prop, send **05** affix, e-mail, haste, newel, pin up, place, put up, shaft, stake, strut **06** assign, attach, column, locate, office, picket, pillar, report, second **07** airmail, appoint, display, forward, letters, packets, parcels, publish, situate, station, stick up, support, upright, vacancy **08** announce, baluster, banister, delivery, dispatch, junk mail, packages, palisade, position, standard, transfer, transmit **09** advertise, broadcast, circulate, mail-coach, make known, publicize, put on duty, situation, snail mail, stanchion **10** assignment, direct mail, employment, packet-boat, Post Office **11** appointment, surface mail **12** all-up service, postal system, recorded mail **13** postal service **14** communications, correspondence, electronic mail, first-class mail, registered mail **15** second-class mail, special delivery

• keep someone posted
06 fill in, inform **12** keep informed, keep up to date **13** keep in the loop

postal order
02 PO

postcard
02 pc

poster
02 ad **04** bill, sign **05** solus **06** advert, notice **07** placard, sticker **08** bulletin, play bill, show bill **12** announcement **13** advertisement

posterior
03 ass, bum **04** back, butt, hind, rear, rump, seat, tail **05** after, later **06** behind, bottom, dorsal, hinder, jacksy, latter **07** ensuing, jacksie **08** backside, buttocks, haunches, rearward **09** following, hinder end, posterity, posticous **10** subsequent, succeeding **12** hindquarters

posterity
04 seed **05** heirs, issue **07** progeny **08** children, mokopuna **09** offspring, posterior **10** succession, successors **11** descendants

posthaste
06 at once, pronto, speedy **07** hastily, quickly, swiftly **08** directly, full tilt, promptly, speedily **09** immediate **11** double-quick, immediately **12** straightaway, with all speed

postman, postwoman
04 post **06** postie **07** courier, mailman **11** mail-carrier, mail handler **12** postal

worker **13** letter-carrier **15** delivery officer

post-mortem
02 PM **06** review **07** autopsy **08** analysis, autopsia, necropsy **10** dissection, necroscopy **11** examination

Post Office
02 PO **03** GPO **04** BFPO

postpone
04 stay, wait **05** defer, delay, frist, refer, table, waive **06** freeze, put off, retard, shelve **07** adjourn, do later, prolong, put back, rejourn, sleep on, suspend **08** hold over, mothball, postpose, prorogue, protract, put on ice, withhold **09** carry over, sleep on it, stand over **10** pigeonhole, reschedule **11** subordinate **13** procrastinate

postponed
05 on ice **06** frozen, put off **07** shelved **08** deferred, held over **09** adjourned, suspended **10** in abeyance, protracted **11** carried over, pigeonholed **15** on the back burner

postponement
04 stay **05** delay **06** freeze, put-off **07** respite **08** deferral **09** deferment **10** moratorium, suspension **11** adjournment, prorogation **13** backwardation

postscript
02 PS **03** PPS **07** codicil **08** addendum, addition, appendix, epilogue **09** afterword **10** supplement **12** afterthought

postulate
05 axiom, claim, posit **06** assume **07** advance, lay down, presume, propose, suppose **08** nominate, petition, theorize **09** stipulate **10** assumption, postulatum, presuppose, put forward **11** hypothesize, stipulation

posture
03 set **04** pike, pose, site, view **05** guard, mudra, stand, strut **06** affect, belief, motion, sprawl, stance **07** bearing, gesture, opinion, outlook, show off **08** attitude, carriage, position **09** arabesque, decubitus, defensive, offensive, put on airs, viewpoint **10** decumbence, decumbency, deportment, standpoint **11** counter-view, disposition, point of view **12** attitudinize **15** strike attitudes

postwoman *see* **postman, postwoman**

posy
05 motto, poesy, spray **07** bouquet, corsage, nosegay **08** affected **09** sentiment **10** buttonhole **12** tussie mussie

pot
02 po **03** box, can, cup, jar, pan, pat, tea, urn **04** bank, bowl, fund, lota, olla, pool, stew, test, vase **05** basin, crewe, crock, cruse, kitty, lotah, purse **06** aludel, bowpot, caster, chatti, chatty, pipkin, pocket, pottle, tajine, teapot, tipple, trivet, trophy, vessel **07** marmite, pitcher, planter, pothole, reserve **08** boughpot, cauldron, crucible, gallipot, plantpot, pot-au-feu **09** casserole, coffee pot, flowerpot **10** chamberpot, receptacle **11** earthenware, manufacture **13** potentiometer

See also **cannabis**

potable
04 safe **05** clean **08** beverage **09** drinkable **10** fit to drink

potassium
01 K

potato
03 alu, yam **04** aloo, chat, spud **05** boxty, early, tater, tatie **06** batata, camote, murphy, pratie, tattie **07** scallop, scollop

Potatoes include:

04 Cara, chat, seed, ware
05 praty, Sante, Saxon, sweet
06 camote, Estima, kidney, kumara
07 Desiree
09 Charlotte, Kerr's Pink, Maris Peer
10 Duke of York, King Edward, Maris Piper
12 Golden Wonder
15 Pentland Javelin

pot-bellied
03 fat **05** kedge, kedgy, kidge, obese, tubby **06** portly **07** bloated, paunchy **09** corpulent, distended **10** abdominous, gor-bellied, overweight

pot-belly
03 gut, pot **05** belly **06** paunch **08** tunbelly **09** beer belly, bow window, spare tyre **11** corporation

potency
04 kick, sway **05** force, might, power, punch **06** energy, muscle, vigour **07** cogency, control **08** capacity, efficacy, strength **09** authority, headiness, influence, potentate, potential, puissance **12** potentiality, powerfulness **13** effectiveness **14** persuasiveness **15** efficaciousness

potent
06 active, cogent, mighty, prince, strong, virile **07** dynamic, pungent **08** dominant, eloquent, forceful, powerful, puissant, vigorous **09** effective, energetic, potentate **10** commanding, compelling, convincing, impressive, persuasive **11** efficacious, influential **12** intoxicating, overpowering **13** authoritative

potentate
04 czar, king, tsar, tzar **05** chief, mogul, queen, ruler **06** despot, dynast, huzoor, leader, prince, tyrant **07** emperor, empress, monarch **08** autocrat, dictator, overlord **09** chieftain, sovereign **10** panjandrum **11** head of state

potential
◇ *anagram indicator*
04 gift **05** flair **06** future, hidden, latent, likely, powers, talent **07** ability, budding, dormant, promise, virtual, would-be **08** aptitude, aspiring, capacity, implicit, inherent, possible, powerful, probable **09** concealed, embryonic, promising, resources **10** capability, developing, unrealized **11** efficacious, possibility, prospective, undeveloped

potentiality
05 power **07** ability, potence, potency, promise **08** aptitude, capacity, prospect **09** potential **10** capability, likelihood, virtuality **13** possibilities

potentially
◇ *anagram indicator*
07 in posse **08** latently, possibly, probably **09** dormantly, virtually **10** implicitly, inherently, in potentia **15** in all likelihood

potion
04 brew, dose **05** drink, tonic **06** elixir **07** draught, mixture, philtre **08** beverage, medicine, potation **10** concoction

potpourri
04 olio **06** jumble, medley **07** melange, mixture **08** mishmash, pastiche **09** confusion, patchwork, selection **10** assortment, collection, hodgepodge, hotchpotch, miscellany **11** gallimaufry, olla-podrida, smorgasbord

potter
04 muck, poke **05** amble, daker **06** dacker, daidle, daiker, dawdle, dodder, fettle, footle, loiter, niggle, pootle, putter, tiddle, tinker, toddle **07** plotter, plouter, plowter **09** mess about **10** dilly-dally

• **potter about**
05 truck **06** humbug, muddle **09** fart about, fool about, mess about, muck about, play about **10** fart around, fool around, mess around, muck around, play around **11** fiddle about, tinker about **12** fiddle around, tinker around **13** do nothing much

pottery
04 bank

Pottery includes:

04 Ming, Tang, Wade
05 Bizen, china, Crown, Delft, Poole
06 basalt, bisque, Dunoon, flambé, Hummel, Jasper, Parian, Sèvres
07 biscuit, ceramic, Dresden, faience, Meissen, redware
08 ceramics, Coalport, crockery, maiolica, majolica, rakuware, Rookwood, slipware
09 agateware, bone china, creamware, Davenport, delftware, hard-paste, ironstone, Jackfield, pearlware,

porcelain, red figure, saltglaze, soft-paste, stoneware, tin-glazed, Worcester
10 Jasper ware, lead-glazed, lustre ware, Parian ware, Queen's ware, terra cotta, Wemyss ware
11 black figure, earthenware, Florian ware, pâte-sur-pâte, Portmeirion, soufflé ware, spatter ware
12 Royal Doulton, transfer ware, Wedgwood ware
13 Claremont ware, Hazledene ware, Staffordshire, tortoiseshell, willow pattern
14 ironstone china
15 cauliflower ware, Royal Crown Derby, Wedgwood pottery

Pottery makers include:

03 **Fry** (Laura), **Rie** (Dame Lucie)
04 **Boyd** (Arthur), **Boyd** (Merric), **Vyse** (Charles), **Wood** (Aaron), **Wood** (Enoch), **Wood** (John), **Wood** (Ralph), **Wood** (Ralph, Jnr), **Wyse** (Henry Taylor)
05 **Adams** (Truda), **Adams** (William), **Amour** (Elizabeth), **Cliff** (Clarice), **Coper** (Hans), **Finch** (Alfred William), **Korin** (Ogata), **Leach** (Bernard), **Mason** (Miles), **Moore** (Bernard), **Perry** (Grayson)
06 **Cardew** (Michael), **Carter** (Truda), **Dwight** (John), **Hamada** (Shoji), **Kenzan** (Ogata), **Murray** (William Staite), **Taylor** (William Howson)
07 **Astbury** (John), **Britton** (Alison), **Doulton** (Sir Henry), **Execias**, **Exekias**, **Forsyth** (Gordon), **Fritsch** (Elizabeth), **Gardner** (Peter), **Grotell** (Maija), **Palissy** (Bernard), **Twyford** (Joshua)
08 **Fujiwara** (Kei), **Robineau** (Adelaide), **Wedgwood** (Josiah), **Whieldon** (Thomas), **Yamamoto** (Toshu)
09 **Kaneshige** (Toyo), **Moorcroft** (William)
10 **Euphronios**

Pottery terms include:

04 kiln, raku, slip
05 delft, glaze, model
06 basalt, enamel, figure, firing, flambé, ground, jasper, lustre, sagger
07 celadon, ceramic, crazing, faience, fairing
08 armorial, bronzing, flatback, maiolica, majolica, monogram, slip-cast
09 china clay, cloisonné, creamware, grotesque, ironstone, overglaze, porcelain, sgraffito, stoneware
10 art pottery, maker's mark, spongeware, terracotta, underglaze
11 crackleware, earthenware, scratch blue
12 blanc-de-chine
13 Staffordshire, Willow pattern
15 mandarin palette

See also **porcelain**

potty

◇ *anagram indicator*
03 ape, fey, mad **04** avid, bats, daft, fond, gyte, keen, loco, nuts, wild **05** barmy, batty, buggy, crazy, daffy, dippy, dotty, flaky, gonzo, loony, loopy, manic, nutty, petty, queer, silly, wacko, wacky, wiggy **06** ardent, crazed, cuckoo, fruity, insane, maniac, mental, raving, red-mad, screwy **07** bananas, barking, berserk, bonkers, cracked, devoted, frantic, lunatic, meshuga, zealous **08** crackers, demented, deranged, dingbats, doolally, frenetic, frenzied, gazunder, maniacal, trifling, unhinged, unstable **09** disturbed, fanatical, lymphatic, psychotic, up the wall **10** bestraught, chamberpot, distracted, distraught, frantic mad, infatuated, off the wall, off your nut, out to lunch, passionate, stone-crazy, unbalanced **11** not all there, off the rails, off your head **12** enthusiastic, mad as a hatter, off your chump, round the bend **13** off your rocker, of unsound mind, out of your head, out of your mind, out of your tree, round the twist **14** off your trolley, wrong in the head **15** non compos mentis, out of your senses

pouch

03 bag, sac, tip **04** poke, sack, spur **05** bursa, cecum, purse, scrip **06** caecum, ovisac, pocket, wallet **07** papoose, sporran **08** codpiece, pappoose, reticule **09** container, marsupium, spleuchan **10** receptacle **11** gaberlunzie **12** diverticulum

poultry

Poultry and game birds include:

03 hen
04 duck, teal
05 goose, quail, snipe
06 grouse, pigeon, turkey, wigeon
07 chicken, ostrich, pochard
08 pheasant, woodcock
09 partridge, ptarmigan
10 guinea fowl, woodpigeon

See also **chicken**; **duck**; **game**

pounce

04 dart, dive, drop, fall, grab, jump, leap, pink **05** bound, lunge, punch, swoop **06** ambush, attack, dive on, fall on, jump on, powder, snatch, spring, strike, thrust **07** assault, descend, swoop on **08** puncture, sandarac, sprinkle **09** descend on, sandarach **10** cuttle-bone **12** take unawares **13** catch off guard, catch unawares **14** take by surprise

pound

01 L **02** as, lb **03** bar, pen, pun, sov **04** bang, bash, beat, bray, drum, fold, mash, pace, pelt, plod, pond, punt, quid, thud, walk, yard **05** crush, grind, lay on, libra, nevel, oncer, pownd, smash, squid, stamp, stomp, throb, thump, tramp, tread **06** batter, bruise, corral, hammer, nicker, pestle, powder, pummel, shower, strike, trudge **07** balance, confine, contund, contuse, enclose, iron man, penfold, pinfold, pulsate, smacker **08** compound, levigate **09** comminute, enclosure, granulate, palpitate, pound coin, pulverize, smackeroo, sovereign, triturate **12** jimmy-o'goblin **13** pound sterling

pour

03 jet, ren, rin, run, tip **04** emit, flow, gush, hush, leak, ooze, rain, rush, spew, teem **05** crowd, drain, flood, issue, serve, spill, spout, spurt, swarm **06** course, decant, stream, throng **07** cascade, come out, let flow, pour out **08** disgorge, make flow, pelt down, sprinkle, teem down **09** discharge **10** bucket down, disembogue **15** rain cats and dogs

• **pour forth**
04 gush, vent, well

• **pour out**
04 lave

pout

03 bib **04** lour, mope, moue, poot, sulk, tout, towt **05** blain, boody, poult, scowl **06** brassy, glower **07** grimace **08** long face, make a lip **09** make a moue, pull a face

poverty

04 lack, need, want **06** dearth, penury **07** beggary, paucity **08** distress, hardship, poorness, poortith, scarcity, shortage **09** depletion, indigence, necessity, privation **10** bankruptcy, deficiency, inadequacy, insolvency, meagreness, shabbiness **11** deprivation, destitution, locust-years **13** impecuniosity, insufficiency, pennilessness **14** impoverishment

poverty-stricken

04 poor **05** broke, needy, skint, stony **07** obolary, squalid **08** bankrupt, beggared, dirt-poor, indigent, strapped **09** destitute, flat broke, penniless, penurious **10** cleaned-out, distressed, stony-broke **11** impecunious **12** impoverished, on your uppers **13** in Queer Street **14** on your beam-ends

powder

04 beat, blue, bran, bray, dust, kohl, mash, must, pulv, salt, seed, talc **05** cover, crush, grind, moust, muist, smalt, smash, strew **06** farina, grains, pestle, pounce, pulvil, saline **07** alcohol, araroba, scatter, smeddum **08** amberite, coal dust, levigate, magnesia, pemoline, pulvilio, pulville, sprinkle, woodmeal **09** comminute, granulate, pulverize, pulvillio, triturate, wood flour **10** icing sugar, ivory-black, thimerosal **11** mould-facing, washing-blue **13** efflorescence, platinum black

powdered

04 semé **05** semée **06** seméed

powdery

03 dry **04** ashy, fine **05** dusty, loose, mealy, sandy **06** chalky, floury, grainy, ground, mealie **07** crumbly, friable **08** granular, levigate, powdered **09** pulverous **10** granulated, pulverized **11** pulverulent **12** efflorescent

power
01 P **03** arm, eon, say, vis **04** aeon, mana, pull, rule, sway, watt **05** clout, force, index, juice, might, oomph, right, state, teeth **06** energy, muscle, nation, people, vigour **07** ability, command, control, country, faculty, licence, mastery, potency, warrant **08** capacity, clutches, dominion, exponent, strength **09** authority, influence, intensity, potential, privilege, supremacy **10** ascendancy, capability, competence, domination, superpower **11** prerogative, sovereignty **12** forcefulness, potentiality, powerfulness **13** authorization, effectiveness

Power stations include:

06 Huntly
07 Benmore
08 Bankside, Dounreay, Sizewell, Yallourn
09 Battersea, Chernobyl, Dungeness, Manapouri, Windscale
10 Sellafield
11 Wallerawang
12 Marsden Point
14 Snowy Mountains
15 Three Mile Island

• **have sufficient power**
03 can
• **having enough power**
04 able
• **the powers that be**
04 them **09** the system **14** the authorities

powerful
03 hot **04** high **05** burly, gutty, hardy, tough **06** brawny, cogent, mighty, potent, punchy, robust, strong, studly **07** intense, leading, telling, winning **08** dominant, forceful, forcible, mightful, muscular, puissant **09** effective, energetic, knock-down, prevalent, strapping **10** commanding, compelling, convincing, impressive, noticeable, persuasive, prevailing **11** all-powerful, efficacious, exceedingly, high-powered, influential **12** overwhelming **13** authoritative

powerfully
04 hard, high **06** highly, strong **08** cogently, forcibly, mightily, potently, strongly **09** tellingly **10** forcefully, vigorously **12** convincingly, impressively, persuasively

powerless
04 numb, weak **05** frail, unfit **06** feeble, infirm, unable **07** unarmed **08** benumbed, disabled, helpless, impotent **09** castrated, hamstrung, incapable, paralysed, toothless **10** impuissant, vulnerable, weak-handed **11** debilitated, defenceless, ineffective, ineffectual **13** incapacitated

practicability
03 use **05** value **07** utility **09** handiness, viability **10** usefulness **11** feasibility, operability, possibility, workability **12** practicality, workableness

practicable
02 on **06** doable, viable **08** feasible, operable, passable, possible, workable **09** practical, realistic **10** achievable, attainable **11** functioning, performable

practical
04 real **05** handy **06** active, actual, strong, useful **07** applied, hands on, skilled, trained, virtual, working **08** everyday, feasible, in effect, ordinary, sensible, suitable, workable, workaday **09** effective, efficient, essential, hard-nosed, pragmatic, qualified, realistic **10** functional, hard-boiled, hard-headed, proficient **11** applicative, commonsense, down-to-earth, experienced, practicable, pragmatical, serviceable, utilitarian **12** accomplished, businesslike, matter-of-fact **14** bread-and-butter
• **practical joke**
03 gag **04** feat, hoax, jape, joke, scam **05** antic, caper, prank, stunt, trick **06** frolic **07** fast one, frame-up, leg-pull **09** booby trap **11** apple-pie bed

practicality
05 sense **06** basics **07** realism, utility **08** practice **09** soundness **10** experience, pragmatism, usefulness **11** common sense, feasibility, nitty-gritty, workability **12** nuts and bolts **13** practicalness **14** practicability, serviceability

practically
06 all but, almost, nearly **07** morally **08** in effect, sensibly, well-nigh **09** just about, virtually **10** pretty much, pretty well, rationally, reasonably **11** essentially, in principle **13** fundamentally, pragmatically, realistically **14** matter-of-factly

practice
03 ism, job, net, ure, use, way **04** firm, wont, work **05** drill, habit, study, trade, usage **06** action, career, custom, dry run, effect, method, policy, system, try-out, warm-up **07** company, pursuit, reality, routine, work-out **08** business, dummy run, exercise, plotting, scheming, training, trickery **09** actuality, following, operation, procedure, rehearsal, tradition **10** convention, employment, experience, occupation, profession, run-through **11** application, partnership, performance, preparation **13** establishment
• **out of practice**
05 rusty **07** disused **10** out of habit **11** unpractised **13** disaccustomed, out of the habit
• **put into practice**
03 use **05** apply **07** perform **08** exercise, put to use **09** make use of **13** put into action, put into effect

practise
02 do **03** use **04** plot **05** apply, drill, study, train **06** effect, follow, go over, polish, pursue, refine, repeat, tamper, work at, work on **07** execute, observe, perfect, perform, prepare **08** carry out, engage in, exercise, frequent, maintain, rehearse **09** go through, implement, prosecute, undertake **10** run through **15** put into practice

practised
03 old **04** able **05** adept **06** expert, traded, versed **07** knowing, skilful, skilled, trained, veteran **08** finished, masterly, seasoned **09** prevalent, qualified **10** consummate, proficient **11** experienced **12** accomplished, experimented **13** knowledgeable

practitioner
03 ace, pro **04** buff, doer **05** crack **06** expert, master, pundit **07** dab hand, maestro, old hand **08** virtuoso **09** authority **10** practician, proficient, specialist **12** professional

pragmatic
05 edict **08** busybody, sensible **09** efficient, hard-nosed, practical, realistic **10** hard-headed, meddlesome **11** opinionated, utilitarian **12** businesslike, matter-of-fact **13** unsentimental

pragmatism
07 realism **08** ad hocery, humanism **10** unidealism **11** opportunism **12** practicalism, practicality **14** hard-headedness, utilitarianism **15** instrumentalism

pragmatist
07 realist **08** humanist **11** opportunist, utilitarian **12** practicalist

praise
03 los, rap **04** hail, hery, laud, loos, puff, rave, sell, tout, wrap **05** adore, bless, blurb, carol, cheer, cry up, exalt, extol, glory, herry, herye, roose **06** admire, eulogy, homage, honour, talk up, thanks **07** acclaim, applaud, bouquet, build up, commend, crack up, flatter, glorify, hosanna, magnify, ovation, promote, tribute, worship **08** accolade, applause, appraise, approval, bouquets, cheering, devotion, emblazon, encomium, eulogium, eulogize, flattery, plaudits, rave over, set forth **09** adoration, adulation, laudation, panegyric, recognize **10** admiration, compliment, hallelujah, wax lyrical **11** acknowledge, approbation, recognition, speak well of, testimonial **12** commendation, congratulate, pay tribute to, thanksgiving **13** glorification, speak highly of **14** congratulation
• **expression of praise**
07 hosanna **08** alleluia **10** halleluiah, hallelujah

praiseworthy
04 fine **06** worthy **08** laudable, sterling **09** admirable, deserving, estimable,

excellent, exemplary, reputable
10 creditable, honourable
11 commendable

praising
09 adulatory, approving, laudative, laudatory, panegyric **10** eulogistic, favourable, flattering, plauditory, worshipful **11** approbatory, encomiastic, promotional
12 commendatory **13** complimentary
14 congratulatory, recommendatory

pram
05 buggy, praam **08** bassinet, stroller
09 Baby Buggy®, pushchair **12** baby carriage, perambulator

prance
◇ *anagram indicator*
04 jump, leap, romp, skip **05** bound, brank, caper, dance, frisk, prank, stalk, strut, swank, titup, vault **06** canary, cavort, curvet, frolic, gambol, jaunce, jaunse, parade, spring, tittup
07 caracol, prankle, show off, swagger, trounce **08** caracole

prank
03 jig, rig **04** fold, gaud, joke, lark, reak, reik **05** antic, caper, pleat, stunt, trick
06 escape, frolic, prance, pranck, vagary, wedgie **07** prancke **08** capering, escapade, fredaine, prancing
11 monkey shine **13** practical joke

prankster
05 joker, rogue **06** hoaxer, jester
07 funster **08** quipster **09** trickster
14 practical joker

praseodymium
02 Pr

prat
03 ass, mug, nit, oaf **04** berk, clot, dope, dork, fool, geek, jerk, nerd, twit
05 chump, clown, dumbo, dunce, idiot, ninny, pratt, prick, twerp, wally
06 cretin, dimwit, dum-dum, muppet, nitwit, sucker **07** fat-head, halfwit, pillock, plonker **08** buttocks, imbecile, innocent, numskull **09** birdbrain, ignoramus, lamebrain, simpleton, thickhead **10** nincompoop **11** knuckle-head
See also **bottom**

prattle
03 gab, gup, jaw, yap **04** chat, talk
06 babble, drivel, gabble, gossip, hot air, jabber, patter, rattle, tattle, witter
07 blabber, blather, blether, chatter, gabnash, nashgab, prating, twaddle, twattle, twitter **08** chitchat, nonsense
09 bavardage, gibberish **11** foolishness

prattler
06 gossip, magpie, rattle, talker, tatler
07 babbler, blether, gabbler, tattler, windbag **09** chatterer, loudmouth
10 chatterbox **12** blabbermouth

pray
03 ask, beg, bid, say **05** adore, crave, daven, plead, thank **06** call on, invoke, praise, talk to **07** beseech, beseeke, confess, entreat, implore, prithee, prythee, request, solicit, speak to, worship **08** petition **09** imprecate
10 be at prayer, say a prayer, supplicate
11 commune with **14** say your prayers, wrestle with God

prayer
03 act, ave, cry **04** bead, bede, bene, plea **06** appeal, litany, mantra, novena, orison, praise **07** collect, request, worship **08** devotion, doxology, entreaty, petition, suffrage
09 adoration, communion
10 confession, fellowship, invocation
11 imprecation **12** intercession, supplication, thanksgiving

Prayers include:

02 Om
03 act
05 adhan, Ardas, grace, salat, Shema
06 Amidah, Gloria, Rosary, Yizkor
07 Angelus, khotbah, khutbah
08 Agnus Dei, Ave Maria, Habdalah, Hail Mary, Havdalah, Kaddhish, Kol Nidre, shahadah
09 Confiteor, Our Father
10 Benedictus, Lychnapsia, Magnificat, requiescat
11 Lord's Prayer, Paternoster, Sursum Corda
12 Divine Office, Kyrie eleison, Nunc Dimittis
15 act of contrition

• **call to prayer**
04 azan

prayer-book
06 mahzor, missal, primer, siddur
07 liturgy, machzor, ordinal, primmer
08 breviary, Triodion **09** euchology, formulary **11** euchologion, service-book

preach
04 urge **05** teach **06** advise, exhort, sermon **07** address, deliver, lecture
08 admonish, advocate, harangue, moralize, proclaim, prophesy
09 inculcate, preachify, predicate, recommend, sermonize **10** apostolize, evangelize **11** give a sermon, pontificate **15** spread the gospel

preacher
05 molla **06** mollah, moolah, mullah, parson, ranter **07** apostle, holy Joe, martext, prophet **08** homilist, minister, pulpiter, sermoner, spintext
09 Boanerges, clergyman, gospeller, itinerant, moralizer, predicant, predikant, pulpiteer, sermoneer
10 ecclesiast, evangelist, Holy Roller, licentiate, missionary, revivalist, sermonizer, tub-thumper **11** Bible-basher, devil-dodger, lay preacher, probationer **12** Bible-pounder, Bible-thumper, circuit rider, pontificater, tent preacher **13** field preacher, local preacher, televangelist **15** open-air preacher

preaching
05 dogma **06** gospel, pulpit
07 evangel, kerygma, message, sermons **08** doctrine, homilies, precepts, prophecy, teaching
09 predicant **10** evangelism, homiletics **11** exhortation, instruction, sermonizing, tub-thumping **12** Bible-bashing **13** pontificating, tent preaching

preachy
02 pi **05** pious **08** didactic, dogmatic, edifying **09** homiletic, hortatory, pharisaic, pietistic, religiose
10 moralistic, moralizing, pontifical
11 exhortatory, sermonizing
13 pontificating, sanctimonious, self-righteous **14** holier-than-thou

preamble
05 proem **06** lead-in **07** preface, prelude **08** exordium, foreword, overture, prologue **11** preparation
12 introduction, prolegomenon
13 preliminaries

prearrange
07 diarize, prepare, pre-plan
08 organize, schedule **09** plan ahead
12 predetermine

prearranged
03 set

precarious
◇ *anagram indicator*
04 iffy **05** dicey, dicky, dodgy, hairy, risky, shaky **06** chancy, unsafe, unsure, wobbly **07** dubious, trickle
08 doubtful, insecure, ticklish, unstable, unsteady **09** dangerous, hazardous, uncertain, unsettled
10 touch and go, unreliable, vulnerable
11 treacherous **12** supplicating, undependable **13** unpredictable

precariously
◇ *anagram indicator*
07 riskily, shakily **08** unsafely, unstably
10 insecurely, unreliably, unsteadily
11 dangerously, hazardously
13 unpredictably

precaution
04 care **07** caution **08** forewarn, prudence, security **09** foresight, insurance, provision, safeguard
10 protection, providence, safety belt
11 forethought, preparation
12 anticipation **13** attentiveness
14 circumspection, farsightedness

precautionary
06 safety **07** prudent **08** cautious
09 judicious, provident **10** far-sighted, preventive, protective **11** preliminary, preparatory **12** preventative

precede
04 head, lead **06** forego, herald
07 forerun, preface, prelude, prevene, prevent, usher in **08** antecede, antedate, go before **09** come first, go ahead of, harbinger, introduce
10 anticipate, come before **14** take precedence

precedence
03 pas **04** lead, rank **05** place
08 eminence, priority **09** seniority,

supremacy **10** ascendancy, first place, preference, right of way
11 preaudience, pre-eminence, superiority **12** pride of place
• **take precedence over**
09 take place **10** come before, take rank of

precedent
04 case, lead **05** model, token
07 example, pattern **08** exemplar, instance, paradigm, parallel, standard
09 criterion, yardstick

preceding
04 past **05** above, prior, supra
06 former **07** earlier, leading
08 anterior, previous **09** aforesaid, foregoing, precedent **10** antecedent, precursive, prevenient **11** preliminary
14 aforementioned

precept
03 law **04** rule **05** axiom, canon, maxim, motto, order **06** charge, decree, dictum, rubric, saying
07 command, mandate, statute
08 doctrine, sentence **09** direction, directive, guideline, institute, ordinance, principle **10** convention, injunction, regulation
11 commandment, instruction

precinct
04 area, land, mall, zone **05** bound, close, court, lands, limit, verge
06 milieu, sector, vihara **07** confine, quarter, section, temenos
08 boundary, building, district, division, environs, galleria, locality, purlieus, vicinity **09** buildings, enclosure, food court, peribolos, peribolus, surrounds
13 neighbourhood **14** shopping centre

preciosity
06 chichi **08** tweeness **11** affectation, floweriness, marivaudage
13 artificiality **14** over-refinement
15 pretentiousness

precious
04 dear, fine, nice, rare, twee **05** ditsy, ditzy, grand, loved, tatty **06** adored, chichi, choice, costly, dainty, prized, valued **07** beloved, darling, dearest, flowery, revered **08** affected, idolized, mannered, valuable **09** cherished, contrived, egregious, expensive, extremely, favourite, priceless, simulated, treasured **10** artificial, dearbought, fastidious, high-priced
11 inestimable, overrefined, pretentious **12** confoundedly
• **precious stone** *see* **gem**

precipice
04 crag, drop **05** bluff, brink, cliff, krans, kranz, scarp, steep **06** escarp, height, krantz **08** precepit **09** cliff face, sheer drop **10** escarpment

precipitate
04 hurl, rash **05** brief, cause, fling, flock, hasty, heave, hurry, quick, rapid, shoot, speed, swift, throw **06** abrupt, flocks, hasten, induce, plunge, sludge, speedy, sudden, thrust **07** advance, bring on, frantic, further, hurried, quicken, speed up, trigger, violent
08 expedite, headlong, heedless, occasion, reckless **09** breakneck, hot-headed, impatient, impetuous, impulsive, magistery **10** accelerate, bring about, indiscreet, unexpected
11 precipitant, precipitous

precipitately
06 rashly **07** hastily, quickly, rapidly
08 abruptly, headlong, suddenly
09 violently **10** recklessly **11** frantically, impetuously, impulsively
12 unexpectedly

precipitation

Precipitation includes:

03 dew, fog
04 hail, mist, rain, snow
05 sleet
06 shower
07 drizzle
08 downpour, rainfall, snowfall
09 rainstorm, snowflake

See also **ice**; **snow**; **weather**

precipitous
04 high **05** sharp, sheer, steep **06** abrupt, sudden **07** steepup **08** headlong, steepeup, vertical **10** steepdowne
11 steepedowne **13** perpendicular

précis
05 sum up, table **06** digest, résumé, sketch **07** abridge, epitome, outline, run-down, shorten, summary
08 abstract, compress, condense, contract, synopsis **09** epitomize, summarize, synopsize **10** abbreviate, compendium, conspectus
11 abridgement, contraction, encapsulate **12** abbreviation, condensation **13** encapsulation

precise
03 dry **04** nice, prim, very **05** exact, fixed, razor, right, rigid, tight **06** actual, formal, minute, narrow, strict
07 buckram, careful, correct, express, factual, finical, literal, pointed, starchy
08 accurate, clear-cut, definite, detailed, distinct, explicit, faithful, preceese, priggish, punctual, rigorous, specific, succinct, surgical
09 authentic, identical **10** blow-by-blow, fastidious, meticulous, particular, scrupulous **11** ceremonious, punctilious, puritanical, unambiguous, unequivocal, word-for-word
13 conscientious

precisely
03 yes **04** just, slap, to a T, true
05 plumb, quite, right, sharp, smack
06 agreed, bang on, dead on, indeed, just so, spot-on **07** clearly, exactly
08 minutely, of course, on the dot, strictly, verbatim, you got it
09 certainly, correctly, literally
10 absolutely, accurately, distinctly, that's right **11** by the squire, on the button, word for word

precision
04 care **06** detail, rigour **08** accuracy, neatness **09** exactness **10** exactitude
11 correctness, preciseness, reliability
12 distinctness, explicitness, faithfulness **13** particularity
14 fastidiousness, meticulousness, scrupulousness **15** punctiliousness

preclude
03 bar **04** stop **05** avoid, check, debar, estop **06** hinder **07** exclude, inhibit, obviate, prevent, rule out **08** prohibit, restrain **09** eliminate, foreclose, forestall

precocious
04 fast **05** ahead, early, quick, smart
06 bright, clever, farand, gifted, mature
07 farrand, farrant, forward
08 advanced, far ahead, talented
09 brilliant, developed, premature
11 auld-farrant **13** old for your age

preconceive
06 assume, expect, ideate **07** imagine, picture, presume, project **08** conceive, envisage **09** visualize **10** anticipate, presuppose **12** predetermine

preconception
04 bias, idea **06** notion **09** prejudice, prenotion **10** assumption, conjecture
11 expectation, presumption
12 anticipation, prejudgement
14 predisposition, presupposition

precondition
04 must **09** condition, essential, necessity **10** sine qua non
11 requirement, stipulation
12 prerequisite

precursor
04 sign **05** usher **06** herald **07** pioneer, prelude **08** ancestor, forebear, way-maker **09** harbinger, messenger
10 antecedent, forerunner, indication, progenitor **11** morning star, predecessor, trailblazer **13** curtain-raiser

precursory
05 prior **07** warning **08** anterior, previous **09** preceding, prefatory, preludial, prelusive, prodromal
10 antecedent, precursive, prevenient
11 preliminary, preparatory
12 introductory **13** preambulatory

predator *see* **bird**; **cat**; **spider**

predatory
06 greedy, lupine **07** hunting, preying, wolfish **08** covetous, ravaging, thieving **09** marauding, pillaging, predative, rapacious, raptorial, voracious, vulturine, vulturous
10 avaricious, despoiling, plundering, predaceous, predacious **11** acquisitive, carnivorous, deleterious, destructive, raptatorial

predecessor
08 ancestor, forebear **09** precursor
10 antecedent, antecessor, forefather, forerunner, progenitor

predestination
03 lot **04** doom, fate **07** destiny **11** reprobation **14** foreordination

predestine
04 doom, fate, mean **06** intend **07** destine **08** foredoom, pre-elect **09** preordain **10** foreordain **12** predestinate, predetermine

predetermined
03 set **05** fated, fixed **06** agreed, doomed **07** settled **08** arranged, destined, ordained **11** prearranged, predestined **12** foreordained

predicament
03 box, fix, jam **04** cart, hole, mess, pass, spot, stew **06** crisis, hiccup, pickle, plight, scrape, taking **07** dilemma, impasse, trouble **08** chancery, hot water, how-d'ye-do, quandary **09** deep water, emergency, situation, tight spot **10** praemunire **12** kettle of fish

predicate
04 aver, avow, base, rest **05** build, found, imply, posit, state **06** affirm, assert, avouch, ground, preach **07** contend, declare, premise **08** maintain, proclaim **09** establish, postulate **11** be dependent

predict
03 bet **04** cast **05** augur **06** divine **07** foresay, foresee, portend, presage, project, warrant **08** forecast, foreshew, foreshow, foretell, prophesy **09** auspicate, forespeak **10** vaticinate **11** second-guess **13** prognosticate

predictable
04 sure **05** trite, usual **06** likely, odds-on **07** certain **08** expected, foregone, foreseen, knee-jerk, probable, reliable **09** customary **10** dependable, imaginable, on the cards, unoriginal **11** anticipated, foreseeable **12** unsurprising

prediction
03 bet **06** augury **07** fortune **08** forecast, prophecy, soothsay **09** horoscope, prognosis **10** divination, prognostic **11** auspication, soothsaying **14** fortune-telling **15** prognostication

predictive
07 augural **09** prophetic **10** diagnostic, divinatory, prognostic **11** foretelling **12** anticipating

predilection
04 bent, bias, love **05** fancy, taste **06** liking **07** leaning **08** affinity, fondness, penchant, soft spot, tendency, weakness **09** affection **10** enthusiasm, partiality, preference, proclivity, propensity **11** inclination **14** predisposition

predispose
04 bias, make, move, sway **06** affect, induce, prompt **07** dispose, incline **08** persuade **09** influence, prejudice **10** make liable

predisposed
05 prone, ready **06** biased, liable, minded **07** subject, willing **08** amenable, disposed, inclined, prepared **09** agreeable **10** favourable, prejudiced **11** susceptible **12** not unwilling, well-disposed

predisposition
04 bent, bias **07** leaning **08** penchant, tendency **09** liability, prejudice, proneness **10** likelihood, preference, proclivity, propensity **11** disposition, inclination, willingness **12** potentiality, predilection **13** vulnerability **14** susceptibility

predominance
04 edge, hold, rain, sway **05** power, raine, reign **06** weight **07** control, mastery, numbers **08** dominion, hegemony **09** dominance, influence, supremacy, upper hand **10** ascendancy, leadership, prepotence, prepotency, prevalence **11** paramountcy, prepollence, prepollency, superiority **13** preponderance

predominant
04 main **05** chief, prime **06** master, potent, ruling, strong **07** capital, leading, primary, supreme **08** dominant, forceful, powerful **09** ascendant, ascendent, important, in control, paramount, principal, sovereign **10** prevailing **11** controlling, influential, most obvious **12** preponderant **13** most important **14** most noticeable, preponderating **15** in the ascendancy

predominantly
06 mainly, mostly **07** as a rule, chiefly, largely, overall, usually **08** above all, commonly **09** generally, in general, in the main, primarily **10** by and large, especially, on the whole **11** principally **14** for the most part

predominate
04 rule, tell **05** reign **06** obtain **07** prevail **08** dominate, outweigh, override, overrule **09** outnumber, transcend **10** overshadow **12** preponderate, rule the roast **15** be in the majority

pre-eminence
04 fame, palm **06** renown, repute **08** majority, prestige **09** supremacy **10** excellence, prominence **11** distinction, paramountcy, sovereignty, superiority **12** peerlessness, predominance **13** matchlessness, transcendence **15** incomparability

pre-eminent
03 gun **04** arch, star **05** chief, first, grand, great **06** famous, unique **07** eminent, extreme, leading, palmary, supreme, topping **08** foremost, renowned, singular, superior **09** excellent, first-rate, matchless, palmarian, prominent, unmatched **10** inimitable, unequalled, unrivalled **11** exceptional, outstanding, superlative, unsurpassed **12** incomparable, transcendent **13** distinguished, most important

pre-eminently
04 only **07** notably **08** paravant, signally **09** eminently, paravaunt, primarily, supremely **10** especially, inimitably, peerlessly, singularly, strikingly **11** exclusively, matchlessly, principally **12** emphatically, incomparably, particularly, surpassingly **13** conspicuously, exceptionally, par excellence, superlatively

pre-empt
05 seize, usurp **06** assume, secure, thwart **07** acquire, prevent, replace **08** arrogate, supplant **09** forestall **10** anticipate **11** appropriate

preen
03 pin **04** bask, deck, do up, trim, whet **05** adorn, array, clean, exult, gloat, groom, pique, plume, pride, primp, prink, proin, proyn, prune, slick **06** doll up, proign, proine, proyne, smooth, tart up **07** dress up, trick up **08** beautify, prettify, spruce up, trick out **12** congratulate

preface
04 open **05** begin, index, proem, start **06** launch, prefix, prolog **07** epistle, precede, prelims, prelude **08** exordium, foreword, lead up to, preamble, prologue **09** introduce **11** avant-propos, frontmatter **12** introduction, prolegomenon **13** preliminaries

prefatory
07 opening **08** exordial, proemial **09** preludial, prelusive, prelusory **10** antecedent, precursory **11** explanatory, prefatorial, preliminary, preparatory **12** introductory, prolegomenal **13** preambulatory

prefect
05 grave **07** monitor **08** praefect **09** commander, prepostor **10** magistrate, praepostor, prepositor, supervisor **13** administrator

prefer
03 opt **04** back, file, pick, want, wish **05** adopt, bring, elect, exalt, fancy, go for, lodge, place, press, raise **06** choose, desire, favour, honour, move up, opt for, select **07** advance, elevate, pick out, present, promote, support **08** advocate, plump for **09** recommend, single out **10** aggrandize, like better **11** be partial to, would rather, would sooner

preferable
05 nicer **06** better, chosen **08** favoured, superior **09** advisable, desirable, preferred **11** more desired, recommended **12** advantageous

preferably
05 first **06** rather, sooner **07** ideally

09 for choice 10 from choice, if possible, much rather, much sooner 12 by preference 13 for preference

preference
03 fad 04 bent, bias, kink, mark, pick, will, wish 05 fancy 06 choice, desire, liking, option 07 leaning 08 cup of tea, druthers, forehand, priority
09 favourite, selection 10 partiality, precedence 11 favouritism, first choice, inclination, pre-election
12 predilection 14 discrimination

• **in preference to**
06 before 08 by choice 09 for choice, in place of, instead of 10 from choice, rather than

preferential
06 better, biased 07 partial, special
08 favoured, partisan, superior
10 favourable, privileged
12 advantageous

preferment
04 rise 06 step up 07 dignity
09 elevation, prelation, promotion, upgrading 10 betterment, exaltation
11 advancement, furtherance, improvement 14 aggrandizement

preferred
03 pet 06 choice, chosen 07 desired
08 approved, favorite, favoured, selected 09 favourite, predilect
10 authorized, sanctioned
11 recommended

prefigure
04 bode, mean, type 05 augur
06 signal 07 portend, predict, presage, promise, signify, suggest 08 indicate, prophesy 10 foreshadow
13 prognosticate

pregnancy
06 cyesis 09 family way, gestation, gravidity 10 conception 11 parturition
12 child-bearing, impregnation
13 fertilization 14 being with child

pregnant
04 full, gone, rich 05 clear, great, heavy, in pig, in pup, pithy, quick, witty
06 cogent, filled, gravid, in calf, in foal, loaded 07 charged, fertile, fraught, obvious, pointed, replete, teeming, telling, weighty 08 eloquent, enceinte, fruitful, preggers, swelling, with calf, with foal 09 expectant, expecting, in the club, in trouble, inventive, momentous, up the duff, up the pole, with child, with young 10 big-bellied, convincing, expressive, fertilized, meaningful, parturient, productive, suggestive, up the spout, up the stick
11 impregnated, significant 12 great-bellied 14 in the family way

prehistoric
03 old 05 early 06 Minoan 07 ancient, archaic, Ogygian 08 earliest, obsolete, outmoded, Pelasgic, primeval 09 out-of-date, primaeval, primitive
10 antiquated, primordial 11 out of the ark 12 antediluvian 14 before the flood

prejudge
06 assume 07 presume 09 forejudge, prejudice 10 anticipate, presuppose
11 prejudicate 12 predetermine

prejudice
03 mar 04 bias, harm, hurt, load, loss, ruin, sway 05 slant, spoil, wreck
06 ageism, colour, damage, hinder, impair, injure, injury, racism, sexism, weight 07 bigotry, distort, incline
08 classism, endanger, jaundice, misogyny 09 condition, detriment, influence, injustice, preoccupy, undermine 10 chauvinism, impairment, partiality, predispose, preference, prepossess, unfairness, xenophobia 11 intolerance, misanthropy, prejudicate
12 anticipation, anti-Semitism, disadvantage, one-sidedness, partisanship, prejudgement
13 preoccupation 14 discrimination
15 be detrimental to

prejudiced
06 ageist, biased, loaded, racist, sexist, unfair, unjust, warped 07 bigoted, ex parte, insular, partial, slanted 08 one-sided, partisan, weighted 09 blinkered, distorted, illiberal, jaundiced, parochial
10 chauvinist, influenced, intolerant, subjective, xenophobic 11 anti-Semitic, conditioned, predisposed, prejudicial 12 chauvinistic, narrow-minded, prepossessed
14 discriminatory

prejudicial
07 harmful, hurtful, noxious
08 damaging, inimical 09 injurious
11 deleterious, detrimental
12 unfavourable 15 disadvantageous

preliminary
04 test 05 early, first, pilot, prior, proem, start, trial 06 basics
07 advance, initial, opening, preface, prelude, primary 08 earliest, exordial, exordium, foreword, preamble, prodrome 09 beginning, inaugural, prefatory, rudiments 10 groundwork, precursory, qualifying 11 exploratory, formalities, foundations, preparation, preparative, preparatory
12 experimental, introduction, introductory, prolegomenon

prelude
05 proem, start 06 entrée, herald, opener, verset 07 intrada, opening, preface 08 exordium, foreword, overture, preamble, prodrome, prologue 09 beginning, harbinger, induction, praeamble, precursor
10 forerunner, praeludium
11 preliminary, preparation
12 commencement, introduction, prolegomenon 13 curtain-raiser

premature
04 prem, rash, soon 05 early, hasty
07 preemie, too soon 08 ill-timed, previous, timeless, too early, untimely
09 impetuous, impulsive, precocial
10 praecocial 11 inopportune, precipitate 13 ill-considered, jumping the gun

prematurely
05 early 06 rashly 07 hastily, too soon
08 too early, untimely 11 impetuously, impulsively 12 incompletely

premeditated
06 wilful 07 planned 08 intended, prepense, propense 09 conscious, contrived 10 calculated, considered, deliberate, preplanned 11 cold-blooded, intentional, prearranged
12 aforethought 13 predetermined

premeditation
06 design 07 purpose 08 planning, plotting, scheming 09 intention
11 forethought 12 aforethought, deliberation 13 determination
14 deliberateness, prearrangement

premier
03 top 04 head, main 05 chief, first, prime 07 highest, initial, leading, primary, supreme 08 cardinal, earliest, foremost, original 09 paramount, principal 10 chancellor, pre-eminent
13 chief minister, first minister, prime minister

Premiers of New Zealand:

03 **Fox** (William)
04 **Grey** (Sir George), **Hall** (John), **Weld** (Frederick Aloysius)
05 **Stout** (Sir Robert), **Vogel** (Sir Julius)
06 **Domett** (Alfred), **Pollen** (Daniel), **Seddon** (Richard John), **Sewell** (Henry)
08 **Atkinson** (Sir Harry Albert), **Ballance** (John), **Stafford** (Edward William), **Whitaker** (Frederick)
10 **Waterhouse** (George Marsden)

See also **prime minister**

première
05 debut 07 opening 10 first night
12 first showing, opening night

premise
05 basis, lemma, posit, state 06 assert, assume, prefix, reason, thesis 07 lay down 08 argument 09 assertion, postulate, predicate, statement, stipulate 10 assumption, hypothesis, presuppose, take as true
11 hypothesize, proposition, supposition 14 presupposition

premises
04 site 05 place 06 estate, office
07 grounds 08 building, property
13 establishment

premium
02 ap, pm 05 bonus, prize 06 bounty, reward 07 grassum 08 extra sum, interest, key money 09 insurance, surcharge 10 instalment 11 extra charge 12 an arm and a leg, overcharging 14 regular payment
15 daylight robbery

• **at a premium**
04 rare 06 scarce 08 above par
12 hard to come by, like gold dust 13 in great demand, in short supply

• **put a premium on**
06 favour **08** hold dear, treasure **10** appreciate **12** regard highly, value greatly **15** set great store by

premonition
04 fear, idea, omen, sign **05** hunch, worry **07** anxiety, feeling, portent, presage, specter, spectre, warning **09** intuition, misgiving, suspicion **10** foreboding, gut feeling, prevention, sixth sense **11** forewarning **12** apprehension, funny feeling, presentiment

preoccupation
05 thing **06** hang-up **07** concern, reverie **08** fixation, interest, oblivion **09** obsession, prejudice **10** absorption, enthusiasm, hobby-horse **11** abstraction, daydreaming, distraction, engrossment, pensiveness **12** heedlessness, one-track mind **13** obliviousness, prepossession, wool-gathering **15** bee in your bonnet, inattentiveness

preoccupied
06 intent **07** engaged, faraway, fixated, pensive, taken up **08** absorbed, distrait, heedless, immersed, involved, obsessed **09** engrossed, oblivious, wrapped up **10** abstracted, distracted **11** daydreaming **12** absent-minded **13** deep in thought

preoccupy
03 eat **04** bias **05** eat up **06** absorb, engage, fixate, obsess, occupy, take up **07** involve **09** prejudice **10** prepossess

preordain
04 doom, fate **07** destine **10** foreordain, prearrange, predestine **12** predestinate, predetermine

preparation
◇ *anagram indicator*
04 plan, prep **05** study **06** basics, lotion, potion, supply **07** address, mixture **08** assembly, coaching, compound, cosmetic, homework, medicine, planning, practice, revision, training **09** equipping, provision, readiness, rudiments, spadework **10** concoction, foundation, groundwork, production **11** application, arrangement, composition, development, mise en place **12** construction, organization **13** preliminaries

preparatory
05 basic **07** initial, opening, primary **09** prefatory **10** antecedent, elementary, precursory **11** fundamental, preliminary, rudimentary **12** introductory
• **preparatory to**
06 before **07** prior to **10** previous to **11** in advance of **15** in expectation of

prepare
◇ *anagram indicator*
02 do **03** fix, mix **04** boun, busk, cock, edit, make, plan **05** bowne, coach, draft, dress, equip, prime, set up, study, teach, tee up, train **06** adjust, attire, cooper, devise, digest, draw up, fit out, gear up, rig out, supply, warm up **07** arrange, compose, concoct, fashion, produce, provide, psych up **08** assemble, contrive, exercise, get ready, instruct, organize, practise **09** construct, make ready **10** pave the way **11** put together **12** get into shape **13** throw together **14** set the scene for
• **prepare yourself**
12 gird yourself **13** brace yourself, steel yourself **15** fortify yourself, gird up your loins

prepared
◇ *anagram indicator*
03 fit, set **04** yare **05** fixed, ready **07** in order, planned, waiting, willing **08** arranged, disposed, inclined **09** organized **11** predisposed
• **prepared with**
03 à la

preparedness
05 order **07** fitness **08** procinct **09** alertness, readiness **10** expectancy **11** preparation **12** anticipation

preponderance
04 bulk, mass, sway **05** force, power **06** weight **08** dominion, majority **09** dominance, supremacy **10** ascendancy, domination, lion's share, overweight, prevalence **11** superiority **12** predominance **13** extensiveness, greater number

preponderant
06 larger **07** greater **08** dominant, foremost, superior **09** important **10** overriding, overruling, prevailing **11** controlling, predominant, significant

preponderate
04 rule, tell **07** prevail **08** dominate, outweigh, override, overrule **09** outnumber, weigh with **11** predominate **13** turn the scales **14** turn the balance **15** be in the majority

prepossessing
04 fair **06** taking **07** amiable, lovable, winning, winsome **08** alluring, charming, engaging, fetching, handsome, inviting, likeable, loveable, magnetic, pleasing, striking **09** appealing, beautiful **10** attractive, bewitching, delightful, enchanting **11** captivating, fascinating, good-looking

preposterous
◇ *anagram indicator*
◇ *reversal indicator*
05 crazy **06** absurd **07** asinine, foolish **08** farcical, shocking **09** ludicrous, monstrous, senseless **10** impossible, incredible, irrational, monstruous, outrageous, ridiculous **11** intolerable, nonsensical, unthinkable **12** unbelievable, unreasonable

preposterously
08 absurdly **10** incredibly, shockingly **11** intolerably, ludicrously **12** outrageously, ridiculously, unbelievably, unreasonably

prerequisite
04 must **05** basic, vital **06** needed **07** needful, proviso **08** required **09** condition, essential, mandatory, necessary, necessity, requisite **10** imperative, obligatory, sine qua non **11** fundamental, requirement **12** precondition **13** indispensable, qualification

prerogative
03 due **05** claim, droit, right **06** choice, purvey **07** liberty, licence, royalty **08** immunity, sanction **09** advantage, authority, exemption, privilege **10** birthright **11** entitlement **12** carte blanche

presage
04 bode, omen, sign **05** abode, augur **06** augury, herald, reveal, threat, warn of **07** bespeak, betoken, point to, portend, portent, predict, promise, signify, warning, warrant **08** announce, forebode, forecast, foretell, forewarn, indicate, threaten **09** adumbrate, be a sign of, foretoken, harbinger, precursor **10** foreboding, forerunner, foreshadow, indication, prognostic **11** forewarning, premonition **12** presentiment **13** foreshadowing, prefiguration, prognosticate, signification **15** prognostication

Presbyterian
04 Whig

prescience
08 prophecy **09** foresight, prevision **11** second sight **12** clairvoyance, precognition **13** foreknowledge, propheticness **14** far-sightedness

prescient
06 divine **07** psychic **08** divining **09** far-seeing, prescious, prophetic **10** discerning, divinatory, far-sighted, perceptive **11** clairvoyant, foreknowing, foresighted, previsional

prescribe
03 act, fix, set **04** rule **05** lapse, limit, order **06** advise, decree, define, direct, enjoin, impose, ordain **07** appoint, command, confine, dictate, lay down, require, specify **09** stipulate

prescribed
03 set **07** decreed **08** assigned, laid down, ordained **09** formulary, prescript, specified, statutory **10** regulation, statutable, stipulated

prescription
04 drug **05** scrip **06** advice, recipe, remedy, script **07** formula, mixture **08** leechdom, medicine **09** direction, guideline, optometry, treatment **10** concoction, guidelines **11** instruction, preparation **14** recommendation

prescriptive
05 rigid **08** didactic, dogmatic

09 customary, normative
10 preceptive 11 dictatorial, legislating, prescribing 13 authoritarian

presence
03 air 04 aura, face 05 being, ghost, poise 06 appeal, person, shadow, spirit 07 bearing, company, dignity, phantom, spectre 08 assembly, carriage, charisma, nearness, Shekinah, vicinity, visitant
09 closeness, demeanour, existence, magnetism, occupancy, proximity, residence, Shechinah 10 apparition, appearance, attendance, attraction
11 personality, propinquity
13 companionship, neighbourhood, self-assurance 14 self-confidence

• **in the presence of**
02 by

• **presence of mind**
04 cool 05 poise 06 aplomb
08 calmness, coolness 09 alertness, composure, sangfroid 10 equanimity
11 self-command 13 self-assurance
14 self-possession, unflappability
15 level-headedness

present
02 pr 03 box, gie, now, tip 04 gift, give, here, host, near, perk, pres, show
05 apply, award, being, endow, grant, mount, offer, put on, ready, stage, there
06 at hand, bestow, bounty, cadeau, confer, convey, depict, donate, extend, favour, moment, nearby, prefer, submit, tender, to hand 07 compère, current, deliver, display, douceur, entrust, exhibit, freebie, handout, hold out, instant, perform, picture, porrect, portray, pressie, prezzie, proffer, propine 08 announce, describe, donation, existent, existing, gratuity, hand over, largesse, offering, organize
09 attending, available, delineate, endowment, immediate, introduce, make known, represent, sweetener
10 present-day, put forward
11 benefaction, close at hand, demonstrate 12 bring forward, characterize, contemporary, contribution, in attendance, put on display

• **at present**
03 now 05 today 06 the now 07 just now 09 currently 10 at this time 11 at the moment

• **for the present**
03 now 06 for now, pro tem 12 for the moment 13 in the meantime 15 for the time being

• **present yourself**
05 arise, occur, pop up 06 appear, arrive, attend, crop up, emerge, happen, show up, turn up 11 come to light, materialize

• **the present day**
03 now 05 today 08 nowadays
09 currently 10 at this time, here and now

presentable
04 neat, tidy 05 clean, smart
06 decent, spruce 08 passable
09 quite good, tolerable 10 acceptable
11 respectable 12 satisfactory
14 smartly dressed

presentation
04 form, show, talk 05 award
06 format, launch, layout, object, speech, system 07 address, display, lecture, program, recital, seminar, showing, staging 08 awarding, bestowal, donating, exterior, granting, mounting 09 collation, conferral, packaging, programme, rendition, structure, unveiling 10 appearance, exhibition, presenting, production
11 arrangement, investiture, making known, performance 12 disquisition, introduction, organization
13 demonstration, poster session
14 representation

present-day
02 AD 06 latest, living, modern
07 current, present 08 existing, up-to-date 11 fashionable 12 contemporary

presenter
02 MC 04 host 05 emcee 06 anchor
07 compère 08 frontman
09 anchorman, announcer
10 postulator 11 anchorwoman, sportcaster 12 sportscaster
See also **radio**; **television**

presentiment
04 fear 05 hunch 07 feeling, presage
08 bad vibes, bodement, forecast
09 intuition, misgiving 10 foreboding, presension 11 expectation, forethought, premonition
12 anticipation, apprehension, forebodement

presently
03 now 04 enow, soon 05 in a mo
06 pronto, the now 07 by and by, in a tick, shortly 08 directly, in a jiffy 09 at present, currently, in a minute, in a moment, in a second, ipso facto, these days 10 before long, inevitably 11 at the moment, immediately, necessarily
12 in a short time 13 in a short while

preservation
06 repair, safety, upkeep 07 defence, keeping, storage, support
08 guarding, security 09 retention, upholding 10 protection 11 cold storage, maintenance, reservation, safekeeping 12 conservation, continuation, freeze-drying, perpetuation, safeguarding
13 refrigeration

preserve
03 can, dry, jam, tin 04 area, corn, cure, hain, keep, salt, save 05 candy, chase, chill, field, guard, jelly, lay up, realm, salve, smoke, store 06 bottle, cocoon, defend, domain, embalm, forest, freeze, keep up, kipper, konfyt, pickle, retain, season, secure, shield, sphere, uphold 07 care for, confect, kyanize, protect, put down, reserve, shelter, sustain 08 chow-chow, conserve, continue, creosote, maintain
09 desiccate, freeze-dry, look after, marmalade, powellize, safeguard, sanctuary 10 perpetuate, safari park, speciality, take care of
11 commemorate, game reserve, quick-freeze, reservation 13 nature reserve

preside
03 run 04 head, lead, rule 05 chair
06 direct, govern, head up, manage
07 conduct, control 08 moderate
09 hold court, officiate 10 administer
12 be in charge of, be in the chair, be the chair of, call the shots, take the chair 15 be the chairman of

president
01 P 04 boss, dean, head, Pres, prex
05 chief, prexy, ruler 06 leader, preses
07 manager, praeses, speaker
08 director, governor 09 commodore, moderator, principal 10 chancellor, chief-baron, controller 11 chief barker, Earl Marshal, head of state 13 Dean of Faculty, Earl Marischal 15 Grand Pensionary

Presidents include:

03 **Moi** (Daniel arap), **Rau** (Johannes), **Zia** (Muhammad)
04 **Amin** (Idi), **Díaz** (Porfirio), **Khan** (Ayub), **Ozal** (Turgut), **René** (France-Albert), **Rhee** (Syngman), **Tito** (Josip Broz)
05 **Ahmed** (Shehabuddin), **Assad** (Hafez al-), **Banda** (Hastings), **Botha** (P W), **Havel** (Vaclav), **Heuss** (Theodor), **Klerk** (F W de), **Mbeki** (Thabo), **Menem** (Carlos), **Obote** (Milton), **Perón** (Juan), **Perón** (Martínez de), **Putin** (Vladimir), **Ramos** (Fidel), **Sadat** (Anwar el-)
06 **Aideed** (Mohammed), **Aquino** (Corazon), **Banana** (Canaan), **Bao Dai**, **Bhutto** (Zulfikar Ali), **Biswas** (Abdur Rahman), **Calles** (Plutarco Elías), **Castro** (Fidel), **Chirac** (Jacques), **Ciampi** (Carlo Azeglio), **Gaulle** (Charles de), **Geisel** (Ernesto), **Herzog** (Chaim), **Juárez** (Benito), **Kruger** (Paul), **Kuchma** (Leonid), **Lahoud** (Émile), **Marcos** (Ferdinand), **Mobutu**, **Mugabe** (Robert), **Nasser** (Gamal Abdel), **Nathan** (Sellapan Ramanathan), **Ortega** (Daniel), **Pierce** (Franklin), **Préval** (René), **Rahman** (Ziaur), **Renner** (Karl), **Santos** (José Eduardo dos), **Somoza** (Anastasio), **Somoza** (Luis), **Valera** (Éamon de), **Vargas** (Getúlio), **Walesa** (Lech)
07 **Atatürk** (Mustapha Kemal), **Batista** (Fulgencio), **Bolívar** (Simón), **Cardoso** (Fernando Henrique), **Demirel** (Süleyman), **Estrada** (Joseph Ejercito), **Gaddafi** (Muammar), **Gemayel** (Amin), **Gromyko** (Andrei), **Habibie** (Jusuf), **Hussein** (Saddam), **Iliescu** (Ion), **Khatami** (Sayed Ayatollah Mohammad), **Mancham** (James), **Mandela** (Nelson), **Masaryk** (Thomás), **Mubarak** (Hosni),

Nkrumah (Kwame), Parnell (Charles Stewart), Sampaio (Jorge), Suharto (Thojib N J), Sukarno (Ahmed), Tudjman (Franjo), Weizman (Ezer), Yanayev (Gennady), Yeltsin (Boris), Zhivkov (Todor)
08 Andropov (Yuri), Aristide (Jean-Bertrand), Bani-Sadr (Abolhassan), Brezhnev (Leonid), Chamorro (Violeta), Childers (Erskine), Cosgrave (William Thomas), Duvalier (François 'Papa Doc'), Duvalier (Jean-Claude 'Baby Doc'), Fujimori (Alberto), Galtieri (Leopoldo), Griffith (Arthur), Karadzic (Radovan), Kenyatta (Jomo), Khamenei (Sayed Ali), Kravchuk (Leonid), MacMahon (Patrice de), Makarios (Cyprus Enosis), McAleese (Mary), Mengistu (Haile Mariam), Museveni (Yoweri), Napoleon, Pinochet (Augusto), Poincaré (Raymond), Pompidou (Georges), Rawlings (Jerry), Robinson (Mary), Waldheim (Kurt), Weizmann (Chaim), Zia Ul-Haq (Muhammad)
09 Ceausescu (Nicolae), Chernenko (Konstantin), Gorbachev (Mikhail), Ho Chi Minh, Kim Il-sung, Kim Jong Il, Mao Zedong, Milosevic (Slobodan), Narayanan (Kocheril Raman), Pilsudski (Józef), Sun Yat-Sen
10 Alessandri (Arturo), Betancourt (Rómulo), Hindenburg (Paul von), Jaruzelski (Wojciech), Jiang Zemin, Khrushchev (Nikita), Kubitschek (Juscelino), Mannerheim (Carl Gustav, Baron von), Mitterrand (François), Najibullah (Mohammad), Rafsanjani (Ali Akbar Hashemi), Stroessner (Alfredo), Voroshilov (Kliment)
13 Paz Estenssoro (Víctor)
14 Mobutu Seze Seko
15 Giscard d'Estaing (Valéry)

Presidents of the United States of America:

03 Abe, Ike, Ron
04 Bill, Bush (George), Bush (George W), Ford (Gerald R), Polk (James K), Taft (William H)
05 Adams (John), Adams (John Quincy), Buren (Martin van), Grant (Ulysses S), Hayes (Rutherford B), Nixon (Richard M), Tyler (John)
06 Arthur (Chester A), Carter (Jimmy), Hoover (Herbert), Monroe (James), Pierce (Franklin), Reagan (Ronald), Taylor (Zachary), Truman (Harry S), Wilson (Woodrow)
07 Clinton (Bill), Harding (Warren G), Jackson (Andrew), Johnson (Andrew), Johnson (Lyndon B), Kennedy (John F), Lincoln (Abraham), Madison (James)
08 Buchanan (James), Coolidge (Calvin), Fillmore (Millard), Garfield (James A), Harrison (Benjamin), Harrison (William Henry), McKinley (William)
09 Cleveland (Grover), Jefferson (Thomas), Roosevelt (Franklin D), Roosevelt (Theodore)
10 Eisenhower (Dwight D), Washington (George)

press
02 AP, UP **03** AAP, CUP, hug, jam, lie, mob, OUP, sit, vex **04** airn, bear, cram, iron, mash, pack, push, roll, urge **05** beset, clasp, crowd, crush, flock, force, grasp, hacks, horde, hurry, knead, pinch, plead, print, stamp, stuff, surge, swarm, troop, worry, wring **06** caress, closet, coerce, compel, cuddle, demand, enfold, exhort, harass, lean on, nuzzle, papers, praise, smooth, squash, strain, stress, strive, throng, thrust **07** afflict, besiege, call for, depress, embrace, entreat, express, flatten, implore, imprint, oppress, push for, reports, reviews, squeeze, swing it, thrutch, trample, trouble, urgency **08** articles, bookcase, campaign, compress, coverage, expedite, fast-talk, insist on, petition, pressmen, pressure, push down, soft-soap, the media **09** constrain, criticism, hold close, importune, multitude, news media, paparazzi, reporters, smooth out, sweet-talk, treatment **10** journalism, newspapers, pressurize, presswomen, supplicate **11** Fleet Street, journalists, pull strings, push forward, rotary press **12** fourth estate, newspapermen **13** photographers, printing press, put pressure on **14** correspondents, newspaperwomen, put the screws on **15** printing-machine, the fourth estate, turn the screws on

See also **news**

• **press close**
04 serr **05** serre
• **press forward**
04 push, spur, urge **05** drive
• **member of the press** *see* **journalist**
• **press on**
04 go on, toil **05** crowd **06** plod on **07** carry on, go ahead, peg away, proceed **08** continue, plug away, slog away, toil away **09** keep going, persevere, soldier on, stick at it **10** keep trying, press ahead

pressed
04 laid, lain **06** forced, pushed, rushed **07** bullied, coerced, hard-run, hurried, lacking, short of **08** harassed **09** pressured **10** bludgeoned, browbeaten, railroaded **11** constrained, deficient in, pressurized **15** having too little, not having enough

pressing
03 key **05** acute, vital **06** urgent **07** burning, crucial, exigent, serious **08** critical, crowding **09** demanding, essential, important **10** imperative **11** importunate **12** high-priority

pressman *see* **journalist**

pressure
01 P **04** heat, load, push **05** aggro, bully, drive, force, power, press, stamp **06** burden, coerce, compel, demand, duress, hassle, lean on, oblige, strain, stress, weight **07** dragoon, problem, swing it, tension, trouble, urgency **08** bludgeon, browbeat, bulldoze, bullying, coercion, crushing, fast-talk, railroad, soft-soap **09** adversity, constrain, heaviness, squeezing, sweet-talk **10** compulsion, constraint, difficulty, harassment, impression, obligation, pressurize **11** compression, constraints, pull strings **13** put pressure on **14** put the screws on
• **blood pressure**
02 BP **03** ABP
• **extreme/high/low pressure**
02 EP, HP, LP
• **measurement of pressure**
02 mb, Pa **03** atm, bar, psi **04** torr **05** barye **06** pascal **07** megabar **08** microbar, millibar **10** atmosphere

pressurize
05 bully, drive, force, press **06** coerce, compel, lean on, oblige **07** dragoon, swing it **08** bludgeon, browbeat, bulldoze, fast-talk, pressure, railroad, soft-soap **09** constrain, sweet-talk **11** pull strings **12** put the acid on **13** put pressure on **14** put the screws on

prestige
04 fame, mana **05** charm, izzat, kudos, magic **06** credit, esteem, honour, regard, renown, status **07** glamour, stature **08** eminence, standing **09** authority, influence **10** ascendancy, importance, reputation **11** distinction

prestigious
05 great **06** famous **07** eminent, exalted **08** blue-chip, esteemed, imposing, juggling, renowned, up-market **09** deceitful, important, prominent, reputable, respected, well-known **10** celebrated, impressive **11** high-ranking, illustrious, influential **13** distinguished

presumably
06 I guess **07** no doubt **08** I presume, probably **09** doubtless, seemingly **10** apparently, most likely, very likely **11** doubtlessly **15** in all likelihood

presume
04 dare **05** infer, think **06** assume, deduce, take it **07** believe, go so far, imagine, suppose, surmise, venture **09** undertake **10** make so bold, presuppose, take as read **11** hypothesize **14** take for granted, take the liberty **15** have the audacity
• **presume on**
05 trust **06** bank on, rely on **07** count on, exploit **08** depend on **15** take advantage of

presumption
03 lip **04** gall, neck **05** cheek, guess, mouth, nerve, sauce **06** belief

07 opinion, surmise **08** assuming, audacity, boldness, chutzpah, temerity **09** arrogance, assurance, brass neck, deduction, impudence, inference, insolence, upsetting **10** assumption, conjecture, effrontery, hypothesis, likelihood **11** forwardness, probability, supposition **12** impertinence **13** outrecuidance **14** presupposition

presumptive
06 likely **07** assumed **08** believed, credible, expected, inferred, possible, probable, supposed **09** designate, plausible **10** believable, reasonable, understood **11** conceivable, conjectural, prospective **12** hypothetical

presumptuous
04 bold **05** cocky, fresh, lippy, pushy, saucy **06** cheeky, mouthy **07** forward **08** arrogant, cocksure, impudent, insolent **09** audacious, bigheaded, conceited **11** impertinent **12** over-familiar **13** over-confident

presuppose
05 imply, posit **06** accept, assume **07** premise, presume, suppose **08** consider **09** postulate **11** necessitate **14** take for granted

presupposition
06 belief, theory **07** premise, premiss **10** assumption, hypothesis **11** presumption, supposition **13** preconception

pretence
03 act, lie **04** mask, ruse, sham, show, veil, wile **05** bluff, cloak, cover, feint, front, guise **06** acting, deceit, excuse, façade, faking, humbug, posing, veneer **07** charade, daubery, display, pretext **08** feigning, trickery **09** deception, falsehood, false show, hypocrisy, invention, posturing, semblance, showiness **10** appearance, masquerade, play-acting, pretension, profession, simulation **11** affectation, dissembling, fabrication, make-believe, ostentation **12** false colours **13** dissimulation **15** pretentiousness

pretend
03 act, kid **04** fake, mime, play, sham **05** bluff, claim, feign, frame, kiddy, let on, offer, put on **06** affect, allege, assume, semble **07** imagine, play-act, profess, purport, purpose, put it on, suppose **08** indicate, simulate **09** dissemble, fabricate, imaginary **10** put on an act **11** counterfeit, impersonate, make believe **15** pass yourself off

pretended
04 fake, sham **05** bogus, false, moody, put on **06** avowed, phoney, pseudo **07** alleged, assumed, feigned, pretend **08** affected, so-called, specious, spurious, supposed, vizarded **09** imaginary, professed, purported, soi-disant **10** artificial, fictitious, ostensible, self-styled **11** counterfect, counterfeit **14** supposititious

pretender
06 suitor **07** claimer, would-be **08** aspirant, claimant **09** candidate

pretension
04 airs, show **05** claim **06** demand, vanity **07** conceit, pretext **08** ambition, pretence **09** hypocrisy, pomposity, showiness **10** aspiration, profession, purporting **11** affectation, floweriness, ostentation **12** snobbishness **13** dissimulation, magniloquence **14** self-importance **15** pretentiousness

pretentious
03 big, OTT **04** fine, twee **05** false, large, pseud, showy **06** chichi, phoney, pseudo, shoddy, uppish **07** kitschy, pompous, tinhorn **08** affected, fantoosh, immodest, inflated, mannered, pseudish, snobbish **09** ambitious, bombastic, conceited, elaborate, flaunting, grandiose **10** artificial, flamboyant, over-the-top **11** exaggerated, extravagant **12** high-sounding, magniloquent, ostentatious, vainglorious **13** overambitious, self-important

pretentiously
07 showily **08** uppishly **09** pompously **10** snobbishly **12** artificially, flamboyantly **14** ostentatiously **15** self-importantly

pretentiousness
04 show, side **05** swank **06** chichi, kitsch, posing **08** flummery, grandeur, paraffle, pretence, pretense, pseudery **09** posturing **10** flatulence, flatulency, floridness, pretension, uppishness **11** flamboyance, floweriness, ostentation **13** ambitiousness, theatricality **14** attitudinizing

preternatural
07 no'canny, unusual **08** abnormal **11** exceptional **12** supernatural **13** extraordinary

pretext
04 hook, mask, plea, ploy, ruse, sham, show, veil **05** cloak, cloke, color, cover, guise, salvo, stale **06** colour, excuse **07** off-come, umbrage **08** occasion, pretence, pretense **09** semblance **10** appearance, pretension, red herring **13** alleged reason

prettify
04 deck, do up, gild, trim **05** adorn **06** bedeck, doll up, tart up **07** deck out, garnish, trick up **08** beautify, decorate, ornament, trick out **09** embellish, smarten up

prettily
06 neatly, nicely **08** daintily **09** elegantly, winsomely **10** charmingly, engagingly, gracefully, pleasantly, pleasingly **11** beautifully **12** attractively, delightfully

pretty
04 cute, fair, fine, neat, nice, twee, very **05** bonny, grand, purty, quite **06** bonnie, clever, comely, dainty, fairly, incony, lovely, rather, tricky **07** elegant, fairway, inconie, not half, winsome **08** charming, delicate, engaging, graceful, handsome, keepsake, keepsaky, pleasant, pleasing, somewhat, stalwart **09** appealing, beautiful, extremely, ingenious, tolerably **10** attractive, decorative, delightful, knick-knack, moderately, personable, reasonably **11** commendable, good-looking, substantial **12** chocolate-box, considerable **13** prepossessing

prevail
03 win **04** ring, rule **05** avail, occur, reign **06** abound, have it, obtain, win out **07** conquer, succeed, triumph **08** be common, be normal, hold sway, overcome, override, overrule, persuade, perswade **09** be current, be present **10** be accepted, win through **11** be customary, carry the day, gain mastery, predominate **12** be victorious, preponderate **14** gain ascendancy

• **prevail upon**
03 win **04** rule, sway, urge **06** induce, lean on, prompt **07** incline, win over **08** convince, persuade, pressure, soft-soap, talk into **09** influence, sweet-talk **10** bring round, pressurize **11** pull strings

prevailing
03 set **04** main **05** chief, usual **06** common, ruling **07** average, current, general, in style, in vogue, popular, supreme **08** accepted, dominant, powerful, reigning **09** ascendant, customary, effective, in fashion, most usual, prepotent, prevalent, principal **10** compelling, mainstream, most common, widespread **11** controlling, established, fashionable, influential, predominant **12** preponderant

prevalence
03 ren, rin, run **04** hold, rule, sway **07** mastery, primacy **08** currency, ubiquity **09** frequency, profusion **10** acceptance, ascendancy, commonness, popularity, regularity **11** commonality **12** omnipresence, predominance, universality **13** order of the day, pervasiveness, preponderance

prevalent
03 set **04** rife **05** usual **06** common, vulgar **07** current, endemic, general, popular, rampant, regnant **08** accepted, dominant, enzootic, epidemic, everyday, frequent, powerful **09** customary, extensive, pervasive, universal **10** prevailing, ubiquitous, victorious, widespread **11** established

prevaricate
03 lie **05** cavil, dodge, evade, hedge, mudge, shift **06** waffle **07** deceive, deviate, pervert, quibble, shuffle, whiffle **09** be evasive, pussyfoot, stonewall **10** equivocate, transgress

12 shilly-shally, tergiversate 13 sit on the fence

prevarication
03 fib, lie 04 fibs 06 deceit 07 evasion, fibbing, untruth 08 pretence 09 cavilling, deception, falsehood, half-truth, quibbling 12 equivocation, pussyfooting 13 falsification 14 tergiversation 15 shilly-shallying

prevaricator
04 liar 06 dodger, evader, fibber, Jesuit 07 casuist, sophist 08 caviller, deceiver, quibbler 09 hypocrite 10 dissembler 11 equivocator, pettifogger

prevent
02 sa' 03 bar, let 04 balk, foil, halt, help, keep, save, stop 05 avert, avoid, block, check, debar, deter, stimy 06 arrest, hamper, hinder, impede, stimie, stymie, thwart 07 fend off, head off, inhibit, obviate, precede, ward off 08 hold back, keep from, obstruct, preclude, prohibit, restrain, stave off 09 foreclose, forestall, frustrate, intercept 10 anticipate 11 hold in check

prevention
03 bar 05 check 07 balking, empeach, foiling, halting, impeach 08 obstacle 09 arresting, avoidance, exclusion, hampering, hindrance, obviation, safeguard 10 deterrence, fending off, heading off, hinderance, impediment, precaution, preclusion, staving off, warding off 11 elimination, frustration, obstruction, premonition, prophylaxis 12 anticipation 13 contraception

preventive
05 block 06 remedy, shield 08 obstacle 09 deterrent, hindrance, safeguard 10 impediment, inhibitory, pre-emptive, prevenient, prevention, protection, protective 11 neutralizer, obstruction, obstructive 12 anticipatory, preventative, prophylactic 13 counteractive, precautionary

previous
02 ex- 04 past 05 prior 06 before, former 07 earlier, one-time, quondam 08 sometime 09 erstwhile, foregoing, preceding, premature 10 antecedent

previously
04 erst, fore, once 05 afore 06 before 07 already, earlier 08 formerly, hitherto, until now 09 at one time, earlier on, erstwhile, in the past 10 beforehand, heretofore

prey
03 mug 04 game, kill 05 booty, ravin, soyle 06 quarry, rapine, target, victim 07 afflict, fall guy, plunder, spreagh 08 distress 11 depredation

• prey on
03 con, eat 04 hunt, kill 05 bleed, catch, haunt, prowl, seize, worry 06 burden, devour, feed on, fleece, plague 07 exploit, live off, moth-eat, oppress, predate, raven on, torment, trouble, vampire 08 distress, hang over, pounce on 09 depredate, weigh down 15 take advantage of

price
02 pr 03 fee, sum 04 bill, cost, fare, levy, rate, toll 05 prise, prize, value, worth 06 amount, assess, charge, figure, outlay, result, reward 07 expense, forfeit, payment, penalty 08 appraise, estimate, evaluate, expenses, valorize 09 quotation, sacrifice, valuation 10 assessment 11 consequence, expenditure 12 consequences, preciousness 13 fix the price at, set the price at

• at any price
09 at any cost, à tout prix 15 whatever it takes, whatever the cost

• at a price
04 dear 09 expensive 11 at a high cost 12 at a high price

• fix price
03 peg

priceless
04 dear, rare, rich 05 comic, funny 06 costly, prized 07 amusing, a scream, killing, riotous 08 precious, unvalued, valuable 09 cherished, expensive, hilarious, treasured 10 invaluable 11 inestimable 12 incalculable, incomparable 13 inappreciable, irreplaceable, side-splitting

pricey
04 dear 05 steep 06 costly 07 sky-high 09 excessive, expensive 10 exorbitant, high-priced 11 over the odds 12 costing a bomb, extortionate 15 costing the earth, daylight robbery

prick
03 dot, jab, jag, pin 04 acme, bite, bore, brod, brog, cloy, gash, hole, itch, mark, nick, pain, pang, peak, prod, prog, slit, stab 05 harry, point, punch, rowel, smart, spike, sting, thorn, worry, wound 06 accloy, gnaw at, harass, incite, pierce, plague, prey on, target, tingle, twinge 07 pinhole, prickle, torment, trouble 08 distress, puncture, smarting 09 perforate 11 perforation

• prick up your ears
06 attend 09 lend an ear 10 take note of 12 pay attention, take notice of 13 listen eagerly 15 listen carefully, pin back your ears

prickle
03 nip 04 barb, itch, pang, spur, tine 05 point, prick, prong, smart, spike, spine, sting, thorn 06 needle, tingle, twinge 07 acantha, aculeus, itching, spicula 08 smarting, stinging 09 sensation 11 formication 12 paraesthesia 14 pins and needles

prickly
04 edgy, hard 05 armed, jaggy, ratty, rough, spiky, spiny, tough 06 barbed, crabby, grumpy, on edge, shirty, spiked, thorny, touchy, tricky 07 bearded, brambly, bristly, grouchy, pronged, stroppy 08 aculeate, delicate, echinate, scratchy 09 aculeated, crotchety, difficult, echinated, irritable, sensitive 10 acanaceous 11 bad-tempered, complicated, problematic, thin-skinned, troublesome 12 acanthaceous 13 problematical, short-tempered

prickly pear
04 tuna 05 nopal 07 opuntia 09 Indian fig

pride
03 ego, joy 05 prime 06 flower, honour, mettle, vanity 07 conceit, delight, dignity, disdain, egotism, elation, stomach 08 pleasure, smugness, snobbery 09 arrogance, proudness, self-image, self-worth, splendour 10 exuberance, self-esteem 11 haughtiness, ostentation, presumption, self-conceit, self-respect 12 boastfulness, magnificence, satisfaction, triumphalism 13 bigheadedness, gratification 14 self-importance 15 pretentiousness

• pride and joy
03 joy 04 best, pick 05 élite, glory 06 finest, flower 07 darling, delight 10 choice part, select part 14 apple of your eye, crème de la crème, pick of the bunch

• pride yourself on
05 vaunt 07 exult in, glory in, revel in 09 brag about, crow about 10 boast about 11 take pride in 13 plume yourself, preen yourself 15 flatter yourself

priest
01 P 02 Pr 03 Eli 05 Aaron, clerk, Zadok 06 cleric, Elijah, Elisha, father, orator 07 prelate, secular 08 man of God 09 churchman, clergyman 10 hierophant, woman of God 11 churchwoman, clergywoman 12 ecclesiastic 13 man of the cloth 15 woman of the cloth

Priests include:

02 HP, PP
04 abbé, arch, curé, high, lama, papa, pope
05 bonze, druid, magus, mambo, padre, rabbi, vicar
06 deacon, flamen, Levite, lucumo, parish, parson, pastor, shaman, zymite
07 Brahman, patrico, pontiff, Pythian, tohunga
08 bacchant, corybant, hierarch, minister, neophyte, seminary, Syriarch
09 bacchanal, confessor, deaconess, lack-Latin, oratorian, patercove, presbyter
10 arch-flamen, masspriest, seminarian, seminarist
11 hedge-parson, hedge-priest
12 concelebrant, Redemptorist

priestess
03 nun 05 mambo 06 abbess, Pythia, sister, vestal 07 beguine, Pythian

08 canoness, prioress **09** bacchante, deaconess, Pythoness, religious **11** clergywoman

priesthood
08 the cloth **09** the church **10** full orders, hierocracy, holy orders, priestship **11** the ministry **12** the pastorate **13** sacerdotalism

priestly
07 Aaronic **08** clerical, hieratic, pastoral **09** Aaronical, canonical **10** priestlike, sacerdotal **14** ecclesiastical

prig
05 filch, prude, thief **06** haggle, tinker **07** coxcomb, entreat, holy Joe, killjoy, old maid, puritan **09** importune, Mrs Grundy, precisian **10** goody-goody, holy Willie

priggish
04 prim, smug **05** prude **06** stuffy **07** prudish, starchy **10** goody-goody **11** puritanical, strait-laced **12** narrow-minded **13** sanctimonious, self-righteous **14** holier-than-thou

prim
03 mim **04** smug **05** fussy, mimsy **06** demure, formal, mimsey, neaten, prissy, proper, quaint, stuffy **07** perjink, precise, primsie, prudish, starchy **08** priggish **10** fastidious, fuddy-duddy, governessy, old-maidish, particular **11** puritanical, strait-laced **12** primigravida **13** schoolmarmish

primacy
07 command **08** dominion **09** dominance, seniority, supremacy **10** ascendancy, leadership, paramouncy **11** pre-eminence, sovereignty, superiority

prima donna
04 diva **10** female lead **11** leading lady, moody person **14** leading soprano

primaeval *see* **primeval, primaeval**

primal
04 main **05** basic, chief, first, major, prime **07** central, highest, initial, primary **08** earliest, greatest, original, primeval **09** paramount, primaeval, primitive, principal **10** primordial **11** fundamental, primigenial, primogenial

primarily
◇ *head selection indicator*
05 first **06** mainly, mostly **07** chiefly, firstly **09** basically, in essence, in the main **10** especially **11** essentially, principally **12** nothing if not, particularly **13** fundamentally, predominantly **15** in the first place

primary
04 main **05** basic, chief, first, prime **06** direct, simple **07** capital, highest, initial, leading, opening, radical, supreme **08** cardinal, dominant, earliest, foremost, greatest, original, primeval, ultimate **09** beginning, elemental, essential, first-hand, paramount, primaeval, primitive, principal **10** elementary, idiopathic, primordial **11** fundamental, predominant, rudimentary **12** introductory

primate
06 bishop **07** Bigfoot **10** archbishop

Primates include:

03 ape
04 mico
05 chimp, drill, human, indri, jocko, lemur, loris, orang, pigmy, pongo, pygmy, satyr
06 aye-aye, baboon, bonobo, chacma, colugo, dog-ape, galago, gelada, gibbon, indris, macaco, malmag, monkey, sifaka, wou-wou, wow-wow
07 gorilla, hoolock, jacchus, macaque, meercat, meerkat, nagapie, siamang, tarsier, wistiti
08 bushbaby, great ape, hylobate, mandrill, marmoset, mongoose, night-ape
09 babacoote, catarhine, hamadryad, orang-utan, prosimian
10 angwantibo, catarrhine, chimpanzee, protohuman, silverback
11 homo sapiens, orang-outang
12 Cynocephalus, ourang-outang, paranthropus
13 Galeopithecus, Kenyapithecus
15 pygmy chimpanzee

See also **ape**; **monkey**

prime
03 top **04** acme, best, fang, fill, main, peak **05** bloom, brief, chief, coach, equip, gen up, phang, pride, train **06** charge, choice, clue up, fill in, flower, gear up, height, heyday, inform, notify, select, zenith **07** blossom, classic, highest, leading, premier, prepare, primary, quality, supreme, typical **08** best part, foremost, get ready, maturity, original, pinnacle, standard, top-grade **09** excellent, first-rate, make ready, principal **10** first-class, perfection, pre-eminent **11** culmination, predominant **12** paradigmatic, prototypical **14** characteristic, quintessential

prime minister
02 PM **05** dewan, diwan **07** premier **08** quisling **09** Taoiseach **10** chancellor **11** Grand Vizier **13** chief minister, first minister

Prime Ministers of Australia:

04 **Cook** (Joseph), **Holt** (Harold), **Page** (Earle), **Reid** (George)
05 **Bruce** (Stanley), **Forde** (Francis Michael), **Hawke** (Bob), **Lyons** (Joseph)
06 **Barton** (Edmund), **Curtin** (John), **Deakin** (Alfred), **Fadden** (Arthur), **Fisher** (Andrew), **Fraser** (Malcolm), **Gorton** (John), **Howard** (John), **Hughes** (Billy), **McEwen** (John), **Watson** (Chris)
07 **Chifley** (Ben), **Keating** (Paul), **McMahon** (William), **Menzies** (Robert), **Scullin** (James), **Whitlam** (Gough)

Prime Ministers of Canada:

04 **King** (William Lyon Mackenzie)
05 **Abbot** (John J C), **Clark** (Joseph)
06 **Borden** (Robert), **Bowell** (Mackenzie), **Tupper** (Charles), **Turner** (John)
07 **Bennett** (R B), **Laurier** (Wilfrid), **Meighen** (Arthur), **Pearson** (Lester B), **Trudeau** (Pierre)
08 **Campbell** (Kim), **Chrétien** (Jean), **Mulroney** (Brian), **Thompson** (John S D)
09 **Macdonald** (John A), **Mackenzie** (Alexander), **St Laurent** (Louis)
11 **Diefenbaker** (John G)

Prime Ministers of New Zealand:

04 **Bell** (Francis), **Kirk** (Norman Eric), **Nash** (Walter), **Ward** (Joseph)
05 **Clark** (Helen), **Lange** (David), **Moore** (Mike)
06 **Bolger** (James), **Coates** (Gordon), **Forbes** (George William), **Fraser** (Peter), **Massey** (William), **Palmer** (Geoffrey), **Savage** (Michael Joseph), **Seddon** (Richard)
07 **Holland** (Sidney), **Muldoon** (Robert), **Rowling** (Wallace), **Shipley** (Jenny)
08 **Holyoake** (Keith), **Marshall** (John Ross)
09 **Hall-Jones** (William), **Mackenzie** (Thomas)

See also **premier**

Prime Ministers of the United Kingdom:

04 **Bute** (John Stuart, Earl), **Eden** (Sir Anthony), **Grey** (Charles Grey, Earl), **Home** (Alec Douglas-Home, Earl), **Peel** (Robert), **Pitt** (William)
05 **Blair** (Tony), **Cecil** (Robert), **Derby** (Edward Stanley, Earl), **Heath** (Ted), **Major** (John), **North** (Frederick North, Lord)
06 **Attlee** (Clement), **Pelham** (Henry), **Wilson** (Harold)
07 **Asquith** (Herbert), **Baldwin** (Stanley), **Balfour** (Arthur), **Canning** (George), **Grafton** (Augustus Henry Fitzroy, Duke), **Russell** (John, Lord), **Walpole** (Robert)
08 **Aberdeen** (George Hamilton-Gordon, Lord), **Bonar Law** (Andrew), **Disraeli** (Benjamin), **Goderich** (Frederick John Robinson, Viscount), **Perceval** (Spencer), **Portland** (William Henry Cavendish Bentinck, Duke), **Rosebery** (Archibald Philip Primrose, Earl), **Thatcher** (Margaret, Lady)
09 **Addington** (Henry), **Callaghan** (James, Lord), **Churchill** (Sir Winston), **Gladstone** (William), **Grenville** (George), **Grenville** (William Wyndham, Lord),

Liverpool (Robert Jenkinson, Earl), MacDonald (Ramsay), Macmillan (Harold), Melbourne (William Lamb, Viscount), Newcastle (Thomas Pelham-Holles, Duke), Salisbury (Robert Gascoyne-Cecil, Marquess), Shelburne (William Petty-Fitzmaurice, Earl)
10 Devonshire (William Cavendish, Duke), Palmerston (Henry John Temple, Viscount), Rockingham (Charles Watson Wentworth, Marquess), Wellington (Arthur Wellesley, Duke), Wilmington (Spencer Compton, Earl)
11 Chamberlain (Neville), Douglas-Home (Alec), Lloyd George (David)
17 Campbell-Bannerman (Henry)

Prime Ministers of other countries include:

02 Nu (U)
03 Ito (Hirobumi)
04 Meir (Golda), Moro (Aldo), Tojo (Hideki)
05 Ahern (Bertie), Assad (Hafez al-), Azaña (Manuel), Aznar (José María), Banda (Hastings Kamuzu), Barak (Ehud), Barre (Raymond), Begin (Menachem), Botha (Louis), Botha (P W), Craxi (Bettino), Desai (Morarji), Faure (Edgar), Hoxha (Enver), Juppé (Alain), Khama (Sir Seretse), Laval (Pierre), Lynch (Jack), Malan (Daniel), Nehru (Jawaharlal), Obote (Milton), Pasic (Nikola), Peres (Shimon), Prodi (Romano), Putin (Vladimir), Rabin (Yitzhak), Sadat (Anwar el-), Singh (Manmohan), Smith (Ian), Smuts (Jan), Spaak (Paul Henri)
06 Bhutto (Benazir), Bhutto (Zulfikar Ali), Briand (Aristide), Bruton (John), Castro (Fidel), Chirac (Jacques), Fabius (Laurent), Gandhi (Indira), Gandhi (Rajiv), Gaulle (Charles de), Hun Sen, Jospin (Lionel), Li Peng, Manley (Michael), Mugabe (Robert), Neguib (Mohammed), O'Neill (Terence, Lord), Pétain (Philippe), Pol Pot, Pombal (Sebastião de Carvalho, Marquês de), Rahman (Sheikh Mujibur), Rhodes (Cecil), Shamir (Yitzhak), Sharif (Nawaz), Sharon (Ariel), Thiers (Adolphe)
07 Berisha (Sali), Cresson (Édith), Gasperi (Alcide de), Halifax (Charles Montagu, Earl of), Haughey (Charles), Hertzog (J B M), Kosygin (Alexei), Lubbers (Ruud), Molotov (Vyacheslav), Nkrumah (Kwame), Nyerere (Julius), Vorster (John), Yeltsin (Boris)
08 Ben Bella (Ahmed), Bismarck (Otto, Fürst von), Bulganin (Nikolai), Daladier (Édouard), de Valera (Éamon), González (Felipe), Kenyatta (Jomo), Mahathir (bin Mohamad), Nakasone (Yasuhiro), Poincaré (Raymond), Pompidou (Georges), Quisling (Vidkun), Reynolds (Albert), Vajpayee (Atal Bihari), Verwoerd (Hendrik), Zapatero (José Luis Rodríguez)
09 Andreotti (Giulio), Ben-Gurion (David), Hashimoto (Ryutaro), Kim Il-sung, Kim Jong Il, Mussolini (Benito), Netanyahu (Binyamin), Stanishev (Sergei)
10 Balkenende (Jan Peter), Berlusconi (Silvio), Clemenceau (Georges), Fitzgerald (Garrett), Jaruzelski (Wojciech), Lee Kuan Yew
11 Verhofstadt (Guy)
12 Bandaranaike (S W R D), Chernomyrdin (Viktor)
13 Brookeborough (Basil Brooke, Viscount)

primer
05 Donat, Donet **06** manual **08** prodrome, textbook **09** absey-book, detonator, prodromus **12** introduction

primeval, primaeval
03 old **05** basic, early, first **06** inborn, innate, primal **07** ancient, natural, Ogygian **08** earliest, inherent, original **09** intuitive, primitial, primitive **10** primordial **11** instinctive, prehistoric **12** autochthonal

primitive
02 ur- **03** pro- **04** wild **05** crude, early, first, naive, rough **06** primal, savage, simple **07** ancient, natural, primary, radical **08** backveld, earliest, original, primeval **09** barbarian, primaeval **10** aboriginal, antiquated, elementary, primordial, uncultured **11** fundamental, rudimentary, uncivilized, undeveloped **12** antediluvian, old-fashioned, protomorphic **15** unsophisticated

primly
07 fussily **08** prissily, stuffily **09** prudishly

primordial
03 old **05** early, first **07** ancient **08** earliest, original, primeval **09** primaeval, primitive **11** instinctive, prehistoric, rudimentary **12** autochthonal, protomorphic

primp
04 tidy **05** groom, preen **06** doll up, tart up **07** brush up, dress up, smarten **08** beautify, spruce up, titivate

prince
01 P **02** Pr **03** mir, ras **04** amir, duke, khan, king, lord, raja, rana **05** ameer, chief, Mirza, nawab, nizam, queen, rajah, ruler, Tunku **06** leader, lucumo, potent, sharif, sherif, Tengku **07** infante, monarch, shereef **08** archduke, atheling, gospodar, hospodar, maharaja, tetrarch **09** Beelzebub, maharajah, potentate, princekin, princelet, royal duke, sovereign **10** princeling, Upper Roger **13** prince consort **14** porphyrogenite

Princes include:

03 Hal
04 Igor, Ivan, John (of Gaunt)
05 Edgar (the Atheling), Harry, Henry (the Navigator), James
06 Albert, Andrew, Arthur, Edward, Edward (the Black Prince), Philip
07 Charles, Michael (of Kent), Rainier, Richard, William
08 Llywelyn, Vladimir
09 Ferdinand
11 James Stuart
15 Alexander Nevski, Bernhard Leopold

Prince Edward Island
02 PE

princely
04 huge, vast **05** grand, noble, regal, royal **06** lavish, superb **07** immense, liberal, mammoth, massive, prenzie, stately **08** colossal, enormous, en prince, generous, glorious, handsome, imperial, imposing, majestic, splendid **09** bounteous, sovereign, sumptuous **10** impressive, large-scale, stupendous, tremendous **11** magnanimous, magnificent **12** considerable

princess
04 lady, rani **05** begum, ruler **07** infanta, monarch **09** potentate, sovereign **11** archduchess **13** crown princess

Princesses include:

02 Di
03 Ida
04 Anne
05 Alice, Diana, Fiona, Grace, Regan
06 Salome
07 Eudocia, Eugenie, Goneril, Jezebel, Matilda
08 Beatrice, Caroline, Cordelia, Margaret
09 Alexandra, Charlotte, Elizabeth, Stephanie
10 Pocahontas
11 Anna Comnena

principal
03 key **04** arch, boss, head, main **05** chief, first, major, money, prime, ruler **06** assets, leader, rector **07** capital, central, decuman, highest, leading, manager, primary, supreme, truncal **08** cardinal, director, dominant, especial, foremost, in charge, mistress **09** essential, paramount **10** capital sum, controller, headmaster, pre-eminent **11** controlling, head teacher **12** capital funds, headmistress **13** most important **14** superintendent

principality
05 duchy, realm, Wales **06** empire, Monaco, Orange **07** Andorra, dukedom, earldom, kingdom, Muscovy **08** dominion, Walachia **09** archduchy, princedom, sultanate, Wallachia **10** dependency, federation, grand duchy, palatinate, principate **11** archdukedom **12** protectorate **13** confederation, Liechtenstein

principally
06 mainly, mostly **07** chiefly **08** above all **09** capitally, in the main, primarily **10** especially **12** particularly **13** predominantly **14** for the most part

principle
03 key, law **04** code, germ, idea, root, rule, seed, soul **05** axiom, basis, canon, creed, dogma, geist, maxim, Sakti, tenet, truth **06** dictum, ethics, honour, morals, origin, reason, Shakti, source, spirit, theory, virtue **07** brocard, decency, element, formula, precept, probity, theorem **08** doctrine, morality, rudiment, scruples, standard **09** beginning, component, criterion, essential, headstone, institute, integrity, postulate, rationale, rectitude, standards **10** classicism, conscience, golden rule, groundwork, primordial, principium, seminality **11** fundamental, proposition, uprightness **12** classicalism

• in principle
07 ideally **08** in theory **09** in essence **10** en principe **13** theoretically

principled
04 just **05** moral **06** decent **07** ethical, upright **08** virtuous **09** righteous **10** high-minded, honourable, scrupulous **11** respectable, right-minded **13** conscientious

print
04 copy, etch, font, lith, mark, oleo, snap, type **05** fount, issue, mould, photo, stamp **06** design, record, run off, strike **07** bromide, edition, engrave, impress, imprint, letters, picture, publish, replica **08** aquatint, put to bed, register, snapshot, typeface **09** aquatinta, engraving, facsimile, footprint, lettering, newspaper, oleograph, reproduce, strike off **10** characters, exactitude, impression, lithograph, photograph, typescript **11** fingerprint **12** reproduction

See also **painter**

• in print
07 in stock **09** available, published **10** obtainable **13** in circulation

• out of print
02 op **07** sold out **10** out of stock **11** unavailable **12** off the market, unobtainable

printer
• instruction to printer
04 dele, hash, stet **05** caret

printing

Printing methods include:

03 CTP
05 laser, litho
06 ink-jet, offset, screen
07 etching, gravure
08 intaglio
09 bubble-jet, collotype, engraving
10 silk-screen, xerography
11 die-stamping, duplicating, flexography, letterpress, lithography, rotary press, stencilling, twin-etching
12 lino blocking, thermography
13 colour-process, electrostatic
14 photoengraving
15 computer-to-plate, copper engraving

Printing and publishing terms include:

02 em, en
03 CTP, TLS, TPS
04 bulk, case, CMYK, copy, demi, font, kern, laid, logo, sewn, stet, text, tint, trim, type, typo
05 bleed, caret, chase, cloth, cover, flong, forme, litho, moiré, press, proof, quoin, roman, widow, zinco
06 galley, gutter, indent, italic, jacket, mackle, margin, matrix, octavo, orphan, Ozalid®, quarto, take in, unsewn, web-fed
07 bromide, carding, cast-off, compose, dot gain, end even, foiling, leaders, leading, literal, opacity, Pantone®, reprint, strip in, woodcut
08 bad break, bold face, Linotype®, logotype, misprint, Monotype®, mottling, offprint, spoilage, strike-on, take over, typeface, type spec
09 backing-up, catchword, condensed, duodecimo, finishing, Intertype®, letterset, lower-case, makeready, newsprint, overprint, run-around, sans serif, signature, trim marks, type scale, upper-case, web offset
10 back margin, collograph, column inch, compositor, dot-etching, dustjacket, feathering, first proof, hard hyphen, imposition, impression, large print, manuscript, perfecting, ragged left, see-through, soft hyphen, stereotype, typescript
11 drum printer, electrotype, initial caps, line printer, ragged right, running head, running text, typesetting, typographer
12 author's proof, character set, expanded type, flat-bed press, inking roller, machine proof, registration, specimen page
13 composing room, cylinder press, image printing, justification, printing press, small capitals, wood engraving
14 relief printing, thermal printer
15 camera-ready copy

See also **typeface**

printmaker *see* **painter**

prior
05 elder **06** former **07** earlier **08** previous **09** foregoing, preceding **10** antecedent, magistrate

• prior to
03 pre **04** till, up to **05** until **06** before **09** preceding **11** earlier than, in advance of

priority
04 rank **07** the lead **09** essential, main thing, seniority, supremacy **10** first place, paramountcy, precedence, preference, right of way **11** pre-eminence, requirement, superiority **12** first concern, highest place, pole position, primary issue, top of the tree **13** supreme matter

priory
05 abbey **06** friary **07** convent, nunnery **08** cloister, priorate **09** béguinage, monastery **14** religious house

prise
03 pry **04** lift, move **05** force, hoist, jemmy, lever, raise, shift **06** winkle **08** dislodge, leverage, purchase

prison
03 bin, can, HMP, jug, pen, pit **04** bird, brig, cage, cell, coop, gaol, jail, nick, quad, quod, stir, tank **05** choky, clink, gulag, kitty, limbo **06** bagnio, chokey, cooler, inside, lock-up, lumber **07** bull pen, confine, custody, dungeon, enclose, hoosgow, slammer **08** bastille, big house, hoosegow, porridge, restrain, the hulks, the joint **09** bridewell, calaboose, detention, jailhouse, Lob's pound, massymore **10** guardhouse **11** confinement **12** imprisonment, penitentiary **15** detention centre

Prisons include:

04 Maze
05 Fleet, Pozzi
06 Albany, Attica, Folsom
07 Brixton, Feltham, Newgate
08 Alcatraz, Bastille, Belmarsh, Dartmoor, Holloway, Long Kesh, Lubyanka, Sing Sing
09 Fremantle, Parkhurst, the Scrubs
10 San Quentin, Wandsworth
11 Hanoi Hilton, Pentonville, Strangeways
12 Devil's Island, Rikers Island, Robben Island
13 Tower of London
14 Wormwood scrubs

prisoner
03 con, lag, POW **05** lifer, trust **06** détenu, inmate, old lag, trusty **07** captive, convict, culprit, détenue, hostage, passman **08** detainee, internee, jailbird, yardbird **10** recidivist **13** prisoner of war, state prisoner

prissily
06 primly **07** fussily **08** stuffily **09** prudishly

prissy
04 prim **05** fussy **06** demure, formal, proper, stuffy **07** finicky, po-faced, precise, prudish, starchy **08** priggish **09** squeamish **10** effeminate, fastidious, old-maidish, particular **11** puritanical, strait-laced **13** schoolmarmish

pristine
04 pure **05** clean, first, fresh **06** former, primal, unused, virgin **07** initial,

primary 08 earliest, original, primeval, unspoilt 09 primaeval, primitive, unchanged, undefiled, unspoiled, unsullied, untouched 10 immaculate, primordial 11 primigenial, uncorrupted

privacy
07 private, privity, retreat, secrecy
08 solitude 09 isolation, quietness, seclusion 10 retirement
11 concealment, privateness
12 independence 13 sequestration
15 confidentiality

private
03 own, Pte, Pvt 04 swad 05 alone, aside, close, privy, quiet, Tommy
06 closed, closet, gunner, hidden, remote, secret, swaddy 07 postern, privacy, soldier, special, squaddy
08 domestic, familiar, homefelt, hush-hush, intimate, isolated, personal, reserved, retiring, secluded, separate, singular, solitary, squaddie
09 concealed, exclusive, innermost, top secret, withdrawn 10 classified, commercial, free-market, individual, particular, privatized, privileged, unofficial 11 clandestine, enlisted man, independent, introverted, out-of-the-way, sequestered, Tommy Atkins, undisturbed 12 confidential, off the record 13 intraparietal, self-contained, self-governing, single soldier
14 denationalized, free-enterprise, private soldier 15 non-governmental, self-determining

• **in private**
07 sub rosa 08 in camera, in secret, secretly 09 privately 12 in confidence
14 confidentially 15 behind the scenes

• **private detective** *see* **detective**

privateer
06 marque, pirate 07 brigand, corsair, cruiser, sea wolf 09 buccaneer, sea robber 10 filibuster, freebooter

private eye *see* **detective**

privately
05 aside 06 inside, within 07 at heart, privily, sub rosa 08 deep down, in camera, in secret, inwardly, secretly
09 in private 10 personally, to yourself
12 in confidence, under the rose
13 deep inside you 14 confidentially

privation
04 lack, loss, need, want 06 misery, penury 07 poverty 08 distress, hardship 09 austerity, indigence, neediness, suffering 10 affliction
11 deprivation, destitution

privilege
03 due 05 honor, prise, right, title
06 honour, octroi, patent 07 benefit, faculty, freedom, liberty, licence
08 immunity, priority, sanction
09 advantage, authority, commodity, exemption, franchise 10 birthright, concession, seignorage 11 entitlement, prerogative, seigniorage
12 dispensation, status symbol

privileged
04 rich 05 élite 06 exempt, immune, ruling, secret 07 private, special, wealthy 08 excepted, favoured, honoured, hush-hush, powerful
09 chartered, indulgent, top secret
10 advantaged, authorized, classified, sanctioned, unofficial 12 confidential, off the record

privy
02 WC 03 bog, can, lav, loo 04 Ajax, kazi 05 dunny, gents', heads, jakes, siege 06 cloaca, closet, ladies', secret, toilet, urinal 07 cottage, crapper, draught, latrine, private
08 familiar, intimate, lavatory, rest room, washroom 09 cloakroom, garderobe 10 powder room, thunderbox 11 water closet 12 draught-house, smallest room 14 comfort station

• **privy to**
04 in on 06 wise to 07 aware of
09 clued up on 10 apprised of, genned up on 11 cognizant of 13 informed about 14 in the know about

prize
03 aim, cup, lot, pie, top 04 best, gain, goal, gree, hope, loot, love, palm, plum, tern 05 award, booty, great, honor, match, medal, plate, price, purse, stake, value 06 desire, esteem, honour, revere, reward, spoils, stakes, trophy 07 capture, cherish, jackpot, laurels, pennant, perfect, pillage, plunder, premium, seizure, winning
08 accolade, champion, hold dear, leverage, pickings, purchase, smashing, terrific, top-notch, treasure, winnings 09 excellent, first-rate, treasured 10 appreciate
11 outstanding, wooden spoon
12 award-winning, prize-winning
13 think highly of 14 out of this world
15 set great store by

See also **award**

prize-winner
03 dux 05 champ 06 winner
08 champion, prizeman 09 cup-winner, medallist 10 prizewoman

See also **Nobel Prize**

pro
03 ace, aye, for 06 expert, master, wizard 07 backing, dab hand, old hand
08 virtuoso 09 authority
10 consultant, in favour of, past master, prostitute, specialist, supporting
12 practitioner, probationary, professional

See also **prostitute**

probability
04 odds 06 chance 07 chances
08 prospect 10 likelihood, likeliness
11 expectation, possibility

probable
06 likely, odds-on 07 seeming 08 a fair bet, apparent, credible, expected, feasible, possible 09 plausible
10 believable, forseeable, on the cards
11 anticipated, predictable 12 to be expected

probably
04 like 05 maybe 06 belike, likely
07 perhaps 08 a fair bet, arguably, possibly 09 doubtless, like as not
10 most likely, presumably 11 as like as not, it looks like 13 as likely as not, the chances are 15 in all likelihood

probation
04 test 05 proof, trial 07 testing
09 noviciate 10 test period
11 supervision, trial period
14 apprenticeship

probationer
04 tiro 05 pupil 06 novice, rookie
07 amateur, learner, recruit, student, trainee 08 beginner, neophyte, newcomer, stibbler 09 greenhorn, noviciate 10 apprentice, raw recruit

probe
04 bore, feel, poke, prod, sift, tent, test
05 check, drill, plumb, sound, study, style 06 device, go into, pierce, search, stilet, stylet, tracer 07 analyse, examine, explore, inquest, inquire, inquiry 08 analysis, look into, research, scrutiny, searcher 09 penetrate
10 instrument, scrutinize
11 examination, exploration, investigate 13 investigation
14 scrutinization

Space probes include:

04 Luna
06 Viking
07 Galileo, Mariner, Pioneer, Voyager
09 Messenger
10 Deep Impact
14 Cassini–Huygens

probity
05 worth 06 equity, honour, virtue
07 honesty, justice 08 fairness, fidelity, goodness, morality 09 integrity, rectitude, sincerity 11 uprightness
12 truthfulness 13 righteousness
14 honourableness 15 trustworthiness

problem
◇ *anagram indicator*
02 BO 03 fix, sum 04 bore, boyg, drag, hole, knot, mess, pain, pest, prob, snag
05 facer, issue, poser, thing, worry
06 bother, enigma, hassle, indaba, matter, pickle, plight, puzzle, riddle, unruly 07 dilemma, toughie, trouble, wrinkle 08 irritant, nuisance, quandary, question, vexation
09 annoyance, conundrum, dichotomy, difficult, tight spot
10 conclusion, delinquent, difficulty, irritation, mind-bender 11 brainteaser, dire straits, disobedient, predicament, troublesome 12 brain-twister, complication, intransigent, recalcitrant, unmanageable
13 Chinese puzzle, inconvenience, pain in the neck 14 no-win situation, uncontrollable 15 thorn in your side

See also **economics**; **environment**

problematic
◇ *anagram indicator*
04 hard, moot **06** thorny, tricky **07** awkward, dubious **08** doubtful, involved, puzzling **09** debatable, difficult, enigmatic, intricate, uncertain **10** a minefield, perplexing **11** a can of worms, troublesome **12** questionable **13** problematical

procedure
02 op **03** way **04** move, play, step **05** drill, means **06** action, course, custom, fetich, fetish, method, policy, scheme, system **07** conduct, fetiche, formula, measure, process, routine, tactics **08** practice, strategy, technics **09** mechanics, operation, technique **11** advisedness, methodology, performance **12** plan of action **13** modus operandi **14** course of action

proceed
02 go, on **03** put **04** come, fand, flow, fond, go on, make, pass, rake, stem, sway, yead, yede, yeed **05** arise, begin, ensue, get on, issue, start, trace **06** come on, derive, follow, happen, move on, pass on, result, spring **07** advance, carry on, emanate, go ahead, press on, prosper **08** continue, progress **09** go forward, originate, prosecute, take steps **10** make a start **11** get under way, make your way, set in motion
- **proceed with difficulty**

04 limp

proceedings
04 acta, case, diet **05** deeds, moves, steps, trial **06** action, annals, doings, events, report **07** account, affairs, lawsuit, matters, minutes, process, records, reports **08** archives, business, dealings, measures, ongoings **10** activities, happenings, litigation, manoeuvres, operations, procedures **12** transactions **14** course of action

proceeds
04 gain **05** motza, yield **06** avails, income, motser, profit, return **07** produce, profits, returns, revenue, takings **08** earnings, receipts **12** intromission

process
◇ *anagram indicator*
03 way **04** mode, sort, step **05** alter, edict, means, stage, train, treat **06** action, change, course, growth, handle, manner, method, refine, system **07** advance, changes, convert, prepare **08** attend to, deal with, movement, practice, progress **09** evolution, formation, narrative, operation, procedure, technique, transform **10** proceeding **11** development, progression
- **in the process of**

05 being **11** in the making **13** in preparation, in the course of, in the middle of

procession
03 run **04** demo, file, pomp, walk **05** corso, march, train **06** column, course, exequy, parade, series, stream **07** cortège, funeral, pageant, triumph **08** Moharram, Muharram, Muharrem, progress, sequence **09** cavalcade, motorcade **10** succession **11** hunger march **13** demonstration, manifestation

proclaim
03 ask, bid, cry **04** ring, show, sing **05** knell, sound **06** affirm, blazon, herald, notify, out-ask, preach, summon **07** declare, enounce, give out, profess, protest, publish, testify, trumpet **08** announce, denounce, indicate **09** advertise, broadcast, circulate, make known, preconize, pronounce, show forth **10** annunciate, annuntiate, apostolize, promulgate **11** blaze abroad

proclamation
03 ban **04** oyes, oyez, rule **05** banns, edict, order **06** decree, notice **07** command, kerygma, placard **08** proclaim **09** broadcast, hue and cry, indiction, manifesto, preaching **11** affirmation, circulation, declaration, publication **12** announcement, annunciation, notification, promulgation, proscription **13** advertisement, order of the day, pronouncement **14** pronunciamento

proclivity
04 bent, bias **07** leaning **08** penchant, tendency, weakness **09** liability, proneness **10** liableness, propensity **11** disposition, inclination **12** predilection **14** predisposition

procrastinate
05 dally, defer, delay, stall **06** put off, retard **07** prolong **08** postpone, protract **09** temporize **10** dilly-dally **11** play for time **12** drag your feet

procrastination
08 deferral, delaying, stalling **10** cunctation **11** temporizing **12** dilatoriness **13** dilly-dallying **15** delaying tactics

procreate
04 sire **05** beget, breed, spawn **06** father, mother **07** produce **08** conceive, engender, generate, multiply **09** propagate, reproduce

proctor
04 prog **08** proggins

procure
03 buy, get, win **04** earn, find, gain, hire, hook, pimp, sort **05** ponce **06** come by, hustle, induce, obtain, pander, pick up, secure **07** acquire, provide, solicit **08** purchase **09** get hold of, importune **10** lay hands on **11** appropriate, requisition

procurer
04 bawd, hoon, mack, pimp **05** madam, ponce **06** broker, pander **07** hustler **08** fancy man, mackerel, panderer **09** procuress, solicitor **11** fleshmonger, whoremonger

prod
03 awl, dig, jab, job **04** brod, butt, goad, move, poke, push, spur, stir, urge **05** egg on, elbow, goose, nudge, prick, probe, punch, shove **06** incite, prompt, skewer, thrust **08** motivate, reminder, stimulus **09** encourage, prompting, stimulate **10** motivation **13** encouragement

prodigal
06 lavish, wanton, waster **07** copious, profuse, wastrel **08** profuser, reckless, spendall, unthrift, wasteful **09** bounteous, bountiful, excessive, exuberant, luxuriant, sumptuous, unsparing, unthrifty **10** big spender, immoderate, profligate, squanderer **11** extravagant, improvident, intemperate, spendthrift, squandering

prodigality
05 waste **06** excess, plenty, wastry **07** abandon, wastery **08** richness **09** abundance, amplitude, profusion **10** exuberance, lavishness, luxuriance, profligacy, wantonness **11** copiousness, dissipation, squandering **12** extravagance, immoderation, intemperance, recklessness, wastefulness **13** bounteousness, plenteousness, sumptuousness, unthriftiness

prodigious
04 huge, vast **05** giant **07** amazing, immense, mammoth, massive, unusual **08** abnormal, colossal, enormous, fabulous, gigantic, striking, terrific **09** fantastic, monstrous, startling, wonderful **10** astounding, gargantuan, impressive, inordinate, marvellous, miraculous, monumental, phenomenal, portentous, remarkable, staggering, stupendous, tremendous **11** exceptional, spectacular **12** immeasurable **13** extraordinary **14** flabbergasting

prodigiously
06 vastly **09** amazingly, immensely, massively, unusually **10** remarkably **11** wonderfully **12** astoundingly, impressively, phenomenally, staggeringly **13** exceptionally, fantastically, spectacularly

prodigy
05 freak **06** genius, marvel, phenom, rarity, wonder **07** miracle, monster, portent **08** moniment, monument, virtuoso, whizz kid **09** curiosity, sensation **10** mastermind, phenomenon, wonderwork, wunderkind **11** child genius, gifted child, phaenomenon, wonder child

produce
◇ *anagram indicator*
04 bear, crop, eggs, food, give, grow, kind, make, show **05** beget, breed, build, cause, crops, dig up, evoke, fruit,

issue, mount, offer, put on, raise, stage, stuff, throw, wheel, yield **06** create, direct, effect, extend, get out, invent, manage, output, put out, supply, upcome **07** advance, arrange, compose, deliver, develop, execute, exhibit, fashion, furnish, harvest, perform, prepare, present, product, proffer, provide, provoke **08** assemble, bring out, engender, generate, increase, knock out, occasion, organize, proceeds, products, put forth, result in **09** construct, fabricate, originate **10** bring about, bring forth, come up with, foodstuffs, give rise to, put forward, vegetables
11 commodities, demonstrate, give birth to, manufacture, put together
12 bring forward **13** dairy products

producer
04 hand **05** maker **06** farmer, grower
07 manager **08** director, generant
09 generator, presenter, régisseur
10 impresario, undertaker
12 manufacturer

See also **director**

product
04 item, work **05** fruit, goods, issue, wares, yield **06** effect, legacy, output, result, return, upshot **07** article, outcome, produce, spin-off
08 artefact, creation, offshoot **09** by-product, commodity, invention, offspring, outgrowth **10** end-product, production **11** consequence, merchandise, producement

production
◇ *anagram indicator*
04 film, play, show, work **05** drama, fruit, opera, revue, yield **06** fruits, making, output, return **07** concert, harvest, musical, returns, staging
08 assembly, building, creation, mounting **09** direction, extension, formation, producing **10** management
11 achievement, composition, development, fabrication, manufacture, origination, performance, preparation
12 construction, organization, presentation, productivity
13 manufacturing

productive
04 busy, rich **06** fecund, useful
07 fertile, gainful, teeming **08** creative, fructive, fruitful, pregnant, prolific, valuable, vigorous **09** effective, efficient, energetic, inventive, rewarding **10** beneficial, generative, profitable, worthwhile **11** increaseful, procreative **12** constructive, fructiferous, high-yielding

productivity
05 yield **06** output **08** capacity, work rate **10** efficiency, production
12 fruitfulness **14** productiveness

profanation
05 abuse **06** misuse **08** violence
09 blasphemy, sacrilege, violation
10 debasement, defilement, perversion **11** desecration
12 dishonouring

profane
03 lay **04** foul **05** abuse, crude
06 coarse, debase, defile, filthy, misuse, unholy, vulgar **07** abusive, godless, impious, pervert, pollute, secular, unclean, ungodly, violate, worldly **08** temporal **09** desecrate, misemploy **10** foul-spoken, idolatrous, irreverent, unhallowed
11 blasphemous, contaminate, foul-mouthed, irreligious **12** sacrilegious, unsanctified **13** disrespectful, unconsecrated

profanity
04 oath **05** abuse, curse **07** cursing, impiety **08** swearing **09** blasphemy, expletive, obscenity, sacrilege, swear-word **10** execration **11** imprecation, irreverence, malediction, profaneness
14 four-letter word

profess
03 own **04** aver, avow **05** admit, claim, state **06** affirm, allege, assert **07** certify, confess, confirm, declare, make out, pretend, purport **08** announce, maintain, proclaim **09** dissemble
10 lay claim to **11** acknowledge

professed
06 avowed **07** alleged, would-be
08 apparent, declared, so-called, supposed **09** certified, confirmed, pretended, purported, soi-disant
10 ostensible, proclaimed, self-styled
12 acknowledged **13** self-confessed

profession
03 job **04** line, post **05** claim, craft, trade **06** avowal, career, métier, office
07 calling **08** averment, business, position, pretence, vocation
09 admission, assertion, situation, statement, testimony **10** confession, employment, line of work, occupation, walk of life **11** affirmation, appointment, declaration
12 announcement
15 acknowledgement

professional
03 ace, pro **04** able **05** adept, buppy, maven, mavin, whizz, yuppy
06 expert, master, wizard, yuppie
07 dab hand, maestro, old hand, regular, skilful, skilled, trained
08 educated, licensed, masterly, virtuoso **09** authority, competent, dexterous, efficient, practised, qualified **10** consultant, past master, proficient, specialist **11** experienced
12 accomplished, businesslike, practitioner **13** knowledgeable

professor
02 RP **03** don, STP **04** dean, prof
05 chair, hodja, khoja **06** fellow, khodja, reader, regent **07** adjoint, provost **08** academic, emeritus, lecturer **09** principal **12** intellectual
13 head of faculty **14** vice chancellor

proffer
04 hand **05** offer **06** extend, submit, tender **07** advance, hold out, present, propose, suggest **09** volunteer

proficiency
05 knack, skill **06** talent **07** ability, aptness, finesse, mastery **08** aptitude
09 adeptness, dexterity, expertise, technique **10** capability, competence, experience **11** skilfulness
14 accomplishment

- **level of proficiency**

03 dan **05** grade

proficient
03 apt **04** able, wise **05** adept
06 clever, expert, gifted, useful
07 capable, skilful, skilled, trained
08 masterly, talented **09** competent, effective, efficient, qualified **10** past master **11** experienced
12 accomplished, passed master

profile
02 CV **04** biog, form, line, vita
05 cameo, chart, graph, lines, shape, study **06** figure, purfle, résumé, review, sketch, survey, talweg **07** contour, diagram, drawing, outline, thalweg
08 analysis, half-face, portrait, side view, template, vignette **09** biography, half-cheek **10** silhouette
11 description, examination
15 curriculum vitae, thumbnail sketch

- **high profile**

08 exposure **10** prominence, visibility
12 the limelight, the spotlight **15** public attention

- **keep a low profile**

06 lie low **12** escape notice, hide yourself **14** avoid publicity

profit
03 pay, use **04** boot, gain, gelt, perk, vail **05** avail, bonus, bunce, gravy, gross, serve, value, worth, yield
06 excess, income, margin, return
07 benefit, bestead, improve, killing, rake-off, revenue, surplus, takings, vantage **08** dividend, earnings, fast buck, increase, interest, proceeds, receipts, winnings **09** advantage, commodity, make money **10** bottom line, percentage, perquisite, usefulness
11 improvement **13** make megabucks
15 line your pockets, make loadsamoney

- **profit by, profit from**

03 use **04** milk **07** exploit, utilize
08 cash in on **12** capitalize on, put to good use **15** take advantage of, turn to advantage

- **share of profit**

03 lay

profitable
03 fat **05** juicy, utile **06** paying, plummy, useful **07** gainful, helpful, payable **08** behovely, economic, fruitful, valuable **09** available, expedient, lucrative, rewarding
10 beneficial, commercial, in the black, productive, successful, worthwhile
11 moneymaking **12** advantageous,

remunerative **13** advantageable, cost-effective

profitably
08 usefully, valuably **10** fruitfully **12** beneficially, commercially, economically, productively, successfully

profiteer
06 extort, fleece **07** exploit **09** exploiter, racketeer **10** overcharge **11** extortioner **12** extortionist **13** make a fast buck **14** make a quick buck

profiteering
09 extortion **10** Rachmanism **12** exploitation, racketeering

profitless
04 idle, vain **06** futile **07** useless **08** gainless, wasteful **09** fruitless, pointless, thankless, to no avail, worthless **10** unavailing **11** ineffective, ineffectual, to no purpose **12** unproductive, unprofitable **14** unremunerative

profligacy
05 waste **06** excess **09** abundance, depravity, profusion **10** corruption, debauchery, degeneracy, immorality, lavishness, wantonness **11** dissipation, libertinism, prodigality, promiscuity, squandering, unrestraint **12** extravagance, improvidence, recklessness, wastefulness **13** dissoluteness, unthriftiness **14** licentiousness

profligate
04 rake, roué **05** loose **06** wanton, waster, wicked **07** corrupt, Don Juan, immoral, wastrel **08** defeated, depraved, prodigal, reckless, wasteful **09** abandoned, debauched, debauchee, dissolute, excessive, libertine, reprobate **10** Corinthian, degenerate, dissipated, immoderate, iniquitous, licentious, overthrown, squanderer **11** extravagant, improvident, promiscuous, spendthrift, squandering **12** unprincipled

profound
03 sea **04** deep, wise **05** abyss, great, ocean **06** marked **07** erudite, extreme, intense, learned, radical, serious, sincere, weighty **08** absolute, abstruse, complete, esoteric, thorough **09** extensive, heartfelt, recondite, sagacious **10** deep-seated, discerning, exhaustive, thoughtful **11** far-reaching, penetrating **12** impenetrable **13** philosophical, thoroughgoing

profoundly
04 deep **06** deeply, keenly **07** acutely, greatly **08** heartily **09** extremely, intensely, seriously, sincerely **10** thoroughly

profundity
05 depth **06** acumen, wisdom **07** insight **08** learning, sagacity, severity, strength **09** erudition, extremity, intensity **11** penetration, perspicuity, seriousness **12** abstruseness, intelligence, perspicacity, profoundness **14** perceptiveness

profuse
04 rich **05** ample **06** lavish **07** copious, fulsome, liberal **08** abundant, generous **09** excessive, luxuriant, plentiful, unsparing **10** immoderate, inordinate, over the top, unstinting **11** extravagant, large-handed, overflowing **12** colliquative, overabundant **13** superabundant

profusely
08 lavishly **09** copiously, liberally **10** abundantly **11** unsparingly **12** immoderately, unstintingly **13** extravagantly

profusion
04 glut, lots, riot, tons **05** heaps, loads, waste **06** excess, lavish, plenty, wealth **07** surplus **08** plethora **09** abundance, multitude, plenitude **10** profligacy **11** copiousness, prodigality, superfluity **12** extravagance **13** unsparingness **14** superabundance

progenitor
05 stock **06** father, mother, parent, source, tupuna **07** founder **08** ancestor, begetter, forebear **09** precursor **10** antecedent, forefather, forerunner, instigator, originator, procreator **11** predecessor **12** primogenitor

progeny
04 burd, race, seed **05** breed, issue, stock, young **06** family, scions **07** lineage **08** children, increase, mokopuna **09** offspring, posterity, quiverful **10** generation **11** descendants

prognosis
07 outlook, surmise **08** forecast, prospect **09** diagnosis **10** assessment, evaluation, prediction, projection **11** expectation, forecasting, speculation **15** prognostication

prognosticate
05 augur **06** divine, herald **07** betoken, portend, predict, presage **08** forebode, forecast, foretell, indicate, prophesy, soothsay **09** harbinger **10** foreshadow

prognostication
04 omen **07** surmise **08** forecast, precurse, prophecy **09** horoscope, prejudice, prejudize, prognosis **10** prediction, projection **11** expectation, speculation

programme
04 book, list, plan, show **05** lay on **06** agenda, course, design, line up, line-up, map out, scheme **07** arrange, episode, itemize, listing, project, work out **08** calendar, schedule, syllabus **09** broadcast, formulate, simulcast, timetable **10** curriculum, prearrange, production, prospectus **11** performance **12** plan of action, presentation, transmission **13** order of events

See also **radio**; **television**

programming *see* **language**

progress
02 go **03** ren, rin, run, way **04** gain, go on, grow, sail **05** bloom, going **06** better, career, come on, course, growth, mature, thrive **07** advance, blossom, circuit, develop, headway, improve, journey, onwards, passage, proceed, prosper, recover, shape up, success **08** continue, distance, flourish, increase, movement, traverse **09** come along, evolution, go forward, promotion, upgrading **10** betterment, forge ahead, periegesis, proceeding, procession **11** advancement, development, improvement, make headway, make strides, make your way, move forward, progression, step forward **12** breakthrough, continuation, make progress, steps forward **14** be getting there **15** forward movement

• **in progress**
02 on **06** on foot **07** en train, going on, in train, on-going **08** on the way, under way **09** happening, occurring **10** continuing, proceeding **11** not finished, on the stocks **12** not completed **13** in preparation, in the pipeline

• **make progress**
04 roll

progression
05 chain, cycle, order, train **06** course, motion, series, stream, string **07** advance, headway, passage, process **08** movement, progress, pub-crawl, sequence **10** paraphonia, precession, resolution, succession **11** advancement, development **12** direct motion **15** forward movement

progressive
04 left, prog **06** modern **07** creator, deviser, dynamic, go-ahead, gradual, growing, liberal, pioneer, radical **08** advanced, left-wing, reformer **09** advancing, developer, innovator, reformist **10** avant-garde, continuing, developing, escalating, increasing, innovative, modernizer, originator **11** enlightened, trailblazer, up-and-coming **12** accelerating, enterprising, fresh thinker, intensifying **13** revolutionary **14** forward-looking **15** forward-thinking

progressively
07 forward **08** bit by bit, by stages, forwards, in stages **09** by degrees, gradually, piecemeal **10** step by step **12** hand over hand, increasingly **14** little by little

prohibit
03 ban, bar **04** stop, veto **06** defend,

enjoin, forbid, hamper, hinder, impede, outlaw **07** exclude, injunct, prevent, rule out **08** obstruct, preclude, restrict **09** interdict, proscribe

prohibited
05 taboo **06** banned, barred, vetoed **07** illegal **08** verboten **09** embargoed, forbidden, off-limits **10** contraband, disallowed, proscribed **11** interdicted

prohibition
03 ban, bar **04** tabu, veto **07** embargo, forbode **08** negation **09** exclusion, forbiddal, interdict **10** constraint, forbidding, injunction, prevention **11** forbiddance, obstruction, restriction **12** disallowance, interdiction, proscription

prohibitionist
03 dry **09** pussyfoot **11** teetotaller **12** abolitionist

prohibitive
05 steep **07** sky-high **09** excessive **10** exorbitant, forbidding, impossible, repressive **11** prohibiting, prohibitory, restraining, restrictive, suppressive **12** extortionate, preposterous, proscriptive

project
03 job, jut **04** cast, hurl, idea, kick, plan, sail, task, work **05** bulge, chuck, fling, gauge, jetty, throw **06** beetle, design, devise, expect, extend, intend, jut out, launch, map out, notion, propel, reckon, reflex, scheme, screen **07** obtrude, predict, propose, venture **08** activity, campaign, contract, estimate, exercise, forecast, outstand, overhang, proposal, protrude, stand out, stick out, workshop **09** calculate, discharge, programme **10** assignment, conception, enterprise, occupation **11** externalize, extrapolate, undertaking **12** predetermine

projectile
04 ball, bomb, shot **05** shell **06** bullet, mortar, rocket, tracer **07** grenade, missile **08** case-shot, fireball **09** ballistic, impelling **13** guided missile

projecting
05 proud **08** beetling, exserted **09** exsertile, extrusive, extrusory, obtrusive, prominent **10** protrudent, protruding, protrusive **11** overhanging, sticking out

• **projecting part**
03 arm, ear, fin **04** nose, tang

projection
03 cam, cog, jut, lug, nab, out, rag **04** beak, nose, peak, plan, sail, sill, spur, tusk **05** bulge, ledge, prong, ridge, sally, scrag, shelf, snout, spike, strap, tooth **06** calcar, corner, design, nozzle, outjet, outjut, relief, tongue **07** jutting, process **08** estimate, forecast, overhang, oversail, planning **09** dentation, reckoning **10** estimation, prediction, prominence, promontory **11** calculation, computation, excrescence, expectation, orthography **12** protuberance **13** extrapolation

proletarian
06 common **08** ordinary, plebeian **12** working-class

proletariat
03 mob **04** herd **05** plebs **06** lumpen, masses, proles, rabble **08** canaille, riff-raff **09** commoners, hoi polloi **10** commonalty **11** rank and file, third estate **12** common people, lower classes, working class **13** great unwashed

proliferate
05 breed **06** expand, extend, rocket, spread, thrive **07** build up, burgeon **08** escalate, flourish, increase, multiply, mushroom, snowball **09** intensify, reproduce **11** grow quickly **15** increase rapidly

proliferation
06 spread **07** build-up **08** increase **09** expansion, extension, rocketing **10** escalation **11** duplication, ecblastesis, mushrooming, snowballing **13** concentration, rapid increase **14** multiplication **15** intensification

prolific
04 rank **06** broody, fecund **07** copious, fertile, profuse **08** abundant, fruitful **09** luxuriant, plentiful **10** productive **11** fertilizing **12** reproductive

prolix
04 long **05** prosy, wordy **07** diffuse, lengthy, tedious, verbose **08** rambling, tiresome **09** prolonged, rigmarole **10** digressive, discursive, long-winded, pleonastic, protracted

prolixity
06 length **08** longueur, pleonasm, rambling, verbiage **09** prosiness, verbosity, wandering, wordiness **10** boringness **11** diffuseness, tediousness, verboseness **13** copia verborum **14** discursiveness, long-windedness

prologue
05 index, proem **07** preface, prelude **08** exordium, foreword, preamble **09** introduce, prooemion, prooemium **11** preliminary, prolegomena **12** introduction

prolong
05 delay **06** extend, linger **07** drag out, draw out, respite, spin out, stretch, sustain **08** continue, elongate, lengthen, postpone, prorogue, protract **10** perpetuate, stretch out

prolongation
04 tail **08** appendix, urostyle **09** extension, gonophore **10** androphore, carpophore, stretching, trichogyne **11** lengthening, protraction **12** continuation, perpetuation

promenade
04 pier, prom, turn, walk **05** front, mosey, paseo, strut **06** airing, parade, stroll **07** saunter, swagger, terrace, walkway **08** breather, seafront **09** boulevard, esplanade, polonaise, walkabout **10** sally forth **11** perambulate **14** constitutional

promethium
02 Pm

prominence
03 rib **04** boss, bump, crag, cusp, fame, hump, lump, name, note, rank, rise **05** bulge, cliff, crest, mound, torus **06** height, renown, rising, tragus, weight **07** jutting, mastoid, process, stature **08** eminence, emphasis, headland, pinnacle, prestige, standing, swelling **09** celebrity, elevation, greatness **10** antitragus, colliculus, embossment, importance, projection, prominency, promontory, protruding, reputation, top billing **11** distinction, pre-eminence **12** pride of place, protuberance **15** conspicuousness, illustriousness

• **into prominence**
02 up

prominent
03 top **04** main **05** A-list, chief, noted **06** famous, goggle, marked **07** bulging, eminent, jutting, leading, notable, obvious, popular, salient **08** beetling, foremost, renowned, striking **09** acclaimed, egregious, important, obtrusive, respected, to the fore, well-known **10** celebrated, jutting out, noticeable, pre-eminent, projecting, protrudent, protruding, protrusive **11** conspicuous, eye-catching, high-profile, illustrious, outstanding, protuberant, standing out, sticking out **12** unmistakable **13** distinguished, unmistakeable

promiscuity
06 laxity **09** depravity, looseness **10** debauchery, immorality, profligacy, protervity, wantonness **11** dissipation **13** dissoluteness **14** licentiousness, permissiveness, sleeping around

promiscuous
◇ *anagram indicator*
04 fast **05** loose, mixed, slack **06** casual, random, wanton **07** immoral **08** sluttish, swinging **09** abandoned, debauched, dissolute, haphazard **10** accidental, dissipated, licentious, profligate **12** of easy virtue **14** indiscriminate, sleeping around

promise
03 vow **04** avow, bond, hand, hete, hint, oath, sign, word **05** augur, flair, hecht, hight, swear, vouch **06** assure, behote, commit, denote, engage, hint at, pledge, plight, talent **07** ability, behight, betoken, betroth, compact, presage, signify, suggest, warrant **08** aptitude, contract, covenant, evidence, indicate, look like **09** assurance, be a sign of, committal,

guarantee, potential, undertake **10** capability, commitment, engagement, indication, suggestion, take an oath **11** expectation, undertaking **12** give your word, word of honour **13** pollicitation **15** give an assurance

• promised land

04 Zion **06** Canaan, heaven, Utopia **07** Elysium **08** El Dorado, paradise **09** Shangri-la **13** Elysian fields

See also **heaven**

promising

04 able, rosy **06** bright, gifted, likely **07** budding, hopeful **08** talented, towardly **09** favorable **10** auspicious, favourable, optimistic, propitious **11** encouraging, up-and-coming

promissory note

02 pn **03** IOU

promontory

03 hoe, nab **04** bill, cape, head, mull, naze, ness, spur **05** bluff, cliff, point, ridge **08** eminence, foreland, headland **09** peninsula, precipice **10** projection, prominence

promote

03 aid, ren, rin, run **04** back, help, hype, make, plug, push, sell, urge **05** boost, exalt, raise **06** assist, foster, honour, market, move up, peddle, prefer, puff up **07** advance, elevate, endorse, espouse, forward, further, nurture, sponsor, support, upgrade **08** advocate, champion **09** advertise, encourage, publicize, recommend, stimulate **10** aggrandize, popularize **11** merchandize **12** contribute to, kick upstairs

promoter

07 pleader, speaker, sponsor **08** advocate, champion, exponent, upholder **09** furtherer, projector, proponent, spokesman, supporter **10** campaigner, evangelist, vindicator **11** spokeswoman **12** spokesperson

promotion

02 ad **04** hype, puff, rise **05** promo **06** advert, move-up, payola, remove, urging **07** backing, puffery, pushing, support, venture **08** advocacy, boosting, campaign, espousal, plugging, speeding **09** elevation, fostering, marketing, prelation, publicity, upgrading **10** exaltation, preferment, propaganda **11** advancement, advertising, development, furtherance **12** contribution **13** advertisement, encouragement **14** aggrandizement, recommendation

prompt

02 OP **03** cue **04** help, hint, jolt, lead, make, move, prod, spur, urge **05** alert, cause, eager, early, frack, impel, quick, rapid, ready, sharp, swift **06** bang on, dead on, direct, elicit, incite, induce, on time, remind, speedy, spot-on, sudden, timely **07** exactly, inspire, instant, premove, produce, provoke, willing **08** expedite, motivate, occasion, on the dot, promptly, punctual, reminder, result in, stimulus **09** call forth, encourage, immediate, instigate, refresher, stimulate **10** give rise to, pernicious, punctually, responsive **11** expeditious, to the minute **12** unhesitating **13** encouragement, instantaneous

prompting

04 hint, urge **06** advice, motion, urging **07** jogging, pushing **08** pressing, pressure, prodding, reminder **09** influence, reminding **10** admonition, assistance, incitement, persuasion, protreptic, suggestion **13** encouragement

promptly

03 pdq, tit **04** asap, tite, tyte **05** sharp, tight **06** bang on, dead on, on time, pronto, spot-on, titely, yarely **07** exactly, lightly, quickly, smartly, swiftly **08** chop-chop, directly, on target, on the dot, speedily **09** forthwith, instantly, like a shot, posthaste, yesterday **10** punctually **11** immediately, to the minute **12** in short order **14** unhesitatingly, without more ado **15** before you know it, pretty damn quick

promptness

05 haste, speed **08** alacrity, dispatch **09** alertness, briskness, eagerness, quickness, readiness, swiftness **10** expedition **11** promptitude, punctuality, willingness

promulgate

05 issue **06** decree, notify, spread **07** declare, promote, publish **08** announce, proclaim **09** advertise, broadcast, circulate, make known, publicize **10** make public **11** communicate, disseminate

promulgation

08 issuance **11** declaration, publication, publicizing **12** announcement, proclamation, promulgating **13** communication, dissemination

prone

03 apt **04** bent, flat **05** eager, given, ready **06** homily, liable, likely **07** subject, tending, willing **08** disposed, face down, inclined, proclive **09** prostrate, recumbent, stretched **10** full-length, horizontal, procumbent, vulnerable **11** predisposed, susceptible

proneness

04 bent, bias **07** aptness, leaning **08** penchant, tendency, weakness **09** liability **10** proclivity, propensity **11** disposition, inclination **14** susceptibility

prong

03 tip **04** fang, fork, spur, tang, tine **05** grain, point, spike, tooth **10** projection

pronounce

◇ *homophone indicator*

03 say **04** give, pass, vote **05** judge, mouth, sound, speak, utter, voice **06** affirm, assert, decree, stress, tongue **07** bring in, declare, deliver, express **08** announce, proclaim, vocalize **09** enunciate **10** adjudicate, articulate

pronounceable

07 sayable, vocable **09** speakable, utterable **10** enunciable **11** articulable, expressible

pronounced

◇ *homophone indicator*

05 broad, clear, thick **06** marked, strong **07** decided, evident, obvious **08** definite, distinct, positive, striking, terrible **10** noticeable **11** conspicuous **12** unmistakable **13** unmistakeable

pronouncement

05 edict **06** decree, dictum **09** assertion, ipse dixit, judgement, manifesto, statement **11** declaration **12** announcement, notification, proclamation, promulgation **14** pronunciamento

pronunciation

06 accent, saying, speech, stress **07** diction, voicing **08** delivery, orthoepy, uttering **09** elocution, phonetics **10** inflection, intonation, modulation **11** enunciation **12** articulation, vocalization

proof

02 ap **04** pull, slip, test **05** assay, issue, prief, repro, tight **06** galley, priefe, strong, upshot **07** outcome, proofed, testing, treated, warrant, witness **08** argument, evidence **09** bombproof, fireproof, foolproof, leakproof, probation, rainproof, repellent, resistant, testimony, windproof **10** argumentum, childproof, experience, impervious, smoking gun, soundproof, validation, waterproof **11** attestation, bulletproof, tamperproof **12** confirmation, impenetrable, invulnerable, verification, weatherproof **13** certification, corroboration, demonstration, documentation **14** authentication, substantiation **15** impenetrability, invulnerability

• adduce as proof

04 cite

prop

03 leg, set **04** lean, post, rest, stay **05** brace, punch, rance, shaft, shore, sprag, staff, stand, stick, stilt, stoop, stoup, strut, stull, truss **06** anchor, brooch, column, crutch, hold up, pillar, steady, tiepin, uphold **07** balance, bolster, bunting, fulcrum, shore up, studdle, support, sustain, upright **08** buttress, mainstay, maintain, property, underpin, underset, upholder **09** bolster up, crippling, propeller, stanchion, supporter **10** underwrite **11** clothes-pole, point d'appui, proposition **14** flying buttress

propaganda
04 hype **08** Agitprop, ballyhoo **09** promotion, publicity **11** advertising, information **12** brainwashing **14** disinformation, indoctrination

propagandist
07 plugger **08** advocate, promoter **09** canvasser, proponent, publicist **10** evangelist **11** pamphleteer **12** hot gospeller, proselytizer **13** indoctrinator

propagandize
06 preach, uphold **07** promote, win over **08** advocate, argue for, champion, persuade, press for, talk into **09** brainwash, re-educate **10** pressurize **11** campaign for **12** indoctrinate

propagate
04 grow, pipe **05** beget, breed, layer, spawn **06** spread **07** diffuse, produce, promote, propage, provine, publish, traduce **08** generate, increase, multiply, proclaim, seminate, transmit **09** broadcast, circulate, procreate, publicize, reproduce **10** distribute, promulgate **11** communicate, disseminate, proliferate

propagation
06 spread **08** breeding, increase, spawning **09** diffusion, promotion, spreading **10** generation **11** circulation, procreation **12** distribution, promulgation, reproduction, transmission **13** communication, dissemination, proliferation **14** multiplication

propel
02 ca' **03** caa', leg, oar, row **04** loft, move, pole, pump, punt, push, sail, send, swim, waft **05** drive, force, impel, power, scull, shoot, shove, wheel **06** launch, paddle, thrust **07** project **09** frogmarch **11** push forward

propeller
03 fan **04** prop, vane **05** helix, rotor, screw **06** pusher **07** tractor **08** airscrew, thruster **09** tail rotor, tilt-rotor

propensity
04 bent, bias **06** foible **07** aptness, leaning **08** penchant, tendency, weakness **09** liability, proneness, readiness **10** proclivity **11** disposition, inclination **14** predisposition, susceptibility

proper
01 U **03** ain, due, own **04** prim, real, true, very **05** exact, right **06** actual, comely, decent, dueful, formal, goodly, kosher, polite, seemly, strict **07** correct, dewfull, fitting, genteel, genuine, gradely, precise, prudish, refined **08** accepted, accurate, decorous, graithly, ladylike, orthodox, peculiar, singular, suitable, thorough **09** befitting, out-and-out, shipshape **10** acceptable **11** appropriate, comme il faut, established, exceedingly, gentlemanly, respectable **12** conventional, well-becoming

properly
04 duly **05** right **07** exactly, gradely, rightly **08** actually, entirely, graithly, strictly, suitably **09** correctly, extremely, fittingly, precisely **10** acceptably, accurately, flawlessly, unerringly **11** faultlessly, respectably **13** appropriately **14** conventionally

• properly so called
04 true

property
03 fee **04** gear, land, mark, prop **05** acres, fonds, goods, house, means, quirk, trait **06** assets, estate, houses, living, riches, things, wealth **07** capital, clobber, effects, feature, fitness, holding, quality **08** chattels, holdings, premises **09** affection, attribute, buildings, ownership, propriety, resources, substance **10** belongings, real estate **11** appropriate, peculiarity, possessions **12** idiosyncrasy **13** individuality, paraphernalia **14** characteristic

prophecy
06 augury **07** message **08** forecast **09** preaching, prognosis **10** divination, prediction **11** second sight, soothsaying **12** vaticination **14** fortune-telling **15** prognostication

prophesy
05 augur **06** preach **07** foresee, predict **08** forecast, foretell, forewarn **10** vaticinate **13** prognosticate

prophet, prophetess
04 seer **05** sibyl **06** oracle **07** tipster, völuspa **10** forecaster, foreteller, soothsayer **11** clairvoyant, vaticinator **13** fortune-teller **14** prognosticator

Prophets and prophetesses include:

02 Is
03 Dan, Hag, Hos, Isa, Jer, Jon, Mic, Nah, Sam
04 Amos, Ezek, Joel, Obad, Zeph
05 Hosea, Jonah, Micah, Moses, Nahum
06 Barton (Elizabeth), Daniel, Elijah, Elisha, Haggai, Isaiah, Nathan, Samuel, St John
07 Ezekiel, Malachi, Obadiah
08 Jeremiah, Mohammed, Muhammad, Nehemiah
09 al-Mokanna, Zephaniah, Zoroaster
11 Zarathustra
12 the Nun of Kent
13 the Maid of Kent
14 John the Baptist

• prophet of doom
08 doomster, Jeremiah **09** Cassandra, doomsayer, pessimist **11** doomwatcher **12** doom merchant

prophetic
03 fey **05** vatic **06** mantic **07** augural, fateful **08** oracular **09** fatidical, oraculous, presaging, prescient, sibylline, vaticidal **10** divinatory, predictive, prognostic **11** apocalyptic, forecasting **13** foreshadowing

prophylactic
04 safe **06** condom, rubber, sheath **07** Femidom®, johnnie, scumbag, treacle **09** deterrent **10** inhibitory, precaution, pre-emptive, preventive, protective **11** obstructive **12** anticipatory, female condom, French letter, immunization, preservative, preventative **13** contraceptive, counteractive, precautionary, viper's bugloss

propinquity
03 tie **05** blood **07** kinship **08** affinity, nearness, relation, vicinity **09** adjacency, closeness, proximity **10** connection, contiguity **11** affiliation, kindredness, kindredship **12** relationship **13** consanguinity, neighbourhood

propitiate
06 pacify, soothe **07** appease, mollify, placate, satisfy **09** reconcile **10** conciliate

propitiation
09 atonement, pacifying, placation **11** appeasement, peacemaking **12** conciliation, pacification **13** mollification **14** reconciliation

propitiatory
08 soothing **09** appeasing, assuaging, expiatory, pacifying, placative, placatory **10** mollifying **11** peacemaking **12** conciliatory, pacificatory, propitiative **14** reconciliatory

propitious
04 rosy **05** happy, lucky **06** benign, bright, kindly, timely **08** friendly, gracious **09** favorable, fortunate, opportune, promising, wholesome **10** auspicious, beneficial, benevolent, favourable, prosperous, reassuring **11** encouraging **12** advantageous, well-disposed

proponent
06 backer, friend, patron **08** advocate, champion, defender, exponent, favourer, partisan, proposer, upholder **09** apologist, proposing, supporter **10** enthusiast, propounder, subscriber, vindicator

proportion
03 cut **04** bulk, mass, part, size **05** depth, quota, ratio, scale, share, split, whack, width **06** amount, extent, height, length, volume **07** analogy, balance, breadth, measure, portion, segment **08** capacity, division, fraction, graduate, quotient, symmetry **09** magnitude **10** dimensions, percentage **11** temperature **12** distribution, measurements, relationship **14** correspondence, slice of the cake

proportional
04 even **08** logistic, relative, relevant **09** analogous, equitable **10** comparable, consistent, equivalent, logistical **12** commensurate **13** corresponding, proportionate

proportionally
06 evenly 07 pro rata 10 comparably, relatively 14 commensurately 15 correspondingly, proportionately

proposal
03 bid 04 plan 05 offer, terms 06 design, motion, scheme, tender 07 project 08 overture, supposal 09 manifesto, programme 10 resolution, suggestion 11 proposition 12 presentation 14 recommendation

propose
03 aim, bid, pop 04 face, mean, moot, move, name, plan, talk, vote 05 offer, place, put up, slate, table 06 design, intend, motion, submit, tender 07 advance, bethink, bring up, imagine, present, proffer, propone, purpose, suggest, suppose 08 advocate, converse, nominate, propound, put forth 09 discourse, enunciate, introduce, recommend 10 ask to marry, have in mind, put forward 14 pop the question 15 plight your troth

proposition
03 job 04 pass, plan, prop, task 05 offer 06 accost, come-on, motion, scheme, tender, theory 07 advance, premise, project, solicit, theorem, venture 08 activity, approach, disjunct, overture, proposal 09 alternant, manifesto, programme, universal 10 hypothesis, suggestion 11 make a pass at, subcontrary, undertaking 14 recommendation

propound
03 put, set 04 move, pose 06 submit 07 advance, contend, lay down, present, propone, propose, purpose, suggest 08 advocate, set forth 09 postulate 10 put forward

proprietary
03 pty

proprietor, proprietress
04 lord 05 owner 06 patron 07 esquire 08 landlady, landlord, zemindar 09 landowner, possessor, publisher 10 deed holder, freeholder, landholder 11 leaseholder, proprietrix, title-holder 12 entrepreneur
See also **newspaper**

propriety
05 mense 07 aptness, decency, decorum, fitness, manners, modesty, p's and q's, quality 08 breeding, civility, courtesy, delicacy, elegance, elegancy, property, protocol, standard 09 character, etiquette, ownership, punctilio, rectitude, rightness 10 bienséance, convention, politeness, refinement, seemliness 11 correctness, good manners 12 becomingness, ladylikeness, social graces, suitableness, the done thing 14 respectability, social niceties 15 appropriateness, gentlemanliness

propulsion
04 push 05 drive, power 06 thrust 07 impetus, impulse 08 momentum, pressure, traction 09 impulsion 10 propelment 11 motive force 12 driving force

pro rata
06 evenly 10 comparably, relatively 14 commensurately, proportionally 15 correspondingly, proportionately

prosaic
03 dry 04 dull, flat, tame 05 banal, bland, stale, trite, vapid 06 boring 07 humdrum, mundane, routine, vacuous 08 everyday, ordinary, workaday 09 hackneyed 10 monotonous, pedestrian, uninspired, unpoetical 11 commonplace, uninspiring 12 matter-of-fact 13 unimaginative

prosaically
05 dully 07 blandly 09 mundanely 10 ordinarily 12 monotonously 13 uninspiringly 15 unimaginatively

proscribe
03 ban, bar 04 damn, doom 05 black, exile, expel 06 banish, deport, forbid, outlaw, reject 07 boycott, censure, condemn, embargo, exclude 08 denounce, disallow, prohibit 09 blackball, interdict, ostracize 10 expatriate 13 excommunicate

proscription
03 ban, bar 05 exile 07 barring, boycott, censure, damning, embargo 08 ejection, eviction, outlawry 09 exclusion, expulsion, interdict, ostracism, rejection 10 banishment 11 deportation, prohibition 12 condemnation, denunciation, expatriation, proclamation 15 excommunication

prosecute
02 do 03 sue, try 05 chase 06 accuse, charge, indict, pursue, summon 07 arraign, proceed, process 08 litigate 10 put on trial 11 take to court 12 bring charges 13 prefer charges

prosecution
05 trial 08 charging 10 accusation, indictment, litigation 11 impeachment 13 taking to court 15 bringing charges

prosecutor
02 DA, PF 06 fiscal 08 quaestor 10 avvogadore 11 prosecutrix 12 Lord Advocate 13 judge advocate 14 advocate-depute

proselyte
07 convert, recruit 08 neophyte 09 new person 10 catechumen 11 new believer 13 changed person

proselytize
07 convert, win over 08 persuade 10 bring to God, evangelize 12 make converts, propagandize 15 spread the gospel

Proserpina
10 Persephone

prosody

Prosody terms include:

04 foot, iamb
05 canto, envoy, epode, ictus, Ionic, metre, paeon
06 choree, dactyl, dipody, dizain, laisse, miurus, rondel, sonnet
07 ballade, caesura, couplet, distich, elision, pantoum, pyrrhic, rondeau, Sapphic, spondee, strophe, triolet, tripody, triseme, trochee, virelay
08 anapaest, choriamb, cinquain, eye rhyme, Pindaric, quatrain, tribrach, trimeter
09 anacrusis, assonance, catalexis, dispondee, ditrochee, free verse, half-rhyme, hexameter, macaronic, monometer, monorhyme, rime riche, tetrapody
10 amphibrach, amphimacer, blank verse, consonance, enjambment, galliambic, heptameter, pentameter, rhyme royal, tetrameter, villanelle
11 Alcaic verse, alexandrine, broken rhyme, linked verse, long-measure, septenarius
12 alliteration, antibacchius, Leonine rhyme, Pythian verse, sprung rhythm
13 abstract verse, feminine rhyme, heroic couplet, hypermetrical, internal rhyme
14 feminine ending, masculine rhyme, rime suffisante
15 feminine caesura, masculine ending, poulters' measure

prospect
04 face, hope, nose, odds, seek, view 05 quest, scene, sight, vista, visto 06 aspect, chance, future, search, survey 07 chances, examine, explore, fossick, inspect, look for, lookout, opening, outlook, promise 08 belle vue, likeness, panorama 09 landscape, spectacle, viewpoint 10 likelihood 11 expectation, opportunity, perspective, possibility, probability 12 anticipation

prospective
04 -to-be 06 coming, future, likely 07 awaited, would-be 08 aspiring, destined, expected, hoped-for, imminent, intended, possible, probable 09 designate, potential 11 anticipated, approaching, forthcoming

prospectus
04 list, plan 06 scheme 07 leaflet, outline 08 brochure, pamphlet, syllabus, synopsis 09 catalogue, manifesto, programme 10 conspectus, literature 11 description 12 announcement

prosper
04 boom, thee 05 bloom, get on 06 do well, flower, thrive 07 advance, blossom, burgeon, proceed, succeed 08 flourish, get ahead, grow rich, progress 09 get on well 11 turn out well

12 be successful, make progress, make your pile 13 hit the big time, hit the jackpot 14 go up in the world 15 get on in the world

prosperity
04 boom, good 06 clover, luxury, plenty, riches, thrift, wealth 07 fortune, success, welfare 08 sunshine
09 affluence, wellbeing 10 bed of roses, easy street 11 good fortune, lap of luxury, the good life 14 the life of Riley
• **spell of prosperity**
02 up 04 boom

prosperous
04 fair, rich 05 blest, lucky, sleek
06 well in 07 blessed, bonanza, booming, opulent, thrifty, wealthy, well-off 08 affluent, blooming, thriving, well-to-do 09 fortunate
10 burgeoning, felicitous, successful, well-heeled, well-to-live
11 flourishing, rolling in it

prostitute
03 pro, pug, tom 04 bawd, dell, drab, moll, punk, road, stew, tart 05 brass, broad, poule, quail, quiff, stale, tramp, trull, wench, whore 06 betray, bulker, callet, debase, demean, floosy, floozy, geisha, harlot, hooker, misuse, mutton, plover 07 cheapen, cocotte, degrade, devalue, floosie, floozie, hetaera, hetaira, hostess, hustler, lorette, pervert, polecat, profane, rent-boy, trollop, venture 08 bona-roba, call-girl, dolly-mop, magdalen, misapply, strumpet 09 courtesan, courtezan, hackneyed, hierodule, loose fish, mercenary, sacrifice, sex worker
10 cockatrice, convertite, fancy woman, loose woman, rough trade, vizard-mask 11 fallen woman, fille de joie, laced mutton, night-walker, poule de luxe, public woman, working girl
12 fille des rues, scarlet woman, street-walker 13 grande cocotte
14 lady of the night, woman of the town

prostitution
04 vice 07 the game, whoring
08 harlotry, whoredom 10 social evil
13 street-walking

prostrate
03 sap 04 fell, flat, laid, ruin, tire 05 all-in, crush, drain, level, prone 06 bushed, fallen, lay low, pooped 07 crushed, exhaust, fatigue, flatten, laid low, wear out, whacked, worn out 08 dead beat, flatling, flatlong, helpless, overcome, tired out, trailing 09 exhausted, flatlings, knock down, lying down, lying flat, overthrow, overwhelm, paralysed, pooped out, powerless 10 devastated, horizontal, procumbent
11 defenceless, overwhelmed, tuckered out
• **prostrate yourself**
05 kneel 06 cringe, grovel, kowtow, submit 07 bow down 13 abase yourself

prostration
03 bow 05 grief 06 kowtow
07 despair 08 collapse, kneeling, weakness 09 abasement, dejection, obeisance, paralysis, weariness
10 depression, desolation, exhaustion, submission 11 despondency
12 genuflection, helplessness
15 slough of despond

protactinium
02 Pa

protagonist
04 hero, lead 06 banker, leader
07 heroine 08 adherent, advocate, champion, exponent, mainstay
09 principal, proponent, supporter, title role 10 prime mover 12 moving spirit 13 leading figure, leading player, main character 14 chief character, standard-bearer

protean
◇ *anagram indicator*
07 amoebic, mutable 08 variable, volatile 09 many-sided, mercurial, multiform, versatile 10 changeable, inconstant 11 polymorphic 12 ever-changing, polymorphous

protect
◇ *containment indicator*
04 keep, save 05 cover, guard
06 defend, escort, screen, secure, shield 07 buckler, care for, harbour, shelter, support, warrant 08 bestride, conserve, enshield, keep safe, preserve, savegard 09 look after, ring-fence, safeguard, watch over
10 overshadow, strengthen, take care of

protected
06 immune

protection
03 lee 04 care, egis, ward, wing
05 aegis, bield, cover, guard
06 armour, asylum, buffer, charge, refuge, safety, screen, shield 07 barrier, buckler, bulwark, custody, defence, defense, shelter 08 security, umbrella, wardship 09 insurance, patronage, safeguard 11 concubinage, defensative, maintenance, safekeeping
12 conservation, entrenchment, guardianship, intrenchment, preservation
• **in protection from**
04 agin 07 against

protective
04 wary 06 condom 07 careful
08 armoured, covering, fatherly, maternal, motherly, paternal, vigilant, watchful 09 defensive, fireproof, shielding, windproof 10 insulating, possessive, sheltering, waterproof
14 over-protective

protector
03 pad 04 faun 05 guard 06 buffer, father, keeper, minder, patron, regent, screen, shield 07 bolster, buckler, counsel, cushion, gardant
08 advocate, champion, Cromwell, defender, guardant, guardian, pectoral
09 bodyguard, safeguard
10 benefactor, protectrix 11 patron saint, protectress 12 father-figure

protégé, protégée
04 ward 05 pupil 06 charge 07 student
08 disciple, follower 09 dependant, discovery 11 blue-eyed boy 14 white-headed boy

protein

Proteins include:

03 TSP, TVP
04 zein
05 abrin, actin, opsin, prion, renin
06 avidin, casein, cyclin, enzyme, fibrin, globin, gluten, kinase, lectin, leptin, myosin, papain, pepsin, rennin
07 albumen, albumin, elastin, gliadin, histone, hordein, insulin, plasmin, sericin, trypsin, tubulin
08 aleurone, amandine, collagen, cytokine, ferritin, gliadine, globulin, glutelin, integrin, lysozyme, protease, thrombin
09 apoenzyme, fibrillin, invertase, isomerase, luciferin, myoglobin, phaseolin, prolamine, protamine, sclerotin
10 calmodulin, complement, conchiolin, dystrophin, factor VIII, fibronogen, interferon
11 angiostatin, angiotensin, haemoglobin, interleukin, lipoprotein, plasminogen, transferrin, tropomyosin
12 immunoglobin, neurotrophin, proteoglycan
13 ceruloplasmin, lactoglobulin

protest
03 vow 04 avow, demo, fuss, riot
05 abhor, argue, demur, gripe, hikoi, march, sit in, sit-in 06 affirm, appeal, assert, attest, avowal, insist, object, obtest, oppose, outcry, picket, reject, squawk, strike, whinge, work-in
07 boycott, contend, declare, dissent, profess, reclaim, scruple, testify
08 announce, complain, demurral, disagree, insist on, maintain, proclaim, speak out 09 assertion, complaint, deprecate, down tools, exception, objection, take issue 10 contention, disapprove, go on strike, opposition, work to rule, work-to-rule
11 affirmation, attestation, declaration, demonstrate, disapproval, kick up a fuss, mass meeting, remonstrate
12 announcement, disagreement, hunger strike, proclamation, protestation, remonstrance
13 demonstration, remonstration, take exception
• **expression of protest**
01 O 02 oh 03 say, why 04 come, I say!, what 07 come now 08 come come

protestation
03 vow 04 oath 06 avowal, outcry, pledge 07 dissent, protest

09 assurance, complaint, objection, statement, testimony 10 profession 11 affirmation, declaration 12 asseveration, disagreement, remonstrance 13 expostulation, remonstration

protester
05 rebel 06 picket 07 opposer, striker 08 agitator, mutineer, objector, opponent 09 dissenter, dissident 10 complainer 11 Remonstrant 12 demonstrator

protocol
02 IP 03 FTP, TCP, WAP 04 HTTP, IMAP, kawa, MIDI 05 TCP/IP 06 custom 07 decorum, manners, p's and q's 08 good form 09 etiquette, procedure, propriety 10 civilities, convention 11 formalities 15 code of behaviour

prototype
04 type 05 model 06 mock-up 07 example, pattern 08 exemplar, original, paradigm, standard 09 archetype, precedent

protract
06 extend, linger 07 drag out, draw out, prolong, spin out, sustain 08 continue, lengthen, postpone, protrude 09 keep going 10 make longer, stretch out

protracted
04 long 07 endless, lengthy, spun out 08 drawn-out, extended, livelong, overlong 09 postponed, prolonged 12 interminable, long-drawn-out, stretched out

protrude
03 jut, pop 04 peer, poke, pout 05 bulge, stick, strut 06 beetle, exsert, extend, goggle, jut out, strout 07 extrude, obtrude, poke out, project 08 protract, stand out, stick out 11 come through

protruding
05 goofy, proud 06 astrut 07 jutting 09 exsertive, extrusive, extrusory, obtrusive, prominent, underhung 10 jutting out, protrudent, protrusive 11 protuberant, sticking out

protrusion
03 jag, jut 04 bump, knob, lump 05 bulge 06 hernia 07 pedicle, process 08 shoulder, swelling 09 obtrusion, outgrowth 10 projection, staphyloma 11 cephalocele, eventration, meningocele 12 exophthalmia, exophthalmos, exophthalmus, protuberance 13 encephalocele

protuberance
03 bud, nub 04 ball, boss, bulb, bump, hump, knap, knob, lump, nurl, teat, wame, wart, welt 05 bulge, caput, ergot, gemma, inion, knurl, mount, nodus, tuber, whelk 06 casque, nipple, paunch, pimple, tumour, venter, wallet 07 condyle, crankle, mamelon, mamilla, papilla, process 08 mammilla, pot-belly, swelling, tubercle 09 apophysis, beer belly, outgrowth 10 bulging-out, projection, prominence, protrusion 11 excrescence

protuberant
04 full 05 proud 06 astrut, rotund 07 bottled, bulbous, bulging, bunched, gibbous, jutting, popping, swollen 08 beetling, swelling 09 exsertive, extrusive, extrusory, prominent 10 protrudent, protruding, protrusive

proud
04 brag, glad, smug, vain 05 cocky, dicty, grand, happy, noble, stout 06 dickty, lordly, snooty, superb, worthy 07 content, haughty, jutting, notable, pleased, pompous, stately, stuck-up, sublime 08 arrogant, boastful, fearless, glorious, honoured, imposing, jumped-up, misproud, pleasing, proudful, puffed up, scornful, snobbish, splendid, swelling, thrilled, top-proud 09 bigheaded, cockhorse, conceited, contented, delighted, dignified, gratified, hubristic, imperious, memorable, prominent, red-letter, satisfied, untamable, wonderful 10 complacent, gratifying, high-handed, honourable, jutting out, marvellous, projecting, satisfying 11 egotistical, magnificent, outstanding, overbearing, overweening, protuberant, sticking out, toffee-nosed, walking tall 12 high-spirited, presumptuous, supercilious 13 high and mighty, self-important, self-satisfied 14 full of yourself, self-respecting

proudly
04 brag 06 smugly, vainly 08 snootily 09 haughtily 10 arrogantly, boastfully 11 bigheadedly, conceitedly, contentedly, delightedly, with delight 14 appreciatively

provable
08 testable 09 evincible 10 attestable, verifiable 11 confirmable 12 corroborable, demonstrable 13 establishable

prove
03 try 04 shew, show, test, trie 05 argue, check 06 attest, pan out, prieve, suffer, try out, verify 07 analyse, bear out, certify, confirm, darrain, darrayn, deraign, examine, justify, make out, qualify, stand up, turn out 08 darraign, darraine, document, evidence, validate 09 ascertain, be the case, bring home, come about, darraigne, determine, establish, eventuate, transpire 10 experience 11 corroborate, demonstrate 12 authenticate, substantiate 13 bear witness to

proven
05 tried, valid 06 proved, tested 07 checked 08 accepted, attested, definite, reliable, verified 09 authentic, certified, confirmed, undoubted 10 dependable 11 established, trustworthy 12 corroborated

provenance
06 origin, source, spring 10 birthplace, derivation 11 provenience

provender
03 kai 04 chow, eats, fare, feed, food, grub, nosh, tuck 05 scoff 06 fodder, forage, stores, tucker, viands 07 aliment, edibles, pabulum, pasture, provand, provend, rations 08 eatables, proviant, supplies, victuals 09 groceries, repasture 10 foodstuffs, provisions, sustenance 11 comestibles

proverb
03 saw 05 adage, axiom, gnome, maxim, motto 06 byword, dictum, saying 07 parable, precept 08 aphorism, paroemia 10 apophthegm, whakatauki

proverbial
05 famed 06 famous 07 typical 08 accepted, infamous, renowned 09 axiomatic, customary, legendary, notorious, well-known 10 archetypal 11 traditional 12 acknowledged, conventional, time-honoured

provide
◇ *anagram indicator*
02 do 03 add 04 give, lend, suit 05 allow, besee, bring, cater, equip, lay on, offer, put on, serve, state, stock, yield 06 afford, fit out, impart, kit out, outfit, purvey, supply 07 compare, furnish, lay down, plan for, prepare, present, require, specify 09 stipulate, take steps 10 anticipate, arrange for, contribute, prepare for 11 accommodate 12 make plans for, take measures 13 make provision 15 take precautions

• **provide for**
04 fend, keep 05 besee, cover, do for, endow 07 support, sustain 08 maintain 09 look after 10 take care of

provided
02 so 05 given 06 sobeit 08 as long as, assuming, so long as 09 presuming 10 in the event 11 on condition 14 with the proviso

providence
04 care, fate, luck 06 thrift, wisdom 07 caution, destiny, economy, fortune 08 disaster, God's will, prudence, sagacity 09 foresight, judgement 11 forethought 13 judiciousness 14 circumspection, far-sightedness

provident
06 frugal 07 careful, prudent, thrifty 08 cautious 09 judicious, sagacious 10 economical, far-sighted 11 circumspect

providential
05 happy, lucky 06 timely 07 welcome 09 fortunate, opportune 10 convenient, fortuitous, heaven-sent

providentially
07 happily, luckily **11** coveniently, fortunately, opportunely
12 fortuitously

provider
05 angel, donor, giver **06** earner, funder, patron, source **07** sponsor
08 mainstay, supplier **09** supporter
10 benefactor, wage-earner
11 breadwinner

providing
02 if **05** given **08** as long as, assuming, provided **09** presuming **10** in the event
11 on condition **14** with the proviso

province
04 area, dorp, duty, line, nome, role, zone **05** field, realm, reame, shire, state
06 charge, circar, colony, county, domain, office, pigeon, region, sircar, sirkar, sphere **07** concern, eparchy, mudiria, rectory, satrapy, vilayet
08 business, district, function, mudirieh **09** backwater, backwoods, eparchate, territory, the sticks
10 department, dependency, the boonies **12** patriarchate, the boondocks **14** responsibility
15 middle of nowhere

Canadian provinces and territories:

05 Yukon
06 Quebec
07 Alberta, Nunavut, Ontario
08 Labrador, Manitoba
10 Nova Scotia
12 New Brunswick, Newfoundland, Saskatchewan
14 Yukon Territory
15 British Columbia
18 Prince Edward Island
20 Northwest Territories
23 Newfoundland and Labrador

Ireland's ancient provinces:

06 Ulster
07 Munster
08 Connacht, Leinster

New Zealand provinces:

05 Otago
06 Nelson
08 Auckland, Taranaki, Westland
09 Fiordland, Hawke's Bay, Northland, Southland
10 Canterbury, Wellington
11 Marlborough

South African provinces:

07 Gauteng, Limpopo
09 Free State, North West
10 Mpumalanga
11 Eastern Cape, Western Cape
12 KwaZulu-Natal, Northern Cape

provincial
04 hick **05** local, naive, rural, yokel
06 narrow, rustic **07** country, hayseed, insular, limited, peasant **08** mofussil, outlying, regional, suburban
09 hillbilly, home-grown, parochial, presidial, small-town **10** intolerant, parish-pump, unpolished **11** small-minded **12** narrow-minded **13** inward-looking **14** country bumpkin
15 unsophisticated

provincialism
08 localism **10** insularity, Patavinity
11 regionalism **12** parochialism, sectionalism **13** provinciality

provision
04 food, plan, step, term **05** rider, stock, store, stuff **06** clause, giving, stocks, stores, supply, viands
07 measure, proviso, rations, service
08 eatables, services, supplies, victuals
09 allowance, amenities, condition, equipping, foodstuff, groceries, resources, stouthrie **10** concession, facilities, furnishing, outfitting, precaution, stoutherie, sustenance
11 arrangement, contingency, preparation, requirement, stipulation
12 contribution **13** qualification, specification

provisional
05 Provo **06** pro tem **07** interim, stopgap **09** makeshift, temporary, tentative **11** conditional, pencilled in
12 transitional

provisionally
06 pro tem **07** interim **09** meanwhile
11 temporarily, tentatively **15** for the time being

proviso
04 term **05** rider **06** clause **07** strings
09 condition, provision **10** limitation
11 requirement, reservation, restriction, stipulation **13** qualification

provocation
04 dare **05** cause, taunt **06** injury, insult, motive, reason **07** affront, grounds, offence **08** angering, enraging, stimulus, vexation
09 annoyance, challenge, eliciting, grievance **10** generation, incitement, inducement, irritation, motivation, production **11** aggravation, inspiration, instigation, stimulation
12 exasperation **13** justification

provocative
04 sexy **05** tarty **06** erotic **07** abusive, galling, piquant, teasing **08** alluring, annoying, arousing, exciting, inviting, tempting **09** insulting, in-yer-face, offensive, seductive **10** in-your-face, irritating, outrageous, suggestive
11 aggravating, challenging, infuriating, stimulating, tantalizing, titillating
12 exasperating

provocatively
06 sexily **08** sexually **10** alluringly, annoyingly, erotically, invitingly, temptingly **11** offensively, seductively
12 outrageously, suggestively
13 infuriatingly **14** exasperatingly

provoke
03 bug, vex **04** goad, miff, move, nark, prod, rile, spur, stir **05** anger, annoy, cause, egg on, evoke, get at, pique, rouse, sound, taunt, tease **06** appeal, elicit, enrage, entice, excite, harass, hassle, incite, induce, insult, kindle, madden, needle, nettle, offend, prompt, summon, wind up **07** incense, inflame, inspire, produce, promote
08 drive mad, engender, generate, irritate, motivate, occasion
09 aggravate, call forth, challenge, infuriate, instigate, stimulate, tantalize
10 drive crazy, exacerbate, exasperate, give rise to **12** drive bananas **13** make sparks fly **14** drive up the wall

provoking
06 irking, vexing **07** agaçant, galling, irksome **08** agaçante, annoying, tiresome **09** maddening, offensive, vexatious **10** irritating **11** aggravating, infuriating, obstructive, stimulating
12 exasperating

prow
03 bow **04** bows, fore, head, nose, ship, stem **05** front, prore **07** valiant
08 cut-water, forepart

prowess
04 grit, guts **05** nerve, pluck, skill, spunk **06** bottle, daring, genius, talent, valour **07** ability, bravery, command, courage, heroism, mastery
08 aptitude, audacity, facility
09 adeptness, dexterity, expertise, gallantry, vassalage **10** adroitness, attainment, capability **11** intrepidity, proficiency, skilfulness **12** fearlessness
13 dauntlessness **14** accomplishment

prowl
04 hunt, lurk, nose, roam, rove
05 creep, lurch, mouse, prole, proll, proul, range, ratch, skulk, slink, sneak, snoke, snook, snoop, snowk, stalk, steal **06** cruise, patrol, search
08 scavenge **14** move stealthily

prowler
06 patrol, proler, roamer **07** proller, prouler, stalker **08** tenebrio
09 nighthawk, scavenger

proximity
08 nearness, vicinity **09** adjacency, closeness **10** contiguity **11** propinquity
13 juxtaposition, neighbourhood

proxy
05 agent **06** deputy, factor **07** stand-in
08 attorney, delegate **09** surrogate
10 substitute **14** representative
• **by proxy**
02 pp

prude
04 prig **07** old maid, puritan **09** Mrs Grundy **10** goody-goody, schoolmarm

prudence
04 care **05** Metis **06** policy, saving, thrift, wisdom **07** caution, economy
08 planning, sagacity, wariness
09 canniness, foresight, frugality, good sense, husbandry, judgement, vigilance **10** discretion, precaution, providence **11** advisedness, common sense, forethought, happy medium,

heedfulness, penny-wisdom
12 cautiousness, preparedness
13 judiciousness **14** circumspection, far-sightedness **15** circumspectness

prudent
04 ware, wary, wise **06** frugal, shrewd
07 careful, politic, thrifty **08** cautious, discreet, sensible, vigilant **09** judicious, provident, sagacious **10** discerning, economical, far-sighted
11 circumspect, ware and wise, well-advised, wise-hearted
13 considerative

prudently
06 warily, wisely **08** sensibly, shrewdly
09 advisedly, carefully **10** discreetly, vigilantly **11** providently
12 economically, far-sightedly

prudery
08 primness **09** Grundyism
10 prissiness, puritanism, strictness, stuffiness **11** overmodesty, starchiness
12 priggishness **13** squeamishness
14 old-maidishness

prudish
04 prim **05** mimsy **06** demure, mimsey, prissy, proper, stuffy **07** po-faced, starchy **08** overnice, priggish, pudibund **09** squeamish, Victorian
10 goody-goody, old-maidish, overmodest **11** puritanical, strait-laced
12 narrow-minded **13** schoolmarmish, ultra-virtuous

prune
03 cut, lop **04** clip, dock, pare, plum, sned, snip, spur, trim **05** preen, proin, proyn, shape, shred **06** cut off, dehorn, prewyn, proign, proine, proyne, pruine, reduce, reform, switch **07** cut back, shorten **08** prunello **10** French plum

prurient
04 blue, lewd **05** dirty **06** erotic, smutty **07** itching, lustful, obscene
08 desirous, indecent **09** lecherous, salacious **10** cupidinous, lascivious, libidinous **11** voyeuristic
12 concupiscent, pornographic

pry
03 dig **04** nose, peep, peer, poke, toot
05 delve, prise, snoop **06** ferret, meddle **07** gumshoe, intrude
08 prodnose **09** interfere
10 stickybeak **12** put your oar in
14 poke your nose in **15** stick your nose in

prying
04 nosy **05** nosey, peery **06** snoopy, spying **07** curious, peering
08 meddling, snooping **09** intrusive
10 meddlesome **11** inquisitive, interfering

psalm
02 Ps **03** Psa **04** hymn, poem, song
05 chant, paean, tract **06** choral, prayer, proper, venite **07** cantate, chorale, introit, tractus **08** canticle, Jubilate, Miserere **09** neckverse
10 paraphrase

psalm tune
04 tone

pseud
04 sham **05** false, fraud, poser
06 humbug, phoney, poseur, trendy
11 pretentious

pseudo
04 fake, mock, sham **05** bogus, false, pseud, quasi- **06** ersatz, phoney
08 spurious **09** imitation, pretended, ungenuine **10** artificial **11** counterfeit, pretentious

pseudonym
05 alias **06** anonym **07** allonym, pen-name **09** false name, incognito, stage name **10** nom de plume **11** assumed name, nom de guerre

Pseudonyms include:

03 Day (Doris), Pop (Iggy), Tey (Josephine)
04 Alda (Alan), Bell (Acton), Bell (Currer), Bell (Ellis), Cage (Nicolas), Dors (Diana), Ford (Ford Madox), Gish (Lillian Diana), Hite (Shere), Holm (Sir Ian), John (Sir Elton), Lulu, Lynn (Dame Vera), Piaf (Edith), Reed (Lou), Rhys (Jean), Ross (Diana), Saki, Sand (George), West (Dame Rebecca), West (Nathanael), Wood (Natalie), York (Susannah)
05 Allen (Woody), Bizet (Georges), Black (Cilla), Bowie (David), Caine (Sir Michael), Clark (Petula), Cline (Patsy), Dylan (Bob), Eliot (George), Flynn (Errol), Garbo (Greta), Gorky (Maxim), Grant (Cary), Grant (Richard E), Hardy (Oliver), Henry (O), Holly (Buddy), Jason (David), Keith (Penelope), Lanza (Mario), Leigh (Vivien), Loren (Sophia), Moore (Demi), Moore (Julianne), Niven (David), Queen (Ellery), Ryder (Winona), Scott (Ronnie), Seuss (Dr), Smith (Stevie), Solti (Sir Georg), Stern (Daniel), Sting, Twain (Mark), Wayne (John), Welch (Raquel)
06 Bacall (Lauren), Bardot (Brigitte), Berlin (Irving), Brooks (Mel), Burton (Richard), Conrad (Joseph), Crosby (Bing), Curtis (Tony), Fields (Dame Gracie), Foster (Jodie), France (Anatole), Gibbon (Lewis Grassic), Harlow (Jean), Heston (Charlton), Irving (Sir Henry), Jolson (Al), Keaton (Diane), Laurel (Stan), London (Jack), Lugosi (Bela), McBain (Ed), Mirren (Helen), Monroe (Marilyn), Morton (Jelly Roll), Neeson (Liam), Orwell (George), Peters (Ellis), Rogers (Ginger), Salten (Felix), Sapper, Scales (Prunella), Simone (Nina), Spacey (Kevin), Steele (Tommy), Turner (Lana), Turner (Tina), Waters (Muddy), Weldon (Fay), Wesley (Mary), Wonder (Stevie)
07 Andrews (Dame Julie), Bachman (Richard), Bennett (Tony), Bogarde (Sir Dirk), Bronson (Charles), Carroll (Lewis), Deneuve (Catherine), Dinesen (Isak), Douglas (Kirk), Gardner (Ava), Garland (Judy), Hepburn (Audrey), Higgins (Jack), Holiday (Billie), Jacques (Hattie), Karloff (Boris), Kincaid (Jamaica), Le Carré (John), Lindsay (Robert), Lombard (Carole), Matthau (Walter), Mercury (Freddie), Michael (George), Miranda (Carmen), Molière, Montand (Yves), Novello (Ivor), Richard (Sir Cliff), Robbins (Harold), Russell (Lillian), Shepard (Sam), Swanson (Gloria), Wyndham (John), Wynette (Tammy)
08 Bancroft (Anne), Coltrane (Robbie), Coolidge (Susan), Costello (Elvis), Crawford (Joan), Dietrich (Marlene), Gershwin (George), Gershwin (Ira), Goldberg (Whoopi), Hayworth (Rita), Kingsley (Ben), MacLaine (Shirley), Ma Rainey, Pickford (Mary), Robinson (Edward G), Sly Stone, Stanwyck (Barbara), Stoppard (Tom), Voltaire, Williams (Tennessee)
09 Bernhardt (Sarah), Bo Diddley, Charteris (Leslie), Fairbanks (Douglas), Lancaster (Burt), Leadbelly, Offenbach (Jacques), Streisand (Barbra), Valentino (Rudolph)
10 Howlin' Wolf, Washington (Dinah), Westmacott (Mary)
11 Springfield (Dusty)

pshaw
03 och

psych
• psych out
03 cow **05** alarm, appal, bully, daunt, get to, scare, throw, upset **06** coerce, compel, dismay, lean on, menace, rattle
07 overawe, terrify, warn off
08 browbeat, bulldoze, domineer, frighten, pressure, unsettle
09 terrorize, tyrannize **10** intimidate, pressurize **13** put off balance, turn the heat on **14** put the screws on
• psych yourself up
13 brace yourself, nerve yourself, steel yourself **14** gear yourself up, pluck up courage, work yourself up

psyche
04 mind, self, soul **05** anima
06 pneuma, spirit **09** awareness, inner self, intellect **10** inmost self
11 personality **12** intelligence, subconscious **13** consciousness, heart of hearts, individuality, innermost self, understanding **15** deepest feelings

psychiatrist
06 shrink **07** analyst **08** alienist
09 therapist **10** head doctor, psychiater
12 headshrinker, psychologist, trick cyclist **13** psychoanalyst
14 psychoanalyser **15** man in a white coat, psychotherapist

Psychiatrists and psychoanalysts include:

04 **Beck** (Aaron), **Jung** (Carl), **Rank** (Otto)
05 **Adler** (Alfred), **Clare** (Anthony), **Freud** (Anna), **Freud** (Sigmund), **Fromm** (Erich), **Jones** (Ernest), **Klein** (Melanie), **Lacan** (Jacques), **Laing** (Ronald David), **Meyer** (Adolf), **Reich** (Wilhelm), **Szasz** (Thomas)
06 **Berger** (Hans), **Bowlby** (John), **Hitzig** (Julius), **Snyder** (Solomon)
07 **Bleuler** (Eugen), **Erikson** (Erik), **Persaud** (Raj)
08 **Maudsley** (Henry), **Sullivan** (Harry Stack), **Wernicke** (Carl)
09 **Alexander** (Franz), **Alzheimer** (Alois), **Kraepelin** (Emil), **Menninger** (Karl), **Rorschach** (Hermann)
11 **Krafft-Ebing** (Richard, von)
13 **Wagner-Jauregg** (Julius)

See also **psychology**

psychic

04 seer **05** augur **06** medium, mental, mystic, occult, oracle **07** diviner, prophet **08** mystical, telepath **09** cognitive, emotional, spiritual, visionary **10** mind-reader, prophetess, soothsayer, telepathic **11** clairvoyant, telekinetic **12** extrasensory, intellectual, supernatural **13** fortune-teller, psychological **14** spiritualistic

psychoanalyst *see* **psychiatrist**

psychological

06 mental, unreal **08** cerebral **09** cognitive, emotional, imaginary **10** conceptual, irrational, subjective **11** theoretical, unconscious **12** all in the mind, intellectual, subconscious **13** psychosomatic

psychologically

08 mentally **11** cognitively, emotionally **12** conceptually, subjectively **13** theoretically, unconsciously **14** intellectually

psychology

04 mind **06** habits, make-up **07** mindset, motives **08** conation, hedonics, psychics **09** attitudes **10** child-study, gestaltism **12** pneumatology **14** metapsychology, study of the mind **15** mental chemistry

Branches of psychology include:

03 bio
04 para
05 child, depth, neuro, sport
06 health, social
07 abnormal, clinical, criminal, forensic
08 hedonics
09 cognitive, narrative
10 industrial, structural
11 educational
12 evolutionary, experimental, occupational
13 developmental, environmental, psychobiology, psychometrics, transpersonal
14 organizational, psychoanalysis
15 psychopathology

Psychology theories include:

07 atomism, Gestalt, Jungian
08 Adlerian, Freudian, Jamesian, Lacanian
09 cognitive, Pavlovian
10 functional, humanistic, Skinnerian, structural
11 behavioural, personality
13 connectionism, functionalism, structuralism
14 associationism, psychoanalytic

Psychological conditions and disorders include:

06 autism, manias
07 agnosia, bulimia, phobias
08 dementia, neurosis, paranoia
09 addiction, anhedonia, Asperger's, psychosis, Tourette's
10 abreaction, Alzheimer's, blindsight, depression, dysmorphia, Munchausen, sociopathy
11 kleptomania, psychopathy
12 hypochondria
13 acatamathesia, battle fatigue, schizophrenia
15 anorexia nervosa, bipolar disorder

Psychological therapies include:

03 art
05 drama, group, hypno
06 colour, psycho
07 Gestalt
08 aversion
09 cognitive
10 regression
11 behavioural, counselling
12 electroshock
13 interpersonal, person-centred, psychodynamic

Psychologists include:

04 **Bain** (Alexander)
05 **Binet** (Alfred), **James** (William), **Pratt** (Joseph Gaither), **Rhine** (Joseph Banks)
06 **De Bono** (Edward), **Kinsey** (Alfred Charles), **Morris** (Robert Lyle), **Murphy** (Gardner), **Piaget** (Jean), **Pinker** (Steven), **Terman** (Lewis Madison)
07 **Cattell** (Raymond Bernard), **Eysenck** (Hans Jürgen), **Skinner** (Burrhus Frederic)
09 **Thorndike** (Edward Lee)
10 **Wertheimer** (Max)

See also **psychiatrist**

psychopath

06 madman, maniac, psycho **07** lunatic **08** madwoman **09** mad person, psychotic, sociopath

psychopathic

03 mad **06** insane, psycho **07** lunatic **08** demented, deranged, maniacal **09** psychotic **10** unbalanced

psychosomatic

06 unreal **09** imaginary **10** irrational, subjective **12** all in the mind **13** psychological

psychotic

03 fey **04** bats, gyte, loco, nuts, wild **05** barmy, batty, buggy, crazy, daffy, dippy, dotty, flaky, gonzo, loony, loopy, manic, nutty, potty, queer, wacko, wacky, wiggy **06** crazed, cuckoo, fruity, insane, maniac, mental, raving, red-mad, screwy **07** bananas, barking, berserk, bonkers, cracked, frantic, lunatic, meshuga **08** crackers, demented, deranged, dingbats, doolally, frenetic, frenzied, maniacal, unhinged, unstable **09** disturbed, lymphatic, up the wall **10** bestraught, distracted, distraught, frantic-mad, off the wall, off your nut, out to lunch, stone-crazy, unbalanced **11** not all there, off the rails, off your head **12** mad as a hatter, off your chump, round the bend **13** off your rocker, of unsound mind, out of your head, out of your mind, out of your tree, round the twist **14** off your trolley, wrong in the head **15** non compos mentis, out of your senses

ptarmigan

04 rype

pub *see* **public house**

puberty

05 teens, youth **08** maturity **09** growing up **10** pubescence **11** adolescence **12** teenage years **14** young adulthood

public

03 out **04** fans, open **05** civic, civil, crowd, known, overt, plain, state **06** buyers, common, famous, masses, nation, people, social, tavern, voters **07** country, eminent, exposed, federal, general, obvious, patrons, popular, society **08** audience, citizens, communal, everyone, national, official, populace **09** available, clientèle, community, consumers, customers, followers, important, multitude, prominent, published, respected, universal, well-known **10** accessible, celebrated, collective, electorate, government, population, recognized, spectators, supporters, widespread **11** illustrious, influential, unconcealed **12** acknowledged, nationalized, unrestricted **13** international

• in public

06 openly **08** publicly **09** in the open **10** in full view **11** for all to see

public house

02 PH **03** bar, inn, pub **04** houf, howf **05** grill, hotel, houff, house, howff, local, table **06** boozer, lounge, saloon, shanty, tavern **07** brewpub, canteen, counter, potshop, shebeen, taproom, wine bar **08** ale house, bona fide, groggery, hostelry **09** brasserie, free house, gin palace, jerry-shop, lounge bar, lush-house **12** watering-hole

Public house names include:

04 Bell, Bull, Ship, Swan
05 Crown, Globe

06 Anchor, Castle, George, New Inn, Plough
07 Railway, Red Lion
08 Green Man, Nags Head, Royal Oak, Victoria
09 Black Bull, Cross Keys, King's Arms, King's Head, White Hart, White Lion, White Swan
10 Black Horse, Golden Lion, Queen's Head, Wheatsheaf, White Horse
12 Fox and Hounds, Rose and Crown
13 Hare and Hounds, Prince of Wales
14 Coach and Horses
15 George and Dragon

publican
04 host **06** barman **07** barmaid, tapster **08** hotelier, landlady, landlord, mine host, taverner **09** barperson, bartender, innkeeper, tax farmer **11** hotel-keeper **12** saloon-keeper, tax collector

publication
04 book, buik, buke **05** daily, forum, issue, title **06** serial, volume, weekly **07** booklet, fanzine, journal, leaflet, monthly, release **08** brochure, handbill, hardback, magazine, pamphlet, printing **09** newspaper, paperback, quarterly, reporting **10** disclosure, half-yearly, newsletter, periodical, production, publishing **11** circulation, declaration, festschrift **12** announcement, broadcasting, distribution, notification, proclamation
• **prepare for publication**
04 edit

publicity
03 air **04** hype, plug, puff **05** boost **06** splash **07** acclaim, build-up, réclame **08** ballyhoo **09** attention, limelight, marketing, notoriety, promotion **10** propaganda **11** advertising
• **publicity agent**
02 PA

publicize
04 hype, plug, push **05** blaze **06** market **07** promote **08** announce, headline **09** advertise, broadcast, make known, spotlight **10** make public, promulgate **11** disseminate

public-spirited
08 generous **09** unselfish **10** altruistic, charitable **12** humanitarian **13** conscientious, philanthropic **15** community-minded

public transport *see* **transport**

publish
03 run **04** vent **05** carry, issue, print, sound **06** delate, import, notice, notify, pirate, poster, put out, report, reveal, spread **07** declare, diffuse, divulge, gazette, placard, produce, release **08** announce, bring out, disclose, evulgate, proclaim, put about, put forth, set forth **09** advertise, broadcast, celebrate, circulate, divulgate, fulminate, give forth, make known, paperback, paragraph, publicize, serialize, syndicate **10** distribute, make public, promulgate **11** communicate, disseminate
See also **printing**

Publishers and imprints include:

02 DK
03 CUP, OUP, Pan
04 Reed
05 Corgi, Letts, Orion
06 Europa, Puffin, Viking, Virago
07 A&C Black, Berlitz, Cassell, Collins, Longman, Merriam, Methuen, Pearson, Picador, Pimlico, Usborne
08 BBC Books, Chambers, Everyman, Flamingo, Gollancz, Ladybird, Larousse, Michelin, Palgrave
09 Allen Lane, Black Swan, Blackwell, Doubleday, Harlequin, Heinemann, Macmillan, Routledge
10 Allen & Unwin, Bloomsbury, Bodley Head, Faber & Faber, Hutchinson, McGraw-Hill, Paul Hamlyn, Scholastic, Times Books, Transworld
11 Bantam Press, Bertelsmann, Fodor Guides, Rand McNally, Random House, Rough Guides
12 André Deutsch, Butterworths, Chatto & Windus, Edward Arnold, Fourth Estate, Jonathan Cape, Lonely Planet, Mills and Boon, Penguin Books, Reed Elsevier, Sweet & Maxwell, Thames & Hudson
13 AOL/Time Warner, Atlantic Books, Hachette Livre, HarperCollins, Reader's Digest, Little, Brown & Co, Secker & Warburg, Simon & Schuster
14 Canongate Books, Chambers Harrap, Chrysalis Books, Hodder Headline, Springer-Verlag
15 Houghton Mifflin, Mitchell Beazley

pucker
04 fold, ruck, shir **05** pleat, purse, shirr **06** cockle, crease, furrow, gather, ruckle, ruffle **07** crinkle, crumple, screw up, shrivel, wrinkle **08** compress, contract **09** agitation, confusion **11** corrugation

puckered
05 pursy **06** plissé, rucked **07** bullate, creased, ruckled **08** gathered, wrinkled

puckering
04 shir **05** shirr

puckish
03 sly **06** impish **07** naughty, playful, roguish, teasing, waggish **08** sportive **09** whimsical **10** frolicsome **11** mischievous

pudding
03 pie, pud **04** tart **05** sweet **06** afters, pastry **07** dessert
See also **cake**; **dessert**

puddle
03 dub, sop **04** pant, pool, slop, soss, sump **05** flush, plash, plesh **06** muddle **07** muddler, plashet

puddock
04 frog, toad

puerile
05 inane, silly **07** babyish, foolish, trivial **08** childish, immature, juvenile, trifling **09** infantile **10** adolescent **13** irresponsible

Puerto Rico
03 PRI

puff
02 ad **04** blow, drag, draw, fuff, gasp, gulp, gust, huff, pant, plug, pull, push, suck, toke, waff, waft, waif **05** blast, extol, flaff, pluff, skiff, smoke, swell, whiff, whift **06** breath, expand, flatus, flurry, market, praise, wheeze **07** breathe, commend, draught, inflate, promote **09** advertise, marketing, promotion, publicity, publicize **10** homosexual **11** ostentation **12** commendation **13** advertisement
• **puff out**
03 bag, sag **04** bulb, hump **05** belly, bloat, bulge, heave, swell **06** bepuff, billow, blouse, dilate, expand **07** balloon, distend, enlarge, project **08** protrude

puffed
06 done in, winded **07** gasping, panting **08** inflated **09** distended, exhausted **10** breathless **11** out of breath
• **puffed up**
05 bloat, elate, proud **06** pluffy **07** swollen, ventose **08** arrogant, prideful **09** bigheaded **13** high and mighty, self-important, swollen-headed **14** full of yourself

puffin
08 rock-bird, Tom-noddy **09** sea parrot **10** Fratercula **11** Tammie Norie

puffy
05 pursy **07** bloated, dilated, swollen **08** engorged, enlarged, inflated, puffed up **09** bombastic, distended **10** oedematous

pugilism
04 ring **06** boxing **07** the ring **08** fighting, fistiana, the fancy **11** the noble art **12** the prize-ring **13** prize-fighting **15** the noble science

pugilist
03 ham, pug **05** boxer **07** bruiser, fighter **12** prize-fighter

pugnacious
07 hostile **09** bellicose, combative **10** aggressive **11** bad-tempered, belligerent, contentious, hot-tempered, quarrelsome **12** antagonistic, disputatious **13** argumentative

puke
03 cat **04** barf, boke, honk, sick, spew **05** heave, retch, vomit **06** emesis, emetic, sick up **07** bring up, chuck up, chunder, fetch up, throw up, upchuck **08** disgorge, parbreak, retching **10** egurgitate **11** regurgitate

pull
03 lug, rip, row, tow, tug **04** drag, draw, fire, haul, jerk, lure, raid, sole, sowl, suck, sway, tear, turn, yank **05** charm, clout, heave, pluck, power, proof, soole, sowle, steal, tempt, trail, tweak **06** allure, arrest, damage, entice, muscle, pull in, pull up, remove, snatch, sprain, strain, twitch, uproot, weight, wrench **07** attract, bring in, draught, draw out, extract, pull out, root out, stretch, take out **08** exertion, withdraw **09** advantage, dislocate, influence, magnetism, magnetize **10** allurement, attraction, resistance **12** drawing power, forcefulness

• **pull apart**
03 pan **04** part, pick, slam **05** slate **06** attack **07** run down **08** demolish, distrain, separate **09** criticize, dismantle, dismember, take apart, tear apart **11** pick holes in **12** pick to pieces, pull to pieces, take to pieces, tear to shreds **15** do a hatchet job on

• **pull back**
04 draw **06** retire **07** back out, retreat **08** draw back, fall back, withdraw **09** disengage

• **pull down**
07 destroy, unbuild **08** bulldoze, demolish, take down **09** dismantle, knock down **10** dilapidate **15** raze to the ground

• **pull in**
03 nab **04** book, bust, draw, earn, halt, lure, make, nick, park, stop **05** clear, run in, seize **06** allure, arrest, arrive, be paid, collar, detain, draw in, entice, pull up, rake in **07** attract, bring in, capture, collect, receive **08** take home **09** apprehend **15** take into custody

• **pull off**
05 pluck **06** detach, fulfil, manage, remove, rip off **07** achieve, succeed, take off, tear off **08** bring off, carry off, carry out, separate **10** accomplish

• **pull out**
04 quit **05** leave **06** depart, desert **07** abandon, back out, draw out, move out, pluck up, retreat **08** evacuate, withdraw

• **pull through**
05 rally **07** improve, recover, survive, weather **09** get better **10** recuperate **11** come through **12** get well again

• **pull together**
04 draw **05** rally **06** team up **09** co-operate **11** collaborate **12** work together

• **pull up**
04 balk, halt, park, stop **05** baulk, blame, brake, chide, scold **06** arrest, berate, carpet, draw up, pull in, rebuke, uproot, uptear **07** censure, lecture, reprove, tell off, tick off **08** admonish, draw rein, pull over **09** castigate, criticize, eradicate, reprimand **10** take to task **11** come to a halt **14** read the riot act

• **pull yourself together**
11 snap out of it **15** buck up your ideas, control yourself

pulled up
02 pu

pulley
04 swig

pullover
03 top **06** jersey, jumper, woolly **07** sweater, tank top **10** sweatshirt **11** windcheater

pulp
03 pap **04** beat, gush, mash, mush, must, pith **05** chyme, cream, crush, flesh, gloop, paste, pound, purée, shred, slush **06** bathos, marrow, pomace, squash **07** furnish **08** nonsense, schmaltz **09** corniness, liquidize, nostalgia, pulverize, triturate **10** sloppiness, tenderness **11** mawkishness, romanticism **12** chemical wood, emotionalism **14** sentimentalism, sentimentality

pulpit
03 tub **04** ambo, dais, desk, tent, wood **05** stand **06** mimbar, minbar, podium **07** lectern, rostrum, soapbox **08** platform **11** three-decker

pulpy
04 soft **05** mushy, pappy **06** fleshy, sloppy **07** baccate, crushed, squashy **09** succulent

pulsate
04 beat, drum, thud **05** pound, pulse, throb, thump **06** hammer, quiver **07** vibrate **09** oscillate, palpitate

pulsating
07 pulsing **09** pulsatile, pulsative, pulsatory, vibratile, vibrating, vibrative **11** oscillating, palpitating

pulsation
04 beat **05** ictus, throb **07** beating **09** heartbeat, throbbing, vibration **11** oscillation, palpitation **12** vibratiuncle

pulse
03 dal, pea **04** bean, beat, daal, dahl, dhal, drum, gram, thud, tick **05** pound, throb, thump **06** legume, rhythm, stroke, thrill **07** beating, flutter, pulsate, vibrate **08** drumming, pounding, sphygmus, thudding, thumping **09** calavance, caravance, pulsation, throbbing, vibration **11** oscillation

See also **bean**

pulverize
◇ *anagram indicator*
04 mill, pulp **05** crush, grind, pound, smash **06** bruise, defeat, hammer, powder, squash, thrash **07** crumble, destroy **08** demolish, vanquish **09** comminute, triturate **10** annihilate **12** contriturate

puma
05 tiger **06** cougar **07** couguar, panther **09** catamount **12** mountain lion

pummel
◇ *anagram indicator*
03 fib, hit **04** bang, beat, soak **05** knock, pound, punch, thump **06** batter, hammer, pommel, strike

pump
03 jet **04** draw, gush, push, quiz, send **05** drain, drive, force, grill, spout, spurt, surge **06** bowser, inject, siphon **08** inflater, inflator **09** grease gun, hydropult **11** interrogate **12** cross-examine **13** cross-question **14** put the screws on

See also **footwear**

• **pump out**
05 drain, empty **06** siphon **07** bail out, draw off **08** force out

• **pump up**
04 fill **06** blow up, puff up **07** inflate **08** increase

pumpkin
06 cashaw, cushaw **07** pompion, pumpion **12** Jack-o'-lantern **14** Queensland blue **15** vegetable marrow

pun
03 ram **04** quip **05** pound **06** clinch **07** quibble **08** equivoke **09** calembour, equivoque, jeu de mots, witticism **10** pundigrion **11** paronomasia, play on words **13** double meaning, play upon words **14** double entendre

punch
03 bop, box, cut, die, fib, hit, jab, job, mat, zap **04** bash, biff, bite, blow, boff, bore, bust, clip, cuff, dong, hole, kick, plug, poke, prod, slug, sock, wind **05** black, check, clout, drill, drive, force, knock, power, prick, rumbo, stamp, thump, verve **06** energy, impact, pierce, pounce, pummel, stingo, strike, thwack, vigour, wallop, whammy **07** king hit, panache, pizzazz **08** keypunch, puncture, strength **09** bolo punch, perforate **10** roundhouse **11** coup de poing, make a hole in, sucker-punch **12** bunch of fives, counter-punch, forcefulness, fourpenny one **13** effectiveness **15** knuckle sandwich

punch-drunk
05 dazed, dizzy, woozy **06** groggy **07** reeling **08** confused, unsteady **09** befuddled, slap-happy, stupefied **10** staggering

punch-up
03 row **05** brawl, fight, scrap, set-to **06** dust-up, fracas, ruckus, shindy **07** scuffle **08** argument, ding-dong **10** free-for-all **12** stand-up fight

punchy
05 dazed, zappy **06** lively, strong **07** dynamic **08** forceful, incisive, powerful, spirited, vigorous **09** effective **10** aggressive

punctilio
05 pique, punto **06** detail, nicety, puncto **08** ceremony, delicacy **09** exactness, fine point, formality, precision **10** convention, exactitude,

particular, refinement, strictness **11** distinction, finickiness, preciseness **13** particularity **14** meticulousness, scrupulousness **15** punctiliousness

punctilious
04 prim **05** exact, fussy, picky **06** choosy, formal, picked, proper, strict **07** careful, finicky, precise **08** punctual **10** meticulous, nit-picking, particular, pernickety, scrupulous **11** ceremonious, persnickety **13** conscientious

punctiliously
07 exactly **09** carefully, precisely **12** meticulously, scrupulously **15** conscientiously

punctual
05 early, exact, on cue **06** on time, prompt **07** precise **08** on the dot, up to time **09** well-timed **10** bang on time, dead on time, in good time **11** punctilious

punctuality
09 readiness **10** promptness, regularity, strictness **11** promptitude

punctually
05 sharp **06** bang on, dead on, on time, prompt, spot-on **07** exactly **08** on the dot, promptly, up to time **09** precisely **11** on the button, on the stroke, to the minute **13** on the stroke of

punctuate
04 stop **05** break, point **06** pepper **07** break up **08** sprinkle **09** emphasize, interject, interrupt **10** accentuate **11** intersperse

punctuation

Punctuation marks include:

04 dash, star
05 colon, comma
06 hyphen, period, quotes
07 solidus
08 asterisk, brackets, ellipsis, full stop
09 backslash, semicolon
10 apostrophe
11 parentheses, speech marks
12 question mark
13 oblique stroke
14 inverted commas, quotation marks, square brackets
15 exclamation mark

puncture
◇ *insertion indicator*
03 cut **04** bite, bore, flat, hole, leak, nick, slit **05** burst, prick, spike **06** holing, pierce, pounce **07** blow-out, deflate, flatten, let down, put down, rupture **08** centesis, flat tyre, piercing **09** humiliate, penetrate, perforate, spinal tap **11** make a hole in, perforation

pundit
04 buff, guru, sage **05** maven, mavin **06** expert, gooroo, master, savant **07** adviser, maestro, teacher **09** authority

pungency
03 nip **04** bite, kick, tang **05** oomph, point, power, sting **07** pizzazz, sarcasm **08** mordancy, strength **09** sharpness, spiciness **10** causticity, trenchancy **11** pepperiness **12** incisiveness **13** strong flavour

pungent
03 hot **04** acid, fell, keen, racy, salt, sour, tart **05** acrid, acute, fiery, nippy, sharp, spicy, tangy **06** biting, bitter, strong **07** burning, caustic, cutting, mordant, painful, peppery, piquant, pointed **08** aromatic, incisive, piercing, poignant, powerful, scathing, stinging **09** sarcastic, trenchant **11** penetrating

punish
◇ *anagram indicator*
03 log **04** beat, cane, fine, flog, gate, hang, harm, lash, slap, sort, whip **05** abuse, scold, scour, shend, smack, spank, visit, wreak **06** amerce, batter, damage, defeat, ground, hammer, misuse, pay out, strafe, straff, thrash **07** chasten, correct, crucify, justify, knee-cap, rough up, scourge, sort out, trounce **08** chastise, decimate, imprison, keelhaul, maltreat, masthead, penalize, serve out **09** castigate, strappado **10** come down on, discipline **11** bring to book **12** come down upon, give it laldie **14** bring to justice, make someone pay, throw the book at **15** give someone hell, make an example of

• **be punished**
03 pay

punishable
07 illegal **08** criminal, culpable, unlawful **10** chargeable, indictable **11** blameworthy, convictable

punishing
04 hard **05** cruel, harsh **06** severe, taxing, tiring **07** arduous, testing **08** crushing, grinding, grueling, wearying **09** crippling, demanding, fatiguing, gruelling, strenuous **10** burdensome, exhausting **12** backbreaking

punishment
04 harm, pine, toco, toko **05** force, impot **06** damage, ill-use, injury **07** deserts, penalty, revenge **08** ferocity, sentence **10** correction, discipline, imposition, storminess, turbulence **11** retribution **12** chastisement, maltreatment **13** rough handling **15** short sharp shock

Punishments include:

04 cane, fine, gaol, jail, rope
05 exile, lines, strap
06 gating, hiding, prison
07 beating, belting, borstal, capital, flaying, hitting, jankers, lashing, the cane, the rack, the rope
08 corporal, demotion, flogging, slapping, smacking, solitary, spanking, the birch, whipping
09 chain gang, detention, exclusion, execution, expulsion, grounding, larruping, probation, scourging, strappado, the stocks, thrashing, torturing
10 banishment, cashiering, decimation, defrocking, internment, leathering, suspension, the slipper, unfrocking
11 confinement, deportation, house arrest, keelhauling, knee-capping, mastheading, penal colony
12 confiscation, dressing-down, imprisonment
13 horsewhipping, incarceration, sequestration
14 transportation
15 excommunication, walking the plank

• **place of punishment**
04 cang, gaol, Hell, jail, tron **05** Hades, trone **06** cangue, prison, sin bin **07** borstal, dungeon, gallows, pillory, tumbrel, tumbril **08** scaffold, solitary, Tartarus **09** black hole, cart's-tail, the stocks **10** little-ease **11** penal colony **12** cucking stool, whipping-post

See also **prison**

punitive
04 hard **05** cruel, harsh, penal, stiff **06** severe **08** crushing **09** crippling, demanding, gruelling, punishing **10** burdensome, chastising, corrective, vindictive **11** castigatory, retaliatory, retributive, vindicatory **12** disciplinary

punter
03 guy **04** chap **05** bloke **06** backer, better, client, fellow, person **07** gambler, wagerer **08** consumer, customer **10** individual **11** handicapper

puny
04 tiny, weak **05** frail, minor, petty, scram, small, weary **06** feeble, little, measly, puisne, puisny, sickly **07** pimping, shilpit, stunted, trivial **08** piddling, reckling, trifling **10** diminutive, undersized **11** undeveloped **13** inexperienced, insignificant **14** underdeveloped **15** inconsequential

pupil
01 L **04** coed, prep, ward **05** cadet **06** alumna, bursar, day-boy, grader, junior, novice, old boy, preppy, senior **07** alumnus, ashrama, boarder, day-girl, learner, monitor, old girl, prefect, protégé, scholar, student **08** beginner, bluecoat, disciple, grey-coat, praefect, protégée, schoolie **09** classmate, schoolboy, St Trinian **10** abiturient, academical, apprentice, charity-boy, day-boarder, day-scholar, gymnasiast, schoolgirl, Wykehamist **11** charity-girl, class-fellow, Westminster **12** pupil teacher **13** apple of the eye, kindergärtner **14** kindergartener, parlour-boarder

• **former pupil**
02 OB **06** alumna, old boy **07** alumnus, old girl

puppet
04 doll, dupe, gull, Judy, pawn, tool **05** Punch, puppy **06** mammet, maumet, mawmet, mommet, motion, poppet, stooge **07** cat's-paw, Guignol **08** creature, quisling **09** dependant, fantoccio, rod puppet **10** fantoccino, figurehead, hand puppet, instrument, Jack of Lent, marionette, mouthpiece **11** glove puppet, Punchinello **12** finger puppet

puppy
03 pup **05** whelp **06** lapdog **08** young dog

purchase
03 buy, get, win **04** deal, earn, gain, grip, hold **05** asset, booty, goods, grasp, price, prise, prize **06** assets, obtain, pay for, pick up, secure, snap up, strive **07** acquire, bargain, emption, procure, seizure, shop for **08** foothold, holdings, invest in, leverage, property **09** advantage **10** go shopping, investment, possession **11** acquisition, possessions, splash out on

purchaser
05 buyer, hirer **06** client, emptor, patron, vendee **07** shopper **08** consumer, customer **11** perquisitor

pure
03 net, pur **04** fair, fine, free, good, holy, meer, mere, neat, nett, puer, real, true **05** clean, clear, fresh, moral, noble, sheer, snowy, solid, total, utter, white **06** chaste, decent, honest, kosher, modest, purity, refine, simple, virgin, worthy **07** aseptic, cleanly, cleanse, genuine, natural, perfect, sincere, sterile, unmixed, upright, utterly **08** absolute, abstract, academic, complete, flawless, germ-free, heavenly, hygienic, innocent, pristine, sanitary, spotless, straight, thorough, undrossy, unsoiled, virginal, virginly, virtuous **09** authentic, blameless, downright, essential, excellent, incorrupt, righteous, Saturnian, snow-white, spiritous, stainless, unalloyed, undefiled, undiluted, unsullied **10** antiseptic, completely, homozygous, honourable, immaculate, intemerate, sterilized, uninfected, unpolluted **11** conjectural, disinfected, speculative, theoretical, unblemished, unmitigated, unqualified **12** unadulterate **13** unadulterated **14** heavenly-minded, uncontaminated

pure-bred
07 blooded **08** pedigree, true-born, true-bred **09** pedigreed, pure-blood **11** full-blooded, pure-blooded **12** thoroughbred

purée
03 dal **04** fool **06** coulis, hummus, kissel, humous **07** houmous **08** hoummous **10** baba ganouj **11** baba ganoush **12** baba ghanouzh

purely
04 just, only **06** merely, simply, solely, wholly **07** totally, utterly **08** chastely, entirely **09** unmixedly **10** absolutely, completely, thoroughly **11** exclusively, wonderfully **15** unconditionally

purgative
05 aloes, enema, jalap, purge, salts, yapon, yupon **06** cacoon, emetic, ipecac, yaupon **07** calomel, drastic, jalapin, purging, rhubarb **08** aperient, elaterin, evacuant, laxative, lenitive **09** cathartic, cleansing, colocynth, croton oil, physic nut **10** abstersive, cholagogue, depurative, eccoprotic, Epsom salts, hiera-picra, higry-pigry, number nine **11** bitter aloes, cathartical, chrysarobin, ipecacuanha **12** black draught **13** diacatholicon **14** hickery-pickery

purgatory
04 hell **05** agony, swamp **06** misery, ordeal, ravine **07** anguish, purging, torment, torture **09** cleansing, expiatory **12** hopelessness, wretchedness

purge
03 rid **04** kill, oust, soil, work **05** clear, eject, expel, scour **06** depose, purify, remove **07** absolve, clarify, cleanse, dismiss, expiate, ousting, removal, root out, wipe out **08** absterge, clean out, clear out, disposal, ejection, get rid of **09** catharize, cleansing, eradicate, expulsion, expurgate, purgative, witch hunt **10** rooting-out **11** eradication, exterminate **13** extermination

purification
05 purge **06** lustre **07** elution, lustrum **08** cleaning **09** catharsis, cleansing, epuration, purgation **10** absolution, depuration, filtration, fumigation, lustration, redemption, refinement **11** sublimation **12** desalination, disinfection, sanitization, zone refining **13** deodorization **14** reverse osmosis, sanctification **15** decontamination

purify
03 try **04** clay, fine **05** clean, purge, scrub **06** distil, filter, redeem, refine, retort, shrive **07** absolve, chasten, clarify, cleanse, epurate, expurge, freshen, furbish, mundify, rectify, sublime **08** chastise, defecate, depurate, filtrate, fumigate, lustrate, sanctify, sanitize **09** catharize, deodorize, disinfect, expurgate, sterilize, sublimate, sublimize **10** circumcise **13** decontaminate

purifying
06 fining **07** lustral, purging **08** refining **09** cathartic, cleansing, purgative **10** depurative, lustration **11** cathartical, expurgation **12** purificatory **13** mundificative

purism
08 Atticism, pedantry **09** austerity, formalism, fussiness, orthodoxy, restraint **10** classicism, strictness **13** over-precision **14** fastidiousness

purist
05 fussy **06** pedant, strict **07** finicky **08** captious, pedantic, puristic, quibbler, stickler **09** dogmatist, formalist, nit-picker, over-exact, quibbling **10** fastidious, literalist, nit-picking **11** over-precise **12** precisionist **13** hypercritical **14** over-fastidious, over-meticulous, over-particular, uncompromising

puritan
04 prig **05** prude **06** zealot **07** fanatic, killjoy, pietist **08** Cromwell, Ironside, moralist, rigorist **09** Ironsides, precisian, Roundhead **10** goody-goody, spoilsport **14** disciplinarian

puritanical
04 prim **05** rigid, stern, stiff **06** proper, severe, strict, stuffy **07** ascetic, austere, bigoted, precise, prudish, puritan, zealous **09** fanatical **10** abstemious, goody-goody, moralistic **11** round-headed, strait-laced **12** disapproving, narrow-minded **14** disciplinarian

puritanism
07 bigotry **08** primness, rigidity, severity, zealotry **09** austerity, propriety, sternness, stiffness **10** abstinence, asceticism, fanaticism, narrowness, self-denial, strictness **11** prudishness **12** priggishness, rigorousness **14** abstemiousness, self-discipline

purity
04 pure **05** truth **06** candor, honour, orient, virtue **07** candour, clarity, decency, honesty **08** chastity, goodness, morality, nobility, pureness, sanctity **09** chiarezza, cleanness, clearness, freshness, innocence, integrity, rectitude, sincerity, virginity **10** perfection, simplicity, worthiness **11** cleanliness, genuineness, uprightness **12** authenticity, flawlessness, virtuousness **13** blamelessness, untaintedness, wholesomeness

• **person of purity**
04 lily

purlieus
06 bounds, limits **07** borders, fringes, suburbs **08** confines, environs, vicinity **09** outskirts, perimeter, periphery, precincts **12** surroundings **13** neighbourhood

purloin
03 bag, rob **04** lift, nick, take, whip **05** annex, filch, pinch, steal, swipe **06** finger, nobble, pilfer, pocket, remove, rip off, snitch, thieve **07** cabbage, snaffle **08** abstract, scrounge, souvenir **10** run off with **11** appropriate **12** make away with

purple

Purples include:

04 anil, plum, puce, puke
05 lilac, mauve, pansy, prune
06 cerise, damson, indigo, maroon, violet
07 fuchsia, fuschia, heather, magenta, purpure

08 amethyst, burgundy, hyacinth, lavender, mulberry
09 aubergine
11 royal purple

purport
04 bear, gist, idea, mean, seem, show **05** claim, drift, imply, point, sense, tenor, theme **06** allege, assert, convey, denote, import, intend, pose as, spirit, thrust **07** bearing, betoken, declare, express, meaning, portend, pretend, profess, purpose, signify, suggest
08 indicate, maintain, proclaim, tendency **09** direction, substance
11 implication **12** significance

purportedly
09 allegedly, dubiously **10** apparently, doubtfully, ostensibly, putatively, reportedly, supposedly **13** by all accounts

purpose
03 aim, end, use **04** gain, goal, good, hope, idea, mean, plan, talk, wish, zeal
05 basis, drive, point, teleo-, telos, value **06** aspire, decide, design, desire, effect, intend, motive, object, reason, result, settle, target, vision **07** benefit, outcome, propose, purport, resolve
08 ambition, backbone, converse, devotion, firmness, function, meditate, tenacity **09** advantage, constancy, determine, intention, objective, principle, rationale **10** aspiration, dedication, doggedness, motivation, resolution, usefulness **11** application, contemplate, persistence
12 conversation, perseverance
13 determination, justification, steadfastness

• **on purpose**
08 à dessein, by design, wilfully
09 knowingly, purposely, wittingly
11 consciously **12** deliberately
13 intentionally **14** premeditatedly

purposeful
04 firm **06** dogged **07** decided
08 constant, positive, purposed, resolute, resolved **09** steadfast, tenacious **10** deliberate, determined, persistent, unwavering **11** persevering, unfaltering **12** single-minded, strong-willed

purposefully
10 resolutely **11** steadfastly, tenaciously
12 persistently, unwaveringly
13 perseveringly, unfalteringly
14 single-mindedly

purposeless
04 vain **05** empty **06** wanton
07 aimless, useless, vacuous
08 goalless, needless **09** pointless, senseless, shapeless, unmeaning
10 gratuitous, motiveless, objectless, unasked-for **11** nonsensical, thoughtless, uncalled-for, unnecessary

purposely
08 by design, wilfully **09** expressly, knowingly, on purpose **10** designedly
11 consciously **12** calculatedly, deliberately, specifically
13 intentionally **14** premeditatedly

purse
◇ *containment indicator*
04 bung, fisc, fisk, gift, prim **05** award, burse, close, funds, means, money, pouch, prize **06** pocket, pucker, reward, wallet **07** coffers, present, tighten, wrinkle **08** compress, contract, crumenal, finances, money-bag, treasury **09** exchequer, resources, spleuchan **10** pocketbook **12** draw together, porte-monnaie **13** press together

pursuance
07 pursuit **08** pursuing **09** discharge, effecting, execution, following
10 completion, fulfilment
11 achievement, performance, prosecution **12** effectuation
14 accomplishment

pursue
03 dog, sew, sue **04** hunt, seek, tail
05 chace, chase, harry, hound, stalk, track, trail **06** aim for, follow, harass, hold to, keep on, keep up, persue, pursew, shadow, try for **07** carry on, conduct, go after, perform, poursew, poursue, run down **08** aspire to, continue, engage in, follow up, hunt down, maintain, practise, run after
09 give chase, make after, persecute, persist in, prosecute, search for, strive for **10** whore after **11** inquire into, investigate, persevere in, work towards **12** have your goal **15** apply yourself to

pursuit
03 aim **04** goal, hunt, line, suit
05 caper, chase, chevy, chivy, craft, hobby, quest, trade, trail **06** attain, chivvy, search **07** hot trod, hunting, pastime, pursual, tailing **08** activity, interest, poursuit, pursuing, stalking, tracking, vocation **09** endeavour, following, hue and cry, poursuitt, pursuance, shadowing, specialty
10 aspiration, employment, occupation, speciality **11** continuance, persistence, wildfowling
12 perseverance **13** investigation

purvey
04 sell **05** cater, stock **06** deal in, pass on, retail, spread, supply **07** furnish, provide, publish, trade in, victual
08 put about, transmit **09** propagate, provision, publicize **11** communicate, disseminate

purveyor
06 dealer, seller, trader, vendor
08 manciple, provedor, provider, providor, provisor, retailer, stockist, supplier **09** provedore **10** propagator, proveditor, victualler **11** proveditore, transmitter **12** communicator, disseminator

pus
06 matter **07** quitter, quittor, seropus
09 diapyesis, discharge **11** suppuration

push
02 go **03** jog, put, ram **04** birr, bunt, butt, cram, goad, horn, hype, jolt, plug, poke, pole, prod, raid, spur, urge
05 boost, bully, drive, dunch, dunsh, egg on, elbow, foray, force, impel, knock, nudge, onset, press, shove
06 charge, coerce, effort, energy, firing, hustle, incite, jostle, market, notice, papers, peddle, plunge, propel, ramrod, squash, the axe, thrust, vigour
07 advance, assault, company, depress, impulse, promote, sacking, squeeze, the boot, the chop **08** ambition, dynamism, invasion, persuade, press for, pressure, the elbow, vitality **09** advertise, constrain, discharge, dismissal, encourage, incursion, influence, manhandle, offensive, onslaught, publicize, your cards **10** enterprise, get-up-and-go, initiative, pressurize
12 forcefulness **13** determination
14 marching orders, put the screws on

• **push around**
05 bully **06** pick on **07** torment
09 terrorize, victimize **10** intimidate

• **push off**
04 move, scat **05** leave, scram **06** beat it, depart, go away **07** buzz off, scarper
08 clear off, clear out, run along, shove off **09** make a move, push along
10 make tracks

• **push on**
04 go on, toil, urge **06** plod on
07 advance, carry on, go ahead, peg away, press on, proceed **08** continue, plug away, slog away, toil away **09** keep going, persevere, soldier on, stick at it
10 keep trying

pushed
06 hard-up, rushed **07** harried, hurried, pinched, pressed, short of
08 harassed, strapped **09** stretched
11 hard-pressed **13** under pressure
14 in difficulties

pushover
03 mug **04** dupe, gull **05** cinch
06 doddle, picnic, stooge, sucker
07 fall guy **08** duck soup, walkover, weakling **09** easy touch, soft touch
10 child's play **11** piece of cake, sitting duck **13** sitting target

pushy
04 bold **05** bossy, brash **07** forward
08 arrogant, assuming, forceful
09 ambitious, assertive **10** aggressive
11 impertinent **12** presumptuous
13 over-confident, self-assertive

pusillanimity
08 timidity, weakness **10** cravenness, feebleness **11** fearfulness, gutlessness, poltroonery **12** cowardliness, timorousness **13** spinelessness

pusillanimous
04 weak **05** timid **06** craven, feeble, scared, yellow **07** chicken, fearful, gutless, wimpish **08** cowardly, timorous **09** spineless, weak-kneed
11 lily-livered **12** faint-hearted, mean-spirited **14** chicken-hearted

pussyfoot
03 pad **05** creep, hedge, prowl, slink, steal **06** tiptoe **09** mess about **10** equivocate **11** prevaricate **12** tergiversate **14** prohibitionist

pustule
04 boil, pock **05** ulcer **06** blotch, fester, papule, pimple **07** abscess, blister, whitlow **08** eruption **09** carbuncle, whitehead **10** uredosorus

put
02 do **03** add, bet, fix, lay, pin, pit, say, set **04** cast, dump, flow, give, have, hurl, levy, park, post, push, rank, rest, risk, sink, sort, turn, word **05** affix, apply, class, couch, drive, exact, force, frame, gauge, grade, group, guess, impel, offer, place, plonk, speak, spend, stake, stand, state, throw, utter, voice **06** append, assert, assign, attach, call on, chance, charge, commit, convey, demand, devote, gamble, impose, impute, incite, invest, locate, oblige, phrase, reckon, reduce, render, repose, set out, settle, submit, tender, thrust **07** arrange, ascribe, bumpkin, connect, convert, deposit, dispose, express, inflict, lay down, present, proceed, proffer, propose, require, set down, situate, station, subject, suggest, venture, work out **08** classify, dedicate, estimate, position, propound, set forth **09** attribute, constrain, establish, formulate, greenhorn, lay before, pronounce, set before, translate, transport **10** categorize, contribute, transcribe **11** guesstimate **12** bring forward

• **put about**
04 tell **06** spread **07** publish **08** announce, distress **09** circulate, make known **11** disseminate

• **put across**
06 convey **07** clarify, explain, express, get over, put over **08** bring off, spell out **09** get across, make clear **11** bring home to, communicate **12** get through to **14** make understood

• **put aside**
04 keep, save, stow **05** hoard, lay by, put by, set by, stash, store **06** retain, shelve **07** reserve **08** lay aside, salt away, set apart, set aside **09** stockpile **12** put to one side **13** keep in reserve

• **put away**
03 eat **04** down, jail, keep, kill, save, stow, wolf **05** drink, eat up, lay by, put by, scoff, snarf, store, waive **06** bang up, commit, devour, guzzle, lock up, pack up, retain, tuck in **07** cashier, certify, confine, consume, divorce, reserve, swallow **08** imprison, lay aside, put aside, renounce, send down, set aside **09** polish off, stockpile **11** incarcerate **13** keep in reserve

• **put back**
05 defer, delay, remit **06** freeze, return, shelve, tidy up **07** adjourn, clear up, replace, repulse, restore, suspend **08** postpone, put on ice, tidy away **09** clear away, reinstate **10** reschedule **13** procrastinate **14** take a raincheck

• **put down**
03 fix, lay, log **04** alay, drop, kill, laid, list, snub, stop **05** abase, aleye, allay, blame, crush, enter, lower, plonk, quash, quell, shame, sneap **06** attach, charge, defeat, humble, reckon, record, slight, squash **07** ascribe, confute, deflate, degrade, destroy, jot down, mortify, repress, set down, silence, squelch, surpass **08** belittle, note down, outshine, register, stamp out, suppress, underlay **09** attribute, deprecate, disparage, humiliate, write down **10** put to sleep, transcribe **12** take down a peg

• **put forward**
03 lay, run **04** move, pose, urge **05** offer, table **06** assign, obtend, prefer, submit, tender **07** advance, present, proffer, propone, propose, suggest **08** nominate **09** hold forth, introduce, recommend

• **put in**
◇ *insertion indicator*
03 fit **05** enter, input **06** insert, submit **07** install, present **09** introduce

• **put in for**
05 order **06** ask for **07** request **08** apply for **11** requisition, write off for **14** fill in a form for

• **put off**
03 fob, fub **04** daff, doff **05** daunt, defer, delay, deter, lay by, shift **06** dismay, divert, shelve, sicken **07** adjourn, confuse, deflect, dismiss, respite, suspend **08** dissuade, distract, nauseate, postpone, put on ice, turn away **09** sidetrack, talk out of, turn aside **10** demoralize, disconcert, discourage, dishearten, intimidate, reschedule **13** procrastinate **14** take a raincheck

• **put on**
02 do **03** add, don **04** fake, give, robe, sham, wear **05** affix, apply, feign, lay on, mount, place, stage, try on **06** affect, assume, attach, impose, plug in, supply, turn on **07** connect, dress in, get into, perform, present, pretend, produce, provide, start up, throw on **08** activate, organize, simulate, slip into, switch on **10** change into **11** make believe **12** get dressed in **13** get dolled up in

• **put out**
03 irk **04** dout, faze, hurt **05** anger, annoy, douse, dowse, issue, snuff, upset, utter **06** bother, offend, quench **07** dismiss, disturb, extinct, perturb, provoke, publish, smother, trouble **08** announce, bring out, disclose, impose on, irritate, stamp out, unsettle **09** broadcast, circulate, infuriate, make known **10** discommode, disconcert, exasperate, extinguish, mistrysted **13** inconvenience

• **put through**
06 manage **07** achieve, execute, process **08** bring off, complete, conclude, finalize **10** accomplish

• **put together**
04 join **05** build, frame, marry **06** cobble, made up, make up **07** compile, concoct **08** assemble **09** carpenter, construct **11** fit together **13** piece together

• **put up**
◇ *reversal down indicator*
03 inn, pay **04** give **05** build, erect, float, house, lodge, offer, raise, sling, stake **06** bump up, choose, hike up, invest, jack up, pledge, supply **07** advance, propose, provide, sheathe, shelter, suggest **08** assemble, compound, escalate, increase, nominate **09** construct, recommend **10** put forward **11** accommodate, give a room to

• **put upon**
07 exploit **08** impose on **13** inconvenience, take liberties **14** take for granted **15** take advantage of

• **put up to**
04 goad, urge **05** egg on **06** incite, prompt **08** persuade **09** encourage

• **put up with**
04 bear, lump, take, wear **05** abide, allow, brook, stand **06** accept, endure, suffer **07** stomach, swallow **08** stand for, tolerate **13** take lying down

putative
07 alleged, assumed, reputed **08** presumed, reported, supposed **10** reputative **11** conjectural, theoretical **12** hypothetical, suppositious **13** suppositional

put-down
03 dig **04** gibe, snub **05** sneer **06** insult, rebuff, slight **07** affront, sarcasm **11** humiliation **13** disparagement, slap in the face

put-off
04 curb **06** damper, excuse **07** evasion **08** obstacle **09** deterrent, hindrance, restraint **10** constraint **12** disincentive, postponement **14** discouragement

putrefaction
03 rot **05** decay, mould **06** fungus, mildew, sepsis **07** rotting **08** going bad **09** perishing, putridity **11** putrescence **13** decomposition

putrefy
03 rot **05** addle, decay, go bad, mould, spoil, stink, taint **06** fester, perish **07** corrupt **08** gangrene **09** decompose **11** deteriorate

putrescent
07 rotting **08** decaying, mephitic, stinking **09** festering, perishing **10** putrefying **11** decomposing

putrid
03 bad, off **04** foul, rank **05** addle, fetid **06** addled, foetid, mouldy, rancid, rotten, turned **07** corrupt, decayed, tainted **08** decaying, polluted, stinking **10** decomposed, disgusting **11** decomposing **12** contaminated

put-upon
04 used **06** abused **09** exploited, imposed on **10** maltreated, persecuted **14** inconvenienced

puzzle
◇ *anagram indicator*
04 beat, crux, pose **05** brood, floor, poser, stump, think **06** baffle, bemuse, enigma, fickle, figure, gravel, kittle, ponder **07** bumbaze, confuse, dilemma, flummox, mystery, mystify, nonplus, paradox, perplex, problem, stagger, tickler **08** bewilder, confound, consider, entangle, intrigue, meditate, mull over, muse over, question
09 bamboozle, fascinate
10 complicate, deliberate, mind-bender, perplexity **11** brainteaser
12 bewilderment, brain-twister
13 metagrobolize **14** beat your brains, rack your brains, think hard about

Puzzles include:

04 maze, quiz
05 logic, rebus
06 hanjie, jigsaw, kakuro, riddle, sudoku
07 anagram, hangman, sorites, tangram
08 acrostic, wordgame
09 crossword, conundrum
10 alphametic, cryptogram, Rubik's Cube®, wordsearch
12 magic pyramid

• puzzle out
03 get **04** suss **05** crack, solve
06 decode **07** clear up, resolve, sort out, suss out, unravel, work out
08 decipher, think out, untangle
09 figure out **13** metagrabolize, metagrobolize, piece together **15** find the answer to

puzzled
04 lost **05** at sea **06** beaten **07** at a loss, baffled, floored, in a haze, stumped
08 confused **09** flummoxed, mystified, perplexed **10** bamboozled, bewildered, confounded, nonplussed

puzzlement
05 doubt **06** wonder **08** surprise
09 confusion **10** bafflement, perplexity
11 incertitude, uncertainty
12 astonishment, bewilderment, doubtfulness **13** bamboozlement, mystification **14** disorientation
• expression of puzzlement
02 ha **03** hah, hey, huh **04** anan, anon
05 heigh **06** indeed

puzzling
05 queer, trick **06** arcane, knotty, posing **07** bizarre, cryptic, curious, strange, unclear **08** abstruse, baffling, involved, mystical, peculiar, riddling, tortuous **09** ambiguous, confusing, damnedest, enigmatic, equivocal, intricate **10** misleading, mysterious, mystifying, perplexing, Sphynx-like
11 bewildering, enigmatical, mind-bending **12** impenetrable, inexplicable, labyrinthine, mind-boggling, unfathomable
13 unaccountable

pygmy
03 elf, toy, wee **04** baby, tiny **05** atomy, dwarf, elfin, small **06** midget, minute, pocket **07** manikin, Negrito, stunted
08 dwarfish, half-pint, Tom Thumb
09 miniature, minuscule, pint-sized, thumbling **10** diminutive, fingerling, homunculus, undersized **11** hop-o'-my-thumb, Lilliputian

pyramid
05 stack **08** teocalli, ziggurat, zikkurat

pyromaniac
04 pyro **07** firebug **08** arsonist **10** fire-raiser, incendiary

Q
03 cue **06** Quebec **13** trichosanthin

Qatar
01 Q **02** QA **03** QAT

quack
04 fake, sham **05** bogus, false, fraud, pseud **06** cowboy, crocus, doctor, humbug, phoney **07** empiric
08 impostor, so-called, spurious, supposed, swindler **09** charlatan, pretended, pretender, trickster
10 fraudulent, medicaster, mountebank
11 counterfeit, masquerader, quacksalver, saltimbanco, unqualified

quackery
04 sham **05** fraud **06** humbug
09 imposture, phoniness
10 empiricism **11** fraudulence
12 charlatanism **13** mountebankery, mountebankism

quadrangle
04 quad **05** court, plaza **06** piazza, square **08** cloister **09** courtyard, enclosure, esplanade

quaff
04 down, gulp, swig **05** booze, drain, drink, swill **06** guzzle, imbibe, quaich, tipple **07** carouse, draught, swallow, toss off **08** drink off **09** crush a cup, knock back

quagmire
03 bog, fen, fix **04** hole, mess, mire, quag **05** marsh, swamp **06** morass, pickle, slough **07** dilemma, problem
08 entangle, hot water, quandary, wagmoire **09** deep water, quicksand, tight spot **10** perplexity

quail
05 colin, cower, daunt, quake, shake, whore **06** blench, caille, cringe, falter, flinch, recoil, shiver, shrink, subdue
07 decline, shudder, shy away, slacken, tremble **08** back away, bobwhite, draw back, hemipode, languish, percolin, pull back **09** partridge

quaint
◇ *anagram indicator*
03 odd **04** fine, twee **05** droll, funky, queer, sweet **06** queint, whimsy
07 bizarre, cunning, curious, skilful, strange, unusual, whimsey
08 charming, fanciful, old-world
09 ingenious, whimsical **10** antiquated, attractive, auld-farand, olde-worlde
11 picturesque **12** old-fashioned

quaintly
05 oddly **09** curiously, strangely, unusually **10** charmingly
11 whimsically **12** attractively
13 picturesquely

quaintness
05 charm **11** unusualness
13 whimsicalness **14** attractiveness
15 picturesqueness

quake
◇ *anagram indicator*
04 move, rock, sway **05** heave, quail, shake, throb **06** didder, dither, quiver, shiver, tremor, wamble, wobble
07 pulsate, shudder, tremble, vibrate
08 convulse

qualification
05 rider, skill **06** caveat, degree
07 ability, diploma, fitness, proviso
08 aptitude, capacity, training
09 allowance, condition, exception, exemption, provision **10** adaptation, adjustment, capability, competence, limitation **11** certificate, eligibility, proficiency, reservation, restriction, stipulation, suitability **12** modification
13 certification **14** accomplishment

Qualifications include:

02 AB, AM, AS, BA, BD, BE, BL, BM, BS, DC, DD, DS, IB, MA, MB, MD, MS
03 BAI, BAS, BCh, BCL, BDS, BEd, BRE, BSc, ChB, ChM, CSE, DCh, DCL, DDS, DEd, DPh, DSc, DTh, EdB, EdD, FPC, LHD, LLB, LLD, LLM, MBA, MCh, MDS, MEd, MSc, NVQ, ONC, OND, PhD, ScB, ScD, SCE, SVQ, ThD, VMD
04 BAgr, BCom, BEng, B ès L, B ès S, BLit, BMus, BTEC, BVM&S, DEng, DIng, DLit, DMus, GCSE, GNVQ, LitB, LitD, MBSc, MCom, MDSc, MMus, MusB, MusD
05 BArch, BComm, BLitt, BPhil, DLitt, DPhil, LittB, LittD, Lower, MEcon, MLitt, MPhil, MTech
06 A level, BAgric, BPharm, degree, DTheol, Higher, MPharm, O grade, O level
07 AS level
10 eleven-plus, Lower grade, School Cert
11 Higher grade, Legum doctor
12 Doctor of Laws, Master of Arts, Master of Laws
13 Advanced level, Bachelor of Law, Doctor of Music, Legum magister, Master of Music, Ordinary grade, Ordinary level, Standard grade
14 Advanced Higher, Artium Magister, Bachelor of Arts, Bachelor of Laws, Magister Artium
15 Bachelor of Music, Doctor of Letters, Doctor of Science, Doctor of Surgery, Master of Letters, Master of Science, Master of Surgery, Medicinae Doctor

qualified
03 fit **04** able, meet **05** adept
06 expert, fitted **07** bounded, capable, guarded, limited, skilful, skilled, trained **08** cautious, eligible, equipped, licensed, modified, prepared, reserved, talented
09 certified, chartered, competent, efficient, equivocal, practised
10 contingent, proficient, restricted
11 conditional, experienced, provisional **12** accomplished, professional **13** circumscribed, knowledgeable

qualify
03 fit **04** ease, pass, vary **05** abate, allow, alloy, coach, equip, limit, prove, teach, train **06** adjust, define, ground, lessen, modify, permit, reduce, soften, temper, weaken **07** appease, certify, confirm, delimit, empower, entitle, license, prepare, warrant
08 classify, diminish, graduate, instruct, mitigate, moderate, restrain, restrict, sanction **09** alleviate, authorize, be allowed, contemper, make ready **10** be eligible, capacitate, habilitate **12** characterize **15** make conditional

quality
01 Q **02** it **04** cast, kind, make, mark, rank, sort, type **05** class, grade, level, merit, skill, trait, value, worth
06 aspect, make-up, manner, nature, status, timbre **07** calibre, feature, variety **08** eminence, property, standard **09** attribute, character, condition **10** excellence, profession, refinement **11** distinction, peculiarity, pre-eminence, superiority
14 accomplishment, characteristic
• **quality assurance**
02 QA

qualm
04 fear **05** doubt, worry **07** anxiety, concern, scruple **08** disquiet
09 hesitancy, misgiving **10** hesitation, reluctance, uneasiness
11 compunction, uncertainty
12 apprehension **14** disinclination

quandary
03 fix, jam **04** hole, mess **06** muddle, pickle **07** dilemma, impasse, problem

09 confusion, tight spot 10 difficulty, perplexity 11 predicament
12 bewilderment

quantify
05 count, weigh 06 number
07 measure, specify 08 evaluate
09 calculate, calibrate, determine, enumerate

quantity
02 qt 03 lot, qty, sum 04 area, bulk, deal, dose, lots, many, mass, much, part, size, tons 05 heaps, loads, quota, reams, scrap, share, total 06 amount, extent, length, masses, number, oodles, stacks, volume, weight
07 breadth, content, expanse, measure, portion 08 capacity, fragment 09 aggregate, allotment, extension, magnitude 10 proportion

See also **measurement**

• in equal quantities
01 ā 02 āā 03 ana

• small quantity
04 curn, drib, lock

• unknown quantity
01 X, Y, Z

quarantine
09 detention, isolation, lazaretto, quarenden, quarender 10 quarrender
11 quarrington, segregation

quarrel
03 jar, row, wap 04 beef, feud, miff, slam, spat, tiff, tift, whid 05 argue, brawl, broil, cavil, chide, clash, fault, fight, flite, flyte, knock, run-in, scrap, set-to, slate 06 barney, bicker, breach, breeze, bust-up, charge, differ, dust-up, fracas, fratch, jangle, quar'le, quarry, ruffle, rumble, schism, square, strife
07 brattle, cast out, censure, contend, dispute, dissent, fall out, outcast, outfall, punch-up, wrangle
08 argument, conflict, disagree, squabble, vendetta 09 caterwaul, complaint, criticize, have words, objection 10 contention, difference, differency, difficulty, dissension, falling-out 11 altercation, controversy, disputation, pick holes in 12 be at variance, disagreement, pull to pieces
13 exchange blows, exchange words, find fault with, part brass rags, shouting match, slanging match 15 be at loggerheads

quarrelling
06 at odds, rowing, strife 07 discord, feuding, warring 08 fighting, variance
09 bickering, scrapping, wrangling
10 at variance, contending, contention, discordant, disharmony, dissension, squabbling 11 altercation, disputation, dissentient 12 argy-bargying
13 argumentation, at loggerheads
14 vitilitigation

quarrelsome
06 chippy 07 scrappy, stroppy
09 bellicose, camstairy, camsteary, debateful, irascible, irritable
10 camsteerie, pugnacious
11 belligerent, contentious, hot-tempered, ill-tempered
12 cantankerous, disputatious
13 argumentative 14 ready for a fight

quarry
04 game, goal, kill, mark, prey
05 chase, curry, prize, spoil 06 currie, object, target, victim 07 quarrel
08 stone pit 09 glory hole, slaughter

quarter
01 E, N, q, S, W 02 qr, qu 03 pad 04 airt, area, digs, east, hand, part, pity, post, side, spot, west, zone 05 board, grace, house, lodge, mercy, north, place, point, put up, quart, rooms, south
06 billet, favour, fourth, ghetto, medina, pardon, region, sector
07 Moorery, section, shelter, station, two bits 08 barracks, clemency, district, division, domicile, dwelling, leniency, locality, lodgings, province, quartern, vicinity 09 direction, residence, territory 10 compassion, habitation, indulgence
11 accommodate, forgiveness
13 accommodation, neighbourhood

See also **compass**

quarterly
02 qu 04 quar 12 three-monthly

quarters
04 camp 05 house 06 ghetto
07 lodging

See also **accommodation**

quartz
04 jasp 05 flint, prase 06 jasper, morion 07 crystal 08 amethyst, tiger eye 09 buhrstone, burrstone, cacholong, cairngorm, carnelian, cornelian, goldstone, tiger's eye
10 avanturine, aventurine, chalcedony
11 rock crystal 12 Bohemian ruby, Spanish topaz 14 Bristol-diamond, cairngorm-stone 15 occidental topaz

quash
04 void 05 annul, crush, quell
06 cancel, defeat, repeal, revoke, scotch, squash, subdue 07 nullify, rescind, reverse 08 abrogate, override, overrule, overturn, set aside, suppress
09 overthrow 10 invalidate, put an end to 11 countermand

quaver
03 sob 05 break, quake, shake, throb, trill, waver 06 quiver, tremor, warble, wobble 07 flicker, flutter, pulsate, shudder, tremble, tremolo, vibrate, vibrato 09 oscillate, trembling, vibration 10 eighth note 11 quaveriness

quay
03 kay, key 04 dock, pier 05 jetty, levee, wharf 07 harbour

queasiness
06 nausea 07 gagging 08 retching, sickness, vomiting 11 airsickness, biliousness, carsickness, seasickness
12 sick headache 14 motion sickness, travel sickness 15 morning sickness

queasy
03 ill 04 sick 05 dizzy, faint, giddy, green, queer, rough 06 groggy, uneasy, unwell 07 bilious 08 nauseous, sickened 09 hazardous, nauseated, squeamish, unsettled 10 fastidious, out of sorts, scrupulous 15 under the weather

Quebec
01 Q 02 QC

queen
01 Q, R 02 ER, FD, HM, Qu, VR 03 VIR
04 idol, rani 05 belle, charm, ranee, ruler, Venus 06 beauty, prince, Brenda, regina 07 consort, empress, majesty, monarch 08 princess 09 sovereign
11 head of state

Queens include:

03 Mab
04 Anne, Anne (of Cleves), Emma, Grey (Jane, Lady), Joan (of Navarre), Mary, Mary (Queen of Scots), Mary (of Teck), Parr (Catherine)
05 Maeve, Maria, Marie (de Médici), Sheba
06 Boleyn (Anne), Esther, Hearts, Himiko, Howard (Catherine), Louisa, Nzinga, Salote, Silvia, Soraya
07 Beatrix, Eleanor (of Aquitaine), Eleanor (of Castile), Juliana, Macbeth (Lady), Seymour (Jane), Titania, Zenobia
08 Adelaide, Berenice, Boadicea, Boudicca, Caroline (of Ansbach), Caroline (of Brunswick), Clotilda (St), Gloriana, Isabella (of Castile), Kristina, Margaret (St), Margaret (of Anjou), Philippa (of Hainault), Victoria
09 Alexandra, Artemisia, Brunhilde, Catherine (de Médici), Catherine (of Aragon), Catherine (of Braganza), Christina, Cleopatra, Elizabeth, Fredegond, Margrethe, Mary Tudor, Nefertiti, Semiramis, Woodville (Elizabeth)
10 Hatshepsut, Lakshmi Bai, Wilhelmina
13 Margaret Tudor
14 Henrietta Maria
15 Charlotte Sophia, Marie Antoinette

queenly
05 grand, noble, regal, royal 06 august
07 reginal, stately, sublime 08 gracious, imperial, majestic, splendid
09 dignified, imperious, sovereign
11 monarchical

queer
◇ *anagram indicator*
03 gay, ill, mar, odd, rum 04 camp, foil, harm, iffy, ruin, sick 05 botch, butch, cheat, dizzy, faint, fishy, funny, giddy, quare, rough, shady, spoil, upset, weird, wreck 06 Fifish, impair, quaint, queasy, shifty, stymie, thwart, unwell
07 bizarre, curious, deviant, dubious, lesbian, strange, suspect, unusual
08 abnormal, bisexual, doubtful,

endanger, peculiar, puzzling, ridicule, singular, uncommon **09** eccentric, frustrate, irregular, unnatural **10** homosexual, jeopardize, mysterious, outlandish, out of sorts, remarkable, suspicious, unorthodox **11** counterfeit, light-headed **13** extraordinary, funny peculiar **14** unconventional **15** under the weather

queerness
06 oddity **11** abnormality, bizarreness, curiousness, peculiarity, singularity, strangeness, unorthodoxy, unusualness **12** eccentricity, irregularity, uncommonness **13** anomalousness, unnaturalness

quell
03 die **04** alay, calm, hush, kill, rout, stay **05** abash, abate, aleye, allay, crush, quash, quiet **06** defeat, pacify, perish, soothe, squash, stifle, subdue **07** appease, conquer, put down, silence, slaying, subside **08** mitigate, moderate, overcome, suppress, vanquish **09** alleviate, overpower **10** disconcert, extinguish, put an end to, spiflicate **11** spifflicate

quench
04 cool, sate, stop **05** douse, slake **06** put out, sloken, stanch, stifle **07** destroy, satiate, satisfy, slocken, smother, staunch **08** snuff out, stamp out **10** extinguish

querulous
04 sour **05** cross, fussy, ratty, testy **06** shirty **07** carping, fretful, grouchy, peevish **08** captious, critical, petulant **09** fractious, grumbling, irascible, irritable, plaintive **11** complaining **12** cantankerous, discontented, dissatisfied, fault-finding

query
01 Q **02** qy **03** ask **05** doubt, qualm **06** quaere, qualms **07** dispute, inquire, inquiry, problem, quibble, suspect **08** distrust, mistrust, question **09** challenge, suspicion **10** disbelieve, hesitation, scepticism, uneasiness **11** quarrel with, reservation, uncertainty **12** question mark **13** be sceptical of, throw doubts on

quest
03 aim **04** bark, goal, hunt, yelp **06** search, voyage **07** crusade, inquiry, journey, mission, purpose, pursuit, seeking, venture **08** ringdove **09** adventure **10** enterprise, expedition, pilgrimage, wood pigeon **11** exploration, undertaking **13** investigation

• in quest of
03 for, out **06** out for **08** questing **10** hunting for **11** in pursuit of **12** harking after, searching for, seeking after, trying to find **14** trying to obtain

question
01 Q **02** Qu **03** ask **04** chin, poll, pose, pump, quiz **05** demur, doubt, grill, issue, point, poser, probe, query, theme, topic **06** debate, matter, motion, quaere, riddle, teaser **07** debrief, discuss, dispute, enquiry, erotema, eroteme, examine, inquire, inquiry, problem, scruple, subject **08** argument, converse, erotesis, proposal **09** backspeer, backspeir, catechize, challenge, conundrum, interview, objection **10** difficulty, disbelieve, discussion **11** controversy, interrogate, investigate, proposition, uncertainty **12** conversation, cross-examine, peradventure, point at issue **13** cross-question, interrogation, interrogatory **15** have doubts about, have qualms about

• in question
07 at issue **09** concerned **14** being discussed **15** under discussion

• out of the question
06 absurd **10** impossible, ridiculous **11** unthinkable **12** unacceptable, unbelievable

• without question
07 on trust **11** immediately **14** unhesitatingly, unquestionably, without arguing

questionable
◇ *anagram indicator*
04 iffy **05** fishy, shady, vexed **07** dubious, immoral, suspect **08** arguable, doubtful, improper, unproven **09** debatable, equivocal, uncertain, unsettled **10** at question, disputable, suspicious **11** problematic **12** undetermined **13** controversial, problematical

questioner
07 doubter, sceptic **08** agnostic, examiner, inquirer **09** catechist **10** catechizer, inquisitor, quizmaster **11** disbeliever, interrogant, interviewer **12** interlocutor, interrogator, investigator **14** question-master

questionnaire
04 form, quiz, test **06** survey **11** opinion poll **14** market research

queue
03 row **04** file, line, tail **05** chain, order, train **06** back up, column, fall in, in line, line up, series, string **07** pigtail **08** sequence, tailback **09** breadline, crocodile, form a line **10** form a queue, procession, succession, wait in line **11** stand in line **13** concatenation

quibble
03 pun **04** carp, quip **05** cavil, dodge, query, quirk **06** haggle, niggle, peck at, snatch **07** brabble, nit-pick, protest, quiblin, quiddit, quillet **08** equivoke, pettifog, quiddity **09** complaint, criticism, equivoque, objection **10** equivocate, nit-picking, split hairs **11** prevaricate **12** carriwitchet, equivocation, pettifogging **13** avoid the issue, find fault with, prevarication

quibbler
07 casuist, niggler, sophist **08** caviller, chicaner **09** nit-picker **11** equivocator, pettifogger **12** hair-splitter

quibbling
07 carping, evasive **08** captious, critical, niggling, overnice **09** ambiguous, casuistic, cavilling, chicanery, chicaning **10** nit-picking **12** equivocating, pettifogging **13** hair-splitting, logic-chopping, word-splitting

quick
03 hot, pdq **04** fast, keen, rath, soon, yare **05** agile, alive, brief, brisk, flash, hasty, nifty, nippy, rapid, rathe, ready, sharp, smart, swift, zippy **06** astute, clever, dapper, living, mobile, nimble, presto, prompt, shrewd, speedy, sudden **07** cursory, express, flutter, hurried, instant, rapidly, schnell **08** expedite, fleeting, pregnant, shifting **09** immediate, receptive, sensitive, sprightly **10** discerning, perceptive, responsive **11** expeditious, intelligent, perfunctory, quick-witted, sharp-witted **12** without delay **13** instantaneous **15** pretty damn quick, quick off the mark

quicken
04 stir, whet **05** couch, hurry, rouse, speed **06** arouse, excite, hasten, incite, kindle, revive, stir up **07** advance, animate, enliven, hurry up, inspire, refresh, speed up **08** activate, dispatch, energize, expedite, revivify **09** galvanize, instigate, stimulate **10** accelerate, couch grass, invigorate, reactivate, revitalize, strengthen **11** precipitate **12** reinvigorate

quickly
04 cito, fast, soon, vite **05** apace, quick, slick, swith **06** presto, pronto **07** briskly, express, hastily, rapidly, readily, smartly, swiftly **08** abruptly, promptly, smartish, speedily **09** cursorily, hurriedly, instantly, like a shot, like smoke, overnight, posthaste **11** at the double, immediately, prestissimo **12** a mile a minute, lickety-split, with dispatch **13** expeditiously, perfunctorily **14** at a rate of knots, hell for leather, unhesitatingly **15** instantaneously, like the clappers

quickness
05 speed **06** acumen **07** agility **08** celerity, keenness, rapidity **09** acuteness, alertness, briskness, hastiness, immediacy, nimblesse, readiness, sharpness, swiftness **10** astuteness, expedition, nimbleness, promptness, shrewdness, speediness, suddenness **11** penetration, promptitude **12** intelligence **13** precipitation **15** quick-wittedness

quick-tempered
05 fiery, testy **06** snappy, touchy **07** waspish **08** choleric, petulant, shrewish, volcanic **09** excitable, explosive, impatient, impulsive, irascible, irritable, splenetic **11** hot-tempered, quarrelsome **13** temperamental

quick-witted
04 keen **05** acute, alert, sharp, smart, witty **06** astute, bright, clever, crafty, shrewd **09** ingenious, wide-awake **10** perceptive **11** intelligent, penetrating, ready-witted, resourceful **12** nimble-witted **15** quick off the mark

quid
01 L **03** sov **04** chew, oner **05** libra, pound, squid **06** guinea, nicker **07** smacker **09** sovereign, substance **12** jimmy-o'goblin **13** pound sterling

See also **pound**

quid pro quo
04 swap **07** damages **08** exchange, trade-off **09** mutuality, tit for tat **10** equivalent **11** co-operation, equivalence, give-and-take, reciprocity **12** compensation, remuneration **13** reciprocation

quiescent
04 calm **05** inert, quiet, still **06** asleep, at rest, latent, placid, serene, silent **07** dormant, passive, resting **08** inactive, peaceful, sleeping, tranquil **09** reposeful **10** in abeyance, motionless, untroubled **11** undisturbed

quiet
01 p **02** QT, sh **03** dry, low, shy **04** calm, ease, hush, loun, lown, lull, meek, mild, pale, rest, soft **05** doggo, faint, lound, lownd, muted, peace, shtum, sober, still, stoic, stumm **06** gentle, hushed, lonely, low-key, pastel, placid, repose, secret, serene, settle, shtoom, shtumm, silent, sleepy, stilly, subtle **07** appease, easeful, muffled, orderly, private, schtoom, silence, subdued **08** composed, discreet, isolated, man-to-man, peaceful, personal, reserved, reticent, retiring, secluded, serenity, taciturn, tranquil **09** inaudible, introvert, noiseless, quietness, soundless, stillness, withdrawn **10** indistinct, phlegmatic, restrained, thoughtful, untroubled **11** inoffensive, sequestered, undisturbed, unexcitable, unflappable **12** confidential, off-the-record, peacefulness, tranquillity, unfrequented, woman-to-woman **13** imperturbable, noiselessness, soundlessness, unforthcoming, without a sound **15** uncommunicative, undemonstrative

See also **silence**

quieten
04 calm, dull, hush, mute **05** lower, quell, quiet, shush, sober, still **06** deaden, muffle, pacify, reduce, shut up, smooth, soften, soothe, stifle, subdew, subdue **07** compose, silence **08** calm down, diminish **12** tranquillize

quietly
01 p **04** loun, lown, soft **05** lound, lownd, still **06** calmly, gently, meekly, mildly, mutely, softly **08** modestly, placidly, secretly, silently **09** inaudibly, privately **10** peacefully, tranquilly **11** noiselessly, soundlessly **12** deliberately **13** unobtrusively **15** surreptitiously

quietness
04 calm, hush, lull **05** peace, quiet, still **06** repose **07** inertia, silence **08** calmness, dullness, quietude, serenity **09** composure, placidity, stillness **10** inactivity, quiescence **12** peacefulness, tranquillity **14** uneventfulness

quietude
04 calm, hush, rest **05** peace, quiet **06** repose **07** ataraxy, silence **08** ataraxia, calmness, coolness, serenity **09** composure, placidity, quietness, stillness **10** equanimity, sedateness **11** restfulness **12** peacefulness, tranquillity

quietus
03 end **05** death **06** demise **07** decease, release **08** dispatch, quashing **09** death-blow, discharge, silencing **10** extinction **11** acquittance, coup de grâce, death-stroke, elimination **15** finishing stroke

quilt
05 doona, duvet, twilt **06** downie, kantha, thrash **07** comfort **08** bedcover, coverlet **09** bedspread, comforter, eiderdown **11** counterpane **12** counterpoint **14** patchwork quilt

quince
03 bel **04** bael, bhel **06** feijoa **08** japonica **11** chaenomeles, queene-apple

quinine
04 kina **05** china, quina **08** cinchona, kinakina **09** quinquina **10** chinachina, quinaquina

quinsy
06 angina **08** cynanche, prunella **09** squinancy **11** tonsillitis

quintessence
04 core, gist, pith, soul **05** heart **06** elixir, kernel, marrow, spirit **07** essence, extract, pattern **08** exemplar, quiddity **10** embodiment **12** distillation **15** personification, sum and substance

quintessential
05 ideal **06** entire **07** perfect, typical **08** complete, ultimate **09** essential **10** consummate, definitive **12** archetypical, prototypical

quip
03 gag **04** gibe, jest, joke **05** crack, quirk **06** retort, zinger **07** epigram, quibble, riposte **08** one-liner **09** wisecrack, witticism **10** knick-knack, pleasantry **12** carriwitchet

quirk
03 way **04** kink, quip, turn, whim **05** fluke, freak, habit, knack, thing, trait, trick, twist **06** foible, hang-up, oddity, vagary **07** caprice, feature, quibble **09** curiosity, mannerism, obsession **11** peculiarity **12** eccentricity, idiosyncrasy **14** characteristic

quirkiness
06 oddity **07** anomaly **08** zaniness **09** wackiness, weirdness **10** aberration, freakiness **11** abnormality, bizarreness, peculiarity, singularity, strangeness, unorthodoxy **12** eccentricity, freakishness, idiosyncrasy **13** nonconformity **14** capriciousness

quirky
◇ *anagram indicator*
03 odd **04** wild, zany **05** barmy, drôle, droll, funky, funny, kinky, queer, wacky, weird **06** far-out, freaky, way-out, whimsy **07** bizarre, curious, deviant, oddball, strange, uncanny, unusual **08** aberrant, abnormal, atypical, crackers, freakish, original, peculiar, singular, uncommon **09** different, eccentric, irregular, whimsical **10** capricious, off the wall, outlandish, remarkable **11** exceptional **13** extraordinary, idiosyncratic **14** unconventional

quisling
05 Judas **06** puppet **07** traitor **08** betrayer, renegade, turncoat **12** collaborator **14** fifth columnist

quit
02 go **03** end, rid **04** drop, exit, free, part, stop, void **05** avoid, cease, clear, leave, quite, quyte, repay, shift, stash **06** acquit, decamp, depart, desert, desist, give up, go away, pack in, quight, resign, retire, vacate **07** abandon, abstain, forsake, requite **08** leave off, renounce, withdraw **09** surrender **10** chicken out, relinquish **11** discontinue

quite
03 all, yes **04** full, just, real, tout, very **05** clean, clear, fully, right, sheer **06** depart, enough, fairly, indeed, quight, rather, really, resign, wholly **07** absolve, exactly, totally, utterly **08** actually, entirely, every bit, somewhat **09** every whit, perfectly, precisely **10** absolutely, completely, moderately, reasonably, relatively **12** to some degree, to some extent **13** comparatively

• **not quite**
◇ *tail deletion indicator*
06 almost, nearly

quits
04 even, meet **05** equal, evens, level **06** square

• **call it quits**
04 stop **05** cease **08** break off **09** make peace **10** call it a day **11** discontinue **12** stop fighting **14** bury the hatchet **15** lay down your arms

quitter
03 pus, rat **06** skiver **07** shirker **08** apostate, defector, deserter, recreant, renegade **10** delinquent

quiver
◇ *anagram indicator*
05 quake, shake, throb **06** active, bicker, nimble, quaver, shiver, thrill, tingle, tremor, wobble **07** feather, flicker, flutter, pulsate, shudder, tremble, twinkle, vibrate **08** flichter **09** oscillate, palpitate, pulsation, vibration **11** oscillation, palpitation

quixotic
06 errant **07** Utopian **08** fanciful, romantic **09** impetuous, impulsive, unworldly, visionary **10** chivalrous, idealistic, starry-eyed **11** extravagant, fantastical, unrealistic **13** impracticable

quiz
03 eye **04** hoax, pump, test, yo-yo **05** grill, smoke, trail **07** examine, monocle **08** question **09** bandalore **11** competition, examination, interrogate, questioning **12** cross-examine **13** cross-question, interrogation, questionnaire

Radio and television quiz shows include:

02 QI
03 3–2–1
05 15 to 1
08 Bullseye, Eggheads
09 Countdown, Odd One Out, Small Talk
10 Mastermind, Masterteam, Screen Test
11 Call My Bluff, Catchphrase, Give Us a Clue, Just a Minute, Spot the Tune, The Food Quiz, The News Quiz, What's My Line?
12 Ask the Family, Blockbusters, Bognor or Bust, Face the Music, Fifteen to One, Going for Gold, Lucky Numbers, Name That Tune, Strike It Rich, Take Your Pick, Telly Addicts, Winning Lines
13 Blankety Blank, Bob's Full House, Going for a Song, Strike It Lucky
14 Brain of Britain, Family Fortunes, The Weakest Link, Wheel of Fortune, Winner Takes All
15 Double Your Money, The Price Is Right

quizzical
06 amused **07** amusing, baffled, comical, curious, mocking, puzzled, teasing **08** humorous, sardonic **09** inquiring, mystified, perplexed, satirical, sceptical **11** questioning

quizzically
06 askant **07** askance **09** curiously, mockingly **11** inquiringly, sceptically **13** questioningly

quoit
04 coit, disc, disk, ring
See also **buttocks**

• target in quoits
03 hub, pin, tee

quota
03 cut **04** part **05** share, slice, whack **06** quotum, ration **07** portion **09** allowance **10** allocation, assignment, contingent, percentage, proportion **11** slice of cake **14** numerus clausus

quotation
03 bid, tag **04** cost, line, rate **05** piece, price, quote **06** charge, figure, tender **07** cutting, excerpt, extract, listing, passage, remnant **08** allusion, citation, estimate **09** reference, selection **14** locus classicus

quote
04 cite, coat, cote, echo, name **05** coate **06** adduce, allege, drag up, recall, recite, repeat **07** examine, mention, refer to **08** allude to **09** recollect, reproduce **10** scrutinize

quoted
05 cited **06** stated **08** reported **09** instanced **10** referred to, reproduced **13** forementioned **14** above-mentioned

quotidian
05 daily **06** common, normal **07** diurnal, regular, routine **08** day-to-day, everyday, habitual, ordinary, repeated, workaday **09** customary, recurrent **11** bog-standard, commonplace **12** run-of-the-mill

R

R
02 ar **05** Romeo

rabbi

Chief Rabbis include:

04 **Hart** (Aaron), **Lyon** (Hart)
05 **Adler** (Hermann), **Adler** (Nathan), **Hertz** (J H), **Sacks** (Jonathan)
06 **Brodie** (Israel)
09 **Hirschell** (Solomon)
10 **Jakobovits** (Immanuel, Lord)
12 **Tevele Schiff** (David)

rabbit
03 bun, doe **04** buck, cony, go on, talk
05 bunny, coney, daman, drone, hyrax
06 dassie, dodder, wander, wibble
07 go-devil, maunder **08** confound
09 give forth **11** bunny rabbit

Rabbits and hares include:

03 fox, lop, Rex, tan
04 jack, pika, rock, sage
05 brown, Dutch, hotot, sable, satin, swamp, water
06 Alaska, Angora, Arctic, Havana, oar-lap, Polish, silver, tapeti, Vienna
07 Argente, Belgian, Flemish
08 European, riverine, snowshoe
09 Harlequin, Himalayan
10 chinchilla, cottontail, New Zealand, Van Beveren
11 black silver, English spot, Rhinelander

• **rabbit on**
03 gab, yap **04** go on **06** babble, natter, waffle, witter **07** blather, blether, chatter, maunder **08** witter on **09** go on and on, maunder on

rabble
03 mob, tag **04** herd, rout **05** crowd, horde, meiny, plebs **06** gabble, masses, meiney, meinie, menyie, proles, raffle, ragtag, rascal, tagrag, throng
07 doggery **08** canaille, populace, riff-raff, varletry **09** colluvies, hoi polloi, rascaille, rascality **10** clamjamfry
11 clanjamfray, proletariat, rank and file
12 clamjamphrie, common people, raggle-taggle **13** great unwashed

rabble-rouser
08 agitator **09** demagogue, firebrand
10 incendiary, ringleader, tub-thumper
12 troublemaker

rabble-rousing
10 stirring up **11** tub-thumping
13 troublemaking

Rabelaisian
04 lewd, racy **05** bawdy, gross
06 coarse, earthy, ribald, risqué, vulgar
08 indecent **09** exuberant, satirical
11 extravagant, uninhibited
12 unrestrained

rabid
03 mad **04** wild **06** ardent, crazed, raging **07** berserk, bigoted, burning, extreme, fervent, frantic, furious, violent, zealous **08** frenzied, maniacal
09 fanatical, ferocious, obsessive
10 hysterical, intolerant, irrational
11 hydrophobic, overzealous, unreasoning **12** narrow-minded

rabies
05 lyssa **08** rabidity **09** rabidness
11 hydrophobia

race
03 cut, fly, ren, rin, run, sex, zap, zip
04 bolt, clan, dart, kind, line, rach, rase, raze, rush, seed, slit, tear, zoom
05 blood, breed, chase, erase, genus, house, hurry, pluck, quest, ratch, scoot, slash, speed, stock, trial, tribe
06 career, colour, family, gallop, ginger, hasten, nation, people, snatch, stirps, strain **07** contest, dynasty, kindred, lineage, rivalry, scratch, species
08 ancestry, go all out, piquancy
09 parentage **10** accelerate, contention, extraction, get a move on
11 competition, ethnic group, get cracking, racial group, run like hell
15 take part in a race

Races include:

02 TT
04 Oaks
05 Derby, Leger
06 Le Mans
07 St Leger
08 Boat Race, Milk Race, RAC Rally
09 Grand Prix
11 Admiral's Cup, America's Cup, Breeder's Cup, Giro d'Italia, the Classics
12 Melbourne Cup, Tour de France
13 Diamond Sculls, Grand National, Kentucky Derby, Tourist Trophy
14 Greyhound Derby, London Marathon
15 Indianapolis 500, Monte Carlo rally, New York Marathon

Race types include:

03 ski
04 arms, dash, road, sack
05 cycle, horse, motor, relay, space, yacht
06 keirin, rowing, slalom, sprint
07 harness, hurdles, pancake, pursuit, regatta, walking
08 downhill, marathon, scramble, speedway, stock car, swimming, trotting
09 Grand Prix, greyhound, motocross, motor-race, time trial, walkathon
10 cyclo-cross, Formula One, motorcycle, track event
11 donkey derby, egg-and-spoon, three-legged, wheelbarrow
12 cross-country, steeplechase

racecourse
03 lap **04** turf **05** track **06** course, dromos **07** circuit **08** speedway
09 racetrack **10** hippodrome

Racecourses include:

03 Ayr
04 York
05 Ascot, Epsom
07 Aintree, Chester, Newbury, Sandown, Warwick
08 Goodwood, Wetherby
09 Doncaster, Leicester, Newcastle, Newmarket, Towcester
10 Cheltenham, Epsom Downs, Flemington, Longchamps, Pontefract
11 Haydock Park, Kempton Park, Musselburgh, Sandown Park, Thistledown
12 Hamilton Park

racehorse
05 neddy, stiff **06** mudder, novice
07 no-hoper **08** cocktail, outsider, yearling **12** morning glory, thoroughbred

See also **horse**

racial
04 folk **06** ethnic, tribal **07** genetic
08 national **09** ancestral, inherited
12 ethnological, genealogical

raciness
03 pep **04** zest **06** energy **07** pizzazz
08 dynamism, lewdness, ribaldry
09 animation, bawdiness, crudeness, freshness, indecency, vulgarity
10 coarseness, ebullience, indelicacy, liveliness, smuttiness **11** naughtiness, zestfulness **12** exhilaration
14 suggestiveness

racing

Horse racing-related terms include:

03 dam
04 colt, firm, foal, form, good, hard, head, mare, nose, odds, sire, soft, stud, tote, trip, turf, yard

05 evens, fence, field, filly, going, heavy, owner, place, silks, stake
06 chaser, faller, jockey, length, maiden, novice, odds-on, pull up, sprint, stable, stayer, tic-tac, weight
07 classic, furlong, gelding, meeting, tipster, trainer
08 blinkers, handicap, hurdling, juvenile, outsider, racecard, stallion, standard, stewards, yearling, yielding
09 ante-poste, bookmaker, favourite, group race, non-runner, pacemaker, short head
10 all-weather, bumper race, flat racing, listed race, parade ring, stakes race
11 accumulator, connections, handicapper, hunter chase, pattern race, photo finish, Triple Crown, winning post
12 handicap race, National Hunt, starting gate, steeplechase, thoroughbred, weighing room
14 conditions race
15 stewards' enquiry

Formula One Grand Prix circuits include:

05 Imola, Monza
06 Sakhir, Sepang, Suzuka
07 Bahrain
08 Istanbul, Shanghai
10 Albert Park, Hockenheim, Interlagos, Magny-Cours, Monte Carlo
11 Hungaroring, Nurburgring, Silverstone
12 Indianapolis
13 Francorchamps

Formula One motor racing teams include:

05 Honda
06 Toyota
07 Ferrari, McLaren, Midland, Red Bull, Renault
08 Williams
09 BMW Sauber, Toro Rosso
10 Super Aguri
13 Red Bull Racing

Motor racing drivers, motorcyclists and associated figures include:

04 **Foyt** (A J), **Hill** (Damon), **Hill** (Graham), **Hunt** (James), **Ickx** (Jacky), **Moss** (Stirling)
05 **Alesi** (Jean), **Clark** (Jim), **Clark** (Roger), **Hulme** (Denny), **Lauda** (Niki), **McRae** (Colin), **Olsen** (Ole), **Petty** (Richard), **Prost** (Alain), **Rossi** (Valentino), **Sainz** (Carlos), **Senna** (Ayrton), **Unser** (Al), **Unser** (Bobby)
06 **Ascari** (Alberto), **Berger** (Gerhard), **Briggs** (Barry), **Button** (Jensen), **Doohan** (Michael), **Dunlop** (Joey), **Fangio** (Juan), **Irvine** (Eddie), **Lawson** (Eddie), **Mauger** (Ivan), **Piquet** (Nelson), **Sheene** (Barry), **Walker** (Murray)
07 **Brabham** (Sir Jack), **Brundle** (Martin), **Ferrari** (Enzo), **Fogarty** (Carl), **Guthrie** (Janet), **Mäkinen** (Tommi), **Mansell** (Nigel), **McLaren** (Bruce), **Mikkola** (Hannu), **Roberts** (Kenny), **Rosberg** (Keke), **Rosberg** (Nico), **Segrave** (Sir Henry), **Stewart** (Sir Jackie), **Surtees** (John)
08 **Agostini** (Giacomo), **Andretti** (Mario), **Campbell** (Donald), **Campbell** (Sir Malcolm), **Hailwood** (Mike), **Häkkinen** (Mika), **Hawthorn** (Mike), **Oldfield** (Barney), **Williams** (Sir Frank)
09 **Blomqvist** (Stig), **Chevrolet** (Louis), **Coulthard** (David), **Earnhardt** (Dale), **Kankkunen** (Juha)
10 **Fittipaldi** (Emerson), **Schumacher** (Michael), **Schumacher** (Ralf), **Villeneuve** (Jacques)
12 **Rickenbacker** (Eddie)

Motor racing-related terms include:

03 lap, pit
04 apex, grid, oval, pits, pole, T-car
05 apron, shunt
06 out lap, slicks
07 chicane, cockpit, hairpin, marshal, pace car, paddock, pit lane, pit stop, stagger, steward
08 dirty air, drafting, fishtail, lollipop, outbrake, pit board, straight
09 Brickyard, parade lap, parc fermé, safety car, telemetry
10 back marker, gravel trap, qualifying, racing line, run-off area, slipstream, team orders
11 braking zone, pit straight, victory lane
12 formation lap, pole position
13 launch control, scrutineering, start straight, stop-go penalty, superspeedway
14 finish straight

racism

04 bias **08** jingoism **09** apartheid, prejudice, racialism **10** chauvinism, xenophobia **14** discrimination **15** racial prejudice

racist

04 Nazi **05** bigot **07** bigoted **09** racialist **10** chauvinist, intolerant **13** discriminator **14** discriminatory

rack

04 bink, hack, haik, hake, heck, pain, tear **05** agony, crash, creel, drift, drive, flake, frame, pangs, shake, shelf, stand, touse, touze, towse, towze, track, wrack, wrest, wring **06** extort, harass, harrow, holder, misery, strain, stress, wrench **07** afflict, agonize, anguish, crucify, distort, oppress, remnant, stretch, support, torment, torture, trestle **08** convulse, distress, lacerate, vertebra **09** framework, structure, suffering, vengeance **10** affliction, excruciate, overstrain, punishment **11** destruction, devastation, persecution, portmanteau **13** umbrella stand

- **on the rack**

06 in pain **07** in agony **09** in trouble, suffering **10** in distress **11** under stress **13** under pressure **14** in difficulties

- **rack your brains**

05 study **09** think hard **11** concentrate, think deeply **13** put your mind to

racket

03 bat, con, din, job, row **04** fuss, game, rort, scam **05** dodge, fraud, noise, trick **06** fiddle, hubbub, outcry, rattle, scheme, tumult, uproar **07** clamour, swindle, yelling **08** business, shouting, snowshoe **09** commotion, deception, gold brick **10** hullabaloo, hurly-burly, occupation **11** dissipation, disturbance, pandemonium **14** responsibility

racketeering

05 fraud **08** cheating, fiddling, fleecing, stealing, stinging **09** extortion, swindling **10** chiselling, defrauding, ripping off **12** overcharging **14** taking for a ride **15** cooking the books

raconteur

07 relater **08** narrator, reporter **09** describer **10** anecdotist, chronicler **11** commentator, storyteller

racquet *see* **racket**

racy

04 blue, rude **05** bawdy, crude, dirty, peppy, salty, spicy, witty, zippy **06** coarse, lively, ribald, risqué, smutty, vulgar **07** buoyant, dynamic, naughty, piquant, pungent, zestful **08** animated, indecent, spirited, vigorous **09** ebullient, energetic, off-colour, sparkling, vivacious **10** boisterous, fast-moving, indelicate, suggestive **12** enthusiastic

radar

- **radar image**

04 blip

- **radar signal**

04 echo **05** angel

raddled

◇ *anagram indicator*

05 drawn, gaunt **06** wasted **07** haggard, in a mess, unkempt, worn out **11** dishevelled **15** the worse for wear

radiance

03 joy **04** glow **05** bliss, gleam, light, sheen, shine **06** lustre **07** delight, ecstasy, elation, glitter, rapture **08** pleasure **09** beaminess, happiness, radiation, splendour **10** brightness, brilliance, effulgence, luminosity, refulgence **12** resplendence **13** incandescence

radiant

05 beamy, happy, lit up **06** bright, elated, joyful **07** beaming, beamish, glowing, lambent, pleased, shining **08** blissful, ecstatic, gleaming, glorious, luminous, splendid **09** brilliant, delighted, effulgent, refulgent, sparkling **10** glittering, in raptures, profulgent **11** illuminated, magnificent, on cloud nine, over the moon, resplendent **12** incandescent **15** in seventh heaven, on top of the world

radiate
03 ray **04** beam, emit, glow, pour, shed **05** gleam, issue, shine **06** branch, spread **07** diffuse, diverge, emanate, give off, scatter, send out **08** disperse **09** oscillate, send forth, spread out **10** divaricate **11** disseminate

radiation
04 rays **05** waves **08** emission **09** emanation **12** transmission

Radiation includes:

02 ir, UV
03 UVA, UVB, UVC, UVR
04 beta, hard, heat, soft
05 alpha, gamma, light, X-rays
06 cosmic
07 Hawking, visible
08 Cerenkov, gamma ray, infrared, ionizing
09 black body
10 background, black light, insolation, microwaves, radio waves, synchroton
11 ultraviolet
12 beta particle
13 alpha particle
14 bremsstrahlung
15 electromagnetic

• **radiation unit**
03 rad, rem, rep

radical
03 rad, red **04** amyl, aryl, dyad, root **05** allyl, basic, butyl, cetyl, group, hexad, hexyl, monad, rebel, total, triad, utter, vinyl, yippy **06** acetyl, benzal, benzil, benzyl, entire, heptad, innate, ligand, methyl, native, pentad, phenyl, propyl, tetrad, yippie **07** benzoyl, carbene, drastic, extreme, fanatic, Jacobin, natural, oxonium, primary, radicle **08** absolute, ammonium, carbonyl, carboxyl, complete, glyceryl, glycosyl, hydroxyl, inherent, left-wing, militant, original, profound, reformer, sweeping, thorough **09** elemental, essential, extremist, fanatical, intrinsic, isopropyl, primitive, reformist **10** deep-seated, elementary, exhaustive, nitro-group, rebellious, vinylidene **11** benzylidine, far-reaching, fundamental, methyl group, phosphonium, rudimentary **13** comprehensive, ferricyanogen, ferrocyanogen, revolutionary, thoroughgoing **14** fundamentalist

radio
08 wireless

Radio stations include:

03 LBC, XFM
04 Kiss
06 Jazz FM, Kiss FM, Radio 1, Radio 2, Radio 3, Radio 4
08 Five Live
09 BBC London, Capital FM, Classic FM, Radio Five, Talksport
11 Virgin Radio
12 World Service
13 Radio Caroline, Radio Scotland
15 Radio Luxembourg

Radio programmes include:

02 PM
04 ITMA
05 Today
10 Home Truths, The Archers, Woman's Hour
11 Just a Minute, You and Yours
12 Any Questions?, Poetry Please, Start the Week
13 Book at Bedtime, Pick of the Week, Round the Horne, The World at One
14 Brain of Britain
15 It's That Man Again

See also **quiz**

• **on the radio**
◇ *homophone indicator*
02 DJ **10** disc jockey

• **radio presenter**
02 DJ **10** disc jockey

Radio presenters include:

04 **Mayo** (Simon), **Peel** (John), **Ross** (Jonathan), **Tong** (Pete)
05 **Cooke** (Alistair), **Evans** (Chris), **Stern** (Howard), **Vance** (Tommy), **Wogan** (Terry), **Young** (Sir Jimmy)
06 **Harris** (Bob), **Jensen** (Kid), **Lamacq** (Steve), **Lamarr** (Mark), **Lawley** (Sue), **Moyles** (Chris), **Murray** (Jenni), **Savile** (Sir Jimmy), **Travis** (Dave Lee), **Walker** (Johnnie), **Whiley** (Jo), **Wright** (Steve)
07 **Edmonds** (Noel), **Everett** (Kenny), **Freeman** (Alan 'Fluff'), **Keillor** (Garrison), **Kershaw** (Andy), **Pickles** (Wilfred), **Plomley** (Roy), **Redhead** (Brian), **Tarrant** (Chris)
08 **Anderson** (Marjorie), **Campbell** (Nicky), **Humphrys** (John), **Metcalfe** (Jean), **Westwood** (Tim)
09 **Blackburn** (Tony), **MacGregor** (Sue), **Radcliffe** (Mark)
10 **Gambaccini** (Paul), **Hardcastle** (William)
11 **Nightingale** (Annie)

radioactive
03 hot

radish
05 mooli, runch **06** daikon **08** Raphanus

radium
02 Ra

radon
02 Rn

raffish
04 loud **05** cheap, gaudy, gross, showy **06** casual, coarse, flashy, garish, jaunty, rakish, sporty, tawdry, trashy, vulgar **07** dashing, uncouth **08** bohemian, careless, improper **09** dissolute, tasteless **10** dissipated, flamboyant **12** devil-may-care, disreputable, meretricious

raffle
04 draw **05** notch, sweep **06** jumble, lumber, rabble, tangle **07** crumple, lottery, rubbish, tombola **08** riff-raff **10** sweepstake

raft
04 heap **05** balsa, crowd, float **09** catamaran **11** Carley float

rag
◇ *anagram indicator*
03 kid, lap, rib, row, tat **04** bait, duds, flag, fray, goof, haze, jeer, mock, sail, slut, tatt **05** argue, cloth, clout, lapje, scold, scrap, shred, taunt, tease, towel **06** badger, banter, duster, lappie, tagrag, tatter, wallop **07** duddery, flannel, garment, remnant, torment, wrangle **08** farthing, ridicule **09** newspaper, schmutter **10** floorcloth, paper money, raggedness **12** handkerchief

See also **newspaper**

• **bunch of rags**
03 mop

ragamuffin
04 waif **05** gamin, ragga **06** urchin **11** guttersnipe **14** tatterdemalion **15** tatterdemallion

ragbag
03 mix **04** olio **05** salad **06** jumble, medley **07** mixture **08** mishmash, pastiche, slattern **09** confusion, potpourri **10** assemblage, assortment, hodgepodge, hotchpotch, miscellany **11** olla-podrida **14** omnium-gatherum

rage
◇ *anagram indicator*
03 ire **04** bait, bate, bayt, fume, fury, ramp, rant, rave, tear **05** anger, craze, flame, flood, go mad, mania, paddy, party, radge, storm, vogue, wrath **06** ardour, frenzy, raving, see red, seethe, temper, tumult **07** bluster, explode, madness, passion, rampage, tantrum, thunder, violent **08** boil over, paroxysm, violence **09** blow a fuse, do your nut, raise hell, spit blood **10** hit the roof, paddy-whack **11** blow a gasket, blow your top, flip your lid, go up the wall, lose your rag **12** blow your cool, lose your cool, spit feathers **14** foam at the mouth **15** fly off the handle, go off the deep end

• **all the rage**
02 in **03** now **04** cool **06** trendy **07** in vogue, popular, stylish **08** the craze **10** the in thing **11** fashionable

ragged
◇ *anagram indicator*
04 poor, rag'd, rent, torn **05** duddy, holey, ragde, rough, tatty **06** duddie, frayed, jagged, raguly, ripped, rugged, shabby, shaggy, tagrag, uneven, untidy **07** erratic, in holes, notched, scruffy, tattery, unkempt, worn-out **08** indented, indigent, serrated, tattered **09** destitute, in tatters, irregular **10** down and out, down-at-heel, fragmented, straggling, threadbare **12** disorganized

14 tatterdemalion 15 falling to pieces, tatterdemallion

raging

03 mad 04 amok, wild 05 amuck, angry, irate, rabid 06 fuming, ireful, raving, stormy 07 enraged, furious, violent 08 flagrant, frenzied, furibund, incensed, seething, wrathful
09 turbulent 10 infuriated, tumultuous
11 fulminating

raid

02 do 04 bust, loot, pull, road, rode, rush, sack 05 blitz, foray, onset, rifle, sally, storm, swoop 06 assail, attack, bodrag, charge, forage, hold-up, inroad, invade, maraud, sortie, strike
07 air raid, assault, break-in, descent, pillage, plunder, ram-raid, ransack, robbery, set upon, spreagh 08 dawn raid, invasion 09 break into, descend on, excursion, incursion, onslaught, sneak-raid 12 Baedeker raid

raider

05 crook, shark, thief 06 looter, pirate, robber, viking 07 brigand, invader, villain 08 attacker, criminal, marauder, pillager 09 plunderer, ransacker

rail

03 bar 04 flow, gush, jeer, mock, rung, sora, spar 05 abuse, cloak, decry, raile, rayle, scoff 06 attack, banter, Rallus, revile 07 arraign, censure, garment, inveigh, protest, upbraid 08 denounce, reviling, ridicule 09 castigate, criticize, fulminate 10 slang-whang, vituperate, vociferate 11 neckerchief

railing

04 rail 05 fence, rails 06 paling, pulpit
07 barrier, fencing, manrope, parapet, pushpit 08 parclose, raillery
09 fireguard 10 balustrade

raillery

04 joke 05 chaff, irony, sport 06 banter, joking, satire 07 jeering, jesting, kidding, mockery, ragging, railing, ribbing, teasing 08 badinage, diatribe, dicacity, repartee, ridicule
09 chiacking, invective 10 persiflage, pleasantry

railway

02 Ry 03 rly, Rwy 04 line, rail 05 rails, track 08 railroad

Railways include:

01 L
02 el
03 cog, ell
04 rack, ship, tube
05 cable, light, metro, model
06 garden, scenic, siding, subway
07 cutting, express, freight, tramway
08 cable-car, electric, elevated, main line, monorail, mountain
09 funicular, goods line, InterCity®, trunk line
10 branch line, broad gauge, feeder line
11 crémaillère, narrow gauge, underground
12 rapid transit
13 high-speed line, passenger line, rack-and-pinion, standard gauge

Railway-related terms include:

02 CN
03 ABC, ATC, ATP, bay, cab, car, CPR, EWS, GWR, lie, LMS, LNE, lye, RMT, rod, RPC, SRA, Sta, tie, TOC, van
04 APEX, bank, crew, dock, dome, frog, halt, LNER, RUCC, slot, SPAD, spur, stay, TPWS
05 aisle, berth, bogey, bogie, brake, brute, coach, coupé, crank, depot, diner, grate, guard, local, Mogul, shunt, T-rail, train, wagon
06 banker, boiler, branch, buffer, coaler, diesel, gricer, hopper, piston, points, porter, reefer, saloon, siding, stoker, target, tender, tunnel, up-line, waggon, Y-track
07 ballast, banking, bay-line, buckeye, bulgine, butcher, caboose, cocopan, cutting, drag-bar, drawbar, entrain, fettler, firebox, fireman, hostler, lineman, locoman, network, off-peak, Pullman, railage, railbed, railbus, railcar, railman, roadbed, signals, sleeper, station, tank car, turnout, viaduct, whistle, yardman
08 box-wagon, Bradshaw, brakeman, brake van, bullgine, cant-rail, carriage, catenary, choo-choo, corridor, coupling, crosstie, down-line, draw-gear, firehole, fire-tube, fly-under, horse box, junction, live-rail, loop-line, main line, manrider, motorail, motorman, overpass, pilotman, platform, puff-puff, rack rail, railcard, railhead, roomette, side-line, smokebox, subgrade, terminus, trackage, trackbed, wagon-lit
09 brakesman, buffet car, checkrail, concourse, conductor, couchette, crossover, cross-sill, day return, dining-car, drag-chain, fishplate, footboard, footplate, funicular, goods line, goods yard, guardrail, guard's van, interrail, iron horse, jerkwater, lengthman, overshoot, palace-car, parlor car, plate rail, pointsman, rail-borne, rail-motor, railwoman, second man, sidetrack, signal box, signalman, slip-coach, steam pipe, tank wagon, third rail, train mile, trunk line, turntable, vestibule, wheelbase
10 baggage-car, brake block, branch line, broad-gauge, centre-rail, draught-bar, embankment, Eurotunnel, feeder line, griddle car, home-signal, lengthsman, locomotive, luggage-van, parlour car, platelayer, Pullman car, railroader, railwayman, smokestack, steam brake, supersaver, surfaceman, switchback, tank engine, zone-ticket
11 compartment, gandy dancer, goods engine, left-luggage, people mover, pilot engine, rack railway, railroad car, ship railway, side cutting, sleeping car, strap-hanger, throatplate, track-walker, underbridge, underground, vacuum brake, whistle stop
12 double-header, driving wheel, engine-driver, euroterminal, footplateman, loading gauge, rolling stock, running board, shunting yard, station house, trainspotter
13 conductor rail, dead man's pedal, level crossing, sleeping coach, standard gauge, stationmaster, through-ticket
14 dead man's handle, shuttle service, superelevation
15 marshalling yard

See also **train**

- **railway station**

Railway stations include:

05 Crewe
06 Euston
08 Victoria, Waterloo, Waverley
09 St Pancras
10 Gare de Lyon, Gare du Nord, Kings Cross, Marylebone, Paddington, Piccadilly
11 Penn Station
12 Charing Cross, Gare St Lazare, Grand Central, Hauptbahnhof, Montparnasse
15 Clapham Junction, Gare d'Austerlitz, Liverpool Street

See also **London**

rain

03 wet 04 pelt, pour, roke, sile, smir, smur, spet, spit, teem, weep 05 blash, brash, raine, reign, smirr, storm, water
06 bucket, deluge, mizzle, shower, squall, volley 07 drizzle, skiffle, torrent
08 down-come, downfall, downpour, pour down, rainfall, sprinkle
09 raindrops, rainstorm, sunshower
10 bucket down, cloudburst, Scotch mist, tipple down 12 thunderstorm
13 precipitation, the clouds open
15 rain cats and dogs

rainbow

03 arc, bow 04 arch, iris 05 prism
06 bruise, dew-bow, fog-bow, irised, sunbow 07 moon-bow 08 irisated, spectral, spectrum 09 arc-en-ciel, prismatic, steelhead, water gall
10 iridescent, opalescent, variegated, weather gaw 11 rainbow-like, weather gall 13 kaleidoscopic

Colours of the rainbow:

03 red
04 blue
05 green
06 indigo, orange, violet, yellow

raincoat

03 mac 04 mack, mino 08 Burberry®
09 macintosh 10 mackintosh

rainy

03 wet 04 damp, soft 05 moist

06 hyetal, watery 07 drizzly, pluvial, showery 08 pluviose, pluvious 09 inclement

raise
◇ *reversal indicator*
02 up 03 get 04 buoy, grow, jack, levy, lift, moot, rear, rise, stir 05 amass, boost, breed, build, cairn, cause, elate, erect, evoke, exalt, extol, hoist, leave, mount, put up, rally, rouse, set up, utter, weigh 06 araise, arayse, arouse, broach, bump up, create, excite, gather, hike up, hold up, jack up, lift up, muster, obtain, push up, step up, stir up, take up, uplift 07 advance, amplify, augment, bring up, collect, develop, educate, elevate, enhance, heave up, magnify, nurture, present, produce, provoke, recruit, suggest, upgrade 08 activate, assemble, escalate, heighten, increase, purchase 09 construct, cultivate, establish, institute, intensify, introduce, propagate 10 accumulate, give rise to, put forward, strengthen 11 get together

raised
◇ *reversal down indicator*
05 cameo 06 relief 07 applied, relievo 08 appliqué, elevated, embossed

rake
03 hoe 04 comb, hunt, roam, roué 05 amass, graze, level, rifle, scour, slope, track 06 gather, gay dog, harrow, lecher, scrape, search, smooth, strafe, straff, string, wanton 07 collect, incline, journey, pasture, playboy, ransack, rummage, scratch, swinger 08 buckrake, hedonist, Lothario, muck-rake, prodigal, rakehell 09 debauchee, dissolute, horse rake, libertine 10 accumulate, degenerate, profligate, sensualist 11 spendthrift, stubble rake 14 pleasure-seeker

• rake in
03 net 04 earn, make, reap 05 fetch, gross 06 haul in, pull in 07 bring in, get paid, receive

• rake up
05 dig up, raise 06 drag up, remind, revive 07 bring up, mention 08 dredge up 09 introduce

rake-off
03 cut 04 part 05 share, slice 07 portion 10 percentage, proportion

rakish
05 loose, natty, sharp, smart 06 breezy, casual, dapper, flashy, jaunty, sinful, snazzy, sporty 07 dashing, immoral, raffish, stylish 08 debonair, depraved, prodigal 09 abandoned, debauched, dissolute, lecherous, libertine 10 degenerate, dissipated, flamboyant, licentious, nonchalant, profligate 11 adventurous 12 devil-may-care

rally
04 demo, rely 05 group, march, unite 06 banter, gather, morcha, muster, perk up, pick up, really, reform, revive, summon 07 collect, convene, get well, improve, marshal, meeting, recover, regroup, renewal, reunion, revival, round up 08 assemble, assembly, comeback, jamboree, mobilize, organize, recovery 09 gathering, get better, re-enforce 10 assemblage, bounce back, conference, congregate, convention, reassemble, recuperate, reorganize, resurgence 11 be on the mend, convocation, get together, improvement, mass meeting, pull through 12 band together, come together, gain strength, recuperation 13 bring together, demonstration

ram
03 hit, jam, pun, tup 04 beat, bump, butt, cram, dash, drum, pack, slam, stem, tamp 05 Aries, crash, crowd, drive, force, pound, smash, stuff, wedge 06 corvus, hammer, punner, strike, thrust, wether 07 block up, squeeze 08 compress

ramble
◇ *anagram indicator*
03 gas, jaw 04 hike, roam, rove, tour, trek, trip, walk, wind 05 amble, drift, jaunt, range, stray, tramp, troll 06 babble, dodder, natter, rabbit, stroll, waffle, wander, wanton, witter, zigzag 07 blather, blether, chatter, digress, diverge, meander, saunter, traipse 08 bushwalk, rabbit on, straggle, witter on 09 excursion, expatiate 15 go off at a tangent

rambler
05 hiker, rover 06 roamer, walker 07 drifter 08 stroller, wanderer, wayfarer 09 saunterer, traveller 10 bushwalker

rambling
◇ *anagram indicator*
05 wordy 06 errant, vagary 07 verbose 08 errantry, trailing 09 desultory, excursive, sprawling, spreading, wandering 10 circuitous, digressive, disjointed, incoherent, long-winded, roundabout, straggling 12 disconnected, long-drawn-out, periphrastic 14 skimble-skamble

rami
04 rhea 10 China grass, grass cloth

ramification
04 limb 06 branch, effect, result, sequel, upshot 07 outcome 08 offshoot 09 branching, outgrowth 11 consequence, development, implication 12 complication, divarication

ramp
03 rob 04 rage, rise, romp 05 climb, grade, slope 06 ramson, snatch, tomboy 07 incline, swindle 08 gradient 09 acclivity, declivity

rampage
◇ *anagram indicator*
04 fury, rage, rant, rave, rush, tear 05 storm 06 charge, frenzy, furore, mayhem, uproar 07 run amok, run riot, run wild, turmoil 08 violence 09 go berserk 10 rush wildly 11 destruction 13 rush violently

• on the rampage
◇ *anagram indicator*
04 amok, wild 06 wildly 07 berserk, violent 08 frenzied 09 in a frenzy, violently 12 out of control

rampant
◇ *anagram indicator*
◇ *reversal indicator*
04 rank, rife, wild 06 fierce, raging, wanton 07 profuse, rearing, riotous, violent 08 epidemic, pandemic 09 excessive, out of hand, prevalent, unbridled, unchecked 10 widespread 12 high-spirited, out of control, uncontrolled, unrestrained

rampart
04 bank, fort, ring, wall 05 fence, guard 06 abatis, vallum 07 abattis, bastion, bulwark, defence, parapet, rampire 08 security 09 barricade, earthwork 10 breastwork, embankment, stronghold 13 fortification

ramshackle
◇ *anagram indicator*
05 shaky 06 flimsy, ruined, unsafe 07 rickety, run-down 08 decrepit, derelict, unsteady 09 crumbling, neglected, tottering 10 broken-down, jerry-built, tumbledown 11 dilapidated

ranch
04 farm, tear 05 range 06 estate, spread 07 fazenda, station 08 estancia, hacienda, property 09 dude ranch 10 plantation 12 sheep station 13 cattle station

rancid
03 bad, off 04 foul, high, rank, sour 05 fetid, frowy, musty, stale 06 foetid, frowie, putrid, rotten, turned 07 froughy, noisome, noxious 08 overripe 10 malodorous, unpleasant

rancorous
06 bitter 07 acerbic, hostile 08 spiteful, vengeful, venomous, virulent 09 malignant, resentful, splenetic 10 implacable, malevolent, vindictive 11 acrimonious

rancour
04 hate 05 spite, venom 06 animus, enmity, grudge, hatred, malice, spleen 07 ill-will 08 acrimony, sourness 09 animosity, antipathy, hostility, malignity, virulence 10 bitterness, ill-feeling, resentment 11 malevolence 13 resentfulness 14 vindictiveness

rand
01 R

random
◇ *anagram indicator*
04 spot, wild 05 stray 06 casual, chance 07 aimless, freedom 08 sporadic 09 arbitrary, desultory, haphazard, hit-or-miss, irregular, unplanned 10 accidental, at a venture, fortuitous, hit-and-miss, hitty-missy, incidental, stochastic, unarranged 11 purposeless, scattershot

12 uncontrolled, unmethodical, unsystematic **13** serendipitous **14** indiscriminate

• at random

◇ *anagram indicator*

06 hobnob **07** at large **08** at rovers, randomly **09** aimlessly, haphazard **11** arbitrarily, haphazardly, irregularly **12** fortuitously, incidentally, sporadically **13** purposelessly **14** unmethodically **15** à tort et à travers

randomly

◇ *anagram indicator*

08 at random **09** aimlessly **11** arbitrarily, haphazardly, irregularly **12** incidentally, sporadically **13** purposelessly **14** unmethodically

randy

03 hot **04** sexy **05** horny, rudas **06** virago **07** amorous, aroused, goatish, lustful, raunchy, satyric **08** turned-on **09** lecherous **10** boisterous, lascivious **12** concupiscent

range

02 go **03** ren, rin, row, run **04** area, file, kind, line, oven, raik, rank, roam, rove, sort, span, type, vary **05** align, amble, array, carry, chain, class, cover, drift, field, gamut, genus, grade, grass, group, level, orbit, order, reach, ridge, scale, scope, stove, stray, sweep **06** bounds, cooker, domain, draw up, extend, extent, limits, line up, meadow, radius, ramble, series, sierra, sphere, spread, string, stroll, wander **07** arrange, compass, dispose, earshot, grazing, paddock, pasture, purview, species, stretch, variety **08** classify, confines, distance, latitude, province, spectrum **09** amplitude, catalogue, diversity, fluctuate, grassland, pasturage, selection **10** assortment, categorize, cordillera, parameters, pigeonhole, straighten **11** grazing land **12** distribution

See also **mountain**

• range over

04 scur, sker **05** skirr **06** squirr

rangy

05 lanky, leggy, roomy, weedy **06** skinny **08** gangling, rawboned **10** long-legged, long-limbed **11** mountainous

rank

03 row **04** état, file, foul, gree, line, lush, mark, nobs, rate, sort, tier, type, vile **05** acrid, align, caste, class, dense, élite, fetid, grade, gross, group, level, lords, lusty, order, peers, place, range, sheer, stale, toffs, total, utter **06** arrant, coarse, column, degree, draw up, estate, family, foetid, gentry, line up, nobles, putrid, rancid, series, status, string, strong **07** arrange, blatant, dispose, echelon, glaring, peerage, profuse, pungent, station, stratum, swollen, utterly, violent **08** absolute, abundant, classify, complete, division, flagrant, mephitic, nobility, organize, position, shocking, standing, stinking, thorough, vigorous **09** condition, downright, formation, luxuriant, offensive, out-and-out, overgrown, repulsive, revolting, violently **10** categorize, disgusting, graveolent, malodorous, outrageous, unpleasant **11** aristocracy, high society, unmitigated, unqualified **12** disagreeable, evil-smelling **14** classification

Air force ranks:

05 major
07 captain, colonel, general
08 corporal, sergeant
10 air marshal
11 aircraftman
12 air commodore, aircraftsman, group captain, major general, pilot officer
13 aircraftwoman, flying officer, wing commander
14 aircraftswoman, air vice-marshal, flight sergeant, squadron leader, warrant officer
15 air chief marshal, first lieutenant
16 brigadier general, flight lieutenant, second lieutenant
17 lieutenant colonel, lieutenant general
19 leading aircraftsman
20 general of the air force
21 leading aircraftswoman
25 marshal of the Royal Air Force

Army ranks:

05 major
07 captain, colonel, general, marshal, private
08 corporal, sergeant
09 brigadier
10 bombardier, lieutenant
12 field marshal, major general
13 lance-corporal, staff sergeant
14 warrant officer
15 first-lieutenant, lance-bombardier
16 brigadier-general, general of the army, second-lieutenant
17 lieutenant colonel, lieutenant-general

Naval ranks:

06 ensign, rating, seaman
07 admiral, captain
09 captain RN, commander, commodore
10 able seaman, lieutenant, midshipman
11 rear admiral, vice-admiral
12 fleet admiral, petty officer
13 leading seaman, sublieutenant
14 warrant officer
16 commodore admiral
17 admiral of the fleet, chief petty officer
19 lieutenant-commander
21 lieutenant junior grade

See also **nobility**; **police**

• other ranks

02 OR

• rank and file

03 mob **04** herd **05** crowd, plebs **06** masses, proles, rabble **08** populace, riff-raff, soldiers **09** hoi polloi **10** grass-roots **11** ordinary men, proletariat **12** common people **15** private soldiers

rankle

03 bug, irk, vex **04** gall, rile **05** anger, annoy, peeve **06** fester, nettle, poison **08** embitter, irritate **11** get your goat **13** get on your wick, get up your nose, get your back up **14** get your blood up **15** get on your nerves

rank-smelling

04 olid

ransack

04 comb, fish, hunt, loot, raid, rake, ripe, sack **05** harry, rifle, scour, strip **06** maraud, ravage, search **07** despoil, pillage, plunder, rummage **09** depredate, devastate, go through, ranshakle **10** ranshackle **13** turn inside out **14** rummage through, turn upside down

ransom

04 free **05** atone, money, price **06** buy off, pay-off, redeem, rescue **07** deliver, freedom, payment, release, set free **08** liberate **09** atonement **10** liberation, redemption **11** deliverance, restoration, setting free **15** buy the freedom of

rant

03 cry **04** rand, rave, roar, yell **05** mouth, shout, storm **06** bellow, crying, tirade **07** bluster, bombast, declaim, oration, roaring, yelling **08** diatribe, harangue, rhetoric, shouting, tear a cat, tub-thump **09** hold forth, philippic **10** slang-whang, tear the cat, vociferate **11** declamation, rant and rave **12** vociferation

rap

03 hit, pan, tap **04** bang, blow, clip, cuff, flak, grab, knap, rail, slam, whit, wrap **05** blame, boost, clout, crime, flick, flirt, knock, ragga, scold, slate, stick, swear, thump, whack **06** batter, hammer, hip-hop, patter, punish, rattle, rebuke, snatch, strike, yanker **07** censure, commend, gangsta, reprove, run down, slating, testify **08** knocking, slamming **09** castigate, criticize, reprimand **10** come down on, punishment **11** acclamation, castigation, pick holes in **12** pull to pieces, tear to pieces, tear to shreds

• take the rap

08 pay for it **10** be punished **12** face the music, take the blame **14** get it in the neck

rapacious

06 greedy **07** preying, wolfish, wolvish **08** esurient, grasping, ravening, ravenous, uncaring, usurious **09** marauding, predatory, voracious, vulturine, vulturish, vulturous

10 avaricious, insatiable, plundering **12** extortionate

• rapacious person

04 kite

rapacity

05 greed, usury **07** avarice, avidity **08** voracity **09** esurience, esuriency, vulturism **10** greediness **11** wolfishness **12** graspingness, ravenousness **13** predatoriness, rapaciousness, shark's manners, voraciousness **14** insatiableness

rape

03 rob **04** loot, raid, sack **05** abuse, navew, strip **06** defile, rapine, ravage, ravish **07** assault, despoil, looting, outrage, pillage, plunder, ransack, sacking, seizure, violate, vitiate **08** coleseed, date rape, deflower, gang rape, gang-rape, maltreat, ravaging, spoliate, violence **09** depredate, devastate, stripping, transport, violation **10** defilement, plundering, ransacking, ravishment, spoliation **11** depredation, devastation **12** despoliation, maltreatment **13** sexual assault, statutory rape **15** assault sexually

rapid

03 pdq **04** fast **05** brisk, chute, hasty, nifty, quick, shoot, shute, swift, zippy **06** lively, prompt, speedy **07** express, hurried, stickle **08** headlong **09** splitting **11** expeditious, precipitate **13** like lightning **15** pretty damn quick

rapidity

04 rush **05** haste, hurry, speed **08** alacrity, celerity, dispatch, velocity **09** briskness, fleetness, quickness, swiftness **10** expedition, promptness, speediness **11** promptitude **15** expeditiousness, precipitateness

rapidly

04 fast **05** quick **06** pronto **07** briskly, hastily, like fun, quickly, swiftly **08** promptly, speedily **09** hurriedly **11** at the double, like winking **12** a mile a minute, lickety-split **13** expeditiously, precipitately **14** at a rate of knots, hell for leather **15** like the clappers

rapine

04 prey, rage, raid, rape **05** raven, ravin **06** ravine **07** looting, sacking, seizure **08** ravaging **09** stripping, transport, violation **10** defilement, plundering, ransacking, ravishment, spoliation **11** depredation, devastation **12** despoliation

rapport

04 bond, link **07** empathy, harmony **08** affinity, relation, sympathy **10** connection **12** relationship **13** understanding

rapprochement

07 détente, reunion **09** agreement, softening **13** harmonization, reconcilement **14** reconciliation

rapt

06 intent, way-out **07** charmed, gripped **08** abducted, absorbed, ecstatic, ravished, snatched, thrilled **09** bewitched, delighted, enchanted, engrossed, entranced **10** captivated, enraptured, enthralled, fascinated, spellbound **11** preoccupied, rhapsodical, transported **12** concentrated

rapture

03 joy **05** bliss **07** delight, ecstasy, elation **08** euphoria, felicity, paroxysm **09** cloud nine, happiness, transport **10** enragement, exaltation **11** delectation, enchantment **12** exhilaration **13** seventh heaven, top of the world

• go into raptures

04 fire, gush, rave **05** drool **06** excite, praise **07** enthuse, inspire **08** motivate **10** bubble over, effervesce, wax lyrical

rapturous

05 happy **06** joyful, joyous **07** exalted **08** blissful, ecstatic, euphoric, ravished **09** delighted, entranced, overjoyed, rhapsodic **11** dithyrambic, on cloud nine, over the moon, tickled pink, transported **12** enthusiastic **15** in seventh heaven, on top of the world

rare

◇ *anagram indicator*

04 seld, thin **05** early **06** choice, geason, scarce, sparse, superb **07** curious, unusual **08** precious, sporadic, superior, uncommon **09** excellent, exquisite, matchless, recherché, underdone **10** far between, infrequent, remarkable **11** exceptional, outstanding, superlative **12** incomparable, like gold dust, unparalleled **13** extraordinary, one in a million **15** thin on the ground

rarefied

04 high, thin **05** noble **06** select, subtle **07** private, refined, special, sublime, tenuous **08** esoteric, tenuious **09** exclusive **10** attenuated

rarely

04 seld **06** hardly, little, seldom **08** choicely, scarcely **10** hardly ever, once in a way **12** infrequently, occasionally, once in a while, scarcely ever, sporadically **13** spasmodically **14** intermittently **15** once in a blue moon

raring

04 keen **05** eager, ready **07** itching, longing, willing **09** desperate, impatient **12** enthusiastic

rarity

03 gem **04** find **05** curio, pearl **06** marvel, wonder **08** scarcity, shortage, thinness, treasure **09** curiosity, nonpareil **10** sparseness **11** infrequency, strangeness, unusualness **12** uncommonness **14** collector's item

rascal

03 imp **04** loon, lown **05** devil, lorel, losel, lowne, rogue, scamp, skelm, smaik **06** lozell, rabble, schelm, skelum, tinker, toerag, varlet **07** a bad hat, cullion, hallian, hallion, hallyon, knavish, lorrell, skellum, villain, wastrel **08** scalawag, schellum, spalpeen, vagabond, wretched **09** rascaille, scallawag, scallywag, scoundrel, skeesicks, son of a gun **10** ne'er-do-well, rascallion, scapegrace **11** rapscallion **13** mischief-maker **14** good-for-nothing, two-for-his-heels

rascally

03 bad, low **04** base, evil, mean **06** arrant, wicked **07** crooked, hangman, knavish, roguish, vicious **09** dishonest, reprobate **10** villainous **11** furciferous, mischievous, scoundrelly **12** disreputable, unscrupulous **14** good-for-nothing

rash

◇ *anagram indicator*

03 run **04** dash, drag, fast, itch, rush, tear, wave **05** flood, hasty, heady, hives, slash, spate, stick **06** deluge, madcap, plague, series, unwary **07** rosacea, roseola, torrent **08** careless, epidemic, eruption, headlong, heat rash, heedless, madbrain, outbreak, reckless, temerous **09** audacious, dare-devil, foolhardy, hot-headed, impetuous, imprudent, impulsive, over-hasty, pompholyx, premature, unguarded, urticaria **10** headstrong, ill-advised, indiscreet, irritation, madbrained, nettlerash, unthinking **11** adventurous, furthersome, hare-brained, harum-scarum, hasty-witted, precipitate, temerarious **13** ill-considered, inconsiderate

rashly

07 hastily **08** headlong, unwarily **09** on impulse **10** carelessly, heedlessly, recklessly **11** audaciously, impetuously, imprudently, impulsively, over-hastily **12** indiscreetly **15** without thinking

rashness

08 audacity, hazardry, temerity **09** brashness, hastiness, incaution **10** imprudence **12** carelessness, heedlessness, indiscretion, precipitance, precipitancy, recklessness **13** foolhardiness, impulsiveness, precipitation **14** incautiousness **15** adventurousness, thoughtlessness

rasp

03 bug, jar, rub **04** file, risp, sand **05** croak, grate, grind, peeve, scour **06** abrade, cackle, scrape, squawk **07** grating, scratch, screech **08** grinding, irritate **09** excoriate, harshness, raspberry **10** hoarseness **15** get on your nerves

rasping

05 gruff, harsh, husky, raspy, rough **06** croaky, filing, hoarse **07** grating, jarring, raucous **08** creaking, croaking, gravelly, scratchy **10** stridulant

rat
03 rot, spy **04** blab, blow, fink, mole, nark, nose, shop, sing, stag, vole **05** dob on, grass, hutia, Judas, peach, puppy, sneak, snout, split **06** agouta, betray, canary, finger, fizgig, gopher, inform, ratton, rumble, snitch, squeal, tell on **07** peacher, stoolie, traitor **08** approver, Arvicola, betrayer, denounce, informer, musk-cavy, promoter, renegade, sand mole, snitcher, squeaker, squealer, tell-tale, turncoat **09** bandicoot, informant, sycophant, water vole, whisperer **10** discoverer, supergrass **11** incriminate, stool pigeon **12** cutting grass **13** strike-breaker, whistle-blower

rate
03 fee, MPH, pay, ret, sum, tax **04** cess, cost, deem, duty, hire, mode, pace, rank, time, toll **05** allot, basis, chide, class, count, grade, judge, merit, price, prize, ratio, scale, scold, speed, sum up, tempo, value, weigh, worth **06** admire, amount, assess, charge, degree, esteem, extent, figure, manner, rating, reckon, regard, tariff **07** adjudge, deserve, justify, measure, payment, reprove, respect, tallage, warrant, weigh up **08** appraise, classify, consider, estimate, evaluate, relation, standard, velocity **09** calculate **10** be worthy of, categorize, estimation, percentage, proportion **12** be entitled to, have a right to
See also **scold**

• **at any rate**
05 at all **06** anyhow, anyway **07** at least **09** in any case **10** at the least, in any event, regardless **12** nevertheless

rather
03 gay, gey, yes **04** a bit, more, some, very **05** quite **06** a bit of, fairly, indeed, pretty, sooner, sort of **07** a little, instead **08** by choice, slightly, somewhat **09** for choice **10** from choice, moderately, much rather, much sooner, noticeably, preferably, relatively **12** by preference, to some degree, to some extent **13** for preference, significantly

ratification
08 approval **10** validation **11** affirmation, endorsement **12** confirmation **13** authorization, certification, corroboration **14** authentication, seal of approval **15** stamp of approval

ratify
02 OK **04** amen, seal, sign **06** affirm, strike, uphold **07** agree to, approve, certify, confirm, endorse, warrant **08** legalize, sanction, validate **09** authorize, establish, preconize **10** homologate **11** corroborate, countersign **12** authenticate

rating
02 AB **04** mark, rank **05** class, grade, order, score **06** degree, status **07** grading, placing, ranking, set-down **08** category, position, standing **09** adjudging, appraisal **10** assessment, evaluation **14** classification

ratio
04 rate **05** index **07** balance, portion **08** fraction, quotient, relation, symmetry **09** allowance **10** percentage, proportion **11** correlation **12** relationship **14** correspondence

ration
03 lot **04** food, part, save **05** allot, issue, limit, point, quota, share **06** amount, budget, stores, supply, viands **07** control, deal out, dole out, hand out, helping, measure, mete out, portion **08** allocate, conserve, dispense, restrict, supplies, victuals **09** allotment, allowance, apportion, divide out **10** allocation, distribute, foodstuffs, iron ration, measure out, percentage, proportion, provisions **11** compo ration

rational
04 sane, wice, wise **05** lucid, sober, sound **06** normal **07** logical, prudent **08** balanced, cerebral, grounded, sensible, thinking **09** cognitive, judicious, realistic, reasoning, sagacious **10** Apollonian, discursive, reasonable **11** circumspect, clear-headed, enlightened, intelligent, well-founded **12** intellectual **13** philosophical, ratiocinative **15** in your right mind

rationale
05 basis, logic **06** motive, reason, theory, thesis **07** grounds, purpose, reasons **09** principle, reasoning **10** hypothesis, motivation, philosophy **11** explanation, raison d'être

rationalization
06 excuse **08** excusing, updating **11** explanation, vindication **12** streamlining **13** justification, modernization **14** reorganization

rationalize
04 trim **06** excuse, update **07** explain, justify **09** cut back on, modernize, vindicate **10** account for, pragmatize, reorganize, streamline **11** cut out waste, explain away

rationally
06 sanely **07** lucidly **08** sensibly **09** logically, prudently **10** reasonably, thinkingly **11** judiciously, sagaciously, without bias **13** intelligently **15** philosophically

rattle
◇ *anagram indicator*
03 jar, rap **04** bang, bump, faze, jolt, reel, tirl **05** alarm, clang, clank, clink, knock, shake, upset **06** bounce, hurtle, jangle, jingle, put off, put out, racket, ruckle **07** clapper, clatter, confuse, disturb, fluster, jarring, jolting, shaking, sistrum, unnerve, vibrate **08** clanking, clinking, irritate, unsettle **09** crepitate, vibration **10** disconcert **13** tintinnabulum **15** throw off balance

• **rattle off**
04 list **06** recite, repeat **07** reel off **10** run through **11** list quickly

• **rattle on**
03 gab **04** yack **05** prate **06** cackle, gabble, jabber, natter, witter **07** blether, chatter, chunter, prattle **08** rabbit on

ratty
05 angry, cross, short, testy **06** peeved, snappy, touchy, untidy **07** annoyed, crabbed, grouchy, unkempt **08** wretched **09** impatient, irritable **13** short-tempered

raucous
04 loud **05** harsh, husky, noisy, rough, rusty, sharp **06** hoarse, raucid, shrill **07** grating, jarring, rasping **08** piercing, strident **10** discordant, scratching, screeching **11** ear-piercing

raunchy
04 lewd, sexy **05** bawdy **06** earthy, erotic, nubile, shabby, slinky **07** sensual **08** alluring, arousing, inviting **09** desirable, provoking, salacious, seductive **10** attractive, suggestive, voluptuous **11** flirtatious, provocative, stimulating, titillating **12** pornographic

ravage
◇ *anagram indicator*
04 loot, raze, ruin, sack **05** harry, havoc, level, spoil, wreck **06** damage, maraud **07** despoil, destroy, looting, pillage, plunder **08** demolish, lay waste, wreckage **09** depredate, devastate, ruination **10** desolation, ransacking, spoliation **11** depredation, destruction, devastation **12** despoliation, leave in ruins

ravaged
◇ *anagram indicator*
06 spoilt **07** war-torn, war-worn, wrecked **08** desolate **09** destroyed, ransacked, shattered, war-wasted **10** battle-torn, devastated

rave
◇ *anagram indicator*
02 do **03** cry **04** bash, fume, hail, orgy, rage, rant, roar, yell **05** crazy, disco, extol, go ape, go mad, party, shout, storm, taver **06** babble, bellow, blow up, jabber, ramble, rave-up, see red, seethe, sizzle, taiver **07** acclaim, blow-out, enthuse, explode, knees-up, thunder **08** boil over, carousal, ecstatic, freak out, praising **09** blow a fuse, do your nut, excellent, go bananas, go berserk, laudatory, raise hell, rapturous, wonderful **10** be mad about, favourable, hit the roof, talk wildly, wax lyrical **11** blow a gasket, blow your top, celebration, flip your lid, go up the wall, have kittens, infatuation, lose your rag, rant and rave **12** blow your cool, enthusiastic, fly into a rage, lose your cool, throw a wobbly **13** throw a tantrum **14** acid-house

party, foam at the mouth, go into raptures, lose your temper **15** fly off the handle, get all steamed up, go off the deep end

raven
03 jet **04** Grip, inky, prey **05** black, crake, dusky, ebony, ravin, sable **06** corbie, rapine **07** preying **08** jet-black **09** coal-black

ravenous
06 greedy, hungry **07** starved, wolfish, wolvish **08** famished, starving **09** rapacious, voracious **10** insatiable, plundering, very hungry

rave-up
02 do **04** bash, orgy **05** party **06** thrash **07** blow-out, debauch, shindig **08** carousal **11** celebration

ravine
03 gap, lin **04** gill, khor, khud, linn, nala, pass, prey **05** abyss, cañon, chine, flume, ghyll, gorge, goyle, grike, gryke, gulch, gully, heuch, heugh, kloof, nalla, nulla **06** arroyo, canyon, clough, coulée, gullet, gulley, nallah, nullah, rapine **07** preying **09** purgatory

See also **gorge**

raving
◇ *anagram indicator*
03 mad **04** wild **05** barmy, batty, crazy, loony, loopy **06** insane, maniac, mental **07** berserk, furious **08** demented, deranged, frenzied **09** delirious **10** barking mad, frantic-mad, hysterical, irrational, unbalanced **12** round the bend **13** out of your mind, round the twist

ravings
06 drivel, yammer **07** prattle, rubbish, twaddle **08** nonsense **09** gibberish **10** balderdash, mumbo-jumbo **12** gobbledygook

ravish
04 rape **05** abuse, charm, force **06** abduct, defile **07** assault, bewitch, delight, enchant, enthral, oppress, outrage, overjoy, violate **08** entrance, maltreat, stuprate, suppress **09** captivate, enrapture, fascinate, spellbind **11** constuprate **15** assault sexually, force yourself on

ravishing
06 lovely, raping **07** radiant **08** alluring, charming, dazzling, gorgeous, stunning **09** beautiful, seductive **10** bewitching, delightful, enchanting **11** enthralling **12** transporting

raw
03 new, red, wet **04** bare, cold, damp, hard, open, sore **05** basic, bleak, blunt, chill, crude, crudy, cruel, frank, fresh, green, harsh, naive, naked, nippy, plain, rough, wersh **06** biting, bitter, bloody, brutal, callow, candid, chafed, chilly, grazed, strong, tender **07** abraded, exposed, intense, natural, scraped, tartare **08** freezing, ignorant, immature, piercing, uncooked, ungenial **09** outspoken, realistic, scratched, sensitive, unrefined, unskilled, untrained, untreated, untutored, unwrought **10** excoriated, forthright, true-to-life, unfinished, unprepared **11** unpractised, unprocessed **13** inexperienced

ray
02 re **04** beam, hint, look **05** array, dirty, dress, flash, gleam, glint, manta, roker, shaft, skate, spark, trace **06** defile, glance, streak, stream **07** flicker, glimmer, homelyn, radiate, torpedo, twinkle **09** cramp-fish, thornback **10** indication, sea vampire, suggestion

raze
04 fell, race, rase, ruin **05** erase, graze, level, wreck **06** scrape, slight **07** destroy, flatten **08** bulldoze, demolish, pull down, tear down **09** dismantle, knock down

razor
04 keen **05** sharp **06** shaver **07** precise **09** cut-throat **11** cutting edge

re
03 are, ray **05** about **09** regarding **10** concerning **12** with regard to **14** on the subject of **15** with reference to

reach
03 bay, fax, hit, rax, win **04** call, come, deal, gain, hand, hent, hold, make, pass, ring, shot, span, take **05** ambit, get at, get to, grasp, phone, power, range, retch, scope, seize, touch **06** amount, arrive, attain, come at, come to, extend, extent, go up to, snatch, spread, strike **07** achieve, command, compass, contact, control, get onto, project, speak to, stretch, write to **08** amount to, arrive at, artifice, come up to, continue, distance, go down to, latitude, make it to **09** authority, extension, get hold of, go as far as, influence, telephone **10** come down to, stretch out **12** get through to, jurisdiction **14** get in touch with **15** communicate with

See also **retch**

• **reach down**
03 dip

• **reach out**
04 push

react
◇ *anagram indicator*
03 act **04** defy **05** rebel, reply **06** answer, behave, oppose, resist, rise up **07** dissent, respond **08** kick back, retroact **09** retaliate **11** acknowledge, reciprocate

reaction
05 reply, stink **06** answer, recoil, reflex **08** backlash, backwash, feedback, kickback, response, reversal **09** reversion, swing-back **11** retaliation **12** repercussion **13** counteraction, reciprocation **14** antiperistasis, counterbalance **15** acknowledgement

reactionary
◇ *anagram indicator*
◇ *reversal indicator*
06 Junker **07** Bourbon, diehard, redneck **08** mandarin, rightist, Sadducee **09** right-wing, young fogy **10** Neandertal, young fogey **11** Neanderthal, right-winger, traditional **12** conservative, Neandertaler **13** Neanderthaler **14** Neanderthal man, traditionalist **15** backward-looking

read
03 maw, rad **04** look, name, scan, show, skim **05** solve, speak, study, teach, utter **06** advise, browse, decode, glance, look at, peruse, recite, record, saying **07** counsel, declaim, declare, deliver, dip into, display, examine, expound, learned, measure, perusal **08** abomasum, browsing, construe, decipher, indicate, pore over, register, scanning, scrutiny, skimming **09** interpret **10** comprehend, scrutinize, understand **11** leaf through **12** flick through, thumb through **13** browse through **14** interpretation

• **read aloud**
◇ *homophone indicator*

• **read into**
05 infer **06** deduce, reason **08** construe **09** interpret **12** misinterpret

readable
05 clear **07** legible **08** gripping **09** enjoyable **10** easy to read **11** captivating, enthralling, interesting, stimulating **12** decipherable, entertaining, intelligible, worth reading **13** unputdownable **14** comprehensible, understandable

reader
06 hearer, lector, taster **08** audience, bookworm, epistler, lectress, lecturer, listener **09** addressee, epistoler, prelector **10** pocketbook **13** bibliophagist

readership
08 audience, regulars **09** following **11** subscribers

readily
04 soon **06** easily, freely, gladly **07** eagerly, happily, lightly, quickly, rapidly, swiftly **08** promptly, smoothly, speedily, with ease **09** willingly **12** effortlessly **14** unhesitatingly

readiness
04 ease **05** alert, skill **07** fitness **08** alacrity, aptitude, facility, gameness, keenness, rapidity **09** eagerness, handiness, quickness **10** promptness **11** inclination, preparation, promptitude, willingness **12** availability, preparedness

• **in readiness**
05 ready **06** on call **07** at point **08** at a point, at points, prepared **09** available, on standby **10** standing by **11** at all points, on full alert **13** in preparation

reading
04 scan, text **05** piece, study **06** figure, lesson, record **07** display, edition, lection, passage, perusal, recital, section, version **08** browsing, decoding, register, scrutiny
09 rendering, rendition **10** indication, inspection, recitation **11** deciphering, examination, measurement
13 understanding **14** interpretation
• **variant reading**
02 vl

reading-desk
04 ambo **07** lectern

ready
02 go **03** apt, fit, set **04** boun, cash, easy, free, game, keen, near, ripe, yare **05** alert, bound, bowne, close, eager, equip, handy, happy, order, prest, prime, prone, quick, rapid, sharp, swift **06** all set, astute, at hand, clever, direct, on hand, prompt, speedy, to hand
07 about to, addrest, ad manum, arrange, attired, dressed, forward, pleased, prepare, present, scratch, waiting, willing **08** arranged, disposed, equipped, finished, geared up, hard cash, inclined, liable to, likely to, organize, pregnant, prepared
09 addressed, available, completed, dexterous, fitted out, immediate, organized, psyched up, rigged out
10 accessible, convenient, discerning, perceptive, pernicious, ready money, the needful **11** predisposed, resourceful, within reach
12 enthusiastic, on the point of, on the verge of, unhesitating **14** argent comptant
• **at the ready**
03 set **06** all set, poised **08** prepared
09 mobilized

real
04 rial, ryal, sure, trew, true **05** quite, right, royal, truly, utter, valid **06** actual, dinkum, honest, proper, really, thingy
07 certain, dinki-di, dinky-di, factual, fervent, genuine, sincere **08** absolute, bona fide, complete, concrete, dinky-die, existing, material, official, physical, positive, rightful, tangible, thorough, truthful, unfabled **09** authentic, heartfelt, immovable, occurring, simon-pure, unfeigned, veritable
10 fair dinkum, legitimate, sure-enough, unaffected **11** substantial, substantive **12** from the heart

realign
◇ *anagram indicator*
09 reshuffle **10** straighten

realism
06 sanity **08** saneness **09** actuality
10 naturalism, pragmatism, televérité
11 genuineness, naturalness, rationality
12 authenticity, cinéma vérité, faithfulness, lifelikeness, practicality, sensibleness, truthfulness

realistic
04 real, true **05** close, vivid
07 genuine, graphic, logical, natural
08 detached, faithful, lifelike, rational, real-life, sensible, truthful
09 authentic, hard-nosed, objective, practical, pragmatic **10** figurative, hard-boiled, hard-headed, true-to-life, unromantic **11** commonsense, down-to-earth, level-headed **12** businesslike, clear-sighted, matter-of-fact
13 unsentimental

realistically
05 truly **07** vividly **08** sensibly
09 genuinely, logically **10** faithfully, rationally, truthfully **11** graphically, objectively, practically **12** figuratively
13 authentically, pragmatically
14 unromantically **15** unsentimentally

reality
04 fact **05** truth **06** effect, verity
07 realism **08** positive, real life, validity
09 actuality, certainty, existence, real world, thingness **10** thinginess
11 genuineness, materiality, tangibility, thingliness **12** authenticity, corporeality **14** substantiality
• **in reality**
05 truly **06** indeed, in fact, really **07** for real, in truth **08** actually **09** in earnest
10 in practice **12** in actual fact, in all but name **13** in point of fact **15** as a matter of fact

realization
04 gain **05** grasp **06** making
07 earning, selling **08** clearing, fetching **09** awareness **10** acceptance, cognizance, completion, fulfilment, perception **11** achievement, discernment, performance, recognition **12** appreciation, apprehension, consummation
13 actualization, comprehension, consciousness, understanding
14 accomplishment, implementation
• **expression of realization**
03 why

realize
03 get, net, see **04** earn, gain, make, twig **05** clear, fetch, glean, grasp, learn
06 accept, effect, encash, fulfil, obtain, take in **07** achieve, bring in, catch on, discern, perform, produce, sell for
08 complete, cotton on, discover, perceive, register, tumble to
09 actualize, apprehend, ascertain, implement, recognize **10** accomplish, appreciate, articulate, bring about, comprehend, concretize, consummate, effectuate, understand
11 see the light **13** become aware of

really
03 way **04** very **05** quite, rally, truly
06 highly, indeed, in fact, quight, simply, surely, verily **08** actually, honestly, in effect, severely
09 certainly, extremely, genuinely, intensely, sincerely **10** absolutely, positively, remarkably, straight up, thoroughly **11** undoubtedly **13** as large as life, categorically, exceptionally

realm
04 area, land **05** field, orbit, reame, reign, state, world **06** domain, empire, region, sphere **07** country, kingdom, royalty **08** monarchy, province, queendom **09** territory **10** department
12 principality

reap
03 cut, get, mow, win **04** crop, gain, swap, swop **05** shear **06** derive, garner, gather, obtain, secure **07** acquire, collect, harvest, realize, receive

rear
◇ *reversal indicator*
◇ *tail selection indicator*
03 end **04** back, grow, hind, last, lift, loom, rise, rump, soar, tail **05** breed, erect, hoist, nurse, raise, rouse, set up, stern, tower, train **06** behind, bottom, foster, hinder, hold up, lift up, parent, rise up, stir up, take up **07** bring up, build up, care for, educate, elevate, nurture, tail-end **08** backside, buttocks, hindmost, instruct, lavatory, rearmost **09** cultivate, look after, originate, posterior
See also **toilet**

rearrange
◇ *anagram indicator*
04 vary **05** alter, rejig, shift **06** adjust, change **07** reorder **08** rejigger
09 reshuffle **10** reposition, reschedule
11 consolidate

reason
03 aim, end, wit **04** case, goal, mind, nous **05** argue, basis, brain, cause, color, infer, logic, sense, solve, think
06 colour, debate, deduce, excuse, ground, induce, motive, object, reckon, remark, sanity, wisdom
07 defence, discuss, examine, grounds, impetus, premise, pretext, purpose, resolve, thought, warrant, work out
08 argument, cogitate, conclude, converse, gumption, occasion, think out **09** cerebrate, discourse, encheason, incentive, intellect, intention, judgement, rationale, reasoning, syllogize **10** inducement, moderation, motivation, proportion
11 common sense, explanation, raison d'être, ratiocinate, rationality
12 intelligence, use your brain
13 comprehension, consideration, justification, ratiocination, understanding **15** intellectuality
• **reason with**
04 coax, move, urge **08** persuade
09 argue with, plead with **10** debate with **11** discuss with, expostulate
15 remonstrate with
• **within reason**
10 moderately **12** in moderation, within bounds, within limits **15** with self-control

reasonable
02 OK **03** low **04** fair, just, okay, sane, wise **05** sound **06** modest, viable
07 average, logical **08** credible, moderate, possible, rational, reasoned, sensible **09** judicious, plausible, practical, sagacious, tolerable,

wholesome **10** acceptable **11** competitive, inexpensive, intelligent, justifiable, well-advised **12** satisfactory **13** no great shakes **14** understandable, well-thought-out

reasonably
02 OK **04** okay **05** quite **06** fairly, rather, wisely **08** passably, sensibly, somewhat **09** plausibly, tolerably **10** adequately, moderately, rationally **13** intelligently

reasoned
05 clear, sound **07** logical **08** rational, sensible **09** judicious, organized **10** methodical, systematic **14** well-thought-out

reasoning
04 case **05** logic, proof **07** ijtihad, thought **08** analysis, argument, thinking **09** casuistry, deduction, induction, rationale, syllogism, synthesis **10** hypothesis, philosophy **11** cerebration, supposition **13** argumentation, ratiocination **14** interpretation **15** rationalization

reassemble
◇ *anagram indicator*
05 rally **07** rebuild **09** re-enforce **11** reconstruct

reassurance
05 cheer **06** urging **07** coaxing, comfort, succour **08** cheering **10** heartening, incitement, motivation, persuasion **11** consolation, exhortation, inspiration, stimulation **13** encouragement
See also **encouragement**

reassure
05 brace, cheer, nerve, rally **06** buoy up, stroke **07** bolster, cheer up, comfort, confirm, hearten, inspire **08** inspirit, reinsure **09** cosy along, encourage

rebate
04 dull **05** abate, blunt **06** rabbet, reduce, refund **08** decrease, discount **09** allowance, deduction, reduction, repayment

rebel
◇ *anagram indicator*
04 defy, riot **06** flinch, mutine, mutiny, oppose, recoil, resist, revolt, rise up, shrink **07** aginner, beatnik, defiant, disobey, dissent, heretic, run riot, shy away **08** agitator, apostate, mutineer, mutinous, pull back, recusant, revolter **09** dissenter, guerrilla, insurgent **10** malcontent, rebellious, schismatic **11** disobedient, turn against **12** malcontented, paramilitary **13** insubordinate, nonconformist, revolutionary **14** freedom fighter **15** insurrectionary

Rebels include:

04 Aske (Robert), Ball (John), Cade (Jack), Kett (Robert)
05 Lalor (Peter)
06 Fawkes (Guy)
09 Glendower (Owen)
10 Engelbrekt

See also **revolutionary**

rebellion
04 coup, riot **06** heresy, mutine, mutiny, revolt, rising **07** dissent, treason **08** defiance, uprising **09** coup d'état **10** insurgence, insurgency, opposition, resistance, revolution **12** disobedience, insurrection **15** insubordination

Rebellions include:

03 Rum
07 Fifteen, Whiskey
08 Jacobite
09 Forty-Five
10 the Fifteen
12 Easter Rising, the Forty-Five
14 Eureka Stockade

rebellious
◇ *anagram indicator*
◇ *reversal indicator*
06 unruly **07** defiant, rioting **08** mutinous **09** insurgent, malignant, obstinate, rebelling, resistant, seditious **10** disorderly, refractory **11** disobedient, intractable **12** contumacious, recalcitrant, ungovernable, unmanageable **13** insubordinate, revolutionary **15** insurrectionary

rebirth
07 renewal, revival **11** reawakening, renaissance, restoration **12** regeneration, rejuvenation, resurrection, risorgimento **13** reincarnation **14** revitalization

rebound
04 fail **05** carom **06** bounce, double, recoil, re-echo, resile, result, return, spring **07** bricole, redound **08** backfire, ricochet **09** boomerang, carambole, reflexion, throw back **10** backfiring, bounce back, reflection, spring back **11** reverberate **12** defeat itself, repercussion **13** reverberation **14** score an own goal **15** be self-defeating, come home to roost

rebuff
03 cut **04** snub **05** check, noser, spurn **06** refuse, reject, rubber, slight **07** decline, put down, put-down, refusal, repulse, set-down, squelch **08** brush-off, spurning, turn down **09** knock back, rejection, repudiate **10** discourage **11** counterbuff, one in the eye, repudiation **12** cold shoulder, cold-shoulder **13** slap in the face **14** a flea in your ear, discouragement, kick in the teeth

rebuild
◇ *anagram indicator*
06 reform, remake **07** re-edify, remodel, restore **08** renovate **09** reaedifye, refashion **10** reassemble **11** reconstruct **12** haussmannize, rehabilitate

rebuke
04 rate, slap, snub, trim **05** blame, check, chide, sauce, scold, score, stick **06** carpet, earful, lesson, talk to, threap, threep **07** censure, lecture, reproof, reprove, rollick, speak to, tell off, tick off, trounce, upbraid **08** admonish, call down, keelhaul, reproach, restrain, scolding, trimming **09** carpeting, castigate, dress down, go crook at, go crook on, objurgate, pitch into, raspberry, reprimand **10** admonition, go to town on, rollicking, telling-off, ticking-off **11** castigation, comeuppance, remonstrate **12** countercheck, dressing-down, give an earful **13** remonstration, tear off a strip **14** throw the book at **15** give someone hell

rebut
05 elide, quash, repel **06** defeat, negate, recoil, refute **07** confute, explode **08** disprove, overturn **09** discredit **10** invalidate **12** give the lie to

rebuttal
06 defeat **08** disproof, negation **09** overthrow **10** refutation **11** confutation **12** invalidation

recalcitrance
08 defiance **09** obstinacy **10** wilfulness **11** waywardness **12** disobedience, stubbornness **13** unwillingness **14** refractoriness **15** insubordination

recalcitrant
06 unruly, wilful **07** defiant, wayward **08** contrary, renitent, stubborn **09** obstinate, unwilling **10** refractory **11** disobedient, intractable **12** contumacious, ungovernable, unmanageable, unsubmissive **13** insubordinate, unco-operative **14** uncontrollable

recall
◇ *reversal indicator*
05 annul, evoke **06** call up, cancel, go over, memory, repeal, revoke, summon **07** nullify, reclaim, rescind, retract, retreat, think of, unswear **08** abrogate, call back, dredge up, recision, remember, summon up, withdraw **09** annulment, bring back, order back, recollect, reminisce **10** abrogation, call to mind, retraction, revocation, summon back, withdrawal **11** countermand, remembrance, think back to **12** cancellation, recollection **13** nullification, order to return **14** countermanding

recant
04 deny **05** unsay **06** abjure, disown, recall, revoke **07** disavow, rescind, retract **08** abrogate, disclaim, forswear, renounce, unpreach, withdraw **09** repudiate **10** apostatize

recantation
06 denial, revoke **08** apostasy, palinode, palinody **09** disavowal **10** abjuration, disclaimer, disownment, revocation, withdrawal **11** repudiation **12** renunciation, retractation

recapitulate
05 recap, sum up **06** go over, repeat, review **07** recount, restate, run over **09** reiterate, summarize

recapitulation
06 review **07** summary **08** epanodos **09** summing-up **10** repetition **11** reiteration, restatement, summarizing

recast
◇ *anagram indicator*
05 alter **06** modify, revamp, revise, rework **07** rewrite **08** rephrase, revision

recce
04 case, scan **05** probe **06** patrol, search, spy out, survey **07** examine, explore, inspect, observe **08** check out, scouting, scrutiny **10** expedition, inspection, scrutinize **11** examination, exploration, investigate, observation, reconnoitre **13** investigation, reconnoitring **14** reconnaissance

recede
◇ *reversal indicator*
03 ebb **04** drop, fade, sink, wane **05** abate **06** go back, lessen, retire, return, shrink **07** decline, dwindle, fall off, regress, retreat, slacken, subside **08** decrease, diminish, move away, withdraw **10** retrograde

receipt
03 pay, rec **04** chit, note, rept, slip, stub **05** gains, paper, recpt, tally **06** chitty, docket, income, recipe, return, ticket **07** gaining, getting, profits, returns, takings, voucher, warrant **08** capacity, delivery, deriving, earnings, proceeds, turnover **09** obtaining, quittance, receiving, reception **10** acceptance **11** acquittance, counterfoil, dock-warrant **13** money received **14** deposit-receipt **15** acknowledgement, proof of purchase

receive
◇ *containment indicator*
03 get **04** bear, draw, gain, hear, hold, take **05** admit, fence, greet, latch, let in **06** accept, come by, derive, gather, obtain, pick up, suffer, take up **07** acquire, be given, collect, contain, embrace, harbour, inherit, react to, sustain, undergo, welcome **08** meet with, perceive **09** apprehend, encounter, entertain, entertake, go through, respond to **10** experience, learn about **11** accommodate, take on board **12** be informed of, find out about

receiver
03 tap **05** donee, fence, radio, tuner **07** catcher, grantee, handset, legatee **08** assignee, receptor, wireless **09** apparatus, recipient, televisor **10** radiopager **11** beneficiary **13** satellite dish **14** stamp collector **15** direction-finder, superheterodyne

recent
03 low, new **04** late **05** fresh, novel, young **06** latest, latter, modern **07** current **08** ci devant, neoteric, up-to-date **09** latter-day **10** neoterical, present-day **11** Post-Glacial **12** contemporary **13** up-to-the-minute

recently
04 late **05** newly **06** lately, of late **07** freshly **09** yesterday **10** not long ago **13** a short time ago

receptacle
04 bath, sink **05** bosom, purse **06** holder, vessel **09** container, reservoir **10** repository **11** conceptacle, reservatory **12** receptaculum

reception
02 do **04** bash **05** beano, levee, party **06** accoil, at-home, durbar, pick-up, rave-up, ruelle, social **07** ovation, receipt, reunion, shindig, welcome **08** assembly, function, greeting, occasion, reaction, response **09** admission, gathering, treatment **10** acceptance, assumption, bel-accoyle, bon accueil, recipience, recipiency **11** get-together, recognition **12** entertaining **13** entertainment **15** acknowledgement

receptive
04 open **05** quick **07** willing **08** amenable, flexible, friendly, pregnant **09** recipient, sensitive, welcoming **10** accessible, favourable, hospitable, interested, open-minded, responsive **11** suggestible, susceptible, sympathetic **12** approachable, open to reason **13** accommodating

recess
◇ *reversal indicator*
03 bay, cwm **04** apse, bole, bunk, cove, ingo, nook, rest **05** ambry, awmry, bower, break, heart, hitch, niche, oriel, press, sinus **06** alcove, almery, aumbry, awmrie, bowels, bunker, cavity, cirque, closet, corner, corrie, depths, exedra, hollow, indent, locule **07** adjourn, exhedra, holiday, innards, loculus, mortice, mortise, outshot, reaches, respite, time off, time out **08** cupboard, interior, interval, playtime, vacation **09** blank door, breaktime, embrasure, embrazure, seclusion, sepulcher, sepulchre **10** depression, penetralia, retirement **11** blank window, columbarium, indentation **12** confessional, intermission

recession
05 crash, slide, slump **06** trough **07** decline, failure **08** collapse, downturn, shake-out **10** depression, withdrawal **15** economic decline

recherché
04 rare **06** arcane, choice, exotic, select **07** obscure, refined, tenuous **08** abstruse, esoteric **10** far-fetched

recipe
01 r **03** rec, way **04** dish, take **05** guide, means **06** method, system **07** formula, process, receipt **09** procedure, technique **10** directions **11** ingredients **12** instructions, prescription

recipient
05 donee **06** vessel **07** grantee, legatee **08** assignee, donatory, receiver **09** receiving, receptive **10** suscipient **11** beneficiary

reciprocal
05 joint **06** mutual, reflex, shared **07** inverse **08** requited, returned **09** commutual, exchanged, reflexive **10** equivalent, quid pro quo **11** alternating, correlative, give-and-take **13** complementary, corresponding **14** interdependent **15** interchangeable

reciprocate
04 swap **05** equal, match, repay, reply, trade **06** return **07** requite, respond **08** exchange **09** alternate, do the same **10** correspond **11** interchange **12** give in return

reciprocity
08 exchange **09** isopolity, mutuality **11** alternation, equivalence, give-and-take **14** correspondence **15** interdependence

recital
04 show **06** report **07** account, concert, reading, telling **08** relation **09** narration, rendering, rendition **10** recitation, repetition **11** commination, declamation, description, enumeration, performance, solmization **14** interpretation

recitation
03 ave **04** poem, tale **05** piece, story, verse **07** passage, reading, recital, telling **09** monologue, narration, rendering **10** party piece **11** incantation, performance

recite
04 scan, tell **05** chant, chime, daven, speak **06** chaunt, relate, repeat **07** declaim, deliver, itemize, narrate, perform, recount, reel off **08** say aloud **09** enumerate, improvise, rattle off **10** articulate, rhapsodize **11** improvisate

reckless
◇ *anagram indicator*
04 rash, wild **05** brash, hasty, perdu, ton-up **06** madcap, perdue **07** wildcat **08** careless, heedless, kamikaze, mindless, tearaway **09** blindfold, daredevil, desperate, foolhardy, imprudent, negligent, rantipole, rechlesse, retchless **10** ill-advised, incautious, indiscreet **11** harum-scarum, inattentive, precipitate, temerarious, thoughtless **12** devil-may-care **13** irresponsible

recklessly
◇ *anagram indicator*
06 rashly **07** hastily **09** full fling, like water **10** carelessly, mindlessly

11 desperately, negligently
13 irresponsibly, thoughtlessly

recklessness
06 Bayard 07 madness 08 rashness
09 incaution 10 imprudence, negligence 11 desperation, gallowsness, inattention
12 carelessness, heedlessness, mindlessness 13 foolhardiness
15 thoughtlessness

reckon
03 sum 04 call, deem, make, rate
05 add up, class, count, fancy, gauge, guess, judge, place, sum up, tally, think, total, value, vogue 06 assess, assume, esteem, expect, figure, impute, number, regard 07 account, believe, compute, imagine, put down, suppose, surmise, think of, work out 08 appraise, consider, estimate, evaluate, look upon
09 calculate, designate, enumerate, figure out 10 conjecture

• **reckon on**
04 face 06 bank on, expect, rely on
07 count on, foresee, hope for, plan for, trade on, trust in 08 depend on, figure on 10 anticipate, bargain for 14 take for granted 15 take into account

• **reckon with**
04 cope, deal, face 05 treat 06 expect, handle 07 foresee, plan for
08 consider 10 anticipate, bargain for
15 take into account

• **reckon without**
06 ignore 08 overlook 09 disregard, not expect, not notice 13 fail to think of

• **to be reckoned with**
05 great 06 mighty, strong 07 weighty
08 forceful, powerful 09 important
10 formidable 11 influential, significant
12 considerable

reckoning
03 due, tab 04 bill, doom, tale, time
05 count, datal, lawin, score, tally, total
06 charge, lawing, number, paying
07 account, daytale, opinion, payment
08 addition, counting, estimate
09 appraisal, damnation, judgement
10 assessment, estimation, evaluation, fellowship, imputation, punishment, settlement, working-out
11 calculation, computation, enumeration, retribution

reclaim
04 tame 05 waste 06 appeal, assart, polder, recall, redeem, regain, rescue
07 get back, recover, restore, salvage
08 civilize, retrieve, take back, wildness 09 claim back, recapture, reinstate 10 regenerate, submersion

reclamation
06 rescue 07 salvage 08 recovery
09 regaining, retrieval 11 restoration
12 regeneration 13 reinstatement

recline
03 lie 04 bend, loll, rest 06 lounge, repose, sprawl 07 incline, lie down
08 lean back 09 recumbent 10 stretch out

recluse
04 monk 05 loner 06 anchor, hermit
07 ascetic, eremite, stylite
08 anchoret, enclosed, monastic, retiring, secluded, solitary
09 anchoress, anchorite, solitaire
10 monastical, solitarian
11 monasterial

reclusive
07 ascetic, recluse 08 eremitic, isolated, monastic, retiring, secluded, solitary 09 withdrawn 10 anchoritic, cloistered, hermitical 11 sequestered

recognition
06 honour, recall, reward, salute, thanks 07 grating, knowing, placing, respect 08 allowing, approval, sanction, spotting 09 admission, awareness, detection, discovery, gratitude, knowledge 10 acceptance, admittance, cognizance, confession, perception, validation
11 endorsement, realization, remembrance 12 appreciation, recognizance, recollection, thankfulness 13 consciousness, understanding 14 identification
15 acknowledgement

recognize
03 ken, own, see, wit 04 know, nose, spot, tell 05 admit, adopt, allow, grant, place 06 accept, acknow, honour, notice, recall, reward, salute
07 approve, concede, confess, discern, endorse, not miss, pick out, realize, respect 08 identify, perceive, remember, sanction, validate
09 apprehend, be aware of, recollect
10 appreciate, call to mind, legitimate, not mistake, understand
11 acknowledge, know by sight 13 be conscious of, be thankful for

recoil
◇ *reversal indicator*
03 shy 04 kick 05 quail, react, rebut
06 falter, flinch, recule, resile, revert, shrink, spring 07 misfire, rebound, recoyle, recuile, redound, retreat, shy away 08 backfire, backlash, draw back, jump back, kickback, move back, reaction, requoyle, undertow, withdraw 09 boomerang
10 degenerate, resilience, resiliency, spring back 11 reverberate
12 repercussion 15 come home to roost

recollect
◇ *anagram indicator*
◇ *reversal indicator*
05 think 06 recall 07 bethink
08 récollet, remember, summon up
09 reminisce 10 call to mind

recollection
◇ *anagram indicator*
06 memory, recall 08 souvenir
09 anamnesis 10 impression
11 remembrance 12 reminiscence

recommend
04 move, plug, tout, urge, wish
05 guide 06 advise, commit, exhort, inform, praise, preach 07 advance, approve, commend, consign, counsel, endorse, propose, suggest
08 advocate, set forth, vouch for 10 put forward

recommendation
03 tip 04 plug 06 advice, coupon, praise, urging 07 counsel 08 advocacy, approval, blessing, good word, guidance, proposal, sanction
09 reference 10 suggestion
11 endorsement, testimonial
12 commendation, exhortations
14 special mention

recompense
03 fee, pay 05 repay, wages
06 amends, answer, return, reward
07 damages, guerdon, payment, redress, requite, satisfy 08 requital
09 indemnify, make up for, reimburse, repayment 10 compensate, remunerate, reparation 11 restitution
12 compensation, remuneration, remuneratory, satisfaction
13 consideration, gratification
15 indemnification

reconcile
04 mend, wean 05 agree, atone
06 accept, accord, adjust, attone, make up, pacify, regain, remedy, settle, square, submit, upknit 07 appease, compose, mollify, patch up, placate, rectify, resolve, reunite 08 face up to, put right 09 harmonize, make peace
10 conciliate, propitiate, shake hands
11 accommodate 12 come to accept, reconsecrate 13 bring together, make your peace 14 bury the hatchet

reconciliation
05 peace 06 accord 07 détente, harmony, reunion 08 squaring
09 agreement, atonement
10 adjustment, compromise, resolution, settlement, syncretism
11 appeasement, explanation, harmonizing 12 conciliation, pacification, propitiation
13 accommodation, mollification, rapprochement

recondite
04 dark, deep 06 arcane, hidden, secret 07 obscure, retired 08 abstruse, esoteric, involved, mystical, profound
09 concealed, difficult, intricate
10 mysterious 11 complicated

recondition
◇ *anagram indicator*
03 fix 05 refit, renew 06 repair, revamp
07 remodel, restore 08 overhaul, renovate 09 refurbish

reconfigure
◇ *anagram indicator*

reconnaissance
04 scan 05 probe, recce, recco, reccy
06 patrol, search, survey 08 scouting, scrutiny 09 discovery 10 expedition, inspection 11 examination, exploration, observation
13 investigation, reconnoitring

reconnoitre
04 case, scan **05** probe, recce, scout **06** patrol, spy out, survey **07** examine, explore, inspect, observe **08** check out, remember **10** scrutinize **11** investigate

reconsider
06 modify, review, revise **07** rethink **08** reassess **09** re-examine, think over **10** think twice **13** think better of

reconsideration
06 review **07** rethink **09** fresh look **12** reassessment **13** re-examination **14** second thoughts

reconstitute
◇ *anagram indicator*

reconstruct
◇ *anagram indicator*
04 redo **06** recast, reform, remake, revamp **07** rebuild, remodel, restore **08** make over, recreate, renovate **09** refashion, reproduce **10** reassemble, regenerate, reorganize **11** recondition, re-establish

record
02 CD, EP, LP **03** can, cut, log, rec **04** best, burn, case, data, disc, disk, edit, file, -gram, keep, list, make, mark, mono, note, read, show, tape **05** album, chart, diary, elpee, enrol, enter, entry, notes, score, trace, video, vinyl **06** annals, career, enroll, manage, memoir, memory, minute, obtain, report, single **07** account, achieve, chalk up, display, dossier, express, fastest, history, journal, lay down, logbook, minutes, myogram, narrate, notch up, produce, put down, release, set down, supreme, swinger, tracing, witness **08** aerogram, annalize, archives, best ever, calendar, cassette, complete, document, evidence, indicate, inscribe, kymogram, memorial, MiniDisc®, preserve, protocol, rap sheet, register, reminder, take down **09** anemogram, catalogue, celebrate, chronicle, documents, recording, testimony, videotape, write down **10** accomplish, background, enregister, instrument, memorandum, seismogram, tape-record, top-ranking, transcribe, unequalled **11** compact disc, fastest time, meteorogram, photography, put on record, remembrance, sphygmogram, superlative, track record, unsurpassed, world record **12** personal best, unparalleled, without equal, world-beating **13** documentation **14** autoradiograph, record-breaking **15** best performance, curriculum vitae

See also **recording**

• **off the record**
07 private, sub rosa **09** privately **10** unofficial **12** confidential, unofficially **14** confidentially

• **on record**
04 ever **05** noted **06** on file **10** documented **11** written down **13** publicly known

recorder
03 VCR, VTR **05** clerk, video **06** marker, scorer, scribe **07** diarist, Walkman® **08** annalist, black box, CD burner **09** archivist, DVD burner, flûte-à-bec, historian, registrar, secretary **10** chronicler, Dictaphone® **11** chronologer, fipple flute, score-keeper, tape machine **12** English flute, remembrancer, stenographer, tape recorder **13** video recorder **14** cassette-player

recording

Recordings include:

02 45, 78, CD, EP, LP
03 DAT, DVD, MP3, vid
04 disc, mono, tape, tele
05 album, video, vinyl
06 record, single, stereo
08 cassette, MiniDisc®
09 audiotape, phonogram, video disc, videotape
11 compact disc, compact disk, long-playing
12 extended play, magnetic tape
13 microcassette, video cassette

recount
04 tell **05** refer **06** depict, detail, impart, recite, relate, repeat, report, run off, unfold **07** account, narrate, portray **08** describe, rehearse **09** reminisce **11** communicate

recoup
05 repay **06** refund, regain **07** get back, recover, recruit, win back **08** claw back, make good, retrieve **09** indemnify, reimburse, repossess **10** compensate, recompense

recourse
04 flow **06** access, appeal, choice, option, refuge, remedy, resort, return, way out **09** turning to **10** recurrence, withdrawal **11** alternative, possibility

• **have recourse to**
03 use **04** take **06** betake, employ, turn to **07** utilize **08** exercise, resort to **09** make use of **10** fall back on **15** avail yourself of

recover
◇ *anagram indicator*
04 cure, heal, mend **05** amend, rally **06** attain, pick up, recoup, recure, redeem, regain, rescue, retake, revive **07** fetch up, get back, get over, get well, improve, reclaim, recoure, recower, recruit, recycle, replevy, restore, salvage, win back **08** overcast, replevin, retrieve **09** come round, get better, recapture, repossess **10** ameliorate, bounce back, convalesce, feel better, recuperate **11** be on the mend, get stronger, pull through, revendicate **12** gain strength **13** turn the corner

recovered
04 over

recovery
05 rally **06** pick-up, recure, regain, rescue, upturn **07** healing, mending, recover, revival, salvage, upswing **08** comeback, rallying **09** recapture, recouping, recycling, regaining, retrieval **10** second wind **11** improvement, reclamation, restoration **12** amelioration, recuperation, regeneration, repossession **13** convalescence, convalescency, dead-cat bounce **14** electrowinning, rehabilitation **15** reconvalescence

recreate
◇ *anagram indicator*
05 amuse, renew **07** refresh **09** replicate, reproduce **11** reconstruct **12** reinvigorate

recreation
03 fun, rec **04** game, play **05** hobby, sport **07** leisure, pastime **08** pleasure **09** amusement, diversion, enjoyment **10** relaxation **11** distraction, refreshment **12** intermission **13** entertainment **14** leisure pursuit **15** leisure activity

recrimination
06 retort **07** quarrel **08** comeback, reprisal **09** bickering **10** accusation **11** retaliation **13** counter-attack, countercharge

recruit
02 AR **03** yob **04** levy, tiro **05** draft, enrol, raise, rooky, sprog **06** engage, enlist, gather, muster, nig-nog, novice, nozzer, obtain, rookie, sign up, swabby, take on **07** acquire, convert, draftee, learner, procure, renewal, restore, trainee **08** assemble, beginner, headhunt, initiate, mobilize, newcomer, unionize, yardbird **09** conscript, greenhorn, reinforce, replenish **10** apprentice, new entrant, talent-spot **11** put together, restoration **12** reinvigorate **13** reinforcement

recruitment
05 press **08** drafting, engaging **09** enlisting, enrolment, signing-up **10** engagement **12** conscription, mobilization

rectification
09 amendment **10** adjustment, correction, making good **11** improvement, reformation **12** putting right, setting right

rectify
03 fix **04** cure, mend **05** amend, emend, right **06** adjust, better, reform, remedy, repair **07** correct, improve, redress **08** make good, put right, set right **10** ameliorate **11** dephlegmate

rectitude
06 honour, virtue **07** decency, honesty, justice, probity **08** goodness, morality **09** exactness, integrity, rightness **11** correctness, uprightness **12** straightness **13** righteousness **14** scrupulousness

recto
02 ro

rector
01 R **04** Rect **06** parson

recumbent
04 flat **05** lying, prone **06** supine
07 leaning, recline, resting
08 lounging, reclined **09** lying down, prostrate, reclining, sprawling
10 horizontal

recuperate
04 mend **05** rally **06** pick up, revive
07 get well, improve, recover **09** get better **10** bounce back, convalesce
11 be on the mend, get stronger, pull through **13** turn the corner

recuperation
05 rally **06** recure, upturn **07** healing, mending, revival **08** rallying, recovery
11 improvement, restoration
12 amelioration **13** convalescence, convalescency **14** rehabilitation
15 reconvalescence

recur
03 ren, rin, run **05** prime **06** repeat, return, revert **07** persist **08** reappear
09 come round **11** happen again, perseverate **12** repeat itself **14** come round again

recurrence
06 return, rhythm **08** paroxysm, recourse **09** flashback, reversion
10 appearance, regularity, repetition, restenosis, revolution **11** persistence
12 alliteration, continuation, reminiscence **14** redintegration

recurrent
◇ *reversal indicator*
07 chronic, regular **08** cyclical, frequent, habitual, periodic, repeated
09 continual, recurring **10** persistent, repetitive **12** intermittent

recycle
◇ *anagram indicator*
04 save **05** re-use **07** reclaim, recover, salvage **09** reprocess

red
◇ *anagram indicator*
01 c **04** cent, comb, redd, rede, rosy
06 florid, refuse, rubric **07** clear up, flaming, flushed, glowing, leftist, reddish, rubbish, vacated **08** blushing, inflamed, rubicund **09** bloodshot, Bolshevik, communist, rubescent, rufescent, socialist **10** erubescent, shamefaced, testaceous
11 carbuncular, disentangle, embarrassed, incarnadine, lateritious, sanguineous **12** Cain-coloured
13 revolutionary

Reds include:

04 guly, pink, rose, ruby, rust, wine
05 brick, gules, henna, ruddy
06 auburn, cerise, cherry, claret, damask, ginger, maroon, minium, modena, murrey, rufous, russet, Titian, tomato, Tyrian
07 carmine, carroty, cramesy, crimson, fuschia, lobster, nacarat, scarlet, stammel, vermeil
08 beetroot, blood-red, brick-red, burgundy, cardinal, chestnut, cinnabar, cramoisy, sanguine
09 carnation, solferino, vermilion
10 Chinese red, coccineous, coquelicot, terracotta
11 burnt sienna, incarnadine, sang-de-boeuf

• **in the red**
04 bust **05** broke **06** in debt
08 bankrupt **09** in arrears, insolvent, overdrawn, penniless **10** on the rocks, owing money **12** impoverished, on your uppers **13** gone to the wall **14** on your beam ends

• **red and inflamed**
03 raw

• **see red**
05 go mad **07** explode **08** boil over
09 do your nut **10** hit the roof
11 become angry, blow your top, lose your rag **12** blow your cool, fly into a rage, lose your cool **14** lose your temper **15** fly off the handle

red-blooded
05 lusty, manly **06** hearty, lively, robust, strong, virile **08** vigorous
09 masculine

redcap
02 MP

redden
03 rud **04** gild, rosy, ruby **05** blush, flush, go red **06** colour, rubefy
07 crimson, scarlet, suffuse

reddish
03 red **04** pink, rosy **05** ruddy, sandy
06 flushy, ginger, rufous, russet
08 pyrrhous, rubicund **09** bloodshot, gingerous, rufescent

• **reddish brown**
03 bay **04** rust, sore **06** russet

redecorate
04 do up, redo **09** refurbish

redeem
03 buy **04** cash, free, save **05** lowse, trade **06** acquit, cash in, change, offset, ransom, recoup, regain, rescue
07 absolve, buy back, convert, deliver, expiate, get back, reclaim, recover, release, reprive, repryve, salvage, set free, trade in **08** atone for, exchange, liberate, outweigh, repreeve, reprieve, retrieve **09** discharge, make up for, repossess **10** emancipate, recuperate, repurchase **13** compensate for **14** give in exchange **15** remove guilt from

redemption
06 ransom, rescue **07** freedom, release, trade-in **08** exchange, recovery **09** atonement, expiation, retrieval, salvation **10** fulfilment, liberation, reparation, repurchase
11 deliverance, reclamation
12 compensation, emancipation, repossession **13** reinstatement

redeploy
◇ *anagram indicator*

redevelop
◇ *anagram indicator*

redevelopment
◇ *anagram indicator*

red-handed
07 napping **08** in the act, off-guard, on the hop, unawares **10** by surprise **12** in the very act

redistribute
◇ *anagram indicator*

redistribution
◇ *anagram indicator*

redness
03 rud **04** glow, heat **05** flush

redolent
07 odorous, scented **08** aromatic, fragrant, perfumed **09** evocative, remindful **10** suggestive **11** reminiscent
13 sweet-smelling

redoubtable
05 awful **06** mighty, strong **07** fearful, valiant **08** dreadful, fearsome, powerful, resolute, terrible
10 formidable

redound
04 cast, tend **05** ensue, surge
06 effect, result, return **07** conduce, rebound, reflect **08** overflow
10 contribute

redraft
◇ *anagram indicator*
06 revise, rework **07** rewrite

redress
03 aid **04** help **05** amend, right
06 adjust, avenge, reform, relief, remead, remede, remedy, remeid
07 balance, correct, justice, payment, rectify, requite, restore **08** put right, readjust, regulate, requital
09 atonement **10** assistance, compensate, correction, recompense, reparation **11** restitution
12 compensation, satisfaction
15 indemnification

reduce
◇ *tail deletion indicator*
02 ax **03** axe, cut, put **04** alay, clip, diet, dock, ruin, slim, trim **05** abate, adapt, aleye, allay, annul, drive, force, halve, lower, scant, slake, slash **06** absorb, adjust, deduct, demote, dilute, draw in, humble, impair, lessen, master, rebate, shrink, subdue, weaken **07** conquer, curtail, cut back, cut down, deflate, degrade, deplete, devalue, disband, shorten, thicken **08** beat down, come down, condense, contract, decrease, diminish, discount, downsize, make less, minimize, mitigate, moderate, overcome, restrict, separate, step down, take down, vanquish, wear down, wind down **09** bring down, comminute, deoxidate, deoxidize, downgrade, go on a diet, humiliate, knock down, overpower, translate,

water down **10** abbreviate, de-escalate, impoverish, lose weight **11** make smaller, weight-watch **12** disintegrate **13** whittle away at **14** take the edge off

reduction
◇ *tail deletion indicator*
03 cut **04** drop, fall, loss, wear **06** rebate **07** cutback, decline **08** batement, clipping, decrease, discount, drawdown **09** allowance, deduction, lessening, narrowing, shrinkage, weakening **10** concession, correction, diminution, downsizing, hatchet job, limitation, moderation, rebatement, shortening **11** compression, contraction, curtailment, devaluation, discounting, restriction, subjugation, subtraction **12** abbreviation, condensation, depreciation, minimization

redundancy
04 boot, push, sack **05** cards, elbow **06** excess, firing, notice, papers **07** jotters, removal, sacking, surplus **08** cheville, pleonasm **09** discharge, dismissal, expulsion, laying-off, prolixity, tautology, verbosity, wordiness **10** downsizing, exuberance, exuberancy, repetition **11** superfluity, uselessness **12** outplacement **14** marching-orders

redundant
05 extra, fired, wordy **06** excess, otiose, padded, sacked **07** copious, jobless, laid off, surging, surplus, verbose **08** unneeded, unwanted **09** dismissed, excessive, out of work **10** pleonastic, unemployed **11** inessential, overflowing, repetitious, superfluous, unnecessary **12** periphrastic, tautological **13** supernumerary

redwood
07 big tree, sequoia

re-edit
◇ *anagram indicator*

reef
03 cay, key **04** bank, motu, scar **05** ridge, scaur, shoal **06** skerry **07** bombora, sandbar **08** sandbank **10** square knot

• **reefer**
05 coral

See also **cannabis**

reek
03 hum **04** fume, honk, ming, niff, pong **05** fetor, fumes, odour, reech, smell, smoke, stink, whiff **06** exhale, stench, vapour **08** malodour, mephitis **09** effluvium **10** exhalation

reel
◇ *anagram indicator*
03 din **04** pirn, rock, roll, spin, sway, swim **05** fling, lurch, pitch, spool, swift, swirl, twirl, waver, wheel, whirl, wince, winch **06** bobbin, falter, gyrate, rattle, totter, wobble **07** revolve, stagger, stumble **08** hoolican **09** eightsome, hoolachan **10** multiplier

• **reel off**
04 list **06** recite, repeat **09** rattle off **10** run through **11** list quickly

refashion
◇ *anagram indicator*
06 adjust, reform, rehash **07** convert, rebuild **11** reconstruct

refer
04 cite, mean, send **05** apply, guide, point, quote, remit **06** advert, allude, appeal, assign, belong, commit, direct, hand on, hint at, look at, look up, pass on, permit, relate, turn to **07** bring up, concern, consult, deliver, mention, pertain, put over, speak of, touch on **08** describe, indicate, relegate, resort to, transfer **09** recommend, represent, reproduce **10** be relevant

• **refer to**
03 see

referee
03 ref, ump **05** judge, zebra **06** umpire **07** arbiter, mediate **08** linesman, mediator **09** arbitrate, intercede **10** adjudicate, arbitrator **11** adjudicator, commissaire, referendary

reference
03 ref **04** hint, note **05** mensh **06** regard, remark, source, squint **07** bearing, mention, respect **08** allusion, citation, footnote, innuendo, instance, relation **09** authority, character, quotation **10** connection, pertinence, retrospect **11** credentials, endorsement, testimonial **12** illustration **13** applicability **14** recommendation

• **with reference to**
02 re **05** about **07** apropos **09** as regards, regarding **10** concerning, relating to, relevant to, respecting **11** referring to **12** with regard to **13** in the matter of, with respect to **14** on the subject of

referendum
04 poll, vote **06** survey, voting **10** plebiscite

referral
07 sending **08** handover, pointing, transfer **09** direction, handing on, passing on

refine
◇ *anagram indicator*
03 try **04** fine, hone, pure, sift, test **05** clear, exalt, treat **06** distil, filter, polish, purify, rarefy, repure, strain **07** chasten, clarify, cleanse, elevate, improve, perfect, process **08** chastise, civilize, freebase, repurify **09** cultivate, elaborate, sublimize, subtilize **11** cut and carve **12** spiritualize

Products and byproducts of refining include:

03 tar
05 sugar
07 asphalt, bitumen, treacle
08 molasses
11 golden syrup

See also **fuel**; **hydrocarbon**; **sugar**

refined
04 fine, pure **05** Attic, civil, clear, couth, exact, horsy **06** gentle, horsey, inland, picked, polite, subtle, urbane **07** classic, courtly, elegant, foppish, genteel, precise, stylish, treated **08** Augustan, cultured, cutglass, delicate, educated, filtered, gracious, ladylike, polished, precious, purified, rarefied, well-bred **09** civilized, distilled, processed, sensitive, spiritual **10** cultivated **11** gentlemanly **12** well-mannered **13** gentlewomanly, sophisticated **14** discriminating

refinement
05 grace, style, taste **06** nicety, polish **07** culture, exility, finesse **08** addition, breeding, chastity, civility, delicacy, elegance, elegancy, subtlety, urbanity **09** amendment, gentility, technique **10** alteration, subtleness **11** cultivation, elaboration, good manners, improvement **12** amelioration, modification **14** discrimination, sophistication

refit
◇ *anagram indicator*
04 mend **05** renew **06** repair, revamp **07** furbish **08** facelift, renovate **09** refurbish **10** renovation

reflect
◇ *reversal indicator*
04 cast, chew, echo, mull, muse, shed, show **05** brood, dwell, glass, glint, image, shine, study, think **06** advise, depict, mirror, ponder, reveal **07** bespeak, display, exhibit, express, imitate, portray, redound, scatter, tarnish **08** cogitate, consider, disgrace, indicate, manifest, meditate, mull over, ruminate, send back **09** bounce off, cerebrate, discredit, repercuss, reproduce, speculate, throw back **10** chew the cud, deliberate **11** communicate, contemplate, demonstrate, reverberate **14** give a bad name to, put in a bad light

reflection
◇ *reversal indicator*
04 baby, echo, idea, life, slur, view **05** blame, image, shame, study **06** belief, musing, reflex **07** censure, display, eidolon, feeling, opinion, rebound, thought **08** disgrace, feelings, likeness, reproach, thinking **09** aspersion, criticism, discredit, disrepute, portrayal, snowblink, viewpoint **10** cogitation, epiphonema, expression, impression, indication, meditation, rumination **11** cerebration, mirror image, observation **12** deliberation, repercussion **13** consideration, contemplation, demonstration, manifestation

reflective
06 dreamy **07** pensive **08** absorbed

09 pondering, reasoning
10 cogitating, meditative, ruminative, thoughtful 12 deliberative
13 contemplative

reflex
06 direct 07 natural, project
08 autotomy, knee-jerk, unwilled
09 automatic, re-entrant
10 expression, mechanical, reciprocal, re-entering 11 instinctive, involuntary, spontaneous 13 manifestation
14 Babinski effect, uncontrollable
15 without thinking

reform
◇ *anagram indicator*
04 mend 05 amend, prune, purge
06 anneal, better, change, repair, revamp, revise 07 correct, disband, dismiss, improve, rebuild, rectify, redress, remodel, restore, shake up, shake-up 08 chastise, renovate, revision 09 amendment, refashion, transform 10 ameliorate, betterment, correction, rebuilding, regenerate, renovation, reorganize
11 improvement, reconstruct, remodelling, restoration
12 reconstitute, rehabilitate
13 rectification, revolutionize
14 reconstruction, rehabilitation, reorganization

reformat
◇ *anagram indicator*

reformation
◇ *anagram indicator*
08 progress, revision 09 amendment
10 renovation 11 improvement, restoration 12 amelioration, palingenesis, regeneration
13 rectification 14 rehabilitation

reformer
03 rad 06 mucker 07 Hussite, liberal, Lollard, Owenite, radical 08 do-gooder, Lutheran 09 Calvinist, reformado, Wyclifite, Zwinglian
10 Wycliffite 11 progressive
12 Pestalozzian 13 bleeding heart, revolutionary, whistle-blower

Reformers include:

03 Hus (Jan)
04 Huss (John), Knox (John), Mill (John Stuart), Owen (Robert)
05 Perón (Evita)
06 Calvin (John), Luther (Martin), Wiclif (John), Wyclif (John)
07 Stanton (Elizabeth Cady), Wycliff (John), Zwingli (Huldreich), Zwingli (Ulrich)
08 Wicliffe (John), Wycliffe (John)
10 Pestalozzi (Johann)
11 Wilberforce (William)

refractory
05 balky, surly, tough 06 mulish, sturdy, unruly, wilful 07 defiant, naughty, restive 08 perverse, stubborn
09 difficult, obstinate, resistant
10 headstrong, rebellious
11 contentious, disobedient, intractable 12 cantankerous, contumacious, disputatious, recalcitrant, unmanageable 13 fire-resistant, unco-operative
14 uncontrollable

refrain
03 bob, tag 04 curb, fa la, juba, keep, quit, song, stop, tune 05 avoid, cease, forgo, spare, wheel 06 burden, chorus, desist, eschew, fading, fa la la, forego, give up, melody, strain 07 abstain, burthen, ducdame, forbear, hold off
08 faburden, falderal, leave off, overcome, overture, renounce, repetend, response, restrain, rum-ti-tum, surcease, withhold 09 do without, hemistich, supersede, tirra-lyra, turnagain, undersong
10 epistrophe, ritornello, tirra-lirra
11 rumti-iddity 12 rumpti-iddity

refresh
03 jog 04 cool, prod, stir 05 brace, renew, slake 06 arouse, prompt, refect, remind, repair, repose, revive
07 enliven, fortify, freshen, restore
08 activate, energize, recreate, revivify
09 reanimate, recomfort, stimulate
10 exhilarate, invigorate, rejuvenate, revitalize 11 refocillate 12 reinvigorate

refreshing
03 new 04 cool 05 fresh, novel
06 caller 07 bracing, welcome
08 original, reviving 09 different, inspiring 10 energizing, freshening, not another, unexpected 11 inspiriting, refrigerant, stimulating 12 exhilarating, invigorating 15 thirst-quenching

refreshment
03 tea 04 bait, food 05 drink, snack
06 drinks, repast 07 elevens, renewal, revival 09 elevenses, four-hours, refection, twalhours 10 freshening, recreation, sustenance 11 reanimation, restoration, stimulation, water of life
12 food and drink, invigoration
14 reinvigoration, revitalization

refreshments
04 eats, food, grub, nosh 06 drinks, snacks, tucker 07 aliment, titbits
08 eatables 09 elevenses 10 provisions, sustenance 12 food and drink

refrigerate
03 ice 04 cool 05 chill 06 freeze
08 keep cold

refuge
04 dive, hole, holt, home 05 haven
06 asylum, burrow, harbor, island, resort 07 harbour, hideout, hospice, retreat, shelter 08 bolthole, funkhole, hideaway, security 09 sanctuary
10 protection, stronghold, subterfuge
11 sheet anchor 13 place of safety

refugee
05 exile, reffo 06 émigré 07 escapee, runaway 08 fugitive 10 contraband
12 asylum seeker 15 displaced person, stateless person

refulgent
06 bright 07 beaming, lambent, radiant, shining 08 gleaming, lustrous
09 brilliant, irradiant 10 glistening, glittering 11 resplendent

refund
05 repay 06 rebate, return 07 imburse, pay back, restore 08 give back
09 reimburse, repayment
10 redisburse 13 reimbursement

refurbish
◇ *anagram indicator*
04 do up, mend 05 refit 06 repair, revamp 07 re-equip, remodel, restore
08 overhaul, renovate 10 redecorate
11 recondition

refurbishment
◇ *anagram indicator*
07 doing-up 09 refitting, repairing, revamping 10 renovation
11 recondition, restoration
12 redecoration

refusal
02 no 04 veto 06 denial, nay-say, rebuff 07 repulse 08 negation, spurning 09 knock-back, raspberry, rejection 11 repudiation, turning-down, withholding 12 incompliance, non-admission, nothing doing 13 non-acceptance 14 nolo episcopari

• **first refusal**
06 choice, option 11 opportunity
13 consideration 15 right of purchase

refuse
◇ *anagram indicator*
03 jib, red 04 bran, deny, junk, marc, nill, rape, redd, scum 05 draff, dregs, dross, flock, husks, offal, repel, say no, spurn, trash, waste 06 debris, litter, naysay, pass up, rebuff, reject, resist, scoria, sewage 07 decline, garbage, offscum, rubbish, sullage 08 leavings, renounce, tailings, turn down, withhold 09 knock back, repudiate, riddlings, throw back 11 offscouring
12 kitchen-stuff, offscourings, rejectamenta 13 draw the line at, shake your head 14 dig your heels in

refutation
08 disproof, elenchus, negation, rebuttal 09 overthrow 11 confutation

refute
04 deny, meet 05 rebut, refel
06 negate 07 confute, counter, reprove, silence 08 disprove, redargue
09 discredit, overthrow 12 deny strongly, give the lie to

regain
04 find 06 recoup, retake 07 get back, reclaim, recover, win back 08 recovery, retrieve, return to, take back
09 recapture, reconcile, repossess

regal
05 noble, royal 06 kingly, lordly
07 queenly, stately 08 imperial, majestic, princely, sceptred
09 sceptered, sovereign 11 magnificent

regale
03 ply 05 amuse, feast, serve
06 divert, junket 07 delight, gratify,

kitchen, refresh **09** captivate, entertain, fascinate

regard
03 eye, see **04** care, deem, gaum, gorm, heed, look, love, mark, note, rate, view **05** gauge, judge, point, think, value, watch **06** aspect, behold, detail, esteem, follow, gaze at, hold of, honour, look at, look on, matter, notice, repute, tender **07** believe, concern, imagine, observe, respect, set down, subject, suppose, weigh up
08 appraise, approval, consider, estimate, listen to, look upon, relation, respects, sympathy **09** affection, attention, deference, greetings, intention, reference **10** admiration, advertence, advertency, bear in mind, best wishes, estimation, good wishes, particular, retrospect, scrutinize
11 approbation, compliments, contemplate, observation, salutations
12 take notice of **13** consideration
14 loving kindness, pay attention to
15 give the once-over, take into account
• with regard to, in regard to
02 re **04** as to **05** about, anent
07 apropos, vis-à-vis **09** as regards, in terms of **10** as concerns, concerning
12 in relation to **13** with respect to
14 on the subject of **15** with reference to

regardful
05 aware **07** careful, dutiful, heedful, mindful **08** noticing, watchful
09 attentive, observant **10** respectful, respective, thoughtful **11** circumspect, considerate

regarding
02 re **04** as to **05** about **07** apropos, vis-à-vis **09** as regards **10** concerning, in regard to **12** in relation to, with regard to **13** when it comes to, with respect to **14** on the subject of **15** with reference to

regardless
◇ *deletion indicator*
06 anyhow, anyway **08** careless, heedless **09** at any cost, negligent, unmindful **10** at any price, neglectful
11 come what may, inattentive, indifferent, nonetheless, respectless, unconcerned **12** disregarding, irregardless, nevertheless, no matter what **13** inconsiderate

regenerate
◇ *anagram indicator*
05 renew **06** change, revive, uplift
07 refresh, renewed, restore
08 inspirit, reawaken, rekindle, renovate, revivify **09** reproduce, twice-born **10** invigorate, rejuvenate, revitalize **11** reconstruct, re-establish
12 reconstitute, reinvigorate

regenerated
◇ *anagram indicator*
03 new

regeneration
07 renewal **10** neogenesis, renovation
11 reformation, restoration
12 morphallaxis, palingenesis, rejuvenation, reproduction
13 homomorphosis **14** reconstitution, reconstruction, reinvigoration **15** re-establishment

regime
03 way **04** diet, fast, rule **05** order, reign **06** method, system
07 command, control, formula, pattern, regimen, routine **08** practice, schedule, tyrannis **09** direction, procedure, programme **10** abstinence, government, leadership, management
11 kleptocracy **13** establishment
14 administration **15** short sharp shock

regiment
04 army, band, body, crew, gang
05 group **06** cohort, pultun, tercio
07 battery, brigade, company, platoon
08 squadron

Army regiments include:

02 RA, RE, TA
03 SAS
04 REME
05 Kings, Paras
06 London
07 Gurkhas, Lowland
08 Cheshire
09 Fusiliers, Parachute, Royal Tank
10 Black Watch, Life Guards, Royal Irish, Royal Scots, Royal Welsh
11 Highlanders, Horse Guards, Irish Guards, Scots Guards, Welsh Guards
12 Army Air Corps, Close Support, Green Howards, Green Jackets, Gurkha Rifles, Rifle Brigade, Royal Anglian, Royal Hussars, Royal Lancers, Royal of Wales
13 Artists' Rifles, Light Dragoons, Light Infantry, Staffordshire
14 General Support, Royal Artillery, Royal Engineers
15 Grenadier Guards, Rifle Volunteers, Territorial Army

regimented
06 strict **07** ordered **09** organized, regulated **10** controlled, methodical, systematic **11** disciplined
12 standardized, systematized

region
01 E **03** end **04** area, belt, high, land, part, wild, zona, zone **05** ambit, bundu, burgh, duchy, field, manor, orbit, place, range, realm, reame, scope, shire, state, tract, waste, wilds, world **06** county, domain, empire, estate, garden, ghetto, parish, riding, sector, sphere **07** borough, climate, country, diocese, emirate, expanse, granary, heavens, hundred, kingdom, mission, quarter, section, suburbs, terrain **08** autonomy, badlands, district, division, dominion, foreland, interior, province, time zone
09 backwoods, bailiwick, climature, continent, goldfield, heartland, inner city, outskirts, periphery, territory
10 borderland, hemisphere, playground, wilderness
11 breadbasket, God's country, reservation, terra ignota
12 municipality, principality, subcontinent **13** catchment area, neighbourhood **14** God's own country, postal district, terra incognita

Regions include:

03 Zug
04 Jura, León, Midi, Ruhr, Vaud
05 Angus, Dixie, Gower, Lazio, Liège, Loire, Marne, Namur, Norte, Otago, Rhine, Rhône, Rioja, Somme, Taupo, Tyrol, Urals
06 Acadia, Alsace, Apulia, Aragón, Argyll, Azores, Bayern, Beiras, Burgos, Centro, Crimea, Hessen, Iberia, Latium, Lisboa, Molise, Mt Cook, Murcia, Nelson, Ozarks, Puglia, Savoie, Saxony, Sicily, Top End, Umbria, Valais, Veneto, Vosges, Wanaka
07 Abruzzo, Algarve, Almería, Ardenne, Bavaria, Bohemia, Borders, Brabant, Castile, Corsica, Drenthe, Galicia, Hainaut, Jutland, La Loire, La Rioja, Liguria, Limburg, Lucerne, Madeira, Marches, Midwest, Moselle, Navarra, Navarre, Picardy, Riviera, Rotorua, Ruapehu, Shannon, Siberia, Silesia, Thurgau, Tuscany, Utrecht, Venetia, Waikato, Zeeland
08 Alentejo, Alicante, Ardennes, Asturias, Auvergne, Bretagne, Brittany, Burgundy, Calabria, Calvados, Campania, Canaries, Cataluña, Caucasus, Charente, Chechnya, Dalmatia, Dordogne, Eastland, Flanders, Grampian, Hebrides, Holstein, Lappland, Limousin, Lombardy, Lorraine, Manawatu, Normandy, Picardie, Piedmont, Provence, Pyrenees, Rust Belt, Saarland, Sardinia, Taranaki, Trentino, Val d'Oise, Valencia, Wallonia, Wanganui
09 Andalucía, Andalusia, Aquitaine, Bible Belt, Bourgogne, Cantabria, Carinthia, Castellón, Catalonia, Champagne, Charentes, Côte d'Azur, Deep South, Fiordland, Flevoland, Friesland, Groningen, Gulf Coast, Hawkes Bay, Highlands, Languedoc, Maritimes, Neuchâtel, Northland, Pomerania, Red Centre, Rhineland, Schleswig, Snowdonia, Southland, Southwest, The Burren, Thuringia, Trossachs, Wairarapa, West Coast
10 Appalachia, Basilicata, Canterbury, Coromandel, Costa Brava, Gelderland, Graubünden, Great Lakes, Horowhenua, New England, Overijssel, Palatinate, Westphalia
11 Bay of Plenty, Black Forest, Brandenburg, Central Belt, Costa Blanca, Costa del Sol, Costa Dorada, Extremadura, Great Plains, Île-de-France, Marlborough, Mid-Atlantic, Zuid-Holland
12 American West, Bay of Islands,

Noord-Brabant, Noord-Holland, The Kimberley
13 Barossa Valley, Basque Country, Brecon Beacons, Canary Islands, Emilia-Romagna, Middle America, Pays-de-la-Loire
14 Castile and Leon, Channel Islands, Snowy Mountains
15 Balearic Islands, Bernese Oberland, Eastern Seaboard

See also **council**; **county**; **department**; **district**; **electorate**; **geography**; **province**; **state**

• in the region of
03 odd **04** near, some **05** about, circa **06** around, nearly **07** close to, loosely, roughly **09** just about, not far off, rounded up **10** give or take, more or less, round about **11** approaching, rounded down **13** approximately, or thereabouts, something like **14** in round numbers **15** in the vicinity of

regional
05 local, zonal **08** district **09** localized, parochial, sectional **10** provincial

register
03 log, say, tax **04** cast, file, list, mark, note, poll, read, roll, show, tone **05** album, clock, diary, enrol, enter, files, index, notes, range, voice **06** annals, betray, book in, docket, enlist, enroll, ledger, lidger, muster, record, regest, reveal, roster, sign on, turn in **07** almanac, check in, diptych, display, exhibit, express, journal, listing, notitia, put down, set down, terrier **08** archives, cadastre, indicate, inscribe, manifest, menology, obituary, schedule, take down **09** cartulary, catalogue, chronicle, directory, enrolment, matricula, registrar **10** enregister, enrollment **11** demonstrate, matriculate, patent-rolls **12** put in writing, transfer book

registrar
05 clerk **07** actuary **08** annalist, greffier, official, recorder, register **09** archivist, secretary **10** cataloguer, chronicler **11** protocolist, protonotary **12** prothonotary, sheriff clerk **13** administrator

registration
04 list, rego **05** reggo **06** noting, record **07** logging **08** entering, register **09** enrolment, recording, signing-on **10** checking-in **11** inscription

regress
◇ *reversal indicator*
03 ebb **04** wane **05** lapse **06** recede, return, revert **07** re-entry, relapse, retreat **09** backslide, retrocede, reversion **10** degenerate, retrogress **11** deteriorate

regret
03 rew, rue **04** weep **05** grief, mourn, shame **06** bemoan, desire, grieve, lament, relent, repent, sorrow **07** be sorry, deplore, remorse **08** had-I-wist **09** deprecate, feel sorry, penitence **10** bitterness, contrition, repentance **11** compunction **12** be distressed, feel bad about, self-reproach **14** be disappointed, disappointment

• expression of regret
02 ay **03** ach, och **04** alas **05** alack, ewhow **06** if only **07** out upon **09** alack-a-day

regretful
03 sad **05** sorry **06** rueful **07** ashamed **08** contrite, penitent **09** repentant, sorrowful **10** apologetic, remorseful **12** disappointed

regrettable
03 sad **05** sorry, wrong **06** too bad **07** unhappy, unlucky **08** shameful **09** upsetting **10** deplorable, ill-advised, lamentable **11** disgraceful, distressing, unfortunate **13** disappointing, reprehensible

regrettably
04 alas **05** sadly **08** sad to say **09** unhappily, unluckily, worse luck **11** sad to relate **13** unfortunately

regular
03 set **04** even, flat **05** daily, fixed, level, loyal, swell, usual **06** common, giusto, hourly, normal, proper, smooth, stated, steady, strict, weekly, yearly **07** average, canonic, certain, classic, correct, monthly, orderly, private, routine, typical, uniform **08** approved, balanced, constant, everyday, frequent, habitual, official, ordinary, orthodox, periodic, rhythmic, standard, standing, thorough **09** canonical, customary, out-and-out, permanent, recurring, unvarying, veritable **10** consistent, methodical, periodical, systematic, unchanging **11** commonplace, established, symmetrical **12** conventional, evenly spread, professional, time-honoured **13** well-organized

regularly
◇ *hidden alternately indicator*
05 often **10** frequently **13** like clockwork

regulate
◇ *anagram indicator*
03 run, set **04** rule, tune **05** align, aline, guide, order **06** adjust, baffle, direct, govern, handle, manage, settle, square **07** arrange, balance, conduct, control, monitor, oversee **08** moderate, modulate, organize **09** supervise **10** administer **11** superintend, synchronize

regulation
02 AR **03** act, law, set **04** code, rule **05** by-law, edict, fixed, order, usual **06** bye-law, curfew, decree, dictum, dosage, normal, pusser, ruling **07** command, control, dictate, precept, statute **08** accepted, guidance, official, orthodox, required, standard **09** customary, direction, directive, mandatory, ordinance, principle, procedure, statutory **10** management, obligatory, prescribed **11** commandment, requirement, supervision **12** dispensation **13** pronouncement **14** administration **15** superintendence

regurgitate
04 puke, spew **05** heave, retch, vomit **06** posset, repeat, sick up, spit up **07** bring up, fetch up, regorge, restate, throw up **08** disgorge, ruminate, say again **09** reiterate, tell again **12** recapitulate

rehabilitate
04 mend, save **05** clear, rehab, renew **06** adjust, redeem, reform **07** convert, rebuild, restore **08** renovate **09** normalize, reinstate **11** recondition, reconstruct, re-establish, reintegrate **12** reconstitute, reinvigorate

rehash
◇ *anagram indicator*
05 alter, rejig **06** change, rework **07** restate, rewrite **08** rejigger **09** rearrange, refashion, rejigging, reshuffle, reworking **11** restatement **13** rearrangement

rehearsal
05 drill **06** dry run **07** hersall, reading, recital **08** band-call, dummy run, exercise, practice, trial run, woodshed **09** narration **10** repetition, run-through **11** enumeration, preparation, read-through, walk-through

rehearse
05 block, drill, train **06** go over, recite, relate, repeat, try out **07** narrate, pour out, prepare, recount **08** block out, practise **09** enumerate, pour forth **10** run through

reign
04 rain, ring, rule, sway **05** exist, occur, power, raine, rayne, realm **06** be king, domain, empire, govern, obtain **07** be queen, command, control, kingdom, prevail **08** dominion, hold sway, monarchy **09** be in power, be present, influence, Silver Age, supremacy **10** ascendancy, be in charge, government **11** be in command, be in control, pontificate, predominate, sovereignty **12** predominance **14** be in government, sit on the throne

reigning
05 world **06** ruling **07** current, in power, present, regnant **09** governing, in command, in control, incumbent, presiding **10** victorious

reimburse
05 repay **06** refund, return **07** pay back, restore **08** give back **09** indemnify **10** compensate, recompense, remunerate

reimbursement
06 refund **09** indemnity, repayment **10** recompense **12** compensation

rein
04 curb, halt, hold, stop **05** brake, check, limit **06** answer, arrest, bridle

07 control, harness **08** hold back, reindeer, restrain, restrict
09 overcheck, restraint **11** restriction

• free rein
07 freedom, liberty **08** free hand
10 free-for-all **11** blank cheque, open slather **12** carte blanche, laissez-faire

reincarnation
07 rebirth, samsara **12** palingenesis
14 metempsychosis

reindeer
04 deer, rein **06** tarand **07** caribou

Father Christmas's reindeer:

05 Comet, Cupid, Vixen
06 Dancer, Dasher, Donner
07 Blitzen, Prancer, Rudolph

reinforce
◊ *containment indicator*
04 line, prop, stay **05** brace, shore, steel
06 beef up, harden, stress, supply
07 augment, enforce, fortify, recruit, stiffen, support, toughen **08** buttress, increase, renforce **09** emphasize, re-enforce, underline **10** strengthen, supplement **11** consolidate

reinforcement
04 help, prop, stay **05** brace, shore
06 back-up **07** recruit, support
08 addition, buttress, emphasis, increase, reserves **09** hardening
10 supplement **11** auxiliaries, enlargement **12** augmentation
13 amplification, fortification, re-enforcement, strengthening
15 supplementaries

reinstate
06 recall, return **07** replace, reseize, restore **08** give back **09** reappoint, reinstall **11** re-establish **12** rehabilitate

reinstatement
06 recall, return **10** giving-back, reposition **11** replacement, restoration
15 re-establishment

reiterate
04 ding **05** recap, resay **06** repeat, retell, stress **07** iterate, restate
08 rehearse **09** emphasize
10 ingeminate **12** recapitulate

reject
◊ *reversal indicator*
03 bin, nix, pip **04** cast, deny, dice, jilt, kill, spin, veto **05** repel, scrap, spurn, trash **06** rebuff, recuse, refuse, second
07 cast off, cast-off, condemn, decline, despise, discard, dismiss, exclude, failure, forsake, outcast, repulse, say no to **08** athetize, brush off, disallow, disclaim, jettison, renounce, set aside, throw out, turn away, turn down
09 eliminate, knock back, reprobate, repudiate, throw away **10** disapprove
11 give the push **13** kick into touch
14 throw overboard, turn your back on
15 wash your hands of

rejection
04 push, veto **05** spurn **06** denial, rebuff
07 heave-ho, refusal **08** brush-off, turn-down **09** athetesis, declining, dismissal, exclusion, knock-back
10 discarding **11** elimination, jettisoning, reprobation, repudiation, turning-down **12** cold shoulder, renunciation **14** Dear John letter

rejig
◊ *anagram indicator*
07 re-equip, shake up **09** modernize, rearrange **10** reorganize, streamline
11 rationalize, restructure

rejoice
03 joy **05** exult, glory, revel **07** be happy, delight, gladden, triumph **08** be joyful, jubilate **09** be pleased, celebrate, make merry, whoop it up
10 jump for joy **11** be delighted **12** take pleasure

rejoicing
03 joy **05** glory **07** delight, elation, ovation, revelry, triumph **08** euphoria, gladness, jubilant, pleasure **09** festivity, happiness **10** exaltation, exultation, jubilation **11** celebration, merrymaking

rejoin
◊ *anagram indicator*
04 quip **05** reply **06** answer, retort
07 respond, riposte **08** repartee

rejoinder
04 quip **05** reply **06** answer, retort
07 riposte **08** comeback, repartee, response

rejuvenate
05 renew **06** revive **07** refresh, restore
08 recharge, rekindle, revivify
09 freshen up, reanimate
10 regenerate, revitalize
12 reinvigorate

rejuvenation
07 renewal, revival **11** restoration, shunamitism **12** regeneration
14 reinvigoration, revitalization

relapse
04 fail, sink, weed, weid **05** lapse
06 revert, weaken, worsen **07** decline, regress, setback **08** fall away
09 backslide, reversion, weakening, worsening **10** degenerate, recurrence, regression, retrogress **11** backsliding, deteriorate, hypostrophe
13 deterioration, retrogression

relate
04 ally, join, link, rede, tell **05** apply, fable, refer, story **06** couple, detail, empart, impart, recite, report
07 compare, concern, connect, feel for, narrate, pertain, present, recount, respect **08** describe, hit it off, identify
09 appertain, associate, bring back, correlate, delineate, discourse, empathize, get on with, make known
10 be relevant, sympathize, understand **11** communicate **12** have a rapport **13** get on well with **14** have a bearing on

related
03 kin, rel **04** akin **05** joint, of kin
06 affine, agnate, allied, kinred, linked, mutual **07** affined, cognate, kindred
08 narrated, referred, relevant
09 connected, pertinent **10** affiliated, associated, correlated **11** concomitant
12 accompanying, interrelated
14 consanguineous, interconnected
15 of the same family

relation
03 kin, rel, sib **04** bond, link, term
05 ratio **06** affine, family, regard, rellie
07 bearing, kindred, kinsman, linking, rapport, recital, respect **08** alliance, kinsfolk, relative **09** connexion, kinswoman, narrative, reference, relevance, statement **10** collateral, comparison, connection, pertinence, similarity **11** affiliation, application, correlation, information
12 relationship **13** interrelation
14 correspondence, correspondency
15 interconnection, interdependence
See also **narrative**; **relative**

relations
03 kin, sex **05** folks, terms, union
06 coitus, family **07** affairs, coition, contact, kindred, kinsman, liaison, quarter, rapport, rellies **08** contacts, dealings, intimacy, kinsfolk
09 kinswoman, relatives **10** copulation, love-making **11** connections, interaction, intercourse
12 associations, consummation, relationship **14** communications
15 carnal knowledge

relationship
03 kin, tie **04** bond, link, ties **05** blood, fling, ratio, thing, tie-up **06** affair
07 account, kinship, liaison, rapport, romance, sibship **08** affinity, alliance, intimacy, parallel **09** chemistry, closeness **10** connection, flirtation, friendship, love affair, proportion, similarity **11** association, correlation

• end relationship
04 dump, jilt **07** break up, divorce, split up

relative
03 kin, rel **06** family, rellie **07** germane, kindred, kinsman, related **08** apposite, kinsfolk, moderate, parallel, relation, relevant **09** connected, connexion, dependant, dependent, kinswoman, pertinent **10** applicable, comparable, connection, reciprocal, respective
11 appropriate, comparative, correlative **12** commensurate, interrelated, proportional
13 corresponding, proportionate

Relatives include:

02 ex
03 bro, dad, mom, mum, sis, son
04 aunt, gran, heir, nana, twin, wife
05 aunty, daddy, mummy, nanna, nanny, niece, uncle
06 auntie, cousin, ex-wife, father, german, godson, grampa, granny, mother, nephew, parent, sister, spouse
07 brother, grandad, husband, partner, sibling, stepdad, stepmum, stepson

08 daughter, godchild, grandson
09 ex-husband, godfather, godmother, stepchild
10 grandchild, half-sister, stepfather, stepmother, step-parent, stepsister, twin-sister
11 first cousin, foster-child, god-daughter, grandfather, grandmother, grandparent, half-brother, stepbrother, twin-brother
12 foster-parent, second cousin, stepdaughter
13 grand-daughter

relatively
05 quite 06 fairly, rather 08 somewhat 12 by comparison, in comparison 13 comparatively

relax
◇ *anagram indicator*
03 veg 04 calm, ease, fall, rest 05 abate, chill, loose, lower, remit, slump 06 cool it, lessen, loosen, reduce, relent, sedate, soften, unbend, unknit, unrein, unwind, veg out, weaken 07 ease off, mollify, resolve, slacken, unbrace, unclasp, unpurse 08 calm down, chill out, de-stress, diminish, kick back, loosen up, moderate, wind down 09 hang loose, lighten up 10 liberalize, take it easy 12 tranquillize 13 let yourself go, put your feet up 14 take things easy 15 let your hair down

relaxation
03 fun 04 rest 05 let-up 06 easing, repose 07 détente, leisure, relâche 08 chill-out, pleasure 09 abatement, amusement, enjoyment, lessening, loosening, reduction, softening, unwinding, weakening 10 autogenics, meditation, misericord, moderation, recreation, slackening 11 délassement, distraction, loosening up, misericorde, refreshment 13 entertainment

relaxed
◇ *anagram indicator*
04 calm, cool, easy 05 loose 06 at ease, atonic, casual, comodo, unbent 07 commodo, languid, restful 08 carefree, composed, downbeat, informal, laid-back, toneless, unbraced, unstrung 09 collected, easy-going, graspless, leisurely, unhurried 11 comfortable, uninhibited 12 happy-go-lucky

relay
◇ *anagram indicator*
04 send, time, turn 05 carry, shift, spell, stint 06 hand on, pass on, period, spread, supply 07 message 08 dispatch, transmit 09 broadcast, circulate, programme 11 communicate 12 transmission 13 communication

release
04 free, undo 05 exeem, exeme, issue, let go, loose, remit, untie 06 acquit, convey, excuse, exempt, launch, let off, let-off, loosen, reveal, unbind, unlock, unveil 07 absolve, acquite, deliver, divulge, freedom, liberty, present, publish, relieve, set free, slacken, unchain, unclasp, unleash, unloose 08 acquight, announce, bulletin, disclose, liberate, uncouple, unfasten 09 acquittal, circulate, discharge, disengage, exemption, exonerate, make known, quitclaim, quittance, remission, surrender, unshackle 10 absolution, disclosure, distribute, emancipate, liberation, make public, publishing, relinquish, revelation 11 acquittance, declaration, deliverance, enlargement, exoneration, manumission, publication 12 announcement, emancipation, proclamation 13 make available

relegate
05 eject, exile, expel, refer 06 assign, banish, demote, deport, reduce 07 consign, degrade, entrust 08 delegate, dispatch, sideline, transfer 09 downgrade 10 expatriate 12 Stellenbosch

relent
04 ease, melt 05 abate, allow, let up, relax, yield 06 give in, regret, repent, soften, unbend, weaken 07 die down, ease off, give way, melting, slacken, slowing 08 moderate 09 come round 10 capitulate 14 change your mind

relentless
04 grim, hard 05 cruel, harsh, stern 06 fierce 08 pitiless, ruthless 09 cut-throat, incessant, merciless, punishing, unceasing 10 implacable, inexorable, inflexible, persistent, unflagging, unyielding 11 cold-hearted, hard-hearted, remorseless, unforgiving, unrelenting, unremitting 14 uncompromising

relevance
07 aptness, bearing 10 pertinence 11 suitability 12 appositeness, significance 13 applicability 15 appropriateness

relevant
03 apt 04 live 06 german, proper 07 apropos, fitting, germane, related 08 apposite, material, relative, suitable 09 congruous, pertinent 10 admissible, applicable, to the point 11 appropriate, significant 12 proportional, to the purpose

reliability
07 honesty 09 certainty, constancy, integrity, precision 10 steadiness 12 faithfulness 13 dependability 14 responsibility 15 trustworthiness

reliable
04 safe, sure, true 05 solid, sound, white 06 honest, stable, tested, trusty 07 certain, devoted, dutiful, regular, staunch 08 bankable, constant, credible, faithful 09 unfailing 10 dependable 11 predictable, responsible, trustworthy, well-founded 12 well-grounded 13 authoritative, conscientious 14 copper-bottomed

reliance
05 faith, trust 06 belief, credit 09 assurance 10 confidence, conviction, dependance, dependence

relic
05 scrap, shell, token, trace 06 corpse, fossil, relict 07 antique, memento, relique, remains, remanié, remnant, vestige 08 artefact, fragment, heirloom, holdover, keepsake, moniment, monument, reminder, souvenir, survival 09 antiquity 11 remembrance

relief
03 aid 04 alms, cure, help, rest
05 break, let-up, locum, proxy
06 back-up, easing, remedy, repose, rescue, saving, succor, supply
07 comfort, redress, release, relievo, reserve, respite, rilievo, stand-by, stand-in, succour, support 08 allaying, breather, calmness, easement, soothing 09 abatement, assuaging, diversion, happiness, lessening, reduction, remission, surrogate
10 assistance, mitigation, palliation, relaxation, substitute, sustenance, understudy 11 alleviation, consolation, deliverance, reassurance, refreshment, replacement 12 interruption

• **expression of relief**
04 phew, whew 06 wheugh 08 thank God 12 thank heavens 13 thank goodness

relieve
03 aid 04 beet, bete, cure, ease, feed, free, heal, help, save, stop 05 abate, allay, break, expel, pause, spare, spell 06 assist, excuse, exempt, lessen, reduce, remove, rescue, soften, soothe, succor 07 assuage, bestead, break up, comfort, console, deliver, dismiss, release, replace, set free, slacken, succour, support, sustain 08 liberate, mitigate, palliate, reassure, unburden 09 alleviate, discharge, interrupt, punctuate 10 stand in for, substitute 11 discontinue 12 bring to an end, take over from 14 take the place of

relieved
04 glad 05 eased, happy 07 cheered, pleased 08 thankful 09 refreshed 10 encouraged

religion
04 code 05 creed, dogma, faith 07 beliefs 08 doctrine 12 belief system

Religions include:

03 Bon, Zen
04 Shi'a
05 Amish, Baha'i, Druze, Islam, Sunni
06 Sufism, Taoism, voodoo
07 animism, Baha'ism, Essenes, Jainism, Jesuits, Judaism, Lamaism, Moonies, Opus Dei, Orphism, Quakers, Saivism, Saktism, Sikhism
08 Baptists, Buddhism, Druidism, Hasidism, Hinduism, paganism, Tantrism, Wahhabis
09 Ahmadiyya, Cabbalism, Calvinism,

Methodism, Mithraism, Mormonism, occultism, Parseeism, shamanism, Shintoism, Vedantism, Waldenses
10 Adventists, Brahmanism, Evangelism, Gnosticism, Iconoclasm, Puritanism, Soka Gakkai
11 Anabaptists, Anglicanism, Catholicism, Creationism, Freemasonry, Hare Krishna, Lutheranism, Manichaeism, Scientology, Zen Buddhism
12 Albigensians, Christianity, Confucianism, Nestorianism, Unitarianism
13 Church in Wales, Protestantism, Reform Judaism, Salvation Army
14 Fundamentalism, Oxford Movement, Pentecostalism, Rastafarianism, Rosicrucianism, Society of Jesus, Ultramontanism, Zoroastrianism
15 ancestor-worship, Church of England, Presbyterianism

religious

02 pi **03** pia **04** holy **05** godly, pious
06 devout, divine, sacred, strict
07 serious **08** reverent, rigorous
09 believing, committed, doctrinal, righteous, spiritual **10** devotional, God-fearing, meticulous, practising, scriptural, scrupulous **11** church-going, theological **13** conscientious

See also **Bible**; **festival**; **scripture**; **service**; **symbol**

Religious buildings include:

04 Kaba
05 Ka'aba
06 Kasbah
07 Abu Mena, al-Azhar
08 Pantheon
09 Abu Simbel, Acropolis, Borobudur, Eye Temple, Kinkakuji, Parthenon, Propylaea, Sacred Way, Sun Temple, Temple Bar
10 Blue Mosque, Erechtheum, Harimandir, Sacré Coeur
11 Ajanta caves, Ellora caves, Erechtheion, Great Sphinx, Hagia Sophia, Temple Mount, Wailing Wall, Western Wall, York Minster
12 Boyana Church, Ely Cathedral, Golden Temple, Great Pyramid, Monte Cassino, Norton Priory, Pagan temples, Temple of Hera, Temple of Isis, Watton Priory
13 Cordoba Mosque, Dome of the Rock, Horyuji Temple, Kailasa Temple, Muhammad's Tomb, Rila Monastery, Vézelay Church
14 Belém Monastery, Dilwara temples, Golden Pavilion, Kazan Cathedral, Mahamuni Pagoda, My Son Sanctuary, Reims Cathedral, Ripon Cathedral, Sagrada Familia, Suleiman Mosque, Temple of Amon-Ra, Temple of Apollo, Temple of Athena, Temple of Heaven, Ummayyad Mosque, Wells Cathedral
15 Aachen Cathedral, Amiens Cathedral, Chavín de Huantar, Durham Cathedral, Exeter Cathedral, Ggantija temples, Pyramid of Cheops, Pyramid of the Sun, Shwe Dagon Pagoda, Shwezigon Pagoda, Speyer Cathedral, Temple of Artemis, Temple of Hathoor, Temple of Solomon, Temple of Somnath

See also **abbey**; **cathedral**; **worship**

Religious figures include:

03 **Fry** (Elizabeth), **Hus** (Jan), **Roy** (Ram Mohan)
04 **Bede** (St, 'the Venerable'), **Eddy** (Mary), **Huss** (John), **John** (of Leyden), **King** (Martin Luther), **Knox** (John), **Penn** (William), **Pire** (Dominique), **Shaw** (Anna Howard), **Tutu** (Desmond), **Weil** (Simone)
05 **Amman** (Jacob), **Booth** (William), **Condé** (Louis Prince de), **Farel** (Guillaume), **Grove** (Sir George), **Jesus**, **Keble** (John), **Lao Zi**, **Lewis** (Clive Staples), **Mahdi** (El), **Paley** (William), **Paris** (Matthew), **Smith** (Joseph), **Soper** (Donald, Lord), **Waite** (Terry), **Young** (Brigham)
06 **Arnold** (of Brescia), **Baxter** (Richard), **Becket** (St Thomas à), **Besant** (Annie), **Boehme** (Jakob), **Borgia**, **Browne** (Robert), **Browne** (Sir Thomas), **Buddha**, **Bunyan** (John), **Calvin** (John), **Christ**, **Gandhi** (Mohandas), **Garvey** (Marcus), **Graham** (Billy), **Hillel**, **Hutter** (Leonhard), **Jowett** (Benjamin), **Julian** (of Norwich), **Kempis** (Thomas à), **Lao-tzu**, **Luther** (Martin), **Mather** (Cotton), **Mesmer** (Franz Anton), **Olcott** (Colonel Henry Steel), **Pilate** (Pontius), **Raikes** (Robert), **Ridley** (Nicholas), **Rogers** (John), **Sieyès** (Emmanuel Joseph Comte), **Tetzel** (Johann), **Wesley** (John)
07 **Aga Khan**, **al-Banna** (Hassan), **Ayeshah**, **Buchman** (Frank), **Coligny** (Gaspard de), **Cranmer** (Thomas), **Crowley** (Aleister), **Erasmus** (Desiderius), **Falwell** (Jerry), **Fénelon** (François), **Hubbard** (L Ron), **Jackson** (Jesse), **Latimer** (Hugh), **Mahatma**, **Müntzer** (Thomas), **Paisley** (Reverend Ian), **Photius**, **Russell** (Charles Taze), **Russell** (Jack), **Sithole** (Reverend Ndabaningi), **Spooner** (William Archibald), **Steiner** (Rudolf), **Tyndale** (William), **William** (of Malmesbury), **William** (of Ockham), **William** (of Tyre), **Wishart** (George), **Zwingli** (Huldreich)
08 **Agricola** (Johann), **Andrewes** (Lancelot), **Barabbas**, **Buchanan** (George), **Caiaphas**, **Khomeini** (Ayatollah Ruhollah), **Mahavira** (Vardhamana), **Mohammed**, **Muhammad**, **Pelagius**, **Rasputin** (Grigoriy), **Selassie** (Emperor Haile), **Williams** (Roger), **Wycliffe** (John)
09 **Akhenaten**, **Bar Kokhba** (Simon), **Blavatsky** (Madame Helena), **Confucius**, **Dalai Lama**, **Guru Nanak**, **Joan of Arc** (St), **McPherson** (Aimee Semple), **Niemöller** (Martin), **Zoroaster**
10 **Belshazzar**, **Fateh Singh** (Sant), **Huntingdon** (Selina Hastings, Countess of), **Manichaeus**, **Savonarola** (Girolamo), **Swedenborg** (Emmanuel), **Torquemada** (Tomás de), **Whitefield** (George)
11 **Bodhidharma**, **Jesus Christ**, **Prester John**, **Ramakrishna**, **Wilberforce** (William)
12 **Krishnamurti** (Jiddu)
13 **Judas Iscariot**
15 **Francis of Assisi (St)**

Religious officers include:

03 nun
04 dean, guru, imam, monk, pope
05 abbot, canon, elder, friar, imaum, kohen, padre, prior, rabbi, rebbe, swami, vicar
06 abbess, bishop, clergy, curate, deacon, father, mullah, parson, pastor, priest, rector
07 muezzin, prelate, proctor
08 cardinal, chaplain, minister, preacher
09 ayatollah, clergyman, Dalai Lama, deaconess, Monsignor, Tashi Lama
10 archbishop, archdeacon, arch-priest, chancellor
11 clergywoman, Panchen Lama
14 mother superior

See also **archbishop**; **cardinal**; **missionary**; **pope**; **theologian**

Religious orders include:

04 IBVM, Sufi
05 Taizé
06 Culdee, Essene, Jesuit, Loreto, Marist
07 Jesuits, Marists, Rifaite
08 Buddhist, Capuchin, Grey nuns, Minorite, Trappist, Ursuline
09 Barnabite, Capuchins, Carmelite, Dominican, Marianist, Mawlawite, mendicant, Salesians, Trappists, Ursulines
10 Bernardine, Carmelites, Carthusian, Celestines, Cistercian, Conventual, Dominicans, Franciscan, Gilbertine, Grey friars, Norbertine, Oratorians, Poor Clares
11 Augustinian, Benedictine, Black friars, Camaldolite, Carthusians, Cistercians, Franciscans, Ignorantine, Sylvestrine, White friars
12 Augustinians, Austin friars, Benedictines
13 Society of Mary
14 Knights Templar, Sisters of Mercy, Society of Jesus

See also **monastery**; **sect**

• religious education

02 RE, RI

religiously
08 strictly **10** rigorously **11** doctrinally, spiritually **12** meticulously, scrupulously **13** theologically **15** conscientiously

relinquish
04 cede, drop, part, quit **05** cease, demit, forgo, let go, waive, yield **06** desert, desist, forego, give up, resign **07** abandon, abstain, discard, forsake, give out, release, retreat **08** abdicate, hand over, part with, renounce **09** repudiate, surrender **11** discontinue

reliquary
04 chef, tope **09** encolpion **10** tabernacle

relish
03 sar **04** gout, gust, like, love, lust, tang, zest **05** adore, charm, enjoy, gusto, sauce, savor, smack, spice, taste, tooth **06** bumalo, degust, flavor, palate, pickle, savour, vigour **07** botargo, bummalo, chutney, delight, flavour, garnish, kitchen, rellish, revel in, stomach **08** appetite, bumaloti, caponata, opsonium, piquancy, pleasure, vivacity **09** appetizer, bummaloti, condiment, delight in, enjoyment, seasoning **10** appreciate, Bombay duck, experience, flavouring, liveliness **12** appreciation, satisfaction
• **lose relish**
04 pall

relocate
02 go **04** move **05** leave **06** go away, remove **08** move away, transfer, up sticks **09** move house **13** change address

reluctance
07 dislike **08** aversion, distaste, loathing **09** hesitancy, renitency **10** hesitation, opposition, repugnance, resistance **12** backwardness **13** indisposition, recalcitrance, unwillingness **14** disinclination

reluctant
03 shy **04** loth, slow **05** loath **06** averse **08** backward, grudging, hesitant, loathful, renitent **09** resisting, squeamish, unwilling **10** indisposed, struggling **11** disinclined **14** unenthusiastic

rely
04 bank, lean, rest **05** count, trust **06** be sure, depend, reckon **07** swear by

remain
02 be **03** lie **04** bide, keep, last, rest, stay, wait **05** abide, abode, await, dwell, leave, stand, stick, tarry **06** endure, linger, stay on **07** climate, persist, prevail, subsist, survive **08** continue, outstand **09** hang about, stand good **10** be left over, hang around, stay behind **11** stick around

remainder
04 lave, rest **06** excess **07** balance, remains, remanet, remnant, residue, surplus **08** remanent, residuum, vestiges **09** carry-over, leftovers **11** superfluity

remaining
03 odd **04** last, left, over **05** other, spare **06** unused **07** abiding, lasting, remnant, unspent **08** left over, remanent, residual **09** lingering, surviving **10** persisting, unfinished **11** outstanding

remains
03 ash **04** body, dust, rest, ruin **05** ashes, bones, dregs, ruins **06** corpse, crumbs, debris, relics, scraps, traces **07** cadaver, carcase, residue **08** dead body, detritus, leavings, oddments, remnants, vestiges **09** fragments, leftovers, reliquiae, remainder, reversion **11** odds and ends

remake
◇ *anagram indicator*
06 mutate **07** rebuild **09** modernize, reproduce, transmute **11** reconstruct **12** metamorphose

remark
03 hit, say **04** barb, jeer, note, quip, shot **05** ad-lib, sally, state **06** assert, insult, notice, reason **07** clanger, comment, declare, mention, observe, opinion **08** brickbat, cynicism, intimacy, one-liner, remarque **09** assertion, gallantry, pronounce, reference, statement, stricture, utterance, witticism **10** commentary, reflection, trivialism **11** commonplace, declaration, discourtesy, non sequitur, observation **12** obiter dictum **13** pronouncement **14** noteworthiness **15** acknowledgement

remarkable
◇ *anagram indicator*
03 odd **04** fine, rare, some, tall, unco **06** signal **07** amazing, notable, strange, unusual **08** singular, striking, uncommon **09** damnedest, important, memorable, momentous, prominent **10** hellacious, impressive, inimitable, miraculous, noteworthy, phenomenal, pre-eminent, surpassing, surprising **11** conspicuous, exceptional, outstanding, significant **12** considerable, unbelievable **13** distinguished, extraordinary
• **remarkable thing**
04 lulu

remarkably
04 unco **08** signally, uncommon **09** unusually **10** uncommonly **12** considerably, surprisingly **13** exceptionally, outstandingly, significantly **15** extraordinarily

remedy
◇ *anagram indicator*
03 fix **04** cure, ease, heal, help, mend, sort **05** azoth, dinic, salve, solve, tonga, treat **06** answer, bicarb, nosode, physic, posset, recure, relief, remead, remede, remeid, repair, soothe **07** arcanum, control, correct, nostrum, panacea, plaster, rectify, redress, relieve, restore, sort out, therapy **08** antidote, cephalic, corn-cure, leechdom, lungwort, medicine, mitigate, pilewort, put right, solution, specific **09** echinacea, eyebright, Galenical, hoarhound, horehound, magistery, prescript, salvarsan, treatment **10** catholicon, corrective, counteract, medicament, medication, reparation, simillimum, tarantella **11** oil of cloves, restorative **12** panpharmacon **13** antiscorbutic, antispasmodic, viper's bugloss **14** countermeasure, white horehound

remember
03 mem **04** keep, mark, mind **05** evoke, learn, place, think **06** honour, recall, record, remind, retain **07** mention, think of **08** hark back, look back, memorize, summon up **09** celebrate, recognize, recollect, reminisce, think back **10** bear in mind, call to mind **11** commemorate, hold against, reconnoitre **12** learn by heart, pay tribute to **13** send greetings **14** commit to memory, send best wishes, send good wishes **15** send your regards

remembrance
04 mind **05** relic, token **06** memory, recall, record **07** memento, thought **08** keepsake, memorial, monument, reminder, souvenir **09** nostalgia, sovenance **10** memorandum, retrospect **11** recognition, recordation, testimonial **12** recollection, reminiscence **13** commemoration

remind
04 hint **05** evoke, nudge **06** call up, prompt **08** remember, take back **10** call to mind **11** bring to mind **13** jog your memory **14** make you think of, put you in mind of

reminder
04 hint, memo, note, prod **05** nudge, token **06** prompt **07** memento **08** keepsake, souvenir **09** red letter **10** memorandum, phylactery, prompt-note, suggestion, verbal note **11** aide-mémoire, remembrance **12** reality check

reminisce
06 recall, review **08** hark back, look back, remember **09** recollect, think back **10** retrospect

reminiscence
06 memoir, memory, recall, review **08** anecdote **10** reflection **11** remembrance **12** recollection **13** retrospection
• **collection of reminiscences**
03 ana

reminiscent
08 redolent **09** evocative, nostalgic, remindful **10** suggestive

remiss
03 lax **04** slow **05** slack, tardy **06** casual, sloppy **07** wayward

08 careless, culpable, dilatory, heedless, slipshod 09 forgetful, negligent, unmindful 10 neglectful 11 inattentive, indifferent, slack-handed, thoughtless 13 lackadaisical

remission
03 ebb 04 lull 05 let-up 06 excuse, pardon, repeal 07 amnesty, release, respite 08 decrease, remittal, reprieve 09 abatement, acquittal, annulment, discharge, exemption, lessening, reduction, remitment, weakening 10 abrogation, absolution, diminution, indulgence, indulgency, moderation, relaxation, rescinding, revocation, slackening, suspension 11 alleviation, exoneration, forgiveness 12 cancellation 13 acceptilation

remit
03 pay 04 mail, post, send 05 abate, brief, refer, relax, scope, untax 06 cancel, desist, direct, give up, orders, pardon, pass on, repeal, revoke, settle 07 forward, release, rescind, suspend 08 abrogate, dispatch, hold over, set aside, transfer, transmit 10 guidelines, overslaugh 12 instructions 13 authorization 14 responsibility

remittance
03 fee 07 payment, sending 08 dispatch 09 allowance, remitment 13 consideration

remnant
03 bit, end, tag 04 butt, fent, rump 05 piece, scrap, shred, trace, wrack 06 offcut 07 balance, oddment, outlier, remains, residue, vestige, witness 08 fragment, leftover, remanent 09 quotation, remainder, remaining 12 odd-come-short

remodel
◇ *anagram indicator*
04 turn 05 adapt, alter, renew, shape 06 adjust, change, mutate, reform 07 convert, furbish, rebuild 08 renovate 09 modernize, refurbish, transform 11 recondition, reconstruct 12 metamorphose

remonstrance
07 protest, reproof 08 petition 09 complaint, exception, grievance, objection, reprimand 10 opposition 12 protestation 13 expostulation 14 representation

remonstrate
05 argue, gripe 06 object, oppose 07 dispute, dissent, protest 08 complain 09 challenge 11 demonstrate, expostulate 13 take issue with 15 take exception to

remorse
03 rew, rue 04 bite, pity, ruth, worm 05 grief, guilt, shame 06 regret, sorrow 08 ayenbite, had-I-wist 09 penitence 10 contrition, mitigation, repentance, ruefulness 11 compunction 12 contriteness, self-reproach 13 bad conscience

remorseful
03 sad 05 sorry 06 guilty, rueful 07 ashamed 08 contrite, penitent 09 chastened, regretful, repentant, sorrowful 10 apologetic 11 guilt-ridden 12 compunctious, on a guilt trip 13 compassionate

remorseless
04 hard 05 cruel, harsh, stern 06 savage 07 callous 08 inhumane, pitiless, ruthless 09 merciless 10 implacable, inexorable, relentless, unmerciful 11 hard-hearted, undeviating, unforgiving, unrelenting, unremitting, unstoppable 12 unremorseful

remorselessly
07 cruelly, harshly 08 savagely 09 callously 10 implacably, inexorably, ruthlessly 11 mercilessly 12 relentlessly 13 unremittingly

remote
03 far, out 04 back, long, poor, slim 05 aloof, faint, inapt, small 06 far-off, lonely, meagre, slight, upland 07 devious, distant, dubious, faraway, outback, outside, removed, slender 08 backveld, detached, doubtful, isolated, outlying, reserved, secluded, unlikely 09 not matter, ungermane, unrelated, up the bush, withdrawn 10 extraneous, immaterial, improbable, inapposite, in the mulga, irrelative, irrelevant, negligible, out of place, peripheral, tangential, uninvolved, up the mulga 11 back-country, god-forsaken, in the sticks, off the point, out-of-the-way, standoffish, unconcerned, unconnected, unimportant, up the Boohai 12 inaccessible, inapplicable, inconsequent, long-distance 13 beside the mark, inappropriate, insignificant 14 beside the point, inconsiderable, unapproachable 15 having no bearing, not coming into it, uncommunicative

removable
07 movable 09 separable 10 detachable, eradicable 12 transferable

removal
04 boot, move, push, sack 05 elbow, shift 06 firing, murder 07 ousting, purging, sacking 08 ablation, deletion, disposal, ejection, eviction, riddance, shifting 09 abolition, clearance, departure, discharge, dismissal, expulsion, taking-off, uprooting 10 conveyance, deposition, detachment, displacing, evacuation, extraction, relegation, relocation, taking away, withdrawal 11 subtraction, transferral 12 dislodgement, obliteration, transference, transporting 14 transportation

remove
03 nip, rid 04 dele, doff, fire, flit, lift, move, oust, pick, sack, shed, take, void, weed 05 amove, carry, eject, eloin, erase, evict, expel, purge, raise, shift, strip 06 ablate, convey, cut off, cut out, delete, depose, detach, efface, eloign, excise, extort, get out, go away, lop off, remble, rub out, unseat 07 abolish, absence, boot out, cart off, cashier, cast out, collect, destroy, dismiss, edge out, expurge, extract, pull off, pull out, put away, removal, take off, take out, tear off 08 amputate, cross out, dislodge, disloign, displace, estrange, get rid of, relegate, relocate, separate, subtract, take away, throw out, transfer, withdraw 09 discharge, eliminate, go off with, strike out, translate, transport 10 blue-pencil, obliterate 11 deaccession

remunerate
03 pay 05 repay 06 reward 07 redress 09 indemnify, reimburse 10 compensate, recompense

remuneration
03 fee, pay 04 sold 05 solde, wages 06 income, profit, reward, salary 07 payment, stipend 08 earnings, retainer 09 emolument, indemnity, repayment 10 honorarium, recompense, remittance 12 compensation 13 reimbursement

remunerative
04 rich 06 paying 07 gainful 08 fruitful 09 lucrative, rewarding 10 profitable, worthwhile 11 moneymaking

renaissance
07 new dawn, rebirth, renewal, revival 08 new birth 09 awakening 10 renascence, resurgence 11 reawakening, re-emergence, restoration 12 reappearance, regeneration, rejuvenation, resurrection, Risorgimento 13 recrudescence

renascent
06 reborn 07 renewed, revived 09 born again, redivivus, resurgent 10 reanimated, reawakened, re-emergent 11 resurrected

rend
03 rip 04 rent, rive, stab, tear 05 break, burst, sever, smash, split, wring 06 cleave, divide, pierce, to-rend 07 rupture, shatter 08 fracture, lacerate, separate, splinter 09 tear apart 10 dilacerate

render
◇ *anagram indicator*
02 do 03 gie, pay, put, try 04 give, make, melt, play, show, sing, turn 05 leave, yield 06 change, depict, give up, make up, return, submit, supply, tender 07 clarify, deliver, display, exhibit, explain, furnish, perform, present, proffer, provide 08 describe, give back, hand over, manifest 09 cause to be, interpret, represent, reproduce, surrender, translate 10 contribute, transcribe

rendering
04 crib, show 05 gloss 06 acting

07 reading, version **09** portrayal, rendition, rewording **10** appearance, paraphrase, production, rephrasing **11** explanation, metaphrasis, performance, translation **12** presentation **13** transcription **14** interpretation, representation, simplification **15** transliteration

rendezvous
02 RV **04** date, meet **05** haunt, rally, tryst, venue **06** gather, muster, resort **07** collect, convene, meeting **08** assemble, converge **10** engagement **11** appointment, assignation **12** come together, meeting-place **13** trysting-place

rendition
05 gloss **07** reading, version **08** delivery **09** depiction, execution, portrayal, rendering, rewording, surrender **10** paraphrase, rephrasing **11** arrangement, explanation, performance, translation **12** construction, presentation **13** transcription **14** interpretation, simplification **15** transliteration

renegade
◇ *anagram indicator*
03 rat **05** rebel **06** outlaw **07** runaway, traitor **08** apostate, betrayer, defector, deserter, disloyal, mutineer, mutinous, recreant, runagate, turncoat **09** dissident **10** backslider, perfidious, rebellious, traitorous, unfaithful **11** backsliding, treacherous **13** tergiversator

renege
04 deny, pike **05** renig, welsh **06** refuse **07** default, renague, renegue **08** renounce **09** backslide, repudiate **10** apostatize **13** cross the floor

renegotiate
◇ *anagram indicator*

renew
◇ *anagram indicator*
03 new **04** mend, stum **05** boost, refit **06** extend, reform, reline, repair, repeat, reseat, resume, revive **07** brush up, prolong, refresh, remodel, replace, reprise, reprize, restart, restate, restock, restore, retrace **08** continue, innovate, overhaul, reaffirm, recreate, renforce, renovate **09** modernize, refurbish, reiterate, replenish, transform **10** invigorate, recommence, regenerate, rejuvenate, revitalize **11** recondition, re-establish, resuscitate **12** reconstitute, reinvigorate

renewal
05 flush **06** repair **07** rebirth, recruit, revival **08** new birth, nidation **09** recruital **10** kiss of life, re-creation, renovation, repetition, resumption **11** continuance, reiteration, restatement **12** instauration, regeneration, rejuvenation, resurrection **13** reaffirmation, refurbishment, replenishment, resuscitation **14** recommencement, reconditioning, reconstitution, reconstruction, reinvigoration, revitalization, revivification

renounce
03 cut **04** deny, reny, shun **05** forgo, renay, reney, renig, spurn, waive **06** abjure, desist, disown, eschew, forego, forsay, give up, pass up, recant, recede, refuse, reject, renege, resign, revolt **07** abandon, abstain, discard, disgown, foresay, forsake, put away, renague, renegue **08** abdicate, abnegate, disclaim, forswear, sign away, swear off **09** repudiate, surrender **10** declare off, disinherit, disprofess, relinquish **14** forisfamiliate **15** wash your hands of

renovate
◇ *anagram indicator*
04 do up **05** refit, renew **06** reform, repair, revamp **07** furbish, improve, remodel, restore **08** overhaul **09** modernize, refurbish, translate **10** redecorate, regenerate **11** recondition **12** rehabilitate **13** give a facelift

renovation
05 refit **06** repair **07** renewal **08** facelift **11** improvement, restoration **13** modernization, refurbishment **14** reconditioning

renown
04 bays, fame,, mana, mark, note **05** glory, kudos, rumor **06** esteem, honour, luster, lustre, repute, rumour **07** acclaim, stardom **08** eminence, prestige **09** celebrate, celebrity **10** prominence, reputation **11** distinction, pre-eminence **15** illustriousness

renowned
05 famed, noted **06** fabled, famous **07** eminent, notable **08** of repute **09** acclaimed, prominent, splendent, well-known **10** celebrated, illustrate, pre-eminent **11** illustrious, prestigious **13** distinguished

rent
◇ *anagram indicator*
03 fee, let, rip **04** cost, farm, gale, hire, mail, rate, ript, take, tare, tear, tore, torn **05** cuddy, gavel, lease, riven, split **06** let out, rental, ripped, screed, sublet **07** charter, divided, fissure, hire out, payment, rent out, revenue, severed **08** lacerate, purchase, ruptured **09** lacerated, torn apart **11** ripped apart

renunciation
06 denial **07** kenosis, waiving **08** giving up, shunning, spurning **09** disowning, forsaking, rejection, surrender **10** abdication, abnegation, abstinence, desistance, discarding, disclaimer **11** abandonment, disclaiming, recantation, repudiation **13** disinheriting **14** relinquishment, self-abnegation

reorder
◇ *anagram indicator*
04 edit **09** rearrange, transpose

reorganize
◇ *anagram indicator*
05 rejig **07** shake up **09** modernize, rearrange **10** streamline **11** rationalize, restructure **12** reconstitute

repackage
◇ *anagram indicator*

repair
◇ *anagram indicator*
02 go **03** fix, sew **04** darn, form, heal, mend, move, nick, turn **05** order, patch, refit, renew, shape, state **06** adjust, doctor, fettle, kilter, make up, remead, remede, remedy, remeid, remove, resort, retire, return, tinker **07** mending, patch up, rectify, redress, refresh, restore, service **08** maintain, make good, overhaul, put right, renovate, revivify, stitch up, withdraw **09** concourse, condition **10** adjustment, reparation **11** improvement, maintenance, restoration, wend your way **12** preservation, working order

reparable
07 curable, savable **10** corrigible, remediable, restorable **11** recoverable, rectifiable, retrievable, salvageable

reparation
04 boot **06** amends, remead, remede, remedy, remeid, repair **07** damages, redress, renewal **08** requital, solatium **09** atonement, indemnity **10** assythment, recompense **11** restitution **12** compensation, propitiation, satisfaction

repartee
03 wit **06** banter, retort **07** jesting, riposte **08** backchat, badinage, wordplay **09** bantering, cross-talk, witticism **11** give and take

repast
04 feed, food, meal **05** board, lunch, snack, table **06** spread **08** victuals **09** collation, refection **11** nourishment
See also **meal**

repatriate
04 oust **05** exile, expel **06** banish, deport **09** extradite, ostracize, transport

repay
03 pay **04** apay, quit **05** appay, quite, quyte, yield **06** avenge, quight, rebate, refund, return, reward, settle, square **07** pay back, requite, revenge **09** get back at, quittance, reimburse, retaliate **10** compensate, recompense, remunerate **11** get even with, reciprocate **12** settle up with **14** settle the score

repayment
06 amends, rebate, refund, reward **07** payment, redress, revenge **08** requital **09** tit for tat, vengeance **10** recompense, reparation **11** eye for an eye, restitution, retaliation, retribution **12** compensation, remuneration **13** reciprocation, reimbursement

repeal
04 lift, void **05** annul, quash, unlaw **06** abjure, cancel, recall, recant, revoke **07** abolish, nullify, repress, rescind, retract, reverse **08** abrogate, quashing, reversal, set aside, withdraw **09** abolition, annulment **10** abrogation, invalidate, rescinding, rescission, revocation, withdrawal **11** countermand, rescindment **12** cancellation, invalidation **13** nullification

repeat
◇ *repetition indicator*
03 rep, rpt **04** copy, echo, redo **05** ditto, labor, quote, recap, recur, renew, rerun, thrum **06** do over, go over, labour, parrot, patter, recite, record, re-echo, relate, replay, reshow, retail, retell, reword, run off, screed **07** confirm, divulge, iterate, persist, recount, replica, reprise, reprize, restate **08** redouble, rehearse, remurmur, say again **09** celebrate, circulate, do to death, duplicate, reiterate, replicate, reproduce, reshowing **10** repetition **11** duplication, perseverate, rebroadcast, reduplicate, restatement **12** recapitulate, reproduction **14** recapitulation

repeated
◇ *repetition indicator*
07 regular **08** constant, frequent, multiple, periodic **09** continual, recurrent, recurring **10** persistent, reiterated, rhythmical **12** repercussive

repeatedly
◇ *repetition indicator*
05 often **10** frequently **11** over and over **12** time and again **13** again and again, time after time

repel
◇ *reversal indicator*
05 check, fight, parry, rebut, spurn **06** offend, oppose, rebuff, refuse, reject, resist, revolt, sicken **07** beat off, decline, disgust, hold off, repulse, turn off, ward off **08** beat back, drive off, fight off, nauseate, push back **09** drive back, force back, keep at bay, repudiate **11** make you sick **13** be repugnant to **15** turn your stomach

repellent
04 foul, grim, vile **05** nasty **06** horrid **07** hateful, obscene **08** shocking **09** abhorrent, loathsome, obnoxious, offensive, repugnant, repulsive, revolting, sickening **10** abominable, despicable, disgusting, nauseating, off-putting, unpleasant **11** distasteful, rebarbative **12** contemptible, disagreeable **13** objectionable

• **insect repellent**
04 deet **07** camphor

repent
03 rue **04** turn **06** lament, recant, regret, relent, sorrow **07** be sorry, confess, deplore, reptant **08** do a U-turn **09** be ashamed **10** be contrite **11** be converted, feel remorse, see the light **14** beat your breast

repentance
03 rue **05** grief, guilt, ruing, shame, U-turn **06** regret, rueing, sorrow **07** penance, remorse **08** metanoia **09** penitence **10** confession, contrition, conversion **11** compunction, recantation

repentant
05 sorry **06** guilty, rueful **07** ashamed, attrite **08** contrite, penitent **09** chastened, regretful, sorrowful **10** apologetic, remorseful

repercussion
04 echo **06** effect, recoil, result, ripple **07** rebound, spin-off **08** backlash, backwash **09** shock wave **10** reflection, side-effect **11** consequence **13** reverberation

repertoire
04 list **05** range, stock, store **06** supply **07** reserve **09** repertory, reservoir **10** collection, repository

repetition
◇ *repetition indicator*
04 echo, rote **05** troll **06** answer, repeat, return **07** copying, echoing, quoting, reprise **08** iterance **09** echolalia, iteration, rehearsal, replicate, tautology **10** recurrence, redundancy **11** duplication, epanalepsis, reiteration, restatement, superfluity **12** reappearance **14** recapitulation

repetitious
04 dull **05** windy, wordy **06** boring, prolix **07** tedious, verbose **08** unvaried **09** redundant **10** long-winded, monotonous, pleonastic, unchanging **12** pleonastical, tautological

repetitive
04 dull **05** samey **06** boring **07** tedious **08** unvaried **09** automatic, iterative, recurrent **10** mechanical, monotonous, unchanging **14** soul-destroying

rephrase
06 recast, reword **07** rewrite **10** paraphrase **13** put another way **14** ask differently, say differently **15** put in other words

repine
04 beef, fret, moan, mope, pine, sulk **05** brood **06** grieve, grouch, grouse, grudge, lament, murmur **07** grumble **08** complain, languish

replace
◇ *anagram indicator*
04 oust **06** act for, change, follow, hang up, refund, return **07** pre-empt, put back, relieve, replant, restore, succeed **08** deputize, displace, exchange, make good, supplant **09** come after, fill in for, reinstate, supersede **10** stand in for, substitute **11** re-establish **14** take the place of

replaceable
09 throwaway **10** disposable, expendable **12** exchangeable **13** biodegradable, non-returnable, substitutable **15** interchangeable

replacement
05 proxy **06** fill-in, supply **07** bionics, reserve, stand-in **09** spare part, successor, surrogate **10** jury-rudder, substitute, understudy **12** arthroplasty, substitution

replenish
04 fill **05** renew, stock, top up **06** fill up, make up, people, refill, reload, supply **07** furnish, provide, recruit, refresh, replace, restock, restore **08** recharge

replenishment
06 supply **07** filling, renewal **09** provision, refilling **10** recharging, restocking, supplyment **11** replacement, restoration

replete
04 full **05** sated **06** filled, full up, gorged, jammed **07** brimful, charged, chocker, crammed, glutted, implete, stuffed, teeming, well-fed **08** brimming, satiated **09** abounding, chock-full, jam-packed **11** chock-a-block, well-stocked **12** well-provided

repletion
04 glut **07** satiety **08** fullness, plethora **09** plenitude, satiation **11** superfluity **12** completeness, overfullness **14** superabundance

replica
04 copy, spit **05** clone, dummy, model **06** repeat **08** gold disc, gold disk **09** duplicate, facsimile, imitation **10** immortelle **12** reproduction

replicate
03 ape **04** copy **05** clone, mimic, reply **06** follow, repeat **08** recreate **09** duplicate, reproduce **10** repetition **11** reduplicate

reply
04 echo **05** duply, react **06** answer, come in, rejoin, retort, return, triply **07** counter, respond, riposte **08** come back, comeback, reaction, rebutter, repartee, response, surrebut, talk back **09** drink-hail, quadruply, rejoinder, replicate, retaliate, surrejoin, write back **11** acknowledge, reciprocate, replication, retaliation, surrebutter **12** surrejoinder, triplication **13** counter-signal **15** acknowledgement

report
◇ *homophone indicator*
03 air, cry, rat, rpt **04** bang, boom, buzz, fame, file, item, name, news, note, rept, shop, shot, tale, talk, tell, word **05** blast, brief, bruit, cover, crack, crash, grass, noise, piece, relay, split, state, story, voice **06** cahier, convey, credit, detail, esteem, furphy, gossip, honour, notify, pass on, record, relate, renown, repute, return, rumour, squeal, tell on, update **07** account, article,

declare, divulge, dossier, give out, hearsay, message, minutes, narrate, opinion, publish, recount, stature, stool on, whisper, write-up **08** announce, blue book, bulletin, complain, describe, disclose, document, inform on, proclaim, register, relation, set forth, standing **09** appraisal, broadcast, celebrity, character, chronicle, circulate, delineate, explosion, judgement, narrative, statement, testimony **10** assessment, communiqué, evaluation, inspection, reputation, stenograph **11** communicate, compte rendu, declaration, delineation, description, distinction, examination, information **12** announcement, press release, procès-verbal
13 communication, reverberation

reportedly
◇ *homophone indicator*
09 allegedly **10** apparently, ostensibly, putatively, supposedly **13** by all accounts

reporter
03 cub **04** hack **05** press **06** leg-man
07 fireman, Jenkins **08** leg-woman, newshawk, pressman **09** announcer, columnist, newshound, roundsman
10 journalist, newscaster, news-writer, presswoman, tripehound
11 commentator **12** newspaperman
13 correspondent
14 newspaperwoman

repose
03 kef, kif, lay, lie, put, set **04** affy, calm, ease, kaif, laze, lean, rest **05** lodge, peace, place, poise, quiet, relax, sleep, store **06** aplomb, invest **07** confide, deposit, dignity, entrust, recline, respite, slumber **08** calmness, quietude, serenity **09** composure, night-rest, quietness, stillness
10 equanimity, inactivity, relaxation
11 restfulness **12** tranquillity **14** self-possession

reposition
◇ *anagram indicator*
05 shift **09** rearrange

repository
03 urn **04** bank, mart, safe, tomb
05 depot, store, vault **06** museum
07 archive, dustbin, spicery
08 magazine, treasury **09** confidant, container, repertory, salvatory, sepulchre, warehouse **10** collection, depository, promptuary, receptacle, storehouse

reprehensible
03 bad, ill **04** base **06** errant, erring, remiss **07** ignoble **08** blamable, culpable, shameful, unworthy
10 censurable, delinquent, deplorable
11 blameworthy, condemnable, disgraceful, opprobrious
13 discreditable, objectionable

represent
◇ *anagram indicator*
02 be **03** act, set **04** draw, mark, mean, show **05** act as, enact, evoke, refer
06 act for, allege, denote, depict, embody, figure, render, sketch, typify
07 display, exhibit, express, perform, picture, portray, present **08** amount to, appear as, describe, speak for, stand for **09** appear for, character, depicture, designate, epitomize, exemplify, personify, sculpture, symbolize
10 constitute, illustrate **11** deputize for
12 characterize, correspond to **13** act on behalf of **14** act in the name of, be equivalent to **15** speak on behalf of

representation
◇ *anagram indicator*
02 MP **04** bust, icon, ikon, play, show
05 envoy, image, model, proxy, stage
06 deputy, reflex, report, shadow, sketch, statue **07** account, drawing, picture, protest, request, showing, stand-in **08** delegate, likeness, petition, portrait, prospect
09 complaint, depiction, depicture, pictogram, portrayal, spectacle, spokesman, statement, tablature
10 allegation, ambassador, councillor, delegation, deputation, mouthpiece, production, thermoform
11 Congressman, delineation, description, explanation, performance, presentment, restoration, spokeswoman **12** cross-section, illustration, presentation, remonstrance, reproduction, spokesperson **13** Congresswoman, expostulation, tableau vivant
14 reconstruction, representative

representative
02 MP **03** rep **05** agent, envoy, proxy, rider, usual, vakil **06** bagman, chosen, deputy, exarch, normal, sample, vakeel
07 drummer, elected, stand-in, typical
08 delegate, devolved, elective, salesman, specimen, symbolic
09 appointed, delegated, exemplary, nominated, spokesman, traveller
10 ambassador, archetypal, authorized, councillor, delegation, deputation, emblematic, exhibitive, indicative, mouthpiece, saleswoman
11 congressman, salesperson, spokeswoman **12** ambassadress, commissioned, commissioner, illustrative, representant, spokesperson **13** decentralized, heir-portioner **14** characteristic **15** knight of the road

repress
◇ *containment indicator*
04 cork, curb **05** check, crush, quash, quell, sit on, sneap **06** cork up, master, muffle, repeal, stifle, subdue
07 control, inhibit, oppress, put down, reprime, silence, sit upon, smother, swallow **08** bottle up, dominate, domineer, hold back, keep back, keep down, overcome, restrain, suppress, vanquish **09** overpower, subjugate
11 bite your lip

repressed
06 hung-up, pent-up **07** uptight
09 inhibited, withdrawn **10** frustrated
11 introverted **14** self-restrained

repression
07 control, gagging, tyranny
08 coercion, crushing, muffling, quashing, quelling, stifling
09 despotism, restraint **10** censorship, constraint, domination, inhibition, oppression, smothering **11** holding-back, subjugation, suffocation, suppression **12** dictatorship

repressive
05 cruel, harsh, tough **06** severe, strict
08 absolute, coercive, despotic
10 autocratic, dominating, oppressive, tyrannical **11** dictatorial **12** totalitarian
13 authoritarian

reprieve
05 let-up, spare **06** acquit, let off, pardon, redeem, relief, rescue
07 amnesty, forgive, relieve, reprive, reprove, respite **08** abeyance, repreeve, show pity **09** abatement, deferment, remission, show mercy
10 suspension **12** postponement
13 let off the hook **15** stay of execution

reprimand
04 jobe, lace **05** blame, check, chide, scold, slate, targe **06** berate, bounce, carpet, earful, rebuke, rocket, see off
07 bawl out, catch it, censure, chew out, go off at, lambast, lecture, reproof, reprove, rouse on, tell off, tick off, wigging **08** admonish, lace into, lambaste, reproach **09** carpeting, castigate, criticize, dress down, pull apart, schooling, take apart, talking-to
10 admonition, telling-off, ticking-off, upbraiding **11** castigation **12** dressing-down **13** call to account, tongue-lashing **14** bring to account, slap on the wrist **15** smack on the wrist

reprisal
05 prize **06** ultion **07** redress, reprise, reprize, revenge **08** requital
09 recaption, recapture, tit for tat, vengeance **11** eye for an eye, retaliation, retribution
12 compensation **13** counter-attack, recrimination

reprise
03 act **04** play, sing **05** prize, put on, renew **06** relate, repeat **07** copying, echoing, narrate, perform, quoting, reissue **08** iterance, reprisal
09 iteration, recapture, rehearsal
10 repetition **11** reiteration, restatement **12** compensation
14 recapitulation

reproach
04 blot, slur, twit, wite, wyte **05** blame, braid, chide, scold, scorn, shame, shend, slate, smear, stain, taunt, touch, wight **06** bounce, carpet, defame, earful, rebuke, rocket, see off, stigma, upcast **07** bawl out, blemish, catch it, censure, chew out, condemn, nayword, obloquy, reproof, reprove,

tell off, tick off, upbraid, wigging **08** admonish, contempt, disgrace, dishonor, ignominy, repriefe, scolding **09** carpeting, criticism, criticize, discredit, dishonour, disparage, dispraise, disrepute, dress down, mispraise, pull apart, reprehend, reprimand, take apart, talking-to **10** admonition, cri de coeur, disrespect, imputation, opprobrium, reflection, telling-off, ticking-off **11** degradation, disapproval **12** condemnation, dressing-down **13** find fault with **14** slap on the wrist **15** smack on the wrist

• **term of reproach**

03 gib **04** runt **05** besom, bisom, madam **06** ronyon, truant **07** Cataian, Catayan, runnion **09** rigwiddie, rigwoodie

reproachful

08 critical, scolding, scornful **09** reproving **10** censorious, upbraiding **11** castigating, disgraceful, disparaging, opprobrious **12** disappointed, disapproving, fault-finding

reprobate

03 bad, rep **04** base, rake, roué, vile **05** knave, rogue, scamp **06** damned, disown, rascal, reject, sinful, sinner, wicked, wretch **07** censure, corrupt, dastard, immoral, villain **08** criminal, depraved, evildoer, hardened, vagabond **09** abandoned, dissolute, miscreant, scallywag, scoundrel, shameless, wrongdoer **10** degenerate, ne'er-do-well, profligate **11** reprobative, reprobatory **12** condemnatory, incorrigible, troublemaker, unprincipled **13** mischief-maker

reprocess

◇ *anagram indicator*

07 recycle

reproduce

◇ *anagram indicator*

03 ape **04** copy, echo, redo **05** breed, cline, clone, match, mimic, print, refer, spawn, Xerox® **06** follow, mirror, pirate, remake, render, repeat **07** emulate, enlarge, express, gemmate, imitate, reflect **08** autotype, generate, multiply, recreate, refigure, simulate **09** bear young, duplicate, facsimile, give birth, photocopy, Photostat®, phototype, procreate, propagate, replicate **10** hectograph, regenerate, transcribe **11** proliferate, reconstruct

reproduction

04 copy, hi-fi, mono **05** clone, print, repro, Xerox® **06** ectype, piracy **07** edition, picture, replica **08** breeding, monogeny, monogony **09** duplicate, facsimile, imitation, photocopy, Photostat® **10** amphimixis, generation, viviparism **11** gamogenesis, monogenesis, procreation, propagation, replication **12** regeneration **14** multiplication, representation

reproductive

03 sex **06** sexual **07** genital **08** prolific **10** generative **11** procreative, progenitive, propagative

reproof

04 rate **05** shame, sloan **06** earful, lesson, rebuke, rocket, sermon **07** censure, jarring, lecture, upbraid, wigging **08** berating, disgrace, disproof, repriefe, reproach, reproval, scolding **09** carpeting, criticism, reprimand, reproving, schooling, talking-to **10** admonition, correption, telling-off, ticking-off, upbraiding **11** castigation **12** condemnation, dressing-down, reprehension **14** curtain lecture, disapprobation, slap on the wrist **15** smack on the wrist

• **expression of reproof**

03 now, tut **04** come, toot, tuts **05** toots **06** tut-tut **07** come now, now then **08** come come

reprove

03 rap **04** rate **05** chide, scold, slate **06** berate, bounce, carpet, rebuke, refute, see off, take up **07** bawl out, catch it, censure, chew out, condemn, lecture, rouse on, tell off, tick off, upbraid **08** admonish, call down, disprove, reprieve, reproach **09** castigate, criticize, dress down, pull apart, reprehend, reprimand, take apart **10** take to task

reptile

Reptiles include:

04 croc, tegu
05 gator
06 caiman, cayman, garial, gavial, mugger, turtle
07 gharial, hicatee, snapper, tuatara
08 aligarta, galapago, hiccatee, matamata, stinkpot, teguexin, terrapin, tortoise
09 alligarta, alligator, crocodile, hawksbill, mud turtle, sea turtle
10 loggerhead, musk turtle
11 green turtle, leatherback
13 giant tortoise, water tortoise
14 leathery turtle, snapping turtle
15 hawksbill turtle

See also **animal**; **dinosaur**; **lizard**; **snake**

republic

Republics include:

03 USA
04 Chad, Cuba, Fiji, Iran, Iraq, Laos, Mali, Peru, Togo
05 Benin, Burma, Chile, China, Congo, Egypt, Gabon, Ghana, Haiti, India, Italy, Kenya, Malta, Nauru, Niger, Palau, Sudan, Syria, Yemen
06 Angola, Brazil, Cyprus, France, Greece, Guinea, Guyana, Israel, Latvia, Malawi, Mexico, Panama, Poland, Russia, Rwanda, Taiwan, Turkey, Uganda, Zambia
07 Albania, Algeria, Armenia, Austria, Belarus, Bolivia, Burundi, Croatia, Ecuador, Estonia, Finland, Georgia, Germany, Hungary, Iceland, Ireland, Lebanon, Liberia, Moldova, Myanmar, Namibia, Nigeria, Romania, Senegal, Somalia, Tunisia, Ukraine, Uruguay, Vanuatu, Vietnam
08 Botswana, Bulgaria, Cameroon, Colombia, Djibouti, Ethiopia, Honduras, Kiribati, Maldives, Mongolia, Pakistan, Paraguay, Portugal, Slovakia, Slovenia, Sri Lanka, Suriname, Tanzania, Zimbabwe
09 Argentina, Cape Verde, Costa Rica, East Timor, Guatemala, Indonesia, Lithuania, Macedonia, Mauritius, Nicaragua, San Marino, Singapore, The Gambia, Venezuela
10 Azerbaijan, Bangladesh, El Salvador, Kazakhstan, Kyrgyzstan, Madagascar, Mauritania, Mozambique, North Korea, Seychelles, South Korea, Tajikistan, Uzbekistan
11 Burkina Faso, Côte d'Ivoire, Philippines, Sierra Leone, South Africa, Switzerland
12 Guinea-Bissau, Turkmenistan
13 Czech Republic, Western Sahara
15 Marshall Islands

See also **country**

repudiate

04 deny **05** repel **06** abjure, desert, disown, nochel, reject, revoke **07** abandon, cast off, disavow, discard, divorce, forsake, notchel, rescind, retract, reverse **08** denounce, disclaim, renounce **09** disaffirm **10** disprofess **14** turn your back on

repudiation

06 denial **09** disavowal, disowning, rejection **10** abjuration, disclaimer, retraction **11** recantation **12** renunciation **13** disaffirmance **14** disaffirmation

repugnance

05 odium **06** hatred, horror, nausea, revolt **07** allergy, disgust, dislike **08** aversion, distaste, loathing **09** abhorring, antipathy, repulsion, revulsion **10** abhorrence, reluctance, repugnancy **11** reluctation **13** inconsistency

See also **disgust**; **distaste**

repugnant

04 foul, vile **05** alien **06** averse, horrid, odious **07** adverse, hateful, hostile, noisome, opposed **08** inimical **09** abhorrent, loathsome, obnoxious, offensive, repellent, resisting, revolting, sickening, unwilling **10** abominable, disgusting, nauseating **11** distasteful **12** antagonistic, antipathetic, incompatible, inconsistent, unacceptable **13** contradictory, objectionable

repulse

04 foil, snub **05** check, refel, repel,

spurn **06** defeat, rebuff, refuse, reject **07** beat off, disdain, failure, put back, refusal, reverse **08** spurning **09** disregard, drive back, rejection **11** repudiation **14** disappointment

repulsion
06 action, effect, hatred **07** disgust **08** aversion, distaste, loathing **09** disrelish, revulsion **10** abhorrence, repellence, repellency, repugnance **11** detestation, raison d'être

repulsive
04 cold, foul, icky, loth, ugly, vile **05** gross, loath, nasty **06** horrid, odious **07** hateful, heinous, hideous, squalid **08** reserved, shocking **09** abhorrent, loathsome, obnoxious, offensive, repellent, repelling, repugnant, revolting, sickening **10** abominable, despicable, disgusting, forbidding, nauseating, off-putting, unpleasant **11** distasteful **12** contemptible, disagreeable, evil-favoured, unattractive **13** objectionable, reprehensible

repulsively
10 abominably, despicably, shockingly **11** obnoxiously **12** disagreeably, disgustingly, nauseatingly, unpleasantly **13** objectionably

reputable
04 good, gude, guid **06** honest, worthy **07** upright **08** esteemed, reliable, virtuous **09** admirable, estimable, excellent, respected **10** creditable, dependable, honourable **11** respectable, trustworthy **12** of good repute, of high repute **13** well-thought-of **14** irreproachable

reputation
03 los, rep **04** fame, loos, name, note, pass, rank **05** image, izzat, voice **06** credit, esteem, honour, infamy, renown, repute, status **07** opinion, respect, stature **08** estimate, good name, position, prestige, standing **09** celebrity, character, notoriety **10** estimation **11** distinction **12** good standing **14** respectability

repute
04 fame, name, odor **05** odour, rumor, savor, stock **06** esteem, regard, renown, report, rumour, savour **07** stature **08** good name, standing **09** celebrity **10** estimation, reputation **11** distinction

• of doubtful repute
03 shy

reputed
03 dit **04** held, said **06** judged **07** alleged, assumed, seeming, thought **08** apparent, believed, presumed, putative, reckoned, regarded, rumoured, supposed **09** estimated **10** considered, ostensible, reputative

reputedly
09 allegedly, seemingly **10** apparently, ostensibly, supposedly **12** reputatively **13** by all accounts

request
03 ask, beg, hit **04** boon, call, plea, seek, suit, wish **05** apply, order **06** adjure, appeal, ask for, behest, demand, desire, invite, prayer **07** beseech, bespeak, call for, call out, entreat, require, send for, solicit **08** apply for, entreaty, petition, pleading, put in for **09** impetrate **10** invitation, supplicate, write in for **11** application, imploration, petitioning, requisition, write off for **12** solicitation, supplication

require
03 ask **04** draw, lack, make, miss, need, take, want, will, wish **05** crave, exact, force, order **06** call on, compel, demand, desire, direct, enjoin, entail, govern, oblige **07** call for, command, involve, requere, request, solicit **08** insist on, instruct **09** be short of, constrain, stipulate **11** necessitate **13** be deficient in

required
03 set **05** vital **06** needed **07** advised **08** demanded **09** essential, mandatory, necessary, requisite **10** compulsory, obligatory, prescribed, stipulated **11** recommended, unavoidable

requirement
04 fike, lack, must, need, term, want **06** demand **07** proviso **08** occasion **09** condition, essential, necessity, provision, requisite **10** obligation, sine qua non **11** desideratum, stipulation **12** precondition, prerequisite **13** qualification, specification

requisite
03 due, set **04** must, need **05** vital **06** needed **07** needful **08** required **09** condition, essential, implement, mandatory, necessary, necessity **10** compulsory, obligatory, prescribed, sine qua non **11** desideratum, requirement, stipulation **12** desiderative, precondition, prerequisite **13** indispensable, qualification, specification

requisition
03 use **04** call, take **05** order, press, seize **06** demand, indent, occupy **07** request, seizure, summons **08** put in for, take over, takeover **10** commandeer, confiscate, occupation **11** application, appropriate **12** confiscation **13** appropriation, commandeering

requital
06 amends, pay-off, return **07** payment, quittal, redress **09** indemnity, quittance, repayment **10** recompence, recompense, reparation **11** restitution, retribution **12** compensation, satisfaction **15** indemnification

requite
03 pay **04** apay, quit **05** repay **06** avenge, pay off, return, reward **07** redress, respond, satisfy **08** even up on, requight **09** reimburse, retaliate **10** compensate, recompense, remunerate **11** reciprocate **14** counterbalance

rescind
04 void **05** annul, quash **06** cancel, negate, recall, repeal, revoke **07** cut away, nullify, retract, reverse **08** abrogate, overturn, set aside **10** invalidate **11** countermand

rescission
06 recall, repeal **08** negation, reversal, voidance **09** annulment **10** abrogation, retraction, revocation **11** rescindment **12** cancellation, invalidation **13** nullification

rescue
04 free, save **05** pluck **06** ransom, redeem, relief, reskew, reskue, saving **07** deliver, freeing, recover, release, relieve, reprive, repryve, salvage, set free **08** bring off, liberate, recovery, repreeve, reprieve, retrieve **09** extricate, salvation **10** emancipate, liberation, redemption **11** deliverance **12** emancipation

research
03 res **04** test **05** probe, study, tests **06** assess, review, search **07** analyse, examine, explore, inquiry, inspect, postdoc, testing **08** analysis, look into, scrutiny **10** assessment, experiment, groundwork, inspection, scrutinize **11** examination, exploration, fact-finding, investigate **13** investigation **15** experimentation

researcher
06 boffin **07** analyst, student **08** inquirer **09** inspector **11** field worker **12** investigator

resemblance
04 like **05** image, match **06** parity **07** analogy **08** affinity, likeness, nearness, parallel, sameness **09** agreement, assonance, closeness, congruity, facsimile, homophyly **10** appearance, comparison, conformity, likelihood, similarity, similitude, uniformity **11** parallelism **13** comparability **14** correspondence

resemble
04 echo **05** favor, mimic **06** be like, depict, favour, mirror **07** compare **08** approach, look like, parallel **09** duplicate, take after **11** be similar to

resent
04 envy **06** grudge **07** dislike, stomach **08** begrudge, object to **09** be angry at, grumble at, take amiss **12** have a derry on **13** take offence at, take umbrage at **15** feel aggrieved at, feel bitter about, take exception to

resentful
04 hurt **05** angry, irked **06** bitter, ireful, miffed, peeved, piqued, put out **07** envious, jealous, wounded **08** grudging, incensed, offended, spiteful **09** aggrieved, indignant,

irritated, malicious **10** embittered, stomachful, stomachous, vindictive **13** in high dudgeon

resentment
03 ire **04** envy, hurt, miff **05** anger, derry, pique, snuff, spite **06** grudge, malice **07** dudgeon, ill-will, offence, umbrage **08** bad blood, ill blood, jealousy, vexation **09** animosity, annoyance, hostility **10** bad feeling, bitterness, ill-feeling, irritation **11** displeasure, high dudgeon, indignation **12** hard feelings **14** vindictiveness

reservation
03 res, rez **04** park **05** demur, doubt, order, qualm, salvo, tract **06** doubts, qualms, safety, saving, upkeep **07** booking, defence, enclave, keeping, proviso, reserve, scruple, storage, support **08** guarding, homeland, preserve, scruples, security **09** condition, hesitancy, misgiving, retention, sanctuary, upholding **10** engagement, hesitation, limitation, misgivings, protection, scepticism **11** appointment, arrangement, maintenance, safekeeping, stipulation **12** conservation, continuation, perpetuation, preservation, safeguarding **13** arrière-pensée, qualification **14** advance booking, prearrangement, second thoughts

• **without reservation**
07 utterly **08** entirely, outright **09** gloves-off **10** completely **11** boots and all **12** unreservedly **14** unhesitatingly, wholeheartedly

reserve
02 TA **03** AVR, ice, MNR, res, RNR **04** area, bank, book, fund, help, hold, keep, park, pool, RNVR, save **05** cache, defer, delay, extra, hoard, order, proxy, spare, stock, store, tract **06** backup, engage, fill-in, put off, retain, secure, shelve, supply **07** adjourn, backlog, earmark, enclave, modesty, savings, shyness, stand-in, support, suspend **08** coldness, coolness, distance, hold back, hold over, keep back, Landwehr, lay aside, postpone, preserve, set apart, set aside, Wavy Navy **09** aloofness, auxiliary, reservoir, restraint, reticence, ring-fence, sanctuary, secondary, stockpile, successor, surrogate **10** accumulate, additional, arrange for, arrière-ban, detachment, limitation, prearrange, remoteness, substitute, understudy **11** alternative, auxiliaries, replacement, reservation, restriction **12** accumulation, put on one side, put to one side **13** secretiveness, self-restraint **14** reinforcements **15** supplementaries

• **in reserve**
02 by **05** spare **06** in hand, stored, to hand, unused **07** in petto, in store **08** set aside **09** available, in pectore

reserved
03 shy **04** cold, cool, held, kept **05** aloof, close, meant, saved, taken **06** booked, modest, remote, silent **07** distant, engaged, on appro, ordered, private, retired, strange **08** arranged, backward, cautious, destined, intended, retained, reticent, retiring, set aside, taciturn **09** diffident, earmarked, repulsive, secretive, spoken for, withdrawn **10** designated, restrained, unsociable **11** introverted, prearranged, standoffish **12** unresponsive **13** self-contained, unforthcoming **14** unapproachable **15** uncommunicative

reservoir
03 vat **04** bank, fund, lake, loch, pond, pool, sump, tank, well **05** basin, stock, store **06** gilgai, header, holder, source, supply **07** cistern, gas tank, ghilgai, hot well, urinary **08** fountain, reserves **09** container, inkholder, stockpile, wind chest **10** header tank, receptacle, repository, steam chest **11** reservatory **12** accumulation

resettle
◇ *anagram indicator*
07 migrate **08** emigrate **09** immigrate **10** transplant

reshape
◇ *anagram indicator*
05 alter **06** adjust, modify, mutate **07** convert **12** metamorphose

reshuffle
◇ *anagram indicator*
05 shift **06** change, revise **07** realign, regroup, shake up, shake-up, shuffle **08** revision, upheaval **09** rearrange **10** regrouping, reorganize **11** interchange, realignment, restructure **12** redistribute **13** rearrangement, restructuring **14** redistribution, reorganization

reside
03 lie, sit **04** hive, keep, live, rest, stay **05** abide, board, dwell, exist, house, lodge **06** inhere, occupy, remain, settle **07** hang out, inhabit, sojourn **09** be present **10** be inherent **11** be contained

residence
03 pad, res **04** digs, flat, hall, home, nest, seat, stay **05** abode, house, lodge, manor, place, villa **06** des res, palace **07** cottage, domicil, lodging, mansion, sojourn **08** domicile, dwelling, lodgings, mansonry, quarters **09** apartment, residency **10** habitation, mansionary, praetorium, presidency, second home **11** country seat, inhabitance, inhabitancy, squarsonage, summerhouse **12** country house **13** dwelling-place **14** winter quarters

resident
05 guest, local **06** client, inmate, ledger, leiger, lieger, live-in, lodger, tenant **07** citizen, dweller, en poste, gremial, leidger, patient, resiant, resider, settled **08** dwelling, inherent, living-in, occupant, occupier **09** commorant, permanent, sojourner, transient **10** inhabitant, inhabiting, stationary **11** householder **13** neighbourhood

residential
07 exurban **08** commuter, suburban **09** dormitory

residual
03 net **06** excess, unused **07** surplus **08** left-over **09** reliquary, remaining **10** unconsumed

residue
04 coke, gunk, lees, rest **05** dregs, extra, mazut, pitch, scrap, snuff **06** excess, mazout, pomace, slurry **07** asphalt, astatki, balance, clinker, remains, remnant, surplus, tankage, vinasse **08** charcoal, mine dump, overflow, residuum **09** asphaltum, carry-over, leftovers, remainder **10** difference, racemation, terra rossa **11** apiezon oils **12** caput mortuum

resign
04 quit **05** demit, forgo, leave, waive, yield **06** forego, give up, retire, submit, vacate **07** abandon, entrust, forsake, throw up **08** abdicate, forelend, renounce, step down **09** stand down, surrender **10** relinquish

• **resign yourself**
03 bow **05** yield **06** accept, comply, submit **09** acquiesce **11** come to terms

resignation
06 notice **07** waiving **08** giving-up, patience, stoicism, yielding **09** defeatism, demission, departure, passivity, surrender **10** abdication, acceptance, compliance, retirement, submission **12** acquiescence, renunciation, standing-down, stepping-down **13** non-resistance **14** reconciliation, relinquishment

• **expression of resignation**
04 well **05** ho-hum **07** heigh-ho

resigned
07 passive, patient, stoical **08** yielding **09** defeatist **10** reconciled, submissive **11** acquiescent, unresisting **12** unprotesting **13** long-suffering, philosophical, uncomplaining

resignedly
09 patiently, stoically **12** submissively **15** philosophically, uncomplainingly

resilience
04 give, kick **06** bounce, recoil, spring **07** granite **08** buoyance, buoyancy, strength **09** hardiness, toughness **10** bounciness, elasticity, plasticity, pliability, suppleness **11** flexibility, springiness **12** adaptability **14** unshockability

resilient
05 hardy, tough **06** bouncy, strong, supple **07** buoyant, elastic, plastic, pliable, rubbery, springy **08** flexible **09** adaptable, recoiling, springing **10** rebounding **11** unshockable **13** irrepressible

resin
03 lac 04 aloe, hing, kino 05 alkyd, aloes, amber, animé, copal, damar, elemi, epoxy, pitch, rosin, Saran®, vinyl 06 balsam, conima, dammar, dammer, guaiac, mastic, storax 07 acrylic, caranna, carauna, copaiba, copaiva, gamboge, hashish, jalapin, ladanum, mastich, Perspex®, shellac, xylenol 08 Araldite®, Bakelite®, cannabin, galbanum, guaiacum, hasheesh, kauri gum, olibanum, opopanax, propolis, retinite, sandarac, scammony, sweet gum 09 asafetida, courbaril, elaterite, sagapenum, sandarach, tacamahac, tacmahack 10 asafoetida, assafetida, euphorbium, turpentine 11 assafoetida, gum ammoniac, podophyllin 12 Canada balsam, frankincense, gum sandarach 13 Burgundy pitch, spirit varnish, thermoplastic

resist
04 buck, curb, defy, face, fend, halt, stem, stop, wear 05 avoid, check, fight, repel 06 battle, combat, defend, hinder, impede, jack up, oppose, refuse, thwart 07 contend, counter, deforce, prevent, weather 08 confront, fight off, obstruct, restrain, stick out, struggle 09 stand up to, withstand 10 counteract, gainstrive 12 stand against 14 hold out against

resistance
01 R 04 drag, kick, pull 05 fight, stand 06 battle, combat 07 refusal 08 defiance, fighting, struggle 09 avoidance, contumacy, hindrance, impedance, repulsion, restraint, thwarting 10 contention, impediment, opposition, prevention 11 contumacity, counter-time, obstruction 12 counter-stand, withstanding 13 confrontation, counteraction, intransigence 14 antiperistasis

• **passive resistance**
09 passivism 10 satyagraha 11 vis inertiae

resistant
04 anti- 05 proof, stiff, tough 06 immune, strong 07 defiant, opposed, viscous 08 renitent 09 unwilling, windproof 10 impervious, shellproof, shockproof, unaffected, unyielding, waterproof 12 antagonistic, intransigent, invulnerable 13 unsusceptible

resolute
03 set 04 bold, firm 05 fixed, hardy, stout, tough 06 dogged, intent, steady, strong, sturdy 07 adamant, decided, diehard, earnest, granite, serious, staunch 08 constant, obdurate, resolved, stalwart, stubborn 09 dauntless, dedicated, obstinate, steadfast, tenacious, unbending, undaunted 10 determined, flat-footed, inflexible, relentless, unswerving, unwavering, unyielding 11 persevering, unflinching 12 single-minded, strong-willed

resolutely
06 firmly 08 steadily, strongly 09 adamantly, earnestly, seriously, staunchly 10 inflexibly, resolvedly, stubbornly 11 dauntlessly, obstinately, steadfastly 12 relentlessly, unswervingly, unwaveringly 13 unflinchingly 14 single-mindedly

resolution
◇ *anagram indicator*
03 res 04 rede, zeal 05 point 06 answer, decree, motion, result 07 courage, finding, granite, melting, resolve, solving, thought, verdict 08 analysis, boldness, decision, devotion, firmness, solution, tenacity 09 constancy, judgement, willpower 10 abreaction, commitment, dedication, doggedness, intentness, sorting out, working out 11 declaration, earnestness, persistence, proposition, seriousness, unravelling 12 perseverance 13 determination, disentangling, inflexibility, steadfastness

resolve
◇ *anagram indicator*
03 fix, vow 04 melt, zeal 05 lapse, patch, relax, solve, untie 06 answer, assure, bottle, decide, detail, divide, inform, pecker, reduce, settle 07 analyse, analyze, break up, convert, courage, itemize, sort out, sublate, talk out, unravel, work out 08 boldness, conclude, devotion, dissolve, firmness, separate, settle on, tenacity 09 anatomize, break down, constancy, decompose, determine, dissipate, factorize, transform, willpower 10 commitment, dedication, doggedness, intentness 11 disentangle, earnestness, persistence, seriousness 12 disintegrate, perseverance 13 determination, inflexibility, steadfastness, straighten out 14 make up your mind, sense of purpose

resonance
05 depth 08 fullness, richness, sonority, strength, vibrancy 09 plangency 10 mesomerism, resounding 12 canorousness 13 reverberation

resonant
04 deep, full, rich 06 fruity, plummy, strong 07 booming, echoing, ringing, vibrant 08 canorous, plangent, sonorous 10 pear-shaped, resounding 11 reverberant 13 reverberating

resonate
04 boom, echo, ring 05 sound 06 re-echo 07 resound, thunder 11 reverberate

resort
◇ *anagram indicator*
02 go 03 spa, use 04 dive, draw, seek, spot, step 05 apply, frame, haunt, trade, visit 06 appeal, center, centre, chance, course, lounge, museum, option, refuge, repair, revert 07 doggery, measure 08 frequent, recourse 09 concourse, dude ranch, frequency, patronize, thronging 10 rendezvous, sanatorium, sanitarium 11 alternative, night-cellar, possibility 12 health resort 13 holiday centre 14 course of action, stamping-ground

Resorts include:

04 Nice, Rhyl
05 Aspen, Davos
06 Cairns, Cannes, St Ives, St-Malo, Whitby
07 Funchal, Margate, Newquay, Torquay, Ventnor, Zermatt
08 Alicante, Aviemore, Benidorm, Biarritz, Chamonix, Honolulu, Klosters, Marbella, Montreux, Penzance, Skegness, St Helier, St Moritz, St-Tropez, Weymouth
09 Albufeira, Blackpool, Galveston, Gold Coast, Kitzbühel, Lanzarote, Morecambe, Nantucket
10 Baden Baden, Bondi Beach, Costa Brava, Eastbourne, Lake Placid, Long Island, Miami Beach, Monte Carlo, Windermere
11 Bognor Regis, Bournemouth, Bridlington, Cleethorpes, Coney Island, Costa Blanca, Costa del Sol, Costa Dorada, Gran Canaria, Grand Bahama, Palm Springs, Scarborough
12 San Sebastian, Santa Barbara, Waikiki Beach
13 Great Yarmouth, Southend-on-Sea
15 Martha's Vineyard, Weston-super-Mare

See also **spa**

• **in the last resort**
06 at last 07 finally 08 after all, in the end 10 eventually, ultimately 13 fundamentally, sooner or later

• **resort to**
03 use 04 seek 06 employ, invoke, turn to 07 utilize 08 exercise, frequent 09 make use of 10 fall back on 14 have recourse to 15 avail yourself of

resound
04 boom, echo, ring 05 sound 06 re-echo 07 thunder, vibrate 08 resonate 11 reverberate

resounding
04 full, loud, rich 05 great, vocal 07 booming, echoing, notable, reboant, ringing, roaring, vibrant 08 decisive, emphatic, plangent, resonant, rumorous, sonorous, striking, thorough 09 memorable, resonance 10 conclusive, impressive, remarkable, resonating, thunderous 11 outstanding 13 reverberating

resource
03 wit 04 fund, pool 05 funds, means, money, power, store 06 assets, course, device, fodder, resort, riches, source, supply, talent, wealth 07 ability, capital, reserve 08 artifice, holdings, property, reserves, supplies 09 expedient, ingenuity, materials, stockpile 10 capability, chevisance, enterprise, initiative 11 contrivance, imagination,

wherewithal **12** accumulation **13** inventiveness **15** resourcefulness

resourceful
04 able **05** fendy, sharp, witty **06** adroit, bright, clever **07** capable **08** creative, original, talented **09** ingenious, inventive, versatile **10** innovative **11** imaginative, quick-witted **12** enterprising

resourceless
06 feeble **07** useless **08** feckless, helpless, hopeless **09** shiftless **10** inadequate

respect
03 way **04** duty, face, heed, obey **05** facet, honor, point, sense, value **06** admire, aspect, detail, esteem, follow, fulfil, homage, honour, matter, notice, praise, regard, revere **07** bearing, devoirs, feature, observe, regards, worship **08** adhere to, consider, courtesy, relation, venerate **09** approve of, attention, deference, greetings, obeisance, reference, reverence **10** admiration, appreciate, best wishes, cognizance, comply with, connection, good wishes, high regard, particular, politeness, veneration **11** approbation, compliments, high opinion, recognition, salutations **12** appreciation **13** attentiveness, consideration, show regard for, think highly of **14** characteristic, pay attention to, thoughtfulness **15** set great store by, take into account

• **title of respect, word of respect**
01 U **03** Esq, oom, sir **04** Esqr, tuan **05** hodja, honor, khoja, molla **06** father, gaffer, honour, khodja, kumari, mollah, moolah, mullah **07** Bahadur, effendi, esquire **08** holiness, talapoin **10** burra sahib, worshipful

• **with respect to**
02 of, on, re **03** for, wrt **04** as to **05** about **07** apropos **09** as regards **10** concerning, in regard to **12** in relation to, with regard to **14** on the subject of **15** with reference to

respectability
07 decency, honesty **09** gentility, integrity **10** worthiness **11** uprightness **15** trustworthiness

respectable
02 OK **04** fair, good, neat, nice, tidy **05** clean **06** decent, honest, not bad, seemly, worthy **07** savoury, upright **08** adequate, all right, clean-cut, decorous, mediocre, menseful, passable, superior **09** dignified, reputable, respected, sponsible, tolerable **10** above-board, acceptable, fairly good, honourable, reasonable, salubrious **11** appreciable, clean-living, presentable, trustworthy **12** considerable

respected
06 valued **07** admired **08** esteemed **12** highly valued **14** highly esteemed, highly regarded **15** thought highly of

respectful
05 civil **06** humble, polite **07** courtly, dutiful **08** reverent **09** courteous, regardful **11** deferential, reverential, subservient **12** well-mannered

respectfully
07 civilly **08** mannerly, politely **10** reverently **11** courteously **13** deferentially, reverentially

respecting
05 about **07** vis-à-vis **09** regarding **10** concerning **11** considering, in respect of **12** with regard to **13** with respect to

respective
03 own **07** heedful, several, special, various **08** personal, relative, relevant, separate, specific **09** regardful **10** individual, particular **11** considerate **13** corresponding **14** discriminating

respectively
06 in turn **08** one by one **09** severally, specially **12** individually, particularly, specifically **15** correspondingly, in the order given

respite
03 gap **04** halt, lull, rest, stay **05** break, delay, frist, let-up, pause, truce **06** give up, hiatus, put off, recess, relief **07** leisure, prolong **08** breather, interval, reprieve **09** abatement, breathing, cessation, deferment, remission **10** moratorium, relaxation, suspension **11** adjournment **12** intermission, interruption, postponement **14** breathing space

resplendent
06 bright **07** beaming, fulgent, radiant, shining **08** dazzling, gleaming, glorious, luminous, lustrous, splendid **09** brilliant, effulgent, irradiant, refulgent **10** glittering **11** magnificent **13** splendiferous

respond
04 rise **05** react, reply **06** answer, behave, rejoin, retort, return **07** counter **10** answer back **11** acknowledge, reciprocate

response
03 tic **04** echo, rise **05** reply, touch **06** answer, retort, return **07** riposte **08** comeback, feedback, reaction **09** rejoinder **10** phototaxis **11** respondence **15** acknowledgement

responsibility
04 baby, care, duty, onus, role, task **05** blame, fault, guilt, power, trust **06** affair, burden, charge, pidgin, racket **07** concern, honesty **08** business, maturity **09** adulthood, authority, soundness, stability **10** obligation **11** culpability, reliability **13** answerability, dependability **14** accountability **15** trustworthiness

responsible
04 sane **05** adult, sober, sound **06** guilty, honest, liable, mature, stable, steady **07** at fault, leading, to blame **08** culpable, managing, powerful, rational, reliable, sensible, solidary **09** executive, high-level, important **10** answerable, dependable, in charge of, reasonable **11** accountable, blameworthy, controlling, in control of, level-headed, trustworthy **13** authoritative, conscientious, correspondent **14** decision-making

responsibly
08 honestly, reliably, sensibly, steadily **10** dependably, rationally, reasonably **15** conscientiously

responsive
04 open **05** alert, alive, awake, aware, quick, sharp **06** with it **08** amenable, reactive, sentient, swinging **09** answering, excitable, on the ball, receptive, sensitive, teachable **10** perceptive, respondent, stimulable, switched on **11** forthcoming, susceptible, sympathetic **12** responsorial **13** correspondent **14** impressionable

responsiveness
05 mouth **08** openness **09** alertness, awareness **11** sensitivity **13** receptiveness **14** susceptibility

rest
03 alt, lie, nap, sit, veg **04** base, calm, doze, ease, halt, hang, last, laze, lean, lull, noon, prop, rely, stay, stop **05** break, cease, hinge, light, pause, quiet, relax, sleep, smoko, spell, stand **06** alight, anchor, bottom, cradle, depend, endure, excess, feutre, fewter, holder, lounge, others, recess, remain, repose, settle, siesta, snooze, steady, veg out **07** balance, be based, breathe, holiday, leisure, lie down, lie-down, persist, recline, relâche, remains, remnant, residue, respite, sit down, slumber, support, surplus, time off **08** breather, continue, idleness, interval, quietude, remnants, residuum, vacation **09** anchorage, cessation, interlude, leftovers, remainder, sabbatism, stillness **10** inactivity, quiescence, quiescency, relaxation, standstill, take breath, take it easy **12** intermission, tranquillity **13** put your feet up **14** breathing space, motionlessness

• **and the rest**
07 and so on **08** et cetera, et ceteri **10** and so forth

• **lay to rest**
04 bury **05** inter

• **rest upon**
04 ride

restaurant

Restaurant types include:

04 café, caff
05 diner, grill, NAAFI
06 bistro, buffet, chippy, pull-in
07 canteen, carvery, chipper, milk bar, taverna, tea room, tea shop
08 creperie, mess room, pizzeria, snack-bar, sushi bar, taqueria, teahouse

09 brasserie, burger bar, cafeteria, coffee bar, dining-car, grill room, refectory, trattoria
10 dining room, health food, rotisserie, steakhouse
11 eating-house, greasy spoon, sandwich bar, self-service
12 drivethrough, Internet café, luncheonette, motorway café
13 transport café
15 fish-and-chip shop, ice-cream parlour

Restaurants include:

06 The Ivy
07 El Bulli
09 L'Escargot
10 Paul Bocuse, Savoy Grill, The Fat Duck
11 The Wolseley
12 Gordon Ramsay, Heinz Winkler, The River Café, Waterside Inn
15 Les Pres d'Eugenie, Patrick Guilbaud

Fast food restaurant chains include:

03 KFC
06 Wendy's
08 Pizza Hut, Taco Bell
09 Harvester, McDonald's
10 Burger King, Dairy Queen, Little Chef
12 Domino's Pizza, Dunkin' Donuts, Hard Rock Café, Pizza Express
13 Baskin-Robbins, Harry Ramsden's
14 Subway Sandwich

restaurateur *see* **chef**

restful
04 calm **05** quiet, still **06** placid, serene **07** calming, languid, relaxed **08** peaceful, relaxing, soothing, tranquil **09** leisurely, unhurried **11** comfortable, undisturbed

restitution
06 amends, refund, return **07** damages, redress, restore **08** requital **09** indemnity, repayment, restoring **10** recompense, reparation **11** restoration **12** compensation, remuneration, satisfaction **13** reimbursement **15** indemnification

restive
04 edgy **05** inert, jumpy, resty, tense **06** on edge, uneasy, unruly, wilful **07** anxious, fidgety, fretful, nervous, restiff, uptight, wayward **08** agitated, restless **09** fidgeting, impatient, obstinate, turbulent, unsettled **10** hot-mouthed, refractory **12** recalcitrant, unmanageable **13** undisciplined **14** uncontrollable

restiveness
10 turbulence, unruliness, wilfulness **11** waywardness **12** restlessness

restless
◇ *anagram indicator*
04 edgy, toey **05** jumpy **06** broken, on edge, uneasy, unruly **07** agitato, anxious, fidgety, fretful, jittery, nervous, restive, unquiet, uptight, worried **08** agitated, disquiet, troubled **09** disturbed, fidgeting, impatient, sleepless, turbulent, unsettled **10** changeable, wanrestful **13** uncomfortable

restlessly
09 anxiously, fretfully, nervously **11** impatiently, turbulently

restlessness
04 fike **05** hurry **06** bustle, fidget, unrest **07** anxiety, jitters, turmoil **08** activity, disquiet, dynamism, edginess, insomnia, movement **09** agitation, dysphoria, gate fever, jumpiness **10** fitfulness, inquietude, transience, turbulence, uneasiness **11** disturbance, fretfulness, inconstancy, instability, jactitation, nervousness, restiveness, spring fever, worriedness **12** fermentation **13** heebie-jeebies, unsettledness

restoration
◇ *anagram indicator*
06 repair, return **07** recruit, renewal, revival **08** recovery **09** recruital **10** kiss of life, rebuilding, renovation **11** refreshment, replacement, restitution **12** instauration, refurbishing, rejuvenation **13** reinstatement **14** reconstitution, reconstruction, rehabilitation, reinstallation, revitalization **15** re-establishment

restore
◇ *anagram indicator*
03 fix **04** do up, heal, mend, stet **05** renew **06** reform, repair, return, revamp, revive **07** build up, rebuild, recover, recruit, redress, refresh, replace, retouch **08** give back, hand back, refigure, re-impose, renovate, retrieve, revivify, undelete **09** reanimate, redeliver, re-enforce, refurbish, reinstate, restitute **10** bring round, redecorate, rejuvenate, revitalize, strengthen **11** recondition, reconstruct, re-establish, reintegrate, reintroduce, restitution **12** reconstitute, redintegrate, rehabilitate, reinvigorate

restrain
◇ *containment indicator*
03 bit, dam, tie **04** bank, bind, curb, heft, hold, jail, keep, rein, stay, stop **05** bound, chain, check, still, stint, trash **06** arrest, behold, bridle, coerce, detain, fetter, forbid, govern, hinder, hold in, hopple, impede, keep in, prison, rebuke, strain, subdue, tether **07** abstain, chasten, cohibit, confine, contain, control, impound, inhibit, injunct, manacle, prevent, refrain, repress, tighten **08** bottle up, chastise, compesce, conclude, hold back, hold down, imprison, keep back, keep down, obstruct, regulate, restrict, suppress, withhold **09** immanacle, temperate **10** hamshackle **11** hold captive, hold in check, keep in check

restrained
03 dry **04** calm, cold, cool, mild, soft **05** aloof, muted, quiet, sober **06** chaste, formal, low-key, modest, severe, steady, subtle **07** captive, classic, ordered, refined, relaxed, subdued **08** discreet, measured, moderate, reserved, ritenuto, tasteful **09** forbidden, temperate **10** abstemious, controlled **11** unemotional, unobtrusive **14** self-controlled, self-restrained **15** uncommunicative

restraint
03 dam, lid, tie **04** curb, grip, hold, rein, stay **05** block, bonds, check, cramp, limit, stint, trash **06** bridle, chains, duress, limits **07** barrier, bondage, control, fetters, measure, reserve **08** coercion, prudence **09** captivity, hindrance **10** constraint, inhibition, limitation, moderation, prevention **11** confinement, restriction, self-control, suppression **12** countercheck, imprisonment, restrictions, straitjacket **13** judiciousness **14** self-discipline

restrict
◇ *containment indicator*
03 tie **04** bind, curb, fast, hold **05** bound, cramp, hem in, limit, pinch, scant, stint, thirl **06** go slow, hamper, hinder, impede, ration **07** astrict, combine, confine, contain, control, curtail, inhibit, peg down, tighten **08** handicap, localize, regulate, restrain, straiten, strangle **09** condition, constrain, constrict, demarcate **15** draw in your horns, pull in your horns

restricted
05 close, small, tight **06** closed, narrow, secret, strict **07** bounded, cramped, limited, private **08** confined **09** exclusive, parochial, regulated **10** controlled **11** constricted

restriction
03 ban **04** curb, rule **05** bound, check, limit, stint **06** burden, chains, ration **07** confine, control, embargo, proviso, reserve **08** handicap **09** condition, restraint, stricture **10** constraint, limitation, regulation **11** stipulation **13** qualification

restructure
05 rejig **07** shake up **09** modernize, rearrange **10** reorganize, streamline **11** rationalize

result
03 end, sum, win **04** flow, make, mark, stem, turn **05** arise, ensue, event, fruit, grade, issue, occur, score **06** answer, derive, effect, emerge, evolve, finish, follow, fruits, happen, pan out, pay-off, revert, sequel, spring, upshot **07** develop, emanate, outcome, proceed, product, rebound, spin-off, verdict **08** decision, reaction **09** by-product, come out of, corollary, culminate, eventuate, judgement,

terminate **10** conclusion, end-product, resolution, side effect **11** consequence, implication, termination **12** repercussion

resultant
07 ensuing **09** following, resulting **10** consequent, subsequent

resume
04 go on **06** reopen, take up **07** carry on, proceed, restart **08** continue, re-occupy, take back **09** reconvene, summarize **10** begin again, recommence, start again **11** rejuvenesce, take up again

résumé
02 CV **05** recap **06** digest, précis, review, sketch, wrap-up **07** epitome, outline, run-down, summary **08** abstract, overview, pirlicue, purlicue, synopsis **09** breakdown **14** recapitulation **15** curriculum vitae

resumption
06 sequel **07** re-entry, renewal, reprise, restart **09** reopening **10** proceeding, resurgence **11** epanalepsis **12** continuation **14** recommencement **15** re-establishment

resurgence
06 return **07** rebirth, revival **10** renascence, resumption **11** re-emergence, renaissance **12** re-appearance, resurrection, risorgimento **13** recrudescence **14** revivification

resurrect
05 renew **06** revive **07** restore **08** disinter **09** bring back, re-install **10** reactivate, revitalize **11** re-establish, reintroduce, resuscitate **13** restore to life **15** bring back to life

resurrection
06 return **07** rebirth, renewal, revival **08** comeback **09** anastasis **10** resurgence **11** renaissance, restoration **12** reappearance **13** resuscitation **14** revitalization **15** re-establishment

resuscitate
04 save **05** renew **06** rescue, revive **07** quicken, restore **08** revivify **09** reanimate, resurrect **10** bring round, revitalize **12** reinvigorate

resuscitated
07 revived **08** restored **09** redivivus **11** resurrected **12** redintegrate **13** redintegrated

resuscitation
03 CPR **07** renewal, revival **10** quickening **11** restoration **12** resurrection, revitalizing **14** reinvigoration, revivification

retain
◇ *containment indicator*
03 pay, ret **04** grip, heft, hire, hold, keep, save **05** brief, grasp **06** employ, engage, keep on, keep up, recall **07** contain, occlude, reserve **08** conserve, continue, contract, hang on to, hold back, maintain, memorize, preserve, remember **09** recollect **10** bear in mind, call to mind, commission, hold fast to, keep hold of, keep in mind

retainer
03 fee **05** valet **06** lackey, menial, vassal **07** advance, deposit, footman, jackman, samurai, servant **08** domestic, follower **09** attendant, dependant, supporter **10** galloglass **11** gallowglass **12** retaining fee

retaliate
06 avenge **07** hit back, pay home **09** fight back, get back at **10** strike back **11** get even with, reciprocate, take revenge **13** counter-attack **14** get your own back, pay someone back

retaliation
06 retort, talion, ultion **07** revenge **08** reprisal **09** retorsion, retortion, tit for tat, vengeance **10** quid pro quo **11** eye for an eye, lex talionis, like for like, retribution **13** an eye for an eye, counter-attack, reciprocation

retard
03 lag **04** curb, slow **05** brake, check, delay, tardy **06** belate, hinder, hold up, impede **07** slacken **08** handicap, obstruct, postpone, restrict, slow down **10** decelerate **11** put a brake on **12** incapacitate **13** put the brake on

retardation
03 lag **05** delay **07** slowing **08** dullness, impeding, slowness **09** hindering, hindrance **10** deficiency, hysteresis, incapacity, inhibition, retardment **11** obstruction **12** incapability **14** mental handicap

retch
03 gag **04** barf, boak, bock, boke, keck, puke, reck, spew **05** heave, reach, vomit **06** sick up, strain **07** chuck up, fetch up, throw up **08** disgorge **11** regurgitate **13** heave the gorge

retching
04 heft, keck **06** nausea, puking **07** gagging, spewing **08** reaching, vomiting **12** vomiturition

retention
05 gripe **06** saving **07** custody, holding, keeping **09** hanging-on, holding on **11** continuance, keeping hold, maintenance **12** preservation

rethink
06 modify, review, revise **08** forthink, reassess **09** re-examine, think over **10** reconsider, think twice **13** think better of

reticence
07 reserve, silence **08** muteness **09** quietness, restraint **10** diffidence **11** taciturnity **13** secretiveness

reticent
03 shy **05** quiet **06** silent **08** boutonné, reserved, taciturn **09** boutonnée, diffident, inhibited, secretive **10** restrained **11** close-lipped, tight-lipped **12** close-mouthed, close-tongued **13** unforthcoming **15** uncommunicative

reticule *see* **bag**

retinue
04 many, port, tail **05** aides, meiny, staff, suite, train **06** escort, meiney, meinie, menyie **07** cortège, sowarry **08** equipage, servants, sowarree **09** comitatus, entourage, followers, following, personnel **10** attendancy, attendants

retire
◇ *reversal indicator*
02 go **03** den **04** move, step **05** leave **06** bow out, decamp, depart, go away, recede, resign, return **07** go aside, retreat, scratch **08** draw back, step down, stop work, withdraw **09** leave work **10** give up work, retirement **11** stop working **14** lick your wounds

retired
◇ *reversal indicator*
02 ex- **03** ret, rtd **04** past, retd **06** former **07** private **08** emeritus, secluded, solitary **09** recondite, withdrawn **11** sequestered

retirement
04 exit **06** recess **07** bedtime, privacy, retreat **08** solitude **09** departure, obscurity, seclusion **10** loneliness, withdrawal **11** recluseness, resignation

retiring
◇ *reversal indicator*
03 coy, shy **05** quiet, timid **06** humble, modest **07** bashful, recluse **08** reserved, reticent **09** diffident, shrinking **10** retreating, unassuming **11** unassertive, unobtrusive **12** self-effacing

retort
04 quip **05** reply, sally **06** answer, clinch, rejoin, return, zinger **07** counter, floorer, respond, riposte, squelch **08** backword, comeback, outfling, repartee, response, turn upon **09** rejoinder, retaliate, squelcher, throw back, wisecrack **11** retaliation

retract
◇ *reversal indicator*
04 deny **05** unsay **06** abjure, cancel, disown, draw in, move in, recant, renege, repeal, revoke **07** disavow, rescind, reverse, unspeak, unswear **08** abrogate, disclaim, draw back, move back, pull back, renounce, take back, withdraw **09** repudiate

retreat
◇ *reversal indicator*
03 den, mew **04** flee, lair, nest, neuk, nook, quit, rout **05** arbor, haven, leave, lodge, tower **06** alcove, arbour, ashram, asylum, bug out, decamp,

depart, flight, recede, recoil, recule, reduit, refuge, retire, shrink **07** back off, give way, harbour, hideout, privacy, recoyle, recuile, redoubt, retrait, retrate, shelter **08** crawfish, draw back, fall back, funkhole, growlery, hideaway, pull back, pull-back, retraict, retraite, solitude, turn back, turn tail, withdraw **09** back-pedal, climb down, climb-down, departure, hermitage, katabasis, sanctuary, seclusion **10** disadvance, evacuation, give ground, ivory tower, retirement, withdrawal **11** drawing-back, falling-back, pulling-back **12** beat a retreat, hibernaculum, interglacial, interstadial

retrench
03 cut **04** pare, save, trim **05** limit, prune **06** lessen, reduce **07** curtail, cut back, husband **08** decrease, diminish, slim down **09** economize **15** tighten your belt

retrenchment
03 cut **07** cutback, economy, pruning, run-down **09** reduction, shrinkage **11** contraction, cost-cutting, curtailment, cutting back

retribution
03 utu **05** karma **06** reward, talion **07** justice, Nemesis, payment, redress, revenge **08** reprisal, requital **09** reckoning, repayment, vengeance, vengement **10** punishment, recompense **11** just deserts, retaliation **12** compensation, satisfaction

retrieve
04 mend, read, save **05** fetch **06** access, recoup, redeem, regain, remedy, repair, rescue, return **07** get back, read out, reclaim, recover, restore, salvage **08** make good **09** bring back, recapture, repossess **11** put to rights

retro
03 old **04** past **05** passé **06** bygone, former, period **07** antique, old-time **10** olde-worlde **12** old-fashioned **13** in period style

retrograde
◇ *reversal indicator*
06 recede **07** inverse, regrede, reverse **08** backward, contrary, downward, negative **09** declining, reverting, worsening **10** retrogress **11** deteriorate **12** degenerating **13** deteriorating, retrogressive

retrogress
◇ *reversal indicator*
03 ebb **04** drop, fall, sink, wane **06** recede, retire, return, revert, worsen **07** decline, regress, relapse, retreat **08** withdraw **09** backslide **10** degenerate, retrograde **11** deteriorate **12** degeneration

retrogression
03 ebb **04** drop, fall **06** return **07** decline, regress, relapse **09** worsening **10** recidivism, regression **13** deterioration **14** retrogradation

retrospect
06 regard, review, survey **08** look back **09** hindsight **10** reflection **11** remembrance **12** afterthought, recollection, thinking back **13** re-examination

• in retrospect
◇ *reversal indicator*
11 looking back **12** on reflection, thinking back **13** retroactively, with hindsight **15** retrospectively

retrospective
◇ *reversal indicator*
11 ex post facto, retro-active **14** retro-operative **15** backward-looking

retrospectively
11 ex post facto, looking back **12** in retrospect, on reflection, thinking back **13** retroactively, with hindsight

return
◇ *reversal indicator*
03 ret **04** data, form, gain, turn **05** equal, match, recur, remit, repay, reply, yield **06** answer, go back, income, profit, record, refund, rejoin, render, report, retort, retour, revert, reward **07** account, benefit, bring in, counter, declare, deliver, get back, pay back, put back, redound, regress, replace, requite, respond, restore, revenue, riposte, takings **08** announce, come back, comeback, come home, delivery, document, exchange, give back, hand back, hand down, interest, proceeds, reappear, recourse, requital, send back, take back, turn away, turn back **09** advantage, backtrack, come again, do the same, pronounce, recursion, reimburse, reinstate, repayment, reversion, round-trip, statement **10** correspond, giving-back, home-coming, recompense, recurrence, taking-back **11** handing-back, happen again, reciprocate, replacement, restoration **12** reappearance **13** reciprocation, reinstatement

• in return
◇ *reversal indicator*
08 mutually **10** in exchange, in response **12** equivalently, reciprocally

• point of no return
07 Rubicon

Réunion
03 REU

re-use
◇ *anagram indicator*
07 recycle **12** reconstitute

revamp
◇ *anagram indicator*
04 do up **05** refit **06** recast, repair, revise **07** rebuild, restore **08** overhaul, renovate **09** modernize, refurbish **11** recondition, reconstruct **12** rehabilitate

reveal
◇ *anagram indicator*
04 ingo, leak, show, tell **05** let on **06** betray, bewray, descry, expose, impart, let out, unfold, unmask, unveil **07** confess, display, divulge, exhibit, express, ingoing, lay bare, let slip, presage, publish, throw up, unbosom, uncover, unearth, unshale **08** announce, decipher, disbosom, disclose, discover, give away, manifest, proclaim, unshadow **09** broadcast, make aware, make known, publicize, undeceive **10** make public **11** communicate **12** blow the lid on, bring to light, expose to view, lift the lid on **15** take the wraps off

revealing
05 sheer **06** daring, low-cut **08** giveaway, telltale **10** diaphanous, indicative, revelatory, see-through **11** significant

revel
◇ *anagram indicator*
02 do **03** fug, joy **04** bask, crow, gala, orgy, rave, riot, wake **05** comus, enjoy, gloat, glory, lap up, party, roist, spree **06** rave-up, relish, savour, shivoo, thrive, wallow **07** carouse, debauch, delight, indulge, knees-up, large it, rejoice, roister, royster **08** carousal, live it up **09** bacchanal, celebrate, festivity, luxuriate, make merry, night-rule, whoop it up **10** have a party, saturnalia **11** celebration, have it large, merrymaking, take delight **12** raise the roof, take pleasure **13** jollification **14** push the boat out **15** paint the town red

revelation
04 fact, leak, news, show **06** detail, vision **07** display **08** betrayal, epiphany, exposure, giveaway **09** admission, eye-opener, unmasking, unveiling **10** apocalypse, confession, disclosure, divulgence, exhibition, expression, revealment, uncovering, unearthing **11** information, publication **12** announcement, broadcasting, proclamation **13** communication, manifestation

reveller
05 raver **07** roister, royster **08** bacchant, carouser, corybant **09** bacchanal, party-goer, roisterer, wassailer **10** celebrator, goodfellow, merrymaker, roaring boy **12** bacchanalian **14** pleasure-seeker

revelry
03 fun **04** riot **05** party, reels **07** jollity, wassail **08** carousal **09** festivity **10** debauchery **11** celebration, festivities, merrymaking **12** celebrations **13** jollification

revenge
03 get, utu **05** repay **06** avenge, pay off, ultion **07** hit back, redress, wreak of **08** avenging, reprisal, requital, revanche, serve out, vendetta **09** fight back, get back at, retaliate, tit for tat, vengeance **10** avengement, punishment **11** eye for an eye, get even with, retaliation, retribution **12** satisfaction, settle a score **14** get

your own back, pay someone back **15** take vengeance on

revengeful
06 bitter **08** pitiless, spiteful, vengeful, wreakful **09** malicious, malignant, merciless, resentful, vengeable **10** implacable, malevolent, unmerciful, vindictive **11** unforgiving, vindicative

revenue
04 fisc, fisk, gain, rent **05** yield **06** income, profit, return **07** profits, rewards, takings **08** incoming, interest, proceeds, receipts **09** patrimony, primitiae

reverberate
04 boom, echo, ring **06** recoil, re-echo **07** rebound, reflect, resound, vibrate **08** resonate **09** repercuss

reverberation
04 echo, wave **06** effect, recoil, result, ripple **07** rebound, ringing **09** re-echoing, resonance, shock wave, vibration **10** reflection, resounding **11** consequence, replication **12** repercussion

revere
04 fear **05** adore, exalt **06** admire, esteem, honour **07** idolize, respect, worship **08** look up to, venerate **09** reverence **11** pay homage to **13** think highly of

reverence
03 awe **04** fear **05** adore, dread **06** admire, esteem, hallow, homage, honour, revere **07** idolism, overawe, respect, worship **08** devotion, venerate **09** adoration, deference, obeisance **10** admiration, exaltation, high esteem, necrolatry, veneration **11** acknowledge, bibliolatry **13** ecclesiolatry

reverent
04 awed **05** pious **06** devout, humble, loving, solemn **07** adoring, devoted, dutiful **08** admiring, obeisant **10** respectful **11** deferential, reverential, worshipping

reverie
05 study **06** musing, trance **08** daydream **10** brown study **11** abstraction, daydreaming, inattention **13** preoccupation, woolgathering

reversal
◇ *reversal indicator*
02 un- **04** blow, swap **05** check, delay, knock, trial, upset, U-turn **06** defeat, mishap, repeal **07** failure, problem, reverse, setback, turning, undoing **08** exchange, hardship, negation **09** about face, adversity, annulment, inversion, revulsion, turnabout, turnround, volte-face **10** affliction, difficulty, misfortune, rescinding, revocation, turnaround **12** cancellation, misadventure **13** nullification **14** countermanding, disappointment

reverse
◇ *reversal indicator*
04 back, blow, pile, rear, swap, turn, undo **05** alter, annul, check, delay, quash, tails, trial, up-end, upset, verso, woman **06** cancel, change, defeat, invert, mishap, negate, repeal, return, revert, revoke, stroke **07** backset, counter, failure, inverse, problem, regress, rescind, retract, retreat, setback, transit **08** backward, contrary, converse, exchange, flip-flop, flipside, hardship, inverted, opposite, overrule, overturn, renverse, reversal, set aside, withdraw **09** adversity, back-pedal, backtrack, disaffirm, other side, overthrow, transpose, turn round, underside **10** affliction, antithesis, backhanded, difficulty, invalidate, misfortune, transverse, turn around **11** change round, countermand, vicissitude **12** misadventure **13** move backwards **14** disappointment, drive backwards, put back to front, turn upside-down

reversion
◇ *reversal indicator*
06 return **07** atavism, escheat, regress **09** puerilism, throwback **10** giving-back, regression, taking-back **11** handing-back, hypostrophe, restoration **13** reinstatement, retrogression

revert
◇ *reversal indicator*
04 fall **05** lapse, recur **06** a tempo, fall in, go back, recoil, resort, result, resume, return **07** cut back, regress, relapse, reverse, run wild, try back **08** fail safe **09** throw back, turn again **10** retrogress

review
◇ *anagram indicator*
◇ *reversal indicator*
03 pan **04** crit, view **05** judge, slate, study, weigh **06** appeal, assess, go over, notice, rating, report, revise, size up, survey **07** analyse, discuss, examine, inspect, journal, rethink, weigh up, write up, write-up **08** analysis, appraise, critique, evaluate, magazine, reassess, reviewal, revision, scrutiny **09** appraisal, comment on, criticism, criticize, judgement, recension, re-examine, summing-up **10** assessment, commentary, evaluation, periodical, reconsider, re-evaluate, retrospect, scrutinize **11** examination, take stock of **12** reassessment, recapitulate, re-evaluation, tour d'horizon **13** re-examination **14** recapitulation **15** reconsideration

reviewer
05 judge **06** critic **07** arbiter **08** essayist, observer **11** commentator, connoisseur

revile
04 hate, rail **05** abuse, libel, scorn, smear **06** defame, malign, missay, vilify **07** despise, inveigh, miscall, slander, traduce **08** reproach **09** denigrate **10** blackguard, calumniate, vituperate

revise
◇ *anagram indicator*
03 Rev **04** cram, edit **05** alter, amend, emend, learn, mug up, study **06** change, go over, modify, peruse, recast, revamp, review, reword, rework, swot up, update **07** correct, recense, redraft, rewrite **08** bone up on, memorize, optimize **09** expurgate, re-examine **10** reconsider **13** think better of

revision
03 Rev **06** change, recast, review **07** editing **08** homework, learning, studying, swotting, updating **09** amendment, recasting, recension, rereading, reworking, rewriting **10** alteration, correction, diorthosis, emendation, memorizing **12** modification **13** re-examination **14** reconstruction

revitalize
05 renew **06** revive **07** refresh, restore **08** revivify **09** reanimate, resurrect **10** reactivate, rejuvenate **12** reinvigorate

revival
04 Romo **06** upturn **07** Odinism, rebirth, renewal, upsurge **08** comeback, wakening **09** awakening, lightning **10** quickening, resurgence **11** neopaganism, reawakening, renaissance, restoration **12** resurrection, risorgimento **13** resuscitation, the kiss of life **14** reintroduction, revitalization **15** re-establishment

revive
04 wake **05** rally, renew, rouse **06** awaken, rake up, relive **07** animate, cheer up, comfort, quicken, recover, refresh, restore **08** reawaken, rekindle, revivify **09** reanimate, resurrect **10** bring round, invigorate, reactivate, revitalize **11** re-establish, reintroduce, resuscitate **12** reinvigorate

• **revivers**
10 Epsom salts

revivify
05 renew **06** repair, revive **07** refresh, restore **08** inspirit **09** reanimate **10** invigorate, reactivate, revitalize **11** resuscitate

reviving
05 tonic **07** bracing, cordial **11** reanimating, revivescent, revivifying, reviviscent, stimulating **12** enheartening, exhilarating, invigorating, refreshening, regenerating **13** resuscitative **14** reinvigorating

revocation
06 repeal, revoke **08** negation, quashing, reversal, revoking **09** abolition, annulment, repealing

10 rescinding, rescission, retraction, revokement, withdrawal **11** countermand, repudiation **12** cancellation, invalidation, retractation **13** nullification **14** countermanding

revoke
04 lift **05** annul, check, quash, recal, renig **06** cancel, negate, recall, recant, renege, repeal, unpray **07** abolish, nullify, renague, renegue, rescind, retract, reverse, unshoot, unshout **08** abrogate, withdraw **09** unpredict **10** invalidate, revocation **11** countermand

revolt
◇ *anagram indicator*
04 coup, riot, rise **05** rebel, repel, shock **06** defect, mutiny, offend, putsch, resist, rise up, rising, sicken **07** disgust, dissent, fall off, outrage **08** apostasy, fall away, futurism, nauseate, uprising **09** breakaway, coup d'état, defection, Jacquerie, rebellion, revulsion, secession **10** revolution, scandalize, take up arms **12** insurrection **13** expressionism **15** Romantic Revival, the Paris Commune, turn your stomach

revolting
◇ *anagram indicator*
02 up **04** foul, vile **05** grody, nasty **07** hateful, heinous **08** horrible, shocking **09** abhorrent, appalling, insurgent, loathsome, obnoxious, offensive, repellent, repugnant, repulsive, sickening **10** abominable, disgusting, nauseating, off-putting **11** distasteful **13** reprehensible

revolution
◇ *anagram indicator*
◇ *reversal indicator*
04 coup, roll, spin, turn **05** cycle, orbit, round, wheel, whirl **06** change, circle, mutiny, putsch, revolt, rising **07** circuit, inqilab, revolve **08** gyration, mutation, rotation, upheaval, uprising **09** cataclysm, coup d'état, rebellion, sex change **10** innovation, insurgence, revolvency **11** reformation **12** insurrection **13** metamorphosis **14** transformation

Revolutions include:

04 July
06 French
07 October, Russian
08 American, Cultural, February, Glorious
10 Industrial
12 Agricultural

revolutionary
◇ *anagram indicator*
◇ *reversal indicator*
03 new, red **04** trot **05** novel, rebel **07** drastic, radical **08** complete, Leninist, mutineer, mutinous **09** anarchist, Bolshevik, different, extremist, insurgent, Menshevik, seditious **10** avant-garde, filibuster, innovative, rebellious, Sandinista, subversive, Trotskyist, Trotskyite **11** anarchistic, progressive, sansculotte **12** experimental **13** revolutionist, thoroughgoing **14** ground-breaking **15** insurrectionary, insurrectionist

Revolutionaries include:

03 Che
04 Biko (Steve), Cade (Jack), Kett (Robert), Marx (Karl)
05 Allen (Ethan), Fanon (Frantz), Gorky (Maxim), Henry (Patrick), Kirov (Sergey), Lenin (Vladimir Ilyich), Marat (Jean Paul), Paine (Tom), Radek (Karl), Rykov (Alexey), Sands (Bobby), Sucre (Antonio José de), Tyler (Wat), Villa (Pancho)
06 Arafat (Yasser), Baader (Andreas), Barras (Paul François Jean Nicolas, Comte de), Castro (Fidel), Corday (Charlotte), Danton (Georges), Fawkes (Guy), Fuller (Margaret), Hébert (Jacques René), Kassem (Abdul Karim), Madero (Francisco), Moreno (Mariano), Qassim (Abd al-Krim), Stalin (Joseph), Zapata (Emiliano)
07 Bakunin (Mikhail), Barnave (Antoine), Blanqui (Auguste), Bolívar (Simón), Catesby (Robert), Goldman (Emma), Guevara (Che), Mandela (Nelson), Meinhof (Ulrike Marie), Princip (Gavrilo), Sandino (Augusto César), Savimbi (Jonas), Tallien (Jean Lambert), Trotsky (Leon), Wallace (William)
08 Abu Nidal, Bin Laden (Osama), Bukharin (Nikolay), Hereward (the Wake), Kerensky (Alexander), Lilburne (John), Mirabeau (Honoré Gabriel Riqueti, Comte de), Proudhon (Pierre Joseph), Santerre (Antoine Joseph), Zinoviev (Grigoriy)
09 Christian (Fletcher), Garibaldi (Giuseppe), Guillotin (Joseph), Kropotkin (Knyaz Peter), Luxemburg (Rosa), Mao Zedong, Nana Sahib, Plekhanov (Georgi), Saint-Just (Louis de), Spartacus, Sun Yat-Sen
10 Delescluze (Charles), Desmoulins (Camille)
11 Jiang Jieshi, Robespierre (Maximilien de)
13 Chiang Kai-Shek, Paz Estenssoro (Víctor)

revolutionize
06 reform **09** transform **10** reorganize **11** restructure, transfigure **14** turn upside-down

revolve
02 go **03** ren, rev, rin, run **04** move, spin, turn **05** orbit, pivot, think, twist, wheel, whirl **06** circle, gyrate, hang on, ponder, return, rotate, swivel, turn on **07** focus on, hinge on, turning **08** centre on, roll back **10** circumduct, revolution **11** circumvolve **13** concentrate on

revolver
03 gat, gun, rod **04** Colt®, iron **05** rifle **06** airgun, pistol **07** bulldog, firearm, handgun, shooter, shotgun **10** peacemaker, six-shooter **12** shooting iron

revolving
07 turning **08** gyrating, gyratory, rotating, spinning, whirling **12** peristrephic

revulsion
04 hate **06** hatred, nausea, recoil, revolt **07** disgust, dislike **08** aversion, distaste, loathing **09** repulsion **10** abhorrence, repugnance, withdrawal **11** abomination, detestation
See also **disgust**; **distaste**

reward
03 pay **04** gain, meed, wage **05** bonus, medal, merit, prise, prize, repay, wages, yield **06** bounty, desert, honour, pay-off, profit, quarry, return **07** benefit, guerdon, payment, premium, present, requite, salvage, testern, warison **08** consider, decorate, requital, sanction, warrison **09** head money, recognize, reguerdon, repayment **10** compensate, decoration, punishment, recompense, remunerate **11** just deserts, retribution **12** compensation, remuneration

rewarding
08 edifying, fruitful, pleasing, valuable **09** enriching, lucrative **10** beneficial, fulfilling, gratifying, productive, profitable, satisfying, worthwhile **11** retributive **12** advantageous, remunerative

rewording
04 edit **08** revision **09** rewriting **10** metaphrase, paraphrase, rephrasing **11** metaphrasis

rework
◇ *anagram indicator*
04 edit **05** alter, amend, emend **06** change, go over, modify, peruse, recast, revamp, review, revise, reword, update **07** correct, recense, redraft, rewrite **09** expurgate, re-examine, refashion **10** reconsider **13** think better of

rewrite
◇ *anagram indicator*
04 edit **05** emend, tweak **06** recast, revise, reword, rework **07** correct, redraft, rescore **08** inscribe, rescript

Rex
01 R

rhea
03 Ops **04** rami **05** nandu, ramee, ramie **06** nandoo, nhandu

rhenium
02 Re

rhesus
02 Rh

rhetoric
07 bombast, fustian, oratory, periods

09 eloquence, hyperbole, pomposity, prolixity, verbosity, wordiness
10 oratorical 11 speechcraft
13 magniloquence 14 grandiloquence, long-windedness

rhetorical
05 grand, showy, wordy 06 florid, prolix 07 aureate, flowery, pompous, verbose 09 bombastic, high-flown, insincere, stylistic 10 artificial, flamboyant, long-winded, oratorical
11 declamatory, pretentious
12 Churchillian, high-sounding, magniloquent 13 grandiloquent

Rhetorical devices include:

03 pun
05 irony, trope
06 aporia, bathos, climax, simile, zeugma
07 auxesis, epigram, erotema, litotes, meiosis, paradox
08 anaphora, chiasmus, diallage, diegesis, ellipsis, epanodos, erotetic, innuendo, metaphor, metonymy, oxymoron, parabole, symploce
09 asyndeton, cataphora, dissimile, epizeuxis, euphemism, hendiadys, hypallage, hyperbole, increment, prolepsis, syllepsis, tautology
10 abscission, anastrophe, anticlimax, antithesis, apostrophe, dysphemism, enantiosis, epanaphora, epiphonema, epistrophe, metalepsis, synchrysis, synecdoche
11 anacoluthon, anadiplosis, antiphrasis, antonomasia, catachresis, enumeration, epanalepsis, hypostrophe, hypotyposis, paraleipsis, parenthesis
12 alliteration, antimetabole, epanorthosis, onomatopoeia
13 amplification, dramatic irony, epanadiplosis, mixed metaphor, vicious circle
14 antimetathesis, double entendre, figure of speech
15 pathetic fallacy, personification

rheumatoid arthritis
02 RA

rhino *see* **money**

Rhode Island
02 RI

rhodium
02 Rh

rhubarb
03 rot, row 05 Rheum 06 rumpus
08 nonsense, pie-plant, squabble
09 rhapontic

rhyme
03 ode 04 poem, rime, song, tink
05 chime, ditty, rhime, verse
06 crambo, jingle, poetry, rhythm, verses 07 couplet 08 limerick
09 harmonize 13 versification

Rhymes include:

03 end, eye
04 half, head, male, near, rich, tail
05 slant, vowel
06 female, riding, tailed
08 feminine, internal
09 assonance, identical, masculine, pararhyme, rime riche
10 apocopated, cynghanedd, rhyme royal
13 rime suffisant

rhythm
04 beat, flow, lilt, stot, time 05 metre, pulse, rhyme, swing, tempo, throb
06 accent 07 cadence, cadency, harmony, measure, numbers, pattern
08 movement 09 voltinism

rhythmic
04 go-go 06 metric, steady
07 flowing, lilting, pulsing, regular
08 metrical, periodic, repeated
09 pulsating, throbbing 10 rhythmical
• **rhythmic pattern**
04 raga, tala 05 talea

rib
03 bar 04 band, bone, cord, gill, vein, wale, welt, wife 05 costa, groin, nerve, ogive, ridge, shaft, tease 06 cutlet, lierne, purlin 07 feather, futtock, nervure, ribbing, support
08 moulding, pork-chop, ridicule
09 tierceron 10 mutton chop 13 cross-springer 14 pleurapophysis

ribald
03 low 04 base, blue, lewd, mean, racy, rude 05 bawdy, gross 06 coarse, earthy, filthy, ribaud, risqué, smutty, vulgar 07 jeering, mocking, naughty, obscene, rybauld 08 derisive, indecent 09 off-colour, satirical
10 irreverent, licentious, scurrilous
11 foul-mouthed, Rabelaisian
13 disrespectful

ribaldry
04 smut 05 filth 07 jeering, lowness, mockery 08 baseness, derision, raciness, ribaudry, rudeness
09 bawdiness, grossness, indecency, obscenity, rybaudrye, vulgarity
10 coarseness, earthiness, scurrility, smuttiness 11 naughtiness
14 licentiousness

ribbing
06 banter 07 baiting, goading, kidding, mocking, ragging, teasing
08 annoying, ridicule, taunting
09 badgering 11 provocation

ribbon
03 jag, pad, tie 04 band, cord, line, pads, sash, tape 05 braid, cloth, flash, shred, strip, tenia 06 caddis, cordon, ferret, fillet, radula, riband, streak, stripe, taenia, tassel, tatter 07 caddice, caddyss, elastic, hatband, ribband, tieback 08 hair-band, headband, quilling, streamer 09 petersham, sword knot 10 cordon bleu, ticker tape
11 multistrike, watchspring

rice
04 reis, twig 05 paddy 07 arborio, zizania 09 brushwood

rich
03 fat 04 busy, deep, fine, full, high, lush, oily, oofy, warm 05 ample, fatty, flush, grand, heavy, juicy, ritzy, spicy, sweet, tasty, vivid 06 absurd, active, bright, costly, creamy, fecund, fruity, ironic, lavish, lively, loaded, mellow, monied, ornate, packed, strong
07 copious, fertile, intense, moneyed, opulent, profuse, replete, rolling, savoury, steeped, vibrant, wealthy, well-off 08 abundant, affluent, eventful, exciting, fruitful, gorgeous, luscious, palatial, precious, prolific, resonant, sonorous, splendid, valuable, well-to-do 09 abounding, brilliant, delicious, elaborate, expensive, laughable, luxurious, pecunious, plenteous, plentiful, priceless, sumptuous 10 filthy rich, full-bodied, in the money, outrageous, productive, prosperous, ridiculous, well-heeled
11 made of money, magnificent, mellifluous, overflowing, rolling in it
12 preposterous, rhinocerical, stinking rich, unreasonable, well-provided, well-supplied 13 full-flavoured 15 with money to burn

riches
04 dosh, gold, loot, pelf 05 brass, bread, dough, gravy, lolly, lucre, means, money, ready, smash 06 assets, greens, mammon, moolah, stumpy, wealth
07 fortune, readies, scratch, shekels
08 greenies, opulence, property, treasure 09 affluence, megabucks, resources, substance 10 prosperity
11 filthy lucre, spondulicks 12 the necessary

richly
04 well 05 fully 08 floridly, lavishly, properly, strongly, suitably
09 elegantly, opulently 10 completely, gorgeously, palatially, splendidly, thoroughly 11 elaborately, expensively, exquisitely, luxuriously, sumptuously
13 appropriately

richness
05 depth, taste 07 fatness 08 business, elegance, fullness, loudness, oiliness
09 abundance, fattiness, fertility, heaviness, intensity, juiciness, provision, resonance, splendour
10 creaminess, excitement, lavishness, liveliness, luxuriance, mellowness
12 eventfulness, magnificence
13 exquisiteness, luxuriousness, plentifulness, sumptuousness

rickety
◇ *anagram indicator*
05 crazy, shaky 06 feeble, flimsy, wobbly 07 tottery 08 decrepit, derelict, insecure, unstable, unsteady
10 broken-down, jerry-built, ramshackle 11 dilapidated

ricochet
03 bob, dap 04 jump, leap, stot
05 bound, carom, stoit, throw
06 bounce, recoil, spring 07 rebound
10 bounce back, spring back

rid
04 free, quit **05** clear, expel, purge, shift **06** purify, remove **07** cleanse, deliver, relieve **08** unburden **11** disencumber

• **get rid of**
04 cast, dump, junk **05** chuck, ditch, eject, expel, scrap, shake, shunt **06** remove, see off, unload **07** abolish, deep-six, discard **08** choke off, chuck out, clear off, clear out, down with, jettison, railroad, shake off, shrug off, throw out **09** dispose of, eliminate, eradicate, get shot of, throw away **10** do away with, put an end to **12** dispense with, make away with

riddance
06 relief **07** freedom, release, removal **08** disposal, ejection **09** clearance, expulsion, purgation **11** deliverance, elimination **13** extermination

riddle
03 mar **04** fill, koan, sift **05** guess, poser, sieve, solve **06** enigma, filter, infest, pepper, pierce, puzzle, strain, teaser, winnow **07** charade, cribble, mystery, pervade, problem **08** permeate, puncture **09** conundrum, logogriph, perforate **10** conclusion, mind-bender **11** brainteaser **12** brain-twister

ride
02 go **03** sit **04** burn, lift, move, road, rode, spin, surf, trip, trot **05** cycle, drive, jaunt, pedal, steer **06** gallop, handle, manage, outing, saddle, travel **07** bobsled, control, journey, overlap **08** bestride, dominate, progress **09** bobsleigh, promenade **12** steeplechase

rider
02 PS **05** biker, bikie **06** hussar, jockey, knight **07** dragoon, eventer **08** horseman, reinsman **09** corollary **10** cavalryman, equestrian, horsewoman, showjumper **11** mosstrooper **12** equestrienne, horse soldier

ridge
02 ås **03** bur, hoe, rib, rig **04** balk, band, bank, burr, drum, edge, hill, kame, keel, list, lump, nurl, rand, reef, wale, welt **05** arête, baulk, costa, crest, esker, halse, hause, hawse, knurl, ledge, linch, raphe, torus **06** crista, ripple, saddle **07** corn rig, crinkle, drumlin, hogback, hummock, linchet, lynchet, wrinkle, yardang **08** eminence, hog's back, sastruga **09** knife-edge, razorback **10** escarpment, promontory **12** superciliary, thank-you-ma'am

ridicule
03 guy, kid, rag, rib **04** gibe, goof, jeer, jest, josh, mock **05** chaff, irony, mimic, queer, scoff, scorn, smoke, sneer, taunt, tease **06** banter, deride, parody, poo-poo, satire, send up **07** crucify, jeering, lampoon, laugh at, mockery, pillory, reticle, sarcasm, teasing **08** badinage, derision, laughter, pooh-pooh, reticule, satirize, taunting **09** absurdity, burlesque, humiliate, make fun of, poke fun at **10** caricature, make game of **11** make a game of **12** depreciation **13** have a game with, poke mullock at

ridiculous
◇ *anagram indicator*
04 rich **05** crazy, droll, funny, silly **06** absurd, mental, stupid **07** comical, damfool, foolish, risible **08** derisory, farcical, humorous, shocking **09** facetious, hilarious, laughable, ludicrous **10** cockamamie, incredible, outrageous **11** nonsensical **12** contemptible, preposterous, unbelievable

ridiculously
◇ *anagram indicator*
08 absurdly **09** laughably **10** incredibly, shockingly **11** ludicrously **12** outrageously, surprisingly, unbelievably, unreasonably **14** preposterously

rife
06 common, raging **07** current, general, rampant, teeming **08** abundant, epidemic, frequent, swarming **09** abounding, extensive, prevalent **10** ubiquitous, widespread **11** overflowing, predominant

riff-raff
03 mob **04** raff, scum **05** dregs, scaff **06** rabble, raffle **07** rubbish **08** canaille, rent-a-mob **09** hoi polloi, scaff-raff **12** undesirables

rifle
◇ *anagram indicator*
02 M1 **03** gun, gut, rob, SLR **04** loot, pick, sack **05** fusil, strip **06** burgle, injure, maraud, Mauser, musket, search, weapon **07** bandook, bundook, carabin, carbine, despoil, express, firearm, Martini, pillage, plunder, ransack, rummage, shotgun **08** Armalite®, carabine, disarray, firelock, petronel **09** chassepot, flintlock **10** Lee Enfield, Winchester® **11** elephant gun **12** Martini-Henry

rift
03 gap, row **04** feud, hole, slit **05** belch, break, chink, cleft, crack, fault, fight, space, split **06** breach, cavity, cleave, cranny, schism **07** crevice, fissure, opening **08** argument, conflict, division, fracture **10** alienation, difference, separation **11** altercation **12** disagreement, estrangement

rig
◇ *anagram indicator*
03 kit **04** cook, fake, garb, gear **05** dress, equip, fit up, forge, prank, ridge, set up, trick, twist **06** clothe, doctor, fiddle, fit out, frolic, gunter, jack-up, outfit, tackle **07** distort, falsify, massage, pervert, swindle **08** fittings, fixtures **09** apparatus, equipment, machinery, structure **10** manipulate, tamper with **12** misrepresent **13** accoutrements

• **rig out**
03 fit **04** garb, robe, trim, wear **05** array, dress, equip, get up, put on **06** attire, clothe, fit out, kit out, outfit, supply **07** dress up, furnish, get into, provide, trick up, turn out **08** accoutre, trick out **09** make ready

• **rig up**
05 build, dress, equip, erect, fit up, fix up **07** arrange, knock up **08** assemble **09** construct, improvise **11** put together **13** throw together **14** cobble together

right
01 r **02** OK, rt **03** due, fit, fix, oke **04** fair, good, just, lien, okay, real, Tory, true, user, well **05** claim, droit, exact, legal, moral, power, quite, sound, truth, utter, valid **06** actual, avenge, bang-on, direct, equity, ethics, fairly, honest, honour, justly, lawful, pronto, proper, repair, seemly, settle, spot on, virtue, wholly **07** charter, correct, ethical, exactly, factual, fitting, freedom, genuine, honesty, justice, licence, precise, rectify, redress, stand up, totally, upright, utterly, warrant **08** absolute, accepted, accurate, approved, becoming, business, complete, directly, entirely, fairness, goodness, legality, morality, properly, put right, sanction, slap bang, straight, suitable, thorough, true-blue, virtuous **09** all the way, authentic, authority, by the book, correctly, desirable, equitable, factually, impartial, integrity, like a shot, opportune, precisely, privilege, propriety, rectitude, righteous, rightness, right-wing, territory, title deed, veritable, vindicate, yesterday **10** absolutely, acceptable, accurately, admissible, auspicious, birthright, completely, convenient, favourable, favourably, honourable, lawfulness, permission, preferable, principled, propitious, put in order, reasonable, straighten **11** appropriate, entitlement, immediately, opportunity, prerogative, reactionary, straightway, uprightness **12** advantageous, conservative, impartiality, satisfactory, the done thing, truthfulness, without delay **13** perpendicular, righteousness, straighten out **14** as the crow flies, characteristic, satisfactorily **15** before you know it, in a straight line

• **by rights**
06 de jure, justly **07** legally, rightly **08** lawfully, properly **09** correctly **10** in fairness, rightfully **11** justifiably **12** legitimately

• **in the right**
09 justified, warranted **10** vindicated

• **put to rights, set to rights**
03 fix **04** sort **05** fix up **06** remedy, settle **07** correct, rectify **10** put in order, straighten **13** straighten out

• **right away**
03 now **04** ASAP **06** at once, pronto **08** directly, in a jiffy, promptly

09 forthwith, instantly, like a shot, yesterday **11** immediately **12** straight away, without delay **13** from the word go **15** before you know it

• right-hand man, right-hand woman
02 PA **04** aide **06** deputy, helper **08** henchman **09** assistant, man Friday, number two, secretary **10** girl Friday, henchwoman, lieutenant, understudy **11** backroom boy, helping hand, henchperson, subordinate **12** backroom girl **15** second-in-command

• right of way
04 lead, rank **08** eminence, priority **09** seniority, supremacy **10** first place, precedence, preference **11** pre-eminence, superiority

• within your rights
07 allowed **08** entitled **09** justified, permitted **10** reasonable

righteous
04 fair, good, just, pure **05** legal, moral, valid **06** honest, lawful, proper, worthy **07** ethical, saintly, sinless, upright **08** virtuous **09** blameless, equitable, excellent, excusable, guiltless, incorrupt, justified, warranted **10** acceptable, defensible, God-fearing, honourable, law-abiding, legitimate, reasonable **11** explainable, justifiable, supportable, well-founded **14** irreproachable

righteousness
06 dharma, equity, honour, purity, virtue **07** honesty, justice, probity **08** goodness, holiness, morality **09** integrity, rectitude **11** ethicalness, uprightness **12** faithfulness **13** blamelessness **14** sanctification

rightful
03 due **04** just, real, true **05** legal, valid **06** de jure, lawful, proper **07** correct, genuine **08** bona fide, suitable **10** authorized, legitimate

rightfully
06 de jure, justly **07** legally, rightly **08** by rights, lawfully, properly **09** correctly **11** justifiably **12** legitimately

rightly
04 well **06** fairly, justly **07** legally, morally **08** by rights, lawfully, properly **09** correctly, equitably, fittingly **10** reasonably **11** justifiably **12** legitimately **13** appropriately

rigid
03 set **04** firm, hard **05** fixed, harsh, stern, stiff, stony, tense **06** ramrod, severe, starch, strict **07** austere, hard-set, spartan **08** cast-iron, rigorous, stubborn **09** inelastic, stringent, tramlined, unbending **10** inflexible, invariable, unyielding **11** unalterable, unrelenting **12** intransigent **14** uncompromising

rigidity
06 fixity **08** hardness, obduracy **09** obstinacy, stiffness **10** stringency **12** immovability, immutability, inelasticity, stubbornness, unsuppleness **13** immutableness, inflexibility, intransigence **14** intractability

rigmarole
04 fuss, to-do **06** bother, hassle, jargon, ragman **07** carry-on, palaver, process, ragment, twaddle **08** nonsense **09** gibberish **11** performance, riddle-me-ree

rigorous
04 firm, hard **05** close, exact, harsh, rigid, stern, tough **06** severe, strait, strict **07** ascetic, austere, precise, spartan, violent **08** accurate, exacting, straight, streight, thorough **09** laborious, stringent, unsparing **10** meticulous, scrupulous **11** painstaking, punctilious **12** intransigent **13** barrack square, conscientious **14** uncompromising

rigorously
06 strait **07** exactly **08** straight, streight **09** precisely **10** accurately, thoroughly **12** meticulously, scrupulously **13** painstakingly, punctiliously

rigour
05 trial **06** ordeal **08** accuracy, firmness, hardness, hardship, rigidity, severity **09** austerity, exactness, harshness, precision, privation, sternness, stiffness, suffering, toughness **10** strictness, stringency **11** preciseness **12** thoroughness **13** inflexibility, intransigence **14** meticulousness **15** punctiliousness

rig-out
03 kit **04** garb, gear, togs **05** dress, get-up, habit **06** livery, outfit, things **07** apparel, clobber, clothes, costume, raiment, uniform **08** clothing, garments

rile
◇ *anagram indicator*
03 bug, irk, vex **04** roil **05** anger, annoy, peeve, pique, upset **06** hassle, nettle, put out, wind up **07** agitate, hack off, tick off **08** brass off, irritate **09** aggravate, cheese off, drive nuts **10** drive crazy, exasperate **11** get your goat **12** drive bananas **13** get on your wick, get up your nose, get your back up, make sparks fly **14** drive up the wall, get your blood up, give you the hump **15** get on your nerves, get your dander up

rill *see* **brook**

rim
03 lip **04** brim, edge, ring, shoe, wood **05** apron, bezel, brink, chimb, chime, chine, felly, helix, rymme, skirt, velum, verge **06** border, felloe, fiddle, girdle, margin, strake **08** membrane **10** peritoneum **13** circumference

rind
04 bark, husk, peel, rine, rynd, skin, zest **05** crust, gourd, shell **06** citron **07** epicarp, outside **09** crackling **10** integument, orange peel

ring
01 O **03** mob, rim **04** area, band, bell, belt, buzz, call, cell, club, crew, dial, ding, disc, disk, echo, gang, gird, halo, hoop, link, loop, peal, sing, tang, ting, toll, tore **05** arena, atoll, chime, clang, clink, group, hem in, knell, phone, reach, reign, round, sound, torus **06** cage in, call up, cartel, circle, clique, collar, girdle, jingle, keeper, league, re-echo, ring up, signet, terret, territ, tingle, tinkle, torret, turret **07** annulet, annulus, circlet, circuit, combine, coterie, enclose, resound, society, vibrate **08** alliance, ding-dong, encircle, proclaim, pugilism, resonate, sorority, surround **09** enclosure, encompass, gathering, give a bell, give a buzz, phone call, syndicate, telephone **10** fraternity **11** association, give a tinkle, reverberate, wedding band **12** circumscribe, organization **14** tintinnabulate

• prize ring
02 PR

• ring of wagons
04 laer **06** corral, laager

ringleader
05 chief **06** brains, leader **08** fugleman **09** spokesman **10** bell-wether, mouthpiece **11** spokeswoman **12** spokesperson

ringlet
04 curl, lock

rinse
03 dip, wet **04** sind, synd, wash **05** bathe, clean, flush, swill **06** sloosh **07** cleanse, wash out **09** flush away, wash clean

riot
◇ *anagram indicator*
03 row **04** fray, hoot, orgy, rage, rant, rave, rout, show, tear **05** brawl, fight, laugh, mêlée, rebel, revel, storm **06** affray, charge, fracas, hubbub, mutiny, rave-up, revolt, rise up, rising, scream, strife, tumult, uproar **07** anarchy, display, quarrel, rampage, revelry, run amok, run riot, run wild, turmoil, whoobub **08** disorder, feasting, flourish, hubbuboo, partying, race riot, uprising **09** commotion, confusion, go berserk, rebellion **10** debauchery, exhibition, indulgence, insurgence, rush wildly, turbulence **11** disturbance, lawlessness, merrymaking **12** extravaganza, insurrection **14** go on the rampage

• run riot
◇ *anagram indicator*
04 rage, rant, rave, tear **05** storm **06** charge **07** rampage, run amok, run wild **09** go berserk **10** rush wildly **14** go on the rampage

riotous
◇ *anagram indicator*
04 loud, wild **05** noisy, rowdy **06** unruly, wanton **07** lawless, roaring,

violent **08** mutinous **10** boisterous, disorderly, ragmatical, rebellious, tumultuous, uproarious
12 ungovernable, unrestrained
13 insubordinate **14** uncontrollable
15 insurrectionary

riotously
◇ *anagram indicator*
05 ariot **06** loudly, wildly **07** noisily
12 tumultuously **14** uncontrollably

rip
◇ *anagram indicator*
03 cut **04** coop, gash, hack, hole, rend, rent, ripp, slit, tear **05** burst, shred, slash, split **06** ladder **07** handful, rupture **08** cleavage, lacerate, separate
• rip off
02 do **03** con, rob **04** dupe **05** cheat, steal, sting, trick **06** diddle, fleece
07 defraud, exploit, swindle **09** gold-brick **10** overcharge

ripe
03 fit **05** grope, grown, ready, right
06 mature, mellow, search, timely
07 forward, perfect, ransack, ripened
08 complete, drop-ripe, finished, in season, rare-ripe, seasoned, spoiling, suitable, thorough **09** developed, excellent, excessive, opportune, premature, ratheripe, under-ripe
10 auspicious, favourable, fully grown, propitious **11** spoiling for
12 advantageous **14** fully developed

ripen
03 age **06** mature, mellow, season
07 develop **13** gather to a head
14 come to maturity **15** bring to maturity

rip-off
03 con **04** scam, swiz **05** cheat, fraud, sting, theft **06** diddle **07** robbery, swindle **08** cheating, con trick, stealing
09 gold brick **12** exploitation
15 daylight robbery

riposte
04 quip **05** reply, sally **06** answer, rejoin, retort, return **07** respond
08 comeback, repartee, response
09 rejoinder **11** reciprocate

ripple
◇ *anagram indicator*
04 curl, eddy, flow, fret, pirl, purl, ring, wave **06** babble, burble, crease, effect, gurgle, jabble, pucker, result, riffle, ruffle, wimple **07** crumple, lapping, ripplet, wavelet, whimple, wrinkle
08 undulate **09** shock wave
10 crispation, undulation
11 consequence, disturbance
12 repercussion **13** reverberation

rise
◇ *reversal down indicator*
02 up **03** sty, try **04** buoy, flow, go up, grow, head, hill, leap, lift, loom, riot, soar, stie, stye **05** arise, begin, climb, get up, issue, mount, pluff, prove, raise, rebel, slope, start, swell, tower
06 appear, ascend, ascent, come in, defect, emerge, growth, harden, jump up, leap up, mutiny, origin, resist, revolt, rising, rocket, source, spring, upturn, volume **07** advance, attempt, climb up, dissent, emanate, improve, incline, prosper, react to, respond, slope up, soaring, stand up, upsurge
08 approach, commence, escalate, increase, occasion, overgrow, progress, response, spring up, surmount, towering **09** acclivity, ascendant, ascendent, elevation, get higher, increment, intensify, originate, promotion **10** be promoted, do your best, escalation, take up arms
11 advancement, get out of bed, improvement, move upwards, upward slope **12** amelioration, make progress
13 exert yourself, get to your feet
14 aggrandizement
• give rise to
◇ *reversal down indicator*
04 make **05** cause, evoke, raise, spawn
06 create, effect, elicit, induce, lead to, prompt **07** bring on, inspire, produce, provoke **08** engender, generate, persuade **09** influence, originate
10 bring about

risible
05 comic, droll, funny **06** absurd
07 amusing, comical **08** farcical, humorous **09** hilarious, laughable, ludicrous **10** ridiculous **11** rib-tickling
13 side-splitting

rising
◇ *reversal down indicator*
04 bull, hill, riot, rise **06** émeute, origin, revolt, uprest, uprise, uprist
07 growing, soaring **08** emerging, mounting, naissant, swelling, uprising
09 advancing, ascendant, ascendent, ascending, assurgent, insurgent
10 increasing, prominence, revolution
11 approaching **12** insurrection, intensifying

risk
04 dare, dice, fear **05** flier, peril, stake, throw **06** chance, danger, gamble, hazard, impawn, threat **07** imperil, venture **08** chance it, endanger, jeopardy **09** adventure **10** go for broke, jeopardize, self-danger
11 possibility, speculation, take a chance, uncertainty **12** lay on the line, play with fire, put on the line **13** put in jeopardy
• against all risks
03 aar
• at the risk of
02 on

risky
04 iffy **05** dicey, dodgy, hairy
06 chancy, risqué, touchy, tricky, unsafe
07 chancey **08** high-risk, perilous
09 dangerous, hazardous, uncertain
10 precarious, touch-and-go
11 venturesome

risqué
04 blue, racy, rude **05** adult, bawdy, crude, dirty, risky, saucy, spicy
06 coarse, earthy, fruity, ribald, smutty
07 naughty **08** immodest, improper, indecent **09** off-colour **10** indelicate, suggestive **14** near the knuckle

rite
03 act **04** bora, form, orgy **05** pawaw, right, usage **06** custom, office, powwow, ritual, symbol **07** dry Mass, liturgy, service, worship **08** ceremony, practice **09** formality, ordinance, procedure, sacrament **10** ceremonial, commixtion, commixture, dry service, initiatory, observance **11** subincision
12 confirmation, superstition

ritual
03 act, set **04** form, rite, wont **05** habit, usage **06** Agadah, cultus, custom, fetich, fetish, formal, lavabo **07** fetiche, Haggada, liturgy, routine, sacring, service **08** ceremony, habitual, Haggadah, lavatory, practice, trumpery **09** customary, custumary, formality, formulary, ordinance, procedure, sacrament, solemnity, tradition **10** ceremonial, consuetude, convention, mumbo-jumbo, observance, prescribed, procedural
11 apotropaism, celebration, traditional
12 conventional, prescription
14 consuetudinary

ritualistic
06 formal, ritual, solemn **07** festive, stately **08** official **09** customary, dignified, formulaic, formulary
10 ceremonial **11** traditional

ritzy
04 posh, rich **05** cushy, grand, plush
06 costly, de luxe, glitzy, lavish, swanky
07 elegant, opulent, stylish **08** affluent, pampered, splendid **09** expensive, luxurious, sumptuous **11** comfortable, magnificent **13** self-indulgent, well-appointed

rival
03 vie **04** mate, peer, vier **05** equal, match, touch **06** fellow, oppose
07 emulate, nemesis, opposed, paragon, partner, vie with **08** corrival, opponent, opposing, parallel
09 adversary, competing, contender
10 antagonist, challenger, collateral, competitor, contestant, in conflict, opposition **11** compare with, compete with, competitive, conflicting, contend with, measure up to **12** in opposition
13 in competition

rivalry
05 vying **06** strife **07** contest
08 conflict, rivality, struggle
09 emulation **10** antagonism, contention, corrivalry, in-fighting, opposition **11** competition
12 corrivalship **15** competitiveness

riven
04 rent **05** split **07** divided, severed
08 ruptured **09** torn apart **11** ripped apart

river
01 R **03** lee, rio **05** flood
11 watercourse

River and watercourse types include:

02 ea
03 cut, pow, sny
04 beck, burn, flow, khor, kill, lake, lane, nala, rill, snye, wadi, wady
05 bourn, brook, canal, creek, delta, ditch, drain, firth, flume, fresh, frith, inlet, mouth, nalla, nulla, rhine, shott, whelm
06 arroyo, broads, influx, nallah, nullah, rapids, rillet, runnel, source, spruit, stream
07 channel, estuary, freshet, riveret, rivulet, torrent
08 affluent, brooklet, effluent, influent, waterway
09 anabranch, backwater, billabong, confluent, headwater, streamlet, tributary
10 confluence, head-stream, millstream, streamling
11 trout stream, water splash
12 distributary, embranchment, water-channel
14 mountain stream

Rivers include:

02 Ob, Po
03 Ain, Axe, Bug, Cam, Dee, Don, Ems, Esk, Exe, Fal, Fly, Han, Ill, Inn, Lea, Lee, Lim, Lot, Mun, Nid, Our, Red, San, Tay, Taz, Ure, Usk, Váh, Wye
04 Aare, Adur, Aire, Amur, Arno, Avon, Bann, Cher, Coco, Dart, East, Ebro, Eden, Elbe, Gail, Hong, Isis, Kemi, Lena, Nene, Neva, Nile, Oder, Ohio, Ouse, Oxus, Ping, Ravi, Ruhr, Saar, Spey, Swan, Taff, Tees, Test, Towy, Tyne, Ural, Vaal, Wear, Yalu, Yare
05 Adige, Argun, Benue, Boyne, Cauca, Chari, Clyde, Congo, Donau, Douro, Fleet, Forth, Glåma, Indus, Jumna, Loire, Marne, Meuse, Mosel, Neath, Negro, Neman, Niger, Peace, Pearl, Pecos, Plata, Plate, Rhine, Rhône, Saône, Seine, Snake, Somme, Tagus, Tamar, Teifi, Tiber, Tisza, Trent, Tweed, Volga, Volta, Weser, Yukon, Zaire
06 Amazon, Angara, Brazos, Chenab, Clutha, Danube, Dnestr, Escaut, Fraser, Gambia, Ganges, Grande, Hudson, Humber, Irtysh, Jhelum, Jordan, Kagera, Kistna, Kolyma, Liffey, Mekong, Mersey, Murray, Orange, Ottawa, Pahang, Paraná, Ribble, Salado, Severn, Seyhan, Sutlej, Thames, Tigris, Tornio, Ubangi, Vltava, Wabash, Yamuna, Yellow
07 Alpheus, Darling, Dnieper, Garonne, Glommen, Helmand, Huang He, Huang Ho, Lachlan, Limpopo, Lualaba, Madeira, Marañón, Maritsa, Narmada, Orinoco, Pechora, Potomac, Salween, Schelde, Selenga, Sénégal, Shannon, Tarim He, Ucayali, Uruguay, Vistula, Waikato, Yangtze, Yenisei, Zambezi
08 Arkansas, Blue Nile, Canadian, Colorado, Columbia, Delaware, Dniester, Dordogne, Missouri, Okavango, Paraguay, Tunguska, Wanganui, Zhu Jiang
09 Churchill, Crocodile, Euphrates, Great Ouse, Irrawaddy, Mackenzie, Rio Grande, Tennessee, White Nile
10 Albert Nile, Bass Strait, Des Plaines, Sacramento, San Joaquin, Shenandoah, St Lawrence, Walla Walla
11 Mississippi, Shatt al-Arab
12 Murrumbidgee, Saskatchewan, Victoria Nile

Mythical rivers include:

04 Alph, Styx
05 Lethe
07 Acheron, Alpheus, Cocytus, Oceanus
08 Achelous, Eridanos
10 Phlegethon

• river valley
04 wadi, wady **05** water **07** wind gap

rivet
04 grip **05** clink **06** absorb, arrest, clinch, excite **07** engross, enthral **08** intrigue **09** captivate, fascinate
• fix rivet
04 pane, pean, peen, pein, pene

riveting
08 exciting, gripping, hypnotic, magnetic **09** absorbing, arresting **10** engrossing **11** captivating, enthralling, fascinating, interesting **12** spellbinding

road
03 via **04** raid, ride, rode, tour **06** course **07** railway, roadway **09** dismissal, incursion **10** journeying, prostitute, travelling

Road types include:

01 A, B, C, E
02 Rd, St
03 Ave, way
04 drag, high, lane, mews, pass, ring, side, slip, toll
05 alley, byway, close, gated, Roman, route, strip, track, trunk
06 avenue, bypass, parade, rat run, relief, strand, street, subway
07 beltway, dead end, flyover, freeway, highway, off ramp, parkway, private, through
08 alleyway, autobahn, causeway, clearway, crescent, cul-de-sac, metalled, motorway, overpass, red route, short cut, speedway, trackway, turnpike
09 autoroute, boulevard, bridleway, cart track, dirt track, esplanade, green lane, promenade, underpass
10 autostrada, bridlepath, cloverleaf, expressway, interstate, unmetalled
11 gravel track, scenic route, single track
12 mountain pass, superhighway, thoroughfare, unclassified
14 gyratory system
15 dual-carriageway

Roads include:

02 A1, M1, M2, M3, M4, M5, M6, M8, M9
03 M25, M40, M62
07 Route 66, Westway
08 Fosse Way, Highway 1, Silk Road
09 Appian Way, Burma Road, Highway 61
10 Cassian Way, Dere Street, Khyber Pass
12 El Camino Real, King's Highway, Périphérique, Sturt Highway
13 North Circular, South Circular, Stuart Highway, Watling Street
14 Great Ocean Road, Great River Road, Le Périphérique, Pacific Highway

roadhouse *see* **public house**

roam
04 rake, rove, trek, walk **05** amble, drift, prowl, range, raven, stray, tramp, wheel **06** ramble, stroam, stroll, travel, wander **07** meander **08** ambulate, squander, traverse **09** wandering **11** perambulate, peregrinate

roar
03 cry **04** bawl, bell, boom, hoot, howl, roin, rore, rote, rout, yell **05** blare, crash, laugh, royne, shout **06** bellow, guffaw, holler, rumble, scream, shriek **07** break up, thunder **08** crease up **09** fall about **14** split your sides **15** laugh like a drain

roaring
04 full, loud, rich **05** great **07** bluster, booming, echoing, notable, ringing, riotous, vibrant **08** decisive, emphatic, resonant, sonorous, striking, thorough **09** memorable **10** conclusive, impressive, remarkable, resonating, resounding, thunderous **11** outstanding **13** reverberating

roast
04 bake, rost **05** brown, parch, swale, swayl, sweal, sweel **06** banter **07** torrefy **08** barbecue **11** decrepitate

rob
02 do **03** mug, pad, rub **04** blag, fake, loot, mill, nick, raid, ramp, roll, sack **05** berob, bunco, bunko, cheat, flimp, heist, pluck, reave, reive, rifle, screw, stiff, sting **06** burgle, do over, hijack, hold up, pirate, rip off **07** bereave, defraud, deprive, despoil, pillage, plunder, ransack, stick up, swindle **08** highjack, knock off, turn over **09** depredate, steal from

robber
04 Tory **05** cheat, fraud, rover, thief **06** bandit, con man, dacoit, dakoit, latron, looter, mugger, pirate, raider **07** brigand, burglar, cateran, ladrone, pandoor, pandour, stealer **08** hijacker, swindler **09** embezzler, plunderer **10** highjacker, highwayman, land-pirate, roberdsman, robertsman **11** motor-bandit
See also **thief**

robbery
04 blag, raid, toby **05** fraud, heist, theft **06** hold-up, piracy, rip-off, snatch **07** break-in, dacoity, dakoiti, larceny, low toby, mugging, pillage, plunder, stick-up, swindle **08** burglary, high toby, stealing **09** dacoitage, latrociny, pilferage **10** plundering **11** latrocinium **12** embezzlement, smash-and-grab **13** housebreaking

robe
04 garb, gown, vest, wrap **05** camis, camus, drape, dress, habit, talar **06** attire, chimer, clothe, dolman, khalat, khilat, killut, kimono, peplos, peplus, purple **07** apparel, cassock, chimere, chrisom, costume, kellaut, wrapper **08** bathrobe, christom, parament, peignoir, vestment, wardrobe **09** housecoat, nightgown **10** palliament **12** chrisom-cloth, dressing-gown

Robert
03 Bob, Rob **05** Bobby **06** Bobbie, Rabbie, Robbie

Robin Hood *see* **legend**

robot
05 golem **06** cyborg, zombie **07** android, machine, nanobot **08** telechir **09** automaton

robust
03 fit, raw **04** hale, iron, rude, well **05** crude, hardy, sonsy, stout, tough **06** coarse, direct, earthy, hearty, ribald, risqué, rugged, sonsie, strong, sturdy **07** healthy, sthenic **08** athletic, forceful, muscular, powerful, stalwart, thickset, vigorous **09** energetic, strapping, well-built **10** able-bodied, no-nonsense **11** down-to-earth **15** straightforward, tough as old boots

rock
◇ *anagram indicator*
03 AOR, jow, tip **04** cill, coin, crag, daze, reef, reel, roll, sill, stun, sway, tilt, toss, trap, tuff, whin **05** crack, lurch, pitch, shake, shock, stone, swing **06** danger, pebble, totter, wobble **07** astound, boulder, diamond, distaff, outcrop, shoggle, stagger, startle **08** astonish, bewilder, hard core, obstacle, surprise, take back, undulate **09** dumbfound, oscillate **12** move to and fro

See also **singer**

Rocks include:

02 aa
03 ore
04 coal, lava, marl
05 chalk, chert, flint, shale, slate
06 basalt, gabbro, gneiss, gravel, marble, schist
07 breccia, granite
08 dolerite, hornfels, obsidian, porphyry
09 argillite, greywacke, limestone, sandstone, soapstone
10 greenstone, serpentine
11 pumice stone
12 conglomerate

• on the rocks
06 doomed, failed, in a fix, in a jam **07** failing, in a hole, in a mess **08** hopeless, in pieces, in shreds, slipping, unstable **09** in a bad way, in a scrape, penniless **11** at an impasse **12** in difficulty **14** in difficulties

rocket
02 V-1, V-2 **04** soar, wald, weld **05** onion, retro, tower **06** rucola **07** arugula, missile, shoot up **08** Congreve, escalate, roquette, thruster **09** reprimand **10** flying bomb, projectile **13** guided missile, launch vehicle **15** increase quickly, St Barbara's cress

rocky
◇ *anagram indicator*
04 hard, weak **05** rough, shaky, stony, tipsy **06** craggy, flinty, pebbly, rugged, wobbly **08** unstable, unsteady, wobbling **09** difficult, tottering, uncertain **10** staggering, unpleasant, unreliable **14** unsatisfactory

rococo
04 bold **05** showy **06** florid, ornate **07** baroque, flowery **08** fanciful, rocaille, vigorous **09** decorated, elaborate, exuberant, fantastic, grotesque, whimsical **10** convoluted, flamboyant **11** embellished, extravagant, overwrought **13** overdecorated, overelaborate **15** churrigueresque

rod
03 bar, cue, lug **04** calm, came, cane, mace, pole, reed, rood, spit, twig, vare, wand **05** baton, shaft, staff, stave, stick, strut, swits **06** pistol, switch **07** ellwand, probang, sceptre, scollop, tringle **08** caduceus, metewand, meteyard, revolver, stanchel, stancher **09** metestick, stanchion

See also **gun**

rodent

Rodents include:

03 rat
04 cavy, cony, hare, paca, pika, vole
05 aguti, coypu, mouse
06 agouti, beaver, ferret, gerbil, gopher, hog-rat, jerboa, marmot, rabbit
07 cane rat, hamster, lemming, meerkat, muskrat, ondatra, potoroo
08 black rat, brown rat, capybara, chipmunk, dormouse, hampster, hedgehog, musquash, sewer rat, squirrel, tucutuco, viscacha, water rat
09 bandicoot, groundhog, guinea pig, porcupine, water vole, woodchuck
10 chinchilla, fieldmouse, prairie dog, springhaas, springhase
11 kangaroo rat, red squirrel, spermophile
12 grey squirrel, harvest mouse

roe
04 melt, milt, raun, rawn **06** caviar, cavier **07** caviare **08** caviarie

roentgenium
02 Rg

rogue
◇ *anagram indicator*
05 cheat, crook, drôle, fraud, gipsy, Greek, gypsy, hempy, knave, scamp **06** con man, donder, limmer, rascal, scally, terror, varlet **07** skellum, vagrant, villain, wastrel, wrong 'un **08** deceiver, dummerer, palliard, swindler **09** fraudster, miscreant, prankster, reprobate, scallywag, scoundrel, son of a gun **10** disruptive, ne'er-do-well, rascallion, slip-string **11** mischievous, rapscallion **12** hedge-creeper **14** good-for-nothing

roguish
04 arch **05** hempy, shady **06** cheeky, impish, wicked **07** crooked, knavish, playful, waggish **08** criminal, espiègle, rascally **09** deceitful, deceiving, dishonest, swindling **10** confounded, coquettish, fraudulent, frolicsome, rascal-like, slip-string, villainous **11** mischievous **12** unprincipled, unscrupulous

roister
04 brag, romp **05** boast, revel, strut **06** frolic **07** bluster, carouse, large it, rollick, swagger **09** blusterer, celebrate, make merry, whoop it up **11** have it large **15** paint the town red

roisterer
06 buster, ranter **07** boaster, roister **08** braggart, carouser, reveller **09** blusterer, swaggerer

roisterous
04 loud, wild **05** noisy, rowdy **09** clamorous, exuberant **10** boisterous, disorderly, uproarious **12** obstreperous

role
03 bit, fat, job **04** duty, lead, part, post, task **05** cameo, place, stead **08** capacity, function, name part, position **09** cameo-part, character, portrayal, situation **11** comprimario **12** principal boy, spear carrier **13** character part, impersonation **14** representation

roll
◇ *anagram indicator*
02 go **03** bap, bun, ren, rin, rob, run, wad **04** bind, boom, bowl, coil, curl, drum, echo, file, flow, fold, furl, list, move, pass, peal, reel, roar, rock, spin, sway, toss, turn, waul, wawl, wind, wrap **05** crush, cycle, dandy, index, level, lurch, pitch, press, spool, start, swell, swing, trill, twirl, twist, wheel, whirl **06** annals, billow, bobbin, census, elapse, enfold, enwrap, gyrate, rafale, record, rental, roller, roster, rotate, rumble, scroll, smooth, tumble, volley, volume, volute, wallow, wander, welter **07** envelop, flatten, go round, grumble,

notitia, reeling, resound, revolve, rocking, rouleau, stagger, swagger, terrier, thunder, tossing, trindle, trundle **08** crescent, cylinder, gyration, pitching, register, rotation, schedule, undulate **09** billowing, catalogue, chronicle, directory, inventory, press down, resonance, turn round **10** muster-file, revolution, undulation **11** reverberate **13** reverberation

See also **bread**

• roll in
04 come **06** appear, arrive, blow in, come in, flow in, pour in, rush in, show up, turn up **07** flood in **09** be present **10** be received

• rolling in it
04 rich **05** flush **06** loaded **07** moneyed, wealthy, well-off **08** affluent, well-to-do **10** filthy rich, in the money, prosperous, well-heeled **11** made of money **12** stinking rich **15** with money to burn

• roll up
04 furl **06** arrive, gather **07** convene **08** assemble **10** congregate, intervolve

roller
02 RR **07** trundle **10** Rolls-Royce®

rollicking
◇ *anagram indicator*
05 merry, noisy **06** banzai, frisky, hearty, jaunty, jovial, joyous, lively, rebuke, rocket **07** censure, chiding, lecture, playful, reproof, romping **08** berating, carefree, harangue, reproach, roisting, scolding, spirited, sportive **09** cavorting, exuberant, reprimand, sprightly, talking-to **10** boisterous, frolicsome, rip-roaring, roisterous, telling-off, upbraiding **12** devil-may-care, dressing-down, light-hearted **13** swashbuckling

rolling
◇ *anagram indicator*
06 goggle, waving **07** heaving, surging **08** rippling, undulant **10** undulating, volutation

roll-on roll-off
04 ro-ro

roly-poly
03 fat **05** buxom, plump, podgy, pudgy, round, tubby **06** barrel, chubby, rotund **07** rounded **10** butterball, overweight

Roman

Roman emperors:

03 Leo
04 Geta, Nero, Otho, Zeno
05 Carus, Gaius, Galba, Nerva, Titus
06 Avitus, Decius, Gallus, Julian, Philip, Probus, Trajan, Valens
07 Carinus, Florian, Gordian, Gratian, Hadrian, Marcian, Maximin, Maximus, Severus, Tacitus
08 Aemilian, Arcadius, Augustus, Aurelian, Balbinus, Caligula, Claudius, Commodus, Constans, Domitian, Galerius, Honorius, Licinius, Macrinus, Majorian, Maximian, Numerian, Olybrius, Pertinax, Tiberius, Valerian
09 Anthemius, Caracalla, Gallienus, Hostilian, Maxentius, Procopius, Vespasian, Vitellius
10 Diocletian, Elagabalus, Magnentius, Quintillus, Theodosius
11 Constantine, Constantius, Julius Nepos, Lucius Verus, Valentinian
13 Antoninus Pius, Libius Severus
14 Didius Julianus, Marcus Aurelius
15 Romulus Augustus
16 Alexander Severus, Petronius Maximus, Septemius Severus

Roman kings:

07 Romulus
12 Ancus Marcius
13 Numa Pompilius
14 Servius Tullius
15 Tullus Hostilius
17 Tarquinius Priscus
18 Tarquinius Superbus

Romans include:

04 **Cato, Livy, Ovid**
05 **Lucan, Pliny**
06 **Antony** (Mark), **Brutus, Cicero** (Marcus Tullius), **Horace, Pilate** (Pontius), **Pompey, Seneca, Vergil, Virgil**
07 **Atticus** (Titus Pomponius), **Cassius, Juvenal, Martial, Plautus** (Titus Maccius), **Roscius, Tacitus, Terence**
08 **Agricola** (Gnaeus Julius), **Catilina** (Lucius Sergius), **Catiline, Catullus** (Gaius Valerius), **Claudian, Gracchus** (Tiberius Sempronius), **Lucretia**
09 **Agrippina, Lucretius, Spartacus, Suetonius**
10 **Coriolanus** (Gaius), **Quintilian**
14 **Marcus Antonius**

See also **god**, **goddess**; **mythology**; **numeral**

romance
03 lie, see, woo **04** date, gest, tale **05** amour, charm, chase, court, fling, geste, idyll, novel, story, thing **06** affair, colour, legend, whimsy **07** crusade, fantasy, fiction, glamour, liaison, mystery, passion, Romanic, romaunt **08** intrigue **09** adventure, fairytale, fantasize, go out with, love story, melodrama, overstate, sentiment **10** attachment, exaggerate, excitement, fairy story, love affair **11** fascination **12** bodice-ripper, go steady with, relationship **15** romantic fiction

Romania
02 RO **03** ROU

romantic
04 fond, wild **05** soppy **06** dreamy, Gothic, loving, sloppy, tender **07** amorous, dreamer, idyllic, utopian **08** exciting, fanciful, idealist, quixotic, stardust, unlikely **09** fairytale, fantastic, imaginary, legendary, visionary **10** fictitious, idealistic, improbable, lovey-dovey, mysterious, optimistic, passionate, starry-eyed **11** extravagant, fascinating, impractical, sentimental, unrealistic **14** sentimentalist

romantically
06 fondly **08** lovingly, tenderly **09** amorously **10** excitingly, fancifully **12** mysteriously, passionately **13** extravagantly, impractically, sentimentally **14** idealistically, optimistically **15** unrealistically

Rome *see* **hill**

Romeo
01 R **05** lover **06** gigolo **07** Don Juan **08** Casanova, Lothario **09** ladies' man **10** lady-killer

romp
03 rig **04** lark, play, ramp, skip **05** caper, frisk, hempy, revel, sport, spree **06** cavort, frolic, gambol, hoiden, hoyden, tomboy **07** roister, rollick

rondo
04 rota

roof
05 vault **06** canopy **07** ceiling, rigging, shelter **08** covering, dwelling **11** culmination

Roof types include:

03 hip
04 bell, dome, flat, helm, ogee, span
05 gable
06 cupola, French, lean-to, saddle
07 gambrel, mansard, monitor, pitched
08 flat roof, imperial, pavilion, sawtooth, thatched
09 onion dome
10 imbricated, saucer dome
12 geodesic dome, sloped turret
13 conical broach
14 gable-and-valley, pendentive dome

• hit the roof
05 go mad **06** blow up, see red **07** explode **08** boil over, freak out **09** do your nut **11** blow your top, flip your lid, go up the wall, lose your rag **12** blow your cool, lose your cool **15** fly off the handle, go off the deep end

roof-gutter
04 roan, rone **05** rhone **08** roanpipe, ronepipe

rook
01 R **02** do **03** con **04** bilk, crow **05** cheat, squab, sting **06** castle, diddle, fleece, rip off **07** defraud, swindle **09** card-sharp, gold-brick, simpleton **10** overcharge **12** take for a ride

room
02 rm **03** ben, but, end, oda **04** area, seat **05** range, scope, space, stead **06** chance, extent, leeway, margin, volume **07** expanse, legroom **08** capacity, headroom, latitude, occasion **09** allowance, elbow-room **10** Lebensraum **11** appointment, compartment, opportunity

Rooms include:

02 WC
03 bed, box, day, den, loo
04 ante, bath, cell, dark, hall, loft, play, rest, sick, tack, wash, work
05 attic, board, cabin, class, cloak, court, foyer, front, games, green, guard, guest, lobby, music, porch, salon, spare, staff, state, stock, store, study
06 cellar, common, dining, engine, family, larder, living, locker, lounge, lumber, office, pantry, rumpus, saddle, strong, studio, toilet
07 boudoir, buttery, chamber, control, cubicle, drawing, fitting, kitchen, landing, laundry, lecture, library, meeting, morning, nursery, parlour, reading, seminar, sitting, smoking, utility, waiting
08 assembly, basement, chambers, changing, dressing, lavatory, scullery, workshop
09 breakfast, dormitory, mezzanine, reception, sun lounge
10 consulting, laboratory, recreation
11 kitchenette, lounge-diner
12 conservatory, kitchen-diner
15 en suite bathroom

• have room for
04 stow

roomy
04 wide **05** ample, broad, large, rangy **07** sizable **08** generous, sizeable, spacious **09** capacious, extensive **10** commodious, voluminous

root
03 fix, nub, rad, set, tap, yam **04** axis, base, core, germ, grub, hail, home, moor, more, pull, seat, seed, spur, stem **05** basis, cause, cheer, embed, fount, heart, radix, shout, stick, tuber **06** anchor, bottom, etymon, family, fasten, ground, kernel, nuzzle, origin, radish, reason, sinker, source **07** applaud, calamus, cheer on, essence, ginseng, implant, nucleus, origins, parsnep, parsnip, radical, radicle, rhizome, rummage, snuzzle, support, turbith, turpeth, vetiver **08** entrench, heritage, radicate, scammony **09** beginning, encourage, establish, principle **10** background, beginnings, birthplace, derivation, foundation **11** fundamental **12** fountainhead, sarsaparilla **13** starting point

• put down roots
09 set up home **10** settle down **12** make your home

• root and branch
06 wholly **07** finally, totally, utterly **08** complete, entirely, thorough **09** radically **10** completely, thoroughly

• root around
03 dig, pry **04** hunt, nose, poke **05** delve **06** burrow, ferret, forage **07** rummage

• root out
06 dig out, remove, uproot **07** abolish, destroy, outweed, uncover, unearth **08** discover, get rid of **09** clear away, eliminate, eradicate, extirpate **10** put an end to **11** exterminate

• take root
08 take hold **11** become fixed **15** establish itself

rooted
04 deep, felt, firm **05** fixed, rigid **06** deeply **07** radical **08** radicate **09** confirmed, ingrained, radicated **10** deep-seated, entrenched **11** established

rootless
04 free **06** moving **07** nomadic **08** carefree, drifting, floating, homeless **09** itinerant, transient, unsettled, wandering **14** of no fixed abode

rootstock
04 race **05** orris

rope
03 tie **04** bind, jeff, lash, moor, stay **05** hitch, lasso **06** fasten

Rope types include:

03 guy, tow
04 cord, drag, fall, head, line, seal, stay, tack, vang, warp
05 brace, cable, lasso, noose, widdy
06 bridle, halter, hawser, hobble, lariat, runner, strand, string, tackle, tether
07 bobstay, bowline, cordage, cringle, halyard, lanyard, lashing, marline, mooring, outhaul, painter, ratline
08 buntline, clew-line, dockline, downhaul, dragline, gantline
09 hackamore

• know the ropes
05 learn **06** master **12** know the drill, know the score **13** know what's what

• rope in
06 engage, enlist **07** involve **08** inveigle, persuade, talk into

ropy, ropey
04 duff, poor **05** rough **06** unwell **07** stringy **08** below par, inferior **09** deficient, glutinous, off colour **10** inadequate **11** substandard **14** not up to scratch, unsatisfactory

rose
03 riz **04** geum, Jack, moss **05** avens, brere, briar, brier **07** Bourbon, monthly, paragon, rosette **08** noisette, primrose **09** crampbark, eglantine, perpetual, remontant **10** erysipelas, floribunda, water elder **12** snowball tree **13** cranberry bush, cranberry tree

• rose fruit
03 hep, hip

rosette
04 chou, rose **06** rosace, rosula **07** cockade **13** wedding favour **14** provincial rose

rosin
05 resin, roset, rosit, rozet, rozit **09** colophony

roster
04 list, roll, rota **05** index **07** listing **08** register, schedule **09** directory

rostrum
04 beak, bema, dais **05** stage **06** podium **08** platform

rosy
03 red **04** pink, rose **05** fresh, ruddy, sunny **06** bright, florid **07** auroral, flushed, glowing, hopeful, reddish, roseate, rose-red **08** aurorean, blooming, blushing, cheerful, inflamed, rose-hued, roselike, rose-pink, rubicund **09** bloodshot, promising **10** auspicious, favourable, optimistic, reassuring **11** encouraging, rose-scented **12** rose-coloured **14** healthy-looking

rot
◇ *anagram indicator*
03 rat, ret **04** blah, bosh, bunk, halt, joke, rait, rate, rust, tosh **05** decay, go bad, go off, hooey, mould, spoil, taint, tease **06** bluing, bunkum, drivel, fester, go sour, humbug, kibosh, kybosh, perish, piffle **07** baloney, blueing, corrode, corrupt, crumble, garbage, hogwash, putrefy, rhubarb, rubbish **08** claptrap, cobblers, collapse, malarkey, Merulius, nonsense **09** corrosion, decompose, moonshine, poppycock **10** codswallop, corruption, degenerate **11** deteriorate **12** disintegrate, putrefaction **13** decomposition, deterioration **14** disintegration

rota
04 list, roll **05** canon, index, rondo, round **06** course, roster **07** listing, routine **08** register, schedule **09** directory

rotary
07 turning **08** gyrating, gyratory, rotating, spinning, whirling **09** revolving **10** roundabout

rotate
◇ *reversal indicator*
04 reel, roll, spin, turn **05** pivot, rabat, whirl **06** gyrate, swivel **07** go round, rabatte, revolve, twiddle **09** alternate, move round, spin round, turn about, turn round **10** change face **11** interchange, reciprocate, take in turns **13** take it in turns

rotation
04 spin, turn **05** cycle, orbit, round, whirl **06** swivel **07** turning **08** gyration, sequence, spinning, whirling **10** revolution, succession, swivelling **11** alternation

rote

• learn by rote
08 memorize **11** learn off pat **14** commit to memory **15** learn from memory, learn off by heart

rotten
◇ *anagram indicator*
03 bad, ill, off, rat **04** evil, foul, mean, poor, poxy, punk, rank, ropy, sick, sour **05** awful, dirty, fetid, lousy, manky, nasty, putid, ropey, rough **06** addled, bloody, crummy, damned, darned,

dashed, foetid, grotty, guilty, mouldy, poorly, putrid, spoilt, unwell, wicked **07** beastly, blasted, corrupt, decayed, flaming, gone off, immoral, rotting, tainted, unsound **08** blinking, blooming, decaying, dratting, dreadful, flipping, horrible, inferior, infernal, low-grade, stinking, terrible, wretched **09** dishonest, off colour, putrefied **10** confounded, decomposed, despicable, inadequate, mouldering, putrescent, unpleasant **12** contemptible, unprincipled **13** dishonourable **14** disintegrating

rotter
03 cad, cur, pig, rat **04** fink, heel **05** beast, louse, rogue, swine **07** bounder, dastard, stinker **08** blighter **09** scoundrel **10** blackguard

rotund
03 fat **04** full, rich **05** heavy, obese, plump, podgy, round, stout, tubby **06** chubby, fleshy, portly **07** bulbous, orotund, rounded, spheral, spheric **08** globular, resonant, roly-poly, sonorous **09** corpulent, orbicular, rotundate, spherical, spherular **10** impressive **12** magniloquent **13** grandiloquent

roué
04 rake **06** lecher, wanton **08** rakehell **09** debauchee, libertine **10** profligate, sensualist

rough
◇ *anagram indicator*
03 ill, ned, row, yob **04** curt, hard, hazy, rude, sick, thug, wild **05** asper, basic, blunt, bully, bumpy, crude, cruel, dirty, draft, gruff, gurly, hairy, harsh, hasty, husky, lousy, lumpy, model, nasty, noisy, plain, quick, raggy, raspy, rocky, rowdy, ruggy, rusty, scaly, sharp, stern, stony, tough, tousy, touzy, towsy, towzy, vague, yobbo **06** brutal, choppy, coarse, craggy, grotty, hoarse, jagged, lively, mock-up, poorly, raucle, rotten, ruffle, rugged, severe, shaggy, sketch, stormy, uneven, unkind, unwell, vulgar **07** bristly, bruiser, brusque, brutish, cursory, drastic, extreme, general, gnarled, grained, hirsute, inexact, of a sort, of sorts, outline, prickly, rasping, raucous, ruffian, sketchy, throaty, unkempt, unshorn, violent **08** agitated, aspirate, below par, croaking, forceful, gravelly, guttural, hooligan, impolite, muricate, scabrous, scratchy, strident, unbroken, ungentle, unshaven **09** difficult, energetic, estimated, harrowing, imprecise, iron-sided, irregular, merciless, muricated, off colour, primitive, roughneck, turbulent, unfeeling, unhealthy, unrefined **10** aggressive, astringent, boisterous, broadbrush, discordant, disorderly, hard-handed, incomplete, unfinished, unpleasant, unpolished **11** approximate, belligerent, insensitive, ramgunshoch, rudimentary, tempestuous, uncivilized **12** tiger country, unelaborated **15** under the weather

• **rough out**
05 draft **06** mock up, sketch **07** outline **11** draw in rough **14** give a summary of

• **rough up**
03 mug **04** bash, do in **06** beat up **08** maltreat, mistreat **09** manhandle **10** knock about

rough-and-ready
05 basic, crude, plain **06** bodgie, make-do, simple **07** hurried, sketchy, stop-gap **09** makeshift, unrefined **10** unpolished **11** approximate, provisional

rough-and-tumble
05 brawl, fight, mêlée, scrap **06** affray, dust-up, fracas, rumpus **07** punch-up, scuffle **08** struggle

roughen
◇ *anagram indicator*
04 chap, hack, rasp, stab **05** chafe, graze, rough, scuff, spray **06** abrade, ruffle **07** coarsen, harshen, spreaze, spreeze **08** asperate, spreathe, spreethe, unsmooth **09** granulate

roughly
◇ *anagram indicator*
01 c **02** ca **03** cir **04** circ **05** about, circa **06** around, nearly, wildly **07** close to, cruelly, harshly, loosely, noisily, rowdily, toughly **08** brutally, unkindly **09** just about, not far off, rounded up, violently **10** forcefully, give or take, more or less, round about **11** approaching, mercilessly, rounded down **12** boisterously **13** approximately, energetically, insensitively, in the region of, or thereabouts, something like **14** in round figures, in round numbers **15** in the vicinity of

roughneck
04 lout, thug **05** rough, rowdy, tough, yobbo **06** keelie **07** bruiser, ruffian **08** bully boy, hooligan, larrikin

roulade
03 run **05** trill

round
◇ *anagram indicator*
◇ *containment indicator*
◇ *reversal indicator*
01 O **03** fat, lap, orb **04** ball, band, beat, bend, bout, coil, disc, disk, full, game, heat, hoop, past, path, ring, rota, tour, walk **05** about, ample, cycle, flank, globe, globy, level, plump, rough, route, scope, skirt, stage, stout **06** around, beyond, bypass, candid, chubby, circle, course, curved, honest, patrol, period, portly, rotund, series, sphere, sphery **07** all over, circlet, circuit, discoid, globate, go round, rounded, routine, session, whisper **08** circular, cylinder, disclike, framed by, globular, hooplike, milk-walk, move past, sequence, sonorous, spheroid, to and fro, vigorous **09** corpulent, discoidal, enclosing, estimated, finish off, full-orbed, globelike, imprecise, orbicular, spherical, unsparing **10** ball-shaped, disc-shaped, encircling, enveloping, everywhere, indirectly, on all sides, ring-shaped, succession, throughout, to all parts **11** approximate, cylindrical, on every side, plain-spoken, surrounding, travel round, unqualified **12** circuitously, encompassing, everywhere in, here and there, on all sides of, to all parts of **13** on every side of **15** in all directions

• **round about**
01 c **02** ca **03** cir **04** circ **05** about, circa **06** around, nearly **07** close to, loosely, roughly **09** just about, not far off, rounded up **10** give or take, more or less **11** approaching, rounded down **13** approximately, in the region of, or thereabouts, something like **14** in round numbers **15** in the vicinity of

• **round off**
03 cap, end **04** turn **05** close, crown **06** finish, parcel, top off **08** complete, conclude **09** finish off

• **round on**
05 abuse **06** attack, turn on **07** lay into, set upon

• **round up**
04 herd **05** group, rally **06** gather, muster **07** collect, marshal **08** assemble **13** bring together

roundabout
05 plump **06** rotary **07** devious, evasive, oblique, waltzer, winding **08** indirect, tortuous, twisting **10** circuitous, meandering **12** merry-go-round, periphrastic **13** traffic circle **14** circumlocutory **15** circumambagious

roundly
06 openly **07** bluntly, frankly, sharply **08** fiercely, severely **09** intensely, violently **10** completely, forcefully, rigorously, thoroughly, vehemently **11** outspokenly

round-up
05 rally, rodeo **06** muster, précis, survey **07** herding, summary **08** assembly, overview **09** collation, gathering **10** collection **11** marshalling **14** bang-tail muster

rouse
◇ *anagram indicator*
04 call, fire, firk, move, rear, send, stir, wake, yerk **05** abray, amove, anger, awake, evoke, flush, get up, impel, raise, roust, set up, shake, start, steer, stire, styre, unbed, waken **06** abrade, abraid, arouse, awaken, bumper, call up, excite, incite, induce, kindle, ruffle, stir up, summon, turn on, wake up, whip up, work up **07** agitate, disturb, inflame, knock up, provoke, shake up **08** carousal, enkindle, irritate, reveille **09** galvanize, instigate, look alive, stimulate, suscitate

rousing
05 brisk, great **06** lively, moving **07** beating, violent, wakeful

08 exciting, spirited, stirring, vigorous 09 awakening, inspiring 10 incitation 11 stimulating 12 electrifying, exhilarating 13 heart-stirring 14 spirit-stirring

rout
04 beat, fuss, grub, herd, lick, pack, riot, roar, rowt 05 brawl, chase, crush, flock, snore 06 bellow, defeat, dispel, flight, grub up, hammer, rabble, thrash, turn up 07 beating, clamour, clobber, conquer, retreat, scatter, trounce, turn out 08 conquest, drubbing, stampede, vanquish 09 discomfit, hurricane, overthrow, shoot down, slaughter, subjugate, thrashing, trouncing 11 disturbance, put to flight, subjugation, walk all over

route
03 run, way 04 beat, line, path, road, send, tail, walk 05 round, trail 06 avenue, bypass, convey, course, direct 07 airline, circuit, forward, journey, passage, transit 08 delivery, despatch, dispatch, main line, sideline 09 direction, itinerary, milk round 10 flight path, navigation 11 long paddock 12 wallaby track

routine
03 act, run, rut, way, yak 04 dull, rota, wont 05 banal, chain, chore, drill, habit, heigh, ho-hum, lines, order, piece, round, spiel, usage, usual 06 boring, common, custom, groove, method, normal, patter, regime, schtik, shtick, system, wonted 07 formula, heigh-ho, humdrum, jogtrot, milk run, mundane, pattern, schtick, tedious, typical 08 day-to-day, everyday, familiar, habitual, heich-how, ordinary, practice, schedule, standard, tiresome, workaday 09 customary, hackneyed, mechanics, procedure, programme, treadmill, unvarying 10 monotonous, unoriginal 11 journey-work, performance, perfunctory, predictable 12 conventional, run-of-the-mill 13 institutional 14 bread-and-butter

routinely
07 usually 08 commonly, normally 09 regularly, typically 10 habitually 11 customarily 14 conventionally

rove
◇ *anagram indicator*
04 roam 05 drift, range, stray 06 cruise, ramble, stroll, wander 07 meander, traipse 08 stravaig 09 gallivant, wandering 11 go walkabout

rover
05 Gypsy, nomad 06 nomade, pirate, ranger, robber 07 drifter, rambler, seacock, vagrant 08 gadabout, wanderer 09 itinerant, transient, traveller 10 stravaiger

row
03 din, oar, rag 04 bank, deen, file, line, pull, rank, roll, tier, tiff 05 argue, brawl, chain, fight, noise, queue, rammy, range, rough, scold, scrap, set-to 06 assail, bicker, column, dust-up, fracas, hubbub, racket, rumpus, series, shindy, splore, string, stroke, tumult, uproar 07 bobbery, clamour, dispute, quarrel, ruction, shindig, wrangle 08 argument, conflict, rebuking, remigate, scolding, sequence, squabble 09 commotion 10 falling-out 11 altercation, arrangement, controversy, disturbance 12 disagreement 13 slanging match

• in a row
04 arew, arow 06 in turn, serial 09 on the trot 10 back to back 12 continuously, sequentially, successively 13 consecutively 15 uninterruptedly

rowan
04 sorb

rowdy
03 yob 04 loud, lout, wild 05 money, noisy, rorty, rough, tough, yahoo, yobbo 06 apache, blowsy, blowzy, keelie, unruly 07 brawler, hoodlum, lawless, riotous, ruffian, stroppy 08 hooligan, larrikin, tearaway 09 bovver boy 10 boisterous, brat packer, disorderly 12 obstreperous, unrestrained

rower
03 oar 06 stroke 07 oarsman, sculler 09 oarswoman, stroke oar

rowing

Rowing-related terms include:

03 bow, cox, rig
04 crew, easy, four, gate, keel, loom, pair, quad, rate, skeg, span, wash
05 blade, catch, coxed, drive, eight, pitch, scull, shell, stern
06 boatie, button, collar, gunnel, length, puddle, rating, rigger, skying, stroke
07 bowside, coxless, gunwale, regatta, row over, sculler
08 coxswain, paddling, rowlocks
09 ergometer, head races, outrigger, slide seat, stretcher
10 catch a crab, feathering, pivot point, strokeside
11 double scull, single scull, the Boat Race
13 getting spoons
15 jumping the slide

• rowing boat
04 four, pair 05 eight

royal
04 king, real, rial, ryal 05 grand, queen, regal 06 august, kingly, prince, regius, superb 07 queenly, stately 08 imperial, imposing, kinglike, majestic, princely, princess, splendid 09 basilical, queenlike, sovereign 10 impressive 11 magnificent, monarchical

royally
07 grandly, greatly 08 superbly 10 splendidly 11 wonderfully 12 impressively, tremendously 13 magnificently

royalty
08 residual

rub
◇ *anagram indicator*
03 dub, pat, rob, wax 04 buff, faze, fret, snag, soap, wipe 05 apply, catch, chafe, clean, curry, emery, grate, grind, hitch, knead, pinch, put on, rosin, scour, scrub, shine, smear, stone, towel 06 abrade, buff up, caress, fondle, fridge, impede, liquor, nuzzle, polish, rubber, scrape, smooth, spread, stroke, work in 07 burnish, flannel, furbish, massage, problem, rub-down, scratch, snuzzle, trouble 08 drawback, irritate, kneading, obstacle, soft-soap 09 embrocate, hindrance, triturate 10 difficulty, impediment

• rub along
04 cope 05 get by, get on 06 manage 08 get along

• rub down
03 dry 04 wash, wisp 05 clean, curry 06 smooth, sponge 07 massage 08 wash down

• rub in
06 harp on, stress 08 insist on 09 emphasize, highlight, underline 10 make much of

• rub off on
05 alter 06 affect, change 09 influence, transform 14 have an effect on

• rub out
04 do in, kill 05 erase 06 cancel, delete, efface, murder 07 bump off 09 eliminate, finish off, liquidate 10 do away with, obliterate, put to death 11 assassinate

• rub up the wrong way
03 bug, get, irk, vex 05 anger, annoy, get to, peeve 06 needle, niggle, wind up 08 irritate 11 get your goat 13 get up your nose

rubber

Rubber types and trees include:

03 ule
04 buna, cold, foam, hard, hule, pará, root
05 butyl, crêpe, hevea, India, Lagos, sorbo
06 sponge
07 ebonite, guayule, seringa
08 Funtumia, neoprene, Silastic®
09 camelback, vulcanite
10 caoutchouc, gum elastic, mangabeira
14 high-hysteresis

rubberneck
04 gape, gawk, gawp, view 05 stare, watch 06 goggle, look at 07 tourist

rubbish
◇ *anagram indicator*
03 red, rot, tat 04 blah, bosh, bull, bunk, cack, crap, dirt, gash, grot, guff, junk, kack, mush, redd, tosh 05 balls, bilge, brock, chaff, culch, dreck, dross, garbo, hokum, hooey, pants, scrap, stuff, trade, trash, tripe, truck, waste 06 bunkum, cultch, debris, drivel, litter,

piffle, raffle, refuse, rubble **07** baloney, eyewash, garbage, gubbins, hogwash, mullock, rhubarb, twaddle
08 bulldust, claptrap, cobblers, detritus, malarkey, nonsense, riff-raff, tommyrot, trashery, trumpery **09** bull's wool, gibberish, moonshine, mouthwash, poppycock, sweepings
10 balderdash, clamjamfry, codswallop, excrementa, tomfoolery
11 clanjamfray **12** clamjamphrie, gobbledegook, gobbledygook

rubbish heap
03 tip **04** coup, cowp, dump, toom
06 midden **08** laystall **09** scrapheap
13 kitchen midden

rubbishy
05 cheap, junky, petty, tatty, tripy
06 cruddy, crummy, grotty, paltry, shoddy, tawdry, tinpot, trashy, tripey
08 gimcrack, inferior, riff-raff **09** third-rate, throw-away, valueless, worthless
10 low-quality, second-rate
14 unsatisfactory

rubble
04 muck **05** ruins, waste, wreck
06 debris **07** moellon, remains, rubbish **08** hard core, wreckage
09 fragments

rubidium
02 Rb

ruby
05 agate, balas, blood **06** redden
09 starstone **12** pigeon's-blood

ruction
03 din, row **04** fuss, rout, to-do
05 brawl, noise, scrap, storm **06** fracas, racket, ruffle, rumpus, uproar **07** carry-on, dispute, protest, quarrel, rookery, trouble **09** commotion, hue and cry, kerfuffle **11** altercation, disturbance

ruddy
03 red **04** rosy **05** fresh **06** bloody, blowsy, blowzy, bright, cherry, darned, dashed, florid, rubric **07** blasted, crimson, flushed, glowing, healthy, reddish, rubious, scarlet **08** annoying, blooming, blushing, flipping, infernal, rubicund, sanguine, sunburnt
10 confounded **11** carnationed, flammulated **12** apple-cheeked, high-coloured

rude
◇ *anagram indicator*
04 blue, curt, lewd **05** basic, bawdy, crude, dirty, gross, harsh, nasty, rough, sharp, short **06** abrupt, cheeky, coarse, filthy, ribald, risqué, robust, rugged, simple, smutty, sudden, vulgar
07 abusive, bestial, boorish, brusque, ill-bred, naughty, obscene, peasant, uncivil, uncouth, violent **08** barbaric, churlish, ignorant, impolite, improper, impudent, indecent, insolent
09 barbarian, giant rude, goustrous, insulting, makeshift, offensive, primitive, salacious, startling, unrefined, unskilled, untutored, unwrought **10** heathenish, illiterate, indelicate, uncultured, uneducated, unexpected, unpleasant, unpolished
11 bad-mannered, bad-tempered, ill-mannered, impertinent, near the bone, rudimentary, uncivilized, undeveloped
12 disagreeable, discourteous
13 disrespectful, rough-and-ready
14 near the knuckle

rudely
06 curtly **07** harshly **08** abruptly, suddenly **09** abusively, brusquely
10 impolitely, impudently, insolently
12 disagreeably, unexpectedly, unpleasantly **14** discourteously
15 disrespectfully

rudeness
05 abuse **09** barbarism, Gothicism, impudence, insolence, rusticity **10** bad manners, disrespect, ill manners, incivility **11** discourtesy, grossièreté, uncouthness **12** impertinence, impoliteness **14** unpleasantness

rudimentary
03 pro- **05** basic, crude, rough
06 simple **07** initial, primary, reduced, seminal **08** inchoate **09** embryonic, embryotic, essential, imperfect, makeshift, primitive, remaining, surviving, vestigial **10** elementary, incomplete, primordial
11 abecedarian, fundamental, undeveloped **12** functionless, introductory **13** rough-and-ready
15 unsophisticated

rudiments
03 ABC **05** abcee, absey **06** basics
08 elements **10** beginnings, essentials, principles **11** foundations
12 fundamentals **15** first principles

rue
03 rew **04** pity, Ruta **05** mourn
06 bemoan, bewail, grieve, lament, regret, repent, sorrow **07** be sorry, deplore, harmala **09** herb-grace
10 repentance, thalictrum **11** be regretful, herb-of-grace **14** feel remorse for

rueful
03 sad **05** sorry **06** dismal, woeful
07 doleful, piteous, pitiful **08** contrite, grievous, mournful, penitent, pitiable
09 plaintive, regretful, repentant, sorrowful, woebegone **10** apologetic, deplorable, lugubrious, melancholy, remorseful **15** self-reproachful

ruff
03 ree **04** band, pope, slam **05** frill, reeve, rough, trump **06** fraise, ruffle, tippet **07** applaud, elation, partlet
08 applause **09** blackfish
10 excitement

ruffian
03 ned, yob **04** hoon, lout, thug
05 brute, bully, rogue, rough, rowdy, tough, yobbo **06** Apache, brutal, rascal, thuggo, toerag **07** bruiser, hoodlum, sweater, villain, violent
08 bully-boy, hooligan, larrikin, plug-ugly **09** bovver boy, bully-rook, cut-throat, desperado, lager lout, miscreant, roughneck, ruffianly, scoundrel **10** highbinder **11** trailbaston

ruffle
◇ *anagram indicator*
03 bug, irk, vex **04** fold, line, rile, ruff, tuck **05** anger, annoy, frill, pleat, rough, rouse, upset **06** bustle, crease, fringe, furrow, gather, hassle, nettle, pucker, put out, rattle, ripple, rumple, snatch, tangle, tousle, tumult, wind up
07 agitate, bluster, confuse, crinkle, crumple, falbala, flounce, fluster, flutter, perturb, quarrel, swagger, trouble, valance, wrinkle **08** brass off, dishevel, disorder, irritate, struggle, trimming **09** aggravate, agitation, annoyance, cheese off, drive nuts, encounter, pantalets **10** disarrange, discompose, drive crazy, exasperate
11 pantalettes **12** drive bananas
13 make sparks fly **14** drive up the wall

rug
03 mat, rya, tug, wig **04** felt, haul, kali, snug **05** kelim, kilim, pilch, share, throw **06** carpet, khilim, Kirman, numdah, secure, toupee, toupet
07 bergama, doormat, flokati, matting
08 bergamot, covering, underlay
09 hairpiece, prayer mat, underfelt
11 buffalo robe **13** floor-covering, Persian carpet

See also **carpet**

rugby
02 RL, RU

Rugby League teams and nicknames include:

04 Eels, Reds
05 Bears, Bulls, Kiwis, Lions, Storm
06 Eagles, Giants, Hull FC, Kumuls, Rhinos, Sharks, Tigers, Wolves
07 Blue Sox, Broncos, Cowboys, Dragons, Knights, Raiders
08 Bulldogs, Panthers, Roosters, Warriors, Wildcats
09 Kangaroos, Rabbitohs, Tomahawks
10 Lionhearts
11 Bravehearts, Leeds Rhinos, St Helens RFC
13 Bradford Bulls, London Broncos, Widnes Vikings, Wigan Warriors
15 Irish Wolfhounds, Leigh Centurions, Les Chanticleers, Salford City Reds

Rugby League-related terms include:

02 RL
03 try
04 back, feed, lock, pack, prop, punt
05 dummy, put-in, scrum
06 centre, hooker, in-goal, tackle, winger
07 dropout, forward, hand-off, knock on, offload, offside, penalty, try line
08 blood bin, drop goal, free-kick, front row, full-back, gain line, goal line, half-back, handover, open side, scissors, sidestep, stand-off, turnover
09 blind side, dummy half, field goal,

place kick, scrum-half
10 charge down, conversion, five-eighth, penalty try, up and under, zero tackle
11 forward pass, grubber kick, play-the-ball, sixth tackle, touch-in-goal
12 dead-ball line, loose forward, three-quarter
13 loose-head prop
14 acting half-back
15 twenty-metre line

Rugby players include:

03 Fox (Neil)
04 Hare (William Henry 'Dusty'), Hill (Richard), John (Barry), Lomu (Jonah), Sole (David), Tait (Alan), Wood (Keith)
05 Batty (Grant), Bevan (Brian), Botha (Naas), Ellis (William Webb), Lydon (Joe), Meads (Colin), Price (Graham), Rives (Jean-Pierre), Sella (Philippe)
06 Andrew (Rob), Blanco (Serge), Boston (Billy), Brooke (Zinzan), Calder (Finlay), Cotton (Fran), Craven (Danie), Davies (Jonathan), Gibson (Mike), Irvine (Andy), Kirwan (John)
07 Bennett (Phil), Campese (David), Carling (Will), Duckham (David), Edwards (Gareth Owen), Edwards (Shaun), Farrell (Andy), Gregory (Andy), Guscott (Jeremy), Jenkins (Neil), Laidlaw (Roy), McBride (Willie John), Meninga (Mal), O'Reilly (Tony)
08 Beaumont (Bill), Hastings (Gavin), Millward (Roger), Scotland (Ken), Slattery (Fergus), Sullivan (Jim), Williams (John Peter Rhys 'JPR'), Williams (John 'JJ'), Woodward (Sir Clive)
09 Dallaglio (Lawrence), Farr-Jones (Nick), McGeechan (Ian), Underwood (Rory), Wilkinson (Jonny)
10 Rutherford (John)
11 Fitzpatrick (Sean)
12 Starmer-Smith (Nigel)

Rugby Union teams and nicknames include:

04 Oaks, Reds
05 Lelos, Lions, Pumas, Wasps
06 Eagles
07 Canucks, Dragons
08 Brumbies, Les Bleus, Los Teros, Saracens, Waratahs
09 All Blacks, Bath Rugby, Wallabies
10 Gli Azzurri, Gloucester, Harlequins, Leeds Tykes, Sale Sharks, Springboks
11 London Irish
14 Cherry Blossoms
15 Leicester Tigers

Rugby Union-related terms include:

02 RU
03 gas, tee, try
04 back, cite, feed, hack, lock, mark, maul, pack, ping, prop, ruck
05 clear, drive, dummy, phase, put-in, scrum, touch, wheel
06 centre, hooker, in-goal, jumper, sevens, tackle, uglies, winger
07 back row, binding, box kick, dropout, flanker, fly hack, fly-half, forward, hand-off, knock on, lifting, line-out, offload, offside, recycle, restart, try line
08 blood bin, crossing, drop goal, free-kick, front row, full back, gain line, goal line, half-back, miss move, open side, scissors, scrum cap, set piece, sidestep, standoff, turnover
09 back three, blind side, breakdown, crash ball, front five, grand slam, place kick, scrum-half, second row, tap tackle, third half, tight five, touchline, twenty-two
10 charge down, conversion, pack leader, penalty try, tap penalty, touch judge, up and under
11 cover tackle, forward pass, grubber kick, number eight, outside half, pushover try, ten-man rugby, triple crown, up the jumper, wing forward
12 dead-ball line, inside centre, loose forward, three-quarter
13 dummy scissors, loose-head prop, outside centre, tight-head prop
14 against the head
15 truck and trailer

rugged

04 firm, rude, wild **05** bumpy, burly, hardy, rocky, rough, stark, stony, tough **06** craggy, jagged, knaggy, knotty, robust, shaggy, sinewy, stormy, strong, sturdy, uneven **07** gnarled, uncouth **08** furrowed, muscular, resolute, stalwart, vigorous **09** iron-bound, irregular, tenacious, well-built **10** determined, unwavering **11** unflinching **13** weather-beaten

ruggedly

07 rockily, roughly, starkly, toughly **08** strongly, unevenly **10** muscularly, vigorously **11** irregularly

ruin

◇ *anagram indicator*
03 mar **04** cook, dish, do in, doom, fall, harm, heap, Hell, loss, raze, sink **05** botch, break, chaos, crash, crush, decay, do for, folly, fordo, havoc, smash, spoil, whelm, wreck **06** banjax, damage, debris, defeat, injure, jigger, mess up, penury, perish, ravage, relics, rubble, traces, unmake **07** carcase, carcass, cripple, destroy, failure, remains, screw up, scupper, scuttle, shatter, subvert, undoing **08** bankrupt, collapse, demolish, detritus, disaster, down-come, downfall, lay waste, remnants, shambles, vestiges, wreckage **09** breakdown, devastate, disrepair, fragments, indigence, overthrow, overwhelm, perdition, ruination, seduction, shipwreck **10** bankruptcy, demolition, impoverish, insolvency, subversion, wreak havoc **11** destruction, devastation **12** do violence to, make bankrupt **13** make insolvent **14** bouleversement, disintegration

• **in ruins**
04 sunk **06** ruined **07** damaged, ruinate, wrecked **08** decrepit **09** destroyed **10** broken-down, devastated, ramshackle, tumbledown **11** dilapidated **12** falling apart

ruination

04 fall **05** decay, havoc **06** damage, defeat **07** failure, undoing **08** collapse, downfall, wreckage **09** breakdown, disrepair, overthrow **11** destruction, devastation **14** disintegration

ruined

◇ *anagram indicator*
See **bankrupt**

ruinous

05 waste **06** ruined **07** damaged, decayed, in ruins, wrecked **08** decrepit, tottered **09** crippling, destroyed, excessive, shattered **10** broken-down, calamitous, devastated, disastrous, exorbitant, immoderate, ramshackle **11** cataclysmic, devastating, dilapidated **12** catastrophic, extortionate, unreasonable

ruinously

11 excessively **12** exorbitantly, immoderately, unreasonably **14** extortionately

rule

01 r **03** law, raj **04** dash, find, form, lead, line, norm, rain, ring, sway, wont **05** axiom, canon, guide, habit, judge, maxim, norma, order, power, raine, reign, sutra, tenet, truth **06** custom, decide, decree, direct, govern, manage, method, regime, rubric, ruling, settle, squier, squire, truism **07** command, conduct, control, dictate, formula, lay down, mastery, ordinar, plummet, precept, prevail, resolve, routine, royalty, statute **08** dominate, dominion, kingship, ordinary, practice, protocol, regulate, standard, thearchy **09** authority, criterion, determine, direction, establish, guideline, gynocracy, hagiarchy, influence, mobocracy, officiate, ordinance, prescript, principle, procedure, pronounce, queenship, supremacy **10** adjudicate, administer, convention, corrective, government, leadership, mastership, ochlocracy, prevalence, regulation **11** be in control, commandment, gubernation, instruction, preside over, restriction, sovereignty, stratocracy, tridominium **12** call the shots, jurisdiction **14** administration

• **as a rule**
06 mainly **07** usually **08** normally **09** generally, in general, in the main **10** by and large, on the whole, ordinarily **14** for the most part

• **collection of rules**
03 pie, pye **04** code

• rule out
03 ban **06** forbid, reject **07** dismiss, exclude, prevent **08** disallow, preclude, prohibit **09** eliminate

ruler

Rulers include:

03 aga, mir, oba
04 amir, czar, duce, emir, head, jarl, kaid, khan, king, ksar, lord, meer, naik, raja, rana, rani, ratu, shah, tsar, tzar
05 begum, mpret, nawab, nizam, queen, rajah, ratoo
06 atabeg, atabek, caesar, caliph, consul, Führer, gerent, kaiser, leader, mikado, prince, regent, satrap, sheikh, shogun, sultan
07 czarina, emperor, empress, monarch, pharaoh, sultana, toparch, tsarina, viceroy
08 governor, maharani, overlord, padishah, princess, suzerain
09 commander, maharajah, potentate, president, sovereign
10 controller
11 gouvernante, head of state
15 governor-general

See also **emperor**; **empress**; **king**; **monarch**; **president**; **prime minister**; **queen**

ruling
04 main **05** chief **06** decree **07** finding, leading, supreme, verdict **08** decision, dominant, in charge, judgment, reigning **09** governing, in control, judgement, principal, sovereign **10** commanding, resolution **11** controlling, on the throne, predominant **12** adjudication **13** pronouncement **15** most influential

rum
◇ *anagram indicator*
03 odd **04** good **05** droll, funny, queer, tafia, weird **06** taffia **07** Bacardi®, bizarre, cachaça, curious, strange, suspect, unusual **08** abnormal, demerara, freakish, peculiar, singular **10** suspicious **13** funny-peculiar

rumble
04 boom, roar, roll **05** grasp, groan **06** lumber, mutter **07** grumble, quarrel, thunder **11** disturbance, reverberate **13** reverberation

rumbustious
04 loud, wild **05** noisy, rough, rowdy **06** robust, unruly, wilful **07** wayward **08** roisting **09** clamorous, exuberant **10** boisterous, disorderly, refractory, roisterous, uproarious **12** obstreperous, unmanageable

ruminant
10 meditative

Ruminants include:

02 ox
03 cow
04 goat
05 camel, sheep
06 musk ox
07 giraffe
08 antelope, cavicorn
09 pronghorn

See also **cattle**; **antelope**

Stomachs of ruminants include:

05 bible, rumen
06 bonnet, fardel, paunch
09 king's-hood, manyplies, rennet-bag, reticulum

ruminate
04 muse **05** brood, think **06** ponder **07** reflect **08** chew over, cogitate, consider, meditate, mull over **10** chew the cud, deliberate **11** contemplate

rummage
03 tat **04** fish, hunt, junk, root, stir **05** delve, rifle, touse, touze, towse, towze, wroot **06** ferret, forage, jumble, powter, search **07** examine, explore, fossick, ransack **08** overhaul, turn over, upheaval **09** bric-à-brac, commotion **10** poke around, root around **11** odds and ends **13** search through

rumour
03 cry, say **04** buzz, fame, goss, hint, kite, news, talk, tell, word **05** bruit, noise, on-dit, say-so, sough, story, voice **06** breeze, canard, furphy, gossip, murmur, outcry, renown, report, repute, speech **07** clamour, hearsay, publish, scandal, tidings, whisper **08** put about **09** circulate, grapevine **10** bruit about **11** bruit abroad, fama clamosa, information, noise abroad, scuttlebutt, speculation, underbreath **12** tittle-tattle **13** bush telegraph

rump
03 ass, bum, can **04** butt, coit, dock, duff, prat, rear, seat, tail, tush **05** booty, croup, fanny, nache, natch, podex, quoit, stern, trace **06** behind, bottom, breech, croupe, haunch, heinie **07** keister, remains, remnant, residue, vestige **08** backside, buttocks, derrière, haunches **09** fundament, leftovers, posterior, remainder, uropygium **12** hindquarters

rumple
04 fold **05** crush, touse, touze, towse, towze **06** crease, pucker, ruffle, tousle, tumble **07** crinkle, crumple, derange, scrunch, wrinkle **08** dishevel, disorder

rumpus
03 row **04** fuss, rout **05** brawl, noise **06** fracas, furore, ruckus, shindy, tumult, uproar **07** bagarre, rhubarb, ruction **08** brouhaha **09** commotion, confusion, kerfuffle, shemozzle, shimozzle **10** disruption, schemozzle, shlemozzle **11** disturbance

run
◇ *anagram indicator*
01 r **02** do, go **03** cut, hit, jet, jog, own, pen, ply, ren, rin, rip, set, sty, use, way **04** bolt, call, coop, dart, dash, drip, emit, flee, flow, fold, fuse, gash, goal, go on, gush, hare, have, head, hole, hunt, keep, kind, last, lauf, lead, leak, line, lope, mark, melt, move, need, pass, pour, race, ride, road, roll, romp, rush, show, slip, slit, snag, sort, spew, spin, take, tear, tend, trip, trot, type, work, yard **05** bleed, brush, carry, chain, chase, class, corso, cross, cycle, drive, enter, glide, hurry, incur, issue, jaunt, point, pound, print, range, reach, round, route, scoot, score, shoal, slash, slide, speed, spell, split, spurt, stand, track, trill **06** become, career, chance, charge, convey, course, curdle, demand, direct, elapse, extend, follow, fulfil, gallop, hasten, ladder, manage, outing, period, pierce, schuss, scurry, series, spread, sprint, stream, string, thrust, travel **07** average, be valid, carry on, cascade, clamour, compete, conduct, contend, control, execute, feature, include, journey, operate, oversee, paddock, passage, perform, possess, proceed, promote, publish, revolve, roulade, run away, scamper, scarper, scutter, scuttle, shuttle, smuggle, stretch, trickle, variety **08** be played, be staged, carry out, category, continue, distance, function, maintain, organize, overflow, pressure, progress, regulate, sequence, step on it, traverse **09** be mounted, broadcast, challenge, coagulate, discharge, enclosure, excursion, free use of, give a lift, give a ride, implement, supervise, transport, undertake **10** administer, be in effect, be produced, co-ordinate, flight path, prevalence, succession, take part in **11** be performed, be presented, communicate, opportunity, superintend **12** be in charge of **13** be in control of, be in operation **15** travel regularly

• in the long run
06 at last **08** in the end **10** eventually, ultimately

• on the run
04 free **07** at large, escaped, pursued **08** on the lam **09** at liberty **10** on the loose, unconfined **11** running away **14** trying to escape

• run across
04 meet **07** run into **08** bump into **09** encounter **10** chance upon, come across **12** meet by chance

• run after
04 tail **05** chase **06** follow, pursue

• run along
04 scat **05** be off, leave **06** go away **07** buzz off, scarper **08** clear off, off you go **09** on your way **10** off with you **11** away with you

• run along the ground
04 taxi

• run away
03 cut **04** bolt, bunk, flee, lift, nick **05** avoid, dodge, elope, evade, filch, leave, pinch, scapa, steal **06** beat it, decamp, desert, escape, ignore, pocket, run off, scarpa **07** abscond, make off, neglect, nick off, purloin, scarper, vamoose **08** cheese it, clear off, overlook **09** coast home,

disregard, do a runner, skedaddle, win easily **10** brush aside **11** appropriate, make off with, walk off with **12** win hands down **13** make a run for it **14** shut your eyes to, take no notice of, turn your back on

• **run down**

03 cut, hit, pan **04** bust, drop, slag, slam, tire, trim **05** knock, slate, weary **06** attack, defame, pooped, reduce, strike, weaken **07** curtail, exhaust, rubbish, run over, slag off, whacked **08** belittle, decrease, denounce, lose time **09** criticize, cut back on, denigrate, disparage, knackered, knock down, knock over **12** pull to pieces, tear to pieces

• **run for it**

03 fly **04** bolt, flee **05** scram **06** escape **07** do a bunk, make off, retreat, scarper, vamoose **09** skedaddle **11** give leg bail

• **run in**

03 nab **04** bust, jail, lift, nail, nick **05** pinch **06** arrest, collar, pick up **09** apprehend

• **run into**

03 hit, ram **04** face, meet **05** crash, equal **06** come to, strike **07** add up to **08** amount to, bump into **09** encounter, run across **10** chance upon, come across, experience **11** collide with **12** meet by chance **13** come up against

• **run off**

04 bolt, copy **05** elope, print, Xerox® **06** decamp, escape, repeat **07** abscond, make off, produce, recount, run away, scarper **09** duplicate, photocopy, Photostat®, skedaddle

• **run off with**

04 lift, nick **05** filch, pinch, steal **06** pocket **07** purloin **08** take away **09** elope with **11** appropriate, make off with, run away with, walk off with **12** make away with

• **run on**

04 go on, last **05** reach **06** extend **07** carry on **08** continue

• **run out**

02 ro **03** end **04** fail, leak **05** cease, close, dry up **06** elapse, expire, finish **07** exhaust, give out **08** be used up **09** terminate **10** be finished **11** be exhausted

• **run out on**

04 dump, jilt **05** chuck, ditch, leave **06** desert, maroon, strand **07** abandon, forsake **09** walk out on **15** leave in the lurch

• **run over**

03 hit **04** flow, heat **05** recap **06** go over, repeat, review, strike, survey **07** run down **08** overflow, practise, rehearse **09** knock down, overthrow, reiterate **10** run through **12** recapitulate

• **run through**

04 read **05** spend, waste **06** review, survey **07** examine, exhaust, run over **08** practise, rehearse, squander **09** dissipate, go through **11** fritter away, read through

• **run to**

05 equal, total **06** afford, come to **07** add up to **08** amount to **12** have enough of

• **run together**

03 mix **04** fuse, join **05** blend, merge, unite **06** concur, mingle **07** combine **08** coalesce **09** commingle **10** amalgamate

runaway

04 wild **05** fugie, loose **06** flight, truant **07** escaped, escapee, escaper, refugee **08** deserter, fugitive **09** absconder **11** loup-the-dyke **12** out of control, uncontrolled

run-down

03 cut, ill **04** drop, weak **05** dingy, peaky, recap, seedy, tired, weary **06** grotty, résumé, review, shabby, sketch, unwell **07** cutback, decline, drained, outline, summary, worn-out **08** analysis, briefing, decrease, decrepit, fatigued, synopsis **09** enervated, exhausted, neglected, reduction, unhealthy **10** broken-down, ramshackle, run-through, tumble-down, uncared-for **11** curtailment, debilitated, dilapidated

rune

03 ash, wen, wyn **04** aesc, wynn

run-in

05 brush, fight, set-to **06** dust-up, tussle **07** dispute, quarrel, wrangle **08** approach, argument, skirmish **11** altercation, contretemps **13** confrontation

runnel *see* **brook**

runner

03 ski **04** scud, skid, slip, stem, tout **05** agent, blade, miler, racer, shoot, slide, slipe, sprig **06** bearer, jogger, sprout, stolon **07** athlete, courier, courser, harrier, slipper, tendril **08** fugitive, offshoot, smuggler, sprinter **09** flagellum, lampadist, messenger, racehorse, sarmentum **10** competitor **11** participant **13** dispatch rider

• **do a runner**

02 go **04** exit, quit **05** scoot **06** decamp, depart, go away, hook it, set out **07** do a bunk, pull out, push off, take off, vamoose **08** clear off, shove off, up sticks **09** disappear, push along **10** make tracks **13** sling your hook, take your leave **15** take French leave

• **runners**

05 field

running

◇ *anagram indicator*

04 easy **05** hasty **06** charge, in a row, moving, racing **07** conduct, contest, control, current, cursive, flowing, jogging, ongoing, rushing, working **08** constant, unbroken **09** candidacy, ceaseless, direction, incessant, itinerant, on the trot, operation, perpetual, shortlist, sprinting, stampede, unceasing **10** contention, continuous, leadership, management, regulation, successive **11** competition, consecutive, controlling, discharging, functioning, performance, supervision **12** co-ordination, in succession, organization **13** uninterrupted **14** administration **15** superintendency

runny

◇ *anagram indicator*

05 fluid **06** liquid, melted, molten, watery **07** diluted, flowing **09** liquefied

run-of-the-mill

02 OK **04** fair, so-so **06** common, normal **07** average **08** everyday, mediocre, middling, ordinary **09** tolerable **11** bog standard, not up to much **12** unimpressive, unremarkable **13** no great shakes, unexceptional **14** common-or-garden **15** undistinguished

rupture

◇ *anagram indicator*

04 rend, rent, rift, tear **05** break, burst, crack, sever, split **06** breach, bust-up, cut off, divide, hernia, rhexis, schism **07** quarrel **08** breaking, bursting, division, fracture, puncture, scissure, separate **09** amniotomy **10** falling-out, separation **12** disagreement, estrangement

rural

04 hick **06** forane, rustic, sylvan, upland **07** bucolic, country, peasant, predial **08** agrarian, agrestic, mofussil, pastoral, praedial **09** bucolical, uplandish **11** countryside **12** agricultural **13** cracker-barrel

ruse

04 hoax, plan, plot, ploy, sham, wile **05** blind, dodge, stall, trick **06** device, scheme, tactic **08** artifice **09** deception, imposture, manoeuvre, stratagem **10** subterfuge

rush

03 fly, ren, rin, rip, run **04** belt, bolt, bomb, call, dart, dash, fall, flaw, flow, gush, lash, leap, need, pelt, push, race, raid, rash, star, stir, tear **05** fling, flood, haste, hurry, onset, press, run at, scour, shoot, spate, speat, speed, starr, storm, surge **06** attack, bustle, career, charge, demand, flurry, gallop, hasten, random, sprint, streak, stream, strike **07** assault, cariere, clamour, defraud, quicken, speed up, tantivy, urgency, viretot **08** activity, despatch, dispatch, pressure, rapidity, scramble, stampede **09** commotion, make haste, onslaught, star grass, swiftness **10** accelerate, excitement, get a move on, hurly-burly, overcharge, shave-grass, spring tide, starr grass **11** run like hell **13** precipitation **14** hive of activity **15** hustle and bustle

rushed

04 busy, fast **05** brisk, hasty, quick, rapid, swift **06** hectic, prompt, urgent

07 cursory, hurried 08 careless
09 emergency 11 expeditious, superficial

Russia
03 RUS

Russian cities and notable towns include:

04 Omsk
05 Kazan
06 Moscow, Moskva, Samara
07 Irkutsk
08 Novgorod
09 Archangel, Volgograd
11 Archangelsk, Chelyabinsk, Novosibirsk, Rostov-on-Don, Vladivostok
12 Ekaterinburg, St Petersburg
13 Yekaterinburg
15 Nizhniy Novgorod

Russian
04 czar, tsar, tzar 05 Lenin, Putin, Raisa
07 czarina, Trotsky, tsarina, Yeltsin
08 czaritsa, Rasputin, tsaritsa
09 Gorbachev

Russians include:

05 Khant
06 Buryat, Ostyak
07 Bashkir, Cossack
08 Siberian
09 Muscovite
10 Volga Tatar

rust
03 rot 05 decay, dross, stain, uredo
07 corrode, decline, ferrugo, oxidize, tarnish 09 corrosion, oxidation, verdigris 11 deteriorate

rust-coloured
03 red 05 brown, rusty, sandy, tawny
06 auburn, copper, ginger, russet, titian
07 coppery, gingery, reddish
08 chestnut 10 rubiginose, rubiginous
11 ferruginous 12 ferrugineous, reddish-brown

rustic
◇ *anagram indicator*
03 hob, oaf 04 boor, carl, clod, hick, hind, rude 05 bacon, borel, churl, clown, crude, Hodge, plain, rough, rural, swain, yokel 06 borrel, clumsy, coarse, forest, hodden, oafish, russet, simple, sylvan 07 artless, awkward, boorish, borrell, bucolic, bumpkin, Corydon, country, culchie, hayseed, peasant, uncouth, woollen
08 backveld, clownish, homespun, pastoral, Strephon 09 bucolical, chawbacon, graceless, hillbilly, Hobbinoll, ingenuous, maladroit, unrefined, uplandish 10 bogtrotter, clodhopper, countryman, indelicate, provincial, uncultured 11 clodhopping, countrified, countryside
12 countrywoman 13 country cousin, cracker-barrel 15 unsophisticated

rustle
◇ *anagram indicator*
04 raid, sigh 05 steal, swish 06 bustle, fissle, hustle, whoosh 07 crackle, whisper 08 crepitus, rustling, susurrus
09 crinkling, susurrate 10 whispering
11 crepitation, susurration

• rustle up
04 make 07 scare up 10 get quickly
11 get together, put together
14 prepare quickly, provide quickly

rusty
03 red 04 dull, poor, weak 05 brown, dated, rough, sandy, stale, stiff, tawny
06 auburn, copper, ginger, russet, rusted, titian 07 coppery, gingery, raucous, reddish 08 chestnut, corroded, creaking, impaired, outmoded, oxidized, time-worn
09 deficient, obstinate, tarnished
10 aeruginous, antiquated, rubiginose, rubiginous 11 discoloured, ferruginous, rust-covered, unpractised
12 ferrugineous, old-fashioned, reddish-brown, rust-coloured 13 out of practice

rut
05 ditch, gouge, grind, habit, track
06 furrow, groove, gutter, system, trough 07 channel, humdrum, pattern, pothole, routine 09 treadmill, wheelmark 10 daily grind, wheel track
11 indentation 12 same old place, same old round

ruthenium
02 Ru

rutherfordium
02 Rf

ruthless
04 fell, grim, hard 05 cruel, harsh, stern
06 brutal, fierce, savage, severe
07 callous, inhuman, vicious
08 felonous, pitiless 09 barbarous, cut-throat, dog-eat-dog, Draconian, ferocious, heartless, merciless, unfeeling, unsparing 10 hard-bitten, implacable, inexorable, relentless, unmerciful 11 hard-hearted, remorseless, third-degree, unforgiving, unrelenting

ruthlessly
06 grimly 07 cruelly, harshly
08 brutally, fiercely, savagely, severely
09 callously 10 inexorably, pitilessly
11 mercilessly, unfeelingly
12 unmercifully 13 hard-heartedly, remorselessly

Rwanda
03 RWA

S

S
02 es **03** ess **06** sierra

• S-shape
04 ogee **08** swan neck

Sabbath
01 S **03** Sat, Sun **06** Sunday **07** Shabbat **08** Saturday

sable
03 jet **04** dark, inky **05** black, dusky, ebony, raven **06** darken, pitchy, sombre **08** midnight, zibeline **09** coal-black, pitch-dark, zibelline **10** pitch-black

sabotage
◇ *anagram indicator*
03 mar **04** ruin **05** spoil, wreck **06** damage, impair, ratten, thwart, weaken **07** cripple, destroy, disable, disrupt, scupper **08** spoiling, wrecking **09** crippling, disabling, rattening, undermine, vandalism, vandalize, weakening **10** disruption, impairment **11** destruction **12** incapacitate

sac
03 bag, pod **04** cyst **05** bursa, pouch, theca **06** ink-bag, pocket, vesica **07** bladder, capsule, saccule, vesicle **08** aerostat, cisterna, follicle, tympanum, vesicula **09** lithocyst, spore case **10** air-bladder, nematocyst, sporangium, vitellicle **11** gall bladder, pericardium **12** diverticulum

saccharine
05 gushy, mushy, soppy, sweet **06** sickly, sloppy, sugary, syrupy **07** cloying, dulcite, dulcose, honeyed, maudlin, mawkish **08** dulcitol **09** oversweet, schmaltzy **10** nauseating **11** sentimental, sickly-sweet

sachet
03 bag **04** pack **06** packet **07** musk-bag, package **08** envelope, musk-ball, scent bag, wrapping **09** container **12** bouquet garni

sack
◇ *anagram indicator*
◇ *deletion indicator*
03 axe, bag, bed, can, mat, rob **04** fire, loot, muid, pack, raid, rape, raze, ruin **05** cards, gunny, level, pouch, rifle, spoil, strip, waste **06** budget, firing, lay off, maraud, notice, papers, pocket, rapine, ravage, razing, remove, the axe **07** boot out, despoil, destroy, dismiss, dust bag, jotters, looting, pillage, plunder, sacking, satchel, the boot, the chop, the push **08** demolish, earth-bag, lay waste, the elbow **09** depredate, desecrate, devastate, discharge, dismissal, hop-pocket, levelling, marauding, select out **10** give notice, plundering, the heave-ho **11** depredation, desecration, destruction, devastation, send packing **12** despoliation **13** make redundant **14** marching orders

sacrament
04 rite **05** order **06** ritual **07** mystery, nagmaal, penance **08** ceremony, practice **09** communion, Eucharist, ordinance **10** holy orders, observance **11** institution **13** Holy Communion **14** extreme unction

sacred
04 holy **05** godly **06** divine, secure **07** blessed, devoted, revered, sainted, saintly **08** accursed, defended, hallowed, heavenly, priestly **09** dedicated, protected, religious, respected, spiritual, venerable **10** devotional, inviolable, sacrosanct, sanctified **11** consecrated, impregnable, untouchable **14** ecclesiastical

sacredness
08 divinity, holiness, sanctity **09** godliness, solemnity **11** saintliness **13** inviolability, sacrosanctity **15** invulnerability

sacrifice
◇ *deletion indicator*
04 loss **05** forgo, let go, offer **06** forego, gambit, give up, victim **07** abandon, forfeit, offer up, sacrify **08** giving-up, hecatomb, immolate, lustrate, oblation, offering, renounce **09** holocaust, martyrize, molochize, sacrifide, slaughter, surrender **10** immolation, juggernaut, lustration, relinquish **11** abandonment, destruction, sin-offering, taurobolium **12** propitiation, renunciation **13** acceptilation, burnt-offering, heave-offering, heave-shoulder, suovetaurilia **14** blood-sacrifice

sacrificial
06 votive **07** atoning **08** oblatory, piacular **09** expiatory **10** reparative **12** propitiatory

sacrilege
06 heresy **07** impiety, mockery, outrage **09** blasphemy, profanity, violation **10** disrespect, irreligion **11** desecration, irreverence, profanation

sacrilegious
06 unholy **07** godless, impious, profane, ungodly **09** heretical **10** irreverent **11** blasphemous, desecrating, irreligious, profanatory **13** disrespectful

sacrosanct
06 sacred, secure **08** hallowed **09** protected, respected **10** inviolable **11** impregnable, untouchable

sad
◇ *anagram indicator*
02 wo **03** low, woe **04** blue, down, dull, glum **05** dowie, dusky, fed up, grave, heavy, mesto, sated, sober, sorry, staid, stiff, upset **06** dismal, doughy, gloomy, sedate, tragic **07** doleful, earnest, joyless, painful, pitiful, serious, tearful, unhappy, wistful **08** constant, dejected, downcast, grievous, lovesick, mournful, pathetic, pitiable, poignant, shameful, subtrist, touching, tragical, wretched **09** depressed, heart-sore, long-faced, miserable, sorrowful, sportless, steadfast, upsetting, woebegone **10** calamitous, deplorable, depressing, despondent, disastrous, distressed, lamentable, melancholy, rock bottom **11** crestfallen, disgraceful, distressing, downhearted, low-spirited, regrettable, unfortunate **12** at rock bottom, disconsolate, heart-rending, heavy-hearted, in low spirits **13** grief-stricken, heartbreaking **14** down in the dumps

Sadat
05 Anwar

sadden
05 upset **06** deject, dismay, grieve **07** attrist, depress **08** cast down, contrist, dispirit, distress **09** bring down **10** discourage, dishearten **14** break your heart, drive to despair, get someone down

saddle
03 col, pad, tax **04** land, load, seat, sell **05** panel, pilch, selle **06** burden, charge, impose, lumber **07** kajawah, pigskin, pillion **08** encumber

sadism
05 spite **07** cruelty **08** savagery **09** barbarity, brutality **10** bestiality, inhumanity **11** callousness, malevolence, viciousness **12** ruthlessness **13** heartlessness, sado-masochism, schadenfreude, unnaturalness

sadist
05 brute **06** abuser, savage, terror **07** monster **08** molester, torturer **09** barbarian

sadistic
05 cruel **06** brutal, savage **07** bestial, inhuman, vicious **08** pitiless **09** barbarous, merciless, perverted, unnatural

sadly
◇ *anagram indicator*
04 alas **08** dismally, gloomily, sad to say **09** miserably, tearfully, unhappily, unluckily, weepingly, worse luck **10** dejectedly **11** regrettably, sad to relate, sorrowfully **12** despondently **13** unfortunately **14** heavy heartedly

sadness
03 woe **04** pain **05** grief **06** dismay, misery, pathos, regret, sorrow **07** tragedy, waeness **08** distress, glumness **09** bleakness, dejection, heartache, poignancy **10** depression, desolation, dismalness, gloominess, low spirits, melancholy, misfortune, sombreness **11** despondency, dolefulness, joylessness, tearfulness, unhappiness, Weltschmerz **12** mournfulness, wretchedness **13** cheerlessness, contristation, sorrowfulness **14** lugubriousness

safe
04 fine, good, hunk, sure **05** ambry, awmry, chest, peter, sound, timid, tried, vault **06** almery, aumbry, awmrie, coffer, condom, honest, immune, intact, proven, secure, tested, unhurt **07** cash box, certain, guarded, keister, prudent, upright **08** all right, cautious, defended, harmless, non-toxic, reliable, unharmed **09** innocuous, protected, sheltered, strongbox, undamaged, uninjured, unscathed **10** dependable, deposit box, depository, home and dry, honourable, repository **11** circumspect, impregnable, in good hands, out of danger, responsible, trustworthy **12** conservative, invulnerable, non-poisonous, safe and sound, safe as houses, unassailable **13** out of harm's way, unadventurous, with whole skin **14** copper-bottomed, uncontaminated, unenterprising

safe-conduct
04 jark, pass **06** convoy, permit **07** licence, warrant **08** passport **09** safeguard **13** authorization, laissez-passer

safeguard
05 cover, guard **06** defend, screen, secure, shield, surety **07** defence, protect, shelter **08** preserve, security **09** assurance, guarantee, insurance, look after, palladium **10** precaution, preventive, protection, take care of **11** safe-conduct **12** preservative, preventative

safekeeping
04 care, ward **05** trust **06** charge **07** custody, keeping **08** wardship **10** protection **11** supervision **12** guardianship, surveillance

safely
06 surely **08** securely **11** impregnably, out of danger, without harm, without risk **13** out of harm's way, without injury

safety
05 cover **06** refuge **07** shelter, welfare **08** fail-safe, immunity, safeness, security **09** safeguard, sanctuary, soundness **10** preventive, protection, protective **11** reliability **12** harmlessness, preventative **13** dependability, precautionary **14** impregnability **15** trustworthiness

sag
03 bag, dip, low **04** bend, drop, fail, fall, flag, flop, give, hang, sink, slip, swag, wilt **05** droop, slide, slump **06** falter, weaken **07** decline, spinach, subside **08** downturn, low point **09** dwindling, reduction **10** depression **11** hang loosely

saga
04 Edda, epic, epos, tale, yarn **05** story **06** epopee **07** history, romance **08** epopoeia **09** adventure, chronicle, narrative, soap opera **11** roman fleuve

sagacious
03 fly **04** able, sage, wary, wily, wise **05** acute, canny, quick, sharp, smart **06** astute, shrewd **07** knowing, prudent, sapient **09** judicious, wide-awake **10** discerning, far-sighted, insightful, long-headed, perceptive, percipient **11** intelligent, long-sighted, penetrating **13** perspicacious

sagacity
05 sense **06** acumen, wisdom **07** insight **08** judgment, prudence, sapience, wariness, wiliness **09** acuteness, canniness, foresight, judgement, sharpness **10** astuteness, shrewdness **11** discernment, knowingness, penetration, percipience **12** perspicacity **13** judiciousness, understanding

sage
04 guru, wise **05** canny, clary, elder, hakam, orval, rishi **06** astute, expert, master, Nestor, oracle, pundit, salvia, saulge, savant, tohunga **07** knowing, learned, mahatma, politic, prudent, sapient, Solomon, teacher, wise man **08** sensible, wiseacre **09** authority, judicious, maharishi, sagacious, wise woman **10** discerning, wise person **11** intelligent, philosopher **13** knowledgeable, perspicacious

The Seven Sages:

04 Bias (of Priene in Caria)
05 Solon (of Athens)
06 Chilon (of Sparta), Thales (of Miletus)
08 Pittacus (of Mitylene)
09 Cleobulus (tyrant of Lindus in Rhodes), Periander (tyrant of Corinth)

sagely
04 ably **06** wisely **07** acutely, quickly, sharply **08** astutely, shrewdly **09** knowingly, prudently **11** judiciously **12** discerningly, perceptively **13** intelligently **15** perspicaciously

saggy
03 lax **04** limp, weak **05** loose, slack **06** droopy, feeble, floppy **07** falling, sagging **08** drooping, dropping

said
◇ *homophone indicator*
03 quo', sed **04** quod **05** quoth

sail
03 fan, fly, ply, rag, van **04** boat, scud, ship, skim, soar, Vela, waft, wing **05** coast, float, glide, pilot, plane, steer, sweep, yacht **06** cruise, embark, put off, voyage **07** captain, go by sea, sea wing, set sail, skipper **08** navigate, put to sea **09** leave port **11** travel by sea, weigh anchor

Sails include:

03 jib, lug, rig, sky, top, try
04 fore, gaff, head, kite, main, moon, stay, stun
05 drift, genoa, royal, smoke, sprit, storm
06 bonnet, canvas, course, jigger, lateen, mizzen, square, stuns'l
07 foretop, gaff-top, jury rig, maintop, spanker, spencer
08 forestay, gennaker, storm try, studding
09 crossjack, foreroyal, moonraker, spinnaker, stargazer
10 Bermuda rig, fore-and-aft, main course, skyscraper, topgallant
13 fore-and-aft rig
14 fore-topgallant

• **part of a sail**
04 bunt, luff, nock, reef **05** belly **06** bonnet

• **sail into**
05 shoal **06** attack, let fly, turn on **07** assault, lay into **08** set about, tear into

• **sail through**
10 pass easily **11** romp through **15** succeed in easily

sailing
07 boating **08** yachting

Sailing-related terms include:

04 beat, gybe, helm, jibe, port
05 abaft, fetch, lay up
06 astern, course, leeway, upwind, yawing
07 backing, bearing, beating, heeling, lee helm, running, tacking
08 downwind, port tack, reaching, under way, windward
09 alongside, laying off, letting go, starboard
10 broad reach, casting off, close

reach, going about, ready about!
11 close-hauled, coming about, goose-winged, steerage way
12 sail trimming, spilling wind
13 across the wind, hard on the wind, starboard tack
15 fixing a position, stepping the mast, taking soundings

sailor

Sailor types include:

02 AB, OS, PO
03 cox, gob, mid, tar
04 hand, jack, mate, salt, tarp, Wren
05 bosun, janty, limey, matlo, middy, pilot, rower
06 bargee, hearty, jaunty, lascar, marine, master, matlow, pirate, purser, rating, sea boy, seadog, seaman, swabby, topman, Triton
07 boatman, captain, crewman, Jack tar, jauntie, mariner, matelot, oarsman, old salt, sculler, shipman, skipper, waister
08 Argonaut, cabin boy, coxswain, deck hand, helmsman, leadsman, seafarer, shipmate, water dog, water rat
09 boatswain, buccaneer, fisherman, galiongee, greenhand, navigator, sailor-man, sea lawyer, shellback, steersman, tarpaulin, yachtsman
10 able rating, able seaman, bluejacket, liberty-man, midshipman, tarpauling
11 foremastman, leatherneck, tarry-breeks, yachtswoman
12 able seawoman
13 canvas-climber

Sailors include:

04 **Ahab** (Captain), **Byng** (George), **Byng** (John), **Cook** (James), **Diaz** (Bartolomeu), **Gama** (Vasco da), **Hood** (Samuel, Viscount), **Howe** (Richard, Earl), **Kidd** (William), **Ross** (Horatio), **Ross** (Sir James Clark), **Ross** (Sir John), **Spee** (Count Maximilian von)
05 **Adams** (Will), **Blake** (Robert), **Bligh** (William), **Cabot** (John), **Cabot** (Sebastian), **Doria** (Andrea), **Drake** (Sir Francis), **Hawke** (Edward, Lord), **Henry** (the Navigator), **Jones** (Paul), **Peary** (Robert Edwin), **Tromp** (Maarten)
06 **Baffin** (William), **Beatty** (David, Earl), **Benbow** (John), **Bering** (Vitus), **Dönitz** (Karl), **Fisher** (John, Lord), **Hudson** (Henry), **Nelson** (Horatio, Viscount), **Nimitz** (Chester), **Ruyter** (Michiel Adriaanzoon de), **Tasman** (Abel Janszoon), **Vernon** (Edward)
07 **Barentz** (William), **Decatur** (Stephen), **Fitzroy** (Robert), **Hawkins** (Sir John), **Hawkyns** (Sir John), **Kolchak** (Alexander), **Lord Jim**, **Marryat** (Captain Frederick), **Pytheas**, **Raleigh** (Sir Walter), **Selkirk** (Alexander), **Tirpitz** (Alfred von), **Weddell** (James)
08 **Beaufort** (Sir Francis), **Columbus** (Christopher), **Cousteau** (Jacques Yves), **Elvström** (Paul), **Jellicoe** (John Rushworth, Earl), **Magellan** (Ferdinand), **Pitcairn** (Robert), **Sandwich** (Edward Montagu, Earl of), **Vespucci** (Amerigo)
09 **Christian** (Fletcher), **Frobisher** (Sir Martin), **Grenville** (Sir Richard), **MacArthur** (Dame Ellen), **St Vincent** (John Jervis, Earl of), **Vancouver** (George)
10 **Chichester** (Sir Francis), **Erik the Red**, **Villeneuve** (Pierre de)
11 **Collingwood** (Cuthbert, Lord), **Elphinstone** (George Keith, Viscount Keith), **Mountbatten** (Louis, Earl)
12 **Bougainville** (Louis Antoine, Comte de), **Knox-Johnston** (Sir Robin), **Themistocles**

See also **admiral**; **pirate**; **ship**

• sailors

02 MN, RM, RN **03** RAN, RFA, RYA, RYS
04 navy

saint

01 S **02** St **03** Ste **04** hagi-, holy, sant **05** angel, hagio-, saunt **06** hallow, patron, santon **07** tutelar **08** tutelary **11** patron saint **13** guardian saint

Saints include:

03 **Ivo**, **Leo**
04 **Adam**, **Anne**, **Bede**, **Gall**, **Joan** (of Arc), **John**, **John** (Chrysostom), **John** (of the Cross), **John** (the Baptist), **Jude**, **Lucy**, **Luke**, **Mark**, **Mary**, **Mary** (Magdalene), **Paul**, **Zita**
05 **Agnes**, **Aidan**, **Alban**, **Amand**, **Basil** (the Great), **Bruno** (of Cologne), **Clare**, **Cyril**, **Cyril** (of Alexandria), **David**, **Denis**, **Edwin**, **Giles**, **James**, **Louis**, **Paula**, **Peter**, **Titus**, **Vitus**
06 **Albert** (the Great), **Andrew**, **Anselm**, **Antony**, **Antony** (of Padua), **Aquila**, **Cosmas**, **Damian**, **Dismas**, **Edmund**, **Edmund** (Campion), **Edward** (the Martyr), **Fiacre**, **George**, **Helena**, **Hilary** (of Poitiers), **Jerome**, **Joseph**, **Joseph** (of Arimathea), **Justin**, **Martha**, **Martin**, **Monica**, **Oliver**, **Oliver** (Plunket), **Oswald**, **Philip**, **Prisca**, **Robert**, **Simeon**, **Teresa** (of Avila), **Thomas**, **Thomas** (Aquinas), **Thomas** (Becket), **Thomas** (More), **Thomas** (à Becket), **Ursula**
07 **Adamnan**, **Ambrose**, **Anthony**, **Anthony** (of Padua), **Barbara**, **Bernard** (of Clairvaux), **Bernard** (of Menthon), **Bridget**, **Cecilia**, **Clement**, **Columba**, **Crispin**, **Cyprian**, **Dominic**, **Dorothy**, **Dunstan**, **Erasmus**, **Francis** (Romulus), **Francis** (Xavier), **Francis** (of Assisi), **Francis** (of Sales), **Gabriel**, **Gregory** (of Nazianzus), **Gregory** (of Tours), **Gregory** (the Great), **Isidore** (of Seville), **Leonard**, **Matthew**, **Michael**, **Pancras**, **Patrick**, **Stephen**, **Swithin**, **Theresa** (of Lisieux), **Timothy**, **Vincent** (de Paul), **Wilfrid**
08 **Albertus** (Magnus), **Angelico**, **Barnabas**, **Benedict** (of Nursia), **Boniface**, **Cuthbert**, **Genesius**, **Ignatius** (of Loyola), **Irenaeus**, **Lawrence**, **Margaret**, **Matthias**, **Nicholas**, **Polycarp**, **Veronica**, **Vladimir**, **Walpurga**
09 **Alexander**, **Alexander** (Nevsky), **Augustine** (of Canterbury), **Augustine** (of Hippo), **Catherine**, **Genevieve**, **Homobonus**, **Honoratus**, **John Bosco**, **John of God**, **Kentigern**, **Ladislaus**, **Methodius**, **Sebastian**, **Valentine**, **Wenceslas**
10 **Appollonia**, **Athanasius**, **Bernadette**, **Crispinian**, **John Fisher**, **Stanislaus**, **Thomas More**, **Wenceslaus**
11 **Bonaventure**, **Christopher**
12 **Justin Martyr**
13 **Martin of Tours**, **Thomas Apostle**, **Thomas Aquinas**
14 **Albert the Great**, **Francis de Sales**, **Francis of Paola**
15 **Aquila and Prisca**, **Cosmas and Damian**, **Francis of Assisi**, **Gregory the Great**, **Our Lady of Loreto**, **Raymond Nonnatus**

St Helena

03 SHN

St Kitts and Nevis

03 KNA, SCN

saintliness

05 faith, piety **06** purity, virtue **08** chastity, goodness, holiness, morality, sanctity **09** godliness, innocence **10** asceticism, devoutness, sanctitude, self-denial **11** blessedness, sinlessness, uprightness **12** selflessness, spirituality, spotlessness **13** blamelessness, righteousness, self-sacrifice, unselfishness

St Lucia

02 WL **03** LCA

saintly

04 good, holy, pure **05** godly, moral, pious **06** devout, worthy **07** angelic, blessed, ethical, sinless, upright **08** innocent, spotless, virtuous **09** believing, blameless, religious, righteous, saintlike, spiritual **10** God-fearing

St Vincent and the Grenadines

02 WV **03** VCT

sake

03 aim **04** gain, goal, good, saki **05** cause **06** behalf, object, profit, reason, regard **07** account, benefit, purpose, respect, welfare **08** interest **09** advantage, objective, wellbeing **13** consideration

salacious

04 blue, lewd, salt **05** bawdy, horny, randy **06** carnal, coarse, erotic, fruity,

ribald, smutty, steamy, wanton
07 lustful, obscene, raunchy, ruttish
08 improper, indecent, prurient
09 lecherous **10** lascivious, libidinous, lubricious, scurrilous **12** concupiscent, pornographic

salaciousness
08 lewdness **09** bawdiness, indecency, obscenity, prurience **10** smuttiness, steaminess **11** lustfulness, pornography **13** concupiscence, lecherousness **14** lasciviousness

salad
◇ *anagram indicator*

Salads include:

04 herb, rice, slaw
05 fruit, Greek, green, pasta
06 Caesar, potato, tomato
07 mesclum, mesclun, niçoise, Russian, seafood, tabouli, Waldorf
08 coleslaw, couscous
09 mixed leaf, tabbouleh, three bean
11 bulgar wheat
15 mustard and cress

Salad ingredients include:

03 egg, ham, nut
04 meat, tuna
05 bacon, chard, cress, olive
06 borage, carrot, celery, endive, lovage, potato, rocket, tomato
07 anchovy, arugula, chicken, chicory, crouton
08 bacon bit, beetroot, cold meat, coleslaw, cucumber
09 boiled egg, corn-salad, green bean, new potato, radicchio, sweetcorn
10 cos lettuce, lollo rosso, mayonnaise, salad cream, watercress
11 salad burnet, spring onion
12 cherry tomato, lamb's lettuce, round lettuce
13 hard-boiled egg, roasted pepper, salad dressing
14 iceberg lettuce, sundried tomato

See also **lettuce**

Salad dressings include:

06 Caesar, French
07 Italian, Russian
10 blue cheese, mayonnaise, salad cream
11 vinaigrette
14 Thousand Island

salamander
03 olm **07** axolotl **08** mudpuppy **10** hellbender **12** springkeeper

salaried
04 paid **05** waged **11** emolumental, remunerated, stipendiary **12** emolumentary

salary
03 fee, pay **05** screw, wages **06** income **07** stipend **08** earnings **09** allowance, emolument **10** honorarium **12** remuneration

sale
04 deal, seal, vend, vent **05** trade **06** wicker, willow **07** selling, traffic, vending **08** disposal **09** marketing **10** bargaining **11** transaction

Sales include:

04 boot, fair, work
06 autumn, bazaar, forced, garage, jumble, market, online, public, spring, summer, winter
07 auction, car-boot, charity, January, private, rummage, warrant
08 bazumble, clearing, cold call, e-auction, tabletop
09 clearance, end-of-line, mail order, mid-season, pre-season, remainder, telesales, trade show
10 exhibition, exposition, fleamarket, open market, second-hand
11 bring-and-buy, closing-down, end of-season, on-promotion, stocktaking
12 bargain offer, church bazaar, grand opening, of the century, special offer
13 online auction
14 pyramid selling
15 of bankrupt stock

• **for sale**
06 on sale, to sell **07** in stock **09** available, up for sale **10** in the shops, obtainable, up for grabs **11** for purchase, on the market **12** wanted to sell

• **sale or return**
03 SOR

saleable
08 vendible **09** desirable **10** marketable **11** sought-after **12** merchantable

salesperson
03 rep **05** clerk **07** shop-boy **08** salesman, shop-girl **09** salesgirl, saleslady **10** salesclerk, saleswoman, shopkeeper **13** sales engineer, shop assistant **14** representative, sales assistant

salient
04 main **05** bulge, chief **06** signal **07** leaping, obvious, saltant **08** striking **09** arresting, important, principal, prominent, springing **10** noticeable, pronounced, remarkable **11** conspicuous, outstanding, significant

saliva
04 foam, spit **05** drool, spawl, water **06** phlegm, slaver, sputum **07** dribble, spittle **13** expectoration

sallow
03 wan **04** pale, sale, seal **05** adust, ashen, pasty, sally, sauch, saugh, waxen **06** pallid, sickly, willow, yellow **07** anaemic **09** jaundiced, unhealthy, yellowish **10** colourless, goat-willow

sally
04 dash, jest, joke, quip, raid, rock, rush, sway, trip **05** amble, bound, crack, drive, erupt, foray, issue, jaunt, mosey, surge **06** attack, bon mot, breeze, charge, escape, frolic, outing, retort, sallee, sallow, sortie, stroll, thrust, wander **07** assault, outrush, riposte, saunter, venture **08** escapade **09** excursion, incursion, offensive, promenade, wisecrack, witticism **10** jeu d'esprit, projection **11** snatch squad

salmon
03 fry, lax, lox **04** chum, cock, coho, kelt, keta, masu, mort, parr **05** cohoe, nerka, smolt, sprod **06** baggit, dorado, grilse, kipper, ligger, samlet **07** bluecap, gravlax, kokanee, quinnat, redfish, salamon, shedder, skegger, sockeye **08** blueback, humpback, rockfish, springer **09** blackfish, brandling, bull trout, gravadlax **10** fingerling, ouananiche **12** Oncorhynchus

salt
02 AB **03** sal, tar, wit, zip **04** corn, cure, dear, leap, saut, zest **05** briny, punch, rapid, salty, sault, smack, taste **06** marine, rating, relish, sailor, saline, salted, savour, seaman, vigour **07** flavour, mariner, pungent, saltish, sea-salt **08** brackish, interest, merum sal, mordancy, piquancy, pungency, seafarer **09** expensive, salacious, seasoning, waterfall **10** liveliness, trenchancy **11** acclimatize **14** sodium chloride

Salts include:

05 azide
06 aurate, borate, folate, halite, iodate, iodide, malate, oleate
07 bay salt, caprate, citrate, cyanate, ferrate, formate, lactate, maleate, nitrate, nitrite, oxalate, sorbate, tannate, toluate, viscose
08 arsenite, benzoate, butyrate, caproate, chlorate, chloride, chromate, plumbate, pyruvate, rock salt, silicate, stearate, sulphate, sulphide, sulphite, tartrate, vanadate, xanthate
09 ascorbate, bath salts, carbamate, carbonate, glutamate, manganate, molybdate, periodate, phosphate, phthalate, solar salt, succinate, table salt
10 antimonite, bichromate, dichromate, Epsom salts, liver salts, salicylate
11 bicarbonate, health salts, persulphate, sal volatile
12 borosilicate, permanganate, Rochelle-salt
13 smelling salts

• **salt away**
04 bank, hide, save **05** amass, cache, hoard, stash **07** collect, put away, store up **08** put aside, set aside **09** stockpile **10** accumulate

• **take with a pinch of salt, take with a grain of salt**
08 hesitate, question **10** disbelieve **14** have misgivings **15** have hesitations, not fully believe

salty
04 racy, salt **05** briny, spicy, tangy, witty **06** lively, saline, salted **07** mordant, piquant, savoury **08** animated, brackish, exciting, vigorous **09** trenchant **11** salsuginous, stimulating

salubrious
06 benign, decent **07** healthy **08** hygienic, pleasant, salutary, sanitary **09** healthful, wholesome **10** beneficial, refreshing **11** respectable **12** health-giving, invigorating

salutary
04 good **06** timely, useful **07** healthy, helpful **08** hygienic, sanitary, valuable **09** practical, wholesome **10** beneficial, profitable, refreshing **12** advantageous, health-giving, invigorating

salutation
03 ave, hat **04** g'day, hail, skol **05** jambo, skoal **06** homage, prosit, salaam, salute **07** address, all-hail, ave Mary, good-day, good-den, good-e'en, wassail, welcome **08** ave Maria, good-even, greeting, Hail Mary, regreets, respects **09** goodnight, obeisance, reverence, time of day **10** excitement, good-morrow **11** good-evening, good-morning **13** good afternoon
See also **greeting**

salute
03 bow, cap, nod **04** hail, mark, move, wave **05** coupé, greet, halse, salue, salvo **06** banzai, coupee, homage, honour **07** address, gesture, half-cap, present, tribute, welcome **08** greeting, Sieg Heil **09** celebrate, handshake, recognize, reverence **11** acknowledge, celebration, present arms, recognition **12** pay tribute to **15** acknowledgement, make your manners

salvage
04 save **05** salve **06** redeem, repair, rescue, retain, savage, saving **07** get back, raising, reclaim, recover, restore **08** conserve, preserve, recovery, retrieve **09** regaining, retrieval **10** recuperate **11** reclamation, restoration **12** regeneration **13** reinstatement

salvation
06 rescue, saving **08** lifeline **10** liberation, redemption **11** deliverance, reclamation, soteriology **12** preservation

salve
03 saw **04** balm, calm, ease, hail, heal **05** cream, smear **06** anoint, lotion, remedy, soothe **07** clear up, comfort, explain, lighten, relieve, salvage **08** greeting, liniment, ointment **09** harmonize, vindicate **10** medication **11** application, embrocation, preparation

salver
04 dish, tray **05** plate **06** server, waiter **07** charger, platter **08** trencher

samarium
02 Sm

same
02 ae, do, id **03** ilk, one **04** idem, like, self, twin, very, ylke **05** alike, ditto, equal, samey, thick, thilk **06** all one, as much, mutual, thicky **07** similar, uniform **08** matching, selfsame, unvaried **09** duplicate, identical, unchanged, unvarying **10** carbon copy, changeless, comparable, consistent, equiparate, equivalent, reciprocal, synonymous, unchanging, unvariable **11** the very same **12** the aforesaid **13** corresponding, one and the same, substitutable, the above-named **15** interchangeable

• **all the same**
03 but, yet **05** still **06** anyhow, anyway, even so **07** however **09** in any case **10** by any means, for all that, in any event, not but what, regardless, tout de même **11** by some means, nonetheless **12** nevertheless **15** birds of a feather, notwithstanding

• **the same as**
02 iq **08** idem quod

sameness
06 déjà vu, tedium **07** oneness **08** ding-dong, equality, identity, likeness, monotone, monotony **09** dead-level, mannerism **10** repetition, similarity, uniformity **11** consistency, duplication, resemblance **13** identicalness, indistinction, invariability **14** changelessness, predictability **15** standardization

samey
04 same **05** alike **07** similar, tedious, uniform **09** identical **10** monotonous, unchanging **11** predictable **12** cookie-cutter

Samoa
02 WS **03** WSM

sample
◇ *hidden indicator*
03 sip, try **04** blad, cast, core, sign, test, type **05** dummy, match, model, piece, pilot, taste, toile, trial **06** muster, swatch, taster, try out **07** examine, example, inspect, pattern, typical **08** instance, prospect, sampling, specimen, transect **09** breakbeat, foretaste, scantling **10** assay-piece, experience, indication **12** cross-section, illustration, illustrative **13** demonstration, demonstrative **14** representative **15** depleted uranium

sanatorium
03 san **06** clinic **07** sick bay **08** hospital **09** infirmary **10** health farm, sanitarium **12** health centre, health resort **13** medical centre

sanctification
05 piety **06** purity **08** devotion, holiness **09** godliness **10** sacredness **11** blessedness **12** spirituality **13** righteousness

sanctify
04 back, wash **05** allow, bless, exalt **06** anoint, hallow, permit, purify, ratify **07** absolve, approve, cleanse, confirm, endorse, license, support, warrant **08** accredit, canonize, dedicate, make holy, sanction, set apart **09** authorize **10** consecrate, legitimize, make sacred, underwrite

sanctimonious
02 pi **04** holy, smug **05** pious **08** priggish, superior, unctuous **09** pietistic **10** goody-goody, moralizing **11** pharisaical **12** hypocritical **13** self-righteous **14** holier-than-thou

sanctimoniousness
04 cant **06** humbug **07** pietism **08** saintism, smugness **09** hypocrisy **10** moralizing, pharisaism **11** complacency, preachiness **12** priggishness, unctuousness **13** righteousness

sanction
02 OK **03** ban, oke **04** back, fiat, okay **05** allow **06** permit, ratify **07** approof, approve, backing, boycott, confirm, embargo, endorse, go-ahead, licence, license, penalty, support, sustain, warrant **08** accredit, approval, royalize, sanctify, sentence, suffrage, thumbs-up **09** agreement, authority, authorize, deterrent **10** green light, legitimize, permission, punishment, underwrite **11** approbation, countenance, endorsement, prohibition, restriction **12** confirmation, ratification, subscription **13** accreditation, authorization

sanctity
05 grace, piety **06** purity, virtue **08** devotion, goodness, holiness **09** godliness, saintship **10** sacredness **11** blessedness, saintliness **12** spirituality **13** inviolability, religiousness, righteousness, sacrosanctity **14** sanctification

sanctuary
04 area, park **05** altar, frith, girth, grith, haven, tract **06** asylum, church, oracle, refuge, safety, shrine, temple **07** Alsatia, chancel, enclave, hideout, reserve, retreat, sanctum, shelter **08** delubrum, hideaway, immunity, preserve, security **09** holy place, nymphaeum, privilege, sacrarium, safeguard **10** frithsoken, protection, tabernacle **11** reservation **12** holy of holies **14** place of worship

sanctum
03 den **05** study **06** refuge, shrine **07** hideout, retreat **08** hideaway **09** cubbyhole, holy place, sanctuary **12** holy of holies

sand
04 grit, rock **05** beach, sands, shore **06** desert, strand **08** seashore **10** wilderness

• **sand dune, sand dunes**
03 erg **04** areg, dene, down, seif

06 barkan **07** barchan, barkhan
08 barchane

sandal
04 geta, zori **05** jelly, thong **06** galosh, golosh, Jandal® **07** chappal, galoche, talaria **08** flip-flap, flip-flop, huarache, slipslop **09** alpargata **12** calceamentum

sandalwood
05 algum, almug **06** santal **07** sanders
08 quandang, quandong, quantong
10 buffalo-nut **11** sanderswood
13 Barbados pride

sandarac
04 arar

sandbank
02 ås **03** bar, key **04** dune, kaim, kame, reef **05** esker, hurst, shelf, shoal
07 sand bar, yardang **08** sandhill
10 harbour-bar
• opening between sandbanks
03 gat

sand-eel
04 grig, lant **05** lance **06** launce

Sandhurst
03 RMA **04** RMAS

sandpiper
03 ree **04** knot, ruff **05** reeve, terek
06 dunlin, ox-bird, willet **07** sea lark
08 peetweet, redshank, sand-lark, sand-peep, sea snipe **10** greenshank, sanderling, yellowlegs

sandstone
04 grit **05** fakes **06** arkose, dogger, faikes, Flysch, kingle **07** hassock
08 sand-flag **09** bluestone, firestone, greensand, gritstone, holystone, quartzite, tile stone **10** brownstone
13 millstone grit

sandwich
◇ *containment indicator*
03 bap, BLT, wad **04** roti, wrap **05** butty, piece, round **06** burger, hoagie, sarney, sarnie **07** toastie **09** submarine
10 jeely piece **11** intercalate, three-decker **12** double-decker **14** croque-monsieur

sandy
◇ *dialect indicator*
03 red **04** Scot **05** light, rusty, tawny
06 auburn, ginger, gritty, Titian, yellow
07 coppery, gingery, reddish, yellowy
08 sabulose, sabulous **09** gingerous, psammitic, yellowish **10** arenaceous
13 reddish-yellow

sane
04 wice, wise **05** lucid, sober, sound
06 formal, normal, stable **07** herself, himself **08** all there, balanced, moderate, rational, sensible, yourself
09 judicious **10** reasonable **11** level-headed, of sound mind, responsible, right-minded **12** compos mentis, well-balanced **15** in your right mind

sangfroid
04 cool **05** nerve, poise **06** aplomb, phlegm **08** calmness, coolness
09 assurance, composure
10 dispassion, equanimity
11 nonchalance, self-control
12 indifference **14** cool-headedness, self-possession, unflappability

sanguinary
04 gory, grim **05** cruel **06** bloody, brutal, savage **08** bloodied, pitiless, ruthless **09** merciless, murderous
12 bloodthirsty

sanguine
03 red **04** gory, pink, rosy **05** fresh, ruddy **06** ardent, bloody, florid, lively
07 assured, buoyant, flushed, hopeful, roseate, unbowed **08** animated, blood-red, cheerful, rubicund, spirited
09 confident, expectant, unabashed
10 optimistic **13** over-confident
14 over-optimistic

sanitary
04 pure **05** clean **07** aseptic, healthy, sterile **08** germ-free, hygienic
09 wholesome **10** antiseptic, salubrious, unpolluted **11** disinfected
14 uncontaminated

sanitize
05 clean **06** filter, purify, refine
07 cleanse, clean up, freshen
08 fumigate **09** deodorize, disinfect, expurgate, sterilize **13** decontaminate, make palatable **14** make acceptable
15 make presentable

sanity
04 mind **05** sense **06** health, reason, wisdom **08** lucidity, prudence
09 good sense, normality, soundness, stability **11** common sense, rationality
13 balance of mind, judiciousness
14 responsibility **15** level-headedness, right-mindedness, soundness of mind

San Marino
03 RSM, SMR

Santa Claus
06 St Nick **10** St Nicholas **11** Kris Kringle **12** Kriss Kringle **15** Father Christmas

São Tomé and Príncipe
02 ST **03** STP

sap
03 box, git, mug, nit **04** clot, fink, fool, jerk, ooze, prat, sura, twit **05** bleed, drain, erode, idiot, juice, moron, toddy
06 energy, impair, nitwit, reduce, trench, vigour, weaken **07** deplete, essence, exhaust **08** diminish, enervate, enfeeble, imbecile, palm wine, vitality, wear away, wear down
09 lifeblood, palm-honey, undermine
10 debilitate, karyolymph, plant fluid, vital fluid

sapi-utan
04 anoa

sapling
05 plant **06** tellar, teller, tiller **08** ash-plant, flittern **09** ground-ash, ground oak

sapper
02 RE

sarcasm
04 jibe, wipe **05** irony, scorn **06** gibing, satire **07** acidity, mockery
08 acrimony, contempt, cynicism, derision, mordancy, ridicule, scoffing, sneering **09** invective **10** bitterness, resentment, trenchancy
12 spitefulness
• expression of sarcasm
03 gee

sarcastic
04 acid **05** sarky, sharp, snide, witty
06 biting **07** acerbic, caustic, cutting, cynical, jeering, mocking, mordant, pungent, satiric **08** derisive, derisory, incisive, ironical, sardonic, scathing, scoffing, scornful, sneering, taunting
09 invective, satirical **10** back-handed, Juvenalian, Voltairian **11** disparaging
12 sharp-tongued

sarcastically
09 cynically, jeeringly **10** ironically, scathingly, scornfully, tauntingly
11 satirically

sardonic
03 dry, wry **05** cruel **06** biting, bitter
07 acerbic, cynical, jeering, mocking, mordant **08** derisive, scornful, sneering **09** heartless, malicious, sarcastic **11** acrimonious
12 contemptuous

sash
03 obi **04** belt **05** lungi, scarf, shash
06 girdle **07** baldric, burdash, chassis
08 baldrick, cincture **09** waistband
10 cummerbund

Saskatchewan
02 SK

sassy
04 pert **05** fresh, lippy, saucy
06 brazen, cheeky, mouthy **07** forward
08 impudent, insolent **09** audacious
11 impertinent **12** overfamiliar
13 disrespectful

Satan
05 devil **06** Belial **07** Abaddon, arch-foe, Lucifer, Old Nick, Shaitan
08 Apollyon, the Devil, the Enemy
09 arch-enemy, arch-felon, arch-fiend, Beelzebub, leviathan **10** the Evil One, the serpent, the Tempter **12** the Adversary **13** the old serpent
14 Mephistopheles

satanic
04 dark, evil **05** black **06** damned, sinful, wicked **07** demonic, hellish, inhuman **08** accursed, devilish, diabolic, fiendish, infernal **09** satanical
10 abominable, diabolical, iniquitous, malevolent, sulphurous

sate
04 cloy, fill, glut **05** gorge, satay, slake
06 accloy, sicken, stodge **07** gratify, satiate, satisfy, surfeit **08** overfill, saturate

sated
03 sad

satellite
04 aide, moon **06** colony, lackey, minion, planet, puppet, vassal **07** moonlet **08** adherent, disciple, dominion, follower, hanger-on, parasite, province, retainer, sidekick, smallsat **09** attendant, dependant, spaceship, sycophant **10** dependency, spacecraft **11** subordinate **12** orbiting body, protectorate, space station

Satellites include:

03 CAT
04 ECHO
05 Astra, TIROS
06 Oshumi, Rohini
07 Asterix, Horizon, Sputnik, Transit
08 Explorer, INMARSAT, Intelsat, Prospero
09 Early Bird, Long March
11 Black Knight

See also **moon**

satiate
04 cloy, fill, glut, jade, sate **05** gorge, slake, stuff **07** engorge, glutted, satisfy, surfeit **08** nauseate, overfeed, overfill

satiety
07 surfeit **08** cloyment, fullness **09** repletion, satiation **10** saturation **11** repleteness **12** over-fullness, satisfaction **13** gratification **14** overindulgence

satire
03 wit **04** jeer, skit **05** irony, satyr, spoof, squib **06** glance, parody, send-up, taxing **07** lampoon, Pasquil, Pasquin, sarcasm, Sotadic, take-off **08** raillery, ridicule, Sotadean, travesty **09** burlesque, invective **10** caricature, mazarinade **12** mickey-taking **15** comedy of manners

satirical
06 biting, bitter **07** abusive, acerbic, caustic, cutting, cynical, mocking, mordant **08** derisive, incisive, ironical, sardonic, Swiftian, taunting **09** invective, sarcastic, trenchant **10** irreverent, ridiculing **12** Archilochian

satirist
05 satyr **06** mocker, satire **07** Pasquil, Pasquin **08** parodist **09** lampooner, pasquiler, ridiculer **10** cartoonist, lampoonist, pasquilant **11** pasquinader **12** caricaturist

Satirists include:

03 **Loy** (Myrna)
04 **Cech** (Svatopluk), **Isla** (José Francisco de), **Pope** (Alexander)
05 **Börne** (Ludwig), **Brown** (Thomas), **Cooke** (Ebenezer), **Ellis** (George), **Larra** (Mariano José de), **Meung** (Jean de), **Nashe** (Thomas), **Nesin** (Aziz), **Swift** (Jonathan)
06 **Butler** (Samuel), **Giusti** (Giuseppe), **Horace**, **Lucian**, **Murner** (Thomas), **Pindar** (Peter), **Wolcot** (John)
07 **Barclay** (John), **Juvenal**, **Marston** (John), **Mencken** (Henry Louis), **Persius**, **Régnier** (Mathurin), **Thurber** (James)
08 **Apuleius** (Lucius), **Beerbohm** (Max), **Fischart** (Johann), **Lucilius** (Gaius), **Rabelais** (François)
09 **Churchill** (Charles), **Delavigne** (Casimir), **Junqueiro** (Ablio Manuel Guerra), **Petronius** (Arbiter), **Whitehead** (Paul)
10 **Mandeville** (Bernard)
12 **Konstantinov** (Aleko)

See also **comedian**

satirize
04 mock **06** deride, parody, send up **07** lampoon, Pasquil, Pasquin, take off **08** ridicule **09** burlesque, criticize, make fun of, poke fun at **10** caricature

satisfaction
03 pay **04** ease **05** pride **06** amends, change, liking **07** comfort, content, damages, delight, payment, redress **08** pleasure, requital **09** atonement, enjoyment, happiness, indemnity, quittance, wellbeing **10** conviction, fulfilment, recompense, reparation, settlement, suffisance **11** complacence, complacency, contentment, restitution, vindication **12** compensation **13** gratification, reimbursement **15** indemnification

satisfactorily
06 nicely **08** passably **10** acceptably, adequately, favourably **11** competently **12** sufficiently

satisfactory
02 OK **03** A-OK, oke **04** fair, fine, nice, okay, well **05** sweet **06** cushty, proper **07** atoning, average **08** adequate, all right, passable, suitable **09** competent, copacetic, copasetic, favorable, kopasetic **10** acceptable, convincing, favourable, sufficient, tickety-boo **11** tickettyboo, up to scratch, up to the mark

satisfied
04 full, paid, smug, sure **05** happy, sated **07** certain, content, pleased, replete **08** pacified, positive, satiated **09** contented, convinced, persuaded, reassured **13** self-satisfied

satisfy
03 pay **04** apay, fill, meet, sate, stay **05** agree, appay, serve, slake **06** answer, assure, defray, fulfil, please, quench, settle, supply **07** appease, assuage, content, delight, gratify, indulge, placate, qualify, requite, satiate, suffice, surfeit **08** convince, live up to, persuade, reassure **09** discharge, indemnify **10** comply with **13** be adequate for, compensate for **15** be sufficient for

satisfying
04 cool **06** enough, far-out, square, way-out **07** filling **08** cheering, pleasing **10** convincing, fulfilling, gratifying, harmonious, persuasive, refreshing **11** pleasurable **12** satisfactory

saturate
03 wet **04** fill, glut, sate, soak **05** flood, imbue, souse, steep **06** drench **07** pervade, suffuse, surfeit **08** overfill, permeate, waterlog **09** surcharge **10** impregnate **14** make wet through

saturated
05 drunk **06** imbued, soaked, sodden, soused **07** flooded, soaking, sopping, steeped **08** drenched, dripping, suffused, wringing **09** permeated **11** impregnated, waterlogged

saturation
06 sating **07** filling, soaking **08** flooding, glutting **09** pervading, satiation, suffusion **10** permeation

Saturday
03 Sat

Saturn
06 Cronus

saturnine
04 dour, dull, glum **05** grave, heavy, moody, stern **06** dismal, gloomy, morose, severe, sombre **07** austere **08** taciturn **09** withdrawn **10** melancholy, phlegmatic, unfriendly **15** uncommunicative

satyr
05 silen **06** satire **07** silenus **08** satirist, woodwose **09** orang-utan, woodhouse

sauce
03 dip, lip **04** sass **05** brass, cheek, mouth, nerve **06** rebuke, relish **08** audacity, backchat, belabour, dressing, pertness, rudeness **09** condiment, flippancy, freshness, impudence, insolence, sauciness **10** brazenness, cheekiness, disrespect, flavouring **11** irreverence, presumption **12** impertinence, malapertness

Sauces include:

02 HP®
03 jus, red, soy
04 fish, hard, mint, mole, soja, soya, wine
05 apple, bread, brown, caper, cream, curry, fudge, garum, gravy, melba, pesto, salsa, satay, shoyu, white
06 catsup, cheese, chilli, coulis, fondue, fu yung, hoisin, mornay, nam pla, oxymel, oyster, panada, reform, tamari, tartar, tomato, tommy K
07 catchup, custard, Daddies®, harissa, ketchup, nuoc mam, passata, rouille, sabayon, soubise, supreme, Tabasco®, tartare, velouté
08 barbecue, béchamel, bigarade, chasseur, marinara, piri-piri, salpicon, yakitori
09 béarnaise, black bean, bolognese, carbonara, chocolate, cranberry, demi-glace, espagnole, Marie Rose, remoulade, Worcester
10 avgolemono, chaudfroid,

Cumberland, mayonnaise, mousseline, napoletana, puttanesca, salad cream, salsa verde, stroganoff
11 bourguignon, buerre blanc, hollandaise, horseradish, vinaigrette
12 brandy butter, sweet-and-sour
13 crème anglaise, salad dressing
14 Worcestershire

saucepan
03 pan, pot, wok **05** fryer **06** chafer, goblet, vessel **07** milk pan, skillet **08** pancheon **09** casserole, container, frying-pan **12** double boiler

saucy
04 pert, rude **05** fresh, lippy, peart, piert, sassy **06** brazen, cheeky, fruity, gallus **07** forward, gallows **08** flippant, impudent, insolent, malapert **10** disdainful, irreverent, lascivious **11** impertinent **12** presumptuous **13** disrespectful

Saudi Arabia
02 SA **03** SAU

saunter
04 walk **05** amble, daker, mooch, mosey, shool, shule **06** dacker, daiker, dander, dauner, dawdle, dawner, ramble, shoole, stroll, toddle, wander **07** daunder, meander **09** promenade **10** knock about **11** knock around **14** constitutional

sausage

Sausages include:

04 beef, lamb, lola, pork
05 blood, liver, Lorne, Lyons, snags, weeny, wurst
06 banger, bumbar, garlic, hot dog, kishke, lolita, mumbar, polony, salami, summer, weenie, Wiener, wienie
07 abruzzo, baloney, Bologna, boloney, cabanos, chorizo, corn dog, kabanos, klobasa, merguez, saveloy, zampone
08 cervelat, chaurice, chourico, cocktail, drisheen, kielbasa, linguica, peperoni, Toulouse
09 andouille, bierwurst, blutwurst, boerewors, bratwurst, chipolata, cotechino, lap cheong, loukanika, pepperoni, saucisson
10 bauerwurst, boudin noir, cervellata, Cumberland, knackwurst, knockwurst, liverwurst, mortadella
11 boudin blanc, boudin rouge, frankfurter, Wienerwurst
12 andouillette, black pudding, Lincolnshire

savage
04 bite, boor, claw, fell, grim, maul, slam, tear, wild **05** beast, brute, churl, cruel, feral, harsh, slate **06** attack, bloody, brutal, fierce, immane, mangle **07** beastly, furious, inhuman, monster, rubbish, run down, salvage, untamed, vicious, wild man **08** barbaric, denounce, lacerate, pitiless, ruthless, sadistic, terrible, warrigal **09** barbarian, barbarous, cut-throat, dog-eat-dog, ferocious, merciless, murderous, primitive, wild woman **10** go to town on, wild person **11** pick holes in, uncivilized **12** bloodthirsty, catamountain, cat o' mountain, pull to pieces, pull to shreds, tear to pieces, tear to shreds **14** undomesticated **15** do a hatchet job on

savagely
07 cruelly, harshly **08** brutally, fiercely **09** viciously **10** pitilessly, ruthlessly **11** barbarously, ferociously, mercilessly **12** barbarically

savagery
06 ferity, sadism **07** cruelty **08** ferocity, wildness **09** barbarism, barbarity, brutality, roughness **10** bestiality, fierceness, inhumanity **11** brutishness, viciousness **12** pitilessness, ruthlessness **13** mercilessness, murderousness, primitiveness

savant
04 guru, sage **06** master, pundit **07** learned, scholar **09** authority **10** mastermind **11** philosopher **12** accomplished, intellectual, man of letters **14** woman of letters

save
02 sa' **04** free, hain, hold, keep, safe **05** guard, hoard, lay up, put by, spare, stash, store **06** budget, but for, except, export, gather, hinder, redeem, rescue, retain, screen, shield, snudge, unless **07** bail out, collect, cut back, deliver, obviate, prevent, protect, reclaim, recover, release, reserve, salvage, set free, use less **08** conserve, cut costs, excepted, keep safe, liberate, preserve, put aside, retrieve, set aside, sock away **09** apart from, aside from, be thrifty, economize, except for, excluding, safeguard, stockpile **10** buy cheaply **11** not counting **13** scrimp and save **14** live on the cheap **15** get someone out of, tighten your belt

saving
03 cut **04** fund **05** store **06** frugal, thrift **07** bargain, capital, careful, economy, nest egg, sparing, thrifty **08** discount, reserves **09** excepting, redeeming, reduction, resources, salvatory **10** economical, mitigating, preserving, protecting, qualifying **11** extenuating, investments, reservation **12** compensating, compensatory, conservation, preservation

saviour
04 Jesu **05** Jesus **06** Christ **07** Messiah, rescuer **08** champion, defender, Emmanuel, guardian, Mediator, redeemer **09** deliverer, Lamb of God, liberator, protector **11** emancipator

savoir-faire
04 tact **05** poise **07** ability, finesse, knowhow **08** urbanity **09** assurance, diplomacy, expertise **10** capability, confidence, discretion **11** social grace **12** social graces **14** accomplishment

savour
03 sar **04** hint, like, odor, sair, salt, tang, zest **05** aroma, enjoy, odour, scent, smack, smell, speak, spice, taste, touch, trace **06** relish, repute, resent, season **07** bouquet, flavour, perfume, revel in, suggest **08** piquancy, seem like **09** delight in, fragrance **10** appreciate, smattering, suggestion **14** enjoy to the full, take pleasure in, taste to the full

savoury
04 tapa **05** gusty, salty, sapid, snack, spicy, tangy, tapas, tasty, yummy **06** canapé, gustie, nibble, samosa, spiced **07** gustful, piquant, scrummy **08** aigrette, aromatic, fragrant, luscious **09** appetizer, delicious, palatable **10** appetizing **11** amuse-bouche, amuse-gueule, bonne-bouche, flavoursome, hors d'oeuvre, respectable, scrumptious **13** mouthwatering

savvy
03 sly **04** keen, know, wily **05** acute, alert, canny, sharp, skill, smart **06** artful, astute, callid, clever, crafty, shrewd **07** cunning, know-how, knowing **09** judicious, observant, sagacious **10** calculated, discerning, far-sighted, perceptive, understand **11** calculating, intelligent, well-advised **13** knowledgeable, perspicacious **14** discriminating

saw
03 mot, say, sow **05** adage, axiom, gnome, maxim, salve **06** byword, decree, dictum, saying **07** epigram, proverb **08** aphorism **10** apophthegm **11** commonplace

Saws include:

03 jig, rip
04 band, fret, hack, hand
05 bench, chain, panel, tenon
06 coping, rabbet, scroll
07 compass, pruning
08 circular, crosscut
09 radial-arm
11 power-driven

say
◇ *homophone indicator*
02 eg **03** add, put, saw **04** read, sway, tell, vote, word **05** assay, claim, clout, drawl, grunt, guess, imply, judge, orate, order, power, reply, speak, state, utter, voice **06** affirm, allege, answer, assert, assume, convey, mutter, phrase, recite, reckon, rejoin, remark, render, repeat, report, retort, reveal, rumour, speech, weight **07** comment, declare, deliver, divulge, exclaim, express, imagine, mention, observe, opinion, perform, presume, respond, signify, suggest, suppose, surmise **08** announce, disclose, estimate, indicate, instruct, intimate, maintain, rehearse **09** authority, ejaculate, enunciate, influence, pronounce **10** articulate, for

example **11** come out with, communicate, turn to speak **12** put into words **13** approximately, chance to speak

• that is to say
02 ie, sc **03** viz **05** id est, to wit **06** namely, that is **09** c'est-à-dire, videlicet **12** in other words

saying
◇ *homophone indicator*
03 mot, saw **04** cant, dict, read, rede, reed, word **05** adage, axiom, gnome, maxim, motto, reede **06** bon mot, byword, cliché, dictum, phrase, remark, slogan, wisdom **07** diction, epigram, fadaise, precept, proverb **08** aphorism, apothegm, overword **09** platitude, quotation, rusticism, statement **10** apophthegm, expression **11** catch phrase **12** word of wisdom **13** household word, pearl of wisdom

say-so
02 OK **04** word **06** dictum, rumour **07** backing, consent, go-ahead, hearsay **08** approval, sanction, thumbs-up **09** agreement, assertion, assurance, authority, guarantee **10** green light, permission **11** affirmation **12** asseveration, ratification **13** authorization

scab
03 rat **08** blackleg **13** strike-breaker

scabies
04 itch **05** psora

scaffold
05 stage, tower **06** gantry, gibbet **07** catasta, gallows, hanging, sustain, the rope **08** platform **09** framework **11** scaffolding

scald
04 burn, leep, plot, poet, sear **05** brand, ploat, scaud, skald **06** paltry, scabby, scorch, scurfy **07** blister **09** cauterize

scalding
07 boiling, burning **08** steaming **09** piping hot **10** blistering **12** extremely hot

scale
04 coat, film, go up, leaf, scan **05** climb, crust, flake, gamme, gamut, layer, level, Libra, mount, order, palea, plate, range, ratio, reach, scope, scurf, shell, skail, weigh **06** ascend, degree, extent, furfur, gunter, ladder, lamina, plaque, series, shin up, spread, squama, tartar **07** clamber, coating, compass, conquer, deposit, measure, ranking **08** escalade, register, scramble, sequence, spectrum, surmount **09** hierarchy, limescale **10** graduation, proportion **11** calibration, progression **12** encrustation, pecking order, relative size **15** measuring system

• scale down
04 drop **06** lessen, reduce, shrink **07** cut back, cut down **08** contract, decrease, make less

• scale up
05 boost, raise **06** bump up, expand, hike up, step up **07** augment, build up, develop, enhance, further, improve **08** increase **09** intensify **10** accumulate, strengthen

scaliness
06 furfur **08** dandruff **09** flakiness, leprosity **10** scurfiness, squamation, squamosity **12** scabrousness

scallop
03 dag **04** clam, gimp, mush **05** grill **06** pecten **07** queenie **08** coquille

scaly
05 flaky, rough **06** branny, scabby, scurfy, shabby **07** leprose, leprous **08** lepidote, scabrous, scarious, squamate, squamose, squamous **09** furfurous **10** squamulose **12** desquamative, desquamatory, furfuraceous

scam
03 con **04** game **05** dodge, fraud, trick **06** fiddle, racket, rip-off, scheme **07** swindle **08** business **09** deception, gold brick

scamp
03 imp **05** devil, losel, rogue **06** fripon, monkey, rascal, skelum, wretch **07** skellum **08** blighter, scalawag, schellum, spalpeen, vagabond **09** reprobate, scallawag, scallywag **10** highwayman **12** troublemaker **13** mischief-maker **14** good-for-nothing, whippersnapper

scamper
03 fly, ren, rin, run **04** dart, dash, lamp, race, romp, rush **05** hurry, scoot, scoup, scowp **06** decamp, frolic, gambol, hasten, scurry, sprint **07** scuttle, skitter **08** scramble

scan
03 con, kon **04** read, skim, test **05** check, climb, conne, judge, probe, scale, spell, study, sweep **06** go over, review, search, survey **07** CAT scan, examine, inspect, run over **08** glance at, scrutiny **09** interpret, screening **10** inspection, run through, scrutinize, sector scan **11** examination, flip through, investigate, leaf through **12** flick through, thumb through **13** browse through, investigation, scintilliscan **14** run your eye over

scandal
04 blot, dirt, -gate, pity, slur **05** libel, shame, shock, smear, stain **06** defame, furore, gossip, outcry, uproar **07** calumny, obloquy, offence, outrage, rumours, slander **08** disgrace, ignominy, reproach **09** black mark, discredit, dishonour **10** defamation, dirty linen, opprobrium **11** crying shame **12** dirty laundry, dirty washing **13** embarrassment

scandalize
05 appal, repel, shock **06** dismay, insult, offend, revolt **07** affront, disgust, horrify, outrage, slander **08** disgrace

scandalmonger
06 gossip, tattle **07** defamer, tattler **08** busybody, quidnunc, traducer **09** muck-raker **10** talebearer **11** calumniator, Nosey Parker, sweetie-wife **12** gossip-monger

scandalous
05 gamey, juicy **06** untrue **07** blatant **08** flagrant, improper, infamous, shameful, shocking, unseemly **09** appalling, atrocious, libellous, malicious, monstrous **10** abominable, defamatory, outrageous, scurrilous, slanderous **11** disgraceful, opprobrious, sensational, unspeakable **12** disreputable **13** dishonourable

Scandinavian
05 Norse

Scandinavians include:

04 Dane, Finn
05 Swede
06 Norman, viking
08 Norseman
09 Icelander, Norwegian, Varangian

scandium
02 Sc

scanner

Scanners include:

02 CT
03 CAT, PET
04 body, SPET
07 barcode, flatbed
10 Emi-Scanner®

scant
04 bare, jimp **05** short, stint **06** barely, jimply, little, measly, reduce, slight, sparse **07** limited, minimal, sparing **08** exiguous, restrict, scantily, scarcity **09** deficient, hardly any **10** inadequate, little or no **12** insufficient

scantily
06 barely, poorly **08** meagrely, scarcely, skimpily, sparsely **11** deficiently **12** inadequately **14** insufficiently

scanty
03 low, shy **04** bare, hard, poor, thin **05** brief, light, scant, short, skimp, spare **06** little, meagre, narrow, scrimp, skimpy, sparse **07** limited, scrimpy **08** exiguous **09** deficient, penurious **10** inadequate, restricted **12** insufficient **13** insubstantial

scapegoat
05 bunny, patsy **06** stooge, sucker, victim **07** fall guy **11** whipping-boy

scar
04 mark, wipe **05** brand, cliff, hilum, scare, scaur, shock, spoil, wound **06** blotch, damage, deface, injure, injury, keloid, lesion, stigma, trauma, ulosis **07** blemish, desmoid, pockpit **08** cicatrix, pockmark, sword-cut **09** cicatrice, cicatrize, discolour, disfigure **10** cicatricle, defacement, stigmatize, traumatize **11** cicatricula, leaf-cushion **12** cicatrichule, parrot-wrasse **13** disfigurement **14** discolouration

scarce
03 few **04** dear, rare **05** scant, tight **06** meagre, scanty, sparse **07** lacking, sparing, unusual **08** uncommon **09** deficient, not enough, too little **10** inadequate, infrequent **12** insufficient, like gold dust **13** in short supply

• **make yourself scarce**
05 scoot **06** go fast **07** dash off **08** run for it, rush away **10** make tracks **12** leave quickly **15** take to your heels

scarcely
03 not **05** uneth **06** barely, hardly, uneath **08** no sooner, not at all, only just, scantily, scrimply, uneathes, unnethes **12** certainly not **13** definitely not

scarcity
04 lack, want **05** scant **06** dearth, famine, rarity **07** paucity **08** exiguity, rareness, shortage **09** scantness **10** deficiency, scantiness, sparseness **11** infrequency **12** uncommonness **13** insufficiency, niggardliness

scare
04 scar, scat, shoo **05** alarm, appal, daunt, gally, gliff, glift, panic, scaur, shock, skear, skeer, start **06** affray, dismay, fright, horror, menace, rattle, scarre, terror **07** perturb, petrify, startle, terrify, unnerve **08** frighten, hysteria, threaten **09** terrorize **10** intimidate, make afraid, scare silly **11** fearfulness **12** put the wind up **14** make frightened

scarecrow
04 bogy **05** bogle, sewel **06** boggle, malkin, mawkin, shewel **07** boggard, boggart **09** galli-crow, gally-crow **10** crow-keeper **11** galli-bagger, galli-beggar, gally-bagger, gally-beggar, potato bogle, tattiebogle

scared
03 rad **05** cowed **06** afraid, shaken **07** alarmed, anxious, chicken, fearful, jittery, nervous, panicky, quivery, worried **08** startled, unnerved **09** petrified, terrified **10** frightened, terrorized **11** in a blue funk **13** having kittens, panic-stricken, scared to death **14** terror-stricken

scaremonger
08 alarmist **09** Cassandra, jitterbug, pessimist **11** doomwatcher **13** prophet of doom

scarf
10 chaplaincy

Scarfs, veils and other head cloths include:

04 caul, doek, haik, hyke, rail, sash, veil
05 curch, fichu, haick, hejab, hijab, pagri, shawl, stole, volet, whisk
06 chadar, chador, cravat, haique, kiss-me, madras, rebozo, screen, tippet, turban, weeper, wimple
07 belcher, chaddar, chaddor, chuddah, chuddar, dopatta, dupatta, foulard, kufiyah, modesty, muffler, necktie, orarium, puggery, puggree, whimple, yashmak
08 babushka, chrismal, kaffiyeh, kalyptra, keffiyeh, kerchief, mantilla, neckatee, puggaree, vexillum
09 comforter, headcloth, headscarf, muffettee
10 fascinator, headsquare, lambrequin
11 kiss-me-quick, neckerchief, nightingale

scarlet
03 red **06** redden, vermil **07** vermeil, vermell, vermily **08** cardinal **09** vermeille, vermilion

scarper
02 go **04** bolt, flee, flit **05** leave, scram **06** beat it, decamp, depart, escape, vanish **07** abscond, bunk off, do a bunk, run away, vamoose **08** clear off, run for it **09** disappear, skedaddle **10** hightail it **13** make a run for it

scary
05 eerie, hairy **06** creepy, skeary, skeery, spooky **08** alarming, chilling, daunting, fearsome, shocking, timorous **10** disturbing, forbidding, formidable, horrifying, petrifying, terrifying **11** frightening, hair-raising **12** intimidating, white-knuckle **13** bloodcurdling, spine-chilling

scathing
04 acid **05** harsh **06** biting, bitter, brutal, fierce, savage, severe **07** caustic, cutting, mordant **08** critical, scornful, stinging **09** ferocious, sarcastic, trenchant, unsparing, vitriolic, withering **11** detrimental, devastating

scatter
◇ *anagram indicator*
03 dot, sow **05** blind, fling, flurr, scail, scale, shake, skail, strew **06** berley, burley, dispel, divide, litter, shower, spread **07** break up, diffuse, disband, disject, scamble, shatter, spatter **08** disperse, disunite, separate, splutter, sprinkle, squander **09** bescatter, broadcast, dissipate **10** dispersion, scattering, sprinkling **11** backscatter, disseminate, intersperse **12** disintegrate **14** cast to the winds **15** fling to the winds, throw to the winds

scatterbrained
05 ditsy, ditzy, dizzy **06** scatty **08** carefree, careless **09** airheaded, forgetful, frivolous, impulsive, slaphappy **10** unreliable **11** empty-headed, hare-brained, inattentive, thoughtless **12** absent-minded **13** irresponsible, wool-gathering **14** feather-brained

scattering
03 few **07** break-up, handful, poor-oot, pour-out **10** dispersion, smattering, sprinkling **12** disgregation

scatty
◇ *anagram indicator*
10 abstracted **11** empty-headed, hare-brained, harum-scarum **12** absent-minded **14** scatterbrained

scavenge
04 hunt, rake **06** forage, search **07** cleanse, look for, rummage **08** scrounge

scavenger
04 dieb, hyen **05** hyena, raker **06** hyaena, jackal **07** forager, gorcrow, scaffie, vulture **08** caracara, night-man, rummager, scavager **09** scrounger **13** lion's provider

scenario
04 plan, plot **05** scene, state **06** résumé, scheme, script **07** outline, summary **08** sequence, synopsis **09** programme, situation, storyline **10** continuity, projection, screenplay **13** circumstances **14** state of affairs

scene
03 act, set **04** area, clip, fuss, part, show, site, spot, to-do, veil, view **05** arena, drama, field, place, scena, sight, stage, vista **06** circus, furore, locale, milieu, screen **07** context, curtain, display, episode, outlook, pageant, picture, scenery, setting, tableau, tantrum **08** backdrop, division, incident, locality, location, outburst, panorama, position, prospect **09** commotion, induction, kerfuffle, landscape, situation, spectacle **10** background, exhibition, proceeding, speciality **11** environment, performance, streetscape, whereabouts **13** tableau vivant **14** area of activity, area of interest **15** three-ring circus

• **behind the scenes**
06 within **08** secretly **09** backstage, in private, privately **10** on the quiet, out of sight **11** not in public **15** surreptitiously

• **scenes**
04 play

scenery
03 set **04** view **05** décor, scene, vista **07** film set, outlook, scenary, setting, terrain **08** backdrop, panorama, prospect **09** landscape **10** background **11** mise-en-scène **12** surroundings

scenic
05 grand **06** pretty **08** striking **09** beautiful, panoramic **10** attractive, impressive **11** picturesque, spectacular **12** awe-inspiring, breathtaking

scent
04 nose, odor, sent, vent, waft **05** aroma, fumet, odour, sense, smell, sniff, spoor, trace, track, trail **06** detect **07** bouquet, cologne, discern, essence, fumette, nose out, perfume **08** perceive, sniff out **09** fragrance, recognize, redolence **11** toilet water **12** eau-de-cologne **13** become aware of, eau-de-toilette

scented
04 rank **07** roseate **08** aromatic, fragrant, perfumed **13** sweet-smelling

sceptic
05 cynic **07** atheist, doubter, scoffer **08** agnostic **10** questioner, unbeliever **11** disbeliever, rationalist **14** doubting Thomas

sceptical
07 cynical, dubious, infidel **08** academic, doubtful, doubting, hesitant, scoffing **10** hesitating, suspicious, Voltairian **11** distrustful, incredulous, mistrustful, pessimistic, questioning, unbelieving, unconvinced **12** disbelieving

scepticism
05 doubt **07** atheism, dubiety **08** cynicism, distrust, nihilism, unbelief **09** disbelief, hesitancy, pessimism, Sadducism, suspicion **10** Pyrrhonism **11** agnosticism, incredulity, rationalism, Sadduceeism **12** doubtfulness

• expression of scepticism
02 ha **04** umph **09** away you go! **11** away with you! **12** pigs might fly

sceptre
03 rod **05** baton, staff **06** bauble

schedule
04 book, form, list, plan, time **05** diary, slate, table **06** agenda, assign, scheme **07** appoint, arrange **08** calendar, organize, syllabus **09** catalogue, inventory, itinerary, programme, timetable **10** enschedule

• behind schedule
04 late **07** overdue **10** behindhand, behind time **11** running late

• on schedule
05 on tap **06** on time **07** on track **08** on course, on target **15** according to plan

• place in schedule
04 slot **06** window

schema
03 map **04** form, plan **05** chart, shape **06** design, figure, layout, scheme, sketch **07** diagram, outline, profile, tracing **09** lineament **11** delineation **13** configuration

schematic
07 graphic **08** symbolic **10** simplified **12** diagrammatic, illustrative

scheme
◇ *anagram indicator*
03 gin, key, map **04** dart, game, idea, plan, plat, plot, ploy, ruse **05** angle, chart, draft, frame, shape, shift, table **06** bubble, design, device, devise, layout, method, schema, sketch, system, tactic **07** collude, connive, diagram, nostrum, outline, pattern, project, tactics, work out **08** conspire, contrive, escapade, intrigue, pedigree, platform, practice, practise, proposal, schedule, strategy **09** blueprint, machinate, manoeuvre, procedure, programme, stratagem, underplot **10** conspiracy, manipulate, mastermind, suggestion **11** arrangement, delineation, disposition, proposition, pull strings **12** machinations **13** configuration **14** course of action

schemer
03 fox **07** plotter, wangler **08** conniver, deceiver **09** contriver, intrigant, intriguer **10** intrigante, intriguant, machinator, mastermind, politician, wire-puller **11** intriguante, Machiavelli **13** éminence grise, Machiavellian, wheeler-dealer

scheming
03 sly **04** foxy, wily **06** artful, crafty, tricky **07** cunning, devious **08** practice, slippery **09** conniving, deceitful, designing, insidious, underhand **11** calculating, duplicitous **12** manipulative, unscrupulous **13** Machiavellian

schism
04 rift, sect **05** break, group, split **06** breach **07** discord, faction, rupture **08** disunion, division, scission, splinter **09** severance **10** detachment, separation **12** estrangement

schismatic
05 rebel **08** apostate, renegade, seceding **09** breakaway, heretical **10** dissenting, separatist **12** secessionist

schmaltz
04 glop, gush, mush, pulp **05** slush **09** soppiness **10** sloppiness **11** mawkishness, romanticism **12** emotionalism **14** sentimentality

scholar
01 L **02** BA, MA **05** clerk, pupil **06** day-boy, expert, pundit, savant **07** artsman, bookman, Dantist, day-girl, egghead, Grecian, learner, Maulana, Pauline, savante, student **08** academic, bookworm, boursier, disciple, Saxonist, schoolie, Semitist, taberdar **09** authority, Gothicist, schoolboy, schoolman, Talmudist **10** Carthusian, day-scholar, mastermind, postmaster, scholastic, schoolgirl **11** philosopher, schoolchild **12** intellectual, man of letters **14** woman of letters **15** person of letters

scholarly
06 school **07** bookish, clerkly, erudite, learned **08** academic, highbrow, lettered, literate, studious, well-read **09** clerklike **10** analytical, scholastic, scientific **12** intellectual **13** conscientious, knowledgeable

scholarship
05 award, burse, grant **06** wisdom **07** bursary **08** learning **09** education, endowment, erudition, knowledge, schooling **10** exhibition, fellowship **11** learnedness, Orientalism

scholastic
06 subtle **07** bookish, learned, precise, teacher **08** academic, lettered, literary, pedantic **09** pedagogic, scholarly, schoolman **10** analytical **11** educational

school
02 GS **03** gam, pod, Sch, set **04** club, coed, high, prep, scul, sect **05** class, coach, drill, flock, group, guild, prime, scull, shoal, teach, train, troop, tutor, verse **06** circle, clique, infant, junior, league, pupils, sculle **07** academy, college, company, coterie, educate, faction, faculty, madrasa, prepare, primary, society, yeshiva **08** admonish, division, instruct, madrasah, madrassa, seminary, students, yeshivah **09** institute, madrassah, medresseh, palaestra, secondary **10** assemblage, department, discipline, foundation, kohanga reo, university **11** association, institution, pedagoguery **12** indoctrinate

Schools include:

03 LSE
04 Eton
05 Rugby, Slade
06 Ascham, Fettes, Harrow, Te Aute
07 Loretto, Roedean, St Paul's
08 Bluecoat, Hogwarts
09 Cranbrook
10 Ampleforth, Grange Hill, Greyfriars, Shrewsbury, Stonyhurst, St Trinian's, The Friends, Winchester
11 Abbotsleigh, Giggleswick, Gordonstoun, Marlborough, Perth Modern, Westminster
12 Chalet School, Charterhouse, Linbury Court, Malory Towers, Marcia Blaine
13 Dotheboys Hall, James Ruse High, Queen Victoria
14 Fort Street High, Geelong Grammar, The Kings School
15 Merchant Taylors'

See also **art**; **educational**

schoolboy, schoolgirl *see* **pupil**

schooling
05 drill **07** reproof, tuition **08** coaching, guidance, learning, teaching, training **09** education, grounding, reprimand **10** discipline **11** instruction, preparation **12** book-learning **14** indoctrination

schoolteacher
06 master **07** dominie, teacher **08** educator, mistress, schoolie **09** pedagogue **10** instructor, schoolmarm **12** schoolmaster **14** schoolmistress

schooner
04 tern **12** fore-and-after

science
03 art, sci **05** skill **09** dexterity, expertise, knowledge, technique **10** discipline, technology **11** proficiency **14** specialization

Sciences include:

04 agri, food, life
05 earth
06 botany

07 anatomy, biology, ecology, geology, medical, natural, physics, zoology
08 chemurgy, computer, domestic, dynamics, genetics, robotics
09 acoustics, astronomy, chemistry, dietetics, economics, materials, mechanics, pathology, political, sociology
10 biophysics, entomology, geophysics, graphology, hydraulics, metallurgy, mineralogy, morphology, physiology, psychology, toxicology, veterinary
11 aeronautics, archaeology, behavioural, climatology, cybernetics, diagnostics, electronics, engineering, linguistics, mathematics, meteorology, ornithology, ultrasonics
12 aerodynamics, agricultural, anthropology, astrophysics, biochemistry, geochemistry, geographical, macrobiotics, microbiology, pharmacology
13 environmental
14 geoarchaeology, nuclear physics, radiochemistry, thermodynamics
15 electrodynamics, space technology

See also **science fiction** *under* **fiction**

scientific
05 exact 07 orderly, precise
08 accurate, thorough 09 regulated, scholarly 10 analytical, controlled, methodical, systematic
12 mathematical 13 demonstrative
See also **law**

Scientific concepts include:

04 area, heat, mass, time, work
05 force, power
06 energy, length, stress, torque, volume
07 density
08 enthalpy, momentum, pressure, velocity
09 frequency, impedance, reactance, viscosity
10 admittance, plane angle, solid angle
11 capacitance, conductance, power factor, susceptance, temperature
12 acceleration, electric flux, illumination, luminous flux, magnetic flux, permeability, permittivity
13 electric force, kinetic energy, moment of force
14 electric charge, mass rate of flow, self inductance, surface tension
15 angular momentum, electric current, moment of inertia, potential energy, velocity of light

Scientific instruments include:

06 strobe
07 coherer, vernier
08 barostat, cryostat, rheocord, rheostat
09 decoherer, heliostat, hodoscope, hydrostat, hygrostat, image tube, microtome, slide rule, telemeter, tesla coil, thyratron, zymoscope
10 centrifuge, collimator, eudiometer, heliograph, humidistat, hydrophone, hydroscope, hygrograph, iconoscope, microscope, nephograph, pantograph, radarscope, radiosonde, tachograph, teinoscope, thermostat
11 chronograph, fluoroscope, stactometer, stauroscope, stroboscope, transformer, transponder, tunnel diode
12 dephlegmator, electrosonde, oscillograph, oscilloscope, spectroscope
13 Geiger counter, phonendoscope, tachistoscope
14 absorptiometer, image converter, interferometer, torsion balance
15 electromyograph, telethermoscope

scientist
05 brain 06 boffin, doctor, expert, genius 07 analyst, ologist, planner, thinker 08 designer, engineer, inventor 09 intellect, magnetist 10 alchemist, mastermind, researcher 11 backroom-boy 12 entomologist, experimenter, intellectual, investigator, technologist 14 explorationist, research worker
See also **anatomy**; **anthropology**; **archaeology**; **astronomer**; **bacteriology**; **biochemistry**; **biology**; **botany**; **chemist**; **computer**; **economist**; **engineer**; **genetics**; **geography**; **inventor**; **mathematics**; **palaeontologist**; **physics**; **physiology**; **psychology**; **zoology**

scintilla
03 bit, jot 04 atom, hint, iota, mite, spot, whit 05 grain, piece, scrap, shred, spark, speck, trace 07 modicum, remnant, snippet 08 fragment, particle, skerrick

scintillate
04 wink 05 blaze, flash, gleam, glint, shine, spark 07 glisten, glitter, sparkle, twinkle 09 coruscate

scintillating
05 witty 06 bright, lively 07 shining
08 animated, dazzling, exciting, flashing 09 brilliant, ebullient, sparkling, twinkling, vivacious
10 glittering 11 stimulating
12 exhilarating, invigorating

scion
03 imp 04 cion, heir, sien, syen, twig
05 child, graft, plant, seyen, shoot, sient, sprig 06 branch, sprout
08 offshoot 09 offspring, successor
10 descendant 11 engraftment

scissors
06 cizers, forfex, shears 13 pinking shears

scoff
03 dor, eat, rib 04 bolt, chow, eats, food, gall, geck, gibe, grub, gulp, jeer, jibe, meal, mock, nosh, rail, tuck, wolf 05 binge, knock, scaff, scorn, scran, snarf, sneer, taunt, tease 06 deride, devour, gall at, geck at, gobble, guzzle, nosh-up, revile 07 consume, despise, laugh at, mockery, plunder, poke fun, put away 08 belittle, eatables, pooh-pooh, ridicule 09 disparage, finish off, nutriment, nutrition 10 foodstuffs, provisions, sustenance 11 comestibles, nourishment, subsistence
12 refreshments

scoffing
07 cynical, mocking 08 derisive, derisory, fiendish, scathing, sneering, taunting 09 sarcastic 11 disparaging
14 Mephistophelic
15 Mephistophelean, Mephistophelian

scold
03 jaw, nag, rag, row, wig, yap 04 Fury, rage, rant, rate, yaff 05 blame, brawl, chide, flite, flyte, go off, shrew, slang, vixen 06 berate, blow up, callet, dragon, rattle, rebuke, virago, yankie
07 censure, earbash, go off at, jawbone, lambast, lecture, reprove, rouse on, speak to, start on, tell off, tick off, trimmer, upbraid 08 admonish, harridan, reproach, spitfire, tear into, Xantippe 09 brimstone, castigate, go crook at, henpecker, objurgate, reprimand, start in on, take apart, termagant 10 take to task
11 clapperclaw 15 give it to someone

scolding
03 row 05 doing 06 dirdam, dirdum, earful, rating, rebuke 07 chiding, hearing, lecture, reproof, rollick, wigging 08 jobation, sasarara, siserary, slanging 09 carpeting, jawbation, reprimand, sassarara, sisserary, talking-to, termagant 10 earbashing, earwigging, telling-off, ticking-off, upbraiding 11 castigation, throughgaun 12 dressing-down, through-going

scombroid fish
04 seer, seir

scoop
03 dig, dip, lap 04 bail, coup, grab, lade, pale 05 empty, gouge, ladle, spoon 06 bailer, bucket, dipper, exposé, hollow, latest, remove, scrape, shovel 07 helping, portion
08 excavate, ladleful, spoonful
09 exclusive, sensation 10 revelation
11 inside story

scoot
03 run, zip 04 belt, bolt, dart, dash, rush, scud, tear 05 hurry, scout, shoot
06 beat it, career, scurry, sprint, squirt, tootle 07 scarper, scuttle, vamoose
09 skedaddle

scope
03 aim, VDU, way 04 area, play, room, span, wale 05 ambit, field, orbit, range, reach, realm, remit, round, space, sweep, swing, verge 06 cinema, domain, extent, leeway, limits, scouth, scowth, sphere 07 breadth, compass,

display, freedom, liberty, monitor, purpose, purview **08** capacity, confines, coverage, latitude
09 dimension, elbow-room
11 opportunity **12** spaciousness

scorch
03 fry **04** burn, char, plot, sear
05 adust, blast, dry up, parch, ploat, roast, scald, scath, singe, slash, swale, swayl, sweal, sweel **06** birsle, scaith, scathe, sizzle, skaith, wither
07 blacken, frizzle, scowder, shrivel, torrefy **08** scouther, scowther
09 discolour

scorching
05 blast **06** baking, red-hot, torrid
07 boiling, burning, searing
08 roasting, sizzling, tropical
09 withering **10** blistering, scowdering, sweltering **11** scouthering
12 extremely hot

score
02 XX **03** cut, get, law, net, rit, run, set, sum, win **04** case, earn, gain, gash, hail, hits, line, lots, make, mark, nick, ritt, runs, slit **05** adapt, basis, count, facts, goals, gouge, graze, hosts, issue, marks, notch, put on, slash, tally, total, truth, write **06** aspect, attain, crowds, droves, groove, grudge, incise, indent, masses, matter, points, reason, record, result, scotch, scrape, shoals, swarms, target, the gen, twenty **07** account, achieve, arrange, be one up, chalk up, concern, dispute, engrave, grounds, legions, motives, myriads, notch up, outcome, quarrel, scratch, subject
08 argument, hundreds, incision, millions, question, register
09 complaint, enumerate, grievance, reckoning, situation, thousands, what's what **10** instrument, keep a tally, multitudes, the picture **11** explanation, have the edge, orchestrate **12** be successful **13** hit the jackpot **14** state of affairs **15** the whole picture

- **even the score**

06 avenge **07** get back **09** retaliate
14 settle the score

- **score off**

09 humiliate **11** have the edge **12** get one over on

- **score out**

05 erase **06** cancel, delete, efface, remove **07** expunge **08** cross out
09 strike out **10** obliterate

scorn
04 geck, mock, shun, spit, zing
05 blurt, spurn **06** deride, rebuff, refuse, reject, scorch, slight **07** crucify, despise, disdain, disgust, dismiss, laugh at, mockery, sarcasm, scoff at, sneer at, sniff at **08** contempt, derision, mesprise, mesprize, misprise, misprize, ridicule, sneering **09** contumely, disparage **10** look down on
11 haughtiness **12** scornfulness
13 disparagement

scornful
07 haughty, jeering, mocking
08 arrogant, derisive, sardonic, scathing, scoffing, sneering
09 insulting, sarcastic, slighting
10 disdainful, dismissive **11** disparaging
12 contemptuous, supercilious

scornfully
09 haughtily **10** arrogantly, derisively, scathingly, sneeringly **11** slightingly, witheringly **12** disdainfully, dismissively
13 disparagingly **14** contemptuously, superciliously

scorpion
07 Scorpio **08** ballista, pedipalp
11 Eurypterida

Scot
◇ *dialect indicator*
03 Mac **04** Gael
See also **Scottish**

scotch
04 gash, halt, maim, ruin, stop
05 block, quash, score, strut, wedge, wreck **07** scupper, scuttle **09** frustrate
10 put an end to, put a stop to **11** put the lid on **12** bring to an end **13** pull the plug on

scot-free
04 safe **05** clear **06** unhurt **07** untaxed
08 shot-free, unharmed
09 undamaged, uninjured, unrebuked, unscathed **10** unpunished
12 unreproached **13** unreprimanded
15 without a scratch

Scotland *see* **council**; **town**

Scotsman *see* **Scot**; **Scottish**

Scottish
◇ *dialect word indicator*
See also **monarch**

Scottish first names include:

03 Ian, Rab, Rae
04 Doug, Euan, Ewan, Ewen, Greg, Iain, Iona, Isla, Jess, Jock
05 Ailsa, Angus, Arran, Blair, Calum, Clyde, Colin, Craig, Isbel, Logan, Lorna, Lorne, Sandy
06 Aileen, Callum, Dougie, Elspet, Gordon, Gregor, Hamish, Kelvin, Lilias, Mhàiri, Rabbie, Ranald, Vanora
07 Cameron, Douglas, Elspeth, Malcolm
08 Campbell, Catriona

Scottish clans include:

04 Ross
05 Baird, Bruce, Grant, Innes, Munro, Scott
06 Brodie, Buchan, Dunbar, Duncan, Dundas, Eliott, Elliot, Forbes, Fraser, Gordon, Graeme, Graham, Irvine, Irving, Lennox, Mackay, Macnab, Macrae, Moffat, Monroe, Murray, Napier, Ogilvy, Ramsay, Stuart
07 Balfour, Cameron, Douglas, Macduff, Maclean, Macleod, Macneil, Malcolm, Ogilvie, Stewart, Wallace
08 Anderson, Campbell, Drummond, Ferguson, Hamilton, Macaulay, MacInnes, Macneill, Oliphant, Sinclair, Stirling, Urquhart
09 Armstrong, Colquhoun, Fergusson, Henderson, Johnstone, MacAlpine, MacAndrew, MacArthur, MacCallum, Macdonald, Macgregor, Macintosh, Macintyre, Mackenzie, Mackinnon, Macmillan, Nicholson, Robertson
10 Macdonnell, Macdougall, Mackintosh, Macpherson, Sutherland
11 MacAllister, MacLauchlan, MacLaughlan, Macnaughton

scoundrel
03 cur, dog, rat **04** scab **05** cheat, hound, louse, rogue, scamp, swine
06 donder, louser, rascal, rotter, scally
07 bounder, dastard, ruffian, stinker, villain **08** blighter, spalpeen, vagabond
09 miscreant, reprobate, scallywag
10 blackguard, hounds-foot, ne'er-do-well **14** good-for-nothing

scour
◇ *anagram indicator*
03 rub **04** comb, drag, full, hunt, rake, scur, sker, wash, wipe **05** clean, flush, purge, scout, scrub, skirr, skirt
06 abrade, forage, polish, punish, scrape, search, squirr **07** burnish, cleanse, ransack, rummage **08** clear out **14** turn upside-down

scourge
04 bane, beat, cane, evil, flog, lash, whip **05** birch, curse, flail, strap, trial
06 burden, menace, plague, punish, switch, terror, thrash **07** afflict, penalty, torment, torture **08** chastise, nuisance, scorpion **09** devastate, flagellum
10 affliction, discipline, misfortune, punishment **13** cat-o'-nine-tails
14 disciplinarium **15** thorn in your side

scout
03 cub, spy **04** case, hunt, look, mock, seek **05** flout, probe, recce, rover, scoot, sixer, snoop, spial, watch
06 beaver, escort, person, search, spying, spy out, survey **07** explore, inspect, look for, lookout, observe, pickeer, scourer, spotter, wolf cub
08 check out, outrider, scurrier, vanguard **09** recruiter, scurriour
10 discoverer, tenderfoot
11 investigate, reconnoitre, voortrekker
12 advance guard **13** talent spotter

scowl
04 lour, pout **05** frown, glare, gloom, lower **06** glower **07** grimace **09** black look, dirty look, overgloom **13** look daggers at

scrabble
◇ *anagram indicator*
03 dig, paw **04** claw, grub, root
05 grope **06** scrape, scrawl
07 clamber, scratch **08** scramble

scraggy
◇ *anagram indicator*
04 bony, lean, thin **05** gaunt, lanky
06 skinny, wasted **07** angular, scrawny,

unkempt **08** raw-boned **09** emaciated, irregular **10** straggling **14** undernourished

scram
04 bolt, flee, puny, quit, scat **05** leave, scoot **06** beat it, depart, get out, go away **07** buzz off, do a bunk, scarper, vamoose **08** clear off, clear out, shove off, withered **09** disappear, skedaddle **15** take to your heels

scramble
◇ *anagram indicator*
03 mix, ren, rin, run, vie **04** dash, muss, push, race, rush **05** climb, crawl, grope, hurry, mêlée, mix up, musse, scale, vying **06** battle, bustle, hasten, hustle, infuse, jockey, jostle, jumble, muddle, scurry, strive, swerve, tussle **07** clamber, compete, contend, disturb, grabble, rat race, scaling, scamble, shuffle **08** scrabble, sprattle, stampede, struggle **09** commotion, confusion **10** free-for-all **11** competition, disorganize

scrap
03 axe, bit, ort, rag, row **04** atom, bite, bits, drop, dump, glim, iota, junk, mite, part, shed, snap, tiff **05** argue, brawl, crumb, crust, ditch, fight, grain, patch, piece, scrip, set-to, shard, sherd, shred, trace, waste **06** battle, bicker, bundle, cancel, dust-up, fracas, morsel, sliver, splore, stitch, tatter, verset **07** abandon, break up, discard, dispute, fall out, punch-up, quarrel, remains, remnant, residue, scissel, scissil, scuffle, snippet, vestige, wrangle **08** argument, chuck out, demolish, disagree, fraction, fragment, get rid of, jettison, leavings, leftover, mouthful, particle, quantity, skerrick, squabble, write off **09** leftovers, scrapings, throw away **11** odds and ends, odds and sods **12** disagreement **13** bits and pieces
• **on the scrap heap**
06 dumped **07** ditched **08** rejected **09** discarded, forgotten, redundant **10** jettisoned, written off

scrape
03 cut, fix, hoe, paw, rub **04** bark, clat, claw, file, hole, mess, rake, rase, rasp, raze, skin **05** claut, clean, curet, erase, flesh, grate, graze, grind, scalp, scart, scour, scrab, scuff, shave, shred **06** abrade, hobble, pickle, plight, remove, splore **07** curette, descale, dilemma, scratch, snapper, trouble **08** abrasion, distress, scrabble, wrong box **09** curettage, shemozzle, shimozzle, tight spot **10** difficulty, praemunire, schemozzle, shlemozzle **11** predicament
• **scrape by**
05 get by, skimp **06** eke out, scrimp **13** muddle through
• **scrape through**
08 just pass **09** barely win **11** only just win **13** just succeed in
• **scrape together**
07 round up, scuffle **11** get together **12** pool together **15** just manage to get

scrappy
◇ *anagram indicator*
05 bitty **06** untidy **07** sketchy **08** slapdash, slipshod **09** piecemeal **10** disjointed, incomplete **11** belligerent, fragmentary, quarrelsome, superficial **12** disconnected, disorganized

scraps
04 odds **05** brock, trash **08** dog's-meat

scratch
◇ *anagram indicator*
◇ *deletion indicator*
03 cut, rit, rub **04** cash, clat, claw, etch, gash, line, mark, nick, race, rase, ritt, skin, tear **05** claut, curry, Devil, fluke, gouge, graze, rough, scart, score, scrab, scram, scrat, scuff, tease, wound **06** abrade, casual, incise, scramb, scrape, scrawm, streak **07** engrave **08** abrasion, lacerate, scrabble **09** haphazard, impromptu **10** improvised, laceration, ready money **11** clapperclaw, unrehearsed **13** rough-and-ready
• **up to scratch**
02 OK **08** adequate **09** competent, tolerable, up to snuff **10** acceptable, good enough, reasonable **11** up to the mark **12** satisfactory

scrawl
03 jot, pen **06** doodle **07** dash off, jot down, scratch, writing **08** scrabble, scribble, squiggle **10** cacography **11** handwriting **12** write quickly **14** bad handwriting

scrawny
04 bony, lean, thin **05** lanky **06** meagre, skinny, sparse **07** angular, scraggy, scranny **08** raw-boned, underfed **09** emaciated **14** undernourished

scream
03 cry, eek, wit **04** bawl, hoot, howl, riot, roar, wail, yawp, yell, yelp **05** comic, joker, laugh, shout **06** holler, shriek, squawk, squeal **07** screech **08** comedian **09** character **13** cry blue murder **15** shout blue murder

screech
03 cry **04** howl, yell, yelp **06** screak, scream, shriek, squawk, squeal **07** scraich, scraigh, screich, screigh, scriech, scritch, shriech, shritch, skreigh, skriech, skriegh, ululate

screen
03 net, VDU, vet **04** grid, hide, mask, mesh, scan, show, sift, sort, test, veil **05** blind, check, chick, cloak, cover, front, gauge, grade, grill, guard, scope, shade, sieve **06** awning, canopy, defend, façade, filter, grille, purdah, riddle, sconce, shield, shroud **07** conceal, cribble, curtain, divider, examine, monitor, netting, picture, present, process, protect, reredos, shelter **08** abat-jour, disguise, evaluate, parclose, traverse **09** broadcast, dashboard, faceplate, partition, reredorse, reredosse, safeguard **10** camouflage, protection **11** concealment, investigate, room-divider **12** clothes-horse
• **screen off**
04 hide **06** divide **07** conceal, protect **08** fence off, separate **09** divide off, partition **11** separate off **12** partition off

screenwriter *see* **playwright**

screw
◇ *anagram indicator*
03 fix, pay, pin, rob **04** bolt, brad, milk, nail, tack, turn, wind **05** bleed, cheat, clamp, force, rivet, twist, wages, wrest, wring **06** adjust, burgle, extort, fasten, pucker, salary **07** defraud, distort, extract, squeeze, tighten, wrinkle **08** compress, contract, fastener, pressure **09** constrain, skinflint **10** pressurize **12** extortionist
• **put the screws on**
05 force **06** coerce, compel, lean on **07** dragoon **09** constrain, strongarm **10** pressurize
• **screwed up**
05 upset **06** hung up **07** mixed up, muddled, puzzled **08** confused, messed up **09** disturbed, perplexed **10** bewildered, disordered, distracted, distraught **11** disoriented, maladjusted
• **screw up**
04 knot, ruin **05** botch, spoil, twist **06** bungle, cock up, mess up, pucker **07** contort, crumple, disrupt, distort, louse up, squinch, stuff up, tighten, wrinkle **08** contract, summon up **09** mishandle, mismanage **11** make a hash of

screwy
◇ *anagram indicator*
03 mad, odd **04** daft **05** batty, crazy, dotty, nutty, queer, tipsy, weird **08** crackers **09** eccentric **12** round the bend **13** round the twist

scribble
03 jot, pen **05** write **06** doodle, scrawl **07** dash off, jot down, scratch, writing **08** bescrawl, scrabble, squiggle **10** bescribble, cacography **11** handwriting **14** bad handwriting

scribbler
04 hack **06** writer **09** ink-jerker, pen-pusher, pot-boiler **10** ink-slinger **11** inkhorn-mate, verse-monger **12** paper-stainer

scribe
04 hack **05** clerk, write **06** author, incise, mallam, penman, writer **07** copyist **08** recorder, reporter **09** pen-pusher, scrivener, secretary **10** amanuensis **11** transcriber **12** calligrapher, hierographer

scrimmage
03 row **04** fray, riot **05** brawl, bully, fight, mêlée, rouge, scrap, scrum, set-to **06** affray, bovver, dust-up, shindy **07** scuffle **08** skirmish, squabble, struggle **10** free-for-all **11** disturbance

scrimp
04 save **05** limit, pinch, skimp, stint **06** barely, reduce, scanty, scrape **07** curtail, shorten, stinted **08** restrict **09** cut back on, economize **15** tighten your belt

script
02 MS **04** book, copy, hand, Jawi, text **05** Cufic, Kufic, lines, ronde, words **06** Arabic, nagari **07** letters, linear A, linear B, writing **08** dialogue, Gurmukhi, libretto, longhand, nastalik, nasta'liq, Sumerian **09** minuscule **10** devanagari, manuscript, screenplay **11** calligraphy, Cypro-Minoan, handwriting, running-hand **14** rustic capitals, shooting script

• insert into script
03 cue

scripture
02 RE, RI

Religious writings include:

02 NT, OT
05 Bayan, Bible, Koran, Qur'an, sutra, Torah, Vedas, Zohar
06 Gemara, gospel, Granth, Hadith, I Ching, Kojiki, Mishna, Talmud, Tantra
07 epistle, Li Ching, Puranas, Shari'ah
08 Haft Wadi, Halakhah, Ramayana, Shu Ching
09 Adi Granth, Apocrypha, Chuang-tzu, Chu'un Ch'iu, Decalogue, Digambara, Hexateuch, scripture, Shih Ching, Tripitaka
10 Heptateuch, Lotus Sutra, Nohon Shoki, Pentateuch, Svetambara, Tao-te-ching, Upanishads, Zend-Avesta
11 Bardo Thodol, Mahabharata
12 Bhagavad Gita, Kitab al-Aqdas, Milindapanha, New Testament, Old Testament
14 Dead Sea Scrolls, Mahayana Sutras, Revised Version
15 Ten Commandments

See also **Bible**

scroll
04 curl, list, roll **05** draft, paper, scrow, Sefer, Torah **06** mezuza, scrowl, stemma, Thorah, volume, volute **07** mezuzah, scrowle **08** cartouch, makimono, megillah, rocaille, schedule **09** cartouche, inventory, parchment **10** monkey tail, phylactery, Sefer Torah

Scrooge
05 crowd, miser **06** meanie **07** niggard, squeeze **08** tightwad **09** skinflint **10** cheapskate **12** money-grubber, penny-pincher

scrounge
03 beg, bum **04** blag **05** cadge **06** bludge, borrow, scunge, sponge **07** purloin

scrounger
03 bum **05** mooch, mouch **06** beggar, cadger, scunge **07** bludger, moocher, sponger **08** borrower, parasite **10** freeloader

scrub
◇ *deletion indicator*
03 axe, rub **04** bush, drop, wash, wipe **05** brush, clean, scour, shrub **06** cancel, delete, drudge, forget, give up, purify **07** abandon, abolish, cleanse, garigue, thicket **08** garrigue **09** backwoods, brushwood, exfoliate, holystone, scrubland **10** improvised, undersized **11** discontinue, undergrowth **13** insignificant

scruff
04 nape **05** scuff, scuft

scruffy
◇ *anagram indicator*
05 daggy, dirty, messy, seedy **06** grotty, ragged, scurvy, shabby, sloppy, untidy **07** run-down, squalid, unkempt, worn-out **08** dog-eared, slovenly, sluttish, tattered **09** ungroomed **10** bedraggled, down-at-heel, slatternly **11** dishevelled **12** disreputable

• scruffy person
03 dag **04** slob **06** scruff

scrum
04 ruck

scrumptious
05 tasty, yummy **06** morish **07** moreish, scrummy **08** gorgeous, luscious **09** delicious, exquisite, succulent **10** appetizing, delectable, delightful **11** magnificent **13** mouthwatering

scrunch
04 chew, mash **05** champ, crush, grate, grind, screw, twist **06** crunch, squash **07** crumple, screw up **09** crumple up

scruple
03 scr **04** balk **05** demur, doubt, qualm, stick **06** boggle, ethics, morals, shrink **07** protest, stickle **08** hesitate, hold back, question **09** disbelief, misgiving, objection, standards, vacillate **10** difficulty, hesitation, perplexity, principles, reluctance, think twice, uneasiness **11** be reluctant, compunction, reservation, vacillation **13** point of honour **14** second thoughts

scrupulous
04 nice **05** exact, moral **06** honest, minute, queasy, queazy, spiced, strict, tender **07** careful, ethical, precise, upright **08** captious, rigorous, thorough **09** religious **10** fastidious, honourable, meticulous, principled **11** painstaking, punctilious **13** conscientious **14** high-principled

scrutinize
04 coat, cote, scan, sift **05** coate, probe, quote, study **06** go over, peruse, search **07** analyse, canvass, examine, explore, inspect, run over **08** look over **09** go through **10** run through **11** investigate, look through

scrutiny
05 probe, study **06** search **07** canvass, check-up, close-up, inquiry, perusal **08** analysis, docimasy **10** inspection **11** examination, exploration **13** investigation

scud
03 fly **04** blow, dart, East, gust, race, sail, skim, slap **05** shoot, speed, spoom, spoon

scuff
03 rub **04** cuff, drag **05** brush, graze, scuft **06** abrade, scrape, scruff **07** scratch

scuffle
◇ *anagram indicator*
03 hoe, row **04** fray **05** brawl, clash, fight, scrap, set-to **06** affray, cuffle, dust-up, rumpus, tussle **07** bagarre, contend, grapple, punch-up, quarrel, scarify, shuffle **08** pull caps, struggle **09** commotion **11** come to blows, disturbance **14** rough-and-tumble

sculpt
◇ *anagram indicator*
03 cut, hew **04** cast, form **05** carve, model, mould, shape **06** chisel **07** fashion **09** represent, sculpture

• he/she sculpted
02 sc **08** sculpsit

sculptor
05 hewer, mason **06** artist, carver, caster **07** moulder, plastic **08** figurist, modeller **09** chiseller, craftsman **10** sculptress **11** craftswoman, stone-carver

Sculptors include:

03 **Arp** (Hans), **Ray** (Man)
04 **Bell** (John), **Bone** (Phyllis), **Caro** (Sir Anthony), **Gabo** (Naum), **Gill** (Eric), **King** (Philip), **Mach** (David), **Rude** (François)
05 **Andre** (Carl), **Bacon** (John), **Beuys** (Joseph), **Cragg** (Tony), **Davey** (Grenville), **Frink** (Dame Elisabeth), **Johns** (Jasper), **Koons** (Jeff), **Manzú** (Giacomo), **Moore** (Henry), **Myron**, **Rodin** (Auguste), **Smith** (David Roland), **Story** (William)
06 **Calder** (Alexander), **Canova** (Antonio), **Cousin** (Jean), **Deacon** (Richard), **Hatoum** (Mona), **Kapoor** (Anish), **Marini** (Marino), **Pisano** (Andrea), **Pisano** (Giovanni), **Robbia** (Luca della), **Scopas**, **Walker** (Dame Ethel)
07 **Bernini** (Gianlorenzo), **Cellini** (Benvenuto), **Christo**, **Duchamp** (Marcel), **Epstein** (Sir Jacob), **Gormley** (Antony), **Klinger** (Max), **Longman** (Evelyn), **Millett** (Kate), **Phidias**, **Samaras** (Lucas)
08 **Boccioni** (Umberto), **Brancusi** (Constantin), **Chadwick** (Lynn), **Ghiberti** (Lorenzo), **Hepworth** (Dame Barbara), **Landseer** (Sir Edwin), **Paolozzi** (Eduardo Luigi), **Pheidias**, **Tinguely** (Jean)
09 **Borromini** (Francesco), **Bourgeois** (Louise), **Donatello**, **Oldenburg** (Claes), **Roubiliac** (Louis François), **Whiteread** (Rachel)

10 Giacometti (Alberto), Polyclitus, Praxiteles, Schwitters (Kurt), Verrocchio (Andrea del)
11 Della Robbia (Luca), Goldsworthy (Andy)
12 Jeanne-Claude, Michelangelo
14 Gaudier-Brzeska (Henri)
15 Leonardo da Vinci

sculpture
◇ *anagram indicator*

Sculpture types include:

04 bust, cast, head, herm, kore
05 group
06 bronze, effigy, figure, kouros, marble, relief, statue
07 carving, kinetic, telamon, waxwork
08 caryatid, Daibutsu, figurine, maquette, moulding
09 bas-relief, statuette
10 high-relief
11 plaster cast

Sculptures and statues include:

04 Adam, Kore, Zeus
05 Angel, Cupid, David, House, Medea, Moses, Pietà, Torso
06 Balzac
07 Bacchus, Genesis, Liberty, Lincoln, Mercury, Merzbau, Spiders, The Kiss, The Wall
08 Cantoria, Ecce Homo, Eggboard, Have Pity!, Mahamuni, Piscator
09 A Universe, Seated Man, Slate Cone
10 Discobolus, Doryphorus, Double Talk, Ledge Piece, Orange Bath, Running Man, Single Form, The Thinker
11 Gomateswara, Kiss and Tell, Pierced Form, Spear Bearer, Venus de Milo
12 Cactus People, Elgin Marbles, Feast of Herod
13 Discus Thrower, Fallen Warrior, People in a Wind, Veduggio Sound
14 Cosimo de' Medici, Fontana Magiore, Horse Lying Down, Japanese War God, Sailing Tonight, The Age of Bronze, The Gates of Hell, The Three Graces
15 Angel of the North, Athena Promachos, Buddhas of Bamian, Christ in Majesty, Figure and Clouds, Giant Clothespin, Madonna and Child, Recumbent Figure

scum
04 dirt, film, foam, slag **05** dregs, dross, froth, layer, plebs, spume, trash **06** mantle, mother, rabble **07** rubbish, sullage **08** covering, pellicle, riff-raff, sandiver **09** epistasis, glass-gall **10** impurities **12** undesirables **13** great unwashed **14** dregs of society, lowest of the low

scupper
03 axe **04** foil, kill, ruin, sink **05** do for, wreck **06** cock up, defeat, mess up **07** destroy, disable, louse up, screw up, scuttle, torpedo **08** demolish, submerge **09** overthrow, overwhelm

scurf
05 scald, scale **06** furfur, scruff **07** furfair **08** dandriff, dandruff **09** flakiness, scaliness **12** scabrousness

scurfy
05 flaky, lepra, scald, scaly **06** scabby, scurvy **07** leprose, leprous, scabrid **08** lepidote, scabrous, scarious **09** furfurous **11** scaberulous **12** furfuraceous

scurrility
05 abuse **07** obloquy **08** foulness, rudeness **09** grossness, indecency, invective, nastiness, obscenity, vulgarity **10** coarseness **11** abusiveness **12** vituperation **13** offensiveness **14** scurrilousness

scurrilous
04 foul, rude **06** coarse, vulgar **07** abusive, obscene, Sotadic **08** indecent, Sotadean **09** insulting, libellous, offensive, salacious **10** defamatory, Fescennine, scandalous, slanderous **11** disparaging **12** vituperative

scurry
03 fly, ren, rin, run **04** dart, dash, race, rush, scud, scur, sker, skim, trot **05** hurry, scoot, scour, skirr, whirl **06** beetle, bustle, flurry, hasten, skurry, sprint, squirr **07** scamper, scutter, scuttle, skelter **08** bustling, scramble **09** beetle off **10** scampering **15** hustle and bustle

scurvy
03 bad, low **04** base, mean, vile, yaws **05** dirty, scall, sorry **06** abject, rotten, scurfy, shabby **07** ignoble, low-down, pitiful, roynish, scruffy **08** whoreson **09** worthless **10** despicable **12** contemptible **13** dishonourable

scuttle
◇ *anagram indicator*
03 hod, ren, rin, run **04** rush, scud **05** hurry **06** bustle, hasten, scurry **07** scamper, scuddle, scutter, skuttle **08** scramble, scrattle **09** purdonium

scythe
03 mow **11** bushwhacker
• **part of scythe**
04 sned **05** snath, snead **06** snathe, sneath

sea
03 mer **04** deep, host, main, mass, salt, tide **05** briny, ocean, swell, waves **06** afloat, marine **07** aquatic, expanse, oceanic **08** maritime **09** abundance, multitude, profusion, roughness, saltwater, seafaring **11** large number

Seas include:

03 Med, Red
04 Aral, Azov, Dead, East, Java, Kara, Ross, Sulu
05 Banda, Black, Coral, Crete, Irish, Japan, North, Timor, White
06 Aegean, Baltic, Bering, Celtic, Flores, Inland, Ionian, Laptev, Nan Hai, Scotia, Tasman, Yellow
07 Andaman, Arabian, Arafura, Barents, Caspian, Celebes, Dong Hai, Galilee, Marmara, Okhotsk, Solomon, Weddell
08 Adriatic, Amundsen, Beaufort, Bismarck, Hebrides, Huang Hai, Labrador, Ligurian, McKinley, Sargasso
09 Caribbean, East China, Greenland, Norwegian
10 Philippine, Setonaikai, South China, Tyrrhenian
11 Yam Kinneret
12 East Siberian
13 Mediterranean
14 Bellingshausen

See also **moon**; **ocean**
• **at sea**
◇ *anagram indicator*
04 lost **06** adrift, afloat **07** baffled, puzzled **08** confused **09** mystified, perplexed **10** bewildered **11** disoriented **12** disorganized **13** disorientated

seabird *see* **bird**

seaborgium
02 Sg

sea bream
03 sar, tai **05** porgy, sargo **06** braise, braize, porgie, sargos, sargus **07** old wife **08** tarwhine

seafaring
05 naval **06** marine **07** oceanic, sailing **08** maritime, nautical, sea-going **10** ocean-going

seafood

Seafood and seafood dishes include:

04 bisk, clam, crab
05 prawn, squid, sushi, whelk
06 bisque, cockle, mussel, oyster, paella, scampi, shrimp, winkle
07 abalone, lobster, octopus, risotto, scallop, tempura, toheroa
08 calamari, coquille, crawfish, crevette, marinara, zarzuela
09 jambalaya, king prawn, surf'n'turf
10 tiger prawn
11 clam-chowder, Dublin prawn, fritto misto, fruits de mer, langoustine, tiger shrimp
13 bouillabaisse, Norway lobster, prawn cocktail
14 Dublin Bay prawn

See also **crustacean**; **fish**; **mollusc**

seahorse
06 tangie, walrus **08** pipefish **09** hippodame, sea dragon **11** hippocampus, lophobranch

seal
04 chop, cork, jark, lute, plug, seel, shut, stop **05** bulla, close, O-ring, plumb, puppy, sigil, stamp, tie up **06** cachet, clinch, enseal, fasten, obsign, ratify, secure, settle, signet, stop up, wicker, willow **07** close up, confirm, consign, enclose, stopper, tar-seal, tighten, ziplock **08** bachelor,

conclude, finalize, insignia, set apart **09** assurance, footprint, obsignate **10** impression, imprimatur, shake hands, waterproof **11** attestation, counterseal **12** confirmation, make airtight, ratification **14** authentication, make watertight

Seals include:

03 fur
04 grey, hair, harp, monk
05 otary, phoca, silky
06 common, hooded, ribbon, sea dog, sealch, sealgh, selkie, silkie
07 harbour, sea bear, sea calf, sea lion, Weddell
08 Atlantic, elephant, seecatch
09 crab-eater, Greenland, whitecoat
10 saddleback, sea leopard
11 sea elephant

• in the place of the seal
02 LS **11** loco sigilli

• seal off
03 cap **06** cut off, fasten **07** block up, isolate, shut off **08** close off, fence off **09** cordon off, segregate **10** quarantine

sealed
04 shut **06** closed, corked **07** plugged **08** hermetic **09** sigillate **10** hermetical, watertight **12** draught-proof

seam
04 fell, join, line, lode, saim, vein, weld **05** joint, layer, quilt, raphe, seame **06** grease, suture, thread **07** closure, joining, stratum, wrinkle **08** cartload, edge coal, junction, wayboard **09** stitching **10** weighboard **12** dorsal suture **15** middle-stitching

seaman
02 AB **03** Kru, tar **04** Kroo **06** merman, sailor **07** killick, killock

See also **sailor**

sea-mist
04 haar

sea-monster
03 orc **04** cete **05** Phoca **06** kraken **07** ziffius **08** seahorse **09** leviathan, rosmarine, sea satyre, wasserman, whirlpool **11** hippocampus

See also **monster**

seamy
03 low **04** dark **05** nasty, rough **06** sleazy, sordid **07** squalid **09** unsavoury **10** unpleasant **12** disreputable

sear
03 dry, fry **04** burn, char, seal, sere, wilt **05** brand, brown, dry up, parch, seare, singe **06** scorch, sizzle, wither **07** burning, shrivel **08** withered **09** cauterize

search
03 pry **04** comb, fish, hunt, rake, ripe, scur, seek, sift, sker **05** check, frisk, grope, probe, quest, rifle, scour, sieve, skirr, sweep **06** ferret, forage, squirr, survey **07** enquire, enquiry, examine, explore, fossick, inquire, inquiry, inspect, look for, pursuit, ransack, rifling, rummage **08** prospect, research, scrutiny **09** cast about, go through, ranshakle **10** inspection, ransacking, ranshackle, scrutinize **11** examination, exploration, investigate, look through **12** perquisition **13** investigation, perscrutation, turn inside-out **14** turn upside-down

• in search of
07 seeking **09** in quest of **10** looking for **11** in pursuit of **12** searching for **15** on the lookout for

• search me
05 dunno **09** I don't know, it beats me, I've no idea **12** ask me another **15** I haven't got a clue, you've got me there

• search out
04 scan **06** ferret **07** explore **08** indigate **10** run to earth **11** run to ground

searching
04 home, keen **05** alert, close, quest, sharp **06** intent, minute, trying **07** probing **08** piercing, thorough **09** observant **10** discerning **11** penetrating, prospecting **13** inquisitional **14** strand-scouring

searing
05 cruel **06** brutal, fierce, savage, severe **07** blazing, burning, extreme, intense, mordant **08** scathing **09** ferocious, scorching, trenchant, vitriolic **10** unbearable **11** devastating **12** insufferable

seaside
05 beach, coast, sands, shore **06** strand **08** seashore

season
03 age **04** fall, salt, seal, seel, seil, sele, span, term, tide, time **05** inure, pep up, phase, prime, ripen, savor, spell, spice, train, treat **06** harden, haysel, master, mature, mellow, period, savour, temper **07** flavour, prepare, toughen **08** festival, interval, moderate, tone down **09** condiment, condition **10** add herbs to, add sauce to, fence month, summertide, summertime **11** add pepper to, add relish to **13** add flavouring

Seasons include:

03 dry, wet
04 high, open
05 close, rainy, silly
06 autumn, closed, spring, summer, winter
07 festive, holiday, monsoon
08 breeding, shooting
12 Indian summer

• in season
02 in **07** growing **09** available **10** obtainable **11** on the market

seasonable
04 tidy **06** timely, timous **07** fitting, timeous, welcome **08** suitable **09** opportune, well-timed **10** convenient, forehanded, tempestive **11** appropriate **12** providential

seasoned
03 old **04** salt **06** mature, spiced **07** veteran **08** cayenned, hardened **09** practised, toughened, weathered **10** habituated, well-versed **11** conditioned, established, experienced, long-serving **12** acclimatized **13** battle-scarred, weather-beaten

seasoning
04 salt **05** herbs, salad, sauce, spice **06** pepper, relish, spices **07** salting **08** dressing, duxelles **09** condiment **10** celery salt, flavouring, weathering **11** fines herbes

See also **herb**

seat
03 fit, fix, hub, pew, put, see, set, sit **04** axis, base, form, hold, home, pouf, sell, site, sofa, sunk, take **05** abode, bench, cause, chair, heart, house, perch, place, sedes, selle, siege, slide, stall, stool, swing, villa **06** bottom, centre, dukery, ground, humpty, locate, origin, pouffe, reason, saddle, settle, source, throne **07** capital, contain, deposit, footing, install, mansion, pillion, sitting, station **08** location, position, sociable, tribunal **09** faldstool, residence, situation **10** foundation, metropolis, strapontin **11** accommodate, have room for, reservation, stately home **12** confessional, headquarters, rumble-tumble

See also **chair**

seating
04 room **05** seats **06** chairs, places **13** accommodation

sea trout
04 peal, peel **05** sewen, sewin **06** finnac **07** finnack, finnock, herling, hirling

seaweed

Seaweeds include:

03 ore, red
04 agar, alga, kelp, kilp, nori, tang, ulva, ware
05 arame, domoi, dulse, fucus, kombu, laver, varec, vraic, wrack
06 fucoid, tangle, varech, wakame
07 oarweed, oreweed, redware, sea lace, sea moss, seaware
08 agar-agar, bull kelp, gulfweed, porphyra, rockweed, sargasso, seawrack, whipcord
09 carrageen, coralline, coral weed, driftweed, Irish moss, Laminaria, nullipore, sargassum, seabottle, sea girdle, sea tangle, thongweed
10 badderlock, carragheen, Ceylon moss, green laver, sea lettuce, see whistle, tangleweed
11 purple laver, sea furbelow
12 bladderwrack, peacock's tail, phaeophyceae, Rhodophyceae

See also **alga, algae**

secede
04 quit **05** break, leave **06** resign, retire **08** separate, split off, withdraw **09** break away **10** apostatize **12** disaffiliate **14** turn your back on

seceders
04 cave

secession
05 break, split **06** revolt, schism **08** apostasy, seceding **09** breakaway, defection **10** withdrawal **14** disaffiliation

secluded
03 shy **05** close **06** cut off, hidden, lonely, remote, secret **07** private, recluse, retired, shadowy **08** in purdah, isolated, purdahed, shut away, solitary, umbratic **09** claustral, cloistral, concealed, sheltered, withdrawn **10** cloistered **11** out-of-the-way, sequestered, umbratilous **12** unfrequented

seclusion
04 nook **06** bypath, hiding, purdah, recess **07** byplace, privacy, retreat, secrecy, shelter **08** bolt hole, retiracy, solitude **09** hermitage, isolation, reclusion, sequester **10** remoteness, retirement, withdrawal **11** concealment, recluseness **13** sequestration

second
01 s **02** mo **03** aid, sec **04** back, beta, help, jiff, move, next, send, tick, twin **05** extra, flash, jiffy, lower, other, shift, spare, trice, vouch **06** assign, assist, backer, back up, back-up, change, deputy, double, helper, lesser, minute, moment **07** advance, another, approve, endorse, forward, further, helpful, instant, promote, support **08** inferior, relocate, repeated, transfer **09** agree with, alternate, assistant, attendant, duplicate, encourage, favouring, following, secondary, supporter, twinkling **10** additional, subsequent, succeeding, supporting **11** alternative, split second, subordinate **12** right-hand man **13** supplementary **14** right-hand woman **15** second-in-command

• **second to none**
04 best **06** superb **07** supreme **08** peerless **09** brilliant, matchless, nonpareil, paramount **10** inimitable, unrivalled **11** superlative, unsurpassed **12** incomparable, without equal **13** beyond compare, nulli secundus **15** without parallel

secondary
05 extra, lower, minor, spare **06** back-up, deputy, feeder, lesser, relief, second **07** derived, reserve **08** delegate, indirect, inferior, Mesozoic **09** ancillary, auxiliary, resulting **10** derivative, subsidiary, supporting **11** alternative, subordinate, unimportant **12** non-essential

second-class
01 B **08** inferior, mediocre **10** second-best, second-rate, uninspired **11** indifferent, unimportant, uninspiring **15** undistinguished

second-hand
03 old **04** used, worn **08** borrowed, indirect, pre-owned **09** nearly-new, obliquely, secondary, vicarious **10** derivative, hand-me-down, indirectly **11** reach-me-down **12** incidentally, tralaticious, tralatitious **13** formerly owned **14** on the grapevine

second-in-command
06 backer, deputy, helper **09** assistant, attendant, number two, supporter **12** right-hand man **14** right-hand woman

secondly
03 too **04** also, next **06** as well **07** besides, further **08** moreover **09** what's more **10** in addition **11** furthermore **12** additionally **14** into the bargain

second-rate
04 poor, ropy **05** cheap, crook, lousy, ropey, tacky **06** grotty, lesser, shoddy, tawdry, tinpot **08** inferior, low-grade, mediocre **10** second-best, uninspired **11** second-class, substandard, unimportant, uninspiring **15** undistinguished

secrecy
04 dern **05** dearn, wraps **07** hidling, hidlins, mystery, privacy, privity, silence, stealth **08** disguise, hidlings **09** seclusion **10** camouflage, confidence, covertness **11** concealment, furtiveness **12** hugger-mugger, stealthiness **15** confidentiality

secret
03 key, sly **04** code, dark, deep, dern, rune **05** close, dearn, hushy, privy **06** answer, arcane, closet, covert, cut off, enigma, hidden, inward, lonely, mystic, occult, recipe, remote, unseen **07** arcanum, covered, cryptic, formula, furtive, hidling, hidlins, mystery, nostrum, private, retired, unknown **08** abstruse, back-door, discreet, esoteric, hidlings, hush-hush, isolated, secluded, shrouded, shut away, sneaking, solitary, solution, stealthy **09** concealed, disguised, recondite, sensitive, sheltered, tête-à-tête, top secret, underhand **10** backstairs, classified, cloistered, confidence, mysterious, restricted, undercover, unrevealed **11** camouflaged, clandestine, inside story, know-nothing, out-of-the-way, sequestered, underground, undisclosed, unpublished **12** confidential, hugger-mugger, Naples yellow, unfrequented, unidentified **13** hole-and-corner, private matter, surreptitious **14** cloak-and-dagger **15** between you and me, under-the-counter

• **in secret**
07 in petto, on the qt, privily, quietly **08** covertly, in camera, on the sly, secretly **09** furtively, in pectore, in private, privately **10** on the quiet, stealthily, under cover, unobserved **12** hugger-mugger, in confidence, subterranean **13** clandestinely **14** confidentially **15** surreptitiously

• **secret agent**
03 spy **04** Bond, mole **05** scout **07** snooper **10** enemy agent **11** double agent **12** foreign agent **14** fifth columnist **15** undercover agent

secretary
02 PA **03** Sec **04** Secy, temp **05** clerk **06** munshi, scribe, typist **07** famulus **08** moonshee **09** assistant, man Friday, town clerk **10** amanuensis, chancellor, girl Friday, secretaire **11** protonotary **12** person Friday, prothonotary, stenographer

secrete
04 bury, emit, hide, leak, ooze, take, veil **05** cache, cover, exude, leach, water **06** screen, secern, shroud **07** conceal, cover up, emanate, excrete, give off, lactate, produce, release, send out **08** disguise, salivate **09** discharge, sequester, stash away **11** appropriate

secretion
04 lerp **05** sebum, slime **06** liquor, oozing, pruina, smegma, succus **07** cerumen, hormone, leakage, osmosis, release **08** autacoid, emission, honeydew **09** discharge, emanation, exudation, incretion, lactation, recrement **10** osmidrosis, production, royal jelly, secernment **12** lachrymation

secretive
03 sly **04** cagy, deep **05** cagey, close, quiet **06** intent **07** cryptic **08** reserved, reticent, taciturn **09** enigmatic, withdrawn **11** tight-lipped **13** unforthcoming **15** uncommunicative

secretively
07 quietly **08** silently **10** reticently, taciturnly **13** enigmatically

secretly
05 close **06** dernly **07** dearnly, on the qt, privily, quietly **08** covertly, in camera, in secret, on the sly **09** furtively, in private, privately **10** on the quiet, stealthily, under-board, under cover, unobserved **11** underground **12** in confidence **13** clandestinely **14** confidentially **15** surreptitiously

sect
03 sex **04** camp, clan, cult, wing **05** group, order, party **06** church, school **07** cutting, faction **08** division **09** tradition **11** subdivision **12** denomination **13** splinter group

Religious sects include:

05 Amish
07 Ahmadis, Cathars, Moonies, Shakers, Zealots

09 Ahmadiyya, Lubavitch
10 Mennonites
11 Hare Krishna, Therapeutae

See also **sectarian**

sectarian
04 Babi **05** Amish, Babee, bigot, Cynic, hodja, khoja, rigid, Saiva, Yezdi
06 Berean, Cathar, Dunker, khodja, Marist, Moonie, Mormon, Mucker, narrow, Ophite, ranter, Sabian, Seeker, Senusi, Shaiva, Shiite, Tunker, Wahabi, Yezidi, Zabian, zealot **07** Adamite, Alawite, Baptist, bigoted, Cainite, Dunkard, extreme, fanatic, hillmen, insular, Ismaili, Karaite, limited, Senussi, Tsabian, Wahabee, Wahhabi, Yezidee, Zezidee **08** Calixtin, cliquish, Darbyite, dogmatic, Donatist, Dukhobor, Familist, hillfolk, Mandaean, Maronite, Mendaite, partisan, Pharisee, Senoussi, Stundist **09** Calixtine, dogmatist, Doukhobor, Encratite, exclusive, extremist, factional, fanatical, Harmonist, Harmonite, Hesychast, hidebound, Israelite, Mennonite, Nasoraean, parochial, Paulician
10 anabaptist, Holy Roller, Karmathian, prejudiced, separatist **11** abecedarian, Albigensian, Black Muslim, Campbellite, doctrinaire, Hare Krishna, Lubavitcher, Plymouthist, Plymouthite, Sandemanian **12** denomination, Muggletonian, narrow-minded
13 convulsionary, fractionalist, Hemerobaptist, Perfectionist, Philadelphian, Schwenkfelder
14 denominational, Schwenkfeldian
15 Christadelphian, Plymouth Brother

section
01 s **03** bit **04** area, part, sect, unit, wing, zone **05** conic, piece, share, slice
06 branch, region, sector **07** article, chapter, passage, portion, segment
08 campfire, district, division, fraction, fragment **09** Caesarean, Caesarian, component, induction, paragraph
10 department, instalment
11 subdivision
• **all sections**
02 AS

sectional
05 class, local **06** racial **07** divided, partial **08** regional, separate
09 exclusive, factional, localized, sectarian **10** individual, separatist

sector
04 area, gore, part, zone **05** field
06 branch, octant, region **07** quarter, section, sextant **08** category, district, division, precinct, quadrant
11 subdivision

secular
03 lay **05** civil, state **06** age-old, layman **07** agelong, earthly, profane, worldly **08** temporal **12** non-religious, non-spiritual

secure
◇ *containment indicator*
03 bag, bar, fix, get, pin, pot, rug, tie, win **04** bolt, bond, fast, firm, gain, hunk, land, lash, lock, moor, nail, safe, shut, sure, take, vest **05** chain, close, cover, fixed, guard, happy, quoin, rivet, solid, tie up, tight **06** anchor, assure, attach, closed, come by, defend, ensure, fasten, immune, line up, locked, lock up, obtain, screen, sealed, shield, stable, steady, sturdy, take up
07 acquire, assured, certain, confirm, endorse, padlock, procure, protect, relaxed, settled, sponsor, warrant
08 careless, definite, fastened, make fast, make safe, reliable, shielded, unharmed **09** confident, contented, establish, fortified, get hold of, guarantee, immovable, protected, reassured, safeguard, sheltered, steadfast, undamaged **10** batten down, conclusive, dependable, home and dry, strengthen, underwrite
11 comfortable, established, impregnable, make certain, self-assured, well-founded **13** make certain of, out of harm's way, self-confident

securely
06 firmly, safely, stably **07** tightly
08 robustly, steadily, strongly, sturdily
09 immovably **11** impregnably, out of danger, steadfastly

security
03 wad, wed **04** care, ease, gage, gilt, lock **05** cover **06** anchor, asylum, pledge, refuge, safety, surety
07 caution, custody, defence
08 guaranty, immunity, warranty
09 assurance, certainty, guarantee, insurance, safeguard, sanctuary
10 collateral, confidence, conviction, precaution, protection, safeguards
11 peace of mind, precautions, safe-keeping **12** carelessness, positiveness, preservation, surveillance **14** over-confidence **15** invulnerability

sedan
05 chair **06** jampan, litter **09** palanquin

sedate
03 sad **04** calm, cool, dull **05** douce, grave, noble, quiet, relax, sober, staid, stiff **06** demure, pacify, proper, seemly, serene, solemn, soothe, worthy
07 earnest, serious **08** calm down, composed, decorous, tranquil
09 collected, dignified, unruffled
10 deliberate, slow-moving, unexciting
11 quieten down, unflappable
12 tranquillize **13** imperturbable

sedately
05 nobly **06** calmly **07** quietly, soberly
08 demurely, serenely, worthily
09 earnestly, seriously **10** decorously
11 with dignity **12** deliberately
13 imperturbably

sedative
06 downer, opiate **07** anodyne, calming **08** lenitive, narcotic, quietive, relaxing, soothing **09** calmative, composing, soporific **10** depressant
11 barbiturate **12** sleeping-pill
13 tranquillizer **14** tranquillizing

Sedatives and tranquillizers include:

06 Amytal®, Ativan®, Valium®
07 codeine, Librium®, lupulin
08 diazepam, Nembutal®, Rohypnol®, tetronal, thridace
09 barbitone, clozapine, lorazepam, Temazepam
10 clonazepam
11 amobarbital, deserpidine, laurel-water, scopalamine, thalidomide
12 meprobramate, methaqualone, promethazine
14 chloral hydrate, cyclobarbitone, pentobarbitone, phenobarbitone

sedentary
05 still **06** seated **07** sessile, sitting
08 immobile, inactive, unmoving
09 desk-bound **10** stationary

sedge

Sedges include:

04 star
05 Carex, chufa, starr
07 bulrush, papyrus
08 clubrush, sawgrass, tiger nut
09 deergrass
13 umbrella plant, water chestnut

sediment
03 lee **04** lees, silt, warp **05** crust, dregs, feces, grout, varve **06** bottom, faeces, fecula **07** bottoms, deposit, grounds, residue **08** residuum
09 turbidite **10** deposition, hypostasis
11 precipitate **13** coffee grounds

sedition
06 mutiny, revolt **07** treason
09 agitation, rebellion, treachery
10 disloyalty, subversion
11 fomentation **12** insurrection
13 rabble-rousing **15** insubordination

seditious
08 disloyal, factious, inciting, mutinous
09 agitating, dissident, fomenting
10 rebellious, refractory, subversive, traitorous **13** insubordinate, rabble-rousing, revolutionary
15 insurrectionist

seduce
◇ *insertion indicator*
04 jape, lure, pull, ruin, undo, vamp
05 charm, tempt, wrong **06** allure, betray, chat up, entice **07** attract, beguile, corrupt, debauch, deceive, deprave, ensnare, mislead **08** bejesuit, dishonor, inveigle **09** dishonour **10** get into bed, lead astray **12** make a play for
15 take advantage of

seducer
04 goat, rake, wolf **05** flirt, Romeo
06 undoer **07** charmer, Don Juan
08 betrayer, Casanova, deceiver, lady's man, Lothario **09** ladies' man, libertine, womanizer **11** philanderer

seduction
04 lure, ruin **05** charm **06** allure, appeal, come-on **09** deception
10 allurement, attraction, corruption,

enticement, misleading, temptation **11** beguilement

seductive
04 sexy **06** honied, luring, sultry **07** honeyed **08** alluring, arousing, charming, enticing, inviting, tempting **09** appealing, beguiling, deceiving **10** attractive, bewitching, come-hither, misleading **11** captivating, flirtatious, provocative, tantalizing, temptatious **12** honey-tongued, irresistible

seductress
04 vamp **05** Circe, siren **07** Delilah, Lorelei **09** temptress **11** femme fatale

sedulous
04 busy **08** constant, diligent, resolved, tireless, untiring **09** assiduous, laborious **10** determined, persistent, unflagging **11** industrious, painstaking, persevering, unremitting **13** conscientious

see
01 C, v **02** la, lo **03** ask, Ely, get **04** date, deek, deem, ecce, espy, know, lead, look, mark, meet, note, seat, show, spot, take, vide, view **05** court, get it, grasp, judge, learn, sight, think, usher, visit, voilà, watch **06** behold, decide, escort, fathom, follow, go with, look at, notice, regard, take in **07** consult, diocese, discern, find out, foresee, glimpse, imagine, inquire, make out, observe, picture, predict, realize, reflect, run into, speak to, take out, witness **08** bump into, consider, discover, envisage, forecast, identify, perceive **09** accompany, apprehend, ascertain, determine, encounter, go out with, interview, latch onto, lay eyes on, recognize, set eyes on, visualize **10** anticipate, appreciate, chance upon, clap eyes on, come across, comprehend, confer with, cotton onto, experience, get a look at, understand **11** distinguish, investigate **12** catch sight of **15** keep company with

See also **diocese**

• see about
02 do **03** fix **06** manage, repair **07** arrange, sort out **08** attend to, consider, deal with, organize **09** look after **10** take care of

• see around
◇ *containment indicator*

• see through
06 fathom, hang in, rumble **07** persist, realize, support, sustain **08** continue, stick out **09** encourage, get wise to, keep going, not give up, penetrate, persevere **10** get through, understand **14** not be taken in by **15** not be deceived by

• see to
02 do **03** fix **04** mind **06** ensure, manage, repair **07** arrange, sort out **08** attend to, deal with, make sure, organize **09** look after **10** take care of **11** make certain

seed
03 egg, nut, pea, pip, pit, sow, urd **04** bean, corn, dust, germ, moit, mote, ovum, race, root **05** argan, carvy, cause, child, grain, heirs, lupin, ovule, piñon, semen, spawn, sperm, start, stone, young **06** bonduc, embryo, family, kernel, lentil, lupine, origin, powder, reason, source **07** genesis, nucleus, reasons **08** chickpea, children, peaberry, sprinkle, young one **09** beginning, fruit body, jequirity, offspring, sword-bean, young ones **10** successors **11** descendants **12** fruiting body, spermatozoon **13** jequirity bean, water chestnut

• go to seed, run to seed
04 bolt **05** decay **07** decline, go to pot **08** get worse, go to hell **10** degenerate, go downhill **11** deteriorate, go to the dogs **14** go down the tubes

• seed covering
03 bur, ear **04** aril, burr, husk

seediness
05 decay, scuzz **09** dirtiness **10** shabbiness, untidiness **11** squalidness **12** dilapidation

seedy
◇ *anagram indicator*
03 ill **04** sick **05** dirty, mangy, ribby, rough, tatty **06** ailing, chippy, crummy, groggy, grotty, mangey, maungy, poorly, shabby, sleazy, untidy, unwell **07** run-down, scruffy, squalid **08** decaying **09** off-colour **10** out of sorts **11** dilapidated **15** under the weather

seek
03 aim, ask, beg, try **04** cast, hunt, want **05** chase, court **06** aspire, desire, follow, gun for, invite, lay out, pursue, resort, search, strive **07** attempt, enquire, entreat, examine, hunt for, inquire, look for, mole out, request, solicit **08** petition, prospect **09** endeavour, look after, search for, try to find

seeker
05 chela, hound **06** novice **07** student, zetetic **08** disciple, enquirer, inquirer, searcher

seem
04 feel, look **05** befit, sound **06** appear, semble **08** look like **11** pretend to be, show signs of, strike you as **12** come across as **13** have the look of

seeming
05 quasi- **06** pseudo **07** assumed, outward, surface **08** apparent, external, semblant, specious, supposed **09** pretended **10** ostensible, semblative **11** superficial

seemingly
09 allegedly, outwardly **10** apparently, ostensibly **12** on the surface **13** on the face of it, superficially

seemly
03 fit **04** meet, nice **06** comely, decent, honest, proper, suited **07** fitting **08** becoming, decorous, handsome, maidenly, suitable **09** befitting **10** attractive **11** appropriate, comme il faut, respectable

seep
04 drip, leak, oose, ooze, sipe, soak, sype, well **05** drain, exude **07** dribble, trickle **08** permeate **09** percolate

seepage
04 leak **06** oozing **07** leakage, osmosis **08** dripping **09** exudation **11** percolation

seer
04 seir **05** augur, sibyl **07** prophet, seeress, spaeman, wise man **08** spaewife **10** prophetess, soothsayer

seesaw
04 yo-yo **05** pitch, swing **06** teeter **08** wild mare **09** alternate, fluctuate, oscillate

seethe
◇ *anagram indicator*
04 boil, fizz, foam, fume, rage, rise, teem **05** froth, go ape, storm, surge, swarm, swell **06** blow up, bubble, buller, see red, simmer **07** be angry, be livid, explode, ferment **08** boil over, smoulder **09** be furious, blow a fuse **10** be incensed, be outraged, effervesce **11** blow a gasket, go ballistic **12** blow your cool, lose your cool **14** foam at the mouth **15** fly off the handle, go off the deep end

see-through
05 filmy, gauzy, sheer **06** flimsy **08** gossamer **09** gossamery **11** translucent, transparent

segment
03 bit, pig **04** exon, link, lith, part, ring **05** cut up, femur, halve, joint, piece, slice, split, urite, wedge **06** divide, scliff, skliff, somite, telson **07** article, isomere, overlay, portion, section, uromere **08** division, metamere, separate **09** anatomize, propodeon, prothorax, sternebra **10** arthromere, metathorax, proglottid, proglottis, trochanter **11** compartment **12** articulation

segregate
06 cut off **07** exclude, isolate, seclude **08** separate, set apart **09** keep apart, ostracize, sequester **10** dissociate, quarantine

segregation
09 apartheid, isolation **10** quarantine, separation **12** dissociation, setting apart **13** sequestration **14** discrimination

seize
◇ *containment indicator*
03 bag, cly, nab, nap **04** bone, grab, grip, hend, hold, nail, snap, take **05** annex, catch, ceaze, cleek, grasp, latch, reach, sease, seaze, seise, usurp

06 abduct, areach, arrest, attach, attain, clutch, collar, graple, hijack, kidnap, nobble, ravish, snatch, tackle 07 capture, forhent, grapple, impound, possess, prehend 08 forehent 09 apprehend, deprehend, get hold of, lay hold of, lay hold on, penetrate 10 commandeer, confiscate, grab hold of, lay hands on, take hold of 11 appropriate, catch hold of, requisition, sequestrate

• seize on
04 grab 07 exploit 08 fasten on 12 grasp eagerly

• seize up
03 jam 04 stop 06 go phut, pack up 07 conk out 09 break down 11 malfunction, stop working

seizure
03 fit 04 grab, rape 05 catch, prise, prize, spasm 06 arrest, attack, extent, hijack, rapine, taking 07 capture, seysure 08 paroxysm, purchase, reprisal, wingding 09 abduction, distraint, snatching 10 annexation, attachment, convulsion, pre-emption 12 apprehension, confiscation 13 appropriation, commandeering, sequestration

seldom
04 rare 06 rarely 07 unoften 10 hardly ever, infrequent 12 infrequently, occasionally, scarcely ever 15 once in a blue moon

select
03 top 04 best, cull, pick, posh, sort 05 elect, élite, prime 06 choice, choose, favour, finest, invite, opt for, prefer 07 appoint, extract, limited, special, supreme 08 decide on, selected, settle on, superior 09 excellent, exclusive, first-rate, single out 10 cherry-pick, first-class, hand-picked, privileged 11 high-quality 12 make choice of

selection
04 blad, pick 05 blaud, range 06 choice, dim sum, line-up, medley, option 07 Auslese, palette, variety 09 anthology, cold table, potpourri 10 assortment, collection, miscellany, preference 11 smörgåsbord

selective
05 fussy, picky 06 choosy 07 careful, finicky 10 discerning, fastidious, particular, pernickety 11 persnickety 14 discriminating

selectively
08 by choice 09 carefully 12 discerningly, particularly 14 differentially, preferentially

Selene
04 Luna

selenium
02 Se

self
01 I 03 ego, own, sel 04 same, sell, soul, very 05 atman, seity 06 person 08 identity 09 identical, number one, the real me 10 inner being, yours truly 11 body and soul, personality 13 heart of hearts

self-assembly
03 DIY 07 kit-form 08 flat-pack 13 prefabricated

self-assertive
05 bossy, perky, pushy 07 pushing 08 forceful, immodest 10 aggressive, commanding, high-handed, peremptory 11 dictatorial, domineering, heavy-handed, overbearing, overweening 13 authoritarian

self-assurance
06 aplomb 09 assurance, cockiness 10 confidence 11 assuredness 12 cocksureness, positiveness 14 overconfidence, self-confidence, self-possession

self-assured
05 cocky 07 assured 08 cocksure 09 confident 13 overconfident, self-collected, self-confident, self-possessed 14 sure of yourself

self-centred
07 selfish 09 egotistic 10 egocentric 11 egotistical, self-seeking, self-serving 12 narcissistic, self-absorbed 14 self-interested

self-confidence
03 ego 05 poise 06 aplomb 07 opinion 09 assurance, composure 10 confidence 12 positiveness, self-reliance 13 self-assurance

self-confident
04 bold, cool 07 assured 08 cocksure, composed, fearless, positive 09 confident, unabashed 11 self-assured, self-reliant 13 self-possessed

self-conscious
03 coy, shy 05 timid 07 awkward, bashful, nervous 08 blushing, insecure, retiring, sheepish, timorous 09 diffident, ill at ease, shrinking 10 shamefaced 11 embarrassed 12 self-effacing 13 uncomfortable

self-contained
02 s/c 05 quiet 07 private 08 discrete, reserved, separate 09 secretive 11 independent, self-reliant 12 free-standing 14 self-sufficient

self-control
04 cool 06 temper 07 dignity, encraty 08 calmness, patience 09 composure, restraint, willpower 10 self-denial, temperance 11 self-mastery 13 self-restraint 14 self-discipline

• lose self-control
04 flip, snap 05 break

self-defence *see* **martial art**

self-denial
10 asceticism, moderation, temperance 12 selflessness 13 self-sacrifice, unselfishness 14 abstemiousness, self-abnegation

self-discipline
07 resolve 09 willpower 11 persistence, self-control, self-mastery 13 determination

self-employed
06 casual 08 part-time 09 freelance, temporary 10 consultant, out-of-house 11 independent

self-esteem
03 ego 05 pride 07 conceit, dignity 09 self-image, self-pride 10 self-regard 11 amour-propre, self-respect 13 self-assurance 14 self-confidence

self-evident
05 clear, plain 07 obvious 08 manifest 09 axiomatic 10 undeniable 11 inescapable 14 unquestionable

self-explanatory
05 clear, plain 07 obvious 10 accessible, easy-to-read 11 self-evident 12 approachable, easy-to-follow, intelligible 14 comprehensible, understandable

self-glorification
07 egotism 09 egotheism 14 self-admiration, self-exaltation

self-governing
04 free 09 autonomic, sovereign 10 autonomous 11 independent 15 self-determining

self-government
06 swaraj 08 autarchy, autonomy, home rule 09 democracy 11 sovereignty 12 independence 15 self-sovereignty

self-importance
04 pomp 06 vanity 07 conceit, donnism 09 arrogance, cockiness, pomposity, pushiness 10 pretension 11 pompousness, self-opinion 13 bigheadedness, bumptiousness, conceitedness 15 self-consequence

self-important
04 coxy, vain 05 cocky, proud, pushy 06 chesty, cocksy 07 pompous 08 arrogant, egoistic 09 bigheaded, bumptious, conceited, egotistic, strutting 10 portentous, swaggering 11 egotistical, overbearing, pragmatical, pretentious, swell-headed 13 consequential, swollen-headed 14 self-consequent

self-indulgence
06 excess 08 hedonism 10 high living, profligacy, sensualism 11 dissipation 12 extravagance, intemperance 13 dissoluteness

self-indulgent
06 wanton 09 dissolute 10 dissipated, hedonistic, immoderate, profligate 11 extravagant, intemperate 15 pleasure-seeking

self-interest
04 self 08 self-love 10 expediency, self-regard 11 selfishness, self-serving

selfish
04 mean **06** greedy **07** miserly **08** covetous **09** egotistic, mercenary **10** egocentric **11** calculating, egotistical, self-centred, self-seeking, self-serving **13** inconsiderate **14** self-interested

selfishly
08 greedily **12** ungenerously **13** egotistically **14** egocentrically **15** inconsiderately, only for yourself

selfishness
05 greed **06** egoism **07** egotism **08** meanness, self-love **10** self-regard **11** self-seeking, self-serving **12** self-interest **15** self-centredness

selfless
08 generous **09** unselfish **10** altruistic **11** magnanimous, self-denying **13** philanthropic **15** self-sacrificing

selflessness
08 altruism **10** generosity, self-denial **11** magnanimity **12** philanthropy **13** self-sacrifice, unselfishness

self-possessed
04 calm, cool **06** poised **07** assured **08** composed, together **09** collected, confident, unruffled **11** self-assured, unflappable **13** self-collected

self-possession
04 cool, head **05** nerve, poise **06** aplomb **08** calmness, coolness **09** assurance, composure, sangfroid **10** confidence **11** self-command **13** collectedness, self-assurance **14** self-confidence, unflappability

self-reliance
07 autarky **11** self-support **12** independence **14** self-sustenance **15** self-sufficiency, self-sustainment

self-reliant
08 autarkic **10** autarkical **11** independent **14** self-sufficient, self-supporting, self-sustaining

self-respect
05 pride **07** dignity **10** self-esteem, self-regard **11** amour-propre **13** self-assurance **14** self-confidence

self-restraint
07 encraty **08** patience **09** willpower **10** continence, continency, moderation, self-denial, temperance **11** forbearance, self-command, self-control **14** abstemiousness, self-discipline, self-government

self-righteous
02 pi **04** smug **05** pious **08** priggish, superior **09** pietistic **10** complacent, goody-goody, moralistic **11** pharisaical **12** hypocritical **13** sanctimonious **14** holier-than-thou

self-righteousness
09 goodiness, piousness **10** pharisaism **12** priggishness **14** goody-goodiness **15** pharisaicalness

self-sacrifice
08 altruism **10** generosity, self-denial **12** selflessness **13** unselfishness **14** self-abnegation

self-satisfaction
05 pride **08** smugness **11** complacency, contentment **12** self-approval **15** self-approbation

self-satisfied
04 smug **05** proud **08** puffed up **10** complacent **13** self-righteous

self-seeking
07 selfish **09** careerist, mercenary, on the make **10** self-loving **11** acquisitive, calculating, gold-digging, self-serving **12** self-endeared **13** opportunistic **14** fortune-hunting, self-interested

self-styled
07 would-be **08** so-called **09** pretended, professed, soi-disant **10** self-titled **13** self-appointed

self-sufficient
11 independent, self-reliant **13** self-contained **14** self-supporting, self-sustaining

self-supporting
11 independent, self-reliant **13** self-financing **14** self-sufficient, self-sustaining

self-willed
05 elvan, elven **06** cussed, elfish, elvish, wilful **07** froward, willful **08** perverse, stubborn **09** obstinate, pig-headed **10** headstrong, refractory **11** intractable, opinionated, stiff-necked **12** bloody-minded, ungovernable **15** self-opinionated

sell
04 flog, hawk, hype, mart, push, seat, self, tout, vend, vent **05** carry, cry up, go for, selle, shift, stock, trade, trick **06** barter, betray, deal in, export, handle, import, market, peddle, praise, retail, saddle, smouch **07** auction, chaffer, let-down, promote, trade in, win over **08** exchange, persuade, retail at **09** advertise, deception, dispose of, traffic in **10** be priced at, bring round **11** merchandize **13** get support for **14** disappointment, get approval for

• **sell out**
04 fail **05** rat on **06** betray, fink on **07** stool on **08** run out of **11** be exhausted, double-cross **12** be out of stock, have none left **13** stab in the back

seller
06 trader, vendor **08** huckster, merchant, stockist, supplier

• **seller's opinion**
02 so

selling
07 dealing, trading, traffic, vending **09** marketing, promotion, vendition **11** trafficking **12** salesmanship, transactions **13** merchandizing

selvage
04 list, roon, rund **05** royne

semblance
03 air **04** copy, garb, idol, life, look, mask, show, sign **05** front, ghost, guise, image **06** aspect, façade, veneer **07** seeming **08** likeness, pretence, pretense **10** apparition, appearance, likelihood, similarity, similitude, simulacrum **11** resemblance

semen
03 cum **04** come, gism, jism, jizz, seed **05** sperm, spoof, spunk **06** jissom **09** ejaculate **12** seminal fluid

semi-liquid
04 slab **05** slimy **06** blashy, globby

seminal
05 major **08** creative, germinal, original, seminary **09** formative, important **10** generative, innovative, productive **11** imaginative, influential, rudimentary

seminar
05 class, forum **07** lecture, meeting, session **08** colloquy, tutorial, workshop **09** symposium **10** colloquium, conference, convention, discussion, study group

seminary
03 Sem **06** school **07** academy, college, nursery, yeshiva **08** yeshivah **09** institute **10** theologate **11** institution **15** training college

send
04 beam, cast, emit, fire, hurl, mail, make, move, post, turn **05** drive, fling, grant, radio, relay, remit, shoot, swash, throw **06** arouse, commit, convey, direct, excite, get off, launch, propel, thrill, turn on **07** address, consign, deliver, forward, project **08** despatch, dispatch, redirect, televise, transmit **09** broadcast, cause to be, discharge, give a buzz, give a kick, messenger, stimulate **11** communicate **12** put in the mail, put in the post **14** give pleasure to

• **send away**
04 hunt, pack, void **05** drive **07** dismiss, pack off **08** despatch, dispatch

• **send for**
05 get in, order **06** summon **07** call for, command, request

• **send forth**
04 beam, pour **05** fling, shoot, speed **08** expedite **09** discharge

• **send off**
04 ship **06** let fly, set off **08** despatch, dispatch, order off **12** order to leave

• **send up**
◇ *reversal down indicator*
04 mock **05** mimic **06** parody **07** imitate, take off **08** ridicule, satirize

send-off
05 start **07** goodbye, push-off **08** farewell **09** departure **11** leave-taking

send-up
04 skit **05** spoof **06** parody, satire **07** mockery, take-off **09** burlesque, imitation **10** mickey-take

Senegal
02 SN **03** SEN

senile
03 old **04** aged, gaga **06** doited, doitit **07** failing **08** confused, decrepit **09** doddering, senescent

senility
03 eld **04** eild **06** dotage, old age **07** anility, paracme **08** caducity **09** infirmity **10** senescence **11** decrepitude **14** senile dementia **15** second childhood

senior
02 Sr **03** Sen, Snr **04** aîné, sire **05** aînée, chief, doyen, elder, first, major, older **06** higher **07** ancient, doyenne **08** superior **11** high-ranking

• **senior citizen**
03 OAP **09** pensioner **10** golden ager **12** coffin-dodger **13** retired person **15** old-age pensioner

seniority
03 age **04** rank **06** status **08** priority, standing **09** ancientry, antiquity, signeurie **10** importance, precedence **11** superiority

sensation
03 hit, wow **04** aura, itch, stir **05** sense, vibes **06** furore, pit-pat, splash, thrill, tingle, winner **07** emotion, feeling, outrage, pitapat, prickle, scandal, success, symptom, triumph **08** goneness, pitty-pat **09** agitation, awareness, commotion **10** Empfindung, excitement, impression, perception **13** consciousness

sensational
04 gamy, pulp **05** gamey, juicy, lurid, shock **06** superb, yellow **07** amazing **08** dramatic, drop-dead, exciting, fabulous, galvanic, gorgeous, shocking, smashing, stirring, terrific **09** excellent, fantastic, revealing, startling, thrilling, wonderful **10** astounding, horrifying, impressive, incredible, marvellous, scandalous, staggering **11** exceptional, spectacular **12** breathtaking, electrifying, melodramatic **15** blood-and-thunder

sense
03 wit **04** feel, gist, mind, nous, wits **05** brain, drift, grasp, logic, point, savvy, tenor **06** brains, detect, divine, import, intuit, notice, nuance, pick up, reason, wisdom **07** ability, discern, faculty, feeling, meaning, observe, opinion, purport, purpose, realize, suspect **08** gumption, judgment, perceive, prudence **09** awareness, be aware of, direction, intuition, judgement, recognize, sensation, substance **10** appreciate, cleverness, comprehend, definition, denotation, experience, impression, perception, understand **11** common sense, discernment, implication, sensibility **12** appreciation, apprehension, intelligence, significance **13** be conscious of, comprehension, consciousness, judiciousness, understanding **14** interpretation, reasonableness

• **in this sense**
02 hs **08** hoc sensu

• **make sense of**
05 grasp **06** fathom **07** make out **09** figure out **10** comprehend, make much of, understand

senseless
03 mad, out **04** daft, numb, surd **05** batty, crazy, dotty, inane, silly **06** absurd, futile, insane, stupid, unwise **07** fatuous, foolish, idiotic, moronic, out cold, stunned **08** deadened, mindless **09** illogical, insensate, ludicrous, pointless, unfeeling **10** insensible, irrational, ridiculous **11** meaningless, nonsensical, purposeless, unconscious **12** unreasonable **13** anaesthetized, load of rubbish **14** load of nonsense

sense-organ
03 ear, eye **04** nose, palp **06** tongue **09** sensillum **15** mechanoreceptor

sensibility
05 taste **07** feeling, insight **08** delicacy, emotions, feelings **09** awareness, intuition, sentiment **10** sentiments **11** discernment, sensitivity **12** appreciation **13** sensitiveness, sensitivities **14** perceptiveness, responsiveness, sentimentality, susceptibility

sensible
04 sane, wise **05** aware, sharp, sober, solid, sound, tough, witty **06** clever, mature, shrewd, strong **07** evident, logical, prudent, working **08** everyday, ordinary, rational, wise-like **09** judicious, practical, realistic, sagacious, sensitive, wholesome **10** discerning, far-sighted, functional, no-nonsense, perceptive, reasonable, responsive, vulnerable **11** appreciable, clear-headed, commonsense, down-to-earth, hard-wearing, intelligent, level-headed, perceptible, serviceable, susceptible, well-advised **14** commonsensical

• **sensible of**
07 alive to, aware of **09** mindful of **11** cognizant of, conscious of, convinced of, observant of, sensitive to **13** understanding **14** acquainted with

sensibly
06 wisely **07** handily **08** cleverly, shrewdly, strongly, suitably, usefully **09** logically, prudently **10** rationally, reasonably **11** judiciously, practically, sagaciously, serviceably **12** functionally **13** realistically

sensitive
04 fine, soft **05** aware, exact, quick **06** kittly, tender, touchy, tricky **07** awkward, brittle, careful, fragile, precise, tactful **08** delicate, discreet, reactive, sentient **09** cold-short, difficult, emotional, irritable **10** diplomatic, discerning, perceptive, responsive, sensitized, vulnerable **11** considerate, problematic, susceptible, sympathetic, thin-skinned **12** appreciative, highly strung **13** controversial, hyperesthetic, temperamental **14** hyperaesthesic, hyperaesthetic, impressionable, well-thought-out

sensitivity
07 algesia **08** delicacy, esthesia, fineness, softness, sympathy **09** aesthesia, aesthesis, awareness, fragility **11** discernment **12** appreciation, radiesthesia, reactiveness **13** receptiveness, vulnerability **14** perceptiveness, responsiveness, susceptibility

sensual
04 lewd, sexy **05** brute, gross, horny, randy **06** animal, bodily, brutal, carnal, erotic, sexual, sultry **07** fleshly, lustful, swinish, worldly **08** embodied, physical **09** lecherous, pandemian **10** licentious, voluptuary, voluptuous **12** encarnalized **13** self-indulgent

sensuality
08 lewdness, pleasure, sexiness **09** animalism, carnality, eroticism, prurience **10** debauchery, profligacy **11** gourmandize, libertinism, lustfulness **13** lecherousness, salaciousness **14** lasciviousness, licentiousness, voluptuousness

sensuous
04 lush, rich **08** pleasant, pleasing **09** aesthetic, luxurious, sumptuous **10** gratifying, voluptuous **11** pleasurable

sensuously
06 lushly, richly **11** luxuriously, pleasurably, sumptuously **12** gratifyingly, voluptuously

sentence
03 swy **04** bird, doom, time **05** curse, judge, lifer, maxim, order **06** decree, period, punish, ruling **07** condemn, opinion, verdict **08** aphorism, decision, judgment, penalize, porridge **09** judgement **10** adjudgment, punishment **11** adjudgement **12** condemnation **13** pronouncement **15** pass judgement on

sententious
05 brief, pithy, short, terse **06** gnomic **07** canting, compact, concise, laconic, pointed, pompous, preachy **08** succinct **09** axiomatic **10** aphoristic, moralistic, moralizing **11** judgemental **12** epigrammatic **13** sanctimonious

sentient
04 live **05** aware **06** living **07** feeling, sensile **08** reactive **09** conscious, sensitive **10** responsive

sentiment
04 idea, posy, view **05** maxim, slops **06** belief, hobnob, pledge **07** emotion,

feeling, opinion, romance, thought **08** attitude, judgment, softness **09** judgement **10** persuasion, tenderness **11** mawkishness, point of view, romanticism, sensibility **14** sentimentality **15** soft-heartedness

sentimental
05 corny, gooey, gucky, gushy, hokey, mushy, soppy, weepy, yucky, yukky **06** gloopy, loving, sickly, sloppy, slushy, sugary, tender, too-too **07** boy-girl, gushing, maudlin, mawkish, missish, treacly **08** cornball, pathetic, romantic, rose-pink, shmaltzy, touching **09** emotional, nostalgic, rosewater, schmaltzy **10** lovey-dovey, Wertherian **11** soft-hearted, tear-jerking **12** affectionate, chocolate-box **13** lackadaisical

sentimentality
03 goo, yuk **04** gush, mush, pulp, yuck **05** gloop, slush **06** bathos **07** feeling, shmaltz, treacle **08** schmaltz **09** corniness, nostalgia, sentiment **10** sloppiness, tenderness **11** mawkishness, romanticism, sensibility **12** emotionalism **14** sentimentalism

sentry
05 guard, watch **06** centry, picket **07** lookout, vedette **08** sentinel, watchman **09** out-sentry

separable
08 distinct, dividant, dividual, partible **09** different, divisible, removable **10** detachable, particular **11** independent **15** distinguishable

separate
03 red, sep, try **04** comb, part, redd, shed, sort, twin **05** alone, apart, break, sever, shear, split, twine **06** cut off, demark, depart, detach, divide, reduce, remove, secede, single, sunder, sundry, winnow **07** break up, discerp, disjoin, dislink, dispart, diverge, divided, divorce, isolate, seclude, several, sort out, split up **08** abstract, break off, detached, discreet, discrete, disperse, dissever, distinct, distract, disunite, divorced, isolated, offprint, prescind, set apart, solitary, uncouple, withdraw **09** come apart, demarcate, different, disengage, dismantle, disparate, disunited, intervene, keep apart, partition, segregate, single out, take apart, uncombine, unrelated **10** autonomous, disconnect, disjointed, dissociate, individual, particular, segregated, unattached **11** disentangle, independent, part company, unconnected **12** disaffiliate, disconnected **15** become estranged

separated
05 apart **06** parted, remote **07** divided, split up **08** isolated, separate, sundered **09** disunited **10** dissociate, poles apart, segregated **12** disconnected, poles asunder **13** disassociated, discontinuous

separately
05 alone, apart **06** singly **07** asunder, divisim **08** one by one **09** in several, severally **10** absolutely, discretely, personally **12** individually **13** independently **14** discriminately

separating
07 parting, sifting **08** abducent, dividing, divisive **09** isolating, precisive **10** discretive **11** intervening, segregating **12** partitioning **13** disengagement

separation
03 gap **04** gulf, rift **05** split **06** schism, wrench **07** break-up, divorce, freedom, parting, split-up **08** avulsion, dialysis, disunion, dividing, division, farewell, interval, solution **09** apartheid, isolation, severance **10** detachment, divergence, uncoupling **11** demarcation, demarkation, disjunction, distinction, leave-taking, segregation **12** disgregation, disseverment, dissociation, estrangement **13** disconnection, disengagement **14** centrifugation

separatist
05 rebel **08** apostate, renegade, seceding **09** breakaway, dissenter, heretical **10** dissenting, schismatic **11** Independent **12** secessionist

separatists
03 ETA

September
03 Sep **04** Sept

septic
06 putrid **08** infected, poisoned **09** festering **10** putrefying **11** suppurating **12** putrefactive

sepulchral
03 sad **04** deep **05** grave **06** dismal, gloomy, hollow, morbid, solemn, sombre, woeful **07** charnel **08** funereal, mournful **09** cheerless **10** lugubrious, melancholy **11** sepulchrous

sepulchre
04 tomb **05** grave, vault **06** burial, entomb **09** mausoleum **10** repository **11** burial place

sequel
03 end **05** issue, suite **06** pay-off, result, upshot **07** outcome **08** follow-up, sequence **09** after-clap, followers **10** conclusion, successors **11** consequence, development **12** consequences, continuation

sequence
03 run, set **04** line, suit **05** chain, cycle, order, track, train **06** course, series, string **10** procession, succession **11** arrangement, consequence, progression

sequester
04 take **05** seize **06** detach, remove **07** impound, isolate, seclude, shut off **08** alienate, insulate, set apart, set aside, shut away **09** seclusion **10** commandeer, confiscate **11** appropriate, sequestrate

sequestered
05 quiet **06** lonely, remote **07** outback, private, retired **08** isolated, secluded **10** cloistered **11** out-of-the-way **12** unfrequented

sequestrate
04 take **05** seize **07** impound **09** sequester **10** commandeer, confiscate **11** appropriate

seraphic
04 holy, pure **06** divine, serene **07** angelic, saintly, sublime **08** beatific, blissful, heavenly, innocent **09** celestial **10** seraphical

Serbia and Montenegro
03 SCG, YUG

serenade
04 wake **07** horning **08** chivaree, shivaree **09** charivari

serendipitous
05 happy, lucky **06** chance **09** fortunate **10** accidental, fortuitous, unexpected

serendipity
04 luck **06** chance **07** fortune **08** accident, fortuity **11** coincidence, good fortune

serene
04 calm, cool **05** clear, quiet, still **06** placid, serein **07** halcyon **08** composed, peaceful, seraphic, tranquil **09** unclouded, unruffled **10** seraphical, untroubled **11** undisturbed, unflappable **12** tranquillize **13** imperturbable

serenely
06 calmly **07** quietly **08** placidly **10** peacefully, tranquilly **13** imperturbably

serenity
04 calm, cool **05** peace **06** repose **08** calmness, quietude **09** composure, placidity, quietness, stillness **12** peacefulness, tranquillity **14** unflappability

serf
05 helot, slave, thete, thirl **06** thrall **07** bondman, servant, villein **08** adscript, bondmaid, bondsman **09** bond-slave, bondwoman **10** bondswoman **11** bondservant

sergeant
02 PS **03** NCO, Sgt **04** Cuff, Serg, Troy **05** Bilko, chips, sarge, Sergt **06** Buzfuz **08** havildar

series
03 row, run, ser, set **04** line **05** chain, cycle, early, order, train **06** catena, course, stream, string **07** library **08** bead-roll, pedigree, sequence **10** succession **11** arrangement, progression **13** concatenation

• new series
02 NS

serious
03 bad, big, sad 04 deep, dour, grim, tidy 05 acute, ample, grave, great, heavy, large, quiet, sober, staid, stern 06 honest, lavish, no joke, severe, solemn, somber, sombre, urgent 07 crucial, earnest, genuine, pensive, sincere, sizable, weighty 08 abundant, critical, generous, grievous, perilous, pressing, sizeable, worrying 09 dangerous, difficult, important, long-faced, momentous, plentiful, unsmiling 10 humourless, precarious, thoughtful, unlaughing 11 far-reaching, preoccupied, significant, substantial 12 considerable, life-and-death 13 consequential, of consequence

seriously
04 very 05 badly, jolly 06 highly, really, sorely 07 acutely, awfully, for real, gravely, greatly, utterly 08 severely, solemnly, terribly 09 au sérieux, decidedly, earnestly, extremely, intensely, sincerely, unusually 10 critically, dreadfully, grievously, remarkably, thoroughly, uncommonly 11 dangerously, exceedingly, excessively, frightfully, joking apart, joking aside 12 immoderately, inordinately, terrifically, thoughtfully, unreasonably 13 distressingly, exceptionally 15 extraordinarily

seriousness
06 moment, weight 07 gravity, urgency 08 gravitas, sobriety 09 solemnity, staidness, sternness 10 importance, sedateness 11 earnestness 12 significance 14 humourlessness

sermon
03 ser 04 talk 06 homily, preach 07 address, karakia, khotbah, khotbeh, khutbah, lecture, message, oration, reproof 08 harangue 09 discourse, talking-to 10 preachment 11 declamation, exhortation

serow
04 thar

serpent
05 lamia, snake 06 ellops 08 basilisk, sea snake 09 ouroboros 10 cockatrice

See also **snake**

serpentine
05 snaky 06 ophite 07 coiling, crooked, sinuous, snaking, winding 08 asbestos, tortuous, twisting 09 ophiolite, snakelike 10 chrysotile, meandering, retinalite 12 serpentiform

serrated
06 jagged, pinked 07 notched, sawlike, toothed 08 indented, saw-edged 09 crenulate 10 crenulated, saw-toothed, serrulated 11 serratulate 12 diprionidian 14 monoprionidian

serried
05 close, dense 06 massed 07 compact, crowded 08 close-set 13 close together

servant
03 boy, man 04 drug, help, jack 06 drudge, helper 07 subject 08 hireling 09 ancillary, assistant, attendant 10 ministrant

Servants include:

03 fag, gip, gyp
04 char, chef, cook, hind, maid, page
05 boots, carer, daily, groom, nanny, slave, valet, wench
06 au pair, barman, batman, butler, chokra, garçon, haiduk, lackey, menial, ostler, skivvy, tweeny, waiter
07 barmaid, bellboy, bellhop, cleaner, equerry, flunkey, footman, gossoon, pageboy, steward, tapsman
08 charlady, coachman, dogsbody, domestic, factotum, handmaid, henchman, home help, house boy, retainer, scullion, servitor, turnspit, waitress, wet nurse
09 chauffeur, errand boy, governess, housemaid, lady's maid, seneschal
10 chauffeuse, handmaiden, henchwoman, manservant, stewardess
11 body servant, boot-catcher, chambermaid, henchperson, housekeeper, kitchen-maid, parlour-maid
12 domestic help, scullery maid
13 care assistant, lady-in-waiting, livery-servant
14 commissionaire

serve
◇ *anagram indicator*
02 do, ka 03 ace, act, aid, kae, let 04 deal, help, sair, wait 05 avail, valet 06 answer, assist, attend, dish up, fulfil, lackey, supply, wait on 07 benefit, deliver, dish out, dole out, further, give out, lacquey, perform, present, provide, satisfy, succour, suffice, support, undergo, work for, work out, worship 08 carry out, complete, function, wait upon 09 be of use to, discharge, go through 10 distribute, minister to, take care of 11 do the work of 12 be employed by 13 be of benefit to, be of service to, do a good turn to

• serve up
◇ *reversal down indicator*

service
02 RN 03 ace, fee, job, let, RAF, use 04 army, duty, help, navy, rite, sorb, tune, turn, work 05 check, usage 06 course, duties, forces, go over, labour, repair, ritual 07 amenity, benefit, repairs, utility, worship 08 activity, air force, business, ceremony, disposal, facility, function, maintain, military, overhaul, resource 09 advantage, ordinance, sacrament, servicing 10 assistance, employment, expediting, observance, usefulness 11 maintenance, performance, recondition 12 availability

Religious services include:

04 Mass
06 matins
07 baptism, evening, funeral, morning, wedding
08 compline, evensong, High Mass, marriage, memorial
09 communion, Eucharist
10 bar mitzvah, bat mitzvah, dedication
11 christening, Christingle, Lord's Supper, nuptial Mass, remembrance, Requiem Mass
12 confirmation, Midnight Mass, thanksgiving
13 Holy Communion, Holy Matrimony
14 First Communion, morning prayers
15 harvest festival

• in service
05 in use 07 working 09 operative 10 functional 11 in operation 12 in regular use 14 in working order

• of service
06 useful 07 helpful 09 of benefit 10 beneficial, profitable 12 advantageous

• on active service
03 oas

• out of service
04 phut 05 kaput 06 broken, faulty, kaputt 08 out of use, packed up 09 conked out, defective 10 not working, on the blink, on the fritz, out of order

serviceable
04 good 05 plain, tough 06 simple, strong, usable, useful 07 durable, helpful 08 availful, sensible 09 effective, efficient, practical, unadorned 10 beneficial, commodious, convenient, dependable, functional, profitable 11 hard-wearing, utilitarian 12 advantageous

serviceman *see* **aircraftsman**; **sailor**; **soldier**

servicemen *see* **air force**; **army**; **navy**

servile
03 low 04 base, mean 05 lowly, slimy 06 abject, humble, menial, vassal 07 fawning, slavish, subject 08 cringing, toadying, unctuous 09 groveling 10 controlled, grovelling, obsequious, submissive 11 bootlicking, subservient, sycophantic

servility
05 slime 07 fawning 08 baseness, meanness, toadyism 09 abjection 10 abjectness, grovelling, sycophancy 11 bootlicking, slavishness 12 subservience, unctuousness 13 self-abasement 14 obsequiousness, submissiveness

serving
05 share 06 amount, ration 07 bowlful, helping, portion 08 plateful, spoonful 11 ministering

servitude
05 bonds **06** chains, thrall **07** bondage, peonage, peonism, serfdom, slavery **08** thirlage, thraldom **09** obedience, vassalage **10** stillicide, subjection, villeinage **11** enslavement, subjugation

sesame
03 til **04** beni, teel **05** benne, benni **06** semsem **07** gingili, jinjili **08** gingelly

session
04 bevy, sesh, Sess, term, time, year **05** bevvy, drill, shoot, spell **06** clinic, grog-on, grog-up, period, séance **07** hearing, meeting, sitting, stretch **08** assembly, semester **09** scrimmage, talkathon **10** conference, discussion **11** church court, down-sitting

See also **term**

• be in session
03 set, sit

• close a session
04 rise

set
◇ *anagram indicator*
02 TV **03** dip, dot, fix, gel, kit, lay, lot, pit, ply, put **04** band, bulb, cake, club, dump, firm, gang, give, jell, knit, look, name, park, plan, rate, rest, sink, stud, turn **05** adapt, apply, array, batch, befit, begin, cause, class, crowd, embed, fixed, frame, grant, group, jelly, lodge, mount, pitch, place, plant, plonk, posit, radio, ready, rigid, scene, score, set up, stage, stake, start, stick, stock, telly, usual, value, wings, write **06** adjust, agreed, all set, assign, become, choose, circle, clique, create, decide, devise, direct, formal, go down, harden, impose, incite, insert, lead to, locate, ordain, outfit, prompt, select, series, set off, set out, settle, strict, vanish **07** agree on, appoint, arrange, bearing, compose, confirm, congeal, consign, coterie, decided, decline, deposit, dispose, faction, install, lay down, posture, prepare, produce, provide, regular, resolve, routine, scenery, setting, settled, sharpen, situate, specify, station, stiffen, subside, thicken, trigger **08** allocate, arranged, backdrop, category, conclude, delegate, equipped, everyday, finished, get ready, habitual, occasion, ordained, organize, position, prepared, propound, put right, regulate, result in, schedule, sequence, solidify, sprinkle, standard **09** appointed, coagulate, completed, customary, designate, determine, direction, disappear, establish, harmonize, ingrained, make ready, organized, prescribe, scheduled, specified, stipulate, variegate **10** assemblage, assortment, background, become firm, become hard, bring about, collection, compendium, complement, co-ordinate, deliberate, determined, entrenched, expression, give rise to, inaugurate, inflexible, prescribed, television, trigger off **11** crystallize, established, inclination, intentional, mise-en-scène, orchestrate, prearranged, stereotyped, synchronize, traditional **12** conventional **13** predetermined **14** bring into being

• set about
05 begin, frame, start **06** attack, tackle **08** commence, embark on **09** get down to, undertake

• set against
05 weigh **06** assail, divide, oppose **07** balance, compare **08** alienate, contrast, disunite, estrange **09** juxtapose

• set apart
04 seal **06** divide, ordain **07** mark off, reserve **08** put aside, separate **09** segregate, sequester **11** distinguish, peculiarize **12** put on one side, put to one side **13** differentiate, make different

• set aside
04 keep, save **05** allot, annul, break, lay by, put by **06** cancel, ignore, reject, repeal, revoke, select **07** discard, earmark, put away, reserve, reverse **08** abrogate, discount, keep back, lay aside, mothball, overrule, overturn, put aside, separate, set apart **09** sequester, slight off, stash away, supersede **10** give over to **13** keep in reserve

• set back
◇ *reversal indicator*
04 cost, slow **05** check, delay **06** hinder, hold up, impede, retard, thwart **07** reverse **08** surprise

• set down
03 lay **04** drop, land, note, snub, take **05** judge, pitch, state **06** affirm, assert, depose, encamp, esteem, record, regard **07** ascribe, deposit, lay down **08** note down **09** attribute, discharge, establish, formulate, prescribe, stipulate, subscribe, write down **12** put in writing

• set forth
03 say **04** shew, show **05** leave, state **06** depart, praise, record, set off, set out **07** clarify, declare, display, exhibit, explain, expound, present, publish **08** describe, start out **09** delineate, elucidate, explicate, recommend

• set in
◇ *insertion indicator*
04 come **05** begin, inset, start **06** arrive **08** commence

• set off
05 begin, leave, light, start **06** blow up, depart, ignite, prompt, set out **07** commend, display, enhance, explode, show off, trigger **08** activate, contrast, detonate, heighten, initiate, set forth, start out, touch off **09** encourage, intensify **10** trigger off **11** set in motion, take the road **14** counterbalance **15** throw into relief

• set on
03 mug, out, sic, tar **04** bent, firm, sick, sool **05** fixed, go for, tarre **06** attack, beat up, dogged, intent, strong, turn on **07** assault, dead set, decided, lay into, set upon **08** fall upon, hell-bent, resolute, resolved, stubborn **09** insistent, steadfast, tenacious **10** determined, persistent, purposeful, unwavering **11** persevering, unflinching **12** single-minded, strong-minded, strong-willed **14** uncompromising

• set out
◇ *anagram indicator*
03 put **04** boun, laid **05** adorn, begin, bowne, leave, start **06** depart, lay out, set off, strike **07** arrange, display, exhibit, explain, expound, present, take off **08** describe, start out

• set up
◇ *reversal down indicator*
02 up **03** rig **04** form, rear, trap **05** array, begin, build, erect, fit up, found, frame, pitch, raise, sport, start **06** create, settle **07** arrange, compose, dispose, elevate, mounted, prepare **08** assemble, initiate, organize **09** construct, establish, institute, introduce **10** constitute, inaugurate **11** incriminate **13** accuse falsely **14** bring into being

setback
◇ *reversal indicator*
04 blip, blow, snag **05** check, delay, hitch, knock, upset **06** blight, defeat, hiccup, hold-up, rebuff, whammy **07** problem, relapse, reverse **08** body blow, hiccough, reversal **09** hindrance, throwback **10** difficulty, impediment, misfortune **11** obstruction **14** disappointment, stumbling-block

settee
04 sofa **05** couch, futon, squab **06** canapé, day-bed, lounge **07** bergère, dos-à-dos, sofa bed **09** bed-settee, davenport, tête-à-tête **12** chesterfield

setter
01 I **02** me **03** spy **07** dropper

• setter's
04 mine

See also **crossword**

setting
04 site, vail **05** frame, scene **06** chaton, locale, milieu, period **07** context, framing, monture, scenery **08** fixation, location, mounting, position **09** placement **10** background **11** environment, mise-en-scène, perspective **12** surroundings

setting-up
05 start **08** creation, founding **09** inception **10** foundation, initiation **11** institution **12** inauguration, introduction **13** establishment

settle
03 fix, pay **04** drop, fall, foot, kill, land, lite, live, nest, perk, rest, sink, stun **05** agree, bench, clear, fix up, ledge, light, lodge, lower, order, perch, pitch, plant, quiet, solve, state **06** accept, adjust, alight, ante up, choose, clinch, decide, defray, go down, occupy, people, repose, reside, square **07** agree on, appoint, arrange,

compact, compose, confirm, cough up, descend, discuss, dispose, fork out, inhabit, install, patch up, resolve, subside **08** colonize, come down, complete, conclude, decide on, organize, populate, regulate, settle up, square up **09** determine, discharge, establish, light upon, reconcile **10** compromise, put in order **12** make your home, put down roots **13** do the business

• **settle down**
05 still **06** shut in, soothe **07** compose, quieten **08** calm down **09** buy a house, get down to, gravitate **10** get married **12** buckle down to, put down roots, start a family **13** concentrate on, knuckle down to **15** apply yourself to, make comfortable

settlement
◇ *anagram indicator*
02 pa **03** pah, utu **04** camp, fine, post **05** truce **06** bustee, colony, hamlet **07** kibbutz, manyata, outpost, payment, sinking, village **08** clearing, contract, decision, defrayal, manyatta, ordering, presidio **09** agreement, Ausgleich, bandobast, Botany Bay, bundobust, clearance, community, discharge, rancherie **10** completion, conclusion, encampment, occupation, patching up, plantation, population, resolution, subsidence **11** arrangement, down-sitting, liquidation, termination **12** colonization, lake dwelling, organization, satisfaction **13** accommodation, establishment **14** reconciliation

settler
07 bushman, incomer, new chum, pilgrim, pioneer, planter **08** colonist, newcomer, shagroon, squatter **09** colonizer, immigrant, inhabiter, Varangian **10** pure Merino **11** beachcomber, Cromwellian **12** frontiersman **14** frontierswoman

set-to
03 row **04** bout, spat **05** brush, fight, scrap **06** barney, bust-up, dust-up, fracas **07** contest, quarrel, wrangle **08** argument, conflict, exchange, squabble **09** argy-bargy **11** altercation **12** disagreement **13** slanging-match

set-up
◇ *reversal down indicator*
06 format, system **08** business **09** framework, structure **10** conditions **11** arrangement, composition, disposition **12** organization **13** circumstances

seven
01 S **03** VII **06** heptad, Pleiad **08** hebdomad **09** septenary

Seven Against Thebes

The Seven Greek champions who attacked Thebes:

06 Tydeus
08 Adrastus, Capaneus
09 Polynices
10 Amphiaraus, Hippomedon
13 Parthenopaeus

Seven Deadly Sins *see* **sin**

seven hills of Rome *see* **hill**

Seven Sisters colleges *see* **university**

seventeen
04 XVII

seventy
03 LXX

Seven Wonders of the World *see* **wonder**

sever
03 cut, end, hew, nip **04** chop, hack, part, pith, rend **05** break, cease, split **06** cleave, cut off, detach, divide, lop off, nip off **07** chop off, disjoin, divorce, tear off **08** alienate, amputate, break off, dissever, dissolve, disunite, estrange, separate **09** disbranch, terminate **10** disconnect, dissociate **13** cut the painter

several
04 a few, many, some **06** divers, sundry **07** diverse, various **08** assorted, distinct, separate **09** a number of, different, disparate, quite a few **10** individual, particular

severally
06 apiece, singly **08** seriatim **10** discretely, separately **12** individually, in particular, particularly, respectively, specifically

severe
03 bad, ill **04** cold, dour, grim, hard **05** acute, cruel, eager, grave, harsh, penal, plain, rigid, sharp, snell, sober, stark, stern, tough **06** fierce, modest, morose, shrewd, simple, strict, strong, taxing, trying **07** arduous, ascetic, austere, caustic, drastic, extreme, intense, serious, spartan, violent **08** Catonian, critical, Draconic, exacting, forceful, grievous, grinding, perilous, pitiless, powerful, rigorous, ruthless **09** agonizing, dangerous, demanding, difficult, Draconian, Dracontic, inclement, merciless, punishing, splitting, stringent, swingeing, unadorned, unbending, unsmiling, unsparing **10** astringent, burdensome, forbidding, functional, hard-handed, inexorable, iron-fisted, iron-handed, relentless, tyrannical, unbearable **11** strait-laced, undecorated **12** businesslike, disapproving, excruciating **13** Rhadamanthine, unembellished, unsympathetic

severely
04 hard, sore **05** badly **06** coldly, dourly, grimly, hardly, sorely **07** acutely, gravely, harshly, sharply, sternly **08** bitterly, strictly **09** extremely, intensely **10** critically, rigorously **11** dangerously **14** disapprovingly

severity
05 wrath **06** rigour **07** gravity **08** bareness, coldness, grimness, hardness, strength **09** acuteness, austerity, extremity, harshness, intensity, plainness, sharpness, sternness, toughness **10** asceticism, fierceness, severeness, simplicity, spartanism, strictness, stringency **11** seriousness **12** forcefulness, pitilessness, ruthlessness, ungentleness **13** mercilessness

sew
03 hem, run, sue **04** bind, darn, mend, ooze, seam, tack, whip, work **05** baste, drain **06** needle, stitch **08** overcast, overhand **09** embroider **10** buttonhole, whipstitch **12** saddle-stitch

sewage
04 soil **07** sullage

sewer
04 sure **05** drain, shore, sough **06** cloaca, needle, tailor

sex
01 f, m **04** male **05** union **06** allure, coitus, female, gender, libido **07** coition, glamour **08** congress, embraces, intimacy, sexiness **09** magnetism, sex appeal, sexuality **10** commixtion, copulation, lovemaking, sensuality **11** fornication, intercourse **12** consummation, desirability, reproduction, **13** seductiveness **14** voluptuousness **15** carnal knowledge, sexual relations

sex appeal
02 it, SA **05** oomph

sexless
01 n **06** neuter **07** asexual, unsexed **08** unsexual **10** undersexed, unfeminine **11** unmasculine **15** parthenogenetic

sexton
06 fossor, verger **09** caretaker, sacristan **10** grave-maker **11** grave-digger

sexual
03 sex **05** gamic **06** carnal, coital, erotic **07** genital, raunchy, sensual **08** venereal **11** procreative **12** reproductive

sexuality
04 lust **06** desire **08** sexiness, virility **09** carnality, eroticism **10** sensuality, sexual urge **12** sexual desire **14** voluptuousness **15** sexual instincts

sexy
04 phat **06** erotic, nubile, slinky, steamy **07** raunchy, sensual **08** alluring, arousing, beddable, exciting, inviting, tempting **09** desirable, provoking, salacious, seductive **10** attractive, suggestive, voluptuous **11** fascinating, flirtatious, provocative, stimulating, titillating **12** pornographic

Seychelles
02 SY **03** SYC

shabbily
08 rottenly, unfairly **09** scruffily **10** despicably, shamefully **11** inelegantly **12** contemptibly, disreputably, unacceptably **13** dishonourably, unfashionably

shabby
03 low **04** mean, poky, worn **05** cheap, dingy, dirty, dowdy, faded, mangy, oorie, ourie, owrie, pokey, scaly, seedy, tacky, tatty **06** frayed, mangey, maungy, paltry, poking, ragged, rotten, scurvy, shoddy, unfair **07** raunchy, run-down, scruffy, squalid, worn-out **08** dog-eared, low-lived, shameful, tattered, unworthy **09** moth-eaten, out at heel **10** broken-down, despicable, down-at-heel, flea-bitten, ramshackle, threadbare, tumbledown **11** dilapidated, in disrepair **12** contemptible, disreputable, unacceptable **13** discreditable, dishonourable

shack
03 hut **04** dump, hole, shed **05** cabin, hovel, hutch **06** lean-to, shanty

shackle
03 tie **04** bind, bond, gyve, iron, rope **05** chain, limit **06** couple, fetter, hamper, hobble, impede, secure, tether, thwart **07** darbies, inhibit, manacle, trammel **08** encumber, handcuff, handicap, obstruct, restrain, restrict **09** bracelets, constrain, hamstring, hindrance, restraint **10** constraint, fetterlock, hamshackle **11** encumbrance, obstruction, restriction

shad
05 allis **06** allice, twaite

shade
03 dim, hue, tad **04** cast, dash, dusk, hide, hint, part, tint, tone, ugly, veil **05** blind, cloud, color, cover, ghost, gloom, swale, tinge, touch, trace, umbra, visor, vizor **06** amount, awning, canopy, colour, darken, degree, memory, nuance, screen, shadow, shield, shroud, spirit **07** conceal, curtain, dimness, obscure, parasol, phantom, protect, shadows, shelter, spectre, umbrage, variety **08** bongrace, covering, darkness, gloaming, overcast, reminder, sunblind, sunshade, tincture, twilight, umbrella **09** gradation, inumbrate, murkiness, obscurity, represent, semblance, shadiness, suspicion **10** apparition, difference, gloominess, overshadow, protection, suggestion **12** semi-darkness **14** block light from

See also **black**; **blue**; **colour**; **dye**; **green**; **grey**; **orange**; **pigment**; **pink**; **purple**; **rainbow**; **red**; **white**; **yellow**

- **a shade**

04 a bit **06** a touch, a trace, rather **07** a little, a trifle **08** slightly

- **put in the shade**

03 top **04** beat **05** dwarf, excel **07** eclipse, outrank, surpass **08** outclass, outshine

- **shade off**

04 melt, pass **05** blend **07** gradate **10** intergrade

shadow
03 dog, pal **04** dusk, hide, hint, pall, scog, scug, skug, stag, tail **05** cloud, cover, ghost, gloom, image, scoog, scoug, shade, shape, stalk, trace, trail, umbra, watch **06** blight, darken, follow, screen, shield, sleuth, spirit, typify, unreal **07** dimness, feigned, obscure, outline, remnant, sadness, shelter, trouble, umbrage, vestige **08** darkness, follower, gloaming, overhang, penumbra, sidekick, twilight **09** companion, detective, obscurity, remainder, suspicion **10** foreboding, overshadow, protection, silhouette, suggestion **11** tenebrosity **12** semi-darkness **14** Brocken spectre, representation

- **a shadow of your former self**

07 apology, remnant, vestige **13** poor imitation, weaker version

- **without a shadow of a doubt**

05 truly **06** surely **07** clearly, no doubt **08** of course **09** assuredly, certainly, doubtless **10** most likely **11** indubitably, undoubtedly **12** indisputably, without doubt **14** unquestionably

shadowy
03 dim **04** dark, hazy **05** faint, murky, shady, vague **06** gloomy, unreal **07** ghostly, obscure, phantom, unclear **08** ethereal, illusory, nebulous, secluded, spectral, symbolic **09** dreamlike, imaginary, tenebrose, tenebrous **10** ill-defined, indistinct, intangible, mysterious, tenebrious **11** crepuscular, umbratilous **13** indeterminate, unsubstantial

shady
03 dim **04** cool, dark, iffy **05** bosky, fishy, leafy **06** bowery, louche, opaque, shaded, shifty, veiled **07** clouded, covered, crooked, dubious, obscure, shadowy, suspect, umbrose, umbrous **08** screened, shielded, shrouded, sinister, slippery **09** dishonest, protected, tenebrose, tenebrous, umbratile, underhand, unethical **10** caliginous, mysterious, suspicious, tenebrious, umbrageous, unreliable **11** umbratilous, umbriferous **12** disreputable, questionable, unscrupulous **13** untrustworthy

shaft
03 ash, bar, fil, pit, ray, rod **04** beam, butt, dart, duct, dupe, fill, flue, fust, hilt, pole, sink, stem, tige, well **05** arbor, arrow, scape, shank, stale, stalk, stave, steal, steel, steil, stele, stick, stock, stulm, winze **06** handle, pencil, pillar, rachis, scapus, steale, tunnel **07** missile, passage, swindle, upright, winning **08** hoistway **09** truncheon

shaggy
04 rag'd **05** bushy, hairy, nappy, ragde, tousy, touzy, towsy, towzy **06** horrid, ragged, woolly **07** crinose, hirsute, unkempt, unshorn **09** mop-headed **10** long-haired **11** dishevelled

shake
◇ *anagram indicator*
03 jog, wag, wap **04** bump, faze, jerk, jolt, pump, rock, roll, shog, stir, sway, wave **05** alarm, alert, crack, heave, lower, quake, rouse, shock, split, swing, throb, trill, upset, waver, wield, wring **06** bounce, didder, dindle, dinnle, dismay, dodder, happen, hustle, jigger, jiggle, joggle, jostle, judder, justle, lessen, moment, quiver, rattle, reduce, shiver, summon, totter, trillo, twitch, weaken, wobble **07** agitate, concuss, disturb, fissure, perturb, quaking, rocking, shake up, shoggle, shoogle, shudder, tremble, unnerve, vibrate **08** brandish, convulse, diminish, distress, flourish, frighten, unsettle **09** oscillate, shivering, throbbing, trembling, undermine, vibration **10** convulsion, discompose, intimidate, shuddering, unsettling **11** disturbance, oscillation

- **shake a leg**

05 hurry **07** hurry up **08** step on it **10** get a move on, look lively **11** get cracking **15** get your skates on

- **shake off**

04 heal, lose, mend **05** elude, rally **06** escape, pick up, revive **07** get away, get over, get well, improve **08** dislodge, get rid of, outstrip, shrug off **09** get better **10** bounce back, convalesce, feel better, recuperate **11** be on the mend, get away from, give the slip, leave behind, outdistance, pull through, recover from **12** gain strength **13** turn the corner

- **shake up**

03 mix **05** alarm, rouse, shock, upset **06** jumble, rattle **07** disturb, succuss, unnerve, upbraid **08** distress, unsettle **09** rearrange, reshuffle **10** reorganize **11** restructure

Shakespeare
02 WS **07** the Bard **13** The Swan of Avon

Shakespeare's characters include:

03 Hal (Prince), Nym, Sly (Christopher)
04 Ajax, Anne (Lady), Dull, Fool (The), Ford (Mistress), Hero, Iago, John (Don), John (King), Kate, Kent (Earl of), Lear (King), Moth, Page (Mistress), Puck, Snug
05 Ariel, Bagot, Belch (Sir Toby), Bushy, Celia, Diana, Edgar, Feste, Flute, Gobbo (Launcelot), Green, Julia, Maria, Nurse, Paris (Count), Pedro (Don), Regan, Romeo, Snout, Speed, Timon, Titus, Viola
06 Alonso, Angelo, Antony (Mark), Armado (Don Adriano de), Audrey, Banquo, Bianca, Bottom (Nick), Brutus, Cassio, Cloten, Cobweb, Dromio, Duncan (King), Edmund,

Emilia, Fabian, Hamlet, Hecate, Hector, Helena, Henry V (King), Hermia, Imogen, Jaques, Juliet, Launce, Marina, Oberon, Oliver (de Bois), Olivia, Orsino, Oswald, Pistol, Pompey, Porter, Portia, Quince, Silvia, Thisbe, Ursula, Verges, Yorick
07 Adriana, Antonio, Berowne, Bertram (Count of Rousillon), Caliban, Capulet, Cesario, Claudio, Costard, Fleance, Goneril, Gonzalo, Henry IV (King), Henry VI (King), Horatio, Hotspur, Iachimo, Jessica, Laertes, Lavinia, Leontes, Lepidus, Lorenzo, Luciana, Macbeth, Macbeth (Lady), Macduff, Malcolm, Mariana, Martext (Sir Oliver), Miranda, Nerissa, Octavia, Ophelia, Orlando, Othello, Paulina, Perdita, Proteus, Pyramus, Quickly (Mistress), Shallow, Shylock, Sycorax, Theseus, Titania, Troilus
08 Bardolph, Bassanio, Beatrice, Benedick, Benvolio, Charmian, Claudius, Cordelia, Cressida, Dogberry, Falstaff (Sir John), Florizel, Fluellen, Ganymede, Gertrude, Hermione, Isabella, Laurence (Friar), Lucretia, Lysander, Malvolio, Mercutio, Montague, Pandarus, Parolles, Pericles, Polonius, Prospero, Rosalind, Rosaline, Stephano, Trinculo
09 Aguecheek (Sir Andrew), Antigonus, Cleopatra, Collatine, Cornelius, Cymbeline, Demetrius, Desdemona, Enobarbus, Ferdinand, Ferdinand (King of Navarre), Frederick (Duke), Henry VIII (King), Hippolyta, Hortensio, Katharina, Katharine (Princess of France), Nathaniel (Sir), Petruchio, Polixenes, Richard II, Sebastian, Valentine, Vincentio (Duke)
10 Antipholus (of Ephesus), Antipholus (of Syracuse), Collatinus, Coriolanus, Fortinbras, Gloucester (Earl of), Holofernes, Jaquenetta, Richard III, Starveling, Tarquinius, Touchstone
11 Mustard-seed, Peasblossom, Rosencrantz
12 Guildenstern, Julius Caesar, Three Witches
15 Robin Goodfellow, Titus Andronicus

Shakespeare's plays:

06 Hamlet, Henry V
07 Macbeth, Othello
08 King John, King Lear, Pericles
09 Cymbeline, Henry VIII, Richard II
10 Coriolanus, Richard III, The Tempest
11 As You Like It
12 Julius Caesar, Twelfth Night
13 Timon of Athens
14 Henry IV Part One, Henry IV Part Two, Henry VI Part One, Henry VI Part Two, Romeo and Juliet, The Winter's Tale
15 Titus Andronicus
16 Henry VI Part Three, Love's Labours Lost
17 Measure for Measure, The Comedy of Errors
18 Antony and Cleopatra, Troilus and Cressida
19 Much Ado About Nothing, The Merchant of Venice, The Taming of the Shrew
20 All's Well That Ends Well
21 A Midsummer Night's Dream, Hamlet, Prince of Denmark
22 The Merry Wives of Windsor
23 The Two Gentlemen of Verona

shake-up
08 upheaval **09** reshuffle
11 disturbance **13** rearrangement, restructuring **14** reorganization

shaky
◇ *anagram indicator*
04 weak **05** dicky, loose, quaky, rocky, wonky **06** coggly, cranky, dickey, flimsy, wobbly **07** dubious, quavery, rickety, suspect, tottery, unsound
08 insecure, unstable, unsteady, wavering **09** doddering, faltering, quivering, tentative, tottering, trembling, tremulous, uncertain, unfounded **10** precarious, staggering, ungrounded, unreliable **11** unsupported
12 questionable **13** untrustworthy

shale
04 husk, till **05** blaes, fakes, shell
06 blaise, blaize, faikes **09** torbanite
12 porcellanite **14** Kupferschiefer

shall
02 'll

shallow
03 ebb **04** bank, flat, flew, flue, idle
05 empty, fleet, petty, shoal **06** flimsy, shoaly, simple, slight, spread
07 foolish, surface, trivial **08** ignorant, skin-deep, trifling **09** frivolous, insincere **11** meaningless, superficial, unscholarly **13** rattle-brained **14** one-dimensional

sham
◇ *anagram indicator*
03 cod **04** copy, fake, hoax, idol, mock
05 bogus, cheat, dummy, false, feign, fraud, mimic, pseud, put on, put-on, snide **06** affect, con man, humbug, phoney, pseudo, shoddy, stumer
07 feigned, forgery, imitate, pretend
08 deceiver, fakement, feigning, imposter, impostor, pretence, pretense, simulate, spurious, swindler
09 brummagem, charlatan, dissemble, gold brick, imitation, imposture, pinchbeck, pretended, pretender, simulated, synthetic **10** artificial, pasteboard, simulation **11** counterfeit, make believe, make-believe, mock-modesty, synthetical **12** impersonator

shaman
05 pawaw **06** healer, powwow
07 angekok, tohunga **08** angekkok, magician, sorcerer **11** medicine man, witch doctor **13** medicine woman

shamble
04 drag, limp **06** doddle, falter, hobble, scrape, toddle **07** bauchle, scamble, shuffle

shambles
04 mess **05** chaos, havoc, wreck
06 bedlam, muddle, pigsty **07** anarchy
08 abattoir, butchery, disarray, disorder, madhouse **09** confusion **10** slaughtery
14 slaughterhouse **15** disorganization

shambling
05 loose **06** clumsy **07** awkward
08 lurching, ungainly, unsteady
09 lumbering, shuffling **10** disjointed
13 unco-ordinated

shambolic
05 messy **07** chaotic, muddled
08 confused **10** in disarray
12 disorganized **14** all over the shop

shame
03 fie, fye, out, sin **04** alas, pity
05 abash, aidos, guilt, pudor, shend, stain, sully, taint **06** ashame, debase, humble, infamy, rebuke, show up, stigma, too bad **07** bad luck, beshame, degrade, modesty, mortify, remorse, reproof, scandal **08** confound, disgrace, dishonor, ignominy, repriefe, reproach, ridicule **09** confusion, discredit, dishonour, disrepute, embarrass, humiliate **10** misfortune, opprobrium, put to shame
11 bashfulness, compunction, degradation, humiliation
13 embarrassment, mortification
14 disappointment, shamefacedness
• **put to shame**
05 shend **06** humble, rebuke, show up
07 eclipse, mortify, surpass, upstage
08 disgrace, outclass, outshine, outstrip **09** embarrass, humiliate

shamefaced
05 sorry **06** guilty **07** abashed, ashamed **08** blushing, contrite, penitent, pudibund, red-faced, sheepish **09** mortified, regretful
10 apologetic, humiliated, remorseful
11 embarrassed **13** uncomfortable

shameful
03 low **04** base, foul, mean, poor, vile
06 wicked **07** heinous, ignoble, shaming **08** indecent, shocking, unworthy **09** atrocious, pudendous
10 abominable, inglorious, mortifying, outrageous, scandalous **11** disgraceful, humiliating, ignominious
12 contemptible, embarrassing
13 discreditable, dishonourable, reprehensible

shamefully
10 shockingly **11** atrociously
12 confoundedly, outrageously, scandalously **13** disgracefully, ignominiously, reprehensibly
14 embarrassingly

shameless
05 brash **06** brazen, wanton
07 blatant, corrupt, defiant **08** blattant, browless, depraved, flagrant,

hardened, immodest, improper, impudent, indecent, insolent, unseemly, unshamed **09** abashless, audacious, bald-faced, barefaced, dissolute, frontless, unabashed, unashamed, unbashful **10** brass-faced, impenitent, indecorous, unbecoming, unblushing **11** ithyphallic, unregretful, unrepentant **12** incorrigible, unprincipled

shamelessly
09 blatantly, defiantly **10** immodestly, improperly, indecently **11** unashamedly **12** incorrigibly

shanty
03 hut **04** shed **05** bothy, cabin, hovel, hutch, shack **06** chanty, lean-to **07** chantey, chantie, shantey

• **shanty town**
06 favela **10** bidonville

shape
◇ *anagram indicator*
03 air, cut, hew **04** cast, form, look, make, plan, trim, turn **05** adapt, alter, block, build, carve, forge, frame, guide, guise, image, lines, model, mould, state **06** adjust, aspect, create, define, design, devise, direct, embody, fettle, figure, format, health, kilter, modify, sculpt **07** conduce, develop, fashion, outline, pattern, prepare, produce, profile, purpose, remodel, whittle **08** contours, likeness, organize, physique, regulate **09** character, condition, construct, determine, influence, sculpture, semblance, structure **10** apparition, appearance, silhouette **11** accommodate **13** configuration

See also **circle**; **figure**; **triangle**

• **shape up**
06 come on **07** develop, improve **08** flourish, progress **09** take shape **11** make headway, move forward **12** make progress

• **take shape**
03 gel **04** form **06** inform **11** become clear, materialize **12** come together **14** become definite

shapeless
◇ *anagram indicator*
05 dumpy **07** chaotic **08** deformed, formless, indigest, nebulous, unformed, unframed **09** amorphous, irregular, misshapen **11** purposeless, undeveloped, unfashioned **12** unstructured **13** unfashionable **15** ill-proportioned

shapely
04 neat, tidy, trig, trim **06** comely, gainly, pretty **07** elegant, featous **08** feateous, featuous, graceful **09** well-set-up **10** attractive, curvaceous, forehanded, voluptuous, well-formed, well-turned **11** clean-limbed

shard
03 bit, gap **04** chip, part **05** piece, scrap, sherd **06** shiver, sliver **08** fragment, particle, splinter

share
03 cut, due, lot, rug **04** divi, part, snap, snip, sock **05** allot, divvy, halve, quota, snack, split, whack **06** assign, common, divide, finger, ration **07** carve up, deal out, dole out, give out, go Dutch, hand out, partake, portion, rake-off, section **08** allocate, dividend, division, go halves, interest, ordinary, share out **09** allotment, allottery, allowance, apportion, bank-stock, co-portion **10** allocation, contingent, distribute, percentage, plough-iron, proportion **11** go halvesies, participate **12** compare notes, contribution, go fifty-fifty, have a share in **14** slice of the cake

• **share out**
05 allot, split **06** assign **07** divvy up, give out, hand out, mete out **08** divide up **09** apportion, parcel out **10** distribute

• **shareholder**
09 ploughman

shark
05 crook **07** fleecer, sharper, slicker, sponger **08** man-eater, operator, parasite, swindler **11** extortioner **12** extortionist **13** wheeler-dealer

Sharks include:

03 cat, fox, saw
04 blue, bull, mako
05 blind, dusky, ghost, lemon, night, nurse, sagre, swell, tiger, whale, zebra
06 beagle, carpet, goblin, salmon, school, sea cat
07 basking, bramble, dogfish, leopard, requiem, sleeper, soupfin
08 blacktip, grey reef, mackerel, thresher, whitetip
09 angelfish, epaulette, Greenland, man-eating, porbeagle, sand tiger, sevengill, sharpnose, wobbegong
10 Colclough's, great white, hammerhead, Portuguese, shovelhead
11 ragged-tooth, smooth-hound

sharp
03 fit, sly **04** able, acid, cold, curt, edgy, fine, gleg, keen, neat, sour, tart, tidy, wily **05** acidy, acrid, acute, alert, brisk, clear, crisp, cruel, eager, edged, harsh, natty, nifty, quick, rapid, razor, smart, snell, spiky, stark, tangy, tight **06** abrupt, acidic, artful, astute, barbed, biting, bitter, bright, clever, crafty, fierce, hungry, jagged, marked, severe, shrewd, snappy, strong, sudden **07** acerbic, brusque, burning, caustic, cunning, cutting, elegant, exactly, extreme, hairpin, hurtful, intense, nipping, piquant, pointed, pungent, stylish, varment, varmint, violent **08** abruptly, all there, clear-cut, definite, distinct, freezing, incisive, on the dot, peracute, piercing, poignant, promptly, sardonic, scathing, serrated, shooting, stabbing, stinging, suddenly, venomous, vinegary **09** deceptive, dishonest, malicious, observant, on the ball, precisely, sarcastic, trenchant, vitriolic, voiceless **10** astringent, discerning, knife-edged, needle-like, perceptive, punctually, razor-edged, razor-sharp, unexpected **11** acrimonious, fashionable, intelligent, penetrating, quick-witted, well-defined **12** twenty-twenty, unexpectedly

sharpen
03 set **04** edge, file, hone, keen, whet **05** frost, grind, point, stone, strop **09** acuminate

sharp-eyed
08 hawk-eyed, noticing **09** eagle-eyed, observant **10** perceptive **11** keen-sighted **12** eagle-sighted

sharply
05 smack **06** curtly **07** acutely, clearly, harshly, quickly, rapidly, starkly, tightly **08** abruptly, bitterly, fiercely, markedly, suddenly **09** brusquely **10** definitely, distinctly, venomously **12** unexpectedly **13** acrimoniously, sarcastically, vitriolically

sharpness
04 edge, whet **05** venom **06** acuity, acumen **07** clarity, cruelty, sarcasm, vitriol **08** keenness, severity **09** acuteness, crispness, eagerness, harshness, intensity, precision **10** astuteness, definition, fierceness, shrewdness **11** brusqueness, discernment, observation, penetration **12** incisiveness **14** perceptiveness

shatter
◇ *anagram indicator*
04 bust, dash, ruin, star **05** blast, break, burst, crack, craze, crush, smash, split, upset, wreck **06** shiver **07** destroy, explode, scatter **08** demolish, fragment, overturn, splinter **09** devastate, overwhelm, pulverize **10** disappoint, smithereen **14** break your heart

shattered
◇ *anagram indicator*
05 all in, weary **06** broken, done in, pooped, zonked **07** crushed, worn out **08** dead beat, dog-tired, tired out **09** exhausted, fagged out, knackered, plastered, pooped out **10** devastated **11** overwhelmed, ready to drop, tuckered out

shattering
06 severe **08** crushing, damaging, smashing **10** paralysing **11** devastating **12** overwhelming

shave
03 cut **04** barb, crop, pare, trim **05** brush, graze, plane, shear, touch **06** barber, fleece, paring, scrape **07** plunder

• **close shave**
09 close call, near touch **10** close thing, narrow miss **11** lucky escape **12** narrow escape

Shaw
03 GBS

shawl
04 wrap **05** scarf, stole, tozie **06** afghan, tonnag, zephyr **07** blanket, dopatta, dupatta, tallith, whittle **08** pashmina, shatoosh, turnover **09** shahtoosh **10** India shawl **11** prayer shawl **12** Kashmir shawl, Paisley shawl

she
01 a **03** her **04** elle
See also **girl**

sheaf
04 gait, garb **05** bunch, garbe, gerbe, truss **06** armful, bundle **07** dorlach

shear
03 cut **04** clip, crop, trim **05** shave, strip **06** barber, fleece **07** scissor, tonsure **08** clipping, separate **09** penetrate

sheath
04 case **05** ocrea, shard, shell, theca, volva **06** casing, cocoon, condom, ochrea, rubber, sleeve, vagina **07** johnnie, root cap, velamen **08** covering, envelope, scabbard, urceolus, vaginula, vaginule, wrapping **09** epidermis **10** caddis-case, coleoptile, endodermis, neurilemma, neurolemma, rhinotheca, thumbstall, zoothecium **11** perineurium **12** French letter, perichaetium, prophylactic, rhamphotheca

shed
◇ *deletion indicator*
03 hut, mew, sow **04** cast, drop, emit, give, molt, part, pour, skeo, skio **05** hovel, linny, moult, shack, shine, spend, spill, spilt, throw **06** impart, lean-to, linhay, linney, remove, shower, slough **07** cast off, diffuse, discard, emitted, fall off, let fall, parting, radiate, scatter, send out, shippen, shippon **08** building, disperse, get rid of, give away, outhouse, separate, skillion **10** besprinkle
• **shed tears**
03 sob **04** bawl, howl, wail, weep **05** whine **06** snivel **07** blubber, whimper **09** be in tears **14** burst into tears, cry your eyes out

sheen
05 gleam, gloss, shine, water **06** bright, luster, lustre, patina, polish **07** burnish, shimmer, shining, sparkle, varnish **08** radiance **09** beautiful, shininess **10** brightness, brilliance

sheep
03 ewe, hog, joe, keb, mug, ram, teg, tup, yeo, yow **04** fold, hogg, lamb, tegg, yowe **05** crone, flock, yowie **06** bident, gimmer, hidder, hirsel, hogget, lamber, theave, wether, woolly **07** jumbuck, twinter **08** hoggerel **09** shearling **10** bell-wether, woollyback

Sheep include:

03 Rya
04 Dala, Gute, Soay
05 ammon, ancon, aodad, Jacob, Lleyn, Lonck, Masai, Rygja, Texel, Tunis, urial
06 aoudad, Arcott, argali, Awassi, Balwen, Beltex, bharal, burhel, burrel, Dorper, Galway, Masham, merino, muflon, Romney
07 Barbary, bighorn, burrell, burrhel, caracul, Cheviot, Colbred, Gotland, karakul, Karaman, Lincoln, Loghtan, Loghtyn, mouflon, Romanov, Roussin, Ryeland, St Croix, Steigar, Suffolk, Tibetan, Vendeen
08 Columbia, Cotswold, herdwick, Katahdin, Loaghtan, Meatlinc, moufflon, Ouessant, Peliquey, Portland, Shetland, thinhorn, troender
09 blackface, Charolais, Costentin, Leicester, Marco Polo, Southdown, Teeswater
10 Charollais
11 Wensleydale
15 Border Leicester

• **flock of sheep**
04 fold, trip

sheepish
05 silly **07** abashed, ashamed, foolish **09** chastened, mortified **10** shamefaced **11** embarrassed **13** self-conscious, uncomfortable

sheepskin
04 napa, roan **05** basan, Mocha, nappa **06** mouton, shammy, skiver **07** chamois, morocco **11** wash leather **13** shammy leather
• **sheepskin coat**
07 posteen, zamarra, zamarro **08** poshteen **10** Afghan coat

sheer
04 bend, fine, flat, full, main, mere, pure, rank, thin, turn, veer **05** blank, clear, drift, gauzy, light, plumb, quite, sharp, shift, stark, steep, swing, total, utter **06** abrupt, bright, flimsy, simple, swerve **07** deflect, deviate, diverge, perfect **08** absolute, complete, delicate, gossamer, thorough, unbroken, vertical **09** deviation, downright, out-and-out, unmingled, veritable **10** diaphanous, see-through, vertically **11** precipitous, translucent, transparent, unmitigated, unqualified **12** unadulterate **13** perpendicular, thoroughgoing, unadulterated, unconditional

sheet
03 cel, sht, web **04** cell, coat, film, leaf, page, pane, sail, sill, skin, slab **05** cover, folio, layer, panel, piece, plate, reach, sweep **06** lamina, shroud, veneer **07** blanket, blotter, coating, expanse, overlay, stratum, stretch, surface **08** bed linen, covering, membrane, pamphlet **09** Celluloid®, newspaper **10** broadsheet

shelf
03 bar **04** bank, bink, rack, reef, sill, step **05** bench, ledge, shoal, stage **06** shelve, shrine **07** bracket, counter, retable, sand bar, terrace **08** credence, credenza, informer, sandbank, shelving **11** mantelpiece, mantelshelf **12** chimney piece
• **on the shelf**
06 single **09** on your own, unmarried **10** spouseless, unattached **15** without a partner

shell
◇ *anagram indicator*
◇ *ends deletion indicator*
03 pod **04** body, bomb, case, clam, hull, husk, mail, rind, shot **05** blitz, chank, conch, cowry, crust, frame, ormer, shale, shard, sheal, sheel, shiel, shill, shuck, testa **06** attack, bullet, casing, cockle, cowrie, fire on, mussel, pellet, sea pen **07** admiral, barrage, bombard, carcase, carcass, chassis, cochlea, grenade, limacel, missile, scallop, scollop **08** carapace, covering, sea acorn, skeleton, univalve **09** explosive, framework, Midas's ear, structure, turbinate **10** integument, projectile **11** globigerina **12** pelican's-foot
• **shell money**
04 peag, peak **06** wakiki, wampum **10** wampumpeag
• **shell out**
04 ante, give **05** pay up, spend **06** ante up, donate, expend, lay out, pay out **07** cough up, fork out **08** disburse **10** contribute

shellfish
• **young shellfish**
04 spat

See also **fish**; **mollusc**; **seafood**

shelter
◇ *containment indicator*
03 cot, lee **04** cote, hide, loun, lown, roof, scog, scug, skug, tent **05** bield, bivvy, bothy, cover, guard, haven, house, hovel, lound, lownd, put up, scoog, scoug, shade **06** asylum, bunker, covert, defend, dugout, harbor, maimai, refuge, safety, sconce, screen, shadow, shield, shroud, wiltja **07** conceal, defence, embower, harbour, imbower, lodging, protect, retreat, roofing **08** security, snow-hole **09** coverture, safeguard, sanctuary, screening **10** overshadow, protection **11** accommodate, cold harbour, weather-fend **13** accommodation

sheltered
03 lee **04** cosy, loun, lown, snug, warm **05** lound, lownd, quiet, shady **06** shaded **07** covered, retired, sharded **08** isolated, screened, secluded, shielded **09** protected, reclusive, unworldly, withdrawn **10** cloistered, in the shade

shelve
04 halt **05** defer, ledge, shelf, shunt, slope **06** put off **07** incline, suspend **08** lay aside, mothball, postpone, put aside, put on ice **09** sidetrack **10** pigeonhole

shepherd
04 Acis, herd, lead **05** guide, steer, swain, usher **06** convoy, escort, feeder, pastor, tar-box **07** conduct, herdboy, herdess, marshal **08** guardian, herdsman **09** herd-groom, protector **11** flockmaster, shepherd boy, shepherdess **12** shepherdling

sheriff
06 grieve, lawman, shirra **07** bailiff **08** landdros, shireman, viscount **09** landdrost **10** shire-reeve

sherry
04 fino **05** Xeres **06** doctor **07** amoroso, oloroso, sherris **08** Montilla **10** manzanilla **11** amontillado, Bristol-milk
• **sherry glass**
06 copita **08** schooner

shield
05 cover, fence, guard, pelta, shade, targe **06** buckle, defend, screen, shadow **07** buckler, bulwark, defence, forfend, mantlet, protect, rampart, shelter, support, ward off **08** keep safe, mantelet, plastron **09** protector, safeguard **10** escutcheon, protection

shift
◇ *anagram indicator*
03 rid **04** core, move, post, quit, sell, slip, span, tack, time, tour, turn, vary, veer, warp, work **05** alter, budge, carry, cimar, cymar, evade, relay, smock, spell, stint, swing, U-turn **06** adjust, change, fidget, go away, hirsle, manage, modify, period, put off, remove, swerve, switch, wrench **07** chemise, consume, removal, stretch, swallow **08** artifice, dislodge, displace, get rid of, movement, pis aller, relocate, transfer **09** cutty-sark, expedient, fluctuate, rearrange, transpose, variation **10** alteration, relocation, reposition **11** contrivance, fluctuation, lodging turn, prevaricate **12** displacement, modification, tergiversate **13** rearrangement, transposition

shiftless
04 idle, lazy **05** inept **07** aimless **08** feckless, goalless, indolent, slothful **11** incompetent, ineffectual, inefficient, unambitious **12** resourceless **13** directionless, irresponsible, lackadaisical **14** good-for-nothing, unenterprising

shifty
◇ *anagram indicator*
04 iffy, wily **05** shady **06** crafty, louche, tricky **07** cunning, devious, dubious, evasive, furtive **08** scheming, slippery **09** deceitful, dishonest, underhand **10** contriving **11** duplicitous **13** untrustworthy

shilling
01 s **03** bob, hog **06** deaner, teston **09** twalpenny **11** shovelboard, twalpennies, twelve-penny **12** shuffleboard

shilly-shally
05 waver **06** dither, falter, seesaw, teeter **08** hesitate, hum and ha **09** fluctuate, hem and haw, mess about, vacillate **10** dilly-dally **11** prevaricate, vacillation **12** be indecisive, indecisively **13** sit on the fence **14** whittie-whattie

shimmer
◇ *anagram indicator*
04 glow, haze, play **05** gleam, glint **06** lustre **07** flicker, glimmer, glisten, glitter, sparkle, twinkle **10** glistening **11** iridescence, scintillate

shimmering
◇ *anagram indicator*
05 shiny **07** glowing, shining **08** gleaming, luminous, lustrous **09** chatoyant **10** avanturine, aventurine, glistening, glittering, iridescent **12** incandescent

shin
03 sin **04** soar **05** climb, mount, scale, shoot, skink, swarm **06** ascend, shinny **07** clamber **08** scrabble, scramble

shine
03 rub, wax **04** beam, buff, dash, emit, glow, lamp, leam, leme, star **05** brush, excel, flash, glare, glaze, gleam, glint, gloss, light, party, rub up, sheen, skyre **06** beacon, come up, dazzle, lustre, patina, polish, shindy **07** burnish, effulge, flicker, give off, glimmer, glisten, glitter, radiate, shimmer, sparkle, twinkle **08** lambency, radiance, resplend, stand out **09** irradiate **10** brightness, effulgence, incandesce **11** be brilliant, be excellent **12** be pre-eminent, luminescence, phosphoresce **13** be outstanding, incandescence

shingle
06 chesel, chisel

shingles
04 zona **06** zoster **12** herpes zoster

shininess
05 gleam, sheen, shine **06** lustre, polish **07** burnish, glitter **10** brightness, effulgence, glossiness

shining
04 glow, neat **05** beamy, glary, light, lucid, moony, nitid, sheen **06** bright, candid, glossy, golden, lucent, marble, starry **07** aeneous, beaming, eminent, fulgent, glowing, lamping, leading, perfect, radiant **08** flashing, gleaming, glinting, glooming, glorious, luminous, lustrous, relucent, rutilant, splendid **09** brilliant, effulgent, excellent, sparkling, splendent, twinkling **10** celebrated, flickering, glistening, glittering, pre-eminent, profulgent, shimmering **11** conspicuous, illustrious, magnificent, outstanding, resplendent **12** incandescent **13** distinguished **14** phosphorescent

shiny
05 raven, silky, sleek **06** bright, glossy, sheeny **07** shining **08** gleaming, lustrous, polished **09** burnished **10** glistening, shimmering

ship
04 boat, post, send **05** craft **06** embark, vessel **07** send off **08** aircraft

Ship and boat types include:

01 E, Q, U
02 el, mv, NS, SS, TB
03 air, ark, bum, cat, cog, cot, day, dow, fly, gig, gun, HMS, hoy, ice, jet, kit, man, MTB, mud, pig, RMS, row, sub, tow, tub, tug, USS, war
04 bark, brig, buss, cock, cott, dhow, dory, falt, fire, flag, flat, fold, four, grab, HMAS, HMCS, hulk, hush, junk, keel, koff, life, long, mail, maxi, pair, pink, pont, post, pram, prau, proa, prow, punt, ro-ro, saic, scow, show, snow, surf, tall, tern, tilt, Turk, waka, well, wind, yawl, zulu
05 aviso, barca, barge, botel, butty, cabin, canal, canoe, casco, coble, coper, crare, dandy, dingy, drake, ferry, funny, guard, gulet, hatch, horse, house, jolly, kayak, ketch, laker, light, liner, motor, oiler, peter, pilot, plate, power, praam, prahu, prore, razee, river, rotor, saick, scout, scull, seine, shell, shore, skiff, slave, sloop, smack, speed, stake, steam, store, swamp, tanka, track, tramp, troop, umiak, wager, waist, whale, whiff, xebec, yacht, zabra
06 advice, argosy, banker, barque, bateau, battle, bethel, bireme, caique, carvel, castle, coaler, cobble, cockle, codder, coffin, convoy, cooper, crayer, cutter, dingey, dinghy, dogger, dragon, droger, dromon, drover, dugout, flying, galiot, galley, gay-you, hooker, hopper, jigger, lateen, launch, lorcha, lugger, masula, monkey, mother, narrow, nuggar, oomiac, oomiak, packet, paddle, pedalo, pirate, prison, puffer, pulwar, puteli, randan, reefer, rowing, runner, sailer, saique, sampan, sandal, sanpan, school, schuit, schuyt, settee, slaver, tanker, tartan, torpid, trader, turret, wangan, wangun, wherry
07 assault, Berthon, birlinn, budgero, capital, caravel, clipper, coaster, collier, consort, coracle, corsair, cruiser, currach, curragh, dredger, drifter, drogher, dromond, factory, felucca, four-oar, frigate, gabbard, gabbart, galleon, galliot, Geordie, gondola, landing, liberty, lighter, lymphad, man-o'-war, mistico, mudscow, mystery, nacelle, oomiack, pair-oar, passage, patamar, pearler, pinnace, piragua, pirogue, polacca, pontoon, sailing, scooter, shallop, sharpie, sponger, steamer, tartane, torpedo, trawler, trireme, vedette, victory, wanigan, warship, weather

08 bilander, billyboy, budgerow, car ferry, corocore, corocoro, corvette, dahabieh, dispatch, eight-oar, galleass, galliass, gallivat, hospital, hoveller, Indiaman, ironclad, log-canoe, longship, mackinaw, man-of-war, masoolah, massoola, merchant, monohull, montaria, periagua, pleasure, repeater, row barge, runabout, sally-man, schooner, skipjack, smuggler, Spaniard, training, trimaran, water bus, woodskin
09 bomb-ketch, Bucentaur, catamaran, commodore, container, dahabeeah, dahabiyah, dahabiyeh, daysailer, daysailor, destroyer, firefloat, flying jib, freighter, herringer, Hollander, hydrofoil, klondiker, klondyker, lapstrake, lapstreak, leviathan, long-liner, minelayer, monoxylon, motoscafo, multihull, Norwegian, oil-burner, oil tanker, outrigger, privateer, randan gig, receiving, sallee-man, speedster, steamship, store ship, submarine, surf canoe, transport, two-decker, two-master, vaporetto, well smack
10 armour-clad, bomb-vessel, brigantine, free-trader, hovercraft, icebreaker, minehunter, quadrireme, seal-fisher, tea clipper, trekschuit, triaconter, victualler, windjammer
11 bulk carrier, cockleshell, dreadnought, galley-foist, merchantman, minesweeper, motor launch, penteconter, purse-seiner, quinquereme, sallee-rover, salmon coble, side-wheeler, steam launch, steam packet, steam vessel, submersible, three-decker, three-master, victualling, wooden horse
12 cabin cruiser, deepwaterman, double-decker, East-Indiaman, line-of-battle, screw steamer, single-decker, square-rigger, stern-wheeler, tangle-netter, tramp steamer, troop carrier
13 Canadian canoe, paddle steamer, revenue cutter, roll-on roll-off
14 Flying Dutchman, ocean-greyhound, turbine steamer
15 aircraft-carrier, floating battery, logistics vessel

Ships include:

03 QE2
04 Ajax, Argo, Hood, Nina
05 Argus, Maine, Pinta
06 Beagle, Bounty, Cathay, Oriana, Pequod, Renown
07 Alabama, Amistad, Belfast, Blücher, Olympic, Pelican, Potomac, Repulse, Tirpitz, Titanic, Victory
08 Ark Royal, Bismarck, Canberra, Fearless, Graf Spee, Intrepid, Iron Duke, Mary Rose, Royal Oak
09 Adventure, Aquitania, Britannia, Britannic, Carinthia, Cutty Sark, Discovery, Endeavour, Gipsy Moth, Gneisenau, Lexington, Lusitania, Mayflower, Normandie, Queen Mary, Sheffield, Téméraire, Terranova
10 Golden Hind, Hispaniola, Invincible, Mauretania, Prinz Eugen, Resolution, Santa Maria, Washington
11 Dawn Treader, Dreadnought, Illustrious, Scharnhorst
12 African Queen, Great Britain, Great Eastern, Great Western, Marie Celeste
13 Prince of Wales
14 Flying Dutchman, Queen Elizabeth
15 Admiral Graf Spee, General Belgrano, Queen Elizabeth 2

Ship parts include:

03 bow, box, oar, rig
04 beam, brig, brow, bunk, cant, deck, head, hold, hull, keel, mast, poop, port, prow, sail
05 berth, bilge, cabin, cable, cleat, davit, hatch, hawse, stern, wheel, winch
06 anchor, bridge, fender, fo'c'sle, funnel, galley, gunnel, hawser, rigger, rudder, tiller
07 bollard, bulwark, caboose, capstan, counter, gangway, gun deck, gunwale, hammock, landing, quarter, rowlock, top deck, transom
08 binnacle, boat deck, bulkhead, hatchway, main deck, poop deck, porthole, wardroom
09 afterdeck, chart room, crosstree, crow's nest, forecabin, gangplank, lower deck, radio room, stanchion, starboard, stateroom, waterline
10 boiler room, engine room, figurehead, flight deck, forecastle, pilot house, stabilizer
11 chain locker, paddle wheel, quarter deck
12 companion way, Plimsoll line
13 promenade deck
14 superstructure
15 companion ladder

Ships' crewmen and officers include:

02 AB
04 mate
06 master, purser
07 captain, steward
08 cabin-boy, ship's boy
09 first mate
10 able rating, able seaman

See also **sailor**

shipping

Shipping forecast areas:

04 Sole, Tyne
05 Dover, Forth, Lundy, Malin, Wight
06 Bailey, Biscay, Dogger, Faroes, Fisher, Humber, Thames, Viking
07 Fastnet, FitzRoy, Forties, Rockall, Shannon
08 Cromarty, Fair Isle, Hebrides, Irish Sea, Plymouth, Portland
09 Trafalgar
10 Finisterre
11 German Bight, North Utsire, South Utsire
16 South-East Iceland

• shipping order

02 so

shipshape

04 neat, tidy, trig, trim **06** proper, spruce **07** orderly **11** well-planned **12** businesslike, spick and span **13** well-organized, well-regulated

shirk

04 balk, duck, funk, shun **05** avoid, baulk, dodge, evade, skive, slack **06** bludge **07** goof off, soldier **08** get out of **09** duck out of, duckshove, gold-brick **10** play truant, shrink from **12** wriggle out of

shirker

05 idler, piker, poler, shirk **06** dodger, loafer, skiver, truant **07** bludger, goof-off, quitter, slacker, sneak-up, soldier **08** absentee, embusqué, layabout **09** gold brick **10** duckshover, malingerer **12** carpet-knight

shirt

01 T **04** sark, serk **05** kurta, parka **06** caftan, camese, camise, kaftan, khurta **07** dasheki, dashiki, partlet **08** guernsey, subucula

shiver

◇ *anagram indicator*

03 bit **04** chip, grew, grue **05** break, crack, flake, piece, quake, shake, shard, shred, shrug, smash, split, start **06** didder, dither, quiver, sliver, tremor, twitch **07** chitter, flutter, frisson, shatter, shaving, shudder, tremble, vibrate **08** cold sore, fragment, splinter **09** disshiver, palpitate, vibration **10** smithereen **11** smithereens

shivery

04 cold **05** ourie **06** chilly **07** brittle, chilled, nervous, quaking, quivery, shaking, trembly **08** fluttery, shuddery **09** trembling

shoal

03 bar, mob, ren, rin, run **04** bank, mass, reef **05** flock, group, horde, shelf, swarm **06** school, throng **07** schoole, shallow **08** sandbank **09** multitude **10** assemblage

shock

◇ *anagram indicator*

03 jar, mat, mop **04** blow, daze, head, jerk, jolt, mane, mass, numb, shog, stun, turn **05** amaze, appal, crash, knock, repel, shake, shook, sixty, start, stook, upset **06** dismay, fright, horror, impact, offend, poodle, revolt, sicken, stound, stownd, tangle, thatch, trauma, whammy **07** agitate, astound, disgust, horrify, jarring, outrage, perturb, scandal, stagger, startle, stupefy, unnerve **08** astonish, bewilder, bowl over, confound, disquiet, distress, gross out, nauseate, paralyse, surprise, unsettle **09** bombshell, collision, dumbfound, knock back, take aback **10** scandalize, traumatize **11** thunderbolt **12** perturbation **13** consternation, rude awakening **15** bolt from the blue

• **shock absorber**

04 oleo **07** oleo leg, snubber

• **shock treatment**

03 ECT, EST

• **shocked**

06 aghast

shocking

04 foul, vile **05** awful **06** daring **07** épatant, ghastly, hideous **08** dreadful, horrible, horrific, terrible **09** abhorrent, appalling, atrocious, execrable, frightful, loathsome, monstrous, offensive, repugnant, repulsive, revolting, sickening **10** abominable, deplorable, detestable, diabolical, disgusting, horrifying, nauseating, outrageous, perturbing, scandalous, unbearable, unsettling **11** disgraceful, disquieting, distressing, intolerable, unspeakable

shockingly

08 terribly **10** abominably, deplorably, dreadfully, unbearably **11** appallingly, atrociously, frightfully, repulsively, revoltingly, sickeningly **12** disgustingly, outrageously, scandalously **13** disgracefully

shoddy

◇ *anagram indicator*

04 poor, ropy, sham **05** cheap, crook, ropey, tacky, tatty **06** tawdry, trashy **07** rag-wool, rubbish **08** careless, gimcrack, inferior, jimcrack, rubbishy, slapdash, slipshod **09** cheapjack, third-rate **10** devil's dust, second-rate **11** poor-quality

shoe *see* **footwear**

shoemaker

04 snab, snob **05** sutor **06** cosier, cozier, soutar, souter, sowter **07** cobbler, crispin **08** cordiner **09** bootmaker **10** cordwainer

shoemaking

08 cobblery, cobbling **10** bootmaking **14** the gentle craft

shoot

03 aim, bud, fly, gun, hit, imp, lob, pop, pot, rod, tip, zap, zip **04** belt, bolt, cast, chit, cyme, dart, dash, dump, film, fire, germ, grow, hurl, kick, kill, plug, poot, pout, race, rush, slip, snap, tear, twig, wand, whip, whiz **05** blast, chute, fling, graft, hurry, loose, pluff, rapid, scion, scoot, shell, slide, spear, speed, spire, spray, sprig, start, throw, tower, video, whisk, wound **06** branch, charge, direct, hurtle, injure, launch, let fly, let off, propel, sprint, sprout, streak, strike, sucker **07** bombard, burgeon, cutting, gun down, mow down, pick off, project, shoot up, snipe at, stretch, tendron **08** detonate, go all out, offshoot, open fire **09** bring down, discharge, germinate, spindling **10** get a move on, photograph **11** crystallize, precipitate

shooter *see* **gun**; **gunman**

shop

03 buy, get, rat **05** grass, split, store **06** betray, pick up, prison, squeal, tell on **07** stool on **08** emporium, imprison, inform on, purchase **09** buy things, stock up on **10** go shopping **11** tell tales on **12** retail outlet **13** do the shopping

Shop types include:

01 e
02 op, PX
03 toy
04 book, chip, deli, farm, grog, shoe, tuck
05 baker, dairy, dress, offie, phone, stall, sweet, video
06 barber, bazaar, bookie, bottle, chippy, corner, draper, grocer, market, online, record, tailor
07 betting, butcher, charity, chemist, chipper, clothes, florist, saddler
08 boutique, hardware, jeweller, milliner, pharmacy, takeaway
09 bookmaker, drugstore, newsagent, outfitter, stationer, superette
10 candy store, chain store, electrical, fishmonger, health-food, ironmonger, mini-market, off-licence, pawnbroker, post office, radio and TV, second-hand, superstore
11 bottle store, fish and chip, five-and-dime, greengrocer, haberdasher, hairdresser, hypermarket, launderette, online store, opportunity, supermarket, tobacconist
12 cash-and-carry, confectioner, delicatessen, general store, indoor market
13 computer store, farmers' market
15 department store

French shops include:

05 tabac
08 boutique, épicerie
09 boucherie, librairie
10 bijouterie, confiserie, fromagerie, parfumerie, pâtisserie, rôtisserie
11 boulangerie, charcuterie
12 chocolaterie, grand magasin, poissonnerie

Shops include:

03 BHV
04 Tati
05 Macy's
07 Hamleys, Harrods, Jenners, Liberty
08 Tiffany's
09 Century 21, Printemps
10 FAO Schwarz, Selfridge's
11 Le Bon Marché
13 Bloomingdale's, Harvey Nichols, La Samaritaine
15 Bergdorf Goodman, Fortnum and Mason, Saks Fifth Avenue

shopkeeper

05 owner **06** dealer, trader **07** manager **08** merchant, retailer, salesman, stockist **09** bourgeois, boxwallah, tradesman **10** proprietor, saleswoman **11** storekeeper, tradeswoman **13** counter-jumper **14** counter-skipper

shopper

05 buyer **06** client **08** consumer, customer **09** purchaser

shore

04 bank, hold, prop, sand, stay, warn **05** beach, brace, coast, drain, front, offer, rance, sands, sewer **06** hold up, menace, prop up, rivage, strand **07** seaside, shingle, support **08** buttress, lakeside, littoral, seaboard, seashore, threaten, underpin **09** foreshore, promenade, reinforce, waterside **10** strengthen, waterfront **11** threatening

shorebird

04 knot **06** dunlin, ox-bird **07** sea lark **08** sand-lark, surfbird

See also **bird**

shorn

03 cut **04** bald **06** polled, shaved, shaven **07** crew-cut, cropped **08** deprived, stripped **09** beardless

short

◇ *tail deletion indicator*

03 low, shy, wee **04** curt, neat, poor, rude **05** blunt, brief, crisp, dumpy, gruff, hasty, pithy, quick, scant, sharp, small, squat, swift, teeny, terse, tight **06** abrupt, curtly, direct, little, meagre, petite, scanty, scarce, slight, snappy, sparse, stubby, teensy **07** briefly, brittle, brusque, compact, concise, cursory, lacking, limited, passing, summary, uncivil, wanting **08** abridged, abruptly, fleeting, impolite, pint-size, snappish, succinct, suddenly **09** condensed, curtailed, deficient, ephemeral, fugacious, minuscule, momentary, pint-sized, shortened, temporary, transient, truncated **10** aphoristic, compressed, diminutive, evanescent, inadequate, short-lived, summarized, to the point, transitory **11** abbreviated, Lilliputian **12** abbreviation, discourteous, insufficient, unexpectedly

• **fall short**

05 fault, under **09** be lacking **12** be inadequate **14** be insufficient

• **in short**

04 once **05** in sum **06** in fine **07** at a word, briefly, in a word, in brief, to sum up **09** concisely, in one word **11** in a few words, in a nutshell, summarizing **12** in conclusion

• **little short of**

02 on **07** towards

• **short of**

03 bar, but **04** save **05** low on, under **06** but for **07** barring, besides, lacking, missing, short on, wanting **08** less than, omitting **09** apart from, aside from, except for, excepting, excluding, other than, pushed for **10** leaving out, this side of **11** deficient in, not counting

shortage
04 lack, need, shtg, want **06** dearth, drouth **07** absence, deficit, drought, paucity, poverty, wantage **08** scarcity **09** shortfall, skills gap **10** deficience, deficiency, inadequacy
13 insufficiency

shortcoming
03 sin **04** flaw **05** fault **06** defect, foible **07** failing, frailty **08** drawback, weakness **09** weak point
12 imperfection

shorten
◇ *tail deletion indicator*
03 cut **04** clip, crop, dock, pare, trim
05 check, prune, sum up **06** lessen, reduce, take up **07** abridge, curtail, cut down, scantle **08** compress, condense, contract, decrease, diminish, pare down, truncate
09 epitomize, telescope **10** abbreviate
11 make shorter **13** become shorter

shortened
◇ *tail deletion indicator*
03 cut **06** curtal **07** curtate
08 abridged **09** condensed
10 abbreviate, abstracted, contracted, summarized **11** abbreviated
12 abbreviatory

shortfall
04 lack, loss **07** arrears, default, deficit
08 shortage **10** deficiency

shorthand
02 s/h **11** phonography, stenography, tachygraphy **12** Speedwriting®

short-lived
05 brief, short **07** passing
08 caducous, fleeting, volatile
09 ephemeral, fugacious, momentary, temporary, transient **10** evanescent, transitory **11** impermanent

shortly
◇ *tail deletion indicator*
04 soon **06** curtly, rudely **07** bluntly, briefly, by and by, gruffly, sharply, tersely
08 abruptly, directly, in a while
09 brusquely, presently, uncivilly
10 before long, impolitely
14 discourteously, in a little while

shorts
07 baggies, cut-offs **08** Bermudas, hot pants

short-sighted
04 rash **05** hasty **06** myopic, unwise
08 careless, heedless **09** impolitic, imprudent **10** ill-advised, unthinking
11 improvident, injudicious, near-sighted, thoughtless **13** ill-considered, uncircumspect

short-staffed
11 shorthanded **12** understaffed
13 below strength

short-tempered
05 fiery, ratty, testy **06** crusty, touchy **07** grouchy **08** choleric **09** crotchety, impatient, irascible, irritable
10 crotcheted **11** bad-tempered, hot-tempered **13** quick-tempered

short-winded
05 puffy, pursy **07** gasping, panting, puffing, purfled **10** breathless

shot
◇ *anagram indicator*
02 go **03** ace, aim, fix, get, hit, jab, lob, peg, pop, pot, shy, try **04** ball, bang, bash, burl, dink, dose, dram, kick, putt, scot, slug, snap, stab, turn **05** blast, crack, fling, guess, image, moiré, photo, pluff, print, range, reach, set-up, shoat, shote, slide, snipe, spell, throw, whack **06** bullet, corner, effort, gunner, header, hunter, jumper, pellet, ruined, shotte, sitter, sniper, strike, stroke
07 attempt, gunfire, missile, mottled, payment, pelican, penalty, picture, shooter, watered **08** advanced, marksman, moon-ball, snapshot
09 discharge, endeavour, explosion, injection, mitraille **10** ammunition, cannonball, iridescent, markswoman, photograph, point-blank, projectile, variegated **11** inoculation, vaccination
12 contribution, immunization, transparency

• call the shots
04 head, lead **06** direct, head up, manage **07** command **09** give a lead, supervise **10** be in charge **15** wear the trousers

• good shot
07 deadeye

• like a shot
06 at once **07** eagerly, quickly
09 instantly, willingly **11** immediately
12 without delay **14** unhesitatingly

• not by a long shot
04 ne'er **05** never, no way **07** in no way
08 not at all **09** by no means
12 certainly not **13** not in the least

• shot in the arm
04 lift **05** boost **06** fillip, uplift
07 impetus **08** stimulus **11** fresh talent
13 encouragement

• shot in the dark
05 guess **09** guesswork, wild guess
10 blind guess, conjecture
11 speculation

shoulder
04 bear, hump, push **05** carry, elbow, force, press, shove, spald, spall, spaul
06 accept, assume, jostle, spalle, spauld, take on, thrust **07** support, sustain **09** undertake **10** coathanger
13 heave-offering

• give someone the cold shoulder
03 cut **04** shun, snub **05** blank, shame, spurn **06** humble, ignore, insult, rebuff, rebuke, slight, squash **07** mortify, put down **08** brush off **09** disregard, humiliate **13** slap in the face **14** kick in the teeth

• rub shoulders with
07 mix with **08** meet with **10** hobnob with **13** associate with, hang about with, socialize with **14** fraternize with, hang around with, knock about with
15 knock around with

• shoulder to shoulder
06 united **07** closely **08** together
10 hand in hand, in alliance, side by side
13 co-operatively **15** working together

shout
03 bay, cry **04** bawl, call, howl, roar, rort, yawp, yell **05** cheer, claim, clame, jodel, round, stand, treat, yodel, yodle
06 bellow, cry out, heckle, holler, scream, shriek, squawk **07** barrack, call out, exclaim, glory be, sing out
11 acclamation, rant and rave, stand a round **12** buy drinks for, conclamation
14 raise your voice

Shouts and cries include:

02 io
03 hup, nix
04 euoi, evoe, fall, fore, haro, I-spy, rivo, shoo, sola
05 chevy, chivy, evhoe, evohe, havoc, heigh, holla, hollo, hooch, huzza
06 banzai, chivvy, eureka, halloa, halloo, harrow, hoicks, yoicks
07 glory be, heureka, kamerad, tally-ho, tantivy
08 alleluia, gardyloo, Geronimo, harambee
09 scaldings, stop thief!
10 halleluiah, hallelujah, view-halloo, westward ho!

See also **war cry** *under* **war**

shouting
03 hue

shove
04 bump, bung, jolt, push **05** barge, crowd, drive, elbow, force, press
06 jostle, propel, thrust **07** thrutch
08 shoulder

• shove off
04 scat **05** hop it, leave, scoot, scram
06 beat it, depart, go away **07** buzz off, do a bunk, get lost, push off, rack off, scarper, vamoose **08** choof off, clear off, clear out, run for it **09** skedaddle

shovel
03 dig, van **04** heap, main, move, peel
05 clear, scoop, shift, shool, spade
06 bucket, dredge **07** backhoe, dust-pan **08** excavate **09** excavator
13 backhoe loader

show
◇ *hidden indicator*
03 air, con **04** come, expo, fair, give, lead, mean, pose, shew, sign, take, wear **05** array, front, guide, guise, offer, prove, sight, steer, teach, usher
06 affair, appear, arrive, attend, chance, depict, direct, escort, expose, façade, parade, record, reveal, set out, turn up
07 clarify, conduct, display, divulge, exhibit, explain, expound, express, panache, pizzazz, portray, present, produce, showing, signify, staging, suggest, uncover **08** disclose, evidence, illusion, indicate, instruct, manifest, point out, pretence, register

09 accompany, elucidate, exemplify, make clear, make known, make plain, operation, programme, semblance, showiness, spectacle **10** appearance, be evidence, exhibition, exposition, illustrate, impression, indication, play-acting, production, profession **11** affectation, arrangement, demonstrate, flamboyance, make it clear, make visible, materialize, opportunity, ostentation, performance, proceedings, undertaking **12** extravaganza, organization, plausibility, presentation **13** bear witness to, demonstration, entertainment, exhibitionism, manifestation **14** representation, window dressing

• **show off**

◇ *anagram indicator*

04 brag **05** boast, pronk, strut, swank, vapor **06** flaunt, hot-dog, parade, set off, vapour **07** display, enhance, exhibit, swagger **08** brandish, flourish **09** advertise **10** grandstand, put on an act **11** demonstrate **15** show to advantage

• **show up**

04 come **05** lodge, shame **06** appear, arrive, bewray, expose, hand in, reveal, turn up, unmask **07** lay bare, let down, mortify, uncloak **08** disgrace, pinpoint **09** embarrass, highlight, humiliate **10** put to shame **11** make visible, materialize

showdown

05 clash **06** climax, crisis **07** face-off **10** dénouement **11** culmination **13** confrontation, moment of truth

shower

◇ *anagram indicator*

04 fall, hail, heap, load, pang, pelt, play, pour, rain, scat, scud, skit **05** drift, pound, skatt, spray, water **06** attack, deluge, lavish, pelter, pepper, stream, volley **07** barrage, scowder, torrent **08** inundate, rainfall, scouther, scowther, sprinkle **09** aspersion, avalanche, drizzling, overwhelm **10** kitchen tea, sprinkling **13** thunder-shower

See also **meteor**

showiness

05 glitz, swank **07** glitter, pizzazz, varnish **09** ritziness **10** flashiness, razzmatazz **11** flamboyance, ostentation **12** razzle-dazzle **15** pretentiousness

showing

04 expo, show **06** record **07** account, display, staging **08** evidence, symbolic **09** endeictic, ostensive, statement **10** appearance, exhibition, impression, indicative, revelatory **11** descriptive, elucidative, explanatory, explicatory, performance, significant, track record **12** illustrative, presentation **13** demonstrative **14** representation, representative **15** past performance

showing-off

05 swank **07** egotism, swagger **08** boasting, bragging **09** vainglory **10** peacockery **11** braggadocio **13** exhibitionism

showjumper *see* **equestrian**

showman

07 show-off **09** performer, publicist **10** impresario, ring-master **11** entertainer **14** self-advertiser

show-off

05 poser **06** poseur **07** boaster, egotist, know-all, peacock, swanker **08** braggart **09** swaggerer **13** exhibitionist

showy

03 gay **04** fine, loud **05** brave, fancy, flash, flory, gaudy, ritzy, spicy, viewy **06** branky, brassy, dressy, flashy, flossy, garish, glitzy, ornate, swanky, tawdry **07** buckeye, dashing, pompous, splashy, stylish **08** fantoosh, gorgeous, sparkish, specious, tinselly **10** bling-bling, flamboyant, glittering **11** conspicuous, pretentious **12** ostentatious

shred

03 bit, cut, jot, rag, rip, tag **04** atom, chop, iota, mite, snip, spot, tear, whit, wisp **05** cut up, grain, grate, piece, prune, rip up, scrap, slice, speck, taver, trace **06** agnail, cut off, paring, ribbon, screed, sliver, taiver, tatter, tear up **07** frazzle, mammock, modicum, mummock, peeling, remnant, snippet, vestige **08** clipping, fragment, hangnail, julienne, particle

shrew

03 nag **04** Fury, Kate, tana **05** bitch, curse, scold, shrow, sorex, vixen **06** dragon, Tupaia, virago **07** muskrat, sondeli **08** banxring, harridan, spitfire **09** bangsring, henpecker, Katharina, termagant, Xanthippe **10** petrodrome

shrewd

03 sly **04** arch, evil, hard, keen, wily, wise **05** acute, alert, canny, savey, savvy, sharp, smart **06** argute, artful, astute, biting, callid, clever, crafty, keenly, savvey, severe, shrowd **07** cunning, gnostic, hurtful, knowing, prudent **08** piercing, shrewish, spiteful, vixenish **09** judicious, observant, sagacious **10** calculated, discerning, far-sighted, formidable, hard-headed, ill-natured, long-headed, perceptive **11** calculating, intelligent, mischievous, well-advised **12** cut-and-thrust, sharp-sighted **13** perspicacious **14** discriminating, ill-conditioned

shrewdly

05 slyly **06** wisely **07** cannily **08** argutely, artfully, astutely, cleverly, craftily **09** knowingly, unhappily **11** judiciously, sagaciously **12** far-sightedly, perceptively **15** perspicaciously

shrewdness

05 grasp **06** acumen, wisdom **08** astucity, gumption, prudence, sagacity **09** acuteness, callidity, canniness, judgement, sharpness, smartness **10** astuteness **11** discernment, knowingness, penetration **12** intelligence, perspicacity **14** perceptiveness

shrewish

06 shrewd **07** nagging, peevish **08** captious, petulant, scolding, vixenish **09** querulous, termagant **10** henpecking, ill-natured, wasp-tongu'd **11** bad-tempered, complaining, ill-humoured, ill-tempered, quarrelsome **12** discontented, fault-finding, sharp-tongued

shriek

03 cry **04** howl, wail, yell, yelp **05** pling, shout, skirl **06** cry out, scream, scrike, shreek, shreik, shrike, squawk, squeal **07** screech, screich, screigh, scriech, shright, shritch, skreigh, skriech, skriegh **08** screamer **09** caterwaul **11** exclamation **15** exclamation mark

shrill

04 high, keen **05** acute, sharp **06** argute, treble **08** piercing, screechy, strident **09** screaming **10** screeching **11** ear-piercing, high-pitched, penetrating **12** ear-splitting

shrimp

05 krill, prawn **06** squill **07** squilla **08** crevette **09** Euphausia, schizopod **10** stomatopod

shrine

04 dome, fane, tope **05** chest, darga, image, stupa **06** chapel, church, dagaba, dagoba, pagoda, scrine, scryne, temple, vimana **07** cabinet, martyry **08** delubrum, feretory, marabout **09** holy place, sanctuary **10** tabernacle **11** sacred place

shrink

04 balk, dare, nirl, shun **05** cling, cower, crine, quail, shrug, wince **06** blench, cringe, flinch, gizzen, lessen, narrow, recoil, reduce, retire, shy off, swerve, wither **07** atrophy, drop off, dwindle, fall off, give way, retreat, shorten, shrivel, shy away, wrinkle **08** back away, contract, decrease, diminish, draw back, withdraw **09** cower away, start back **10** constringe, withdrawal **11** contraction, grow smaller **12** psychiatrist **13** become smaller **15** have qualms about

shrivel

03 dry **04** burn, nirl, sear, welk, wilt **05** cling, crine, dry up, parch **06** blight, gizzen, pucker, scorch, shrink, wither **07** dwindle, frizzle, wrinkle **08** pucker up **09** dehydrate, desiccate

shrivelled

03 dry **04** sere **06** gizzen, shrunk **07** dried up, wizened **08** puckered, shrunken, withered, wrinkled, writhled **09** emaciated **10** desiccated

shroud
03 fog, lop **04** hide, pall, veil, wrap
05 cloak, cloth, cloud, cover, shade
06 branch, mantle, screen, sindon, swathe **07** blanket, clothes, conceal, envelop, garment, shelter
08 cerement, covering, enshroud, loppings **09** cerecloth
12 graveclothes, winding-sheet

shrouded
06 hidden, veiled **07** cloaked, clouded, covered, swathed, wrapped
09 blanketed, concealed, enveloped
10 enshrouded

shrub
04 bush **07** arboret

Shrubs include:

03 box, ivy, til
04 coca, hebe, nabk, Rosa, rose
05 brere, briar, brier, broom, buaze, buchu, bucku, bwazi, holly, lilac, nebek, peony, yucca
06 azalea, daphne, laurel, mallow, mimosa, nebbuk, nebeck, privet, sesame
07 arbutus, Banksia, boronia, bramble, dogwood, fuchsia, heather, jasmine, phlomis, rhatany, spiraea, weigela
08 barberry, berberis, bilberry, buddleia, camellia, clematis, euonymus, gardenia, japonica, krameria, laburnum, lavender, magnolia, musk rose, viburnum, wistaria, wisteria
09 beach plum, bean caper, eucryphia, firethorn, forsythia, hydrangea
10 bitter-king, buffalo-nut, buttonbush, mock orange, witch hazel
11 calycanthus, cotoneaster, honeysuckle
12 blackcurrant, buffalo-berry, rhododendron
13 Barbados pride, butcher's broom, mountain avens

See also **plant**

shrug
• **shrug off**
06 ignore **07** dismiss, neglect **08** brush off **09** disregard **14** take no notice of

shrunken
05 gaunt **06** shrunk, wasted
07 reduced **09** emaciated
10 cadaverous, contracted, shrivelled, sphacelate **11** sphacelated

shudder
04 grew, grue **05** creep, grise, heave, quake, shake, shrug, spasm **06** judder, quiver, shiver, tremor **07** frisson, tremble, vibrate **08** convulse
10 convulsion

shuffle
◇ *anagram indicator*
03 mix **04** drag, limp, make, pack
05 dodge, hedge, mix up, scuff, stack
06 doddle, falter, hobble, jumble, riffle, scrape, switch, toddle **07** confuse, evasion, patch up, scuffle, shamble
08 artifice, disorder, intermix, jumble up, scramble, shauchle **09** rearrange, reshuffle **10** move around, reorganize
11 shift around **12** tergiversate

shun
◇ *deletion indicator*
03 shy **04** snub **05** avoid, elude, evade, evite, spurn **06** eschew, ignore
09 attention, ostracize **11** shy away from **12** cold-shoulder, keep away from, steer clear of

shunt
04 move, take **05** bring, budge, carry, crash, fetch, shift, swing **06** bypass, mishap, shelve, switch **08** relocate, transfer **09** sidetrack, transport, transpose

shut
02 to **03** bar **04** bolt, jail, lock, seal, slam, spar, tine **05** close, latch, put to, shoot, steek **06** cage in, closed, coop up, fasten, immure, intern, lock up, secure **07** confine **08** imprison
11 incarcerate, put the lid on
• **shut down**
04 halt, stop **05** cease, close, scram
07 suspend **09** close down, switch off, terminate **10** inactivate **11** discontinue
• **shut in**
04 cage **05** box in, embar, hem in, imbar **06** cage in, empale, immure, impale, keep in **07** confine, enclose, fence in, inclose, occlude **08** imprison, restrain **10** encloister
• **shut off**
06 cut off **07** exclude, isolate, occlude, seclude **08** obstruct, separate
09 segregate, switch off
• **shut out**
03 bar **04** fend, hide, mask, veil
05 cover, debar, exile **06** banish, outlaw, screen **07** conceal, cover up, exclude, lock out **08** block out
09 ostracize
• **shut up**
03 gag, pen **04** hush, jail, lock, pent
05 cabin, close, frank, quiet **06** bang up, cage in, clam up, closet, coop up, encage, hush up, immure, incage, intern, lock up **07** confine, keep mum, quieten, silence **08** imprison, pipe down **09** endungeon **11** incarcerate
14 hold your tongue

shutter
05 blind, shade **06** douser, louver, louvre, screen **07** scuttle **08** abat-jour, jalousie

shuttle
03 ply, run **05** flute, shunt **06** seesaw, travel **07** commute, shottle
09 alternate **10** go to and fro
11 shuttlecock **13** netting-needle

shy
03 coy, jib **04** cagy, gibe, shot, shun, toss, wild **05** cagey, chary, fling, mousy, squab, throw, timid **06** demure, modest, mousey, scanty, skeigh
07 attempt, bashful, indrawn, nervous, startle, strange **08** backward, cautious, farouche, hesitant, reserved, reticent, retiring, secluded, timorous, willyard, willyart **09** diffident, inhibited, shrinking, withdrawn **10** suspicious
11 embarrassed, introverted **12** self-effacing, unproductive **13** self-conscious
• **fight shy of**
04 shun **05** avoid, spurn **06** eschew
12 steer clear of
• **shy away**
03 jib **04** balk, buck, rear **05** avoid, quail, spook, start, wince **06** flinch, recoil, shrink, swerve **07** startle
08 back away

shyly
05 coyly **06** cagily **07** charily, timidly
09 bashfully **10** cautiously, hesitantly, reticently **11** diffidently **15** self-consciously

shyness
07 coyness, modesty **08** caginess, timidity **09** chariness, hesitancy, mousiness, reticence, timidness
10 constraint, diffidence, inhibition
11 bashfulness, nervousness
12 timorousness **13** embarrassment

SI

SI prefixes include:

03 exa
04 atto, deca, deci, giga, kilo, mega, nano, peta, pico, tera
05 centi, femto, hecto, micro, milli, yocto, yotta, zepto, zetta

sibling
04 twin **06** german, sister **07** brother

sibyl
04 seer **06** oracle, Pythia **07** seeress, völuspa **09** pythoness, sorceress, wise woman **10** prophetess

sick
◇ *anagram indicator*
03 ill **04** weak **05** angry, black, bored, chase, crook, cruel, fed up, gross, rough, seedy, tired, weary **06** ailing, feeble, groggy, laid up, pining, poorly, puking, queasy, sickly, unwell, vulgar
07 airsick, annoyed, bilious, carsick, enraged, heaving, macabre, seasick, set upon **08** diseased, gruesome, nauseous, retching, vomiting
09 disgusted, hacked off, mortified, nauseated, off colour, spewing up, tasteless, uncle Dick **10** browned off, cheesed off, in bad taste, indisposed, out of sorts, throwing up, travel-sick
11 disgruntled **12** disappointed, sick and tired **15** under the weather
• **be sick**
03 ail, gag **04** barf, puke, spew, spue
05 heave, retch, vomit **07** fetch up, throw up **10** feel queasy **12** feel nauseous

sicken
03 ail, get **05** appal, catch, repel
06 pick up, put off, revolt **07** develop, disgust, turn off **08** contract, nauseate

09 become ill, succumb to **10** go down with **12** come down with **13** become ill with **15** turn your stomach

sickening
04 foul, vile **08** nauseous, shocking **09** appalling, loathsome, offensive, repellent, repulsive, revolting **10** chunderous, disgusting, nauseating, off-putting **11** distasteful **12** cringe-making, cringeworthy **14** stomach-turning

sickly
03 wan **04** pale, puly, sick, weak **05** faint, frail, gushy, mushy, soppy, sweet, wersh **06** ailing, donsie, feeble, infirm, morbid, pallid, slushy, sugary, syrupy, weakly **07** anaemic, bilious, cloying, insipid, languid, mawkish, pimping, queachy, queechy **08** delicate **09** revolting, schmaltzy, unhealthy, washed out **10** indisposed, nauseating **14** valetudinarian

sickness
03 bug, mal **04** dwam, puna **05** dwalm, dwaum, qualm, virus **06** malady, nausea, puking **07** ailment, disease, heaving, illness, soroche, surfeit **08** disorder, retching, vomiting **09** complaint, ill-health, infirmity, spewing up **10** affliction, queasiness, throwing up **11** airsickness, biliousness, carsickness, seasickness **13** indisposition **14** motion sickness, travel sickness **15** morning sickness

side
◇ *ends selection indicator*
01 L, R **02** 11, XI, XV **03** end, rim **04** area, bank, camp, edge, face, hand, jamb, left, long, page, sect, team, teme, view, wing, zone **05** angle, brink, cause, facet, flank, limit, minor, party, right, shore, slant, verge **06** aspect, border, eleven, fringe, lesser, margin, region, sector **07** faction, fifteen, lateral, oblique, profile, quarter, section, surface **08** boundary, district, division, flanking, interest, marginal, sidelong, sideward, sideways **09** arrogance, direction, periphery, secondary, viewpoint **10** department, incidental, standpoint, subsidiary **11** point of view, subordinate **13** neighbourhood, splinter group
See also **football**

• **at the side of**
02 by

• **both sides**
◇ *ends selection indicator*

• **change sides**
06 defect **08** come over

• **from side to side**
04 over **06** across

• **side by side**
06 jugate **07** abreast **10** collateral **11** cheek by jowl, neck and neck **14** heads and thraws **15** next to each other

• **side-effect**
04 echo **06** effect, recoil, result, ripple **07** outcome, rebound, spin-off **08** backwash **09** aftermath, by-product **11** consequence **12** repercussion **13** reverberation

• **side with**
04 back **06** favour, prefer **07** support, vote for **08** join with **09** agree with **10** team up with **13** be on the side of **15** give your backing, give your support

• **take someone's side**
04 back, help **06** favour, prefer **07** support, vote for **08** join with, motivate **09** encourage **13** be on the side of **14** sympathize with

sideline
04 game, omit **05** eject, exile, expel, hobby, sport **06** banish, demote, deport **07** degrade, exclude, pastime, pursuit **08** interest, relegate, transfer **09** amusement, diversion, downgrade, second job **10** expatriate, recreation, relaxation **13** entertainment **14** divertissement, leisure pursuit **15** leisure activity

sidelong
06 covert, secret, tilted **07** oblique, sloping **08** indirect, sideward, sideways **13** surreptitious

side-splitting
05 funny **07** amusing, a scream, comical, killing, riotous **08** farcical, humorous **09** hilarious, laughable **10** hysterical, uproarious

sidestep
04 duck **05** avoid, dodge, elude, evade, shirk, skirt **06** bypass **09** give a miss **10** circumvent **14** find a way around

sidetrack
05 shunt **06** divert **07** deflect, head off **08** distract **12** lead away from

sideways
04 side **07** askance, athwart, lateral, oblique, slanted **08** crabwise, edgeways, edgewise, indirect, sidelong, sideward **09** laterally, obliquely, sidewards, to the side **14** from side to side

siding
03 lie, lye **04** spur **07** turnout **09** sidetrack

sidle
04 edge, inch **05** creep, slink, sneak

siege
04 dung, rank, seat **05** class, privy, sedge **06** throne **07** leaguer **08** blockade **09** obsession, offensive **11** besiegement, distinction **12** encirclement **13** beleaguerment

Sieges include:

04 Acre, Metz, Troy, Waco
05 Alamo, Derry, Kuito, Paris, Rouen
06 Janina, London, Quebec, Toulon, Vienna
07 Antioch, Bristol, Granada, Lucknow, Orléans
08 Damascus, Drogheda, Limerick, Mafeking, Roxburgh, Sarajevo, Syracuse, The Alamo
09 Barcelona, Jerusalem, Kimberley, Ladysmith, Leningrad, Silistria, Singapore, Vicksburg
10 Charleston, Kut al-amara, Montevideo, Sevastopol
12 Tenochtitlán
14 Balcombe Street, Constantinople, Entebbe Airport, Iranian Embassy, Munich Olympics, Spaghetti House

sierra
01 S

Sierra Leone
03 SLE, WAL

siesta
03 nap **04** doze, rest **05** sleep **06** catnap, repose, snooze **10** forty winks, relaxation **12** afternoon nap

sieve
03 sye **04** sift, sort, tems **05** temse **06** bolter, filter, girdle, remove, riddle, screen, searce, search, sifter, strain, winnow **07** boulter, cribble, griddle, trommel **08** colander, separate, strainer

sift
03 try **04** bolt, sort, tems **05** boult, probe, sieve, study, temse **06** filter, garble, review, riddle, screen, searce, search, strain, winnow **07** analyse, cribble, discuss, examine **08** pore over, separate **10** scrutinize **11** investigate

sigh
04 moan **05** heave, sithe, sough, swish **06** besigh, exhale, grieve, lament, rustle **07** breathe, crackle, suspire, whisper **08** complain **09** susurrate

• **sigh for**
03 cry **04** long, pine, weep **05** mourn, yearn **06** grieve, lament **08** languish **13** cry for the moon

sight
03 eye, see **04** bead, espy, look, show, spot, vane, view **05** range, scene, skill, visor **06** beauty, behold, fright, glance, marvel, seeing, vision, wonder **07** amenity, discern, display, eyesore, feature, glimpse, insight, make out, observe, perusal **08** eyesight, judgment, landmark, perceive, prospect **09** beholding, curiosity, judgement, spectacle, splendour **10** appearance, estimation, exhibition, perception, visibility **11** distinguish, monstrosity, observation **12** ability to see, conspectuity, sense of sight **13** field of vision, range of vision **14** faculty of sight **15** place of interest

Ways of describing sight impairment include:

06 myopic
08 purblind
09 amaurotic, cataracts, half-blind, sand-blind, snow-blind
10 astigmatic, far-sighted, night-blind, nyctalopic, presbyopic, stone-blind

11 blind as a bat, colour-blind, hemeralopic, long-sighted, near-sighted
12 glaucomatous, short-sighted, trachomatous
13 hypermetropic

• **catch sight of**
03 see, spy **04** espy, mark, note, spot, view **05** watch **06** look at, notice
07 discern, glimpse, make out
08 identify, perceive **09** recognize, set eyes on **10** clap eyes on
• **lose sight of**
04 omit **06** forget, ignore **07** neglect
08 overlook, put aside **09** disregard
12 slip your mind **14** fail to remember
• **set your sights on**
05 aim at **06** seek to **07** plan for
08 intend to **09** strive for **11** work towards **13** aspire towards

sightless
05 blind **07** eyeless **08** unseeing
09 invisible, unsighted, unsightly
10 visionless

sightseer
07 tourist, tripper, visitor
10 rubberneck **12** excursionist, holidaymaker

sign
01 V **03** act, nod, tag **04** bode, clue, code, hint, levy, logo, mark, omen, shew, show, wave, wink, word
05 badge, board, draft, enrol, frank, proof, raise, sigil, stamp, token, trace, write **06** action, attest, augury, banner, beckon, caract, cipher, effigy, emblem, engage, enlist, ensign, figure, gather, marker, motion, muster, notice, obelus, obtain, poster, ratify, signal, sign up, symbol, take on **07** acquire, ale-bush, ale-pole, betoken, bus stop, earnest, endorse, express, gesture, glimmer, initial, insigne, placard, pointer, portent, presage, promise, recruit, symptom, witness **08** ale-stake, assemble, evidence, headhunt, ideogram, indicate, inscribe, insignia, mobilize, movement, signpost **09** autograph, character, conscript, harbinger, ideograph, indicator, sacrament, subscribe **10** death-token, denotement, foreboding, indication, suggestion, talent-spot, three balls **11** barber's pole, communicate, countersign, forewarning, gesticulate, phraseogram, put together, recognition, significant **12** shilling mark
13 gesticulation, manifestation
14 representation **15** prognostication
See also **zodiac**

• **from the sign**
02 DS **08** dal segno
• **sign over**
06 convey **07** consign, deliver, entrust
08 make over, transfer, turn over
09 surrender
• **sign up**
04 hire, join **05** enrol **06** employ, engage, enlist, join up, sign on, take on
07 recruit **08** register **09** volunteer
15 join the services

signal
◇ *anagram indicator*
04 clue, hint, mark, show, sign, toll, waff, waft **05** alert, recal, token
06 beckon, convey, famous, gryfon, maroon, motion, recall, target, tip-off
07 eminent, express, gesture, griffin, griffon, gryphon, message, notable, pointer, signify, symptom, warning
08 evidence, glorious, indicate, intimate, striking **09** important, memorable, momentous, telegraph
10 impressive, indication, intimation, noteworthy, remarkable
11 communicate, conspicuous, exceptional, gesticulate, outstanding, significant **13** distinguished, extraordinary

Signals and warnings include:

03 cue, gun, nod, pip, SOS
04 bell, buoy, fire, flag, gong, home, honk, horn, pips, taps, toot, wave, wink
05 alarm, bugle, flare, knell, larum, light, pager, robot, shout, siren, vigia
06 beacon, buzzer, hooter, klaxon, mayday, rocket, tattoo, tocsin, war cry, winker
07 bleeper, car horn, foghorn, go-ahead, red card, red flag, torpedo, whistle
08 car alarm, diaphone, drumbeat, high sign, password, red alert, red light, reveille
09 alarm-bell, detonator, fire alarm, indicator, larum-bell, Morse code, signal box, storm cone, Very light, watch fire, watchword, white flag
10 alarm clock, amber light, Bengal fire, curfew bell, green light, hand signal, heliograph, lighthouse, Lutine bell, smoke alarm, time signal, yellow card, yellow flag
11 Bengal light, bicycle bell, gale warning, smoke signal, starter's gun, storm signal, trafficator, trumpet call, warning shot
12 burglar alarm, final warning, storm warning, warning light
13 Belisha beacon, flashing light, personal alarm, police whistle, security alarm, signal letters, traffic lights
14 distress signal
15 semaphore signal

signature
01 X **03** sig, tag **04** hand, mark, name
05 cross, frank, sheet **08** initials
09 autograph, theme song, theme tune
10 criss-cross, sign-manual
11 endorsement, inscription, John Hancock **12** subscription

significance
04 gist, pith **05** ethos, force, point, sense **06** import, matter, slight, weight
07 essence, meaning, message, purport **08** interest **09** magnitude, relevance, solemnity **10** importance, inwardness **11** consequence, implication, seriousness
12 implications **13** consideration

significant
03 big, key **04** sign **05** vital **06** cosmic, marked, of note **07** crucial, fateful, meaning, ominous, serious, telling, weighty **08** critical, eloquent, material, pregnant, relevant, senseful, symbolic
09 important, memorable, momentous **10** expressive, indicative, meaningful, noteworthy, suggestive
11 appreciable, symptomatic
12 considerable **13** consequential

significantly
07 notably, vitally **09** crucially, knowingly, meaningly **10** critically, eloquently, materially, noticeably, remarkably **11** appreciably, perceptibly
12 considerably, expressively, meaningfully, suggestively

signify
04 mark, mean, show **05** count, imply, skill, spell **06** bemean, convey, denote, import, matter, signal **07** betoken, connote, declare, exhibit, express, magnify, portend, suggest **08** indicate, intimate, proclaim, stand for, transmit
09 be a sign of, importune, make waves, represent, symbolize **10** be relevant **11** be important, carry weight, communicate **13** have influence **14** be of importance **15** be of consequence

signpost
04 clue, sign **06** marker **07** placard, pointer, waypost **08** handpost
09 guidepost, indicator **10** fingerpost, indication

silence
03 gag **04** calm, hush, lull, mute
05 abate, burke, peace, quell, quiet, still **06** deaden, muffle, muzzle, stifle, subdue **07** clamour, infancy, put down, quieten, reserve, secrecy **08** calmness, cut short, dumbness, muteness, oblivion, suppress **09** cough down, dumbfound, quietness, reticence, stillness **10** quiescence, strike dumb
11 taciturnity **12** peacefulness, tranquillity, wordlessness
13 noiselessness, secretiveness, soundlessness, voicelessness **14** altum silentium, speechlessness
• **expressions invoking silence**
02 sh, st **03** mum, shh **04** hist, hush, tace **05** dry up, peace, quiet, shush, whish, whist **06** belt up, shut up, wheesh, whisht, wrap up **07** wheesht
08 button it, give over, pack it in, pipe down **09** say no more **10** enough said, keep shtoom, stay shtoom **11** give it a rest **12** cut the cackle, put a sock in it, shut your face **13** hold your peace, shut your mouth **14** hold your tongue, not another word
See also **quiet**

silent
03 mum **04** calm, dumb, hush, mute
05 dummy, muted, quiet, shtum, still, stumm, tacit, whist **06** hushed,

shtoom, shtumm, sullen, whisht **07** implied, schtoom, sulking, wheesht **08** implicit, peaceful, reserved, reticent, taciturn, tuneless, unspoken, unvoiced, wordless **09** conticent, inaudible, mumchance, noiseless, quiescent, secretive, soundless, voiceless **10** creepmouse, dumbstruck, speechless, tongue-tied, understood **11** inoperative, obmutescent, tight-lipped, unexpressed **12** languageless

silently
06 calmly, dumbly, mutely, stilly **07** quietly, tacitly, unheard **08** ex tacito **09** inaudibly **10** wordlessly **11** noiselessly, quiescently, soundlessly **12** speechlessly, without a word

silhouette
04 form **05** shape **06** shadow **07** contour, outline, profile, skyline **08** stand out **09** configure, delineate **11** configurate, delineation **12** shadow figure **13** configuration

silicon
02 Si

silk
02 KC, QC **03** bur **04** burr **05** crape, moire, satin, surah, tulle **06** crepon, faille, pongee, sendal **07** alamode, challie, challis, marabou, organza, ottoman, taffeta **08** boulting, marabout, prunella, prunelle, prunello, taffetas **09** barrister, filoselle, grenadine **10** peau de soie **11** Canton crepe **12** bolting cloth, King's Counsel, moire antique **13** Queen's Counsel

• **silk yarn**
04 tram **08** chenille **09** organzine

silky
04 fine, seal, soft **05** sleek **06** glossy, satiny, selkie, silken, silkie, smooth **07** velvety **08** lustrous **09** sericeous **10** diaphanous

silliness
◇ *anagram indicator*
05 folly **06** idiocy **08** daftness, rashness **09** absurdity, barminess, frivolity, inaneness, looniness, loopiness, pottiness, stupidity **10** immaturity **11** fatuousness, foolishness **12** childishness, recklessness **13** foolhardiness, frivolousness, irrationality, ludicrousness, pointlessness, senselessness **14** ridiculousness **15** meaninglessness

silly
◇ *anagram indicator*
03 nit **04** berk, clot, daft, dope, dumb, fool, rash, soft, twit **05** apish, barmy, bunny, dazed, dilly, dizzy, dotty, dumbo, goose, idiot, inane, inept, loopy, ninny, nutty, potty, seely, wally **06** absurd, cuckoo, dotish, drippy, duffer, feeble, humble, nitwit, simple, spoony, stupid, unwise **07** fatuous, foolish, halfwit, idiotic, missish, puerile, spooney, strange, stunned **08** childish, harmless, immature, pitiable, reckless **09** airheaded, brainless, foolhardy, frivolous, hen-witted, ignoramus, illogical, imprudent, ludicrous, pointless, senseless, simpleton **10** irrational, nincompoop, ridiculous, silly-billy **11** defenceless, hair-brained, hare-brained, injudicious, meaningless, nonsensical, thoughtless **12** feeble-minded, preposterous, unreasonable **13** irresponsible, unintelligent **14** feather-brained, scatterbrained

silt
03 mud **04** ooze **06** sludge **07** deposit, residue, sullage **08** alluvium, illuvium, sediment **10** brick-earth

• **silt up**
03 dam **04** clog **05** block, choke **06** clog up **07** block up, congest

silvan
05 leafy **06** forest, wooded **08** arcadian, forestal, forested, woodland **09** arboreous, forestine **11** tree-covered

silver
02 Ag **05** plate, snowy **06** albata, argent, siller **07** bonanza, cutlery **08** pale grey **11** whitish-grey **12** British plate, greyish-white

similar
04 akin, like **05** alike, close, samey **07** related, uniform **08** such like **09** analogous, semblable **10** coincident, comparable, equivalent, homologous, resembling **11** homogeneous, much the same **13** corresponding

similarity
06 kinred **07** analogy, kindred, kinship **08** affinity, homogeny, likeness, relation, sameness **09** agreement, closeness **10** conformity, congruence, similitude, uniformity **11** concordance, equivalence, homogeneity, isomorphism, parallelism, resemblance **13** comparability, compatibility **14** correspondence

similarly
08 likewise **09** by analogy, uniformly **12** in the same way **14** by the same token **15** correspondingly

similitude
07 analogy, parable **08** affinity, likeness, relation, sameness **09** agreement, closeness, semblance **10** comparison, congruence, likelihood, similarity, uniformity **11** equivalence, parallelism, resemblance **13** comparability, compatibility **14** correspondence

simmer
04 boil, burn, fume, rage, stew **06** bubble, seethe **08** smoulder **10** boil gently, cook gently

• **simmer down**
06 lessen **07** subside **08** calm down, cool down **15** become less angry, collect yourself, control yourself

simpering
03 coy **05** silly **06** smirky **07** missish **08** affected, giggling **13** schoolgirlish, self-conscious

simple
04 bald, easy, mean, mere, open, slow **05** afald, basic, blunt, clear, crude, cushy, green, lucid, naive, naked, plain, seely, sheer, silly, sorry, stark **06** a cinch, aefald, afawld, candid, direct, honest, semple, soigné, stupid **07** a doddle, aefauld, artless, austere, classic, foolish, gullish, idiotic, low-tech, natural, onefold, sincere, soignée, spartan, unfussy **08** Arcadian, backward, homespun, innocent, inornate, no-frills, ordinary, retarded, semplice **09** a cakewalk, a pushover, a walkover, boastless, credulous, easy as pie, easy-peasy, Galenical, guileless, ingenuous, primitive, Saturnian, unadorned, unlearned, unskilled **10** effortless, elementary, half-witted, unaffected, uninvolved **11** incomposite, inelaborate, Mickey Mouse, open-and-shut, rudimentary, unambiguous, undecorated **12** a piece of cake, feeble-minded, inartificial, simple-minded, unsuspecting **13** low technology, rough and ready, uncomplicated, unembellished, unpretentious **14** comprehensible, understandable, unsophisticate **15** straightforward, unsophisticated

simple-minded
03 twp **05** dopey, goofy, idiot **06** simple, stupid **07** artless, foolish, idiotic, moronic, natural **08** backward, imbecile, innocent, retarded **09** brainless, cretinous, dim-witted **12** addle-brained, feeble-minded **14** not the full quid **15** unsophisticated

simpleton
03 daw, mug **04** clot, dolt, dope, dupe, flat, fool, gaby, loon, poop, rook, simp, tony, twit, zany **05** booby, bunny, cokes, dunce, goose, idiot, moron, ninny, noddy, patsy, spoon, sumph, twerp **06** gander, Johnny, nincom, nincum, nitwit, noodle, simple, stupid **07** dawcock, dullard, gomeral, gomeril, jackass, Johnnie, juggins, mafflin **08** Abderite, flathead, imbecile, maffling, numskull, shot-clog, softhead, wiseacre, woodcock **09** blockhead, Gothamist, Gothamite, greenhorn, nicompoop **10** green goose, hoddy-doddy, nickumpoop, nincompoop **11** ninny-hammer

See also **fool**

simplicity
04 ease **06** purity **07** candour, clarity, honesty, naiveté, naivety **08** easiness, facility, lucidity, openness, simplism **09** frankness, gracility, innocence, niaiserie, plainness, restraint, rusticity, simplesse, sincerity, starkness **10** clean lines, directness, simpleness

11 artlessness, naturalness
13 guilelessness 14 elementariness
15 intelligibility

simplification
09 reduction 10 paraphrase
11 abridgement, explanation
13 clarification 14 interpretation, popularization

simplify
06 reduce 07 abridge, clarify, explain, sort out, unravel 08 decipher, make easy, untangle 09 interpret 10 make easier, paraphrase, popularize, streamline 11 disentangle 14 make accessible

simplistic
03 pat 04 naif 05 naive 06 facile, simple 07 shallow 08 sweeping
10 oversimple 11 superficial
14 oversimplified

simplistically
06 simply 07 naively 08 facilely
09 shallowly 13 superficially

simply
04 just, only 05 quite, truly 06 easily, merely, purely, really, solely, wholly
07 clearly, lucidly, plainly, totally, utterly
08 directly, semplice 09 naturally, obviously, shallowly, tout court
10 absolutely, altogether, completely, positively, undeniably 11 simpliciter
12 intelligibly, unreservedly, without doubt 14 unquestionably
15 unconditionally

Simpson
02 OJ 04 Bart, Lisa 05 Homer, Marge
06 Maggie, Wallis

simulate
03 act 04 copy, echo, fain, fake, mock, sham 05 faine, fayne, feign, mimic, put on 06 affect, assume, parrot
07 feigned, imitate, pretend, reflect
08 parallel 09 duplicate, reproduce
11 counterfeit, make believe

simulated
04 fake, faux, mock, sham 05 bogus, put-on 06 phoney, pseudo
07 assumed, feigned, man-made
08 spurious 09 imitation, insincere, pretended, synthetic 10 artificial, substitute 11 inauthentic, make-believe

simultaneous
05 simul 08 parallel 10 coexistent, coinciding, concurrent, synchronic
11 concomitant, synchronous
15 coinstantaneous, contemporaneous

simultaneously
06 at once 07 at one go 08 in unison, together 09 all at once, at one time
10 in parallel 11 all together 13 at the same time, synchronously
14 synchronically

sin
03 err 04 debt, evil, fall, pity, shin, sine
05 crime, error, fault, folly, guilt, lapse, shame, since, stray, wrong 06 offend
07 badness, do wrong, go wrong, impiety, misdeed, offence, offense
08 go astray, iniquity, trespass
09 misbehave 10 commit a sin, immorality, sinfulness, transgress, wickedness, wrongdoing
11 ungodliness 12 misdemeanour
13 fall from grace, transgression
15 irreligiousness, unrighteousness

The Seven Deadly Sins:

04 envy, lust
05 anger, greed, pride, sloth, wrath
06 acedia
07 accidie, avarice
08 gluttony
12 covetousness

since
02 as 03 ago, sin 04 past, sens, sine, sith, syne, ygoe 05 after, agone, being, until 06 seeing, sithen 07 because, owing to, sithens, through 08 sithence, until now 09 following 10 inasmuch as, seeing that 11 as a result of, on account of 12 from that time, subsequent to 13 from the time of
15 considering that, from the time that

sincere
04 open, pure, real, true 05 afald, frank
06 aefald, afawld, candid, dinkum, direct, hearty, honest, simple, single
07 aefauld, artless, cordial, dinki-di, earnest, fervent, genuine, natural, serious, unmixed, up front 08 bona fide, truthful 09 guileless, heartfelt, ingenuous, unfeigned 10 above board, fair dinkum, heart-whole, no-nonsense, unaffected 11 plain-spoken, true-hearted, trustworthy, undesigning
12 plain-hearted, wholehearted
13 simple-hearted, single-hearted, unadulterated 15 straightforward

sincerely
05 truly 06 entire, really, simply
08 honestly 09 earnestly, genuinely, in earnest, seriously 10 truthfully
11 unfeignedly 12 unaffectedly
14 wholeheartedly

sincerity
05 truth 06 candor, honour, purity
07 candour, honesty, probity, realtie
08 openness 09 frankness, integrity
10 directness 11 artlessness, earnestness, genuineness, seriousness, uprightness 12 truthfulness
13 guilelessness, ingenuousness
15 trustworthiness

sinecure
05 cinch 06 doddle, picnic 07 plum job 08 cushy job 10 gravy train, soft option 11 money for jam 15 money for old rope

sinewy
04 wiry 05 burly 06 brawny, robust, strong, sturdy 07 nervous, stringy
08 athletic, muscular, stalwart, vigorous 09 strapping

sinful
03 bad 04 evil 05 wrong 06 erring, fallen, guilty, unholy, wicked
07 corrupt, immoral, impious, ungodly
08 criminal, depraved, wrongful
10 iniquitous 11 irreligious, unrighteous

sinfulness
03 sin 05 guilt 07 impiety 08 iniquity, peccancy 09 depravity 10 corruption, immorality, wickedness 11 peccability, ungodliness 13 transgression
15 unrighteousness

sing
03 hum 04 lilt, pipe, rant, ring, scat, slur 05 carol, chant, chirp, croon, jodel, trill, yodel, yodle 06 chaunt, chorus, intone, quaver, record, second, squall, squeal, strain, warble 07 confess, measure, perform, whistle
08 serenade, vocalize 09 celebrate
13 burst into song

• **sing out**
03 cry 04 bawl, call, yell 05 cooee, peach, shout 06 bellow, cry out, holler, inform

Singapore
03 SGP

singe
04 burn, char, sear 05 swale, swayl, sweal, sweel 06 scorch, swinge
07 blacken, scowder 08 scouther, scowther

singer

Singer types include:

03 pop
04 alto, bard, bass, diva, folk, wait
05 carol, mezzo, opera, tenor
06 chorus, treble
07 crooner, pop star, soloist, soprano, warbler
08 baritone, barytone, castrato, choirboy, falsetto, minstrel, songster, vocalist
09 balladeer, chanteuse, choirgirl, chorister, contralto, precentor, sopranist
10 prima donna, songstress, troubadour
11 Heldentenor
12 counter-tenor, mezzo-soprano
13 basso profondo, basso profundo

See also **bird**

Singers include:

03 **Day** (Doris)
04 **Cole** (Nat 'King'), **Lynn** (Dame Vera), **Piaf** (Edith)
05 **Lloyd** (Marie), **Paige** (Elaine)
06 **Atwell** (Winifred), **Bassey** (Dame Shirley), **Church** (Charlotte), **Crosby** (Bing), **Fields** (Dame Gracie), **Jolson** (Al), **Lauder** (Sir Harry), **Lillie** (Beatrice), **Steele** (Tommy)
07 **Andrews** (Dame Julie), **Garland** (Judy), **Miranda** (Carmen), **Robeson** (Paul), **Secombe** (Sir Harry), **Sinatra** (Frank)

08 Bygraves (Max), Liberace
09 Belafonte (Harry), Chevalier (Albert)

Classical singers include:

04 Butt (Dame Clara), Lind (Jenny), Popp (Lucia), Tear (Robert)
05 Baker (Dame Janet), Craig (Charles), Evans (Sir Geraint), Ewing (Maria), Field (Helen), Gigli (Beniamino), Lanza (Mario), Lenya (Lotte), Melba (Dame Nellie), Patti (Adelina), Pears (Sir Peter)
06 Bowman (James), Callas (Maria), Caruso (Enrico), Davies (Ryland), Deller (Alfred), Kirkby (Emma), Norman (Jessye), Terfel (Bryn), Turner (Dame Eva), Van Dam (José)
07 Baillie (Dame Isobel), Bartoli (Cecilia), Caballé (Montserrat), Domingo (Plácido), Ferrier (Kathleen), Garrett (Lesley), Hammond (Dame Joan), Lehmann (Lotte), Nilsson (Birgit), Vickers (Jon)
08 Carreras (José), Flagstad (Kirsten), Te Kanawa (Dame Kiri)
09 Chaliapin (Fyodor), Forrester (Maureen), McCormack (John), Pavarotti (Luciano)
10 Söderström (Elisabeth), Sutherland (Dame Joan)
11 Schwarzkopf (Dame Elisabeth)
12 De Los Angeles (Victoria)

Folk singers, musicians and bands include:

03 Gow (Niel)
04 Baez (Joan), Bain (Aly), Reid (Robert)
05 Sharp (Cecil James), Simon (Paul)
06 Browne (Ronnie), Fisher (Archie), Foster (Stephen Collins), Fraser (Marjory Kennedy), Mackay (Charles), Martyn (John), Nairne (Carolina), Pogues, Runrig, Seeger (Pete)
07 Burgess (John Davey), Cassidy (Eva), Clannad, Donegan (Lonnie), Donovan, Gaughan (Dick), Guthrie (Woody), MacColl (Ewan), Robeson (Paul), Skinner (James Scott), Thomson (George)
08 Marshall (William), Morrison (Van), O'Donnell (Daniel), Rafferty (Gerry)
09 Dubliners, Henderson (Hamish), Leadbelly, Robertson (Jeannie), The Pogues
10 Williamson (Roy)

Jazz singers and musicians include:

03 Guy (Buddy), Ory (Kid)
04 Cole (Nat 'King'), Getz (Stan), Kidd (Carole), King (B B), Monk (Thelonius), Pine (Courtney), Shaw (Artie)
05 Baker (Chet), Basie (Count), Corea (Chick), Davis (Miles), Evans (Gil), Hines (Earl), Jones (Quincy), Krupa (Gene), Laine (Dame Cleo), Roach (Max), Scott (Ronnie), Smith (Bessie), Smith (Tommy), Sun Ra, Tatum (Art), Young (Lester)
06 Barber (Chris), Bechet (Sidney), Blakey (Art), Domino (Fats), Dorsey (Tommy), Garner (Errol), Gordon (Dexter), Herman (Woody), Hodges (Johnny), Hooker (John Lee), Joplin (Scott), Kenton (Stan), Miller (Glenn), Mingus (Charles), Morton (Jelly Roll), Oliver (King), Parker (Charlie), Powell (Bud), Simone (Nina), Tracey (Stan), Walker (T-Bone), Waller (Thomas 'Fats'), Waters (Muddy)
07 Bennett (Tony), Broonzy (Big Bill), Brubeck (Dave), Charles (Ray), Coleman (Ornette), Goodman (Benny), Hampton (Lionel 'Hamp'), Hancock (Herbie), Hawkins (Coleman), Holiday (Billie 'Lady Day'), Hot Five, Ibrahim (Abdullah), Jackson (Milt), Jarrett (Keith), Johnson (James Price), Metheny (Pat), Mezzrow (Mezz), Rollins (Sonny), Shorter (Wayne), Vaughan (Sarah)
08 Adderley (Cannonball), All Stars, Calloway (Cab), Coltrane (John), Eldridge (Roy), Franklin (Aretha), Gershwin (George), Hot Seven, Marsalis (Wynton), Mulligan (Gerry), Peterson (Oscar)
09 Armstrong (Louis 'Satchmo'), Christian (Charlie), Dankworth (Sir John), Ellington (Duke), Gillespie (Dizzy), Grappelli (Stephane), Henderson (Fletcher), Leadbelly, Lunceford (Jimmie), Lyttelton (Humphrey), Reinhardt (Django), Teagarden (Jack)
10 Fitzgerald (Ella), McLaughlin (John), Thielemans (Toots), Washington (Dinah)
11 Beiderbecke (Bix), Howling Wolf
12 Jazz Warriors

Opera singers include:

03 Mei (Lanfang)
04 Lind (Jenny), Pons (Lily), Popp (Lucia), Tear (Robert), Ward (David)
05 Allen (Sir Thomas), Baker (Dame Janet), Evans (Sir Geraint), Ewing (Maria), Freni (Mirella), Gedda (Nicolai), Gigli (Beniamino), Gobbi (Tito), Horne (Marilyn), Jones (Dame Gwyneth), Kollo (René), Kraus (Alfredo), Lanza (Mario), Luxon (Benjamin), Melba (Dame Nellie), Patti (Adelina), Pears (Sir Peter), Pinza (Ezio), Price (Leontyne), Siepi (Cesare), Sills (Beverly), Teyte (Dame Maggie)
06 Bowman (James), Callas (Maria), Caruso (Enrico), Davies (Ryland), Dawson (Peter), Deller (Alfred), de Luca (Giuseppe), Farrar (Geraldine), García (Manuel), Garden (Mary), Harper (Heather), Hotter (Hans), Ludwig (Christa), Minton (Yvonne), Norman (Jessye), Reszke (Jean de), Scotto (Renata), Studer (Cheryl), Tauber (Richard), Terfel (Bryn), Turner (Dame Eva), Van Dam (José)
07 Barstow (Dame Josephine), Bartoli (Cecilia), Caballé (Montserrat), Domingo (Placido), Farrell (Eileen), Ferrier (Kathleen), Garrett (Lesley), Jurinac (Sena), Lehmann (Lilli), Lehmann (Lotte), Migenes (Julia), Milanov (Zinka), Nilsson (Birgit), Stratas (Teresa), Tebaldi (Renata), Tibbett (Lawrence), Traubel (Helen), Vickers (Jon)
08 Anderson (Marian), Berganza (Teresa), Bergonzi (Carlo), Björling (Jussi), Carreras (José), Dernesch (Helga), Flagstad (Kirsten), Lawrence (Marjorie), Melchior (Lauritz), Piccaver (Alfred), Ponselle (Rosa), Schumann (Elisabeth), Seefried (Irmgard), Te Kanawa (Dame Kiri)
09 Berberian (Cathy), Brannigan (Owen), Chaliapin (Feodor), Christoff (Boris), Della Casa (Lisa), Del Monaco (Mario), Forrester (Maureen), Hendricks (Barbara), McCormack (John), McCracken (James), Pavarotti (Luciano)
10 Galli-Curci (Amelita), Los Angeles (Victoria de), Martinelli (Giovanni), Söderström (Elisabeth), Sutherland (Dame Joan), Tetrazzini (Luisa)
11 Schwarzkopf (Dame Elisabeth)
12 de los Angeles (Victoria), Shirley-Quirk (John)
14 Fischer-Dieskau (Dietrich)

Pop and rock singers, musicians and bands include:

02 U2
03 ELO, Eno (Brian), Jam, Lee (Peggy), Pop (Iggy), REM, Yes
04 Abba, AC/DC, B52s, Baez (Joan), Blur, Bush (Kate), Cash (Johnny), Cher, Cray (Robert), Crow (Sheryl), Cure, Devo, Dion (Celine), Dury (Ian), Gaye (Marvin), Joel (Billy), John (Sir Elton), Khan (Chaka), King (Carole), Kiss, Lulu, Piaf (Edith), Pulp, Reed (Lou), Ross (Diana), Rush, Sade, Shaw (Sandie), UB40, Vega (Suzanne), Wham!
05 Adams (Bryan), Berry (Chuck), Black (Cilla), Bolan (Marc), Bowie (David), Brown (James), Byrds, Byrne (David), Carey (Mariah), Clash, Cohen (Leonard), Davis (Sammy, Junior), Doors, Dylan (Bob), Ferry (Bryan), Flack (Roberta), Haley (Bill, and the Comets), Jarre (Jean-Michel), Jones (Grace), Jones (Tom), Kinks, Lewis (Jerry Lee), Melua (Katie), Moyet (Alison), Oasis, Queen, Simon (Carly), Simon (Paul), Smith (Patti), Starr (Ringo), Twain (Shaniah), Verve, Waits (Tom), White (Barry), Wings, Young (Neil), Zappa (Frank), ZZ Top
06 Atwell (Winifred), Bassey (Shirley), Cocker (Joe), Cooper (Alice), Crosby (Bing), Damned, Denver (John), Domino (Fats), Eagles,

Easton (Sheena), Fields (Dame Gracie), Jolson (Al), Joplin (Janis), Knight (Gladys, and the Pips), Lauper (Cyndi), Lennon (John), Lennox (Annie), Marley (Bob), Midler (Bette), Newman (Randy), Palmer (Robert), Pitney (Gene), Pogues, Police, Prince, Richie (Lionel), Sedaka (Neil), Simone (Nina), Smiths, Summer (Donna), Taylor (James), The Who, Turner (Tina), Wonder (Stevie)
07 Animals, Beatles, Bee Gees, Blondie, Bon Jovi, Charles (Ray), Clapton (Eric), Cochran (Eddie), Collins (Phil), Diamond (Neil), Diddley (Bo), Donovan, Gabriel (Peter), Garland (Judy), Genesis, Hendrix (Jimi), Hollies, Houston (Whitney), Jackson (Janet), Jackson (Michael), Madonna, Mercury (Freddie), Michael (George), Minogue (Kylie), Monkees, Orbison (Roy), Osmonds, Pickett (Wilson), Presley (Elvis), Redding (Otis), Richard (Sir Cliff), Santana (Carlos), Shadows, Sinatra (Frank), Squeeze, Stevens (Cat), Stewart (Rod), Vincent (Gene), Warwick (Dionne)
08 Coldplay, Costello (Elvis), Franklin (Aretha), Green Day, Harrison (George), Liberace, Mitchell (Joni), Morrison (Van), New Order, Oldfield (Mike), Robinson (Smokey), Vandross (Luther), Van Halen, Williams (Robbie)
09 Aerosmith, Beach Boys, Chevalier (Albert), Garfunkel (Art), Kraftwerk, McCartney (Paul), Motorhead, Pink Floyd, Radiohead, Roxy Music, Simply Red, Status Quo, Steely Dan, Streisand (Barbra), The Pogues, Thin Lizzy
10 Carpenters, Deep Purple, Def Leppard, Duran Duran, Eurythmics, Guns 'n' Roses, Iron Maiden, Moody Blues, Portishead, Pretenders, Sex Pistols, Shangri-las, Spice Girls, Stranglers
11 Armatrading (Joan), Culture Club, Cypress Hill, Dire Straits, Human League, Joy Division, Judas Priest, Led Zeppelin, Public Enemy, Simple Minds, Springfield (Dusty), Springsteen (Bruce), Temptations
12 Black Sabbath, Dead Kennedys, Fleetwood Mac, Grateful Dead, Talking Heads
13 Little Richard, Rolling Stones, Spandau Ballet
14 Everly Brothers, Pointer Sisters, Public Image Ltd
15 Neville Brothers

single
03 ane, one **04** free, lone, only, poor, sole, solo, thin, unit, weak **05** afald, alone, small, unwed **06** aefald, afawld, honest, one run, simple, slight, unique, versal **07** aefauld, one-fold, simplex, sincere **08** by itself, celibate, distinct, isolated, man-to-man, one-to-one, separate, singular, solitary, unbroken, unshared **09** available, exclusive, on your own, undivided, unmarried **10** by yourself, determined, individual, one and only, particular, unattached, uncombined **12** woman-to-woman **14** person-to-person

• single out
04 pick **05** hit on **06** choose, pick on, select **07** hit upon, isolate **08** decide on, hand-pick, identify, pinpoint, separate, set apart **09** highlight, victimize **11** distinguish, separate out

single-handed
04 solo **05** alone **07** unaided **09** on your own **10** by yourself, unassisted **11** independent, without help **13** independently, unaccompanied

single-minded
03 set **05** afald, fixed **06** aefald, afawld, dogged **07** aefauld, devoted, onefold **08** resolute, tireless **09** committed, dedicated, ingenuous, obsessive, steadfast **10** determined, unswerving, unwavering **11** persevering, undeviating **12** monomaniacal

singly
04 only **05** alone **06** solely **08** one by one **10** distinctly, one at a time, on their own, separately, singularly **12** individually **13** independently

singular
01 s **03** odd **04** sing **05** queer **06** proper, single, unique **07** curious, eminent, private, strange, unusual **08** atypical, peculiar, uncommon **09** eccentric **10** noteworthy, pre-eminent, remarkable **11** conspicuous, exceptional, out-of-the-way, outstanding **12** unparalleled **13** extraordinary

singularity
05 quirk, twist **06** oddity **07** oddness, oneness **09** queerness **10** uniqueness **11** abnormality, curiousness, peculiarity, strangeness **12** eccentricity, idiosyncrasy, irregularity **13** individuality, particularity

singularly
06 singly **07** notably **08** signally **09** bizarrely, strangely, unusually **10** especially, peculiarly, remarkably, uncommonly **12** particularly, pre-eminently, prodigiously, surprisingly **13** conspicuously, exceptionally, outstandingly **15** extraordinarily

sinister
01 L **02** lh **04** dark, evil, left **05** cruel, shady **06** Gothic, louche, malign, wicked **07** harmful, ominous, unlucky, vicious **08** menacing **09** underhand **10** disturbing, forbidding, malevolent, misleading, portentous, terrifying **11** disquieting, frightening, threatening **12** inauspicious

sink
◇ *anagram indicator*
03 bog, dig, dip, ebb, lay, pay, pot, sag, set **04** bore, damn, dive, drop, fade, fail, fall, flag, foil, fund, mire, risk, ruin, slip **05** abate, basin, bason, decay, drill, drive, droop, drown, embed, lapse, let in, lower, merge, put in, shaft, slump, stoop, wreck **06** cloaca, devall, engulf, fall in, go down, insert, invest, jawbox, lay out, lessen, plough, plunge, settle, vanish, weaken, worsen **07** abandon, abolish, capsize, conceal, decline, degrade, descend, destroy, dwindle, founder, go lower, go to pot, go under, immerse, plummet, put down, scupper, scuttle, subside, succumb, venture **08** cesspool, collapse, decrease, demolish, diminish, excavate, submerge, suppress **09** devastate, disappear, gravitate, penetrate **10** degenerate, go downhill **12** draught-house

sinless
04 pure **08** innocent, virtuous **09** faultless, guiltless, undefiled, unspotted, unsullied **10** immaculate, impeccable **11** unblemished, uncorrupted

sinner
08 criminal, evil-doer, offender **09** miscreant, reprobate, wrongdoer **10** backslider, impenitent, malefactor, trespasser **12** transgressor

sinuous
04 ogee, wavy **05** lithe **06** curved, slinky **07** bending, coiling, curling, curving, sinuate, turning, weaving, winding, wriggly **08** tortuous, twisting **10** meandering, serpentine, undulating

sip
03 sup **04** drop, sowp, tiff, tift **05** drink, taste **06** sample, sipple **08** delibate, mouthful, spoonful **11** drink slowly

sir
02 Sr **03** Dan, Don **04** baas, Herr, stir, tuan **05** bwana, sahib, Señor **06** Mister, Signor, sirrah, stirra **07** lording, mynheer, Signior, Signore, stirrah **08** Monsieur

siren
04 vamp **05** alarm, Circe, syren **06** hooter, tocsin **07** charmer, Delilah, foghorn, Lorelei, mermaid **08** car alarm **09** fire alarm, temptress **10** seductress **11** femme fatale **12** burglar alarm **13** moaning minnie, personal alarm, security alarm

sissy *see* **cissy**

sister
02 Sr **03** nun, sib, sis **04** siss **05** titty **06** abbess, fellow, friend, german, vowess **07** comrade, partner, sibling **08** prioress, relation, relative **09** associate, colleague, companion **10** full sister, half-sister, twin-sister **11** blood-sister

sit
02 do **03** fit, lie, put **04** bear, hang, hold, meet, pass, pose, rest, seat, take **05** befit, brood, clock, model, perch, place, press, roost, serve, squat, stand,

weigh **06** gather, locate, reside, settle **07** consult, contain, convene, deposit, sit down, situate **08** assemble, be seated, position, study for, take part **09** be a member, squat down **10** deliberate, take part in **11** accommodate, be a member of, be in session, have room for **12** have space for, take your seat

• **sit back**
05 relax **09** do nothing **15** not be involved in

• **sit in on**
04 join **05** watch **06** attend **07** observe **11** be present at

• **sit on**
04 ride **05** brood, cover

• **sit upright**
04 perk

site
03 lot, put, set **04** area, plot, seat, spot **05** place, scene, venue **06** ground, locate **07** install, posture, setting, situate, station, website **08** locality, location, platform, position **09** situation

sitting
04 seat **05** spell **06** assize, clutch, period, seated, sejant **07** hearing, meeting, sejeant, session **08** assembly, brooding, sederunt **12** consultation

sitting room
06 lounge, parlor, sitter **07** day room, parlour **08** anteroom **09** front room **10** living room **11** drawing room **13** reception room

situate
03 put, set **04** site **05** place **06** locate **07** install, station **08** position **12** circumstance

situation
03 job, lie **04** case, post, rank, seat, site, spot **05** place, score, set-up, state **06** locale, milieu, office, status **07** affairs, climate, picture, setting, station **08** juncture, locality, location, position, scenario **09** condition **10** conditions, employment **11** appointment, environment, predicament, state of play **12** lie of the land, what's going on **13** circumstances **14** state of affairs

six
02 VI **04** sice, size **05** hexad **06** senary, sestet **07** sestett **08** sestette **09** half-dozen **10** half-a-dozen

six-footer *see* **insect**

sixpence
04 kick, zack **05** tizzy **06** bender, tanner, tester, teston **07** testern, testril **08** testrill

sixteen
03 XVI

sixty
02 LX

sizable, sizeable
05 hefty **06** decent, goodly **07** biggish, largish **08** generous **11** fairly large, respectable, substantial **12** considerable

size
04 area, bulk, mass **05** range, scale **06** amount, assize, extent, height, length, volume **07** bigness, expanse, measure **08** quantity, vastness **09** allowance, dimension, greatness, immensity, largeness, magnitude **10** dimensions **11** measurement, proportions **12** measurements

• **size up**
04 rate **05** gauge, judge **06** assess **07** measure, suss out, weigh up **08** appraise, estimate, evaluate

sizeable *see* **sizable, sizeable**

sizzle
03 fry **04** hiss, sear, spit **06** scorch **07** crackle, frizzle, sputter

skate
03 ray **04** rink **06** rocker

See also **ice skating**

skeletal
05 drawn, gaunt **06** wasted **07** haggard **08** shrunken **09** emaciated, fleshless, unfleshed **10** cadaverous **11** skin-and-bone **13** hollow-cheeked

skeleton
04 plan **05** atomy, basic, bones, draft, frame **06** lowest, sketch **07** anatomy, minimum, outline, reduced, support **08** corallum, smallest **09** bare bones, blueprint, framework, polyzoary, structure, tentorium **10** coenosteum **11** polyzoarium **12** endoskeleton

sketch
03 act **04** draw, line, plan, skit, turn **05** draft, paint, rough, scene, skiff, spoof, trick **06** aperçu, depict, design, memoir, parody, pencil, précis, résumé, satire, send-up, visual **07** cartoon, croquis, diagram, draught, drawing, ébauche, modello, outline, portray, profile, summary, take-off **08** abstract, block out, bozzetto, esquisse, platform, rough out, scenario, skeleton, synopsis, vignette **09** bare bones, bare facts, burlesque, delineate, framework, programme, represent, rough idea, thumbnail **10** caricature, designment, main points, pencilling, prospectus **11** delineation, description **12** mickey-taking **13** prosopography **14** representation **15** thumbnail sketch

sketchily
07 hastily, roughly, vaguely **08** patchily **09** cursorily **11** imperfectly **12** inadequately, incompletely **13** perfunctorily

sketchy
◇ *anagram indicator*
05 bitty, crude, hasty, rough, vague **06** meagre, patchy, slight **07** cursory, scrappy **09** defective, deficient, imperfect **10** inadequate, incomplete, unfinished, unpolished **11** perfunctory, provisional, superficial **12** insufficient

skew
04 awry, bias **05** slant, twist, weigh **06** biased, colour **07** distort, falsify, oblique **09** obliquity **12** asymmetrical, misrepresent

skewer
04 prod **05** kebab **06** skiver **09** brochette

skier

Skiers include:

04 Hess (Erika)
05 Cranz (Christl), Killy (Jean Claude), Maier (Hermann), Tomba (Alberto)
06 Dahlie (Björn), Figini (Michela), Sailer (Toni), Wenzel (Hanni)
07 Edwards (Eddie 'The Eagle'), Klammer (Franz), Nykänen (Matti), Simpson (Myrtle)
08 Kostelic (Janica), Nykaenen (Matti), Stenmark (Ingemar), Walliser (Maria)
09 Schneider (Vreni), Smetanina (Raisa)
10 Girardelli (Marc), Moser-Pröll (Annemarie), Zurbriggen (Pirmin)

skiing

Skiing events include:

05 grass, mogul, relay, speed
06 aerial, alpine, nordic, slalom, sprint, super-g
07 jumping, pursuit
08 combined, downhill, halfpipe
09 classical, dual mogul, freestyle, snowboard
11 giant slalom
12 cross-country

Skiing-related terms include:

04 gate
05 daffy, glide, inrun, piste, split
06 basket, big air, edging, kicker, k point, outrun, p point, schuss
07 grip wax, hairpin, harries, kick wax, takeoff
08 glide wax, table top, Telemark
09 freestyle, large hill, mass start, Steilhang, V-position
10 Hahnenkamm, helicopter, normal hill
11 egg position, scramble leg, spread eagle
12 starting gate, tuck position, vertical gate
13 backscratcher, critical point, herringboning

skilful
03 hot, sly **04** able, deft, good, hend, mean, wise **05** adept, canny, handy, smart **06** adroit, artful, clever, expert, gifted, quaint, skeely, versed **07** capable, cunning, knowing, learned, skilled, trained **08** dextrous, masterly, tactical, talented, well-seen **09** competent, dexterous, efficient, ingenious, practised **10** diplomatic, proficient, well-versed **11** experienced, industrious, workmanlike **12** accomplished,

diplomatical, professional **14** nimble-fingered

skilfully
04 ably, well **06** deftly, yarely **07** capably, handily **08** cleverly, expertly **11** competently **12** proficiently

skill
03 art **04** chic, feat, hand **05** craft, knack, power, savey, savvy, sight, touch **06** matter, reason, savvey, talent **07** ability, cunning, finesse, know-how, mastery, quality, science, signify **08** aptitude, artifice, deftness, facility, training **09** adeptness, expertise, handiness, knowledge, smartness, technique **10** adroitness, cleverness, competence, efficiency, experience, expertness **11** proficiency, skilfulness **12** intelligence **14** accomplishment, discrimination **15** professionalism

skilled
04 able, good **05** adept **06** expert, gifted **07** capable, skilful, trained **08** complete, masterly, schooled, talented **09** competent, efficient, practised, qualified **10** consummate, proficient **11** experienced **12** accomplished, professional

skim
03 fly **04** ream, sail, scan, skip **05** brush, cream, float, glide, graze, plane, skate, skiff, touch **06** bounce **07** run over, skitter, take off **08** glance at, separate **09** despumate **10** hydroplane, run through **11** flip through, leaf through, look through, read quickly **12** flick through, thumb through **13** browse through

skimp
05 pinch, spare, stint **06** scanty, scrimp **08** withhold **09** cut back on, economize **10** be mean with, cut corners **12** be economical **15** tighten your belt

skimpy
04 mean, thin **05** brief, short, small, tight **06** meagre, measly, scanty, sparse, stingy **07** miserly, sketchy **08** beggarly, exiguous **09** niggardly **10** inadequate **12** insufficient **13** insubstantial

skin
03 pod **04** drum, fell, film, flay, hide, hull, husk, peel, pelt, rind, rine **05** cover, crust, graze, layer, strip **06** casing, fleece, scrape **07** coating, outside, surface, swindle **08** covering, membrane, tegument **10** complexion, integument

Skin parts include:

04 derm, hair, hide, pore
05 cutis, derma
06 corium, dermis
07 cuticle, papilla
09 epidermis
10 sweat gland
11 lower dermis
12 hair follicle
14 sebaceous gland

Skin diseases and conditions include:

02 EB, XP
04 acne, boba, buba, rash, yaws
05 favus, tinea, warts
06 eczema, herpes, ulcers
07 anthrax, gum rash, leprosy, scabies
08 dandruff, melanoma, ringworm
09 keratosis, psoriasis
10 dermatitis, dermatosis, framboesia
11 prickly heat
12 athlete's foot, button scurvy

• by the skin of your teeth
06 barely **08** narrowly, only just **10** a near thing, by a whisker **11** a close thing

skin-deep
05 empty **07** outward, shallow, surface **08** external **10** artificial **11** meaningless, superficial **13** superficially

skinflint
05 miser, screw **06** meanie **07** niggard, Scrooge **08** tightwad **09** flay-flint **11** cheeseparer **12** penny-pincher

skinny
04 lean, thin **07** scraggy, scrawny **08** skeletal, underfed **09** emaciated **11** skin-and-bone **12** tight-fitting **14** undernourished

skip
◇ *anagram indicator*
◇ *deletion indicator*
03 bob, cut, hop **04** dart, jump, leap, miss, omit, pass, race, rush, tear **05** bound, caper, dance, dodge, flisk, frisk, slipe **06** bounce, cavort, gambol, prance, spring, tittup **07** captain, miss out, scamper, skipper, trounce **08** dumpster, leave out, overleap, overskip, ricochet **10** bottle bank **11** move quickly

skirmish
05 argue, brawl, brush, clash, fight, mêlée, scrap, set-to **06** affray, battle, combat, dust-up, fracas, tussle **07** contend, dispute, fall out, pickeer, punch-up, quarrel, scuffle, wrangle **08** argument, conflict, scarmoge **09** encounter **10** engagement, velitation **11** altercation, escarmouche **13** confrontation, running battle

skirt
03 hug, rim **04** coat, edge, gore, kilt, maxi, mini, tutu **05** avoid, evade, flank, woman, women **06** border, bypass, circle, margin, piupiu **07** go round, midriff **08** lava-lava, wrapover **09** move round, petticoat **10** circumvent, wraparound **13** find a way round **14** circumnavigate

skit
03 act **04** hoax, turn **05** scene, spoof **06** parody, satire, send-up, sketch **07** take-off **09** burlesque **10** caricature **12** mickey-taking

skittish
03 coy **05** jumpy **06** fickle, frisky, lively, skeigh, wanton **07** fidgety, kitteny, nervous, playful, restive **08** startish, unsteady, volatile **09** excitable, frivolous, kittenish **10** changeable **11** light-headed **12** highly-strung

skittles
04 pins **05** bowls, kails **07** tenpins **08** ninepins **10** kettle-pins, kittle-pins **11** skittle-pins **13** tenpin bowling

skive
04 idle, laze **05** dodge, evade, shirk, skulk, slack **07** bunk off, goof off **08** malinger **09** avoid work **12** swing the lead

skiver
05 idler **06** dodger, loafer, skewer **07** goof-off, shirker, slacker **09** do-nothing **10** malingerer

skivvy *see* **servant**

skulduggery
08 trickery **09** chicanery, duplicity, swindling **10** hanky-panky **11** fraudulence, shenanigans **12** machinations **13** double-dealing, jiggery-pokery **15** underhandedness

skulk
03 pad **04** hide, lurk, lusk **05** creep, miche, mooch, mouch, prowl, shool, shule, slide, slink, sneak, steal **06** loiter, shoole **08** malinger **09** lie in wait, pussyfoot

skunk
04 atoc, atok **05** zoril **06** zorino **07** polecat, zorilla, zorille, zorillo

sky
03 air **04** blue, lift **05** azure, carry, space **06** welkin **07** ambient, heavens, the blue, weather **08** empyrean **09** firmament **10** atmosphere **12** upper regions **13** vault of heaven

skyscraper
10 tower block **14** sliver building

slab
03 mud, tab **04** blad, hawk, hunk, lump, pane, slat, tile, turf **05** blaud, block, board, brick, chunk, dalle, piece, plate, slate, slice, stela, stele, table, wedge, wodge **06** bunker, ice pan, ledger, lidger, marble, marver, metope, mihrab, peever, planch, plaque, quarry, sheave, tablet **07** briquet, portion, viscous **08** capstone **09** briquette **10** altar-stone, superaltar **11** paving-stone **12** drawing board, Moabite stone, plasterboard

slack
◇ *anagram indicator*
03 lax **04** ease, give, idle, lash, lazy, limp, play, room, slow, veer **05** baggy, dodge, loose, quiet, shirk, skive, surge, tardy **06** excess, flabby, leeway, lessen, reduce, remiss, sloppy, softly **07** flaccid, get less, hanging, languid, neglect, relaxed, sagging, slacken

08 careless, decrease, diminish, flapping, flexible, inactive, malinger, moderate, slapdash, slow down, sluggish 09 easy-going, looseness, negligent, nerveless, partially 10 neglectful, permissive 11 inattentive, promiscuous 12 become slower 13 spare capacity 14 insufficiently

slacken

• slacken off

04 ease, slow 05 abate, relax 06 lessen, loosen, reduce 07 ease off, get less, release 08 decrease, diminish, forslack, moderate, slow down 10 take it easy 12 become slower

slacker

05 idler 06 loafer, skiver 07 dawdler, shirker 08 embusqué, layabout 10 malingerer 12 clock-watcher 14 good-for-nothing

slag

• slag off

04 mock, slam 05 abuse, knock, slate 06 berate, deride, insult, malign 07 lambast, run down 08 lambaste 09 criticize

slake

03 mud 04 daub, lick, sate 05 abate, allay, slime, smear 06 deaden, quench, reduce, sloken 07 assuage, gratify, hydrate, moisten, mudflat, satiate, satisfy, slacken, slocken, subside 08 mitigate, moderate 10 extinguish

slam

03 pan 04 bang, clap, dash, hurl, ruff, slag, slap, swap, swop 05 clash, crash, fling, slate, smash, throw, thump, trump 06 attack 07 censure, rubbish, run down, slag off 08 denounce 09 criticize 12 pull to pieces, tear to pieces, tear to shreds 13 find fault with 15 do a hatchet job on

slander

03 mud 04 slur 05 libel, smear 06 defame, malign, missay, vilify 07 asperse, calumny, obloquy, scandal, traduce 08 backbite, badmouth, vilipend 09 aspersion, denigrate, disparage, sclaunder 10 backbiting, calumniate, defamation, detraction, fling mud at, muck-raking, scandalize, sling mud at, throw mud at 11 denigration, mudslinging, speak evil of, traducement 12 evil-speaking, vilification 13 disparagement, smear campaign 14 cast aspersions

slanderous

05 false 06 untrue 07 abusive 08 damaging 09 aspersive, aspersory, insulting, libellous, malicious 10 backbiting, calumnious, defamatory 12 calumniatory, venom'd-mouth'd

slang

04 cant 05 argot, chain, lingo, scold 06 jargon, patois, patter 07 cockney 09 vulgarism 10 mumbo-jumbo, vituperate, watch chain 11 criminalese, doublespeak 12 gobbledygook 13 colloquialism

slanging match

03 row 04 spat 05 set-to 06 barney 07 dispute, quarrel 08 argument 09 argy-bargy 11 altercation 13 shouting match

slant

03 dip 04 bend, bias, jibe, lean, list, ramp, skew, spin, tilt, view, warp 05 angle, bevel, pitch, slash, slope, splay, twist 06 camber, chance, colour, glance, shelve, sklent, weight 07 be askew, distort, incline, leaning, oblique, opinion, sloping 08 attitude, diagonal, emphasis, gradient 09 embrasure, embrazure, obliquity, prejudice, viewpoint 10 distortion 11 inclination, point of view 12 forward slash, one-sidedness

slanting

05 askew, bevel, slope 06 aslant, tilted 07 asklent, dipping, leaning, listing, oblique, sloping, tilting 08 at a slant, diagonal 09 inclining 11 on an incline

slap

03 hit, set 04 bang, biff, blow, clap, cuff, daub, dead, scud, slam, snub, sock, spat, swap, yank 05 apply, clout, pandy, plonk, plumb, plump, punch, right, skelp, smack, spank, stick, thump, twank, whack 06 breach, buffet, clatch, make-up, pierce, rebuke, sclaff, spread, strike, wallop 07 clobber, exactly, plaster, put down, set down 08 directly, slap-bang, straight, suddenly 09 precisely, violently 10 paddy-whack 11 strike hands

• slap in the face

04 blow, snub 06 insult, rebuff, rebuke 07 affront, put-down, repulse 09 indignity, rejection 11 humiliation

• slap on the wrist

04 flak 05 blame, stick 06 earful, rebuke 07 censure, slating 08 knocking, slamming 09 carpeting, reprimand 10 punishment, rollicking, telling-off, ticking-off 11 castigation, comeuppance 12 dressing-down

slapdash

◇ *anagram indicator*

04 rash 05 hasty, messy 06 clumsy, sloppy, untidy 07 hurried, offhand 08 careless, slipshod, slovenly 09 haphazard, negligent, roughcast 10 disorderly, last-minute 11 perfunctory, thoughtless 14 thrown-together

slap-happy

05 dazed, giddy, woozy 06 casual 07 reeling 08 reckless, slapdash 09 haphazard, hit-or-miss 10 boisterous, nonchalant, punch-drunk 12 happy-go-lucky 13 irresponsible

slapstick

05 farce 06 comedy 09 horseplay, low comedy 10 buffoonery, custard pie, knockabout, tomfoolery

slap-up

06 lavish, superb 08 princely, splendid 09 elaborate, excellent, first-rate, luxurious, sumptuous 10 first-class 11 magnificent, superlative

slash

03 axe, cut, jag, rip 04 curb, gash, hack, race, rase, rash, raze, rend, rent, slit, snip, tear 05 knife, prune, score, slant, slice 06 reduce, scorch, stroke 07 curtail, oblique, solidus, urinate, virgule 08 decrease, diagonal, incision, lacerate 09 carbonado 10 laceration, separatrix 12 forward slash

See also **urinate**

slate

03 cam, pan, rag 04 calm, caum, ragg, slag, slam, slat 05 abuse, blame, knock, scold, set on 06 berate, killas, rebuke, sklate 07 censure, propose, rubbish, run down, slag off 08 schedule, tomahawk 09 alum-shale, criticize, pull apart, reprimand, spilosite 10 black chalk, tabula rasa 11 sclate-stane 12 pull to pieces, tear to pieces, tear to shreds 14 Knotenschiefer 15 do a hatchet job on

• size of roofing slate

04 lady 05 peggy, queen, small 06 double 07 duchess 08 countess, princess 09 small lady 11 marchioness, viscountess

slatternly

05 dirty, dowdy 06 frowzy, frumpy, sleazy, sloppy, untidy 07 unclean, unkempt 08 frumpish, slipshod, slovenly, sluttish 10 bedraggled

slaughter

04 beat, best, drub, kill, lick, rout, slay 05 halal, worst 06 battue, defeat, hallal, hammer, murder, outwit, subdue, thrash 07 butcher, carnage, clobber, conquer, killing, murther, outplay, trounce 08 butchery, massacre, outsmart, overcome, vanquish 09 bloodbath, bloodshed, holocaust, liquidate, mactation, overpower, overwhelm, sacrifice, subjugate 10 annihilate, put to death 11 exterminate, liquidation, meat packing 12 annihilation 13 extermination, have the edge on 14 get the better of, putting to death

slaughtered

◇ *anagram indicator*

See **drunk**

slaughterhouse

08 abattoir, butchery, shambles

Slav

04 Serb, Sorb, Wend 05 Sclav 06 bohunk

See also **European**

slave

03 boy 04 esne, serf, slog, toil 05 grind, sweat, theow 06 abject, addict, drudge, labour, lackey, maroon, menial, sclave, skivvy, thrall, vassal 07 bondman, captive, odalisk, predial,

servant, villein **08** bondmaid, bondsman, Mameluke, odalique, praedial **09** bond-slave, bondwoman, Gibeonite, odalisque
10 bondswoman, contraband
11 bondservant, galley slave **15** work your guts out

slave-driver
05 bully **06** despot, tyrant **08** autocrat, dictator, martinet **09** oppressor
10 taskmaster

slaver
05 drool, spawl **06** drivel **07** dribble, slobber, spittle **08** salivate
09 beslobber

slavery
04 yoke **06** thrall **07** bondage, serfdom **08** drudgery, nativity, slabbery, thraldom **09** captivity, servitude, thralldom, vassalage
11 bond-service, enslavement, enthralment, subjugation
12 enthrallment

slavish
03 low **04** mean, meek **06** abject, menial, strict **07** fawning, literal, servile
08 cringing **09** imitative, laborious
10 grovelling, obsequious, submissive, uninspired, unoriginal **11** deferential, subservient, sycophantic
13 unimaginative

slavishly
06 meekly **08** strictly **12** submissively, unoriginally **13** unresistingly
15 unimaginatively

slay
04 kill **06** murder, rub out **07** butcher, destroy, execute **08** despatch, dispatch, massacre **09** eliminate, slaughter **10** annihilate **11** assassinate, exterminate

slaying
05 quell **06** murder **07** killing
08 butchery, despatch, dispatch, massacre **09** mactation, slaughter
11 destruction, elimination
12 annihilation **13** assassination, extermination

sleazy
03 low **05** grody, seedy, tacky
06 crummy, sleezy, sordid **07** corrupt, squalid **10** slatternly **12** disreputable

sledge
03 bob **04** dray, luge, pulk, sled
05 pulka, slide, slipe, train **06** hurdle, pulkha, Ski-doo®, sleigh **07** bobsled, dogsled, kibitka, travois **08** toboggan
09 bobsleigh **10** fore-hammer
11 hurly-hacket, skeleton bob
12 sledgehammer

sleek
04 calm, smug, soft **05** glide, shiny, silky, slick, smalm, smarm **06** glossy, oilily, silken, smooth, soothe **07** stylish
08 lustrous, smoothly, thriving
10 prosperous **11** insinuating, well-groomed

sleep
03 kip, nap, ziz **04** bunk, doss, doze, rest, zizz **05** death, dover, go off
06 catnap, drowse, nod off, repose, siesta, snooze **07** bye-byes, drop off, shut-eye, slumber **08** be asleep, crash out, dormancy, doss down, drift off, flake out, REM sleep **09** hibernate
10 fall asleep, forty winks **11** have a snooze, hibernation **12** get some sleep
13 sleep like a log **14** have forty winks
15 go out like a light

• go to sleep
03 kip **04** dove, doze **05** go off
06 catnap, nod off, snooze **07** doze off, drop off **08** crash out, drift off, fall over
10 fall asleep **14** have forty winks

• put to sleep
06 sopite **07** destroy, put down

sleepily
06 slowly **07** heavily, quietly, wearily
08 drowsily, torpidly **09** languidly
10 inactively, sluggishly **13** lethargically

sleepiness
06 torpor **07** languor **08** doziness, lethargy **09** drowsihed, heaviness, oscitancy **10** drowsihead, drowsiness, oscitation, somnolence, somnolency

sleeping
04 idle **06** asleep **07** dormant, passive, unaware **08** abeyance, becalmed, dormient, inactive, off guard
10 slumbering **11** daydreaming, hibernating, inattentive **12** spine-bashing

sleepless
05 alert, awake **07** wakeful **08** restless, vigilant, watchful **09** disturbed, insomniac, wide-awake **10** unsleeping

sleeplessness
08 insomnia **11** wakefulness
12 insomnolence

sleepwalker
10 somnambule **11** night-walker
12 noctambulist, somnambulist

sleepwalking
12 noctambulism, somnambulism
13 somnambulance
14 noctambulation, somnambulation

sleepy
04 dull, slow **05** heavy, quiet, still, tired, weary **06** drowsy, lonely, torpid
07 languid, slumbry **08** comatose, hypnotic, inactive, isolated, peaceful, sleepery, sluggish, slumbery, soporose, soporous, tranquil **09** lethargic, slumbrous, somnolent, soporific
10 languorous, slumberous
11 lethargical, sequestered, undisturbed **12** unfrequented

sleeve
03 arm **04** bush **05** brass, gigot, gland, liner **06** drogue, manche **08** wind cone

sleigh
04 dray, luge **05** pulka, slide, slipe, train
06 Ski-doo®, sledge **07** bobsled, dogsled, kibitka, travois **08** toboggan
09 bobsleigh **10** snowmobile **11** hurly-hacket, skeleton bob

sleight of hand
05 magic, skill **08** artifice, trickery
09 deception, dexterity **10** adroitness
11 legerdemain **12** manipulation

slender
04 fine, jimp, lean, slim, thin, trim
05 faint, scant, small, swank **06** feeble, flimsy, little, meagre, narrow, remote, scanty, slight, svelte **07** gracile, tenuous, thready, willowy
08 exiguous, graceful, tenuious
09 deficient, sylphlike, willowish
10 inadequate **12** insufficient
14 inconsiderable

sleuth
04 dick, tail **05** track, trail **06** shadow
07 gumshoe, tracker **09** detective, Pinkerton **10** bloodhound, private eye
See also **detective**

slice
◇ *hidden indicator*
03 cut **04** chip, chop, fade, hunk, part, slab **05** carve, chunk, crisp, cut up, lunch, piece, round, sever, share, shive, slash, swipe, wafer, wedge, whack, whang **06** cantle, collop, croûte, divide, rasher, runner, sheave, sliver
07 frustum, helping, portion, scallop, scollop, section, segment, shaving, tranche **08** doorstep, separate
09 allotment **10** allocation **14** slice of the cake

slick
04 deft, easy, glib, trim **05** quick, sharp, sheen, shiny, sleek, smart, suave
06 adroit, deftly, glibly, glossy, polish, smarmy, smooth, tidy up, urbane
07 quickly, skilful **08** masterly, polished, smoothly, unctuous
09 dexterous, efficient, insincere, plausible, well-oiled **10** altogether, persuasive, simplistic **11** streamlined
12 professional **13** smooth-talking, smooth-tongued, sophisticated, well-organized **14** smooth-speaking

slide
◇ *anagram indicator*
03 ski **04** drop, fall, skid, skim, slip
05 chute, coast, glide, lapse, mount, plane, shoot, skate **06** decamp, hirsle, ice run, lessen, plunge, runner, sledge, worsen **07** decline, descend, descent, falling, plummet, relapse, slidder, slither **08** decrease, get worse, glissade, landslip, toboggan
10 depreciate, go smoothly
11 deteriorate, diapositive
12 depreciation, move smoothly, transparency **13** helter-skelter

slight
03 cut, pet **04** raze, slim, slur, snub, thin
05 elfin, frail, light, minor, petty, scant, scorn, small, spurn, wispy **06** dainty, flimsy, ignore, insult, little, meanly, minute, modest, offend, paltry, petite, rebuff, single, smooth, subtle
07 affront, despise, disdain, fragile,

neglect, sketchy, sleight, slender, tenuous, trivial **08** brush-off, contempt, delicate, misprise, misprize, overlook, rudeness, tenuious, trifling **09** disparage, disregard **10** diminutive, disrespect, negligence, negligible **11** discourtesy, unimportant **12** cold shoulder, cold-shoulder, indifference **13** imperceptible, inappreciable, insignificant, insubstantial, slap in the face **14** inconsiderable, kick in the teeth **15** inconsequential

slighting
07 abusive **08** mesprise, mesprize, misprise, misprize, scornful **09** insulting, offensive **10** belittling, defamatory, derogatory, disdainful, neglectful, slanderous **11** disparaging **12** supercilious **13** disrespectful **15** uncomplimentary

slightly
04 a bit **05** quite **06** rather **07** a little, a trifle, halfway, lightly **08** somewhat **12** to some degree, to some extent

slim
03 axe **04** diet, lean, poor, thin, trim **05** faint, leggy, lower, scant, small **06** crafty, flimsy, lessen, little, meagre, reduce, remote, scanty, shrink, slight, svelte, weaken **07** curtail, cut back, cut down, slender, tenuous, willowy **08** contract, decrease, downsize, graceful, make less, minimize, moderate, restrict, sylphine, sylphish, wind down **09** bring down, go on a diet, sylphlike, willowish **10** inadequate, lose weight **11** make smaller **12** insufficient **14** inconsiderable

slime
03 goo, mud **04** gunk, mess, muck, ooze, yuck **05** slake **06** matter, sludge **07** bitumen

slimy
04 miry, oily, oozy **05** gucky, muddy **06** glairy, greasy, limous, mucous, sludgy, smarmy, sticky **07** servile, viscous **08** creeping, glareous, slippery, toadying, unctuous **09** glaireous, uliginose, uliginous **10** disgusting, grovelling, obsequious **11** sycophantic **12** ingratiating

sling
03 lob, shy **04** band, give, hang, hurl, loop, pass, toss **05** bribe, chuck, fling, heave, pitch, put up, scarf, strap, sweep, swing, throw **06** dangle, prusik **07** bandage, support, suspend **08** ballista, catapult, selvagee **09** parbuckle

slink
04 lean, lurk, mean, slip **05** creep, droop, miche, prowl, sidle, skulk, sneak, steal **07** starved

slinky
04 lean **05** sleek, tight **07** sinuous **08** clinging **09** skin-tight **12** close-fitting, tight-fitting **13** figure-hugging

slip
◇ *anagram indicator*
03 don, err, ren, rin, run **04** boob, cast, chit, drop, fall, flub, goof, note, shim, sink, skid, skip, trip, wear **05** creep, error, fault, glide, jupon, lapse, leash, paper, piece, plant, put on, scape, scrap, skate, slide, slink, slive, slump, sneak, steal, strip **06** booboo, cave in, cock-up, coupon, escape, howler, kirtle, lapsus, piping, plunge, pull on, runner, sledge, slip-up, worsen **07** bloomer, blunder, clanger, cutting, decline, failure, get into, go to pot, incline, mistake, plummet, scedule, slidder, slither, stumble, take off, voucher **08** decrease, get worse, omission, quickset, schedule **09** disengage, landslide, oversight, petticoat **10** change into, descendant, underskirt **11** certificate, change out of, deteriorate, galley proof, go to the dogs **12** get dressed in, indiscretion, lapsus calami **13** lapsus linguae **14** go down the tubes, lapsus memoriae **15** lose your balance, lose your footing

• a slip of a
04 slim, thin **05** small, young **06** slight **07** fragile, slender **08** delicate

• give someone the slip
04 duck **05** dodge **08** flee from, shake off **10** escape from **11** get away from, run away from **14** break loose from

• let slip
04 balk, blab, leak, miss, tell **05** baulk **06** betray, let out, reveal, squeal **07** divulge **08** disclose, give away, overslip **13** spill the beans **15** give the game away

• slip away
05 evade **06** elapse

• slip up
03 err **04** boob, fail, goof **05** botch, fluff **06** bungle, cock up, goof up **07** blunder, deceive, go wrong, screw up, stumble **08** get wrong **10** disappoint **12** make a mistake, miscalculate

slipper
04 muil, mule, pump **06** loafer, panton, sandal **07** baboosh, babuche **08** babouche, flip-flop, mocassin, moccasin, pabouche, pantable, pantofle, slip-shoe **09** houseshoe, pantoffle, pantoufle **13** carpet-slipper

slippery
◇ *anagram indicator*
03 icy, wet **04** foxy, glib, glid, oily **05** false, slime, slimy **06** clever, crafty, glassy, greasy, shifty, skiddy, slippy, smarmy, smooth **07** cunning, devious, elusive, evasive, glidder, slither **08** glibbery, gliddery, perilous, sliddery, slithery, two-faced, unstable **09** dangerous, deceitful, dishonest, lubricous, uncertain **10** lubricious, perfidious, unreliable **11** duplicitous, treacherous **13** unpredictable, untrustworthy

slipshod
◇ *anagram indicator*
03 lax **06** casual, sloppy, untidy **08** careless, slapdash, slovenly **09** negligent **12** disorganized

slip-up
04 boob, flub, goof, slip **05** error, fault **06** booboo, cock-up, howler **07** bloomer, blunder, clanger, failure, mistake **08** omission **09** oversight **12** indiscretion

slit
03 cut, rip, rit **04** fent, gash, loop, loup, peep, race, rend, rent, ritt, sipe, slot, snip, tear, vent **05** knife, lance, slash, slice, spare, speld, split **06** pierce **07** fissure, opening, pertuse **08** aperture, incision, loophole, pertused **09** pertusate, pertusion **10** buttonhole **11** placket-hole

slither
04 skid, slip, worm **05** creep, glide, slide, slink, snake **08** slippery

sliver
03 bit **04** chip, rove **05** flake, piece, scrap, shard, shred, slice, wafer **06** paring, shiver **07** shaving **08** fragment, splinter

slob
03 mud, oaf, yob **04** boor, lout, ooze **05** churl **06** sloven, sludge **07** mud-flat **08** layabout **10** philistine **14** good-for-nothing

slobber
04 slop **05** drool **06** drivel, slaver **07** dribble **08** salivate **14** foam at the mouth

slog
03 hit **04** bash, belt, hike, plod, slug, sock, toil, trek, work **05** clout, graft, grind, slave, slosh, smite, sweat, thump, tramp **06** effort, labour, strike, trudge, wallop **08** exertion, struggle, work hard **09** peg away at, persevere **10** plug away at, sweat blood **13** plough through **15** work till you drop

slogan
03 cry **04** logo **05** chant, motto **06** jingle, splash, war cry **07** tag line **08** slughorn **09** battle-cry, catchword, slughorne, watchword **10** shibboleth **11** catch phrase, rallying cry **12** back to basics

sloop
03 hoy **05** dandy, smack **06** cutter

slop
05 slosh, slush, spill **06** puddle, splash **07** slather, slobber, spatter **08** overflow, slattern, splatter, wash away **09** policeman

slope
03 bow, dip, lie, tip **04** bank, brae, cant, drop, fall, heel, kant, lean, rake, ramp, rise, tilt **05** pitch, slant, splay, verge **06** ascent, aslant, breast, decamp, escarp, glacis, shelve **07** decline, descent, incline, upgrade **08** fall away, shelving, slanting **09** acclivity, disappear, downgrade, watershed **11** inclination

• slope off
06 decamp, go away **08** slip away, sneak off **09** steal away **12** leave quietly

sloping
03 dip **05** askew, slant **06** angled, canted, supine **07** canting, leaning, oblique, tilting **08** at a slant, bevelled, inclined, shelving, sidelong, slanting **09** acclivous, declivous, inclining **11** acclivitous, declivitous

sloppily
07 hastily, messily **08** untidily **09** hurriedly **10** carelessly **11** haphazardly **15** lackadaisically

sloppy
◇ *anagram indicator*
03 wet **05** baggy, corny, gooey, gucky, gushy, hasty, messy, muddy, mushy, runny, slack, soggy, soppy **06** clumsy, liquid, sickly, slushy, sozzly, untidy, watery **07** gushing, hurried, maudlin, mawkish, splashy **08** careless, romantic, slapdash, slattery, slipshod, slovenly **09** haphazard, hit-or-miss, schmaltzy **10** amateurish, wishy-washy **11** sentimental **12** disorganized **13** lackadaisical

slosh
◇ *anagram indicator*
03 hit **04** bash, beat, biff, pour, slap, slog, slop, slug, sock, wade **05** clout, punch, spray, swash, swipe, thump **06** shower, splash, strike, thwack, wallop **08** flounder

slot
03 bar, fit, gap, put **04** bolt, hole, slit, spot, time, vent **05** crack, niche, notch, place, space, track **06** assign, groove, insert, tracks, window **07** channel, install, opening, vacancy **08** aperture, position **10** pigeonhole

sloth
02 ai **04** unau **06** acedia, torpor **07** accidie, inertia, mylodon **08** idleness, laziness, mylodont **09** fainéance, indolence, slackness **10** inactivity **12** listlessness, slothfulness, sluggishness

slothful
04 idle, lazy **05** inert, slack, sweer, sweir **06** sweert, sweirt, torpid **07** skiving, sweered, workshy **08** fainéant, inactive, indolent, listless, sluggish **09** do-nothing

slouch
04 bend, loll **05** droop, hunch, mooch, slump, stoop **06** lounge **07** shamble, shuffle **08** drooping

Slovakia
02 SK **03** SVK

Slovenia
03 SLO, SVN

slovenly
◇ *anagram indicator*
05 dirty, messy **06** sloppy, untidy **07** scruffy, unclean, unkempt **08** careless, slattery, slipshod, sluttish **09** slammakin **10** slammerkin, slatternly **12** disorganized

slow
03 dim, twp **04** daft, dead, dull, dumb, lash, late, lazy, poky **05** delay, dense, dopey, gross, largo, lento, loath, pokey, quiet, slack, tardy, thick, unapt **06** adagio, averse, boring, obtuse, retard, sleepy, stupid **07** andante, delayed, glacial, gradual, lagging, slacken, slack up, tedious **08** creeping, dawdling, dilatory, hesitant, measured, plodding, retarded, sluggish, stagnant, tiresome **09** larghetto, leisurely, lingering, loitering, ponderous, prolonged, reluctant, slacken up, unhurried, unwilling, wearisome **10** deliberate, dull-witted, indisposed, lentissimo, protracted, slow-motion, slow-moving, slow-witted, uneventful **11** disinclined **12** long-drawn-out **13** at a snail's pace, time-consuming, unintelligent, uninteresting **14** slow off the mark **15** slow on the uptake

• slow down
04 curb, stem **05** brake, check, delay, relax **06** detain, do less, ease up, hold up, relent, retard, wait up **08** calm down, chill out, handicap, hold back, keep back, restrict **09** hang loose **10** decelerate, take it easy **11** reduce speed **12** throttle back, throttle down **14** put the brakes on

• slowing down
03 rit **04** rall **08** ritenuto **10** ritardando **11** rallentando

• slow up
04 rein

slowly
05 largo, lento **06** adagio, lazily **08** steadily **09** by degrees, gradually, larghetto, leisurely **10** lentissimo, ploddingly, sluggishly **11** ponderously, unhurriedly **13** at a snail's pace **14** little by little **15** slowly but surely

sludge
03 mud **04** gunk, mire, muck, ooze, silt, slag, slob, slop **05** dregs, gunge, mudge, slime, slush, swill **07** residue **08** sediment

slug
04 bash, boff, gulp, oner, swat **05** douse, dowse, limax, one-er, slosh, souse, swash **06** bullet, lander, wallop, wunner **07** lounder, swallow **08** Linotype®, sea lemon **10** bêche-de-mer

sluggish
04 dull, idle, lazy, slow **05** heavy, inert, resty, tardy **06** jacent, torpid **07** languid **08** inactive, indolent, lifeless, listless, slothful **09** apathetic, lethargic, somnolent **10** languorous, phlegmatic, slow-moving **12** unresponsive

sluggishness
05 sloth **06** apathy, lentor, phlegm, torpor **07** inertia, languor **08** dullness, lethargy, slowness **09** fainéance, heaviness, indolence, lassitude **10** drowsiness, somnolence, stagnation **12** listlessness, slothfulness

sluice
04 wash **05** drain, flush, inlet, koker, sasse, slosh, sluse, slush, swill **06** drench, outlet **07** channel, cleanse, conduit, passage **08** irrigate, lock gate, penstock **09** floodgate, water gate

slum
05 hovel **06** favela, ghetto **07** rookery **10** shanty town **11** cabbagetown **15** across the tracks

slumber
03 kip, nap **04** doze, rest **05** sleep, sloom **06** drowse, repose, snooze **07** shut-eye **08** lethargy **10** forty winks

slummy
05 dirty, seedy **06** sleazy, sordid **07** decayed, run-down, squalid **08** wretched **10** ramshackle **11** overcrowded

slump
03 low, sag **04** bend, drop, fail, fall, flop, loll, sink **05** crash, droop, flump, plump, slide, stoop **06** go down, lounge, plunge, slouch, trough, worsen **07** decline, failure, plummet, subside **08** collapse, decrease, downturn, lowering, nosedive **09** downswing, recession, worsening **10** depression, go downhill, stagnation **11** deteriorate, devaluation **13** deterioration

slur
04 blot, blur **05** cheat, libel, smear, stain **06** insult, mumble, slight, stigma **07** affront, calumny, slander, stumble **08** besmirch, disgrace, innuendo, ligature, reproach, splutter **09** aspersion, discredit, disparage **11** insinuation **13** disparagement **14** speak unclearly

slush
04 gush, mush, pulp, slop, snow **05** slosh, sposh, swash **06** lapper, lopper **07** wet snow **08** schmaltz **09** soppiness **10** sloppiness **11** mawkishness, melting snow, romanticism **12** emotionalism **14** sentimentality

slut
04 drab, slag, tart **05** bitch, hussy **06** clatch, drazel, hooker, pussel, puzzle, sloven **07** floozie, pucelle, trollop **08** dolly-mop, scrubber, slattern, slummock **09** dratchell **10** loose woman, prostitute **11** draggle-tail

See also **prostitute**

sly
03 fly **04** foxy, leer, slee, wily **05** canny, carny, peery, smart **06** artful, astute, carney, clever, covert, crafty, expert, impish, secret, shifty, shrewd, sleeky, sneaky, subtle, tricky **07** cunning, devious, furtive, illicit, knowing, roguish, sleekit **08** guileful, scheming, stealthy, weaselly **09** conniving, insidious, secretive, underhand

11 clandestine, mischievous
13 surreptitious

• **on the sly**

07 on the qt 08 covertly, in secret, secretly 09 furtively, in private, privately 10 stealthily, under cover
13 clandestinely, underhandedly
15 surreptitiously

• **sly person**

03 tod 04 coon 06 weasel

slyly

◇ *anagram indicator*

07 cannily 08 artfully, covertly, shrewdly 09 cunningly, deviously, furtively 10 stealthily
13 underhandedly 15 surreptitiously

smack

03 box, hit, pat, tap 04 bang, belt, biff, blow, clap, cuff, dash, hint, kiss, like, slap, sock, tack, tang, thud, zest
05 clout, crack, crash, enjoy, evoke, plumb, punch, right, smell, spank, speck, spice, taste, thump, tinge, touch, trace, twang, whack, whiff
06 bawley, flavor, heroin, hint at, hooker, nuance, relish, savour, smatch, smouch, strike, thwack, wallop
07 clobber, coaster, exactly, flavour, revel in, sharply, smacker, suggest
08 directly, intimate, piquancy, savour of, slap-bang, straight 09 delight in, precisely 10 absolutely, appreciate, impression, intimation, paddy-whack, suggestion 11 bring to mind, remind you of 13 give a hiding to 14 take pleasure in 15 put over your knee

See also **hit**; **kiss**

• **smack your lips**

05 enjoy 06 relish, savour 09 delight in, drool over 10 anticipate

smacker *see* **kiss**

small

◇ *deletion indicator*

01 S 03 low, sma, wee 04 mean, mini, pink, poky, puny, tiny 05 bitsy, diddy, dwarf, minor, petty, pinky, short, teeny, tiddy, totty, young 06 broken, dilute, humble, little, meagre, minute, narrow, paltry, peerie, peewee, petite, pinkie, pocket, scanty, single, slight, stupid, teensy, tottie 07 ashamed, compact, cramped, crushed, foolish, ignoble, limited, slender, trivial 08 confined, deflated, degraded, delicate, dwarfish, pint-size, trifling 09 disgraced, miniature, minuscule, pint-sized
10 diminutive, humiliated, inadequate, negligible, ungenerous, unimposing
11 embarrassed, microscopic, pocket-sized, unimportant 12 insufficient, teensy-weensy 13 inappreciable, infinitesimal, insignificant
14 inconsiderable

small-minded

04 mean 05 petty, rigid 06 biased, little
07 bigoted, insular 09 cat-witted, hidebound, illiberal, parochial
10 intolerant, prejudiced, ungenerous
12 narrow-minded

smallness

07 exility, fewness, paucity 08 tininess
09 small size 10 littleness, minuteness, slightness 11 compactness, parvanimity 12 microcephaly
14 diminutiveness

small-time

05 minor, petty 08 piddling 09 no-account 10 small-scale 11 unimportant
13 insignificant 15 inconsequential

smarminess

07 suavity 08 oiliness, toadying
09 servility 10 sycophancy, unctuosity
12 unctuousness 14 obsequiousness

smarmy

04 oily 05 suave 06 smooth
07 fawning, servile 08 crawling, toadying, unctuous 10 obsequious
11 bootlicking, sycophantic
12 ingratiating

smart

01 U 03 nip 04 ache, bite, burn, chic, cool, fine, flip, hurt, neat, pacy, pert, posh, smug, tidy, trim 05 acute, brisk, dandy, gemmy, janty, jemmy, kooky, natty, nifty, nobby, pacey, prick, ritzy, saucy, sharp, slick, smoke, spiff, sting, swank, sweat, swish, throb, tippy, witty
06 astute, brainy, bright, clever, dapper, glitzy, jaunty, kookie, larney, modish, pusser, shrewd, snappy, snazzy, spiffy, spruce, swanky, tiddly, tingle, twinge
07 crabbit, elegant, stylish, swagger, tiddley 08 all there, rattling, sprauncy
09 expensive, on the ball, vivacious
11 fashionable, intelligent, presentable, well dressed, well-groomed 13 well-turned-out

• **smart alec**

07 know-all, wise guy 08 wiseacre
09 smartarse 10 clever dick 11 clever clogs, smartyboots, smartypants

smarten

04 tidy 05 clean, groom, primp, prink
06 neaten, polish, spruce, tidy up
08 beautify, make neat, make tidy, spruce up

smartly

06 neatly, tidily 07 briskly, hastily, nattily, quickly, rapidly, readily, swiftly 08 abruptly, directly, promptly, snazzily, speedily 09 elegantly, hurriedly, instantly, stylishly
11 fashionably, immediately, presentably 14 unhesitatingly
15 instantaneously

smash

◇ *anagram indicator*

02 go 03 hit, run, wow 04 bang, bash, bump, cash, dash, ruin 05 break, crack, crash, crush, drive, knock, prang, thump, wreck 06 bingle, defeat, pile-up, plough, shiver, strike, winner
07 collide, destroy, shatter, smash-up, success, triumph 08 accident, demolish, knockout, smash hit, splinter, squabash, stramash
09 collision, pulverize, sensation
12 disintegrate

smashing

05 great, super 06 superb 07 dashing
08 crushing, fabulous, terrific
09 excellent, fantastic, first-rate, wonderful 10 first-class, marvellous, shattering, stupendous, tremendous
11 magnificent, sensational, superlative
12 exhilarating

smattering

03 bit 04 dash 06 basics, smatch
07 modicum 08 elements
09 rudiments 10 sprinkling

smear

03 dab, gum, oil, pay, rub, tar, wax
04 blot, blur, coat, daub, gaum, gild, gorm, lard, lick, mark, slap, slur, soot, spot 05 blood, cover, libel, patch, pitch, salve, slake, slime, smalm, smarm, stain, sully, taint 06 anoint, bedaub, blotch, defame, grease, malign, slairg, smudge, spread, streak, vilify 07 blacken, obloquy, plaster, slander, slather, slubber, splodge, splotch, tarnish, treacle 08 badmouth
09 aspersion 10 calumniate, defamation, muck-raking, turpentine
11 false report, mudslinging
12 vilification

smell

03 fug, hum 04 funk, fust, gale, guff, ming, must, niff, nose, odor, pong, ponk, reek 05 aroma, fetor, odour, scent, sniff, snuff, stink, trace, whiff
06 miasma, savour, stench 07 bouquet
08 malodour, mephitis, pungency
09 fragrance, redolence

Particular smells include:

02 BO
04 feet, musk, rose
05 basil, booze, ozone, smoke, spice
06 cheese, coffee, garlic, nutmeg, pepper
07 alcohol, camphor, incense, menthol, perfume, vanilla
08 bergamot, lavender
09 body odour, patchouli, pot pourri, woodsmoke
10 eucalyptus, peppermint
11 wintergreen

smelly

03 bad, off 04 foul, high, nosy, olid, rank, ripe 05 fetid, nosey, olent, pongy
06 foetid, mingin, putrid 07 honking, humming, noisome, reeking
08 mephitic, stinking 10 malodorous
12 foul-smelling 14 strong-smelling

smile

04 beam, grin, leer 05 drink, laugh, smirk, sneer, treat 06 favour, giggle, simper, smoile, smoyle, titter
07 chuckle, snigger 11 be all smiles

smirk

04 grin, leer, trim 05 sneer 06 simper, spruce 07 grimace, snigger

smitten

05 beset, épris 06 éprise, in love, struck 07 charmed, hard-hit, plagued
08 beguiled, burdened, obsessed,

troubled **09** afflicted, attracted, bewitched, enamoured **10** bowled over, captivated, infatuated **12** enthusiastic

smock
04 slop **05** frock, shift **07** chemise, smicket
• **lady's smock**
05 spink **09** cardamine **12** cuckoo flower

smog
03 fog **04** haze, mist **05** fumes, smoke **06** vapour **07** exhaust **09** pea-souper, pollution

smoke
03 dry, fog, gas **04** cure, draw, fume, lunt, mist, puff, quiz, reek, roke, smog **05** fumes, reast, reest, reist, smart, smoor **06** draw on, puff on, smudge, suffer, thrash, vapour **07** exhaust, light up, smother, tear gas **08** preserve, ridicule, smoulder **09** London ivy
See also **cigarette**; **tobacco**

smoky
04 dark, grey, hazy **05** black, foggy, fuggy, grimy, murky, peaty, reeky, sooty **06** cloudy, rechie, reechy, reekie, smoggy, smudgy **07** reechie **10** suspicious

smooch
03 hug, pet **04** hold, kiss, neck, snog **05** clasp, nurse **06** caress, cuddle, enfold, fondle, nestle **07** embrace, snuggle **08** canoodle

smooth
03 aid, dub **04** calm, ease, easy, even, file, flat, glib, help, iron, mild, rich, roll, sand, smug, snod, soft, trim **05** allay, bland, brent, dress, filed, float, flush, grind, level, plane, press, shiny, silky, sleek, slick, sooth, still, suave, sweet, terse, thick **06** assist, classy, creamy, fluent, glassy, glossy, legato, mature, mellow, pacify, polish, serene, silken, simple, sleeky, smarmy, soothe, steady, urbane **07** appease, assuage, elegant, equable, even out, fawning, flatten, flatter, flowing, mollify, plaster, regular, rub down, sleekit, slicken, uniform, velvety, worsted **08** blandish, calm down, charming, crawling, glabrate, glabrous, hairless, levigate, mitigate, palliate, peaceful, polished, rhythmic, slippery, tranquil, unbroken, unctuous **09** agreeable, alleviate, burnished, encourage, plausible, press down, unruffled **10** continuous, effortless, facilitate, horizontal, make easier, persuasive, unwrinkled **11** legatissimo, like a mirror, mellifluent, mellifluous, plaster down, problem-free, trouble-free, undisturbed **12** ingratiating, plain sailing **13** full-flavoured, over-confident, smooth-talking, sophisticated, uninterrupted **14** clear the way for **15** straightforward

smoothly
06 calmly, easily, evenly, legato, mildly **07** cleanly, equably, sleekly, slickly, voluble **08** fluently, serenely, steadily **10** peacefully, pleasantly, soothingly, swimmingly, tranquilly **11** legatissimo **12** effortlessly

smoothness
04 ease, flow **05** shine **06** finish, polish, rhythm **07** fluency
08 calmness, evenness, facility, flatness, serenity, softness
09 levelness, lubricity, silkiness, sleekness, stillness **10** efficiency, glassiness, regularity, steadiness
11 velvetiness **12** unbrokenness
14 effortlessness

smooth-talking
04 glib **05** bland, slick, suave **06** facile, smooth **09** plausible **10** flattering, persuasive **12** conciliatory **13** silver-tongued

smother
04 damp, hide, wrap **05** choke, cover, smoke, smoor, smore, snuff
06 cocoon, dampen, muffle, put out, shroud, stifle, welter **07** conceal, envelop, oppress, overlie, repress
08 damp down, inundate, keep back, smoulder, strangle, suppress, surround, throttle **09** overwhelm, suffocate
10 asphyxiate, extinguish
11 suffocation

smoulder
04 boil, burn, foam, fume, rage
05 smoke **06** fester, seethe, simmer
07 smother

smudge
04 blot, blur, daub, mark, soil, spot
05 dirty, smear, stain **06** blotch, offset, smouch, smutch, streak **07** blacken, blemish **08** besmirch **09** dirty mark, make dirty

smug
04 neat, prim **05** sleek, steal **06** hush up, smooth, spruce **08** priggish, smirking, superior, unctuous
09 conceited **10** complacent **13** self-righteous, self-satisfied **14** holier-than-thou

smuggle
03 owl, ren, rin, run **05** steal **07** bootleg

smuggler
04 mule **05** owler **06** runner
07 courier **10** bootlegger, drug-runner, free-trader, moonshiner
13 contrabandist

smutty
04 blue, lewd, racy, rude **05** bawdy, crude, dirty, gross **06** coarse, filthy, fruity, ribald, risqué, sleazy, vulgar
07 obscene, raunchy **08** improper, indecent, prurient **09** off colour, salacious **10** indelicate, suggestive
12 pornographic

snack
04 bite, gorp, meze, snap, tapa, wrap
05 bever, butty, chack, fours, lunch, share, tapas, taste **06** buffet, crisps, nacket, nibble, nocket, snatch, supper, tidbit, titbit **07** bar meal, elevens, fourses, nibbles, zakuska **08** bar lunch, pick-me-up, sandwich, scroggin, trail mix **09** appetizer, bite to eat, Bombay mix, elevenses, light meal **11** amuse-bouche, hors d'oeuvre, refreshment
12 potato crisps, refreshments **15** pork scratchings

snaffle
03 bag, nab, win **04** gain, grab, grip, nail, pull, take **05** grasp, pluck, seize, steal, swipe, wrest **06** arrest, clutch, collar, secure, wrench **07** bridoon, capture, purloin, snabble **08** pounce on **09** get hold of **10** take hold of
11 make off with

snag
03 bug, jag, nog, rip **04** hole, sneb, snub, tear **05** catch, hitch, stump
06 banger, ladder, obtain, secure, snubbe **07** problem, sausage, setback
08 drawback, obstacle **10** difficulty
12 complication, disadvantage
13 inconvenience **14** stumbling-block

snail
05 crawl, helix **06** dodman, nerite
08 escargot, wallfish **09** hodmandod, wing shell

snake
04 bend, drag, loop, naga, wind, worm
05 creep, curve, twine **06** drudge, ramble, spiral, wretch, zigzag
07 deviate, meander, serpent **08** Joe Blake, ophidian

Snakes include:

03 asp, boa, rat, sea
04 boma, bull, corn, file, hoop, king, milk, naga, Naia, Naja, pine, pipe, ring, rock, sand, seps, tree, whip, worm
05 adder, black, blind, brown, cobra, coral, Elaps, grass, green, krait, mamba, racer, tiger, viper, water
06 carpet, dipsas, dugite, ellops, flying, gaboon, garter, gopher, indigo, karait, python, ribbon, smooth, taipan
08 anaconda, cerastes, colubrid, cylinder, jararaca, jararaka, mocassin, moccasin, pit viper, ringhals, rinkhals, sucurujú
09 berg-adder, boomslang, coachwhip, hamadryad, hamadryas, king cobra, puff adder, river-jack
10 bandy-bandy, bushmaster, copperhead, death adder, dendrophis, fer-de-lance, Gabon viper, massasauga, sidewinder
11 constrictor, cottonmouth, diamondback, gaboon viper, horned viper, massasauger, rattlesnake
12 carpet python
13 diamond python, water moccasin
14 boa constrictor, river-jack viper

snap
03 nip, pic **04** bark, bite, chop, film, grip, knap, shot, snip, span, take, tick, time, whit **05** break, catch, cheat, click,

clink, crack, flick, gnash, grasp, growl, hanch, photo, print, scrap, seize, share, shoot, snack, snarl, snick, spell, split, still, stint **06** abrupt, bark at, fillip, period, record, retort, snatch, sudden **07** crackle, earring, give way, growl at, instant, offhand, picture, sharper, snarl at, stretch **08** collapse, fracture, separate, snapshot, splinter **09** crepitate, immediate, lash out at, on-the-spot **10** photograph, unexpected **14** speak angrily to, speak sharply to

• snap up
03 nab **04** grab **05** grasp, pluck, seize **06** pick up, snatch **08** pounce on **10** buy quickly

snappy
04 chic, edgy **05** brisk, cross, hasty, natty, quick, ratty, smart, testy **06** crabby, crusty, lively, modish, snazzy, touchy, trendy **07** brusque, crabbed, elegant, grouchy, stroppy, stylish **08** polished, up-to-date **09** crotchety, energetic, irascible, irritable **10** ill-natured **11** bad-tempered, fashionable, ill-tempered **13** instantaneous, quick-tempered, short-tempered, up-to-the-minute

• make it snappy
05 hurry **06** buck up **07** hurry up **08** go all out, jump to it, step on it **09** come along, look sharp, shake a leg **10** look lively **11** get cracking **15** get your skates on

snare
◇ *containment indicator*
03 gin, net, web **04** grin, hook, toil, trap, weel, wire **05** catch, fraud, noose, seize, toils **06** cobweb, engine, entrap, spring, trepan **07** capture, ensnare, pitfall, springe **08** lime-twig **09** spider web **10** allurement, temptation **12** entanglement

snarl
◇ *anagram indicator*
04 bark, girn, gnar, gurn, howl, knar, knot, snap, snar, yelp **05** gnarl, gnarr, growl, ravel, twist **06** enmesh, jumble, muddle, tangle **07** confuse, embroil, ensnare, entwine, grumble **08** complain, entangle **09** lash out at **10** complicate **13** show your teeth

snarl-up
04 mess **05** mix-up **06** jumble, muddle, tangle **08** gridlock **09** confusion **10** traffic jam **12** entanglement

snatch
03 bag, bit, nab, nip, rap, win **04** gain, glom, grab, grip, nail, part, pull, race, ramp, rase, snap, snip, take **05** catch, grasp, piece, pluck, reach, seize, snack, spell, steal, swipe, whift, wrest **06** abduct, clutch, collar, gobble, kidnap, ruffle, secure, twitch, wrench **07** claucht, claught, quibble, robbery, section, segment, snippet **08** fraction, fragment, pounce on **09** get hold of **10** kidnapping, smattering, take hold of **11** make off with **13** take as hostage

snazzy
05 jazzy, ritzy, showy, smart **06** flashy, snappy, sporty, with it **07** dashing, raffish, stylish **08** swinging **10** attractive, flamboyant **11** fashionable **13** sophisticated

sneak
03 pad, rat **04** lurk, mole, peak, shop, slip **05** creep, grass, prowl, quick, sidle, skulk, slide, slink, snoke, snook, snowk, split, steal **06** covert, cringe, secret, snitch, spirit, squeal **07** furtive, grass on, smuggle, stoolie, stool on **08** informer, inform on, squealer, stealthy, surprise, tell-tale **09** tell tales **11** clandestine, stool pigeon **13** surreptitious, whistle-blower

sneaking
04 mean **06** hidden, secret **07** furtive, lurking, nagging, private, sleekit **08** grudging, niggling, unvoiced, worrying **09** crouching, intuitive, underhand **10** persistent, suppressed **11** sheep-biting, unexpressed **13** surreptitious, uncomfortable

sneaky
03 low, sly **04** base, mean **05** nasty, shady, snide **06** shifty **07** cunning, devious, furtive, low-down **08** cowardly, guileful, slippery **09** deceitful, dishonest, malicious, unethical **10** unreliable **12** contemptible, disingenuous, unscrupulous **13** double-dealing, untrustworthy

sneer
04 gibe, grin, jeer, mock **05** laugh, scoff, scorn, smirk, taunt **06** deride, insult, slight, twitch **07** disdain, mockery, snicker, snigger **08** derision, ridicule **10** look down on **12** curl your lips

sneeze
05 neese, neeze **07** atishoo

sneezing
12 sternutation

snicker
05 laugh, neigh, sneer **06** giggle, nicker, titter **07** chortle, chuckle, snigger, snirtle

snide
04 base, mean, sham **05** nasty **06** biting, unkind **07** caustic, cynical, hurtful, jeering, mocking **08** derisive, scathing, scoffing, scornful, sneering, spiteful, taunting **09** dishonest, malicious, sarcastic **10** derogatory, ill-natured **11** counterfeit, disparaging

sniff
04 hint, nose, sent, vent **05** aroma, scent, shmek, smell, snift, snuff, trace, whiff **06** inhale, nuzzle, snivel **07** breathe, schmeck, sniffle, snifter, snuffle **10** impression, intimation, suggestion **11** get a whiff of

• sniff at
04 mock, shun, vent **05** scorn, spurn **06** deride, refuse, reject, slight **07** disdain, dismiss, laugh at, scoff at, smell at, sneer at **08** overlook **09** disparage, disregard **10** look down on

sniffy
06 snobby **07** haughty **08** scoffing, scornful, sneering, snobbish, superior **10** disdainful **12** contemptuous, supercilious **13** condescending

snifter *see* **dram**

snigger
05 laugh, smirk, sneer **06** giggle, nicher, nicker, titter **07** chortle, chuckle, snicker, whicker

snip
03 bit, cut **04** clip, crop, dock, nick, slit, snap, trim **05** notch, piece, prune, scrap, share, shred, slash, sneck, snick, steal **06** incise, snatch, tailor **07** bargain, good buy, snippet **08** clipping, discount, fragment, giveaway **09** certainty, reduction **12** special offer **13** value for money

snipe
04 fool, walk, wisp **05** scape **06** attack **09** criticism, criticize **12** heather-bleat **14** heather-bleater, heather-bluiter, heather-blutter

sniper
06 haiduk **08** partisan **09** guerrilla, irregular, terrorist **11** bushwhacker, franc-tireur, guerrillero **14** freedom fighter

snippet
03 bit **04** part, snip **05** piece, scrap, shred **06** snatch **07** cutting, portion, section, segment **08** clipping, fragment, particle

snivel
03 cry, sob **04** bawl, blub, cant, moan, weep **05** sniff, snift, whine **06** whinge **07** blubber, grizzle, sniffle, snuffle, whimper

snivelling
06 crying **07** moaning, weeping, whining **09** grizzling, sniffling, snuffling, whingeing **10** blubbering, whimpering

snob
04 scab **05** swank **07** bighead, cobbler, élitist, high-hat, parvenu **08** blackleg, townsman **09** shoemaker **13** social climber

snobbery
04 airs, side **05** pride **07** disdain **09** arrogance, loftiness **10** pretension, snootiness, uppishness **11** haughtiness, superiority **12** snobbishness **13** airs and graces, condescension **15** pretentiousness

snobbish
05 dicty, lofty, proud **06** dickty, snobby, snooty, uppish, uppity **07** haughty, stuck-up **08** affected, arrogant, jumped-up, superior **10** disdainful, hoity-toity, toffee-nose **11** patronizing, pretentious, toffee-nosed

12 supercilious **13** condescending, high and mighty

snog
03 hug, pet **04** hold, kiss, neck
05 clasp, nurse **06** caress, cuddle, enfold, fondle, nestle, smooch
07 embrace, snuggle **08** canoodle

snoop
03 pry, spy **04** nose **05** sneak
06 meddle **07** gumshoe, meddler, Paul Pry, snooper **08** busybody, meddling
09 interfere **11** Nosey Parker
12 interference, put your oar in
14 poke your nose in, stick your oar in
15 stick your nose in

snooper
03 pry, spy **05** snoop **07** meddler, Paul Pry **08** busybody **11** Nosey Parker
12 eavesdropper

snooty
05 lofty, proud **06** snobby, uppity
07 haughty, stuck-up **08** affected, arrogant, jumped-up, snobbish, superior **10** disdainful, hoity-toity
11 patronizing, pretentious, toffee-nosed **12** supercilious
13 condescending, high and mighty

snooze
03 kip, nap **04** calk, doze **05** caulk, dover, sleep **06** catnap, nod off, repose, siesta **07** drop off, shut-eye, slumber **10** forty winks **14** have forty winks

snout
03 neb **04** beak, nose **05** sword, trunk
06 muzzle, nozzle, snitch **07** gruntle, tobacco **08** informer **09** cigarette, proboscis, schnozzle
See also **nose**

snow
03 ice **05** linen **06** heroin, whiten, winter **07** cocaine **08** blizzard, morphine, snowfall **09** snowdrift, snowstorm **10** snowflakes **12** snow flurries

Snow types and formations include:

03 red
04 corn, crud, firn, névé
05 drift, flake, sleet, slush
06 powder, sludge, yellow
07 cornice, flaught
08 sastruga
09 avalanche, spindrift

See also **ice**

snowman
04 yeti **06** frosty

snub
03 cut **04** knob, shun, slap, snag, sneb, snib, stop, stub **05** blank, check, frump, shame, sloan, sneap, snool, spurn
06 humble, ignore, insult, rebuff, rebuke, slight, squash **07** affront, heave-ho, mortify, put down, put-down, set-down, squelch **08** brush off, brush-off **09** disregard, humiliate
11 down-setting, humiliation **12** cold shoulder, cold-shoulder **13** slap in the face **14** give the heave-ho, kick in the teeth

snuff
04 stop, vent **06** pulvil, rappee, sneesh
• **snuff out**
03 end **04** kill **05** choke, crush, douse, erase **06** put out, quench, remove, stifle **07** abolish, blow out, destroy, smother **08** suppress **09** eliminate, eradicate **10** dampen down

snug
03 rug **04** cosh, cosy, cozy, snod, warm
05 comfy, tight **06** couthy, homely, secure **07** compact, couthie
08 friendly, intimate **09** sheltered, skintight **11** comfortable **12** close-fitting **13** figure-hugging

snuggle
03 hug **04** cose **06** cozy up, cuddle, curl up, nestle, nuzzle **07** croodle, embrace

snugly
06 cosily, warmly **07** tightly
08 securely **11** comfortably

so
02 as **03** sae, sic, soh, sol **04** ergo, thus, well **05** hence **06** soever
08 insomuch, likewise, provided
09 therefore, thereupon **10** thereafter
11 accordingly

soak
03 mop, ret, sog, sop, wet **04** beat, buck, rait, rate, sipe, sype **05** bathe, imbue, souse, steep **06** drench, embrue, guzzle, imbrue, infuse, pummel, seethe, sodden, sponge
07 embrewe, immerse **08** macerate, marinate, permeate, saturate, submerge **09** drenching, penetrate
10 overcharge
See also **drunkard**

soaking
03 sop **05** steep **06** sluicy, soaked, sodden **07** sopping **08** drenched, dripping, wringing **09** saturated, streaming **10** sopping wet, wet through **11** waterlogged **15** soaked to the skin

soap
04 ball, cake, curd **05** money
06 sudser, tablet **07** flannel, flatter
08 flattery, washball **09** soap opera
12 shaving-stick

Soaps include:

03 Lux®
04 Dove®, hard, soft
05 glass, Pears®, sugar
06 liquid, marine, saddle, toilet, yellow
07 Castile, coal-tar, shaving, Spanish, Windsor
08 carbolic, mountain, olive-oil
09 Palmolive®
10 coconut-oil

Soap operas include:

06 Dallas
07 Dynasty, The Bill
08 Casualty
09 Brookside, Emmerdale, Holby City, Hollyoaks, River City
10 EastEnders, Neighbours, The Archers
11 Home and Away

soar
03 fly **04** rise, sore, wing, zoom
05 climb, fly up, glide, mount, plane, soare, tower **06** ascend, rocket, sorrel, spiral **07** take off **08** escalate
09 skyrocket **15** increase quickly

sob
03 cry, sab **04** bawl, blub, howl, weep, yoop **06** boohoo, snivel **07** blubber, singult, snotter **09** shed tears

sober
02 TT **03** dry, sad **04** calm, cool, dark, drab, dull, poor, sane **05** douce, grave, plain, quiet, staid **06** demure, feeble, sedate, serene, severe, solemn, sombre, steady **07** austere, earnest, serious, subdued **08** composed, moderate, rational, teetotal
09 abstinent, dignified, drying out, practical, realistic, temperate, unexcited, unruffled **10** abstemious, on the wagon, reasonable, restrained, thoughtful, unliquored **11** clear-headed, level-headed, unconcerned
12 off the bottle **13** dispassionate, sober as a judge **14** self-controlled, stone-cold sober
• **sober up**
06 dry out **10** sleep it off **13** clear your head

sobriety
07 gravity **08** calmness, coolness
09 composure, restraint, soberness, solemnity, staidness **10** abstinence, moderation, sedateness, steadiness, temperance **11** seriousness, teetotalism **13** self-restraint
14 abstemiousness **15** level-headedness

sobriquet, soubriquet
03 tag **04** name, term **05** label, style, title **06** handle **07** epithet
08 cognomen, monicker, nickname
11 appellation, designation
12 denomination

so-called
07 alleged, nominal, would-be
08 supposed **09** pretended, professed, purported, soi-disant **10** ostensible, self-styled

soccer *see* **football**

sociability
10 affability, chumminess, cordiality
12 congeniality, conviviality, friendliness **14** gregariousness
15 neighbourliness

sociable
04 maty, warm **05** matey **06** chummy, clubby, folksy, genial, social **07** affable, cordial **08** clubable, familiar, friendly, outgoing **09** clubbable, convivial, extrovert **10** accessible, gregarious,

hospitable **11** companiable, conversable, neighbourly **12** approachable **13** companionable

social
02 do **04** bash **05** civic, dance, group, party **06** at-home, common, public, rave-up, thrash **07** blow-out, general, knees-up, leisure **08** communal, function, sociable, societal **09** amusement, community, convivial, gathering, organized **10** collective, gregarious, neighborly, sociologic **11** get-together, neighbourly, sympathetic **12** recreational, sociological **13** entertainment

• **social insect**
03 ant **05** queen

• **social standing**
04 rank **05** class **11** consequence

socialism
07 leftism, Marxism **08** Leninism **09** communism, Stalinism, welfarism **10** Trotskyism **12** collectivism

socialist
03 red, Soc **04** pink, Trot **05** pinko **06** commie, leftie **07** leftist **08** hard-left, left-wing **09** Bolshevik, communist, Menshevik, welfarist **10** left-winger, Trotskyist, Trotskyite **11** parlour pink

socialize
03 mix **05** go out **06** hobnob, mingle **08** converse **09** entertain **10** be sociable, fraternize, meet people **11** get together **12** meet socially

society
01 S **03** Soc **04** band, body, club, nobs, tong **05** élite, group, guild, toffs, union **06** circle, gentry, league, nation, people, public, swells **07** company, culture, mankind **08** alliance, humanity, nobility, sorority **09** community, humankind, human race, top drawer **10** federation, fellowship, fraternity, friendship, population, sisterhood **11** aristocracy, association, brotherhood, camaraderie, corporation, high society, the smart set **12** civilization, organization, upper classes **13** companionship, polite society, Sloane Rangers, the upper crust

Societies include:

03 BCS, BPS, CSP, ENS
04 BNES, BRCS
05 ASLEF, Royal
06 burial, choral, Dorcas
07 benefit, Camorra
08 affluent, building, friendly, Red Cross

sock
04 drub, hose, tabi **06** argyle, Argyll, thrash **08** half-hose, knee-high **11** ploughshare

socket
03 pod **04** hose, jack, ouch, port **05** hosel, point **06** budget, eye-pit, keeper **07** eyehole, hot shoe, torulus **08** alveolus **10** lampholder, power point, tabernacle

sod
04 delf, fail, turf **05** delph, divot, scraw, sward **06** ground

sodden
03 wet **04** miry **05** boggy, soggy **06** boiled, doughy, marshy, poachy, soaked **07** drookit, soaking, sopping **08** drenched **09** saturated **11** waterlogged

sodium
02 Na

sofa

Sofas include:

05 couch, divan, futon, squab
06 canapé, day bed, litter, lounge, settee, sunbed
07 bergère, casting, dos-à-dos, lounger, sofa bed
09 banquette, bed-settee, davenport, tête-à-tête, twoseater
10 sun lounger
11 studio couch
12 chaise-longue, chesterfield

soft
01 B, p **02** mp, pp **03** dim, lax, low **04** easy, fool, hold, kind, lash, mild, pale, waxy, weak **05** bland, cushy, downy, faint, fuffy, furry, light, milky, mulch, mulsh, mushy, muted, piano, pulpy, quiet, rainy, silky, sweet **06** crumby, doughy, dulcet, fleecy, gentle, gently, hushed, low-key, mellow, pastel, pliant, shaded, silken, smooth, sonant, spongy, supple, tender, voiced **07** cottony, diffuse, ductile, elastic, flowing, fungous, lenient, liberal, pillowy, plastic, pliable, quietly, springy, squashy, squishy, subdued, unsized, velvety **08** cushiony, delicate, diffused, flexible, generous, merciful, pleasant, soothing, squelchy, tolerant, yielding **09** easy-going, forgiving, indulgent, luxurious, malleable, melodious, sensitive, spineless, whispered **10** bituminous, effeminate, forbearing, mezzo-piano, permissive, pianissimo, prosperous, restrained, successful, unarmoured **11** a bed of roses, comfortable, mellifluous, soft-hearted, sympathetic, unprotected **12** affectionate, dough-kneaded

• **soft in the head**
04 daft **05** barmy, dotty, loopy, nutty, potty **06** stupid, unwise **07** foolish, puerile **08** childish, immature **09** senseless **13** irresponsible, unintelligent

• **soft spot**
06 liking **08** fondness, penchant, weakness **10** fontanelle, partiality, proclivity

soften
03 pad, ret **04** blet, calm, cree, ease, melt, rait, rate, soak **05** abate, lower, malax, quell, relax, still, water **06** digest, lessen, mellow, muffle, reduce, relent, soothe, subdue, temper **07** appease, assuage, cushion, lighten, liquefy, mollify, quicken, unsteel **08** calm down, diminish, dissolve, humanize, macerate, malaxate, mitigate, moderate, modulate, palliate, tone down **09** alleviate, emolliate **10** intenerate

• **soften up**
04 melt **06** disarm, weaken **07** win over **08** butter up, persuade, soft-soap **10** conciliate

soft-hearted
04 kind **06** gentle, tender **08** generous **10** benevolent, charitable **11** sentimental, sympathetic, warm-hearted **12** affectionate **13** compassionate, tender-hearted

softly-softly
06 low-key **07** careful, patient **08** cautious, delicate, indirect **09** tentative **10** diplomatic, restrained **11** circumspect

soft-pedal
06 go easy, subdue **08** minimize, moderate, play down, tone down

soggy
03 wet **04** damp **05** boggy, heavy, moist, pulpy, soppy **06** marshy, soaked, sodden, spongy, sultry, swampy **07** soaking, sopping **08** drenched, dripping **09** saturated **10** sopping wet, spiritless **11** waterlogged

soil
04 clay, dirt, dung, dust, foul, lair, land, loam, mire, smut, spot, tash **05** black, dirty, earth, filth, humus, mould, muddy, smear, solum, stain, sully **06** befoul, damage, defile, fatten, ground, region, sewage, smudge **07** begrime, country, pollute, slubber, tarnish **08** besmirch **09** territory **10** terra firma

soiled
05 dingy, dirty, grimy, manky, tarry **06** grubby **07** spotted, stained, sullied **08** maculate, polluted **09** tarnished

sojourn
04 rest, stay, stop **05** abide, dwell, lodge, tarry, visit **06** reside **08** stopover **09** tarriance **10** tabernacle **13** peregrination

Sol
06 Helios

solace
05 allay, cheer **06** relief, soften, soothe **07** comfort, console, succour, support **08** mitigate, pleasure **09** alleviate, amusement **10** condolence **11** alleviation, consolation

soldier
03 ant, Joe, man, vet **04** swad **05** shirk **06** swaddy **07** shirker, veteran **10** red herring

Soldier types include:

02 GI
03 NCO

04 merc, para, peon
05 cadet, poilu, tommy
06 ensign, gunner, hussar, lancer, marine, sapper, sentry, sniper, troops
07 dragoon, fighter, officer, orderly, private, recruit, regular, terrier, trooper, warrior
08 commando, fusilier, partisan, rifleman
09 centurion, conscript, guardsman, guerrilla, irregular, mercenary, minuteman
10 cavalryman, serviceman
11 infantryman, legionnaire, paratrooper, Territorial
12 sharpshooter

Soldiers include:

02 **Li** (Hongzhang)
03 **Cid** (El), **Lee** (Robert E), **Ney** (Michel), **Wet** (Christian de), **Zia** (Muhammad)
04 **Alba** (Ferdinand Alvarez de Toledo, Duke of), **Alva** (Ferdinand Alvarez de Toledo, Duke of), **Cade** (Jack), **Foch** (Ferdinand), **Haig** (Alexander), **Haig** (Douglas, Earl), **Jodl** (Alfred), **John** (Don), **Khan** (Ayub), **Röhm** (Ernst), **Tojo** (Hideki)
05 **Allen** (Ethan), **Bader** (Sir Douglas), **Barak** (Ehud), **Botha** (Louis), **Bowie** (James), **Bruce** (Robert), **Cimon**, **Clive** (Robert, Lord), **Dayan** (Moshe), **Essex** (Robert Devereux, Earl of), **Gates** (Horatio), **Grant** (Ulysses S), **Inönü** (Ismet), **Monck** (George), **Murat** (Joachim), **Perón** (Juan), **Pride** (Sir Thomas), **Rabin** (Yitzhak), **Smuts** (Jan), **Sucre** (Antonio José de), **Sully** (Maximilien de Béthune, Duc de), **Timur**, **Zhu De**
06 **Anders** (Wladyslaw), **Antony** (Mark), **Arnold** (Benedict), **Blamey** (Sir Thomas Albert), **Brutus** (Marcus Junius), **Butler** (Benjamin Franklin), **Caesar** (Julius), **Cortés** (Hernán), **Custer** (George Armstrong), **Dundee** (John Graham, Viscount of), **Dunois** (Jean d'Orléans Comte), **Edward** (the Black Prince), **Egmont** (Graaf van Gavre), **Ershad** (Hossain Muhammad), **Eugene** (of Savoy), **Franco** (Francisco), **Gaulle** (Charles de), **Gordon** (Charles George), **Granby** (John Manners, Marquis of), **Greene** (Nathanael), **Ireton** (Henry), **Keitel** (Wilhelm), **Marius** (Gaius), **Moltke** (Helmuth, Graf von), **Napier** (Robert, Lord), **Nasser** (Gamal Abd al-), **Neguib** (Mohammed), **Patton** (George), **Pétain** (Philippe), **Pompey**, **Prokop** (the Bald), **Raglan** (Fitzroy James Henry Somerset, Lord), **Rahman** (Ziaur), **Revere** (Paul), **Rommel** (Erwin), **Rupert** (Prince), **Scipio** (Publius Cornelius), **Vauban** (Sebastien le Prestre de), **Wavell** (Archibald, Earl), **Zhukov** (Giorgiy)
07 **Agrippa** (Marcus Vipsanius), **Allenby** (Edmund, Viscount), **Almagro** (Diego de), **Artigas** (José Gervasio), **Atatürk** (Mustapha Kemal), **Baldwin**, **Bazaine** (Achille), **Bedford** (John of Lancaster, Duke of), **Blücher** (Gebbard Leberecht von Fürst von), **Bourbon** (Charles), **Boycott** (Charles Cunningham), **Bradley** (Omar Nelson), **Cadogan** (William, Earl), **Cassius**, **Coligny** (Gaspard de), **Dreyfus** (Alfred), **Fairfax** (Thomas, Lord), **Farnese** (Alessandro), **Gaddafi** (Muammar), **Gemayel** (Bashir), **Hunyady** (János Corvinus), **Jackson** (Thomas Jonathan), **Kolchak** (Alexander), **Kutuzov** (Mikhail, Knyaz), **Lambert** (John), **Masséna** (André), **Maurice** (Prince), **Metaxas** (Ioannis), **Mortier** (Edouard Adolphe Casimir Joseph), **Pizarro** (Francisco), **Ptolemy**, **Roberts** (Frederick, Earl), **Sherman** (William Tecumseh), **St Leger** (Barry), **Tancred**, **Turenne** (Henri de la Tour d'Auvergne, Vicomte de), **Vendôme** (Louis Joseph Duc de), **Warwick** (Richard Neville, Earl of), **William** (Prince of Orange), **Wrangel** (Pyotr, Lord)
08 **Agricola** (Gnaeus Julius), **Alvarado** (Pedro de), **Anglesey** (Henry William Paget, Marquis of), **Antonius** (Marcus), **Arminius**, **Badoglio** (Pietro), **Bentinck** (William, Lord), **Boadicea**, **Burgoyne** (John), **Burnside** (Ambrose Everett), **Campbell** (Sir Colin), **Cardigan** (James Thomas Brudenell, Earl of), **Cromwell** (Oliver), **Eichmann** (Adolf), **Ginckell** (Godert de), **Guiscard** (Robert), **Hamilton** (James, Duke of), **Harrison** (William Henry), **Hereward** (the Wake), **Horrocks** (Sir Brian), **Ironside** (William, Lord), **Itúrbide** (Agustín de), **Lawrence** (Thomas Edward), **Lucullus** (Lucius Licinius), **MacMahon** (Marie Edme Patrice Maurice de), **Marshall** (George Catlett), **Mengistu** (Haile Mariam), **Montfort** (Simon de), **Montrose** (James Graham, Marquis of), **Napoleon**, **Nobunaga** (Oda), **Pershing** (John Joseph), **Potemkin** (Grigoriy), **Pugachev** (Emelyan), **Seleucus**, **Sheridan** (Philip Henry), **Sikorski** (Wladyslaw), **Skorzeny** (Otto), **Stanhope** (James, Earl), **Tokugawa** (Ieyasu), **Valdivia** (Pedro de), **Wolseley** (Garnet, Viscount), **Xenophon**, **Yamagata** (Prince Aritomo), **Zia Ul-Haq** (Muhammad)
09 **Alexander** (Harold, Earl), **Antonescu** (Ion), **Bonaparte** (Jérôme), **Carausius** (Marcus Aurelius Mausaeus), **Cavendish** (William), **Garibaldi** (Giuseppe), **Gneisenau** (August, Graf Neithardt von), **Hasdrubal**, **Hideyoshi** (Toyotomi), **Kim Il-sung**, **Kitchener** (Herbert, Earl), **Lafayette** (Marie Joseph, Marquis de), **MacArthur** (Douglas), **Miltiades**, **Spartacus**
10 **Abercromby** (Sir Ralph), **Alanbrooke** (Alan Francis Brooke, Viscount), **Alcibiades**, **Auchinleck** (Sir Claude), **Belisarius**, **Clausewitz** (Karl von), **Cornwallis** (Charles, Marquis), **Cumberland** (William, Duke of), **Eisenhower** (Dwight D), **Germanicus**, **Hindenburg** (Paul von), **Karageorge**, **Montgomery** (Bernard, Viscount), **Schlieffen** (Alfred, Graf von), **Stroessner** (Alfredo), **Voroshilov** (Kliment), **Washington** (George), **Wellington** (Arthur Wellesley, Duke of)
11 **Baden-Powell** (Robert, Lord), **Black Prince**, **Genghis Khan**, **Marlborough** (John Churchill, Duke of), **Mohammed Ali**, **Münchhausen** (Baron von)
12 **Ptolemy Soter**, **Stauffenburg** (Claus, Graf von)
13 **Fabius Maximus** (Quintus), **Rouget de Lisle** (Claude Joseph)
14 **Pinochet Ugarte** (Augusto)
15 **Scipio Africanus** (Publius Cornelius), **Seleucus Nicator**

• **soldier on**
06 hang on, hold on, keep on, remain
08 continue, keep at it, plug away
09 keep going, persevere, stick at it
11 hang in there
• **soldiers**
02 OR, RE, TA **03** GIs **04** army
06 legion **08** garrison

sole

03 one **04** lone, only, palm, pull, sill, slip, sowl **05** alone, capon, clump, mered, soole, sowle **06** meered, single, thenar, unique **07** uniform **08** singular, solitary **09** exclusive, scaldfish **10** individual

solecism

04 boob **05** error, gaffe, lapse **06** booboo, howler **07** blunder, faux pas, mistake **08** cacology **09** absurdity, gaucherie, indecorum **11** anacoluthon, impropriety, incongruity

solely

04 just, only **05** alone **06** merely, simply, singly **08** entirely, uniquely **09** allenarly **10** completely **11** exclusively **14** single-handedly

solemn

02 po **04** awed, glum **05** grand, grave, pious, sober, state **06** august, devout, formal, honest, owlish, ritual, sedate, sombre **07** earnest, genuine, po-faced, pompous, serious, sincere, stately **08** imposing, majestic **09** committed, dignified, momentous, venerable **10** ceremonial, impressive, portentous, thoughtful **11** ceremonious, reverential **12** awe-inspiring, wholehearted

solemnity

04 rite **06** ritual **07** dignity, gravity **08** ceremony, grandeur, sanctity **09** formality **10** ceremonial, observance, sacredness

11 celebration, earnestness, proceedings, seriousness, stateliness 13 momentousness 14 impressiveness, portentousness

solemnize
04 keep 06 honour 07 dignify, observe, perform 09 celebrate 11 commemorate

solemnly
07 gravely, soberly 08 formally 09 earnestly, seriously 10 faithfully

sol-fa *see* **note**

solicit
03 ask, beg, sue, woo 04 bash, drum, pray, seek, tout 05 apply, court, crave, plead 06 accost, ask for, hustle, incite, manage 07 accoast, beseech, canvass, conduct, entreat, implore, request, require 08 apply for, petition 09 importune 10 supplicate 11 proposition

solicitor
02 QC, SL, WS 03 Att, Sol, SSC 04 Atty, Solr, tout 06 lawyer 08 advocate, attorney, law agent, recorder 09 barrister, canvasser 10 crown agent

solicitous
05 eager 06 caring, uneasy 07 anxious, careful, earnest, jealous, worried, zealous 08 troubled 09 attentive, concerned 11 considerate 12 apprehensive

solicitude
04 care, cark, fear 05 worry 06 regard 07 anxiety, concern, trouble 08 disquiet 10 uneasiness 13 attentiveness, consideration 15 considerateness

solid
04 firm, hard, pure, real 05 cubic, dense, gross, sober, sound, thick, valid 06 cogent, decent, square, stable, strong, sturdy, trusty, worthy 07 compact, cubical, durable, genuine, serious, unmixed, upright, wealthy, weighty 08 concrete, reliable, sensible, tangible, unbroken, unvaried 09 steadfast, unalloyed, unanimous, undivided, well-built 10 compressed, continuous, dependable, holosteric, unshakable, upstanding 11 level-headed, long-lasting, respectable, substantial, trustworthy, unshakeable, well-founded 12 well-grounded 13 authoritative, unadulterated, uninterrupted

solidarity
05 unity 06 accord 07 concord, harmony 08 cohesion 09 agreement, consensus, soundness, stability, unanimity 10 team spirit 11 camaraderie 13 esprit de corps 14 like-mindedness

solidify
03 gel, set 04 cake, clot, jell 06 go hard, harden 07 congeal 09 coagulate, corporify 10 become hard 11 crystallize

soliloquy
06 homily, sermon, speech 07 address, lecture, monolog, oration 09 monologue

solitary
03 one 04 lone, monk, sole 05 alone, loner 06 hermit, lonely, remote, single 07 ancress, ascetic, dernful, eremite, recluse, retired, stylite 08 dearnful, desolate, isolated, lonesome, lone wolf, monastic, secluded, separate 09 anchoress, anchorite, reclusive, untrodden, unvisited, withdrawn 10 by yourself, cloistered, friendless, hermitical, monastical, unsociable 11 introverted, monasterial, out-of-the-way, sequestered 12 inaccessible, Jimmy Woodser, unfrequented 13 companionless, individualist

solitude
07 privacy 09 aloneness, isolation, seclusion 10 desolation, loneliness, remoteness, retirement, singleness 12 introversion, lonesomeness 13 reclusiveness, unsociability 14 friendlessness

solo
04 aria, ayre, lone 05 alone, break, récit 06 single 07 cadenza 09 on your own 10 by yourself, unattended, unescorted 12 single-handed 13 unaccompanied

Solomon Islands
03 SLB

solution
◇ *anagram indicator*
02 aq 03 fix, gel, key, lye, mix, sol 05 blend, brine 06 answer, liquid, liquor, remedy, result, saline, way out 07 cure-all, formula, mixture, panacea, solvent 08 compound, emulsion, quick fix 09 rationale, unfolding 10 resolution, suspension 11 elucidation, explanation, unravelling 12 decipherment 13 clarification 15 disentanglement

solve
◇ *anagram indicator*
04 read, undo, work 05 crack, guess, loose, untie 06 answer, assoil, fathom, puzzle, remedy, riddle, settle, unbind, unfold 07 clarify, clear up, explain, expound, rectify, resolve, unravel, work out 08 decipher, put right, solution, think out, unriddle 09 figure out, interpret, puzzle out 11 disentangle 12 think through

solvent
04 DMSO 05 ether, sound 06 dioxan, toluol 07 benzine, dioxane, toluene 08 alcahest, alkahest, methanol, terebene 09 able to pay, banana oil, detergent, financial, menstruum, out of debt 10 chloroform, extractant, in the black, in the clear, unindebted 11 cyclohexane 12 banana liquid, creditworthy, ethyl acetate, nitromethane, salt of sorrel 14 banana solution, petroleum ether 15 propylene glycol, trichloroethane

solver
11 solutionist

• solvers
02 ye 03 you

Somalia
02 SO 03 SOM

sombre
03 dim, sad 04 dark, drab, dull 05 dingy, grave, morne, shady, sober 06 dismal, gloomy, morose, solemn 07 doleful, joyless, obscure, serious, shadowy, subfusc, subfusk 08 funereal, mournful 09 depressed 10 lugubrious, melancholy

some
◇ *hidden indicator*
03 any, few, one 04 they 07 certain, several 10 remarkable 11 outstanding, such-and-such 12 considerable

somebody
03 one, VIP 04 name, star 05 mogul, nabob 06 bigwig, quidam 07 big shot, magnate, notable, someone 08 big noise, big wheel, luminary 09 celebrity, dignitary, personage, superstar 10 panjandrum 11 heavyweight 13 household name

someday
05 later 06 one day 07 by and by, later on 08 sometime 10 eventually, ultimately 11 in due course 13 sooner or later 14 one of these days

somehow
◇ *anagram indicator*
06 in a way 11 by some means, come what may 15 by hook or by crook, one way or another

someone *see* **somebody**

somersault
◇ *anagram indicator*

sometime
02 ex 04 late, then 06 former, one day 07 earlier, one-time, quondam, retired, someday 08 emeritus, formerly, previous 09 erstwhile, in the past 10 occasional, previously 11 another time

sometimes
07 at times 08 off and on, on and off 09 somewhile 10 now and then, on occasion, otherwhile, somewhiles 11 now and again, on occasions, otherwhiles 12 every so often, occasionally, once in a while 14 from time to time

somewhat
04 a bit 05 kinda, quite 06 a bit of, fairly, kind of, pretty, rather, sort of 07 a little 08 slightly 10 moderately, relatively 12 to some degree, to some extent

somnolent
04 dozy 06 drowsy, sleepy, torpid 08 comatose, oscitant 09 half-awake, heavy-eyed, soporific

Somnus
06 Hypnos

son
01 s **03** boy, lad **04** fils **05** child, lewis
06 epigon, filius, laddie, native
07 epigone **08** disciple **09** offspring
10 descendant, inhabitant

Sons include:

04 **Abel**, **Amis** (Martin), **Bush** (George W), **Cain**, **Esau**, **Pitt** (William)
05 **Dumas** (Alexandre), **Groan** (Titus), **Harry** (Prince), **Isaac**, **Jacob**, **Milne** (Christopher Robin), **Morel** (Paul), **Waugh** (Auberon)
06 **Andrew** (Prince), **Edward** (Prince), **Gandhi** (Rajiv), **Hamlet**, **Joseph**
07 **Absalom**, **Charles** (Prince), **Douglas** (Michael), **Hotspur**, **Laertes**, **Oedipus**, **Simpson** (Bart), **William** (Prince)
08 **Benjamin**, **Dimbleby** (David), **Dimbleby** (Jonathan), **Florizel**, **Pontifex** (Ernest)
09 **Dumas fils**
10 **Duke of York**
11 **Jesus Christ**
13 **Prince of Wales**
14 **Pitt the Younger** (William)

• **son of**
01 M', O' **02** Mc **03** Mac

song

Songs include:

03 air, art, fit, lay, oat, ode, pop, pub, war
04 aria, bird, duet, folk, glee, hymn, lied, lilt, love, pean, rock, rune, tune
05 blues, carol, catch, chant, dirge, ditty, elegy, lyric, paean, plain, psalm, torch, yodel
06 amoret, anthem, ballad, chorus, gospel, jingle, lieder, lyrics, melody, number, shanty
07 calypso, cantata, canzone, chanson, descant, lullaby, refrain, requiem, wassail
08 bird call, canticle, canzonet, madrigal, serenade, threnody
09 barcarole, cantilena, dithyramb, epinikion, roundelay, spiritual
10 plainchant, recitative
11 bothy ballad, chansonette, rock and roll
12 epithalamium, nursery rhyme

See also **poem**

Pop songs include:

03 Bad
04 1999, Gold, Help!, True
05 Clair, Diana, Faith, Layla, My Way, Relax, Shout
06 Apache, Atomic, The End, Vienna, Volare
07 Delilah, D.I.V.O.R.C.E., Hey Jude, Holiday, Imagine, Jamming, Let It Be, Rat Trap, Respect, Sailing, Starman
08 Answer Me, Antmusic, At the Hop, Baby Love, Downtown, Love Me Do, Mamma Mia, Our House, Parklife, Peggy Sue, The Boxer, The Model, Thriller, Wannabee, Waterloo
09 Albatross, Dance Away, I Feel Love, Maggie May, Metal Guru, Penny Lane, Praise You, Release Me, Something, Stand By Me, Wild Thing, Yesterday
10 All Shook Up, Annie's Song, Band of Gold, Billie Jean, Blue Monday, Bye Bye Baby, House of Fun, King Creole, Lazy Sunday, Living Doll, Millennium, Moving On Up, Night Fever, Perfect Day, Purple Haze, Reet Petite, Ring of Fire, Wonderwall
11 All Right Now, American Pie, Back for Good, Baker Street, Cathy's Clown, Firestarter, From Me to You, Glad All Over, Golden Brown, I Got You Babe, I'm Not in Love, Light My Fire, Like a Virgin, Lily the Pink, Mrs Robinson, Oliver's Army, Space Oddity, Tainted Love, Voodoo Chile
12 All or Nothing, Bat Out of Hell, Born in the USA, Born to be Wild, Come on Eileen, Common People, Dancing Queen, Eleanor Rigby, God Only Knows, Material Girl, No Woman No Cry, The Birdy Song, West End Girls
13 Blueberry Hill, Brass in Pocket, Design for Life, Don't You Want Me, Into the Groove, It's Not Unusual, It's Now or Never, Jailhouse Rock, Last Christmas, Long Tall Sally, Mary's Boy Child, Mull of Kintyre, Oh, Pretty Woman, Only the Lonely, Pinball Wizard, Summer Holiday, Tears in Heaven
14 20th Century Boy, A Hard Day's Night, Blue Suede Shoes, Good Vibrations, Karma Chameleon, Stand By Your Man, Sunny Afternoon, That'll Be the Day, The Power of Love, Waterloo Sunset, White Christmas, Wonderful World
15 Baby One More Time, Begin the Beguine, Blowin' in the Wind, Candle in the Wind, Careless Whisper, Congratulations, God Save the Queen, Heartbreak Hotel, Hotel California, I Shot the Sheriff, Jumpin' Jack Flash, Killing me Softly, Love is all Around, Paperback Writer, Puppet on a String, Rivers of Babylon, Unchained Melody, When I Fall In Love, Yellow Submarine

See also **musical**

• **song and dance**
03 ado **04** flap, fuss, stir, to-do **05** hoo-ha, tizzy **06** bother, furore, pother, tumult **09** commotion, kerfuffle
11 performance

songster
06 singer **07** crooner, soloist, warbler
08 minstrel, vocalist **09** balladeer, chanteuse, chorister **10** troubadour

songwriter

Songwriters and lyricists include:

03 **Pop** (Iggy)
04 **Bart** (Lionel), **Cahn** (Sammy), **Cash** (Johnny), **Hart** (Lorenz), **John** (Sir Elton), **Kern** (Jerome), **Reed** (Lou), **Rice** (Sir Tim)
05 **Berry** (Chuck), **Brown** (James), **Cohan** (George Michael), **Davis** (Miles), **Dylan** (Bob), **Holly** (Buddy), **Loewe** (Frederick), **Simon** (Paul), **Smith** (Tommy), **Sousa** (John Philip), **Swann** (Donald), **Weill** (Kurt)
06 **Berlin** (Irving), **Coward** (Sir Noël), **Fields** (Dorothy), **Joplin** (Scott), **Lennon** (John), **Lerner** (Alan Jay), **Marley** (Bob), **Mercer** (Johnny H), **Morton** (Jelly Roll), **Oliver** (King), **Parker** (Charlie), **Porter** (Cole), **Seeger** (Pete), **Waller** (Thomas 'Fats'), **Warren** (Harry)
07 **Collins** (Phil), **Dickson** (Barbara), **Donovan**, **Gilbert** (Sir Wiliam), **Guthrie** (Woody), **Hendrix** (Jimi), **Loesser** (Frank), **MacColl** (Ewan), **Mancini** (Henry), **Novello** (Ivor), **Orbison** (Roy), **Rodgers** (Richard), **Romberg** (Sigmund)
08 **Coltrane** (John), **Costello** (Elvis), **Gershwin** (George), **Mitchell** (Joni), **Morrison** (Van), **Sondheim** (Stephen)
09 **Bernstein** (Leonard), **Ellington** (Duke), **Faithfull** (Marianne), **Gillespie** (Dizzy), **McCartney** (Sir Paul)
10 **Carmichael** (Hoagy)
11 **Armatrading** (Joan), **Hammerstein** (Oscar), **Lloyd Webber** (Andrew, Lord), **Springsteen** (Bruce)

sonorous
04 full, loud, rich **05** round **07** orotund, ringing, rounded **08** plangent, resonant, sounding **09** high-flown, ororotund **10** full-voiced, resounding
11 full-mouthed **12** full-throated, high-sounding **13** grandiloquent

soon
04 anon **05** early, quick **06** pronto, timely **07** betimes, ere long, in a tick, just now, readily, shortly **08** in a hurry, in a jiffy, in no time **09** any minute, in a minute, in a moment, presently, willingly **10** before long **12** any minute now, in a short time, without delay
13 in no time at all **14** in a little while, in a moment or two, round the corner
15 in the near future

• **as soon as**
04 once, when **07** whene'er
08 directly, eftsoons, whenever
10 right after **11** immediately, in the wake of **13** directly after

sooner
06 before, rather **07** earlier, instead
08 by choice **09** for choice, in advance
10 beforehand, from choice, much rather, preferably **12** by preference
13 for preference

• **no sooner than**
06 barely, hardly **08** only just, scarcely

• **sooner or later**
06 at last **07** finally **08** after all, at length, in the end **10** eventually, ultimately **11** in due course **12** in the long run, subsequently

soot
04 coom, smut **05** colly **06** smutch **08** gas black **09** lampblack

soothe
04 balm, calm, coax, ease, hush, lull **05** accoy, allay, quiet, salve, sleek, still **06** augury, back up, cajole, pacify, settle, smooth, soften, temper **07** appease, assuage, comfort, compose, confirm, flatter, mollify, quieten, relieve, support **08** blandish, calm down, mitigate, palliate **09** alleviate **10** settle down **11** quieten down **12** foretokening, tranquillize

soothing
04 soft **05** balmy **06** anetic, gentle **07** anodyne, calming, easeful, lenient, restful **08** balsamic, lenitive, relaxing **09** assuasive, demulcent, emollient, paregoric **10** palliative

soothsayer
04 seer **05** augur, sibyl **07** Chaldee, diviner, prophet **08** Chaldaic, haruspex **10** foreteller, prophetess **14** prognosticator

sophisticated
04 cool, gold **05** couth, slick, suave **06** hi-tech, inland, subtle, urbane **07** complex, elegant, refined, stylish, worldly **08** advanced, cultured, delicate, high-tech, joined-up, polished, seasoned, space-age **09** civilized, elaborate, executive, expensive, falsified, intricate **10** cultivated **11** adulterated, complicated, experienced, worldly wise **12** cosmopolitan **13** state-of-the-art **15** highly developed

sophistication
05 poise **07** culture, finesse **08** elegance, urbanity **10** experience **11** savoir-faire, savoir-vivre, worldliness

sophistry
07 fallacy, quibble, sophism **08** elenchus **09** casuistry, choplogic **10** paralogism **14** false reasoning

soporific
06 hypnic, opiate, sleepy **07** poppied, Seconal® **08** hypnotic, narcotic, sedative **09** dormitive, somnolent **10** poppy water **11** anaesthetic **12** sleeping pill **13** sleep-inducing, tranquillizer **14** benzodiazepine, sleeping tablet, tranquillizing

soppy
03 wet **04** daft, soft, wild **05** corny, crazy, gooey, mushy, silly, soggy, weepy **06** cheesy, gloopy, sloppy, slushy **07** cloying, maudlin, mawkish, wimpish **08** drenched **09** schmaltzy **10** lovey-dovey **11** sentimental **13** overemotional

soprano
01 S **03** sop **05** mezzo **06** treble **08** castrato

sorcerer
04 mage **05** magus, witch **06** magian, voodoo, wizard **07** angekok, warlock **08** angekkok, magician **09** enchanter, sorceress **10** reim-kennar **11** enchantress, necromancer **13** thaumaturgist

sorcery
05 charm, magic, spell, wicca **06** voodoo **07** pisheog **08** diablery, malefice, pishogue, witching, wizardry **09** diablerie, warlockry **10** black magic, necromancy, witchcraft **11** enchantment, incantation, thaumaturgy

sordid
03 low **04** base, foul, mean, vile **05** dirty, grimy, mucky, seamy, seedy **06** filthy, scungy, shabby, sleazy, soiled, tawdry **07** corrupt, debased, immoral, miserly, squalid, stained, unclean **08** degraded, grasping, shameful, wretched **09** abhorrent, debauched, dishonest, mercenary, niggardly **10** degenerate, despicable **11** ignominious, self-seeking **12** disreputable **13** dishonourable

sore
03 cut, raw, red **04** bite, boil, gall, hard, hurt, sair **05** angry, blain, botch, chafe, felon, graze, grief, nasty, nerve, ulcer, upset, vexed, wound **06** aching, bitter, chafed, fester, lesion, miffed, peeved, scrape, shiver, sorrel, tender, the raw, touchy **07** abscess, annoyed, anthrax, bruised, burning, eagerly, hurting, injured, painful, quittor, wounded **08** abrasion, grievous, inflamed, offended, reddened, severely, smarting, stinging, swelling **09** afflicted, aggrieved, irritable, irritated, painfully, resentful, sensitive **10** affliction, cheesed off, distressed, grievously, laceration **12** inflammation **13** distressingly

sorely
04 much **06** highly **07** greatly, notably **08** markedly, very much **09** extremely **10** noticeably, powerfully, remarkably **11** exceedingly **13** significantly, substantially

sorrel
03 oca **04** soar, sore **05** soare, sorel **06** oxalis, sorell **07** bilimbi, sourock **08** shamrock, sourwood **09** carambola, sour-gourd

sorrow
03 rew, rue, woe **04** moan, pain, pine, pity, ruth, weep **05** be sad, grief, mourn, night, sorra, trial, worry **06** bemoan, bewail, dolour, grieve, lament, misery, regret, repent **07** agonize, anguish, feel sad, remorse, sadness, trouble **08** distress, hardship, mourning **09** dejection, heartache, suffering, tristesse **10** affliction, compassion, contrition, heartbreak, misfortune **11** be miserable, lamentation, tribulation, unhappiness, Weltschmerz **12** wretchedness **13** feel miserable

See also **grief**

sorrowful
02 wo **03** sad, wae, woe **05** sorry, trist, woful **06** dismal, rueful, triste, woeful **07** baleful, careful, doleful, painful, piteous, ruthful, tearful, unhappy, wailful **08** dejected, grievous, mournful, wretched **09** afflicted, depressed, miserable, woebegone **10** lamentable, lugubrious, melancholy **11** distressing, heartbroken **12** disconsolate, heart-rending, heavy-hearted

sorry
◇ *anagram indicator*
02 wo **03** bad, sad, woe **04** mean, poor **05** moved, upset **06** dismal, rueful, simple **07** ashamed, pitiful, pitying, unhappy **08** contrite, grievous, pathetic, penitent, shameful, wretched **09** concerned, miserable, regretful, repentant, worthless **10** apologetic, distressed, remorseful, shamefaced **11** distressing, guilt-ridden, sympathetic, unfortunate **12** contemptible, heart-rending **13** compassionate, understanding

• **be sorry for**
03 rew, rue **06** repent **08** forthink

sort
◇ *anagram indicator*
03 fit, ilk, lot, set **04** beat, geld, kind, make, race, rank, sift, type **05** agree, allot, befit, brand, breed, class, genre, genus, grade, group, order, stamp, style, woman **06** accord, adjust, assign, divide, family, kidney, manner, nature, parcel, person, punish, screen, select **07** arrange, company, consort, dispose, fashion, procure, provide, quality, species, variety **08** category, classify, organize, separate **09** catalogue, character, segregate **10** categorize, collection, distribute, put in order **11** description, systematize **12** denomination

• **out of sorts**
◇ *anagram indicator*
03 ill **04** mean, sick, weak **05** crook, cross, dicky, frail, narky, nohow, ratty, rough, seedy **06** ailing, crabby, crummy, feeble, groggy, grumpy, infirm, laid up, poorly, queasy, rotten, shirty, snappy, unwell **07** crabbed, grouchy, in a huff, in a mood, in a sulk, run down, run-down, stroppy **08** below par, choleric, diseased, nohowish **09** bedridden, crotchety, fractious, impatient, in a bad way, irritable, off-colour, unhealthy **10** in a bad mood **11** bad-tempered **13** mops and brooms, quick-tempered **14** down in the dumps, down in the mouth **15** under the weather

• **sort of**
◇ *anagram indicator*
04 a bit **05** kinda, quite **06** fairly, kind of, pretty, rather **07** a little **08** slightly, somewhat **10** moderately, relatively **12** to some degree, to some extent

• **sort out**
04 rank **05** class, grade, group, order,

solve **06** choose, divide, select **07** arrange, clear up, resolve, work out **08** classify, organize, put right, separate **09** segregate **10** categorize, put in order

sortie
04 raid, rush **05** foray, sally, swoop **06** attack, charge **07** assault, outfall **08** invasion **09** offensive

so-so
02 OK **04** fair **06** not bad **07** average, neutral **08** adequate, mediocre, middling, moderate, ordinary, passable **09** tolerable **11** indifferent, respectable **12** run-of-the-mill **13** no great shakes, unexceptional **14** comme ci comme ça, fair to middling **15** undistinguished

soubriquet *see* **sobriquet, soubriquet**

sought-after
02 in **03** big, hip, hot, now **04** cool **05** liked **06** modish, trendy, wanted **07** admired, desired, popular **08** approved, favoured, in demand, in favour **09** favourite, well-liked **10** all the rage **11** fashionable **13** in great demand

soul
02 ba, ka **03** âme, ego, man **04** alma, life, mind **05** anima, model, shade, woman **06** person, pneuma, psyche, reason, spirit **07** element, epitome, essence, example, feeling, passion **08** creature, humanity, inner man, sympathy **09** character, inner self, intellect **10** compassion, embodiment, human being, individual, inner being, inner woman, tenderness, vital force **11** inspiration, sensitivity **12** appreciation **13** heart of hearts, understanding **15** personification

soulful
06 moving **08** eloquent, mournful, profound **09** emotional, heartfelt, sensitive **10** expressive, meaningful

soulless
04 cold, dead, mean **05** bleak, cruel, empty **06** unkind **07** callous, ignoble, inhuman **08** lifeless **09** unfeeling **10** mechanical, spiritless **11** dehumanized **12** mean-spirited **13** characterless, uninteresting, unsympathetic **14** soul-destroying

sound
◇ *homophone indicator*
03 din, fit, say, voe **04** deep, firm, goad, good, hale, look, mean, safe, sane, seem, tend, test, toll, tone, trig, true, vibe, well **05** firth, fiord, fjord, gauge, go off, inlet, noise, plumb, probe, radio, right, sense, solid, swoon, tease, tenor, utter, valid, voice, whole **06** appear, cogent, deeply, fathom, intact, notion, proven, robust, secure, severe, strait, strong, sturdy, timbre, unhurt **07** channel, declare, earshot, estuary, examine, express, extreme, feeling, greatly, healthy, inspect, intense, logical, measure, passage, perfect, provoke, publish, resound, serious, weighty **08** announce, complete, orthodox, proclaim, profound, rational, reliable, resonate, severely, thorough, unbroken, very much, vigorous **09** enunciate, excellent, extremely, intensely, judicious, pronounce, resonance, seriously, undamaged, uninjured, very great, wholesome **10** articulate, completely, dependable, impression, profoundly, reasonable, thoroughly, unimpaired, vigorously **11** disease-free, implication, in good shape, investigate, reverberate, substantial, trustworthy, well-founded **12** in fine fettle, in good health, sound as a bell, well-grounded **13** authoritative, reverberation **15** in good condition

Sounds include:
03 cry, hum, pip, pop, sob, tap
04 bang, beep, boom, buzz, chug, clap, echo, fizz, hiss, honk, hoot, moan, peal, ping, plop, ring, roar, sigh, slam, snap, thud, tick, ting, toot, wail, whiz, yell, yoop
05 blare, blast, bleep, chime, chink, chirm, clack, clang, clank, clash, click, clink, clunk, crack, crash, creak, drone, grate, groan, knock, plonk, skirl, slurp, smack, sniff, snore, snort, swish, throb, thump, twang, vroom, whine, whirr, whish, whizz, whoop
06 bubble, crunch, gabble, gollar, goller, gurgle, hiccup, jangle, jingle, murmur, patter, rattle, report, rumble, rustle, scrape, scream, sizzle, splash, squeak, squeal, tinkle, whoosh
07 brattle, chatter, clatter, crackle, explode, graunch, grizzle, pitapat, screech, squelch, thunder, whimper, whistle
08 splutter
11 taratantara

Animal sounds include:
03 baa, bay, caw, coo, kaw, low, mew, moo, wee, yap
04 bark, bell, blat, bray, bump, crow, hiss, honk, hoot, howl, purr, roar, woof, yawp, yelp, yowl
05 bleat, cheep, chirp, cluck, crake, croak, groin, growl, grunt, miaow, neigh, pewit, quack, scape, snarl, tweet
06 bellow, cackle, gobble, heehaw, peewit, squawk, squeak, warble, whinny
07 chirrup, gruntle, looning, screech, trumpet, twitter, whicker
09 caterwaul

Geographical sounds include:
03 Hoy, Rum
04 Bute, Calf, Crow, Deer, Eigg, Holm, Iona, Jura, King, Mull, Papa, Rock, Yell
05 Barra, Canna, Cross, Exuma, Gigha, Inner, Islay, Luing, Puget, Sanda, Shuna, Sleat
06 Breton, Harris, Norton, Pabbay, Raasay, Ramsey, Sanday, Shiant, Turner
07 Arisaig, Bardsey, Caswell, Cuillin, Gairsay, McMurdo, Milford, Pamlico, St Mary's
08 Auskerry, Bluemull, Breaksea, Colgrave, Doubtful, Kotzebue, Taransay
09 Albemarle, Casiguran, Currituck, Eynhallow, Lancaster, Shapinsay
10 Chandeleur, Cumberland, Kilbrannan, King George, Long Island, New Georgia, Possession
11 Mississippi, Roes Welcome
12 Prince Albert
13 Prince William

• **by the sound of it**
◇ *homophone indicator*
• **sound measure/unit**
02 dB **03** bel **04** phon, sone **07** decibel, phoneme, segment **09** kilohertz
• **sound out**
03 ask **04** pump **05** probe **06** survey **07** canvass, examine, suss out **08** question, research **11** investigate

soundly
04 fast **05** fully, quite, tight **06** deeply **07** greatly, solidly, totally, utterly, validly **08** entirely, securely, severely, very much **09** downright, extremely, intensely, logically, perfectly, seriously **10** absolutely, completely, dependably, profoundly, reasonably, thoroughly, vigorously **15** authoritatively

soundtrack
10 theme music

soup
◇ *anagram indicator*

Soups include:
03 dal, pea, pho
04 cawl, crab, dhal, game, miso
05 adrak, blaff, broth, egusi, gumbo, locro, misua, rasam, snert, stock
06 ajiaco, asapao, barley, birria, bisque, borsch, cocido, congee, fennel, guacho, harira, lentil, noodle, oxtail, pazole, posole, potage, potato, reuben, sambar, tomato, turtle, won ton
07 borscht, chicken, chowder, tarator, turbana
08 borschch, broccoli, callaloo, chirmole, consommé, ful nabed, gazpacho, halászlé, julienne, mondongo, mushroom, okroshka, sancocho, solianka, split pea
09 asparagus, bird's nest, cacciucco, Clanallen, escabeche, fasolatha, pea and ham, pepperpot, picadillo, quimbombo, royal game, rozsolnyk, shark's fin, tom kha gai, white foam
10 avgolemono, caldo verde, minestrone, mock turtle, mole de olla, sauerkraut, superkanja, watercress
11 clam chowder, cock-a-leekie, cullen skink, French onion, gaeng

som kai, gaeng som pla, Scotch broth, tom yam goong, vichyssoise
12 bouneschlupp, brown Windsor, cockieleekie, guriltai shul, mulligatawny
13 bouillabaisse, chicken noodle, cream of tomato, potato and leek, stracciatella
14 lentil and bacon
15 Queen Anne's broth

sour
03 bad, off **04** acid, rank, tart, tiff, tift, turn **05** acerb, acidy, aygre, eager, heavy, nasty, ratty, sharp, spoil, surly, tangy, wersh **06** acetic, bitter, canker, crusty, morose, rancid, shirty, strong, turned **07** acerbic, acetous, austere, crabbed, curdled, envenom, grouchy, peevish, pungent, subacid **08** alienate, churlish, embitter, verjuice, vinegary **09** acidulent, acidulous, resentful **10** disenchant, embittered, exacerbate, exasperate, make bitter, unpleasant **11** acrimonious, bad-tempered, ill-tempered **12** disagreeable, inharmonious, unsuccessful

source
03 urn **04** font, head, mine, rise, root, well, ylem **05** cause, fount, radix, start, stock **06** author, origin, sourse, spring, supply, whence **07** surging **08** wellhead **09** authority, beginning, generator, good hands, informant, principle, rootstock, water head **10** derivation, originator, primordium, provenance, springhead, wellspring **11** fons et origo **12** commencement, fountainhead

sourpuss
04 crab **05** grump, shrew **06** grouse, kvetch, misery, whiner **07** killjoy, whinger **08** buzzkill, grumbler **10** crosspatch **14** dog in the manger

souse
03 dip, ear, sou **04** dash, duck, dunk, sink, soak, wash **05** douse, plump, smite, souce, sowce, sowse, steep, thump **06** drench, impact, pickle, plunge, sowsse, strike **07** ducking, immerse, impinge **08** drunkard, marinade, marinate, saturate, submerge, suddenly **09** drenching

south
◇ *tail selection down indicator*
01 S **02** So **03** Sth **04** Midi

South Africa
02 SA, ZA **03** RSA, ZAF **04** S Afr

South African
02 SA **04** S Afr

South America *see* **America**; **god, goddess**

South Carolina
02 SC

South Dakota
02 SD **04** S Dak

south-east, south-eastern
02 SE

southern
01 S **05** south **07** austral **09** southerly **10** meridional

south-west, south-western
02 SW

souvenir
05 relic, steal, token **06** trophy
07 memento, purloin, relique
08 keepsake, reminder
11 remembrance

sovereign
01 K, L, Q **02** ER, HM **03** bar, sov **04** king, quid, tsar **05** chief, crown, pound, queen, royal, ruler, squid **06** canary, couter, kingly, nicker, prince, ruling, shiner, sovran, utmost **07** emperor, empress, extreme, monarch, queenly, smacker, supreme, thick'un **08** absolute, autocrat, dominant, imperial, majestic, princely **09** paramount, potentate, principal, unlimited **10** autonomous, self-ruling, unequalled, unrivalled **11** independent, outstanding, predominant **12** jimmy-o'goblin **13** pound sterling, self-governing
See also **king**; **queen**

sovereignty
03 raj **04** sway **07** primacy, royalty **08** autonomy, chiefdom, dominion, imperium, kingship, regality, synarchy **09** chiefship, princedom, queenship, supremacy **10** ascendancy, domination, suzerainty **11** condominium, pre-eminence **12** independence **13** thalassocracy, thalattocracy **14** rangatiratanga, self-government

sow
03 elt, saw **04** gilt, seed, yelt **05** drill, lodge, plant, strew **06** spread
07 bestrew, implant, scatter
08 disperse, seminate **09** broadcast
10 distribute, inseminate
11 disseminate
See also **pig**

sozzled
◇ *anagram indicator*
05 happy, merry, tight, tipsy **06** blotto, tiddly **07** drunken, pickled, squiffy, tiddley **09** crapulent, plastered **10** inebriated **11** intoxicated

spa
06 spring **07** Kurhaus

Spas include:

03 Dax
04 Bath
05 Baden, Baños, Epsom, Sochi, Vichy
06 Aachen, Boston, Buxton, Ilkley, Trebon
07 Lourdes, Malvern, Matlock
08 Carlsbad, Shearsby, Woodhall
09 Bad Elster, Droitwich, Harrogate, Marienbad, Velingrad
10 Baden Baden, Cheltenham, Leamington
11 Bad Dürrheim, Scarborough
12 Strathpeffer
13 Aix-la-Chapelle, Knaresborough
14 Tunbridge Wells

space
02 em, en **03** gap **04** area, lung, play, room, seat, span, time, void **05** array, blank, break, chasm, order, place, range, scope, shift, spell, stint, sweep **06** cosmos, extent, galaxy, lacuna, leeway, margin, period, volume **07** arrange, be apart, dispose, expanse, opening, stretch **08** capacity, interval, latitude, omission, set apart, space out, universe **09** amplitude, clearance, deep space, elbow-room, expansion, string out **10** empty space, interstice, Lebensraum, outer space, put in order, stretch out **11** the Milky Way **12** intermission **13** accommodation

Space travel-related terms include:

03 bus, ELV, ESA, ISS, LOX, LRV, MCC
04 NASA
05 abort, flyby, orbit
06 CAPCOM, drogue, G force, hydyne, launch, module, rocket
07 booster, coolant, docking, lift-off, mission, payload, re-entry, shuttle, vidicon
08 attitude, blast-off, free-fall, fuel cell, fuel tank, lunanaut, moonwalk, nose cone, sloshing
09 astronaut, cosmonaut, hydrazine, launch pad, light year, lunarnaut, spaceship, space suit
10 heat shield, pogo effect, propellant, rendezvous, spacecraft, space probe, trajectory
11 lunar module, solar system, zero gravity
12 ascent module, launch window, lunar landing, man on the moon, microgravity, space station
13 command module, descent module, jet propulsion, launch vehicle, space sickness
14 escape velocity, mission control, weightlessness
15 re-entry corridor

Spacecraft include:

02 LM
03 ISS, LEM, Mir
06 Skylab, Tardis
07 Gemini 4, Vostok 1, Vostok 5, Vostok 6
08 Apollo 11, Apollo 13, Apollo 17, Columbia, Freedom 7, Nostromo, Red Dwarf, Sputnik 1, Sputnik 2, Voskhod 1, Voskhod 2
09 Discovery, Endeavour, Liberator, Pioneer 10, Shenzhou V
10 Challenger, USS Voyager
11 Fireball XL5, Heart of Gold
12 SS Discovery 1, Thunderbird 3, Thunderbird 5
13 Moonbase Alpha, USS Enterprise

See also **probe**

spaceman, spacewoman *see* **astronaut**

spacious
03 big **04** huge, open, vast, wide **05** ample, broad, large, roomy **07** immense, sizable **08** palatial, sizeable **09** capacious, expansive, extensive, uncrowded **10** commodious

spade
01 S **03** loy **04** pick, spay, spit **05** graft, slane, spado, spayd **06** paddle, pattle, pettle, spayad, tuskar, tusker **07** cas crom, tushkar, tushker, twiscar **08** caschrom **09** flaughter **11** paddle-staff **12** breastplough
• **spades**
01 S

spadework
06 labour **08** drudgery, homework **10** donkey-work, foundation, groundwork **11** preparation **15** preliminary work

Spain
01 E **03** ESP **06** España
• **in Spain**
◇ *foreign word indicator*

span
04 arch, last, link, term, time, yoke **05** cover, cross, fresh, piece, range, reach, scope, spell, vault **06** bridge, extend, extent, length, period, spread, wind up **07** compass, include, measure, overlay, stretch **08** bestride, distance, duration, interval, traverse **09** encompass **10** overbridge

spangle
01 O **06** sequin **07** glitter **09** paillette

Spaniard
03 don

spaniel
04 mean **07** fawning

Spaniels include:

03 toy
04 land
05 field, water
06 cocker, Sussex
07 clumber
08 Blenheim, papillon, springer
10 Irish water, Maltese dog
11 King Charles

Spanish *see* **day**; **month**; **number**

spank
03 tan **04** cane, slap **05** smack, whack **06** paddle, strike, thrash, thwack, wallop **07** slipper **15** put over your knee

spanking
04 fast, fine, very **05** brand, brisk, quick, scuds, smart, swift **06** lively, snappy, speedy **07** exactly, totally, utterly **08** gleaming, spirited, striking, vigorous **09** energetic **10** absolutely, completely, paddy-whack, positively, strikingly **12** invigorating

spanner
03 key **06** wrench **12** monkey wrench

spar
03 bar, box **04** gaff, pole, rail, shut, spat, tiff **05** argue, scrap, sprit **06** barite, bicker, fasten, rafter, ricker, steeve **07** barytes, contend, contest, dispute, fall out, quarrel, wrangle, wrestle **08** bowsprit, cryolite, mainboom, skirmish, squabble **09** outrigger **10** martingale **11** torpedo boom **12** swinging-boom, wollastonite **13** rhodochrosite

spare
04 bony, free, gash, give, hain, lank, lean, over, save, slim, thin **05** allow, avoid, extra, gaunt, grant, guard, hoard, scant, skimp, stint **06** afford, defend, frugal, let off, meagre, modest, pardon, scanty, secure, skimpy, skinny, unused **07** forbear, forgive, leisure, not harm, protect, provide, refrain, release, reserve, scraggy, scrawny, slender, sparing, surplus **08** buckshee, leftover, part with, reprieve, unwanted, withhold **09** auxiliary, do without, emergency, remaining, safeguard, subsecive **10** additional, subsidiary, take care of, unoccupied **11** show mercy to, superfluous **12** dispense with **13** manage without, supernumerary, supplementary **15** all skin and bones
• **to spare**
05 extra **06** unused **07** surplus **08** left over **09** in reserve, remaining
• **with little to spare**
04 fine **06** narrow

sparing
05 canny, mingy, scant **06** frugal, meagre, scarce, stingy, strait **07** careful, miserly, prudent, thrifty **09** penurious **10** economical **11** close-fisted, tight-fisted

sparingly
06 nighly **08** frugally, meagrely, scrimply, stingily **09** carefully, prudently **12** economically

spark
03 bit, jot **04** atom, beau, funk, hint, iota **05** flake, flame, flare, flash, gleam, glint, lover, scrap, spunk, touch, trace **06** kindle **07** animate, bluette, flaught, flicker, glimmer, sparkle, vestige **08** skerrick **09** scintilla **10** suggestion **11** electrician
• **spark off**
04 stir **05** cause, start **06** excite, incite, kindle, prompt, set off **07** inspire, provoke, trigger **08** occasion, start off, touch off **09** stimulate **10** give rise to, trigger off **11** precipitate

sparkle
03 vim **04** beam, brio, dash, fire, fizz, glow, life, zest **05** flash, gleam, glint, shine, spark **06** bubble, dazzle, energy, spirit **07** be witty, emicate, flicker, glimmer, glisten, glister, glitter, pizzazz, shimmer, twinkle **08** be bubbly, be lively, radiance, vitality, vivacity **09** animation, coruscate, emication **10** be animated, be spirited, brilliance, ebullience, effervesce, enthusiasm, get-up-and-go, liveliness **11** be ebullient, be vivacious, coruscation, scintillate **13** scintillation **14** be effervescent, be enthusiastic

sparkling
05 fizzy, witty **06** bubbly, lively **07** emicant **08** aglitter, animated, flashing, gleaming, spritzig **09** brilliant, frizzante, pétillant, twinkling **10** carbonated, glistening, glittering **11** coruscating, scintillant **12** effervescent **13** scintillating
• **make sparkling**
09 carbonate

sparrow
04 tody **05** sprug **06** mossie **07** dunnock, pinnock, spadger, titling **08** accentor, prunella, ricebird **09** paddy-bird **11** whitethroat **13** hedge-accentor

sparse
04 rare, thin **06** meagre, scanty, scarce, slight **07** scrawny **08** scattery, sporadic **09** scattered **10** infrequent

sparsely
08 meagrely, scantily, scarcely, slightly **12** sporadically

spartan
05 bleak, hardy, harsh, plain **06** frugal, severe, simple, strict **07** ascetic, austere, harmost, joyless, laconic **08** rigorous **09** stringent, temperate **10** abstemious **11** disciplined, self-denying **12** militaristic

spasm
03 fit, tic **04** bout, grip, jerk **05** burst, cramp, crick, gripe, spell, start, thraw, throe, throw, tonus **06** access, attack, clonus, frenzy, hippus, throwe, twitch **07** seizure, trismus **08** eruption, outburst, paroxysm **10** blepharism, convulsion, tonic spasm **11** clonic spasm, contraction, laryngismus **12** childcrowing

spasmodic
◇ *anagram indicator*
05 jerky **06** fitful **07** erratic, spastic **08** periodic, sporadic **09** irregular **10** convulsive, occasional **12** intermittent

spasmodically
08 off and on, on and off **11** now and again **12** occasionally, periodically, sporadically **14** intermittently

spate
04 flow, rush **05** flood, speat **06** deluge, series **07** torrent **10** outpouring

spatter
◇ *anagram indicator*
03 jap **04** daub, jaup, soil **05** dirty, spray **06** bedaub, dabble, shower, splash **07** bestrew, scatter, speckle, splodge **08** splatter, sprinkle **09** bespatter **10** besprinkle

spawn
03 fry, roe **04** blot, make, redd, seed, spat, spit, teem **05** brood, cause, culch,

sperm **06** create, cultch, lead to **07** bring on, produce **08** engender, generate **09** offspring, originate **10** bring about, give rise to

spay
03 fix **04** geld **05** spade, spayd **06** doctor, neuter, spayad **08** castrate **09** sterilize **10** emasculate

speak
◇ *homophone indicator*
03 gab, say, yak **04** chat, mang, pipe, talk, tell, word **05** argue, sound, state, utter, voice **06** witter **07** address, chatter, declaim, declare, discuss, expound, express, lecture, mention **08** converse, describe, harangue, platform **09** enunciate, hold forth, pronounce **10** articulate **11** communicate **13** have a word with

• **speak angrily**
04 pelt

• **speak for**
06 act for **08** stand for **09** represent **15** speak on behalf of

• **speak of**
05 voice **07** discuss, mention, refer to **13** make mention of **15** make reference to

• **speak out**
03 ope **04** open **06** defend **07** protest, support **11** say publicly, speak openly

• **speak tediously**
05 prose

• **speak to**
04 warn **05** scold **06** accost, attest, bounce, carpet, rebuke **07** address, bawl out, discuss, lecture, rouse on, tell off, tick off, upbraid **08** admonish **09** dress down, go crook at, pull apart, reprimand, take apart **10** go to town on **11** bring to book **13** have a word with **14** throw the book at **15** give someone hell

• **speak up**
06 defend **07** protest, support **10** talk loudly **11** say publicly, speak openly **14** raise your voice, talk more loudly

speaker
05 mouth **06** orator, talker, woofer **07** tweeter **08** lecturer, top tweet **09** spokesman, subwoofer **10** mouthpiece, prolocutor **11** first person, spokeswoman **12** spokesperson

spear
03 ash, gad, gig **04** dart, gade, gaid, pike, pile, reed **05** lance, pilum, spire, stick **06** glaive, gleave, waster **07** assagai, assegai, harpoon, javelin, leister, trident **08** assegaai, gavelock, lancegay **09** boar-spear, demi-lance, fish-spear, handstaff, truncheon **12** burn the water

spearhead
03 van **04** head, lead **05** front, guide **06** launch, leader **07** pioneer **08** initiate, overseer, vanguard **09** front line **11** cutting edge, trailblazer **15** leading position

special
◇ *anagram indicator*
01 S **02** sp **05** exact, major **06** choice, select, unique **07** notable, precise, unusual **08** detailed, intimate, peculiar, singular, specific **09** different, dividuous, exclusive, important, memorable, momentous, red-letter **10** individual, noteworthy, particular, remarkable **11** distinctive, exceptional, outstanding, significant **13** distinguished, extraordinary **14** characteristic

specialist
06 brains, expert, master **07** attaché **08** boutique **09** authority **10** consultant **11** connoisseur **12** professional

Specialists include:

03 vet
07 Arabist, biblist, cambist, chemist
08 alienist, apiarist, aquarist, arborist, botanist, canonist
09 archivist, biblicist, biologist, Braillist, campanist, Celticist
10 aerologist, aeronomist, agrologist, agronomist, algebraist, algologist, batologist, biochemist, bryologist
11 carpologist
12 apiculturist, bibliopolist, biophysicist, bioscientist, cerographist, choreologist
13 acupuncturist, agrobiologist, anagrammatist, arachnologist, archaeologist, calligraphist, campanologist, carcinologist, chirographist
14 aerodynamicist, anthropologist, bacteriologist, chalcographist
15 agriculturalist, arboriculturist, biopsychologist, biotechnologist

See also **medical**

speciality
03 bag **04** gift **05** field, forte **06** talent **07** feature **08** strength **09** specialty **11** area of study **12** field of study

specialization
05 focus **12** special study **13** concentration **14** special subject **15** special interest

specialize
05 major, study **06** follow **07** focus on, major in, specify **13** concentrate on, differentiate

specially
◇ *anagram indicator*
07 express **08** uniquely **09** expressly **10** distinctly, explicitly **11** exclusively **12** in particular, particularly, specifically

species
02 sp **03** spp **04** kind, sort, type **05** breed, class, genus, group **07** variety **08** category **10** collection **11** description

specific
03 set **05** exact, fixed **07** express, limited, precise, special, trivial **08** clear-cut, concrete, definite, detailed, explicit **10** determined, particular **11** unambiguous, unequivocal, well-defined

specifically
07 clearly, exactly, plainly **09** expressly, specially **10** definitely, distinctly **11** exclusively **12** in particular, particularly **13** unambiguously

specification
04 item, spec **06** detail, naming **07** listing **09** condition, statement **10** particular **11** delineation, description, designation, instruction, requirement, stipulation **13** qualification

specify
04 cite, list, name **05** limit, state **06** assign, define, detail, set out **07** frutify, itemize, mention **08** describe, indicate, spell out **09** delineate, designate, enumerate, stipulate **10** condescend, specialize **13** particularize **14** condescend upon

specimen
04 copy, sort, swab, type **05** assay, model, piece **06** person, sample **07** example, exhibit, pattern **08** exemplar, instance, paradigm **12** illustration **14** representative

specious
04 fair **05** false, showy **06** untrue **07** pageant, unsound **08** imposing **09** beautiful, casuistic, deceptive, fair-faced, plausible, sophistic **10** fallacious, misleading **11** sophistical

speck
03 bit, dot, fat, jot, pip **04** atom, blot, flaw, iota, mark, mite, mote, peep, spek, spot, whit **05** bacon, fault, fleck, grain, peepe, shred, stain, trace **06** defect, sheave, tittle **07** blemish, floater, spangle, speckle **08** particle

speckled
03 gay **05** mealy **06** dotted, mealie, spotty, ticked **07** brinded, brindle, dappled, flecked, mottled, spotted **08** brindled, freckled, stippled **09** fleckered, sprinkled **11** lentiginous **13** trout-coloured

spectacle
04 shew, show **05** scene, sight **06** marvel, object, parade, wonder **07** display, pageant, picture **09** bullfight, curiosity, pageantry, raree-show **10** exhibition, outspeckle, phenomenon **11** performance **12** extravaganza, son et lumière

spectacles
02 OO **05** specs **06** specks **07** glasses, goggles, lorgnon **08** bifocals, cheaters, gig-lamps, horn-rims **09** barnacles, glass eyes, lorgnette, preserves, trifocals **10** eyeglasses, sunglasses, varifocals **13** granny glasses, pebble-glasses **14** National Health, pinhole glasses

spectacular
04 show **05** grand **06** daring
07 amazing, display, opulent, pageant
08 dazzling, dramatic, glorious, splendid, striking, stunning
09 colourful, spectacle **10** exhibition, flamboyant, impressive, remarkable, staggering **11** astonishing, eye-catching, magnificent, outstanding, resplendent, sensational
12 breathtaking, extravaganza, ostentatious **13** extraordinary

spectacularly
09 amazingly **10** gloriously, remarkably, strikingly, stunningly
12 impressively, staggeringly
13 astonishingly, magnificently, outstandingly, sensationally
15 extraordinarily

spectator
06 viewer **07** watcher, witness
08 beholder, looker-on, observer, onlooker, passer-by **09** bystander, ringsider **10** eyewitness, groundling, rubberneck, supervisor, wallflower

spectral
05 eerie, weird **06** spooky **07** ghostly, phantom, shadowy, uncanny
08 eldritch **09** phantosme, unearthly
11 disembodied, incorporeal
12 supernatural **13** insubstantial

spectre
04 fear **05** bogle, dread, ghost, larva, shade, spook **06** bodach, Empusa, menace, shadow, spirit, threat, vision, wraith **07** phantom **08** phantasm, presence, revenant, visitant
09 phantosme **10** apparition

spectrum
05 gamme, prism, range **07** rainbow
10 after-image

speculate
04 muse, risk, view **05** guess
06 gamble, hazard, wonder
07 examine, imagine, observe, reflect, suppose, surmise, venture **08** cogitate, consider, meditate, theorize
10 conjecture, deliberate
11 contemplate, hypothesize

speculation
04 risk, spec **05** flier, flyer, guess
06 gamble, hazard, theory, vision, wisdom **07** flutter, surmise, theoric, venture, viewing **08** gambling, ideology, observer **09** adventure, guesswork, theorique **10** conjecture, hypothesis, theorizing **11** imagination, supposition **12** deliberation
13 consideration, contemplation, flight of fancy **14** a shot in the dark

speculative
04 iffy **05** dicey, risky, vague **06** chancy
08 abstract, academic, notional, unproven **09** hazardous, tentative, theoretic, uncertain **10** indefinite
11 conjectural, theoretical
12 hypothetical, transcendent
13 suppositional, unpredictable

speculator
04 bear, bull **05** piker **07** gambler, lookout **08** boursier, watchman
09 pinhooker **10** adventurer, land-jobber **11** adventuress, speculatist, speculatrix, stockjobber **12** money-spinner

speech
◇ *anagram indicator*
◇ *homophone indicator*
03 say **04** rant, talk **05** lingo, spiel, voice **06** accent, homily, jargon, korero, parole, patter, rumour, saying, sermon, tirade, tongue **07** address, dialect, diction, lecture, mention, message, oration **08** colloquy, delivery, dialogue, diatribe, harangue, language, parlance **09** discourse, elocution, monologue, philippic, soliloquy, utterance **11** enunciation
12 articulation, conversation
13 communication, pronunciation

Parts of speech include:

01 a, n, v
02 vb, vi, vt
03 adj, adv, art
04 noun, prep, verb
06 adnoun, adverb, gerund, plural, prefix, suffix
07 article, pronoun
08 singular
09 adjective, gerundive
10 common noun, connective, copulative, participle, proper noun
11 conjunction, phrasal verb, preposition
12 abbreviation, interjection
13 auxiliary verb
14 transitive verb
15 definite article, relative pronoun

• **speech defect**
04 lisp **07** stammer, stutter
10 impediment

speechless
03 mum **04** dumb, mute **06** aghast, amazed, silent **07** shocked
08 unworded **09** astounded, voiceless
10 dumbstruck, struck dumb, tongue-tied **11** dumbfounded, obmutescent
12 inarticulate, languageless, lost for words **13** thunderstruck

speed
01 v **02** AS **03** bat, mph **04** belt, clip, dash, fare, knot, pace, pelt, race, rate, rush, tear, zoom **05** haste, hurry, tempo, whisk **06** career, cruise, gallop, hasten, hurtle, sprint **07** quicken, succeed, success **08** alacrity, celerity, despatch, dispatch, momentum, rapidity, step on it, velocity **09** bowl along, quickness, swiftness
10 accelerate, promptness
11 amphetamine **12** acceleration, step on the gas **14** step on the juice
15 expeditiousness, put your foot down

• **increase speed**
03 gun **10** accelerate, give the gun

• **speed up**
05 hurry **06** hasten, open up, spur on, step up **07** advance, forward, further, promote, quicken **08** expedite, go faster, step on it **09** stimulate
10 accelerate, facilitate **11** drive faster, gather speed, pick up speed, precipitate, put on a spurt **12** gain momentum, step on the gas **14** step on the juice **15** put your foot down

speedily
04 fast, post **06** pronto **07** betimes, hastily, on wings, quickly, rapidly, swiftly **08** in a hurry, promptly
09 hurriedly, posthaste **11** at the double
12 a mile a minute, lickety-split
13 expeditiously **14** at a rate of knots, hell for leather **15** like the clappers

speedwell
06 hen-bit **08** bird's-eye, fluellin, neckweed, veronica **09** brooklime

speedy
03 pdq **04** fast **05** hasty, nippy, quick, rapid, swift, zappy, zippy **06** nimble, prompt **07** cursory, express, hurried, summary **09** immediate, posthaste
11 expeditious, precipitate **15** pretty damn quick

spell
02 go **03** fit, hex, jag, ren, rin, run
04 bout, mean, mojo, pull, rest, rune, rung, scan, scat, span, tack, term, time, turn **05** augur, charm, imply, magic, patch, shift, skatt, spurt, stint, trick, weird **06** allure, course, extent, grigri, herald, lead to, lesson, period, season, signal, snatch, trance, whammy
07 cantrip, enchant, glamour, innings, portend, presage, promise, relieve, session, signify, sorcery, stretch, suggest **08** amount to, greegree, grisgris, indicate, interval, splinter, witchery **09** discourse, influence, magnetism **10** attraction, open sesame
11 abracadabra, bewitchment, conjuration, contemplate, enchantment, fascination, incantation, paternoster **12** drawing power, entrancement, supplication

• **cast a spell on**
05 charm **07** attract, bewitch, enchant, encharm, enthral **09** captivate, fascinate, mesmerize

• **spell out**
06 detail **07** clarify, explain, specify
09 elucidate, emphasize, make clear, stipulate

spellbinding
08 gripping, riveting **10** bewitching, enchanting, entrancing **11** captivating, enthralling, fascinating, mesmerizing

spellbound
04 rapt **07** charmed, gripped, riveted
09 bewitched, enchanted, entranced
10 captivated, enraptured, enthralled, fascinated, hypnotized, mesmerized, transfixed **11** transported

spelling
02 sp **11** orthography

spend
02 do **03** use **04** blow, fill, kill, live,

pass, shed, ware **05** apply, put in, use up, waste **06** devote, employ, expend, finish, invest, lay out, occupy, pay out, take up **07** consume, cough up, exhaust, fork out, fritter, outwear, stump up **08** contrive, disburse, shell out, squander **09** splash out, while away **14** spend like water

spendthrift
06 waster **07** wastrel **08** prodigal, profuser, unthrift, wasteful **10** high-roller, profligate, squanderer **11** extravagant, improvident, scattergood, squandering

spent
04 gone, used **05** all in, weary **06** bushed, done in, effete, fagged, pooped, used up, zonked **07** drained, wearied, whacked, worn out **08** burnt out, consumed, dead beat, dog-tired, expended, finished, jiggered, overworn, tired out, weakened **09** exhausted, fagged out, knackered, pooped out, shattered **11** debilitated, tuckered out

sperm
04 eggs **05** brood, semen, spawn **06** gamete **07** sex cell **08** germ cell **09** offspring **10** spermaceti **11** spermatozoa **12** seminal fluid, spermatozoon

spew
04 barf, emit, gush, puke **05** belch, issue, retch, spurt, vomit **06** sick up **07** bring up, chuck up, chunder, fetch up, spit out, throw up **08** disgorge **11** regurgitate

sphere
03 orb, set **04** area, ball, band, rank **05** class, crowd, field, globe, group, orbit, range, realm, round, scope, world **06** circle, clique, domain, extent, planet **07** compass, globule **08** capacity, function, province, universe **09** territory **10** department, discipline, speciality

spherical
05 round **06** global, rotund **07** globate, globoid, globose **08** globular **09** orbicular **10** ball-shaped **11** globe-shaped

spice
03 pep, zap, zip **04** kick, life, mull, stir, tang, vary, zest **05** gusto, hot up, liven, pep up, rouse, touch **06** buck up, colour, jazz up, perk up, relish, savour, stacte, stir up **07** animate, enliven, liven up **08** brighten, energize, ginger up, piquancy, tincture, vitalize **09** diversify, seasoning **10** excitement, flavouring, invigorate, sweetmeats **11** put life into

See also **herb**

spick and span
04 neat, tidy, trim **05** clean **06** spruce **08** polished, scrubbed, spotless, well-kept **09** shipshape **10** immaculate **11** uncluttered

spicy
03 hot **04** blue, racy, tart **05** adult, juicy, sharp, showy, tangy **06** ribald, risqué **07** peppery, picante, piquant, pointed, pungent, raunchy **08** aromatic, fragrant, improper, indecent, seasoned, unseemly **09** flavoured **10** indecorous, indelicate, scandalous, suggestive **11** flavoursome, near the bone, sensational **12** well-seasoned **14** near the knuckle

spider
07 beastie, spinner

Spiders and arachnids include:

03 red
04 bird, mite, tick, wolf
05 bolas, money, water, zebra
06 diadem, epeira, katipo, mygale, violin
07 araneid, harvest, hunting, jumping, limulus, redback
08 huntsman, scorpion, trapdoor
09 funnel-web, harvester, phalangid, tarantula
10 black widow, cheesemite, harvestman, saltigrade
11 harvest mite, harvest tick
12 book-scorpion, whip scorpion
13 horseshoe crab

spiel
04 line **05** pitch **06** patter, speech **07** oration, recital **11** sales patter

spies *see* **spy**

spignel
03 meu **09** baldmoney

spike
03 add, ear, gad, nib **04** barb, brod, cloy, drug, lace, nail, spit, tang, tine **05** beard, chape, mix in, point, prick, prong, rowel, spear, spick, spine, spire, stake, stick **06** catkin, impale, reject, skewer, spadix **07** bayonet, pricket **09** dosshouse, frustrate, strobilus **10** filopodium, projection **11** contaminate **13** Anglo-Catholic

spill
03 ren, rin, run, tip **04** drip, fall, flow, kill, leak, pour, shed, slop, well **05** scail, scale, skail, spile, taper, throw, upset, waste **06** escape, oozing, run out, tumble **07** cropper, destroy, fidibus, leakage, leaking, run over, scatter, seepage, seeping, slatter, swatter **08** accident, disgorge, overflow, overturn, spillage, spilling **09** discharge, pipe-light **11** lamplighter, percolation, pipe-lighter **13** candle-lighter

• **spill the beans**
03 rat **04** blab, tell **05** grass, split **06** inform, squeal, tell on **07** tell all **11** blow the gaff **15** give the game away

spin
◇ *anagram indicator*
03 cut, run **04** flap, play, reel, ride, tell, tizz, trip, turn **05** drive, jaunt, panic, spirt, state, swirl, tizzy, twirl, twist, wheel, whirl, whirr **06** circle, dither, gyrate, hurtle, invent, make up, outing, relate, rotate, swivel **07** draw out, dream up, fluster, go round, journey, narrate, revolve, twizzle **08** gyration, rotation **09** agitation, commotion, fabricate, pirouette, turn about, turn round **10** revolution

• **spin doctor**
03 pro **07** spinner

• **spin out**
06 extend, pad out **07** amplify, prolong **08** lengthen, protract, wiredraw **09** keep going

• **spin round**
04 gyre, purl

spindle
03 pin, rod **04** axis, axle, spit **05** arbor, fusee, fuzee, pivot, staff, verge

spindly
04 long, thin **05** lanky, weedy **06** gangly, skinny **07** spidery **08** fusiform, gangling, skeletal **09** attenuate **10** attenuated **14** spindle-shanked

spine
04 barb, grit, guts **05** chine, pluck, quill, spike, spunk, thorn **06** bottle, dorsum, mettle, needle, rachis, spirit **07** bravery, bristle, courage, prickle, rhachis, spinule **08** backbone, spiculum, strength **09** fortitude, Jew's-stone, ridge bone, vertebrae **10** resolution **12** spinal column **13** determination **15** ichthyodorulite, ichthyodorylite, vertebral column

spine-chilling
05 eerie, scary **06** spooky **10** horrifying, terrifying **11** frightening, hair-raising **13** bloodcurdling

spineless
03 wet **04** soft, weak **05** cissy, milky, timid, wussy **06** feeble, yellow **07** chicken, wimpish **08** boneless, cowardly, muticous, timorous **09** weak-kneed **10** indecisive, irresolute, spiritless, submissive **11** ineffective, lily-livered, vacillating **12** faint-hearted, invertebrate

spin-off
06 effect, result **10** side effect **11** consequence **12** repercussion **13** reverberation

spinster
07 old maid

spiny
05 spiky **06** briery, thorny **07** prickly, spinose, spinous, thistly **08** spicular **09** acanthoid, acanthous, perplexed, spiculate **11** spiniferous, spinigerous, troublesome **12** acanthaceous

spiral
04 coil, dive, go up, gyre, rise, soar, wind **05** climb, helix, screw, spire, twist, whorl **06** circle, coiled, gyrate, plunge, rocket, volute, wreath **07** cochlea, helical, plummet, voluted, whorled, winding, wreathe **08** circular, cochlear, curlicue, dive-bomb,

escalate, gyroidal, increase, nosedive, scrolled, tailspin, twisting, volution **09** cochleate, corkscrew, skyrocket **10** cochleated **11** convolution, drop rapidly, fall rapidly **15** decrease quickly

spire
03 tip, top **04** coil, cone, peak, reed **05** crest, crown, point, shoot, spear, spike, spyre, stalk, tower **06** belfry, broach, flèche, spiral, sprout, summit, turret **07** shoot up, steeple **08** pinnacle

spirit
02 ka **03** air, div, fay, imp, nix, pep, zip **04** atua, brio, deev, deva, fire, gist, grit, guts, jinn, kick, life, mind, mood, nixy, soul, zeal, zest **05** angel, anima, cheer, demon, devil, drift, fairy, fiend, force, genie, ghost, jinni, monad, nixie, pluck, sense, shade, spook, spunk, tenor, verve **06** ardour, bottle, breath, djinni, energy, humour, jinnee, kidnap, make-up, mettle, morale, psyche, shadow, sprite, temper, vigour, wraith **07** bravery, courage, essence, feeling, meaning, mindset, outlook, phantom, pizzazz, purport, quality, sparkle, spectre **08** attitude, backbone, feelings, presence, revenant, tendency, visitant, vivacity **09** animation, breathing, character, élan vital, elemental, encourage, inner self, kidnapper, principle, substance, willpower **10** apparition, atmosphere, complexion, enterprise, enthusiasm, inner being, liveliness, motivation, resolution, vital force **11** disposition, frame of mind, implication, state of mind, temperament **13** dauntlessness, determination **14** characteristic

See also **mythical**

• spirit away
05 carry, seize, steal, whisk **06** abduct, convey, kidnap, remove **07** capture, purloin, snaffle **08** abstract

spirited
04 bold, gamy, racy **05** fiery, gamey, gutty **06** active, ardent, feisty, gallus, lively, plucky, spunky **07** dashing, gallows, valiant, zealous **08** animated, resolute, spanking, stomachy, valorous, vigorous **09** confident, energetic, sparkling, vivacious **10** courageous, determined, mettlesome, passionate, sprightful, stomachful, stomachous **12** high-spirited

spiritless
03 low **04** cold, dead, dowf, dull, poor, tame, weak **05** amort, soggy **06** craven, droopy, jejune, mopish, torpid **07** anaemic, hilding, languid, unmoved **08** dejected, enervate, lifeless, listless **09** apathetic, bloodless, depressed, exanimate, inanimate **10** despondent, dispirited, lacklustre, melancholy, wishy-washy **11** sprightless **12** faint-hearted, muddy-mettled **14** unenthusiastic

spirit-level
04 vial

spirits
04 ginn, jinn, mood **05** djinn, hooch **06** humour, liquor, temper **07** alcohol **08** attitude, emotions, feelings **09** firewater, moonshine **11** strong drink, temperament **12** strong liquor, the hard stuff

Spirits include:

03 gin, kir, rum, rye
04 feni, grog, ouzo, raki, sake
05 fenny, Pimm's®, vodka
06 brandy, cognac, eggnog, geneva, grappa, kirsch, mescal, mezcal, pastis, Pernod®, poteen, Scotch, whisky
07 aquavit, Bacardi®, bitters, bourbon, Campari, dark rum, genever, pink gin, sloe gin, tequila, whiskey
08 Armagnac, Calvados, eau de vie, Hollands, hot toddy, sambucca, schnapps, vermouth, white rum, witblits
09 apple-jack, aqua vitae, framboise, golden rum, mirabelle, slivovitz, spiced rum
10 malt whisky, usquebaugh
11 gold tequila, Hollands gin, peach brandy
12 añejo tequila
13 peach schnapps, silver tequila
15 reposado tequila

See also **cocktail**; **liqueur**

spiritual
04 aery, holy **05** aerie, witty **06** clever, divine, sacred **07** psychic **08** ethereal, heavenly **09** pneumatic, psychical, religious, unfleshly, unworldly **10** devotional, immaterial, intangible **11** incorporeal **12** metaphysical, otherworldly, supernatural, transcendent **14** ecclesiastical

spit
03 dig, gob, yex **04** fuff, hawk, hiss, hook, jack, rasp, slag, spet, yesk **05** drool, eject, issue, spade, spawl, spawn, spume, sword **06** bespit, broach, phlegm, saliva, skewer, slaver, sputum **07** dribble, replica, spittle, sputter **08** broacher, emptysis, spadeful, splutter, turnspit **09** brochette, discharge, smoke-jack **10** rotisserie **11** expectorate **13** expectoration

• spitting image
04 twin **05** clone **06** double, ringer **07** picture, replica **08** dead spit, likeness **09** lookalike **10** dead ringer **13** exact likeness

spite
03 irk, vex **04** evil, gall, hate, hurt **05** annoy, upset, venom, wound **06** grudge, hatred, injure, malice, maugre, offend, put out, rancor, spight, thwart **07** ill-will, maulgre, provoke, rancour **08** irritate **09** animosity, hostility, ill nature, malignity, vengeance **10** bitterness, ill-feeling, resentment **11** malevolence **12** hard feelings, spitefulness **13** maliciousness **14** vindictiveness

• in spite of
03 for **04** with **06** malgré, maugre **07** against, defying, despite, maulgre **08** after all, malgrado **11** in the face of **12** nevertheless, regardless of, undeterred by **13** be that as it may **15** notwithstanding

spiteful
05 catty, cruel, nasty, petty, snide **06** barbed, bitchy, bitter, shrewd, wicked **07** cattish, hostile, vicious, waspish **08** vengeful, venomous, viperish **09** cat-witted, malicious, malignant, rancorous, resentful **10** ill-natured, malevolent, vindictive **11** ill-disposed **12** evil-tempered

spitefully
07 cruelly **08** bitchily, bitterly **10** venomously **11** maliciously, resentfully **12** malevolently, vindictively

spitting image *see* **spit**

splash
◇ *anagram indicator*
03 jap, lap, wet **04** beat, dash, daub, jaup, plop, show, slop, soss, spat, spot, stir, wade, wash **05** bathe, blash, blaze, break, burst, patch, plash, slosh, slush, smack, spray, stain, surge, swash, touch **06** batter, bedash, blazon, buffet, dabble, effect, flaunt, flouse, floush, impact, jabble, paddle, plunge, shower, sozzle, splish, splosh, spread, squirt, streak, strike, wallow **07** beating, display, exhibit, plaster, scatter, slatter, spatter, splatch, splodge, splotch, splurge, swatter, trumpet **08** splatter, sprinkle, squatter **09** publicity, publicize, sensation **10** excitement, impression **11** ostentation

• splash out
05 spend **07** lash out, splurge **08** invest in **13** be extravagant **14** push the boat out

spleen
03 pip **04** bile, gall, lien, melt, milt **05** anger, miltz, mirth, pique, spite, venom, wrath **06** animus, hatred, malice **07** boredom, caprice, ill-will, impulse, rancour, stomach **08** acrimony **09** animosity, bad temper, hostility, ill-humour, malignity **10** bitterness, melancholy, resentment **11** biliousness, malevolence, peevishness **12** spitefulness **14** vindictiveness

splendid
04 braw, fine, rich **05** bonny, grand, great, jolly, super **06** bonnie, bright, divine, lavish, superb **07** gallant, glowing, opulent, radiant, stately, sublime, supreme **08** dazzling, fabulous, glorious, gorgeous, imposing, lustrous, pontific, renowned, terrific **09** admirable, brilliant, effulgent, excellent, luxurious, refulgent, sumptuous, wonderful **10** celebrated, first-class, glittering, impressive, marvellous, pontifical,

remarkable **11** exceptional, illustrious, magnificent, outstanding, resplendent **13** distinguished

splendidly
07 grandly **08** superbly **09** admirably **10** remarkably **11** brilliantly, wonderfully **12** impressively, marvellously **13** exceptionally, magnificently, outstandingly

splendour
04 glow, pomp, show **05** éclat, gleam, glory, pride **06** dazzle, finery, fulgor, luster, lustre, luxury **07** display, fulgour, majesty, panache **08** ceremony, flourish, grandeur, opulence, radiance, richness **09** solemnity, spectacle **10** brightness, brilliance **12** magnificence, resplendence **13** sumptuousness **15** illustriousness

splenetic
04 acid, sour **05** angry, cross, ratty, testy **06** bitchy, crabby, morose, sullen, touchy **07** bilious, crabbed, fretful, peevish **08** choleric, churlish, petulant, spiteful **09** envenomed, irascible, irritable, irritated, rancorous **10** melancholy **11** atrabilious, bad-tempered

splice
◇ *anagram indicator*
03 tie **04** bind, join, knit, mesh **05** braid, graft, marry, plait, unite **06** fasten **07** connect, entwine **09** interlace **10** intertwine, interweave

• get spliced
03 wed **10** get hitched, get married, tie the knot **13** take the plunge **15** plight your troth

splinter
03 bit **04** chip, flaw **05** break, flake, piece, shard, shred, skelf, smash, spale, spall, spalt, speel, spelk, spell, split **06** cleave, paring, shiver, sliver, splint **07** crumble, flinder, shatter, shaving, spicula, spicule **08** flinders, fracture, fragment **11** smithereens **12** disintegrate **15** break into pieces

split
◇ *insertion indicator*
03 cut, gap, rat, rip **04** chop, dual, open, part, rend, rent, rift, rive, shop, slit, tear **05** allot, break, burst, cleft, crack, grass, halve, leave, peach, sever, shake, share, slash, spall, spalt, wreck **06** betray, bisect, breach, broken, cleave, cloven, divide, rumble, schism, shiver, sliver, spring, sprung, squeal, stitch, tell on **07** break up, break-up, carve up, cracked, crevice, disband, discord, disrupt, divided, divorce, divulge, dole out, fissure, hand out, rupture, spalted, stool on, twofold **08** allocate, bisected, cleavage, crevasse, disunion, disunite, division, inform on, ruptured, separate, set apart, share-out, splinter **09** apportion, fractured, parcel out, partition **10** alienation, difference, dissension, distribute, divergence, separation **11** incriminate, part company **12** estrangement **14** dissociate from **15** become alienated, become estranged

• split up
04 part **06** divide **07** break up, disband, divorce **08** separate **11** get divorced, part company

split-up
07 break-up, divorce, parting **10** alienation, separation **12** estrangement

spoil
◇ *anagram indicator*
03 end, gum, mar, mux, pie, ret, rot **04** baby, cook, foul, game, harm, hurt, kill, rait, rate, ruin, sour, turn **05** bitch, blunk, bodge, booty, botch, bribe, decay, go bad, go off, gum up, louse, queer, strip, taint, upset, wreck, wrong **06** boodle, coddle, cosset, curdle, damage, deface, deform, foul up, go sour, impair, injure, mangle, mess up, murder, pamper, poison, prizes, quarry, wash up **07** bauchle, bitch up, blemish, butcher, corrupt, deprive, despoil, destroy, distort, indulge, louse up, pillage, plunder, pollute, screw up, tarnish, viciate, vitiate **08** distaste, go rotten, mutilate **09** decompose, disfigure, spoon-feed, vulgarize **10** impairment, obliterate, spoliation **11** contaminate, deteriorate, mollycoddle, overindulge, prejudicate **12** acquisitions, become rotten, put a damper on **15** cast a shadow over, pour cold water on

• spoil for
07 long for **08** be keen on, yearn for **10** be eager for, be intent on

spoils
04 gain, haul, loot, swag **05** booty, bribe **06** boodle, damage, prizes, profit, trophy **07** benefit, pillage, plunder, spulzie, the game **08** pickings, winnings **10** impairment, spoliation **11** spolia opima **12** acquisitions, despoliation

spoilsport
04 nark **06** damper, misery, wowser **07** killjoy, meddler **08** buzzkill **10** wet blanket **11** party-pooper **14** dog in the manger

spoke
04 rung **06** radius

spoken
◇ *homophone indicator*
03 sed **04** oral, said, told **06** stated, verbal, voiced **07** uttered **08** declared, phonetic, viva voce **09** expressed, unwritten

spokesman, spokeswoman
05 agent, mouth, voice **06** broker, orator **07** foreman **08** delegate, mediator **09** forewoman, go-between **10** arbitrator, foreperson, mouthpiece, negotiator, prolocutor **12** intermediary, propagandist, spokesperson **14** representative

sponge
03 beg, bum, mop **04** mump, swab, wash, wipe **05** cadge, clean, mooch, mouch, shool, shule **06** bludge, borrow, loofah, shoole, spunge, sucker **07** monaxon, zimocca **08** bedeguar, drunkard, freeload, hanger-on, parasite, quandang, quandong, quantong, scrounge, victoria **09** glass-rope, hyalonema, sea orange **13** mermaid's glove, sulphur sponge

See also **drunkard**

• sponge cake
06 coburg, trifle **09** lamington, madeleine, Swiss roll **11** lady's finger **12** lady's fingers **14** charlotte russe

• sponge spicule
06 hexact, sclere, tylote **07** monaxon, pentact, rhabdus, tetract, triaxon **08** polyaxon, tetraxon, triaxial **09** polyaxial, spiraster

sponger
03 bum **06** beggar, bummer, cadger **07** bludger, moocher **08** borrower, hanger-on, parasite, scambler **09** scrounger **10** freeloader, smell-feast

spongy
◇ *anagram indicator*
04 fozy, soft **05** light **06** poachy, porous **07** drunken, elastic, fungous, springy, squashy **08** cushiony, yielding **09** absorbent, cushioned, resilient **10** absorptive, cancellate, cancellous **11** cancellated

sponsor
04 back, fund **05** angel, vouch **06** backer, friend, gossip, patron, surety **07** finance, promise, promote, support **08** bankroll, promoter, stand for **09** godfather, godmother, guarantee, guarantor, patronize, subsidize, supporter, susceptor **10** subsidizer, undertaker, underwrite **11** be a patron of, underwriter

sponsorship
03 aid **05** funds, grant **07** backing, finance, subsidy, support **09** patronage, promotion **10** assistance **11** endorsement **12** financial aid

spontaneity
07 impulse **08** instinct **11** naturalness **13** improvisation **15** extemporization, instinctiveness

spontaneous
04 free **06** reflex **07** natural, willing **08** free-will, knee-jerk, unbidden, unforced, untaught **09** automatic, autonomic, extempore, impromptu, impulsive, unplanned, unstudied, voluntary **10** ultroneous, unprompted **11** instinctive, uncompelled, unrehearsed **12** unhesitating **14** unpremeditated **15** spur of the moment

spontaneously
05 ad-lib **06** freely **09** extempore, impromptu, on impulse, unplanned, willingly **10** off the cuff, unprompted

11 impulsively, voluntarily
13 instinctively 15 of your own accord

spoof
03 con 04 fake, game, hoax, joke
05 bluff, prank, trick 06 parody, satire, send-up 07 lampoon, leg-pull, mockery, take-off 08 travesty
09 burlesque, deception 10 caricature

spooky
05 eerie, scary, weird 06 creepy
07 ghostly, macabre, uncanny
08 chilling 09 unearthly 10 mysterious
11 frightening, hair-raising
12 supernatural 13 spine-chilling

spool
04 pirn, reel 06 bobbin 07 trundle

spoon
05 court, labis, ladle, scoop 07 spatula
08 cochlear 09 cochleare, courtship, simpleton

spoon-feed
04 baby 05 spoil 06 cosset, pamper
07 indulge 10 featherbed
11 mollycoddle, overindulge

sporadic
06 random, uneven 07 erratic
08 episodic, isolated 09 irregular, scattered, spasmodic 10 episodical, infrequent, occasional 12 intermittent

sporadically
08 off and on, on and off 10 now and then 11 now and again 12 occasionally, periodically 13 spasmodically
14 intermittently

sport
◇ *anagram indicator*
03 fun, gig 04 game, jest, joke, laik, lake, play, wear 05 amuse, mirth, wager
06 banter, frolic, humour, joking, trifle
07 display, exhibit, jesting, kidding, mockery, pastime, show off, teasing
08 activity, exercise, pleasure, ridicule, sneering, squander 09 amusement, dalliance, diversion, plaything
10 recreation 13 entertainment

See also **athletics**; **American football**; **Australian football**; **baseball**; **boxing**; **competition**; **cricket**; **football**; **golf**; **gymnastics**; **ice hockey**; **race**; **rugby**; **stadium**; **tennis**

Sports include:

04 golf, judo, polo, pool
05 bowls, darts, fives, rugby
06 boules, boxing, discus, diving, futsal, hockey, karate, kung fu, luging, Nascar®, pelota, quoits, rowing, shinty, skiing, slalom, soccer, squash, tennis
07 angling, aquafit, archery, camogie, cricket, croquet, curling, fencing, fishing, gliding, hunting, hurling, jogging, jujitsu, keep-fit, netball, putting, running, sailing, shot put, snooker, surfing, walking
08 aerobics, baseball, biathlon, canoeing, climbing, football, handball, high-jump, hurdling, lacrosse, long-jump, pétanque, ping-pong, rounders, shooting, swimming, trotting, yachting
09 athletics, badminton, billiards, bobsleigh, decathlon, go-karting, ice-hockey, pole vault, pot-holing, sky-diving, tae kwon do, triathlon, water polo, wrestling
10 basketball, drag-racing, gymnastics, ice-skating, pentathlon, real tennis, skin-diving, triple-jump, volleyball
11 cycle racing, horse-racing, motor racing, show-jumping, table-tennis, tobogganing, water-skiing, windsurfing
12 aqua aerobics, cross-country, orienteering, pitch and putt, rock-climbing, snowboarding, speed skating, trampolining
13 bungee jumping, coarse fishing, roller-skating, tenpin bowling, weightlifting
14 downhill skiing, Gaelic football, mountaineering, speedway racing, stock-car racing
15 greyhound-racing

Sports equipment includes:

03 bow, cue, fly, jig, mat, net, oar, ski, tee
04 bail, bait, beam, bolt, bowl, épée, foil, gaff, hook, jack, lure, mask, mitt, nets, pins, puck, rack, reel, rest, rope, shot, wood
05 arrow, boule, brush, caman, chalk, float, rings, sabre, stump, table, trace
06 bridge, discus, fly rod, hammer, hurley, priest, spider, wicket
07 cue ball, fly reel, javelin, keep-net, netball, snorkel
08 aqualung, baseball, crossbow, football, gang-hook, golfball, golf club, ice-skate, punch-bag, ski stick, toboggan, water-ski
09 disgorger, face-guard, gum shield, punch-ball, rugby ball, sailboard, snow board, surfboard
10 basketball, cricket bat, fishing-rod, hockey ball, roller boot, skateboard, speed skate, tennis ball, trampoline, volleyball
11 balance beam, baseball bat, bowling ball, boxing glove, cricket ball, fishing-line, hockey skate, hockey stick, in-line skate, paternoster, pommel horse, racket press, rollerblade, roller-skate, shuttlecock, snooker ball, spinning rod, springboard
12 billiard ball, curling stone, golfing glove, isometric bar, parallel-bars, tennis racket
13 catcher's glove, horizontal bar, vaulting horse
14 ice-hockey stick
15 badminton racket

Sports positions include:

04 lock, slip, wing
05 cover, gully, mid-on, point, rover
06 batter, centre, goalie, hooker, libero, long on, mid-off, setter, winger
07 batsman, catcher, fine leg, flanker, fly-half, fly slip, forward, leg slip, long leg, long off, number 8, pitcher, ruckman, sweeper, torpedo
08 attacker, backstop, defender, fullback, halfback, left back, left wing, long stop, short leg, split end, third man, tight end, wing back
09 deep cover, deep point, first base, first slip, left field, left guard, leg gulley, mid-wicket, right back, right wing, ruck rover, scrum-half, short stop, square leg, third base, third slip
10 back pocket, cover point, defenceman, extra cover, goal attack, goalkeeper, goaltender, inside left, left tackle, midfielder, point guard, right field, right guard, second base, second slip, silly mid-on, silly point, wing attack
11 centre field, deep fine leg, full-forward, goal defence, goal shooter, inside right, left forward, prop forward, quarterback, right tackle, silly mid-off, wing defence
12 left half-back, power forward, right forward, short fine leg, small forward, stand-off half, wicketkeeper
13 backward point, centre-forward, deep mid-wicket, deep square leg, forward pocket, half-back flank, loosehead prop, right half-back, shooting guard, tighthead prop
14 centre half-back, deep extra cover, left corner-back, short mid-wicket
15 left half-forward, right corner-back, short extra cover

sporting
◇ *anagram indicator*
04 fair, just 06 decent, modest
08 ladylike 10 honourable, reasonable
11 considerate, gentlemanly, respectable 13 sportsmanlike

sportive
03 gay 05 ludic, merry 06 frisky, jaunty, lively, wanton 07 amorous, coltish, playful, toysome 08 gamesome, prankish, skittish 09 kittenish, ludicrous, sprightly, vivacious
10 frolicsome, rollicking

sportsperson
04 blue, jock

Sportspeople include:

04 **Bird** (Larry), **Dean** (Christopher), **Khan** (Jahangir), **Lowe** (John), **Nudd** (Bob), **Witt** (Katerina)
05 **Curry** (John), **Davis** (Fred), **Davis** (Joe), **Davis** (Steve), **Ender** (Kornelia), **Kelly** (Sean), **O'Neal** (Shaquille), **Spitz** (Mark), **White** (Jimmy)
06 **Briggs** (Karen), **Bryant** (David), **Davies** (Sharron), **Fraser** (Dawn), **Hendry** (Stephen), **Jordan** (Michael), **LeMond** (Greg), **Malone** (Karl), **Merckx** (Eddy), **Pulman** (John), **Wilkie** (David), **Wilson** (Jocky)

07 Allcock (Tony), Bristow (Eric), Cousins (Robin), Gretzky (Wayne), Harding (Tonya), Higgins (Alex 'Hurricane'), Hinault (Bernard), Johnson (Earvin 'Magic'), O'Reilly (Wilfred), Reardon (Ray), Rodnina (Irina), Torvill (Jayne), Zaitsev (Aleksandr)
08 Boardman (Chris), Indurain (Miguel), Kerrigan (Nancy), Redgrave (Sir Steve), Williams (Rex)
09 Cipollini (Mario), Hazelwood (Mike)
10 Barrington (Jonah)
11 Abdul-Jabbar (Kareem), Chamberlain (Wilt 'the Stilt'), Weissmuller (Johnny)

See also **athlete**; **Australian football**; **baseball**; **boxer**; **chess**; **cricket**; **footballer**; **golfer**; **gymnastics**; **horseman, horsewoman**; **motor**; **mountaineering**; **rugby**; **skier**; **tennis**

sporty
03 fit **04** loud **05** natty, showy **06** casual, flashy, jaunty, lively, snazzy, trendy **07** outdoor, stylish **08** athletic, informal **09** energetic

spot
03 bit, dot, eye, fix, jam, pin, pip, see, zit **04** area, bite, blob, blot, blur, boil, daub, drop, espy, flaw, fret, give, hole, lend, mail, mark, meal, mess, moil, mold, mole, peep, plot, pock, show, site, slot, smut, soil, some, sore, time, turn **05** cloud, fleck, freak, hilum, naeve, nerve, nevus, niche, patch, peepe, place, plook, plouk, point, pupil, scene, speck, stain, sully, swale, taint **06** blotch, descry, detect, garden, little, locale, locate, macula, morsel, naevus, notice, papula, papule, pickle, pimple, plight, recess, scrape, smudge, splash, stigma **07** airtime, blemish, discern, flecker, freckle, lentigo, make out, observe, ocellus, opening, pick out, pustule, setting, spangle, speckle, splodge, splotch, tarnish, trouble **08** fenestra, identify, locality, location, maculate, position, quandary **09** birthmark, blackhead, freckling, programme, recognize, reprehend, situation **10** cicatricle, death-token, difficulty, maculation **11** cicatricula, performance, predicament, small amount **12** catch sight of, cicatrichule **13** discoloration

• **on the spot**
02 in **04** down, next **05** alert **06** at once, pronto **07** quickly **08** directly, in a jiffy, promptly, right now, speedily, sur place **09** forthwith, instantly, like a shot, right away **10** this minute **11** immediately, this instant **12** straight away, there and then, without delay **13** straightforth, with a siserary **14** unhesitatingly, without more ado **15** before you know it, instantaneously, without question

• **spot-on**
04 true **05** close, exact, right **06** bang on, dead-on, strict **07** correct, factual, precise **08** accurate, definite, detailed, explicit, flawless, specific, unerring **09** excellent, faultless, on the nail **10** on the money **11** on the button

spotless
04 pure **05** clean, white **06** chaste, virgin **07** shining **08** gleaming, innocent, unmarked, virginal **09** blameless, faultless, snow-white, unstained, unsullied, untainted, untouched **10** immaculate **11** unblemished **12** spick and span **14** irreproachable

spotlight
04 baby, fame, spot **05** brute **06** stress **07** feature, focus on, point up **08** emphasis, interest **09** attention, emphasize, highlight, limelight, notoriety, public eye, underline **10** accentuate, foreground, illuminate **15** draw attention to, public attention, throw into relief

spotted
03 gay **04** pied **06** dotted, macled, parded, spotty **07** brindle, dappled, flecked, guttate, macular, mottled, piebald **08** brindled, guttated, maculose, polka-dot, speckled

spotty
04 pied, poxy **05** acned, bitty **06** dotted, measly, patchy, pimply, uneven **07** blotchy, dappled, erratic, flecked, mottled, piebald, pimpled, spotted, varying **08** speckled **12** inconsistent

spouse
04 feer, fere, mate, wife **05** feare, fiere, hubby **06** missus, pheere **07** consort, husband, partner **09** companion, other half **10** better half

spout
03 jet **04** blow, emit, flow, go on, gush, pawn, pour, rant, rose, spew **05** chute, erupt, mouth, orate, shoot, spiel, spray, spurt, surge **06** geyser, nozzle, outlet, squirt, stream, stroup, waffle, witter **07** bespout, declaim **08** disgorge, fountain, gargoyle, pawnshop, rabbit on, spout off, witter on **09** discharge, expatiate, hold forth, sermonize **10** spout forth, waterspout **11** pontificate

sprain
03 hip **04** pull, rick, turn **05** crick, stave, twist, wrest, wrick **06** injure, wrench **09** dislocate **12** shoulder slip

sprat
04 brit, Jack **06** garvie **07** garvock **08** brisling

sprawl
04 flop, loll **05** slump, trail **06** lounge, ramble, repose, slouch, spread **07** recline, scamble, stretch **08** sprangle, straggle

spray
◇ *anagram indicator*
03 jet, wet **04** Alar®, foam, gush, Mace®, mist, posy, scud, twig **05** froth, shoot, spout, sprig, spume, swish **06** branch, drench, mister, shower, spritz, squirt, wreath **07** aerosol, bouquet, corsage, diffuse, drizzle, garland, nosegay, scatter, spatter, sprayer **08** aigrette, atomizer, disperse, moisture, mothball, nebulize, spray gun, sprinkle, vaporize **09** aspersion, nebulizer, spindrift, sprinkler, squirt gun, vaporizer **10** golden rose, propellant, spoondrift, waterspout **11** disseminate **13** water-sprinkle

spread
◇ *anagram indicator*
03 air, lay, ren, rin, run, set, sow, ted **04** coat, grow, laid, open, span, teer, walk **05** apply, cover, feast, flare, layer, order, party, put on, ranch, reach, scale, smear, spray, strew, sweep, swell, treat, widen **06** dilate, dinner, effuse, expand, extend, extent, fan out, lay out, mantle, repast, slairg, smooth, sprawl, unfold, unfurl, unroll **07** advance, arrange, banquet, blow-out, broaden, compass, develop, diffuse, enlarge, expanse, go round, open out, overlay, publish, radiate, scatter, stretch **08** disperse, escalate, extended, get round, increase, mushroom, swelling, transmit **09** advertise, broadcast, circulate, diffusion, displayed, expansion, large meal, make known, percolate, propagate, publicize, spill over **10** dispersion, distribute, escalation, gain ground, grow bigger, make public, promulgate **11** communicate, development, dinner party, disseminate, mushrooming, proliferate, propagation **12** become bigger, broadcasting, distribution, transmission **13** communication, dissemination, proliferation

Spreads include:

03 jam
04 marg, oleo, pâté
05 honey, marge
06 butter
07 Marmite®, Nutella®
08 dripping, Vegemite®
09 butterine, lemon curd, margarine, marmalade
11 lemon cheese
12 peanut butter
13 oleomargarine

spree
03 bat, bum, jag **04** bout, bust, orgy, tear **05** binge, blind, fling, revel, skite, skyte **06** bender, junket, randan, razzle, splore **07** blinder, carouse, debauch, splurge **08** jamboree **12** razzle-dazzle

sprig
04 brad, stem, twig **05** bough, scion, shoot, spray **06** branch

sprightly
04 airy, spry **05** agile, brisk, perky **06** active, blithe, gallus, hearty, jaunty, lively, nimble, sprack **07** gallows, ghostly, playful **08** animated, cheerful,

spirited **09** energetic, mercurial, vivacious **10** frolicsome, spirituous **12** light-hearted

spring
◇ *anagram indicator*
03 eye, gin, hop, lep, spa **04** bend, bolt, come, dawn, give, grow, hair, jump, leap, Lent, open, rise, root, skip, stem, stot, voar, ware, warp, well **05** arise, basis, bound, burst, cause, copse, crack, dance, issue, prime, shoot, spang, split, start, vault, youth **06** appear, bounce, derive, emerge, energy, geyser, origin, pounce, recoil, salina, source, spirit, sprout, strain **07** descend, develop, emanate, explode, proceed, rebound **08** balneary, brine-pan, brine-pit, buoyancy, wellhead **09** animation, beginning, briskness, originate **10** bounciness, elasticity, liveliness, resilience, wellspring **11** black smoker, flexibility, springiness, undergrowth **12** cheerfulness, fountainhead **14** reveal suddenly

• **spring up**
04 grow, rise **05** start **06** upblow **07** develop, shoot up **08** fountain, mushroom, sprout up **11** proliferate **13** come into being **14** appear suddenly

springtime *see* **spring**

springy
05 crisp, lofty **06** bouncy, spongy **07** buoyant, elastic, rubbery, squidgy, tensile **08** flexible, stretchy, tensible **09** resilient

sprinkle
◇ *anagram indicator*
03 dot, set **04** drop, dust, salt, sand, seed, sift **05** flake, flour, spang, spray, strew, sugar **06** dredge, pepper, pounce, powder, shower, sparge, splash **07** asperge, sawdust, scatter, spairge, spatter, trickle **08** beflower, disponge, dispunge, lavender, strinkle **09** bespatter, diversify **10** scowdering **11** aspersorium, scouthering

sprinkling
03 few **04** dash **05** touch, trace **07** baptism, dusting, handful, scatter, sifting, trickle **08** sprinkle **09** admixture, aspersion **10** scattering, smattering

sprint
03 fly, run, zip **04** belt, dart, dash, race, tear **05** scoot, shoot **06** career, scurry

sprite
03 elf, imp, pug **04** bogy, puck **05** bogle, dryad, fairy, gnome, kelpy, naiad, nymph, pixie, pouke, sylph **06** goblin, kelpie, spirit **07** apsaras, brownie, spright **10** apparition, leprechaun **11** water spirit

sprout
03 bud **04** chit, germ, grow **05** scion, shoot, spire, spirt **06** come up, spring **07** develop, tendron **08** put forth, spring up **09** germinate, pullulate, turnip top **10** descendant

spruce
04 chic, cool, neat, smug, trim **05** brisk, natty, nifty, Picea, sleek, smart, smirk, spiff, Tsuga **06** dapper, snazzy, spiffy, sprush **07** band-box, elegant, finical, hemlock, smarten **11** well-dressed, well-groomed **13** well-turned-out

• **spruce up**
04 tidy **05** groom, preen, primp **06** neaten, tart up, tidy up **08** titivate **09** smarten up

spry
05 agile, alert, brisk, nippy, peppy, quick, ready **06** active, nimble, supple **09** energetic, sprightly

spud *see* **potato**

spume
04 fizz, foam, head, scum, spit, suds **05** froth, yeast **06** lather **07** bubbles **13** effervescence

spunk
04 grit, guts **05** heart, match, nerve, pluck, spark **06** bottle, fire up, mettle, spirit, tinder **07** courage **08** backbone, chutzpah, gameness **09** touchwood, toughness **10** resolution

spur
04 goad, heel, limb, poke, prod, stud, urge **05** drive, ergot, impel, prick, prong, rowel, spica, spike, strut **06** branch, calcar, fillip, hasten, incite, induce, motive, offset, prompt, propel, Rippon, siding, spurne **07** impetus **08** motivate, stimulus **09** encourage, incentive, star wheel, stimulant, stimulate **10** incitement, inducement, motivation, projection, protrusion **12** embranchment, protuberance **13** encouragement

• **on the spur of the moment**
08 suddenly **09** extempore, impromptu, on impulse, on the spot **10** upon the gad **11** impetuously, impulsively **12** unexpectedly **13** spontaneously, thoughtlessly **15** without planning

spurious
◇ *anagram indicator*
03 bad, dog **04** fake, mock, sham **05** bogus, cronk, false **06** forged, phoney, pseudo **07** bastard, feigned **08** pseudish **09** contrived, deceitful, imitation, pretended, simulated, trumped-up **10** adulterate, adulterine, apocryphal, artificial, fraudulent **11** counterfeit, make-believe **12** illegitimate **14** supposititious

spurn
04 kick, snub, trip **05** scorn, tread **06** ignore, rebuff, reject, slight **07** condemn, despise, disdain, repulse, say no to **08** turn away, turn down **09** disregard, repudiate **10** look down on **12** cold-shoulder

spurt
03 fit, jet **04** boak, bock, boke, gush, kick, pour, pump, rush, spin, well **05** burst, erupt, issue, shoot, spate, spray, start, surge **06** access, skoosh, squirt, stream **07** welling **08** eruption, increase **10** outpouring

spy
03 eye, see **04** espy, look, mole, nark, spie, spot, tout, wait **05** agent, plant, scout, spial, spook, spyal **06** beagle, descry, notice, setter, shadow, survey **07** discern, glimpse, make out, observe, sleeper, snooper **08** discover, emissary, mouchard **10** enemy agent **11** double agent, secret agent, under-espial **12** catch sight of, foreign agent **13** intelligencer **14** fifth columnist **15** undercover agent

Spies include:

03 Pym (Magnus)
04 Bond (James), Hale (Nathan), Hiss (Alger)
05 André (John), Blake (George), Blunt (Anthony Frederick), Fuchs (Klaus Emil Julius), Karla, Szabo (Violette), Wynne (Greville)
06 Howell (James), Philby (Kim), Smiley (George), Tubman (Harriet), Vidocq (Eugène François), Werner (Ruth)
07 Burgess (Guy Francis de Moncy), Maclean (Donald)
08 Lonsdale (Gordon Arnold), Mata Hari
09 Carstares (William), Rosenberg (Ethel), Rosenberg (Julius)
10 Cairncross (John)

• **spies**
02 MI **03** CIA, KGB, MI5, MI6 **05** Stasi **06** Mossad

• **spy on**
04 tout **05** watch **07** observe **10** keep tabs on **11** keep an eye on **14** observe closely

spymaster
01 M

squabble
03 row **04** spat, tiff, tift **05** argue, brawl, clash, fight, scrap, set to, set-to **06** barney, bicker **07** dispute, quarrel, rhubarb, wrangle **08** argument **09** have words **12** disagreement

squad
03 set **04** band, crew, gang, team, unit **05** force, group, troop **06** outfit **07** brigade, company, platoon

squadron
03 red, RYS, sqn **04** blue **10** escadrille

squalid
03 low **04** foul, mean, vile **05** dingy, dirty, grimy, mucky, nasty, ribby, seedy **06** filthy, grotty, grubby, sleazy, slummy, sordid, untidy **07** obscene, run-down, unclean, unkempt **08** improper, shameful, slovenly, wretched **09** neglected, offensive, repulsive **10** broken-down, Dickensian, disgusting, ramshackle, uncared-for, unpleasant **11** dilapidated, disgraceful

squall
03 cry **04** blow, drow, gale, gust, howl,

moan, wail, wind, yell, yowl **05** groan, storm **06** flurry **07** sumatra, tempest **08** williwaw **09** hurricane, windstorm

squally
04 wild **05** blowy, gusty, rough, windy **06** stormy **07** gustful **08** blustery **09** turbulent **10** blustering **11** tempestuous

squalor
04 dirt, slum **05** decay, filth, grime **07** neglect, skid row **08** dung-heap, dung-hill, foulness, meanness, skid road **09** dinginess, dirtiness, griminess, muckiness **10** filthiness, grubbiness, sleaziness **11** squalidness, uncleanness **12** wretchedness

squander
04 blow, blue, lash, muck, roam **05** spend, sport, waste **06** bezzle, expend, gamble, lavish, misuse, mucker, plunge, wander **07** consume, fritter, scamble, scatter, slather, splurge **08** disperse, fool away, misspend, straggle **09** dissipate, sport away, throw away **10** muddle away **11** fritter away, splash out on

square
01 S, T **02** sq **03** fit, pay **04** even, fair, full, just, quad, rule, suit, true **05** adapt, agree, align, bribe, canon, exact, fogey, level, match, order, plaza, scarf, solid, tally **06** accord, adjust, dinkum, equity, evenly, fairly, honest, settle, tailor **07** balance, conform, diehard, ethical, fitting, genuine, honesty, quarrel, resolve, solidly, swagger, upright **08** complete, directly, fairness, honestly, old fogey, put right, regulate, set right, settle up, standard, straight, suitable, thick-set **09** conformer, criterion, equitable, harmonize, headscarf, make equal, reconcile **10** above-board, conformist, correspond, dissension, fuddy-duddy, honourable, on the level, quadrangle, satisfying, straighten, town square **11** marketplace, rectangular, right-angled, strait-laced, unequivocal **12** buttoned-down, conservative, market square, old-fashioned **13** perpendicular, quadrilateral, stick-in-the-mud **14** traditionalist **15** be congruous with, conventionalist

Squares include:
03 Red
05 Times
06 Sloane
07 Central, Madison, People's
08 Berkeley, Victoria
09 Leicester, Tiananmen, Trafalgar
10 Bloomsbury, Washington
12 Covent Garden

squarely
04 bang, dead, just **05** plumb, right, smack **07** exactly **08** directly, straight **09** precisely **12** unswervingly

squash
03 jam **04** mash, pack, pulp, snub **05** crowd, crush, grind, pound, press, quash, quell, smash, stamp **07** distort, flatten, put down, silence, squeeze, squelch, squidge, trample **08** compress, macerate, suppress **09** dilutable, humiliate, pulverize, squeezing **10** annihilate

squashy
04 soft **05** mushy, pappy, pulpy **06** spongy **07** sopping, springy, squidgy, squishy **08** squelchy, yielding **10** squelching

squat
03 sit **04** bend, ruck **05** croup, dumpy, fubby, fubsy, hunch, kneel, podgy, pudgy, short, stoop **06** chunky, crouch, croupe, hunker, pyknic, stocky, stubby **07** squabby **08** thickset **09** crouching **10** hunker down **12** absquatulate, Humpty-dumpty

squawk
03 cry, nag **04** beef, carp, crow, fuss, hoot, moan, yelp **05** bitch, bleat, croak, gripe, groan, growl, grump, whine **06** cackle, grouch, grouse, object, scream, shriek, squeal, whinge **07** carry on, grumble, protest, scrauch, scraugh, screech **08** complain **09** bellyache, criticize, find fault **11** kick up a fuss, raise a stink **15** have a bone to pick

squeak
03 eek **04** peep, pipe **05** cheep, chirk, creak, whine **06** inform, squeal **07** confess

squeal
03 cry, rat, wee **04** howl, shop, sing, tell, wail, yell, yelp **05** grass, shout, sneak, split, stool **06** betray, inform, scream, shriek, snitch, squawk **07** screech, sell out **08** complain **09** tell tales

squeamish
03 coy **04** sick **06** queasy, queazy **07** finicky, mawkish, missish, prudish **08** delicate, nauseous **09** nauseated **10** fastidious, particular, scrupulous **11** punctilious, strait-laced **12** mealy mouthed

squeeze
◇ *containment indicator*
03 hug, jam, nip, ram **04** cram, grip, hold, mash, milk, pack, pulp, push, shoe, suck **05** bleed, chirt, clasp, crowd, crush, force, grasp, gripe, juice, pinch, press, shove, stuff, sweat, twist, wedge, wrest, wring **06** clutch, cuddle, enfold, extort, fleece, jostle, lean on, mangle, scruze, squash, strain, thrust **07** embrace, extract, rubbing, scrooge, scrouge, squidge, thrutch, tighten **08** compress, pressure, sandwich, scrowdge, shoehorn, wring out **09** boyfriend, hold tight **10** congestion, girlfriend, pressurize **14** put the screws on

squid
01 L **04** quid **05** pound **06** loligo, nicker **07** ink-fish, smacker **08** calamari, calamary **10** sleeve fish

squiffy
◇ *anagram indicator*
05 happy, merry, tight, tipsy **06** blotto, tiddly **07** drunken, pickled, sozzled, tiddley **09** crapulent, plastered **10** inebriated **11** intoxicated

squint
03 aim **04** awry, cast, gaze, glee, gley, hint, peep, peer, pink, scan **05** askew, blink, twire **06** aslant, glance, gledge, gleyed, skelly, squiny **07** crooked, glimpse, oblique, skellie, squinny **08** cockeyed, cross-eye, indirect, strabism, tendency, walleyed **09** obliquely, off-centre, skew-whiff **10** hagioscope, side-glance, strabismic, strabismus **11** look askance **12** sideways look

squire
04 rule **05** canon **06** attend, donzel, escort, Junker, squier **08** scutiger, squarson **12** armour-bearer

squirm
◇ *anagram indicator*
04 move, worm **05** shift, twist **06** fidget, wiggle, writhe **07** agonize, wriggle **08** flounder, squiggle

squirrel
03 bun **04** skug, vair **05** hoard **06** gopher, suslik, taguan **07** meercat, meerkat **08** chipmuck, chipmunk **09** chickaree **10** prairie dog **11** flickertail, spermophile

• **squirrel away**
04 hide, save **05** hoard, lay in, lay up, put by, store **06** save up **07** conceal, put away, stock up **08** salt away, set aside **09** stash away, stockpile

• **squirrel's nest**
04 cage, dray, drey

squirt
03 jet **04** emit, gush, pour, spew, well **05** chirt, eject, expel, issue, scoot, shoot, spirt, spout, spray, spurt, surge **06** scoosh, skoosh, stream **07** spew out **09** discharge, ejaculate

• **sea squirt**
08 ascidian, cunjevoi

Sri Lanka
02 CL **03** LKA

stab
02 go **03** cut, jab, try **04** ache, bash, dirk, fork, gash, gore, kris, pain, pang, pink, push, shot **05** crack, essay, knife, prick, prong, slash, spasm, spear, stick, throb, whirl, wound **06** injure, injury, pierce, skewer, thrust, twinge **07** attempt, bayonet, poniard, venture **08** incision, puncture, stiletto, transfix **09** endeavour

• **stab in the back**
06 betray **07** deceive, let down, sell out, slander **08** inform on **11** double-cross

stabbing
05 acute, sharp **07** knifing, painful **08** piercing, shooting, stinging **09** throbbing

stability
06 fixity, fixure **07** balance **08** firmness, solidity **09** constancy, soundness **10** durability, regularity, secureness, steadiness, sturdiness, uniformity **11** reliability **15** unchangeability

stabilize
03 fix, peg **06** firm up, freeze, secure, steady **07** balance, support **08** equalize, valorize **09** establish **10** keep steady, make stable **11** make uniform

stable
04 barn, fast, firm, sure **05** fixed, solid, sound, stall **06** secure, static, steady, strong, sturdy **07** abiding, durable, lasting, regular, uniform **08** balanced, constant, enduring, reliable, together **09** permanent **10** deep-rooted, dependable, invariable, unchanging, unswerving, unwavering **11** established, long-lasting, substantial, well-founded **12** unchangeable **13** self-balancing

• stablehand
06 ostler

stack
03 lot **04** fill, flue, heap, load, many, mass, pile, rick, ruck, save, tons, vent **05** amass, clamp, heaps, hoard, loads, mound, piles, shaft, stash, stock, store **06** funnel, gather, granum, masses, oodles **07** chimney **08** assemble **09** a good deal, stockpile **10** accumulate, a great deal, collection **12** accumulation, a large amount, great numbers

stadium
04 bowl, park, ring **05** arena, field, pitch, track, venue **06** ground **08** coliseum **09** colosseum, velodrome **11** sports field **12** amphitheatre, sports ground

Sports stadia and venues include:

04 Oval
05 Ascot, Epsom, Ibrox, Imola, Lords, Monza, Troon
06 Henley, Le Mans
07 Aintree, Anfield, Daytona, Olympia, San Siro, The Oval
08 Highbury, Sandwich
09 Cresta Run, Edgbaston, Longchamp, Muirfield, Newmarket, St Andrews, The Belfry, Turnberry, Villa Park, Wimbledon
10 Brooklands, Carnoustie, Celtic Park, Cheltenham, Elland Road, Fairyhouse, Headingley, Hockenheim, Interlagos, Meadowbank, Millennium, Monte Carlo, Twickenham
11 Belmont Park, Brands Hatch, Hampden Park, Murrayfield, Old Trafford, Royal Lytham, Sandown Park, Silverstone, The Crucible, The Rose Bowl, Trent Bridge, Windsor Park
12 Goodison Park, Texas Stadium, Wembley Arena
13 Azteca Stadium, Caesar's Palace, Crystal Palace, Heysel Stadium, Royal Birkdale, The Albert Hall, White Hart Lane
14 Anaheim Stadium, Churchill Downs, Stamford Bridge, Wembley Stadium
15 Bernabeu Stadium, Cardiff Arms Park, Flushing Meadows, Maracana Stadium

staff
03 man, rod **04** cane, crew, mace, pike, pole, prop, team, wand, work **05** baton, crook, cross, equip, stave, stick **06** burden, crutch, cudgel, occupy, stanza, supply, taiaha, warder **07** bourdon, crosier, crozier, operate, provide, scepter, sceptre, support, workers **08** arbalest, ash-plant, manpower, officers, pastoral, teachers **09** employees, personnel, truncheon, workforce **10** alpenstock **11** secretariat **12** secretariate **13** establishment **14** human resources

stag
03 dog **04** colt, male **05** royal, staig **06** follow, humble, hummel, shadow **07** brocket, knobber **08** imperial, informer, stallion **10** ten-pointer

stage
02 do **03** lap, leg, pin **04** dais, give, step, tier, time, trek **05** apron, arena, field, floor, lay on, level, mount, phase, point, put on, realm, scene, shelf, stand **06** direct, length, period, podium, sphere, storey **07** arrange, perform, present, produce, rostrum, setting, soapbox **08** backdrop, division, engineer, juncture, organize, platform, scaffold **10** background **11** orchestrate, put together, stage-manage

• the stage
03 rep **05** drama **07** theatre, the play **09** dramatics, theatrics, the boards **11** Thespian art **12** show business **13** the footlights

stagecoach
03 fly **05** dilly **09** diligence

stagger
◇ *anagram indicator*
04 reel, rock, roll, step, stot, stun, sway **05** amaze, lurch, pitch, shake, shock, stoit, waver **06** bumble, daidle, falter, recoil, recule, teeter, totter, wintle, wobble **07** astound, blunder, nonplus, recoyle, recuile, stoiter, stotter, stupefy **08** astonish, bowl over, confound, hesitate, keel over, surprise, titubate, wavering **09** dumbfound, overwhelm **11** flabbergast

staggered
◇ *anagram indicator*
05 dazed **06** amazed **07** shocked, stunned **08** open-eyed, startled **09** astounded, surprised **10** astonished, bewildered, bowled over, confounded, gobsmacked, taken aback **11** dumbfounded **12** lost for words **13** flabbergasted, knocked for six

staggering
◇ *anagram indicator*
06 groggy **07** amazing, rolling **08** dramatic, shocking, stunning **09** titubancy **10** astounding, stupefying, surprising, titubation, unexpected, unforeseen **11** astonishing **12** mind-boggling

stagnant
04 dull, foul, slow **05** dirty, dying, inert, quiet, stale, still **06** filthy, smelly, torpid **08** brackish, inactive, moribund, sluggish, standing **09** lethargic, unflowing, unhealthy **10** motionless

stagnate
03 rot **04** idle, rust **05** decay **06** fester **07** decline, putrefy **08** languish, vegetate **09** do nothing **10** degenerate **11** deteriorate **14** become stagnant

staid
03 sad **04** calm, prim **05** grave, quiet, sober, stiff **06** demure, formal, proper, sedate, solemn, sombre, steady **07** serious, starchy **08** composed, decorous **09** permanent **12** buttoned-down **13** serious-minded

stain
03 dye **04** blot, mail, mark, meal, mote, slur, smit, soil, spot, tint **05** bedye, black, chica, chico, cloud, color, dirty, henna, paint, shame, smear, sully, taint, tinge **06** blotch, chicha, colour, damage, embrue, imbrue, injure, injury, marble, smirch, smudge, smutch **07** attaint, blacken, blemish, corrupt, embrewe, inkspot, soilure, splodge, splotch, tarnish, varnish **08** besmirch, Congo red, discolor, disgrace, maculate, sanguine **09** discolour, dishonour, osmic acid, pollution, soiliness **10** ensanguine, trypan blue **11** contaminate **12** methyl violet, picrocarmine **13** Coomassie Blue®, discoloration **14** discolouration

stair, stairs
04 ghat, pair, trap, vice **05** ghaut, grece, scale, sweep **06** perron, stayre **07** caracol **08** caracole, escalier, turnpike **09** escalator, forestair **10** backstairs, scale stair **11** common stair **12** companionway, winding stair **13** scale and platt, turnpike stair **14** apples and pears, escalier dérobé, scale staircase **15** companion ladder, moving staircase, spiral staircase

stake
02 go **03** bet, peg, pot, put, rod, set, tie, vie **04** ante, gage, hold, mise, pale, pawn, pile, play, pole, post, prop, race, rest, risk, stob **05** brace, claim, prize, put in, put on, put up, share, spike, spile, stang, state, stick, tie up, wager **06** assert, chance, demand, fasten, gamble, hazard, hold up, loggat, paling, picket, pierce, piquet, pledge, prop up, secure, tether **07** concern, contest, declare, picquet, support, venture **08** interest, standard, winnings **09** establish **10** investment, lay claim to **11** competition, involvement, requisition

• **stake out**
05 watch **06** define, survey **07** delimit, mark off, mark out, outline, reserve **08** stake off **09** demarcate **11** keep an eye on

stakes
03 bet **04** pool
• **row of stakes**
04 wear, weir **05** orgue **06** paling, zareba, zariba, zereba, zeriba **07** zareeba **08** estacade, palisade, stockade **09** worm fence

stale
03 dry, off, old **04** flat, hard, lure, sour **05** banal, blown, corny, fusty, jaded, musty, shaft, stalk, stock, tired, trite, urine **06** handle, mouldy **07** gone off, insipid, pretext, tainted, urinate, worn-out **08** clichéed, hardened, overused **09** hackneyed, tasteless, worthless **10** uninspired, unoriginal **11** commonplace, stereotyped **12** cliché-ridden, overfamiliar, run-of-the-mill **13** platitudinous

stalemate
03 tie **04** draw, halt **07** impasse **08** blockade, deadlock, stand-off, zugzwang **10** standstill **15** Mexican standoff

stalk
03 bun, kex **04** haft, hunt, keck, pace, rush, seta, stem, step, tail, twig, walk **05** chase, haunt, kecks, march, quill, shaft, shoot, spire, stale, stipe, strig, track, trail, trunk **06** bennet, branch, follow, kecksy, keksye, pursue, shadow, stride **07** pedicel, pedicle, petiole **08** peduncle **09** creep up on, give chase, track down **10** sporophore

See also **stem**

stall
03 bay, pen, pew **04** bulk, coop, crib, ruse, slow, staw, trap **05** booth, decoy, defer, delay, dwell, hedge, kiosk, place, stand, table, trick **06** corral, hold up, induct, put off, stable, travis, trevis **07** counter, cowshed, cubicle, install, shamble, surface, surfeit, sutlery, treviss, tribune **08** fauteuil, flypitch, horse box, obstruct, platform, postpone, put on ice, slow down **09** enclosure, news-stand, stasidion, stonewall, temporize **10** equivocate, standstill **11** compartment, play for time **12** drag your feet

stallion
04 stag **05** staig **06** cooser, cusser, entire **07** cuisser, kestrel, staniel, stannel, stanyel **09** courtesan, stud horse **10** stonehorse

stalwart
05 burly, hardy, loyal, stout **06** brawny, daring, pretty, robust, rugged, steady, strong, sturdy, trusty **07** buirdly, devoted, staunch, valiant **08** athletic, faithful, intrepid, muscular, reliable, resolute, vigorous **09** committed, stalworth, steadfast, strapping **10** dependable, determined **11** indomitable

stamina
04 grit, guts **05** fiber, fibre, force, power **06** bottom, energy, vigour **07** stamens **08** strength **09** endurance, fortitude **10** resilience, resistance **12** staying power

stammer
03 hum **04** lisp **06** babble, falter, gibber, mumble **07** stumble, stutter **08** hesitate, splutter **12** speech defect

stamp
03 cut, die, fix, tag **04** beat, cast, coin, form, kind, mark, mash, mint, pulp, seal, sort, type **05** brand, breed, crush, grind, label, mould, pound, press, print, punch, tread **06** cachet, emboss, enface, incuse, preace, prease, signet, squash, stramp, strike **07** engrave, fashion, impress, imprint, mintage, preasse, quality, trample, variety **08** hallmark, identify, inscribe **09** character, designate, signature **10** categorize, definitive, impression, tripudiate **11** attestation, description **12** characterize **13** authorization

Famous and rare stamps include:

08 Bull's eye, Penny Red
09 Basel dove, Penny Blue
10 Mount Athos, Penny Black, Red Mercury, Scinde Dawk, VR official
11 Jenny invert, St Louis bear
12 Inverted swan
13 Black Honduras, Inverted Jenny, Uganda Cowries

• **stamp out**
03 end **04** curb, kill **05** crush, quash, quell **06** quench, scotch **07** destroy, put down **08** suppress **09** eliminate, eradicate, extirpate **10** extinguish, put an end to

stampede
03 fly, ren, rin, run **04** dash, flee, race, rout, rush, tear **05** shoot **06** charge, flight, gallop, onrush, sprint **07** debacle, scatter **09** breakaway **10** scattering **12** sauve qui peut

stance
04 line **05** angle, slant, stand **06** policy, stanza **07** bearing, opinion, posture, stretch **08** attitude, carriage, position **09** viewpoint **10** deportment, standpoint **11** point of view

stanch
03 dam **04** halt, plug, stay, stem, stop **05** allay, block, check, loyal **06** arrest, hearty, quench, trusty **07** styptic, zealous **08** constant **09** floodgate, seaworthy **10** watertight

stand
02 be **03** bin, nef, put, set **04** base, bear, bier, case, dais, desk, hold, line, park, post, rack, rise, wait **05** abide, allow, angle, bipod, booth, brook, erect, exist, frame, get up, place, plant, shelf, slant, stage, stall, stool, table, up-end **06** cradle, endure, locate, obtain, policy, remain, stance, suffer, tripod **07** be erect, be valid, counter, dumpbin, monopod, opinion, prevail, stand up, station, stomach, support, sustain, swallow, tribune, undergo, weather **08** attitude, cope with, guéridon, live with, monopode, pedestal, platform, position, stillage, stilling, stillion, stoppage, tolerate **09** be in force, be upright, put up with, viewpoint, withstand **10** be in effect, experience, resistance, standpoint **11** point of view **12** be on your feet, straighten up **13** get on your feet, get to your feet **14** rise to your feet
• **stand by**
04 back **06** affirm, defend, hold to, uphold **07** stick by, support **08** adhere to, champion, side with **10** stand up for, stick up for
• **stand down**
04 quit **06** give up, resign, retire **08** abdicate, step down, withdraw
• **stand for**
04 bear, mean **05** allow, brook **06** denote, endure **07** betoken, signify, stomach **08** indicate, tolerate **09** put up with, represent, symbolize
• **stand in for**
07 replace **08** cover for **10** understudy **11** deputize for **13** substitute for **14** hold the fort for, take the place of
• **stand out**
04 show **06** extend, jut out, strout **07** jump out, poke out, project **08** stick out **09** be obvious **11** catch the eye **12** be noticeable **13** be conspicuous, stick out a mile
• **stand up**
04 jilt, rise, wash **05** get up **06** cohere, hold up **07** let down, upstare **09** hold water **10** fail to meet **11** remain valid **12** straighten up **13** get to your feet **14** rise to your feet
• **stand up for**
06 adhere, defend, uphold **07** protect, stand by, support **08** champion, fight for, side with **10** stick up for **13** remain loyal to
• **stand up to**
04 defy, face **05** brave **06** endure, oppose, resist **08** confront, face up to **09** challenge, withstand

standard
03 par, set, std **04** base, code, flag, mark, norm, rate, rule, type **05** basic, color, ethic, fixed, gauge, grade, guide, ideal, level, model, moral, norma, stock, usual **06** banner, colors, colour, ensign, normal, pennon, sample, square, staple **07** average, classic, colours, example, labarum, measure, pattern, pennant, popular, quality, regular, routine, scruple, typical **08** accepted, approved, exemplar, gonfalon, habitual, official, ordinary, orthodox, paradigm, streamer, vexillum **09** archetype, benchmark, criterion, customary, guideline, horsetail, principle, yardstick **10** definitive, prevailing, recognized, touchstone **11** established, Lesbian

rule, requirement **12** conventional **13** authoritative, specification

standard-bearer
06 cornet, ensign **07** alférez, ancient **08** standard **09** vexillary **11** gonfalonier

standardize
08 equalize, regiment **09** normalize **10** homogenize, regularize, stereotype **11** mass-produce, systematize

stand-in
03 sub **04** temp **05** locum, proxy **06** deputy, second **08** delegate, stuntman **09** surrogate **10** stuntwoman, substitute, understudy **11** pinch-hitter **14** representative **15** second-in-command

standing
04 foul, rank **05** dirty, erect, fixed, stale, still **06** filthy, repute, smelly, status **07** footing, lasting, rampant, regular, settled, station, up-ended, upright **08** brackish, duration, eminence, position, repeated, stagnant, vertical **09** existence, permanent, perpetual, seniority, unflowing, unhealthy **10** experience, motionless, on your feet, reputation **11** continuance, established **13** perpendicular

stand-off
03 tie **04** draw, halt **07** impasse **08** blockade, deadlock **10** five-eighth, standstill

standoffish
04 cold, cool **05** aloof **06** remote **07** distant **08** detached, reserved **09** withdrawn **10** unfriendly, unsociable **14** unapproachable **15** uncommunicative

standpoint
05 angle, slant **06** stance **07** station **08** position **09** viewpoint **11** perspective, point of view **12** vantage point

standstill
03 jam, jib **04** halt, lull, rest, stop **05** pause, stall, stand, tie-up **06** hold-up, log jam **07** dead-set, impasse **08** deadlock, dead stop, gridlock, stoppage, unmoving **09** cessation, stalemate **10** dead-finish, stationary, still-stand

• **to a standstill**
02 up **04** down

staple
03 key **04** main **05** basic, chief, major, sadza, vital **06** matoke **07** leading, matooke, primary, stapple, stopple **08** foremost, plantain, standard **09** essential, fastening, important, necessary, principal **11** fundamental, ship biscuit **13** indispensable

star
03 orb, sun **04** idol, lead, moon, nova **05** celeb, major, shine **06** bigwig, famous, planet, shiner, sphere **07** big name, big shot, leading **08** asterisk, asteroid, luminary, talented **09** bespangle, brilliant, celebrity, paramount, personage, principal, prominent, satellite, superstar, well-known **10** celebrated, leading man, pre-eminent **11** illustrious, leading lady **12** heavenly body, leading light **13** celestial body, household name

Stars include:

03 Dog, sun
04 Mira, nova, Pole, Vega
05 Deneb, Dubhe, Merak, North, Rigel, Spica
06 meteor, Pollux, pulsar, quasar, Sirius
07 Alphard, Antares, Canopus, Capella, falling, neutron, Polaris, Procyon
08 Achernar, Arcturus, Barnard's, red dwarf, red giant, shooting
09 Aldebaran, Alderamin, Fomalhaut, supernova
10 Beta Crucis, Betelgeuse, brown dwarf, supergiant, white dwarf
11 Alpha Boötis, Alpha Crucis, Delta Cephei
12 Alpha Doradus
13 Alpha Centauri
15 Proxima Centauri

See also **constellation**

starboard
01 R **05** right

starchy
04 prim **05** staid, stiff **06** formal, stuffy **07** precise **11** ceremonious, punctilious, strait-laced **12** conventional

stare
04 dare, gape, gawk, gawp, gaze, gorp, look, ogle **05** glare, watch **06** glower, goggle **07** fisheye, outface **08** starling **10** rubberneck

• **be staring you in the face**
09 be blatant **13** be conspicuous, be very obvious, stick out a mile

starfish
07 asterid **08** asteroid **09** stellerid **10** asteridian, bipinnaria, fivefinger **11** fivefingers, stelleridan **13** crown of thorns

stark
04 bald, bare, grim, pure **05** bleak, blunt, clean, clear, empty, harsh, plain, quite, sharp, sheer, stern, stiff, total, utter **06** arrant, barren, dreary, gloomy, severe, simple, wholly **07** austere, obvious, totally, utterly **08** absolute, clear-cut, complete, desolate, distinct, entirely, flagrant, forsaken, starkers, thorough **09** downright, out-and-out, unadorned **10** absolutely, altogether, completely, consummate, depressing, stark-naked, start-naked **11** undecorated, unmitigated, unqualified **13** unembellished

stark-naked
04 nude **05** naked, stark **06** unclad **08** en cuerpo, in the raw, starkers, stripped **09** in the buff, in the nude, undressed **15** in the altogether

start
◇ *head selection indicator*
03 bug, fit, gin, law, off, set **04** dart, dawn, fire, jerk, jump, leap, make, open, roll **05** abray, arise, begin, birth, braid, break, burst, debut, found, get-go, go-off, issue, leave, onset, rouse, set up, shoot, spasm, spurt, wince **06** abrade, abraid, appear, boggle, create, depart, flinch, kick in, launch, origin, outset, recoil, set off, set out, shrink, spring, turn on, twitch **07** combust, getaway, jump-off, kick off, kick-off, opening, pioneer, trigger **08** activate, commence, conceive, embark on, fire away, get going, initiate, outburst **09** beginning, emergence, establish, inception, instigate, institute, introduce, originate, set on foot **10** convulsion, embark upon, foundation, inaugurate, initiation, trigger off **11** get cracking, get under way, institution, origination **12** commencement, inauguration, introduction **13** come into being **14** bring into being **15** get things moving

• **did not start, fail to start**
◇ *head deletion indicator*

starter
◇ *head selection indicator*
04 meze, whet **05** tapas **06** bhajee, canapé, entrée, relish **08** antepast, apéritif, cocktail **09** appetizer **11** first course, hors d'oeuvre **13** prawn cocktail

starting point
03 tee **04** base **06** origin **07** scratch **08** terminus **11** springboard

startle
03 shy **04** rock **05** alarm, amaze, scare, shock, spook, start, upset **06** affray **07** agitate, astound, disturb, perturb **08** astonish, frighten, surprise, unsettle **11** make you jump

startling
06 sudden **07** épatant **08** alarming, dramatic, galvanic, shocking **10** astounding, staggering, surprising, unexpected, unforeseen **11** astonishing **12** electrifying **13** extraordinary

starvation
04 pine **05** death **06** famine, hunger **07** fasting **10** famishment **12** malnutrition **13** extreme hunger

starve
03 die **04** clem, deny, diet, fast, pine **05** faint **06** famish, hunger, perish, sterve **07** atrophy, deprive **11** deteriorate

starving
05 dying, faint **06** hungry **08** famished, ravenous, underfed **10** very hungry **14** undernourished

stash
04 fund, heap, hide, mass, pile, quit, stop, stow **05** cache, hoard, lay up, store **06** closet, desist, save up **07** conceal, reserve, secrete **08** salt

away **09** reservoir, stockpile **10** collection **12** accumulation, squirrel away

state

◇ *homophone indicator*

03 put, say **04** aver, case, état, flap, land, name, pomp, tell **05** endow, glory, panic, phase, realm, shape, stage, tizzy, utter, voice **06** affirm, assert, bother, canopy, dither, estate, formal, nation, plight, public, report, reveal, set out, settle, status, tizwas **07** council, country, declare, dignity, display, divulge, express, fluster, install, kingdom, majesty, pompous, present, specify, stately **08** announce, ceremony, disclose, grandeur, national, official, position, proclaim, property, republic **09** condition, establish, formulate, make known, situation, splendour, statement, territory **10** articulate, ceremonial, federation, government, parliament, promulgate **11** authorities, communicate, magnificent, predicament **12** governmental **13** circumstances, Establishment, parliamentary **14** administration

See also **province**

Australian states and territories:

02 NT, SA, WA
03 ACT, NSW, QLD, TAS, VIC
08 Tasmania (TAS), Victoria (VIC)
10 Queensland (QLD)
13 New South Wales (NSW)
14 South Australia (SA)
16 Western Australia (WA)
17 Northern Territory (NT)
26 Australian Capital Territory (ACT)

Australian state residents' nicknames:

08 Top Ender
09 cornstalk, Croweater, gumsucker, Taswegian
10 sandgroper
11 Territorian, Vandemonian
12 bananabender
13 Apple Islander
14 Cabbage Patcher
15 Cabbage Gardener

Indian states and union territories:

03 Goa
05 Assam, Bihar, Delhi
06 Kerala, Orissa, Punjab, Sikkim
07 Gujarat, Haryana, Manipur, Mizoram, Tripura
08 Nagaland
09 Jharkhand, Karnataka, Meghalaya, Rajasthan, Tamil Nadu
10 Chandigarh, West Bengal
11 Daman and Diu, Lakshadweep, Maharashtra, Pondicherry, Uttaranchal
12 Chhattisgarh, Uttar Pradesh
13 Andhra Pradesh, Madhya Pradesh
15 Himachal Pradesh, Jammu and Kashmir
16 Arunachal Pradesh
17 Andaman and Nicobar
19 Dadra and Nagar Haveli

US states:

04 Iowa, Ohio, Utah
05 Idaho, Maine, Texas
06 Alaska, Hawaii, Kansas, Nevada, Oregon
07 Alabama, Arizona, Florida, Georgia, Indiana, Montana, New York, Vermont, Wyoming
08 Arkansas, Colorado, Delaware, Illinois, Kentucky, Maryland, Michigan, Missouri, Nebraska, Oklahoma, Virginia
09 Louisiana, Minnesota, New Jersey, New Mexico, Tennessee, Wisconsin
10 California, Washington
11 Connecticut, Mississippi, North Dakota, Rhode Island, South Dakota
12 New Hampshire, Pennsylvania, West Virginia
13 Massachusetts, North Carolina, South Carolina
18 District of Columbia

US state abbreviations and zip codes:

02 **AK** (Alaska), **AL** (Alabama), **AR** (Arkansas), **AZ** (Arizona), **CA** (California), **CO** (Colorado), **CT** (Connecticut), **DC** (District of Columbia), **DE** (Delaware), **FL** (Florida), **GA** (Georgia), **HI** (Hawaii), **IA** (Iowa), **ID** (Idaho), **IL** (Illinois), **IN** (Indiana), **KS** (Kansas), **KY** (Kentucky), **LA** (Louisiana), **MA** (Massachusetts), **MD** (Maryland), **ME** (Maine), **MI** (Michigan), **MN** (Minnesota), **MO** (Missouri), **MS** (Mississippi), **MT** (Montana), **NC** (North Carolina), **ND** (North Dakota), **NE** (Nebraska), **NH** (New Hampshire), **NJ** (New Jersey), **NM** (New Mexico), **NV** (Nevada), **NY** (New York), **OH** (Ohio), **OK** (Oklahoma), **OR** (Oregon), **PA** (Pennsylvania), **RI** (Rhode Island), **SC** (South Carolina), **SD** (South Dakota), **TN** (Tennessee), **TX** (Texas), **UT** (Utah), **VA** (Virginia), **VT** (Vermont), **WA** (Washington), **WI** (Wisconsin), **WV** (West Virginia), **WY** (Wyoming)
03 **Ala** (Alabama), **Ark** (Arkansas), **Del** (Delaware), **Fla** (Florida), **Ill** (Illinois), **Ind** (Indiana), **Nev** (Nevada), **Tex** (Texas), **Wis** (Wisconsin), **W Va** (West Virginia), **Wyo** (Wyoming)
04 **Ariz** (Arizona), **Colo** (Colorado), **Conn** (Connecticut), **Kans** (Kansas), **Mass** (Massachusetts), **Mich** (Michigan), **Minn** (Minnesota), **Miss** (Mississippi), **Mont** (Montana), **N Dak** (North Dakota), **Nebr** (Nebraska), **N Mex** (New Mexico), **Okla** (Oklahoma), **Oreg** (Oregon), **S Dak** (South Dakota), **Tenn** (Tennessee), **Wash** (Washington)
05 **Calif** (California)

US state nicknames:

08 **Bay State** (Massachusetts), **Gem State** (Idaho)
09 **Beef State** (Nebraska), **Corn State** (Iowa), **Free State** (Maryland), **Old Colony** (Massachusetts)
10 **Aloha State** (Hawaii), **First State** (Delaware), **Peach State** (Georgia), **Sioux State** (North Dakota)
11 **Beaver State** (Oregon), **Coyote State** (South Dakota), **Creole State** (Louisiana), **Empire State** (New York), **Garden State** (New Jersey), **Golden State** (California), **Gopher State** (Minnesota), **Little Rhody** (Rhode Island), **Nutmeg State** (Connecticut), **Show Me State** (Missouri), **Silver State** (Nevada), **Sooner State** (Oklahoma), **Sunset State** (Oklahoma)
12 **Beehive State** (Utah), **Buckeye State** (Ohio), **Bullion State** (Missouri), **Chinook State** (Washington), **Diamond State** (Delaware), **Granite State** (New Hampshire), **Hawkeye State** (Indiana), **Heart of Dixie** (Alabama), **Hoosier State** (Indiana), **Old Line State** (Maryland), **Prairie State** (Illinois), **Tar Heel State** (North Carolina)
13 **Big Sky Country** (Montana), **Camellia State** (Alabama), **Equality State** (Wyoming), **Keystone State** (Pennsylvania), **Land of Lincoln** (Illinois), **Lone Star State** (Texas), **Magnolia State** (Mississippi), **Mainland State** (Alaska), **Mountain State** (West Virginia), **Old North State** (North Carolina), **Palmetto State** (South Carolina), **Pine Tree State** (Maine), **Sunshine State** (Florida, New Mexico, South Carolina), **Treasure State** (Montana)
14 **Bluegrass State** (Kentucky), **Evergreen State** (Washington), **Great Lake State** (Michigan), **Jayhawker State** (Kansas), **North Star State** (Minnesota), **Panhandle State** (West Virginia), **Sagebrush State** (Nevada), **Volunteer State** (Tennessee), **Wolverine State** (Michigan)
15 **Centennial State** (Colorado), **Plantation State** (Rhode Island), **The Last Frontier** (Alaska)
16 **Flickertail State** (North Dakota), **Grand Canyon State** (Arizona), **Peace Garden State** (North Dakota)
17 **America's Dairyland** (Wisconsin), **Constitution State** (Connecticut), **Land of Enchantment** (New Mexico), **Land of Opportunity** (Arkansas)
18 **Green Mountain State** (Vermont), **Mother of Presidents** (Virginia)

• **in a state**

05 het up, upset **07** anxious, hassled, in a stew, ruffled, worried **08** agitated, in a tizzy, troubled, worked up **09** flustered **10** distressed **13** panic-stricken

• state of affairs
03 job **04** case **05** scene **06** crisis, plight, status **07** posture **08** juncture, position **09** condition, situation **11** predicament **12** kettle of fish, lie of the land **13** circumstances

stately
05 grand, lofty, noble, proud, regal, royal **06** august, solemn **07** courtly, elegant, pompous **08** glorious, graceful, imperial, imposing, majestic, measured, splendid **09** dignified, mausolean **10** ceremonial, deliberate, impressive, majestical **11** ceremonious, magnificent

statement
04 note **05** state, story, table **06** exposé, report, verbal **07** account, preface **08** averment, bulletin, manifest, relation **09** assertion, testimony, utterance **10** communiqué, disclosure, divulgence, revelation, white paper **11** affirmation, declaration, enunciation, presentment **12** announcement, constatation, presentation, press release, procès-verbal, proclamation, promulgation **13** communication **14** representation

state-of-the-art
02 in **03** hip, new **04** cool **05** fresh, novel **06** hi-tech, latest, modern, modish, recent, trendy, with it **07** complex, go-ahead, in vogue, present **08** advanced, high-tech, space-age, up-to-date **09** inventive, the latest **10** futuristic, innovative, newfangled, present-day **11** complicated, cutting edge, modernistic, progressive **12** contemporary **13** up-to-the-minute **14** forward-looking **15** highly developed

statesman, stateswoman
03 GOM **06** leader **08** diplomat, wealsman **10** homme d'état, politician **11** grand old man **14** elder statesman

See also **politician**

static
05 fixed, inert, still **06** stable, steady **07** resting **08** constant, immobile, unmoving **09** unvarying **10** changeless, motionless, stationary, unchanging **11** undeviating **13** at a standstill, Maginot-minded

station
03 lay, set, Sta **04** base, camp, farm, halt, post, rank, seat, send, site, stop **05** class, depot, grade, level, place, plant, point, rowme, stand **06** assign, centre, locate, office, status **07** appoint, channel, habitat, install, quarter **08** exchange, garrison, location, position, standing, terminus **09** establish, fare-stage **10** wavelength **11** park-and-ride, place of duty, whistle stop **12** headquarters **13** establishment, stopping-place

See also **London**; **police station**; **power**; **radio**; **railway station** *under* **railway**

stationary
05 fixed, inert, still **06** at rest, ledger, lidger, moored, parked, static **07** resting, sessile, settled **08** constant, immobile, standing, unmoving **09** sedentary **10** motionless, standstill **13** at a standstill

stationery

Stationery items include:

03 ink, pen, pin
04 file
05 diary, label, ruler, toner
06 eraser, folder, marker, pencil, rubber, staple, Tipp-Ex®
07 blotter, Blu-Tack®, divider, file tab, Filofax®, memo pad
08 calendar, cash book, envelope, Jiffy bag®, notebook, scissors, stamp pad
09 card index, clipboard, desk diary, flip chart, index card, notepaper, paper clip, Sellotape®, wall chart
10 calculator, drawing pin, filing tray, floppy disk, graph paper, paper knife, Post-it note®, ring binder, rubber band
11 account book, address book, bulldog clip, carbon paper, elastic band, rubber stamp, treasury tag
12 adhesive tape, computer disk, copying paper, pocket folder, printer label, printer paper, writing paper
13 expanding file, lever arch file, paper fastener, printer ribbon, tape dispenser
14 document folder, document wallet, manila envelope, spiral notebook, suspension file, window envelope
15 cartridge ribbon, correcting paper, correction fluid, headed notepaper, pencil-sharpener

statue
02 ka **04** bust, head, idol, kore, tiki **05** gnome, image, torso **06** bronze, effigy, figure, kouros, xoanon **07** carving, stookie **08** acrolith, colossus, figurine, monument **09** sculpture, statuette **10** polychrome **11** garden gnome, whole-length **14** representation

See also **sculpture**

statuesque
04 tall **05** regal **07** stately **08** handsome, imposing, majestic **09** dignified **10** impressive

stature
04 fame, rank, size **06** height, inches, renown, weight **08** attitude, eminence, prestige, standing, tallness **09** elevation, loftiness **10** importance, prominence, reputation **11** consequence

status
04 rank **05** class, grade, level, state **06** degree, weight **07** quality, station **08** eminence, position, prestige, standing **09** character, condition **10** importance, reputation **11** consequence, distinction **14** territoriality

statute
03 act, law **04** rule **05** edict, ukase **06** assize, decree **07** Riot Act **09** capitular, enactment, ordinance **10** lex scripta, regulation, written law **13** interlocution, Septennial Act **15** act of parliament

staunch
04 firm, halt, plug, stay, stem, stop, sure, true **05** allay, block, check, loyal, sound, stout **06** arrest, hearty, quench, stanch, strong, trusty **07** devoted, styptic, zealous **08** constant, faithful, reliable, resolute, yeomanly **09** committed, floodgate, seaworthy, steadfast **10** dependable, watertight **11** trustworthy

staunchly
06 firmly **08** yeomanly **10** implacably, resolutely **11** steadfastly **12** unswervingly **13** unfalteringly, unflinchingly

stave
03 bar, lag, rod **05** break, shaft, staff **06** sprain, stanza **07** break up

• stave off
04 foil **05** avert, avoid, parry, repel **07** deflect, fend off, prevent, repulse, ward off **08** keep back **09** keep at bay, turn aside

stay
04 curb, halt, hold, keep, last, live, prop, rest, sist, stop, wait, wire **05** abide, abode, allay, await, block, board, brace, cease, check, defer, delay, dwell, lodge, pause, put up, quell, strut, tarry, visit **06** arrest, desist, detain, endure, hinder, linger, put off, remain, reside, settle **07** adjourn, appease, control, holiday, persist, prevent, satisfy, shoring, sojourn, stay put, support, suspend **08** buttress, continue, obstacle, obstruct, postpone, prorogue, put on ice, reprieve, restrain, stopover, suppress, vacation **09** deferment, endurance, hang about, remission, restraint, stanchion **10** hang around, suspension **11** continuance, discontinue, take a room at **12** postponement **13** reinforcement

staying power
04 grit, guts **05** fibre, force, power, steel **06** bottom, energy, vigour **07** stamina **08** strength **09** endurance, fortitude **10** resilience, resistance

steadfast
03 sad **04** fast, firm **05** fixed, loyal **06** intent, manful, stable, steady, strong, sturdy **07** staunch **08** constant, faithful, reliable, resolute **09** dedicated, immovable **10** dependable, implacable,

unswerving, unwavering
11 established, perseverant, persevering, unfaltering, unflinching
12 single-minded, stout-hearted

steadily
06 calmly, evenly **07** soberly
08 sensibly **09** regularly, seriously
10 constantly, rationally **12** all year round, on an even keel **13** round the clock **15** uninterruptedly

steady
03 fix **04** calm, even, firm, rest
05 brace, check, fixed, relax, sober, staid, still, usual **06** poised, secure, soothe, stable, subdue **07** balance, compose, control, regular, serious, settled, support, uniform **08** balanced, constant, habitual, reliable, resolute, restrain, sensible, unbroken, unmoving
09 boyfriend, ceaseless, customary, immovable, incessant, perpetual, rock-solid, stabilize, steadfast, unexcited, unvarying **10** consistent, controlled, dependable, girlfriend, motionless, persistent, unchanging, unvariable, unwavering **11** consistence, consistency, established, industrious, unexcitable, unfaltering, unflappable, unremitting **12** on an even keel, tranquillize, well-balanced
13 imperturbable, uninterrupted
14 self-controlled

steak
05 T-bone **08** pope's eye **09** entrecôte
11 porterhouse **13** Chateaubriand

steal
03 bag, cly, dip, lag, mag, nap, nim, nip, rob **04** blag, bone, crib, duff, glom, knap, lift, magg, mill, nick, pick, pull, slip, smug, snip, take, whip **05** annex, boost, bribe, creep, filch, heist, hoist, miche, mooch, mouch, pinch, poach, purse, shaft, shank, slide, slink, sneak, steel, steil, stele, swipe, theft
06 abduct, burgle, convey, finger, handle, hijack, kidnap, nobble, pickle, pilfer, pocket, rip off, rustle, scrump, skrimp, skrump, snatch, snitch, steale, thieve, tiptoe, twitch **07** bargain, break in, cabbage, good buy, knock up, purloin, slither, smuggle, snaffle
08 abstract, discount, embezzle, giveaway, half-inch, high-jack, knock off, liberate, peculate, scrounge, shoplift, souvenir **09** condiddle, duckshove, go off with, reduction, relieve of **10** burglarize, plagiarize, run off with **11** appropriate, make off with, pick a pocket, walk off with **12** make away with, special offer **13** value for money **14** help yourself to, misappropriate

stealing
05 swipe, theft **06** piracy, snatch
07 break-in, larceny, mugging, nicking, robbery, stick-up **08** burglary, filching, pinching, poaching, thievery, thieving
09 pilferage, pilfering, sprechery
10 peculation, plagiarism, purloining, spreaghery **11** shoplifting
12 embezzlement, smash-and-grab
13 appropriation

stealth
05 theft **07** secrecy, slyness
10 covertness, sneakiness
11 furtiveness **12** stealthiness
15 unobtrusiveness

• by stealth
08 stowlins **09** stownlins **10** à la dérobée, stolenwise

stealthily
05 slyly **08** covertly, secretly **09** by stealth, cunningly, furtively, stownlins
10 à la dérobée, stolenwise
15 surreptitiously

stealthy
03 sly **05** mousy, quiet **06** covert, mousey, secret, sneaky **07** catlike, cunning, furtive **09** secretive, underhand **11** clandestine, unobtrusive
13 surreptitious

steam
04 haze, mist, roke **05** force **06** energy, exhale, spirit, vapour, vigour
07 stamina **08** activity, dampness, moisture, momentum, outdated
09 eagerness **10** enthusiasm, exhalation, liveliness **11** water vapour
12 condensation, old-fashioned

• get steamed up
07 explode **08** boil over, get angry, get het up **09** blow a fuse, do your nut
10 get annoyed, get excited, hit the roof
11 have kittens, lose your rag **12** blow your cool, fly into a rage, get flustered, lose your cool **15** fly off the handle

• let off steam
08 sound off **13** let yourself go **15** air your feelings

• steam up
05 fog up **06** mist up

• under your own steam
05 alone **07** unaided **10** by yourself
11 without help **13** independently

steamer
02 SS **03** str, USS **06** packet, puffer
09 propeller, steamboat, steamship, vaporetto, whaleback **10** packet-boat, packet-ship, paddle-boat **11** side-wheeler, steam-packet, steam vessel
12 screw steamer **13** paddle steamer
14 ocean-greyhound

steaming
◇ *anagram indicator*

See **drunk**

steamy
03 hot **04** blue, damp, hazy, sexy
05 close, humid, misty, muggy, stewy
06 erotic, sticky, sultry, sweaty
07 amorous, gaseous, lustful, raunchy, sensual, vapoury **08** steaming, vaporous **09** seductive, vapourish
10 lubricious, passionate, sweltering, vaporiform

steed
03 nag **04** hack, jade, sted **05** horse, mount, stedd, stede **06** stedde
07 charger **09** Rosinante

steel
05 brace, nerve, psych, shaft, shank, steal, steil, stele, sword **06** handle, harden, steale **07** fortify, prepare, toughen **15** trustworthiness

steely
04 firm, grey, hard **05** harsh **06** strong
08 blue-grey, pitiless, resolute
09 merciless, steel-blue
10 determined, inflexible, unyielding
13 steel-coloured

steep
03 sop **04** bold, buck, damp, dear, fill, high, mask, plot, soak, stey **05** bathe, bluff, brent, brine, embay, imbue, lofty, sharp, sheer, souse, stiff **06** abrupt, costly, drench, imbrue, infuse, pickle, rennet, seethe, steepy, sudden
07 arduous, cragged, ensteep, extreme, immerse, moisten, pervade, stickle, suffuse **08** headlong, macerate, marinate, permeate, saturate, submerge, vertical
09 difficult, excessive, expensive
10 exorbitant, incredible, inordinate, overpriced, over the top, precipiced
11 acclivitous, declivitous, exaggerated, exponential, high-pitched, precipitous, uncalled-for
12 extortionate, unreasonable
13 perpendicular

steeple
05 spire, tower **06** belfry, turret
11 rood-steeple **12** spire-steeple

steeply
07 rapidly, sharply **08** abruptly, suddenly

steer
03 con, cox **04** beef, cann, conn, helm, lead, stir, stot, tack **05** drive, guide, pilot, usher **06** direct, govern, steare
07 conduct, control **08** navigate

• steer clear of
04 shun **05** avoid, dodge, evade, skirt
06 bypass, escape, eschew
10 circumvent **12** keep away from

stem
03 dam, pin, ram **04** axis, beam, bine, cane, come, corm, culm, curb, flow, halm, halt, plug, race, runt, stop, tail, tamp **05** arise, block, check, haulm, issue, shaft, shank, shoot, stalk, stock, trunk **06** arrest, bamboo, branch, breast, derive, family, oppose, resist, spring, stanch **07** contain, develop, emanate, hop-vine, staunch **08** kail-runt, peduncle, restrain **09** originate
11 pipe-stapple, pipe-stopple **14** have its origins

stench
04 niff, pong, reek **05** odour, smell, stink, whiff **06** miasma **08** mephitis

stentorian
04 full, loud **06** strong **07** booming, ringing, vibrant **08** carrying, powerful, resonant, sonorous, strident
10 thundering, thunderous
13 reverberating

step
03 act, fix, pas, peg **04** deed, gait, gree, gris, move, pace, rank, rung, trip, walk **05** glide, grade, grece, grees, grese, grice, grise, grize, level, notch, phase, point, print, stage, stair, stamp, stile, titup, trace, track, tramp, tread **06** action, degree, effort, gradin, greece, greese, griece, pit-pat, remove, stride, tittup **07** advance, gradine, grecian, measure, pitapat, process, shuffle, stempel, stemple, twinkle **08** démarche, footfall, footstep, greesing, gressing, halfpace, movement, pitty-pat, progress **09** expedient, footprint, gradation, manoeuvre, procedure **10** impression, proceeding **11** development, pas de basque, progression **14** course of action

See also **dance**

• **in step**
08 in accord, in unison, together **09** in harmony **11** in agreement

• **out of step**
06 at odds **09** not in step **13** at loggerheads **14** in disagreement

• **step by step**
06 slowly **08** bit by bit, gradatim **09** gradually **13** progressively **14** little by little, one step at a time

• **step down**
04 quit **05** leave **06** resign, retire **08** abdicate, withdraw **09** stand down **14** give up your post

• **step in**
07 intrude, mediate **09** arbitrate, intercede, interfere, interrupt, intervene

• **step up**
05 boost, raise **07** augment, build up, speed up **08** escalate, increase **09** intensify **10** accelerate

• **watch your step**
07 look out **08** take care, watch out **09** be careful **11** be attentive **12** mind how you go

stereotype
03 tag **04** cast **05** label, model, mould **06** cliché, stereo **07** formula, pattern **08** typecast **09** formalize **10** categorize, convention, pigeonhole **11** mass-produce, standardize **15** conventionalize, fixed set of ideas

stereotyped
05 banal, corny, fixed, stale, stock, tired, trite **07** cliché'd **08** clichéed, overused, standard **09** hackneyed **10** threadbare, unoriginal **12** cliché-ridden, conventional, mass-produced, standardized, unchangeable **13** platitudinous, stereotypical

sterile
03 dry **04** arid, bare, pure, vain **05** clean, moory, stale **06** barren, futile **07** aseptic, moorish, useless **08** abortive, acarpous, germ-free, germless, infecund, lifeless **09** fruitless, infertile, pointless **10** antiseptic, sterilized, unfruitful, uninfected, uninspired, unyielding **11** disinfected, ineffectual **12** unproductive, unprofitable **13** unimaginative **14** uncontaminated

sterility
06 atocia, purity **07** asepsis **08** futility **09** cleanness, impotence **10** barrenness, inefficacy **11** infertility, unfecundity, uselessness **12** disinfection **13** fruitlessness, pointlessness **14** unfruitfulness **15** ineffectiveness

sterilize
04 geld, spay **05** clean **06** doctor, neuter, purify, retort **07** cleanse **08** castrate, fumigate **09** autoclave, disinfect **13** make infertile

sterling
03 ace, stg **04** mean, neat, pure, real, ster, true **05** brill, great, sound **06** worthy **07** genuine **08** smashing, standard, starling, terrific, top-notch **09** authentic, excellent **10** first-class **11** superlative **12** second to none **14** out of this world

stern
04 back, grim, hard, helm, iron, poop, rear, rump, star, tail **05** cruel, harsh, rigid, stark, starn, tough **06** ramrod, severe, sombre, strict **07** austere, tail end **08** exacting, rigorous **09** demanding, Draconian, stringent, unsmiling, unsparing **10** forbidding, inflexible, relentless, tyrannical, unyielding **11** unrelenting **13** authoritarian

sternly
06 grimly **07** cruelly, harshly **08** severely, sombrely, strictly **10** inflexibly **12** forbiddingly, relentlessly

Stevenson
03 RLS

stew
◇ *anagram indicator*
03 fix, jug **04** boil, cook, fret, fuss, hash, hole **05** daube, salmi, stove, sweat, tizzy, worry **06** bother, braise, burgoo, paella, pother, ragout, salmis, scouse, simmer, tajine, tizwas **07** agonize, cholent, chowder, fluster, goulash, haricot, navarin, stovies, swelter, tzimmes **08** matelote, mulligan, pot-au-feu, zarzuela **09** agitation, carbonade, carbonado, casserole, cassoulet, Irish stew, lobscouse, potpourri, succotash **10** carbonnade, lob's course, maconochie, prostitute **11** olla-podrida, ratatouille, slumgullion **13** bouillabaisse

steward
05 dewan, diwan, reeve **06** bailie, butler, commis, factor, waiter **07** bailiff, baillie, foreman, maître d', marshal, mormaor **08** khansama, manciple, official, overseer, waitress **09** attendant, caretaker, custodian, khansamah, major-domo, seneschal, sommelier **10** air hostess, stewardess, supervisor **11** chamberlain **12** maître d'hôtel **14** homme d'affaires **15** flight attendant

stick
03 fix, gad, gum, jab, jam, jut, lay, pin, put, set **04** bear, bind, bond, clog, drop, flak, fuse, glue, grip, hang, hold, join, last, poke, push, rest, site, stab, stay, stop, tack, tape, trap, twig, weld, yard **05** abide, abuse, affix, blame, cling, dwell, paste, place, prick, spear, stand, tally **06** adhere, attach, branch, cement, clog up, endure, fasten, impale, insert, linger, locate, pierce, remain, rocket, secure, solder, switch, thrust **07** carry on, confine, deposit, install, persist, reproof, scruple, set down, stomach, swallow **08** continue, position, protrude, puncture, tolerate, transfix **09** criticism, hostility, penetrate, put up with **10** punishment **11** come to a halt **12** dressing-down **13** get bogged down

Sticks include:

02 ko
03 bat, lug, rod
04 cane, club, cosh, pike, pole, post, wand, whip
05 baton, billy, birch, crook, lathi, staff, stake, waddy
06 alpeen, crutch, cudgel, hockey, kierie, tripod
07 sceptre, walking, woomera
08 bludgeon, cocktail
09 truncheon
10 alpenstock, knobkerrie, shillelagh

• **stick at**
04 balk **05** demur, doubt, pause **06** keep at, recoil, stop at **07** persist, scruple **08** continue, hesitate, plug away **09** persevere **10** shrink from **13** draw the line at

• **stick by**
04 back **06** defend, hold to, uphold **07** stand by, support **08** adhere to, champion, side with **10** stand up for, stick up for

• **stick it out**
07 persist **08** continue, keep at it, plug away **09** persevere **11** hang in there **13** grin and bear it

• **stick out**
04 perk **05** bulge **06** extend, jut out, tongue **07** poke out, project **08** protrude **09** be obvious **12** be noticeable **13** be conspicuous

• **stick to**
04 obey **06** accept, follow, fulfil, hold to, keep to, uphold **07** abide by, agree to, observe, respect, stand by **08** adhere to, carry out, submit to **09** conform to, discharge **10** comply with, toe the line **11** go along with, go by the book

• **stick up for**
06 defend, uphold **07** protect, stand by, support **08** champion, fight for **10** speak up for, stand up for **13** take the part of, take the side of

• **the sticks**
04 bush, wops **05** scrub **07** boonies,

hickdom, outback, wop-wops **08** backveld, yokeldom **09** backwoods, boondocks **10** back-blocks **11** remote areas, up the Boohai **13** end of the earth **15** middle of nowhere

sticker
03 bur **04** tine

stickiness
03 goo **04** gaum, gorm, tack **09** glueyness, gooeyness, gumminess, tackiness, viscidity **10** syrupiness **12** adhesiveness **13** glutinousness

stick-in-the-mud
05 fogey **06** fossil, square **08** fogeyish, old fogey, outmoded **09** Victorian **10** antiquated, back number, fossilized, fuddy-duddy **12** antediluvian, buttoned-down, conservative **13** unadventurous

stickler
03 nut **06** backer, maniac, pedant, purist, second, umpire **07** fanatic, fusspot **08** mediator **09** regulator **10** fussbudget **12** precisianist **13** perfectionist, quarterdecker

sticky
04 limy **05** chewy, close, dauby, gluey, gooey, goopy, gummy, humid, jammy, muggy, tacky, tough **06** claggy, clammy, clarty, clingy, cloggy, gummed, smeary, stodgy, sultry, sweaty, thorny, tricky, viscid **07** awkward, viscous **08** adhesive, delicate, ticklish **09** difficult, glutinous, sensitive, tenacious **10** oppressive, sweltering, unpleasant **12** embarrassing

• **sticky substance**
03 goo, gum **04** glit, goop, gunk, lime **05** gunge **06** viscin **08** mucilage, propolis

stiff
03 rob **04** cold, dead, firm, hard, prim, taut, very **05** brisk, cheat, dense, fresh, harsh, large, rigid, solid, stark, stoor, stour, sture, tense, thick, tight, tough, windy **06** aching, chilly, corpse, formal, murder, potent, severe, stowre, strict, strong, tiring **07** arduous, austere, awkward, certain, drastic, extreme, pompous, stilted, unlucky, viscous **08** decorous, exacting, forceful, hardened, priggish, reserved, rigorous, stubborn, vigorous **09** alcoholic, arthritic, demanding, difficult, Draconian, excessive, extremely, inelastic, laborious, resistant, rheumatic, stringent, unbending **10** ceremonial, formidable, inflexible, solidified, unyielding **11** ceremonious, challenging, constrained, rheumaticky, standoffish **12** intoxicating, pertinacious

stiffen
03 gel, set **04** jell **05** brace, stark, steel, tense **06** harden, starch **07** congeal, fortify, tense up, thicken, tighten **08** ankylose, solidify **09** anchylose, bandoline, coagulate, reinforce, Trubenise, Trubenize® **10** strengthen

stiff-necked
05 proud **06** formal **07** haughty **08** arrogant, stubborn **09** obstinate, pig-headed, unnatural **11** opinionated **12** contumacious **14** uncompromising

stifle
04 curb, funk, hush **05** check, choke, crush, quash, quell, stive **06** dampen, deaden, hush up, keep in, muffle, subdue **07** repress, silence, smother, swallow **08** gulp back, gulp down, hold back, restrain, scomfish, strangle, suppress **09** constrain, suffocate **10** asphyxiate, extinguish

stigma
04 blot, mark, note, pore, scar, slur, spot **05** brand, shame, stain, taint **07** blemish **08** disgrace, spiracle **09** dishonour

stigmatize
04 mark, note **05** brand, label, shame, stain **06** vilify **07** blemish, condemn **08** demonize, denounce, disgrace, vilipend **09** discredit

still
03 but, e'en, ene, yet **04** calm, deep, even, hush, kill, mild **05** abate, accoy, allay, inert, peace, quiet **06** always, distil, even so, hushed, pacify, serene, settle, silent, smooth, soothe, static, subdue, though **07** appease, assuage, however, quieten, quietly, restful, silence **08** although, constant, immobile, inactive, lifeless, moderate, peaceful, restrain, serenity, stagnant, tranquil, unmoving, until now **09** continual, noiseless, quiescent, quietness, sedentary, stillness, unruffled **10** constantly, for all that, inactively, motionless, stationary, stock-still, unstirring **11** nonetheless, undisturbed **12** nevertheless, peacefulness, tranquillity, tranquillize, up to this time **13** in spite of that, in spite of this, noiselessness **15** notwithstanding

• **be still**
03 lie **04** hush, rest **06** remain, repose

stillness
04 calm, hush, rest **05** peace, quiet **06** repose **07** silence **08** calmness, coolness, quietude, serenity **09** composure, placidity, quietness **10** equanimity, sedateness **11** restfulness **12** peacefulness, tranquillity

stilted
05 stiff **06** forced, wooden **08** laboured, mannered **09** unnatural **10** artificial **11** constrained

stimulant
01 E **03** kat, qat **04** khat **05** betel, chile, chili, tonic, upper **06** chilli, cinder **07** caffein, cardiac, digoxin, ecstasy, guaraná, pep pill, reviver **08** caffeine, coramine, doxapram, excitant, incitant, lobeline, pemoline, pick-me-up **09** analeptic, cantharis, dance drug, digitalin, nux vomica, sassafras, whetstone **11** nikethamide, purple heart, restorative, winter's bark **13** dexamfetamine, smelling salts **14** dexamphetamine **15** methamphetamine

stimulate
03 fan, jog **04** fire, goad, hype, spur, urge **05** gee up, hop up, impel, rouse **06** arouse, buck up, excite, fillip, hype up, incite, induce, kindle, prompt, whip up **07** animate, hearten, inflame, inspire, provoke, quicken, trigger **08** activate, irritate, motivate **09** challenge, encourage, instigate **10** potentiate, trigger off

stimulating
07 bracing, piquant, rousing **08** excitant, exciting, galvanic, stirring **09** inspiring, provoking, stimulant **10** intriguing, suggestive **11** interesting, provocative **12** exhilarating

stimulation
06 ginger **07** arousal **08** kindling **09** animation, prompting **10** excitement, incitement, irritation, motivation, quickening **11** inspiration, instigation, provocation **13** encouragement

stimulus
03 jog **04** goad, jolt, kick, prod, push, spur, whet **05** drive, sting **06** fillip **07** impetus **09** incentive **10** incitement, inducement **11** provocation **12** shot in the arm **13** encouragement

sting
02 do **03** con, nip, rob **04** barb, bite, burn, edge, goad, hurt, lurk, pain, pole, scam, tang **05** annoy, cheat, fraud, point, prick, smart, spite, stang, trick, upset, wound **06** diddle, fiddle, fleece, grieve, injure, injury, malice, needle, nettle, offend, racket, rip off, rip-off, tingle **07** aculeus, deceive, defraud, incense, piercer, provoke, sarcasm, swindle, torment **08** distress, irritate, pungency, stimulus, trickery, urticate **09** deception, gold brick, gold-brick, heartache, sharpness **10** causticity, exasperate, incitement, irritation **11** causticness, viciousness **12** incisiveness, take for a ride **13** double-dealing, sharp practice

stinging
05 smart, urent **07** burning, hurtful, piquant **08** aculeate, poignant, smarting, tingling, urticant, wounding **09** aculeated, injurious, offensive **10** irritating **11** distressing

stingy
04 hard, mean, near **05** close, mingy, tight **06** hungry, skimpy, snippy **07** costive, miserly, niggard, save-all **09** niggardly, penurious **11** bad-tempered, tight-fisted **12** candle-paring, cheeseparing, parsimonious **13** penny-pinching

stink
03 hum, row **04** flap, fuss, guff, honk, ming, niff, pong, reek, stir, suck **05** be bad, hoo-ha, odour, smell **06** bother, furore, hassle, stench **07** be awful, be nasty, fluster, trouble **08** bad smell, malodour, mephitis **09** commotion, foul smell **12** be despicable, be unpleasant, song and dance

stinker
03 cur, dog, rat **04** scab **05** cheat, hound, louse, rogue, scamp, swine **06** fulmar, horror, louser, petrel, plight, rascal, rotter **07** bounder, dastard, problem, ruffian, shocker, villain **08** blighter, stinkard, vagabond **09** miscreant, reprobate, scallywag, scoundrel **10** blackguard, difficulty, impediment, ne'er-do-well **11** predicament **14** good-for-nothing

stinking
03 bad **04** foul, vile **05** awful, fetid, nasty, niffy, pongy **06** foetid, mingin', rotten **07** humming, minging, stenchy **08** terrible **10** disgusting, unpleasant **12** contemptible

stint
03 bit **04** bout, save, stop, time, turn **05** allot, cease, check, limit, pinch, quota, scant, share, shift, skimp, spare, spell, stent **06** period, scrimp **07** scantle, skimp on, stretch **08** begrudge, restrain, restrict, withhold **09** allowance, apportion, economize, restraint **11** restriction

stipend
03 ann **05** annat, grant **06** income, salary **07** alimony, annuity, benefit, payment, pension **08** expenses **09** allowance **10** assistance **11** maintenance **12** contribution

stipulate
06 demand **07** article, lay down, provide, require, set down, specify **08** covenant, insist on **09** guarantee

stipulation
05 point, rider **06** clause, demand **07** proviso **08** contract **09** condition, postulate, provision **11** requirement **12** precondition, prerequisite **13** specification

stir
◇ *anagram indicator*
03 ado, jee, jog, mix, wag **04** beat, flap, fuss, moot, move, to-do, turn, whip **05** blend, budge, churn, hoo-ha, pique, quich, raise, rouse, shake, shift, steer, stire, tizzy, touch **06** affect, bustle, excite, flurry, muddle, prison, puddle, quatch, quetch, quitch, quiver, racket, riffle, rustle, thrill, tumult, twitch, uproar **07** agitate, clutter, disturb, ferment, flutter, inspire, provoke, quinche, rummage, tempest, torment, tremble **08** activity, disorder, movement **09** agitation, commotion, kerfuffle, sensation **10** excitement **11** disturbance **12** song and dance
See also **prison**

• stir up
03 jog **04** fire, poke, rear, spur, wake **05** amove, awake, drive, impel, poach, raise, rouse, roust, waken **06** arouse, awaken, excite, incite, kindle, prompt, racket, rustle **07** agitate, animate, disturb, inflame, inspire, provoke, quicken, rummage **08** motivate **09** electrify, encourage, galvanize, instigate, stimulate

stirring
◇ *anagram indicator*
04 live **05** heady **06** lively, moving **07** emotive, rousing, working **08** dramatic, exciting, spirited **09** animating, inspiring, thrilling **11** impassioned, stimulating **12** exhilarating, intoxicating

stitch
03 hem, sew **04** darn, mend, seam, tack **06** repair **09** embroider
See also **embroidery**

• stitch up
03 con **04** shop, trap **05** fit up, grass, plant, set up **06** rumble, suture **07** swindle **11** double-cross, incriminate **13** stab in the back

stock
03 box, log, set **04** cows, fund, heap, keep, line, name, pack, pigs, pile, post, race, sell, team **05** banal, basic, block, blood, bonds, breed, cache, carry, equip, fumet, funds, goods, herds, hoard, money, plant, range, sheep, store, stump, talon, tired, trite, trunk, usual, wares **06** assets, cattle, common, credit, deal in, family, flocks, handle, horses, kit out, market, repute, shares, source, strain, supply, trough **07** animals, average, capital, descent, fumette, furnish, holding, kindred, lineage, opinion, plenish, provide, regular, reserve, routine, species, stretch, trade in, variety, worn-out **08** accoutre, ancestry, clichéed, equities, good name, ordinary, overused, pedigree, pressure, quantity, standard, standing, stoccado **09** amassment, customary, equipment, essential, genealogy, hackneyed, inventory, livestock, parentage, portfolio, provision, relatives, reservoir, selection, stockpile, traffic in **10** assortment, background, collection, estimation, extraction, investment, repertoire, reputation, securities **11** commodities, farm animals, merchandise, merchandize, stereotyped, traditional **12** accumulation, conventional, run-of-the-mill

• in stock
06 on sale **07** for sale **09** available **11** on the market **12** on the shelves

• stock up
03 buy **04** fill, heap, load, save **05** amass, buy up, hoard, lay in, store **06** fill up, gather, heap up, pile up **07** put away, stack up, store up **08** put aside, salt away **09** provision, replenish, stash away, stockpile **10** accumulate

• take stock
06 assess, review, size up, survey **07** weigh up **08** appraise, estimate, evaluate, reassess **09** re-examine **10** re-evaluate

stockade
06 zareba, zariba, zereba, zeriba **07** zareeba

stocking
05 nylon, stock **06** hogger, moggan **07** popsock, spattee **08** boothose, knee-high **10** understock **11** netherstock
See also **sock**

stockings
04 hose **07** hold-ups, legwear **11** netherlings

stockpile
04 fund, heap, keep, pile, save **05** amass, cache, hoard, stock, store **06** gather, heap up, pile up **07** put away, reserve, store up **08** put aside **09** amassment, reservoir **10** accumulate **12** accumulation

stock-still
05 inert, still **06** static **08** immobile, inactive, unmoving **10** motionless, stationary, unstirring

stocky
05 broad, dumpy, short, solid, squat **06** blocky, chunky, stubby, stumpy, sturdy **07** nuggety **08** thickset **11** mesomorphic

stodgy
04 dull **05** heavy, solid, staid **06** boring, formal, leaden, solemn, stuffy, turgid **07** filling, starchy, tedious **08** laboured **10** fuddy-duddy, spiritless, unexciting, uninspired **11** substantial **12** indigestible **13** unimaginative **14** unenterprising

stoical
04 calm, cool **07** patient **08** resigned **09** accepting, impassive **10** forbearing, phlegmatic **11** indifferent, unemotional, unexcitable **13** dispassionate, imperturbable, long-suffering, philosophical, uncomplaining **14** self-controlled **15** self-disciplined

stoicism
07 ataraxy **08** ataraxia, calmness, fatalism, patience **09** fortitude, stolidity **10** acceptance, dispassion, philosophy **11** forbearance, impassivity, resignation **12** indifference **13** long-suffering **14** unexcitability

stoke
04 tend **09** add coal to, add fuel to, add wood to **11** keep burning **12** feed with fuel

stokes
01 S

stolen
03 hot **04** bent **05** taken **06** nicked, swiped **07** nobbled, punched

08 pilfered 09 ill-gotten, purloined, ripped off 10 knocked off

• **stolen goods**

03 tom 04 crib, loot, soup, waif 05 cheat, theft 07 stealth 08 tweedler 09 stouthrie 10 stoutherie, tomfoolery

stolid

02 po 04 dull, slow 05 beefy, heavy 06 bovine, solemn, wooden 07 lumpish, po-faced 08 blockish 09 apathetic, impassive 10 phlegmatic 11 indifferent, unemotional, uninspiring 13 unimaginative

stomach

03 gut, maw, tum 04 bear, craw, guts, puku, read, take, vell, zest 05 abide, belly, bible, bingy, brook, gorge, pride, rumen, stand, taste, tummy 06 bonnet, desire, digest, endure, fardel, hunger, inside, liking, omasum, paunch, relish, rennet, resent, spirit, spleen, suffer, tum-tum, venter 07 abdomen, courage, gizzard, insides, passion 08 abomasum, appetite, pot-belly, submit to, tolerate 09 approve of, king's-hood, manyplies, put up with, rennet-bag, reticulum 10 little Mary, psalterium 11 bread basket, corporation, disposition, inclination 13 determination

See also **ruminant**

• **without stomach**

◇ *middle deletion indicator*

stomach ache

05 colic 06 gripes, gut rot 09 bellyache, dyspepsia, tummy ache 12 hypochondria 13 grass staggers 15 stomach staggers

stone

02 st 03 gem, pip, pit, rag, set 04 flag, hone, plum, rock, seed, sett, slab 05 jewel, lapis 06 cobble, gibber, gonnie, goolie, kernel, mirror, pebble, yonnie 07 boondie, boulder, brinnie 08 endocarp, gemstone, sardonyx, testicle 09 flagstone, headstone, tombstone 10 concretion, gravestone

See also **birth**; **gem**; **rock**

stoned *see* **drunk**

stonewall

03 lie 05 dodge, evade, hedge, shift 06 waffle 07 deceive, quibble, shuffle 09 be evasive, pussy-foot 10 equivocate 11 prevaricate 12 shilly-shally 13 sit on the fence

stony

03 icy 04 cold, hard 05 blank, rigid, rocky, stern 06 chilly, frigid, frosty, gritty, pebbly, severe, steely 07 adamant, callous, deadpan, hostile, petrous, shingly 08 gravelly, obdurate, pitiless 09 heartless, lapideous, merciless, unfeeling 10 inexorable, petrifying, poker-faced, unfriendly 11 indifferent, unforgiving 12 unresponsive 14 expressionless

stooge

04 butt, dupe, feed, foil, pawn 06 drudge, lackey, puppet 07 cat's paw, fall guy 08 henchman 09 scapegoat 11 subordinate

stool

05 coppy, stand 06 buffet, sunkie, tripod 07 creepie, cricket, taboret, tumbrel, tumbril 08 stillage, tabouret

stoop

03 bow, sag 04 bend, curb, duck, lean, lout, lowt, poke, post, prop, sink 05 courb, deign, droop, hunch, kneel, lower, porch, slump, squat, steep, stoep, stope, stoup, swoop 06 bucket, cringe, crouch, patron, resort, slouch, stoope, submit 07 bending, decline, descend, descent, ducking, incline 08 hunching, lowering, verandah 09 go so far as, go so low as, supporter, vouchsafe 10 condescend 11 inclination 13 condescension, lower yourself

stop

03 bar, can, dit, end 04 bung, cork, halt, hold, kick, kill, live, plug, poop, quit, rein, rest, seal, sist, snub, stap, stay, stem 05 block, board, break, cease, check, choke, close, cover, dwell, embar, imbar, lodge, media, pause, put up, snuff, sprag, stage, stall, stash, stimy, tarry, visit 06 anchor, arrest, cut off, desist, detain, devall, draw up, finish, hinder, impede, keep up, pack in, pack up, rein in, reside, scotch, settle, stanch, stimie, stop up, stymie, thwart, wind up 07 abandon, bus stop, chuck it, close up, occlude, prevent, refrain, sojourn, station, staunch, suspend 08 conclude, draw rein, give over, hold hard, knock off, leave off, obstacle, obstruct, pack it in, pack it up, restrain, stopover, stoppage, suppress, terminus, withhold 09 cessation, diaphragm, fare stage, foreclose, frustrate, hindrance, intercept, interrupt, obstruent, punctuate, terminate 10 conclusion, standstill 11 come to an end, come to a rest, destination, discontinue, termination 12 bring to an end, bring to a rest, interruption 13 stopping-place 14 discontinuance 15 discontinuation

See also **organ**

• **expressions ordering a stop**

02 ha, ho, wo 03 hoa, hoh 04 easy, proo, pruh, toho, whoa 05 avast

stopgap

05 shift 06 resort 09 emergency, expedient, impromptu, makeshift, temporary 10 improvised, substitute 11 provisional 12 expediential 13 improvisation, rough-and-ready

stopover

04 rest, stop 05 break, visit 07 layover, sojourn, stop-off 13 overnight stay

stoppage

03 cut, jam 04 blin, halt, stop 05 check, choke, hitch, sit-in, stand, stick 06 arrest, freeze, hartal, hold-up, outage, pull-up, strike 07 closure, embargo, removal, shut-off, walk-out 08 asphyxia, blackout, blockage, decrease, discount, obstacle, shutdown, stayaway 09 allowance, breakdown, cessation, deduction, hindrance, occlusion, reduction, taking off 10 inhibition, standstill, taking away, withdrawal 11 haemostasis, obstruction, subtraction, suppression, termination 12 heart failure, interruption 14 discontinuance 15 discontinuation

stopper

03 tap 04 bung, cork, plug, seal 06 spigot 07 stopple 08 screwtop

storage

• **computer storage**

03 RAM, ROM

store

03 lot 04 bank, barn, fund, heap, keep, load, mine, pack, save, shop, stow 05 cache, hoard, house, lay by, lay in, lay up, stash, stock, stuff, value 06 coffer, esteem, garner, gather, larder, panary, plenty, supply, vintry 07 buttery, collect, deposit, furnish, keeping, lay down, put down, reserve 08 cupboard, minimart, multiple, put aside, quantity, salt away, treasury 09 abundance, amassment, livestock, provision, reservoir, stockpile, storeroom, warehouse 10 accumulate, chain store, corner shop, depository, groceteria, repository, storehouse 11 hypermarket, stock up with, sufficiency, supermarket 12 accumulation, retail outlet, squirrel away 15 department store

• **set store by, lay store by**

05 value 06 admire, esteem 13 think highly of 14 consider highly

storehouse

04 barn, fund, hold, silo 05 depot, étape, vault 06 cellar, garner, larder, pantry, pataka, wealth 07 armoury, arsenal, buttery, granary 08 dene-hole, elevator, entrepot, magazine, treasury 09 repertory, thesaurus, warehouse 10 depository, repository 12 conservatory

storey

04 deck, flat, tier 05 attic, étage, floor, level, stage 06 flight 07 stratum 08 basement, bel étage, entresol 09 triforium 10 clearstory, clerestory, downstairs, first floor 11 ground floor

stork

06 argala, jabiru 08 adjutant, shoebill 09 whale-head 10 saddlebill

storm

◇ *anagram indicator*

03 row 04 fume, rage, rand, rant, rave, roar, rush, stir, tear, to-do 05 shout, stamp 06 assail, attack, charge, furore, outcry, rumpus, seethe, tumult, uproar 07 assault, clamour, explode, flounce, turmoil 08 brouhaha, outbreak, outburst, paroxysm 09 agitation, commotion, kerfuffle, offensive,

onslaught **10** hit the roof **11** disturbance **12** lose your cool **14** foam at the mouth

Storms include:

03 ice, sea, sun
04 dust, gale, hail, line, rain, sand, snow
05 buran, devil
06 baguio, calima, haboob, meteor, pelter, squall
07 cyclone, monsoon, Shaitan, tempest, thunder, tornado, typhoon, violent
08 blizzard, downpour, magnetic
09 bourasque, dust devil, hurricane, whirlwind
10 cloudburst, electrical

stormy
◇ *anagram indicator*
04 foul, wild **05** dirty, gusty, rainy, rough, windy, wroth **06** choppy, raging, rugged, unruly, wintry **07** gustful, squally, wintery **08** blustery, oragious, stormful **09** inclement, turbulent **10** boisterous, passionate **11** tempestuous

story
03 bar, fib, gag, lie, rib **04** baur, bawr, epic, idyl, item, joke, myth, plot, saga, tale, tier, yarn **05** fable, floor, idyll, novel, rumor, theme **06** legend, record, relate, report, rumour, serial, storey **07** account, article, episode, fantasy, feature, fiction, history, recital, romance, shocker, untruth **08** anecdote, jeremiad, nouvelle, oratorio, phantasy, relation, thriller **09** chronicle, falsehood, narrative, statement, storyline **10** allegation, Munchausen, rib-tickler **11** fabrication, historiette, Munchhausen **12** old wives' tale, spine-chiller

See also **novel**; **tale**

storyteller
04 bard, liar **06** author, writer **08** narrator, novelist, romancer, tell-tale **09** raconteur **10** anecdotist, chronicler, raconteuse

stout
03 big, fat **04** bold, tall **05** beefy, brave, bulky, burly, cobby, gutsy, hardy, heavy, lusty, obese, plump, proud, solid, thick, tough, tubby **06** brawny, entire, fierce, fleshy, gritty, heroic, manful, plucky, portly, robust, spunky, stanch, stocky, strong, stuffy, stuggy, sturdy **07** durable, gallant, hulking, staunch, valiant **08** arrogant, athletic, chopping, enduring, fearless, forceful, intrepid, muscular, resolute, stalwart, stubborn, thickset, valorous, vigorous **09** corpulent, dauntless **10** courageous, determined, embonpoint, overweight, unyielding **11** substantial

stoutly
06 boldly **07** toughly **08** fiercely, strongly **09** staunchly **10** fearlessly, resolutely

stove
03 Aga **04** kiln, oven, stew **05** grill, range **06** cockle, cooker, heater, Primus® **07** caboose, chaufer, furnace **08** chauffer, hothouse, pot-belly **09** gas cooker, kitchener **10** base-burner, calefactor, salamander **12** cooking-range

stow
◇ *containment indicator*
04 cram, crop, load, pack **05** place, stash, store, stuff **06** bundle **07** deposit, put away **11** flemish down

• **stow away**
04 hide, snug, tuck **05** put up **07** put away **14** travel secretly **15** conceal yourself

straggle
03 gad, lag **04** roam, rove, tail **05** amble, drift, range, stray, trail **06** loiter, ramble, sprawl, spread, wander **07** scatter, vagrant **08** sprangle, squander **09** string out **10** dilly-dally

straggly
05 loose **06** random, untidy **07** aimless **08** drifting, rambling, straying **09** irregular, spreading, strung out **10** straggling **12** disorganized

straight
03 het, str **04** even, fair, flat, gain, just, neat, pure, slap, tidy, true **05** blunt, frank, level, right, smack, spang **06** at once, candid, decent, direct, honest, normal, pronto, square, unbent **07** aligned, bluntly, clearly, frankly, in order, orderly, plainly, settled, sincere, unmixed, upright **08** accurate, arranged, balanced, candidly, directly, faithful, honestly, promptly, reliable, slap-bang, unbroken, uncurved, vertical **09** downright, instantly, on the trot, organized, outspoken, right away, shipshape, tramlined, unbending, uncurving, undiluted **10** consistent, continuous, forthright, honourable, horizontal, law-abiding, point-blank, successive, unswerving, upstanding **11** consecutive, immediately, outspokenly, rectilineal, rectilinear, respectable, trustworthy, undeviating **12** continuously, conventional, forthrightly, heterosexual, orthotropous, successively, without delay **13** consecutively, unadulterated, uninterrupted **14** as the crow flies **15** straightforward, uninterruptedly

• **off the straight**
04 agee, ajee **08** cockeyed

• **straight away**
03 now **06** at once, pronto **08** directly, like that **09** instantly, right away **11** immediately, incontinent **12** just like that, there and then, without delay **13** incontinently

straighten
◇ *anagram indicator*
04 tidy, yelm **05** align, dress, order, range, yealm **06** adjust, neaten, tidy up, unbend **07** arrange, stretch **08** put right **10** put in order **12** make straight **14** become straight

• **straighten out**
06 extend, settle, tidy up **07** clear up, correct, realign, rectify, resolve, sort out, untwist **08** put right **10** put in order, regularize **11** disentangle

• **straighten up**
05 stand **07** stand up **10** stand erect **12** stand upright

straightforward
04 easy, even, open **05** clear, frank, pakka, plain, pucka, pukka **06** candid, direct, honest, simple **07** genuine, jannock, sincere, up-front **08** no frills, truthful **09** outspoken **10** child's play, elementary, forthright, on the level, penny-plain, point-blank, unexacting **11** undemanding, undesigning **12** a piece of cake **13** plain-speaking, uncomplicated, without frills

strain
03 air, fit, rax, sye, tax, try, tug, way **04** aria, fitt, hurt, kind, play, pull, race, rack, rick, seil, sift, sile, sing, song, sort, tear, tire, tune, type, vein, work **05** blood, breed, drain, drive, exert, fitte, force, fytte, heave, labor, music, point, press, retch, shear, sieve, sound, stock, theme, trace, trait, twist, worry, wrick, wring **06** burden, demand, duress, effort, extend, family, filter, goggle, injure, injury, labour, melody, purify, riddle, screen, sprain, spring, streak, stress, stripe, strive, tauten, weaken, wrench **07** anxiety, descent, distend, element, embrace, express, fatigue, lineage, measure, overtax, quality, squeeze, stretch, tension, tighten, variety **08** ancestry, compress, elongate, exertion, go all out, overwork, pedigree, pressure, restrain, separate, struggle, tendency **09** endeavour, offspring, percolate, suspicion, tiredness, weariness **10** exhaustion, extraction, proclivity, suggestion **11** disposition **12** do your utmost **14** beyond the limit, characteristic, push to the limit **15** make every effort

strained
05 drawn, false, heavy, stiff, tense **06** forced, sprung, uneasy, wooden **07** awkward, intense **08** laboured **09** intensive, unnatural, unrelaxed **10** artificial, non-natural **11** constrained, embarrassed **13** self-conscious, uncomfortable

strainer
03 sye **04** seil, sile, tems **05** sieve, siler, tammy, temse **06** filter, milsey, riddle, screen, sifter **08** colander **09** cullender

strait
02 St **03** fix, gat, gut, jam **04** belt, hole, kyle, mess **05** close, inlet, needy, sound, tight **06** crisis, narrow, pickle, plight, strict **07** channel, closely, dilemma, narrows, poverty, tighten, tightly **08** distress, hardship, narrowly, rigorous, straight, streight, strictly

09 emergency, extremity 10 difficulty, perplexity, rigorously 11 hard-pressed, predicament 13 embarrassment

Straits include:

03 Rae
04 Adak, Bass, Cook, Haro, Irbe, Kara, Palk, Pitt, Soya
05 Banks, Bohai, Cabot, Canso, Davis, Dease, Dover, Kerch, Korea, Luzon, Menai, Osumi, Sunda, Tatar
06 Bering, Dundas, Etolin, Fisher, Hecate, Hormuz, Hudson, Lombok, Solent, Sunday, Tablas, Taiwan, Tokara, Torres, Vitiaz
07 Balabac, Chatham, Dampier, Denmark, Florida, Formosa, Foveaux, Georgia, Le Maire, Makasar, Malacca, McClure, Messina, Mindoro, Otranto, Polillo, Rosario, Tsugaru
08 Bosporus, Clarence, Karimata, Kattegat, Mackinac, Magellan, Makassar, Shelikof, Tsushima, Victoria
09 Belle Isle, Bonifacio, Bosphorus, Gibraltar, Great Belt, La Pérouse, Linapacan, Van Diemen
10 Juan de Fuca, Little Belt
11 Dardanelles
12 Bougainville, Investigator
13 San Bernardino
14 Northumberland, Queen Charlotte
15 Dolphin and Union

straitened
04 poor 07 limited, reduced
09 difficult 10 distressed, restricted
11 embarrassed 12 impoverished

strait-laced
04 prim 06 narrow, proper, strict, stuffy
07 prudish, starchy, uptight
08 priggish, unstuffy 09 tight-lace
10 moralistic, tight-laced 11 puritanical
12 narrow-minded 13 prim and proper

strand
03 ply 04 kemp, lock, sand, wire, wisp
05 beach, fibre, front, piece, sands, shore, tress, twist 06 bundle, factor, gutter, length, maroon, sliver, string, strond, thread 07 element, feature, monofil, rivulet 08 filament, multifil, seashore 09 component, foreshore
10 ingredient, waterfront
11 homopolymer 12 optical fibre
13 multifilament 14 vascular bundle

stranded
07 aground, beached, wrecked
08 forsaken, grounded, helpless, marooned 09 abandoned, penniless
10 high and dry, in the lurch
11 shipwrecked 14 left in the lurch

strange
◇ *anagram indicator*
03 new, odd, rum, shy 04 unco
05 alien, crazy, fraim, fremd, funny, kinky, novel, queer, silly, unked, unket, unkid, wacky, weird 06 exotic, freaky, fremit, stupid, unreal 07 bizarre, curious, foreign, oddball, offbeat, surreal, uncanny, uncouth, unknown, untried, unusual 08 abnormal, peculiar, selcouth, singular, straunge, uncommon, unversed, wondrous
09 eccentric, estranged, fantastic, irregular, unheard-of, wonderful, wonderous 10 mysterious, mystifying, off the wall, outlandish, perplexing, remarkable, surprising, unexpected, unfamiliar 11 exceptional, unexplained 12 inexplicable, unaccustomed, unacquainted
13 extraordinary

strangely
◇ *anagram indicator*
05 oddly 07 weirdly 08 wondrous
09 bizarrely, curiously, unusually, wonderous 10 abnormally, peculiarly, remarkably, singularly, uncommonly
12 inexplicably, unexpectedly
13 exceptionally

strangeness
01 S 06 oddity 07 oddness 08 eeriness
09 queerness 10 exoticness
11 abnormality, bizarreness, peculiarity, singularity, uncanniness
12 eccentricity, irregularity

stranger
04 unco 05 alien, fraim, fremd, guest
06 fremit, frenne 07 incomer, pilgrim, visitor 08 newcomer, outsider
09 foreigner, non-member 10 new arrival

• a stranger to
10 unversed in 14 unaccustomed to, unfamiliar with 15 inexperienced in

strangle
03 gag 04 kill 05 check, choke
06 impede, keep in, stifle 07 garotte, garrote, inhibit, repress, smother
08 garrotte, hold back, restrain, suppress, thrapple, thropple, throttle
09 bowstring, constrict, suffocate
10 asphyxiate 11 strangulate

strap
03 tab, tie 04 band, beat, belt, bind, cord, flog, hang, jess, lash, rein, taws, whip 05 leash, sling, strop, tawse, thong, truss 06 barber, credit, fasten, muzzle, secure 07 bandage, leather, scourge 08 backband, selvagee
10 watchguard

strapping
03 big 05 beefy, burly, hefty, hunky, husky 06 brawny, robust, strong, sturdy 07 hulking 08 chopping, swanking 09 thrashing, two-handed, well-built

stratagem
04 coup, plan, plot, ploy, ruse, wile
05 dodge, fetch, guile, guyle, trick
06 device, feeler, scheme, tactic
08 artifice, intrigue, maneuver, trickery
09 deception, malengine, manoeuvre
10 subterfuge 11 counter-plot, machination 12 ruse de guerre

strategic
03 key 05 vital 07 crucial, planned, politic 08 critical, decisive, tactical
09 essential, important 10 calculated, commanding, deliberate, diplomatic
11 strategical

strategy
03 ESS 04 plan 06 design, policy, scheme 07 maximin, minimax, tactics
08 approach, game plan, planning, schedule 09 blueprint, procedure, programme 11 generalship, geostrategy 12 plan of action 14 shark repellent

stratification
07 bedding, ranking, sorting
08 division, layering 09 gradation, hierarchy 10 graduation
14 categorization, classification

stratum
03 bed 04 lode, post, rank, seam, tier, vein 05 caste, class, grade, group, layer, level, table 06 region 07 bracket, cap rock, coal-bed, day-coal, station
08 category, wayboard 09 Corallian
10 weighboard 14 stratification

straw
04 halm, wase 05 chaff, haulm, strae
06 buntal, litter, thatch 07 stubble
08 strammel, strummel

• bundle of straw, bundles of straw
04 wisp, yelm 05 truss, yealm
06 kemple

• straw hat
04 hive 06 basher, boater 07 leghorn
09 coolie hat, Dunstable 10 balibuntal

stray
◇ *anagram indicator*
03 err, odd, tag 04 lost, roam, rove, waff, waif 05 amble, drift, freak, range, traik 06 casual, chance, common, estray, ramble, random, wander, wilder
07 deviate, digress, diverge, erratic, get lost, go wrong, meander, roaming, saunter 08 alleycat, drifting, go astray, homeless, isolated, maverick, straggle, stravaig, stray cat, stray dog
09 abandoned, forwander, scattered, straggler, wandering, wander off
10 accidental, exorbitate, occasional
15 go off at a tangent, go off the subject

streak
03 fly 04 band, belt, dart, dash, daub, lace, line, mark, race, rach, roll, rush, tear, time, vein, waif, wake, wale, wave, weal, zoom 05 flash, fleck, freak, layer, ratch, smear, speed, spell, stint, stria, strip, sweep, touch, trace, vibex, whizz
06 beat it, gallop, hurtle, period, ribbon, scurry, smudge, sprint, strain, strake, stripe, stroke 07 element, scarper, scratch, stretch, striate, vamoose, whistle 09 skedaddle

streaked
05 lined 06 banded, barred, hawked, hawkit, veined 07 brinded, brindle, flecked, streaky, striate, striped
08 brindled 09 fleckered 11 tear-stained

stream
03 fly, jet, pow, ren, rin, run 04 beck, burn, flap, flow, gush, kill, lake, lane,

nala, pour, rill, rush, shed, tide, well **05** brook, burst, creek, crowd, drift, float, flood, issue, nalla, nulla, river, spill, spout, surge, trail **06** course, deluge, efflux, gutter, nallah, nullah, rillet, streel, volley **07** cascade, current, flutter, rivulet, torrent **08** affluent, influent, tendency **09** tributary **10** outpouring, succession **11** watercourse

streamer
04 flag, vane **05** plume **06** banner, ensign, fallal, pennon, pinnet, ribbon **07** bandrol, pennant **08** banderol, bannerol, gonfalon, standard, vexillum **09** banderole, bannerall

streamlined
05 sleek, slick **06** smooth **07** well-run **08** graceful **09** efficient, organized **10** modernized, time-saving **11** aerodynamic **12** rationalized **13** smooth-running, up-to-the-minute

street
02 St **03** rue, way **04** gate, lane, road **06** avenue **12** thoroughfare

See also **London**; **New York**; **Paris**; **road**

• man in the street, woman in the street
07 Joe Blow **09** Joe Bloggs, Joe Public, Mr Average **10** Joe Sixpack, Mrs Average **13** average person, average punter **14** ordinary person **15** ordinary citizen

streetwalker *see* **prostitute**

strength
04 bant, bent, gift, grit, guts, iron, main, thew **05** asset, brawn, clout, depth, force, forte, might, nerve, point, power, sinew, thing, truth, vigor **06** ardour, energy, fizzen, foison, fusion, health, métier, muscle, spirit, talent, vigour, weight **07** ability, bravery, cogency, courage, fitness, fushion, passion, potence, potency, stamina, urgency **08** aptitude, fervency, firmness, keenness, pungency, solidity, validity **09** advantage, fortitude, hardiness, influence, intensity, sharpness, solidness, soundness, specialty, stoutness, toughness, vehemence, vividness **10** brute force, complement, durability, resilience, resistance, resolution, robustness, speciality, sturdiness **11** athleticism, graphicness, persistence, strong point **12** forcefulness, might and main **13** assertiveness, determination, effectiveness **14** impregnability, persuasiveness

• lose strength
04 fade, pall **05** faint, waste **08** wind down

• on the strength of
07 based on **09** because of **10** by virtue of **11** on account of **12** on the basis of

strengthen
03 arm, man **04** fish, line, stay **05** brace, cleat, edify, force, rally, serve, sinew, steel, wharf **06** anneal, back up, beef up, harden, munite, picket, piquet, prop up, turn up **07** afforce, bolster, build up, confirm, fortify, hearten, nourish, picquet, protect, refresh, restore, shore up, stiffen, support, toughen **08** buttress, heighten, increase **09** encourage, intensify, reinforce **10** invigorate, work-harden **11** consolidate, corroborate **12** substantiate

strenuous
04 bold, hard, keen, warm **05** eager, heavy, tough **06** active, taxing, tiring, uphill, urgent **07** arduous, earnest, weighty, zealous **08** forceful, resolute, spirited, tireless, vigorous **09** demanding, difficult, energetic, gruelling, laborious, tenacious **10** blistering, determined, exhausting **13** indefatigable

strenuously
06 boldly **08** actively **10** forcefully, resolutely, tirelessly, vigorously **11** tenaciously

stress
◇ *anagram indicator*
04 beat, birr, rack **05** brunt, force, ictus, shear, value, worry **06** accent, burden, hassle, repeat, strain, trauma, weight **07** anxiety, point up, straits, tension, trouble **08** distress, emphasis, hardship, pressure, priority **09** distraint, emphasize, highlight, spotlight, underline **10** accentuate, difficulty, exaggerate, importance, underscore, uneasiness **12** accentuation, apprehension, significance, thermal shock

stressed
04 edgy **05** jumpy, tense **06** on edge, strong, uneasy **07** anxious, fidgety, jittery, keyed up, nervous, uptight, worried **08** emphatic, restless, strained **09** screwed up **10** distraught, emphatical **11** overwrought, stressed out **12** apprehensive **13** under pressure

stressful
05 tense **06** uneasy **07** charged, fraught **08** strained, worrying **10** nail-biting **12** high-pressure, nerve-racking

stretch
03 rax, ren, rin, run, tax, try **04** area, last, line, pull, push, rack, span, term, test, time **05** offer, perch, range, reach, space, spell, stint, sweep, tract, widen **06** bouncy, expand, extend, extent, go up to, lay out, length, period, pliant, return, spread, strain, streek, supple, tauten, unfold, unroll **07** broaden, buoyant, draw out, elastic, expanse, hold out, plastic, pliable, present, proffer, project, prolong, rubbery, springy, tighten **08** come up to, continue, distance, elongate, flexible, go down to, lengthen, protract, reach out, straucht, straught, stretchy, yielding **09** challenge, extension, go as far as, make wider, resilient, spread out, stimulate **10** come down to, exaggerate, make longer, straighten **11** become wider, elasticated, stretchable **12** become longer, exaggeration, put demands on **13** extensibility

• stretch out
05 crane, reach, relax **06** extend, intend, put out, sprawl, string **07** hold out, lie down, recline

• stretch your legs
06 stroll **08** exercise **09** move about, promenade, take a walk **10** go for a walk, take the air **13** take a breather

stretcher
04 rack **06** gurney, litter

strew
03 sow **04** lard, rush, snow, toss **05** level, straw, strow **06** litter, spread **07** bestrew, scatter **08** bespread, disperse, sprinkle **10** besprinkle

stricken
03 hit **06** struck **07** injured, smitten, wounded **08** affected **09** afflicted

strict
04 firm, hard, true **05** clear, close, exact, harsh, rigid, stern, tight, total, tough, utter **06** giusto, narrow, proper, severe, strait **07** austere, literal, precise, regular **08** absolute, accurate, clear-cut, complete, faithful, intimate, orthodox, rigorous, straight, streight **09** Draconian, religious, stringent **10** inflexible, iron-fisted, iron-handed, meticulous, no-nonsense, particular, restricted, scrupulous **11** hard and fast **13** authoritarian, barrack square, conscientious, thoroughgoing **14** disciplinarian, uncompromising

strictly
04 only **06** firmly, purely, strait, wholly **07** sternly, totally **08** narrowly, properly, severely, straight, straitly, streight, uniquely **10** absolutely, completely, definitely, in every way, inflexibly, positively, rigorously **11** exclusively **13** categorically, unambiguously, unequivocally **14** in every respect, unquestionably

• strictly speaking
07 exactly **09** literally, precisely **11** to the letter

strictness
06 rigour **08** accuracy, firmness, rigidity, rigorism, severity **09** austerity, exactness, harshness, precision, rigidness, sternness **10** stringency **12** rigorousness **13** barrack square, stringentness **14** meticulousness, scrupulousness

stricture
04 flak **05** blame, bound, limit **06** rebuke **07** binding, censure, closure, confine, control, reproof **09** criticism, restraint, tightness **10** constraint, strictness **11** restriction **13** animadversion

stride
04 lamp, lope, pace, sten, step, walk

05 stalk, stend, tread **06** stroam **07** advance, galumph **08** bestride, gallumph, movement, progress, straddle **10** overstride **11** progression

• **take something in your stride**
11 do blindfold, make light of **14** cope with easily, deal with easily, think nothing of

strident
04 loud **05** harsh, rough **06** shrill, urgent **07** booming, grating, jarring, rasping, raucous, roaring **08** clashing, jangling **09** clamorous, unmusical **10** discordant, screeching, stentorian, stridulant, thundering, vociferous

strife
03 row **04** bate, feud **05** sturt **06** barrat, battle, brigue, combat, debate, hassle, mutiny **07** bargain, conteck, contest, discord, dispute, ill-will, quarrel, rivalry, trouble, warfare **08** argument, conflict, fighting, friction, striving, struggle, variance **09** animosity, bickering, hostility, wrangling **10** contention, dissension, ill-feeling **11** controversy, quarrelling **12** colluctation, contestation, disagreement

strike
03 bop, box, cob, fix, hit, lam, pat, ram, rap, tip, wap, zap **04** bang, beat, belt, biff, blad, blow, buff, chap, chip, clap, coin, cuff, dart, deal, draw, feel, find, fist, flog, gowf, hook, knee, look, neck, pane, pash, pean, peck, peen, pein, pene, pole, raid, rush, seem, slam, slap, slat, sock, swap, swop, take, toll, tonk, trap, yerk **05** adopt, bandh, blast, blaud, catch, chime, clout, crash, douse, dowse, fight, impel, knock, lower, plump, pound, prang, print, punch, reach, shoot, sit-in, slant, smack, smite, sound, souse, spank, stamp, storm, swipe, thump, touch, whack **06** affect, affrap, alight, ambush, appear, assail, assume, attack, batter, blight, broach, buffet, cancel, charge, clinch, come to, dawn on, delete, go-slow, hammer, hit out, mutiny, paddle, poleax, ratify, revolt, sclaff, set out, settle, smooth, stroke, take on, thrash, thwack, wallop **07** achieve, afflict, agree on, assault, bewitch, clobber, come out, compute, deliver, embrace, impinge, impress, inflict, occur to, percuss, poleaxe, protest, torpedo, uncover, unearth, walk out, walk-out **08** arrive at, come upon, describe, discover, estimate, look like, pounce on, register, set about, settle on, siderate, stayaway, stoppage, stop work, storming, strickle **09** dismantle, down tools, encounter, événement, interpose, penetrate, surrender **10** bird impact, chance upon, come to mind, constitute, happen upon, work to rule, work-to-rule **11** collide with **13** have the look of

• **on strike**
03 out

• **strike back**
07 hit back **09** fight back, get back at, retaliate **11** get even with, reciprocate **14** get your own back, pay someone back

• **strike down**
04 fell, kill, ruin, slay **05** smite **06** murder **07** afflict, destroy **11** assassinate

• **strike out**
03 paw **05** erase **06** cancel, delete, efface, remove, rub out **08** cross out **09** strike off **10** obliterate **13** strike through

• **strike up**
05 begin, start **07** kick off **08** commence, initiate **09** establish, instigate, introduce

strike-breaker *see* **scab**

striking
04 bold, dash, fine **06** pretty, strike **07** beating, evident, obvious, salient, visible **08** dazzling, distinct, frappant, gorgeous, sizzling, spanking, stunning **09** arresting, beautiful, distingué, glamorous, memorable **10** attractive, distinguée, impressive, incidental, noticeable, percussion, percutient, photogenic, remarkable **11** astonishing, conspicuous, eye-catching, good-looking, outstanding **13** extraordinary

string
01 G **03** row, tie **04** cord, file, hang, hoax, lace, line, link, loop, nete, rake, rope, yarn **05** cable, chain, chord, drove, fibre, leash, queue, quint, sling, strap, tie up, train, twine **06** column, fasten, humbug, number, series, strand, stream, thairm, thread **07** connect, elastic, festoon, suspend **08** lichanos, nicky-tam, paramese, paranete, sequence, shoelace **10** procession, succession

• **string along**
04 dupe, fool, hoax **05** bluff **06** humbug **07** deceive, mislead **09** co-operate, play false **12** put one over on, take for a ride

• **string out**
06 extend, fan out, wander **08** disperse, lengthen, protract, space out, straggle **09** spread out **10** stretch out

• **strings of a lyre**
04 mese, nete **05** trite **06** hypate **08** lichanos, paramese, paranete **09** parhypate

• **string up**
03 top **04** hang, kill, kilt **05** lynch, run up, truss **15** send to the gibbet

• **with no strings attached**
13 unconditional

stringency
06 rigour **07** demands **08** firmness **09** exactness, toughness **10** strictness **12** rigorousness **13** inflexibility

stringent
04 firm, hard **05** harsh, rigid, tight, tough **06** severe, strict **07** binding, extreme **08** exacting, rigorous **09** demanding **10** inflexible **14** uncompromising

stringy
04 ropy, wiry **05** chewy, ropey, tough **06** sinewy **07** fibrous, gristly **08** leathery

strip
03 bar, bit, gut, jib, rig **04** area, band, bare, bark, belt, bend, doff, flay, gear, husk, lath, list, loot, peel, pull, rand, roon, rund, sash, skin, slat, slip, tack, tirl, tirr, togs, welt, zona, zone **05** clear, empty, get-up, ledge, linch, piece, pluck, press, royne, ruler, shear, shred, shuck, spoil, strap, thong, tract, unrip **06** denude, devest, divest, expose, extent, lardon, outfit, peeler, ribbon, rig-out, screed, splent, spline, splint, straik, strake, stripe, stroke, swathe, things, uncase, unload **07** clobber, clothes, colours, deprive, despoil, disrobe, expanse, feather, flaught, flitter, fumetto, lardoon, lay bare, parking, peeling, pillage, plunder, ransack, stretch, tear off, uncover, undress **08** airstrip, clean out, clothing, degrease, flake off, separate, unclothe **09** dismantle, excoriate, pull apart, take apart **10** disfurnish, dispossess, striptease **11** disassemble **12** straightedge, take to pieces **13** swaddling-band

stripe
03 bar **04** band, belt, blow, lash, line, list, pale, snip, zone **05** flash, fleck, guard, slash, strip, vitta, whelk **06** ribbon, straik, strain, strake, streak **07** chevron, endorse **09** laticlave, pin-stripe

striped
06 banded, barred, pirnie, pirnit, stripy **07** bausond, guarded, streaky, vittate **08** endorsed, streaked, striated **10** variegated **11** finch-backed

stripling
03 boy, lad **05** youth **07** young 'un **08** teenager **09** fledgling, youngster **10** adolescent **11** hobbledehoy

strive
03 try, tug, vie **04** toil, work **05** bandy, fight, force, heave, press **06** aspire, battle, combat, engage, follow, labour, pingle, preace, prease, resist, strain **07** attempt, bargain, compete, contend, contest, enforce, preasse, try hard, wrestle **08** campaign, do battle, endeavor, purchase, struggle **09** endeavour, persevere **10** do your best **11** give your all **12** do your utmost **13** exert yourself

stroke
03 cut, hit, pat, pet, rub **04** beat, bell, belt, biff, blow, coup, dash, dint, hand, jole, joll, jowl, line, milk, move, push, shot, slap, touk, tuck, whet **05** boast, chuck, cross, ictus, joule, knock, pulse, scoop, shock, smack, spasm, strip, sweep, swipe, thump, touch, trait,

whack **06** action, attack, buffet, caress, fondle, glance, motion, stound, stownd, strike, struck, thwack, tittle, wallop **07** clobber, flatter, massage, nobbler, outlash, reverse, reverso, seizure, solidus, strooke, upright, whample **08** collapse, flourish, movement **09** encourage, grand coup **10** back-hander, coup d'éclat, pile-driver, sideration, thrombosis **11** achievement **12** punto reverso, punto riverso, repercussion **14** accomplishment

See also **swimming**

stroll
04 turn, walk **05** amble, troll **06** bummel, dander, dauner, dawdle, dawner, lounge, ramble, toddle, wander **07** daunder, meander, saunter **08** ambulate **10** go for a walk **14** constitutional **15** stretch your legs

stroller
06 walker **07** dawdler, flâneur, rambler, vagrant **08** wanderer **09** itinerant, pushchair, saunterer

strong
01 f **03** fit, hot, str **04** able, bull, deep, firm, full, hale, keen, rank, sour, very, well, yald **05** beefy, brave, burly, clear, eager, great, gross, gutsy, hardy, heady, heavy, lusty, nappy, pithy, sharp, solid, sound, spicy, stiff, stout, thewy, tough, valid, vivid, wight, yauld **06** active, ardent, biting, brawny, cogent, fierce, marked, mighty, potent, robust, rugged, secure, severe, sinewy, sturdy, trusty, urgent **07** devoted, doughty, durable, evident, fervent, graphic, healthy, intense, marrowy, obvious, piquant, pollent, pungent, telling, violent, weighty **08** athletic, cast-iron, clear-cut, decisive, definite, forceful, forcible, grievous, muscular, numerous, positive, powerful, profound, resolute, stalwart, stressed, vehement, vigorous **09** assertive, committed, competent, confident, effective, efficient, excelling, heavy-duty, plausible, resilient, resistant, steadfast, strapping, undiluted, well-built **10** aggressive, compelling, convincing, courageous, determined, emphasized, fast-moving, formidable, hogen-mogen, passionate, persistent, persuasive, pronounced, reinforced, remarkable **11** efficacious, hard-wearing, long-lasting, substantial **12** concentrated, enthusiastic, single-minded, strong-minded, strong-willed **13** well-protected **14** highly seasoned **15** highly flavoured

• **strong point**
04 bent, gift **05** asset, forte, thing **06** métier, talent **08** aptitude, strength **09** advantage, specialty **10** speciality

strongarm
06 terror **07** violent **08** bully-boy, bullying, coercive, forceful, physical, thuggish **10** aggressive, oppressive **11** threatening **12** intimidatory

strongbox
04 safe **05** chest, vault **06** coffer **07** cash box **10** deposit box, depository, repository

stronghold
04 aery, eyry, fort, hold, holt, keep **05** aerie, ayrie, eyrie, tower **06** castle, center, centre, refuge **07** bastion, citadel, outpost **08** fastness, fortress, hill-fort

strongly
06 deeply, firmly **07** durably, solidly, toughly **08** markedly **09** intensely **10** definitely, forcefully, muscularly, positively, powerfully, resolutely **11** resiliently **12** athletically **13** substantially

strong-minded
04 firm **08** resolute **09** steadfast, tenacious, unbending **10** determined, iron-willed, unwavering **11** independent **12** strong-willed **14** uncompromising

strong-willed
06 wilful **07** wayward **08** obdurate, stubborn **09** obstinate **10** inflexible, refractory, self-willed **11** intractable **12** intransigent, recalcitrant

strontium
02 Sr

stroppy
05 ratty, rowdy **06** shirty **07** awkward, bolshie **08** perverse **09** difficult, unhelpful **10** refractory **11** bad-tempered, quarrelsome **12** bloody minded, cantankerous, obstreperous **13** unco-operative

structural
06 design **07** organic **08** tectonic **09** edificial **11** formational **14** constructional, organizational **15** configurational

structure
◇ *anagram indicator*
04 form, make **05** build, frame, set-up, shape **06** design, fabric, make-up, system **07** arrange, build up, chassis, edifice **08** assemble, building, erection, organize **09** construct, formation, framework **10** contexture **11** arrangement, composition **12** architecture, conformation, constitution, construction, organization **13** configuration

struggle
◇ *anagram indicator*
03 tug, vie, war **04** agon, camp, toil, work **05** agony, brawl, clash, fight, pains, scrum **06** battle, combat, effort, engage, hassle, labour, ruffle, strain, strife, strift, strive, tussle **07** agonize, compete, contend, contest, grapple, problem, scuffle, trouble, try hard, tuilyie, tuilzie, warfare, wrestle **08** conflict, exertion, flounder, skirmish, slugfest, sprangle **09** encounter, handgrips, luctation, scrimmage, scrummage **10** difficulty, do your best **11** competition, give your all, hostilities **12** do your utmost **13** exert yourself, passage of arms

strumpet *see* **prostitute**

strut
03 jet **04** cock, prop, spur **05** brank, bulge, dwang, glory, major, pronk, raker, stalk, swank **06** flaunt, parade, prance, scotch, strout, strunt **07** nervure, peacock, swagger **08** protrude, stanchel, stancher, tail boom **09** stanchion

stub
03 end **04** butt, grub, snub, stob **05** stump **06** dog-end, fag end, snubbe **07** remnant **11** counterfoil

stubborn
05 rigid, stiff, stoor, stour, stout, sture **06** dogged, mulish, ornery, stowre, thrawn, wilful **07** adamant **08** obdurate, obstacle, perverse **09** difficult, hidebound, obstinate, opinioned, pig-headed, rigwiddie, rigwoodie, tenacious, unbending **10** headstrong, inflexible, inveterate, persistent, refractory, self-willed, unyielding **11** intractable, opinionated, stiff-necked **12** cantankerous, contumacious, intransigent, opinionative, pertinacious, recalcitrant, stiff-hearted, strong-willed, unmanageable **14** overdetermined, uncompromising **15** not open to reason, stubborn as a mule

See also **obstinate**

stubbornly
08 doggedly, wilfully **10** inflexibly, perversely **11** obstinately, pig-headedly, tenaciously **12** persistently **14** intransigently

stubby
05 dumpy, short, squat **06** chunky, stumpy **08** thickset

stuck
04 fast, firm **05** fixed, glued **06** beaten, jammed, joined, rooted **07** at a loss, baffled, stalled, stumped **08** cemented, embedded, fastened, immobile **09** perplexed, unmovable **10** bogged down, nonplussed **13** at your wits' end

• **get stuck into**
05 begin, start **06** tackle **08** embark on, set about **09** get down to

• **stuck on**
05 mad on **06** fond of, keen on, nuts on **07** sweet on **09** wild about **10** crazy about, dotty about **12** obsessed with **14** infatuated with

stuck-up
05 proud **06** snooty, uppish **07** haughty **08** arrogant, snobbish, toplofty **09** bigheaded, conceited **10** hoity-toity **11** patronizing, toffee-nosed, toploftical **12** supercilious **13** condescending, high and mighty

stud
03 seg, set **04** boss, knob, nail, race, spur, stop, tack **05** pitch, prick, rivet, stump **06** popper **07** clinker **08** doornail **11** pop-fastener **12** clip-fastener, snap-fastener **13** press fastener

studded
03 set **06** dotted **07** flecked, spotted, starred **08** mamillar, spangled, speckled **09** mamillary, scattered, sprinkled **10** bejewelled, bespangled, icy-pearled, ornamented **12** star-spangled

student
01 L **04** semi, soph **05** bejan, pupil, semie, softa, welly **06** bejant, bursar, medico, premed, tosher, wellie **07** alumnus, bookman, fresher, grinder, learner, scarfie, scholar, Templar, trainee **08** disciple, freshman, premedic **09** collegian, schoolboy, semi-bajan, sophomore **10** apprentice, green welly, schoolgirl **11** collegianer, probationer **12** extensionist, postgraduate **13** undergraduate
• **student group**
03 NUS

studied
05 voulu **06** forced, versed, wilful **07** planned **08** affected, designed, well-read **09** conscious, contrived, unnatural **10** artificial, calculated, deliberate, purposeful **11** intentional **12** premeditated **13** over-elaborate

studio
06 school **07** atelier, bottega, gallery **08** workroom, workshop

studious
05 eager **07** bookish, careful, earnest, serious **08** academic, diligent, sedulous, thorough **09** assiduous, attentive, scholarly **10** deliberate, meticulous, reflective, thoughtful **11** hard-working, industrious **12** intellectual

study
03 con, den, dig, kon **04** cram, muse, plod, read, scan, swot, work, zeal **05** conne, essay, learn, mug up, paper, train **06** bone up, devise, digest, office, peruse, ponder, read up, report, review, revise, studio, survey, thesis **07** analyse, article, examine, inquiry, library, major in, perusal, reading, reflect, reverie, subject, thought **08** analysis, bone up on, consider, cramming, critique, homework, instruct, interest, learning, meditate, pore over, research, revision, scrutiny, swotting, workroom **09** attention, monograph, workplace **10** deliberate, inspection, scrutinize **11** contemplate, examination, inclination, investigate, lucubration, preparation, prolegomena, scholarship **12** propaedeutic **13** consideration, contemplation, investigation

Subjects of study include:

02 D&T, IT
03 art, ICT, law, PSE
04 PHSE
05 craft, dance, drama, music, sport
06 botany, design
07 anatomy, biology, driving, ecology, fashion, fitness, geology, history, physics, pottery, science, zoology
08 commerce, eugenics, genetics, heraldry, medicine, penology, politics, theology
09 astrology, astronomy, chemistry, cosmology, economics, education, erotology, ethnology, forensics, geography, languages, logistics, marketing, mechanics, mythology, pathology, shorthand, sociology, surveying, web design
10 humanities, journalism, literature, metallurgy, philosophy, physiology, psychology, publishing, statistics, technology, visual arts
11 accountancy, agriculture, archaeology, calligraphy, citizenship, dressmaking, electronics, engineering, linguistics, mathematics, metaphysics, meteorology, ornithology, photography, the Classics, typewriting
12 anthropology, architecture, horticulture, lexicography, media studies, oceanography, pharmacology
13 gender studies, home economics, librarianship, marine studies, women's studies
14 food technology, leisure studies, natural history, social sciences, word processing
15 building studies, business studies, computer studies, creative writing, hotel management

stuff
03 jam, kit, pad, ram, wad **04** clog, cram, crap, fill, gear, hoax, lard, line, load, pack, pang, push, sate, stap, stow, trig, tuck **05** binge, blash, block, cloth, crowd, farce, force, fudge, goods, gorge, items, money, press, shove, squab, store, wedge **06** bung up, fabric, gobble, guzzle, liquor, matter, pig out, steeve, stodge, tackle, things, thrust **07** bombast, clobber, essence, filling, furnish, luggage, objects, rubbish, satiate, squeeze, woollen **08** articles, compress, garrison, gross out, material, nonsense, obstruct, stuffing **09** equipment, furniture, materials, provision, substance **10** belongings, gormandize **11** overindulge, possessions **13** paraphernalia

stuffing
◇ *containment indicator*
◇ *hidden indicator*
05 farce, kapok **07** bombast, farcing, filling, packing, padding, pudding, wadding **08** dressing, quilting, stopping **09** deafening, forcemeat, taxidermy

stuffy
04 dull, prim **05** close, fuggy, fusty, heavy, muggy, musty, staid, stale, stiff, stivy, stout, sulky **06** dreary, frowsy, frowzy, poking, stodgy, sturdy, sultry **07** airless, pompous, starchy **08** stifling **10** fuddy-duddy, oppressive **11** strait-laced, suffocating **12** buttoned-down, conventional, old-fashioned, unventilated **13** uninteresting

stultify
04 dull, numb **05** blunt **06** negate, stifle, thwart **07** nullify, smother, stupefy **08** hebetate, suppress **10** invalidate

stumble
◇ *anagram indicator*
03 err **04** fall, peck, reel, slip, trip **05** lapse, lurch, stoit **06** falter, hamble **07** blunder, founder, snapper, stagger, stammer, stotter, stutter **08** flounder, hesitate, titubate **09** false step **10** disconcert **15** lose your balance
• **stumble across, stumble on**
04 find **08** discover **09** encounter **10** chance upon, come across, happen upon

stumbling-block
03 bar **04** snag **06** hurdle **07** barrier, scandal **08** obstacle **09** hindrance **10** difficulty, impediment **11** obstruction **12** Becher's Brook

stump
03 end, leg, nog, peg **04** butt, dare, foil, more, runt, snag, stob, stub, stud **05** floor, scrag, stock, stool, trunk **06** baffle, defeat, dog-end, fag end, outwit, puzzle, wicket **07** confuse, flummox, mystify, nonplus, perplex, remains, remnant, staddle, stubble **08** bewilder, confound **09** bamboozle, challenge, dumbfound, tortillon
• **stump up**
03 pay **05** pay up **06** ante up, chip in, donate, pay out **07** cough up, fork out **08** hand over, shell out **10** contribute

stumped
02 st **05** stuck **07** baffled, floored, stymied **09** flummoxed, perplexed **10** bamboozled, nonplussed

stumpy
04 cash **05** dumpy, heavy, nirly, short, squat, thick **06** chunky, nirlie, stocky, stubby **07** stubbed **08** thickset

stun
02 KO **04** daze, kayo **05** amaze, devel, dover, knock, shock, stonn, stoun, Taser® **06** abrade, bruise, deafen, devvel, settle, stonne, stound **07** astound, confuse, stagger, stupefy **08** astonish, bedeafen, bewilder, bowl over, confound, knock out, overcome **09** dumbfound, overpower **11** flabbergast, knock for six

stunned
04 numb **05** dazed, silly **06** aghast, amazed, stupid **07** floored, in a daze, shocked **09** astounded, staggered, stupefied **10** astonished, devastated,

gobsmacked **11** dumbfounded **13** flabbergasted

stunner
02 KO **03** wow **05** peach, siren **06** beauty, looker, lovely **07** charmer, cracker, dazzler, smasher **08** knockout **09** sensation **10** eye-catcher, good-looker, heart-throb **11** femme fatale

stunning
05 great **06** dazing, lovely **07** amazing **08** dazzling, drop-dead, fabulous, gorgeous, smashing, striking **09** beautiful, brilliant, ravishing, wonderful **10** impressive, incredible, marvellous, remarkable, staggering, stupefying **11** sensational, spectacular **12** stupefaction **13** extraordinary

stunningly
09 amazingly **10** fabulously, gorgeously, remarkably, strikingly **11** beautifully, brilliantly, wonderfully **12** impressively, marvellously, staggeringly **13** spectacularly **15** extraordinarily

stunt
03 act **04** curb, deed, feat, hype, nirl, ramp, slow, stop, turn **05** check, dwarf, stock, trick **06** action, arrest, hamper, hinder, impede, retard, wheeze **07** exploit, inhibit **08** restrict **10** enterprise **11** performance

stunted
04 puny, tiny **05** nirly, small **06** little, nirlie **07** dwarfed, scroggy, scrubby **08** dwarfish, scroggie, scrubbed, withered **10** diminutive, undersized, wanthriven

stupefaction
04 daze **06** wonder **08** blackout, numbness, stunning **09** amazement **10** amazedness, bafflement **12** astonishment, bewilderment, state of shock **13** senselessness

stupefy
04 daze, drug, dull, mull, numb, stun **05** amaze, dozen, hocus, shock **06** bemuse, benumb, drowse, fuddle, mither, moider **07** astound, moither, stagger **08** bowl over, etherize, knock out, somniate **09** devastate, dumbfound **11** knock for six

stupendous
04 huge, vast **06** killer, superb **07** amazing, immense **08** colossal, enormous, fabulous, gigantic, stunning **09** fantastic, wonderful **10** astounding, marvellous, phenomenal, prodigious, staggering, tremendous **12** breathtaking, overwhelming **13** extraordinary

stupid
◇ *anagram indicator*
03 dim, jay, mad, twp **04** dopy, dull, dumb, rash, slow **05** barmy, brute, crass, crazy, dazed, dense, divvy, dopey, doted, dovie, dunny, flaky, foggy, goofy, gross, inane, looby, loony, loopy, muddy, potty, silly, stupe, thick **06** absurd, boring, bovine, donsie, facile, futile, groggy, lumpen, owlish, tavert, wooden **07** damfool, doltish, donnard, donnart, donnerd, donnert, fatuous, foolish, glaiket, glaikit, idiotic, insulse, lunatic, moronic, puerile, stunned, taivert, witless **08** anserine, backward, besotted, blockish, Boeotian, boobyish, clueless, donnered, gaumless, gormless, mindless, sluggish **09** brainless, fat-witted, foolhardy, half-assed, imbecilic, laughable, ludicrous, pointless, senseless, stupefied **10** beef-witted, dull-witted, fatbrained, half-witted, ill-advised, indiscreet, insensible **11** beef-brained, blunt-witted, clay-brained, conceitless, hair-brained, hare-brained, heavy-headed, injudicious, meaningless, nonsensical, not all there, thickheaded, unconscious **12** feeble-minded, hammer-headed, muttonheaded, simple-minded, sodden-witted, thick-skulled, woodenheaded **13** chuckle-headed, irresponsible, pudding-headed, semiconscious, thick as a plank **15** slow on the uptake

stupidity
05 folly **06** bêtise, idiocy, lunacy, torpor **07** dimness, duncery, fatuity, goosery, inanity, madness, naivety **08** dopiness, doziness, dullness, dumbness, futility, insanity, rashness, slowness **09** absurdity, asininity, bruteness, crassness, denseness, insulsity, oscitancy, puerility, silliness, thickness **10** crassitude, imbecility, ineptitude, obtuseness **11** fatuousness, foolishness, glaikitness **12** indiscretion **13** brainlessness, foolhardiness, ludicrousness, pointlessness, senselessness **14** impracticality

• **expression of stupidity**
03 doh, duh

stupidly
◇ *anagram indicator*
07 inanely, sillily **08** absurdly **09** fatuously, foolishly **10** mindlessly **12** unthinkingly **13** irresponsibly

stupor
04 coma, daze **06** torpor, trance **07** inertia **08** blackout, lethargy, numbness, oblivion **12** state of shock, stupefaction **13** insensibility **15** unconsciousness

sturdy
03 gid **04** dunt, firm **05** burly, giddy, hardy, husky, rough, solid, stout **06** hearty, mighty, robust, rugged, steeve, stieve, stocky, strong, stuffy **07** durable, staunch, violent **08** athletic, lubberly, muscular, powerful, resolute, stalwart, turnsick, vigorous, well-made **09** impetuous, obstinate, steadfast, tenacious, well-built **10** determined, refractory **11** flourishing, substantial

sturgeon
04 huso **05** elops **06** beluga, ellops **07** osseter, sevruga, sterlet **10** shovelnose

stutter
04 lisp **06** falter, mumble **07** sputter, stammer, stumble **08** hesitate, splutter **12** speech defect

style
◇ *anagram indicator*
03 cut, dub, pen, tag, way **04** call, chic, dash, form, hand, kind, make, mode, name, sort, term, tone, type, vein **05** adapt, flair, genre, index, label, shape, taste, tenor, title, trend, vogue **06** custom, design, gnomon, luxury, manner, method, phrase, polish, tailor, wealth **07** address, comfort, diction, entitle, fashion, panache, pattern, pointel, pointer, produce, variety, wording **08** approach, category, elegance, grandeur, language, phrasing, urbanity **09** affluence, designate, smartness, suaveness, technique **10** appearance, denominate, dressiness, expression, refinement **11** flamboyance, methodology, stylishness **14** sophistication

• **in the style of**
03 à la **05** after, -esque

stylish
03 fly **04** chic, posh **05** janty, natty, nifty, ritzy, sharp, showy, smart, swish **06** chichi, classy, dressy, jaunty, modish, snappy, snazzy, sporty, trendy, urbane **07** à la mode, dashing, elegant, in vogue, refined, voguish **08** polished **11** fashionable **13** sophisticated

stylus
03 gad, pen **04** hand **05** index, probe, style **06** needle **07** pointer **08** graphium

stymie
04 balk, foil **05** stump **06** baffle, defeat, hamper, hinder, hogtie, impede, puzzle, thwart **07** flummox, mystify, nonplus, snooker **08** confound **09** bamboozle, frustrate, interfere

styptic
06 amadou, matico, stanch **07** staunch **10** astringent **11** haemostatic

suave
04 glib **05** bland, civil **06** polite, smooth, urbane **07** affable, refined, worldly **08** charming, debonair, polished, unctuous **09** agreeable, civilized, courteous **10** soft-spoken **13** sophisticated

suavity
05 charm **08** civility, courtesy, urbanity **09** blandness **10** politeness, refinement, smoothness **11** worldliness **12** agreeability, unctuousness **14** sophistication

sub
04 dues, gift, lend, temp **05** agent, locum, proxy, U-boat **06** deputy, fill-in, relief, supply **07** advance, payment, reserve, stand-by, stand-in, stopgap

08 donation, offering 09 makeshift, surrogate 10 substitute, understudy 11 locum tenens, pinch-hitter, replacement 12 contribution, subscription 13 membership fee

subaquatic
07 subaqua 08 demersal, undersea 09 submarine, submersed 10 subaqueous, underwater

subatomic particle *see* **particle**

subconscious
02 id 03 ego 04 deep, mind 05 inner 06 hidden, latent, psyche 08 super-ego 09 innermost, inner self, intuitive, repressed 10 inner being, subliminal, suppressed, underlying 11 instinctive, unconscious 15 unconscious self

subcontract
07 farm out 08 delegate 09 outsource 11 contract out 12 give to others, pass to others

subdue
03 cow 04 adaw, damp, mate, tame 05 accoy, allay, break, charm, check, crush, daunt, quail, quash, quell 06 defeat, do down, humble, master, mellow, pacify, reduce, soften, starve, step on, stifle, subact, subdew, take in 07 achieve, chasten, conquer, control, crucify, daunton, mortify, overrun, quieten, repress, subject 08 chastise, moderate, overcome, restrain, suppress, vanquish 09 overpower, soft-pedal, subjugate 10 bring under, discipline 12 put a damper on 14 get the better of 15 gain mastery over

subdued
03 dim, sad 04 soft 05 grave, muted, quiet, sober, still 06 abated, hushed, low-key, pastel, shaded, silent, solemn, sombre, subtle 07 captive, passive, serious, submiss 08 dejected, delicate, downcast, lifeless, softened 09 depressed, noiseless, toned-down, unexcited 10 restrained 11 crestfallen, unobtrusive 13 irrepressible 14 down in the dumps

subject
03 apt, put, sub 04 case, open, subj 05 bound, field, issue, liege, motif, point, prone, theme, thirl, topic 06 affair, aspect, client, expose, ground, liable, likely, matter, native, subdew, subdue, submit, vassal, victim 07 caitive, captive, citizen, exposed, hanging, lay open, patient, resting, servant, servile 08 amenable, business, disposed, inferior, liegeman, national, obedient, question, resident 09 dependant, dependent, depending, guinea pig, subjugate, substance, underling 10 answerable, cognizable, contingent, discipline, inhabitant, subjugated, submissive, underlying, vulnerable 11 accountable, area of study, conditional, constrained, participant, subordinate, subservient, susceptible 12 field of study
See also **study**

subjection
06 chains, defeat 07 bondage, mastery, slavery 08 exposure, question, shackles 09 captivity, servitude, vassalage 10 discipline, domination, oppression 11 enslavement, subjugation

subjective
06 biased 07 bigoted 08 personal 09 emotional, intuitive 10 individual, nominative, prejudiced 11 instinctive 13 idiosyncratic, introspective

subjugate
04 tame 05 crush, quell 06 defeat, master, reduce, subdue, thrall 07 conquer, enslave, oppress 08 overcome, suppress, vanquish 09 overpower, overthrow 14 get the better of 15 gain mastery over

sublimate
04 turn 05 exalt 06 divert, purify, refine 07 alcohol, channel, elevate, flowers 08 heighten, redirect, transfer 09 transmute

sublime
04 high 05 exalt, grand, great, lofty, noble, utter 06 august, winged 07 Dantean, exalted, extreme, intense, supreme 08 complete, elevated, empyreal, glorious, heavenly, imposing, majestic 09 celestial, Dantesque, spiritual 10 majestical 11 magnificent 12 transcendent

subliminal
06 hidden 09 concealed 11 unconscious 12 subconscious, subthreshold

submarine
03 sub 05 U-boat 06 hoagie, X-craft 07 pigboat

submerge
03 dip 04 bury, dive, duck, dunk, sink, take 05 drown, flood, swamp, whelm 06 deluge, engulf, go down, plunge 07 conceal, immerse, plummet 08 implunge, indrench, inundate, overflow, submerse, suppress 09 overwhelm 12 go under water 13 put under water

submerged
04 sunk 06 hidden, sunken, unseen, veiled 07 cloaked, drowned, swamped 08 immersed, obscured 09 concealed, inundated, submersed 10 underwater

submission
05 entry 06 assent, tender 07 tabling 08 averment, giving in, meekness, offering, proposal 09 agreement, assertion, deference, obedience, passivity, statement, surrender, tendering 10 compliance, confession, suggestion 11 resignation 12 acquiescence, capitulation, contribution, introduction, presentation, resignedness, subscription 13 subordination 14 submissiveness

submissive
04 meek, weak 06 docile, humble, supine 07 passive, patient, servile, subdued 08 biddable, obedient, resigned, yielding 09 compliant, malleable 10 weak-willed 11 acquiescent, deferential, downtrodden, reverential, subordinate, subservient, unresisting 12 ingratiating, self-effacing 13 accommodating, uncomplaining

submissively
06 humbly, meekly, weakly 09 cap in hand, passively, patiently 10 obediently 13 deferentially, subserviently 15 uncomplainingly

submit
03 bow, put 04 aver, bend, move 05 agree, argue, claim, defer, lower, offer, posit, refer, state, stoop, table, yield 06 accede, assert, comply, expose, give in, permit, prefer, render, resign, send in, tender 07 consent, give way, lay down, passage, present, proffer, propose, subject, succumb, suggest, violate 08 propound 09 acquiesce, introduce, lay before, subscribe, surrender 10 bow the knee, capitulate, come to heel, kiss the rod, put forward 11 bend the knee, come to terms, subordinate 12 knuckle under 13 bite the bullet 15 lay down your arms

subnormal
03 low 04 slow 08 backward, inferior, retarded 11 below normal 12 below average, feeble-minded

subordinate
◇ *juxtaposition down indicator*
04 aide 05 lower, lowly, minor, under 06 deputy, junior, lesser, menial, second, skivvy, stooge, submit, vassal 07 subject 08 dogsbody, inferior, marginal, offsider, servient, sidekick 09 ancillary, assistant, attendant, auxiliary, dependant, dependent, secondary, subaltern, underling 10 submissive, subsidiary, underlying 11 lower in rank, subservient 12 lower-ranking, second fiddle 14 understrapping

subordination
09 servitude 10 dependence, subjection, submission 11 inferiority 12 subservience

subscribe
04 back, give, sign, take 05 agree 06 answer, assent, chip in, donate, pledge, submit 07 approve, endorse, fork out, support 08 advocate, shell out, sign up to 10 contribute, underwrite 12 buy regularly 13 take regularly 15 pay for regularly

subscriber
06 member 08 customer 13 regular reader

subscription
04 dues, gift 06 assent 07 payment 08 donation, offering, sanction

09 signature 10 abonnement, submission 11 endorsement 12 contribution 13 membership fee

subsequent
04 next 05 later 06 future 07 ensuing 09 following, resulting 10 consequent, succeeding 12 postliminary

subsequently
05 after, later 09 afterward 10 afterwards 12 consequently

subservience
08 humility 09 deference, obedience, servility, servitude 10 subjection 11 dutifulness 12 acquiescence 13 subordination 14 submissiveness

subservient
05 lower, minor 06 junior, lesser 07 fawning, servile, slavish, subject 08 inferior, toadying, unctuous 09 ancillary, auxiliary, dependent, secondary 10 obsequious, submissive, subserving, subsidiary 11 bootlicking, deferential, subordinate, sycophantic 12 ingratiating, instrumental, subalternate 13 less important

subside
03 ebb 04 adaw, drop, ease, fall, lull, sink, wane 05 abate, let up, lower, quell, slake, sound, swoon, swoun 06 cave in, lessen, quench, recede, settle, swound 07 assuage, decline, descend, die down, dwindle, founder, quieten, slacken 08 collapse, decrease, diminish, dissolve, get lower, moderate, peter out, pipe down

subsidence
03 ebb, sag 04 swag 07 decline, descent, sinking 08 collapse, decrease, settling 09 abatement, lessening 10 diminution, settlement, slackening 12 de-escalation, detumescence

subsidiary
02 by 03 bye 04 part, side, wing 05 minor 06 aiding, branch, feeder, lesser 07 section 08 division, offshoot 09 accessory, adjective, affiliate, ancillary, assistant, auxiliary, secondary, succursal 10 additional, collateral, supporting 11 subordinate, subservient 12 contributory 13 supplementary

subsidize
03 aid 04 back, fund 07 endorse, finance, promote, sponsor, support 08 invest in 10 underwrite 12 contribute to 14 give a subsidy to

subsidy
03 aid 04 help 05 grant 07 backing, finance, funding, headage, support 09 allowance 10 assistance, investment, subvention 11 endorsement, sponsorship 12 contribution, underwriting

subsist
04 last, live 05 exist 06 endure, remain 07 consist, hold out, survive 08 continue

subsistence
04 food, keep 06 living 07 aliment, rations, support 08 survival 09 existence 10 livelihood, provisions, sustenance 11 continuance, maintenance, nourishment

substance
03 sum 04 body, gist, mass, meat, pith, quid, text 05 basis, being, force, means, money, power, stuff, theme, topic, truth 06 amount, assets, burden, entity, fabric, ground, import, matter, medium, riches, wealth, weight 07 essence, fortune, meaning, reality, subject 08 material, property, solidity, validity 09 actuality, affluence, influence, marijuana, resources 10 foundation, prosperity 11 consistence, consistency, materiality, tangibility 12 concreteness, corporeality, significance 13 subject matter 14 meaningfulness

substandard
04 poor 05 crook 06 shoddy 07 damaged 08 below par, inferior 09 imperfect 10 inadequate, second-rate 12 unacceptable 14 not up to scratch

substantial
03 big 04 firm, hard, main, real, rich, tidy, true 05 ample, basic, bulky, great, large, solid, sound, stout, tough 06 actual, hearty, pretty, stable, strong, sturdy 07 central, durable, filling, notable, primary, sizable, wealthy, weighty 08 affluent, cast-iron, concrete, enduring, existing, generous, inherent, material, powerful, sizeable, tangible, valuable, well-to-do 09 corporeal, essential, heavy-duty, important, intrinsic, principal, well-built 10 meaningful, measurable, prosperous, remarkable, successful, worthwhile 11 fundamental, influential, significant 12 considerable

substantially
06 mainly 07 at heart, largely 08 in effect 09 in the main 10 materially 11 essentially 12 considerably 13 fundamentally, significantly 14 to a great extent

substantiate
05 prove 06 back up, embody, uphold, verify 07 bear out, confirm, support 08 validate 11 corroborate 12 authenticate

substantive
02 sb 04 noun, real 05 solid, subst, valid 07 factual 08 concrete, material 09 intrinsic 11 fundamental, substantial

substitute
03 sub 04 -ette, heir, lieu, swap, temp 05 agent, cover, locum, proxy, vicar 06 acting, change, deputy, double, ersatz, fill in, fill-in, relief, supply, switch 07 commute, fig leaf, relieve, replace, reserve, stand-by, stand in, stand-in, stopgap 08 deputize, exchange, replacer, take over 09 alternate, makeshift, prorector, subrogate, surrogate, temporary 10 changeling, proproctor, understudy, use instead 11 alternative, interchange, locum tenens, pinch-hitter, replacement 12 act instead of 14 take the place of

substitution
04 swap 06 change, switch 08 exchange, novation, swapping 09 switching 10 delegation, innovation, resolution 11 interchange, replacement

subsume
03 add 04 hold 05 add in, admit, cover, enter, put in 06 embody, insert, take in 07 contain, count in, embrace, enclose, include, swallow 08 comprise, take over 09 encompass, introduce 10 comprehend 11 incorporate

subterfuge
04 hole, ploy, ruse, wile 05 dodge, trick 06 excuse, refuge, scheme 07 evasion, off-come, pretext 08 artifice, intrigue, pretence 09 creep-hole, deception, duplicity, expedient, manoeuvre, stratagem 11 deviousness, machination

subtle
◇ *anagram indicator*
03 sly 04 deep, fine, mild, nice, wily 05 faint 06 artful, astute, clever, crafty, low-key, minute, shrewd, slight, subtil, suttle, tricky 07 complex, cunning, devious, elusive, implied, refined, tactful, tenuous 08 abstruse, delicate, dextrous, discreet, indirect, profound, rarefied, ticklish 09 dexterous, insidious, intricate, sophistic, strategic, toned-down 10 impalpable, indefinite, indistinct, scholastic 11 overrefined, sophistical, understated 13 sophisticated 14 discriminating

subtlety
05 guile, skill 06 acumen, nicety, nuance 07 cunning, finesse, quillet, slyness 08 delicacy, sagacity, wiliness 09 acuteness, faintness, intricacy, mutedness, suttletie 10 artfulness, astuteness, cleverness, craftiness, refinement 11 deviousness, discernment 14 discrimination, indefiniteness, indistinctness, sophistication

subtly
◇ *anagram indicator*
05 slyly 06 mildly, suttly 07 faintly 08 artfully, astutely, cleverly 09 cunningly, deviously, tenuously 10 indirectly 11 deceitfully 12 indefinitely, indistinctly

subtract
04 dock, take 05 debit 06 deduct, remove 07 detract 08 diminish, take away, withdraw, withhold

suburb
04 burb 08 banlieue, faubourg, purlieus, suburbia 09 dormitory, outskirts 12 commuter belt

13 bedroom suburb, dormitory town
15 dormitory suburb, residential area

suburban
04 dull 06 narrow 07 insular
08 commuter 09 bourgeois, parochial
10 provincial 11 middle-class, residential 12 conventional, narrow-minded 13 unimaginative
14 common-or-garden

subversive
07 riotous, traitor 08 quisling
09 dissident, seditious, terrorist, weakening 10 disruptive, incendiary, traitorous, treasonous 11 destructive, seditionist, treacherous, undermining
12 discrediting, inflammatory, troublemaker 13 revolutionary, troublemaking 14 fifth columnist, freedom fighter

subvert
04 raze, ruin 05 upset, wreck
06 debase, poison 07 corrupt, deprave, destroy, disrupt, pervert, vitiate 08 confound, demolish, overturn, sabotage 09 overthrow, undermine 10 demoralize, invalidate
11 contaminate

subway
04 dive, tube 05 metro 06 tunnel
09 underpass 11 underground

succeed
04 fare, work 05 cut it, ensue, fadge, get on, reach, speed 06 answer, attain, come on, do well, follow, fulfil, make it, manage, result, thrive, walk it, win out
07 achieve, crack it, devolve, inherit, make out, prevail, prosper, pull off, realize, replace, triumph, turn out, work out 08 approach, bring off, carry out, complete, flourish, get there, go places, make good, take over 09 come after, win the day 10 accomplish, get results, strike gold, take effect, win through 11 come through, squeeze home 12 be successful, make the grade, steal the show, turn up trumps
13 hit the jackpot 14 fall on your feet, land on your feet, take the place of

• **succeed to**
06 accede, assume 07 inherit, replace
08 come into, take over 09 enter upon, supersede

succeeding
04 next 05 later 06 coming, to come
07 ensuing 09 following 10 hereditary, subsequent, successive

success
02 go, up 03 hit, VIP, win, wow
04 fame, luck, riot, star 05 celeb, fluke, smash 06 bigwig, upshot, winner
07 big name, big shot, fortune, sell-out, triumph, victory 08 eminence, sequence, smash hit, somebody, speeding 09 celebrity, happiness, sensation 10 attainment, bestseller, completion, fulfilment, prosperity, succession 11 achievement, realization
12 box-office hit 13 coup de théâtre, flash in the pan, flying colours
14 accomplishment, positive result

• **expression of success**
03 Jai 05 bingo 06 eureka, hurrah
07 heureka, hey pass 09 hey presto

successful
03 top 05 boffo, lucky, socko
06 famous 07 booming, leading, popular, thriven, wealthy, winning
08 affluent, fruitful, thriving, unbeaten
09 fortunate, lucrative, rewarding, well-known 10 home and dry, productive, profitable, prosperous, riding high, satisfying, triumphant, victorious 11 bestselling, flourishing, moneymaking 12 chart-busting

successfully
04 fine, well 05 great 08 famously
09 feliciter 10 swimmingly
11 beautifully 12 victoriously

succession
03 run 04 flow, line 05 chain, cycle, order, train 06 course, series, string
08 pedigree, sequence 09 accession, attaining, elevation, posterity
10 assumption, procession, survivance
11 continuance, inheritance, progression 12 continuation

• **in succession**
06 in a row, in turn 07 by-and-by, en suite, running 08 seriatim, straight
09 on the trot 12 sequentially, successively 13 consecutively
15 uninterruptedly

successive
06 serial 07 running, sequent
09 following 10 hereditary, sequential, succeeding 11 consecutive

successively
07 running 09 on the trot 12 in succession, sequentially
13 consecutively 15 uninterruptedly

successor
04 heir 05 coarb 06 co-heir, comarb, epigon, relief 07 epigone, khalifa
08 khalifah 09 inheritor, succeeder
10 descendant, next in line, substitute
11 beneficiary, replacement

succinct
05 brief, crisp, pithy, short, terse
07 compact, concise, in a word, summary 08 Laconian 09 condensed
10 to the point 12 close-fitting

succinctly
07 briefly, crisply, in a word, in brief, pithily, tersely 09 compactly, concisely
10 to the point

succour
03 aid 04 help 05 nurse 06 assist, foster, relief 07 comfort, help out, relieve, support 08 befriend
09 encourage 10 assistance, minister to 11 helping hand 13 ministrations

succulent
04 lush, rich 05 juicy, moist, sappy, tasty 06 cactus, fleshy, mellow 08 ice plant, luscious, spekboom, stapelia
09 echeveria, kalanchoe
11 sempervivum 13 mouthwatering

succumb
03 die 04 fall 05 catch, die of, yield
06 give in, pick up, submit 07 die from, give way 08 collapse, contract
09 surrender 10 capitulate, go down with 12 knuckle under

suck
04 draw, pull 05 drain 06 absorb, blot up, draw in, hoover, imbibe, soak up, sponge, suckle 07 exhaust, extract, suction

• **suck up to**
04 fawn 05 creep, toady 06 grovel
07 flatter, truckle 10 ingratiate 11 curry favour

sucker
03 mug, sap 04 butt, dupe, fool
05 graft, leech, patsy, sweet, toady
06 sponge, stooge, tellar, teller, tiller, victim 07 cat's-paw, muggins, osculum
08 lollipop, parasite, pushover, surculus 10 acetabulum

suckle
04 feed 05 nurse 07 nourish 08 wet-nurse 10 breastfeed

suction
07 sucking 08 draining 09 absorbing, drawing-in 10 extraction

Sudan
03 SDN, SUD

sudden
04 fast, rash, snap 05 ferly, flash, hasty, quick, rapid, sharp, swift 06 abrupt, prompt, speedy 07 hurried, quantum
08 dramatic, meteoric 09 extempore, immediate, impetuous, impulsive, overnight, startling 10 improvised, surprising, unexpected, unforeseen
11 subitaneous 13 instantaneous, unanticipated 15 spur-of-the-moment

suddenly
03 pop 04 slap, swap, swop 05 souse
06 astart, subito 07 asudden, at a blow, quickly, sharply 08 abruptly, unwarely
09 all at once, extempore
11 immediately 12 à l'improviste, all of a sudden, out of the blue, unexpectedly 13 with a siserary 14 at one fell swoop, in one fell swoop, without warning 15 instantaneously

suddenness
05 haste 09 hastiness 10 abruptness
11 hurriedness 13 impulsiveness
14 unexpectedness

suds
04 beer, foam 05 froth 06 lather
07 bubbles 09 soapiness

sue
03 beg 05 court, plead 06 appeal, charge, follow, indict, pursue, summon
07 beseech, entreat, implead, process, solicit 08 petition 09 prosecute 11 beg for a fool, take to court 12 bring to trial

suffer
◇ *anagram indicator*
03 die, let, pay 04 ache, bear, feel,

have, hurt **05** abide, allow, gripe, incur, prove, stand, thole **06** endure, grieve, permit, sorrow **07** agonize, support, sustain, undergo **08** be in pain, meet with, tolerate **09** go through, put up with **10** experience **11** be afflicted

suffering
◇ *anagram indicator*
04 hurt, pain, pine **05** agony, trial **06** misery, ordeal, plight **07** anguish, hurting, passion, torment, torture **08** distress, hardship **09** adversity, afflicted, endurance **10** affliction, discomfort **12** wretchedness

suffice
02 do **05** serve **06** answer **07** content, satisfy **08** be enough **09** measure up **10** be adequate, fit the bill **11** fill the bill **12** be sufficient

sufficiency
05 store **06** enough, plenty **07** satiety **08** adequacy, bellyful **09** abundance **10** competence, competency **11** sufficience **12** adequateness

sufficient
04 enow, good **05** ample **06** decent, enough, plenty **08** adequate **09** competent, effective **12** satisfactory

• **a sufficient quantity**
02 qs **15** quantum sufficit

suffocate
05 choke, smoke, smoor, smore, stive **06** stifle **07** oppress, smother **08** strangle, throttle **10** asphyxiate **12** be breathless **14** make breathless

suffrage
04 vote **06** prayer **08** sanction **09** franchise **11** right to vote **15** enfranchisement

suffuse
03 dip **04** gild **05** bathe, cover, flood, imbue, steep, tinge **06** colour, infuse, mantle, redden, spread **07** pervade **08** permeate **09** transfuse

sugar
03 LSD **05** money, sweet **06** heroin **08** flattery

Sugars include:

03 gur
04 beet, cane, date, goor, loaf, lump, milk, palm, spun, wood
05 brown, fruit, grape, icing, maple, syrup, white
06 aldose, barley, caster, castor, golden, hexose, invert, ketose, xylose
07 glucose, glycose, jaggery, lactose, maltose, mannose, pentose, refined, sucrose, treacle
08 demerara, dextrose, fructose, levulose, molasses, powdered
09 arabinose, galactose, laevulose, raffinose, trehalose, unrefined
10 granulated, saccharose
12 crystallized
13 confectioner's

sugary
05 corny, gushy, mushy, soppy, sweet **06** sickly, sloppy, slushy, syrupy **07** gushing, maudlin, mawkish, sugared **08** touching **09** emotional, schmaltzy, sweetened **10** lovey-dovey, saccharine **11** sentimental

suggest
04 hint, move, vote **05** evoke, float, imply, smack, smell, table, tempt **06** advise, allude, hint at, prompt, savour, submit **07** connote, counsel, present, propose, smack of, smell of **08** advocate, envisage, indicate, intimate, nominate **09** insinuate, recommend **10** come up with, put forward **11** bring to mind **12** bring forward

suggestion
04 hint, idea, kite, note, plan, ring, wind **05** smack, touch, trace, twang, whiff **06** motion **07** pointer, wrinkle **08** allusion, innuendo, proposal **09** prompting, prompture, suspicion **10** incitement, indication, intimation, submission, temptation **11** implication, insinuation, proposition **12** aesthesiogen **13** piece of advice **14** recommendation

suggestive
04 blue, lewd **05** bawdy, dirty **06** ribald, risqué, sexual, smutty **07** meaning **08** immodest, improper, indecent, redolent **09** evocative, off-colour **10** expressive, indelicate, indicative **11** provocative, reminiscent, stimulating, titillating

suicide
06 suttee **07** seppuku **08** felo de se, hara-kiri, hari-kari **10** self-murder **11** ending it all, parasuicide **12** self-violence **13** happy dispatch, self-slaughter **14** self-immolation **15** killing yourself, self-destruction, topping yourself

• **commit suicide**
08 end it all **11** top yourself **12** do yourself in, kill yourself, take your life **14** commit hari-kari **15** take your own life

suit
03 fit, gee, hit, set **04** case, meet **05** agree, apply, befit, besit, cause, clubs, do for, match, queme, suite, trial **06** action, answer, attire, become, drapes, effeir, effere, hearts, outfit, please, series, spades, square **07** contest, costume, crawler, dispute, fashion, flatter, furnish, gratify, lawsuit, overall, process, provide, pursuit, satisfy, suffice **08** argument, clothing, diamonds, ensemble, petition, sequence, tailleur **09** agree with, courtship, plus fours, tally with **10** complement, fit the bill, go well with, litigation, look good on, qualify for **11** fill the bill, proceedings, prosecution **12** set of clothes **13** be suitable for, harmonize with **14** be acceptable to, be applicable to **15** be convenient for

Suits include:

01 g
03 cat, dry, Mao, NBC, sun, wet
04 body, Eton, jump, play, swim, zoot
05 drape, dress, noddy, pants, shell, siren, sleep, space, sweat, track, union
06 boiler, diving, flying, lounge, monkey, riding, safari, sailor, tsotsi
07 bathing, leisure, penguin, trouser
08 birthday, business, pressure, skeleton, sleeping

suitability
07 aptness, fitness **09** congruity, rightness **10** competence, competency, congruence, congruency, timeliness **11** convenience, fittingness **12** appositeness **13** opportuneness **14** correspondence, correspondency **15** appropriateness

suitable
03 apt, due, fit **04** able, good **05** right **06** giusto, liable, proper, seemly, suited **07** fitting **08** adequate, agreeing, all right, apposite, becoming, decorous, relevant **09** agreeable, befitting, competent, congruent, consonant, in keeping, opportune, pertinent **10** acceptable, applicable, compatible, convenient, well-suited **11** appropriate, well-matched **12** satisfactory

suitably
05 fitly, quite **06** as well **08** properly **09** fittingly **10** acceptably **11** accordingly **13** appropriately

suitcase
03 bag **04** case, port **05** trunk **06** valise **07** holdall **09** flight bag, portfolio, travel bag **10** vanity-case **11** attaché case, hand-luggage, portmanteau **12** overnight-bag

suite
03 set **04** flat, tail **05** court, rooms, train **06** ballet, escort, sequel, series **07** partita, retinue **08** chambers, sequence, servants **09** apartment, cassation, entourage, followers, furniture, household, retainers **10** attendants, collection, set of rooms **11** hospitality **12** divertimento

suitor
04 beau **05** lover, swain, wooer **07** admirer **08** follower, young man **09** boyfriend, pretender **10** petitioner, pretendant, pretendent **11** detrimental

sulk
03 dod, pet **04** dort, huff, miff, mood, mope, mump, pout **05** boody, brood, grump, pique **06** grouse, temper **07** bad mood **08** be miffed **09** bad temper, be in a huff **13** pull a long face

• **the sulks**
03 pet **04** dods, hump, tout, towt **05** glout, grump **06** glumps, strunt **07** strunts

sulkily
07 crossly, moodily **08** morosely, sullenly **10** grudgingly **11** resentfully

sulky
05 aloof, cross, huffy, humpy, moody, pouty, ratty **06** glumpy, grouty, grumpy, jinker, miffed, moping, morose, put out, stuffy, sullen **07** pettish
08 brooding, grudging, stunkard
09 resentful **10** out of sorts, unsociable
11 bad-tempered, disgruntled
13 gumple-foisted

sullen
04 dark, dour, dull, glum, grim, sour
05 black, cross, heavy, moody, sulky, surly **06** broody, dismal, dogged, gloomy, leaden, morose, silent, solein, sombre **07** lumpish, mumpish
08 churlish, farouche, perverse, stubborn, stunkard **09** cheerless, obstinate, resentful, simpleton
11 black-browed **15** uncommunicative

sullenly
06 glumly, sourly **07** crossly, moodily, sulkily **08** gloomily, morosely
10 churlishly, stubbornly **11** obstinately, resentfully

sullenness
05 gloom **08** brooding, glumness, sourness **09** glowering, heaviness, moodiness, sulkiness, surliness
10 moroseness

sully
03 mar **04** soil, spot **05** dirty, spoil, stain, taint **06** assoil, befoul, damage, darken, defile, smirch, smutch
07 blemish, distain, pollute, tarnish
08 besmirch, disgrace **09** dishonour
11 contaminate

sulphur
01 S **09** brimstone

sultan, sultana
06 despot, fiddle, raisin, sharif, sherif, soldan **07** shereef **08** padishah
09 Grand Turk **12** Grand Signior
13 Grand Seignior

sultanate
04 Oman **06** Brunei

sultry
03 hot **04** sexy **05** close, humid, lurid, muggy, soggy **06** sticky, stuffy
07 airless, sensual, sweltry **08** alluring, stifling, tempting **09** seductive
10 attractive, indelicate, oppressive, passionate, sweltering, voluptuous
11 provocative, suffocating

sum
03 add **05** penny, score, tally, total, whole **06** amount, answer, height, number, result **07** summary
08 entirety, quantity, sum total
09 abatement, aggregate, carry-over, exemplify, reckoning, summarize, summation **10** completion, remittance
11 culmination
• **large sum**
04 pots **11** golden hello **12** a king's ransom, a pretty penny **15** golden handshake
• **small sum**
04 dime **05** groat, penny **08** pittance

• **sum up**
03 add **04** foot, wind **05** close, compt, count, gauge, recap **06** assess, embody, review, size up, upknit
08 conclude, consider, evaluate
09 epitomize, exemplify, inventory, summarize **11** encapsulate
12 recapitulate **14** put in a nutshell

summarily
07 hastily, swiftly **08** abruptly, promptly, speedily **09** forthwith
11 arbitrarily, immediately
12 peremptorily, without delay
13 expeditiously

summarize
03 pot, sum **05** recap, sum up
06 docket, minute, précis, resume, review, sketch **07** abridge, outline, shorten **08** abstract, condense, pirlicue, purlicue **09** epitomize, synopsize **10** abbreviate
11 encapsulate

summary
02 CV **04** curt, plan **05** brief, creed, hasty, recap, short, summa, swift
06 aperçu, digest, direct, docket, précis, prompt, résumé, review, speedy, summar, wrap-up **07** cursory, docquet, epitome, instant, minutes, offhand, outline, rundown, sylloge, tabloid **08** abstract, argument, overview, succinct, synopsis
09 arbitrary, condensed, immediate, summation, summing-up
10 compendium, conspectus, Hitopadesa, main points, memorandum, peremptory
11 abridgement, aide-mémoire, compendious **12** balance-sheet, condensation, without delay **13** bank statement, instantaneous, unceremonious **14** recapitulation
15 abstract of title, curriculum vitae

summerhouse
06 gazebo **08** pavilion **09** belvedere, root house **11** garden-house

summit
◇ *head selection indicator*
03 top **04** acme, acro-, apex, head, peak, pike **05** crest, crown, glory, point, spire, talks **06** apogee, climax, height, vertex, zenith **07** hilltop, meeting **08** pinnacle **09** sublimity
10 conference, discussion
11 culmination, negotiation
12 altaltissimo, consultation

summon
03 bid **04** buzz, call, cite, gong, hail, hist, hoop, page, ring, sist, toll, warn
05 knell, order, rally, rouse, shake, whoop **06** accite, arouse, beckon, call up, demand, drum up, gather, invite, muster, ring up, work up **07** call out, conjure, convene, convent, convoke, history, pluck up, provoke, screw up, send for, trumpet, whistle
08 assemble, mobilize, muster up
09 challenge, preconize, recollect
• **summon up**
05 evoke, rally, rouse **06** arouse, gather, muster, revive, work up
07 convene, pluck up, screw up
08 assemble, mobilize **09** recollect
10 call to mind

summons
04 call, writ **05** bluey, cital, order, rouse
06 gather, what ho, wo ha ho
07 warning, war note, whistle
08 citation, monition, reveille, subpoena **09** challenge **10** arrière-ban, injunction, invocation **11** clarion call, curtain call **12** gathering-cry
13 parking ticket **14** interpellation

sumptuous
04 dear, rich **05** grand, plush **06** costly, de luxe, lavish, slap-up, superb
07 opulent **08** gorgeous, palatial, princely, splendid **09** expensive, luxurious **11** extravagant, magnificent

sun
01 S **03** day, tan **04** bake, bask, star, year **05** brown, light **07** daystar
08 daylight, eye of day, insolate, sunbathe, sunlight, sunshine
• **sun god**
02 Ra, Re **03** Sol **05** Horus, Surya
06 Apollo, Helios, Tammuz
07 Phoebus

sunbathe
03 sun, tan **04** bake, bask **05** brown
07 sunbake **08** insolate

sunburnt
03 red **05** brown, burnt **07** peeling
08 inflamed **09** blistered **10** blistering
13 weather-beaten

Sunday
01 S **03** Sun

sunder
03 cut **04** chop, part **05** sever, split
06 cleave, divide, sundra, sundri
07 disally, sundari **08** dissever, disunite, separate **09** dissunder

sundry
04 a few, some **06** divers, varied
07 diverse, several, various
08 assorted, separate **09** different
13 miscellaneous

sunk
◇ *anagram indicator*
03 pad **04** bank, deep, lost
06 doomed, failed, in a fix, in a jam, ruined **07** done for **08** finished, knee-deep **09** submerged **10** up the creek, up the spout

sunken
05 drawn, laigh, lower **06** buried, hollow **07** concave, haggard, lowered
08 hollowed, recessed **09** cellarous, depressed, submerged

sunless
04 dark, grey, hazy **05** bleak **06** cloudy, dismal, dreary, gloomy, sombre
08 overcast **09** cheerless
10 depressing

sunlight
03 sun **05** light **08** daylight, sun's rays
12 natural light

sunny
04 fine, glad **05** clear, happy, merry **06** blithe, bouncy, bright, bubbly, cheery, genial, joyful, sunlit **07** beaming, buoyant, hopeful, radiant, smiling, summery **08** cheerful, pleasant, sunshiny **09** brilliant, cloudless, unclouded **10** optimistic **12** light-hearted

sunrise
04 dawn **05** sun-up **06** aurora, orient **07** morning **08** cock-crow, daybreak, daylight **10** break of day, first light **11** crack of dawn

sunset
04 dusk **07** evening, sundown **08** gloaming, twilight **09** nightfall **10** close of day

sup *see* **eat**; **dine**

super
03 ace **04** cool, good!, mega, neat **05** brill, great **06** lovely!, superb, wicked **08** glorious, peerless, smashing, terrific, top-notch **09** excellent, matchless, wonderful **10** delightful, marvellous **11** magnificent, outstanding, sensational **12** incomparable

superannuated
03 old **04** aged **06** past it, senile **07** elderly, retired **08** decrepit, moribund, obsolete **10** antiquated **12** pensioned off **13** put out to grass

superb
03 ace **04** fine, neat, posh **05** brill, grand, great, proud **06** choice, lavish **07** haughty **08** clipping, dazzling, fabulous, gorgeous, jim-dandy, smashing, splendid, superior, terrific **09** admirable, brilliant, excellent, exquisite, first-rate, wonderful **10** first-class, impressive, marvellous, remarkable, unrivalled **11** fantabulous, magnificent, outstanding, superlative, unsurpassed **12** breathtaking

supercilious
05 lofty, proud **06** lordly, overly, snooty, snotty, snouty, uppish, uppity **07** haughty, stuck-up **08** arrogant, cavalier, insolent, jumped-up, scornful, superior **09** imperious **10** disdainful, hoity-toity, toffee-nose **11** high-sighted, overbearing, patronizing, toffee-nosed **12** contemptuous, vainglorious **13** condescending

superficial
◇ *containment indicator*
05 hasty, outer **06** casual, facile, slight **07** alleged, cursory, hurried, outside, outward, passing, seeming, shallow, sketchy, surface, trivial **08** apparent, careless, cosmetic, exterior, external, skin-deep, slapdash **09** frivolous, surficial **10** ostensible, peripheral **11** lightweight, perfunctory **13** insignificant **14** one-dimensional

superficiality
09 lightness **10** simplicity, slightness, triviality **11** externality, shallowness **13** frivolousness, worthlessness

superficially
07 outward **08** casually, skin-deep **09** hurriedly, outwardly, seemingly **10** apparently, carelessly, externally, ostensibly **12** on the surface

superfine
03 sup **04** supe **05** super **09** rosewater

superfluity
04 glut **05** extra **06** excess **07** surfeit, surplus **08** pleonasm, plethora **09** overflush, superflux **10** exuberance, overgrowth, redundancy, surplusage **13** excessiveness **14** superabundance

superfluous
05 extra, spare, waste **06** de trop, excess, frilly, otiose **07** surplus, to spare **08** needless, unneeded, unwanted **09** excessive, redundant, remaining **10** excrescent, fifth-wheel, gratuitous, prolixious **11** at a discount, uncalled-for, unnecessary, unwarranted **13** supernumerary

superhuman
03 god **04** hero **05** great **06** bionic, divine, heroic **07** goddess, immense **09** herculean **10** paranormal, phenomenal, prodigious, stupendous **12** supernatural **13** extraordinary, preternatural

superimpose
03 add **05** lay on, put on **07** lay over, overlay **08** transfer **10** overstrike

superintend
03 run **05** steer **06** direct, handle, manage **07** control, inspect, oversee **08** overlook **09** supervise **10** administer **12** be in charge of **13** be in control of

superintendence
04 care **06** charge, survey **07** control, running **08** episcopy, guidance **09** direction, oversight **10** government, inspection, management **11** supervision **12** surveillance **14** administration

superintendent
04 boss, Supt **05** chief, super **06** gaffer, viewer, warden **07** curator, manager **08** curatrix, director, governor, overseer **09** conductor, inspector, intendant **10** controller, provincial, supervisor **13** administrator

superior
03 sup **04** boss, fine, over **05** chief, elder, fancy, lofty, prime, prize, upper **06** better, choice, de luxe, higher, la-di-da, lordly, select, senior, snooty, uppish, uppity **07** foreman, generic, greater, haughty, manager, premium, quality, stuck-up, upstage **08** director, jumped-up, lah-di-dah, overlord, snobbish, top-notch **09** admirable, excellent, exclusive, first-rate, high-class, high-grade, high-toned, paramount, preferred, principal, top-drawer, top-flight, top-sawyer **10** disdainful, first-class, supervisor, unrivalled **11** exceptional, good-quality, high-quality, outstanding, patronizing, pretentious, toffee-nosed **12** higher in rank, supercilious, transcendent **13** condescending, distinguished, par excellence

• **without superior**
04 odal, udal **07** alodial, topless **08** allodial

superiority
04 edge, gree, lead **07** numbers **08** eminence **09** advantage, dominance, supremacy **10** ascendancy, mastership **11** pre-eminence **12** predominance

superlative
03 ace, -est, sup **04** best **05** brill **06** superl **07** highest, supreme **08** greatest, peerless, unbeaten **09** brilliant, excellent, first-rate, matchless **10** consummate, first-class, unbeatable, unrivalled **11** magnificent, outstanding, unsurpassed **12** transcendent, unparalleled

supermarket
08 minimart **09** superette **10** superstore **11** hypermarket **12** cash-and-carry

supernatural
03 fay, fey, fie **05** eerie, magic, weird **06** hidden, mystic, occult **07** ghostly, magical, phantom, psychic, uncanny **08** abnormal, daemonic, daimonic, eldritch, mystical **09** spiritual, unnatural, witchlike **10** miraculous, mysterious, paranormal **12** metaphysical, otherworldly **13** hyperphysical, preternatural **14** transcendental
See also **occult**

supernumerary
04 orra **05** extra, spare **06** excess **07** surplus **09** excessive, redundant **11** superfluous **13** extraordinary

supersede
04 oust **05** usurp **06** desist, remove **07** discard, refrain, replace, succeed **08** displace, override, set aside, supplant **12** Stellenbosch, take over from **14** take the place of

supersonic transport
03 AST, SST

superstition
04 myth **05** magic **07** fallacy **08** delusion, illusion **10** Aberglaube **11** apotropaism **12** old wives' tale

superstitious
05 false **06** freety, freity **08** delusive, illusory, mythical **10** fallacious, groundless, irrational

supervise
03 run **04** edit **05** guide, nanny, targe, watch **06** direct, handle, manage, umpire **07** conduct, control, inspect, monitor, oversee **08** bear-lead **09** look after, watch over **10** administer,

invigilate **11** keep an eye on, preside over, superintend **12** be in charge of **13** be in control of

supervision
04 care, duty **06** charge **07** control, running **08** guidance **09** direction, oversight **10** inspection, management **11** instruction **12** surveillance **14** administration **15** superintendence

supervisor
04 boss **05** chief **06** umpire, warden **07** foreman, manager, monitor, proctor, steward **08** director, governor, overseer **09** forewoman, inspector, roundsman, spectator **10** brewmaster, foreperson, sheep-biter, toolpusher **11** floorwalker, invigilator **12** floor manager **13** administrator **14** superintendent

supervisory
09 executive **10** managerial, overseeing **11** directorial **14** administrative, superintendent

supine
03 sup **04** flat, idle, lazy, weak **05** bored, inert **06** torpid **07** languid, passive, sloping, upright **08** careless, heedless, inactive, inclined, indolent, listless, resigned, slothful, sluggish **09** apathetic, lethargic, negligent, prostrate, recumbent, spineless **10** horizontal, spiritless **11** indifferent, unresisting **12** uninterested

supper
03 tea **04** mass **05** snack **06** dinner, hawkey, hockey, horkey **07** nagmaal **10** rere-supper **11** aftersupper, evening meal

supplant
04 oust **05** usurp **06** cut out, remove, topple, unseat, uproot **07** pre-empt, replace **08** displace **09** overthrow, supersede **12** take over from **14** take the place of

supple
05 agile, leish, lithe, lofty, wanle **06** limber, pliant, souple, wandle, wannel, whippy **07** bending, elastic, fawning, plastic, pliable, sinuous **08** flexible, graceful, yielding **09** willowish **10** stretching **11** loose-limbed **12** loose-jointed **13** double-jointed

supplement
02 PS **03** eik, eke, SCP, sup, TES, TLS **04** mend, supp **05** add-on, add to, annex, boost, extra, relay, rider, suppl, top up **06** eke out, extend, fill up, insert, make up, sequel, supply **07** augment, codicil, help out, pull-out **08** addendum, addition, additive, appendix, increase, salt lick, schedule **09** Beta fibre, reinforce, sooterkin **10** Beres drops, complement, Incaparina, postscript, suppletion

supplementary
05 added, extra **06** bolt-on, second **07** ripieno **08** attached **09** ancillary, auxiliary, corollary, expletory, secondary, suppliant **10** additional **12** accompanying **13** complementary

suppliant
07 begging, craving **09** imploring **10** beseeching, entreating **11** importunate, reinforcing **12** supplicating **13** supplementary

supplicant
06 suitor **07** pleader **09** applicant, postulant, suppliant **10** petitioner

supplicate
04 pray **05** plead **06** appeal, invoke **07** beseech, entreat, request, solicit **08** petition

supplication
04 plea, suit **06** appeal, orison, prayer **07** request **08** entreaty, petition, pleading, rogation **10** invocation **11** conjuration, imploration, obsecration **12** solicitation

supplicatory
06 humble **07** begging **09** imploring, precative, precatory **10** beseeching **11** imprecatory, petitioning, postulatory **12** supplicating

supplier
05 donor **06** dealer, seller, vendor **08** provider, retailer **09** connexion, outfitter **10** connection, wholesaler **11** contributor

supply
◇ *anagram indicator*
03 due, fit, gas **04** bank, crop, feed, fill, find, food, fund, give, heap, help, lend, load, mass, pile, sell, temp, wood **05** cache, endew, endow, endue, equip, grant, grist, hoard, indew, indue, labor, plumb, serve, stake, stock, store, yield **06** amount, donate, fit out, labour, occupy, outfit, output, plenty, purvey, source, stores **07** furnish, plenish, produce, proffer, provide, rations, reserve, satisfy, service, victual **08** minister, quantity **09** equipment, materials, reinforce, replenish, reservoir, stockpile **10** contribute, cornucopia, provisions, substitute, supplement **11** necessities **15** cut and come again

support
◇ *juxtaposition down indicator*
03 aid, arm, bra, cup, leg, tee **04** abet, axle, back, base, bear, care, feed, food, fund, help, keep, pier, pole, post, prop, raft, rest, root, skid, stay **05** brace, carry, grant, truss **06** assist, back up, be with, corset, crutch, defend, endure, foster, hold up, pillar, prop up, ratify, relief, second, uphold, verify **07** backing, bear out, bolster, capital, care for, comfort, confirm, defence, endorse, espouse, finance, funding, further, loyalty, nourish, promote, run with, shore up, sponsor, subsidy, sustain, trestle **08** advocate, approval, be behind, befriend, be kind to, buttress, champion, document, donation, espousal, evidence, maintain, motivate, skeleton, strength, sympathy, underpin, validate **09** bolster up, encourage, look after, patronage, provision, reinforce, subsidize **10** allegiance, assistance, foundation, friendship, motivation, protection, provide for, rally round, strengthen, sustenance, take care of, underwrite, validation **11** corroborate, foundations, maintenance, sponsorship, subsistence **12** authenticate, be in favour of, confirmation, contribute to, contribution, moral support, ratification, substantiate, substructure, underpinning, verification **13** encouragement **14** authentication, be supportive to, give strength to, substantiation, sympathize with **15** give a donation to, take the weight of, tower of strength

• **be supported**
04 live, rest **05** float

• **expression of support**
03 olé

supporter
◇ *juxtaposition down indicator*
03 bra, fan, leg **04** ally, beam, belt, foot, prop **05** angel, donor, stoop, voter **06** braces, friend, helper, patron, pillar, second **07** apostle, booster, partner, sponsor **08** adherent, advocate, champion, co-worker, defender, follower, henchman, janizary, militant, promoter, seconder, upholder **09** apologist, crossbeam **10** ideologist, well-wisher **11** contributor, sympathizer **12** bottle-holder, understander

supporting
03 pro- **06** behind

supportive
06 caring **07** helpful **08** positive **09** attentive, sensitive **10** comforting, reassuring **11** affirmative, encouraging, sympathetic **13** understanding **14** on someone's side

suppose
02 if **03** say **04** take **05** fancy, guess, imply, infer, judge, opine, posit, sepad, think **06** assume, devise, expect, reckon, uphold **07** believe, dare say, imagine, presume, propose, put case, require, surmise, warrant **08** conceive, conclude, consider, perceive **09** calculate, postulate **10** conjecture, presuppose, put the case **11** expectation, hypothesize **14** take for granted

supposed
07 alleged, assumed, feigned, reputed **08** believed, imagined, presumed, putative, reported, rumoured, so-called **11** conjectured **12** hypothetical **14** supposititious

• **supposed to**
07 meant to **09** obliged to **10** expected to, intended to, required to

supposedly
09 allegedly **10** apparently, ostensibly,

putatively, reportedly **13** by all accounts

supposing that
02 if

supposition
02 if **04** idea **05** guess **06** notion, theory **07** fiction, opinion, surmise **10** assumption, conjecture, hypothesis **11** postulation, presumption, speculation **14** presupposition

suppress
04 kill, sink, stay, stop **05** burke, check, choke, crush, elide, mince, quash, quell, sit on **06** cancel, censor, hold in, hush up, ravish, squash, stifle, subdue **07** conceal, contain, control, cushion, inhibit, put down, repress, silence, sit upon, smother, squelch **08** black out, blank out, block out, gulp back, gulp down, hold back, moderate, restrain, stamp out, strangle, submerge, throttle, vanquish, vote down, withhold **09** choke back, choke down **10** put an end to **11** clamp down on, crack down on, keep in check, strangulate **14** knock on the head, put the tin hat on, put the tin lid on

suppression
05 check **07** cover-up, elision **08** blackout, crushing, ischuria, quashing, quelling, stoppage **09** clampdown, crackdown, epistasis **10** censorship, ecthlipsis, extinction, inhibition, smothering **11** comstockery, concealment, dissolution, elimination, prohibition, termination

suppurate
04 ooze, weep **06** fester, gather **08** maturate **09** discharge

suppuration
03 pus **09** diapyesis, festering, mattering, pyorrhoea

supremacy
04 rule, sway **05** power **07** control, mastery, primacy **08** dominion, hegemony, lordship, regalism **09** dominance **10** ascendancy, domination **11** paramountcy, pre-eminence, sovereignty **12** predominance

supreme
03 sup, top **04** best, head, last, Supr **05** chief, final, first, grand, prime **06** sudder, utmost **07** extreme, highest, leading, sublime **08** crowning, foremost, greatest, imperial, peerless, ultimate **09** excellent, first-rate, matchless, paramount, principal, sovereign **10** consummate, first-class, pre-eminent, prevailing **11** culminating, predominant, superlative, unsurpassed **12** incomparable, second-to-none, transcendent, world-beating

supremely
04 very **06** highly, really **07** acutely, greatly, utterly **08** severely **09** decidedly, extremely, intensely, unusually **10** remarkably, thoroughly, uncommonly **11** exceedingly, excessively, sovereignly **12** inordinately, terrifically **13** exceptionally **15** extraordinarily

sure
02 OK **03** yes **04** fast, fine, firm, okay, safe **05** bound, clear, loyal, pakka, pucka, pukka, right, sewer, solid **06** agreed, indeed, secure, siccar, sicker, stable, steady, tested **07** assured, certain, decided, precise **08** accurate, all right, definite, faithful, of course, positive, reliable, sure-fire, unerring, very well **09** certainly, confident, convinced, effective, foolproof, steadfast, undoubted, unfailing **10** dependable, guaranteed, home and dry, inevitable, infallible, sure-footed, undeniable, unwavering **11** efficacious, irrevocable, trustworthy, undoubtedly, unfaltering **12** indisputable, never-failing, safe as houses, unmistakable **14** unquestionable

• **for sure**
06 indeed **07** clearly, plainly **09** certainly, obviously **10** absolutely, definitely, for certain, positively, undeniably **11** indubitably, undoubtedly **12** unmistakably, without doubt **13** categorically **14** unquestionably **15** without question

• **make sure**
04 look **05** check **06** assure, ensure, insure, secure, verify **07** betroth, confirm **09** ascertain, guarantee **11** make certain

• **make sure of having**
03 see

surely
05 syker **06** firmly, safely, siccar, sicker **07** no doubt **09** assuredly, certainly **10** definitely, inevitably, inexorably **11** confidently, doubtlessly, indubitably, undoubtedly **12** without doubt **14** unquestionably

surety
04 bail, bond **06** borrow, pledge, safety **07** caution, deposit, hostage, sponsor, warrant **08** bondsman, security, warranty **09** assurance, cautioner, certainty, frithborh, guarantee, guarantor, indemnity, insurance, mortgagor, safeguard **10** undertaker

surface
03 top **04** area, face, rise, side, skin **05** arise, outer, plane **06** appear, come up, emerge, façade, veneer **07** outside, outward **08** aerofoil, apparent, covering, exterior, external, reappear **11** come to light, materialize, superficial

• **on the surface**
04 upon **09** seemingly **10** apparently, externally, ostensibly **13** at first glance, superficially

surfeit
04 cram, fill, glut, staw **05** gorge, stall, stuff **06** excess, gutful **07** gorging, satiate, satiety, surplus **08** bellyful, cloyment, gluttony, overcloy, overfeed, overfill, plethora **09** repletion, satiation **11** overfulness, repleteness, superfluity **14** overindulgence, superabundance

surge
03 jaw **04** eddy, flow, gush, jerk, pour, rise, roll, rush, wave **05** break, heave, spike, sweep, swell, swirl, waves, whelm **06** billow, efflux, roller, seethe, stream, upgush, uprush, wallow, welter **07** breaker, pouring, redound, upsurge, upswing **08** escalate, increase **09** transient **10** escalation **15** intensification

surgeon
02 BS, ch, CM, DS, MS **03** BCh, ChB, ChM, DCh, LCh, MCh, vet **04** surg **05** LChir **06** doctor, extern, intern **07** externe, interne **08** orthopod, sawbones **09** trephiner **10** chirurgeon **11** lithotomist **12** lithotritist **13** lithotriptist **14** lithontriptist

Surgeons include:

04 **Bell** (Sir Charles), **Mayo** (Charles Horace), **Reed** (Walter)
05 **Broca** (Paul Pierre), **Paget** (Sir James)
06 **Carrel** (Alexis), **Cooper** (Sir Astley), **Hunter** (John), **Lister** (Joseph, Lord), **Treves** (Sir Frederick), **Yacoub** (Sir Magdi)
07 **Barnard** (Christiaan), **Burkitt** (Denis Parsons), **Cushing** (Harvey Williams), **MacEwen** (Sir William), **McIndoe** (Sir Archibald)
08 **Beaumont** (William), **Billroth** (Theodor), **Charnley** (Sir John)

See also **doctor**; **medical**

• **sea surgeon**
04 tang **06** doctor **10** doctor-fish

surgery
03 ops

Surgery types include:

06 biopsy
07 keyhole, nose job, plastic
08 cosmetic, elective, facelift, lobotomy
09 Caesarean, colostomy, open-heart, sex change, skin graft, spare-part, tummy tuck
10 autoplasty, cordectomy, iridectomy, laparotomy, lumpectomy, mastectomy, nip and tuck, phlebotomy, thymectomy, transplant, varicotomy
11 angioplasty, cryosurgery, enterostomy, gastrectomy, laparoscopy, mammoplasty, rhinoplasty, splenectomy, tracheotomy, trepanation
12 appendectomy, circumcision, corneal graft, hysterectomy, laryngectomy, microsurgery, neurosurgery, tonsilectomy, tracheostomy, trephination
13 adenoidectomy, prostatectomy, psychosurgery, stomatoplasty,

thyroidectomy, tonsillectomy
14 appendicectomy, coronary bypass, pancreatectomy, reconstructive
15 cholecystectomy, thoracocentesis

Surgery-related terms include:

02 op
04 CABG, seam
05 couch, curet, donor, graft, stoma, taxis, truss
06 canula, domino, dossil, garrot, hobday, lancet, post-op, reduce, stitch, trepan, trocar
07 cannula, catling, curette, forceps, garotte, myotome, operate, scalpel, section, theatre, torsion
08 ablation, adhesion, bistoury, cannular, capeline, centesis, clinical, compress, cosmesis, crow-bill, curarine, écraseur, garrotte, incision, incisure, invasive, trephine
09 abduction, autograft, cannulate, capelline, collodion, crow's-bill, curettage, depressor, dermatome, diastasis, enucleate, operation, osteotome, piggyback, resection, retractor, tamponade, tamponage, tenaculum
10 deligation, diorthosis, discussion, guillotine, lithotrite, lithotrity, osteoclast
11 anaesthetic, arthrodesis, autoplastic, cannulation, curettement, decapsulate, exteriorize, incarnation, laparoscope, lithotripsy, lithotritor, prosthetics
12 fenestration, lithotripter, lithotriptor, lunar caustic, paracentesis, scarificator, short circuit, tissue-typing
13 cyclodialysis, decompression, herniorrhaphy, operating room, post-operative, premedication, under the knife
14 embryo transfer, operating table

surgical *see* **medical**

Suriname
03 SME, SUR

surly
04 grum **05** bluff, cross, cynic, gruff, gurly, stoor, stour, sture, sulky, testy **06** crusty, grumpy, morose, stowre, sullen **07** brusque, crabbed, cynical, grouchy, haughty, uncivil **08** churlish **09** crotchety, irascible **10** ill-natured, refractory, ungracious **11** bad-tempered **12** cantankerous

surmise
04 idea **05** fancy, guess, infer, opine **06** assume, deduce, notion **07** imagine, opinion, presume, suppose, suspect, thought **08** conclude, consider **09** deduction, inference, speculate, suspicion **10** allegation, assumption, conclusion, conjecture, hypothesis **11** possibility, presumption, speculation, supposition

surmount
03 top **04** rise, rush **05** crest **06** breast, exceed, master **07** conquer, get over, surpass **08** overcome, superate, vanquish **09** transcend **11** prevail over, triumph over

surpass
03 cap, top **04** bang, beat, ding, pass, whap, whop **05** excel, outdo, outgo **06** better, exceed, overgo **07** eclipse, outbrag, outpeer, overtop, paragon, put down **08** go beyond, outclass, outrival, outshine, outstrip, surmount, underlay **09** transcend **10** overshadow, tower above **12** beat to sticks, leave for dead **13** knock spots off

surpassing
04 rare **07** corking, supreme, topping **08** frabjous **09** bettering, exceeding, matchless **10** inimitable, phenomenal, unrivalled **11** exceptional, outstanding, unsurpassed **12** incomparable, transcendent **13** extraordinary

surplice
04 sark **05** cotta, ephod, stole **06** rochet

surplus
04 glut, over, plus **05** extra, spare **06** excess, unused **07** balance, o'ercome, overage, residue, surfeit **08** left over, overcome, overplus, owrecome, wine lake **09** carry-over, leftovers, redundant, remainder, remaining **11** superfluity, superfluous

surprise
03 wow **04** drop, find, stun **05** alert, amaze, seize, shock, start **06** dismay, expose, unmask, wonder **07** astound, confuse, find out, nonplus, stagger, startle **08** astonish, bewilder, blow away, bowl over **09** amazement, bombshell, burst in on, curveball, surprisal, take aback **10** disconcert, revelation, wonderment **11** flabbergast, incredulity, knock for six, thunderbolt **12** astonishment, bewilderment **13** catch in the act, catch unawares **14** catch red-handed **15** bolt from the blue

• **expression of surprise**
01 O **02** ah, eh, ha, ho, my, oh **03** aha, coo, cor, gee, god, hah, hoa, hoh, law, lor, man, oho, ooh, ook, say, wow **04** dear, egad, gosh, hech, igad, I say, Jeez, lawk, lord, losh, odso, phew, well, what, whew, yike **05** arrah, blimy, fancy, gadso, glory, godso, golly, hallo, hello, hullo, Jeeze, Jesus, lawks, lordy, lumme, lummy, ma foi, mercy, musha, my God, my hat, never, wowee, yikes, zowie **06** blimey, by Jove, Christ, cricky, crikey, cripes, crumbs, dear me, gemini, geminy, gemony, heaven, indeed, jiminy, my word, oh dear, wheugh, whoops, zounds **07** bless me, brother, caramba, cravens, crickey, crimine, crimini, crivens, deary me, gee whiz, glory be, good-now, heavens, jeepers, stone me, too much **08** crivvens, dearie me, good-lack, goodness, gorblimy, gracious, I declare, man alive, stroll on, well well **09** blood oath, cor blimey, fancy that, good grief, gorblimey, I never did, Jesus wept, mercy on us, son of a gun **10** conscience, gracious me, Great Scott, hell's bells, hell's teeth, hoity-toity, upon my soul, upon my word, well I never **11** bless my soul, good heavens, to think of it **12** good gracious, heavens above, my conscience, strike a light, well I declare **13** Gordon Bennett, just think of it, stone the crows **14** it's a small world **15** jeepers creepers

surprised
05 agape **06** amazed **07** shocked, stunned **08** jiggered, startled **09** astounded, staggered **10** astonished, gobsmacked, nonplussed, speechless **11** dumbfounded, open-mouthed **12** lost for words **13** flabbergasted, thunderstruck

surprising
◇ *anagram indicator*
05 funny **07** amazing, strange **08** shocking, stunning **09** obreption, startling, wonderful **10** astounding, incredible, remarkable, staggering, unexpected, unforeseen **11** astonishing, jaw-dropping, unlooked-for **13** extraordinary

surprisingly
◇ *anagram indicator*
07 funnily **09** amazingly, strangely **10** incredibly, remarkably, stunningly **11** wonderfully **12** staggeringly, unexpectedly **13** astonishingly **15** extraordinarily

surrender
04 cede, quit **05** forgo, waive, yield **06** bail up, forego, give in, give up, remise, render, resign, strike, submit, turn in **07** abandon, cession, concede, enfeoff, kamerad, let go of, release, succumb, waiving **08** abdicate, renounce, yielding **09** rendition, sacrifice, surrendry **10** abdication, capitulate, relinquish, submission **11** abandonment, leave behind, resignation **12** capitulation, lower the flag, renunciation **13** cessio bonorum, strike the flag **14** relinquishment **15** lay down your arms, throw in the towel, throw in your hand

surreptitious
03 fly, sly **06** covert, hidden, secret, sneaky, veiled **07** furtive **08** stealthy **09** underhand **10** behind-door, subreptive **11** clandestine **12** unauthorized

surrogate
05 proxy **06** deputy **07** stand-in **10** substitute **11** replacement **14** representative

surround
◇ *containment indicator*
03 lap, orb, rim **04** brim, edge, gird, halo, moat, pack, ring, zone **05** beset, bound, brink, hedge, hem in, limit,

round, verge, water **06** begird, border, bounds, edging, empale, encase, enhalo, fringe, garter, girdle, impale, incase, invest, margin, picket, piquet **07** besiege, compass, confine, embosom, enclave, enclose, enround, envelop, environ, fence in, go round, imbosom, inclose, picquet, rampart, setting **08** cincture, confines, encircle, overflow, palisade, stockade **09** encompass, perimeter, periphery **10** circumvent, water about **11** close in upon **13** circumference, circumvallate

surrounding
◇ *containment indicator*
06 gherao, nearby **07** ambient **08** adjacent **09** adjoining, bordering **10** encircling **12** encompassing, neighbouring

surroundings
05 scene **06** milieu **07** context, element, habitat, setting **08** ambience, environs, locality, vicinity **10** background **11** environment, mise en scène **12** circumstance **13** neighbourhood

surveillance
04 care **05** check, watch **06** charge, spying **07** control **08** scrutiny **09** direction, vigilance **10** inspection, monitoring, regulation **11** observation, stewardship, supervision **12** guardianship, suicide watch **15** superintendence

survey
03 map, spy **04** form, plan, plot, poll, quiz, scan, test, view **05** chart, level, probe, recce, study, sweep **06** assess, look at, review, size up **07** examine, inspect, measure, observe, overeye, surview **08** appraise, consider, episcopy, estimate, evaluate, look over, once-over, overview, perceive, prospect, research, scrutiny, traverse **09** appraisal, summing-up, supervise, valuation **10** assessment, conspectus, inspection, plane-table, scrutinize **11** contemplate, examination, measurement, opinion poll, reconnoitre, triangulate **12** Domesday book, Doomsday book, tour d'horizon **13** consideration, perambulation, questionnaire, triangulation **14** market research, reconnaissance **15** superintendence

surveyor
02 CS **08** assessor, examiner, overseer **09** geodesist, inspector

survival
06 coping **08** hangover, leftover, managing **09** endurance, existence **10** will to live **11** continuance, persistence, withholding **12** perseverance, staying power

survive
04 cope, last, live, stay **05** exist, rally **06** endure, live on, make it, manage, remain **07** die hard, hold out, live out, outlast, outlive, persist, recover, weather **08** be extant, continue **09** withstand **10** get through **11** come through, live through, pull through

susceptibility
07 feeling **08** openness, tendency, weakness **09** liability, proneness **10** proclivity, propensity **11** gullibility, sensitivity **13** sensibilities, vulnerability **14** predisposition, responsiveness, suggestibility **15** defencelessness

susceptible
04 open, weak **05** given, prone **06** at risk, liable, tender **07** capable, patient, subject **08** disposed, gullible, inclined **09** credulous, easily led, receptive, sensitive **10** responsive, vulnerable **11** defenceless, impressible, predisposed, suggestible **14** impressionable

suspect
◇ *anagram indicator*
03 sus **04** fear, feel, iffy, suss **05** dodgy, doubt, fancy, fishy, guess, infer, smoke, sniff, snuff **07** believe, dubious, jalouse, misdeem, suppose, surmise **08** be wary of, conclude, consider, distrust, doubtful, jealouse, misdoubt, mistrust **09** debatable, mislippen, smell a rat, speculate, suspicion **10** conjecture, have a hunch, inadequate, suspicious, unreliable **11** misconceive **12** insufficient, questionable **13** be uneasy about **15** have doubts about, have qualms about

suspend
04 hang, hold, side, stay **05** cease, debar, defer, delay, expel, swing **06** arrest, dangle, ground, hang up, put off, recess, remove, shelve **07** adjourn, dismiss, entrain, exclude, keep out, shut out, unfrock **08** disperse, postpone, prorogue, put on ice, sideline, stand off **09** interrupt **10** pigeonhole **11** discontinue **13** put in abeyance

suspended
06 put off **07** delayed, hanging, pendent, pending, pensile, shelved **08** dangling, deferred, put on ice **09** postponed **10** underslung

suspense
05 doubt, poise **07** anxiety, tension **09** cessation, deferring **10** excitement, expectancy, indecision, insecurity **11** expectation, nervousness, uncertainty **12** anticipation, apprehension, doubtfulness, intermission

• in suspense
06 on edge **07** eagerly, keyed up **09** anxiously **11** expectantly **13** on tenterhooks **15** with bated breath

suspension
03 sol **04** foam, mist, stay **05** break, delay **07** removal, respite **08** abeyance, abeyancy, deferral **09** cessation, debarment, deferment, dismissal, exclusion, expulsion, grounding, remission **10** inhibition, moratorium, unfrocking **11** adjournment, standing-off **12** intermission, interruption, postponement **14** pseudosolution

suspicion
03 sus **04** dash, hint, idea, suss **05** doubt, hunch, qualm, shade, sniff, tinge, touch, trace **06** belief, breath, notion, qualms, shadow **07** caution, feeling, glimmer, inkling, opinion, soupçon, surmise, suspect, umbrage **08** distrust, misdoubt, mistrust, paranoea, paranoia, wariness **09** chariness, intuition, misgiving, scintilla **10** conjecture, intimation, misdeeming, misgivings, scepticism, sixth sense, suggestion **12** apprehension, funny feeling

suspicious
◇ *anagram indicator*
03 odd **04** iffy, suss, wary **05** chary, dodgy, fishy, funny, queer, shady, smoky **06** guilty, shifty, uneasy, unsure **07** dubious, strange, suspect **08** doubtful, peculiar **09** dishonest, equivocal, irregular, sceptical **10** misdeeming, suspectful, suspecting **11** distrustful, mistrustful, unbelieving **12** apprehensive, disbelieving, questionable

suspiciously
05 oddly **06** warily **07** shadily **09** dubiously, strangely **10** doubtfully **11** dishonestly, sceptically **12** questionably **13** distrustfully, mistrustfully, unbelievingly **14** apprehensively, disbelievingly

Sussex
• division of Sussex
04 rape

sustain
03 aid **04** bear, buoy, face, feed, help, hold, prop, ride **05** abide, carry, stand **06** assist, buoy up, endure, foster, hold up, keep up, prop up, suffer, upbear, uphold, upstay **07** aliment, carry on, comfort, endorse, nourish, nurture, prolong, receive, relieve, ride out, support, suspend, undergo **08** continue, happen to, maintain, protract, sanction, scaffold **09** encourage, go through, keep going, underbear **10** experience, provide for, sustentate **14** give strength to

sustained
06 steady, tenuto **07** ongoing **08** constant **09** perpetual, prolonged, sostenuto **10** continuing, continuous, protracted **11** unremitting **12** long-drawn-out

sustenance
04 fare, food, grub, nosh **05** scoff **06** viands **07** aliment, support **08** victuals **09** autophagy, provender, refection **10** autophagia, livelihood, provisions **11** comestibles, maintenance, nourishment, subsistence, sufficience

svelte
04 slim **05** lithe **06** lissom, urbane **07** elegant, shapely, slender, willowy **08** graceful, polished **09** sylphlike **13** sophisticated

swag
03 sag **04** drum, sway **05** bluey **07** bed roll, festoon, matilda, plunder **10** depression, subsidence

swagger
04 brag, cock, crow, roll, show **05** boast, brank, pronk, smart, strut, swank, vapor **06** parade, prance, ruffle, square, vapour **07** bluster, panache, roister, royster, show off **08** parading, prancing, tigerism **09** arrogance **11** ostentation **12** go over the top

swallow
◇ *containment indicator*
03 buy, eat, pop **04** bear, bolt, down, gulp, slug, swig, take **05** abide, abyss, ariel, drink, gorge, gulch, quaff, scoff, shift, stand, thole, trust **06** accept, devour, endure, englut, gobble, guzzle, ingest, martin, Progne, stifle, take in, throat, up with **07** believe, consume, contain, fall for, martlet, repress, smother, stomach, subsume, take off **08** down with, gobble up, gulp down, hold back, martinet, suppress, tolerate **09** knock back, polish off, put up with, worry down **11** be certain of, house martin
• **swallow hole**
04 sink **06** dolina, doline **07** swallet **08** sinkhole
• **swallow up**
06 absorb, enfold, engulf **07** engulph, envelop, ingulph, overrun **08** take over **09** overwhelm **10** assimilate **11** ingurgitate

swamp
03 bog, fen, mud, vly **04** mire, quag, sink, vlei **05** beset, cowal, flood, Lerna, Lerne, marsh **06** deluge, Dismal, drench, engulf, morass, muskeg, slough **07** besiege, bog down, Dismals, wash out **08** inundate, loblolly, overload, quagmire, saturate, submerge, waterlog **09** overwhelm, purgatory, quicksand, swampland, weigh down

swampy
03 wet **04** miry **05** boggy, fenny, soggy **06** marshy, quaggy **07** paludal **08** squelchy **09** uliginose, uliginous **11** waterlogged

swan
03 cob, pen **04** Leda **06** cygnet, Cygnus

Swans include:

04 mute
05 black
07 Bewick's, whooper
08 whooping
09 trumpeter, whistling

swank
04 brag, show, swot **05** agile, boast, pronk, smart, strut **06** parade, pliant **07** conceit, display, posture, show off, slender, swagger **08** bragging **09** vainglory **10** showing-off **11** ostentation **12** attitudinize, boastfulness **13** conceitedness, preen yourself **15** pretentiousness

swanky
04 posh, rich **05** fancy, flash, grand, plush, ritzy, showy, smart, swish **06** de luxe, flashy, lavish, plushy **07** stylish **09** exclusive, expensive, glamorous, luxurious, sumptuous **11** fashionable, pretentious **12** ostentatious

swap, swop
◇ *anagram indicator*
03 hit **04** blow, flop, slam **05** bandy, plump, smite, trade **06** barter, strike, stroke, switch **07** traffic **08** exchange, suddenly, trade-off **09** transpose **10** substitute **11** interchange **12** substitution **13** transposition

sward
03 sod **04** turf

swarm
03 fry, mob **04** army, bike, body, byke, cast, herd, host, mass, nest, pack, shin, teem **05** crowd, drove, flock, flood, horde, shoal, surge, troop **06** abound, colony, hotter, myriad, stream, swerve, throng **08** offshoot **09** multitude **10** congregate
• **be swarming with**
08 abound in **13** be crowded with, be overrun with, be teeming with **14** be crawling with, be hotching with, be thronged with **15** be bristling with

swarthy
04 dark **05** black, brown, dusky **06** tanned **08** blackish **11** black-a-vised, dark-skinned

swashbuckling
04 bold **06** daring, robust **07** dashing, gallant **08** exciting, spirited **09** dare-devil **10** courageous, flamboyant, swaggering **11** adventurous

swat
03 hit **04** biff **05** lunge, swipe, whack **06** strike, wallop **07** fly-flap, lash out

swathe
03 lap **04** bind, fold, furl, wind, wrap **05** cloak, drape **06** enwrap, shroud **07** bandage, envelop, sheathe, swaddle **08** enshroud, wrapping

sway
04 bend, lean, reel, rock, roll, rule, shog, swag, swee, swey, veer, wave **05** clout, hoist, lurch, power, sally, shake, swale, swing, thraw, wield **06** affect, direct, divert, govern, induce, swerve, swinge, teeter, titter, totter, waddle, wobble **07** command, control, convert, incline, proceed, reeling, rocking, shoogie, shoogle, stagger, win over **08** convince, dominate, dominion, hegemony, overrule, persuade, rotation **09** authority, dominance, fluctuate, influence, oscillate, supremacy, vacillate **10** ascendancy, bring round, government, leadership **11** fluctuation, oscillation, prevail upon, sovereignty **12** jurisdiction, predominance **13** preponderance
• **hold sway**
04 rule **05** reign **07** prevail **09** have power **10** wield power **13** exercise power, have authority, have influence, lay down the law

Swaziland
02 SD **03** SWZ

swear
03 eff, rap, vow **04** aver, avow, cuss, damn, oath **05** abuse, blind, curse **06** abjure, adjure, affirm, assert, attest, depose, insist, invoke, objure, pledge **07** declare, promise, testify **08** be on oath, forswear, maledict **09** blaspheme, imprecate, overswear **10** asseverate, take an oath **11** be under oath, eff and blind, take the oath **12** damn and blast **14** abjure the realm, pledge yourself, turn the air blue, use bad language **15** promise solemnly
• **swear by**
06 rely on **07** trust in **08** depend on **09** believe in **11** have faith in **14** put your faith in

swearing
07 cursing, cussing **08** language **09** blasphemy, profanity **10** coprolalia, expletives **11** bad language **12** foul language, imprecations, maledictions **14** strong language

swear-word
04 cuss, oath **05** curse **08** cussword, swearing **09** blasphemy, expletive, obscenity, profanity **11** bad language, imprecation **12** foul language **14** four-letter word

sweat
04 drip, flap, fuss, toil **05** chore, exude, panic, smart, sudor, tizzy, worry **06** dither, effort, labour, lather, sudate, tizwas **07** anxiety, fluster, secrete, soldier, swelter **08** drudgery, hidrosis, moisture, perspire, sudation **09** agitation, cold sweat, death-damp, mucksweat **10** osmidrosis, perspirate, stickiness **11** bloody-sweat, diaphoresis **12** perspiration, sweat buckets **13** sweat like a pig

sweaty
04 damp **05** moist **06** clammy, sticky **08** forswatt, sudorous, sweating **10** perspiring

Sweden
01 S **03** SWE

sweep
03 arc, fly **04** bend, drag, dust, lash, move, pass, poke, push, race, roll, sail, scud, skim, soop, span, sway, tear, wash, whip, wipe **05** besom, broom, brush, clean, clear, curve, drive, elbow, force, glide, range, scoop, scope, shove, sling, surge, swath, swing, swipe, swoop, vista, whisk **06** action,

extent, glance, hurtle, jostle, onrush, remove, search, stroke, swathe, thrust, vacuum **07** clean up, clear up, compass, ensweep, expanse, gesture, impetus, stretch **08** besom out, movement, overrake, snowball, vastness **09** besom away, clearance, curvature, immensity, sooterkin **10** blackguard, pump-handle **11** move quickly **13** spread quickly

• **sweep under the carpet**
04 hide **06** hush up **07** conceal, cover up **08** suppress **09** gloss over, paper over

sweeper
05 broom **06** libero

sweeping
04 sway, wide **05** broad, swing **06** global **07** blanket, general, radical, rubbish **08** thorough **09** extensive, universal, wholesale **10** simplistic **11** far-reaching, wide-ranging **12** all-embracing, all-inclusive **13** comprehensive, thoroughgoing **14** across-the-board, indiscriminate, oversimplified

sweepstake
04 draw **05** sweep, Tatts **07** lottery **08** gambling **11** sweepstakes, Tattersall's

sweet
03 pud **04** cute, dear, easy, icky, kind, mild, pure, ripe, soft, soot, twee **05** balmy, candy, clean, clear, dolce, fresh, glacé **06** afters, benign, dulcet, gentle, kindly, lovely, mellow, pretty, sickly, sugary, syrupy, tender **07** amiable, beloved, candied, darling, dessert, honeyed, lovable, musical, odorous, pudding, sweetie, tuneful, winning, winsome **08** adorable, all right, aromatic, charming, engaging, fragrant, gracious, likeable, loveable, luscious, perfumed, pleasant, pleasing, precious, redolent **09** agreeable, ambrosial, appealing, beautiful, cherished, delicious, melodious, sweetened, sweetmeat, treasured, wholesome **10** attractive, confection, delightful, euphonious, harmonious, saccharine **11** mellifluous, odoriferous, sickly sweet **12** affectionate, ingratiating, satisfactory, sweet-scented **13** confectionery, sweet-sounding

Sweets include:

03 gum, ice
04 jube, Mars®, mint, rock
05 fudge, halva, jelly
06 bonbon, confit, humbug, jujube, nougat, tablet, toffee
07 alcorza, caramel, fondant, gumdrop, lozenge, pomfret, praline, truffle, wine gum
08 acid drop, bull's eye, confetti, lollipop, marzipan, noisette, pastille, pear drop
09 chocolate, jelly baby, jelly bean, lemon drop, liquorice
10 candyfloss, chewing-gum, gobstopper, peppermint
11 aniseed ball, barley sugar, marshmallow, toffee apple
12 butterscotch, dolly mixture
13 Edinburgh rock, fruit pastille
14 pineapple chunk, Turkish delight

See also **cake**; **dessert**

• **sweet on**
06 fond of, keen on, liking **08** mad about **09** far gone on **10** crazy about **12** ravished with **14** infatuated with

sweetbread
03 bur **04** burr

sweeten
04 ease **05** honey, sugar **06** mellow, pacify, soften, soothe, temper **07** appease, cushion, mollify, relieve **08** mitigate **09** alleviate **10** add sugar to, edulcorate

sweetheart
02 jo **03** joe **04** beau, dear, dona, duck, girl, lass, love **05** bonny, donah, flame, leman, lover, Romeo, swain, toots **06** amoret, bonnie, steady, suitor, sweety, tootsy **07** admirer, beloved, darling, sweetie **08** Dulcinea, follower, lady-love, truelove, young man **09** betrothed, boyfriend, inamorata, inamorato, valentine, young lady **10** girlfriend

sweetly
04 soot **05** dolce, soote **06** easily, evenly, in tune, kindly, softly **08** lovingly, mellowly, smoothly, steadily, tenderly **09** tunefully, winsomely **10** charmingly, dolcemente, pleasantly **11** melodiously **12** delightfully, effortlessly, euphoniously, harmoniously **14** affectionately

sweetness
04 love **05** aroma, charm, sirup, syrup **07** douceur, euphony, harmony **08** kindness **09** balminess, dulcitude, fragrance, freshness, saccharin **10** amiability, loveliness, mellowness, saccharine, succulence, sugariness, tenderness **11** sweet temper, winsomeness **12** lusciousness, mellifluence, pleasantness

sweet-smelling
05 balmy **07** odorous **08** aromatic, fragrant, perfumed, redolent **09** ambrosial **11** odoriferous **12** sweet-scented

swell
03 bag, don, fop, sea **04** beau, blab, boll, bulb, bulk, dude, grow, hove, huff, lord, plim, posh, puff, rise, toff, wave **05** adept, belly, berry, blast, bloat, bulge, bunch, dandy, elate, farce, grand, great, heave, mount, plump, raise, ritzy, smart, surge **06** bigwig, billow, blow up, de luxe, dilate, expand, extend, fatten, flashy, louden, puff up, step up, strout, swanky, tumefy, volume, wallow **07** augment, balloon, distend, enlarge, ferment, heaving, incline, inflate, stylish, tumesce **08** belly out, escalate, heighten, increase, mushroom, outswell, snowball **09** backwater, cockscomb, excellent, exclusive, intensify, intumesce, loudening, roughness, skyrocket, wonderful **10** accelerate, distension, grow larger, undulation **11** enlargement, fashionable, proliferate

swelling
03 sty **04** boil, boll, bulb, bump, gall, knob, knot, lump, node, stye **05** bulge, heave, mouse, nodus, proud, tuber, tumor **06** bruise, nodule, pimple, rising, torose, torous, tumour, venter **07** blister, chancre, pillowy, tympany, vesicle **08** nodosity, pulvinus, scirrhus, tubercle **09** chilblain, gathering, puffiness **10** distension, tumescence, turgescent **11** enlargement, tumefaction **12** inflammation, intumescence, protuberance

sweltering
03 hot **05** humid, muggy, stewy **06** baking, clammy, steamy, sticky, sultry, torrid **07** airless, boiling **08** roasting, sizzling, stifling, tropical **09** scorching **10** oppressive **11** suffocating

swerve
03 wry **04** bend, lean, skew, sway, swee, swey, turn, veer, warp **05** faint, sheer, shift, stray, swarm, swing, twist **06** shrink, wander **07** deflect, deviate, diverge, incline, inswing **08** outswing, scramble **09** deviation **10** deflection

swift
04 fast **05** agile, brief, brisk, fleet, hasty, nippy, quick, rapid, ready, short, wight **06** abrupt, flying, lively, nimble, prompt, speedy, sudden, winged **07** express, flighty, hurried **09** feathered, immediate, screecher **10** pernicious **11** dispatchful, expeditious, tiger-footed **13** screech-martin

swiftly
04 fast **05** apace **07** express, hotfoot, quickly, rapidly **08** promptly, speedily **09** hurriedly, instantly, posthaste **10** at full tilt **11** double-quick **13** expeditiously

swiftness
05 speed **08** alacrity, celerity, despatch, dispatch, rapidity, velocity **09** fleetness, immediacy, quickness, readiness **10** expedition, promptness, speediness, suddenness **13** immediateness, instantaneity

swill
◇ *anagram indicator*
04 gulp, swig, wash **05** drain, drink, quaff, rinse, slops, waste **06** gargle, guzzle, imbibe, refuse, sluice **07** consume, hogwash, pigwash, swallow, toss off **08** pig's-wash, pigswill **09** knock back, scourings

• swill out
05 clean, flush, rinse **06** drench, sluice **07** cleanse, wash out **08** wash down

swim
◇ *anagram indicator*
03 bob, dip, fin, ren, rin, run **04** soom, swan, whim **05** bathe, crawl, float **06** paddle **07** snorkel **08** take a dip **09** strike out **10** tread water

swimmer *see* **fish**

swimming
◇ *anagram indicator*

Swimming strokes include:

03 fly
05 crawl
07 trudgen
09 back crawl, butterfly, dog-paddle, freestyle
10 backstroke, front crawl, sidestroke
11 doggy-paddle
12 breaststroke
15 Australian crawl

Swimming- and diving-related terms include:

02 IM
03 fly, rip
04 pike, tuck
05 block, boost, entry, scull, split
06 inward, layout, length, medley
07 forward, reverse
08 armstand, backward, flamingo
09 ballet leg, eggbeater, elevation
10 tumble turn
11 dolphin kick, flutter kick, rocket split
12 combined spin
13 negative split
14 continuous spin
15 backstroke flags

Swimmers and divers include:

04 Klim (Michael), Otto (Kristin), Rose (Murray), Webb (Matthew)
05 Crapp (Lorraine), Curry (Lisa), Ender (Kornelia), Evans (Janet), Gould (Shane), Gross (Michael), Lewis (Hayley), Riley (Samantha), Spitz (Mark)
06 Biondi (Matt), Davies (Sharron), Durack (Fanny), Ederle (Gertrude), Fraser (Dawn), Loader (Danyon), O'Neill (Susie), Phelps (Michael), Thorpe (Ian), Wilkie (David)
07 Goodhew (Duncan), Hackett (Grant), Perkins (Kieren), Wickham (Tracey)
08 Champion (Malcolm), Charlton (Boy), De Bruijn (Inge), Louganis (Greg), Streeter (Alison), Van Wisse (Tammy), Williams (Esther)
09 Armstrong (Duncan), Kellerman (Annette)
11 Beaurepaire (Sir Frank), Weissmuller (Johnny)

• swimming organ
03 oar **05** ctene

swimming costume *see* **swimsuit**

swimmingly
06 easily **08** smoothly, very well **12** successfully **13** like clockwork, without a hitch

swimming-pool
04 lido **05** baths **10** natatorium **11** leisure pool **12** swimming-bath, swimming-pond **13** swimming-baths

swimsuit
03 tog **04** togs **05** tanga, thong **06** bikini, cossie, trunks **07** bathers, maillot, tankini **08** monokini, one-piece **11** bathing suit **12** bathing dress **14** bathing costume **15** swimming costume

swindle
02 do **03** con, gyp, rig **04** beat, chiz, dupe, fake, have, lurk, ramp, rook, scam, skin, take **05** bunco, bunko, cheat, chizz, fraud, gouge, grift, let in, mulct, pluck, shaft, sting, trick, twist **06** bucket, chouse, diddle, fiddle, fleece, hustle, nobble, racket, rip off, rip-off **07** con game, deceive, defraud, exploit, skelder, tweedle **08** clean-out, con trick, fakement, sell a pup, stitch up, trickery **09** bamboozle, deception, financier, gold brick, gold-brick, sell smoke **10** overcharge **12** put one over on, take for a ride **13** double-dealing, sharp practice

swindler
03 con, leg **04** hood, rook **05** cheat, crook, fraud, rogue, shark **06** chouse, con man, escroc, rascal **07** fiddler, grifter, hoodlum, hustler, magsman, slicker, spieler **08** blackleg, con woman, impostor **09** charlatan, chiseller, con artist, fraudster, trickster **10** mountebank **12** bunko-steerer

swine
03 hog, pig **04** boar, boor **05** beast, brute, rogue **06** rascal **09** scoundrel **14** good-for-nothing

• bit of a swine
03 ham **05** bacon

swing
◇ *anagram indicator*
03 fix, get **04** bend, hang, hurl, jive, lean, make, move, rock, shog, spin, sway, swee, swey, turn, vary, veer, wave, wind **05** curve, fix up, pivot, scope, set up, shift, sling, sweep, twist, wheel, whirl **06** change, dangle, excite, motion, rhythm, rotate, stroke, swerve, waving **07** achieve, arrange, attract, control, impetus, incline, shoogie, vibrate **08** brandish, fishtail, movement, organize, sweeping **09** fluctuate, oscillate, pendulate, variation, vibration **11** fluctuation, oscillating, oscillation

swingeing
04 huge **05** great, harsh, heavy **06** severe **07** drastic, extreme, serious **08** thumping **09** Draconian, excessive, punishing, stringent **10** exorbitant, oppressive **11** devastating **12** extortionate

swinging
◇ *anagram indicator*
03 hip **06** lively, modern, trendy, with it **07** dynamic, hanging, stylish, swaying, turning **08** exciting, up-to-date **10** jet-setting **11** fashionable, oscillatory **12** contemporary **13** up-to-the-minute

swipe
03 hit **04** biff, blow, gulp, lift, nick, slap, sock, swat, whip, wipe **05** clout, filch, lunge, pinch, slice, smack, steal, swath, whack **06** pilfer, strike, stroke, wallop **07** lash out, purloin

swirl
◇ *anagram indicator*
04 curl, eddy, purl, spin, wind **05** churn, twirl, twist, wheel, whirl **07** agitate, revolve, swizzle **09** circulate **10** tourbillon **11** tourbillion

swish
04 cane, flog, lash, posh, wave, whip **05** birch, flash, grand, plush, ritzy, smart, swell, swing, swirl, twirl, whirl, whisk, whizz **06** de luxe, rustle, swanky, swoosh, thrash, whoosh **07** elegant, stylish, whistle **08** brandish, flourish **09** exclusive, sumptuous **11** fashionable

switch
◇ *anagram indicator*
◇ *reversal indicator*
03 put, rod **04** beat, cane, jerk, lash, swap, turn, twig, veer, whip **05** birch, lever, prune, relay, shift, shoot, shunt, thong, trade, tress, whisk **06** barter, beat up, branch, button, change, divert, gain-up, scutch, toggle, twitch **07** control, convert, deflect, deviate, replace **08** cryotron, exchange, reversal **09** about-turn, rearrange, transpose **10** alteration, changeover, substitute **11** interchange, on-off device, replacement **12** substitution **13** chop and change **14** circuit-breaker

• switch off
03 cut **07** shut off, turn off, turn out **08** flick off **09** close down **11** stop working

• switch on
05 put on **06** set off, turn on **07** flick on, operate **08** activate **10** trigger off

Switzerland
02 CH **03** CHE

swivel
04 spin, turn **05** pivot, twirl, wheel **06** gyrate, rotate **07** revolve **09** pirouette

swollen
04 rank **05** bloat, puffy, tumid **06** bolled, bollen, gourdy, turgid **07** blabber, bloated, bulbous, bulging, dilated, distent, gibbose, gibbous **08** blubbery, engorged, enlarged, expanded, hydropic, inflamed, inflated, puffed up **09** blubbered, distended, tumescent **11** incrassated

swoop
04 dive, drop, fall, rush **05** lunge, souse,

stoop **06** attack, plunge, pounce **07** descend, descent **09** onslaught

• **at one fell swoop**

07 in one go **08** suddenly **09** all at once, at one time, by one blow **13** on one occasion **15** by a single action

swop *see* **swap, swop**

sword

03 war **04** spit

Swords include:

03 fox
04 back, épée, foil, simi
05 bilbo, blade, brand, broad, court, estoc, kukri, saber, sabre, short, skean, skene, small, steel
06 espada, glaive, hanger, katana, kirpan, rapier, sweard, Toledo, waster
07 curtana, curtaxe, gladius, hunting, Morglay, shabble, spurtle, whinger, yatagan
08 claymore, curtalax, damaskin, falchion, schläger, scimitar, spadroon, whiniard, whinyard, white arm, yataghan
09 curtalaxe, damascene, damaskeen, damasquin, Excalibur
10 damasceene
12 spurtle-blade, toasting fork, toasting iron

See also **dagger**; **knife**

• **cross swords**

05 argue, fight **06** bicker **07** contend, contest, dispute, quarrel, wrangle **08** be at odds, disagree **15** be at loggerheads

sworn

07 devoted, eternal **08** attested **09** confirmed **10** implacable, inveterate, relentless

swot

03 mug **04** cram, work **05** learn, mug up, study, swank **06** bone up, revise **08** memorize

sybarite

07 epicure, playboy **08** hedonist, parasite **09** bon vivant, epicurean, pleasurer **10** sensualist, voluptuary **14** pleasure-seeker

sybaritic

04 easy **07** sensual **09** epicurean, luxurious, parasitic **10** hedonistic, voluptuous **13** self-indulgent **14** pleasure-loving **15** pleasure-seeking

sycophancy

07 fawning **08** cringing, flattery, toadyism **09** adulation, kowtowing, servility, truckling **10** grovelling, toad-eating **11** bootlicking, slavishness **14** backscratching, obsequiousness, oleaginousness

sycophant

05 slave, toady **06** fawner, yes-man **07** crawler, cringer, placebo, sponger **08** claqueur, hanger-on, parasite, truckler **09** flatterer, groveller, toad-eater **10** bootlicker **12** cookie-pusher **13** apple polisher, backscratcher

sycophantic

05 slimy **06** smarmy **07** fawning, servile, slavish **08** cringing, toadying, unctuous **09** truckling **10** flattering, grovelling, obsequious, oleaginous, toad-eating **11** bootlicking, parasitical, time-serving **12** ingratiating **13** sycophantical **14** backscratching

syllabus

03 syl **04** plan **05** table **06** course **07** outline **08** schedule **09** programme **10** curriculum

syllogism

08 argument **09** abduction, deduction, enthymeme **11** epicheirema, proposition

sylph-like

04 slim **05** lithe **06** slight, svelte **07** elegant, slender, willowy **08** graceful **11** streamlined

sylvan *see* **silvan**

symbiotic

07 epizoan, epizoic **09** commensal, epizootic **10** endophytic, synergetic **11** co-operative, interactive **14** interdependent

symbol

04 mark, rune, sign, type **05** creed, image **06** figure **09** character, ideograph **14** representation

Symbols include:

01 A, Å, @, B, C, ©, D, e, F, g, H, I, J, K, L, M, N, O, P, Q, R, ®, S, T, U, V, W, X, Y, Z
02 Ac, Ag, Al, Am, Ar, As, At, Au, Ba, BB, Be, Bh, Bi, Bk, Bq, Br, Ca, Cd, Ce, Cf, Cl, Cm, Co, CQ, Cr, Cs, Cu, Db, Ds, Dy, Er, Es, Eu, Fe, ff, Fm, Fr, Ga, Gd, Ge, Gy, Ha, He, Hf, Hg, HH, Ho, Hs, Hz, In, Ir, kg, Kr, La, Li, lm, Lr, Lu, Lw, lx, Md, Mg, Mn, Mo, Mt, MV, Na, Nb, Nd, Ne, Ni, No, Np, Oe, Os, Pa, Pb, Pd, Pm, Po, Pr, Pt, Pu, Ra, Rb, Re, Rf, Rg, Rh, Rn, Ru, Sb, Sc, Se, Sg, Si, Sm, Sn, Sr, Sv, Ta, Tb, Tc, Te, Th, Ti, Tl, Tm, Wb, Xe, Yb, Zn, Zr
03 BBB, dBA, kat, LXX, mol, rad
04 icon, ikon, logo
05 badge, brand, crest, motif, token, totem
06 cipher, emblem, smiley, uraeus
08 caduceus, ideogram, insignia, logogram, monogram, swastika
09 pentagram, trademark, watermark
10 coat of arms, hieroglyph, pictograph
12 yellow ribbon

Religious symbols include:

02 Om
03 IHC, IHS
04 ankh, fish, yoni
05 cross, linga
06 chakra, filfot, fylfot, lingam
07 Ik Onkar, mandala, menorah, yin-yang
08 crescent, swastika
11 Christingle, star of David

See also **element**

symbolic

05 token **07** shadowy, typical **10** emblematic, figurative, meaningful, symbolical **11** allegorical, significant **12** illustrative, metaphorical **14** representative

symbolically

07 as a sign **09** as a symbol **10** as an emblem **11** by this token **12** figuratively **14** emblematically

symbolize

04 mean, type **05** agree **06** denote, emblem, figure, symbol, typify **07** betoken, combine, express, present, signify **08** stand for **09** epitomize, exemplify, personate, personify, represent

symmetrical

03 sym **04** even **07** dimeric, regular, uniform **08** balanced, parallel **10** consistent, harmonious **11** well-rounded, zygopleural **12** isobilateral, proportional, right-and-left **13** actinomorphic, corresponding

symmetry

07 balance, harmony **08** evenness **09** agreement, congruity **10** proportion, regularity, uniformity **11** consistency, parallelism, proportions **14** correspondence

sympathetic

04 kind, soft, warm **06** caring, genial, kindly, social, tender **07** feeling, pitying **08** friendly, likeable, pleasant, sociable, tolerant **09** agreeable, concerned, congenial, consoling, simpatico **10** comforting, compatible, favourable, interested, like-minded, solicitous, supportive **11** considerate, encouraging, kind-hearted, neighbourly, warm-hearted **12** affectionate, appreciative, well-disposed **13** commiserating, commiserative, companionable, compassionate, sympathetical, understanding

sympathetically

06 kindly, warmly **09** feelingly, pityingly **11** consolingly, sensitively **12** comfortingly, responsively, supportively **13** warm-heartedly **14** appreciatively **15** compassionately, understandingly

sympathize

03 rap **04** pity **07** care for, comfort, condole, console, feel for **09** empathize, encourage, respond to **10** appreciate, correspond, understand **11** commiserate, show concern **12** be supportive, feel sorry for, identify with, show interest

sympathizer

03 fan **06** backer **07** admirer **08** adherent, condoler, partisan **09** supporter **10** copperhead, well-wisher **15** fellow-traveller

sympathy
04 pity **05** aroha **06** accord, solace, warmth **07** comfort, empathy, harmony, rapport, support **08** affinity, approval, kindness **09** agreement, closeness **10** compassion, tenderness **11** approbation, condolences, consolation, correlation, Weltschmerz **12** appreciation **13** commiseration, consideration, encouragement, fellow-feeling, understanding
14 correspondence, thoughtfulness
15 warm-heartedness

• **expression of sympathy**
02 ah, aw **04** dear **05** shame, sorry, there **06** dear me, oh dear, too bad
07 deary me **08** dearie me, good-lack
09 hard lines, tough luck **10** hard cheese

symptom
03 sym **04** mark, note, sign **05** fever, hives, rigor, token **06** signal **07** anxiety, display, feature, hard pad, warning
08 evidence, merycism, necrosis, prodrome **09** ketonuria, prodromus, rosetting **10** diagnostic, expression, indication, nettle rash, prognostic
11 hydrophobia, proteinuria
13 demonstration, epiphenomenon, malabsorption, manifestation
14 characteristic
See also **disease**

symptomatic
07 typical **10** associated, indicative, suggesting, suggestive
14 characteristic

synagogue
04 shul **06** temple

synchronize
04 sync, tune **05** synch

syndicate
04 bloc, ring **05** group, judge **06** cartel
07 censure, combine, council
08 alliance **11** association, combination

synonymous
07 similar, the same **09** identical
10 comparable, equivalent, tantamount **13** corresponding, substitutable **15** interchangeable

synopsis
05 recap **06** digest, précis, résumé, review, schema, sketch **07** outline, run-down, summary **08** abstract
09 summation **10** abridgment, compendium, conspectus, tabulation
11 abridgement **12** condensation
14 recapitulation

synthesis
05 alloy, blend, union **06** fusion
07 amalgam, welding **08** compound, pastiche **09** anabolism, composite
11 coalescence, combination, integration, pantheology, unification
12 amalgamation, glycogenesis
13 individuation

synthesize
04 fuse, weld **05** alloy, blend, merge, unify, unite **07** combine **08** coalesce, compound **09** integrate
10 amalgamate

synthetic
◇ *anagram indicator*
03 syn **04** fake, faux, mock, sham
05 bogus **06** ersatz, pseudo **07** man-made, plastic **09** imitation, simulated
10 artificial **12** manufactured

Syria
03 SYR

syrup
03 rob **05** sirup **06** orgeat **07** glucose, linctus, treacle **08** quiddany
09 cocky's joy, diacodion, diacodium, grenadine, moskonfyt **10** capillaire, maple syrup

syrupy
05 corny, gushy, mushy, soppy, sweet, weepy **06** loving, sickly, sloppy, slushy, sugary **07** gushing, honeyed, maudlin, mawkish **08** pathetic, romantic
09 emotional, oversweet, schmaltzy, sweetened **10** lovey-dovey, saccharine
11 sentimental, sickly sweet, tear-jerking **12** affectionate

system
03 way **04** mode, plan, rule, them
05 logic, means, order, set-up, usage
06 method, scheme **07** network, process, routine **08** approach, practice
09 apparatus, framework, mechanism, procedure, structure, technique
11 arrangement, methodology, orderliness **12** co-ordination, organization **13** modus operandi, the government **14** classification, the authorities **15** systematization, the powers that be

systematic
07 logical, ordered, orderly, planned
08 habitual, methodic **09** efficient, organized **10** methodical, scientific, structured **11** intentional, well-ordered, well-planned **12** businesslike, standardized, systematized **13** well-organized

systematize
04 plan **05** order **06** codify **07** arrange, dispose **08** classify, organize, regiment, regulate, tabulate
09 methodize, structure
10 schematize **11** make uniform, rationalize, standardize

T

T
03 tee, toc **04** tock **05** tango

TA
10 volunteers **15** Territorial Army

tab
03 fob, tag **04** bill, cost, drug, flap, pill **05** check, label, strap, tally **06** marker, tablet, ticket **07** Ecstasy, sticker, trimmer **08** ring pull, tabulate **09** cigarette, tabulator

• keep tabs on
07 observe **11** keep an eye on **12** watch closely

tabby
04 girl, wavy **05** woman **06** banded, stripy **07** brindle, mottled, striped **08** brindled, streaked **10** variegated

table
03 bar **04** chow, diet, dish, fare, food, grub, list, menu, move, nosh, plan, slab, tuck **05** bench, chart, graph, index, layer, panel, stand **06** figure, record, submit **07** diagram, picture, propose, suggest, worktop **08** register, schedule, syllabus, tabulate **09** catalogue, committee, inventory, programme, timetable **10** put forward, speciality, tabulation **12** string-course **13** entertainment

Tables include:

03 bed, loo, tea, top
04 bird, card, desk, draw, drum, high, pier, pool, sand, side, sofa, work
05 altar, board, lunch, night
06 bureau, coffee, dining, dinner, dolmen, gaming, inking, lowboy, picnic, teapoy, toilet, vanity
07 capstan, console, counter, cricket, drawing, draw-top, dresser, gateleg, snooker, trestle, writing
08 billiard, credence, credenza, draw-leaf, dressing, drop-leaf, guéridon, mahogany, pembroke, piecrust
09 breakfast, communion, operating, refectory
10 dissecting, gate-legged, greencloth, occasional
12 council-board
13 bonheur-du-jour

Tableware includes:

03 cup, jug, mug
04 bowl
05 ashet, cruet, plate
06 goblet, saucer, teacup, teapot, tureen
07 creamer, milk jug, platter, tumbler
08 cream jug, flatware, mazarine, rice bowl, salt mill
09 coffee cup, coffee pot, gravy boat, pasta bowl, pasta dish, pepper pot, salad bowl, sauceboat, side plate, soup plate, sugar bowl, toast rack, wineglass
10 bread plate, butter dish, cereal bowl, cruet-stand, pepper mill, salt shaker, soup tureen
11 butter plate, cheese plate, dessert bowl, dessert dish, espresso cup, serving bowl, serving dish
12 dessert plate, mazarine dish, pudding-plate
13 mazarine plate
14 serving platter

• inner table
04 home

tableau
05 scene **07** diorama, picture **08** vignette **09** portrayal, spectacle **13** tableau vivant **14** representation

tableland
04 mesa, puna **05** Karoo **06** Karroo **07** plateau

tablet
01 E **03** pad, tab **04** ball, dove, pill, slab **05** album, benny, bolus, panel, plate, stela, stele **06** abacus, caplet, marker, pellet, plaque, Roofie, tabula, troche **07** capsule, diptych, lozenge, sleeper, surface **08** monument, triglyph **09** medallion, tablature, wobbly egg **10** osculatory, tabula rasa **11** purple heart **12** disco biscuit, Rosetta stone

tabletalk
03 ana

tabloid *see* **newspaper**

taboo
03 ban **04** tabu, tapu, veto **05** curse **06** banned, vetoed **08** anathema, ruled out **09** exclusion, forbidden, interdict, ostracism, restraint **10** prohibited, proscribed, sacrosanct **11** prohibition, restriction, unthinkable **12** interdiction, proscription, unacceptable **13** unmentionable

tabulate
03 tab **04** list, sort **05** chart, index, order, range, table **06** codify **07** arrange **08** classify **09** catalogue **10** categorize, tabularize **11** systematize

tabulation
07 listing, sorting, tabling **08** indexing, ordering **11** arrangement, cataloguing **14** categorization, classification

tacit
06 silent **07** implied **08** implicit, inferred, unspoken, unstated, unvoiced, wordless **10** understood **11** unexpressed

taciturn
04 cold, dumb, mute **05** aloof, quiet **06** silent **07** distant **08** detached, reserved, reticent **09** withdrawn **10** of few words **11** tight-lipped, untalkative **12** close-mouthed **13** unforthcoming **15** uncommunicative

tack
03 add, fix, pin, sew, tag, way **04** line, nail, path, plan, take, turn, veer **05** affix, annex, baste, catch, lease, smack, spell **06** append, attach, attack, course, fasten, method, policy, sleaze, staple, stitch, swerve, tactic, tenure, tingle, zigzag **07** bearing, go about, heading, process, tintack **08** approach, club-haul, strategy **09** come about, direction, procedure, technique, thumbtack **10** drawing-pin, stickiness **12** change course, line of action **14** course of action **15** change direction

See also **horse**

tackle
◇ *containment indicator*
03 cat, rig, try **04** chin, foul, gear, grab, halt, sack, stop, take, whip **05** begin, block, catch, grasp, hoist, seize, stuff, tools **06** attack, burton, garnet, handle, jigger, outfit, pulley, take on, things **07** address, attempt, clobber, deflect, go about, harness, have a go, rigging, weapons **08** attend to, confront, deal with, embark on, face up to, obstruct, set about, wade into **09** apparatus, challenge, encounter, equipment, get down to, intercept, trappings, undertake **10** clew-garnet, get to grips, ground-hold, implements, take hold of **11** come to grips, grapple with, topping lift **12** interception, intervention **13** accoutrements, paraphernalia **14** get to grips with **15** apply yourself to, come to grips with

tacky
03 wet **04** naff **05** dingy, gaudy, gluey, gooey, gummy, messy, tatty **06** flashy, grotty, ragged, shabby, shoddy, sleazy, sloppy, sticky, tawdry, untidy, vulgar **07** kitschy, scruffy **08** adhesive, plimsoll, tattered **09** tasteless **10** threadbare

tact
05 skill **07** finesse **08** delicacy,

judgment, prudence, subtlety **09** dexterity, diplomacy, judgement **10** adroitness, discretion, perception **11** discernment, savoir-faire, sensitivity, tactfulness **13** consideration, judiciousness, understanding **14** thoughtfulness

tactful

06 adroit, polite, subtle, tender **07** careful, politic, prudent, skilful **08** delicate, discreet, kid-glove **09** judicious, sensitive **10** diplomatic, discerning, perceptive, thoughtful **11** considerate **12** diplomatical **13** understanding

tactfully

08 politely, tenderly **09** carefully, prudently, skilfully **10** delicately, discreetly **11** judiciously, sensitively **12** thoughtfully **14** diplomatically

tactic

03 way **04** move, plan, ploy, ruse **05** means, moves, shift, trick **06** course, device, method, policy, scheme **07** audible **08** approach, campaign, game plan, hardball, soft sell, strategy **09** expedient, manoeuvre, procedure, stratagem **10** manoeuvres, subterfuge **12** line of attack **14** course of action, full-court press

tactical

05 smart **06** adroit, artful, clever, shrewd **07** cunning, planned, politic, prudent, skilful **09** judicious, strategic **10** calculated

tactician

05 brain **07** planner **08** diplomat, director **10** campaigner, mastermind, politician, strategist **11** co-ordinator **12** orchestrator

tactless

04 rude **05** crass, rough **06** clumsy, gauche, unkind **07** awkward, hurtful **08** careless, impolite, unsubtle **09** impolitic, imprudent, maladroit, unfeeling **10** blundering, indelicate, indiscreet **11** injudicious, insensitive, thoughtless **12** discourteous, undiplomatic **13** inappropriate, inconsiderate

tactlessness

08 rudeness **09** bad timing, gaucherie **10** clumsiness, crassitude, indelicacy, ineptitude, maladdress **11** boorishness, discourtesy **12** impoliteness, indiscretion **13** insensitivity, maladroitness **15** thoughtlessness

tadpole

08 polliwig, polliwog, pollywig, pollywog **09** porwiggle

tag

03 add, dag, dub, tab, tig **04** call, flap, mark, name, note, slip, tack, term **05** affix, aglet, annex, badge, label, maxim, moral, motto, quote, shred, strap, style, tally, title **06** adjoin, aiglet, anklet, append, attach, cliché, dictum, docket, fasten, phrase, rabble, saying, ticket **07** entitle, epithet, kabaddi, proverb, refrain, remnant, sticker **08** allusion, bracelet, christen, identify, nickname **09** designate, quotation **10** aglet babie, expression, Kimball tag **11** aiguillette, description, stock phrase, treasury tag **12** identity disc **14** identification

• tag along

04 tail **05** trail **06** follow, shadow **09** accompany

tail

◇ *tail selection indicator*

03 dog, end, fan, fud, uro- **04** back, flag, herd, rear, rump, scut **05** brush, queue, stalk, stern, suite, track, trail, train **06** behind, bottom, follow, pursue, shadow, shamus, sleuth **07** gumshoe, limited, rear end, retinue **08** backside, buttocks, cynosure, straggle **09** appendage, detective, extremity, posterior **10** conclusion, private eye **11** termination **12** investigator

• part of tail

03 fin **04** dock

• tail back

03 jam **04** line **05** queue **06** back up

• tail off

03 die **04** drop, fade, wane **06** die out **07** decline, drop off, dwindle **08** decrease, fall away, peter out, taper off

• turn tail

04 bolt, flee **06** beat it, decamp, escape **07** abscond, run away, scarper **09** skedaddle

tailback

03 row **04** file, line, tail **05** queue, train **06** backup, column **09** crocodile **10** procession

tailor

◇ *anagram indicator*

03 cut, fit **04** dung, snip, suit, trim **05** adapt, alter, darzi, flint, mould, shape, style **06** adjust, cutter, modify, sartor, teller **07** convert, fashion, modiste, whipcat **08** clothier, costumer, seamster **09** costumier, couturier, customize, outfitter **10** dressmaker, prick-louse, seamstress, whipstitch **11** accommodate, personalize **13** prick-the-louse

tailor-made

05 ideal, right **06** fitted, suited **07** bespoke, perfect **08** tailored **11** custom-built **13** made-to-measure

taint

◇ *anagram indicator*

04 blot, flaw, harm, ruin, soil, spot, wilt **05** dirty, fault, muddy, shame, smear, smoke, spoil, stain, sully, tinge **06** befoul, blight, damage, defect, defile, infect, injure, mildew, poison, stigma, weaken, wither **07** blacken, blemish, corrupt, deprave, envenom, pollute, tarnish **08** disgrace **09** attainder, contagion, dishonour, infection, pollution **10** adulterate, corruption **11** contaminate **12** adulteration **13** contamination

Taiwan

02 RC **03** TWN

Tajikistan

02 TJ **03** TJK

take

◇ *containment indicator*

01 r **02** do **03** bag, buy, eat, fet, get, nim, rec, use, win **04** bear, bite, book, deem, draw, fall, fett, gain, gate, give, grab, grip, haul, have, help, hent, hire, hold, last, lead, lift, need, nick, note, pick, read, rent, seat, show, twig, view, work **05** abide, admit, adopt, angle, begin, bring, carry, catch, charm, cheat, drink, drive, ferry, fetch, filch, grasp, guide, learn, lease, pinch, scoff, seize, slant, stand, steal, study, teach, think, use up, usher, visit, whisk, yield **06** abduct, accept, aspect, assume, attain, become, betake, blight, choose, clutch, come by, convey, decide, deduct, demand, derive, detect, devour, endure, engage, escort, fathom, follow, freeze, gather, guzzle, handle, imbibe, income, ingest, inhale, kidnap, obtain, occupy, pay for, profit, pursue, recipe, reckon, regard, remove, return, secure, select, snatch, strike, suffer, tuck in **07** achieve, acquire, be given, believe, bewitch, call for, capture, conduct, conquer, consume, contain, deceive, deliver, detract, examine, execute, extract, find out, go along, major in, measure, mistake, observe, perform, portray, presume, procure, profits, purloin, react to, receive, require, returns, revenue, set down, stomach, succeed, suppose, swallow, swindle, takings, undergo **08** attitude, be taught, carry off, consider, cope with, cotton on, deal with, discover, look upon, proceeds, purchase, receipts, remember, research, settle on, shepherd, submerge, subtract, surprise, take away, tolerate, vanquish **09** accompany, apprehend, ascertain, captivate, determine, eliminate, establish, fathom out, gate-money, get hold of, lay hold of, put up with, respond to, transport, undertake, viewpoint, withstand **10** bear in mind, comprehend, confiscate, drive along, experience, photograph, standpoint, take effect, understand **11** accommodate, acknowledge, appropriate, be effective, frame of mind, have room for, necessitate, perspective, point of view, subscribe to, travel along **12** have space for, vantage point **13** be efficacious **14** interpretation, produce results **15** have a capacity of

• let him/her take

03 cap

• take after

04 echo **06** be like, favour, mirror **08** look like, resemble, surprise **11** be similar to

• take against
06 oppose **07** despise, dislike **08** object to **12** disapprove of

• take apart
03 nag, pan **04** carp, slag, slam **05** blame, knock, slate, snipe **06** attack **07** analyse, censure, condemn, nit-pick, rubbish, run down, slag off **08** badmouth, denounce, separate **09** criticize, dismantle, disparage **10** come down on, go to town on **11** disassemble, pick holes in **12** disapprove of, pull to pieces, put the boot in, take to pieces, tear to shreds **13** find fault with, tear a strip off **15** do a hatchet job on, pass judgement on

• take back
04 deny **05** evoke **06** call up, recant, regain, remind, resume, retake, return **07** get back, reclaim, replace, restore, retract **08** disclaim, give back, hand back, renounce, send back, withdraw **09** repossess, repudiate **12** eat your words **14** make you think of, put you in mind of

• take down
04 note, raze **05** level, lower **06** record, reduce, remove **07** demount, get down, put down, set down **08** demolish, pull down **09** dismantle, write down **10** put on paper, transcribe **11** disassemble, make a note of

• take in
◇ *containment indicator*
03 con, lap **04** dupe, fool **05** admit, cheat, cover, grasp, trick **06** absorb, digest **07** contain, deceive, embrace, include, mislead, realize, receive, shelter, swindle, welcome **08** comprise, hoodwink **09** bamboozle, encompass **10** appreciate, assimilate, comprehend, understand **11** accommodate, incorporate

• take off
◇ *deletion indicator*
02 go **03** ape, fly **04** bolt, doff, drop, flee, mock, rise, shed, soar, work **05** climb, leave, mimic, mount, strip **06** ascend, decamp, deduct, depart, detach, divest, do well, make it, parody, remove, send up **07** abscond, bunk off, catch on, discard, imitate, lift off, prosper, pull off, run away, scarper, succeed, tear off, undress **08** discount, flourish, go places, satirize, subtract, take away, throw off **09** disappear, do a runner, skedaddle **10** caricature, strike gold **11** impersonate **12** get undressed **13** become popular, hit the jackpot **14** become airborne

• take on
◇ *containment indicator*
◇ *juxtaposition indicator*
04 copy, face, hire, kill **05** enrol, fight **06** accept, assume, defeat, employ, engage, enlist, escort, oppose, retain, tackle **07** acquire, destroy, extract, recruit, vie with **08** get angry, get upset **09** entertain, make a fuss, undertake **11** compete with, contend with

• take out
03 fix, see, zap **04** dele, do in, draw, kill **05** set up, shoot, waste **06** be lent, borrow, cut out, defeat, delete, detach, escort, except, excise, get out, go with, murder, remove, rub out **07** arrange, bump off, butcher, destroy, execute, extract, pull out, wipe out, work out **08** blow away, despatch, dispatch, knock off, massacre, organize, settle on **09** accompany, eliminate, finish off, go out with, have a loan, liquidate, polish off **10** do away with, put to death **11** assassinate, exterminate **14** use temporarily

• take over
05 adopt **06** buy out **07** subsume **10** run the show **12** take charge of **13** gain control of

• take to
04 like **05** begin, start **08** commence, set about **09** undertake **10** appreciate, launch into **12** become keen on, find pleasant **14** find attractive

• take up
◇ *insertion indicator*
◇ *reversal down indicator*
03 use **04** fill, lift, rear **05** adopt, begin, raise, start, use up **06** absorb, accept, assume, engage, occupy, pick up, pursue, resume **07** agree to, carry on, consume, engross **08** commence, continue, embark on **10** monopolize **13** hang about with **14** knock about with **15** get involved with

take-off
05 spoof **06** ascent, flight, flying, parody, send-up **07** lift-off, mimicry **08** climbing, drawback, scramble, travesty **09** departure, imitation **10** caricature **13** impersonation

takeover
04 coup **06** buyout, merger **09** coalition **11** combination **12** amalgamation **13** incorporation

taking
04 gain, gate **05** yield **06** income, plight **07** profits, returns, revenue, winning, winsome **08** alluring, catching, charming, earnings, engaging, fetching, pickings, pleasing, proceeds, receipts, winnings **09** agitation, appealing, beguiling, gate-money **10** attractive, compelling, delightful, enchanting, infectious, intriguing, perplexity **11** bewitchment, captivating, fascinating **13** prepossessing

tale
03 bam, fib, lie, toy **04** epic, gest, hoax, myth, rede, reed, saga, talk, yarn **05** blood, fable, geste, novel, porky, reede, roman, spiel, story, total, weird **06** legend, number, report, rumour **07** account, fabliau, Märchen, mystery, novella, odyssey, parable, romance, untruth, whopper **08** allegory, anecdote, jeremiad, sob story **09** discourse, fairytale, falsehood, folk story, narrative, reckoning, storiette, storyette, tall story, tradition **10** fairy story, hair-raiser **11** fabrication **12** old wives' tale, superstition **14** traveller's tale

talent
04 bent, feel, gift, nous **05** flair, forte, knack, power, skill, talon **06** genius **07** ability, aptness, faculty **08** aptitude, capacity, facility, ingenium, long suit, new blood, strength **09** endowment **11** disposition, showmanship, strong point **12** shot in the arm

talented
04 able, deft **05** adept **06** adroit, clever, gifted **07** capable, skilful **08** artistic **09** brilliant, versatile **10** proficient **11** well-endowed **12** accomplished

talisman
04 idol, ju-ju **05** charm, totem **06** amulet, fetish, mascot, symbol, telesm **07** abraxas, periapt **10** phylactery

talk
03 gab, gas, jaw, rap, say, yak **04** blab, bull, cant, chat, tell, yack **05** grass, haver, lingo, moody, mouth, noise, noyes, orate, parle, slang, speak, spiel, utter, voice, words **06** babble, confab, confer, debate, devise, gossip, haggle, havers, jabber, jargon, jaw-jaw, korero, natter, parley, rabbit, report, rumour, sermon, speech, squeal, yabber **07** address, baloney, bargain, blether, boloney, chatter, chinwag, clatter, confess, dialect, discuss, earbash, express, hearsay, lecture, malarky, meeting, oration, palaver, prattle, seminar, twaddle **08** badinage, chitchat, conclave, converse, dialogue, flimflam, haggling, idiolect, inform on, language, malarkey **09** discourse, gibberish, interview, negotiate, symposium, tell tales, tête-à-tête, utterance **10** articulate, balderdash, bargaining, conference, discursion, discussion, namby-pamby **11** communicate, negotiation **12** consultation, conversation, disquisition, tittle-tattle **13** rabbit and pork, spill the beans, spread rumours **15** give the game away

• foolish talk
04 bosh **05** haver **06** havers

• impudent talk
03 lip **08** slack jaw

• talk back
06 retort **07** riposte **09** retaliate **10** answer back, be cheeky to **12** answer rudely

• talk big
04 brag, crow **05** boast, swank, vaunt **07** bluster, show off **10** exaggerate

• talk down to
07 despise **09** patronize **10** look down on

• talk into
04 coax, sway **07** win over **08** convince, persuade **09** encourage **10** bring round

• talk nonsense
03 gum, rot **04** jive **05** bleat, haver **06** havers

• talk out of
04 stop **05** deter **06** put off **07** prevent **08** dissuade **10** discourage

talkative
04 gash **05** gabby, gassy, talky, vocal, wordy **06** chatty, mouthy **07** gossipy, verbose, voluble **09** expansive, garrulous **10** long-winded, loquacious, unreserved **11** forthcoming, long-tongued **13** communicative

talker
05 prose **06** orator, tatler **07** speaker, tattler, twaddle **08** lecturer **09** chatterer **10** chatterbox, motormouth **11** speechmaker **12** blatherskite, bletherskate, communicator **14** bletheranskate

talking-to
06 rebuke, rocket **07** lecture, reproof, wigging **08** reproach, scolding **09** carpeting, criticism, reprimand **10** telling-off, ticking-off **12** dressing-down

tall
03 big **04** hard, high, long **05** giant, great, lanky, lofty, stout, taunt **06** absurd, taxing, towery, trying **07** doughty, dubious, sky-high, soaring **08** elevated, exacting, gigantic, towering, unlikely **09** bombastic, demanding, difficult, overblown **10** far-fetched, improbable, incredible, remarkable **11** challenging, exaggerated, implausible **12** preposterous, unbelievable

tallness
06 height **07** stature **08** altitude **09** loftiness, procerity

tally
03 add, fit, sum, tab, tag **04** list, nick, roll, stub, suit, tick **05** adapt, add up, agree, count, label, match, score, stick, stock, tie in, total **06** accord, concur, credit, figure, reckon, record, square, ticket **07** account, conform **08** coincide, register **09** calculate, duplicate, harmonize, nickstick, reckoning **10** correspond **11** counterfoil, counterpart, enumeration

tame
03 pet **04** calm, curb, dull, flat, lame, mail, meek, weak **05** bland, break, quell, train, vapid **06** boring, bridle, docile, entame, feeble, gentle, humble, master, mellow, pacify, soften, subdue, temper, wonted **07** amenage, break in, conquer, humdrum, insipid, reclaim, repress, subdued, tedious, trained **08** amenable, biddable, broken in, domestic, lifeless, mansuete, obedient, overcome, suppress **09** kids' stuff, subjugate, tractable, wearisome **10** accustomed, cultivated, discipline, house-train, manageable, spiritless, submissive, unexciting, uninspired **11** bring to heel, disciplined, domesticate, uninspiring, unresisting **12** domesticated **13** unadventurous, uninteresting **14** unenterprising

tamper
03 fix, rig **04** work **05** alter **06** bishop, damage, doctor, fiddle, juggle, meddle, monkey, temper, tinker **07** falsify **08** contrive, medicate, practise **09** interfere, mess about, muck about, undermine **10** manipulate **11** interpolate **12** put your oar in **14** poke your nose in, stick your oar in **15** stick your nose in

tan
04 bark, beat, belt, cane, flay, flog, lash, whip **05** beige, birch, brown, clout, spank, strap, tawny, whack **06** bronze, thrash, wallop **07** go brown, tangent **09** turn brown **10** light brown, make darker **12** become darker **14** yellowish brown

tang
03 pep **04** barb, bite, edge, hint, kick, ring **05** aroma, point, prong, punch, scent, smack, smell, spice, spike, sting, taste, tinge, touch, trace, whiff **06** savour **07** flavour **08** overtone, piquancy, pungency **09** sharpness **10** sea-surgeon, suggestion

tangible
04 hard, real **05** solid **06** actual **07** evident, tactile, visible **08** concrete, definite, manifest, material, palpable, physical, positive **09** corporeal, touchable **11** discernible, perceptible, substantial, well-defined **12** unmistakable

tangle
◇ *anagram indicator*
03 mat, ore, web **04** coil, fank, knot, maze, mesh, mess, nest, taut, tawt, trap **05** catch, mix-up, ravel, skein, snarl, twist **06** burble, enmesh, entrap, fankle, hamper, icicle, jumble, muddle, raffle **07** confuse, embroil, ensnare, involve, perplex, snarl-up **08** argument, conflict, convolve, entangle, mess with **09** confusion, drift-weed, embroglio, imbroglio, implicate, interlace, labyrinth, Laminaria **10** intertwine, intertwist, interweave, perplexity, wilderness **11** convolution, embroilment, intertangle **12** complication, entanglement

tangled
◇ *anagram indicator*
05 messy **06** knotty, matted **07** complex, haywire, jumbled, knotted, mixed up, muddled, snarled, tousled, twisted **08** confused, involved, tortuous **09** entangled, intricate **10** convoluted **11** complicated, dishevelled

tango
01 T

tangy
04 acid, tart **05** fresh, sharp, spicy **06** biting, strong **07** piquant, pungent

tank
03 vat **04** pond, pool, stew **05** basin **06** defeat, header, panzer, refuel, thrash **07** cistern, sponson, whippet **08** aquarium, flush-box, sponsing **09** baptistry, container, gasholder, gasometer, reservoir, Valentine **10** baptistery, receptacle, septic tank, shield pond **11** armoured car **12** precipitator **13** shielding pond **15** armoured vehicle

tanning material
04 puer, pure **07** valonea, valonia **08** vallonia

tantalize
04 bait, balk, mock **05** taunt, tease, tempt **06** allure, entice, lead on, thwart **07** beguile, provoke, torment, torture **09** frustrate, titillate **10** disappoint

tantalum
02 Ta

tantamount
05 equal **08** as good as **09** the same as **10** equivalent, synonymous **12** commensurate

tantrum
03 fit, pet **04** fury, rage **05** paddy, scene, storm **06** blow-up, temper, wobbly **07** flare-up **08** hissy fit, outburst, paroxysm, tirrivee, tirrivie **10** conniption **11** fit of temper

Tanzania
03 EAT, TZA

tap
03 bob, bug, hit, pat, rap, tat, tip, tit, top, use **04** beat, blip, bung, cock, drum, milk, mine, plug, tack, tick, touk, tuck **05** bleed, chuck, drain, knock, spout, touch, valve **06** broach, draw on, faucet, pierce, pirate, pit-pat, quarry, siphon, spigot, strike, stroup **07** bibcock, draw off, exploit, monitor, percuss, petcock, pitapat, stopper, utilize, wiretap **08** draw upon, listen to, pitty-pat, receiver, stopcock **09** light blow, make use of **10** listen in on **11** eavesdrop on **15** listening device, take advantage of

• on tap
05 handy, ready **06** at hand, on hand **09** available **10** accessible

tape
03 tie **04** band, bind, seal **05** stick, strip, video **06** fasten, record, ribbon, secure, string **07** binding **08** cassette **09** audiotape, recording, Sellotape®, videotape **10** gaffer tape, Scotch tape®, sticky tape, tape-record **11** masking tape, video-record **12** adhesive tape, magnetic tape, passe-partout **13** audio cassette, tape-recording, video cassette **14** video recording

taper
04 fade, nose, slim, thin, wane, wick **05** spill **06** acumen, candle, die off, lessen, narrow, reduce **07** die away, dwindle, tail off, thin out **08** decrease,

diminish, make thin, peter out, wax light **09** attenuate **10** become thin, make narrow **12** become narrow

tapir
04 anta **07** sladang **08** seladang

tar
05 set on **06** maltha, sailor
11 pissasphalt
See also **sailor**

• **smear with tar**
03 pay

• **tar derivative**
05 furan, indol, pitch **06** cresol, furane, indene, indole, phenol, picene, retene, xylene **07** acridin, aniline, benzene, indulin, naphtha, picamar, skatole, styrene **08** acridine, cerulein, creasote, creosote, heavy oil, induline, nigrosin, pyridine, safranin **09** carbazole, coumarone, nigrosine, primuline, safranine **10** anthracene, benzpyrene **11** creosote oil, naphthalene, phenanthene

tardily
04 late **06** slowly **09** belatedly
10 sluggishly **12** late in the day, unpunctually **13** not before time **15** at the last minute

tardiness
05 delay **08** dawdling, lateness, slowness **11** belatedness
12 dilatoriness, sluggishness
13 unpunctuality **15** procrastination

tardy
03 lag **04** late, slow **05** slack **06** retard
07 belated, delayed, overdue
08 backward, dawdling, dilatory, retarded, sluggish **09** loitering
10 behindhand, last-minute, unpunctual **12** eleventh-hour
15 procrastinating

tare
01 t **04** tine, weed **05** vetch **06** darnel

target
03 aim, end **04** butt, game, goal, mark, prey, seek **05** aim at **06** aim for, object, quarry, try for, victim **07** purpose
08 ambition, bull's eye **09** intention, objective **11** destination **14** have as your goal

• **centre of target**
03 pin **04** bull **06** carton **08** bull's-eye

• **on target**
05 exact **06** bang on, on time, spot-on
07 precise **08** accurate, on course
10 on schedule **15** according to plan

tariff
03 tax **04** duty, levy, menu, rate, toll
06 excise, zabeta **07** charges, customs
08 schedule **09** price list **10** bill of fare
13 list of charges

tarnish
03 dim, mar **04** blot, dull, film, rust, soil, spot **05** spoil, stain, sully, taint
06 befoul, darken, impair, patina
07 blacken, blemish, corrode
08 besmirch **09** discolour
10 blackening **13** discoloration

taro
04 coco, eddo **05** cocco **07** dasheen

tarry
03 lag **04** bide, leng, rest, stay, stop, wait **05** abide, await, dally, delay, pause
06 dawdle, linger, loiter, remain, stay on
07 sojourn

tart
03 pie, pro, tom **04** acid, bawd, drab, flan, moll, slut, sour **05** brass, broad, patty, quiff, sharp, tangy, tramp, wench, whore **06** biting, bitter, geisha, harlot, hooker, pastry, quiche **07** acerbic, caustic, cocotte, cutting, floozie, hetaera, hostess, hustler, lorette, piquant, pungent, rent-boy, strudel, tartlet, trollop **08** call girl, incisive, magdalen, mirliton, sardonic, scathing, scrubber, strumpet, vinegary
09 acidulous, charlotte, courtesan, croquante, hierodule, loose fish, sarcastic, trenchant **10** astringent, fancy woman, loose woman, prostitute, rough trade, vizard-mask
11 fallen woman, fille de joie, night-walker, poule de luxe, working girl
12 fille des rues, scarlet woman, street-walker **13** grande cocotte **14** lady of the night, woman of the town

• **tart up**
06 doll up **07** dress up, smarten
08 decorate, renovate **09** embellish, smarten up **10** redecorate

tartar
05 scale, Tatar **08** beeswing, calculus

task
03 job, tax **04** darg, duty, pain, snap, toil, work **05** chore, grind, stint
06 burden, charge, errand, killer, labour, pensum **07** mission, stretch
08 activity, business, exercise, hard time, trauchle **09** challenge, job of work, soft thing **10** assignment, commission, employment, engagement, enterprise, imposition, occupation **11** piece of work, undertaking

• **take to task**
04 slam **05** blame, knock, scold, slate
06 attask, pull up, rebuke **07** censure, chapter, lecture, reprove, tell off, tick off, upbraid **08** reproach **09** criticize, reprimand

Tasmania
03 Tas **06** Tassie

taste
03 bit, eat, sar, sip, try **04** bent, bite, dash, drop, feel, gout, know, meet, pree, tang, test **05** enjoy, fancy, grace, piece, smack, style **06** choice, desire, hunger, liking, morsel, nibble, polish, relish, sample, savour, thirst, titbit
07 culture, decorum, discern, finesse, flavour, leaning, make out, soupçon, undergo **08** appetite, breeding, elegance, fondness, judgment, mouthful, penchant, perceive
09 encounter, etiquette, hankering, judgement, propriety **10** experience, partiality, perception, preference, refinement **11** cultivation, discernment, distinguish, inclination, sensitivity, stylishness **12** appreciation, predilection, tastefulness
13 differentiate **14** discrimination

Tastes include:

03 hot
04 acid, sour, tart
05 acrid, bland, fishy, meaty, nutty, salty, sapid, sharp, spicy, sweet, tangy
06 acidic, bitter, citrus, creamy, fruity, sugary
07 insipid, peppery, piquant, pungent, savoury
08 vinegary
11 bittersweet

tasteful
05 smart, tasty **06** dainty, pretty
07 correct, elegant, refined, stylish
08 artistic, charming, cultured, delicate, graceful, gracious, pleasing, polished **09** aesthetic, beautiful, exquisite, judicious **10** cultivated, fastidious, harmonious, restrained, well-judged **14** discriminating

tastefully
07 smartly **09** elegantly, stylishly
10 charmingly, delicately, graciously
11 beautifully, exquisitely, judiciously
12 artistically, harmoniously

tasteless
04 dull, flat, loud, mild, naff, rude, thin, weak **05** bland, cheap, crass, crude, gaudy, plain, showy, stale, tacky, vapid, wersh **06** boring, flashy, garish, kitsch, tawdry, vulgar, watery **07** insipid, insulse, uncouth, wearish **08** improper, tactless, unseemly **09** graceless, inelegant, unfitting, unsavoury
10 indiscreet **11** flavourless, watered-down **13** uninteresting

tasting
05 assay, smack, trial **07** testing
08 sampling **09** gustation
10 assessment

tasty
04 nice **05** spicy, sweet, tangy, yummy
06 morish **07** gustful, moreish, piquant, savoury **08** luscious, tasteful
09 delicious, flavorous, palatable, succulent, toothsome **10** appetizing, attractive, delectable **11** flavoursome, interesting, scrumptious
13 mouthwatering

tatter

• **in tatters**
03 rag **06** broken, in bits, in rags, ragged, ruined **07** in ruins, wrecked
08 in pieces, in shreds **09** destroyed, in ribbons, shattered **10** devastated

tattered
◇ *anagram indicator*
04 torn **05** tatty **06** frayed, ragged, ripped, shabby **07** scruffy
10 threadbare **14** tatterdemalion
15 tatterdemallion

tattie *see* **potato**

tattler
04 blab **06** gossip **08** busybody, tell-tale **09** chatterer **10** newsmonger, talebearer, tale-teller **12** rumour-monger **13** scandalmonger

tattoo
03 tat **04** moko, tatu **06** tattow
08 drumming

taunt
03 dig, rib **04** bait, barb, gibe, gird, goad, jeer, jest, jibe, jive, mock, twit **05** fling, sneer, tease **06** deride, insult, revile **07** catcall, censure, mockery, provoke, sarcasm, teasing, torment **08** brickbat, derision, reproach, ridicule, taunting **09** make fun of, poke fun at **11** provocation

taut
03 mat **05** rigid, stiff, tense, tight **06** tangle, tensed **07** anxious, fraught, worried **08** strained **09** stretched, tightened, unrelaxed **10** contracted

tautological
05 wordy **07** verbose **09** redundant **10** pleonastic, repetitive **11** superfluous

tautology
08 pleonasm **09** iteration, verbosity **10** redundancy, repetition **11** duplication, perissology, superfluity **14** repetitiveness

tavern
03 bar, inn, pub **04** bush, dive **05** fonda, joint, local **06** boozer, Kneipe, public **08** alehouse, hostelry, tap-house **09** roadhouse **10** night-house, trust-house **11** night-cellar, public house

taw
03 tew **04** ally, flog, whip **05** alley, thong

tawdry
05 cheap, fancy, gaudy, showy, tacky, tatty **06** cheapo, flashy, garish, vulgar **07** chintzy **08** tinselly, trumpery **09** tasteless **10** glittering **11** gingerbread

tawny
03 tan **04** fawn **05** khaki, sandy **06** fulvid, golden, yellow **07** fulvous **08** xanthous **11** golden brown

tax
03 aid, lot, sap, try **04** cess, duty, levy, load, rate, scot, sess, soak, test, tire **05** drain, exact, stent, weary, weigh **06** assess, burden, charge, demand, impose, impost, strain, stress, tariff, weaken, weight **07** exhaust, stretch, wear out **08** encumber, enervate, overload, pressure **09** agistment, weigh down **10** accusation, assessment, imposition **12** contribution **13** make demands on

Taxes include:

02 PT
03 GST, sur, VAT
04 geld, gelt, PAYE, poll, scat, skat, toll
05 rates, scatt, tithe
06 excise, income
07 airport, council, customs, gabelle
08 property, Rome-scot
09 death duty, head money, insurance
10 capitation, estate duty, value added
11 corporation, inheritance, Peters' pence
12 capital gains, pay as you earn
15 capital transfer, community charge

• **tax collectors**
02 IR **03** IRS

taxi
03 cab **06** fiacre, samlor **07** Joe Baxi, minicab, taxicab **09** hansom-cab **10** hackney cab **12** hackney coach **15** hackney carriage

taxing
04 hard **05** heavy, tough **06** satire, tiring, trying **07** censure, onerous, testing, wearing **08** draining, exacting, wearying **09** demanding, punishing, stressful, wearisome **10** burdensome, enervating, exhausting

taxman
02 IR **03** IRS

tea
03 cha, tay **04** char **05** cuppa **06** tisane **07** Rosy Lee **08** infusion, Rosie Lee, stroupan **09** stroupach
See also **cannabis**

Teas and herbal teas include:

03 ice, kat, qat
04 beef, bush, chai, herb, iced, khat, mate, mint, sage
05 Assam, black, bohea, brick, caper, China, congo, fruit, green, hyson, lemon, pekoe, senna, yerba
06 Ceylon, congou, herbal, oolong, oulong
07 cambric, instant, jasmine, lapsang, redbush, rooibos, rosehip, Russian, twankay
08 camomile, Earl Grey, Lady Grey, souchong, switchel
09 breakfast, chamomile, gunpowder
10 Darjeeling
11 orange pekoe
13 decaffeinated
15 lapsang souchong

teach
03 con, kon **04** cram, larn, lear, leir, lere, read, show, take **05** coach, conne, din in, drill, edify, guide, leare, learn, train, tutor, verse **06** advise, direct, ground, impart, inform, parrot, preach, school **07** counsel, din into, educate, lecture, perfect **08** accustom, disciple, hammer in, instruct **09** brainwash, condition, enlighten, foreteach, inculcate, pedagogue **10** discipline, hammer into, potty-train **11** demonstrate, give lessons **12** indoctrinate

teacher
03 rav **04** Miss **05** guide **07** dominie, prophet **08** educator, schoolie **09** pedagogue, schoolman **10** instructor, scholastic **12** demonstrator, instructress **13** gerund-grinder

Teacher types include:

03 AST, don
04 dean, form, guru, head
05 barbe, coach, molla, rabbi, rebbe, tutor, usher
06 docent, doctor, duenna, fellow, gooroo, mallam, master, mentor, mollah, moolah, mullah, munshi, pedant, pundit, reader, school, supply
07 acharya, adviser, crammer, starets, staretz, student, trainer
08 lecturer, mistress, moonshee, sol-faist
09 governess, maharishi, mnemonist, pedagogue, preceptor, principal, professor, rebbetzin, reception
10 counsellor, deputy head, headmaster, head of year, instructor, paedotribe, schoolmarm
11 housemaster, preceptress, upper school
12 demonstrator, headmistress, mademoiselle, middle school, pastoral head, posture-maker, private tutor, schoolmaster
13 housemistress, nursery school, posture-master, primary school
14 schoolmistress, senior lecturer
15 college lecturer, secondary school

Teachers include:

04 **Beck** (Madame), **Eyre** (Jane), **Hart** (Sheba), **King** (Anna), **Lamb** (Michael), **Nunn** (Sir Percy), **Wilt** (Henry)
05 **Brill** (Miss), **Chips** (Mr), **Crane** (Edwina), **Crick** (Tom), **Dixon** (Jim), **Doyle** (Patrick), **Handy** (Charles Brian), **Henri** (Frances), **Levin** (Sam), **Odili**, **Snape** (Severus)
06 **Alcott** (Bronson), **Angelo** (Albert), **Arnold** (Thomas), **Brodie** (Miss Jean), **Coppin** (Fanny Marion Jackson), **Cotton** (George Edward Lynch), **Covett** (Barbara), **Graham** (Martha), **Grimes** (Captain), **Gyatso** (Geshe Kelsang), **Hagrid** (Rubeus), **Harris** (Crocker), **Hillel**, **Hornby** (A S), **Ramsay** (Dunstan), **Solent** (Wolf)
07 **Darling** (Sir James Ralph), **Eckhart** (Miss), **Enketei** (Mira), **Fischer** (Marcus), **Keating** (John), **Krishna**, **Lowther** (Gordon), **Matthay** (Tobias), **Mr Chips**, **Mulcahy** (Henry), **Peecher** (Emma), **Porpora** (Nicola), **Saville** (Colin), **Squeers** (Wackford), **Vaughan** (Barbara), **Wackles** (Sophy)
08 **Bridgman** (Laura Dewey), **Caldwell** (George), **Chipping** (Mr), **Doubloon** (Maggie), **Lewisham** (George), **Prodicus**, **Sullivan** (Anne)
09 **Batchelor** (Barbie), **Bellgrove** (Professor), **Braidwood** (Thomas), **Hartright** (Walter), **Headstone** (Bradley), **Strasberg** (Lee)
10 **Dumbledore** (Albus), **Leadbetter**

(David), Madame Beck, Madam Hooch, McGonagall (Minerva), Protagoras
12 Pennyfeather (Paul), Stanislavsky
13 M'Choakumchild (Mr)

• teachers
03 ATL, NUT **06** NASUWT

teaching
04 lair, lare, lore, TEFL, TESL **05** dogma, tenet, TESOL **06** loring, wisdom **07** precept, tuition **08** doctrine, pedagogy **09** didactics, education, principle, tradition **10** pedagogism **11** instruction, instructive, pedagoguism

team
02 11, XI, XV **03** set **04** band, crew, gang, pair, side, yoke **05** brood, bunch, chain, group, shift, squad **06** équipe, line-up, litter, outfit, pick-up, stable, troupe **07** company, offence, offense, turn-out **08** equipage

National team nicknames in Australia and New Zealand include:

05 Opals
07 Boomers, Olyroos
08 Matildas
09 All Blacks, All Whites, Kangaroos, Socceroos, Wallabies
10 Hockeyroos
11 Kookaburras, Silver Ferns

See also **Australian football**; **baseball**; **basketball**; **cricket**; **football**; **racing**; **rugby**

• team up
04 join, yoke **05** match, unite **06** couple **07** combine **09** co-operate **10** join forces **11** collaborate **12** band together, come together, work together

teamwork
10 fellowship, team spirit **11** co-operation, joint effort **12** co-ordination **13** collaboration, esprit de corps

tear
03 fly, nip, rag, ren, rin, rip, run, zap, zip **04** bead, belt, blob, bolt, bomb, claw, dart, dash, gash, grab, hole, plow, pull, race, rage, rash, rend, rent, rive, rush, slip, slit, snag, tire, yank, zing, zoom **05** hurry, pluck, ranch, scoot, seize, sever, shoot, shred, slash, speed, split, spree, vroom, whizz, wound, wrest **06** career, charge, divide, gallop, injure, injury, ladder, mangle, plough, screed, snatch, sprint, sunder, tatter, unroot **07** eye-drop, mammock, rupture, scratch **08** lacerate, mutilate, step on it **09** pull apart, water drop **10** break apart, laceration, mutilation

• in tears
03 sad **05** upset, weepy **06** crying **07** sobbing, tearful, wailing, weeping **09** emotional, sorrowful **10** blubbering, distressed, whimpering

• tear down
07 destroy **08** demolish, pull down **09** dismantle, knock-down

tearaway
05 rough, rowdy, tough **06** madcap, rascal **07** hoodlum, hothead, ruffian **08** hooligan, reckless **09** daredevil, impetuous, roughneck **10** delinquent **14** good-for-nothing

tearful
03 sad, wet **05** misty, moist, upset, weepy **06** crying **07** doleful, in tears, sobbing, weeping **08** mournful **09** emotional, sorrowful, upsetting **10** blubbering, distressed, lachrymose, whimpering **11** distressing

tease
◇ *anagram indicator*
03 kid, mag, rag, rib, rot, vex **04** bait, chip, gibe, goad, goof, grig, josh, mock, nark, tose, toze **05** annoy, chaff, kiddy, sound, taunt, teaze, toaze, touse, touze, towse, towze, worry **06** badger, banter, bother, chiack, chyack, needle, pester, plague, wind up **07** mamaguy, perplex, provoke, torment **08** back-comb, irritate, ridicule **09** aggravate, have a go at, make fun of, poke fun at, tantalize

technetium
02 Tc

technical
06 expert **07** applied **09** practical **10** artificial, electronic, industrial, mechanical, scientific, specialist **11** specialized **12** computerized, professional **13** technological

technically
11 practically **12** mechanically **14** electronically, professionally, scientifically **15** technologically

technician
06 fitter **08** engineer, mechanic, operator **09** machinist, operative, rocketeer **11** mechanician, vision mixer **12** phlebotomist, radiographer

technique
03 art, way **04** mode **05** craft, ELISA, knack, means, skill, style, touch, trick **06** course, manner, method, system **07** ability, fashion, knowhow, mastery, technic **08** approach, artistry, delivery, facility, technics **09** animation, dexterity, execution, expertise, procedure, serialism **10** capability, holography, millefiori, rag-rolling **11** performance, proficiency, skilfulness **12** oil immersion **13** craftsmanship, modus operandi

technology
• appropriate technology, alternative technology
02 AT
• information technology
02 IT **08** infotech **11** informatics

tedious
04 drab, dull, flat, long **05** a drag, banal, prosy, samey, weary **06** boring, draggy, dreary, dreich, tiring **07** humdrum, irksome, operose, prosaic, routine **08** lifeless, long-spun, tiresome, unvaried, wearying **09** laborious, wearisome **10** dragsville, long-winded, monotonous, unexciting, uninspired **11** balls-aching **12** long-drawn-out, run-of-the-mill **13** uninteresting

• tedious person
04 bore **06** foozle

tedium
03 rut **05** ennui **07** boredom, routine **08** banality, drabness, dullness, monotony, sameness, vapidity **09** prosiness **10** dreariness **11** irksomeness, tediousness **12** lifelessness **14** monotonousness

tee
01 T

teem
04 bear, brim, pour, rain **05** burst, crawl, empty, spawn, swarm **06** abound, be full **07** bristle, produce **08** increase, multiply, overflow, pelt down **09** pullulate **10** bucket down **11** chuck it down, proliferate **15** rain cats and dogs

teeming
04 full **05** alive, great, thick **06** packed **07** copious, crowded, replete **08** abundant, brimming, bursting, childing, crawling, fruitful, numerous, pregnant, seething, swarming **09** bristling, chock-full, plentiful **11** chock-a-block, overflowing, pullulating

teenage
05 young **08** immature, juvenile, teenaged, youthful **10** adolescent

teenager
03 boy, Mod, yob **04** girl, teen **05** minor, youth **06** rocker **07** sharpie **08** juvenile **09** rangatahi **10** adolescent, bobbysoxer, junior miss, young adult **11** teeny-bopper, young person **13** emerging adult

teeny
03 wee **04** tiny **06** minute, teensy, teenty, titchy **07** teentsy **09** miniature, minuscule **10** diminutive, teeny-weeny **11** microscopic **12** teensy-weensy

teeter
◇ *anagram indicator*
04 reel, rock, roll, sway **05** lurch, pitch, pivot, shake, waver **06** seesaw, totter, wobble **07** balance, stagger, tremble **08** hesitate **09** vacillate

teeth

Teeth include:

03 cap, dog, egg, eye, gag, gam, jaw
04 baby, back, buck, fang, fore, gold, milk, mill, tush, tusk, wang, wolf
05 cheek, colt's, crown, false, first, molar, plate, store, sweet, upper
06 bridge, canine, chisel, corner, cuspid, wisdom
07 denture, grinder, incisor, scissor, snaggle
08 bicuspid, dentures, impacted, premolar

09 milk-molar, permanent, sectorial, serration
10 carnassial, first molar, masticator, molendinar, third molar
11 multicuspid, second molar
12 snaggletooth
13 first premolar
14 central incisor, lateral incisor, second premolar

teetotal
02 TT **05** sober **06** tee-tee **08** complete **09** abstinent, out-and-out, temperate **10** abstemious, on the wagon

teetotaller
02 TT **06** tee-tee, wowser **09** abstainer, nephalist, Rechabite **10** non-drinker **12** water-drinker

telegram
03 fax **04** wire **05** cable, telex **09** cablegram, radiogram, telegraph **11** night letter, Telemessage®

telegraph
04 send, wire **05** cable, telex **06** signal **08** telegram, transmit **10** radiograph **11** teleprinter **12** Telautograph® **14** radiotelegraph

• telegraph office
02 TO

telepathy
03 ESP **10** sixth sense **11** mind-reading, second sight **12** clairvoyance

telephone
03 tel **04** buzz, call, dial, ring, tele- **05** phone **06** blower, call up, ring in, ring up **07** contact, handset, hot line **08** receiver **09** give a bell, give a buzz, make a call **10** get in touch **11** give a tinkle

• on the telephone
◇ *homophone indicator*

telescope
03 cut **04** trim, tube **05** crush, optic, scope **06** reduce, shrink, squash **07** abridge, compact, curtail, shorten, squeeze **08** compress, condense, contract, spyglass, truncate **09** binocular, optic tube, reflector, refractor **10** abbreviate, binoculars, concertina, equatorial **11** perspective **13** prospect-glass

televise
03 air **04** beam, show **05** cable, put on, relay **06** screen **08** transmit **09** broadcast

television
02 TV **03** box, set **04** tele, tube **05** cable, telly **06** the box **07** the tube **08** boob tube, idiot box, receiver **09** goggle-box **11** cablevision, small screen **13** narrowcasting

Television programme types include:

04 news, soap
05 anime, drama
06 repeat, sitcom
07 cartoon, phone-in, reality
08 bulletin, chat show, docusoap, game show, quiz show
09 panel game, soap opera
11 documentary
12 makeover show

Television channels include:

02 E4
03 ABC, CNN, Fox, HBO, MTV, NBC, QVC, S4C, VH1
04 BBC1, BBC2, BBC3, BBC4, CBBC, CNBC, Five, ITV1, ITV2, ITV3
06 Sky One
07 Fox News, History, Sky News
08 BBC World, Cbeebies, Channel 4, FilmFour, Living TV
09 al-Jazeera, BBC News 24, Bloomberg, Discovery, Eurosport, Sky Movies, Sky Sports
11 Nickelodeon

Television programmes include:

02 ER, QI
03 CSI, QED
04 GMTV, M*A*S*H
05 Arena, Bread, Kojak, LA Law, Shaft
06 Batman, Bottom, Cheers, Dallas, Hi-De-Hi, Lassie, Minder, Mr Bean, Quincy, Sharpe, Tiswas
07 Bagpuss, Blake's 7, Columbo, Dynasty, Frasier, Friends, Holiday, Horizon, Lovejoy, Maigret, Mr Magoo, Omnibus, Poldark, Pop Idol, Rainbow, Rawhide, Spender, Taggart, The Bill, The Word, Tonight, Top Gear
08 'Allo 'Allo, Baywatch, Bergerac, Casualty, Dad's Army, Eldorado, Faking It, NYPD Blue, Panorama, Porridge, Red Dwarf, Roseanne, Seinfeld, Sgt Bilko, Star Trek, Stingray, The Saint, Time Team, Trumpton, Watchdog, Wife Swap
09 Andy Pandy, Blind Date, Blue Peter, Brookside, Countdown, Doctor Who, Dr Kildare, Emmerdale, Father Ted, Happy Days, Heartbeat, Holby City, Hollyoaks, I Love Lucy, Jackanory, Miami Vice, News at Ten, Newsnight, Newsround, Parkinson, South Park, That's Life, The X Files, Twin Peaks, Up Pompeii!
10 Ally McBeal, Big Brother, Blackadder, Crossroads, Deputy Dawg, EastEnders, Gladiators, Grandstand, Grange Hill, Howards' Way, Jim'll Fix It, Kavanagh QC, Masterchef, Mastermind, Miss Marple, Neighbours, On the Buses, Pebble Mill, Perry Mason, Play School, Postman Pat, Quatermass, Rising Damp, The Goodies, The Monkees, The Sweeney, The Waltons, The Wombles, The X-Factor, Wacky Races
11 Animal Magic, Call My Bluff, Catchphrase, Come Dancing, Crackerjack, Fame Academy, Give Us a Clue, Ground Force, Hawaii Five-O, Home and Away, Juke Box Jury, Life on Earth, Teletubbies, The Avengers, The Fast Show, The Fugitive, The Good Life, The Prisoner, The Simpsons, Tom and Jerry, What's My Line?, Yes, Minister
12 As Time Goes By, Blockbusters, Candid Camera, Citizen Smith, Fawlty Towers, Fifteen to One, It's a Knockout, Knots Landing, Melrose Place, Moonlighting, Mork and Mindy, Open All Hours, Peak Practice, Points of View, Question Time, Sesame Street, Terry and June, The Young Ones, Thunderbirds, Top of the Pops
13 A Touch of Frost, Blankety Blank, Bob the Builder, Breakfast Time, Emmerdale Farm, Hamish Macbeth, Ivor the Engine, Little Britain, Match of the Day, May to December, Muffin the Mule, Pinky and Perky, Ready, Steady, Go, Sex and the City, Songs of Praise, Spitting Image, Steptoe and Son, The Likely Lads, The Liver Birds, The Lone Ranger, The Muppet Show, The Sky at Night, The Two Ronnies, The World at War, Whicker's World
14 Animal Hospital, Ballykissangel, Cagney and Lacey, Captain Pugwash, Charlie's Angels, Family Fortunes, Gardener's World, Inspector Morse, Murder, She Wrote, My Friend Flicka, Record Breakers, The Flintstones, The Frost Report, The Weakest Link, This Is Your Life, Tomorrow's World, To the Manor Born, Wheel of Fortune, Worzel Gummidge
15 Birds of a Feather, Camberwick Green, Hill Street Blues, Midsomer Murders, One Man and His Dog, Ready Steady Cook, Remington Steele, Starsky and Hutch, The Addams Family, The Big Breakfast, The Man from UNCLE, The New Statesman, The Price is Right, The Twilight Zone, Watch with Mother, You've Been Framed

See also **quiz**

Television presenters include:

03 **Ant** (Anthony McPartlin), **Dec** (Declan Donnelly)
04 **Muir** (Frank), **Ross** (Jonathan)
05 **Aspel** (Michael), **Black** (Cilla), **Bragg** (Melvyn, Lord), **Evans** (Chris), **Frost** (Sir David), **James** (Clive), **Moore** (Sir Patrick), **Negus** (Arthur), **Wogan** (Terry)
06 **Carson** (Johnny), **Norden** (Denis), **Norman** (Barry), **Paxman** (Jeremy), **Rayner** (Claire), **Savile** (Sir Jimmy)
07 **Andrews** (Eamon), **Bellamy** (David), **Edmonds** (Noel), **Forsyth** (Bruce), **Kennedy** (Sir Ludovic), **Madeley** (Richard), **Rantzen** (Esther), **Starkey** (David), **Tarrant** (Chris), **Wheldon** (Sir Huw), **Whicker** (Alan), **Winfrey** (Oprah)
08 **Bakewell** (Joan), **Campbell** (Nicky), **Finnigan** (Judy), **Stoppard** (Miriam), **Sullivan** (Ed)
09 **Ant and Dec** (Anthony McPartlin/Declan Donnelly), **Magnusson** (Magnus), **Parkinson** (Michael)

10 Titchmarsh (Alan)
12 Attenborough (Sir David)
14 Richard and Judy (Richard Madeley/Judy Finnigan)

• television system
03 PAL 10 flat-screen 13 closed circuit

tell
03 bid, rat, say, see 04 blab, shop, show, talk 05 alter, brief, count, drain, grass, order, speak, state, story, utter
06 advise, affect, assure, betray, change, charge, decree, direct, gossip, impart, inform, notify, recite, relate, report, reveal, sketch, squeal, tattle, unfold 07 apprise, command, confess, declare, dictate, discern, divulge, exhaust, explain, let know, make out, mention, narrate, portray, recount, require, versify 08 acquaint, announce, count out, denounce, describe, disclose, discover, identify, inform on, instruct, perceive, proclaim
09 authorize, broadcast, delineate, elucidate, make known, recognize, tell apart, tell tales, transform
10 comprehend, understand 11 blow the gaff, communicate, distinguish
12 discriminate 13 differentiate, spill the beans, take its toll of 14 give the low-down, have an effect on 15 give the game away

• tell off
04 slam 05 chide, knock, scold, slate
06 berate, bounce, carpet, rebuke, see off 07 bawl out, catch it, censure, chew out, lecture, reprove, tick off, upbraid
08 reproach 09 dress down, pull apart, reprimand, take apart 14 give a talking-to

teller
05 clerk, griot 06 banker, tailor, tellar, tiller 07 cashier, sapling 09 bank clerk, raconteur, treasurer 10 Munchausen, raconteuse 11 Munchhausen

telling
06 cogent, marked 07 pointed
08 powerful 09 effective, narration, narrative, numbering, revealing
10 convincing, impressive, meaningful, persuasive 11 instruction, significant

telling-off
03 row 06 earful, rebuke, rocket
07 chiding, lecture, reproof, wigging
08 reproach, scolding 09 carpeting, reprimand, talking-to 10 bawling-out, ticking-off, upbraiding 11 castigation
12 dressing-down 14 kick in the pants, slap on the wrist 15 smack on the wrist

tell-tale
03 spy 05 clype, grass, sneak
06 buzzer, snitch 07 stoolie, tattler
08 blabbing, give-away, informer, snitcher, squealer 09 betraying, revealing 10 indicating, meaningful, noticeable, revelatory, suggestive, tale-teller, tattle-tale 11 perceptible, secret agent 12 unmistakable 15 snake in the grass

tellurium
02 Te

telly *see* **television**

temerity
04 gall 05 cheek, nerve 06 daring
08 audacity, boldness, rashness
09 impudence 10 effrontery
11 presumption 12 impertinence, recklessness 13 impulsiveness

temper
03 wax 04 alay, calm, cool, fury, mood, rage, tone, trim, tune 05 aleye, allay, alloy, anger, assay, blood, delay, paddy, radge, scene, storm 06 adjust, anneal, attune, harden, humour, lessen, master, meddle, modify, nature, reduce, season, soften, soothe, tamper, weaken 07 assuage, bad mood, chasten, flare-up, fortify, passion, roughen, tantrum, toughen
08 attitude, calmness, comeddle, mitigate, moderate, palliate, tone down 09 alleviate, annoyance, character, composure, condition, fireworks, ill-humour, petulance
10 resentment, strengthen
11 disposition, fit of temper, frame of mind, self-control, state of mind, temperament 12 constitution, irritability, pyrotechnics, tranquillity

See also **bad-tempered**

• lose your temper
05 go mad 06 see red 07 explode
08 boil over, freak out, get angry
09 blow a fuse, do your nut, go bananas, go up a wall, raise hell 10 hit the roof 11 blow a gasket, blow your top, flip your lid, get up in arms, go up the wall, lose your rag 12 blow your cool, fly into a rage, lose your cool, throw a wobbly 13 get aggravated, have a hissy fit, hit the ceiling, throw a tantrum 14 foam at the mouth 15 fly off the handle, get all steamed up, go off the deep end

temperament
04 bent, mood, soul 05 blood, humor
06 humour, kidney, make-up, mettle, nature, phlegm, spirit, temper
07 climate, outlook 08 attitude, tendency 09 character, composure, fieriness, moodiness, tempering
10 complexion, compromise, impatience, touchiness, volatility
11 disposition, frame of mind, personality, sensitivity, state of mind
12 constitution, excitability, idiosyncrasy, irritability
13 explosiveness, hot-headedness, red-headedness

temperamental
05 fiery, moody 06 inborn, innate, touchy 07 natural 08 artistic, inherent, neurotic, petulant, volatile
09 emotional, excitable, explosive, hot-headed, impatient, ingrained, irritable, mercurial, sensitive 10 capricious, congenital, hot-blooded, passionate, unreliable 12 highly strung 13 over-emotional, over-sensitive, unpredictable 14 constitutional, hypersensitive

temperamentally
08 innately 09 basically, naturally
10 inherently 13 fundamentally

temperance
08 sobriety 09 austerity, restraint
10 abstinence, continence, moderation, self-denial 11 prohibition, self-control, teetotalism 13 self-restraint 14 abstemiousness, self-discipline

temperate
04 calm, fair, mild 05 balmy, sober
06 gentle, stable 07 clement, equable
08 balanced, composed, moderate, pleasant, sensible, teetotal
09 abstinent, agreeable, continent
10 abstemious, controlled, reasonable, restrained 11 self-denying 12 even-tempered 14 self-controlled, self-restrained

temperature
01 t 04 temp 05 fever 07 mixture
10 proportion 12 constitution

tempest
04 gale 05 storm 06 furore, squall, tumult, uproar 07 cyclone, ferment, tornado, turmoil, typhoon
08 upheaval 09 bourasque, commotion, hurricane 11 disturbance

tempestuous
04 high, wild 05 gusty, rough, windy
06 fierce, heated, raging, stormy, wrathy 07 furious, intense, squally, violent 08 blustery, feverish
09 turbulent 10 boisterous, passionate, tumultuous 11 impassioned
12 uncontrolled

template
03 jig 04 form, mold 05 frame, model, mould 06 master, matrix 07 pattern, profile 08 strickle 09 blueprint, prototype 10 master page, stylesheet
12 cookie-cutter

temple
03 wat 04 fane, naos 06 church, haffet, haffit, mandir, mosque, pagoda, shrine
07 mandira 08 teocalli 09 joss house, sanctuary, synagogue 10 tabernacle
14 place of worship

See also **religious**; **worship**

tempo
04 beat, pace, rate, time 05 agoge, metre, pulse, speed, throb 06 rhythm
07 cadence, measure 08 movement, velocity

temporal
04 good 05 civil 06 carnal, mortal, timely 07 earthly, fleshly, profane, secular, worldly 08 material
11 terrestrial 12 temporaneous

temporarily
06 for now, pro tem 07 briefly 08 for a time 10 fleetingly 11 momentarily, transiently 12 in the interim, transitorily
15 for the time being

temporary
05 brief **06** fill-in, pro tem **07** Band-aid®, interim, passing, stopgap **08** fleeting, temporal **09** ephemeral, fugacious, makeshift, momentary, provisory, short-term, transient **10** evanescent, short-lived, transitory **11** impermanent, provisional **12** temporaneous **14** extemporaneous

temporize
05 delay, pause, stall **08** hang back **09** hum and haw **10** equivocate **11** play for time **12** tergiversate **13** procrastinate

tempt
03 woo **04** bait, bayt, coax, draw, lure, tice **05** assay, educe, egg on **06** allure, cajole, entice, incite, induce, invite **07** attempt, attract, dispose, incline, provoke, suggest **08** inveigle, persuade **09** tantalize

temptation
04 bait, draw, lure, pull **05** snare, trial **06** allure, appeal, urging **07** attempt, coaxing **08** cajolery **09** influence, seduction, tentation **10** allurement, attraction, cloven hoof, enticement, incitement, inducement, invitation, invitement, persuasion, suggestion

tempting
04 sexy **08** alluring, enticing, inviting **09** lickerish, liquorish, seductive **10** appetizing, attractive **11** tantalizing **13** mouthwatering

temptress
04 vamp **05** Circe, flirt, siren **06** Dalila **07** Dalilah, Delilah, Lorelei **08** coquette **09** sorceress **10** seductress **11** enchantress, femme fatale

ten
01 X **02** 10 **05** decad **06** decade, dectet, denary

tenable
05 sound **06** viable **08** arguable, credible, feasible, rational **09** plausible **10** believable, defendable, defensible, reasonable **11** justifiable, supportable **12** maintainable

tenacious
04 fast, firm **05** tight, tough **06** claggy, dogged, grippy, secure, sticky **07** adamant **08** adhesive, clinging, cohesive, obdurate, resolute, stubborn **09** obstinate, retentive, steadfast **10** determined, persistent, purposeful, relentless, unshakable, unswerving, unyielding **11** persevering, unshakeable **12** intransigent, single-minded

tenacity
04 guts, hold **05** force, power **07** resolve **08** fastness, firmness, obduracy, solidity, strength **09** diligence, obstinacy, solidness, toughness **10** doggedness, resolution **11** application, persistence, pertinacity, staunchness **12** forcefulness, perseverance, resoluteness, stubbornness **13** determination, inflexibility, intransigence, steadfastness **14** indomitability

tenancy
05 lease **06** tenure **07** holding, renting **09** leasehold, occupancy, residence **10** incumbency, occupation, possession

tenant
04 ryot **05** baron, dwell, gebur, thane **06** farmer, lessee, mailer, occupy, raiyat, renter, socman **07** cottier, métayer, socager, sokeman **08** gavelman, occupant, occupier, resident, suckener **09** incumbent, pendicler **10** inhabitant, landholder **11** householder, leaseholder

- **be a tenant**

03 sit

tend
02 go **03** aim, ren, rin, run **04** bear, bend, grow, head, herd, keep, lamb, lead, lean, make, mind, move, wait **05** dress, groom, guard, nurse, offer, point, see to, serve, sound, verge, watch **06** affect, attend, escort, handle, invite, manage, wait on **07** care for, conduce, hearken, incline, nurture, protect **08** attend to, be liable, maintain, wait upon **09** cultivate, gravitate, look after, watch over **10** be inclined, minister to, take care of **11** keep an eye on **13** show a tendency

tendency
03 set **04** bent, bias, turn **05** drift, trend **06** course, genius, levity **07** aptness, bearing, conatus, heading, leaning **08** movement **09** direction, liability, proneness, readiness **10** partiality, proclivity, propensity **11** disposition, inclination **14** predisposition, susceptibility

tendentious
06 biased **07** at issue **08** disputed, doubtful **09** debatable, polemical **10** disputable **11** contentious **12** questionable **13** controversial

tender
03 bid, new, raw, red **04** care, fond, give, kind, nesh, plan, pram, sair, soft, sore, warm, weak **05** chary, coins, early, frail, green, juicy, money, offer, praam, price, value, young **06** aching, callow, caring, dainty, extend, feeble, fleshy, gentle, humane, kindly, loving, regard, render, submit **07** advance, amoroso, amorous, beloved, bruised, cherish, concern, fragile, painful, pinnace, present, proffer, propose, suggest **08** currency, delicate, estimate, fondness, footsore, generous, immature, inflamed, merciful, pathetic, proposal, romantic, smarting, youthful **09** banknotes, easy to cut, emotional, evocative, quotation, sensitive, soft-paste, succulent, throbbing, volunteer **10** affettuoso, benevolent, easy to chew, scrupulous, submission, suggestion, vulnerable **11** considerate, proposition, sentimental, soft-hearted, sympathetic **12** affectionate **13** compassionate, inexperienced, tender-hearted **14** impressionable

tender-hearted
04 fond, kind, mild, warm **06** benign, caring, gentle, humane, kindly, loving **07** feeling, pitying **08** merciful **09** sensitive **10** benevolent, responsive **11** considerate, kind-hearted, sentimental, soft-hearted, sympathetic, warm-hearted **12** affectionate **13** compassionate

tenderly
06 fondly, gently, warmly **08** lovingly **10** affettuoso, generously **11** emotionally, sensitively **12** benevolently, romantically **13** considerately, sentimentally **14** affectionately **15** compassionately, sympathetically

tenderness
04 ache, care, love, pain, pity **05** mercy, youth **06** aching, liking, warmth **07** feeling, rawness **08** bruising, delicacy, devotion, fondness, humanity, kindness, softness, soreness, sympathy, weakness **09** affection, fragility, frailness, greenness, juiciness, sweetness **10** attachment, callowness, compassion, feebleness, gentleness, humaneness, immaturity, irritation, succulence **11** amorousness, benevolence, painfulness, sensitivity **12** delicateness, inexperience, inflammation, youthfulness **13** consideration, sensitiveness, vulnerability **14** loving-kindness, sentimentality **15** soft-heartedness, warm-heartedness

tendon
05 sinew **06** leader, paxwax **09** hamstring **11** aponeurosis, heart-string

tenet
04 rule, view **05** canon, credo, creed, dogma, maxim **06** belief, thesis **07** opinion, precept **08** doctrine, teaching **09** principle **10** adiaphoron, conviction **11** presumption **14** article of faith

Tennessee
02 TN **04** Tenn

tennis
10 jeu de paume **12** sphairistike

Tennis players include:

04 **Ashe** (Arthur), **Borg** (Björn), **Cash** (Pat), **Graf** (Steffi), **Hoad** (Lew), **King** (Billie Jean), **Ryan** (Elizabeth), **Wade** (Virginia)
05 **Budge** (Don), **Bueno** (Maria), **Court** (Margaret), **Evert** (Chris), **Jones** (Ann), **Laver** (Rod), **Lendl** (Ivan), **Lloyd** (Chris), **Perry** (Fred), **Roche** (Tony), **Seles** (Monica), **Stich** (Michael), **Vilas** (Guillermo), **Wills** (Helen)

06 **Agassi** (Andre), **Austin** (Tracy), **Barker** (Sue), **Becker** (Boris), **Cawley** (Evonne), **Drobny** (Jaroslav), **DuPont** (Margaret), **Edberg** (Stefan), **Gibson** (Althea), **Henman** (Tim), **Hewitt** (Lleyton), **Hingis** (Martina), **Hopman** (Harry), **Kramer** (Jack), **Murray** (Andy), **Rafter** (Pat), **Tilden** (Bill)
07 **Borotra** (Jean), **Brookes** (Sir Norman Everard), **Connors** (Jimmy), **Emerson** (Roy), **Federer** (Roger), **Godfree** (Kitty), **Lacoste** (Rene), **Lenglen** (Suzanne), **Maskell** (Dan), **McEnroe** (John), **Nastase** (Ilie), **Novotna** (Jana), **Renshaw** (Willie), **Sampras** (Pete), **Sedgman** (Frank), **Shriver** (Pam)
08 **Capriati** (Jennifer), **Connolly** (Maureen 'Little Mo'), **Gonzales** (Pancho), **Krajicek** (Richard), **Newcombe** (John), **Rosewall** (Ken), **Rusedski** (Greg), **Sabatini** (Gabriela), **Williams** (Serena), **Williams** (Venus)
09 **Davenport** (Lindsay), **Goolagong** (Evonne), **Sharapova** (Maria), **Woodforde** (Mark)
10 **Ivanisevic** (Goran), **Kafelnikov** (Yevgeny), **Kournikova** (Anna), **Wills Moody** (Helen), **Woodbridge** (Todd)
11 **Navratilova** (Martina)
15 **Goolagong Cawley** (Evonne)

Tennis-related terms include:

03 ace, ATP, let, lob, LTA, set, WTA
04 love, pass
05 AELTC, break, deuce, drive, fault, rally, serve, slice, smash
06 return, umpire, volley, winner
07 ballboy, net cord, runback
08 backhand, ballgirl, baseline, drop shot, forehand, line call, love game, midcourt, net judge, overhead, overrule, set point, tie-break, wood shot
09 advantage, backcourt, baseliner, break back, foot fault, forecourt, hold serve, line judge, mini-break, sweet spot, tramlines, two-handed
10 break point, cross court, deuce court, match point
11 block volley, double fault, service game, service line
12 approach shot, ground stroke, mixed doubles, service court
13 second service
14 advantage court, serve and volley

tenor
01 T **03** aim, way **04** feck, gist, path **05** drift, point, sense, theme, trend, Trial **06** burden, course, intent, spirit **07** essence, meaning, purport, purpose, texture **08** tendency **09** direction, substance

tense
01 t **04** edgy, taut, work **05** brace, drawn, heavy, jumpy, rigid, stiff, tight **06** narrow, on edge, strain, taught, uneasy **07** anxious, charged, fidgety, fraught, jittery, keyed up, nervous, stiffen, stretch, tighten, uptight, worried **08** contract, exciting, restless, strained, worrying **09** inflexion, screwed up, stressful, stretched **10** distraught, inflection, nail-biting **11** overwrought, stressed out **12** apprehensive, nerve-racking **13** under pressure

Grammatical tenses include:

02 pt
03 pat
04 past
06 aorist, future
07 perfect, present
08 preterit
09 imperfect, preterite
10 pluperfect
11 conditional, past perfect
12 gnomic aorist, past historic
13 future perfect
14 present perfect
15 paragogic future

tensely
08 in a state, uneasily **09** anxiously, nervously, worriedly **10** restlessly **11** stressed out **14** apprehensively

tension
04 feud **05** clash, worry **06** nerves, strain, stress, strife, unrest, wobbly **07** anxiety, discord, dispute, ill-will, jitters, quarrel, willies **08** conflict, disquiet, distress, edginess, friction, pressure, rigidity, suspense, tautness, variance **09** agitation, antipathy, hostility, stiffness, straining, tightness **10** antagonism, contention, dissension, opposition, stretching, uneasiness **11** butterflies, nervousness **12** apprehension, collywobbles, disagreement, hypertension, restlessness **13** confrontation, heebie-jeebies

• equal tension
08 isotonic

• high tension
02 HT

• low tension
02 LT

• premenstrual tension
03 PMT

• surface tension
01 T

tent
04 camp, heed **05** probe

Tents include:

03 box, ger, gur, mat
04 bell, dome, kata, tilt, tipi, yurt
05 bivvy, black, frame, lodge, ridge, tepee, tupik, yourt
06 big top, canopy, canvas, teepee, tunnel, wigwam
07 conical, marquee, touring, trailer, yaranga
10 single hoop, tabernacle
11 hooped bivvy
12 sloping ridge, sloping wedge
13 barrel-vaulted, crossover pole

• tent village
04 duar **05** douar, dowar

tentacle
03 arm **04** horn **06** feeler **12** hectocotylus

tentative
04 test **05** pilot, timid, trial **06** unsure **08** cautious, doubtful, hesitant, unproven, wavering **09** diffident, faltering, peirastic, uncertain, undecided **10** indefinite **11** conjectural, exploratory, provisional, speculative, unconfirmed **12** experimental **13** to be confirmed

tentatively
06 on spec **07** timidly **08** gingerly **10** cautiously, doubtfully, hesitantly **12** indefinitely **13** peirastically, provisionally, speculatively **14** experimentally

tenterhooks
• on tenterhooks
05 eager **07** anxious, excited, keyed up, nervous, waiting **08** watchful **09** expectant, impatient **10** in suspense **15** with bated breath

tenuous
04 fine, hazy, slim, thin, weak **05** shaky, vague **06** flimsy, slight, subtle **07** dubious, fragile, slender **08** delicate, doubtful, rarefied **09** recherché **10** indefinite **12** questionable **13** insubstantial

tenure
03 fee, feu **04** tack, term, time **05** lease, tenor **06** papacy, socage **07** burgage, fee-farm, holding, popedom, soccage, tenancy **08** frank-fee, steelbow, vavasory, venville **09** commendam, gavelkind, leasehold, occupancy, pastorate, priorship, rabbinate, residence, sokemanry, villenage **10** archontate, cottierism, government, habitation, incumbency, occupation, possession, villeinage **12** frankalmoign **13** knight service **14** proprietorship, subinfeudation

tepee
04 tent, tipi

tepid
03 lew **04** cool **07** warmish **08** lukewarm **09** apathetic **11** half-hearted, indifferent **14** unenthusiastic

terbium
02 Tb

term
03 dub, end, tag **04** call, fees, name, span, time, word **05** bound, close, costs, label, limit, point, rates, space, spell, style, title **06** clause, course, detail, finish, period, phrase, prices, season, tariff **07** charges, entitle, epithet, footing, proviso, session, stretch **08** boundary, duration, fruition, interval, locution, position, semester, standing, terminus **09** condition, designate, provision, relations, trimester **10** conclusion, denominate, expression, particular **11** appellation, culmination, designation, restriction,

stipulation **12** denomination, relationship **13** qualification, specification

Terms and sessions include:

04 Lent
06 Easter, Hilary
07 Trinity
10 Michaelmas

• come to terms
06 accept, submit **08** compound **10** articulate **11** accommodate **12** come to accept **14** resign yourself
• in terms of
09 as regards **10** in regard to **12** in relation to, with regard to **13** with respect to
• on good terms
02 in

terminal
◇ *tail selection indicator*
03 end, VDU **04** last, pole, POST, RJET **05** acute, depot, dying, fatal, final, limit **06** deadly, ending, garage, lethal, mortal, utmost **07** console, extreme, killing, monitor, station **08** boundary, desinent, keyboard, last stop, limiting, railhead, terminus, ultimate **09** confining, extremity, incurable **10** concluding **11** desinential, termination, untreatable, workstation **12** end of the line
• terminal part
03 cap **06** cloaca, rectum **12** sigmoid colon **14** sigmoid flexure

terminally
07 fatally **08** lethally, mortally **09** incurably **11** malignantly

terminate
03 end **04** fall, stop **05** abort, cease, close, issue, lapse **06** cut off, expire, finish, result, run out, wind up **07** dismiss **08** complete, conclude, dissolve, leave off **10** put an end to **11** come to an end, discontinue **12** bring to an end

termination
03 end **05** close, finis, issue **06** demise, effect, ending, expiry, finale, finish, result **07** success **08** abortion, boundary, naricorn **09** cessation **10** completion, conclusion, dénouement **11** consequence **15** discontinuation

terminology
05 terms, words **06** jargon **08** language **10** glossology, vocabulary **11** expressions, phraseology **12** nomenclature

terminus
◇ *tail selection indicator*
03 end **04** goal **05** close, depot, limit **06** garage, target **07** station **08** boundary, terminal **09** extremity **11** air terminal, destination, termination **12** end of the line **13** starting-point

termite
03 ant **07** duck-ant, royalty, wood ant **08** white ant **09** woodlouse

Terra
04 Gaia

terrace
03 Ter **04** Terr **05** beach, bench, linch, shelf **06** offset, perron, tarras **07** balcony, sun deck, veranda **08** barbette, crescent, platform, verandah **09** promenade **10** undercliff

terrain
04 land **06** ground **07** country, terrane, terrene **09** landscape, territory **10** topography **11** countryside

terrapin
04 emys **06** slider **08** redbelly **11** diamondback **13** water tortoise

terrestrial
04 land **06** global, layman **07** earthly, mundane, terrene, worldly **09** subastral, tellurian

terrible
◇ *anagram indicator*
03 bad, big, ill **04** foul, grim, naff, poor, poxy, ropy, sick, vile, weak **05** awful, great, large, lousy, nasty, pants, ropey, sorry **06** aching, crappy, crummy, faulty, gloomy, guilty, horrid, in pain, poorly, severe, unwell **07** ashamed, extreme, fearful, hateful, hideous, intense, notable, painful, serious, tearing, the pits, unhappy, useless **08** contrite, diseased, dreadful, gruesome, hopeless, horrible, horrific, inferior, mediocre, pathetic, pokerish, shocking **09** abhorrent, appalling, defective, deficient, frightful, harrowing, imperfect, monstrous, obnoxious, offensive, repulsive, revolting, third-rate **10** abortional, apologetic, despondent, disgusting, hellacious, inadequate, indisposed, outrageous, pronounced, remorseful, second-rate, shamefaced, unpleasant **11** a load of crap, distressing, exceptional, incompetent, ineffective, substandard, unspeakable **12** unacceptable **14** a load of garbage, a load of rubbish, unsatisfactory **15** under the weather

terribly
◇ *anagram indicator*
04 evil, much, very **06** evilly **07** awfully, greatly **09** decidedly, extremely, seriously **10** thoroughly **11** desperately, exceedingly, frightfully

terrier
04 roll **08** register, rent-roll **09** inventory **11** territorial

Terriers include:

03 fox
04 bull, Skye
05 cairn, foxie, Irish, Welsh
06 Border, Boston, Scotch, Scotty, Westie, Yorkie
07 pit bull, Scottie, Tibetan
08 Aberdeen, Airedale, Doberman, Scottish, Sealyham, wire-hair
09 Kerry blue, schnauzer, Yorkshire
10 Australian, Bedlington, Manchester, wire-haired
11 Jack Russell
12 West Highland
13 Dandie Dinmont
15 American pit bull

terriers
02 TA

terrific
03 ace **04** cool, huge, mega, neat, wild **05** brill, crack, great, large, super, triff **06** superb, wicked **07** amazing, awesome, crucial, extreme, hell of a, intense **08** dreadful, enormous, fabulous, gigantic, smashing **09** brilliant, excellent, excessive, fantastic, wonderful **10** marvellous, prodigious, remarkable, stupendous, terrifying, tremendous **11** frightening, magnificent, outstanding, sensational **12** breathtaking **13** extraordinary **14** out of this world

terrifically
04 very **05** jolly **06** highly, really **07** acutely, awfully, greatly, utterly **08** severely, terribly **09** decidedly, extremely, intensely, unusually **10** dreadfully, remarkably, thoroughly, uncommonly **11** exceedingly, excessively, frightfully **12** immoderately, inordinately, unreasonably **13** exceptionally **15** extraordinarily

terrified
04 awed **06** aghast, scared **07** alarmed **08** appalled, dismayed **09** horrified, petrified **10** frightened **11** in a blue funk, intimidated, scared stiff **12** horror-struck **13** having kittens, panic-stricken, scared to death

terrify
04 fear, gast, numb **05** alarm, appal, ghast, grise, panic, scare, shock **06** agrise, agrize, agryze, dismay, rattle **07** horrify, petrify **08** affright, frighten, paralyse **09** terrorize **10** intimidate, scare stiff **12** put the wind up

territorial
04 area **05** zonal **08** district, domainal, regional **09** localized, sectional **11** topographic **12** geographical

territorials
02 TA

territory
03 Ter **04** area, land, mark, Terr, turf, zone **05** field, state, tract **06** county, domain, region, sector **07** abthane, apanage, country, outland, terrain **08** appanage, backyard, district, outlands, preserve, province, sheikdom, toparchy, township **09** khedivate, sheikhdom **10** dependency, home ground, khediviate, possession, Reichsland **11** trusteeship **12** jurisdiction
See also **province**; **state**

terror
03 bug **04** bogy, fear **05** alarm, bogle, demon, devil, dread, fiend, panic, poker, rogue, shock **06** dismay, fright,

horror, rascal **07** bugbear, monster **08** affright, blue funk, tearaway **09** cold sweat, scarecrow, terrorism **10** amazedness **11** trepidation **12** intimidation **13** consternation

terrorist
06 bomber, gunman, player **07** butcher **08** agitator, assassin, attacker, militant **09** aggressor, anarchist, assailant, guerrilla **11** seditionist **13** revolutionary **14** freedom fighter, fundamentalist, urban guerrilla

• **terrorist militia**
02 SA

terrorize
04 prey **05** alarm, bully, scare, shock **06** coerce, menace **07** horrify, oppress, petrify, terrify **08** browbeat, frighten, threaten **09** strongarm **10** intimidate **12** put the wind up

terse
04 curt **05** blunt, brief, crisp, pithy, short **06** abrupt, gnomic, smooth, snappy **07** brusque, compact, concise, laconic **08** clean-cut, incisive, succinct **09** condensed **10** elliptical, to the point **12** epigrammatic, monosyllabic

test
03 MOT, pix, pyx, sap, SAT, try, van **04** Esda, exam, load, pass, quiz, tire **05** assay, check, drain, exact, probe, proof, prove, study, testa, touch, trial, trier, weary **06** assess, burden, dry run, impose, ordeal, prieve, sample, screen, strain, try out, try-out, verify, weaken **07** analyse, check-up, examine, exhaust, inspect, reagent, scratch, stretch, wear out **08** analysis, appraise, audition, check out, crucible, encumber, enervate, evaluate, overload, prospect, sounding, trial run **09** challenge, criterion, probation, questions, testimony, time trial **10** assessment, evaluation, experience, experiment, inspection, pilot study, scrutinize, shibboleth **11** examination, exploration, investigate **13** investigation, make demands on, questionnaire **14** scrutinization

See also **examination**

• **stand the test**
04 wash

testament
02 NT, OT **04** Test, will **05** proof **07** earnest, tribute, witness **08** covenant, evidence **09** testimony **11** attestation **13** demonstration **15** exemplification

testicles
04 nuts **05** balls, groin **07** cojones, doucets, dowsets, gooleys, goolies **08** cobblers, knackers, lamb's fry **12** family jewels

testify
03 rap **04** avow, show **05** state, swear, vouch **06** affirm, assert, attest, back up, depone, verify **07** certify, confirm, declare, endorse, speak to, support **08** proclaim **09** establish **11** bear witness, corroborate, demonstrate **12** give evidence, substantiate

testimonial
04 chit **06** chitty **07** tribute **09** character, reference **10** credential **11** certificate, endorsement **12** commendation **14** recommendation

testimony
05 proof **06** attest, report **07** support, tribute, witness **08** evidence **09** affidavit, assertion, statement **10** deposition, indication, profession, submission **11** affirmation, attestation, declaration **12** confirmation, verification **13** corroboration, demonstration, manifestation

testy
05 cross, ratty **06** crusty, grumpy, shirty, snappy, sullen, tetchy, touchy **07** crabbed, fretful, peevish, stroppy, waspish **08** captious, petulant, snappish **09** crotchety, impatient, irascible, irritable, splenetic **11** bad-tempered, quarrelsome **12** cantankerous **13** quick-tempered, short-tempered

tetchy
05 ratty **06** crusty, grumpy, shirty, touchy **07** grouchy, peevish, teachie **08** scratchy, snappish **09** crotchety, irascible, irritable **11** bad-tempered **13** short-tempered

tête-à-tête
03 jaw **04** chat, talk **06** confab, natter, secret **07** twasome, twosome **08** chitchat, dialogue **10** face to face **12** a quattr'occhi, confidential, conversation, heart-to-heart

tether
03 tie **04** bind, bond, cord, lash, lead, line, rope **05** chain, hitch, leash, tie up **06** fasten, fetter, picket, piquet, secure **07** manacle, picquet, shackle **08** restrain **09** fastening, restraint

Teutonic
03 Ger **04** Teut **05** Dutch **06** German **08** Germanic

Texas
02 TX **03** Tex

text
04 body, book **05** Bible, issue, point, theme, topic, verse, words **06** matter, source **07** chapter, content, passage, reading, set book, subject, wording **08** libretto, sentence, textbook **09** paragraph **10** main matter **11** boilerplate **13** subject matter

texture
03 web **04** feel, wale, woof **05** grain, touch, weave **06** fabric, finish, tissue **07** quality, surface, weftage **09** character, structure, texturize **10** appearance **11** composition, consistency **12** constitution

Thailand
01 T **03** THA

thallium
02 Tl

thank
03 owe **06** credit **07** aggrate, remercy **09** recognize **10** appreciate, be grateful **11** acknowledge **13** say thank you to

thankful
07 obliged, pleased **08** beholden, grateful, indebted, relieved **09** contented **12** appreciative

thankfulness
09 gratitude **10** obligation **12** appreciation, indebtedness

thankless
07 useless **09** fruitless **10** ungrateful, unrequited, unrewarded **11** unrewarding **12** unprofitable, unrecognized **13** unappreciated **14** unacknowledged

thanks, thank you
02 ta **05** mercy **06** cheers, credit **08** bless you, gramercy, thank you **09** gratitude **10** many thanks **11** much obliged, recognition **12** appreciation, gratefulness, thanksgiving **13** thank-offering **14** acknowledgment **15** acknowledgement

• **thanks to**
05 due to **07** owing to, through **09** because of **11** as a result of, on account of

that
02 as, so, yt **03** how, yon **04** such **05** which **07** because

• **that French**
03 que, qui

• **that is, that's**
02 dh, ie **05** id est **09** das heisst

thatching
04 atap, reed **05** attap

thaw
04 melt, warm **05** de-ice, fresh, relax **06** heat up, soften **07** defrost, liquefy **08** defreeze, dissolve, loosen up, unfreeze **09** uncongeal

the
01 t' **02** ye

• **the French**
02 la, le **03** les

• **the German**
03 das, der, die

• **the Italian**
01 i **02** il, la, le

• **the Spanish**
02 el, la **03** las, los

theatre
04 hall, shop **05** drama **06** cinema **08** the stage **09** dramatics, playhouse, theatrics, the boards **10** opera house **11** Thespian art **12** amphitheatre, show business **13** the footlights

See also **cinema**

Theatres include:

03 Pit
04 Rose, Swan
05 Abbey, Globe, Lyric, Savoy

06 Albery, Apollo, Donmar, Lyceum, Old Vic, Palace, Queen's
07 Adelphi, Aldwych, Almeida, Garrick, Gielgud, Mermaid, Olivier, Phoenix
08 Barbican, Broadway, Coliseum, Crucible, Dominion, Festival, National, Young Vic, Ziegfeld
09 Cottesloe, Criterion, Drury Lane, Haymarket, Lyttelton, Palladium, Playhouse
10 Royal Court
11 Comedy Store, Duke of York's, Her Majesty's, Moulin Rouge, Royal Lyceum, Shaftesbury
12 Covent Garden, Sadler's Wells, Theatre Royal, Winter Garden
13 Folies Bergère, Prince of Wales, The Other Place, The Roundhouse
14 Barbican Centre
15 Donmar Warehouse, London Palladium

Theatre parts include:

03 box, pit, set
04 area, drop, flat, grid, loge
05 apron, decor, flies, house, logum, spots, stage, wings
06 border, bridge, circle, floats, floods, lights, loggia, scruto, stalls
07 balcony, catwalk, curtain, cut drop, gallery, leg drop, rostrum, the gods, upstage
08 backdrop, coulisse, trapdoor
09 backstage, cyclorama, downstage, forestage, green room, mezzanine, open stage, tormentor
10 auditorium, footlights, fourth wall, ghost light, prompt side, proscenium
11 drop-curtain, house lights, upper circle
12 orchestra pit
13 safety curtain
14 opposite prompt, proscenium arch, revolving stage
15 proscenium doors

Theatre-related terms include:

02 BS, LX, OB, OP, PS
03 act, cue, fée, fly, gel, rep, run, vis, yok
04 call, cast, flat, grid, juve, loge, plot, pong, rake, tabs, wash, yock
05 actor, ad lib, angel, aside, derig, dry up, fit-up, genre, get-in, lines, lodge, props, re-rig, scene, spike, usher
06 baffle, chorus, corpse, critic, double, dry ice, Equity, flyman, fringe, get-out, make-up, miscue, places, prompt, review, script, walk-on
07 actress, costume, curtain, dresser, matinee, pittite, preview, project, rhubarb, rigging, scenery, tableau, upstage, West End
08 audience, audition, blackout, block out, Broadway, business, coulisse, dialogue, director, duologue, entr'acte, interval, libretto, overture, pass door, play-goer, producer, ring down, thespian, wardrobe, white out
09 backlight, backstage, beginners, box office, break a leg, chaperone, curtain up, cyclorama, double act, downstage, footlight, full house, limelight, monologue, periaktos, programme, rehearsal, repertory, soliloquy, soubrette, spotlight, stage crew, stage door, stage hand, stage left, usherette, visual cue
10 book-holder, dénouement, first night, followspot, fourth wall, get the bird, in the wings, prompt book, prompt copy, prompt desk, prompt side, stagecraft, stage right, understudy, walk-around
11 bastard side, centre stage, curtain call, curtain time, die the death, greasepaint, house lights, iron curtain, leading lady, off-Broadway, quick change, read-through, stage fright, top one's part, wind machine
12 breeches part, breeches role, first-nighter, front of house, intermission, jeune premier, juvenile lead, monstre sacré, principal boy, prompt corner, prompt script, stage manager, travesty role
13 bastard prompt, curtain-raiser, curtain speech, grande vedette, jeune première, safety curtain
14 dress rehearsal, opposite prompt, special effects
15 genteel business, opposite bastard

See also **director**

• theatre award

04 Tony

theatrical

◇ *anagram indicator*
03 OTT **04** camp **05** showy, stagy **06** forced, scenic, unreal **07** actorly, pompous **08** actorish, actressy, affected, dramatic, mannered, overdone, thespian **09** emotional **10** artificial, histrionic, over the top **11** exaggerated, extravagant **12** histrionical, melodramatic, ostentatious

Theatrical forms include:

03 Noh
04 mime, play
05 farce, opera, revue
06 Absurd, ballet, circus, comedy, fringe, kabuki, masque, puppet, street
07 cabaret, Cruelty, mummery, musical, pageant, tableau, tragedy
08 duologue, operetta
09 burlesque, melodrama, monologue, music hall, pantomime
10 in-the-round
11 black comedy, kitchen-sink, miracle play, mystery play
12 Grand Guignol, morality play, Punch and Judy
13 fringe theatre, musical comedy, puppet theatre, street theatre
14 comedy of menace
15 comedy of humours, comedy of manners, legitimate drama

Thebes *see* **Seven Against Thebes**

theft

03 job **04** blag, crib **05** fraud, heist, steal, sting, swipe, touch **06** mainor, rip-off, stouth, walk-in **07** larceny, lifting, mugging, nicking, pilfery, robbery, stealth, stick-up, swiping **08** burglary, filching, nobbling, pinching, plagiary, rustling, stealing, thieving **09** autocrime, pilferage, pilfering, stouthrie, swindling **10** purloining, stoutherie, stouthrief **11** kleptomania, shoplifting **12** embezzlement, smash-and-grab

them

02 'em **03** hem **04** some

thematic

08 notional **09** taxonomic **10** conceptual **14** classificatory

theme

03 peg **04** gist, idea, song, talk, text, tune **05** essay, lemma, motif, paper, story, topic, topos **06** burden, matter, melody, mythos, mythus, thesis, thread **07** burthen, essence, keynote, o'ercome, subject, subtext **08** argument, overcome, owrecome **09** leitmotif, leitmotiv **11** composition **12** dissertation **13** subject matter

then

03 now, tho, too **04** also, next, soon, syne, thus **05** after, and so **06** as well **07** besides, further **08** moreover **09** as a result, therefore, whereupon **10** afterwards, at that time, by that time, in addition **11** accordingly, at that point, furthermore, in those days **12** additionally, at a later date, at that moment, consequently, subsequently

theocracy

04 Zion **08** thearchy

theologian

02 DD **03** ThD **06** divine **09** schoolman

Theologians include:

03 **Eck** (Johann), **Ela** (Jean-Marc)
04 **Baur** (Ferdinand Christian), **Bede** ('the Venerable', St), **John** (of Damascus, St), **More** (Henry), **Otto** (Rudolf), **Paul** (St)
05 **Arius**, **Barth** (Karl), **Buber** (Martin), **Colet** (John), **Cyril** (of Alexandria, St), **Llull** (Ramón), **Mbiti** (John S), **Paley** (William), **Pusey** (Edward Bouverie), **Young** (Thomas)
06 **Alcuin**, **Anselm** (St), **Butler** (Joseph), **Calvin** (John), **Hooker** (Richard), **Jansen** (Cornelius), **Jerome** (St), **Mather** (Increase), **Newman** (John Henry, Cardinal), **Ockham** (William of), **Origen**, **Pascal** (Blaise), **Rahner** (Karl)
07 **Abelard** (Peter), **Aquinas** (St Thomas), **Arnauld** (Antoine), **Bernard** (of Clairvaux, St), **Clement** (of Alexandria), **Cyprian** (St), **Eckhart** (Johannes), **Edwards** (Jonathan), **Gregory** (of Nazianzus,

St), **Gregory** (of Nyssa), **Grotius** (Hugo), **Lombard** (Peter), **Sankara**, **Spinoza** (Baruch), **Tillich** (Paul Johannes), **William** (of Ockham)
08 **Arminius** (Jacobus), **Berengar** (of Tours), **Bultmann** (Rudolf Karl), **Chalmers** (Thomas), **Cudworth** (Ralph), **Eusebius**, **Ignatius** (of Loyola, St), **Irenaeus** (St), **Sprenger** (Jacob)
09 **Augustine** (St), **Bessarion** (John), **Nagarjuna**, **Söderblom** (Nathan)
10 **Athanasius** (St), **Bellarmine** (St Robert), **Bonhoeffer** (Dietrich), **Duns Scotus** (John), **Macquarrie** (John), **Rosenzweig** (Franz), **Schweitzer** (Albert), **Swedenborg** (Emanuel), **Tertullian**, **Weizsäcker** (Karl Heinrich)
11 **Bonaventure** (St), **Kierkegaard** (Sören Aabye)
12 **Justin Martyr** (St)
14 **Schleiermacher** (Friedrich)

theological
06 divine **09** doctrinal, religious **10** scriptural **12** hierological **14** ecclesiastical

theology
08 divinity **09** dogmatics **14** school-divinity

theorem
04 rule **06** dictum **07** formula **09** deduction, postulate, principle, statement **10** hypothesis **11** proposition

theoretical
04 pure **05** ideal **07** a priori, on paper **08** abstract, academic, armchair, notional **10** conceptual **11** conjectural, doctrinaire, speculative **12** hypothetical **13** suppositional

theoretically
07 a priori, ideally, on paper **08** in theory **09** nominally, seemingly **10** notionally **11** in principle **12** conceptually **14** hypothetically

theorize
05 guess **07** suppose **08** propound **09** formulate, postulate, speculate **10** conjecture **11** hypothesize

theory
03 ism, law **04** idea, plan, view **05** guess **06** notion, scheme, system, thesis **07** opinion, surmise **08** proposal **09** principle, rationale **10** assumption, conjecture, hypothesis, philosophy **11** abstraction, postulation, presumption, speculation, supposition

Theories include:

03 GUT, TOE
04 game
05 chaos
06 atomic, number, string
07 Big Bang, quantum
09 collision, Darwinism, evolution
10 panspermia, relativity
11 catastrophe
12 Grand Unified, Milankovitch
14 plate tectonics
15 butterfly effect

• in theory
07 a priori, ideally, on paper **09** seemingly **10** notionally **11** in principle **12** conceptually **13** in the abstract, theoretically **14** hypothetically

therapeutic
04 good **05** tonic **06** curing **07** healing **08** curative, remedial, salutary, sanative **09** medicinal **10** beneficial, corrective **11** restorative **12** advantageous, ameliorative, health-giving

therapy
04 cure **05** tonic **06** remedy **07** healing **09** treatment **12** therapeutics

Therapies include:

02 OT
03 art, CST, HRT, LDT, ORT, sex
04 drug, play, zone
05 aroma, chemo, drama, group, hydro, hypno, music, photo, radio, reiki
06 beauty, family, physio, primal, psycho, retail, speech
07 electro, Gestalt, Rolfing, shiatsu
08 aversion
09 behaviour, cognitive, herbalism
10 homeopathy, osteopathy, regression, ultrasound
11 acupressure, acupuncture, biofeedback, homoeopathy, irradiation, moxibustion, naturopathy, reflexology
12 chiropractic, craniosacral, electroshock, faith healing, horticulture, occupational, reminiscence
13 confrontation, dream analysis, heat treatment

See also **psychological**

there
04 ecco **06** yonder

thereabouts
05 about **07** roughly **12** near that date **13** approximately **14** near that number

thereafter
02 so **04** next, upon **09** after that **10** afterwards **11** accordingly **12** subsequently **13** after that time

therefore
02 so **04** ergo, then, thus **05** and so, argal **06** forthy, so then **09** as a result **11** accordingly **12** consequently **13** for that reason

thereupon
02 so **06** withal **08** with that, with this **11** immediately

thesaurus
05 Roget **07** lexicon **08** synonymy, treasury, wordbook **10** dictionary, repository, storehouse, vocabulary, wordfinder **12** encyclopedia

these
04 thir

thesis
04 idea, view **05** essay, paper, theme, topic **06** theory **07** opinion, premise, subject **08** argument, position, proposal, treatise **09** monograph, statement **10** contention, hypothesis **11** composition, proposition **12** disquisition, dissertation

thick
03 big, fat, hub **04** daft, deep, dull, dumb, fast, full, slow, this, warm, wide **05** broad, bulky, close, dense, dippy, dopey, focus, foggy, gross, gruff, heart, heavy, husky, lumpy, midst, murky, rough, solid, soupy, stiff, stout **06** centre, chunky, creamy, croaky, filled, grouty, hoarse, marked, middle, opaque, packed, simple, smoggy, strong, stupid, turbid, unfair **07** chocker, closely, clotted, compact, crowded, foolish, muffled, obvious, rasping, teeming, thicket, thickly, throaty, unclear, viscous, woollen **08** abundant, brimming, bursting, close-set, crawling, croaking, definite, frequent, gormless, gravelly, guttural, intimate, numerous, striking, swarming **09** abounding, brainless, bristling, condensed, dim-witted, excessive, semi-solid, squabbish **10** coagulated, frequently, indistinct, noticeable, pronounced **11** chock-a-block, overflowing, substantial **12** concentrated, impenetrable **13** thick as a plank, unintelligent

thicken
03 gel, set **04** cake, clot, curd, jell, meal **05** upset **06** curdle, reduce **07** congeal, stiffen **08** condense, solidify **09** coagulate **10** incrassate, inspissate **13** make more solid **15** become more solid

thickening
04 roux **08** clubbing **09** callosity **14** hyperkeratosis **15** atherosclerosis, middle-age spread, primitive streak

thicket
04 bosk, wood **05** brake, brush, copse, cover, grove, shola **06** bosket, greave, maquis, queach **07** bosquet, coppice, spinney **08** chamisal, fernshaw, reed-rand, reed-rond **09** canebrake, chaparral, salicetum **10** dead-finish **11** bramble-bush

thickhead
03 git, oaf **04** berk, clot, dope, dork, fool, geek, prat, twit **05** chump, dummy, dunce, idiot, moron, ninny, twerp **06** dimwit, nitwit **07** buffoon, fathead, halfwit, pinhead **08** imbecile, numskull **09** blockhead **10** nincompoop

thick-headed
04 dumb, slow **05** barmy, dense, dopey, loony, loopy, potty, thick **06** obtuse, stupid **07** asinine, doltish, foolish, idiotic, moronic **08** gormless **09** brainless, dim-witted, imbecilic **10** dull-witted, slow-witted **11** blockheaded, not all there **13** thick as a plank **15** slow on the uptake

thickness
03 bed, ply **04** band, body, bulk, coat, film, loft, seam, vein **05** layer, sheet, width **06** extent, lamina **07** breadth, density, deposit, stratum **08** diameter **09** bulkiness, closeness, solidness, viscosity **11** consistency, pachydermia **14** third dimension

thickset
05 beefy, bulky, burly, dense, heavy, solid, squat **06** brawny, robust, stocky, strong, sturdy **07** nuggety, squabby **08** muscular, powerful **09** well-built **12** heavily built

thick-skinned
05 tough **06** inured **07** callous **08** hardened **09** hard-nosed, unfeeling **10** hard-boiled, impervious **11** insensitive **12** case-hardened, invulnerable **14** pachydermatous **15** tough as old boots

thief
05 crook **06** magpie, nicker **07** filcher, stealer, tea leaf **08** larcener, pilferer **09** Autolycus, larcenist, plunderer **12** kleptomaniac

Thieves and robbers include:

03 dip, pad
04 bung, coon, file, prig, Tory, wire, yegg
05 diver, fraud, heist, kiddy, rover, sneak
06 bandit, bulker, chummy, con man, dacoit, dakoit, dipper, hotter, ice man, latron, lifter, limmer, looter, mugger, nipper, pirate, raider, robber
07 abactor, blagger, booster, brigand, burglar, cateran, cosh boy, footpad, hoister, ladrone, land-rat, nobbler, nut-hook, pandoor, pandour, poacher, prigger, rustler, twoccer, whizzer, yeggman
08 cly-faker, cutpurse, hijacker, huaquero, rapparee, river-rat, swindler
09 area-sneak, cracksman, embezzler, fraudster, pick-purse, ram-raider, sea robber
10 cat-burglar, gully-raker, highjacker, highwayman, horse-thief, land-pirate, man-stealer, pickpocket, roberdsman, robertsman, shoplifter, sneak thief, water thief
11 motor-bandit, poddy-dodger, safe-breaker, safe-cracker, snatch-purse, snow-dropper, stair-dancer
12 appropriator, baby-snatcher, cattle duffer, cattle-lifter, housebreaker, sheep-stealer, snow-gatherer
13 highway robber
15 resurrectionist, resurrection man

thieve
03 bag, lag, rob **04** blag, lift, nick, pull, whip **05** cheat, filch, heist, hoist, pinch, poach, steal, swipe **06** burgle, nobble, pilfer, rip off **07** plunder, purloin, snaffle, swindle **08** abstract, embezzle, knock off, peculate **10** run off with **11** make off with **14** misappropriate

thieving
05 theft **06** piracy **07** crooked, larceny, lifting, mugging, nicking, pugging, robbery **08** banditry, burglary, filching, stealing, thievery **09** dishonest, furacious, larcenous, pilferage, pilfering, predatory, rapacious **10** fraudulent, peculation, plundering, ripping off **11** crookedness, knocking off, sheep-biting, shoplifting **12** embezzlement **13** light-fingered **14** sticky-fingered

thievish
07 crooked, furtive **08** thieving **09** dishonest, furacious, larcenous, predatory, rapacious, theftuous **10** fraudulent **13** light-fingered, tarry-fingered **14** nimble-fingered, sticky-fingered

thin
04 bony, fine, lame, lank, lean, poor, rare, slim, soft, trim, weak **05** faint, filmy, gaunt, gauzy, lanky, light, quiet, runny, scant, sheer, spare, wispy **06** dilute, feeble, flimsy, lessen, meagre, narrow, paltry, rarefy, reduce, refine, scanty, scarce, single, skimpy, skinny, slight, sparse, svelte, wasted, watery, weaken **07** diluted, dwindle, scraggy, scrawny, slender, spindly, tenuous, weed out **08** anorexic, decrease, delicate, diminish, gossamer, rarefied, scrannel, shrunken, skeletal, straggly, tenuious, tinkling **09** attenuate, defective, deficient, emaciated, paper-thin, scattered, untenable, wafer-thin, water down **10** attenuated, diaphanous, inadequate, see-through, wishy-washy **11** high-pitched, implausible, lightweight, thin as a rake, translucent, transparent, underweight **12** inconclusive, unconvincing **13** insubstantial **14** make more watery, undernourished

• **on thin ice**
06 at risk, unsafe **08** insecure **10** in jeopardy, precarious, vulnerable **12** open to attack

thing
02 it **03** act, aim, bag, job **04** baby, bent, bias, body, deed, fact, fear, feat, gear, idea, item, love, task, togs, tool **05** chore, court, event, fancy, gismo, goods, mania, point, stuff, taste, tools, trait, waldo **06** action, affair, aspect, attire, desire, detail, device, dinges, doodah, entity, factor, fetish, gadget, hang-up, horror, liking, matter, notion, object, phobia, tackle, thingy **07** apparel, article, baggage, clobber, clothes, concept, council, dislike, effects, element, episode, exploit, feature, leaning, luggage, machine, problem, quality, thought, whatsit **08** activity, affinity, assembly, aversion, clothing, creature, cup of tea, fixation, fondness, garments, idée fixe, incident, oddments, penchant, property, soft spot, tendency, thingamy, weakness **09** affection, apparatus, attribute, condition, equipment, happening, implement, mechanism, obsession, proneness, situation, substance, thingummy **10** attraction, belongings, instrument, occurrence, parliament, partiality, particular, phenomenon, possession, preference, proceeding, proclivity, propensity, speciality **11** arrangement, bits and bobs, contrivance, eventuality, inclination, odds and ends, possessions, undertaking, what you like **12** appreciation, circumstance, one-track mind, predilection, thingummybob, thingummyjig, what's-its-name **13** bits and pieces, paraphernalia, preoccupation **14** characteristic, responsibility, what-d'you-call-it, what turns you on

• **the thing**
03 hip **04** cool **06** latest, modish, trendy **07** current, in vogue, popular **09** in fashion, the latest **10** all the rage **11** fashionable

think
04 deem, feel, hold, muse, seem **05** brood, cense, guess, judge, opine **06** design, esteem, expect, figure, intend, look on, ponder, reason, recall, reckon, regard, review **07** believe, conceit, foresee, imagine, presume, purpose, reflect, suppose, surmise, thought, weigh up **08** chew over, cogitate, conceive, conclude, consider, envisage, estimate, meditate, mull over, remember, ruminate **09** calculate, cerebrate, determine, recollect, sleep on it, take stock, visualize **10** anticipate, assessment, cogitation, conjecture, deliberate, evaluation, meditation, reflection **11** concentrate, contemplate **12** deliberation **13** consideration, contemplation

• **think better of**
06 revise **07** rethink **10** reconsider, think again, think twice **11** get cold feet **13** decide not to do

• **think much of**
04 rate **05** prize, value **06** admire, esteem, reckon **07** respect **10** set store by **13** think highly of

• **think nothing of**
13 consider usual **14** consider normal

• **think over**
06 digest, ponder **07** weigh up **08** chew over, consider, meditate, mull over, ruminate **11** contemplate, reflect upon

• **think up**
06 create, design, devise, invent **07** concoct, dream up, imagine **08** conceive, contrive **09** visualize

thinkable
06 likely **08** feasible, possible **09** cogitable **10** imaginable, reasonable, supposable **11** conceivable

thinker
04 sage **05** brain **07** scholar **08** theorist **09** intellect **10** ideologist, mastermind, philosophe **11** philosopher **12** theoretician

thinking
04 idea, view **06** theory **07** logical, opinion, outlook, thought **08** cultured, judgment, position, rational, sensible, thoughts **09** appraisal, judgement, reasoning **10** analytical, assessment, conclusion, evaluation, meditative, philosophy, reflective, thoughtful **11** conclusions, intelligent **12** excogitation, intellectual **13** contemplative, philosophical, sophisticated

thin-skinned
04 soft **06** tender, touchy **07** prickly **08** snappish **09** irritable, sensitive **10** vulnerable **11** easily upset, susceptible **14** hypersensitive

third-rate
03 bad **04** naff, poor, poxy, ropy **05** awful, lousy, pants, ropey **06** crappy, crummy, shoddy **07** botched, the pits, useless **08** inferior, low-grade, mediocre, pathetic, slipshod, terrible **10** low-quality **11** a load of crap, indifferent, poor-quality, substandard **13** cheap and nasty **14** a load of garbage, a load of rubbish, not up to scratch, unsatisfactory

thirst
03 yen **04** long, lust, want **05** crave, yearn **06** desire, drouth, hanker, hunger, thrist, thrust **07** aridity, craving, drought, dryness, longing, passion **08** appetite, keenness, yearning **09** eagerness, hankering **11** drouthiness, have a yen for, parchedness, thirstiness

thirsty
03 dry **04** adry, arid, avid, keen **05** dying, eager **06** greedy, hungry **07** athirst, burning, craving, drouthy, gasping, itching, longing, parched, thristy **08** desirous, droughty, hydropic, yearning **09** hankering, thirsting **10** dehydrated

thirteen
04 XIII

thirty
03 XXX

this
03 hic, hoc

Thomas
03 Tom

thong
03 taw **04** band, belt, cord, lash, lore, riem **05** strap, strip, whang **06** Jandal® **07** latchet **08** flip-flop **11** shoe latchet

thorium
02 Th

thorn
04 barb **05** doorn, point, prick, spike, spine **06** needle **07** acantha, aculeus, bristle, prickle

thorny
05 armed, dicey, sharp, spiky, spiny, tough, vexed **06** barbed, briery, knotty, sticky, tricky, trying **07** awkward, bristly, complex, irksome, pointed, prickly, spinose, spinous **08** delicate, ticklish, worrying **09** acanthous, difficult, harassing, intricate, upsetting **10** convoluted **11** problematic, troublesome

thorough
04 deep, full, good, pure **05** close, pakka, pucka, pukka, sheer, sound, total, utter **06** damned, entire, narrow, proper **07** careful, in-depth, ingoing, perfect, radical, regular, through **08** absolute, complete, rigorous, sweeping **09** downright, efficient, extensive, intensive, out-and-out, searching **10** exhaustive, methodical, meticulous, resounding, scrupulous, widespread **11** down-the-line, painstaking, unmitigated, unqualified **12** all-embracing, all-inclusive **13** comprehensive, conscientious, thoroughgoing

thoroughbred
07 blooded, pur sang **08** pedigree, pure-bred **09** pedigreed, pure-blood **11** full-blooded, pure-blooded **12** high-spirited

thoroughfare
03 way **04** road **05** corso **06** access, avenue, street **07** highway, passage, roadway **08** broadway, motorway, turnpike **09** boulevard, concourse **10** passageway **12** king's highway

thoroughgoing
04 deep, full, pure **05** sheer, total, utter **06** entire, strict **07** careful, in-depth, perfect **08** absolute, complete, deep-dyed, outright, rigorous, sweeping **09** downright, extensive, intensive, out-and-out **10** exhaustive, methodical, meticulous, scrupulous, widespread **11** painstaking, unmitigated, unqualified **12** all-embracing, all-inclusive **13** comprehensive **14** uncompromising

thoroughly
02 up **03** out **04** well **05** à fond, fully, good-o, quite **06** good-oh, mortal **07** soundly, totally, utterly **08** entirely, even-down **09** carefully, downright, every inch, inside out, perfectly, throughly **10** absolutely, completely, sweepingly **11** assiduously, back to front, efficiently, intensively **12** exhaustively, meticulously, scrupulously, well and truly **13** painstakingly, root and branch **15** comprehensively, conscientiously

those
03 tho **04** thae, them, they

though
02 if **03** but, yet **05** still, while **06** even if, even so **07** granted, however **08** allowing, although **09** admitting **10** all the same, for all that **11** nonetheless **12** nevertheless **15** notwithstanding

thought
03 aim **04** care, heed, hint, hope, idea, idée, mind, muse, plan, view **05** dream, fancy, grief, study, think, touch, trace **06** belief, design, musing, notion, pensée, reason, regard, theory **07** anxiety, conceit, concept, concern, feeling, gesture, opinion, purpose **08** judgment, kindness, prospect, scrutiny, sympathy, thinking **09** appraisal, attention, intention, judgement, pondering, reasoning **10** aspiration, assessment, cogitation, compassion, conception, conclusion, conviction, estimation, meditation, reflection, resolution, rumination, solicitude, tenderness **11** cerebration, expectation, point of view **12** anticipation, deliberation **13** consciousness, consideration, contemplation, introspection **14** thoughtfulness **15** considerateness

thoughtful
04 deep, kind, wary **05** quiet **06** caring, dreamy, solemn, tender **07** careful, heedful, helpful, mindful, pensive, prudent, serious, wistful **08** absorbed, cautious, profound, sobering, studious, thinking **09** attentive, unselfish **10** abstracted, cogitative, conceitful, methodical, pensieroso, reflective, solicitous **11** considerate, sympathetic **13** compassionate, considerative, contemplative, in a brown study, introspective, lost in thought

thoughtfully
06 deeply **07** quietly **08** dreamily **09** carefully, helpfully, mindfully, pensively, seriously, wistfully **10** cautiously, profoundly **11** unselfishly **12** methodically, reflectively **13** considerately **15** compassionately, contemplatively, introspectively, sympathetically

thoughtless
04 rash, rude, vain **05** hasty, silly **06** remiss, stupid, unkind, unwise **07** étourdi, foolish, selfish **08** carefree, careless, étourdie, heedless, impolite, mindless, reckless, tactless, uncaring **09** blindfold, frivolous, imprudent, negligent, unfeeling **10** ill-advised, incogitant, indiscreet, unthinking, unweighing **11** giddy-headed, improvident, inattentive, insensitive, light-headed, precipitate **12** absent-minded, undiplomatic **13** ill-considered, inconsiderate

thoughtlessly
06 rashly, rudely **08** stupidly **09** foolishly **10** carelessly, impolitely, recklessly, tactlessly **11** unfeelingly **12** indiscreetly **13** inattentively, insensitively **15** inconsiderately

thousand
01 G, K, M **04** thou **05** grand, mille **07** chiliad **09** millenary

thrall
04 grip, serf **05** hands, power, slave

07 bondage, control, enslave, serfdom, slavery **08** clutches, enslaved, thraldom **09** servitude, vassalage **10** subjection **11** enslavement, subjugation

thrash
02 do **03** hit, lam, pay, tan **04** beat, belt, cane, drub, flog, jerk, lace, lash, lick, rout, rush, sock, tank, toss, trim, whap, whip, whop **05** bless, cream, crush, dress, flail, party, paste, pound, quilt, smoke, spank, swish, targe, towel, whack, whale **06** beat up, defeat, donder, hammer, larrup, lather, punish, raddle, thresh, wallop, writhe **07** clobber, lambast, lay into, leather, scourge, swaddle, trounce **08** beat up on, demolish, lambaste, vanquish, work over **09** dress down, horsewhip, marmelize, overwhelm, pulverize, slaughter, surcingle **11** walk all over **13** have the edge on
• **thrash out**
06 debate, settle **07** discuss, hash out, resolve **09** hammer out, negotiate **11** clear the air

thrashing
04 rout **05** doing, laldy **06** caning, defeat, hiding, laldie, wiping **07** beating, belting, lamming, lashing, licking, pasting, tanking, tanning, whaling **08** crushing, dressing, drubbing, flogging, quilting, strap-oil, whacking, whipping, whopping **09** hammering, strapping, towelling, trouncing, walloping **10** clobbering, leathering, punishment **12** chastisement, dressing-down

thread
03 end **04** ease, inch, line, move, pass, plot, push, silk, wind, yarn **05** braid, drift, fibre, Lurex®, motif, seton, shoot, strip, tenor, theme, thrid, thrum, twine, twist, weave **06** course, lingel, lingle, needle, strand, streak, string, suture **07** meander, subject, worsted **08** filament **09** direction, storyline **14** train of thought

threadbare
03 old **04** bare, poor, worn **05** corny, stale, stock, tatty, tired, trite **06** frayed, meagre, ragged, shabby **07** napless, scruffy, worn-out **08** overused, overworn, tattered, well-worn **09** hackneyed, moth-eaten **11** commonplace, stereotyped **12** cliché-ridden

threat
04 omen, risk **05** peril, stick **06** danger, hazard, menace **07** portent, presage, war drum, warning **08** big stick **09** blackmail, ultimatum **10** foreboding **11** commination **12** brutum fulmen, denunciation **14** enemy at the door

threaten
03 cow, vow **04** burn, loom, mint, warn **05** augur, bully, flank, shore **06** extort, impend, lean on, loom up, menace, scorch **07** imperil, portend, presage, scowder, warn off **08** approach, browbeat, endanger, forebode, hang over, look like, scouther, scowther **09** blackmail, comminate, terrorize **10** be imminent, foreshadow, intimidate, jeopardize, pressurize, push around **11** lift a hand to **13** be in the offing **14** lift your hand to, put the screws on

threatening
04 grim, ugly **05** lurid, nasty, shore **07** bravado, looming, ominous, warning **08** frowning, imminent, menacing, minatory, sinister **09** impending, minacious **10** broodiness, cautionary, forbidding, foreboding **11** commination, comminative **12** denunciatory, inauspicious, intimidatory
• **threatening character**
04 omen

three
03 III, ter-, tri- **04** tern, tray, trey, trio **05** leash, prial, triad **06** parial **07** pairial, triplet **09** pair-royal
• **Three Wise Men** *see* **wise man** *under* **wise**

threesome
04 trio **05** triad **06** triple, triune, troika **07** trilogy, trinity, triplet **08** triptych **11** triumvirate

thresh
03 hit **04** flog, jerk, rush, toss **05** flail, swish **06** thrash, writhe

threshold
04 cill, dawn, door, sill **05** brink, entry, limen, start, verge **06** outset **07** doorway, opening **08** door-sill, doorstep, entrance **09** beginning, inception **12** commencement **13** starting-point

thrice *see* **three**

thrift
04 gain **06** saving **07** economy, savings, sea pink **08** prudence, sea grass **09** frugality, husbandry, parsimony **10** prosperity, providence **11** carefulness **12** conservation **14** sea gillyflower

thriftless
06 lavish **08** prodigal, wasteful **09** imprudent, unthrifty **10** profligate **11** dissipative, extravagant, improvident, spendthrift

thrifty
04 wary **05** fendy **06** frugal, saving **07** careful, prudent, sparing **09** husbandly, provident **10** conserving, economical, prosperous **12** parsimonious

thrill
03 gas, joy **04** bang, buzz, dirl, glow, kick, move, stir **05** flush, pulse, rouse, shake, thirl, throb **06** arouse, charge, dindle, dinnle, excite, pierce, quiver, shiver, tingle, tremor **07** delight, feeling, flutter, frisson, pulsate, shudder, tremble, vibrate **08** pleasure **09** adventure, electrify, galvanize, sensation, stimulate, vibration **10** excitement, exhilarate, the shivers **11** give a buzz to, give a kick to, stimulation

thrilling
07 quaking, rousing, shaking, vibrant **08** electric, exciting, gripping, riveting, stirring, tinglish **09** shivering, trembling, vibrating **10** rip-roaring, shuddering **11** hair-raising, sensational, stimulating **12** action-packed, electrifying, exhilarating, soul-stirring **13** heart-stirring

thrive
02 do **04** boom, gain, grow, thee **05** bloom **06** come on, do well, profit **07** advance, blossom, burgeon, develop, prosper, succeed **08** flourish, increase **11** make headway **12** make progress

thriving
04 well **07** booming, growing, healthy, wealthy **08** affluent, blooming **10** blossoming, burgeoning, developing, prosperous, successful **11** comfortable, flourishing

throat
04 crag, craw **05** gorge, halse, hause, hawse **06** fauces, gullet **07** pharynx, swallow, trachea, weasand **08** prunella, thrapple, thropple, throttle, windpipe **10** oesophagus, the Red Lane
• **part of throat**
04 gula

throaty
03 low **04** deep **05** gruff, husky, thick **06** hoarse **07** rasping, raucous **08** croaking, guttural **12** full-throated

throb
◇ *anagram indicator*
04 beat, drum, jump, pant, quop **05** pound, pulse, thump **06** stound, stownd, tingle **07** pulsate, vibrate **08** drumming, pounding, thumping **09** heartbeat, palpitate, pulsation, vibration **11** palpitation

throe
03 fit **04** pain, pang, stab **05** agony, spasm, thraw **07** anguish, seizure, torture, travail **08** distress, paroxysm **09** deid-thraw, suffering **10** convulsion
• **in the throes of**
08 busy with **12** in the midst of **13** in the middle of, wrestling with **14** in the process of, struggling with **15** preoccupied with

thrombosis
03 DVT **08** apoplexy, coronary **09** blood clot **11** heart attack

throne
03 see **04** gadi, seat **05** exalt, siege, stool **07** tribune **08** cathedra, enthrone, kingship, lavatory **09** mercy-seat **12** bed of justice
See also **toilet**

throng
03 jam, mob **04** bevy, busy, cram, fill,

herd, host, mass, pack **05** bunch, crowd, crush, flock, horde, press, swarm **06** jostle, preace, prease, thrang **07** besiege, crowded, preasse **08** converge, crowding, intimate **09** multitude **10** assemblage, congregate, mill around **12** congregation, grex venalium

throttle
03 gag, gun **05** check, choke, scrag **06** keep in, stifle **07** inhibit, silence, smother **08** hold back, restrain, strangle, suppress, thrapple, thropple, wiredraw **09** suffocate **10** asphyxiate **11** accelerator, strangulate

through
02 by, in **03** per, tra-, via **04** done, yond, yont **05** among, clear, due to, ended, fully, using **06** across, direct, during **07** between, by way of, clear of, express, non-stop, owing to, totally **08** entirely, finished, thanks to **09** because of, by means of, completed, connected, throughly **10** by virtue of, completely, terminated, thoroughly, throughout, to the end of **11** as a result of, on account of **12** continuously **13** until the end of, with the help of **15** all the way across, uninterruptedly, without a break in

• **through and through**
05 fully **06** wholly **07** totally, utterly **08** entirely, to pieces **09** to the core **10** altogether, completely, thoroughly **11** all to pieces **12** unreservedly **13** to the backbone **14** in every respect **15** from top to bottom

throughout
04 over **05** along **06** during, widely **07** all over **08** all round **09** up and down **10** all through, completely, everywhere, in all parts **11** extensively, in every part **12** in the whole of, ubiquitously **13** in every part of, in the course of

throughput
05 yield **06** fruits, output, return **07** harvest, outturn, product, turnout **10** production **11** manufacture **12** productivity

throw
◇ *anagram indicator*
02 go **03** hip, lob, peg, put, shy, wap **04** blow, bung, cast, dash, emit, faze, fell, flip, give, host, hurl, lose, puck, putt, scat, send, shed, shot, toss, turn, whap, whop, work, yerk **05** chuck, ditch, fling, floor, force, heave, lay on, pitch, put on, skatt, sling, spang, spasm, spill, upset, whang, while **06** baffle, bemuse, direct, launch, propel, purler, put out, rattle, unseat, upcast, wheech, wuther **07** arrange, confuse, disturb, execute, give off, operate, perform, perplex, produce, project, radiate, unhorse, whither **08** astonish, catapult, confound, dislodge, jaculate, occasion, organize, overturn, paroxysm, surprise, switch on, unsaddle **09** bring down, discomfit, dumbfound, prostrate **10** disconcert **11** cause to fall, move quickly

See also **wrestling**

• **throw away**
04 blow, dump, lose **05** ditch, scrap, waste **06** reject **07** discard **08** chuck out, get rid of, jettison, squander, throw out **09** chuck away, dispose of **11** fritter away **12** dispense with

• **throw headlong**
04 purl

• **throw off**
04 cast, drop, shed **05** elude **06** divest **07** abandon, cast off, discard, discuss **08** get rid of, jettison, shake off **10** escape from

• **throw out**
04 cast, dump, emit **05** ditch, eject, evict, expel, exude, fling, scrap **06** reject, unseat **07** bring up, diffuse, discard, dismiss, emanate, give off, mention, produce, project, radiate, refer to, send out, turf out, turn out **08** distance, distract, jettison, point out, turn down **09** introduce, throw away **10** disconcert, speak about **12** dispense with

• **throw over**
04 drop, jilt, quit **05** chuck, leave **06** desert, reject **07** abandon, discard, forsake **10** finish with

• **throw up**
03 gag **04** barf, jack, puke, quit, spew, toss **05** heave, leave, retch, vomit **06** cast up, give up, jack in, pack in, resign, reveal, sick up **07** abandon, bring up, chuck in, chuck up, chunder, fetch up, upchuck **08** disgorge, renounce **10** relinquish **11** regurgitate

throwaway
05 cheap **06** casual **07** offhand, passing **08** careless **10** disposable, expendable, undramatic, unemphatic **13** biodegradable, non-returnable

throwback
06 return **07** setback **09** reversion **10** taking back **11** restoration **13** reinstatement, retrogression

thrush
04 chat **05** mavis, sprue, veery **06** missel, sylvia, Turdus **07** antbird, redwing, wagtail **08** throstle **09** fieldfare, olive-back, ring ouzel, solitaire, stormcock **10** bush-shrike, missel-bird **12** throstle-cock

thrust
03 dig, jab, jam, pop, put, ram, ren, rin, run **04** bear, butt, chop, dash, foin, gist, poke, pote, prod, prog, push, rash, side, sock, stab, stap, stop, tilt, urge **05** crowd, drift, drive, foist, force, impel, lunge, pitch, poach, point, power, press, shove, stick, stuck, tenor, theme, wedge **06** burden, impose, motive, muscle, muzzle, pierce, plunge, potche, propel, saddle, thirst **07** aventre, essence, impetus, impulse, inflict, intrude, message, thrutch **08** encumber, momentum, pressure, protrude **09** have-at-him, penetrate, substance **10** imbroccata **11** pertinacity **13** determination

thrustplane
04 sole

thud
04 bang, bash, beat, dump, plod, wham **05** clonk, clump, clunk, crash, flump, knock, smack, thump **06** bounce, wallop **07** thunder

thug
04 goon **05** rough, tough, yobbo **06** bandit, goonda, killer, mugger, robber, thuggo, tsotsi **07** cosh boy, gorilla, hoodlum, ruffian, villain **08** assassin, gangster, hooligan, murderer, plug-ugly **09** cut-throat, phansigar, roughneck

thuggery
05 abuse **06** murder **07** killing **08** atrocity, butchery, foul play, violence **09** brutality, vandalism **10** inhumanity **11** hooliganism, viciousness

thulium
02 Tm

thumb
04 inch **06** pollex

• **thumb through**
04 scan, skim **06** peruse **08** glance at **11** flip through, leaf through **12** flick through **13** browse through

thumbnail
05 brief, pithy, quick, short, small **07** compact, concise **08** succinct **09** miniature

thumbs-down
02 no **06** rebuff **07** refusal **08** negation, turn down **09** rejection **11** disapproval

thumbs-up
02 OK **03** yes **07** go-ahead **08** approval, sanction **10** acceptance, green light **11** affirmation **13** encouragement

thump
03 box, cob, dad, dod, hit, rap **04** bang, beat, blow, bonk, bump, cuff, daud, dawd, ding, dong, dump, dunt, paik, slap, thud, tund, whap, whop **05** clout, clunk, crash, knock, pound, punch, smack, souse, throb, whack **06** batter, hammer, pummel, strike, thrash, thwack, wallop **07** bethump, pulsate, trounce **09** palpitate

thumping
03 big **04** huge, mega, very **05** great **06** highly, really, severe **07** extreme, greatly, immense, intense, mammoth, massive, titanic **08** colossal, enormous, gigantic, severely, terrific, towering, whopping **09** excessive, extremely, intensely, seriously, swingeing, unusually **10** exorbitant, gargantuan, impressive, monumental, remarkably, thundering, tremendous **12** tremendously

thunder
03 cry **04** bang, bawl, boom, clap, howl, peal, roar, roll, yell **05** blast, crack, crash, shout **06** bellow, holler, rumble, scream, shriek **07** clamour, foulder, resound **08** crashing, intonate, outburst **09** explosion, fulminate, upthunder **11** reverberate **13** reverberation **14** raise your voice

thundering
04 very **05** great **06** really, tonant **07** greatly **08** enormous, severely **09** excessive, extremely, intensely, unusually **10** altitonant, foudroyant, monumental, remarkable, tremendous **11** unmitigated

thunderous
04 loud **05** noisy **07** booming, roaring **08** rumbling **09** deafening **10** resounding, tumultuous **12** ear-splitting **13** reverberating

thunderstruck
05 agape, dazed **06** aghast, amazed **07** floored, shocked, stunned **09** astounded, flummoxed, paralysed, petrified, staggered **10** astonished, bowled over, nonplussed **11** dumbfounded, open-mouthed **12** wonder-struck **13** flabbergasted, knocked for six **14** wonder-stricken

Thursday
02 Th **03** Thu **04** Thur **05** Thurs

thus
02 so **04** ergo, then **05** hence **08** like this **09** as follows, in this way, therefore **11** accordingly **12** consequently, frankincense

• **thus far**
05 so far **07** up to now **08** until now **09** up till now **13** up to this point **14** up to the present

thwack
03 hit **04** bash, beat, blow, cuff, flog, slap **05** clout, smack, thump, whack **06** buffet, strike, wallop

thwart
03 pip **04** balk, foil, stop **05** baulk, block, check, crimp, cross, spite, stimy, thraw **06** across, baffle, banjax, defeat, hamper, hinder, hogtie, impede, nobble, oppose, stimie, stymie **07** adverse, athwart, pre-empt, prevent, snooker, stonker **08** conflict, obstruct, perverse, traverse **09** crosswise, forestall, frustrate, hindrance **10** transverse **11** frustration **12** cross-grained **13** put the skids on

tic
04 jerk **05** spasm **06** twitch **13** tic douloureux

tick
02 mo **03** dot, jar, pat, sec, tap **04** beat, line, mark, tock, work, worm **05** check, click, flash, jiffy, tally, trice, trust **06** choose, credit, minute, moment, second, select, stroke, whimsy **07** instant **08** indicate, tick-tock **09** twinkling **10** crib-biting

• **tick off**
04 mark, pick **05** check, chide, prick, scold **06** bounce, carpet, rebuke, see off, select **07** bawl out, catch it, chew out, reprove, rollick, rouse on, tell off, upbraid **08** call down, check off, indicate, reproach **09** dress down, go crook at, go crook on, pull apart, reprimand, take apart **10** go to town on **13** tear off a strip **14** throw the book at **15** give someone hell, put a tick against

ticker
05 clock, heart, watch **08** examiner

ticket
03 tag **04** card, pass, slip, stub **05** carte, check, label, token **06** ballot, coupon, docket, permit, return **07** licence, sticker, voucher, warrant **09** pass-check **11** certificate, counterfoil **12** lunch voucher **13** authorization **15** luncheon voucher

• **ticket seller**
04 tout

tickle
04 beat, nice **05** amuse, touch **06** divert, excite, kittle, please, stroke, thrill, tingle **07** delight, gratify, perplex **08** insecure, interest, ticklish, unstable **09** entertain, stimulate, titillate

ticklish
04 nice **05** dodgy, risky **06** kittly, knotty, subtle, thorny, touchy, tricky **07** awkward, trickle **08** critical, delicate, unchancy, unstable **09** difficult, hazardous, sensitive **10** precarious **11** problematic

tiddly *see* **drunk**

tide
03 ebb, ren, rin, run, sea **04** flow, flux, neap, tied, time **05** drift, flood, tenor, trend, water **06** course, happen, season, spring, stream **07** current **08** festival, movement, sea-water, tendency **09** direction **10** rising tide **11** opportunity

• **sudden rise of tide**
04 bore, eger **05** eagre

• **tide over**
03 aid **04** help **06** assist **07** help out, sustain **09** keep going **10** see through **11** help through

tidily
06 just so, neatly **07** in order, in place, orderly, smartly **12** immaculately, methodically **14** systematically

tidings
03 gen **04** dope, news, word **06** advice, report **07** message **08** bulletin **09** greetings **11** information **12** intelligence **13** communication

tidy
◇ *anagram indicator*
02 do **03** red **04** fair, good, neat, redd, trim **05** ample, clean, groom, kempt, large, order, plump, primp, slick, smart, spick **06** comely, fettle, neaten, redd up, spruce **07** arrange, band-box, brush up, clean up, clear up, in order, ordered, orderly, shapely, sizable, smarten, tiddley **08** clear out, generous, sizeable, spruce up, well-kept **09** declutter, efficient, organized, shipshape **10** immaculate, methodical, seasonable, square away, straighten, systematic **11** respectable, substantial, uncluttered, well-groomed, well-ordered **12** businesslike, considerable, spick-and-span, straighten up **13** clear the decks, straighten out

tie
03 fix **04** band, bind, bond, clip, curb, draw, duty, join, knot, lace, lash, link, moor, rope, tape **05** chain, cramp, limit, strap, unite **06** attach, be even, copula, couple, fasten, hamper, hinder, impede, oblige, ribbon, secure, tether **07** be equal, confine, confirm, connect, kinship, liaison, necktie, shackle **08** dead heat, deadlock, ligature, restrain, restrict **09** constrain, fastening, hindrance, restraint, stalemate **10** allegiance, commitment, connection, constraint, friendship, limitation, obligation **11** affiliation, be all square, restriction **12** relationship **13** be neck and neck

Ties include:

03 bow
04 bolo, neck
05 ascot, dicky, stock
06 clip-on, cravat, dickey, dickie, kipper, string
07 overlay, owrelay, soubise
08 bootlace, kerchief
09 neckcloth, solitaire, steenkirk, waterfall
10 tawdry lace
11 neckerchief

• **tie down**
03 fix **05** limit **06** hamper, hinder **07** confine **08** restrain, restrict **09** constrain

• **tied up**
04 busy

• **tie in with**
08 relate to **09** agree with, fit in with **13** correlate with **15** be connected with

• **tie together**
04 knit **05** fagot **06** faggot

• **tie up**
04 bind, do up, lash, moor, rope, seal **05** cable, chain, truss **06** attach, bail up, commit, engage, fasten, invest, ligate, occupy, secure, settle, string, tether, wind up, wrap up **07** connect, engross, Gordian, reserve **08** conclude, finalize, keep busy, restrain **09** terminate **11** spread-eagle **15** make unavailable

tie-in
04 link **05** tie-up **06** hook-up **07** liaison **08** relation **10** connection **11** affiliation, association **12** co-ordination, relationship

tier
03 row **04** band, bank, belt, deck, line, rank, tire, zone **05** floor, layer, level, stage, story **06** gradin, storey

07 echelon, gradine, stratum
09 bleachers

tie-up

04 bond, link 05 tie-in 07 analogy, mooring 08 alliance, parallel, relation 09 reference 10 connection, stand-still
11 association, correlation
12 entanglement, relationship
13 interrelation 14 correspondence

tiff

03 pet, row, sip 04 dram, huff, miff, sour, spat, sulk 05 dress, drink, lunch, scrap, set-to, stale, words 06 barney, dust-up, temper 07 dispute, quarrel, tantrum 08 squabble, trick out 09 ill-humour 10 difference, falling-out
12 disagreement

tiger

04 puma 06 jaguar 07 leopard, stripes 08 man-eater 11 Machaerodus, Machairodus

tight

◇ *anagram indicator*
04 even, fast, firm, hard, mean, near, neat, pang, snug, taut, trig, trim
05 close, dodgy, drunk, fixed, harsh, merry, rigid, stiff, tense, tipsy, tough
06 at once, narrow, scanty, scarce, sealed, secure, severe, stingy, stoned, strict, tiddly, tricky 07 awkward, compact, concise, cramped, legless, limited, miserly, precise, sloshed, smashed, soundly, sozzled 08 airtight, clenched, delicate, hermetic, promptly, rigorous, strained, tanked up
09 competent, dangerous, difficult, niggardly, not enough, plastered, skin-tight, stretched, stringent, too little, well-oiled 10 compressed, hard-fought, impervious, inadequate, inflexible, restricted, soundproof, watertight 11 constricted, intoxicated, neck and neck, problematic, tight-fisted, well-matched 12 close-fitting, impenetrable, insufficient, parsimonious 13 evenly matched, figure-hugging, in short supply, penny-pinching

tighten

03 fix 04 swig 05 brace, cinch, close, cramp, crush, screw, swift, tense
06 beef up, fasten, firm up, narrow, pull up, secure, strait, take in, tauten, wind up 07 squeeze, stiffen, stretch
08 heighten, increase, make fast, restrain, rigidify, straiten 09 constrict, pull tight, toughen up 10 constringe, strengthen 12 make stricter

tight-fisted

04 mean 05 mingy, tight 06 stingy
07 miserly, sparing 08 grasping
09 niggardly 10 fast-handed
12 parsimonious 13 penny-pinching

tight-lipped

03 mum 04 mute 05 quiet 06 silent
08 reserved, reticent, taciturn
09 secretive 11 close-lipped 12 close-mouthed 13 unforthcoming
15 uncommunicative

till

02 to 03 dig, ear, ere, set 04 EPOS, farm, up to, work 05 peter, shale, until 06 plough 07 cash box, through, towards 08 checkout, rotavate, rotovate 09 cultivate 10 all through, cash drawer 11 boulder clay 12 cash register 13 up to the time of

tilt

03 hut, tip 04 bank, cant, cock, duel, heel, just, kant, lean, list, peak, ride, rock, rush, spar, tent, toss, trip
05 angle, clash, cover, fight, joust, pitch, slant, slope 06 attack, awning, camber, careen, charge, combat, jostle, justle, thrust 07 contend, contest, dispute, incline 08 attitude, heel over, tilt yard 09 encounter, pas d'armes 10 tournament 11 inclination

• **at full tilt**

06 all out 07 flat out 08 very fast 10 at full pelt, at top speed 11 at full blast, at full speed, very quickly 13 with full force

timber

03 log, rib 04 balk, beam, lath, pole, rung, spar, tree, wale, wood 05 baulk, board, build, karri, maple, plank, trees
06 forest, lumber, wooden 07 bunting, chesnut, templet 08 chestnut, stumpage, template, woodland
09 beechwood, sapodilla, unmusical
10 afrormosia, swing-stock 11 palmyra wood

See also **tree**; **wood**

• **measurement of timber** *see* **measurement of wood** *under* **wood**

• **timber carrier**

04 gill, jill

timbre

04 ring, tone 05 clang, color, klang, sound 06 colour, tamber 07 quality
08 tonality 09 resonance
10 klangfarbe, tone colour 12 voice quality

time

01 t 03 fix, set 04 aeon, beat, date, life, mora, peak, sith, span, term, tide
05 clock, count, meter, metre, point, space, spell, stage, tempo, while
06 adjust, heyday, rhythm 07 arrange, control, measure, session, stretch
08 duration, instance, interval, juncture, lifespan, occasion, regulate, schedule 09 calculate, programme, timetable 15 fourth dimension

Times and periods of time include:

02 am, pm
03 age, day, eon, era, min
04 dawn, dusk, fall, hour, morn, noon, week, year
05 epoch, month, night, sun-up, today
06 autumn, decade, midday, minute, moment, morrow, period, season, second, spring, summer, sunset, winter
07 bedtime, century, chiliad, daytime, evening, instant, midweek, morning, quarter, sunrise, teatime, tonight, weekday, weekend
08 eternity, high noon, lifetime, tomorrow, twilight
09 afternoon, decennium, fortnight, light-year, midsummer, nightfall, night-time
10 generation, millennium, nanosecond, yesteryear
11 long-weekend, microsecond, millisecond
12 quinquennium
13 the early hours, wee small hours

Time zones include:

02 AT, CT, ET, MT, PT
03 AST, BST, CET, CST, EET, EST, GMT, HST, MST, PST, WET
04 AKST, CYST, HAST, WAST, WEST
08 zulu time
10 Alaska Time
11 Central Time, Eastern Time, Pacific Time
12 Atlantic Time, Mountain Time
13 Greenwich Time

See also **geology**

• **after expected time**

04 late

• **ahead of time**

05 ahead, early 06 sooner 07 earlier, in front, up front 09 in advance
10 beforehand, previously

• **ahead of your time**

03 new 05 novel 07 radical 10 avant-garde, innovative 11 progressive
12 experimental 13 revolutionary

• **all the time**

05 among 06 always 07 forever, nonstop 08 all along 10 constantly
11 continually, incessantly, perpetually
12 continuously, interminably
15 twenty-four-seven

• **at all times**

03 e'er 04 ever 12 early and late

• **at any time**

03 e'er 04 ever, once, onst 07 anytime

• **at one time**

04 once 07 long ago 08 formerly 10 at one point, previously 11 in times past
14 simultaneously

• **at the proper time**

04 duly

• **at the right time**

03 pat

• **at the same time**

03 but, yet 04 then 05 still 06 anyway, at once, even so 07 however
08 meantime, together 09 meanwhile
10 for all that, in parallel 11 all together, nonetheless 12 concurrently, nevertheless 14 simultaneously 15 in the same breath, notwithstanding

• **at times**

06 whiles 08 off and on, on and off
09 sometimes 10 now and then 11 now and again, on occasions 12 every so often, occasionally 14 from time to time

• **behind the times**

03 old 04 past 05 dated 06 old hat
08 obsolete 09 out of date 10 fuddy-duddy, oldfangled 11 god-forsaken
12 god-forgotten, old-fashioned, out of fashion 13 unfashionable

• behind time
04 late **05** tardy **06** behind **07** delayed, overdue **10** unpunctual **14** behind schedule
• brief space of time
02 mo **03** bit, sec, wee
• common time
01 C
• fit time
03 tid
• former times
03 eld **04** yore
• for the time being
06 for now, pro tem **07** just now **08** meantime, right now **09** at present, meanwhile, presently **10** pro tempore **11** at the moment, temporarily **12** for the moment **13** for the present, in the meantime
• from time to time
07 at times **09** sometimes **10** now and then, on occasion **11** ever and anon, now and again, still and end **12** every so often, occasionally, once in a while, periodically, sporadically, still and anon **13** spasmodically **14** intermittently **15** every now and then
• in good time
05 early **06** indeed, on time, timely, timous **07** betimes, timeous **08** timously **09** timeously **10** punctually **11** ahead of time **14** bright and early **15** ahead of schedule, with time to spare
• in time
06 on time **10** eventually, not too late, punctually **11** early enough
• on time
05 sharp **06** bang on, dead on, spot on, spot-on **07** exactly **08** on the dot, promptly, punctual **09** precisely **10** on schedule, punctually
• opportune time
04 seal, seel, seil, sele
• play for time
05 delay, stall **08** hang fire, hesitate **09** stonewall, temporize **10** filibuster **12** drag your feet **13** procrastinate
• taking extra time
04 lean
• time after time
05 often **09** many times **10** frequently, repeatedly **11** recurrently **12** time and again **13** again and again **15** on many occasions

time-honoured
03 old **05** fixed, usual **06** age-old **07** ancient **08** historic **09** customary, venerable **10** accustomed **11** established, traditional **12** conventional **15** long-established

timeless
07 abiding, ageless, endless, eternal, lasting **08** enduring, ill-timed, immortal, unending, untimely **09** deathless, immutable, permanent, premature **10** changeless, unchanging **11** everlasting **12** imperishable **14** indestructible

timely
04 soon **05** early **06** prompt **08** punctual, suitable, temporal **09** opportune, well-timed **10** convenient, felicitous, propitious, seasonable, tempestive **11** appropriate **14** at the right time

times
01 X

timetable
03 fix, set **04** list, rota **05** diary, set up **06** agenda, roster **07** arrange, diarize, listing **08** calendar, schedule **09** programme **10** curriculum

time-worn
03 old **04** aged, worn **05** dated, hoary, lined, passé, rusty, stale, stock, tired, trite **06** ragged, ruined, shabby **07** ancient, cliché'd, outworn, run-down, worn out **08** bromidic, clichéed, decrepit, dog-eared, well-worn, wrinkled **09** hackneyed, out of date, weathered **10** broken-down, threadbare

timid
03 shy **05** cissy, pavid, wimpy **06** afraid, modest, mousey, scared, yellow **07** bashful, chicken, fearful, gutless, nervous, wimpish **08** cowardly, retiring, timorous **09** shrinking, spineless **10** frightened, hen-hearted, irresolute, meticulous **11** lily-livered **12** apprehensive, faint-hearted **13** pigeon-hearted, pusillanimous **14** chicken-hearted, chicken-livered

timidity
04 fear **07** shyness **09** cowardice **11** bashfulness, fearfulness **13** pusillanimity

timorous
03 coy, shy **04** eery **05** aspen, eerie, mousy, scary, timid **06** afraid, aspine, modest, mousey, scared, scarey **07** bashful, fearful, meacock, nervous **08** cowardly, retiring **09** diffident, shrinking, tentative, trembling, tremulous **10** frightened, irresolute **12** apprehensive, faint-hearted **13** pusillanimous, unadventurous

tin
02 Sn **03** can **05** money **06** paltry **09** argentine, Dutch oven
See also **money**

tincture
02 or **03** dye, fur, hue, Sol **04** bufo, dash, hint, tint **05** aroma, imbue, metal, scent, shade, smack, spice, stain, tinge, touch, trace **06** arnica, colour, elixir, infuse, season, smatch **07** flavour, sericon, suffuse **08** laudanum, permeate **09** seasoning **10** suggestion **12** friar's balsam

tine
03 bay, bez **04** lose, shut, snag, tare, teen, tiny, tray, trey, trez **05** point, prong, royal, spike, spire **06** kindle, perish **07** bay-tine, enclose **08** brow-tine, surroyal, trey-tine **09** bay-antler **10** affliction, brow-antler, trey-antler **11** crown antler

tinge
03 bit, dye, eye **04** cast, dash, drop, hint, tang, tint, wash **05** imbue, pinch, shade, smack, stain, taint, tinct, touch, trace **06** colour **07** flavour, suffuse **08** encolour, tincture **09** encrimson **10** smattering, sprinkling, suggestion

tingle
04 glow, itch, ring **05** prick, sting, thirl, throb **06** dindle, dinnle, quiver, shiver, thrill, tickle, tinkle, tremor **07** itching, prickle, tremble, vibrate **08** stinging, tickling **09** prickling **10** gooseflesh **12** goosepimples **14** pins and needles

tingling
04 dirl **05** sting **06** dindle, dinnle **07** prickly

tinker
03 toy **04** play, prig, tink **05** caird, fixer, Gypsy **06** dabble, fiddle, hawker, meddle, mender, pedlar, potter, rascal, repair, tamper, trifle **07** botcher, bungler, didakai, didakei, didicoi, didicoy, tinkler **08** diddicoy **09** fool about, itinerant, mess about **10** fool around, mess around

tinkle
04 bell, buzz, call, ding, peal, ring **05** chime, chink, clink **06** jangle, jingle, tingle **07** urinate **09** phone call

tinny
04 thin **05** cheap, harsh, lucky **06** flimsy, jingly **07** jarring **08** jangling, metallic **09** cheapjack **11** high-pitched, poor-quality **13** insubstantial

tinpot
03 bad **04** poor, ropy **05** awful, ropey **06** crummy, paltry, shoddy **07** useless **08** inferior, mediocre, pathetic, rubbishy, slipshod **09** defective, imperfect **10** low-quality, second-rate **11** incompetent, substandard **13** insignificant **14** unsatisfactory

tinsel
04 loss, sham, show **05** cheap, gaudy, showy **06** flashy, tawdry, trashy **07** display, glitter, spangle **08** frippery, gimcrack, specious **09** clinquant, gaudiness **10** garishness, pretension, triviality **11** flamboyance, ostentation, superficial **12** meretricious, ostentatious **13** artificiality, worthlessness **14** insignificance **15** meaninglessness

tint
03 dye, hew, hue **04** cast, tone, wash **05** color, rinse, shade, stain, taint, tinct, tinge, touch, trace **06** affect, colour, streak **08** tincture

tinware
04 tole

tiny
03 wee **04** mini **05** diddy, small, teeny, weeny **06** little, midget, minute, petite, pocket, slight, teensy **08** dwarfish, trifling **09** itsy-bitsy, itty-bitty, miniature, minuscule, pint-sized **10** diminutive, fractional, negligible,

teeny-weeny **11** Lilliputian, microscopic **13** infinitesimal, insignificant **14** circumstantial

tip

◇ *head selection indicator*

03 cap, end, nap, nib, tap, top **04** acme, apex, bung, cant, clue, dump, gift, give, hand, head, hint, horn, lean, list, noop, pass, peak, perk, pour, tell, tilt, toom, toss, vail, warn **05** bonus, crown, dodge, empty, point, pouch, shoot, slant, spill, trick, upset, vales **06** advice, advise, convey, gryfon, inform, midden, reward, summit, tip off, tip-off, topple, unload **07** capsize, caution, cumshaw, douceur, griffin, griffon, gryphon, incline, pointer, pour out, present, propine, slender, staithe, suggest, warning, wrinkle **08** bonamano, forecast, forewarn, gratuity, overturn, pinnacle, slag heap, surmount **09** backshish, bakhshish, baksheesh, buonamano, extremity, pourboire **10** backsheesh, perquisite, refuse-heap, remunerate, suggestion, topple over **11** information, rubbish-heap **13** gratification **14** recommendation

tip-off

◇ *head deletion indicator*

04 clue, hint, wire **07** pointer, warning **10** suggestion **11** information

tipple

03 bib, pot **04** down, dram, swig **05** booze, drink, paint, quaff, usual **06** imbibe, liquor, poison **07** alcohol, indulge **09** knock back **12** regular drink **14** favourite drink

tippler

03 sot **04** lush, soak, wino **05** alkie, dipso, drunk, toper **06** bibber, boozer, sponge **07** drinker, tosspot, winebag **08** drunkard, maltworm **09** inebriate **11** dipsomaniac, hard drinker

tipsy

◇ *anagram indicator*

03 wet **04** awry **05** askew, bosky, drunk, happy, lushy, merry, moony, muzzy, nappy, oiled, rocky, tight, totty, woozy **06** mellow, screwy, slewed, sprung, squiff, tiddly **07** a pip out, screwed, squiffy, tiddled **08** cockeyed, glorious, pleasant, top-heavy **09** a peepe out, well-oiled **10** a peg too low **15** the worse for wear

tirade

04 rant **05** abuse **06** laisse **07** lecture **08** diatribe, harangue, outburst **09** invective, monorhyme, philippic **11** fulmination **12** admonishment, denunciation

tire

03 tax **04** bore, cook, drop, flag, tyre **05** drain, dress, sew up, train, use up, weary **06** attire, bejade, strain, tucker, volley **07** apparel, breathe, exhaust, fatigue, tire out, wear out **08** enervate, outweary, pinafore **09** broadside, equipment, furniture, headdress

tired

03 old **04** beat, jack, sick **05** all in, blown, bored, corny, fed up, jaded, rough, stale, trite, weary **06** bushed, drowsy, pooped, sleepy, wabbit, zonked **07** cliché'd, drained, shagged, wappend, wearied, whacked, worn-out **08** clichéed, dead-beat, dog-tired, dog-weary, fatigate, fatigued, flagging, outspent **09** enervated, exhausted, fagged out, forjaskit, forjeskit, hackneyed, knackered, pooped out, shattered, washed-out **10** clapped-out, shagged out, war-wearied, world-weary **11** ready to drop, tuckered out **12** sick and tired, world-wearied

tireless

08 diligent, resolute, untiring, vigorous **09** energetic, unwearied **10** determined, unflagging **11** industrious **13** indefatigable, inexhaustible

tirelessly

10 diligently, resolutely, untiringly, vigorously **13** energetically, indefatigably

tiresome

04 dull **05** weary **06** boring, gallus, tiring, trying **07** gallows, humdrum, irksome, routine, tedious **08** annoying **09** fatiguing, laborious, vexatious, wearisome **10** irritating, monotonous, prolixious, unexciting **11** troublesome **12** exasperating **13** uninteresting

tiring

04 hard **05** stiff, tough **06** taxing **07** arduous **08** draining, exacting, wearying **09** demanding, difficult, fatiguing, laborious, strenuous, wearisome **10** enervating, exhausting

tiro, tyro

05 pupil **06** novice **07** learner, starter, student, trainee **08** beginner, freshman, initiate, neophyte **09** greenhorn, novitiate **10** apprentice, catechumen, tenderfoot

tissue

03 web **04** mesh, suet, tela **05** gauze, stuff, weave **06** fabric, matter **07** Kleenex®, network, texture **08** gossamer, material **09** structure, substance, variegate **10** aerenchyma, interweave, mesenchyme **11** toilet paper **12** facial tissue, sclerenchyma, toilet tissue

titan

05 Atlas, giant **06** Helios **08** colossus, Hercules, Hyperion, superman **09** leviathan **10** Prometheus

titanic

04 huge, vast **05** giant, jumbo **06** mighty **07** immense, mammoth, massive **08** colossal, enormous, gigantic, towering **09** cyclopean, herculean, monstrous **10** monumental, prodigious, stupendous **11** mountainous

titanium

02 Ti

titbit

05 scrap, snack, treat **06** dainty, morsel **08** delicacy **09** appetizer **11** bonne-bouche

tit for tat

03 hat **06** in kind, titfer **07** revenge **08** reprisal, requital **10** quid pro quo **11** blow for blow, counterblow, counterbuff, lex talionis, like for like, retaliation **13** an eye for an eye, countercharge

tithe

03 pay, tax **04** duty, give, levy, rate, rent, toll **05** disme, teind, tenth **06** assess, charge, impost, take in, tariff **07** tribute **08** decimate, hand over **10** assessment

titillate

05 tease **06** arouse, excite, thrill, tickle, turn on **07** provoke **08** interest, intrigue **09** stimulate, tantalize

titillating

04 lewd, sexy **05** lurid **06** erotic **07** naughty, teasing **08** arousing, exciting **09** seductive, thrilling **10** intriguing, suggestive **11** captivating, interesting, provocative, sensational, stimulating

titivate

05 groom, preen, primp, prink **06** doll up, make up, tart up **07** touch up **09** refurbish, smarten up

title

03 dub, tag **04** book, call, game, head, name, rank, term, work **05** claim, crown, deeds, label, match, prize, right, style **06** credit, eponym, handle, legend, office, stakes, status, trophy **07** caption, contest, credits, dukedom, entitle, epithet, heading, laurels **08** headline, monicker, nickname, position, subtitle **09** designate, honorific, ownership, privilege, pseudonym, sobriquet **10** nom-de-plume, soubriquet **11** appellation, competition, designation, entitlement, inscription, prerogative, publication **12** championship, denomination **13** form of address **14** proprietorship

Titles include:

01 M, U
02 Dr, Mr, Ms
03 bey, Dan, Dom, Don, Mrs, Pir, Rav, Reb, Rex, san, Sir, Sri, Ven
04 amir, Aunt, babu, bhai, Capt, Dame, Devi, Doña, emir, Frau, Herr, Imam, Lady, Lord, Ma'am, Miss, Prof, sama, Sant, Shri, tuan
05 baboo, begum, ghazi, hodja, khoja, Madam, Mirza, molla, padre, pasha, Rebbe, Señor, Swami, Uncle
06 Doctor, Father, khodja, kumari, Madame, Master, Mister, mollah, moolah, Mother, mullah, Regina, Señora, Signor, Sister, Tuanku
07 Bahadur, Brother, Captain, Colonel,

effendi, esquire, Signior, Signora , Signore
08 Fräulein, Highness, memsahib, Mistress, Monsieur, Señorita, Viscount
09 Monsignor, Professor, Signorina, Signorino, Your Grace
10 burra sahib
11 Monseigneur, Your Majesty, Your Worship
12 Mademoiselle
15 Right Honourable

titter
04 mock, sway **05** laugh, te-hee **06** cackle, giggle, tee-hee, totter **07** chortle, chuckle, snicker, snigger, whicker

tittle-tattle
03 jaw, yak **04** chat, idle, yack **06** babble, cackle, gossip, natter, rumour, witter **07** blather, blether, chatter, hearsay, prattle, twaddle **08** chitchat, rabbit on, yack-yack **09** tell tales **10** yackety-yak

titular
05 token **06** formal, puppet **07** nominal **08** honorary, official, putative, so-called **10** in name only, self-styled

to
01 t' **02** at, au, of, on **03** à la, aux, for, tae **04** near, till, unto **05** until **06** before, beside **07** against, as far as, forward, towards

toad
04 bufo, pipa **07** paddock, puddock **10** natterjack

toadstool *see* **mushroom**

toady
04 fawn, sook, zany **05** crawl, creep **06** cringe, fawner, grovel, jackal, kowtow, lackey, minion, sucker, suck up, yes-man **07** crawler, flatter, flunkey, Jenkins, truckle **08** bootlick, butter up, hanger-on, parasite, suck-hole, toadfish, truckler **09** flatterer, groveller, sycophant **10** bootlicker, tuft-hunter **11** curry favour, kiss the feet, lick-platter, lickspittle **12** bow and scrape

to and fro
◇ *palindrome indicator*

toast
04 bake, heat, warm **05** brown, crisp, drink, grill, roast **06** birsle, heat up, honour, pledge, salute, scorch, warm up **07** drink to, tribute **08** barbecue, brindisi, scouther **09** sentiment **10** best wishes, compliment, salutation **11** compliments

See also **cheers**

tobacco
04 burn, chaw, chew, pipe, plug, quid, weed **05** bacco, baccy **07** the weed

Tobacco and tobacco preparations include:

04 capa, shag
05 régie, snout, snuff, snush, twist
06 burley, dottle, rappee, return, sneesh
07 caporal, chewing, Latakia, nail-rod, perique, pigtail
08 bird's-eye, canaster, honeydew, short-cut, Virginia
09 broad-leaf, cavendish, flue-cured, mundungus, strip-leaf

Tobacco pipes include:

03 cob
04 bong, clay
05 briar, brier, cutty, hooka, peace, water
06 dudeen, hookah, kalian
07 calumet, chibouk, chillum, corncob, dudheen, nargile, nargily
08 calabash, narghile, narghily, nargileh, nargilly
09 chibouque, narghilly
10 meerschaum
12 churchwarden, hubble-bubble
13 woodcock's-head

toboggan
04 dray, luge **05** pulka, slide, slipe, train **06** Ski-doo®, sledge, sleigh **07** bobsled, dogsled, kibitka, travois **09** bobsleigh **11** hurly-hacket, skeleton bob

today
03 now **06** the day **07** just now, this day **08** nowadays, right now **09** these days **11** this evening, this morning, this very day **12** at this moment **13** the present day, this afternoon **14** the present time

toddle
04 reel, rock, sway **05** lurch, shake, waver **06** falter, teeter, totter, waddle, wobble **07** saunter, stagger, stumble **14** move unsteadily, walk unsteadily

toddler
04 trot

to-do
03 ado **04** flap, fuss, stew, stir **05** hoo-ha **06** bother, bustle, flurry, furore, rumpus, tumult, unrest, uproar **07** quarrel, ruction, turmoil **08** brouhaha, razmataz **09** agitation, commotion **10** excitement, hullabaloo, razzmatazz **11** disturbance, performance, razzamatazz

toe
04 kick **05** digit **06** hallux, tootsy **07** dewclaw, tootsie **09** prehallux **12** tootsy-wootsy

together
03 cum **04** calm, cool **05** as one, atone, on end **06** attone, in a row, stable, united **07** as a team, jointly **08** composed, in unison, mutually, sensible **09** all at once, at one time, in company, in concert, on the trot, organized, pari passu **10** back to back, hand in hand, side by side **11** down-to-earth, level-headed, unflappable **12** collectively, concurrently, continuously, in succession, successively, well-adjusted, well-balanced **13** at the same time, consecutively, in conjunction, well-organized, without a break **14** as a partnership, commonsensical, simultaneously **15** in collaboration, working together

• come together
03 gel **04** jell, meet **05** close, rally **07** collect, convene **10** amalgamate

Togo
02 TG **03** TGO

toil
03 net, tew, tug **04** grub, moil, slog, trap, work **05** graft, grind, labor, slave, snare, sweat, swink, yakka **06** drudge, effort, labour, murder, strive, yacker, yakker **07** fatigue, murther, slaving, travail, turmoil **08** drudgery, drudgism, exertion, hard work, industry, plug away, struggle **09** persevere **10** contention, donkey-work **11** application, elbow grease **12** push yourself **14** Hercules' choice **15** work like a Trojan

toiler
05 navvy, slave **06** drudge, menial, worker **07** grafter, slogger **08** labourer **09** struggler, workhorse **10** workaholic

toilet
02 WC **03** APC, bog, can, lat, lav, loo **04** dike, head, john, kazi, toot, tout **05** dunny, Elsan®, heads, jacks, lavvy, potty **06** lavabo, throne, urinal **07** cludgie, cottage, crapper, latrine **08** bathroom, lavatory, outhouse, Portaloo®, rest room, superloo, the gents', washroom **09** cloakroom, necessary, the ladies' **10** facilities, powder room, reredorter, throne room, thunderbox **11** convenience, earth-closet, water closet **12** dressing-room, smallest room **14** comfort station, little boys' room, necessary house, necessary place **15** Parliament House

toilsome
04 hard **05** tough **06** severe, taxing, uphill **07** arduous, painful, tedious, toiling, toylsom **08** tiresome **09** difficult, fatiguing, herculean, laborious, strenuous, toylesome, wearisome **10** burdensome **12** backbreaking

token
04 clue, disc, mark, seal, sign, slug **05** check, index, jeton, proof, scrip, staff **06** coupon, emblem, hollow, jetton, pledge, signal, slight, symbol **07** counter, memento, minimal, nominal, portent, tessera, voucher, warning **08** cosmetic, evidence, keepsake, memorial, moniment, monument, reminder, souvenir, symbolic **09** insincere, precedent, sacrament, triumphal **10** abbey-piece, emblematic, expression, indication, plague-spot **11** perfunctory, recognition, remembrance, superficial **12** abbey-counter, recognizance **13** demonstration, manifestation **14** representation

told
◇ *homophone indicator*

tolerable
02 OK **04** fair, so-so **06** not bad **07** average **08** adequate, all right, bearable, mediocre, middling, ordinary, passable **09** endurable, tollolish **10** acceptable, fairly good, not much cop, reasonable, sufferable **11** indifferent **12** run-of-the-mill, satisfactory **13** no great shakes, unexceptional

tolerably
06 enough, fairly **08** bearably **10** acceptably, adequately, ordinarily, reasonably **12** sufficiently **13** indifferently

tolerance
04 give, play **05** swing **06** lenity **07** laxness, stamina **08** leniency, patience, sympathy **09** allowance, clearance, endurance, fortitude, toughness, variation **10** good-humour, indulgence, liberalism, resilience, resistance, toleration **11** fluctuation, forbearance, magnanimity **13** understanding **14** open-mindedness, permissiveness **15** broad-mindedness

tolerant
03 lax **04** fair, soft **06** decent **07** lenient, liberal, patient **08** catholic, enduring, mellowed **09** compliant, easy-going, forgiving, indulgent **10** charitable, forbearing, open-minded, permissive **11** broad-minded, free and easy, kind-hearted, magnanimous, sympathetic **12** unprejudiced **13** long-suffering, understanding

tolerate
04 bear, have, take, wear **05** abear, abide, admit, allow, stand, thole **06** accept, endure, pardon, permit, suffer **07** condone, indulge, receive, stomach, swallow, warrant **08** sanction **09** put up with **11** countenance

toleration
06 lenity **07** laxness, stamina **08** leniency, patience, sanction, sympathy **09** allowance, endurance, fortitude, toughness **10** acceptance, indulgence, liberalism, resilience, resistance, sufferance **11** forbearance, magnanimity **13** understanding **14** open-mindedness, permissiveness **15** broad-mindedness

toll
03 bar, due, fee, jow, tax **04** call, cost, duty, harm, jole, joll, jowl, levy, loss, lure, peal, pike, rate, ring, warn **05** chime, clang, death, decoy, joule, knell, price, sound **06** charge, damage, demand, herald, injury, octroi, signal, strike, tariff **07** payment, penalty, pierage, pontage, scavage, tallage, tollage **08** announce, hardship **09** streetage, suffering **13** adverse effect

tomb
04 bury, cist **05** crypt, death, grave, speos, vault **06** burial, dolmen, entomb, heroon, marble, shrine, tholus **07** funeral, mastaba, reposit **08** catacomb, cenotaph, hypogeum, monument, sacellum **09** hypogaeum, mausoleum, sepulcher, sepulchre, sepulture **10** repository **11** burial-place, sarcophagus **13** Holy Sepulchre

tomboy
04 ramp, romp **05** hempy **06** hoiden, hoyden

tombstone
05 stone **06** marble **08** memorial, monument **09** headstone **10** gravestone **12** through-stane, through-stone **13** memorial stone

tomcat
03 gib

tome
03 tom **04** book, opus, work **06** volume

tomfoolery
03 tom **05** hooey, larks **06** idiocy **07** inanity, rubbish, trifles **08** clowning, mischief, nonsense **09** horseplay, jewellery, ornaments, silliness, stupidity **10** buffoonery, carrying on, skylarking **11** foolishness, shenanigans **12** childishness, larking about, messing about

ton
01 t **03** tun **07** fashion

tone
03 air, hue **04** cast, feel, mood, note, suit, tint, tune, vein **05** blend, drift, force, match, pitch, shade, sound, style, tenor, tinge, twang **06** accent, colour, effect, go with, humour, manner, spirit, stress, temper, timbre, volume **07** quality **08** attitude, emphasis, strength, tincture, tonality **09** character, harmonize **10** co-ordinate, expression, go well with, inflection, intonation, modulation **12** accentuation

• high tone
03 alt

• tone down
03 dim **06** dampen, reduce, soften, subdew, subdue, temper **07** assuage, lighten **08** mitigate, moderate, play down, restrain **09** alleviate, soft-pedal

• tone up
04 buck, trim **05** brace **06** buck up, tune up **07** freshen, shape up, touch up **08** brighten, limber up **09** sharpen up **10** invigorate

toneless
03 dim **04** dull, grey **05** faded **07** neutral, relaxed **08** listless, tuneless **09** soundless, unmusical **10** colourless **11** unmelodious **12** unexpressive **14** expressionless

Tonga
03 TON

tongue
04 cant, doab, lick, rasp, spit, talk, vote **05** argot, clack, idiom, lingo, slang, utter, voice **06** glossa, jargon, lingua, patois, radula, red rag, speech **07** clapper, dialect **08** language, parlance **09** discourse, pronounce, utterance **10** articulate, vernacular **12** articulation

See also **language**

tongue-tied
04 dumb, mute **06** silent **08** wordless **09** voiceless **10** dumbstruck, speechless **11** mush-mouthed **12** inarticulate, lost for words, tongue-tacked

tonic
01 t **05** boost, final **06** bracer, fillip, saloop **07** cordial, home key, keynote **08** pick-me-up, roborant **09** analeptic, refresher, stimulant **11** restorative **12** shot in the arm **15** fundamental note

See also **note**

too
03 tae **04** also, over, very **06** as well, overly, unduly **07** besides **08** likewise, moreover **09** extremely **10** in addition **11** excessively, furthermore **12** inordinately, ridiculously, unreasonably

tool
03 cut **04** dupe, over, pawn, work, yoke **05** agent, chase, gismo, means, shape, tanto **06** agency, device, gadget, medium, minion, puppet, stooge, troppo, weapon **07** cat's-paw, fashion, flunkey, machine, utensil, vehicle **08** artefact, decorate, hireling, ornament **09** apparatus, appliance, implement **10** instrument, over-the-top **11** contraption, contrivance **12** intermediary

Tools include:

02 ax
03 awl, axe, gad, hod, hoe, loy, saw, sax, van
04 adze, burr, card, celt, file, fork, froe, goad, hawk, jack, mace, mall, maul, peel, pick, plow, prod, prog, rake, rasp, risp, rule, snap, spud, vice
05 auger, bevel, clamp, dolly, drill, level, plane, punch, snips, spade, steel, tongs
06 bodkin, chaser, chisel, dibber, dibble, fuller, gimlet, hammer, jig-saw, mallet, mortar, needle, pestle, pliers, plough, sander, scutch, scythe, shears, shovel, sickle, trowel, wrench
07 bolster, bradawl, chopper, cleaver, crowbar, forceps, fretsaw, hacksaw, handsaw, hay fork, jointer, mattock, nail gun, pick-axe, pincers, scalpel, scriber, stapler, swingle, T-square
08 billhook, chainsaw, dividers, penknife, scissors, spraygun, tenon-saw, thresher, tommy bar, tweezers
09 grass-rake, jack-plane, pitchfork, plumb-line, secateurs, set-square
10 jackhammer, paper-knife, protractor

11 brace and bit, crochet hook, paper-cutter, pocket-knife, screwdriver, spirit level
12 angle grinder, caulking-iron, digging stick, pruning-knife, sledgehammer, socket-wrench, wirestripper
13 pinking-shears, pruning-shears, soldering-iron

See also **gardening**; **saw**

tooth
03 cog, jag **05** crena, prong, taste **06** dentil, joggle, relish **08** appetite, denticle **09** interlock, serration **10** serrations **13** denticulation

See also **teeth**

toothsome
04 nice **05** sweet, tasty, yummy **06** dainty, morish **07** moreish, savoury, scrummy **08** luscious, pleasant, tempting **09** agreeable, delicious, palatable **10** appetizing, attractive, delectable **11** flavoursome, scrumptious **13** mouthwatering

top
◇ *head selection indicator*
02 up **03** cap, cop, lid, nun, tip **04** acme, apex, beat, best, comb, cork, head, kill, lead, main, peak, roof, rule, tuft **05** chief, cover, crest, crown, excel, first, outdo, prime, ridge, shirt, smock, upper **06** apogee, better, blouse, climax, coppin, exceed, finest, finish, height, jersey, jumper, ruling, summit, T-shirt, upmost, upward, utmost, vertex, zenith **07** cacumen, command, eclipse, garnish, highest, leading, maximum, premier, premium, spinner, stopper, supreme, surpass, sweater, tank top, topmost, topsail, topspin **08** crowning, decorate, dominant, foremost, greatest, outshine, outstrip, pinnacle, pullover, superior, surmount, tee shirt, very good **09** be first in, finish off, paramount, principal, sovereign, transcend, uppermost **10** pre-eminent, sweatshirt **11** culminating, culmination **12** highest point

See also **cut**

• **over the top**
03 OTT **05** undue **06** lavish **07** extreme, too much **08** a bit much **09** excessive **10** exorbitant, immoderate, inordinate **11** extravagant, uncalled-for **12** unreasonable

• **top and tail**
◇ *ends deletion indicator*

• **top off**
◇ *head deletion indicator*

• **top up**
05 add to, boost **06** fill up, refill, reload **07** augment **08** increase, recharge **09** replenish **10** supplement

topi
03 hat **04** sola **05** solah **07** sola hat **10** sola helmet

topic
04 head, text **05** issue, place, point, theme, topos **06** matter, thesis **07** subject **08** argument, question **09** hot button **10** hobby-horse, touch-me-not **11** commonplace, hardy annual, old chestnut **12** talking point **13** subject matter

topical
05 local **06** recent **07** current, popular **08** familiar, relevant, up-to-date **10** newsworthy **12** contemporary **13** up-to-the-minute

topless
◇ *head deletion indicator*

topmost
03 top **05** first, upper **06** apical **07** highest, leading, maximum, supreme **08** dominant, foremost, loftiest, supernal **09** paramount, principal, uppermost

top-notch
02 A1 **03** ace, top **04** cool, fine, mega **05** crack, prime, super **06** superb, way-out, wicked **07** leading, premier, radical, supreme **08** peerless, splendid, superior **09** admirable, excellent, first-rate, matchless, top-flight **10** first-class **11** exceptional, outstanding, superlative **12** second-to-none **14** out of this world

topping
◇ *juxtaposition down indicator*
05 crust **07** tipping **08** arrogant **09** excellent, wonderful

topple
◇ *anagram indicator*
03 tip **04** fall, oust **05** upset **06** totter, tumble, unseat **07** capsize, dismast, tip over **08** collapse, dethrone, displace, fall over, keel over, overturn **09** bring down, knock down, knock over, overthrow **11** overbalance

top-secret
06 secret **07** private **08** hush-hush, intimate, personal **09** sensitive **10** classified, restricted **12** confidential, off-the-record

topsy-turvy
◇ *anagram indicator*
05 messy **06** untidy **07** chaotic, jumbled, mixed-up **08** confused **09** confusion, inside out **10** disorderly, in disorder, upside down **11** disarranged, in confusion **12** disorganized, looking-glass, tapsalteerie, tapsieteerie

torch
04 burn, link, tead, wisp **05** brand, flare, light, teade **06** ignite, lampad **07** cresset, roughie **08** arsonist, flambeau, splinter **09** firebrand, set alight, set fire to, set on fire **10** flashlight **11** put a match to

torment
◇ *anagram indicator*
03 vex **04** bane, pain, pest, pine **05** agony, annoy, curse, grill, hound, tease, worry, wrack **06** badger, bother, harass, harrow, misery, ordeal, pester, plague **07** afflict, agitate, anguish, bedevil, crucify, furnace, Gehenna, provoke, scourge, torture, trouble **08** distress, irritate, nuisance, vexation **09** annoyance, martyrdom, persecute, suffering, tantalize **10** affliction, harassment, irritation **11** persecution, provocation **13** pain in the neck **15** thorn in the flesh

torn
◇ *anagram indicator*
03 cut **04** rent, slit **05** split **06** ragged, ribbon, ripped, unsure **07** divided, enriven **08** lacerate, wavering **09** dithering, lacerated, uncertain, undecided **10** in two minds, irresolute **11** vacillating

tornado
04 gale **05** storm **06** squall **07** cyclone, monsoon, tempest, twister, typhoon **09** hurricane, whirlwind **10** waterspout

torpedo
03 ray **05** wreck **07** tin fish **09** cramp-fish **11** electric ray

torpid
04 dead, dull, lazy, numb, slow **05** inert **06** drowsy, sleepy, supine **07** dormant, passive **08** deadened, inactive, indolent, lifeless, listless, sluggish **09** apathetic, lethargic, nerveless, somnolent **10** insensible, languorous **11** lethargical

torpor
05 sloth **06** acedia, apathy, stupor **07** inertia, languor **08** dullness, hebetude, laziness, lethargy, numbness, slowness **09** indolence, inertness, passivity, stupidity, torpidity **10** drowsiness, inactivity, sleepiness, somnolence **12** lifelessness, listlessness, sluggishness

torrent
04 gush, rush **05** flood, spate, storm **06** deluge, stream, volley **07** barrage, blatter, cascade **08** downpour, outburst **10** inundation

torrential
05 heavy **07** driving, pelting, teeming **10** inundating, persistent **11** pouring down **13** bucketing down

torrid
03 hot **04** arid, sexy **06** desert, erotic, red-hot, steamy **07** amorous, blazing, boiling, parched **08** scorched, sizzling, stifling, tropical **09** scorching, waterless **10** blistering, passionate, sweltering

torsk
04 cusk

tortoise
06 gopher **07** hicatee, testudo **08** galapago, hiccatee, terrapin

tortuous
◇ *anagram indicator*
06 zigzag **07** curving, devious,

sinuous, winding **08** indirect, involved, twisting **09** ambagious, Byzantine **10** circuitous, convoluted, meandering, roundabout, serpentine **11** complicated

torture

◇ *anagram indicator*

03 fry, gip, gyp **04** pain, pine **05** abuse, agony, worry, wrack **06** harrow, martyr, misery, murder, plague, punish **07** afflict, agonize, anguish, crucify, murther, trouble **08** distress, ill-treat, mistreat **09** martyrdom, persecute, suffering, tantalize **10** affliction, excruciate, punishment **11** forcipation, persecution **12** excruciation, ill-treatment, mistreatment

Torture forms and instruments include:

03 gin, saw
04 boot, cage, pear, rack
05 brank, gadge, irons, jougs, screw, wheel
06 carcan, engine, harrow, picana, shabeh, spider, stocks, turcas
07 bilboes, boiling, cat's paw, hooding, picquet, pillory, pincers, scourge, stoning, torment
08 bootikin, branding, garrotte, knotting, pendulum, pressing, shin vice, trip-hook
09 bastinado, gauntlets, gridirons, picketing, scarpines, strappado, treadmill
10 brazen bull, cattle prod, impalement, iron collar, iron maiden, Judas scale, pilliwinks, spiked hare, starvation, suspension, thumbscrew, treadwheel
11 cave of roses, forcipation, German chair, head crusher, Judas cradle, keelhauling, knee-capping, squassation, thumbscrews, wooden horse
12 ball and chain, ducking-stool, flesh tearers, scold's bridle, shrew's fiddle, skull crusher, Spanish chair, water torture
13 cat-o'-nine-tails, electric shock, heretic's forks, Spanish mantle
14 Austrian ladder, devil-on-the-neck, disembowelment, drunkard's cloak
15 confession chair

Tory

01 C **03** Con **04** blue **07** tantivy **08** Abhorrer **12** Conservative

toss

◇ *anagram indicator*

03 bum, lob, shy, tip **04** birl, cant, cast, flip, hurl, jerk, jolt, loft, perk, puck, rock, roll, sway **05** bandy, brank, chuck, drink, fling, heave, lurch, pitch, shake, sling, throw **06** bridle, dandle, slight, sprawl, squirm, thrash, tumble, welter, writhe **07** agitate, blanket, canvass, flutter, wriggle **09** commotion, confusion

tot

03 dop, nip, sum **04** baby, dram, mite, shot, slug, swig **05** bairn, child **06** finger, infant **07** measure, swallow, toddler

See also **add**; **baby**; **drink**

• **tot up**

03 add, sum **05** add up, count, mount, tally, total **06** reckon **07** compute, count up, mount up **09** calculate

total

03 add, all, lot, sum, tot **04** full, make, mass, rank **05** add up, count, gross, reach, sheer, sum up, tot up, utter, whole **06** all-out, amount, come to, entire, reckon **07** count up, full-out, perfect, pur sang **08** absolute, amount to, complete, entirety, integral, outright, subtotal, thorough, totality **09** aggregate, downright, out-and-out **10** consummate, grand total, undisputed **11** unmitigated, unqualified **13** comprehensive, thoroughgoing, unconditional

totalitarian

08 despotic, one-party **09** tyrannous **10** monocratic, monolithic, omnipotent, oppressive **11** dictatorial **12** undemocratic **13** authoritarian

totality

03 all, sum **05** total, whole **06** cosmos **07** pleroma **08** entirety, fullness, universe **09** aggregate, wholeness **10** entireness, everything **12** completeness

totally

05 fully, quite **06** wholly **07** utterly **08** entirely, outright **09** perfectly **10** absolutely, completely, thoroughly **11** boots and all, undividedly **12** consummately, undisputedly **13** unmitigatedly **14** wholeheartedly **15** comprehensively, unconditionally

totter

◇ *anagram indicator*

04 reel, rock, roll, sway **05** lurch, shake, waver **06** daddle, dodder, falter, hotter, quiver, teeter, titter, topple, waddle, wobble **07** be shaky, stagger, stumble, tremble **10** be insecure, be unstable, be unsteady **12** be precarious **14** move unsteadily

touch

03 art, bit, dab, eat, hit, jot, nie, pat, pet, tap, tat, tig, use, way **04** abut, blow, dash, draw, feel, hand, harm, hint, hold, kiss, make, meet, move, nigh, nose, palm, palp, skim, spot, stir, take **05** bribe, brush, cheat, cover, drink, equal, flair, grain, graze, knack, match, pinch, point, reach, rival, skiff, skill, smack, speck, spice, stamp, style, taste, theft, tinge, trace, trait, upset, verge, weave, whiff, wound **06** adjoin, affect, aspect, attain, better, border, broach, caress, come to, detail, devour, finger, finish, fondle, handle, injure, little, manner, method, molest, muzzle, nicety, pierce, pocket, regard, sadden, smatch, strike, stroke, tickle **07** ability, concern, consume, contact, disturb, feature, impinge, impress, inspire, involve, knuckle, mention, minutia, rapport, receive, refer to, soupçon, speak of, surface, taction, texture, touch up **08** addition, allude to, approach, come near, deal with, fineness, remark on **09** dexterity, direction, influence, suspicion, tactility, technique **10** connection, suggestion, touchstone **11** association **12** lay a finger on, put a finger on **13** communication, craftsmanship, hold a candle to **14** be contiguous to, correspondence, have an effect on, have an impact on **15** come into contact

• **touch down**

04 land **05** rouge **06** come in **11** come to earth **12** come in to land

• **touch off**

04 fire **05** begin, cause, light **06** arouse, foment, ignite, set off **07** actuate, inflame, provoke, trigger **08** detonate, initiate, spark off **10** trigger off

• **touch up**

03 tat **04** tatt **06** revamp **07** brush up, enhance, improve, patch up, perfect, retouch **08** polish up, renovate, round off **09** finish off

touch-and-go

04 dire, near **05** close, dodgy, hairy, risky **06** sticky, tricky **07** offhand, parlous **08** critical, perilous **09** dangerous, hazardous, uncertain **10** precarious **12** nerve-racking

touchdown

07 arrival, landing **08** coming in **14** coming in to land

touched

03 mad **04** daft **05** barmy, batty, crazy, dotty, loopy, moved, nutty, upset **06** insane **07** bonkers, stirred **08** affected, deranged, inspired **09** disturbed, eccentric, impressed **10** influenced, unbalanced

touchiness

09 bad temper, petulance, surliness, testiness **10** grumpiness, tetchiness **11** crabbedness, grouchiness, peevishness, pettishness **12** captiousness, irascibility, irritability

touching

03 sad **05** hongi **06** libant, moving, tender **07** attaint, darshan, piteous, pitiful, tangent **08** handball, pathetic, pitiable, poignant, stirring, tangency **09** affecting, emotional, fingering, upsetting **10** concerning, contiguous, disturbing, impressive **11** cloud-topped **12** cloud-kissing, heart-rending **13** heartbreaking

touchstone

04 norm, test **05** gauge, guide, model, proof **07** measure, pattern **08** standard, template **09** benchmark, criterion, yardstick **11** Lydian stone

touchwood

04 funk, monk, punk **05** spunk **09** matchwood

touchy
04 edgy, sore **05** cross, huffy, miffy, mifty, risky **06** badass, chippy, feisty, grumpy, ornery, snuffy, tricky
07 awkward, crabbed, grouchy, huffish, peevish, prickly **08** badassed, captious, delicate **09** difficult, irascible, irritable, sensitive **11** bad-tempered, problematic, thin-skinned
13 controversial, over-sensitive, quick-tempered

tough
03 fit, nut, yob **04** firm, grim, hard, lout, thug **05** brute, bully, burly, butch, chewy, hardy, harsh, rigid, rough, rowdy, solid, stern, stiff, teuch, teugh, yobbo **06** badass, ballsy, keelie, knotty, robust, rugged, severe, sticky, strict, strong, sturdy, taxing, thorny, uphill
07 adamant, arduous, callous, durable, fibrous, gristly, rubbery, ruffian, unlucky, vicious, violent, viscous
08 badassed, baffling, criminal, exacting, hardened, hooligan, leathery, muscular, plug-ugly, puzzling, resolute, stalwart, vigorous **09** bovver boy, cut-throat, difficult, hardnosed, laborious, lager lout, obstinate, resilient, resistant, roughneck, strenuous, tenacious, violently, well-built **10** determined, disorderly, inflexible, perplexing, refractory, unpleasant, unyielding
11 distressing, intractable, troublesome, unfortunate
12 aggressively **13** uncomfortable
14 tough as leather, uncompromising

toughen
04 neal **05** brace **06** anneal, harden
07 fortify, stiffen **09** reinforce
10 strengthen **12** make stricter, substantiate

toughness
04 grit, guts **08** firmness, obduracy, strength, tenacity **09** hardiness
10 resilience, resistance, ruggedness, sturdiness **13** determination, inflexibility

toupee
03 jiz, rug, wig **04** gizz **05** caxon, jasey, major **06** bagwig, bobwig, Brutus, peruke, tie-wig **07** buzz-wig, periwig, Ramilie, spencer **08** postiche
09 hairpiece **10** scratch-wig
14 transformation

tour
◇ *anagram indicator*
02 do **03** van **04** hike, ride, road, rode, trip **05** drive, jaunt, round, tramp, visit
06 course, outing **07** circuit, explore, go round, journey **08** roadshow, sightsee **09** barnstorm, excursion, walkabout **10** expedition, inspection
11 travel round **12** drive through
13 peregrination **14** journey through

tourist
05 emmet **06** tourer **07** grockle, tripper, visitor, voyager **09** sightseer, sojourner, traveller **10** day-tripper, rubberneck **12** excursionist, globetrotter, holidaymaker

• **tourist attraction** *see* **Africa**; **America**; **Asia**; **Australia**; **Canada**; **Europe**; **London**; **Middle East**; **New York**; **New Zealand**; **Paris**

tournament
04 meet, seed **05** basho, event, jerid, joust, match **06** jereed, series
07 contest, meeting, tourney
08 carousel **09** carrousel **10** round robin **11** bridge-drive, competition
12 championship

tousled
06 untidy **07** ruffled, rumpled, tangled, tumbled, unkempt **08** messed up
10 disordered, in disarray
11 disarranged, dishevelled

tout
03 all, ask, pet **04** hawk, hype, plug, pout, push, seek, sell **05** blast, every, plier, trade, watch, whole **06** appeal, barker, inhale, market, peddle, praise, runner, toilet **07** commend, endorse, promote, solicit **08** petition
09 advertise **11** workwatcher

tow
03 lug, tug **04** drag, draw, haul, pull, rope **05** track, trail **09** transport
• **in tow**
08 in convoy **10** by your side
12 accompanying

towards
02 to **03** for **04** near **05** about, anent, -wards **06** almost, nearly **07** close to, nearing **09** regarding **10** concerning, on the way to **11** approaching **12** to help pay for, with regard to **13** with respect to

tower
03 cap, top **04** loom, rear, rise, sail, soar
05 excel, mount, shoot **06** ascend, exceed **07** eclipse, surpass **08** dominate, overlook **09** transcend **10** overshadow
See also **tug**

Tower types include:

04 bell, fort, gate, keep, mill, peel, rood, shot
05 block, broch, clock, ivory, minar, pagod, round, spire, Texas, watch, water
06 belfry, castle, church, column, donjon, gopura, nurhag, pagoda, turret
07 bastion, citadel, conning, control, cooling, lookout, minaret, mirador, nuraghe, steeple
08 barbican, bastille, brattice, fortress, hill-fort, martello, scaffold
09 belvedere, campanile, smock mill, tower mill
10 skyscraper, stronghold
11 demi-bastion
13 fortification

Towers include:

02 CN
03 AMP, Sky
04 Pisa
05 Babel, Clock, Macau, Sears, Seoul, Tokyo
06 Big Ben, Dragon, Eiffel, Kiev TV, London, Riga TV, Tahoto
07 Alma-Ata, Leaning, Olympic, Praha TV, Yueyang
08 Tallin TV, Tashkent, Tengwang
09 Blackpool, Donauturm, Ostankino, Tianjin TV
10 Collserola, Liberation
11 Fernsehturm, The Euromast, Yellow Crane
12 Petronas Twin, Stratosphere
15 Oriental Pearl TV

• **tower of strength**
04 prop **06** pillar **07** support
08 mainstay **09** supporter **12** friend in need

towering
04 high, tall **05** great, lofty **07** extreme, soaring, sublime, supreme **08** colossal, elevated, gigantic, imposing
10 impressive, inordinate, monumental, surpassing, unrivalled
11 magnificent, outstanding
12 incomparable, overpowering
13 extraordinary

town
04 burg, city, dorp, toun **05** borgo, bourg, burgh, urban **06** favela, Podunk, pueblo **07** borough, new town, suburbs, village **08** township
09 enclosure, outskirts, urban area
10 county town, market town, metropolis, settlement **11** conurbation
12 municipality **13** urban district

County towns include:

03 Ayr
04 Mold, Wick, York
05 Banff, Cupar, Derry, Elgin, Lewes, Nairn, Omagh, Perth, Truro
06 Armagh, Brecon, Durham, Exeter, Forfar, Lanark, London, Oakham, Oxford
07 Appleby, Bedford, Belfast, Bristol, Cardiff, Chester, Denbigh, Dornoch, Ipswich, Kinross, Lerwick, Lincoln, Matlock, Morpeth, Newport, Norwich, Peebles, Preston, Reading, Renfrew, Selkirk, Taunton, Warwick, Wigtown
08 Aberdeen, Barnsley, Beverley, Cardigan, Carlisle, Cromarty, Dingwall, Dumfries, Greenlaw, Hereford, Hertford, Jedburgh, Kingston, Kirkwall, Monmouth, Pembroke, Rothesay, Stafford, Stirling
09 Aylesbury, Beaumaris, Cambridge, Dolgellau, Dumbarton, Newcastle
10 Haddington, Huntingdon, Linlithgow, Manchester, Montgomery, Nottingham, Presteigne, Shrewsbury, Stonehaven, Trowbridge, Winchester
11 Clackmannan, Downpatrick, Enniskillen, Northampton
12 Kircudbright
13 Middlesbrough, Northallerton

English towns include:

03 Ely
04 Bath, Bury, Hove, Hull, York
05 Ascot, Corby, Cowes, Crewe, Derby, Dover, Epsom, Ewell, Hythe, Leeds, Lewes, Luton, Otley, Poole, Ripon, Rugby, Truro, Wells, Wigan
06 Barnet, Bexley, Bodmin, Bolton, Bootle, Boston, Buxton, Darwen, Dudley, Durham, Exeter, Harlow, Harrow, Ilkley, Jarrow, Kendal, London, Ludlow, Oakham, Oldham, Oundle, Oxford, Slough, St Ives, Stroud, Torbay, Warley, Whitby, Widnes, Wirral, Woking, Yeovil
07 Andover, Arundel, Ashford, Bedford, Berwick, Bristol, Brixham, Burnley, Chatham, Cheddar, Chester, Crawley, Croydon, Dorking, Evesham, Exmouth, Gosport, Grimsby, Halifax, Harwich, Haworth, Helston, Horsham, Ipswich, Keswick, Lincoln, Malvern, Margate, Matlock, Morpeth, Newport, Norwich, Padstow, Preston, Reading, Redruth, Reigate, Royston, Runcorn, Salford, Stilton, Sudbury, Swindon, Taunton, Telford, Tilbury, Torquay, Ventnor, Walsall, Wantage, Warwick, Watford, Windsor
08 Abingdon, Barnsley, Basildon, Beverley, Bradford, Brighton, Carlisle, Coventry, Dartford, Falmouth, Grantham, Hastings, Hatfield, Hereford, Hertford, Kingston, Knowsley, Minehead, Newhaven, Nuneaton, Penzance, Plymouth, Ramsgate, Redditch, Richmond, Rochdale, Sandwell, Solihull, Spalding, Stafford, St Albans, Stamford, St Helens, Thetford, Westbury, Weymouth, Worthing
09 Aldeburgh, Aldershot, Ambleside, Ashbourne, Axminster, Aylesbury, Blackburn, Blackpool, Bletchley, Bracknell, Cambridge, Dartmouth, Doncaster, Gateshead, Gravesend, Greenwich, Guildford, Harrogate, King's Lynn, Lancaster, Leicester, Lichfield, Liverpool, Lowestoft, Lyme Regis, Maidstone, Morecambe, Newcastle, Newmarket, Rochester, Rotherham, Salisbury, Sheerness, Sheffield, Sherborne, Southport, Southwold, St Austell, Stevenage, Stockport, Stratford, Wakefield, Worcester
10 Birkenhead, Birmingham, Bridgwater, Bromsgrove, Buckingham, Canterbury, Chelmsford, Cheltenham, Chichester, Colchester, Darlington, Dorchester, Eastbourne, Felixstowe, Folkestone, Gillingham, Gloucester, Hartlepool, Huntingdon, Kenilworth, Kensington, Launceston, Letchworth, Maidenhead, Manchester, Nottingham, Pontefract, Portsmouth, Scunthorpe, Shrewsbury, Sunderland, Tewkesbury, Warrington, Washington, Whitehaven, Winchester
11 Bognor Regis, Bournemouth, Cirencester, Cleethorpes, Farnborough, Glastonbury, High Wycombe, Northampton, Scarborough, Shaftesbury, Southampton
12 Chesterfield, Clacton-on-Sea, Great Malvern, Huddersfield, Loughborough, Macclesfield, Milton Keynes, North Shields, Peterborough, South Shields, Stoke-on-Trent, West Bromwich
13 Bury St Edmunds, Ellesmere Port, Great Yarmouth, Kidderminster, Leamington Spa, Littlehampton, Lytham St Anne's, Middlesbrough, Saffron Walden, Southend-on-Sea, West Bridgford, Wolverhampton
14 Ashby-de-la-Zouch, Bishop Auckland, Chipping Norton, Hemel Hempstead, Henley-on-Thames, Stockton-on-Tees, Tunbridge Wells
15 Ashton-under-Lyne, Barrow-in-Furness, Burton upon Trent, Sutton Coldfield, Weston-Super-Mare

Northern Irish towns include:

05 Derry, Larne, Newry, Omagh
06 Antrim, Armagh, Bangor, Lurgan
07 Belfast, Lifford, Lisburn
08 Limavady, Portrush, Strabane
09 Ballymena, Banbridge, Coleraine, Cookstown, Dungannon, Portadown
10 Ballyclare, Ballymoney
11 Downpatrick, Enniskillen, Londonderry, Magherafelt, Newtownards, Portstewart
13 Carrickfergus

Scottish towns include:

03 Ayr
04 Oban, Tain, Wick
05 Alloa, Banff, Elgin, Keith, Kelso, Nairn, Perth, Scone, Troon
06 Alness, Dunbar, Dundee, Dunoon, Forfar, Girvan, Glamis, Hawick, Huntly, Irvine, Lanark, Thurso
07 Airdrie, Alloway, Braemar, Dornoch, Falkirk, Glasgow, Golspie, Gourock, Lerwick, Mallaig, Paisley, Peebles, Portree, Selkirk
08 Aberdeen, Arbroath, Banchory, Dalkeith, Dingwall, Dumfries, Dunblane, Fortrose, Giffnock, Greenock, Hamilton, Jedburgh, Kirkwall, Montrose, Stirling, Ullapool
09 Ardrossan, Callander, Clydebank, Dumbarton, Edinburgh, Inverness, Inverurie, Kingussie, Kirkcaldy, Lockerbie, Peterhead, Pitlochry, Prestwick, St Andrews, Stornoway, Stranraer
10 Coatbridge, Dalbeattie, Galashiels, Glenrothes, Kilmarnock, Kincardine, Linlithgow, Livingston, Motherwell, Newtonmore, Stonehaven
11 Blairgowrie, Campbeltown, Cowdenbeath, Crianlarich, Cumbernauld, Dunfermline, Fort William, Fraserburgh, Grangemouth, Gretna Green, Invergordon, John o'Groats, Port Glasgow
12 Auchterarder, East Kilbride, Lochgilphead
13 Castle Douglas, Kirkcudbright, Kirkintilloch
14 Grantown-on-Spey

Welsh towns include:

04 Bala, Mold, Rhyl
05 Barry, Conwy, Tenby, Tywyn
06 Bangor, Brecon, Ruthin
07 Cardiff, Cwmbrân, Denbigh, Harlech, Newport, Newtown, Swansea, Wrexham
08 Aberdare, Barmouth, Bridgend, Cardigan, Chepstow, Ebbw Vale, Hay-on-Wye, Holyhead, Lampeter, Llanelli, Monmouth, Pembroke, Pwllheli, Rhayader, St David's, Treorchy
09 Aberaeron, Carnarvon, Colwyn Bay, Dolgellau, Fishguard, Llandudno, Llangefni, Pontypool, Prestatyn, Welshpool
10 Caernarfon, Caerphilly, Carmarthen, Llandovery, Llangollen, Pontypridd, Porthmadog, Port Talbot
11 Abergavenny, Abertillery, Aberystwyth, Builth Wells, Machynlleth
12 Milford Haven
13 Haverfordwest, Merthyr Tydfil

See also **city**; **United Kingdom**

• **mushroom town**
04 camp

• **open space in town**
04 lung

town-dweller
03 cit **05** towny **07** burgher, citizen, oppidan **08** townsman, urbanite **10** townswoman

township
02 tp **04** deme, vill **06** parish **07** village **09** community

toxic
06 deadly, lethal **07** baneful, harmful, noxious **08** poisoned **09** dangerous, poisonous, unhealthy

See also **poison**

toy
04 jest, play, whim **05** dally, flirt, knack, model, sport, trick **06** bauble, beaker, fiddle, gewgaw, paddle, tinker, trifle **07** reduced, replica, trinket **08** crotchet **09** automaton, mess about, miniature, plaything **10** knick-knack, mess around, small-scale **12** reproduction

Toys include:

03 ark, gun, top
04 ball, bike, dart, doll, farm, fort, game, gonk, kite, Lego®, Sega®, XBox®, yo-yo

05 coral, Dinky®, slide, swing, teddy, trike
06 cap-gun, garage, go-kart, guitar, paints, pop-gun, puzzle, rattle, rocker, seesaw, tea set
07 balloon, bicycle, box-kite, crayons, Digimon®, dreidel, drum set, Frisbee®, Game Boy®, marbles, Meccano®, ocarina, Play-Doh®, Pokémon®, rag doll, sandpit, scooter, shoofly, soft-toy, tumbler, Turtles®
08 catapult, doll's cot, football, GameCube®, golliwog, hula-hoop, Matchbox®, mirliton, model car, model kit, Nintendo®, Noah's ark, pedal-car, pinwheel, skipjack, squeaker, Subbuteo®, train set, tricycle, windmill
09 Action Man®, aeroplane, bandalore, Care Bears, doll's pram, gyroscope, playhouse, pogo stick, Sindy doll®, swingball, teddy bear, video game, whirligig
10 baby-walker, Barbie doll®, doll's buggy, doll's house, fivestones, hobby-horse, kewpie doll, musical box, pantograph, peashooter, Plasticene®, Rubik's Cube®, Scalextric®, skateboard, Steiff bear, Super Mario®, tin soldier, toy soldier, trampoline, typewriter, weather box, Wendy house
11 baby-bouncer, glove puppet, PlayStation®, shape-sorter, spacehopper, spinning top, stroboscope, Tantalus cup, thaumatrope, tiddly winks, water pistol, wheel of life
12 action figure, boxing-gloves, computer game, executive toy, jack-in-the-box, jigsaw puzzle, kaleidoscope, model railway, mountain bike, My Little Pony, paddling-pool, Power Rangers®, praxinoscope, rocking-horse, skipping-rope, walkie-talkie, weather house
13 Bob the Builder®, building block, climbing-frame, modelling clay, Newton's cradle, sewing machine, Space Invaders®, Tiny-Tears doll®
14 activity centre, bucket and spade, building-blocks, building-bricks, Cartesian devil, Cartesian diver, electronic game, Paddington Bear, Powerpuff Girls®

trace
03 bit, dog, jot, map, way **04** calk, copy, dash, draw, dreg, drop, find, hint, hunt, mark, move, plan, scar, seek, show, sign, spot, walk **05** chart, dig up, draft, pinch, relic, savor, scent, smack, spoor, stalk, tinge, token, touch, track, tract, trail, whiff, write **06** course, depict, derive, detect, engram, follow, fossil, pursue, record, savour, shadow, sketch **07** analyse, mark out, outline, proceed, remains, remnant, run down, soupçon, thought, uncover, unearth, vestige **08** chalk out, describe, discover, engramma, evidence, footmark, generate, moniment, monument, traverse **09** delineate, footprint, scintilla, suspicion, track down **10** hide or hair, impression, indication, suggestion **11** counterdraw, hide nor hair

track
03 dog, pug, ren, rin, run, way **04** beat, hunt, line, loke, mark, path, race, rack, rail, rake, road, sent, sign, slot, tail, tram, trod, wake **05** chase, drift, orbit, piste, route, scent, spoor, stalk, trace, tract, trade, trail, tread, troad, trode
06 course, follow, groove, ground, inside, pursue, riding, runway, shadow, sleuth, troade **07** circuit, footing, monitor, portage, tramway
08 argument, cycleway, footmark, footstep, sequence, sideline, speedway, traverse **09** cyclepath, footprint **10** serpentine, trajectory

See also **athletics**

• **keep track of**
04 plot **05** check, grasp, trace, watch
06 follow, record **07** monitor, observe, oversee **10** keep up with, understand
11 keep an eye on

• **lose track of**
04 miss **06** forget **08** misplace **13** lose touch with **15** lose contact with

• **make tracks**
02 go **04** dash **05** leave, scram **06** beat it, depart **07** dash off, make off
09 disappear **10** hit the road **15** leave footprints

• **off the beaten track**
06 remote **07** private **08** isolated, outlying, secluded **11** god-forsaken, in the sticks, out-of-the-way
12 unfrequented

• **on track**
06 on time **08** on course, on target
10 on schedule

• **track down**
04 find **05** catch, dig up, trace
06 detect, expose, turn up **07** capture, nose out, run down, uncover, unearth
08 discover, hunt down, sniff out
09 ferret out **10** run to earth **11** run to ground

• **tracks**
02 Ry

tract
03 lot **04** area, dene, plot, vast, zone
05 clime, essay, monte, trace, track
06 desert, extent, homily, region, sermon **07** booklet, expanse, leaflet, quarter, stretch, terrain **08** brochure, district, pamphlet, tractate, treatise
09 discourse, monograph, territory
12 disquisition, dissertation

tractable
04 tame **05** tawie **06** docile, pliant
07 pliable, willing **08** amenable, biddable, obedient, towardly, tractile, workable, yielding **09** compliant, malleable, treatable **10** governable, manageable, submissive
11 complaisant, persuadable
12 controllable

traction
04 drag, grip, pull **07** draught, drawing, haulage, pulling **08** adhesion, friction
09 telferage **10** propulsion, telpherage

tractor
03 cat **07** backhoe, pedrail, skidder
09 bulldozer **13** backhoe loader
14 traction engine

trade
02 go **03** art, buy, job, ply, ren, rin, run, way **04** deal, line, mart, sell, swap, work **05** craft, skill, track, trail, tread
06 barter, buying, career, course, custom, market, métier, mister, occupy, peddle, resort, switch **07** bargain, calling, dealing, rubbish, selling, traffic
08 business, commerce, exchange, medicine, merchant, peddling, practice, sideline, transact, treading, vocation **09** carpentry, clientele, customers, marketing **10** contraband, do business, employment, line of work, occupation, profession
11 commodities, merchandize, shopkeeping, trafficking
12 transactions

trademark
04 logo, mark, name, sign **05** badge, brand, crest, label, quirk, stamp
06 emblem, symbol **07** feature
08 hallmark, insignia **09** attribute, brand name, idiograph, tradename
10 brand label, speciality **11** peculiarity
12 idiosyncrasy **14** characteristic, typical quality **15** proprietary name

tradename
02 TN **05** brand, label

trader
05 bania, buyer, plier **06** banian, banyan, broker, dealer, seller, vendor
07 higgler, peddler **08** marketer, merchant, pitchman, retailer, supplier
09 barrow boy, marketeer, tradesman
10 easterling, shopkeeper, trafficker, wholesaler **11** tradeswoman

tradesman, tradeswoman
05 buyer **06** dealer, seller, trader, vendor, worker **07** artisan
08 mechanic, merchant, retailer
09 craftsman **10** journeyman, shopkeeper **11** craftswoman

tradition
03 way **04** rite **05** habit, usage
06 belief, cabala, custom, kabala, legend, praxis, ritual **07** cabbala, kabbala, qabalah, routine
08 ceremony, folklore, kabbalah, practice **10** convention, observance
11 institution

traditional
03 old, set **04** folk, oral **05** fixed, usual
06 age-old **07** old-line, pompier, routine **08** habitual, historic
09 customary, traditive, unwritten
10 accustomed, ceremonial
11 established **12** conservative, conventional, time-honoured, tralaticious, tralatitious **15** long-established

traditionalist
07 diehard **08** old fogey, old guard, old-liner **09** formalist **11** reactionary **12** conservative **13** stick-in-the-mud **15** conventionalist

traduce
04 slag **05** abuse, decry, knock, smear **06** defame, insult, malign, revile, vilify **07** asperse, blacken, detract, run down, slag off, slander **08** transmit **09** denigrate, deprecate, disparage, propagate, translate **10** calumniate, depreciate **12** misrepresent

traducer
06 abuser **07** defamer, knocker, smearer **08** asperser, vilifier **09** detractor, slanderer **10** denigrator, deprecator, disparager, mud-slinger **11** calumniator

traffic
03 buy **04** cars, deal, sell **05** queue, trade, truck **06** barter, hold-up, peddle **07** bargain, contact, dealing, freight, trade in, trading **08** business, commerce, dealings, exchange, gridlock, intrigue, peddling, shipping, tailback, vehicles **09** negotiate, relations, transport **10** congestion, do business, passengers, traffic jam **11** commodities, intercourse, trafficking **13** communication **14** transportation

trafficker
05 agent **06** broker, dealer, monger, seller, trader **07** peddler **08** marketer, merchant, supplier **11** distributor **12** merchandizer

tragedy
04 blow **06** buskin **08** calamity, disaster **09** adversity **10** affliction, misfortune **11** catastrophe, unhappiness

tragic
◇ *anagram indicator*
03 sad **04** dire **05** awful, fatal **06** deadly **07** unhappy, unlucky **08** buskined, dreadful, ill-fated, pathetic, pitiable, shocking, terrible, Thespian, wretched **09** appalling, miserable, sorrowful **10** calamitous, deplorable, disastrous **11** unfortunate **12** catastrophic **13** heartbreaking

tragically
07 awfully **08** terribly **10** dreadfully, shockingly, wretchedly **11** appallingly

trail
◇ *juxtaposition indicator*
03 dog, lag, tow, way **04** drag, draw, fall, hang, haul, hunt, path, pull, road, sign, tail, wake **05** chase, droop, marks, piste, reach, route, scent, spoor, stalk, sweep, trace, track, trade, train **06** dangle, dawdle, extend, follow, linger, loiter, pursue, ramble, runway, shadow, sleuth, stream, streel, trapes **07** abature, draggle, traipse **08** footpath, straggle, tag along, trauchle **09** footmarks **10** footprints

• destroy trail
04 foil

• trail away
04 fade, sink **06** lessen, shrink, weaken **07** die away, dwindle, subside, tail off **08** decrease, diminish, fade away, fall away, melt away, peter out, taper off, trail off **09** disappear

trailblazer
06 leader **07** founder, pioneer **09** developer, innovator **10** discoverer, pathfinder **13** ground-breaker

train
◇ *anagram indicator*
03 aim, set **04** drag, file, line, lure, path, sack, tail, tire **05** breed, chain, coach, court, drill, flier, flyer, focus, groom, learn, level, local, longe, lunge, order, point, staff, study, suite, teach, track, trail, tutor **06** allure, cafila, column, convoy, direct, ground, kafila, lesson, nuzzle, school, series, sledge, stream, string **07** bring up, caffila, caravan, cortège, educate, improve, prepare, process, retinue, work out **08** be taught, choo-choo, exercise, instruct, practise, puff-puff, rehearse, sequence **09** be trained, entourage, followers, following, household, inculcate **10** attendants, be prepared, discipline, procession, succession **11** progression **12** indoctrinate **13** concatenation

Train types include:

01 Q
02 up
03 APT, HST, owl, TGV, way
04 boat, down, loco, mail, milk
05 goods, hover, mixed, paddy, steam
06 bullet, diesel, Maglev
07 baggage, express, freight, through
08 cable-car, corridor, monorail, push-pull
09 aerotrain, excursion, high-speed, Intercity®, manriding
10 locomotive
12 Freightliner®
13 accommodation
14 shuttle service
15 steam locomotive

Trains include:

06 Rocket, Thomas
07 Mallard, The Ghan
09 The A-Train
13 Indian Pacific, Orient Express, Trans-Siberian
14 Flying Scotsman
15 Hogwarts Express

trained
03 fit **08** schooled **10** discerning **11** experienced

trainee
01 L **02** AT, ET **04** tiro **05** cadet, pupil **06** intern, novice **07** interne, learner, student **08** beginner **10** apprentice **11** probationer

trainer
02 PT **05** coach, tutor **06** mentor **07** handler, teacher **08** educator **10** instructor
See also **footwear**; **horseman, horsewoman**

training
◇ *anagram indicator*
02 PT **03** CAT, CBT **05** drill **07** lessons, nurture, tuition, workout **08** coaching, exercise, learning, pedagogy, practice, teaching, tutoring **09** education, grounding, schooling **10** bringing up, discipline, tirocinium, upbringing, working-out **11** instruction, preparation **14** apprenticeship

• out of training
04 soft

• youth in training
04 page

traipse
03 gad **04** plod, slog, trek **05** trail, tramp, trape **06** slouch, trudge **08** slattern

trait
04 thew **05** quirk, touch, trick **06** stroke **07** feature, quality **08** property **09** attribute **11** peculiarity **12** idiosyncrasy **14** characteristic

traitor
03 dog **05** Judas, kulak **07** nithing **08** betrayer, deceiver, defector, deserter, informer, proditor, quisling, renegade, traditor, treacher, turncoat, two-timer **09** traitress, treachour **11** backstabber, treachetour **12** collaborator, double-dealer **13** double-crosser **14** fifth columnist

traitorous
05 false **06** untrue **08** apostate, disloyal, renegade **09** faithless, seditious **10** perfidious, unfaithful **11** treacherous, treasonable **13** dishonourable, double-dealing **14** double-crossing

trajectory
04 line, path **05** orbit, route, track, trail **06** course, flight **10** flight path

trammel
◇ *anagram indicator*
03 bar, net, tie **04** bond, clog, curb, rein **05** block, catch, chain, check **06** enmesh, entrap, fetter, hamper, hinder, hobble, impede **07** capture, confine, ensnare, inhibit, shackle **08** entangle, handicap, obstacle, restrain, restrict **09** hindrance, restraint **10** impediment **14** stumbling-block

tramp
03 bum **04** hike, hobo, plod, roam, rove, slag, slut, step, tart, trek, walk **05** caird, jakey, march, piker, rogue, stamp, stomp, stump, trail, tread, tromp, wench, whore **06** dosser, hooker, ramble, sloven, toerag, truant, trudge, vagrom, walker, whaler **07** dingbat, floater, floozie, gangrel, swagger, swagman, tinkler, traipse, trample, trollop, vagrant **08** clochard, cursitor, derelict, footslog, scrubber, slattern, straggle, stroller, vagabond

09 landloper, sundowner, toeragger 10 down-and-out, loose woman, prostitute 11 rinthereout, scatterling, Weary Willie 12 hallan-shaker 15 knight of the road

trample
04 foil 05 crush, poach, potch, stamp, tramp, tread, tromp 06 insult, squash, stramp 07 flatten, hobnail 08 override, ride down

trance
04 daze 05 dream, spell 06 stupor, transe 07 ecstasy, rapture, reverie 08 entrance 09 catalepsy 12 somnambulism 15 unconsciousness

tranche
03 cut 04 part 05 block, piece, slice, wedge 06 length 07 portion, section, segment 10 instalment

tranquil
04 calm, cool, easy 05 quiet, still 06 hushed, placid, sedate, serene, silent 07 pacific, relaxed, restful 08 composed, laid-back, peaceful 09 reposeful, unexcited 10 untroubled 11 undisturbed, unflappable 12 even-tempered 13 imperturbable, unimpassioned 14 disimpassioned

tranquillity
03 lee 04 calm, hush, rest 05 peace, quiet 06 repose 07 ataraxy, silence 08 ataraxia, calmness, coolness, quietism, quietude, serenity 09 composure, placidity, quietness, stillness 10 equanimity, sedateness 11 restfulness 12 peacefulness

tranquillize
04 calm, lull 05 quell, quiet, relax 06 opiate, pacify, sedate, serene, soothe 07 compose 09 narcotize

tranquillizer
06 downer, opiate 07 bromide 08 narcotic, quietive, sedative 09 calmative 10 depressant 11 barbiturate 12 sleeping pill

See also **sedative**

transact
02 do 05 enact 06 handle, manage, settle 07 carry on, conduct, execute, perform 08 carry out, conclude, despatch, dispatch 09 discharge, negotiate, prosecute 10 accomplish

transaction
03 job 04 deal, deed 06 action, affair, annals, doings, gamble, matter, record 07 affairs, bargain, minutes, passage, reports 08 business, concerns, debt swap, goings-on, handling, straddle 09 agreement, discharge, enactment, execution 10 enterprise, proceeding, put-through, settlement, swap option 11 arrangement, negotiation, proceedings, undertaking 12 control event, part-exchange, publications

transactions
02 tr 07 affairs, dealing, journal, memoirs

transcend
04 beat 05 excel, outdo 06 exceed 07 eclipse, surpass 08 go beyond, outshine, outstrip, overstep, surmount 09 rise above 11 leave behind

transcendence
09 greatness, sublimity, supremacy 10 ascendancy, excellence, paramouncy 11 paramountcy, pre-eminence, superiority 12 predominance 13 matchlessness, transcendency 15 incomparability

transcendent
07 sublime, supreme 08 numinous, peerless 09 excellent, excelling, ineffable, matchless, spiritual 10 superhuman, surpassing 11 magnificent, superlative 12 incomparable, supernatural, transcending, unparalleled 13 unsurpassable

transcendental
05 vague 08 mystical 09 excelling, spiritual 10 mysterious 12 metaphysical, otherworldly, supereminent, supernatural, transcending 13 preternatural

transcribe
04 copy, note 06 copy up, record, render 07 Braille, copy out, rewrite, write up 08 take down, write out 09 reproduce, translate 13 transliterate

transcript
04 copy, note 05 tenor 06 record, tenour 07 version 09 duplicate 10 manuscript 11 translation 12 reproduction 13 transcription 15 exemplification, transliteration

transcription
07 version 10 writing-out 11 translation 12 reproduction, transumption 15 transliteration

transfer
◇ *anagram indicator*
02 ET 03 EFT, PET, PMT 04 deed, flit, GIFT, hand, move, pass, take, turn, ZIFT 05 carry, grant, ladle, remit, shift 06 assign, change, convey, pounce, remove 07 consign, pipette, removal 08 alienate, give over, hand over, handover, movement, relocate, sign away, sign over, transmit 09 negotiate, transhume, transport, transpose 10 assignment, changeover, conveyance, relocation, transplant 12 displacement, transduction, transference, transmission 13 transposition

transfigure
◇ *anagram indicator*
05 alter, exalt, morph 06 change 07 convert, glorify 08 idealize 09 transform, translate, transmute 11 apotheosize 12 metamorphose

transfix
04 hold, spit, stun 05 rivet, spear, spike, stick 06 empale, impale, pierce, skewer 07 bestick, engross, petrify 08 paralyse 09 fascinate, hypnotize, mesmerize, spellbind 10 run through

transform
◇ *anagram indicator*
04 turn 05 adapt, alter, morph, renew 06 absorb, change, mutate, reform 07 commute, convert, lithify, rebuild, receive, remodel, resolve 08 disclose 09 sovietize, translate, transmute, transpose 10 trans-shape, transverse 11 reconstruct, transfigure 12 decentralize, metamorphose, transmogrify 13 revolutionize 15 unprotestantize

transformation
◇ *anagram indicator*
03 wig 06 change, reform 07 turning 08 dilation, mutation, petalody, phyllody, reaction, rotation, sepalody 09 reflexion, sea change, variation 10 alteration, conversion, dilatation, metaplasia, metastasis, reflection, revolution 11 reformation, translation 13 metamorphosis, transmutation 15 theriomorphosis, transfiguration

transfuse
05 imbue 06 instil 07 pervade, suffuse 08 permeate, transfer

transgress
03 err, sin 04 defy 05 break, lapse 06 breach, exceed, offend 07 disobey, violate 08 encroach, infringe, overstep, trespass 09 misbehave 10 contravene 11 prevaricate

transgression
03 sin 04 debt, slip 05 crime, error, fault, lapse, scape, wrong 06 breach, escape 07 misdeed, offence, offense 08 iniquity, peccancy, trespass 09 overgoing, violation 10 infraction, peccadillo, wrongdoing 12 disobedience, encroachment, infringement, misbehaviour, misdemeanour, overstepping 13 contravention

transgressor
05 felon 06 debtor, sinner 07 culprit, villain 08 criminal, evil-doer, offender 09 miscreant, wrongdoer 10 delinquent, lawbreaker, malefactor, trespasser

transience
07 brevity 08 caducity, fugacity 09 briefness, shortness 11 evanescence 12 ephemerality, fleetingness, fugitiveness, impermanence 13 deciduousness, temporariness 14 transitoriness

transient
05 brief, fleet, short 06 bubble, flying 07 passing 08 fleeting, volatile 09 ephemeral, fugacious, momentary, short-term, temporary 10 evanescent, short-lived, transitory 11 impermanent 13 summer-seeming

transistor
03 FET

transit
05 route **06** travel **07** haulage, journey, passage, reverse **08** carriage, crossing, movement, shipment, transfer
10 conveyance, journeying, pass across **11** culmination
14 transportation
• **in transit**
05 by air, by sea **06** by rail, by road
07 en route **08** on the way **10** travelling

transition
04 flux, leap, move **05** shift **06** change, switch **07** passage, passing
08 movement, progress **09** evolution, metabasis **10** alteration, changeover, conversion, metastasis, unbecoming
11 composition, development, progression **12** transitional
13 metamorphosis, rite of passage, transmutation **14** transformation

transitional
05 fluid **07** interim, passing
08 changing, twilight **09** temporary, unsettled **11** provisional
12 evolutionary, intermediate
13 developmental

transitory
05 brief, fleet, short **06** flying
07 passing **08** fleeting **09** deciduous, ephemeral, fugacious, momentary, short-term, temporary, transient
10 evanescent, fly-by-night, short-lived **11** impermanent

translate
◇ *anagram indicator*
◇ *foreign word indicator*
03 put **04** move, turn **05** alter, shift
06 change, decode, encode, reduce, render, reword **07** conster, convert, English, explain, improve, traduce
08 construe, decipher, relocate, renovate, simplify, transfer
09 enrapture, interpret, transform, transmute, transport **10** metaphrase, paraphrase, transcribe **12** transmogrify
13 transliterate

translation
◇ *anagram indicator*
03 key **04** crib, move, pony **05** gloss, horse, shift **06** change, motion
07 version **08** transfer **09** rendering, rendition, rewording **10** alteration, conversion, metaphrase, paraphrase, rephrasing, traduction **11** explanation, metaphrasis **12** transumption
13 metamorphosis, transcription, transmutation **14** interpretation, simplification, transformation
15 transliteration

translator
02 tr **03** CLT **07** exegete, glosser, Rhemist **08** dragoman, linguist, polyglot **09** Englisher, exegetist, glossator **10** glossarist, metaphrast, paraphrast **11** interpreter, paraphraser

translucent
05 clear **06** limpid **08** lancelet, pellucid **10** diaphanous, membranous, see-through, translucid
11 membraneous, transparent
13 membranaceous

transmigration
07 rebirth **13** reincarnation
14 metempsychosis, Pythagoreanism, transformation

transmission
04 show **06** entail, signal, spread
07 beaming, episode, message, passage, sending **08** carriage, despatch, dispatch, relaying, shipment, transfer **09** broadcast, diffusion, imparting, programme, simulcast, transport **10** convection, conveyance, production, trajection **11** consignment, performance **12** broadcasting, presentation, transference
13 communication, dissemination, transmittance
• **end of transmission**
04 over **10** over and out

transmit
03 fax **04** beam, bear, buzz, pass, pipe, send **05** carry, modem, radio, relay, remit **06** convey, hand on, impart, pass on, report, send on, spread
07 conduct, consign, diffuse, forward, mediate, message, network, radiate, send out, traduce, traject **08** despatch, dispatch, hand down, telecast, televise, transfer **09** broadcast, propagate, satellite, transport **11** communicate, disseminate, interrogate

transmute
◇ *anagram indicator*
05 alter **06** change, remake
07 convert, permute, sublime
08 transmew **09** alchemize, permutate, sublimate, transform, translate, transmove **10** transverse
11 transfigure **12** metamorphose, transmogrify

transparency
05 photo, slide, water **07** clarity, picture **08** openness, overhead
09 clearness, filminess, frankness, gauziness, limpidity, plainness, sheerness **10** candidness, directness, limpidness, patentness, photograph
11 obviousness, pellucidity
12 apparentness, distinctness, explicitness, pellucidness, translucence, translucency
13 translucidity **14** diaphanousness, forthrightness **15** perspicuousness, unambiguousness

transparent
04 open **05** clear, filmy, gauzy, lucid, plain, sheer, white **06** candid, direct, limpid, patent, watery **07** evident, hyaline, hyaloid, obvious, tiffany, visible
08 apparent, distinct, explicit, manifest, pellucid **10** colourless, diaphanous, forthright, noticeable, see-through **11** discernible, perceptible, translucent, unambiguous, undisguised, unequivocal **12** semipellucid, transpicuous, unmistakable
15 straightforward

transparently
07 clearly, plainly **08** patently
09 evidently, obviously **10** distinctly, explicitly, noticeably **11** discernibly, perceptibly **12** unmistakably
13 unambiguously, unequivocally

transpire
05 arise, ensue, occur, prove
06 appear, befall, exhale, happen
07 come out, turn out **09** come about, take place **10** come to pass **11** become known, be disclosed, come to light
14 become apparent

transplant
04 move **05** graft, repot, shift
06 remove, uproot **07** replant
08 displace, plant out, relocate, resettle, transfer **12** cluster graft

transport
◇ *anagram indicator*
02 MT **03** AST, fit, lag, put, ren, rin, run, SST **04** bear, haul, move, rail, rape, rush, ship, take, waft **05** bliss, bring, carry, cycle, exile, fetch, shift, witch
06 convey, deport, frenzy, ravish, remove, thrill **07** delight, ecstasy, elation, freight, haulage, medevac, overjoy, rapture, removal, traject, transit, vehicle **08** carriage, entrance, euphoria, shipment, shipping, transfer
09 captivate, carry away, electrify, enrapture, spellbind, translate
10 conveyance **12** exhilaration
13 seventh heaven, transportance
14 transportation
See also **travel**; **vehicle**

Public transport includes:

03 bus, cab
04 taxi, tram, tube
05 ferry, metro, train
07 omnibus, railway, trolley
10 stage-coach, trolleybus
11 park-and-ride, underground
12 light railway

transportation
07 airlift, freight, haulage, railage, removal, traffic, transit, waftage
08 carriage, shipment, shipping, transfer **09** fishyback **10** conveyance

transported
◇ *anagram indicator*
04 rapt **05** piped **08** traveled
09 rhapsodic, travelled

transpose
◇ *anagram indicator*
02 tr **04** move, swap, turn **05** alter, shift
06 change, invert, switch **07** convert, reorder **08** exchange, flip-flop, transfer
09 rearrange, transform **10** substitute
11 interchange, metathesize
13 anagrammatize

transverse
05 cross **06** thwart **07** oblique, reverse
08 diagonal **09** crossways, crosswise, transform **10** overthwart **11** transversal

trap
◇ *containment indicator*
03 gin, gob, net, pit, pot **04** drop, dupe,

fall, grin, hook, lime, lock, lure, mesh, ploy, ruse, take, toil, weel, wile **05** bazoo, catch, creel, decoy, fault, mouth, noose, plant, snare, spell, sting, toils, trick **06** ambush, bunker, corner, danger, device, enmesh, entrap, hazard, tangle **07** beguile, capture, confine, deceive, ensnare, flytrap, gin trap, mantrap, mist-net, pin down, pitfall, putcher, rat-trap, springe **08** artifice, cakehole, catch-pit, deadfall, fall-trap, inveigle, putcheon, trapdoor, traphole, trickery **09** booby-trap, deception, mouse-trap, snaphance, stratagem **10** catch-basin, dig a pit for, potato trap, snaphaunce, snaphaunch, subterfuge

See also **carriage**

trapped

◇ *insertion indicator*

05 duped, stuck **06** caught, netted, snared **07** tricked **08** ambushed, beguiled, cornered, deceived, ensnared **09** inveigled **10** surrounded **11** in by the week

trapper

06 hunter **08** covering, huntsman, voyageur **12** backwoodsman, frontiersman

trappings

04 gear **05** dress **06** finery, livery, things **07** clothes, panoply, raiment **08** fittings, fixtures, housings **09** equipment, furniture, ornaments, trimmings **10** adornments, fripperies **11** accessories, decorations, furnishings **13** accoutrements, paraphernalia **14** accompaniments

trash

◇ *anagram indicator*

03 mar, pan, rot **04** blah, bosh, bull, bunk, carp, dust, guff, junk, ruin, scum, sink, slam **05** balls, blame, break, check, decry, dreck, dregs, hooey, knock, leash, slate, smash, snipe, spoil, tripe, waste, wreck **06** attack, drivel, grunge, harass, kitsch, litter, rabble, ravage, refuse, scraps, trudge **07** baloney, censure, condemn, destroy, eyewash, garbage, hogwash, rhubarb, rubbish, run down, shatter, torpedo, wear out **08** badmouth, canaille, demolish, denounce, malarkey, nonsense, riff-raff, trashery, write off **09** criticize, denigrate, devastate, disparage, excoriate, gibberish, moonshine, sweepings, trashtrie, vandalize **10** balderdash, come down on, go to town on, vituperate **11** pick holes in **12** disapprove of, gobbledygook, offscourings, pull to pieces, put the boot in, tear to shreds, undesirables **13** find fault with, play havoc with, tear a strip off **15** do a hatchet job on, pass judgement on

trashy

04 naff **05** cheap **06** crappy, flimsy, kitsch, paltry, shabby, shoddy, tawdry, tinsel **07** kitschy **08** inferior, rubbishy **09** cheap-jack, third-rate, worthless **12** meretricious

trauma

04 hurt, jolt, pain **05** agony, grief, shock, upset, wound **06** damage, injury, lesion, ordeal, strain, stress **07** anguish, torture **08** disorder, distress, upheaval **09** suffering **11** disturbance

traumatic

07 harmful, hurtful, painful **08** shocking, wounding **09** agonizing, injurious, stressful, upsetting **10** disturbing, unpleasant **11** distressing, frightening

traumatize

04 daze, hurt, numb, stun **05** amaze, appal, shock, upset **06** dismay, grieve, offend **07** astound, horrify, outrage, stagger, startle, stupefy **08** distress, paralyse

travail

04 slog, toil **05** grind, sweat, tears **06** effort, labour, strain, stress, throes, travel **07** travois, trouble **08** distress, drudgery, exertion, hardship **09** suffering **10** birth-pangs, childbirth **11** labour pains, tribulation

travel

02 go **03** ren, rin, run **04** meve, move, pass, ride, roam, rove, tour, trip, tube, walk, wend, wing **05** cover, cross, vroom, wagon, wheel **06** ramble, troupe, voyage, waggon, wander **07** advance, conduct, explore, impetus, journey, passage, proceed, touring, tourism, travail, trolley, wayfare **08** go abroad, progress, traverse **09** excursion, make a trip **10** expedition, go overseas, journeying, travelling, wanderings **11** make your way, see the world, sightseeing **13** globetrotting

See also **space**

Travel methods and forms include:

- **03** bus, fly, row, ski
- **04** bike, hike, punt, ride, sail, tour, trek, trip, walk
- **05** cycle, drive, jaunt, march, motor, pilot, skate, steam, visit
- **06** aviate, cruise, flight, outing, paddle, ramble, safari, voyage
- **07** commute, holiday, journey, mission, shuttle
- **09** excursion, freewheel, hitch-hike, migration, orienteer
- **10** expedition, pilgrimage
- **11** exploration

traveller

03 rep **05** agent, Gypsy, hiker, nomad, rider, tramp **06** bagman, spacer, tinker, tourer, viator **07** aviator, bushman, drifter, drummer, migrant, rambler, tourist, tripper, vagrant, voyager **08** aviatrix, commuter, explorer, roadster, salesman, seafarer, spaceman, wanderer, wayfarer **09** itinerant, passenger, peregrine, sightseer **10** commercial, saleswoman, spacewoman **11** salesperson **12** excursionist, globetrotter, holidaymaker **14** representative **15** knight of the road

travelling

◇ *anagram indicator*

04 road, rode **06** mobile, moving, roving **07** migrant, nomadic, roaming, sailing, touring, vagrant **08** homeless **09** itinerant, itinerary, migrating, migratory, on the move, on the road, unsettled, wandering, wayfaring **11** peripatetic

travel-worn

05 tired, weary **07** seasick, waygone, wayworn **08** footsore **09** jet-lagged **10** saddle-sore **11** travel-weary

traverse

03 lap, ply, ren, rin, run **04** deny, ford, pace, plod, race, ride, roam, span, walk, wear, wind, wing **05** cover, cross, motor, range, stump, trace, track, tramp **06** bridge, denial, oppose, overgo, parade, screen, thwart, voyage, wander **07** barrier, curtain, descend, dispute, examine, measure, oblique, parapet **08** consider, crossing, go across, pass over, progress, walk over **09** adversity, go through, negotiate, partition **10** contradict, crosspiece **11** obstruction, pass through, peregrinate **12** travel across **13** contradiction, travel through

travesty

04 sham **05** farce, spoof **06** parody, send-up, wind-up **07** apology, mockery, take-off **08** disguise **09** black mass, burlesque, tall story **10** caricature, corruption, distortion, perversion

trawl

04 comb, hunt, sift, wade **06** search **07** look for **11** investigate

treacherous

03 icy **05** dirty, false, Punic, risky, snaky **06** guiled, trappy, unsafe, untrue **08** disloyal, perilous, slippery **09** dangerous, deceitful, faithless, hazardous, two-timing **10** perfidious, precarious, traitorous, unfaithful, unreliable **11** duplicitous **12** backstabbing, false-hearted **13** double-hearted, hollow-hearted, untrustworthy **14** double-crossing

treacherously

07 falsely **08** mala fide **10** disloyally **11** deceitfully, faithlessly **12** perfidiously

treachery

07 treason **08** bad faith, betrayal, sabotage, trahison **09** duplicity, falseness, Judas kiss, perfidity, two-timing **10** disloyalty, hollowness, infidelity, Punic faith **11** fides Punica, traitorhood **12** backstabbing **13** deceitfulness, double-dealing, faithlessness **14** double-crossing, unfaithfulness

tread
02 go **04** beat, form, gait, hike, pace, plod, step, trek, walk **05** clamp, clump, crush, dance, march, press, spurn, stamp, trace, track, trade, tramp **06** squash, stramp, stride, trudge, walk on **07** chalaza, flatten, footing, oppress, trample **08** business, copulate, footfall, footmark, footstep **09** footprint, press down **11** cicatricula

• **tread on someone's toes**
03 irk, vex **04** hurt **05** annoy, upset **06** bruise, injure, offend **07** affront **08** infringe **10** discommode, disgruntle **13** inconvenience

treason
06 mutiny **07** perfidy **08** sedition, trahison **09** duplicity, rebellion, treachery **10** disloyalty, subversion **11** lese-majesty, leze-majesté, leze-majesty, perduellion, traitorhood **12** disaffection **14** traitorousness

treasonable
05 false **08** disloyal, mutinous **09** faithless, seditious **10** perfidious, rebellious, subversive, traitorous, unfaithful

treasure
03 gem **04** cash, gems, gold, love **05** adore, cache, guard, hoard, money, prize, value **06** dote on, esteem, jewels, revere, riches, taonga, wealth **07** cherish, darling, fortune, idolize, worship **08** hold dear, preserve **09** valuables **11** masterpiece, pride and joy **13** think highly of **14** crème de la crème

treasurer
06 bursar, fiscal, purser **07** cashier, steward **08** quaestor **10** camerlengo, camerlingo, cash-keeper **11** purse-bearer

treasury
04 bank, fisc, fisk **05** cache, chest, funds, hoard, money, store, vault **06** assets, camera, corpus **07** bursary, capital, coffers **08** finances, revenues **09** exchequer, resources, thesaurus **10** repository, storehouse

treat
◇ *anagram indicator*
02 do **03** buy, fun, rub, tar, tub, use, vat, vet, wax **04** cure, gift, give, heal, tend, view, wine, worm **05** amuse, apply, besee, cover, dress, feast, lay on, nurse, paint, party, prime, put on, serve, smear, stand, study, waste, wheel **06** doctor, handle, manage, outing, parley, pay for, regale, regard, review, thrill **07** banquet, care for, delight, discuss, present, provide, take out **08** attend to, consider, deal with, medicate, pleasure, spread on, surprise **09** amusement, cover with, enjoyment, entertain, excursion, look after, negotiate, poeticize, tartarize **10** indulgence, minister to, pay the bill **11** celebration, foot the bill, negotiation **13** behave towards, entertainment, gratification

treatable
07 curable **08** moderate, operable **09** medicable, reparable, tractable **10** reformable, remediable **11** rectifiable

treatise
05 essay, ethic, paper, study, summa, tract **06** Cybele, system, thesis **07** pandect **08** Almagest, lapidary, pamphlet, prodrome, tractate **09** cosmology, discourse, festilogy, festology, monograph **10** arithmetic, dendrology, exposition, halieutics **11** gnomonology **12** disquisition, dissertation

treatment
◇ *anagram indicator*
03 EST, use **04** care, cure, deal **05** doing, usage **06** action, demean, notice, reason, remedy **07** affront, conduct, dealing, demaine, demayne, demeane, healing, measure, nursing, quarter, regimen, surgery, therapy **08** cosmesis, coverage, dealings, handling **09** behaviour, discursus, going-over **10** asepticism, discussion, management, medicament, medication, observance **12** manipulation, therapeutics **13** antisepticism **14** discountenance

treaty
04 bond, deal, pact **05** peace **06** pledge **07** bargain, compact, concord **08** alliance, assiento, contract, covenant, entreaty, protocol **09** agreement, concordat **10** convention, engagement **11** negotiation **12** pacification

Treaties and agreements include:

03 **Edo** (Treaty of)
04 **Jay's** (Treaty), **Rome** (Treaty of), **SALT**
05 **Baden, Dover** (Treaty of), **Ghent** (Treaty of), **Kyoto** (accord), **Lyons** (Treaty of), **Paris** (Treaties of), **Union**
06 **Amiens** (Treaty of), **Berlin** (Treaty of), **London** (Treaties of), **Madrid** (Treaty of), **Passau** (Treaty of), **Poland** (Partitions of), **Tilsit** (Treaties of), **Vienna** (Treaties of)
07 **Barrier** (Treaties), **Dresden** (Treaty of), **Nanjing** (Treaty of), **Nystadt** (Treaty of), **Tianjin** (Treaty of), **Utrecht** (Peace of)
08 **Brussels** (Treaty of), **Kanagawa** (Treaty of), **Lausanne** (Treaty of), **Pyrenees** (Treaty of the), **Tientsin** (Treaty of)
09 **Bucharest** (Treaties of), **Hay-Herrán** (Treaty), **Karlowitz** (Treaty of), **Pressburg** (Treaty of), **St Germain** (Treaty of)
10 **Adrianople** (Treaty of), **Anglo-Iraqi** (Treaty), **Maastricht** (Treaty), **Magna Carta, Paris Pacts, San Stefano** (Treaty of), **Versailles** (Treaty of), **Warsaw Pact, Washington** (Treaty of), **Westphalia** (Peace of)
11 **Fort Stanwix** (Treaties of), **Locarno Pact, Vereeniging** (Peace of), **Westminster** (Treaty of)
12 **Brest-Litovsk** (Treaty of), **Lateran Pacts**
13 **North Atlantic** (Treaty), **Social Chapter, Triple Entente**
14 **Hague Agreement, Hoare-Laval Pact**
15 **Entente Cordiale, Munich Agreement**

treble
04 high **05** sharp **06** piping, shrill, triple **07** soprano **09** threefold **11** high-pitched

tree
04 bush, limb, spar **05** shrub **06** corner, wooden **07** gallows **08** pedigree

See also **palm**; **pine**; **rubber**

Tree types include:

03 nut
04 palm
05 covin, fruit
06 bonsai, citron, citrus, forest, timber
07 conifer, dwarfed
08 hardwood, softwood
09 broad-leaf, Christmas, deciduous, evergreen
10 ornamental

Trees include:

02 bo, ti
03 ash, asp, bay, bel, box, elm, fig, fir, gum, ita, jak, koa, may, nim, oak, sal, tea, ule, yew
04 acer, akee, arar, atap, bito, coco, cola, dali, dhak, dika, dita, eugh, gean, holm, hule, ilex, jack, kola, lime, lind, mate, mowa, neem, nipa, olea, ombu, palm, pear, pine, plum, poon, rata, rimu, shea, sorb, teak, teil, toon, upas, yang
05 ackee, afara, alder, apple, aspen, assai, balsa, beech, birch, cacao, carob, cedar, china, ebony, elder, fruit, guava, hazel, holly, karri, kauri, larch, lemon, lilac, lotus, mango, maple, morus, olive, papaw, peach, pecan, piñon, pipal, plane, rowan, salix, thorn, tulip, yucca
06 acacia, almond, bamboo, banana, banyan, baobab, bonsai, cashew, cassia, cherry, damson, gingko, jarrah, laurel, linden, papaya, pawpaw, poplar, prunus, quince, rubber, sapele, spruce, walnut, willow
07 apricot, Banksia, blue gum, conifer, cork oak, cypress, dogwood, hickory, quassia, redwood, sequoia, wych elm
08 chestnut, date palm, Dutch elm, ghost gum, hardwood, hawthorn, hornbeam, mahogany, mandarin, mangrove, mulberry, oleaster, softwood, sycamore, tamarisk
09 araucaria, blackwood, Chile pine, crab apple, deciduous, evergreen, jacaranda, kauri-pine, leylandii, melaleuca, paperbark, persimmon, Scots pine, stone pine,

whitebeam, wych-hazel
10 blackthorn, breadfruit, cottonwood, Douglas fir, eucalyptus, ornamental, sandalwood, witch hazel
11 bottle brush, bristlecone, coconut palm, copper beech, false acacia, golden larch, London plane, mountain ash, pussy willow, silver birch, silver maple
12 monkey puzzle, Monterey pine, Wellingtonia
13 angel's trumpet, horse chestnut, Japanese maple, sweet chestnut, weeping willow
14 cedar of Lebanon, Lombardy poplar
15 bristlecone pine

• abounding in trees
04 elmy, oaky, piny
• clump of trees
03 mot **04** mott **05** bluff, copse, motte, plump **06** spinny **07** spinney
• embedded tree
04 snag
• isolated tree
04 ombu
• tree stump
04 runt
• tree trunk
03 log **04** bole, butt, stud **06** ricker

tree-planted walk
04 xyst **06** xystos, xystus

trek
04 drag, hike, plod, roam, rove, slog, trip, walk, yomp **05** march, stage, tramp **06** ramble, safari, trudge
07 journey, migrate, odyssey, traipse
09 migration **10** expedition

trellis
03 net **04** grid, mesh **05** grate **06** grille
07 grating, lattice, network, treille
08 espalier **09** framework
11 latticework **12** reticulation

tremble
◇ *anagram indicator*
04 rock **05** quake, shake **06** dither, dodder, hotter, judder, quaver, quiver, shiver, tremor, wobble, wuther
07 shudder, vibrate, whither
09 vibration **13** tremulousness

trembling
◇ *anagram indicator*
04 yips **06** quaver, shakes **07** quaking, rocking, shaking **09** juddering, quavering, quivering, shivering, tremulous, vibration **10** heart-quake, shuddering **11** oscillation, trepidation

tremendous
04 huge, vast **05** great **06** wicked
07 amazing, corking, howling, immense, massive **08** colossal, dreadful, enormous, gigantic, smashing, terrific, towering
09 wonderful **10** formidable, impressive, incredible, marvellous, prodigious, remarkable, stupendous, thundering **11** exceptional, sensational, spectacular **13** extraordinary **14** out of this world

tremendously
04 very **06** highly, really **07** acutely, awfully, greatly, utterly **08** severely
09 decidedly, extremely, intensely, unusually **10** remarkably, thoroughly, uncommonly **11** exceedingly, excessively, frightfully
12 immoderately, inordinately, terrifically, unreasonably
13 exceptionally **15** extraordinarily

tremor
05 quake, shake, shock **06** dindle, dinnle, quaver, quiver, shiver, thrill, wobble **07** shudder, temblor, tremble
09 agitation, foreshock, marsquake, moonquake, quavering, trembling, vibration **10** earthquake, titubation

tremulous
◇ *anagram indicator*
05 aspen, jumpy, shaky, timid **06** afraid, aspine, scared **07** anxious, excited, fearful, jittery, nervous, quivery, shaking, trembly **08** agitated, timorous, unsteady, wavering
09 quavering, quivering, shivering, trembling, vibrating **10** frightened

trench
03 cut, fur, pit, sap **04** dike, dyke, foss, furr, grip, leat, leet, line, moat, rill
05 boyau, ditch, drain, fosse, gripe, verge **06** border, furrow, gullet, gutter, trough **07** channel, cunette, slidder
08 encroach, entrench, parallel, waterway **09** earthwork **10** excavation
12 entrenchment
See also **ocean**

trenchant
05 acute, blunt, clear, sharp, terse
06 astute, biting **07** acerbic, caustic, cutting, mordant, pungent **08** clear-cut, distinct, emphatic, forceful, incisive, scathing, vigorous
09 effective **10** forthright, no-nonsense, perceptive **11** penetrating, unequivocal **13** perspicacious

trend
03 fad **04** bend, bent, flow, look, mode, rage, tide, turn, wind **05** craze, drift, style, vogue **06** course, downer, latest
07 bearing, current, fashion, leaning
08 downturn, tendency **09** bandwagon, consensus, direction, downswing
10 mainstream, rising tide **11** inclination, radical chic **13** name of the game

trendsetter
05 model **06** leader, new man
07 pioneer **08** new woman
09 innovator, modernist, modern man
11 modern woman, trailblazer
12 avant-gardist **13** avant-gardiste, groundbreaker

trendy
02 in **03** hip, now **04** cool **05** funky, natty **06** groovy, latest, modish, snazzy, with it **07** right-on, stylish, voguish **10** all the rage **11** fashionable
13 up-to-the-minute

trepidation
04 fear **05** alarm, dread, worry
06 dismay, fright, nerves, qualms, tremor, unease **07** anxiety, emotion, jitters, shaking **08** disquiet
09 agitation, cold sweat, quivering, trembling **10** excitement, misgivings, uneasiness **11** butterflies, nervousness, palpitation
12 apprehension, perturbation
13 consternation

trespass
03 sin **05** poach, wrong **06** invade, offend **07** impinge, intrude, offence, violate **08** encroach, infringe, invasion, obdurate, poaching **09** intrusion, violation **10** transgress, wrongdoing
12 encroachment, infringement, misdemeanour **13** contravention, transgression

trespasser
06 sinner **07** burglar, poacher
08 criminal, evil-doer, intruder, offender **10** delinquent, encroacher
12 transgressor

tress
04 curl, hair, lock, tail **05** braid, bunch, plait, swits **06** strand, switch **07** pigtail, ringlet **08** trammels

trial
03 try **04** bane, case, exam, pest, test
05 assay, check, cross, dummy, grief, pilot, probe, study **06** appeal, assess, assize, bother, burden, dry run, hassle, misery, ordeal, sample, screen, trinal, try out, try-out **07** analyse, approof, attempt, contest, examine, hearing, inquiry, lawsuit, retrial, scratch, testing, test run, trouble **08** appraise, audition, distress, dummy run, endeavor, evaluate, hardship, nuisance, practice, tribunal, vexation **09** adventure, adversity, annoyance, endeavour, probation, rehearsal, selection, suffering, threefold **10** affliction, experiment, litigation, temptation
11 approbation, competition, cross to bear, examination, exploratory, investigate, provisional, tribulation
12 cause célèbre, experimental, probationary **13** pain in the neck
14 experiment with **15** thorn in the flesh

triangle

Triangles include:

05 right
07 Bermuda, eternal, Pascal's, scalene, similar, warning
09 cocked hat, congruent, isosceles, spherical
11 acute-angled, equilateral, right-angled
12 obtuse-angled

triangular
08 trigonal, trigonic **09** trigonous
10 three-sided, trilateral, triquetral
11 triquetrous **13** three-cornered
14 triangle-shaped
• triangular piece
04 gair, gare, gore **05** fichu, godet

tribal
05 class, group **06** ethnic, family, native **08** gentilic **09** sectional **10** indigenous

tribe
03 iwi, rod **04** clan, hapu, race, sept **05** blood, breed, caste, class, group, house, ngati, stock **06** branch, family, nation, people **07** dynasty **08** division **11** ethnic group

Tribes of Israel:

03 Dan, Gad
05 Asher, Judah
06 Reuben, Simeon
07 Ephraim, Zebulun
08 Benjamin, Issachar, Manasseh, Naphtali

See also **Aboriginal**; **African**; **American**; **Asian**; **European**

tribulation
03 woe **04** blow, care, pain **05** curse, grief, trial, worry **06** burden, misery, ordeal, sorrow **07** anxiety, reverse, travail, trouble **08** distress, hardship, vexation **09** adversity, heartache, suffering **10** affliction, misfortune **11** unhappiness **12** wretchedness

tribunal
03 bar, EAT **04** rota **05** bench, court, trial **07** hearing **09** Areopagus, committee **11** examination, inquisition **12** confessional **13** kangaroo court

tribune
04 bema

tributary
04 fork **05** bogan, river **06** branch, feeder, stream **08** influent **09** confluent **10** head-stream **12** contributing

tribute
03 due, fee, tax **04** cain, duty, gift, kain, levy, scat, skat, toll **05** gavel, paean, proof, scatt **06** charge, credit, eulogy, homage, honour, praise, tariff **07** payment, pension, present, respect **08** accolade, applause, encomium, evidence, good word, offering, Rome-scot **09** drift-land, gratitude, panegyric, Rome-penny **10** compliment, dedication **11** good opinion, high opinion, Peter's pence, recognition, testimonial **12** commendation, contribution **15** acknowledgement

trice
02 mo **03** sec **04** haul, tick **05** flash, jiffy, shake **06** minute, moment, pulley, second **07** instant **09** twinkling

trichosanthin
01 Q

trick
◇ *anagram indicator*
02 do **03** art, con, fix, fob, fun, gag, kid, rig, tip, toy **04** dupe, fake, feat, flam, fool, gift, gull, hang, have, hoax, jape, joke, mock, pass, pawk, ploy, rook, ruse, scam, sell, sham, trap, trim, turn, vice, wile **05** antic, bluff, bogus, caper, cheat, cozen, dodge, false, flair, fraud, glaik, gleek, knack, plant, prank, quirk, skill, skite, skyte, spell, stall, stunt, watch **06** adroit, antick, begunk, chouse, deceit, delude, device, diddle, double, ersatz, forged, frolic, genius, have on, illude, juggle, lead on, mirage, outwit, palter, rip-off, secret, shavie, take in, talent **07** ability, anticke, antique, beguile, chicane, deceive, defraud, faculty, fantasy, fast one, feigned, frame-up, knowhow, leg-pull, mislead, pliskie, roughie, skylark, slinter, swindle, trinket, wrinkle **08** artifice, capacity, doubling, facility, flimflam, gimcrack, hoodwink, illusion, jimcrack, prestige, skin game, subtlety **09** deception, defective, expedient, gold brick, imitation, manoeuvre, mousetrap, stratagem, technique, underplot **10** apparition, artificial, capability, hocus-pocus, pleasantry, subterfuge, subtleness, under-craft, unreliable **11** conjuration, counter-cast, counterfeit, galliardise, hornswoggle, legerdemain, monkey shine, pull one over **12** starting hole, take for a ride, trick of light **13** double-shuffle, practical joke, sleight of hand **14** pull a fast one on, three-card monte

• **number of tricks**
03 nap **04** book, slam

• **trick out**
04 do up, fard, tiff **05** adorn, array **06** attire, bedeck, doll up, tart up **07** dress up, trick up **08** decorate, ornament, spruce up

trickery
04 trap **05** fraud, guile **06** deceit, ropery, slight **07** cantrip, cunning, dodgery, jookery, joukery, sleight **08** artifice, cheating, illusion, jugglery, practice, pretence, wiliness **09** chicanery, deception, duplicity, imposture, stratagem, swindling **10** conveyance, dishonesty, hanky-panky, hocus-pocus, imposition, shenanigan, subterfuge **11** contrivance, legerdemain, shenanigans, skulduggery **12** skullduggery **13** double-dealing, funny business, jiggery-pokery, sleight of hand **14** joukery-pawkery, monkey business **15** smoke and mirrors

trickle
03 ren, rin, run **04** drib, drip, drop, leak, ooze, seep **05** exude **06** filter, gutter **07** dribble, driblet, drizzle, dropple, seepage **08** dribblet, ticklish **09** percolate **10** flow slowly, precarious

trickster
04 hood, rook **05** cheat, fraud, joker, rogue, shark **06** con man, dodger, hoaxer, rascal **07** cozener, diddler, hoodlum, hustler, tricker **08** con woman, deceiver, impostor, swindler **09** artificer, charlatan, con artist, fraudster, pretender, tregetour **10** dissembler, mountebank **11** illy whacker

tricky
◇ *anagram indicator*
03 sly **04** foxy, wily **05** dicey, dodgy, elvan, elven, nasty **06** artful, crafty, elfish, elvish, knotty, pretty, shifty, subtle, thorny **07** awkward, cunning, devious, finicky **08** delicate, scheming, slippery, ticklish **09** deceitful, difficult, sensitive **11** complicated, legerdemain, problematic

tried
06 proved, proven, tested **07** trusted **08** reliable **10** dependable **11** established, trustworthy

trifle
03 bit, fig, toy **04** dash, doit, drop, fool, iota, play, song, spot **05** dally, flirt, sport, straw, touch, trace, wally **06** bauble, dabble, daidle, faddle, fiddle, fisgig, fizgig, frivol, geegaw, gewgaw, little, meddle, niggle, paddle, palter, peddle, piffle, pingle, potter, tiddle, trivia, wanton **07** flamfew, fribble, nothing, old song, quiddle, trinket **08** falderal, fal de rol, flea-bite, folderol, niffnaff, whim-wham **09** bagatelle, mess about, plaything **10** dilly-dally, knick-knack, mess around, triviality **11** fiddlestick, inessential, small amount **12** fiddle-faddle **13** play the wanton

trifling
04 idle **05** empty, minor, petty, potty, seely, silly, small **06** faddle, fallal, futile, paltry, slight **07** fooling, foolish, puerile, shallow, trivial **08** baubling, boy's play, childish, fiddling, frippery, immoment, nonsense, nugatory, piddling, piffling **09** dalliance, desipient, fribbling, fribblish, frivolous, whifflery, worthless **10** negligible **11** superficial, unimportant **12** fiddle-faddle **13** insignificant **14** inconsiderable **15** inconsequential

trigger
04 spur **05** catch, cause, lever, start **06** elicit, prompt, set off, switch **07** produce, provoke **08** activate, generate, initiate, spark off, stimulus, touch off **09** day-length **10** bring about **11** set in action, set in motion

trill
04 lilt, pipe, roll, sing **05** flute, shake, twirl **06** quaver, warble **07** trundle

trim
◇ *head deletion indicator*
◇ *tail deletion indicator*
03 cut, dub, fit, fur, lop, net, way **04** barb, chop, clip, cool, crop, dink, dock, edge, face, form, lace, neat, nett, pare, slim, snip, snod, tidy, tosh, trig **05** adorn, array, braid, cheat, dress, frill, guard, natty, order, prune, roach, ruche, shape, shave, shear, slick, smart, smirk, state, tight, trick **06** adjust, border, dapper, donsie, edging, fettle, fit out, fringe, health, humour, neaten, plight, reduce, smooth, snazzy, spruce, svelte, temper, thrash, tidy up, trimly

07 arrange, balance, compact, curtail, cut down, festoon, fitness, garnish, orderly, slender **08** clean-cut, contract, decorate, decrease, diminish, fittings, ornament, trimming, well-kept **09** condition, cut back on, embellish, scale down, shipshape, underbear **10** decoration **11** clean-limbed, disposition, in good order, presentable, streamlined, well-dressed, well-groomed **12** spick-and-span **13** well-turned-out

trimming
03 end **04** gimp, gymp, trim **05** braid, extra, frill, guard, guimp, robin **06** border, edging, fringe, paring, piping, robing **07** cascade, cutting, falbala, garnish, macramé, macrami, marabou **08** clipping, frou-frou, furbelow, marabout **09** accessory, adornment, balancing, garniture, passement **10** decoration **11** fimbriation **13** accompaniment, embellishment, ornamentation, passementerie

Trinidad and Tobago
02 TT **03** TTO

trinket
04 seal **05** bijou, charm, jewel, trick **06** bauble, doodad, doodah, geegaw, gewgaw, trifle **07** flamfew, trankum **08** delicacy, gimcrack, kickshaw, ornament, whim-wham **09** bagatelle, kickshaws **10** knick-knack **11** whigmaleery **12** whigmaleerie

trio
05 triad **06** triune, troika **07** musette, trilogy, trinity, triplet **08** terzetto, triunity **09** threesome **10** triplicity **11** triumvirate

See also **three**; **threesome**

trip
◇ *anagram indicator*
03 hop, ren, rin, run **04** buzz, fall, flip, high, hurl, kilt, link, ride, sail, skip, slip, spin, tilt, tour **05** caper, dance, dream, drive, error, flock, foray, gaffe, jaunt, jolly, lapse, slide, spurn, waltz, whirl **06** booboo, bummer, gambol, howler, outing, sortie, spring, tiptoe, tootle, totter, tumble, vision, voyage **07** bloomer, blunder, clanger, fantasy, faux pas, journey, mistake, stagger, stumble **08** freak-out, illusion **09** excursion, false step **10** apparition, expedition, experience, inaccuracy **13** hallucination **15** lose your footing

• **trip up**
04 trap **05** catch, snare, trick **06** ambush, outwit, waylay **07** ensnare **08** catch out, fall over, outsmart, surprise **09** wrongfoot **10** disconcert **15** throw off balance

tripe
03 rot **04** blah, bosh, guff, tosh **05** balls, hooey, trash **06** bunkum, drivel **07** baloney, eyewash, garbage, hogwash, inanity, rhubarb, rubbish, twaddle **08** claptrap, entrails, malarkey, nonsense, tommyrot **09** bullswool, moonshine, poppycock **10** balderdash

triple
04 trio **05** third, triad **06** treble, triune, troika **07** perfect, trilogy, trinity, triplet **08** three-ply, three-way, triunity **09** threefold, threesome **10** sdrucciola, three times, tripartite, triplicate, triplicity **11** triumvirate

tripod
03 cat, pod **06** trivet **08** triangle **09** brand-iron

tripper
07 grockle, tourist, voyager **09** sightseer, traveller **12** excursionist, holidaymaker

trite
04 dull, worn **05** banal, corny, stale, stock, tired **06** beaten, common **07** cliché'd, routine, worn-out **08** clichéed, cornball, ordinary, overdone, overused, overworn, tritical, truistic, well-worn **09** hackneyed, rinky-dink **10** threadbare, uninspired, unoriginal **11** commonplace, Mickey Mouse, novelettish, predictable, stereotyped, well-trodden **12** run-of-the-mill **13** platitudinous

tritium
01 T **13** heavy hydrogen

triton
03 eft **04** evet, newt

triumph
03 hit, joy, win **04** beat, coup, crow, feat, pomp **05** exult, gloat, glory, paean, revel, trump **06** defeat, insult **07** conquer, elation, mastery, pageant, prevail, prosper, rejoice, succeed, success, swagger, victory **08** conquest, dominate, jubilate, overcome, overcrow, vanquish, walkover **09** celebrate, exultance, exultancy, festivity, happiness, overwhelm, rejoicing, sensation, win the day **10** attainment, exultation, jubilation, observance **11** achievement, celebration, gain mastery **12** masterstroke **13** flying colours **14** accomplishment

• **expression of triumph**
02 ha, ho, io **03** aha, hah, hey, hoa, hoh, Jai, oho, olé **04** ha-ha **05** heigh, there **06** yippee **07** so there

triumphant
05 proud **06** elated, joyful **07** crowing, winning **08** boastful, exultant, gloating, glorious, jubilant **09** cock-a-hoop, rejoicing, triumphal **10** conquering, successful, swaggering, victorious **11** celebratory **12** prize-winning

trivia
03 pap **06** Hecate **07** details, trifles **08** minutiae **12** trivialities **13** irrelevancies **14** technicalities

trivial
04 bald **05** banal, dinky, minor, petty, small, trite **06** flimsy, frothy, little, measly, paltry **08** everyday, gimcrack, piddling, piffling, snippety, trifling **09** frivolous, quibbling, rinky-dink, small beer, worthless **10** incidental, negligible, peppercorn, vernacular **11** commonplace, meaningless, unimportant **12** cutting no ice, pettifogging **13** insignificant, no great shakes **14** inconsiderable **15** inconsequential, of no consequence

triviality
06 detail, trifle **07** nothing **08** banality, frippery, nonsense, pretence **09** frivolity, pettiness, puerility, smallness **10** nothingism **11** foolishness **12** technicality, unimportance **13** worthlessness **14** insignificance **15** meaninglessness

trivialize
07 devalue, scoff at **08** belittle, minimize, play down **09** underplay **10** depreciate, undervalue **12** Hollywoodize **13** underestimate

troglodyte
04 wren **11** cave-dweller

troll
03 elf **04** drow, harl, jinn, roll, rove, spin, trow **05** dwarf, gnome, pooka **06** allure, goblin, ramble, stroll **07** trundle **08** trolling **09** circulate **10** repetition

trolley
04 corf **05** bogey, bogie, brute, dolly, truck **07** tramcar **09** caddie car **10** caddie cart, traymobile **11** dinner-wagon

trollop
03 pro, pug, tom **04** bawd, dell, drab, moll, punk, road, stew, tart **05** brass, broad, quail, quiff, stale, tramp, trull, wench, whore **06** bulker, callet, geisha, harlot, hooker, mutton, plover **07** cocotte, floozie, hetaera, hostess, hustler, lorette, polecat, rent-boy, venture **08** bona-roba, callgirl, dolly-mop, magdalen, strumpet **09** courtesan, hierodule, loose fish **10** cockatrice, convertite, fancy woman, loose woman, prostitute, rough trade, vizard-mask **11** fallen woman, fille de joie, laced mutton, night-walker, poule de luxe, public woman, working girl **12** fille des rues, painted woman, scarlet woman, street-walker **13** grande cocotte **14** lady of the night, woman of the town

troop
02 go, tp **03** mob **04** army, band, body, crew, gang, herd, kern, pack, team, turm, unit, walk **05** bunch, crowd, flock, group, horde, kerne, march, squad, swarm, turme **06** parade, school, stream, throng, troupe, trudge **07** cavalry, company, consort, convoys, gunners, militia, traipse **08** assemble, brigades, division, fighters, military, platoons, soldiers, squadron **09** commandos, fusiliers, gathering,

multitude, regiments, squadrons **10** assemblage, contingent, paratroops, servicemen **11** armed forces, infantrymen **12** paratroopers, servicewomen

trophy

03 cup, pot **05** award, prize **06** spoils **07** laurels, memento **08** souvenir **10** silverware

Trophies include:

02 TT
05 FA Cup
06 Fed Cup
07 Auld Mug, Gold Cup, Grey Cup, Uber Cup
08 Davis Cup, Ryder Cup, The Ashes, World Cup
09 Aresti Cup, Curtis Cup, Thomas Cup, Walker Cup
10 Masters Cup, Solheim Cup, Stanley Cup, Winston Cup
11 Admiral's Cup, America's Cup, Eschborn Cup, Kinnaird Cup, McCarthy Cup
12 Camanachd Cup, Lugano Trophy
13 Heisman trophy, Leonard Trophy, Sam Maguire Cup
14 Continental Cup, Jesters' Club Cup
15 Champions Trophy, Lilienthal Medal, Louis Vuitton Cup, Nascar Nextel Cup, Scotch Whisky Cup

See also **award**

tropical

03 hot **05** humid **06** steamy, sultry, torrid **07** boiling, very hot **08** stifling **09** luxuriant **10** boiling hot, figurative, sweltering

trot

03 jog, ren, rin, run **04** crib, pace **05** crone **06** bustle, canter, scurry **07** dogtrot, heigh-ho, jogtrot, passage, scamper, scuttle, tripple **08** heigh-how

• **on the trot**

04 busy **06** in a row, in turn **10** back to back **12** continuously, sequentially, successively **13** consecutively **15** uninterruptedly

• **trot out**

06 adduce, drag up, recite, relate, repeat **07** bring up, exhibit **08** bring out, rehearse **09** reiterate **12** bring forward

troubadour

04 poet **06** singer **08** jongleur, mariachi, minstrel, trouvère, trouveur **09** balladeer, cantabank **11** Minnesinger

trouble

◇ *anagram indicator*

03 ado, ail, dog, fix, jam, noy, vex, woe **04** care, fash, fuss, gram, heat, mess, moil, pain, rile, work **05** annoy, grame, grief, kaugh, muddy, pains, sturt, trial, upset, visit, weigh, worry **06** barrat, bother, burden, corner, cumber, defect, effort, harass, hassle, hatter, kiaugh, molest, pickle, put out, sadden, scrape, shadow, shtook, shtuck, strife, tsuris, tumult, unease, unrest **07** afflict, agitate, ailment, anxiety, concern, disease, disturb, failure, illness, mismake, perplex, perturb, problem, schtook, schtuck, thought, torment, travail, tsouris **08** disorder, disquiet, distress, exercise, exertion, fighting, hardship, headache, hot water, irritate, nuisance, problems, shutdown, stalling, stopping, struggle, upheaval, vexation **09** adversity, agitation, annoyance, attention, breakdown, commotion, complaint, heartache, packing-up, suffering, tight spot, weigh down **10** affliction, conking-out, cutting-out, difficulty, disability, discommode, disconcert, irritation, misfortune, solicitude, uneasiness **11** botheration, disturbance, malfunction, tribulation **13** inconvenience, make the effort **14** solicitousness, thoughtfulness

troubled

◇ *anagram indicator*

05 tense, upset **06** afraid, on edge, uneasy **07** anxious, fearful, fretful, nervous, uptight, worried **08** agonized, bothered, dismayed, strained **09** concerned, disturbed, ill at ease, perturbed **10** disquieted, distracted, distraught, distressed, frightened **11** overwrought **12** apprehensive **14** hot and bothered

troublemaker

05 mixer **07** inciter, stirrer **08** agitator **09** bovver boy **10** incendiary, instigator, ringleader **12** rabble-rouser **13** mischief-maker

troublesome

◇ *anagram indicator*

04 hard **05** pesky, rowdy, spiny **06** infest, plaguy, taxing, thorny, tricky, trying, unruly **07** awkward, brickle, irksome, plaguey, testing **08** annoying, exacting, fashious, tiresome **09** demanding, difficult, laborious, turbulent, vexatious, wearisome, worrisome **10** bothersome, disturbing, irritating, perturbing, plaguesome, rebellious **11** importunate, mischievous **12** incommodious, inconvenient **13** insubordinate, unco-operative

trough

03 gum, hod, tie, tye **04** crib, duct **05** chute, ditch, drain, flame, gully, hutch, shoot, shute, stock, trunk **06** backet, feeder, furrow, groove, gutter, hollow, hopper, manger, sluice, straik, strake, trench, valley **07** channel, conduit, launder **08** sheep-dip **09** sand table **10** depression **12** seasoning-tub **13** feeding trough **14** watering-trough

trounce

04 beat, best, drub, lick, rout **05** crush, paste, thump **06** defeat, hammer, harass, indict, punish, rebuke, thrash, wallop **07** clobber, shellac **09** overwhelm, slaughter

troupe

03 set **04** band, cast **05** group, troop **06** ballet **07** company

trouper

05 actor **06** player **07** artiste, old hand, veteran **08** thespian **09** performer **10** theatrical **11** entertainer

trousers

04 bags, daks, keks **05** cords, jeans, kecks, Levis®, longs, pants, trews **06** Capris, chinos, denims, shorts, slacks, trouse **07** gauchos, nankins, trouses **08** bloomers, breeches, bumsters, flannels, nankeens, overalls, trossers, trowsers **09** corduroys, dungarees, moleskins, strossers **10** Capri pants, cargo pants, drainpipes, Oxford bags, spongebags **12** innominables, reach-me-downs **14** indescribables, inexpressibles

• **part of trousers**

03 fly

trout

04 peal, peel **05** sewen, sewin **06** finnac **07** finnack, finnock, herling, hirling, rainbow **08** gillaroo, whitling **09** steelhead **10** fingerling, squeteague

Troy

01 t **05** Ilium

truancy

07 absence, jigging, skiving, wagging **08** shirking **11** absenteeism, French leave, malingering

truant

03 jig, kip, wag **04** bunk **05** dodge, hooky, idler, miche, mitch, mooch, shirk, skive **06** absent, desert, dodger, hookey, skiver **07** goof off, missing, runaway, shirker, vagrant **08** absentee, deserter, malinger, skive off **09** play hooky **10** malingerer, play the wag, play truant

truce

03 pax **04** lull, rest, stay **05** break, fains, let-up, peace **06** barley, fains I **07** respite, treague **08** fainites, interval **09** armistice, ceasefire, cessation **10** moratorium, suspension **12** intermission, pacification

truck

02 PU **03** HGV, ute, van **04** skip, tram **05** bogey, bogie, chore, dolly, float, lorry, trade, wagon **06** bakkie, barter, crummy, dumper, pick-up, tipper, waggon **07** bargain, contact, rubbish, traffic, trolley, trundle, utility **08** business, commerce, dealings, exchange **09** honey-cart, persevere, relations **10** connection, honey-wagon, juggernaut **11** association, honey-waggon, intercourse **12** curtain-sider, utility truck **13** communication **14** utility vehicle

truculence

08 defiance, rudeness, violence **09** hostility, pugnacity **11** bellicosity **12** belligerence, disobedience

14 aggressiveness 15 bad-temperedness, quarrelsomeness

truculent
04 rude 05 cross, cruel 06 fierce, savage, sullen 07 defiant, hostile, violent 09 bellicose, combative 10 aggressive, pugnacious 11 bad-tempered, belligerent, contentious, disobedient, ill-tempered, quarrelsome 12 antagonistic, discourteous, obstreperous 13 argumentative, disrespectful

trudge
03 pad 04 haul, hike, plod, slog, toil, trek, vamp, walk 05 clump, march, stump, tramp, trash 06 labour, lumber, stodge, taigle, trapes 07 shuffle, splodge, splotch, traipse, trudger 10 pad the hoof

true
04 fast, firm, flat, just, leal, real, trew, very 05 close, exact, loyal, plumb, right, sooth, truly, truth, valid 06 actual, dinkum, honest, proper, trusty, truthy 07 correct, devoted, dinki-di, exactly, factual, genuine, precise, rightly, sincere, staunch, typical 08 absolute, accurate, constant, faithful, honestly, properly, reliable, rightful, straight, truthful, unerring 09 authentic, corrected, correctly, dedicated, perfectly, precisely, steadfast, veracious, veritable, veritably 10 accurately, dependable, fair dinkum, faithfully, honourable, legitimate, truthfully, undeniable, unerringly 11 conformable, true-hearted, trustworthy, veraciously

• **hold true**
02 go

true-blue
04 true 05 loyal 06 trusty 07 devoted, diehard, staunch 08 constant, faithful, orthodox 09 committed, confirmed, dedicated 10 unwavering 12 card-carrying 13 dyed-in-the-wool 14 uncompromising

truism
05 axiom, truth 06 cliché 07 bromide 09 platitude 11 commonplace

truly
04 fegs, full, real, true, very 05 quite 06 certes, indeed, in fact, really, simply, surely, verily 07 exactly, greatly, in truth, rightly, soothly 08 actually, honestly, of a truth, on my word, properly 09 certainly, correctly, extremely, genuinely, in reality, precisely, sincerely, soothlich, veritable 10 constantly, definitely, on my honour, truthfully, undeniably 11 indubitably, steadfastly, undoubtedly 13 exceptionally, o' my conscience, without a doubt 14 upon conscience

trump
03 cap, top 04 ruff 05 blast, outdo 06 allege 07 deceive, eclipse, surpass, triumph, trumpet, upstage 08 Jew's-harp, outshine 13 knock spots off

• **trump up**
04 fake 06 cook up, create, devise, invent, make up 07 concoct, falsify 08 contrive 09 fabricate

trumped-up
04 fake 05 bogus, faked, false 06 made-up, phoney, untrue 08 cooked-up, invented, spurious 09 concocted, contrived, falsified 10 fabricated

trumpery
05 cheap, nasty, showy 06 flashy, shabby, shoddy, tawdry, trashy 07 mockado, rubbish, useless 08 rubbishy, trifling 09 valueless, worthless 10 pasteboard 12 meretricious

trumpet
03 bay, cry, lur 04 call, horn, lure, parp, roar, toot, tuba 05 blare, blast, bugle, chide, clang, conch, shell, shout, sound, trump 06 bellow, cornet, corona, herald, lituus, sennet, summon, tucket 07 alchemy, alchymy, buccina, clarino, clarion, corolla, salpinx, tantara 08 announce, denounce, proclaim, ram's horn, trombone 09 advertise, broadcast, celebrate, last trump 11 taratantara 12 watering-call

• **blow your own trumpet**
04 brag, crow 05 boast, skite, swank 07 show off, talk big 09 loudmouth 15 blow your own horn

trumps

• **ace of trumps**
03 tib

• **no trumps**
02 NT

truncate
03 cut, lop 04 clip, crop, dock, maim, pare, trim 05 prune 06 reduce 07 curtail, shorten 08 cut short, diminish 10 abbreviate

truncheon
04 club, cosh 05 baton, billy, carve, staff, stick 06 batoon, billie, cudgel 09 shillalah 10 billystick, knobkerrie, nightstick, shillelagh

trundle
04 bowl, chug, hoop, roll, spin 05 trill, troll, truck, twirl 06 castor, cruise, roller 07 trindle 09 freewheel

trunk
03 box, leg, log 04 body, bole, bulk, butt, case, nose, runt, stem, tube 05 chest, crate, frame, shaft, snout, stalk, stick, stock, torso 06 coffer 08 Saratoga, sea chest, suitcase 09 proboscis, telescope 10 pea-shooter 11 portmanteau

truss
03 pad, tie 04 bind, hang, pack, prop, stay, wrap 05 brace, joist, shore, strap, strut 06 bundle, corbel, fasten, lace up, pack up, pinion, secure, tether, tuck up 07 bandage, binding, dorlach, make off, support 08 bundle up, buttress, muffle up, string up 09 principal

trust
03 EZT, VCT 04 affy, care, duty, give, hope, tick, trow 05 faith 06 assign, assume, bank on, belief, charge, commit, credit, expect, rely on 07 believe, combine, confide, consign, count on, custody, entrust, imagine, presume, suppose, surmise, swear by 08 be sure of, credence, delegate, depend on, fidelity, reliance, turn over 09 assurance, believe in, certainty 10 commitment, confidence, conviction, dependance, dependence, obligation, protection, street cred 11 expectation, safekeeping, trusteeship 12 guardianship 14 put your trust in, responsibility

trustee
02 tr 05 agent 06 keeper 08 assignee, executor, guardian 09 custodian, executrix, fiduciary 10 depositary 13 administrator

trusting
05 naive 06 unwary 08 gullible, innocent, trustful 09 confiding, credulous, ingenuous, unguarded 12 unsuspecting 13 unquestioning

trustworthiness
05 steel 07 honesty, loyalty 08 devotion 09 integrity, stability 10 commitment 11 reliability 12 faithfulness, sensibleness 13 dependability, steadfastness 14 honourableness, responsibility 15 faithworthiness, level-headedness

trustworthy
04 safe, true 05 loyal, sound 06 honest, stable, trusty 07 devoted, ethical, staunch, upright 08 faithful, reliable, sensible 09 authentic, committed, steadfast 10 creditable, dependable, honourable, principled 11 level-headed, responsible 14 good as your word

trusty
04 firm, true 05 loyal, solid 06 honest, stanch, steady, strong 07 staunch, upright 08 faithful, reliable 09 greatcoat 10 dependable, supportive 11 responsible, trustworthy 15 straightforward

truth
04 fact, true 05 axiom, facts, maxim, right, sooth 06 honour, truism, verity 07 candour, honesty, loyalty, realism, reality 08 accuracy, fidelity, validity, veracity 09 actualité, actuality, constancy, exactness, frankness, home truth, integrity, knowledge, precision, principle, rightness, sincerity 10 cold turkey, legitimacy 11 correctness, genuineness, historicity, uprightness 12 authenticity, faithfulness, truthfulness 14 honourableness, the gospel truth

• **in truth**
05 sooth, troth, truly 06 indeed, in fact,

really, surely, troggs **07** insooth, soothly **08** actually, en vérité, forsooth, honestly, in effect **09** assuredly, in reality, soothlich **10** to be honest **11** truth to tell **12** in actual fact **13** if truth be told, in point of fact **15** as a matter of fact

truthful
04 open, true **05** exact, frank, right, sooth, valid **06** candid, honest **07** correct, factual, precise, sincere **08** accurate, faithful, reliable, soothful, straight **09** realistic, soothfast, veracious, veridical, veritable **10** forthright, veridicous **11** trustworthy

truthfully
05 truly **06** openly **08** honestly, reliably **09** correctly, factually, precisely, sincerely **10** accurately, faithfully

truthfulness
06 verity **07** candour, honesty **08** openness, veracity **09** frankness, sincerity **11** uprightness **12** straightness **13** righteousness

try
02 go **03** aim, sap, tax **04** bash, fand, fond, hear, pree, pull, seek, shot, sift, stab, test, tire **05** annoy, assay, crack, drain, essay, fling, judge, prove, taste, tempt, trial, weary, whirl **06** choice, effort, purify, refine, render, sample, strain, stress, strive, try out, weaken **07** afflict, attempt, examine, exhaust, extract, have a go, inspect, stretch, turn out, undergo, venture, wear out **08** appraise, evaluate, irritate, purified **09** appraisal, endeavour, give it a go, have a bash, have a shot, have a stab, undertake **10** evaluation, experience, experiment, have a crack **11** investigate **13** make demands on

• try out
04 test **05** taste, try on **06** sample **07** inspect **08** appraise, check out, evaluate **10** have a pop at, take a pop at

trying
04 hard **05** tough, trial **06** severe, taxing **07** arduous, testing **08** annoying, tiresome **09** demanding, difficult, searching, stressful, vexatious, wearisome **10** bothersome, irritating **11** aggravating, distressing, troublesome **12** exasperating

• trying situation
03 cow

tub
03 dan, keg, kid, kit, tun, vat **04** back, bath, butt, cask, cowl, kier **05** basin, keeve, kieve, stand **06** barrel, bucket, pulpit **07** bathtub, bran-pie, bran tub, salt-fat, washtub **08** ash-leach, hogshead, lucky dip, salt-foot, swill-tub **09** container

tubby
03 fat **05** buxom, obese, plump, podgy, pudgy, stout **06** chubby, portly, rotund **07** paunchy **08** roly-poly **09** corpulent **10** overweight **15** well-upholstered

tube
03 CRT, vas **04** duct, hose, pipe, vein **05** inlet, shaft, spout, trunk **06** outlet, tubing **07** channel, conduit, snorkel **08** aircraft, cylinder **09** capillary **13** television set, umbilical cord

See also **London**

tuber
03 set **04** coco, eddo **05** cocco **06** jicama, mashua, potato, yautia **08** earth-nut **10** seed potato **11** sweet potato **13** water chestnut

tuberculosis
02 TB **05** lupus **08** phthisis, scrofula **11** consumption **12** pearl disease

tubular
04 pipy **05** piped, tubal, tubar **06** tubate **07** quilled **08** pipelike, tubelike, tubiform, tubulate, tubulous, vasiform

tuck
03 tap **04** beat, chow, cram, ease, eats, fold, food, grub, kilt, nosh, push **05** meals, pleat, scoff, scrab, snack, stuff **06** crease, gather, hamper, insert, pucker, rapier, ruffle, snacks, stroke, thrust **08** eatables **11** comestibles **12** gird yourself

• tuck away
04 hide, save **05** hoard, store **06** save up **07** conceal **09** stash away

• tuck in, tuck into
◇ *insertion indicator*
03 eat, sup **04** dine **05** eat up, feast, gorge, scoff **06** devour, gobble **08** wolf down **11** eat heartily

• tuck in, tuck up
04 kilt **05** truss **06** fold in, wrap up **07** cover up **08** make snug, put to bed **09** fold under **15** make comfortable

Tuesday
02 Tu **03** Tue **04** Tues

tuft
03 dag, top **04** coma, hank, knop, knot, lock, tait, tate, tuzz, wisp **05** beard, brush, bunch, clump, crest, flock, plume, quiff, scopa, swits, truss, tuffe, whisk **06** dallop, dollop, goatee, pencil, pompom, pompon, switch, tassel, toorie, tourie, tuffet **07** cluster, cowlick, daglock, fetlock, flaught, floccus, hassock, pompoon, scopula, topknot, tussock **08** aigrette, corn silk, dislodge, fascicle, imperial, plumelet **09** fascicule, flocculus, scalp lock **10** fasciculus **12** witches' broom

tug
03 lug, pug, rug, tit, tow **04** drag, draw, haul, jerk, pull, rive, tire, toil, yank **05** heave, pluck **06** jigger, strain, strive, wrench **07** saccade, tow boat, tracker

tuition
05 grind **07** lessons **08** coaching, guidance, teaching, training, tutelage **09** education, schooling **11** instruction **12** guardianship

tumble
◇ *anagram indicator*
04 dive, drop, fall, flop, reel, roll, sway, toss, trip **05** heave, lurch, pitch, slide, touse, touze, towse, towze **06** jumble, plunge, rumple, topple, tousle, touzle, trip up, unseat, welter **07** decline, plummet, stumble **08** collapse, decrease, dishevel, disorder, fall over, nosedive **09** knock down, overthrow, tumble-dry **10** disarrange, somersault, throw about **12** fall headlong

• tumble to
03 get **04** suss, twig **05** grasp, savvy **07** realize **08** perceive **09** latch on to **10** comprehend, cotton on to, understand **13** become aware of, get the picture

tumbledown
◇ *anagram indicator*
05 shaky **06** ruined, unsafe **07** crumbly, rickety, ruinous **08** decrepit, unstable, unsteady **09** crumbling, tottering **10** broken-down, ramshackle **11** dilapidated **14** disintegrating

tumbler
03 cup, mug **05** glass **06** beaker, goblet **07** acrobat, gymnast, tumbrel **10** water glass **13** contortionist, drinking-glass **15** jerry-come-tumble

tumid
06 turgid **07** bloated, bulbous, bulging, flowery, fulsome, pompous, stilted, swollen **08** affected, enlarged, inflated, puffed up **09** bombastic, distended, grandiose, high-flown, overblown, tumescent **10** euphuistic **11** pretentious, protuberant **12** magniloquent **13** grandiloquent

tummy
03 gut **05** belly **06** inside, paunch **07** abdomen, insides, stomach **08** pot-belly **11** bread basket, corporation

tumour
03 -oma **04** lump, onco- **06** cancer, growth **08** neoplasm, swelling **09** turgidity **10** malignancy

Tumours include:

05 gumma, myoma, Wilm's
06 epulis, glioma, lipoma, myxoma
07 adenoma, angioma, fibroma, myeloma, sarcoma
08 lymphoma, melanoma, teratoma, xanthoma
09 carcinoma, papilloma, syphiloma
10 meningioma
11 astrocytoma, rodent ulcer
12 glioblastoma, mesothelioma, osteosarcoma
13 neuroblastoma
14 retinoblastoma

tumult
◇ *anagram indicator*
03 din, row **04** coil, riot, rore, rout, stir **05** babel, brawl, chaos, deray, hurly, noise, stoor, stour, surge, whirl **06** affray, bedlam, bustle, fracas, hubbub, mutiny, racket, romage, ruffle, rumpus, stowre, strife, unrest, uproar **07** brattle, clamour, ferment, turmoil **08** disarray, disorder, shouting,

stramash, upheaval, williwaw **09** agitation, commotion, confusion, hurricane **10** hullabaloo, hurly-burly, rabblement **11** disturbance, pandemonium **12** pandaemonium

tumultuous
04 loud, wild **05** noisy, rowdy **06** fierce, hectic, raging, stormy, unruly **07** excited, fervent, riotous, violent **08** agitated, frenzied, restless, troubled, vehement **09** clamorous, deafening, disturbed, troublous, turbulent **10** boisterous, disorderly, hurly-burly, tumultuary **12** uncontrolled

tumulus
03 how, low **04** howe, mote **05** motte **06** barrow

tune
03 air, set, toy **04** ayre, dump, lilt, note, port, rant, song, tone, toon **05** adapt, dance, ditty, loure, motif, pitch, round, theme, utter **06** adjust, attune, choral, chorus, jingle, maggot, melody, spring, strain, temper **07** express, hunt's-up, melisma, ragtime **08** folk-tune, regulate, saraband, serenade **09** harmonize, sarabande, siciliano, signature, theme song, theme tune **10** light-o'-love **11** schottische, synchronize **13** melodiousness, signature tune

• **change your tune**
14 change your mind

• **in tune with**
04 true **07** d'accord **12** agreeing with, in accord with **13** in harmony with **14** in sympathy with **15** in agreement with

• **out of tune**
04 ajar **05** false **06** at odds, off-key **07** jarring, untuned **08** distuned, mistuned, out of key, scordato **11** disagreeing

tuneful
04 tuny **06** catchy, mellow **07** melodic, musical, tunable **08** pleasant, sonorous, tuneable **09** agreeable, melodious **10** euphonious, harmonious **11** mellifluous

tuneless
05 harsh **06** atonal, silent **08** clashing **09** dissonant, unmelodic, unmusical **10** discordant, unpleasant **11** cacophonous, horrisonant, unmelodious **12** disagreeable

tungsten
01 W

tunic
05 ao dai, kurta **06** blouse, camese, camise, chiton, kabaya, kameez, khurta, kirtle, tabard, taberd **07** choroid, tunicle **08** chorioid **09** laticlave **12** chorioid coat

tuning device
03 peg **08** magic eye

Tunisia
02 TN **03** TUN

tunnel
03 dig, sap **04** bore, flue, head, hole, mine **05** cundy, drift, qanat, shaft **06** burrow, condie, subway, syrinx **07** chimney, gallery, incline, passage **08** excavate, wormhole **09** penetrate, undermine, underpass **10** passageway

Tunnels include:

03 Aki, Box
05 Keijo, Rokko
06 FATIMA, Fréjus, Fucino, Haruna, Hoosac, Kanmon, Mersey, Moffat, Seikan, Thames
07 Arlberg, Cascade, Channel, Chunnel, Holland, Laerdal, Øresund, Simplon, Vereina
08 Apennine, Flathead, Hokuriku, Hyperion, Lierasen, Nakayama, Posilipo, Tronquoy
09 Dayaoshan, Eupalinus, Furka Base, Mont Blanc
10 Chesbrough, Dai-shimizu, Gorigamine, Lotschberg, Qinling I-II, Rogers Pass, St Gotthard
11 Kilsby Ridge, Mt MacDonald, Shin shimizu, Tower Subway
12 Detroit River, Moscow subway
13 Great Apennine, Iwate Ichinohe, Severomuyskiy
14 NEAT St Gotthard, Romeriksporten
15 Monte Santomarco, Orange-Fish River

tunny
04 tuna **13** horse mackerel

turban
05 mitre, pagri, toque **06** tulban **07** puggery, puggree, turband, turbant, turbond **08** puggaree, tulipant **09** turribant

turbid
03 dim **04** foul, hazy **05** dense, foggy, fuzzy, muddy, murky, riley, roily, thick **06** cloudy, drumly, impure, opaque **07** clouded, muddled, unclear **08** confused, feculent **09** turbulent, unsettled **10** disordered, incoherent

turbulence
◇ *anagram indicator*
05 chaos, storm **06** buller, tumult, unrest **07** boiling, turmoil **08** disorder, upheaval **09** agitation, commotion, confusion, roughness **10** disruption **11** instability, pandemonium

turbulent
◇ *anagram indicator*
04 wild **05** noisy, rough, rowdy **06** choppy, raging, stormy, unruly **07** foaming, furious, riotous, violent **08** agitated, blustery, confused, factious, mutinous, unstable **09** in turmoil, unbridled, unsettled **10** boisterous, disordered, disorderly, outrageous, rebellious, tumultuous **11** combustious, tempestuous **12** obstreperous **13** insubordinate, undisciplined

turf
03 sod **04** clod, fail, feal, lawn, terf **05** divot, gazon, glebe, grass, green, patch, scraw, sward, terfe **06** gazoon **07** flaught **09** territory **12** putting green

• **turf out**
04 fire, oust, sack **05** eject, elbow, evict, expel **06** banish, remove **07** dismiss, kick out, turn out **08** chuck out, fling out, throw out **09** discharge **10** dispossess **14** give the elbow to

turgid
07 dilated, flowery, fulsome, pompous, stilted, swollen, turgent **08** affected, inflated **09** bombastic, grandiose, high-flown, overblown **11** extravagant, pretentious **12** magniloquent, ostentatious **13** grandiloquent

Turkey
02 TR **03** TUR

Turkmenistan
02 TM **03** TKM

Turks and Caicos Islands
03 TCA

turmoil
◇ *anagram indicator*
03 din, row **04** dust, moil, stir, toil **05** chaos, noise, stoor, stour **06** bedlam, bustle, flurry, hubbub, pother, pudder, stowre, tumult, uproar **07** ferment, trouble **08** disarray, disorder, disquiet, upheaval **09** agitation, commotion, confusion **10** turbulence **11** disturbance, pandemonium, tracasserie **12** pandaemonium **13** Sturm und Drang **14** the devil and all

• **place of turmoil**
04 hell **11** Pandemonium **12** Pandaemonium

turn
◇ *anagram indicator*
◇ *reversal indicator*
01 U **02** go **03** act, aim, fit, jar, lot, rev, say, set, uey **04** bash, bend, bent, bias, bout, cast, form, grow, loop, make, move, pass, reel, roll, send, shot, slew, slue, sour, spin, stab, time, veer, wind **05** adapt, alter, apply, crack, curve, cycle, drift, drive, focus, go bad, go off, hinge, issue, mould, pivot, point, round, scare, shape, shift, shock, spell, spoil, start, stint, swing, trend, trick, twirl, twist, whirl **06** adjust, appeal, attend, become, chance, change, circle, corner, crisis, curdle, depend, direct, divert, do a uey, favour, fright, gyrate, invert, manner, modify, mutate, period, render, resort, return, rotate, spiral, swerve, swivel, take up **07** benefit, convert, deflect, develop, deviate, fashion, go round, heading, illness, leaning, remodel, reverse, revolve, routine, service, winding **08** aptitude, come to be, courtesy, exigency, give back, good deed, gyration, hand over, kindness, nauseate, occasion, reversal, rotation, round off, surprise, tendency, transfer **09** chuck a uey, deviation, direction, faintness, infatuate, performer, transform, translate, transmute,

variation **10** alteration, appearance, difference, divergence, make rancid, propensity, revolution **11** culmination, inclination, nervousness, opportunity, performance, vicissitude **12** become rancid, have recourse, metamorphose **13** act of kindness **15** go round and round

• **to a turn**

07 exactly **09** correctly, perfectly, precisely **12** to perfection

• **turn against**

07 dislike **08** distrust **12** disapprove of **13** make hostile to **15** become hostile to

• **turn aside**

04 daff **05** avert, parry, swits, twist **06** depart, divert, put off, swerve, switch **07** askance, deflect, deviate, diverge, diverse, fend off, reverse, ward off **08** withdraw **09** sidetrack

• **turn away**

05 avert **06** depart, refuse, reject, return **07** decline, deflect, deviate **08** move away, send away **09** discharge **12** cold shoulder, cold-shoulder

• **turn back**

◇ *reversal indicator*

05 clock, repel **06** go back, return, revert, revolt **07** reflect, retreat **09** drive back, force back, retrovert

• **turn down**

04 bend, mute, veto **05** lower, spurn **06** double, invert, lessen, muffle, rebuff, reduce, refuse, reject, soften **07** decline, quieten **08** decrease **09** knock back, repudiate **11** make quieter

• **turn in**

04 sell, shop **05** dob in, enter, grass, rat on **06** betray, give in, give up, hand in, invert, retire, return, rumble, submit, tell on, tender **07** deliver, go to bed, let down, sack out, sell out, split on, stool on **08** denounce, give back, go back on, hand over, inform on, register, renege on, squeal on **09** hit the hay, surrender, walk out on **10** hit the sack **11** double-cross, turn traitor **12** be disloyal to **13** stab in the back **14** be unfaithful to, break faith with

• **turn of events**

06 affair, result **07** outcome **08** incident **09** happening **10** occurrence, phenomenon

• **turn off**

04 bore, hang, kill, quit, stop **05** leave, repel **06** divert, offend, put off, sicken, unplug **07** deviate, disgust, dismiss, pull off, shut off, turn out **08** alienate, complete, nauseate, shut down **09** branch off, displease, switch off **10** depart from, disconnect, discourage, disenchant **11** turn against

• **turn of phrase**

05 idiom, style **06** saying **07** diction **08** locution, metaphor **10** expression, foreignism **11** phraseology

• **turn on**

04 plug **05** put on, start **06** arouse, attack, excite, fall on, hang on, please, plug in, rest on, ride on, thrill **07** attract, connect, hinge on, lay into, round on, set upon, start on, start up **08** activate, depend on, switch on **09** start in on, stimulate **14** be contingent on

• **turn out**

02 go **03** try **04** come, fire, make, rout, sack, sort, trie **05** clear, dress, eject, empty, end up, ensue, evict, expel, fadge, issue, prove **06** appear, arrive, attend, banish, become, bounce, clothe, deport, emerge, happen, muster, pan out, result, show up, turn up, unplug **07** develop, dismiss, drum out, fall out, kick out, present, produce, succeed, turf out, turn off **08** assemble, chuck out, churn out, clean out, clear out, throw out **09** be present, come about, discharge, eventuate, fabricate, switch off, transpire **10** disconnect **11** manufacture

• **turn over**

◇ *reversal down indicator*

02 TO **03** rob **04** flip, mill, mull, roll **05** upend, upset, volve **06** assign, invert, pass on, ponder, tumble **07** capsize, consign, deliver, examine, reverse, start up **08** consider, hand over, keel over, meditate, mull over, overturn, roll over, ruminate, transfer **09** reflect on, surrender, think over **10** deliberate, think about, turn turtle **11** contemplate

• **turn up**

◇ *reversal down indicator*

02 go **03** act, dig **04** bash, bend, bias, cock, come, find, loop, plow, root, rout, shew, show, spin, stab, time **05** crack, curve, cycle, dig up, drift, raise, round, scare, shift, shock, spell, stint, trend, twirl, twist, whirl, wroot **06** appear, arrive, attend, cast up, chance, change, circle, corner, expose, fright, grub up, invert, look up, period, plough, reveal, show up, swivel **07** amplify, disgust, disturb, illness, leaning, routine, subsoil, turn out, uncover, unearth **08** disclose, discover, gyration, increase, occasion, reversal, rotation, tendency **09** be present, deviation, direction, faintness, intensify, performer, variation **10** alteration, appearance, difference, divergence, make louder, propensity, revolution, strengthen **11** inclination, materialize, nervousness, opportunity, performance **12** bring to light

turncoat

03 rat **04** fink, scab **07** seceder, traitor **08** apostate, blackleg, defector, deserter, renegade, renegate **10** backslider **11** Vicar of Bray **13** tergiversator

turned

◇ *reversal indicator*

03 off **04** sour **06** soured **08** reversed **09** fashioned **10** upside down

turning

◇ *anagram indicator*

◇ *reversal indicator*

04 bend, fork, turn **05** curve **07** shaping, turn-off, winding **08** junction, reversal, rotation **09** deviation **10** conversion, crossroads **14** transformation

turning-point

04 crux, turn **06** crisis, moment, tropic **08** solstice **09** watershed **10** crossroads **13** moment of truth **14** critical moment, decisive moment

turnip

04 neep **05** navew, swede **07** tumshie **09** breadroot **10** dunderhead

turnout

04 gate, gear, team, togs **05** array, crowd, dress, get-up **06** attire, muster, number, outfit, output, siding, strike, things **07** clobber, clothes, display, striker **08** assembly, audience **09** gathering **10** appearance, assemblage, attendance **12** congregation

turnover

◇ *reversal indicator*

04 flow **05** yield **06** bridie, change, income, output, volume **07** outturn, profits, revenue **08** business, movement **10** production **11** replacement **12** productivity, transference

turpitude

04 evil **07** badness **08** baseness, foulness, iniquity, vileness, villainy **09** depravity **10** corruption, degeneracy, immorality, sinfulness, wickedness **11** corruptness, criminality, viciousness **13** nefariousness **14** flagitiousness

tusk

03 gam **04** tush **05** torsk

tussle

03 vie **04** bout, fray **05** brawl, fight, mêlée, scrap, scrum, set-to, touse, touze, towse, towze **06** battle, dust-up, fracas, tousle, touzle **07** compete, contend, contest, grapple, punch-up, scuffle, tuilyie, tuilzie, wrestle **08** conflict, scramble, struggle **09** scrimmage **10** contention **11** competition

tutelage

03 eye **04** care **05** aegis **06** charge **07** custody, tuition **08** guidance, teaching, wardship **09** education, patronage, schooling, vigilance **10** protection **11** instruction, preparation **12** guardianship

tutor

04 abbé, guru **05** coach, drill, guide, teach, train **06** direct, mentor, school **07** control, dominie, educate, lecture, teacher **08** educator, governor, guardian, instruct, lecturer **09** governess, preceptor, supervise **10** discipline, instructor, répétiteur, supervisor **11** preceptress **12** schoolmaster

tutorial

05 class **06** lesson **07** guiding, seminar, teach-in **08** coaching, didactic, teaching **09** educative, educatory **13** instructional

Tuvalu
03 TUV

TV *see* **television**

twaddle
03 rot **04** blah, bosh, bunk, guff, tosh **05** balls, hooey, stuff, trash **06** bunkum, drivel, gabble, gossip, hot air, piffle, tattle, waffle **07** baloney, eyewash, fadaise, garbage, hogwash, inanity, rhubarb, rubbish, twattle **08** blathers, blethers, claptrap, malarkey, nonsense, slipslop, tommyrot **09** bullswool, moonshine, poppycock **10** balderdash **12** gobbledygook

tweak
◇ *anagram indicator*
03 fit, nip, tug **04** jerk, pull, suit **05** adapt, pinch, twist **06** adjust, change, modify, tuning, twinge, twitch **07** fitting, shaping, squeeze **08** fine-tune, revision **09** agitation, amendment, arranging **10** adaptation, adjustment, alteration, conversion, fine-tuning, perplexity **11** accommodate, rearranging, remodelling **12** modification **13** accommodation, rearrangement **15** make adjustments

twee
04 cute **05** sweet **06** cutesy, dainty, pretty, quaint **08** affected, precious **11** sentimental

twelve
02 dz **03** doz, XII **05** dozen **06** zodiac

Twelve Days of Christmas *see* **Christmas**

twenty
02 XX

twice
◇ *repetition indicator*
02 bi-, di- **03** bin-, bis **06** doubly

twiddle
◇ *anagram indicator*
04 turn **05** twirl, twist **06** adjust, fiddle, finger, rotate, swivel, wiggle **07** twitter **08** ornament

• **twiddle your thumbs**
08 kill time **13** kick your heels **15** have nothing to do

twig
03 get, see **04** reis, rice, whip, with **05** birch, grasp, shoot, spray, sprig, stick, swits, twist, withe, withy **06** branch, fathom, fettle, rumble, switch, wattle, wicker **07** catch on, fashion, observe, ramulus, realize, sarment **08** cotton on, offshoot, perceive, tumble to **10** comprehend, understand
See also **understand**

twilight
03 dim, ebb **04** dusk, last **05** dying, final, gloom **06** ebbing, sunset **07** decline, dimness, evening, obscure, partial, shadowy **08** cockshut, demi-jour, evenfall, gloaming, glooming, owl-light **09** crepuscle, darkening, declining, half-light **10** crepuscule, indefinite **11** crepuscular **12** transitional **15** Götterdämmerung

twin
04 dual, join, link, mate, pair, part, yoke **05** clone, gemel, match **06** couple, double, fellow, paired, ringer **07** combine, couplet, deprive, matched, twofold **08** didymous, likeness, matching, parallel, separate **09** corollary, duplicate, identical, lookalike **10** complement, dead ringer, equivalent **11** counterpart, symmetrical **13** corresponding

Twins include:

04 Esau, Gibb (Maurice), Gibb (Robin), Kray (Reggie), Kray (Ronnie)
05 Diana, Jacob, Remus, Viola, Waugh (Mark), Waugh (Steve)
06 Apollo, Bunker (Chang), Bunker (Eng), Castor, Dromio (of Ephesus), Dromio (of Syracuse), Pollux
07 Artemis, Piccard (Auguste), Piccard (Jean-Felix), Romulus, Stanley (Francis), Stanley (Freelon), Weasley (Fred), Weasley (George)
08 Hercules, Iphicles, Louis XIV, Philippe
09 O'Sullivan (Isabel), O'Sullivan (Pat), Sebastian
10 Antipholus (of Ephesus), Antipholus (of Syracuse), Tweedledee, Tweedledum

twine
04 bend, coil, cord, curl, knit, loop, part, wind, wrap, yarn **05** braid, plait, twist, weave **06** spiral, string, tangle, thread **07** deprive, entwine, wreathe, wriggle **08** encircle, separate, surround, whipping **09** intorsion, intortion **10** intertwine

twinge
04 ache, grip, pain, pang, stab **05** cramp, pinch, prick, spasm, throb, throe, twang, tweak **06** stitch, twitch **08** shooting

twinkle
◇ *anagram indicator*
04 wink **05** blink, flash, gleam, glint, light, shine, twink **06** quiver **07** flicker, glimmer, glisten, glitter, shimmer, shining, sparkle, vibrate **09** coruscate, twinkling **11** coruscation, scintillate **13** scintillation

twinkling
◇ *anagram indicator*
02 mo **03** sec **04** jiff, tick, wink **05** flash, jiffy, nitid, shake, trice, twink **06** bright, minute, moment, no time, second **07** instant, shining, winking **08** blinking, flashing, gleaming, polished **09** short time, sparkling **10** flickering, glimmering, glistening, glittering, shimmering **11** coruscating **13** scintillating, scintillation

twirl
◇ *anagram indicator*
04 coil, curl, spin, turn, wind **05** pivot, trill, twist, wheel, whirl, whorl **06** gyrate, rotate, spiral, swivel **07** revolve, trundle, twiddle, twizzle **08** gyration, rotation **09** pirouette **10** revolution **11** convolution **12** tirlie-wirlie

twirling
◇ *anagram indicator*
05 gyral **07** pivotal **08** gyratory, pivoting, rotating, rotatory, spinning, whirling **09** revolving **10** swivelling **11** pirouetting

twist
◇ *anagram indicator*
03 arc, cue **04** bend, coil, cord, curl, flaw, kink, loop, rick, roll, rove, skew, slew, slue, spin, turn, twig, warp, whim, wind **05** alter, angle, braid, break, curve, freak, plait, quirk, screw, slant, twine, twirl, weave, wrest, wrick, wring **06** change, defect, deform, foible, garble, oddity, rotate, spiral, sprain, squirm, strain, strand, swivel, tangle, thread, wamble, wigwag, wimple, wreath, wrench, writhe, zigzag **07** contort, distort, entwine, falsify, pervert, revolve, swindle, torsion, twizzle, whimple, wreathe, wriggle **08** entangle, misquote, misshape, squiggle, surprise, wresting **09** misreport, turnabout, variation **10** aberration, contortion, distortion, intertwine, perversion **11** convolution, peculiarity **12** idiosyncrasy, imperfection, misrepresent

• **twist someone's arm**
05 bully, force **06** coerce, lean on **07** dragoon **08** bulldoze, persuade **10** intimidate, pressurize **14** put the screws on

twisted
◇ *anagram indicator*
03 odd **04** wavy **05** kinky, thraw **06** thrawn, thrown, warped **07** deviant, sinuous, strange, tortile, winding **08** peculiar, squiggly **09** contorted, perverted, unnatural

twister
04 gale **05** cheat, crook, fraud, rogue, storm **06** con man, phoney, squall **07** cyclone, monsoon, tempest, tornado, typhoon **08** con woman, deceiver, swindler **09** con artist, hurricane, scoundrel, trickster, whirlwind **10** blackguard

twisty
06 zigzag **07** curving, sinuous, winding **08** indirect, tortuous **10** circuitous, meandering, roundabout, serpentine

twit
03 ass, git **04** berk, clot, dope, dork, fool, geek, goop, nerd, nerk, prat **05** chump, clown, dweeb, idiot, ninny, twerp **06** nig-nog, nitwit **07** airhead, halfwit, plonker, saphead, twitter **08** imbecile **09** blockhead, simpleton **10** nincompoop **11** knuckle-head **13** proper Charlie

twitch
◇ *anagram indicator*
03 tic, tig, tit, tug **04** jerk, jump, pull, yips **05** blink, pluck, shake, spasm, start, tweak **06** quiver, shiver, snatch, tremor **07** flutter, the yips, tremble **09** vellicate **10** convulsion

twitchy
04 edgy **05** het up, jerky, jumpy, nervy, shaky, tense **06** on edge, uneasy **07** anxious, fidgety, in a stew, jittery, keyed up, nervous, panicky, restive, uptight, wound up **08** agitated, in a sweat, in a tizzy **12** apprehensive

twitter
03 cry, gab **04** chat, sing, song **05** cheep, chirp, tweet **06** babble, gabble, gossip, jabber, jargon, warble, witter **07** blather, blether, chatter, chirrup, chitter, prattle, twaddle, whistle **08** chirping, tweeting **09** palpitate **10** chirruping

two
02 II **04** pair **05** deuce, twain **06** couple
• **the two**
04 both

two-faced
05 false, lying **07** devious **09** deceitful, insincere **10** Janus-faced, perfidious **11** dissembling, duplicitous, treacherous **12** hypocritical **13** double-dealing, untrustworthy

twofold
04 dual, twin **05** duple **06** bifold, binary, double, duplex **07** twafald, twifold, twyfold **09** duplicate

two-master
04 buss

twosome
03 duo **04** duet, pair **06** couple **09** tête-à-tête

two-up
03 swy **05** swy-up **07** swy game

two-wheeler
04 cart

Tyche
07 Fortuna

tycoon
05 baron, mogul **06** fat cat **07** magnate, supremo **08** big noise **09** big cheese, financier, moneybags **10** capitalist **12** entrepreneur, moneyspinner **13** industrialist

Tyler
03 Wat

Tyneside
02 NE

type
◇ *anagram indicator*
03 ilk, key, set **04** face, font, form, hair, kind, make, mark, norm, sort **05** brand, breed, class, fount, genre, genus, group, model, order, print, stamp, style **06** emblem, letter, number, strain, symbol **07** epitome, example, letters, numbers, pattern, species, symbols, variety **08** category, exemplar, insignia, original, printing, specimen, standard, typeface **09** archetype, character, exemplify, lettering, prefigure, prototype, symbolize, typewrite **10** characters, embodiment, foreshadow **11** description, designation, subdivision **12** anticipation, quintessence **13** foreshadowing **14** classification
• **confused type**
02 pi **03** pie, pye
• **type size**
03 gem **04** body, pica **05** canon **06** minion **07** brevier, English **09** bourgeois, Columbian, nonpareil **10** longprimer **11** emerald type, Great Primer

typeface

Typefaces include:

05 Arial
06 Bell MT, Impact, Lucida, Modern, Tahoma
07 Courier, Curlz MT, Marlett, MS Serif, Verdana
08 Garamond, Jokerman, MS Gothic, MS Mincho, Playbill, Rockwell, Webdings
09 Colonna MT, Wide Latin, Wingdings
10 Arial Black, Courier New, Lucida Sans
11 Baskerville, Book Antiqua, Comic Sans MS, MS Sans Serif, Poor Richard, Trebuchet MS
13 Century Gothic, Lucida Console, Times New Roman
14 Franklin Gothic
15 Bookman Old Style

typhoon
05 storm **06** squall, typhon **07** cyclone, tempest, tornado, twister **09** hurricane, whirlwind

typical
04 trew, true **05** model, stock, typal, typic, usual **06** normal, Podunk **07** average, classic **08** ordinary, orthodox, standard, true-bred **10** archetypal, emblematic, figurative, indicative, stereotype **11** distinctive **12** conventional, illustrative, run-of-the-mill **13** typographical **14** characteristic, quintessential, representative

typically
07 as a rule, usually **08** normally **09** routinely **10** habitually, ordinarily **11** classically, customarily

typify
05 image **06** embody, imbody, shadow **08** indicate **09** epitomize, exemplify, personify, represent, symbolize **10** foreshadow, illustrate **11** encapsulate, foresignify **12** characterize

tyrannical
05 cruel, harsh **06** lordly, severe, strict, unjust **08** absolute, despotic, Neronian, ruthless, satrapal, tyrannic **09** arbitrary, imperious **10** autocratic, despotical, high-handed, oppressive, peremptory, repressive **11** dictatorial, domineering, magisterial, overbearing **12** overpowering, totalitarian, unreasonable **13** authoritarian

tyrannize
04 lord **05** bully, crush **06** coerce **07** dictate, enslave, oppress, repress **08** browbeat, domineer, suppress **09** subjugate, terrorize **10** intimidate, lord it over

tyranny
07 cruelty, liberty **08** severity **09** autocracy, despotism, harshness, injustice **10** absolutism, domination, oppression, strictness **12** dictatorship, ruthlessness **13** imperiousness **14** high-handedness

tyrant
05 bully, pewee **06** despot, peewee **08** autocrat, dictator, martinet **09** oppressor, tyranness **10** absolutist, taskmaster **11** slave-driver **13** authoritarian

See also **despot**

tyro *see* **tiro, tyro**

U

U
07 uniform **10** upper-class

ubiquitous
06 common, global **08** frequent
09 pervasive, universal
10 everywhere, ubiquarian, wall-to-wall **11** ever-present, omnipresent

ubiquity
09 frequency **10** commonness, popularity, prevalence
12 omnipresence, universality
13 pervasiveness

Uganda
03 EAU, UGA

ugliness
04 evil **06** danger, horror, menace
08 disgrace, enormity, vileness
09 deformity, nastiness, plainness
10 homeliness, horridness
11 heinousness, hideousness, monstrosity **12** unloveliness
13 frightfulness, offensiveness, repulsiveness, unsightliness
14 unpleasantness

ugly
◇ *anagram indicator*
04 evil, foul, loth, vile **05** grave, loath, nasty, plain **06** gorgon, grotty, homely, horrid, oughly, ouglie, unfair
07 hideous, hostile, ogreish
08 alarming, deformed, horrible, ill-faced, ill-faste, ill-faurd, plug-ugly, shocking, sinister, terrible, unlovely
09 dangerous, frightful, grotesque, loathsome, misshapen, monstrous, obnoxious, offensive, repulsive, revolting, ugly as sin, unsightly
10 disgusting, ill-looking, ill-natured, unpleasant **11** disquieting, ill-favoured, threatening **12** disagreeable, evil-favoured, unattractive
13 objectionable **15** unprepossessing

UK *see* **United Kingdom**

Ukraine
02 UA **03** UKR

ulcer
04 boil, noma, sore **05** issue, rupia
06 aphtha, canker, fester **07** abscess, bedsore, fistula, sycosis **08** open sore
09 impostume **10** plague-sore, ulceration **11** peptic ulcer **13** varicose ulcer **14** decubitus ulcer

ulster
02 NI **04** coat

ulterior
06 covert, hidden, secret **07** private, remoter, selfish **08** personal
09 concealed, secondary
10 underlying, unrevealed
11 undisclosed, unexpressed

ultimate
◇ *tail selection indicator*
03 end, ult **04** best, last, peak **05** basic, final, ideal **06** height, summit, utmost
07 closing, epitome, extreme, highest, maximum, perfect, primary, radical, supreme, topmost **08** eventual, furthest, greatest, last word, limiting, remotest, terminal **09** elemental
10 concluding, perfection, the mostest
11 chef d'oeuvre, culmination, fundamental, masterpiece, summum bonum, superlative **12** consummation
14 daddy of them all

ultimately
◇ *tail selection indicator*
03 ult **06** at last **07** finally **08** after all, in the end **09** basically, primarily
10 eventually **13** fundamentally, sooner or later **15** in the last resort

ultra-
05 extra **09** extremely, unusually
10 especially, remarkably **11** excessively
13 exceptionally **15** extraordinarily

ultraviolet
02 UV

ululate
03 cry, sob **04** hoot, howl, keen, moan, wail, weep **05** mourn **06** holler, lament, scream **07** screech

umbrage
• **take umbrage**
06 be hurt, resent **07** be angry, be upset **08** be miffed, be put out, get huffy **09** be annoyed **10** be insulted, be offended, feel put out **11** take offence
13 be exasperated, take exception
14 take personally

umbrella
05 aegis, cover, **06** agency **08** auspices
09 en tout cas **10** protection

Umbrellas and parasols include:

04 gamp, mush
05 dumpy
06 brolly, chatta
07 gingham
08 marquise, mushroom, ombrella, sunshade, umbrello
09 en tout cas
11 bumbershoot

umpire
03 ref, ump **05** judge **06** odd-man
07 arbiter, control, daysman, mediate, oddsman, referee **08** linesman, mediator, moderate, oversman, stickler
09 arbitrate, birlieman, byrlaw-man, moderator **10** adjudicate, arbitrator
11 adjudicator
See also **cricket**

umpteen
06 plenty **08** millions, numerous, very many **09** a good many, countless, thousands **11** innumerable

UN *see* **United Nations**

unabashed
04 bold **06** brazen **07** blatant
09 abashless, confident, unashamed, undaunted **10** undismayed **11** bold as brass, unconcerned **13** in countenance, unembarrassed

unable
04 weak **05** unfit **06** cannot
08 impotent **09** incapable, powerless
10 inadequate, unequipped
11 incompetent, ineffectual, unqualified

unabridged
04 full **05** uncut, whole **06** entire
08 complete **10** full-length
11 uncondensed, unshortened
12 unexpurgated

unacceptable
04 non-U **05** wrong **07** a bit off
09 obnoxious, offensive, unwelcome
10 unpleasant, unsuitable
11 intolerable, undesirable
12 disagreeable, inadmissible
13 beyond the pale, disappointing, objectionable **14** unsatisfactory

unaccommodating
05 rigid **08** perverse, stubborn
09 obstinate, unbending **10** inflexible, unyielding **11** disobliging
12 intransigent **13** uncomplaisant, unco-operative **14** uncompromising

unaccompanied
04 lone, solo **05** alone, secco
06 lonely, silent, single **09** on your own
10 by yourself, unattended, unescorted **12** single-handed

unaccountable
03 odd **04** free **05** queer **06** immune
07 bizarre, curious, strange, unusual
08 baffling, peculiar, puzzling, singular, uncommon **09** insoluble, unheard-of
10 mysterious **11** astonishing
12 impenetrable, inexplicable, unfathomable **13** extraordinary, not answerable, unexplainable **14** not responsible

unaccountably
09 strangely **10** bafflingly, incredibly, puzzlingly **12** inexplicably, miraculously, mysteriously, mystifyingly **13** unexplainably

unaccustomed
03 new **06** unused, unwont **07** strange, unusual **08** uncommon, unwonted, wontless **09** different, inusitate **10** remarkable, surprising, unexpected, unfamiliar **11** unpractised **12** unacquainted **13** extraordinary, inexperienced, unprecedented

unacquainted
06 unused **07** strange, unknown, unusual **08** ignorant **10** unfamiliar, uninformed **12** unaccustomed **13** inexperienced

unadorned
04 bald, bare **05** plain, stark **06** severe, simple **07** undight **08** homespun **10** restrained **11** undecorated, unvarnished **12** unornamented **13** unembellished **15** straightforward

unadulterated
04 neat, pure, real, true **05** sheer, solid, total, utter **06** simple **07** genuine, natural, perfect, sincere, unmixed **08** absolute, complete, flawless, straight, thorough **09** authentic, downright, unalloyed, undiluted **11** unmitigated, unqualified **14** unsophisticate **15** unsophisticated

unaffected
04 real, true **05** naive, plain **06** candid, honest, immune, simple **07** artless, genuine, natural, sincere, unmoved **08** unspoilt **09** guileless, ingenuous, unaltered, unchanged, untouched **10** impervious, unassuming **11** indifferent, unconcerned **13** unpretentious **15** straightforward, unsophisticated

unafraid
05 brave **06** daring **08** fearless, intrepid, unfeared **09** confident, dauntless, undaunted **10** courageous, unshakable **11** unshakeable **13** imperturbable

unalterable
05 final, fixed, rigid **09** immovable, immutable, permanent **10** inflexible, invariable, unchanging, unyielding **11** hard and fast, reverseless **12** unchangeable

unaltered
04 as is **09** invariant

unanimity
05 unity **06** accord, unison **07** concert, concord, harmony **09** agreement, consensus **10** congruence **11** concurrence, consistency **14** like-mindedness

unanimous
05 as one, joint, solid **06** common, united **08** in accord **09** concerted **10** concordant, consistent, harmonious, like-minded **11** in agreement **12** single-minded

unanimously
05 as one **06** nem con **08** as one man **09** in concert, of one mind, unopposed **10** conjointly **12** with one voice **15** by common consent

unannounced
06 abrupt, chance, sudden **07** amazing, unusual **09** startling **10** accidental, fortuitous, surprising, unexpected, unforeseen **11** astonishing, unlooked-for **13** unanticipated, unpredictable

unanswerable
05 final **08** absolute **10** conclusive, unarguable, undeniable **11** irrefutable **12** indisputable, irrefragable **13** incontestable

unanswered
04 open **05** vexed **07** in doubt **09** undecided, unsettled **10** unrequited, unresolved, up in the air

unappetizing
07 insipid **09** tasteless, unsavoury **10** off-putting, unexciting, uninviting, unpleasant **11** distasteful, unappealing, unpalatable **12** disagreeable, unattractive **13** uninteresting

unapproachable
04 cold, cool **05** aloof **06** remote **07** distant **08** reserved **09** withdrawn **10** forbidding, unfriendly, unsociable **11** standoffish **12** inaccessible, unresponsive **15** uncommunicative

unapt
04 slow **05** inapt, unfit **08** unfitted, unsuited, untimely **10** inapposite, malapropos, unsuitable **12** inapplicable, unseasonable **13** inappropriate

unarmed
04 bare, open, weak **05** inerm, naked **07** exposed **08** helpless **10** unweaponed, vulnerable **11** defenceless, unprotected

unashamed
04 open **06** direct, honest **07** blatant **08** bashless **09** shameless, unabashed **10** impenitent **11** unconcealed, undisguised, unrepentant

unasked
08 unbidden, unsought, unwanted **09** uninvited, voluntary **10** unrequired **11** spontaneous, unannounced, unrequested, unsolicited

unassailable
05 sound **06** proven, secure **08** absolute, positive **09** well-armed **10** conclusive, invincible, inviolable, undeniable **11** impregnable, irrefutable **12** indisputable, inexpugnable, invulnerable **13** incontestable, well-fortified

unassertive
03 shy **04** meek **05** mousy, quiet, timid **06** mousey **07** bashful **08** backward, retiring, timorous **09** diffident **10** unassuming **12** self-effacing

unassuming
03 shy **04** meek **05** quiet **06** demure, humble, modest, simple **07** natural **08** reticent, retiring **10** restrained **11** unassertive, unobtrusive **12** self-effacing, underbearing **13** unpretentious

unattached
04 free **05** loose **06** single **08** detached **09** available, fancy-free, footloose, on your own, unengaged, unmarried **10** by yourself, with no ties **11** independent, uncommitted **12** unaffiliated

unattended
05 alone **07** ignored **08** forsaken **09** abandoned, forgotten, neglected, unguarded, unwatched **10** unescorted **11** disregarded **12** unsupervised **13** unaccompanied

unattractive
04 ugly **05** plain, warby **06** grungy, homely, skanky **08** ill-faurd, uncomely, unlovely **09** offensive, repellent, unsavoury, unsightly, unwelcome **10** disgusting, off-putting, unexciting, uninviting, unpleasant **11** distasteful, ill-favoured, unappealing, undesirable, unpalatable **12** disagreeable, unappetizing **13** no oil painting, objectionable **15** not much to look at, unprepossessing

unauthorized
07 illegal, illicit **08** unlawful **09** forbidden, irregular **10** prohibited, unapproved, unlicensed, unofficial **11** unchartered, unwarranted **12** illegitimate, unsanctioned

unavailing
04 vain **06** beaten, failed, futile, losing **07** sterile, unlucky, useless **08** abortive, defeated, luckless, nugatory, thwarted **09** fruitless **10** frustrated **11** ineffective, unfortunate **12** unprevailing, unproductive, unprofitable, unsuccessful

unavoidable
04 sure **05** fatal, fated **07** certain **08** destined, required **09** mandatory, necessary **10** compulsory, inevitable, inexorable, obligatory **11** ineluctable, inescapable, predestined

unaware
04 deaf **05** blind **07** witless **08** heedless, ignorant, wareless **09** in the dark, oblivious, unknowing, unmindful, unwitting **10** insentient, uninformed, with no idea **11** incognizant, unconscious **12** unsuspecting **13** unenlightened

unawares
05 aback **07** unwares **08** abruptly, off guard, on the hop, suddenly **09** in the dark, red-handed **10** by surprise, mistakenly, unprepared **11** insidiously, unknowingly, unwittingly

12 accidentally, à l'improviste, unexpectedly, unthinkingly
13 inadvertently, unconsciously
15 unintentionally

unbalanced
◇ *anagram indicator*
03 mad 05 barmy, crazy 06 biased, insane, mental, uneven, unfair, unjust
07 erratic, lunatic, unequal, unsound
08 crackers, demented, deranged, doolally, lopsided, one-sided, partisan, unstable, unsteady 09 disturbed, stir-crazy 10 irrational, prejudiced
11 dysharmonic, inequitable, mentally ill 12 asymmetrical, round the bend
13 round the twist 14 wrong in the head

unbearable
06 too bad 07 too much 08 the limit
10 importable 11 intolerable, unendurable 12 excruciating, insufferable, the last straw, unacceptable 13 insupportable

unbeatable
04 best 07 supreme 09 excellent, matchless, rock-solid 10 invincible
11 indomitable, unstoppable
13 unconquerable, unsurpassable

unbeaten
07 supreme, unbowed, winning
09 unsubdued 10 triumphant, undefeated, victorious 11 unconquered, unsurpassed 12 unvanquished

unbecoming
08 improper, indecent, infra dig, unseemly, unworthy 09 unfitting, unseeming, unsightly 10 indecorous, indelicate, misseeming, unladylike, unsuitable 11 unbefitting 12 ill-beseeming, unattractive
13 inappropriate, ungentlemanly
15 infra dignitatem

unbeknown
• **unbeknown to**
07 unknown 09 unheard of
10 unrealized 11 unperceived
13 unbeknownst to

unbelief
05 doubt 07 atheism 09 disbelief
10 scepticism 11 agnosticism, incredulity

unbelievable
06 unreal 07 amazing 08 unlikely
10 far-fetched, impossible, improbable, incredible, outlandish, remarkable, staggering 11 astonishing, implausible, incredulous, unthinkable
12 preposterous, unconvincing, unimaginable 13 extraordinary, inconceivable

unbelievably
09 amazingly 10 incredibly
12 outlandishly, unimaginably
13 inconceivably 15 extraordinarily

unbeliever
06 zendik 07 atheist, doubter, infidel, sceptic 08 agnostic 11 disbeliever, nullifidian 14 doubting Thomas

unbelieving
07 dubious, infidel 08 doubtful, doubting 09 miscreant, sceptical
10 suspicious 11 distrustful, incredulous, nullifidian, unconvinced, unpersuaded 12 disbelieving

unbend
04 thaw, undo 05 relax 06 uncoil, uncurl 08 loosen up, unbuckle, unbutton, unfasten, unfreeze
10 straighten

unbending
04 firm 05 aloof, rigid, stern, stiff, tough
06 formal, severe, strict 07 distant
08 Catonian, hardline, relaxing, reserved, resolute, stubborn
10 forbidding, formidable, inflexible, unyielding 12 intransigent
14 uncompromising

unbiased
04 fair, just 06 candid 07 neutral
08 balanced 09 equitable, impartial, objective 10 even-handed, fair-minded, open-minded, uncoloured
11 independent 12 uninfluenced, unprejudiced 13 disinterested, dispassionate

unbidden
04 free 07 unasked, willing
08 unforced, unwanted 09 uninvited, unwelcome, voluntary 10 unprompted
11 spontaneous, unsolicited

unbind
04 free, undo 05 loose, solve, untie
06 loosen, unyoke 07 release, set free, unchain, unloose 08 liberate, unfasten, unfetter, unloosen 09 unshackle

unblemished
04 pure 05 clear, white 07 perfect
08 flawless, spotless, unflawed
09 unspotted, unstained, unsullied, untainted 10 immaculate
11 untarnished 13 unimpeachable
14 irreproachable

unblinking
04 calm, cool 06 steady 07 assured
08 composed, fearless, unafraid
09 impassive 10 unwavering
11 emotionless, unemotional, unfaltering, unflinching, unshrinking
13 imperturbable

unblushing
04 bold 06 amoral, brazen 07 blatant
08 immodest, impudent 09 shameless, unabashed, unashamed
13 unembarrassed 15 conscience-proof

unborn
06 coming, future, to-come
07 awaited, in utero 08 expected, unyeaned 09 embryonic
10 subsequent, succeeding 11 non-existent

unbosom
04 bare, tell 05 admit 06 let out, reveal
07 confess, confide, divulge, lay bare, pour out, tell all, uncover 08 disclose, unburden

unbounded
04 vast 07 endless 08 infinite
09 boundless, limitless, unbridled, unchecked, unlimited
12 immeasurable, unconfinable, uncontrolled, unrestrained, unrestricted

unbreakable
05 solid, tough 06 rugged, strong
07 durable 09 resistant, toughened
10 adamantine 11 infrangible
12 shatterproof 14 indestructible

unbridled
04 wild 07 rampant, riotous
08 unbitted, uncurbed 09 excessive, unchecked 10 immoderate, licentious, profligate, ungoverned 11 intemperate
12 uncontrolled, unrestrained
13 unconstrained

unbroken
04 wild 05 rough, sheer, solid, whole
06 entire, in a row, intact, single
07 endless, non-stop, unbroke, untamed 08 complete, constant, seamless, unbeaten 09 ceaseless, incessant, perpetual, unceasing, undivided, unmatched 10 continuate, continuous, successive, unequalled, unrivalled 11 progressive, unremitting, unsurpassed 13 uninterrupted
14 undomesticated

unburden
04 bare, tell 05 admit 06 let out, reveal
07 cast off, confess, confide, divulge, lay bare, offload, pour out, tell all, uncover 08 disclose 09 discharge

unbutton
04 undo

uncalled-for
07 unasked 08 needless, unsought
09 unwelcome 10 gratuitous, undeserved, unprompted, unprovoked
11 unjustified, unnecessary, unsolicited, unwarranted

uncannily
05 oddly 08 spookily 09 bizarrely, strangely 10 incredibly, remarkably
11 unnaturally 12 mysteriously
14 supernaturally 15 extraordinarily

uncanny
03 odd 05 eerie, queer, weird
06 creepy, spooky, unsafe 07 bizarre, strange 08 eldritch, pokerish
09 fantastic, unearthly, unnatural, wanchancy 10 incredible, mysterious, remarkable, wanchancie
11 exceptional 12 supernatural
13 extraordinary, preternatural, unaccountable

uncared-for
07 run-down, squalid 08 derelict, deserted, forsaken, stranded, untended, untilled, unweeded
09 abandoned, neglected, overgrown
11 dilapidated, disregarded, undervalued, unhusbanded
12 uncultivated, unmaintained
13 unappreciated

uncaring
04 cold **07** callous, unmoved **09** unfeeling **11** indifferent, unconcerned **12** uninterested **13** inconsiderate, marble-hearted, unsympathetic **14** marble-breasted

unceasing
07 endless, non-stop, undying **08** constant, unbroken, unending **09** ceaseless, continual, continued, incessant, perpetual **10** continuous, persistent, relentless **11** everlasting, never-ending, unrelenting, unremitting

unceremonious
04 rude **06** abrupt, casual, direct, sudden **07** off-hand, relaxed **08** familiar, impolite, informal, laid-back, sans gêne **09** easy-going **10** unofficial **11** undignified **12** discourteous **13** disrespectful

uncertain
◇ *anagram indicator*
04 iffy, open **05** dicey, dodgy, risky, shaky, vague **06** chancy, fitful, slippy, unsure **07** chancey, dubious, erratic, unclear, unknown, vagrant, various **08** doubtful, hesitant, insecure, slippery, unsteady, variable, wavering **09** hazardous, irregular, undecided, unsettled **10** ambivalent, changeable, inconstant, indefinite, in two minds, of two minds, precarious, touch-and-go, unreliable, unresolved, up in the air **11** speculative, unconfirmed, unconvinced, vacillating **12** equivocating, in the balance, questionable, undetermined **13** indeterminate, unforeseeable, unpredictable

uncertainly
05 shyly **06** warily **07** timidly **09** dubiously, haltingly **10** delayingly, doubtfully, hesitantly, in two minds, waveringly **11** reluctantly, sceptically, tentatively, unwillingly **12** indecisively, irresolutely, stammeringly, stutteringly **13** half-heartedly, vacillatingly

uncertainty
02 if **05** doubt, qualm **06** qualms **07** dilemma **09** ambiguity, confusion, misgiving, riskiness, vagueness **10** hesitation, insecurity, perplexity, puzzlement, scepticism, uneasiness **11** ambivalence, contingency **12** bewilderment, irresolution, peradventure **13** unreliability

unchallengeable
05 final **07** sacless **08** absolute **10** conclusive **11** impregnable, irrefutable **12** inappellable, indisputable, irrefragable **13** incontestable

unchangeable
05 final, fixed **07** eternal **08** constant **09** immutable, permanent **10** changeless, invariable, unchanging **11** stereotyped **12** irreversible **14** intransmutable

unchanging
04 same **06** steady **07** abiding, eternal, lasting **08** constant, enduring **09** permanent, perpetual, phaseless, steadfast, unvarying **10** changeless, invariable

uncharitable
04 hard, mean **05** cruel, harsh, stern **06** severe, unkind **07** callous **09** unfeeling **10** unfriendly, ungenerous **11** hard-hearted, insensitive, unchristian, unforgiving **13** unsympathetic **15** uncompassionate

uncharted
03 new **05** alien **06** virgin **07** foreign, strange, unknown **09** unplumbed **10** unexplored, unfamiliar, unsurveyed **12** undiscovered

unchaste
04 lewd **05** frail, light, loose **06** fallen, impure, wanton **07** defiled, immoral, wappend **08** depraved, immodest **09** dishonest, dissolute **10** licentious **11** light-heeled, promiscuous

unchecked
03 raw **04** wild **06** unruly **07** rampant, riotous, violent **08** uncurbed, unreined **09** unbridled **10** boisterous, unhindered **12** uncontrolled, unrestrained **13** undisciplined

uncivil
04 curt, rude **05** gruff, surly **06** abrupt, coarse **07** bearish, boorish, brusque, ill-bred, uncouth **08** churlish, impolite, unseemly **09** menseless **10** ungracious, unmannerly **11** bad-mannered, ill-mannered **12** discourteous **13** disrespectful

uncivilized
04 wild **05** rough **06** savage **07** boorish, brutish, heathen, salvage, uncouth, untamed **08** barbaric, impolite **09** barbarian, barbarous, primitive, unrefined **10** antisocial, heathenish, illiterate, tramontane, uncultured, uneducated **13** unenlightened **15** unsophisticated

unclassifiable
05 vague **07** elusive **08** doubtful **09** uncertain **10** ill-defined, indefinite, indistinct **11** indefinable, undefinable **13** indescribable, indeterminate **14** unidentifiable

unclassified
05 basic, known **06** lowest, public **07** general, minimal, minimum **08** official, revealed, ungraded **09** disclosed, published **11** on the record **12** unrestricted **14** for publication

uncle
03 eme, oom **10** pawnbroker

Uncles include:

03 Bob, Joe, Pio, Sam, Tom
05 Henry, Lynch (Andrew), Remus, Silas, Vanya
06 Domkin (George), Fester, Jasper (John), Julius, Shandy (Toby), Wilson (Arthur)
07 Flowers (Philip), Forsyte (Old Jolyon), Trotter (Albert), Quentin
08 Bulgaria, Claudius, McCaslin (Buck), McCaslin (Buddy)
09 Cobbleigh (Tom), Old Jolyon
10 Richard III
11 Pumblechook
15 Richard the Third

unclean
03 bad **04** evil, foul, lewd **05** dirty, grimy **06** filthy, grubby, impure, soiled, wicked **07** corrupt, defiled, profane, sullied, tainted **08** ordurous, polluted **10** unhygienic **11** adulterated, unwholesome **12** contaminated

unclear
03 dim **04** hazy, iffy **05** foggy, vague **06** unsure **07** dubious, obscure **08** doubtful **09** ambiguous, equivocal, non liquet, uncertain, unsettled **10** convoluted, indefinite, indistinct **12** undetermined

unclothed
04 bare, nude **05** naked **06** unclad **08** disrobed, in the raw, starkers, stripped **09** in the buff, undressed **10** stark-naked **15** in the altogether

uncomfortable
04 cold, hard, mean **05** tense, unked, unket, unkid **06** on edge, uneasy **07** anxious, awkward, cramped, nervous, painful, worried **08** troubled **09** disturbed, ill at ease **10** disquieted, distressed, ill-fitting, irritating **11** discomfited, embarrassed **12** disagreeable **13** self-conscious

uncommitted
04 free **07** neutral **08** floating **09** available, fancy-free, footloose, undecided **10** non-aligned, unattached, uninvolved **11** non-partisan **12** free-floating

uncommon
◇ *anagram indicator*
03 odd **04** rare, seld, very **05** queer **06** scarce **07** bizarre, curious, notable, special, strange, unusual **08** abnormal, atypical, peculiar, singular, striking **10** infrequent, remarkable, remarkably, unfamiliar **11** distinctive, exceptional, out of the way, outstanding **12** like gold dust **13** extraordinary **15** thin on the ground

uncommonly
◇ *anagram indicator*
04 seld, very **06** rarely, seldom **09** extremely, strangely, unusually **10** abnormally, peculiarly, remarkably, singularly **12** infrequently, occasionally, particularly **13** exceptionally, outstandingly

uncommunicative
03 shy **04** curt **05** aloof, brief, close, quiet **06** silent **08** reserved, reticent,

retiring, taciturn **09** diffident, secretive, withdrawn **10** buttoned-up, unsociable **11** tight-lipped **12** unresponsive **13** unforthcoming

uncomplicated
◇ *anagram indicator*
04 easy **05** clear **06** direct, simple **10** uninvolved **11** undemanding **15** straightforward

uncompromising
04 firm **05** rigid, stiff, tough **06** gritty, strict **07** diehard **08** hardline, obdurate, stubborn **09** hard-faced, hardshell, immovable, obstinate, out-and-out, unbending **10** inexorable, inflexible, unyielding **12** intransigent **15** unaccommodating

unconcealable
05 clear, plain **07** obvious **08** manifest **09** insistent **13** irrepressible **14** insuppressible, uncontrollable

unconcealed
04 open, pert **05** frank, naked, overt **06** patent, public **07** blatant, evident, obvious, visible **08** admitted, apparent, manifest, unveiled **09** unashamed **10** noticeable **11** conspicuous **12** ill-concealed, undissembled **13** self-confessed **15** undistinguished

unconcern
06 apathy **09** aloofness **10** detachment, negligence, remoteness **11** callousness, disinterest, insouciance, nonchalance **12** indifference **13** pococurantism

unconcerned
04 cool **05** aloof, sober **06** casual, remote **07** callous, distant, relaxed, unmoved **08** carefree, careless, composed, detached, not fussy, uncaring **09** apathetic, impartial, not fussed, oblivious, unruffled, unworried **10** complacent, insouciant, nonchalant, uninvolved, untroubled **11** indifferent, pococurante, unperturbed **12** uninterested **13** disinterested, dispassionate, unsympathetic

unconditional
04 full, pure **05** total, utter **06** entire **07** plenary **08** absolute, complete, definite, outright, positive, termless **09** categoric, downright, out-and-out, unlimited **10** conclusive, unreserved **11** categorical, unequivocal, unqualified **12** unrestricted, wholehearted **13** thoroughgoing

unconditionally
05 fully **06** purely **07** totally **08** entirely **10** absolutely, completely **11** simpliciter **12** unreservedly **13** categorically, unequivocally **14** wholeheartedly

unconfirmed
08 ignorant, unproved, unproven **10** unratified, unverified **14** uncorroborated **15** unauthenticated, unsubstantiated

unconformity
12 irregularity **13** disconformity, discontinuity

uncongenial
08 unsuited **09** unsavoury **10** discordant, unfriendly, uninviting, unpleasant **11** displeasing, distasteful, unappealing **12** antagonistic, antipathetic, disagreeable, incompatible, unattractive **13** unsympathetic

unconnected
07 foreign **08** confused, detached, separate **09** illogical, unrelated **10** disjointed, incoherent, irrational, irrelevant, unattached **11** independent, off the point **12** disconnected **13** inappropriate, unco ordinated **14** beside the point

unconquerable
08 enduring **09** ingrained **10** inveterate, invincible, unbeatable, unyielding **11** indomitable, insuperable **12** irresistible, overpowering, undefeatable **13** irrepressible **14** insurmountable

unconscionable
06 amoral, unholy **07** extreme, ungodly **08** criminal **09** excessive, unearthly, unethical **10** exorbitant, immoderate, inordinate, outrageous **11** extravagant **12** preposterous, unpardonable, unprincipled, unreasonable, unscrupulous **13** unjustifiable, unwarrantable

unconscious
03 out **04** deaf **05** blind, dazed **06** asleep, innate, latent, put out, reflex, zonked **07** drugged, fainted, in a coma, out cold, stunned, unaware, witless **08** comatose, heedless, ignorant, knee-jerk, lifeless **09** automatic, collapsed, concussed, impulsive, oblivious, passed out, repressed, senseless, unmindful, unwitting **10** accidental, blacked out, insensible, knocked out, subliminal, suppressed, unthinking **11** inadvertent, incognizant, inconscient, inconscious, instinctive, involuntary **12** subconscious **13** unintentional **14** dead to the world, out for the count

• **render unconscious**
04 stun **06** lay out, put out **07** garotte, garrote **08** garrotte, knock out

unconsciously
10 heedlessly, insensibly **11** impulsively, obliviously, unmindfully, unwittingly **12** accidentally, subliminally, unthinkingly **13** automatically, inadvertently, instinctively, involuntarily **15** unintentionally

unconsciousness
04 coma, doze **05** faint, sleep **06** snooze, torpor, trance **08** blackout, daydream, narcosis, numbness **12** inconscience, stupefaction **13** insensibility

unconstraint
07 abandon, freedom **08** openness **09** unreserve **10** liberality, relaxation **11** unrestraint **12** laissez-faire

uncontrollable
03 mad **04** wild **06** strong, unruly **07** furious, violent **08** absolute **10** disorderly **11** intractable **12** indisputable, out of control, ungovernable, unmanageable **13** irrepressible

uncontrolled
◇ *anagram indicator*
04 wild **06** random, randon, unruly **07** rampant, riotous, runaway, violent **08** uncurbed **09** unbridled, unchecked **10** boisterous, unhindered, unmastered **12** unrestrained **13** undisciplined

unconventional
◇ *anagram indicator*
03 odd **04** rare, zany **05** gipsy, gypsy, spacy, wacky, weird **06** far-out, freaky, fringe, spacey, way-out **07** bizarre, oddball, offbeat, radical, unusual **08** abnormal, bohemian, freakish, original, uncommon **09** different, eccentric, irregular, left-field **10** avant-garde, individual, long-haired, unorthodox **11** alternative, uncustomary **12** experimental **13** idiosyncratic

unconvincing
04 lame, weak **05** fishy **06** farfet, feeble, flimsy **07** dubious, suspect **08** doubtful, unlikely **10** far-fetched, improbable **11** implausible **12** questionable

uncooked
03 raw **09** au naturel

unco-operative
04 rude **07** awkward, cubbish, stroppy **08** stubborn **09** obstinate, unhelpful **10** unpleasant **12** bloody-minded

unco-ordinated
◇ *anagram indicator*
05 inept **06** clumsy **07** awkward **08** bumbling, bungling, ungainly **09** maladroit **10** disjointed, ungraceful **11** clodhopping

uncork
04 open, undo **05** clear, crack **06** broach, expose, unseal **07** uncover **08** push open **09** break open, burst open, force open, prise open, slide open

uncouth
◇ *anagram indicator*
04 rude **05** crude, rough **06** clumsy, coarse, gauche, rugged, rustic, unrude, vulgar **07** awkward, boorish, loutish, unknown **08** impolite, improper, ungainly, unseemly **09** graceless, rough-hewn, unrefined **10** uncultured, unfamiliar, ungraceful **11** bad-mannered, ill-mannered, uncivilized **12** uncultivated **15** unsophisticated

uncover
04 bare, leak, open, peel, rake, show

05 dig up, strip, unlid 06 detect, exhume, expose, reveal, unheal, unhele, unmask, unrake, unveil, unwrap 07 dismask, divulge, lay bare, lay open, unearth 08 disclose, discover, unbonnet, unshroud 09 make known, unsheathe 12 bring to light 13 blow the lid off, lift the lid off, take the lid off

uncritical
05 naive 07 unfussy 08 gullible, trusting 09 accepting, credulous, incurious 11 superficial, unselective 12 undiscerning 13 unquestioning 14 non-judgemental

unctuous
04 glib, oily 05 slick, suave 06 creamy, greasy, smarmy, smooth 07 fawning, gushing, servile 09 insincere, pietistic, plausible 10 obsequious 11 sycophantic 12 ingratiating 13 sanctimonious

uncultivated
03 new 04 wild 05 feral, rough, waste 06 desert, fallow, incult 07 natural, wilding 11 unhusbanded

uncultured
04 hick, rude 05 crude, ocker, rough 06 coarse, incult, rustic 07 boorish, ill-bred, uncouth 09 barbarous, unrefined 10 philistine 11 uncivilized 12 uncultivated 14 unintellectual 15 unsophisticated

undaunted
04 bold 05 brave 07 impavid, unbowed 08 fearless, intrepid, resolute, unafraid 09 dauntless, steadfast, unalarmed 10 courageous, undeterred, undismayed, unflagging 11 indomitable 13 undiscouraged

undecided
04 moot, open 05 vague 06 unsure 07 dubious, in doubt, unknown 08 doubtful, hesitant, wavering 09 debatable, dithering, uncertain, unsettled 10 ambivalent, indecisive, indefinite, in two minds, irresolute, of two minds, unresolved, up in the air 11 uncommitted 12 equivocating, in the balance 13 unestablished

undecorated
05 plain, stark 06 severe, simple 07 austere 08 inornate 09 classical, unadorned 10 functional 12 unornamented 13 unembellished

undefeated
07 supreme, unbowed, winning 08 unbeaten 09 unsubdued 10 triumphant, victorious 11 unconquered, unsurpassed 12 unvanquished

undefended
04 open 05 naked 07 exposed, unarmed 09 pregnable, unguarded 10 vulnerable 11 defenceless, unfortified, unprotected

undefiled
04 pure 05 clean, clear 06 chaste, intact, virgin 07 sinless 08 flawless, spotless, unsoiled, virginal 09 inviolate, unspotted, unstained, unsullied 10 immaculate, intemerate 11 unblemished

undefined
04 hazy 05 vague 06 woolly 07 inexact, shadowy, tenuous, unclear 08 formless, nebulous 09 imprecise 10 ill-defined, indefinite, indistinct 11 unexplained, unspecified 13 indeterminate

undemonstrative
04 cold, cool 05 aloof, stiff 06 formal, remote 07 distant 08 reserved, reticent 09 impassive, withdrawn 10 phlegmatic, restrained 11 unemotional 12 unresponsive 15 uncommunicative

undeniable
04 sure 05 clear 06 patent, proven 07 certain, evident, obvious 08 definite, manifest, positive 09 excellent, hard facts, undoubted 11 beyond doubt, indubitable, irrefutable 12 indisputable, unmistakable 13 incontestable 14 beyond question, unquestionable 15 unexceptionable

undeniably
09 certainly 10 definitely, positively 11 beyond doubt, indubitably, undoubtedly 12 indisputably, unmistakably 14 beyond question, unquestionably

undependable
06 fickle 07 erratic 08 unstable, variable 09 mercurial, uncertain 10 capricious, changeable, inconstant, unreliable 11 fair-weather, treacherous 12 inconsistent 13 irresponsible, unpredictable, untrustworthy

under
◇ *juxtaposition down indicator*
04 down, less 05 below, lower 06 within 07 beneath 08 downward, junior to, less than, under par 09 lower than 10 inferior to, underneath 11 secondary to, subordinate 13 subordinate to, subservient to

underclothes *see* **underwear**

undercover
03 sly 06 covert, hidden, secret 07 furtive, private 08 hush-hush, stealthy 09 concealed 11 clandestine, underground 12 confidential, intelligence 13 surreptitious

undercurrent
04 aura, hint 05 drift, sense, tinge, trend 07 feeling, flavour 08 movement, overtone, tendency, underset, undertow 09 underflow, undertone 10 atmosphere, suggestion

undercut
04 mine 05 filet 08 excavate, gouge out, scoop out, underbid 09 hollow out, undermine, undersell 10 tenderloin, underprice 11 undercharge 14 charge less than

underdog
04 prey 05 loser 06 victim 07 outcast 08 outsider 09 little man 11 unfortunate, weaker party 12 the exploited

underdone
04 rare 09 half-baked

underestimate
07 dismiss 08 belittle, minimize, misjudge, play down 09 disparage, sell short, underrate 10 look down on, trivialize, undervalue 12 miscalculate

undergarment *see* **underwear**

undergo
04 bear 05 enjoy, stand 06 endure, suffer 07 sustain, weather 08 submit to, tolerate, underlie 09 go through, put up with, withstand 10 experience 11 pass through

underground
04 tube 05 metro 06 buried, covert, hidden, secret, subway, sunken 07 covered, furtive, illegal, radical 08 secretly 09 concealed, hypogeous 10 avant-garde, hypogaeous, subversive, undercover, unofficial, unorthodox 11 alternative, below ground, clandestine 12 experimental, subterranean 13 revolutionary, surreptitious 15 below the surface

Underground and metro transport systems include:

01 T
04 BART, DART
07 the Tube
09 Chicago El, Rome Metro
10 City Circle, Paris Métro
11 Berlin S-Bahn, Berlin U-Bahn, Madrid Metro, Munich S-Bahn, Munich U-Bahn
13 New York Subway
15 Clockwork Orange, Washington Metro

See also **London**

undergrowth
05 brush, scrub 06 briars, bushes, shrubs, spring 07 bracken, thicket 08 brambles 09 brushwood, shrubbery, underwood 10 vegetation 11 ground cover

underhand
03 sly 05 shady 06 crafty, secret, shonky, sneaky 07 crooked, devious, furtive, immoral, oblique 08 improper, scheming, sinister, sneaking, stealthy 09 deceitful, deceptive, dishonest, unethical 10 backstairs, fraudulent 11 clandestine, unobtrusive 12 unscrupulous 13 hole-and-corner, surreptitious

underline
04 mark 06 stress 07 point up 09 emphasize, highlight, italicize 10 accentuate, foreground, underscore 15 draw attention to

underling
05 slave **06** lackey, menial, minion, nobody **07** flunkey, servant
08 hireling, inferior, munchkin, weakling **09** nonentity **11** subordinate

underlying
04 root **05** basal, basic **06** hidden, latent, veiled **07** lurking, primary, subject
08 inherent **09** concealed, essential, intrinsic, subjacent **10** elementary
11 fundamental, subordinate

undermine
03 dig, mar, sap **04** mine **05** erode
06 damage, impair, injure, tunnel, weaken **07** cripple, destroy, handbag, subvert, vitiate **08** excavate, sabotage, undercut, wear away **09** underwork
14 make less secure

undernourished
06 hungry **07** starved **08** anorexic, underfed **09** anorectic
12 malnourished

underprivileged
04 poor **05** needy **06** in need, in want
08 deprived **09** destitute, oppressed
10 in distress **11** impecunious
12 impoverished **13** disadvantaged

underrate
07 dismiss **08** belittle, inferior
09 disparage, downgrade, extenuate, sell short **10** depreciate, look down on, undervalue **13** underestimate

under-secretary
02 US

undersell
03 cut **05** slash **06** reduce **08** mark down, play down, undercut
09 disparage, sell short **10** depreciate, understate **11** undercharge

undershirt
04 vest **06** semmit **07** singlet, surcoat

undersized
03 wee **04** puny, tiny **05** dwarf, pygmy, scrub, small, teeny **06** little, minute, teensy **07** runtish, stunted **08** pint-size
09 atrophied, miniature, pint-sized
11 underweight **14** underdeveloped
15 achondroplastic

understand
03 dig, get, see **04** gaum, gorm, hear, know, read, take, twig **05** catch, click, get it, grasp, imply, learn, savey, savvy, think **06** accept, assume, fathom, follow, gather, make of, rumble, savvey, take in **07** believe, comfort, discern, elusive, feel for, get wise, make out, presume, realize, support, suppose, suss out **08** conceive, conclude, contrive, cotton on, perceive, tumble to **09** apprehend, empathize, enter into, figure out, interpret, latch onto, penetrate, recognize **10** appreciate, comprehend, sympathize
11 commiserate, make sense of **12** feel sorry for, get a handle on, get the hang of, identify with, know the ropes **13** get the message, get the picture, the penny drops

• failure to understand
04 anan, anon

understandable
05 clear, lucid, plain **06** direct
07 natural **08** expected **10** acceptable, accessible, admissible, penetrable, reasonable **11** transparent, unambiguous **12** intelligible, unsurprising **14** comprehensible, self-explaining **15** self-explanatory, straightforward

understanding
03 ken **04** gaum, gorm, head, idea, kind, pact, view, with **05** grasp, sense, trust **06** accord, belief, loving, notion, tender, uptake, wisdom **07** bargain, comfort, command, compact, conceit, empathy, entente, feeling, harmony, insight, lenient, opinion, patient, support **08** sympathy, tolerant
09 agreement, awareness, forgiving, hindsight, intellect, judgement, knowledge, sensitive **10** compassion, discerning, forbearing, impression, perception, supportive, thoughtful
11 arrangement, considerate, consolation, discernment, intelligent, sympathetic **12** appreciation, apprehension, intelligence
13 commiseration, compassionate, comprehension **14** interpretation

understate
07 dismiss **08** belittle, minimize, play down **09** soft-pedal, underplay
11 make light of

understated
04 mild **05** faint **06** low-key, subtle
07 implied **08** indirect **09** toned-down
10 indefinite, indistinct

understatement
07 litotes, meiosis **09** dismissal, restraint **12** minimization, underplaying

understood
05 tacit **07** assumed, implied
08 accepted, familiar, implicit, inferred, presumed, unspoken, unstated
09 unwritten **11** transparent

understudy
05 locum **06** deputy, double, fill-in, relief **07** reserve, stand-in **10** substitute
11 replacement

undersurface
03 pad **04** sole **05** belly **08** intrados, pavilion **09** gastraeum

undertake
03 try **05** agree, begin **06** accept, assume, pledge, tackle, take on
07 attempt, promise, receive
08 commence, contract, covenant, deal with, embark on, perceive, set about, shoulder **09** endeavour, get down to, guarantee, set in hand, underfong **10** enterprise, take in hand
13 put your hand to, set your hand to
14 commit yourself, get to grips with, grasp the nettle, turn your hand to
15 apply yourself to

undertaker
06 editor, surety **07** sponsor
08 compiler, upholder **09** mortician, projector, publisher **10** contractor
12 entrepreneur **15** funeral director

undertaking
03 job, vow **04** call, plan, task, word
06 affair, effort, pledge, scheme
07 attempt, emprise, project, promise, venture, warrant **08** business, campaign, contract, warranty
09 assurance, challenge, endeavour, guarantee, operation **10** commitment, enterprise **12** enterprising

undertone
04 aura, hint **05** tinge, touch, trace
06 murmur **07** feeling, flavour, whisper
09 undernote, undersong
10 atmosphere, intimation, suggestion
11 connotation **12** undercurrent

undervalue
07 disable, dismiss **08** disprize, minimize, misjudge, misprise, misprize
09 disparage, sell short, underrate
10 depreciate, look down on
13 underestimate

underwater
06 sunken **08** demersal, demersed, immersed, undersea, undertow
09 submarine, submerged
10 subaquatic, subaqueous

underwear
06 smalls, undies **08** grundies, lingerie, scanties, skivvies, underset
09 innerwear **10** underlinen
11 underthings **12** underclothes
13 underclothing, undergarments
14 unmentionables

Underwear includes:

03 bra
04 body, coms, jump, slip, vest
05 bania, cimar, combs, cymar, jupon, pants, shift, tanga, teddy, thong, tunic
06 banian, banyan, basque, briefs, corset, garter, girdle, knicks, semmit, skivvy, teddie, trunks
07 chemise, drawers, G-string, hosiery, linings, panties, singlet, spencer, Y-fronts
08 bloomers, camisole, chuddies, frillies, knickers, subucula, thermals
09 brassière, crinoline, jockstrap, long johns, petticoat, stockings, union suit, wyliecoat
10 suspenders, underdress, underpants, undershirt, underskirt
11 boxer shorts, directoires, undershorts
12 body stocking, camiknickers, combinations
13 liberty bodice, suspender-belt
14 French knickers

underweight
04 thin **08** underfed **10** undersized
11 half-starved **14** undernourished

underworld
03 Dis, pit **04** Ades, fire, hell **05** abyss,

below, Hades, Sheol **06** Erebus, the mob, Tophet **07** Abaddon, Acheron, Gehenna, inferno **08** gangland, Tartarus **09** down there, Malebolge, perdition **10** other place, subterrene **11** nether world, underground **12** lower regions **13** bottomless pit, criminal world **14** organized crime **15** abode of the devil, infernal regions

underwrite
04 back, fund, sign **05** write **06** insure **07** approve, confirm, endorse, finance, initial, sponsor, support **08** sanction **09** authorize, guarantee, subscribe, subsidize **11** countersign

undesirable
04 foul **05** nasty **08** disliked, riff-raff, unwanted **09** obnoxious, offensive, repugnant, unwelcome **10** unpleasant, unsuitable **11** distasteful, unwished-for **12** disagreeable, unacceptable **13** objectionable

undeveloped
04 rude **06** latent, neuter **07** dwarfed, stunted **08** immature, inchoate, unformed **09** embryonic, infantile, potential, unfledged **10** developing, primordial, Third World **12** less advanced **14** underdeveloped

undignified
06 clumsy **07** foolish **08** improper, ungainly, unseemly **09** inelegant **10** indecorous, unbecoming, unsuitable **13** inappropriate

undiluted
04 neat, pure **05** heady, sheer, utter **06** strong **07** unmixed **08** straight, unspoilt **09** unalloyed, unblended **11** unmitigated, unqualified **12** concentrated

undisciplined
◇ *anagram indicator*
04 wild **06** unruly, wanton, wilful **07** wayward **08** unsteady **09** untrained **10** unreliable, unschooled **11** disobedient **12** disorganized, obstreperous, uncontrolled, unrestrained, unsystematic **13** unpredictable

undisguised
04 bald, open **05** frank, naked, overt, stark, utter **06** patent **07** blatant, evident, genuine, obvious **08** apparent, explicit, manifest, outright, unmasked, unveiled **09** unadorned **11** transparent, unconcealed **12** undissembled **13** thoroughgoing

undisguisedly
06 openly **07** frankly, overtly **08** outright, patently **09** blatantly, obviously **12** unreservedly **13** transparently

undisputed
04 fact, sure **07** certain **08** accepted, unargued **09** undoubted **10** conclusive, recognized, undeniable **11** indubitable, irrefutable, uncontested **12** acknowledged, indisputable, unchallenged, unquestioned

undistinguished
04 so-so **05** banal, plain **06** common **07** ordinar, plebean **08** everyday, inferior, mediocre, nameless, ordinary, plebeian **10** not much cop, pedestrian **11** indifferent, not up to much **12** run-of-the-mill, unimpressive, unremarkable **13** no great shakes, unexceptional

undisturbed
04 calm, even **05** quiet **06** placid, serene **07** equable **08** composed, tranquil, wakeless **09** collected, quietsome, unruffled, untouched **10** motionless, unaffected, untroubled **11** unconcerned, unperturbed **13** uninterrupted

undivided
03 one **04** full **05** solid, total, whole **06** entire, intact, single, united **07** serious, sincere **08** combined, complete, unbroken **09** dedicated, exclusive, unanimous **10** individual, unreserved **11** individuate, pro indiviso, unqualified **12** concentrated, wholehearted

undo
◇ *anagram indicator*
03 dup, mar **04** free, open, poop, ruin **05** annul, crush, loose, poupe, quash, solve, spoil, untie, unzip, upset, wreck **06** cancel, defeat, loosen, offset, repeal, revoke, seduce, unbend, unclew, unhook, unlace, unlock, unwind, unwork, unwrap **07** destroy, nullify, release, retract, reverse, shatter, subvert, undight, unravel, unshape **08** overturn, separate, set aside, unbuckle, unbutton, unfasten **09** disanoint, undermine **10** invalidate, neutralize, obliterate **11** disentangle

undoing
◇ *anagram indicator*
04 ruin **05** shame **06** defeat **07** opening **08** collapse, disgrace, downfall, reversal, weakness **09** defeature, overthrow, ruination **10** defeasance **11** destruction, unfastening

undomesticated
04 wild **05** feral **06** savage **07** natural, untamed **11** uncivilized **12** ferae naturae

undone
◇ *anagram indicator*
04 left, lost, open **05** loose **06** adrift, opened, ruined, untied **07** ignored, omitted, seduced, unlaced **08** annulled, betrayed, unlocked **09** destroyed, forgotten, neglected, unwrought **10** incomplete, passed over, unbuttoned, unfastened, unfinished **11** outstanding, uncompleted, unfulfilled **14** unaccomplished
• **come undone**
03 run

undoubted
04 sure **06** patent **07** certain, obvious **08** definite **10** undisputed **11** indubitable, irrefutable, uncontested, undesirable **12** acknowledged, indisputable, unchallenged, unquestioned **14** unquestionable

undoubtedly
04 sure **06** surely **07** no doubt **08** of course **09** assuredly, certainly, doubtless **10** definitely, manifestly, no question, undeniably **11** beyond doubt, indubitably **12** unmistakably, without doubt **14** unquestionably

undreamed-of
07 amazing **08** undreamt **09** unheard-of **10** incredible, miraculous, unexpected, unforeseen, unhoped-for, unimagined **11** astonishing, unsuspected **13** inconceivable

undress
04 peel, shed **05** strip **06** devest, divest, nudity, remove, streak, uncase, unrobe **07** discase, disrobe, peel off, take off **08** disarray, unclothe **09** disattire, nakedness **10** déshabillé, dishabille **11** make unready **13** get your kit off

undressed
04 nude **05** naked **08** disrobed, en cuerpo, in the raw, starkers, stripped, untented **09** in the buff, self-faced, unclothed **10** stark-naked **12** not a stitch on **15** in the altogether

undue
07 extreme **08** improper, needless **09** excessive, obtrusive **10** immoderate, inordinate, undeserved **11** exaggerated, extravagant, superfluous, uncalled-for, unjustified, unnecessary, unwarranted **12** unreasonable **13** inappropriate

undulate
04 roll, wave, wavy **05** heave, surge, swell **06** billow, ripple **07** vibrate **11** rise and fall

undulating
04 wavy **05** waved **06** undate **07** rolling, sinuous **08** flexuose, flexuous, rippling, undulant, undulose, undulous **09** billowing, up-and-down **10** undulatory

unduly
◇ *anagram indicator*
03 too **04** over **08** overmuch **10** wrongfully **11** excessively, obtrusively **12** immoderately, inordinately, unreasonably **13** exaggeratedly, unjustifiably, unnecessarily

undutiful
05 slack **06** remiss **08** careless, disloyal, unfilial **09** negligent **10** defaulting, delinquent, neglectful

undying
07 abiding, eternal, lasting **08** constant, immortal, infinite,

unending, unfading **09** deathless, perennial, permanent, perpetual, unceasing **10** continuing **11** everlasting, sempiternal **12** imperishable, undiminished **14** indestructible

unearth
04 find **05** dig up **06** detect, dig out, exhume, expose, reveal **07** uncover **08** discover, disinter, excavate **12** bring to light

unearthly
05 eerie, weird **06** absurd, creepy, unholy **07** ghostly, phantom, strange, uncanny, ungodly **08** eldritch **09** appalling, celestial, unheard-of **10** horrendous, outrageous **12** otherworldly, preposterous, supernatural, unreasonable **13** preternatural, spine-chilling **14** unconscionable

unease
05 alarm, doubt, worry **06** qualms **07** anxiety, dis-ease **08** disquiet **09** agitation, misgiving, suspicion **10** discomfort, inquietude, uneasiness **11** nervousness **12** apprehension, perturbation

uneasily
04 hard

uneasiness
05 alarm, doubt, qualm, worry **06** qualms, unease **07** anxiety, dis-ease, malaise, misease, trouble **08** disquiet **09** agitation, dysphoria, misgiving, suspicion **10** discomfort, inquietude, solicitude **11** nervousness **12** apprehension, perturbation **14** distemperature, solicitousness **15** dissatisfaction

uneasy
◇ *anagram indicator*
04 edgy **05** nervy, shaky, tense, upset **06** on edge, queasy, queazy, unsure **07** alarmed, anxious, fidgety, jittery, keyed up, nervous, restive, twitchy, unquiet, worried, wound up **08** agitated, disquiet, insecure, restless, strained, troubled, worrying **09** disturbed, ill at ease, impatient, perturbed, troubling, unnerving, unrestful, unsettled **10** disquieted, disturbing, perturbing, unsettling **11** disquieting **12** apprehensive **13** disconcerting, uncomfortable

uneconomic
10 loss-making **12** uncommercial, unprofitable **15** non-profit-making

unedifying
04 idle

uneducated
06 unread **08** ignorant, untaught **09** benighted, lack-Latin, unlearned **10** illiterate, philistine, uncultured, uninformed, unschooled **12** uncultivated

unemotional
04 cold, cool **05** bland **06** stolid **08** detached, reserved **09** apathetic, bloodless, impassive, objective, unfeeling **10** phlegmatic **11** indifferent, passionless, unexcitable **12** phlegmatical, unresponsive **13** dispassionate **15** undemonstrative

unemphatic
08 downbeat **10** played-down **11** underplayed, understated, unobtrusive **12** soft-pedalled **14** unostentatious

unemployed
04 idle **07** jobless, laid off, unwaged **08** workless **09** on the dole, out of work, redundant **10** unoccupied

unending
07 endless, eternal, undated, undying **08** constant **09** ceaseless, continual, incessant, perpetual, unceasing **10** continuous **11** everlasting, never-ending, unremitting **12** interminable **13** thorough-going, uninterrupted

unendurable
10 shattering, unbearable **11** intolerable **12** insufferable, overwhelming **13** insupportable

unenthusiastic
04 cool, damp **05** blasé, bored **07** neutral, unmoved **08** lukewarm **09** apathetic, Laodicean **10** nonchalant **11** half-hearted, indifferent, unimpressed **12** uninterested, unresponsive

unenviable
09 dangerous, difficult, thankless **10** unpleasant **11** uncongenial, undesirable **12** disagreeable **13** uncomfortable

unequal
06 biased, uneven, unfair, unjust, unlike **07** not up to, varying **08** lopsided, unfitted, unsuited **09** different, disparate, excessive, incapable, irregular, unmatched **10** dissimilar, inadequate, unbalanced **11** incompetent, inequitable, unqualified **12** asymmetrical, not cut out for **14** discriminatory

unequalled
06 unique **07** supreme **08** peerless, unbeaten, unpeered **09** matchless, nonpareil, paramount, unmatched **10** inimitable, pre-eminent, surpassing, unrivalled **11** exceptional, unpatterned, unsurpassed **12** incomparable, transcendent, unparalleled

unequivocal
05 clear, plain **06** direct, square **07** evident, express **08** absolute, definite, distinct, explicit, outright, positive, straight **10** unreserved **11** categorical, unambiguous, unqualified **12** unmistakable **15** straightforward

unequivocally
06 firmly **07** clearly **08** directly **10** definitely, distinctly, explicitly, positively **12** unmistakably **13** unambiguously **14** unquestionably

unerring
04 dead, sure **05** clean, exact **07** certain, perfect, uncanny **08** accurate, inerrant **09** faultless, unfailing **10** impeccable, infallible

unerringly
04 bang, dead **10** accurately, infallibly **11** unfailingly

unethical
04 evil **05** shady, wrong **06** wicked **07** illegal, illicit, immoral **08** improper **09** dishonest, underhand **12** disreputable, unprincipled, unscrupulous **13** dishonourable **14** unprofessional

uneven
◇ *anagram indicator*
03 odd **05** bumpy, jerky, lumpy, rough, ruggy, stony **06** coarse, craggy, fitful, jagged, patchy, rugged, spotty, unfair **07** crooked, erratic, ruffled, rumpled, streaky, unequal **08** lopsided, one-sided, scratchy, unsteady, variable **09** inequable, irregular, spasmodic **10** accidented, changeable, ill-matched, unbalanced **11** fluctuating, inequitable **12** asymmetrical, inconsistent, intermittent

uneventful
04 dull **05** quiet **06** boring **07** humdrum, routine, tedious **08** everyday, ordinary, unvaried **10** monotonous, unexciting **11** commonplace, unmemorable **12** run-of-the-mill, unremarkable **13** unexceptional, uninteresting

unexampled
05 novel **06** unique **09** unheard-of, unmatched **10** unequalled **11** unpatterned **12** incomparable, unparalleled **13** unprecedented **15** never before seen

unexceptionable
04 mild, safe **05** bland **08** harmless, innocent **09** excellent, innocuous, peaceable **10** undeniable **11** inoffensive **15** unobjectionable

unexceptional
04 so-so **05** usual **06** common, normal **07** average, typical **08** everyday, mediocre, ordinary **10** not much cop **11** indifferent, not up to much, unmemorable **12** run-of-the-mill, unimpressive, unremarkable **13** no great shakes **15** undistinguished

unexcitable
04 calm, cool **06** serene **07** relaxed **08** composed, laid-back **09** contained, easy-going, impassive **10** phlegmatic **11** passionless **13** dispassionate, imperturbable, self-possessed, unimpassioned

unexpected
◇ *anagram indicator*
04 snap **05** shock **06** abrupt, chance, sudden, unware, unwary, wonder

07 amazing, unhoped, unusual, unwarie 08 emergent, unweened 09 inopinate, startling 10 accidental, fortuitous, surprising, unforeseen 11 astonishing, unlooked-for 13 unanticipated, unpredictable

unexpectedly
◇ *anagram indicator*
06 unware 08 abruptly, by chance, suddenly, unawares, unwarely 11 ex improviso 12 accidentally, à l'improviste, fortuitously, out of the blue, phenomenally, refreshingly, surprisingly 13 unpredictably 14 without warning

unexpressive
05 blank 06 vacant 07 deadpan 08 immobile 09 impassive 11 emotionless, inscrutable 12 inexpressive 13 inexpressible 14 expressionless

unfading
04 fast 07 abiding, durable, lasting, undying 08 constant, enduring, fadeless 09 evergreen, unfailing 12 imperishable 13 immarcescible

unfailing
04 sure, true 05 loyal 06 steady 07 certain, staunch, undying 08 constant, faithful, reliable, unerring, unfading 09 steadfast 10 dependable, infallible 12 indefectible, inexhaustive 13 inexhaustible

unfair
◇ *anagram indicator*
04 bent, foul, ugly 05 crook, shady, thick 06 biased, unjust 07 a bit off, bigoted, crooked, partial, slanted 08 one-sided, partisan, weighted, wrongful 09 arbitrary, deceitful, dishonest, unethical, unmerited 10 prejudiced, unbalanced, undeserved 11 inequitable, uncalled-for, unwarranted 12 below the belt, over the score, unprincipled, unreasonable, unscrupulous 14 discriminatory

unfairly
◇ *anagram indicator*
04 foul 07 wrongly 08 biasedly, unjustly 09 illegally, partially 10 improperly, unlawfully 11 dishonestly, inequitably 12 unreasonably

unfairness
04 bias 05 cross 07 bigotry, unright 08 inequity, misusage 09 injustice, prejudice 10 partiality 12 one-sidedness, partisanship 14 discrimination 15 inequitableness

unfaithful
05 false 06 fickle, unleal, untrue 07 godless 08 cheating, disloyal 09 deceitful, dishonest, faithless, insincere, two-timing 10 adulterous, inconstant, perfidious, unreliable 11 duplicitous, treacherous, unbelieving 13 double-dealing, untrustworthy

unfaltering
04 firm 05 fixed 06 steady 08 constant, resolute, tireless, untiring 09 steadfast, unfailing 10 unflagging, unswerving, unwavering, unyielding 11 unflinching 12 pertinacious 13 indefatigable

unfamiliar
◇ *anagram indicator*
03 new 05 alien, novel 07 curious, foreign, strange, uncouth, unknown, unusual 08 selcouth, uncommon, unversed 09 different, uncharted, unskilled 10 unexplored, uninformed 11 unpractised 12 unaccustomed, unacquainted, unconversant 13 inexperienced

unfashionable
03 out 04 lame 05 daggy, dated, dowdy, passé 06 démodé, old hat, square 08 obsolete, outmoded, unmodish 09 out of date, shapeless, unpopular 10 antiquated 12 old-fashioned, out of fashion

unfasten
04 open, undo 05 loose, unbar, unfix, unpin, untie, unzip 06 detach, loosen, unbend, unhasp, unlock, unwrap 07 unclasp, unloose, untruss 08 separate, unbuckle, uncouple, unloosen 10 disconnect

unfathomable
04 deep 06 hidden 07 abysmal 08 abstruse, baffling, esoteric, profound 09 unplumbed, unsounded 10 bottomless, fathomless, mysterious, unknowable 11 inscrutable, unsoundable 12 immeasurable, impenetrable, inexplicable 14 indecipherable

unfavourable
03 bad, ill 04 foul, poor 07 adverse, hostile, ominous, unlucky 08 contrary, critical, inimical, negative, untimely, untoward 09 ill-suited 10 prejudiced, unfriendly 11 in a bad light, inopportune, threatening, unfortunate, unpromising 12 discouraging, inauspicious, unseasonable 15 disadvantageous, uncomplimentary

unfavourably
03 ill 05 badly 06 poorly 09 adversely, in bad part, in ill part, unhappily 10 negatively 13 unfortunately, unpromisingly

unfeeling
04 cold, hard 05 cruel, harsh, stony 06 brutal 07 callous, inhuman 08 hardened, pitiless, uncaring 09 heartless, merciless 10 impassible, iron-headed, iron-witted 11 hard-hearted, insensitive, iron-hearted 13 unsympathetic

unfeigned
04 pure, real 05 frank 07 genuine, natural, sincere 08 unforced 09 heartfelt 10 unaffected 11 spontaneous 12 undissembled, wholehearted

unfettered
04 free 09 chainless, unbridled, unchecked 10 unconfined, unhampered, unhindered, unshackled 11 uninhibited 12 unrestrained, untrammelled 13 unconstrained

unfinished
◇ *tail deletion indicator*
05 crude, rough 06 undone 07 lacking, sketchy, wanting 08 half-done, inchoate 09 deficient, imperfect, incondite 10 incomplete 11 uncompleted, unfulfilled 14 unaccomplished

unfit
◇ *anagram indicator*
04 weak 05 inapt 06 feeble, flabby, impair, unable, unmeet 07 unequal, useless 08 decrepit, disabled, improper, unsuited 09 condemned, incapable, unhealthy, untrained 10 inadequate, ineligible, out of shape, unprepared, unsuitable 11 debilitated, ill-equipped, incompetent, ineffective, unqualified 12 disqualified 13 inappropriate, incapacitated 14 out of condition

unflagging
05 fixed 06 steady 07 staunch 08 constant, tireless, untiring 09 assiduous, unceasing, unfailing 10 persistent, unswerving 11 persevering, undeviating, unfaltering, unremitting 12 never-failing, single-minded 13 indefatigable

unflappable
04 calm, cool 07 equable 08 composed, laid-back 09 collected, easy-going, impassive, supercool, unruffled, unworried 10 phlegmatic 11 level-headed, unexcitable 13 imperturbable, self-possessed

unflattering
05 blunt 06 candid, honest 08 critical 09 outspoken 10 unbecoming 12 unattractive, unfavourable 15 uncomplimentary, unprepossessing

unflinching
04 bold, firm, sure 05 fixed 06 steady 07 staunch 08 constant, resolute, stalwart, unshaken 09 steadfast 10 determined, unblenched, unblinking, unswerving, unwavering 11 unblenching, unfaltering, unshrinking

unflinchingly
04 fast 06 boldly, firmly 08 steadily 09 staunchly 10 resolutely 11 steadfastly 12 unswervingly, unwaveringly 13 unfalteringly, unshrinkingly

unfold
04 grow, open, show, tell, undo 06 deploy, emerge, evolve, extend, relate, result, reveal, spread, unclew, uncoil, unfurl, unroll, untuck, unwrap 07 clarify, develop, display, explain, flatten, narrate, open out, present, uncover, unravel, work out

08 describe, disclose, shake out, undouble **09** come about, elaborate, explicate, interpret, make known, spread out **10** disenvelop, disinvolve, illustrate, straighten, stretch out **13** straighten out

unforeseen
06 casual, sudden **07** amazing, unusual **09** startling **10** surprising, unexpected **11** astonishing, unavoidable, unlooked-for, unpredicted **13** unanticipated, unpredictable

unforgettable
07 notable, special **08** historic, striking **09** important, indelible, memorable, momentous **10** impressive, noteworthy, remarkable **11** distinctive, exceptional, significant **13** extraordinary

unforgivable
08 shameful **10** deplorable, outrageous **11** disgraceful, inexcusable, intolerable **12** contemptible, indefensible, unpardonable **13** reprehensible, unjustifiable

unforgiven
10 unabsolved, unredeemed **11** unrepentant **12** unregenerate

unfortunate
◇ *anagram indicator*
03 ill **04** evil, poor **05** tough **06** doomed **07** adverse, hapless, ruinous, unhappy, unlucky **08** hopeless, ill-fated, ill-timed, luckless, untimely, untoward, wretched **09** ill-omened **10** calamitous, deplorable, disastrous, ill-advised, lamentable, unpleasant, unsuitable **11** evil-starred, injudicious, inopportune, misfortuned, regrettable **12** disaventrous, unfavourable, unsuccessful **13** inappropriate, misadventured **14** disadventurous **15** disadvantageous

unfortunately
◇ *anagram indicator*
04 alas **05** sadly **08** sad to say **09** unhappily, unluckily, worse luck **11** regrettably, sad to relate **13** I am sorry to say

unfounded
04 idle **05** false **08** baseless, spurious, unproven **09** trumped-up **10** bottomless, fabricated, groundless **11** conjectural, unjustified, unsupported **14** uncorroborated **15** unsubstantiated

unfrequented
04 lone **06** lonely, remote, untrod **08** deserted, desolate, isolated, secluded, solitary, untraded, wasteful **09** untrodden, unvisited **11** god-forsaken, sequestered, uninhabited

unfriendly
04 cold, cool, sour **05** aloof, chill, fraim, fremd, surly **06** chilly, fremit, frosty, frozen, unkind, wintry **07** distant, hostile, wintery **08** inimical, strained, unkindly **10** aggressive, unpleasant, unsociable **11** ill-disposed, quarrelsome, standoffish, uncongenial, unwelcoming **12** antagonistic, disagreeable, inauspicious, inhospitable, inimicitious **13** unneighbourly **14** unapproachable

unfrock
06 demote, depose, ungown **07** degrade, dismiss, suspend

unfruitful
04 arid **06** barren **07** sterile **08** infecund **09** exhausted, fruitless, infertile **10** unprolific **11** infructuous, unrewarding **12** impoverished, unproductive, unprofitable

unfurl
04 grow, open, undo **05** break **06** emerge, evolve, extend, result, spread, uncoil, unfold, unroll, unwrap **07** develop, display, flatten, open out, uncover, unravel, work out **09** come about, spread out **10** straighten, stretch out **13** straighten out

ungainly
◇ *anagram indicator*
05 gawky **06** clumsy, gauche, ungain **07** awkward, loutish, uncouth **08** gangling, unwieldy **09** awkwardly, inelegant, lumbering, maladroit **10** ungraceful **13** unco-ordinated

ungodly
05 world **06** sinful, wicked **07** corrupt, godless, immoral, impious, profane **08** depraved, unsocial **09** unearthly **10** horrendous, iniquitous, outrageous **11** blasphemous, intolerable, irreligious **12** preposterous, unreasonable **14** unconscionable

ungovernable
04 wild **06** unruly **10** disorderly, masterless, rebellious, refractory, ungoverned **12** unmanageable **14** uncontrollable, unrestrainable

ungracious
04 rude **07** boorish, ill-bred, mesquin, offhand, uncivil **08** churlish, impolite, mesquine **09** graceless **10** ungraceful, unhandsome, unmannerly **11** bad-mannered, disgracious **12** discourteous **13** disrespectful

ungrateful
04 rude **07** ingrate, irksome, selfish, uncivil **08** heedless, impolite **09** thankless **10** ungracious, unthankful **11** ill-mannered **12** disagreeable **14** unappreciative

unguarded
04 rash **06** unwary **07** exposed, foolish **08** careless, heedless, off guard **09** foolhardy, impolitic, imprudent, lippening, unweighed **10** incautious, indiscreet, undefended, unscreened, unthinking, vulnerable **11** defenceless, inadvertent, inattentive, thoughtless, unpatrolled, unprotected **12** undiplomatic **13** ill-considered, uncircumspect

ungulate
03 cow **04** deer **05** horse, takin, tapir **06** hoofed **09** Dinoceras **10** Deinoceras, mesohippus, rhinoceros, rhinocerot **11** rhinocerote **12** hippopotamus, Uintatherium **13** Palaeotherium, Titanotherium

unhappily
◇ *anagram indicator*
04 alas **05** sadly **08** sad to say, shrewdly **09** unluckily, worse luck **11** maliciously, regrettably, sad to relate **12** unfavourably **13** unfortunately **14** unsuccessfully

unhappy
◇ *anagram indicator*
03 low, sad **04** blue, down, glum **05** fed up, inapt, upset **06** clumsy, gloomy **07** awkward, hapless, unlucky **08** dejected, downcast, ill-fated, luckless, mournful, tactless **09** depressed, ill-chosen, long-faced, miserable, sorrowful, woebegone **10** despondent, dispirited, ill-advised, ill-starred, melancholy, unsuitable **11** crestfallen, injudicious, mischievous, unfortunate **12** disconsolate, infelicitous **13** inappropriate **14** down in the dumps

unharmed
04 safe **05** sound, whole **06** intact, unhurt **09** undamaged, uninjured, unscathed, untouched

unhealthy
03 ill **04** sick, weak **05** crook, frail, pasty **06** ailing, feeble, infirm, morbid, poorly, sickly, unwell **07** harmful, invalid, noxious, unsound **08** diseased, epinosic **09** dangerous, injurious, unnatural **10** indisposed, insalutary, insanitary, unhygienic, unsanitary **11** debilitated, detrimental, unwholesome **12** insalubrious

unheard-of
03 new **06** unsung **07** obscure, unknown, unusual **08** shocking **09** offensive **10** outrageous, unfamiliar, unheralded **11** exceptional, undreamed-of, unthinkable **12** preposterous, unacceptable, unbelievable, undiscovered, unimaginable **13** extraordinary, inconceivable, unprecedented

unheeded
07 ignored, unnoted **08** unminded, untented **09** disobeyed, forgotten, neglected, unnoticed **10** overlooked, unobserved, unremarked **11** disregarded

unhelpful
04 rude **06** rustic, touchy **07** awkward, boorish, cubbish, loutish, prickly, stroppy **08** stubborn **09** irritable, obstinate **10** unpleasant **11** disobliging, obstructive, troublesome **12** bloody-minded **13** oversensitive, unco-operative **15** unaccommodating

unheralded
06 unsung **08** surprise **09** unnoticed **10** unexpected, unforeseen **11** unannounced **12** unadvertised, unproclaimed, unpublicized, unrecognized

unhesitating
05 ready **06** prompt **07** instant **08** implicit **09** automatic, confident, immediate **10** unwavering **11** spontaneous, unfaltering **12** wholehearted **13** instantaneous, unquestioning

unhinge
05 craze, upset **06** madden **07** confuse, derange, unnerve **08** disorder, distract, drive mad, unsettle **09** unbalance

unhinged
03 mad **04** nuts **05** barmy, crazy, loony, loopy, nutty, potty **06** insane **07** berserk, bonkers, frantic, lunatic **08** confused, demented, deranged **09** delirious, disturbed, unsettled **10** disordered, distraught, irrational, out to lunch, unbalanced **11** not all there **12** round the bend **13** off your rocker, of unsound mind, out of your mind, round the twist **15** non compos mentis

unholy
◇ *anagram indicator*
04 evil **06** sinful, wicked **07** corrupt, godless, immoral, impious, ungodly **08** depraved, dreadful, shocking, terrible **09** unearthly, unnatural **10** horrendous, iniquitous, outrageous **11** blasphemous, irreligious **12** unreasonable **14** unconscionable

unhook
04 free, undo **05** loose, untie **06** loosen **07** release **08** unfasten

unhoped-for
10 incredible, surprising, unexpected, unforeseen **11** undreamed-of, unlooked-for **12** unbelievable, unimaginable **13** unanticipated

unhurried
04 calm, easy, slow **06** sedate **07** relaxed **08** laid-back **09** easy-going, leisurely **10** deliberate

unhurt
02 OK **04** okay, safe **05** sound, whole **06** intact **08** all right, unharmed **09** uninjured, unscathed, untouched **12** whole-skinned

unhygienic
04 foul **05** dirty **06** filthy, impure **07** dirtied, noisome, noxious, unclean **08** feculent, infected, infested, polluted **09** unhealthy **10** insanitary **11** unhealthful, unsanitized **12** contaminated, insalubrious **13** disease-ridden

unidentified
06 secret **07** obscure, strange, unknown, unnamed **08** nameless, unmarked **09** anonymous, incognito **10** mysterious, unfamiliar **12** unclassified, unrecognized

unification
05 union **06** enosis, fusion, merger **07** uniting **08** alliance **09** coalition **10** federation **11** coalescence, combination, integration **12** amalgamation **13** confederation, incorporation

uniform
01 U **03** rig **04** even, flat, garb, like, same, sole, suit **05** alike, dress, equal, habit, level, robes **06** livery, outfit, smooth, stable, steady **07** costume, equable, regalia, regular, similar **08** constant, insignia, of a piece, unbroken **09** identical, unvarying **10** consistent, invariable, monotonous, throughout, unchanging **11** homogeneous, regimentals, undeviating

uniformity
06 tedium **08** drabness, dullness, evenness, flatness, monotony, sameness **09** constancy **10** regularity, similarity, similitude **11** homogeneity **12** homomorphism **13** invariability

unify
03 mix **04** bind, fuse, join, weld **05** blend, merge, unite **07** combine **08** coalesce **09** integrate **10** amalgamate **11** consolidate **12** come together **13** bring together

unifying
06 unific **07** henotic, uniting **11** combinatory, esemplastic, reconciling **13** consolidative

unimaginable
07 amazing **08** unlikely **09** fantastic, unheard-of **10** far-fetched, impossible, incredible, outlandish, staggering **11** astonishing, implausible, undreamed-of, unthinkable **12** mind-boggling, preposterous, unbelievable, unconvincing **13** extraordinary, inconceivable

unimaginative
03 dry **04** dull, tame **05** banal, samey, stale, usual **06** barren, boring **07** mundane, prosaic, routine **08** lifeless, ordinary **09** hackneyed **10** flat-footed, pedestrian, unexciting, uninspired, unoriginal **11** predictable **12** matter-of-fact

unimpaired
05 sound **06** entire, intact **08** integral
• remain unimpaired
04 last

unimpeachable
07 perfect **08** reliable, spotless **09** blameless, faultless **10** dependable, immaculate, impeccable **11** unblemished **12** unassailable **14** irreproachable, unquestionable **15** unchallengeable

unimpeded
04 free, open **05** clear **08** all-round **09** unblocked, unchecked **10** unhampered, unhindered **11** uninhibited **12** unrestrained, untrammelled **13** unconstrained

unimportant
04 idle **05** light, minor, petty **06** slight **07** trivial **08** marginal, nugatory, peddling, trifling **09** minuscule, no big deal, secondary, small-time, worthless **10** immaterial, incidental, irrelevant, negligible, peripheral **11** down-the-line, Mickey Mouse **12** inconsequent **13** insignificant, insubstantial, no great shakes **14** inconsiderable **15** inconsequential, of no consequence

unimpressive
04 dull **06** common **07** average **08** mediocre, ordinary **10** unexciting, unimposing **11** commonplace, indifferent **12** unremarkable **13** unexceptional, uninteresting, unspectacular **15** undistinguished

uninhabited
04 lone **05** empty **06** desert, lonely, vacant **08** deserted, desolate, wasteful **09** abandoned, unpeopled, unsettled **10** unoccupied **11** unpopulated

uninhibited
04 free, open **05** frank **06** candid, rave-up **07** natural, relaxed **08** informal **09** abandoned, liberated, outspoken **10** unreserved **11** spontaneous **12** uncontrolled, unrestrained, unrestricted **13** unconstrained **15** unself-conscious

uninspired
04 dull **05** samey, stale, stock, trite **06** boring **07** humdrum, pompier, prosaic **08** ordinary **10** flat-footed, pedestrian, unexciting, unoriginal **11** commonplace, indifferent, uninspiring **13** unexceptional, unimaginative, uninteresting **15** undistinguished

uninspiring
03 dry **04** dull, flat, tame **05** ho-hum, samey, stale, trite **06** boring, dreary, jejune, tiring **07** humdrum, insipid, prosaic, routine, tedious **08** tiresome, unvaried **10** long-winded, monotonous, uneventful, unexciting **11** commonplace, repetitious, stultifying **13** institutional, unimaginative, uninteresting **14** soul-destroying

unintelligent
04 dull, dumb, slow **05** dense, silly, thick **06** obtuse, stupid **07** fatuous, foolish, witless **08** gormless **09** brainless **10** half-witted, unthinking **11** empty-headed, unreasoning

unintelligible
07 complex, garbled, jumbled, muddled, obscure **08** involved, puzzling **09** illegible, scrambled **10** incoherent, mysterious, unreadable **11** complicated, double Dutch **12** impenetrable, inarticulate, unfathomable **14** indecipherable

unintentional
08 careless **09** unplanned, unwilling, unwitting **10** accidental, fortuitous, unintended **11** inadvertent, involuntary, unconscious
12 uncalculated **14** unpremeditated

uninterested
05 blasé, bored **07** distant **08** listless
09 apathetic, impassive, incurious
10 uninvolved **11** indifferent, pococurante, unconcerned
12 unresponsive **14** not giving a damn, not giving a hoot, not giving a toss, unenthusiastic

uninteresting
03 dry **04** drab, dull, flat, tame
05 samey, stale **06** boring, dreary
07 humdrum, prosaic, tedious
08 tiresome **09** incurious, wearisome
10 monotonous, pedestrian, uneventful, unexciting **11** indifferent, uninspiring **12** unimpressive

uninterrupted
06 steady **07** endless, non-stop
08 constant, peaceful, straight, unbroken, unending **09** ceaseless, continual, continued, incessant, sustained, unceasing **10** continuous
11 undisturbed, unremitting

uninvited
07 unasked **08** unbidden, unsought, unwanted **09** unwelcome
11 unsolicited

uninviting
09 offensive, repellent, repulsive, unsavoury **10** forbidding, off-putting, unpleasant **11** distasteful, unappealing, undesirable, unwelcoming
12 disagreeable, unappetizing, unattractive

uninvolved
04 free **06** dégagé **09** fancy-free, footloose, unengaged **10** unattached, unhampered, unhindered
11 independent, uncommitted
12 untrammelled

union
01 U **04** club, yoke **05** blend, close, unity **06** accord, cement, fusion, league, merger **07** harmony, joining, mixture, uniting, wedding, wedlock
08 alliance, juncture, marriage, nuptials, spousage **09** agreement, coalition, espousals, matrimony, synthesis, unanimity **10** consortium, couplement, federation, trade union, Zollverein **11** association, cementation, coadunation, coalescence, combination, concurrence, confederacy, conjugation, conjunction, unification
12 amalgamation **13** confederation, consolidation **14** conglutination

See also **rugby**

Unions include:

02 AU, CU, EU
03 AUT, CDU, CGT, CWU, EIS, EMU, FBU, GMB, ITU, NFU, NUJ, NUM, NUS, NUT, RFU, RMT
04 BIFU, CCCP, TGWU, UEFA, USSR, ZANU, ZAPU
05 BECTU, T and G
06 Amicus, Soviet, UNISON
07 African
08 European

unionist
01 U **02** UU

unique
03 one **04** lone, only, sole **05** alone
06 one-off, single **07** unusual
08 peerless, singular, solitary
09 matchless, nonpareil, unmatched
10 inimitable, one and only, one of a kind, pre-eminent, sui generis, unequalled, unrivalled **11** idiographic
12 incomparable, unparalleled
13 unprecedented

uniquely
04 only **06** singly, solely **08** by itself, markedly **09** specially **10** inimitably, peculiarly, peerlessly, remarkably, singularly **11** in its own way, matchlessly
12 incomparably **13** distinctively

unison
05 unity **06** accord **07** concert, concord, harmony **09** agreement, unanimity **11** co-operation

• **in unison**
08 in chorus **09** in harmony
10 homophonic **11** in agreement **13** at the same time, in co-operation
14 simultaneously **15** at the same moment

unit
03 ace, one **04** item, part **05** corps, force, piece, squad, whole **06** entity, module, patrol, system **07** brigade, element, portion, section, segment
08 assembly **09** component, task force **10** detachment, individual
11 constituent

See also **measurement**; **military**; **measurement of pressure** *under* **pressure**; **unit of weight** *under* **weight**

unite
03 fay, lap, tie, wad, wed **04** ally, band, fuse, join, knit, knot, link, lock, meng, ming, pool, weld **05** blend, clasp, close, joint, marry, menge, merge, twist, unify **06** cement, cleave, couple, embody, imbody, splice **07** accrete, combine, conjoin, connect, consort
08 coalesce, copulate, federate
09 associate, coadunate, conjugate, co-operate, synoecize
10 amalgamate, close ranks, join forces
11 confederate, consolidate, incorporate **12** concorporate, conglutinate, pull together
15 consubstantiate, make common cause

united
01 U **03** one **04** ment **05** meint, meynt
06 agreed, allied, menged, minged, pooled **07** unified **08** combined, conjoint, in accord **09** concerted, conjoined, corporate, unanimous
10 affiliated, collective, like-minded
11 amalgamated, conjunctive, co-operative, in agreement
12 incorporated **13** concorporated

United Arab Emirates
03 ARE, UAE

United Kingdom
02 UK

See also **prime minister**

UK cities include:

03 Ely
04 Bath, York
05 Derby, Leeds, Newry, Ripon, Truro, Wells
06 Armagh, Bangor, Dundee, Durham, Exeter, London, Oxford
07 Belfast, Bristol, Cardiff, Chester, Glasgow, Lincoln, Lisburn, Newport, Norwich, Preston, Salford, Swansea
08 Aberdeen, Bradford, Carlisle, Coventry, Hereford, Kingston, Plymouth, St Albans, St David's, Stirling
09 Cambridge, Edinburgh, Inverness, Lancaster, Leicester, Lichfield, Liverpool, Newcastle, Salisbury, Sheffield, Wakefield, Worcester
10 Birmingham, Canterbury, Chichester, Gloucester, Manchester, Nottingham, Portsmouth, Sunderland, Winchester
11 Londonderry, Southampton, Westminster
12 Brighton
13 Wolverhampton

UK landmarks include:

04 Fens, Tyne
06 Big Ben, Exmoor, Mersey, Severn, Thames
07 Avebury, Glencoe, Needles, Snowdon
08 Balmoral, Bass Rock, Ben Nevis, Dartmoor, Land's End, Loch Ness
09 Cape Wrath, Chilterns, Cotswolds, Helvellyn, London Eye, New Forest, Offa's Dyke, Royal Mile, Snowdonia, Tay Bridge
10 Beachy Head, Cader Idris, Holy Island, Ironbridge, Kew Gardens, Loch Lomond, Lough Earne, Lough Neagh, Stonehenge, The Gherkin, Windermere
11 Arthur's Seat, Canary Wharf, Forth Bridge, Hever Castle, Isle of Wight, John O'Groats, Leeds Castle, Lizard Point, Menai Bridge, Old Man of Hoy, Scafell Pike, York Minster
12 Antonine Wall, Brighton Pier, Castle Howard, Cheddar Gorge, Forest of Dean, Hadrian's Wall, Hampton Court, Humber Bridge, Lake District, Peak District, Seven Sisters, Severn Bridge
13 Arundel Castle, Blue John Caves, Brecon Beacons, Bridge of Sighs, Hatfield House, Liver Building,

Norfolk Broads, Robin Hood's Bay, Royal Pavilion, Tower of London, Warwick Castle, Windsor Castle
14 Blackpool Tower, Blenheim Palace, Giant's Causeway, Holyrood Palace, Inverary Castle, Isle of Anglesey, Sherwood Forest, Stirling Castle, Wells Cathedral
15 Angel of the North, Bodleian Library, Caledonian Canal, Cerne Abbas Giant, Chatsworth House, Edinburgh Castle, Flamborough Head, Grand Union Canal, Post Office Tower, St Michael's Mount

See also **town**

United Nations

United Nations members:

04 Chad, Cuba, Fiji, Iran, Iraq, Laos, Mali, Oman, Peru, Togo
05 Benin, Chile, China, Congo, Egypt, Gabon, Ghana, Haiti, India, Italy, Japan, Kenya, Libya, Malta, Nauru, Nepal, Niger, Palau, Qatar, Samoa, Spain, Sudan, Syria, Tonga, Yemen
06 Angola, Belize, Bhutan, Brazil, Canada, Cyprus, France, Greece, Guinea, Guyana, Israel, Jordan, Kuwait, Latvia, Malawi, Mexico, Monaco, Norway, Panama, Poland, Russia, Rwanda, Sweden, Turkey, Tuvalu, Uganda, Zambia
07 Albania, Algeria, Andorra, Armenia, Austria, Bahrain, Belarus, Belgium, Bolivia, Burundi, Comoros, Croatia, Denmark, Ecuador, Eritrea, Estonia, Finland, Georgia, Germany, Grenada, Hungary, Iceland, Ireland, Jamaica, Lebanon, Lesotho, Liberia, Moldova, Morocco, Myanmar, Namibia, Nigeria, Romania, Senegal, Somalia, St Lucia, Tunisia, Ukraine, Uruguay, Vanuatu, Vietnam
08 Barbados, Botswana, Bulgaria, Cambodia, Cameroon, Colombia, Djibouti, Dominica, Ethiopia, Honduras, Kiribati, Malaysia, Maldives, Mongolia, Pakistan, Paraguay, Portugal, Slovakia, Slovenia, Sri Lanka, Suriname, Tanzania, Thailand, Zimbabwe
09 Argentina, Australia, Cape Verde, Costa Rica, East Timor, Guatemala, Indonesia, Lithuania, Macedonia, Mauritius, Nicaragua, San Marino, Singapore, Swaziland, The Gambia, Venezuela
10 Azerbaijan, Bangladesh, El Salvador, Kazakhstan, Kyrgyzstan, Luxembourg, Madagascar, Mauritania, Mozambique, New Zealand, North Korea, Seychelles, South Korea, Tajikistan, The Bahamas, Uzbekistan
11 Afghanistan, Burkina Faso, Côte d'Ivoire, Philippines, Saudi Arabia, Sierra Leone, South Africa, Switzerland
12 Guinea-Bissau, Turkmenistan
13 Czech Republic, Liechtenstein, United Kingdom
14 Papua New Guinea, Solomon Islands, The Netherlands
15 Marshall Islands, St Kitts and Nevis
16 Brunei Darussalam, Equatorial Guinea
17 Antigua and Barbuda, Dominican Republic, Trinidad and Tobago
18 São Tomé and Príncipe, United Arab Emirates
19 Serbia and Montenegro
20 Bosnia and Herzegovina
21 United States of America
22 Central African Republic
25 St Vincent and the Grenadines
27 Federated States of Micronesia
28 Democratic Republic of the Congo

United States of America

02 US **03** USA

See also **president**

US cities include:

02 LA, NY
03 NYC
05 Boise, Dover, Miami, Salem
06 Albany, Austin, Boston, Dallas, Denver, Helena, Juneau, Pierre, St Paul, Topeka
07 Atlanta, Augusta, Chicago, Concord, Detroit, Houston, Jackson, Lansing, Lincoln, Madison, Memphis, New York, Olympia, Phoenix, Raleigh, Santa Fe, Seattle, Trenton
08 Bismarck, Cheyenne, Columbia, Columbus, Hartford, Honolulu, Las Vegas, Portland, Richmond, San Diego
09 Annapolis, Baltimore, Des Moines, Frankfort, Milwaukee, Nashville
10 Baton Rouge, Carson City, Charleston, Harrisburg, Little Rock, Los Angeles, Montgomery, Montpelier, New Orleans, Pittsburgh, Providence, Sacramento, San Antonio, Washington
11 New York City, Springfield, Tallahassee
12 Indianapolis, Oklahoma City, Philadelphia, Salt Lake City, San Francisco, Washington DC
13 Jefferson City

US landmarks include:

05 Yukon
07 Capitol, Rockies
08 Colorado, Lake Erie, Missouri, Mt Elbert, Mt Vernon, Pentagon, Yosemite
09 Graceland, Hollywood, Hoover Dam, Lake Huron, Milwaukee, Mt Rainier
10 Everglades, Great Lakes, Joshua Tree, Mt McKinley, Mt Rushmore, Mt St Helens, Sears Tower, White House
11 Grand Canyon, Lake Ontario, Liberty Bell, Mississippi, Pearl Harbor, Space Needle, Yellowstone
12 Appalachians, Carnegie Hall, Lake Michigan, Lake Superior, Niagara Falls
13 Great Salt Lake
14 Brooklyn Bridge, Monument Valley, Rocky Mountains
15 Lincoln Memorial, Statue of Liberty

See also **president**; **state**

unity

03 one **05** peace, union **06** accord **07** concert, concord, harmony, oneness **09** agreement, consensus, integrity, unanimity, wholeness **10** solidarity **11** unification **12** amalgamation, togetherness

universal

01 U **03** all **05** total, whole **06** common, cosmic, entire, global, varsal, versal **07** general **08** all-round, catholic, ecumenic **09** unlimited, worldwide **10** ecumenical, ubiquitous **11** omnipresent **12** all-embracing, all-inclusive **13** comprehensive **14** across-the-board

universality

08 entirety, totality, ubiquity **10** commonness, generality, prevalence **11** catholicity **12** completeness, predominance **14** generalization

universally

06 always **09** uniformly **10** everywhere, invariably **12** ubiquitously

universe

03 all **05** world **06** cosmos, nature **07** heavens **08** creation, everyone **09** firmament, macrocosm **14** the sum of things

university

01 U **03** uni **07** academy, college, varsity **08** academia **09** institute **11** polytechnic

Ivy League universities:

04 Yale
05 Brown
07 Cornell, Harvard
08 Columbia
09 Dartmouth, Princeton
12 Pennsylvania

Seven Sisters colleges:

05 Smith
06 Vassar
07 Barnard
08 Bryn Mawr
09 Radcliffe, Wellesley
12 Mount Holyoke

Universities include:

02 OU
03 LSE, MIT, UCL
04 City, Open, UCLA
05 Aston, Keele, UMIST
06 Brunel, Durham, Leiden, Napier, Oxford
07 Caltech, Warwick
08 Ann Arbor, Berkeley, Sorbonne, Stanford
09 Cambridge, St Andrews
10 De Montfort, Heriot-Watt

12 Robert Gordon, Thames Valley
13 Royal Holloway
14 Trinity College
15 California State, Imperial College, Juilliard School

See also **college**

• at university
02 up

unjust
05 wrong 06 biased, unfair, wanton 07 partial, unequal 08 one-sided, partisan, wrongful, wrongous 10 iniquitous, prejudiced, undeserved 11 inequitable, unjustified, unrighteous 12 unreasonable

unjustifiable
05 undue 09 excessive 10 immoderate, outrageous 11 inexcusable, uncalled-for, unwarranted 12 indefensible, unacceptable, unforgivable, unpardonable, unreasonable

unkempt
◇ *anagram indicator*
05 messy, ratty, rough, tousy, touzy, towsy, towzy 06 frowsy, frowzy, scungy, shabby, sloppy, untidy 07 rumpled, scraggy, scruffy, squalid, tousled 08 scraggly, slobbish, slovenly, uncombed 09 mal soigné, shambolic, ungroomed 10 disordered, scraggling, unpolished 11 dishevelled

unkind
04 mean 05 cruel, harsh, nasty, snide 06 bitchy, shabby 07 callous, inhuman, vicious 08 inhumane, pitiless, ruthless, spiteful, uncaring, unkindly 09 heartless, malicious, unfeeling 10 malevolent, unfriendly 11 cold-hearted, disobliging, hard-hearted, insensitive, thoughtless 12 uncharitable 13 inconsiderate, unsympathetic

unkindness
05 spite 07 cruelty 08 meanness 09 harshness 10 ill-feeling, inhumanity 11 callousness 13 insensitivity, maliciousness 14 unfriendliness 15 hard-heartedness

unknowable
06 untold 08 infinite 12 incalculable, unfathomable, unimaginable 13 unconditioned, unforeseeable, unpredictable 15 unascertainable

unknowing
06 chance, unwist 07 unaware 08 ignorant 09 unplanned, unwitting 10 accidental, unintended, unthinking 11 inadvertent, involuntary, unconscious 12 unsuspecting 13 unintentional

unknown
01 X, Y, Z 03 ign, new 04 dark 05 alien 06 hidden, occult, secret, unkent, untold 07 foreign, obscure, strange, unnamed 08 nameless, unkenned 09 anonymous, concealed, incognito, uncharted, unheard-of 10 mysterious, substance x, undivulged, unexplored, unfamiliar, unrevealed 11 undisclosed 12 undiscovered, unidentified

unlawful
06 banned 07 illegal, illicit, vicious 08 criminal, non licet, outlawed, wrongful 09 forbidden 10 prohibited, unlicensed 12 illegitimate, unauthorized, unsanctioned 13 against the law

unleash
04 free 05 let go, loose, untie 07 deliver, release, set free, unloose 08 let loose, untether

unless
03 but 04 less, nisi, save 06 except 07 without

unlettered
08 ignorant, untaught 09 unlearned, untutored 10 illiterate, uneducated, unlessoned, unschooled

unlike
06 unlich 07 difform, diverse, opposed, unequal, various 08 distinct, opposite 09 as against, different, disparate, divergent, unconform, unrelated 10 contrasted, dissimilar, ill-matched 11 as opposed to 12 dissimilar to, incompatible, in contrast to 13 different from, heterogeneous 14 out of character

unlikely
◇ *anagram indicator*
04 last, slim 05 faint, fishy, small 06 farfet, remote, slight, unlike 07 distant, dubious, outside, suspect 08 doubtful 09 fictional 10 far-fetched, improbable, improbably, incredible, suspicious, unexpected, unsuitable 11 implausible, unpromising 12 questionable, unbelievable, unconvincing, unimaginable 13 inconceivable 14 inconsiderable 15 unprepossessing

unlimited
◇ *ends deletion indicator*
04 full, vast 05 great, total 06 untold 07 endless, immense 08 absolute, complete, infinite 09 boundless, countless, extensive, limitless, shoreless, unbounded, unchecked, unimpeded, universal 10 indefinite, unconfined, unhampered 11 confineless, illimitable, unqualified 12 immeasurable, incalculable, uncontrolled, unrestricted 13 inexhaustible, unconditional, unconstrained 15 all-encompassing

unload
04 dump 05 empty, strip 06 remove, unlade, unpack, unship, vacate 07 disload, offload, relieve 08 unburden, uncharge 09 disburden, discharge, unfraught 10 disburthen

unlock
04 free, open, undo 05 unbar 06 unbolt 07 release, unlatch 08 disclose, unfasten

unlooked-for
05 lucky 06 chance 08 surprise 09 fortunate 10 fortuitous, surprising, unexpected, unforeseen, unhoped-for 11 undreamed-of, unpredicted, unthought-of 13 unanticipated

unloved
05 hated 06 dumped 07 spurned 08 detested, disliked, forsaken, loveless, rejected, unwanted 09 neglected, unpopular 10 uncared-for

unluckily
04 alas 05 sadly 08 sad to say 09 unhappily, worse luck 11 regrettably, sad to relate 13 I am sorry to say, unfortunately

unlucky
04 poor 05 black, stiff, tough 06 cursed, donsie, doomed, jinxed, wicked 07 adverse, hapless, infaust, ominous, unhappy 08 ill-fated, luckless, sinister, unchancy, untoward, wretched 09 ill-omened, mischancy, miserable, wanchancy 10 calamitous, disastrous, ill-starred, left-handed, unpleasant, wanchancie 11 star-crossed, unfortunate, unpromising 12 catastrophic, inauspicious, unfavourable, unpropitious, unsuccessful 14 down on your luck 15 disadvantageous

unmanageable
04 wild 05 bulky 06 gallus, unruly, wanton 07 awkward, gallows, ropable, unhandy, unweldy 08 ropeable, unwieldy 09 difficult, wieldless 10 cumbersome, disorderly, refractary, refractory, weeldlesse 11 intractable, troublesome 12 incommodious, inconvenient, obstreperous, recalcitrant, ungovernable 13 impracticable 14 uncontrollable

unmanly
03 wet 04 base, soft, weak 05 cissy, weedy, wussy 06 craven, effete, feeble, yellow 07 wimpish 08 cowardly, womanish 09 weak-kneed 10 effeminate, namby-pamby 11 lily-livered 13 dishonourable 14 chicken-hearted

unmannerly
04 rude 07 boorish, ill-bred, low-bred, uncivil, uncouth 08 impolite 09 graceless, misleared 10 ungracious 11 bad-mannered, ill-mannered 12 badly-behaved, discourteous 13 disrespectful

unmarried
04 free, lone 05 unwed 06 maiden, single 08 celibate, divorced 09 available, on your own, separated 10 unattached 11 partnerless

unmask
04 bare, show 06 detect, expose, reveal, show up, unveil 07 uncloak, uncover, unvisor 08 disclose, discover, unvizard

unmatched
03 odd **04** orra **06** unique **07** supreme **08** peerless **09** matchless, nonpareil, paramount **10** consummate, unequalled, unexampled, unfellowed, unrivalled **11** unparagoned, unsurpassed **12** incomparable, unparalleled **13** beyond compare

unmentionable
05 taboo **08** immodest, indecent, shameful, shocking **09** forbidden **10** abominable, scandalous, unpleasant **11** disgraceful, unspeakable, unutterable **12** embarrassing

unmerciful
04 hard **05** cruel **06** brutal **07** callous **08** pitiless, ruthless, sadistic, uncaring **09** heartless, merciless, spareless, unfeeling, unsparing **10** implacable, relentless **11** remorseless, unrelenting

unmethodical
06 random **07** muddled **08** confused **09** desultory, haphazard, illogical, irregular **10** disorderly **11** unorganized **12** unsystematic **13** unco-ordinated

unmindful
03 lax **04** deaf **05** blind, slack **06** remiss **07** unaware **08** careless, heedless **09** forgetful, negligent, oblivious, unheeding **10** neglectful, regardless **11** inattentive, indifferent, unconscious

unmistakable
04 sure **05** clear, frank, plain **06** patent **07** blatant, certain, decided, evident, glaring, obvious **08** clear-cut, definite, distinct, explicit, manifest, positive, striking, univocal **10** pronounced, undeniable **11** conspicuous, indubitable, unambiguous, unequivocal, well-defined **12** indisputable **14** beyond question, unquestionable

unmistakably
06 surely **07** clearly, plainly **08** proclaim **09** blatantly, certainly, evidently, obviously **10** definitely, distinctly, manifestly, undeniably **11** doubtlessly, indubitably **12** indisputably, without doubt **13** conspicuously, unambiguously, unequivocally **14** unquestionably **15** without question

unmitigated
04 grim, pure, rank **05** harsh, sheer, utter **06** arrant **07** intense, perfect **08** absolute, complete, outright, thorough, unabated, unbroken **09** downright, out-and-out **10** consummate, persistent, relentless, unmodified, unredeemed, unrelieved **11** unqualified, unrelenting, unremitting **12** unalleviated, undiminished **13** thoroughgoing

unmixed
03 net, raw **04** mere, neat, nett, pure **07** sincere **09** unallayed **12** unadulterate, uncompounded **13** unadulterated

unmoved
04 calm, cold, firm **06** steady **07** adamant, dry-eyed **08** resolute, resolved, unshaken **09** impassive, unbending, unchanged, unfeeling, unstirred, untouched **10** determined, inflexible, unaffected, unwavering **11** indifferent, unconcerned, undeviating, unimpressed **12** unresponsive **13** dispassionate

unnamed
04 anon **05** house **09** anonymous

unnatural
◇ *anagram indicator*
03 odd **05** false, queer, stiff **06** farfet, forced, formal, staged, unholy, wooden **07** bizarre, feigned, fustian, heinous, inhuman, pompous, stilted, strange, uncanny, unusual **08** abnormal, absonant, affected, freakish, kindless, laboured, peculiar, strained, uncommon, unkindly **09** anomalous, contrived, insincere, irregular, monstrous, perverted **10** artificial, disnatured, far-fetched, forcedness, monstruous **11** constrained, stiff-necked **12** cataphysical, supernatural **13** against nature, extraordinary, self-conscious, unspontaneous

unnaturally
◇ *anagram indicator*
05 oddly **08** unkindly **09** strangely, unusually **10** abnormally, peculiarly, uncommonly **11** irregularly **15** extraordinarily

unnecessarily
10 needlessly **11** excessively **12** immoderately **13** superfluously

unnecessary
06 wasted **08** needless, unneeded, unwanted **09** excessive, redundant **10** expendable, gratuitous, unrequired **11** dispensable, inessential, superfluous, uncalled-for **12** non-essential, tautological

unnerve
05 alarm, daunt, scare, shake, unman, upset, worry **06** deject, dismay, put out, rattle, weaken **07** fluster, perturb, shake up **08** confound, disquiet, frighten, unsettle **10** demoralize, disconcert, discourage, dishearten, intimidate

unnoticed
06 unseen **07** ignored **08** unheeded **09** neglected **10** overlooked, unobserved, unremarked **11** disregarded **12** undiscovered, unrecognized

unobstructed
04 fair, open **05** plain

unobtrusive
05 quiet **06** humble, low-key, modest **07** subdued **08** retiring **09** underhand **10** restrained, unassuming **11** unassertive **12** self-effacing, unaggressive, unnoticeable **13** inconspicuous, unpretentious **14** unostentatious

unobtrusively
06 humbly **07** on the QT, quietly **08** modestly **10** on the quiet **15** inconspicuously, surreptitiously, unpretentiously

unoccupied
04 free, idle, room, void **05** empty, waste **06** otiose, vacant **07** jobless **08** deserted, forsaken, inactive, workless **09** at liberty, désoeuvré **10** disengaged, unemployed **11** uninhabited, unpopulated

unofficial
04 curb, kerb **05** black **06** fringe **07** illegal, private **08** informal, personal **10** undeclared, unratified **11** alternative, unconfirmed **12** confidential, off-the-record, unauthorized **15** unauthenticated

unoriginal
05 stale, trite **06** copied **07** cribbed, derived, slavish **09** hackneyed, ready-made **10** derivative, second-hand, uninspired **11** predictable **12** cliché-ridden **13** unimaginative

unorthodox
◇ *anagram indicator*
03 new **04** cult, zany **05** fresh, novel **06** fringe, way-out **07** unusual **08** abnormal, creative **09** eccentric, heterodox, irregular, left-field **10** innovative, off the wall **11** alternative **13** nonconformist **14** unconventional

unpaid
03 due **04** free **05** owing **06** unfeed **07** overdue, payable, pending, pro bono, unwaged **08** honorary **09** remaining, unsettled, voluntary **10** unsalaried **11** outstanding, uncollected **14** pro bono publico, unremunerative

unpalatable
05 nasty **06** bitter **07** insipid **08** inedible **09** offensive, repellent, repugnant, uneatable, unsavoury **10** disgusting, unpleasant **11** distasteful **12** disagreeable, unappetizing, unattractive

unparalleled
04 rare **06** unique **07** supreme **08** peerless **09** matchless, unmatched **10** unequalled, unrivalled **11** exceptional, superlative, unsurpassed **12** incomparable, without equal **13** beyond compare, unprecedented

unpardonable
08 shameful, shocking **10** deplorable, outrageous, scandalous **11** disgraceful, inexcusable **12** indefensible, irremissible, unforgivable **13** reprehensible, unjustifiable **14** unconscionable

unperturbed
04 calm, cool **06** placid, poised,

serene **08** composed, tranquil **09** collected, impassive, unexcited, unruffled, unworried **10** untroubled **11** undisturbed, unflappable, unflinching, unflustered **13** self-possessed

unpleasant
03 bad **04** foul, grim, mean, rude, sour **05** awful, crook, nasty, surly **06** filthy, mingin', stinky, ungain, unkind **07** drastic, hostile, minging, noisome **08** impolite **09** offensive, repugnant, repulsive, traumatic **10** aggressive, disgusting, ill-natured, unfriendly **11** bad-tempered, distasteful, quarrelsome, troublesome, undesirable, unpalatable **12** disagreeable, discourteous, unappetizing, unattractive **13** objectionable

unpleasantness
04 fuss **05** upset **06** bother, furore **07** scandal, trouble **08** bad blood **09** annoyance, esclandre, nastiness **10** bad feeling, ill-feeling **13** embarrassment

unpolished
04 bare, rude **05** crude, rough **06** coarse, vulgar **07** sketchy, uncouth, unfiled, unkempt **08** agrestic, home-bred, unpolite, unworked **09** unrefined **10** provincial, uncultured, unfinished **11** uncivilized, unfashioned **12** uncultivated **13** rough and ready, wild and woolly **15** unsophisticated

unpopular
05 hated **07** avoided, ignored, shunned, unloved **08** detested, disliked, rejected, unwanted **09** neglected, unwelcome **10** friendless **11** undesirable **12** unattractive **13** unfashionable, unsought-after

unprecedented
03 new **07** unheard, unknown, unusual **08** abnormal, freakish, original, uncommon **09** unheard-of **10** remarkable, unequalled, unexampled, unrivalled **11** exceptional **12** unparalleled **13** extraordinary, revolutionary

unpredictable
◇ *anagram indicator*
06 chance, fickle, random, slippy **07** erratic **08** slippery, unstable, variable, volatile **09** mercurial **10** capricious, changeable, inconstant, unexpected, unreliable **12** incalculable **13** unforeseeable

unprejudiced
04 fair, just **08** balanced, detached, unbiased **09** impartial, objective **10** even-handed, fair-minded, open-minded, uncoloured **11** enlightened, non-partisan, unpossessed **12** cosmopolitan **13** dispassionate

unpremeditated
07 offhand **09** extempore, impromptu, impulsive, unplanned **10** fortuitous, off-the-cuff, unprepared **11** spontaneous, unmeditated, unrehearsed **13** unintentional **15** spur-of-the-moment

unprepared
03 raw **05** ad-lib, crude **07** napping, unready **09** half-baked, surprised, unplanned, unwilling **10** flat-footed, improvised, incomplete, off-the-cuff, unfinished, unpurvaide, unpurveyed **11** ill-equipped, spontaneous, unrehearsed **12** unsuspecting **14** on the wrong foot

unprepossessing
04 ugly **05** plain **06** homely **08** ordinary, unlikely, unlovely **10** forbidding, unexciting, unpleasing **11** indifferent, unappealing **12** unattractive, unremarkable **13** unexceptional, uninteresting **15** undistinguished

unpretentious
05 plain **06** homely, honest, humble, modest, simple **07** natural **08** discreet, ordinary **10** penny-plain, unaffected, unassuming **11** unobtrusive **14** unostentatious **15** straightforward

unprincipled
07 corrupt, crooked, devious, immoral **09** deceitful, dishonest, reprobate, underhand, unethical **10** profligate **12** uninstructed, unscrupulous **13** discreditable, dishonourable **14** unprofessional

unproductive
03 dry, shy **04** arid, dead, idle, lean, poor, vain, yeld, yell **05** blank, waste **06** barren, futile, otiose **07** sterile, useless **09** fruitless, infertile, worthless **10** unfruitful **11** ineffective, unrewarding **12** unprofitable **13** inefficacious **14** unremunerative

unprofessional
03 lax **06** casual, sloppy **08** improper, inexpert, unseemly **09** negligent, unethical, unskilled, untrained **10** amateurish, indecorous **11** incompetent, inefficient **12** inadmissible, unacceptable, unprincipled, unscrupulous **13** inexperienced

unprofitable
04 lean **08** bootless

unpromising
06 gloomy **07** adverse, ominous **08** doubtful, unlikely **10** depressing **11** dispiriting **12** discouraging, inauspicious, unfavourable, unpropitious

unprotected
04 open, soft **05** naked **06** liable **07** exposed, unarmed **08** helpless **09** uncovered, unguarded **10** unattended, undefended, unshielded, vulnerable **11** defenceless, unfortified, unsheltered

unprovable
12 unverifiable **14** indemonstrable, indeterminable, undemonstrable **15** unascertainable

unqualified
05 inapt, round, total, unfit, utter **07** amateur, perfect, plenary **08** absolute, complete, outright, positive, thorough **09** downright, incapable, out-and-out, unallayed, untrained **10** consummate, ineligible, unlicensed, unprepared, unreserved, unsuitable **11** categorical, ill-equipped, incompetent, unequivocal, unmitigated **12** unrestricted, wholehearted **13** inexperienced, unconditional

unquestionable
04 sure **05** clear **06** patent **07** certain, obvious **08** absolute, definite, flawless, manifest **09** faultless **10** conclusive, undeniable **11** indubitable, irrefutable, self-evident, unequivocal **12** indisputable, unchallenged, unmistakable **13** incontestable **14** beyond question

unquestionably
06 firmly **07** clearly **08** directly **09** certainly **10** definitely, distinctly, explicitly, manifestly, positively **11** indubitably, irrefutably **12** unmistakably **13** unambiguously, unequivocally

unquestioning
08 implicit **11** unqualified **12** questionless, unhesitating, wholehearted **13** unconditional

unravel
◇ *anagram indicator*
04 fray, free, undo **05** solve **06** evolve, unknit, unknot, unwind **07** clear up, explain, resolve, sort out, work out **08** separate, untangle **09** extricate, figure out, interpret, penetrate, puzzle out **11** disentangle **13** straighten out

unreadable
07 complex, garbled, jumbled, muddled, obscure **08** involved, puzzling **09** illegible, scrambled **10** incoherent, mysterious **11** complicated, double Dutch **12** impenetrable, inarticulate, unfathomable **14** indecipherable, unintelligible

unreal
04 fake, faux, mock, sham **05** false, phony **06** aerial, ersatz, hollow, made-up, phoney, shadow, untrue **07** amazing, bizarre, phantom, pretend **08** aeriform, fanciful, illusive, illusory, mythical, nebulous, notional **09** fairytale, fantastic, imaginary, legendary, moonshiny, phantosme, storybook, synthetic, visionary, whimsical **10** artificial, chimerical, fictitious, immaterial, incredible, ungrounded **11** Disneyesque, make-believe, non-existent **12** hypothetical, unbelievable **13** insubstantial

unrealistic
08 quixotic, romantic, wild-eyed

10 idealistic, impossible, unworkable
11 impractical, theoretical
12 unreasonable 13 impracticable
14 over-optimistic

unreality
09 irreality, phoniness 10 hollowness, phoneyness 11 bizarreness, make-believe 12 fancifulness, illusoriness, nebulousness, non-existence
13 artificiality, imaginariness

unreasonable
03 mad, OTT 05 silly, steep, undue
06 absurd, biased, stupid, unfair, unjust
07 foolish, froward, obscene 08 a bit much, exacting, perverse 09 arbitrary, excessive, expensive, illogical, ludicrous, senseless 10 exorbitant, far-fetched, headstrong, immoderate, iniquitous, irrational, outrageous, over the top, scandalous 11 extravagant, nonsensical, opinionated, uncalled-for, unchristian, unjustified, unrealistic, unwarranted 12 extortionate, inconsistent, preposterous, unacceptable 13 unco-operative, unjustifiable

unreasoning
04 wild 05 brute, crazy, silly 06 absurd, unwise 07 brutish, foolish, invalid, unsound 09 arbitrary, beastlike, illogical, senseless 10 groundless, irrational, ridiculous 11 implausible, nonsensical 12 inconsistent, unreasonable 14 beside yourself

unrecognizable
07 altered, changed 09 disguised, incognito 10 unknowable
12 incognizable 14 unidentifiable

unrecognized
06 unseen 07 ignored 08 unheeded
09 neglected, unnoticed 10 overlooked, unobserved, unremarked
11 disregarded 12 undiscovered

unrefined
03 raw 05 blunt, crude, rough
06 coarse, earthy, rustic, vulgar
07 bestial 09 rough-hewn, untreated
10 uncultured, unfinished, unpolished, unpurified 11 unprocessed
12 uncultivated 15 unsophisticated

unregenerate
06 sinful, wicked 07 natural
08 hardened, obdurate, stubborn
09 abandoned, obstinate, shameless
10 impenitent, persistent, refractory, unreformed 11 intractable, unconverted, unrepentant
12 incorrigible, recalcitrant

unrelated
06 unlike 07 foreign 08 distinct, separate 09 different, disparate
10 dissimilar, extraneous, irrelevant
11 independent, off the point, unconnected 12 inconsequent, relationless, unassociated 14 beside the point

unrelenting
05 cruel, stern 06 steady 07 endless
08 constant, pitiless, ruthless, unabated, unbroken 09 ceaseless, continual, incessant, merciless, perpetual, unceasing, unsparing
10 continuous, implacable, inexorable, relentless, unmerciful
11 remorseless, unforgiving, unremitting 12 intransigent
14 uncompromising

unreliable
◇ *anagram indicator*
04 iffy 05 dodgy, false, trick 06 fickle, shonky 07 unsound 08 doubtful, fallible, in-and-out, mistaken, slippery, unstable 09 deceptive, erroneous, sieve-like, uncertain 10 fly-by-night, inaccurate 11 implausible
12 disreputable, questionable, unconvincing, undependable
13 irresponsible, temperamental, untrustworthy

unremitting
08 constant, tireless, unabated, unbroken 09 assiduous, ceaseless, continual, continued, incessant, intensive, perpetual, unceasing
10 continuous, relentless
11 irremissive, remorseless, unrelenting
13 indefatigable

unrepentant
07 callous 08 hardened, obdurate
09 confirmed, shameless, unabashed, unashamed 10 impenitent
12 incorrigible, unapologetic, unregenerate

unrequited
07 ignored, snubbed, spurned
08 rejected 09 discarded, neglected
10 unanswered 11 not returned
12 unrecognized 14 unacknowledged, unreciprocated

unreserved
04 free, full, open 05 frank, total
06 candid, direct, entire 08 absolute, complete, explicit, outgoing, unbooked 09 extrovert, outspoken, talkative, unlimited 10 forthright
11 uninhibited, unqualified, whole-footed 12 heart-to-heart, unhesitating, unrestrained, unrestricted, wholehearted 13 communicative, demonstrative, unconditional

unreservedly
03 out 05 fully 07 totally, utterly
08 entirely, outright 09 out-and-out
10 absolutely, completely
14 unhesitatingly, wholeheartedly
15 unconditionally

unresisting
04 meek 06 docile 07 passive
08 obedient 09 unsisting
10 submissive

unresolved
04 moot 05 vague, vexed 07 pending
08 doubtful, unsolved 09 undecided, unsettled 10 indefinite, irresolute, unanswered, up in the air
12 undetermined 13 problematical

unresponsive
04 cool 05 aloof 06 frigid 07 unmoved
08 echoless 09 apathetic, withdrawn
10 unaffected 11 indifferent
12 uninterested 13 unsympathetic

unrest
◇ *anagram indicator*
05 worry 06 unease 07 discord, protest, turmoil 08 disorder, disquiet
09 agitation, commotion, rebellion
10 discontent, dissension, uneasiness
11 disturbance 12 disaffection, perturbation, restlessness
15 dissatisfaction

unrestrained
◇ *anagram indicator*
04 free, wild 05 frank, loose 06 hearty, lavish, wanton 07 natural, rampant, unyoked 08 impotent 09 abandoned, libertine, unbounded, unbridled, unchecked 10 boisterous, immoderate, inordinate, unbuttoned, unfettered, unhindered, unlaboured, unreserved 11 extravagant, full-frontal, intemperate, uninhibited, unrepressed
12 uncontrolled 13 irrepressible, unconstrained, wild and woolly

unrestricted
◇ *anagram indicator*
04 free, open 05 clear 06 public
08 absolute, open door 09 chainless, unbounded, unimpeded, unlimited, unopposed 10 free-for-all, unhindered, unreserved
12 discretional, unobstructed
13 discretionary, unconditional

unripe
05 green 07 unready 08 immature
09 unripened 11 out of season, undeveloped

unrivalled
07 supreme 08 peerless 09 matchless, nonpareil, unmatched, untouched
10 inimitable, unequalled
11 superlative, unsurpassed
12 incomparable, unparalleled, without equal 13 beyond compare

unruffled
04 calm, cool, even 05 level 06 serene, smooth 08 composed, peaceful, tranquil 09 collected 10 untroubled
11 undisturbed, unperturbed
13 imperturbable

unruly
◇ *anagram indicator*
04 rag'd, wild 05 ragde, rowdy
06 stormy, wanton, wilful 07 lawless, riotous, rulesse, wayward
08 mutinous, ruleless, torn-down
09 camstairy, camsteary, turbulent
10 camsteerie, disorderly, disruptive, headstrong, rebellious, refractary, refractory 11 disobedient, intractable
12 obstreperous, recalcitrant, ungovernable, unmanageable
13 insubordinate, undisciplined
14 uncontrollable

unsafe
05 dicey, fishy, hairy, risky 06 chancy

07 exposed, uncanny, unsound
08 high-risk, insecure, perilous, unstable 09 dangerous, hazardous, uncertain 10 precarious, unreliable, vulnerable 11 defenceless, treacherous

unsaid
08 unspoken, unstated, unvoiced
09 unuttered 10 undeclared
11 unexpressed, unmentioned
12 unpronounced

unsatisfactory
04 lame, poor, ropy, tame, weak
05 empty, lousy, rocky, ropey, wrong
06 faulty 08 inferior, mediocre
09 defective, deficient, imperfect, off-colour 10 inadequate, unsuitable
11 displeasing, frustrating
12 insufficient, unacceptable, unsatisfying 13 disappointing, dissatisfying

unsavoury
05 nasty 06 sordid 07 squalid
09 obnoxious, offensive, on the nose, repellent, repugnant, repulsive, revolting, sickening, tasteless
10 disgusting, nauseating, unpleasant
11 distasteful, undesirable, unpalatable
12 disagreeable, disreputable, unappetizing, unattractive
13 objectionable

unscathed
04 safe 05 sound, whole 06 intact, unhurt 08 unharmed 09 undamaged, uninjured, untouched 13 with whole skin

unscramble
◇ *anagram indicator*
06 decode 08 decipher

unscrupulous
07 corrupt, crooked, immoral
08 improper, ruthless 09 dishonest, shameless, unethical 10 Rottweiler, unscrupled, villainous 12 unprincipled
13 dishonourable 14 unconscionable

unseasonable
08 ill-timed, mistimed, untimely
10 malapropos, out of place, seasonable, unsuitable 11 inopportune
12 intempestive 13 inappropriate

unseasoned
05 green 08 unprimed 09 unmatured, untreated 10 unprepared, untempered

unseat
04 oust 05 throw 06 depose, remove, topple, unship 07 dismiss, unhorse
08 dethrone, dishorse, dismount, displace, unsaddle 09 discharge, overthrow

unseemly
◇ *anagram indicator*
05 undue 06 indign 07 uncivil
08 improper, uncomely, unhonest
09 unrefined 10 ill-looking, indecorous, indelicate, unbecoming, unhandsome, unsuitable
11 unbefitting, undignified
12 disreputable 13 discreditable, inappropriate

unseen
06 hidden, uneyed, veiled 07 cryptic, lurking, obscure 09 concealed, invisible, unnoticed 10 unbeholden, undetected, unobserved
11 unobtrusive 13 inexperienced

unselfish
04 kind 05 noble 07 liberal
08 generous, selfless 10 altruistic, charitable, open-handed, single-eyed
11 magnanimous, self-denying
12 humanitarian 13 disinterested, philanthropic 14 public-spirited, self-forgetting 15 self-sacrificing

unsentimental
05 tough 09 hard-faced, hardnosed, practical, pragmatic, realistic, unfeeling 10 hard-headed, iron-headed, unromantic 11 hard as nails, level-headed, unemotional

unserviceable
02 U/S

unsettle
◇ *anagram indicator*
04 faze 05 feese, feeze, phase, phese, shake, throw, unfix, upset 06 bother, pheese, pheeze, rattle, ruffle
07 agitate, confuse, disturb, fluster, perturb, trouble 09 discomfit, unbalance 10 discompose, disconcert
11 destabilize

unsettled
◇ *anagram indicator*
04 edgy, open 05 fazed, owing, shaky, tense, upset 06 futile, on edge, queasy, queazy, roving, shaken, uneasy, unpaid
07 aimless, anxious, fidgety, lawless, overdue, payable, vagrant 08 agitated, confused, deserted, desolate, doubtful, drifting, goalless, insecure, rambling, restless, troubled, unguided, unnerved, unstable, unsteady, vagabond, variable 09 abandoned, disturbed, flustered, in arrears, pointless, turbulent, uncertain, undecided, unpeopled, wandering
10 changeable, inconstant, irresolute, undirected, unoccupied, unresolved, up in the air 11 disoriented, outstanding, purposeless, to be decided, undiscussed, uninhabited, unmotivated, unpopulated
12 indetermined, in the balance, undetermined 13 directionless, unpredictable 14 in a state of flux

unshakable, unshakeable
04 firm, sure 05 fixed 06 stable
07 staunch 08 constant, resolute
09 immovable, steadfast 10 determined, unswerving, unwavering 11 well-founded 12 unassailable

unsightly
04 ugly 07 hideous 09 repugnant, repulsive, revolting 10 off-putting, unpleasant 11 carbuncular
12 disagreeable, unattractive
15 unprepossessing

unskilful
03 bad 05 inept 06 clumsy, gauche
07 awkward 08 bungling, fumbling, inexpert, unartful, untaught
09 maladroit, unskilled, untrained
10 amateurish, uneducated, unhandsome, untalented
11 incompetent, unpractised, unqualified 13 inexperienced
14 unprofessional

unskilled
04 rude 06 simple, ungain 07 unwitty
08 inexpert 09 unperfect, untrained
10 amateurish 11 incompetent, unpractised, unqualified
13 inexperienced 14 unprofessional

unsociable
04 cold, cool 05 aloof 06 chilly
07 distant, hostile 08 reserved, retiring, solitary, taciturn 09 reclusive, withdrawn 10 insociable, unfriendly
11 introverted, standoffish, uncongenial 12 inhospitable
13 unforthcoming, unneighbourly
15 uncommunicative, uncompanionable

unsoiled *see* **unsullied**

unsolicited
07 unasked 08 unsought, unwanted
09 sponte sua, uninvited, unwelcome, voluntary 10 gratuitous, unasked-for
11 spontaneous, uncalled-for, unrequested

unsophisticated
03 jay 04 naif 05 basic, crude, naive, plain 06 direct, native, simple
07 artless, genuine, natural, verdant
08 cornball, corn-pone, innocent
09 childlike, guileless, ingenuous, small-town, unrefined, unworldly
10 provincial, unaffected, uninvolved
11 rudimentary, undeveloped
13 inexperienced, unadulterated, uncomplicated, unpretentious
15 straightforward

unsound
◇ *anagram indicator*
03 ill 04 weak 05 false, frail, shaky, wonky 06 ailing, broken, faulty, flawed, hollow, rotten, unsafe, unwell, wobbly 07 damaged, injured, invalid, rickety 08 delicate, deranged, diseased, insecure, unhinged, unstable, unsteady 09 dangerous, defective, erroneous, illogical, unfounded, unhealthy, untenable
10 disordered, fallacious, ill-founded, unbalanced, unreliable
11 unwholesome

unsparing
04 hard 05 harsh, round, stern
06 lavish, severe 07 drastic, liberal, profuse 08 abundant, generous, rigorous, ruthless, slashing
09 bountiful, merciless, plenteous
10 implacable, munificent, open-handed, relentless, ungrudging, unmerciful, unstinting 11 unforgiving
14 uncompromising

unspeakable
05 awful 08 dreadful, horrible,

nameless, shocking, terrible
09 appalling, execrable, frightful, monstrous, nefandous **10** horrendous
11 unthinkable, unutterable
12 unbelievable, unimaginable
13 inconceivable, indescribable, inexpressible, unmentionable

unspeakably
07 awfully **08** terribly **11** appallingly, frightfully, unthinkably, unutterably
12 horrendously, unbelievably, unimaginably **13** inconceivably, indescribably, inexpressibly

unspecified
05 vague **07** obscure, unknown, unnamed **09** uncertain, undecided, undefined **10** indefinite, mysterious
12 undetermined, unidentified

unspectacular
04 dull **06** boring, common **07** average
08 mediocre, ordinary, plodding
10 unexciting **12** unimpressive, unremarkable **13** uninteresting

unspoilt
07 natural, perfect **08** pristine, unharmed **09** preserved, unchanged, undamaged, untouched
10 unaffected, unimpaired
11 unblemished **15** unsophisticated

unspoken
04 mute **05** tacit **06** silent, unsaid
07 assumed, implied **08** implicit, inferred, unstated, wordless
09 unuttered, voiceless **10** undeclared, understood **11** unexpressed

unstable
◇ *anagram indicator*
03 mad **04** nuts, weak **05** barmy, batty, crazy, daffy, dippy, dodgy, loony, loopy, moody, nutty, risky, shaky **06** fitful, infirm, insane, labile, mental, slippy, tickle, unsafe, wankle, wobbly
07 bananas, bonkers, brittle, bruckle, erratic, flighty, meshuga, rickety, unsound **08** crackers, deranged, insecure, instable, ricketty, shifting, slippery, ticklish, unhinged, unstayed, unsteady, variable, volatile, wavering
09 disturbed, mercurial, tottering, unsettled **10** capricious, changeable, inconstant, off balance, off the wall, out to lunch, precarious, unbalanced, unreliable **11** fluctuating, light-minded, off your head, unballasted, vacillating
12 inconsistent, round the bend **13** off your rocker, round the twist, unpredictable, untrustworthy **14** off your trolley, wrong in the head

unsteady
◇ *anagram indicator*
05 dotty, giddy, shaky, totty, warby
06 cranky, groggy, titupy, unsafe, wambly, wavery, wobbly **07** doddery, rickety, tittupy **08** insecure, skittish, unstable, variable, waverous
09 irregular, tottering, versatile
10 flickering, inconstant, precarious, unreliable **11** light-headed, treacherous, unballasted

• be unsteady
04 flit **05** waver **06** coggle, wobble
09 vacillate

unstinting
04 full **05** ample, large **06** lavish
07 liberal, profuse **08** abundant, generous, prodigal **09** abounding, bountiful, plentiful, unsparing
10 munificent, ungrudging

unstoppable
07 undying **08** unending **09** unceasing
10 inevitable **11** unavoidable, unrelenting, unremitting **13** without a let-up

unsubstantial
04 airy **07** shadowy **10** cloud-built

unsubstantiated
07 dubious **08** unproved, unproven
09 debatable **10** disputable, unattested, unverified
11 unconfirmed, unsupported
12 questionable **13** unestablished
14 uncorroborated

unsuccessful
04 lost, sour, vain **06** beaten, failed, futile, losing **07** bungled, fumbled, sterile, unlucky, useless **08** abortive, defeated, luckless, thwarted, washed-up **09** fruitless **10** frustrated, miscarried, trade-falne, unavailing
11 ineffective, ineffectual, trade-fallen, unfortunate **12** unproductive, unprofitable

unsuitable
05 amiss, inapt, inept, unapt, unfit
08 improper, unlikely, unseemly, unsorted, unsuited **09** unfitting
10 inapposite, ineligible, malapropos, out of place, unbecoming
11 incongruent, incongruous
12 incompatible, inconvenient, infelicitous, unacceptable
13 inappropriate

unsullied
04 pure **05** clean **06** intact **07** perfect
08 pristine, spotless, unsoiled
09 stainless, undefiled, unspoiled, unspotted, unstained, untainted, untouched **10** immaculate
11 unblackened, unblemished, uncorrupted, untarnished

unsung
07 obscure, unknown **08** unhailed
09 anonymous, forgotten, neglected, unpraised **10** overlooked, unhonoured
11 disregarded, unacclaimed
12 uncelebrated, unrecognized
14 unacknowledged

unsure
05 vague **07** dubious, unknown
08 doubtful, hesitant, insecure, wavering **09** dithering, sceptical, tentative, uncertain, undecided
10 ambivalent, indefinite, in two minds, irresolute, precarious, suspicious **11** uncommitted, unconvinced, unpersuaded
12 equivocating **13** untrustworthy

unsurpassed
07 supreme **08** unbeaten **09** matchless, unmatched **10** surpassing, unequalled, unexcelled, unrivalled **11** exceptional, superlative **12** incomparable, second-to-none, transcendent, unparalleled
13 state-of-the-art

unsurprising
08 expected, forecast, foreseen, hoped-for, promised **09** looked-for, predicted, wished-for **10** forseeable
11 anticipated, predictable

unsuspecting
05 naive **06** simple, unwary
07 unaware **08** gullible, innocent, off guard, trustful, trusting **09** credulous, ingenuous **11** unconscious
12 unsuspicious

unswerving
04 firm, sure, true **05** fixed **06** direct, steady **07** devoted, staunch
08 constant, resolute, untiring
09 dedicated, immovable, steadfast
10 unflagging, unwavering
11 undeviating, unfaltering **12** single-minded

unsympathetic
04 cold, hard **05** cruel, harsh, stony
06 unkind **07** callous, hostile, inhuman, unmoved **08** pitiless, soulless, uncaring **09** hard-faced, heartless, unfeeling, unpitying **11** hard as nails, hard-hearted, ill-disposed, indifferent, insensitive, unconcerned
12 antagonistic, unresponsive

unsystematic
06 random, sloppy, untidy **07** chaotic, jumbled, muddled **08** confused, slapdash **09** haphazard, illogical, irregular, shambolic, unplanned
10 disorderly **11** unorganized
12 disorganized, unmethodical, unstructured **13** unco-ordinated
14 indiscriminate

untamed
04 wild **05** feral **06** fierce, savage
07 haggard, salvage **08** unmanned
09 barbarous **10** unmellowed, untameable **14** undomesticated

untangle
04 undo **05** solve **07** resolve, unravel, work out **09** extricate **11** disentangle
13 straighten out

untarnished
04 pure **05** clean **06** bright, intact
07 glowing, shining **08** polished, pristine, spotless, unsoiled, unspoilt
09 burnished, stainless, unbraided, unspotted, unstained, unsullied
10 immaculate, impeccable
11 unblemished **13** unimpeachable

untenable
05 rocky, shaky **06** flawed **07** unsound
09 illogical, intenable **10** fallacious
11 inexcusable **12** indefensible, unreasonable **13** insupportable, unjustifiable, unsustainable
14 unmaintainable

unthinkable
06 absurd **08** shocking, unlikely **09** illogical, unheard-of **10** impossible, improbable, incredible, outrageous, staggering **11** implausible, incogitable **12** preposterous, unbelievable, unimaginable, unreasonable **13** inconceivable

unthinking
04 rash, rude **06** unkind, vacant **08** careless, heedless, impolite, knee-jerk, tactless **09** automatic, impulsive, negligent, Pavlovian **10** incogitant, indiscreet, mechanical **11** insensitive, instinctive, involuntary, thoughtless, unconscious **12** undiplomatic, unrespective **13** inconsiderate

unthinkingly
06 rashly, rudely **08** stupidly **09** foolishly **10** carelessly, impolitely, recklessly, tactlessly **11** unfeelingly **12** indiscreetly **13** inattentively, insensitively, thoughtlessly **15** inconsiderately

untidily
07 dirtily, messily **08** sloppily **09** scruffily **10** disorderly, sluttishly **11** chaotically **12** topsy-turvily **13** shambolically **15** like a dog's dinner

untidy
◇ *anagram indicator*
04 foul **05** dirty, messy, ratty, tatty **06** sloppy **07** chaotic, haywire, jumbled, muddled, raunchy, rumpled, scruffy, unkempt **08** slipshod, slovenly, sluttish **09** cluttered, shambolic **10** bedraggled, disorderly, slatternly, topsy-turvy **11** dishevelled **12** disorganized, unsystematic

untie
04 free, undo **05** loose, solve **06** loosen, unbind, unknit, unknot, unwrap **07** release, resolve, unhitch, untruss **08** unfasten

until
02 to **04** till, unto, up to **05** hasta, prior, while **06** before, up till **07** prior to **08** as late as **11** earlier than, up to the time

untimely
05 early **07** awkward **08** ill-timed, immature, timeless **09** importune, premature **10** malapropos, unsuitable **11** inopportune, prematurely, unfortunate **12** inauspicious, inconvenient, infelicitous, intempestive, unseasonable, unseasonably **13** inappropriate, inopportunely

untiring
06 dogged, steady **07** devoted, staunch **08** constant, resolute, tireless **09** dedicated, incessant, tenacious, unceasing, unfailing **10** determined, persistent, unflagging **11** persevering, unfaltering, unremitting **13** indefatigable

untold
08 infinite **09** boundless, countless, uncounted **10** unnumbered, unreckoned **11** innumerable, measureless, uncountable, undreamed-of, unutterable **12** immeasurable, incalculable, unimaginable **13** inconceivable, indescribable, inexhaustible, inexpressible

untouched
04 safe **06** intact, unhurt, virgin **08** pristine, unharmed **09** unaltered, unchanged, undamaged, uninjured, unscathed, unstirred **10** unaffected, unimpaired, unrivalled **11** unimpressed

untoward
05 amiss **07** adverse, awkward, froward, ominous, unlucky **08** annoying, contrary, ill-timed, improper, unseemly, untimely, worrying **09** unfitting, vexatious **10** disastrous, indecorous, irritating, unbecoming, unexpected, unsuitable **11** inopportune, troublesome, unfortunate **12** inauspicious, inconvenient, unfavourable, unpropitious **13** inappropriate

untrained
03 raw **06** unbred **07** amateur **08** inexpert, untaught **09** unskilled **10** uneducated, unschooled **11** incompetent, unpractised, unqualified **13** inexperienced, undisciplined **14** unprofessional

untried
03 new **05** novel **08** unproved, untested **10** innovative, innovatory **11** exploratory **12** experimental **13** unestablished

untroubled
04 calm, cool **06** placid, serene, steady **08** composed, peaceful, tranquil **09** impassive, unexcited, unruffled, unstirred, unworried **11** unconcerned, undisturbed, unflappable, unflustered, unperturbed **14** inapprehensive

untrue
◇ *anagram indicator*
05 false, wrong **06** made-up, mythic **07** inexact, untruly **08** disloyal, mistaken, mythical, two-faced **09** deceitful, deceptive, dishonest, erroneous, incorrect, legendary, trumped-up, two-timing **10** fabricated, fallacious, fraudulent, inaccurate, misleading, perfidious, unfaithful, unofficial, untruthful **11** inauthentic **12** untruthfully **13** untrustworthy

untrustworthy
05 false **06** fickle, sleeky, slippy, unsure, untrue **08** disloyal, slippery, two-faced, untrusty **09** deceitful, dishonest, faithless **10** capricious, fly-by-night, unfaithful, unreliable, untruthful **11** duplicitous, treacherous **12** disreputable **13** dishonourable

untruth
03 fib, lie **04** crap, tale **05** false, lying, porky, story **06** deceit **07** falsity, fiction, perjury, whopper **09** falsehood, falseness, invention, tall story **10** inveracity **11** fabrication, made-up story **14** unfaithfulness, untruthfulness

untruthful
05 false, lying **06** untrue **07** crooked **08** invented, two-faced **09** deceitful, dishonest, erroneous, fictional, insincere **10** fabricated, fallacious, mendacious **11** unveracious **12** hypocritical

untutored
06 simple **07** artless **08** ignorant, inexpert, unversed **09** unlearned, unrefined, untrained **10** illiterate, uneducated, unlessoned, unschooled **11** unpractised **12** uninstructed **13** inexperienced **15** unsophisticated

untwine
06 uncoil, unwind **07** unravel, untwist **10** disentwine

untwist
05 ravel, unlay **06** detort, uncoil, unwind **07** unravel, untwine

unused
03 new **04** idle **05** blank, clean, extra, fresh, spare **06** maiden **07** surplus, unusual **08** left over, pristine, untapped, unwonted **09** available, remaining, untouched **10** unemployed, unfamiliar **11** unexploited, unpractised **12** unaccustomed, unacquainted **13** inexperienced

unusual
◇ *anagram indicator*
03 odd **04** rare, unco **05** freak, kinky, queer, weird **06** exotic, freaky, unwont **07** bizarre, curious, offbeat, special, strange **08** abnormal, atypical, freakish, peculiar, singular, uncommon, unwonted **09** anomalous, different, eccentric, irregular **10** phenomenal, remarkable, surprising, unexpected, unfamiliar, unorthodox **11** exceptional, out of the way **12** unacquainted **13** extraordinary, unprecedented **14** unconventional

See also **strange**

unusually
◇ *anagram indicator*
04 very **05** oddly **08** devilish **09** bizarrely, curiously, extremely **10** especially, peculiarly, remarkably, singularly **11** exceedingly **12** particularly, prodigiously, tremendously **13** exceptionally **15** extraordinarily

unutterable
07 extreme **09** egregious, ineffable, nefandous **11** unspeakable **12** overwhelming, unimaginable **13** indescribable, inexpressible

unvarnished
04 bare, pure **05** frank, naked, plain, sheer, stark **06** candid, honest, simple **07** sincere **09** unadorned **11** undisguised **13** unembellished **15** straightforward

unveil
04 bare **06** betray, expose, reveal, unmask **07** divulge, lay bare, lay open, uncover **08** disclose, discover **09** make known **11** disenshroud **12** bring to light **13** take the lid off

unwanted
05 extra **06** otiose **07** outcast, surplus, useless **08** rejected, unneeded **09** discarded, redundant, undesired, uninvited, unwelcome **10** unrequired **11** superfluous, unnecessary, unsolicited

unwarranted
05 wrong **06** unjust **10** gratuitous, groundless, undeserved, unprovoked **11** inexcusable, uncalled-for, unjustified, unnecessary **12** indefensible, unreasonable **13** unjustifiable

unwary
04 rash **05** hasty **08** careless, heedless, off guard, reckless **09** imprudent, unguarded **10** incautious, indiscreet, unthinking **11** thoughtless

unwashed
04 dark, dull, foul, miry **05** black, dirty, dusty, grimy, manky, messy, mucky, muddy, slimy, sooty, yucky **06** chatty, clarty, cloudy, cruddy, filthy, greasy, grotty, grubby, grungy, scungy, shabby, soiled **07** clouded, defiled, grufted, scruffy, squalid, stained, sullied, unclean **08** polluted, unsoaped **09** tarnished **10** flea-bitten, insanitary, unhygienic
• **the great unwashed**
05 plebs **06** the mob **07** the herd **08** riff-raff, the crowd **09** the crowds, the masses, the rabble **12** the hoi polloi **13** the lower class **14** the proletariat, the rank and file **15** the common people, the lower classes, the working class

unwavering
06 steady, sturdy **07** staunch **08** resolute, unshaken, untiring **09** dedicated, rock-solid, steadfast, tenacious **10** consistent, determined, unflagging, unshakable, unswerving **11** down-the-line, undeviating, unfaltering, unshakeable **12** single-minded **13** unquestioning

unwelcome
08 excluded, rejected, unwanted, worrying **09** uninvited, unpopular, upsetting **10** unpleasant **11** distasteful, undesirable, unpalatable **12** disagreeable, unacceptable

unwell
03 bad, ill **04** ropy, sick **05** badly, crook, dicky, queer, ropey, rough, unfit, warby **06** ailing, groggy, poorly, sickly **07** run down **09** in a bad way, off-colour, unhealthy **10** indisposed, out of sorts **15** under the weather

unwholesome
03 bad, wan **04** evil, junk, pale **05** pasty **06** morbid, pallid, sickly, wicked **07** anaemic, harmful, immoral, noxious, tainted, unsound **08** epinosic **09** degrading, depraving, poisonous, unhealthy **10** corrupting, insalutary, insanitary, perverting, unhygienic **12** demoralizing, innutritious, insalubrious

unwieldy
05 bulky, hefty **06** clumsy **07** awkward, hulking, massive, weighty **08** cumbrous, ungainly **09** ponderous **10** cumbersome **12** incommodious, inconvenient, unmanageable

unwilling
04 loth, slow **05** loath **06** averse **07** opposed **08** backward, grudging, hesitant, loathful **09** reluctant, repugnant, resistant **10** indisposed **11** disinclined **13** unintentional **14** not having any of, unenthusiastic

unwillingness
08 nolition, slowness **09** hesitancy, objection **10** reluctance **12** backwardness, loathfulness **13** indisposition **14** disinclination

unwind
◇ *anagram indicator*
03 veg **04** undo **05** chill, relax **06** cool it, unclew, uncoil, unreel, unroll, unwrap, veg out **07** slacken, unravel, unreave, untwist **08** calm down, chill out, wind down **09** hang loose **10** take it easy **11** disentangle **13** let yourself go, put your feet up **14** take things easy **15** let your hair down

unwise
◇ *anagram indicator*
04 rash **05** silly **06** insane, stupid, unredy **07** foolish, unready **08** reckless **09** foolhardy, ill-judged, impolitic, imprudent, senseless **10** ill-advised, indiscreet **11** improvident, inadvisable, inexpedient, injudicious, thoughtless **12** short-sighted **13** ill-considered, irresponsible

unwitting
06 chance **07** unaware **09** unknowing, unplanned, unweeting **10** accidental, unintended, unthinking **11** inadvertent, involuntary, unconscious **12** unsuspecting **13** unintentional

unwonted
04 rare **07** strange, unusual **08** atypical, peculiar, singular, uncommon **09** unheard-of **10** infrequent, unexpected, unfamiliar **11** exceptional, uncustomary **12** unaccustomed **13** extraordinary

unworldly
05 green, naive **08** gullible, innocent **09** ingenuous, spiritual, visionary **10** idealistic **11** impractical **12** metaphysical, otherworldly **13** inexperienced **14** transcendental **15** unsophisticated

unworried
08 composed, downbeat **09** collected, unabashed, unruffled **10** undismayed, untroubled **11** unperturbed

unworthy
04 base **06** indign, shabby **07** ignoble **08** improper, inferior, shameful, unseemly, wanwordy **09** unfitting, worthless **10** despicable, ineligible, unbecoming, undeserved, unsuitable **11** disgraceful, incongruous, unbefitting, undeserving **12** contemptible, disreputable **13** discreditable, dishonourable, inappropriate **14** unprofessional

unwritten
04 oral **05** tacit **06** verbal **08** accepted, implicit, unpenned **09** customary **10** recognized, understood, unrecorded **11** traditional, word-of-mouth **12** conventional

unwrought
03 raw **04** live, rude

unyielding
04 firm, grim, hard **05** rigid, solid, stern, stiff, stout, tough **06** marble **07** adamant, granite, staunch **08** hardline, obdurate, resolute, stubborn **09** immovable, inelastic, iron-bound, obstinate, steadfast, unbending **10** determined, implacable, inexorable, inflexible, relentless, rock-ribbed, unwavering **11** intractable, unrelenting **12** intransigent, pertinacious **14** uncompromising

unzip
04 free, open, undo **06** detach, loosen, unhook, unpack, unwind **07** release **08** separate **10** decompress

up
◇ *reversal down indicator*

up-and-coming
05 eager **07** pushing **09** ambitious, assertive, go-getting, promising **12** enterprising

up and down
◇ *palindrome indicator*

upbeat
04 rosy **06** bright, cheery **07** bullish, buoyant, hopeful **08** cheerful, positive **09** promising **10** favourable, heartening, optimistic **11** encouraging **14** forward-looking

upbraid
04 twit **05** chide, scold, storm **06** berate, rebuke, upbray **07** censure, reproof, reprove, shake up **08** admonish, reproach **09** castigate, criticize, go crook at, go crook on, reprimand **10** exprobrate

upbringing
04 care **07** nurture, raising, rearing,

tending **08** breeding, teaching, training **09** education, parenting **10** bringing-up **11** cultivation, instruction

upcoming
04 near **05** close **06** at hand, coming **07** looming **08** imminent, in the air, on the way **09** impending **11** approaching, forthcoming, in the offing **12** on the horizon **13** about to happen, almost upon you **14** round the corner **15** fast approaching

update
05 amend, renew **06** revamp, revise **07** correct, upgrade **08** renovate **09** modernize

up-front
04 free, open **05** bluff, blunt, early, first, frank, plain **06** candid, direct, honest, sooner **07** advance, earlier, genuine, initial, primary, sincere **08** explicit, straight, truthful **09** downright, in advance, initially, outspoken **10** beforehand, forthright **11** hard-hitting, plain-spoken **12** introductory **15** straightforward

upgrade
05 raise **06** better, uphill, uprate **07** advance, elevate, enhance, improve, promote **09** modernize **10** ameliorate, make better

upheaval
05 chaos, upset **06** romage, uplift, upturn **07** rummage, shake-up, turmoil, upthrow **08** disorder, shake-out **09** confusion, overthrow **10** disruption, earthquake, revolution **11** disturbance

uphill
04 hard **05** tough **06** ascent, taxing, tiring **07** arduous, onerous, upgrade **09** ascending, difficult, gruelling, laborious, punishing, strenuous, wearisome **10** burdensome, exhausting

uphold
04 back, keep **06** defend, hold to **07** confirm, endorse, fortify, justify, promote, stand by, stand to, support, sustain, warrant **08** advocate, champion, maintain **09** vindicate **10** strengthen **11** countenance

upkeep
04 care, keep **06** outlay, repair **07** oncosts, running, support **08** expenses **09** overheads **10** sustenance **11** expenditure, maintenance, subsistence **12** conservation, preservation, running costs **14** operating costs

uplift
◇ *reversal down indicator*
04 draw, lift **05** boost, edify, elate, exalt, heave, hoist, raise **06** better, lift up, mark-up, refine **07** advance, collect, elevate, improve, inspire, raising, upgrade, upthrow **08** civilize, increase, upheaval **09** cultivate, elevation, enlighten **10** ameliorate, betterment, enrichment, refinement **11** advancement, cultivation, edification, enhancement, improvement **13** enlightenment

upmarket
04 fine, high **05** prime, prize **06** choice, de luxe, select **07** quality, upscale **08** prestige, superior, top-notch **09** admirable, excellent, exclusive, expensive, first-rate, high-class, reputable, top-flight **10** first-class, respectful, unrivalled **11** exceptional, good-quality, prestigious **13** distinguished, par excellence

upper
03 top **04** high, over **06** higher, senior **07** eminent, exalted, greater, loftier, topmost **08** elevated, superior **09** important, uppermost

• upper hand
04 edge, sway **07** control, mastery **08** dominion, eminence, forehand **09** advantage, dominance, supremacy **10** ascendancy, domination **11** superiority

upper-class
01 U **04** posh **05** élite, noble **06** plummy, swanky **07** toffish **08** cutglass, high-born, well-born, well-bred **09** exclusive, high-class, patrician, top-drawer **11** blue-blooded **12** aristocratic

uppermost
03 top **04** main **05** chief, first, major **07** highest, leading, primary, supreme, topmost **08** dominant, foremost, greatest, loftiest **09** paramount, principal **10** pre-eminent **11** predominant

uppity
05 cocky **06** swanky **07** stuck-up **08** affected, arrogant, assuming, snobbish **09** bigheaded, bumptious, conceited **10** hoity-toity **11** impertinent, overweening, toffee-nosed **12** presumptuous, supercilious **13** self-important

upright
04 good, just **05** erect, moral, noble, sheer, steep, white **06** decent, honest, supine, worthy **07** ethical **08** straight, vertical, virtuous **09** elevation, reputable, righteous **10** high-minded, honourable, principled, upstanding **11** respectable, trustworthy, verticality **13** at right angles, incorruptible, perpendicular

• set upright
04 cock, rear **05** erect **10** straighten

uprising
◇ *reversal down indicator*
06 mutiny, putsch, revolt, rising **08** intifada **09** coup d'état, overthrow, rebellion **10** insurgence, revolution **12** insurrection

uproar
03 din **04** flaw, hell, riot **05** noise, raird, rammy, reird **06** bedlam, clamor, dirdam, dirdum, émeute, fracas, furore, hubbub, mayhem, outcry, racket, randan, rumpus, tumult **07** clamour, garboil, ruction, turmoil, whoobub **08** brouhaha, disorder, hubbuboo **09** commotion, confusion, imbroglio **10** hullabaloo, rough music, turbulence **11** pandemonium **12** insurrection, katzenjammer, Pandaemonium **13** collieshangie

uproarious
04 loud, wild **05** noisy, rowdy **07** killing, riotous **08** confused **09** clamorous, deafening, hilarious **10** boisterous, hysterical, rip-roaring, rollicking, rowdy-dowdy **11** rib-tickling **12** unrestrained **13** side-splitting

uproot
04 weed **05** rip up **06** pull up, remove **07** destroy, root out, weed out, wipe out **08** displace, supplant **09** eradicate **11** averruncate

upset
◇ *anagram indicator*
◇ *reversal down indicator*
03 bug, eat, tip **04** coup, cowp, hurt, purl **05** het up, shake, shock, spill, worry **06** bother, chew up, choked, dismay, grieve, gutrot, gutted, jangle, malady, put out, ruffle, sadden, shaken, take on, tip out, topple, upcast **07** agitate, ailment, annoyed, anxious, break up, capsize, confuse, disrupt, disturb, fluster, grieved, illness, jealous, overset, perturb, reverse, shake up, shake-up, trouble, unhappy, unnerve, uptight, worried **08** agitated, bothered, confused, dismayed, disorder, disquiet, distress, in a state, irritate, overturn, renverse, sickness, surprise, troubled, unsteady, upheaval, worked up **09** aggrieved, agitation, complaint, disturbed, flustered, in a bad way, knock over, mess about, overthrow, perturbed, shattered, unsettled **10** discompose, disconcert, disruption, distressed, mess around, traumatize, tumble over **11** coup the cran, destabilize, discomposed, disorganize, disturbance **12** disconcerted, perturbation, play hell with **13** play havoc with **14** discomboberate, discombobulate

upsetting
◇ *anagram indicator*
08 alarming, assuming, worrying **09** conceited, overthrow, startling **10** disturbing, off-putting, perturbing, unsettling **11** distressing, frightening, overturning, presumption **13** disconcerting

upshot
03 aim, end **05** issue, loose, proof **06** finish, pay-off, result, sequel **07** outcome, success **10** conclusion, dénouement **11** consequence, culmination

upside down
◇ *reversal down indicator*
05 upset **06** turned **07** chaotic,

inverse, jumbled, muddled, up-ended **08** confused, inverted, messed up, upturned **10** disordered, in disarray, overturned, resupinate, topsy-turvy, wrong way up **11** wrong side up **13** heels o'er gowdy, heels over head

• turn upside down
05 up-end, upset **06** invert, mess up **07** disturb, whemmle, whomble, whommle, whummle **08** demolish **09** overthrow **10** make untidy, topsy-turvy **11** disorganize **13** turn inside out

upstage
03 top **04** beat, best **05** dwarf, excel, outdo **07** eclipse, outrank, surpass **08** outclass, outshine, outstrip, superior **09** transcend **10** overshadow, put to shame **11** stand-offish **13** put in the shade

upstanding
04 firm, good, true **05** erect, moral **06** honest, strong **07** ethical, upright **08** virtuous **10** four-square, honourable, principled **11** trustworthy **13** incorruptible

upstart
06 nobody **07** parvenu **08** jumped-up, mushroom **09** arriviste **10** new-fangled **12** nouveau riche **13** social climber

upsurge
04 gain, hike, rise **05** boost, surge **06** growth, spread, step-up, upturn **07** advance, build-up **08** addition, increase **09** expansion, extension, increment, rocketing **10** escalation **11** development, enlargement, heightening, mushrooming, snowballing **12** augmentation, skyrocketing **13** proliferation **15** intensification

uptight
04 edgy **05** angry, nervy, tense **06** hung-up, on edge, uneasy **07** anxious, prickly **09** irritated **11** strait-laced **12** conventional

up-to-date
02 in **03** hip, new, now, rad **04** cool, gear **06** groovy, latest, modern, recent, trendy, with it **07** à la page, current **08** space-age, swinging **09** in fashion, prevalent **10** all the rage, present-day **11** fashionable, in the groove **12** contemporary **13** state-of-the-art, up to the minute

• bring up-to-date
09 modernize

upturn
◇ *anagram indicator*
◇ *reversal down indicator*
04 rise **05** boost **07** revival, upsurge, upswing **08** increase, recovery, upheaval **10** betterment **11** disturbance, improvement **12** amelioration

upward, upwards
◇ *reversal down indicator*
03 top **06** rising, uphill **07** going up **08** moving up **09** ascending

• upwards of
04 over **05** above **08** more than **09** exceeding **10** higher than, in excess of

uranium
01 U

urban
04 city, town **05** civic **07** built-up, oppidan **09** inner-city, municipal **12** metropolitan **13** megalopolitan

urbane
05 civil, suave **06** smooth **07** elegant, refined **08** cultured, debonair, mannerly, polished, well-bred **09** civilized, courteous **10** cultivated **12** well-mannered **13** sophisticated

urbanity
04 ease **05** charm, grace **06** polish **07** culture, suavity **08** civility, courtesy, elegance **10** eutrapelia, refinement, smoothness **11** cultivation, worldliness **12** mannerliness **14** sophistication

urchin
03 elf, imp, kid **04** brat, waif **05** child, gamin, rogue **06** rascal **07** mudlark **08** hedgehog, hurcheon, townskip **09** hunchback **10** ragamuffin **11** guttersnipe

urge
03 beg, hie, nag, yen **04** goad, hist, itch, need, prod, push, spur, wish **05** chevy, chirp, chivy, drive, egg on, fancy, force, impel, plead, press **06** advise, appeal, chivvy, compel, desire, excite, exhort, hasten, incite, induce, libido, threap, threep **07** beseech, counsel, enforce, entreat, impetus, implore, impulse, incense, longing, procure **08** advocate, persuade, perswade, yearning **09** cacoethes, constrain, eagerness, encourage, instigate, prompting, recommend, stimulate **10** compulsion **11** inclination

• urge on
02 ca' **03** caa', egg, hie **04** edge, mush, spur **05** whoop, yoick **06** compel, giddap, giddup, halloa, halloo, hoicks, whet on, yoicks **07** giddy-up **09** instigate **11** whet forward

urgency
04 need **05** haste, hurry, press **06** preace, prease, stress **07** gravity, preasse **08** clamancy, exigency, instance, instancy, pressure, priority **09** extremity, necessity **10** importance **11** importunity, seriousness **14** imperativeness

urgent
04 dire **05** acute, eager, grave, prior, vital **07** crucial, earnest, exigent, instant, serious **08** critical, emergent, pressing, strident **09** emergency, essential, immediate, important, importune, insistent, necessary, strenuous **10** compelling, imperative, persistent, persuasive **11** top-priority

urinate
02 go **03** pee, wee, wet **04** leak, whiz **05** slash, stale, urine, whizz **06** pee-pee, piddle, tiddle, tinkle, wee-wee, widdle **07** relieve **09** make water, micturate, pass water, take a leak **11** spend a penny **12** be taken short, ease yourself **13** be caught short **15** relieve yourself

urn
04 olla **07** kitchen, ossuary, samovar **08** the Ashes **09** ballot box

Uruguay
01 U **03** ROU, Uru, URY

US
◇ *dialect word indicator*

usable
05 valid **07** current, working **08** fit to use **09** available, practical **10** functional **11** exploitable, operational, serviceable

usage
03 law, use, way **04** form, mode, rule **05** habit, idiom, style **06** custom, method, usance **07** control, meaning, practic, routine, running **08** handling, parlance, practice **09** etiquette, formalism, modernism, operation, procedure, tradition, treatment **10** consuetude, convention, employment, expression, management, regulation **11** application, institution, phraseology, terminology **12** way of writing **13** way of speaking

use
◇ *anagram indicator*
02 do **03** end, ply, try, ure **04** call, good, help, milk, need, work **05** abuse, apply, avail, bleed, cause, enjoy, point, right, spend, treat, usage, value, waste, wield, worth **06** custom, demand, draw on, employ, expend, follow, handle, misuse, object, profit, resort **07** ability, benefit, consume, exhaust, exploit, observe, operate, purpose, service, utilize **08** accustom, cash in on, deal with, exercise, impose on, occasion, practise, put to use, resort to **09** advantage, go through, habituate, make use of, manoeuvre, necessity, operation, privilege, regularly **10** employment, get through, imposition, manipulate, permission, usefulness **11** application, utilization **12** exploitation, manipulation, mistreatment **13** bring into play **15** take advantage of

• used to
06 wont to **07** given to, prone to **08** inured to **10** adjusted to, at home with **11** practised in **12** accustomed to, familiar with, habituated to, in the habit of, no stranger to **14** acclimatized to

• use up
◇ *reversal down indicator*
03 sap **04** burn, take **05** drain, spend, waste **06** absorb, devour, finish, peruse, work up **07** consume, deplete,

eat into, exhaust, fritter, tire out
08 squander **09** go through

used
◇ *anagram indicator*
04 wont, worn **05** usual **06** expert, soiled **07** cast-off **08** dog-eared, pre-owned **09** customary, nearly-new
10 hand-me-down, second-hand
11 experienced

useful
04 able **05** handy, nifty **06** expert
07 helpful, skilful, skilled **08** behovely, fruitful, valuable **09** competent, effective, practical, practised, rewarding **10** all-purpose, beneficial, convenient, functional, productive, proficient, profitable, worthwhile
11 experienced, serviceable
12 advantageous **14** general-purpose

usefulness
03 use **04** good, help **05** avail, value, worth **06** profit **07** benefit, fitness, service, utility **08** efficacy
09 advantage **10** efficiency
11 convenience **12** practicality
13 functionality **15** serviceableness

useless
◇ *anagram indicator*
03 bad, dud **04** bung, idle, poor, ropy, vain, void, weak **05** awful, kaput, lousy, ropey **06** futile, grotty, no good
07 botched **08** bootless, frippery, hopeless, pathetic, terrible, unusable
09 fruitless, half-assed, incapable, pointless, to no avail, unhelpful, worthless **10** broken-down, clapped-out, effectless, unavailing, unworkable
11 impractical, incompetent, ineffective, ineffectual, inefficient
12 unproductive, unprofitable
13 inefficacious **14** a load of garbage, a load of rubbish, good-for-nothing

uselessness
08 futility, idleness **09** inutility
10 ineptitude **12** hopelessness, incompetence **14** impracticality, ineffectuality **15** ineffectiveness

usher
04 lead, show **05** guide, macer, pilot, steer **06** direct, escort **07** chobdar, conduct, marshal **08** Black Rod, huissier **09** accompany, assistant, attendant, introduce, usherette
10 doorkeeper
• **usher in**
06 herald, launch, ring in **07** precede
08 announce, initiate **09** introduce
10 inaugurate **13** pave the way for
14 mark the start of

usual
05 stock **06** common, normal, wonted
07 average, general, ordinar, regular, routine, typical **08** accepted, customed, everyday, expected, familiar, habitual, ordinary, orthodox, standard **09** customary
10 accustomed, exceptless, recognized, regulation
11 commonplace, established, predictable, traditional
12 conventional **13** unexceptional

usually
03 usu **06** mainly, mostly **07** as a rule, chiefly **08** commonly, normally
09 generally, in the main, on average, regularly, routinely, typically **10** by and large, habitually, on the whole, ordinarily **13** traditionally **14** for the most part

usurer
05 gripe **07** Shylock **09** loan-shark
10 gombeen-man, note-shaver
11 money-lender **12** extortionist

usurp
04 take **05** annex, seize, steal
06 assume **08** arrogate, supplant, take over **10** commandeer **11** appropriate

usury
06 excess **07** gombeen **08** interest
09 extortion **12** money-lending

Utah
02 UT

utensil
04 tool **06** device, gadget
09 apparatus, appliance, implement
10 instrument **11** contrivance

Kitchen utensils include:

03 bin, pan, wok
04 etna, fork
05 corer, ladle, mouli, sieve, tongs, whisk
06 baster, bun tin, grater, juicer, karahi, mincer, peeler, shears, sifter, skewer, stoner, tureen, zester
07 blender, cake tin, cleaver, cocotte, flan tin, grinder, loaf tin, milk pan, ramekin, skillet, skimmer, spatula, steamer, terrine
08 blini pan, breadbin, colander, crêpe pan, cruet set, egg-timer, grill pan, ham stand, herb mill, mandolin, pie plate, saucepan, scissors, stockpot, tea caddy, teaspoon, wine rack
09 bain marie, blowtorch, brochette, can-opener, casserole, corkscrew, dough hook, egg slicer, fish slice, fondue set, frying pan, gravy boat, mezzaluna, muffin tin, paella pan, pie funnel, punch bowl, sharpener, spice rack, tin-opener, toast rack
10 breadboard, breadknife, butter dish, cook's knife, egg coddler, egg poacher, fish kettle, jelly mould, knife block, liquidizer, mixing bowl, nutcracker, pasta ladle, pasta maker, pepper mill, quiche dish, rice cooker, rolling pin, slow cooker, steak knife, storage jar, table knife, tea infuser, waffle iron, wine cooler
11 baking sheet, boning knife, butter knife, cheese board, cheese knife, cooling rack, garlic press, melon baller, omelette pan, oyster knife, pastry board, pastry brush, potato ricer, roasting pan, sandwich tin, soufflé dish, tea strainer, thermometer, wooden spoon
12 bottle opener, butter curler, carving knife, cheese slicer, deep-fat fryer, dessert spoon, egg separator, flour dredger, icing syringe, measuring jug, nutmeg grater, palette knife, pastry cutter, potato masher, pudding basin, pudding mould, salad spinner, serving spoon, yoghurt maker
13 butcher's block, chopping-board, draining spoon, food processor, ice-cream scoop, kitchen scales, lemon squeezer, preserving pan
14 measuring spoon, pressure cooker, straining spoon, vegetable knife
15 grapefruit knife, meat thermometer, mortar and pestle

utilitarian
05 lowly **06** useful **08** sensible
09 effective, efficient, practical, pragmatic **10** convenient, functional
11 down-to-earth, serviceable
13 unpretentious

utility
03 use, ute **04** good, help, tool **05** avail, value, worth **06** profit **07** benefit, fitness, service **08** efficacy
09 advantage **10** efficiency, usefulness
11 convenience **12** practicality
15 serviceableness

utilize
03 use **05** adapt **06** employ **07** exploit
08 put to use, resort to **09** make use of
13 turn to account **15** take advantage of

utmost
03 end, top **04** best, last, most, peak
05 final **07** extreme, hardest, highest, maximum, supreme **08** farthest, furthest, greatest, remotest, ultimate
09 outermost, paramount
11 furthermost

Utopia
04 Eden **05** bliss **06** heaven **07** Elysium
08 paradise **09** Shangri-la **12** Garden of Eden **13** heaven on earth, seventh heaven

Utopian
04 airy **05** dream, ideal **07** Elysian, perfect, wishful **08** fanciful, illusory, romantic **09** fantastic, imaginary, visionary **10** chimerical, idealistic, unworkable **11** impractical

utter
◇ *homophone indicator*
03 say **04** dead, emit, pass, pure, rank, talk, tell, vend, vent **05** outer, plain, sheer, sound, speak, stark, state, total, voice **06** accent, arrant, entire, goddam, put out, reveal, tongue
07 declaim, declare, deliver, divulge, express, extreme, goddamn, perfect
08 absolute, announce, complete, monotone, outright, positive, proclaim, thorough, vocalize
09 downright, enunciate, goddamned, out-and-out, pronounce, verbalize
10 articulate, consummate
11 categorical, come out with, unmitigated, unqualified **12** put into words **13** thoroughgoing

utterance
03 cry **04** talk, word **05** drawl, mouth, voice **06** remark, speech, tongue **07** comment, inanity, opinion **08** delivery, prophecy **09** outgiving, prolation, speech act, statement **10** expression, outpouring **11** declaration, enunciation **12** announcement, articulation, proclamation **13** pronouncement

utterly
03 dog **04** dead, pure, rank **05** fully, plumb, stark **06** goddam, wholly **07** goddamn, totally **08** entirely **09** downright, goddamned, perfectly, to the wide **10** absolutely, completely, thoroughly **13** categorically

U-turn
03 uey **07** wheelie **08** reversal **09** about-turn, backtrack, volte-face

Uzbekistan
02 UZ **03** UZB

V

V
03 vee **06** victor

vacancy
03 gap, job **04** hole, post, room **05** blank, place **07** inanity, leisure, opening, vacuity **08** idleness, position **09** blankness, emptiness, situation **10** inactivity **11** opportunity

vacant
04 free, void **05** blank, empty, inane **06** absent, dreamy, unused **07** deadpan, vacuous **08** deserted, gaumless, gormless, not in use, unfilled **09** abandoned, available **10** unoccupied, unthinking **11** inattentive, uninhabited **12** absent-minded **14** expressionless

vacate
04 quit **05** annul, leave, waive **06** unload **07** abandon **08** evacuate, withdraw

vacated
03 red **04** redd

vacation
03 vac **04** hols, long, rest, trip **05** break, leave **06** recess **07** holiday, leisure, non-term, time off, vacance, voiding **08** furlough, holidays **12** intermission

vaccinate
03 jab, jag **07** protect, syringe **08** immunize **09** inoculate

vaccination
03 jab **04** dose, shot **09** injection **11** inoculation **12** immunization

vacillate
◇ *anagram indicator*
04 halt, sway, wave **05** haver, waver **06** didder, dither, teeter, waffle, wobble **07** whiffle **08** hesitate **09** fluctuate, oscillate, temporize **11** back and fill **12** shilly-shally, tergiversate **14** blow hot and cold, go back and forth

vacillating
◇ *anagram indicator*
06 feeble **08** hesitant, waffling, wavering **09** spineless, uncertain **10** indecisive, irresolute, unresolved, willy-nilly **11** oscillating **15** shilly-shallying

vacillation
◇ *anagram indicator*
06 waffle **08** wavering, wobbling **09** dithering, hesitancy **10** hesitation, indecision **11** fluctuation, inconstancy **12** irresolution, shilly-shally **13** temporization **14** indecisiveness, tergiversation **15** shilly-shallying

vacuity
04 void **05** space **06** apathy, hollow, vacuum **07** inanity **08** idleness **09** blankness, emptiness **11** nothingness, vacuousness **12** listlessness

vacuous
04 idle, void **05** blank, empty, inane **06** stupid, vacant **07** foolish **08** unfilled **09** apathetic **11** empty-headed **14** expressionless

vacuum
03 gap, vac **04** void **05** chasm, space **06** Hoover®, lacuna **07** vacuity **09** emptiness **11** nothingness

• **vacuum flask**
05 dewar **07** Thermos®

vagabond
03 bum **04** hobo **05** caird, nomad, piker, rogue, rover, scamp, tramp **06** beggar, dosser, rascal, roving **07** dingbat, floater, gadling, gangrel, migrant, outcast, vagrant **08** clochard, cursitor, palliard, runabout, runagate, straggle, wanderer **09** itinerant, landloper, sundowner, unsettled **10** down-and-out, land-louper **11** rinthereout, scatterling, Weary Willie **12** hallan-shaker **15** knight of the road

vagary
04 whim **05** fancy, prank, quirk **06** fegary, humour, megrim, whimsy **07** caprice **08** crotchet, rambling **10** digression

vagrancy
08 nomadism **09** wandering **10** itinerancy, travelling **12** homelessness, rootlessness

vagrant
◇ *anagram indicator*
03 bum **04** hobo **05** caird, derro, rogue, scamp, tramp **06** beggar, dosser, rascal, roving, truant, vagrom, walker **07** drifter, erratic, floater, gangrel, nomadic, roaming, tinkler **08** cursitor, homeless, rootless, straggle, stroller, vagabond, wanderer **09** itinerant, landloper, shiftless, uncertain, unsettled, wandering **10** inconstant, land-louper, travelling **11** rinthereout, scatterling **12** gang-there-out, hallan-shaker, rolling stone **14** circumforanean **15** circumforaneous

vague
◇ *anagram indicator*
03 dim, lax **04** hazy **05** faint, foggy, fuzzy, loose, misty, rough, woozy **06** unsure, wander, woolly **07** blurred, evasive, general, inexact, obscure, of a sort, of sorts, shadowy, sketchy, unclear **08** nebulous, yonderly **09** ambiguous, amorphous, imprecise, uncertain, undefined, unfocused **10** ill-defined, indefinite, indistinct, out of focus, unspecific **11** approximate, generalized **12** undetermined, woolly-minded **13** indeterminate **14** transcendental

vaguely
◇ *anagram indicator*
05 dimly **07** faintly **08** slightly, vacantly **09** distantly, inexactly, obscurely **11** imprecisely **14** absent-mindedly

vagueness
07 dimness **08** haziness **09** ambiguity, faintness, fuzziness, looseness, obscurity **10** generality, impression, woolliness **11** imprecision, uncertainty **12** inexactitude

vain
04 idle **05** empty, proud, vogie, waste **06** devoid, futile, hollow, snooty **07** foppish, haughty, stuck-up, useless **08** abortive, affected, arrogant, nugatory, vaporous, wasteful **09** bigheaded, conceited, coxcombic, fruitless, pointless, worthless **10** coxcomical, groundless, peacockish, sleeveless, swaggering, unavailing **11** coxcombical, egotistical, empty-headed, pretentious, swell-headed, thoughtless **12** narcissistic, ostentatious, unproductive, unprofitable **13** high and mighty, self-important, swollen-headed

• **in vain**
04 no go **06** vainly **07** in waste **09** fruitless, to no avail, uselessly **10** for nothing **11** fruitlessly **13** ineffectually **14** unsuccessfully

vainglorious
04 vain **05** cocky, proud **06** swanky **07** crowing **08** arrogant, boastful, bragging, puffed up **09** bigheaded, conceited **10** swaggering **11** egotistical **13** swollen-headed **14** self-flattering

vainly
04 no go **07** for vain, to no end **09** to no avail, uselessly **10** for nothing **11** fruitlessly **13** ineffectually **14** unsuccessfully

vale *see* **farewell**; **valley**

valediction
05 adieu, aloha **06** shalom, so long **07** goodbye, send-off **08** farewell **11** leave-taking **14** shalom aleichem

valedictory
04 last **05** final **07** parting **08** farewell **10** apopemptic

valet
03 man **06** Jeeves, lackey **07** lacquey **10** manservant **11** body servant **14** valet de chambre

valetudinarian
04 weak **05** frail **06** feeble, infirm, sickly, weakly **07** invalid **08** delicate, neurotic **13** hypochondriac

valiant
04 bold, prow **05** brave **06** heroic, mighty, plucky, strong **07** gallant, staunch **08** fearless, intrepid, valorous **09** audacious, dauntless **10** courageous, determined **11** indomitable, lion-hearted, redoubtable **12** stout-hearted

valiantly
06 boldly **07** bravely **08** pluckily **09** gallantly, staunchly **10** fearlessly, heroically, intrepidly **11** audaciously, dauntlessly, indomitably **12** courageously **14** stout-heartedly

valid
04 good, just **05** legal, sound **06** cogent, lawful, proper, strong **07** binding, genuine, logical, weighty **08** bona fide, credible, licensed, official **09** authentic, available, effectual **10** accredited, applicable, approbated, legitimate, meaningful, reasonable **11** justifiable, substantial, well-founded **12** acknowledged, well-grounded

validate
06 attest, ratify, verify **07** certify, confirm, endorse **08** accredit, legalize **09** authorize, formalize **10** underwrite **11** corroborate **12** authenticate, substantiate

validation
11 attestation, endorsement **12** confirmation, ratification **13** accreditation, authorization, corroboration, formalization **14** authentication

validity
05 force, logic, point, vigor **06** vigour, weight **07** cogency, grounds **08** legality, strength **09** authority, soundness, substance **10** lawfulness, legitimacy **14** justifiability

valley
03 cwm, den, ria **04** comb, dale, dean, dell, dene, gill, glen, park, vale, wadi, wady **05** combe, coomb, griff, grike, gryke, gulch, heuch, heugh, slade, Tempe, water **06** clough, coombe, dingle, graben, griffe, hollow, strath, Tophet, trough **07** Gehenna, wind gap **09** re-entrant

valorous
04 bold **05** brave **06** heroic, plucky **07** doughty, gallant, valiant **08** fearless, intrepid, stalwart **09** dauntless **10** courageous, mettlesome **11** lion-hearted **12** stout-hearted

valour
05 value, worth **06** mettle, spirit, virtue **07** bravery, courage, heroism, prowess **08** boldness, valiance, valiancy, war-proof **09** fortitude, gallantry **11** doughtiness, intrepidity **12** fearlessness **15** lion-heartedness

valuable
04 dear **05** noble **06** costly, golden, prized, useful, valued, worthy **07** helpful **08** fruitful, precious **09** cherished, deserving, expensive, important, priceless, treasured **10** beneficial, invaluable, profitable, worthwhile **12** advantageous, constructive

valuation
05 price, prise, prize, stent, value **06** extent, survey **08** estimate **09** appraisal, expertise **10** assessment, evaluation **11** stocktaking **12** appraisement

value
03 use **04** cost, gain, good, prys, rate **05** merit, price, prize, worth **06** admire, assess, esteem, ethics, morals, profit, survey **07** benefit, cherish, respect, revere, utility **08** appraise, efficacy, estimate, evaluate, hold dear, treasure **09** advantage, standards **10** appreciate, excellence, importance, principles, usefulness **11** put a price on **12** desirability, significance **15** set great store by

• **of little value**
03 low **05** cheap **06** common

• **something of little value**
04 damn **06** button, trifle **10** boondoggle

valued
04 dear **05** loved **06** priced, prized **07** beloved **08** esteemed **09** cherished, respected, treasured **14** highly regarded

valueless
04 naff, poor **05** cheap **06** futile, paltry, trashy **07** trivial, useless **08** nugatory, rubbishy, trifling, unusable **09** pointless, worthless **10** unavailing **11** ineffectual, meaningless, unimportant **13** insignificant

valve

Valves include:

04 ball, blow, gate, side, tube
05 bleed, choke, clack, diode, heart, slide
06 escape, mitral, mixing, needle, poppet, puppet, safety, triode, ventil
07 exhaust, petcock, seacock, snifter, tetrode
08 bicuspid, bistable, cylinder, dynatron, snifting, throttle, turncock
09 air-intake, butterfly, induction, injection, magnetron, non-return, semilunar, thyratron
10 Eustachian, thermionic

vamp
05 Circe, flirt, siren **06** trudge **07** charmer, Delilah, Lorelei, patch up **08** coquette **09** temptress **10** seductress **11** enchantress, femme fatale

van
02 RV **03** ute **04** wing **05** lorry, truck, wagon **06** camper, pick-up, waggon **07** caravan, minivan, trailer, utility **08** carriage, vanguard **09** advantage, Dormobile®, meat wagon, motor home, Winnebago® **10** baggage-car, black Maria, freight-car, mobile home, panel truck **11** patrol-wagon, railroad car **12** pantechnicon, utility truck **14** utility vehicle

vanadium
01 V

vandal
03 yob **04** lout, thug **05** rough, rowdy, tough **06** locust, mugger **07** hoodlum, mobster, ravager, ruffian, wrecker **08** hooligan **09** bovver boy, desolater, despoiler, ransacker **10** delinquent, demolisher **11** annihilator

vandalize
◇ *anagram indicator*
04 ruin, sink **05** break, smash, trash, wreck **06** ravage **07** destroy, shatter, torpedo **08** demolish, write off **09** devastate

vane
03 fan, web **04** fane, wing **05** blade, plume **07** dogvane **08** windsail **11** weathercock

vanguard
03 van **04** fore, lead **05** front **09** forefront, front line, spearhead **10** firing line

vanish
04 exit, fade **05** faint, ghost, leave **06** depart, die out, exhale **07** emanate, evanish, fade out **08** disperse, dissolve, evanesce, fade away, melt away, peter out **09** disappear, evaporate, fizzle out **11** go up in smoke **12** end up in smoke **13** dematerialize

vanity
04 airs, pomp **05** folly, pride **07** conceit, egotism, foppery **08** futility, idleness, self-love, vainesse, vainness **09** arrogance **10** narcissism, pretension, snootiness, triviality **11** affectation, haughtiness, ostentation, self-conceit **12** extravagance **13** bigheadedness, conceitedness, dressing-table

vanquish
04 beat, drub, lick, rout **05** crush, paste, quell, smash, thump **06** defeat,

hammer, humble, master, subdue, thrash **07** clobber, conquer, repress, trounce **08** confound, overcome **09** overpower, overwhelm, subjugate **10** annihilate **11** triumph over **15** make mincemeat of

Vanuatu
03 VUT

vapid
04 dull, flat, limp, weak **05** banal, bland, stale, trite **06** boring, flashy, jejune, watery **07** insipid, tedious, vacuous **08** lifeless, tiresome **10** colourless, wishy-washy **11** uninspiring

vaporous
04 fumy, vain **05** foggy, misty **06** flimsy, fumous, steamy **07** gaseous **08** fanciful, halitous **10** chimerical **13** insubstantial

vapour
03 fog **04** brag, damp, fume, haze, mist, reek, roke **05** boast, fumes, smoke, steam **06** breath **07** halitus, show off, swagger **09** evaporate **10** exhalation

variable
01 X, Y, Z **03** var **04** Mira **05** Algol **06** factor, fickle, fitful, uneven **07** moonish, mutable, Protean **08** flexible, shifting, unstable, unsteady, wavering **09** fluxional, irregular, parameter **10** changeable, fluxionary, inconstant **11** chameleonic, fluctuating, vacillating **13** pulsating star, temperamental, unpredictable

variance
04 odds **06** strife **07** discord, dispute, dissent **08** conflict, division **09** deviation, dichotomy, variation **10** alteration, difference, dissension, divergence **11** discrepancy **12** disagreement **13** inconsistency

• **at variance**
03 odd **06** at odds, at outs **07** arguing **08** clashing **09** differing, out of step **10** in conflict **11** conflicting, disagreeing, quarrelling **13** at loggerheads **14** in disagreement

variant
◇ *anagram indicator*
03 var **05** rogue **07** derived, deviant, variate, varying, version **08** modified **09** changeful, character, different, divergent, variation **11** alternative, diversified

variation
◇ *anagram indicator*
05 pulse **06** change **07** fluxion, novelty, variant, variety, varying **08** variance **09** departure, deviation, diversity, saltation **10** alteration, alternance, difference, inflection, modulation **11** discrepancy, fluctuation **12** orthogenesis

varied
◇ *anagram indicator*
05 dedal, mixed **06** daedal, motley, sundry **07** diverse, various **08** assorted **09** different **10** accidented **11** wide-ranging **12** multifarious **13** heterogeneous, miscellaneous

variegated
◇ *anagram indicator*
04 pied **05** jaspe, paned, vairé **06** broken, motley, veined **07** brocked, brockit, clouded, dappled, marbled, mottled, various **08** distinct, speckled, streaked **09** checkered, chequered, dapple-bay, harlequin, proud-pied **10** poikilitic **12** varicoloured **13** multicoloured, parti-coloured, party-coloured

variety
◇ *anagram indicator*
03 var **04** brew, kind, make, sort, type **05** brand, breed, class, color, range **06** change, colour, medley, strain **07** mixture, species **08** category **09** diversity, pot-pourri, variation **10** assortment, collection, difference, miscellany, subspecies **11** versatility **12** multiplicity **13** dissimilarity **14** classification

various
◇ *anagram indicator*
04 many **05** mixed **06** motley, sundry, unlike, varied **07** diverse, several, varying **08** assorted, distinct **09** different, differing, disparate, uncertain **10** changeable, dissimilar, variegated **11** diversified **13** heterogeneous, miscellaneous

varnish
03 lac **04** coat, dope **05** glair, glaze, gloss, japan, resin **06** dammar, dammer, enamel, lacker, mastic, polish, veneer **07** coating, lacquer, mastich, shellac **08** kauri gum, shell-lac **10** lacquering, nail enamel, nail polish **12** French polish, Japan lacquer, vernis martin **13** etching ground

vary
◇ *anagram indicator*
04 hunt **05** alter, clash, range, spice, waver **06** change, depart, differ, modify **07** deviate, diverge, inflect, qualify, variate **08** be at odds, disagree, modulate **09** alternate, diversify, embellish, fluctuate, oscillate, permutate, transform **12** metamorphose

vase
03 jar, jug, urn **04** ewer **05** diota, flask **06** hydria, luster, lustre, vessel **07** amphora, Canopus, pitcher, potiche **09** moon flask **10** Canopic jar, Canopic urn, cornucopia

vassal
03 man **04** serf **05** liege, slave **06** client, thrall **07** bondman, servile, subject, villein **08** bondsman, liegeman, retainer **09** dependant **11** bondservant, subordinate

vassalage
03 fee **04** fief **07** bondage, prowess, serfdom, slavery **08** thraldom **09** servitude **10** dependence, subjection, villeinage **11** subjugation

vast
04 huge **05** great **07** immense, massive **08** colossal, cyclopic, enormous, far-flung, gigantic, infinite, sweeping **09** boundless, cyclopean, cyclopian, extensive, limitless, monstrous, unlimited **10** monumental, tremendous **11** appreciable, never-ending **12** considerable, immeasurable

vastly
06 hugely **07** greatly **09** immensely, massively **10** enormously, infinitely **11** boundlessly, extensively, limitlessly **12** immeasurably **13** without limits

vat
03 fat, tub **04** back, case, keir, kier, tank **05** cuvée, keeve, stand **06** barrel, girnel, tan-pit **07** wine fat **08** pressfat

Vatican City
01 V **03** VAT

vault
◇ *anagram indicator*
04 arch, dome, jump, leap, over, roof, span, tomb, vaut **05** bound, clear, crypt, embow, vaute, vawte **06** cavern, cellar, cupola, heaven, hurdle, spring **07** concave **08** leap-frog **09** cul-de-four, mausoleum, wagon roof **10** depository, repository, strongroom, undercroft, wine-cellar **11** safe-deposit **13** safety-deposit

vaunt
03 gab **04** brag, crow **05** boast, swank **06** flaunt, parade **07** exult in, show off, trumpet **08** vanguard **15** blow your own horn

veer
04 cast, tack, turn, wind **05** sheer, shift, slack, swing, wheel **06** broach, change, pay out, swerve, wester **07** box-haul, deviate, diverge, norther, peel off, souther, whiffle **09** come round

vegetable

Vegetables include:

03 oca, pea, yam
04 bean, cole, eddo, kale, leek, neep, okra, sium, spud, taro, wort
05 chard, choko, cress, gumbo, laver, mooli, onion, swede
06 bhindi, carrot, celery, chives, chocho, daikon, endive, fennel, garlic, lentil, manioc, marrow, pepper, potato, radish, rocket, sorrel, squash, tomato, turnip
07 avocado, bok choy, cabbage, cardoon, cassava, chayote, chicory, lettuce, pak choi, parsnip, pumpkin, salsify, shallot, skirret, spinach, tapioca
08 baby corn, beetroot, borecole, broccoli, capsicum, celeriac, cucumber, eggplant, finochio, kohlrabi, leaf beet, mushroom, red onion, soya bean, zucchini
09 artichoke, asparagus, aubergine,

bean shoot, broad bean, calabrese, courgette, finocchio, mange tout, petit pois, red pepper, Romanesco, sweetcorn
10 bean sprout, butter bean, French bean, lollo rosso, red cabbage, runner bean, swiss chard, watercress
11 cauliflower, Chinese leaf, green pepper, lady's finger, spring onion, sweet potato
12 marrow-squash, savoy cabbage, summer squash, turnip greens, winter squash, yellow pepper
13 ladies' fingers
14 Brussels sprout, Chinese cabbage, globe artichoke
15 vegetable marrow

See also **bean**

vegetarian
05 vegan, vegie **06** veggie **08** ovo-lacto **09** lactarian **11** Pythagorean

vegetate
04 idle **07** moulder **08** go to seed, languish, stagnate **09** do nothing, rusticate **10** degenerate **11** deteriorate

vegetation
04 sudd **05** flora, plant, trees **06** plants **07** flowers, herbage, verdure, vesture **08** greenery, savagery

vehemence
04 fire, heat, zeal **05** force, power, verve **06** ardour, energy, fervor, vigour, warmth **07** fervour, passion, urgency **08** emphasis, fervency, strength, violence **09** animation, intensity **10** enthusiasm **12** forcefulness

vehement
03 hot **04** keen, warm **05** eager **06** ardent, fervid, fierce, heated, strong, urgent **07** earnest, fervent, intense, violent, zealous **08** animated, emphatic, forceful, forcible, powerful, spirited, vigorous **10** passionate, thunderous **11** impassioned **12** enthusiastic

vehicle
05 means, organ **06** agency, medium **07** channel **09** mechanism, transport **10** conveyance, instrument

Vehicles include:

03 bus, cab, car, cat, fly, gig, HGV, tip, ute, van
04 arba, biga, bike, boat, cart, drag, dray, duck, ekka, hack, Jeep®, kago, kart, scow, ship, sled, solo, tank, taxi, tram, trap, tube, wain
05 araba, coach, cycle, lorry, plane, stage, sulky, train, truck, Vespa®, wagon
06 bakkie, camper, hansom, hearse, Humvee®, jalopy, jinker, landau, litter, Maglev, sidecar, sledge, sleigh, surrey, tandem, troika, tuk tuk
07 bicycle, caravan, dog-cart, minibus, minivan, omnibus, phaeton, Pullman, ricksha, scooter, sleeper, tractor, trailer, Transit®, trishaw
08 barouche, brougham, Cape cart, golf cart, monorail, rickshaw, toboggan, tricycle, wagon-lit
09 bobsleigh, buck-wagon, charabanc, motorbike
10 boneshaker, four-in-hand, jinricksha, jinrikisha, juggernaut, motorcycle, post-chaise, Scotch cart, sedan-chair, service car, stagecoach, trolleybus
11 caravanette, jinrickshaw, steam-roller
12 double-decker, pantechnicon
13 fork-lift truck, penny-farthing
15 hackney-carriage

See also **aircraft**; **bicycle**; **car**; **carriage**; **ship**

International Vehicle Registration codes include:

01 A (Austria), B (Belgium), C (Cuba), D (Germany), E (Spain), F (France), G (Gabon), H (Hungary), I (Italy), J (Japan), K (Cambodia), L (Luxembourg), M (Malta), N (Norway), P (Portugal), Q (Qatar), S (Sweden), T (Thailand), V (Vatican City), Z (Zambia)
02 AL (Albania), AM (Armenia), AZ (Azerbaijan), BD (Bangladesh), BF (Burkina Faso), BG (Bulgaria), BH (Belize), BR (Brazil), BS (The Bahamas), BW (Botswana), BY (Belarus), BZ (Belize), CH (Switzerland), CI (Côte d'Ivoire), CL (Sri Lanka), CO (Colombia), CR (Costa Rica), CU (Cuba), CY (Cyprus), CZ (Czech Republic), DK (Denmark), DY (Benin), DZ (Algeria), EC (Ecuador), ES (El Salvador), ET (Egypt), FL (Liechtenstein), FR (Faroe Islands), GB (Great Britain), GE (Georgia), GH (Ghana), GR (Greece), HK (Hong Kong), HR (Croatia), IL (Israel), IR (Iran), IS (Iceland), JA (Jamaica), KS (Kyrgyzstan), KZ (Kazakhzstan), LB (Liberia), LS (Lesotho), LT (Lithuania), LV (Latvia), MA (Morocco), MC (Monaco), MD (Moldova), MK (Macedonia), MS (Mauritius), MW (Malawi), NA (Netherlands Antilles), NL (Netherlands), NZ (New Zealand), PA (Panama), PE (Peru), PK (Pakistan), PL (Poland), PY (Paraguay), QA (Qatar), RA (Argentina), RB (Benin), RC (Taiwan), RG (Guinea), RH (Haiti), RI (Indonesia), RL (Lebanon), RM (Madagascar), RN (Niger), RO (Romania), RP (Philippines), RU (Burundi), SA (Saudi Arabia), SD (Swaziland), SK (Slovakia), SN (Senegal), SO (Somalia), SU (Belarus), SY (Seychelles), TG (Togo), TJ (Tajikistan), TM (Turkmenistan), TN (Tunisia), TR (Turkey), TT (Trinidad and Tobago), UA (Ukraine), UZ (Uzbekistan), VN (Vietnam), WD (Dominica), WG (Grenada), WL (St Lucia), WS (Samoa), WV (St Vincent and the Grenadines), YV (Venezuela), ZA (South Africa), ZW (Zimbabwe)
03 AFG (Afghanistan), AND (Andorra), ARM (Armenia), AUS (Australia), BDS (Barbados), BIH (Bosnia and Herzegovina), BOL (Bolivia), BRN (Bahrain), BRU (Brunei), BUR (Myanmar), CAM (Cameroon), CDN (Canada), DOM (Dominican Republic), EAK (Kenya), EAT (Tanzania), EAU (Uganda), EAZ (Tanzania), EST (Estonia), ETH (Ethiopia), FIN (Finland), FJI (Fiji), GAB (Gabon), GBA (Alderney), GBG (Guernsey), GBJ (Jersey), GBM (Isle of Man), GBZ (Gibraltar), GCA (Guatemala), GUY (Guyana), HKJ (Jordan), IND (India), IRL (Ireland), IRQ (Iraq), KWT (Kuwait), LAO (Laos), LAR (Libya), MAL (Malaysia), MEX (Mexico), MGL (Mongolia), MOC (Mozambique), NAM (Namibia), NAU (Nauru), NEP (Nepal), NGR (Nigeria), NIC (Nicaragua), PNG (Papua New Guinea), RCA (Central African Republic), RCB (Republic of Congo), RCH (Chile), RGB (Guinea-Bissau), RIM (Mauritania), RMM (Mali), ROK (South Korea), ROU (Uruguay), RSM (San Marino), RUS (Russia), RWA (Rwanda), SCG (Serbia and Montenegro), SGP (Singapore), SLO (Slovenia), SME (Suriname), SUD (Sudan), SVN (Slovenia), SYR (Syria), TCH (Chad), USA (United States of America), WAG (The Gambia), WAL (Sierra Leone), WAN (Nigeria), YAR (Yemen), ZRE (Democratic Republic of the Congo)

veil
04 caul, film, hide, mask, mist, vail, vele **05** blind, burka, burqa, cloak, cover, scarf, scene, shade, veale, velum, volet **06** boorka, canopy, chadar, chador, kiss-me, mantle, purdah, shroud, sudary, weeper, wimple **07** bourkha, chaddar, chaddor, chuddah, chuddar, conceal, cover up, curtain, humeral, modesty, obscure, veiling, whimple, yashmak **08** chrismal, covering, disguise, kalyptra, mantilla, sudarium **09** encurtain **10** camouflage, lambrequin **11** concealment, kiss-me-quick

See also **scarf**

veiled
06 covert, hidden, masked, secret **07** cloaked, covered, obscure **08** indirect, shrouded **09** concealed, disguised **13** surreptitious

vein
03 rib **04** lode, mode, mood, seam, tone, vena **05** costa, nerve, style, tenor, varix **06** cavity, humour, marble, strain, streak, stripe **07** fissure, nervure, stratum **08** stringer **11** blood vessel, disposition, inclination, temperament

Veins and arteries include:

05 aorta, iliac, renal, ulnar
06 portal, radial, thread, tibial
07 basilic, carotid, coeliac, femoral, frontal, gastric, hepatic, jugular, organic, precava, saphena, splenic
08 axillary, brachial, coronary, postcava, praecava, superior, temporal, varicose, vena cava
09 popliteal, pulmonary, spermatic
10 innominate, mesenteric, subclavian
11 common iliac
14 anterior tibial
15 brachiocephalic, posterior tibial

veined
05 jaspe **06** venose, venous **07** marbled **08** streaked **10** reticulate, variegated

velocity
01 v **04** pace, rate **05** speed **08** celerity, rapidity **09** fleetness, quickness, swiftness

• **velocity constant**
01 k

velvet
05 gains, panne **06** dévoré, vellet, velour, velure **07** mockado, velours **08** chenille, suedette, winnings **09** three-pile

venal
04 bent **06** venous **07** buyable, corrupt **08** bribable, grafting **09** mercenary **10** simoniacal **11** corruptible

vendetta
04 feud **06** enmity **07** quarrel, rivalry **08** bad blood **09** blood-feud

vendor
06 seller, trader **07** butcher, camelot **08** merchant, salesman, stockist, supplier

veneer
04 mask, show **05** front, gloss, guise, layer **06** façade, fineer, finish **07** coating, display, surface **08** covering, pretence **09** grass-moth **10** appearance, lamination

venerable
03 Ven **04** aged, Bede, wise **06** august **07** revered **08** esteemed, honoured **09** dignified, respected, venerated **10** worshipped

venerate
04 fear **05** adore **06** esteem, honour, revere **07** iconize, respect, worship **09** reverence

veneration
03 awe **05** dulia, honor **06** esteem, honour, latria **07** douleia, respect, worship **08** devotion **09** adoration, aniconism, reverence, sublimity **10** hyperdulia, Mariolatry, Maryolatry **12** symbololatry

Venezuela
02 YV **03** VEN

vengeance
03 utu **04** harm **05** curse, wrack, wreak **07** revenge **08** mischief, reprisal, requital **09** extremely, vengement **10** avengement **11** exceedingly, retaliation, retribution

• **with a vengeance**
05 fully **07** flat out, greatly **09** furiously, like crazy, to the full, violently **10** forcefully, powerfully, thoroughly, vigorously **11** exceedingly, to the utmost, with a wanion **12** with a witness **13** energetically **14** to a great degree, to a great extent **15** with a wild wanion

vengeful
08 avenging, punitive, spiteful **09** rancorous **10** implacable, revengeful, vindictive **11** retaliatory, retributive

venial
05 minor **06** slight **07** trivial **08** trifling **09** excusable **10** forgivable, negligible, pardonable **11** permissible **13** insignificant

venom
04 hate **05** spite, toxin, virus **06** enmity, malice, poison **07** envenom, ill-will, rancour, swelter **08** acrimony **09** animosity, hostility, poisonous, virulence **11** malevolence

venomous
05 fatal, toxic **06** bitter, deadly, lethal **07** baleful, baneful, noxious, vicious **08** spiteful, viperish, viperous, virulent **09** malicious, malignant, poisonous, rancorous **10** malevolent, vindictive

vent
03 air, gap **04** duct, emit, flue, hole, pipe, sale **05** salse, scent, sniff, snuff, utter, voice, wreak **06** crenel, escape, let out, market, outlet, smoker **07** airhole, chimney, express, opening, orifice, passage, pour out, publish, release **08** aperture, blowhole, breather, emission, spiracle, vomitory **09** discharge, solfatara **10** mud volcano **11** black smoker, let off steam, take it out on **14** counter-opening

ventilate
03 air, fan **04** cool **06** aerate, debate, winnow **07** discuss, express, freshen

ventilation
06 airing **07** cooling **08** aeration **10** freshening

venture
03 put **04** dare, jump, luck, mint, risk, sink **05** assay, fling, foray, stake, throw, wager **06** chance, gamble, hazard, venter, ventre **07** advance, exploit, imperil, presume, pretend, project, suggest **08** be so bold, endanger, make bold **09** adventure, endeavour, operation, promotion, speculate, volunteer **10** enterprise, prostitute, put forward **11** speculation, undertaking **14** take the liberty

venturesome
04 bold **05** brave, risky **06** daring, plucky **07** doughty **08** fearless, intrepid, spirited **09** audacious, daredevil, dauntless **10** courageous **11** adventurous **12** enterprising

venue *see* **stadium**

venus
04 clam **05** cohog **06** copper, Hesper, quahog, venery, vesper **07** Lucifer, quahaug **08** Hesperus **09** Aphrodite, round clam **11** evening star, morning star

veracious
04 true **05** exact, frank **06** honest **07** factual, genuine **08** accurate, credible, faithful, truthful

veracity
05 truth **07** candour, honesty, probity **08** accuracy **09** frankness, integrity, rectitude **10** exactitude **12** truthfulness

veranda
05 lanai, porch, stoep, stoop **06** piazza **07** decking, gallery, terrace, viranda, virando

verbal
◇ *homophone indicator*
04 oral, said **05** abuse, vocal **06** insult, spoken **07** literal, uttered, voluble **09** invective **10** articulate, linguistic **11** word-of-mouth

verbalize
03 say **04** tell, word **05** speak, state, utter, voice **06** assert, convey, report **07** declare, get over, put over **08** announce, point out **09** enunciate, formulate, pronounce, put across **10** articulate, put in words **11** communicate, give voice to **12** put into words

verbatim
07 closely, exactly **09** literally, precisely **11** to the letter, word for word

verbiage
06 waffle **07** wordage, wording **08** pleonasm **09** prolixity, verbosity **10** repetition **11** periphrasis, perissology **14** circumlocution

verbose
05 gassy, windy, wordy **06** prolix **07** diffuse, voluble, wordish **09** garrulous **10** long-winded, loquacious, pleonastic **12** periphrastic **14** circumlocutory

verbosity
08 verbiage **09** garrulity, loquacity, prolixity, windiness, wordiness **10** logorrhoea, multiloquy **14** long-windedness, loquaciousness

verdant
04 lush **05** fresh, green, leafy, virid **06** virent **11** viridescent

verdict
05 vardy **06** ruling, verdit **07** finding, opinion **08** decision, judgment, recovery, sentence **09** judgement **10** assessment, conclusion **12** adjudication, rough justice

verdure
05 grass **07** foliage, greenth, herbage, leafage **08** greenery, verdancy, viridity **09** freshness, greenness **12** viridescence

verge
03 rim, rod **04** brim, edge, pale, tend **05** brink, limit, merge, point, range, scope, slope, touch, virge **06** border, edging, margin, trench **07** horizon, incline **08** boundary, precinct **09** threshold **11** long paddock **12** jurisdiction

• **verge on**
04 near **08** approach, border on **11** come close to, tend towards

verification
05 audit, proof **08** checking **10** validation **11** attestation **12** ascertaining, confirmation, constatation **13** corroboration **14** authentication, substantiation

verify
05 audit, check, prove **06** attest **07** bear out, confirm, support **08** accredit, validate **09** ascertain **11** corroborate **12** authenticate, substantiate

verisimilitude
07 realism **09** semblance **10** likeliness **11** credibility, resemblance, ring of truth **12** authenticity, plausibility **13** vraisemblance

veritable
04 fair, rank, real, true **05** right, sheer, utter **06** actual **07** genuine, perfect, regular **08** absolute, complete, outright, positive, thorough **09** out-and-out **10** consummate **11** unmitigated

verity
05 sooth, truth **07** reality **08** validity, veracity **09** actuality, soundness **12** authenticity, truthfulness

vermin

Vermin include:

03 rat
04 lice, mice, moth
05 louse, mouse
06 pigeon, weevil
09 cockroach

See also **rodent**

Vermont
02 VT

vermouth
02 It **06** French **07** Cinzano®, Martini®

vernacular
05 idiom, lingo, local **06** common, jargon, native, speech, tongue, vulgar **07** dialect, endemic, popular, trivial **08** informal, language, parlance **09** idioticon **10** colloquial, indigenous **12** vulgar tongue

Veronica
04 Hebe **09** speedwell

versatile
◇ *anagram indicator*
05 handy **07** Protean **08** all-round, flexible, unsteady, variable **09** adaptable, many-sided **10** adjustable, all-purpose, changeable **12** multifaceted, multipurpose

verse
01 v **04** line, rime, sijo, vers **05** haiku, Ionic, meter, metre, rhyme **06** heroic, jingle, poetry, riddle, stanza **07** doggrel, elegiac, iambics, Leonine, pennill, stichos, strophe, versify **08** doggerel, elegiacs, glyconic, singsong, trochaic, versicle **09** amphigory, vers libre **11** acatalectic, septenarius **12** Archilochian, nursery rhyme **13** vers de société, vers d'occasion, versification

versed
02 up **04** deep, read **06** strong, traded, turned **07** learned, perfect, skilled, studied, versant **08** deep-read, familiar, overseen, reversed, scienced, seasoned **09** competent, practised **10** conversant, proficient **11** experienced **13** knowledgeable

versifier
04 poet **06** rhymer, verser **07** poetess, rhymist **09** metrifier, poetaster, poeticule, rhymester **10** verse-maker, verse-smith **11** verse-monger **12** versificator

version
◇ *anagram indicator*
02 EV, NV, RV **04** form, kind, sort, type **05** cover, Itala, model, style **06** design, report, Rev Ver, Targum, update **07** account, edition, reading, turning, variant **08** rough cut **09** microcosm, portrayal, rendering **10** adaptation, paraphrase **11** translation **14** interpretation, King James Bible

versus
01 v **02** vs **06** facing **07** against, playing **08** opposing **09** as against, instead of **10** rather than **11** as opposed to **12** in contrast to **14** in opposition to

vertex
03 top **04** acme, apex, peak **05** crown **06** apogee, height, summit, zenith **08** pinnacle **09** extremity **12** highest point

vertical
05 apeak, apeek, erect, on end, plumb, sheer **07** upright **10** straight up, upstanding **13** perpendicular

vertigo
06 megrim **09** dizziness, giddiness, wooziness **15** light-headedness

verve
03 zip **04** brio, dash, élan, life **05** force, gusto **06** energy, relish, spirit, vigour, whammo **07** fervour, passion, pizzazz, sparkle **08** vitality, vivacity **09** animation **10** enthusiasm, liveliness

very
01 v **02** ae **03** e'er, way **04** ever, fell, mega, mere, pure, real, same, self, très, true, unco **05** assai, awful, dooms, exact, hefty, ideal, jolly, molto, plain, quite, sheer, stiff, truly, utter **06** actual, as hell, damned, deeply, dogged, ever so, highly, mighty, pretty, proper, really, simple **07** acutely, all that, awfully, genuine, good and, gradely, greatly, hell of a, hellova, helluva, majorly, only too, passing, perfect, precise **08** bitching, devilish, graithly, selfsame, spanking, stinking, suitable, terribly, uncommon **09** eminently, extremely, identical, unusually **10** absolutely, abundantly, incredibly, not a little, remarkably, uncommonly **11** exceedingly, excessively **12** particularly, unbelievably

vessel
03 ark, jar, jug, pot, tun, vat **04** boat, bowl, ewer, ship **05** craft, plate **06** barque, holder **07** airship, pitcher, vassail, vessail **09** container **10** receptacle

See also **container**; **ship**

vest
03 bib **04** garb, robe **05** drape, dress, endow, grant, lodge **06** bestow, clothe, confer, invest, semmit, supply **07** descend, devolve, empower, entrust, garment, singlet **08** sanction, vestment **09** authorize, waistcoat **10** undershirt **11** sequestrate

Vesta
06 Hestia

vestibule
04 hall **05** entry, foyer, lobby, porch **06** atrium, exedra **07** exhedra, hallway, narthex, portico, pronaos, tambour **08** anteroom, entrance **09** forecourt **11** oeil-de-boeuf **12** entrance hall

vestige
04 hint, mark, sign **05** print, scrap, shred, token, touch, trace, track, whiff **06** relics **07** glimmer, inkling, remains, remnant, residue **09** footprint, remainder, suspicion **10** impression, indication

vestigial
07 reduced **09** remaining, surviving **10** incomplete **11** rudimentary, undeveloped

vestment
04 vest **09** vestiment

Clerical vestments include:

03 alb
04 cope, cowl, hood
05 amice, cotta, ephod, frock, habit, mitre, scarf, stole
06 mantle, rochet, saccos, sakkos, tippet, wimple
07 biretta, cassock, chimere, humeral, maniple, pallium, soutane, tallith, tunicle
08 chasuble, dalmatic, mozzetta, rational, scapular, skullcap, surplice, yarmulka
09 dog-collar, phelonion

10 Geneva gown, omophorion, phaelonion, sticharion
11 Geneva bands, humeral veil
12 superhumeral
14 clerical collar

vet
04 scan **05** audit, check **06** review, screen, survey **07** examine, inspect **08** appraise, check out **10** scrutinize **11** investigate

vetch
03 ers **04** tare, tine **05** fitch

veteran
03 old, pro **05** adept **06** expert, master **07** old hand, warrior **08** old-timer, seasoned **09** old stager, practised **10** campaigner, pastmaster, proficient **11** experienced, long-serving **13** battle-scarred, old campaigner

veto
03 ban, nix **05** block **06** forbid, negate, reject **07** embargo, rule out **08** disallow, negative, prohibit, turn down **09** blackball, interdict, proscribe **10** thumbs-down **11** prohibition **12** proscription

vex
03 bug, noy **04** fret, haze, hump, rile **05** annoy, grief, spite, upset, worry **06** bother, enrage, excess, grieve, harass, hassle, molest, needle, pester, put out, rankle, wind up **07** afflict, agitate, chagrin, discuss, disturb, hack off, perturb, provoke, tick off, torment, trouble **08** bepester, brass off, distress, irritate **09** aggravate, cheese off **10** exasperate

vexation
03 noy **04** bind, bore, fury, pain **05** anger, pique, upset, worry **06** bother, plague **07** chagrin **08** headache, irritant, nuisance **09** annoyance **11** aggravation, frustration **12** exasperation **14** disappointment

See also **annoyance**

vexatious
05 pesky **06** noyous, plaguy, trying, vexing **07** irksome, nagging, nimious, peevish, plaguey, teasing **08** annoying, fashious, worrying **09** pestilent, provoking, upsetting, worrisome **10** bothersome, burdensome, irritating, tormenting **11** aggravating, infuriating, pestiferous, troublesome **12** exasperating

vexed
04 moot, sore **05** irate, riled, tough, upset **06** knotty, miffed, narked, peeved, put out, tricky **07** annoyed, awkward, debated, hassled, nettled, ruffled, worried **08** agitated, bothered, confused, disputed, harassed, provoked, troubled **09** contested, difficult, disturbed, flustered, in dispute, irritated, perplexed **10** aggravated, displeased, infuriated **11** exasperated

viability
10 expedience **11** feasibility, possibility, workability **12** practicality **13** achievability **14** practicability, reasonableness

viable
05 sound **08** feasible, operable, possible, workable **10** achievable, commercial **11** practicable, sustainable

vibes
04 aura, feel **08** ambience, emotions, feelings **10** atmosphere, vibrations

vibrancy
02 go **04** life, zest **05** oomph **06** energy, spirit, vigour **07** pizzazz, sparkle, stamina **08** strength, vitality, vivacity **09** animation **10** exuberance, get-up-and-go, liveliness

vibrant
05 vivid **06** bright, lively **07** dynamic **08** animated, electric, resonant, spirited, striking, vigorous **09** brilliant, colourful, energetic, sparkling, thrilling, vibrating, vivacious **12** electrifying

vibrate
◇ *anagram indicator*
03 jar **04** dirl, ring, sway **05** quake, shake, swing, thirl **06** dindle, dinnle, hotter, judder, quiver, shimmy, shiver, thrill, tingle **07** flutter, pulsate, resound, shudder, tremble, twinkle **08** brandish, resonate, undulate **09** oscillate, pendulate **11** reverberate

vibration
03 jar **04** dirl **05** pulse, quake, throb **06** dindle, dinnle, hotter, judder, quiver, shimmy, thrill, tremor **07** diadrom, flutter, frisson, shaking **08** fremitus **09** juddering, pulsation, resonance, trembling **10** resounding **11** oscillation, seismic wave **12** seismic shock **13** reverberation, tremulousness

vicar
03 Rev, Vic **06** cleric, curate, deputy, parson, pastor, priest, rector **08** chaplain, minister, preacher, reverend **09** clergyman **10** arch-priest, substitute **11** clergywoman **15** perpetual curate

vicarious
06 acting **08** indirect **09** surrogate **10** empathetic, second-hand **11** substituted

vice
03 sin **04** evil, flaw, grip, tool **05** fault, screw **06** defect, foible **07** blemish, buffoon, failing **08** bad habit, iniquity, weakness **09** depravity, evil-doing **10** bestiality, degeneracy, immorality, profligacy, wickedness, wrongdoing **12** besetting sin, imperfection **13** transgression

vice versa
02 vv **09** inversely **10** conversely, oppositely **12** contrariwise, reciprocally

vicinity
04 area **08** district, environs, locality, nearness **09** precincts, proximity **11** propinquity **12** surroundings **13** neighbourhood

vicious
03 bad **04** foul, mean, vile **05** catty, cruel, nasty **06** bitchy, brutal, faulty, fierce, impure, lethal, morbid, savage, wicked **07** heinous, immoral, violent **08** depraved, impaired, mistaken, spiteful, unlawful, venomous, virulent **09** barbarous, dangerous, ferocious, malicious, malignant **10** malevolent, vindictive **11** bad-tempered

viciously
06 wildly **07** cruelly **08** brutally, fiercely, lethally, savagely **09** violently

viciousness
05 spite, venom **06** malice **07** cruelty, rancour **08** ferocity, savagery **09** brutality, depravity, viciosity, virulence, vitiosity **10** bitchiness, wickedness **11** malevolence **12** spitefulness

vicissitude
04 turn **05** shift, twist **06** change **07** weather **08** mutation **09** deviation, variation **10** alteration, revolution **11** alternation, fluctuation

victim
04 butt, dupe, fool, host, mark, prey **05** patsy **06** martyr, muggee, nebish, quarry, sucker, target **07** fall guy, nebbich, nebbish **08** casualty, fatality, murderee, paranoic, soft mark, sufferer **09** paranoeic, paranoiac, sacrifice, scapegoat **11** sitting duck **13** sitting target

• **fall victim to**
05 catch **07** develop, fall for **08** contract **09** succumb to **10** fall prey to **11** be taken in by **12** be attacked by, be deceived by, be overcome by **14** be stricken with **15** become a target of

victimize
03 con **04** dupe, fool, rook **05** bully, cheat, frame, shaft, sting, trick **06** fleece, pick on, prey on, rip off **07** deceive, defraud, exploit, swindle **08** hoodwink, stitch up **09** bamboozle, persecute **11** have it in for

victor
01 V **05** champ, first **06** top dog, winner **08** bangster, champion **09** conqueror **10** vanquisher **11** pancratiast, prize-winner **13** victor ludorum

Victoria
02 VR **03** Vic **04** Nike

victorious
03 top **05** first **07** winning **08** champion, unbeaten **09** prevalent **10** conquering, successful, triumphant **11** vanquishing **12** prize-winning

victory
01 V **02** VE, VJ **03** Jai, win **04** gree, Nike **07** mastery, success, triumph, winning

08 conquest, squeaker, walk-away, walkover **09** checkmate, landslide **11** subjugation, superiority, triple crown

• sign of victory
01 V

victuals
04 chow, eats, food, grub, nosh, tuck **05** bread, scran **06** stores, viands **07** aliment, edibles, rations, vittles **08** eatables, supplies **10** provisions, sustenance **11** comestibles

vie
03 bid **05** fight, rival, stake **06** strive **07** compare, compete, contend, contest, declare **08** corrival, struggle **09** challenge

Vietnam
02 VN **03** VNM

view
02 Vw **03** see **04** espy, idea, look, scan **05** angle, judge, range, scene, sight, study, vista, watch **06** aspect, belief, descry, gaze at, look at, notion, regard, review, sketch, survey, vision **07** account, examine, feeling, glimpse, inspect, observe, opinion, outlook, picture, purpose, thought, witness **08** attitude, consider, eyesight, panorama, perceive, portrait, prospect, scrutiny **09** intention, judgement, landscape, portrayal, sentiment, spectacle **10** appearance, assessment, conviction, estimation, impression, inspection, perception, scrutinize **11** contemplate, examination, expectation, observation, perspective **13** contemplation, range of vision

• in view of
07 whereas **11** considering **13** bearing in mind

• on view
05 shown **06** on show **07** showing **09** displayed, exhibited, on display, presented **10** made public

viewer
07 goggler, watcher **08** observer, onlooker **09** inspector, spectator

viewpoint
05 angle, slant **06** stance **07** feeling, opinion **08** attitude, position, prospect **10** standpoint **11** observatory, perspective, point of view

vigil
04 wake **05** watch **07** lookout **08** stake-out, watching **10** deathwatch **11** wakefulness **12** pernoctation

vigilance
05 guard, watch **07** caution **09** alertness **11** carefulness, guardedness, observation, wakefulness **12** watch and ward, watchfulness **13** attentiveness **14** circumspection

vigilant
05 alert, awake, aware **07** careful, jealous, wakeful **08** cautious, wakerife, watchful **09** Argus-eyed, attentive, observant, wide-awake **10** on the watch, unsleeping **11** circumspect, on your guard **12** on the lookout, on the qui vive

vigilante
05 guard, watch **07** lookout **08** sentinel, watchman **10** armed guard **11** watchperson **13** Guardian Angel, security guard

vignette
03 act **04** plan, turn **05** cameo, draft, scene **06** design, sketch **07** diagram, drawing, outline **08** abstract, skeleton **14** representation

vigorous
◇ *anagram indicator*
04 go-go, hard, rank **05** alive, brisk, green, hefty, lusty, round, sound, stout, tough, vital, vivid, young **06** active, bouncy, lively, manful, punchy, raucle, robust, rugged, sprack, strong, vegete **07** dynamic, healthy, intense, lustick, nervous **08** animated, athletic, forceful, forcible, lustique, muscular, powerful, spirited, swanking, youthful **09** energetic, gymnastic, strenuous **11** flourishing, full-blooded, gymnastical

vigorously
◇ *anagram indicator*
04 hard **06** lively **07** briskly, eagerly, lustily **08** heartily, strongly **09** in a big way **10** forcefully, like billy-o, powerfully **11** like billy-oh, strenuously **12** like old boots **13** energetically

vigour
03 pep, vim, zip **04** bant, birr, brio, dash, élan, fire, pith **05** flush, force, gusto, heart, might, moxie, oomph, power, verve **06** energy, health, spirit, stingo **07** pizzazz, potency, stamina **08** activity, dynamism, strength, virility, vitality, vivacity **09** animation, toughness **10** liveliness, robustness **12** forcefulness **13** vivaciousness

vile
◇ *anagram indicator*
03 bad, low **04** base, evil, foul, mean, vild **05** nasty, vilde **06** horrid, impure, paltry, scurvy, sinful, wicked **07** beastly, corrupt, debased, earthly, noxious, scabbed, vicious **08** depraved, horrible, infamous, wretched **09** appalling, degrading, loathsome, miserable, obnoxious, offensive, repugnant, repulsive, revolting, sickening, villanous, worthless **10** degenerate, despicable, detestable, disgusting, iniquitous, nauseating, scandalous, unpleasant, villainous **11** disgraceful, distasteful **12** contemptible, disagreeable

vileness
04 evil **06** infamy **07** outrage **08** baseness, foulness, meanness, ugliness **09** depravity, nastiness, profanity, turpitude **10** corruption, degeneracy, wickedness **11** noxiousness **13** offensiveness

vilification
03 mud **05** abuse **07** calumny **09** aspersion, contumely, criticism, invective **10** defamation, revilement, scurrility **11** denigration, mud-slinging **12** calumniation, vituperation **13** disparagement

vilify
04 slag, slam **05** abuse, decry, knock, slate, smear, snipe **06** berate, debase, defame, malign, revile **07** asperse, rubbish, run down, slag off, slander, traduce **08** badmouth, denounce, vilipend **09** denigrate, disparage **10** calumniate, stigmatize, vituperate

village
03 vil **04** dorp, duar, gram, vill, wick **05** aldea, douar, dowar, kraal, thorp **06** hamlet, kainga, thorpe **07** clachan, endship, kampong, kirkton, outport **08** kirk town, township **09** borghetto, community, rancheria **10** Chautauqua, settlement

villain
04 base **05** baddy, bravo, devil, heavy, knave, rogue **06** baddie, rascal, wretch **07** low-born, villein **08** criminal, escapado, evildoer, scelerat **09** miscreant, reprobate, scelerate, scoundrel, wrongdoer **10** malefactor

Villains include:

04 Case, Cass (Dunstan), Hyde (Mr), Iago
05 Bates (Norman), Doone (Carver), Queeg (Captain), Regan
06 Lecter (Dr Hannibal), Oswald, Silver (Long John)
07 Antonio, Bateman (Patrick), Blofeld (Ernst), Goneril
08 Cornwall (Duke of), Injun Joe
09 Voldemort (Lord)
10 Darth Vader, Goldfinger (Auric), Richard III
12 Aaron the Moor
14 Bonnie and Clyde, Sauron the Great

villainous
03 bad **04** evil, vile **05** cruel **06** gallus, sinful, wicked **07** debased, gallows, heinous, inhuman, roguish, vicious **08** criminal, depraved, fiendish, terrible **09** miscreant, nefarious, notorious **10** degenerate, detestable, iniquitous **11** disgraceful, opprobrious

villainy
03 sin **04** vice **05** crime **07** badness, knavery, roguery **08** atrocity, baseness, disgrace, iniquity **09** depravity, rascality, turpitude **10** wickedness **11** criminality, delinquency

vindicate
04 free **05** clear, right, salve **06** acquit, assert, avenge, uphold, verify **07** absolve, darrain, darrayn, deraign, justify, warrant **08** advocate, champion, darraign, darraine, maintain **09** darraigne, exculpate, exonerate **11** corroborate

vindication
07 apology, defence, defense, support **08** apologia, theodicy **09** assertion **10** apologetic **11** exculpation, exoneration, extenuation **12** compurgation, verification **13** justification **14** substantiation

vindictive
08 punitive, spiteful, vengeful, venomous **09** malicious, rancorous **10** implacable, malevolent, revengeful **11** retributive, unforgiving, vindicative

vine
06 muscat **08** grape ivy, heartpea, muscadel, muscatel **09** ayahuasco, heartseed **10** wonga-wonga **12** winter cherry

vinegar
05 eisel **06** alegar, eisell, energy, vigour **07** souring **08** wood acid **10** acetic acid

vintage
03 cru, era, old **04** best, crop, fine, ripe, time, wine, year **05** epoch, prime **06** choice, gather, mature, origin, period, select **07** classic, harvest, quality, supreme, veteran **08** enduring, superior **09** gathering **11** high-quality

viol
02 gu **03** gju, gue **05** quint, rebec **06** quinte, rebeck

viola
04 alto **05** gamba, pance, pansy **06** paunce, pawnce, violet

violate
◇ *anagram indicator*
04 rape **05** abuse, break, flout, fract, wreck **06** breach, defile, invade, molest, offend, ravish **07** debauch, defiled, despoil, disobey, disrupt, disturb, infract, outrage, profane, vitiate **08** infringe, stuprate **09** desecrate, dishonour **10** contravene, transgress **13** interfere with

violation
◇ *anagram indicator*
04 rape **05** abuse, crime **06** breach, mopery **07** offence, outrage **08** invasion, trespass **09** injustice, sacrilege, vitiation **10** defilement, disruption, infraction, spoliation, stupration **11** desecration, profanation **12** infringement, private wrong **13** breach of trust, contravention, transgression

violence
04 fury, rage, rape **05** force, might, power, wrath **06** frenzy, injury, tumult **07** cruelty, outrage, passion **08** ferocity, fighting, foul play, savagery, severity, strength, wildness **09** bloodshed, brutality, intensity, roughness, vehemence **10** aggression, fierceness, turbulence **11** hostilities, profanation **12** forcefulness

violent
◇ *anagram indicator*
03 het, hot **04** high, rage, rank, rude, wild **05** acute, cruel, fiery, force, great, harsh, heady, hefty, rough, sharp, tough **06** brutal, fierce, savage, severe, stormy, strong, sturdy **07** drastic, extreme, flaming, furious, intense, riotous, rousing, ruffian, vicious **08** dramatic, forceful, forcible, maddened, powerful, slap-bang, towering, vehement **09** ferocious, hot-headed, impetuous, murderous, turbulent **10** aggressive, headstrong, outrageous, passionate, tumultuous **11** destructive, devastating **12** bloodthirsty, excruciating, ungovernable, unrestrained **15** blood-and-thunder

violently
◇ *anagram indicator*
04 rank, slap **05** amain, tough **06** wildly **07** cruelly, greatly, sharply **08** brutally, fiercely, savagely, severely, slap-bang, strongly **09** extremely, intensely, viciously **10** powerfully **11** ferociously, hot-headedly, impetuously **12** aggressively, dramatically **14** uncontrollably, with a vengeance

violin
02 gu **03** gju, gue, kit **05** Amati, strad **06** catgut, fiddle, leader **07** chikara **10** Stradivari **12** Stradivarius

• **violin part**
03 nut, rib **04** back, neck, soul **05** belly, f-hole, table **06** bridge, button **07** bass-bar **08** purfling **09** sound post **11** fingerboard

VIP
03 nib, pot **04** lion, star **06** bigwig, top dog **07** big name, big shot, magnate, notable **08** big noise, luminary, somebody **09** big cheese, celebrity, dignitary, personage **11** heavyweight

viper
03 asp **05** adder **08** cerastes, mocassin, moccasin **09** berg-adder, river-jack **10** fer-de-lance **11** rattlesnake

virago
04 fury **05** randy, scold, shrew, vixen **06** amazon, dragon, gorgon, randie, tartar **08** harridan **09** battle-axe, brimstone, termagant, Xanthippe

virgin
03 new **04** girl, maid, pure **05** fresh, Virgo **06** chaste, intact, maiden, modest, vestal **07** Madonna, pucelle **08** celibate, maidenly, spotless, unspoilt, virginal **09** stainless, undefiled, unsullied, untainted, untouched **10** immaculate, unattained **11** unblemished, unexploited

virginal
04 pure **05** fresh, snowy, white **06** chaste, vestal, virgin **08** celibate, maidenly, pristine, spotless **09** stainless, undefiled, untouched **10** immaculate **11** uncorrupted, undisturbed **15** parthenogenetic

Virginia
02 VA

Virgin Islands
02 VI **03** BVI, VGB, VIR

virginity
05 honor **06** cherry, honour, purity, virtue **08** chastity, pucelage **09** innocence **10** chasteness, maidenhead, maidenhood

virile
05 lusty, macho, manly **06** potent, robust, rugged, strong **08** forceful, muscular, vigorous **09** masculine, strapping **10** red-blooded

virility
06 energy, vigour **07** manhood, potency **08** machismo **09** manliness **10** ruggedness **11** masculinity

virtual
07 implied **08** implicit, in effect, virtuous **09** effective, essential, potential, practical **11** prospective **12** in all but name

virtually
06 almost, nearly **08** as good as, in effect **09** in essence **10** more or less **11** effectively, practically **12** in all but name, to all intents

virtue
04 good, plus **05** asset, merit, vertu, worth **06** credit, dharma, honour, valour, vertue **07** benefit, honesty, probity, quality **08** efficacy, goodness, morality, strength **09** advantage, attribute, rectitude, virginity **10** excellence, worthiness **11** saving grace **14** accomplishment, high-mindedness

The seven virtues:

04 hope
05 faith
07 charity, justice
08 prudence
09 fortitude
10 temperance

• **by virtue of**
07 by way of, owing to **08** by dint of, thanks to **09** because of, by means of **11** on account of **13** with the help of

virtuosity
05 éclat, flair, skill **06** finish, polish **07** bravura, finesse, mastery, panache **08** artistry, wizardry **09** expertise **10** brilliance

virtuoso
06 expert, genius, master **07** maestro, prodigy, skilful **08** dazzling, masterly **09** brilliant, excellent

virtuous
04 good **05** moral **06** chaste, decent, graced, honest, worthy **07** angelic, ethical, upright, virtual **08** innocent **09** blameless, continent, exemplary, righteous **10** honourable, upstanding **11** clean-living, respectable **12** squeaky-clean **13** incorruptible, unimpeachable **14** above suspicion, high-principled, irreproachable **15** beyond suspicion

virulence
05 spite, venom **06** hatred, malice, poison, rancor, spleen **07** rancour, vitriol **08** acrimony, toxicity
09 hostility, malignity **10** antagonism, bitterness, malignancy
11 malevolence, viciousness
14 vindictiveness

virulent
05 fatal, toxic **06** bitter, deadly, lethal, severe **07** extreme, hostile, intense, vicious, waspish **08** spiteful, venomous
09 injurious, malicious, malignant, poisonous, rancorous, vitriolic
10 blistering, malevolent, pernicious, vindictive **11** acrimonious

virus

Viruses include:

03 CDV, DNA, EBV, flu, FLV, HIV, HPV, pox, pro, RNA
04 arbo, cold, ECHO, filo, HTLV, myxo, rota
05 Ebola, flavi, hanta, irido, lenti, parvo, phage, retro, rhino
06 baculo, calici, cowpox, herpes, papova
07 oncorna, picorna, polyoma, variola
08 morbilli, Vaccinia
09 Coxsackie, influenza, papilloma
10 hepatitis A, hepatitis B, hepatitis C, Lassa fever, leaf mosaic
11 Epstein-Barr
13 bacteriophage, parainfluenza
14 human papilloma
15 canine distemper

visa
04 pass, visé **06** carnet, docket, permit
07 licence, warrant **08** passport, sanction **09** green card **10** permission
11 endorsement, safe-conduct
13 authorization, laissez-passer
14 permis de séjour

vis-à-vis
06 facing **08** opposite **09** as regards
10 face-to-face **11** over against **12** in relation to

viscera
04 guts **06** bowels, vitals **07** giblets, innards, insides **08** entrails, gralloch, harigals **09** harigalds **10** intestines

viscous
04 slab **05** gluey, gooey, gummy, stiff, tacky, thick, tough **06** glairy, mucous, sticky, viscid **07** treacly, viscose
08 glareous **09** glaireous, glutinous, resistant **10** gelatinous
12 mucilaginous

Vishnu *see* **incarnation**

visible
04 open **05** clear, overt, plain
06 patent, visual **07** evident, exposed, in sight, obvious, showing
08 apparent, manifest, palpable
10 aspectable, in evidence, noticeable, observable **11** conspicuous, discernible, perceivable, perceptible, unconcealed, undisguised
12 recognizable **15** distinguishable

visibly
06 openly **07** clearly, overtly, plainly
08 patently **09** evidently, obviously
10 manifestly, noticeably
11 perceptibly **13** conspicuously

vision
04 idea, look, view **05** dream, ghost, ideal, image, sight **06** glance, mirage, seeing, wraith **07** aisling, chimera, fantasy, imagine, insight, phantom, picture, spectre **08** daydream, delusion, eyesight, illusion, phantasm
09 foresight, intuition, phantosme
10 apparition, conception, perception, revelation **11** fata Morgana, imagination, mental image
13 hallucination, mental picture **14** far-sightedness **15** optical illusion

visionary
04 aery, seer **05** aerie **06** dreamy, mystic, unreal **07** dreamer, prophet, utopian **08** airdrawn, fanciful, idealist, illusory, quixotic, romantic, theorist
09 fantasist, imaginary, moonshiny, prophetic **10** daydreamer, Don Quixote, far-sighted, idealistic, ideologist, ivory-tower, perceptive **11** impractical, translunary, unpractical, unrealistic
13 impracticable, rainbow-chaser

visit
03 gam, see **04** call, chat, mump, stay, stop, take **05** curse, haunt, pop in, smite **06** call by, call in, call on, come by, drop by, look in, look up, plague, punish, stop by, stop in, take in, wait on
07 afflict, examine, inflict, inspect, sojourn, stop off, trouble **08** call in on, drop in on, frequent, go and see, go over to, stay with, stop in at, stop over, wait upon **09** call round, come round, excursion, first-foot, go round to, house call, stop off at **10** salutation, stop over at **13** spend time with

visitation
05 trial, visit **06** blight, ordeal
08 calamity, disaster, haunting
10 appearance, infliction, inspection, punishment **11** catastrophe, examination **13** manifestation

visitor
05 guest **06** caller **07** company, tourist
08 manuhiri, stranger **09** traveller
12 holidaymaker **13** bird of passage

visor
05 sight **06** mesail, mezail, umbrel, umbril **07** umbrere **08** umbriere

vista
04 view **05** scene **06** avenue, vision
07 outlook **08** enfilade, panorama, prospect **11** perspective

visual
05 optic **06** ocular, visive **07** optical, visible **08** specular **10** observable

visualize
03 see **07** imagine, picture
08 conceive, envisage, envision

vital
03 key **05** alive, basic **06** lively, living, urgent, zoetic **07** animate, crucial, dynamic, vibrant **08** animated, critical, decisive, forceful, spirited, vigorous
09 energetic, essential, important, necessary, requisite, vivacious
10 imperative, life-giving, quickening
11 fundamental, significant
12 invigorating, life-and-death
13 indispensable

vitality
02 go **03** sap, zap **04** life, zest, zing
05 juice, oomph **06** bounce, energy, fizzen, foison, spirit, vigour **07** fushion, pizzazz, sparkle, stamina, vivency
08 strength, vivacity **09** animation
10 exuberance, get-up-and-go, liveliness **13** vivaciousness

vitally
08 urgently **09** crucially **10** critically, decisively **11** essentially, importantly
13 fundamentally, significantly

vitamin

Vitamins include:

01 A, B, C, D, E, G, H, K, P
06 biotin, citrin, niacin
07 adermin, aneurin, retinol, thiamin
08 carotene, thiamine
09 folic acid, menadione
10 calciferol, pyridoxine, riboflavin, tocopherol
11 menaquinone, pteroic acid
12 ascorbic acid, bioflavonoid, linoleic acid
13 linolenic acid, nicotinic acid, phylloquinone
14 cyanocobalamin, dehydroretinol, ergocalciferol, phytomenadione
15 cholecalciferol, pantothenic acid, vitamin B complex

vitiate
03 mar **04** harm, rape, ruin **05** blend, spoil, sully, taint **06** blight, debase, defile, impair, injure, mucker, weaken
07 blemish, corrupt, debauch, deprave, devalue, nullify, pervert, pollute, violate **09** undermine
10 adulterate, invalidate
11 contaminate

vitriolic
06 biting, bitter **07** abusive, acerbic, caustic, mordant, vicious **08** sardonic, scathing, venomous, virulent
09 malicious, trenchant
11 acrimonious, destructive
12 vituperative

vituperate
03 nag **04** slag, slam **05** abuse, blame, knock, slang, slate **06** berate, rebuke, revile, vilify **07** censure, rubbish, run down, slag off, upbraid
08 denounce, reproach **09** castigate
10 blackguard

vituperation
04 flak **05** abuse, blame, stick
07 censure, obloquy **08** diatribe, knocking, reproach **09** contumely, invective, philippic, reprimand
10 revilement, rubbishing, scurrility

11 castigation, objurgation, slagging-off **12** vilification

vituperative
05 harsh **07** abusive **08** sardonic, scornful **09** insulting, withering **10** belittling, censorious, derogatory, scurrilous **11** fulminatory, opprobrious **12** calumniatory, denunciatory

vivacious
05 jolly, merry, smart **06** bright, bubbly, chirpy, lively **08** animated, cheerful, spirited, sportive **09** ebullient, in spirits, long-lived, sparkling, sprightly **12** effervescent, high-spirited, light-hearted

vivacity
02 go **03** fiz, zap **04** brio, élan, fizz, life, zing **05** oomph **06** energy, spirit, vigour **07** pizzazz, sparkle, spirits **08** activity, dynamism, vitality **09** animation, merriness **10** ebullience, liveliness **13** effervescence

vivid
04 live, rich, vive **05** clear, lurid, sharp **06** bright, lively, strong **07** dynamic, eidetic, glaring, glowing, graphic, intense, vibrant **08** animated, dazzling, distinct, dramatic, lifelike, powerful, spirited, striking, vigorous **09** brilliant, colourful, graphical, memorable, pictorial, realistic **11** picturesque

vividly
06 richly **07** clearly **08** brightly, strongly **09** intensely, memorably, vibrantly **10** distinctly, powerfully **11** brilliantly, graphically **12** dramatically, flamboyantly

vividness
04 glow, life **05** color **06** colour **07** clarity, realism **08** lucidity, radiance, strength **09** intensity, sharpness **10** brightness, brilliancy, refulgence

viz
02 ie, sc **04** scil, sciz **05** to wit **06** namely, that is **08** scilicet **09** videlicet **11** that is to say **12** in other words, specifically

vocabulary
04 cant **05** idiom, lexis, vocab, words **07** lexicon **08** glossary, language, wordbook **09** idioticon, thesaurus **10** dictionary **11** nomenclator **12** Basic English, nomenclature

vocal
◇ *homophone indicator*
04 oral, said, sung **05** blunt, frank, noisy **06** phonal, shrill, spoken, voiced **07** uttered **08** eloquent, strident **09** expressed, outspoken, talkative **10** articulate, expressive, forthright, resounding, vociferous

vocalize
03 air, say **04** sing, tell, vent, word **05** speak, state, utter, voice **06** assert, convey, report **07** declare, express, get over, put over **08** announce, intimate, point out **09** enunciate, formulate, pronounce, put across, ventilate, verbalize **10** articulate **11** communicate, give voice to **12** put into words

vocally
10 eloquently, stridently **12** articulately, expressively, forthrightly

vocation
03 job **04** line, post, role, work **05** craft, trade **06** career, métier, office **07** calling, mission, pursuit **08** business **10** employment, occupation, profession

vociferous
04 loud **05** blunt, frank, noisy, vocal **08** shouting, strident, vehement **09** clamorous, outspoken **10** forthright, thundering **12** obstreperous

vociferously
06 loudly **07** bluntly, frankly, noisily, vocally **10** stridently, vehemently **11** outspokenly

vogue
03 fad **04** mode, rage **05** craze, style, taste, trend **06** custom **07** fashion, the rage **08** the thing **09** the latest **10** popularity **11** fashionable

• in vogue
02 in **06** modish, trendy, with it **07** current, popular, stylish, voguish **09** prevalent **11** fashionable **13** up-to-the-minute

voice
03 air, say, vox **04** alto, bass, cast, pipe, tone, view, vote, will, wish **05** elect, mezzo, mouth, organ, sound, taish, tenor, utter, words **06** airing, assert, convey, medium, report, rumour, singer, speech, taisch, talk of, throat, tongue, treble **07** acclaim, appoint, declare, divulge, express, mention, opinion, soprano, speak of **08** approval, castrato, decision, disclose, falsetto, language, nominate **09** contralto, enunciate, utterance, verbalize **10** articulate, expression, give tongue, inflection, instrument, intonation, mouthpiece, reputation **11** contra-tenor, Heldentenor **12** articulation, counter-tenor, mezzo-soprano

void
03 gap **04** emit, lack, null, vain, want **05** abyss, annul, avoid, belch, blank, chasm, clear, drain, eject, empty, inane, inept, space **06** cancel, cavity, devoid, hollow, lacuna, remove, vacant, vacuum **07** dismiss, drained, emptied, invalid, lacking, nullify, opening, rescind, send out, useless, vacuity **08** abnegate, annulled, defecate, deserted, evacuate, nugatory, send away, unfilled **09** blankness, cancelled, clear away, discharge, emptiness, nullified, worthless **10** invalidate, unoccupied, unutilized **11** ineffectual

volatile
◇ *anagram indicator*
05 giddy, Latin **06** fickle, fitful, lively **07** erratic, flighty **08** fleeting, restless, skittish, unstable, unsteady, variable, volcanic **09** explosive, irregular, mercurial, transient, unsettled, up and down **10** capricious, changeable, inconstant, short-lived **11** light-winged **13** temperamental, unpredictable

volatility
09 shakiness **10** fickleness, fitfulness, insecurity **11** flightiness, fluctuation, inconstancy, instability, uncertainty, variability **12** irresolution, unsteadiness **13** unreliability **14** capriciousness, changeableness, precariousness

volcano
05 salse **08** spitfire **15** burning mountain

Volcanoes include:

03 Apo, Awu, Usu
04 Etna, Fuji, Laki, Taal
05 Hekla, Kenya, Mayon, Pelée, Thera, Thira, Unzen
06 Ararat, Erebus, Hudson, Katmai, Sangay
07 Jurullo, Kilauea, Rainier, Ruapehu, Surtsey, Tambora, Vulcano
08 Cotopaxi, Krakatoa, Mauna Kea, Mauna Loa, Pinatubo, St Helens, Tarawera, Vesuvius
09 Aconcagua, Coseguina, El Chichon, Helgafell, Karisimbi, Lamington, Paricutín, Pichincha, Santorini, Stromboli, Tongariro
10 Bezymianny, Chimborazo, Galunggung, La Soufrire, Lassen Peak, Tungurahua
11 Kilimanjaro, Nyamuragira
12 Citlaltépetl, Ixtaccihuatl, Klyuchevskoy, Popocatèpetl
13 Nevado del Ruiz, Ojos del Salado, Soufrire Hills, Volcán El Misti
14 Cerro Incahuasi
15 Haleakala Crater

vole
08 Arvicola, water dog, water rat **10** water mouse **11** meadow mouse

volition
04 will **06** choice, option **07** purpose **08** choosing, election, free will, velleity **10** preference, resolution **13** determination

• of your own volition
06 freely **08** by choice **09** purposely, willingly **11** consciously, voluntarily **12** deliberately **13** intentionally, spontaneously **15** of your own accord

volley
04 hail, tire **05** blast, burst, round, salvo **06** flight, shower **07** barrage, platoon **08** cannonry **09** cannonade, discharge, fusillade **11** bombardment

volte-face
◇ *reversal indicator*
05 U-turn **08** reversal **09** about-face, about-turn, turnabout **13** enantiodromia

voluble
06 chatty, fluent, verbal **07** twining,

verbose **09** garrulous, talkative **10** articulate, changeable, loquacious **11** forthcoming

volume
01 v **03** tom, vol **04** body, book, bulk, code, mass, rise, roll, size, tome **05** codex, noise, sound, space, swell **06** amount, scroll **07** omnibus **08** capacity, decibels, loudness, quantity, solidity **09** aggregate, amplitude **10** dimensions **11** publication

voluminous
03 big **04** full, huge, vast **05** ample, bulky, large, roomy **08** spacious **09** billowing, capacious

voluntarily
06 freely **08** by choice, by my will **09** purposely, willingly **12** deliberately **13** intentionally **15** of your own accord

voluntary
03 vol **04** free **06** unpaid, votive, willed **07** willing **08** designed, free-will, optional, postlude, unforced **09** volunteer **10** deliberate, gratuitous, purposeful, ultroneous, unsalaried, without pay **11** intentional, spontaneous, unsolicited

volunteer
03 vol **05** offer **06** tender **07** advance, proffer, propose, suggest **08** activist, do-gooder, fencible **09** home guard, reformado, voluntary **10** put forward **11** come forward, helping hand, step forward **15** voluntary worker

• **volunteers**
02 TA **03** AVR, CDV, UVF, VAD **04** RNVR

voluptuary
07 playboy **08** hedonist, sybarite **09** bon vivant, bon viveur, debauchee, epicurean, libertine **10** profligate, sensualist **14** pleasure-seeker

voluptuous
05 buxom **06** sultry **07** opulent, sensual, shapely **08** enticing, luscious, sensuous **09** luxurious, seductive **10** curvaceous, effeminate, goloptious, goluptious, hedonistic **11** full-figured **13** self-indulgent

vomit
03 cat **04** barf, boak, bock, boke, honk, puke, sick, spew, spue **05** heave, retch **06** be sick, emetic, sick up **07** bring up, chuck up, chunder, fetch up, throw up, upchuck **08** disgorge, parbreak **10** egurgitate **11** regurgitate

vomiting
04 puke, sick **06** emesis, puking **07** barfing, spewing **08** ejection, parbreak, retching, sickness **10** chundering, sick as a dog **11** hyperemesis **12** anacatharsis, haematemesis **13** regurgitation **15** morning sickness

voracious
04 avid **06** greedy, hungry **07** swinish **08** edacious, gourmand, ravening, ravenous **09** devouring, rapacious **10** gluttonous, insatiable, omnivorous, prodigious, voraginous

voracity
05 greed **06** hunger **07** avidity, edacity **08** rapacity **12** ravenousness

vortex
04 eddy **05** whirl **09** maelstrom, whirlpool, whirlwind **10** tourbillon **11** tourbillion

votary
06 addict **07** devotee, Paphian, sectary **08** adherent, bacchant, believer, disciple, follower **10** worshipper

vote
01 X **02** no **03** aye, nay, yea, yes **04** poll **05** elect, go for, put in, voice **06** ballot, choose, opt for, return **07** declare, propose, re-elect, suggest, write-in **08** division, election, plump for, suffrage **09** franchise **10** plebiscite, referendum **11** ballot paper, show of hands **12** go to the polls **15** enfranchisement

• **vote in**
04 pick **05** adopt, co-opt, elect, voice **06** choose, opt for, prefer, return, select **07** appoint, vote for **08** decide on, plump for **09** designate, determine

• **vote out**
04 oust **06** demote, remove, topple, unseat **07** boot out, dismiss, turf out **08** dethrone, displace **09** overthrow

voter
02 no **03** nay, yea, yes **04** vote **05** fagot **06** faggot **07** burgher, citizen **08** balloter, colonist, outvoter **10** franchiser, free person, ten-pounder **11** constituent **13** floating voter

vouch
• **vouch for**
04 back **06** affirm, assert, assure, avouch, uphold, verify **07** certify, confirm, endorse, support, swear to, warrant **08** attest to, speak for **09** answer for, guarantee **10** asseverate

voucher
02 LV **04** chit, note **05** paper, token **06** chitty, coupon, ticket **07** warrant **08** document **09** book token, gift token **11** youth credit

vouchsafe
04 cede, give **05** deign, grant, vouch, yield **06** accord, bestow, beteem, confer, impart **07** beteeme **09** guarantee **10** condescend

vow
03 vum **04** avow, hest, hete, oath **05** heast, hecht, hight, swear **06** affirm, behote, bename, devote, heaste, pledge **07** behight, profess, promise, protest **08** dedicate **09** nuncupate, undertake **11** nuncupation **12** give your word

vowel
01 a, e, i, o, u

• **vowel sound**
05 schwa

voyage
04 sail, tour, trip **06** course, cruise, safari, travel **07** journey, odyssey, passage, traffic, travels **08** crossing, put to sea, shipping, traverse **10** enterprise, expedition, navigation **12** rough passage **13** middle passage

Vulcan
10 Hephaestus

vulgar
03 low **04** lewd, loud, naff, rude, vulg **05** bawdy, broad, cheap, crude, dirty, flash, gaudy, rough, showy, tacky, tarty, usual **06** coarse, common, filthy, flashy, garish, glitzy, kitsch, public, ribald, risqué, tawdry **07** boorish, general, ill-bred, obscene, plebean, popular, uncouth, upstart **08** banausic, gorblimy, impolite, improper, indecent, low-lived, ordinary, plebeian **09** customary, gorblimey, hoi polloi, low-minded, off-colour, offensive, pandemian, prevalent, tasteless, unrefined **10** indecorous, indelicate, suggestive, threepenny, uncultured, vernacular **11** commonplace, distasteful, near the bone, picturesque **12** ostentatious **13** cheap and nasty **15** unsophisticated

vulgarian
04 pleb, snob **05** tiger **07** plebean, tigress **08** plebeian

vulgarity
07 crudity **08** ribaldry, rudeness **09** crudeness, gaudiness, indecency **10** coarseness, garishness, tawdriness **11** ostentation

vulnerable
◇ *anagram indicator*
04 open, weak **06** tender **07** exposed **08** helpless, high-risk, in danger, insecure, wide open **09** powerless, pregnable, sensitive, unguarded **11** defenceless, susceptible, unprotected **12** open to attack **15** exposed to danger

vulture
05 gripe, grype, urubu **06** condor **08** aasvogel, zopilote **09** gallinazo, gier-eagle, ossifrage **11** carrion crow, lammergeier, lammergeyer **13** turkey buzzard

W
07 double-u, whiskey **09** double-you

wacky
◇ *anagram indicator*
03 odd **04** daft, wild, zany **05** crazy, goofy, loony, loopy, nutty, silly
06 screwy **07** bonkers, erratic, offbeat
09 eccentric **10** irrational
13 unpredictable

wad
03 bun, pad **04** ball, cake, hunk, lump, mass, plug, roll **05** block, chunk, marry, wodge **06** bundle, dossil, pledge
07 pledget **08** sandwich, security

wadding
06 filler, lining **07** batting, filling, packing, padding **08** stuffing **10** cotton wool **14** quilting-cotton

waddle
04 rock, sway **06** clumsy, daidle, hoddle, toddle, totter, wobble **07** shuffle

wade
02 go **04** ford, roll **05** cross, lurch
06 paddle, splash, wallow, welter
08 flounder, traverse
• wade in
05 set to **06** tear in **07** pitch in
08 launch in **10** get stuck in **11** wade through **12** trawl through **13** plough through

wader, wading bird *see* **bird**

wafer
04 host, seal **05** matza, matzo
06 matzah, matzoh

waffle
04 guff, wave **05** gofer, waver
06 babble, gaufer, gaufre, gopher, hot air, jabber **07** blather, blether, padding, prattle **08** blathers, blethers, nonsense, rabbit on, witter on **09** vacillate, verbosity, wittering, wordiness
10 cotton wool **11** vacillation
12 gobbledygook

waft
04 blow, puff, turn, wave, wing
05 carry, drift, float, glide, scent, whiff
06 beckon, breath, breeze, winnow
07 current, draught **08** transmit
09 transport

wag
◇ *anagram indicator*
03 bob, nod, wit **04** fool, lick, move, rock, stir, sway, walk, wave **05** clown, comic, droll, joker, shake, swing, troll
06 fellow, gagman, jester, quiver, truant, waggle, wiggle, wobble
07 flutter, vibrate **08** banterer, brandish, comedian, humorist
09 oscillate

wage
03 fee, pay, war **04** gage, hire, levy, meed **05** bribe, screw **06** battle, hazard, pledge, pursue, reward, salary
07 carry on, conduct, contend, execute, imprest, payment, pension, returns, stipend **08** earnings, engage in, penny-fee, pittance, practise
09 allowance, emolument, undertake
10 recompense, wage-packet
12 compensation, remuneration

wager
03 bet, lay, wad, wed **04** gage, punt, risk **05** put on, sport, stake **06** chance, gamble, hazard, pledge **07** flutter, lay odds, venture **09** speculate
11 speculation **14** gaming contract

waggish
04 arch **05** droll, funny, merry, witty
06 facete, impish, jocose **07** amusing, comical, jesting, jocular, playful, puckish, risible, roguish **08** humorous, sportive **09** bantering, facetious
10 frolicsome **11** mischievous

waggle
◇ *anagram indicator*
03 wag **04** wave **05** shake **06** bobble, jiggle, wiggle, wobble **07** flutter
09 oscillate **12** niddle-noddle

wagon
03 car, van **04** cart, corf, drag, dray, wain **05** buggy, float, gambo, hutch, lorry, train, truck **06** boxcar, camion, hopper, telega **07** caisson, chariot, cocopan, flatcar, fourgon, gondola, kibitka, tank car, tartana **08** carriage, democrat, schooner **09** low-loader
10 freight-car, luggage-van **15** prairie schooner
• on the wagon
02 TT **06** tee-tee **08** teetotal

waif
04 puff, weft **05** stray, wefte **06** orphan, streak, urchin **07** wasting **09** foundling, neglected, wandering **10** ragamuffin

wail
02 io **03** cry, sob **04** howl, keen, moan, weep, yowl **05** groan **06** bemoan, lament, yammer **07** ululate, vagitus, weeping **08** complain **09** complaint, ululation

waistcoat
04 vest **05** gilet **06** bodice, bolero, jerkin **07** surcoat

wait
03 spy **04** bide, halt, hold, rest, stay, tend **05** abide, await, delay, lurch, pause, stand, tarry, watch **06** ambush, attend, escort, expect, hang in, hang on, hold-up, linger, remain, sit out, taihoa **07** stand by **08** hang fire, hesitate, hold back, interval, sentinel, watchman **09** bide tryst, hang about
10 hang around, hesitation **12** bide your time **13** lick your chops
• wait on
03 see **04** tend **05** serve **06** attend
07 work for **08** attend to **09** look after
10 minister to, take care of

waiter, waitress
04 host, tray **05** Nippy **06** busboy, butler, carhop, commis, garçon, mousmé, Nippie, salver, server
07 busgirl, hostess, maître d', mousmee, pannier, steward, waitron
08 watchman **09** attendant, sommelier
10 stewardess **12** maître d'hôtel

waive
04 cede **05** avoid, defer, evade, forgo, yield **06** forego, give up, ignore, reject, resign, vacate **07** abandon, forsake, put away **08** postpone, renounce, set aside **09** do without, surrender
10 relinquish **12** dispense with, strain a point

waiver
08 deferral **09** remission, surrender
10 abdication, disclaimer
11 abandonment, resignation
12 postponement, renunciation
14 relinquishment

wake
04 fire, goad, path, prod, rear, rise, stir, warn, wash, whet **05** alert, arise, awake, egg on, get up, rouse, track, trail, train, vigil, waken, watch, waves
06 arouse, awaken, come to, excite, notify, revive, signal, stir up **07** animate, funeral **08** activate, backwash, festival, lichwake, lykewake, serenade
09 aftermath, galvanize, reanimate, stimulate **10** bring round, death-watch
11 make aware of **13** become aware of
15 make conscious of

wakeful
04 wary **05** alert **06** waking
07 heedful, rousing **08** restless, vigilant, wakerife, watchful, waukrife
09 attentive, awakening, insomniac, observant, sleepless **10** unsleeping

wakefulness
05 vigil **08** insomnia **09** vigilance

12 restlessness, watchfulness
13 attentiveness, sleeplessness

waken
04 fire, rise, stir, wake, whet 05 awake, evoke, get up, rouse 06 arouse, awaken, excite, ignite, kindle, stir up, waking 07 animate, enliven, quicken 08 activate 09 galvanize, stimulate

Wales *see* **council**; **town**

walk
03 lag, leg, pad, wag, way 04 beat, foot, gait, hike, hump, lane, lead, limp, mall, move, pace, path, pawn, plod, step, trek, trog, turn, xyst, yomp 05 allée, alley, amble, drive, flock, guide, march, paseo, round, route, steps, stump, track, trail, tramp, tread, usher 06 avenue, behave, depart, escort, foot it, hoof it, pasear, ramble, rounds, sashay, spread, stride, stroll, trapes, trudge, xystos, xystus 07 alameda, berceau, circuit, conduct, gallery, passage, pathway, saunter, terrace, traipse, walkway 08 ambulate, carriage, footpath, frescade, go on foot, pavement, shepherd, sidewalk, traverse, withdraw 09 accompany, boulevard, circulate, disappear, esplanade, promenade 10 ambulatory, pad the hoof, pipe-opener
11 perambulate 13 hunting-ground, pedestrianize 15 stretch your legs

• **walk off with, walk away with**
03 bag, nip 04 lift, nick, whip 05 filch, pinch, steal, swipe 06 nobble, pocket 07 knock up, snaffle 08 knock off, liberate, souvenir 09 duckshove, go off with, relieve of 10 run off with 11 make off with 14 help yourself to

• **walk of life**
04 area, line 05 arena, field, trade
06 career, course, métier, sphere
07 calling, pursuit 08 activity, vocation
10 background, occupation, profession

• **walk out**
05 leave 06 mutiny, revolt, strike
07 protest 08 stop work 09 down tools
10 go on strike

• **walk out on**
04 dump, jilt 06 desert 07 abandon, forsake 08 run out on 15 leave high and dry, leave in the lurch

• **walk over**
05 abuse, cross 06 misuse 07 oppress
08 ill-treat, impose on, traverse
09 profiteer, trample on 10 manipulate
12 take for a ride 13 take liberties
14 play off against, pull a fast one on
15 take advantage of

• **walk unsteadily**
04 halt, stot 06 daddle, hobble, paddle, totter 07 shamble, stumble

walker
03 ped 05 hiker 06 fuller, ganger
07 rambler, vagrant 08 forester
09 ambulator 10 colporteur, pedestrian 11 stick insect

walking-stick
04 cane 05 waddy 06 kebbie, waddie
07 hickory 08 ash-plant
10 blackthorn 11 Malacca-cane
12 Penang-lawyer
See also **stick**

walk-out
06 revolt, strike 07 protest
08 stoppage 09 rebellion

walkover
02 WO 05 cinch 06 doddle 07 easy win, laugher 08 cakewalk, pushover
10 child's play 11 easy victory, piece of cake

walkway
04 lane, path, road 07 passage, pathway 08 footpath, pavement, sidewalk 09 esplanade, promenade

wall
02 wa' 04 mure

Wall types include:

03 dam, sea
04 dike, dyke
05 block, brick, death, fence, hedge, inner, mural, party
06 bailey, cavity, garden, paling, screen, shield
07 barrier, bulwark, curtain, divider, parapet, rampart, sea-wall
08 abutment, bulkhead, buttress, dry-stone, obstacle, palisade, stockade
09 barricade, enclosure, partition, retaining
10 embankment
11 breeze-block, load-bearing, outer bailey
13 fortification, stud partition
14 flying buttress

Walls include:

05 Great
06 Berlin
07 Wailing, Western
08 Antonine, Hadrian's

• **go to the wall**
04 fail, flop, fold 05 slump 06 finish, go bust 07 founder, go under 08 collapse
09 break down 11 come to an end, fall through 12 disintegrate 13 come to nothing

• **wall in**
03 pen 04 cage, hold, ring, wrap
05 bound, fence, frame, hedge, hem in
06 circle, corral, shut in 07 close in, confine, enclose, envelop 08 encircle, surround 09 encompass
10 circummure 12 circumscribe

wallaby
06 quokka, tammar 13 brush kangaroo

wallet
04 case 05 pouch, purse 06 folder, holder 08 bill-fold, notecase, pochette
10 pocketbook

wallop
03 hit, lam 04 bash, beat, beer, belt, blow, bonk, drub, kick, lick, rout, swat, whop 05 clout, crush, paste, pound, punch, smack, swipe, thump, whack
06 batter, buffet, defeat, gallop, hammer, pummel, strike, thrash, thwack 07 clobber, heavily, noisily, trounce 08 flounder, vanquish
See also **beer**; **blow**

wallow
03 lie 04 bask, blow, loll, roll, wade
05 enjoy, glory, heave, lurch, revel, surge 06 muddle, relish, splash, tumble, well up, welter 07 delight, indulge, slubber 08 flounder
09 luxuriate

walrus
05 morse 06 sea cow 08 seahorse
09 rosmarine

wan
04 dark, pale, took, weak 05 ashen, bleak, faint, lurid, pasty, waxen, weary, white 06 feeble, gained, gloomy, pallid, sickly 07 anaemic, ghastly 08 mournful 09 washed out, whey-faced 10 colourless
11 discoloured

wand
03 rod 04 mace, twig, vare 05 baton, sprig, staff, stick 06 batoon 07 sceptre, thyrsus 08 caduceus 09 goldstick

wander
◇ *anagram indicator*
03 err, gad 04 moon, rave, roam, roll, rove, veer, wend 05 amble, drift, mooch, mouch, prowl, range, ratch, stray, taver, vague, wheel 06 babble, cruise, depart, gibber, maraud, mither, moider, ramble, streel, stroam, stroll, swerve, taiver, wilder 07 deviate, digress, diverge, maunder, meander, moither, pilgrim, saunter, swan off, traipse 08 aberrate, bewilder, divagate, go astray, squander, straggle, stravaig, traverse, turn away 09 bat around, excursion, expatiate, forwander, kick about, moon about
10 kick around, moon around, pilgrimage, ratch about
11 extravagate, lose your way, peregrinate, vagabondize 12 stooge around, talk nonsense 14 walk the streets

wanderer
04 waif 05 Gypsy, nomad, rover, stray
06 nomade, ranger 07 drifter, erratic, pilgrim, rambler, vagrant, voyager
08 prodigal, stroller, vagabond, wayfarer 09 itinerant, straggler, traveller 12 rolling stone

wandering
03 gad 04 roam, rove, waff, waif
05 drift, error 06 errant, erring, flight, roving 07 erratic, journey, meander, nomadic, odyssey, strayed, travels, vagrant 08 aberrant, drifting, errantry, homeless, rambling, rootless, vagabond, voyaging 09 departure, deviation, erroneous, evagation, excursion, itinerant, migratory, strolling, unsettled, walkabout, wayfaring 10 aberration, digression, divergence, journeying, meandering, solivagant, travelling 11 extravagant, noctivagant, peripatetic

13 peregrination, peregrinatory
14 circumforanean
15 circumforaneous

wane
03 dim, ebb 04 drop, fade, fail, fall, sink, welk 05 abate, decay, droop, welke 06 fading, lessen, shrink, vanish, weaken, wither 07 atrophy, decline, dwindle, failure, sinking, subside
08 contract, decrease, diminish, fade away, peter out, taper off
09 abatement, dwindling, lessening, weakening 10 diminution, subsidence
11 contraction, tapering off
12 degeneration
• on the wane
06 ebbing, fading 08 dropping, moribund 09 declining, dwindling, lessening, subsiding, weakening, withering 11 obsolescent, on the way out, tapering off 12 degenerating, on the decline 13 deteriorating, on its last legs

wangle
03 fix 04 work 06 fiddle, manage, scheme 07 arrange, falsify, finagle, pull off 08 contrive, engineer
09 manoeuvre 10 manipulate
12 wheel and deal

want
04 lack, like, lust, miss, mole, need, pine, will, wish 05 covet, crave, fancy
06 besoin, dearth, defect, demand, desire, hunger, penury, pining, thirst
07 absence, blemish, call for, craving, hope for, long for, longing, paucity, pine for, poverty, require 08 appetite, coveting, feel like, scarcity, shortage, yearn for, yearning 09 be without, hunger for, indigence, privation, thirst for 10 deficiency, desiderate, feebleness, inadequacy, scantiness
11 destitution, requirement 13 be deficient in, insufficiency

wanting
03 for 04 less, poor 05 needy, short
06 absent, faulty 07 lacking, missing, without 08 amissing, desirous
09 defective, deficient, imperfect
10 inadequate 11 substandard
12 insufficient, unacceptable
13 disappointing 14 not up to scratch, unsatisfactory

wanton
◇ *anagram indicator*
03 gay, rig 04 idle, lewd, nice, rake, rash, roué, slut, tart, wild 05 cadgy, whore 06 frisky, frolic, harlot, impure, jovial, kidgie, lecher, toyish, trifle, unjust, unruly 07 amorous, Don Juan, immoral, riggish, smicker, toysome, trifler, trollop, twigger 08 arrogant, Casanova, immodest, insolent, petulant, prodigal, reckless, skittish, sportive, strumpet 09 abandoned, arbitrary, debauchee, dissipate, dissolute, lecherous, libertine, malicious, merciless, pointless, shameless 10 capricious, cork-heeled, dissipated, gratuitous, groundless, lascivious, malevolent, prostitute, unprovoked, voluptuary
11 extravagant, promiscuous
12 unmanageable, unrestrained
13 self-indulgent, undisciplined, unjustifiable

war
04 army 05 clash, excel, fight, worse, worst 06 combat, defeat, enmity, stoush, strife, strive 07 contend, contest, ill-will, make war, wage war, warfare 08 campaign, conflict, fighting
09 bloodshed 10 antagonism, contention, take up arms 11 cross swords, hostilities 13 confrontation

War types include:

03 hot
04 cold, germ, holy
05 blitz, civil, jihad, total, trade, world
06 ambush, attack, battle, jungle, nerves, trench
07 assault, limited, nuclear, private
08 chemical, intifada, invasion, skirmish, struggle
09 attrition, guerrilla
10 asymmetric, biological, blitzkrieg, engagement, manoeuvres, resistance
11 bombardment
12 asymmetrical, state of siege
13 armed conflict, counter-attack

Wars include:

03 Cod
04 1812, Boer, Gulf, Iraq, Sikh, Zulu
05 Chaco, Dutch, Great, Maori, Opium, Punic, Roses, World
06 Afghan, Balkan, Barons', Gallic, Indian, Korean, Six-Day, Trojan, Vendée, Winter
07 Bishops', Crimean, Italian, Mexican, Pacific, Persian, Servile, Vietnam
08 Crusades, Football, Iran-Iraq, Peasants', Religion, Ten Years'
09 Black Hawk, Falklands, Yom Kippur
10 Devolution, Jenkins' Ear, Napoleonic, Peninsular, Queen Anne's, Seven Years', Suez Crisis
11 Arab-Israeli, Eighty Years', Indian Civil, King Philip's, Thirty Years'
12 English Civil, Hundred Years', Independence, King William's, Russian Civil, Russo-Finnish, Russo-Turkish, Spanish Civil
13 American Civil, Grand Alliance, Russo-Japanese
14 Boxer Rebellion, Franco-Prussian, Indian Uprising, July Revolution, Triple Alliance
15 Easter Rebellion

See also **battle**

• war cry
04 hoop, word 05 havoc, whoop
06 banzai, slogan 07 war song
08 Geronimo 09 alalagmos, battle-cry, watchword 11 rallying-cry
• war god
03 Tiu, Tiw, Tyr 04 Mars 08 Quirinus

warble
03 cry 04 call, sing, song 05 carol, chirl, chirp, trill, yodel 06 quaver, record, relish 07 chirrup, rellish, twitter

ward
04 area, care, fend, room, unit, zone
05 guard, minor, parry, pupil, spike, watch 06 charge 07 cubicle, custody, lookout, protégé, quarter 08 district, division, precinct, protégée
09 apartment, dependant, maternity
10 protection, sanatorium, sanitarium
11 compartment 12 guardianship
• ward off
04 fend, wear, weir 05 avert, avoid, block, dodge, evade, parry, repel
06 defend, shield, thwart 07 beat off, deflect, fend off, forfend 08 stave off, turn away 09 drive back, forestall, turn aside 11 averruncate

warden
06 keeper, ranger, regent, warder
07 curator, janitor, steward
08 bearward, guardian, meter man, overseer, sentinel, watchman
09 caretaker, concierge, constable, custodian, meter maid, protector
10 gatekeeper, supervisor
11 housekeeper, lollipop man
12 lollipop lady 13 administrator, lollipop woman 14 superintendent

warder
05 guard, screw 06 jailer, keeper, warden 08 wardress 09 beefeater, custodian 13 prison officer

wardrobe
04 robe 06 attire, closet, locker, outfit
07 almirah, apparel, armoire, cabinet, clothes 08 cupboard, garments
09 garderobe

warehouse
04 hong, shed 05 depot, store
06 bodega, godown, lock-up 07 store up 08 entrepot 09 goods shed, stockroom 10 depository, repository, storehouse 11 freight shed

wares
05 goods, stock, stuff 07 brokery, pedlary, produce 08 ironware, products 11 charcuterie, commodities, merchandise

warfare
03 war 04 arms 05 blows 06 battle, combat, strife 07 contest, discord, feuding 08 campaign, conflict, fighting, struggle 10 contention
11 hostilities 13 confrontation, passage of arms

warily
06 cagily 07 charily 08 gingerly, uneasily, with care 09 carefully, guardedly 10 cautiously, hesitantly, vigilantly, watchfully 12 suspiciously
13 circumspectly, distrustfully
14 apprehensively

wariness
04 care 06 cautel, unease 07 caution
08 caginess, distrust, prudence, wariment 09 alertness, attention,

foresight, hesitancy, suspicion, vigilance **10** discretion **11** carefulness, heedfulness, mindfulness **12** apprehension, watchfulness **14** circumspection

warlike
07 hawkish, hostile, martial **08** cavalier, militant, military **09** bellicose, combative **10** aggressive, battailous, pugnacious, unfriendly **11** belligerent **12** antagonistic, bloodthirsty, militaristic, warmongering

warlock
05 demon, witch **06** wizard **08** conjurer, magician, sorcerer **09** enchanter **11** necromancer

warm
03 het, hot, lew, sun **04** beat, fine, heat, kind, luke, melt, rich, stir, thaw **05** angry, balmy, calid, close, eager, fresh, rouse, sunny, tepid, toast **06** ardent, caring, excite, genial, hearty, heated, heat up, kindly, lively, loving, mellow, please, reheat, tender, toasty **07** affable, amiable, amorous, animate, beating, cheer up, cordial, delight, earnest, enliven, excited, fervent, glowing, intense, liven up, sincere, thermal, zealous **08** cheerful, friendly, interest, lukewarm, make warm, relaxing, vehement, well-to-do **09** harassing, heartfelt, stimulate, strenuous, temperate **10** hospitable, indelicate, passionate **11** comfortable, kind-hearted, sympathetic **12** affectionate, enthusiastic **15** put some life into

• **warm to**
11 begin to like

• **warm up**
04 heat **07** prepare **08** exercise, limber up, loosen up

warm-blooded
04 rash **06** ardent, lively **07** earnest, fervent **08** spirited **09** emotional, excitable, impetuous, vivacious **10** hot-blooded, passionate **11** endothermic, homothermal, homothermic **12** enthusiastic, homothermous, idiothermous

warm-hearted
04 kind **06** ardent, genial, hearty, kindly, loving, tender **07** cordial **08** generous **11** kind-hearted, sympathetic **12** affectionate **13** compassionate, tender-hearted

warmonger
04 hawk **09** aggressor **10** militarist **12** sabre-rattler

warmth
04 care, fire, glow, heat, love, zeal **05** ardor, flame **06** ardour **07** fervour, hotness, passion, unction **08** fervency, kindness, sympathy, warmness **09** affection, eagerness, intensity, sincerity, vehemence **10** compassion, cordiality, enthusiasm, kindliness, tenderness **11** hospitality **12** friendliness

warn
03 vor **04** tell, urge **05** alert, awarn, shore **06** advise, exhort, forbid, inform, notify, rebuke, summon, tip off **07** caution, command, counsel, let know, portend, presage, reprove, warrant **08** admonish, forewarn, instruct **09** factorize, premonish, reprimand **10** give notice **13** sound the alarm **14** put on your guard

warning
04 call, hint, omen, sign, wire **05** alarm, alert **06** advice, augury, caveat, lesson, notice, signal, threat, tip-off **07** caution, counsel, example, ominous, portent, presage, summons **08** monition, monitory **10** admonition, admonitory, cautionary, wake-up call, yellow card **11** information, premonition, premonitory, threatening **12** notification **13** advance notice

See also **signal**

• **expression of warning**
03 nix, now **04** cave, fore, gang, mind **06** timber **07** Achtung, you wait! **08** gardyloo **09** scaldings

warp
◇ *anagram indicator*
04 bend, bent, bias, cast, kink, turn **05** kedge, quirk, throw, twist **06** buckle, defect, deform, spring, swerve **07** contort, corrupt, deviate, distort, entwine, pervert **08** miscarry, misshape **09** deviation **10** contortion, distortion, perversion **11** deformation **12** irregularity

warrant
04 able, back, fiat, keep, warn **05** allow, proof, sepad, swear **06** affirm, assure, avouch, behote, defend, excuse, pardon, permit, pledge, uphaud, uphold **07** approve, behight, call for, caption, certify, consent, declare, defence, deserve, empower, endorse, entitle, justify, licence, license, precept, predict, presage, promise, protect, require, support, voucher **08** defender, detainer, guaranty, mittimus, sanction, security, transire, vouch for, warranty **09** answer for, assurance, authority, authorize, consent to, diligence, execution, guarantee, underclay, vouchsafe **10** commission, permission, underwrite, validation **11** necessitate **12** bench-warrant, death warrant, fugie-warrant, peace-warrant **13** authorization, justification, search warrant **14** lettre de cachet

• **warrant officer**
02 WO **03** CSM, RSM **04** bos'n **05** bosun **09** boatswain

warrantable
05 legal, right **06** lawful, proper **09** allowable, estimable, excusable, necessary **10** defensible, reasonable **11** accountable, justifiable, permissible

warranty
04 bond **06** pledge **08** contract, covenant, evidence **09** assurance, guarantee **11** certificate **13** authorization, justification

warring
◇ *anagram indicator*
05 at war **07** hostile, opposed **08** fighting, opposing **09** combatant, embattled **10** contending **11** belligerent, conflicting **14** at daggers drawn

warrior
05 brave, ghazi **06** Amazon, haiduk, wardog, warman **07** berserk, fighter, heyduck, soldier, warlock, warwolf **08** champion, warhorse **09** berserker, combatant **11** fighting man

warship
03 cog, ram **06** galley **07** cruiser, man-o'-war **08** man-of-war **09** blockship, destroyer, first-rate **10** battleship, turret ship **11** capital ship, dreadnaught, dreadnought, torpedo boat **13** battle-cruiser

wart
03 wen **04** lump **06** anbury, growth **07** verruca **09** keratosis, papilloma **10** angleberry **11** excrescence **12** protuberance

wary
04 cagy, ware **05** alert, aware, cagey, chary, leery, tenty **06** tentie **07** careful, guarded, heedful, prudent, thrifty **08** cautious, vigilant, watchful **09** attentive, wide-awake **10** on the alert, suspicious **11** circumspect, distrustful, on your guard **12** on the lookout **14** circumspective

wash
03 fen, lap, lip, mop, wet **04** bath, beat, coat, dash, flow, hold, lave, lick, roll, sind, slop, soak, synd, wave, wipe **05** bathe, clean, layer, marsh, rinse, scrub, souse, stain, stick, sujee, surge, sweep, swell, swill **06** douche, lotion, shower, sloosh, soogee, soogie, soojey, splash, sponge, stream **07** cleanse, coating, launder, laundry, moisten, shampoo, stand up, washing **08** cleaning, swab down **09** cleansing, freshen up, have a bath, have a wash, hold water **10** be accepted, laundering, pass muster **11** be plausible, carry weight, have a shower **12** bear scrutiny, be believable, be convincing, get cleaned up **15** bear examination

• **wash your hands of**
07 abandon **08** give up on

washed-out
03 wan **04** flat, pale **05** all in, ashen, drawn, faded, spent, weary **06** pallid **07** anaemic, drained, haggard, worn-out **08** blanched, bleached, dog-tired, fatigued, tired-out **09** exhausted, knackered **10** colourless, lacklustre **14** dead on your feet

Washington
02 WA **04** Wash

washout
04 flop, mess **06** fiasco **07** debacle,

failure **08** disaster **11** lead balloon **14** disappointment

wasp

05 vespa **06** hornet **07** gallfly **08** ruby-tail **09** cuckoo fly, mud dauber, velvet ant **12** yellow jacket

waspish

05 cross, testy **06** bitchy, crabby, grumpy, touchy **07** crabbed, grouchy, peevish, prickly **08** captious, critical, petulant, snappish, spiteful, virulent **09** crotchety, irascible, irritable **11** bad-tempered, ill-tempered **12** cantankerous

wastage

04 loss **05** decay **07** atrophy **08** draining, marasmus **10** emaciation, exhausting **11** dissipation, squandering **12** degeneration **14** frittering away

waste

◇ *anagram indicator*

03 nub **04** bare, blow, crud, gash, kill, knub, lose, loss, pass, pine, rape, raze, ruin, sack, slag, vain, wild **05** abuse, bleak, drain, dregs, dross, empty, erode, extra, husks, offal, scrap, slops, spend, spill, spoil, trash **06** barren, debris, desert, dismal, dreary, expend, injure, lavish, litter, misuse, ravage, refuse, shrink, slurry, unused, wither **07** atrophy, consume, despoil, destroy, exhaust, garbage, neglect, pillage, rubbish, ruinous, shrivel, splurge, useless **08** cast away, desolate, effluent, emaciate, lay waste, left-over, misspend, rejected, squander, unwanted **09** depredate, devastate, dissipate, go through, leftovers, profusion, recrement, throw away, worthless **10** desolation, devastated, dilapidate, get through, impoverish, unoccupied **11** consumption, destruction, dissipation, expenditure, fritter away, offscouring, prodigality, prodigalize, squandering, superfluous, uninhabited **12** extravagance, offscourings, uncultivated, unproductive, unprofitable, wastefulness **13** supernumerary **14** misapplication **15** become emaciated

See also **kill**

wasted

◇ *anagram indicator*

04 high, lost, weak **05** drunk, gaunt, spent **07** useless, war-worn, worn-out **08** ill-spent, needless, shrunken, weakened, withered **09** atrophied, emaciated, exhausted, washed-out **10** shrivelled, squandered, unrequired **11** unexploited, unnecessary **12** down the drain

wasteful

04 vain **06** lavish **07** ruinous **08** desolate, prodigal, wastfull, wastrife **09** unthrifty, wasterife **10** profitless, profligate, thriftless **11** extravagant, improvident, spendthrift, uninhabited **12** uneconomical, unfrequented

wasteland

04 fell, void, wild **05** waste, wilds **06** desert **07** thwaite **08** badlands **09** emptiness **10** barrenness, wilderness

wasting

05 tabes **07** atrophy **08** marasmic, marasmus, phthisis, syntexis **09** cirrhosis, consuming, symptosis **10** colliquant, destroying, emaciating, enfeebling, tabescence **11** colliquable, consumption, consumptive, devastating, tabefaction **12** colliquative, contabescent

wastrel

04 waif **05** idler, waste **06** feeble, loafer, refuse, skiver **07** goof-off, lounger, shirker **08** layabout **09** lazybones **10** malingerer, ne'er-do-well, profligate **11** spendthrift **14** good-for-nothing

watch

03 eye, nit, see, spy **04** espy, heed, keep, mark, mind, nark, note, scan, tend, tout, view, wait, wake, ward **05** await, clock, flock, guard, scout, spial, vigil **06** follow, gape at, gaze at, look at, look on, look to, notice, peer at, regard, shadow, survey, ticker **07** inspect, look out, lookout, monitor, observe, outlook, overeye, protect, stare at **08** repeater, sentinel, take care, take heed, tick-tick **09** alertness, attention, be careful, look after, timepiece, vigilance **10** inspection, keep tabs on, stemwinder, take care of, wristwatch **11** chronometer, contemplate, keep an eye on, observation, superintend, supervision **12** pay attention, pernoctation, surveillance, watchfulness

See also **clock**

• watch out

04 mind **06** notice **07** keep nit, look out **08** cockatoo, stand nit **10** be vigilant **12** keep a lookout **13** stand cockatoo

• watch over

04 mind, tend, ward **05** guard **06** defend, shield **07** protect, shelter **08** preserve, sentinel, shepherd **09** look after, supervise **10** take care of **11** keep an eye on **14** stand guard over

watchdog

07 monitor **08** guard dog, guardian, house-dog **09** custodian, inspector, ombudsman, protector, regulator, vigilante **10** scrutineer **11** housekeeper

watcher

03 spy **05** Argus **06** viewer **07** lookout, witness **08** audience, looker-on, observer, onlooker **09** spectator **10** eyewitness, televiewer

watchful

04 wary **05** alert, chary **07** guarded, heedful **08** cautious, open-eyed, vigilant, wakerife, waukrife **09** adviceful, attentive, avizefull, observant, wide awake **10** suspicious **11** circumspect, on your guard **12** on the lookout, on the qui vive

watchfulness

07 caution **08** wariness **09** alertness, attention, dragonism, suspicion, vigilance **10** observance **11** heedfulness **12** cautiousness **13** attentiveness **14** circumspection, suspiciousness

watchman

04 wait **05** guard **06** waiter **07** Charley, Charlie, rug gown, wakeman **08** chokidar, night-man **09** caretaker, chowkidar, custodian **10** speculator **13** security guard

watchword

03 cry **05** maxim, motto **06** byword, signal, slogan **07** nayword, tag line **08** buzz word, password **09** battle-cry, catchword, magic word, principle **10** shibboleth **11** catchphrase, rallying-cry

water

02 aq, ea **03** eau, sea, wet **04** aqua, hose, lake, rain, soak **05** class, douse, drink, flood, ocean, river, spray **06** dampen, drench, lustre, saliva, stream **07** current, moisten, quality, torrent **08** flooding, irrigate, moisture, saturate, sprinkle, surround **09** Adam's wine **10** excellence **12** transparency

See also **lake**; **river**; **sea**

Mineral water brands include:

05 Evian®
06 Buxton®, Ty Nant®, Vittel®, Volvic®
07 Perrier®
08 Aqua Pura®
10 Strathmore®
13 Pennine Spring®, San Pellegrino®
14 Highland Spring®

• hold water

04 hold, wash, work **05** stand, stick **06** cohere, hold up **07** stand up **08** convince, ring true **09** make sense **10** be accepted **11** be plausible, carry weight, pass the test, remain valid **12** bear scrutiny, be believable, be convincing **15** bear examination

• water carrier

06 bhisti **07** bheesty, bhistee **08** Aquarius, bheestie

• water down

03 mix **04** thin **06** dilute, soften, weaken **07** qualify **08** mitigate, moderate, play down, tone down **09** attenuate, soft-pedal **10** adulterate

watercourse

04 burn, khor, lead, nala, rean, reen, wadi **05** brook, canal, ditch, drain, nalla, nulla, rhine, rhyne, river, shott, whelm **06** arroyo, nallah, nullah, spruit, stream **07** channel **09** sunk fence **12** water-channel

See also **river**

waterfall

03 lin **04** drop, fall, foss, linn, salt **05** chute, falls, force, rapid, sault, shoot, shute, spout **06** lasher, rapids

07 cascade, chignon, necktie, torrent **08** cataract, overfall **10** salmon leap

Waterfalls include:

05 Angel, Della, Glass, Pilao, Tysse
06 Boyoma, Iguaçu, Krimml, Ormeli, Ribbon, Tugela
07 Mtarazi, Niagara, Stanley, Thukela
08 Cuquenán, Gavarnie, Gullfoss, Itatinga, Kaieteur, Takkakaw, Victoria, Wallaman, Yosemite
09 Churchill, Dettifoss, Giessbach, Multnomah, Staubbach
10 Cleve-Garth, Sutherland, Wollomombi
11 Reichenbach, Trummelbach
12 Cusiana River, Paulo Alfonso, Silver Strand
13 Mardalsfossen, Tyssetrengane, Upper Yosemite, Vestre Mardola

waterproof, waterproof material
03 mac **04** mack **05** loden **06** anorak, arctic, cagoul, camlet, coated, kagool, kagoul, poncho **07** Barbour®, cagoule, camelot, jaconet, kagoule, oilskin, proofed, slicker, tanking **09** damp-proof, macintosh, sou'wester, tarpaulin **10** impervious, mackintosh, rubberized, tarpauling, trench coat, watertight **11** Barbour® coat, gutta-percha, impermeable **12** antigropelos **13** antigropeloes, Barbour® jacket **14** water-repellent, water-resistant

watertight
04 firm **05** sound **06** sealed, stanch **07** staunch **08** airtight, flawless, hermetic **09** foolproof **10** waterproof **11** impregnable **12** indisputable, unassailable

watery
03 wet **04** damp, thin, weak **05** blear, eager, fluid, moist, runny, soggy, vapid, washy **06** bleary, liquid, serous, sloppy **07** aqueous, diluted, hydrous, insipid, shilpit **08** hydatoid, skinking, squelchy **09** tasteless **10** wishy-washy **11** adulterated, flavourless, transparent, watered-down

wave
◇ *anagram indicator*
03 sea, waw **04** curl, flap, flow, foam, rash, rush, sign, stir, surf, sway, waff, waft, wawe **05** crimp, drift, float, flood, flote, froth, hover, shake, surge, sweep, swell, swing, trend, waver **06** beckon, billow, comber, direct, quiver, ripple, roller, signal, stream, waffle **07** breaker, current, decuman, feather, flutter, gesture, impulse, soliton, tide rip, upsurge, wavelet **08** backwash, brandish, flourish, increase, indicate, movement, outbreak, tendency, undulate, whitecap **09** tidal wave, vacillate **10** crispation, supersonic, undulation, white horse **11** beachcomber, gesticulate, ground swell

• **make waves**
12 cause trouble **13** disturb things, stir up trouble

• **wave aside**
05 spurn **06** reject, shelve **07** dismiss **08** set aside **09** disregard **10** brush aside **15** pour cold water on

• **wave down**
06 summon **08** flag down **12** signal to stop

waver
◇ *anagram indicator*
04 reel, rock, sway, vary, wave **05** haver, shake **06** change, didder, dither, falter, seesaw, teeter, totter, waffle, wobble **07** give way, stagger, tremble **08** hesitate **09** fluctuate, hum and haw, oscillate, vacillate **10** equivocate **11** be undecided **12** shilly-shally

waverer
07 doubter, haverer, wobbler **08** ditherer **14** shilly-shallier

wavering
◇ *anagram indicator*
04 wavy **05** shaky **07** dithery, stagger **08** doubtful, doubting, firmless, havering, hesitant **09** ambiguous, dithering, hesitance, hesitancy **10** hesitation, indecision, in two minds, of two minds **11** vacillatory **12** double-minded **15** shilly-shallying

wavy
04 undé **05** curly, curvy, oundy, undee **06** nebulé, nebuly, repand, ridged, undate, wiggly, zigzag **07** curling, curving, rippled, sinuate, sinuous, undated, winding **08** sinuated, undulate, wavering **09** snow goose **10** flamboyant, undulating, undulatory **11** fluctuating

wax
03 say **04** cere, grow, kiss, pela, rise, seal, talk, tell **05** mount, speak, state, swell, utter, voice, widen **06** become, expand, extend, spread **07** address, broaden, cerumen, declaim, declare, develop, enlarge, express, fill out, magnify, passion **08** converse, increase, paraffin **09** enunciate, get bigger, hold forth, pronounce **10** articulate **11** communicate

waxen
03 wan **04** pale **05** ashen, livid, white **06** pallid **07** anaemic, ghastly, whitish **09** bloodless **10** colourless

waxy
04 soft **05** irate, pasty, waxen **06** pallid **07** cereous **08** incensed **09** ceraceous **11** impressible **14** impressionable

way
◇ *anagram indicator*
01 E, N, S, W **02** Rd, St, Wy **03** far, via **04** gate, lane, mode, path, plan, road, rode, room, tool, very, will, wise, wont **05** habit, lines, means, route, scope, state, style, track, trait, usage, weigh **06** access, avenue, course, custom, esteem, manner, method, nature, really, street, system, temper **07** channel, conduct, fashion, highway, journey, passage, pathway, process, respect, roadway **08** approach, district, position, practice, progress, strategy **09** behaviour, condition, direction, mannerism, procedure, technique **10** instrument **11** disposition, peculiarity, personality, temperament **12** idiosyncrasy, thoroughfare **14** characteristic, course of action **15** instrumentality

• **all the way**
02 up **04** thro, thru **07** through **08** straight

• **by the way**
02 ob **03** BTW **06** obiter **07** apropos **09** en passant, in passing **11** secondarily **12** incidentally **14** by the same token **15** à propos de bottes, parenthetically

• **either way**
◇ *palindrome indicator*

• **give way**
02 go **03** sag **04** bend, cede, sink **05** break, burst, crack, yield **06** cave in, fall in, give in, relent, shrink, spring, submit, swerve **07** concede, subside, succumb **08** collapse, fall back, withdraw **09** give place, surrender **10** capitulate, give ground **12** disintegrate

• **make your way**
04 wend **06** travel **07** journey

• **on the way**
07 en route **09** in transit

• **quickest way**
07 beeline

• **under way**
05 afoot, begun, going **06** moving **07** started **08** in motion **10** in progress **11** in operation, progressing **12** off the ground

• **way of life**
04 life **05** world **08** position **09** lifestyle, situation **12** modus vivendi

• **ways and means**
04 cash **05** funds, tools **07** capital, methods **08** capacity, reserves **09** procedure, resources **10** capability **11** wherewithal

• **whichever way you look at it**
◇ *palindrome indicator*

wayfarer
05 Gypsy, nomad, rover **06** viator, walker **07** pilgrim, swagger, swagman, trekker, voyager **08** traveler, wanderer **09** itinerant, journeyer, piepowder, traveller **12** globetrotter

wayfaring
06 roving **07** nomadic, walking **08** drifting, rambling, voyaging **09** itinerant, wandering **10** journeying, travelling **11** peripatetic

waylay
03 lay **05** belay, catch, seize **06** accost, ambush, attack, hold up **07** set upon, stick up **08** obstruct, surprise **09** intercept **10** buttonhole **12** lie in wait for

way-out
04 lost, rapt, wild **05** crazy, wacky, weird **06** exotic, far-out, freaky **07** bizarre, off-beat, unusual **09** eccentric, excellent, fantastic, left-field **10** avant-garde, outlandish,

unorthodox **11** exceptional, progressive **12** experimental **14** unconventional

wayward

06 fickle, unruly, wilful **07** peevish **08** contrary, obdurate, perverse, stubborn **09** irregular, obstinate **10** capricious, changeable, headstrong, rebellious, refractory, self-willed **11** disobedient, intractable, loup-the-dyke **12** contumacious, incorrigible, ungovernable, unmanageable **13** insubordinate, unpredictable

waywardness

08 obduracy **09** contumacy, obstinacy **10** perversity, unruliness, wilfulness **12** contrariness, disobedience, perverseness, stubbornness **14** rebelliousness **15** insubordination

weak

01 W **03** dim, low **04** dull, fade, gone, lame, poor, puny, soft, thin **05** cissy, faint, frail, milky, runny, shaky, weedy **06** debile, facile, faulty, feeble, flimsy, infirm, meagre, pallid, sickly, single, slight, unable, watery **07** brickle, diluted, exposed, fragile, insipid, lacking, muffled, stifled, unsound, useless, worn out **08** cowardly, delicate, fatigued, impotent **09** defective, deficient, enervated, exhausted, forceless, imperfect, powerless, spineless, strung out, tasteless, unguarded, unhealthy, untenable **10** effeminate, fizzenless, foisonless, fusionless, inadequate, indecisive, indistinct, irresolute, unstressed, vulnerable **11** adulterated, debilitated, defenceless, fushionless, impressible, ineffectual, unprotected **12** inconclusive, invertebrate, unconvincing **13** imperceptible **14** inconsiderable, valetudinarian

weaken

03 sap **04** fade, fail, flag, kill, pall, thin, tire **05** abate, appal, craze, delay, droop, lower, taint **06** deduct, dilute, ease up, impair, lessen, reduce, soften, temper **07** cripple, disable, dwindle, exhaust, give way, unnerve **08** diminish, enervate, enfeeble, entender, intender, mitigate, moderate, paralyse, soften up **09** extenuate, undermine, water down **10** debilitate, disconcert, effeminate, effeminize **12** incapacitate **13** disinvigorate **14** take the edge off

weakening

06 easing, fading, waning **07** failing **08** dilution, flagging, lowering **09** abatement, dwindling, lessening, reduction **10** enervation, impairment, moderation **11** extenuation, frontolysis, undermining **12** debilitation, diminishment, enfeeblement

weakling

03 wet **04** drip, tonk, weed, wimp, wuss **05** cissy, mouse, wally **06** coward **07** dilling, doormat, milksop **08** softling, underdog **09** underling **10** namby-pamby

weakly

06 feebly, lamely **07** faintly, frailly **08** slightly **09** tenuously **10** helplessly **11** implausibly, powerlessly **12** dispiritedly, indecisively, pathetically **13** ineffectively

weak-minded

04 daft **07** pliable **09** compliant, spineless, weak-kneed **10** irresolute, submissive **11** complaisant, persuadable, persuasible **12** faint-hearted **13** pusillanimous

weakness

04 flaw **05** doubt, fault, folly **06** defect, dotage, foible, liking **07** acrasia, apepsia, blemish, cachexy, failing, frailty, languor, passion **08** azoturia, cachexia, debility, delicacy, fondness, frailtee, penchant, soft spot, trembles **09** frailness, impotence, infirmity, lassitude, weak point **10** deficiency, effeminacy, enervation, feebleness, flimsiness, incapacity, myasthenia, proclivity **11** dubiousness, inclination, paraparesis, shortcoming, tenuousness, uncertainty, unsoundness **12** Achilles' heel, delicateness, doubtfulness, enfeeblement, imperfection, phonasthenia, predilection, unlikelihood, unlikeliness **13** improbability, powerlessness, vulnerability **14** far-fetchedness, implausibility, predisposition **15** ineffectiveness, second childhood

weal

04 mark, scar, wale, welt **05** bends, ridge, wheal, wound **06** streak, stripe **07** welfare **08** cicatrix **09** cicatrice, contusion **12** commonwealth **14** the sum of things

wealth

04 cash, ease, mass, pelf **05** funds, goods, lucre, means, money, store **06** assets, bounty, estate, mammon, plenty, riches **07** capital, finance, fortune, fulness, tallent, warison **08** fullness, opulence, property, richesse, treasure, treasury, warrison **09** abundance, affluence, plenitude, profusion, resources, substance, wellbeing **10** cornucopia, prosperity **11** copiousness, loadsamoney, possessions

wealthy

04 oofy, posh, rich **05** flush, pluty, solid **06** fat-cat, loaded **07** moneyed, opulent, well-off **08** affluent, well-to-do **10** filthy rich, prosperous, well-heeled **11** comfortable, made of money, rolling in it, substantial **12** stinking rich

weapon

03 arm

Weapons include:

03 bow, gas, gun, Uzi
04 bomb, Colt®, cosh, dirk, épée, foil, ICBM, Mace®, mine, pike, Scud
05 arrow, billy, bolas, CS gas, H-bomb, knife, lance, Luger®, panga, rifle, sabre, sling, spear, sword, Taser®, vouge
06 airgun, cannon, cudgel, dagger, Exocet®, glaive, jambok, magnum, Mauser, mortar, musket, pistol, rapier, rocket, six-gun, taiaha, tomboc
07 assegai, balista, bayonet, bazooka, bomblet, Bren gun, caltrop, halberd, harpoon, longbow, machete, pole-axe, poniard, sjambok, sten gun, stun gun, tear-gas, torpedo
08 air rifle, atom bomb, ballista, blowpipe, calthrop, catapult, chemical, claymore, crossbow, field gun, howitzer, landmine, nail bomb, nerve gas, nunchaku, oerlikon, partisan, revolver, scimitar, shuriken, stiletto, threshel, time-bomb, tomahawk, tommy gun
09 automatic, battleaxe, boomerang, Mills bomb, smart bomb, truncheon, turret-gun
10 bowie knife, broadsword, flick-knife, gatling gun, machine-gun, mustard gas, napalm bomb, peashooter, shillelagh, six-shooter
11 Agent Orange, blunderbuss, bow and arrow, cluster-bomb, daisy-cutter, depth-charge, hand grenade, kalashnikov, neutron bomb, submunition, water pistol
12 bunker buster, flame-thrower, hydrogen bomb, quarterstaff
13 Cruise missile, knuckleduster, submachine-gun
14 incendiary bomb, rocket-launcher
15 thermobaric bomb, Winchester® rifle

See also **dagger**; **gun**; **knife**; **missile**; **sword**

wear

◇ *insertion indicator*
03 air, don, fly, rub, use **04** bear, edge, fray, have, pack, pass, show, stub **05** carry, dress, erode, grind, guide, mount, put on, spend, sport, waste, weary **06** abrade, accept, affect, assume, attire, become, damage, endure, have on, outfit **07** believe, clothes, conduct, consume, corrode, costume, display, dress in, erosion, exhaust, exhibit, fashion, service, utility **08** abrasion, clothing, friction, garments, tolerate, traverse **09** corrosion **10** durability, employment, usefulness **11** be clothed in, be dressed in, deteriorate, wear and tear **12** become weaker **13** become thinner, deterioration **14** fray at the edges

• wear down

05 erode, grind **06** abrade, impair, lessen, reduce **07** attrite, consume, corrode, degrade, rub away

08 diminish, macerate, overcome, soften up 09 grind down, undermine 10 chip away at

• **wear off**

03 ebb 04 fade, fray, wane 05 abate 06 lessen, weaken 07 dwindle, subside 08 decrease, diminish, peter out 09 disappear

• **wear on**

04 go by, go on, pass 06 elapse

• **wear out**

03 sap 04 fray, mush, tire 05 break, drain, erode, trash, use up, waste 06 harass, impair, peruse, strain, stress 07 consume, exhaust, fatigue, frazzle, knacker, knock up, tire out 08 enervate, forspend, overteem 09 forespend 11 deteriorate, wear through

wearily

07 tiredly 08 drowsily, sleepily 10 listlessly 11 unexcitedly 13 lethargically

weariness

05 ennui 07 fatigue, languor 08 lethargy 09 lassitude, tiredness 10 drowsiness, enervation, exhaustion, sleepiness 11 prostration, Weltschmerz 12 listlessness, taedium vitae

• **expression of weariness**

04 hech 07 heigh-ho

wearing

◇ *containment indicator*

02 in 06 taxing, tiring, trying 07 erosive, irksome 08 tiresome 09 consuming, fatiguing, wearisome 10 durability, exhausting, oppressive 12 exasperating

wearisome

04 dull 06 boring, dreary, trying 07 humdrum, irksome, tedious, wearing 08 annoying, tiresome, weariful 09 fatiguing, vexatious 10 bothersome, burdensome, exhausting, monotonous 11 troublesome 12 exasperating

weary

03 bug, fag, irk, sap, tax 04 bore, cloy, fade, fail, jade, puny, tire 05 all in, annoy, bored, drain, ennui, jaded, tired 06 aweary, betoil, burden, bushed, done in, drowsy, harass, pooped, sicken, sleepy, zonked 07 drained, exhaust, fatigue, tedious, tire out, wear out, whacked, worn out 08 awearied, dead beat, dog-tired, dog-weary, enervate, fatigued, forweary, half-dead, irritate, tiresome, toil-worn, trauchle, wiped out 09 exhausted, fagged out, knackered, overweary, pooped out, ramfeezle, think long, unexcited 10 brassed off, browned off, cheesed off, debilitate, exasperate 11 tuckered out 12 bored to tears, sick and tired, uninterested 14 unenthusiastic

wearying

06 taxing, tiring, trying 07 wearing 08 draining 09 fatiguing, wearisome 10 exhausting

weasel

04 mink 05 stoat, taira, tayra 06 grison, marten 07 whitret 08 whittret 09 delundung, wolverene, wolverine 10 whitterick

weather

03 dry, set, sky 04 gain, pass 05 brave, slope, stand 06 endure, expose, harden, resist, season, suffer 07 climate, dryness, outlook, ride out, survive, toughen 08 forecast, humidity, overcome, stick out, surmount, windward 09 rise above, sunniness, windiness, withstand 10 cloudiness, conditions, get through 11 come through, live through, pull through, temperature

Weather phenomena include:

03 fog, ice
04 gale, hail, haze, mist, rain, smog, snow, thaw, wind
05 cloud, frost, sleet, slush, storm
06 breeze, deluge, shower, squall
07 chinook, cyclone, drizzle, drought, mistral, monsoon, rainbow, tempest, thunder, tornado, twister, typhoon
08 black ice, downpour, heatwave, sunshine
09 hoar frost, hurricane, lightning, snowstorm, whirlwind

See also **cloud**; **ice**; **precipitation**; **snow**; **storm**; **wind**

• **under the weather**

03 ill 04 ropy, sick 05 crook, drunk, lousy, queer, ropey, rough, seedy 06 ailing, groggy, grotty, poorly 08 below par, hung over, nauseous 09 off-colour, squeamish 10 indisposed, out of sorts 15 the worse for wear

weave

◇ *anagram indicator*

03 rya, web 04 cane, fuse, knit, lace, spin, wind 05 braid, merge, plait, tweel, twill, twist, unite 06 create, damask, make up, plight, tissue, zigzag 07 compose, entwine, inweave, texture 08 contrive 09 construct, fabricate, interlace, interwork 10 criss-cross, intercross, intertwine, interweave 11 put together

weaver

04 loom

weaver bird

04 taha 06 bishop, ox-bird, quelea 09 grenadier 10 zebra finch 11 Java sparrow

web

03 mat, net 04 knot, mesh, plot, tela, trap, vane, weft 05 skein, snare 06 tangle 07 complex, lattice, netting, network, texture, webbing 08 intrigue, lacework, mesh-work, vexillum 11 fabrication, interlacing, latticework

wed

03 wad 04 ally, fuse, join, link, yoke 05 blend, marry, merge, unify, unite, wager 06 pledge, splice 07 combine, espouse 08 coalesce, security 09 commingle 10 get hitched, get married, get spliced, interweave, take to wife, tie the knot 13 take the plunge 14 lead to the altar, lead up the aisle

wedded

06 joined, wifely 07 marital, married, nuptial, spousal 08 conjugal 09 connubial, husbandly 11 matrimonial

wedding

05 union 06 bridal, huppah, mating 07 chuppah, nuptial, wedlock 08 espousal, hymeneal, hymenean, marriage, nuptials, spousage 09 espousals, matrimony 11 epithalamic, matrimonial 15 marriage service

See also **anniversary**; **marriage**

wedge

03 fit, gad, gib, jam, key, ram 04 cram, lump, pack, push, trig 05 block, chock, chunk, cleat, crowd, force, lodge, piece, quoin, stuff, wodge 06 cotter, scotch, thrust 07 blaster, feather, squeeze 08 doorstop, triangle 09 space band, whipstock

wedlock

05 union 08 marriage 09 matrimony 13 holy matrimony

Wednesday

03 Wed 04 Weds

wee

03 pee, sma 04 leak, tiny 05 small, teeny, urine, weeny 06 little, midget, minute, teensy 07 urinate 09 itsy-bitsy, miniature, minuscule 10 diminutive, negligible, teeny-weeny 11 Lilliputian, microscopic 13 insignificant

weed

03 hoe 04 tare

Weeds include:

03 ers
04 dock, moss
05 daisy, vetch
06 fat hen, oxalis, spurge, yarrow
07 bracken, ragweed, ribwort
08 bindweed, duckweed, knapweed, self-heal
09 chickweed, coltsfoot, dandelion, ground ivy, groundsel, horsetail, knotgrass, liverwort, pearlwort, snakeweed, speedwell, sun spurge
10 cinquefoil, common reed, couch grass, curled dock, deadnettle, sow thistle, thale cress
11 ground elder, meadow grass, petty spurge, salad burnet, white clover
12 annual nettle, rough hawkbit, sheep's sorrel
13 common burdock, field wood rush, large bindweed, pineapple weed, small bindweed
14 common plantain, shepherd's purse
15 broad-leaved dock, burnet saxifrage, common chickweed, creeping thistle, greater plantain,

lesser celandine, perennial nettle, stemless thistle

See also **cannabis**; **seaweed**; **tobacco**

• weed out
05 purge **06** remove **07** isolate, root out **08** get rid of **09** eliminate, eradicate, extirpate

weedkiller
06 diquat **08** atrazine, Paraquat®, simazine **09** herbicide, weedicide **10** glyphosate **11** glufosinate, graminicide **14** sodium chlorate

weedy
03 wet **04** puny, thin, weak **05** frail, lanky, wussy **06** feeble, skinny **07** insipid, scrawny, wimpish **08** gangling **09** weak-kneed **10** undersized

week
01 w **03** ouk **04** oulk

weekly
09 by the week, every week, once a week **10** hebdomadal **11** hebdomadary **12** hebdomadally

weep
03 cry, sob **04** bawl, blub, drip, leak, moan, ooze, pipe, rain, seep, wail **05** droop, exude, greet, mourn, whine **06** beweep, boo-hoo, greete, grieve, lament, snivel **07** blubber, outweep, whimper **09** be in tears, shed tears **11** pipe your eye

weepy
04 oozy **05** teary **06** crying, labile **07** sobbing, tearful, weeping **08** greeting, sob-stuff **09** melodrama **10** blubbering, lachrymose, tear-jerker **11** sentimental

weigh
03 sit, way **04** ride **05** loose, poise, raise, scale, worry **06** burden, ponder **07** afflict, balance, depress, examine, get down, oppress, perpend, trouble **08** bear down, consider, evaluate, mull over, unanchor **09** disanchor, ponderate, reflect on, think over **10** deliberate, meditate on **11** contemplate **13** have a weight of **14** tip the scales at

• weigh down
04 load **05** pease, peaze, peise, peize, peyse, poise, worry **06** burden **07** afflict, depress, get down, oppress, trouble **08** bear down, outweigh, overload **09** press down, weigh upon

• weigh up
05 scale **06** assess, ponder, size up **07** balance, compare, discuss, examine **08** chew over, consider, evaluate, mull over **09** think over **10** deliberate **11** contemplate

weighing machine
04 tron **05** trone **06** bismar **09** steelyard

weight
01 w **02** wt **03** agw, gvw **04** bias, bulk, duty, gr wt, last, lead, load, mark, mass, nt wt, onus, pith, sway, tare **05** angle, clout, flesh, force, pease, peaze, peise, peize, peyse, poise, power, slang, slant, twist, value, wecht, worry **06** burden, impact, moment, scales, slight, strain **07** ballast, gravity, oppress, plummet, tonnage, trouble **08** gravitas, handicap, live load, poundage, pressure, quantity **09** authority, heaviness, influence, prejudice, substance, unbalance, weigh down **10** importance, importancy, ponderance, ponderancy **11** avoirdupois, consequence, encumbrance **12** significance **13** consideration, preponderance **14** impressiveness, responsibility

See also **boxing**

• unit of weight
01 g, k, l, t **02** as, cg, ct, dg, gm, gr, hg, kg, lb, mg, oz, st **03** cwt, grt, kat, kin, kip, mna, oke, tod, ton, wey **04** boll, gram, kati, khat, kilo, mina, obol, pood, rotl, seer, tola, unce **05** candy, carat, catty, kandy, katti, liang, maneh, maund, ounce, picul, pikul, pound, stone, tical, todde, tonne **06** candie, carrat, cental, denier, dirhem, fother, gramme, kantar, shekel, talent **07** centner, lispund, scruple **08** decigram, lispound **09** centigram, milligram **10** decigramme **11** centigramme, milligramme

weightless
04 airy **05** light **11** imponderous **13** insubstantial

weighty
05 bulky, grave, great, heavy, hefty, solid, vital **06** severe, solemn, taxing **07** crucial, massive, onerous, pesante, serious **08** critical, exacting, pregnant, worrying **09** demanding, difficult, important, momentous, ponderous **10** burdensome **11** influential, significant, substantial **13** authoritative, consequential

weir
03 pen **04** wear **05** cauld, garth, guard **06** lasher **07** ward off **09** fish-garth

weird
◇ *anagram indicator*
03 odd, rum **04** doom, eery, fate **05** charm, eerie, queer, spell, witch **06** creepy, far-out, spooky, way-out, weyard **07** bizarre, destine, ghostly, strange, uncanny, weyward **08** eldritch, forewarn, freakish, peculiar, witching **09** grotesque, happening, left-field, unearthly, unnatural **10** mysterious **12** supernatural **13** preternatural

weirdly
06 eerily **08** spookily **09** bizarrely, strangely **11** unnaturally **12** mysteriously **14** supernaturally

weirdo
03 dag, nut **04** card, case, cure, geek, kook, loon, wack **05** crank, flake, freak, loony **06** nutter **07** cupcake, dingbat, nutcase, oddball, odd fish **08** crackpot **09** character, eccentric, fruitcake, queer fish **14** fish out of water

welcome
◇ *containment indicator*
04 free, hail, meet **05** greet **06** accept, salute **07** acclaim, embrace, karanga, popular, powhiri, proface, receive **08** glad hand, greeting, haeremai, pleasant, pleasing **09** agreeable, approve of, ben venuto, desirable, gratulate, reception, red carpet **10** acceptable, acceptance, delightful, gratifying, refreshing, salutation, salutatory **11** acclamation, appreciated, hospitality **13** be pleased with **15** be satisfied with

welcoming
04 cosy, warm **06** genial, hearty **07** affable, cordial, earnest **08** amicable, cheerful, friendly, homelike, pleasant, relaxing, sociable **09** agreeable, gemütlich, heartfelt, open-armed **10** hospitable **11** comfortable, stimulating, warm-hearted **12** affectionate, invigorating, wholehearted

weld
04 bind, bond, fuse, join, link, pile, seal, seam, wald **05** braze, joint, seize, unite, wield **06** cement, solder **07** connect **09** dyer's-weed **10** mignonette, yellow-weed **11** dyer's rocket **15** dyer's-yellowweed

welfare
04 good, heal, weal **05** hayle, state **06** health, income, profit **07** benefit, comfort, fortune, payment, pension, sick pay, success **08** interest, security **09** advantage, allowance, happiness, soundness, wellbeing **10** commonweal, prosperity **14** social security

well
02 my, OK, so **03** eye, far, fit, jet, lor, sae, spa **04** ably, bien, eddy, fine, flow, font, good, gush, ooze, pool, pour, rise, rush, seep, weel **05** aweel, fitly, flood, fount, fully, good-o, issue, lucky, right, sound, spout, spurt, surge, swell, wally **06** atweel, cavity, deeply, easily, fairly, geyser, good-oh, highly, kindly, proper, robust, source, spring, stream, strong, supply, warmly **07** adeptly, clearly, closely, cockpit, fortune, greatly, happily, healthy, luckily, Mickery, rightly, spouter, trickle **08** all right, brim over, decently, expertly, fountain, genially, pleasing, probably, properly, suitably, thriving, very much, wellhead **09** advisable, agreeable, agreeably, carefully, certainly, correctly, fittingly, fortunate, glowingly, reservoir, skilfully, to a wonder, water hole **10** able-bodied, abundantly, adequately, admiringly, completely, favourably, generously, hospitably, intimately, pleasantly, profoundly, rigorously, splendidly, thoroughly, very likely, wellspring **11** approvingly, comfortable, comfortably,

competently, conceivably, effectively, efficiently, excellently, flourishing, fortunately, intensively **12** considerably, conveniently, in good health, proficiently, prosperously, satisfactory, successfully, sufficiently, watering hole **13** hale and hearty, industriously, quite possibly, substantially, weeping spring **14** satisfactorily, to a great extent **15** comprehensively

• **as well**

03 als, and, tae, too **04** also, both **06** to boot **07** besides **08** moreover **10** in addition **11** furthermore **14** into the bargain

• **as well as**

09 along with, including **12** in addition to, not to mention, over and above, together with **14** to say nothing of

• **well done**

04 euge **05** bravo **06** encore, hurrah **08** congrats, good show **13** à la bonne heure **15** congratulations

well-advised

04 wise **05** sound **06** shrewd **07** politic, prudent **08** sensible **09** judicious, sagacious **10** far-sighted, reasonable **11** circumspect, long-sighted

well-balanced

04 even, sane **05** level, sober, sound **06** sorted, stable **08** balanced, rational, sensible, together **10** harmonious, reasonable **11** level-headed, symmetrical, well-ordered **12** well-adjusted

well-behaved

04 good **06** polite, orderly **08** mannerly, obedient **09** compliant **10** good as gold, respectful **11** considerate, co-operative **12** under control, well-mannered

wellbeing

04 good **06** health, wealth **07** comfort, welfare **09** eudaemony, happiness **10** eudaemonia, good health

well-bred

05 civil **06** polite, urbane **07** gallant, genteel, refined **08** cultured, ladylike, mannerly **09** courteous **10** cultivated, upper-crust **11** blue-blooded, comme il faut, gentlemanly **12** aristocratic, well-mannered **13** well-brought-up

well-built

05 beefy, burly, stout **06** brawny, strong, sturdy **08** muscular **09** strapping

well-deserved

03 due **04** just, meet **07** condign, merited **08** deserved, rightful **09** justified **11** appropriate

well-disposed

06 toward **07** healthy **08** amicable, friendly, towardly **09** agreeable, well-aimed **10** benevolent, favourable, well-minded, well-placed **11** sympathetic **12** well-arranged

well-dressed

04 chic, neat, tidy, trim **05** natty, smart **06** dapper, spruce **07** elegant, stylish **11** fashionable, well-groomed

well-founded

03 fit **05** right, sound, valid **06** proper **08** sensible **09** plausible, warranted **10** acceptable, reasonable **11** justifiable, sustainable

well-groomed

04 neat, tidy, trim **05** smart **06** dapper, soigné, spruce **07** soignée **11** well-dressed **13** well-turned-out

well-heeled

04 oofy, posh, rich **05** flush, solid **06** fat-cat, loaded **07** moneyed, opulent, wealthy, well-off **08** affluent, well-to-do **10** filthy rich, prosperous **11** comfortable, made of money, rolling in it, substantial **12** stinking rich

well-informed

02 up **06** au fait, sussed **07** clued-up **09** au courant

well-known

04 name **05** famed, noted, usual **06** common, famous, notour, of note **07** eminent, notable **08** familiar, renowned **09** notorious **10** celebrated, proverbial **11** illustrious, widely-known

well-mannered

05 civil **06** polite, urbane **07** gallant, genteel, refined **08** cultured, ladylike, mannerly, well-bred **09** bien élevé, courteous **10** cultivated, upper-crust **11** blue-blooded, gentlemanly **12** aristocratic, house-trained **13** well-brought-up

well-nigh

05 welly **06** all but, almost, nearly **09** just about, virtually **11** practically

well-off

04 bein, bien, rich **05** flush, lucky **06** loaded, monied **07** moneyed, wealthy **08** affluent, thriving, well-to-do **09** fortunate **10** filthy rich, forehanded, in the money, prosperous, successful, well-heeled **11** comfortable, made of money, rolling in it **12** stinking rich **15** with money to burn

well-read

07 studied **08** cultured, educated, lettered, literate **12** well-informed **13** knowledgeable

Wells

02 HG

well-spoken

05 clear **06** fluent **08** coherent, eloquent **10** articulate **13** well-expressed

well-thought-of

07 admired, revered **08** esteemed, honoured **09** respected, venerated **10** looked up to **14** highly regarded

well-to-do

04 oofy, posh, rich, warm **05** flush **06** fat-cat, loaded **07** moneyed, wealthy, well-off **08** affluent **10** filthy rich, prosperous **11** comfortable, made of money, rolling in it, substantial **12** stinking rich

well-versed

02 up **06** au fait **07** trained **08** deep-read, familiar **10** acquainted, conversant **11** experienced **13** knowledgeable

well-wisher

03 fan **06** friend **09** supporter **10** well-willer **11** sympathizer

well-worn

04 worn **05** corny, stale, stock, tired, trite **06** frayed, ragged, shabby **07** cliché'd, scruffy, worn-out **08** clichéed, overused, timeworn **09** hackneyed **10** threadbare, unoriginal **11** commonplace, stereotyped **13** battle-scarred

welsh

01 W **02** do **05** cheat **06** diddle **07** defraud, swindle

Welsh first names include:

03 Dai, Huw, Nye, Wyn
04 Aled, Alun, Ceri, Dewi, Enid, Eryl, Evan, Glyn, Gwen, Gwyn, Ifor, Ioan, Owen, Rees, Rhys, Siôn
05 Carys, Cerys, Dilys, Dylan, Elwyn, Emlyn, Emrys, Ffion, Gavin, Haydn, Howel, Hywel, Idris, Ieuan, Lloyd, Madoc, Megan, Nerys, Olwen, Olwin, Olwyn, Rhian, Tudor
06 Dafydd, Delyth, Dilwyn, Eirian, Eirlys, Eluned, Gareth, Gaynor, Gladys, Glenda, Glenys, Glynis, Gwenda, Gwilym, Howell, Mervyn, Morgan, Olwyne
07 Aneirin, Aneurin, Bronwen, Brynmor, Eiluned, Geraint, Gwenyth, Gwillym, Gwyneth, Myfanwy, Myrddin, Peredur, Vaughan
08 Angharad, Llewelyn, Meredith, Morwenna, Rhiannon
09 Gwendolen, Gwenllian

See also **county**; **town**

welt

03 dry **04** beat, blow, lash, mark, scar, weal **05** ridge, world, wound **06** streak, stripe, wither **08** cicatrix **09** cicatrice, contusion

welter

03 web **04** mess, roll, toss, wade **05** heave, lurch, pitch **06** jumble, muddle, splash, tangle, wallow **07** smother **08** flounder, mish-mash **09** confusion **10** hotchpotch

wend *see* **Slav**

• **wend your way**

02 go **04** hike, move, plod, walk **05** amble **06** travel, trudge, wander **07** meander, proceed **08** progress **11** make your way

west

01 W **03** Mae **08** New World, Occident **10** Occidental

• **go west**
◇ *reversal indicator*
03 die **06** perish **11** be destroyed **12** be dissipated

western
01 W **06** ponent **07** westlin
10 occidental

Western Sahara
03 ESH

West Virginia
02 WV **03** W Va

wet
03 dip, wat **04** damp, dank, dram, drip, fool, jerk, moil, nerd, rain, soak, soft, sour, wash, weak, weed, weet, wimp, wuss **05** bewet, cissy, douse, flood, humid, idiot, imbue, madid, moist, muggy, rainy, softy, soggy, soppy, spray, steep, swamp, sweat, tipsy, wally, water, weedy **06** beweep, clammy, daggle, dampen, drench, drippy, effete, embrue, feeble, imbrue, liquid, madefy, slippy, sloppy, sluice, soaked, sodden, soused, splash, spongy, watery **07** debauch, draggle, drizzle, embrewe, milksop, moisten, pouring, raining, showery, soaking, sopping, squidgy, tearful, teeming, wetness, wimpish **08** bedabble, bedrench, dampness, drenched, dripping, humidity, irrigate, moisture, pathetic, saturate, slippery, sprinkle, timorous, weakling, wringing **09** drizzling, irriguous, moistness, saturated, spineless **10** clamminess, imbruement, irresolute, namby-pamby, sopping wet **11** ineffective, ineffectual, madefaction, waterlogged
12 condensation

• **wet behind the ears**
03 new, raw **05** green, naive **06** callow
08 gullible, immature, innocent
09 untrained **13** inexperienced

• **wet patch** *see* **sea**

wetness
03 wet **04** damp **05** water **06** liquid
08 dampness, dankness, humidity, moisture **09** sogginess **10** clamminess, rising damp, soddenness
12 condensation

whack
03 box, cut, hit, lot, rap **04** bang, bash, beat, belt, biff, blow, cuff, part, slap, sock **05** clout, quota, share, smack, stint, thump **06** buffet, murder, strike, stroke, thrash, wallop **07** attempt, clobber, portion, rake-off **08** division **09** allowance, parcel out **10** allocation, percentage, proportion **14** slice of the cake

whacking
04 huge, mega, vast **05** giant, gross, jumbo **07** beating, immense, mammoth, massive, socking, Titanic, whaling **08** almighty, colossal, enormous, gigantic, great big, plonking, whopping **09** ginormous, humongous, monstrous, thrashing, walloping **10** astronomic, gargantuan, large-scale, prodigious, stupendous, tremendous **11** God-almighty
12 considerable

whale
05 Cetus **06** thrash

Whales include:

03 fin, orc, sei
04 blue, grey, orca
05 black, minke, pigmy, piked, pilot, right, sperm, white
06 baleen, beaked, beluga, caa'ing, finner, killer
07 bowhead, dolphin, finback, grampus, Layard's, narwhal, rorqual, toothed
08 humpback, porpoise
09 Greenland, grindhval, razorback, whalebone
10 bottlenose, humpbacked
11 bottle-nosed, false killer
12 river dolphin, strap-toothed
13 common rorqual, Risso's dolphin, sulphur-bottom
15 gangetic dolphin, harbour porpoise

wharf
03 kay, key **04** dock, pier, quay **05** jetty
06 marina, staith **07** staithe
08 dockyard, quayside **12** landing-stage

what
02 eh, my

what's-its-name
05 gismo, thing **06** doings, doodad, doodah, doofus, jigger, thingy
07 doobrey, doobrie, whatnot, whatsit
08 thingamy **09** doohickey, jigamaree, jiggumbob, thingummy, timenoguy
12 thingummybob, thingummyjig
14 what-d'you-call-it
15 whatchamacallit

wheat
04 corn **05** durum, emmer, fitch, rivet, spelt **06** bulgur, sharps **07** bulghur, einkorn **08** amelcorn, semolina, Triticum

wheedle
03 cog **04** blag, coax, draw **05** carny, charm, court **06** cajole, carney, cozy up, cuiter, entice, induce, phrase, whilly **07** beguile, flatter, tweedle, win over **08** butter up, inveigle, persuade, soft-soap, talk into **09** sweet-talk, whillywha **10** whillywhaw

wheel
◇ *reversal indicator*
04 disc, hoop, reel, ring, roam, roll, spin, turn **05** dolly, orbit, pivot, ratch, rhomb, snail, swing, truck, twirl, whirl **06** circle, dollar, gyrate, roller, rotate, sheave, swivel, wander **07** bicycle, go round, refrain, revolve, trindle, trochus, trolley, truckle **08** encircle, gyration, rotation, tricycle **10** revolution

Wheels include:

03 big, cog, fly
04 buff, cart, gear, idle, mill, worm
05 bedel, bevel, crown, drive, idler, sakia, wagon, water
06 castor, charka, escape, Ferris, paddle, prayer, sakieh
07 balance, driving, fortune, potter's, ratchet, sakiyeh
08 roulette, spinning, sprocket, spur gear, steering
09 Catherine
13 spinning jenny, throwing table, whirling-table

• **at the wheel**
07 driving, turning **08** in charge, steering **09** at the helm, directing, heading up, in command, in control
11 responsible **14** behind the wheel

wheeze
03 gag **04** gasp, hiss, idea, joke, pant, plan, ploy, rasp, ruse **05** antic, cough, crack, prank, story, stunt, trick, whiss
06 scheme **07** whaisle, whaizle, whistle, wrinkle **08** anecdote, chestnut, one-liner **11** catchphrase
13 practical joke

whelp
03 cub, pup **05** puppy **07** brachet
08 bratchet

whereabouts
04 site **05** place **08** location, position, vicinity **09** situation

wherewithal
04 cash, dosh, loot **05** brass, bread, dough, funds, gravy, lolly, means, money, ready, smash **06** greens, moolah, stumpy **07** capital, readies, scratch, shekels **08** greenies, supplies
09 megabucks, necessary, resources
11 spondulicks

whet
04 edge, file, hone, stir **05** grind, preen, rouse **06** arouse, awaken, excite, incite, kindle, stroke **07** provoke, quicken, sharpen **08** appetize, increase
09 stimulate, titillate **11** scythe-stone

whiff
04 gust, hint, puff, reek **05** aroma, blast, cigar, jiffy, odour, scent, smell, sniff, stink, touch, trace **06** breath, inhale, stench **07** draught, glimpse, soupçon **09** cigarette, suspicion
10 suggestion

while
02 as **04** span, time, when **05** spell, throw, until **06** period, season
07 stretch, whereas **08** although, interval **09** the whilst **13** in the middle of

• **while away**
03 use **04** pass **05** spend, use up
06 devote, occupy

whim
03 fad, toy **04** flam, idea, kink, swim, urge **05** crank, craze, fancy, flisk, freak, quirk **06** humour, maggot, megrim, notion, vagary, whimsy **07** caprice, conceit, impulse, passion, whimsey
08 crotchet **11** whigmaleery
12 whigmaleerie

whimper
03 cry, sob **04** mewl, moan, pule, weep **05** groan, whine **06** snivel, whinge **07** grizzle, sniffle

whimsical
03 fay, fey, fie, odd **05** dotty, droll, fairy, funny, queer, weird **06** quaint, quirky, whimsy **07** baroque, curious, playful, toysome, unusual **08** fanciful, peculiar **09** crotchety, eccentric, fantastic, impulsive **10** capricious, crotcheted **11** Disneyesque, fantastical, mischievous **13** unpredictable

whimsy
03 odd **04** tick, whim **05** droll, funny, weird **06** fisgig, fizgig, quaint, quirky **07** curious, playful, unusual **08** fanciful, peculiar **09** eccentric, whimsical **10** changeable **13** unpredictable

whine
03 cry, sob **04** beef, carp, moan, pule, wail **05** bleat, gripe, groan **06** grouch, grouse, kvetch, peenge, whinge, yammer **07** grizzle, grumble, wheenge, whimper **08** complain **09** bellyache, complaint

whinge
04 beef, carp, moan **05** greet, gripe, groan, winge **06** grouse, peenge **07** grumble, wheenge **08** complain **09** bellyache, complaint

whip
◇ *anagram indicator*
03 cat, fly, mix, tan, tat, taw **04** beat, belt, cane, crop, dart, dash, firk, flay, flit, flog, goad, hide, jerk, lash, prod, pull, push, rush, spur, stir, tear, urge, whap, whop, yank **05** birch, braid, drive, flash, knout, outdo, quirt, rouse, steal, strap, swish, thong, whack, whang, whisk **06** beat up, breech, defeat, driver, feague, incite, larrup, prompt, punish, snatch, switch, thrash, wallop **07** agitate, chabouk, cowhide, instant, kurbash, overlay, provoke, rawhide, scourge, sjambok **08** ash-plant, bullwhip, chastise, coachman, kourbash, overcast, vapulate **09** bullwhack, castigate, coachwhip, flagellum, horsewhip, instigate, longe whip, lunge whip, stock whip **10** black snake, discipline, flagellate, riding-crop **11** hunting-crop, hunting-whip, lunging whip, overcasting **13** cat-o'-nine-tails

• **whip up**
◇ *anagram indicator*
04 beat **06** arouse, excite, foment, incite, kindle, stir up, work up **07** agitate, inflame, provoke, psych up **09** instigate, stimulate

whippersnapper
03 imp **05** scamp **06** nipper, rascal **07** upstart, whiffet **08** whipster **09** pipsqueak, scallywag **11** hobbledehoy **14** snipper-snapper

whipping
05 knout **06** caning, defeat, hiding, laldie **07** beating, belting, lashing, tanning **08** birching, flogging, spanking **09** scourging, thrashing, walloping **10** punishment **11** castigation, overcasting **12** flagellation

whirl
◇ *anagram indicator*
04 daze, eddy, reel, roll, spin, tirl, turn **05** pivot, round, swing, swirl, twirl, twist, waltz, wheel **06** bustle, circle, flurry, gyrate, hubbub, jumble, muddle, rotate, series, swivel, tumult, uproar **07** revolve **08** gyration, rotation **09** agitation, commotion, confusion, giddiness, pirouette, turn round **10** hurly-burly, revolution, succession **12** circumgyrate, merry-go-round

• **give something a whirl**
03 try **06** strive **07** attempt, have a go, venture **09** endeavour, have a bash, have a lash, have a shot, have a stab **10** have a crack **11** give it a burl

whirlpool
04 eddy, gulf, weal, weel, weil, wiel **05** gurge **06** vortex **08** sea purse, swelchie **09** Charybdis, maelstrom

whirlwind
04 eddy, rash **05** babel, chaos, hasty, noise, quick, rapid, swift **06** bedlam, furore, hubbub, speedy, tumult, typhon, uproar, vortex **07** anarchy, clamour, cyclone, tornado, turmoil, typhoon **08** headlong, madhouse **09** commotion, confusion, impetuous, impulsive, lightning, sand-devil **10** hullabaloo, tourbillon **11** pandemonium, tourbillion, white squall

whisk
◇ *anagram indicator*
03 fly, mix, zip **04** beat, belt, bolt, bomb, dart, dash, dive, lash, pelt, race, rush, stir, tear, tuft, whid, whip, wipe **05** brush, flick, hurry, scoot, shoot, speed, sweep, swish, whist **06** beater, chowri, chowry, hasten, switch, twitch **07** panicle **09** egg beater **12** swizzle-stick

whiskey
01 W

whisky
04 dram, half **05** hooch **06** hootch **08** the grain **09** aqua vitae, good stuff, the cratur **10** barley-bree, barley-broo, usquebaugh **11** barley-broth, mountain dew, the Auld Kirk, water of life

Whiskies include:

03 rye
04 malt
06 poteen, red-eye, Scotch
07 blended, Bourbon, potheen, spunkie
08 peat-reek, sour mash
09 moonshine
10 cornbrandy, corn whisky, single malt, tanglefoot
12 the real McCoy
13 the real Mackay
14 chain lightning, tarantula juice

whisper
03 bur **04** burr, buzz, hark, hint, hiss, sigh **05** round, sough, tinge, trace, whiff **06** breath, gossip, mumble, murmur, mutter, report, rumour, rustle, tittle, whisht **07** breathe, divulge, soupçon, wheesht **08** innuendo, intimate, low voice, susurrus **09** insinuate, soft voice, suspicion, susurrate, undertone **10** quiet voice, say quietly, suggestion **11** insinuation, pig's whisper **12** speak quietly, stage whisper **14** whittie-whattie

whistle
04 call, ping, pipe, sing, song, sowf **05** cheep, chirp, siren, sowff, sowth, whiss **06** hooter, siffle, throat, warble **07** catcall, summons, tweedle, warbler, wheeple **09** quail-call, quail-pipe

whit
03 bit, jot, rap **04** atom, dash, drop, fico, haet, ha'it, hate, hoot, iota, mite, snap, spot **05** aught, crumb, grain, piece, pinch, point, scrap, shred, speck, straw, trace **06** little **07** modicum, red cent **08** fragment, particle

white
03 wan **04** hoar, leuc-, leuk-, pale, pure **05** ashen, hoary, leuco-, leuko-, light, moral, pasty, waxen **06** albino, bright, honest, pallid **07** albumen, anaemic, niveous, upright **08** innocent, reliable, spotless, virtuous **09** blameless, bloodless, burnished, stainless, undefiled **10** auspicious, colourless, favourable, honourable, immaculate **11** transparent, unblemished, unburnished **12** light-skinned

Whites include:

04 ecru, grey, lily, opal, whey
05 cream, ivory, milky, snowy
06 argent, creamy, pearly, silver
08 magnolia
09 champagne, lily-white, snow-white
11 silver-white

white-collar
06 office **08** clerical, salaried **09** executive, non-manual **12** professional

whiten
03 cam **04** calm, caum, fade, pale, snow **06** blanch, bleach **08** dealbate, etiolate, pipeclay **09** whitewash

whitewash
04 beat, best, drub, -gate, hide, lick **05** crush, paste **06** granny, hammer, thrash **07** clobber, conceal, cover up, cover-up, grannie, trounce **08** suppress **09** calcimine, deception, gloss over, Kalsomine® **10** camouflage **11** concealment, make light of **13** defeat utterly

whittle
03 cut, hew, use **04** fret, pare, trim **05** carve, erode, peach, shape, shave, use up **06** reduce, scrape **07** blanket, consume, eat away **08** diminish, wear away **09** undermine

whole
03 all, fit, lot, sum **04** full, hale, mint, unit, well **05** piece, sound, total, uncut **06** entire, entity, healed, intact, strong, unhurt **07** healthy, perfect
08 complete, ensemble, entirety, fullness, integral, sum total, totality, unbroken, unedited, unharmed
09 aggregate, inviolate, undamaged, undivided, uninjured **10** altogether, completely, everything, in one piece, unabridged **11** full-blooded
• **on the whole**
06 mostly **07** as a rule **08** all in all
09 generally, in general, in the main
10 by and large **13** predominantly
14 for the most part

wholehearted
04 real, true, warm **06** hearty
07 devoted, earnest, genuine, sincere, zealous **08** complete, emphatic
09 committed, dedicated, heartfelt, unfeigned **10** passionate, unreserved, unstinting **11** boots and all, unqualified
12 enthusiastic

wholeheartedly
06 warmly **08** heartily **09** genuinely, sincerely **10** completely
12 emphatically, passionately, unreservedly

wholesale
04 mass **05** broad, great, total **06** en bloc **07** in gross, massive, totally
08 outright, sweeping **09** extensive, massively **11** extensively, far-reaching, wide-ranging **12** all-inclusive
13 comprehensive **14** indiscriminate
15 comprehensively

wholesome
04 good, pure **05** clean, moral, sound, sweet **06** decent, proper **07** bracing, ethical, healthy, helpful, holesom
08 edifying, healsome, holesome, hygienic, physical, remedial, salutary, sanitary, sensible, virtuous
09 healthful, improving, righteous, uplifting **10** beneficial, healthsome, honourable, nourishing, nutritious, propitious, reasonable, refreshing, salubrious **11** respectable
12 invigorating, squeaky-clean

wholly
03 all **04** only **05** clear, fully, quite **06** in toto, purely **07** sheerly, totally, utterly
08 entirely **09** perfectly, tout à fait
10 absolutely, altogether, completely, thoroughly **11** exclusively **14** in every respect **15** comprehensively

whoop
02 ho! **03** cry **04** hoop, hoot, roar, yell
05 cheer, shout **06** holler, hurrah, scream, shriek

whopper
03 fib, lie **05** fable, giant, whale
07 cracker, mammoth, monster, plumper, slapper, stonker, swapper, swinger, swopper, untruth
08 colossus, scrouger **09** falsehood, leviathan, tall story **10** fairy story, socdolager, sogdolager **11** fabrication, sockdolager, sockdoliger, sockdologer
12 hippopotamus, slockdolager
See also **lie**

whopping
03 big **04** huge, mega, vast **05** giant, great, jumbo, large **07** immense, mammoth, massive, whaling
08 almighty, enormous, gigantic, great big, plonking, slapping, whacking
09 ginormous, humongous, thrashing, walloping **10** monumental, prodigious, staggering, tremendous **11** God-almighty **13** extraordinary

whore
03 pro, pug, tom **04** bawd, dell, drab, hoor, moll, punk, road, stew, tart
05 brass, broad, quail, quiff, stale, tramp, trull, wench **06** bulker, callet, geisha, harlot, hooker, mutton, plover
07 cocotte, floozie, hetaera, hostess, hustler, lorette, Paphian, pinnace, polecat, rent-boy, trollop, venture
08 bona-roba, callgirl, dolly-mop, magdalen, strumpet **09** courtesan, hierodule, loose fish **10** cockatrice, convertite, fancy woman, loose woman, prostitute, rough trade, vizard-mask **11** fallen woman, fille de joie, laced mutton, night-walker, poule de luxe, public woman, working girl
12 fille des rues, scarlet woman, street-walker **13** grande cocotte **14** lady of the night, woman of the town
See also **prostitute**

whorehouse
03 kip **04** crib, stew **06** bagnio, bordel
07 brothel, Corinth **08** bordello, cathouse, hothouse, red light
10 bawdy-house, flash-house
12 knocking-shop, leaping-house
13 sporting house, vaulting-house
14 house of ill fame **15** disorderly house

whorl
04 coil, loop, turn **05** helix, twirl, twist
06 spiral, volute, vortex **07** calicle, calycle, corolla **08** calycule, gyration, verticil, volution **09** corkscrew
11 convolution

wicked
◇ *anagram indicator*
03 ace, bad, def, fab, ill, rad **04** cool, evil, foul, mean, mega, neat, vile, wick
05 awful, boffo, brill, cruel, felon, nasty, wrong **06** divine, fierce, groovy, guilty, impish, severe, sinful, unholy, unkind, way-out **07** amazing, corrupt, crucial, debased, harmful, heinous, immoral, intense, naughty, radical, roguish, ungodly, unlucky, vicious **08** clinking, depraved, devilish, dreadful, fabulous, heavenly, perverse, rascally, shameful, spiteful, stonking, terrible, terrific **09** abandoned, admirable, atrocious, brilliant, difficult, dissolute, egregious, excellent, fantastic, felonious, high-viced, injurious, miscreant, nefarious, offensive, scelerate, worthless **10** abominable, evil-minded, facinorous, flagitious, iniquitous, not half bad, scandalous, unpleasant, villainous **11** distressing, facinerious, mischievous, sensational, the business, troublesome, unrighteous **12** black-hearted, second to none, unprincipled **14** out of this world

wickedness
03 ill, sin **04** evil **06** naught **07** impiety, pravity, villany **08** atrocity, enormity, evilness, foulness, iniquity, vileness, villainy **09** amorality, depravity, reprobacy **10** corruption, immorality, sinfulness **11** abomination, corruptness, heinousness
12 devilishness, fiendishness, shamefulness **13** dissoluteness
15 unrighteousness

wickerwork
05 ratan **06** rattan, wattle, wicker
10 basket-work, wattle-work

wide
01 w **04** full, vast, wily **05** ample, baggy, broad, fully, great, loose, roomy
06 astray, astute, remote **07** dilated, distant, general, immense
08 expanded, extended, spacious
09 all the way, capacious, extensive, off course, off target **10** completely, off the mark **11** far-reaching, wide-ranging
12 latitudinous **13** comprehensive
15 to the full extent

wide-awake
04 keen, wary **05** alert, aware, sharp
06 astute, roused **07** heedful, wakened
08 vigilant, watchful **09** conscious, observant, on the ball **10** fully awake, on the alert, on your toes **11** quick-witted **12** on the qui vive

wide-eyed
04 open **05** dazed, frank, fresh, naive
06 amazed, simple **07** angelic, artless, natural, shocked, stunned **08** dewy-eyed, gullible, innocent, open-eyed, startled, trustful, trusting
09 astounded, childlike, credulous, guileless, ingenuous, staggered, surprised, unworldly **10** astonished, bewildered, bowled over, confounded, gobsmacked, taken aback
11 dumbfounded, open-mouthed
12 lost for words, unsuspecting
13 flabbergasted, inexperienced, knocked for six, thunderstruck
15 unsophisticated

widely
07 broadly **09** generally **11** extensively
15 comprehensively

widen
06 dilate, expand, extend, flanch, let out, spread **07** broaden, distend, enlarge, flaunch, stretch **08** increase

wide-open
04 open, wide **06** gaping, spread
07 exposed **09** outspread
10 vulnerable **11** defenceless, susceptible, unfortified, unprotected
12 outstretched

wide-ranging
05 broad **08** sweeping, thorough **09** extensive, important, momentous, universal **10** widespread **11** far-reaching, scattershot, significant **13** comprehensive, thoroughgoing

widespread
04 rife **05** broad **06** common, global **07** general, prolate **08** far-flung, sweeping **09** extensive, pervasive, prevalent, universal, unlimited, wholesale **10** wall-to-wall **11** far-reaching

widow
04 sati **05** widdy **06** relict, suttee **07** bereave, dowager **08** feme sole, war widow **10** grass widow **11** hempen widow **12** queen dowager

width
01 w **04** beam, span **05** girth, range, reach, scope **06** extent **07** breadth, compass, measure **08** diameter, latitude, wideness **09** amplitude, broadness, largeness, thickness **13** extensiveness

wield
03 ply, use **04** gain, have, hold, play, rule, sway, wave, weld, wild, wind **05** apply, enjoy, exert, shake, sownd, swing **06** employ, handle, manage **07** command, control, possess, utilize **08** brandish, exercise, flourish, maintain **10** manipulate

wife
01 w **02** ux **03** rib **04** dame, frau, lady, mate **05** bride, dutch, femme, queen, woman **06** missis, missus, spouse, vahine, wahine **07** consort, hostess, old lady, partner **08** helpmate, helpmeet, princess **09** child-wife, companion, concubine, first lady, other half **10** better half, her indoors, stepmother **11** little woman, sister-in-law **12** kickie-wickie, married woman **13** daughter-in-law **14** the little woman

wig
03 jiz, tie **04** gizz, jasy, jazy **05** caxon, Irish, jasey, major, scold, syrup **06** bagwig, bobwig, Brutus, peruke, tie-wig, toupee, toupet **07** buzz-wig, periwig, Ramilie, scratch, spencer **08** perruque, postiche, Ramilies, Ramillie **09** hairpiece, Ramillies **10** full-bottom, scratch-wig **14** transformation

wiggle
03 wag **04** jerk **05** shake, twist **06** jiggle, squirm, twitch, waggle, writhe **07** wriggle

wild
◇ *anagram indicator*
03 mad, shy **04** bush, daft, keen, nuts, rash **05** angry, crazy, feral, livid, messy, myall, nutty, potty, rough, rowdy, waste, weald, wield **06** absurd, barren, casual, chance, choppy, desert, ferine, fierce, fuming, gallus, raging, random, rugged, savage, stormy, unruly, untame, untidy, unwise **07** agitato, aimless, bananas, berserk, blazing, bonkers, brutish, enraged, excited, fervent, foolish, frantic, furious, gallows, lawless, natural, rampant, riotous, ropable, salvage, tousled, uncouth, unkempt, untamed, violent, wayward **08** agitated, agrestal, blustery, chimeric, demented, desolate, fanciful, forsaken, frenzied, incensed, reckless, romantic, ropeable, terrific, unbroken, uncombed, vehement, warragal, warragle, warragul, warrigal **09** agrestial, arbitrary, barbarous, enjoyable, fanatical, fantastic, ferocious, foolhardy, haphazard, hit-or-miss, imprudent, impulsive, irregular, primitive, turbulent, unsettled **10** accidental, boisterous, chimerical, disordered, disorderly, distracted, distraught, fortuitous, hopping mad, incidental, infuriated, irrational, licentious, outrageous, passionate, ridiculous **11** approximate, dishevelled, extravagant, fantastical, impractical, purposeless, tempestuous, uncivilized, uninhabited, unpopulated **12** enthusiastic, ferae naturae, inhospitable, out of control, preposterous, unconsidered, uncontrolled, uncultivated, ungovernable, unmanageable, unrestrained **13** impracticable, serendipitous, undisciplined, uninhabitable **14** beside yourself, indiscriminate, skimble-skamble, uncontrollable, undomesticated

• **run wild**
◇ *anagram indicator*
04 lamp, riot **05** feral **07** rampage

wild animal *see* **animal**

wilderness
05 waste, wilds **06** desert, jungle **09** wasteland

wild flower *see* **flower**

wildlife
05 fauna **07** animals

wildly
◇ *anagram indicator*
07 angrily, noisily **08** absurdly, casually **09** aimlessly, defiantly, foolishly, furiously, riotously **10** recklessly **11** arbitrarily, chaotically, haphazardly **12** anarchically, boisterously, outrageously, rebelliously, ridiculously **13** extravagantly, fantastically, irresponsibly **14** preposterously, uncontrollably, unmethodically, unrestrainedly

wilds
06 desert **07** outback **09** the sticks, wasteland **10** the boonies, wilderness **11** remote areas **12** the boondocks **15** the back of beyond

wiles
05 fraud, guile, ploys, ruses **06** deceit, dodges, tricks **07** cunning, devices **08** cheating, trickery **09** chicanery, deception **10** artfulness, craftiness, manoeuvres, stratagems, subterfuge **12** contrivances

wilful
06 dogged, mulish **07** planned, wayward, willing **08** contrary, obdurate, perverse, stubborn, willyard, willyart **09** conscious, obstinate, pig-headed, voluntary **10** calculated, deliberate, determined, headstrong, inflexible, refractory, self-willed, unyielding **11** intentional, intractable **12** intransigent, premeditated **14** uncompromising

will
02 'll **03** aim, way **04** lust, mind, Self, want, wish **05** fancy, leave, order **06** astray, choice, choose, compel, confer, decree, desire, devise, direct, intend, option, ordain, pass on **07** at a loss, command, feeling, purpose, require, resolve **08** attitude, bequeath, decision, hand down, pass down, pleasure, transfer, volition **09** dispose of, intention, testament, willpower **10** bewildered, discretion, preference, resolution **11** disposition, inclination, prerogative **13** determination **14** purposefulness

William
02 Wm **04** Bill, Will **05** Billy, Willy

willing
02 on **04** game, glad, keen **05** eager, happy, prone, ready **06** chosen **07** content, pleased, up for it **08** amenable, biddable, disposed, inclined, prepared, so-minded **09** agreeable, compliant, volitient, voluntary **10** consenting, favourable **11** co-operative, intentional **12** enthusiastic, well-disposed

willingly
04 leve, lief, soon **05** lieve **06** freely, gladly **07** eagerly, happily, readily **08** by choice, in a hurry **09** like a shot **10** cheerfully **11** voluntarily **12** nothing loath **14** unhesitatingly

willingness
04 will, wish **06** desire, favour **07** consent **08** volition **09** agreement, readiness **10** compliance, enthusiasm **11** disposition, inclination **12** complaisance **13** agreeableness

will-o'-the-wisp
06 min min **07** fen-fire, spunkie **08** wildfire **09** nightfire **11** fatuous fire, ignis fatuus **12** Jack-o'-lantern **13** friar's lantern

willow
04 sale, seal **05** osier, salix, sauch, saugh, withy **06** sallow

willowy
04 slim, tall **05** lithe **06** limber, lissom, supple, svelte **07** slender **08** flexible, graceful **09** lithesome, sylph-like

willpower
04 grit, will **05** drive **07** resolve **10** commitment, doggedness,

resolution **11** persistence, self-command, self-control, self-mastery **13** determination **14** self-discipline, strength of will

willy-nilly
08 by chance, perforce, randomly **10** carelessly **11** arbitrarily, haphazardly, irregularly, necessarily, of necessity **12** compulsorily, nolens volens **14** unmethodically

wilt
03 ebb, sag, wot **04** fade, fail, flag, flop, sink, wane, woot **05** droop, faint, taint **06** lessen, weaken, wither **07** dwindle, shrivel **08** diminish, grow less, languish

wily
03 fly, sly **04** foxy, wide **05** sharp **06** artful, astute, crafty, shifty, shrewd, tricky **07** crooked, cunning, versute **08** cheating, guileful, scheming **09** deceitful, deceptive, designing, underhand **10** intriguing, streetwise

wimp
03 wet **04** clot, drip, fool, jerk, nerd, tonk, weed, wuss **05** clown, softy, wally **07** milksop **10** namby-pamby

wimpish
03 wet **04** soft, weak **05** cissy, weedy, wussy **06** drippy, effete, feeble **08** pathetic, timorous **09** spineless **10** irresolute, namby-pamby **11** ineffective, ineffectual

win
03 get, net, pot **04** earn, gain, mine **05** carry, catch, penny, reach **06** allure, attain, effect, obtain, open up, result, secure **07** achieve, acquire, collect, conquer, mastery, prevail, procure, receive, succeed, success, triumph, victory **08** atchieve, carry off, conquest, overcome, persuade **09** come first, win the day **10** accomplish, strike gold **11** come in first, finish first, squeeze home **12** be victorious, come out on top, turn up trumps, win hands down **13** hit the jackpot, squeak through **14** achieve success

• win over
04 sway **05** bribe, charm **06** allure, engage, nobble **07** attract, buy over, convert **08** convince, persuade, win round **09** influence, talk round **10** bring round, conciliate **11** prevail upon

wince
04 jerk, jump, kick, reel **05** cower, quail, start **06** blench, cringe, flinch, recoil, roller, shrink **08** draw back **09** pull a face

wind
◇ *anagram indicator*
02 go **03** air **04** bend, burp, coil, curl, furl, gale, gust, haul, hint, loop, puff, reel, roll, turn, veer, wrap **05** blast, curve, hoist, snake, twine, twist, weave, wield **06** breath, breeze, enfold, ramble, spiral, writhe, zigzag **07** bluster, conceit, current, deviate, draught, meander, turning, wreathe, wriggle **08** encircle **10** air-current, flatulence, suggestion **12** twist and turn

Winds include:

04 berg, bise, bora, east, föhn, helm
05 Eurus, north, Notus, trade, zonda
06 Auster, Boreas, buster, doctor, El Niño, levant, samiel, simoom, zephyr
07 Aquilon, austral, chinook, cyclone, etesian, gregale, khamsin, meltemi, mistral, monsoon, pampero, sirocco, tornado, twister
08 Argestes, Favonian, Favonius, libeccio, westerly, williwaw
09 harmattan, hurricane, nor'wester, snow eater, southerly
10 Cape doctor, Euroclydon, prevailing, tramontana, wet chinook, willy-willy
11 anticyclone
15 southerly buster

• get wind of
07 learn of **08** discover **09** hear about **12** find out about **13** become aware of

• in the wind
06 likely **08** expected, probable **10** on the cards **13** about to happen

• put the wind up
05 alarm, daunt, panic, scare, spook **06** boggle, rattle **07** agitate, perturb, startle, unnerve **08** frighten **10** discourage **13** sound the alarm

• wind down
04 slow, stop **05** chill, relax **06** cool it, ease up, lessen, reduce, unwind **07** decline, dwindle, subside **08** calm down, chill out, diminish, slow down **09** hang loose, lighten up **10** slacken off, take it easy **11** come to an end, quieten down **12** bring to an end **13** let yourself go, put your feet up **14** take things easy **15** let your hair down

• wind up
03 end, kid, rib **04** fool, furl, goof, span, stop **05** anger, annoy, close, end up, hoist, tease, trick, uptie **06** excite, finish, settle **07** agitate, tighten **08** conclude, finalize, finish up, irritate **09** close down, liquidate, make fun of, terminate **10** disconcert **12** bring to an end, find yourself **13** bring to a close **15** pull someone's leg

windbag
04 bore **06** gasbag, gossip **07** blether, boaster **08** bigmouth, braggart

winded
06 puffed **07** panting **09** out of puff, puffed out **10** breathless **11** out of breath

windfall
04 find **05** manna **06** caduac **07** bonanza, godsend, jackpot **12** stroke of luck **13** treasure-trove

winding
◇ *anagram indicator*
04 mazy, turn **06** creeky, spiral **07** bending, coiling, crankle, crooked, curving, devious, sinuate, sinuous, turning, twining **08** flexuose, flexuous, indirect, sinuated, tortuous, twisting **09** meandrian, meandrous **10** circuitous, convoluted, meandering, roundabout, serpentine **11** anfractuous **12** serpentinous **14** crinkle-crankle

window
05 light **07** opening

Windows include:

03 bay, bow
04 pane, rose, sash, shop
05 oriel
06 dormer, French, lancet, louvre, Norman, screen, ticket
07 compass, lucarne, sliding
08 astragal, bull's eye, casement, fanlight, porthole, skylight
09 decorated, mullioned, patio door
10 windscreen
11 oeil-de-boeuf
12 double-glazed, early English, quarterlight, stained glass
13 double-glazing, perpendicular
14 Catherine wheel
15 secondary-glazed

windpipe
05 pipes **06** larynx, throat **07** pharynx, trachea, weasand **08** thrapple, thropple, throttle **11** weasand-pipe

windswept
04 open **05** bleak, blowy, messy, windy **06** barren, untidy **07** exposed, in a mess, ruffled, tousled, unkempt **08** desolate **09** windblown **10** disordered **11** dishevelled, unprotected, unsheltered

windward
04 luff **07** weather

• beat to windward
04 turn, work **06** laveer

• to windward
02 up **05** aloof **08** a-weather

windy
04 wild **05** blowy, gusty, nervy, timid, wordy **06** afraid, breezy, on edge, prolix, scared, stormy, turgid, uneasy **07** anxious, chicken, nervous, pompous, squally, ventose, verbose **08** blustery, rambling, stressed **09** bombastic, garrulous, windswept **10** frightened, long-winded **11** tempestuous

wine
02 en- **03** eno-, oen-, oin-, vin **04** oeno-, oino-, vino

Wines include:

03 Dão, dry, red, sec
04 Asti, brut, Cava, fino, hock, port, rosé, sack, Sekt, Tent
05 blush, bombo, Douro, Fitou, Gamay, house, Mâcon, Médoc, plonk, Rioja, Soave, straw, sweet, Syrah, table, Tavel, Tokay, tonic, white
06 Alsace, Barolo, Barsac, Beaune, canary, claret, grappa, Graves, Malaga, Malbec, Merlot, mulled, Muscat, Pontac, sherry, Shiraz
07 alicant, Amarone, Auslese, Barbera,

Bunyuls, Chablis, Chianti, Cinsaut, demi-sec, Madeira, Margaux, Marsala, moselle, oloroso, Orvieto, retsina, sangria, vintage, Vouvray
08 Alicante, Bordeaux, Brunello, bucellas, Burgundy, Carignan, Cinsault, Dolcetto, Frascati, Garnacha, Glühwein, Grenache, house red, jerepigo, Kabinett, Malvasia, Marsanne, Montilla, Muscadet, muscatel, Nebbiolo, New World, Palomino, Pauillac, Pinotage, Pornerol, Riesling, Rousanne, ruby port, Sancerre, Sauterne, Sémillon, Spätlese, Spumante, St Julien, Vermouth
09 Bardolino, Carignane, champagne, Colombard, dry sherry, fortified, Frizzante, Hermitage, Lambrusco, Langue d'Oc, Minervois, Pinot Gris, Pinot Noir, Sauternes, sparkling, St-Émilion, Tarragona, tawny port, Trebbiano, Ugni Blanc, white port, Zinfandel
10 Barbaresco, Beaujolais, Chambertin, Chardonnay, Constantia, Grignolino, house white, Manzanilla, Mateus Rosé, Monastrell, Muscadelle, Piesporter, Pinot Blanc, Sangiovese, Verdicchio, vinho verde
11 alcohol-free, amontillado, Chenin Blanc, Niersteiner, Pinot Grigio, Pouilly-Fumé, Rüdesheimer, Steinberger, sweet sherry, Tempranillo, vintage port
12 Blanc de Noirs, Côtes du Rhône, Johannisberg, medium sherry, Pedro Ximénez, Ruby Cabernet, Tinta Barroca, Valpolicella
13 Blanc de Blancs, Cabernet Franc, Château Lafite, Liebfraumilch, Montepulciano, Pouilly-Fuissé
14 Crémant d'Alsace, Crémant de Loire, Lacrima Christi, Sauvignon Blanc
15 Crozes-Hermitage, Gewürztraminer, lachryma Christi

Wine-bottle sizes include:

06 flagon, magnum
08 jeroboam, rehoboam
09 balthazar
10 methuselah, salmanazar
11 Marie-Jeanne
14 nebuchadnezzar

See also **bottle**

• **wine-grower**
05 viner **08** vigneron

wine glass
05 flute, glass **06** goblet **07** balloon **08** schooner **09** straw-stem

wing
02 el **03** ala, arm, fan, fly, set, van **04** flit, move, part, pass, race, sail, side, soar, vane, waft, zoom **05** alula, flank, flock, glide, group, hurry, penny, pinna, right, speed **06** annexe, branch, circle, flight, hasten, pinion, travel **07** adjunct, coterie, faction, section, segment **08** grouping **09** extension, liverwing **10** attachment **11** parascenium

• **wing it**
04 vamp **05** ad-lib **06** busk it **09** play by ear **11** extemporize **15** speak off the cuff

wingless
◇ *ends deletion indicator*

wink
04 pink **05** blink, eliad, flash, gleam, glint **06** eyliad, illiad, moment, second **07** connive, eyeliad, flicker, flutter, glimmer, glitter, instant, nictate, sparkle, twinkle **08** oeillade **09** nictation, nictitate **10** glimmering **11** nictitation, split second

• **wink at**
06 ignore **07** condone, neglect **08** overlook, pass over **09** disregard **14** take no notice of **15** turn a blind eye to

winkle
04 pupu, worm **05** flush, force, prise **07** draw out, extract **09** extricate

winner
03 ace, dux **05** champ **06** top dog, victor **08** champion, prizeman **09** conqueror, medallist **10** prizewoman, vanquisher **11** prizewinner, title-holder, world-beater **13** Nobel laureate

winning
02 up **05** sweet **06** lovely **07** amiable, winsome **08** alluring, charming, engaging, fetching, pleasing, unbeaten **09** beguiling, endearing **10** attractive, bewitching, conquering, delightful, enchanting, persuasive, successful, triumphant, undefeated, victorious **11** captivating, vanquishing **13** prepossessing

winnings
05 booty, gains, prize **06** prizes, spoils, velvet **07** jackpot, profits, takings **08** proceeds **10** prize money

winnow
03 fan, fly, van **04** comb, cull, flap, part, sift, sort, waft **06** divide, screen, select **07** diffuse, flutter **08** separate **09** ventilate

winsome
05 sweet **06** comely, lovely, pretty **07** amiable **08** alluring, charming, cheerful, engaging, fetching, pleasant, pleasing **09** appealing, beguiling, endearing **10** attractive, bewitching, delectable, delightful, enchanting **11** captivating **13** prepossessing

wintry
03 icy, raw **04** cold, cool **05** bleak, harsh, snowy **06** arctic, biting, chilly, dismal, frosty, frozen, hiemal, stormy **07** brumous, glacial, hostile **08** desolate, freezing, hibernal, piercing **09** cheerless **10** Decemberly, unfriendly **11** Decemberish

wipe
03 dab, dry, mop, rub **04** blow, dust, jibe, null, scar, swab **05** brand, brush, clean, clear, dicht, dight, erase, purge, scrub, sweep, swipe **06** cancel, forget, reject, remove, sponge, strike **07** cleanse, deterge, expunct, expunge, sarcasm, take off **08** absterge, get rid of, take away **09** eliminate, eradicate **12** handkerchief

• **wipe out**
03 zap **04** kill, null, raze **05** erase, purge, sweep, waste **06** efface, murder, rub out, sponge **07** abolish, blot out, destroy, expunct, expunge **08** blow away, decimate, demolish, massacre **09** eliminate, eradicate, extirpate, liquidate, polish off **10** annihilate, obliterate **11** exterminate

wire
04 bind, coil **05** cable, snare **06** aerial, needle, tip-off **07** connect, protect, support, warning **08** telegram **09** telegraph, telephone **10** pickpocket **11** information **13** finishing line

wire-pulling
04 pull **05** clout **08** intrigue, plotting, scheming **09** influence **10** conspiring **12** manipulation

wiry
04 lean, wavy **05** rough, tough **06** coarse, sinewy, strong **08** muscular

Wisconsin
02 WI **03** Wis

wisdom
05 sense **06** genius, reason, sanity **07** insight **08** learning, prudence, sagacity, sapience **09** erudition, foresight, judgement, knowledge **10** astuteness, experience **11** common sense, discernment, penetration, skilfulness, speculation **12** intelligence **13** comprehension, enlightenment, judiciousness, understanding **14** circumspection

wise
03 way **04** sage, wice **05** aware, godly, pious, sound, weise, weize, witty **06** astute, clever, manner, owlish, shrewd **07** erudite, knowing, learned, politic, prudent, sapient, skilful **08** discreet, educated, informed, rational, sensible **09** judicious, sagacious **10** discerning, far-sighted, perceptive, proficient, reasonable **11** circumspect, common-sense, enlightened, experienced, intelligent, long-sighted, well-advised **12** well-informed **13** knowledgeable, sophisticated, understanding

• **put wise**
04 tell, warn **05** alert **06** clue in, fill in, inform, notify, tip off, wise up **07** apprise **10** intimate to **15** put in the picture

• **wise man**

The Three Wise Men:

06 Caspar
08 Melchior
09 Balthasar

See also **sage**

wiseacre
03 owl **05** Solon **07** wise guy **08** wiseling **09** Gothamite, smart alec **10** clever dick **11** smartypants

wisecrack
03 gag, pun **04** barb, gibe, jest, joke, quip **05** funny **06** in-joke **08** one-liner **09** witticism

wisely
06 sagely **07** clearly, soundly **08** sensibly, shrewdly **09** advisedly, knowingly **10** rationally **11** sagaciously **12** perceptively **13** intelligently

wish
03 ask, bid, wis, yen **04** hope, know, long, lust, need, pine, urge, want, whim, will, wist **05** covet, crave, fancy, order, yearn **06** aspire, desire, direct, hanker, hunger, liking, prefer, thirst **07** believe, bewitch, bidding, command, craving, longing, request, require **08** fondness, instruct, yearning **09** hankering, recommend **10** aspiration, preference **11** inclination, instruction, malediction

• **best wishes**
04 best **08** mazeltov, well-wish **09** good-speed

wishy-washy
04 flat, pale, thin, weak **05** bland, vapid **06** feeble, sloppy, watery **07** diluted, insipid, vanilla **09** tasteless **10** namby-pamby **11** ineffective, ineffectual, watered-down **12** milk-and-water

wisp
04 lock, tuft, wase **05** flock, piece, plume, shred, twist **06** strand, thread

wispy
04 fine, thin **05** faint, frail, light **06** flimsy, slight **07** fragile **08** delicate, ethereal, gossamer, straggly **10** attenuated **13** insubstantial

wistful
03 sad **06** dreamy, intent, musing **07** earnest, forlorn, longing, pensive, wishful **08** dreaming, mournful, yearning **09** regretful **10** meditative, melancholy, reflective, thoughtful **12** disconsolate **13** contemplative

wistfully
05 sadly **09** forlornly, longingly, pensively **10** mournfully **11** plaintively **12** thoughtfully

wit
03 wag **04** know, mind, nous, salt **05** comic, joker, sense **06** banter, brains, esprit, gagman, humour, levity, reason, wisdom **07** discern, insight, marbles, sparkle **08** badinage, comedian, concetto, drollery, gumption, humorist, merum sal, repartee, sagacity, satirist **09** Attic salt, bel esprit, eutrapely, faculties, funniness, ingenuity, intellect, invention, judgement, mother wit, recognize, wittiness **10** astuteness, cleverness, eutrapelia, jocularity, liveliness, shrewdness **11** common sense, imagination, information, waggishness **12** homme d'esprit, intelligence **13** facetiousness, understanding

witch
04 mage, wich, wych **05** crone, magus **08** magician

Witches, witch doctors and wizards include:

03 hag, hex
05 Hecat, lamia, sibyl, weird
06 Hecate, magian, mganga, shaman, voodoo, wisard, zendik
07 angekok, carline, sangoma, warlock, wise man
08 angekkok, conjurer, marabout, night-hag
09 enchanter, galdragon, occultist, pythoness, sorceress, wise woman, witch-wife
10 besom-rider, craigfluke, reim-kennar
11 enchantress, gyre-carline, medicine man, necromancer, thaumaturge
12 Weird Sisters
13 thaumaturgist

Witch- and wizard-related terms include:

03 hex
04 mojo, muti, wart
05 charm, coven, goety, magic, spell, wicca
06 cackle, potion, Sabbat, voodoo, voudou
07 cantrip, gramary, hag-seed, pricker, Sabbath, sorcery
08 black art, black cat, cauldron, diablery, familiar, gramarye, pishogue, wizardry
09 diablerie, enchanted, occultism, the occult, witch's hat
10 black magic, broomstick, divination, necromancy, witchcraft
11 apotropaism, conjuration, enchantment, incantation, thaumaturgy, the black art, witch-finder
12 witching hour
14 Walpurgis night

witchcraft
03 obi **04** obia **05** magic, obeah, spell, wicca **06** makatu, voodoo **07** myalism, sorcery **08** wizardry **09** occultism, the occult **10** black magic, divination, necromancy **11** conjuration, enchantment, incantation, the black art

witch doctor
06 mganga, shaman **07** angekok, sangoma **08** magician, marabout **11** medicine man **13** medicine woman

witch hunt
08 hounding **09** hue and cry **11** McCarthyism

with
◇ *juxtaposition indicator*
01 w **02** by, in, of **03** cum, mit **04** avec **05** among, using **06** beside, having **08** together **09** including **10** containing, possessing **13** accompanied by **14** in the company of

withdraw
◇ *deletion indicator*
02 go **04** pull, walk **05** annul, leave, unsay **06** abjure, call in, cancel, cry off, depart, detach, go away, opt out, recall, recant, recede, recoil, remove, repair, retire, revoke, secede, shrink **07** abolish, back out, call off, deflect, draw out, drop out, extract, give way, go aside, inshell, nullify, pull out, rescind, retract, retreat, scratch, subduce, subduct, take out **08** disclaim, draw back, evacuate, fall back, pull away, pull back, separate, step down, subtract, take away, take back **09** turn aside **10** declare off, shrink back **11** contract out, discontinue **14** absent yourself

withdrawal
03 tap **04** exit **06** exodus, recall, shrink **07** Dunkirk, removal, retiral, retreat **08** backword, delivery, pullback, recourse **09** breakaway, departure, disavowal, recession, revulsion, secession **10** abjuration, disclaimer, drawing out, evacuation, extraction, retirement, revocation, subduction, taking away **11** abstraction, drawing back, falling back, pulling back, recantation, repudiation, subtraction **13** disengagement

withdrawn
03 shy **05** aloof, quiet **06** hidden, remote, silent **07** distant, private, retired **08** alienate, detached, isolated, reserved, retiring, secluded, solitary, taciturn **09** introvert, shrinking **10** unsociable **11** introverted, out-of-the-way **12** unresponsive **13** unforthcoming **15** uncommunicative

wither
03 die, dry **04** fade, sear, sere, wane, welk, welt, wilt **05** arefy, blast, decay, droop, dry up, taint, waste **06** blight, die off, gizzen, perish, scorch, shrink, weaken **07** decline, destroy, dwindle, miff off, mortify, shrivel **08** fade away, languish **09** disappear, humiliate **12** disintegrate

withering
06 deadly, fading **08** autumnal, blasting, scathing, scornful, snubbing, wounding **09** blighting, scorching **10** marcescent, mortifying **11** destructive, devastating, humiliating **12** contemptuous, death-dealing

withhold
◇ *deletion indicator*
04 curb, hide, keep, stop **05** check **06** deduct, detain, refuse, retain **07** conceal, control, decline, forbear, repress, reserve **08** hold back, keep back, postpone, restrain, subtract, suppress **11** keep in check

within
◇ *hidden indicator*
◇ *insertion indicator*
02 in **04** into **05** intra **06** entire, herein, inside **07** indoors, not over **08** inside of, inwardly **09** in reach of **10** enclosed by **12** surrounded by

with it
02 in **03** hep, hip **04** cool **05** funky, natty, ritzy, vogue **06** glitzy, groovy, modern, modish, snazzy, trendy
08 up-to-date **10** all the rage
11 fashionable, progressive
12 contemporary **13** up-to-the-minute

without
◇ *containment indicator*
01 a-, x **02** an-, ex, w/o **03** sen **04** less, sans, sine **06** beyond, except, unless
07 lacking, needing, outside, wanting
08 free from, in need of **09** not having, outwardly **10** deprived of

withstand
04 bear, defy, face **05** brave, fight, stand **06** endure, hinder, oppose, resist, take on, thwart **07** hold off, hold out, last out, survive, weather
08 confront, cope with, tolerate, tough out **09** put up with, stand fast, stand firm, stand up to **10** tough it out **14** hold your ground **15** stand your ground

witless
04 daft, dull, nuts **05** barmy, crazy, inane, loony, loopy, nutty, potty, silly
06 cuckoo, mental, raving, stupid
07 bonkers, foolish, idiotic, moronic, unaware **08** doolally, gaumless, gormless, mindless **09** cretinous, imbecilic, senseless, up the wall
10 half-witted **11** empty-headed, off the rails, unconscious **12** mad as a hatter, off your chump **13** off your rocker, unintelligent **14** wrong in the head

witness
03 see **04** mark, note, show, sign, view
05 prove, see in, teste, watch **06** affirm, attest, depose, evince, expert, look on, notice, obtest, record, verify, viewer
07 bear out, confirm, endorse, observe, support, testify, vouchee, watcher **08** deponent, evidence, looker-on, observer, onlooker, perceive, speak for, validate
09 attestant, authority, bystander, spectator, testifier, testimony
10 eyewitness, man of skill **11** bear witness, compurgator, corroborate, countersign **12** be evidence of, give evidence

• **bear witness**
04 aver, show **05** prove **06** adjure, affirm, assert, attest, evince, record, verify **07** certify, confirm, declare, display, endorse, testify **08** evidence, manifest, vouch for **10** asseverate
11 corroborate, demonstrate

witter
04 chat **06** babble, drivel, gabble, gossip, jabber, patter, rattle **07** blather, blether, chatter, twaddle, twattle, twitter

witticism
03 hit, pun **04** jibe, joke, quip **06** bon mot **07** epigram, riposte **08** one-liner, repartee **09** impromptu, wisecrack
10 jeu d'esprit, pleasantry **11** play on words
See also **joke**

wittingly
08 by design, wilfully **09** knowingly, on purpose, purposely, studiedly, willingly
10 designedly **11** consciously
12 calculatedly, deliberately
13 intentionally

witty
04 wise **05** comic, droll, funny, light, salty, smart **06** clever, lively
07 amusing, jocular, lambent, waggish
08 discreet, fanciful, humorous, original, pregnant, sensible **09** brilliant, conceited, facetious, ingenious, sarcastic, sparkling, spiritual, spirituel, whimsical **11** coruscating, sharp-witted, spirituelle

wizard
03 ace, hex **04** good, star, whiz
05 adept, great, super, witch
06 expert, genius, master, superb, wisard **07** hotshot, maestro, prodigy, warlock, wise man **08** conjurer, magician, smashing, sorcerer, terrific, virtuoso **09** brilliant, enchanter, enjoyable, fantastic, occultist, wonderful **10** delightful, marvellous, tremendous **11** necromancer, sensational, thaumaturge
See also **witch**

wizened
04 thin, worn **05** lined **07** dried up, gnarled **08** shrunken, withered, wrinkled **10** shrivelled

wobble
◇ *anagram indicator*
04 rock, sway **05** quake, shake, waver
06 coggle, dither, dodder, quaver, quiver, seesaw, teeter, totter, tremor, wabble **07** precess, quaking, shoggle, stagger, tremble, vibrate **08** hesitate
09 fluctuate, oscillate, vacillate, vibration **11** oscillation **12** shilly-shally, unsteadiness, wibble-wobble

wobbly
◇ *anagram indicator*
05 shaky, wonky **06** uneven, unsafe
07 doddery, rickety **08** unstable, unsteady **09** doddering, quavering, teetering, tottering, trembling
10 unbalanced

Wodehouse
02 PG

woe
02 wo **03** sad, wae **04** bale, dool, dule, pain **05** agony, curse, doole, gloom, grief, sorry, tears, trial **06** burden, misery, sorrow, tsuris **07** anguish, sadness, trouble, tsouris **08** calamity, disaster, distress, hardship, wretched
09 adversity, dejection, heartache, suffering **10** affliction, depression, heartbreak, melancholy, misfortune
11 tribulation, unhappiness
12 wretchedness

woebegone
03 sad **04** blue **06** gloomy **07** doleful, forlorn, tearful **08** dejected, downcast, mournful, troubled, wretched **09** long-faced, miserable, sorrowful
10 dispirited, lugubrious **11** crestfallen, downhearted, tear-stained
12 disconsolate **13** grief-stricken
14 down in the mouth

woeful
◇ *anagram indicator*
03 bad, sad **04** mean, poor **05** awful, cruel, lousy, sorry, waefu' **06** feeble, gloomy, paltry, rotten, tragic, waeful
07 doleful, unhappy, waesome
08 dreadful, grieving, grievous, hopeless, mournful, pathetic, pitiable, shocking, terrible, wretched
09 afflicted, appalling, miserable, sorrowful **10** calamitous, deplorable, disastrous, inadequate, lamentable
11 disgraceful, distressing
12 catastrophic, disconsolate, heart-rending **13** disappointing, heartbreaking

woefully
05 sadly **07** awfully, lousily
08 gloomily, pitiably, terribly
09 dolefully, forlornly, miserably, unhappily **10** deplorably, dreadfully, hopelessly, lamentably, mournfully, shockingly, tragically, wretchedly
11 appallingly **12** disastrously, pathetically **13** disgracefully
14 disconsolately

wolf
04 lobo **05** Romeo **06** coyote, lecher
07 Don Juan, Isegrim, seducer
08 Casanova, Isengrim **09** ladies' man, thylacine, womanizer **10** lady-killer
11 philanderer

• **wolf down**
04 bolt, cram, gulp **05** gorge, scoff, stuff **06** devour, gobble **07** put away
08 pack away

woman
01 w **03** bit, chi, gin, hag, hen, her, she, Tib, tit **04** baby, bint, bird, chai, doll, fair, feme, frau, girl, jane, Judy, lady, lass, maid, Mary, minx, mort, peat, puss, sort, tart, wife **05** belle, biddy, broad, chick, cutie, cutty, dolly, femme, fille, filly, flirt, hussy, lover, madam, peach, popsy, quean, randy, wench **06** au pair, blowze, cummer, damsel, female, geisha, gillet, jillet, kimmer, lassie, maiden, moppet, number, ogress, sheila, shiksa, tomboy, tottie, wahine
07 bag lady, fiancée, mystery, nymphet, partner, reverse **08** mistress, princess
09 charwoman, dolly bird, plain Jane
10 bit of stuff, Cinderella, girlfriend, sweetheart **11** beauty queen
12 bachelorette, bobby-dazzler
See also **girl**

• first woman
03 Eve **07** Pandora

• good woman
01 S **02** St **04** sant **05** Saint

womanhood
05 woman **08** maturity **09** adulthood, womankind, womenfolk, womenkind
10 muliebrity, womenfolks

womanizer

Womanizers and libertines include:

04 goat, lech, rake, roué, wolf
05 letch, Romeo
06 gay dog, lecher
07 Don Juan, seducer, wastrel
08 Casanova, Lothario, Lovelace, palliard, rakehell
09 debauchee, ladies' man, libertine, reprobate, voluptary
10 Corinthian, lady-killer, profligate, sensualist
11 gay deceiver, philanderer

womanly
04 kind, warm **06** female, tender
07 shapely **08** feminine, ladylike, motherly, womanish **10** effeminate, well-formed

women

• excluding women
04 stag

• Women's Institute
02 WI

See also **woman**

wonder
03 awe **04** gape, marl, muse **05** doubt, ferly, marle, query, sight, think
06 admire, marvel, ponder, puzzle, rarity **07** cruller, inquire, miracle, prodigy, reflect **08** be amazed, meditate, pleasure, question, surprise
09 amazement, curiosity, nonpareil, spectacle, speculate **10** admiration, conjecture, phenomenon, stand in awe, wonderment **11** ask yourself, be astounded, be surprised, fascination
12 astonishment, be astonished, bewilderment **13** be dumbfounded
14 be lost for words

The Seven Wonders of the World:

15 Pyramids of Egypt
16 Colossus of Rhodes
18 Pharos of Alexandria
21 Statue of Zeus at Olympia
23 Hanging Gardens of Babylon
24 Mausoleum of Halicarnassus, Temple of Artemis at Ephesus

• expression of wonder
01 O **02** oh **03** god, wow **04** gosh, whew **05** wowee **06** heyday, wheugh
07 good-now **08** gracious **09** Jesus wept **13** stone the crows

wonderful
03 ace, def, fab, old, rad **04** boss, cool, keen, mean, mega, neat **05** beaut, boffo, brill, bully, crack, dicty, dilly, great, hunky, jammy, lummy, socko, super, triff **06** castor, divine, famous, far-out, geason, groovy, mighty, peachy, superb, way-out, wicked, wizard **07** amazing, awesome, capital, classic, crucial, elegant, épatant, magical, mirable, radical, ripping, stellar, strange, tipping, topping, triffic, trimmer **08** champion, clinking, fabulous, glorious, heavenly, jim-dandy, knockout, smashing, spiffing, splendid, stonking, stunning, terrific, top-notch **09** admirable, brilliant, copacetic, excellent, fantastic, righteous, startling **10** astounding, delightful, incredible, marvellous, not half bad, phenomenal, remarkable, staggering, stupendous, surprising, tremendous **11** astonishing, fantabulous, magnificent, outstanding, sensational **12** second to none
13 extraordinary **14** out of this world

wonderfully
06 purely **09** amazingly, extremely
10 incredibly **12** phenomenally, terrifically, tremendously, unbelievably
13 fantastically

wonky
04 awry, weak **05** amiss, askew, shaky, wrong **06** wobbly **07** crooked, unsound **08** unsteady **09** skew-whiff

wont
03 use, way **04** fain, rule, used **05** given, habit **06** custom **07** routine **08** inclined, practice **10** accustomed, habituated

wonted
04 tame **05** daily, usual **06** common, normal **07** regular, routine **08** familiar, frequent, habitual **09** customary
10 accustomed, habituated
12 conventional

woo
03 wow **04** seek **05** chase, court
06 pursue **07** address, attract, look for, romance **09** cultivate, encourage
10 make love to, pay court to **13** seek the hand of

wood
03 mad, wud **04** bowl, hyle, shaw, tree
05 copse, cross, grove, hurst, trees, woods, xylem **06** fierce, forest, planks, pulpit **07** coppice, furious, spinney, thicket **08** woodland **10** plantation

See also **forest**; **golf club**; **timber**

Woods include:

03 ash, box, cam, elm, fir, nut, oak, ply, red, sap, yew
04 bass, cord, cork, deal, ebon, fire, hard, iron, lana, lime, pine, pink, pulp, rose, sasa, soft, teak
05 alder, apple, balsa, beech, black, brush, cedar, drift, ebony, green, hazel, heart, larch, maple, match, olive, peach, plane, ramin, satin, tiger, torch, tulip, utile, white, zebra
06 acacia, bamboo, bitter, brazil, candle, cherry, cotton, linden, lumber, obeche, orange, padauk, pedauk, poplar, rubber, sandal, sapele, spruce, timber, veneer, walnut, willow
07 Amboina, bubinga, hickory, palmyra, quassia
08 amaranth, chestnut, cocobolo, hornbeam, kindling, mahogany, red lauan, seasoned, silky oak, sycamore
09 chipboard, hardboard, jacaranda, quebracho
10 afrormosia, Douglas fir, paper birch
11 black cherry, lignum vitae, purple heart, tulip poplar, white walnut, yellow birch
13 sweet chestnut

• measurement of wood
04 cord **05** stere **06** fathom, square
08 standard **09** board-foot, decastere, decistere **10** hoppus foot **15** hoppus cubic foot

• out of the woods
04 safe **06** secure **10** home and dry, in the clear **11** out of danger **12** safe and sound **15** out of difficulty

• piece of wood
03 cat, log **04** beam, chip, lath, slat
05 block, board, dwang, plank, split, staff, wedge **06** batten, billet, fillet, flitch, loggat, planch, timber, tipcat
07 bunting **08** splinter **09** four-by-two, scantling, two-by-four

wooded
05 woody **06** sylvan **08** forested, nemorous, timbered **09** arboreous
11 arboraceous, tree-covered

wooden
04 dull, hard, slow, tree **05** blank, empty, heavy, rigid, stiff, treen, woody
06 clumsy, leaden, stodgy, stupid, timber, vacant **07** awkward, deadpan, stilted, vacuous **08** lifeless, ligneous
09 graceless, impassive, inhibited, unnatural **10** insensible, spiritless
11 emotionless, unemotional
12 unresponsive **14** expressionless

woodland
04 bush, wood **05** copse, grove, trees, woods **06** forest, miombo, timber
07 boscage, boskage, coppice, spinney, thicket **10** plantation

woodpecker
05 Picus **06** yaffle, yucker **07** awlbird, flicker, piculet, witwall **08** hickwall, rainbird **10** yaffingale

wood sorrel
03 oca **06** oxalis **08** shamrock

woody
05 bosky **06** sylvan, wooded, wooden, xyloid **08** forested, ligneous **11** tree-covered

wool
02 oo **03** ket **04** coat, down, hair, kemp, noil, yarn **05** flock, llama, noils
06 Angora, botany, fleece, jersey, pelage, staple, two-ply, vicuña
07 floccus, morling **08** cashmere, mortling, shatoosh **09** shahtoosh, strouding **13** linsey-woolsey

• pull the wool over someone's eyes
03 con **04** dupe, fool **05** trick

06 delude, take in 07 deceive
08 hoodwink 09 bamboozle 12 pull a swiftie, put one over on 14 pull a fast one on

wool-gathering
06 dreamy 11 day-dreaming, distraction, inattention 12 absent-minded 13 forgetfulness, preoccupation

woollen fabric *see* **fabric**

woolly
04 hazy 05 downy, foggy, fuzzy, hairy, sheep, vague, woozy 06 cloudy, fleecy, fluffy, frizzy, jersey, jumper, lanate, lanose, shaggy 07 blurred, muddled, sweater, unclear, woollen 08 cardigan, confused, floccose, nebulous, pullover
10 flocculent, ill-defined, indefinite, indistinct 12 woolly-haired

woozy
05 dazed, dizzy, rocky, tipsy, vague
06 wobbly, woolly 07 bemused, blurred, fuddled 08 confused, unsteady 09 befuddled, nauseated
11 light-headed

word
03 gen, mot, put, say, vow 04 book, chat, dope, hint, info, name, news, oath, sign, talk, term, text, will
05 couch, order, speak, state, write
06 advice, decree, gossip, honour, lyrics, notice, phrase, pledge, remark, report, rumour, saying, script, signal, war cry 07 account, command, comment, explain, express, flatter, go-ahead, hearsay, low-down, mandate, message, palabra, promise, scandal, tidings, vocable, warning, whisper
08 bulletin, dispatch, libretto, password, thumbs-up 09 assertion, assurance, guarantee, statement, tête-à-tête, utterance, watchword
10 communiqué, discussion, expression, green light
11 commandment, declaration, designation, information, instruction, speculation, undertaking
12 consultation, conversation, intelligence 13 communication
See also **speech**

• **have words**
03 row 05 argue 06 bicker 07 dispute, quarrel 08 disagree, squabble

• **in a word**
07 briefly, in brief, in short, to sum up
09 concisely, to be brief 10 succinctly
11 in a nutshell, summarizing 14 to put it briefly

• **in other words**
02 ie 05 id est 06 that is

• **word for word**
06 verbal 07 closely, exactly, literal
08 ad verbum, verbatim 09 literally, precisely 10 accurately

wordiness
06 waffle 07 wordage 08 verbiage
09 garrulity, loquacity, prolixity, verbosity 10 logorrhoea
11 diffuseness, perissology, verboseness 13 garrulousness 14 long-windedness 15 verbal diarrhoea

wording
04 text 05 style, tenor, words
07 diction, wordage 08 language, phrasing, speaking, verbiage
09 subtitles, utterance, verbalism
10 expression 11 phraseology, terminology 13 choice of words

word-perfect
05 exact 06 spot-on 08 accurate, faithful 13 letter-perfect

wordplay
03 pun, wit 04 puns 07 punning
08 repartee 10 witticisms
11 paronomasia

wordy
05 windy 06 phrasy, prolix 07 diffuse, verbose 08 rambling 09 garrulous
10 discursive, long-winded, loquacious

work
◇ *anagram indicator*
02 do, go, op 03 art, dig, fag, fix, hat, job, ply, ren, rin, run, sew, tut, use
04 ache, acts, book, char, deed, duty, edge, farm, form, fuss, guts, line, make, mill, move, opus, plan, play, poem, shop, slog, take, task, tick, till, toil
05 cause, chore, craft, drive, field, graft, guide, knead, model, mould, parts, piece, plant, purge, shape, shift, skill, slave, study, trade, trick 06 action, cajole, career, charge, create, doings, drudge, effect, effort, fiddle, go well, handle, labour, manage, métier, oeuvre, strain, wangle 07 achieve, actions, arrange, calling, control, execute, factory, fashion, ferment, foundry, innards, mission, operate, peg away, perform, process, prosper, pull off, pursuit, squeeze, succeed, travail, trouble, writing 08 business, contrive, creation, drudgery, engineer, exercise, exertion, function, have a job, industry, movement, painting, plug away, treatise, vocation, workings, workshop
09 cultivate, embroider, influence, machinery, manoeuvre, mechanism, penetrate 10 accomplish, assignment, be employed, bring about, commission, embroidery, employment, livelihood, manipulate, occupation, production, profession
11 achievement, be effective, composition, elbow grease, pull strings, undertaking, workmanship
12 be successful, working parts
13 exert yourself, installations
14 accomplishment, be satisfactory, earn your living, line of business, responsibility 15 slog your guts out

• **bit of work**
01 J 03 erg 05 joule 08 therblig

• **day's work**
04 darg 05 stent, stint 06 man-day
07 journey

• **the works**
06 the lot 10 everything 11 the whole lot 15 the whole shebang

• **work out**
04 dope, plan, toil 05 drill, serve, solve, total, train 06 come to, deduce, devise, evolve, finish, go well, invent, pan out, warm up 07 add up to, arrange, clear up, come out, develop, dope out, exhaust, expiate, keep fit, prosper, resolve, sort out, succeed, turn out
08 amount to, contrive, exercise, organize, practise 09 calculate, construct, elaborate, figure out, formulate, puzzle out 10 understand
11 be effective, put together

• **work up**
03 tew 04 meng, ming, move, spur, whet 05 menge, reach, rouse, use up
06 arouse, excite, expand, incite, kindle, stir up, subact 07 achieve, agitate, animate, build up, ferment, inflame 08 generate, summon up
09 elaborate, instigate, stimulate

workable
06 doable, viable 08 feasible, possible
09 practical, realistic 11 practicable

workaday
04 dull 06 common 07 average, humdrum, mundane, prosaic, routine, toiling, work-day, working
08 everyday, familiar, ordinary
09 labouring, practical
11 commonplace 12 run-of-the-mill

worker
03 ant, bee 04 hand, peon, temp
06 coater, Indian, key man, legger, toiler
07 artisan, grinder, ouvrier, workman
08 employee, grisette, labourer, mechanic, ouvrière, strapper, stuccoer
09 craftsman, midinette, operative, salaryman, tradesman, workhorse, workwoman 10 mechanical, painstaker, railroader, wage-earner, workaholic, working man
11 breadwinner, craftswoman, proletarian, tradeswoman
12 Gastarbeiter, willing horse, working woman 13 member of staff

workforce
03 men 05 hands, staff 06 labour
07 workers 08 manpower, skeleton
09 employees, personnel, shop floor
10 workpeople 11 labour force
14 human resources

working
◇ *anagram indicator*
02 on 03 pit 04 guts, live, mine
05 going, parts, shaft, waste, works
06 action, active, in a job, in work, manner, method, quarry, system
07 innards, process, routine, running
08 diggings, employed, movement
09 endeavour, labouring, machinery, mechanism, operating, operation, operative 10 in business
11 excavations, functioning, operational 12 up and running, working parts 13 installations 14 in working order

workman, workwoman
04 hand, hobo 05 hunky, navvy
06 beamer, glazer, master, worker

07 artisan 08 apron-man, employee, gunsmith, labourer, mechanic
09 artificer, craftsman, operative, prud'homme, stage hand
10 journeyman, surfaceman
11 craftswoman 12 manual worker, tradesperson

workmanlike
05 adept 06 expert 07 careful, skilful, skilled 08 masterly, thorough
09 competent, efficient 10 proficient
11 painstaking 12 businesslike, professional, satisfactory

workmanship
03 art 04 work 05 craft, skill 06 finish
07 facture, tooling 08 artifice, artistry
09 execution, expertise, handiwork, technique 10 handicraft
11 manufacture 13 craftsmanship

workmate
03 lad 08 co-worker 09 associate, colleague 10 work-fellow, yoke-fellow
12 fellow-worker

workout
05 drill 06 warm-up 08 aerobics, exercise, practice, training
10 gymnastics, isometrics
11 eurhythmics, limbering up
13 callisthenics

workshop
03 lab 04 mill, shop 05 class, forge, plant, works 06 garage, smithy, studio
07 atelier, factory, seminar
08 plumbery, smithery, workroom
09 cooperage, symposium
10 laboratory, study group 11 machine-shop, rigging-loft 15 discussion group

work-shy
04 idle, lazy, lusk, slow 05 inert, slack, tardy 06 laesie, lither, torpid
07 languid, luskish 08 bone-idle, fainéant, inactive, indolent, slothful, sluggish 09 lethargic 10 languorous, slow-moving 14 good-for-nothing

workwoman *see* **workman, workwoman**

world
03 age, era, man, orb 04 area, days, life, star, vale 05 class, earth, epoch, field, globe, group, realm, times 06 cosmos, domain, nature, people, period, planet, public, sphere, system 07 kingdom, mankind, reality, section, society
08 creation, division, everyone, humanity, province, universe
09 everybody, existence, humankind, human race, situation, way of life
10 department, experience, population 11 environment
12 heavenly body

World heritage sites include:

03 Bam, Omo, Taï
04 Agra, Bath, Graz, Lima, Manú, Pisa, Riga, San'a, Troy, Tyre
05 Aksum, Awash, Berne, Bosra, Copán, Cuzco, Delos, Galle, Hatra, Kandy, Lyons, Ohrid, Paris, Petra, Quito, Siena, Sucre, Uluru
06 Abomey, Aleppo, Amazon, Assisi, Bassae, Byblos, Cyrene, Darién, Delphi, Durham, Göreme, Kakadu, Naples, Oporto, Orkney, Paphos, Potosí, Puebla, Sangay, Sousse, Thebes, Toledo, Treves, Venice, Verona, Vienna, Warsaw
07 Abu Mena, Avebury, Avignon, Baalbek, Caracas, Djemila, Garamba, Gwynedd, Holy See, Olympia, San Juan, Segovia, St Kilda, Vicenza, Virunga
08 Agra Fort, Alhambra, Altamira, Carthage, Chartres, Damascas, Durmitor, Florence, Ghadamès, Hattusas, Mount Tai, Palenque, Pyramids, Pyrénées, Sabratha, Salvador, Salzburg, Shark Bay, Sigiriya, Stari Ras, Taj Mahal, Timbuktu, Valletta, Würzburg
09 Abu Simbel, Auschwitz, Ayutthaya, Dubrovnik, Edinburgh, Epidaurus, Greenwich, Gros Morne, Huascarán, Jerusalem, Mesa Verde, Nemrut Dag, Parthenon, Serengeti
10 El Escorial, Everglades, Generalife, Hierapolis, Hildesheim, Ironbridge, Monte Albán, Monticello, Persepolis, Pont du Gard, Stonehenge, Versailles
11 Ajanta caves, Danube Delta, Ellora caves, Gorée Island, Hagia Sophia, Leptis Magna, Machu Picchu, Madara Rider, Mohenjo-daro, Quedlinburg, Teotihuacán, Vatican City, Western Wall, Westminster, Yellowstone
12 Altamira Cave, Ancient Kyoto, Fraser Island, Hadrian's Wall, Koguryo Tombs, Mont-St-Michel, Santo Domingo, The Great Wall
13 Fontainebleau, Fontenay Abbey, Great Zimbabwe, Rila Monastery, Tower of London
14 Aldabra Islands, Blenheim Palace, Elephanta caves, Fountains Abbey, Giant's Causeway, Heraion of Samos, Imperial Palace
15 Aachen Cathedral, Amiens Cathedral, Ironbridge Gorge, Kasbah of Algiers, Kathmandu Valley, Nubian monuments, Speyer Cathedral, Statue of Liberty

• **on top of the world**
05 happy 06 elated, joyful 08 ecstatic, euphoric, exultant, jubilant, thrilled
09 delighted, exuberant, overjoyed, rapturous 10 enraptured, in raptures
11 exhilarated, high as a kite, on cloud nine, over the moon, tickled pink
14 pleased as Punch 15 in seventh heaven

• **out of this world**
02 ET 03 ace, rad 04 cool, mean, mega, neat 05 brill, great 06 divine, superb, way-out, wicked 07 crucial, radical 08 fabulous, heavenly, smashing, stonking, stunning, terrific
09 excellent, fantastic, wonderful
10 delightful, incredible, marvellous, phenomenal, remarkable
11 sensational 12 second to none, unbelievable 13 indescribable

worldly
06 carnal, greedy, mortal, urbane
07 earthly, knowing, mondain, mundane, outward, profane, secular, selfish, terrene 08 covetous, grasping, material, mondaine, physical, temporal
09 ambitious, corporeal 10 avaricious, streetwise 11 experienced, terrestrial, unspiritual, worldly-wise
12 cosmopolitan 13 materialistic, sophisticated

worldly-wise
06 shrewd, urbane 07 cynical, knowing, worldly 10 cultivated, perceptive, streetwise 11 experienced
12 cosmopolitan 13 sophisticated

worldwide
06 global 07 general, mondial
08 catholic 09 universal 10 ubiquitous
11 transglobal 13 international

worm
04 grub 05 snake 06 dragon, maggot, squirm 07 remorse

Worms include:

03 eel, lug, pin, rag
04 flat, hook, tape
05 arrow, earth, fluke, leech, round
06 peanut, ribbon, thread
07 annelid, bristle
08 sea mouse
10 blood fluke, liver fluke

worn
03 old 04 bare, used 05 all in, drawn, jaded, spent, tatty, tired, trite, weary
06 bushed, done in, frayed, ragged, shabby 07 haggard, thumbed, worn-out 08 careworn, dog-tired, fatigued, strained, tattered 09 exhausted, hackneyed, in tatters, knackered
10 threadbare 13 weather-bitten

• **worn out**
03 old 04 beat, gone, past, used 05 all in, banal, corny, rough, seedy, stale, stock, tacky, tatty, tired, trite, warby, weary 06 bushed, common, done in, épuisé, failed, frayed, pooped, ragged, shabby, wasted, zonked 07 cliché'd, épuisée, to-worne, traikit, useless, wearied, whacked, worn-out
08 clichéed, dead-beat, decrepit, dog-tired, dog-weary, forfairn, overused, tattered, time-worn, tired out
09 bedridden, disjaskit, exhausted, geriatric, hackneyed, knackered, moth-eaten, pooped out, shattered, washed-out, worm-eaten 10 broken-down, clapped-out, overworked, pedestrian, shagged out, threadbare, uninspired, unoriginal, yawn-making
11 commonplace, ready to drop, stereotyped, tuckered out, wearing thin 12 cliché-ridden, journey-bated, overscutched, run-of-the-mill 13 on its last legs, platitudinous, unimaginative

worried
◇ *anagram indicator*
04 worn 05 het up, tense, upset, wired

06 afraid, on edge, uneasy 07 anxious, fearful, fretful, haunted, in a stew, jittery, nervous, uptight 08 agonized, bothered, dismayed, in a tizzy, strained, troubled 09 concerned, disturbed, ill at ease, perturbed 10 disquieted, distracted, distraught, distressed, frightened 11 overwrought 12 apprehensive 14 beside yourself, hot and bothered 15 a bundle of nerves

worrisome
05 hairy, scary 06 vexing 07 irksome 08 insecure, worrying 09 agonizing, upsetting, vexatious 10 bothersome, disturbing, nail-biting, perturbing 11 disquieting, distressing, frightening, troublesome

worry
◇ *anagram indicator*
03 bug, dog, eat, nag, tew, tiz, vex 04 bite, care, faze, fear, frab, fret, gnaw, pest, stew 05 annoy, choke, deave, deeve, devil, eat up, feese, feeze, go for, harry, phase, phese, sweat, tease, tizzy, touse, touze, towse, towze, trial, upset 06 attack, badger, bother, burden, hang-up, harass, hassle, misery, niggle, pester, pheese, pheeze, pingle, plague, savage, strain, stress, tear at, unease, worrit 07 agitate, agonize, anguish, anxiety, concern, disturb, perturb, problem, tension, torment, trouble 08 disquiet, distress, headache, irritate, nuisance, unsettle, vexation 09 aggravate, agitation, annoyance, be anxious, misgiving 10 be troubled, irritation, perplexity 11 disturbance, fearfulness 12 apprehension, be distressed, perturbation 13 consternation 14 responsibility
• **expression of worry**
04 uh-oh, yike 05 yikes 06 cripes

worrying
05 hairy, scary 06 trying, uneasy 07 anxious, weighty 08 alarming, niggling 09 agonizing, harassing, upsetting, worrisome 10 disturbing, nail-biting, perturbing, unsettling 11 disquieting, distressing, troublesome

worsen
04 sink, slip 06 weaken 07 decline, go to pot 08 get worse, heighten, increase 09 aggravate, intensify 10 degenerate, exacerbate, go downhill 11 deteriorate 13 go down the tube 14 go down the tubes

worsening
05 decay 07 decline 10 pejoration 12 degeneration, exacerbation 13 deterioration, retrogression

worship
02 Wp 04 laud, love, puja 05 adore, deify, exalt, extol, glory 06 admire, homage, honour, Ibadat, praise, prayer, pray to, regard, revere 07 adulate, dignity, glorify, idolize, opus Dei, prayers, respect 08 adultery, devotion, geolatry, idolatry, naturism, religion, satanism, venerate 09 adoration, adulation, aniconism, devotions, diabolism, laudation, pyrolatry, reverence, snake cult 10 astrolatry, bardolatry, exaltation, eye-service, heliolatry, iconolatry, litholatry, ophiolatry, reputation, veneration 11 angelolatry, be devoted to, deification, idolization, physiolatry, theriolatry 13 anthropolatry, glorification, thaumatolatry

Places of worship include:

03 wat
04 fane, kirk, shul
05 abbey, gompa
06 bethel, chapel, church, mandir, masjid, mosque, pagoda, shrine, temple, vihara
07 chantry, convent, minster
08 gurdwara
09 cathedral, monastery, synagogue
10 tabernacle
12 meeting-house

See also **abbey**; **religious**

worshipful
02 Wp 04 awed, Wpfl 05 pious 06 devout, humble, loving, solemn 07 adoring, devoted, dutiful 08 admiring, obeisant 10 respectful 11 deferential, reverential

worshipper *see* **believer**

worst
03 war 04 beat, best, drub, lick 05 crush, paste, smash, thump 06 damage, defeat, hammer, master, subdue, thrash 07 clobber, conquer, trounce 08 overcome, pessimal, pessimum, vanquish 09 devastate, overpower, overthrow, slaughter, subjugate, whitewash 10 annihilate 13 run rings round 14 get the better of 15 make mincemeat of

worth
02 be 03 use 04 cost, gain, good, help, rate 05 avail, carat, merit, price, value, virtu 06 become, carrat, credit, desert, happen, profit, virtue 07 benefit, deserts, quality, service, utility 08 eminence, meriting, repaying, valuable 09 advantage, deserving, substance 10 assistance, excellence, excellency, importance, justifying, usefulness, warranting, worthiness 11 possessions 12 significance

worthily
04 well 08 laudably, reliably, valuably 09 admirably 10 creditably, honourably 11 commendably

worthless
03 bad, bum, low 04 base, junk, naff, orra, poor, punk, raca, vile, waff 05 blown, cheap, junky, light, sorry, tripy 06 abject, cruddy, crummy, draffy, drossy, futile, naught, no good, ornery, paltry, trashy, tripey 07 corrupt, drunken, ignoble, mauvais, nothing, shotten, trivial, useless 08 beggarly, castaway, draffish, gimcrack, jimcrack, mauvaise, nugatory, rubbishy, sixpenny, trifling, twopenny, unusable, unworthy, wanwordy, wretched 09 brummagem, cheap-jack, no-account, pointless, valueless 10 despicable, unavailing, unprizable 11 ineffectual, littleworth, meaningless, stramineous, unimportant 12 contemptible 13 insignificant 14 good-for-nothing, not worth shucks
• **worthless thing**
03 mud 04 dirt, grot 05 nyaff 06 fag end 10 catchpenny

worthlessness
07 ambs-ace, ames-ace 08 futility 09 cheapness 11 lack of worth, nothingness, unusability, uselessness 13 pointlessness 15 ineffectualness, meaninglessness

worthwhile
04 good 05 tanti 06 useful, worthy 07 gainful, helpful, of value 08 valuable 09 estimable, rewarding 10 beneficial, productive, profitable 11 justifiable 12 advantageous, constructive

worthy
03 fit, VIP 04 good, name 05 moral, noble 06 big gun, bigwig, decent, honest, honour, top dog 07 big shot, notable, upright 08 big noise, laudable, luminary, reliable, somebody, top brass, valuable, virtuous 09 admirable, big cheese, deserving, dignitary, estimable, excellent, personage, reputable, righteous 10 creditable, excellence, honourable, notability, worthwhile 11 appropriate, commendable, meritorious, respectable, trustworthy 12 praiseworthy

would
01 'd

would-be
04 keen 05 eager 07 budding, hopeful, longing, wannabe, wishful 08 aspiring, striving 09 ambitious, soi-disant 10 optimistic 12 endeavouring, enterprising

wound
◇ *anagram indicator*
03 cut, hit, pip 04 ache, bite, blow, dunt, gash, harm, hurt, pain, scar, sore, stab, tear, vuln, win't 05 bless, graze, grief, saber, sabre, shock, shoot, slash, touch, upset 06 damage, grieve, injure, injury, insult, lesion, offend, pierce, slight, trauma 07 anguish, mortify, scratch, torment 08 distress, lacerate, puncture, sword-cut 09 vulnerate 10 heartbreak, laceration, traumatism, traumatize

wow
03 boy, cor

wrack
◇ *anagram indicator*
05 wreck 07 remnant, seaweed, torment, torture 08 wreckage 09 vengeance 10 punishment 11 destruction, devastation

wraith
05 ghost, shade, spook 06 double, spirit 07 phantom, spectre 08 revenant 10 apparition, astral body 12 doppelgänger

wrangle
03 rag, row 04 herd, spar, spat, tiff 05 argue, clash, fight, scrap, set-to 06 argufy, barney, bicker, cample, cangle, debate, dust-up, hassle, jangle, tussle 07 brabble, brangle, contend, contest, dispute, fall out, punch-up, quarrel, wrestle 08 argument, disagree, ergotize, squabble 09 altercate, argy-bargy, bickering, have it out, have words 10 digladiate 11 altercation, controversy, cross swords 12 disagreement 13 have it out with, slanging match 15 be at loggerheads, have a bone to pick

wrap
◇ *containment indicator*
03 hap, lap, rug, wap 04 bind, cape, fold, hide, mail, pack, robe, roll, snug, wind 05 amice, boost, cloak, cover, scarf, shawl, sheet, stole, throw 06 clothe, cocoon, emboss, encase, enfold, mantle, muffle, parcel, roll up, shroud, swathe, wimple 07 commend, embrace, enclose, envelop, flannel, immerse, involve, obscure, package, snuggle, swaddle, whimple 08 bemuffle, bundle up, enswathe, entangle, gift-wrap, inswathe, parcel up, surround 09 clingfilm, night-rail 11 acclamation

• **wrap up**
03 end, hap 04 mail 05 dry up 06 belt up, bundle, enfold, infold, pack up, parcel, shut up, wind up 07 be quiet, package 08 complete, conclude, gift-wrap, muffle up, parcel up, pipe down, round off 09 finish off, terminate 11 dress warmly, give it a rest 12 put a sock in it 13 bring to a close, shut your mouth 14 hold your tongue 15 wear warm clothes

wrapper
04 case 05 cover, folio, paper 06 casing, jacket, sheath, sleeve 08 covering, envelope, Jiffy bag®, wrapping 09 packaging 10 dust jacket

wrapping
04 case, foil 05 paper 06 carton, swathe 07 tinfoil, wrapper 08 envelope, Jiffy bag® 09 packaging 10 bubble pack, Cellophane® 11 blister card, blister pack, envelopment, silver paper

wrapt *see* **rapt**

wrath
03 ire 04 fury, rage 05 anger, angry 06 ardour, choler, spleen, temper 07 passion 09 annoyance 10 bitterness, irritation, resentment 11 displeasure, indignation 12 exasperation

wrathful
03 mad 05 angry, cross, irate, ratty, spewy, wroth 06 bitter, choked, ireful, raging 07 crooked, enraged, furious, ropable, stroppy, uptight 08 burned up, furibund, hairless, in a paddy, incensed, up in arms 09 in a lather, indignant, raving mad, seeing red, ticked off 10 aggravated, displeased, hopping mad, infuriated 11 disgruntled, fit to be tied 12 on the warpath

wreak
04 harm, vent 05 cause 06 avenge, bestow, create, damage, effect, punish 07 execute, express, inflict, unleash 08 carry out, drive out, exercise 09 vengeance 10 bring about, perpetrate, punishment

wreath
03 lei 04 band, loop, ring 05 crown, torse 06 anadem, circle 07 chaplet, circlet, coronet, festoon, garland 09 snowdrift 10 civic crown

wreathe
04 coil, turn, wind, wrap 05 adorn, crown, twine, twist, wring 06 enfold, enwrap, shroud 07 contort, entwine, envelop, festoon 08 decorate, encircle, surround 10 intertwine, interweave

wreck
◇ *anagram indicator*
03 gum, mar 04 crab, loss, mess, ruin, sink 05 break, gum up, mouse, smash, split, spoil, trash, wrack 06 cast up, debris, pieces, ravage, rubble 07 chicken, destroy, disable, flotsam, handbag, remains, shatter, torpedo, undoing 08 breaking, cast away, demolish, derelict, disaster, neurotic, smashing, stramash, write off, write-off 09 devastate, fragments, ruination, shipwreck 10 basket-case, demolition, disruption, shattering 11 bag of nerves, destruction, devastation 13 play havoc with 14 bundle of nerves

wreckage
◇ *anagram indicator*
04 ruin 05 lagan, ligan, wrack 06 debris, pieces, rubble 07 flotsam, remains 08 detritus 09 fragments

wrench
03 fit, rip, tug 04 ache, blow, jerk, pain, pang, pull, rick, tear, yank 05 force, shock, twist, wrest, wring 06 sorrow, sprain, strain 07 distort, sadness, spanner 08 upheaval 09 uprooting

wrest
03 win 04 pull, rack, take, turn 05 force, screw, seize, thraw, twist, wring 06 sprain, strain, wrench 07 distort, extract, pervert 10 distortion 12 misinterpret

wrestle
03 vie 05 argue, fight 06 battle, combat, debate, strive, tussle, wraxle, writhe 07 bulldog, contend, contest, dispute, grapple, scuffle, wrangle, wriggle 08 struggle

wrestling
◇ *anagram indicator*

Wrestling holds and throws include:

03 hug
04 lock
06 grovet, nelson, souple, suplex
07 bear hug, buttock, hip-lock
08 arm throw, body lock, headlock, scissors
09 ankle lace, body throw
10 Boston crab, full nelson, hammerlock
11 backbreaker, scissor hold
12 cross-buttock, scissors hold, stranglehold
14 grand amplitude

Wrestling-related terms include:

03 hug, mat, pin
04 bout, fall, hold, open, sumo
05 judge
06 action, bridge, souple
07 default, referee
08 arm throw, body lock, chairman, exposing, reversal, takedown
09 ankle lace, body throw, bridge out, freestyle, grapevine, gut wrench, passivity
10 arm control, Greco-Roman
13 central circle, cross-body ride, passivity zone
14 danger position, grand amplitude, protection area
15 double-leg tackle, single leg tackle, technical points

wretch
03 rat 04 worm 05 being, devil, exile, miser, rogue, snake, swine 06 insect, rascal, vassal 07 cullion, outcast, ruffian, scroyle, villain 08 blighter, creature, recreant, vagabond 09 miscreant, miserable, rakeshame, scoundrel 10 peelgarlic, pilgarlick, rascallion 11 rapscallion 14 good-for-nothing

wretched
◇ *anagram indicator*
02 wo 03 bad, low, sad, woe 04 base, mean, poor, vile 05 awful, ratty, seely, sorry, woful 06 abject, bloody, cursed, damned, darned, dashed, effing, gloomy, odious, paltry, rascal, woeful, wretch 07 blasted, doleful, flaming, forlorn, hapless, hateful, piteous, pitiful, unhappy, unlucky 08 annoying, blinking, blooming, dejected, downcast, dratting, dreadful, fiendish, flipping, hopeless, horrible, inferior, infernal, pathetic, pitiable, shameful, shocking, terrible 09 appalling, atrocious, depressed, life-weary, loathsome, miserable, worthless 10 confounded, deplorable, despicable, detestable, distraught, distressed, melancholy, outrageous, unpleasant 11 crestfallen, unfortunate 12 contemptible, disconsolate 13 broken-hearted

wretchedly
05 sadly 07 awfully, lousily

08 gloomily, pitiably, terribly, woefully 09 dolefully, forlornly, miserably, unhappily 10 deplorably, dreadfully, hopelessly, lamentably, mournfully, shockingly, tragically 11 appallingly 12 disastrously, pathetically 13 disgracefully 14 disconsolately

wriggle
04 bend, duck, edge, jerk, shun, turn, wind, worm 05 crawl, dodge, elude, evade, hedge, shirk, sidle, slink, snake, twine, twist 06 escape, eschew, jiggle, squirm, twitch, waggle, wamble, wiggle, writhe, zigzag 07 forbear, wrestle 08 get out of, get round, scriggle, sidestep, squiggle 09 extricate, give a miss, manoeuvre 10 body-swerve, circumvent 11 abstain from, refrain from, run away from 12 keep away from, stay away from, steer clear of

wring
04 coil, hurt, pain, rack, rend, stab, tear 05 exact, force, pinch, screw, thraw, twist, wound, wrest 06 coerce, extort, harrow, injure, mangle, pierce, wrench, writhe 07 distort, extract, squeeze, torture, wreathe 08 distress, lacerate

wrinkle
03 tip 04 fold, idea, line, lirk, plow, ruck, seam 05 frown, ridge, rivel, whelk 06 crease, furrow, gather, notion, plough, pucker, ruckle, ruck up, ruffle, rumple, runkle, trench, wimple 07 crankle, crimple, crinkle, crumple, frounce, frumple, shrivel, whimple 08 unsmooth 09 corrugate 10 suggestion, unevenness 11 corrugation

wrinkled
04 ropy 05 crêpy, ropey 06 crepey, crimpy, ridged, rucked, rugate, rugose, rugous 07 creased, crinkly, furrowy, puckery, ruffled, rumpled, wizened, wrinkly, wrizled 08 crankled, crinkled, crumpled, frounced, furrowed, puckered, rivelled, writhled 09 chamfered 10 corrugated

wrist
06 carpus 11 shackle-bone

writ
04 tolt 05 brief, sci fa 06 capias, decree, elegit, extent, venire 07 dedimus, latitat, precept, process, summons, warrant 08 mandamus, mittimus, noverint, replevin, subpoena 09 nisi prius 10 certiorari, court order, devastavit, distringas, inhibition, injunction, law-burrows, praemunire 11 fieri facias, jury-process, quo warranto, scire facias, supersedeas, supplicavit 12 habeas corpus, quare impedit, venire facias 13 ad inquirendum, audita querela

write
03 pen 04 copy, note 05 carve, chalk, draft, print, trace 06 create, decree, draw up, indite, pencil, record, scrawl, scribe, scrive 07 compose, dash off, engrave, jot down, put down, screeve, scrieve, set down 08 foretell, inscribe, note down, register, scribble, sling ink, take down 09 character, poeticize, transpose 10 correspond, transcribe, underwrite 11 communicate, make a note of

• **write off**
05 annul, crash, smash, wreck 06 cancel, delete 07 destroy, nullify, smash up, wipe out 08 amortize, cross out, demolish 09 disregard 11 forget about

writer
03 pen 06 author 12 man of letters 14 woman of letters

Writers include:

04 bard, hack, poet
05 clerk
06 author, editor, fabler, penman, pen-pal, rhymer, scribe
07 copyist, diarist
08 annalist, composer, essayist, lyricist, novelist, penwoman, reporter, satirist
09 columnist, dramatist, historian, pen-friend, penpusher, scribbler, sonneteer, web author
10 biographer, chronicler, copywriter, journalist, librettist, playwright
11 contributor, ghost writer, storyteller
12 leader-writer, poet laureate, scriptwriter, stenographer
13 calligraphist, correspondent, court reporter, fiction writer, lexicographer
14 autobiographer
15 technical author, technical writer

See also **author**; **biography**; **chef**; **diary**; **essay**; **fable**; **historian**; **journalist**; **lexicographer**; **literary**; **playwright**; **poet**; **satirist**

• **the writer**
02 me

• **this writer**
01 I

write-up
05 study 06 rating, report, review, survey 08 analysis, critique, scrutiny 09 appraisal, criticism, judgement, recension, summing-up 10 assessment, commentary, evaluation 11 examination

writhe
◇ *anagram indicator*
03 wry 04 coil, curl, jerk, toss, wind 05 thraw, twist, wring 06 squirm, thrash, thresh, wiggle 07 contort, distort, wrestle, wriggle 08 scriggle, struggle 10 intertwine 12 twist and turn

writing
02 MS 03 pen 04 dite, fist, hand, opus, text, work 05 entry, print, prose, words 06 scrawl, script, volume 08 document, scribble 10 manuscript, penmanship 11 calligraphy, composition, handwriting, publication

Writing instruments include:

03 nib, pen
04 Biro®, reed
05 quill
06 crayon, dip pen, pencil, stylus
07 cane pen
08 brailler, CD marker, steel pen
09 ballpoint, eraser pen, ink pencil, marker pen
10 felt-tip pen, lead-pencil, rollerball, typewriter
11 board marker, fountain pen, highlighter
12 cartridge pen, writing brush
13 laundry marker, Roman metal pen, word-processor
14 calligraphy pen, coloured pencil
15 permanent marker

Writings include:

04 blog, book, news, poem, tale
05 diary, drama, essay, lyric, paper, story, study
06 annals, letter, memoir, record, report, review, satire, script, sketch, sonnet, thesis, weblog
07 account, apology, article, epistle, feature, history, journal, parable, profile
08 apologia, critique, treatise, yearbook
09 biography, chronicle, criticism, discourse, editorial, life story, monograph, narrative, statement, technical
10 commentary, literature, propaganda, scientific, travelogue
11 confessions, copywriting, documentary
12 dissertation
13 autobiography, legal document
14 correspondence
15 advertising copy, curriculum vitae, newspaper column

See also **alphabet**; **scripture**

written
06 penned 07 drawn up, set down 08 recorded 09 pen-and-ink 10 documental, documented 11 documentary, transcribed

wrong
◇ *anagram indicator*
01 X 03 bad, bum, sin 04 awry, back, bent, evil, harm, tort 05 abuse, amiss, badly, crime, crook, error, false, inapt, spoil 06 astray, curved, damage, delict, faulty, guilty, impair, injure, injury, inside, seduce, sinful, unfair, unjust, wicked 07 abusion, abusive, crooked, defraud, illegal, illicit, immoral, in error, inverse, misdeed, off base, off beam, offence, reverse, to blame, twisted, unright, wrongly 08 contrary, criminal, faultily, improper, inequity, iniquity, inverted, mistaken, opposite, trespass, unlawful, unseemly 09 defective, dishonest, dishonour, erroneous, felonious, grievance, imprecise, incorrect, inexactly, injustice, off target, unethical, unfitting 10 fallacious, immorality, improperly, inaccurate,

inapposite, indecorous, iniquitous, malapropos, mistakenly, out of order, sinfulness, unfairness, unsuitable, up the spout, wickedness, wrongdoing **11** blameworthy, erroneously, imprecisely, incongruous, incorrectly, misinformed, unjustified
12 inaccurately, infelicitous, infringement, unlawfulness
13 dishonourable, hardly the time, inappropriate, reprehensible, transgression, wide of the mark
14 hardly the place, unconventional, unsatisfactory

• go wrong

04 fail, miss **05** stray **06** go phut, pack up **07** conk out, pervert, seize up **08** backfire, collapse, go astray, walk awry **09** break down, not make it
11 come to grief, come unglued, come unstuck, malfunction, stop working
12 come a cropper, go on the blink, go on the fritz **13** become unstuck, come to nothing **14** be unsuccessful

• in the wrong

04 harm, hurt **05** abuse, cheat
06 guilty, ill-use, injure, malign **07** at fault, in error, oppress, to blame **08** ill-treat, maltreat, mistaken, mistreat
09 discredit, dishonour
11 blameworthy **12** misrepresent

wrongdoer

05 felon **06** sinner **07** culprit
08 criminal, evildoer, offender
09 miscreant **10** delinquent, lawbreaker, malefactor, trespasser
12 transgressor

wrongdoing

03 sin **04** evil, miss **05** crime, error, fault **06** felony **07** misdeed, offence **08** iniquity, mischief
09 misfaring **10** immorality, maleficent, maleficial, sinfulness, wickedness
11 delinquency, lawbreaking, maleficence, malfeasance
13 transgression

wrongful

04 evil **05** wrong **06** unfair, unjust, wicked **07** illegal, illicit, immoral
08 criminal, improper, tortious, unlawful **09** dishonest, injurious, unethical **11** blameworthy, unjustified, unwarranted **12** illegitimate
13 dishonourable, reprehensible

wrongfully

03 ill **06** unduly **08** unfairly, unjustly
09 illegally, illicitly, immorally
10 criminally, improperly
11 dishonestly, unethically **13** against the law **14** illegitimately

wrongly

◇ *anagram indicator*
05 amiss, badly **07** athwart, in error
09 by mistake **10** mistakenly
11 erroneously, incorrectly
12 inaccurately

wrought

◇ *anagram indicator*
04 made **06** beaten, formed, ornate, shaped **08** hammered **09** decorated, fashioned **10** decorative, ornamental, ornamented **12** manufactured

• wrought up

05 upset **07** anxious, nervous, ruffled, worried **08** agitated, in a tizzy, troubled, unnerved **09** disturbed, flustered, in a lather, unsettled
10 distraught **12** disconcerted

wry

03 dry **05** askew, canny, cross, droll, pawky, thraw, witty **06** bitter, ironic, swerve, thrawn, uneven, warped, writhe **07** contort, crooked, mocking, pervert, twisted **08** deformed, perverse, sardonic, scoffing
09 contorted, distorted, sarcastic
10 distortion, ill-natured

Wyoming

02 WY **03** Wyo

X
02 ex **03** chi, ten **04** xray

xenon
02 Xe

xenophobia
06 racism **09** racialism, xenophoby **13** ethnocentrism **15** ethnocentricity

xenophobic
06 racist **09** parochial, racialist **12** ethnocentric **13** ethnocentrist

Xerox®
04 copy **05** print **06** run off **09** duplicate, facsimile, photocopy, Photostat®, reproduce

xylophone
07 gamelan, marimba **08** sticcado, sticcato **09** xylorimba **12** metallophone

Xmas
02 Xm **04** Noel, Yule **05** Nowel **06** Crimbo, Nowell **08** Chrissie, Nativity, Yuletide **09** Christmas **13** Christmas-tide, Christmas-time

X-ray, xray
01 X **08** skiagram **09** angiogram, mammogram, pyelogram, radiogram, sialogram, skiagraph, X-ray image **10** mammograph, radiograph, röntgen ray **11** shadowgraph **13** encephalogram **14** encephalograph, X-ray photograph

Y
03 wye **06** yankee

yacht
02 MY **04** maxi, scow **06** dragon **07** cruiser **08** keelboat **10** knockabout

yack
03 gab, jaw, yap **04** blah, chat, rant **06** babble, confab, gossip, harp on, hot air, jabber, tattle **07** blather, chatter, chinwag, prattle, twattle **08** witter on, yack-yack **11** yackety-yack

yam
06 camote **09** breadroot, Dioscorea **11** sweet potato

yank
◇ *anagram indicator*
03 tug **04** blow, haul, jerk, pull, slap **05** heave **06** snatch, wrench

yankee
01 y

yap
03 cur, gab, jaw **04** bark, fool, yelp **05** mouth, nyaff, scold **06** babble, jabber, natter, yatter **07** bumpkin, chatter, prattle **08** witter on

yard
01 y **02** yd **03** Hof, ree **04** mews, quad, reed **05** court, garth, meuse **06** garden **08** knackery **09** courtyard **10** quadrangle, rick-barton **13** barrack square, cloister-garth

yardstick
05 gauge, scale **07** measure **08** standard **09** benchmark, criterion, guideline **10** comparison, touchstone

yarn
03 abb **04** gimp, gymp, line, tale, tram, wool **05** fable, fibre, guimp, lisle, story, twist **06** Angora, bouclé, cotton, crewel, mohair, saxony, strand, thread, two-ply, zephyr **07** four-ply, genappe, textile, worsted **08** anecdote, chenille, wheeling **09** Crimplene®, fibroline, fingering, organzine, tall story **10** water twist **11** fabrication

yawn
04 gant, gape **08** oscitate

yawning
04 huge, vast, wide **06** drowsy, gaping **08** wide-open **09** cavernous, oscitancy **10** oscitation

yaws
04 boba, buba **10** framboesia **12** button scurvy

yea *see* **yes**

year
01 a, y **02** yr **03** sun **11** twelvemonth **12** calendar year

Years include:

03 gap
04 leap
05 great, lunar, solar
06 fiscal, Hebrew, Julian, Sothic
07 natural, perfect, tropica
08 academic, Platonic, sidereal
09 canicular, financial
10 sabbatical
11 anomalistic, equinoctial
12 astronomical
14 ecclesiastical

See also **animal**

• **many years**
03 age, eon, era **04** aeon **05** calpa, decad, kalpa, yonks **06** decade, lustre, pentad **07** century, chiliad, lustrum **08** triennia **09** centenary, decennary, decennium, great year, millenary, millennia, septennia, triennial, triennium **10** centennial, millennium, quadrennia, septennium **11** bimillenary, quadrennium, quinquennia **12** donkey's years, quinquennium

• **in the year**
01 a **02** an **04** anno

• **in this year**
02 ha **07** hoc anno

• **year in, year out**
09 endlessly, regularly **10** repeatedly **11** continually **12** monotonously, persistently, time and again **13** again and again

yearbook
06 annual

yearling
03 hog **05** stirk

yearly
02 pa **05** per an **06** annual **07** per year **08** annually, per annum **09** every year, once a year, perennial **11** perennially

yearn
03 yen **04** ache, earn, erne, itch, long, pant, pine, sigh, want, wish **05** covet, crave, fancy, green, grein **06** desire, hanker, hunger, thirst **08** languish **09** think long

yearning
◇ *anagram indicator*
03 yen **04** wish **05** fancy **06** desire, hanker, hunger, pining, rennet, thirst **07** craving, longing, panting, wistful **09** hankering **11** nympholepsy

yeast
04 barm, bees, cell, yest **06** leaven, torula **13** Saccharomyces

yell
03 cry **04** bawl, howl, roar, yeld, yelp, yowl **05** shout, tiger, whoop **06** barren, bellow, cry out, holler, scream, shriek, squall, squeal **07** screech, yelloch **08** skelloch **12** unproductive

yellow
04 nesh, soft, weak, yolk **05** faint, mangy, timid **06** coward, cowish, craven, flaxen, fulvid, sallow, scared **07** chicken, citrine, fearful, fulvous, gutless, jittery, luteous, meacock, nithing, unmanly, wimpish, xanthic **08** clay-bank, cowardly, icterine, timorous, unheroic, xanthous **09** dastardly, spineless, vitellary, vitelline, weak-kneed **10** flavescent, spiritless **11** icteritious, lily-livered, milk-livered, sensational, sulphureous **12** faint-hearted, weak-spirited, white-livered, xanthochroic **13** pusillanimous, yellow-bellied **14** chicken-hearted, chicken-livered

Yellows include:

02 or
04 buff, gold, sand
05 amber, khaki, lemon, maize, ochre, peach, tawny, topaz
06 auburn, canary, fallow, golden, sienna, sulfur
07 mustard, saffron, sulphur
08 daffodil, primrose
10 chartreuse, light-brown
11 straw-colour

yellowhammer
04 yite **08** yeldring, yeldrock, yoldring

yelp
03 bay, cry, yap, yip **04** bark, yawp, yell, yowl **05** boast, nyaff, quest **06** squeal

Yemen
03 YAR, YEM

yen
01 Y **02** Yn **04** itch, lust, urge **05** thing, yearn **06** desire, hunger **07** craving, longing, passion **08** yearning **09** hankering

yeoman
04 exon **07** goodman **09** beefeater

yes
01 I **02** ay, OK **03** aye, yah, yea, yep **04** okay, ou ay, sure, yeah **05** jokol, quite, right, uh-huh, yokul **06** agreed, and how, indeed, ja wohl, rather

07 quite so 08 all right, of course, very well 09 certainly 10 absolutely, by all means, definitely 11 affirmative

yes-man
05 toady 06 lackey, minion 07 crawler 09 sycophant, toad-eater 10 bootlicker

yet
03 but, now, too 04 also, even 05 as yet, by now, howbe, so far, still 06 anyway, by then, even so 07 already, besides, further, howbeit, however, thus far 08 hitherto, moreover, until now 09 up till now 10 all the same, for all that, heretofore, in addition, up till then 11 furthermore, just the same, nonetheless 12 nevertheless, up to this time 14 into the bargain 15 notwithstanding

• as yet
05 so far 07 thus far, till now, up to now 08 hitherto 13 up to this point

yield
◇ *anagram indicator*
03 bow, net, pan, pay, sag 04 bear, bend, cede, crop, duck, earn, fall, give, haul, meal, vail 05 admit, agree, allow, defer, fetch, forgo, grant, gross, repay 06 accede, accord, afford, cave in, comply, forego, give in, give up, income, output, permit, profit, render, resign, return, reward, submit, supply 07 abandon, bring in, concede, consent, deliver, furnish, give out, give way, harvest, produce, product, provide, revenue, succumb, takings 08 abdicate, earnings, fructify, generate, give over, part with, proceeds, renounce 09 acquiesce, fructuate, give place, surrender 10 bring forth, capitulate, give ground, knock under, relinquish 11 admit defeat, go along with 12 knuckle under 14 resign yourself 15 throw in the towel

yielding
◇ *anagram indicator*
04 easy, give, soft 05 buxom 06 facile, flabby, pliant, quaggy, spongy, supple 07 ductile, elastic, pliable, springy 08 amenable, biddable, flexible, obedient, obliging 09 compliant, complying, resilient, tractable 10 compliance, submissive 11 acquiescent, complaisant, unresisting 13 accommodating

yob, yobbo
03 hob, lob, oaf, oik 04 boor, calf, clod, coof, cuif, dolt, gawk, hick, hoon, jake, lout, slob, swad 05 yahoo, yobbo 06 lubber 07 bumpkin, hallion, lumpkin 08 bull-calf, loblolly 09 barbarian, lager lout, roughneck 10 clodhopper 11 chuckle-head, hobbledehoy

yobbish
04 rude 05 crude, gawky, gruff, rough 06 coarse, oafish, rustic, vulgar 07 boorish, doltish, ill-bred, loutish, uncouth 08 bungling, churlish, ignorant, impolite 09 unrefined 10 uneducated, unmannerly 11 clodhopping, ill-mannered, uncivilized

yobbo *see* **yob, yobbo**

yoke
03 bow, tie 04 bond, join, link, span, team, tool 05 hitch, thing, union, unite 06 burden, couple, halter, inspan, object, square 07 bondage, bracket, connect, enslave, harness, slavery, tyranny 08 coupling 09 servility, servitude 10 oppression 11 enslavement, subjugation

yokel
04 boor, hick, jake, Jock, rube 06 joskin, rustic 07 bucolic, hayseed, peasant 09 hillbilly 10 clodhopper 13 country cousin 14 country bumpkin

you
01 U 02 du, tu 03 Sie 04 thee, vous

• you and me
02 us, we

young
03 fry, kid, new 04 baby 05 brood, early, green, issue, jeune, small 06 babies, family, infant, junior, litter, little, recent, youthy 07 ageless, growing, progeny, teenage, youthly 08 childish, children, immature, juvenile, under age, vigorous, youthful 09 beardless, childlike, fledgling, miniature, offspring, unfledged 10 adolescent, fledgeling, little ones 11 undeveloped 13 inexperienced 15 in the first flush

See also **animal**

younger
02 yr 04 less 05 chota 06 junior 10 latter-born

youngster
03 boy, cub, kid, lad, tot 04 brat, girl, gyte, lass, teen, tyke, wean 05 bairn, bimbo, child, smout, sprog, youth 06 nipper, rug rat, shaver 07 hellion, protegé, subteen, tiny tot, toddler, young 'un 08 teenager, young man 10 adolescent, ankle-biter, knave-bairn, young adult, young woman 11 young person

your
02 yr 03 thy

• yours
05 thine

• yours truly
02 me 06 myself 09 tout à vous

youth
03 boy, kid, lad 04 colt, lout, lowt, page, teen, yoof 05 child, prime, teens 06 Adonis, childe, chylde, gunsel, infant, keelie, kipper, spring 07 boyhood, homeboy, juvenal, May-lord 08 calf-time, girlhood, homegirl, juvenile, springal, teenager, the young, young man 09 childhood, freshness, greenhorn, hot-rodder, lager lout, salad days, springald, stripling, youngster 10 adolescent, immaturity, recentness, young adult 11 adolescence, hobbledehoy, leaping-time, teeny-bopper, young people 12 inexperience, teenage years

youthful
04 spry 05 fresh, young 06 active, boyish, lively, tender, vernal 07 buoyant, girlish 08 blooming, childish, immature, juvenile, vigorous 09 sprightly, youngling, youngthly 13 inexperienced, well-preserved 14 bread-and-butter 15 in the first flush

youthfulness
06 vigour 08 spryness, vivacity 09 freshness 10 juvenility, liveliness 12 juvenileness 13 sprightliness, vivaciousness

yowl
03 bay, cry 04 bawl, howl, wail, yawl, yell, yelp 06 squall 07 screech, ululate 09 caterwaul

ytterbium
02 Yb

yttrium
01 Y

yuck
02 fy 03 yuk 04 itch, yech

yucky
04 foul 05 dirty, gross, itchy, messy, mucky 06 filthy, grotty, grungy, sickly 08 horrible 09 revolting 10 disgusting, unpleasant

Yukon Territory
02 YT

Z

Z
03 zed, zee **04** Zulu **06** izzard

Zambia
01 Z **03** RNR, ZMB

zany
◇ *anagram indicator*
03 odd **04** daft **05** crazy, droll, funny, kooky, toady, wacky **06** absurd **07** amusing, bizarre, comical **08** clownish, merryman **09** eccentric, screwball, simpleton **10** ridiculous

Zanzibar
03 EAZ

zap
03 hit **04** do in, kill **05** erase, force, shoot **06** rub out, strike **07** bump off, correct, destroy, wipe out **08** vitality **09** finish off

zeal
04 fire, zest **05** gusto, study, verve **06** ardour, energy, fervor, spirit, vigour, warmth **07** bigotry, fervour, passion **08** devotion, keenness **09** eagerness, intensity, vehemence, zelotypia **10** commitment, dedication, enthusiasm, fanaticism **11** earnestness **12** propagandism

zealot
05 bigot **07** fanatic, radical, zealant **08** militant, partisan **09** extremist **10** enthusiast **11** eager beaver

zealous
04 keen, warm **05** eager, fiery **06** ardent, fervid, gung-ho, stanch **07** bigoted, burning, devoted, diehard, earnest, fervent, intense, staunch **08** militant, spirited **09** committed, dedicated, fanatical, strenuous **10** passionate **11** impassioned, true-devoted **12** enthusiastic, wholehearted **14** enthusiastical

zealously
06 keenly **07** eagerly **08** ardently **09** earnestly, fervently, instantly, staunchly **11** fanatically **12** passionately

zenith
01 z **03** top **04** acme, apex, peak **06** apogee, climax, height, summit, vertex **07** optimum **08** meridian, pinnacle **09** high point **11** culmination **12** highest point

zero
01 O, z **03** nil, zip **04** blob, duck, love, null **05** nadir, zilch, zippo **06** bottom, cipher, cypher, naught, nought **07** nothing **08** duck's egg, goose-egg **12** absolute zero

• zero in on
05 fix on **06** aim for **07** focus on, head for, level at, train on **08** centre on, direct at, home in on, pinpoint **10** converge on **13** concentrate on

zest
04 husk, peel, rind, rine, skin, tang, zeal, zing **05** crust, gusto, shell, spice, taste **06** relish, savour, vigour **07** epicarp, flavour **08** appetite, interest, keenness, piquancy **09** eagerness, enjoyment **10** enthusiasm, exuberance, integument, liveliness **11** joie de vivre

Zeus
07 Jupiter

zigzag
03 yaw **04** tack, wind **05** curve, snake, twist **07** crooked, meander, sinuous, vandyke, winding **08** indented, traverse, twisting **10** meandering, serpentine **14** crinkle-crankle

Zimbabwe
02 ZW **03** ZWE

zinc
02 Zn

zing
02 go **03** pep, zip **04** brio, dash, élan, life, zest **05** oomph, punch, scorn **06** energy, spirit, vigour **07** pizzazz, sparkle **08** vitality **09** animation, criticize **10** enthusiasm, get-up-and-go, liveliness **11** joie de vivre

zip
01 O **02** go **03** fly, pep **04** belt, dash, élan, life, pelt, race, rush, tear, whiz, zero, zest, zing, zoom **05** drive, flash, gusto, hurry, oomph, punch, scoot, shoot, speed, verve, vroom, whisk, whizz **06** energy, spirit, vigour, whoosh **07** nothing, pizzazz, sparkle **08** vitality **10** enthusiasm, get-up-and-go, liveliness **13** slide fastener

See also **United States of America**

zirconium
02 Zr

zither
06 cither **07** cithern, cittern, kantela, kantele **08** autoharp

zodiac
04 year **07** baldric **08** baldrick **09** baudricke

Zodiac signs:

03 Leo, Ram
04 Bull, Crab, Fish, Goat, Lion
05 Aries, Libra, Twins, Virgo
06 Archer, Cancer, Gemini, Pisces, Scales, Taurus, Virgin
07 Balance, Scorpio
08 Aquarius, Scorpion
09 Capricorn
11 Sagittarius, Water-bearer
12 Water-carrier

zone
01 z **04** area, belt, zona **05** tract **06** girdle, region, sector, sphere **07** section, stratum **08** district, province **09** territory

zoo
06 aviary **08** aquarium **09** menagerie **10** animal park, safari park **14** zoological park

zoology

Branches of zoology include:

07 ecology, zoonomy, zootaxy
08 cetology, oecology
09 acarology, hippology, mammalogy, ophiology, therology
10 autecology, conchology, embryology, entomology, limacology, malacology, morphology, nematology
11 arachnology, herpetology, ichthyology, insectology, myrmecology, ornithology
12 gnotobiology, parasitology, protozoology, zoopathology
13 helminthology, neuroethology, palaeozoology, zoophysiology
14 archaeozoology
15 lepidopterology

Zoologists include:

03 **Pye** (John David)
04 **Beer** (Sir Gavin Rylands de), **Mayr** (Ernst Walter), **Owen** (Savi)
05 **Fabre** (Jean Henri), **Hubel** (David Hunter), **Krebs** (Sir John), **Krogh** (August), **Kühne** (Wilhelm)
06 **Darwin** (Charles), **Flower** (Sir William Henry), **Frisch** (Karl von), **Kinsey** (Alfred), **Lorenz** (Konrad Zacharias), **Morris** (Desmond John), **Müller** (Johannes Peter), **Newton** (Alfred), **Pavlov** (Ivan)
07 **Agassiz** (Louis), **Audubon** (John James), **Dawkins** (Richard), **Durrell** (Gerald), **Galvani** (Luigi), **Hodgkin** (Sir Alan Lloyd), **Mantell** (Gideon Algernon), **Medawar** (Sir Peter Brian), **Wallace** (Alfred Russel)
08 **Hamilton** (William Donald), **Linnaeus** (Carolus)
09 **Aristotle**, **Schaudinn** (Fritz

Richard), **Tinbergen** (Nikolaas)
10 **Kettlewell** (Henry Bernard David)
11 **Sherrington** (Sir Charles Scott)
12 **Wigglesworth** (Sir Vincent Brian), **Wynne-Edwards** (Vero Copner)

zoom

03 fly, zap, zip **04** belt, buzz, dash, dive, pelt, race, rush, soar, tear, whiz **05** flash, shoot, speed, vroom, whirl **06** hurtle, streak **08** go all out

zulu

01 Z

- **Zulu warriors**

04 impi

Crossword Completer

How to Use the Crossword Completer

The Crossword Completer section of this book includes over 370,000 entries.

Ranging from 4 to 15 letters, these entries are arranged by length and then alphabetically according to the alternate letters. The first instance of each combination of alternate letters is highlighted in bold. For ease of reference the Completer section is divided into two parts:

- The first part gives entries where the *odd* letters are checked (and therefore known), starting with **a_a_**. Within this group the entries run in alphabetical order of the unknown (unchecked) letters (abac, à bas, Adam ...). After **a_a_** comes **a_b_**, etc, until all the four-letter entries have been dealt with. After the four-letter entries come the five-letter entries (**a_a_a** and so on), and the section eventually finishes with **z_r_p_i_t_n_r_y**.
- The second part gives entries where the *even* letters are checked (and therefore known), beginning with **_a_a** and eventually ending with **_z_n_a_i_d_s_r_**.

For quick and easy reference there is a clear indication on each page of the length of entries, and the alternate letters (up to a maximum of six characters) of the first and last entry on that page.

The Completer section is based on *Chambers Words for Crosswords and Wordgames*, and thus includes all the bold words (of 4 to 15 letters) from *The Chambers Dictionary* (2003). The only omissions are entries including numbers, entries including slashes or ellipses, symbols, some offensive terms, some abbreviations and some duplicate phrases (such as 'abstinence from' where 'abstinence' is already present). These few deletions, made for reasons of space, have been carefully selected to ensure that only terms unlikely ever to occur as a crossword clue solution have been removed. As *The Chambers Dictionary* does not include -ise and -isation variants of -ize and -ization in compounds and phrases, they are not included here.

Alongside the wealth of vocabulary from *The Chambers Dictionary* you will also find encyclopedic material, primarily names of events, people and places, from other Chambers crossword resources.

To retain information which may help with crossword clues, words are listed as they appear in the dictionary; words genuinely beginning with a capital can therefore be recognized. Where a word can be spelled with or without an initial capital letter, often with different meanings, this is shown by the symbol ✧. The use of this symbol also denotes words which may be spelled with one or more capital letters; hence, aloe vera/Aloe Vera is included only as ✧aloe vera.

Accents have been retained to distinguish between separate word meanings (eg pate and pâté) or to reflect the foreign origin of the word. Registered trade names have also been noted. Hyphenated and unhyphenated forms are shown, again as they reflect different meanings or usages. All these devices will help the solver to track down words and meanings. Hyphens, apostrophes, spaces and the like do not, of course, count in the total number of letters.

Words Arranged According to Odd Letters

For Words Arranged According to Even Letters see p 1461

4 – odd

abac
à bas
Adam
Adar
adaw
afar
agar
Ahab
ajar
Ajax
alae
Alan
alap
Alar®
alar
alas
alay
amah
anal
anan
ana's
anas
apay
Arab
arak
Aran
arar
asap
åsar
atap
aval
away
ayah
azan
✧abba
abbé
Abby
albe
ambo
arba
acct
ance
arch
arco
asci
AC/DC
Addy
✧aida
aide
AIDS
Andy
Ards
Audi®
awdl
abed
Abel
Aber
abet
acer
Aden
Ades
a few
aged
agee
agen
ages
ahem
ajee
akee
✧alec
Aled
alee
alef
alew
Alex
amen
Amex
anew
✧apex
area
ared
areg
Ares
aret
arew
Aten
aver
Aves
awed
axel
axes
Azed
affy
alfa
Aggy
alga
Algy
Angy
argh
Argo
ache
achy
agha
ashy
Abib
abid
a bit
acid
Adil
adit
agin
agio
akin
alif
alit
amid
amie
Amin
amir
amis
anil
anis
Apia
Apis
aria
arid
aril
aris
Asia
as if!
as is
at it
avid
axil
axis
ayin
alky
ankh
able
ably
alls
✧ally
amla
arle
aula
auld
axle
acme
agma
✧alma
alme
alms
ammo
an mo
arms
army
Asma
acne
Agni
aîné
ain't
Ainu
amn't
✧anna
Anne
anno
a one
arna
aune
✧aunt
awny
Abos
Acol
ados
aeon
agog
agon
ahoy
alod
aloe
aloo
alow
amok
Amos
anoa
anon
anow
apod
a-row
arow
as of
atoc
atok
atom
atop
avos
avow
AWOL
axon
Alph
Alps
acre
adry
aero
aery
Afra
✧afro
Agra
airn
airs
airt
airy
'Arry
aura
awry
ayre
aesc
also
apse
Apso
arsy
✧asst
acta
aitu
alto
anta
ante
anti
arty
Asti
Atty
auto
abut
a due
ague
alum
Alun
anus
Apus
aqua
arum
Arun
Atum
arvo
abye
acyl
amyl
aryl
azym
adze
Baal
baas
bead
beak
beam
bean
bear
beat
beau
bhai
bias
blab
blad
blae
blag
blah
blat
blay
boab
boak
boar
boat
brad
brae
brag
brak
Bram
✧bran
bras
brat
braw
bray
buat
baba
✧babe
Babi
Babs
babu
baby
boba
bobs
buba
✧bubo
✧bach
back
beck
bice
bock
buck
Badb
bade
✧bede
Bedu
bide
bidi
bode
body
budo
bael
Beeb
beef
been
beep
beer
bees
beet
bhel
bien
bier
bleb
bled
blee
blet
blew
bley
Boer
bred
bree
✧bren
brer
brew
byes
baff
baft
biff
boff
buff
bufo
bagh
bags
bego
biga
bigg
bogy
baht
boho
buhl
bail
bait
bein
blin
blip
blit
boil
Brie
brig
brim
brio
✧brit
buik
baju
bake
Baku
bike
Biko
boke
boko
buke
byke
bald
bale
Bali
balk
ball
balm
Balt
balu
bell
belt
bile
bilk
✧bill
bold
bole
Böll
boll
bolo
✧bolt
bulb
bulk
✧bull
bema
boma
bomb
bumf
bump
banc
✧band
bane
bang
bani
bank
bant
bend
bene
beni
benj
Benn
bent
bind
bine
bing
bink
bins
bint
bona
bond
bone
bong
bonk
Bonn
bony
Brno
buna
✧bund
bung
bunk
buns
bunt
biog
bios
blob
bloc
blot
blow
boob
booh
✧book
bool
boom
boon
boor
boot
brod
brog
broo
brow
buoy
bapu
✧barb
✧bard
bare
barf
Bari
bark
barm
barn
barp
bars
Bart
bere
berg
berk
berm
Bern
Bert
bird
birk
birl
Biro®
birr
Birt
bora
bord
bore
Borg
born
Boro
Bors
bort
brrr
burb
burd
burg
burk
burl
burn
burp
burr
✧bury
byre
base
bash
bask
bass
bast
Bess
✧best
bise
bish
bisk
bosh
bosk
bo's'n
bos'n
boss
bush
busk
buss
bust
busy
bate
✧bath
bats
batt
beta
bete
bête
beth
bite
bito
bitt
bote
both
bots
bott
✧bute
butt
byte
baud
bauk
baur
blub
blue
✧blur
Blut
bouk
boun
bout
Brum
brut
bevy
bawd
bawl
bawn
bawr
bowl
bowr
bows
Bixa
boxy
baye
bays
bayt
boyg
boyo
boys
Bryn
bozo
buzz
ceas
✧chad
Chae
chaf
chai
chal
✧cham
chap
char
chat
chaw
✧chay
ciao
clad
clag
clam
clan
clap
clat
claw
clay
coal
coat
co-ax
coax
✧crab
crag
✧cram
cran
crap
craw
cyan
czar
caba
Cebu
Ciba
cobb
Cuba
cube
ceca
coca
coch
cock
coco
cade
cadi
cede
cedi
cide
coda
code
Caen
CBer
chef
✧cher
chew
chez
ciel
clef
cleg
✧clem
Cleo
clew
coed
cred
✧cree
crew
cued
cafe
café
caff
C of E
coff
C of I
C of S
coft
cuff
cage
cagy
coho
✧cain
ceil
✧chic
chid
chik
chin
chip
chit
chiv
chiz
Clio
clip
coif
coil
coin
coir
coit
crib
crim
crit
cuif
cuit
cake
caky
Coke®
✧coke
coky
calf
Cali
calk
call
calm
calp
calx
cell
✧celt
cill
✧cola
cold
cole
✧coll
Colm
Colt®
colt
coly
cull
culm
cult
✧cama
came
camp
coma
comb
come
Como
comp
coms
cyma
cyme
cane
cang
cann
cans
can't
cant
cany
cens
cent
C-in-C
cine
ciné
con'd
cond
cone
conf
coni
conk
conn
Cono
cony
choc
chon
chop
chou
✧chow
cion
clod
clog
clop
clot
clou
clow
cloy
coof
cook
cool
coom
coon
co-op
coop
coot
croc
crop
✧crow
capa
✧cape
capi
capo
cope
Copt
copy
Cara
carb
card
care
cark
✧carl
Caro
carp
carr
cart
CD-RW
cere
Ceri
cero
cert
ciré
cirl
Cora
cord
core
corf
✧cork
corm
corn
curb
curd
cure
curé
curl
curn
curr
curt
casa
case
✧cash
cask
Cass
cast
cess
cist
cose
cosh
coss
cost
cosy
cush
cusk
cusp
cuss
cyst
cate
Cats
CCTV

Words marked ✧ can also be spelled with one or more capital letters

cete
cite
cito
cits
✧city
cote
coth
cott
cute
cyte
cauf
cauk
caul
caum
caup
chub
chug
chum
chut
club
clue
coup
cour
crud
crue
crus
✧crux
Cava
cave
cavy
cive
cove
cawk
cowl
cowp
cows
Cixi
coxa
coxy
coze
cozy
daal
D-day
dead
deaf
✧deal
dean
dear
deaw
dhai
dhak
dhal
dial
Dian
doab
doat
drab
drad
drag
dram
drap
drat
draw
dray
duad
dual
duan
duar
dwam
dyad
Dyak
dabs
debt
dibs
do by
dubs
dace
deck
✧deco
dice
dich
✧dick
dict
dock
duce
duck
duct
Dada
dado
Didi
✧dido
dodo
dods
dude
duds
deed
deek
deem
deen
deep
deer
deet
deev
dieb
died
dies
✧diet
Dieu
doek
doen
doer
does
dree
dreg
drek
✧drew
drey
duel
dues
duet
dyed
dyer
daff
daft
deft
defy
doff
duff
Dufy
dags
digs
doge
dogs
dogy
✧dahl
Doha
dohs
dzho
Dáil
dais
deid
deil
do in
do-in
doit
drib
drip
dojo
daks
deke
dika
dike
duke
dyke
dale
✧dali
dalt
dele
delf
deli
dell
delt
Dili
dill
dole
doll
dolt
dule
✧dull
duly
dame
damn
damp
dams
deme
demo
demy
dime
dome
domy
✧duma
dumb
dump
Dana
Dane
dang
dank
dant
Danu
dene
dent
deny
dine
ding
dink
dino
dint
Doña
dona
done
dong
Dons
don't
Dr No
dune
dung
dunk
dunt
dyne
dhol
dhow
diol
Dior
doob
dook
dool
doom
door
drop
drow
duos
✧dept
dopa
dope
dopy
dupe
Dard
dare
darg
✧dari
dark
darn
d'art
dart
dere
derm
dern
derv
dire
dirk
dirl
dirt
Dora
Doré
dork
dorm
dorp
dorr
dort
dory
dura
dure
durn
duro
dash
desk
disa
disc
dish
disk
diss
dose
dosh
doss
dost
dush
dusk
dust
data
date
dita
dite
ditt
ditz
dote
doth
doty
duty
daub
daud
daur
daut
deus
douc
Doug
do up
doup
dour
dout
drub
drug
drum
Druz
Dave
Davy
deva
Devi
Devo
diva
dive
divi
✧dove
dawd
dawk
✧dawn
dawt
Dewi
dewy
dowd
dowf
dowl
✧down
dowp
dows
dowt
dixi
dixy
doxy
✧days
daze
doze
dozy
ecad
Edam
egad
egal
El Al
élan
Elat
eoan
Esau
et al
état
Euan
Evan
Ewan
exam
eyas
Elba
each
ecce
ecco
eech
etch
Edda
eddo
✧eddy
Esda
Edel
Eden
eger
emeu
enew
épée
eten
even
ever
evet
Ewen
ewer
exec
exes
eyed
eyes
edge
edgy
eggy
Eigg
ergo
ergs
euge
eugh
eche
✧echo
echt
epha
erhu
ethe
Edie
edit
Efik
E-fit®
egis
emir
emit
Enid
Eoin
epic
✧eric
Erik
Erin
Eris
Evie
evil
✧exit
ekka
elks
Esky®
eale
eely
eild
Ella
Elle
egma
Elma
elmy
✧emma
Emmy
Edna
eine
erne
esne
✧etna
eyne
eaon
ebon
ecod
Egon
enow
epos
Eros
Eton
euoi
evoe
exon
eyot
espy
expo
eard
earl
earn
ecru
eery
eorl
euro
eyra
eyre
eyry
Ezra
ease
✧east
easy
else
Erse
erst
esse
eath
eats
Efta
Esth
Elul
eruv
étui
exul
eev'n
eevn
Elva
envy
Edwy
emys
Eryl
feal
fear
feat
fiar
Fiat®
fiat
flab
flag
flak
flam
flan
flap
flat
flaw
flax
flay
foal
foam
frab
frae
frag
frap
✧frau
fray
face
fact
feck
fico
foci
fuci
fade
fado
fady
Fido
fee'd
feed
feel
feer
feet
fief
flea
fled
flee
fleg
flew
flex
fley
foen
foes
Fred
free
fret
Frey
fuel
faff
fife
fuff
fegs
✧figo
fogy
fugu
Fahd
Fehm
föhn
faik
fail
fain
fair
faix
feis
flic
flip
flit
flix
foid
foil
foin
fris
frit
friz
Fiji
Fuji
Fuji®
fake
fike
fiky
fyke
fa la
fa-la
fall
falx
fell
felt
file
fill
film
filo
fils
fold
folk
full
fyle
fame
feme
fume
fumy
fand
fane
fang
fank
fend
feni
fent
find
fine
fini
fink
Finn
fino
fond
fone
font
fund
fung
funk
feod
floc
floe
flog
flop
flor
flow
Floy
food
fool
✧foot
froe
✧frog
from
frow
fard
fare
farl
farm
faro
fere
ferm
fern
fire
firk
firm
firn
fora
forb
Ford®
✧ford
fore
fork
form
fort
furl
furr
✧fury
fyrd
fash
fast
fess
fest
fisc
✧fish
fisk
fist
foss
fusc
fuse
fuss
fust
fate
feta
fete
fête
fett
fitt
faun
faux
feud
flub
flue
flux
foud
foul
four
fave
five
fawn
fowl
foxy
Faye
faze
fizz
fozy
fuze
fuzz
g'day
geal
gean
gear
geat
ghat
glad
glam
G-man
gnar
gnat
gnaw
goad
goaf
goal
Goan
go at
✧goat
grab
grad
Graf
gram
gran
grat
gray
Graz
Guam
guan
guar
gyal
Gabi
gaby
gibe
gobi
gobo
go by
go-by
goby
gybe
geck
guck
gade
gadi
Gide
God's
gods
gude
Gaea
Gael
geed
geek
geep
Geëz
ghee
gied
gien
gled
glee
gleg
glei
✧glen
gley
goel
goer
goes
goey
gree
gren
grew
grey
Gwen
gaff
gift
Gifu
goff
guff
gaga
gage
giga
Gigi
Gogl
go-go
gogo
guga
Gaia
gaid
Gail
gain
gair
gait
geit
glia
glib
glid
glim
Glis
glit
go in
go it
✧grid
grig
grim
grin
grip
gris
grit
guid
gajo
gala
✧gale
✧gall
geld
gelt
gila
gild
gill
gilt
gold
gole
✧golf
golp
gula
gule
✧gulf
gull
gulp
guly
gamb
game
gamp
gamy
Gems
gimp
gump
gymp
gane
gang
gant
Gdns
gena
gene
gêne
Genl
gens
✧gent
genu
Gina
ging
gink
ginn
gone
gong
Gonk®
gonk
gunk
Günz
gyny
gaol
geos
gios
glob
glom
glop
glow
good
goof
gool
go on
goon
goop
goor
grog
grot
grow
Györ
gape
gapó
garb
gare
gart
Gary
gere
germ
Gers
Gert
gird
girl
girn

✧giro
girr
girt
gore
gorm
gorp
gory
gurl
gurn
guru
gyre
gyro
gash
gasp
gast
gest
gism
gist
gosh
Goss
gush
gust
gate
gath
geta
Gita
gite
gîte
Goth
guts
gyte
gaud
Gaul
gaum
gaun
gaup
gaur
geum
glue
glug
glum
glut
gnus
gouk
go up
gout
goût
grub
grue
grum
Grus
gave
give
gyve
gawd
gawk
gawp
gowd
gowf
gowk
gowl
gown
Gaye
Glyn
Goya
goys
Gwyn
Gaza
gaze
gazy
gizz

Gozo
haaf
haar
head
heal
heap
hear
heat
hoar
hoas
hoax
✧hebe
hobo
hack
hech
heck
hick
hock
huck
hade
hadj
hide
haem
haet
heed
heel
hied
hoed
hoer
hued
huer
Huey
hyen
haff
haft
heft
✧hi-fi
huff
hagg
high
hogg
hogh
huge
Hugh
Hugo
hugy
ha-ha
he-he
hohs
haik
hail
hain
✧hair
ha'it
heid
heil!
heir
hoik
huia
huis
haji
hajj
haka
hake
hike
hoke
hoki
hyke
hale
half
hall

halm
halo
Hals
halt
held
hele
he'll
✧hell
helm
Help!
help
hila
hild
hili
hill
hilt
hold
hole
Holi
holm
holp
hols
holt
holy
hula
hule
hulk
✧hull
hyla
hyle
hame
heme
hemp
home
✧homo
Homs
homy
huma
humf
hump
hymn
hand
hang
Hani
✧hank
ha'n't
hend
hent
hind
hing
hint
hond
hone
hong
honk
hung
hunk
hunt
'hood
hood
hoof
✧hook
hoon
hoop
hoot
hapu
hept
hipt
hope
Hopi
hops

hype
hypo
hard
hare
Hari
hark
harl
harm
harn
haro
harp
hart
Hera
herb
herd
here
herl
herm
hern
✧hero
Herr
hers
hery
hire
hora
hore
✧horn
hors
hurl
hurt
hash
hask
hasp
hast
hesp
Hess
hest
hish
his'n
hisn
hiss
hist
hose
hoss
✧host
hush
husk
huso
huss
hate
hath
hete
heth
hote
Hutu
haud
haul
haut
houf
hour
hout
have
hive
Hova
✧hove
hawk
hawm
hewn
howe
howf
howk

howl
hiya
hoya
hwyl
haze
hazy
hizz
igad
ikat
✧imam
Iran
Iraq
I say!
Ivan
I-way
Iyar
Ibby
Igbo
inby
Inca
inch
itch
Indy
ibex
iced
Icel
icer
idea
idée
idem
✧ides
ilea
ilex
Ines
Inez
item
iffy
info
Iago
Inga
Inge
ingo
ings
imho
Iain
ibis
ilia
inia
in it
irid
iris
Isis
iwis
ixia
Ickx
icky
ilka
inky
idle
idly
illy
inly
Isla
isle
it'll
iamb
Irma
inns
Iona
isn't
Iynx

Ibos
icon
idol
Ifor
ikon
in on
Ipoh
iron
Ivon
Ivor
impi
I-spy
in re
inro
iure
Iasi
in se
inti
into
iota
Iowa
idyl
ivy'd
jean
jeat
jiao
Joan
jibe
jobe
juba
jube
✧jack
✧jock
joco
jade
Jodi
Jody
Jude
judo
✧judy
jeel
Jeep®
jeer
Jeez
Joel
joes
✧joey
J-pen
✧jeff
jiff
juga
jugs
Jehu
✧john
jail
Jain
join
ju-ju
juju
✧jake
joke
joky
juke
jell
jill
jilt
jole
joll
jolt
Jule
July

jamb
Jima
jimp
jomo
jump
✧jane
jann
jink
jinn
jinx
Joni
June
Jung
junk
Juno
✧junr
✧jynx
jook
jape
jark
jarl
jerk
jird
✧jura
jure
jury
jasp
jass
jasy
✧jess
jest
Jesu
jism
✧josh
✧joss
just
jato
jeté
jota
✧jute
jaup
jouk
jour
Java
Java®
jive
Jove
juve
Jawi
✧jaws
jowl
Jixi
jazy
jazz
Jozy
kcal
khaf
khan
khat
Klan
knag
knap
knar
koan
krab
ksar
kyat
Kaba
kibe
Kobe
kobo

keck
kick
kade
kadi
kudu
keek
keel
keen
keep
Kiel
kier
✧kiev
Klee
knee
knew
koel
koff
kago
kagu
✧kohl
kaid
kaie
kaif
kail
kaim
kain
keir
knit
kris
kaka
kaki
keks
koka
kuku
kale
✧kali
kell
kelp
✧kelt
kild
kill
kiln
✧kilo
kilp
kilt
✧kola
Köln
kolo
kula
kyle
✧kama
kame
kami
kemb
kemp
kana
kang
Kano
kans
✧kant
keno
✧kent
kina
kind
kine
king
kink
kino
kond
konk
kuna

kynd
kyne
kaon
khor
knob
knop
knot
know
Knox
kook
Kroo
kaph
kepi
kept
kipe
✧kipp
koph
kype
kara
kark
Karl
kart
kerb
kerf
kern
kero
kirk
kirn
kora
✧kore
Kurd
kuri
Kurt
kuru
kesh
kest
kish
✧kiss
kist
koss
kata
Kate
Kath
kati
Katy
keta
kite
kith
Kota
koto
kyte
khud
knub
knur
✧knut
kava
kiva
kiwi
Kaye
kayo
Keys
kazi
kuzu
lead
leaf
Leah
leak
leal
leam
✧lean
leap

✧lear
leat
Liam
Lian
liar
Lias
load
loaf
loam
loan
luau
lyam
lobe
lobi
lobo
lube
lace
lack
lacy
lech
lice
lich
lick
loch
loci
lock
loco
luce
luck
Lucy
Lada®
lade
✧lady
Leda
Lide
lido
lode
Lódz
Lüda
ludo
laer
leek
leep
leer
lees
leet
lied
lief
lien
lier
lieu
lues
lwei
left
life
lift
lo-fi
loft
luff
lags
Lego®
loge
Logi
logo
logs
logy
luge
Lugh
lehr
laic
laid

laik
lain
lair
leir
Leix
loid
loin
loir
Lois
luit
lake
lakh
laky
leke
like
loke
Loki
✧luke
la-la
lill
Lilo®
lilt
lily
Lola
loll
lull
✧lulu
Lyle
lama
✧lamb
lame
lamé
lamp
leme
✧lima
limb
lime
limn
limo
limp
limy
loma
Lomé
lome
Lomu
luma
lump
✧lyme
lana
✧land
lane
✧lang
lank
lant
lanx
Lena
lend
leng
leno
lens
✧lent
Lina
lind
✧line
ling
link
linn
lino
lint
liny
Linz

lone
long
✧luna
Lund
lune
lung
lunk
lunt
lyne
Lynn
✧lynx
Laos
León
Leos
✧lion
loof
look
loom
loon
loop
loor
loos
✧loot
Lvov
Lyon
Lapp
lipa
lope
Lara
lard
lare
lari
lark
larn
lere
lerp
lira
lire
lirk
✧lord
lore
lorn
lory
lure
lurk
Lyra
lyre
lase
lash
lass
last
lese
'less
less
lest
Lisa
Lise
lisk
✧lisp
'list
list
lose
losh
loss
löss
lost
lush
lusk
lust
lyse
late

lath
lati
lats
Leto
Lett
lite
lith
lota
lote
loth
loti
loto
lots
lute
lutz
lyte
laud
lauf
loud
loun
loup
lour
lout
lava
lave
leva
leve
Levi
levy
live
Livy
love
lawk
lawn
lewd
lowe
lown
lowt
luxe
laze
lazo
lazy
leze
Liza
ma'am
maar
Maat
mbar
mead
meal
mean
meat
mnas
moan
moat
M-way
myal
Macc
Mace®
mace
mack
mica
mice
✧mick
mico
moch
mock
much
✧muck
made
Medb
Mede
✧midi
mode
modi
✧mods
Maev
meed
meek
✧meer
meet
mien
mzee
miff
muff
mage
magg
✧magi
mags
mega
Moho
mohr
Maia
maid
maik
mail
maim
main
mair
mein
moil
moit
muid
muil
muir
✧mojo
make
mako
✧mike
moke
moki
moko
Malé
male
✧mali
mall
malm
malt
mela
meld
mell
melt
mild
mile
milk
mill
milo
milt
mola
✧mold
✧mole
✧moll
molt
moly
mule
✧mull
mama
meme
memo
mime
mome
mumm
mump
mana
mand
mane
mang
mani
Mann
mano
Manú
Manx
many
mend
mene
meng
meno
ment
menu
✧mina
mind
mine
✧ming
Mini®
mini
mink
mino
mint
minx
miny
✧mona
'mong
mong
monk
mono
Mons
mony
munt
myna
meow
mhos
mood
Moog®
mooi
mook
mool
✧moon
moop
✧moor
moot
muon
mips
mope
Mopp
mopy
mara
marc
mard
mare
marg
✧mark
marl
marm
Marq
Mars
mart
Marx
✧mary
merc
mere
meri
merk
merl
Mira
mire
miri
mirk
Miró
mirs
mirv
miry
mora
More!
more
morn
Moro
mort
mure
murk
murl
Myra
masa
mase
mash
mask
✧mass
mast
masu
mesa
mese
mesh
✧mess
mise
miso
✧miss
mist
mose
mosh
✧moss
most
Musa
✧muse
mush
musk
muso
muss
must
mate
maté
math
✧matt
maty
Meta
mete
Metz
mite
mitt
mity
MOT'd
mote
✧moth
mott
✧motu
mute
muti
mutt
myth
✧maud
Maui
maul
maun
moue
moup
meve
move
mawk
mawr
mewl
mews
mowa
mown
maxi
mixt
mixy
moxa
✧maya
✧mayo
moya
moyl
maze
mazy
meze
mézé
mizz
moze
mozz
muzz
naam
naan
✧neal
neap
near
neat
Noah
Noam
nyas
nabk
nabs
nibs
nach
neck
nice
✧nick
nock
nada
nide
nidi
node
nodi
nude
need
neem
neep
ne'er
nief
✧noel
✧noël
noes
naff
nife
niff
nuff
naga
nigh
nogg
no go
Naha
Naia
naif
naïf
naik
nail
nain
Nair
neif
Neil
ne is
noil
Naja
Nike
nuke
nala
Nell
n'ill
nill
Nola
nole
noll
null
✧name
nemn
nimb
noma
nome
numb
✧nana
nene
Nina
✧nine
Nona
none
nong
no-no
non-U
naos
neon
nook
noon
noop
napa
nape
✧nipa
nope
Nupe
Nara
narc
nard
nare
nark
nary
nerd
nerk
Nero
nirl
Nora
nori
norm
Norn
nurd
nurl
nurr
NASA
Nash
nesh
ness
nest
nisi
nose
nosh
nosy
Nato
nete
nets
nett
Nita
nite
n'ote
no'te
note
not-I
nott
nuts
neuk
neum
noul
noun
noup
nous
nout
nave
✧navy
névé
nevi
nova
news
newt
nowl
nown
nowt
nowy
next
nixy
naze
Nazi
Oban
odal
ogam
okay
Olaf
Olav
Oman
Omar
opah
opal
oral
Oran
ou ay
oval
ombu
ombú
orby
once
orca
ouch
odds
olds
oldy
obey
odea
Odes
ogee
OKed
Olea
oleo
omen
✧omer
oner
op-ed
open
oven
over
owed
Owen
ower
oxen
oxer
oyer
oyes
oyez
oafs
Offa
offy
oofy
orfe
Olga
orgy
Oahu
oche
Otho
obia
obit
odic
Odie
Odin
Oeic
Ohio
olid
olio
omit
otic
Ovid
Oaks
oaky
ogle
oils
oily
olla
only
orle
Oslo
ould
oulk
Oulu
Owls
owly
Ogma
ouma
oink
oint
oons
oont
oboe
obol
Obon
obos
odor
Oxon
Ogpu
olpe
oops
oppo
oupa
ouph
oary
ogre
okra
orra
ourn
ours
owre
oast
odso
Omsk
onst
oose
oosy
or so
ossa
Ossi
oust
oath
oats
oaty
octa
Oita
okta
onto
orts
✧otto
outs
onus
opus
ovum
odyl
onyx
oryx
ooze
oozy
orzo
ouzo
Ozzy
paan
peag
peak
peal
pean
pear
peas
peat
phat
Piaf
plan
plap
plat
play
prad
pram
prat
prau
pray
Ptah
pyat
peba
paca
✧pace
pack
paco
pact
pacy
pech
peck
Pécs
pecs
✧pica
pice
pick
pics
Pict
pock
poco
puce
✧puck
pads
pudu
peek
peel
peen
peep
peer
phew
pied
pier
piet
plea
pleb
pled
poem
poet
pree
prep
prex
prey
puer
pyet
puff
✧page
pegh
Pegu
pogo
pugh
paid
paik
pail
pain
pair
pais
pein
Phil
phiz
plié
plim
prig
prim
puir
puja
peke
pika
pike
poke
poky
puke
puku
puky
pale
Pali
pall
palm
palp
paly
pela
✧pele
pelf
pell
pelt
pila
pile
pili
pill
Pils
✧pole
polk
✧poll
polo
polt
poly
pula
pule
puli
pulk
pull
✧pulp
puls
pulu
puly
pimp
pome
po-mo
pomp
puma
pump
pumy
pand
pane
pang
pant
pend
pene
peni
penk
pent
piña
pine
ping
pink
pint
piny
✧pond
pone
pong
ponk
pons
pont
pony
puna
punk
punt
puny
pyne
peon
phoh
phon
phot
pion
pioy
plod
plop
plot
plow
ploy
pood
poof
✧pooh
pook
pool
poon
poop
poor
poot
proa
prob
✧prod
prof
prog
prom
proo
prop
pros
prow
pyot
✧papa
pape
pepo
pipa
pipe
pipi
pipy
✧pope
pops
pupa
Pará
para
pard
pare
✧park
parp
parr
part
père
peri
perk
Perl
perm
pern
perp
pert
Peru
perv
pirl
pirn
pore
pork
porn
port
pory
pure
puri
purl
purr
pyre
pyro
pash
pass
past
peso
pest
Pisa
pisé
pish
pose
posé
posh
poss
post
posy
psst
push
puss
pate
pâté
path
Pete
pita
pith
Pitt
pity
pote
pots
pott
putt
putz
paua
✧paul

pbuh
phut
pium
Pius
plug
plum
plus
pouf
pouk
pour
pout
Prue
pruh
pave
pavé
Pavo
pawa
pawk
pawl
pawn
pown
pixy
poxy
pays
Phyl
Pnyx
prys
Pu Yi
pize
pozz
✧**quad**
quag
quat
quay
qadi
quep
quey
Q-Tip®
quid
quin
quip
quit
quiz
quod
quop
qoph
read
reak
real
ream
rean
reap
rear
rial
road
roam
roan
roar
ryal
Ryan
rabi
'robe
robe
rube
ruby
raca
race
rach
rack
racy
reck

Rect
rice
rich
✧rick
ricy
roch
✧rock
ruck
rade
rads
redd
rede
redo
Reds
ride
rode
rudd
rude
Ryde
reed
reef
reek
reel
reen
✧rhea
riel
riem
roed
rued
raff
raft
reft
rife
riff
rift
ruff
ryfe
raga
rag'd
rage
ragg
ragi
rags
regd
rego
Riga
rigg
Rahu
raid
raik
rail
rain
rait
reif
reik
rein
reis
roil
roin
ruin
raja
roji
rake
raki
raku
reke
roke
roky
rukh
ryke
rale

râle
rely
rile
rill
role
rôle
Rolf
roll
rule
ruly
Rama
rami
ramp
Rams
rima
rime
rimu
rimy
✧roma
Rome
Romo
romp
rume
✧rump
✧**rana**
✧rand
rang
rani
rank
rant
rend
Rene
René
Reno
✧rent
reny
rind
rine
ring
rink
Rona
rone
rong
ront
rund
rune
rung
runs
runt
rynd
rhos
riot
rood
roof
rook
room
roon
roop
root
ryot
rape
rapt
repo
repp
reps
ripe
ripp
ript
rope
ropy
rype

rare
rore
ro-ro
rort
✧rory
rurp
ruru
rase
rash
rasp
rast
resh
rest
rise
risk
risp
Riss
Rosa
rose
rosé
Ross
rost
rosy
rusa
✧ruse
rusé
✧rush
rusk
Russ
rust
rata
rate
rath
rats
ratu
retd
rete
Rita
rite
ritt
Ritz
✧rota
rote
Roth
roti
rotl
Ruta
✧ruth
raun
Rhun
rhus
roué
roul
roum
roup
rout
roux
rave
Ravi
Revd
riva
rive
rivo
rove
rawn
rowt
Rhyl
Rhys
Raza
raze
razz

riza
Saab®
saag
Saam
scab
scad
scag
scam
scan
scar
scat
scaw
seal
seam
✧sean
Seaq
sear
Seat®
seat
Sfax
shad
shag
shah
sham
✧shan
shat
✧shaw
shay
sial
Sian
skag
skat
skaw
slab
slae
slag
slam
slap
slat
Slav
slaw
slay
snab
snag
snap
snar
soak
soap
soar
Soay
spae
Spam®
spam
span
spar
spat
spaw
spay
spaz
stab
stag
stap
star
stat
staw
stay
swab
swad
swag
swam
swan

swap
swat
sway
Saba
sibb
subs
sybo
sack
sech
seco
sect
Secy
sice
sich
sick
soca
sock
such
suck
syce
✧**sade**
sida
side
Sids
soda
sudd
suds
seed
seek
seel
seem
seen
seep
seer
shea
she'd
shed
Shem
Shep
she's
shes
shet
shew
sien
skeg
skeo
skep
sker
skew
sled
slee
slew
sley
✧smee
smew
sneb
sned
snee
spec
sped
spek
✧spet
spew
sted
stem
✧sten
step
stet
stew
stey
sued

suer
suet
Suez
swee
swey
syen
safe
Safi
sift
sofa
Sofi
soft
Sufi
saga
sage
sago
sagy
sego
sigh
sign
so-ho
soho
saic
said
sail
saim
sain
sair
seif
seik
seil
seir
Shia
shim
shin
ship
shir
shiv
ski'd
skid
skim
skin
skio
skip
skis
skit
'slid
slid
✧slim
slip
slit
smir
smit
snib
snig
snip
snit
soil
spie
spin
spit
spiv
stie
stir
suid
suit
swig
swim
swiz
Sejm
sijo

soja
sake
saké
✧saki
✧sekt
sika
sike
Sikh
soke
Suke
sukh
Suky
syke
sale
salp
salt
seld
sele
self
sell
sild
sile
silk
sill
silo
silt
sola
sold
sole
soli
solo
sulk
✧sulu
sama
same
Sami
samp
semé
semi
shmo
sima
simi
simp
Soma®
✧soma
some
sumo
sump
sumy
San'a
sand
sane
sang
sank
sans
✧sant
sena
send
sene
sens
sent
sind
Síne
sine
sing
sinh
sink
sone
✧song
✧sung
suni

sunk
sunn
sync
synd
syne
scog
scop
✧scot
scow
shod
shoe
shog
shoo
✧shop
shot
show
Sion
Siôn
skol
slob
sloe
slog
slop
slot
slow
smog
snob
snod
snog
snot
snow
sook
soom
soon
soop
soor
soot
spod
spot
stoa
stob
stop
stot
stow
swob
swop
swot
seps
sept
sipe
soph
supe
Supt
sype
Sara
✧sard
sari
✧sark
scry
sera
Serb
sere
serf
serk
serr
Shri
sire
✧siri
skry
sora
✧sorb

sord
sore
sori
sorn
sort
spry
sura
surd
sure
surf
sa sa
sash
sass
sese
sesh
sess
siss
sist
so so
so-so
soss
Susa
suss
✧susu
Susy
sate
sati
seta
Seth
sett
Sita
site
sith
✧**saul**
saut
✧scud
scug
scul
scum
scup
scur
scut
shul
'shun
shun
shut
Sium
skua
skug
slub
slue
slug
slum
slur
slut
smug
smur
smut
snub
✧snug
souk
✧soul
soum
soup
✧sour
sous
sout
spud
spue
spun
spur

stub
stud
stum
stun
swum
save
Siva
Suva
sawn
sewn
shwa
sowf
sowl
sowm
sown
sowp
✧**saxe**
sext
sexy
says
scye
Skye
skyr
snye
soya
stye
Styx
size
sizy
Suzy
Taal
T-bar
tea'd
tead
teak
teal
team
Tean
tear
teat
thae
Thai
than
thar
that
thaw
tian
tiar
toad
to a T
trad
tram
trap
trat
tray
tsar
tuan
twae
twal
'twas
tway
tzar
tabi
tabu
to-be
✧toby
tuba
✧tube
tace
tach
tack

taco
tact
tech
tice
✧tich
tick
Tico
Toc H
tock
toco
tuck
tedy
tide
tidy
to-do
tody
tyde
tael
ta'en
tee'd
teed
teel
teem
teen
teer
Thea
thee
them
then
Theo
thew
they
tied
tier
toea
toed
toey
tree
tref
trek
très
tret
trew
T Rex
trey
trez
twee
Taff
teff
tiff
tift
toff
toft
tofu
tufa
tuff
tuft
tags
tegg
tegu
tige
toga
toge
Togo
to go
togs
taha
tahr
tehr
toho
Tshi

tail
tait
teil
tein
thig
thin
thir
this
toil
trie
trig
trim
trin
trio
trip
Trix
twig
twin
twit
Tojo
taka
take
taki
taky
tika
tike
tiki
toke
toko
tyke
tala
talc
tale
tali
talk
tall
tela
teld
tele
tell
telt
tile
till
tilt
tola
told
tole
toll
tolt
✧tolu
Tula
tule
tame
tamp
Tema
teme
temp
tems

✧time
tomb
tome
tump
tymp
tana
ta'ne
tane
T'ang
✧tang
tanh
tank
tend
tene
tent
Tina
tind
tine
ting
tink
tint
tiny
tone
tong
Toni
tonk
tons
✧tony
tuna
tund
tune
tuny
tyn'd
tynd
✧tyne
thon
Thor
thou
took
tool
toom
toon
toot
trod
trog
tron
✧trot
trow
✧troy
tapa
tape
taps
tapu
tipi
tipt
tope
topi
topo

tops
Tupi
Tupí
type
typo
tara
tare
tarn
taro
tarp
tart
terf
term
tern
thro
thro'
thru
tire
tirl
tiro
tirr
torc
tore
tori
torn
torr
tort
Tory
turf
Turk
turm
turn
tyre
tyro
tash
task
tass
tbsp
Tess
test
tosa
tose
tosh
toss
tost
tush
tusk
ta-ta
✧tate
tath
Tati
tatt
tatu
tête
teth
tite
titi
Tito

tits
tote
Toto
tuts
✧tutu
tyte
taut
thud
thug
Thun
thus
touk
toun
tour
tout
✧true
trug
tava
tawa
taws
tawt
town
towt
towy
taxa
taxi
text
trye
tryp
tizz
toze
tuzz
udal
Umar
unau
upas
Ural
urao
Utah
utas
umbo
unbe
upby
unce
unci
unco
unde
undé
undo
urdé
Urdu
urdy
ulex
urea
used
user
uses
Utes

uvea
upgo
urge
Unio
✧unit
Unix
uric
utis
Ugli®
ugly
umma
ulna
udon
udos
✧ufos
upon
umph
upsy
Ursa
USSR
unto
uh-uh
Uruk
urus
ulva
urva
V-day
veal
vial
voar
vibe
vibs
✧**vice**
vade
Veda
vide
veep
veer
vied
vier
✧view
vlei
vagi
✧vega
Vigo
Vehm
vail
vain
vair
veil
vein
void
vril
vale
vali
✧vela
veld
vele

vell
vild
vile
vill
vola
vole
volk
volt
vuln
vvll
vamp
vane
vang
vant
vena
vend
vent
vina
vine
vino
vint
viny
viol
vrow
vara
vare
vary
Vera
verb
vers
vert
very
vire
virl
✧**vasa**
vase
vast
vest
visa
vise
visé
Voss
vatu
veto
✧vita
vite
vote
vaut
viva
vive
vivo
vext
vizy
Waac
Waaf
weak
weal
wean

wear
Wham!
wham
whap
what
woad
wrap
wack
Waco
wice
wich
✧wick
wock
wych
wadd
wade
wadi
wadt
wady
wide
weed
week
weel
weem
ween
weep
weet
whee
when
whe'r
whet
whew
whey
wiel
Wien
woes
✧wren
Wafd
waff
waft
weft
wife
wage
Wuhu
waid
waif
wail
✧wain
wait
weid
weil
weir
whid
✧whig
whim
whin
whip
whir

✧whit
whiz
writ
waka
wake
✧wakf
weka
woke
wald
wale
wali
walk
wall
Walt
waly
weld
welk
we'll
✧well
✧welt
✧wild
wile
wili
will
wilt
wily
wold
wolf
wull
wame
wemb
wimp
womb
wan'd
wand
wane
wang
want
wany
✧wend
went
wind
wine
wing
wink
winn
wino
win't
winy
wonk
won't
wont
wynd
wynn
whoa
who'd
whom
whop

who's
whot
whow
wood
woof
wool
woon
woo't
woot
wept
wipe
✧**waqf**
ward
ware
wark
warm
warn
warp
wart
wary
we're
were
wert
wire
wiry
✧word
wore
work
worm
worn
wort
Würm
wase
wash
✧wasp
wast
✧west
✧wise
wish
wisp
wist
wost
wuss
wate
wats
watt
weta
wite
with
wits
wots
wyte
wauk
waul
waur
whup
wave
wavy

we've
wive
wove
wawe
wawl
wowf
waxy
wexe
Wuxi
ways
Xian
Xmas
X-ray
✧xray
Xema
Xosa
xyst
yead
yeah
yean
year
yuan
yack
yech
YMCA
yock
yuca
yuck
YWCA
yede
yode
yodh
ybet
yeed
ylem
Yves
yaff
yuft
Yagi
yegg
yoga
yogh
yogi
yuga
Yugo®
yo-ho
ywis
yike
ylke
yoke
yuke
yuko
yuky
yald
Yale®
yale
y'all
yeld

yelk
yell
yelm
yelp
yelt
yill
yold
yolk
✧yule
Yama
yomp
yump
✧**yang**
✧yank
yond
yoni
yont
yunx
ygoe
yoof
yoop
yapp
yips
ympe
ympt
✧**yard**
yare
yarn
yarr
yerd
yerk
yird
yirk
yore
✧york
yurt
yesk
yes's
yest
yate
yeti
yett
yite
yaud
yaup
yeuk
you'd
youk
your
yeve
yawl
yawn
yawp
yaws
yawy
yowe
yowl
yo-yo

zeal
zebu
Zibo
zobo
zobu
Zach
✧zack
Zico
zoea
ziff
Zift
zein
zoic
zila
Zola
✧zulu
zimb
zyme
Zanu
zany
Zena
Zend
zinc
zine
zing
zona
zone
zonk
Zuni
Zuñi
Zion
zoom
zoon
Zapu
zupa
Zara
zarf
zero
Zorb®
zori
zurf
zest
zati
zeta
zite
ziti
'zbud
Zeus
zouk
zeze
zizz

5 – odd

abaca
abaya
Adana
afara
Agama
Agana
alapa
anana
Aqaba

araba
asana
aband
afald
aland
Åland
apaid
apayd
award

abase
abate
adage
agape
a'gate
agate
agave
agaze
alate

amate
amaze
apace
apage
arame
avale
awake
aware
awave

alang
abash
✧awash
abaci
acari
agami
Amati
aback
abask

alack
at all
avail
alarm
again
Al Ayn
amain
awarn
Alamo

alaap
Adams
adays
amass
Anaïs
aways
abaft
adapt
agast

apart
avant
avast
await
alary
Araby
ataxy
✧**albee**
amble

album
Alban
amban
amber
arbor
ambos
abbot
ambit
at bat

at-bat
abbey
ambry
Accra
aecia
arced
abcee
ancle
ancon

Alcis
arcus
ascus
✧**ascot**
accoy
Archy
aldea
Ardea
ardeb

Asdic
aided
Addie
addle
Andie
ao dai
ard-ri
ardri
Abd-al
Abdul
add-in
add-on
Aidan
Aiden
Auden
addio
add to
audio
add up
adder
aider
alder
and/or
ardor
aedes
aidos
Andes
Ardas
audit
addax
Adela
Akela
Alexa
ameba
areca
arena
Areta
Avena
acerb
ahead
amend
an-end
aread
aredd
abele
Adèle
Agene®
agene
akene
aleye
amene
anele
arede
arere
arête
aleph
à demi
Adeni
Alesi
Azeri
Aleck
apeak
apeek
a-week
Adeel
areal
aweel
abeam
adeem
aweto
aheap

ayelp
abear
afear
ameer
anear
arear
avens
adept
agent
ahent
aleft
alert
ament
anent
apert
aren't
arett
avert
à deux
aiery
apery
arefy
Alfie
awful
as for
affix
algid
Aggie
✧algae
Angie
✧angle
argue
aygre
aggri
algal
Algol
angel
argal
argil
argol
algum
algin
argan
argon
aggro
Anglo
Aegir
agger
anger
auger
augur
aegis
Angus
Argos
✧argus
avgas
✧**angst**
argot
aught
aggry
angry
Aphra
ad hoc
aphid
ashen
abhor
achar
Asher
aphis
Århus
✧ashes

Athos
ashet
as how
agila
akita
aliya
Amina
Anila
anima
Anita
Arica
Arita
Ávila
ahind
abide
afire
agile
Alice
alike
A-line
aline
alive
amice
amide
amine
anile
anime
animé
anise
arise
A-side
aside
avine
avise
avize
axile
azide
azine
aging
a-wing
ahigh
Amish
anigh
apish
arish
acini
Aditi
alibi
amici
apiol
✧ariel
axial
apism
axiom
✧**alien**
align
anion
apian
Arian
Arien
Asian
avian
avion
axion
amigo
aviso
abies
adiós
agios
alias
amiss

Aries
Arius
agist
ahint
A-list
ariot
atilt
adieu
acidy
amity
atimy
alkyd
ackee
alkie
ankle
Arkle
alkyl
anker
asker
akkas
ankus
askew
Ailsa
ad lib
ad-lib
adlib
aulic
abled
allod
aglee
Ailie
all-be
allée
Allie
Allah
auloi
aflaj
allel
allyl
Allan
Allen
all in
all-in
Aslan
Aalto
all-to
all-up
abler
allis
✧arles
✧atlas
aulos
ablet
aglet
allot
ablow
aglow
allow
agley
allay
alley
alloy
allez
Ahmad
Ahmed
armed
almug
almah
almeh
armil
aumil

ad-man
adman
admin
✧amman
✧ammon
atman
axman
armor
admit
armet
admix
awmry
amnia
apnea
acned
awned
aînée
Annie
annal
annul
Adnan
amnio
Arnor
awner
Agnes
Alnus
Annis
annat
Annot
arnut
Agnew
as now
annex
annoy
aunty
agora
aloha
Anona
aroba
aroma
A-bomb
azoic
abord
acold
à fond
agood
ahold
aloed
aloud
A-road
aroid
avoid
axoid
abode
abore
above
adobe
adore
afore
agoge
agone
alone
alowe
amove
anode
anole
apode
arose
atoke
at one
atone

awoke
azole
azote
aloof
along
among
azoth
aioli
aïoli
acock
awork
aboil
afoul
atoll
Acorn®
acorn
adorn
adown
ab ovo
à go-go
à gogo
apoop
amour
aloes
abort
about
adopt
afoot
aloft
amort
aport
ayont
a'body
agony
anomy
atomy
atony
atopy
✧**alpha**
aspic
ample
✧apple
appui
ampul
appal
appel
✧**aspen**
appro
as per
asper
at par
al più
Ampex®
amply
appay
apply
appuy
aorta
atria
Afric
auric
acred
acrid
adrad
adred
aerie
agree
aurae
ayrie
aargh
arrah

aurei
April
aural
Avril
✧**abram**
abrim
ad rem
Aaron
abrin
agrin
apron
Arran
atrip
airer
aurar
Abrus
acres
après
✧arras
arris
auras
afrit
✧amrit
arrêt
arrow
abray
array
Aisha
Aosta
at sea
Aysha
aisle
assai
adsum
Aksum
Assam
arson
Aesop
aesir
apsis
arsis
asses
absit
asset
assot
absey
assay
antra
antic
artic
✧attic
Aztec
antae
antre
anti-g
aitch
artal
artel
actin
act on
acton
astun
act up
attap
actor
after
altar
alter
antar
aster
astir

attar
actus
altos
Attis
autos
Artex®
antsy
aptly
artsy
Abuja
abuna
alula
Anura
Aruna
adunc
agued
abune
abuse
acute
alure
amuse
azure
aguti
amuck
ahull
azurn
adult
adust
azury
abuzz
anvil
arval
arvos
advew
Ahvaz
aswim
ajwan
Alwin
Alwyn
Aswan
Anwar
as was
alway
asway
as why
auxin
adyta
avyze
azyme
abysm
Aryan
abyss
as yet
as-yet
azygy
Anzac
aizle
brava
bwana
beard
bland
blaud
board
braid
brand
beare
blade
Blake
blame
blare
blasé

blate
blaze
brace
brake
brame
brave
braze
buaze
bhang
beach
beath
blash
brach
brash
bhaji
braai
Bragi
bravi
bwazi
✧**black**
blank
brack
brank
be-all
brail
brawl
blain
Boann
brain
brawn
beano
✧bravo
Blair
by air
beads
beans
beaus
blaes
brass
braws
✧**beast**
beaut
blast
blatt
boart
boast
bract
brast
beaux
beady
beaky
beamy
braky
braxy
Bubka
bobac
Babee
✧bible
bobak
✧**babel**
babul
bobol
bubal
baboo
bebop
bob up
Babur
Bibby
✧bobby
bubby
bacca

bocca
becke
bocce
✧boche
✧**bacon**
bacco
bucko
buchu
bucku
baccy
Becky
biccy
bedad
bided
badge
bedye
bodge
bodle
budge
bedel
bedim
Baden
bid in
bidon
bid up
budos
bidet
bedew
baddy
badly
✧biddy
buddy
Breda
bield
bleed
blend
bread
breed
by-end
brede
breme
brere
breve
beech
beedi
bleak
break
B cell
bream
breem
bleep
blear
breer
beefs
bless
bleat
blent
blest
✧brent
Brest
Brett
beefy
beery
BAFTA
buffa
bifid
buffe
befog
buffi
boffo
buffo

by far
buffs
befit
baffy
bigha
begad
bigae
bogie
bogle
bugle
bags I
bagel
begem
begum
began
✧begin
begun
bogan
big up
begar
bogus
Bagot
begat
beget
begot
bight
bigot
baggy
biggy
bogey
boggy
buggy
bohea
Baha'i
Bahai
Behar
Bihar
bohos
bahut
baisa
baiza
Beira
blind
build
baize
beige
blite
blive
Boise
bribe
✧bride
brine
brisé
brize
B-side
brief
ba'ing
being
boing
bring
blini
blink
boink
brick
brink
brisk
Buick®
brill
bairn
Brian
blimp

Words marked ✧ can also be spelled with one or more capital letters

briar
brier
✧**bliss**
B-list
blist
built
buist
blimy
briny
✧**blitz**
bajra
bajri
✧**bajan**
Bajau
bijou
baked
bikie
bekah
baken
baker
biker
bokos
balsa
belga
Bella
✧bulla
balk'd
belee
belie
✧belle
bilge
bulge
bulse
belah
belch
balti
Belém
balun
Balbo
✧baloo
Balto
bilbo
baler
Balor
balas
balls
bells
bolas
bolos
bolts
bolus
B flat
below
bylaw
bolix
baldy
balky
bally
balmy
belay
belly
bilby
bilgy
billy
bulgy
bulky
bully
bemad
bemud
bombe
bombé

bumph
Bambi
bimbo
bombo
bumbo
bumps
bumpy
banda
✧bania
banya
benga
Binca®
bonza
bunia
bunya
B and B
boned
Bände
benne
binge
bonce
bonie
bonne
bonze
bunce
bunje
Banff
bandh
bench
bunch
benni
Benxi
bindi
Bondi
banal
Benin
banco
banjo
bingo
bongo
bunco
bunko
boner
bands
bangs
Banks
banns
bonds
bones
bonus
Banat
benet
✧**bantu**
bundu
bandy
bendy
✧benny
benty
bingy
bonny
Bundy®
bungy
bunjy
✧bunny
✧bunty
biota
Brona
blond
blood
boord
broad

brond
brood
biome
bloke
blore
boose
booze
broke
brose
be off
booth
broch
brogh
broth
Baoji
booai
block
brock
✧brook
broil
brool
bloom
broom
blown
brown
bloop
biogs
boobs
books
boots
biont
bloat
boost
Bronx
blowy
booay
booby
boody
booky
boomy
booty
boozy
biped
bipod
bepat
buppy
barca
Barra
burka
Burma
burqa
bursa
berob
baric
boric
bored
barbe
barge
barre
barré
barye
Berne
birle
birse
borde
boree
borne
borné
burke
burse
berth

birch
birth
burgh
borak
beryl
borel
baron
boron
buran
burin
Byron
bardo
borgo
buroo
burro
bar-b-q
borer
barbs
bards
Bart's
Biros
bords
Boris
Burns
Byrds
beret
buret
burnt
burst
borax
bardy
barky
barmy
Barry
beray
berry
birsy
burly
burry
Basra
basta
Bosra
✧**basic**
based
Basle
basse
baste
besee
bosie
Bosch
bassi
✧**basij**
basal
✧basil
besom
bisom
bosom
basan
basen
basin
bason
bison
boson
bo'sun
bosun
Busan
basho
basso
basto
bases
basis

buses
beset
besit
besot
bussu
bassy
Bessy
bosky
bossy
busby
✧bushy
busky
busty
batta
Botha
Butea
betid
bathe
bitte
botte
butte
batch
bitch
botch
✧butch
batik
betel
botel
butyl
baton
béton
buteo
biter
baths
batts
bitos
bitts
butut
battu
Botox®
batty
Betsy
✧betty
bitsy
bitty
bothy
botty
butty
bhuna
blurb
bluid
bound
bourd
blude
bouge
boule
bouse
Bruce
brûlé
brume
brute
bluff
bourg
blush
bough
brush
baulk
blunk
bourn
Bruin
Bruno

✧**blues**
blunt
blurt
boult
bruit
brunt
brust
bludy
bluey
bousy
bovid
bevue
bevel
bavin
Bevin
bever
bevvy
bivvy
bowed
Bowie
bowne
bowse
bewig
bowel
bow in
bower
bowes
bowls
bewet
bowat
bowet
bawdy
byway
buxom
boxen
box in
box up
✧**boxer**
boxty
bayle
Boyle
Blyth
Bayan
Bryan
buy in
buy-in
buy up
boyar
buyer
boyos
bayou
boyau
Bazza
bezel
bazoo
bazar
bozos
Bizet
bizzy
buzzy
Caaba
chana
chara
chaya
Ciara
Clara
coarb
craic
chard
Claud
cease

ceaze
chace
chafe
chape
chare
chase
chave
clade
clame
Clare
clave
coate
crake
crame
crane
crape
crare
crate
crave
craze
chaff
clang
✧craig
clash
coach
crash
coati
chack
✧chalk
chank
chark
clack
clank
crack
crank
crawl
Chaim
charm
chasm
claim
chain
chaco
claro
champ
clamp
clasp
cramp
chair
charr
Clair
Chams
chaos
✧chaps
chars
claes
class
crabs
craps
crass
chaft
chant
chart
clart
claut
coact
coapt
✧coast
craft
chary
clary
coaly

crapy
crazy
cobia
cobra
cobza
cabob
cubeb
caboc
cubic
cable
cabré
coble
cabal
cibol
Cobol
cabin
Cuban
caber
cabas
Cebus
Cabot
cubit
cabby
cobby
cubby
cocoa
cycad
cache
cycle
cacti
cocci
cecal
Cecil
cecum
cacao
cocco
cyclo
cocos
cocky
codec
cadee
cadge
cadie
cadre
codon
cedar
cider
coder
cyder
cedis
cadet
codex
caddy
cadgy
cuddy
Cádiz
caeca
✧cheka
chela
crena
✧**creed**
caese
✧chère
clepe
cleve
creme
crème
crême
crepe
crêpe
Crete

✧crewe
ctene
cheth
Czech
check
cheek
cleck
cleek
clerk
creak
✧creek
creel
cream
clean
Cleon
Creon
chemo
✧credo
cheap
cheep
cleep
creep
cheer
clear
chess
Crees
cress
cheat
chert
chest
cleat
cleft
crept
crest
chevy
chewy
crepy
crêpy
Cufic
cuffo
caged
cogie
cogue
✧**cigar**
CS gas
cagot
ci-gît
cagey
ciggy
cohab
cohoe
cohog
cohen
cohos
ceiba
Chiba
chica
✧china
Chita
cnida
chimb
climb
caird
child
cried
chide
✧chile
chime
chine
chiné
chive

clime
cline
clipe
Clive
crime
crine
crise
chief
cliff
cling
cuing
chich
crith
cuish
ceili
chili
chick
chink
chirk
click
clink
crick
chiel
chill
chirl
chirm
cairn
Chian
coign
Cairo
chiao
chico
chimo
chino
chimp
chirp
crimp
crisp
chirr
crier
Chios
chips
cries
chirt
clift
✧clint
clipt
C-list
chiru
chivy
chizz
✧**cajun**
cokes
cakey
calla
calpa
Celia
cella
cilia
colza
celeb
colic
calid
calve
Celie
Chloe
calif
C clef
colog
culch
Calum

celom
Colum
✧**colin**
Colón
colon
'cello
cello
color
calfs
calms
culet
calix
calyx
culex
cylix
calmy
coley
colly
cully
culty
comma
comic
cumec
comae
combe
cymae
combi
camel
comal
caman
Cimon
cumin
cameo
campo
combo
commo
compo
cimar
comer
cymar
camas
camis
✧camus
combs
comms
✧comus
cymas
✧**comet**
compt
cimex
campy
comby
comfy
commy
Cymry
canna
conga
conia
c and b
conic
✧cynic
canid
canoe
cense
congé
conne
conte
✧conté
C and G
caneh
cinch

conch
canal
Canon®
canon
cañon
conin
Cynon
can do
can-do
canto
cento
condo
✧congo
conto
convo
caner
Conor
Canis
cents
conus
can it
canst
cinct
Candu
C and W
✧**candy**
canny
canty
Cindy
coney
conky
Conwy
cundy
chota
clomb
coomb
cromb
chord
cloud
cooed
crowd
chode
choke
chore
chose
cloke
clone
close
clote
clove
cloye
cloze
cooee
crome
crone
crore
croze
ca' off
choof
cloff
cloth
choli
chock
chook
cloak
✧clock
clonk
croak
crock
cronk
crook

ceorl
✧**choom**
cloam
clown
croon
✧crown
choco
choko
chomp
clomp
cloop
croup
choir
clour
chops
✧cross
Crows
chott
chout
cloot
clout
co-opt
coopt
coost
Croat
croft
crost
crout
choux
choky
cooey
cooky
cooly
coomy
crony
copra
cuppa
copec
✧**cupid**
caple
copse
Capri
cippi
capul
copal
cupel
capon
Copán
Cipro®
caper
coper
capos
capot
caput
cop it
capex
coppy
copsy
capiz
Carla
carta
ceria
circa
curia
Carib
carob
ceric
cored
Carré
carse
carte

carve
cerge
cerne
Circe
corbe
corse
curie
curse
curve
curch
cardi
carpi
cerci
cirri
corgi
corni
✧**carol**
coral
Cyril
carom
CD-
ROM
coram
Corin
cargo
corno
corso
curio
carap
carer
corer
curer
cards
Carys
Ceres
Chris
circs
cords
corps
Cyrus
carat
caret
Corot
curat
curet
curst
Corfu
cornu
carex
carby
cardy
Carly
carny
carry
carvy
certy
corky
corny
curdy
curly
curny
curry
curvy
costa
cosec
cusec
caste
cesse
coste
cusum
casco

cisco
Cosmo
César
costs
coset
✧**cissy**
cushy
cotta
cutie
catch
cutch
cetyl
cital
cut in
cut-in
cutin
cyton
cutto
cut up
cut-up
cater
citer
cates
Cetus
cutis
cut it
Cathy
catty
cutey
cutty
causa
chufa
crura
Chubb®
courb
crumb
cauld
could
courd
'cause
cause
chuse
chute
coudé
coupe
coupé
coure
crude
cruse
cruve
chuff
clung
couch
cough
couth
crush
caulk
chuck
chunk
cluck
clunk
cruck
churl
cruel
churn
chump
clump
crump
churr
cruor
clubs

count
court
cruet
crust
crudy
crusy
civic
coved
cavie
cuvée
cavel
cavil
civil
Cavan
coven
covin
caver
cover
civet
covet
civvy
covey
cowed
crwth
cowal
cowan
cower
Cowes
cowry
coxed
coxae
coxal
caxon
Coxes
chynd
chyle
chyme
Clyde
clype
cry up
crypt
coypu
coyly
cozen
Cuzco
Dhaka
Diana
drama
Duala
deare
deave
Diane
DNase
✧drake
drape
drave
Duane
dwale
Dwane
draff
dwarf
dwang
death
D-mark
drank
do-all
drail
drawl
dwaal
dwalm
dwaum

dearn
drain
drawn
diazo
Draco
dealt
diact
draft
drant
deary
deawy
diary
Debra
dobra
Debye
Dubhe
debag
debug
Dubai
debel
dob in
Dobro®
debar
debur
debus
dibbs
debit
debut
début
✧**debby**
dobby
Dacca
dacha
Decca®
dicta
decad
diced
decal
ducal
decko
decor
décor
dicer
docks
ducks
dicht
dicot
docht
ducat
decay
decoy
decry
dicey
✧dicky
dicty
duchy
ducky
Dodge®
dodge
dedal
dados
didos
dodos
didst
daddy
diddy
doddy
dodgy
duddy
dweeb
dread

deere
deeve
diene
drere
doeth
dreck
dwell
dream
due to
drear
dregs
dress
duets
doest
drent
drest
duett
dwelt
deedy
defer
do for
defat
daffy
Dagda
dagga
dogma
dogie
degum
Dagon
dig in
doggo
dig up
✧**degas**
dight
digit
daggy
doggy
dohyo
dried
daine
de-ice
drice
✧drive
dwile
dwine
doing
D-ring
dying
drink
drill
deism
deign
djinn
daiko
drier
dries
daint
deist
doilt
drift
daily
dairy
daisy
deify
✧deity
doily
drily
Dijon
dojos
dekko
Dakar

daker
diker
dyker
Dukou
Delia
Della
✧delta
dolia
dolma
dulia
dalle
delve
dolce
dulse
delph
Delhi
dilli
Dalek
Dylan
dildo
Dilip
dolor
delfs
Delos
Dilys
dalet
Dalit
delft
dally
delay
dilly
Dolby®
dolly
dully
dumka
demob
demic
domed
damme
domoi
domal
daman
Damon
deman
demon
✧**dumbo**
damar
demur
dimer
demos
dumps
demit
dempt
dampy
dimly
dumky
dummy
dumpy
dinna
donga
Donna
Deneb
D and C
dinic
Danae
dance
Dante
dense
dinge
donee
✧donne

donné
dunce
Dinah
donah
dunch
dunsh
Donal
denim
danio
dingo
dunno
denar
dinar
diner
Donar
donor
Denis
Denys
Donus
denet
Donat
Donet
donut
dancy
dandy
Danny
denay
Denny
dingy
Dinky®
dinky
dungy
dunny
diota
doona
droob
dhole
diode
doole
drôle
drome
drone
drove
droog
dhobi
dhoti
duomi
drook
drouk
dholl
droil
droll
drool
doorn
drown
dsobo
dsomo
duomo
droop
dooms
drops
dross
do out
droit
doomy
doozy
drony
duple
depth
Dipak
dip in

dipso
dip up
doper
duper
depot
dippy
dopey
duply
duppy
darga
derma
dorsa
Durga
durra
daric
Doric
dared
dorad
darre
dirge
dirke
doree
dorse
daraf
derig
derth
darzi
Derek
dural
diram
durum
Dürer
dares
darts
Doras
Doris
dorts
duros
durst
darcy
darky
deray
✧derby
✧derry
dirty
dorky
dormy
dorty
durgy
duroy
desse
disme
doseh
Dyson
disco
desex
dishy
dusky
dusty
dated
doted
ditch
✧dutch
Datuk
datal
Datel®
dital
dotal
datum
Datin
ditto

dater
deter
doter
detox
ditsy
ditty
ditzy
dotty
doula
douma
doura
✧**druid**
daube
deuce
douce
douse
drupe
✧druse
Druze
dough
drunk
douar
dault
daunt
doubt
dauby
drusy
druxy
David
dived
Davie
dovie
devel
✧devil
daven
Devon
divan
Davao
diver
✧dover
Davos
Dives
davit
dévot
divot
duvet
divvy
downa
dowed
dowie
dowle
dowse
dowel
dewan
diwan
dewar
dowar
dower
Down's
✧downs
dowdy
downy
dowry
dixie
dryad
Dayak
dayan
doyen
dry up
dryer
daynt

doyly
dryly
dazed
dozed
dizen
dozen
dazer
dozer
dizzy
eland
Éfaté
elate
enate
erase
étage
étape
evade
e-la-mi
en ami
✧**e-mail**
email
enarm
Erato
Elaps
enact
epact
exact
exalt
erbia
embed
embog
embar
ember
embus
elbow
embow
embox
embay
El Cid
emcee
elchi
excel
escot
Eddic
ended
Eddie
endue
ek dum
eldin
Emden
end-on
end up
eider
elder
ex div
ex-div
endew
endow
edema
enema
emend
exeme
elemi
Eyeti
exeem
eye up
emeer
evens
egest
eject
elect

erect
event
evert
ewest
exeat
exert
elegy
emery
enemy
every
Effie
elfin
enfix
edged
eagle
eagre
eigne
egg on
ergon
eager
Edgar
edger
eggar
egger
Eiger
Elgar
eight
ergot
Ethna
ethic
ephod
Ethne
evhoe
ephah
ethal
Ethel
Ethyl®
ethyl
ephor
ether
ethos
ewhow
Eliza
✧erica
Evita
eniac
eliad
edile
elide
elite
élite
esile
evite
✧exile
exine
e-zine
eying
Edith
erick
Elian
exies
edict
evict
exist
edify
Emily
eejit
enjoy
eikon
eskar
esker

Eolic
Ellie
Ellen
Emlyn
Eblis
éclat
Eilat
Emmie
elmen
emmer
Emmys
emmet
emmew
enmew
Ernie
ennui
Ernst
Ebola
Epona
éloge
elope
emote
emove
epode
erode
erose
evohe
evoke
exode
emong
Enoch
epoch
E coli
enoki
e-book
ebook
enorm
eloin
✧**elops**
Etons
E-boat
epopt
ebony
elogy
epoxy
eupad
elpee
expel
expos
expat
empty
eared
Edred
erred
eerie
eyrie
✧**earth**
enrol
Errol
error
eyrir
Emrys
épris
euros
Eurus
earst
egret
early
Elroy
easle
Elsie

ensue
Essie
easel
eisel
eusol
Epsom
Elsan®
elsin
eosin
Essen
easer
ensew
Essex
ensky
essay
entia
extra
estoc
eathe
ettle
Eytie
extol
eaten
eat in
Elton
Estyn
ettin
estro
eat up
estop
eater
enter
ester
entry
Eruca
exurb
equid
educe
elude
elute
emule
emure
enure
étude
exude
equal
enurn
equip
Equus
educt
eruct
erupt
exult
envoi
eeven
elvan
elven
erven
elver
eaves
elves
Elvis
envoy
etwee
Edwin
Elwyn
etyma
Egypt
Enzed
flava
franc

fa'ard
fraud
feare
flake
flame
flare
frame
frate
flaff
Flash®
flash
frati
flack
flank
flask
frack
✧frank
flail
frail
flamm
fraim
flawn
flair
fiars
flats
frass
feart
feast
fract
flaky
flamy
flary
flawy
flaxy
foamy
fable
fibre
fibro
fiber
fabby
fubby
fubsy
facia
faced
fiche
fecal
focal
FA Cup
facer
feces
ficos
ficus
focus
fucus
facet
fecht
fecit
fichu
fadge
fidge
fudge
fed up
fader
fados
✧fides
faddy
Freda
frena
Freya
field
fiend

freed
fremd
Freud
feese
feeze
fiere
fleme
frère
flesh
fresh
fleck
freak
fleam
foehn
Freon®
fuero
fleer
✧fleur
freer
flews
fient
✧fleet
freet
freit
faery
fiery
✧**fifth**
fifer
fifty
fuffy
fogle
fugie
fugle
fugue
fugal
Fagin
fig up
fog up
Fagus
figos
fagot
fight
fogou
fogey
foggy
fuggy
Fehme
fried
faine
flite
frize
fling
Frigg
faith
frith
flick
flisk
frisk
frill
feign
Ffion
flimp
flier
friar
frier
fains
flies
fries
faint
feint
flint

flirt
flitt
foist
frist
fairy
fritz
frizz
fakie
faker
fakir
fakes
fella
folia
felid
filed
false
fille
folie
F-clef
filch
filth
falaj
felon
folio
filar
filer
Felis
films
folks
filet
Felix
felly
felty
filly
filmy
foley
folly
fully
famed
femme
femal
femur
fomes
fumes
fumet
fonda
fence
finch
Fanti
fundi
fungi
fanal
final
fanon
fango
fungo
finer
fenks
fines
finis
finks
finos
fonds
funds
fancy
✧fanny
fendy
fenny
finny
fonly
fundy

funky
funny
Fiona
✧flora
flota
fiord
fjord
✧flood
Floyd
frond
f-hole
flote
Frome
frore
froze
feoff
flong
flosh
froth
flock
frock
Fionn
flown
frorn
frown
Flo-Jo
floor
flour
floss
foots
float
flout
front
✧frost
flory
foody
footy
frory
frowy
farad
Farid
fired
farce
farle
farse
✧force
forge
forme
forte
furze
Farah
firth
✧forth
furth
farci
Farsi
fermi
feral
forel
fural
furol
✧**forum**
furan
Fargo
fordo
forgo
Faruq
farer
firer
furor
first

forex
farcy
ferly
ferny
ferry
firry
foray
forby
forky
✧forty
furry
furzy
festa
✧fossa
fesse
Feste
fosse
fusee
fasci
fasti
fusil
Fusus
fishy
fisty
fussy
fusty
fatwa
fetta
fetwa
fated
fetid
fitte
fytte
Fatah
fetch
fitch
fatal
fetal
fit in
futon
fatso
fit up
fit-up
f-stop
fetor
Fates
fetus
fatly
fatty
fitly
✧**fauna**
faurd
fluid
found
Fauré
Fauve
Fiume
fluke
flume
✧flute
foulé
fluff
flung
faugh
✧flush
fouth
frush
flunk
Fluon®
flump
frump

feuar
fluor
flurr
fours
fault
Faust
fouat
fouet
fount
fruit
frust
fluey
fluky
fluty
fovea
✧**favel**
favor
fever
fiver
favus
fives
fowth
fowls
fixed
foxed
foxie
Fuxin
fix up
fixer
Foxes
fayne
fayre
flype
flyte
foyle
foyne
Flymo®
fry-up
flyer
foyer
fryer
fly at
fly-by
fazed
fuzee
fezes
fizzy
fuzzy
Ghana
grama
grana
guana
guava
gland
grand
guard
geare
glacé
glade
glare
glaze
go ape
✧grace
grade
grame
grape
grate
grave
graze
graff
gnash

graph
ghazi
glaik
gnarl
graal
grail
glaum
ghayn
gnawn
grain
Grapo
guaco
guano
graip
grasp
glair
glaur
gnarr
Ghats
glans
✧glass
goals
goats
grass
ghast
ghaut
giant
graft
✧grant
Glaux
glady
glary
glazy
goary
goaty
grapy
gravy
gabba
go bad
gable
gobbi
gibel
Gabon
gobbo
gebur
giber
gibus
gobos
✧gabby
gecko
gucky
gadge
gadje
gadso
godso
Gadus
godet
god it
giddy
godly
go dry
Geeta
Greta
gleed
greed
gyeld
geese
glebe
glede
grebe
grece

Words marked ✧ can also be spelled with one or more capital letters

grège
grese
greve
Guelf
goeth
gleek
Greek
gleam
glean
Glenn
✧green
grein
grebo
grego
gee up
grees
guess
Ghent
ghest
gleet
glent
goest
great
greet
guest
Gueux
geeky
gleby
goety
gaffe
go far
gofer
gigue
Giggs
gigot
gaita
grind
guild
glide
glike
grice
gride
grike
grime
gripe
grise
grize
✧guide
guile
guise
gliff
grief
griff
going
Grieg
grith
glisk
glial
grill
guiro
guimp
grips
grits
gaitt
geist
glift
glint
grift
griot
grist
guilt

gaily
grimy
grisy
glitz
Gijon
gajos
Galba
galea
Golda
gelid
Galle
Golde
golpe
G-clef
gulag
galah
gulch
gulph
golem
Galen
galop
gular
Giles
gilts
gules
✧**galut**
gilet
gulet
gally
gelly
gilly
gilpy
goldy
golly
gulfy
gully
gamba
gamma
✧gemma
gompa
gumma
gamic
go mad
gamme
gimme
Gamal
gemel
gimel
Gomel
gamin
gambo
gombo
✧gumbo
gum up
gamer
games
gamut
gemot
gamay
gamey
gammy
gemmy
gimpy
gummy
ganja
✧genoa
gonia
gonna
genic
gonad
genie

genre
gunge
gynae
gynie
ganch
genii
genal
genom
Genro
gonzo
genip
gen up
go nap
goner
G and S
gents
genus
gonys
✧**g and t**
✧genet
genty
✧ginny
gundy
gungy
gunny
gynny
groma
geoid
goold
geode
globe
glode
glove
gloze
gnome
goose
grone
grope
✧grove
Geoff
go off
go-off
groof
grouf
glogg
Gooch
ghoul
growl
gloom
groom
groan
groin
grown
good-o
gloop
group
gloss
goods
gross
ghost
gloat
glout
go out
groat
grout
globy
glory
goody
gooey
✧goofy
gooly

goopy
goosy
grody
grosz
gopak
gopik
Gopal
gaper
gapes
gapós
gappy
gipsy
guppy
gypsy
garda
Gerda
go red
gored
garbe
garre
gerbe
gerle
gerne
gorge
gorse
gurge
garth
gerah
girth
garni
goral
gyral
garum
giron
gyron
✧**garbo**
giros
gyrus
Garry
Gerry
girly
Gorky
gormy
gorsy
gurly
gurry
gusla
gesse
geste
gosse
gusle
gusli
gesso
gismo
gusto
gases
gosht
gaspy
gassy
gushy
gusty
gotta
gutta
gated
get in
get on
Gatso®
get-go
get up
get-up
gator

getas
get at
get it?
get by
gutsy
gutty
Gouda
✧goura
glued
gourd
gauge
gauje
gauze
glume
gouge
grufe
grume
gruff
Gough
Gaudí
Gauri
gruel
gluon
grump
gluer
gauss
✧**gault**
gaunt
giust
grunt
g-suit
gaucy
gaudy
gaumy
gauzy
gluey
gouty
Gavle
gavel
Gavin
given
giver
gowan
Gower
gawcy
gawky
gawsy
Gayle
goyle
gryce
gryde
gryke
grype
guyle
guyse
glyph
gayal
ghyll
goyim
geyan
gayer
grypt
guyot
Gazza
gazal
gazon
gazoo
gizmo
gazar
gazer
heald

heard
hoard
heame
heare
heave
✧**heath**
Huari
heads
heaps
Hyads
heart
heast
hiant
hoast
heady
heapy
heavy
hoary
hable
heben
hobos
habit
hobby
hubby
hacek
hocus
Hecat
hecht
hodja
✧hydra
hedge
Hodge
hadji
hadal
hydro
heder
hider
Hoder
Hades
hadn't
hadst
hedgy
hyena
heeze
H-beam
hiems
heedy
hefte
Hefei
hefty
huffy
hafiz
Hague
Hegel
hogan
hogen
Hagar
hight
hog it
ho-hum
hi-hat
Hohot
Haida
Haifa
Heine
hoise
hying
Haikh
haith
heigh
Haiti

Heidi
haick
hoick
heist
hoist
haiku
haily
hairy
hejra
hijra
hejab
hijab
hajji
Hekla
hakam
hakim
hokum
hiker
hokku
hokey
halfa
halma
halva
Helga
Hilda
holla
hylic
halo'd
Halle
Hallé
halse
halve
helve
hyleg
hilch
halal
hilum
halon
Helen
hallo
Hello!
hello
hillo
hollo
hullo
haler
hilar
halfs
halos
hilts
hilus
helot
Holst
✧**helix**
Haley
hilly
Holby
holey
holly
hulky
hully
✧**hamza**
humic
humid
homie
homme
✧**humph**
hamal
hemal
he-man
hem in

human
✧hymen
himbo
✧**homer**
humor
Hamas
homos
humus
hammy
hempy
homey
humpy
Hansa
henna
Honda®
h and c
hance
Hanse
hence
henge
Henle
hinge
hynde
hanch
hunch
hangi
Hanoi
Henri
Hindi
hongi
Honan
Hanno
hanap
honer
✧honor
hands
hunks
Hindu
handy
hanky
henny
✧henry
hinny
honey
honky
hunky
✧**haoma**
hoo-ha
hooka
H-bomb
hoord
hyoid
hoove
hooch
hoosh
hoo-oo
H-hour
hoofs
Hoops
hoots
hooey
hooky
hooly
hypha
hippo
hop up
hepar
hoper
hyper
Hopis
hypos

hop it
haply
happy
hippy
hoppy
hdqrs
herma
hurra
Herod
hired
herse
herye
Horae
horde
horme
horse
harsh
horah
horal
haram
harem
harim
Harun
heron
Huron
hirer
hards
harns
herms
hi-res
Horus
hurds
horst
✧hurst
✧**hyrax**
✧**hardy**
harpy
✧harry
herby
herry
horny
horsy
hurly
hurry
hertz
hasta
Hosea
hosta
Hasid
hosed
haste
Hesse
Husni
hosel
Hasan
hosen
hyson
hoses
husks
husos
hasn't
hashy
hasty
hushy
husky
hussy
Hatra
hutia
hi-tec
hithe
hythe

hatch
hitch
hotch
hutch
✧**hotel**
hit on
hoten
het up
hot up
hater
hit it
Hatty
Hetty
hotly
Hausa
hauld
hound
hause
haute
✧house
houff
haugh
heuch
heugh
hough
houri
haulm
hours
hault
haunt
hevea
havoc
Havel
hovel
haven
hoven
haver
hiver
hover
haves
hives
Hovas
hewed
hawse
howbe
howre
howff
hewgh
Howel
Hywel
how so?
howso
how-to
hewer
hawks
howdy
hexad
hexyl
hayle
Haydn
huzza
✧**hazel**
hazan
✧hizen
hazer
huzzy
Ilana
Itala
Ivana
Isaac
izard

image
inane
irade
irate
✧**imari**
Iraqi
Iwaki
in all
✧**imaum**
inarm
Idaho
igapó
imago
idant
in alt
inapt
Italy
imbed
in bud
imbue
inbye
Isbel
imbar
in-box
incle
Incan
in-car
incur
incus
incut
itchy
✧**india**
Indra
Indic
iodic
indie
indue
indri
indol
Indus
indew
index
Irena
ileac
idea'd
in eye
Irene
Iceni
ideal
ileal
I-beam
ileum
inerm
ice up
ileus
ident
id est
inept
inert
infra
in fun
infer
in few
infix
ingle
ingan
ingot
ichor
Ibiza
✧**iliac**
Isiac

Words marked ✧ can also be spelled with one or more capital letters

Iliad
ivied
imide
imine
icing
Irish
idiom
✧ilium
Ilian
inion
Ixion
Iai-do
Inigo
idiot
Idist
icily
Injun
inked
inkle
ink in
icker
inker
illth
Islam
igloo
idler
Iblis
inlet
islet
in-law
inlay
Islay
iambi
Izmir
immit
immew
immix
Ionia
✧**ionic**
I-and-I
✧**inner**
innit
I know
✧**idola**
Ilona
Imola
inorb
Isold
iMode®
in one
in-off
iroko
irons
irony
ivory
in pig
impel
ippon
in pup
impis
impot
input
imply
ihram
in rem
Idris
Ibrox
issue
imshi
issei
in sum

Ibsen
inset
imshy
intra
ictic
istle
ixtle
ictal
Intal®
intil
intro
in two
iftar
inter
ictus
inula
inure
in use
Idunn
Ieuan
inurn
Inuit
inust
Isuzu®
Invar®
inwit
idyll
Iyyar
izzat
jhala
jnana
jeans
jibba
jebel
jiber
jabot
Jacob
jocko
jacks
Jedda
jaded
Jodie
judge
Judie
Judah
jodel
✧**judas**
Jeeze
jeely
Joely
✧**jaffa**
jiffy
jugal
jugum
jäger
jagir
jigot
jaggy
jehad
jihad
Jaina
Jaime
juice
joint
joist
juicy
jokol
joker
jakes
jokey
Julia

jelab
Julie
Jilin
jello
jalap
julep
jelly
jolly
jolty
Jemma
jambe
Jamie
Jamal
Jamil
jambo
jumbo
jumar
✧**james**
jumps
jambu
jammy
jemmy
✧jimmy
jimpy
jumby
jumpy
Jenna
junta
Jonah
jinni
Jinan
✧**jingo**
junco
junto
Janis
Janus
jinns
Janet
janty
✧jenny
Jinny
jonty
junky
Jools
✧**japan**
jupon
japer
jarta
jirga
Jared
jerid
jarul
jural
joram
jorum
juror
jurat
jerky
✧jerry
jaspe
jaspé
Jesse
Josie
Jason
Jesus
jésus
jasey
Jessy
jeton
✧jotun
jatos

jetty
jutty
jeune
joule
joual
jougs
jaunt
joust
javel
Javan
jiver
jivey
jawed
jewel
jawan
jowar
Jewry
jowly
joyed
Joyce
jazzy
Kaaba
kaama
khaya
koala
knave
kiang
klang
krang
kyang
khadi
khaki
khazi
knack
knarl
kraal
Keats
krans
kvass
kiaat
kraft
krait
kranz
kabab
kabob
kebab
kebob
Kabul
koban
kacha
Kochi
kecks
kedge
kidge
Kodak®
kidel
kid on
kid-on
kiddo
kudos
kydst
kudzu
kedgy
kiddy
keema
kheda
Kiera
kwela
knead
knee'd
kneed

keeve
kieve
kreng
keech
kneel
knell
Kreon
knelt
Kafka
kofta
Kufic
kefir
kagos
kight
kahal
kohen
Kahlo
knife
knive
✧koine
KOing
Keith
knish
kaiak
krill
kails
Klimt
kokra
kikoi
kukri
kokum
koker
kalpa
✧**kylie**
kyloe
kalif
kulfi
kulak
kelim
kilim
kulan
kylin
Kelso
kilos
kolos
kylix
✧**kelly**
kelpy
kelty
kiley
kilty
kamme
kamik
Kamal
kembo
kimbo
Khmer
Kumar
kamis
kemps
Kamet
kempt
kombu
kempy
✧**kanga**
Kanta
Kenna
Kenya
kinda
Konya
kente

kynde
kenaf
kaneh
kanji
Kanak
Khnum
kinin
kendo
ken-no
Kenzo
kunar
Kings
kinos
kanzu
✧**kandy**
Kenny
kindy
kinky
khoja
krona
króna
knowe
krone
kloof
koori
kiosk
knock
knoll
khoum
known
kroon
Kyoto
knosp
kaons
Kwok's
knout
Kuo-yü
kooky
kappa
kippa
koppa
kopje
kapok
kopek
Koper
Kipps
kaput
Karla
karma
kerma
Korda
korma
Kurma
kurta
kerne
kerve
kurre
Kyrie
karri
kirri
Karaj
Kursk
Karen
Karin
Kiran
Koran
✧**karoo**
Koror
kurus
karat
karst

Kirov
karsy
karzy
Kerry
Korky
kasha
Kasim
kisan
✧**kesar**
Katya
Katie
kithe
Kitwe
kythe
ketch
kutch
katti
katal
kitul
kit up
kotos
kotow
Kathy
✧kitty
kaugh
Kauai
kauri
knurl
knurr
klutz
kevel
Kevan
Kevin
keyed
kayle
kbyte
kayak
key in
key up
Kayes
kayos
Kazak
Kazan
kazoo
Lhasa
✧liana
llama
liard
leare
lease
leave
leaze
liane
loave
lyase
liang
leach
leash
loach
loath
laari
learn
llano
leads
loads
leant
leapt
least
liart
loast
lyart

leady
leafy
leaky
leany
leary
leavy
loamy
labda
labia
labra
✧libra
Libya
Lubna
lobed
label
libel
Laban
labor
liber
Libor
lobar
labis
lobus
Libby
lobby
Lucia
Lycra®
laced
Le Cid
lucid
Locke
lucre
lycée
lichi
lo-cal
local
locum
Lucan
licks
locks
locos
locus
Lucas
luces
lacet
licht
licit
lacey
leccy
✧lucky
Lydia
ludic
laded
ladle
ledge
lodge
ledum
laden
Ladin
loden
lidos
ludos
ledgy
leese
leeze
Liège
liege
lieve
leech
lie in
lie-in

lie up
leear
Leeds
loess
leery
lie by
luffa
lefte
lifer
lefty
lofty
logia
logic
legge
ligge
ligne
logie
legal
logum
lagan
ligan
✧logan
log in
log-in
login
log on
log-on
logon
lug in
lager
leger
liger
Luger®
luger
Lagos
✧logos
leg it
legit
light
leggy
lahar
✧**laika**
Leica®
Leila
laird
loipe
lying
laigh
laith
Leigh
leish
Leith
Laius
loins
lairy
✧laity
laksa
lakin
liken
likin
laker
liker
Lalla
lilac
Lille
lolog
laldy
Lally
lolly
lamia
lemma

Lemna
limma
lamed
lumme
lymph
✧**limbi**
lemel
leman
lemon
limen
lumen
✧**limbo**
lemur
limes
limos
lumas
lam it
limit
limax
lammy
limey
lummy
lumpy
Lanza
Linda
linga
longa
Lynda
linac
lined
lance
lande
longe
lunge
Lynne
lanch
linch
lunch
lynch
✧**lanai**
lenti
lungi
Lendl
Lenin
linen
linin
Lando
lento
lingo
liner
loner
lunar
lenes
lenis
lenos
lines
links
Linus
longs
Linux
lanky
Lenny
Lindy
liney
lingy
linny
linty
Lundy
L-dopa
Leona
loofa

Lloyd
loord
leone
loose
Lao Zi
Laois
loofs
looks
loons
Lyons
looby
loony
loopy
lepra
lepta
lepid
lipid
lapje
lapse
lapel
lupin
lap up
leper
loper
lapis
Lepus
lipas
✧lupus
lippy
La Paz
larva
Lerna
Lorca
Lorna
loric
lyric
lurid
large
Larne
Lerne
Lorne
lurve
larch
lurch
✧**lurgi**
loral
lorel
larum
✧**loran**
largo
lares
laris
Larus
liras
Lords
loris
Lurex®
lardy
larky
Larry
Leroy
lordy
lorry
lurgy
lurry
lyssa
lisle
los'te
lassi
losel
lysol

losen
lysin
lasso
laser
loser
lists
lysis
Liszt
lassu
lossy
lushy
lusty
lytta
lotic
lytic
lated
lathe
latke
latte
let be
Lethe
lithe
litre
lythe
latch
letch
lotah
lathi
litai
laten
Latin
let in
let on
Luton
let go
litho
lotto
let up
let-up
lit up
later
liter
luter
laths
litas
lotos
✧lotus
latex
lathy
Letty
Lauda
✧laura
laund
lound
Louie
loupe
loure
louse
lauch
laugh
leuch
leugh
lough
Louth
lauds
✧louis
loury
lousy
lavra
Livia
lived
livid
levee
livre
level
levin
liven
✧**laver**
lever
liver
livor
lover
lavas
Levis®
lives
lovat
lavvy
lovey
luvvy
lownd
Lewie
lowne
lowse
lawin
lowan
lower
lawks
Lewes
✧lewis
lawny
lowly
Lowry
Luxor
lexis
Lexus®
luxes
laxly
Layla
loyal
lay in
lay on
lay up
lay-up
layer
lay by
lay-by
lazzi
lozen
Luzon
lazzo
lazar
meal'd
mear'd
meane
meare
mease
✧**meath**
Miami
miaul
myall
miasm
Mt Apo
means
meant
miaow
mealy
meany
meaty
moble
Mr Big
Mabel
mebos
mob it
mobby
Macha
Mecca
micra
✧mocha
mucid
macle
miche
Moche
Micah
Mâcon
macon
mucin
Macao
macho
macro
micro
mucro
macer
mucor
micas
micos
mocks
mucus
macaw
✧**micky**
mochy
mucky
Medea
media
mudra
Madoc
✧medic
Médoc
madid
✧**madge**
Médée
medle
midge
mudge
modii
medal
modal
model
✧**madam**
modem
Medan
mid-on
moder
mudir
Midas
modus
'midst
midst
Medau
Middx
madly
middy
midgy
muddy
Meena
Moera
Maeve
mieve
mneme
my eye
Mbeki
✧**mafia**
mafic
ma foi
✧mufti
miffy
mifty
Magda
magma
magic
My God!
Magog
✧**mogul**
Megan
mug up
maggs
✧magus
magot
might
moggy
muggy
mahua
mahwa
mahoe
Mahdi
Mehdi
mohel
mohur
my hat!
mbira
Moira
maile
Maine
Máire
maire
maise
maize
moire
moiré
meith
Màiri
Meiji
maiko
mains
meint
moist
muist
meiny
Mainz
mujik
✧**major**
mojos
mikra
Makah
makar
✧maker
makos
mokos
Malta
malva
melba
Melia
milia
molla
mulga
malic
melic
mêlée
mille
mulse
milch
mulch
mulsh
malik
melik
molal
Malin
melon
Milan
Malmo
Malmö
milko
molto
malar
miler
milor
molar
Mylar®
Melos
✧miles
milos
molas
Myles
mol wt
mulct
mal vu
malax
Malay
malty
melty
milky
✧molly
muley
miltz
mamba
mamma
momma
mimic
mamee
Mamie
mambo
mimer
Mimir
memos
Mimus
Momus
mumps
mamey
mammy
mimsy
mommy
mummy
mumsy
manga
mania
manna
✧manta
many a
Mensa
Monza
Munda
manic
maned
monad
Mande
mange
manse
menge
mense
minae
mince
minke
monte
maneh
mensh
month
✧munch
mynah
Minsk
manul
monal
minim
mango
manto
mento
mondo
mongo
✧mungo
Munro
manor
minar
miner
✧minor
moner
✧**manes**
Manis
manos
manus
mends
minas
✧minos
minus
✧monas
monos
manat
✧manet
Monet
muntu
Mandy
mangy
manky
manly
Manny
manty
mingy
minty
✧money
monty
Muntz
moola
myoma
myoid
moose
moove
myope
M-roof
mooch
Maori
mooli
mhorr
mools
myops
moody
mooly
moony
moory
moped
maple
Mopti
mop up
mop-up
moper
mopes
mopus
mopey
moppy
mopsy
maqui
✧**maria**
marka
Mirza
✧moria
Morna
morra
murra
murva
Myrna
marid
mered
Murad
marae
marge
Marie
marle
merge
merle
merse
morne
morné
✧morse
murre
Morag
marah
✧march
✧marsh
mirth
morph
myrrh
marri
Merak
merel
meril
Meryl
moral
morel
mural
maron
mirin
moron
Myron
Margo
morro
Murdo
maror
marls
mores
Moros
Morus
Marat
Marot
merit
morat
mpret
murex
mardy
marly
marry
✧mercy
merry
mirly
✧moray
murky
murly
murry
massa
misca'
✧missa
Mosca
Musca
musha
mesic
music
mused
massé
mesne
Moshe
musse
musth
Masai
Musci
Musak
mesal
mesel
Mosel
Mosul
Masan
mason
meson
mesto
misdo
misgo
mosso
maser
miser
muser
misos
Moses
musos
muset
musit
mashy
massy
masty
meshy
messy
missy
misty
mosey
mossy
mushy
musky
mussy
musty
matza
Mitla
motza
metic
meted
moted
muted
matte
metre
mitre
motte
✧**metif**
motif
match
mitch
mutch
matai
metal
metol
motel
✧**matin**
moten
muton
matlo
matzo
me-too
✧metro
✧métro
motto
mater
meter
miter
motor
maths
meths
Metis
✧métis
✧motus
motet
matey
Matty
Mitty
motey
mothy
motty
Maura
maund
mould
mound
Maude
mauve
meuse
mouse
mvule
mouch
mouth
Mouli®
mouli
mourn
mouls
moult
✧mount
moust
Mt Usu
mauby
mousy
movie
maven
mavin
mover
✧**mavis**
mowra
mowed
mower
mawky
My Way
mixed
moxie
✧**maxim**
mixen
mix-in
mix up
mix-up
mixer
mix it
Moyra
maybe
mbyte
✧moyle
Mayan
Mayon
mayor
mayn't
mayst
meynt
Mazda®
mezze
Muzak®
muzak
mizen
mezzo
mazer
mazut
muzzy
ngana
Nuada
Nuala
nyala
neafe
Neale
nyaff
'neath
neath
Niamh
Naafi
Niall
✧**ngaio**
nabla
nubia
nabob
noble
nebek
nebel
Nobel
Nabis
Nabby
nobby
nobly
nubby
nucha
nicad
nache
nacre
niche
✧**nicol**
Nicam
nacho
Nicky
Nadia
nudge
nudie
nidal
nodal
nadir
nidor
nidus
nodus
✧**neddy**
noddy
nuddy
neemb
neeld
no end
naeve
neele
neese
neeze
niece
nieve
Noele
naevi
needs
needy
niffy
nifty
nugae
Nigel
✧**negro**
nagor
✧niger
✧**negus**
night
naggy
✧**nahal**
nihil
Nahum
ne has
Nehru
nohow
naira
naiad
naive
naïve
neive
n mile
noise
nying
neigh
Naias
noils
neist
'noint
noint
noisy
no joy
nakfa
naked
Nikon®
naker
nikau
nalla
nulla
nylon
nelis
Nilot
✧**nelly**
nomic
named
nomad
nymph
nimbi
nomoi
Neman
no-man
nomen
numen
Nampo
namer
Namur
Nîmes
nomos
nempt
Nimby
✧**nanna**
✧ninja
nonce
ninth
ninon
N and Q
✧**nones**
no-no's
no-nos
nonet
nandu
Nancy
nanny
ninny
nonny
Nantz

Words marked ✧ can also be spelled with one or more capital letters

Ndola
Njord
Niobe
no one
no-one
noose
Naomi
Ngoni
Nkomo
nooky
nappa
nappe
Nepal
nopal
nip in
napoo
neper
Nupes
nepit
nappy
✧nippy
nary a
nerka
Nerva
noria
✧norma
Norna
narre
nerve
Norse
✧nurse
Norah
✧north
narco
naras
narcs
nares
narks
Nerys
Norns
narky
nerdy
nervy
nirly
Nessa
Nesta
nyssa
nosed
nisse
nashi
Neski
nisei
Nasik
nasal
Nisan
noser
nisus
nasty
nosey
Netta
nitid
noted
nitre
natch
notch
✧**natal**
notal
notum
niton
not on
nitro

not up
niter
noter
nates
Notus
natty
✧netty
nitry
nitty
nutty
n'ould
nould
neume
noule
Nguni
nouns
naunt
Nauru
nouny
novae
naval
navel
nevel
nival
novel
novum
never
nevus
novas
navew
navvy
nawab
nowed
newie
ngwee
newel
✧nowel
no-win
ne was
newly
newsy
no way
noway
nixie
noxal
Nixon
nixer
Naxos
nexus
nixes
n-type
Nayar
noyes
noyau
✧**nizam**
nazir
Omaha
omasa
Osaka
of age
orate
Osage
ovate
obang
orang
Omagh
orach
okapi
Omani
okays
✧**op art**

orant
otaku
oracy
otary
ovary
orbed
ombre
ombré
ombus
ombús
oobit
orbit
oubit
ox-bot
ox-bow
oh boy!
on cue
owche
occam
Ofcom
orcin
Oscan
occur
oncer
Oscar®
✧oscar
oncus
Orcus
op cit
oucht
oidia
oldie
ovdim
olden
older
✧order
on-dit
oddly
omega
opera
oleic
ogee'd
ogeed
on end
oread
obese
opepe
or ere
ox-eye
obeah
obeli
ozeki
odeum
oleum
ocean
odeon
olein
one-er
or e'er
oleos
ouens
olent
overt
Ovett
onely
offie
offal
Oxfam
offer
off it
orgia

orgic
orgue
Ofgem
ob-gyn
oggin
organ
ought
oshac
ochre
ogham
ocher
other
ochry
Omiya
Oriya
Ouija®
ouija
ogive
ojime
olive
on ice
opine
ovine
oxide
oxime
OD'ing
OK'ing
OKing
O-ring
owing
oribi
oriel
odism
odium
opium
onion
Orion
osier
olios
obiit
odist
ovist
Oujda
on-job
objet
oakum
oaken
of kin
oaker
✧ocker
onkus
oiled
✧**ollie**
oflag
omlah
Orlon®
orlop
oxlip
ogler
oiler
owler
owlet
ollav
Otley
ogmic
ohmic
osmic
oomph
ormer
ounce
own up

owner
ornis
of new
oundy
Onora
of old
ovoid
ohone
ozone
on-off
oboli
ovoli
ovolo
odour
ology
ouphe
orpin
oppos
ocrea
oared
Ohrid
oorie
ourie
owrie
omrah
Oprah
orris
o'erby
ossia
Ossie
ousel
Oisin
opsin
Orson
owsen
oases
Oasis®
✧oasis
Ossis
onset
✧**ostia**
Optic®
optic
octad
ootid
outed
outré
octal
Oftel
oaten
often
opt in
Orton
ortho
outdo
outgo
on tap
oater
opter
ottar
otter
outer
oxter
oaths
octet
on tow
outby
of use
ovule
oculi
orval

oaves
Olwen
Olwin
Olwyn
Ofwat
Oryza
odyle
Oryol
Ozzie
ouzel
ouzos
playa
plaza
poaka
Praia
prana
plaid
peace
Peake
peare
pease
peaze
phage
phare
phase
✧place
plage
'plane
plane
plate
poake
prase
prate
phang
prang
peach
plash
Plath
poach
piani
plack
plank
prank
pearl
plasm
praam
psalm
plain
prawn
✧**piano**
Plato
peart
plait
plant
plast
pratt
prahu
peaky
peaty
peavy
platy
praty
pzazz
pubic
pubes
pubis
pacha
Picea
picra
pucka
paced

pecke
picul
pecan
pacer
pacos
Picus
Pecht
picot
pacey
piccy
picky
pocky
✧**padma**
Padua
podia
pudic
padle
padre
podge
pudge
pi-dog
pedal
podal
✧**pedro**
pudor
pedes
podex
✧**paddy**
poddy
podgy
puddy
pudgy
pudsy
pieta
✧pietà
presa
piel'd
piend
plead
pseud
peece
peepe
peeve
phene
phese
piece
pièce
plebe
prese
preve
preif
plesh
paean
paeon
pheon
pleon
preen
preon
piezo
pheer
Piers
plebs
✧press
P-Celt
piert
P-Kelt
pleat
prent
prest
peeoy
peery

piety
poesy
predy
premy
prexy
puffy
pagod
pagle
pogge
pagri
pugil
pygal
pagan
pager
pages
Peght
pight
pig it
✧**peggy**
✧piggy
pigmy
puggy
pygmy
pshaw
paisa
plica
✧prima
Priya
plied
poind
pried
Paige
paire
peise
peize
poise
price
pride
prime
prise
prize
prief
pling
plink
prick
prink
phial
prial
prill
Priam
prism
prion
psion
primo
primp
plier
prier
prior
pains
pairs
plies
paint
point
print
poilu
pricy
primy
privy
pi-jaw
pakka
pukka

piked
poked
pekoe
pokie
pikul
pokal
pekan
piker
poker
puker
pokey
pukey
palea
palla
Palma
pelma
pelta
pilea
polka
pulka
palae
Pelée
polje
pulse
pilaf
pilch
palki
palpi
pilei
pilum
pylon
polio
pulmo
polyp
piler
polar
poler
puler
palas
Pales
piles
pills
pilus
polis
polos
polys
palet
pilot
Palau
pilau
pilaw
pilow
✧**phlox**
Pulex
palay
pally
palmy
palsy
poley
✧polly
pulpy
pampa
pombe
pumie
Pomak
pumas
pommy
panda
panga
Penda
penna

Penza
✧pinna
✧pinta
Pinza
ponga
punga
punka
panic
Punic
paned
pance
panne
pence
penie
penne
ponce
punce
pinch
✧punch
panel
penal
panim
piñon
P and O
panto
pingo
pinko
pinto
pongo
punto
p and p
pin-up
pants
penes
penis
✧**pinot**
panax
pandy
pansy
panty
penny
piney
pinky
pinny
poncy
poney
pongy
ponty
punky
punty
✧**phoca**
pooja
pooka
Poona
psora
proud
pyoid
'phone
phone
pioye
Poole
poove
probe
proke
prole
prone
prore
prose
prove
proof
plong

prong
pooch
paoli
poori
Prodi
plonk
plook
plouk
pronk
proll
proul
prowl
pro-am
proem
proin
proyn
paolo
photo
promo
proso
Proto®
Provo
pions
pious
pools
props
psoas
ploat
poort
peony
phony
piony
poovy
prosy
proxy
Pippa
poppa
piped
pupae
Pepsi®
papal
pipal
pipul
pupal
pupil
pep up
pop-up
paper
✧piper
pepos
Pepys
pipes
pupas
pipit
papaw
pappy
peppy
pippy
poppy
popsy
puppy
pique
piqué
Parca
parka
Parma
Perca
porta
parge
parle
parse

perce
per se
perse
perve
porge
Porte
puree
purée
purge
purse
pirog
parch
perch
Perth
porch
pardi
parki
Parsi
parti
perai
pirai
parol
peril
poral
pyral
Purim
Perón
purin
pareo
porno
parer
porer
Paris
Paros
parts
Pyrus
perst
pareu
perdu
Purex
Pyrex®
pardy
parky
parly
parry
party
Percy
perdy
perky
✧perry
pervy
✧porgy
porky
porty
purpy
pursy
purty
pasha
pasta
passé
paste
piste
posse
pusle
Pasch
Pesah
pashm
Pusan
paseo
pesto
poser
pesos
posit
paspy
pasty
pesky
pisky
posey
pushy
pussy
Patna
Petra
✧pitta
pated
putid
patte
patté
petre
patch
pitch
potch
putti
petal
paten
patin
piton
potin
Putin
put in
put-in
put on
put-on
patio
potoo
potto
putto
pot up
put up
put-up
pater
petar
✧peter
paths
Pott's
petit
patly
✧patsy
✧patty
petty
pithy
potty
put by
putty
Paula
plumb
✧**pound**
pause
plume
✧pouke
poule
poupe
Pruce
prude
prune
pluff
plush
pouch
pluck
plunk
Pluto
plump
poulp
poult
poupt
prunt
plumy
pouty
Pavia
paved
pavid
pavan
paven
pavin
paver
pavis
pivot
pownd
pewee
powre
powan
powin
power
Powys
pewit
pawaw
pawky
powny
pixie
pixel
✧**pyxis**
phyla
payed
paysd
payee
peyse
phyle
poyse
pryse
p-type
psych
Pwyll
pay in
pay up
psyop
payer
pryer
poynt
pay TV
pizza
puzel
Pozzo
pozzy
quayd
quake
quale
quare
quaff
quash
quasi
quack
quark
quail
qualm
quair
quant
quart
quaky
qibla
qubit
quena
queme
queue
quell
quean
✧queen
quern
queyn
queer
Q-Celt
Q-Kelt
quest
query
Q-ship
quina
quine
quire
quite
quiff
quich
qui-hi
quick
quirk
quill
quipo
Quito
quids
quits
quiet
quilt
quint
quirt
quist
quipu
Qajar
qanat
quota
quoad
quote
quoif
quoth
quonk
quoll
quoin
Quorn®
Q-boat
Q-sort
quoit
qursh
Qoran
Qur'an
Quran
Qasim
Qatar
quyte
reata
riata
ruana
Roald
reame
reate
reave
roate
reach
roach
realm
rearm
realo
reaks
reals
reams
rears
roads
react
reast
riant
roast
ready
reamy
roary
Rubia
rabic
rebec
rabid
rebid
✧**rebbe**
roble
ruble
✧**rabbi**
rubai
Rubik
rebel
Rabin
robin
Robyn
rub in
rubin
rub up
re-bar
rebus
Ribes
robes
Rubus
✧**rabat**
rebut
robot
rybat
ribby
recta
rache
recce
Roche
ruche
recti
recal
racon
ricin
recco
recto
recap
racer
recur
ricer
races
rocks
récit
richt
reccy
ricey
Ricky
✧rocky
Radha
redia
Rudra
redid
radge
ridge
rudie
radii
radon
redan
Rodin
radio
rodeo
redip
radar
rider
rudas
radix
redox
redux
reddy
redly
ridgy
Roddy
ruddy
Rheia
rueda
reede
reeve
rieve
reech
✧**rheum**
reels
reest
reedy
reeky
rifle
rifte
ruffe
refel
refer
Rufus
refit
rifty
ragga
regma
rigid
ragde
ragee
régie
rogue
regal
Rigel
Rigil
rigol
Regan
reggo
rag up
rig up
rager
regar
regur
rigor
✧roger
right
raggy
roguy
rugby
ruggy
rehab
Rohan
raita
raird
reird
raile
✧raine
raise
reive
rhime
✧rhine
ruing
Reich
reiki
reign
Rhian
rhino
rails
rains
Reims
reins
ruins
reist
roist
rainy
reify
roily
re-jig
rejig
rajah
Rajni
rejón
Rajiv
rakee
raker
roker
rekey
relic
relie
rille
rolag
Ralph
ruler
Rolls
✧rules
relet
✧**relax**
rally
relay
Riley®
riley
rumba
Romic
rimed
ramee
ramie
rimae
rymme
ramal
romal
rumal
ramen
ramin
reman
remen
✧roman
Ruman
rumen
✧**romeo**
rumbo
remap
rimer
rumor
ramus
Remus
ramet
remit
remex
remix
Rumex
rammy
rumly
rummy
rumpy
R and A
renga
R and B
runic
runed
rance
ranee
range
ranke
Renée
renne
rente
rinse
ronde
ronne
ronte
renig
ranch
runch
renal
renin
ronin
run in
run-in
run on
run-on
rondo
Roneo®
roneo
run up
run-up
R and R
rands
ranks
rings
renew
✧**randy**
rangy
renay
reney
rindy
run by
runny
runty
Rhoda
Rhona
Rioja
roosa
rhomb
rhone
roose
ruoti
roofs
rooms
✧roots
roost
rhody
roofy
rooky
roomy
roopy
rooty
repla
rupia
rapid
roped
raphe
raphé
rupee
repel
ripen
Ripon
repro
rap up
rip up
raper
riper
roper
ryper
repos
repot
repay
reply
ropey
roque
roric
rorid
rorie
roral
rural
rerun
ro-ros
rorty
✧**rasta**
rusma
rased
rosed
rasae
rasse
Rosie
rishi
Rossi
rösti
resin
risen
rosin
riser
risus
roses
resat
reset
resit
roset
rosit
raspy
resay
resty
risky
rushy
rusty
ratha
retia
rated
rathe
retie
ratch
retch
rotch
ratel
rotal
ratan
rat on
rutin
ratio
ratoo
✧retro
rater
rotor
rates
Rett's
rotis
rotls
✧**ratty**
retry
ritzy
rutty
rhumb
round
reuse
rouge
roule
rouse
route
rough
routh
Rouen
roust
roupy
rived
revie
revue
✧**ravel**
revel
rival
rivel
raven
ravin
riven
rev up
raver
river
Rover®
rover
revet
rivet
rownd
rowme
rewth
rowth
rowel
✧**rowan**
rowen
rower
rewax
rawly
rowdy
rhyta
rayed
rayle
rayne
rhyme
rhyne
royne
rayah
riyal
royal
rayon
Reye's
royst
razed
razee
razoo
razor
rozet
rozit
scala
scapa
shama
shaya
scald
scand
scaud
shand
shar'd
shard
skald
slaid
spald
spard
spayd
staid
stal'd
stand
sward
Saame
scale
'scape
scape
scare
seame
seare
sease
seaze
shade
shake
shale
shame
Shane
shape
share
shave
skate
slade
slake
slane
slate
slave
smaze
snake
snare
soare
Soave
space
spade
spake
spale
spane
spare
spate
stade
stage
stake
stale
stane
stare
state
stave
suave
swage
swale
sware
scaff
scarf
snarf
staff
swarf
Shang
slang
spang
staig
stang
swang
scath
shash
slash
smash
snash
snath

Words marked ✧ can also be spelled with one or more capital letters

staph
stash
swash
swath
scapi
Shani
spahi
Stasi
✧swami
Swazi
shack
shank
shark
skank
slack
smack
smaik
snack
snark
spank
spark
stack
stalk
stank
stark
swack
swank
scail
scall
shall
shawl
skail
small
snail
snarl
spall
spaul
spawl
stall
swayl
shalm
shawm
smalm
smarm
spasm
swarm
sdayn
sharn
Shaun
Shawn
slain
✧spain
spawn
stain
starn
swain
shako
spado
scalp
scamp
scarp
scaup
sharp
stamp
swamp
scaur
spaer
stair
starr
scads
shaps

snaps
stars
stays
swabs
swats
scant
✧scart
scatt
shaft
shakt
shalt
sha'n't
shan't
skart
skatt
slant
smalt
Smart®
smart
spalt
spart
start
swapt
swart
snafu
scaly
scary
seamy
shady
shaky
shaly
slaty
snaky
snary
soapy
spacy
Stacy
stagy
swaly
spazz
sabra
sable
Sabme
sabre
sybbe
syboe
subah
Sabmi
Sabal
✧sibyl
✧sybil
sebum
sabin
saber
sober
suber
sabot
Sebat
sybow
subby
Sacha
sacra
socle
sucre
sycee
shchi
Sochi
succi
Sicel
Sican
secco

sicko
socko
socks
sucks!
sadza
sidha
Sudra
sodic
sided
sadhe
Sadie
sedge
sidle
sedum
Sodom
sedan
Sidon
Sudan
saddo
Seder
sider
sudor
sedes
sadhu
sadly
sedgy
soddy
sudsy
scena
Sheba
Shema
sheva
Siena
stela
'scend
scend
seeld
shend
sherd
sield
snead
✧speed
speld
spend
stead
stedd
steed
stend
scene
shere
siege
sieve
skene
smeke
Speke
stede
stele
steme
stere
Steve
suede
suède
✧swede
sheaf
shelf
skelf
swerf
skegg
sieth
sheik
sleek

smeek
smeik
sneak
sneck
speak
speck
spelk
steak
steek
sheal
sheel
she'll
shell
✧she'ol
✧sheol
skell
smell
snell
speal
speel
spell
steal
✧steel
steil
stell
sweal
sweel
swell
skelm
sperm
steam
steem
sdein
see in
sheen
shewn
skean
skein
spean
stean
steen
stein
stern
Svein
Sweyn
spero
steno
sheep
skelp
sleep
sneap
steep
sweep
shear
sheer
skear
skeer
smear
sneer
spear
speer
speir
stear
steer
swear
sweer
sweir
skeos
specs
speos
steps

stews
sceat
scent
sheet
shent
sient
skeet
sleet
slept
smelt
speat
spelt
spent
stent
stept
sweat
sweet
swelt
swept
seedy
seely
seepy
spewy
stewy
suety
Sofia
softa
Sufic
Sefer
so far
sofar
Sofis
softs
Sufis
softy
sigla
sigma
segue
segol
sigil
sagum
Sagan
Sigyn
segno
segar
soger
sugar
segos
signs
sight
Ségou
saggy
soggy
schwa
sahib
sehri
schul
schmo
sohur
suhur
saiga
Saiva
✧shiva
✧spica
spina
stipa
Suita
stilb
shied
skied
spied

stied
saice
saine
seine
seise
seize
shine
shire
shive
skite
skive
slice
slide
'slife
slime
slipe
slive
Smike
smile
smite
snide
snipe
spice
spide
spike
spile
spine
spire
spite
stile
stime
stipe
stire
stive
suite
swine
swipe
swire
swive
skiff
sniff
spiff
stiff
sling
sting
suing
✧swing
saith
Shiah
slish
smith
stich
swish
swith
sci-fi
saick
shirk
skink
slick
slink
smirk
snick
spick
spink
stick
stink
stirk
swink
shiel
shill
skill

skirl
spial
spiel
spill
still
swill
swirl
seism
scion
Skien
Sligo
skimp
stirp
shier
shirr
shiur
skier
skirr
slier
smirr
Sails
shies
skies
skios
slips
snips
spies
sties
Swiss
swits
saint
saist
shift
shirt
skint
skirt
slipt
snift
snirt
spilt
spirt
stilt
stint
suint
✧swift
seity
shily
shiny
skiey
skivy
slily
slimy
snipy
soily
spicy
spiky
spiny
spiry
stimy
stivy
✧**spitz**
sujee
sajou
sakia
Sakta
Sukie
sokah
Sakai
Sakti
Sikel
soken

saker
syker
sekos
salpa
salsa
sella
selva
silva
sol-fa
sulfa
sylva
✧**salic**
salad
silo'd
solid
salle
salse
salue
salve
selle
solde
solve
selah
solah
sylph
salmi
soldi
Solti
sulci
salal
Salem
Salim
sclim
Selim
sklim
solum
✧**salon**
✧silen
solan
Solon
Salmo
salto
✧salvo
soldo
sulfo
salep
salop
shlep
siler
solar
soler
salts
Seles
selfs
sells
Silas
silos
soles
solos
solus
sulks
salet
splat
✧split
Sclav
salix
silex
✧**sally**
salty
silky
silly

silty
Solly
splay
sulky
sully
samba
Samoa
summa
sumac
semée
semie
Somme
sumph
sampi
shmek
samel
simul
saman
samen
semen
Simon
soman
sambo
sum up
simar
symar
Samos
semis
somas
sumos
Samit
samfu
samey
Sammy
Sana'a
sansa
Senga
✧senna
sensa
senza'
Sonia
Sonya
Sunna
Sun Ra
Sinic
sonic
synod
sense
sente
since
singe
sonce
sonde
sonne
sonse
synch
synth
senti
Sindi
Sunni
Sunil
sanko
sunup
✧**señor**
sonar
sands
senes
sinus
sinew
✧**sandy**
senvy

Sindy
sinky
sonny
sonsy
sunny
saola
scopa
shola
Shona
Skoda®
stoma
✧**stoic**
scold
shoed
sloid
sloyd
snood
stond
stood
sword
scone
✧scope
score
shone
shope
shore
shote
shove
slope
slove
✧smoke
smore
smote
snoke
snore
soole
soote
✧spode
spoke
spore
stoae
stoke
stole
stone
stope
store
stove
swore
scoff
skoff
spoof
scoog
scoug
stong
Shoah
slosh
✧sloth
sooth
sposh
shogi
shoji
stoai
Suomi
shock
shook
smock
snoek
snook
snowk
spook
stock

stonk
stook
stork
scowl
Seoul
shoal
shool
skoal
snool
spoil
spool
stool
sloom
spoom
storm
scorn
shoon
shorn
shown
sloan
spoon
stoln
stonn
stoun
stown
swoln
swoon
sworn
swoun
slo-mo
smoko
✧**scoop**
scoup
scowp
sloop
snoop
stoep
stomp
stoop
stoup
swoop
scour
shoer
smoor
spoor
stoor
stour
Scops
Scots
shoes
slops
spots
stoas
stoss
scoot
Scott
scout
'sfoot
shoat
shoot
short
shott
✧shout
sloot
smolt
smoot
smout
smowt
snoot
snort
✧snout

Words marked ✧ can also be spelled with one or more capital letters

spoot
sport
spout
stoat
stoit
stout
swopt
shoyu
Sioux
showy
slopy
smoky
✧snowy
sooty
stogy
stony
story
sepia
septa
sopra
supra
sapid
sepad
Sophi
sepal
sapan
sop up
sapor
sopor
super
sappy
sepoy
Sophy
soppy
serra
sorda
sorra
stria
surra
Surya
Syria
scrab
scrub
shrub
serac
sérac
✧seric
siroc
sared
sarod
scrod
shred
sprad
spred
sprod
strad
saree
sarge
scrae
scree
serge
serre
serve
soree
spree
sprue
strae
surge
serif
scrag
scrog

shrug
sprag
sprig
sprog
sprug
strag
strig
Sarah
Sirah
sirih
surah
✧syrah
serai
Shrek
skrik
strak
seral
soral
sorel
sural
scram
scrim
scrum
serum
strim
strum
Saran®
sarin
scran
serin
seron
✧siren
skran
syren
sargo
servo
sordo
sorgo
scrap
scrip
sirup
strap
strep
strip
strop
syrup
saros
sarus
serfs
Serps
sorus
scrat
Sergt
sprat
sprit
strut
✧surat
scraw
screw
scrow
serow
shrew
shrow
sprew
straw
strew
strow
sorex
sarky
scray
serry

sorry
spray
stray
stroy
surfy
surgy
surly
Sasha
sessa
sasse
Susie
sushi
sisal
sasin
Susan
sysop
sassy
sesey
sissy
Sitra
Sitta
sutra
sated
Satie
setae
sithe
sythe
setal
shtum
Satan
satin
set in
set on
seton
sit in
sit-in
sit on
set-to
Sotho
set up
set-up
sit up
sit-up
satyr
sitar
Soter
sutor
situs
satay
set by
sit by
sauba
sauna
scuba
scuta
Shula
shura
sputa
stupa
slubb
slurb
squab
squib
Stubb
slued
sound
squad
squid
sauce
sauté
'scuse

scuse
scute
shule
shute
sluse
souce
souse
spule
spume
stupe
sture
scuff
scurf
snuff
stuff
slung
squeg
stung
swung
sauch
saugh
shush
slush
snush
sough
✧south
Saudi
scudi
sculk
shuck
skulk
skunk
slunk
snuck
spunk
stuck
stunk
scull
skull
stull
stulm
stumm
shuln
spurn
scudo
sculp
slump
slurp
stump
scuds
shuls
Spurs
stubs
sault
saunt
scuft
shunt
sluit
souct
spurt
squat
squit
stunt
sturt
saucy
saury
soupy
spumy
study
scuzz
squiz

saved
savin
seven
Sivan
saver
savor
sever
siver
syver
savey
✧savoy
savvy
sawed
sewed
sowed
sownd
sowce
sowle
sowne
sowse
sowff
sawah
sowth
sewel
sewen
sewin
Suwon
sew up
sawer
sewer
sowar
sower
Sawny
sexed
sixte
sixth
Saxon
sexer
sixer
sixty
sayid
styed
sayne
skyre
skyte
slype
soyle
spyre
style
styme
styre
styte
says I
styli
spyal
sayon
seyen
say-so
stylo
swy-up
sayer
shyer
skyer
slyer
styes
sayst
shyly
skyey
slyly
Soyuz
sized

sizel
sizar
sizer
thana
tiara
tra-la
teaed
teade
tease
teaze
thane
toaze
trace
trade
trape
trave
tzade
thang
twang
teach
trash
tuath
thagi
thali
tragi
tsadi
thack
thank
track
traik
twank
T-rail
trail
trawl
thaim
train
✧twain
tramp
teals
traps
trass
T-cart
toast
tract
trait
trant
tratt
tuart
teary
thawy
toady
Tracy
tabla
tibia
tabid
tubed
table
tubae
tubal
✧**tabun**
taboo
tabor
tubar
✧tuber
tabes
tabus
tubas
Tebet
Tibet
Tobit
tabby

Tibby
tubby
ticca
tache
Tyche
tical
✧**tacan**
tacho
tacos
Ticos
tocos
tacet
tacit
tacky
techy
tichy
ticky
todde
tidal
Tudor
to-dos
teddy
tiddy
today
toddy
theca
thema
Thera
theta
trefa
trema
theic
teend
they'd
tread
treed
trend
tweed
teene
thebe
theme
there
these
thete
'twere
thelf
treif
teeth
theek
treck
tweak
T-cell
tweel
therm
thegn
tie-in
toe-in
treen
'tween
the go
tee up
thesp
tie up
tie-up
twerp
their
tweer
teens
thews
Trees
tress

trews
theft
treat
trest
tweet
Taegu
theow
teeny
thewy
tafia
tuffe
✧**taffy**
toffy
tufty
tagma
tugra
toga'd
toged
togue
tigon
tog up
tiger
tight
taggy
te-hee
taiga
taira
Thira
Trina
tui na
tuina
teind
third
✧triad
tried
trild
thine
toile
toise
tribe
trice
tride
trike
trine
tripe
trite
twice
twine
twire
twite
thief
triff
thing
tying
taish
thigh
Trish
thick
thilk
think
trick
twink
thill
thiol
thirl
✧trial
trill
'twill
twill
twirl
tuism

Teian
tyiyn
taiko
Taino
twirp
✧**trier**
trior
twier
tails
teins
toils
Trias
trios
✧twins
'taint
taint
trist
twilt
twist
'twixt
tripy
Trixy
twiny
Tajik
tikka
takhi
Tikal
taken
takin
token
Tokyo
taker
toker
tokos
✧**tokay**
talea
talma
✧talpa
telia
Tilda
Tilia
Tulsa
Talib
telic
tell'd
tiled
telae
tilde
tulle
tilth
teloi
talak
taluk
tilak
talon
telco
tulip
talaq
talar
taler
tiler
tolar
tyler
talas
tales
talks
talus
telos
to let
telex
talcy

talky
tally
telly
✧tilly
Tampa
Tomba
temed
timed
timid
tumid
Temne
Tempe
temse
tempi
Tomsk
tamal
Tamil
tamin
✧timon
toman
tempo
timbó
Tamar
tamer
timer
Timor
Timur
tumor
tamis
✧times
timps
'tempt
tempt
✧**tammy**
Timmy
✧tommy
tummy
tumpy
✧**tanga**
Tania
✧tanka
tanna
Tanya
tenia
✧tinea
✧tonga
tonic
tunic
tined
toned
tuned
tyned
tenge
tenné
tense
tenue
tinge
tonne
tynde
tench
tenth
tangi
tanti
tondi
tonal
tenon
✧**tango**
tanto
tenno
tondo
ton-up

tenor
toner
tuner
tongs
tonus
Tonys
tunas
Tunis
tenet
tinct
Tunku
tangy
tanky
tansy
tenny
tenty
tinny
tinty
toney
tunny
Thora
trona
Troic
tronc
thou'd
troad
T-bone
thole
those
trode
troke
trone
trope
trove
thong
Thoth
tooth
troth
tholi
trock
thowl
troll
thorn
Troon
thorp
tromp
troop
two-up
twoer
thous
tools
toots
thoft
troat
trout
tappa
Typha
topic
typic
tepid
tepee
topee
tuple
tophi
topoi
topek
tupek
tupik
tepal
typal
tapen

tap-in
tip in
typto
tap up
tip-up
top up
top-up
taper
tapir
toper
tapas
tapis
topos
typos
tapet
tippy
tipsy
Topsy
topaz
toque
tuque
terga
terra
throb
taroc
toric
thrid
tired
tyred
targe
tarre
terce
terfe
terne
terse
thrae
three
throe
Tiree
torse
torte
turme
Torah
torch
tarsi
terai
torii
torsi
Turki
tarok
terek
torsk
thrum
toran
Torun
Turin
tyran
✧**torso**
turbo
Turco
Tariq
taros
teras
teres
terms
terts
✧tiros
torus
turfs
turps
tyros
tarot
Turku
thraw
threw
throw
tardy
tarry
tarty
terry
turfy
tesla
Tessa
testa
Tosca
tasse
taste
teste
Tisri
Tyson
Tasso
tasar
Taser®
taser
'tisn't
tasty
testy
toshy
tossy
tushy
tusky
tetra
tatie
tithe
title
titre
tutee
tythe
✧**titch**
tetri
Tutsi
tutti
total
totem
✧**titan**
titup
tot up
Tatar
tater
titer
tutor
Tatts
Titus
tatou
tatty
titty
totty
tutty
thuja
thuya
tsuba
Tsuga
thumb
tauld
taube
taupe
Thule
touse
touze
truce
teuch
teugh
touch
tough
truth
truck
trunk
trull
Truro
thump
trump
Tours
truss
taunt
trust
tousy
touzy
Trudy
truly
tavah
Tavel
taver
Tevet
tawie
tawse
towse
towze
tewel
towel
tawer
tower
tewit
to wit
tawny
towny
towsy
towzy
toxic
taxed
Taxol®
Texel
taxon
Texan
toxin
taxer
taxor
taxes
taxis
Taxus
✧texas
texts
tayra
thyme
thymi
tiyin
toyon
try on
try-on
toyer
tryer
twyer
tryst
thymy
tazza
tazze
tozie
tizzy
Urawa
ukase
urate
usage
umami
urali
urari
unarm
Urals
unapt
unary
umbra
unbed
unbid
umbre
upbye
unbag
Uzbeg
Uzbek
umbel
✧**urban**
umber
unbar
umbos
upbow
unbox
✧**uncle**
uncap
ulcer
uncos
uncus
uncut
undid
undee
undée
undue
urdee
urdée
undug
undam
udder
under
ulema
urena
ureic
U-bend
up-end
upend
uneth
uteri
ureal
uveal
uredo
use up
urent
usen't
upsee
unfed
up for
unfit
unfix
ugged
ungod
ungag
ungum
urger
unget
ungot
uh-huh
unhip
usher
unhat
Utica
unite
urine
urite
utile
umiak
urial
✧**union**
Uniat
unify
✧unity
upjet
unked
unkid
unket
unled
unlid
upled
uhlan
unlet
unlit
unlaw
unlay
uplay
ummah
Uxmal
ulmin
unman
urman
Ulmus
unmet
unmew
usnea
urned
ulnae
urnal
ulnar
U-boat
U-bolt
upped
unpeg
unpen
unpin
upper
umpty
unpay
Ugric
Ulric
unred
unrid
unrig
uprun
unrip
U-trap
unsod
upsee
Ulsan
urson
Ursus
unset
upset
unsew
unsex
unsay
upsey
ultra
untie
uptie
uptak
until
Ultan
untin
up top
utter
untax
uvula
usure
U-tube
usual
U-turn
usurp
uhuru
Uluru
urubu
usury
unwed
unwon
unwet
unwit
ulyie
ulzie
unzip
Vaasa
vraic
viand
veale
Vlach
vealy
vibes
vibex
vacua
vocab
vocal
vicar
voces
vichy
Vedda
vodka
Vedic
video
Vidar
Vedas
VE day
VJ day
voddy
Vaduz
veena
V-neck
veery
viewy
vifda
vigia
vague
vegie
vogie
✧vogue
vagal
vigil
✧**vegan**
vigor
vagus
VX gas
vuggy
Vehme
V-chip
voilà
vairé
voice
voile
vying
V-sign
vails
vairy
veily
veiny
Vijay
vakil
vakas
✧**villa**
volta
volva
vulva
valid
valse
value
valve
vilde
volae
volte
volve
villi
velum
Volvo®
vulgo
valor
velar
volar
vales
Vilas
valet
veldt
volet
vomer
vomit
V and A
vinca
vaned
venae
venge
venue
venal
vinal
vinyl
venom
venin
Vanir
viner
✧**venus**
vinos
vinew
veney
Vinay
✧**viola**
viold
vroom
vrouw
vapid
vapor
viper
✧**varna**
virga
varec
virid
varve
verge
verse
verve
virge
Verdi
viral
varan
verso
vireo
Virgo
varus
vires
virus
verst
vertu
virtu
varix
vardy
verry
Vespa®
vespa
✧vesta
vista
visie
visne
Vesak
vasal
vison
visto
visor
visit
vasty
vitta
vatic
vitae
vetch
vital
voter
vitas
Vitis
Vitus
vitex
vaute
vouge
vouch
vault
vaunt
voulu
vivda
vivid
viver
vives
vivat
vowed
vawte
vowel
vower
vexed
voxel
vixen
vexer
vozhd
vezir
vizir
vizor
weamb
✧**weald**
weave
✧whale
whare
wrate
wharf
whang
wrath
whack
wrack
wrawl
whaup
whaur
wraps
wrapt
wrast
weary
weber
webby
✧**wicca**
wacke
wacko
wecht
wacky
wicky
wedge
wodge
width
widen
Wodan
Woden
wader
✧**widow**
waddy
wedgy
widdy
wield
weeke
weete
where
whelk
wreak
wreck
wheal
wheel
whelm
wheen
whelp
whear
weeds
weeks
wheat
wheft
wrest
waefu'
weedy
weeny
weepy
wefte
wifie
woful
wafer
waged
✧**wagon**
✧wigan
wager
wages
✧**wight**
Wuhan
wahoo
weird
waide
waite
waive
weise
weize
while
whine
✧white
write
whiff
wring
weigh
Which?
which
whish
whilk
whisk
wrick
whirl
whirr
wrier
waits
Weil's
whiss
waift
waist
whift
whipt
whist
wrist
whiny
✧whity
whizz
waked
waken
woken
waker
wakes
walla
wilga
wilja
Wilma
Walid
welke
Wilde
Wolfe
wolve
Wolof
✧**welch**
✧welsh
✧**waldo**
wilco
✧**waler**
✧**wales**
walks
walls
Wells
wilds
wiles
wills
welkt
✧**wally**
walty
✧welly
✧willy
wolly
waltz
wamed
✧**woman**
women
wamus
wimpy
womby
Wanda
wanna
winna
wonga
waned
wanle
wanze
wince
winge
winze
Wynne
wench
winch
wongi
wants
winds
✧wings
winos
waney
wanly
wanty
Wendy
wenny
windy
winey
wingy
wonky
wooed
woold
whole
whore
whose
who've
wroke
wrote
wrong
woosh
wroth
who'll
whorl
whoso
whoop
wooer
✧**woods**
whoot
whort
wroot
woody
woofy
woozy
wootz
wiper
✧**wired**
world
Warne
warre
worse
wersh
worth
wirer
wares
wires
words
works
✧worms
warst
worst
wurst
warby
warty
wordy
wormy
worry
waste
Wessi
Wesak
Wasim
wasn't
✧**wu shu**
✧wushu
washy
waspy
wispy
wussy
withe
watch
witch
witan
Wotan

watap
water
wetly
withy
witty
would
wound
wauff
wrung
✧waugh
waulk
waved
woven
waver
waves
wives
wavey
wowee
waxed
waxen
woxen
wax up
waxer
Wayne
why, so
wryer
wryly
wizen
wazir
xoana
xebec
xylic
xylol
xylyl
xylem
xenia
xenon
Xhosa
X-body
xeric
Xeres
Xyris
Xerox®
xysti
x-axis
yeard
ysame
yealm
yearn
years
Yeats
yeast
yrapt
ya-boo
yobbo
yabby
yacca
yucca
yacht
yucky
yodle
yodel
yield
yfere
yrent
yogic
yogin
yager
Yahve
Yahwe
✧yahoo
yrivd
ylike
yoick
yojan
yakka
yokel
yokul
Yukon
yikes
Yakut
yakow
yukky
yclad
ycled
yulan
yolky
yamen
Yemen
yummy
yenta
yince
yrneh
yonks
ycond
ybore
Y-moth
ymolt
ytost
yapok
Yupik
yapon
yupon
yappy
yippy
✧yuppy
yarfa
yarta
yerba
Yerma
ydrad
ydred
yarto
Ypres
yeses
yesty
yauld
you're
youse
you've
young
youth
you'll
yourn
yours
yourt
yeven
yowie
yewen
yawey
yawny
y-axis
Yezdi
zabra
zebra
zebub
zebec
Zyban®
zibet
zocco
Z-bend
zoeae
zoeal
zoeas
zygal
zigan
zygon
Zahra
Zohar
zaire
zaïre
zoism
zoist
zakat
Zelda
zilch
zamia
zymic
zimbi
✧zombi
zaman
zambo
zanja
zonda
zineb
Zenic
zoned
zante
zanze
zinke
zonae
zonal
zinco
zincy
zingy
zinky
zooea
zooid
zhomo
zooks
zoons
zloty
zoppa
zip-in
zip-on
zupan
✧zippo
zoppo
zap up
zip up
zappy
zippy
Zarqa
zerda
zirna
Zorba
zurna
zoril
zorro
zeros
zoris
zesty
ZZ Top
Zhu De
✧zowie
z-axis
zayin
zizel
zuzim
zazen

6 – odd

Abadan
Agadah
agapae
anabas
ananas
Arafat
atabal
ataman
avatar
anarch
awatch
AD and C
Amanda
abased
abated
acater
acates
agapes
agazed
A J Ayer
alated
Amabel
anadem
Aranea
atabeg
atabek
awaked
awaken
awayes
azalea
Agatha
Agatho
✧apache
apathy
abatis
acacia
acarid
adagio
Adamic
Agadic
Agadir
agamic
agamid
agaric
alalia
Alaric
Arabic
arabin
arabis
aralia
Aramis
à ravir
ataxia
ataxic
Azania
Alaska
ananke
afawld
anally
arable
availe
avails
avaunt
abator
acajou
amadou
amatol
✧amazon
analog
Aragon
Avalon
à l'abri
Agassi
araise
arayse
as also
abattu
acanth
anatta
anatto
a salti
avanti
abacus
acarus
alarum
asarum
Avarua
abbacy
Abbado
albedo
aubade
ambler
Aubrey
albugo
ambage
albeit
Alboin
albums
Albany
albino
Albion
✧albert
ambery
anbury
auburn
abbess
ambush
at best
albata
albite
arbute
arbour
abbeys
arctan
ascian
aucuba
accede
arcade
Arcady
Aachen
accrew
arched
✧archer
✧arches
arcked
accoil
Alcaic
Alcuin
Archie
archil
arcsin
✧arctic
ancile
archly
ancome
accend
accent
Ancona
arcana
arcane
arcing
ascend
ascent
accloy
anchor
arccos
archon
accept
auceps
accord
ancora
access
accost
accuse
accite
accrue
aecium
alcove
am-dram
Andean
audial
abdabs
abduce
abduct
addict
adduce
adduct
addeem
addled
Andrea
Andrew
Audrey
aldrin
aedile
and all
audile
addend
add-ins
add-ons
aidant
aiding
Aldine
Andine
ardent
addoom
and how!
Andros
audios
aldern
aldose
aidful
ardour
acetal
akedah
alegar
apeman
axeman
agency
alerce
amerce
aperçu
areach
agenda
amende
A level
A-level
Alexei
Alexej
apexes
abeigh
alegge
anergy
avenge
aweigh
Aretha
Ayesha
abelia
acedia
acetic
alevin
✧alexia
alexic
alexin
Alexis
amebic
✧amelia
Amélie
anemia
anemic
anetic
avenir
Averil
axenic
Adella
age-old
anelli
anerly
areola
areole
ageing
apedom
Avedon
awetos
Aleppo
a tempo
afeard
à terre
Aveira
aweary
ageism
ageist
apepsy
a-per-se
at ease
averse
Alecto
amenta
aneath
aseity
Avesta
✧avenue
à l'envi
acetyl
aye aye
aye-aye
Arezzo
affear
affrap
affray
affect
affyde
affeer
affied
affret
Alfred
affair
au fait
aefald
affine
al fine
au fond
as from
affirm
afford
afflux
Aegean
✧afghan
Anghar
arghan
Augean
angico
aiglet
angled
angler
arguer
argufy
algoid
Anguis
Angela
Angelo
✧angola
argala
argali
arguli
argyle
Argyll
Aegina
angina
argand
argent
Anglos
Al Gore
angary
✧angora
Asgard
augury
argosy
✧august
algate
angsty
argute
augite
Argive
at gaze
achkan
Aphrah
ash-can
ashlar
ash-pan
Ashraf
ashram
Achebe
aphids
ash-key
ashler
Ashley
awheel
a wheen
achage
Alhagi
aphtha
ash-bin
ash-pit
ashake
as hell
awhile
ashame
at home
at-home
achene
aching
aphony
ashine
at hand
Athena
Athene
Athens
a'thing
Ashdod
athrob
awhape
adhere
ashery
ashore
Ashura
a'where
aghast
alidad
aliyah
animal
apical
Ativan®
avital
akimbo
a piece
apiece
abided
aliped
apices
arisen
Aviles
avised
axises
alight
anight
aright
acidic
adipic
Alicia
avidin
acidly
afield
aridly
arilli
avidly
axilla
alisma
Amiens
azione
Alison
Amidol®
amigos
Asimov
avisos
apiary
ariary
aviary
ahimsa
amidst
ariosi
arioso
arista
aristo
aviate

abitur
acinus
adieus
adieux
Amicus
anicut
animus
abject
adjoin
abjure
adjure
adjust
ack-ack
aikido
acknew
ankled
anklet
auklet
alkali
Ankole
aikona
alkane
alkene
alkyne
askant
Atkins
acknow
ackers
Ankara
askari
arkose
arkite
ask out
afloat
agleam
all-day
allice
anlace
allude
Aelred
Aileen
allied
allies
all-red
asleep
allege
anlage
Aglaia
all-hid
aslake
allele
aflame
aplomb
ablins
adland
ailing
all one
allons
aslant
abloom
aslope
allure
ablest
ablush
at last
ablate
aplite
atlatl
ablaut
all but
allium

all out
all-out
alleys
ablaze
asmear
almuce
as much
armada
armlet
aim off
Armagh
✧almain
armpit
aumail
awmrie
aemule
Akmola
Almany
almond
Armani
as many
admire
almery
armory
armure
Asmara
aumbry
Aymara
ad-mass
admass
almost
at most
acmite
almous
armful
armour
awmous
Aeneas
anneal
annual
Aonian
Annaba
Alnico®
Annecy
arnica
apnoea
Arnhem
aunter
alnage
agnail
✧auntie
Anneka
Annika
annals
annuli
Arnold
auntly
agname
Annona
awning
amnion
agnise
adnate
agnate
adnoun
Arnaut
adnexa
annexe
agnize
aboral
Adonai

agorae
agoras
ajowan
amoral
anodal
anorak
apodal
atokal
atonal
avowal
axonal
azonal
amoeba
amorce
at once
avouch
at odds
Abomey
adored
adorer
amoret
apogee
apozem
atoner
avocet
avoset
avowed
avower
avoyer
awoken
Azores
anough
Adonia
Adonic
Adonis
Aeolic
agogic
agonic
alogia
anodic
anomic
anomie
anoxia
anoxic
aporia
atocia
✧atomic
atonic
atopic
azonic
azotic
abolla
✧apollo
arolla
azolla
aborne
abound
a-going
agoing
amount
anoint
à point
aroint
around
aroynt
agorot
a pox on
aboard
adoors
amours
Anoura

avoure
avowry
ahorse
Alonso
arouse
abouts
agouta
agouti
agouty
at outs
Acorus
Aeolus
amomum
amoove
anonym
azo dye
appeal
appear
alpaca
aspect
aspick
alpeen
apples
applet
appaid
appair
au pair
ampule
✧alpine
Alpini
Alpino
append
arpent
aspine
approx
ampere
ampère
apport
aspire
asport
appose
aspout
appayd
asquat
acquit
abroad
adread
Adrian
aerial
airbag
air-car
air dam
airgap
air-gas
airman
air-sac
airway
aortal
arrear
Arrian
atrial
aerobe
arroba
Africa
arrack
arrect
awrack
abrade
arride
afreet
agreed

air-bed
'Arriet
Auriel
Azrael
adrift
aurify
abrégé
agrégé
Auriga
abraid
adroit
afraid
aortic
airily
Abroma
afront
airing
arrant
awrong
Auriol
abrupt
Atropa
air-arm
air-dry
✧aurora
Aurore
across
afresh
agrise
aorist
arrest
arrish
at rest
at risk
at-risk
aurist
aerate
amrita
aurate
Aarhus
Airbus®
air-gun
Atreus
atrium
aureus
aurous
arrive
acrawl
arrows
arrowy
arroyo
abrazo
agrize
agryze
Anshan
as such
aisled
answer
Austen
Auster
assign
abseil
arshin
assail
assoil
Aussie
Austin
Austin®
alsike
Anselm
assume

awsome
absent
arsine
assent
alsoon
absorb
absurd
adsorb
assart
assert
assort
assure
assess
assist
ansate
assets
assott
at stud
assize
actual
Altman
amtman
Amtrak
antiar
antral
astral
astray
at that
attrap
antick
antics
attach
attack
aether
✧althea
Alt key
Anthea
anthem
anther
antler
as then
Astrex
Attlee
Altaic
Altair
✧antlia
Antrim
Astrid
attain
attrit
astely
Attila
asthma
autumn
actant
acting
anting
Antony
Astana
astone
astony
attend
attent
attone
attune
act for
action
ant cow
astoop
author
acture

afters
altern
antara
artery
astare
astart
astern
astert
attire
attorn
artist
attask
attest
autism
aptote
astute
Actium
act out
ante up
antrum
artful
Arthur
astrut
auteur
active
alteza
alulae
alulas
aoudad
abuser
acumen
aludel
amulet
amused
amuser
abulia
agutis
Anubis
anuria
Aquila
alumna
alumni
Amun-Re
aburst
aguise
aguish
avulse
acuity
aguize
advice
abvolt
advene
✧advent
alvine
adverb
advert
advise
atweel
atween
atwain
as well
at will
An Wang
aswing
aswoon
Atwood
adward
adware
aswarm
aswirl
ayword

atwixt
always
Amytal®
any day
anyway
any old
any one
anyone
anyhow
azygos
adytum
amylum
asylum
Aizoon
bhajan
bharal
Bharat
bhavan
biaxal
blazar
bear by
Bianca
✧blanch
blanco
branch
boards
braide
Brando
Brandt
brandy
beaded
beaked
beaker
beamer
bearer
beaten
beater
beaver
bhagee
bhajee
biased
bladed
blader
blades
blamed
blazed
blazer
blazes
boatel
boater
bracer
braces
brayer
brazen
beachy
blashy
brashy
Baalim
beanie
beat it
boatie
boat it
✧brazil
blacks
branks
branky
beadle
beagle
bragly
brails
branle

brawly
Brahma
Brahmi
Brahms
baaing
Beaune
brains
brainy
branny
brawny
beacon
beanos
blazon
Brasov
bravos
braird
✧blaise
braise
brassy
Beatty
beauty
bhakti
bratty
bear up
beat up
beat-up
blague
Braque
blaize
braize
bablah
bobcat
babaco
babied
bibber
bobbed
bobber
bubkes
buboes
Babbie
Babbit
Bobbie
bobbin
bobwig
babble
babbly
bobble
bobbly
bob-fly
bubble
bubbly
bebung
baboon
Byblos
by-blow
Babism
Babist
bibful
buccal
Buchan
backed
backer
backet
Becker
✧becket
bicker
bucker
bucket
bocage
bach it
bichir

bickie
buckie
bacula
becall
becalm
buckle
became
become
beckon
biceps
backra
becurl
bicarb
bicorn
buckra
back up
back-up
backup
Bochum
buck up
badman
bedlam
bedpan
bedral
bodrag
bedeck
beduck
bodach
bodice
bedide
bedyde
badder
✧badger
bedded
bedder
bed-key
bedyed
bidden
bidder
bodger
bodied
bodies
budded
budger
✧budget
bodega
✧buddha
baddie
bedrid
bedsit
✧beduin
Biddie
bodgie
bodkin
budgie
bedell
boddle
bodily
buddle
bedung
bident
biding
boding
bedrop
badass
bedash
bedust
bedaub
bedbug
bed out
bedaze
beegah
beenah
bye-law
bleach
blench
breach
breech
bieldy
blende
Brenda
beeper
beeves
beezer
Bremen
brevet
brewer
Brecht
beedie
brewis
bleaky
breeks
bee fly
✧beetle
bregma
blenny
Boeing
brenne
brehon
✧breton
bleary
breare
breast
breese
breath
beef up
beer-up
brew up
brew-up
baetyl
bye-bye
breeze
breezy
befoam
buffer
buffet
biffin
boffin
baffle
befall
befeld
befell
bifold
befana
befool
before
biform
by-form
beflum
befoul
bagman
beggar
begnaw
big cat
bogman
bogoak
buggan
bagged
bag-net
begged
Big Ben
bigger
bogies
bugged
bugler
buglet
begift
beg off
Baggio
baggit
bagnio
baguio
bagwig
beguin
béguin
biggie
biggin
bigwig
buggin
begild
boggle
bigamy
begone
begunk
big end
bogong
bugong
bygone
big pot
big toe
big top
begird
begirt
Bogart
bog ore
Bogotá
bagful
big-bud
big bug
big gun
bug out
bug-out
bigeye
bogeys
behead
bahada
behalf
beheld
behold
by half
behind
bohunk
by hand
behoof
Bihari
Bahasa
behest
behote
behave
behove
behowl
Bairam
baizas
bridal
bhindi
bailee
bailer
bailey
baiter
beigel
blimey
boiler
briber
briefs
bridge
blight
blithe
bright
bailie
bainin
blinis
✧bridie
Brigid
Brigit
blinks
bricky
brisky
bailli
bridle
✧briony
bailor
Briton
✧briard
briery
bhisti
blintz
bail up
Beirut
brigue
bajada
bejade
bajree
bejant
bijoux
by Jove
Bokmål
bukshi
bakkie
baking
B B King
biking
bikini
bakery
bekiss
Balaam
Balkan
ballad
ballan
ballat
balsam
Balzac
beldam
Belial
Bilbao
bilian
bulbar
Bulgar
bullae
Baluch
belace
bolide
Balder
baleen
balker
balled
ballet
belied
belief
belier
belled
belted
belter
bilges
bilker
billed
billet
bolden
bolled
bollen
bolter
bulbed
bulbel
bulger
bulker
buller
bullet
beluga
bolshy
baldie
✧baltic
bel air
Belgic
✧billie
bollix
bulbil
belike
baldly
boldly
belamy
bulimy
Belone
belong
by-lane
byline
balboa
ballon
ballot
ballow
Belloc
✧bellow
bilbos
billon
billow
Bolton
bolt-on
belfry
Boléro
bolero
ballsy
balata
belate
boleti
ball up
ballup
belaud
belt up
bulbul
bulgur
bulk up
belive
belove
bylive
Biloxi
billy-o
Belize
bemean
bemoan
bombax
Bombay
bum bag
bumbag
bum rap
bemock
bammed
bammer
✧bembex
bombed
bomber
bum-bee
bummed
bummel
bummer
bumper
✧bembix
bemoil
bumkin
Bamako
bumalo
✧bumble
bummle
Bimana
bamboo
bampot
bimbos
bombos
bumbos
bemire
bemuse
bemete
bemaul
bump up
Bombyx
bandar
✧banian
banjax
Bannat
bantam
✧banyan
banzai
Bengal
benzal
bin-bag
binman
bonsai
buntal
Bunyan
bonobo
banded
banged
banger
banker
banket
banned
banner
banter
bended
bendee
bender
bennet
binder
binger
binned
bonded
bonder
bonnet
bonzer
bungee
bungey
bunjee
bunker
✧bunsen
bunted
✧bunter
Buñuel
benign
bindhi
✧binghi
bunchy
bandit
bangin'
Benjie
ben-oil
Benoît
benzil
✧bonnie
bonxie
bungie
bunjie
bunnia
Bunnie
bun tin
bunyip
Bangla
bangle
bingle
bundle
bungle
bename
benumb
bon ami
by-name
byname
banana
bin-end
boning
bandog
bang on
Bangor
banjos
benzol
bonbon
bongos
bon mot
bon ton
buncos
bunion
bunkos
Bengpu
binary
bon gré
banish
Benesh
bonism
bonist
Banate
binate
bonito
Bangui
bang up
bang-up
Banjul
bank up
Banquo
Ben-Hur
ben-nut
bonduc
bunkum
bunk-up
benzyl
baobab
Bao Dai
Bhopal
biogas
boohai
brogan
blobby
blotch
broach
bronco
brooch
Blonde®
blonde
bloody
boorde
broads
broody
biogen
blokey
blowed
blower
booker
boomer
booted
bootee
Boötes
boozed
boozer
boozey
broken
broker
brolga
brough
broché
bionic
biopic
biotic
biotin
blowie
blow in
blow-in
blow it
B-movie
boodie
boogie
bookie
book in
bootie
bromic
blocks
blocky
boorka
Brooke
boodle
Bootle
brolly
bloomy
blow me
broomy
bhoona
browny
Baotou
Biopol®
booboo
boo-boy
boo-hoo
biopsy
blouse
blowse
blowsy
booksy
broose
browse
browst
browsy
blotto
blotty
Brontë
blow up
✧blow-up
boot up
brogue
buoy up
blowze
blowzy
bronze
bronzy
brouze
by-play
bo-peep
bopper
bepuff
bepelt
by-plot
bypass
by-past
bepity
bypath
barkan
barman
barrat
Barsac
Berean
bordar
✧boreal
Boreas
bureau
burial
burlap
Burman
bursae
bursal
bursar
byrlaw
byroad
barock
Baruch
borsch
Bursch
boride
barbed
barbel
barber
barbet
barded
bargee
barken
barker
barley
Barnes
✧barnet
✧barney
barred
barrel
barren
barret
barter
Berber
✧bergen
berley
berret
birder
birken
birler
bordel
border
boreen
Borges
Borneo
borrel

Words marked ✧ can also be spelled with one or more capital letters

burden
burgee
burger
burhel
buried
burler
burley
burned
burner
burnet
burpee
burrel
bereft
barege
barège
borage
✧bertha
berthe
Barbie®
barbie
bardic
Barkis
barrio
✧berlin
Bernie
Bertie
birdie
birkie
Borgia
burdie
burn in
burn-in
byrnie
barely
barfly
Barolo
birsle
burble
burgle
bireme
barong
barony
borane
boring
Bardot
barrow
Bartók
barton
baryon
borgos
borrow
borzoi
burbot
burgoo
Burgos
burros
burrow
✧burton
byroom
Baresi
barish
barite
baryta
berate
borate
buriti
by rote
barful
barium
barque
burn up

burn-up
baraza
bashaw
Bassae
bespat
bestad
bestar
Biscay
bismar
Bissau
busbar
busman
byssal
basics
basuco
bisect
beside
✧baseej
basher
basket
basnet
basset
baster
Bastet
beseem
beseen
besped
bested
bister
bosker
bosket
bossed
bushed
bushel
busied
busked
busker
busket
busses
busted
bustee
✧buster
besigh
✧bosche
Bastia
besoin
bespit
Bessie
bestir
Bosnia
buskin
busk it
basalt
basely
bastle
busily
bustle
bosoms
bosomy
basant
basing
besing
besung
busing
bash on
bassos
bastos
bespot
Besson
bestow
bishop

bisson
bosbok
✧boston
busboy
besort
bistre
bistro
Basuto
Basutu
boshta
✧basque
besmut
bestud
bisque
bust up
bust-up
byssus
bateau
✧batman
betray
bitmap
Botham
bothan
betide
bather
batler
batlet
batted
battel
batten
batter
beteem
bethel
betted
better
bitser
bitted
bitten
bitter
bother
bo tree
butler
butter
by then
betcha
bitchy
botchy
betoil
betrim
bite in
bittie
bothie
butt in
betake
battle
Betula
botfly
bottle
buttle
Batumi
betime
by-time
bating
betony
biting
✧botany
botoné
butane
but-end
butene
bathos

batoon
betook
betrod
bettor
bittor
bottom
buteos
button
bêtise
betoss
batata
bututs
battue
bittur
Beulah
Bhutan
brumal
brutal
brumby
bounce
bouncy
brunch
bluidy
bounds
bouget
boules
Boulez
Bruges
Brunei
Brunel
brunet
bruter
bouffe
bludge
bluggy
blunge
Brugge
bouche
bouché
bought
brushy
bludie
bougie
Brücke
bauble
bluely
bouclé
boulle
bluing
bourne
boubou
bouton
bauera
beurre
beurré
blurry
bluesy
bluish
✧bourse
bruise
✧bounty
Brutus
bovver
Bovril®
bovine
bovate
bivium
bewray
bowman
bow-oar
bowsaw

Bowlby
bawbee
bawler
bawley
beweep
bowget
bowled
bow leg
bowler
✧bowser
bowyer
bewail
bowfin
bowsie
bow tie
bawble
bowels
bowing
bow-boy
bowpot
bowwow
bewept
bawdry
beware
✧bowery
byword
by-work
bow out
boxcar
box-day
box van
baxter
Bexley
box-bed
boxing
Buxton
boxful
buy off
✧beyond
✧bryony
buying
Boyson
✧bayard
boyish
bay rum
boyaux
buy out
buyout
bazaar
bezoar
buzzer
bezzle
bezant
bizone
byzant
bazazz
bezazz
bizazz
chadar
chagan
chalan
charas
chazan
Ciaran
cravat
clambe
crabby
crambo
chance
chancy
Clancy

clatch
cranch
cratch
Claude
chafer
chalet
châlet
Chanel
chapel
chared
charet
chaser
claret
claver
claves
clawed
clayed
clayey
coaler
coatee
coater
coaxer
crases
✧crater
craven
craver
crayer
crazed
chaffy
chaufe
chauff
change
charge
chargé
claggy
craggy
cha-cha
coachy
Chadic
Charis
Chasid
clavie
clavis
crania
crasis
cyanic
cyanin
chalky
chapka
charka
cranky
czapka
cradle
craple
crawly
chacma
chammy
charms
chasmy
clammy
chaîné
chains
chaunt
cranny
chador
Charon
chaton
clamor
claros
Cracow
craton

crayon
chappy
cramps
crampy
chakra
charry
Claire
chaise
chasse
chassé
classy
clause
coarse
chaeta
chafts
chanty
charta
charts
chaste
chatta
chatti
chatty
clarts
clarty
clasts
coaita
crafty
crants
chat up
clam up
clap up
claque
cratur
cabman
cabobs
cubica
cablet
cobber
✧cobweb
cubbed
cubage
cabbie
cabrie
cabrio
cabrit
cobric
cuboid
cybrid
cabala
cobalt
cobble
Cybele
cabana
Cabiri
coburg
cyborg
✧cubism
cubist
cobnut
coccal
cicada
cachet
cocked
✧cocker
cocket
cycler
coccid
Cochin
cyclic
cyclin
cackle

cecils
Cecily
cicala
cicale
✧cicely
cockle
cachou
cacoon
coccos
cocoon
cuckoo
cyclos
cicero
cocksy
cecity
cicuta
cactus
coccus
cock up
cock-up
cyclus
coccyx
cadeau
caduac
Cod War
cadger
codded
codder
codger
cudden
cudgel
codify
caddie
caddis
Cedric
codlin
cuddie
cuddin
cedula
coddle
cuddle
cuddly
cadent
coding
cedarn
cidery
codist
Cadmus
ca' down
caecal
✧caesar
Ceefax®
chelae
chenar
chetah
coeval
credal
Cretan
clench
cleuch
coerce
creach
cheder
chenet
cheven
chevet
chewer
chewet
clever
crenel
crepey

crewel
cyeses
cierge
clergy
cleugh
creagh
cleché
✧crèche
chemic
chenix
Cherie
chesil
chevin
chewie
cleric
clevis
credit
✧cretic
cretin
cue bid
cyesis
checky
cheeky
creaky
Creeks
creeky
✧creole
chemmy
cleome
creamy
creant
cueing
coelom
✧credos
cremor
crepon
cresol
cheapo
cheapy
Cheops
creepy
cuerpo
cheers!
cheery
cherry
chèvre
cheese
cheesy
crease
creasy
creese
creesh
cueist
cherty
chesty
create
cuesta
caecum
Caelum
cheque
chequy
cherub
cherup
chew up
clew up
cleave
cleeve
caftan
coffed
coffee
coffer

coffin
cuffin
cafila
coffle
cuffle
cafard
Caffre
✧cognac
Cagney
cogged
cogger
cygnet
cage in
ciggie
coggie
cagily
coggle
coggly
caging
cogent
cagoul
Cygnus
cahier
cohoes
coheir
cohune
cahoot
cohere
cohorn
cohort
cohosh
co-host
caimac
caiman
chinar
Chirac
chiral
chital
climax
clinal
cnidae
coital
crinal
Crimbo
chiack
chinch
clinch
childe
ceiled
chided
chider
chiles
chimer
chimes
Chinee
chisel
chives
coiner
crikey
crimen
cripes
crises
cuiter
cliffy
clingy
cringe
chicha
chi-chi
chichi
✧chi-rho
cliché

chilis
chip in
chitin
clinic
clitic
clivia
coin it
crisis
critic
chinks
cricky
caille
chicle
chicly
chield
chilli
chilly
criblé
Cairns
client
coigne
criant
chibol
chicon
chigoe
chikor
chinos
Chiron
chiton
clip-on
coinop
chippy
chirpy
crimpy
Cripps
Crispa
crisps
crispy
chigre
chirre
chiasm
crissa
cuisse
chintz
chitty
clifty
clints
crista
caique
caïque
chiaus
chin up
clique
cliquy
Cnicus
coitus
crinum
chivvy
cojoin
cajole
caking
calcar
callan
Callao
Callas
calpac
celiac
cellae
cellar
collar
Colmar

coltan
call by
colobi
calico
cilice
cultch
calced
calces
calker
caller
callet
calmed
calver
calves
calxes
celled
collet
Colley
colter
Culdee
culler
cullet
culmen
culter
culver
calefy
caligo
colugo
caltha
Calais
calcic
calkin
callid
call in
Calvin
Celtic
coldie
collie
cullis
cultic
calmly
coldly
calami
calima
column
Celina
colons
colony
call on
callop
callow
cellos
collop
caliph
✧calory
celery
colure
calash
Callum
call up
call-up
callus
calque
cilium
coleus
colour
cultus
combat
Comsat®
cymbal
come by

comice
comedo
comedy
comodo
camber
Camden
camlet
camper
cimier
combed
comber
commer
compel
comper
cumber
cummer
camsho
cambia
come in
come it
comfit
commie
commis
commit
commix
cummin
cymoid
Cymric
cample
camply
comble
comely
comply
cumuli
cement
✧coming
Comino
cameos
camion
✧campos
combos
come on
come-on
common
commos
commot
compos
compot
camera
cembra
comarb
comart
camash
camass
camese
camise
comose
cymose
camote
co-mate
comate
comity
camp up
campus
come up
comous
cymous
Canaan
cancan
cannae
Cantal

cantar
canvas
centai
cental
centas
confab
con man
Conrad
Conran
cuneal
Canuck
conics
Canada
cañada
cancel
✧cancer
canker
Canley
canned
cannel
canner
Cannes
canted
canter
censer
center
cinder
conder
confer
congee
conger
conjee
conker
conned
conner
convex
convey
cunner
canthi
concha
conche
conchs
conchy
Candia
candid
candie
condie
confit
confix
congii
Connie
conoid
candle
cangle
canola
cantle
canula
cinema
conima
canine
caning
conine
candor
cannon
cannot
canton
cantor
cantos
canyon
censor
centos

cineol
condom
condor
condos
congou
Connor
con-rod
contos
convoy
canapé
canopy
Cynips
canard
canary
cendré
centra
centre
centry
contra
conure
Canute
cenote
canful
cangue
cantus
census
centum
cinque
concur
consul
Consus
choral
clonal
crotal
coombe
Crosby
choccy
choice
cloaca
crotch
crouch
chorda
cloddy
cloudy
ca' over
choked
choker
chokey
choler
chorea
choree
chosen
closed
closer
closet
Cloten
cloven
clover
cloves
cloyed
cooker
cooler
cooper
coosen
cooser
cronet
crowed
chough
cloggy
clough
chocho

cloche
clothe
Clotho
cloths
croche
cholic
chop in
✧chopin
choria
choric
clonic
Clovis
cookie
coolie
cool it
coosin
cootie
Chonju
chocko
croaky
cholla
clodly
coolly
choana
cooing
Crohn's
chokos
croton
choppy
croppy
croupe
croupy
chokra
chokri
chowri
chowry
choose
choosy
chouse
crosse
crouse
Cloots
clotty
coolth
coonty
croûte
chop up
chorus
clog up
clonus
cloqué
cook up
coop up
crocus
Cronus
crop up
croove
capias
captan
cupman
copeck
caplet
capped
capper
cipher
copied
copier
copped
copper
copter
cupped

cupper
cypher
cy pres
cop off
caplin
capric
caprid
Capris
capsid
coppin
Coptic
cupric
cup-tie
cyprid
cypris
copple
copula
cupola
cupule
coping
captor
capita
✧capote
copita
capful
cippus
cop out
cop-out
cupful
✧cyprus
coquet
carfax
carman
carnal
carpal
carrat
cercal
cereal
circar
corban
Corfam®
corral
corsac
curial
cursal
curtal
caribe
carack
caract
Carica
curacy
corody
carder
careen
career
caries
Carmel
Carmen
carnet
carney
carpel
carper
carpet
carrel
carsey
cartel
✧carter
carved
carvel
carven
carver

cermet
certes
corbel
corded
corked
corker
cormel
cornea
corned
cornel
corner
cornet
corset
Cortes
Cortés
cortex
corvée
corves
corvet
curfew
curiet
curled
curler
curlew
curney
curpel
cursed
curser
curved
curves
curvet
carafe
Cardin
Carlie
Carrie
cerris
cervid
cervix
corbie
corgis
corkir
corrie
corvid
currie
Carola
Carole
caroli
cerule
circle
corals
curdle
curtly
curule
✧carême
chroma
chrome
chromo
corymb
✧carina
caring
corona
Cyrene
carbon
carboy
care of
carfox
carhop
carlot
Carlow
carrot
Carson

carton
ceroon
cordon
corsos
curios
cursor
ceriph
curara
curare
curari
caress
Caruso
cerise
ceruse
chrism
Christ
corpse
curtsy
cerate
cerite
curate
carpus
cercus
cereus
cerium
cerous
circus
cirque
cirrus
corium
cork up
cormus
cornua
corpus
✧corvus
curium
curl up
cursus
corozo
coryza
casbah
cashaw
Caspar
✧casual
Cosmas
costae
costal
co-star
cushat
cushaw
casaba
cosech
cashew
casket
casted
caster
cesser
cisted
cosher
cosier
cosmea
cosset
costed
coster
cusped
cussed
cusser
casein
cash in
✧cassia
Cassie
Cassio
cassis
Cissie
cistic
cosmic
cossie
cuspid
cystic
cystid
castle
cosily
costly
casing
casino
cosine
cascos
Caslon
cast on
✧castor
cestos
ciscos
cosmos
C P Snow
custom
✧custos
casern
Castro
cesura
cesure
cushty
cash up
casque
cast up
cesium
cestui
cestus
cissus
cistus
costus
cosy up
cuscus
Cathal
Cathar
Cathay
cat-lap
catnap
citral
coteau
cottar
cotwal
cytode
catnep
cither
cotted
cotter
cutler
cutlet
cutter
citify
cityfy
cut off
cut-off
catcht
catchy
cutcha
Cathie
catkin
catnip
citric
citrin
cottid
cytoid
catalo
cattle
citole
cotyle
cutely
cuttle
catena
cetane
cation
citron
cotton
cuttoe
citess
cotise
cutesy
cytase
cytisi
catgut
catsup
✧citrus
cottus
cut out
cut-out
caudad
caudal
causal
chukar
coucal
cougar
crural
chubby
clubby
crumbs
crumby
church
clunch
clutch
crunch
crutch
chuddy
Cluedo®
cruddy
caudex
cauker
caules
causen
causer
causey
cautel
cauter
cauves
C-cubed
coulée
couped
coupee
couper
couter
cruces
crumen
cruset
cruxes
chuffy
Cruyff
caught
couché
couthy
caulis
clue in
clusia
coulis
cousin
coutil
crusie
chucks
chukka
chunky
clucky
clunky
caudle
couple
cruels
chummy
crummy
chukor
cou-cou
coupon
clumps
clumpy
crumpy
clumsy
course
cruise
county
crusta
crusty
caucus
crud up
cruive
caveat
caviar
civics
cavier
cave in
cave-in
caving
covent
coving
covyne
cavern
cavort
covary
covers
covert
cavass
civism
cavity
cowman
cowpat
cawker
cowled
cowpea
cowage
cowrie
cawing
cowboy
cowpox
✧coward
cowish
Cow Gum®
Caxton
cayman
chyack
chylde
clypei
cry off
Cayuga
cry aim
crying
Ceylon
chypre
cayuse
coyish
coyote
crypto
coypus
cry out
cozier
cizers
drabby
drag by
diarch
deaden
deader
deafen
dealer
deaner
diadem
dialed
diaper
doater
dragée
draped
draper
drapes
drapet
drawee
drawer
drazel
draffy
dwarfs
draggy
deathy
drachm
dearie
deasil
deawie
diacid
diapir
draw in
dualin
dyadic
deadly
deafly
dearly
diable
doable
drably
dually
dyable
dear me
dharma
Deanna
Deanne
dharna
Dianne
draunt
deacon
dead on
dead-on
dialog
diatom
diaxon
diazos
drag on
✧dragon
Dralon®
draw on
drappy
dearth
drafts
drafty
dial-up
drag up
draw up
diamyl
dabbed
dabber
debted
debtee
dibbed
dibber
dobbed
dobber
dubbed
Debbie
debris
débris
dobbie
✧dobbin
dubbin
Dublin
dabble
debile
dibble
debunk
debtor
debark
do bird
debase
debosh
deboss
debate
de-blur
dybbuk
Declan
decoct
decade
decide
decode
dacker
decked
decker
decree
decrew
dectet
Dicken
dicker
dickey
docken
docker
docket
ducker
decaff
dacoit
✧deccie
deceit
✧dickie
decoke
decile
deckle
docile
decamp
décime
decane
decani
decant
decent
dicing
docent
Dacron®
deckos
Dickon
doctor
da capo
decarb
decare
decern
decury
dicast
dacite
dickty
Docete
dictum
dactyl
dodman
deduce
deduct
dadoed
dadoes
didder
didoes
dodded
dodder
Dodgem®
dodger
dodoes
dudder
dudeen
Dudley
dodkin
duddie
daddle
diddle
doddle
Dodoma
dedans
did won
DVD-ROM
dudish
dudism
dude up
do down
daedal
deejay
Deepak
djembe
dreich
drench
dreads
duende
deemed
deepen
diesel
dieses
dieter
djebel
dzeren
die off
dredge
dreggy
deepie
diesis
drecky
deeply
duello
dreamt
dreamy
doesn't
duenna
dyeing
daemon
Daewoo®
Dieppe
dièdre
dreare
dreary
dressy
duetti
duetto
duetts
die out
dueful
daftar
defeat
defrag
defray
deface
defect
Dafydd
de fide
defied
defier
deflex
differ
doffer
duffel
duffer
daftie
daftly
deffly
defile
deftly
duffle
defame
defend
define
deform
defast
defus'd
defuse
defoul
duff up
defuze
degras
dog-ear
dog tag
dagaba
dagoba
dagger
degree
digged
digger
dog-bee
dogged
✧dogger
dog-hep
dogleg
dégagé
doggie
dog-hip
Duggie
daggle
Dugald
digamy
dog-end
dugong
diglot
dogfox
dog-ape
degust
digest
dogate
dugite
dégoût
dig out
dugout
dahlia
dehorn
dehort
daiker
daimen
de-icer
doiled
doited
drivel
driven
driver
duiker
doings
daimio
deific
deixis
doitit
daidle
djinni
daikon
daikos
daimon
drippy
Deidre
driest
dainty
drifty
deject
de jure
déjà vu
diktat
dakoit
dik-dik
duke it
dekkos
dikkop
dukery
dikast
Dakota
Dalian
Dallas
Delian
dollar
dolman
dolmas
delice
delict
deluce
delude
dalles
Del key
delver
delves
dolmen
dulcet
deluge
delphs
Dulcie
Dalila
dolent
✧dolina
doline
dallop
dalton
Delroy
dildoe
dildos
dollop

delope
dalasi
delish
daleth
delate
delete
Delyth
dilate
dilute
Duluth
Delius
dolium
doll up
dolour
de luxe
Dilwyn
Damian
Dammam
dammar
demean
démodé
Damien
dammed
dammer
damned
dampen
damper
damsel
demies
dimmed
dimmer
dumper
damage
dammit
demain
dimwit
domain
damply
dimble
dimple
dimply
dumbly
dumple
demand
dement
domino
Dympna
damson
dump on
demark
demure
damask
demise
demiss
demist
dumose
demote
dimity
domett
dim out
dim-out
dim sum
dum-dum
dumdum
dumous
Danaan
denial
dental
dinnae
Donmar
donnat
Duncan
denude
dynode
dancer
dancey
dander
danger
Daniel
denied
denier
dennet
dentel
dentex
Denver
dinged
dinger
dinges
dingey
dinned
dinner
donder
donkey
donned
donnée
Donner
donnés
donzel
Dundee
dunder
✧dunker
dunned
dinghy
Danzig
Dennis
dentil
dentin
Denzil
done in
Donnie
donsie
dunlin
dandle
dangle
dangly
dindle
dingle
dinnle
Donald
dongle
denims
dynamo
doning
Danaoi
danios
✧danton
donjon
donnot
dun-cow
Dunlop
denary
De Niro
donary
Danish
Danisk
Denise
dynast
Danite
denote
donate
dunite
dengue
dinful
dingus
dinkum
de novo
deodar
dioxan
doodad
doodah
drop by
droich
doofer
dooket
doomed
do over
droger
drover
drongo
dioxin
doolie
dromic
Dromio
drop in
drop-in
drosky
dhooly
doodle
drolly
droome
Dionne
Diodon
doocot
doo-doo
doo-wop
dromoi
dromon
dromos
duomos
✧**droopy**
dropsy
drossy
drowse
drowsy
dhooti
drouth
doofus
drogue
✧**dipsas**
depict
dipody
dapper
diplex
dip-net
dipped
✧dipper
✧dopper
duplet
duplex
doppie
dapple
dipole
dopily
daphne
depend
depone
dopant
doping
deploy
diploe
diplon
Dipnoi
dipsos
dupion
depart
deport
dupery
depose
depute
deputy
diquat
Daqing
Dardan
dargah
derham
dermal
der Tag
dirdam
dirham
Dorcas
Dorian
dorsal
Durban
durbar
durgan
Durham
durian
Deryck
direct
deride
dirndl
✧dorado
Darién
darken
darkey
darned
darnel
darner
darred
Darren
darter
Darwen
dirhem
Doreen
dormer
dorsel
dorser
Dorset
dorter
Durres
dirige
Dardic
Darwin
derail
dermic
dermis
derris
dormie
Dorrie
durrie
dargle
darkle
darkly
dartle
dernly
Dervla
dor-fly
dirams
daring
durant
during
Dermot
durion
dartre
dorise
Dorism
duress
derate
Darius
dirdum
dor-bug
dorsum
durdum
derive
darcys
dorize
desman
disbar
discal
dismal
disman
dismay
distal
dossal
De Sica
dosi-do
✧**dasher**
deseed
des res
dished
dishes
Disney
dispel
dossel
dosser
dusken
duster
design
dosage
dassie
desmid
distil
dossil
Dustin
desalt
disple
duskly
disomy
desine
desyne
despot
discos
Dr Slop
descry
desert
desire
desorb
disarm
dysury
desist
disuse
disbud
✧discus
diseur
dish up
dust-up
disown
dittay
detach
detect
dither
ditted
dotted
dutied
dotage
detail
detain
dittit
Dottie
ditali
dottle
do time
dating
Datong
detent
détenu
detune
ditone
dotant
doting
de trop
dittos
dot-com
dotcom
datary
datura
detort
dotard
detest
dotish
Datsun®
detour
dative
Dougal
dauber
dauner
deuced
doucet
douser
douter
drupel
drudge
druggy
douche
dought
doughy
dautie
Douala
double
doubly
dourly
drumly
douane
deuton
dhurra
drum up
Devdan
device
divide
devvel
devein
devoid
devoir
devall
Divali
Davina
divine
diving
dévoré
divers
divert
devest
devise
divest
dovish
devote
dévote
duvets
devour
devout
dyvour
dewlap
dowlas
dawner
downed
downer
dowser
dowset
dawtie
Downie®
dawdle
Dewali
dewily
Diwali
do well
dewani
dowlne
dew-bow
dawbry
deworm
dawish
dewitt
✧**dexter**
dry ice
✧**dryads**
✧**day bed**
doyley
Dryden
duyker
day off
dry off
dry ski
day-fly
Day-Glo
dayglo
day-old
dry-fly
day one
drying
day-boy
Dayton
dry bob
dry rot
dryish
day out
dry out
dry run
dizain
dazzle
dozens
dozing
elance
enarch
eparch
exarch
elanet
elated
elater
E-layer
enamel
erased
eraser
evader
examen
eyalet
Elaeis
egally
enable
epaule
Elaine
Evadne
enamor
etalon
elapse
écarté
ex ante
en beau
embace
embody
emblem
Euboea
embail
emblic
emboil
ecbole
embale
emball
embalm
emboly
embank
Eubank
en bloc
Edberg
Egbert
embark
embers
embase
emboss
embost
embusy
embrue
erbium
embryo
eschar
encode
escudo
excide
elchee
Escher
eschew
esc key
etcher
exceed
encage
eucain
Euclid
encalm
encamp
excamb
Eocene
escroc
escrol
escrow
escape
except
encore
escarp
escort
euchre
encase
encash
encyst
excess
excise
excuse
excite
encave
endear
end man
Esdras
eddied
eddoes
Eddaic
endrin
eidola
end-all
eident
elding
ending
ex dono
Eddery
endart
endure
enduro
eadish
eddish
eldest
em dash
en dash
endoss
end use
endite
endive
enemas
evejar
egence
egency
elench
éperdu
eleven
evener
Exeter
eyelet
emerge
energy
exergy
Edenic
Egeria
elegit
emesis
emetic
emetin
eremic
eyelid
eye-pit
Eyetie
evenly
eterne
exeunt
eyeing
elevon
ere now
erenow
exempt
✧**epeira**
exedra
emerse
even so
ever so
egesta
ejecta
émeute
eke out
Erebus
even up
exequy
eye-cup
eyeful
enerve

Evelyn
effray
efface
effect
en face
enface
Eiffel
enfree
ewftes
effigy
effeir
enfold
enfant
effere
effort
enfire
enform
effuse
elfish
effete
en fête
efflux
elf cup
engram
engobe
Eagles
eaglet
eggler
erg-ten
eughen
ewghen
engage
engagé
edgily
Engels
engild
engulf
edging
engine
Eugene
egg box
egg-box
eggnog
engaol
eggery
engird
engirt
engore
eighth
eights
eighty
ergate
eggcup
englut
El Gîza
ephebe
ephebi
ethics
echoed
echoer
echoes
echoey
echoic
ethnic
enhalo
exhale
exhume
ethane
ethene
ethyne
Ethiop
exhort
echium
Elijah
epical
Evipan®
eriach
evince
ebitda
epimer
eringo
Elisha
elicit
elixir
Emilia
exilic
edible
enisle
evilly
✧enigma
Edison
editor
Elinor
✧epigon
epilog
epizoa
émigré
eo ipso
Erinys
enjoin
enjamb
Ed Koch
Eskimo
Eolian
eyliad
enlace
enlock
Eilidh
eel-set
Eileen
eulogy
éclair
en l'air
esloin
Ealing
enlink
ellops
enlard
eclose
enlist
eolith
enlevé
Emmies
Eamonn
Eamunn
Edmund
ermine
Esmond
Exmoor
emmesh
enmesh
enmity
emmove
enmove
ennead
Etnean
esnecy
Eunice
eunuch
ennage
El Niño
eonism
Ernest
ennuyé
ecomap
enodal
euouae
evovae
Elodea
eloper
emoter
enoses
epopee
eposes
eroded
evoker
Exocet®
exogen
eloign
enough
epocha
Ecofin
Elohim
enosis
epodic
erotic
exodic
exomis
exonic
exotic
étoile
Evonne
exopod
egoism
egoist
Eloisa
Eloise
egoity
econut
évolué
✧exodus
evolve
eponym
exonym
espial
expect
espada
espied
expugn
esprit
empale
expand
expend
employ
euphon
empare
emparl
empart
empery
✧empire
expert
expire
expiry
export
El Paso
✧empusa
empuse
expose
exposé
ear-cap
earlap
earwax
Eirian
enrobe
Edrich
eirack
enrace
enrich
earner
étrier
enrage
enragé
Eartha
earthy
earwig
eureka
eerily
em rule
enroll
en rule
Euro-MP
earing
enrank
enring
errand
errant
erring
earbob
earcon
enroot
enrapt
Europa
Europe
egress
éprise
errata
earful
Evreux
Eirlys
enseal
enseam
ensear
exsect
eassel
✧easter
Elspet
ensued
ensign
eassil
elshin
essoin
easily
eisell
ensile
Essene
ensure
exsert
ensate
ersatz
ease up
ensoul
essive
entrap
estray
entice
either
entrée
entrez
eothen
esteem
Esther
eat off
eatage
eatche
eltchi
entail
entoil
eathly
extold
entame
entomb
eating
Eithna
Eithne
extant
extend
extent
extine
Eftpos
ectopy
ectype
eatery
entera
entire
extern
extirp
extort
eftest
extasy
entêté
entity
estate
eat out
estrus
eutaxy
eluder
Eluned
Études
emulge
emunge
écurie
epulis
ekuele
eluant
eluent
equant
equine
elutor
équipe
Eluard
épuisé
evulse
eluate
equate
✧equity
envied
envier
Elvira
elvish
ex voto
enwrap
enwall
enwomb
Edwina
enwind
eh whow
Edward
emydes
eryngo
etymic
etypic
etymon
Eeyore
elytra
enzian
Eozoic
eczema
enzyme
enzone
evzone
Eozoon
fracas
flabby
flambé
fiancé
fiasco
flanch
France
franco
fratch
feared
flamed
flamen
flamer
flares
flaser
flawed
flaxen
flayed
F-layer
flayer
framed
framer
frater
flaggy
flange
flashy
Flavia
flavin
frazil
featly
flatly
fiaunt
flaune
flaunt
fraena
flacon
flagon
flavor
fragor
flappy
frappé
fiacre
fratry
fraise
fealty
flatty
feague
flatus
franzy
Fabian
fabled
fabler
fibbed
fibber
fibred
fob off
fub off
fabric
fibril
fibrin
fibula
Fablon®
fibros
facial
fecial
facade
✧façade
facies
factis
fucoid
facile
facula
feckly
fecula
fickle
fo'c'sle
facing
fecund
factor
fictor
facete
factum
fidget
fodder
fade in
fade-in
faddle
fiddle
fiddly
fuddle
fading
fi donc!
✧fedora
fade up
fade-up
fadeur
faecal
foeman
foetal
fierce
fleece
fleech
fleecy
flench
fletch
✧french
fresco
fleadh
Freddy
faeces
feeder
feeler
flewed
foemen
fledge
fledgy
flèche
fleshy
faerie
feel in
féerie
feerin
flemit
foetid
fremit
Freyja
freaky
feeble
feebly
freely
feeing
frenne
Fresno
flexor
foetor
fueros
fleury
flense
freest
fiesta
freety
freity
fretty
feed up
feel up
foetus
free up
frenum
freez'd
freeze
frenzy
Fafnir
Fifers
Fifish
fogman
fogram
fagged
figged
fogged
fogger
fogies
fag end
faggot
fog-bow
fog-dog
fegary
figure
fogash
fugato
fig out
fogeys
Führer
Fehmic
Faisal
Friday
flinch
flitch
Frieda
faikes
failed
foiled
frisée
fridge
fringe
fringy
flight
fricht
fright
fail in
frigid
flicks
flisky
friska
frisky
faible
faille
fainly
fairly
foible
frills
frilly
friand
friend
faitor
feijoa
foison
frigot
frijol
fripon
frivol
friary
fains I
flimsy
faints
fainty
feints
feisty
flinty
flirty
frieze
frizzy
Fijian
fajita
Fokker
fakery
fikery
fikish
fallal
fellah
filial
foliar
✧fulham
fullam
fullan
fulmar
Felice
falces
fallen
faller
falser
falter
feller
felter
filler
fillet
filter
folder
fuller
filthy
fall in
fall-in
felsic
fill in
fill-in
fillip
filmic
fold in
folkie
fulfil
fulgid
fulvid
fa la la
feline
felony
filing
falcon
fallow
felloe
✧fellow
filfot
folios
follow
fulgor
full-on
fylfot
filtre
fulcra
filose

folksy
folate
filius
fill up
fill-up
fold up
folium
full up
fumado
fumage
family
female
fimble
fumble
famine
foment
femora
femurs
famish
fumets
famous
fumous
fantad
fan-tan
Fenian
fenman
Finbar
Fingal
fingan
finial
finjan
Finlay
finnac
finnan
fin-ray
Fintan
fontal
fungal
fanded
fanged
fan-jet
fannel
fanner
Fantee
fenced
fencer
fender
fennec
fennel
finder
fineer
finger
Finley
finned
finner
Finney
fonded
funded
funder
funnel
Fangio
Finnic
fundie
funkia
finsko
fangle
fankle
finale
finals
finely
Finola

fondle
fondly
fining
fanboy
fandom
fangos
fanion
fantod
fantom
fynbos
finery
finish
funest
finite
fan out
fondue
fundus
fun fur
fungus
fun run
feodal
florae
floral
floras
flocci
floods
Fronde
Flores
floret
flotel
flowed
flower
footed
footer
froren
frozen
✧froggy
frothy
fiorin
florid
florin
foodie
footie
foot it
frolic
frowie
flocks
footle
foozle
frorne
flow-on
floppy
floury
footra
floosy
flossy
flouse
floush
froise
frowst
frowsy
floats
floaty
Flotta
frosty
floozy
frowzy
fipple
faquir
ferial
Fermat

firman
forbad
forçat
forgat
formal
Forman
format
Fornax
forrad
forray
forsay
furcal
foreby
far ben
fardel
farden
Fareed
farfet
farmer
Faroes
farren
ferrel
ferret
firmer
Forbes
forced
forcer
forces
forfex
forger
forget
forked
forker
formed
former
forpet
forren
fortes
furder
Furies
furred
far-off
forage
forego
forthy
for why
forwhy
furphy
farcin
farm-in
ferric
fervid
firkin
forbid
fordid
formic
fornix
forpit
forrit
fortis
✧ferula
ferule
firmly
for all
furole
forums
farand
farina
ferine
firing
forane

forint
for one
furane
farrow
fervor
firlot
forgot
forhoo
forhow
formol
for now
furrow
far cry
furore
forest
ferity
Farouk
far-out
Fergus
fire up
firm up
fork up
fureur
furfur
for aye
forbye
formyl
festal
fiscal
fossae
fast by
fasces
fasten
faster
fester
✧fisher
✧fishes
fossed
✧foster
fusser
fustet
fascia
fascio
fisgig
fistic
fossil
fusain
fustic
fastly
fissle
fusile
fossor
fusion
fustoc
fescue
fess up
Fushun
fat cat
fat-cat
fatwa'd
fatwah
fetial
fetich
fat hen
✧father
fatted
fatten
fatter
fetter
fitted
fitter

fother
fitché
fitchy
fatsia
fettle
futile
Fatima
fathom
fatsos
future
fetish
fitful
fit out
fit-out
faucal
faunae
faunal
faunas
feudal
frugal
fruict
fauces
faucet
flugel
flügel
flukey
fluted
fluter
fouter
frutex
fluffy
flushy
fought
flunky
foully
fluent
fautor
frumpy
feutre
flurry
foutra
foutre
foussa
faulty
fluate
fourth
fousty
fruits
fruity
frusta
Faunus
flub up
foul up
foul-up
foveae
foveal
five Ks
favela
✧favell
favism
favose
favour
favous
fawner
fewmet
fewter
✧fowler
fox-bat
fixing
foxing
fixure

fixate
fixity
fixive
Faysal
flyman
flyway
✧flysch
flying
frying
fu yung
fly rod
fly ash
fly out
fezzed
fezzes
fizzed
fizzen
fizzer
fizgig
fizzle
fuzzle
Fuzhou
ghazal
Graeae
Graham
Graiae
guaiac
grabby
glance
grande
guards
geared
ghazel
glazed
glazen
glazer
gnawed
gnawer
goatee
graben
graced
Graces
grader
grapey
grated
grater
graved
gravel
graven
graver
Graves'
✧graves
grazer
grange
guango
glacis
goalie
Gracie
gradin
Gräfin
Grania
gratin
gratis
gravid
glaiks
gladly
gnarly
graile
grakle
graple
grayle

glammy
Graeme
gramma
gramme
Grammy
goanna
graine
grains
grainy
granny
geason
Glagol
glamor
guacos
guanos
grappa
gharri
gharry
glairy
glaury
Gdansk
glassy
grassy
graith
Granta
Granth
graste
gear up
giaour
glam up
gradus
granum
glaive
Gladys
Granya
gib-cat
gubbah
go back
gabbed
gabber
gabled
gablet
gibbed
gibber
gibbet
giblet
gobbed
gobbet
gobies
goblet
goboes
gubbed
go bail
gobiid
goblin
gabble
gobble
go bang
gobang
Gobind
gobony
go bung
gabion
gaboon
gibbon
gabbro
go bush
go bust
go cold
geckos
go-cart

giddap
goddam
god day
gadded
gadder
gadget
Gadhel
gidgee
gidjee
godded
god-den
godden
gadgie
gadoid
geddit
godwit
gadfly
guddle
Gideon
godson
Godard
giddup
Gudrun
go down
go-down
godown
geegaw
gherao
✧greece
Glenda
greedy
Gwenda
gee-gee
geezer
Gheber
gleyed
Gueber
gledge
greige
Goethe
Gaelic
goetic
greyly
gleamy
geeing
✧greens
greeny
grebos
gregos
guenon
Guelph
Ghebre
Guebre
ghesse
gneiss
go easy
✧grease
greasy
greese
ghetto
gleety
Greats
greete
gee hup
Gnetum
gleave
greave
Glenys
guffaw
gaffer
gifted

goffer
guffie
Gefion
gagman
gigman
gagged
gagger
gigged
giglet
goglet
gag-bit
giggit
gagaku
gaggle
giggle
giggly
gigolo
goggle
goggly
go gold
guggle
giglot
go home
go hang
go hard
guitar
glitch
griece
gainer
gaiter
glider
Glires
Goidel
goiter
gricer
grices
Grimes
griper
gripes
grivet
✧guider
guiled
guiler
✧guinea
guiser
guizer
griffe
gringo
geisha
gaijin
gainly
glibly
grille
grimly
griple
grisly
glioma
grison
guidon
guiros
grippe
grippy
goitre
grigri
'gainst
gainst
griesy
grilse
gaiety
go into
gritty

guilty
gain-up
Griqua
grieve
glitzy
Gujrat
go-kart
Galway
gilgai
golias
gollan
gollar
Gullah
gelada
gallet
galley
gelded
gelder
gelled
gilded
gilden
gilder
gillet
gilpey
golden
golfer
goller
gulden
guller
gullet
gulley
gulper
gylden
galage
galago
✧gallic
Gallio
gilgie
gillie
Goldie
Gullit
galant
galena
go long
galiot
gallon
gallop
gallow
galoot
gollop
galère
galore
Gelert
galosh
gelosy
golosh
✧galuth
gelati
gelato
gallus
gilcup
Gollum
go live
✧galaxy
gemmae
gemman
gimbal
gimmal
gymbal
gymmal
gambet
gammer
gemmed
gemmen
gimlet
gimmer
gimmes
gummed
gambir
gambit
gymnic
gomoku
gamble
gamely
gamine
gaming
✧gemini
geminy
gemony
gambol
gammon
gimmor
gumbos
Gemara
gombro
gamash
gamesy
gamete
gomuti
gomuto
gumnut
genial
gingal
gunman
gunyah
gander
ganger
gannet
gansey
gender
gennel
gennet
gentes
✧ginger
ginned
ginnel
ginner
gunned
gunnel
gunner
gunsel
gunter
gynney
ginkgo
Gandhi
gung-ho
gun-shy
ganoid
ganoin
gingko
gangly
gentle
gently
gingle
Ginola
genome
✧gentoo
Gondor
gonion
gun dog
gantry
genera
gentry
Ganesa
Ganesh
gunite
gangue
gang up
✧genius
✧geneva
global
gnomae
globby
grouch
goonda
gaoler
globed
gloved
glover
glower
gnomes
gnoses
goober
gooier
gooley
gooney
gooses
goosey
go over
grocer
gromet
groper
groser
groset
grovel
grovet
grower
George
Georgy
groggy
grough
geodic
globin
✧gloria
gnomic
gnosis
goolie
Gromit
goodly
google
googly
grooly
growly
gloomy
Grodno
ground
groyne
Grozny
gnomon
good-oh
googol
gooroo
grog-on
gloopy
groupy
gloire
glossa
glossy
grouse
ghosty
Giotto
groats
grotto
grotty
grouty
growth
goof up
grog-up
grow up
groove
groovy
Geomys
grosze
groszy
gapper
gipsen
✧gopher
gypped
gopiks
gaping
gopura
go phut
gypsum
gardai
garial
garjan
garran
✧german
gurrah
✧garuda
garden
garget
garner
garnet
garred
✧garret
✧garter
germen
girded
girder
girnel
girner
gorged
gorget
gorier
gurlet
gurnet
gurney
garage
Gurkha
Garcia
garlic
garvie
gerbil
germin
Gerrie
Gertie
girkin
girlie
girnie
gorgia
gorgio
garble
gargle
Gerald
girdle
gorily
gurgle
goramy
Göreme
gurami
gerent
gerund
goring
gyrant
garbos
garçon
garron
garrot
Geryon
Gordon
✧gorgon
Gerard
garish
gyrose
Gareth
gyrate
gurjun
gyrous
garrya
gasbag
gas cap
gas jar
gasman
gas tap
gas-tar
gossan
guslar
Gustav
gas jet
gasket
gasper
gassed
gasser
gaster
Goshen
goslet
gospel
gusher
gusset
gasify
go soft
gaskin
gaslit
gas oil
gestic
gossib
gossip
✧gussie
gustie
gashly
✧gascon
gismos
go slow
go-slow
gas gun
gateau
gâteau
guttae
gather
getter
gotten
gutsed
gutser
gutted
gutter
gutzer
get off
gotcha
get rid
✧gothic
guttle
gating
gitana
gitano
gutrot
get out
get-out
gutful
grubby
gaunch
grutch
gourde
gourds
gourdy
gaufer
gauger
gauper
gluier
glutei
gluten
grudge
grunge
grungy
gauche
gaucho
gaucie
Gaugin
glumly
grumly
gluing
Gounod
glumps
glumpy
grumph
grumps
grumpy
gaufre
gru-gru
gluish
giusto
gousty
goutte
gaupus
gavial
gavage
give me
giving
Govind
govern
give up
gewgaw
gowlan
gowf-ba'
gawker
gawper
gowfer
gowned
gowpen
Gawain
go well
gowany
go west
gawpus
gaydar
geyser
guyler
Gdynia
glycin
Glynis
grysie
Guyana
gay dog
Gaynor
gay-you
glycol
gryfon
gayest
goyish
gryesy
gozzan
gazebo
gizzen
guzzle
gazump
gazoon
gizmos
hiatal
headed
header
healer
Healey
Heaney
heaped
hearer
heated
heater
heaved
✧heaven
heaver
heaves
hoaxer
Hyades
heathy
hearie
hoagie
hyalin
heaume
hyaena
Haakon
head-on
hearse
hearsy
hoarse
health
hearth
✧hearts
hearty
heaste
head up
hiatus
hobday
hub-cap
Hebrew
Hibees
Hobbes
hoboes
Hebrid
hobbit
hubris
hybrid
hybris
habile
hobble
hebona
haboob
Hebron
hobjob
hobnob
Hobart
Hubert
hubbub
Hecabe
Hecuba
hackee
hacker
hickey
hocker
hockey
hachis
hectic
hackle
hackly
heckle
huckle
✧hector
Hecate
hiccup
hodman
hadden
hedger
hidden
hidder
hodden
hudden
hidage
haddie
hydria
hydric
heddle
✧hoddle
huddle
hiding
hydyne
hadron
Hudson
hydros
Hedera
heders
Hadith
huddup
Hydrus
haemal
heehaw
Hielan'
hiemal
hyetal
heeled
heeler
haemic
haemin
heel in
heezie
Hoenir
hieing
hoeing
Huelva
haffet
haffit
Haggai
hog-rat
hagden
hagged
haglet
✧higher
hogged
hogger
hogget
hog-pen
hugged
Hughes
haggis
hoggin
hogtie
Hughie
haggle
higgle
highly
hugely
Hegang
hagdon
hegira
highth
hagbut
high-up
hognut
haikai
Heimat
hainch
hairdo
hailer
hained
haired
heifer
hoiden
hoised
height
heinie
hoicks
hairst
haiduk
haikus
haique
hijrah
hijack
hejira
Hyksos
hike up
hoke up
hallal
hallan
halvah
heliac
Hellas
hold by
halide
halfen
haloed
haloes
halsed
halser
halter
halver
halves
Hellen
heller
helmed
helmet
helped
helper
hilled
Hillel
hold 'em
holden
holder
holler
Holmes
holpen
haloid
hele in
hold in
hold it!
holmia
holmic
halala
holily
Helena
holing
halloa

halloo
hallos
hallow
Halton
Helios
hellos
hold on
holloa
hollos
hollow
hullos
halers
haleru
Hilary
holism
holist
hylism
hylist
halite
hallux
helium
hold up
hold-up
hole up
hammal
hammam
hamzah
Humean
Humian
hymnal
humect
✧hamlet
hammer
hamper
hemmed
hempen
Humber
hummed
hummel
hummer
humped
✧humpen
humper
Humvee®
hymned
humefy
humify
homage
home in
humlie
hymnic
Himeji
Himiko
hamble
hamuli
homely
homily
humble
humbly
Hamina
hemina
homing
hominy
humane
himbos
hombre
humeri
Hamish
hamose
Humism
Humist
humusy
hamate
Hamite
humite
humpty
hamous
humbug
humhum
hummum
hummus
humour
humous
Handan
hangar
hanjar
Hannah
Henman
handed
Handel
hander
hanged
hanger
hanker
hansel
Henley
henner
hen-pen
hinder
hinged
honied
honker
hunger
hunker
Hun Sen
hunted
hunter
honcho
Honshu
hand-in
hang in
hankie
hen-bit
hennin
Hingis
honkie
Hunnic
handle
hantle
hang on
hansom
Hindoo
Hendry
Honora
hungry
honest
hang up
hang-up
hen run
✧honour
hung up
hunt up
henrys
Henry V
hoo-hah
hookah
hoorah
hooray
hootch
hooded
hoofed
hoofer
hooked
hooker
hookey
hooley
hooper
hooter
hooven
Hoover®
✧hoover
hooves
hoodie
hoof it
hook it
hoop-la
Heorot
hoodoo
hoopoe
hooroo
hook up
hook-up
hep-cat
heptad
huppah
hyphae
hyphal
happed
happen
hapten
hipped
hippen
hipper
hopped
hopper
hyphen
hop-off
haptic
hippic
hippie
hippin
hypnic
hypoid
hop-fly
hopple
hip-hop
hippos
hopdog
Hypnos
hypate
hippus
hype up
hypnum
harman
hartal
herbal
herbar
hereat
hermae
hurrah
hurray
hereby
Horace
harden
hareem
harken
Harlem
Harley®
harmel
harper
harten
Harvey
herbed
herden
herder
Hermes
heroes
herpes
Herren
hersed
Hervey
hirsel
horkey
horned
horner
hornet
horses
horsey
hurden
hurler
hurley
hurter
hirage
Harbin
harmin
Harris
Herbie
herdic
herein
Hermia
hermit
hernia
heroic
heroin
Hornie
horn in
horrid
Harald
hardly
hareld
Harold
herald
hirple
hirsle
hurdle
hurtle
hiring
harbor
harlot
Harlow
harrow
hereof
hereon
heriot
Hermod
heroon
Herzog
horror
horson
Harare
Herero
horary
harass
harish
heresy
hereto
hard-up
Haroun
Hassan
hassar
Hesvan
hussar
haslet
hasten
Hesper
Hester
hosier
hostel
hushed
husher
husked
husker
Hassid
Hestia
hispid
histie
Husain
hussif
hassle
hustle
Hesiod
hyssop
hostry
hush up
hetman
hitman
hot war
hi tech
hatpeg
hatred
hatted
hatter
hether
hither
Hitler
hitter
hotbed
hot key
hotted
hotter
hutted
hit off
hitchy
hatpin
Hattie
hot air
hot-air
hottie
hatbox
Hathor
hot dog
hot-dog
hotpot
hot rod
hetero
hatful
hit out
hot tub
houdah
houdan
haunch
hauler
housel
houses
housey
haught
hourly
haüyne
haulst
haul up
houmus
have in
have it
Havana
haven't
having
have on
have-on
havers
have up
hive up
haw-haw
howdah
Howrah
howzat
hawked
hawker
hawkey
hawser
howe'er
howker
howled
howler
howlet
Hawaii
hawkie
hawkit
howdie
Howell
hewing
how now?
Howard
hexact
hexane
hexene
hexing
hexose
heyday
Hayden
Hayley
haysel
hoyden
haying
hryvna
haybox
Haydon
haymow
hazzan
huzza'd
hazily
hazing
huzoor
hazard
Ibadan
Ibadat
Idaean
in a way
Isaiah
inarch
imager
Images
imaret
✧isabel
inanga
Icaria
isatin
Isatis
✧italic
in arms
imagos
in a row
ita est
Icarus
in a rut
imbibe
imbody
imbrex
inbred
Imbolc
in banc
inbent
in-bond
imbark
in bird
inborn
imbase
imbosk
imboss
imbrue
incubi
incede
inched
inches
incage
inclip
ischia
in calf
in-calf
incult
income
incony
Inchon
incept
ID card
in care
in case
incase
in cash
incest
incise
incuse
incite
incave
incavi
incavo
Indian
indaba
indict
in dock
induce
induct
iodide
in deed
indeed
indign
indigo
indris
indole
indult
indene
indent
induna
iodine
indoor
indart
Indira
Indore
iodise
iodism
indite
iodate
indium
iodous
iodize
ice bag
icecap
ice man
ice pan
ipecac
Imelda
ibexes
ice tea
ideaed
ilexes
✧ice age
iberis
irenic
Iseult
icebox
in esse
ideate
ice out
ice run
ireful
iterum
ice axe
in foal
in-foal
in fact
infect
iffier
infeft
infall
infelt
infill
infold
infula
in full
infame
infamy
infant
inflow
infare
in fere
infere
infirm
inform
infest
infuse
in fits
influx
ingram
ingoes
Ingres
Ingrid
ingulf
ingénu
ingine
It Girl
ingest
ingate
ingrum
in heat
Ishtar
in hock
Ishbel
inhale
inhume
I Ching
in hand
inhoop
inhere
inhaul
iridal
idiocy
ibices
ibidem
ibises
ilices
irides
irised
irises
Ibibio
imidic
iridic
iritic
iritis
icicle
inisle
inject
in-joke
injera
injure
injury
ink-bag
ink-cap
inkpad
ink-sac
ickier
inkier
ink-jet
in kind
inkpot
inkosi
illiad
I'll say!
inlace
inlock
illude
inlier
ill off
ill-off
inlaid
illume
inland
in line
in-line
island
ill-got
illipe
illupi
ill-use
illite
iolite
Iolaus
in love
in-laws
iambic
Ismail
in milk
immane
immune
immure
immask
immesh
in mass
in mesh
inmesh
inmost
inmate
Io moth
iambus
Ionian
Innuit
ignomy
in name
inning
ionone
ignaro

ignore
Irn-Bru®
✧**ionise**
Ionism
Ionist
ignite
innate
ionium
✧**ionize**
isobar
Isolda
Isolde
Imogen
ironer
Isobel
isohel
isomer
iconic
ironic
Isodia
if only
✧**idolon**
irokos
iron-on
isogon
isopod
Idoist
✧**idolum**
in play
impact
in pace
impede
impies
implex
impugn
impair
impala
impale
impend
impone
improv
impark
imparl
impart
import
impure
in part
impish
impose
impost
impute
impave
impawn
inroad
Israel
irrupt
inrush
in rixa
inseam
inspan
instal
instar
insect
inside
inseem
INS key
in step
instep
issuer
Iastic
inship
instil
insole
insula
insult
itself
insane
in sync
insert
in sort
insure
insist
in situ
insoul
it says
in that
in-tray
intact
in-toed
intoed
in tail
intuit
intake
intima
in time
intime
intomb
intend
intent
intine
intone
in tune
intron
intros
intern
intire
in turn
intuse
in toto
intown
inulin
iguana
invade
in view
in vain
invoke
invent
Irvine
invert
invest
invis'd
invite
in vivo
inwrap
inwick
inwall
inwind
in wine
inward
in word
inwork
inworn
Iswara
inwith
inwove
inyala
ivy-tod
izzard
Jeames
Jeanie
Joanie
✧**joanna**
Joanne
jibbah
jubbah
jabber
Jabneh
jibbed
jibber
jobbed
jobber
job off
jabble
job lot
jabers
jabiru
jubate
job out
jackal
jacket
jockey
jack in
jicama
jacana
jaçana
jacent
jocund
jockos
jacksy
jocose
jack up
jack-up
Jacque
Jeddah
Jiddah
Judean
Judica
Judaea
judder
Judges
judogi
Judaic
judoka
jadery
jadish
Judith
Jaeger®
jaeger
jeerer
jeelie
Joelle
Jaffna
Jaguar®
jaguar
jigsaw
jagged
jagger
jigged
jigger
jogged
jogger
jugged
juglet
jaghir
jigjig
jiggle
jiggly
joggle
juggle
jig-jog
jugate
jugful
jug-jug
Jahveh
Johnny
jailer
joiner
juiced
juicer
join in
jailor
Jaipur
join up
jojoba
jujube
jejune
jokily
Julian
jillet
Joleen
jolled
joller
jolley
jolter
✧juliet
jilgie
Jolene
Jolyon
jalopy
J-cloth®
Julius
jamjar
jampan
jimjam
jumbal
jambee
jamber
jammed
jammer
jumper
Jamnia
Jimmie
jumbie
Jamila
jimply
jumble
jumbly
jymold
✧**jemima**
jiminy
jambok
Jambos
jampot
jumbos
jump on
jumart
jambul
jump-up
Jandal®
Janian
jingal
Juneau
Janice
janker
Jansen
jantee
jennet
jinker
jinnee
jinxed
✧junker
junket
Jancis
Jennie
junkie
Jun Xie
jansky
jangle
jangly
jingle
jingly
jungle
jungli
jungly
Janina
Janine
juncos
✧junior
juntos
Jan Hus
juncus
japing
japery
jupati
Jaques
Jarman
jarrah
✧jordan
jarred
jarvey
jereed
jerker
✧jersey
jarvie
Jarvis
jerbil
jerkin
Jervis
jirble
Jeremy
Jerome
jurant
jargon
jarool
Jarrow
jerboa
jurist
jarful
jerque
Jashar
Josiah
Jasher
jasper
jessed
jestee
jester
josher
josser
jaspis
✧jessie
Jesuit
joskin
Justin
jostle
justle
justly
jissom
✧**joseph**
just so
Joshua
jet lag
jetsam
jetted
jitney
jitter
jotted
jotter
jutted
✧**jataka**
jet ski
jet-ski
✧**jötunn**
jetsom
jetson
jetton
Jethro
Jutish
jut out
jaunce
jounce
journo
jaunse
jaunty
J-curve
✧**jovial**
Jovian
jowled
jowler
ja wohl
jawing
jawbox
jawari
jowari
Jewess
Jewish
joypad
✧**jaycee**
joying
joypop
joyful
joyous
jazzer
jezail
jazz up
✧**keasar**
khalat
klatch
knawel
kraken
krater
khanga
kiaugh
knaggy
kwacha
keavie
Khalid
khalif
kharif
Kvasir
Khalka
knacky
✧**klaxon**
Kraków
kia-ora
Khalsa
krantz
khanum
kwanza
keblah
kiblah
kababs
kabobs
kebabs
kebobs
kebbie
kabaka
kabuki
kabala
kabele
Kabyle
kebele
kibble
kobold
kobang
kibosh
kybosh
kibitz
kabaya
kicker
Kuchen
kaccha
kuccha
kick in
kochia
keckle
kecksy
kick-up
keddah
kidnap
Kodiak
kedger
kidded
kidder
kidlet
kidney
kidgie
kidvid
kiddle
kidult
kiddos
kid-fox
Kid Ory
Keegan
Kieran
kvetch
keeker
keeled
keeler
keener
keeper
klepht
keelie
keep in
kie-kie
kierie
keenly
keep on
Kieron
K-meson
Kneipe
kreese
keep up
kaftan
keffel
kafila
Kafiri
Kegels
Kigali
kagool
kagoul
k'thibh
Kahlúa®
kaikai
khilat
knitch
✧**kaiser**
kaizen
keiren
knifer
knives
krises
kainga
keight
knight
keirin
khilim
knicks
Kojiki
Kakadu
kokako
kakapo
Ku Klux
keksye
✧kikuyu
Kalgar
kalian
kalpak
killas
✧**kelper**
kelter
killer
kilted
kilter
Kaluga
kalmia
kalpis
keloid
kelpie
keltie
✧kelvin
Killie
kiltie
kaluki
kalong
kelson
kilerg
kalium
kill up
killut
Kultur
Kalmyk
kamees
kameez
kemper
kimmer
kümmel
kimchi
kamsin
kamala
kamela
kamila
kemple
kimono
kumara
✧kumari
kumiss
kumite
kanban
Kansas
kantar
Kendal
Kenyan
kunkar
Kanuck
Konica®
kanten
kenned
kennel
kenner
kennet
kinder
kinred
kynded
kung fu
kangha
kantha
kanjis
Kennie
✧kentia
kindie
king it
✧**kanaka**
Kandla
kindle
kindly
kingle
kingly
kinkle
kinema
kinone
Ken Hom
kincob
kinase
Kanpur
kunkur
konfyt
koolah
knobby
klooch
knower
kronen
kroner
kyogen
kaolin
kookie
khodja
kgotla
krooni
kroons
koodoo
kronor
Kronos
knotty
krónur
kopeck
kipper
kephir
keppit
koppie
kaputt
Kirman
kirpan
kirtan
Korean
✧kurgan
Kirkby
kirsch
karsey
karter
kermes
kernel
kersey
kirbeh
kurvey
karahi
karait
kark it
karmic
kermis

✧kerria
kirkin'
korkir
karaka
Kerala
kirtle
Karena
Karina
koruna
Karpov
✧karroo
karyon
korero
korora
kaross
karate
karite
Kirsty
Kirkuk
Kyrgyz
✧kasbah
Kaspar
Kosice
Kassel
Kisleu
Kislev
✧kismet
kissel
kisser
kosher
kishke
kiss-me
kosmos
✧kathak
kitbag
kit-car
✧kit-cat
kotwal
kitsch
kitten
kutcha
Kathie
Kittie
kettle
kittle
kittly
katana
ketene
ketone
kiting
kation
katipo
ketose
kit out
kittul
Kaunas
koulan
Kru-man
knubby
Kaunda
Keuper
kludge
knurly
Khulna
kouros
Kru-boy
khurta
klutzy
Kevlar®
kavass
kowhai
Kuwait
kowtow
key man
keypad
keypal
keyway
kayoed
kayoes
Keynes
Kazakh
Luanda
laager
leaded
leaden
leader
leafed
leaker
leaned
leaped
leaper
leaser
leaved
leaven
leaver
leaves
✧loaded
loaden
loader
loafer
loanee
loaner
loaves
leachy
loathe
loathy
lead in
lead-in
lea-rig
leally
leanly
liable
Leanne
learnt
Lianna
Lianne
lead on
lean on
leasow
llanos
liaise
lealty
lean-to
lead up
lead-up
league
labial
lablab
labral
Lib-Lab
Libran
Libyan
Lübeck
libido
labret
lebbek
libber
libken
lobbed
lubber
labrid
Lublin
lubric
labile
lobola
lobolo
lobule
lobuli
libant
lobing
libero
lobose
libate
lobate
Lobito
labium
✧labour
labrum
Labrus
labrys
lactam
lochan
Lucian
laches
lacker
lackey
lecher
lichee
lichen
licker
locker
locket
locoed
locoes
lucken
lychee
lactic
lectin
lochia
lock in
lock-in
luckie
lacily
locale
locule
loculi
locums
lucuma
lucumo
lacing
lacuna
lucent
Lucina
Laclos
lector
lictor
lock on
lucern
locust
Lycosa
locate
Lucite®
lace up
lace-up
lacmus
lock up
lock-up
Lucius
✧lyceum
lechwe
lac-dye
lad mag
Lydian
la-di-da
ladder
ladies
ladies'
ledden
ledged
ledger
lidded
lidger
lodger
ladify
ladyfy
laddie
lading
✧ladino
Ludlow
leeway
lienal
lieder
liefer
lieger
liever
laesie
Leerie
Liebig
loerie
luetic
leetle
lierne
lie low
lifter
lofted
lofter
leftie
lifull
lyfull
lift up
leglan
leg-man
leguan
loggat
log jam
log-man
log-saw
legacy
lagged
laggen
lagger
legged
legger
leglen
leglet
ligger
logged
logger
lugged
lugger
log off
log-off
logoff
laggin
leglin
lignin
loggia
loggie
luggie
ligula
ligule
legume
lagena
lag-end
lagune
legend
ligand
Lugano
luging
lagoon
legion
logion
log-log
loglog
ligure
legist
ligase
legate
legato
ligate
lights
lignum
log-hut
log out
log-out
logout
leg bye
Lahore
laical
laiker
Leiden
leiger
loipen
loiter
luiten
laidly
leipoa
laisse
laid up
lekker
likely
liking
lakish
Lakota
lallan
Lilian
Lilias
lilied
Lillee
Lilley
loller
Lalage
loligo
laldie
Lallie
lalang
lollop
Lalita
Lilith
Lolita
L-plate
Lilium
lolium
Lammas
lampad
lampas
lemmas
lumbar
lum hat
lambda
lamedh
lamber
lammer
limbec
limbed
limber
limmer
limner
limpet
lumber
lumpen
lumper
lambie
lammie
limail
limbic
limpid
lamely
limply
lament
lamina
Lamont
Le Mans
lemans
lemony
liming
loment
lumens
lumina
lumine
Lemnos
✧limbos
lummox
lemurs
lamish
lam out
✧limbus
limous
Lamaze
landau
lineal
linear
lingam
linhay
longan
lunacy
lancer
lances
✧lancet
landed
Länder
lander
Langer
lanner
lender
lenger
lenses
✧lenten
linden
lingel
linger
linker
linnet
linney
linsey
lintel
linter
longer
lunged
lunker
Lynsey
lynxes
lenify
lanugo
linage
lynage
Lancia®
Lennie
lentic
lentil
lintie
lungie
lunyie
lankly
lingle
lonely
longly
lunula
lunule
La Niña
lining
Lennon
lentor
lentos
lenvoy
lingot
London
Lanark
lunary
lanose
linish
lanate
length
lenity
lunate
land up
langue
langur
line up
line-up
lingua
link up
link-up
loofah
✧lionel
lionet
looker
looped
looper
loosen
looten
looter
looves
Leonia
Leonid
Leonie
look in
look-in
loonie
lionly
look up
lookup
Lao-tzu
lipide
lapped
lappel
lapper
lappet
lapsed
lepped
lipped
lippen
lopped
lopper
luppen
lappie
leptin
lipoid
lippie
lupoid
lipoma
Li Peng
loping
lupine
lapdog
laptop
lepton
lipase
Lapith
Laputa
lapful
lapsus
lip out
lupous
loquat
liquid
liquor
Lariam®
lariat
larnax
larvae
larval
Lorcan
lurdan
lorica
lyrics
larder
largen
larker
larney
Lorien
lurden
lurker
lorcha
Larkin
laroid
lord it
lordly
larine
larynx
loring
lardon
largos
loriot
lyrism
lyrist
lorate
lyrate
larrup
lascar
lasher
lasket
laster
Lesley
lessee
lessen
lesser
Lester
Lisbet
lisper
lisses
listed
listel
listen
✧lister
lusher
luster
✧lassie
lesbic
Leslie
Lusaka
lastly
lushly
lasing
losing
lysine
lassos
Lesbos
lesion
lesson
lessor
Lisbon
lissom
Liston
lustra
lustre
lash-up
lasque
Latian
lethal
luteal
let-a-be
lateen
lathee
lathen
lather
latten
latter
lethee
letted
letter
lither
litten
litter
lotted
Luther
lutten
let off
let-off
litchi
latria
Latvia
let rip
Lettic
Lettie
lithia
lithic
Lottie
lutein
lately
let fly
little
La Tène
latent
Latina
Latino
Latona
litany
luting
latron
lithos
lotion
lottos
lettre
latest
latish
lutist
let out
let-out

litmus
lituus
louvar
✧**launce**
launch
lauder
✧laurel
Lauren
Leuven
louden
loupen
louser
louses
louver
lounge
laughy
louche
Laurie
leucin
loupit
lourie
loudly
✧**louvre**
Louisa
Louise
Laurus
lavabo
live by
laveer
levied
lavage
lovage
live in
live-in
love-in
luvvie
lavolt
lively
lovely
✧**levant**
living
loving
livery
lavash
lavish
✧**levite**
levity
law-day
law-man
lawman
low-cal
low-fat
low-tar
lawned
lawyer
low-key
Lawrie
Lowrie
lowsit
lewdly
lawing
lowing
Lawson
lowboy
lowery
lowest
lowish
lawful
low-cut
lexeme
luxury
laxism
laxist
laxity
luxate
lay-day
layman
Leyden
lay off
lay-off
laying
lay low
lay out
layout
lay-bye
lay-bys
Lizzie
lazily
lazuli
lozell
Luzula
✧**lizard**
luzern
meatal
meat-ax
mealer
meawes
meazel
moaner
moated
mganga
meathe
mealie
meanie
mia-mia
meanly
measle
measly
miasma
miasms
meadow
meagre
meatus
mob cap
mob law
mobbed
mobled
mobbie
mabela
mobble
✧mobile
Mabuse
Mobutu
Möbius
machan
Micmac
Mr Chad
macaco
mocock
mocuck
macher
macled
micher
✧mickey
mocker
muchel
✧mucker
Maceio
mochie
muck in
mucoid
mackle
macula
macule
mickle
muchly
muckle
machos
macron
macros
micron
micros
Mt Cook
mucros
mucosa
micate
mucate
mock-up
muck up
muck-up
mucluc
mucous
macoya
madcap
madman
Mad Max
madras
mediae
medial
✧median
medlar
Medway
midday
midway
mudcat
medick
medico
madden
madder
medley
midden
midget
mid-leg
mid-sea
Modred
mudder
mudger
mud hen
madefy
mid-off
modify
mid-age
Madrid
midair
midgie
midrib
mud pie
medaka
mid-sky
meddle
medfly
✧middle
Model T
module
moduli
modulo
muddle
muddly
✧**madame**
madams
✧**medina**
modena
mod con
✧**modern**
Medise
Medism
✧medusa
modest
modish
modist
made up
Madhur
medium
medius
mid-gut
modius
Medize
maenad
Moerae
meeken
meered
maelid
meemie
mnemic
myelin
meekly
meetly
muesli
Mt Etna
mnemon
myelon
Meerut
meet up
Muftat
miffed
✧**maffia**
muffin
Muftis
Mt Fuji
muffle
muflon
my foot!
magian
magmas
✧magyar
moggan
Mughal
Mugabe
maglev
magnes
magnet
maguey
Megger®
mugged
muggee
mugger
megohm
✧**maggie**
magpie
megrim
moggie
magilp
megilp
moguls
mygale
maggot
magnon
Magnox®
magnox
mignon
Megara
magism
megass
mighty
magnum
Magnus
mugful
mahmal
mihrab
Mohock
mehndi
Mahler
Mehmet
mahsir
mohair
mahzor
Mahmud
Mahoun
mahout
✧**mohawk**
maidan
Mai Tai
Moirai
✧**maiden**
mailed
✧mailer
maimed
meiney
moider
moiler
moiser
meishi
mail-in
Maisie
meinie
mainly
maikos
mainor
maigre
moiety
mojoes
✧**majlis**
✧mejlis
majors
Majuro
Makkah
mikvah
make do
make-do
mikado
Meknès
mikveh
Mukden
make it
Makalu
making
make of
mikron
make up
make-up
mike up
mukluk
Malian
mallam
malmag
mellay
mollah
mullah
Multan
Malabo
malice
melick
Milice
Molech
✧moloch
malady
melody
miladi
milady
my lady
Malbec
mallee
mallei
mallet
malted
melder
melted
melter
milden
mildew
milieu
milken
milker
milled
✧miller
✧millet
milsey
milter
molten
mulled
muller
mullet
mulley
Malaga
Málaga
malign
milage
maltha
maleic
malkin
Melvin
Millie
mollie
mildly
Malang
melano
moline
my lane
mallow
mellow
melton
Milton
mal gré
malgre
malgré
milord
My Lord
malism
malist
molest
mulish
malate
maloti
Mel Ott
muleta
milium
Milvus
mulmul
multum
Malawi
Melvyn
mammae
mammal
mimbar
mammee
mammer
mammet
mamzer
member
mimsey
mommet
momzer
mummed
mummer
mumper
memoir
mummia
mumble
moment
mambos
✧mammon
Memnon
memory
mimosa
man-day
mangal
maniac
manoao
Man Ray
manual
Mencap
menial
mensal
mental
minbar
Minoan
minyan
Monday
monial
menace
mensch
Monaco
monact
Monica
Munich
monody
mangel
manger
mangey
manned
manner
manred
mantel
mantes
mender
meneer
menged
menses
mentee
minced
mincer
minded
Mindel
minder
minged
minger
minter
minuet
monger
monied
monies
monkey
montem
minify
munify
manage
manège
menage
ménage
manche
Manchu
manehs
munshi
mandir
mantic
mantid
mantis
menhir
menyie
mingin'
min min
✧minnie
Monsig
mundic
muntin
manuka
mangle
✧manila
mantle
mingle
Manama
minima
mañana
manent
meninx
mining
mandom
mangos
manioc
mantos
mentor
mentos
minion
minnow
Minton
✧mongol
mongos
mungos
Munros
mantra
manure
minors
monera
montre
minish
'mongst
monism
monist
monosy
manati
manito
minute
moneth
munite
Manaus
mancus
manful
manqué
✧mantua
Mensur
mentum
minium
monaul
moneys
moolah
miombo
mooned
mooner
mooter
myogen
Maoris
miosis
miotic
Moonie
muonic
myopia
myopic
myosin
myosis
moo-cow
Maoism
Maoist
Mt Ossa
moorva
mapped
mapper
mopped
mopper
moppet
muppet
map-pin
mopoke
mopily
mopane
mopani
mopery
mopish
Maputo
map out
✧**maquis**
Marcan
margay
Marian
marram
mercat
merman
Miriam
Morgan
Morgan®
morgay
mornay
morsal
mortal
mortar
murlan
murram
✧murray
myriad
Myriam
maraca
Myrica
✧**marcel**
marked
marker
market
marled
marred
martel
marten
marvel
marver
mercer
merger
Meriel
moreen
morgen
morned
morsel
Morven

murder
Muriel
murren
murrey
mirage
murage
Marsha
marshy
Martha
morcha
morpho
murphy
murrha
Marcia
margin
marlin
✧martin
Marvin
merkin
merlin
Mersin
morbid
morkin
Morris®
morris
Murcia
murlin
murrin
Marek's
markka
marble
marbly
merell
merels
merely
merils
morale
morall
morals
morula
✧myrtle
merome
✧marina
marine
merino
Moroni
murena
murine
Marcos
Marion
Marlon
marmot
maroon
marron
marrow
merlon
Merlot
Merton
mirror
Mordor
morion
Mormon
morros
morrow
Merops
marari
marish
Marist
merest
merism
morass
morish
Morisk
morose
merits
miriti
maraud
Marcus
mark up
mark-up
marque
marrum
morbus
morgue
murmur
Myrtus
Martyn
martyr
Mervyn
mescal
mesial
mesian
messan
mishap
mislay
missal
missay
moshav
Mossad
✧muscat
mashed
masher
masked
masker
masses
masted
✧master
Meshed
mestee
misfed
misken
miskey
misled
missee
missel
Misses
misset
✧mister
mosher
Moslem
Mosley
musher
musked
muskeg
musket
mussel
mustee
muster
Masais
mashie
masjid
maslin
massif
mastic
mesail
mess in
misaim
misdid
misfit
mishit
✧missis
✧mosaic
mossie
muscid
Muslim
muslin
mystic
masala
mascle
masula
mistle
mostly
muscle
muscly
muskle
myself
mishmi
Mishna
musang
musing
mustn't
mascon
mascot
Moscow
Mrs Mop
Mt Sion
musk ox
musmon
musrol
Maseru
Masora
Messrs
misère
✧misery
Mysore
misuse
misust
meseta
mesite
mashua
masque
mess up
mess-up
miscue
missus
mist up
mosque
museum
muss up
musive
Matrah
matzah
matzas
met man
mitral
Mt Taal
mutual
matico
motuca
mutuca
matier
matjes
matted
matter
métier
metred
mither
mitten
mothed
mother
motley
motser
mutter
mutuel
metage
matric
matrix
✧mattie
metric
mythic
matoke
matily
metals
mettle
motile
mottle
mutely
mutule
✧matins
mutant
mutine
mutiny
matlos
matlow
matron
matzoh
matzos
matzot
meteor
method
✧métros
motion
motmot
motto'd
mottos
mutton
mythos
metope
mature
Mithra
motory
mutism
metate
motett
mutate
mutuum
mythus
motive
Motown®
methyl
moutan
maundy
moulds
mouldy
maumet
Mauser
mouser
mousey
mouter
maungy
mzungu
mought
mouths
mouthy
mauvin
moujik
moulin
mousie
mousle
mousmé
maunna
mouton
maugre
mousse
Mounty
miurus
muu-muu
maulvi
movies
move in
moving
move up
mawmet
mewses
mawkin
Mowgli
mowing
my word
mawpus
Mexico
Mixtec
maxima
myxoma
Maxine
maxixe
May Day
✧mayday
mayhap
May-dew
mayhem
mayfly
maying
mayest
moyity
✧may bug
mazhbi
mizzen
mezail
mozzie
muzhik
muzaky
mazily
mizzle
mizzly
mozzle
muzzle
mazuma
mezzos
Mt Zion
mazard
Mozart
mazout
mezuza
nyalas
near by
nearby
Nearco
nuance
nhandu
neaped
nearer
neaten
Niamey
neaffe
neanic
niacin
Nyanja
nearly
neatly
ngaios
nyanza
nebeck
Nubuck
nobody
nabbed
nabber
nebbed
neb-neb
nibbed
nebris
nubbin
Nabila
nebula
nebule
nebulé
nebuly
nibble
no-ball
nobble
nubble
nubbly
nubile
nybble
Nyborg
nebish
Nablus
nebbuk
nobbut
nectar
nickar
nuchae
nuchal
nacket
nacred
necked
niched
nicher
nickel
nicker
nochel
nocket
nuclei
nocake
Nacala
nicely
Nicola
Nicole
nucule
Nicene
nocent
nachos
Nichol
no chop
nicish
nicety
nickum
✧noctua
no dice
Nedyet
nidget
nodded
nodder
nudger
nidify
nod off
Neddie
nudnik
noddle
nodule
nudely
Na-Dene
Nadine
niding
nid-nod
nodose
nudism
nudist
nudity
nodous
need-be
naeves
needer
noesis
noetic
needle
needly
nielli
niello
Noelle
naevus
no fear
niffer
no fair
nuffin
naffly
nefast
nuggar
nagged
nagger
nogged
nugget
noggin
nogaku
niggle
niggly
nighly
nagana
Nagano
nigh on
no good
no-good
nagari
negate
nights
nighty
Nagpur
Nagoya
no-hope
nairas
✧naiads
nailed
nailer
noises
Nzinga
naiant
nail up
no joke
nekton
nallah
nilgai
nilgau
nullah
nelies
nilled
✧nellie
✧nelson
no less
Nilote
Nilots
Nemean
no mean
numbat
numdah
numnah
nomade
nomady
nimbed
nimmed
nimmer
numbed
number
Nymphs
nim-oil
namely
nimble
nimbly
numbly
naming
nomina
numina
Nimrod
no more
nomism
numpty
nimbus
Nan Hai
Ninian
✧ninjas
non-fat
Ningbo
Nantes
non-net
no-noes
nonage
non-ego
nankin
nuncio
nuncle
nonane
nandoo
nincom
non-com
non-con
nonary
nanism
nanite
ninety
nincum
nooner
niobic
Nootka
noodle
Nuphar
Napier
Naples
napped
napper
nephew
nipped
✧nipper
nipter
nip off
napkin
Nippie
napalm
Nepali
nipple
napron
Nippon
napery
nepeta
Nippur
narial
narras
nerval
norlan'
normal
✧norman
Norway
nurhag
Narada
Neruda
narked
nerved
nerver
nerves
nirled
Noreen
norsel
nor yet
nurser
nark it!
Narnia
Narvik
✧nereid
nirlie
nirlit
Nordic
neroli
nurdle
nursle
narine
nerine
narcos
nardoo
narrow
Norroy
Nernst
Nerita
nerite
norite
Nereus
Nerium
Nascar®
Nassau
Nissan®
nosean
no-side
nosode
Nasser
nester
nisses
nosher
Naskhi
Neskhi
nastic
Nessie
nestle
nosily
nosing
nasion
Nesiot
Nestor
no-show
nostoc
nostos
nasard
nasute
Nessus
nose up
nosh-up
Nathan
not bad
no-tech
notice
natter
nether
netted
nutlet

Words marked ✧ can also be spelled with one or more capital letters

nutmeg
nutted
nutter
notify
notchy
Nettie
nitric
nitwit
nut oil
nutria
nettle
nettly
no time
natant
nutant
nation
natron
notion
nutjob
natura
✧nature
nitery
notary
notate
nutate
netful
notour
not out
native
nitryl
neural
nougat
nounal
nautch
noulde
✧**nausea**
neuter
Nouméa
naught
nought
nautic
Ngunis
nousle
neuron
Novial
novice
Nevada
Navaho
navaid
Navajo
novels
novena
never a
Nivôse
novate
novity
Newham
new lad
Newman
✧new man
new-sad
✧**new age**
✧new-age
newbie
Newfie
newell
new-old
✧nowell
new sol
newton
Newark

newish
nowise
noways
nix-nie
nextly
naysay
noyade
noyous
nozzer
nuzzer
Nazify
nozzle
nuzzle
Nazism
omasal
on a lay
Osasco
O'Casey
okayed
onager
opaled
✧**orange**
otalgy
orache
ogamic
okapis
oxalic
oxalis
Ozalid®
Oracle®
oracle
orally
ovally
of arms
ozaena
orator
ovator
Onagra
omasum
opaque
oubaas
on bail
Osbert
ox-bird
orbita
orbity
orchat
opcode
orchel
orcein
orchid
orchil
✧orchis
occult
on call
oscula
oscule
occamy
oncome
orcine
oscine
occupy
oecist
oncost
oocyst
oocyte
odd-man
ogdoad
oh dear!
Oldham
old-hat

old man
old-man
ordeal
oodles
old age
Old Vic
ordain
oedema
Old One
✧ondine
onding
odd-job
odd lot
odds-on
old boy
Old Tom
obdure
orders
ordure
oddish
oldest
oldish
oddity
on-dits
on duty
oidium
one day
one-day
one-man
one-way
overby
owerby
Oneida
✧oreads
oreide
overdo
obeyer
O level
O-level
omelet
omened
oneyer
opener
or ever
ox-eyed
one-off
on edge
overgo
obeche
olefin
Onegin
orexis
ocelli
O'Neill
openly
Otello
overly
odeons
one-one
Oberon
ocelot
operon
Oregon
oneyre
obeism
Odense
Odessa
or else
Odette
oleate
omenta

omerta
omertà
owelty
obelus
Olenus
open up
one-two
off-day
off pat
office
olfact
off-key
offset
off-air
Offaly
onfall
on file
offend
offing
off-job
onflow
on foot
on fire
✧oxford
oafish
offish
offcut
offput
orgeat
orgies
ouglie
oughly
oogamy
oogeny
organa
orgone
oxgang
orgasm
oxgate
on heat
oxhead
ochrea
ochrey
on high
on hold
ochone
on hand
ochery
on hire
Ophism
✧**ophite**
obi-man
obital
ogival
ooidal
origan
ovisac
Oviedo
obiter
Oliver!
✧oliver
olivet
orifex
Origen
Olivia
oniric
opioid
origin
Osiris
otitis
oriole

oniony
Oriana
✧orient
orison
ovibos
osiery
obiism
Orissa
otiose
opiate
odious
Ojibwa
object
objure
objets
Orkney
oikist
oak-nut
oilcan
oil-gas
oilman
oil pan
on loan
owl-car
o'clock
oillet
oblige
oology
oil rig
oilily
ollamh
oblong
ogling
on-lend
on-line
online
oolong
oulong
oxland
oilers
oilery
owlery
oblast
owlish
oblate
of late
✧oolite
oolith
oil-cup
oilnut
oomiac
oomiak
oompah
ohmage
ormolu
osmund
Ogmios
osmose
osmate
osmium
osmous
Ormazd
Ormuzd
omnify
ornery
of note
ornate
omnium
oroide
orogen
ozonic

oboist
on oath
Oporto
obolus
orphan
osprey
oppugn
Orphic
orpine
oppose
oar-lap
ocreae
o'erlay
oorial
ourebi
O grade
O-grade
oarage
ourali
orrery
ourari
ogress
ogrish
Oirish
onrush
Ossian
onside
Ofsted
on spec
ouster
oyster
ossify
obsign
ossein
oxslip
on sale
on song
Orsino
on show
op shop
obsess
on-site
osteal
Ostiak
ostial
Ostyak
outbar
outeat
outgas
outlaw
outlay
outman
obtect
on tick
optics
ostler
Ostmen
Ostrea
outher
outjet
outler
outlet
outred
outset
outage
obtain
outbid
outfit
outhit
outlie
outsit

outvie
outwin
outwit
oxtail
outfly
on time
optima
optime
obtend
obtund
octane
Octans
octant
optant
Ostend
ostent
outing
octroi
octuor
option
orthos
out-box
outbox
outfox
outtop
octopi
outcry
obtest
obtuse
out-ask
octett
opt out
opt-out
ostium
outgun
outjut
output
outrun
outsum
octave
octavo
ottava
Ottawa
outbye
ocular
ovular
opuses
oeuvre
oculus
opulus
on view
obvert
ouvert
Orwell
Oswald
Olwyne
onward
oxygen
oxymel
onycha
of yore
oozily
plagal
planar
platan
play at
✧**pearce**
plaice
planch
prance
pranck

peahen
peaked
peavey
phased
Piaget
placed
placer
placet
planer
planet
plated
platen
plater
plates
played
player
prater
prayed
prayer
piaffe
pa'anga
peachy
plashy
poachy
phaeic
phasic
phasis
phatic
placid
placit
play it
pratie
praxis
pranky
pearls
pearly
phalli
prawle
Phasma
plasma
Psalms
✧**plains**
plaint
prajna
peacod
peapod
peason
pharos
pianos
play on
pearst
praise
planta
plaste
peanut
plague
plaguy
plaque
play up
Prague
piazza
public
pebble
pebbly
pachak
po'chay
pochay
packer
packet
pecker
pecten

picked
picker
picket
pocked
pocket
pucker
pacify
pectic
pectin
picnic
picric
pycnic
pickle
puckle
picene
picine
pick on
Pictor
pycnon
PC card
Pecora
picoté
pack up
pactum
pick up
pick-up
pad-nag
padsaw
Paduan
pedlar
podial
padded
padder
pedder
podded
podley
pudden
pudder
pudsey
pidgin
paddle
pedalo
peddle
piddle
puddle
puddly
✧**padang**
pedant
Podunk
pudent
podsol
podzol
Podura
pedate
podite
padauk
padouk
podium
pieman
Pleiad
prefab
prepay
pre-tax
pre-war
plebby
✧**pierce**
pleach
pleuch
preace
preach
pseudo

peeled
peeler
pee-pee
peeper
peeved
peever
peewee
piecen
piecer
preces
prefer
pre-let
premed
preses
preset
preife
peenge
pledge
pleugh
peen in
peerie
peewit
Phemie
phenic
pierid
Pieris
poetic
précis
prefix
prelim
premia
premie
premix
pteria
pterin
Pteris
pyemia
paella
Puebla
✧pueblo
pneuma
preamp
paeony
pieing
pyeing
phenol
phenom
pie-dog
plexor
pretor
pye-dog
preppy
Phèdre
pheere
Pierre
pleura
poetry
pheese
pierst
please
prease
plenty
presto
pretty
peepul
plenum
plexus
pre-buy
precut
pre-nup
prevue
preeve
phenyl
prewyn
pheeze
puffed
puffer
puffin
piffle
poffle
puff up
pig-man
pig-rat
pagoda
pegged
peg leg
pig-bed
pigged
✧piglet
pigpen
piggie
piggin
puggie
puggle
paging
pigsny
pegbox
peg-top
pigeon
pogrom
pug dog
pygarg
Paget's
pigsty
peg out
pig-nut
pignut
pig out
Pahari
plicae
plical
primal
ptisan
Philby
paiock
peinct
✧prince
Prisca
pained
paired
Philem
poised
poiser
priced
pricer
pricey
primer
priser
privet
prized
prizer
priefe
plight
poisha
painim
Philip
paidle
paigle
primly
prisms
prismy
pliant
puisne
puisny
phizog
Poirot
poison
primos
prison
pliers
priory
plissé
priest
prissy
painty
plinth
pointe
points
pointy
paid-up
Primus®
primus
prieve
pajock
pokies
pakeha
pyknic
pukeko
Peking
poking
pakora
Pakhto
Pakhtu
pokeys
paleae
pallae
pallah
Pallas
Palmae
palmar
palpal
✧pelham
pillar
pillau
poleax
pollan
pulsar
pultan
pulwar
palace
Polack
✧police
policy
palkee
palled
pallet
palmed
palmer
palter
pellet
pelmet
pelter
pelves
phloem
pilfer
Pilsen
polder
polled
pollen
poller
pollex
puller
pullet
pulley
pulper
pulsed
pulver
pilaff
palagi
pelage
phlegm
pulkha
palais
pallia
pallid
palmie
peloid
pelvic
pelvis
pile in
pull in
pull-in
pulpit
pulvil
palely
palolo
pilula
pilule
palama
Paloma
paling
piling
Poland
poling
polony
puling
pylons
pallor
pillow
polios
Pol Pot
pull-on
pulton
Pelops
polype
polypi
polyps
paltry
pelory
peltry
palish
pilose
✧polish
palate
pelite
pelota
Pilate
polite
polity
P-plate
palpus
Peleus
Phleum
pileum
pile up
pile-up
pileus
pilous
Pollux
pull up
pull-up
pulque
pultun
poleyn
pampas
Pamyat
pomace
pumice
pomade
pamper
pommel
✧pompey
pummel
pumped
pumper
Pamela
pimple
pimply
pomelo
pumelo
piment
Pomona
pom-pom
pompom
pompon
pomroy
pomato
pump up
pandar
penial
penman
pennae
pennal
pen pal
pentad
Pentax®
Pindar
pineal
pin-man
pinnae
pontal
Punjab
punkah
panick
Punica
panada
pander
paneer
Pangea
pangen
panned
panter
panzer
pencel
penned
penner
pensée
pensel
pincer
pinder
Pinger®
pinger
pinked
pin-leg
pinned
pinner
pinnet
Pinter
poncey
ponder
pongee
pontes
punier
punned
punner
punnet
puntee
punter
pang-fu'
poncho
punchy
pandit
pencil
pensil
✧pinkie
pinnie
pinxit
Pinyin
pongid
✧pontic
pontie
pontil
pundit
penile
penult
pingle
pinole
pintle
punily
✧panama
panini
Penang
pinene
ponent
punany
panton
pantos
pennon
pingos
pinion
pinkos
pintos
pondok
pongos
ponton
puntos
panary
pan-fry
pantry
penury
pinery
panisc
panisk
punish
piñata
pineta
pinite
puncta
puncto
panful
pannus
pan out
pantun
penful
pen-gun
pensum
pent-up
pony up
pentyl
phocae
phocas
✧pholas
phonal
poojah
poonac
Prozac®
✧phoebe
poonce
ploidy
Proddy
phoner
'phones
phones
phoney
phooey
piolet
pioned
pioner
pioney
pioted
plover
pooped
✧pooter
prober
proker
proleg
proler
propel
proper
proser
protea
pro tem
proved
proven
prover
ptoses
pyoner
proofs
plongd
plonge
✧plough
proign
phobia
phobic
phonic
photic
pionic
pookit
probit
profit
prolix
prosit
psocid
psoric
ptosis
plonky
people
poodle
poorly
pootle
Progne
proine
proyne
phonon
photog
photon
photos
poo-poo
✧prolog
promos
Proton®
proton
prompt
Proust
plotty
pronto
Probus
prop up
poogye
propyl
protyl
Papuan
Popian
poplar
papacy
pepper
pipped
popped
✧popper
poppet
pupped
puppet
pop off
pipage
papain
pepsin
peptic
pipe in
pipkin
pippin
poplin
poppit
poprin
Puppis
papula
papule
popple
popply
pepino
piping
Paphos
peplos
popjoy
pop-top
papers
papery
papyri
✧pop art
popery
papish
papism
papist
popish
pupate
pappus
pepful
peplum
peplus
pipe up
pip out
popgun
papaya
pop-eye
✧piquet
Pequod
Parcae
pardal
pariah
parial
Parian
parlay
parral
partan
perfay
phreak
portal
portas
purdah
piracy
✧parade
parody
parcel
parded
parget
parkee
parker
parley
parpen
parrel
parsec
Parsee
parser
parted
parter
percen
perfet
porker
✧porter
Purdey®
purger
purler
purser
pursew
purvey
purify
parage
perogi
pirogi
Pyrrho
pardie
parkie
parkin
partim
parvis
perdie
pereia
perfin
perkin
perk it
permit
Persic
pirnie
pirnit
porgie
Portia
purlin
purpie
peruke
parkly
parole
partly
pertly
portly
purely
purfle
purfly
purple
purply
Pyrola
paramo
parang
parent
paring
perone
piraña
Purana
purine
pyrene
pardon

pardon?
parlor
parrot
parson
parton
period
Pernod®
perron
person
paraph
pyrope
parure
parish
perish
peruse
phrase
phrasy
porism
porose
✧purism
purist
parity
periti
pirate
purity
pyrite
perdue
perk up
persue
porous
pursue
piraya
✧pascal
pasear
postal
Pushan
pass by
Pesach
pesade
posada
passed
passée
passer
pastel
paster
pester
Pisces
pished
posnet
posser
posset
poster
pushed
pusher
pussel
pusser
pashim
passim
pastil
pastis
past it
pistil
possie
postie
postil
Post-it®
pestle
poshly
pesant
Pisano
posing

pass on
pastor
✧pistol
piston
post-op
push on
pastry
Pashto
Pashtu
peseta
Pushto
Pushtu
pass up
passus
poseur
posh up
'possum
Possum®
possum
post up
push-up
pesewa
peshwa
Pathan
pet-day
pitman
pit-pat
pit-saw
pot hat
potman
puteal
pataca
putsch
patted
pattée
patten
patter
patzer
pether
petrel
petted
petter
pitied
pitier
pitted
pitten
pitter
poteen
pother
potted
potter
putted
puttee
putten
putter
putzes
put off
put-off
potage
patchy
pitchy
potche
pathic
pat-lid
patois
Pattie
pet-sit
pot-lid
putois
putrid
puttie

Pythia
Pythic
Pitaka
pattle
pettle
Petula
potale
pottle
puteli
patent
patina
patine
potent
pathos
patios
Patmos
patrol
patron
petrol
pithoi
pithos
potboy
potion
pottos
putlog
✧python
patera
petara
petard
petary
pitara
pituri
puture
pot-ash
potash
potass
Potosí
petite
potato
potful
potgun
put out
put-put
pausal
plural
paunce
paunch
pounce
pounds
pauper
pauser
Phuket
plumed
plused
pluses
pouder
poufed
poules
pourer
pouter
pruner
pluffy
pouffe
plunge
plushy
pouchy
piupiu
plug in
plug-in
poukit
pourie

✧prusik
pyuria
plucky
plummy
pruina
pruine
pluton
plumpy
poulpe
poudre
pousse
prunus
pavage
pavane
paving
pavone
pavior
pavise
pawpaw
phwoah
phwoar
powwaw
pawnce
✧pawnee
pawner
pewter
powder
powney
powter
pownie
powwow
powers
Paxman
paxwax
pay day
psywar
pay bed
pay off
pay-off
✧psyche
✧psycho
paynim
physic
physio
ptyxis
payola
phyllo
psylla
paying
plying
prying
pay-box
phyton
poyson
peyote
pay out
pay-out
phylum
pry out
Poznan
puzzel
pizzle
puzzle
pezant
pazazz
Peziza
pizazz
Quapaw
quasar
quaich
quatch

✧quaker
quaver
quagga
quaggy
quaigh
quango
qualia
quar'le
qualmy
quaint
quahog
quaere
quarry
quanta
quarte
quarto
quartz
queach
quelch
quench
quetch
Q-fever
✧quebec
quelea
queued
queuer
quethe
Queens
queeny
queint
querpo
queasy
queest
qwerty
queazy
qi gong
qigong
quidam
qui tam
✧quince
quitch
quite a
quited
quiver
quiche
quight
quinic
quinie
quirky
quinoa
quinol
quipos
quinsy
quinta
quinte
qui-hye
quinze
qindar
qintar
quotas
quoter
quotes
quotha
quokka
quooke
quoist
quoits
quorum
quotum
Q-train
qasida

Qatari
qiviut
qawwal
Reagan
riancy
Rwanda
reader
reales
reamer
reaper
rearer
reaver
roamer
roarer
rhaphe
read in
read-in
reagin
realia
roadie
roarie
re-ally
really
rearly
realos
reason
realty
reasty
Rialto
read up
rear up
road up
rya rug
ribibe
reback
rebeck
rabbet
rabies
ribbed
riblet
robbed
robber
rubbed
rubber
rubbet
rubied
rubies
rebuff
rubefy
rubify
rub off
rabbin
rabbis
✧rabbit
reboil
Robbie
rubbit
rubric
rebuke
rabble
ribald
robalo
rubble
rubbly
rebind
riband
Ribena®
Robina
robing
Rubens
Rubina

rubine
reboot
ribbon
Rob Roy
rebore
reborn
rebury
Robert
ribose
robust
rabato
rebate
rebato
rebite
rubati
rubato
ribaud
rub out
rubout
rebozo
racial
reckan
rectal
ric-rac
rictal
✧rococo
re-cede
recede
recode
Rachel
racier
racked
racker
racket
recced
recces
recked
richen
riches
ricker
ricket
rickey
rochet
✧rocker
rocket
ruched
Recife
rachis
rechie
rechip
recoil
recoin
Riccia
Richie
racily
recall
recule
richly
rickle
rickly
ruckle
rucola
raceme
Racine
racing
recant
✧recent
racoon
reccos
reckon
rector

rectos
recept
recipe
record
recure
racism
racist
recast
recess
recuse
recite
rack up
recoup
rectum
rectus
rictus
ruck up
ruckus
radial
radian
redcap
Redcar
redeal
red hat
rediae
redial
red-mad
red man
red rag
redraw
rid way
rodman
redact
reduce
redden
redder
redeem
redleg
Red Sea
ridded
ridden
ridder
ridged
ridgel
ridger
Ridley
rodded
Rodney
rudded
rudder
reduit
ride in
ridgil
raddle
radula
reddle
riddle
ruddle
rudely
Rudolf
radome
red ant
redone
rident
✧riding
rodent
roding
radios
red box
red dog
red-dog

red fox
red-hot
red rot
red-top
redtop
ride on
rodeos
rudery
radish
rudish
redate
radium
radius
redbud
redd up
red gum
red mud
red out
Red Rum
red-wud
ride up
redowa
red-eye
reeded
reeden
reeder
reefer
reeler
reeved
riever
roemer
re-echo
reechy
Raetia
re-edit
reekie
rhexis
ruelle
Rheims
rheums
rheumy
rueing
reebok
rhebok
rhetor
reesty
roesti
rhesus
rueful
reflag
reface
refect
✧rafter
reffed
reflet
reflex
refuel
rifler
rifles
ruffed
refuge
raffia
ruffin
rafale
raffle
refill
rifely
riffle
ruffle
refine
re-fund

refund
reflow
refoot
re-form
reform
refuse
refute
reflux
rufous
ragbag
rag day
raglan
ragman
ragtag
reggae
regnal
rug rat
ragged
raggee
reglet
regret
rigged
rigger
roguer
rugged
rugger
regain
Reggie
Reggio
riglin
raggle
raguly
regale
regula
reguli
Regulo®
regulo
rigoll
regime
régime
raging
ragini
regent
✧regina
ragtop
region
regard
regest
rugose
righto
rights
rugate
rag out
rag-out
ragout
regius
rigour
rig out
rig-out
rugous
regive
rehear
reheat
reheel
rehang
rehire
rehash
raiyat
rhinal
raider
railer

raiser
raited
reiter
reiver
ruined
ruiner
rain in
raisin
rein in
rhizic
Roisin
railly
rhinos
Raipur
rein up
Rajkat
reject
rejoin
Rijeka
Rajani
Rajesh
Rajput
rake in
raking
rakery
rakish
rake up
reload
relics
relict
reluct
relide
relied
relief
relier
rilled
rillet
✧rolfer
rolled
✧roller
relaid
rellie
roll in
relume
relent
reline
Roland
ruling
roll on
roll-on
rule OK
relish
✧**relate**
Rallus
rile up
roll up
roll-up
relive
rallye
ramcat
rameal
Ramean
remead
remade
remede
remedy
remuda
ramjet
rammed
rammer
ramper

Ramses
rimmed
Rommel
romper
rummer
Rumper
ramify
romage
remain
remeid
Romaic
rumkin
romaji
remake
ramble
ramuli
remble
rumble
rumbly
rumple
rumply
remand
remind
remint
Rimini
Romani
Romano
Romany
rumens
✧rumina
ramrod
ramson
rom-com
romcom
Romeos
rumbos
re-mark
remark
remora
Ramism
Ramist
ramose
remise
remiss
rimose
Romish
ramate
remote
ramous
ramp up
remoud
rimous
rum bud
rumour
rumpus
remove
Randal
randan
rental
runway
rancel
randem
✧ranger
ranked
ranker
ransel
ranter
ranzel
render
renied
Rennes

rennet
renter
rentes
rinded
ringed
ringer
rinser
rondel
runlet
runnel
runner
runnet
runted
run off
run-off
renege
Ranchi
rancho
rancid
randie
Rankin
rennin
Renoir
ring in
✧runrig
rankle
rankly
ranula
Ranulf
Ronald
rundle
runkle
rename
ranine
rancor
random
randon
ransom
renvoi
renvoy
rondos
ronyon
run low
run dry
Renata
ring up
run out
run-out
✧**renown**
roo bar
ryokan
rhombi
Rhonda
reopen
Rhodes
rioter
roofed
roofer
roomed
roomer
rooted
rooter
rhodic
rhodie
rhotic
Roofie
rookie
roomie
roopit
rootle
riotry

rootsy
root up
✧**repeal**
repeat
replan
replay
rip-rap
riprap
ripsaw
rupiah
repack
ripeck
rypeck
rapids
rapier
rapped
rappee
rappel
rappen
rapper
repped
ripped
ripper
ropier
rip off
rip-off
repugn
✧**raphia**
raphis
repaid
repair
rope in
raptly
repulp
ripely
ripple
ripply
ropily
rapine
raping
repand
repent
repine
repone
roping
raptor
repros
Rippon
report
repure
ropery
Rupert
rapist
repass
repast
repose
repost
repute
replum
rip out
Raquel
roquet
requit
reread
rorter
rarefy
rerail
rarely
raring
re-roof
rarity

rascal
reseal
reseat
réseau
roseal
Roseau
Roshan
resect
rosace
✧**reseda**
réséda
reside
rasher
rasper
raster
reskew
restem
rester
risker
rosier
rosser
roster
rushee
rushen
rusher
rushes
russel
russet
rusted
re-sign
resign
reship
roscid
Ruskin
✧russia
rustic
Russki
Russky
rashly
resale
resell
resile
resole
result
rosily
rosula
rustle
resume
résumé
resent
rising
Rosina
rosiny
rusine
rasure
resorb
resort
rosary
rosery
rostra
rustre
resist
re-site
rosety
rescue
reskue
rise up
risque
risqué
ruscus
ratbag

rattan
rat-tat
retial
retral
ritual
rottan
rather
ratted
ratten
ratter
retree
retted
ritter
rother
rotted
rotten
rotter
rutted
rutter
ratify
rotche
ratlin
rat-pit
retail
retain
retrim
retake
Rothko
✧**rattle**
rattly
retell
retile
rotolo
rotula
rutile
retama
retime
ratine
ratiné
rating
retene
retina
retund
retune
rotund
ration
ratios
ratoon
ratton
retook
retool
retrod
retros
re-type
retard
retire
retort
returf
re-turn
return
✧rotary
retuse
ratite
rotate
rat run
retour
rotgut
Rouman
rhumba
raunch
rounce

rouncy
round B
Reuben
rouser
routed
router
raunge
reurge
raught
rought
roughy
raucid
roupit
raucle
rouble
roucou
reveal
revied
re-view
review
revved
ravage
rivage
rivlin
revoke
revels
revile
revolt
revamp
Ravana
ravin'd
ravine
raving
roving
reverb
✧revere
revers
revert
revery
rivery
ravish
revest
revise
rave-up
rêveur
revive
raw bar
rewrap
rawing
rewind
Rowena
rowing
row-dow
reward
rewire
reword
rework
rawish
rewash
Rex cat
Rexine®
Roxana
Roxane
Riyadh
raylet
rhymed
rhymer
rhythm
✧**royals**
rhyton
ray gun

rizzar
rizzer
rozzer
razzia
razzle
rezone
rizzor
razure
rizard
scalae
scalar
scarab
sea bat
sea cap
sea cat
sea ear
sea fan
sea law
✧seaman
Seamas
sea mat
sea maw
Seanad
searat
seaway
shaman
spayad
stalag
statal
swaraj
scabby
shabby
shamba
slabby
swabby
scarce
scatch
sea ice
sealch
séance
searce
search
slatch
smatch
snatch
stance
stanch
stanck
starch
swatch
shandy
Skanda
stadda
swaddy
swardy
Saanen
scaled
scaler
✧scales
scamel
scapes
scared
scarer
scarey
seabed
Seabee
sea eel
sealed
sealer
seamer
sea mew

Words marked ✧ can also be spelled with one or more capital letters

sea pen
seared
seated
seater
shaded
shader
✧shades
shaked
shaken
✧shaker
shakes
shamed
shamer
shaped
shapen
shaper
shared
sharer
shaved
shaven
shaver
skater
slated
slater
slaver
slavey
slayed
slayer
snarer
soaked
soaken
soaker
soaper
soarer
spaced
spacer
spacey
spader
spahee
sparer
Stacey
staged
stager
stagey
stakes
stamen
stapes
starer
stated
stater
✧states
staved
staves
stawed
stayed
stayer
swayed
swayer
scarfs
Staffa
staffs
sea egg
sealgh
shaggy
slaggy
slangs
slangy
snaggy
sparge
Svarga
Swarga

scathe
Shashi
snathe
spathe
swashy
swathe
swathy
sea air
sea fir
sea pie
sea-pig
Shamir
✧sharia
✧sharif
shavie
sialic
Slavic
soapie
spadix
sparid
spavie
spavin
stadia
stag it
Stalin
stasis
static
statim
statin
stay in
swag it
swan in
shacko
shaikh
skanky
slacks
sparke
sparks
sparky
stalko
stalky
swanky
scally
shalli
smalls
'snails
snaily
snarly
spalle
spauld
stable
stably
stalls
staple
suable
suably
shammy
smalmy
smarmy
spammy
sdaine
shanny
sharny
spaing
spawny
stayne
swanny
scazon
sea boy
sea cob
sea cow

sea dog
sea fog
sea fox
sea god
seahog
season
shadow
shakos
shalom
shalot
shamoy
Sharon
sialon
slalom
spados
stator
Syalon®
scampi
scarpa
scarph
sea ape
sharps
snappy
swampy
scarr'd
scarre
scarry
scaury
shairn
slairg
sparre
sparry
stairs
starry
stayre
sparse
scaith
scanty
scarth
scatty
Shakta
Shakti
shanty
skaith
skarth
smalti
smalto
smarty
snaste
Sparta
sparth
stacte
staith
swarth
swarty
swatty
scapus
Scarus
sea bun
Seamus
shaduf
✧shamus
slap-up
snap up
soak up
statua
statue
status
stay up
swan up
sway up

Shaiva
starve
swarve
sea owl
snazzy
stanza
stanze
stanzo
sabbat
Sabean
Sabian
subman
subway
subact
St Bede
sables
sobbed
subbed
subdew
subfeu
sublet
subsea
subset
syboes
sabkha
so be it
sobeit
subbie
submit
subtil
sobole
✧subtle
subtly
Sabina
Sabine
Subaru®
suborn
suburb
sebate
subito
subdue
subgum
sybows
sacral
siccan
siccar
social
socman
succah
secede
sachem
sachet
sacker
sacred
seckel
secret
sicken
sicker
soccer
socket
Socred
succès
sucked
sucken
sucker
sucket
socage
sickie
suck in
suck-in
seckle

Sicily
sickle
sickly
suckle
secant
second
secund
saccos
seccos
sector
sickos
succor
secern
secure
secesh
sacque
sacrum
sick up
succus
suck up
Saddam
seduce
sadden
sadder
sedged
Sidney
sodden
sodger
sudden
sudder
sudser
Sydney
saddhe
saddhu
siddha
✧siddhi
saddie
sodaic
sodain
saddle
sedile
sodomy
sedent
siding
side-on
sudary
sadism
sadist
sedate
sudate
siddur
sodium
seesaw
Shebat
she-oak
Shevat
stelae
stelar
snebbe
sheuch
sketch
sleech
smeech
speccy
speech
spence
spetch
stench
speedo
speedy
steady

stedde
steddy
steedy
saeter
seeded
seeder
✧seeker
seemer
see red
shekel
shewed
shewel
sieger
skewed
skewer
sleded
slewed
soever
spewer
stereo
✧steven
stewed
stewer
Sweden
sweven
Szeged
Szekel
see off
sheafy
shelfy
sdeign
sheugh
skeigh
sledge
sleigh
Swerga
seethe
scenic
see fit
✧sheria
sherif
specie
step in
step-in
steric
Stevie
sheikh
sleeky
sneaky
specks
specky
seemly
Sheela
✧sheila
shelly
skeely
skelly
smelly
snelly
steale
stealt
steeld
steels
steely
Stella
smegma
steamy
stemma
stemme
scerne
seeing

Sheena
✧sheeny
sienna
steane
sterna
Sterne
Sterno®
sweeny
see you
stenos
step on
sterol
sheepo
sheepy
✧sherpa
sleepy
steepy
steppe
sweepy
shears
'sheart
sheers
✧sherry
✧sierra
skeary
skeery
skerry
smeary
sneery
speary
sperre
steard
steare
steery
sweard
sweert
sweirt
smeuse
sneesh
speiss
sperse
sperst
sceatt
'sdeath
sheath
sheets
sheety
Shelta
shelty
siesta
sleety
sleuth
smeath
smeeth
sneath
suetty
svelte
sweats
sweaty
sweets
✧sweety
see out
skelum
step up
step-up
sheave
shelve
shelvy
sleave
sleeve
steeve

sterve
swerve
Sheryl
sleaze
sleazy
sleezy
sneeze
sneezy
Sifrei
sifter
soften
suffer
soffit
softie
suffix
sifaka
safely
siffle
softly
soft on
safari
Sofism
Sufism
safety
sag bag
saggar
seggar
signal
sagged
sagger
segued
sigher
signer
signet
sogged
sagoin
saguin
sign in
sagely
sagene
seghol
segnos
sign on
✧signor
sugary
sign up
sphear
sahiba
schlep
sphaer
schtik
schuit
Suhair
schelm
schuln
schuls
schema
scheme
sphene
✧sphinx
Stheno
schmoe
school
Sahara
schorl
sphere
sphery
schism
schist
schuss
schout

schuyt
schizo
shibah
shikar
Shiraz
shivah
smilax
spicae
spicas
spinal
spinar
spiral
spital
smirch
snitch
stitch
Switch®
switch
shindy
smiddy
saikei
sailed
sailer
seiner
seised
seiten
seizer
shined
shiner
shiver
shives
skiver
slicer
slided
slider
slimes
slived
sliven
sliver
smiler
smilet
smiley
smiter
snidey
sniper
snipes
snivel
soiled
soirée
spiced
spicer
spider
spiked
spikes
spined
spinel
spinet
spirea
spired
stilet
stipel
stipes
stived
stiver
St Ives
suited
suivez
swiper
swipes
swipey
swivel

Words marked ✧ can also be spelled with one or more capital letters

swivet
sniffy
spiffy
stiffy
stingo
stingy
swinge
swingy
saithe
seiche
'slight
slight
smight
Smiths
smithy
spight
stithy
swishy
seisin
seizin
skip it!
skivie
spiric
✧spirit
stimie
slinky
smirky
sticks
sticky
stinko
stinks
stinky
swink't
scilla
shield
skills
skilly
slimly
stifle
Still's
stilly
swirly
shimmy
stigma
stigme
swimmy
scient
shinne
shinny
skiing
skinny
soigné
spinny
Saigon
sailor
sciroc
Shiloh
shivoo
skibob
Ski-doo®
skidoo
Skiros
ski tow
slip-on
spigot
suitor
shippo
skimpy
skippy
slippy
snippy
stirps
sbirri
sbirro
shirra
smirry
stirra
stirre
saidst
shiest
Shiism
shiksa
shikse
sliest
slimsy
Saints
shifty
Shiite
Shinto
shinty
shirty
snifty
spilth
spinto
stilty
stinty
saique
shin up
ski bum
skin up
ski run
slip up
slip-up
spit up
stir up
skivvy
spivvy
stieve
St John
sejant
sukkah
sakieh
Sikkim
sakkos
Sukkot
salaam
Salian
sallad
sallal
salpae
salpas
selvas
silvae
silvan
silvas
soldan
sol-fa'd
sollar
sulcal
sultan
sylvae
sylvan
sylvas
select
shlock
silica
solace
splice
salade
solidi
solids
Saleem
sallee
sallet
salted
salter
salued
salver
seller
selves
silken
siller
siloed
silver
solder
sol-gel
solgel
soller
solver
spleen
sullen
salify
sclaff
scliff
skliff
spliff
silage
sulpha
sylphy
salmis
salvia
selkie
sell in
sell-in
silkie
Silvia
solein
✧sylvia
saluki
saltly
solely
salami
Salome
solemn
salina
saline
Selene
Selina
silane
silene
✧sileni
silent
sklent
solano
so long
so long!
so-long
splent
spline
splint
sallow
salmon
saloon
saloop
saltos
salvor
✧salvos
'sblood
seldom
sell on
sold on
solion
salary
sclera
sclere
solera
splore
sultry
Salish
splash
splish
splosh
Salote
salute
sclate
sklate
solito
solute
splits
saltus
Seljuk
sell up
silt up
soleus
sulcus
sulfur
saliva
sclave
solive
salewd
samaan
sambal
sambar
Samian
Samoan
sampan
simial
simian
simpai
summae
summar
summat
samech
shmock
shmuck
so much
sumach
samiel
samlet
Samoed
Samuel
seméed
semper
semsem
Semtex®
shmoes
simmer
simnel
simper
somber
summed
summer
samshu
semeia
semmit
simkin
summit
sumpit
samekh
samely
sample
semble
Semele
semple
simile
simple
simply
Somali
St Malo
sememe
Simone
simony
so many
somoni
sambos
samfoo
Samiot
samlor
Samson
Simeon
'simmon
simoom
simoon
summon
symbol
✧samara
sempre
simorg
simurg
sombre
samosa
samite
samiti
Semite
somata
somite
sambur
Samsun
sancai
sandal
sangar
Sangay
sanjak
Sanjay
sanpan
santal
Sendai
sendal
Sinéad
sin tax
sontag
sundae
Sunday
sungar
sunhat
Sunnah
sunray
suntan
syngas
syntan
syntax
Seneca
sonics
Sqn Ldr
sanded
sander
sanies
sansei
sended
sender
sennet
sensed
sensei
senses
singed
singer
sinker
sinned
sinner
sinnet
sinter
sonnet
sunbed
sunder
sundew
sunken
sunket
sunned
sunset
syndet
sanify
senega
sancho
sandhi
sangha
Sindhi
sannie
santim
santir
send in
sennit
sin bin
sin-bin
sink in
sonsie
sunkie
sunlit
syndic
sanely
senile
single
singly
sonant
sankos
santon
Santos
send on
✧senhor
senior
sensor
sindon
sunbow
sundog
sun-god
Syncom
synroc
Sandra
senary
✧señora
sentry
soneri
sundra
sundri
sundry
Senusi
sanity
✧senate
seniti
sonata
sannup
santur
send up
send-up
sensum
sinful
sinewy
Scogan
scopae
✧scopas
Seonag
shofar
shoran
Siouan
slogan
Slovak
Sno-cat
stomal
storax
slobby
snobby
stop by
sconce
scorch
✧scotch
slouch
smooch
smouch
shoddy
swords
scolex
scorer
scores
scoter
shoder
shorer
shores
shovel
shover
showed
shower
sloken
sloven
smoked
smoker
snorer
soogee
soojey
sooner
spoked
spoken
stogey
stoked
stoker
stokes
stoled
stolen
stoned
stonen
stoner
storer
stores
storey
stover
stower
spoffy
shough
✧slough
smoggy
sponge
spongy
stodge
stodgy
stooge
stop-go
storge
sloshy
soothe
sposhy
scolia
scoria
✧scotia
Scotic
shojis
shoo-in
show in
skolia
slot in
smokie
soogie
stogie
stolid
stop in
stotin
Suomic
Skopje
shonky
snooks
spooky
stocks
stocky
shoaly
shoole
should
skolly
slowly
smoile
smoyle
spoils
spoilt
stools
sloomy
stormy
Sloane
spoony
stonne
stound
stownd
swound
swoune
swownd
swowne
sholom
smokos
spot-on
stolon
shoppy
sloppy
✧snoopy
stoope
scours
stoury
stowre
scoosh
scorse
✧scouse
skoosh
sloosh
smouse
spouse
stoush
swoosh
Scotty
scouth
scowth
shorts
shorty
shotte
shouty
smooth
snooty
snorty
snotty
snouty
sports
sporty
spotty
spouty
stotty
stouth
swotty
shogun
show up
slow up
slow-up
snod up
snow up
stop up
snooze
snoozy
sappan
sepmag
septal
sapped
✧sapper
sephen
sepses
septet
sipped
sipper
sippet
sopped
suplex
supped
supper
sypher
sapego
Sappho
sepsis
septic
Sophia
Sophie
sapele
sapple
sipple
supple
supply
supine
siphon
syphon
superb
super G
sapota
sopite
sapful
Sapium
sepium
septum
St Paul
supawn
sequel
sequin
si quis
sardar
screak
scream
serdab
serial
serrae
serran

Words marked ✧ can also be spelled with one or more capital letters

serras
serval
sircar
sirdar
Sirian
sirkar
sirrah
spread
streak
stream
striae
stroam
surtax
Syriac
Syrian
scribe
scrobe
✧scrubs
Strabo
strobe
Sirach
sprack
spruce
strack
strich
strict
struck
scryde
spredd
stride
strode
sardel
sarney
sarsen
screed
screen
scried
scryer
series
server
shreek
shriek
Sir Ken
sirred
sirree
skreen
skryer
sorbet
Sorley
sorner
sorrel
sorted
sorter
sortes
spryer
streek
streel
✧street
surbed
surbet
surfer
surrey
survew
survey
syrtes
scruff
shrift
shroff
strafe
straff
strife

strift
sorage
Strega®
striga
sorgho
Sardis
sarnie
serail
Serbia
serein
shreik
sordid
sortie
spraid
sprain
spruik
spruit
straik
strain
strait
surfie
syrtis
scrike
shrike
strake
strike
stroke
scroll
shrill
sorell
sorely
spryly
stroll
surely
scramb
scrimp
scrump
serums
shrimp
skrimp
skrump
stramp
stroma
stromb
struma
saring
sarong
scrine
scrunt
scryne
serang
Serena
✧serene
serine
shrank
shrine
shrink
shrunk
Sirens
siring
sprang
sprent
✧spring
sprint
sprong
sprung
strand
strene
Strine
string
strond

strong
strung
strunt
✧syrinx
Sargon
sargos
sartor
scroop
sermon
seroon
servos
sorgos
sorrow
sort of
strook
sarape
scrape
script
serape
seraph
seriph
stripe
stripy
syrupy
Sartre
serosa
sprush
strass
stress
Syrism
scruto
sprite
spritz
strata
strath
Strato
Sûreté
surety
sargus
serous
✧shroud
Sirius
sorbus
sprout
✧stroud
stroup
strout
scrive
shrive
✧shrove
strive
strove
scrawl
scrawm
screwy
scrowl
scrows
shrewd
shrowd
sprawl
strawn
strawy
strewn
strown
scraye
Soraya
strays
syrlye
scruze
sashay
Sasebo

sestet
Sisley
sister
sussed
✧system
Saskia
siskin
suslik
seseli
sesame
sasine
seston
sissoo
sastra
sistra
Sathan
satrap
sittar
so that
shtick
shtuck
sateen
settee
setter
sithen
sithes
sitrep
sitter
so then
sotted
sutler
suttee
sythes
set off
set-off
shtchi
Sothic
settle
setule
situla
sutile
suttle
suttly
shtumm
satang
satiny
set pot
set-to's
set-tos
shtook
shtoom
sitcom
Sutton
satara
satire
satori
Saturn
satyra
Satyrs
suture
setose
shtetl
set out
set-out
sit out
sative
Sittwe
scutal
Seumas
Seurat
soutar

squeak
squeal
slubby
snubbe
snubby
Stubbs
stubby
scutch
sluice
sluicy
smutch
source
stucco
sounds
spuddy
squids
sturdy
saucer
sauger
saurel
sautés
souled
souper
soused
souses
souter
squier
stumer
scurfy
snuffy
squiff
stuffy
saulge
scunge
scungy
sludge
sludgy
smudge
smudgy
snudge
spunge
spurge
stuggy
slushy
sought
saulie
shut in
shut-in
SI unit
slum it
squail
studio
stupid
shucks
spunky
sculle
sculls
smugly
snugly
souple
sourly
squall
squill
studly
scummy
slummy
squama
squame
spurne
squint
squiny

sou-sou
stupor
sculpt
slumpy
slurpy
stumps
stumpy
scurry
skurry
slurry
smurry
souari
spurry
square
squire
squirm
squirr
squirt
Stuart
sourse
Sousse
squash
squish
stuns'l
shufti
shufty
smutty
✧**scutum**
shut up
soup up
sputum
scurvy
squawk
spulye
scuzzy
sovran
savvey
Sèvres
✧soviet
savage
Savoie
savant
savine
saving
sevens
savory
severe
severy
savate
save up
savour
so what?
sawder
✧sawney
saw set
sawyer
sowter
sewage
sawpit
sawfly
sawing
sewing
sowans
sowens
sowing
✧siwash
sowsse
Soweto
sow bug
sextan
sexual

six-day
sextet
sex aid
sexfid
sixain
sexily
saxony
sexpot
sexton
sexism
sexist
saxaul
six-gun
Sixtus
✧**skylab**
skyman
skyway
spycam
stylar
styrax
stylet
shy off
says he
scyphi
scythe
sayyid
stymie
Scylla
saying
shying
skying
Smyrna
spying
stying
stylos
sayest
shyest
shyish
skyish
slyest
slyish
spy out
stylus
sazhen
syzygy
sizzle
sozzle
sozzly
sizing
Suzhou
sizism
sizist
size up
tea bag
teabag
thanah
tiara'd
to a man
Trajan
trapan
tsamba
thatch
trance
tzaddi
teamed
teamer
tearer
teasel
teaser
tea set
teated

teazel
thaler
Thales
Thames
thawer
to a tee
tracer
traces
Tracey
traded
trader
trades
Tralee
trapes
travel
Tuareg
twangy
trashy
Thalia
thalis
tragic
travis
thanks
tracks
Tuanku
teagle
teazle
thalli
trauma
teaing
thanna
tranny
trayne
teapot
teapoy
trappy
tea urn
thairm
transe
toasty
twaite
teacup
Teague
team up
tear up
tragus
tebbad
Tib-cat
tibiae
tibial
tibias
Tobias
tabbed
tab key
tabled
tables
tablet
tabret
tabued
tubber
tabefy
Tobago
tubage
Tabriz
Tebbit
Tibbie
tabula
tubule
Tybalt
tubing
taboos

to boot
tabard
taberd
Tibert
to burn
Tyburn
Tebeth
to bits
tubate
tabour
Tobruk
tubful
Tubruq
tic-tac
Ty Cobb
tacked
tacker
tacket
Tactel®
teckel
ticked
ticken
ticker
ticket
tickey
tocher
tucker
tucket
tactic
techie
tocsin
tuck in
tuck-in
tackle
tickle
tickly
Tacoma
to come
techno
Tucana
tachos
Tucson
tycoon
tectum
tuchun
tuck up
tedded
tedder
tidied
tidier
taddie
Tadjik
✧teddie
tidbit
tide it
tiddle
tiddly
tidily
toddle
to date
Te Deum
tedium
Theban
thecae
thecal
the can
the day
the law
thenar
the Ram
the raw

the Way
tietac
toecap
toerag
trepan
thence
thetch
tierce
tiercé
trench
trendy
tweeds
tweedy
tee-hee
teemed
teemer
teepee
tee-tee
teeter
Thebes
the few
the leg
themed
the Net
The Sea
theses
the sex
thewed
thewes
tiered
tmeses
Treves
tee off
tee-off
the off
teethe
✧the who
taenia
Teenie
the lie
Themis
Theria
thesis
thetic
The Wiz
tiepin
tie-wig
tmesis
tremie
trémie
trepid
trevis
Thecla
The Fly
they'll
treble
trebly
tweely
Thelma
therms
teeing
the end
theine
the one
toeing
tweeny
Taejon
tee box
the box
the lot
✧the mob
the now
the Son
tie rod
toetoe
trek-ox
tremor
Trevor
✧the dry
theirs
theory
they're
teensy
theism
theist
tressy
tsetse
tzetse
teenty
treaty
Trento
twenty
The Sun
theave
they've
✧twelve
the axe
tie-dye
tweeze
tzetze
toffee
tuffet
tufted
tufter
taffia
tiffin
to-fall
Teflon®
tofore
tifosi
tifoso
tag day
tagrag
taguan
tagged
taggee
tagger
tegmen
tigged
Tigger
togaed
togged
tugged
tugger
tugrik
tegula
toggle
TV game
tag end
tiglon
tigery
tughra
tights
togate
tog out
tugrug
Tehran
tchick
tahsil
tehsil
tahina
tahini
to hand
T-shirt
Tahiti
Tainan
taipan
Taiwan
thiram
tribal
tricar
trinal
Thisbe
✧trilby
taisch
triact
twitch
triode
tailed
T'aipei
taiver
Taizés
✧thibet
thivel
toiled
toiler
toilet
tri-jet
trimer
tripey
trivet
twicer
twined
twiner
things
thingy
triage
twiggy
twinge
taiaha
t'ai chi
Trisha
twight
Tricia
trifid
trimix
trivia
Trixie
twilit
thicko
thicky
tricky
taigle
taille
thible
thinly
trials
trifle
trigly
trillo
trimly
triple
triply
tuille
twilly
twirly
triene
triune
tyiyns
taikos
tailor
Tainos
toison
toitoi
tricot
trigon
tripod
tripos
✧triton
trippy
thirst
triose
thirty
triste
twisty
thin'un
trip up
trisul
thieve
tailye
tajine
takahe
take in
take-in
take it
taking
token'd
take on
tykish
take up
take-up
tuk tuk
taleae
tallat
tele-ad
telial
tellar
tulban
tulwar
teledu
Toledo
talced
talker
tallet
talweg
telfer
tellen
teller
✧telnet
tiller
tilted
tilter
toller
tolsel
tolsey
Toltec
tolter
tolzey
telega
Telegu
Telugu
talkie
talk-in
tellin
til oil
toluic
talcky
taluka
talant
talent
tiling
toling
Talbot®
talbot
talion
tallot
tallow
telcos
telson
tol-lol
toluol
telary
tilery
telesm
T-cloth
T-plate
tylote
talcum
talk up
✧talmud
telium
✧tellus
tambac
tammar
tam-tam
timbal
tombac
tombak
tomcat
tomial
tymbal
tympan
tamber
tamper
Temnes
tempeh
temper
temsed
timber
tommed
tumefy
tumphy
Tammie
Tamsin
Timmie
tombic
tomtit
tamale
tamely
✧temple
timely
tumble
tumuli
tumult
tamanu
tamine
taming
temene
timing
Tambov
tampon
tempos
timbós
tomboc
tomboy
tompon
tom-tom
✧tamara
tamari
Timaru
timbre
tamise
timist
tomato
Tammuz
timous
tomium
tumour
tum-tum
tankas
tannah
tan vat
tincal
tin can
tindal
tineal
tin hat
tinman
Tongan
tonnag
Tanach
tenace
tan bed
tandem
tanged
tanked
tanker
tanned
tanner
tanrec
Tencel®
tended
tender
tenges
tenner
tenrec
tented
tenter
tenues
tinded
tinder
tinier
tinies
tinker
tinned
tinner
tinsel
tinsey
tinted
tinter
Tonies
tonker
tonlet
tunier
Tunker
tunned
✧tunnel
tangie
✧tankia
tannic
tannin
tan pit
tenail
tennis
tenpin
tentie
tenuis
tineid
tinnie
tone in
tonsil
tune in
tinaja
Tengku
tangle
tangly
tingle
tingly
tinily
tinkle
tinkly
to-name
toneme
tenant
tonant
toning
tuning
tangos
Tannoy®
tannoy
tendon
tennos
tenson
tensor
tenzon
tin god
tinpot
tondos
tonsor
✧tantra
tendre
tenure
tundra
tanist
tonish
tenuti
tenuto
tonite
tangun
tank up
tenour
tinful
tone up
tongue
tundun
tune up
tune-up
Tungus
Thomas
Thorah
thorax
too bad
trocar
Trojan
Troyan
two-way
troade
thowel
tooler
tooter
trover
trowel
taonga
though
troggs
trough
toothy
troche
trophi
trophy
thoria
toonie
toorie
trofie
tropic
two-bit
✧troika
tootle
troely
trolly
troule
two-ply
'twould
thorny
tholoi
tholos
thoron
too too
too-too
trogon
✧thorpe
trompe
troops
troppo
troupe
tooart
Taoism
Taoist
tootsy
trouse
tsotsi
trouts
trouty
tholus
tool up
trotyl
tipcat
Top Cat
top hat
top-hat
topman
Tupian
tapped
tapper
tappet
tipped
tipper
tippet
Tipp-Ex®
Tippex
Tophet
topped
topper
tupped
tepefy
tip off
tip-off
top off
typify
tappit
Tupaia
Topeka
tipple
tipula
topple
tupelo
typing
tiptoe
tiptop
top dog
✧typhon
tephra
tapist
typist
tapeta
tapeti
Top Gun
tophus
top out
typhus
Tarmac®
tarmac
tarnal
tarpan
tarras
tarsal
Tartan®
tartan
✧tartar
Tarzan
tergal
ternal
terrae
Terran
terras
thread
threap
threat
throat
Tor Bay
Torbay
turban
Tyrian
thrice
turaco
teredo
tirade
tarcel
target
tarred
tarsel
tercel
tercet
termer
Termes
terret
three-D
threep
tiroes
torret
torsel
torten
tortes
tureen
turfed
turfen
turkey
turned
✧turner
turret
turves
tyroes
tariff
terefa
thrift
Torify
Toryfy
Tardis
tar pit
tarsia
terbic
tercio
territ
tertia
tirrit
toroid
torpid
torrid
turbid

turbit
turgid
Turkic
turkis
turn in
turn-in
turnip
tartly
termly
thrall
thrill
torula
toruli
turtle
tarand
taring
thrang
threne
throne
throng
Tirana
tiring
torana
to-rend
to-rent
tyrant
Tyrone
tar box
tarboy
tarpon
tarrow
termor
✧terror
torpor
torsos
turbos
turbot
Turcos
turgor
turion
turn on
turn-on
teraph
thrips
torero
T-cross
Teresa
thrash
thresh
thrist
thrush
thrust
torose
tarots
terata
terete
Targum
✧tarsus
tart up
tergum
T-group
torous
torque
Turdus
turn up
turn-up
thrave
thrive
throve
Tarawa
thrawn

throwe
thrown
testae
tiswas
Tuscan
tuskar
tussah
tussal
tisick
tasker
taslet
tassel
tasset
tasted
taster
testee
tester
testes
to seek
tosher
tossed
tossen
tosser
tusked
tusker
tusseh
tusser
tusche
✧tassie
testis
tushie
tussis
tystie
to sell
tussle
tisane
teston
Tishri
tissue
toss up
toss-up
tetrad
✧titian
to-tear
T-strap
tutman
tutsan
tatler
tatter
tether
tetter
titfer
tithed
tither
titled
titler
titles
ti tree
titter
t'other
tother
totted
totter
tutted
tetchy
titchy
tattie
tettix
titbit
tottie
tutrix

tuttis
titoki
tattle
titely
tittle
titule
tatami
tetany
Titans
tattoo
tattow
Titipu
titupy
Tatary
totara
tittup
tote up
tut-tut
Tethys
tetryl
toucan
Truman
thumby
tauten
toupee
toupet
tourer
✧touser
touter
thuggo
trudge
taught
touché
touchy
truthy
taupie
tauric
tautit
thulia
tourie
toutie
tsuris
trunks
tautly
tousle
touzle
truant
tautog
Teuton
Toulon
Thurso
truism
Tz'u Hsi
trusty
Taurus
Tuvalu
tavern
tavers
tavert
tow bar
tow-rag
thwack
tawney
towhee
townee
tow net
✧towser
towage
tawpie
tawtie
tewhit

townie
townly
tawing
towing
Tswana
towmon
tu-whoo
tawdry
tawery
tewart
thwart
toward
towery
taxman
tuxedo
taxied
taxies
Tex-Mex
texter
toxoid
taxeme
taxing
toyman
thymic
Toyama
thyine
tiyins
toying
trying
thymol
toy boy
toy dog
Trygon
tuyère
twyere
thyrse
thyrsi
toyish
Toyota
Toyota®
thymus
try out
try-out
tazzas
tizwas
ujamaa
usance
Uganda
unawed
usager
usages
Ugarit
uracil
Uralic
Urania
uranic
uranin
unable
usable
usably
Ubasti
uraeus
Uranus
uranyl
umbrae
umbral
umbras
unbear
unbias
upbear
up-beat

upbeat
upbray
umbles
umbrel
unbred
umbril
upboil
unbelt
unbolt
unbend
unbent
unbind
unbone
upbind
urbane
unboot
upblow
umbery
unbare
unbark
unborn
unbury
unbusy
unbitt
uncial
unclad
uncock
unclew
uncage
uncoil
upcoil
urchin
uncolt
upcome
uncini
unclog
uncool
uncape
uncope
uncart
uncord
uncork
uncurl
upcurl
uncase
upcast
uncate
uncowl
undead
undeaf
undear
undraw
updrag
updraw
undeck
undock
undies
undoer
undyed
Updike
unduly
undine
undone
undern
undate
update
ureide
uneven
uneyed
ureter
Usenet

unedge
uredia
uremia
uremic
uresis
uretic
used in
user ID
usedn't
unease
uneasy
uberty
uneath
used-up
useful
uterus
uveous
unfact
unfeed
unfree
unfair
unfelt
unfold
upfill
unfine
unfool
upflow
unfirm
unform
unfurl
upfurl
Uffizi
ungear
unglad
ungual
ungues
upgrew
ungain
unguis
ungild
ungilt
ungula
upgang
urgent
urging
upgrow
Ungaro
ungird
ungirt
ungord
Utgard
upgush
unglue
ungyve
ungown
upgaze
unhead
unheal
upheap
unhair
unhele
unhelm
unholy
upheld
uphild
uphill
uphold
unhand
unhang
unhung
uphand

uphang
unhood
unhook
unhoop
uphroe
unhurt
uphurl
unhasp
unhusk
uphaud
unhive
unhewn
unital
urinal
uniped
unisex
✧united
uniter
ulitis
unific
ukiyo-e
ulicon
ulikon
unipod
unison
ubiety
Uniate
ubique
unique
unjust
upkeep
unknit
upknit
unkent
unkind
unking
unknot
unkept
uakari
uckers
unkiss
unlead
unleal
unload
uplead
uplean
upleap
upload
unlace
unlich
unlock
uplock
unlade
uglify
uplift
ullage
unlaid
unlike
uglily
unlime
ulling
unline
unlink
upland
up-line
uplink
uplook
unlord
unlash
unlast
unless

unlost
umlaut
unlive
unlove
unmade
unmeek
unmeet
unmake
upmake
unmoor
unmard
unmiry
unmask
upmost
utmost
unmown
unnail
urning
ulnare
unnest
urnful
unowed
up-over
ulosis
urosis
✧utopia
uropod
unpray
unpack
unpick
unpaid
unpent
upping
unprop
unpope
umpire
uppish
uppity
unplug
Ugrian
unread
unreal
uprear
uproar
unrobe
Ulrica
unredy
unrude
unreel
unrein
unrake
unroll
unrule
unruly
uproll
unrent
unroof
unroot
uproot
unripe
unrope
unrest
uprest
uprise
uprist
uprose
uprush
upryst
uprate
unseal
unseam

unseat
unsnap
unspar
upstay
upsway
upside
✧ulster
unseel
unseen
unshed
unsped
unstep
unsafe
unsoft
unsaid
unship
unspi'd
unsuit
unself
unsold
Ursula
ugsome
unsent
unsung
upsend
ursine
unshod
unshoe
unshot
unstop
unstow
upshot
unsure
unshut
unsoul
unspun
unsewn
unsown
unteam
unthaw
uptear
untack
untuck
urtica
untidy
untied
untrim
uptake
untile
untold
uptalk
up-till
uptilt
ultima
ultimo
untame
untomb
uptime
untent
untune
ultion
untrod
ustion
untorn
unturf
unturn
uptorn
upturn
untrue
up town
uptown

urtext
uvulae
uvular
uvulas
unused
uruses
usurer
Urumqi
ubuntu
unvail
unveil
unweal
unwrap
upwrap
upwaft
unwell
unwill
upwell
unwind
unwont
up-wind
upwind
unwept
unware
unwary
unwire
unwork
unworn
upward
usward
unwise
unwish
unwist
unwive
unyoke
Uzziah
Veadar
viands
vealer
viable
viator
Viagra®
Vibram®
vibrio
Viborg
vibist
vacked
victim
vocals
vocule
vacant
vicuna
vicuña
vector
✧victor
vicary
vacate
vacuum
vidual
vidame
videos
vadose
Vedism
Vedist
veduta
vedute
vee-jay
veejay
viewer
vielle
viewly

Vienna
voguer
voguey
veggie
vagile
vagina
vagrom
vagary
vigoro
vegete
veg out
vigour
Vehmic
vahine
V-shape
vihara
veiled
veined
voiced
voicer
voided
voidee
voider
vainly
Vaisya
Vijaya
Vikram
vakeel
✧viking
vallar
valval
valvar
villan
villar
✧vulcan
vulgar
vulval
vulvar
veloce
valley
valued
valuer
values
valved
vellet
Velsen
velvet
volley
vulned
Vulpes
vilify
volage
vildly
vilely
volume
valine
Volans
volant
volens
vellon
Villon
volvox
Valéry
Velcro®
velure
Volare
volary
volery
valise
volost
valeta

valete
valuta
velate
veleta
volute
valgus
Valium®
vallum
valour
vellum
velour
villus
vulgus
vomica
vamper
Vimule®
vimana
vamose
vomito
✧vandal
venial
Venice
vanned
vanner
Vannes
vendee
vender
veneer
venger
vennel
vented
venter
vendis
ventil
venule
vendor
ven'son
Vanora
venery
venire
ventre
vinery
vintry
vanish
venose
vanity
venite
vendue
venous
vinous
venewe
Vinaya
violer
violet
violin
voodoo
vapour
Vargas
varsal
verbal
vermal
vernal
versal
vorpal
varech
varied
varier
varlet
varved
varvel
verdet

verger
Verges
verier
✧vermes
verrel
verrey
versed
verser
verset
vertex
vervel
verven
vervet
virger
vortex
verify
virago
vorago
verbid
verdin
verdit
Verein
verlig
vermil
vermin
vermis
versin
Virgil
✧virgin
viroid
verily
virile
Varuna
Verona
virent
virino
vorant
✧varroa
verdoy
Vernon
versos
vireos
Virgos
virion
verism
verist
virose
vérité
✧verity
versus
vertue
virous
virtue
vassal
✧vestal
vestas
vista'd
vistal
visual
vesica
✧vesper
vessel
vested
visaed
viséed
visier
visage
viscid
viscin
vastly
visile

Vishnu
vision
vistos
Vasari
vestry
visite
✧viscum
viscus
visive
✧vatman
vittae
vatted
vatter
vetoes
vetted
voteen
vetchy
vitric
vote in
vittle
votary
vatful
votive
vat dye
vaunce
voulge
vaudoo
voudou
vaulty
vaunty
Vivian
Vyvian
Vyvyan
vivace
Vivien
vivres
vivify
vively
vivary
vivers
vowels
vaward
vowess
vexing
vox pop
voyage
voyeur
vizier
vizzie
vizsla
vizard
whanau
weaken
weanel
weaner
wearer
weasel
weaved
weaver
weazen
whaler
whaten
woaded
wharfs
what ho
wrathy
weak in
what if
wrap in
wealk'd
whacko

whacky
weakly
whally
wraxle
whammo
whammy
whatna
weapon
wear on
whatso
wrasse
wealth
wraith
wrap up
wharve
webcam
webbed
web-fed
wabain
wabbit
wabble
wibble
wobble
wobbly
waboom
wiccan
Wu Chao
wacker
wicked
wicken
wicker
wicket
wackos
wadmal
wadded
wadset
wedded
wedder
wedged
widget
Widnes
waddie
wade in
wedgie
widgie
waddle
✧wedeln
widdle
widely
wading
wadmol
waders
widish
whenas
wheech
whence
wrench
wretch
wieldy
weeded
weeder
weeper
weeten
weever
wee-wee
wheyey
wiener
wheugh
wrethe
weenie
weepie

weevil
wienie
Wrekin
whelk'd
whelky
weekly
wheels
wheely
wheare
wherry
wheesh
wheaty
wreath
waeful
whenua
woeful
wheeze
wheezy
wafted
wafter
waffle
waffly
wifely
wafery
wigwag
wigwam
wagged
Wagner
wigged
waggle
waggly
wiggle
wiggly
woggle
waggon
wigeon
wig out
wah-wah
Wahabi
wo ha ho
wahine
Weimar
whidah
Whitby
weirdo
Weirds
wailer
waiter
waiver
whiles
whiner
whiten
whites
✧whitey
writer
whiffy
whinge
whingy
weight
whisht
wright
writhe
whip in
whisky
whilly
whirly
whimmy
whinny
wait on
wait-on
whilom

whippy
whirry
whilst
whimsy
wriest
wristy
wait up
whip up
whizzo
whizzy
wakiki
wakame
waking
Woking
wake up
wake-up
Walian
wallah
will do
Walden
✧walker
walled
waller
wallet
Walter
welder
welter
wilder
willed
willer
willet
willey
wolfer
Wolsey
wolver
wolves
walk-in
walk it
✧wallie
welkin
wellie
well in
Wilkie
Willie
wiltja
wildly
wilily
Weland
waldos
walk-on
wallop
wallow
weldor
willow
Wilton
Walesa
walise
walk-up
wall up
walnut
walrus
well up
wilful
wolf up
wombat
wampee
wombed
wimmin
wamble
wambly
wimble

wimple
woman'd
Wim Kok
womera
wammus
wampum
wampus
wangan
want ad
windac
windas
wander
wannel
wanted
wanter
wended
wincer
wincey
winded
winder
winged
winger
winker
winner
winsey
winter
wonder
wonned
wonted
wunner
want in
Wendic
wing it
Winnie
wandle
wangle
wankle
windle
winkle
winnle
wintle
waning
Winona
woning
Wynona
wandoo
wanion
wanton
✧window
winnow
won ton
winery
wintry
wangun
want up
wind up
wind-up
win out
wooded
wooden
woofed
woofer
woolen
woosel
wroken
woodie
✧woopie
wholly
woolly
wooing
W boson

Words marked ✧ can also be spelled with one or more capital letters

whoops
whoosh
woodsy
wroath
woobut
wood up
wapped
wapper
wippen
wopped
wiping
wapiti
wipe up
war gas
warman
warran
warray
Warsaw
worral
warded
warden
warder
warmed
warmer
warner
warped
warper
warred
warren
warrey
warted
worded
worked
worker
wormed
wormer
worrel
worsen
worser
wurley
waragi
worthy

wire in
work in
work-in
worrit
warble
warily
warmly
warsle
wirily
wortle
weren't
wiring
wardog
war god
Warhol
work on
✧war cry
warmth
warm up
warm-up
wire up
work up
wasabi
washed
washen
washer
wasted
wastel
waster
wastes
Wesker
Wesley
Wessex
✧wester
wisher
wishes
wisket
wash-in
waspie
Wessis
Westie
wisely

wistly
wesand
wisent
✧wisdom
wastry
wisard
wash up
wash-up
wise up
wet bar
witgat
withal
wether
wetted
wetter
wither
witted
witter
wotted
wuther
witchy
wotcha
within
with it
with-it
wattle
wet-fly
wet bob
wet rot
wittol
waters
watery
Watusi
wet out
woundy
wauker
waured
waucht
waught
woubit
wou-wou
waurst

wavily
waving
wavery
wivern
wyvern
wowser
wow-wow
wax-red
waxily
wax end
waxing
waylay
whydah
why-not
weyard
wryest
way-out
wizier
wiz kid
wuzzle
wezand
wizard
Xiamen
X-rated
xoanon
xyloid
xyloma
xylene
xylose
xenial
Xanadu
Xanthe
Xining
xenium
Xhosan
Xerxes
X-craft
xeroma
xyster
xystoi
xystos
xystus

Xavier
Xuzhou
ynambu
yearly
yeasty
yabber
yabbie
yobbos
yacker
yicker
yucker
Yichun
yodler
Y-level
Yvette
yaffle
yagger
yogini
yogurt
yogism
Yahveh
Yahweh
yo-ho-ho
yshend
yah-boo
Yahoos
ypight
yoicks
yojana
yakker
yikker
yaksha
yoking
yukata
yakuza
yelper
yolked
yblent
Y-alloy
yellow
yclept
yplast

yammer
✧yumpie
Yemeni
Yom Tob
yum-yum
✧yankee
yanker
yonder
yonker
yankie
Yangon
yanqui
yeoman
yeomen
Yeovil
ybound
Yvonne
yoo-hoo
yaourt
yapock
yapper
yippee
yipper
yappie
yippie
✧yuppie
yaqona
Yoruba
Yorick
Y-track
yorker
yarpha
Yardie
✧yorkie
ywroke
yarely
ybrent
yarrow
Y-cross
yes-man
yesses
yester

Yasmin
yes-but
yatter
yttria
yttric
you bet
youths
youthy
yautia
you-all
yaupon
yawner
yawper
yowley
Yo-Yo Ma
Yezidi
Yizkor
✧zealot
Zabian
zebeck
zabeta
zoccos
zodiac
zydeco
zaddik
Zidane
zoetic
zaffer
zaftig
zoftig
zufoli
zufolo
zaffre
zigzag
zagged
Zagreb
zigged
zygoma
zygose
zygote
Zainab
zillah

zelant
zeloso
Zimmer®
Zambia
✧zombie
zymoid
zymome
zamang
zambos
zymase
zymite
✧zambuk
Zantac®
Zunian
Zuñian
zander
zinced
zingel
zinger
zinked
zonked
zendik
zinnia
zonoid
zincky
zonula
zonule
zenana
zoning
zincos
zonary
zonure
Zenist
zenith
zonate
zooeal
zoonal
zoom in
zoonic
Z boson
zoozoo
zlotys

zapper
zipped
zipper
zap off
zip-off
ziptop
✧zapata
zip gun
✧zephyr
Zyrian
zareba
zariba
zereba
zeriba
Zurich
zarnec
zeroed
zero in
zorino
zircon
zorros
zarape
zeroth
zester
zoster
zither
zythum
zounds
zeugma
Zouave
Zaynab
zuzzim

7 – odd

Aga saga
Alabama
apadana
Atacama
atalaya
Ayamará
Aramaic
à la page
anatase
apanage
à la main
Arapaho
à jamais
atamans
adamant
agaçant
amarant
ataraxy
à gauche
Ajaccio
a far cry
anarchy
awardee
acaudal
Abaddon

abandon
Aladdin
awarder
awayday
alameda
araneid
at an end
academe
a latere
Araceae
Araneae
a bad egg
acaleph
amateur
Amadeus
anapest
academy
amalgam
Alamgir
abashed
Arachne
Aga Khan
ataghan
al-Azhar
arachis

a bad hat
Acarida
Acarina
amanita
arabica
acarine
Adamite
alanine
Alawite
amabile
amative
apatite
arabise
arabize
avarice
amazing
awaking
Azariah
abaxial
adaxial
anaxial
Arabism
atavism
Acadian
acarian

amation
Arabian
Azanian
acacias
adagios
Ananias
Arabist
a bad job
a mark on
a bad lot
a fat lot
at a blow
anaemia
anaemic
alarmed
acapnia
alannah
Adamnan
against
araroba
acaroid
agamoid
at a word
abalone
alamode

à la mode
anagoge
apagoge
a majori
amakosi
acatour
agamous
at a loss
à tâtons
alamort
amatory
anagogy
analogy
anatomy
anagram
atabrin
Asa Gray
Aral Sea
acantha
ad astra
Agartha
atactic
adapted
acanthi
abactor

adapter
adaptor
abattis
anattos
abature
as a rule
at a push
Atatürk
analyse
analyze
analyst
ambs-ace
arblast
A S Byatt
albedos
ambient
albugos
ambages
ambling
aiblins
albumen
albumin
Albania
albinic
albinos

ambones
ambroid
Ambrose
Alberta
ambered
auberge
Auberon
albergo
arborio
arboret
Abbasid
ambassy
albitic
ambatch
arbiter
arbutus
ambitty
archaic
arcuate
acclaim
arc-lamp
accoast
accablé
aecidia
Alcudia

Arcadia
ascidia
arcaded
accidie
Alcidae
acceder
Alcides
alchera
accrete
Archean
ancress
✧archeus
ancient
alchemy
archery
arch-foe
alcohol
accoied
arctiid
alcaide
archive
ascribe
arcking
auction
Alcaics

alcalde
archlet
accompt
accinge
a sconce
asconce
arcanum
al conto
accents
ancones
arctoid
Alcyone
anchors
anchovy
alcopop
alcorza
ascarid
accurse
Alcoran
ascaris
accurst
accused
accusal
accuser
ascesis

ascetic
ascitic
ascites
anchusa
accrual
account
accourt
ad court
ascaunt
archway
accoyed
accoyld
alcayde
alchymy
alcázar
audible
audibly
adducer
address
aidless
addrest
audient
and that
Andrina
andvile
ard-righ
ardrigh
abdomen
addenda
aidance
al dente
andante
ardency
android
and so on
arduous
add up to
Andorra
andiron
auditor
Abelard
acerate
acetate
amenage
ames-ace
anelace
average
abeyant
agelast
apetaly
ave Mary
a few bob
acerbic
alembic
amender
axe-head
ageless
aweless
Aberfan
anergia
anergic
alength
avenger
aheight
alethic
Ayeshah
America
Amerind
adenine
alepine
alewife

alerion
atelier
Alexius
acetify
amenity
areolae
Ameslan
areolar
areolas
adermin
Avernus
adenoma
adenoid
aneroid
apehood
acerose
acetone
acetose
ale-pole
anemone
awesome
ale-hoof
age-long
agelong
acerous
acetous
alecost
averred
aleuron
✧aneurin
atebrin
amearst
apepsia
Ayeesha
asepses
asepsis
ab extra
amentia
aseptic
Avestic
abetted
averted
aventre
abettal
amental
amentum
Avertin®
Avestan
abetter
abettor
adeptly
alertly
ale-bush
asexual
Avebury
areaway
affear'd
affeard
affeare
aufgabe
affiant
affable
affably
affiche
Anfield
Alfheim
A-effect
affaire
affying
affairs
afflict

alfalfa
awfully
affined
affinal
ad finem
Alfonso
affoord
affront
alfaquí
alforja
afforce
at first
alférez
aefauld
at fault
Al-Fayed
aggrace
aggrade
aggrate
at grade
afghani
algebra
angicos
Al Green
aggress
Algiers
augment
✧anglice
anguine
angling
anguish
Anglian
anglist
anglify
angrily
angekok
angelic
Angolan
angular
angelus
argulus
Angelou
alginic
anginal
angioma
Algeria
argyria
augural
augurer
angerly
algesia
Augusta
✧auguste
algesis
✧arguses
augitic
algates
Angevin
ashrama
at heart
athwart
adhibit
aphides
athleta
achieve
athlete
Achaean
ash-heap
awheels
aphagia
aphthae

atheise
atheize
athrill
atheism
Achaian
atheist
aphelia
Athalia
aphylly
ashamed
aphonia
aphonic
Ashanti
athanor
Ashford
ash-hole
Ashdown
atheous
acharya
adharma
Amharic
acharné
Acheron
adherer
athirst
ashtray
aphasia
aphasic
aphesis
aphetic
aphotic
Achates
Achtung
à cheval
ashiver
Alhazen
agitate
alidade
animate
Aligarh
alizari
✧abigail
agitato
animato
Arimasp
alicant
amiable
amiably
acid dye
Ariadne
abidden
amildar
aniseed
aliment
Aricept®
abide by
agilely
atingle
a-tishoo
atishoo
a-rights
apishly
aniline
asinine
axinite
abiding
animism
✧apician
A Vision
Azilian
Akihito

asinico
animist
ability
acidify
acidity
agility
anility
aridity
avidity
Abidjan
axillae
axillar
arillus
axially
anionic
Asianic
avionic
aliened
alienee
aliunde
Avignon
aginner
alienor
Arizona
acinose
adipose
a bit off
a minori
aciform
aliform
aviform
acinous
a pip out
alimony
aripple
at issue
Ariosto
abiosis
aliases
Arieses
ariosos
ab intra
arietta
abiotic
Asiatic
Amistad
ariette
aristae
aviette
agister
agistor
Alister
aviator
aristos
Avicula
azimuth
aliquot
adjudge
abjoint
adjoint
adjunct
abjurer
adjourn
Anjouan
awkward
asklent
alkalic
alkalis
ack emma
askance
alkanet

anklong
acknown
Alkoran
askaris
askesis
anklung
ask over
aulnage
all-hail
all ears
at least
axle-box
alledge
allseed
allheal
all-seer
allness
ailment
Allegra
✧alleged
allegge
anlagen
allegro
alleger
anlages
all that
awlbird
all-time
allying
ableism
ableist
allelic
Atlanta
aclinic
Allende
allonge
allonym
ailanto
aplanat
aplenty
all-good
all told
all done
all's one
Aalborg
all-work
at large
aileron
allurer
allergy
aplasia
Allison
atlases
ailette
ad litem
ablator
all-star
ally-tor
ally-taw
alluvia
AS level
all over
all-over
allowed
alleyed
allayer
all eyes
Alma-Ata
armband
army ant
ad modum

Asmoday
aimless
armless
armrest
au mieux
alms-fee
armiger
Almaine
armoire
Acmeism
Acmeist
armilla
A A Milne
alms-man
ammonia
Armenia
almanac
ammonal
ad manum
almoner
almonry
armhole
armlock
Almeria
Armoric
almirah
admiral
ammiral
Aymaran
admirer
Aymaras
ammeter
armfuls
armoury
Annabel
annicut
awnless
alnager
Alnwick
annuity
annelid
Agnelli
annular
annulus
annulet
agnamed
agnomen
amniote
aeneous
Arnaout
Aintree
agnosia
amnesia
amnesic
amnesty
annatta
agnatic
Annette
annatto
arnotto
annates
adnexal
annoyed
annoyer
abomasa
abomasi
avocado
amorant
anomaly
apogamy
amoebic

amoebae
amoebas
acouchi
acouchy
avoider
apogeal
apogean
at one go
alonely
anorexy
aloofly
abought
alongst
amongst
apothem
A N Other
another
aconite
adonise
adonize
agonise
agonize
amosite
anodise
anodize
atomise
atomize
azotise
azotize
adoring
abolish
Anouilh
amorini
alodial
asocial
alodium
amorism
Anobium
atomism
✧aeolian
aeonian
amorino
agogics
agonist
amorist
apomict
atomist
Aboukir
aboulia
Avonlea
apollos
apoplex
anosmia
anosmic
acorned
à pointe
as of now
amorosa
apocope
axolotl
amoroso
amorous
apodous
atokous
azotous
apology
à compte
arousal
arouser
anoeses
anoesis

aloetic
anoetic
adopted
abortee
adoptee
à moitié
à portée
✧apostle
apostil
adopter
agoutis
avoutry
apolune
anonyma
acolyte
anodyne
acolyth
Alphard
applaud
appease
at peace
appeach
asprawl
asphalt
aspidia
aspread
adpress
Alpheus
appress
at press
applied
appuied
apprise
apprize
Alphito
applier
appoint
at point
amplify
ampulla
appulse
appalti
appalto
amphora
approve
approof
alphorn
asprout
asperge
asperse
apparel
apperil
aspirin
apports
apparat
Aspasia
al pasto
apposer
ampassy
amputee
ampoule
asphyxy
acquest
acquire
acquite
acquist
asquint
Adriana
air-raid
airward
acreage

airbase
air-lane
air rage
airwave
arriage
aureate
abroach
air-bath
air taxi
airmail
air-rail
air mass
airways
arrears
abreact
abreast
already
aerobic
Arrabal
Aerobus®
Acrobat®
acrobat
aerobot
Acre Bay
auricle
African
aurochs
apricot
abridge
acridin
acridly
airhead
arreede
arriéré
air-bell
air-cell
arriero
airless
agraffe
a trifle
aerogel
acrogen
alright
Abraham
airship
air shot
airshow
à droite
airline
air mile
airside
airtime
'Arryish
airsick
air sign
arraign
air kiss
air-kiss
air miss
airlift
aureity
aurelia
acrylic
Acrilan®
airflow
airglow
air play
aurally
acromia
Ahriman
Aaronic
arrange
adrenal
acronym
aureola
abrooke
airhole
aureole
a priori
airlock
air-cool
airfoil
airboat
airport
agrapha
Agrippa
atropia
atropin
apropos
Atropos
atrophy
Airdrie
aurorae
auroral
airdrop
air-trap
auroras
aircrew
airprox
acrasia
akrasia
atresia
agrised
arrased
agraste
au reste
aerosol
acratic
aerated
aurated
airstop
acroter
aerator
aground
Air Pump
air-pump
atriums
agravic
arrival
arrowed
apraxia
apraxic
✧**abraxas**
arrayal
arrayer
arroyos
abrazos
assuage
asswage
at stake
abstain
apsidal
apsides
assiege
Auslese
austere
arsheen
abscess
assagai
assegai
al segno
assigns
at sight
Aeschna
abscind
abscise
arshine
auspice
✧**aisling**
absciss
absolve
Absalom
assumed
arsenic
absence
absinth
arsenal
arsines
abscond
alsoone
Austria
Austric
assured
✧**austral**
also-ran
assurer
apsaras
Alsatia
ansated
assault
assever
assayer
assizer
assizes
althaea
astrand
abthane
actuate
amtrack
attract
actuary
actable
astable
at table
Antibes
autobus
attaboy
attacca
antacid
anticke
article
attaché
autocue
autocar
Actaeon
Aetnean
Art Deco
Antwerp
antbear
actress
aptness
artless
antient
attuent
antefix
Antigua
antigen
ant-eggs
antigay
antbird
antliae
Astaire
astride
attrite
attuite
at twice
Althing
ant-hill
asteism
antlion
act dido
astrict
attaint
attrist
astelic
astilbe
antilog
astylar
artsman
Artemis
at times
attempt
automat
autumny
actinia
antenna
Antonia
actinic
attonce
actinal
antonym
autonym
actinon
Antonio
attones
anthoid
astroid
asthore
art-song
Antioch
Art Monk
artwork
art form
althorn
aftmost
Anthony
autopsy
antique
apteria
asteria
altered
asterid
alterne
Astarte
apteral
act drop
Antares
Anterus
Art Brut
anthrax
apteryx
actorly
autarky
altesse
artiste
artisan
attaskt
aptotic
astatic
astatki
astound
autovac
ActiveX
antiwar
altezza
abusage
adulate
ajutage
asudden
asunder
Abu Mena
azurean
azulejo
aculeus
acutely
aquafer
aquifer
ague-fit
aquafit
ahungry
acushla
Anushka
alumina
abusive
alunite
amusive
azurine
azurite
amusing
alumish
alumium
abusion
✧**aquilon**
alumnae
alumnus
anurous
aqueous
aquaria
Al Unser
aquatic
abutted
à quatre
abuttal
abutter
arugula
as usual
aquiver
aquavit
alveary
advices
advance
alveole
alveoli
adverse
advised
adviser
advisor
ad vivum
akvavit
at worst
anxiety
anxious
Auxerre
auxesis
auxetic
amylase
Aly Bain
anyways
amygdal
amylene
anywhen
anytime
anywise
✧azymite
acyclic
abysmal
amyloid
anyroad
amylose
any more
azygous
azymous
anybody
abyssal
alyssum
asylums
anziani
Bharati
bradawl
bravado
blatant
blabbed
brabble
bramble
beanbag
Baalbek
blaubok
blabber
beatbox
brambly
braccia
Blanche
braccio
bearcat
bias-cut
branchy
bearded
braided
branded
beardie
board up
bladder
boarder
brander
blandly
by and by
by-and-by
Boateng
brasero
blaze up
braless
beanery
beavery
bravely
bravery
beaufin
beaufet
boat-fly
bhangra
bragged
brangle
blagger
brachia
beached
bear hug
blather
brachet
brashly
Baalite
beading
beaming
bearing
beating
biasing
blazing
boating
bracing
beamish
bearish
beauish
boarish
biaxial
Baalism
brasier
brazier
beamily
beatify
blacken
bracken
blanket
bracket
blackly
blankly
Braille
beagler
brawler
beamlet
Bramley
beadman
boatman
Bradman
Brahman
Brahmin
brained
brawned
braunch
beatnik
bran-new
✧**blarney**
by a nose
beat off
bravoes
bear out
beat out
blawort
bran-pie
bear pit
Beatrix
beam sea
biassed
beats me
bransle
brassie
Brassaï
Branson
brasset
bran tub
blasted
blatted
boasted
beastie
brantle
brattle
blaster
blatter
boaster
beastly
bravura
Bhagwan
Branwen
Babbage
bobtail
babiche
babuche
Baby Doc
Bobadil
babudom
bebeeru
bobbery
Babygro®
babying
bobbing
babyish
bobbish
Babiism
babuism
Babbit's
Babrius
✧**babbitt**
biblist
bobbitt
bubukle
bobsled
Babylon
babbler
bubbler
bobbles
bubalis
Bubalus
Bubbles
bibelot
bubinga
bubonic
Bob Hope
baboosh
bibcock
baby oil
Babesia
baby-sit
babassu
Bob Nudd
baccara
baclava
baccare
baccate
backare
becharm
bicycle
back-end
buckeye
buckeen
Beckett
✧**bacchic**
Bacchae
backhoe
bacchii
Beckham
Bacchus
buccina
backing
bucking
buckish
biccies
bickies
bycoket
bucolic
backlog
bacilli
baculum
bicolor
buckler
backlot
baconer
becloud
bichord
back off
buckoes
back out
back pay
bicorne
Bacardi®
buckram
bucardo
back row
back-row
bécasse
bucksom
backset
backsaw
bucksaw
backsey
bycatch
because
bedward
bedwarf
badmash
bedbath
budmash
bid fair
bedfast
body bag
bidie-in
budgero
budge up
badness
bad news
budless
bad debt
baddest
bed-rest
bodeful
bedight
bad shot
bad show
bedrite
bedside
bedtime
bedding
bidding
bodying
budding
baddish
bedtick
Badajoz
bodikin
bedeman
Bedford
bedsore
bedrock
bed-work
bedroll
bad form
bedroom
budworm
bed down
badious
bedpost
bedropt
bidarka
bederal
bodhran
bodhrán
bad trip
bad luck
✧**bedouin**
bedevil
Bedawin
buddy up
bedazed

bedizen
beerage
brewage
bee balm
beefalo
blewart
blesbok
breccia
Brescia
blended
breaded
breadth
Brendan
bleeder
blender
breeder
breveté
brewers'
brewery
Brer Fox
beet-fly
✧**bren gun**
beer gut
Beecham
beef-ham
brecham
beechen
blether
beehive
bee-kite
beeline
brewing
blemish
brevier
blewits
brevity
break in
break-in
bee-skep
break up
break-up
breaker
bleakly
bee-glue
beer-mat
beesome
bee-moth
brewpub
bleeper
bleared
blessed
bless me!
bheesty
beef tea
Boeotia
bletted
breathe
Beeston
bleater
breathy
Boer War
beeswax
bye-byes
beffana
buffalo
bifocal
buffing
baffler
bifilar
buffoon
Bifrost
beghard
big band
big-band
boggard
bogland
baggage
big game
big name
bugbane
buggane
✧**big bang**
bagwash
big hair
big cats
boggart
bag lady
beggary
bugaboo
Baghdad
bighead
big deal
bogbean
bugbear
bagless
bigness
Big Beat
bigfeet
biggest
big shot
bagpipe
begrime
beguile
beguine
béguine
big time
big-time
bagging
begging
bugging
by going
big fish
biggish
bogyism
baggies
bagnios
baguios
baggily
Big Blue
boggler
Biggles
bogyman
begonia
beginne
bigener
bygones
bug-word
big-note
begloom
bighorn
bog down
Big Four
bog moss
bugloss
✧**bigfoot**
bugwort
begorra
begored
bagarre
big tree
bog iron
bagasse
bigoted
bigotry
bagfuls
Bagpuss
big guns
bug-eyed
Bahrain
by heart
Bahadur
behight
Bahaite
Bahaism
bohrium
Bahaist
Bahamas
behoove
behaved
brigand
brigade
Baisaki
Britart
brioche
blinded
brinded
builded
brindle
build in
build up
build-up
blinder
builder
blindly
buirdly
bride it
boilery
bribery
brimful
briefly
bring in
bring on
bring up
bringer
Bridget
Brighid
blither
brights
blighty
bainite
bailiff
baiting
Beijing
boiling
briming
brinish
British
brinjal
beinked
blinked
brickie
brickle
bricken
brisken
blinker
brisket
briskly
bridled
baillie
bridler
brimmed
brimmer
beignet
bairnly
bricole
boil off
bridoon
bail out
bail-out
bailout
Britpop
briared
briered
britska
bhistee
blintze
bristle
brittle
Bristol
Britten
built-in
built-up
blister
blitter
bristly
brittly
brisure
briquet
britzka
blitzed
Blitzen
bejewel
baklava
Bukhara
beknave
bukshee
bok choy
Bakunin
beknown
bikeway
belgard
bollard
ballade
bal paré
beldame
Beltane
bullace
bullate
bulwark
Balmain
ballant
ballast
Belfast
bull ant
balsamy
biliary
bullary
bilobed
belt bag
belabor
bilobar
bullbat
bold bow
ball-boy
bell-boy
bulk-buy
Baluchi
Bulldog®
bulldog
baladin
bell end
believe
Belleek
balneal
baleful
bulb fly
Bologna
bolshie
bellhop
belcher
bulghur
bellied
bullied
bulgine
balding
balking
balling
belting
belying
billing
bolting
bulging
bulling
baldish
bullish
Bellini
ballium
Belgium
Belgian
billion
bullion
billies
balmily
bulkily
bell jar
bulimia
bulimic
bilimbi
bellman
beltman
billman
bulimus
Belinda
✧**balance**
balancé
Balanus
baloney
boloney
Bellona
biltong
bullock
balloon
bellows
bilboes
bilious
bulbous
bale out
belt out
bulk out
balcony
billowy
bull pen
bull-pup
baldric
Belarus
boleros
balista
boluses
belated
bolo tie
bolster
✧**boletus**
bulrush
Bolivia
✧**beloved**
bi-level
✧**bolivar**
Baldwin
beltway
belayed
billy-oh
bombard
bumbaze
bummalo
by means
bombast
bemedal
bimodal
bamming
bombing
bumming
bumping
bambini
bambino
bumpily
bumpkin
bumbler
bomblet
bimanal
bombora
bump off
bummock
bum roll
bomb out
bum-boat
bump out
bemired
bemused
bumster
bemouth
bemazed
bandana
Band-aid®
band-aid
bin card
Bonnard
bandage
bondage
beneath
bone ash
Bengali
bunraku
bone-bed
bunk bed
bonobos
band-box
binocle
bone-dry
bansela
benzene
banteng
bonkers
Bennett
bandeau
bindery
benefic
baneful
benefit
benight
benthic
bunched
banshee
Bentham
bencher
benthos
bunches
bandied
benzine
Bonaire
bonfire
banding
banging
banking
banning
banting
bending
binding
binning
bonding
bonking
bunting
Bendigo
bandits
bonnily
Ben Okri
Bangkok
bangled
bundler
bungler
bendlet
Benelux
banally
Bentley®
bonamia
benamed
benomyl
bondman
benempt
bynempt
bonanza
bananas
bandora
benzoic
bandore
benzole
bang off
bunk off
Bon Jovi
bandook
bannock
bundook
benzoyl
bone-oil
benzoin
bonjour
bonsoir
banjoes
bang out
bon goût
bandrol
Banares
Benares
✧**banksia**
benison
bonasus
boneset
band-saw
bonitos
bandura
Bandung
Ben Gunn
banquet
Banbury
Bunbury
biodata
brocard
brocade
brocage
brokage
bromate
buoyage
Bronach
Bronagh
biomass
buoyant
bloubok
boombox
boot boy
bronchi
broncho
broncos
bootcut
blotchy
blooded
brodded
Blondie
Blondel
broaden
broider
brooder
blow-dry
broadly
bookend
biotech
Boolean
booze-up
biogeny
brokery
bookful
blowfly
brogged
blowgun
brought
brothel
brochan
biochip
biophor
brother
boodied
boogied
biocide
biotite
bromide
bromine
blowing
booking
booming
boozing
broking
bookish
boorish
bromism
bionics
boonies
boozily
blocked
brocked
block in
brodkin
blocker
brocket
brockit
bootleg
broiler
booklet
boomlet
Bromley
bookman
Boorman
bloomer
brommer
Brownie®
✧brownie
boo-word
biotope
blow off
blow-off
boobook
blot out
blow out
blow-out
book out
boot out
biology
blooper
blowsed
bloosme
booksie
blossom
blouson
Bronson
browser
bloated
blotted
bloater
blotter
booster
Beowulf
biofuel
Bronwen
biotype
blowzed
bronzed
bronzen
bronzer
Buphaga
biplane
byplace
bepearl
bipedal
baptise
baptize
baptism
✧**baptist**
bepaint
bipolar
beprose
bequest
Barbara
bergama
barmaid
Bernard
barbate
barrace
barrage
bereave
burgage
bardash
berdash
burdash
biriani
biryani
barrack
bar tack
bargain
Bormann
Bergamo
bureaus
burlaps

bureaux
Barbary
Barnaby
bursary
byrlady
bark-bed
boracic
baracan
barocco
borscht
bird-dog
boredom
Berbera
Bursera
bur-reed
burweed
bergère
Burmese
berserk
barbell
bar meal
borrell
burrell
barge in
burgeon
barrens
borders
burdens
burgess
bargest
berceau
burp gun
by right
burghal
burghul
burrhel
barchan
barkhan
birchen
burthen
Bircher
birchir
✧burgher
Barthes
berried
bar line
berline
Bernice
bornite
✧barking
barring
birding
birling
burning
burying
burnish
Bernini
birlinn
barrico
burrito
barrier
barrios
Berlioz
barmkin
barilla
burbler
burglar
Burnley
Bergman
birdman
byreman

boronia
Byronic
baronne
Burundi
borings
baronet
barbola
barwood
barcode
bar none
burdock
barn owl
bar-room
Barbour®
burnous
burn out
burn-out
barmpot
✧baroque
Bertram
bar-iron
barista
bartsia
bortsch
biretta
barytic
bursted
Barotse
burette
borstal
baryton
bursten
burst-up
burster
barytes
Barbuda
Bermuda
barbule
bordure
borough
B Traven
Berowne
bergylt
borazon
bastard
bustard
beshame
beslave
bespake
bespate
boscage
boskage
bus lane
bosvark
bestain
bus pass
bass-bar
best boy
best buy
basoche
bush-cat
basidia
bush dog
besides
bespeed
bestead
best end
beseeke
besiege
beseech
bespeak

Boswell
besmear
base fee
bashful
bush-fly
bastide
beshine
bespice
byssine
bashing
basting
bushing
busking
bussing
busting
busying
bestick
ba'spiel
bestial
bestill
busgirl
bossism
bastion
Bosnian
bushido
bustier
bassist
besaint
bossily
Bishkek
bashlik
basilar
bustler
bas-bleu
besomed
bosomed
baseman
best man
✧bushman
basenji
basinet
byssoid
beshone
bespoke
bestorm
bassoon
base out
besport
bespout
bistort
bush pig
bestrid
bistred
bistros
beshrew
bestrew
bostryx
bush tea
Basotho
bus stop
boshter
bushtit
basqued
bascule
bismuth
bestuck
biscuit
bosquet
bit-rate
bit-part
bateaux

Bethany
batable
Bath bun
betided
Beth Din
bottega
betread
butt-end
beteeme
be there
between
bittern
battero
bathers
battels
Batten's
betters
bitless
bitters
butment
battery
butlery
buttery
by the by
betight
bitch up
botch up
botcher
butcher
batch it
but that
but what
Bettina
betaine
bottine
batting
batwing
betting
bitting
by-thing
batfish
bethink
battill
betwixt
betaken
betoken
bottled
botulin
bottle-o
battler
bottler
bathmic
bitumed
batsman
bitumen
betimes
by times
bath mat
botanic
bitonal
butanol
bothole
bettong
betroth
bittock
buttock
bittour
bottoms
buttons
butt out
bottony

buttony
butyric
botargo
by turns
batiste
bathtub
betitle
battuta
bethumb
bethump
bathyal
bruhaha
boutade
Blu-Tack®
Bauhaus
blubbed
blue bag
✧bourbon
blubber
blue box
bluecap
bouncer
bounded
Brundle
bounden
bourdon
bound to
bound up
blunder
✧boulder
bounder
bourder
blue-eye
bluefin
bluffer
blue fox
bluffly
blue gum
bludger
blunger
Bourgas
bruchid
brushed
bauchle
bouchée
brush up
brush-up
Blücher
blucher
blusher
Boucher
brusher
blushet
bauxite
brucine
brucite
blueing
bousing
bruting
blueish
brutish
bruxism
bouvier
brutify
blue jay
bourkha
bruckle
blunker
bouilli
bourlaw
Brummie

brummer
bausond
boudoir
brumous
brusque
baudric
blurred
bourrée
blue-rot
Boursin
bruiser
blue-sky
bluette
bluster
boulter
blue tit
bluntly
bouquet
brulyie
brulzie
Bovidae
bevvied
bivalve
bivious
buvette
bivouac
bow-hand
bow wave
bowyang
bowlder
bowhead
bawbees
bowbent
bowlful
bowshot
bow-tied
bowline
bow-side
bawling
bowling
bawdily
bawdkin
bywoner
bowknot
bewhore
bawcock
bawl out
bowl out
bewitch
by water
box-calf
box-haul
box beam
box seat
box tent
BMX bike
box file
box kite
box-fish
Bexhill
boxwood
boxroom
box-coat
box-tree
box-iron
boxfuls
boy band
buy-back
bay salt
buyable
bay leaf

Brython
bay-line
bay-tine
boy-girl
buy into
bayonet
boyhood
Boyzone
✧boycott
buy a pup
buy over
Bryozoa
buzzard
bazzazz
bezzazz
bizzazz
buzzcut
bez-tine
buzzing
bizonal
bazooka
buzz off
bezique
Bizerta
bizarre
buzz saw
bazouki
buzz-wig
chalaza
chamade
charade
clavate
cranage
cyanate
chapati
Chagall
clarain
charact
clamant
coal-bed
crabbed
chambré
chaebol
chamber
clabber
clamber
crabber
crabbit
coal-box
chalcid
chancre
chancel
chancer
Chaucer
chances
claucht
chancey
Chandra
Claudia
Chaldee
czardom
Claudio
chaddar
chaddor
chalder
cladder
csárdás
czardas
chapess
co-agent
chapeau

chateau
château
cramesy
chametz
chaffer
chamfer
chaufer
charged
clagged
cragged
changer
charger
clanger
clangor
charges
coal gas
claught
Cyathea
cyathia
coachee
clachan
clasher
coacher
crathur
cyathus
czarina
chalice
chamise
Clarice
coalise
Coalite®
coalize
cyanide
cyanine
cyanise
cyanite
cyanize
ceasing
charing
chasing
coaming
coating
craving
crazing
clayish
clarini
coaxial
cranial
charism
cladism
cranium
czarism
Chadian
clarion
chamiso
clarino
clavier
crazier
crazies
chariot
cladist
czarist
charily
charity
clarify
clarity
crazily
charkha
clarkia
cracked
crackle

crankle
crack on
chalk up
crack up
crackup
crank up
clacker
cracker
crack it
crackly
challie
✧charlie
challah
challan
Chaplin
crawler
Chablis
challis
Charles
chamlet
chaplet
✧charley
Crawley
chasmic
charmed
chasmed
clammed
crammed
chasmal
chapman
coalman
charmer
chaumer
claimer
crammer
Cranmer
chained
Clannad
chaunce
chaunge
crannog
craunch
✧channel
charnel
chain up
channer
clapnet
crab-nut
chalone
chayote
cladode
cracowe
claw off
chabouk
coal oil
crab-oil
clamour
chamois
claroes
crap out
chanoyu
champac
chapped
clapped
cramped
crapped
chappie
charpie
crappie
champak
chappal

claypan
crampon
clamper
clapper
clasper
clay-pit
coalpit
coal pot
crampet
crampit
charpoy
charqui
charred
Chabrol
chagrin
classic
Chassid
classed
clausal
chanson
coarsen
chassis
classis
crassly
chaotic
clastic
chatted
chaetae
chantie
Chantal
chattel
coastal
chasten
chanter
chantor
chapter
charter
chatter
clatter
coal tar
✧coaster
coal tit
chantey
chantry
coagula
chalutz
chauvin
cabbala
cabbage
cab-rank
cob wall
cabbagy
cubicle
cubical
Cebidae
Cabrera
cubless
Cobbett
Coblenz
cob pipe
cabling
cubbing
cubbish
Cabeiri
cobbler
Cabinda
✧cabinet
cubhood
caboose
cobloaf
cab-tout

ciboria
Cabiric
cabaret
cubital
cubitus
C G Bruce
cob-swan
cabezon
cachaça
cockade
co-chair
cicadae
cacodyl
cicadas
cockeye
cachexy
cacoepy
Cocagne
cocaine
coctile
cycling
coction
cyclist
cockily
Cecilia
cochlea
cichlid
cockled
cackler
cicalas
cacolet
cacumen
coconut
ca' canny
✧cockney
coccoid
cuckold
cycloid
cyclone
Cecrops
✧cyclops
cocopan
cockpit
cacique
cockshy
cocotte
cecitis
cocoyam
cedrate
cadrans
cadeaux
caducei
codicil
codices
Cedrela
cudweed
Cadmean
cudbear
caddice
cedrine
codeine
codding
codling
caddish
codfish
cadmium
cedilla
codilla
cadelle
codille
coddler

cadenza
cadence
cadency
Caddoan
cedared
✧cidaris
codetta
cadaver
caddyss
chelate
cremate
crenate
cue ball
crew bus
Clew Bay
crew cut
Cheadle
creedal
Cheddar
cheders
crewels
✧clement
credent
Chengdu
Cheng-tu
chéchia
Czechic
Chechen
Chekhov
coeliac
chemise
crevice
cieling
cherish
chewink
cnemial
caesium
chemism
cretism
Caelian
credits
chekist
chemist
Cheviot
coexist
clerisy
checked
cleeked
check in
check-in
check up
check-up
checker
cleekit
clerkly
Caedmon
crewman
creamer
cleanse
creance
chetnik
clean up
clean-up
cleaner
chesnut
cleanly
Cremona
cheloid
ctenoid
chelone
coelome

coehorn
cheroot
chew out
cheapie
creepie
cheapen
cheeper
creeper
cheaply
chetrum
chevron
cheerio
cheer up
clear up
clear-up
cheerer
clearer
cheerly
clearly
Chelsea
cheesed
chessel
creosol
cremsin
creaser
chesses
cresset
creeshy
creatic
chested
crested
cheetah
creatin
creston
cheater
Chester
✧creator
caestus
caesura
caerule
cleruch
coequal
chequer
cherubs
cleaved
chervil
Chesvan
cleaver
café bar
caffein
caffila
coffret
cognate
cage-cup
cognise
cognize
cogging
cogence
cogener
cogency
cagoule
cohabit
cohibit
coherer
chicana
chikara
chicane
climate
coinage
crinate
Chicago

✧chicano
cui malo?
caimans
cuirass
clipart
Coimbra
climbed
cribbed
cribble
climber
cribber
coin box
childed
chidden
childer
✧chindit
childly
✧chimera
Cairene
chimere
✧chinese
Chilean
chime in
clivers
crivens
cliffed
clip-fed
coiffed
chiffon
chiefer
chiefly
chiefry
cringle
chigger
clinger
cringer
cliché'd
cain-hen
chikhor
chip hat
crimina
chiliad
Cainite
caitive
crimine
crinite
cuisine
caitiff
ceiling
chiding
coining
ceilidh
crimini
Chilian
coition
chilies
crinkle
chicken
clicker
clinker
clicket
cricket
crickey
crinkly
chilled
chillum
Caitlín
criollo
chiller
chillis
Chislev

chimley
crimmer
cairned
Chianti
chignon
chimney
cricoid
crinoid
crinose
chip off
chibouk
✧chinook
cui bono?
clip-ons
chicory
chipped
clipped
crimped
chippie
clippie
crimple
cripple
Crippen
✧crispin
chipper
chirper
clipper
crimper
crisper
crisply
chirrup
chiasma
chiasmi
crissum
caisson
crimson
cuisser
chiasms
chipset
clifted
cristae
cuittle
Clinton
chitter
clitter
critter
crittur
chintzy
chi kung
cliquey
chinwag
cajoler
cojones
cajeput
cajuput
coked-up
cake tin
collard
ciliate
collage
collate
calpack
callant
calmant
Calgary
✧calvary
ciliary
colobid
calibre
colibri
Caliban

Calabar
caliber
Celebes
colobus
call-box
call-boy
culicid
caliche
calicle
calycle
calices
calicos
calyces
culices
cylices
Calicut
colicky
celadon
caldera
college
Caltech
✧colleen
Culdees
Colbert
collect
culvert
✧cologne
colugos
culchie
Calchas
culmina
cullied
calcine
calcite
collide
calling
colling
culling
coldish
coltish
cultish
calcium
cultism
cullion
Calvino
collier
Celsius
✧collins
'cellist
cellist
cultist
calcify
calumba
Columba
calomel
columel
Colombo
✧calamus
chlamys
calumet
calumny
colonic
colonel
calando
Calanus
calends
colones
Cellnet®
colloid
calzone
cellose

call off
calzoni
callous
call out
call-out
calipee
cold pig
calypso
caloric
chloric
✧calorie
chloral
caldron
caltrap
caltrop
culprit
celesta
celosia
celeste
colossi
calotte
Colette
culotte
calathi
colitis
cole tit
calluna
cellule
collude
culture
calculi
Calmuck
colours
coloury
caliver
cold war
C S Lewis
calyxes
caloyer
campana
command
compand
compage
compare
comrade
Campari
cembali
cembalo
cymbalo
combats
compass
compact
compart
compast
company
camp-bed
Cimabué
comical
Comecon
cimices
comedic
comedos
commend
compend
commère
compère
compete
compear
compeer
comment
cumbent

campery
come for
camogie
camphor
cumshaw
combine
compile
camping
comping
cambial
cambism
cambium
Comtism
campion
Comtian
cambist
Comtist
camaïeu
Camilla
cimelia
camelid
✧complin
cumulus
✧camelot
complot
come low
complex
camelry
camwood
C E M Joad
camboge
commode
commote
commove
componé
compose
compote
come off
come-off
commodo
✧commons
camp out
comb out
comb-out
come out
comfort
comport
compost
compony
comique
✧camorra
Cumbria
cambric
camerae
cambrel
cameral
camaron
Comoran
cumarin
cameras
Comoros
comfrey
comitia
cometic
comital
cami-top
compter
commune
commute
compute
combust

Words marked ✧ can also be spelled with one or more capital letters

cumquat
cantala
cantata
Candace
cantate
centage
centare
concave
con game
connate
cuneate
cannach
canbank
contain
centavo
Cinzano®
centaur
canvass
cineast
contact
cenacle
conacre
conical
cynical
conidia
Canidae
cantdog
candela
contend
concede
convene
conteck
conceal
congeal
conseil
canteen
concern
condemn
contemn
concedo
confess
conkers
candent
conceit
concent
concept
concert
confect
confest
congest
conject
connect
consent
content
contest
context
convect
convent
convert
cankery
cannery
cindery
conifer
Cynthia
conchae
conchie
conchal
canthus
conches
candida
cantina

candied
Candice
Candide
centile
centime
concise
confide
confine
coniine
connive
convive
✧**canning**
canting
conning
cunning
confirm
cantion
condign
consign
cantico
centimo
candies
congius
consist
convict
cannily
Canajan
canakin
canikin
Conakry
canella
canulae
candler
canulas
cantlet
conflux
canonic
centner
✧**canonry**
Cantona
canzona
✧**concord**
canzone
cineole
condole
condone
connote
console
convoke
cone off
canzoni
candock
conform
conjoin
con moto
candour
contour
cannons
cantons
Connors
consols
concoct
conk out
consort
contort
Canopic
conspue
Canopus
cinerea
conaria
centric

cantred
centred
congree
congrue
cantref
central
control
centrum
cinerin
con brio
cantrip
cane rat
contrat
concrew
canasta
cunette
conster
conatus
cannula
cingula
contund
censure
conduce
confuse
confute
conjure
consume
contuse
censual
conquer
canfuls
concuss
conduct
conduit
consult
can buoy
century
concupy
conjury
condyle
crotala
chorale
cromack
coolant
crombec
Crombie®
cool bag
choc-bar
clobber
clotbur
crowbar
clog box
cool box
cloacae
cloacal
cooncan
clodded
clouded
crowded
chondre
chordae
chordee
croodle
crowdie
coondog
chondri
chordal
Croydon
chobdar
chowder
clowder

crowder
cholera
choreic
close in
close-in
close on
crocein
close to
choke up
close up
close-up
crop-ear
choreus
cholent
close by
closely
clovery
cookery
coopery
chometz
cropful
clogged
clogger
clothed
chochos
clothes
crochet
choc-ice
choline
chopine
chorine
closing
cloying
coolish
chorial
chorism
chorion
chorizo
crosier
crozier
chorist
clocked
crocked
crooked
chookie
cloak in
clock in
clock on
clock up
crock up
chocker
clocker
croaker
crocket
ceòl mór
crowned
choanae
crooner
crowner
crownet
choenix
choroid
cook off
cool off
cookout
crop out
chopped
cropped
croupon
chopper
cropper

crouper
Choisya
crossed
cloison
chooser
crosser
Croesus
Chomsky
choosey
crossly
Croatia
clotted
clouted
chortle
Clootie
coontie
crottle
crow-toe
crottin
croûton
cooktop
crop top
clotter
clouter
crofter
✧**choctaw**
choltry
closure
cloture
croquis
croquet
Chogyal
cap-case
caprate
cupcake
cup mark
cupgall
captain
capable
capably
Cape Cod
capuche
copycat
capuera
cypsela
cuphead
Cepheus
cypress
coppery
copshop
copaiba
copaiva
cup-tied
caprice
caprine
capsize
captive
coppice
cuprite
cyprine
capping
copying
c-spring
cupping
copyism
Capsian
caption
✧cyprian
copyist
Cypriot
caprify

Capella
cupeled
cupola'd
copulae
capelin
cipolin
copular
cupolar
cupular
copulas
capelet
Capulet
co-pilot
copilot
Coppola
caproic
cap rock
copious
cup moss
cuprous
copepod
cap-a-pie
cap-à-pie
caporal
caperer
capital
Capitol
capitan
capstan
capsule
capture
capouch
capfuls
cupfuls
coquina
coquito
cariama
Circaea
curtana
carcake
carcase
carfare
carnage
cartage
cirrate
cordage
cordate
corkage
cornage
corrade
corsage
curtate
curtaxe
curvate
car-wash
currach
curragh
carjack
car park
carrack
cure-all
curtail
certain
curtain
corsair
carcass
corcass
carract
currant
cerebra
carabid

curable
carabin
Cariban
corn bin
carabao
caribou
curaçoa
corncob
caroche
coracle
caracal
caracol
✧caracul
✧**curaçao**
Caracas
carices
Caradoc
corn dog
Corydon
CB radio
carbene
cariere
cortège
carrell
corbeil
corneal
Circean
carve up
carve-up
carneys
carrect
Corbett
cornett
correct
current
cardecu
corbeau
carvery
curtesy
corn-fed
careful
cartful
cornfly
corrida
Corsica
cardiac
carried
curried
carbide
carbine
carline
carmine
cervine
cordite
cornice
corsive
cortile
corvine
cursive
Cardiff
carding
carking
✧carling
carping
carving
cording
corking
curling
cursing
curving
carlish

Cornish
currish
cortili
car-sick
cerrial
cordial
Carlism
carrion
carrier
curlier
currier
curvier
carnies
Carlist
Corfiot
cornist
carnify
certify
cornily
curvity
Ctrl key
coralla
corella
corolla
circled
Carolyn
circlip
circler
curdler
carolus
corylus
circlet
corslet
corn law
caramba
ceramic
chromic
caramel
caromel
ceramal
chromel
cerumen
chromos
cork mat
caranna
Corinna
Corunna
chronic
corsned
carinae
Corinne
coronae
Corinth
coronal
chronon
coranto
Corinto
coroner
carinas
coronas
coronis
coronet
✧**carioca**
cordoba
✧córdoba
corpora
curiosa
car bomb
car-bomb
carload
cirsoid

cariole
carnose
cirrose
corrode
cart off
carlock
cork oak
car pool
car-pool
corn oil
cardoon
cartoon
cargoes
carious
cereous
cirrous
corious
cormous
curious
car-coat
carport
carroty
corrody
cursory
Corypha
coryphe
corn pit
corn rig
card row
cornrow
chrisom
cerasin
ceresin
Christo
✧**christy**
curtsey
carotid
cerated
curette
carotin
curator
caritas
carauna
curcuma
carouse
cornute
cornual
cornuto
carduus
circuit
corrupt
circusy
caravel
corival
caravan
corn van
caraway
cartway
Carlyle
carry on
carry-on
carry up
carry it
corozos
cascara
cassaba
cassata
cassava
✧costard
✧custard
cascade

costate
cuspate
Cossack
casuals
ciseaux
cash-box
cosh boy
cash cow
C K Stead
cistern
costean
coshery
costive
Cushite
cystine
casting
cissing
cosmism
cession
cushion
cassino
cashier
cushier
Cassius
casuist
cosmist
castled
case law
caseman
casemix
casinos
Cestoda
cestoid
cissoid
cystoid
cassone
cestode
custode
cast off
cast-off
cassock
castock
custock
caseous
ciscoes
customs
cast out
C P Scott
castory
custody
cesspit
caserne
castral
cesural
costrel
custrel
cas crom
cistron
Cesario
costume
cithara
cotland
citrate
cot case
cottage
cut-rate
Cathari
catwalk
cut back
cutback
catcall

cattalo
Cathars
cutlass
cattabu
coteaux
citable
cuticle
catechu
citadel
cotidal
cathead
cut dead
Cat's-eye®
cat's-eye
cithern
cittern
cat's-ear
cattery
cutlery
cut-offs
catched
catch me
catchen
catch on
catch up
catchup
catcher
catch it
catbird
catlike
citrine
cottise
cutline
catling
cutting
catfish
cattish
Cataian
cottier
catmint
cattily
catskin
cutikin
catalpa
cotylae
catalog
catelog
Catalan
cat-flap
catalos
cotyles
city man
Catania
cotinga
catenae
catenas
Cotonou
cathood
cottoid
cathode
cathole
cot-folk
cutwork
catworm
cutworm
Citroen®
cottown
cut down
cut-down
cat door
citrous

cuttoes
catboat
cottony
catapan
cat's-paw
coterie
catarrh
cateran
cut drop
caterer
catasta
cytosol
cytisus
cothurn
catsuit
citrusy
cut-over
catawba
CN Tower
cutaway
cat-eyed
Catayan
citizen
caudate
courage
couvade
crusade
chupati
crusado
cruzado
courant
clubbed
crumble
clubber
clumber
Courbet
crumbly
council
churchy
crunchy
could be
cruddle
chuddah
clued-up
chuddar
chunder
couldn't
clupeid
crubeen
couvert
cautery
crudely
chuffed
cludgie
Chungho
crushed
couchee
couchée
couthie
cough up
cougher
crusher
Cluniac
cauline
crucial
Couéism
caution
crucian
crusian
courier
chutist

Couéist
crucify
crudity
chuckie
chuckle
crunkle
chuck in
chuck up
caulker
chukker
clunker
chuck it
courlan
coupler
cruller
cruells
couplet
club-law
chumley
cruelly
cruelty
chummed
clubman
✧chunnel
churn up
chunner
chutney
coulomb
caulome
couloir
crumple
chuppah
clumper
crupper
crumpet
crumply
caudron
churrus
cruores
cruisie
counsel
courser
cruiser
courses
caustic
counted
crustae
crustal
count in
count on
chunter
cluster
clutter
coulter
counter
crustas
country
courtly
coupure
couture
couguar
caviare
cave art
ceviche
CD video
civvies
cavalla
covelet
cavally
cavalry
civilly

caveman
covered
cover in
cover up
cover-up
coveted
cuvette
cavetti
cavetto
cowhand
cowbane
cowhage
cow-calf
cowherb
cowherd
cow-weed
cowbell
cowheel
cowshed
cowbird
cowhide
co-write
cowling
cowfish
cowlick
cowgirl
cowslip
cowpoke
cowtree
cowitch
cow-dung
coxless
coxcomb
caymans
crybaby
clypeal
clypeus
coyness
cryogen
chylify
chymify
cryonic
✧cayenne
cry wolf
cry down
chymous
cryptic
cryptal
crystal
crypton
clyster
coyotes
cryptos
Cy Young
Cézanne
cozener
cazique
deaf aid
diabase
diapase
drayage
dead air
drabble
drabber
drag-bar
drawbar
drabbet
draw-boy
diascia
diarchy
duarchy

dyarchy
dvandva
diandry
dead end
dead-end
deadeye
drawers
dearest
dialect
deanery
drapery
dwarfed
dragged
draggle
draught
drachma
draw hoe
deathly
diamine
diarise
diarize
dealing
dialing
doating
drawing
deasiul
diarial
dualism
diarian
drapier
dialist
diarist
dualist
duality
dialled
dialler
drabler
drawler
dead men
drag-man
drayman
drainer
dragnet
draw-net
dearnly
diamond
Diasone®
Dracone®
dracone
draw off
deasoil
dragoon
diabolo
diazoes
drag out
draw out
drappie
deadpan
dead-pay
diagrid
diadrom
diagram
Dead Sea
dhansak
dead set
dead-set
drastic
dratted
draftee
diaster
drafter

draft ox
Dracula
dwarves
deary me
dialyse
dialyze
dobhash
debacle
débâcle
Debrett
dubiety
débride
debrief
dabbing
dibbing
dobbing
dubbing
dubnium
dabbity
dabbler
dibbler
do brown
dubious
dub poet
Deborah
dibasic
debased
debaser
Debussy
dibutyl
dabster
debater
debitor
debauch
debouch
decease
deciare
declare
dictate
dockage
ducdame
declaim
Duchamp
declass
duck-ant
docible
decibel
dice-box
duck-coy
decidua
decided
decadal
decider
decoder
decreed
✧dickens
duchess
decreet
decagon
decried
deceive
decline
dockise
dockize
ductile
decking
dicking
docking
ducking
ducting
decrial

diction
decrier
dacoity
deckled
decolor
ducally
decimal
decuman
decanal
Diconal®
Di Canio
decency
d'accord
dichord
decrown
doctors
deck out
duck out
du choix
decapod
decuple
decuria
decurve
decorum
Docetic
Docetae
docquet
decayed
decrypt
doddard
didicoi
didicoy
dudgeon
dudheen
Dodgems®
doddery
dodgery
duddery
dadoing
dodging
Dadaism
Dadaist
didakai
didakei
diddler
dedimus
daddock
Diderot
✧die hard
diehard
die game
due date
die back
dieback
die-cast
dietary
dyeable
dreaded
dreidel
Dresden
dreader
duendes
dreadly
deedful
Dreyfus
deep-fet
deep-fry
deer fly
dredger
diethyl
Djemila

dietine
dyeline
drevill
dietist
deedily
doeskin
duelled
dwelled
dueller
dweller
duellos
deerlet
dreamed
dream on
dream up
dreamer
dies non
dyewood
die-work
dye-work
die down
diedral
deep-sea
dressed
dress up
dresser
deep-set
deep-six
duetted
dyester
duettos
die away
die-away
doe-eyed
defraud
deflate
defiant
de facto
defacer
defocus
deficit
deflect
daffing
defying
duffing
defiler
defence
defense
definer
defunct
defrock
difform
defrost
deforce
defaste
diffuse
default
degrade
dogbane
dogeate
dog's age
dogvane
digraph
dog days
dogcart
digicam
dog-head
dog's-ear
digress
doggess
dog-belt

Words marked ✧ can also be spelled with one or more capital letters

doggery
dogship
digging
dogging
dogfish
doggish
dog-sick
dog-tick
dignify
dignity
dogskin
dogsled
digamma
Digynia
digonal
dog on it
dagwood
dogwood
doggone
doghole
dog rose
daglock
dogtown
dogbolt
dog-crab
doggrel
dogtrot
digital
Dog Star
degauss
digoxin
diglyph
dehisce
dribble
djibbah
dribber
dribbly
Deirdre
dwindle
drip-dry
Dhivehi
deiseal
drive-in
drive-by
dyingly
daisied
deified
deicide
driving
deifier
dailies
daimios
doitkin
drink in
drink to
drink up
drinker
Daimler®
driller
driblet
deiform
dripped
deictic
deistic
drip-tip
drifter
drizzle
drizzly
dejecta
dejeune
dukedom
De Klerk
dakoiti
dika-oil
deke out
Dakotas
deltaic
dullard
deleble
delible
Delibes
deluded
dolldom
deluder
Dalyell
delve in
dulness
diluent
doleful
delight
✧**delphic**
delphin
✧dolphin
dallied
dollied
delaine
dulcite
dilling
dollish
doltish
dullish
dulcian
dallier
dollier
dulcify
Dalilah
Delilah
dilemma
delimit
delenda
deltoid
dulcose
doll off
dildoes
dole out
doll out
delapse
deliria
Dolores
dalasis
dulosis
dulotic
dilated
dilutee
delator
dilater
dilator
diluter
dilutor
delouse
deliver
delayed
delayer
demeane
damn all
dum-palm
dumb-ass
dime bag
dumpbin
domical
domicil
demoded
dimness
dimmest
demigod
damages
demaine
damming
damning
damping
dimming
dampish
dimmish
dumpish
Dampier
dumaist
damnify
dimpled
demonic
Dominic
dominee
dominie
démenti
Domingo
dominos
demonry
damfool
dimeric
dambrod
demerge
demerse
dimorph
demirep
demerit
demi-sec
demesne
damosel
Damasus
domatia
✧**demotic**
Demeter
dimeter
demount
demayne
damozel
donnard
Dunkard
dentate
dunnage
Denmark
Dundalk
Danaans
donnart
dunnart
dentary
dingbat
Dunedin
Daniela
donnerd
Dantean
dungeon
danseur
donkeys
données
donnert
densely
duncery
dung-fly
Donegal
Dong Hai
donship
dun-bird
Dunciad
dentine
dunnite
dancing
denying
dinning
Don King
donning
dunning
dankish
donnish
dun-fish
dunnish
Dunkirk
donnism
dinkies
dunlins
Dantist
dentist
dandify
dandily
densify
density
Dansker
dandler
dangler
✧**danelaw**
dynamic
dynamos
din into
dentoid
dine off
dunnock
Don John
dingoes
dine out
dinmont
denarii
dendron
don't say
dynasty
dinette
Donetsk
Dunstan
donator
denture
Don Juan
dan buoy
Donovan
dinky-di
denizen
Dionaea
diorama
deodand
deodate
dioxane
Dioecia
droichy
do or die
do-or-die
drosera
duodena
diocese
Diomede
drone on
doomful
dropfly
drongos
drought
drogher
droshky
diorite
dioxide
D-Notice
dooming
droving
dronish
diorism
drookit
droukit
doodler
droplet
doorman
doormat
dvornik
drowner
drop-net
dromond
duotone
drop off
drop-off
drop out
dropout
duopoly
dropped
dropple
dropper
doobrie
doobrey
deontic
dioptre
do out of
diopter
drostdy
drouthy
droguet
doorway
dopiaza
deplane
deprave
dupable
dépêche
✧**diptera**
deplete
depress
deprive
depside
dip-pipe
dipping
dopping
depaint
dappled
dipolar
Daphnia
daphnid
dip into
Daphnis
diploma
diploid
dapsone
deplore
diphone
dipnoan
diplont
dip-trap
deposal
deposer
deposit
dopatta
dupatta
deplume
diptych
daquiri
dorlach
dorhawk
darrain
darrayn
dormant
durmast
dirt-bed
durable
durably
derider
dorados
dareful
dernful
direful
dureful
de règle
Dorigen
darshan
Derrida
dirtied
dormice
darling
darning
darting
Dorking
darkish
✧dervish
dorkish
✧**derrick**
dornick
deraign
dernier
darbies
darcies
dirtily
duramen
dirempt
derange
durance
dermoid
dariole
Dario Fo
dortour
dirt-pie
dart-sac
duresse
Dorothy
dastard
disband
discard
dismayd
descale
discage
discase
dis-ease
disease
disfame
dispace
disrate
distaff
disbark
dismask
dispark
disrank
de Staël
dismayl
disdain
distain
despair
✧**dismals**
descant
discant
dismast
dispart
distant
disable
dust bag
dustbin
disobey
disedge
dysodil
dos-à-dos
dosi-dos
descend
dispend
distend
disleaf
dasheki
disleal
dishelm
dasheen
discern
discerp
descent
dessert
discept
disgest
disject
disnest
disseat
dissect
dissent
dissert
distent
dishful
dislimb
desmine
despise
despite
destine
discide
dislike
dashing
desking
dishing
distich
duskish
dashiki
dislink
deskill
De Stijl
distill
dislimn
dossier
dismiss
destiny
duskily
dustily
di salto
disally
display
disomic
dustman
dyspnea
desmoid
Desmond
despond
discoed
discoid
discord
disload
dishome
dispone
dispose
disrobe
disyoke
dash off
despoil
disform
disgown
dishorn
disjoin
discoer
dash out
dish out
disport
dispost
disroot
distort
dyslogy
dasypod
dustpan
Dasypus
dashpot
dysuria
dysuric
disprad
dispred
deserve
Désirée
dishrag
desirer
destroy
disused
desktop
disturb
dasyure
discure
diseuse
disjune
dispute
distune
discuss
disgust
disrupt
disavow
distyle
detrain
dot gain
detract
dittany
datable
databus
Dyticus
dithery
dutiful
ditcher
dotting
dottled
détente
détenue
detinue
dittoed
duteous
Detroit
dataria
deterge
dottrel
data set
detrude
datival
do to wit
drubbed
drumble
druidic
daunder
Deus det
douleia
douceur
doucets
daubery
doucely
drugged
druggie
drudger
drugger
drugget
dauphin
doughty
doucine
dourine
daubing
Drusian
drucken
drunken
drum kit
drumlin
doubler
doubles
Douglas
doublet
double-u
drummed
drummer
diurnal
drum out
dhurrie
doubted
daunton
daunter
doubter
duumvir
Deutzia
deviate
deviant
dovecot
davidia
divider
divvied
devoice
devling
doveish
devoirs
dovekie
deviled
devalue
devolve
divulge
develop
devilet
dovelet
devilry
da Vinci
diviner
devious
diverge
diverse
divorce
divorcé
devisee
devisal
divisim
deviser
devisor

divisor
devoted
devotee
duvetyn
dyvoury
divvy up
Devizes
dewfall
downa-do
dewlapt
down-bed
dowable
downbow
dowsets
dowager
DEW line
dawning
dowdily
dawdler
dewclaw
dawn-man
dewanny
dowlney
dew-pond
do wrong
dawcock
dew worm
Dawn Run
dewdrop
dewater
dewfull
dextral
dextran
dextrin
dry land
day care
day name
daytale
dry-wash
daymark
daypack
daysack
drywall
dry Mass
dry-salt
Daya Bay
dry-iced
dryades
dry-cell
day-peep
daywear
dry beer
dryness
drybeat
dry-shod
daytime
day-girl
dry-fist
day lily
daysman
doyenne
Daytona
dry hole
daylong
day book
day-work
dry dock
dry-dock
day-coal
day room
dayboat

dry-foot
day trip
daystar
dry-cure
dry suit
dry-eyed
dizzard
dazedly
dizzied
dizzily
dazzler
dozenth
doze off
emanate
étalage
exarate
emanant
en avant
épatant
ébauche
eparchy
exarchy
étagère
evangel
edaphic
erathem
elative
evasive
examine
evanish
epaxial
etacism
El Aaiún
elation
enation
erasion
evasion
ex animo
edacity
egality
e-mailer
enabler
e-tailer
epaulet
enarmed
Erasmus
epagoge
enamour
example
ex aequo
epacrid
etaerio
epacris
elastic
exalted
elastin
enactor
exacter
exactor
exactly
erasure
evacuee
Emanuel
embraid
emblaze
embrace
embrave
emblema
embread
embrewe
Esbjerg

ebbless
embogue
ebb-tide
ecbolic
embolic
embolus
embroil
embloom
embrown
embargo
embased
embaste
embosom
embassy
embathe
embound
embrute
embowed
embowel
embower
ebb away
embayld
embryon
embryos
enchafe
enchase
enclave
escuage
euclase
exclave
encharm
exclaim
enchain
enclasp
en clair
enchant
etchant
encraty
encoder
escudos
excudit
excreta
excrete
encheer
escheat
excheat
eccrine
escribe
eucaine
eucrite
etching
excel in
escalop
escolar
encomia
excimer
encloud
enclose
escroll
escapee
escaper
ex curia
euchred
excurse
excerpt
excused
excusal
excuser
excited
exciton
exciter

excitor
exclude
encrust
each way
each-way
encrypt
✧endgame
endgate
endlang
endways
Eudocia
endless
endogen
endship
endwise
eddying
eidolon
endplay
endemic
endnote
endzone
endlong
endmost
end up by
endorse
endarch
enderon
endiron
endurer
elderly
end-user
ecdysis
eidetic
end even
endowed
endower
endozoa
enemata
e re nata
ewe-lamb
emerald
elevate
eyebath
eyelash
eyewash
eye bank
eyeball
elegant
E Nesbit
elenchi
Edexcel
éperdue
exegete
ewe-neck
eye-beam
elevens
eyeless
element
Everest
en effet
energic
energid
epergne
exergue
Evesham
Erewhon
eyeshot
elegiac
eyeliad
elegise
elegize

emetine
eremite
eserine
evening
emeriti
ewe-milk
eye-wink
Ezekiel
E-region
etesian
elegist
épéeist
eye-flap
✧eternal
Eleanor
even now
even-odd
eyehole
eyesore
ere long
erelong
eyehook
emerods
even out
eyebolt
exempla
exemple
eye-spot
epeirid
exedrae
eye-drop
eyebrow
emersed
Emerson
erepsin
Electra
Elektra
Eleatic
elected
erected
edental
electro
ejector
✧elector
erecter
erector
eventer
evertor
erectly
execute
elfland
enflame
enframe
effable
effacer
effects
Enfield
enflesh
elf-shot
enfiled
effulge
enfelon
effendi
elfhood
enfeoff
elf-bolt
efforce
enforce
enguard
egg case
engrace

engrave
engraff
eggwash
engrail
engrain
engrasp
eggmass
engraft
ergodic
euglena
egghead
egg cell
El Greco
eggless
engaged
✧engager
egg-bird
erg-nine
English
engulph
egg plum
egg-flip
✧eugenia
eugenic
engined
Eugenie
Eugénie
eugenol
enginer
englobe
engloom
engross
edge out
egg-cosy
en garde
engorge
eagerly
eightvo
ergates
Ephraim
ephebic
ephebes
ephebos
ephebus
exhibit
ethical
echidna
ephedra
exhedra
echoise
echoize
echoing
echoism
echoist
echelon
ephelis
exhumer
enhance
ethanal
ethanol
echinus
ethmoid
ethiops
échappé
etheric
Ephesus
Echiura
exhaust
emicate
emirate
epilate

evirate
evitate
✧epitaph
Emirati
epicarp
emicant
epitaxy
Eriador
epicede
epicene
epigene
evil eye
epigeal
epigean
eminent
evident
exigent
epithem
epithet
edified
edifice
erinite
elitism
élitism
epicism
edition
elision
exilian
edifier
épicier
elitist
élitist
epicist
exility
e-ticket
etiolin
edibles
epizoic
ericoid
epidote
✧epigone
episode
episome
epitome
epitope
✧epigoni
epizoan
epizoon
✧epigons
edit out
Eritrea
epigram
ekistic
eristic
emitted
✧epistle
evictee
edictal
emitter
evictor
epicure
Erinyes
epigyny
enjoyer
Eskuara
Eskimos
ellwand
eelfare
eulogia
ellagic
eclogue

enlight
eel-like
eilding
erl-king
eelworm
eelpout
✧eclipse
ellipse
enlarge
enliven
esloyne
El Mahdi
ermelin
ermined
elmwood
en masse
Ed Moses
Exmouth
ennoble
ennuied
eanling
einkorn
ennuyed
evocate
exocarp
exogamy
écorché
exordia
erotema
eroteme
exoderm
egoless
erodent
esotery
emonges
emongst
epochal
erotica
exotica
epoxied
ebonise
ebonite
ebonize
ecocide
egotise
egotize
emotive
epoxide
erosive
egotism
elogium
erodium
erotism
emotion
erosion
Etonian
exomion
Ebonics
ebonist
egotist
elogist
Elohist
exodist
enounce
eloiner
ecotone
ecology
economy
enomoty
étourdi
ego-trip

e contra
elocute
evolute
evolver
ecotype
emplace
emplane
enplane
expiate
empeach
explain
explant
empyema
ekpwele
empress
express
empight
emptied
empaire
emprise
en prise
espying
emption
emptier
empties
enprint
emptily
expulse
empaler
expanse
expense
expunge
empanel
expunct
explode
explore
exploit
euphony
euphory
eupepsy
emporia
empiric
expired
emperce
euphroe
ex parte
expurge
esparto
emperor
exposed
en poste
exposal
exposer
empathy
expound
emplume
espouse
Euphues
empower
empayre
empty in
en queue
enquire
✧esquire
enquiry
ebriate
Euryale
earbash
earmark
errable
earache

earldom
enrheum
earless
earnest
ebriety
enraged
en règle
earthen
earth up
earshot
earthly
errhine
earning
earring
earpick
earlier
earlies
earplug
earflap
eirenic
enrange
étrenne
errands
Euronet
errancy
ear-bone
ear-hole
earlobe
ebriose
earlock
earn out
Europol
europop
euripus
Egreria
Etruria
eardrum
eardrop
Eurasia
erratic
erratum
Euratom
enround
en route
enrough
enriven
early on
Euscara
enslave
ensnare
Eustace
ensnarl
enstamp
✧ecstasy
eustacy
eustasy
Eusebio
Euskera
East End
Elspeth
enshell
✧eastern
Epstein
ensteep
ensweep
easeful
exscind
en suite
easting
ensuing
eastlin

epsilon
essence
Essenes
ease off
easy-osy
ensurer
East Sea
essayed
enstyle
essoyne
eustyle
essayer
estrade
entrail
entrall
en train
entrain
entrant
extract
extrait
estuary
eatable
Entebbe
enticer
eat lead
esthete
estrepe
extreme
entreat
estreat
extreat
entwine
estoile
estrich
entrism
eat dirt
entrist
entwist
Estella
Estelle
entomic
Estonia
entente
extense
eat into
extinct
entrold
entropy
eutropy
ectopia
ectopic
entopic
ectypal
enteric
eaterie
Euterpe
externe
enteral
enthral
enteron
enterer
eat crow
ectases
ectasis
entasis
entotic
extatic
entêtée
entitle
enthuse
extrude

entrust
estival
estover
eat away
eutexia
ecthyma
entayle
ectozoa
entozoa
educate
emulate
epurate
exudate
epulary
exurbia
equable
exurban
E number
equably
Equidae
Ecuador
elusive
erudite
exuviae
eluvial
exuvial
eluvium
elusion
elution
écuelle
equally
equinia
equinal
equinox
emulous
elusory
emu wren
equerry
épuisée
emulsin
emulsor
eductor
equator
equites
eevning
envying
en ville
envelop
envenom
envious
environ
envault
enwheel
E B White
eryngos
Elysium
Elysian
etymons
elytral
elytrum
elytron
enzymic
Elzevir
flatbed
frabbit
flaccid
fiancée
Francie
flat cap
flatcar
fiascos

Frances
Francis
fratchy
✧flag day
flare up
flare-up
frame-up
flâneur
fratery
fearful
flaffer
flamfew
flagged
flanged
fragged
Feargal
flaught
fraught
feather
flasher
flavine
fragile
flaming
flaring
flaying
foaming
framing
fraying
Flavian
franion
Frazier
foamily
Frankie
flacker
flanker
flacket
flasket
frankly
flatlet
frailly
frailty
flagman
flaunch
flannel
fraenum
flannen
flaunty
flavone
flavour
featous
flat out
flapped
frapped
frappée
frampal
flapper
frantic
flatted
fracted
fractal
flan tin
flatten
feaster
flatter
Fraktur
feature
frazzle
fibbery
fubbery
febrile
fabling

fibbing
fabliau
fabular
fibular
fibroma
fibroid
fibrose
fibroin
fibrous
fibered
Fabergé
fibster
factice
factive
fictile
fictive
faction
fiction
faculae
facular
faculty
focally
faceman
façonné
facings
factoid
face off
face-off
face out
factory
fuchsia
focused
fucused
fuchsin
focuses
fucuses
faceted
fechter
facture
factual
fadable
fidibus
fadedly
fidgets
fidgety
fadaise
faddish
faddism
fideism
faddist
fideist
fuddled
Fidelio
fiddler
fuddler
fiddley
fade out
fade-out
fedarie
federal
fedayee
fee tail
fee-farm
free-arm
feel-bad
feelbad
freebee
freebie
flea-bag
fleeced
fleecer

frescos
Frenchy
fielded
Freddie
fiefdom
freedom
fielder
fretful
fledged
freight
fleshed
freshen
flesher
fresher
freshet
fleshly
freshly
flexile
feeding
feeling
feering
fleeing
Fleming
freeing
✧flemish
flexion
fierily
flecked
freckle
flecker
freckly
fuelled
fueller
feedlot
flehmen
freeman
freemen
Fleance
fresnel
Fiennes
feed off
fuel oil
fie upon
fleapit
fuel rod
Fredrik
fleuron
fleerer
Fuehrer
fleuret
freesia
fretsaw
fretted
fletton
fleetly
frenula
flexure
freeway
freezer
✧fifteen
fifthly
fifties
foggage
fog bank
fig wasp
fog lamp
fogydom
fig leaf
fog-bell
fogless
figment

faggery
figgery
fig-bird
fagging
figging
fogyish
fogyism
fuguist
foggily
fugally
fig roll
foghorn
figwort
figured
fig tree
figural
fagotti
fagotto
fighter
fugatos
fog over
fahlerz
fahlore
frigate
Fridays
friable
fribble
Frisbee®
flip-dog
flinder
fair do's
FT Index
fair-day
friseur
fritfly
fringed
flinger
frigger
flighty
failing
fairing
foiling
fairish
Frisian
fairily
flicker
frisker
frisket
feigned
faience
faïence
friande
frijole
faitour
flip out
flipper
fripper
friarly
Friesic
frisson
fainted
flitted
fritted
flip-top
flitter
foister
fritter
faintly
failure
frisure
friture

flivver
fairway
friezed
frizzed
frizzle
frizzly
fajitas
Fukuoka
falbala
falsafa
falcade
falcate
faldage
filiate
foliage
foliate
fullage
fellahs
folk art
fallacy
Félibre
filabeg
filibeg
✧felicia
felucca
folacin
filacer
Filices
Felidae
filmdom
filberd
fulness
filbert
fulgent
fullest
falsely
full-fed
falafel
felafel
film fan
fall for
Filofax®
fall guy
filcher
full-hot
felsite
fulmine
falling
felting
filling
folding
falsish
filmish
fullish
Fellini
Falkirk
fulfill
falsism
falsies
Follies
falsify
falsity
filemot
Falange
Felinae
filings
felonry
folioed
foliole
foliose
fulsome

fall off
fall-off
file off
fulgour
fulvous
fall out
fall-out
fallout
felwort
fill out
foldout
full-out
felt pen
felspar
✧filaria
fulcrum
Falasha
filasse
film set
filmset
felt tip
falcula
folkway
filazer
fumados
fumbler
famulus
feminal
fimbria
Fumaria
femoral
fumette
fumetti
fumetto
femiter
fomites
fenland
Finland
fan base
fanfare
finback
finnack
fun park
fan mail
fantail
fan palm
fantasm
Finbarr
funfair
fantads
fantast
fine art
fondant
fantasy
finable
funèbre
funicle
finical
finicky
fanteeg
fannell
fin keel
Fonteyn
fingers
finless
fan belt
finagle
finched
Funchal
Fontina
fancied

fanwise
fanzine
fen-fire
fencing
finding
finning
funding
funning
fennish
fineish
Finnish
fancier
funnies
funnily
finikin
Fenella
fan club
fangled
fankled
fine leg
Fénelon
fondler
fontlet
finally
finance
finings
fanfold
fin-toed
fungoid
finnock
fantods
fungoes
fungous
find out
finfoot
funeral
findram
finesse
finnsko
fanatic
fenitar
functor
funster
fan oven
froward
flotage
flowage
footage
flokati
flotant
feodary
footbar
frogbit
footboy
floccus
flooded
fronded
Floréal
flowers
floreat
flowery
foolery
feoffee
foodful
feoffer
feoffor
flogged
frogged
flogger
froughy
Florida
flowing
fooling
footing
foolish
foodism
florist
foot-jaw
frocked
Floella
foozler
froglet
footman
footmen
frogman
flounce
frounce
frown on
flouncy
from off
foo yong
from out
footpad
floored
Florrie
floorer
foot rot
floosie
Flossie
Footsie
flotsam
frowsty
fronted
frosted
floatel
frontal
foot-ton
fronton
floater
foo yung
floruit
food web
footway
floozie
foppery
fopling
foppish
fermata
Ferrara
forlana
furlana
farrand
forward
fardage
fermate
ferrate
forbade
forgave
formate
forsake
furcate
✧furnace
Ferrari®
firearm
forearm
for vain
forwarn
farrago
forzato
forfair
furfair
Far East
farrant
fire ant
formant
firebug
fire-bar
firebox
forecar
faradic
firedog
✧**faraday**
fore-day
fore-end
forfend
forlend
for real
fur seal
farceur
forbear
for fear
farness
forceps
far be it
Far West
ferment
fervent
forfeit
forhent
forlent
fornent
for rent
forwent
farmery
fernery
ferrety
forgery
furmety
forkful
firefly
forager
foregut
farthel
Fareham
farther
further
for that
for show
Formica®
farcied
ferried
ferrite
fertile
forgive
for life
forpine
furtive
farcing
farding
farming
ferning
firring
forging
forming
furring
furbish
furnish
fermium
fermion
foreign
farrier
furrier
✧**forties**
farcify
fortify
furmity
forelie
forsloe
foreleg
fartlek
fortlet
forslow
forelay
fireman
foramen
foreman
foremen
Feronia
for once
fire-new
firwood
for good
far gone
fir cone
forbode
forbore
fordone
forgone
fire off
furlong
forsook
fern-owl
forlorn
forworn
furioso
fervour
ferrous
furious
farmost
farm out
fire out
fork out
furrowy
firepan
firepot
forepaw
fir tree
for free
foreran
forerun
Fortran
foresee
foresaw
foresay
foretop
firstly
farruca
formula
Fortuna
furcula
ferrule
for sure
✧fortune
ferrugo
for ever
forever
faraway
forayer
fusible
fuse box
fast-day
fish-day
fisheye
Fastens
Fastext
fashery
fishery
fish-fag
fishful
fistful
fish-god
fishgig
fascine
festive
fissile
fissive
fasting
fishing
fastish
fossick
fascial
✧**fascism**
fashion
fission
fushion
fustian
✧**fascist**
fishify
fussily
fustily
fasolia
fusilli
fist-law
Fastnet
fish-net
fish-oil
festoon
fuscous
fish out
fusspot
fusarol
fistula
fossula
fissure
fish-way
✧foss way
fat-face
fatback
futhark
fat camp
fetiche
fathead
fathers
fatness
fetters
fitness
fattest
fitment
fittest
fateful
fatigue
fitchée
futchel
fetch up
fetcher
fitchet
fitchew
fatling
fatting
fitting
fattish
fattism
fitlier
fattist
✧**fat city**
fatuity
fettler
fatally
Fatimid
futhorc
fetlock
futhork
futtock
fathoms
fatsoes
fatuous
fat body
fat-free
futures
FitzRoy
fat-lute
foulard
fougade
four-ale
faux ami
foumart
feudary
flubbed
f-number
fluidic
fluidal
foulder
founder
foundry
fluff up
fourgon
flushed
fauchon
flush up
flusher
foughty
flutina
fluxive
fou rire
feuding
fluting
faucial
fluvial
Fauvism
fluxion
faunist
Fauvist
feudist
flutist
flukily
frutify
flunkey
flummox
fluence
fluency
four-oar
frumple
faux pas
fluoric
foudrie
fourses
Flustra
fructed
fruited
fouetté
frustum
fluster
flutter
fruiter
feu-duty
foveate
five-bar
favrile
foveola
foveole
fivepin
favored
fevered
favorer
favours
fewmets
fewness
fawning
fowling
fox-mark
fox-tail
fixable
fixedly
foxship
foxfire
fixings
foxhole
fox-trap
fox-trot
✧foxtrot
fixated
fixture
fox hunt
fox-evil
flybane
fly half
flyback
fly rail
flypast
flyable
flyleaf
flybelt
fly line
flyting
fly-fish
fly high
fly-kick
fly-flap
fly slip
flyblow
fly-slow
fayence
flybook
flyboat
fly open
fly upon
flytrap
flyover
fly swat
flyaway
fuzzbox
fizzgig
fizzing
fuzzily
fazenda
Granada
guaraná
gradate
Grahame
gramash
Guaraní
guarani
guanaco
gramary
Granary®
granary
grabbed
grabble
grab-bag
grabber
gearbox
Glaucus
Giardia
grandma
grandpa
gladded
grandad
guarded
gladdie
grandee
guardee
grandam
gladden
gladdon
graddan
glandes
grandly
glacéed
go ahead
go-ahead
goateed
glad eye
Goanese
glareal
Goa bean
gradely
grapery
gravely
goat-fig
gladful
granfer
grayfly
goat-god
guar gum
granger
guangos
Gwangju
Glasgow
gnathic
graphic
gnathal
✧**gnasher**
Graphis
granita
go aside
gracile
gradine
granite
gratiné
guanine
gearing
glaring
glazing
gnawing
grading
grating
graving
grazing
goatish
guarish
gradini
gharial
glacial
gradino
glacier
glazier
grazier
Gwalior
gladius
gratify
gravity
grackle
glaiket
glaikit
gnarled
Grallae
gravlax
grammar
Grammys
grained
grannie
graunch
grapnel
grannam
grainer
granola
✧**glamour**
gealous
go about
grapple
graupel
grasper
grampus
gnarred
glairin
grassum
glassen
grass up
grasser
glasses
granted
grantee
Granthi
grafter
granter
grantor
ghastly
giantly
giantry
granule
gravure
guayule
gradual
glaived
gabbard
gabnash
go blank
gabbart
giblets
gabfest
gabbing
gibbing
gobbing
gubbing
Gabriel
gubbins
gabelle
Gobelin
gabbler
gobbler
gobioid
gibbose
gibbous
goburra
gabbros
go crazy
go crook
geckoes
godward

God's ape
God save
Gaddafi
gadwall
goddamn
Gadidae
✧godhead
godsend
gudgeon
goddess
godless
gadgety
Godthab
godship
godlike
gadding
gadling
god-king
godling
godlier
giddily
godlily
god's lid
God slot
gadsman
gudeman
godhood
gadroon
godroon
Godfrey
gude-son
godetia
go Dutch
go-devil
giddy-up
Grenada
gregale
grenade
gheraos
Grendel
Gaeldom
guerdon
guereza
gee-gees
Guelfic
gleeful
Gielgud
geechee
greyhen
gee whiz
Grecize
guérite
Goering
greying
greyish
gremial
Grecism
✧grecian
gherkin
grey-lag
gremlin
gleeman
greenie
Gwennie
greenth
gleaner
greener
greenly
glenoid
Geelong
grey owl
glebous
grey-out
Gregory
grecque
ghessed
greisen
greaser
guesser
greisly
greeted
greaten
guesten
great go
greater
greeter
ghettos
greatly
geebung
✧greaves
Gaekwar
Gwenyth
Gift Aid
gaffing
go Fanti
go first
go for it
gag-rein
gagging
gigging
gig mill
goggled
giggler
goggler
giggles
gigolos
goggles
G-agents
Gagarin
gagster
gahnite
Gehenna
guisard
grimace
guidage
Guiyang
gribble
grieced
grinded
griddle
gliadin
glidder
gridder
grinder
guilder
guildry
Guinean
grisely
gainful
griffin
griffon
ghilgai
going on
gringos
Grisham
geishas
guichet
gwiniad
gliding
gricing
griping
✧guiding
guising
grimily
griskin
grilled
grisled
ghillie
Gwillym
griller
glimmer
grimmer
gliomas
Goiânia
grinned
Guignol
grinner
gripped
glimpse
gripple
gripper
goitred
grigris
griesie
gliosis
gainsay
griesly
Grimsby
gristle
glisten
glister
glitter
grifter
gritter
gristly
guipure
griever
Gaikwar
grizzle
grizzly
Gujarat
goliard
golland
galeate
gallate
gill ale
Goliath
goldarn
gallant
galabea
galabia
gold-bug
golf bag
galoche
giltcup
goldcup
gelidly
goldeye
galleon
gulleys
✧gilbert
gallery
gullery
gallfly
galagos
Galahad
gullied
Gallice
gallise
gallize
galling
gelding
gelling
gilding
golfing
goldish
gullish
gold ink
gallium
Gillian
gillion
Gallios
gullies
galliot
✧galilee
Galileo
galumph
galanga
Galenic
gallnut
gill net
galloon
gallows
galopin
galipot
✧galatea
galette
gelatin
Gulf War
gummata
gemmate
gum rash
gambado
gimbals
gymnast
game bag
gemsbok
Game Boy®
gombeen
gemmery
gumshoe
gym shoe
gummite
gemming
gumming
gampish
gemfish
gimmick
Gambian
gambier
gambist
gummily
gamelan
gym slip
gambler
Geminid
Geminis
gamboge
gammock
gumboil
gamboes
gummous
gumboot
gum tree
gambrel
gomeral
gomeril
gumdrop
gametic
gametal
gomutos
gymnura
gemmule
Gin Lane
gunnage
gunwale
Gandalf
gingall
Gonzalo
gang-bye
ganache
gonidia
gonadic
gonidic
gonadal
gunnera
Genoese
ginseng
gun deck
genteel
gunge up
gunless
Gunners
gingery
ginnery
gunnery
gingham
ginshop
gunship
gunshot
ganoine
✧gentile
genuine
gunfire
ganging
ginning
gunning
gingili
gentian
Günzian
gin fizz
ganglia
gantlet
gunplay
genomic
gondola
genlock
gunlock
gun moll
gunroom
gun down
gunboat
gunport
genappe
genipap
generic
gangrel
general
Goneril
gin trap
Ganesha
gangsta
genista
geneses
✧genesis
genuses
gang saw
genetic
genette
genital
genitor
Genevan
gangway
genizah
globate
geofact
geomant
goodbye
grow-bag
goombah
gnocchi
grouchy
Geordie
geoidal
good-den
good-day
good egg
good-e'en
gropers
gooiest
grosert
geodesy
geogeny
goosery
grocery
Georgia
georgic
Georgie
gloried
gloving
glowing
glozing
groping
growing
gnomish
goodish
Grobian
Grotian
grodier
Grolier
goodies
goolies
gnomist
glorify
goofily
Goorkha
grockle
growler
glommed
✧goodman
grommet
groined
grown-up
groaner
grounds
good-now
globoid
grow old
globose
goof off
good oil
glonoin
giocoso
globous
geogony
geology
groupie
grouper
grogram
Glossic
glossal
good-son
gross up
glosser
grouser
grossly
glottic
✧gnostic
glottal
gloater
grouter
glottis
grottos
ghostly
globule
geoduck
grooved
groover
glory be
glory in
gap year
gap site
gypping
guppies
gopuram
garland
gormand
gurnard
garbage
germane
Gervase
germain
Germans
gardant
Germany
gertcha
gyrocar
Guri Dam
gurudom
gory dew
gerbera
✧gorsedd
✧gardens
garment
goriest
gargety
giraffe
garigue
garagey
garpike
girding
garfish
garnish
girlish
guruism
Gordian
Gordius
Gorgias
gorgios
Geraint
gorilla
garbled
girdled
girolle
garbler
girdler
gyrally
Garamba
gironic
gyronic
gerenuk
gyronny
girlond
garrote
garvock
gorcock
garboil
gorsoon
Gorgons
gorcrow
girasol
girosol
garotte
Gore-Tex®
go round
garbure
gestate
go spare
gas mask
gas tank
goshawk
gas main
✧gestapo
gas lamp
✧gestalt
gestant
gas well
Gospels
gashful
gustful
Gasthof
gasahol
gasohol
gas fire
gas-lime
gas pipe
gasping
gas ring
gassing
gosling
gushing
gaskins
gas lift
gaseity
gossipy
Giselle
Gosplan
gas-coke
gas-coal
gossoon
gaseous
gessoes
gasp out
go short
Gosport
Guscott
gastric
gisarme
gastrin
gas trap
gesture
gas-buoy
gas oven
gussy up
Gotland
guttate
gytrash
get back
gateaus
gâteaux
go to bed
get real
gittern
gathers
gutless
gutters
gutsful
gutcher
get shot
göthite
Gatting
getting
G-string
gutsing
gutting
Gatwick
Gothick
guttier
gutsily
gateleg
gateman
get in on
gitanos
gate net
get hold
get down
get lost!
go to pot
go to sea
get it on
get over
go to war
gateway
get away
getaway
goulash
glutaei
gourami
grubbed
grubble
grumble
grubber
grumbly
gouache
go under
gougère
Gruyère
gluteal
glue ear
gluteus
gluiest
gaudery
gauffer
goutfly
gruffly
glugged
gaudgie
gauchos
glucina
gauging
Gaulish
grunion
Gautier
gaudily
glummer
gourmet
grummet
glucose
grumose
goujons
grumous
glue-pot
glutted
grufted
gruntle
glutton
grutten
gaulter
grunter

gauntly
gauntry
Gauguin
give aim
give ear
give off
give out
gavotte
give way
gowland
gownboy
gowpens
go white
gownman
gowaned
go wrong
Gawayne
grysbok
Gwynedd
gay gene
Gwyneth
gayness
grysely
glyphic
✧gryphon
gwyniad
glycine
gaysome
glycose
guy-rope
goyisch
gryesly
glyptic
gizzard
gazebos
gazeful
gazelle
guzzler
gazania
gazooka
✧gazette
headage
heal-all
huanaco
head boy
headcap
hoarder
heave ho!
heave-ho
heavens
heathen
heather
hyacine
hyaline
hyalite
heading
healing
heaping
hearing
heating
heaving
heavier
headily
heavily
hoarily
hearken
headman
Huainan
haaf-net
hyaloid
head off
hear out
headrig
head sea
hoarsen
heads-up
headset
hearsay
hearted
hearten
healthy
heartly
headway
hoatzin
Hebraic
hobnail
habdabs
hibachi
hobodom
hobbish
Hobbism
hoboism
Hobbian
Hobbist
hobbler
hob-a-nob
hebenon
habited
habitué
habitus
H E Bates
habitat
hectare
hackbut
Hock-day
hac lege
hackery
hacking
hack-log
hackler
heckler
hackles
hacklet
hoc anno
✧hackney
Hockney
hoc loco
hickory
hocused
hacksaw
hicatee
hachure
hiccups
hiccupy
hydrate
hydrant
had need
had best
Hodeida
had like
hydride
hedging
hidling
Hadrian
hidlins
hidalga
huddled
hidalgo
hedonic
hydroid
hadrome
haddock
hideous
hydrous
hideout
hydroxy
hederal
hadarim
hydatid
Hieland
hoe-cake
Hielant
heelbar
hueless
heedful
heeling
hoedown
haemony
heeltap
huff-cap
huffish
hafnium
heftily
huffily
huffkin
hafflin
Hofburg
Haggada
haggard
hogward
hog-mane
hogwash
hogback
high bar
highboy
high day
hag-seed
hag-weed
high-end
hogweed
hygiene
hog-deer
highest
hoggery
high-fed
high-hat
hag-ride
hog-line
hogging
hugging
hagfish
haggish
highish
hogfish
hoggish
Hygeian
hog-skin
high-key
hog-plum
haggler
higgler
high-low
highman
highmen
Hyginus
hoghood
hognose
hagdown
hugeous
hagbolt
Hogarth
high-set
high tea
high-top
highway
hahnium
huitain
haircut
heirdom
hairdos
hair-eel
heiress
hair gel
heigh-ho
haining
hei-tiki
Haitian
hairnet
hair oil
heinous
hairpin
heister
hoister
Heimweh
hijinks
halyard
holland
half-ape
holy-ale
hallali
holdall
holla-ho!
Hillary
halibut
holibut
hell-box
Halacha
helical
helicon
half-cap
helices
half-cut
hellcat
Helodea
halidom
holydam
half-day
holiday
holy day
halberd
Hellene
Holbein
Hulsean
halvers
halbert
helpful
Halifax
halogen
Heloise
halling
halting
helping
hilding
holding
hulking
hylding
hellish
holmium
hallian
hallion
hellion
hellier
hyloist
holy Joe
Halakah
halflin
halalas
Hillman®
hillmen
halimot
hell of a
hellova
helcoid
half-one
Holy One
hold off
hillock
holm-oak
holloes
help out
hold out
holdout
hole out
helipad
half-pie
half pay
half-pay
Hilarus
Holy See
holesom
hilltop
holster
halitus
helotry
helluva
hold-ups
halavah
holy war
halfwit
halfway
hallway
helixes
halcyon
hallyon
hummaum
hymnary
homeboy
humidor
humidly
himself
Hammers
Humbert
humogen
homager
Humphry
hemline
hemming
humming
hymning
hymnist
hammily
homolog
homelyn
hamular
hamulus
humbles
hymenia
hominid
hymenal
homonym
H H Munro
humanly
hemiola
hemione
hammock
hemlock
hommock
hummock
hymnody
Homeric
Homerid
humeral
humoral
humdrum
home run
humerus
Hamitic
hamster
Hamburg
Hamhung
Homburg
humbuzz
Honiara
Hansard
hennaed
handaxe
henbane
Honiari
Hans Arp
Hungary
handbag
handcar
hangdog
henpeck
hinge on
Hansen's
hunkers
hennery
handful
handgun
hind-gut
hunch up
honchos
hen-wife
hanging
hinging
honking
hunting
Hunnish
handier
henries
handily
handjar
handled
hindleg
handler
hangman
✧hanuman
hen-toed
hand-off
hang off
Hancock
hen-coop
hand out
hand-out
handout
hang out
hangout
hunt out
hanaper
hundred
Hendrix
handsel
hands-on
hands up
hunt's-up
handset
handsaw
honesty
henotic
Honiton
honours
Hanover
honeyed
Henry VI
Henry IV
hoop-ash
hooters
hoosgow
hoodlum
hoodman
hoolock
hook-pin
hoofrot
hook-tip
hop-yard
heptane
hip bath
hop-sack
hopsack
hop-oast
hyped up
hyped-up
hophead
hapless
hipness
hip-belt
hippest
✧hopeful
hypogea
hip-shot
hopbind
hopbine
hoplite
hop-vine
happing
hipping
hopping
hippish
haptics
hippies
happily
hop-flea
hopples
hip-knob
ha'pence
hyponym
ha'penny
haploid
hypnoid
hip bone
hop-pole
hypnone
hip-roof
hip-lock
haplont
hip-gout
hop-tree
hap'orth
haporth
hypural
heparin
hyperon
Hypatia
hepatic
hepster
hipster
hypoxia
hypoxic
harmala
herbage
her lane
hireage
hersall
harmans
herbary
hirable
hornbug
hard bop
hurlbat
herdboy
hire car
hyraces
haricot
hirudin
herself
Hordeum
hordein
harness
herdess
Hornets
hurleys
harvest
Herbert
horrent
horse it
hartely
harmful
hornful
hurtful
hard-got
harshen
hership
hard hat
hard hit
hard-hit
harshly
harried
hurried
harmine
heroine
heroise
heroize
hircine
harling
herling
herring
hirling
horning
horsing
hurling
hardish
Harwich
hornish
hernial
heroism
hornito
harrier
Harpies
her nibs
heroics
hurdies
harpist
Harriet
herbist
hornist
hardily
horrify
Harijan
hare-lip
hurdler
hurdles
harslet
herblet
hornlet
horn-mad
hard man
herdman
hyrvnia
horn-nut
heronry
hardoke
herbose
hormone
hordock
horn owl
harpoon
harbour
herbous
harmost
hire out
harmony
hard pad
hard-pan
harn-pan
hard roe
hard-run
Hereros
harissa
hérissé
hard-set
haroset
herb tea
heretic
Harstad
hirstie
Horatio
hardtop
heritor
hirsute
hard-won
hyraxes
hurry up
Hertzog
horizon
husband
hastate
his lane
hostage
Hussain
his nabs
hushaby
Hasidic
Hasidim
hisself
has-been
Hussein
hostess
hosiery
hospice
hostile
Hussite
huswife
hashing
hissing
hosting
husking
hashish
hassium

✧hessian
his nibs
hastily
huskily
hush kit
hostler
✧hustler
hoseman
hosanna
hose-net
histoid
histone
hassock
hash out
history
histrio
Heshvan
hatband
hot date
hatrack
hit back
hot wall
hetmans
hatable
hetaera
hothead
hot well
hatless
hotness
hot melt
hot seat
hottest
hutment
hateful
hot shoe
hatchel
hitch up
hatcher
hitcher
hatchet
hotshot
hetaira
Hittite
hot line
hotline
hot-wire
hatting
hitting
hotting
hutting
hottish
hit list
hot flue
hats off
hattock
hotfoot
hutzpah
hit upon
Hotspur
hot spot
hot trod
hot-trod
heteros
hit it up
hatfuls
haulage
hautboy
Hyundai®
heureka
hauberk
hauteur
haughty
housing
houting
heurism
haulier
Housman
hoummos
haul off
haut pas
haunted
haut ton
Houston
haunter
have a go
have-a-go
hive bee
have got
hoveled
havened
havings
have-not
have off
hive off
hive-off
haveour
haviour
have out
haverel
have way
hawkbit
howbeit
✧hawking
howling
hawkish
H G Wells
how come?
hawk owl
hawbuck
however
howdy-do
hexadic
hexagon
hexapla
hexapod
hexarch
hayband
hayward
hayrake
hey pass
hayseed
Huygens
hayride
haywire
hayrick
Hay diet
hryvnya
hay-bote
haycock
hayfork
hayloft
Hey Jude
heyduck
huzzaed
Hazlitt
hazelly
igarapé
imamate
in a daze
in-and-in
I have it
imagery
inanely
irately
Ivanhoe
in a kind
✧imagine
isatine
imaging
✧imagism
itacism
Icarian
Idalian
Iranian
Italian
italics
imagist
Italiot
inanity
Isadora
in a word
Isadore
isagoge
imagoes
in a sort
in a body
in a spot
in antis
in a stew
inaptly
iracund
Iraq War
inboard
imbrast
imbiber
inbreed
inbreak
in brief
inbeing
inbring
in-built
in banco
in blood
imbrown
imburse
inburst
imbosom
imbathe
inbound
imbrute
imbower
inchase
inclasp
incubus
incudes
incline
in chief
ischial
ischium
Iachimo
itchier
incomer
incense
inconie
inconnu
inclose
incross
inch out
inchpin
incipit
incurve
incised
incisor
inciter
include
incrust
incivil
Indiana
indrawn
indraft
indicia
Indocid®
indican
inducer
Indy car
indices
indwell
indwelt
indigos
in drink
indulge
indulin
indoors
in depth
in-depth
indorse
ioduret
indusia
inditer
in doubt
indexal
indoxyl
indexer
indexes
ikebana
Iceland
Ireland
iterate
ice-calk
icepack
iceball
ice fall
inexact
iterant
iceberg
ice fern
ice beer
ice-belt
iced gem
ice show
itemise
itemize
ice fish
ice pick
ice rink
ice hill
Iberian
irenics
ice-blue
ice floe
ideally
ice-cold
ice worm
iceboat
ice-foot
ice spar
ice-free
inearth
Isegrim
ileuses
iced tea
inertia
identic
ileitis
ineptly
inertly
ice cube
ice over
inflame
inflate
infract
in focus
infidel
infield
in flesh
in fieri
iffiest
inflect
Isfahan
inflict
infulae
in folio
infimae
infimum
infanta
infante
in funds
infancy
in front
in force
inforce
✧inferno
infarct
in for it
infuser
infauna
in fault
infaust
in fruit
ingrate
in grain
ingrain
ingraft
ingress
ingoing
ingulph
ingénue
ingener
inglobe
ingrown
ingroup
in gross
ingross
Iggy Pop
ingesta
Ishmael
ichabod
inhabit
inhibit
ichthic
ichthys
ichnite
ich dien
inhaler
in holes
inhuman
inhumer
inherce
inherit
Imhotep
in-house
inhaust
Izhevsk
imitate
irisate
imitant
Isiacal
iliacus
Irideae
irideal
iciness
Irisher
Irishry
iridise
iridize
initial
iridial
Iricism
iridium
iridian
Ibibios
Idi Amin
Isidora
Isidore
Iliescu
idiotic
idiotcy
injoint
injelly
injunct
injurer
ilkaday
ink-feed
in-kneed
inkwell
ickiest
inkiest
inkling
ink-fish
ink-blot
irksome
inkhosi
inkhorn
icky poo
inkspot
inkosis
Inkatha
Irkutsk
ill fame
ill part
illicit
ill seen
illness
illogic
illegal
inlying
ill-will
Islamic
isleman
illapse
ill-bred
ill-used
idlesse
ill luck
ill turn
inlayer
Ismaili
iambics
iambist
immense
immerge
immerse
immoral
ismatic
Ibn Saud
innyard
ignoble
ignobly
inn sign
ionomer
innings
Ian Holm
igneous
innerve
ignorer
ignaros
innards
innerly
Ionesco
ioniser
igniter
Ian Rush
Ian Dury
in no way
ionizer
Iron Age
isobare
isobase
isolate
isobath
isopach
isogamy
in order
isomere
isogeny
isochor
Iwo Jima
ivoried
iconise
iconize
idolise
idolize
ironise
ironize
isoline
ironing
idolism
Ivorian
ivories
idolist
ironist
ivorist
iconify
iron man
ipomoea
isodoma
Isopoda
iron ore
Isodore
isotone
isotope
iron out
isodont
isokont
isonomy
isotopy
iron-pan
isospin
iron-red
isogram
isotron
isoetes
inocula
isotype
isozyme
isohyet
implate
in peace
in phase
inphase
in place
impeach
impearl
implant
impresa
implead
implete
imprese
impregn
in pleno
impress
imprest
impiety
implied
impaint
imprint
in point
in print
impulse
impaler
impalas
impinge
impanel
implode
implore
improve
impious
imperia
imperil
impasse
impaste
in posse
impasto
imposer
imposex
in petto
imputer
Iapetus
impetus
impound
impavid
in power
inquere
inquest
inquire
inquiet
inquiry
inqilab
Israeli
Ibrahim
Igraine
ivresse
inscape
in shape
insnare
in spate
instate
in small
install
in stays
instant
issuant
Insecta
insider
insides
instead
inshell
it seems
inspect
insofar
insigne
in sight
insight
inspire
in spite
inswing
Ipswich
instill
insulae
insulse
insulin
insular
insanie
in synch
insinew
inshore
in store
in-store
insooth
in stock
in short
insipid
insured
insurer
insculp
in style
I ask you!
intrada
in train
in twain
in tears
intrant
intreat
Integra®
integer
ijtihad
intwine
intwist
intimae
intimal
isthmus
intense
intoner
Ictinus
introld
introit
icteric
icterid
interne
inter se
inthral
✧interim
icterus
in terms
ictuses
intrude
in touch
in truth
in trust
intrust
inulase
in utero
Iguvine
inutile
iguanid
iguanas
Iquique
Iquitos
in vacuo

in vadio
invader
in voice
invoice
inveigh
invoker
invalid
involve
invenit
invious
inverse
invitee
in vitro
inviter
invexed
inweave
inwards
in waste
inwoven
I myself
idyllic
ivy-bush
Jean Arp
Jeannie
joannes
jealous
jib sail
jobless
jobbery
jibbing
jobbing
Jobclub
job club
jubilee
jib boom
jib-door
jackass
✧jacobin
jacobus
jackdaw
✧jackeen
jacchus
jockish
Jacklin
Jocelin
Jocelyn
jocular
jackman
jacamar
Jacinta
jacinth
jaconet
✧jockney
jack off
jackpot
Jocasta
jacksie
Jackson
✧jack tar
Jacques
Jacuzzi®
jacuzzi
Jeddart
jadedly
Judaean
juddery
Judaica
jadeite
Judaise
Judaize
Judaism

Judaist
judoist
Jude Law
Jodhpur
j'adoube
Judezmo
Joe Baxi
jeepers
jeering
Joe Blow
jeepney
Joe Soap
Jeffrey
jug band
jug-ears
Juglans
jughead
joggers
jaggery
jaghire
jagging
jigging
jogging
jugging
jiggish
juggins
jigajig
jigajog
joggled
juggler
jugular
jogtrot
jugfuls
John Dee
John Doe
John Gay
John Hop
Jahvism
Johnian
Jahvist
Johanna
Johnnie
John Pym
John Ray
Johnson
Jehovah
joinder
juice up
joinery
joining
Jainism
Jainist
juicily
jai alai
jointed
jointer
jointly
jejunal
jejunum
ju-jitsu
jukebox
jukskei
Jakarta
jellaba
Juliana
jellied
jolling
Jillian
jillion
jellify
jollify

jollily
jollity
jalapic
jalapin
jaloppy
jalouse
jolly up
jollyer
jamdani
jampani
jimjams
jam tart
jump-cut
jamadar
jemadar
jemidar
jambeau
jambeux
Jamaica
jambiya
jemmied
✧jamming
jambier
jumpily
jump jet
jumelle
jumbler
Jumblat
jambone
jump off
jump-off
jambool
jam roll
jump out
✧jim crow
jumbuck
juncate
January
June bug
Janácek
Jane Doe
jankers
Jinzhou
Janeite
jinjili
Jungian
Jenkins
janskys
jungled
jangler
jingler
jinglet
junkman
Jon Snow
jannock
jingoes
juncoes
Jan Oort
juniper
Janetta
Janette
janitor
jonquil
janizar
jeopard
jeofail
jookery
jipyapa
Japheth
Japonic
Jephtha

Jupiter
jury box
Jericho
juridic
jarring
jerking
Jersian
jerkily
jurally
jarkman
juryman
jurymen
jargoon
jerk out
jury-rig
jerquer
jarfuls
jessant
jessamy
jaspery
jestful
Jessica
Justina
jasmine
jussive
justice
Justine
jesting
Jesuits
justify
just now
jus soli
Josette
Jethart
jitters
jet d'eau
jittery
jettied
jet pipe
jetting
jotting
jutting
jetfoil
jet boat
✧j'ouvert
joukery
journal
journos
journey
jauntee
jauntie
jouster
jive-ass
javelin
Java man
✧juvenal
Java Sea
jawfall
Jew's eye
Jew's-ear
jawless
jewfish
jewelry
jawbone
jawhole
jaw-foot
jaywalk
Joycean
joyless
joyride
joyance

jazz age
Jezebel
jazzily
jazzman
jazz-pop
khanate
knaidel
khaddar
knavery
khalifa
kyanise
kyanite
kyanize
Keating
knavish
klavier
khanjar
Khalkha
knacker
Kharkov
knapped
knapple
knapper
knarred
klatsch
khamsin
Kwanzaa
kabbala
kabaddi
Koblenz
Kubrick
kebbock
kibitka
kebbuck
kibbutz
kick-ass
kachcha
kuchcha
ko cycle
kacheri
kachina
kicking
Kuching
kick off
kick-off
kick out
kidding
kidling
Kaddish
kiddier
kiddies
kidskin
kiddush
keelage
Kiel Bay
knee-cap
kneecap
kneidel
Kiev Dam
kneader
knevell
keep fit
keep-fit
khediva
✧khedive
keeling
keening
keeping
kneeled
✧kremlin
kneeler

keep mum
keelman
klezmer
keepnet
Kleenex®
keep off
keep out
knee-pad
knee-pan
keelson
Kherson
knees-up
Knesset
koftgar
kufiyah
keg beer
kagoule
kohanim
Kuh-horn
kahawai
klipdas
Krishna
kainite
knifing
Krilium®
klinker
knicker
keitloa
krimmer
kail-pat
kail-pot
knitted
knittle
keister
knitter
K-Y® jelly
kajawah
kakodyl
kokakos
kikumon
kokanee
Kekrops
kakapos
Kildare
kellaut
kilobit
killcow
killdee
kiln-dry
kolkhoz
Kallima
killing
killick
Killian
killjoy
Kalinin
kalends
kill off
kalooki
killock
kiloton
Kilauea
Kalmuck
Kampala
kamichi
kamseen
Kommers
kemping
kimonos
kimboed
kampong

kamerad
komatik
kumquat
Kannada
kingcup
kingdom
kantela
Kundera
kantele
Kenneth
kennels
kinless
Kennedy
kinchin
kinship
king-hit
kunzite
kenning
Kunming
Kentish
Kennick
Kantism
Kantian
Kantist
kinkily
King Log
kindler
kinglet
king mob
kinsman
Ken Dodd
kongoni
kinfolk
Kinnock
kingpin
kindred
king-rod
kenosis
kinesis
Kenitra
kenotic
kinetic
know-all
knobbed
knobble
khotbah
khotbeh
knobber
knobbly
Kroo-boy
know-how
knowhow
kaoline
knowing
kookily
knock on
knock-on
knock up
knock-up
knocker
Kroo-man
Khoisan
Khonsou
knotted
klootch
knotter
kippage
Kipling
kipskin
kept man
kip down

kopiyka
kopiyok
kurbash
Kursaal
Kurhaus
Karachi
Kartell
kirmess
kerygma
kerogen
Kirghiz
Karaite
kernite
Karling
karting
kerning
kirking
kernish
Kurdish
karaism
✧karakul
kirtled
keramic
kirimon
Koranic
Karenni
karaoke
koreros
Kara Sea
karoshi
karstic
Kirstie
keratin
kirkton
Kirstin
Kerouac
Kushite
Keswick
Kushiro
kishkes
✧kashmir
kiss off
kiss-off
kestrel
✧kashrus
✧kashrut
kithara
Ketubah
kitschy
katydid
kitteny
kitchen
ketchup
Katrina
Katrine
kitling
ketonic
kitenge
kathode
kit-boat
katorga
Kathryn
ketosis
ketotic
knubble
khutbah
knubbly
koumiss
knuckle
knuckly
knurled

kruller
kouprey
Kuwaiti
Kiwanis
Kowloon
keycard
Kayseri
key-desk
keyless
key-seat
keyline
kayoing
key ring
kayaker
key-cold
keyword
keyhole
keynote
krytron
key grip
krypsis
krypton
leafage
leakage
leafbud
lean bow
Leander
leap day
leave be
leave go
llanero
leaders
leafery
leaf fat
loathed
leather
loather
loathly
leading
leafing
leaning
leaping
leasing
leaving
loading
loafing
loaning
leaflet
learned
learner
lianoid
leasowe
lead off
lead-off
lead out
lead-out
leak out
liatris
Liassic
liaison
loaf tin
lean-tos
leasure
✧leaguer
libbard
lubbard
labiate
librate
library
libidos
lobbing

lubfish
Librium®
labella
lobelia
lobular
lobules
lobulus
lobelet
Lobamba
Lebanon
labroid
labrose
lobworm
lobiped
Liberia
✧**liberal**
labarum
liberos
liberty
lobster
lobbyer
Luciana
lac-lake
lactase
lactate
lockage
lack-all
lace bug
Luce Bay
Lycidas
lucidly
Lycaena
Lucrece
lacteal
lectern
Lockean
lackeys
lechery
lockful
✧**lucifer**
lucigen
lacking
Li Ching
licking
lochial
lection
Lockian
Locrian
Lockist
luckily
lockjaw
Lucilla
Lucille
Lachlan
locular
locules
loculus
locally
lace-man
lockman
locoman
lucumos
lacinia
Lucinda
✧**laconic**
Lychnic
lacunae
licence
license
lacunal
lacunar
lychnis
locknut
Lucknow
lucency
lactone
lactose
lich-owl
lock out
lockout
luck out
Lacroix
lycopod
Lacerta
Le Carré
lucarne
✧lucerne
lockram
✧**locusta**
Lacoste
locator
lichtly
licitly
Lactuca
lecture
lecturn
lacquer
lyceums
lacquey
lichway
ladybug
ladycow
Lady Day
lidless
laddery
ladyfly
La Digue
ludship
Luddite
lyddite
lodging
laddish
ladyish
laddism
ladyism
Luddism
Lady Jay
ladykin
Lady Lee
ladanum
✧**ladinos**
ladrone
ladette
Ludovic
leeward
lie hard
laetare
lee gage
lee-lane
lee wave
lie back
lie-abed
Laender
leeze me
lee beam
liefest
lievest
leechee
lee side
lee tide
leering
lie down
lie-down
lie upon
loessic
Laertes
lie over
lift-boy
lifeful
leftish
leftism
leftist
loftily
lift-man
left-off
lift off
lift-off
laggard
lignage
luggage
leg bail
lugsail
leguaan
loggats
legible
legibly
logical
log-head
log-reel
legwear
legless
leg-rest
log-chip
leg-show
leg side
legside
lignite
logline
lagging
Lagting
legging
ligging
logging
Løgting
lugeing
lugging
leggism
loggias
lignify
leg slip
ligular
legally
legumin
logania
logwood
lignose
lughole
legwork
logbook
logroll
legroom
lugworm
✧**leghorn**
ligroin
leg spin
leg-spin
leg-iron
leg drop
lighted
legatee
legitim
lighten
light on
Loghtan
Loghtyn
light up
legator
lighter
legatos
lightly
leg-pull
Le Havre
lairage
lying-in
leidger
lyingly
laithfu'
laicise
laicize
lairise
lairize
laicity
leisler
laid low
laid off
Leitrim
leister
leisure
Leipzig
likable
likably
like fun
Lakshmi
lokshen
lekking
lakelet
like mad
Lake Van
Lollard
Lallans
lullaby
lulibub
lalling
Lillian
Lillias
lily pad
L S Lowry
lambada
lemmata
Limnaea
Lymnaea
Lombard
lamb-ale
limbate
limeade
lumbang
lumbago
lambast
Lyme Bay
lumache
limacel
limaçon
limaces
lum-head
Lumière
Lambeth
limbeck
lampern
lampers
limbers
lambent
lambert
lamp-fly
lamiger
Limoges
lymphad
lempira
lambing
lamming
lamping
lemming
limning
limping
lumping
lompish
lumpish
Lamaism
lampion
Lemnian
Lamaist
lumpily
lambkin
limpkin
lumpkin
lamella
limulus
lamplit
limelit
lomenta
laminae
liminal
lumenal
luminal
lam into
laminar
lampoon
lamboys
limbous
limepit
Lemuria
✧**lemures**
lamprey
lump sum
limosis
limited
lameter
lamiter
limiter
lymiter
limites
lampuka
lampuki
langaha
lantana
linear A
linear B
laniard
lanyard
lindane
lineage
lineate
linkage
linsang
long arm
long-ago
laniary
longbow
linkboy
linocut
linseed
lantern
Linnean
lyncean
✧**lancers**
linters
lengest
lenient
longest
lungful
lanugos
long hop
luncher
lyncher
linchet
lynchet
Lanzhou
lentisc
landing
lending
longing
lunging
longish
lentisk
lentigo
lankily
Lineker
long leg
lanolin
ländler
lunular
land law
landman
lensman
lineman
link man
linkman
linings
lentoid
long off
long-oil
Lincoln
lentous
lingoes
line-out
Londony
long pig
langrel
land-rat
langsam
long sin
Lindsay
Lindsey
lunatic
lunated
Linette
lunette
Lynette
Landtag
✧**long Tom**
long ten
long ton
linctus
land tax
lengthy
✧**lingula**
langued
languid
lingual
languor
languet
laneway
Leonard
leopard
leotard
Luoyang
lion-cub
lioncel
Lyomeri
lioness
loosely
loofful
lyophil
✧**leonine**
lionise
lionize
looning
looping
looting
lionism
lookism
Laotian
Leonian
loobily
Leonora
Leopold
loo roll
Laocoon
look out
lookout
look-see
Leontes
look you
La Plata
✧**lapsang**
Lepidus
lapheld
lip-read
lip-deep
lipless
lap belt
liplike
lapping
lapwing
lipping
lopping
Lappish
lapilli
lupulin
lipemia
leprose
leptome
lapwork
leprous
leptons
leprosy
Laputan
Lapiths
lip-sync
liquate
liqueur
liquefy
Larnaca
larvate
lurdane
Lord Coe
loricae
lyrical
lyricon
Laridae
luridly
lorrell
lernean
largess
large it
larceny
largely
larchen
lurcher
lording
lurking
largish
larkish
Lerwick
larmier
Lord Jim
lordkin
✧**lorelei**
lorimer
La Ronde
lorgnon
Lorenzo
loriner
lardoon
Loretta
lyrated
lorette
L-driver
lyra-way
lastage
losable
Lisbeth
listeth
listful
lustful
lasagna
lasagne
lashing
lasting
lisping
listing
luskish
lustick
✧**lesbian**
lustily
lashkar
last man
lisente
lassoed
lissome
lassock
lassoer
lassoes
lash out
last out
lose out
lustral
lustrum
lustres
Lisette
Lesotho
lispund
Lisburn
lost wax
lose way
lithate
let fall
Lothair
latrant
latices
lethean
lettern
luthern
letters
Lutyens
lathery
lithely
littery
lottery
latchet
lethied
latrine
lattice
let ride
Lettice
lithite
lathing
letting
lotting
Lettish
lithium
Latvian
Lothian
luthier
lithify
Latakia
littlin
let slip
latence
let into
Latiner
Latinus
latency
lithoed
lithoid
let down
let-down
luteous
lateral
literal
Lythrum
Lateran
let drop
lit crit
liturgy
Letitia
Let It Be
litotes
latitat
lettuce
latexes
Louvain
laus Deo
launder
lounder
laundry
Lou Reed
louse up
laurels
Launfal
lounger
loungey
leuchen
leughen
laugher
laugh at
Liuzhou
lauwine
leucine
leucite
louring
lousing
loudish
loutish
La Union
lousily
leucoma
louvred
livable

Words marked ✧ can also be spelled with one or more capital letters

lovable
lavabos
live-box
lived-in
loved up
lividly
love-day
levying
lavolta
livelod
level up
levelly
Lavinia
livener
live off
live oak
live out
lovered
Livorno
leveret
love rat
loverly
levitic
levator
levy war
lawland
lowland
low-paid
law-calf
Low Mass
✧lowveld
low tech
low-tech
low-bell
low gear
low-gear
lawless
lowness
low-rent
low life
low-life
low-rise
low tide
law-list
lowlily
Law Lord
Lew Hoad
law-book
low-born
low-down
low-cost
low toby
low-bred
lowbrow
lewisia
lewdsby
lawsuit
lexical
lexicon
laxness
loxygen
laxator
lay bare
layback
lay wait
lay odds
laytime
ley line
loyally
loyalty
Layamon

lay into
laylock
lay down
lay-down
lay open
lay upon
layered
layette
lay it on
layover
lay away
layaway
lazy-bed
lazy eye
Lizbeth
lozenge
lozengy
Lazarus
lazaret
Mbabane
meat-axe
meal-ark
meander
moanful
meat-fly
myalgia
myalgic
Meacher
Moabite
meaning
mean ill
myalism
meatier
mealies
meatily
maatjes
measled
measles
miasmic
miasmal
meal-man
meat-man
Myanmar
miasmas
meacock
meadowy
meat pie
mean sun
meat-tea
meat-tub
measure
mobbing
mobbish
mobsman
Mubarak
mobster
mace-ale
macramé
mockage
macrami
Michael
Meccano®
mockado
machair
macabre
macacos
macadam
Mica Dam
machete
Macbeth
mochell

muchell
mickery
mockery
mucigen
macchie
machine
miching
mocking
miction
muckier
micella
mycelia
maculae
micelle
Mechlin
macular
macumba
meconic
Mycenae
meconin
mockney
microbe
microns
muck out
macaque
machree
my certy
mucosae
mucosal
mock sun
mycoses
mycosis
mycotic
✧mycetes
Macrura
Macduff
machzor
madrasa
mud lava
Midgard
✧midland
mediate
Midrash
mudbath
mudlark
mudpack
mediant
Mideast
mediacy
medacca
medical
modicum
medicos
mudscow
✧mid-week
midterm
mid-year
madness
maddest
middest
mid-Lent
Midwest
midship
Madeira
muddied
midsize
midwife
midwive
midriff
madding
madling

Midwich
mudfish
muddier
muddily
✧mudéjar
medulla
middle C
medaled
modeled
modelli
modello
mudflap
meddler
modeler
modular
muddler
modulus
medalet
mudflat
mudflow
modally
made man
Madonna
madroña
Modiola
madrone
mud-cone
mudhole
modioli
maddock
mudhook
madzoon
midnoon
midtown
madroño
mid-hour
madwort
midmost
mud-boat
mudwort
madoqua
mudiria
mad-bred
moderne
Madurai
midiron
Mr Darcy
medusae
modiste
✧madison
medusan
medusas
modesty
mud-lump
mud pump
mediums
medevac
Maenads
meercat
mueddin
Mae West
meeting
meemies
meerkat
moellon
myeloma
myeloid
McEnroe
maestri
maestro
muezzin

muffish
maffick
Muftiat
miffily
maffled
muffled
mafalde
mafflin
muffler
Myfanwy
miff off
✧mafiosi
✧mafioso
mofette
magmata
magnate
migrate
migrant
megabar
megabit
magical
Mogadon®
Megaera
magneto
megafog
mug shot
mugshot
mugging
muggish
muggier
Magpies
megrims
muggins
magnify
moguled
magalog
Mogilev
magsman
magenta
mugwort
maggoty
Maghreb
Maghrib
megarad
megaron
megasse
megaton
mightn't
mightst
mugwump
magnums
mugfuls
Meg Ryan
Mahican
✧mohican
mahseer
Mohegan
Mahdism
Mahdist
Mt Hekla
Mahomet
mahonia
mah-jong
✧mahatma
Mahound
mridang
mailbag
mailbox
mail-car
moineau
mail-gig

moither
mailing
maiming
maidish
maidism
maillot
mailman
moidore
mainour
mail-out
maître d'
Maigret
Meissen
meioses
meiosis
myiasis
meiotic
moisten
maintop
maister
meister
maistry
moistly
mailvan
Majorca
major in
majorat
majorly
majesty
makable
mikados
make for
make hay
Mt Kenya
makings
Mikonos
make off
mikrons
make out
mukhtar
make use
make war
make way
mallard
maleate
maltase
mild ale
mileage
Millais
Malraux
miliary
milk bar
malacia
Malachi
malicho
milk cap
milk-cow
melodic
milldam
mylodon
Mole End
Maltese
mill-eye
Molière
meltemi
Malvern
mullein
malleus
milieus
milreis
milieux

mildewy
malefic
Mt Logan
Malthus
malaise
mellite
millime
milvine
malting
melting
milking
milling
meltith
Millian
million
mullion
milkily
mollify
Molokai
Melilla
milk leg
melilot
maltman
milkman
molimen
melanic
Malinke
melange
mélange
Melanie
melanin
Malines
melanos
molinet
Moldova
maltose
mullock
milfoil
Malcolm
Miltown®
mole out
mellowy
milk pan
malaria
Mildred
milk run
millrun
mall rat
mole rat
malarky
melisma
Melissa
Molasse
molossi
malison
milksop
malmsey
malt tea
militia
mulatta
mulcted
mulatto
militar
Miletus
Molotov
mollusc
multure
mollusk
mulmull
M G Lewis
Malayan

Mombasa
mammate
mammary
mimical
mimicry
mamzers
momzers
mummery
mamaguy
Memphis
mummied
mumming
mumpish
mimmick
mumsier
memoirs
mummify
mamilla
mamelon
mumbler
mimulus
momenta
memento
mim-mou'd
mammoth
mammock
mummock
membral
mimosae
mu-meson
mimesis
mimosas
memetic
mimetic
Mt Mayon
mancala
mandala
manyata
Montana
mansard
✧mandate
man-made
miniate
mintage
Mondale
montage
montane
mundane
man jack
man-jack
manjack
manpack
mondain
man-days
manoaos
minyans
Mondays
montant
minable
menu-bar
minibar
minibus
minicab
monacid
manacle
monocle
minicam
menacer
mini-car
Manx cat

monocot
monadic
monodic
Monodon
Mandela
minuend
man-week
Mansell
manteel
Mindelo
montero
man-year
minceur
mynheer
manless
manners
monkeys
manrent
manteau
mongery
monkery
mindful
monofil
Managua
manager
manihoc
menthol
Manchoo
muncher
manchet
Manihot
monthly
mandira
mandioc
mankind
man-like
mannite
man-size
manning
mending
mincing
minding
minging
munting
mannish
monkish
Mancini
minnick
mondial
mansion
mention
munnion
mankier
manlier
mingier
mintier
Mencius
mangily
mundify
muntjac
muntjak
manakin
manikin
minikin
moniker
manilla
Minolta®
monilia
manille
monolog
mangler

mingler
mantlet
manumea
minimal
minimum
Manxman
mint-man
monomer
minimus
manumit
minimax
mint-new
Men Only
mandola
mandora
Mendoza
mineola
mangold
manhood
manhole
mannose
manrope
menfolk
minnock
monsoon
man-hour
mangoes
mantoes
mind out
man-body
monopod
maniple
Manipur
Menorca
mens rea
Minerva
Minorca
monarda
✧menorah
monarch
mandrel
mandril
mineral
mongrel
mantram
minor in
moneron
mantrap
manurer
minaret
mini-sub
menisci
monoski
monosis
mindset
Manaslu
minutia
manatee
minette
Menotti
Minitel
minster
monitor
monster
Munster
Münster
minutes
manitou
monture
mensual
Mantuan

manhunt
minivan
minever
miniver
minivet
man-o'-war
men-o'-war
monaxon
moneyed
moneyer
mind you
moorage
miombos
moonbow
Miocene
mooneye
Mooress
Moorery
moon god
moorhen
moocher
mooring
mooting
moonish
✧moorish
moorill
muonium
moodier
Moonies
moodily
moorlog
moonlet
moonlit
moorman
mootman
maormor
Mjölnir
myosote
myotome
myology
moor-pan
myogram
moon rat
moonset
mooktar
myotube
Mao-suit
mophead
mapless
mappery
mapwise
mapping
mopping
mappist
Mt Pelée
Mt Qogir
Mariana
Marsala
mermaid
Margate
mirbane
muriate
myrbane
murlain
murrain
marcato
Marrano
mormaor
mordant
marybud

mirable
marabou
Merzbau
miracle
moriche
morocco
maracas
murices
Maracay
Muridae
mirador
✧muraena
Marlene
Morpeth
Marvell
murgeon
marrels
margent
martext
mordent
Marceau
morceau
Margery
mercery
mirific
Mr Right
morphia
morrhua
morphic
myrrhic
marshal
myrrhol
Märchen
marcher
markhor
murther
✧marches
morphos
merchet
morphew
Martina
married
marline
Marmite®
marmite
Martine
moraine
morrice
mortice
mortise
murrine
marking
marling
marring
merling
morling
morning
moreish
murkish
Martini®
✧martini
✧martial
Marxism
Marcian
Marmion
Martian
Marxian
mersion
morrion
murrion
marrier

merrier
Marxist
mercify
merrily
mortify
murkily
markkaa
markkas
marbled
morulae
Marilyn
morello
marbler
morular
marbles
merells
morulas
marplot
martlet
morally
Morglay
maremma
marimba
maremme
Mérimée
markman
Maranta
Miranda
Moringa
myringa
moronic
meranti
meronym
Marengo
morendo
mariner
Marinus
merinos
margosa
Marlowe
marmose
mark off
morwong
Murdoch
✧marconi
merfolk
Mormops
mark out
Marjory
marrowy
marl-pit
Moresco
more suo
✧morisco
Marists
morassy
Maratha
Marathi
marital
Marcuse
marquee
morsure
Marburg
marquis
✧mercury
Moravia
Mordvin
murexes
marry up
Marsyas
martyry

maruzze
mascara
mastaba
Mustafa
mislaid
missaid
mustard
massage
message
misdate
misease
misfare
misgave
mismade
mismake
mismate
misname
misrate
mistake
mustang
miscall
misfall
mista'en
miscast
mishapt
musk-bag
musk-cod
musical
musk-cat
Mustela
misdeed
misfeed
mislead
misread
missend
miswend
misdeal
misfell
mis-sell
mistell
misdeem
misseem
misterm
misween
masseur
mishear
missent
miswent
mastery
mistery
mystery
mast-fed
mastful
mistful
museful
Mashhad
moss hag
Messina
mestiza
massive
misfile
misfire
misgive
mislike
mislive
missile
missive
mistime
mastiff
mashing
meshing

missing
misting
moshing
mastich
✧messiah
missish
miskick
misdial
Mosaism
mission
mestizo
Miskito
mistico
messier
mistier
mossier
mushier
muskier
mustier
✧messias
misdiet
messily
mistily
mushily
muskily
mustily
mystify
mess kit
mascled
meseled
muscled
Moselle
mashlam
mashlim
mashlum
mesclum
mashlin
mesclun
Musales
mesally
misally
misplay
mishmee
mashman
musimon
masonic
mesonic
Mishnic
Mishnah
Mt Sinai
mist net
mist-net
misknow
masonry
Mashona
Massora
mastoid
mistold
misword
muscoid
misdone
misgone
misyoke
muscone
muscose
muskone
mistook
misform
Mas-John
Mes-John
misborn

misjoin
Mrs Mopp
misdoer
miss out
miscopy
Muscovy
musk-pod
mosh pit
Masorah
mesarch
mistral
muskrat
misdraw
miserly
musk-sac
must-see
misuser
mash-tub
musette
mash-tun
mess-tin
misstep
meshuga
misrule
mistune
misluck
mesquin
masquer
museums
mesquit
missuit
masculy
moshvei
mash-vat
Mesozoa
methane
matrass
matzahs
metcast
mutable
mutably
metical
maticos
matador
Mt Thera
matweed
mittens
matiest
moth-eat
MOT test
mattery
mothery
mitogen
mutagen
matched
matchup
matcher
Matthew
Mt Thira
matrice
mythise
mythize
matting
methink
mythism
mothier
mattins
metrics
metrist
mythist
Matilda

metaled
mettled
mottled
Mytilus
matelot
metally
metamer
mutanda
Metonic
matinee
matinée
matinal
metonym
mattoid
mottoed
matooke
matzoth
Matlock
mattock
matzoon
matlows
matross
motions
mottoes
mete out
Methody
muttony
metopic
metopon
Mithras
Matisse
✧métisse
mitoses
mitosis
mitotic
matsuri
Matsudo
motivic
mitzvah
métayer
✧metazoa
Maulana
mousaka
moulage
mauvais
maunder
moulder
Maureen
mauvein
maulers
mousery
maulgre
mauther
moucher
mouther
mouth it
Mauriac
Maurice
mauvine
mousing
mousier
Maurist
mousily
mouillé
maudlin
mouflon
mousmee
mourner
mounted
Mountie
moulten

mount up
mounter
movable
movably
Mevlevi
Moviola®
move out
Mawlawi
mawseed
mawther
mawkish
mawkier
mowings
maw-worm
mow down
mowburn
mixable
Mexican
mixed-up
mixedly
✧maxwell
Max Uhle
mixtion
maxilla
maximal
maximum
maximin
Max Born
Max Euwe
mixture
may I add
May-game
may I ask
Mayfair
May laws
May-lady
mayweed
may-bird
Maytime
may-lily
May-lord
maypole
May-morn
may tree
mayoral
mayster
may-duke
mazzard
mizmaze
mezzani
Mazdean
mazeful
muzzier
muzzily
muzzler
Mazeppa
mazurka
Mozarab
Mazarin
mozetta
mezuzah
nuanced
near cut
nearest
Noachic
Nyanjas
naartje
Nabucco
nabbing
nibbing

nebbich
nebbish
niblick
nobbily
Nabokov
nebulae
nebular
nibbler
nobbler
nebulas
nibbles
nictate
nectary
nucleal
Nicaean
nuclein
nucleon
nuclear
nucleus
nacrite
nuclide
necking
niceish
nacelle
nucelli
Nicolas
necklet
no can do
no' canny
Nichola
necrose
nacrous
nocuous
nacarat
Nicosia
necktie
noctuid
noctule
nocturn
NBC suit
nodical
nodding
noduled
nodular
nodally
nodated
no doubt
✧**ne'erday**
Nyerere
needful
Niel Gow
Noetian
needily
needler
niellos
naevoid
nae mows
naebody
naff all
naffing
niftily
no-fines
naff off
no-fault
niggard
nagmaal
neglect
nuggety
negligé
négligé
nagging
nogging
Negrito
nigrify
nigella
niggler
✧**negroid**
✧**negroes**
nagapie
Nigeria
nighted
nightie
negator
nightly
Nahuatl
nihonga
no-hoper
Niigata
nail-bed
naiades
naiveté
naïveté
nailery
naively
naïvely
naivety
naïvety
nail gun
neither
nailing
noir-ish
noirish
naivist
noisily
noisome
Nairobi
nail-rod
nainsel'
nail set
nakedly
niks-nie
nilgais
nilgaus
nylghau
nulling
nullify
nullity
nelumbo
Nilotic
Nilotes
nummary
Namibia
namable
nomadic
name day
✧**numbers**
nimiety
nymphic
nymphae
nymphal
nymphos
nymphet
nymphly
numbing
nombles
numbles
nimonic
nominee
nominal
nimious
numeric
nomarch
nemoral
nombril
numeral
nemesia
namaste
name-son
✧**nemeses**
✧nemesis
nematic
nu-metal
nanobot
non-term
nankeen
non-hero
non-zero
nunnery
nonaged
nonagon
nunship
ninthly
nannied
nandine
nundine
Nanjing
Nanking
Nanning
nunnish
✧**nancies**
nannies
nuncios
non-skid
non-slip
nonplus
nunhood
non-come
nonuple
ninepin
Nynorsk
non-iron
non-drip
non-user
Nanette
Ninette
nonette
nonetti
nunatak
none too
nonetto
non-stop
nonsuch
nonsuit
non-jury
nun buoy
Nineveh
Nunavut
Neogaea
neonate
niobate
neo-Nazi
noonday
Neogene
Niobean
neoteny
niobite
nooning
neolith
niobium
nuoc mam
Neozoic
niobous
neology
noology
nap hand
napless
nippers
Nepthys
napping
nipping
nuptial
nappies
nippily
Nepalis
nephric
nephron
naphtha
nepotic
Neptune
✧**nirvana**
norland
nor'ward
norward
narrate
nervate
Normans
nurhags
nor'-east
norteña
narceen
norteño
nor'-west
nursery
Nurofen®
nuraghe
nuraghi
narwhal
norther
Nerthus
✧**narthex**
nargile
nervine
nursing
nerdish
Norwich
✧**nereids**
nargily
nervily
nartjie
norimon
Neronic
narrow a
Norfolk
narrows
nervous
Nerissa
neritic
nervule
nervure
nurture
Nureyev
Nastase
nosebag
nest box
nest egg
nascent
no sweat
noshery
nestful
nashgab
nosegay
nesting
nastily
nose job
nose-led
Nasalis
nasally
nose out
nose rag
nostril
nostrum
Netcafé
net game
nitrate
nutcase
not half
netball
nutgall
notable
not a bit
notably
notedly
nutmeal
notaeum
nathemo
nattery
not very
nuttery
not a few
notched
notchel
notch up
notcher
not that
Natchez
nitride
nitrile
nitrite
nutlike
nut pine
netting
nithing
nothing
nutting
net-fish
nit-pick
natrium
Nitrian
nattily
nitrify
nuttily
Natalia
Natalie
notelet
net-play
notanda
Nitinol
net cord
nutwood
network
nut-hook
nitroso
nations
nitrous
notions
note-pad
natured
niterie
nut-tree
Niterói
natural
note row
Natasha
notitia
netsuke
no-trump
netizen
noumena
nousell
nouveau
naughty
neurine
neurite
nourice
nourish
nautili
neurism
nautics
nauplii
neuroma
neurone
neutral
neutron
noursle
neuston
Nauruan
Navahos
navvied
Navajos
novalia
novella
Neville
novelle
Novalis
novelty
niveous
navarch
navarin
navarho
never so
Novi Sad
navette
new-laid
Newgate
new-made
✧new wave
✧new-wave
New Hall
newsboy
Newsday
nowhere
✧**new deal**
new peso
New Year
newness
nowness
New Left
✧**new ager**
new chum
now then!
new pice
new rich
newsman
newcome
new look
New York
newborn
new moon
new-mown
new town
new poor
New Ross
Newport
new star
Newbury
Newquay
noxious
nayward
noyance
nayword
noysome
Naziism
Okayama
of an age
oxalate
ouakari
ouabain
on and on
otalgia
orangey
ocarina
of a mind
of a size
on a time
opaline
otarine
oxazine
okaying
Obadiah
odalisk
onanism
oralism
orarium
orarian
orarion
oration
ovarian
ovation
otaries
onanist
oralist
opacity
orality
ovality
odaller
Oral Law
on a roll
opacous
of a sort
✧**oratory**
on appro
oratrix
Onassis
Omayyad
on board
on-board
onboard
oxblood
Osborne
orbital
orbiter
orchard
oscheal
oncogen
osculum
oscular
obconic
orcinol
Oscines
occiput
oncosts
Occitan
occlude
old hand
old maid
old face
old gang
old talk
old-talk
oddball
Old Dart
old salt
old lady
old bean
old dear
odd legs
oddness
oldness
oddment
old chap
old bird
odd-like
old-line
old-time
old wife
on drive
on-drive
odd fish
Old Nick
Old Bill
old girl
oodlins
oddsman
ordinee
ordinal
ordinar
old gold
old rose
old song
old moon
odd jobs
old boot
old fogy
Oedipal
Oedipus
orderer
orderly
ondatra
oldster
odd-even
operand
operate
over age
over-age
overage
overawe
over-all
overall
overarm
oregano
open-air
operant
overact
overbid
overbuy
overdub
overdue
overdye
oreades
open day
open-end
oreweed
overeye
one self
oneself
oneness
overeat
overfed
overfar
overfly
overget
one-shot
overhit
obelise
obelize
olefine
one-time
Owenite
opening
obelisk
Owenism
obelion
Owenian
Owenist
obesity
open-jaw
overjoy
overlie
oleo leg
overlap
ocellar
ocellus
overlay
open-mic
overman
Oceania
Oleanna
oceanic
✧**oceanid**
Oceanus
overnet
oceloid
onefold
operose
one's own
onerous
open out
ore body
overpay
overply
olearia
oneiric
overred
on earth
overran
overren
overrun
over-rev
open sea
oversea
oversee
overset
oversew
oversow
orectic
omental
omentum
one-step
one-stop
open-top
overtop
Orestes
oven-tit
overtax
overtly
overuse
one-eyed
offhand
off-ward

Words marked ✧ can also be spelled with one or more capital letters

off base
offtake
off-ramp
offscum
officer
offices
off-peak
offpeak
off beam
off-beam
offbeat
off line
off-line
offline
offside
off-site
ooftish
off-plan
offence
offense
ox-fence
offload
off-road
off-come
off-fore
off spin
off-spin
od-force
offeree
offer up
offerer
offeror
off duty
off-duty
on guard
orgiast
ouguiya
on-going
ongoing
oogonia
organza
organic
organum
organon
organdy
Ophidia
ochreae
Ophelia
Othello
oghamic
ochroid
ochrous
✧ophitic
ophiura
Okinawa
origane
oxidase
oxidate
origami
oxidant
olivary
Oniscus
olivine
orifice
ovicide
oxidise
oxidize
Odinism
opinion
Osirian
Ovidian
Olivier
Odinist
oligist
oriency
oviform
okimono
ominous
olitory
osiered
omicron
omitted
opiated
omitter
obitual
oviduct
Ojibwas
Oakland
oak gall
oak mast
oak-leaf
oak fern
Orkneys
oakling
oak wilt
oak-wood
oak tree
oak lump
oil sand
oil-cake
oil bath
oil palm
orleans
oilseed
oil seal
oil well
oil-less
oil-belt
onliest
obligee
obliger
obligor
oilbird
owl-like
oil-rich
oil silk
oil mill
oilskin
oolakan
oulakan
Orlando
on-liner
onliner
owl-moth
oblique
obloquy
oil-tree
oil drum
oolitic
only too
oil pump
owl-eyed
osmiate
oomiack
Ohm's law
osmunda
Osmanli
osmious
O C Marsh
osmosis
ommatea
osmotic
omniana
omnibus
omniety
omnific
omneity
oenomel
own goal
of no use
Odonata
obovate
odorate
odorant
obolary
Odoacer
ovoidal
on order
oropesa
orogeny
on offer
oporice
ozonide
ozonise
ozonize
otolith
oxonium
Oxonian
ologist
obovoid
oloroso
odorous
orology
otology
odoured
opossum
odontic
orotund
otocyst
oppidan
Orphean
oppress
Orpheus
of price
Orphism
on paper
orphrey
opposer
oophyte
ocreate
o'ergang
our Lady
oarweed
ourself
oarless
oar fish
ogreish
owrelay
oarsman
orra man
o'erword
o'ercome
oarlock
oersted
on stage
on-stage
ossuary
ossicle
onstead
obscene
on sleep
ossific
on sight
od's life
oustiti
osselet
opsonic
opsonin
on shore
on-shore
onshore
oospore
od's bobs
osseous
obsequy
observe
oestral
oestrum
oestrus
of sorts
osseter
obscure
ostraca
ostraka
outland
outward
oatcake
ostiate
outdare
outdate
outface
outgate
outname
outpace
outrace
outrage
outrate
out-take
outtake
out-half
outlash
outwash
Ostmark
outback
outrank
outtalk
outwalk
outfall
outhaul
outsail
out-wall
on toast
outcast
outlast
outpart
outwait
ostiary
October
optical
octadic
outedge
Otto Dix
ootheca
outweed
oatmeal
outsell
outtell
outwell
on the in
on the go
on the up
outleap
outpeep
outweep
outpeer
outwear
outness
on the QT
outjest
outwent
octofid
out of it
octagon
outshot
outwind
outgive
outhire
outline
outlive
outride
outside
outsize
outwing
ostrich
outfish
outwith
outwick
on trial
orthian
outlier
ortolan
outflow
outplay
optimal
optimum
✧ottoman
osteoma
osteoid
out cold
out loud
ostiole
outcome
outgone
outmode
outmove
outrope
outsole
outvote
outlook
outwork
outworn
outroop
outdoor
outgoer
outpour
outroar
outsoar
Options
outgoes
outfoot
outmost
outport
outpost
outroot
octapla
octopod
octuple
outspan
out upon
octopus
outbred
outbrag
Ontario
outcrop
on terms
orthros
outgrow
outpray
out-tray
octette
outstep
outstay
obtrude
outdure
outgush
outrush
outburn
outturn
outjump
on trust
Octavia
octaval
out-over
octavos
out-owre
outswim
outhyre
oculate
ovulate
opuscle
✧opus Dei
opulent
oculist
oeuvres
opuntia
obviate
ouvrage
Orvieto
ouvrier
obvious
obverse
ouverte
on wings
onwards
oxy-salt
oxyacid
onychia
odylism
Ogygian
oxytone
olycook
olykoek
onymous
Olympia
Olympic
Olympus
Olympus®
✧odyssey
oxyntic
odzooks
placard
placate
platane
✧pharaoh
peasant
play-act
phalanx
peatary
peat bed
prabble
peat bog
Playbus®
play-box
✧playboy
peascod
prancke
✧prancer
placcat
Phaedra
plaided
Play-Doh®
p's and q's
plaudit
play-day
phase in
placebo
prayers
plateau
peatery
playful
piaffer
play hob
peat-hag
peach on
peacher
poacher
plashet
placita
platina
praline
peaking
phasing
placing
plating
playing
prating
praying
planish
Platini
phaeism
pianism
plagium
pianino
pianist
piarist
pravity
prankle
play kip
placket
prank it
phallic
pearled
pearlin
phallin
prawlin
Phar Lap
pearler
✧phallus
playlet
pyaemia
plasmic
ptarmic
pyaemic
phasmid
plasmid
peatman
plasmin
plasmon
planned
praunce
planner
plainly
Pianola®
phacoid
placoid
plafond
play off
play-off
✧peacock
peafowl
platoon
pea soup
pea coat
peak out
play out
playpen
pea-crab
prairie
pea-iron
Prakrit
praiser
praeses
plastic
practic
plaited
plastid
platted
piastre
prattle
phantom
phaeton
Plantin
plaiter
plantar
planter
plaster
platter
praetor
✧psalter
peartly
planula
peanuts
plaguey
planury
play-way
planxty
pharynx
pébrine
pubbing
publish
pebbled
pabulum
pabular
pibroch
puberal
puberty
pubises
P W Botha
pochard
pockard
package
pickaxe
picrate
peccavi
peccant
peccary
pacable
pace car
picador
pace egg
pace-egg
pickeer
pschent
pickery
puckery
✧pacific
pack ice
pectise
pectize
picrite
pycnite
packing
pecking
picking
peckish
Pictish
puckish
pachisi
Puccini
paction
piccies
pickled
✧pucelle
pickler
pickles
piculet
packman
picamar
pickmaw
picante
pectose
pack off
pick off
pickoff
puccoon
piccolo
pochoir
piceous
pace out
pick out
pockpit
pack-rat
Picasso
picotee
picture
picquet
packway
pedrail
pedlary
pedicab
pedicle
pedicel
pidgeon
pedrero
podagra
padding
podding
pudding
padella
podalic
pedaled
paddler
peddler
piddler
puddler
pedalos
pudenda
pudency
padrone
padroni
paddock
padlock
piddock
puddock
pad-tree
podestà
pedesis
pedetic
precava

piebald
prefard
prepaid
pyebald
peerage
phenate
pierage
Pléiade
predate
preface
prefade
prelate
prepare
presage
pre-wash
prepack
prevail
prewarm
predawn
prewarn
peekabo
Pleiads
precast
plenary
prelacy
prelaty
pierced
pre-echo
piercer
preachy
pleaded
pleader
preverb
prebend
prehend
pretend
precede
prevene
pre-sell
preterm
plebean
pre-teen
piece up
peeress
peevers
poetess
precess
precept
prefect
preheat
prelect
present
pretest
pretext
prevent
preyful
pledgee
pledger
pledgor
pledget
pie-shop
poe-bird
Peelite
poetise
poetize
precise
premise
preside
previse
puerile
peeling

peevish
piedish
plenish
prejink
predial
pietism
premium
Pierian
pterion
plenipo
premier
poetics
prelims
premiss
pietist
plenist
predict
preview
plebify
phellem
Peebles
✧pueblos
preemie
pre-empt
paeonic
pfennig
pleroma
plerome
premove
prepone
prepose
peel off
pierogi
precook
precool
predoom
preform
preborn
pleopod
prepped
pleurae
pleural
preoral
pleuron
✧**pierrot**
pleased
pressed
preasse
pressie
press on
press-up
pleaser
plessor
presser
pressor
plectra
P-Celtic
pleated
peep-toe
plectre
Prestel®
Preston
pre-stun
pleater
prestos
paenula
plexure
prelude
prepuce
presume
preludi

prequel
prerupt
pteryla
pie-eyed
prenzie
prezzie
pretzel
pheazar
puff-box
po-faced
piffero
puffery
puffing
puffily
piffler
pigwash
peg back
pigtail
pageant
pageboy
pigfeed
pig-herd
pig-lead
pigweed
pigmean
pygmean
pig-deer
pigmeat
pigment
piggery
puggery
pegging
pigging
pigling
pogoing
pugging
pig-fish
piggish
puggish
pig sick
pig-sick
pug mill
piggies
pig-lily
pigskin
puggled
pigsnie
paginal
pigsney
pigmoid
pygmoid
pug nose
pug-moth
peg down
peg-tops
pigboat
Piggott
pagurid
puggree
pig iron
✧**pegasus**
pightle
pig-jump
peg away
pig-eyed
Pahlavi
Pehlevi
Pohjola
plicate
primage
primate

prisage
private
paisano
poinado
privado
primacy
✧primary
privacy
pliable
pribble
pliably
paiocke
prince's
princox
poinder
primero
primeur
primely
pailful
painful
prigged
prigger
peishwa
prithee
primine
pairing
priming
pairial
pridian
pricier
Phidias
privily
privity
pliskie
prickle
prick in
prick up
prink up
pricker
pricket
prickly
paillon
Phillip
✧**paisley**
primmed
primmer
psionic
pliancy
pair off
pair-oar
✧**priapic**
Priapus
poitrel
Prizren
primsie
poisson
painted
pointed
philtre
pointel
point up
painter
philter
pointer
printer
pointes
point at
primula
pajocke
pyjama'd
pajamas

P D James
pyjamas
pokeful
poke fun
pak choi
pukekos
pikelet
pikeman
pakfong
paktong
pakapoo
Pakhtun
Poltava
polkaed
pollard
pale ale
palmate
palpate
peltate
pileate
pillage
poleaxe
poll-axe
pollaxe
pulsate
pellach
pellack
✧pollack
pillars
peltast
polyact
palmary
palabra
pill bug
pillbox
polacca
polacre
pelican
pile-cap
palm cat
polecat
paludic
paludal
paladin
polyene
pulleys
pollent
pilfery
palmful
pelagic
polygam
polygon
phlegmy
pilcher
palsied
palling
pelting
pilling
polling
pulvini
pallial
pallium
pillion
palmiet
palmist
poloist
pollicy
pulpify
pulpily
Palikir
Palilia

pilular
palolos
polemic
palamae
pollman
Pullman
polymer
✧**phlomis**
polenta
Polonia
polynia
polynya
polonie
✧**pilsner**
pilinut
palooka
polyoma
pallone
palm off
pull off
pellock
pillock
✧pollock
palm oil
palm-oil
pilcorn
pultoon
pileous
pulpous
pile out
pull out
pull-out
pillory
pillowy
Pelopid
polypod
polypes
polypus
peloria
peloric
pyloric
pilgrim
polaron
puldron
Palermo
pelorus
Polaris
pylorus
pilcrow
palfrey
pelisse
pull-tab
pelitic
politic
palette
palatal
peloton
palmtop
P-plater
Pilates
pilotis
paletot
poll tax
poll-tax
pollute
pulture
Palauan
palaver
Palawan
phloxes
palmyra

Polyzoa
palazzi
palazzo
pompano
pemican
pommelé
Pompeii
pampean
pampero
pompelo
pump gun
pimping
pompion
pumpion
pompier
pumpkin
pimpled
pomelos
pimento
pompoon
pompous
pump out
pomfret
pomeroy
pi-meson
pomatum
Pangaea
poniard
pancake
pannage
pen-case
pen name
pennate
pentane
pincase
pinnace
pinnate
pondage
pontage
Panjabi
pindari
Punjabi
pinball
pintail
pintado
pendant
pennant
pentact
pangamy
panacea
panocha
panache
panicle
penuche
pinocle
penuchi
Panicum
panicky
Panadol®
pinhead
pangene
pentene
pink-eye
Pandean
pincers
pandect
pendent
pungent
puniest
ponceau
Panagia

pink gin
punt-gun
penthia
pinched
punch-up
panther
pincher
puncher
ponchos
panchax
Pontiac®
pansied
pennied
pensiv'd
pantile
pantine
pennine
pensile
pensive
pentice
pentise
pin-fire
pontile
pontine
pontiff
panging
panning
panting
pending
penning
pinking
pinning
punning
Penrith
pinfish
pinkish
punkish
pentiti
pannick
pennill
Pentium®
Pandion
Peneian
pension
Pontian
pentito
pannier
panties
pennies
paneity
pontify
punalua
pantler
pingler
Pan-Slav
penally
penalty
penance
paninis
pine nut
✧**pandora**
penfold
pinfold
pinnoed
pandore
pannose
Pantone®
pentode
pentose
pinhole
pan loaf

pinnock
pantoum
pinworm
pin down
pindown
pontoon
pandoor
pandour
pingoes
pinkoes
pongoes
pint-pot
panoply
Pan-Arab
pangram
pan drop
penises
pinetum
punctum
pin it on
pine tar
Pinxter
punster
penates
punctos
pandura
pinnula
pinguid
pinnule
pin tuck
pin curl
penguin
pinguin
panfuls
pin-dust
pin-eyed
pro rata
prosaic
proband
provand
peonage
phonate
probate
proface
profane
prolate
pronate
propage
propale
propane
prorate
probang
pronaoi
proball
pronaos
provant
Pooh-Bah
Phoebus
poor box
plodded
prodded
Proddie
plodder
prodder
Plovdiv
proudly
proverb
proceed
propend
proteid
protend

provend
phoneme
propene
protégé
phone-in
✧protean
protein
pioneer
proneur
process
profess
✧proteus
prowess
project
protect
protest
plovery
poovery
progeny
pronely
Ptolemy
plotful
proffer
pronged
prothyl
✧**prophet**
phocine
plosive
profile
pro-life
proline
✧promise
propine
provide
provine
pioning
prosing
proving
poorish
peonism
phobism
photism
protium
plosion
proviso
proximo
phonics
photics
Photius
pionies
phobist
protist
probity
prodigy
prosify
prosily
prop-jet
plookie
ploukie
plonker
problem
proller
prouler
prowler
peoples
Proclus
poor law
poor-law
prommer
phoenix
pronota
prosoma
photo CD
promote
propone
propose
protore
provoke
prolong
poon-oil
pronoun
pro bono
photo op
poop out
poor-oot
provost
prosody
plopped
propped
prosper
prodrug
program
piously
prootic
plotted
plottie
proctal
plotter
plouter
plowter
proctor
procure
produce
profuse
Profumo
product
propyla
poogyee
protyle
Procyon
pep talk
papable
Papa Doc
popadum
popedom
pop-weed
Papeete
pipless
poppers
pap-meat
Pap test
pup tent
peppery
pipeful
pop-shop
paprika
poppied
pepsine
peptide
peptise
peptize
pipping
popping
pupping
poppish
pupfish
pep pill
Paphian
peptics
pipe-key
papilla
papulae
✧**papilio**
papular
popular
pupilar
papules
papally
pip emma
pupunha
papoose
pappose
peptone
pop song
popsock
popcorn
pappous
pap-boat
puparia
piperic
poperin
paperer
papyrus
pipette
pop star
Papaver
popover
pop-eyed
piquant
pargana
pardale
parpane
partake
percale
percase
pertake
pervade
portage
portate
pur sang
Parvati
pertain
perhaps
parfait
periapt
persant
parable
paracme
Porsche®
pericon
parodic
Paradip
parader
parador
Peredur
parados
peridot
paradox
parpend
perpend
Perseid
portend
Purbeck
Parnell
Purcell
peraeon
Perseus
Piraeus
porpess
portess
parpent
per cent
percept
perfect
perpent
pervert
porrect
portent
parvenu
parafle
porifer
Perugia
piragua
perigee
pirogue
peregal
paragon
perigon
pyrogen
✧**pyrrhic**
parched
perched
percher
✧**porthos**
Pyrrhus
pareira
partita
Perdita
pereira
parried
pardine
partite
parvise
percine
perlite
porcine
purline
parking
parsing
parting
purging
purling
purring
parkish
porcini
perjink
partial
Parsism
per diem
Persism
pereion
Permian
Persian
portion
persico
porrigo
portico
Perrier®
perrier
Persius
porkies
✧**persist**
purlieu
purview
perfidy
perkily
peruked
parella
purfled
pyralid
parelle
parolee
parulis
purples
✧pyralis
✧**partlet**
perplex
parsley
pyramid
portman
paramos
pyramis
Pyramus
piranha
phrenic
Puranic
paranym
paronym
parsnep
parsnip
pardner
partner
Puranas
pará nut
perenty
phrensy
pergola
persona
percoid
purpose
pyrrole
part-off
parrock
partook
porlock
parboil
perform
purloin
parlour
parlous
periods
perlous
persons
portous
percoct
periost
purport
parroty
pork pie
pyropus
parapet
Perspex®
perique
parerga
para-red
Portree
portray
parasol
perusal
phrasal
parison
peruser
phraser
paresis
poroses
porosis
pyrosis
paratha
paretic
parotic
piratic
pyretic
pyritic
parotid
✧**puritan**
paritor
parotis
peritus
pyrites
phratry
✧**purpura**
perturb
parture
perdure
perfume
perfuse
perjure
permute
pertuse
purpure
pursual
pursuer
percuss
parquet
pursuit
perfumy
perjury
periwig
parkway
part way
part-way
pyrexia
pyrexic
✧**parazoa**
passata
Pascale
passade
passage
postage
passado
passant
pessary
piscary
postbag
postbus
postbox
post boy
postdoc
post day
pisheog
pas seul
pastern
Piscean
posteen
postern
paste-up
Pasteur
pastels
possess
pusser's
pestful
pushful
push fit
postfix
post hoc
✧**paschal**
pessima
piscina
passive
pastime
piscine
pismire
passing
pasting
posting
pushing
✧**passion**
Peshito
pasties
peskily
Pasajes
Pushkin
passkey
passman
postman
pesante
Pistoia
pistole
pass off
post off
push off
push-off
pissoir
pass out
passout
push out
push-out
pushpin
pushpit
pushrod
posited
positif
push-tug
Pashtun
positon
Pushtun
Pushtoo
post-tax
pasture
posaune
poseuse
posture
pustule
pascual
Pasquil
Pasquin
pesaunt
post-war
pesewas
put paid
pet hate
pet name
pottage
put case
Pat Cash
potlach
pot bank
put back
patball
pitfall
petrary
patible
potable
potiche
Potsdam
pot herb
pithead
pot-head
pothead
pattern
potheen
patness
Pytheas
patient
pothery
pottery
putrefy
pithful
pitiful
patagia
potager
patched
pitched
putchuk
pitch in
patch up
patch-up
pitch up
potshop
patcher
pitcher
potcher
putcher
pith hat
pot shot
pituita
puttied
Petrine
✧pittite
pituite
patting
petting
pitting
pitying
potting
putting
pettish
✧**patrick**
pit-mirk
pot-sick
patrial
Pittism
pythium
Pythian
patrico
puttier
patriot
petrify
pettily
pithily
✧**patella**
patulin
potamic
Potomac
putamen
patamar
✧**petunia**
patined
patonce
potence
potencé
patency
potency
petiole
pothole
petcock
pothook
putlock
puttock
pit-coal
patroon
put down
put-down
petrous
piteous
put to it
putt out
pit pony
put upon
pit-a-pat
pitapat
paterae
pitarah
Patarin
potoroo
pitprop
pit brow
potassa
petasus
put it on
pit stop
pot luck
pit bull
potfuls
put over
pathway
put away
poulard
plumage
plumate
plusage
plumbic
plumbum
plumb in
plumber
pounced
plumcot
pouncet
paunchy
pouldre
poundal
plunder
poulder
pounder
pluteal
pluteus
Peugeot®
prudent
plumery
prudery
pouffed
plugged
plugger
plunger
pouched
pouther
plushes
plug-hat
paughty
Paulina
Pauline
pausing
plusing
pouring
pouting
pruning
prudish
pluvial
Paulian
prurigo
plumist
paucity
plucked
pluck up
plucker
plunker
plummet
pout net
plumose

plumous
pour out
pour-out
plumpie
plumpen
plumper
Paul Pry
plumply
prussic
plussed
poursue
✧poussin
plusses
poursew
prunted
poulter
poultry
plumula
plumule
pH value
Pevsner
✧pavlova
paviour
poverty
pivoted
pivotal
pivoter
Pawnees
pew-rent
powdery
pawkily
powered
power up
pyxidia
pyxides
pixy-led
paxiuba
paysage
pay cash
pay back
payback
pay cain
Prydain
poynant
payable
pay-desk
payment
psychic
pr'ythee
prythee
psych up
psych-up
psychos
poy-bird
pay-bill
physics
physios
pay dirt
paylist
psyllid
ptyalin
payslip
Phyllis
payload
plywood
payfone
pay home
payroll
pay down
pazzazz
pizzazz
puzzler
quayage
quahaug
quamash
Quapaws
Quakers
quavery
quaffer
quangos
✧quashee
✧quashie
quaking
qualify
quality
quackle
quacker
quannet
quadric
quarrel
quadrat
quassia
quantic
quartic
quantal
quantum
quartan
Q factor
quarter
quartos
quartet
quartzy
qabalah
Qaddish
Quercus
queachy
queechy
queue up
Quechua
queried
queuing
querist
queller
✧queenie
queynie
queen it
queenly
queerly
quetsch
Q-Celtic
Quentin
quester
questor
quetzal
quinate
quidams
quinary
quibble
quinche
quiddle
quiddit
quite so
quivery
Quichua
quinine
qui vive
quiting
quickie
quicken
quickly
quilled
quillai
quiblin
quillon
quillet
quinnat
quinoid
quinone
Quixote
quiesce
quids in
quintic
quilted
quitted
quintal
quittal
quieten
quintan
Quintin
Quinton
quieter
quilter
quitter
quittor
quietus
quintet
quietly
quizzed
quizzer
quizzes
quorate
quondam
quodlin
quoiter
quo jure?
qawwali
real ale
reawake
readapt
rhatany
roadbed
rhabdom
Reardon
Rwandan
rear-dos
rhabdus
reamend
rear-end
road end
reagent
Ruapehu
realgar
reached
roached
road hog
reacher
rhachis
rhaphis
readied
realise
realize
rearise
✧reading
reaming
roading
roaming
roaring
✧realism
realign
readier
reamier
readies
realist
readily
reality
reallie
reallot
roadman
road map
Réaumur
readmit
Rhamnus
reannex
Roanoke
read off
readopt
read out
read-out
reapply
Rhaetia
Rhaetic
realtie
reactor
re-alter
Realtor®
realtor
roaster
road tax
roadway
rebrand
ribband
rebrace
ribcage
reboant
ribible
Rebecca
✧rubicon
Robocop
rebadge
rabidly
ribless
rubbers
robbery
rubbery
rebuild
riblike
ribbing
robbing
rubbing
rubying
rubbish
rabbins
rabbits
rabbity
Rebekah
rebuker
rubella
rabbler
robalos
rabanna
robinia
rubeola
rib bone
rabboni
ribwork
rebloom
rub down
rubdown
ribbons
rubious
ribwort
ribbony
Roberta
ruby-red
rebirth
robusta
Robeson
rebuses
robotic
rabatte
ribston
rebater
rubatos
rebound
rybauld
Ruby Wax
rub away
rebozos
Richard
rechate
réclame
Rachael
Rockall
reclaim
rechart
rock art
rock cod
recycle
race-cup
rococos
recceed
recheck
rock elm
rackets
rickets
raciest
rackett
recheat
rackety
rickety
rockery
reclimb
reccied
receive
recline
recuile
racking
rocking
ruching
rachial
rection
ruction
rockier
Rockies
receipt
rectify
rockily
rocklay
racemic
racemed
recense
Ricinus
recency
reclose
rack off
rock oil
raccoon
racloir
recross
rectory
recipes
recurve
rectrix
ricksha
ricotta
recatch
recital
reciter
rock tar
recluse
recoure
rectums
racquet
re-count
recount
recruit
rocquet
re-cover
recover
recower
raceway
recoyle
✧radiata
red card
red-card
red hand
radiale
radiate
red face
red game
Red Lane
red tape
red-tape
redback
radiant
redraft
ridable
rude boy
reduced
radicle
✧radical
radicel
reducer
radices
redhead
red lead
red seed
redneck
red cell
red deer
redsear
red beds
redness
re-dress
redress
Rodgers
rodless
red cent
reddest
red heat
red meat
redbird
ruddied
red line
red-line
red pine
redrive
red tide
red wine
rodlike
redding
redwing
ridding
ridging
rodding
reddish
redfish
ruddier
ruddily
raddled
radulae
✧red flag
Rudolph
radular
riddler
red clay
rodsman
red snow
red-wood
✧redwood
Red Rose
ride off
red moki
red book
red cock
ruddock
red-cowl
redpoll
redcoat
redroot
ride out
ridered
Red Crag
ruderal
rudesby
ridotto
rodster
radium A
radium B
redound
redoubt
rodeway
re-enact
reedbed
re-endow
ryepeck
roe deer
re-elect
re-erect
reechie
reeding
reefing
reeking
reeling
Rhemish
Rhenish
rhenium
Raetian
reedier
re-exist
Rhemist
re-edify
reedily
ruellia
rheumed
reelman
reel off
rye wolf
rye-roll
rye corn
riempie
re-enter
re-entry
roebuck
re-equip
reflate
reframe
refrain
refract
refocus
refresh
rafters
reflect
refugia
refugee
refried
Rifkind
rafting
reffing
rifling
raffish
ruffian
ruffled
raffler
riffler
ruffler
Raffles
raftman
refined
refiner
refloat
referee
refusal
refuser
refutal
refuter
refound
rufiyaa
regmata
riggald
regrade
regrate
rag-fair
regnant
regrant
rag baby
Rigsdag
rigidly
Rigveda
ragweed
regrede
rag week
regress
regrets
ragment
regreet
raggedy
raggery
roguery
rageful
regrind
ragtime
ragging
rigging
rigling
roguing
rugging
riggish
roguish
regalia
raguled
regulae
regular
✧regulus
regally
regimen
regence
reginal
✧regency
rag-book
ragwork
rag doll
rag-roll
rag-wool
ragworm
rug gown
regroup
ragbolt
ragwort
regorge
regards
regatta
right-oh
righten
right on
right-on
righter
rightly
rag-bush
rag-dust
rehouse
railage
Reigate
ruinate
rein-arm
railbed
railbus
✧rainbow
railcar
raiment
reified
rhizine
railing
raising
raiting
ruining
roinish
✧rainier
reifier
raisiny
railman
Rain Man
rhizoid
rhizome
ruinous
reissue
reinter
roister
railway
rejudge
rejoice
rejoneo
rejones
Rajpoot
rejourn
rokkaku
Riksdag
rakshas
rokelay
Riksmål
rake-off
rikishi
R B Kitaj
release
relearn
Reliant®
reliant
rulable
rollbar

relâche
Rolodex®
relieve
rilievi
relievo
rilievo
relight
rallied
ralline
relying
✧rolfing
rolling
Raleigh
Raleigh®
rellish
rollick
rullion
rallier
rollmop
Relenza®
roll-off
rollock
rullock
rollout
rule out
relapse
relique
rulesse
rules OK
related
roll-top
relater
relator
reliver
relaxed
relaxin
relayed
rum baba
ram-raid
Rimbaud
rampage
remuage
rummage
rampant
rampart
remnant
Rommany
remodel
Ramadan
romneya
rump-end
remueur
rimless
rompers
rumness
rummest
rump-fed
remiges
rum shop
rim-shot
romaika
rampike
rampire
rim-fire
romaine
ramming
ramping
rammish
rompish
rummish
RAM disk
rampick
rampion
remains
rummily
ramakin
ramekin
rumpled
Ramilie
remblai
rambler
ramular
rumbler
ramulus
Romulus
ramenta
Romania
Romanic
remanié
✧romance
Romansh
Romanes
Romanus
remanet
rim lock
rimrock
rameous
ramsons
remerge
remorse
remarry
remercy
Rameses
rematch
ramstam
remould
remount
romaunt
removed
removal
remover
Ronsard
run hard
rundale
ransack
runback
Randall
run past
ringbit
Ranidae
rent-day
ringent
rondeau
renague
renegue
✧röntgen
reneger
ringgit
ranched
rancher
ranchos
run wild
Rankine
run time
ranking
ranting
renning
renying
ringing
rinsing
ronning
running
run high
runtish
runnion
rondino
randier
rangier
rentier
runnier
run riot
randily
rundled
Ranulph
Ronaldo
ringlet
rundlet
runflat
run amok
ringman
run into
Randolf
ring off
rangoli
Rangoon
Runcorn
run down
run-down
rundown
rancour
ring out
run a rig
ring rot
ring taw
rondure
Renault®
run over
renewal
renewer
ringway
run away
runaway
renayed
Roobarb
rootage
Riot Act
rhombic
rhomboi
rhombos
rhombus
rhonchi
root cap
reoccur
Rhondda
reorder
Rood Day
rookery
roomful
riotise
riotize
rioting
roofing
rooting
rookish
rhodium
Rhodian
roomier
rootier
roomily
rooikat
raoulia
rootlet
rhodora
rhodous
riotous
root out
rooftop
rooster
R months
replace
Raphael
rupiahs
replant
reptant
ropable
rapidly
replete
ripieni
ripieno
re-press
repress
ropiest
replevy
replica
replied
raphide
Rappite
reprime
reprise
reprive
reprize
reptile
riptide
rapping
repping
ripping
replier
rippier
Rappist
repaint
repoint
reprint
✧repulse
rippler
ripples
ripplet
repoman
rip into
repiner
repunit
ripcord
reprove
reproof
raploch
rape oil
rapport
repaper
repique
roper-in
reposed
riposte
reposal
reposit
reputed
ripstop
rapture
rupture
ropeway
repryve
requere
request
require
requite
✧requiem
requote
rarebit
reredos
rare gas
rorting
rurally
reroute
rorqual
re-scale
rescale
reshape
restage
restate
roseate
restaff
réseaus
resiant
✧restart
réseaux
rosebud
risible
rose bug
Rosabel
risibly
rosebay
rosacea
rose-cut
residua
residue
Rushdie
resider
rest day
rosiere
respeak
respell
Russell
✧respect
rosiest
russety
restful
riskful
raschel
rosehip
rescind
reseize
respire
respite
restive
restiff
rasping
resting
rusting
Rossini
reskill
Rissian
Roscian
Russian
riskier
rustier
Roscius
riskily
Russify
rustily
rosaker
rosalia
rosella
rusalka
resolve
Rosalie
roselle
Rosy Lee
rosolio
rustler
Rosanna
rosined
resiner
roseola
respond
rescore
restore
rissole
restock
Rostock
rose oil
rusa oil
reshoot
✧rosaria
rose-red
rustred
re-serve
reserve
resurge
rostral
rastrum
rostrum
Rosario
Rasores
respray
Ross Sea
Rosetta
rosette
risotto
rosetty
russula
rescued
re-sound
resound
rescuer
restyle
Rutland
rat race
retrace
retrate
ratpack
rat-tail
retrain
retract
retrait
retiary
ratable
retable
ratably
reticle
rate-cap
retread
Ruthene
ratteen
rathest
re-treat
retreat
rattery
rettery
ratafia
ruthful
rotifer
rotchie
ratchet
retsina
retried
ratline
rut-time
ratling
ratting
retting
rotting
rutting
ratfish
rattish
ruttish
ratfink
rethink
retrial
rattier
ritzier
rattily
ritzily
retaken
retaker
rat-flea
rotulae
rattlin
Ritalin®
rattler
rotolos
rotulas
rotunda
retinae
retinue
retinal
retinol
retinas
rathole
rations
retired
retiree
retiral
✧rat trap
retirer
returns
Ratitae
retitle
rotator
rat-a-tat
retouch
rhubarb
roulade
rousant
raunchy
rounded
roundle
roundel
round on
round up
round-up
rounder
roundly
rouleau
roughie
routhie
roughen
rough in
rough up
rougher
rough it
roughly
reunite
routine
rouming
rousing
routing
reunion
reunify
rouille
raucous
routous
roup out
rout out
reutter
rouster
riviera
rivière
ravager
revving
revying
rivlins
revoker
revalue
revolve
ravelin
revel in
Rivaldo
reviler
rivulet
revelry
rivalry
Ravenna
ravined
revenge
revenue
ravener
ravioli
River Ob
rivered
reverie
reverse
reversi
reverso
River Po
reverer
riveret
revisal
reviser
revisor
revisit
riveted
riveter
rêveuse
revival
reviver
revivor
Rowland
rowable
rawhead
rawness
rawhide
rewrite
reweigh
raw silk
rowdily
rawbone
rewrote
rowlock
rowboat
row port
rewater
rewound
row over
Roxanne
✧reynard
Ray-Bans®
rayless
rhytina
roynish
rhymist
✧royal we
royalet
royally
royalty
Raymond
Reynold
royster
rizzart
rozelle
shahada
sea card
seamaid
sea sand
seaward
smaragd
scalade
scavage
sea dace
sea gate
sea hare
seakale
sea lace
sea lane
seaware
sea wave
soakage
sea calf
siamang
sladang
spa bath
seabank
seahawk
sea lark
seamark
sea wall
scalado
sea wasp
sea haar
sea bass
sea pass
shamans
sealant
sea salt
statant
scabbed
slabbed
stabbed
swabbed
scabble
scamble
shabble
shamble
snabble
sjambok
spag bol
slabber
stabber
swabber
Shabbat
soapbox
shambly
spancel
snatchy
starchy
sraddha
scaldic
Scandic
skaldic
sharded
swarded
staddle

standee
swaddle
scandal
shahdom
Slavdom
stardom
St Aidan
standen
stand in
stand-in
stand on
so-and-so
stand-to
stand up
stand-up
scalder
slander
stander
Spandex®
spandex
shandry
staidly
stand by
stand-by
sea reed
seaweed
scalene
✧siamese
siameze
scaleni
Scafell
sea mell
sea term
sea bean
stave in
scale up
scare up
shake up
shake-up
shape up
shape-up
sea bear
sea legs
Shakers
stamens
starers
starets
sea-beat
sea beet
sea belt
stage it
sealery
shapely
slavery
sparely
stagery
stalely
stately
suavely
staretz
scarfed
scaffie
snaffle
scarf up
staffer
shagged
slagged
snagged
swagged
spangle
swaggie

slanger
spadger
sparger
stagger
swagger
spangly
spathic
slashed
smashed
spathed
stashie
smash-up
slasher
slather
smasher
swasher
stachys
Sharifa
stamina
stasima
seabird
sea wind
sea-fire
sea-like
sealine
sea mile
sea pike
seaside
seawife
stabile
statice
stative
suasive
scaling
sea king
sealing
searing
seating
sea wing
shading
shaking
shaping
sharing
shaving
skating
slating
snaring
soaking
soaring
spacing
sparing
staging
staring
swaling
swaying
sea fish
Shari'ah
slavish
snakish
Spanish
Swahili
sea pink
seasick
spacial
spaniel
spatial
stadial
staniel
Slavism
stadium
statism

sea lion
Shavian
station
suasion
scabies
statics
sea-girt
✧shariat
statist
sea view
scarify
scarily
sea lily
shadily
shakily
Slavify
snakily
soapily
stagily
suavity
shanked
stacked
stalked
shackle
sparkie
sparkle
swankie
slacken
starken
shack up
slack up
stack up
Shankar
sharker
slacker
smacker
spanker
stacker
stalker
swanker
shank it
stacket
slackly
sparkly
starkly
swankey
scaglia
scalled
snarled
stalled
star-led
sea-blue
shawlie
sea slug
shallon
scallop
shallop
snarl up
snarl-up
snarler
stabler
stapler
stables
scarlet
shallot
snail it
starlet
starlit
swallet
✧**shallow**
swallow

shawley
Stanley
spasmic
shammed
slammed
spammed
stammel
slammin'
spaeman
Starman
swagman
star map
scammer
shammer
slammer
spammer
stammer
swarmer
shammes
stannic
scanned
spanned
stained
Shawnee
slàinte
starnie
staunch
stamnoi
stannel
Shannon
scanner
spanner
spawner
stainer
Staines
stamnos
span new
seafood
✧sea lord
sea road
sialoid
sparoid
scatole
sea dove
skatole
seal off
sea wolf
sea-wolf
shadoof
slag off
swan off
sea loch
seacock
sea cook
seafolk
sea coal
seafowl
spa pool
sea foam
sea room
seaworm
sea-born
sea gown
sea-worn
spa town
scazons
sea moss
shakoes
spadoes
sea boat
Sea Goat

seaport
snap out
spaz out
stay out
shadowy
suasory
scarped
slapped
snapped
swapped
scapple
sharpie
stapple
Shar-Pei
scalpel
sharpen
shampoo
scalper
scamper
scarper
scauper
sharper
slapper
snapper
stamper
swamper
swapper
stay put
sharply
scabrid
scarred
sparred
staired
starred
spairge
sparrer
sea fret
sea crow
sparrow
S-matrix
Swansea
seamset
shastra
spastic
scatted
shafted
slanted
slatted
spalted
swatted
scantle
Seattle
smartie
sparthe
spattee
staithe
startle
✧**shaitan**
smarten
✧spartan
start in
start on
start up
start-up
scatter
sea star
shafter
shaster
shatter
slatter
smatter

spatter
starter
swatter
smaltos
scantly
shantey
slantly
smartly
startly
swarthy
scapula
spatula
statued
seasure
spatule
stature
statute
sea lung
sea duck
seagull
sea turn
shakudo
sea dust
Shavuot
starved
scarves
shalwar
sealwax
stanyel
swazzle
stanzos
subbase
sublate
✧**sabbath**
subtack
subtask
Sabians
sebacic
subacid
subadar
subedar
subedit
subhead
subtend
subsere
Sabaean
subdean
subteen
subzero
sabreur
subject
subtext
subvert
sebific
sabkhah
Sabahan
sibship
sabkhat
Sabrina
sublime
subside
subtile
sabbing
sibling
sobbing
subbing
subring
Sabaism
sub divo
submiss
subsist

subsidy
sabella
Sibylla
Sybilla
sibylic
soboles
subplot
subunit
sebundy
sub rosa
sub Jove
sub voce
subzone
subsong
Sabaoth
subcool
subgoal
subsoil
subjoin
sub-aqua
subaqua
saburra
subarea
suberic
subarid
suberin
sober up
suburbs
Sybaris
soberly
sybotic
subatom
sabaton
subfusc
subdued
subduce
subsume
subfusk
subdual
subduer
subduct
subtype
sabayon
saccade
saccate
sackage
soccage
sociate
succade
sucrase
sectary
sickbed
sick bag
sackbut
sick bay
seceder
secreta
succeed
secrete
sockeye
sacless
secrets
success
Sickert
secrecy
society
sackful
socager
saclike
sectile
siclike

succise
sacking
sacring
socking
sucking
sickish
section
suction
sucrier
sacrist
sacrify
siccity
sacella
sickled
seculum
secular
suckler
seconde
secondi
Seconal®
secondo
seconds
succose
suck'ole
sucrose
Succoth
succour
succous
sick-out
succory
St Cyril
securer
Sycorax
sycosis
sacaton
succuba
succumb
saccule
seclude
sacculi
succubi
succuss
sadhana
soda ash
sad sack
sidearm
side-bar
sidebar
side box
seducer
✧sidecar
sadness
saddest
sodaine
saddish
sedilia
saddler
Sod's law
sideman
sidemen
sudamen
Sudanic
Sidonie
St Denis
soda pop
sideral
sudoral
sadiron
Sudbury
steward
seepage

shemale
shebang
Shelagh
Stewart
scenary
seedbed
seeable
sueable
stembok
sherbet
seedbox
stencil
stew-can
stem cup
✧**spencer**
step-cut
sketchy
sleechy
stenchy
shedded
sledded
sleided
speeded
steaded
smeddum
speldin
speed up
speed-up
steed up
shedder
skelder
slender
speeder
spelder
spender
speedos
Sienese
stelene
shereef
shebeen
spelean
seeress
shekels
siemens
stereos
sievert
scenery
Szekely
skepful
sdeigne
stengah
✧**sten gun**
Shergar
skegger
sledger
sleight
seethed
Stephen
seether
shehita
see life
Shemite
sterile
syenite
sheriff
seeding
seeling
seeming
seewing
stewing
Swedish

Words marked ✧ can also be spelled with one or more capital letters

special
sferics
species
✧sheriat
seedily
specify
sheikha
sneaked
speckle
sleeken
sneak-up
sneck up
speak up
sleeker
sneaker
speaker
sleekit
steekit
sleekly
seed-lac
shellac
shelled
smelled
spelled
stealed
steeled
stelled
swelled
skellie
stealth
skellum
seedlip
sheller
smeller
speeler
speller
stealer
stellar
sweller
Szekler
stemlet
sterlet
Shelley
spermic
steamed
stemmed
steamie
steam up
steamer
stemmer
sternal
sternum
Steiner
stepney
sternly
sweeney
steroid
seed-oil
seek out
step out
skepped
stepped
steeple
stemple
stempel
sleep in
sleep on
steepen
stewpan
steep-to
steepup

sweep up
sleeper
steeper
stepper
sweeper
sheepos
✧sherpas
skew-put
stewpot
sleepry
steeply
stearic
sheared
speared
sweered
sierran
stearin
swear in
shearer
smearer
sneerer
steerer
swearer
sherris
sheerly
swear by
spersed
stemson
stepson
Stetson®
Spenser
scepsis
skepsis
speoses
spectra
sweet FA
✧sceptic
✧skeptic
smectic
scented
sheeted
stetted
sweated
swelted
✧sceptre
sheathe
sheltie
spectre
sperthe
✧sweetie
sweeten
scepter
✧shelter
skeeter
skelter
slenter
smelter
specter
spelter
stentor
sweater
swelter
sheaths
sceptry
sheathy
sweetly
sweltry
specula
scedule
sheaved
sleaved

sleeved
see over
shelver
sleever
swerver
sheaves
shelves
St Edwin
sneezer
soft art
sofa bed
suffete
suffect
suffice
sifting
softish
saffian
safrole
Suffolk
soft roe
saffron
Seferis
soft rot
safe sex
soft top
soft-top
suffuse
soft you
saggard
sigmate
signage
saguaro
signary
signeur
segment
suggest
sighful
sagging
sighing
signing
sogging
sugging
✧signior
signify
soggily
sagaman
✧signora
sigmoid
✧signore
sign off
signori
signors
sign out
signory
sugared
sage tea
✧sagitta
sighted
sighter
sagathy
sightly
sagouin
Segovia
spheare
schnaps
sahibah
sphaere
schmeck
schnell
schlepp
schmelz

schlich
schtick
scholia
scholar
schemer
schemas
sphenic
sthenic
schanse
schanze
schoole
schlock
schmock
schnook
schtook
schtoom
schnorr
schloss
schmoes
schools
schmooz
schappe
spheric
sphered
scherzi
spheral
Saharan
scherzo
schisma
schmuck
schtuck
schizos
spiraea
soilage
spicate
spinage
spinate
spinach
shikari
shimaal
sail arm
spirant
skiable
stibble
spit box
ship boy
switchy
skidded
spindle
stiddie
swindge
swindle
shindig
slidden
swidden
Swindon
shidder
skidder
slidder
Skiddaw
spindly
spin-dry
stipend
spireme
seize up
spice up
shiness
Spiders
saidest
shivery
snidely

spicery
spidery
spikery
swinery
skiffle
sniffle
stiffie
shipful
skilful
skinful
stiffen
spiff up
sniffer
sniffly
stiffly
stir-fry
stinged
swigged
shingle
sniggle
swingle
smidgen
smidgin
slinger
snigger
✧stinger
swigger
swinger
stingos
shingly
swing-by
stichic
stishie
stichoi
Swithin
slither
swisher
swither
stichos
Saivite
spilite
stibine
suicide
sailing
seining
seizing
shining
skiving
slicing
sliding
smiling
sniping
soiling
spiling
suiting
swinish
saimiri
stibial
Saivism
stibium
suidian
spirits
ski lift
Shimizu
shinily
slimily
spicily
spikily
spirity
shicksa
sticked

swinked
stickle
slicken
stick in
snick up
stick up
stick-up
shicker
shirker
skinker
slicker
slinker
smicker
smirker
snicker
sticker
stinker
smicket
snicket
stick it
stickit
slickly
smickly
stick by
Ski Club
skid lid
skilled
spilled
stifled
sciolto
shiplap
spieler
spiller
stifler
stiller
swiller
skillet
Shirley
skimmia
seismic
skimmed
slimmed
seismal
✧shipman
shipmen
shimmer
skimmer
slimmer
swimmer
stigmas
shimmey
skinned
✧science
soignée
spignel
skinner
spinner
spinnet
spinney
Spinoza
spiroid
ski pole
spinode
spinose
skim off
slip off
spin off
spin-off
spinous
spin out
spinout

spit out
stir out
shin pad
shipped
skid pad
skipped
slipped
snipped
stipple
swipple
shippen
shippon
skid pan
skidpan
skin-pop
shipper
skipper
slipper
snipper
Scirpus
stirpes
shilpit
skippet
snippet
sciarid
shim rod
shirred
stirred
stirrah
shiurim
stirrup
stirrer
skirret
skid row
scissel
scissil
scissor
Swisses
sciatic
Shiitic
sainted
shifted
skirted
spitted
stilted
stinted
skittle
smittle
snirtle
spirtle
spittle
shittah
shittim
Shilton
smitten
spitten
Stilton®
shift up
shifter
skirter
skitter
slinter
slitter
snifter
spitter
stilter
stinter
swifter
shiatsu
shiatzu
shih tzu

saintly
swiftly
spicula
seizure
soilure
spicule
spinule
stipule
stimuli
ski jump
shipway
slipway
swizzle
Switzer
sejeant
St John's
sojourn
saksaul
sokaiya
Saktism
Sikhism
St Kilda
sokeman
Sekhmet
Sukkoth
sakeret
sakiyeh
Silvana
sultana
salband
sol-faed
saltate
salvage
selvage
solvate
sulcate
sulfate
sullage
syllabi
saltato
soldado
salaams
saltant
salable
soluble
saltbox
salably
St Lucia
silicic
silicle
salicin
silicon
splicer
salices
salicet
saltcat
solicit
splodge
solidum
solidus
solidly
splodgy
self-end
salvete
solfège
salt eel
salfern
saltern
silvern
salient
solvent

Sillery
silver Y
silvery
spleeny
self-fed
salt-fat
St Leger
saligot
silphia
sylphid
sulphur
silk hat
sola hat
salchow
sallied
sullied
saltine
saltire
sulfide
sulfite
sylvine
sylvite
salting
salving
selfing
saltish
selfish
selfism
salpian
Sylvian
saltier
soldier
selfist
soloist
salpinx
salsify
saltily
silkily
sillily
sulkily
salamon
silk-man
Solomon
✧salamis
selenic
splenic
silence
solanum
✧silenus
solanos
Salford
saltoed
sulfone
sylloge
sell off
sell-off
sillock
salmons
salvoes
salt out
sell out
sell-out
sallowy
salmony
soliped
salt pan
salt pit
siliqua
Salique
silique
silurid

splurge
scleral
Salerno
splurgy
silesia
Sulu Sea
self-sow
splashy
solatia
splatch
splotch
soliton
split up
split-up
saluter
Solpuga
St Louis
Sallust
salival
seltzer
samsara
SIM card
summand
summate
Samhain
summary
samadhi
someday
sumless
summery
some few
samshoo
somehow
Samnite
sampire
summing
somnial
semeion
symbion
summist
✧**simpkin**
Somalia
semi-log
sampler
similar
similor
simpler
simular
similes
simplex
shmaltz
seminal
Simenon
seminar
Samiote
shmoose
shmooze
someone
symbole
simious
summons
shmoozy
semiped
semi-pro
Samaria
simarre
simurgh
samurai
Sampras
samisen
samosas
same-sex
✧**sumatra**
sematic
Semitic
somatic
somitic
somital
symptom
semitar
simitar
sumpter
symitar
sambuca
samovar
someway
somewhy
Samoyed
Sankara
Santana
Sinhala
sunward
Santa Fe
sensate
sinkage
sinuate
sondage
sunbake
sunbath
sundari
syntagm
sunlamp
syncarp
Sundays
suntans
sunfast
syngamy
sand bed
sandbag
sand bar
sandbox
sandboy
sanicle
sinical
Senecan
senecio
sand dab
synodic
sine die
synodal
sincere
sondeli
sun deck
sundeck
sand eel
sunbeam
Sinaean
San Remo
sun bear
sanders
sinless
sonless
sunkets
sunless
sunbeat
Sun Belt
✧sunbelt
sintery
songful
send for
sandfly
Senegal
Sankhya
sandhog
synthon
synchro
sonship
sanchos
sun disc
sunbird
sensile
Sonnite
sunlike
Sunnite
sunrise
sunwise
sanding
sending
sensing
singing
sinking
sinning
sunning
sunfish
sun disk
sundial
sensism
Sunnism
San Siro
sonties
sensist
sunnily
sun-clad
singles
singlet
sunglow
sandman
songman
sonance
Songnam
synonym
sonancy
sangoma
✧senhora
San José
sinuose
syncope
send off
send-off
sunroof
sun room
Sandown
sundown
santoor
santour
sanious
sinuous
send out
sing out
synd out
sensory
syntony
sinopia
synapse
synapte
sinopis
sandpit
sunspot
sangria
senarii
suntrap
synergy
Senussi
Senusis
sinuses
synesis
Sinatra
Sinitic
sanctum
senator
Sanctus
sensual
synfuel
San Juan
sunburn
singult
sun cult
sunsuit
synovia
sinewed
synaxis
sinsyne
sun myth
stomata
scopate
Spokane
storage
stowage
stomach
saouari
shofars
Scomber
slobber
swobber
showbox
snow box
shop boy
show biz
showbiz
stoical
snowcap
Scotchy
slouchy
smoochy
snodded
snooded
spondee
spondyl
Snowdon
stooden
scolder
scowder
smolder
sworder
snoddit
Slovene
stone me!
shoneen
stonern
smoke-ho
Spoleto
shore up
stoke up
storeys
soonest
showery
snow-fed
shopful
scoffer
spoofer
scoff at
shoofly
shogged
slogged
shoggle
shoogie
shoogle
showghe
sloughi
Scoggin
shotgun
sloe gin
snow gun
spongin
stopgap
slogger
sponger
stodger
shoggly
shoogly
sloughy
sloshed
Siobhán
shophar
smother
soother
shochet
stop hit
soothly
scoriac
stonied
storied
scoriae
Scotice
slob ice
snow-ice
scoring
shoeing
shoring
showing
sloping
slowing
smoking
snoring
sooping
stoning
stoping
stoving
stowing
slowish
snowish
Suomish
Scotism
spodium
scolion
Scotian
skolion
stories
stovies
Scotist
scorify
Scotify
showily
smokily
snowily
sootily
stonily
snow job
shocked
stookie
snorkel
slocken
stock up
shocker
snooker
stocker
stonker
stooker
spoiled
skollie
stoolie
stollen
swollen
scollop
scowler
spoiler
spooler
shopman
showman
snowman
stormer
swooned
scorner
'swounds
swounds
Sloaney
spooney
scotoma
Sao Tomé
São Tomé
show off
show-off
stop off
stop-off
stopoff
suo loco
show out
slop out
spot out
stop out
stop-out
scotomy
snow pea
scooped
shopped
slopped
stooped
stopped
swopped
stopple
shoe peg
Scorpio
scooper
scorper
shopper
snooper
stomper
stooper
stopper
swopper
shot put
scourge
scourie
scourse
scowrie
snotrag
sporran
scourer
scowrer
spoorer
sponsal
spousal
sponson
scorser
Scouser
smouser
sponsor
shotted
slotted
snouted
spotted
swotted
Scottie
shoe tie
shortie
shottle
snottie
stottie
shorten
shotten
stouten
shoot up
scooter
scouter
shooter
shouter
slotter
snorter
snotter
sporter
spotter
spouter
stoiter
stotter
swotter
shout at
sport it
shortly
stoutly
scopula
sporule
suo jure
São Luis
snoozle
swozzle
snoozer
septate
soprani
suppawn
sapsago
soprano
saphena
saphead
supreme
suprême
supremo
sapless
sapient
✧**sapphic**
septime
sapling
sapping
sipping
sopping
supping
sophism
sophist
sappily
soppily
sapajou
sapples
saponin
sapwood
saprobe
suppose
Sapporo
sepiost
support
Septrin®
Siporex®
septuor
seppuku
sequela
sequent
sequoia
sardana
serfage
seriate
serrate
sirname
sorbate
spreaze
striate
surbase
surbate
surface
surname
sirgang
spreagh
serkali
sarcasm
Syriasm
surpass
servant
screaky
streaky
streamy
strobic
scribal
soroban
scrub up
scriber
scrubby
shrubby
soroche
Saracen
sericin
sericon
sirocco
soredia
spredde
strodle
strudel
serfdom
sarsden
strider
stridor
strides
shreddy
seriema
screeve
scriene
scrieve
seruewe
servewe
shrieve
spreeze
survewe
screech
scriech
shriech
skriech
skriegh
surreal
surgeon
serve up
Serpens
Sargent
sarment
✧serpent
sorbent
spryest
surfeit
surgent
servery
sorcery
streety
surgery
sarafan
serafin
scruffy
strigae
strigil
Striges
shright
spright
scraggy
scroggy
spriggy
syrphid
sorghum
sorehon
sorghos
Syrphus
serried
sardine
service
servile
Servite
sorbite
surmise
survive
sarking
scrying
serving
sirring
sorning
sorting
surfing
surging
scraich
scraigh
screich
screigh
serfish
skreigh
Sorbish
sordini
Sercial
Serbian
Servian
Sorbian
serpigo
sordino
sorrier
sardius
Sergius
straits
spraint
straint
surview
sarkily
sorrily
surdity
surlily
stroken
striker
stroker
surplus

shrilly
strumae
suramin
surfman
scrimpy
scrummy
scrumpy
shrimpy
seringa
✧syringa
saronic
sirenic
springe
strange
surance
syringe
scranch
scrunch
sarangi
shrinal
Surinam
Shriner
strings
strunts
sarsnet
scranny
scrunty
springy
stringy
sarcoma
sarcoid
sarcode
✧scrooge
strooke
sirloin
surloin
sarcous
serious
sort out
surcoat
surtout
Sarapic
Serapic
striped
scrapie
scruple
strophe
strap-on
strip in
scraper
Sarapis
seraphs
Serapis
seropus
stripes
scrappy
strappy
stripey
stroppy
sororal
serosae
serosal
serosas
sorosis
stretta
soritic
strette
✧scratch
scritch
shritch
stretch

stretti
scrotal
stratal
scrotum
stratum
stretto
scrutos
sorites
stratus
Saratov
scrouge
scrauch
scraugh
shrouds
Strauss
shroudy
shrived
strived
shrivel
shriven
striven
shriver
Sir Ivor
striver
screwed
strawed
strewed
strowed
scrowle
strewth
screw in
strawen
screw up
screw-up
screwer
strewer
strower
scrawly
scrawny
sprawly
Seroxat®
Surayya
sprayed
strayed
scroyle
spray-on
sprayer
strayer
sprayey
sustain
sus laws
sassaby
suspend
suspens
sestett
suspect
sestina
sessile
sestine
Sistine
suspire
sossing
sussing
sashimi
session
sassily
Susanna
systole
Sassoon
suss out
sistrum

sosatie
Sesotho
systyle
satiate
setuale
situate
set back
setback
sit back
set sail
setwall
set fair
sitfast
satrapy
Sotadic
so there
setness
sithens
satiety
sutlery
satchel
Satchmo
set fire
setline
sittine
setting
sitting
sotting
sottish
sitella
settled
situlae
settler
settlor
satanic
Satanas
satinet
set down
set-down
sit down
sit-down
set upon
sit upon
sit-upon
satiric
satyric
satyrid
sutured
set free
satyral
sutural
satisfy
so to say
shtetel
shtetls
satsuma
Sat Guru
sausage
scutage
scutate
soutane
sfumato
squeaky
slubbed
snubbed
stubbed
scumble
stubble
stumble
scumbag
scumber

slubber
slumber
snubber
slumbry
squabby
stubbly
stumbly
stucco'd
soupçon
squacco
stuccos
scudded
studded
scuddle
squidge
studdle
souldan
studden
scudder
shudder
sounder
soundly
spun-dry
squaddy
squidgy
sautéed
shut-eye
✧squeeze
Souness
sou'-west
student
stupent
squeezy
stupefy
stuffed
scuffle
shuffle
snuffle
souffle
soufflé
soulful
snuffer
stuffer
snuff it
stuff it
snuffly
squiffy
snugged
smuggle
snuggle
stun gun
slugger
smudger
smugger
snugger
sour gas
stushie
scuchin
slush up
souther
Southey
studied
soubise
spuriae
souming
souring
sousing
sourish
saurian
saucier
studier

SI units
Spurius
squails
studies
studios
saucily
spunkie
spunk up
stuck-up
shucker
skulker
squilla
squalid
squelch
souslik
scudler
sculler
skudler
squalor
squills
squally
scummed
stummed
squamae
stummel
scummer
skummer
slummer
✧sturmer
shunned
stunned
squinch
sputnik
scunner
shunner
spurner
stunner
sturnus
squinny
squinty
sauroid
spumone
shut off
shut-off
spumoni
sourock
sautoir
soukous
spumous
shut out
shutout
spun-out
stub out
stumped
sculpin
skulpin
stump up
scupper
slurper
stumper
square B
slurred
spurred
squared
scurril
soup run
spurrer
squarer
spurrey
squirmy
soursop

squashy
squishy
smutted
stunted
scuttle
shuttle
skuttle
spurtle
squitch
saunter
scutter
shunter
shutter
sputter
stutter
squatty
spurway
squawky
spulyie
snuzzle
spulzie
save-all
savable
Sivaite
Sivaism
Seville
saveloy
savanna
savante
seventh
savings
✧seventy
✧saviour
several
savarin
Severus
Savitri
sevruga
savoury
save you
saw gate
sowback
saw-edge
saw kerf
sawlike
sawfish
sawbill
sawmill
sow-skin
sawn-off
saw-wort
sowarry
sawbuck
sawdust
six-pack
✧sextans
✧sextant
sexed-up
sex cell
sixteen
sexless
sexpert
sextett
sex shop
sixthly
sextile
sixaine
six bits
sixties
Saxonic
sex bomb

sixfold
sexfoil
saxhorn
six-foot
sextuor
scybala
skyward
scytale
sky wave
spyware
stylate
swy game
skyjack
skylark
skysail
sayable
styrene
soy bean
shyness
skyless
slyness
scythed
say when
scyther
scyphus
stymied
skydive
skyline
stylise
stylite
stylize
sky-high
stylish
spy film
sky sign
Stygian
stylist
skyclad
sky blue
sky-blue
styloid
spyhole
shy-cock
Shylock
skyhook
skyborn
sky-bred
smytrie
stypsis
styptic
shyster
seysure
shy away
says you
sizable
sizably
sizeism
sizeist
sozzled
sizzler
Sazerac®
tuatara
tiaraed
twafald
teacake
thanage
thalami
tea ball
travail
to a hair
tea lady

tear bag
traybit
tranced
tranche
tramcar
thatcht
trap-cut
trancey
twaddle
tsaddik
tzaddik
tsardom
tsaddiq
tzaddiq
twaddly
tea lead
trapeze
tea leaf
trade in
trade-in
trade on
trade up
travels
traject
tranect
tracery
tragedy
traffic
tearful
trayful
trangle
twangle
trangam
tear gas
tear-gas
trachea
trashed
teachie
teach-in
tea shop
teacher
tsarina
toadied
teatime
teaming
tearing
teasing
thawing
tracing
trading
tea dish
tsarism
thalian
Tsabian
tsarist
Tianjin
tracked
thankee
trankum
track up
thanker
tracker
traikit
twankay
thallic
trailer
trawler
thallus
trammed
trammel
traumas

Thammuz
trained
trainee
trannie
thannah
trainer
tea rose
twasome
tear off
tea room
tea gown
travois
thaw out
tea cosy
tea-cosy
trapped
traipse
trample
tramper
trapper
tear pit
trampet
tea tree
tea tray
transom
Transit®
transit
toasted
toastie
twattle
toaster
tractor
traitor
tranter
tractus
traduce
tragule
to a turn
thalweg
tramway
to blame
to-brake
tubfast
tobacco
tabrere
Tib's Eve
to-break
tableau
tubeful
tubifex
tabbied
tabbing
tabling
tabuing
tubbing
tubbish
tubfish
tablier
tubbier
✧toby-jug
tabulae
tubulin
tabular
tubular
tabanid
Tabanus
tabinet
tabloid
tabooed
taborin
taborer

tabaret
taboret
Tabasco®
Tabitha
tabetic
Tibetan
tab stop
to-brusd
tabouli
tubfuls
toccata
tuck box
tackety
tactful
tacrine
tactile
tacking
ticking
tachism
tactism
tychism
taction
tackier
techier
tackies
tactics
tachist
tackily
techily
tackled
tackler
tickler
toc emma
technic
tick off
tick out
tuck-out
tectrix
Tacitus
tacitly
tactual
tachyon
to death
tidiest
Tadzhik
tedding
tidying
tiddled
tiddler
toddler
tidally
tiddley
tidings
tadpole
tedious
tide rip
tideway
themata
trehala
the Lamb
Thebaic
Thebaid
the Bard
the Rand
the Yard
teenage
the Cape
the case
thecate
The Face
the game
the same
the tane
trepang
the sack
tieback
tietack
The Fall
the Taal
✧the wall
toenail
trenail
the Wain
the fair
The Oaks
the East
the Manx
The Lady
the many
therapy
tremble
tael bar
treybit
Tees Bay
trembly
tierced
treacle
tiercel
tiercet
treacly
treadle
treddle
tweedle
treader
Tuesday
Theresa
tee-heed
the dead
the weed
the sere
thereof
tie-neck
The Bell
the hell
tie beam
therein
thereon
thereto
the year
Theseus
tieless
thereat
the West
thereby
twelfth
teemful
treague
the chop
the Shop
thether
tee shot
the Big C
theriac
taeniae
the like
✧the line
the Nine
tie line
trenise
teeming
The Ring
toe ring
treeing
the kick
the Bill
the pill
taedium
the Lion
therian
taenias
The Kiss
the pips
the pits
the yips
treviss
T S Eliot
✧the city
trekked
trekker
tweaker
treille
the Klan
the clap
tie clip
toeclip
trellis
the flat
thermic
thermae
thermal
Thermos®
Thermit®
the bomb
the tomb
the good
theroid
the void
the Word
toehold
the robe
the rope
toe poke
✧the book
the Rock
The Fool
trefoil
the form
the Horn
the morn
tie down
Tiepolo
tremolo
toe loop
the dods
the gods
the tops
the Goat
the Crab
theoric
theorem
theorbo
the grip
theurgy
tressed
tressel
treason
Thepsis
they say
theatre
trestle
trental
Trenton
treetop
theater
The Star
treater
tweeter
teentsy
The Cure
the nude
the Gulf
the push
the Bull
the lump
The Quip
the Rump
toe jump
the runs
the dust
The Oval
twelves
tie-dyed
✧tiffany
taffeta
Toffees
taffety
tiffing
tufting
toffish
tagmata
tag tail
tagmeme
tag team
taggers
tagless
tigress
toggery
tegmina
tag line
tigrine
tagging
tigging
togging
tugging
tigrish
tegulae
Tagalog
Tagálog
tegular
tigroid
tugboat
tughrik
tigerly
togated
tighten
tagetes
tightly
tohunga
T-shaped
toheroa
Teheran
tailard
tri-band
tribade
tsigane
tridarn
tribady
trigamy
trinary
tzigany
twin bed
thimble
triable
tribble
Trimble
trilbys
triacid
twin-cam
twiscar
twitchy
triadic
trindle
twiddle
thirdly
twiddly
tail end
Trilene®
trireme
triseme
toisech
triceps
taivert
✧trident
trisect
tripery
tritely
triffic
triffid
toilful
tail fin
tail fly
trigged
twigged
tringle
twiggen
thigger
trigger
twigger
thiggit
Tlingit
trip hop
thither
trishaw
tritide
tailing
T'ai-p'ing
toiling
twining
trilith
Tbilisi
trivial
twibill
tritium
trivium
tuition
✧trinity
thickie
trickle
twinkie
twinkle
trinkum
thicken
thick'un
think-in
think up
thinker
tricker
thickos
thicket
trinket
thickly
trickly
tricksy
twinkly
trilled
twilled
taillie
twigloo
thiller
trifler
twirler
tailles
triblet
triglot
triolet
triplet
twiglet
triplex
trimmed
Triumph®
triumph
thiamin
trimmer
trismus
tzimmes
thinned
twinned
thionyl
trionym
thinner
triones
Tritoma
twifold
trilobe
trisome
tritone
trizone
tail off
✧tripoli
triform
tricorn
Tritons
thin out
trig out
trip out
trifoly
trilogy
tripody
trisomy
tripped
tripple
tripper
trippet
Thimphu
triarch
trigram
Trieste
thiasus
tripsis
twinset
thirsty
trimtab
twin-tub
triatic
tainted
twisted
twitted
thistle
Tristan
twitten
twinter
twister
twistor
twitter
thistly
Tripura
trisula
✧tribune
tribute
triduum
Taiyuan
triduan
thieves
triaxon
tuilyie
tailzie
tuilzie
twizzle
Tijuana
take aim
take air
takable
tiki bar
tektite
tokamak
takings
take off
take-off
take out
takeout
take ten
tallage
tillage
tollage
toluate
talk big
Taleban
Taliban
toll bar
tallboy
telecom
Toledos
til seed
toluene
tallent
taleful
telefax
Telugus
tulchan
telpher
tall hat
tile hat
Tellima
tallied
tillite
talcing
talking
telling
tilling
tilting
tolling
tallish
tallith
Tallinn
Tolkien
Tullian
tallier
talkies
tallies
talcked
tall men
telamon
tollman
taloned
talooka
Telford
talcose
tell off
tall oil
talcous
talk out
teleost
tallowy
tilapia
taliped
tylopod
talipes
talipat
talipot
talaria
tile-red
telergy
taluses
telesis
tyloses
tylosis
Telstar
teletex
Tolstoy
talaunt
✧tilbury
Tel Aviv
tollway
tally-ho
talayot
tambala
tympana
timbale
timpani
tympani
timpano
tympano
Tammany
tympany
tamable
tame cat
timidly
tumidly
tempera
Tempean
timbers
tempest
time gun
tumshie
Tim Rice
tamping
temsing
Tom King
tomming
tampion
tompion
Tampico
tumpier
Tamilic
Tamulic
templed
time lag
temblor
✧templar
tumbler
tumular
tumulus
templet
tomenta
temenos
tamandu
tombola
tempore
tomfool
tombolo
tambour
timeous
✧time out
timbrel
tumbrel
tumbril
tamarin
tamarao
Tom-trot
tamarau
timarau
tamasha
tumesce
to match
✧tempter
✧timothy
tambura
tempura
Tim Hunt
TV movie
time was
tantara
tankard
tanyard
Tynwald
tankage
tannage
tannate
tentage
tinware
tonnage
tunnage
tanbark
tintack
tone arm
tent bed
tenable
tunable
tunably
tunicle
tunicin
tank car
tanadar
tonnell
tangelo
tangent
tiniest
tuniest
tonneau
tannery
tensely
tindery
tendenz
tankful
tentful
tuneful
tent-fly
✧tanagra
tanager
tonight
tent-guy
tinchel
tanghin
tenthly
tan ride
tensile
tensive
tontine
tanking

Words marked ✧ can also be spelled with one or more capital letters

tanling
tanning
tenting
Tenzing
tinging
tinning
tinting
tunning
tannish
tin fish
tonnish
tun-dish
tankini
tondini
tension
tentigo
tondino
✧tangier
tinnier
tenpins
tantivy
tensity
tenuity
tinnily
tangled
tangler
tingler
tinkler
tonally
tonemic
tinamou
tenoner
tenancy
tangoed
tenfold
tenioid
tan ooze
tinfoil
tung oil
tinhorn
tandoor
tenuous
ten-foot
tune out
tantony
tonepad
tent peg
tent pin
tant pis
✧tantric
Tancred
tenured
tendril
tangram
tantrum
tendron
tone row
Tunisia
tonetic
Tiny Tim
tank top
tenutos
tongued
tonsure
tinfuls
taniwha
tintype
two-hand
two-pair
two-part
trouble

toolbag
toolbar
toolbox
twoccer
trodden
thonder
to order
Tuonela
two deep
twoness
Thoreau
thonged
trogged
thought
trophic
toothed
trochee
trochal
thother
✧trochus
thorite
two-line
two-time
tooling
Thomism
thorium
tropism
tromino
tropics
two bits
Thomist
tropist
trocken
toolkit
troelie
troolie
trollop
troller
Troilus
trolley
trommel
toolman
thorned
trounce
two-inch
twofold
twosome
two-tone
two-down
two-four
trot out
two-foot
trooper
trouper
tsouris
✧tootsie
trouser
trouses
Trotsky
trotted
two-step
trotter
trouter
too much
two-eyed
taplash
topsail
tip-cart
topmast
topiary
typebar

topical
typical
tepidly
top deck
top gear
tipless
topless
tip-offs
tap shoe
tappice
topline
topside
tapping
tipping
topping
tupping
tap kick
tipsier
to point
tipsify
tipsily
tippler
tupelos
tapsman
topsman
to-pinch
toponym
tap into
topknot
tapioca
tiptoed
typhoid
top-hole
topsoil
taproom
tip down
top-down
typhoon
typhous
tap bolt
taproot
top boot
topcoat
topmost
topspin
tapered
toparch
taperer
typeset
tapetal
tapetum
tapster
tipster
tapstry
topfull
T-square
tequila
tartana
tar sand
turband
tartane
✧tartare
ternate
terrace
terrane
threave
tornade
torsade
terrain
Torfaen
✧tornado

threads
turbant
Tartary
ternary
thready
throaty
turbary
✧terebra
turacin
turacos
turndun
teredos
term day
tiredly
Tarpeia
tarweed
terpene
terrene
turpeth
tar heel
tar seal
tar-seal
terreen
torpedo
Targets
Turkess
torment
torrent
turgent
tersely
torpefy
torrefy
turnery
terefah
thrifty
torchon
torcher
tormina
tarried
tardive
tartine
tergite
termite
terrine
torsive
tortile
tortive
turbine
turdine
turfite
tarring
turfing
turning
tarnish
tartish
Toryish
turbith
Turkish
termini
tertial
Torvill
terbium
Toryism
ternion
tersion
tertian
tordion
torsion
turdion
tardier
tarrier

tarsier
tartier
terrier
turfier
tercios
tertius
torpids
turkies
tardily
terrify
Turkify
turnipy
Tirpitz
turnkey
torulae
torulin
turtler
torulus
tartlet
thrilly
thrimsa
thrymsa
Tarim He
thrombi
turfman
Turkman
Turkmen
thrummy
throned
Terence
tyranne
Taranto
Toronto
threnos
tyrones
tyranny
turbond
turdoid
turn off
turn-off
turnoff
torgoch
tortoni
tarrock
turmoil
terroir
Terrors
turf out
turn out
turnout
tar spot
toreros
tortrix
tirasse
thristy
thrutch
thretty
torqued
Tartufe
torture
tarbush
through
Tarbuck
Torquil
Tarquin
tartufo
Targums
Torquay
thrived
thriven
thriver

throw in
throw-in
throw up
thrower
turf war
thruway
tostada
testate
to scale
to spare
toshach
Toshack
testacy
test bed
test ban
taskbar
tessera
tassell
testern
tushery
test-fly
tussive
tasking
tasting
testing
tossing
tusking
tastier
testier
tastily
testify
testily
tossily
tushkar
tushker
tussore
tussock
testoon
toss out
tosspot
Tasered
testril
✧testudo
titrate
titlark
tetract
tote bag
tatters
tutress
totient
tattery
tottery
titmice
tatting
tithing
titling
totting
tutting
Titoism
tattier
Titoist
tattily
tattler
titular
tutelar
totally
totemic
TV Times
Titania
tutania
tetanic

✧titanic
tutenag
tetanal
tetanus
✧titanis
totanus
tetrode
titmose
tutwork
tituped
Tataric
to-torne
tatouay
tittupy
trucage
tsunami
touraco
thumbed
truncal
thudded
trundle
thunder
toupeed
✧taurean
Trudeau
trumeau
truffle
thus far
thuggee
trudgen
trudger
thuggos
touched
toughie
touch on
toughen
touch up
touch-up
toucher
teuchat
toughly
taurine
thulite
touring
tousing
trucial
thulium
tourism
tourist
thurify
trunked
truckie
truckle
trucker
tousled
Trullan
Thummim
trueman
Tournai
trunnel
tourney
truancy
trump up
thumper
trumpet
true rib
trussed
trusser
trusses
toustie
trustee

Taunton
taunter
truster
Tavener
taverna
towpath
towable
tow-head
town end
town gas
thwaite
T H White
towline
townish
toweled
Tswanas
towmond
tow rope
tow boat
towmont
towered
to-worne
tow-iron
towards
tax cart
taxable
taxably
taxicab
toxical
tuxedos
taxless
tax disc
textile
taxiing
taxying
texting
toxemia
toxemic
taximan
text-man
tax loss
tax upon
tax-free
texture
textual
taxiway
Toyland
try back
trysail
thyself
toyless
toyshop
thymine
toylike
try-line
thyroid
twyfold
thylose
toysome
toylsom
trypsin
thyrses
thyrsus
tryptic
try it on
tryster
unaware
unaided
um and ah
Ugandan
urachus

unalike
unalive
uralite
uranide
uranite
unaking
uranism
uranium
Uralian
✧uranian
unalist
unasked
udaller
uraemia
uraemic
unaimed
unarmed
una voce
up-along
uranous
unaired
up a tree
uva-ursi
unacted
unaptly
Umayyad
upbraid
umbrage
unbrace
upbrast
umbrere
upbreak
unbless
unblent
unblest
unbegun
unbeget
unbegot
unblind
unbuild
upbuild
unbeing
upbring
Umbrian
unbuilt
unbaked
umbonal
umbones
umbrose
unbroke
unblock
unblown
upblown
umbrous
umbered
Umberto
unburnt
upburst
unbosom
unbated
unbound
upbound
unbowed
uncrate
uncharm
unchain
unclasp
upcoast
unchary
uncheck
unclean

Words marked ✧ can also be spelled with one or more capital letters

unclear
upcheer
uncaged
upclimb
unchild
unction
unclipt
Uccello
uncomfy
uncinus
uncanny
uncloud
unclose
upclose
uncloak
uncrown
uncross
ulcered
uncured
uncurse
uncited
upcatch
uncouth
upchuck
uncivil
uncover
updrawn
undealt
urd bean
undress
undight
undried
undoing
undying
undeify
uddered
underdo
undergo
undated
undrunk
ukelele
useless
urethra
urethan
uredine
uterine
uredium
uberous
uneared
unearth
utensil
uveitic
uneaten
uveitis
unequal
unfaded
unfreed
upfield
unflesh
unfaith
unfiled
unfilde
unfamed
unfumed
unfunny
unfrock
up front
up-front
upfront
unfired
unfussy
unfitly
unfeued
unfound
upflung
unflush
unfixed
unfazed
unguard
upgrade
ungodly
ungreen
unguent
upgoing
unguled
ungulae
urgence
urgency
unglove
ungrown
upgrown
ungored
ungorg'd
ungirth
unglued
ungyved
ungazed
unheard
unhoard
uphoard
upheave
unheart
unhable
unheedy
uphoist
unhuman
unhinge
unhandy
uphoord
unhoped
U-shaped
unhappy
unhired
unhorse
usher in
unherst
unhardy
unhasty
unhitch
unhouse
unitard
uricase
urinate
urinant
unitary
urinary
unidea'd
unideal
ut infra
ulichon
unified
unitise
unitive
unitize
uridine
utilise
utilize
uniting
unition
unifier
unicity
utility
Unicode
urinose
✧uniform
✧unicorn
urinous
unjaded
unjoint
unkempt
unknown
unleash
unlearn
unlucky
unladen
uplying
unlimed
ugly man
unlined
unloose
unlaste
unlatch
unloved
unmeant
upmaker
unmanly
unmoral
unmarry
unmated
unmeted
unmould
unmount
unmoved
unmixed
unneath
unnoble
unnamed
ulnaria
unnerve
unnoted
urnfuls
unorder
Urodela
urodele
uromere
urolith
uxorial
utopism
✧utopian
utopist
unoiled
unowned
urosome
ufology
urology
unoften
Uppsala
unplace
unplait
unpaced
umpteen
unpaged
unpaint
uppiled
unpanel
unpinkt
unpaper
unpared
unpurse
unperch
unposed
unplumb
unplume
unpaved
unqueen
unquiet
unquote
unreave
unready
unraced
utricle
Utrecht
unreeve
unruffe
unright
upright
Ukraine
upraise
unraked
unruled
Utrillo
unrimed
unroost
uprisal
unrisen
uprisen
unrated
unround
uprouse
unrough
unravel
unriven
upriver
unrivet
unroyal
unskan'd
unstaid
unswai'd
upstand
unscale
unshale
unshape
unstate
upscale
upspake
upstage
upstare
upstate
unstack
unsnarl
up-swarm
unslain
upstair
unsmart
upstart
unscary
upsides
unsneck
unspeak
upspeak
unshell
unspell
unsteel
upswell
unshewn
upsweep
unswear
upspear
unshent
unspent
unsweet
unswept
upswept
unsight
unspied
unspide
unsling
upswing
unstick
upskill
unsaint
unspilt
unsolid
upsilon
unsense
Ursinus
unsinew
unsonsy
unsunny
upstood
unsmote
unsoote
unspoke
upspoke
unstock
unshorn
unshown
unsworn
unshoot
unshout
upshoot
ut supra
unsured
upsurge
unstrap
unstrip
unscrew
unsated
unshun'd
unsound
unslung
unstuck
unstuft
unsaved
unsewed
unsexed
unsized
untrace
unteach
up-train
uptrain
untread
uptrend
uptight
untried
untride
untwine
untying
unthink
untwist
untaken
untiled
untamed
up-tempo
untoned
untuned
untenty
untaped
untired
utterer
upthrow
utterly
untruth
untruss
untrust
untruly
untaxed
ululate
ululant
usucapt
ukulele
usuress
unurged
usuring
usually
usurous
usurped
usurper
unusual
Uruguay
unvocal
unvaile
unvoice
upvalue
unvisor
unvital
unvexed
unweave
unweary
unwaged
umwhile
unwrite
upwhirl
unwhipt
unwaked
unweldy
unwoman
unwooed
unwiped
unwarie
unworth
unwares
upwards
unwitch
unwater
unwitty
unwound
upwound
unwrung
unwived
unwoven
unwayed
unyoked
Ulysses
unzoned
vialful
viatica
vialled
via tuta
viaduct
vibrate
vibrato
vibrant
vibices
vibrios
vacuate
viciate
vocable
vocoder
vaccine
vacking
Vectian
vacuist
vacuity
vocalic
vocular
vocally
vicomte
Vicenza
vacance
vicinal
vacancy
vacuole
vacuous
vicious
✧victory
victrix
viceroy
vacatur
victual
vacuums
viduage
Vidicon®
viduity
vedalia
vidimus
Vedanta
videnda
Veddoid
videoed
viduous
vedette
vidette
veering
viewing
V-necked
Vietnam
voetsak
vagrant
vaguely
voguing
voguish
veggies
veganic
vaginae
vaginal
V-agents
vaginas
vegetal
vagitus
vehicle
vihuela
V-shaped
vyingly
Vaishya
veiling
veining
voicing
voiding
veinlet
vaivode
voivode
veinous
voiture
voltaic
valuate
valvate
✧village
voltage
volvate
✧vulgate
vulvate
villain
viliaco
viliago
volcano
Vulcano
Villans
valiant
vallary
villany
volable
voluble
volubil
volubly
validly
villein
valleys
volleys
velvety
veliger
vulpine
volpino
Vilnius
volumed
velamen
valonea
✧valonia
valance
valence
volante
Volundr
valency
villose
Volpone
valgous
villous
Volapük
velaria
velaric
Valerie
✧völuspa
Valetta
volatic
velated
voluted
volutin
valvula
valvule
velouté
vulture
vulturn
velours
vilayet
vampire
vamping
vampish
Viminal
vamoose
vomited
vomitus
ventana
vanward
vantage
vendace
vendage
ventage
vintage
ventail
Vanuatu
vanadic
Vendean
Vincent
venefic
vinegar
V-engine
ventige
vanning
venting
vendiss
vanilla
Vinalia
venally
venomed
Ventnor
vintner
Ventôse
ventose
vin rosé
Van Gogh
vent-peg
vine-rod
ventral
venerer
✧vanessa
vinasse
venison
Venetia
venatic
vingt-un
venator
vanitas
vincula
venture
✧venturi
vinewed
✧vandyke
van Eyck
violate
violent
violist
violone
vapidly
vapours
vapoury
vaquero
variate
Versace
virgate
vervain
verbals
variant
verdant
vernant
versant
varices
verbena
vermeil
vermell
verse in
Vermeer
varment
veriest
variety
viragos
verdite
versine
varying
versing
varnish
vermian
✧version
✧vertigo
vernier
varmint
verdict
varsity
verbify
vermily

Words marked ✧ can also be spelled with one or more capital letters

verminy
versify
verglas
virelay
viremia
veranda
viranda
Virunga
Veronal®
veronal
virando
Varanus
variola
variole
verbose
very own
Virgoan
various
Vermont
verismo
virosis
Vorster
viretot
verruca
verruga
vareuse
verdure
versute
virgule
virtual
vistaed
vassail
vessail
visuals
visible
visibly
vesicae
vesicle
vesical
viscera
Vosgean
vespers
visaged
vis viva
vespine
vestige
vesting
Vosgian
vastity
vespoid
viscose
viscous
visnomy
visored
vestral
visitee
visiter
visitor
vascula
vesture
vis-à-vis
vitiate
vitrage
vittate
vitrail
vitrain
vitraux
✧**vatable**
Vitebsk
Vatican
vitreum

votress
vote for
Vitrina
vitrine
vatting
vetting
vitriol
vitrics
vitrify
vitelli
vitular
vittles
vitally
vitamin
vetkoek
vote out
Vitoria
veteran
vettura
vatfuls
vetiver
vouchee
Vaughan
voucher
vaurien
Vaudois
vaudoux
Vouvray
vaulted
vaunted
vaulter
vaunter
vividly
vivific
Vivaldi
vivamus
vivency
vivaria
✧viverra
vowelly
vexedly
vexilla
vixenly
voyager
Viyella®
vizored
weasand
weazand
Wealden
W H Auden
whate'er
whalery
wharfie
whangee
wrangle
whangam
weather
wearied
wearing
weaving
whaling
weakish
wearish
wearily
whacked
wracked
whacker
whackos
whammed
what not
whatnot

what now?
wear off
wear out
whapped
wrapped
whample
wrapper
whaisle
what's up?
whatsis
whatsit
whatten
wealthy
wharves
whaizle
✧**web page**
webcast
web-like
✧web site
web-site
website
webbing
wabbler
wobbler
web-toed
webworm
webfoot
wabster
✧webster
wu cycle
wych-elm
Wichita
wickiup
wackily
Wicklow
wadmaal
wadable
wide boy
widgeon
wadsett
wide-gab
wadding
wedding
wedging
waddler
widener
wedlock
wadmoll
widower
wheedle
wielder
weekday
weekend
wee-weed
whereof
wherein
whereon
whereso
whereto
whene'er
where'er
waeness
whereas
whereat
weedery
whereby
Wrexham
whether
weeding
weeping
weeting

wheyish
weepily
weevily
whelked
wreaked
wrecked
wreaker
wrecker
wheeled
wheelie
wheeler
whemmle
wheenge
woe unto
waesome
woesome
woe-worn
weed out
wheeple
Wee Free
wherret
woe is me
Wheeson
wheesht
whey tub
whetted
wreathe
wrestle
wheaten
whetter
wrester
wreaths
wren tit
wreathy
wheezle
wheezer
waftage
weftage
wafting
waffler
wofully
wafture
W G Grace
wagtail
wigless
waggery
wiggery
wiglike
wagging
wigging
waggish
waggler
wiggler
✧**wagoner**
wagerer
wightly
wage war
Wahhabi
Wahabee
Weiland
wainage
whipcat
whidded
weirdie
whidder
weirdos
weirdly
weigela
whilere
write in
write-in

write up
write-up
whitely
whiffle
wailful
whiffer
whiffet
whigged
wringed
wriggle
whinger
wringer
wriggly
weighed
weigh in
weigh-in
writhen
weigh up
weigher
whither
weights
weighty
wailing
waiting
whining
whiting
writing
waifish
whitish
whiz kid
wrinkle
whicker
whisker
whisket
✧**whiskey**
wrinkly
wrizled
whirler
whitlow
whimmed
Whitman
waivode
waiwode
woiwode
wait off
whim off
whip out
whipped
whimple
whimper
whipper
whisper
whippet
whirred
whirret
whitret
Whitsun
whipsaw
whimsey
waisted
whirtle
whistle
whittle
written
whip-top
waister
whitter
whittaw
whizzed
whizzer
W E Johns

wakeful
wakeman
wakened
wakener
wallaba
welfare
Walsall
wild ass
wallaby
✧**wolf cub**
wildcat
wild dog
wolf dog
wolf-dog
walleye
Wilhelm
willest
well-fed
wileful
willful
welcher
welsher
walking
walling
welding
welling
wilding
willing
wolfing
wolving
wildish
wolfish
wolvish
William
Wolfian
wallies
✧wellies
willies
wolfkin
Walkman®
wild man
well met
well now
Walpole
welcome
walk off
well off
well-off
Walloon
walk out
walkout
well out
wild oat
willowy
Wilfred
Wilfrid
wall rue
wolfram
well-set
well-won
walkway
welaway
waltzer
wameful
wampish
wimpish
woman it
womanly
wimp out
wimbrel
wannabe

wantage
windage
windbag
wine bag
wine bar
wine box
wind egg
wanness
winkers
wintery
wine fat
wine gum
wanigan
windgun
wind gap
Wyndham
winch in
winch up
wencher
wincher
wongied
wanting
wincing
winding
winking
winning
wonning
wannish
Wendish
wennish
wannion
wendigo
windigo
Windies
windily
wonkily
wing-led
wangler
winkler
winglet
wing nut
wanhope
windore
winsome
Wenlock
windock
winnock
Windows®
windows
want out
wind out
win upon
wondred
windrow
Winesap
wine-sap
Windsor
Winston
win over
wine vat
want-wit
woorara
wood ash
woorali
wood ant
whoobub
whomble
wooable
woodcut
woolded
woolder

woomera
woosell
woolfat
wrong'un
wronger
wrought
wrongly
whoa-hoa
Wyoming
whorish
wholism
wholist
woozily
whorled
woolled
woollen
wood lot
Wroclaw
whommle
woodman
woolman
wood oil
wood owl
wool oil
whopped
whoopee
whooper
whopper
woodrat
woodsia
woolsey
wood tin
wood tar
woofter
whoever
✧**who's who**
woodwax
wappend
wapping
wopping
wipe off
wipe out
wipeout
warrand
warfare
war game
warpage
wordage
warpath
war hawk
warrant
war baby
workbag
wire bar
workbox
worlded
wired up
workday
worldly
warhead
wurleys
wormery
workful
wart hog
warthog
warship
✧worship
Werther
worth it
wergild
worried

warlike
wartime
warding
warling
warming
warning
warping
warring
wording
working
warmish
wordish
Warwick
war film
Wardian
Wormian
Würmian
warrior
worrier
wurlies
wordily
warbler
wireman
workman
warlord
war note
ward off
warn off
warwolf
werwolf
work off
war song
warlock
war loan
war-worn
work out
workout
worm out
worn-out
war drum
wardrop
warison
workshy
worsted
waratah
wiretap
worktop
wireway
wastage
wassail
washday
West End
✧**western**
washers
washery
wastery
wishful
wistful
wise guy
wosbird
washing
wasting
westing
wishing
waspish
wistiti
wispily
westlin
wise man
wash out
wash-out

washout
washpot
washrag
wastrel
washtub
wysiwyg
wetland
wattage
wetware
wetback
wet pack
witwall
wotteth
wet cell
wetness
withers
witless
witness
wettest
wottest
Watteau
wet-shod
watch in
witchen
watch up
watcher
wotcher
watches
watchet
watch it!
wet bike
wetting
witling
witting
wotting
wet fish
wettish

wittily
wattled
wattles
Watford
witloof
wet dock
wet-look
without
watered
waterer
Watutsi
wet suit
wourali
would-be
wound up
wounder
wouldst
wauling
wauring
waulker
whummle
whupped
wavelet
wave off
waverer
waveson
wawling
wax palm
waxwing
waxbill
Wexford
wax moth
waxwork
wax doll
wax tree
waylaid
Wayland

wayward
weyward
wayfare
way back
waymark
W B Yeats
wryneck
wayless
wryness
wayment
wrythen
wayside
waybill
wrybill
waygone
waywode
wayworn
waypost
whyever
waza-ari
Wu Zhaov
Wozzeck
wizened
wazzock
X-factor
x-height
xylogen
xylomas
xylonic
xylenol
Xylopia
xylitol
Ximenes
Xingang
Xenical®
xanthic
xantham

xanthan
xanthin
Xenopus
Xenurus
Xiphias
xiphoid
xerafin
xeromas
xerarch
xerasia
xerosis
xerotic
xerotes
yealdon
year-end
yearner
yobbery
yobbish
yobbism
yibbles
yobboes
yachtie
yachter
Yiddish
yielder
yeggman
yoghurt
Yahvist
Yahwist
yakhdan
ycleap'd
ycleepe
yplight
yelling
yelping
yslaked
Yule log

Yolanda
yelloch
yellows
yellowy
ycleped
yolk sac
Yeltsin
yamulka
Yonkers
yanking
Yangtze
Yaoundé
ymolten
yuppify
yapster
yardage
yardang
yardarm
Yorkish
Yorkist
yardman
Y-fronts
Yerevan
yestern
yeshiva
ypsilon
yashmak
yu-stone
yatagan
yttrium
you wait!
you're on!
youngth
younger
youngly
youthly
younker

you know
yawning
yowling
yew tree
Yezidee
Zealand
zealant
zealful
zoarium
zealous
zebrass
zebrina
zebrine
zabtieh
Zebulun
zebroid
zebrula
zebrule
Zachary
zoccolo
zedoary
Zadkiel
zaddiks
Zhdanov
zoeform
ziffius
zuffoli
zuffolo
Zygaena
zagging
zigging
zygomas
ziganka
zygosis
zygotic
zaitech
Zairean

Zoilean
zoisite
Zoilism
Zoilist
Zwickau
zakuska
zakuski
Zuleika
Zolaism
zillion
zelator
Zulu War
zimocca
Zambezi
zymogen
Zambian
zombify
zampone
Zamboni®
zamponi
zamarra
zamarro
zymurgy
zymosis
zemstva
zymotic
zemstvo
zamouse
✧zambuck
Zincala
Zingana
Zingara
Zingare
Zincali
Zingari
Zincalo
Zingano

Zingaro
Zenobia
zanjero
zincite
zincing
zinking
zanyism
Zantiot
Zennist
zincify
zinkify
zincked
zanella
zonular
zonulet
zincoid
zincode
zone off
zincous
zonated
zoogamy
zootaxy
zooecia
zooidal
zoogeny
zoopery
zeolite
zoolite
zoonite
zoolith
Zionism
Zionist
zoom out
zoogony
zoology
zoonomy
zootomy

zootype
zip-neck
zipping
zaptiah
zaptieh
Zip® disk
zip disk
Ziphius
zip code
ziplock
Zapotec
zap it up
zareeba
zorgite
zeroing
Zorbing
zarnich
zorilla
zorille
zorillo
zorinos
zero-sum
Zostera
zestful
Zosimus
zithern
Zatopek
zetetic
zeuxite
Zeuxian
Zezidee
zizania

8 – odd

agar-agar
amadavat
Aramaean
avadavat
anasarca
apanaged
anabasis
anabatic
ataraxia
ataraxic
abatable
arapaima
anabaena
Arapahos
anapaest
Aramaism
agaçante
à la carte
amaranth
Atalanta
amaracus
Alan Bean
Adam Bede
Alan Bond
Adalbert
anarchal
anarchic
analcime
at anchor
analcite

a raw deal
Alasdair
amandine
acaudate
Araldite®
Araneida
Acalepha
acalephe
academia
academic
agacerie
apatetic
amazedly
Arabella
analemma
amaretti
amaretto
analecta
analects
Agapetus
araceous
araneous
arachnid
as a whole
anathema
a dab hand
anaphora
anaphase
acaridan
Adamical

Agamidae
at an inch
at a pinch
Adamitic
Amarillo
Aganippe
abat-jour
agalloch
acauline
availing
anableps
anaglyph
acaulose
availful
alaiment
alarming
alarmism
alarmist
anaconda
à la volée
araponga
Amazonia
anabolic
anagogic
analogic
anatomic
apagogic
at a point
analogon
analogue

abampere
acarpous
anaerobe
at a price
Anacreon
anatropy
alacrity
Adam's ale
abattoir
acanthin
Alan Tait
Alastair
alastrim
awanting
adaption
a bad turn
a battuta
acanthus
adaptive
Acapulco
abacuses
arapunga
Acajutla
abat-voix
analyser
analyses
analyzer
analysis
analytic
akaryote

ambiance
albacore
albicore
ambience
aubretia
Ambridge
aubrieta
ambulant
arbalest
arbalist
ambulate
Albanian
albiness
albinism
✧ambrosia
Arbroath
Arbor Day
arboreal
alberghi
amberoid
arborist
amberite
arboreta
alburnum
amberous
arborous
Abbaside
asbestic
asbestos
abbatial

arbitral
ambition
at bottom
albitise
albitize
arboured
ambivert
Archaean
arcuated
Alcmaeon
archaise
archaism
archaist
✧archaeus
archaize
Accadian
Arcadian
ascidian
archduke
accident
arcading
aecidium
ascidium
accredit
alchemic
ancients
ad clerum
alcahest
archival
Anchises

archives
arc-light
atchieve
accolade
arcology
Auckland
archlute
arch-mock
ascender
arcanely
accentor
arcanist
archness
anchoret
A J Cronin
accepted
accepter
arch-poet
Al Capone
acceptor
accuracy
ascarids
accorder
accursed
accorage
ascorbic
accurate
Alcestis
accusing
accustom

ancestor
ancestry
alcatras
ascetism
accouter
accoutre
accounts
Arcturus
aich whow
archwise
addebted
abductee
addicted
abdicant
abducent
adducent
abductor
adductor
abdicate
audacity
audience
Andretti
aldehyde
Aldo Moro
ardently
Aldaniti
addendum
androgen
Andropov
Abderian
alderman
Andorran
addorsed
aldermen
Alderney
Andersen
alder-fly
Anderson
Abderite
Addison's
andesine
andesite
and stuff
audit ale
addition
audition
auditory
additive
auditive
abeyance
abeyancy
Adelaide
Arenaria
ave Maria
amenable
amenably
Alemaine
ageratum
areca-nut
acerbate
acerbity
ayenbite
area code
acescent
amelcorn
Aberdeen
anecdote
alebench
ale-berry
avenging
anechoic

amethyst
Arethusa
American
alewives
adenitis
age limit
aperitif
apéritif
aperient
areolate
abetment
averment
ad eundem
agedness
adenomas
adenoids
ameioses
ameiosis
à rebours
alehouse
à l'époque
à peu près
adespota
Averroës
awearied
afebrile
aberrant
aleurone
averring
aneurism
aneurysm
aberrate
age group
à dessein
aseismic
aversely
aversion
abessive
adessive
aversive
agential
a best bet
a-weather
aventail
ale-stake
abetting
Aventine
axe-stone
alert box
aleatory
aperture
aventure
Ames test
aseptate
anestrus
agentive
adequacy
adequate
acervate
affiance
afflated
affrayed
afflatus
affected
affecter
alfresco
affeered
affright
affinity
affronté
affirmer

afferent
afforest
affusion
affluent
Algoa Bay
Angharad
aggraced
alguacil
alguazil
au gratin
arguable
arguably
Augsburg
algicide
algidity
angle bar
Anglesey
angle for
aigrette
argufier
Anglican
anguiped
aiguille
Anguilla
aggrieve
angekkok
✧**angelica**
algology
Angeleno
Angelina
angklung
angulate
argemone
argument
Algonkin
arginine
alginate
✧**argonaut**
aegrotat
angiomas
aeglogue
Algerian
algaroba
auger-bit
augur ill
aegirine
✧algerine
Algernon
algorism
aegirite
argyrite
Augustan
Argestes
augustly
Augustus
argutely
angstrom
Ångström
Ashgabat
ashtanga
aphicide
ad hocery
anhedral
aphidian
ash-leach
achiever
Ashleigh
athletic
ashy-grey
aphthous
an-heires

aphelian
achillea
Achilles
ash-blond
ash-plant
atheling
aphelion
ashaming
Alhambra
achenial
Athenian
achingly
an hungry
an-hungry
athanasy
aphanite
achenium
aphonous
achromat
Achernar
A S Hornby
abhorred
✧abhorrer
atheroma
adherent
atherine
Atherton
aphorise
aphorism
aphorist
aphorize
aphasiac
adhesion
adhesive
athetoid
ash-stand
aphetise
athetise
aphetize
athetize
abidance
agitated
animated
animater
alizarin
animalic
animatic
amicable
amicably
animally
apically
avifauna
agitator
animator
Alicante
aligarta
a piacere
acid drop
akinesia
akinesis
akinetic
Avicenna
anisette
Anicetus
acid-head
alighted
ab initio
acid jazz
arillode
axiology
arilloid

arillary
axillary
arillate
axiality
a bit much
Aviemore
amidmost
avionics
alienage
à bientôt
Ayia Napa
acidness
alienism
alienist
Arianise
Arianism
aridness
avidness
alienate
Adiantum
amiantus
Arianize
amitoses
acidosis
amitosis
amitotic
aniconic
✧**agit-prop**
✧agitprop
apiarian
acid rock
acierage
acid rain
apiarist
aviarist
acierate
acid salt
aliasing
amissing
agiotage
Alistair
aviatrix
aviation
acid test
aristate
acicular
aliquant
a dim view
as it were
arid zone
abjectly
adjacent
Al Jolson
adjuring
adjuster
adjustor
adjutage
adjutant
adjuvant
Akkadian
A V Kidder
ark-shell
alkahest
alkalies
alkalify
alkaloid
alkaline
ask along
alkalise
ankylose
alkalize

Arkansas
Ark Royal
ask for it
acknowne
ankerite
alliance
A Alvarez
aulnager
all-party
ad-libber
allocate
allodial
allodium
allogamy
allegros
allegory
alligate
all the go
all-thing
all there
all-fired
all-fives
all-giver
allnight
all right
all-right
all-risks
all-clear
alleluia
all along
aglimmer
Allen key
Atlantes
Atlantic
Atlantis
all in all
all in one
all-in-one
ailantos
allanite
at length
all roses
All Souls
all found
all-round
all to one
all-fours
allsorts
allspice
allopath
aularian
allergen
allergic
alluring
allerion
aplastic
allusion
aplustre
allosaur
allusive
aflutter
aglitter
all at sea
allotted
allottee
axle-tree
ablation
ablution
All Stars
ablative
allative

alluvial
alluvion
at livery
alluvium
alleycat
alley-taw
alleyway
allaying
alley-oop
alley-tor
all my eye
armgaunt
alms-deed
alms-dish
Asmodeus
armed eye
alms-folk
Armagnac
armigero
Almagest
✧**almighty**
armchair
atmology
army list
atmolyse
Armalite®
atmolyze
armament
ammoniac
Armenian
Arminian
ammonoid
Armenoid
arm in arm
admonish
ammonite
ammonium
Arminius
armorial
arms race
admiring
armorist
admitted
armature
armoured
armourer
army worm
armozeen
armozine
annealer
annually
Anna Ford
Annigoni
abnegate
Annelida
annulled
annalise
annalist
annulose
Annulata
annulate
annalize
Ann Jones
amniotic
abnormal
amnesiac
✧**agnus dei**
agnostic
adnation
agnation
annattos

annotate
announce
annexion
annexure
annoying
abomasal
amorance
à mon avis
apogaeic
apogamic
aromatic
adorable
adorably
amorally
atonally
avowable
avocados
abomasum
abomasus
amoeboid
atom bomb
aboideau
a good bet
a good few
a good job
a good buy
above par
as one man
alopecia
anoretic
anorexia
anorexic
above all
avowedly
amoretti
amoretto
apophyge
apothegm
alogical
atomical
aborigen
agonised
agonized
atomiser
atomizer
aborigin
aconitic
apomixis
apositia
apositic
Anonioni
aconitum
Apolline
Apollyon
Anoplura
axoplasm
apoplexy
acosmism
acosmist
acoemeti
Anointed
anointer
aborning
acorn-cup
apodosis
apologia
amorosos
à volonté
apologue
apospory
à coup sûr
Al Oerter
apocrine
amour fou
apograph
anourous
acoustic
avoision
aboiteau
agouties
avoutrer
anorthic
a pox take
abortion
adoption
amortise
apostasy
apostate
abortive
adoptive
amortize
azoturia
à couvert
✧aloe vera
Apocynum
alphabet
appearer
appeaser
applause
appraise
Al Pacino
aspidium
Apple Mac®
apple-pie
aspheric
amplexus
arpeggio
appriser
apprizer
Amphibia
amphipod
at points
appliqué
ampullae
appalled
appellee
appanage
appendix
alpinism
alpinist
amphorae
amphoras
approval
approach
approver
asphodel
amphoric
asperger
asperges
amperage
aspermia
apperill
apparent
aspirant
aspiring
asperate
asperity
aspirate
asperous
appestat
apposite
ad patres
appetent
appetise
amputate
appetite
appetize
asphyxia
applying
appuying
acquaint
arquebus
acquiral
acquired
acquight
airwards
Adriatic
aerially
Adrianne
Aerobics®
aerobics
aerobomb
abricock
apricock
airscrew
auricled
apractic
Agricola
✧auricula
apricate
atrocity
Air Scout
abridger
Airedale
abradant
acridine
aerodyne
aerodart
acridity
air-bends
Adrienne
agreeing
arrieros
aerofoil
acre-foot
aeriform
Agra Fort
auriform
aerogram
arrogant
abrogate
arrogate
airshaft
Ayrshire
airliner
airtight
aortitis
adroitly
airfield
air rifle
Afro-jazz
Aprilian
aurelian
aerology
agrology
acrolein
airplane
air-plant
Aprilish
acrolith
aerolite
aerolith
Aurelius
Abram-man
acromial
atremble
acrimony
agrémens
agrément
agrimony
atrament
acromion
apron-man
air inlet
arranger
arrantly
aeronomy
agronomy
airiness
aeronaut
apronful
airwoman
✧air force
air-force
air-cover
air-power
aureoled
air-to-air
airborne
air-house
airspace
airspeed
agraphia
agraphic
atrophic
abruptly
atropine
agraphon
atropism
atropous
agrarian
aurorean
Afro-rock
air-brick
aircraft
air-drain
air-brake
airdrome
airframe
airgraph
airbrush
air frost
airdrawn
aerostat
agrestal
arrestee
arrester
acrostic
agrestic
aoristic
apres-ski
après-ski
acrosome
Aura-Soma
arrasene
abrasion
arrestor
abrasive
Amritsar
airstrip
aerotone
aeration
acrotism
arraught
air-built
airburst
au revoir
arrivals
aardvark
à travers
at rovers
aardwolf
atrazine
au second
answerer
absterge
Answer Me
answer to
assiento
Ansafone®
assegaai
assignat
assignee
assigner
assignor
aesthete
aestival
assailer
auspices
abscisin
abscissa
abscisse
absolver
✧absolute
assolute
assemble
assemblé
✧assembly
assuming
Assamese
ad summum
Ausonian
arsenide
absentee
assenter
absinthe
absently
absonant
assonant
assentor
arsonist
arsenate
arsenite
arsonite
assonate
aasvogel
Assyrian
Austrian
abstract
abstrict
absorbed
absorber
asserter
assorted
assorter
absurdly
australe
anserine
assertor
adscript
abstruse
assisted
assister
assassin
assist in
assessor
✧alsatian
assotted
aesculin
Aesculus
assaying
astragal
anteater
art paper
actually
actuator
Art Tatum
antibody
Autobahn
Antabuse®
autocrat
antecede
autocade
alto clef
anticked
articled
articles
attached
attacker
anti-chip
autacoid
autocarp
Atticise
Atticism
astucity
anticous
Arts Club
anticize
Atticize
auto-da-fé
autodyne
antedate
antidote
at the bar
antlered
ants'-eggs
anthelia
anthelix
anthemia
anthemic
anthesis
asthenia
asthenic
At the Hop
actressy
artefact
artifact
artifice
anti-fade
act of God
antefixa
astigmia
autogamy
Antigone
autogeny
attagirl
autogiro
autogyro
anti-hero
autoharp
altrices
anti-icer
astringe
antliate
anti-lock
antilogy
autology
antelope
Antilope
autolyse
autolyze
autumnal
alta moda
attemper
antimony
Altamira
antimere
antimask
automata
automate
astomous
actiniae
actinian
actinias
antennae
antennal
antennas
attentat
actinide
antinode
astonied
attendee
attender
actinoid
antinomy
antonymy
autonomy
art union
actinism
artiness
astonish
antenati
autunite
actinium
actioner
although
as though
Anthozoa
antrorse
arthouse
✧antipode
autopsia
autoptic
antipole
antiphon
antipope
antepast
ante-post
after-tax
alternat
arterial
Asterias
Asturias
attorney
altarage
alter ego
autarchy
asteroid
autarkic
after all
anti-roll
alterant
attiring
altar boy
anterior
anteroom
antiriot

Words marked ✧ can also be spelled with one or more capital letters

attercop
actorish
antirust
apterism
asterisk
asterism
alterity
aftersun
apterium
apterous
aftereye
antistat
✧artesian
actus rei
attested
attester
antiship
antiskid
artistic
autistic
autosome
attestor
antisera
artistry
autosave
altitude
aptitude
attitude
antithet
astutely
autotomy
anti-tank
astatine
antitype
autotype
Antmusic
artfully
art autre
altruism
altruist
actively
antevert
activism
activist
activate
activity
acutance
adularia
amusable
adulator
aquacade
ague-cake
Asunción
aduncate
aduncity
aguacate
aduncous
aqueduct
Amundsen
abundant
amuletic
anuresis
amusedly
azulejos
aculeate
amusette
ad unguem
Abu Dhabi
Abu Nidal
abutilon
a quoi bon?

aluminum
Ayub Khan
arum lily
aqualung
aquiline
abutment
aquanaut
aqua pura
✧**aquarian**
alum-root
aquarist
aquarium
Aquarius
aguishly
avulsion
aquatics
abuttals
abutting
aquatint
adultery
✧**ayurveda**
alveated
advocaat
advocacy
Arvicola
arvicole
✧**advocate**
advanced
alveolar
alveolus
ad verbum
advising
advisory
advoutry
advowson
Aswan Dam
atwitter
auxiliar
aux armes
Amy March
adynamia
adynamic
amygdala
amygdale
amygdule
asyndeta
asynergy
apyretic
apyrexia
anything
anywhere
atypical
anyplace
Aryanise
Aryanize
asystole
Anzac Day
bear away
bearable
bearably
beatable
blamable
blamably
bear arms
bravados
Bramante
Braganza
blah-blah
boatbill
bearbine
blabbing

Bradbury
branched
brancher
bratchet
branchia
bean curd
brancard
Brancusi
braccate
boat deck
brandade
brandied
brand-new
boarding
braiding
bladdery
blandish
Braidism
brandise
brandish
board out
bear down
beat down
brakeman
brake pad
brake van
beam-ends
beavered
blazered
bracelet
brazenly
braseros
brazenry
beat-'em-up
blameful
beauffet
Bradford
boarfish
bragging
braggart
brachial
beach boy
biathlon
boathook
bear hard
Ba'athism
Baathism
Ba'athist
Baathist
beach bum
beach hut
brachium
Boadicea
bearings
beatific
Brasília
brazilin
beak-iron
beau jour
black cap
blackcap
black-cat
black rat
black ice
blackleg
Black Sea
black tea
blank off
black tie
black fly
bean-king

blacking
blanking
black box
blackboy
✧black dog
black-fox
Black Rod
black rot
blacktop
black art
blackish
brackish
black bun
black out
blackout
blank out
black eye
bear-lead
boatload
brailler
beagling
bratling
brawling
beamless
Brahmana
bran-mash
biannual
brain fag
brainiac
brain-pan
brainpan
boat neck
brainbox
brainish
braunite
blazoner
blazonry
brat pack
brat-pack
bratpack
beanpole
beau-pere
Brad Pitt
blanquet
Beatrice
✧boat race
bead-roll
Blairism
Biarritz
Blairite
baasskap
beadsman
bear's ear
bear's-ear
Bradshaw
brass hat
brassica
brass off
bearskin
brassily
biassing
boat-song
boat shoe
brassard
brassart
bracteal
brattice
beam tree
bean tree
beauties
bractlet

beautify
blast off
blast-off
blastoid
boattail
beastily
blastula
blastema
blastoma
blasting
blattant
blatting
boasting
Blantyre
brattish
boastful
bear upon
beat up on
blagueur
Beauvais
bearward
beauxite
beady eye
Bob Hawke
bob major
baby beef
Baby Bell
baby bond
baby boom
baby blue
baby corn
baby doll
Babeeism
baby face
babyfood
bobwheel
babyhood
bobwhite
biblical
bobbinet
bob minor
Babbitry
Babbitt's
bob skate
bobolled
babbling
bobolink
bubaline
babeldom
babelish
babelism
bibulous
Baby Love
bob royal
bebopper
bob-apple
babirusa
Babe Ruth
babushka
baby talk
bibation
bobstays
babouche
Bob Dylan
bobby pin
baccarat
bechance
by chance
bechamel
béchamel
backache

buckaroo
buckayro
backbeat
buckbean
backband
backbond
backbone
backbite
backchat
bicyclic
back-comb
backcast
back door
backdoor
backdrop
back-date
back down
backdown
back edge
bacteria
bacteric
bachelor
buckeroo
backflip
backfall
backfile
backfill
backfire
bacchiac
✧bacchian
back-heel
back-hair
bacchant
backhand
buckhorn
bacchius
beck-iron
bick-iron
Buccinum
bacillar
back-load
bucellas
becalmed
backlift
back-lill
back-lilt
backland
back lane
baculine
buckling
backlash
backless
backlist
baculite
✧**bacillus**
bicolour
Buckley's
becoming
backmost
Baconian
biconvex
by choice
back onto
backpack
back pass
Bactrian
by-corner
buckrake
back room
backroom
bucardos

back-rope
back rest
backside
buckshee
backspin
bicuspid
buckskin
backstop
buckshot
back talk
back time
bucatini
backveld
backward
backword
backwork
backwash
buck-wash
backyard
badlands
bedwards
bedeafen
bedmaker
bad habit
beddable
bed-table
biddable
bad faith
bedabble
body blow
bud-scale
bedrench
budgeree
budgeted
badgerly
budgeros
budgerow
bedeguar
bedaggle
Body Heat
bed-sheet
Buddhism
Buddhist
bed linen
bedright
buddleia
bodyline
bad blood
bodiless
bedplate
bedimmed
bodement
bidental
Bodensee
badinage
bedcover
bedsocks
badmouth
bad apple
Budapest
bad break
bad dream
bid price
bedarken
bedesman
Bode's law
badassed
by design
bodysuit
body shop
bodysurf

bedstead
bedstraw
bed-staff
✧bedouins
Bedivere
body wrap
bodywork
badly off
Buddy Guy
beddy-bye
bedazzle
bee-eater
bresaola
bien-aimé
beefalos
bleuâtre
Beerbohm
boerbull
bleacher
breeched
breeches
beefcake
bread bin
bleeding
blending
breeding
breadnut
Baedeker
breveted
bien-être
bretesse
Breughel
brethren
Brezhnev
beech-oil
Blenheim
beerhall
blethers
beechnut
breviary
breviate
break-jaw
break off
breakoff
breakage
breaking
break-vow
break out
breakout
beetling
bdellium
bregmata
biennial
Biennale
Brezonek
bee-house
breloque
beer pump
bhelpuri
bleep out
bee-bread
blearily
beetroot
breasted
brewster
bheestie
breaskit
blessing
bless you!
bheesite
Boeotian

brettice
breathed
breather
bleating
bletting
Blefuscu
beeswing
beefwood
breezily
breeze up
bifacial
buff-coat
bifocals
befuddle
buffered
befringe
befriend
befallen
baffling
befinned
beflower
befitted
big Daddy
bog-Latin
beggarly
Bagheera
baguette
big wheel
bagpiper
bagpipes
beguiler
bigamist
bigamous
beginner
big money
bignonia
✧big board
big house
big noise
bughouse
bigmouth
begorrah
bigarade
begirded
big stick
begetter
begotten
begrudge
big bucks
bogeyman
bogeyism
beheadal
Bahraini
beholden
beholder
by halves
Bahamian
✧bohemian
behemoth
behappen
behatted
behovely
behavior
boil away
Baisakhi
bailable
bribable
brigalow
bailbond
blimbing
Brisbane

britches
by inches
Blind Bay
bail-dock
Blind Pew
brindled
blindage
blinding
building
blinders
✧brindisi
blind gut
boil down
brideman
brine-pan
bride-bed
brine-pit
bride-ale
brief-bag
brim-full
briefing
baitfish
bring off
Bridgend
bridging
bringing
bring out
blighted
blighter
brighten
blithely
brightly
Brighton
blini pan
brickbat
brinkman
brick-red
brick-tea
blinking
bricking
brick-nog
blinkard
blinkers
briskish
buik-lear
brisling
brimless
bailment
brimming
Brian Eno
beinness
boil over
boilover
brim over
blimpish
Briarean
bailsman
by itself
blissful
bristled
bristols
blistery
briguing
britzska
blizzard
bejabers
Bajocian
bijwoner
bejesuit
Bakelite®
bakemeat

Baker day
bakeware
Ballades
Balearic
balladin
balsamic
Bulgaria
Bulgaric
balladry
bel paese
bel canto
bilabial
bull-beef
buln-buln
bellbind
bell buoy
billbook
bellbird
bullbars
bilobate
belabour
ballclay
ballcock
bull-calf
bald-coot
bellcote
bale-dock
baladine
bulldust
bulldoze
believer
belleter
billeted
balletic
bulletin
balneary
bilberry
balled-up
belle vue
boldface
billfold
bullfrog
bale-fire
billfish
ball game
bullgine
ball-girl
ball-gown
bald-head
billhead
bolthead
bulkhead
bullhead
bolthole
billhook
bull-hoof
bullhorn
billions
billiard
ballista
bull into
bull kelp
balkline
ball mill
bilinear
balanced
balancer
belonger
bilander
bylander
baldness

Balinese
boldness
bullnose
balmoral
Belmopan
balconet
ballonet
balloted
ballotee
bellower
billowed
ballocks
bullocky
Belgorod
bell pull
ball park
ballpark
bell push
baldpate
baldrick
Belgrade
belfried
bullring
ballroom
bell-rope
bolt rope
baluster
bullshot
balestra
Bullseye
bull's-eye
bel étage
belittle
bell tent
bulrushy
Bolivian
beloving
below par
bullwhip
bellwort
bollworm
Bulawayo
ballyrag
billy-can
bullyrag
bully off
bully-off
bellying
bullying
ballyhoo
belly-god
billyboy
bully boy
bully-boy
bullyism
bellyful
belly out
Belizean
bombarde
bemoaner
bummaree
bimbashi
bemuddle
bimbette
bemuffle
bambinos
bump into
bum-clock
bumfluff
bumbling
bumaloti

bimanual
bimanous
bombsite
bum steer
bumsters
by-motive
by my will
bombycid
Banda Sea
bondager
bone-ache
✧benjamin
bankable
bendable
binnacle
bandanna
bungalow
bank-bill
bonibell
bank book
bank barn
band-call
bank card
bone-cave
Benedick
✧benedict
bunodont
Benidorm
bone-dust
bank down
banner ad
bandelet
bannered
banneret
banterer
bonneted
bunkered
Ben Nevis
bankerly
bonsella
banderol
bannerol
bonne foi
bontebok
bandeaux
benefact
benefice
✧boniface
bona fide
bandfish
bonefish
bang goes
benignly
bank giro
benthoal
bonehead
bank-high
bunghole
bunching
Benghazi
bin-liner
bun fight
bone-idle
banditry
banditti
banlieue
bindi-eye
bank loan
bone-lace
bantling
bundling

bungling
buntline
Ben Elton
banalise
boneless
banality
bundle up
banalize
binomial
bone meal
benumbed
bondmaid
bone-mill
bonamani
bonamano
bons mots
Beninois
Beninese
boniness
banknote
Ben Hogan
buncombe
bind over
Benvolio
bonhomie
bento box
banjoist
benzoate
bonspiel
bony pike
Bonar Law
bona-roba
bongrace
bankroll
banxring
bankrupt
bank rate
bandsman
banksman
bondsman
bandster
bangster
banister
beniseed
bank shot
bonassus
bénitier
bang-tail
binaural
banausic
bone up on
bung-vent
bindweed
bentwood
banewort
bendwise
bandyman
bandying
bunny hop
boneyard
bunny hug
bunny-hug
blow away
buoyance
buoyancy
brocaded
brocatel
bookable
bootable
boogaloo
browbeat

blowback
blowball
browband
bloncket
blotched
broacher
bronchia
broccoli
boot camp
bronchos
bioscope
bookcase
book club
bronchus
blood-tax
broad day
✧broadway
brood-sac
book-debt
bloodied
blood-red
bloodfin
blood-wit
bloodily
broodily
brodding
brooding
blood-hot
broidery
broadish
blow down
blowdown
biogenic
brodekin
broken-in
bromelia
bromelin
brokenly
blokedom
biometry
blokeish
booked-up
blowfish
brougham
brogging
boofhead
brouhaha
blowhole
book-hand
boot-hook
biophore
blowhard
brochure
brothers
boothose
biocidal
bootikin
bromidic
boom-iron
bloviate
boot-jack
brockram
blockade
brooklet
blockage
brockage
block-tin
blocking
blockish
brookite
block out
Brooklyn
book-lear
booklice
bootlace
bootlick
blowlamp
bookland
book lung
booklore
bioblast
bioplasm
bioplast
bookless
bootlast
bootless
browless
blooming
bloomers
bloomery
bookmark
book-mate
brown-bag
brown fat
Brownian
brown rat
brown ale
✧browning
Brown Cow
brown rot
brownish
Brownism
Brownist
brownout
✧brown owl
blow over
bionomic
biomorph
book-oath
blowpipe
book-post
biograph
bookrest
bioassay
boot sale
blossomy
browsing
bookshop
boob tube
boortree
boot-tree
bloating
blotting
brow-tine
boom town
blow upon
broguish
bookwork
bookworm
Bronx hat
biolysis
boodying
boobyish
boobyism
bronzify
bronzing
bronzite
biphasic
bepraise
buplever
biphenyl
Baptists
bepommel
Baphomet
bepepper
biparous
bepester
beplumed
bepowder
bequeath
Barnabas
barracan
barbasco
barranca
barranco
Barnard's
barbated
bereaved
bereaven
burganet
berdache
barbaric
byrlakin
barracks
barnacle
Barbados
barrator
bergamot
barratry
Barabbas
bareboat
bareback
Barr body
bird-bolt
barebone
beri-beri
birdbath
burn blue
Burschen
birdcage
borachio
barm cake
birdcall
borecole
baroccos
boracite
barn door
burn down
bargeman
Bergerac
barterer
Berkeley
bird-eyed
bordered
borderer
berberis
bergenia
bargello
bordello
barberry
Burberry®
bargeese
berceuse
barbette
barrette
burletta
barbecue
barbeque
berceaux
Bordeaux
burned up
Born Free
bergfall
barefoot
born fool
barogram
baregine
by rights
berghaan
birthday
berthage
birch fly
borehole
Bornholm
barchane
birthing
birch rod
birthdom
bar chart
barghest
barbican
barbital
bartisan
bartizan
barbicel
bursitis
Bareilly
Barbizon
barricos
burritos
barriers
Bergkamp
bird-lice
bar slide
bird-life
beryllia
birdlike
Bartlemy
bird-lime
bardling
burbling
burglary
barkless
bergmehl
barometz
biramous
baronial
Berenice
baronage
boringly
Birendra
bareness
baroness
burinist
Byronism
barcoded
borrowed
borrower
burgonet
Bardolph
bargoose
burnouse
Baryonyx
bar graph
burgrave
barostat
Burnsian
burnside
Barnsley
birdseed
bardship
birdsong
birdshot
baresark
Burnsite
bird's-eye
burnt-ear
born to be
barathea
borstall
baritone
barytone
bar stool
by return
Bermudan
Bermudas
bar lunch
✧burgundy
barrulet
barouche
Borduria
berg wind
birdwing
barbwire
berrying
biriyani
barnyard
berry bug
Biscayan
Bismarck
bastardy
bestadde
beslaver
bostangi
biscacha
Bassanio
bistable
beshadow
bust a gut
bushbaby
bushbuck
busybody
baseball
best-ball
baseband
baseborn
bass clef
base coin
bisector
basicity
basidial
basidium
bass drum
by-speech
besieger
Bessemer
boss-eyed
beseemly
basketry
bushfire
besognio
best girl
boschbok
bass horn
besmirch
bassinet
besuited
buskined
✧bastille
bestiary
base jump
base-load
Basilian
basilica
basaltic
baseline
bassline
bustling
baselard
baseless
bashless
basilisk
bushmeat
best maid
basement
besoming
besom out
besonian
Besançon
baseness
business
busyness
basanite
basinful
bestowal
bespoken
bestower
bistoury
biscotti
biscotto
base pair
basophil
best part
bespread
bestreak
biserial
bestride
bestrode
bescreen
by-street
base ring
besprent
bush-rope
base rate
bescrawl
bestrewn
bestrown
boss shot
bass tuba
besetter
besotted
Basothos
besmutch
besouled
besought
base unit
basquine
biscuity
bushveld
bass viol
bushwalk
basswood
busywork
bisexual
✧betrayal
betrayer
battalia
bittacle
bite back
bathcube
betacism
Betjeman
by the way
✧bethesda
batteler
battered
batterer
bettered
bathetic
batterie
bitterly
butter up
by the bye
butthead
bitchily
batching
bitching
botching
butching
bitchery
botchery
butcher's
butchery
botritis
battle ax
battle-ax
bit-slice
batology
bottle it
butylene
bottle-oh
bateless
botulism
bateleur
betel nut
bottle up
batement
bathmism
botanise
botanist
baton gun
botanize
batwoman
bottomed
buttocks
bottomry
bathorse
bottom-up
button up
bathrobe
bethrall
bathroom
botargos
buttress
butyrate
beta rays
bitesize
betatron
beta test
beta-test
Bathurst
Batavian
bethwack
batswing
Botswana
beta wave
bothyman
buttyman
bit by bit
botryoid
Botrytis
botryose
brutally
Brumaire
blue baby
blueback
bluebuck

bluebell
blubbing
blue book
blubbery
bluebird
bluecoat
blue-chip
bouncily
bouncing
blue duck
bounding
boundary
Bruneian
Bruce Lee
baudekin
bouderie
Brunella
brunette
blue flag
blue film
blue funk
bouffant
bluff bow
bluefish
blue-grey
bluegill
bludgeon
bourgeon
bluegown
boughten
brush off
brush-off
blushing
brushing
boughpot
blue hare
blushful
Boudicca
bauhinia
bauxitic
boutique
blue john
bruilzie
baubling
blue line
bouillon
blue laws
Blue Nile
blueness
✧bluenose
blue note
Baudouin
bouzouki
Boulogne
boutonné
baudrick
blue ruin
✧baudrons
blurring
baud rate
boursier
Brussels
bruising
bountree
bourtree
blurting
boulting
blustery
bluntish
blurt out
blueweed

bluewing
bevelled
beveller
bivalent
bovinely
Bevin boy
Beverley
beverage
bevatron
bowyangs
bawd-born
bi-weekly
bowlfuls
bewigged
bewailed
by weight
bewilder
bowelled
bowl over
bowsprit
bewetted
box-wagon
Bixaceae
boxthorn
box-pleat
box elder
box-cloth
boxiness
box-lobby
boxboard
box-frame
boy racer
bi-yearly
Boy Scout
bayadère
bayberry
Bayreuth
Bay of Dew
bryology
boy's love
bayonets
boy's play
boyishly
bizcacha
buzzbait
buzz bomb
bozzetti
bozzetto
bezonian
buzz term
buzz word
buzzword
chalazae
chalazal
chalazas
clamancy
charades
clavated
charango
chadarim
chapatis
characid
characin
Clara Bow
chapatti
ciabatta
ciabatte
chambray
claw back
clawback
crabbier

cramboes
clambake
chaebols
coalball
crabbily
clay-bank
crabbing
chapbook
chambers
charcoal
cratches
chance it
chancily
clay-cold
chance on
✧chancery
coat-card
Chaldean
Claudian
✧chandler
Chaldaic
cladding
Claudine
chaldron
chawdron
clapdish
coal dust
Claudius
✧clarence
co-agency
coalesce
clap eyes
clavecin
cranefly
cravenly
czarevna
chamelot
chaperon
chapelry
chapeaux
châteaux
chawed up
crateful
coal-flap
coalface
chauffer
cramfull
chaffing
chaffron
chamfron
claw-foot
chaffery
Cranford
coalfish
cragfast
crawfish
crayfish
craggier
Changsha
clagging
clanging
clangbox
change up
change-up
clangour
coachman
coach-way
crash-mat
crashpad
crachach
cha-chaed

clap hold
coal hole
clashing
coaching
crashing
coach box
coachdog
crash out
cyathium
chamisal
Clarinda
chaliced
chamises
chapiter
Charites
clarinet
claviger
caatinga
coamings
Chasidic
clavicle
charisma
craniums
chamisos
clarinos
Clarissa
craziest
czaritsa
Craniata
craniate
crackjaw
cracknel
crankier
chalkpit
crank pin
crankily
clanking
cracking
clackbox
crackpot
crackers
chalk out
charlock
charlady
crawlier
chaology
challahs
chaplain
crablike
Charlene
chat-line
chatline
cradling
crawling
chapless
clawless
coatless
challoth
Charmian
clammily
clay-mill
charming
claimant
clamming
coalmine
cramming
clay-marl
claymore
charmful
chainman
chainsaw

charneco
chainlet
chaunter
crannied
channels
chauntry
clannish
crab-nuts
Chaco War
charoset
cyanogen
cyanosed
chalonic
cratonic
cyanosis
cyanotic
chaconne
cramoisy
Chappell
clapping
clasping
cramping
crapping
champion
clay pipe
champart
champers
clappers
claspers
Coalport
chappess
chairman
clay road
coatrack
chair-bed
CFA franc
charring
chat room
chayroot
clansman
classman
class war
cragsman
clarsach
classics
Coal Sack
chausses
classify
clanship
clarsair
clap-sill
classily
clausula
coarsely
chat show
claustra
classism
classist
coarsish
chasseur
claptrap
chaptrel
Chartres
crab tree
craftier
chantage
chastely
chattily
craftily
chatting
coasting

coaction
co-author
chattery
clatters
clattery
✧chartism
✧chartist
chastise
chastity
coactive
Chanukah
cyanuret
chasuble
claqueur
coagulum
crab-wood
crabwise
crab-yaws
caboceer
caboched
cabochon
Cub Scout
cable-car
cableway
cobwebby
cabretta
cubiform
cuboidal
cabriole
caballed
caballer
cobaltic
cobbling
cobblers
cobblery
cabalism
cabalist
cobble up
cabin-boy
cob money
caboodle
Cabirian
Cabernet
cyberpet
cybersex
cube root
ciborium
caboshed
cubistic
cabotage
cab-stand
cibation
cubature
cocoa fat
cockaded
Cyclades
cyclamen
Cockayne
Coctaine
cachalot
ciclaton
cockatoo
cocoanut
cockboat
Coca-Cola®
cock-crow
cacodoxy
cycleway
cockerel
cockeyed
cachexia

cachepot
cacafogo
Coccidae
cyclical
✧coccidia
Cocaigne
cochleae
cochlear
cockloft
cacology
cichloid
cockling
cucumber
cacomixl
cocknify
cicinnus
✧cyclopes
cycloses
cecropia
cecropin
cyclonic
cyclopic
cyclosis
cacholot
coco-palm
cocoplum
cucurbit
cicerone
ciceroni
cicisbei
cicisbeo
cockshot
cocksure
cockshut
cockspur
coco-tree
cicatrix
cocktail
cactuses
cachucha
Cocculus
coco-wood
coccyges
codebook
caducean
caducity
caduceus
caducous
codified
codifier
codpiece
co-driver
Cadillac®
codomain
cadenced
codename
ciderkin
cider-and
cedar-nut
cider-cup
cadastre
ci-devant
codeword
crepance
chevalet
crenated
clematis
chewable
coevally
chelator
cremator

Words marked ✧ can also be spelled with one or more capital letters

crevasse
chee-chee
crescent
coercion
coercive
crescive
cleidoic
creodont
cheddite
clew down
crêpe pan
clemency
credence
credenda
cheverel
cheveril
creperie
cleverly
crenelle
Cheyenne
cheveron
Clevedon
cleveite
crevette
cheverye
credenza
Cheshvan
chechako
Cheshire
chemical
clerical
cheliped
clerihew
caecitis
ctenidia
chenille
cheville
credible
credibly
creditor
caesious
crepitus
check-key
creakier
check off
check-off
cheekily
creakily
clecking
check box
clerkdom
checkers
Cherkess
clerkess
clerkish
check out
check-out
checkout
checksum
Chellean
creolian
creolist
creamier
cream tea
cream off
creamily
creamery
cream bun
cream jug
cream-nut
crew neck

cleanser
cleaning
Chemnitz
clean-cut
clean out
clean-out
Cherokee
chew over
coelomic
coenobia
cremosin
cremorne
cretonne
chenopod
creepier
creepily
creeping
cheapish
clearway
clear off
clearage
cheerily
chetrums
cheering
chevrony
clearing
cheerios
cheerful
clear-cut
clear out
clear-out
chessman
Cressida
cheese it
Chepstow
creasote
creosote
crease up
creutzer
creatrix
chestily
cheating
coextend
creatine
cresting
✧creation
C-section
cheaters
cheatery
creature
chestful
chestnut
creative
caesurae
caesural
caesuras
chemurgy
cleruchy
cherubic
cherubim
cherubin
chequers
Coelurus
coenurus
cleavage
cleaving
cleavers
cheewink
cresylic
coenzyme
cofactor

coffered
caffeine
caffeism
cuff link
café noir
cage-bird
cogwheel
Cagliari
cageling
cogently
caginess
cagyness
cognosce
cognomen
cognovit
cogitate
cagework
cohobate
coherent
cohesion
cohesive
caimacam
chicanas
✧chinaman
chip away
climatal
chicaner
China tea
chivaree
clinamen
crinated
climatic
✧china ink
✧chicanos
chinampa
✧chimaera
chiragra
chivalry
cribbled
cribbage
climbing
cribbing
Chimbote
Chibchan
chitchat
coincide
clincher
chin-chin
clip coin
clip-clop
chiccory
childbed
children
childing
childish
Criseyde
chimeric
chimerid
cricetid
criteria
clitella
cribella
crimeful
chiffons
coiffing
chiefdom
chiefery
Clifford
coiffure
chiefess
chiefest

coiffeur
cringing
clithral
clichéed
clip-hook
coinhere
Chichewa
Chisinau
clinical
criminal
critical
cuitikin
chiliasm
chiliast
clinique
critique
chickpea
chick lit
clicking
clinking
chinkara
caillach
chillada
chillies
chillily
chilling
criollos
chinless
chill out
chill-out
chipmuck
chipmunk
cliental
chitosan
clitoral
clitoris
chipotle
chilopod
Caiaphas
Crispian
crimpier
crippled
crippler
crispier
chirpily
chipping
chirping
clipping
clippers
crispate
Chippewa
chirrupy
cribrose
cribrate
cribrous
chiasmas
chiastic
chip shop
chip shot
chiasmus
coistrel
coistril
ceinture
cristate
cliquish
cliquism
crivvens
cribwork
cajolery
cokehead
cake hole

cokernut
cakewalk
call away
coll'arco
calcanea
calcanei
cellarer
cellaret
collagen
collared
calcaria
caldaria
calvaria
colzaoil
culpable
culpably
chloasma
Calvados
collator
collapse
col canto
call back
call-back
celibacy
calibred
colubrid
coloboma
cold boot
cold-boot
call-bird
calabash
celibate
calicoes
calycled
calycoid
calycule
calycine
culicine
cold cuts
cold duck
calidity
caladium
call down
calm down
cul-de-sac
calvered
colleger
caller ID
collegia
culverin
col legno
calceate
cold feet
cult film
Califont®
coliform
cold fish
Caligula
call-girl
colchica
calthrop
cultivar
calliper
collider
cultigen
calcific
calcitic
✧calliope
colliery
call-loan
calflick

cell line
calfless
calf-love
Columban
columnal
columnar
columned
Colombia
Columbia
columbic
calamine
calamint
calamari
calamary
calamite
calamity
Columbus
calendar
colonial
Colonsay
calender
colander
cylinder
calanthe
calendry
cilantro
culinary
calmness
coldness
colonise
colonist
call-note
colonize
call over
calzones
Culloden
collogue
colloque
colloquy
caliphal
cold pack
calypsos
colophon
calipers
calyptra
calipash
Calor Gas®
celeriac
chlordan
chloride
Colorado
Calormen
chlorine
colorant
caltrops
calorist
calcrete
celerity
chlorate
chlorite
cultrate
chlorous
calcspar
cold slaw
cold snap
coleslaw
colossal
coleseed
call sign
calfskin
cold sore

✧coliseum
colossus
calisaya
calathea
culottes
calc-tufa
calc-tuff
calf-time
calltime
colotomy
calutron
calotype
calathus
calcular
cellular
cultural
coleuses
colluder
✧coloured
colourer
cultured
colluvia
colour in
call upon
Calcutta
calculus
colour up
cell wall
cold-weld
coltwood
cold work
cold-work
colewort
cold wave
Calixtin
Calixtus
collyria
cullying
cullyism
come away
commando
cum laude
combated
compages
campaign
campagna
cembalos
cimbalom
cymbalos
compadre
cum-savvy
come back
comeback
comedian
comeddle
come down
comedown
commence
commerce
compesce
cumbered
cumberer
commerge
campfire
camshoch
cam-wheel
camshaft
come high
come home
camphane
camphene

camphine
camphire
compital
combined
compiler
combings
cymbidia
cambiums
Commissr
come into
camaïeux
camp it up
compleat
complect
complice
cameleer
comelier
complied
complier
camellia
cameloid
complain
cameline
✧compline
cameleon
camelish
combless
complish
cumulose
cimolite
complete
cumulate
camomile
cementer
Comanche
campness
ciminite
cementum
camporee
camp oven
comb over
combover
come over
commoner
commoney
composed
composer
Cambodia
commonly
compound
Comsomol
Commodus
Cambrian
Comorian
comprint
Cameroon
compress
comprise
cumbrous
camisade
camisado
camisole
camp-shot
Camisard
campsite
cymatics
comether
camstane
camstone
cemetery
cemitare
cometary
comatose
come true
cymatium
communal
campuses
commuter
computer
come upon
compulse
combwise
cinnabar
contango
Connacht
cannabic
cannabin
cannabis
cinnamic
cuneatic
centavos
cinnamon
Centaurs
centaury
concause
cineaste
cinéaste
cunabula
cenobite
Canicula
cynicism
Canadian
conidial
conodont
conidium
candelas
conveyal
cankered
centeses
conceder
conferee
congener
convener
convexed
conveyer
converge
centesis
congenic
cancelli
convexly
canoeing
convenor
conveyor
cunjevoi
contempt
Canberra
canoeist
condense
contessa
converse
conceity
concepti
concerti
concerto
concetti
concetto
confetti
contents
conceive
conferva
conserve
cine film
coniform
conchoid
cinching
cinchona
canthook
canthari
conchate
candidal
cannibal
conoidal
convince
centinel
confider
confined
confiner
confines
conniver
consider
cannikin
conoidic
canaille
candidly
canfield
✧canticle
canticos
canticoy
centimos
canaigre
centiare
congiary
canticum
continua
continue
continuo
conglobe
conflict
conclude
contline
canalise
conflate
conclave
canalize
cane-mill
con amore
canon law
cynanche
canoness
canonise
canonist
caninity
canonize
cantonal
canzonas
confocal
con woman
Concorde
cantoned
canzonet
centonel
centones
Congo red
consoler
Cantoria
cantoris
canoodle
consommé
confound
conjoint
contorno
concolor
cannonry
concours
centoist
Congoese
convolve
canopied
cineplex
canephor
conspire
cinereal
conarial
conurban
contract
con trick
centrode
canaries
congreet
cancroid
cant-rail
centroid
contrail
contrair
conurbia
contrôlé
centrums
Cinerama®
cancrine
centring
confront
cinerary
confrère
contrary
Canarese
centrism
centrist
✧congress
contrast
contrist
concrete
congrats
contrate
contrite
canorous
conarium
controul
Congreve
contrive
canaster
canister
cynosure
cane-toad
canstick
canities
Constans
constant
conation
✧cenotaph
cincture
constate
construe
conative
cannulae
cannular
cannulas
conjugal
consular
con fuoco
conjunct
confused
conjurer
consumer
cinquain
centuple
conjuror
consumpt
✧conquest
convulse
conducti
consulta
cingulum
Cynewulf
cony-wool
candyman
condylar
candy-ass
Cenozoic
coolabah
chota peg
choragic
chorally
clonally
cookable
coolamon
Cromarty
choragus
crotalum
Crotalus
crow-bill
cookbook
crow boot
crotched
crotchet
choicely
choo-choo
chop-chop
chow-chow
clop-clop
chondral
Cloud Bay
cloudlet
cloudage
chondrin
cloudily
chording
clodding
clouding
cloddish
Chordata
chordate
✧chondrus
crowd out
cool down
close-set
closeted
clovered
choke off
cholemia
choleric
choregic
closed-in
croceate
choregus
close-run
clotebur
croceous
choof off
cropfull
cropfuls
crowfoot
cloth cap
cloth-cap
clothier
clothing
clochard
chokidar
coolibah
coolibar
Coolidge
chorioid
chorisis
cootikin
choliamb
choriamb
C-horizon
chorizos
cloak-bag
croakier
clock off
croakily
clocking
croaking
crockery
Cronkite
clock out
cromlech
cropland
choultry
cloyless
chow mein
cookmaid
cloyment
crown cap
crown saw
chounter
crownlet
cooingly
clowning
crooning
crowning
crown rot
clownery
clownish
coolness
crow over
cromorna
cromorne
crocoite
croupade
croupier
choppily
clodpole
clodpoll
clotpoll
chopping
cropping
choppers
clodpate
croupous
choirman
choirboy
choy-root
cookroom
crossbar
crossway
cropsick
chop suey
cloister
crosslet
cross sea
coonskin
cross-rib
crosstie
crousely
cloysome
crossing
cook shop
crossbow
cross-row
crossish
cross bun
crosscut
cross-eye
Croatian
clotting
crofting
crostini
co-option
co-optive
chorused
crocuses
Cromwell
cookware
cronyism
cephalad
coplanar
cap-paper
cephalic
cephalin
copybook
capybara
cap screw
capuccio
✧capuchin
Cape cart
capacity
cupidity
copperas
cypselae
Coppélia
copy-edit
capoeira
cupreous
Cape Fear
copyhold
Cape Horn
Capridae
Caprinae
capsizal
cup final
capricci
Caprices
cyprides
caprifig
cyprinid
capriole
Cypriote
capsicum
captious
capellet
cupelled
cupolaed
capeline
Copeland
cupeling
copulate
cupulate
copemate
caponier
caponise
caponata
caponize
cup coral
coprosma
cupboard
caproate

Copepoda
cop a plea
copyread
caper-tea
CFP franc
capeskin
capotted
capitula
capitani
capitano
capstone
capitate
Cape Town
capitayn
capsular
capturer
capework
Copaxone®
caprylic
Cape York
coquetry
coquette
coquilla
coquille
coquitos
coq au vin
carraway
Circaean
curtalax
carnauba
carcanet
curvated
care a fig
car radio
caryatic
caryatid
cercaria
carnally
curbable
carcajou
cardamom
cardamon
cariacou
carjacou
currasow
cornacre
curranty
cardamum
carbaryl
cerebral
corn-baby
corn-beef
cerebric
cornball
carabine
corybant
caribous
cerebrum
carucage
coracoid
corncrib
corn-cake
caracole
caracara
care card
Carl Cori
corn-cure
corocore
corocoro
cardcase
carucate
core dump
carceral
Carreras
cervelat
cornetcy
currency
carpeted
corbeled
cornered
corselet
cortexes
curveted
Cordelia
Cornelia
cursedly
car ferry
corsetry
cargeese
cornetti
cornetto
corvette
cardecue
carneous
carve out
Cerberus
corneous
cornflag
carefree
card file
cartfuls
coraggio
card game
caragana
coregent
car-thief
Carthage
carl-hemp
car phone
cornhusk
cardigan
✧cardinal
carnival
cervical
corrival
cortical
Corvidae
Corvinae
curvital
carritch
carnifex
cervices
cervixes
circiter
cirriped
cordiner
corniced
cortices
carriage
corniche
cardioid
carditis
cornific
Carlisle
carriole
cornicle
curricle
corridor
cortisol
cursitor
Corbiere
curliest
curviest
Corfiote
Circinus
curlicue
Carl Jung
corn-kist
Carolean
cartload
cerulean
Coral Rag
carolled
caroller
Coral Sea
cornloft
cerulein
Cyrillic
Carolina
Caroline
circling
cornland
carillon
careless
cordless
coreless
curbless
cureless
corallum
Corn Laws
cornmeal
ceramics
ceramide
cornmill
cerement
ceremony
chromene
coramine
ceramist
chromate
chromite
cornmoth
chromium
chromous
coranach
coronach
carangid
coronoid
Cyrenaic
caringly
caruncle
corantos
coronary
curtness
carinate
coronate
coronium
corundum
Caryocar
cordovan
corporal
corporas
cartouch
cursores
Carl Orff
carbolic
carbonic
cercopid
cargoose
carbonyl
carboxyl
carapace
coryphee
coryphée
carap-oil
corn pone
corn-pone
cornpipe
cartroad
corn rent
curarine
curb-roof
curarise
corn rows
curarize
chrismal
curbside
cerastes
Chris Rea
christen
Chrysler®
Chrissie
✧christie
Christly
cork-sole
corn silk
ceresine
christom
corn snow
curassow
cerusite
Christus
Curitiba
corktree
ceratoid
curatrix
caretake
carotene
cerotype
curatory
curative
carousal
circular
carburet
✧carousel
carouser
cornuted
curculio
curcumin
corduroy
cornutos
circussy
circuity
cernuous
card-vote
cordwain
Cornwall
cordwood
corkwood
careware
careworn
cornworm
carry off
carry-all
carryall
carrying
currying
carrycot
carry out
carry-out
cast away
castaway
cascabel
Castanea
castanet
costated
cashable
casually
casualty
cashback
cast back
casebook
cash-book
cosecant
cash crop
cash card
cash desk
cash down
cast down
cosherer
cosmesis
cosmetic
cussedly
cisterna
cysteine
casteism
cassette
cost-free
cash flow
caschrom
cosmical
cuspidal
Cushing's
Cushitic
cystitis
cushiony
cassinos
cast iron
cast-iron
cuspidor
cushiest
case-load
ciselure
cashless
cast lots
ciseleur
casement
cashmere
casimere
costmary
casemate
cosiness
Casanova
custodes
customed
customer
cesspool
cost push
cost plus
cost-plus
Cesarean
Castries
castrate
castrati
castrato
case-shot
cislunar
cistuses
costumed
costumer
cistvaen
casework
case-worm
cussword
Cathaian
Cathayan
cottaged
cottager
cottagey
cutwater
citrange
citeable
cattalos
cottabus
Cuthbert
cetacean
catechin
catacomb
catechol
cut a deal
cytidine
city desk
cut a dash
catheter
cathexes
cathexis
cutie-pie
cathedra
cot death
cut teeth
cathetus
citreous
citified
cityfied
cat's-foot
city farm
category
catch him
catch-pit
catch-all
catchfly
city hall
catching
cute hoor
cutchery
cut short
catch out
Cottidae
cat-fight
cathisma
Catriona
cytokine
cataloes
cetology
cytology
cotyloid
Catiline
coteline
cut along
cotillon
catalase
catalyse
catalyst
cut glass
cutglass
cattleya
catalyze
cat's-meat
catamite
Catonian
catenoid
catenane
cotenant
cotinine
catenary
cuteness
cutinise
catenate
cutinize
cathodal
cut no ice
cathodic
✧catholic
chthonic
catworks
cotton on
cathouse
cot-house
cut loose
catapult
cataphor
Cotopaxi
cataract
ceterach
cut-price
catering
cateress
cytosome
cytisine
cytosine
cat-stick
cat's-tail
catatony
citation
citatory
cut it out
cotquean
cothurni
cothurns
citrussy
cutpurse
cetywall
Cotswold
caudated
crusader
Crusades
coumaric
coumarin
caudally
causally
clubable
crusados
cruzados
chupatti
courante
crumbier
chubbily
clubbing
clubbish
clubbism
clubbist
clutches
cruncher
crutched
churchly
couscous
chuddies
cauldron
causeway
crumenal
caudexes
causeyed
causerie
clupeoid
crude oil
cruzeiro
club-face

club foot
chugging
clubhead
crush bar
crush hat
Caughley
couchant
couching
coughing
crushing
crumhorn
club-haul
caudices
crucifer
crudités
churinga
crucifix
caudicle
caudillo
caulicle
cousinly
coutille
✧crucible
cousinry
✧coulisse
cruciate
cautious
chuckies
chuckler
chuck off
chunkily
caulking
chunking
chuck out
crueller
clubland
club-line
coupling
churlish
clueless
crummack
crummock
crummier
chummage
chummily
chumming
club moss
churning
churn out
churn-owl
couronne
crumpled
chumping
clumping
clubroom
clubroot
clubrush
club soda
clumsily
coursing
court-day
courtier
courtlet
Courtney
cruet set
crustier
crustily
courting
control
clustery
countess

courtesy
crustose
crustate
count out
count-out
chutzpah
caviarie
cave-bear
cavicorn
cavefish
civil day
civilian
civil law
civil war
✧cavalier
cavilled
caviller
covalent
civilise
civilist
civility
civilize
Cévennes
covenant
Coventry
covinous
caverned
coverlet
coverage
coverlid
coverall
covertly
covering
cover for
cavesson
civet cat
cavitied
cavatina
covetise
cavitate
covetous
cow-leech
cowberry
cowheard
cow-wheat
cow whale
cow shark
co-writer
cow-pilot
cow's lick
cow-plant
cowslip'd
cow cocky
cowhouse
co-worker
cowardly
cowardry
cowgrass
coxalgia
coxiness
coxswain
cly-faker
clypeate
cryogeny
cryolite
cryonics
cayenned
cryostat
coyishly
coystrel
coystril

cryotron
chyluria
cry quits
cozenage
diabasic
dramatic
drawable
Dracaena
diapason
diapause
diamanté
Djakarta
dead-beat
deadbeat
draw back
drawback
drabbler
Drambuie®
dead-bolt
dual band
dead-born
Dearborn
drabbish
dealbate
diarchal
diarchic
diascope
dead-cart
dead cert
draw cuts
dead-deal
dead duck
Diandria
drawdown
diazepam
do a Melba
deadener
diabetes
diademed
diameter
diabetic
diapente
drabette
dead-fall
dead-fire
dealfish
draffish
dwarfish
dwarfism
draw-gear
dragging
draughts
draughty
dead-head
deadhead
dead heat
dead-heat
death cap
death ray
drachmae
drachmai
drachmas
deathbed
dead hand
diaphone
drag hunt
death row
death cup
deathful
dealings
drawings

diapiric
dearie me
diazinon
DNA virus
dead load
dead-lock
deadlock
dead-lift
drag lift
diallage
deadline
dearling
dialling
dragline
diaglyph
diablery
dead loss
draw lots
dead-meat
drammach
drammock
deaf-mute
draw near
drainage
deadness
deafness
dearness
diagnose
drabness
dearnful
diaconal
diagonal
dianodal
dragoman
dragonet
diadochi
diabolic
dialogic
diatomic
diatonic
✧draconic
dragonné
diabolos
deaconry
dialogue
dead-pull
✧diaspora
diaspore
diatribe
drag race
diarrhea
draw rein
dead-rope
diagraph
Dean Rusk
dragsman
dragster
dead spit
deanship
draisene
draisine
dead shot
drag-shot
dram-shop
draft-bar
draw-tube
diastole
diastyle
diastema
diactine
dial tone

diastase
dianthus
draw upon
dead-wall
draw-well
dead-wind
dead wood
dead-wood
dead-work
dialyser
dialyses
dialyzer
dialysis
dialytic
Daboecia
dobber-in
Dubuffet
debugger
dabchick
dobchick
Du Bellay
debelled
dabbling
debility
debunker
Dubonnet
debonair
Doberman
debarred
debt swap
debussed
debasing
do battle
debutant
débutant
dubitate
débouché
deceased
declared
declarer
dichasia
dictator
déclassé
duckbill
dice-coal
dicyclic
dicacity
deciduae
decidual
deciduas
dock-dues
decadent
decedent
decretal
docketed
decrepit
Duchenne
decrease
duchesse
decagram
decigram
deck game
deck hand
duck hook
duck-hawk
declinal
decciver
deck-load
dockland
duckling
ductless

docility
decolour
dochmiac
December
decemvir
duckmole
document
docimasy
decimate
dochmius
decanter
decently
dicentra
doctoral
deck over
dichotic
dicrotic
doctorly
dice-play
Decapoda
decipher
duck-pond
decurved
dichroic
doctrine
decurion
doctress
decorate
decorous
docusoap
dockside
dicastic
decision
deck shoe
duck-shot
decisory
duck's ass
duck soup
decisive
duck-tail
ducatoon
duct tape
Docetism
Docetist
declutch
decouple
duckweed
dactylar
dactylic
Dactylis
decrying
dockyard
didrachm
didactic
dedicant
dedicate
didactyl
doddered
dodderer
diddicoy
✧dedalian
didymium
didymous
Dodonian
didapper
daedalic
Daedalus
Deep Blue
drencher
deep-dyed
dieldrin

dreadful
deep down
diereses
diegesis
dieresis
dietetic
deepfelt
dredge up
deer-hair
deer horn
deer-horn
dies irae
deep kiss
djellaba
deer lick
deep-laid
duelling
dwelling
deedless
duellist
dreamily
dreaming
dreamery
deepmost
dreamful
deer-neck
deepness
daemonic
dye-works
dye-house
deed poll
deer-park
deep-read
Dietrich
drearily
drearing
deemster
dressage
deerskin
dress tie
duelsome
dressing
die-stock
dyestuff
duetting
duettino
duettist
diestrus
✧dielytra
defrayal
defiance
deflater
defrayed
defrayer
deflator
defector
defecate
daft days
deflexed
defreeze
defilade
defaming
defenced
defended
defender
daftness
deftness
definite
deflower
duff over
daffodil

deferral
diffract
deferred
deferrer
deformed
deformer
deferent
deforest
defatted
diffused
diffuser
defluent
dogwatch
degraded
dog-eared
dog-faced
dog Latin
dogmatic
Dogmatix
diggable
dog-daisy
dog's-body
dogsbody
dog'sbane
dog-leech
doggerel
doggedly
✧dogberry
dog-weary
degrease
dog-cheap
dog-wheat
dog-whelk
dog-tired
daggings
diggings
dogfight
dogsleep
dog's life
dog's-meat
digamist
digamous
Dagenham
digynian
degender
dog's-nose
digynous
doggoned
do-gooder
doghouse
dog-louse
dogtooth
dog-trick
dog-grass
digerati
digester
digestif
dogeship
digitise
digitate
digitize
De Gaulle
doggy bag
dahabieh
dihybrid
dihedral
dihydric
dihedron
dehorner
dehorter
drivable
Daihatsu®
dribbler
dribblet
Duisburg
driveway
drip-feed
deisheal
drisheen
deicidal
deifical
drink off
dricksie
drinking
drill bit
drill rig
daidling
drilling
deionise
deionize
daimonic
Djibouti
dripping
drift-way
drift ice
drift net
driftage
driftpin
daintily
daiquiri
Daibutsu
dairyman
dairying
deifying
dejected
Dr Jekyll
déjeuner
dekalogy
dukeling
Dukhobor
dukeship
delta ray
dollared
dolmades
Dalmatia
dalmatic
dalmahoy
delibate
delubrum
delicacy
✧dolichos
delicate
dull-eyed
dal segno
delegacy
diligent
delegate
✧delphian
dollhood
dulcimer
Dulcinea
dulciana
dulcitol
Dalglish
De La Mare
dolomite
dullness
De Lorean®
doldrums
doloroso
dolerite
delirium
dolorous
dalesman
dolesome
delusion
delusory
delusive
dule-tree
dilatant
delation
deletion
dilation
dilution
deletory
dilatory
deletive
dilative
diluvial
diluvian
diluvion
delivery
diluvium
Delaware
dilly bag
dallying
delaying
dolly-mop
dolly tub
damnable
damnably
demeanor
demobbed
dumb-bell
✧democrat
domicile
dumb-cane
damp down
dumb down
dummerer
demagogy
DiMaggio
damaging
domainal
damoisel
demijohn
demi-jour
demology
demilune
dumpling
demolish
demoniac
demonian
domanial
Dominica
Dominick
demander
demanned
demented
domineer
dominoes
dementia
dominant
dominion
dampness
demoness
demonise
demonism
demonist
diminish
dumbness
dominate
dominium
demonize
dumfound
damboard
dum spiro
demersal
demurral
Dr Moreau
demerger
demersed
demurred
demurrer
Dumfries
démarche
demurely
demerara
dimerise
dimerism
dimerous
dimerize
demister
dempster
dumpster
damaskin
damassin
demyship
domestic
demissly
dumbshow
dumosity
Damascus
Domitian
dimetric
dome tent
demotion
demotist
domatium
dimethyl
demiurge
demi-volt
demi-wolf
dummy run
dentated
dungaree
dentalia
dentaria
dunnakin
deniable
deniably
Denebola
dingbats
dung-cart
ding-dong
denudate
ding doun
donnered
Don Revie
Daniella
Danielle
dentelle
duncedom
Don Pedro
Dunleary
danseuse
dancette
dancetté
dancetty
dung-fork
danegeld
danegelt
dungheap
dane-hole
dene-hole
dunghill
dun-diver
denticle
don't-know
Danelagh
dangling
dynamics
dungmere
dynamise
dynamism
dynamist
dynamite
dynamize
dankness
doneness
Dunwoody
Dan Fouts
dandriff
dandruff
dinarchy
dendroid
Dinornis
dendrite
denarius
diner-out
Denis Law
dynastic
dinosaur
DA-Notice
denetted
donation
dynatron
denature
donatary
donatory
donatism
Donatist
denotate
donative
denounce
dentures
Don Budge
do-naught
do-nought
Danewort
dandy-hen
dinky-die
dandyish
dandyism
denazify
Dino Zoff
drop away
dioramic
doolally
doorbell
Dioscuri
dioecism
doorcase
drop dead
drop-dead
drop down
drop-down
diocesan
duodenal
Diomedes
Diogenic
drone fly
duodenum
drop goal
drongoes
Dzongkha
droogish
droughty
Drogheda
dromical
dioritic
drop kick
drop-kick
drooking
drouking
doorknob
drop-leaf
drop lock
drolling
drollery
drollish
drownded
doornail
drowning
duologue
doom-palm
droopily
dropping
doorpost
drop-ripe
doomsday
doomsman
doors-man
doorsman
diopside
doomster
doorstep
dropsied
door-sill
drowsily
doorstop
drop-shot
deontics
dioptric
drop tank
dioptase
drop test
dropwort
dropwise
Dionysia
door-yard
Dionysus
drop zone
depraved
dipsades
Dipsacus
depicter
depictor
dipteral
dipteran
duplexer
diplegia
dapperly
dipteros
diphenyl
dipchick
deprival
depeinct
deprived
dip-slope
depilate
dopamine
dip snuff
dupondii
deponent
dopiness
diplomat
diploidy
diplogen
diplopia
diplopod
diplozoa
dipnoous
departer
deportee
depurant
depurate
dipstick
deputise
deputize
Dipavali
dormancy
Dark Ages
darraign
dermatic
dorsally
darraine
dirt bike
directly
déraciné
director
Doricism
doridoid
darndest
Dartford
dirigent
dirigism
derogate
derailer
dormient
Durmitor
derrière
durukuli
derelict
darkling
dark meat
darkmans
diriment
Dortmund
dart-moth
daring-do
deranged
daringly
darkness
direness
der-doing
dormouse
dirt-poor
dirt road
darkroom
dartrous
dark star
Doris Day
darksome
derision
derisory
derisive
Dorothea
derating
deration
duration
durative
derivate
dire wolf
dirtying
Derby dog
dirty dog

Words marked ✧ can also be spelled with one or more capital letters

Darbyite
Dushanbe
despatch
dispatch
distance
dastardy
discandy
diseased
disgavel
dispathy
dyspathy
desyatin
dishabit
dishable
dismally
Disraeli
distally
disfavor
distaste
disvalue
disabled
dust-ball
disabuse
dust-bath
✧dust bowl
dustcoat
dustcart
dysodile
dysodyle
disadorn
doss down
disbench
dispeace
dispence
deseeded
dishevel
dissever
Disneyfy
disherit
dysgenic
dyslexia
dyslexic
dysmelia
dysmelic
dispense
disperse
disseise
dyspepsy
diskette
disleave
disserve
disseize
disk file
designer
disagree
dysphagy
dust-hole
disthene
deschool
dyschroa
despisal
discinct
distinct
despiser
disliken
despight
dissight
distichs
dispirit
disciple
deselect

displace
displode
desilver
dosology
disclaim
displume
displant
disallow
disclose
disclost
disflesh
diskless
dustless
desolate
dyspneal
disannex
disinter
dyspnoea
dyspneic
desinent
disendow
disenrol
disunion
disinure
duskness
disunite
disunity
disannul
despotat
disloyal
disposal
disvouch
disbowel
discover
dismoded
disponee
disponer
disposed
disposer
disgorge
dislodge
disloign
disponge
despotic
dystocia
dystonia
dystonic
dystopia
discoing
discount
disjoint
dismount
disbosom
discolor
dishonor
discoure
dishorse
dishouse
dissolve
disk pack
disapply
disarray
dispread
describe
destruct
disfrock
disgrace
distract
district
disgrade
descried

deserted
deserter
deserved
deserver
destrier
disarmer
discreet
disorbed
disorder
distrail
distrain
distrait
disproof
de-stress
distress
distrust
discrete
desirous
descrive
disprove
discrown
disprize
disaster
disusage
dust-shot
disjunct
dissuade
disputer
disquiet
dispunge
disburse
disguise
dispurse
disowner
desk-work
dateable
dutiable
détraqué
databank
database
detached
detector
dithecal
ditherer
dotterel
do the job
ditheism
ditheist
duty-free
data flow
datagram
Dutch cap
Dutchman
Dutch War
ditch-dog
Dutch hoe
detrital
detailed
detainee
detainer
detritus
ditokous
dataller
date line
dateline
dateless
datolite
dotingly
detonate
dittoing
duty-paid

date palm
date plum
deterred
daturine
dethrone
date rape
dytiscid
Dytiscus
date tree
dotation
detrusor
dote upon
detoxify
ditty bag
ditty box
drumbeat
drubbing
deuddarn
✧druidess
✧druidism
deuce-ace
douzeper
drupelet
diuresis
diuretic
deucedly
deuteron
drumfire
drumfish
drugging
drudgery
drudgism
druggist
drumhead
daughter
dauphine
doughboy
druthers
doughnut
drunkard
doubling
doubloon
doublure
double up
drummock
drumming
Drum Mass
douanier
dourness
doum-palm
drum roll
daunting
doubting
doubtful
Deus vult
duumviri
duumvirs
deviance
deviancy
deviator
dive-bomb
dovecote
dividual
dividant
dividend
dividing
dividers
dividivi
dove-eyed
dove grey
divagate

dive into
devilled
devilkin
dovelike
Davy lamp
deviling
divalent
devildom
develope
De Valera
deviltry
deviless
devilish
devilism
Devonian
divan-bed
divinify
divinely
divinise
divinity
divinize
divorcee
divorcée
divorcer
diversly
division
divisive
dovetail
duvetine
duvetyne
devotion
devourer
devoutly
divvying
downbeat
down-come
downcast
dewy-eyed
dewberry
down east
downfall
downflow
downhill
downhole
down-home
downhaul
download
dowel-pin
downland
down-line
downlink
dowel-rod
downmost
dewiness
dowfness
dewpoint
downplay
downpipe
downpour
dewormer
dawn raid
downrush
downside
downsize
downtime
down-trod
Dr Watson
downturn
down town
✧downtown
down upon

downwind
downward
downwash
dowdyish
dowdyism
duxelles
doxology
doxapram
dextrine
dextrose
dextrous
doxastic
daytaler
day about
day-level
day shift
dry riser
daylight
day-sight
dry light
dry-bible
dry-clean
dry-plate
day-to-day
day-woman
dey-woman
dry goods
dry-point
dry-roast
drymouth
daybreak
daydream
dayes-man
dry steam
dry-stone
dry-stove
dry-nurse
day by day
doze away
dizygous
dazzling
doziness
dizzying
erasable
evadable
exarchal
enarched
Enard Bay
ecaudate
evanesce
elaterin
elatedly
Eva Perón
evangely
enargite
elaphine
examinee
examiner
evasible
étatisme
emaciate
eradiate
étatiste
edacious
enallage
e-mailing
enabling
e-tailing
enaunter
epagogic
epanodos

examplar
etaerios
Evans Bay
Erastian
exanthem
elastane
enacting
exacting
enaction
exaction
enacture
elastase
enactive
evacuant
evacuate
evaluate
embraced
embracer
embraces
emblazon
embrasor
embodied
embalmer
embolden
embolise
embolism
embolize
embanker
E W Benson
en brosse
embarras
embarked
embarred
emborder
embossed
embosser
embussed
embusqué
embitter
embattle
Ebbw Vale
embryoid
embryons
embezzle
enchased
encharge
exchange
eucharis
encradle
eschalot
excubant
encyclic
eucyclic
eschewal
excretal
eschewer
excreter
ecclesia
✧encaenia
en cuerpo
encierro
encrease
ecce homo
encrinal
eccrisis
eccritic
enclisis
enclitic
encrinic
eucritic
enceinte

Words marked ✧ can also be spelled with one or more capital letters

escalade
escalado
escalier
excelled
esculent
escallop
escalope
eucalypt
encolure
escalate
encolour
encumber
Eichmann
encomion
encomium
encroach
encloser
enclothe
enchoric
en croupe
en croûte
escapade
escapado
encipher
exceptor
escapism
escapist
encircle
escarole
escargot
eucaryon
eucaryot
excerpta
encarpus
excursus
encysted
excesses
excuse me
excuse-me
excision
excusive
excitant
exciting
et cetera
etcetera
et ceteri
excluded
excludee
excluder
excavate
endeared
endpaper
endeavor
endocarp
endodyne
endoderm
Erdgeist
endogamy
endogeny
eldritch
endeixis
endemial
endamage
Endymion
endemism
endanger
endzones
end organ
El Dorado
Eldorado
endorsed
endorsee
endorser
endermic
enduring
endorsor
elder-gun
Eddy Shah
ecdysone
endosarc
endozoic
endozoon
elegance
elegancy
emeraude
eye candy
elevated
eye-water
elevator
eye-salve
Eteocles
elenctic
exercise
elenchus
emendals
ependyma
emendate
even date
even-down
eyes down
ebenezer
even-even
eye level
eye-level
exegesis
exegetic
elements
eleventh
eye of day
evenfall
exergual
emergent
emerging
energise
energize
eyeshade
erewhile
eye-rhyme
elephant
erethism
emetical
eremital
elegiacs
eyepiece
eyeliner
evenings
eyesight
eremitic
elegiast
ébéniste
emeritus
eye-black
eyeglass
evermore
Eleanore
eternise
evenness
eternity
eternize
eye tooth
eye to eye
exemplar
exemplum
eye-drops
execrate
evensong
emersion
eversion
eventual
eventide
electret
electric
erectile
eyestalk
eventing
egestion
ejection
election
electron
electros
erection
evection
exertion
Edentata
edentate
electrum
eventful
egestive
ejective
elective
erective
exertive
exequial
executer
exequies
executor
executry
enervate
emery bag
everyday
✧everyman
everyway
every bit
everyone
effraide
efficacy
effecter
effector
effierce
enfierce
enfeeble
enfreeze
effigies
elf-child
elf-shoot
enfilade
effulged
enflower
enfrosen
elflocks
enforcer
efferent
elf-arrow
enforest
enfested
effusion
effusive
enfetter
effetely
effluvia
effluent
egg dance
engraved
engraven
engraver
ex gratia
engramma
edgebone
Eugubine
edge coal
eagle-ray
eagle-owl
eagle eye
ergogram
engaging
eggshell
egg whisk
egg white
egg timer
engrieve
egg slice
eggplant
edgeless
egg glass
eugenics
engender
engineer
enginery
edginess
eugenism
eugenist
Eugenius
egg-bound
Eggboard
egg tooth
engroove
egg-apple
egg spoon
engorged
edge rail
eggfruit
engirdle
en garçon
eight-day
eight-oar
eighteen
eighties
ergatoid
eighthly
edge tool
eightvos
ergotise
ergotism
ergative
ergotize
engouled
egg purse
edgewise
edgeways
ethnarch
enhearse
ethicise
ethicism
ethicist
ethicize
exhedrae
enhydros
echogram
ethnical
Ethelred
ethology
ethylene
exhalant
echoless
ethylate
ephemera
exhumate
enhancer
enhunger
echinoid
Echinops
Esha Ness
echinate
Ethiopia
Ethiopic
eohippus
ethercap
ethereal
etherial
Ethernet
exhorter
etherify
etherion
etherise
etherism
etherist
ephorate
etherize
Ephesian
echiuran
epigaeal
epigaean
exitance
epitases
epigamic
epitasis
editable
epically
evitable
epifauna
epilator
epinasty
Eridanus
epicalyx
episcope
episcopy
evincive
evil-doer
eminence
eminency
evidence
exigence
exigency
epicedes
evil-eyed
epicedia
epidemic
epimeric
exigeant
episemon
erigeron
epilepsy
epigeous
epithema
epithems
✧epiphany
epiphyte
eligible
eligibly
Eric Idle
exigible
elicitor
eximious
Ewigkeit
etiology
epiploic
epiploon
epiblast
etiolate
Eli Smith
ebionise
ebionism
evilness
Ebionite
erionite
ebionize
epifocal
episodal
✧epigones
epidotic
epilogic
epinosic
epipolic
episodic
epitomic
epitonic
epizoite
epilogue
epicotyl
exit poll
episperm
epispore
Eritrean
emigrant
epigraph
editress
emigrate
epitrite
emissile
emission
emissary
emissive
ekistics
epistler
epistyle
emitting
existent
emiction
eviction
emictory
epidural
exiguity
Epicurus
exiguous
epicycle
edifying
enjoiner
enkindle
elkhound
enkernel
eukaryon
eukaryot
ex libris
ex-libris
eulachan
eclectic
eulachon
éolienne
eulogies
eulogise
eulogist
eclogite
eklogite
eulogium
eulogize
Eulalius
enlumine
eclampsy
eel-spear
ellipses
ecliptic
ellipsis
elliptic
eolipile
eelwrack
enlarged
enlargen
enlarger
eelgrass
enlister
enlist in
eclosion
✧eolithic
eglatere
Emmeline
Emmental
Emmanuel
Edmonton
emmarble
eumerism
enmossed
enneadic
enneagon
Ernie Els
ex nihilo
eo nomine
Einstein
ennuying
eco-label
egomania
exogamic
evocable
exorable
evocator
Elo scale
Eton crop
exorcise
exorcism
exorcist
exorcize
ego ideal
exordial
exordium
erogenic
erotesis
erotetic
esoteric
exoteric
eloigner
emongest
elongate
exophagy
erotical
erodible
emoticon
exoplasm
exosmose
enormity
enormous
ecologic
economic
ecotoxic
epopoeia
exotoxic
exotoxin
exospore
ecofreak

étourdie
exoergic
exocrine
egoistic
Eton suit
ecostate
eloquent
evolvent
eponymic
euonymin
epoxying
euonymus
emphases
emphasis
emphatic
expiable
expiator
especial
empacket
expected
expecter
expedite
empierce
empleach
ekpweles
empyemic
empyesis
Euphemia
espiègle
empressé
espresso
expresso
en prince
explicit
empoison
en pointe
empolder
espalier
expelled
expellee
expeller
espumoso
empanada
expanded
expander
expender
expenses
expunger
exponent
expandor
employed
employee
employer
exploded
exploder
✧explorer
emplonge
euphobia
euphonia
euphonic
euphoria
euphoric
empeople
eupepsia
eupeptic
empyreal
empyrean
exporter
expert in
empurple
expertly
expirant
expiring
espartos
emperise
emperish
euphrasy
emporium
emperize
exposure
empathic
eupatrid
empatron
espousal
espouser
euphuise
✧euphuism
euphuist
euphuize
emptysis
emptying
Esquimau
enquirer
esquisse
ebriated
euro area
Eurobond
Eurocrat
Eurydice
enridged
Earl Grey
earth-bag
earthman
earthwax
earth-fed
earth-pea
Earthsea
Earl Haig
ear-shell
earthily
earphone
earth-hog
earth-nut
Earl Howe
earpiece
earnings
earwiggy
earliest
enrolled
enrollee
enroller
Euroland
Euromart
étranger
étrennes
errantly
erringly
errantry
eeriness
ex re nata
European
en rappel
Europort
europium
Etrurian
eardrops
errorist
Etruscan
Eurasian
Euroseat
Eurostat
écraseur
✧eurythmy
earmuffs
enraunge
enravish
Eurozone
enslaved
enslaver
enswathe
ecstasis
ecstatic
eustatic
Eusebian
Eusebius
eusocial
easy-care
easterly
ens reale
ens per se
ensheath
ensiform
ensigncy
easy-goer
easy game
ensphere
essoiner
enshield
ensilage
eastland
eastling
eastlins
easeless
easy meat
ensample
ensemble
easement
easy mark
eastmost
epsomite
Essencia
Elsinore
easiness
Essenism
essonite
ensconce
easy over
exserted
enshrine
enshroud
East Side
eastward
elsewise
Essex Man
essaying
essayish
essayist
extra jam
entrance
extranet
estrange
entrails
extrados
enthalpy
entr'acte
eatables
estacade
eutectic
enticing
ex tacito
ectoderm
entoderm
entrench
entremes
esteemed
extremer
extremes
enthetic
esthesia
esthetic
Eutheria
entrepot
entrepôt
entresol
entreaty
ectogeny
entailer
estridge
extolled
extoller
entellus
estimate
Ertan Dam
Estonian
entender
extended
extender
estancia
entangle
extensor
estrogen
eutrophy
ectropic
entropic
eutropic
eftsoons
extrorse
estopped
estoppel
entoptic
ettercap
external
externat
enter key
extorter
esterify
enthrall
entirely
entering
enthrone
exterior
esterase
enterate
entirety
ectosarc
extruder
estivate
eutaxite
entry fee
entryism
entryist
ectozoan
entozoal
ectozoic
entozoic
ectozoon
entozoon
educated
educable
educator
emulator
eau de Nil
eau de vie
ecumenic
enuresis
enuretic
emulgent
evulgate
educible
eludible
esurient
exuviate
equalled
equalise
equality
Equuleus
equalize
eburnean
equinity
epulotic
equipped
equipper
equipage
erumpent
emulsify
emulsoid
emulsion
evulsion
emulsive
equities
equitant
exultant
eduction
equation
eruption
eructate
equative
eruptive
equivoke
enviable
enviably
enveigle
envelope
elvanite
environs
en vérité
envassal
envisage
envision
enwallow
euxenite
eryngoes
eryngium
erythema
etypical
Erysimum
epyllion
Epyornis
Egyptian
Enzedder
enzootic
Fragaria
flambeau
flatboat
flatback
flambéed
flabbily
Flaubert
flax-bush
fiascoes
flanched
flax-comb
Francome
Francine
✧frascati
flanch up
francium
fraudful
flag down
frame-saw
flamenco
flamelet
flare off
flânerie
flagella
feateous
flake out
flame gun
flame out
flameout
flare-out
flat file
flat-foot
foalfoot
flatfish
flagging
fragging
Flashman
✧flathead
flashily
flashing
flash ROM
feathery
flashgun
flamingo
flag iris
feasible
feasibly
flatiron
Fraxinus
flapjack
frabjous
frank-fee
✧franklin
fracking
Frankish
frailtee
✧fräulein
flax-lily
✧flatland
flatline
flatling
flatlong
✧fearless
flawless
foamless
frailish
flammule
flax-mill
fragment
flatmate
flaunter
flannels
flatness
flatpack
frampler
flagpole
frampold
flapping
frappant
frapping
flat race
flag rank
flagrant
fragrant
flat rate
flaxseed
flagship
flat spin
fraus pia
fearsome
feast-day
frautage
feasting
flatting
feast-won
fraction
flattery
flat tyre
fracture
flattest
flattish
flautist
feastful
features
flatuses
featuous
flatuous
flag-worm
flatware
flatworm
flatwise
flatways
fob-watch
feblesse
febrific
fibrilla
fabliaux
fabulise
fabulist
fabulous
fabulize
fibromas
fibrosis
fibrotic
faburden
February
face-ache
facially
focaccia
face card
face down
fucoidal
factious
facelift
facilely
feculent
faceless
feckless
focalise
facility
focalize
face mask
factor in
factotum
face pack
focussed
focusing
fuchsine
fuchsite
facetiae
face time
fade away
fiducial
fade down
fade-down
fidgeted

fodderer
fiddious
fedelini
fiddling
fuddling
fadeless
fidelity
federacy
federary
federate
fedayeen
foedarie
feedable
fredaine
free atom
feedback
flea-bane
freeborn
freebase
flea-bite
frescade
fletcher
frescoed
frescoer
frescoes
fiercely
fuel cell
free-cost
free-city
field day
freedman
Freudian
field ice
field bed
field-dew
freedmen
fielding
free drop
fiendish
field gun
Frederic
Frederik
frenetic
feel free
free fall
free-fall
Freefone®
free-form
free gift
feel-good
feelgood
feed-head
freshman
fresh-new
flesh-fly
freehold
free hand
freehand
flesh pot
freshish
flesh out
fresh-run
feelings
flexible
flexibly
fremitus
free kick
freckled
freakish
freakful
freak out

freak-out
freeload
feel like
feed-line
fuelling
feeblish
feetless
free list
fretless
free love
freeness
feed-pump
feed-pipe
Freeport
free port
Freepost®
free ride
fee-grief
free reed
free-reed
fleering
free-soil
fleasome
free-shot
Flextime®
fleeting
fretting
flection
Freetown
flexural
frequent
flexuose
flexuous
frenulum
free vote
free will
free-will
fleawort
freeware
fretwork
frenzied
freezing
freeze-up
fiftieth
fife rail
fiftyish
Fagaceae
fugacity
fugleman
fughetta
fog light
figuline
fog-smoke
fog index
fogbound
figurant
figurine
figurist
figurate
fight off
fight shy
fagoting
fighting
fugitive
fogeydom
fogeyish
fogeyism
fahlband
fricadel
Frimaire
fribbler

flincher
fair copy
fail-dyke
flinders
fainéant
frisette
frizette
flimflam
flip-flap
fair fall
flip-flop
foie gras
fair game
flinging
fling mud
fling out
flichter
flighted
frighten
✧faithful
fainites
Fair Isle
Fair-Isle
frigidly
friskily
frisking
friskful
fair-lead
frillies
frilling
friended
friendly
feigning
fainness
fairness
feijoada
frijoles
Fribourg
fair play
flippant
flipping
frippery
Friesian
flipside
fail safe
fail-safe
flimsily
Friesish
flintify
feistily
flintily
fainting
flirting
flitting
fritting
friction
flittern
flitters
faintish
flirtish
frittata
flix-weed
fairydom
fairyism
fakement
fakirism
Fukuyama
fall away
foldaway
falcated
foliaged

foliated
full-aged
fellahin
F R Leavis
fellable
filially
filmable
foldable
faltboat
foldboat
full beam
fall back
fall-back
full back
full-bore
full-cock
filicide
file copy
✧felicity
felo de se
falderal
False Bay
fulgency
false hem
false leg
filleted
full-eyed
false rib
fal de rol
folderol
faldetta
falsetto
Filberts
fall flat
full-face
folk-free
filiform
fallfish
filefish
feldgrau
filagree
filigree
filmgoer
filthily
filching
full hand
falchion
folk hero
fillibeg
filliped
fillings
felsitic
fallible
fallibly
follicle
fall line
filmland
folkland
folklore
filament
folkmoot
full moon
filander
film noir
filename
full name
fellness
fullness
felinity
felonous
falconer

falconet
fall over
follower
fellowly
folioing
follow on
follow-on
falconry
Falmouth
filioque
follow up
follow-up
full-page
full pelt
full-pelt
Filipina
Filipino
filariae
filarial
filarias
folk rock
fulcrums
filtrate
fulcrate
feldspar
film star
feldsher
full sail
folk song
full stop
fall-trap
Falstaff
folk tale
full tilt
full-tilt
full time
full-time
felstone
folk tune
filatory
filature
full toss
fulgural
fall upon
fumed oak
fumadoes
fumigant
fumigate
fume hood
familial
familiar
fameless
✧familism
Familist
femality
fomenter
feminine
feminise
feminism
feminist
feminity
feminize
fimbrial
femerall
fumarole
fumerole
famished
feme sole
fumosity
femetary
fumatory

fumitory
famously
fan dance
fontanel
fandango
fontange
fantasia
findable
fineable
fundable
fanfaron
fine arts
fentanyl
funebral
finochio
fine comb
fine-draw
fine down
fingered
finnesko
fen-berry
finagler
Fine Gael
Fanagalo
fan wheel
fin whale
funkhole
fannings
findings
fanlight
fencible
fungible
fanciful
fantigue
final say
fine lady
fondling
fangless
finalise
finalism
finalist
fineless
fundless
finality
finalize
finances
font name
fineness
fondness
fungo bat
funboard
fantoosh
funereal
Fanariot
funerary
finesser
finished
finisher
fenestra
feng shui
finespun
finish up
finitude
finitely
fine-tune
function
funguses
Funtumia
Fancy Dan
fancy man
Fundy Bay

funny man
fancying
fool away
frowards
florally
from A to B
from A to Z
football
fool-born
footbath
floccule
flocculi
floscule
food-card
floccose
floodway
frondage
floodlit
flooding
frondent
frondose
froideur
frondeur
✧florence
flowered
flowerer
floweret
Fiorello!
fromenty
footfall
frou-frou
food-fish
frogfish
footgear
Fjorgynn
flogging
frogging
froggery
foothill
foothold
from hell
froth-fly
frothily
frothery
florigen
Florizel
floridly
flotilla
flock-bed
frocking
footling
foozling
frogling
foodless
footless
footmuff
footmark
flounder
frowning
footnote
footpace
footpage
floppily
footpump
footpost
footpath
floor pan
foot-race
footrule
flooring
foot-rope

flourish
footrest
fool's cap
foolscap
footstep
frowster
frog-spit
flox silk
flossing
footslog
footsore
front man
frontman
frontier
frontlet
floatage
frontage
frostily
floatant
floating
front-end
frosting
frontoon
front row
frog test
footwear
footwall
footwell
footwork
footworn
fippence
fermatas
fire away
forwards
forzando
forrader
forsaken
forsaker
furcated
formalin
farfalla
farfalle
farmable
fernally
fordable
forfault
forhaile
formable
formally
firearms
farragos
forfairn
Firdausi
forwaste
firebrat
forebear
fireback
forebode
fore-body
fireball
firebomb
furibund
fernbird
fire-bird
fire-bote
forebitt
fire clay
forecast
feracity
ferocity
furacity

foredeck
faradaic
fire damp
firedamp
fire door
foredoom
faradise
faradism
foredate
firm down
faradize
forgeman
fervency
for mercy
ferreted
ferreter
fire-eyed
force-fed
fire-edge
fore-edge
forget it
forcedly
forkedly
formerly
farnesol
furbelow
for keeps
forweary
farceuse
fornenst
forfeits
furmenty
ferreous
forceful
fire-flag
forefeel
forefeet
form feed
forefelt
forkfuls
forefoot
foregoer
foregone
forehead
forkhead
forehock
for shame
farm hand
farthing
forehand
forehent
forthink
fire-hook
for short
farthest
fire hose
furthest
farcical
fornical
forcipes
forgiven
forgiver
ferriage
ferritic
ferritin
for kicks
fervidly
forcible
forcibly
Fervidor
farriery

furriery
farm into
formiate
fortieth
foreking
foreknow
firelock
forelock
forslack
forelift
fork-lift
forelimb
far-flung
fern land
foreland
forelend
forelent
fireless
firmless
formless
foremean
foramina
firemark
foremast
foremost
Faringee
forinsec
Feringhi
forensic
furuncle
forename
forenoon
farinose
firmness
fire opal
fork over
furlough
forhooie
forborne
fordoing
forgoing
furiosos
far-forth
Far North
Far South
forsooth
Formosus
forepeak
foreplan
forspeak
far-spent
forspend
forspent
fire-plow
forepart
forepast
fireplug
foreread
Furcraea
fore-rank
fire-risk
fortress
fernshaw
forestal
forestay
fireside
foreside
fern-seed
fire-step
foreseen
foreshew

forested
✧forester
fire sign
fireship
foresaid
foresail
foreship
foreskin
fire sale
foreshow
foreslow
forestry
farm team
firetrap
first-day
fire-tube
first aid
first fix
forktail
foretell
foretold
for a time
foretime
feretory
farm-toun
formulae
formular
formulas
furcular
furfural
furfuran
fortuned
forjudge
farouche
furfurol
fortuity
forswear
fireweed
farewell
fire-walk
firewall
forewent
forewind
forewing
forswink
forswunk
firewood
firework
fireworm
firmware
foreward
forewarn
foreword
formwork
forswore
forsworn
forswatt
ferryman
ferrying
farmyard
foreyard
fortyish
farcy-bud
festally
fiscally
fishable
fastback
fastball
fishball
fuss-ball
fish-bone

fish cake
fish-dive
✧**fosse way**
fastener
fosterer
fossette
fast food
fish farm
fusiform
fish-guts
fish-glue
Fasching
fish-hook
fish-hawk
festival
fistical
fissiped
fascicle
fasciola
fasciole
Fascismo
fashions
fistiana
fasciate
Fascista
Fascisti
✧fascists
fashious
fusileer
fusilier
fuselage
fusel-oil
fast lane
fishmeal
fistmele
fastness
fisnomie
fish pond
fusarole
fostress
fish-stew
fishskin
fishtail
fast-talk
fistulae
fistular
fistulas
fossulae
fissured
fastuous
fishwife
fish-weir
fuse wire
fess-wise
fat-faced
feticide
Fête-Dieu
fattener
fatherly
fatigued
fatigues
fatigate
fetch off
fetching
fetch out
fittings
fitliest
futilely
fettling
fatalism
fatalist

fatality
futility
fat mouse
fattrels
✧**futurism**
futurist
futurity
fat stock
fatstock
fitfully
feudally
Foucault
frugally
fougasse
four-ball
flubbing
four bits
faulchin
flue-cure
fluidics
fluidify
founding
fluidise
fluidity
fluidize
four-eyes
fauteuil
fauvette
frumenty
foul fall
fourfold
four-foot
foul-fish
foughten
✧**flushing**
fauchion
flush-box
flush out
frutices
fluxions
Faulkner
flunk out
four-leaf
Fluellen
fluellin
flummery
foulmart
faux-naïf
fluent in
fluently
foulness
faubourg
foul play
four-pack
flue pipe
four-part
frumpish
fluoride
flurried
fluorine
fluorite
foursome
flue stop
✧**faustian**
fruit bat
fourteen
fruitlet
fruit tea
fructify
fruitage
fountain

faultily
fourthly
fruit fly
frustule
frustums
Faustina
fructans
fruiting
fruition
flustery
fluttery
fruitery
fructose
faultful
fountful
fruit-bud
fruitful
fructive
fruitive
fluework
fava bean
fivefold
Favonian
fivepins
feverfew
feverish
favorite
feverous
favoured
favourer
fowl-pest
fewtrils
fawn upon
fox-earth
fixed air
foxberry
foxshark
foxglove
foxiness
foxhound
fox-grape
fox-brush
fixation
fixature
fixative
flymaker
flypaper
flysheet
flywheel
fly whisk
flypitch
fly a kite
fayalite
flyblown
fly-under
fly-tower
flyspray
fly-speck
fly front
fly-drive
fly-tying
fuzz-ball
foziness
Ghanaian
Ghadamès
gravamen
gradatim
guaranis
gradable
gram-atom
guanacos

Words marked ✧ can also be spelled with one or more capital letters

guaranty
guaiacum
gramarye
grabbler
goalball
grabbing
giambeux
Gray code
glaucoma
glancing
gear-case
Graecise
Graecism
glaucous
Graecize
granddad
grand mal
guardian
guardage
glandule
grandame
gladding
guardant
grandson
guard dog
glanders
grand cru
grandeur
gear down
grave-wax
gramercy
glabella
gravelly
glacéing
glareous
grace cup
graceful
grade out
grateful
grape ivy
Graafian
goatfish
graffiti
graffito
graphics
grapheme
glad hand
glad-hand
gnashing
gnashers
goatherd
guacharo
gnathite
graphite
graphium
gravitas
glacises
gratinée
granitic
gladiole
gladioli
gradient
graviton
gracioso
grazioso
glaciate
gladiate
goad into
gracious
goal kick
gralloch
gnarlier
gnatling
goal line
goatling
grayling
gearless
goalless
go all out
Grammies
Grasmere
goat-moth
grainage
graining
gladness
glasnost
gramoche
go-around
gealousy
grappler
grasping
goalpost
go abroad
glam rock
glam-rock
glad rags
glabrate
glabrous
glass jaw
glassman
goadsman
goadster
Graf Spee
glassify
goatskin
grass-oil
glassily
gladsome
glassine
grassing
grass box
Glassite
glassful
goat's-rue
glass eye
Grantham
grattoir
graithly
grafting
giantess
giantism
ghastful
granular
graduand
graduate
gratuity
goatweed
gable end
Gobiidae
gabeller
gabbling
Gobelins
gobble up
gybe mark
gibingly
Gabonese
gabioned
gabbroic
gabbroid
Gaborone
gibbsite
go better
go beyond
Geckones
godwards
God's acre
gad about
gadabout
gude-dame
Gadhelic
gadgetry
God's foot
gado-gado
God's gift
Godthaab
godchild
God-given
godliest
God's life
god-smith
God knows
gadzooks
✧godspeed
Godspell
God squad
Gadarene
gudesire
gudewife
god-awful
Gnetales
grey area
Grenache
gregatim
Goebbels
grey-coat
glee club
greedily
grey-eyed
greffier
grey-fish
greegree
goethite
guerilla
guéridon
Gwen John
Greek way
Greek key
✧greeking
Greekdom
Greek god
Greekish
gleaming
grey mare
green-bag
green ban
green man
green ray
green way
Greenock
Guernica
greenies
greenlet
green tea
✧guernsey
greenfly
gleaning
greening
Grey nuns
greenery
greenish
greyness
greeneye
Grenoble
grey seal
greasies
gneissic
greasily
gleesome
greesing
gressing
guessing
Great War
ghettoes
great fee
Great Sea
great tit
greeting
Great Dog
great toe
great ape
greatest
great auk
great gun
grey wolf
gift-book
giftedly
gefuffle
giff-gaff
go figure
gaff sail
giftshop
gift-wrap
gig-lamps
gigabyte
gigaflop
go-go girl
gaggling
giggling
goggling
Gigantes
gigantic
gaga over
gag-tooth
go-getter
gigawatt
go halves
go hungry
guidance
Grimaldi
grimacer
gainable
guidable
glibbery
guimbard
gliadine
grinding
gliddery
grindery
grind out
Griselda
Grizelda
gaitered
Gaiseric
Goidelic
gridelin
guide dog
Ghiberti
grisette
griseous
guileful
gliffing
griefful
gairfowl
gris-gris
grisgris
goings-on
gainings
gridiron
grill pan
gridlock
grillade
grillage
grilling
gaillard
gainless
glimmery
grimmest
gliomata
grinning
glibness
grimness
Guicowar
grimoire
gripping
goitrous
gripsack
glissade
gainsaid
grissini
grissino
gainsays
grittily
guiltily
gain time
griptape
glittery
grittest
gain upon
go in unto
grievous
glitzier
grizzled
grizzler
glitzily
Gujarati
Gujerati
gill arch
goliardy
galeated
gallabea
gallabia
galvanic
gullable
gillaroo
galbanum
galabeah
galabiah
gulp back
gill beer
golf ball
Galician
galactic
gold card
golf cart
golf club
gall duct
gold disc
gold dust
gelidity
gulp down
gold-ends
galleted
galleria
goldenly
galleass
gold foil
goldfish
gilt-head
Gallican
gallivat
gullible
Galliano
Galliano®
golfiana
gallipot
galliard
Galtieri
galliass
Galilean
gold leaf
gold-leaf
gold lace
gall-less
goldless
gold mine
galangal
galenoid
Galenism
Galenist
galenite
gold note
Galloway
Golconda
galloper
Golgotha
galtonia
galapago
gold rush
Galerius
gelastic
gulosity
Gelasius
goldsize
gilt-tail
gelatine
gelation
galluses
gallumph
Gil Evans
galowses
gulfweed
gull-wing
giltwood
gold wire
goldwork
gall wasp
gold-wasp
gillyvor
gamma ray
gammadia
gammatia
gymnasia
gymnasic
gambados
gemma-cup
game ball
game bird
gamecock
game call
gimme cap
gimme hat
gum resin
gambeson
gambetta
gemmeous
game fish
gymkhana
gumphion
gemshorn
gimmicky
gemology
gambling
game laws
Geminian
go mental
gameness
gaminess
gamyness
geminate
geminous
gammoner
gambogic
gummosis
game plan
gameplay
Gomorrah
gimcrack
gambroon
gamester
gamesome
game show
gematria
gemstone
gumption
gambusia
gym tunic
Gonzales
gunlayer
gunmaker
Gunga Din
genially
gendarme
gonfalon
gonfanon
gene bank
Ginsberg
genocide
gonocyte
gynecium
gonadial
gonidial
gonidium
Gang Days
gondelay
gunmetal
gendered
gingelly
gingerly
gannetry
genned up
ginger up
gene flow
ginkgoes
Gandhian
Gandhism
Gandhist
gingival
Ganoidei
gunfight
gunsight
gentilic
gingkoes
gangliar
ginglymi
gangland
gangling
gantline

gin sling
gunflint
ganglion
gantlope
genomics
Ganymede
gang mill
gunsmith
gin and it
gynandry
goneness
gunpoint
ginhouse
gunhouse
gene pool
Ganapati
gang plug
gentrice
gentrify
generale
gangrene
generant
generate
generous
gangsman
Genesiac
gangster
ganister
gongster
genetics
gunstick
gunstock
genetrix
genitrix
genitals
gunstone
genotype
geniture
genitive
go native
geniuses
gin rummy
Genevese
Genovese
Gondwana
geomancy
globated
geotaxis
globally
growable
Giovanni
geocarpy
geolatry
grosbeak
goofball
gaolbird
✧groschen
good-dame
goose-cap
geometer
good-even
groveled
groveler
goose-egg
geodesic
geodetic
glove box
goosegob
goosegog
geometry
gooped up
Geoffrey
good folk
good form
go on fire
Georgian
Georgics
groggily
Georgina
groo-groo
groggery
geophagy
geophone
geophyte
gloxinia
gloriole
Gloriana
gloriosa
grodiest
grow into
glorious
good-lack
goodlier
glowlamp
growling
growlery
ghoulish
gloomily
gloaming
glomming
glooming
gloomful
grounded
grounden
grounder
groaning
groining
geognost
geognosy
goodness
gooiness
groanful
geologer
geogonic
geologic
geoponic
gnomonic
grouplet
groupage
grow pale
grouping
groupers
groupist
glow plug
grow rich
glossily
glosseme
glossina
good show
grog-shop
glossary
goodsire
grossart
gross out
gross-out
grottoed
grottoes
goodtime
ghosting
grouting
good turn
ghost gum
globular
globulet
globulin
groovily
✧goodwife
goodwill
gromwell
glow-worm
goodyear
glory-pea
geomyoid
glorying
glory box
go places
go public
gypseous
gapingly
gapeseed
gapeworm
gypsydom
gypsyism
garlands
garganey
Garnacha
Germanic
✧germaine
garbanzo
germ cell
gyrodyne
gardener
garreted
✧gardenia
gorgerin
gor-belly
gorgeous
giraffid
garefowl
garaging
garagist
Gershwin
Gurkhali
girlhood
✧germinal
gyroidal
garcinia
garlicky
Garfield
gerbille
garrison
garrigue
gorblimy
garbling
germ line
girtline
gormless
gyrolite
Garamond
Gurinder
gerontic
Girondin
Geronimo
geraniol
goriness
geranium
garroted
Gorgonia
gargoyle
gurgoyle
garboard
garrotte
geropiga
Gertrude
gyrostat
guruship
garishly
girasole
garotted
garotter
gyration
gyratory
Gurmukhi
gurdwara
gardyloo
gas-water
go shares
gossamer
gustable
gestapos
Gustavus
go steady
gas meter
gesneria
gasifier
gastfull
gasiform
gasogene
gas shell
Gasthaus
gas-fired
gossiped
gaslight
gas-tight
gasfield
gossipry
gas-globe
gas black
gust-lock
gasalier
gaselier
gasolier
gasolene
gasoline
gas-plant
gastness
gospodar
gas poker
gasworks
Gisborne
gas-motor
gastraea
gastrula
gas stove
gestural
gossypol
guttated
gettable
get about
get ideas
get ready
gatherer
gatefold
gate-fine
get ahead
get there
guttiest
get a load
get a life
get a line
get along
gateless
go too far
get round
gatepost
get wrong
go to seed
go to show
get it off
go to town
guttural
gate-vein
glutaeal
glucagon
glutaeus
grumbler
glueball
grubbily
grubbing
glutelin
glumella
Giuseppe
goujeers
gruffish
glugging
grudging
Gaucher's
glucinum
grub kick
grueling
Gaullism
Gaullist
gaumless
gourmand
glummest
glumness
grumness
glucosic
grumphie
grumpily
glumpish
✧gaussian
gruesome
grub shop
Gaultier
gauntlet
gauntree
gruntled
glutting
gluttony
grunting
goutweed
✧glühwein
goutwort
gaudy-day
give away
giveaway
give arms
give bail
give into
give it up
gavelman
gavelock
give line
Givenchy
give odds
give over
give rein
governor
give rise
give upon
give vent
gownsman
glyceria
glyceric
glycerin
glycerol
glyceryl
Gay Times
Guyanese
glycogen
glycolic
glyconic
glycosyl
Guyaquil
glyptics
gazpacho
gazeboes
gazogene
gazement
gazunder
gazetted
headache
headachy
Hiawatha
huarache
healable
huanacos
headband
headbang
head-boom
head-butt
head cold
headcase
hoarding
heavenly
headfast
headgear
Huang Hai
head girl
hear, hear!
hoarhead
heath-hen
headhunt
heathens
Heathrow
heathery
heaviest
hyacinth
headlock
headlamp
headland
headline
headlong
headless
headmark
headmost
headnote
heat pump
headrace
headrail
head rent
headring
headroom
headrope
headrest
headsman
headsail
headship
hoarsely
healsome
heat sink
headshot
heatspot
heart cam
hoastman
hearties
heartlet
heartpea
hoactzin
heartily
heart-rot
head-tire
hiatuses
huaquero
headwind
headword
headwork
heat wave
heavy sea
heavy wet
heavy oil
Habdalah
Hyblaean
hobdayed
Hebraise
Hebraism
Hebraist
Habbakuk
Hebraize
hibachis
Hebrides
Hobbiton
hobbitry
Habakkuk
hobbling
habanera
habanero
habañero
hebdomad
hobnobby
hibernal
hub-brake
✧hibiscus
habitual
habitude
hebetude
habitans
habitant
hebetant
hebetate
hubbuboo
hobbyism
hobbyist
hiccatee
hic jacet
hackbolt
hock-cart
Hock-days
hacienda
hackette
hectical
hack into
heckling
hectorer
hiccough
hectorly
hocussed
huckster
hocusing
hacksawn
Hock-tide
hecatomb
hiccuped
hickwall
hackwork
hideaway

 Words marked ✧ can also be spelled with one or more capital letters

hydranth
Hudibras
hedgepig
hydremia
hiddenly
hedgehog
hedge-hop
hedgerow
hidy-hole
hidlings
Hodgkin's
hidalgos
huddle up
hedonics
hedonism
hedonist
hydrogel
hydrogen
hydromel
hadronic
hidrosis
hidrotic
hydropic
hydroski
✧hydrozoa
hydropsy
Hydromys
hydroxyl
hydatoid
had-I-wist
hielaman
hierarch
haematic
haematin
hieratic
hyena dog
heelball
heel-bone
haeremai
heedless
hierurgy
Haftorah
Haft Wadi
Haggadah
Hogmanay
hag-taper
hog-maned
Haggadic
huggable
hog's-back
high-bred
highball
highbrow
high-born
Highbury
high camp
hog-score
hoggerel
hygienic
Huguenot
hagberry
higher-up
hog-reeve
high five
high-five
high gear
high-gear
hogshead
high hand
highjack
high jump
high kick
Hegelian
high life
higgling
✧highland
high-lone
hegemony
High Mass
highmost
✧high noon
✧highness
hugeness
highroad
hog-frame
high-rise
high-risk
high seas
high spec
high sign
high shoe
high spot
high toby
high tech
high-tech
high tide
hightail
high time
high-test
high wire
hair-ball
hairbell
hairband
Huis Clos
Heimdall
hair grip
hairgrip
heighten
Haiphong
heich-how
hairlike
hairline
heirloom
hairless
heirless
✧hail Mary
hair seal
huissier
heirship
hailshot
hoistman
hoistway
hair-tail
hoisting
Hailwood
hair-work
hairworm
hair-wave
hijacker
Hokkaido
Hakodate
Häkkinen
hoky-poky
half a bar
heliacal
Hollands
Helladic
helpable
half anna
hallaloo
holla-hoa!
halfbeak
halfback
hold back
holdback
half-bred
hell-bred
half-ball
hell-bent
half-boot
hell-born
half-butt
hylobate
half-blue
Halachah
holy coat
half-cock
Halachic
helicoid
half-calf
HeLa cell
Holocene
halicore
hole card
hylicism
hylicist
holy city
half-dead
helideck
holydame
half-done
half-door
hall-door
helpdesk
hold down
hull-down
holidays
halteres
halve-net
helmeted
Hellenic
Helvetic
half-face
hillfolk
hell-fire
hellfire
hill-fort
holdfast
hologram
hold good
hell-gate
Holyhead
hellhole
hula-hula
hula hoop
hold hard
hold hard!
half-hose
half-hour
hellicat
hollidam
half-inch
Hilfiger
holdings
Helsinki
halliard
helminth
Halakhah
hell-kite
half loaf
half-loaf
halalled
half-life
halfling
halflins
helpline
Holy Land
helmless
helpless
helpmeet
half-moon
hall-moot
half mark
hallmark
half mast
half-mast
halimote
helpmate
haleness
✧holiness
half-note
helenium
Hal Roach
hallowed
hold over
holdover
✧haliotis
heliosis
hillocky
hollowly
halloumi
heliodor
Heliozoa
hold play
halfpace
holoptic
half-pike
half-pint
half-pipe
heliport
holy-rood
hilarity
Halmstad
helmsman
hold sway
hillside
half step
Holostei
holistic
half-sole
holesome
helistop
half-size
half-tide
hall tree
helotage
Holstein
half-time
half-tint
half-tone
halation
holotype
half-term
helotism
halitous
half-text
halluces
Holy Week
✧holy writ
Holywell
hellward
half-year
holly-oak
Holy Year
Halcyone
holozoic
hummable
hump-back
humpback
home body
home-bred
home-brew
hymn-book
home bird
home-born
home base
homicide
humidify
homodont
homodyne
humidity
hammerer
hammer in
homefelt
home farm
home-fire
homogamy
homogeny
homegirl
Humphrey
home help
home loan
home-life
homology
homaloid
homelike
homelily
homeland
humbling
Hamilton
homeless
homilist
hamulate
humility
Himalaya
home-made
hymeneal
hymenean
hymenial
hum and ha
hominoid
humanoid
homuncle
humanely
homonymy
humanise
humanism
humanist
humanity
hymenium
humanize
hemiolia
hemiolic
hemiopia
hemiopic
homeosis
homeotic
hummocky
homeobox
hemionus
hemipode
home page
hemp-palm
home port
hamartia
✧home rule
humoresk
humorist
humorous
homesick
hampster
hempseed
homespun
home time
ham stand
homotony
himation
homotype
homotypy
hematite
humstrum
home town
humoured
Hamburgh
home unit
homeward
homework
hamewith
home zone
huntaway
hangable
hen-padle
Hanratty
hen party
hang back
hung-beef
handball
handbell
handbill
hunt ball
handbook
hangbird
handclap
Honecker
handcuff
handcart
hand down
hunt down
hinderer
hungerly
hanger-on
handfuls
hindfoot
hang fire
hangfire
handfast
Hans Gram
handgrip
henchman
hindhead
honchoed
hand-held
handheld
handhold
hand-horn
handicap
hangings
hen night
handiest
hung jury
Hanukkah
hand-knit
handknit
Hong Kong
Honolulu
hand line
handling
hand-loom
handless
handlist
hen-flesh
handmade
handmaid
hand-mill
hindmost
hangnail
hangnest
hand over
handover
hang over
hangover
Hannover
hung over
hen-court
hen house
hen roost
hang onto
handplay
hand-pick
hanepoot
hand-post
henequen
henequin
heniquin
hundreds
handrail
hungrily
honorand
honorary
huntress
Honorius
huntsman
hony-seed
hands off
hands-off
honestly
handsome
hand-sewn
Honduran
Honduras
honoured
honouree
honourer
hen-hussy
Hinduise
Hinduism
Hinduize
hindwing
handwork
hindward
honewort
handyman
honey-bag
honey-sac
honey bee
honeydew
Hinayana
honey ant
honeying
honeypot
honeybun
Henry Pye
Hangzhou
hoofbeat
hyoscine
hooked by
hoosegow

Hrothgar
hoolican
hooligan
hoodless
hoofless
hoof-mark
hoodooed
Huon pine
hook shot
hoot-toot
hoodwink
hookworm
heptarch
hipparch
heptagon
hypobole
hypocist
hypoderm
hyphened
hyphenic
hapteron
hopped-up
hypogeal
hypogean
hypogaea
hypogene
hypogyny
hypogeum
hypalgia
hip flask
hopeless
hopingly
hyponymy
haploidy
hypnotee
hypnosis
hypnotic
hip joint
Hyperion
hypernym
Hepatica
hypothec
hepatoma
hipsters
hepatise
hepatite
hepatize
hippuric
Hippuris
hippydom
haqueton
hark away
hereaway
hard-a-lee
herbaged
hard at it
harmalin
herbaria
her paiks
hireable
hurt a fly
hardbeam
hornbeak
hornbeam
hardback
hark back
hark-back
hartbees
herb-beer
hardbake
hardball
harebell
hornbill
herd-book
hornbook
hard coal
Heracles
Heraclid
hyracoid
hard copy
hard-copy
hard card
hard core
hard-core
hard case
hard cash
hard disk
heredity
hired gun
Harleian
horsecar
horseman
horseway
hardened
hardener
herbelet
hard edge
hermetic
herpetic
horsefly
horse bot
horse box
horse-boy
horse hoe
hardface
hornfels
hare-foot
herefrom
hard-fern
Hartford
Hereford
Hertford
here goes!
harigals
horngeld
hiragana
horn gate
hardhead
hardhack
hurcheon
Hirohito
harridan
heroical
harpings
horrific
Horlicks®
heroicly
horrible
horribly
horridly
Hermione
hirrient
hornitos
hereinto
hara-kiri
hari-kari
hard luck
hard left
horologe
horology
heraldic
hard line
hardline
hireling
hurdling
heraldry
harmless
herbless
hornless
hurtless
harambee
herb mill
Hiri Motu
Huronian
Haringey
heronsew
Hartnell
hardness
hereness
harangue
hormonal
harborer
harmonic
hormonic
harlotry
harmosty
hornpipe
horn pout
horn-pout
hard rock
Hereroes
horn-rims
hard soap
hare's-ear
harp seal
✧herdsman
hernshaw
harassed
harasser
haruspex
hardship
heroship
hard sell
herisson
haroseth
Horatian
hardtack
heritage
heritrix
horntail
hard time
herstory
Hercules
hereupon
harrumph
hereunto
herdwick
hardwood
harewood
hardware
hornwork
hornworm
hornwort
herewith
harrying
hurrying
Hertzian
hastated
Hispanic
his paiks
hush-boat
Hasidism
Hasidist
hastener
hosteler
hesperid
Hesperis
✧hysteria
hysteric
has-beens
hostelry
hasheesh
Hesperus
hush-hush
hospital
✧hastings
hustings
Hassidic
histioid
hospitia
hustling
hashmark
hospodar
histogen
historic
hassocky
hosepipe
hose reel
histrion
histrios
hesitant
hesitate
hissy fit
hot hatch
hot-hatch
hot water
hateable
hot pants
hit a blot
hetaerae
hetaeras
hot metal
hot-metal
Hatteria
hitherto
hotted-up
hatchway
hitchily
hatching
hotchpot
hatchery
hot-short
hatchety
hetairai
hetairas
hetairia
hotelier
hôtelier
hat plant
hat-plant
hoteling
hateless
hot blast
hot flash
hot flush
hotplate
hate mail
hot money
hothouse
hit squad
hat trick
hot-brain
haterent
hatbrush
hot press
hot-press
hit it off
hot stuff
hatstand
Hattusas
hatguard
hautbois
house bat
houseman
house-tax
house red
heuretic
house-sit
housefly
houseboy
house-dog
housetop
houseful
hausfrau
hour hand
heuchera
housings
hauriant
haurient
hourlong
housling
Hounslow
haunting
hout-tout
Havdalah
have a fit
have a pop
have back
havocked
have done
havildar
havelock
hovelled
hoveller
hivelike
hiveless
hive-nest
have-nots
Have Pity!
hover-bed
hoverfly
Havering
have to be
hiveward
hawkbell
howl down
Hawke Bay
hawk-eyed
hawthorn
Hawaiian
hawfinch
hawklike
hawk moth
how's that
howitzer
hawkweed
how-d'ye-do
hexafoil
hexagram
hexylene
hexaplar
Hexapoda
hexapody
haymaker
hay fever
hay-de-guy
hey-de-guy
hayfield
hay knife
hey-go-mad
Hay Point
haystack
huzzaing
Hezekiah
hazel hen
hazelnut
haziness
hazardry
Id al-Adha
inarable
I dare say
I daresay
✧isabella
in a sense
Id al-Fitr
imaginal
imaginer
imagines
Italiote
inasmuch
isagogic
inaurate
inaction
ITAR-Tass
inactive
in a hurry
in bianco
imbecile
imbrices
imborder
imbitter
in charge
incubate
incubous
incident
ischemia
ischemic
in cuerpo
increase
increate
inclined
incliner
itchiest
inchmeal
incumber
incoming
in common
in camera
itch-mite
incenser
incensor
incentre
inconnue
incloser
inchoate
in chorus
inceptor
in capite
incurred
incurved
incorpse
incision
incisory
incisure
incisive
incitant
inch-tape
included
ischuria
in course
incivism
itchweed
inch-worm
Indiaman
Indiamen
✧india ink
indebted
indicial
induciae
indictee
indicter
inductee
indocile
indecent
indicant
inductor
indicate
indicium
indrench
iodoform
indigoes
indigoid
indigene
indigent
indigest
indagate
indulger
Indology
indolent
induline
indamine
in demand
in Domino
in denial
in danger
indented
indenter
indentor
indirect
indurate
iodyrite
indusial
industry
indusium
in detail
induviae
induvial
indexing
ice dance
iterance
ice water
ice yacht
Irenaeus
in excess
ice-ledge
in effect
idée fixe
ideogram
Isengrim
ice sheet
ice shelf
irenical
inedited
itemiser
itemizer
icefield
inedible

Words marked ✧ can also be spelled with one or more capital letters

irenicon
ice skate
ice-skate
ideal gas
ice block
ideology
iceblink
ice plant
ice-plant
I tell you
I declare!
idealess
idealise
idealism
idealist
ideality
idealize
inermous
ice lolly
icebound
ice point
ice house
ice apron
inexpert
idem quod
ice cream
ice track
ice craft
ice front
inerrant
inessive
inert gas
inertial
identify
icestone
ideation
ice storm
identity
ideative
irefully
inequity
inflamed
inflamer
inflated
inflater
infrared
infra dig
inflator
inflatus
infobahn
infecund
infector
inficete
inflexed
infefted
infringe
in-flight
infamise
infamous
infamize
infantry
iffiness
infinite
infinity
inferiae
infernal
informal
inferred
informed
informer
infirmly
inferior
infernos
infusion
infusory
infusive
infotech
infaunal
influent
in favour
in gremio
inguinal
ingenium
ingrowth
ingroove
ingather
inhearse
Iphicles
Ishiguro
ichthyic
inholder
inhalant
inhumane
inhumate
inhere in
inherent
ichorous
inhesion
inhauler
imitancy
imitable
imitator
iriscope
idiogram
Irish car
Irishman
Irish Sea
Irish elk
Irishism
inimical
initiate
idiolect
it is said
in itself
idiot box
idiotish
idiotism
✧iniquity
injector
inkberry
ink plant
in kindle
inkiness
inkstand
inkstone
ill-faced
ill-fated
ill-faurd
ill-faste
in league
ill-being
idlehood
ill-timed
ill blood
in lumber
illumine
in limine
Islamise
Islamism
Islamist
Islamite
Islamize
inlander
islander
Iolanthe
Illinois
Islandia
idleness
illinium
ill-spent
illiquid
in liquor
ill-treat
Illyrian
islesman
ill-usage
illision
illusion
illusory
illusive
in little
idle time
illation
illative
illuvial
illuvium
illawara
inlaying
immobile
immodest
immolate
immoment
Immanuel
immanely
immantle
immingle
immanent
imminent
immunise
ilmenite
immanity
imminute
immunity
immunize
immortal
Inmarsat
immersed
immitted
immotile
immature
iambuses
✧innocent
Ionicise
Ionicize
innuendo
ianthine
ignominy
Ian Smith
inner bar
inner ear
inner man
Ian Brady
ignaroes
ignorant
Ignatian
innately
ignition
ignitron
innative
innovate
in no wise
idolater
isolated
isobaric
isogamic
isolable
ibogaine
idolator
isolator
idolatry
ironbark
iron-clad
iron-clay
Iron Duke
Idomeneo
isogenic
isomeric
isometry
iron-gray
iron-grey
isocheim
isochime
iron hand
isochore
isothere
isotherm
isochasm
ironical
idoliser
idolizer
inositol
isodicon
I could go
ironlike
iron lung
isocline
isogloss
isopleth
iron-mail
iron-mole
iron-mine
inornate
isogonal
isopodan
isogonic
isonomic
isotonic
isotopic
isodomon
isomorph
isodomum
isologue
isospory
isocracy
isocryme
isobront
isoprene
isotropy
idocrase
iron-sick
Ironside
iron-sand
Isoptera
isostasy
Iroquois
inoculum
ironwood
ironware
ironwork
ivory-nut
in public
impocket
in pocket
impeding
impudent
impleach
in pieces
impledge
impresse
in plenty
impugner
impaired
impairer
implicit
imprimis
imprison
impolicy
impelled
impeller
impolder
impolite
impannel
impinger
imponent
impanate
impunity
implorer
improper
improver
imperial
imparter
importer
impurely
impurple
in person
imparity
impurity
imperium
impasted
imposter
impishly
imposing
impasto'd
impastos
impostor
inputter
impetigo
impotent
implunge
impluvia
implying
in querpo
inquirer
in reason
irrigate
Imre Nagy
irrision
irrisory
irritant
in return
irritate
instance
instancy
issuance
in spades
inswathe
instable
issuable
issuably
in season
instants
insectan
Issachar
in secret
insucken
insecure
in specie
insignia
insphere
instinct
inspired
inspirer
inspirit
inscient
insulter
insolent
insolate
insulate
insomuch
✧insomnia
Ibsenian
in sunder
insanely
Ibsenism
Ibsenite
insanity
insconce
inscribe
instruct
in series
inserted
inserter
inscroll
inshrine
insurant
instress
insetter
in shtook
insculpt
intranet
intrados
Istabraq
intubate
iotacism
in the bag
in the can
in the raw
in the way
intrench
in the red
in the air
✧intrepid
in the end
in the poo
intifada
integral
intaglio
integrin
intrince
intuited
intrigue
Intelsat
isthmian
intimacy
intimism
intimist
intimate
intimity
intonaco
in tandem
intended
intender
intently
intoning
intonate
Istanbul
intromit
introrse
interlay
internal
interval
interwar
interact
internee
✧internet
interred
interrex
intersex
intorted
intarsia
intermit
intermix
intertie
in thrall
inthrall
icterine
intercom
interior
inter nos
Interpol
interess
interest
intercut
intitule
intruder
inurbane
inundant
inundate
inustion
inveagle
inviable
invecked
invected
inveigle
involved
involute
inventor
in ventre
inverted
inverter
invertin
invertor
invest in
izvestia
invasion
investor
invasive
inviting
Iowa City
in weight
inwardly
idyllian
idyllist
Joan Baez
✧jeanette
Juan Gris
Jean Muir
Joan Miró
jealouse
jealousy
Jean Rook
Jean Rhys
Joan Sims
jabberer
jib sheet
job share
job-share

jobshare
jibbings
jubilant
✧jubilate
Jabalpur
Job's news
Job's post
J M Barrie
jib crane
Jebusite
jobation
jackaroo
jickajog
jack bean
Jacobean
Jacobian
jackboot
Jacobite
Jack Cade
jacketed
jackeroo
jack easy
jockette
Jack-fool
jackfish
jack-high
jack into
Joceline
jaculate
Jacintha
Jacinthe
jocundly
jack pine
jack plug
jocosely
jocosity
jack-tree
✧jacquard
judicial
Judaical
Judaiser
Judaizer
judgment
jodhpurs
Joe Davis
Joe Dante
Joe Blake
Joe Slovo
Joe Louis
Joe Orton
Joe Brown
Joe Lyden
J G Frazer
Jiffy bag®
jigsawed
jog pants
jogpants
jiggered
jaggedly
jigger up
jog along
joggling
juggling
jugglery
jugulate
jig borer
Jugo-Slav
Jugoslav
John Bull
John Byng
John Birt
John Cage
John Cary
John Dory
John Ford
John Hume
John Hunt
John Hurt
John Huss
John Kemp
John Knox
John Kerr
John Lowe
johannes
Jahangir
John Nash
John Pond
John Paul
John Ridd
John Ross
John Venn
Jehovist
John Wain
joinable
jailbait
jailbird
joined-up
juiced up
join-hand
joint-fir
joint-oil
jointing
jointure
jejunely
jejunity
jokingly
jokiness
jokesome
Julia set
jillaroo
jolleyer
julienne
jolthead
jalapeño
jalfrezi
jelutong
jalousie
jelly bag
jelly-pan
jollying
jim-dandy
jampanee
Jim Laker
jumpable
Jam tarts
jump bail
jump ball
jambeaux
jumped-up
Jamaican
jambiyah
jump lead
Jim Clark
jimpness
jambolan
jamboree
jumbo jet
jumboise
jumboize
jimcrack
jump rope
Jim Brown
Jamesian
jump seat
jump ship
jump suit
James Fox
jump shot
jump to it!
jump-turn
jemmying
Jan Mayen
joncanoe
junkanoo
jingbang
junk bond
June drop
junketed
junketer
Jane Eyre
Jungfrau
junk food
Janiform
Januform
Jennifer
jangling
junglist
jongleur
junk mail
Jan Smuts
Junonian
jingoish
jingoism
jingoist
junk-ring
junk shop
Jonathan
janitrix
Jonathon
junction
juncture
junkyard
janizary
jeopardy
Japhetic
Japan wax
japonica
japanned
japanner
Japanese
Japanesy
Japanise
Japanize
✧jeroboam
jury duty
jordeloo
jerrican
jirkinet
jeremiad
Jeremiah
jurymast
jerepigo
jararaca
jararaka
jury room
Jurassic
juristic
jarosite
juratory
jerquing
jerrycan
jestbook
Joscelin
justicer
Jesuitic
Jesuitry
jostling
justness
jetliner
jettison
jet-skier
jet-black
jet plane
jetplane
jato unit
jaundice
jiu-jitsu
journeys
jauntily
jaunting
jovially
juve lead
juvenile
Javanese
Java plum
jive talk
jaw lever
jew's harp
✧jew's-harp
✧jews'-harp
jewelled
jeweller
jewel box
jowing-in
jaw-tooth
Jewishly
joy-wheel
joyrider
joystick
joyfully
joyously
jazz-funk
jazz-rock
jazerant
Krakatoa
krameria
khalifah
khalifat
kyanitic
Kwakiutl
knackers
knackery
knackish
Klaipeda
knapping
Klansman
knapscal
knapsack
khansama
Khartoum
knapweed
Krazy Kat
kabbalah
kabeljou
Kabinett
kibitzer
kickable
kachahri
kick back
kickback
kickball
kickdown
keckling
kickshaw
kick turn
kedgeree
kidology
kid glove
keep away
keep at it
keepable
keelboat
keep back
kielbasa
kvetcher
keep calm
keep cave
knee-deep
keep dark
keep down
knee-high
klephtic
keep hold
kneehole
keeshond
keelhaul
khedival
knee-jerk
kreplach
keelless
keenness
keel over
keep pace
knee sock
keep step
keepsake
keepsaky
knee-stop
kreasote
kreosote
keep tabs
Koestler
kreutzer
keep time
kreatine
keep warm
Keflavik
keftedes
kefuffle
koftgari
kaffiyeh
keffiyeh
koftwork
kohlrabi
kaimakam
khilafat
knife-man
kaiserin
knife-box
knife-boy
keiretsu
knightly
knickers
kail-runt
knittles
knitting
Kristina
knitwear
kailyard
kaka beak
kaka bill
✧kakiemon
kakemono
Ku Kluxer
kala-azar
killadar
Kill Bill
kilobyte
killcrop
killdeer
Kilkenny
kilogram
kilogray
kiln-hole
Kalahari
kolkhozy
keloidal
Kol Nidre
kill line
kalamdan
kalumpit
kalendar
kolinsky
kalinite
kalookie
killogie
kyllosis
kilopond
kalyptra
Kolarian
kill time
kill-time
kalotype
Kalevala
kilovolt
kilowatt
Kaliyuga
kamacite
✧kamadeva
Kimberly
kymogram
kamikaze
kimonoed
✧komondor
Komsomol
komissar
komitaji
Kandahar
Keneally
kangaroo
kinkajou
Kenyatta
kingbolt
kingbird
king crab
king-crow
Ken Kesey
kinsfolk
kingfish
kinghood
kink-host
Kinshasa
kantikoy
King John
kingklip
kinakina
King Kong
King Lear
kinglike
kindlily
kindling
kingling
kindless
kingless
kindness
kenspeck
king pair
kingpost
Kanarese
king's-man
kinesics
Kingsley
kingship
Kingston
king-size
kinetics
Konstanz
Kentucky
kingwood
knowable
✧klondike
✧klondyke
kromesky
knothole
kaolinic
kaoliang
knock off
knocking
Khoikhoi
knockers
knock out
knockout
knotless
knottily
knotting
Klosters
knotweed
knotwork
kephalic
kephalin
kipperer
Kip Keino
kyphosis
kyphotic
kopiykas
Kirkaldy
kirn-baby
Karl Baer
Karl Böhm
korfball
Karl Benz
Kiribati
Karadzic
kernelly
kyrielle
kurveyor
kermesse
kerchief
kirn-milk
Karl Marx
karyotin
kurtosis
Karlsbad
kerbside
Kuroshio
kerosene
kerosine
Kirsteen
karstify
keratoid
karateka
Karitane
keratose
kirk town
Kirkwall
kirkward
kirkyard

Words marked ✧ can also be spelled with one or more capital letters

kissable
Kasparov
Kismaayo
kiss-curl
Kishinev
Kushitic
Kashmiri
✧kashruth
kistvaen
Kate Adie
kottabos
Kate Bush
katakana
Kathleen
ketamine
Kite mark
Kitemark
kite-mark
Katerina
Katowice
kaumatua
kourbash
krumhorn
kauri gum
khuskhus
kouskous
knurling
kawakawa
Kiwanian
kowtower
Kawasaki
Key Largo
key light
kayaking
key-plate
key money
keyboard
key-fruit
key stage
keystone
klystron
key punch
keypunch
keybugle
kazachoc
kazatzka
leaf axil
leasable
loanable
loanback
leaf beet
leafbird
lean-burn
leaf-base
loaf-cake
leaf curl
leave off
leadenly
lease-rod
llaneros
leave out
Llaregub
Llaregyb
lead-free
leaf-fall
leapfrog
Loaghtan
leaching
loathing
leathern
leathers
leathery
leachate
leachour
leachtub
loathful
leavings
leaflike
lead-line
load line
leadless
leafless
learning
leanness
leaf roll
leaprous
leadsman
leaf-scar
loadstar
leaf soil
leaf spot
lead tree
lead time
leadwort
loan word
leap year
Labiatae
labially
Labrador
libraire
labdanum
libeccio
lubberly
libretti
libretto
lobe-foot
La Bohème
Labridae
lubrical
labelled
labeller
libelled
libellee
libeller
libeling
lobeline
lobeless
lability
lobulate
labellum
Lebanese
loblolly
Labor Day
Liberian
Liberace
liberate
laburnum
Liberius
lobotomy
Libitina
libation
lobation
libatory
laboured
labourer
lobbying
lobbyist
lackaday
lock away
lockaway
lockable
lichanos
lace-boot
lacebark
lucidity
Lac Léman
lichened
Lachesis
lichenin
licker-in
Lucretia
lycaenid
Loch Earn
lacteous
✧locofoco
lockfast
lichgate
lock gate
lychgate
lacrimal
lactific
lace into
luck into
lace-leaf
Lucullan
Lucullic
lackland
luculent
localise
localism
localist
lockless
luckless
locality
loculate
lack-love
localize
locomote
laciniae
Laconian
licensed
licensee
licenser
licensor
lacunars
lacunary
lecanora
laciness
laconism
lacunose
Loch Ness
lacunate
Licinius
lacrosse
lockpick
lycopene
lectrice
licorice
lacerant
La Coruna
lectress
lacerate
Lycurgus
locksman
locustae
lockstep
lecithin
Lecythis
location
locution
locutory
lecythus
locative
lecturer
luck upon
lacqueys
locoweed
lichwake
lacewing
lacrymal
lucky bag
lucky dip
Lucky Jim
Lucozade®
Lady Anne
ladybird
lodicula
lodicule
laddered
ladleful
ladle out
ladified
ladyfied
lady fern
Lady Grey
lady-help
ladyhood
lodgings
ladylike
lad's love
lady-love
Lady Muck
lodgment
Ladinity
led horse
luderick
lady's man
lodesman
lodestar
ladyship
lee gauge
liegeman
lie perdu
liegedom
lie heavy
Llewelyn
leechdom
lee shore
lie along
lie under
lie in one
lee-board
loessial
lientery
liftable
lifeboat
liftback
lifebelt
Left Bank
left-bank
lifebuoy
lift down
left face!
lift-girl
lifehold
left-hand
lifelike
lifeline
lifelong
lifeless
leftover
life peer
lift pump
life raft
life-rent
Laforgue
lifespan
lifesome
life-size
lifetime
left wing
left-wing
leftward
life-work
log cabin
luggable
log-canoe
lagnappe
La Guaira
logician
logicise
logicism
logicist
logicize
ligneous
logogram
lug-chair
Lagthing
leggings
lignitic
legal aid
liguloid
Legoland
legalese
legalise
legalism
legalist
log-glass
legality
ligulate
log-slate
legalize
ligament
legendry
lagoonal
leg-woman
legioned
logboard
log-house
leg break
legering
legerity
logistic
light pen
light air
legatine
lighting
legation
ligation
light box
logotype
legatary
ligature
lightish
lightful
light out
logjuice
leg-guard
lah-di-dah
laitance
laid-back
laid bare
loiterer
laired up
Luis Figo
Laingian
lyings-in
Leinster
leisured
laid work
Lake Abbé
Lok Sabha
likeable
likeably
Lake Bled
Lake Biwa
Lake Chad
Lake Como
Lake Erie
Lake Eyre
like fury
like hell
Lake Kivu
✧lakeland
likeness
lakeside
like that
Lake Tana
lekythos
likewake
lykewake
likewalk
lykewalk
lukewarm
likewise
Lollardy
l'allegro
lollipop
Lilliput
✧la-la land
Lilongwe
lolloped
lallygag
lollygag
limnaeid
lumbagos
lampasse
lambaste
Lima bean
Limaceae
limacine
lame duck
lambdoid
lamb down
lambency
lumberer
limnetic
lumberly
lumpenly
limber up
lumpfish
lymphoid
lamphole
lymphoma
lamp-hour
lammiger
limpidly
limekiln
lamellae
lamellar
lamb-like
lambling
limbless
limbmeal
lemon dab
lemon law
lemonade
lamented
lemon tea
lamantin
limonene
luminant
laminary
luminary
lameness
laminose
liminess
limpness
luminist
laminate
limonite
lomentum
luminous
lamppost
lemurian
limerick
lemuroid
lemurine
lamp-room
lampreys
lambskin
Limassol
lamasery
lamb's fry
lime-tree
lime-twig
limiting
limation
limitary
Limousin
Limavady
lima-wood
lime-wood
limewash
lumpy jaw
Linnaean
lentando
lineated
lendable
lineally
linearly
linkable
land-army
Linnaeus
longboat
land bank
lung-book
land crab
lonicera
landdros
lancegay
longeval
lenience
leniency
lancelet
lanceted
lanneret
lingerer
lynx-eyed
lingerie
lungeing
Lancelot
longeron
long face
line feed
landfall
landfill

landform
long-firm
Longford
land-fish
line-fish
lungfish
land girl
long-head
lunkhead
lynch-law
linchpin
long-hair
lynchpin
long home
lone hand
longhand
lynching
lens hood
lunch box
luncheon
lynch mob
land-herd
lanthorn
longhorn
land-haul
long haul
long-haul
lenticel
line item
lenticle
long iron
Longinus
long jump
landlady
long-life
long-legs
lent lily
land-line
lanoline
long-line
linalool
landlord
landless
longlist
lungless
lunulate
langlauf
linoleum
land laws
landmine
liniment
landmark
long mark
landmass
long moss
luna moth
long-nine
lankness
Leninism
Leninist
loneness
longness
Leninite
lunanaut
long odds
Londoner
lone pair
land-poor
lunarian
long robe
landrace
langrage
landrail
land-roll
lunarist
Landsmål
landsman
Langshan
Lenz's law
linesman
long-stay
landside
long side
Landseer
langspel
lingster
linisher
linkster
lintseed
land-ship
landskip
landslip
lantskip
longship
long slip
long suit
lonesome
longsome
lang syne
long shot
long stop
long-stop
long-spun
longspur
linstock
lengthen
long-togs
long-tail
lino tile
long-time
lenition
lunation
Linotype®
Lent term
lincture
long-term
lenitive
lingular
language
linguine
linguini
languish
linguist
longueur
long view
Landwehr
lone wolf
longwall
landwind
landward
lindworm
linkwork
lungworm
lungwort
longwise
long-wave
longways
lindy hop
Leonardo
Leopardi
loo-table
look awry
look back
Léon Blum
loosener
loose end
looker-on
loose box
loose-cut
loosen up
Laoighis
Lion Gate
lyophobe
loophole
lyophile
look here!
Leonidas
lioniser
lionizer
Leo Minor
look into
lionlike
look like
loop-line
look over
loom over
look sick
Leo Esaki
look to be
lap dance
lop-eared
lapsable
lipsalve
lapidify
lapidary
lapidate
lepidote
lappeted
lipaemia
lipogram
lip liner
lopsided
lapelled
lupuline
lip gloss
lopolith
lipomata
leptonic
lap joint
lap-board
Lupercal
leporine
lip brush
lopgrass
liparite
liposome
Lapithae
Laputian
lipstick
lapstone
lip-synch
liquable
liquesce
liquidly
liquidus
loquitur
liquored
liquor up
lernaean
larnakes
larvated
Lorraine
Lord Birt
lyrebird
lyricism
lyricist
loricate
larcener
larderer
largesse
lyriform
Lord Home
Lord Hunt
Lord Hurd
Lord Howe
larrigan
lordings
larrikin
lorikeet
lordlike
lordling
Lord Lyon
lordless
Lord Muck
laryngal
larynges
larynxes
Lord Owen
lordosis
lordotic
larboard
liripoop
liripipe
Lord's Day
lordship
larkspur
Larousse
lyra viol
lyra-viol
lyra-wise
lorry-hop
listable
L'Estaque
Las Vegas
listener
La Spezia
listen in
listeria
listen up
lose face
lysogeny
last-gasp
last heir
lashings
listings
luscious
lustique
lasslorn
listless
lustless
Lysander
losingly
last name
lushness
Les Noces
lissomly
lassoing
lispound
last post
laser pen
lustrums
lustrine
lustring
lustrate
lustrous
lysosome
lost soul
less than
Lusatian
lose time
last word
lysozyme
Letraset®
lethargy
litharge
Lattakia
Lothario
lethally
lettable
lutecium
Lutheran
let me see
lettered
letterer
littered
litreage
latterly
litherly
lothfull
litigant
litigate
latchkey
letching
let slide
little go
lathlike
Little Mo
let alone
let-alone
Lettland
littling
let blood
latently
lateness
Latinise
Latinism
Latinist
lutanist
lutenist
Latinate
Latinity
Latinize
littoral
luteolin
lithoing
lithosol
let loose
literacy
liturgic
literary
literose
laterite
literate
literati
literato
let drive
Lutetian
latitude
let it rip
latitant
lutetium
latewake
late wood
lathyrus
Laurasia
laudable
laudably
Lausanne
laudanum
launcher
Laurence
louvered
leukemia
laureate
Lauretta
lounging
laughter
laugh off
louchely
laughing
laughful
Lough Awe
leucitic
loudness
leucosin
leukosin
Leucojum
louis-d'or
live a lie
leviable
liveable
live axle
loveable
lavaboes
live bait
live-born
lovebird
lovebite
levodopa
lividity
love-drug
live down
love-feat
lavaform
love game
levigate
live it up
love-knot
live load
Lovelace
lovelock
levelled
✧leveller
level off
love life
livelily
lovelily
lava lamp
livelong
livelood
lovelorn
levulose
loveless
level out
lava-lava
Love Me Do
lavement
lavender
✧levanter
lovingly
Lavengro
love nest
laverock
liveried
leverage
live-rail
liver rot
liverish
levirate
love seat
lovesick
love-suit
lavishly
lovesome
love-song
lavation
lavatera
lavatory
levitate
live well
live-well
liveware
live wire
Lowlands
lawmaker
low water
law Latin
Low Latin
Lawrence
lawyerly
law agent
lawgiver
low-lifer
low-lived
low wines
lowlight
low-slung
lewdness
lawcourt
lower lip
lowering
Lewisham
Lewisian
lewdster
lewisson
lewisite
Lewis gun
Low Dutch
lawfully
luxmeter
lexigram
luxurist
luxation
laxative
lux mundi
lixivial
lixivium
lay waste
layabout
Llywelyn
layshaft
lay vicar
ley lines
lay siege
lay claim
lay clerk
loyalism
✧loyalist
lay under
lay an egg
laywoman
layering
lay aside
laystall
lazy jack
lazulite
lozenged

laziness
Lazarist
lazarets
lazurite
Mt Ararat
mbaqanga
meatball
mean-born
meanders
meat-free
meathead
meatiest
meat loaf
measlier
meatless
meal moth
miasmata
miasmous
meanness
meal-poke
meat rack
meagrely
meat safe
meal-tide
meal-tree
mealtime
mean time
meantime
mean-tone
measured
measurer
measures
meatuses
mea culpa
mean well
mealworm
mealy bug
mobocrat
Moby Dick
mobilise
mobility
mobilize
muchacha
muchacho
Meccania
mechanic
moccasin
Michaela
mockable
MacMahon
mocuddum
mackerel
Michelle
MacHeath
Macleaya
muckheap
macahuba
mackinaw
Michigan
machismo
muckiest
micellar
mycelial
muckluck
mucilage
mycology
muculent
maculose
much less
maculate
macallum
mycelium
mock moon
Macanese
muchness
meconate
meconium
mucinous
microbar
microcar
mucrones
microbic
macropod
microdot
microbus
McCarthy
my certie
muck-rake
macaroni
macaroon
macarise
macarism
macerate
macarize
macassar
mocassin
mucosity
mycetoma
Macaulay
macrural
micrurgy
Micrurus
Macavity
muck-worm
madrasah
✧midlands
Mad Maria
medially
medianly
mediator
madrassa
Medibank
mad about
Medicean
midi-coat
mid-ocean
✧medicaid
modicums
medicine
✧medicare
medicate
made dish
medieval
modified
modifier
midships
madrigal
medcinal
midwifed
midwived
midwives
midnight
Medjidie
midfield
muddiest
medullae
medullar
medullas
mudslide
medalled
modelled
modeller
medallic
meddle in
Medellín
Madeline
medaling
meddling
middling
modeling
modellos
mud-clerk
medalist
modalism
modalist
modality
modulate
muddle up
madwoman
modiolar
mid-point
midpoint
madroños
mediocre
madhouse
✧modiolus
mad-apple
made road
mudirieh
madbrain
midbrain
modernly
maderise
moderate
moderato
maderize
medusoid
modestly
modishly
mudstone
meditate
mudpuppy
mudguard
made wine
modiwort
muddying
maenadic
Mt Elbert
Mt Elbrus
Maecenas
myelinic
myelitis
meet in wi'
Mt Egmont
Maeonian
meekness
meetness
myelomas
mnemonic
Muenster
maestros
maestoso
meet with
maffling
mofussil
✧magdalen
magmatic
migraine
migrator
megabuck
megabyte
magician
magicked
megacity
magic eye
megadyne
megadose
magnetar
magnesia
magnetic
magneton
magnetos
McGuffin
megaflop
magnific
muggiest
Magritte
megillah
megalith
magnolia
mignonne
mug-house
megapode
megastar
magister
mageship
magot-pie
mightily
mightest
mightful
megavolt
megawatt
magazine
Mahratta
Mt Hudson
Mahadeva
mahogany
Mahdiism
Mahdiist
Muhammad
Mohammed
mahi-mahi
mah-jongg
mahzorim
Moharram
Muharram
Muharrem
maharaja
maharani
maha yoga
Mahayana
mridanga
mailable
mail-boat
mail bomb
mainboom
muirburn
mail-clad
mail-cart
mail-drag
main drag
main-deck
mail drop
maindoor
maidenly
mailgram
maidhood
maiolica
mainland
main line
mainline
maidless
mainmast
meionite
maid-pale
muir-poot
muir-pout
mailroom
mainstay
mailsack
mainsail
mailshot
moistify
maintain
moisture
maieutic
mainyard
me judice
majolica
Maja Nude
Majorcan
major key
Majorism
Majorite
majority
majestic
make away
make a bed
make a lip
makeable
make bold
makebate
mokaddam
make down
make eyes
make good
make like
makeless
mako-mako
makimono
make over
makeover
make play
Makarios
Makassar
make sail
make sure
Mike Todd
make time
make wing
melt away
Meleager
malvasia
miliaria
mullarky
meltable
millable
Mallarmé
mild beer
molybdic
Moluccas
Milicien
molecule
molecast
maledict
melodica
melodics
mule deer
mylodont
melodeon
melodion
malt-dust
melodise
melodist
malodour
melt down
meltdown
melodize
mal de mer
mildewed
milleped
mole-eyed
mallecho
malvesie
moltenly
mulberry
malleate
multeity
malefice
mala fide
male-fern
milkfish
maligner
malignly
mill girl
Malagash
Malagasy
mill-head
molehill
millhand
mole hunt
milch-cow
millibar
mulligan
Maldives
milliner
milliped
millirem
Mulciber
multiped
mellitic
multifid
multifil
multiple
multi-ply
multiply
millième
millions
milliard
milliare
milliary
multigym
malt-kiln
malt loaf
milk loaf
milklike
milkless
melilite
molality
milkmaid
malt-mill
melamine
malamute
malemute
Mel Smith
malander
malinger
melanoid
melanoma
maleness
melanism
Milanese
mildness
Molinism
Molinist
malonate
melanite
melinite
mylonite
melanous
Moldovan
mulloway
mill over
mull over
Malvolio
miltonia
Miltonic
mellowly
Mulhouse
millpond
malapert
milepost
malarial
malarian
maltreat
Milk Race
millrace
malgrado
malarkey
Mill Reef
millrind
molarity
melismas
Milesian
maltster
molasses
molester
moleskin
mulishly
molossus
malstick
milk-tree
muleteer
melittin
milltail
✧militant
mulattos
military
militate
Mollusca
multurer
Malawian
milk-weed
milk-walk
milkwood
maltworm
milk-warm
milkwort
millwork
moldwarp
malaxage
malaxate
Milky Way
Malaysia
Mammalia
Mamma Mia
Mamma Mia!
memsahib
mimicked
mimicker
membered
mamzerim
momzerim
mamselle
mammetry
Memphian
Memphite

mammifer
mammilla
mumsiest
mamillae
mamillar
mameluco
Mameluke
mumbling
momently
mementos
momentum
memorial
membrane
memorise
memorize
mimester
me myself
mimetite
Mo Mowlam
mummying
Mandaean
Mandalay
maniacal
✧manta ray
mancando
man-eater
mangabey
manna-dew
menhaden
✧mandarin
manganic
Manganin®
minyanim
monoacid
montaria
manually
mendable
menially
mentally
mineable
mondaine
mandator
manna-ash
manyatta
montanto
mandamus
Montague
mung bean
mind-body
manubria
minibike
myna bird
monachal
monocrat
Manichee
monicker
monocled
menacing
manicure
mind-cure
mongcorn
monocarp
mungcorn
minacity
monocyte
Monachus
mine dump
monodont
MiniDisc®
minidish
minidisk
monadism
monodist
mannered
mantelet
many-eyed
Ménière's
mince pie
Monoecia
man-weeks
mannerly
manzello
minneola
Mantegna
monteros
man-years
monteith
manteaus
manteaux
menseful
man of law
man-of-war
men-of-war
man of sin
manifold
manyfold
man of God
maniform
manifest
monkfish
Monaghan
monogram
monogamy
managing
monogeny
monogony
monogyny
monoglot
Mon-Khmer
munchies
manshift
manchego
Mannheim
munchkin
minshuku
man-child
monohull
monkhood
mandioca
manrider
man-sized
mantises
Mandingo
mannikin
manciple
mandible
mantilla
monticle
Montilla
mansions
mannitol
mankiest
manliest
mantissa
mingiest
mintiest
✧monsieur
monokini
menology
monology
mantling
mingling
maneless
mindless
Mona Lisa
monolith
Menelaus
man alive
monomial
monomode
minimums
Menomini
miniment
moniment
monument
muniment
minimart
mint mark
monomark
minimise
minimism
minimist
minimize
Manannan
Menander
meninges
monandry
man to man
mangonel
manpower
mandolin
Mongolia
Mongolic
Monrovia
menfolks
mandorla
man-hours
mansonry
mongoose
mungoose
monopode
minipill
monopole
Monopoly®
monopoly
menopome
manorial
manurial
Mondrian
Montreal
minor key
menarche
Monarcho
monarchy
monorail
mandrake
mandrill
manuring
many-root
Minoress
Montrose
Minorite
minority
Montreux
mangrove
monk seal
Manasseh
minister
mini-skis
monastic
monistic
monosemy
monosome
monosomy
ministry
meniscus
mind's eye
minutiae
Manitoba
minstrel
minutely
monotint
monotone
monotony
monition
munition
Monotype®
monotype
minatory
monetary
monitory
monstera
monetise
menstrua
Minotaur
monitive
monetize
mensural
monaural
mancuses
maneuver
Mensuren
manfully
mansuete
Menevian
menswear
mani wall
mansworn
monaxial
monoxide
money bag
moneyman
money box
monazite
myomancy
myopathy
mootable
moonbeam
moon-ball
moor-band
moon boot
moorburn
moorcock
mooncalf
moot case
moon-eyed
myogenic
moonface
moonfish
moorfowl
moon gate
moot hall
moot-hill
Maori hen
moorings
myositis
Maoridom
moodiest
Maori bug
Mjöllnir
moorland
moonless
myoblast
myosotis
myotonia
myotonic
moon pool
moor-poot
moor-pout
moonrock
moonroof
myograph
moonrise
moonseed
moonshee
moonsail
moonshot
Moon type
moo-juice
moonwalk
moonwort
moody-mad
mappable
mopehawk
mephitic
mephitis
Mephisto
mopingly
mopiness
mopboard
mopishly
mapstick
mopstick
muqaddam
maquette
moquette
mordancy
Margaret
muriated
mariachi
margaric
margarin
muriatic
mortally
Marranos
martagon
Mercator
Mirna Loy
myriapod
Myrna Loy
Murmansk
myriadth
mersalyl
Mirabeau
mortbell
moribund
marabout
Moraceae
Moroccan
miracles
marocain
moroccos
mericarp
merycism
muricate
meridian
Mary Daly
Maradona
Meredith
mire-drum
mark down
mark-down
Mordecai
mergence
Mary Eddy
marketer
Mercedes
Mercedes®
murderee
murderer
murrelet
Marbella
marcella
markedly
martello
Morwenna
Martenot
morceaux
muriform
marigram
mortgage
marigold
maraging
merogony
marchman
marsh-gas
marsh-man
morphean
mort-head
marshier
murphies
marsh tit
merchild
morpheme
merchant
morphine
morphing
murrhine
myrrhine
marchesa
marchese
marchesi
Myra Hess
mirthful
Morpheus
marginal
marzipan
morainal
Morrigan
margined
Marsilea
martinet
morticer
mortiser
markings
marriage
mornings
Marsilia
morainic
morbific
mortific
morbidly
morbilli
Marciano
mirliton
✧myrmidon
merriest
merciful
Mary Jane
moral law
moraller
marbling
Maryland
mortling
morellos
moralise
moralism
moralist
muralist
morality
Merulius
moralize
merum sal
mortmain
merimake
Maronian
marinade
meronymy
marinara
marinera
Marinism
Marinist
miriness
marinate
Maronite
merengue
meringue
marjoram
marmoset
marooner
mirrored
moreover
Marjorie
myriopod
Mercosur
mirepoix
marsport
morepork
mariposa
maroquin
Mary Read
Mary Rose
margrave
marksman
meresman
meristem
mort-safe
marasmic
meristic
myristic
morosely
merosome
murksome
✧moriscos
morosity
marasmus
Moresque
Mark Todd
maritage
Marattia
maritime
mark time
marathon
moratory
Mormugao
marauder
murmurer
mercuric
Mercutio
mortuary
marquess
marquise
Moravian
maravedi
Mordvins
Mirkwood
merryman

✧merry men
moray eel
marry off
martyria
marrying
mismatch
massager
✧mesdames
messages
mismated
mistaken
muscadel
Muscadet
muscatel
mustache
mescalin
moshavim
muscadin
mesially
missable
misfalne
mascaron
massacre
miscarry
mismarry
misfaith
mossback
mass-bell
musk-ball
mass-book
Musaceae
musician
musicker
music pen
Masaccio
mast cell
musicale
moss-crop
music box
mesocarp
musk-cavy
mess deck
musk duck
musk deer
mesoderm
misteach
masseter
miscegen
musterer
misfeign
master it
mesmeric
muster in
misleeke
masterly
misdealt
misbegot
misletoe
misdempt
misheard
mismetre
musketry
masseuse
muster up
moss-flow
miss fire
mess gear
misogamy
misogyny
masthead
mischief
moss hagg
misthink
misshood
misshape
must-have
mestizas
Muscidae
mystical
misgiven
misliker
missives
mistimed
muslined
muslinet
moslings
misdight
mislight
mastitis
miscible
misfield
mistitle
massicot
masticot
Messidor
mestizos
misticos
missilry
messiest
mistiest
mossiest
mushiest
muskiest
mustiest
misbirth
mystique
Mass-John
Mess-John
misplead
Musulman
mashloch
misplace
misalign
misology
muscle in
mosslike
mossland
muscling
misallot
mastless
mesolite
mishmash
messmate
✧mason jar
Mt Sangay
mason bee
Mishnaic
musingly
misandry
misentry
Masonite®
mass noun
masoolah
Massorah
misdoubt
misnomer
mist over
massoola
miscount
misdoing
misdonne
mispoint
mastodon
miscolor
Missouri
Mrs Moore
misroute
misspeak
musk pear
misspoke
misapply
misspell
misspelt
misspend
misspent
musk-plum
misarray
misdread
mistreat
mistrial
miscreed
misorder
misgraff
misgraft
mesaraic
misprint
mess-room
mushroom
✧miserere
mesprise
misprise
✧mistress
mistrust
mistryst
moss rose
musk rose
Masorete
Masoreth
miswrite
masurium
misproud
mesprize
misprize
misusage
mesotron
misstate
muscular
misguide
meshugga
meshugge
messuage
misjudge
mesquine
musquash
mesquite
misquote
mosquito
mostwhat
mesh-work
Mesozoic
methanal
mutually
methadon
methanol
Metabola
mothball
miticide
matachin
muticous
matadora
matadore
metadata
mittened
mutterer
mathesis
motherly
matfelon
mitre box
metafile
mitigant
mitigate
Matthias
mutchkin
mote-hill
matching
matchbox
Mata Hari
Matthews
metrical
mythical
Mathilda
matrices
matrixes
métairie
metritis
methinks
mothiest
mittimus
metalled
motelier
metallic
mytiloid
metaling
mottling
mateless
metalist
matelote
motility
mutilate
metalize
metamere
matamata
Matanzas
mutineer
mutinied
metanoia
metonymy
matiness
muteness
mutandum
mutinous
matronal
motional
meteoric
methodic
matronly
metaphor
metaplot
metopism
metopryl
material
maternal
meter man
motor car
motorial
motorman
motorway
materiel
matériel
Mithraea
motor-jet
Mithraic
motorail
maturely
matgrass
mattress
motorise
motorist
maturate
maturity
motor bus
motorium
motorize
mute swan
mateship
matutine
mutation
mutatory
mutative
Mathurin
mitzvahs
mitzvoth
motivate
motivity
metewand
métayage
methylic
methysis
meteyard
metazoan
metazoic
metazoon
Mauna Kea
Mauna Loa
mauvaise
mouldier
moulding
mouse-ear
mousemat
mousepad
mouterer
mousekin
mauveine
maumetry
mouse-dun
moufflon
mouthier
mouth off
mouchoir
mouchard
mouthful
moulinet
meunière
mousiest
Maudling
Moulmein
mourning
mournful
mausolea
mounseer
moussaka
Mount Tai
✧mountain
moulting
mountant
mounting
Mount Apo
Mount Usu
moveable
moveably
Mevlevis
moveless
movement
movingly
move over
✧maverick
Mawlawis
mawmetry
mawkiest
mawbound
mowburnt
mixed bag
myxedema
mixed bud
maxillae
Maximian
maximums
maximise
maximist
myxomata
Maxim-gun
mixy-maxy
maximize
Max Roach
mixer tap
Max Ernst
Mayology
may bloom
may apple
mayoress
May queen
Mazdaism
Mazdaist
Mazdeism
mozzetta
muzziest
mizzling
mazel tov
mazeltov
mazement
maziness
mazarine
mezereon
mezereum
Mazatlan
mezuzahs
mezuzoth
near beer
Nearctic
Near East
near gale
near-gaun
Noachian
near-hand
neat-herd
near miss
nearness
neatness
nearside
near-silk
Noah's ark
Nebraska
nubecula
noble gas
nobleman
noblemen
noble rot
noble art
noblesse
nubiform
nebbishe
nibbling
Nibelung
nebulise
Nobelist
nobility
nubility
nebulium
nebulous
nobelium
nubilous
nebulize
no chance
neckatee
nectared
neckbeef
neckband
neck-bone
nucleide
nickeled
nickelic
nucleole
nucleoli
nuclease
nucleate
nacreous
neckgear
noctilio
nucellar
necklace
neckline
Nicklaus
nucellus
nick-nack
nocently
nickname
niceness
Nicholas
necrosis
necrotic
necropsy
Nichrome®
nicotian
niceties
nicotine
✧nocturne
noctuary
neckwear
neckweed
nicky-tam
nudicaul
Ned Kelly
nodalise
nodulose
nodality
nodulous
nodalize
nudeness
nidering
nidorous
nodosity
nudities
nidation
nodation
nudation
nieveful
needfire
naething
nielloed
needless
niellist
needment
nuevo sol
neem tree
ne'er-weel
Niflheim
no frills

no-frills
niffnaff
naffness
no-go area
nigh-hand
negligee
negligée
Negrillo
Negritos
Nagaland
niggling
nighness
nigrosin
Nigerian
Nigerien
niger oil
Nagasaki
nightcap
night-hag
nightjar
night-man
night air
night-fly
negation
negatron
night-dog
night-foe
night-ape
negatory
nugatory
night out
negative
night owl
✧nihilism
nihilist
nihility
Nehemiah
no-hitter
nohowish
nuisance
nail bomb
nail down
noisette
noiseful
nail file
nail-head
nail-hole
neighbor
nailless
nainsell
naissant
nainsook
N'Djamena
Nijinsky
naked bed
naked eye
Nile blue
Nell Gwyn
nylghaus
nelumbos
no longer
nullness
nolition
naloxone
nameable
Namibian
name-drop
nomadise
nomadism
nomadize
numberer
nomogram
nomogeny
nymphean
Nymphaea
nymphish
numskull
nomology
nameless
numbness
nominate
numinous
name part
numeracy
Nemertea
nomarchy
numerals
numerary
numerate
nemorous
numerous
namaskar
nomistic
namesake
Nematoda
nematode
no matter
nematoid
nametape
Nembutal®
nummular
nimbused
nimbuses
nimbyism
non-fatal
Nuneaton
non-dairy
non-party
non-metal
Nintendo®
nine-eyes
nankeens
nonsense
ninefold
nine-foot
nunchaku
nine-hole
Nanchang
non-thing
nuncheon
non-white
nennigai
nundinal
nine-inch
non licet
non-rigid
ninjitsu
non-elect
non-claim
nine-mile
non-union
non-entry
non-moral
nonpolar
non-voter
non-ionic
non-toxic
✧nenuphar
nonuplet
ninepins
nan bread
nonesuch
non-issue
nanotube
nanotech
non-stick
nineteen
nineties
nunataks
nonettos
non-human
✧nonjuror
ninjutsu
non-quota
non-event
nannygai
nannying
nannyish
Neogaean
neonatal
neopagan
Neo-Latin
neotenic
neoteric
noometry
neophobe
neophile
neophyte
no object
neon lamp
neoblast
neoplasm
neologic
neotoxin
neoprene
noontide
noontime
neomycin
nip a bung
no picnic
napiform
nuptials
✧napoleon
Nepalese
nepenthe
nepionic
Naperian
nephroid
nephrite
Naphtali
naphthol
nepotism
nepotist
Nur Jahan
normalcy
normally
narrator
Nürnberg
naricorn
nerve gas
Norseman
norteñas
Norweyan
nervelet
nerve net
narceine
nerve end
norteños
nuraghic
Northman
North Sea
narghile
narghily
northing
✧northern
nargileh
nereides
nargilly
narcissi
Nurek Dam
nursling
niramiai
no remedy
Neronian
narcoses
narcosis
narcotic
narrowly
Neritina
nervular
nurtural
nurturer
narquois
nastalik
nasta'liq
nystatin
noseband
nose cone
nosedive
nascence
nascency
nisberry
nose-herb
nescient
nose-leaf
nosology
nestlike
nestling
nasalise
noseless
nasality
noselite
nasalize
neshness
nosiness
no sirree
Nostromo
nose-ring
nuthatch
not-pated
not a bean
notables
nota bene
notebook
Netscape®
notecase
nattered
natterer
nutmeggy
not-being
notified
notifier
natiform
Notogaea
nutshell
notching
not a hope
Nethinim
nutrient
nathless
noteless
natality
notandum
✧national
notional
not to say
nitrogen
nuthouse
nitrosyl
nitroxyl
Netspeak
not a peep
notarial
nutarian
notornis
Nataraja
naturing
naturism
naturist
nit-grass
notarise
nut-grass
nut-brown
notarize
not at all
natation
notation
nutation
natatory
no-trumps
not fussy
natively
nativism
nativist
✧nativity
naumachy
neurally
noumenal
nouvelle
nauseant
noumenon
nauseate
nauseous
Naum Gabo
Nausicaa
nautical
neuritic
neuritis
nautilus
nauplius
neuromas
neuronal
neuroses
neuronic
neuropil
neurosis
neurotic
neutrino
ngultrum
navy blue
navicula
navicert
navigate
novellae
noveldom
navalism
navy list
novelese
novelise
novelish
novelism
novelist
novelize
✧november
novenary
Novgorod
never-was
novercal
navarchy
noverint
Novatian
novation
navvying
navy yard
New Haven
Newhaven
new maths
New Latin
newscast
news desk
nowadays
nowhence
New Delhi
new penny
newsgirl
nowt-herd
newshawk
new dinar
new-risen
New Light
New Right
new birth
newelled
new blood
newsless
new-blown
no wonder
✧new woman
Newcombe
newcomer
Newcomes
new-model
Newtonic
New World
new-found
✧newspeak
New Order
newsreel
new broom
newsroom
New Crete
newishly
New Style
Newsweek
newswire
newly-wed
nox gases
next best
next door
next-door
nextness
naysayer
naythles
Nazarean
Nazarene
Nazareth
Nazarite
Nazirite
on and off
on-and-off
ob and sol
orangery
orangish
Orangism
omadhaun
of a piece
opalised
opalized
of a night
ovaritis
ovariole
odalique
oragious
ovarious
Ozacling®
ovalness
oratorio
oratress
of a truth
Ovaltine®
oracular
opaquely
ombrella
Oxbridge
Orbilius
Orcadian
✧occident
oncidium
orchesis
orchella
oncogene
orchitic
orchitis
orchilla
Otchipwe
occulted
oecology
oncology
occultly
osculant
osculate
oncoming
on camera
once more
Occamism
Occamist
oscinine
once-over
occupied
occupier
occupant
occupate
occurred
occasion
oncotomy
oscitant
oscitate
occlusal
occluder
occlusor
of course
ordnance
Ondaatje
Old Harry
oddments
old thing
old-liner
old-timer
ordainer
Old Light
ordalian
Old Glory
ordalium
on demand
ordinand
ordinant
ordinary

ordinate
old woman
old fogey
Old Poker
Old World
✧old-world
Old Norse
Oedipean
old squaw
oldsquaw
Omdurman
obduracy
old fruit
ordering
obdurate
ordurous
Old Style
old story
old guard
opera hat
overarch
operatic
openable
operable
overalls
operator
oreganos
overbear
overbeat
overboil
overbrim
overbold
overbulk
open book
overblow
overbook
overbrow
ovenbird
overburn
overbusy
overbite
Oleaceae
overclad
overcoat
overcraw
one-acter
opercula
overcall
overcome
overcloy
overcook
over-cool
overcrop
overcrow
open-cast
overcast
overclub
one-idea'd
overdraw
overdoer
overdo it
okey-doke
overdone
open door
open-door
overdose
overdust
open-eyed
omelette
operetta
overfeed
overfree
overfall
overfill
overfold
overfull
overfine
overfond
overfund
overflow
open fire
overfish
overgall
overgang
overgrow
overgive
overhead
overhear
overheat
overhair
overhale
overhold
overhand
overhang
overhent
overhung
overhype
obeahism
overhaul
one-piece
one-liner
one-sided
olefinic
obedient
olefiant
overjump
overkeen
overkeep
overknee
overkill
overkind
overking
overkest
overleaf
overleap
overload
overlock
overlade
Ole Olsen
overlier
oreology
overlaid
overlain
overland
overlend
overlent
overlong
overlook
overlard
✧overlord
one flesh
ocellate
overloud
owerloup
overlive
overmuch
open-mike
open mind
overmast
Oceanian
overneat
overnice
✧oceanids
oleander
overname
one-on-one
openness
open note
oceanaut
one-woman
one-to-one
Ode to Joy
one-horse
open-plan
overplay
overpeer
overpage
overpart
overpass
overpast
overpost
overplus
overread
one-track
overrack
override
overrode
open-reel
overruff
overrake
overrule
overrank
overripe
overrash
over rate
overrate
one or two
orecrowe
over seas
overseas
oversman
overstay
oversway
open side
over side
overside
oleaster
overseen
overseer
overstep
oversail
overskip
overslip
overspin
overswim
one's self
oversell
oversold
obeisant
open shop
over-shoe
overshoe
overshot
oversoul
oversize
overt act
overteem
Oresteia
overtoil
overtrip
overtake
overtalk
overtime
overtone
overtype
one's turn
ore-stare
overtire
overture
overturn
overtask
open town
overview
overveil
overwear
overwrap
overween
overwent
overwind
overwing
ovenwood
openwork
ovenware
overword
overwore
overwork
overworn
overwash
overwise
overyear
one by one
off-wards
off-label
off-sales
official
off-shake
off-shakt
offshoot
offshore
off-white
offsider
off-piste
offended
offender
off and on
off-and-on
off-comer
off-board
off-sorts
off break
offering
offprint
off drive
oafishly
offishly
off-stage
off guard
ongoings
orgulous
oogamous
oogonial
organdie
organise
organism
organist
organity
oogonium
organize
orgasmic
orgastic
ophidian
ochidore
ochreate
ochreous
ox-halide
ocherous
Ochotona
Ophitism
ophiuran
ophiurid
oligarch
opinable
olibanum
origanum
oniscoid
ox-iodide
Olivetan
oximeter
olive oil
orichalc
oliphant
original
opificer
oxidiser
oxidizer
opinicus
oeillade
orielled
orillion
opium den
opiumism
✧oriental
oriented
onion fly
obi-woman
oligomer
oviposit
osier-bed
otiosely
omission
otiosity
omissive
omitting
ouistiti
oviducal
oliguria
oliguric
odiously
obituary
objector
oak egger
Oak Ridge
oak apple
✧ockerism
oil paper
oil gauge
oil paint
oulachon
oil of ben
obligant
obliging
oologist
obligate
obligati
obligato
oil shale
Oklahoma
Oklahoma!
oil-fired
owl-light
oilfield
on liking
oil slick
oil gland
Owl-glass
oilcloth
oiliness
onlooker
obliquid
owl-train
oil press
orlistat
owlishly
oilstone
oblation
oblatory
oblivion
ohmmeter
ommateum
on my word
own-label
osnaburg
omniform
of nights
oenology
ointment
ornament
oenophil
own-brand
ornithic
ornately
omnivore
omnivory
opopanax
ovo-lacto
otoscope
Onondaga
odometer
orogenic
odometry
omophagy
ozoniser
ozonizer
ocotillo
omoplate
Oroonoko
olorosos
odograph
odontoid
odontoma
odontist
omohyoid
omphalic
omphalos
oxpecker
Orpheans
oppugner
oppilate
orpiment
opponent
oophoron
opposing
opposite
owrecome
on record
✧oerlikon
ourology
on remand
Our House
or rather
owreword
Ossianic
obstacle
of secret
obsidian
Oostende
ossified
oosphere
orseille
orsellic
obsolete
opsimath
opsonise
opsonium
opsonize
od's nouns
obsequie
on stream
on-stream
obstruct
observer
on-screen
oystrige
on strike
oestrone
oestriol
oestrous
ossarium
onsetter
obscurer
outdance
outmarch
outmatch
outrance
outwatch
outlands
outwards
outdated
outtaken
outrange
oathable
ostracod
ostracon
ostrakon
outlawry
outcaste
outvalue
optician
oiticica
obtected
outscold
outscore
outscorn
on the jar
on the lam
on the map
on the mat
on the rag
on the way
oothecae
on the ebb
outreach
ostreger
outremer
outreign
outweigh
on the air
on the bit
on the fly
on the sly
on the bot
on the dot
on the hop
on the job
on-the-job
on the nod
out-Herod

outvenom
outlearn
outweary
on the run
out of key
out of cry
out of use
ontogeny
outshine
outthink
outshoot
outrival
obtainer
ofttimes
outrider
outsider
outsides
outsized
outfight
outnight
outright
outsight
osteitis
outfield
orthicon
Otto John
outplace
outsleep
ontology
optology
Ottoline
outflank
outfling
outglare
outclass
outflash
outflush
Ortelius
obtemper
outsmart
optimise
optimism
optimist
optimate
Ottamite
Ottomite
optimize
octantal
octonary
ostinato
ox-tongue
optional
outvoice
orthoses
osteogen
outmoded
outpower
outroper
outvoter
orthosis
orthotic
outworks
outbound
outgoing
outpoint
✧**orthodox**
orthopod
orthoepy
outboard
outdoors
outhouse
outworth
out to out
outspeak
octapody
Octopoda
octuplet
outspeed
octopoid
outspend
outspent
on tiptoe
outsport
octopush
outbreak
outer bar
outprice
on target
outbreed
outdrink
octaroon
octoroon
oat grass
outcross
outgross
outwrest
obturate
outbrave
outdrive
outfrown
outprize
obtusely
obtusity
outstrip
outstand
outstare
optative
obtruder
outguard
outburst
outguess
ottavino
outswear
outdwell
outswell
outswing
outlying
oculated
ocularly
opuscula
opuscule
opulence
Orvietan
ouvrière
on velvet
obvolute
onwardly
ox-warble
Oswestry
onychite
onychium
oxytocic
oxytocin
oxytonic
oxymoron
✧**olympiad**
Olympian
✧**olympics**
Odyssean
Odysseus
ooziness
pia mater
✧**phalange**
placable
placably
playable
platanna
peasanty
Platanus
play back
playback
play ball
playbill
peat bank
platband
playbook
planched
planchet
prancing
placcate
praecava
plaidman
praedial
prandial
play-debt
plaiding
pear drop
plaudite
plaudits
Phaedrus
play down
placeman
place mat
plateman
placemen
platelet
peacenik
✧**phacelia**
planetic
peasecod
placebos
peaberry
plateasm
pianette
placenta
peaceful
phase out
plateaus
plateaux
plateful
poaceous
Piacenza
praefect
play fair
play full
pratfall
play fine
platform
play-goer
plangent
playgirl
pea-chick
peat-hagg
peat-hole
plashing
poaching
pea-viner
Pharisee
platinic
pea-rifle
placidly
pianinos
plagiary
pianiste
placitum
platinum
pratique
plank bed
planking
pranking
plankton
prankish
prankful
peak load
pearlies
phalloid
pea-plant
pearling
pearlins
peatland
pearl ash
phallism
planless
playlist
pearlite
pearl-eye
pharmacy
psalmody
pearmain
pharming
peat moor
play-mare
peat moss
✧psalmist
playmate
psammite
plainant
plaining
planning
plain bob
plainish
plainful
✧**platonic**
peacocky
pea-soupy
pear-push
Prairial
pea-green
peat-reek
prairied
pea-brain
playroom
pia fraus
piassaba
plaister
play safe
peatship
playslip
playsuit
playsome
praising
Praesepe
piassava
plausive
pea-straw
plastral
plastics
practice
practick
practics
Praktica®
pear-tree
plantlet
prattler
plantage
Plantago
plantain
plantule
phantomy
playtime
pea-stone
plaiting
planting
platting
Phaethon
plant pot
plastron
plastery
✧psaltery
phantasm
phantasy
practise
plant out
practive
piacular
planulae
planular
planuria
plaguily
play upon
platysma
platypus
piazzian
publican
publicly
pebbling
pabulous
pubertal
pub-crawl
pabouche
peccancy
packaged
packager
pachalic
peccavis
peccable
po'chaise
pickback
pickerel
picketed
picketer
pocketed
pochette
picker-up
pucker up
pacifier
packfong
pacifism
pacifist
puckfist
pectinal
pectines
pickings
pack it in
Puccinia
pachinko
picnicky
pack it up
pack-load
✧peculiar
picklock
pucelage
peculate
peculium
packmule
pockmark
pick-me-up
pick'n'mix
pecan nut
pectoral
pick over
pycnosis
piccolos
Picariae
picarian
pacarana
pecorino
picaroon
pacation
picotite
pictural
pictures
pichurim
picayune
paduasoy
podiatry
pudibund
pedicled
pediculi
pedicure
podocarp
pudicity
podagral
pedigree
pedagogy
podagric
Podogona
puddings
puddingy
pedalier
pedalled
pedaller
pedaloes
pedology
podology
pedal bin
paddling
pedaling
peddling
piddling
puddling
paddlers
pad-cloth
pediment
pudendal
pedantic
peduncle
pedantry
pudendum
podsolic
pad-horse
pedipalp
paderero
pederero
pederast
podargus
padishah
pedestal
pedately
Paddyism
prenasal
prenatal
Pleiades
prepared
preparer
presager
poematic
prelatic
peekaboo
predator
plenarty
presbyte
✧**preacher**
piercing
prescind
Prescott
preach up
Pheidias
pleading
preadapt
pseudery
pseudish
plebeian
presence
pretence
piecener
phenetic
precepit
premedic
preterit
predella
pre-teens
preceese
prepense
pretense
presents
piece out
preserve
pyengadu
Peer Gynt
pledgeor
preggers
phengite
pierhead
peephole
pie chart
plethora
psephism
psephite
Pieridae
poetical
precinct
Pierides
précised
premised
premises
presidia
presidio
pyelitic
pyelitis
premiums
plenipos
premiere
première
precious
previous
pre-elect
preclude
phelloid
pie-plant
peerless
psellism
pie plate
preamble
piedmont
pied noir
plein-air

Words marked ✧ can also be spelled with one or more capital letters

pfenning
pregnant
piedness
pleonasm
pleonast
prehnite
phenogam
premolar
peen over
phenolic
Pretoria
pteropod
premorse
preppily
prepping
poetries
preorder
pre-print
pie graph
piecrust
pleurisy
pressfat
pressman
press bed
please it
poetship
pheasant
pleasant
pleasing
pressing
peepshow
press box
pression
pleasure
pressure
pleaseth
pressful
'prentice
prentice
pleather
pretties
prettify
prestige
prettily
plectron
plectrum
pretty up
prehuman
plexuses
presumer
prejudge
preludio
prey upon
precurse
peesweep
peetweet
pre-owned
pre-exist
pterylae
phenylic
pterygia
puffball
puffbird
pifferos
puffed up
piffling
puff-puff
pigmaean
pygmaean
pig-faced
pug-faced
puggaree
pig Latin
pygidial
pygidium
pagehood
pugilism
pugilist
Paganini
paganise
paganish
paganism
paginate
paganize
pig-woman
pug-nosed
pegboard
pigeonry
Pago Pago
pagurian
Pegasean
pig swill
pigswill
pig's-wash
Peggy Lee
Peggy Sue
pahoehoe
primatal
philabeg
plicated
Primates
privates
primatic
primally
prizable
paisanos
philamot
privados
pair-bond
princock
prince it
princely
Pliocene
Príncipe
pair case
princess
prie-dieu
poinding
prig down
price tag
price war
primeval
prizeman
prideful
prix fixe
prigging
priggery
priggish
priggism
peishwah
plighted
plighter
philibeg
Philippa
Poitiers
priciest
pyinkado
pricking
prick out
phialled
painless
prismoid
primming
primmest
phinnock
psionics
poignado
peignoir
pliantly
phisnomy
poignant
primness
Philomel
poisoner
prisoner
phimosis
psilocin
psilosis
psilotic
ptilosis
philomot
Psilotum
Priapean
priapism
paitrick
primrose
primrosy
✧prioress
priorate
priority
plimsole
plimsoll
priestly
prissily
puissant
pliosaur
point man
point set
painting
pointing
printing
pristane
Pristina
pristine
paintbox
paint job
painture
pointers
printery
philtrum
point out
print out
printout
print run
pairwise
pyjamaed
pejorate
pike-head
Pekinese
pokerish
Pakistan
Pakhtuns
Pakhtoon
pokeweed
pull away
polyarch
palmated
pileated
pillager
palladia
palladic
Palladio
pelmatic
polyacid
pulza-oil
palpable
palpably
pile arms
polkaing
polka dot
polka-dot
polyaxon
pulsator
pellagra
Polabian
palebuck
pull back
pullback
Polybius
palmchat
pulicide
policies
pull caps
Polycarp
pale-dead
paludine
paludism
paludose
paludous
pelt down
pull down
pull-down
pale-eyed
palleted
palterer
pilferer
✧pilsener
pulsejet
Palmerin
Palme d'Or
palmette
palmetto
paleface
poltfoot
paliform
piliform
✧pelagian
polygala
polygamy
polygene
polygeny
polygony
polygyny
phlegmon
✧polyglot
Pelagius
pillhead
pilchard
pollical
poloidal
pulvinar
palmiped
pelvises
pollices
pulpited
pulpiter
pulsidge
palmitin
pollicie
pollinia
pollinic
polliwig
pulsific
pulvilio
pallidly
pellicle
pulville
pulvilli
pile it on
polliwog
palliard
pulpitry
palliate
pile into
pulpitum
pulvinus
pelology
polemics
Polymnia
pall-mall
pell-mell
pulpmill
palamino
palimony
palomino
polymery
polemise
polemist
palamate
polymath
polemize
Polonian
polo neck
palinode
palinody
Polander
Polanski
pulingly
paleness
polonise
polonism
Palenque
polonium
Polonius
polonize
pillowed
pull over
pullover
pulmones
pulsojet
pulmonic
Pulmotor®
pilhorse
polyonym
palm-play
polypide
polypody
polypoid
Pilipino
polypine
polyphon
polypary
polypite
polypous
polar cap
pultrude
Polaroid®
paltrily
pelerine
pull rank
poltroon
pelorism
polarise
polarity
polarize
Pole Star
palisade
palisado
pilaster
polished
polisher
pollster
Pelasgic
polyseme
polysemy
polysome
polysomy
pile shoe
palestra
pilosity
polish up
palatial
pilotman
politick
politico
politics
palm tree
pilot jet
palstaff
pilotage
politely
✧palatine
polytene
palstave
polluted
polluter
pellucid
polyuria
palm wine
pulpwood
pilework
pile-worm
pilewort
pillworm
pillwort
palewise
pollywig
pollywog
polyzoan
polyzoic
polyzoon
pomwater
pompanos
pumicate
Pompeian
pamperer
pamperos
pompelos
pimiento
pommetty
pump-head
pamphlet
pumphood
P A M Dirac
pemmican
Pompidou
pump iron
pomology
Pamplona
pemoline
pomander
pimentos
pembroke
pump room
pomatoes
pump-well
panda car
pentarch
Penzance
pindaree
pin-maker
pinnated
Punjabee
pangamic
Panhagia
pentadic
Pindaric
pantable
pentacle
pinnacle
pintable
pantalon
✧pentagon
pentanol
pintados
Pandanus
Pandarus
panacean
panicked
panicled
Pinochet
pinscher
pinacoid
penuchle
pinochle
pine cone
panic-buy
ponderal
pendency
penneech
penneeck
pungence
pungency
pince-nez
pink-eyed
ponderer
pandemia
pandemic
Pentelic
panderly
pancetta
Pandects
ponceaux
pang-full
pinafore
panegyry
punch-bag
pinwheel
pinch-hit
penchant
pinching
pancheon
panchion
✧pantheon
puncheon
pinchers
Pentheus
pinchgut
punch out
pannikel
Pan-pipes
pantiled
Pennines
pen-wiper
pinniped
pontifex
penlight

panmixia
panmixis
pannikin
pencil in
pontific
pannicle
pendicle
punditry
pinakoid
panel saw
panel van
punaluan
Pink Lady
panelled
pond-life
penology
panel pin
pond lily
pingling
Penelope
pangless
penalise
penalize
penumbra
penoncel
penknife
pinkness
puniness
pentosan
penwoman
pandowdy
pennoned
pin money
pansophy
pangolin
Panionic
pentomic
pantofle
pinpoint
pundonor
pinboard
penn'orth
panoptic
punt-pole
Ping-Pong®
pancreas
pinprick
punk rock
pencraft
panorama
pentroof
pinkroot
panislam
puntsman
pinaster
Pinkster
punisher
pantsuit
pink slip
pink-slip
ponyskin
pond scum
pint-size
punctual
Pinatubo
panstick
penstock
pine tree
pinotage
ponytail
punctule
penitent
punition
puncture
punitory
punctate
punitive
pendular
pinguefy
pendulum
pondweed
pinewood
pine-wool
penny fee
penny-fee
penny-pig
penny-dog
penny-bun
pholades
profaner
protases
psoralen
prolamin
protasis
protatic
probable
probably
provable
provably
Phocaena
procaine
ptomaine
pronator
propanol
prolapse
prosaism
prosaist
pro tanto
Phoebean
poop deck
plodding
prodding
Proudhon
proudish
proudful
prometal
propenal
prose-man
proseman
Proverbs
proceeds
phone sex
protégée
phonemic
phoner-in
phonetic
progeria
pyogenic
properly
proteome
pyoderma
provedor
propense
protease
protense
proteose
property
proofing
plougher
plough in
phosgene
proggins
plough on
prong-hoe
prophecy
prophage
prophyll
prothyle
poor hand
prophase
prophesy
Phocidae
prodigal
proviral
proximal
Psocidae
procinct
province
profiler
profiter
pro-lifer
promisee
promiser
provided
provider
pyonings
✧photinia
prohibit
prolific
Prosimii
prolixly
proviant
proditor
promisor
providor
provisor
provisos
Protista
Plotinus
provirus
poor-John
plonking
pronking
prowl car
proclaim
prowling
plotless
proclive
poor laws
proemial
phorminx
✧phormium
poorness
prodnose
photomap
pronotal
proposal
photogen
promoter
proposer
provoker
prolonge
Photofit®
photofit
photopia
photopic
propolis
prosodic
protonic
pro forma
pro-forma
profound
propound
promotor
prosopon
protocol
✧protozoa
proto-ore
photopsy
prologue
pronotum
prorogue
Paolozzi
✧prospect
prompter
Prospekt
promptly
plopping
proppant
propping
✧phosphor
piou-piou
pooh-pooh
Prospero
prog rock
protract
prograde
protrude
prodrome
prodromi
prop-root
progress
poor rate
poolside
poor's-box
prostyle
plotting
poortith
prostate
procurer
producer
profuser
promulge
poorwill
poon-wood
propylic
propylon
pappadom
poppadum
pipe bomb
pipe band
pipeclay
pipe-case
pupa-case
pipe down
pepperer
puppetry
pipefuls
pipefish
popehood
poplitic
pop-visit
Popsicle®
Pope Joan
papillae
papillar
pupillar
populace
pupil age
pupilage
pipelike
pipeline
popeling
papilios
papillon
pupilary
papalise
papalism
papalist
papulose
pipeless
populism
populist
populate
papulous
populous
papalize
Pap smear
popinjay
pop-under
pappoose
puppodum
pap-spoon
paper-day
puparial
pipe rack
Pipe Roll
papering
peperino
peperoni
piperine
paperboy
pop group
puparium
Pepysian
papisher
pipe-stem
papistic
popeship
popishly
papistry
pope's eye
pipe-tree
pupation
pop music
pipe-wine
pipework
pipewort
Poppy Day
puppy fat
poppy-oil
puppy-dog
puppydom
puppyish
puppyism
piquancy
piquillo
Parma ham
parlance
pernancy
portance
parlando
partaken
partaker
purdahed
pardalis
perradii
phreatic
portable
persaunt
Pergamon
Portaloo®
perianth
par value
per caput
Pergamum
periagua
portague
periblem
pure-bred
parabola
parabole
periboli
parabema
Pericles
parochin
pork-chop
pericope
pericarp
peracute
peridial
parodied
paradigm
pyridine
paradrop
periderm
✧paradise
parodist
peridote
peridium
pare down
paradoxy
parietal
Parmesan
Perceval
perdendo
parcener
pargeted
pargeter
purse-net
parhelia
parhelic
paroemia
porterly
perceant
purveyor
parterre
permease
perverse
porpesse
portesse
percents
perfecta
perfecti
perfecto
permeate
perseity
parcel up
porteous
purseful
perceive
purified
purifier
paraffin
parafoil
paraffle
porn film
Porifera
port-fire
pyriform
paragram
Paraguay
perigeal
perigean
Phrygian
perogies
pirogies
paragoge
porogamy
perigone
perigyny
Perugino
Parthian
porthole
perching
perchery
Porphyra
✧porphyry
porthors
parchesi
purchase
perthite
pyrrhous
Parsifal
partisan
partitas
partizan
Percidae
Percival
per minas
parritch
porridge
perlitic
partible
particle
Portillo
persicot
porrigos
porticos
portière
Parsiism
perviate
Partitur
pervious
pirlicue
portigue
purlicue
purlieus
parakeet
parallax
parallel
Parolles
perilled
Parklife
paralogy
purslain
parklike
parkland
perilune
porkling
✧portland
purblind
purfling
purslane
purulent
paralyse
parclose
portlast
purplish
pyrolyse
perilous
paralyze
pyrolyze
✧pyramids
parament
paramese
paramour

parental
perineal
peroneal
Pyrenean
paranoea
Pyrenees
paranoia
paranoic
paranoid
perentie
pyrenoid
paronymy
partners
Peronism
Peronist
pertness
phrenism
Piranesi
poriness
pureness
paranete
per annum
perineum
peroneus
Pareoean
personae
personal
personas
portolan
perforce
pardoner
parroted
parroter
pore over
purposed
purposes
parrot it
parsonic
percolin
periodic
periotic
pardon me
parpoint
parrotry
porpoise
portoise
perspire
piri-piri
peripety
periplus
Paraquat®
paroquet
parbreak
pirarucu
portrait
purtraid
parergon
portress
Portrush
perorate
purtrayd
Parisian
pyrostat
parishen
perished
perisher
poristic
Port Said
puristic
piroshki
Pyrosoma
pyrosome
parasang
part-song
phrasing
porn shop
perisarc
parasite
porosity
part-time
pyritise
pyritous
pyritize
Portugal
portulan
persuade
perfumed
perfumer
perjured
perjurer
pertused
Portugee
parousia
purpuric
purpurin
pursuant
pursuing
pore upon
perruque
Portunus
Peruvian
paravail
Port-Vila
paravane
paravant
par avion
pyruvate
perswade
port wine
port-winy
parkward
partwork
pyrexial
peroxide
pyroxyle
pyroxene
paroxysm
party man
parrying
partyism
parazoan
pirozhki
parazoon
passatas
pass away
Peshawar
pastance
pashalik
passable
passably
poseable
postally
passados
✧piscator
Pissarro
paspalum
pass-back
pushbike
push-ball
pass band
passbook
postcode
Postcomm
postcard
push-cart
postcava
Pasadena
postdate
pass down
passer-by
Passeres
paste-eel
pesterer
post-echo
postface
post-free
pisiform
postgrad
pasch-egg
post hole
post horn
pessimal
piscinae
piscinas
pasticci
pastiche
postiche
passible
passibly
pastille
possible
possibly
Poseidon
Peshitta
Peshitto
pessimum
postlude
pis aller
posology
Pasolini
passless
pisolite
pass laws
post mill
pashmina
passment
postmark
puss-moth
posingly
poshness
postnati
pastoral
postoral
Passover
pass over
pistolet
post over
pushover
post-obit
pastorly
pishogue
Pasiphae
post-paid
push-pull
postpone
passport
postpose
post road
pastrami
post ship
poshteen
post time
Pashtuns
positing
Pushtuns
position
positron
positive
post town
pastural
postural
pustular
posturer
Pasquale
pass upon
password
pussy-cat
Puseyism
Puseyite
Petrarch
pittance
potlatch
phthalic
phthalin
pitiable
pitiably
pithball
put about
petechia
poticary
pot metal
patience
pattened
patterer
potterer
pathetic
pettedly
pot-belly
putter-on
pita-flax
petaflop
patagial
patagium
pitchman
putchock
patchily
pita-hemp
patching
pitching
patch box
putcheon
patchery
petchary
potshard
potshare
potsherd
pit viper
Patricia
petrific
phthisic
phthisis
putridly
pettifog
patriate
patellae
patellar
patellas
petalody
petalled
petaloid
pithlike
petaline
petulant
pot plant
pathless
petalism
pithless
pitiless
patulous
petalous
putamina
put on ice
patentee
patently
potently
pathname
patentor
petuntse
pétanque
petuntze
patronal
petiolar
petrosal
pathogen
petioled
petronel
potholer
put to bed
put to sea
petrolic
pythonic
patronne
pot-bound
pothouse
pot roast
pot-roast
put forth
put-up job
paternal
peter-man
peterman
Peter Pan
Peterkin
pityroid
Patarine
Peterloo
paterero
pattress
peter out
put aside
pot ashes
pot-ashes
potassic
put a stop
petit mal
pot stick
pith-tree
potatoes
pot still
pot-still
potstone
petition
potation
petitory
potatory
putative
pot-au-feu
pattypan
Petty Bag
pitty-pat
puttying
plug away
Plutarch
plumaged
plurally
pourable
poulaine
✧plumbago
plumbing
plumb bob
Paul Berg
plumbery
plumbism
plumbate
plumbite
plumbous
plum-cake
pound day
pound net
plum-duff
poundage
pounding
pauldron
pouldron
prudence
plumelet
✧prunella
prunelle
prunello
Paulette
pauseful
plugging
plunging
plughole
pouchful
plumiped
prusiked
plurisie
pruritic
prurient
prurigos
Pluviôse
pluviose
pluvious
pruritus
Paul Klee
pluck off
pluckily
Paul Nash
pruinose
✧plutonic
pauropod
più mosso
plumpish
Paul's-man
Prussian
Prussify
plussage
plus sign
poursuit
plussing
pourtray
poultice
plum tree
plus twos
plumulae
plumular
plug-ugly
pavilion
pavement
pavonian
pavonine
pivot-man
pivoting
pewterer
powdered
pew-chair
powsowdy
power nap
power set
power tea
power-amp
power cut
powerful
pawnshop
pyxidium
pixie hat
poxvirus
pax-board
pax-brede
pixy-ring
phylarch
prytanea
physalia
physalis
pay a call
physeter
phyletic
psychics
pay-sheet
psychoid
payphone
psychism
psychist
psych out
physical
physicky
paynimry
physique
phyllode
phyllody
phylloid
phyllome
phyllary
ptyalise
ptyalism
phyllite
psyllium
ptyalize
pryingly
phytosis
pay round
pay court
Plymouth
peyotism
peyotist
Pozidriv®
pizzeria
puzzling
pezizoid
quad bike
quandang
quandong
quandary
quaverer
Quakerly
quackery
quackish
Quaalude®
quailing
qualming
quagmire
quagmiry
qualmish
quaintly
✧quatorze
quarried

quarrier
quadriga
quatrain
quadrans
quadrant
quadroon
quadrate
quayside
quaestor
quartier
quantify
quartile
quantong
quart-pot
quartern
quarters
quantise
quantity
quartett
quantize
quae vide
quencher
Quebecer
quenelle
queueing
Quechuan
Queen Mab
queen bee
queenlet
queening
queendom
queenite
Queequeg
queerish
queerity
queasily
questant
questing
question
querying
qaimaqam
quibbler
quincunx
quiddler
quiddany
quiddity
quivered
quinella
Quichuan
Quirinal
Quirites
Quirinus
quickset
quick-fix
quirkily
quirkish
quillman
quill-pen
Quillaia
quill-nib
Quillaja
quilling
quisling
quidnunc
quixotic
quixotry
quippish
quit-rent
quinsied
quipster
quiz show
quietude
quintain
quintile
quieting
quilting
quitting
quietism
quietist
quintett
quietive
quizzify
quizzing
quizzery
Q D Leavis
qalamdan
qindarka
quo vadis?
quotable
quotably
quoad hoc
quotient
quoining
quod vide
rear-arch
Ruaraidh
reawaken
rhagades
readable
readably
real beer
road book
reascend
reascent
reaedify
rhabdoid
Ruaidhri
Rwandese
reagency
real food
reaffirm
road game
rhaphide
road hump
reaching
realiser
realizer
readiest
reamiest
read into
readjust
road kill
real life
rear lamp
roadless
rearmice
rearmost
realness
reasoned
reasoner
read-only
rearouse
reappear
roanpipe
road race
Ruairidh
road rage
rear-rank
rearrest
roadsman
rhapsode
rhapsody
roadside
reanswer
roadster
reassign
road sign
reassume
roadshow
reabsorb
reassert
reassure
reassess
Rhaetian
reattach
reattain
realtime
reactant
roasting
reaction
road test
road-test
reactive
readvise
rearward
roadwork
ready-mix
readying
rubicund
rabidity
rubidium
rabbeted
rubified
rub off on
✧rubaiyat
rubrical
rabbiter
rubbishy
✧rabbinic
rabbit on
rabbitry
rubellan
rebelled
rebeller
Rabelais
rabbling
rub along
rebeldom
rebellow
ribaldry
Robin Day
ribbonry
rib-roast
ruby port
reburial
roborant
reborrow
rib-grass
roburite
robustly
ribosome
rebuttal
robotics
rabatoes
rebatoes
rebutted
rebutter
ruby-tail
rabatine
ribstone
rubstone
rebutton
robotise
robotize
ribaudry
ribozyme
rockaway
Richards
recharge
racially
RAC Rally
rectally
rock-alum
rice beer
race-ball
ricebird
rock-bird
rock bass
rice bowl
ricochet
rice cake
rock cake
rock cook
racecard
rock cork
Rochdale
receding
rock dove
racketer
rocketer
Roccella
Rochelle
recceing
recreant
racketry
rocketry
richesse
raclette
recreate
ricketty
rockfall
Rockford
rockfish
racegoer
rice glue
racahout
rock-hewn
receival
rachides
rachises
received
receiver
reclined
recliner
recoiler
rachitic
rachitis
rectitic
rectitis
rachilla
rocaille
ructions
récollet
rich-left
rocklike
reckling
rockling
rock lark
reckless
recommit
rice milk
Richmond
racemise
racemism
racemose
racemate
racemize
recanter
reconvey
recently
recentre
raciness
richness
rectoral
reckoner
reclothe
reckon up
recaptor
receptor
racepath
ricercar
rick-rack
✧recorder
recurred
recurved
rack rail
rack-rent
race riot
rectress
rock rose
rickshaw
ruckseat
rucksack
recessed
recesses
rock salt
recusant
rock song
recision
rice soup
rictuses
recourse
Racovian
recovery
rockweed
rock wood
rock wool
rackwork
rockwork
reccying
rickyard
radiance
radiancy
riddance
red panda
radiated
red-faced
redwater
Rod Laver
red dagga
radialia
radially
red eagle
rideable
radiator
radwaste
radicule
ridicule
radicand
radicant
reducing
redactor
radicate
ride down
red cedar
ridgeway
reddenda
reddendo
✧redeemer
redbelly
Redbeard
redefine
red wheat
red shift
red shank
redshank
redshare
redshire
Red Shirt
redshort
Redditch
red biddy
Red River
red light
red-light
red giant
ruddiest
red algae
redolent
riddling
ridgling
red alert
redeless
radulate
rudiment
Rodentia
red onion
rudeness
radio ham
red coral
radio fix
raddocke
red route
redeploy
red brick
redbrick
redirect
Roderick
Red Cross
radar gun
redargue
Redgrave
redesign
redistil
ridottos
redstart
radiuses
redouble
ride upon
Red Guard
redivide
reduviid
red dwarf
ruddying
rhematic
reedbuck
re-embody
reed-band
reef band
reed-bird
re-embark
rheocord
re-emerge
re-engage
reediest
reef knot
rheology
reedling
Riesling
re-enlist
ryeflour
reed-mace
rhetoric
re-expand
reed pipe
re-export
ryebread
reed-rand
reed-rond
rye grass
rheostat
reed stop
rye-straw
✧roentgen
rheotome
roestone
ruefully
reed-wren
Rh-factor
rifleman
raftered
reflexed
reflexes
rifle pit
reflexly
refreeze
refigure
refugium
Rifaites
refringe
refelled
ruffling
riftless
refunder
refining
refinery
rifeness
reflower
raft-port
referral
reformat
referred
referrer
re-formed
✧reformed
✧reformer
riff-raff
referent
raft-rope
reforest
raftsman
refusnik
refusion
refluent
rag paper
regrater
Ragnarok
Ragnarök
regrator
regicide
rigidify
rigadoon
rigidise
rigidity
rigidize
raggedly
ruggedly

regreets
ragwheel
ragtimer
regainer
regalian
rugelach
reguline
regalism
regalist
regulise
rugulose
regality
regelate
regolith
regulate
regulize
regiment
Rogun Dam
ragingly
Reginald
rag-woman
regional
rag-money
regrowth
Rogerian
rag trade
regarder
rigorism
rigorist
rigorous
register
rugosely
registry
rugosity
regather
right off
ragstone
rigatoni
righting
rogation
right arm
rogatory
rightish
rightism
rightist
rightful
right out
reheater
rehearse
rehoboam
rehandle
Rohypnol
Rohypnol®
raisable
ruinable
rein back
rainband
rainbird
rainbowy
raincoat
railcard
reindeer
raindrop
raindate
raise hob
reinette
rainfall
reinfund
reinform
reinfuse
railhead

Reichian
rein-hand
railings
rhinitis
rainiest
reillume
raillery
railless
rainless
reinless
Rhiannon
re-ignite
rhizobia
raisonné
Rhinodon
rhizopod
rhizopus
reimport
reimpose
railroad
reinsman
reinsert
reinsure
rain tree
roisting
reinvent
reinvest
rainwear
rainwash
reifying
rejecter
rejector
rejigger
rejoicer
rajaship
raja yoga
rakehell
rakshasa
rekindle
rakishly
rollaway
reliance
releasee
releaser
reliable
reliably
rollable
releasor
rollback
roll-call
relucent
relocate
relieved
reliever
relievos
religion
relegate
Rallidae
ruleless
relumine
rillmark
roll-neck
roll over
roll-over
rule over
role-play
relapsed
relapser
roly-poly
relation
relative

relaunch
relevant
relaxant
relaxing
rallying
rallyist
rampancy
rampager
rummager
rampauge
rump bone
Ramadhan
remedial
remediat
remedied
remodify
rumbelow
ramified
ramiform
remigial
Ramsgate
remigate
romp home
ram's-horn
rum shrub
rampired
Ram Singh
rum-ti-tum
Ramilies
REM sleep
Ramillie
rambling
rumbling
ramulose
rumpless
ramulous
remember
Romanian
Roman law
Rumanian
Romansch
Rumansch
Rumonsch
reminder
romancer
romantic
remanent
ruminant
Romanise
Romanish
Romanism
Romanist
ruminate
ramentum
Romanize
rump-post
ramequin
remarked
remarker
rim brake
R R Marett
remarque
remurmur
rumorous
rampsman
Ramesses
remaster
remissly
Rome-scot
remittal
remitted

remittee
remitter
remotely
remittor
remotion
rambutan
rum punch
rumourer
Romeward
Ramayana
rondavel
rondache
rentable
rinsable
runnable
roncador
ring back
ringbolt
ringbone
ring-bark
runabout
ring dial
ring dyke
ringdove
ring down
renderer
renverse
renverst
rinse out
rondeaux
runner-up
rent-free
run after
raniform
reniform
ring fort
renegade
renegado
reneguer
ronggeng
renegate
runagate
ranchman
ringhals
rinkhals
ranching
ranchero
run chart
run short
✧renminbi
rinsings
rinsible
runcible
rondinos
randiest
rangiest
runniest
run along
rindless
ringless
run close
rungless
ringlets
renumber
ring main
run a mile
ring mark
rankness
renforce
ransomer
run for it

randomly
Randolph
re'nforst
renforst
ring pull
rink polo
ronepipe
ranarian
ring road
rent roll
run a risk
ranarium
ringside
ringster
ring-tail
ringtail
ring-time
renitent
ringtone
ring true
renounce
run out on
renovate
renowned
renowner
ring walk
ring wall
renewing
ringwork
ringworm
ringwise
renaying
rendzina
rhodanic
rhopalic
rood beam
root beer
rhomboid
root ball
rhonchal
root crop
reoccupy
rhonchus
reordain
reopener
rootedly
roomette
roomfuls
reoffend
root-fast
riot gear
riot girl
riot grrl
root hair
roothold
Rhodites
reorient
roomiest
rootiest
root-knot
rood loft
rooflike
rootlike
roofless
rootless
roommate
roof rack
roomsome
rood-tree
rooftree
roof tile

ryotwari
rapparee
✧repealer
repeated
repeater
replacer
raphania
ropeable
Raphanus
republic
rape cake
rapacity
rapidity
replevin
ripienos
repreeve
rap sheet
reprisal
raphides
repairer
repriefe
Reptilia
replicon
reprieve
repelled
repeller
rippling
repenter
Rupinder
repining
ripeness
ropiness
reproval
reproach
Raptores
reprover
repeople
riparial
riparian
repartee
reporter
repurify
rope-ripe
reperuse
rephrase
rap group
rapeseed
reposall
rope's end
rope's-end
reposure
repetend
reputing
raptured
rap music
repoussé
rope-walk
ropework
repaying
replying
rope yarn
roquette
requital
required
requirer
requited
requiter
requight
requoyle
rere-arch
rara avis

rare bird
rerecord
rarefied
ruralise
ruralism
ruralist
rurality
ruralize
rere-mice
rareness
rare-ripe
rerevise
rereward
✧rastaman
re-search
research
resiance
rascally
Roseanna
Roseanne
rascasse
resubmit
✧rust belt
rust-belt
rosebush
rosebowl
Rosaceae
rose comb
rest cure
residual
Rusedski
resident
rose drop
rosy drop
residuum
Rasselas
Rosie Lee
respects
rispetti
rispetto
rosefish
Rose Gray
resigned
resigner
rosoglio
rose-hued
rest home
rush hour
rush-hour
rustical
Roskilde
raspings
rispings
riskiest
rustiest
rose knot
resalgar
risaldar
rose leaf
reselect
resolved
resolver
result in
roselike
rushlike
resplend
Rosalind
Rosaline
Roseland
rustling
Rosslare

restless
roseless
rustless
resalute
resolute
risoluto
rosulate
rustle up
resemble
Rosamond
Rosamund
rosemary
rest mass
Rosa Mota
Russniak
resenter
resinify
resinoid
rosin oil
resonant
rashness
resinise
rosiness
resinata
resinate
resonate
rosinate
resinous
resinize
roseolar
restorer
Responsa
response
resupine
rose-pink
rasorial
rosarian
restrict
reserved
reserver
reserves
resorter
resurvey
resorcin
restrain
restring
rush ring
rest room
roseroot
rescript
rose rash
rostrate
risorius
rosarium
resister
resistor
rest stop
resetter
rose tree
rosetted
rise to it
resettle
risottos
russulae
russulas
resource
Rasputin
rescuing
Rosewall
rosewood
retraict

retiarii
rateable
rateably
retrally
ritually
retraite
retraitt
rutabaga
ratsbane
Rutaceae
reticula
reticule
reticent
retrench
ruthenic
rottenly
ratified
ratifier
retiform
Rotifera
rat-rhyme
Rattigan
retailer
retainer
rattiest
ritziest
retrieve
retaking
rattlier
reteller
rattline
rattling
rutilant
riteless
ruthless
retinoid
rat snake
retinula
rotundly
rotenone
retinite
ritenuto
rational
R S Thomas
retroact
ratooner
retrofit
Retrovir®
retrorse
rataplan
Rotarian
retiracy
retarded
retarder
retorted
retorter
returnee
returner
ritornel
roturier
returnik
retiring
ratproof
rathripe
rotor arm
rotgrass
rat's-tail
rot-stone
rotation
rotatory
rotative

rat-guard
rotavate
rotovate
retrying
rhubarby
reusable
rout-cake
roundlet
round off
rounding
round top
round-arm
rounders
roundure
roundish
round out
routeman
routeing
roulette
rouleaus
rouleaux
rough-hew
roughage
rough-dry
roughish
rough cut
rough out
rough-out
Rousseau
rout-seat
revealer
reviewal
reviewer
revved-up
reveille
ravelled
revelled
reveller
revolted
revolter
revolver
rivalled
rivelled
reviling
Rivelino
rivaless
rivalise
revolute
rivality
ravel out
rivalize
revenger
revenges
revenued
revanche
ravingly
rovingly
ravening
revenant
ravenous
rave over
rove-over
reversal
riverman
river-rat
River Tay
River Váh
riverway
reversed
reverser
reverted

river bed
reversis
riverain
River Ems
✧reverend
reverent
riverine
River Inn
reversos
River Don
river god
river-hog
reverist
River Exe
River Wye
ravisher
revision
revestry
revisory
revetted
rivetted
riveting
revivify
reviving
row barge
rowndell
rowdedow
rowelled
raw umber
rewinder
rawboned
row house
Rawlplug®
rewarder
rewarewa
rowdydow
rowdyish
rowdyism
Raynaud's
rhythmal
rhythmed
rhythmic
rhythmus
Rhytisma
Royal Oak
royalise
royalism
✧royalist
rhyolite
royalize
Reynolds
roysting
razmataz
razor cut
razor-cut
scalawag
soakaway
soaraway
stayaway
seawards
scalades
scarabee
scavager
seafarer
sea raven
seawater
staragen
sea marge
Scalaria
shamanic
sparaxis

scalable
scalably
sea eagle
sealable
seamanly
shakable
shamable
shapable
sharable
sparable
statable
stalagma
scalados
sea pansy
snap bean
Starbuck
swayback
scambler
shambles
snap-brim
seat belt
shabbily
soap-ball
stay bolt
slam-bang
slap-bang
stabbing
St Albans
swabbing
shadblow
scabbard
shagbark
slabbery
soapbark
swabbers
shadbush
shadchan
searcher
snatcher
stanchel
stancher
starched
starcher
scarcely
shauchle
shauchly
stanchly
search me
seascape
sea acorn
scarcity
staccato
Sea Scout
Scandian
Shandean
stand pad
stand pat
stand sam
shaddock
spar deck
sea adder
spandrel
swaddler
stand off
stand-off
standoff
spandril
stand oil
scalding
scaldini
scaldino

scandent
slam dunk
slam-dunk
standing
stand low
Standard®
standard
slapdash
soap dish
standish
stardust
scandium
stand out
standout
swan dive
slap down
shake-bag
shake-rag
shareman
space bar
spaceman
spademan
sea beach
sea perch
sea level
slaverer
snake eel
stake net
stamened
stapedes
shake off
stake off
stave off
scavenge
space age
space-age
Swadeshi
sea devil
shale oil
snake-oil
snake-pit
spageric
spare rib
stapelia
sea jelly
snake fly
statedly
slave ant
sea lemon
sea-berry
sea beast
sea heath
scalenus
shake out
shake-out
shameful
share-out
space out
spadeful
stake out
stake-out
stare out
slate axe
Scarface
seamfree
staffage
scarf-pin
scaffold
spatfall
swap file
scarfing

Stafford
Stamford
scarfish
starfish
scarf out
✧shanghai
spanghew
spangled
spangler
spanglet
shaggily
slangily
shagging
slagging
slanging
snagging
swagging
staggard
staggers
slangish
Stan Getz
star-gaze
slag heap
slaphead
scaphoid
shashlik
smash hit
seashell
Swan Hill
scathing
slashing
smashing
stag hunt
swashing
stanhope
sea chart
seashore
staghorn
swanherd
sea chest
spathose
sea shrub
spar-hawk
Scaridae
staminal
Stari Ras
statical
sea piece
Saarinen
shamisen
spadices
spavined
sea-fight
spagiric
spadille
spadillo
suasible
stadiums
shamiana
stasimon
Spaniard
Shafiite
scabious
scarious
spacious
slapjack
star jump
Shark Bay
slack jaw
snack bar
spark gap

shackles
sparkler
sparklet
stalkoes
slack off
spark off
Shanklin
shark oil
sharking
skanking
smacking
spanking
stacking
stalking
swanking
swankpot
starkers
sparkish
spark out
smallsat
Stahlian
stallman
stay lace
small ads
stall-fed
sea cliff
stall off
smallage
stallage
scablike
starlike
Swan Lake
swanlike
small ale
seaplane
shawling
snap-link
snarling
soapland
spalling
span-long
sparling
stabling
stalling
starling
swap line
swayling
scallion
sea floor
shalloon
smallpox
stallion
small arm
small fry
snailery
scarless
seamless
seatless
smallish
soapless
spanless
✧spätlese
stablish
Stahlism
starless
stayless
Scarlett
seablite
shallows
swap meet
scarmoge
smalmily
smarmily
scammony
shamming
slamming
spamming
swarming
swan-mark
shammash
swan neck
sea snail
sea snake
scanning
spanning
spawning
stagnant
staining
swaining
swanning
sea onion
sea snipe
✧stannary
swannery
searness
swainish
stagnate
stannate
stannite
stannous
seasonal
seawoman
sea loach
sea power
sea rover
seasoned
seasoner
shadower
slalomer
spadones
stay over
sea robin
Slavonia
Slavonic
sea holly
seaborne
sea-going
seahound
seamount
seaboard
seacoast
seahorse
sea mouse
shatoosh
sea boots
starosta
starosty
✧seaspeak
swamp gas
swamp oak
Stamp Act
stampede
stampedo
sharp-set
spalpeen
shagpile
snappily
scalping
scalpins
scamping
scarping
Sean Penn
sharping
slapping
snapping
stamping
swapping
shampoo'd
shampoos
seal-pipe
scampish
sharpish
snappish
scalprum
sharp-cut
stamp out
star-pav'd
sea bream
stairway
star-read
star ruby
sea wrack
shabrack
shamrock
sea brief
sea green
sea-green
shagreen
seacraft
snap roll
starrily
seadrome
scarring
seafront
seal ring
seat rent
sparring
starring
shagroon
soaproot
spadroon
span roof
stair rod
sea grape
sea-grape
sea grass
sea froth
scabrous
sea trout
swagsman
soapsuds
sea aster
seamster
slaister
star sign
sealskin
starship
staysail
swan-skin
swanskin
spansule
sparsely
St Anselm
swan song
swansong
scansion
slapshot
snapshot
starspot
swagshop
swan-shot
swap-shop
sparsity
star trap
sea stick
scanties
sea otter
soap tree
startled
startler
slant rig
svastika
swastika
scantily
scattily
scatting
shafting
shantung
slanting
starting
swatting
swaption
stay tape
scattery
sea storm
shattery
slattern
slattery
starters
star turn
Shaktism
smartish
soap test
startish
scantity
scawtite
smaltite
startful
start out
scapulae
scapular
scapulas
spatular
shamuses
statured
statuses
seaquake
seacunny
stay upon
statuary
sea purse
Shabuoth
Shavuoth
starving
sea ivory
Shaivism
Shaivite
spaewife
sea swine
slag wool
soapwort
stalwart
✧star wars
starwort
✧sealyham
scaly-leg
spagyric
sea nymph
stanzoes
stanzaic
subbasal
Sabratha
sabbatic
Sobranje
subcaste
Sobranye
subabbot
subacrid
subucula
subacute
subadult
sub verbo
submerge
subgenre
sublease
submerse
subtense
subverse
subverst
sabre-cut
subgenus
subserve
subagent
subahdar
subchief
subchord
subshrub
subsizar
subtidal
subviral
sublimed
subfield
subtitle
sobriety
sibyllic
subclaim
sabuline
sibilant
subfloor
sabulose
subclass
sibilate
subtlety
subulate
sabulous
Sibelius
sibilous
subimago
subpolar
subsolar
subtotal
subvocal
subzonal
subsonic
subtonic
subtopia
subpoena
subcosta
subequal
saburral
suburban
subtribe
suberect
subtract
subgrade
subtrude
subbreed
suborder
suborner
suburbia
subframe
sobering
subprior
soberise
subcrust
suberise
suberose
subtrist
suberate
✧sybarite
suberous
subgroup
soberize
suberize
sebesten
sabotier
sob stuff
sabotage
substage
substyle
sob story
subitise
sybotism
substate
saboteur
subitize
subaural
subdural
subhuman
sublunar
Subbuteo®
subaudio
subhumid
subduple
subovate
suboxide
sock away
Socrates
saccadic
sacraria
Socratic
sackable
sociable
sociably
socially
sectator
secodont
societal
sickener
socketed
suckener
suckered
sachemic
secretin
Szczecin
sacredly
secretly
sickerly
secretor
sockette
sick flag
suck face
sackfuls
suck-hole
succinct
succinic
sacristy
succinyl
Sicelian
Sicilian
Siculian
sicklied
so called
sacklike
such like
suchlike
sicklily
suckling
Siceliot
sucklers
sackless
sick list
sacellum
sycamine
sycamore
sycomore
Sicanian
Socinian
secondee
seconder
secantly
secondly
secundly
sickness
suchness
sick note
secundum
syconium
sectoral
Suctoria
sack race
sucurujú
securely
sickroom
security
secesher
such that
sack tree
saccular
succubae
succubas
saccules
secluded
sacculus
succubus
suchwise
Sid James
sidearms
sideband
side comb
seducing
seductor
side door
side dish
side drum
sedge fly
suddenly
suddenty
side-foot
soda jerk
sidekick
sidelock
sidalcea
soda-lake
soda lime
sideline
sideling
sidelong
saddlery
sedulity
sodalite
sodality
saddle up
sedulous
side meat
sodamide
sediment

sudamina
sodomise
✧sodomite
sodomize
Sudanese
sidenote
side post
sidepath
sidereal
sideroad
sederunt
siderate
siderite
sudarium
sudorous
sidesman
sidestep
sadistic
sideslip
sideshow
sedately
side tone
sedation
sedition
sudation
sudatory
sedative
Sadducee
siddur-im
siddurim
St David's
side view
sidewalk
sidewall
side wind
sideward
sidewise
sideways
spelaean
seecatch
skew arch
scenario
Sheraton
skewback
stembuck
skewbald
seed bank
spekboom
see about
seed coat
skeechan
sketcher
swelchie
seedcake
stem cell
seed corn
seedcase
speedway
Stendhal
shelduck
steadied
steadier
speldrin
speedily
spendall
steadily
stepdame
sheading
shedding
sledding
speeding
spelding
spending
steading
speed-cop
steady on!
speedful
speed gun
step down
step-down
scelerat
scene bay
sceneman
skeletal
skene-dhu
stereome
skeleton
suedette
siege-gun
shelf ice
seed fern
stem form
Stepford
seed-fish
stedfast
shelf-ful
sleigher
Spergula
Svengali
sledging
Sieg Heil
seething
shedhand
stephane
Stephano
see where
✧shepherd
shechita
scenical
shehitah
Shekinah
specimen
specific
syenitic
Special K
sterigma
speciate
step into
specious
sneaksby
speckled
sneakily
sleeking
sneaking
speaking
sheikdom
sneakish
sneak-cup
sneakeup
speak out
speakout
seed leaf
shedload
shell-lac
steelman
steel pan
seed lobe
shell-ice
✧sherlock
skelloch
stenlock
seemlier
steelmen
stellify
stealthy
seedlike
seedling
shealing
sheiling
shelling
✧shetland
smelling
spelling
sperling
stealing
steeling
stelline
✧sterling
swealing
swelling
steelbow
stellion
swell box
swelldom
swell-mob
seedless
seemless
stemless
swellish
stellate
shellful
shell out
smell out
spellful
spell out
steam car
sperm oil
steamily
steaming
St Edmund
stemming
spermary
stemmata
spermous
Steinway
sternway
sternage
skean-dhu
sternums
steaning
steening
steining
steenbok
steinbok
sternson
seedness
Siennese
Skegness
skewness
shea nuts
sternite
stenosed
stenoses
stenosis
stenotic
step on it
see round
stegodon
sweep-saw
sheep ked
sheep-pen
steepled
sweep-net
sleep off
sheep-dip
steapsin
sleepily
skelping
skepping
sleeping
sneaping
stepping
stewpond
sweeping
seed plot
sheepdog
sheep-pox
sheep-rot
sleepery
sheepish
steepish
sheep run
sleep out
sleepout
steepeup
shearman
smear dab
smear-dab
spearman
skerrick
shearleg
sheerleg
sheer off
swear off
stearage
steerage
shear pin
smearily
shearing
sneering
stearine
steering
swearing
shear-hog
slew rate
stearate
spear gun
seedsman
sneeshan
✧spetsnaz
speisade
sneeshin
sceattas
scent bag
sceptral
spectral
sweet bay
sweet gas
sceptred
sheathed
shea tree
sweet pea
sheet tin
sweet-oil
sweet ale
seed time
steatoma
scenting
sheeting
smelting
stetting
sweating
sweeting
scent box
sweetsop
see stars
sheltery
smeltery
stem turn
sweetish
smectite
spectate
steatite
scentful
spectrum
stentour
sweet gum
specular
Shevuoth
saeculum
speculum
sleeveen
steevely
shelving
sleeving
steeving
swerving
see a wolf
sherwani
stemware
stepwise
Shenyang
seedy-toe
✧spetznaz
sleazily
sneezing
safranin
softback
soft-boil
softball
soft copy
soft-core
softener
sufferer
soften up
softhead
suffixal
sufficer
siftings
soffioni
soft iron
soft loan
soft lens
soft line
softling
sufflate
siffleur
soft meat
soft mark
safeness
softness
safronal
soft rock
suffrage
saffrony
safarist
safe seat
soft soap
soft-soap
Sufistic
soft sell
soft-sell
soft-shoe
soft-slow
soft spot
soft sore
softwood
software
sign away
signaled
signaler
sigmatic
signally
saguaros
sage cock
sagacity
signeted
segreant
segueing
signieur
St Gallen
signless
segolate
sagamore
sageness
sagenite
saginate
sign over
signoria
sago palm
signpost
sugar pea
sugaring
sugar gum
Sigiriya
sigisbei
sigisbeo
sagittal
sightsee
sighting
schläger
schnapps
schmaltz
Schubert
schedule
schiedam
Schwerin
schnecke
schleppy
sphygmic
sphagnum
sphygmus
Sahelian
schiller
St Helier
so help me
St Helena
St Helens
scholion
schellum
scholium
schimmel
scheming
Schumann
schemata
sphinges
sphinxes
sphenoid
sphingid
schantze
schooled
schooner
Schröder
schoolie
schlocky
schmooze
schmoozy
schapska
spherics
spheroid
spherule
scherzos
Schizaea
schizoid
schizont
Srinagar
shikaree
ship a sea
shiralee
shivaree
spicated
spirated
Sri Lanka
sailable
seizable
slidable
spiracle
spirally
suitable
suitably
Shivaism
Shivaite
ski pants
suivante
sailboat
stibbler
shinbone
stilbene
stilbite
sticcado
snitcher
spitcher
stitched
stitcher
switchel
switcher
scincoid
switch on
skincare
spit curl
slipcase
slip-cast
suitcase
spiccato
sticcato
stitch up
stitch-up
shidduch
slip-dock
skin-deep
swindler
skidding
sliddery
slim down
shireman
seine net
shiverer
Spike Lee
spikelet
skive off
smite off
sciaenid
slime pit
Spigelia
spike oil
shigella
snipe fly

Words marked ✧ can also be spelled with one or more capital letters

snivelly
spice box
swine-pox
seicento
spinette
stiletto
swine-sty
smileful
spiteful
stived-up
sniffler
sniffles
sainfoin
stiff bit
Seinfeld
sniffily
sniffing
spiffing
skinfood
slipform
✧spitfire
stiff-arm
sailfish
stiffish
skiagram
stingray
shingled
shingler
shingles
sniggler
sling off
swingbin
stingily
skin game
sling ink
stinging
swigging
swinging
smidgeon
swingism
sling mud
skinhead
sei whale
slightly
swishing
slithery
smithers
smithery
scimitar
suicidal
scilicet
spinifex
spirited
stipites
suitings
spilikin
spilitic
spirilla
spiritus
skipjack
stickjaw
spicknel
stickies
stickler
stick pin
slinkily
smirkily
stickily
skinking
slicking
smirking
sticking
stinking
slipknot
stink pot
stinkpot
stinkard
stickful
stick out
stink bug
stink out
shipload
spillway
shielder
sail loft
spillage
stillage
skin-like
saibling
shieling
shilling
skilling
skiplane
skirling
slimline
spilling
spirling
stifling
stilling
Stirling
suilline
swilling
skillion
stillion
ski slope
saikless
sailless
sciolism
sciolist
shipless
skilless
skinless
soilless
stirless
sciolous
skillful
swill out
swill-tub
skim milk
shipment
skimming
slimming
swimming
shimmery
seismism
skirmish
slimmest
slimmish
shipmate
stigmata
scienced
scienter
spinnies
skinning
spinning
seignior
seignory
spinnery
slimness
stibnite
seigneur
shinny up
spinneys
scirocco
skijorer
skim over
skip over
slip-over
slivovic
sailorly
smilodon
stippled
stippler
slippage
skimpily
shipping
skimping
skipping
slipping
snipping
soil pipe
slippery
snippety
skid road
slip road
sciuroid
sliprail
sciurine
shirring
slip ring
stirring
sailroom
suitress
scirrhus
snip-snap
spinster
swimsuit
scissile
Shiv Sena
swissing
scission
ship's boy
slipshod
slip-shoe
slipslop
scissors
scissure
Swiftian
sciatica
ski stick
shift key
skittles
swiftlet
shirt pin
shiitake
shiftily
shirtily
shifting
shirting
skirting
slitting
spitting
stilting
stinting
saintdom
Skiathos
skiatron
spittoon
stiction
swift fox
ship-tire
snifters
saintess
saintish
saintism
skin test
skittish
stiltish
spin-text
spintext
spicular
stipular
stipuled
sui juris
spiculum
stimulus
skivvies
stievely
spivvery
swimwear
Shinwell
skin wool
shipworm
slipware
sail-yard
shipyard
skip zone
St Julien
St James's
St Jerome
Sikelian
Sikeliot
Sikorski
✧sikorsky
Sikh Wars
sukiyaki
salt away
silladar
saltando
salvager
selvaged
selvagee
sulcated
✧sylvaner
sultanic
Syldavia
syllabic
Sylvania
sylvatic
saleable
saleably
salvable
sellable
solvable
syllable
sol-faing
Salvador
soldados
sol-faism
sol-faist
sell a pup
sillabub
Silvanus
syllabub
syllabus
Salzburg
self-born
saltbush
salt bath
Salic law
selictar
silicide
selected
selectee
silicify
salt cake
silicula
silicule
salicine
silicone
selector
solecise
solecism
solecist
salacity
saliceta
salt-cote
silicate
solicity
silicium
solecize
solidify
solidago
salad oil
salt dome
salading
seladang
solidare
solidary
solidish
solidism
solidist
solidate
solidity
salt down
salience
saliency
solvency
solderer
solleret
selvedge
solfeggi
silverly
sullenly
salt flat
salified
salt-foot
saltfish
silaging
selfheal
sulphide
sylphide
self-help
Solihull
sulphone
sylphine
selfhood
sulphury
sylphish
self-hate
sulphate
sulphite
✧silphium
salvific
Salvinia
sylviine
salpicon
soldiery
sulfinyl
salt-junk
salt lick
self-left
self-life
salt lake
self-like
silk-like
saltless
selfless
self-lost
self-love
self-made
shlemiel
solemnly
salt-mine
selenian
Solonian
splenial
Salonica
selenide
Salinger
silenced
silencer
solander
splinter
solenoid
splendid
Salonika
silently
solanine
splendor
saltness
selfness
soleness
salinity
selenate
selenite
solonets
solonetz
selenium
selenous
splenium
splenius
salmonet
salmonid
selcouth
sulfonyl
✧salopian
shlepper
self-pity
salt plug
salariat
Silurian
solar day
salaried
sclereid
scleroid
siluroid
self-rule
sultrily
sclerema
scleroma
salering
saleroom
sclerose
✧silurist
solarise
solarism
solarist
sclerite
sclerous
solarium
solarize
Salesian
salesman
sales tax
Salishan
seldseen
splasher
Silastic®
silastic
selfsame
solo stop
self-sown
split cap
solstice
solitude
splatter
split-new
split pea
splitted
splitter
splutter
split-off
splotchy
silktail
split pin
split end
solation
solution
sola topi
salutary
solitary
solatium
solutive
saltuses
Seleucid
solpugid
Seleucus
salivary
salivate
silkweed
self-will
saltwort
silkworm
siloxane
sally-man
silky oak
Süleyman
sallying
sullying
salty dog
silly-how
saleyard
sympathy
samsaric
semi-arid
semi-axis
somebody
semibold
semibull
semicoma
so much so
somedeal
somedele
semi-dome
simperer
Sam Neill
summerly
symmetry
somegate
symphile
symphily
Symphyla
symphony
some hope
same here
samphire

Words marked ✧ can also be spelled with one or more capital letters

sumphish
summital
sumpitan
samnitis
somnific
symbiont
summitry
Simbirsk
somniate
semplice
symploce
simplify
sampling
semblant
semilune
semolina
simpling
simulant
Sémillon
samplery
similise
simplism
simplist
symplast
simulate
simulium
shmaltzy
similize
semi-mute
simoniac
semi-nude
Samantha
semantic
semuncia
Seminole
semantra
seminary
sameness
simonist
seminate
semi-opal
sum total
shmoozer
summoner
semiotic
symbolic
sympodia
symposia
Sam Spade
semi-pros
Sumerian
simaruba
✧somerset
sombrely
Semarang
semi-ring
sombrero
St Moritz
samarium
sombrous
semester
sempster
semi-soft
same that
Sumatran
Semitics
sometime
semitone
sumotori
symitare
Semitise
Semitism
Semitist
somatism
somatist
semitaur
Semitize
Sama-Veda
Samaveda
somewhat
somewhen
somewise
someways
samizdat
✧simazine
sandarac
sun dance
sunwards
sangaree
Santarém
senna tea
sin-eater
sinuated
sunbaked
sungazer
sunbathe
santalin
syngamic
sendable
singable
sinkable
syntagma
syntagms
Santa Ana
syncarpy
sandbank
sand blow
songbook
sonobuoy
songbird
sand bath
Sanscrit
synechia
synectic
senecios
sinecure
sand-cast
sinicise
Sinicism
sinicize
synedria
sand-dune
sanidine
sand-dart
send down
sentence
sundered
sunderer
sanserif
Santeria
sinner it
syndesis
syndetic
syntexis
sunbeamy
singeing
Sancerre
San Pedro
sunberry
senseful
sand-flag
son of man
Son of Sam
sand flea
Sinn Fein
song form
songfest
sonogram
sans gêne
sandheap
sunshade
Sondheim
sandhill
sink hole
sinkhole
sunn hemp
sunshine
sunshiny
syndical
sandiver
sentinel
San Diego
Santiago
sindings
syndings
se'nnight
sennight
sunlight
Sinaitic
sinuitis
sensible
sensibly
sensilla
sentient
sun visor
sinciput
Sanskrit
sunblock
sand leek
sanglier
Sinology
sand-like
songlike
senilely
sandling
singling
sun-blind
sunblind
sun-blink
syncline
sand-lark
songless
sunglass
senility
sand mole
Senonian
son-in-law
synanthy
synonymy
saneness
syncopal
santonin
sensoria
sinfonia
syncopic
syntonic
syntonin
sand-peep
synaphea
synapses
synopses
Sinophil
synapsis
synaptic
synopsis
synoptic
sandpump
sand pipe
sinapism
sinopite
Sangraal
Sangreal
sun cream
sungrebe
sun crack
Sangrado
sengreen
sun-dried
sundries
sentry-go
synarchy
Sangrail
synergic
synergid
syndrome
sonorant
sun print
sunproof
sundrops
syngraph
sundress
✧señorita
sonority
senarius
sonorous
sand-star
sinister
songster
Senussis
sinusoid
sand sole
sing-sing
singsong
sandshoe
synastry
sand trap
sanctify
sonatina
sunstone
sanction
sanatory
sanitary
sanitise
sanctity
sanitate
sanative
sanitize
singular
sun-cured
sanguify
sink unit
sinfully
sanguine
sunburnt
Senoussi
sunburst
sensuous
synovial
✧sandwich
sandworm
sandwort
send word
sand wasp
sine wave
syncytia
sandyish
sannyasi
stomatal
stow away
stowaway
show a leg
stomachy
Slovakia
sporadic
stomatic
São Paulo
smokable
storable
stovaine
Sholapur
Show Boat
showboat
slowback
scombrid
shoebill
shop bell
show bill
✧snowball
stopbank
smørbrød
snowboot
slobbery
slow burn
slow-burn
snobbery
snowbird
slobbish
sloebush
snobbish
snobbism
snow bush
snowbush
stop bath
slop bowl
stopcock
stoccado
scorched
scorcher
sloucher
smoocher
snow cone
shot-clog
snow-capt
show card
showcase
spot cash
stoicism
stoccata
sword-law
swordman
spondaic
shoddily
scolding
snowdrop
sword-arm
scordato
sword-cut
showdown
slow down
slowdown
stop down
stowdown
shoreman
stone-mad
stonerag
stoneraw
stone saw
storeman
scoleces
shoveler
sloe-eyed
snow-eyes
storeyed
score off
shove off
slope off
Stone Age
✧stone-age
scolecid
scopelid
Slovenia
snowed in
stone pit
slovenly
stonefly
smokebox
smoke-hos
slovenry
smoke-dry
Smolensk
Scopelus
score out
shore due
smoke out
snowed up
stone axe
scofflaw
scot-free
shot-free
snow flea
snowfall
scoffing
spoofery
scomfish
spoffish
sloughed
sloughis
spongoid
spongily
stodgily
shogging
slogging
shop girl
showgirl
soothsay
shothole
snow-hole
show home
Shoshone
Shoshoni
sloshing
soothing
shoehorn
smothery
slothful
soothful
Scotican
skokiaan
scolices
sporidia
stotinka
stotinki
stolidly
scolioma
slot into
spoliate
scorious
stocious
stotious
showjump
stock car
stockman
spot kick
stockade
spookily
stockily
shocking
smocking
stocking
stonking
shock dog
stockpot
Stockton
spookery
spookish
stockist
shoelace
shoulder
smoulder
shoplift
spoilage
snowlike
Scotland
scowling
shoaling
shouldn't
slobland
snobling
snowline
stowlins
smouldry
shoeless
shouldst
snowless
sootless
spotless
stopless
stop-loss
spoilful
storm jib
stormily
spooming
storming
stormful
spoon-fed
spoonfed
shoe nail
spoonily
scorning
swooning
scoinson
slowness
scornful
spoonful
scotomas
Shotokan
show over
stop over
stopover
scotomia
scotopia
scotopic
Sporozoa
Scorpian
snowpack
scoop net
stoppage

slop pail
slowpoke
sloppily
scooping
shopping
slopping
stooping
stopping
swopping
✧scorpion
Scorpios
Stoppard
scoopful
Scorpius
scourger
scouring
Sjögren's
showroom
shofroth
Scotsman
shop sign
spousage
Scots fir
snowslip
stooshie
spousals
sponsing
shoe shop
slop-shop
snowshoe
sponsion
Scorsese
scout car
scout law
Scottice
scouther
scowther
shoetree
short leg
short sea
shouther
sloetree
smoothen
smoother
Scottify
shoot off
shortage
short-oil
short rib
smoothie
smooth it
shop talk
smoothly
snootily
snottily
sportily
spottily
scouting
shooting
shotting
shouting
slotting
snorting
sporting
spotting
spouting
Storting
swotting
scontion
short ton
spontoon
shortarm
snottery
Scottish
shootist
shortish
stoutish
shoot-out
short cut
short-cut
snootful
sportful
sportive
shogunal
sporular
spot-weld
St Oswald
shopworn
slopwork
slowworm
scolytid
storying
showyard
Scolytus
snowy owl
sforzati
sforzato
smorzato
Sephardi
septaria
sapsagos
sopranos
sapucaia
sapidity
sapience
suppeago
sopheric
sopherim
supremos
septette
supremum
sept-foil
✧sapphics
sapphire
✧sapphism
sapphist
septimal
syphilis
supplial
sepalody
supplied
supplier
supplies
sepaloid
supplely
sepaline
supplant
sepalous
septleva
sepiment
saponify
supinely
saponite
supinate
siphonal
supposal
sapropel
siphonet
supposed
supposer
supposes
siphonic
superman
supermax
supernal
supertax
superadd
sap-green
superjet
superego
superfit
superbly
superior
superloo
superspy
soporose
suppress
separate
superate
saporous
soporous
superbug
supergun
sapi-utan
septuple
sequelae
sequence
sequined
surbahar
sarpanch
sortance
Syriarch
screamer
serrated
spreader
streaked
streaker
streamer
striated
surbased
surbated
surfaced
surfacer
spreathe
Sarmatia
Sarmatic
sarrasin
sarrazin
seriatim
serranid
siriasis
sorbaria
serially
sortable
sargasso
servants
Serranus
serratus
striatum
surf boat
scrabbed
scrubbed
scrubber
Scrabble®
scrabble
scribble
scribbly
strobila
strobile
strobili
saraband
scribing
Strabane
strobing
surfbird
scribism
strabism
Surabaya
surucucu
sprocket
Strachey
stricken
strucken
soricoid
sprackle
sprucely
strickle
strictly
soricine
siroccos
sure card
Syracuse
sericite
suricate
Siricius
spruce up
soredial
surf duck
shredded
shredder
stridden
shraddha
shred-pie
straddle
striddle
stroddle
strident
stradiot
soredium
shrieval
surveyal
sarcenet
sarsenet
screeder
screener
screever
shrieker
shrieved
sorcerer
streeted
screechy
spreethe
sardelle
sergeant
serjeant
sur-reyn'd
Sarpedon
surveyor
surcease
sarmenta
serve its
sirvente
serve out
surgeful
surrebut
seriffed
scrofula
serafile
sure-fire
surffish
scragged
shrugged
spragged
sprigged
shrug off
scroggie
scroggin
seraglio
scraggly
scriggle
scriggly
straggle
straggly
struggle
scrag-end
strigine
Strigops
strigose
strigate
sorehead
serfhood
surgical
surmisal
survival
sardines
services
spruiker
strained
strainer
straiten
surmiser
straicht
straight
streight
Sardinia
sorbitic
sordidly
straitly
surtitle
servient
streigne
servitor
sorbitol
survivor
sorriest
spraints
Sarajevo
strike in
striking
stroking
strike-on
strike up
sur place
surplice
scrolled
stroller
serology
serflike
stroll on!
strelitz
scramjet
scrammed
scrimped
scrummed
shrimper
strammel
Strimmer®
strummed
strummel
strummer
strumpet
scramble
scrimply
scrumple
sortment
scrumpox
scrimure
Sarum use
stramash
strumose
stromata
strombus
strumous
sirenian
springal
serenade
scrannel
shrinker
shrunken
springed
springer
sprinter
stranded
stranger
stringed
stringer
stronger
syringes
syrinxes
scrunchy
strontia
serenely
sprangle
springle
sprinkle
strangle
strinkle
strongly
Suriname
spring on
sirenise
soreness
spryness
sureness
serenata
serenate
serenity
strength
string up
strung up
strongyl
sirenize
sarcomas
surroyal
Sarcodes
sarconet
sermoner
sermonet
sorrowed
sorrower
strooken
sarcodic
sardonic
sermonic
Sorbonne
surmount
surround
sardonyx
scrap-man
Strepyan
strip map
scrapped
scrapper
scripted
scrupler
scruples
shrapnel
strapped
strapper
stripped
stripper
stropped
strip off
seraphic
seraphim
seraphin
strap-oil
strophic
scrapple
scraping
strepent
striping
Strephon
scrape up
Serapeum
strip out
Sartrian
sororial
sororise
surprise
sororate
sorority
sororize
stressed
serfship
stressor
serosity
spritzer
strutted
strutter
stratify
Saratoga
strategy
scratchy
stretchy
spritzig
scrattle
sprattle
spritely
scrutiny
serotine
sorption
serotype
stratose
stratous
stroupan
sprauncy
surquedy
scrouger
shrouded
sorbuses
sprouted
streusel
scrounge
straunge
straucht
straught
serpulid
surculus
stravaig
Serevent®
shriving
striving
screw cap
screw tap
straw-hat
straw man

scrawler
sprawler
scrowdge
strewage
shrewdie
shrewdly
screwing
strewing
strowing
screwtop
screw you
shrewish
screw eye
straying
sorryish
spray gun
Sassanid
sash bolt
sash cord
sesterce
suspence
systemed
systemic
sisterly
suspense
sestette
sestetto
syssitia
sessions
suss laws
sesamoid
Susannah
sassolin
systolic
sesspool
Sisyphus
sastruga
sastrugi
sasarara
siserary
susurrus
sissyish
Sathanas
satrapal
situated
satiable
sitz-bath
set about
setscrew
Sotadean
sithence
sitter-in
sittella
set terms
setter-on
setter-up
setiform
set piece
set-piece
set light
sit tight
set him up
satelles
sitology
settle in
settling
sateless
setulose
settle up
setulous
sit under
se-tenant
satanism
satanist
satanity
set one up
St-Tropez
set going
set point
set forth
set you up
set to two
set apart
Saturday
soterial
sutorial
sutorian
Saturnia
saturnic
saturant
satirise
satirist
satyress
satyrisk
saturate
satirize
set aside
set-aside
shut away
slug-a-bed
squeaker
squealer
soutache
sauba ant
sfumatos
spumante
stubbled
stumbler
squab pie
squabble
stud bolt
slubbing
snubbing
stubbing
studbook
slumbers
slumbery
stubborn
snubbish
squabash
stulchak
snub cube
scutcher
sous-chef
stuccoed
stuccoer
sour-cold
sourcing
squaccos
soundman
squad car
souldier
sturdied
sound off
squaddie
sturdily
scudding
sounding
sourdine
spudding
studding
sound bow
soundbox
squadron
shuddery
Stundism
Stundist
sound out
shut down
shutdown
saucepan
sour-eyed
squeegee
squeezer
souvenir
scutella
souterly
sautéing
Sauterne
saucebox
studenty
souped-up
scuffler
shuffler
snuffler
snuffles
squiffer
stuffily
snuffing
stuffing
snuffbox
soul food
stuff you
snuffers
studfarm
scumfish
slugfest
snuff out
spur gear
smuggled
smuggler
squegger
smudgily
spur-gall
squiggle
squiggly
snugging
sturgeon
saufgard
sluggard
snuggery
sluggish
smuggest
snuggest
southpaw
southsay
South Sea
Shu Ching
souchong
Southend
southing
scuchion
✧southron
slughorn
✧southern
scutiger
shuriken
squailer
stupidly
sauciest
saucisse
spurious
studious
shuck off
shucking
skulking
stunkard
spunk out
skullcap
squaller
squilgee
squelchy
spuilzie
squaloid
souvlaki
sculling
spurling
squalene
scullion
scullery
slumlord
shunless
soulless
spurless
slummock
squamula
squamule
scumming
slumming
stumming
sour mash
soul mate
Squamata
squamate
squamous
squander
squinter
stub-nail
sturnoid
shunning
spurning
stunning
sturnine
smugness
snub nose
snugness
sourness
sauropod
stumpage
sculpsit
stumpily
sculptor
scuppers
sourpuss
scuppaug
slump sum
stump out
spur-rial
spur-ryal
squarial
scurrier
spurrier
squireen
squirrel
squirter
squirage
scurrile
squarely
squirely
slurring
spurring
squaring
squarson
squarish
squiress
stuprate
square up
soul-scat
soul-sick
squasher
stunsail
spun silk
soul-scot
soul-shot
stuntman
scuttler
squatted
squatter
stultify
smuttily
squattle
shunting
shutting
sluttery
sputtery
sluttish
Saururae
scurvily
squawman
squawker
sourwood
studwork
studying
spunyarn
scuzzbag
sovranly
sovranty
sovietic
savagely
savagery
savegard
savagism
✧savannah
seven-day
savingly
suversed
severely
severity
savorous
savoured
savourly
✧savoyard
saw-edged
sawed-off
sawshark
sawblade
sewellel
sawbones
saw-tones
sawhorse
sawtooth
sewer gas
sewer rat
sowbread
sowarree
sewerage
saw frame
sewering
sow-drunk
sawgrass
sawdusty
sexually
saxe blue
sixscore
sixpence
sixpenny
sextette
sixtieth
sexology
Saxonian
Saxondom
Saxonise
Saxonism
Saxonist
sexiness
saxonite
Saxonize
sextolet
sex drive
saxatile
sextuple
soy sauce
skywards
scybalum
soya bean
skyscape
Scythian
say-piece
skydiver
skylight
sky pilot
Sky blues
spy plane
spyglass
soy flour
soya milk
sayonara
spy-money
say sorry
slyboots
styluses
sizeable
sizeably
syzygial
syzygies
sizzling
siziness
suzerain
tear a cat
tear away
tearaway
thanadar
thataway
tea dance
tea caddy
thalamic
Tia Maria®
tearable
tea table
to a fault
tradable
travails
tea wagon
Thanatos
tea party
thalamus
trapball
thatched
✧thatcher
tranchet
trauchle
tear duct
twaddler
T-bandage
tear drop
trapdoor
to and fro
Thaddeus
tear down
trade gap
teaseled
teaseler
traveled
traveler
trade off
trade-off
trapezia
trapezii
tsarevna
thanedom
travelog
teaberry
traverse
trabeate
travesty
tease out
tradeful
toadflax
trapfall
trayfuls
toadfish
team game
twanging
tracheae
tracheal
trashcan
trashman
trashier
tracheid
Toad Hall
trashily
trachoma
teaching
trashery
tea chest
trachyte
tragical
tea fight
traditor
trahison
tsaritsa
tear into
trad jazz
trackman
trackway
thanks be
trackbed
trackage
thanking
tracking
thank God
thank you
thankyou
track rod
thankful
trail-net
trawl-net
T-bar lift
trail off
thalloid
trail mix
traplike
tea plant
Thailand
thalline
trailing

Words marked ✧ can also be spelled with one or more capital letters

tramline
trapline
trawling
tearless
thawless
tea cloth
thallium
thallous
Teasmade®
trammels
tramming
teammate
traumata
train-oil
training
trainers
thatness
Tlalocan
tragopan
tea towel
teaboard
tea house
trappean
trampler
tramping
trapping
teaspoon
trampish
Trappist
tranquil
tea bread
tea break
tramroad
traprock
toadrush
transact
transect
transude
teamster
transfer
transmew
toad spit
transfix
tranship
transmit
transume
tram-stop
transept
transire
toastier
twattler
tractrix
tray-trip
tractile
To Autumn
tjanting
toasting
traction
tractors
tractate
tractive
traducer
trapunto
than whom
teamwork
teamwise
toadying
toadyish
toadyism
tzatziki
to blazes
tubbable
tubicole
tobaccos
Table Bay
table mat
table top
tableaux
table-cut
tableful
tubefuls
tube foot
tubiform
taboggan
toboggan
toboggin
Tubigrip®
tub-thump
tabbinet
tubbiest
tubelike
Tebilise®
tubeless
tabulate
tubulate
Tibullus
tubulous
Tebilize®
Tobin tax
Tübingen
tubenose
tabloidy
to-broken
tabooing
taberdar
Tiberias
tubercle
to borrow
tuberose
Taborite
Tiberius
tuberous
tabashir
to be sure
Tibb's Eve
tabouret
tabourin
to-bruise
tube well
tube worm
tabby cat
tabbying
tick away
tuckahoe
tic-tac-to
tick bird
tick down
tacked-on
tacahout
tactical
tachinid
tachisme
tackiest
techiest
tachiste
tuck into
tocology
tackling
tickling
tactless
ticklish
tuck-mill
techMARK®
to camera
technics
taconite
tick over
tick-over
tectonic
Tychonic
tack room
tacksman
tick shop
tuck shop
tick-tack
tick-tick
tick-tock
tucotuco
tucutuco
taciturn
tac-au-tac
tack-weld
to die for
tide gate
tide lock
tiddlier
tideland
toddling
tideless
tidemill
tidemark
TV dinner
tidiness
tide over
tide race
tidesman
tedisome
tidivate
tidewave
toddy cat
Teddy boy
the fancy
the sauce
toe dance
toe-dance
The Dagda
The Dandy
teenaged
teenager
the Fates
The Waves
✧the basij
thematic
theramin
trematic
the Backs
the balks
the narks
the ranks
The Eagle
the halls
trevally
thebaine
the Wagon
The Wasps
thesauri
The Hague
trembler
trembles
therblig
the above
Theaceae
theocrat
treacher
trencher
Trenches
tree calf
to excess
theodicy
treadler
trendier
tweedier
tweedler
trendily
tweedily
treading
The Idiot
Theodora
Theodore
teem down
Tuesdays
The Derby
the bends
the needy
the ready
the wedge
theremin
the seals
the Weald
the wells
Tremella
The Beano
therefor
The Pearl
the Beast
the Deity
trecento
thereout
The Reeve
The Verve
tree frog
Thetford
tree farm
tree fern
theogony
the which
the chair
the Chalk
the while
teething
the shiny
✧the thing
trephine
tee shirt
The Shire
the chase
thetical
the piece
theriaca
toe-piece
The Birds
The Miser
The Times
The Night
taenioid
the limit
The Kinks
The Field
tredille
the Lions
The Piano
the Widow
taeniate
the filth
the skids
trekking
tweaking
The Iliad
the elect
the slide
✧the blues
the Fleet
The Flies
theology
The Oldie
treelike
tree lily
the Alamo
the blind
tree line
the Flood
The Clerk
teemless
The Clash
thewless
tie clasp
treeless
the cloth
✧the smoke
thermals
thermion
tree moss
thermite
tweenage
treenail
the enemy
theonomy
the Union
tweeness
the known
teetotal
the Horae
the royal
the woman
the goods
tre corde
The Boxer
The Model
the novel
the cough
the works
the pools
the Boyne
the Downs
the downy
The Goons
the joint
the young
✧theropod
toe to toe
toe-to-toe
tremolos
The Doors
the House
the Norse
the Forty
The Month
the North
the South
teetotum
✧thespian
the Apple
trespass
The Dream
The Friar
the great
The Trial
tie-break
the crack
the Creed
the griff
The Frogs
thearchy
theurgic
the Proms
The Tramp
the briny
The Bronx
the drink
theorbos
the grape
the brass
theorise
theorist
the press
the fritz
the trots
the Greys
theorize
the usual
trewsman
tsessebe
Teesside
the Ashes
theistic
treeship
themself
theosoph
treasure
✧treasury
tressure
theatral
tree toad
the other
twenties
theatric
Theatine
The Sting
treating
trey-tine
treatise
the nuddy
the Muses
the mulga
the hulks
the curse
twelvemo
the Twins
the F-word
the twist
The Tyger
tweezers
taffetas
tafferel
tefillah
tefillin
taffrail
taghairm
tog value
tagmemic
teguexin
tegmenta
tug-of-war
taglioni
Tigrinya
tag along
Togolese
tegument
Taganrog
tiger cat
tigerish
tigerism
tiger nut
tiger eye
tightwad
together
tight end
tight ass
tightish
tohu bohu
Tahitian
T H Huxley
tail away
thin away
trimaran
thio-acid
tribadic
tribasic
twin axis
tribally
tridacna
trivalve
tailback
trilbies
tailband
tail boom
twin-born
tail coat
twitcher
Trinculo
third man
third way
twiddler
Third Age
thirding
Triodion
triadist
third eye
tripedal
tripe-man
toiseach
tail ends
toileted
trimeter
trimeric
trisemic
trilemma
taileron
toiletry
toilette
trifecta
triffidy
thin-film
thingamy
thigging
trigging
twigging
tailgate
trichoid
twichild
trichome
Taichung
trichina
triphone
trip-hook
this here
trichord

trichite
Trinidad
tritical
toilinet
tailings
twilight
twi-night
tritiate
te igitur
Triticum
thick ear
thickoes
thickset
trickier
tricklet
twinkler
trickily
triskele
thinking
tricking
trickery
thickish
trickish
thickety
think out
trick out
trial-day
trialled
trilloes
thirlage
triploid
tail-like
tail lamp
trifling
trilling
triplane
tripling
twin-lens
twinling
trillion
triglyph
tailless
toilless
trialism
trialist
triality
tailleur
trial run
trillium
triumvir
tail male
thiamine
trimming
triennia
triangle
thinning
twinning
thinners
thinness
thinnest
thinnish
thisness
trigness
trimness
triunity
trifocal
trigonal
tripodal
trizonal
tailored
trilobed
triforia
trigonic
trisomic
tritonia
Trizonia
tricorne
tricolor
triapsal
thiophen
trippier
trippler
thiophil
trippant
tripping
tailpipe
trippery
tailrace
tribrach
triarchy
tail rope
trigraph
thirster
tailskid
tailspin
Triassic
twinship
thio-salt
toilsome
twigsome
thin-spun
thin-sown
trim size
tric-trac
Tristram
triptych
tristich
teil tree
thirteen
thirties
twist-off
triptane
twisting
twitting
tainture
twittery
triptote
tristful
twin town
triethyl
tribunal
thiourea
tributer
Trimurti
thieving
thievery
thievish
tail wind
toilworn
tripwire
triaxial
trioxide
Trigynia
tricycle
thiazide
thiazole
triazole
thiazine
triazine
Taj Mahal
take away
takeaway
takeable
take arms
take a bow
take a pop
take back
take care
take down
take-down
take fire
take five
take heed
take hold
Tok Pisin
tokology
takamaka
takingly
tokenism
take note
take odds
take over
takeover
take part
take pity
Takoradi
take root
take rise
take ship
take silk
Take That
take wing
talkable
tellable
tillable
tiltable
tollable
tilt-boat
talk back
talkback
toll bait
telechir
toll call
telecoms
telecine
tall copy
telecast
tolldish
talk down
Toltecan
Taliesin
telferic
toll-free
telefilm
talkfest
tilefish
telegram
Taleggio
telegony
tollgate
tile-hung
Talpidae
talliths
talk into
talliate
talukdar
talcking
telemark
telomere
talented
tallness
talk over
talionic
tolbooth
teleplay
Tylopoda
talapoin
thlipsis
tulipant
teleport
telepath
telergic
tolerant
tolerate
talesman
talisman
tall ship
telestic
telesale
teleseme
talk shop
talk show
talkshow
talk tall
telltale
talktime
telethon
teletron
Teletype®
teletext
tellural
Talmudic
telluric
teleview
televise
telework
toleware
tallyman
tallying
tally-ho'd
tally-hos
tilt yard
tambalas
tympanal
timbales
tympanic
Tom Hanks
tameable
Tom Paine
Tom Waits
tympanum
time ball
time bill
time bomb
time code
timecard
timidity
tumidity
tamp down
tamperer
tempered
temperer
timbered
tumefied
time fuse
tomogram
Tom Thumb
tomahawk
tumpiest
Tamilian
time loan
timelier
tomalley
tumble in
temulent
timeline
tumbling
tumpline
temblors
tumulary
tameless
timeless
tombless
template
tumble up
to my mind
timoneer
tamanoir
tameness
Timonise
Timonism
Timonist
tamandua
tomentum
Timonize
temporal
Tom-noddy
Tom Jones
Tom Wolfe
tombolos
tamboura
✧tamworth
tamarack
Timor Sea
timbrel'd
tamarind
timariot
tomorrow
tamarisk
Timorese
temerity
temerous
timorous
tumorous
Tomasina
time slot
tomatoes
tomatoey
tempting
tamburin
time unit
timously
Timbuktu
time warp
time-work
time-worn
tommy bar
tommyrot
tommy gun
time zone
tendance
✧tantalic
Tanzania
tan balls
tannable
tentacle
tuneable
tantalum
✧tantalus
✧tenebrae
✧tenebrio
Tony Benn
tent coat
tunicked
tenacula
ten-score
tenacity
tonicity
Tunicata
tunicate
tone-deaf
tone down
tangency
tendence
tendency
tenpence
tenderer
tinkerer
tinseled
tunneled
tunneler
tenderly
tinselly
tunbelly
tenpenny
tingeing
tin terne
tangelos
tinselry
tanked up
tonneaus
tonneaux
tankfuls
tank farm
tuna fish
Tineidae
tontiner
tangible
tangibly
tenaille
tensible
tondinos
tangiest
tinniest
Tanaiste
tenuious
tinnitus
Tony Lock
tinglier
tangling
tingling
tinkling
tankless
tentless
tinglish
tintless
toneless
tuneless
Tanalith®
tinplate
tonalite
tonality
tenement
tinsmith
tenon saw
tinsnips
tenantry
tininess
tenendum
tentoria
tin works
tangoing
ten-pound
ten to one
tandoori
tangoist
tone poem
tent pole
tenurial
Tenerife
tendrons
tenor cor
tenoroon
tent rope
Tantrism
Tantrist
tenorist
tenorite
Tangshan
Tunisian
tongster
tungsten
tonishly
tanistry
tenesmus
tank trap
tung tree
tenotomy
tinstone
tint tool
tincture
tonsured
Tunguses
tongue it
Tungusic
tonguing
tend upon
tent-work
tentwise
Tennyson
thoracal
thoraces
thoraxes
two-faced
thoracic
troparia
teocalli
troubled
troubler
trombone
twoccing
two-score
trot-cozy
two-edged
two pence
twopence
thole pin
two bells
twopenny
tooled up
Thom Gunn
trogging
thoughts
toothier
trochlea
trophied
trochaic
trochoid
toothily
trochisk
trophesy
two-phase
trochite
toothful
trothful
tropical
two-piece

two-sided
two-timer
two-digit
trominos
teosinte
trollies
trolling
trotline
toodle-oo
Trollope
trollopy
thowless
troilism
troilist
troilite
trollius
trolleys
thornier
thornset
trouncer
✧thorough
two pound
two-horse
troopial
troupial
tool post
toolroom
tool shed
Taoistic
thousand
trossers
trousers
trowsers
troutlet
trottoir
trotting
trouting
trout rod
trotters
troutful
trouvère
trouveur
two by two
tap-dance
tap water
topmaker
tapeable
tappable
tippable
top table
type-body
tapacolo
tapaculo
type case
typecast
tape deck
tapadera
tapadero
tepidity
tuppence
to pieces
top-level
tape echo
tuppenny
top-heavy
typeface
tepified
typified
typifier
top whack
type-high
top-shelf
top-shell
topliner
topsides
toppings
tipsiest
top-slice
topology
typology
tapelike
tapeline
tape loop
tape-lure
tapeless
tapenade
toponymy
Typhoean
top-notch
✧typhonic
taphouse
toplofty
Typhoeus
taper off
toparchy
taper pin
tapiroid
tapering
top brass
top-dress
tephrite
top-proud
tapas bar
tape slap
type spec
tapestry
tap issue
tap stock
tape-tied
tipstaff
top stone
topotype
top quark
top tweet
tapeworm
tipsy key
tippy-toe
topazine
taqueria
tequilla
toquilla
tu quoque
tarlatan
turn away
Tyrtaean
Terrance
Torrance
tar paper
tartaned
tar water
terraced
terraces
threaden
threader
threaten
throated
turbaned
✧tartaric
Tartarie
Terrapin®
terrapin
terraria
threapit
tornadic
tarnally
✧tartarly
targa top
tarragon
Tir nan-Og
Tir-na-nOg
toreador
tornados
tartanry
Tartarus
terrazzo
terebrae
terebras
turn back
turn-back
turnback
throbbed
terebene
terabyte
turf-clad
turncoat
turncock
Turf Club
thridace
tire down
torn-down
turn down
turn-down
Tarpeian
three-man
three-way
targeted
tercelet
Turgenev
turreted
threepit
turmeric
terrella
three-ply
tortelli
torpedos
terzetta
terzetti
terzetto
tarted-up
to ruffl'd
teraflop
tara fern
torchier
tarwhine
torching
Tyrrhene
torchère
Torshavn
Tórshavn
terminal
torminal
toroidal
turbinal
tarsiped
Tarsipes
terminer
tirrivee
turbined
turbines
turnings
tarsioid
terrific
tirrivie
turn it in
terrible
terribly
torpidly
torridly
tortilla
turbidly
turgidly
✧tertiary
tardiest
tartiest
turfiest
turn into
✧terminus
tortious
turn it up
tarakihi
terakihi
Tirolean
Tyrolean
thrilled
✧thriller
Terylene®
tireling
turtling
thraldom
termless
tireless
Tirolese
torulose
tyreless
Tyrolese
thrum cap
thrummed
thrummer
thrombin
Turkmans
Turkmens
tyramine
tiramisu
thrombus
tarantas
Tironian
Turanian
threnode
threnody
thronged
tyrannic
tyrannis
Turandot
tartness
turbo car
turbocar
turbofan
Turcoman
Turkoman
turbojet
turn over
turnover
turlough
tarboosh
tarboush
tortoise
thripses
teraphim
turnpike
thrapple
thropple
tar brush
tartrate
Tiresias
Turk's cap
thrasher
threshel
thresher
thrissel
thruster
turnskin
turnspit
thristle
throstle
turnsole
tiresome
Teresina
tyrosine
teratoid
turn tail
throttle
teratoma
term-time
teru-tero
turn Turk
teratism
torcular
tortured
torturer
✧tartuffe
Targumic
toreutic
tartufos
turn upon
torquate
tortuous
thriving
throw off
throwing
thraward
thrawart
throw mud
throw out
throw-out
throw rug
teriyaki
tarrying
toss away
Tasmania
tastable
testable
testator
Tisha Bov
Test Acts
testamur
testatum
test card
test case
tesserae
tesseral
tasseled
tastevin
tasselly
tessella
taste bud
tasteful
testicle
tastiest
testiest
Tashkent
tuskless
tussocky
testrill
test tube
Tashtego
testudos
taskwork
tetrarch
tetracid
tetradic
tetrapla
tithable
tetragon
tetrapod
tetraxon
titubant
titubate
title bar
to the bad
tattered
titterer
tottered
totterer
tithe-pig
to the nth
Titograd
tetchier
tetchily
tattiest
total war
totalled
tutelage
tattling
titulary
tutelary
totalise
totality
totalize
totemism
totemist
Titanian
tetanoid
tetanise
Titaness
✧titanism
titanate
titanite
titanium
titanous
tetanize
tetronal
tattooed
tattooer
titmouse
Tithonus
titupped
tituping
Tatarian
tutorial
tutorage
tottring
tutoring
tutoress
tutorise
tutorism
tityre-tu
tutorize
totitive
tittuped
titivate
toucanet
Tauranga
touracos
true-bred
true bill
thumbpot
true-born
thumbnut
thumbs up
thumbs-up
true blue
true-blue
truncate
trundler
thudding
thundery
trumeaux
truffled
Truffaut
trudging
trudgeon
thuggery
thuggish
thuggism
touch pad
truchman
teuchter
touchier
truchmen
touch off
touchily
touching
touch-box
toughish
tough guy
tough out
truthful
thurifer
thurible
Trujillo
touristy
truckman
truckler
truckage
trucking
trunking
trunkful
truelove
Thutmose
trunnion
tournure
truantry
tautness
thusness
trueness
tautomer
Teutonic
Toulouse
tautonym
thumping
trumping
trumpery
thump out
Teucrian
Thurrock
tau cross
Thursday
truistic
tsutsumu
trussing
trustier
tau staff
trustily
true time
taunting
trusting
trustful

Tauruses
truquage
truqueur
thuswise
tousy tea
Tuvaluan
tovarich
taverner
tovarish
thwacker
town hall
towelled
toweling
townland
townling
towplane
townless
tow truck
tawdrier
thwarted
thwarter
tawdrily
thwartly
towardly
towering
towns gas
townsman
township
townskip
town talk
tawny owl
taxiarch
tax haven
taxpayer
textbook
Taxaceae
toxicant
toxocara
toxicity
tuxedoes
Taxodium
toxaemia
toxaemic
text-hand
textless
taxonomy
tax point
tax break
taxi rank
taxation
Taxotere®
taxative
textural
textured
textuary
tax exile
Tay-Sachs
thyreoid
tayberry
try a fall
tryingly
toywoman
thyloses
thylosis
thyroxin
try house
Thyestes
thyrsoid
toyishly
Toy Story
thymuses
unabated
unamazed
unawares
upadaisy
unanchor
up-anchor
unaneled
unargued
unaching
Upanisad
unarisen
uralitic
uranitic
unallied
USA Today
una corda
unadored
unatoned
unavowed
unafraid
upas-tree
unartful
unactive
unamused
uranylic
umbrated
unbeaten
unbiased
unblamed
unbraced
umbratic
unbraste
unbacked
unbuckle
unbedded
unbidden
unbodied
unbudded
unboding
unbreech
umble-pie
umbrella
umbrello
umbrette
unbegged
unbaited
unbridle
umbriere
umbellar
unbelief
unbelted
unbolted
unbanded
unbanked
unbended
unbonnet
unbenign
unbundle
urbanely
urbanise
urbanism
urbanist
umbonate
urbanite
urbanity
urbanize
unbloody
unblowed
unbooked
unbroken
unbarbed
unbarked
unbarred
unburden
unburied
unburned
unbereft
unburrow
unbeseem
unbishop
unbathed
unbitted
unbutton
unbrused
unbought
unchancy
uncoated
uncharge
unclassy
unchaste
Uncle Sam
unclench
unchewed
Uncle Tom
upcheard
uncreate
unciform
unco guid
uncoined
uncalled
unculled
uncombed
uncomely
upcoming
uncommon
uncandid
uncinate
uncloudy
unchosen
unclosed
uncloven
uncooked
unclothe
urceolus
uncapped
uncipher
uncurbed
uncurled
uncurved
upcurved
uncaring
ulcerate
ulcerous
uncashed
uncostly
unchurch
unclutch
uncaused
uncaught
upcaught
uncouple
unctuous
uncowled
uncoyned
undraped
undubbed
undecked
undocked
undecent
ut dictum
undeeded
undreamt
undefide
undefied
undriven
US dollar
undulled
undulant
undulose
undelete
undulate
undulous
undammed
undamned
undamped
undimmed
undinted
undinism
undoomed
undrossy
undipped
under-jaw
underlap
underlay
underman
under par
underpay
undersay
under way
underway
underact
underfed
underlet
undersea
underset
under age
under-age
underbid
underdid
underlie
underlip
underpin
underwit
undersky
under-boy
underdog
under tow
undertow
underarm
underuse
udderful
underbuy
undercut
underfur
underrun
undashed
undesert
undouble
undivine
undevout
undazzle
unelated
unending
ureteral
ureteric
unevenly
urethrae
urethral
urethras
urethane
unedited
uredines
uredinia
uteritis
username
unespied
unearned
unerring
uneasily
uneathes
usefully
unenvied
unfeared
unflawed
unframed
unfabled
unfading
unfreeze
unfairly
unfriend
unfilial
unfallen
unfelled
unfilled
unfilmed
unfolded
unfolder
upfollow
unfanned
unfenced
unfunded
unfooted
unfrozen
unformal
unforced
unforged
unformed
unfurred
unforbid
unforgot
unfasten
unfished
unfetter
unfitted
unfeudal
unfought
unfaulty
unfixity
ungeared
unglazed
ungraced
ungraded
ungrazed
upgrader
ungravly
ungifted
unguided
ungainly
unguilty
ungalled
ungilded
ungulate
ungummed
ungenial
ungentle
ungently
urgently
ungloved
unground
upgrowth
ungirded
ungorged
urge that
ungotten
upgather
ungauged
ungiving
ungowned
upheaval
unhealed
unheated
unhearse
unhealth
unhacked
unhedged
unhidden
uphudden
unheeded
unhailed
unhaired
unhalsed
unhelmed
unhelped
unholpen
upholder
unholily
unhallow
unhomely
unhanged
unhinged
unhunted
unhonest
unhooded
unheppen
unharmed
unheroic
ushering
usheress
unhatted
unhatch'd
unhoused
uric acid
up in arms
urinator
univalve
unimbued
unit cell
unit cost
unitedly
universe
unifilar
utiliser
utilizer
unionise
✧unionism
✧unionist
unionize
unilobar
unipolar
unisonal
univocal
unilobed
unironed
unicolor
uninured
uniquely
ubi supra
ubiquity
uniaxial
unicycle
unifying
unjustly
unjoyful
unjoyous
unknight
unkenned
unkennel
unkindly
unkingly
unkissed
unleaded
unleased
unloaded
unloader
unlearnt
unlicked
unlocked
uplocked
unlidded
unlading
uplifted
uplifter
unlikely
unlimber
unlineal
unlinked
uplander
ugliness
unlooked
unloosen
unlopped
Ullapool
unlorded
unlordly
unlisted
unlively
unlovely
unliving
unloving
unlawful
unmoaned
Ulmaceae
unmodish
unmade-up
unmeetly
unmuffle
unmailed
unmaimed
unmaking
upmaking
unmelted
unmilked
unmilled
unmanned
unminded
unmonied
unmantle
unmapped
unmarked
unmarred
upmarket
unmasked
unmasker
unmissed
un-Mosaic
unmoving
unmuzzle
uintaite
unneeded
urnfield
unnaneld
unnerved
unnethes
unnetted
unnative
uroscopy

urodelan
udometer
unobeyed
unopened
Ulothrix
urochord
utopiast
uxorious
uno animo
urologic
upon oath
urostege
urostyle
urostomy
unplaced
unplayed
unpraise
unpacked
unpacker
unpicked
unpreach
unpeeled
unpeered
unpoetic
unpretty
unpained
unpaired
unpoised
unpriced
unprimed
unprized
unpliant
unpoison
unprison
unpriest
umptieth
unpolled
unpulled
unpolish
unpolite
unpanged
unpannel
unpenned
unpinked
unpinned
unproper
unproved
unproven
unpeople
unpurged
upper ten
umpirage
upper lip
unperson
uppercut
unposted
uppishly
unpathed
unpitied
unpruned
umquhile
unquoted
unreaped
upreared
unreally
unreason
unribbed
unrubbed
unracked
unrecked
utriculi
unridden
unriddle
unrifled
unruffle
unrigged
unraised
unreined
upraised
unringed
uprootal
unroofed
unrooted
uprooter
unripped
unrepaid
unrepair
uprising
unrotted
unrotten
unrouged
unroused
unrhymed
unstarch
unscaled
unsealed
unseamed
unseated
unshaded
unshaked
unshaken
unshamed
unshaped
unshapen
unshared
unshaved
unshaven
unslaked
unsoaped
unspared
unstated
unstayed
unswayed
unswathe
unstable
unseason
unshadow
upstairs
unsubtle
unsocial
unsecret
unsicker
unsocket
unsucked
unsodden
unsaddle
up so down
unsteady
ulstered
unseeded
unseemly
unseeing
unsued-to
unsifted
unsafely
unsafety
unsigned
unsphere
unstitch
unsailed
unsained
unseized
unsliced
unsoiled
unsuited
up sticks
unsalted
unsolder
unsolved
unsolemn
Ursuline
unseldom
unsummed
unsensed
unsunned
unsmoked
unspoken
unspoilt
unsmooth
unsapped
unsupple
upstream
unshrubd
unstruck
unsorted
upstroke
unsprung
unstring
unstrung
upsprang
upspring
upsprung
unshroud
unsashed
upsetter
unsettle
unsating
unsluice
unsouled
unsoured
unstuffy
unsought
unsexual
unsexist
unthatch
ultrared
unthawed
untraced
untraded
ultraism
ultraist
untucked
untackle
urticant
urticate
untidily
up to date
up-to-date
untailed
untilled
uptilted
Ustilago
until now
ultimacy
untemper
untombed
untimely
ultimata
ultimate
Ultonian
untanned
untended
untender
untented
untinged
untinned
untangle
untenant
untapped
unthread
untarred
unturned
upturned
unthrift
unturbid
unthrone
untiring
uttering
ulterior
upthrust
utterest
untasted
untested
untether
untitled
up to time
untaught
untruism
untrusty
uptowner
untoward
unusable
unusably
uvularly
unuseful
urushiol
uvulitis
usurious
usurping
usufruct
unviable
unviewed
unveiled
unveiler
unvoiced
unvulgar
unvalued
unvented
unvaried
unversed
unvirtue
unvetted
unvizard
unweaned
unweapon
unwebbed
unwedded
unwieldy
unweeded
unweened
unwifely
unwigged
unwalled
unwilled
unwilful
unwanted
unwinged
unwonted
unwooded
unwarded
unwarmed
unwarned
unwarped
unworded
unworked
unwormed
unworthy
unwarely
unwarily
upwardly
unwashed
unwashen
unwasted
unwished
unwisely
unwisdom
unwetted
unwatery
unyeaned
vraicker
viameter
via media
Vladimir
viaticum
via trita
vibrancy
vibrator
vibratos
vibrissa
vibronic
viburnum
vice-dean
vacherin
vaccinal
vaccinia
vice-king
vicelike
vocalion
viceless
vocalese
vocalise
vocalism
vocalist
vocality
vocalize
vicinage
vacantly
vicenary
vicinity
vacuolar
✧victoria
vicarial
vicarage
vice ring
vicaress
victress
vicarate
vacation
vocation
vocative
victuals
Vichyite
Vadodara
Vodafone®
Vedantic
videndum
videotex
videofit
videoing
view away
viewable
Viet Cong
Vietcong
viewdata
viewless
Viennese
vieux jeu
VHF radio
vagrancy
vagabond
vogueing
vigneron
vignette
vigilant
vagility
vegelate
Vigilius
Vegemite®
vaginula
vaginule
vaginant
veganism
vaginate
vagaries
vagarish
vigorish
vigoroso
vigorous
vagotomy
vegetant
vegetate
vegetive
Vehmique
vehement
voidance
voidable
voir dire
voice box
vainesse
voiceful
voidings
veilless
vainness
voidness
valiance
valiancy
villager
villagio
villatic
volcanic
✧vulcanic
Valhalla
valuable
valuably
vulgarly
villainy
valuator
viliacos
villadom
Voltaire
voltaism
Volscian
velocity
validate
validity
valvelet
velveret
velveted
volleyed
volleyer
valve off
vulsella
Valletta
velleity
Villette
vilified
vilifier
villiaco
villiago
vulvitis
volpinos
velskoen
volplane
velamina
volumise
volumist
volumize
valanced
Valencia
vildness
vileness
vallonia
Vellozia
vilipend
✧valerian
Vila Real
valorise
velarise
valorous
velarium
valorize
velarize
volutoid
volatile
valeting
volitant
volition
volution
velatura
volitate
volitive
valvulae
valvular
valvules
Volsungs
volvulus
Valkyrie
vampiric
vamplate
vambrace
vomerine
vomiting
vomitory
vomitive
Van Halen
vintager
vendange
Vandalic
venially
ventaile
ventayle
vindaloo
vine-clad
vena cava
vanadate
vanadium
vanadous
venidium
veneerer
vendeuse
vendetta
vengeful
Vonnegut
venogram
vine-gall
vinegary
Vanaheim

Words marked ✧ can also be spelled with one or more capital letters

vent-hole
vendible
vendibly
venville
vincible
vine-leaf
vinology
vanillin
vin blanc
vinolent
vaneless
ventless
venality
Vinylite
venomous
vin rouge
Ventolin®
vine-prop
vent-pipe
vent-plug
venereal
venerean
Vanbrugh
ventring
venerate
vent'rous
ventrous
Venusian
vanisher
vanessid
venosity
vinosity
Venetian
Venutian
venation
Vanitory®
vanitory
Van Buren
venturer
vanguard
vanquish
vinculum
vandyked
vineyard
violater
violable
violably
violator
violence
vapidity
vapulate
viperine
vaporise
viperish
vaporous
viperous
vaporize
vapoured
vapourer
vaqueros
variance
verdancy
vartabed
verbatim
variable
variably
verbally
vernally
Verlaine
variceal
viricide
virucide
verecund
varactor
varicose
veracity
voracity
Veracruz
viridian
Varidase®
viridite
viridity
varietal
verse-man
vergence
vergency
verderer
verselet
vertexes
vortexes
verdelho
versed in
viraemia
viraemic
variedly
verderor
varletry
vertebra
varletto
verified
verifier
variform
viragoes
voragoes
virogene
very good
vertical
virginal
vortical
verditer
vermined
vertices
vortices
verbiage
verticil
Virginia
virgin it
vernicle
versicle
virginly
vertigos
verligte
virology
virulent
verbless
virilism
virility
virement
veranda'd
verandah
virandas
✧veronica
virandos
Varanasi
Veronese
Voronezh
variolar
verboten
vermouth
variorum
verkramp
veristic
very same
varistor
verities
veratrin
veratrum
verrucae
verrucas
verrugas
verjuice
verdured
vargueño
verquere
verquire
virtuosa
virtuose
virtuosi
virtuoso
vertuous
virtuous
very well
viscacha
visually
vis major
vassalry
visibles
vesicula
vesicant
vesicate
vesperal
visceral
vasiform
visagist
Visigoth
Vespidae
vestigia
vespiary
vestiary
Vaseline®
vestment
vastness
visional
visioned
visioner
visnomie
✧viscount
Visconti
✧visitant
visiting
vascular
vestural
vestured
vesturer
vasculum
✧vesuvian
Vesuvius
vitiable
vitiator
Vitaceae
vaticide
viticide
vote down
vitreous
Vitalian
vitiligo
vital air
vitellin
vituline
vitalise
vitalism
vitalist
voteless
vitality
vitellus
vitalize
vitamine
vitamin H
Vittoria
votaress
votarist
vitative
vauncing
Vauxhall®
voutsafe
voussoir
vaultage
vauntage
vaulting
vaunting
vauntery
vauntful
vivacity
vividity
vivifier
vivipary
viverrid
vivarium
vivisect
vavasory
vavasour
viva voce
vowelled
vowelise
vowelize
vexillum
vexingly
vixenish
vexation
vexatory
voyageur
vizcacha
vizament
vizirial
vizarded
vizirate
wear away
wearable
wear down
whaleman
weakener
weak-eyed
weaseler
whatever
whale oil
weaselly
what else?
wharf rat
wharfage
wharfing
what for a
weakfish
wrangler
wrathily
wrathful
wear iron
wham into
weariful
whacking
wrackful
what-like
weakling
weanling
wraxling
whamming
weakness
whatness
what next?
weaponed
wrapover
what of it?
weaponry
wrappage
whapping
wrapping
what reck?
wealsman
weak side
what's new?
weak spot
what then?
wear thin
what time
wearying
weary out
wobegone
webwheel
wobbling
wibble on
wickered
wickedly
wadeable
widebody
wideband
wide-eyed
wade into
waddling
wideness
Wodenism
wide open
wide-open
widowman
Wedgwood
Wedgwood®
wretched
wheedler
whenever
wherever
wye-level
wherefor
whereout
whey-face
weel-far'd
weel-far't
weephole
weeviled
weevilly
wreckage
wrecking
wreakful
wreckful
wheelman
wheeling
weedless
weetless
wheel-cut
wheel out
woe worth
wherries
wheat ear
wheatear
wheat eel
wreathed
wreathen
wreather
wrestler
wrest pin
wheat fly
whetting
waesucks
woefully
wheezily
wheezing
W C Fields
wifehood
wifelike
waffling
waffle on
wifeless
wig-maker
wage fund
wig block
wageless
wagon bed
wagonage
wagon-lit
wagon box
wagonful
✧waggoner
wagmoire
wage plug
wage slip
wage work
Wahhabis
Wahabism
Wahabite
Wahiguru
whip away
wait-a-bit
writable
whimbrel
whizbang
whipbird
whinchat
whipcord
weirdies
whidding
weird out
whitecap
Whitelaw
white man
white rat
white wax
white-leg
whitener
White Sea
write off
write-off
white lie
white tie
white-tie
white ale
whitefly
writerly
white ant
Whiteboy
white boy
white-hot
whitepot
while-ere
white arm
white out
white-out
write out
white-eye
whiffled
whiffler
whiffing
wriggler
wring off
whigging
wringing
Whiggery
Whiggish
Whiggism
wring out
writhled
weigh off
weighage
weighing
whip hand
writhing
weigh out
weigh-out
writings
whiniard
whinid'st
whipjack
wrinkled
whisking
whiskers
whiskery
whirlbat
whirl off
waiflike
whiplike
whirling
whitling
Whieldon
wait list
wait-list
whiplash
whipless
Weizmann
whimming
whinnied
whipping
whispery
whirring
waitress
whipster
whitster
Whigship
whimsily
Whin Sill
wainscot
waist bag
whistled
✧whistler
whittler
whittret
wristlet
whiptail
wrist pin
wait upon
whim-wham
Whit week
whipworm
whinyard
whizz kid
whizzing
wakeless
wakening
wakerife
walk away
walk-away
welladay

Words marked ✧ can also be spelled with one or more capital letters

well away
wellaway
wile away
Wallasey
Walhalla
walkable
weldable
willable
wallaroo
walk awry
wild arum
well boat
wild boar
well-bred
wall bars
well-born
wild-born
well curb
wild card
well deck
wild duck
wild-duck
well-doer
well done
well-done
wolf down
walleyed
wildered
wild-eyed
Wolseley®
welter in
walker-on
Wolffian
wildfire
wallfish
wolffish
wildfowl
wild goat
wall game
wellhead
Welshman
well hole
well-hung
Wild Hunt
waldhorn
williwaw
wild iris
walk into
well-knit
wale knot
wall knot
well-kept
wildlife
wolflike
wildland
wolfling
wall-less
weldless
will-less
well-made
walk-mill
walkmill
weldment
wild mare
wall moss
Weldmesh®
well-nigh
wellness
wildness
wiliness
wolf note
wall newt
walk over
walkover
walloper
wallowed
wallower
welcomer
well over
willowed
wild oats
wolf pack
wall pass
well-read
wild rice
well room
waldrapp
Wellsian
well seen
well-seen
wolfskin
wild silk
Will Self
✧wallsend
well-to-do
wall tree
well then
walk tall
wall tile
wild type
Walpurga
wall unit
well up in
wilfully
wall walk
well, well
wildwood
wallwort
well-worn
well-wish
Wild West
Walkyrie
willyard
willyart
waltzing
womblike
wambling
womanise
womanish
womanize
✧wannabee
winnable
Wanganui
wingbeat
wing back
wind band
windblow
windburn
wind cone
wine cask
wing case
wingding
want down
wind down
wind-down
wandered
✧wanderer
wintered
winterer
wondered
wonderer
wingedly
winterly
wanderoo
Winifred
windfall
wind farm
windgall
winchman
Windhoek
wanthill
wind harp
Winnipeg
winnings
wongiing
wine lake
winglike
wangling
windlass
windless
wine list
wingless
wontless
windmill
wanwordy
windowed
wingover
winnowed
winnower
wantonly
win round
wanworth
wine palm
wind pump
windpipe
wind park
wind rock
wine rack
wind-rode
wintrily
windring
wind rose
wondrous
wingspan
windsock
wind side
windsail
windship
wineskin
wing shot
wing-shot
windsurf
windward
wood acid
wool ball
woodbind
✧woodbine
wood-born
woodchat
wood coal
woodcock
woodchip
wool clip
wool comb
wool card
wood duck
wool-dyed
woolding
whomever
whosever
wood-evil
woodenly
whole-hog
whoredom
whoreson
woolfell
wrongful
wrongous
whoa-ho-ho
woodhole
wood ibis
whorlbat
woodlice
woollies
wool-like
woodland
woodlark
woodless
woodmeal
wool mill
wood mite
wooingly
woodness
woodnote
wood opal
woolpack
whoopsie
woodpile
wood pulp
whooping
whopping
woodruff
woodroof
woodrush
woodsman
✧woolsack
woodshed
woolshed
wood sage
woodskin
wood tick
who but he
whodunit
wood wren
woodwale
woodwind
wood wool
Woop Woop
woodward
woodwork
woodworm
woolward
woolwork
wood wasp
woodwose
woodyard
wipe away
wipeable
wiped out
warn away
warragal
wire away
workaday
war dance
warfarer
war-gamer
warfarin
warhable
warragle
workable
workably
war paint
warranty
warragul
workboat
work back
warm boot
warm-boot
wordbook
workbook
wire bird
Würzburg
word bite
work camp
wardcorn
wormcast
wiredraw
word-deaf
World War
world-old
World Cup
warm down
warm-down
warrener
worse off
wardenry
war-weary
warmed-up
workfolk
workflow
workfare
worm gear
weregild
wordgame
workgirl
wire-heel
worthies
wire-hair
wormhole
worthily
Worthing
war whoop
war chest
worthful
warrigal
workings
warrison
war widow
wirricow
worricow
wire into
work into
workload
wartlike
wormlike
warbling
warplane
wire line
wordlore
wareless
wartless
wireless
wordless
workless
war cloud
wariment
wardmote
workmate
wire nail
wariness
warmness
wiriness
work over
work-over
warhorse
wordplay
war trial
wardrobe
war bride
war crime
wardroom
war-proof
workroom
wire rope
wardress
wormseed
wardship
worksome
workshop
wire-sewn
worm tube
work upon
word wrap
workwear
wartweed
workweek
werewolf
wire wool
wormwood
wartwort
wirework
wireworm
wirewove
worky-day
worrying
worrycow
worry out
wurtzite
wash away
wash-away
wistaria
washable
wastable
wiseacre
washball
West Bank
wishbone
washbowl
wash-dirt
wash down
Wesleyan
waste bin
wisteria
westerly
wastelot
washed-up
wasteful
wastfull
washings
wasp-like
wise-like
washland
westland
westlins
wiseling
wish list
westmost
waspnest
wastness
wiseness
wastrife
washroom
West Side
wash sale
wash well
Westwood
washwipe
westward
wish-wash
wetlands
wettable
with calf
withdraw
withdrew
wet meter
withered
witter on
wet lease
wet-lease
with foal
watch cap
watchman
watch key
witch-elm
withheld
withhold
watching
witching
watchbox
watchdog
witchery
watchful
watch out
watch-out
watt-hour
wattling
witeless
wet plate
witblits
wittolly
water bag
water gap
water gas
waterman
water ram
water rat
water tap
waterway
water yam
water ice
water bed
waterhen
water-jet
water key
waterage
water-ski
water fly
watering
water boa
water box
water cow
water dog
water god
waterlog
Waterloo
water lot
water pot
waterpox
waterish
water bug
water bus
water gun
water rug
wet assay
with that
with this
wet nurse

wet-nurse
withwind
Wat Tyler
woundily
wounding
waukmill
whupping
waukrife
waveband
wave down
waveform
wivehood
wavelike
waveless
waviness
Wavy Navy
Waverley
wavering
waverous
wax paper
waxed end
waxberry
wax light
wax plant
waxcloth
waxiness
waxworks
wayfarer
waylayer
way-maker
wayleave
waywiser
way-going
way point
wayboard
waygoose
Weymouth
waybread
way train
wizardly
wizardry
X-ray tube
X-ray unit
xylocarp
xyloidin
xylology
xylomata
Xylonite®
xylonite
xenogamy
Xanthian
xanthein
xanthoma
xanthene
xanthine
Xanthura
xanthate
Xanthium
xanthous
Xantippe
xenolith
Xenophon
xenophya
xenurine
xenotime
xeromata
xeransis
xerantic
xeraphin
yea-sayer
yearbook
yeanling
yearling
yearlong
yearning
yearn for
yachting
Ygdrasil
yodeller
yielding
yoghourt
Yugo-Slav
Yugoslav
✧yahrzeit
Yokohama
yokelish
yakimono
yoke-mate
yoke-toed
yakitori
yokozuna
Yale lock
yeldrock
yeldring
yoldring
✧yuletide
yglaunst
yonderly
Yenglish
Yinglish
Yanomami
Yanomamo
yongthly
yeomanly
yeomanry
ybounden
yarraman
yardbird
yarn-dyed
yersinia
yardland
yard sale
Yorktown
yarmulka
yarmulke
yardwand
yeshivah
yeshivas
yeshivot
ypsiloid
yestreen
yataghan
yttrious
ytterbia
young man
Young Vic
youngest
youngish
young gun
youthful
yourself
zealless
zealotry
Zoanthus
zabaione
zebrinny
zibeline
zuchetta
zuchetto
zecchine
zecchini
zecchino
zucchini
zoccolos
zodiacal
zaddikim
Zedekiah
zoetrope
zigzaggy
zygodont
zygaenid
zygomata
zygotene
ziggurat
Zigeuner
zugzwang
zaibatsu
zwieback
zoiatria
Zakopane
zikkurat
Zola Budd
Zelanian
zylonite
Zalophus
zelatrix
zulu time
Zimbabwe
zombiism
zymology
zamindar
zemindar
zambomba
zampogna
zomboruk
zamarras
zamarros
zemstvos
zindabad
zone axis
zanjeros
Zane Grey
Zanzibar
zingiber
Zantippe
Zentippe
Zantiote
zinckify
zincking
zoneless
zaniness
zenithal
zonation
zoomancy
zoolater
zoopathy
zoolatry
zooscopy
zooecium
zooperal
zoogenic
zoometry
Zoophaga
zoophagy
zoophile
zoophily
zoothome
zoochore
zoochory
Zoophyta
zoophyte
zeolitic
zoolitic
zoonitic
zoogloea
zoom lens
zooblast
zoonoses
zoonomia
zoonomic
zoonosis
zoonotic
zootomic
zootoxin
zoomorph
zoosperm
zoospore
zoograft
zootrope
zoot suit
Zionward
zoocytia
zootypic
zippered
✧zeppelin
zap along
zopilote
zip-front
Zip® drive
zircaloy
zero hour
zero in on
zorillos
zerumbet
zirconia
zirconic
Zircoloy®
zero-rate
zaratite
zarzuela
zero-zero
zastruga
zastrugi
Zhu Jiang
zizyphus

9 – odd

avalanche
à l'abandon
alabamine
atacamite
alalagmoi
alalagmos
agalactia
ataractic
amarantin
alabaster
Amarantus
adamantly
Alan Bates
Alan Clark
anarchise
anarchize
anarchial
anarchism
anarchist
acalculia
avascular
✧araucaria
as accords
as and when
abandoned
abandonee
anandrous
agateware
Araneidae
awareness
abasement
abatement
amazement
Acalephae
acalephan
aware that
asafetida
awakening
academism
academics
academist
Agamemnon
Agapemone
arabesque
analectic
analeptic
amarettos
analgesia
analgesic
abashedly
abashless
abashment
Arachnida
anathemas
at a why-not
arachnoid
anaphoric
✧anacharis
apathetic
apathaton
acaridean
amazingly
acaricide
Adamitism
acaridian
arabinose
acariasis
anabiosis
anabiotic
atavistic
alack-a-day
Alan Knott
available
availably
as all that
at a glance
Anaglypta®
anaplasty
anaclitic
Anacletus
alarm call
alarmedly
alarm-bell
a rainy day
anamneses
anamnesis
amazon ant
at a low ebb
amazonite
anabolite
analogise
analogize
anatomise
anatomize
aragonite
amatorial
anabolism
amatorian
Amazonian
Anatolian
analogist
anatomist
✧ayatollah
analogous
acarology
à la poupée
a cappella
Alan Paton
anaerobic
anabranch
amaurosis
anacruses
anacrusis
amaurotic
amassable
Adar Sheni
amassment
Alan Sugar
Adam's wine
Adam Smith
Adansonia
a vast many
adaptable
apartheid
apartness
apartment
acanthine
abactinal
acanthoid
at a stroke
acanthous
ananthous
avant-goût
Anastasia
anastasis
anastatic
a fast buck
anaptyxis
Atahualpa
ayahuasco
analysand
at any hand
at any rate
amaryllid
amaryllis
at any cost
away you go!
arblaster
Ambleside
Albufeira
ambiguity
ambagious
ambiguous
aubrietia
ambulacra
ambulance
ambulator
album-leaf
Alban Berg
albinoism
albinotic
ambrosial
✧ambrosian
ambrotype
amberjack
Albertina
albertite
aubergine
amber-fish
albarelli
albarello
alburnous
arboreous
ambergris
arboretum
ambassage
ambuscade
ambuscado
ambush bug
albescent
albespine
asbestine
Ambystoma
asbestous
albespyne
arbitrage
arbitrate
arbitrary
arbitress
abbotship
arbitrium
albatross
ambitious
arbovirus
amblyopia
amblyopic
archangel
arcuation
archaiser
archaizer
archducal
archduchy
accedence
accidence
arch-druid
archeress
arch-enemy
asclepiad
accretive
alchemise

alchemize
accretion
asclepias
Asclepios
Asclepius
alchemist
arcsecond
anciently
ancientry
archetype
arch-fiend
arch-felon
alcoholic
Archibald
acclimate
archimage
Archimago
Arctiidae
architect
arctic fox
archivist
acclivity
archilowe
acclivous
archivolt
architype
ancillary
accompany
accumbent
Alcantara®
ascendant
ascendent
ascensive
ascending
arc-en-ciel
accension
✧ascension
accentual
Arctogaea
✧anchorage
anchoveta
anchoress
arctophil
anchor-ice
anchorite
auctorial
Alcyonium
anchor leg
anchor man
anchor-man
archology
archontic
acceptant
acceptive
ancipital
accipiter
alcarraza
ascorbate
ascertain
accordant
Ascaridae
ascarides
according
accordion
accessary
accusable
access eye
accession
archstone
ascospore
accessory
ancestral
ascetical
ascitical
accourage
au courant
accoutred
anchylose
András Fay
andradite
Aldebaran
abdicable
adducible
addictive
adductive
abduction
addiction
adduction
audacious
abdicator
audiencia
addlement
André Gide
addressed
addressee
addresser
addressor
addresses
Andreotti
aldehydic
and things
abdominal
andantino
Audenarde
audiotape
androecia
✧andromeda
audiophil
audio disc
audio disk
Androcles
audio book
andrology
audiology
audiogram
arduously
androgyne
androgyny
audiphone
Aldershot
Alderamin
adderwort
Aldis lamp
andesitic
auditress
auditoria
and twenty
Alexandra
Alexander
Aceraceae
averagely
alewashed
acetamide
Amerasian
arenation
Alemannic
âme damnée
amenaunce
Ametabola
apetalous
asepalous
agelastic
acetabula
alembroth
acescence
acescency
amendable
amendment
anecdotal
Adeodatus
an even bet
âme perdue
âme de boue
Amen glass
avengeful
Amenhotep
Americana
Americano
Amerindic
aperiodic
aperitive
americium
Aretinian
amenities
Alex James
acellular
areolated
areometer
Apennines
adenomata
adenoidal
awesomely
adenosine
ale-conner
anemology
anemogram
Areopagus
ademption
aneuploid
a peepe out
atemporal
Averroism
Averroist
aberrance
aberrancy
a merry pin
ale-draper
Aleurites
area-sneak
areostyle
avertable
avertible
avertedly
adeptness
alertness
apertness
aventaile
awe-strike
azeotrope
agent noun
aleatoric
awe-struck
Apex Trust
asexually
acetylene
affianced
afflation
Alf Ramsay
affective
affecting
affection
affidavit
affrended
affricate
afflicted
affiliate
awfulness
at full sea
au fromage
affronted
affrontee
affrontée
affirmant
affluxion
affluenza
affluence
aggravate
Aegean Sea
Afghan War
algebraic
argy-bargy
Algeciras
aggregate
angle shot
anglesite
anglewise
angleworm
aigre-doux
angle iron
aggressor
augmented
Augmentin®
augmenter
augmentor
anguipede
angriness
anguished
anglicise
anglicize
anglicism
anglicist
anguiform
aggrieved
angel cake
angel hair
angelical
angel shot
argillite
angelfish
Angelenos
angelhood
angularly
angulated
angel dust
Argentina
✧argentine
argentite
Algonkian
Argentino
Algonquin
Argonauts
angiomata
✧anglophil
angiogram
Aegyptian
angophora
Angora cat
augur well
angerless
Apgar test
augurship
Alger Hiss
algarroba
auger-hole
auger-worm
algarrobo
algorithm
Aegisthus
Augustine
Angostura
Argus-eyed
Aphra Behn
ashramite
ashlaring
Ashtaroth
a thick ear
anhydride
anhydrite
anhedonia
anhedonic
anhydrous
aphidious
Ashkenazi
Ashkenazy
ashlering
achaenium
athletics
Ashkhabad
atheistic
Achillean
ash-blonde
aphyllous
Athelstan
ashamedly
ad hominem
achimenes
athematic
Athenaeum
a thin time
anhungred
ashen-grey
Akhenaten
Ashtoreth
Aphrodite
atheology
athrocyte
abhorrent
A D Hershey
abhorring
atheromas
adherence
aphoriser
apheresis
aphorizer
adhesions
arhythmia
arhythmic
athetosic
athetesis
athetosis
athetotic
Acheulean
Acheulian
ash-bucket
A E Housman
avisandum
avizandum
Adis Abeba
agitative
alizarine
animalise
animalize
animating
Anita Hill
animalism
animatism
agitation
animation
animalist
animality
avifaunal
adiabatic
as it comes
Agincourt
Alice band
aliterate
aliteracy
aliveness
alinement
avisement
ami de cour
Avicebrón
alimental
avizefull
acid freak
apiphobia
apishness
a right one
aliphatic
acid house
acid-house
asininely
abidingly
acidified
acidifier
asininity
aciniform
animistic
arillated
aciclovir
axiomatic
alienable
Asian pear
alignment
amianthus
a big noise
Aziz Nesin
alienator
anisogamy
amino acid
adipocere
acidophil
aniconism
aniconist
adiposity
animosity
apivorous
adiaphora
Adi-Granth
amissible
amidships
Aristides
aviatress
agistment
a bit thick
Aristarch
ad interim
Aristotle
aciculate
acidulate
apiculate
acidulent
avirulent
azimuthal
acidulous
alicyclic
adjective
abjection
adjacency
Aljeciras
adjoining
adjunctly
Aujeszky's
adjutancy
adjuvancy
awkwardly
ankle-jack
ankle sock
ankle-boot
ankylosed
alkalosis
ankylosis
All-father
All Saints
alla breve
ad-libbing
at liberty
ad libitum
allocable
allicholy
allocarpy
all serene
all-seeing
all-seater
axle-guard
allograph
allegiant
allograft
allegedly
a plague on
alligarta
allegoric
alligator
Allahabad
all thumbs
all the way
all-ticket
at leisure
All Blacks
Auld Licht
alleluiah
allemande
allomorph
allometry
Atlantean
ailanthus
all-ending
allantoic
allantoid
allantois
allenarly
all ends up
aplanatic
all comers
allcomers
alloplasm
alla prima
arle-penny
allophone
allopathy
allopatry
all square
Aula Regis
allergist
all-or-none
allostery
allis shad

Aylesbury
allotment
allottery
allotting
all at once
allotrope
ablutions
allotropy
ablatival
aflatoxin
all-ruling
alleviate
allow bail
allowable
allowably
allowedly
allowance
auld-warld
allayment
All My Sons
admeasure
army corps
Ahmadabad
alms-drink
armadillo
Almodovar
Ahmadiyya
aimlessly
armigeral
almshouse
armillary
atmolysis
alma mater
atmometer
adminicle
almandine
almond-oil
admonitor
Axminster
admirable
admirably
Armorican
admirance
admissive
armistice
admission
admitting
admit into
asmoulder
alms-woman
admixture
annualise
annualize
annealing
Annabella
Annabelle
Anne Bonny
annectent
Annie Hall
Anne Frank
Anna Freud
abnegator
annuitant
Arnold Bax
annelidan
annulment
annulling
annulated
agnolotti
anno mundi
adnominal
agnominal
amniotomy
Annapolis
anno regni
abnormity
abnormous
Agnes Oaks
adnascent
Aunt Sally
agnatical
Anne Tyler
au naturel
annotator
announcer
ad nauseam
A Universe
annexment
annoyance
avoparcin
Anonaceae
aromatise
aromatize
amoralism
atonalism
adoration
avocation
amoralist
atonalist
amorality
atonality
anomalous
apogamous
Azobacter
amoebaean
avoidable
avoidably
Arondight
abondance
avoidance
à bon droit
a good sort
a good turn
aforehand
aforesaid
aloneness
abodement
atonement
aforetime
at one time
adobe clay
alopecoid
anorectic
anorectal
aloofness
Adolf Loos
alongside
apothecia
anopheles
apophasis
apophyses
apophysis
apophatic
abominate
Anobiidae
adoringly
atoningly
✧aborigine
aconitine
aeolipile
agonising
agonizing
abolition
atomicity
atonicity
agonistic
apodictic
apomictic
atomistic
agonistes
aeolipyle
acock-bill
anosmatic
adornment
a top noise
abounding
amornings
acorn worm
apoenzyme
apocopate
apologise
apologize
apologist
amorosity
amorously
a bob or two
amorphism
amorphous
✧apocrypha
amourette
acoustics
aloes-wood
anoestrum
anoestrus
about-face
about east
abortuary
about-ship
about time
anorthite
apostolic
apostille
a fortiori
adoptious
avouterer
à tout prix
apoptosis
apoptotic
apostatic
about-turn
anovulant
acoluthic
akoluthos
anonymise
anonymize
anonymity
anonymous
agony aunt
alpha wave
alpha rays
applauder
alpha test
alphatest
appealing
appeasing
A J P Taylor
alphasort
appraisee
appraisal
appraiser
asphaltic
asphaltum
asphalter
aspectual
aspidioid
apple-jack
apple-cart
apple-tart
apprehend
ampleness
at present
apple-wife
asplenium
au premier
apple-John
apple tree
adpressed
appressed
arpeggios
applicate
applicant
appliable
amplified
apprising
apprizing
amphibian
amplifier
appliance
Amphipoda
amphibole
amphiboly
amphigory
appointed
appointee
appointer
appointor
amplitude
amphioxus
appellate
appellant
arpillera
appalling
Appaloosa
appendage
appendant
appanaged
aspen-like
alpenglow
alpenhorn
approbate
approving
Aepyornis
amplosome
ampholyte
alpargata
ampersand
amperzand
aspartame
appertain
Asperger's
asparagus
aspersive
aspergill
apportion
aspersion
apparency
aspersoir
aspersory
apparitor
aspirator
apparatus
appetible
appetence
appetency
appetiser
amputator
appetizer
asphyxial
acquiesce
acquitted
acquittal
arrearage
aureately
Afro-Asian
aerialist
aeriality
air-cavity
air-jacket
aerobrake
aerobiont
acrobatic
aerobatic
arracacha
auric acid
auricular
Africaner
atrocious
aerodrome
agreeable
agreeably
a free rein
agreement
agree with
air letter
airy-fairy
aerograph
acrogenic
arrogance
as regards
abrogator
air-piracy
air-minded
arraigner
air pistol
air filter
Afrikaans
Afrikaner
April-fish
April fool
aerolitic
agréments
aeromancy
aerometer
aeromotor
aerometry
air-intake
Aaronical
acronical
acronycal
air-engine
Adrenalin®
adrenalin
acronymic
agronomic
Aaron's rod
Aurangzeb
apriorism
apriorist
apriority
air-pocket
air-cooled
agriology
airworthy
aeroplane
aerophagy
Agrippina
atrophied
abruption
air-splint
✧acropolis
aerophobe
aerophone
acrophony
acropetal
aerophyte
air-bridge
aurorally
aerospace
arris rail
aeroshell
acrospire
aerospike
arrestive
arris tile
arresting
Aerosmith
agrestial
auriscope
après coup
après-goût
aerotrain
airstream
air-strike
acroteria
aerotaxis
a pretty go
air-bubble
air guitar
arrivance
arrivancy
arrivisme
arriviste
arrowhead
arrow-shot
arrow-slit
arrowwood
arrowworm
arrowroot
arrayment
Ausländer
assuasive
assuaging
abstainer
associate
au secours
assiduity
apsidiole
assiduous
Amsterdam
austerely
answer for
austenite
austerity
abscessed
assientos
assuetude
Auschwitz
Aeschylus
aesthesia
aesthesis
aesthetic
Anschluss
aestivate
auspicate
assailant
abstinent
abseiling
abscissae
abscissin
abscissas
abscisses
assoilzie
Ausgleich
assumable
assumably
assumedly
assembler
assumpsit
arseniate
arsenical
assentive
assonance
arsenious
absconder
absorbate
adsorbate
assurable
assuredly
absorbent
adsorbent
assurgent
au sérieux
assertive
absorbing
absurdism
assertion
absurdist
absurdity
Australia
australes
assurance
assertory
apsarases
assistant
absit omen
assaulter
arsy-versy
assayable
absey book
assez bien
astragali
astragals
astraddle
attrahens
attrahent
astrakhan
actualise
actualité
actualize
actuarial
actuation
actualist
actuality
astrantia
attractor
autoclave
Attic salt
autocracy
autocycle
anticline
autocrime
anticking
antichlor
articular
artichoke
antechoir
astichous

astucious
autocross
anticivic
antidotal
Artie Shaw
at the time
anthelion
anthemion
at the fore
at the most
Aethelred
artlessly
authentic
at the full
autoflare
anti-flash
✧**artificer**
autofocus
arty-farty
antefixal
antefixes
autograph
autograft
autoguide
autogamic
antigenic
autogenic
Antigonus
autogiros
autogyros
antihelix
aitchbone
ant thrush
attainder
astringer
attuitive
altricial
attrition
attuition
attribute
antiknock
ante lucem
antelucan
Autolycus
attollens
attollent
artillery
Art Blakey
autolysis
autolytic
autolatry
antimonic
antimeric
✧**artemisia**
asthmatic
automatic
automated
automaton
altimeter
attempter
altimetry
attenuate
attendant
attenuant
antennary
antinodal
antinoise
attentive
attention
actinally
antinomic
antonymic
autonomic
Antoninus
antenatal
antennule
anti-novel
Actinozoa
astrolabe
anthocarp
astronaut
astrofell
authoress
astrophel
Antiochus
authorise
authorize
authoring
authorish
authorial
authorism
actionist
authority
astrodome
aetiology
anthology
astrology
astronomy
AstroTurf®
astrocyte
anthocyan
Altiplano
autophagy
✧**antipodal**
✧**antipodes**
autopoint
autopilot
antiphony
autophoby
autophony
antipapal
autopista
antipasti
antipasto
antipathy
antiquate
antiquark
antiquary
antiquely
antiquity
afterward
aftercare
aftergame
altercate
alternate
aftermath
after-damp
alternant
alterable
anthracic
afterdeck
attorneys
afterheat
alter egos
autarchic
after kind
afterlife
aftertime
altarwise
autarkist
after-clap
afterglow
afterings
altar-tomb
afterword
arteriole
afternoon
aftermost
anthropic
arthropod
autoreply
after-crop
arthrosis
Antarctic
arthritic
arteritis
arthritis
autoroute
apteryxes
autos-da-fé
antispast
actus reus
antiscian
altissimo
autosomal
antisense
artisanal
autoscopy
antiserum
antitrade
antitragi
altitudes
antitheft
autotelic
autotimer
autotroph
antitypic
antitypal
antitrust
antitoxic
autotoxic
antitoxin
autotoxin
astounded
anthurium
auteurism
Arthurian
auteurist
Arthur Mee
Althusser
antivenin
antiviral
antivirus
activator
Antrycide®
adulation
a cut above
adulatory
aquaboard
adumbrate
aquabatic
Aguecheek
avuncular
a quick one
aduncated
abundance
abundancy
aquadrome
acuteness
amusement
aculeated
ahungered
acuminate
aluminate
Abu Simbel
aduki bean
abusively
amusingly
aluminise
aluminize
aluminium
acuminous
aluminous
anucleate
Aqua Libra®
aquilegia
acupoints
aquaplane
aquaphobe
ague-proof
aquarobic
aqua regia
aquariist
aquarelle
à outrance
aquariums
alum-shale
alum-slate
a mug's game
à huis clos
alum-stone
Ayutthaya
adult film
aquatinta
Aquitania
adulthood
adulterer
✧**ayurvedic**
aqua vitae
adviceful
advection
advocator
ad valorem
advantage
adventive
Adventism
Adventist
adventure
alveolate
✧**adversary**
advertent
adversely
advertise
advertize
adverbial
adversity
advisable
advisably
advisedly
advoutrer
auxiliary
auxometer
anxiously
auxotroph
aryballos
amygdalae
amygdalin
Amygdalus
asyndetic
asyndeton
asynergia
arytenoid
anywheres
any old how
acyclovir
abysmally
asymmetry
any amount
amyloidal
Amy Lowell
Amy Dorrit
amylopsin
azygously
asymptote
Arya Samaj
as you were
Aizoaceae
bear a hand
bravadoes
blatantly
brambling
Bradbury's
Bradburys
bearberry
blaeberry
branchery
bias crime
branchiae
branching
branchial
branchlet
branch off
branch out
bean caper
board game
brand name
boardwalk
brandreth
beardless
blandness
brandling
Beardsley
boardroom
board-foot
bladdered
brandered
brand-iron
brake-fade
brake pads
blameable
blameably
blameless
brakeless
brazeless
beakerful
Boanerges
brake shoe
brakesman
blade-bone
bladework
brake drum
beaver rat
blaze away
beanfeast
bear fruit
brangling
✧**beau geste**
brachiate
beach-ball
beachhead
biathlete
beachwear
brashness
beach plum
blatherer
Brachyura
boar-hound
bead-house
boathouse
beau ideal
brazilein
beaminess
beamingly
bearishly
Brazilian
Brazil nut
beatitude
blackband
✧black hand
blackface
blackgame
blackwash
blackjack
black mark
blackball
blackmail
black damp
black bass
black mass
Black Bart
blackhead
blacklead
black bean
black bear
black beer
blackness
blankness
black belt
Blackfeet
blackbird
black bile
blackfish
blacklist
black flag
black-flag
black gold
✧blackwood
✧**black hole**
Black Pope
black book
blackcock
✧black monk
blackpoll
Blackpool
blank door
Blackfoot
black body
black spot
black gram
black drop
Black Iris
black lung
blackbuck
Blackburn
black butt
black swan
beadledom
Braillist
Brahmanic
Brahminic
beau monde
Brahminee
beat music
braincase
brainwave
brainwash
brain-dead
brainless
✧**béarnaise**
brainsick
brainstem
blaspheme
blasphemy
bead-proof
brass band
brassware
beanstalk
boatswain
Bratsk Dam
brassiere
brassière
brass neck
boar-spear
bean shoot
bear's-foot
brasserie
bracteate
beam trawl
boat train
boastless
bractless
blastment
beautiful
beastlike
blast-pipe
brattling
blastulae
blastular
blastulas
blastomas
beastings
beasthood
blast-hole
bracteole
beauteous
bratwurst
beaux yeux
✧**beaux arts**
beady-eyed
bobtailed
Bob Marley
Bob Sawyer
Baby Buggy®
baby bonus
baby blues
babacoote
bibacious
Bible belt
bebeerine
Bob Beamon
baby grand
bob-cherry
baby house
biblicism
biblicist
bobbin net
Bob Gibson
Babbittry
bubble car
bubble gum
bobble hat
bobolling
bobsleigh
bubble-jet
baboonery
baboonish
babirussa

baby tooth
bobby calf
bobbysock
bacharach
beccaccia
buccaneer
Bucharest
beccafico
buccanier
buckayros
bicoastal
backboard
buckboard
backboned
back-bench
back-block
backbiter
back-crawl
back-chain
bicyclist
back-cloth
back-cross
backcourt
bucketful
bacterise
bacterize
bucketing
bacterial
bacterium
bacterian
bacteroid
backfield
backfisch
buck fever
back green
bacchante
✧**bacchanal**
bacchants
buckhound
backing-up
buckishly
bacciform
back issue
bacillary
bucolical
back-light
bicolored
Baculites
bicameral
biconcave
Bucentaur
buck naked
backplate
back-pedal
backpiece
bicipital
backspace
backstage
back-slang
backslash
back-spaul
backstall
backstays
backspeer
backspeir
backsight
backslide
backswing
backshish
buckshish
buckskins
back-shift
✧**buck's fizz**
Buck's Club
backsword
buck's-horn
back story
backtrack
bucktooth
buckthorn
becquerel
buckwheat
buck-wagon
backwoods
backwards
back water
backwater
buckyball
buckytube
bedraggle
bedlamite
bedlamism
bed-jacket
bad sailor
bed-warmer
body board
Bud Abbott
body-check
body clock
bodacious
body-curer
body count
Bo Diddley
budgetary
badger-dog
budgeting
bedfellow
budgerows
bad temper
bad cess to
bed-settee
bed of down
body forth
by default
bodyguard
bodeguero
by degrees
Buddhists
body image
bedridden
bodhi tree
badminton
bedsitter
bedelship
bed-closet
bedimming
bidentate
Bud Powell
bedropped
bed-bottle
bed-worthy
bedspread
bodyshell
bide tryst
beddy-byes
bedazzled
bedizened
bretasche
beefaloes
bee-master
beer belly
beef broth
bleachers
bleachery
bleaching
breeching
breed-bate
breadhead
breadline
breadroom
bread-corn
breadroot
bread tree
bien élevé
breveting
boerewors
beekeeper
brevetted
beefeater
beech mast
bye the bye
beech fern
Brechtian
beechwood
beech tree
bletherer
beer house
brew-house
Beethoven
brevi manu
beeriness
breakback
break rank
break gaol
break jail
break camp
breakfast
breakable
breakneck
bleakness
breakbeat
break wind
break-wind
breaktime
break into
break down
breakdown
break free
break crop
break step
break bulk
break even
break-even
breakeven
break away
breakaway
beetle off
bee-flower
beer money
bregmatic
✧**breton hat**
beef olive
Brehon Law
bier right
bee-orchis
blear-eyed
blessedly
Beersheba
beefsteak
breastfed
beet sugar
breastpin
breathe up
breathful
breathing
breathily
beestings
biestings
Bretwalda
bierwurst
Beelzebub
breezeway
buffaloes
buffet car
buffeting
Baffin Bay
bifoliate
bafflegab
befalling
bifurcate
Bofors gun
bifarious
befortune
buff-stick
befitting
buff-wheel
beggardom
biguanide
beggar-man
beglamour
big screen
big-screen
bugle-band
bugle-call
beglerbeg
bigheaded
bugle-weed
bugle-horn
Big Bertha
big cheese
béguinage
bagginess
bogginess
beggingly
bagpiping
big-ticket
✧**big dipper**
big hitter
beginning
Big-endian
bigeneric
bog cotton
bog spavin
begetting
bagatelle
bog-butter
bug-hunter
bog myrtle
beheading
beholding
buhrstone
behoveful
bahuvrihi
behaviour
brigandry
brigadier
Britannia
Britannic
Brigadoon
bric-à-brac
bricabrac
blind date
blindless
blindness
blind side
blind-side
blindfish
blindfold
blind road
blind coal
blindworm
blind spot
bridemaid
bridecake
baisemain
bridewell
bride's-man
bridesman
brisé volé
briefcase
briefless
briefness
bridgable
beingless
beingness
bring home
bring down
bring over
blighting
brininess
Britisher
Briticise
Briticize
bailiwick
Briticism
brinjarry
brickyard
brickwall
briskness
brick-kiln
brickclay
brickwork
blinkered
brick-dust
bailliage
brilliant
bridleway
bain-marie
Brian Lara
bairn-team
baignoire
bairnlike
bairn-time
bricolage
Britomart
Britoness
brier-wood
brier-root
Brix scale
blissless
britschka
brimstone
brimstony
brittlely
bristling
Brittania
Brittanic
Brittonic
briquette
blizzardy
bijective
bijection
Bujumbura
bakeapple
bakeboard
bake blind
baksheesh
bakehouse
bakhshish
bakestone
balmacaan
Balaam-box
balladeer
balsam fir
bel sangue
baldachin
Balsamina
Balaamite
✧balkanise
✧balkanize
ballabile
balladine
balzarine
Bulgarise
Bulgarize
ballabili
Bulgarian
balladist
balsawood
billabong
bal masqué
Bellatrix
ballasted
baldaquin
beleaguer
Balkan War
✧**bilharzia**
billboard
bull-board
bilabiate
bilobular
✧**balaclava**
bell crank
balection
bolection
bilocular
bulk cargo
Bill Cosby
bile ducts
ball-dress
belt drive
bull-dance
bulldozer
belle-mère
belvedere
bilge keel
believe in
bald eagle
ballerina
ballerine
believing
billeting
belle amie
bolletrie
bulletrie
bilge-pump
bald-faced
boldfaced
bullfight
balefully
bullfinch
bell-glass
✧**bolognese**
Bill Gates
Bill Haley
✧**balthasar**
✧**bolshevik**
✧**balthazar**
balkiness
balminess
bulginess
bulkiness
balkingly
bulgingly
bullishly
billionth
Baltimore
bellibone
bellicose
baldicoot
billiards
Baltic Sea
ballistic
balalaika
bulk large
belemnite
bilimbing
baldmoney
belomancy
bell-metal
bolometer
bolometry
belamoure
Belonidae
bull-nosed
balanitis
bilingual
ballot box
Bill Oddie
balconied
balloting
billowing
bulbosity
Balto-slav
biliously
bulbously
ballpoint
bull point
bell-punch
bolo punch
ball-proof
baldpated
bilirubin
bull snake
bull shark
Bill Sikes
bull's wool
bel esprit
balas ruby
belatedly
bull trout
bolstered
bilateral
biliteral
bolster up
boletuses
bell tower
boliviano
ball valve
bull whale
bullwhack
bald wheat
belly-band
belly tank
bellyache
Ballymena
bully-beef

Billy Liar
belly flop
belly-flop
Bollywood
billycock
bully-rook
Billy Joel
billy goat
bully-tree
Billy Budd
bombardon
bombasine
bombazine
bemoaning
bum-baylie
Bombay mix
bummaloti
bombastic
by my certy
bumper car
be my guest
bumblebee
Bumbledom
bimonthly
bemonster
bumpology
bamboo rat
bamboozle
bombproof
bum around
by mistake
bump-start
bombshell
bombsight
bomb squad
bumptious
bon marché
Bengalese
bank-agent
bengaline
bungaloid
bandalore
Bangalore
bandbrake
bone-black
baneberry
bone china
binocular
bank draft
benedight
bannerall
benne-seed
bonne mine
bantering
bandelier
bonne amie
banderole
bone-earth
bandeiras
Bundesrat
Bundestag
Benbecula
ben venuto
beneficed
bona fides
banefully

benefited
benefit by
bent grass
benignant
benignity
benighted
benighten
benighter
benchmark
bench fees
bench seat
bench test
bench-test
benthonic
bench-hole
Bunthorne
bunkhouse
bon vivant
bon diable
benni-seed
bonnibell
bon viveur
✧bannister
bundle off
bundle out
bonilasse
by no means
by numbers
binominal
banana oil
bon voyage
bingo hall
bandobast
banjolele
bandoleon
bandoneon
bandolero
bandoleer
bandoline
bentonite
benzoline
bandonion
bandolier
bonhommie
bonhomous
bongo drum
Ben Jonson
bundobust
bank paper
bank-paper
bond paper
binervate
Bantry Bay
Banbridge
bandstand
bond-slave
bandshell
banisters
bangsring
band-stone
bondstone
bank-stock
bonetired
banjulele
banausian
binturong
banqueted

banquette
Bantustan
banqueter
bene vobis
bone-weary
bandwidth
band-wheel
bandwagon
bondwoman
bandy-ball
Benny Hill
✧bunny girl
biohazard
buonamani
buonamano
buona sera
blow a well
bioparent
biomarker
blow a fuse
bootblack
book block
broadband
blond-lace
bloodbath
blood oath
blood bank
broadtail
blood-rain
broadways
broadcast
boondocks
blood-feud
broad-leaf
Broad Peak
blood cell
broad bean
bloodless
broadness
blood heat
blood test
blood agar
bloodshed
bloodshot
blood-bird
blood-fine
bloodline
blood-wite
broadside
broadwise
bloodying
broadbill
by-ordinar
bloodwood
bloodworm
broadloom
bloodroot
broad-brim
brondyron
broiderer
broad jump
blood-dust
bloodlust
brood over
blood type
blow-dryer
brokerage
boomerang

bromelain
Broken Bay
be oneself
by oneself
bromeliad
broken man
biogenous
booked-out
biometric
biosensor
boot-faced
brotherly
brochette
biorhythm
biopiracy
booziness
boorishly
biomining
boogieing
brominism
boodie-rat
biodiesel
blockhead
blockship
brooklime
blockhole
block vote
block-book
blockwork
block-coal
block type
booklouse
broomrape
broomball
bloomless
bookmaker
bootmaker
broom-corn
brown bear
brown Bess
brownness
brown rice
brown bill
Björn Borg
brown coal
brown spar
brown lung
bionomics
biologist
Book of Job
bromoform
bookplate
biosphere
book price
Blomqvist
biography
bookstand
boomslang
bookstall
browsable
bookshelf
bookstore
bootstrap
bloatware
book trade
biostable
bioethics
book token
blootered
blowtorch

B rotundum
brogueish
blow-valve
book value
boot virus
booby trap
booby-trap
Bronze Age
beplaster
buprestid
Buprestis
baptismal
baptistry
bipinnate
by-product
bipartite
bipyramid
by-passage
bepatched
bird-alane
burd-alane
burrawang
✧bergamask
born-again
barbascos
barrancos
bargander
berg-adder
bergander
barbarise
barbarize
Barnabite
bursarial
barbarism
Barbadian
barbarian
barbarity
barracker
barnacled
barnacles
byrlaw-man
bargainer
bar magnet
barcarole
bird-alone
barracoon
Barbadoes
barbarous
barbastel
barracuda
barmbrack
birdbrain
Borobudur
bara brith
bare bones
bark-bound
bard-craft
boric acid
berg-cedar
borachios
bark-cloth
barm-cloth
barn dance
barrelage
burger bun
barret-cap
bartender
bordereau
barrelful
Barmecide
berberine

berkelium
berserker
berserkly
barrelled
bargellos
bordellos
barge into
Barcelona
bargepole
burdenous
burned out
barkeeper
burlesque
barperson
barretter
barrefull
barefaced
barograph
baragouin
birth rate
birchbark
birthmark
birth pill
birth sign
barghaist
birthwort
birch tree
Bert Hardy
borghetto
bird-house
barricade
Burkinabé
barricado
barminess
burliness
burningly
burnisher
birlieman
barbitone
bursiform
barricoes
barrister
Burakumin
beryllium
Bartlemew
bark-louse
bird-louse
bird-lover
born mimic
barometer
barometry
Burundian
Barenboim
Bering Sea
baronetcy
✧bergomask
barrow boy
barbotine
borrowing
Borromini
Bardolino
borrow pit
Bernstein
bird's-nest
Berkshire
barasinga
baroscope
burrstone
barnstorm
birdsfoot
burnt sack

bird table
burnt cork
burnt-cork
Barataria
barathrum
barotitis
Bermudian
bar supper
byrewoman
Barry John
bystander
bespangle
bashawism
bossa nova
boss about
bescatter
bespatter
busk after
baseboard
basic salt
bushcraft
boss cocky
bisection
basic slag
basically
base-court
besteaded
bestead by
basketful
beseeched
beseecher
bas-relief
beseeming
besieging
bespeckle
busheller
bushelman
basifugal
bashfully
bush-fruit
basifixed
besognios
boschveld
bisphenol
bush-house
bastinade
bastinado
boskiness
bossiness
bushiness
bismillah
bastioned
besainted
bisulcate
basilical
basilican
basilicon
baseliner
Basil Hume
base-level
besom-head
base metal
bush-metal
basen wide
basin-wide
basinfuls
beslobber
bishopdom
bishopess
Boston ivy
bishopric

bespotted
baseplate
bush pilot
basipetal
biserrate
bus-driver
bestrewed
bush shirt
besetment
besetting
besitting
besotting
beslubber
besmutted
bushwhack
bushwoman
Bath Abbey
✧batrachia
battalion
bethankit
bit-mapped
bath-brick
✧bath chair
beta decay
butadiene
by the yard
butlerage
butterbur
butter-box
buttercup
Buthelezi
battement
butterfat
butterfly
butterine
battening
bettering
bitterish
butternut
better off
bitten off
by the book
butter oil
bitter-pit
butter pat
Beta fibre
batch file
butt hinge
batch loaf
butcherly
bath-house
bathhouse
battle axe
battle-axe
battlebus
battle-cry
Betelgeux
bottleful
bottle gas
Bethlehem
bottle-imp
bottle off
bottle out
bit player
betumbled
but and ben
Botany Bay
botanical
bête noire
betrodden
bottom end

bethought
betrothed
betrothal
batholite
batholith
Bathonian
bottom out
battology
bite or sup
bottoms up
botargoes
bat around
butt-shaft
Bathsheba
bath sheet
bath salts
Bath stone
Batistuta
bath-towel
bethumbed
bytownite
batswoman
Botswanan
butty-gang
bathylite
bathylith
bathybius
Betty Blue
Bhutanese
brutalise
brutalize
brutalism
brutalist
brutality
bourasque
✧bluebeard
blue-black
blue blood
blubbered
Blue Beret
blueberry
boundless
bound up in
blunderer
blue devil
boulevard
brute fact
bruteness
brutelike
bluffness
bluegrass
blue-green
bourgeois
Bruchidae
blushless
blush wine
brush fire
Brunhilde
brushwood
blush-rose
brushwork
brush away
brutishly
brutified
✧brummagem
blue merle
blue mould
blue movie
Brunonian
boutonnée
blueprint

blue poppy
Blue Peter
brusquely
baudricke
blue rinse
blue-rinse
blue shark
blue sheep
Brunswick
blue-skies
bluestone
bluntness
bountiful
bountyhed
Bluetooth®
blustrous
bounteous
blusterer
blue whale
blutwurst
blue water
bower boy
bevel gear
bevelment
bevelling
bivalence
bivalency
bavin wits
bavardage
bivariate
bivariant
bow-backed
bowl along
bow-legged
bowler hat
bowler-hat
bow window
bawdiness
bewailing
bowelling
bowerbird
bowstring
bowstrung
box camera
boxwallah
box canyon
boxkeeper
box office
box-office
box girder
box clever
buxomness
Box and Cox
Boxing Day
box spring
boxercise
box number
Brylcreem®
Boy Scouts
Boyle's law
Bay of Pigs
Blyth Tait
Brythonic
bay window
boy bishop
bay-antler
beyond one
bayoneted
boycotter
Bryophyta
bryophyte

boyfriend
be your age!
bezoardic
buzzingly
Byzantine
Byzantium
bez-antler
bizarrely
char-à-banc
charabanc
Characeae
charangos
Chaka Khan
cranachan
chabazite
cyanamide
chalazion
clavation
chapaties
crab-apple
chaparral
coadapted
cravatted
character
chapatis
ciabattas
clamantly
Clara Butt
clapboard
coal-black
coal-brass
chawbacon
clabby-doo
crabbedly
clapbread
crabbiest
charbroil
chambered
clamber up
chamberer
cranberry
coarctate
chanceful
chalcogen
crab canon
chancroid
chancrous
clay court
Chaldaean
coat-dress
chandlery
Chaldaism
chandelle
Claudette
Clare Hall
châtelain
claret cup
clarendon
chavender
✧chameleon
ceaseless
chapeless
ceasefire
czarevich
claret jug
chaperone
craterous
chaseport
clay eater
crab-eater
cratefuls

chamfrain
crab-faced
coalfield
chauffeur
chaffinch
coat-frock
chamfered
coal-fired
chafferer
crab grass
charge-cap
craggiest
changeful
chargeful
Changchun
chargrill
charge-man
Craigavon
crash-land
clathrate
cha-cha-cha
coachline
crash dive
crash-dive
cha-chaing
clap hands
coachload
coach road
coachwood
coachwork
coach-horn
coach tour
coach bolt
coalhouse
charivari
chariness
craziness
coaxingly
clarified
cyaniding
Chasidism
coalition
clarifier
charities
coaxially
cranially
clarionet
claviform
clavicorn
cladistic
clavicula
coadjutor
chalkface
crankcase
chalk talk
crack baby
crack a can
crackhead
crack-hemp
cracknels
crankness
crankiest
chalklike
crackling
clackdish
cracksman
crack-rope
crack down

crackdown
cradle cap
crawliest
challenge
Charleroi
chapleted
✧charlotte
charlatan
crab-louse
claimable
crammable
charmless
Charmaine
Charminar
coalminer
charmeuse
coal mouse
chain gang
chain mail
charnecos
channeler
chainwork
chain down
chain bolt
chain rule
chain pump
Charolais
chatoyant
charoseth
ceanothus
chaconine
chamomile
Cracovian
coal owner
clamorous
cladogram
clamourer
clafoutis
cyanotype
coal-plate
crampbark
cramp ball
coal plant
clappy-doo
champlevé
champagne
cramp-ring
cramp-fish
champaign
cramp-bone
clamp down
clampdown
cramp-iron
champerty
chairdays
chairlift
cuadrilla
chagrined
chaprassi
chaprassy
cranreuch
coalstand
classmate
clay-slate
classable
classible
classical

Chassidic
crab-sidle
clamshell
classless
crassness
classific
chapstick
crab stick
crabstick
class list
clausulae
clausular
class-book
classroom
crapshoot
chassepot
claustral
claustrum
Ceausescu
chantress
chartless
craftless
craftiest
craft shop
coastline
coastwise
coat tails
Chantilly
craftsman
claytonia
chastened
chastener
craftwork
chart-room
chaetopod
chartered
charterer
chatterer
clatterer
chastiser
chanteuse
clavulate
coadunate
coagulase
coagulate
coagulant
crapulent
chalumeau
Chanukkah
crapulous
charwoman
Charybdis
chalybean
chalybite
crazy bone
crazy golf
cabbalism
cabbalist
cubic yard
cubically
cubic inch
cubic foot
cebadilla
cable-laid
cablecast
Cobdenite

Words marked ✧ can also be spelled with one or more capital letters

Billy Liar
belly flop
belly-flop
Bollywood
billycock
bully-rook
Billy Joel
billy goat
bully-tree
Billy Budd
bombardon
bombasine
bombazine
bemoaning
bum-baylie
Bombay mix
bummaloti
bombastic
by my certy
bumper car
be my guest
bomb-happy
bombilate
bombinate
bumpiness
bomb-ketch
bumblebee
Bumbledom
bimonthly
bemonster
bumpology
bamboo rat
bamboozle
bombproof
bum around
by mistake
bump-start
bombshell
bombsight
bomb squad
bumptious
bon marché
Bengalese
bank-agent
bengaline
bungaloid
bandalore
Bangalore
bandbrake
bone-black
baneberry
bone china
binocular
bank draft
benedight
bannerall
benne-seed
bonne mine
bantering
bandelier
bonne amie
banderole
bone-earth
bandeiras
Bundesrat
Bundestag
Benbecula
ben venuto
beneficed
bona fides
banefully
benefited
benefit by
bent grass
benignant
benignity
benighted
benighten
benighter
benchmark
bench fees
bench seat
bench test
bench-test
benthonic
bench-hole
Bunthorne
bunkhouse
bon vivant
bon diable
benni-seed
bonnibell
bon viveur
bonniness
bendingly
benzidine
bandicoot
✧bannister
bundle off
bundle out
bonilasse
by no means
by numbers
binominal
banana oil
bon voyage
bingo hall
bandobast
banjolele
bandoleon
bandoneon
bandolero
bandoleer
bandoline
bentonite
benzoline
bandonion
bandolier
bonhommie
bonhomous
bongo drum
Ben Jonson
bundobust
bank paper
bank-paper
bond paper
binervate
Bantry Bay
Banbridge
bandstand
bond-slave
bandshell
banisters
bangsring
band-stone
bondstone
bank-stock
bonetired
banjulele
banausian
binturong
banqueted
banquette
Bantustan
banqueter
bene vobis
bone-weary
bandwidth
band-wheel
bandwagon
bondwoman
bandy-ball
Benny Hill
✧bunny girl
biohazard
buonamani
buonamano
buona sera
blow a well
bioparent
biomarker
blow a fuse
bootblack
book block
brow-bound
blotching
bronchial
broadband
blond-lace
bloodbath
blood oath
blood bank
broadtail
blood-rain
broadways
broadcast
boondocks
blood-feud
broad-leaf
Broad Peak
blood cell
broad bean
bloodless
broadness
blood heat
blood test
blood agar
bloodshed
bloodshot
blood-bird
blood-fine
bloodline
blood-wite
broadside
broadwise
bloodying
broadbill
by-ordinar
bloodwood
bloodworm
broadloom
bloodroot
broad-brim
brondyron
broiderer
broad jump
blood-dust
bloodlust
brood over
blood type
blow dryer
brokerage
boomerang
bromelain
Broken Bay
be oneself
by oneself
bromeliad
broken man
biogenous
booked-out
biometric
biosensor
boot-faced
brotherly
brochette
biorhythm
biopiracy
booziness
boorishly
biomining
boogieing
brominism
boodie-rat
biodiesel
blockhead
brookweed
blockship
brooklime
blockhole
block vote
block-book
blockwork
block-coal
block type
booklouse
broomrape
broomball
bloomless
bookmaker
bootmaker
broom-corn
brown bear
brown Bess
brownness
brown rice
brown bill
Björn Borg
brown coal
brown spar
brown lung
bionomics
biologist
Book of Job
bromoform
bookplate
biosphere
book price
Blomqvist
biography
bookstand
boomslang
bookstall
browsable
bookshelf
bookstore
bootstrap
bloatware
book trade
biostable
bioethics
book token
blootered
blowtorch
B rotundum
brogueish
blow-valve
book value
boot virus
booby trap
booby-trap
Bronze Age
beplaster
buprestid
Buprestis
baptismal
baptistry
bipinnate
by-product
bipartite
bipyramid
by-passage
bepatched
bird-alane
burd-alane
burrawang
✧bergamask
born-again
barbascos
barrancos
bargander
berg-adder
bergander
barbarise
barbarize
Barnabite
bursarial
barbarism
Barbadian
barbarian
barbarity
barracker
barnacled
barnacles
byrlaw-man
bargainer
bar magnet
barcarole
bird-alone
barracoon
Barbadoes
barbarous
barbastel
barracuda
barmbrack
birdbrain
Borobudur
bara brith
bare bones
bark-bound
bard-craft
boric acid
berg-cedar
borachios
bark-cloth
barm-cloth
barn dance
barrelage
burger bun
barret-cap
bartender
bordereau
barrelful
Barmecide
berberine
berkelium
berserker
berserkly
barrelled
bargellos
bordellos
barge into
Barcelona
bargepole
burdenous
burned out
barkeeper
burlesque
barperson
barretter
barrefull
barefaced
barograph
baragouin
birth rate
birchbark
birthmark
birth pill
birth sign
barghaist
birthwort
birch tree
Bert Hardy
borghetto
bird-house
barricade
Burkinabé
barricado
barminess
burliness
burningly
burnisher
birlieman
barbitone
bursiform
barricoes
barrister
Burakumin
beryllium
Bartlemew
bark-louse
bird-louse
bird-lover
born mimic
barometer
barometry
Burundian
Barenboim
Bering Sea
baronetcy
✧bergomask
barrow boy
barbotine
borrowing
Borromini
Bardolino
borrow pit
Bernstein
bird's-nest
Berkshire
barasinga
baroscope
burrstone
barnstorm
birdsfoot
burnt sack
bird table
burnt cork
burnt-cork
Barataria
barathrum
barotitis
Bermudian
bar supper
byrewoman
Barry John
bystander
bespangle
bashawism
bossa nova
boss about
bescatter
bespatter
busk after
baseboard
basic salt
bushcraft
boss cocky
bisection
basic slag
basically
base-court
besteaded
bestead by
basketful
beseeched
beseecher
bas-relief
beseeming
besieging
bespeckle
busheller
bushelman
basifugal
bashfully
bush-fruit
basifixed
besognios
boschveld
bisphenol
bush-house
bastinade
bastinado
boskiness
bossiness
bushiness
bismillah
bastioned
besainted
bisulcate
basilical
basilican
basilicon
baseliner
Basil Hume
base-level
besom-head
base metal
bush-metal
basen wide
basin-wide
basinfuls
beslobber
bishopdom
bishopess
Boston ivy
bishopric

bespotted
baseplate
bush pilot
basipetal
biserrate
bus-driver
bestrewed
bush shirt
besetment
besetting
besitting
besotting
beslubber
besmutted
bushwhack
bushwoman
Bath Abbey
✧batrachia
battalion
bethankit
bit-mapped
bath-brick
✧bath chair
beta decay
butadiene
by the yard
butlerage
butterbur
butter-box
buttercup
Buthelezi
battement
butterfat
butterfly
butterine
battening
bettering
bitterish
butternut
better off
bitten off
by the book
butter oil
bitter-pit
butter pat
Beta fibre
batch file
butt hinge
batch loaf
butcherly
bath-house
bathhouse
battle axe
battle-axe
battlebus
battle-cry
Betelgeux
bottleful
bottle gas
Bethlehem
bottle-imp
bottle off
bottle out
bit player
betumbled
but and ben
Botany Bay
botanical
bête noire
betrodden
bottom end
bethought
betrothed
betrothal
batholite
batholith
Bathonian
bottom out
battology
bite or sup
bottoms up
botargoes
bat around
butt-shaft
Bathsheba
bath sheet
bath salts
Bath stone
Batistuta
bath-towel
bethumbed
bytownite
batswoman
Botswanan
butty-gang
bathylite
bathylith
bathybius
Betty Blue
Bhutanese
brutalise
brutalize
brutalism
brutalist
brutality
bourasque
✧bluebeard
blue-black
blue blood
blubbered
Blue Beret
blueberry
boundless
bound up in
blunderer
blue devil
boulevard
brute fact
bruteness
brutelike
bluffness
bluegrass
blue-green
bourgeois
Bruchidae
blushless
blush wine
brush fire
Brunhilde
brushwood
blush-rose
brushwork
brush away
brutishly
brutified
✧brummagem
blue merle
blue mould
blue movie
Brunonian
boutonnée
blueprint
blue poppy
Blue Peter
brusquely
baudricke
blue rinse
blue-rinse
blue shark
blue sheep
Brunswick
blue-skies
bluestone
bluntness
bountiful
bountyhed
Bluetooth®
blustrous
bounteous
blusterer
blue whale
blutwurst
blue water
bovver boy
bevel gear
bevelment
bevelling
bivalence
bivalency
bavin wits
bavardage
bivariate
bivariant
bow-backed
bowl along
bow-legged
bowler hat
bowler-hat
bow window
bawdiness
bewailing
bowelling
bowerbird
bowstring
bowstrung
box camera
boxwallah
box canyon
boxkeeper
box office
box-office
box girder
box clever
buxomness
Box and Cox
Boxing Day
box spring
boxercise
box number
Brylcreem®
Boy Scouts
Boyle's law
Bay of Pigs
Blyth Tait
Brythonic
bay window
boy bishop
bay-antler
beyond one
bayoneted
boycotter
Bryophyta
bryophyte
boyfriend
be your age!
bezoardic
buzzingly
Byzantine
Byzantium
bez-antler
bizarrely
char-à-banc
charabanc
Characeae
charangos
Chaka Khan
cranachan
chabazite
cyanamide
chalazion
clavation
chapaties
crab-apple
chaparral
coadapted
cravatted
character
chapattis
ciabattas
clamantly
Clara Butt
clapboard
coal-black
coal-brass
chawbacon
clabby-doo
crabbedly
clapbread
crabbiest
charbroil
chambered
clamber up
chamberer
cranberry
coarctate
chanceful
chalcogen
crab canon
chancroid
chancrous
clay court
Chaldaean
coat-dress
chandlery
Chaldaism
chandelle
Claudette
Clare Hall
châtelain
claret cup
clarendon
chavender
✧chameleon
ceaseless
chapeless
ceasefire
czarevich
claret jug
chaperone
craterous
chaseport
clay eater
crab-eater
cratefuls
chamfrain
crab-faced
coalfield
chauffeur
chaffinch
coat-frock
chamfered
coal-fired
chafferer
crab grass
charge-cap
craggiest
changeful
chargeful
Changchun
chargrill
charge-man
Craigavon
crash-land
clathrate
cha-cha-cha
crash-test
coachwhip
coach-hire
coachline
crash dive
crash-dive
cha-chaing
clap hands
coachload
coach road
coachwood
coachwork
coach-horn
coach tour
coach bolt
coalhouse
charivari
chariness
craziness
coaxingly
clarified
cyaniding
Chasidism
coalition
clarifier
charities
coaxially
cranially
clarionet
claviform
clavicorn
cladistic
clavicula
coadjutor
chalkface
crankcase
chalk talk
crack baby
crack a can
crackhead
crack-hemp
cracknels
crankness
crankiest
chalklike
crackling
clackdish
cracksman
crack rope
crack down
crackdown
cradle cap
crawliest
challenge
Charleroi
chapleted
✧charlotte
charlatan
crab-louse
claimable
crammable
charmless
Charmaine
Charminar
coalminer
charmeuse
coal mouse
chain gang
chain mail
charnecos
chain-gear
chainless
chainshot
chain pier
channeler
chainwork
chain down
chain bolt
chain rule
chain pump
Charolais
chatoyant
charoseth
ceanothus
chaconine
chamomile
Cracovian
coal owner
clamorous
cladogram
clamourer
clafoutis
cyanotype
coal-plate
crampbark
cramp ball
coal plant
clappy-doo
champlevé
champagne
cramp-ring
cramp-fish
champaign
cramp-bone
clamp down
clampdown
cramp-iron
champerty
chairdays
chairlift
cuadrilla
chagrined
chaprassi
chaprassy
cranreuch
coatstand
classmate
clay-slate
classable
classible
classical
Chassidic
crab-sidle
clamshell
classless
crassness
classific
chapstick
crab stick
crabstick
class list
clausulae
clausular
class-book
classroom
crapshoot
chassepot
claustral
claustrum
Ceausescu
coat-style
crab's-eyes
coastland
coastward
chaetodon
chantress
chartless
craftless
craftiest
craft shop
coastline
coastwise
coat tails
Chantilly
craftsman
claytonia
chastened
chastener
craftwork
chart-room
chaetopod
chartered
charterer
chatterer
clatterer
chastiser
chanteuse
clavulate
coadunate
coagulase
coagulate
coagulant
crapulent
chalumeau
Chanukkah
crapulous
charwoman
Charybdis
chalybean
chalybite
crazy bone
crazy golf
cabbalism
cabbalist
cubic yard
cubically
cubic inch
cubic foot
cebadilla
cable-laid
cablecast
Cobdenite

Cobdenism
cablegram
cabriolet
cobriform
Cuba libre
caballero
caballine
cobaltite
caballing
cobalamin
cabaletta
cabalette
Cuban heel
cabin ship
cabin crew
cabinetry
cybercafé
cybernate
cybernaut
caber toss
cyberpunk
cab-driver
cab-runner
cubby-hole
cyclamate
Cactaceae
cockateel
Cockaigne
cockatiel
cocoa nibs
cachaemia
cachaemic
cocoa-wood
ciclatoun
cock-a-hoop
cock-broth
cacodylic
cacodemon
coco-de-mer
cycle lane
cycle race
cyclepath
cache-sexe
cacoethes
cocked hat
cachectic
coco fibre
cacafuego
cacafogos
cockfight
cockhorse
cyclic AMP
cochineal
cockiness
cocainise
cocainize
cyclizine
cocainism
coccidium
cyclicism
cocainist
cyclicity
cactiform
cochleare
cochleate
cucullate
cocklebur
Cichlidae
cockle hat
cocklaird
Cecil King
cockleman
coculture
cacuminal
cockmatch
cockneyfy
cyclorama
cuckoo-bud
cuckoo bee
cycloidal
cuckoldom
cuckoldly
cuckoldry
cyclopean
cocoonery
cuckoo fly
coccolite
cyclonite
cocooning
coccolith
cyclolith
cyclopian
cacholong
cyclotron
Cyclopses
cock-padle
cacophony
caciquism
cockroach
Ciceronic
cicerones
cockswain
cock's-comb
cockscomb
cocuswood
cocksfoot
cock-shoot
cicatrice
cicatrise
cicatrize
cacotopia
Cuchulain
coccygeal
coccygian
cocky's joy
cuddeehih
cudgelled
cudgeller
codifying
caddie car
caddis fly
cod-fisher
caddishly
cadential
code-named
cedar-bird
cedarwood
cadastral
cadetship
cadaveric
Caesarean
chelaship
cheralite
Caesarism
Caesarian
chelation
cremation
crenation
chevalier
Caesarist
coevality
crematory
cremaster
crenature
Chet Baker
Cherbourg
cheechako
coercible
coercibly
cherchef't
crescendo
crescioni
Cleveland
crenelate
credendum
cleverish
crewelist
crenelled
coeternal
clerecole
crêpe sole
clemently
chevelure
clergyman
chechaqua
chechaquo
clericate
crepitate
clericals
crepitant
chelicera
chewiness
crepiness
cherished
cretinise
cretinize
cretinism
ctenidium
caecilian
Ctesibius
clericity
chemicked
cherimoya
cretinoid
cheliform
cteniform
cretinous
chemistry
chemitype
chemitypy
checkmate
checkrail
checkable
checkrein
creakiest
clerkship
clerklike
clerkling
check-till
checklist
cheekbone
checkbook
checkroom
checkered
clew-lines
cheilitis
creamlaid
cream cake
creamware
creamiest
cream soda
creamwove
cream horn
chermoula
cream puff
Chernobyl
cleanness
cleansing
cleanskin
Chernenko
clean room
cheongsam
chernozem
Coelomata
coenosarc
coelomate
cremocarp
cheloidal
coenobite
crepoline
coenobium
Chekovian
chelonian
Caenozoic
chemostat
coelostat
coenocyte
cheap Jack
✧cheap-jack
cheapness
creepiest
cee-spring
coemption
cheapener
creep-hole
cheap John
creepered
✧cleopatra
cherryade
cherry-bob
clearable
cheerless
clearness
clearwing
clearskin
Chevrolet®
chevroned
clearance
clearcole
cherry-pie
cherry-pit
cherry red
chevrette
clear away
clear-eyed
clepsydra
caen-stone
cheesevat
creatable
creatress
crestless
chest-note
chest tone
cleithral
creatural
Cresta Run
crenulate
crepuscle
caerulean
chemurgic
cleruchia
cherubims
credulity
coequally
credulous
chequered
cleavable
coenzyme Q
coffee bag
coffee bug
coffee bar
coffee cup
cofferdam
coffee pot
coffee set
coffinite
cafetière
cafeteria
cuffuffle
cognately
cognation
cognisant
cognizant
cognitive
cognition
cognomens
cognomina
cigar case
cigarillo
cigar tree
cigarette
cogitable
cogitator
cageyness
cohabitee
cohabiter
coheiress
cohune oil
cohyponym
coherence
coherency
coheritor
cohesible
chinaware
china bark
chicanery
climatise
climatize
chicaning
cnidarian
chirality
china clay
China rose
Chinatown
chinaroot
chiragric
chivalric
china tree
climactic
China jute
climature
chipboard
clipboard
chilblain
climbable
climb down
climb-down
chip-based
chinch bug
chiacking
chincapin
chincough
child care
crib death
childless
childness
childlike
child-wife
childhood
child lock
crime wave
chime bars
Clive Bell
crimeless
Chile pine
chimerism
criterion
chiselled
clitellum
cribellum
chiseller
clitellar
cribellar
cliff-face
cliffhang
chieftain
chiefless
chiefship
chiefling
coiffeuse
clingfish
clingfilm
criminate
ceilinged
chiliagon
chidingly
criticise
criticize
criticism
clinician
cuisinier
chirimoya
chitinoid
chitinous
criminous
chiliarch
clip joint
chickadee
chickweed
chickling
crinklier
chinkapin
chickaree
Chickasaw
cricketer
cailleach
cailliach
chilly bin
chilli dog
chillness
chidlings
chitlings
coin money
clientage
clientele
clientèle
clianthus
Chiang Mai
cairngorm
chipolata
chiyogami
Chico Marx
Crinoidea
crinoidal
chipochia
crinoline
chinovnik
Cainozoic
chirology
chironomy
chiropody
chibouque
clinoaxis
Crimplene®
crispness
crimpiest
crispiest
crippling
clinquant
chiarezza
chiasmata
chinstrap
Cointreau®
chihuahua
cri du chat
clip wings
culpa lata
calcarate
cellarage
call alarm
call a halt
calcaneal
calcaneum
calcanean
calcaneus
Callaghan
calcarine
calmative
Collatine
collative
caldarium
collation
cellarist
collagist
calla lily
cellarman
colcannon
caliatour
cellarous
culpatory
collapsar
calibrate
celebrate
celebrant
calabrese
colubriad
colubrine
celebrity
coldblood
calaboose
calibered
colobuses
calf-bound
cell cycle
Culicidae
cold cream
calyculus
colocynth
calycinal
cilicious
colicroot
colectomy
Colocasia
cold-drawn
caladiums
calfdozer
cullender

called-for
colleague
collegial
collegium
collegian
culver-key
cul-de-four
calcedony
calceated
collected
collector
cold frame
cold front
cold forge
call forth
cole-garth
colchicum
call house
coldhouse
colligate
collimate
culminate
cultivate
culminant
Celtiberi
collinear
callipers
coltishly
calcimine
Calvinism
Celticism
collision
calvities
Calvinist
Celticist
callidity
Cal Ripken
cullionly
calcicole
Callippic
calligram
Celtic Sea
Callistus
calcifuge
celsitude
colliculi
cold light
columbate
columbary
chlamydia
chlamydes
✧columbine
columbite
columbium
Colombian
Columbian
columnist
columella
calamanco
call-money
calembour
chlamyses
colonnade
celandine
colonelcy
call names
calandria
calendric
cylindric
calendrer
coloniser
colonitis
calendula
calenture
colonizer
ciliolate
collocate
colloidal
colcothar
collodion
callosity
caliology
callously
colloquia
collotype
caliphate
calyptera
cellphone
colophony
chlordane
chloracne
Coleridge
calorific
colorific
Coleraine
chlorella
chlorosis
chloritic
chlorotic
cultrated
call round
calmstane
cold start
cold steel
colosseum
✧celestine
celestite
celestial
calmstone
cold-short
coltsfoot
colostomy
colostric
colostrum
cold table
calculate
cellulase
colourant
calculary
colour bar
coloureds
colourful
cellulite
collusive
colourise
colourize
colouring
colluvial
colluvium
collusion
colluvies
colourist
culturist
colour-mag
colourman
celluloid
✧celluloid®
calculose
cellulose
calculous
colour-sup
colourway
calavance
calf whale
cold water
Calixtine
Colwyn Bay
colly bird
collyrium
Collymore
come again?
combatant
come apart
come and go
come-and-go
commander
compander
compandor
commandos
campanero
comradely
companied
campanile
combative
come alive
combating
companing
campanili
companion
come amiss
campanist
cembalist
cymbalist
Cambazola
come along
cymbaloes
come about
✧compasses
compacted
come after
compactor
compactly
campanula
camp-chair
campcraft
Cimicidae
come clean
comically
comic book
comedones
compendia
commendam
campeador
competent
Commelina
Cymbeline
cambering
Cimmerian
campesino
compelled
compeller
commensal
commenter
commentor
camper van
camp-fever
cymagraph
cymograph
camphoric
camsheugh
combinate
comminate
commingle
combining
cymbidium
cambiform
cymbiform
commissar
committed
committee
committal
committer
cambistry
comfiture
comminute
comb jelly
camelback
camel hair
compliant
Camelidae
comeliest
complying
complaint
camel spin
completed
cumulated
completer
complexus
complexly
Camembert
camanachd
Comintern
cement gun
Comanches
cementite
Cominform
comings-in
cameo ware
come of age
commonage
cameo-part
commorant
camcorder
Common Era
campodeid
component
come off it!
✧composite
commoning
come-o'-will
Cambodian
commotion
compotier
commodify
commodity
common law
compound Q
Cambozola®
cameo-role
commodore
✧comforter
composter
composure
cymophane
cyma recta
Cambridge
comprador
Camorrism
Camorrist
camarilla
cameraman
cumbrance
comprisal
camera-shy
camerated
combretum
come round
camisades
camisados
camp-stool
come short
camass-rat
camsteary
comptable
comptible
comitadji
camstairy
comatulid
comptroll
comitatus
✧communard
commutate
computant
come under
communise
communize
communing
computing
✧communism
communion
✧communist
computist
community
camouflet
combustor
commutual
cantabank
Cingalese
concavely
contangos
contadina
cantabile
contadine
contadini
contagium
connation
contagion
contadino
concavity
container
con calore
cantaloup
centaurea
conga drum
Centaurus
canvassed
canvasser
contactor
connature
cant-board
canebrake
cane-chair
conscient
conscribe
conscript
canicular
conically
cynically
conscious
cony-catch
Canada Day
Canada Dry®
cancerate
centenary
cancelbot
contender
conger-eel
canceleer
connexive
centering
centesimi
congenial
Cancerian
connexion
centesimo
cancelier
centenier
congeries
convexity
cancelled
canceller
concealer
concerned
condemned
contemner
contemnor
cancerous
cankerous
cancel out
contemper
conferred
conferral
conferrer
condensed
confessed
condenser
confessor
converser
consensus
contessas
conceited
concerted
congested
connected
contented
contested
concentre
connect up
concenter
connecter
connector
contester
convector
converter
convertor
concentus
conceptus
concertos
confestly
cannelure
confervae
conserver
confervas
canefruit
cane grass
cynegetic
Conchobar
cinchonic
cantharid
cantharis
cantharus
conchitis
candidate
confidant
candidacy
convincer
condiddle
cantilena
centipede
centinell
confide in
confiseur
✧confiteor
canniness
cantiness
condiment
confident
connivent
conticent
✧continent
concisely
cantingly
cunningly
confiding
confining
convivial
concision
condition
conciliar
✧canticles
confirmed
confirmee
confirmer
confirmor
consigned
consignee
consigner
consignor
cincinnus
condignly
cuneiform
canticoys
concierge
centigram
consist in
continued
configure
confiture
continual
continuum
continuer
continuos
concluded
candle-end
canal-cell
confluent
canellini
Candlemas
candlenut
canal-boat
Canaletto
cynomolgi
cynomania
cinematic
canonical
conundrum
cannonade
centonate
connotate
consolate
convocate
consonant
Candomble
Candomblé
cannon bit
concordat
Cantonese

Congolese
centonell
cannoneer
canzonets
condolent
cantonise
cantonize
connotive
cantoning
canyoning
cantorial
censorial
censorian
cannonier
consocies
centonist
conformal
conformer
conjoined
contornos
con dolore
consonous
contoured
concourse
consortia
consorted
contorted
concocter
concoctor
consorter
consolute
convolute
Cynipidae
cane piece
cinephile
canopying
can-opener
canephora
canephore
conspirer
concreate
centre bit
centrical
congruent
centreing
congruity
contralti
contralto
centrally
cineramic
confronté
centriole
cinereous
congruous
cineraria
confrérie
contrasty
cinerator
contrived
contriver
cone shell
canescent
cane sugar
cane-trash
constrain
✧constable
constrict
Constanta
Constance
constancy
cinctured
cunctator
construer
construct
cannulate
cingulate
conjugate
consulage
consulate
conjugant
contumacy
conjure up
contumely
concubine
conducive
contusive
confusing
conjuring
consuming
centurial
connubial
centurion
Confucian
confusion
contusion
Confucius
concurred
✧conqueror
consultee
conductor
consulter
consultor
conductus
centumvir
cone wheat
concyclic
condyloma
condyloid
candytuft
clozapine
crotaline
crotalism
choralist
cholaemia
cholaemic
Cro-Magnon
crowberry
cropbound
crotchety
choiceful
cook-chill
cloacalin
cloacinal
cloudland
cloud base
crowd sail
cloud-capt
cloudless
chondrite
chondrify
clogdance
co-ordinal
coordinal
chondroid
cloudtown
chondrule
cloud over
choleraic
cooperage
co-operate
cooperate
choke back
close call
chokedamp
co-operant
closed-end
closehead
choke-pear
closeness
cloze test
choke line
closeting
coopering
cholelith
clove pink
close-knit
chokebore
clove-hook
chokecoil
choke down
close down
closedown
crop-eared
clove-tree
closed set
choke-full
cholecyst
crowfoots
Chongqing
cloth-yard
cloth-hall
cloth-ears
cloth head
crocheted
crocheter
coonhound
chop-house
chophouse
cookhouse
coolhouse
cloyingly
coolie hat
clonicity
chorionic
chorizont
crosiered
chorister
clock card
crookback
chowkidar
crookedly
croakiest
clockwise
clock-golf
clockwork
cloakroom
chock-full
chop logic
choplogic
crop-marks
crown land
crown-bark
crown gall
crown-head
crownless
crown cork
crownwork
crown-post
chocolate
chocolaty
Croton bug
crocodile
crocosmia
croton oil
chorology
clodpated
crow-quill
choirgirl
choir loft
crossband
cross-fade
croustade
crossjack
cross-talk
crosswalk
crossfall
crossways
croissant
chopsocky
crosshead
crossbeam
crossness
crow-steps
crow's-feet
crow's-nest
crosswind
crossbite
crossfire
crosswise
crossfish
chopstick
cross-kick
cross-link
cross bill
crossbill
cross-sill
crow's-bill
Chomskian
cloisonné
crossroad
crossword
Cookstown
crosstown
Cook's tour
crosswort
crow's-foot
crossbred
crosstree
cloistral
crossette
cross-ruff
crossbuck
crossover
cross-eyed
Chomskyan
clout-nail
clout-shoe
clouterly
chorusing
croquante
croquette
cephalate
capsaicin
captain RN
captaincy
captainry
cephalous
capocchia
Capuchins
capacious
cepaceous
copacetic
capacitor
Cupid's bow
Cape dagga
Cape Dutch
Copper Age
copresent
ciphering
coppering
copperish
cipher key
copsewood
cupbearer
cap verses
Cupressus
captivate
capsid bug
capriccio
cup lichen
coppicing
captivity
cyprinoid
caprifole
caprifoil
capriform
Capricorn
cap pistol
capsicums
capillary
cap sleeve
capelline
cupelling
cipollino
co-polymer
copolymer
cupolated
cap in hand
caponiere
coping-saw
coprolite
coprolith
coprozoic
coprology
copiously
copyright
co-portion
copartner
caparison
caper-bush
copes-mate
Cape smoke
copestone
copasetic
copataine
capotting
copatriot
capitella
capitulum
capitular
capitally
capitanos
capotasto
capsulate
capsulary
cup fungus
capsulise
capsulize
Cape Verde
Cape Wrath
caprylate
coquetted
coquilles
carbamate
curtalaxe
carpaccio
Carl Andre
coriander
Cartagena
Cornaceae
carrageen
carbachol
carbamide
cardamine
carnalise
carnalize
cercariae
curvative
carnalism
curialism
carbanion
carnation
cercarian
circadian
corrasion
curtation
curvation
caryatids
carnalist
cerealist
curialist
carnality
carjacker
corralled
curtailer
curtain up
certainly
certainty
carbazole
currajong
currawong
care about
carvacrol
Cervantes
Cordaites
carnahuba
curvature
cardboard
corkboard
cerebrate
cornbrake
cornbrash
Carabidae
cornbread
Caribbean
cerebella
carabiner
corybants
corkborer
cornborer
Carl Bosch
cerebrums
corncrake
Caracalla
cerecloth
ceraceous
corocoros
corydalis
careenage
correlate
curveball
cursenary
carpet-bed
carpetbag
carpet bug
corner-boy
cerberean
Correggio
✧carmelite
cartelise
cartelize
carpeting
corbeling
curveting
careerism
carpe diem
cartelism
carnelian
Cartesian
cerberian
cornelian
Cordelier
corsetier
Cornelius
careerist
cartelist
cornetist
corbelled
corbeille
Corneille
corner-man
curvesome
corbel off
corbel out
carpet-rod
curvetted
carpenter
corrector
carpentry
correctly
currently
cornemuse
cornflake
cornfield
carefully
cornflour
cerograph
cord grass
Cary Grant
Coregonus
caregiver
cirrhopod
cart-horse
Corchorus
cirrhosis
cirrhotic
cart-house
corfhouse
cartilage
circinate
corticate
curtilage
cardiacal
card index
card-index
cirripede
carbineer
corkiness
corniness
curdiness
curliness
curviness
corrigent
cursively
carpingly
cornichon
currishly

certified
cormidium
carbinier
certifier
cardialgy
cordially
carcinoma
Carnivora
corticoid
carnivore
cortisone
cirriform
cordiform
corniform
curviform
corridors
cursitory
corbicula
curricula
certitude
corollary
care label
Carol Reed
coral weed
coral reef
coral fern
coralline
corallite
corolline
carolling
coral-fish
Corallian
cor blimey
coralloid
coral-rock
ceruleous
coralroot
coralwort
coral spot
coral tree
caroluses
corsleted
Carl Lewis
chromidia
chromogen
chromakey
ceromancy
carambola
carambole
corymbose
chromatic
chromatid
chromatin
chronicle
chronical
Carinthia
carangoid
corantoes
carinated
coronated
coroneted
chronaxie
carbonara
carbon arc
carbonade
carbonate
carronade
cartonage
corporate
Carbonari
carbonado
cormorant
corposant
cursorary
car-bomber
cartouche
care order
corporeal
cornopean
corrodent
carrot fly
carbonise
carbonize
carnotite
corrosive
cursorial
corrosion
carnosity
corporify
curiosity
cursorily
car-pooler
cordon off
carron oil
carpology
cartology
cordotomy
cartogram
carrousel
caryopses
caryopsis
coreopsis
curiously
carbon tax
cargo cult
coryphaei
coryphene
cardpunch
carap-wood
cardphone
curlpaper
corn poppy
carap-nuts
cartridge
corn snake
coruscate
cornstalk
cart's-tail
card-sharp
coruscant
Carl Sagan
Christina
card swipe
caressive
cerussite
Christine
caressing
cerastium
Christian
chrysalid
corn-salad
chrysalis
Christmas
chrysanth
core store
cornstone
curbstone
corkscrew
corn shuck
curettage
cart-track
card-table
ceratodus
curstness
caretaker
core times
ceratitis
carburate
circulate
corrugate
cartulary
carbuncle
corpuscle
corpulent
carfuffle
curfuffle
carburise
carburize
co-routine
curcumine
Carausius
curculios
Cernunnos
corduroys
corrupter
corruptor
circuitry
corruptly
corivalry
caravaned
caravance
caravaner
cartwheel
carrytale
carry back
carry-back
Carlylese
curry-leaf
Carlylean
cordyline
Carlylism
currycomb
carry over
carry-over
carry away
Carl Zeiss
corozo nut
cispadane
Cassandra
cast an eye
Cistaceae
cassareep
castanets
costalgia
casuarina
Costa Rica
cassaripe
casualise
casualize
c'est-à-dire
casualism
caseation
cassation
Castalian
cessation
CT scanner
cost a bomb
cast a vote
cosy along
cast about
co-starred
cascadura
case-bound
caste-mark
casteless
coshering
cosmetics
castellum
castellan
cisternae
cashew nut
casserole
case glass
cosphered
castigate
cuspidate
cassimere
cystidean
cushiness
costively
cassingle
Castilian
coseismic
coseismal
cushioned
cushionet
cespitose
cuspidore
cystiform
cashierer
casuistic
casuistry
case-knife
Castlebar
cast light
cisalpine
cash limit
castle nut
cast loose
cisplatin
c'est la vie
casemaker
casemated
cosmorama
cassonade
Cosmo Lang
cystocarp
cosmonaut
cassowary
customary
Cystoidea
cystocele
castoreum
cosmogeny
customise
customize
cystolith
custodial
custodian
custodier
cassocked
cassoulet
castor oil
cosmogony
cosmology
cystotomy
cosmotron
cosmocrat
cosponsor
cost price
Cashpoint®
cashpoint
casarecci
castrated
cash ratio
castratos
cesarevna
caskstand
cast-steel
case-study
custumary
costumier
cast water
cut capers
Catharine
catharise
catharize
Catharism
Catharist
citharist
Cat Ballou
cat-hammed
cattaloes
catharses
catharsis
cathartic
catabolic
catabasis
cataclasm
catechise
catechize
catechism
catechist
coticular
cuticular
cetaceous
cut across
cut a caper
cataclysm
Cytherean
Catherina
Catherine
cotter-pin
cathedral
cathectic
cut-leaved
catafalco
citigrade
categoric
catchable
catchweed
catchment
catch fire
catch cold
catch hold
catchword
catchpole
catchpoll
cut-throat
catch-crop
cutcherry
catch away
cattiness
cat-rigged
cuttingly
cattishly
cetrimide
cat-witted
cat litter
cat-silver
Catskills
cytokinin
cotyledon
catalogue
cataloger
cotillion
cattleman
catalepsy
catalyser
catalysis
cytolysis
catalytic
cytolytic
côtelette
catalexis
catalyzer
catamenia
catamaran
cytometer
cytometry
catamount
cat-and-dog
cut and dry
cotangent
cotenancy
cutaneous
cut and run
cottonade
cotton bud
city of God
cotton gin
chthonian
cataplasm
cytoplasm
cataplexy
cytopenia
cataphora
catoptric
cataphyll
caterwaul
catarrhal
catarhine
cityscape
city state
cut it fine
catatonia
catatonic
cytotoxic
cytotoxin
cothurnus
Cutty Sark
cutty-sark
citizenry
causalgia
causative
Caucasian
causation
causality
Caucasoid
coumarone
cruzadoes
clubbable
crumbiest
crumblies
chubb-lock
courbaril
crumb-tray
courbette
church-ale
club class
clutch bag
churching
Churchill
churchism
crunchier
crunchily
church key
councilor
churchman
churchway
coup d'oeil
cauldrife
chunder on
coup d'état
cauterant
Clupeidae
causeless
crudeness
cauterise
cauterize
cauterism
cause list
cautelous
cruzeiros
Chungking
courgette
crushable
crush a cup
cauchemar
crush room
cough down
cough drop
couchette
clubhouse
cousinage
churidars
caulinary
coulibiac
crucified
crucifier
caudillos
crucially
cautioner
cautionry
cauliform
cruciform
coulisses
chuckling
chuckhole
chuck-full
caudle cup
coupledom
cruelness
cruellest
crummiest
Chu'un Ch'iu
churnmilk
chunner on
Chuang-tzu
crumpling
churr-worm
chuprassy
caumstane
counselor
caumstone
cruiseway
Coulthard
court card
court hand
courtyard
court case
countback
countable
Crustacea
countless
crustless
court-leet

crustiest
court shoe
countship
courtship
countline
courtlike
courtling
courtlier
Courtelle®
court fool
court-roll
courtroom
count down
countdown
count noun
courteous
clustered
chunter on
clutter up
courtesan
crustated
courtezan
couturier
clubwoman
civically
cave canem
cevadilla
cave-earth
cavalcade
civil year
civil time
covellite
cavilling
civil list
covalency
civilised
civiliser
civilized
civilizer
cavendish
covin-tree
cevapcici
covariant
coverable
cover girl
coverslip
coveralls
cover-slut
cover into
cover note
cavernous
cover crop
coverture
covert way
covetable
cowfeeder
cowdie-gum
cowardice
cowardree
cower away
cowl-staff
coxcombic
coxcombry
ceylanite
cly-faking
cry halves
Clydeside
cryogenic
chymistry
cryometer
Ceylonese
ceylonite
cryoprobe
cryoscope
cryoscopy
cryptical
cryptadia
cryptogam
coyotillo
cryptonym
do a candle
draw a bead
dead-alive
Dramamine®
dramatise
dramatize
Diana Rigg
dramatics
dramatist
diamagnet
Diana Dors
Diana Ross
dramaturg
draw blank
drabbling
drag-chain
dratchell
dead-doing
diandrous
dead drunk
draperied
deadening
deafening
diapering
do a perish
Dianetics®
draperies
drape coat
diametric
diametral
dialectic
dialectal
drape suit
diazeuxis
draughter
draught ox
deathward
death rate
death mask
diaphragm
death-damp
death-bell
death cell
deathless
death-fire
deathlike
death wish
diachylum
diachylon
Diaghilev
deathblow
deathsman
death-song
death roll
diachrony
dray-horse
deathtrap
diathermy
diaphyses
diaphysis
diathesis
diathetic
death star
draghound
deadhouse
death duty
deaminate
diapirism
Dravidian
dualistic
dear knows
diallagic
deadlight
diablerie
deadly sin
dead-level
draw level
dharmsala
dead march
drainable
drainpipe
drain-tile
drawn work
drain-trap
diagnoses
diagnosis
diaconate
dragomans
dialog box
diamonded
deaconess
dragoness
dragonfly
diabolise
diabolize
dialogise
dialogite
dialogize
diatomite
dragonise
dragonize
dragonish
diabolism
diacodium
Draconism
dragonism
diacodion
✧draconian
diabolist
dialogist
diatomist
diabology
dianoetic
✧dracontic
dial-plate
draw-plate
dead point
draw poker
drag-queen
diarrheic
diarrheal
diarrhoea
diatropic
diaereses
diaeresis
diacritic
diatretum
dead's part
draw-sheet
deadstock
Dead Souls
draw-table
diastolic
draftsman
diactinic
diactinal
dead thraw
diastasic
diastasis
diastatic
do a runner
dead-water
diapyesis
diapyetic
Debye unit
debagging
debugging
Dublin Bay
Dubliners
debelling
debenture
dubiosity
Dubrovnik
dubiously
dub poetry
Dobermann
debarrass
debarment
debarring
debossing
debussing
debit card
debatable
dubitable
dubitably
debateful
debutante
débutante
dib-stones
dubitancy
debit note
debauched
debauchee
debaucher
de-blurred
debruised
declarant
dichasial
dichasium
dictation
declaimer
dictatory
dictatrix
déclassée
dictature
duck-board
decubitus
deckchair
dock-cress
decoctive
decoction
decachord
dicacious
deck-cargo
decocture
docudrama
deciduate
decidable
decidedly
decadence
decadency
deciduous
✧**decretals**
dickey bow
decrement
Dick Emery
ducted fan
decretive
decreeing
docketing
decretist
déchéance
decretory
Decagynia
decagonal
decoherer
deckhouse
dacoitage
declinate
declinant
deceitful
diclinism
De Chirico
declivity
ductility
declivous
diclinous
Dr Crippen
decollate
décolleté
✧**decalogue**
decillion
decalcify
decalitre
decilitre
deciliter
decumbent
decemviri
decemvirs
decomplex
decimally
decompose
Decameron
decametre
decimetre
decimator
decimeter
decantate
decennary
decongest
decennial
decennium
decencies
Decandria
decontrol
doctorand
doctorate
dichogamy
doctoress
doctorial
dicrotism
dicrotous
dichotomy
decapodal
decapodan
deceptive
deception
deceptory
decurrent
decursive
dichroite
dichroism
decursion
dichromic
dichromat
doctrinal
decorated
decorator
decussate
decastere
decistere
duck's-meat
dicastery
decastich
decession
Dicksonia
duckshove
duck's-foot
dachshund
decastyle
Dicotylae
decathlon
Docetists
decaudate
decoupage
découpage
decay heat
dictyogen
Dicky Bird
dicky-bird
dactylist
decoy-duck
didrachma
deducible
dodecagon
deductive
deduction
didactics
dedicated
dedicatee
dedicator
dodgeball
doddering
doddipoll
Dadaistic
Didelphia
didelphic
didelphid
Didelphis
Didelphys
Dodonaean
Didynamia
dude ranch
doddypoll
Deepavali
drepanium
✧**daedalian**
dietarian
diet-bread
deerberry
deep-drawn
dreadless
diet-drink
dieselise
dieselize
dietetics
diesel oil
dae-nettle
deep field
deer fence
dies fasti
dies festi
deergrass
dredge-box
deerhound
drerihead
dietician
dietitian
die-sinker
djellabah
dreamland
dream team
dreamless
dreamtime
dreamhole
dreamboat
deer mouse
Die Brücke
deep space
dressmake
dyer's-weed
dyer's-weld
diet sheet
dress form
dress down
dress coat
Deep South
dress suit
deep-toned
duettinos
defrauder
defragger
defraying
defeatism
deflation
defeatist
defiantly
defeature
deficient
defective
defection
defecator
defaecate
duffel bag
dufferdom
different
dufferism
deflexion
deflected
deflector
deflexure
diffident
duffing-up
difficile
difficult
defalcate
defoliate
defoliant
diffluent
defendant
definable
definably
✧**defenders**
definiens
defensive
deflorate
defroster
deferable
deferment
deferring
deformity
deference
defatting
diffusely
diffusive
defluxion
diffusion

defaulter
dog-paddle
dog eat dog
dog-eat-dog
dogmatise
dogmatize
degrading
dog racing
dogmatism
dogmatics
dogmatist
dog-salmon
dogmatory
degree day
doglegged
doggerman
dog fennel
dog-kennel
dog letter
dogshores
dignitary
dogginess
doggishly
dignified
dog violet
dog sledge
dog sleigh
Digambara
do-goodery
do-gooding
do-goodism
dog collar
diglossia
dogs of war
degarnish
dogaressa
degustate
digestive
digestion
digastric
digitalin
digitalis
dog's-tooth
digitiser
digitated
digitizer
dahabeeah
dahabiyah
dahabiyeh
dehydrate
dehiscent
deiparous
driver ant
driveable
drive belt
drive time
drivelled
driveller
drive home
dyingness
dziggetai
drink-hail
drinkable
drillship
drillhole
deinosaur
Deinornis
dei gratia
dripstone
drift-land
drift-sail

deistical
drift-weed
driftless
de integro
driftwood
drift-bolt
deid-thraw
drift tube
dairymaid
Daily Mail
dairy farm
Daily Star
dejection
dejectory
Dr Johnson
dika-bread
Dekabrist
Dukhobors
dyke swarm
dak runner
dulcamara
delta wave
dollar gap
dollarise
dollarize
delta wing
Dalmatian
Dalradian
dulocracy
delicious
Delacroix
doli capax
deludable
dolce vita
delve into
dolefully
delegable
diligence
delighted
delight in
delphinia
Delphinus
dolphinet
dollhouse
Dalai Lama
dolliness
doltishly
dalliance
Dulcitone®
dulcitude
dolomitic
delimiter
Dolomites
delineate
delundung
✧daltonism
Daltonian
delapsion
deliquium
deliriant
dolorific
delirious
doleritic
deliriums
Delftware
dilatable
dilutable
delete key
dilatancy
dilatator
deliverer

deliverly
dill-water
dolly-shop
dolly shot
dolly bird
delay line
dolly girl
Dolayatra
Domdaniel
damnation
dimyarian
demeanour
damnatory
Dumbarton
demobbing
✧democracy
democraty
Damoclean
domiciled
dumb-cluck
dimidiate
demi-deify
demi-devil
damnedest
damselfly
dumbfound
demagogic
demagogue
demi-gorge
dumminess
dumpiness
dumpishly
dim-witted
demulcent
demulsify
demi-lance
demomania
demi-monde
Demi Moore
dementate
demandant
dominical
Dominican
demanding
demanning
Damon Hill
dimension
demand-led
dominance
dominancy
demantoid
dominions
dominator
dime novel
dumb piano
damp-proof
demipique
demarcate
demurrage
dimorphic
demurring
demersion
demisable
✧damascene
damaskeen
demissive
demission
domestics
demystify
dime store
dimissory

damp squib
damasquin
Demetrius
demitasse
dump truck
demiurgic
demiurgus
demi-volte
dungarees
ding-a-ling
dentalium
dentation
Dan Marino
don't ask me!
Dungannon
Doncaster
dune-buggy
Dinoceras
dance band
dance hall
danceable
dunce's cap
denseness
dandelion
danger man
donkey-man
dungeoner
dangerous
Dantesque
dance drug
dannebrog
dinner set
dancettee
dance tune
Dance Away
denigrate
danthonia
dandiacal
dinginess
denyingly
dandified
dentition
densifier
dentiform
dandiprat
dentistry
Dingle Bay
dynamical
dinomania
denominal
dynamiter
dynamotor
dona nobis
dining-car
Dinantian
den mother
Dundonian
dine out on
donor card
Dundreary
dendrimer
dendritic
denitrate
denotable
Dunstable
dinothere
denetting
do-nothing
denitrify
Donatello
denouncer

Dan Quayle
D'Annunzio
Danny Kaye
dandy-cart
dandy-cock
dandy-roll
dandyprat
dandyfunk
Donizetti
door-cheek
dioecious
Dioscorea
Dioscorus
drop-drill
dromedare
dromedary
duodenary
do one's bit
drone-pipe
duodecimo
do one's nut
drove road
doorframe
drop-forge
diosgenin
deoxidate
droningly
dronishly
deoxidise
deoxidize
doohickey
dioristic
dhobi itch
doorknock
doodlebug
doom-laden
drollness
drool over
doornboom
deodorant
deodorise
deodorize
door-plate
drop-press
droppings
droop nose
dropsical
door-stead
drop-scene
drowsihed
doorstone
drop scone
dropstone
dioestrus
doomsayer
dioptrate
dioptrics
doomwatch
Dionysiac
Dionysian
Dionysius
depravity
depictive
depiction
depicture
Dipodidae
deprecate
depredate
deprehend
depletive
depletion

dipterist
dipterous
depletory
depressed
depressor
dip-sector
dope-fiend
depigment
depthless
depth bomb
duplicand
duplicate
dip-circle
duplicity
dapple-bay
depilator
dependant
dependent
depending
dupondius
di penates
diplomate
diplomacy
Dr Proudie
diplotene
Diplopoda
diplozoon
deprogram
diplontic
dipeptide
departing
depurator
departure
deposable
depositor
depasture
diphthong
DIP switch
dipswitch
✧diphysite
De Quincey
darraigne
Dardanian
D'Artagnan
dermatoid
dermatome
Durga-puja
dartboard
Dark blues
dirt cheap
directive
direction
✧directory
directrix
direct tax
duricrust
Dorididae
dare-devil
dermestid
dor-beetle
direfully
dirigible
de rigueur
dirigisme
dirigiste
dark horse
dark-house
dirtiness
derring do
derring-do
derringer

dartingly
dormitive
Darwinism
Darwinian
dormition
Darwinist
dorsiflex
dormitory
Duralumin®
duralumin
darklings
dura mater
doronicum
Dormobile®
derepress
Dordrecht
derisible
dirt track
derivable
derivably
dirty bomb
dirty word
dirty look
dirty work
disparage
disparate
discalced
discandie
dastardly
dismal day
dismayful
dismaying
dissaving
d'escalier
dismality
disparity
disjaskit
dishallow
disdained
disfavour
dispauper
dismantle
Descartes
distantly
dashboard
dust-brand
disc brake
disoblige
dust bunny
desk-bound
deskbound
dust-brush
desecrate
desiccate
desiccant
disaccord
dishcloth
dish-clout
dish-cover
dust cover
disk drive
dust devil
disregard
desperate
desperado
disrepair
dissemble
dismember
dissembly
descended
descender

Words marked ✧ can also be spelled with one or more capital letters

disbelief
disrelish
dysgenics
dispelled
discerner
Desdemona
dispeople
destemper
distemper
dyspepsia
dispensed
dispersal
disseisin
dispenser
disperser
disseisor
dissensus
das heisst
dyslectic
dyspeptic
dystectic
dissected
dissector
✧dissenter
desuetude
disrepute
désoeuvré
disseizin
disseizor
dish-faced
disaffect
disaffirm
designate
designful
designing
dysphagia
dysphagic
dysthymia
dysthymic
dysphonia
dysphonic
dyschroia
disthrone
dysphoria
dysphoric
discharge
dischurch
dysphasia
dysthesia
dysthetic
dosshouse
disshiver
destinate
dissipate
duskiness
dustiness
dissident
distingué
dashingly
distichal
duskishly
dissimile
distilled
distiller
dish it out
dismissal
destitute
disfigure
displease
disfluent
desulphur
desalting
desultory
dysplasia
desolater
desolator
disillude
displayed
displayer
disembark
disemploy
disembody
dose-meter
dosimeter
dosimetry
disimmure
disengage
disentail
disenable
dyspnoeic
dyspnoeal
disinfect
disinfest
disinvent
disinvest
dysentery
disanchor
disinvite
disanoint
desinence
disentomb
disinhume
despotate
dislocate
dissonant
disgodded
dispondee
discoidal
dispose of
discovert
disforest
dishonest
✧discovery
discomfit
disbodied
disposing
dissocial
desmodium
despotism
dystopian
despoiler
discommon
Des Moines
desmosome
discolour
dishonour
dosiology
discourse
distorted
disposure
dissolute
disappear
desipient
dustproof
desirable
describer
desirably
disgracer
discredit
disorient
disprofit
dispraise
distraite
descrying
deserving
disarming
desertion
distraint
disbranch
disproove
desert pea
dystrophy
desert rat
dyscrasia
disprison
disproved
disproval
disproven
dyspraxia
destroyed
destroyer
disesteem
dustsheet
disk store
dust storm
disattire
disattune
dishtowel
despumate
disputant
disturbed
discumber
disturber
disburden
dissuader
dissunder
dishumour
disguised
disbursal
disburser
discusser
disguiser
discursus
disgusted
dislustre
disrupter
disruptor
dispurvey
disavouch
disavowal
dash-wheel
disc wheel
Discworld
dishwater
Dusty Hare
dusty-foot
dittander
dot matrix
detractor
détraquée
duty-bound
detective
detection
datacomms
do to death
✧dithelete
✧dithelism
dithecous
dutifully
dataglove
Dutch barn
Dutch leaf
Dutch wife
Dutch pink
Dutch gold
Dutch doll
Dutch rush
Dutch oven
dottiness
detriment
detrition
dottipoll
datum line
detention
detonator
ditrochee
dittology
D C Thomson
duteously
detergent
determent
deterrent
determine
detersive
deterring
detersion
detorsion
detortion
dethroner
date-stamp
date-shell
date-sugar
detrusion
detox tank
dithyramb
Deucalion
drug abuse
drum brake
drum-belly
druidical
Deusdedit
deuterate
doucepere
douceness
douzepers
deuteride
deuterium
drug fiend
doughball
Doukhobor
doughtily
dough hook
drunkenly
double-axe
double act
double bed
double bar
double dip
double-dip
double-log
doubleton
double top
double-you
drum-major
diurnally
drumstick
drugstore
Doug Scott
drug squad
doubtable
drum table
dauntless
doubtless
diuturnal
duumviral
Drury Lane
deviation
Dave Allen
deviatory
deviceful
David Hare
David Mach
dove-drawn
dividable
dividedly
David Lean
David Hope
David Sole
dividuous
David Hume
David Owen
dove-house
Davy Jones
devaluate
divulgate
devil a bit
devil's-bit
devilment
divellent
devilship
divulsive
devilling
devilfish
divulsion
divalency
devil a one
devil's own
developed
développé
developer
devil-crab
davenport
devonport
divinator
deviously
divergent
diversely
divertive
divorcive
diverging
diverting
diversion
diversify
diversity
Dover sole
devastate
devisable
divisible
divisibly
dove's-foot
divesture
devotedly
devitrify
devotions
devouring
dewlapped
downburst
downforce
downgrade
down-going
down-gyved
dowdiness
downiness
dowelling
down-lying
do wonders
down-quilt
dowerless
downright
downriver
downscale
downstage
downstate
downstair
downswing
downshift
downspout
down south
downsizer
down-train
downtrend
dowitcher
down tools
do without
downthrow
down under
downwards
Dexedrine®
Dixieland
Dixie Dean
dexterity
dexterous
dextrally
dextrorse
daysailer
daysailor
dry-waller
day-labour
drysalter
day school
day-length
day centre
day-nettle
day return
dry sherry
dayr'house
dry lining
dry-fisted
dry skiing
dayflower
Days of Awe
dayspring
day trader
Dryasdust
do you mind?
dizygotic
dizziness
El Alamein
emanative
emanation
evagation
exaration
emanatist
Elaeagnus
emanatory
eparchate
exarchate
exarchist
Ecardines
égarement
erasement
elaterite
elaterium
enamelled
enameller
evangelic
eradicate
evaginate
examinate
exanimate
eradicant
examinant
evasively
examining
evanition
emaciated
Evaristus
epaulette
état-major
epaenetic
epainetic
elaborate
evaporate
enamorado
elaeolite
evaporite
enamoured
en arrière
enactable
exactable
exaltedly
enanthema
exanthema
exactness
exactress
exanthems
enactment
exactment
elastomer
elastance
ejaculate
Eva Turner
evacuator
evaluator
élan vital
embraceor
embracery
embrangle
embracive
embracing
embrasure
embrazure
embedment
embedding
embodying
emblemata
emblemise
emblemize
embreathe
embrittle
emballing
embalming
embellish
embrocate
embroider
embroglio
emblossom
embarrass
Ember-days
Ember-week
embarking
embarring
embargoed
embargoes
emboscata
embassade
embassage

embossing
embussing
embattled
elbow-room
embayment
embryonic
embryonal
embryo-sac
embryotic
embezzler
esclandre
exchanger
Encratite
Encratism
Eucharist
enchanted
enchanter
escabeche
en caballo
excrement
excretive
exceeding
ecclesial
excretion
excretory
encierros
encheason
escheator
✧exchequer
Escoffier
enchilada
escribano
Euclidean
El Chichon
encrinite
encrimson
exculpate
Excalibur
excellent
excelling
encolpium
encolpion
✧excelsior
eucalypti
euchloric
escalator
encompass
encomiast
excambium
excambion
encomiums
encanthis
eccentric
excentric
each other
enchorial
euchology
enclosure
exclosure
exceptant
escapable
excipient
exceptive
excepting
exception
escape key
escopette
escortage
excarnate
excoriate
encurtain
excurrent
excursive
excursion
eucaryote
excerptum
excerptor
excisable
excusable
excusably
excessive
excise law
exciseman
excise tax
excitable
excitably
excitedly
excitancy
etceteras
encourage
excaudate
exclusive
excluding
exclusion
exclusory
encaustic
encounter
excavator
eachwhere
eucryphia
encrypted
endearing
✧endeavour
eudialyte
endoblast
endecagon
endocrine
end-reader
eudaemony
endlessly
end result
eidograph
endogamic
endogenic
endeictic
ex delicto
Eid al-Adha
Eid al-Fitr
endolymph
endemical
endamoeba
endomorph
endomixis
endungeon
endenizen
end for end
endoplasm
endophagy
endophyte
elder hand
endurable
endurably
endorphin
eldership
endurance
eiderdown
eider duck
ecdysiast
endosteal
endosperm
endosteum
endoscope
endosmose
endospore
endoscopy
endotherm
endowment
Ebenaceae
epedaphic
elevating
elevation
edematose
edematous
elevatory
elegantly
exerciser
exercises
emendable
ependymal
emendator
eyeleteer
événement
exegetics
exegetist
ewe-necked
Eye Temple
elevenses
elemental
✧everglade
evergreen
energy gap
energumen
exergonic
emergence
emergency
energetic
energizer
eyeshadow
ewe-cheese
erethitic
elegiacal
eremitism
eye-glance
epeolatry
even money
eternally
eye lotion
eye socket
esemplasy
exemplary
eye splice
exemption
exemplify
eye-opener
execrable
execrably
Epeiridae
eyebright
e-learning
Eve Arnold
eversible
ever such a
eventrate
eventuate
eyestrain
electuary
electable
erectable
eleutheri
electress
erectness
eventless
ejectment
electrise
electrize
eye-string
electrics
electrify
electrode
electoral
executant
eye muscle
executive
execution
executory
executrix
exequatur
edelweiss
every last
everywhen
every whit
every inch
everybody
efficient
effective
effectual
enfreedom
exfoliate
exfoliant
effulgent
effulging
en famille
effortful
efference
E M Forster
effluvial
effluvium
effluxion
effluence
enfevered
Englander
engravery
engraving
englacial
engrained
engrainer
Edgbaston
edged tool
engrenage
eagle-hawk
eaglewood
euglenoid
egg beater
eagle-eyed
ergograph
Englisher
Englishry
Englified
egg slicer
ergomania
ergometer
ergonomic
engine-man
eigentone
engendure
egg powder
engrossed
engrosser
engarland
eagerness
engyscope
eightieth
eightsman
ergataner
eightfold
eightsome
eightfoil
eight-hour
eight-foot
engoûment
englutted
ethnarchy
enhearten
ephialtes
exhibiter
exhibitor
ethically
echidnine
enhydrite
ephedrine
enhydrous
echograph
ethnicism
ethnicity
exhalable
ephelides
Ethelbert
ethologic
echolalia
Ethelwulf
ephemerid
ephemerae
ephemeral
ephemeron
ephemeras
ephemeris
echinacea
enhancive
echinated
ethmoidal
ethnocide
Ethiopian
ethnology
etherical
ephoralty
ethereous
echiuroid
exhausted
exhauster
echeveria
ECHO virus
echovirus
epicardia
Ericaceae
Elisabeth
Elizabeth
Erika Hess
epitaphic
epitapher
epitaxial
emication
epilation
evitation
epifaunal
epigaeous
Epidaurus
epinastic
Edinburgh
evincible
evincibly
episcopal
epic drama
evil-doing
exilement
epimerise
epimerize
epicedial
epicedium
epimerism
epicedian
epidermic
epidermal
epidermis
exigeante
eviternal
Emile Zola
Émile Roux
epineural
epileptic
epicentre
epicenter
eminently
evidently
exigently
epizeuxis
epiphragm
Edith Piaf
epithelia
epiphanic
epiphyses
epiphysis
epithesis
epiphytic
epithetic
epiphytal
epitheton
eliminate
eliminant
epilithic
edificial
epinician
epinicion
epinikian
epinikion
edibility
epilimnia
Elia Kazan
epicleses
epiclesis
etiolated
enigmatic
eriometer
ebionitic
Eric Newby
epidosite
epilogise
epilogize
epitomise
epitomize
editorial
episodial
epilobium
epipolism
epilogist
epitomist
epicormic
epizootic
Emin Pasha
epirrhema
epigraphy
epicritic
Erik Satie
eristical
epistolic
epistoler
epistolet
edictally
epistemic
existence
epistases
epistasis
epistatic
epistaxis
✧epicurean
epicurise
epicurize
epicurism
etiquette
exit value
exit wound
epimysium
epicyclic
epigynous
enjoyable
enjoyably
enjoyment
Eskimo dog
enkindled
eukaryote
eel-basket
ex-librism
ex-librist
eclectics
enlighten
eulogiums
eclampsia
eclamptic
eglantine
ealdorman
ellipsoid
enlivener
Eumycetes
eumelanin
Eumenides
Emmenthal
emmetrope
E W Maunder
enneagram
ennobling
eunuchise
eunuchize
eunuchism
eunuchoid
Ernie Wise
Eindhoven
Ernö Rubik
Ernst Mach
Ernst Abbe
Ernst Udet
Ernst Röhm
Enobarbus
egomaniac
evocative
Elo rating
evocation
exoration
exogamous
evocatory
exorciser
exorcizer
exordiums
exonerate
elopement
esoterica
esoterism
exodermal
exodermis

erogenous
exogenous
ex officio
elongated
ecophobia
esophagus
egotheism
ecothermy
emotively
eroticise
eroticize
emotivism
eroticism
exoticism
emotivist
eroticist
emotivity
emotional
erosional
egotistic
Elohistic
Egon Krenz
emolliate
emollient
e-commerce
exosmosis
exosmotic
eloinment
exoenzyme
economise
economize
exopodite
economism
economics
economies
ecologist
economist
erotology
ecosphere
exosphere
exosporal
écossaise
erostrate
exostoses
exostosis
emolument
evolutive
elocution
evolution
eloquence
elocutory
evolvable
e converso
eponymous
ecosystem
esplanade
emphasise
emphasize
expiation
explainer
expiatory
Euphausia
euphausid
emplastic
emplaster
expectant
expecting
expedient
expediter
expeditor
euphemise
euphemize
expletive
euphemism
euphenics
expletory
expresser
espressos
expressly
empaestic
emplectum
emplecton
espagnole
explicate
en primeur
emptiness
emptional
expellant
expellent
expulsive
expelling
expulsion
emphlyses
emphlysis
espumosos
empennage
exponible
expansile
expansive
expensive
en pension
expansion
empanoply
espionage
euphorbia
euphonise
euphonize
explosive
exploring
euphonism
euphonium
explosion
exploiter
expurgate
expirable
empirical
Empire Day
expertise
expertize
esperance
Esperanto
euphrasia
ecphrasis
ekphrasis
empyreuma
emporiums
expiscate
en passant
exposable
expositor
exposture
expatiate
empathise
empathize
espousals
expounder
emphysema
Esquimaux
esquiress
Esquiline
exquisite
earbasher
Eurocracy
Eurocorps
enrheumed
earnestly
egregious
earthward
earth-bath
earthfall
earthfast
earthling
earth sign
earthflax
Earl Hines
earth-tone
earthwolf
earthwork
earthworm
earthborn
earth-bred
earth-star
eard-house
earliness
earlier on
ébrillade
enrolment
enrolling
errand boy
eirenicon
étrangère
enranckle
erroneous
ebriosity
ear-cockle
Euripides
Europhile
Europhobe
en rapport
Europoort
Ezra Pound
enrapture
Euraquilo
errorless
Eurospeak
egressive
egression
erratical
eurytherm
écritoire
eurytopic
early days
✧eurhythmy
✧early bird
early wood
early door
ecstasied
ecstasise
ecstasize
enstatite
Euskarian
eastabout
eastbound
exsiccate
easy chair
exsiccant
exsection
exsuccous
East-ender
Easter Day
Easter egg
✧easterner
ensheathe
enshelter
easy-going
Eastleigh
eastlings
easy money
essential
easy-peasy
Easy Rider
ensorcell
exsertile
ex-service
exsertion
East River
East Timor
easy terms
easy touch
elsewhere
erstwhile
eastwards
Essex Girl
essayette
estrapade
euthanase
euthanasy
extravert
eutrapely
estranged
estranger
extraught
estuarine
euthanise
euthanize
extradite
extra time
estuarial
estuarian
entralles
entrammel
extrapose
entrapper
extractor
ectoblast
entoblast
establish
ectocrine
Eutychian
eutectoid
entremets
extremest
extremely
entrechat
extremism
eutherian
euthenics
euthenist
extremist
extremity
entrecôte
entre nous
either way
estafette
ectogenic
eat the air
extricate
estrildid
extrinsic
entelechy
extolment
extolling
estimable
estimably
entamoeba
estaminet
extempore
ectomorph
estimator
extenuate
extendant
extensile
extensive
extension
extensity
Elton John
extincted
extrovert
eutrophic
ectropium
entropium
ectropion
entropion
Esthonian
eutropous
extrorsal
estoppage
ectoplasm
estopping
entoptics
entoproct
ectophyte
entophyte
entertake
extirpate
entertain
externals
enterable
Euterpean
extermine
extorsive
extortive
extortion
enter into
exteriors
enter upon
enteritis
estate car
ectotherm
entourage
En-Tout-Cas®
en tout cas
extrusile
extrusive
extrusion
extrusory
eutaxitic
enthymeme
entry form
educative
emulative
exudative
education
emulation
epulation
epuration
épuration
exudation
educatory
Ehud Barak
enunciate
emunction
emunctory
enumerate
exuberate
exuberant
educement
enurement
ecumenism
ecumenics
equifinal
emulgence
elucidate
elusively
eruditely
erudition
esurience
esuriency
eruciform
Eduskunta
enucleate
equalness
ebullient
equalling
equal sign
equaliser
equalizer
eburneous
emulously
equipment
equipoise
equipping
elutriate
equisetic
equisetum
equatable
equitable
equitably
exultance
exultancy
equivocal
equivalve
equivoque
ervalenta
enveloped
envenomed
enviously
envermeil
eavesdrip
eavesdrop
envoyship
enwreathe
Edwin Muir
Edwardian
erythrina
erythrite
erythrism
erythemal
etymology
Esztergom
enzymatic
flambeaus
flambeaux
flatbread
flat broke
flat brush
flaccidly
fraîcheur
fratchety
franchise
flanching
fratching
francolin
flanch out
fraudsman
fraudster
flare path
flamencos
flame-leaf
flameless
flabellum
flagellum
flageolet
fraternal
framework
flap-eared
flame-tree
flare star
flay-flint
fearfully
foam glass
✧franglais
frangible
flaughter
flash card
flashback
flash chip
flash fire
feathered
flashbulb
flashcube
flash tube
frat house
flash burn
flash-over
flagitate
flakiness
foaminess
fragilely
flamingos
flamingly
flaringly
foamingly
fragility
frankness
Frankenia
Frankfort
Frankfurt
frailness
flatliner
flatlings
flammable
fiat money
flaunting
flannelly
Fragonard
flavorful
flavoring
flavonoid
flavorous
flappable
flagrance
fragrance
flagrancy
fragrancy
flatshare
flagstaff
Frans Hals
flagstick
flagstone
flaptrack
franticly
feast-rite
fractious
flatterer
feature in
flatulent

featurely
flax-wench
flat-woven
flag-waver
Franz Marc
Franz Bopp
Franz Boas
Fabianism
Fabianist
fabaceous
fibreless
fibrefill
fabricate
fabricant
febricity
febrility
fibrillae
fibrillin
fibrillar
fibrinoid
fibriform
fibrinous
febricula
febricule
febrifuge
Fibonacci
fibromata
fibroline
fibrolite
fibrocyte
fiberless
face cream
facecloth
face-guard
facsimile
factitive
facticity
factional
fictional
feculence
feculency
focimeter
fecundate
facundity
fecundity
factorage
factorise
factorize
factoring
factorial
factor out
factotums
faceplate
face paint
fact sheet
focussing
face-saver
facetious
face value
fiduciary
fadedness
fudge cake
fidgeting
foddering
faddiness
fideistic
F W de Klerk
fiddle-bow
fuddle-cap
federarie
free agent
fee-faw-fum
Fremantle
feel after
freeboard
fretboard
free-bench
freebooty
feel cheap
French fry
fleeching
fletching
frescoing
frescoist
Frenchify
Frenchman
French pox
field hand
fieldward
fieldfare
field lark
field mark
field test
field-test
fiendlike
field club
fieldsman
Freedonia
fieldvole
field book
fieldwork
field goal
field trip
field gray
field grey
free-diver
Fred Davis
foederati
Frederica
Frederick
Fredegond
free fight
fretfully
fledgling
freighter
fuel gauge
fleshless
freshness
flesh-meat
fleshment
fleshling
flesh-tint
freshen up
freshener
fleshings
fleshhood
flesh-hook
fleshworm
flesh pots
flechette
fléchette
free house
Fred Hoyle
fieriness
feelingly
flexitime
foeticide
fee simple
fleckless
freckling
freelance
free lunch
free-liver
✧free-lover
✧freemason
freephone
Fred Perry
free-rider
free-range
fleurette
free space
free-space
feel small
freesheet
freestone
feedstock
feedstuff
Flensburg
freestyle
Fred T Jane
free trade
free-to-air
fleetness
Fleetwood
fleet-foot
free throw
frequence
frequency
free verse
freewheel
freewoman
freewomen
Free World
feed-water
fiery mine
freezable
frenzical
freeze-dry
freeze out
freeze-out
faff about
fifteenth
fifteener
Fifteen O's
fife-major
fogramite
fogramity
fagaceous
fugacious
fig-pecker
fagged out
fogginess
fugginess
fog signal
faggoting
figurable
figurante
figure out
fight back
fightback
fightable
fagottist
Friday car
fricative
frigatoon
fricassee
fribbling
fribblish
Fairbanks
foilborne
flip chart
flinching
fair catch
friedcake
feiseanna
fainéance
faineancy
fair-faced
fair field
flight bag
faithless
frightful
frithgild
flightily
frithborh
faith cure
fright wig
foiningly
frigidity
frikkadel
feignedly
friending
frivolity
frivolous
flippancy
fripperer
friar's cap
friarbird
Friar Tuck
fair's fair
foies gras
fair trade
fair-trade
faintness
flirt-gill
flintlock
flint corn
fritterer
fair words
✧fairyland
fairy cake
fairy tale
fairytale
fairy tern
fairylike
fairy ring
fairy gold
fairyhood
fairy moss
fairy wren
Fritz Lang
frizzante
fall apart
full and by
fellaheen
fallalery
falcation
filiation
foliation
fall among
fall about
foliature
full board
full blast
full-blast
film badge
Félibrige
full-blood
full-blown
full-bound
full blues
folic acid
full-cream
felicific
Filicales
filaceous
feliciter
full dress
full-dress
folk dance
false card
false-card
false face
false dawn
filter bed
filler cap
fullerene
falseness
faltering
filleting
Folketing
falsehood
false move
falsework
filter out
filler rod
false step
filter tip
falsettos
fulgently
full-faced
full fling
full-front
filigrane
filigrain
filigreed
full-grown
fill-horse
full house
fulminate
fulminant
fillipeen
filminess
falsified
filliping
falsifier
fulfilled
fulfiller
falciform
fulminous
fillister
fill light
Falklands
folkloric
film-maker
full marks
folk music
✧falun dafa
filanders
✧falangism
✧falangist
✧falun gong
felonious
foliolate
full-orbed
fulsomely
full organ
falconine
following
Fallopian
fellow man
foliolose
fulgorous
follow out
filopodia
full point
Filipinas
Filipinos
full pitch
filoplume
filtrable
folk-right
Falernian
full-scale
feldspath
full-speed
filoselle
full split
full-split
full score
faldstool
fall short
folk story
filmstrip
full-timer
falculate
fulgurate
fulgurant
fulgurite
fulgurous
filovirus
folk-weave
full whack
Famagusta
fumigator
Fomalhaut
family man
femineity
fimbriate
fumarolic
famishing
fumatoria
fanfarade
Fongafale
Finlandia
Finlander
fundament
fandangle
fandangos
fantasied
fantasise
fantasize
Fenianism
fantasist
fantailed
fanfarona
fantasque
Fantaisie
fantastic
fantastry
funebrial
finickety
finocchio
finicking
funicular
funiculus
finically
fine-drawn
finger-dry
finger-end
fenceless
fingering
funnelled
funnel-net
fingertip
fan heater
funnel-web
find fault
find-fault
fenugreek
fan-shaped
fanciable
fanciless
funkiness
funniness
fungicide
fungibles
fungiform
fine metal
financial
financier
fining-pot
fungoidal
finnochio
fungosity
fin-footed
fine print
finessing
finishing
font-stone
finish off
fenestral
fanatical
fen-sucked
fun runner
fondue set
funny ha-ha
fancy cake
fanny pack
fancy ball
funny farm
fancy fair
fancy that
fancy-sick
Funny Girl
funny bone
fancywork
fancy-free
frowardly
flotation
footboard
footbrake
food chain
flow chart
floccular
floscular
flocculus
food canal
footcloth
food court
floodgate
floodmark
floodwall
flood lamp
floodtide
flowerage
flower-bed
flower-bud
flowering
flowerpot
Flores Sea
floreated
frog-eater
feoffment
foot fault
footfault
frothless

foothills
froth-fomy
fool-happy
foolhardy
fiochetti
flophouse
Florideae
floridean
flowingly
foolishly
floridity
frolicked
floriform
floristic
floriated
floristry
fioritura
fioriture
frockless
frock-coat
footlight
footloose
frogmarch
flowmeter
frogmouth
flouncing
frown upon
footplate
footprint
foolproof
foot-pound
floor lamp
floorhead
floor show
floor tile
flour mill
floor plan
flour moth
flour bolt
flourishy
fool's mate
footstalk
foot-stall
frogspawn
footsteps
flow sheet
floss silk
fool's gold
flowstone
footstool
foodstuff
frontward
front-page
float tank
front-rank
frost-nail
frontways
floatable
floptical
frontiers
frontless
frostless
frontager
front line
front-line
frontwise
frostbite
frostlike
frost line
frostwork
front door
from where
foppishly
Fermanagh
fire alarm
Fernandel
forwander
forwarder
forwardly
Fortaleza
firmament
foreanent
forgather
formalise
formalize
formative
fortalice
forsaking
formalism
formation
furcation
formalist
formality
forjaskit
farragoes
fur fabric
fire-arrow
formatted
forfaiter
formatter
firebrand
fore-brace
forebrain
fire-blast
foreboder
firebreak
firebrick
form class
forecabin
forecaddy
forecheck
firecrest
foreclose
forecloth
feracious
ferocious
furacious
fore-cited
fork-chuck
forecourt
firedrake
fire drill
force-land
forgeable
fardel-bag
force-feed
farmeress
forceless
forcemeat
forgetful
forgetive
far-seeing
ferreting
forjeskit
forcepses
fermented
fermenter
fermentor
fire-eater
forfeiter
forgetter
fervently
for effect
firefight
firefloat
forefront
fireguard
fire-grate
forage cap
foregleam
foregoing
form genus
for choice
forthwith
forthcome
fore-horse
form horse
furtherer
farmhouse
firehouse
Ferdinand
forcipate
forficate
formicate
fornicate
fortilage
formicant
formicary
forbiddal
forbidden
forbidder
forkiness
furriness
furniment
fertilely
furtively
furnished
furbisher
furnisher
fortified
fertilise
fertilize
forgiving
fortifier
fertility
fervidity
foreigner
fire irons
Forficula
fortitude
furniture
forejudge
foreknown
firelight
fork lunch
feralised
for a laugh
feralized
foraminal
forenight
fortnight
Feringhee
farandine
forensics
forenamed
farandole
firing pin
ferrocene
for toffee
far-sought
furiosity
forlornly
fervorous
furiously
forgotten
ferrotype
farm-place
fireplace
forepoint
fireproof
firepower
forereach
fire-robed
far from it
fare stage
forestage
foreslack
forestall
forestair
for a start
farmstead
forespend
forespeak
foresteal
foreshewn
foresheet
forespent
forest-fly
foresight
forestine
fire-stick
foreskirt
forest law
firestone
foreshore
foreshock
forest-oak
fire-storm
foreshown
forasmuch
first-hand
first name
first-rate
foreteach
fire trail
✧first lady
fernticle
foreteeth
first gear
first chop
first-time
firstling
forethink
foretoken
foretooth
firethorn
first-born
first-foot
first post
foretaste
form tutor
fire truck
formulaic
formulate
fortunate
formulary
formulise
formulize
fortunize
formulism
formulist
furfurole
furfurous
fore-wheel
foreweigh
firewoman
forewoman
forewomen
forswonck
Fort Worth
fireworks
firewater
forky-tail
for my part
forsythia
✧forty-five
ferry-boat
fish-creel
fosterage
Fasten-e'en
fish eagle
fesse-wise
fastening
fostering
fisherman
foster-son
fistfight
fast foods
Fishguard
fish-guano
fish-garth
fascinate
festinate
fustigate
fissipede
fishiness
fussiness
fustiness
festively
fossilise
fossilize
fastigium
festivity
fissility
fossicker
fascicled
fascicles
fashioner
festivous
festilogy
fascistic
fasciated
fasciitis
fascicule
fisticuff
fasciculi
fustilugs
fish-joint
fish knife
fusillade
fish louse
fossorial
fusionism
fusionist
festology
fishplate
fish-spear
fish slice
fish stick
fish-scrap
fast track
fast-track
fossulate
fistulose
fistulous
fish-woman
fishyback
fat-tailed
feticidal
fetichise
fetichize
fetichism
fetichist
fatidical
fetidness
fat-headed
fattening
fatefully
fatigable
fatiguing
fat chance
fattiness
fittingly
fatuitous
fat-witted
fat client
fetlocked
fatiscent
fetishise
fetishize
fetishism
fetishist
fetoscopy
fettucine
fettucini
fatty oils
feudalise
feudalize
feudalism
feudalist
frugalist
feudality
frugality
feudatory
foul-brood
four-by-two
faulchion
Fourcroya
flue-cured
fluidness
foundress
foundling
flûte-à-bec
flute-bird
frusemide
flugelman
feu de joie
fluke-worm
four-flush
flushness
four-horse
four-hours
flukiness
fluxional
frugivore
fruticose
faunistic
fluviatic
feuilleté
fourpence
fourpenny
flurrying
fluorspar
fluoresce
fluorosis
fourscore
fluctuate
Fluothane®
flustrate
fructuate
fruit cage
fruitcake
frustrate
fluctuant
fruit tart
fructuary
Fructidor
fruit beer
faultless
fruitless
faultline
fruitwood
fructuous
fruit body
fruit tree
fruiterer
four-wheel
five-a-side
faveolate
fivepence
fivepenny
favorable
favorably
favorless
fever-heat
fever tree
favourite
fawningly
fixed-rate
fixed idea
fixed odds
fixedness
fixed oils
foxhunter
Fay Weldon
flyweight
fly agaric
fly-fisher
fly-bitten
flying fox
flying jib
frying-pan
fly powder
flyposter
Fay Godwin
flybridge
fly orchis
fly-by-wire
fizziness
fuzziness
fizzle out
gravamina
gradation
guaranies
gravadlax
go against
guacamole
guanazolo
gradatory
guarantee
guarantor
Guayaquil
grandmama
grandpapa
guardrail
guard hair
guardable

grandaddy
guardedly
guard cell
grandness
guardless
guard-ship
guardship
grandsire
guard ring
grand slam
glandular
guardsman
grandiose
guard-book
guardroom
grand coup
Grand Tour
glandered
✧grand prix
grand duke
grand luxe
Grand Turk
grand-aunt
grand jury
guard's van
Guatemala
graveyard
grapeseed
Gravesend
graceless
grapeless
graveless
graveness
grapeshot
grapevine
graveside
gravelled
glabellae
glabellar
grace note
grate upon
gravel-pit
grapetree
gnateater
glaze over
go ape over
Gradgrind
graphical
graphicly
graphemic
gnathonic
guacharos
graphitic
gratinate
gravitate
Gramineae
glaringly
gratingly
goatishly
gratified
granitise
granitite
granitize
gratifier
gracility
gravidity
gladiolus
glacially
granitoid
granivore
gravitron
graciosos
glaciated
✧gladiator
graticule
gratitude
gnarliest
gear-lever
grammatic
goalmouth
Guarnieri
grauncher
grain side
Goa powder
glamorise
glamorize
glamorous
glamour up
Grampians
graspable
graspless
go airside
Goa trance
glaireous
gear ratio
grassland
glass case
glassware
grass-rake
glass-gall
grass carp
goat's-hair
grassless
glass chin
grassbird
glasslike
grass-like
grass line
gear-stick
gearshift
grass-plot
glass-rope
grass rope
grass moth
glasswork
grasshook
glass wool
glass soap
glasswort
glass-crab
grass tree
glassfuls
grassquit
glass eyes
gear train
grantable
ghastness
giantship
gianthood
Giant Pope
giant star
giant rude
ghastfull
granulate
gratulate
gratulant
granulary
go a bundle
granulite
gradually
granuloma
granulose
granulous
graduated
Goa butter
graduator
graywacke
gearwheel
gravy-soup
gravy boat
Gibraltar
gobbeline
gibberish
go begging
Gabrielle
gubbinses
go belly up
go bananas
gabionade
gabionage
Gibeonite
Gibbonian
gibbosity
gibbously
go berserk
gabardine
gaberdine
go between
go-between
go cahoots
go camping
godparent
godfather
goddamned
gadgeteer
godlessly
God's heart
giddiness
godliness
God-gifted
God's light
God-a-mercy
God's nails
God forbid
godmother
gadrooned
godrooned
God's truth
Gnetaceae
Gregarina
gregarine
✧grenadine
gregarian
Grenadian
grenadier
greybeard
Gwendolen
glebe land
gier-eagle
✧grey friar
gleefully
greegrees
grey goose
glengarry
grewhound
greyhound
gaelicise
gaelicize
gmelinite
gaelicism
Greekless
Greekness
Greek fire
Greekling
Greek gift
Greek nose
grey mould
green card
greenhand
Greenland
✧greensand
greengage
greenwash
greenback
greenmail
greenweed
green leek
green bean
greenness
green belt
greenling
Greenwich
gleanings
green road
greenwood
green-bone
greenroom
green corn
green gown
greenhorn
green gram
green crop
Green Isle
green fund
green-eyed
gremolata
glenoidal
Gregorian
guerrilla
greyscale
guessable
grease cup
grease gun
Gneisenau
gneissoid
gneissose
greystone
guesswork
Great Dane
Great Wall
Gaeltacht
Great Week
✧great seal
Great Bear
great year
guest beer
greatness
ghettoise
ghettoize
guestwise
gee-string
guest rope
guest-room
greatcoat
great-aunt
grey whale
greywacke
goffering
gift horse
gift token
gigmanity
gaga about
gigahertz
goggle-box
gigantean
gigantism
go-getting
go hard but
go haywire
gris-amber
guitarist
grimalkin
grisaille
go it alone
guildhall
guildsman
Guildford
grind down
grindhval
grind away
guide card
glide path
guide rail
Guinevere
gripe's egg
guideless
guileless
guinea hen
guideship
Ghibeline
guideline
guide rope
guidebook
guidepost
guinea pig
griefless
grief-shot
gainfully
going rate
goings-out
going-over
griminess
glidingly
gripingly
guilloche
Ghislaine
guillemot
grillwork
grill room
gaillarde
Grimm's law
Gaitskell
glissandi
glissando
gritstone
gainsayer
guiltless
grist-mill
guilt trip
grievance
glitziest
Gujarathi
Gujerathi
go-karting
galravage
gilravage
Galway Bay
goliardic
gallabeah
Golda Meir
gallabiya
galvanise
galvanize
gallabiah
gallabieh
galvanism
galvanist
gallantly
gallantry
gold brick
gold-brick
galabiyah
Gold Coast
goldcrest
galactose
gold-cloth
gold crown
gill cover
gala-dress
gelidness
golden age
golden boy
GoldenEye
golden-eye
gilt-edged
galleried
gelsemine
galleting
gelsemium
Galwegian
goldenrod
Galveston
goldfield
gillflirt
goldfinch
goldfinny
gold-fever
gelignite
gill-house
gallinazo
galliwasp
gallivant
gallingly
✧gallicise
✧gallicize
gallisise
gallisize
✧gallicism
Gallienus
Golgi body
gallinule
gold-laced
golf links
gall midge
gold medal
galumpher
golomynka
goldminer
galengale
galingale
Galenical
galantine
gallonage
gallopade
gallopers
galiongee
Gallophil
gilsonite
galloping
gallooned
gallowses
gold plate
gold-plate
Galápagos
galapagos
gold paint
gold point
gold penny
gill pouch
galdragon
gold rings
goldsmith
goldspink
goldstick
gill slits
goldsinny
gallstone
goldstone
goloshoes
gilt spurs
gold tooth
gully-hole
gally-crow
gamma rays
gemmative
gymnasial
gymnasium
gammadion
gammation
gemmation
gymnasien
gimmalled
gambadoes
gummatous
gymnastic
game chips
Gammexane®
gama grass
gumshield
gomphoses
gomphosis
gumminess
gum-digger
gimmickry
gemel-ring
gaminerie
gammoning
gambogian
gummosity
gambolled
gymnosoph
gemmology
game point
gum arabic
gum dragon
go missing
gemütlich
gumptious
gameyness
Genoa cake
gin palace
genialise
genialize
goniatite
geniality
gendarmes
genealogy
gun barrel
gangboard
gynocracy
gonococci
genocidal
gens de loi
gens de peu
gingerade
ginger ale
gynaeceum

ganderism
gynaecium
gynoecium
genteelly
ginger nut
gynaecoid
gingerous
ginger pop
genuflect
gone goose
Gandhi-ism
genuinely
genning up
gentilise
gentilize
gentilish
gentilism
gentility
gannister
Gene Kelly
gangliate
gene locus
gentleman
gentlemen
ginglymus
ganglions
gunpowder
Gongorism
gondolier
Gongorist
guncotton
gangplank
gang-punch
gonophore
gynophore
generable
generical
gonorrhea
generalia
generally
ginormous
generator
Genistein®
gong-stick
Genesitic
genetical
genitalia
genitalic
genotypic
genitival
gone under
gunrunner
Genevieve
geomancer
go on and on
goosander
grow angry
globalise
globalize
globalism
globalist
geocarpic
geomantic
geotactic
gaolbreak
good-cheap
good cheer
grouchily
glomerate
go over big
gooseherd

goose-neck
goose-wing
groveling
globe fish
goose-fish
goose-girl
geodetics
groceries
geodesist
goose-skin
goose-club
grovelled
groveller
gloves-off
goosefoot
goober pea
grotesque
geometric
geometrid
globe-trot
goose step
goose-step
glomerule
glomeruli
groneful
gloze over
go one's way
goodfaced
good faith
good-faith
goodfella
gaol-fever
Georgiana
good grace
grosgrain
George Fox
good grief
good grief!
Giorgione
georgette
geophilic
geophones
good hands
geophytic
goodiness
goofiness
goopiness
Groningen
glowingly
gropingly
glorified
goodliest
good looks
groomsman
Gros Morne
groundage
ground-ash
goodnight
groundhog
ground ice
grounding
ground ivy
ground-ivy
groundman
groundnut
ground oak
ground run
groundsel
geognosis
geologise
geologize

geologian
geoponics
gnomonics
geologist
globosity
good on you
groupware
groupable
geosphere
gros point
group work
groupwork
geotropic
geography
good-speed
grossness
grossular
good sense
gross loss
glossator
glossitis
good stuff
gloss over
good-sized
gnostical
glottides
ghostlike
growthist
good-timer
ghost word
ghost moth
ghost town
grow tired
good taste
glottises
geostatic
gloat over
globulite
globulous
good value
good-willy
good works
goodyears
Geomyidae
glory hole
gypsy moth
gypsywort
gerfalcon
gyrfalcon
germander
garlandry
germanely
Gorbachev
gargarise
gargarize
Germanice
Germanise
Germanize
Germanish
gargarism
Germanism
germanium
Germanist
geriatric
Gargantua
garbanzos
✧**garibaldi**
gore-blood
Girl Crazy
Géricault
garreteer

gardening
garderobe
garmented
giraffine
giraffoid
Girl Guide
garagiste
girthline
germinate
germinant
Garrincha
garnishee
garnisher
garnishry
girlishly
germicide
garniture
Geraldine
gorilline
gorillian
gorblimey
gorilloid
germ layer
gyromancy
gerundive
gerundial
Girondism
Girondist
Guru Nanak
girandola
girandole
giro order
gorgoneia
gorgonise
gorgonize
garroting
gorgonian
garbology
garrotted
garrotter
gyroplane
germ plasm
girl power
gyroscope
Girl Scout
garotting
garrulity
Garfunkel
garrulous
Gore Vidal
gyrovague
garryowen
gas-carbon
gossamery
gessamine
gestative
goslarite
gustative
gestation
gustation
gestatory
gustatory
gas mantle
gaspereau
gospelise
gospelize
gusseting
gospeller
gas helmet
gas-retort
gas heater

gaspiness
gassiness
gustiness
gaspingly
gushingly
gossiping
gas-filled
gas-fitter
gas-liquor
gasometer
gasometry
gas engine
gastnesse
gasconade
gasholder
Gascoigne
gasconism
gas cooker
gas-cooled
gismology
gas-bottle
gastraeum
gastropub
gastropod
gastritis
gas escape
gas-burner
gossypine
Gossypium
get laldie
Gothamite
guttation
Gothamist
gatecrash
get across
go to court
go the pace
gathering
gettering
guttering
gutter-man
go the vole
go to earth
gutlessly
gather way
gate fever
go to grass
get the law
gatehouse
get wind of
gutsiness
gothicise
gothicize
Gothicism
Gothicist
guts it out
gate-money
Gutenberg
get any joy
go to press
go to prove
get around
go through
Gateshead
go to sleep
get-at-able
gate-tower
gutbucket
gate valve
go to waste
glutamate

glutamine
grub about
grumbling
grund mail
Grundyism
gourd-worm
gaugeable
gaudeamus
glutenous
gauze-tree
gauleiter
gruffness
grudgeful
gaucherie
gauchesco
gaudiness
gauziness
goutiness
glucinium
glutinous
gruelling
glucoside
gruppetti
gruppetto
grubstake
grub screw
gauntness
grunt work
goustrous
glueyness
give a back
give a miss
give a knee
give birth
give chase
give forth
give it a go
gavelkind
given name
givenness
give place
give pause
governall
governess
governing
give voice
gowpenful
gawkiness
gawkihood
go whistle
go wilding
go walkies
gowdspink
go without
Guy Fawkes
geyserite
glyceride
glycerine
gay rights
Guy Gibson
glycoside
glycollic
glycocoll
Glyptodon
Gay-Lussac
gazpachos
Gaziantep
gaze-hound
gizmology
gazetteer
gazetting

headboard
head-crash
headchair
headcloth
Huascarán
head count
heat death
headdress
haanepoot
headframe
hoarfrost
head first
heath bell
heathbird
heathenry
heathcock
heath-fowl
hoarhound
headiness
heaviness
hoariness
healingly
hyalinise
hyalinize
hearkener
headlease
headlight
headliner
headlines
head money
Hyaenidae
hyalonema
headpeace
headpiece
headphone
heatproof
headreach
head-rhyme
headshake
headscarf
headstall
head start
heapstead
headstick
headstone
hoar-stone
headstock
heartland
heartache
heartseed
heart-dear
heartless
heartbeat
heartfelt
healthful
heartling
heartsick
heartsink
healthily
heartikin
heart-bond
heartwood
heartsome
heart-sore
heart-free
hearth rug
hearth-tax
heartburn
head voice
head-woman
headwater

heavy beer
heavy rock
heavy spar
heavy-duty
Hebraical
hobnailed
Hebraiser
Hebraizer
Hebrewess
Hebrewism
Hobbesian
Hebridean
hybridise
hybridize
hybridism
Hebridian
hybridity
hybridoma
Hobbinoll
hybridous
hubristic
hibakusha
habilable
hob-and-nob
hobjobber
hobgoblin
hibernate
habergeon
haberdine
hibernise
hibernize
Hibernian
habituate
habitable
habitably
hobbyless
huckaback
hackamore
hackberry
hecogenin
Ho Chi Minh
hackneyed
hectoring
hectorism
hectogram
huckstery
hocussing
hacksawed
hiccuping
hacqueton
Hacky Sack®
hodmandod
hydrangea
had rather
hydrazine
hydration
hydraulic
hydraemia
hidebound
hiddenite
hedgebill
hodiernal
hedge-bote
hedge-born
had better
hedge fund
hodograph
hydriodic
had liefer
had liever
heddle-eye

hodometer
hodometry
hydrolase
hydrovane
hadrosaur
hydronaut
Hudson Bay
hydrocele
hydroxide
hideosity
hydrosoma
hydrosome
hydrofoil
hydrozoan
hydrozoon
hydrology
hideously
hydroptic
hydrostat
hydropult
hydrolyse
hydrolyte
hydrolyze
hedyphane
Hyderabad
hederated
had as lief
had as good
hodoscope
hydathode
hidey-hole
hierarchy
hieratica
haematite
hieracium
haematoma
haematoid
haecceity
heedfully
heediness
hue and cry
haemocoel
hierology
hyetology
hierogram
hierocrat
haemostat
hierodule
haemocyte
heel-piece
heftiness
huffiness
huffishly
hagiarchy
haggardly
hog badger
Haggadist
high altar
high-blest
high-blown
highchair
high-class
high cross
Hugh Capet
Hugo Capet
high court
high-dried
High Dutch
hygienics
hygienist
hog heaven

✧high-flier
high-flown
✧high-flyer
high-grade
Hugh Grant
high-grown
high horse
hag-ridden
hog-ringer
haggishly
hoggishly
hygristor
high jinks
highlight
Highlands
high-level
hegemonic
Hugh Munro
hygrodeik
hygrophil
hagiology
hygrology
hugeously
hygrostat
high-place
high point
high-proof
high-speed
high table
high-toned
high-taper
high-viced
high words
high water
heir-at-law
hairbrush
haircloth
hairdrier
hairdryer
Heidegger
hair-grass
hairiness
hoi polloi
heinously
hairpiece
hair space
hair slide
hair shirt
hailstone
hailstorm
hairst-rig
hairspray
hairstyle
hair-waver
hairy Mary
hijacking
hold a call
half-adder
Hollander
Halmahera
hallalled
half board
hell-black
half-breed
half-blind
half-baked
hillbilly
half-blood
hell-broth
halobiont
heliborne

Hylobates
half-bound
Helicidae
half-cheek
helictite
holocrine
helically
half-close
half-crown
half-caste
holy-cruel
hold court
✧holocaust
half-dozen
holderbat
✧hellenise
✧hellenize
Hellenism
helvetium
Helvetian
Holmesian
Hellenist
Helvellyn
hellebore
halieutic
half-frame
half-faced
Holyfield
hold forth
holograph
✧holy grail
holy grass
half groat
Holy Ghost
hold hands
half-hardy
hell-hated
half hitch
hellhound
hilliness
haltingly
hellishly
hole in one
half-light
halalling
halflings
half-miler
holing-axe
holloware
Hallowe'en
Hallowmas
heliozoic
heliozoan
hollow out
heliology
heliostat
heliotype
heliotypy
half-plate
half-price
halophile
halophily
halfpence
halfpenny
halophobe
holophote
half-pound
halophyte
holophyte
hylophyte
Haloragis

hilarious
Holarctic
half-round
half-rhyme
half-royal
hallstand
Hallstatt
half-shell
heli-skier
half-shift
hula skirt
half-sword
holystone
heliscoop
halothane
half-track
half-timer
holotypic
hell to pay
holstered
halitosis
halitotic
half-title
half-truth
hellwards
hold water
holy water
holly-fern
Hollywood
hollyhock
holly tree
hylozoism
hylozoist
ham-handed
hemialgia
Himyarite
Home Alone
hamfatter
homebound
homebuyer
humectate
homecraft
humectant
hemicycle
homicidal
humective
home-comer
home-croft
humidness
hamadryad
hamadryas
homoeobox
hammering
hammerkop
hummeller
hammerman
hammer out
homoeosis
homoeotic
hammer-toe
home fries
✧home guard
homograph
homograft
homogamic
home-grown
hemihedry
humdinger
ham-fisted
humiliate
humiliant

humble-bee
homologue
humble pie
humble-pie
humblesse
homiletic
Himalayan
Himalayas
homemaker
✧hamamelis
homomorph
home movie
hymeneals
Hominidae
hymenaeal
hymenaean
humanness
hum and haw
humankind
Human Life
humanlike
H L Mencken
homuncles
homonymic
humongous
humungous
home nurse
homuncule
homunculi
Hemingway
homeopath
homeomery
hymnodist
hummocked
homeowner
hymnology
hemiopsia
home plate
homoplasy
Hemiptera
Homoptera
homophile
homopolar
homophobe
homophone
homophony
homophyly
Homeridae
humorless
home-ruler
humorally
home range
hemispace
homestall
homestead
Hampshire
hemistich
Humpty Doo
hamstring
homotonic
hemitrope
homotypic
homotypal
hemstitch
hamstrung
home truth
homotaxic
homotaxis
Hammurabi
humbugged
hamburger

humbugger
homousian
humbucker
home video
homewards
hen-paddle
hen-paidle
hang a left
Hungarian
hang about
Hank Aaron
hunt after
handbrake
hindbrain
hindberry
Hans Bethe
handclasp
handcraft
handcuffs
hinder-end
hungerful
hankering
Hunterian
henpecked
hanselled
hand glass
hang-glide
handgrips
hunchback
honchoing
hendiadys
handiness
hintingly
handiwork
Henrietta
hen-witted
Hans Krebs
handlebar
hang loose
hansom-cab
hand organ
hand-press
handprint
hand-paper
hundredth
hundreder
hundredor
honorific
hindrance
honoraria
hen-driver
handstand
handshake
handstaff
Hans Sachs
hindsight
handspike
hone-stone
hands down
hands-free
hand-screw
hand's turn
handsturn
hung tiles
hang tough
handtowel
Hindu Kush
hind-wheel
Henry Tate
Henry Vane
honey-cart

Words marked ✧ can also be spelled with one or more capital letters

honey-seed
honey bear
honeyless
Honeyghan
honey-bird
Henry VIII
Henry Wilt
honey-blob
honeycomb
Henry Ford
Henry Wood
Henry More
handywork
honky-tonk
honeymoon
honeypots
hunky-dory
honey-trap
hoolachan
haoma vine
hoof-bound
Hoover Dam
Hooke's law
hooped-pot
hooked rug
hood-mould
hootnanny
hook-nosed
hoodooing
hoofprint
hoop-snake
haphazard
heptarchy
hop-garden
Hipparion
heptapody
hypoblast
hope chest
hypocrite
hypocrisy
hopscotch
hypocotyl
hypocaust
hypoderma
hyphenate
hyphenise
hyphenize
happening
hyphenism
haplessly
hopefully
hypogaeal
hypogaeum
hypogaean
hypogeous
hip-girdle
hippiedom
happiness
hop-picker
hop pillow
hippiatry
hypallage
hypomania
hypomanic
hypinosis
hyponasty
hippodame
hypnoidal
hypnogeny
hypnotise
hypnotize
hypnotism
hypnotist
hip pocket
hop-pocket
hypnotoid
haplology
hippology
hoplology
hypnology
hippocras
haplontic
Hippolyta
hypermart
hypergamy
✧hypericum
hypertext
hyperfine
hyperlink
hyperemia
hyperemic
hyperbola
hyperbole
hyperopia
hypercube
hypernymy
hypostyle
Hepaticae
hepatical
hepatomas
hypotonia
hypotonic
Haphtarah
Haphtorah
hepatitis
hypotaxis
hippurite
hypoxemia
hypoxemic
happy hour
hermandad
harmaline
hortative
herbalism
herbarium
herbarian
hortation
herbalist
Hardaknut
hare along
hereabout
hortatory
herbal tea
harmattan
hark after
hereafter
hardboard
Hart Crane
Heraclean
Heraclius
hard-cured
hard court
hardcover
hard-drawn
hard drive
harmdoing
Hirudinea
Herodotus
horse race
horse rake
horseback
horse nail
horsetail
horse fair
horsehair
Hervey Bay
horse bean
horseless
horsemeat
horseshoe
horsewhip
horsehide
hardening
horse mill
hermetics
horsemint
Harper Lee
hordeolum
horseplay
herpetoid
horsepond
harden off
horned owl
horse boat
horse-foot
Hortensio
harvester
Herpestes
✧harlequin
hard-faced
hard facts
harmfully
hurtfully
herb-grace
hardgrass
herd grass
harigalds
herd-groom
harshness
horehound
hermitage
heroic age
✧hurricane
hurricano
Hormisdas
hurriedly
hardihead
hardiness
hermitess
horniness
horsiness
hardiment
herriment
harbinger
herringer
horrified
herbicide
herbivora
hardihood
herbivore
herbivory
herniated
Heraklion
horologic
horologer
hors la loi
hardliner
hard lines
hartlesse
horn-maker
hard money
hard-metal
horometry
heronshaw
hirundine
hardnosed
harangued
haranguer
harborage
hariolate
Harrogate
Harpo Marx
hercogamy
herkogamy
harmonica
harmonise
Harmonite
harmonize
herborise
herborize
harrowing
harmonium
Harrovian
harmonics
✧harmonist
herborist
hircosity
harpooner
harmotome
harbourer
hardparts
herb Paris
hard-paste
herb Peter
hard right
hard-ruled
Herb Ritts
hare-stane
hare's-tail
hardshell
harp-shell
Hiroshima
harassing
haruspicy
hornstone
horoscope
hartshorn
horn spoon
hare's-foot
horoscopy
hors série
hard sauce
hard stuff
heritable
heritably
heretical
heritress
Hard Times
hors texte
harquebus
hereunder
✧herculean
hirsutism
here we are
hornwrack
hard wheat
hard-wired
hard words
hornyhead
herryment
hercynite
Harry Hill
Hercynian
husbandly
husbandry
histamine
Hispanist
Hesychasm
Hesychast
Haslemere
Hesperian
hysterics
hosteller
hesternal
hysteroid
hospitage
hospitale
hastiness
huskiness
hostilely
hissingly
histidine
Hassidism
hospitium
Hussitism
hispidity
hostility
Heseltine
hostlesse
hush money
hyson-skin
histogeny
hessonite
historism
historian
historify
histology
histogram
hush puppy
Hasdrubal
histrions
hesitance
hesitancy
hesitator
hetmanate
hit parade
hatha yoga
hate crime
hotheaded
Hitlerite
hetaerism
Hitlerism
hetaerist
Hitlerist
✧hottentot
hatefully
hatchback
hatchment
hit the hay
hitch-hike
hatchling
hitch kick
Hitchcock
hatch boat
hut-circle
hetairism
hetairist
hit wicket
hot ticket
hotelling
hôtel-Dieu
hot-and-hot
hit-and-run
hot potato
hot-rodder
hot-dogger
Huttonian
hot to trot
hit for six
hit bottom
hotfoot it
hot spring
heterodox
hit-or-miss
heteronym
heteropod
heterosis
heterotic
hot button
hour-angle
houndfish
housemaid
hause-bane
house-mate
house call
house-carl
house leek
houseless
house-line
housewife
house wine
houselled
house flag
✧household
house-bote
hause-lock
housework
houseroom
houseboat
housecoat
housefuls
house-hunt
house-duty
hourglass
Houyhnhnm
haughtily
heuristic
haut monde
hourplate
haul round
haustella
haustoria
have a care
have a bash
have a ball
have-at-him
have a shot
have a stab
havocking
have cause
have had it
hive-honey
have ideas
have it out
have in tow
hovel-post
have place
haversack
have right
haversine
haverings
hoverport
have round
have wrong
have words
hivewards
hawsepipe
hawsehole
how chance?
Hawthorne
hawkishly
hawk-nosed
howtowdie
howsoever
how are you?
hawksbill
Hawksmoor
hexachord
Hexagynia
hexagonal
hexahedra
hexameter
Hexandria
hexapodal
hexaploid
hexastich
hexastyle
Hexateuch
haymakers
haymaking
hoydenish
hoydenism
hey presto
hay asthma
Haystacks
Hezbollah
Hizbollah
hazardize
hazardous
hazard pay
Hizbullah
in a manner
in a bad way
Ivan Bunin
irascible
irascibly
inaidable
inaudible
inaudibly
imageable
imageless
inaneness
irateness
image tube
in as far as
inaugural
inanimate
imaginary
imagineer
italicise
italicize
imagining
Italicism
inanition
imaginist
inability
imagistic
in a big way
isallobar
Ivan Lendl
inamorata
inamorato
isagogics
Itaipu Dam
in arrears
inaptness
in advance

in any hand
in any case
in any wise
imbrangle
it beats me
imbecilic
in bad part
inbreathe
imbricate
in ballast
imbalance
inbrought
imbroglio
inburning
in-between
ischaemia
ischaemic
incubuses
incubator
incidence
incremate
inclement
increment
incretion
increaser
incognito
in cahoots
ischiadic
itchiness
inclining
ischiatic
inculcate
inculpate
in company
in-company
incumbent
incommode
income tax
incunable
in concert
in context
incentive
incondite
in consort
incensory
inclosure
incapable
incapably
incipient
inceptive
inception
incarnate
incurvate
incertain
incurable
incurably
incorrect
incurrent
incursive
incurring
incursion
incurvity
incurious
incorrupt
incessant
in council
include in
inclusive
including
incaution
inclusion
Indian fig
indraught
Indianise
Indianize
in drawing
✧indian ink
Indianist
Indian red
Indian War
Indo-Aryan
indubious
indocible
inducible
inductile
inductive
indiction
induction
indecency
indecorum
✧indicator
indweller
in default
indignant
indignify
indignity
indigence
indigency
indigo red
indigotin
indagator
indelible
indelibly
indulge in
indulgent
indolence
indolency
indemnify
indemnity
indumenta
iodometry
indention
Indonesia
indenture
indinavir
iodophile
indirubin
indurated
indusiate
indispose
in dispute
in disgust
iddy-umpty
induviate
index case
indexical
indexless
index-link
index fund
ice dancer
Icelandic
Icelander
iterative
iteration
inelastic
inexactly
ice-action
inelegant
I never did!
isenergic
ineffable
ineffably
ideograph
ice diving
irenicism
in epitome
ice-skater
idealless
ideologic
idealogue
ideologue
Ideal Home
I Feel Love
idealiser
idealizer
ideomotor
ice anchor
ice hockey
irenology
ideophone
inebriate
inebriant
inerrable
inerrably
idée reçue
in earnest
inebriety
inerrancy
inebrious
in essence
ileostomy
identical
ineptness
inertness
Identi-Kit
identikit
in extenso
inequable
inerudite
ice bucket
iced water
inflative
inflation
infracted
infractor
infective
infection
infielder
inflexion
inflexure
infringer
inflicter
inflictor
in full cry
in full fig
infilling
infolding
in full rig
infomania
infantile
infantine
inflowing
infuriate
informant
infirmary
inferable
infertile
inferring
infirmity
inference
infortune
infuscate
infusible
in fashion
✧infusoria
infatuate
influxion
influenza
influence
ingrately
ingrained
ingrainer
ingleneuk
ingle-side
inglenook
ingenuity
ingenious
ingenuous
in general
ingrowing
Inguri Dam
ingestive
ingestion
ingluvial
ingluvies
inhibited
inhabiter
inhabitor
inhibiter
inhibitor
ichneumon
in high leg
ichthyoid
inhalator
inhumanly
ichnolite
ichnology
in harness
inherence
inherency
inharmony
inheritor
Iridaceae
imitative
imitation
irisation
it is all up
imidazole
idioblast
Iain Banks
itinerate
itinerant
itineracy
itinerary
idiograph
isinglass
Irish Scot
Irishness
Irish mile
Irish moss
it is hoped
Irish stew
initialed
initially
initiator
idiomatic
Irian Jaya
Isidorian
iridology
iridotomy
idioplasm
idiophone
idiopathy
idiot card
idiot tape
idiotical
idioticon
injective
injection
injurious
injustice
ink pencil
in keeping
ink-jerker
inkholder
irksomely
ink-bottle
ink-eraser
ill-manned
ill-haired
ill nature
illiberal
illicitly
ill-headed
ill-hedded
ill-deedly
ill health
ill become
ill temper
ill-versed
ill office
illegible
illegibly
illogical
illegally
ill-wisher
Islamabad
ill-omened
illuminer
idle money
Islamitic
illimited
Inland Sea
Islington
ill-boding
Isle of Man
Isle of Rum
ill-gotten
illipe oil
ill at ease
ill-judged
ill-humour
idle wheel
idle worms
immediate
immediacy
immodesty
immigrate
immigrant
Ismailiya
Ismailism
Ismailian
immolator
immanacle
immensely
immunogen
Immingham
immensity
immanence
imminence
immanency
imminency
immuniser
immunizer
✧immortals
immersion
immorally
immission
immutable
immutably
ismatical
immitting
immovable
immovably
in my voice
immixture
Iona Abbey
Ian Rankin
Ionian Sea
Innsbruck
innocuity
innocence
innocency
ionic bond
innocuous
Ian McEwan
innuendos
innkeeper
Ian Hislop
in numbers
ion engine
Ian Botham
ionophore
ionopause
inner ward
innervate
inner wall
inner part
ignorable
innerwear
innerness
Ian Wright
inner city
inner-city
ignoramus
ignorance
innermost
inner tube
ionisable
ignescent
ignitable
ignitible
Ian St John
innovator
I know what
innoxious
ionizable
isogamete
isobathic
isolative
isolation
isogamous
isotactic
iron-bound
iso-octane
isosceles
Iron Crown
Iron Cross
iron-cased
isomerase
Idomeneus
isomerise
isomerize
isomerism
in one word
isogenous
isomerous
isometric
in one's way
inorganic
isochimal
isochrone
isochoric
iron horse
isotheral
inopinate
ixodiasis
isoniazid
isoclinic
isoclinal
I could use
iron-miner
isosmotic
iron mould
isoenzyme
iron oxide
isopolity
inodorous
isodomous
isologous
isonomous
isopodous
iconology
Isokontae
isodontal
isokontan
iconostas
isocrymal
inotropic
isotropic
isopropyl
isocratic
iron-sided
Ironsides
ironsmith
ironstone
I don't know
isosteric
isopteran
isostatic
inoculate
Iroquoian
ironworks
ivory gate
ivory-palm
isocyclic
isopycnic
ivory-tree
isohyetal
impeacher
impeccant
impacable
impactite
impactive
impaction
in pectore
impedance
impudence
imprecate
impresari
impleader
implement
imprecise
impletion
implexion
implicate
in private

impliedly
impairing
impellent
impulsive
impelling
impulsion
impolitic
impennate
impendent
impingent
impending
impinging
impundulu
implodent
implosive
improvise
impsonite
imploring
improving
implosion
improbity
impromptu
impiously
important
imperfect
impartial
imperious
imperator
importune
imposable
impassive
in passing
impassion
impastoed
impostume
imposture
impetrate
imputable
imputably
impeticos
impatiens
impatient
in-patient
impetigos
inputting
impotence
impotency
impetuous
input area
impetuses
impounder
imprudent
inpouring
impluvium
impavidly
inpayment
inquinate
inquiline
inquiring
inquietly
inquorate
in reality
irreality
irradiate
irradiant
Israelite
irrigable
irregular
irriguous
irrigator
irrelated
Imran Khan
iprindole
irruptive
irruption
inrushing
irritable
irritably
irritancy
irritator
installed
inshallah
installer
inspanned
instanter
instantly
itsy-bitsy
insectary
insectile
insection
insect net
inside-car
insidious
inside out
ipse dixit
issueless
in special
insheathe
inshelter
inspector
ipso facto
in so far as
Issigonis
insphear'd
instigate
inswinger
inspiring
in spirits
instilled
inscience
institute
insultant
insoluble
insolubly
inselberg
insolvent
insulting
insulsity
insolence
insularly
insulator
insomniac
insensate
insinuate
ifs and ans
insincere
insipidly
insipient
insurable
inscriber
insurgent
in service
in-service
insertion
insurance
insistent
in session
insatiate
insatiety
insetting
in several
in transit
itty-bitty
in the dark
in the main
in the mass
in the cart
in the scud
in the mean
in the wind
in the pink
in the club
in the know
in the road
in the zone
in the dock
in the loop
in the soup
in the buff
in the lump
in the swim
integrand
integrate
integrant
intaglios
integrity
intricate
intrigant
intricacy
intuitive
intuition
intrinsic
intriguer
intellect
Intelpost
intimiste
intumesce
intensate
intendant
intenable
intenible
intensely
intensive
intentive
intension
intention
intensify
intensity
intonator
in trouble
introject
introvert
iatrogeny
in thought
introitus
introduce
in two twos
interlard
interface
interlace
interpage
intervale
interdash
interbank
interrail
internals
icterical
Icteridae
intercede
interfere
intervene
interleaf
interdeal
intervein
intercept
interject
interment
intersect
intersert
intertext
interwind
interdine
interfile
interline
interring
interlink
intorsion
intortion
interdict
internist
interview
Intercity®
intercity
inter alia
interflow
interplay
interknit
interfold
interlope
internode
interpone
interpose
interzone
interlock
interwork
interjoin
interbred
intercrop
interpret
intergrow
interesse
interfuse
interlude
intermure
interrupt
Intertype®
intestate
intestacy
intestine
in tatters
intrusive
intrusion
inumbrate
inunction
inurement
inusitate
inutility
Iguanidae
iguanodon
ibuprofen
Inuktitut
invective
invidious
inveigler
involucre
involucel
invalidly
involuted
inventive
Irvingite
Irvingism
invention
inventory
inviolate
inviolacy
invertase
invariant
Inverness
inversely
inversive
inversion
invisible
invisibly
izvestiya
inwreathe
inwrought
inworking
Ivy League
ivy-leaved
in-yer-face
if you like
Jean Alesi
Jean Bodin
Jean Genet
Jeannette
Joan of Arc
jealously
Juan Perón
Jean Patou
job-master
jabbering
✧jobseeker
job centre
✧jobcentre
job of work
J G Ballard
jubilance
jubilancy
jaborandi
jobernowl
Jebusitic
Job's tears
jobsworth
Jack-a-Lent
jactation
jackalled
Jacobinic
jack-block
jacobuses
Jacobitic
jockey cap
jockeyism
J M Coetzee
Jack Frost
jack-fruit
Jack Hobbs
jackknife
Jack Ketch
Jack Lynch
jocularly
jaculator
joculator
jocundity
jack plane
jacaranda
Jack-slave
jack-staff
jack-stays
jack shaft
jackshaft
Jock Stein
jacksnipe
jacksmith
jackstone
Jock Scott
jock strap
jockstrap
Jack Sprat
jack screw
Jack Straw
jack-straw
Jack-sauce
jockteleg
jack towel
✧jacquerie
jack-up rig
Jacky Ickx
judiciary
judicable
judicious
judicator
jadedness
Judi Dench
judge-made
judgement
judgeship
jade green
Judaistic
Judas kiss
✧judas hole
Judas tree
Joel Cohen
Joe Mercer
jeeringly
Joe Miller
Joe Bloggs
Joe Blakes
Joe Cocker
Joe Greene
Joe Public
jeely nose
Jefferson
jaghirdar
Jo Grimond
jigamaree
Jagannath
✧jugannath
jiggumbob
John Adams
John André
John Arden
John-apple
John Clare
John Cabot
John Colet
John Canoe
John Curry
John Donne
John Dewey
John Elway
John Greig
John Glenn
John Henry
John Inman
John Junor
John Keats
John Keble
John Kanoo
John Locke
John Major
John Mills
John Mayow
Johannean
Johannine
Johnny Reb
Johnny-raw
John O'Hara
John Ogdon
John Piper
John Powys
John Rebus
John Reith
John Soane
John Speke
John Smith
Johnstone
John Tyler
John Wayne
jailbreak
jaileress
juiceless
jail-fever
jailhouse
juiciness
join issue
joint heir
jointless
jointness
jointress
joint will
joint-worm
jointworm
juke-joint
jokesmith
juliet cap
jolleying
jillflirt
jolliness
jolliment
joltingly
jelliform
joliotium
jaloused
jelly baby
jollyhead
jelly bean
jellyfish
jollyboat
jambalaya
jam-packed
Jim Carrey
Jim Baxter
jemminess
jumpiness
jump leads
jambolana
Jim Lovell
James Watt
jump-start
James Dean
James Lind
James Bond
James Hogg
James Cook
James Hook
Jamestown
James Hunt
jemmy open
Jan Palach
Juncaceae
juneating
Juneberry
Junkerdom
junketeer
jenneting
junketing
Jansenism

Junkerism
Jansenist
Junoesque
Jane Fonda
Jena glass
Jin Shin Do®
Jonah word
Jonah Lomu
junkiness
Jennie Lee
Jan Timman
jungle cat
jungle gym
jingo-ring
Jonsonian
juniority
janissary
Janet Reno
janitress
Jenny Lind
jenny-wren
jeoparder
japanning
Japaneses
Jaqueline
jequirity
jerfalcon
Jordanian
juridical
jerkiness
jarringly
jargoneer
jargonise
jargonize
jargonist
jerepigos
Jarlsberg®
Jerusalem
J K Rowling
jurywoman
jurywomen
jerkwater
jerry-shop
Jerry Rice
jessamine
jus mariti
just about
joss-block
jesserant
jasperise
jasperize
jasperous
Jesse Boot
joss house
jaspidean
jestingly
justified
jus civile
Jesuitism
Justinian
justiciar
justifier
jasmonate
Josephine
Joséphine
Jesus wept
joss stick
jet-lagged
jettatura
jitterbug
jet-setter

jut-window
jettiness
juttingly
Jotunheim
jet engine
J J Thomson
jet-driven
jet stream
jetstream
jaundiced
jeu de mots
journeyed
journeyer
jouisance
joviality
juvenilia
jawbation
jaw-fallen
jewel case
jewel-weed
jewellery
jewelling
jewelfish
jawboning
Jew's-pitch
Jew's-stone
Jews' thorn
✧jew's-trump
✧jews'-trump
J M W Turner
juxtapose
jaywalker
Jay Gatsby
Joyce Cary
joylessly
joyriding
jazziness
koala bear
knaidloch
knaveship
khalifate
knavishly
knackered
krakowiak
khansamah
knapscull
knapskull
Kraftwerk
Kubla Khan
kabeljouw
kibbutzim
kick about
kick boxer
kick pleat
kickstand
kickshaws
kick-start
✧kidnapped
kidnapper
kidney ore
kadaitcha
kiddingly
kids' stuff
kidstakes
kiddywink
keep an act
keep at bay
keep a term
knee-cords
keep count
kneidlach

kneadable
knee-drill
klendusic
kieserite
keep faith
klephtism
knee-holly
keep house
khedivate
keelivine
khedivial
knee joint
klezmorim
keep quiet
knee-swell
keep sight
keep track
keep under
keep watch
keelyvine
keepy-uppy
Kagoshima
kahikatea
Kshatriya
knife-edge
kaiserdom
knifeless
knife-rest
knifelike
kaiserism
knife into
klieg eyes
knightage
kniphofia
knickered
Kainozoic
klinostat
Klinsmann
kailyaird
kok-saghyz
kakemonos
Killarney
kilocycle
killdeers
kiln-dried
Kilner jar®
kilderkin
kilohertz
kolkhozes
killingly
killifish
kallitype
kilojoule
kilolitre
kalamkari
kilometre
kalanchoe
Kalsomine®
kilotonne
Kimberley
kymograph
Kim Philby
Kamchatka
Kim Il-sung
Komintern
Kominform
Kim Jong Il
Kama Sutra
Kamasutra
Kampuchea
✧kangaroos

king-apple
Kinkakuji
kent-bugle
kingcraft
king cobra
kink-cough
kingdomed
kennelled
kennelman
kinsfolks
Kentigern
kinkiness
kantikoys
Kandinsky
kentledge
kintledge
kanamycin
kingmaker
kinematic
konimeter
koniology
king prawn
King Priam
king snake
king's-hood
kinescope
koniscope
King Stork
Kingstown
king's evil
King's Lynn
king-sized
kinetical
Kunstlied
kinswoman
kloochman
klondiker
klondyker
knotgrass
kookiness
knowingly
kaolinise
kaolinite
kaolinize
knock back
knock-back
knock-knee
knock cold
knock wood
knock down
knock-down
knock copy
knocker-up
knowledge
knobstick
Kaohsiung
Keplerian
kipper tie
kopasetic
kept woman
Karnataka
Kárpathos
kurrajong
Korean War
Kariba Dam
karabiner
Karl Barth
Kirkcaldy
kerb drill
kermesite
kermes oak

Kurt Gödel
Kartikeya
Kirbigrip®
kirbigrip
Kurt Jooss
karyogamy
karyosome
karyology
karyogram
karyotype
Karl Radek
Karisimbi
kerbstone
Karlsruhe
karateist
keratoses
keratosis
keratitis
kerfuffle
Kurt Weill
kirkyaird
Kerry blue
kirby grip
Kiswahili
kissagram
kiss hands
Kissinger
Kisangani
kissogram
✧kathakali
Katharina
Katharine
Kit Carson
katharsis
katabasis
katabatic
kitschily
Katherine
kittenish
kite-flyer
kitchener
kittiwake
kettleful
Kathmandu
ketonemia
ketonuria
kauri-pine
krummhorn
krummholz
kiwi fruit
Keynesian
kryometer
keyworker
keyboards
keystroke
Kuybyshev
Kozhikode
Lhasa Apso
loaf-bread
Leadbelly
lead colic
leaf cells
lease-band
leaseback
lease-lend
leaderene
leavening
loaferish
leasehold
leaperous
leavenous

lean-faced
lead glass
leaf-green
Llangefni
loathsome
lyam-hound
leafiness
leakiness
loaminess
Leavisite
liability
leafleted
leaf miner
leaf-metal
leaf mould
learnable
learnedly
leaf-nosed
leaporous
lead-paint
leaf-stalk
loan shark
loaf sugar
loadstone
leaf trace
leastways
leastwise
labialise
labialize
labdacism
labialism
librarian
libration
libratory
librairie
Lubeck Bay
libecchio
libeccios
lobectomy
lobscouse
libidinal
librettos
lubricate
lubricant
lubricity
lubricous
labelmate
libellant
labelling
libelling
labelloid
libellous
lobulated
Lob's pound
libertine
liberties
liberally
labyrinth
laborious
liberator
Labour Day
Labourite
labourism
labourist
Lubavitch
lucrative
lactarian
lactation
luctation
Lucia Popp
lack-beard

lucubrate
lack-brain
lock-chain
lucidness
lickerish
lichenism
Lucretius
lichenist
lichenoid
lichenose
lecherous
lichenous
Luc Besson
lace-frame
✧locofocos
Lichfield
luciferin
lace glass
lacy glass
lock horns
lockhouse
lacrimary
luckie-dad
luckiness
lacrimoso
Lochinvar
locellate
local call
Lucullean
Local Hero
local veto
localness
local time
Lucullian
lack-linen
local loop
localiser
lack-Latin
Loch Leven
localizer
lucumones
Loch Morar
locomotor
laciniate
laconical
lacunaria
licensure
lectorate
laccolite
laccolith
locoplant
locuplete
lickpenny
luck-penny
lace-paper
lacerable
lacertine
lacertian
lachrymal
lacerated
Lycosidae
locksmith
locatable
lacquerer
lacrymary
lidocaine
lodiculae
ludically
ludicrous
lodge-gate
lodgement

ladies' man
lodgepole
ladlefuls
Ludditism
loden coat
lady's-maid
Ladislaus
lodestone
lady-smock
lie perdue
liegeless
liege-lord
laevigate
leeringly
Lee Miller
lie in wait
lie at host
lienteric
laevulose
lift a hand
lifeblood
left bower
life class
life cycle
left-click
left-field
life-force
lifeguard
Lofthouse
loftiness
leftovers
life story
life-saver
lifestyle
life-sized
life table
life-weary
left wheel
Luftwaffe
leftwards
laggardly
log tables
lign-aloes
lignaloes
logically
logic bomb
leg before
logograph
logogriph
leg theory
legginess
laggingly
lignified
ligniform
lagrimoso
lagniappe
legal year
logomachy
logomania
lagomorph
legendary
legendist
legionary
logaoedic
Liguorian
logroller
logopedic
logophile
leger bait
Lagerfeld
lager beer
logorrhea
leger line
lager lout
logarithm
legislate
logistics
light-ball
light-fast
logothete
light-year
lightless
lightness
lightship
light show
light time
lightning
light-mill
light into
lighten up
lightsome
light-foot
lights out
light upon
light trap
light bulb
light-dues
leg-puller
leg-cutter
✧lehrjahre
Lohengrin
L P Hartley
loincloth
lairdship
loitering
Leicester
Leigh Hunt
leitmotif
leitmotiv
Leibovitz
laid paper
leisurely
like a shot
like a bird
lake-basin
like crazy
like flies
Lake Garda
Lakshmana
Lake Huron
Lake Nyasa
Lake Onega
Lake Ohrid
Lake poets
Lake Poopó
Lake Patos
like stink
like smoke
Lake Tahoe
Lake Taupo
Lake Volta
like water
Lollardry
Liliaceae
lallation
la lucerne
lollingly
lollipops
lilangeni
lolloping
loll-shrob
lily-white
lampadary
Lombardic
Lemnaceae
lemmatise
lemmatize
lampadist
lampblack
lamebrain
limaceous
Lambegger
lumbering
lumberman
lumber-pie
lambently
Lampedusa
lamp-glass
lyme-grass
lime green
lime-green
lymph node
lymphatic
lime-hound
lyme-hound
lumpiness
limpingly
lumpishly
lambitive
limpidity
lamaistic
lime juice
lamellate
lamplight
limelight
lamelloid
lamellose
lemon balm
lemon tart
laminable
lemon-weed
lemon peel
luminaire
lamenting
lemonfish
luminance
lemonwood
lemon sole
Laminaria
lemon tree
lemon drop
luminesce
limonitic
laminated
lamington
Lymington
laminator
laminitis
lemon curd
Lamb of God
lampooner
limnology
lumbrical
lumbricus
Lambrusco
lampshade
lamb's ears
lamp-shell
lump sugar
Lymeswold®
limestone
lamb'swool
lamaserai
limitable
limitedly
limitless
Limburger
limousine
limewater
lend a hand
line ahead
lend an ear
land agent
lineament
Lon Halévy
linearise
linearize
lineation
lineality
linearity
landaulet
landamman
Lanzarote
Lancaster
longaeval
Long Beach
line block
Lindbergh
long-chain
Longchamp
long-coats
longcloth
long drink
landdamne
line dance
landdrost
long-dated
long dozen
lancejack
longe whip
lunge whip
lingering
longevity
lintelled
lanterloo
lanceolar
lancewood
longevous
long-eared
leniently
Langesund
long-faced
long field
line-fence
land-flood
landforce
landgrave
land grant
line-grove
lung-grown
lunchtime
lanthanum
Lon Chaney
lunch hour
longhouse
lancinate
lankiness
longingly
lanciform
lentiform
longicorn
longitude
line judge
long johns
lend-lease
linoleate
long-liner
land-loper
landloper
lunulated
long-lived
long metre
Lenin Peak
linen-fold
Langobard
Longobard
lineolate
Londonese
Londonise
Londonize
Londonish
Londonism
Londonian
London ivy
✧land of Nod
landowner
langouste
land-plane
land-pilot
lunarnaut
langridge
land-reeve
lunar year
long-range
lincrusta
Land Rover®
landscape
land-shark
Landsmaal
land snail
long sheep
landslide
Landsting
linishing
langspiel
lunisolar
long since
longshore
lintstock
line-storm
land-scrip
Landsturm
long sixes
long-sixes
lunitidal
lengthful
lengthily
lengthman
linctuses
lingulate
Langue d'oc
languidly
languaged
lingually
languette
Len Hutton
longueurs
land-value
lintwhite
long whist
landwards
land-yacht
lookalike
look alive
look after
Léon Bakst
lioncelle
Lyon Court
loose fall
loose-leaf
looseness
loose fish
lyomerous
lookers-on
lion-heart
lyophobic
lyophilic
Laodicean
looniness
loopiness
loop-light
loom large
✧lyonnaise
loon-pants
look-round
look small
look sharp
look smart
lion-tamer
look where
loony left
lap dancer
Laplander
lipectomy
lapidific
lapideous
lapse rate
lip-reader
lippening
Laptev Sea
Lippizana
lippitude
lupulinic
lipolysis
leptotene
leprosery
leprosity
lap-roller
leptosome
lophodont
liposomal
lapstrake
lapstreak
lip-syncer
liquation
loquacity
liquefied
liquefier
laquearia
liquidate
liquidise
liquidize
liquidity
liquorice
liquorish
lardalite
lark about
Largactil®
Lord Astor
Lord Byron
Lord Clark
Lord Clive
lyrically
luridness
largeness
larcenist
larcenous
Lord Forte
larghetto
Lord Hawke
larkiness
larvicide
larvikite
largition
larviform
Lord Lucan
larum-bell
Lord Marks
Lord Mayor
laryngeal
Lord North
lorgnette
Lord Reith
lark's-heel
Lord Steel
Lord Soper
lardy-cake
Larry Bird
lorazepam
L'Escargot
Las Palmas
Les Dawson
lust after
lose caste
lost cause
lose count
last-ditch
Listerise
Listerize
Listerism
Listerian
lustfully
lysigenic
lose heart
lush-house
lustihead
lustiness
lastingly
lispingly
lustihood
lassitude
lossmaker
lysimeter
lissomely
lessoning
list price
Lusophile
laser card
laser disc
lysergide
laser disk
laserwort
last rites
lose sight
lysosomal
last straw
lose track
last thing
Lusitania
let have it
lethargic
L'Étranger
latration
Lotharios
lethality
laticlave
laticifer

lytically
latecomer
litterbug
litter bin
letterbox
latter-day
latter end
litheness
letter-gae
la trenise
lettering
Lutherism
Lutherist
lithesome
letterset
lothefull
latter-wit
latifondi
litigable
litigious
litigator
latch bolt
lithified
luteinise
luteinize
latticini
latticino
lithiasis
lithistid
littleane
little auk
Little Dog
Little Eva
little end
little man
little owl
little toe
Late Latin
Latiniser
Latinizer
lithoidal
latrociny
lithopone
lithotome
luteolous
lithology
lithotomy
lithocyst
Lotophagi
lat spread
liturgics
liturgist
laterally
literally
lateritic
literatim
literator
literatus
Lotus-land
latescent
lutescent
latitancy
Lithuania
lathyrism
Lauraceae
Laura Dern
laudative
laudation
Laurasian
leucaemia
leukaemia
leucaemic
leukaemic
laudatory
Launcelot
launch out
launch pad
Launceton
laundress
loup de mer
launderer
laurelled
lousewort
Lou Gehrig
lounge-bar
laughable
laughably
Lough Derg
laughsome
Leuciscus
lousiness
louringly
loutishly
Laurie Lee
Ljubljana
loudmouth
leuco-base
leuko-base
leucotome
leukotome
leucotomy
leukotomy
leucocyte
leukocyte
Louisiana
✧leviathan
Lev Yashin
love apple
love-arrow
livraison
live birth
love-charm
love child
lividness
love feast
levigable
luvviedom
live in sin
love-juice
lavaliere
levelness
lovelight
levelling
level-coil
level down
lovemaker
love match
loving cup
✧levantine
live on air
loverless
leveraged
liverwing
liveryman
Liverpool
liverwort
liver spot
livery pot
love-shaft
live shell
live steam
livestock
love-story
levitical
Leviticus
love-token
live tally
levitator
live under
✧lowlander
low relief
low-necked
Low German
lawlessly
law centre
Low Church
low-minded
lowlihead
lowliness
lowlights
lawgiving
Lowrie-tod
lawnmower
low-loader
low comedy
lawmonger
low-downer
lawn party
lower-case
lower deck
lower-deck
lowermost
law-writer
Lewis base
Lewis acid
Lowestoft
lawful day
Low Sunday
lexically
loxodrome
loxodromy
Lexington
luxuriate
luxuriant
luxurious
lixiviate
lixivious
leylandii
lay aboard
lay reader
Leyden jar
lay before
layperson
lay rector
lay sister
lay-figure
Loya Jirga
loyalties
lay on load
lay hold on
lay to rest
layer cake
lay eyes on
lazzarone
lazzaroni
lazybones
lazar-like
lazarette
lazaretto
lazy Susan
lazy tongs
lazy-tongs
Mia Farrow
meandrian
meandrous
meandered
Mr Average
meat-eater
moanfully
mealiness
meatiness
meaningly
mealie pap
meat jelly
measliest
miasmatic
meadow-rue
meat plate
meat paste
means test
means-test
measure up
measuring
meat wagon
meanwhile
mob-handed
mobocracy
mobiliser
mobilizer
Maccabean
Maccabees
muchachos
mechanise
mechanize
mechanism
mactation
mechanics
mechanist
mockadoes
muck about
muck-a-muck
mucic acid
micaceous
macédoine
macadamia
Macedonia
muckender
mockernut
Michel Ney
machinate
mochiness
muckiness
machinery
mockingly
machinist
Macmillan
mycologic
machmeter
Mycenaean
macintosh
MacDonald
microcard
microwave
mucronate
micromesh
microchip
microlite
microwire
microlith
micro-mini
microbial
microfilm
macrobian
microbian
macrocode
macrodome
microcode
micropore
microsome
microtome
microtone
macrocosm
microcosm
microform
macrocopy
macrology
microcopy
micrology
microtomy
microgram
microbrew
micropsia
micropump
macro-axis
macrocyte
microcyte
micropyle
mycophagy
Mecoptera
mycorhiza
muck-raker
Mucorales
macaronic
macaronis
McCartney
macerator
mica-slate
mucksweat
mycotoxin
Mycetozoa
micturate
MacGuffin
macrurous
macaw-palm
macaw-tree
machzorim
Media Mail
mud dauber
midlander
mediately
midmashie
Midrashim
mediatise
mediative
mediatize
mediation
mediatory
mediatrix
madrassah
Mad Hatter
mediaeval
medicable
medically
medicinal
mediciner
medicated
medaewart
maddening
madrepore
medresseh
mid-season
mid-heaven
modifying
madrilène
Madrileño
muddiness
midwifery
maddingly
midwifing
midwiving
mid-wicket
médaillon
mud minnow
mydriasis
mydriatic
mid-winter
✧mudéjares
medullate
middle-age
medullary
modal verb
middle ear
madeleine
medalling
modelling
medallion
modillion
medallist
medal play
medalplay
middleman
middlings
Middleton
modulator
midinette
mudlogger
mudhopper
mad-doctor
modernise
modernize
✧modernism
✧modernist
modernity
madarosis
moderator
moderatos
Midas's ear
midi-skirt
midstream
meditated
meditator
midsummer
mud turtle
made woman
Mt Everest
Maeonides
myelomata
mnemonics
mnemonist
Mnemosyne
✧maelstrom
maestosos
muffettee
muffin-cap
muffineer
miffiness
mafficker
muffin man
muffin pan
muffin tin
✧magdalene
Magyarise
Magyarize
migmatite
mugearite
magianism
magmatism
magnalium
Magyarism
migration
migraines
migratory
megabucks
megacycle
magic show
magicking
magically
magic word
megacurie
magic cube
megadeath
Mogadishu
magnesite
magnetise
magnetite
magnetize
magnesium
magnetism
magnesian
magnetics
magnetist
magnetron
Magdeburg
megaflora
megafarad
megafauna
megagauss
megahertz
mugginess
magnified
magnifico
magnifier
Maggie May
magnitude
megajoule
megillahs
megilloth
maggot-pie
megaphone
magistery
megascope
megaspore
megastore
magistral
mag-stripe
mug-hunter
Mahajanga
maharajah
maharanee
maharishi
Mohs scale
mahlstick
Mehitabel
mridamgam
mridangam
mainbrace
mail-coach
maid-child
maidenish
mainframe
Muirfield
meiofauna
mainliner
mailmerge
mail order
mail-order
meibomian

mail-plane
main plane
mainprise
mainsheet
Maidstone
main store
mail-train
moistness
maistring
maieutics
mujahedin
mujahidin
major term
majorship
major mode
major tone
major-domo
majorette
major suit
major axis
majuscule
make a card
make a face
make a back
make a pass
make a meal
make a play
make a bomb
make a move
make after
make a fuss
make faces
make fun of
make haste
make light
Mike Leigh
Mt Kilauea
mako-makos
makimonos
make money
make merry
mekometer
make or mar
make peace
make-peace
make ready
make-ready
mako shark
makeshift
make sense
make terms
Mike Tyson
make water
make waves
mallander
Malvaceae
Meliaceae
maltalent
mulga wire
Milwaukee
mill about
millboard
molybdate
Meliboean
Malebolge
molybdous
Miliciens
malachite
molochise
molochize
molecular

malicious
melocoton
melodrama
melodrame
mole drain
melodious
maladroit
my lee-lane
millenary
malleable
malleably
mallender
millepede
mallee-hen
millerite
Millerian
malleolar
malleolus
millennia
millepore
molten sea
mallemuck
milken-way
maleffect
malt-floor
milk float
milk fever
milk-gland
milk glass
✧malignant
milk gravy
malagueña
malignity
mylohyoid
malt-horse
mill-horse
malt-house
milk-house
multipara
multipack
multitask
multi-wall
Miltiades
millipede
multipede
milkiness
Millicent
millinery
meltingly
Malpighia
mollified
Maldivian
mollifier
mollities
multiplet
multiplex
mullioned
millionth
millimole
multimode
multirole
multifoil
multiform
milligram
Mel Gibson
multiuser
multitude
multihull
melaleuca
milo maize
milk-molar

melomania
melomanic
melampode
milometer
melon-pear
malanders
malingery
malengine
melanomas
melanuria
melanuric
Melanesia
melanosis
melanotic
mylonitic
meliorate
Mallorcan
male order
Melpomene
mal soigné
meliorism
Miltonism
Miltonian
meliorist
meliority
malformed
mill owner
mellow out
Melbourne
Mellotron®
millocrat
malvoisie
milk punch
melaphyre
malgré lui
malgré moi
malarious
Mel Brooks
milk round
melismata
milk shake
milk snake
millscale
mole spade
mild steel
molestful
milk sugar
Molossian
moleskins
Mélisande
Mills bomb
malmstone
milestone
millstone
milk stout
male screw
Milosevic
milk train
Malathion®
melatonin
militancy
milk tooth
mill-tooth
mulattoes
militaria
mal du pays
molluscan
molluskan
milk vetch
millwheel
milk-white

melt-water
meloxicam
malaxator
mollymawk
Malaysian
Malayalam
mammalian
mammalogy
mimicking
Mummerset
mumchance
Memphitic
mumpishly
mummified
memoirism
memoirist
mammillae
mammiform
mummiform
mamillate
mamillary
mamelucos
momentany
momentary
mementoes
momentous
mammonite
mammonish
mammonism
Memnonian
mammonist
mammogram
memorials
memorable
memorably
memoranda
memoriser
memoriter
memorizer
mumpsimus
mimetical
mum-budget
mummy-case
manganate
mental age
mandatary
manhandle
manganese
mundanely
Montaigne
manzanita
mandarine
manganite
monoamine
man-eating
Mondayish
mentalism
Montanism
mentation
miniation
mentalist
Montanist
mendacity
mentality
mundanity
manganous
mandatory
mental set
Manhattan
Mendaites
miniature

montan wax
Mont Blanc
minibreak
manubrial
manubrium
monobasic
monocracy
monocycle
Manichean
monactine
monocline
monachism
Munichism
monachist
monocular
manically
monochord
minacious
monecious
municipal
monocoque
mind-curer
monoceros
manicotti
monodrama
monadical
monodical
minidress
menadione
monadnock
Minnehaha
Minnesang
Minié ball
monkey bag
menseless
mincemeat
mongering
monkeyish
✧mannerism
Mendelism
monkeyism
monoecism
Mendelian
Mindelian
✧mannerist
monkey jar
manzellos
monkey nut
Minnesota
mangetout
monkey pod
monkey pot
monkey run
Monterrey
Mandelson
Montezuma
mannequin
manoeuvre
Mansfield
minefield
Man of Kent
manifolds
mindfully
manifesto
monograph
monogamic
Monogynia
monogenic
menagerie
mynah bird
monthling

Menshevik
mancipate
mendicant
mandiocca
man-minded
manginess
manliness
minginess
Mandingos
mincingly
mannishly
monkishly
mundified
menticide
manriding
✧mandilion
menuisier
mendicity
Monsignor
manticora
manticore
monticule
mint julep
monologic
monologue
monolater
monolatry
Monk Lewis
man-slayer
minelayer
monolayer
monomachy
minim rest
minimally
monomania
✧menominee
menomines
muniments
monomeric
meno mosso
minimiser
manometer
monometer
manometry
minimizer
mining bee
man and boy
man-and-dog
meningeal
Monandria
Mungo Park
mandoline
Mennonite
Mongolise
Mongolize
monzonite
mentoring
mentorial
✧mongolism
Monroeism
Mongolian
Monroeist
monsoonal
mine owner
✧mongoloid
mangouste
mongooses
mangostan
monophase
monoplane
monophagy

mons pubis
monopodia
Menippean
maniplies
manyplies
moniplies
monyplies
monopulse
manipular
monoploid
monoptote
monophony
monopsony
monopitch
menopause
Man Friday
minor term
manor-seat
minirugby
menorrhea
monarchic
man-orchid
monorchid
monarchal
minorship
monorhine
monergism
mongrelly
manurance
minor mode
minor tone
Minervois
minor poet
minareted
Minorites
minor suit
minor axis
monorhyme
mint state
many-sided
monk's seam
mane-sheet
monastery
monostich
minus sign
monoskier
miniskirt
monosomic
meniscoid
monkshood
minestone
Minkstone
miniscule
mint sauce
minuscule
monostyle
Minitrack®
monotreme
monitress
minute gun
monatomic
✧minuteman
monotonic
Monotropa
minutiose
monotroch
monstrous
munitions
monotypic
man-at-arms
menstrual

Words marked ✧ can also be spelled with one or more capital letters

menstruum
manducate
mundungus
Mancunian
Manxwoman
minoxidil
monoxylon
monaxonic
moneybags
moneyless
money belt
money bill
✧mandylion
money clip
money down
moneywort
myocardia
Mao-jacket
moon about
myomantic
moonblind
moot court
moon daisy
mooseyard
Moore's law
Mao Zedong
moon flask
moon-faced
moon-glade
moor grass
moong bean
moot house
Maoriland
Maori Wars
moodiness
myofibril
Maori oven
moon knife
myoglobin
moonlight
moon-loved
myologist
moonphase
moot point
moonquake
✧moonraker
myography
moonscape
moonshine
moonshiny
moonstone
Mt Olympus
mepacrine
mop-headed
map-reader
✧maple leaf
mappemond
mephitism
✧maquisard
marmalade
mermaiden
Myrtaceae
Marrakesh
Mt Ruapehu
mariachis
✧margarita
marcasite
margarine
margarite
marialite
marmarise
marmarize
morganite
mortalise
mortalize
mordacity
mortality
murrained
Myriapoda
merganser
mercaptan
mordantly
mirabilia
mirabelle
Marc Bolan
myrobalan
✧mirabilis
marabunta
miracidia
Maracaibo
Morecambe
mortcloth
moraceous
muricated
Mark Darcy
Mariehamn
mercenary
market-day
✧marketeer
murderess
marmelise
marmelize
mercerise
mercerize
marketing
marcelled
market-led
martelled
marvelled
Marcellus
martellos
market-man
myrmecoid
Marie Rose
Morse code
murderous
merpeople
marker pen
mirifical
marigraph
mortgagee
mortgager
mortgagor
marihuana
marshland
✧March hare
marchpane
marsh hawk
march past
marsh fern
March beer
mirthless
marshiest
march-dike
marshalcy
morphemic
marshwort
murtherer
morphosis
morphetic
morphotic
march-dyke
marginate
marxisant
merciable
merciless
merriness
murkiness
merriment
mortified
mercifide
mortician
mortifier
Mt Rainier
morbidity
martially
Martinmas
mirligoes
Myrmidons
Mardi Gras
meroistic
marijuana
Martlemas
moraliser
myrtle-wax
moralizer
marinière
maranatha
myriorama
marmoreal
marrowfat
Mormonite
marooning
mirroring
marrowish
Mormonism
marrow-men
Marco Polo
Mariology
Maryology
mereology
marrowsky
Mario Puzo
Meropidae
meropidan
marsquake
Mary Quant
Mt Roraima
merbromin
Margrethe
mare's-tail
mare's-nest
mareschal
marischal
Myristica
mere swine
mire-snipe
Marasmius
Mark Spitz
marlstone
merestone
morass ore
mort-stone
Morescoes
✧moriscoes
Mark Twain
Mary Tudor
maritally
moratoria
mercurate
Marcus Fox
mercurise
mercurize
marauding
murmuring
marsupial
✧mercurial
marsupium
mercurous
murmurous
Marquesan
marquises
marquetry
mark-white
Mark Waugh
merry-make
martyrdom
mercy-seat
martyrise
martyrize
martyrium
marry into
mercy on us
merozoite
mismanage
moss agate
mishandle
most an end
mistaught
mustachio
mustaches
Messalina
mescaline
muscadine
muscarine
messaging
misfaring
missaying
mistaking
mescalism
massagist
mashallah
misfallen
Mt Stanley
mess about
mystagogy
mishappen
mishanter
mesoblast
Miss Bates
music case
music rack
music hall
music-hall
misoclere
music-demy
musicking
masochism
masochist
musically
music roll
music room
musaceous
mesic atom
misadvise
misregard
masterate
misbehave
misrelate
mishegaas
masterdom
misleader
miscegene
misbeseem
misdemean
musketeer
misdesert
masterful
messenger
mesmerise
mesmerize
miscegine
musteline
misbelief
mastering
mesmerism
Moslemism
mysteries
mesmerist
misreckon
master-key
musselled
misdeemed
mesne lord
misbecome
musketoon
misreport
muster out
mistemper
misleared
misfeasor
Mrs Beeton
misbestow
Masefield
musefully
musk gland
moss green
mesogloea
moss-grown
mischance
mischancy
misshaped
misshapen
mischarge
moschatel
masthouse
masticate
mussitate
massiness
messiness
mistiness
mossiness
mushiness
muskiness
mussiness
mustiness
misdirect
massively
missilery
missingly
mystified
misgiving
misliking
mosaicism
Muslimism
mysticism
mystifier
mosaicist
mispickel
Mosaic Law
mosaic map
✧messianic
missioner
mislippen
mistigris
✧messieurs
Miss Julie
misplease
misallege
misallied
muscleman
muscle out
mistletoe
mass media
musk melon
misemploy
mesomorph
mushmouth
mason wasp
most noble
misintend
must needs
mesentery
masonried
misoneism
misoneist
misinform
muscovado
mastoidal
Mt Snowdon
Massorete
misgovern
moskonfyt
✧muscovite
Mussolini
Muscovian
miscolour
muscology
museology
Mrs Norris
Moscow Sea
misgotten
mossplant
musk-plant
misspoken
mesopause
musk-pouch
mesophyte
mesophyll
miscreate
miscreant
miserable
miserably
miscredit
mispraise
misprised
Masoretic
misgrowth
miss stays
misesteem
musk-sheep
misassign
musk shrew
meshugaas
misguided
misguider
misguggle
masculine
Mussulman
Mussulmen
musculous
misaunter
mosquitos
Mesa Verde
misavised
massymore
mutualise
mutualize
mutualism
mutualist
mutuality
mitraille
mattamore
methadone
metabolic
metabasis
Matt Busby
metabatic
miticidal
matachina
matachini
motocross
metacarpi
Matt Damon
matterful
mother hen
mothering
muttering
mother lye
metheglin
mitre fold
mitre-wort
moth-eaten
mother wit
Met Office
mitigable
mitogenic
mutagenic
mitigator
matchable
Matthaean
matchless
match play
matchplay
match-cord
matchwood
matchbook
matchlock
metricate
matricide
metricise
metricize
mythicise
mythicize
mythicism
metrician
metrifier
metricist
mythicist
matriliny
mitriform
matrimony
matriarch
metric ton
matricula
metalware
Mytilidae
metalline
metallise
metallize
metalling
metallist
metalloid
metalwork
matelasse
matelassé
mutilator

Metal Guru
metameric
Mutiny Act
mutinying
metonymic
matronage
mythomane
matzo ball
matzo meal
methought
mutton ham
matronise
matronize
meteorite
methodise
methodize
meteorism
Methodism
Methodius
meteorist
✧methodist
motionist
metroplex
motion-man
meteoroid
metronome
meteorous
mythopoet
metrology
mythology
metaphase
metaplasm
metapelet
mothproof
meter maid
motorcade
materials
maturable
motorable
Motorhead
Mithraeum
motor-ship
motorbike
Mithraism
Mithraist
maternity
motor home
motorboat
motoscafi
motoscafo
metestick
mutoscope
mote spoon
motettist
matutinal
Mathurine
Mutsuhito
Mathurins
motivator
methylate
methylene
mateyness
methystic
mould-made
mouldwarp
mouldable
mouldiest
mound-bird
mould-loft
maunderer
mouse hare

mousetail
mouse-deer
mousebird
mouse hole
mousetrap
mouse-hunt
moufflons
mouth-made
mouthwash
mouth harp
mouthpart
mouthable
mouthfeel
mouthless
mouthiest
mouthfuls
moudiwart
mousiness
Mauritian
Mauritius
moudiwort
mournings
mournival
mausoleum
mausolean
maulstick
Mount Taal
mountable
Mounts Bay
moustache
Mount Sion
Mount Zion
Mount Cook
Mount Ossa
Mount Etna
Mount Fuji
moveables
movieland
moviegoer
movie star
move house
moving map
mowdiwart
mawkishly
mowdiwort
mixedness
myxedemic
mixed up in
myxoedema
Max Perutz
Max Aitken
maxillary
Max Planck
maxillula
maximally
maximiser
maximizer
Maxentius
Max Ophuls
myxovirus
Moygashel®
✧may beetle
✧mayflower
mayorship
Mayerling
mayoralty
may as well
Muz Tag Ata
mezzanine
mezza voce
muzziness

muzzle-bag
mizzonite
mezzotint
Mozarabic
Mozartean
Mozartian
Mizushima
naan bread
Naas Botha
no-account
neat-house
nearly man
near point
neat-stall
niaiserie
near touch
near-white
no-brainer
nubeculae
nobleness
noble opal
nobbiness
nebbisher
nobiliary
nobilesse
nebuliser
nebulizer
Nabataean
nectareal
nectarean
nectarine
nectarial
nictation
nectarous
nyctalops
neckcloth
Nicodemus
nickeline
nickelise
nickelize
nickeling
nickelled
nucleolar
nucleolus
nickelous
nucleated
nucleator
Nick Faldo
nictitate
Nickie-ben
noctilios
no chicken
noctiluca
Nicolette
no comment
nicompoop
necrophil
necrotise
necrotize
niccolite
necrology
necrotomy
nocuously
neckpiece
nickpoint
Nicaragua
necessary
nickstick
necessity
nicotiana
nachtmaal

nicotinic
nicotined
Noctuidae
nocturnal
Nocturnes
neckverse
niddering
noddingly
nodulated
Nadir Shah
niderling
noddy suit
neesberry
needfully
neediness
needleful
needle-gun
nielloing
niellated
needle-tin
Niels Bohr
needs must
needy-hood
Nietzsche
niftiness
no flies on
niff-naffy
nefandous
Nefertiti
nefarious
no-fly zone
niggardly
négociant
neglecter
nigricant
negligent
Nigritian
Negrillos
negritude
nigritude
Nigel Benn
negroidal
negrohead
negrophil
nigrosine
negro-corn
Nagarjuna
nightward
negotiate
Night Café
nightmare
night safe
nighthawk
night-walk
nightfall
night-rail
negotiant
night-cart
nightmary
night-bell
nightgear
nightwear
nightless
night-rest
nightbird
nightfire
nightlife
night-line
nightside
night-tide
night-time

nightclub
night-robe
nightlong
night-work
night-fowl
night-soil
nightgown
nightspot
night-crow
night-rule
night duty
Nahum Tate
nuisancer
nail-biter
nailbrush
naiveness
naïveness
noiseless
noises off
neighbour
noisiness
noisomely
nail punch
Neil Young
Nuku'alofa
naked lady
nakedness
naked boys
Niki Lauda
nikau palm
Nile green
nullipara
nullified
nullifier
Nellie Kim
nullipore
nelumbium
Nilometer
Nolan Ryan
nilpotent
no-meaning
namma hole
name after
name brand
nomocracy
namecheck
name-child
number one
number off
Number Ten
number two
nomograph
nymphical
nymphaeum
nymphlike
nymphalid
nymphette
numbingly
numble-pie
nimblesse
nominable
nominally
name names
nominator
nameplate
nemophila
numerable
numerably
numerical
nemertean
nemertine

numeraire
numéraire
nemertian
numerally
numerator
numero uno
no messing
numbskull
nomothete
nummulary
Nemrut Dag
nummuline
nummulite
Nanda Devi
nonpareil
non-paying
non-racial
nunnation
nonparous
non-access
non-verbal
non-member
non-reader
non-lethal
nunneries
non-sexist
non-person
non-return
nun's-flesh
nonagonal
nineholes
Nandi bear
non-linear
non liquet
non placet
nonillion
nonplused
non-smoker
nanometre
nine-metre
nonentity
none other
non-voting
ninepence
ninepenny
non-profit
non troppo
non-driver
non-usager
ninescore
ninetieth
nunataker
nuncupate
nonjuring
nannyghai
nanny goat
neo-Nazism
neoterise
neoterize
neoterism
neoterist
neoteinia
neotenous
neophobia
neophobic
neophilia
neophytic
Neolithic
neopilina
Naomi Wolf
noodledom

neon light
neoplasia
Neo-Gothic
neologise
neologize
neologism
Neocomian
neologian
neonomian
neologist
neocortex
noosphere
neon tetra
neodymium
nephalism
nephalist
nepheline
nephelite
Napierian
nipperkin
nipcheese
nappiness
nippiness
nippingly
Nepenthes
Nipponese
no problem
nephology
nephogram
nephralgy
nephrosis
nephritic
nephrotic
nephritis
naphthene
neptunium
Neptunian
Neptunist
nappy rash
Normandie
narrative
normalise
normalize
Normanise
Normanize
normative
Normanism
narration
nervation
normality
narratory
Norway rat
nor'-easter
nervature
nursemaid
nurse-tend
nerve cell
nerveless
nurselike
nurseling
Norwegian
norseller
nerve cord
Norueyses
nor'-wester
nor'wester
northland
northward
north-east
north-west
North Uist

narghilly
north pole
North Down
northmost
northerly
North Star
nerviness
narcissus
neroli oil
Nuremberg
narcotine
narcotise
narcotize
narrowing
narcotism
narcotist
nervously
Narasimha
Neritidae
nurturant
nostalgia
nostalgic
nystagmic
nystagmus
nosebleed
naseberry
nose candy
Nosferatu
Nissen hut
nose-flute
nastiness
nescience
Nestorian
nostology
nosepiece
nisi prius
no strings
no-strings
Nostratic
Nashville
nose wheel
Nathanael
nitratine
Nathaniel
note a bill
nitration
nuts about
notabilia
notochord
notedness
Notodonta
Notre-Dame
not-headed
natheless
netheless
nutmegged
nutpecker
net-veined
nathemore
nut-weevil
notifying
Notogaeic
Notogaean
notchback
nattiness
nuttiness
nutriment
not likely
net-winged
nitrified
nutritive

nitriding
nutrition
nit-picker
nitwitted
net-player
Notonecta
nutjobber
natrolite
nitro-silk
notionist
not for Joe
networker
notaphily
notepaper
notoriety
nature-god
naturally
nut-wrench
notorious
not proven
Nithsdale
net assets
not a scrap
Nototrema
not a thing
not at home
natatoria
nut cutlet
no-trumper
not fussed
nutbutter
native cat
neuralgia
neuralgic
naumachia
neuration
neural net
naughtily
Neuchâtel
nourisher
neurility
nautiloid
nouriture
nauplioid
neuromata
neuropath
neurochip
neuroglia
neurology
neurotomy
neurogram
neutrally
neutrinos
neutretto
noviciate
Novocaine®
navicular
novodamus
navigable
navigably
navigator
navel ring
novelties
Naval Club
navelwort
noveliser
novelette
novelizer
novennial
✧never land
never mind

nevermore
Navaratra
Navaratri
novus homo
novitiate
new candle
newsagent
newfangle
✧newmarket
new-fallen
New Labour
Newcastle
New Mexico
New Jersey
now of late
newsflash
✧new ageism
newsgroup
New Church
newshound
newsiness
no whither
nowhither
newel post
Newtonian
new dollar
new for old
newsprint
newspaper
new-create
no worries
new critic
news-stand
news-sheet
newstrade
New Guinea
news-value
newswoman
nux vomica
next of kin
noxiously
next world
naysaying
Nazaritic
ovalbumin
on account
on average
of a verity
orangeade
opal glass
Orangeism
Orangeman
orang-utan
orange-tip
ovational
odalisque
onanistic
of all arms
oratorial
✧oratorian
oratorios
on a string
oraculous
orbicular
✧ombudsman
✧ombudsmen
obbligati
obbligato
oubliette
on balance
ombrophil

once again
orchestra
orchestic
oncogenic
Orchideae
orchidist
oscillate
oecologic
occulting
occultism
occultist
oncolysis
oncolytic
oecumenic
oncometer
OncoMouse®
obconical
occupying
occupance
occupancy
occipital
obcordate
occurrent
occurring
oncostman
occasions
oscitancy
occludent
occlusive
occlusion
on draught
Old Bailey
odd man out
✧old master
old school
old-school
Oddfellow
old fellow
on default
Ogden Nash
ordinaire
ordinance
odd one out
Oudenarde
odd-jobber
odd-jobman
odd-lotter
orderless
Old French
order book
order form
on display
old stager
odd number
Old Buddha
old fustic
over again
one-handed
ore-raught
operative
operating
one-nation
operation
overalled
open-armed
overboard
overbuild
overblown
overbound
open-chain
overclass

oleic acid
overcheck
operculum
opercular
overcloud
overcrowd
oleaceous
overcarry
overcatch
open court
overcount
overcover
overdraft
overdress
overdight
overdrive
okey-dokey
overdated
over-exact
open-ended
obeseness
overexert
one-legged
Olenellus
orepearch
one-person
ore-rested
open-field
o're-office
overflown
overflush
overglaze
overgraze
oleograph
overgrain
overgrass
overgreen
overgreat
overgoing
oven glove
overgloom
overgrown
overgorge
overheads
overhaile
overhappy
overhaste
overhasty
open house
obeliscal
overinked
obedience
overissue
overjoyed
overladen
overlying
overlusty
ocellated
Ogen melon
overmerry
overmatch
overmount
one and all
oceanides
overnight
oceanaria
open order
operosely
operosity
onerously
overplast

overpedal
overpress
overpoise
overprice
overprize
overpaint
overprint
overproud
over proof
overproof
overperch
overpitch
overpower
overreach
oven-roast
overreact
overroast
oven-ready
overrider
overruler
olecranal
olecranon
overripen
oleoresin
overstand
open stage
overshade
overstare
overstate
overstaff
overstain
overspend
open-steek
overswell
oversleep
oversteer
overswear
overspent
oversight
overshine
Odelsting
overstink
overspill
open skies
overshirt
overskirt
obeisance
open score
overscore
overstock
over-shoes
overshoot
overstrew
overstuff
overstunk
overstudy
oversexed
oversized
overtrade
overtrain
overtrick
overtaken
overtimer
orestunck
overtones
overtures
overthrow
overtrump
overtrust
overtower
over to you!

overvalue
open-weave
overweary
overwhelm
overwrest
overwrite
overweigh
overwatch
overwater
overwound
offhanded
offsaddle
off camera
officiate
officiant
office boy
olfactive
olfaction
officinal
officious
olfactory
offseason
off-centre
off the air
off the bit
off the map
off chance
off-chance
off the peg
off-the-peg
off limits
off-limits
off kilter
Offenbach
offensive
offending
off-roader
off colour
off-colour
offspring
offerable
Oxfordian
offerings
offertory
obfuscate
off-stream
off-street
off-cutter
off-putter
orgiastic
orgillous
orgone box
organical
organ-bird
organ-pipe
organzine
organelle
organised
organiser
oogenesis
oogenetic
organized
organizer
oughtness
Oshogatsu
on holiday
ophiolite
ophiology
ochlocrat
otherness
otherwise

Ophiuchus
ophiuroid
oricalche
oligarchy
oxidative
oxidation
oviparity
oligaemia
oligaemic
oviparous
oviraptor
olive-yard
olive-back
olivenite
Origenism
Oliverian
Origenist
oviferous
ovigerous
olive drab
olive-drab
olive tree
originate
originals
orificial
opinioned
Oriolidae
oriflamme
Opium Wars
orientate
orienteer
onion-skin
onion dome
onion-eyed
Oligocene
ovibovine
oligopoly
ominously
on impulse
Ohio River
omissible
omittance
oviductal
objective
objection
objectify
objurgate
objet d'art
Ockhamism
Ockhamist
oakenshaw
Orleanism
Orleanist
oil tanker
owl-parrot
On Liberty
on-licence
oil length
oil beetle
oil of cade
Owle-glass
oological
obligator
obligatos
oil filter
oil engine
onlooking
oil colour
orlop deck
obliquely
obliquity
oil string
oil-burner
oblivious
osmic acid
ohmically
osmometer
osmometry
on-message
ommatidia
osmeteria
omnibuses
Osnabrück
oenomania
ornaments
oenomancy
oenometer
oenanthic
oenophile
oenophily
ownerless
ownership
omnirange
Oenothera
ornithoid
obnoxious
Orobanche
obovately
ozonation
odonatist
opobalsam
onomastic
ovo-lactos
otoscopic
opodeldoc
of one mind
ozocerite
ozokerite
ozone hole
of one's own
on one's own
ovotestes
ovotestis
on one's way
omophagia
omophagic
otolithic
ocotillos
orologist
otologist
odorously
ororotund
odourless
otorrhoea
orography
odontalgy
odontomas
orphanage
omphacite
orphanism
orpharion
omphaloid
oppressor
oppugnant
opponency
Orpington
of purpose
on purpose
opportune
opposable
ouroboros
Oort cloud
ourselves
oar-footed
obreption
on request
orris-root
ouroscopy
oarswoman
on stand-by
onslaught
osso bucco
obsecrate
ossicular
oyster-bed
obscenely
obscenity
obstetric
ossifraga
ossifrage
ossifying
obsignate
oast house
obstinate
obstinacy
of Solomon
obsolesce
opsomania
opsimathy
oesophagi
obsequent
obsequial
obsequies
✧observant
obstruent
oestrogen
observing
Oh So Sharp
obsessive
obsession
onsetting
obscurant
obscurely
obscurity
outlander
outwardly
ostracean
outraigne
ostracise
ostracize
out-parish
of that ilk
ostracism
Ostracion
outbacker
outhauler
outlaunce
outlaunch
Ostracoda
outmantle
Octobrist
optic disc
optically
octachord
optic lobe
optic tube
optic axis
on the game
on the make
on the take
on the bash
on the rack
on the ball
on the nail
on the edge
outredden
on the mend
on the beam
ostleress
on the beat
on the line
on the rise
on the side
ottrelite
outrelief
on the wing
on the pill
on the bias
on the club
✧on the road
on the bone
on the dole
on the move
on the nose
on the hoof
on the boil
✧on the town
on the hour
on the spot
on-the-spot
on the broo
on the trot
out-sentry
on the cuff
on the pull
on the turn
out of hand
out of date
out-of-date
out of cash
out of mind
out of line
out of time
out of play
out of work
out-of-work
out-of-town
out-of-door
out-of-body
out of true
out of step
out of tune
out of curl
out of sync
Octogynia
ontogenic
octagonal
octahedra
outside in
outlinear
outsiders
outrigger
out with it!
on thin ice
outgiving
outwitted
outfitter
outskirts
outplacer
ontologic
octillion
optimally
optimiser
octameter
optometer
optimates
optometry
optimizer
oftenness
obtundent
ostensive
octennial
obtention
out-and-out
ostensory
ortanique
Octandria
octonarii
ostinatos
ostiolate
osteopath
osteoderm
orthopedy
osteogeny
outtongue
optronics
orthotics
orthotist
outworker
outjockey
outbounds
outgoings
orthotone
osteotome
Ostrogoth
orthodoxy
osteology
osteotomy
orthoepic
outrooper
outsource
outpourer
outdoorsy
orthoptic
out to stud
out-porter
orthoaxes
orthoaxis
octapodic
octopodes
outspread
outspring
outspoken
octaploid
octoploid
optophone
octopuses
Octopussy
outer ward
outerwear
outcrafty
outermost
obturator
outtravel
outgrowth
Otto Stern
octastich
octastyle
octostyle
outstrain
out at heel
outstrike
outnumber
obtrusive
obtruding
obtrusion
outrunner
outlustre
ottavinos
ovulation
ocularist
ovulatory
obumbrate
opusculum
opulently
obviation
obvolvent
obvoluted
obvention
obviously
obversely
obversion
Orwellian
of warrant
oxygenate
oxygenise
oxygenize
oxygenous
onychitis
ouzel-cock
pranayama
Prajapati
play a part
praeamble
phalangid
phalangal
phalanger
phalanges
placation
planarian
planation
Phanariot
pea jacket
pharaonic
phalarope
play along
play about
placatory
play-actor
peasantry
phalanxes
play by ear
play booty
praecoces
peat-creel
Pratchett
plaid-neuk
playdough
place card
place name
platemark
plate rack
plate rail
peace camp
planetary
peaceable
peaceably
peaked cap
phagedena
pease-meal
peaseweep
peaceless
phaseless
placeless
placement
prayerful
plate-ship
peace pipe
peacetime
plate-like
place kick
peace pill
peace sign
phaseolin
prayer mat
planetoid
piacevole
plate-room
pease-soup
placeboes
played-out
plane tree
peace drug
prayer rug
placentae
placental
placentas
play false
playfully
play-going
play games
plangency
playgroup
peach-palm
peach-blow
peach-wood
peach-tree
playhouse
play havoc
pharisaic
pray in aid
pratingly
prayingly
planisher
platinise
platinize
placidity
platinoid
platinous
placitory
pianistic
platitude
plackless
pranksome
plank down
prankster
pearl-sago
praeludia
pearl-edge
pearlings
pearlwort
pearl-spar
pearl-gray
pearl-grey
pearlised
phalluses
pearlitic
pearl-eyed
pearlized
plasmodia
psalmodic
Phasmidae
ptarmigan
playmaker
psalm-book
plasmatic
pragmatic

psammitic
psalm-tune
plain Jane
plain-Jane
plain-darn
plainness
plain text
plaintful
phaenogam
plaintive
plaintiff
plainsman
plainsmen
praenomen
plain loaf
plainsong
plain cook
plain-cook
plainwork
Planorbis
phacoidal
placoderm
phacolite
piano wire
Platonise
Platonize
phacolith
Platonism
Platonics
pianolist
Platonist
piano roll
pea-souper
phagocyte
Prakritic
play round
pea gravel
peat-spade
praiseach
peat-stack
plausible
plausibly
play-spell
praiseful
phansigar
peat-smoke
plaustral
Praise You
plantable
practical
practicum
plasticky
plantless
psaltress
plant lice
plant-like
plantling
plaything
practolol
plantsman
plant-lore
plastique
practique
psalteria
plastered
plasterer
phantasma
practised
phantosme
plastisol
phantasim
practiser
planuloid
peanut oil
plague-pit
plaquette
play-world
pharyngal
pharynges
pharynxes
public act
public art
public bar
publisher
publicise
publicize
publicist
publicity
public-key
public law
pubescent
pickaback
pickapack
piccadell
pickadell
packaging
piccadill
pickadill
pictarnie
poco a poco
peccantly
pack-cinch
packcloth
pack-drill
pocketful
picketing
pocketing
picket out
pickeerer
packframe
pacificae
pacifical
Puck-hairy
packhorse
pectinate
Pichincha
pectineal
pycnidium
picnicked
picnicker
pactional
Peckinpah
peculator
pacemaker
pockmanky
pecuniary
pecunious
pecan tree
peck order
pectolite
pictorial
pick oakum
pictogram
pick-purse
packstaff
packsheet
pick-thank
pack-train
pack-twine
pick-tooth
pachyderm
pad-saddle
pedicular
✧pediculus
puddening
pedigreed
pedagogic
pedagogue
pedogenic
podagrous
podginess
pudginess
paddle-box
pedalling
pedal-bone
pademelon
padymelon
pedometer
pedantise
pedantize
pedantism
pudendous
Pedipalpi
pedereros
pederasty
pedatifid
paddy-bird
pre-cancel
prelatess
prevalent
phenacite
phenakite
precative
predative
prelatise
prelatize
prelatish
prefacial
prelatial
phenakism
prelatism
predation
prelation
prelatist
plenarily
predacity
prepacked
prevail on
prehallux
precatory
predatory
prefatory
poetaster
poetastry
prelature
premature
presbyope
presbyopy
presbytic
presbyter
prescient
prescribe
preaching
prescript
preachify
preachily
preocular
preschool
pre-echoes
prescious
prescutum
preoccupy
pleadable
pre-adamic
pseudonym
pleadings
pseudopod
pseudaxis
piece rate
paederast
preverbal
pretended
prebendal
pretender
piecemeal
pieceless
precedent
preselect
predefine
pre-senile
preterite
preceding
predesign
phenetics
preterist
pretermit
pre-vernal
prerecord
predevote
piecework
preferred
preferrer
prehensor
paedeutic
presentee
precentor
preceptor
prelector
presenter
preventer
presently
preserver
preserves
pier glass
peer group
phengites
pre-shrink
plethoric
psephitic
✧peel-house
predicate
predicant
predikant
precincts
predigest
predilect
president
precisely
Preminger
peevishly
pieridine
poeticise
poeticize
precipice
precisive
précising
presidial
poeticism
presidium
Pteridium
puerilism
Phenician
precisian
precision
prefixion
prevision
presidios
puerility
Plexiglas®
plexiform
plenipoes
pietistic
prebiotic
predicter
predictor
paediatry
plenilune
plenitude
poeticule
précieuse
prefigure
phellogen
preflight
pre-employ
pneumonia
pneumonic
pre-embryo
pneumatic
pre-emptor
pre-engage
pregnable
pregnance
pregnancy
pleonaste
pleonexia
premosaic
phenolate
pterosaur
pre-loaded
piepowder
peep of day
phenomena
Pleiocene
prepotent
pleiomery
preconise
preconize
premonish
precocial
phelonion
premotion
prenotion
prerosion
pierogies
precocity
prenotify
prepollex
Pteropoda
pheromone
paedology
phenocopy
phenology
poenology
phenol red
pyelogram
precoital
prepostor
pleno jure
phenotype
preoption
pied piper
puerperal
preordain
poetresse
pleuritic
pierrette
pleuritis
press gang
press-gang
pressmark
peep sight
pleaseman
pleasance
pheasants
press book
presswork
pressroom
press upon
pleasurer
pressures
press stud
Pressburg
please you
pier table
plentiful
prettyish
Prestwick
prettyism
plectrons
plenteous
plectrums
✧peel-tower
prejudice
prejudize
prelusive
prenubile
presuming
preludial
preputial
pie funnel
prelusory
precurrer
precursor
pre-exilic
pterygial
pterygium
pterygoid
puff adder
puftaloon
pifferari
pifferaro
puffed out
puffiness
puffingly
puff paste
pegmatite
Pygmalion
pugnacity
pageantry
pigsconce
pignerate
pigheaded
pigmented
pigmental
piggishly
pug-engine
pignorate
pigeon pea
page-proof
pogo stick
pygostyle
page three
page-three
piggyback
piggy bank
✧philander
✧primavera
privateer
philately
plicately
privately
privatise
privative
privatize
primatial
plication
privation
primality
primarily
poinadoes
privadoes
peirastic
plicature
primaeval
poinciana
princedom
Prince Hal
princekin
Priscilla
princelet
principia
principle
principal
princesse
Princeton
prime rate
priceless
prideless
primeness
prime time
prime-time
price ring
prize ring
price list
prize list
Price Code
prime cost
prize crew
paideutic
painfully
plightful
pair-horse
philhorse
primipara
privilege
priciness
primitiae
✧primitive
primitial
primitias
✧philippic
Philister
prickling
prickwood
prick-song
prick spur
phillabeg
phillibeg
phialling
Phillyrea
paillasse
paillette
prismatic
poignancy
philomath
Philomela
philopena

Philomene
Primo Levi
poison gas
poison ivy
poison-nut
poison oak
poisonous
prisonous
philology
poison pen
prison van
philogyny
priorship
primrosed
pair-royal
priestess
Priestley
puissance
priest-rid
puissaunt
point-lace
✧**paintball**
paintable
printable
Psittacus
pointedly
printhead
paintress
pointless
printless
point shoe
print shop
pointillé
pointsman
paintwork
painterly
point duty
primuline
✧**privy seal**
poke borak
pokeberry
Pekingese
Peking man
Pekin duck
pyknosome
pike-perch
poker face
poker work
pikestaff
Pakistani
Pakhtoons
pull a face
pull apart
pillar box
polyarchy
polyandry
pull ahead
palmately
polianite
polyamide
pulsatile
pulsative
polyaxial
✧**palladium**
✧pelmanism
Palladian
palmarian
palmation
palpation
pulsation
pillarist
palladous
pull about
polyamory
pulsatory
pellagrin
pulpboard
Palm Beach
pull baker
polybasic
phlebitis
palace-car
Pulicidae
police dog
phlyctena
pole-clipt
policeman
polyconic
pelecypod
palm court
palm-court
palm civet
Paludrine®
paludinal
pull devil
pilferage
pulse-rate
pulse-wave
pulseless
palletise
palletize
pelletise
pelletize
polverine
pulverine
pulverise
pulverize
pilfering
pelletify
pulverous
palpebral
pollen sac
palaestra
polyester
palmettos
pull faces
Polyfilla®
palafitte
palsgrave
polygraph
Polygamia
polygamic
Polygynia
polygenic
polygonal
polygonum
polyglott
polyhedra
palm-honey
palmhouse
✧pele-house
palmitate
palpitate
pollinate
pulvinate
palpitant
palmipede
pulpiteer
pulpiness
pelvic fin
peltingly
polyimide
pollinium
pallidity
pulvilled
pulvillio
pulvillar
pulvillus
pillicock
pelviform
pellitory
palliasse
palmistry
pulvinule
palilalia
polylemma
palillogy
Palembang
polemical
palominos
poll-money
palampore
palempore
polymeric
polemarch
polymorph
polymasty
polymathy
polymyxin
Polynices
palankeen
polonaise
palanquin
pulp novel
Pulmonata
pulmonate
pulmonary
pillow-cup
pilloried
pillorise
pillorize
polyomino
polyonymy
polyphase
polyphagy
polypidom
pole piece
polyploid
polyphone
polyphony
Polyporus
polyposis
polyptych
polar bear
pilgrimer
polar body
pelorised
polarised
polariser
polar star
pull round
polar axis
palfreyed
pelorized
polarized
polarizer
Pele's hair
palisades
palm sugar
Palestine
Pelasgian
polo shirt
pulpstone
polish off
palustral
polystyle
pilot jack
pilot lamp
palatable
palatably
political
politicos
politicly
polythene
pilotless
pilot fish
pilot flag
polytonal
pilot-boat
polytypic
politique
politesse
Politburo
✧**pele-tower**
pullulate
pollutant
pollutive
pollusion
pollution
polyvinyl
paloverde
palaverer
pole vault
pole-vault
polywater
Polixenes
✧**pollyanna**
polyzoary
polyzonal
polyzooid
pompadour
pomace-fly
pomaceous
pumiceous
pomoerium
pommelled
pummelled
pimpernel
pimientos
pemphigus
pompholyx
pomposity
pompously
pumy stone
pome-water
pump-water
pantagamy
Punjaubee
pentarchy
panhandle
pineal eye
pantaleon
pantalets
pentamery
pinnately
pentangle
panta rhei
Pindarise
Pindarize
pin-making
pennalism
Pindarism
pandation
Pindarist
pinnacled
pintailed
✧**pantaloon**
pentalogy
pentapody
pentalpha
pineapple
pentagram
pennatula
panachaea
Punic Wars
Pinocchio
panicking
piña-cloth
panic-bolt
ponderate
panderess
panderism
pandemian
pannelled
Pan-German
panderous
ponderous
Pentecost
✧**pinkerton**
pendently
pungently
pansexual
pine-finch
Pink Floyd
pinafored
panegoism
panegyric
punch-card
punch-ball
panphobia
pinchbeck
punchline
pantheism
pantheist
pinchfist
panthenol
pinchcock
punchbowl
punch-prop
penthouse
pine-house
panchayat
pinnipede
pannikell
penniless
pinkiness
punkiness
pensively
pantingly
punningly
penninite
pontifice
pantiling
pensility
pencilled
penciller
pendicler
pontianac
pontianak
pensioner
pantihose
pencil-ore
penniform
panniered
panmictic
panoistic
panel game
penal laws
penultima
panelling
penillion
panellist
penal code
Pan-Slavic
pontlevis
Phnom Penh
panama hat
penumbral
pink noise
pen-and-ink
✧**peninsula**
pin and web
pentosane
pennoncel
penholder
pinto bean
pontoneer
pantoffle
pantoufle
pansophic
Pentothal®
pantomime
pentoxide
panlogism
pontonier
pondokkie
pinhooker
pancosmic
pontooner
peneplane
peneplain
panoplied
Pan's pipes
panspermy
pink pound
Pan-Arabic
pen friend
pendragon
panoramic
pantryman
penurious
pancratic
pen-driver
pond snail
punishing
penis envy
penistone
pint-stoup
pants suit
pint-sized
penetrate
punctuate
penetrant
pinstripe
panatella
punctilio
penstemon
penitence
pin it onto
penitency
panettone
panettoni
Pinot Noir
punctured
puncturer
punctated
punctator
pandurate
pendulate
pinnulate
pen-pusher
penduline
penguinry
pendulous
pendulums
pennyland
Penny Lane
penny gaff
penny-bank
penny mail
pentylene
penny-rent
panty line
penny wise
penny ante
penny-ante
pantyhose
penny-post
pennywort
propagate
prosaical
protandry
prosateur
profanely
prolately
promachos
probative
prolamine
prolative
protamine
phonation
probation
prolation
pronation
proration
procacity
profanity
propanone
protanope
phonatory
probatory
pro patria
prolapsus
prolactin
propagule
procaryon
prokaryon
prokaryot
Poor Clare
proactive
proscribe
proscript
proudness
proud-pied
pro re nata
Ptolemaic
phonecard
promenade
phone call
proletary
probeable
proveable
proveably
proseucha
proseuche
Provençal
properdin

proceeder
provender
proneness
phonetise
phonetize
Pooterish
phonetism
Pooterism
prooemium
prooemion
phonemics
phonetics
proxemics
phonetist
procerity
propelled
propeller
proteinic
provedore
prose poem
processed
professed
prowessed
processor
professor
prolepses
prolepsis
proteuses
proleptic
protected
progestin
projector
prorector
prosector
✧protector
✧protester
✧protestor
procedure
prosecute
proselyte
proof-mark
proofread
proofless
proof text
proof coin
proffered
profferer
Pyongyang
ploughboy
ploughing
ploughman
ploughmen
pronghorn
prongbuck
pro-choice
prothalli
prothorax
prothesis
prophetic
prothetic
poorhouse
proximate
provinces
Phonic Ear®
profiteer
phoniness
prosiness
procident
prominent
provident
prolicide
Prosimiae
profiling
profiting
promising
providing
prosimian
provision
profilist
prolixity
proximity
provisoes
proditory
provisory
promissor
psoriasis
probiotic
protistic
psoriatic
poodle-dog
profluent
proclisis
proclitic
proembryo
phonmeter
poor-mouth
pro and con
prognoses
prognosis
proenzyme
prorogate
photo call
provocant
proboscis
protonema
photogene
photocell
propodeum
✧proto team
propodeon
proponent
photogeny
prolonger
photophil
phonolite
prologise
prologize
promotive
protogine
protoxide
provoking
prosodial
promotion
prosodian
photonics
Procopius
prosodist
Prokofiev
pronounce
protozoic
phonopore
provolone
protozoal
protozoan
protozoon
phonology
photocopy
phonogram
photogram
photopsia
proconsul
protostar
Photostat®
provostry
phototube
protoavis
phonotype
photolyse
phototype
prototype
phonotypy
phototypy
protogyny
phosphate
prompt box
phosphene
phosphide
phosphine
phosphite
prompting
plot-proof
prompture
prom queen
procreate
procreant
propriety
prodromic
programme
prodromal
prodromus
pyorrhoea
prop shaft
proustite
Proustian
phossy jaw
poor's-roll
poop scoop
prostrate
Prontosil®
proptosis
prostatic
proctitis
procuracy
pronuncio
promuscis
procureur
procuress
profusely
procuring
profusion
prolusion
prolusory
propulsor
poor white
propylaea
propylene
propylite
prozymite
procyonid
pipe dream
pepper box
puppeteer
peppering
poppering
Popperian
pop record
pepperoni
pepper pot
pepsinate
peptidase
popliteal
pop singer
pepticity
papillate
pupillage
pupillate
papillary
pupillary
pipe-light
pupilship
papilloma
papillose
papillote
papillous
popularly
papillule
pipe-layer
pipe major
piping hot
pipe organ
peptonise
peptonize
pipsqueak
paper-case
paper tape
paperware
paperback
paperbark
paper wasp
paper-reed
paperless
paper-thin
paper-file
papergirl
paper mill
pop artist
paper clip
peperomia
piperonal
paperwork
paper-coal
paper-pulp
paper over
paparazzi
paparazzo
pipe snake
pope's head
pipestone
pope's nose
pipe-track
papeterie
poppy-head
poppy seed
puppyhood
puppy love
poppycock
piquantly
piqué work
pique upon
piquillos
purdah bus
pariah dog
Periander
port a beul
partake in
parrakeet
permanent
per capita
pargasite
percaline
pervasive
portatile
portative
purgative
partaking
phreaking
perradial
pervasion
purgation
perradius
permalloy
✧**purgatory**
Parnassus
per saltum
periaktos
parabrake
periblast
parabolic
periboloi
parabolas
peribolos
peribolus
pure-blood
parabasis
periclase
pyroclast
pericrany
pericycle
✧**paraclete**
Periclean
parochine
pericline
parochial
pyracanth
pericones
parecious
paracusis
Paricutín
parachute
parodical
parodying
peridinia
peridrome
paradores
paradisic
paradisal
peridotic
paradoxal
pyridoxal
pyridoxin
paradoxer
porterage
porcelain
parcenary
perceable
permeable
permeably
persevere
porteress
porbeagle
porrenger
paroemiac
perseline
pargeting
paroemial
Parseeism
parhelion
parcelled
permeance
parge-work
parcel out
peraeopod
per mensem
Pernettya
pargetted
perverted
percental
pargetter
perfecter
perfector
perverter
perfectos
perfectly
persecute
perpetual
perfervid
parleyvoo
perceiver
perfervor
paraffine
purifying
paraffiny
portfolio
poriferal
poriferan
paragraph
pará grass
paragogic
paragogue
peregrine
porogamic
pyrogenic
paregoric
parchedly
Parcheesi®
parchment
Pyrrhonic
perchance
Parthenon
porphyria
percheron
porphyrin
porphyrio
parrhesia
purchaser
perthitic
porthouse
pervicacy
Parminder
perkiness
pursiness
pertinent
porwiggle
porringer
purringly
parricide
partitive
Persicise
Persicize
partition
perdition
partially
persimmon
portioned
persienne
Perpignan
portioner
porticoed
perciform
paroicous
porticoes
parcimony
parsimony
pereiopod
parti pris
permitted
persist in
permitter
partitura
perikarya
parfleche
Pyralidae
paralogia
paralegal
perilling
paralalia
perilymph
Port Limon
purulence
parklands
purulency
paralyser
paralysis
pyrolysis
paralytic
pyrolytic
pyrolater
pyrolatry
Port Louis
paralexia
paralyzer
paramecia
paramedic
pyramidic
pyramidal
pyramidon
pyramides
pyromania
pyromancy
poromeric
paramorph
perimorph
pyramises
paramatta
parameter
perimeter
pyrometer
perimetry
pyrometry
paramount
parentage
perennate
Pyreneans
paranoeic
perinaeum
Pyrenaean
Paranagua
paranoiac
pyreneite
parenting
phrentick
perennial
perennity
paranymph
Peronista
Peronismo
parenesis
phrenesis
phrenetic
phrenitic
perinatal
Port Natal
phrenitis
parsonage
perborate
percolate
perforate

Words marked ✧ can also be spelled with one or more capital letters

periodate
personage
personate
porporate
portolani
portolano
perforans
personals
perforant
parlor car
parrot-cry
purposely
periodise
periodize
personise
personize
purposive
pardoning
parroting
parsonish
purdonium
personify
parrot-jaw
performer
personnel
part-owner
purloiner
Porto Novo
per contra
parroquet
periplast
parapodia
periphery
periptery
pyrophone
periproct
porcpisce
pari passu
peripetia
parapeted
✧peripatus
paraquito
partridge
portreeve
pararhyme
portrayal
portrayer
Port Sudan
parasceve
perisperm
parischan
perishing
periscian
Port Salut
phraseman
periscope
peristome
poroscope
pyroscope
Paris doll
poroscopy
parasitic
parish top
porn squad
peristyle
peritrack
piratical
pyritical
parotides
peritrich
parathion
parity law
part-timer
paratonic
puritanic
✧pyrethrum
pyrethrin
parotitis
parataxis
portulaca
perfusate
permutate
pertusate
perturbed
pursuable
perturber
persuader
purpureal
perfumery
perfusive
porcupine
per curiam
perfusion
pertusion
parbuckle
pursuance
pergunnah
perjurous
percussed
pertussal
percussor
pertussis
parqueted
pirouette
parquetry
Portuguee
perovskia
paravaunt
parkwards
pyroxylic
pyroxylin
pyroxenic
parhypate
party-call
party wall
party line
party-size
Party Time
partygoer
party-jury
pistareen
passament
pistachio
pas d'armes
push along
passadoes
piscatory
piscatrix
pushchair
push-cycle
pass-check
paso doble
poster boy
posset cup
pas de seul
passement
pas de deux
passenger
pas de chat
passepied
passerine
posterior
posterity
Pasternak
paste-down
pesterous
possessed
possess in
possessor
passers-by
post-entry
pushfully
posigrade
posthorse
posthaste
pesthouse
posthouse
passivate
pasticcio
pastiness
pushiness
pestilent
passively
pushingly
pastiches
pesticide
passivism
pessimism
postilion
passivist
pessimist
passivity
postiller
possibles
passioned
passional
pisciform
posticous
pisolitic
pisoliths
Pisanello
postnasal
postnatal
pastorale
pastorate
pastorali
pistoleer
pistolled
pestology
piston rod
postponer
postrider
pass round
push-start
poss-stick
post-synch
pasturage
postulate
pustulate
postulant
pustulant
posturist
pasquiler
pustulous
postviral
postwoman
pass water
pussyfoot
phthalate
phthalein
pot-hanger
Patna rice
Pat Barker
pot-waller
pot barley
pot valour
Pat Rafter
pit-sawyer
pita bread
petechiae
petechial
putschist
put across
Pat Eddery
pothecary
putrefied
pottering
pathetics
patterned
pithecoid
putter-out
patiently
pitifully
pot of gold
pitch-dark
pitch camp
patchable
patchocke
pitch bend
patch test
pitchpine
pitchpipe
pitch into
pitch-pole
patchwork
pitchfork
pitch-poll
pitch upon
pitch-tree
patchouli
patchouly
pituitary
pettiness
pithiness
pottiness
pottingar
pottinger
pityingly
pettishly
petrified
patricide
pethidine
✧petri dish
Petrinism
✧patrician
patriliny
putridity
patricoes
pettitoes
petticoat
patrimony
patriarch
pituitrin
patriotic
patristic
pet-sitter
pot liquor
patellate
pétillant
petulance
petulancy
pottle-pot
potometer
potentate
put on sail
Putonghua
put in mind
potentise
potentize
put on side
potential
put on airs
patent log
patinated
patronage
petiolate
petrolage
patrol car
pot holder
petroleum
pétroleur
patroness
✧pythoness
pathogeny
patronise
patronize
potholing
patrolled
petrolled
patroller
potboiler
Patroclus
patrolman
patio door
pathology
patrology
petrology
potpourri
petrogram
piteously
petiolule
put option
Peter Hall
Peterhead
petersham
paternity
Peter Snow
patercove
Peter Cook
peter-boat
patereros
Peter Buck
potassium
put ashore
put at ease
petit pain
put at risk
petit four
petit pois
potato pit
potato rot
Pitot tube
petit jury
Petruchio
petaurine
petaurist
put-putted
pot-hunter
petty cash
petty whin
petty jury
pluralise
pluralize
pluralism
Poujadism
Pausanias
pluralist
Poujadist
plurality
plumbless
plumbagos
plumb line
pourboire
plumbeous
plumb rule
pounce bag
pounce box
pounching
pounce pot
pound cake
Paul Dacre
pound sign
Paul Dukas
plumdamas
pound coin
Paul Dirac
plunderer
pauperess
pauseless
plumeless
plume-bird
pauperise
pauperize
pauperism
prunellos
plume-moth
plume upon
prudently
pour forth
plus fours
plug gauge
Prudhomme
prud'homme
pouchfuls
pluripara
pausingly
poutingly
prudishly
prusiking
Paulinism
Paulician
Paulinian
Paulinist
prurience
pruriency
paupiette
Paul Jones
pluck down
Prue Leith
Paul Nurse
pousowdie
Plutonism
plutonium
Plutonian
Plutonist
paulownia
Pauropoda
plutology
plutonomy
plutocrat
plumpness
pourpoint
prussiate
poursuitt
Paul Simon
plum-stone
Paul Scott
poussette
pourtrayd
poultfoot
poulterer
plumulate
plumulose
pavonazzo
Pavlovian
Pavarotti
pivotally
powder box
powder keg
pew-fellow
pawkiness
powellise
✧powellite
powellize
Powellism
pew-holder
pew-opener
power base
power pack
powerless
power dive
power-dive
power line
powerplay
power unit
power loom
powerboat
power user
pixie hood
pixilated
pixy-stool
phylarchy
prytaneum
paysagist
pay packet
paymaster
puy lentil
pay-office
psychical
psychogas
psychoses
psychosis
psychotic
physicals
physicism
physician
physicist
physicked
physic nut
Psyllidae
phyllopod
phylogeny
phytogeny
phycology
phytology
phytotomy
phytotron
phycocyan
pay gravel
pay its way
pizzaiola
pizzicato
puzzledom
puzzle out
puzzle-peg
pozzolana
puzzolana

Q Magazine
quand même
Quakerdom
quarenden
quarender
Quakeress
Quaker gun
quavering
Quakerish
Quakerism
quakiness
quakingly
qualified
qualitied
qualifier
qualities
Quasimodo
quail-call
quail-pipe
qualmless
quadrifid
quadrigae
quarrying
quadrella
quadrille
quadruman
quarryman
quadruped
quadruple
quadruply
quarry-sap
quadrate B
quadratic
quaeritur
quadratus
quaesitum
quantical
quartzite
quartzose
quartered
quarterly
quartette
quartetti
quartetto
quenching
quercetum
quercetin
Quebecker
Québecois
queue-jump
querimony
queen-cake
queen's-arm
Queen Mary
queenless
queenship
queen-like
queenside
queen-size
queenfish
Queen Anne
queenhood
queen post
quebracho
queerness
queer fish
questrist
querulous
quetzales
quibbling
quitclaim
quidditch
quiverful
quite a few
quivering
quiverish
quinidine
quirister
quicksand
quickbeam
quickness
quick fire
quick-fire
quicklime
quick time
quickener
quick-born
quickstep
quick-eyed
quillwort
quinoidal
quinoline
quixotism
quinonoid
quinolone
quinquina
quiescent
quietness
quia timet
quittance
quietsome
quintroon
quintuple
quintuply
quintette
quintetti
quintetto
quizzical
qinghaosu
quotative
quotation
quotidian
quotition
quodlibet
Qutb Minar
road agent
Reaganite
Reaganism
read aloud
roadblock
road-borne
roadcraft
Roald Dahl
readdress
reaedifye
rear-dorse
rearguard
Ryan Giggs
reachable
rhachides
rhaphides
reachless
roach clip
rearhorse
rhachises
rhachitis
roadhouse
real image
reanimate
readiness
roaringly
realising
realizing
realistic
reality TV
rear light
realmless
road maker
road metal
rearmouse
road movie
reasoning
rearousal
rhapontic
real price
reappoint
rhamphoid
reapparel
reacquire
rearrange
rhapsodic
roadstead
road sense
reassurer
reactuate
road train
roast beef
reattempt
reactance
real terms
readvance
real wages
roadworks
ready-made
ready-wash
ready meal
Rubiaceae
reboation
rubicelle
rabidness
robber fly
rubberise
rubberize
rabbeting
rebbetzin
rubifying
ruby glass
rabbinate
rubricate
rubbishly
rabbinite
rabbinism
rubrician
rabbinist
rebukable
rebukeful
rebel-like
rubellite
rebelling
rebellion
rub elbows
rib-plough
robe maker
Robin Hood
Robin Cook
rubineous
Rob Andrew
reblochon
Ribbonism
Ribbon-man
reblossom
rebaptise
rebaptize
rebaptism
rebirther
Robert Kee
rubescent
ribosomal
rebatable
rabatment
rebutment
robot-like
rabatting
rebutting
ribattuta
ribaudred
rybaudrye
Richardia
Richard II
réchauffé
rectangle
Rechabite
racialism
raciation
ructation
racialist
reclaimer
raccahout
recharter
rock brake
rock borer
rock-basin
rock-bound
recyclate
rock cress
recyclist
rock candy
rock drill
rocker arm
recherché
racketeer
rocketeer
recrement
Richelieu
ricketily
recreance
recreancy
Rochester
rice field
rice flour
rock flour
Rock fever
rice grain
rock guano
rice grass
recognise
recognize
racegoing
racehorse
rock house
reclinate
recoinage
rockiness
rectified
receiving
reclining
rachidial
rachidian
rectifier
rectitude
recalment
re-collect
recollect
recalesce
rechlesse
recompact
recommend
recumbent
recombine
rock melon
recompose
rocambole
recomfort
rock music
racing bit
racing car
reconvene
raconteur
reconnect
reconvert
reconcile
recondite
reconfirm
recension
Ricinulei
rock'n'roll
reconquer
rectorate
rectocele
rectoress
reckoning
rectorial
rock plant
recipient
rack price
receptive
recaption
reception
rack-punch
rice paper
rock pipit
rock perch
recapture
ricercata
ricercare
rectrices
recurrent
recursive
recording
recurring
recursion
Ricardian
recordist
rich rhyme
rickstand
rock snake
rockshaft
rock socks
Rick Stein
recessive
rickstick
recession
rock-solid
recusance
recusancy
racetrack
recitable
rock tripe
reclusely
reclusive
reclusion
reclusory
recountal
recruital
recruiter
recoveree
recoverer
recoveror
rice water
rockwater
redhanded
radiately
radialise
radialize
radiative
red-tapism
radiation
red-tapist
radiality
red salmon
radiatory
red carpet
red-carpet
red-haired
red rattle
radiantly
reductase
redecraft
reductant
reducible
radicchio
reductive
redaction
reduction
radicular
ridiculer
radically
rudaceous
radicated
ridgeback
red-headed
reddendum
reddendos
red-legged
ridge tile
redeeming
Red Devils
rudbeckia
red-heeled
ridge bone
ridgepole
ridge rope
red pepper
rodgersia
redressal
redresser
red lentil
red-letter
red setter
red riband
red ribbon
ruddiness
redding-up
rodfisher
red-lining
Ruddigore
red diesel
red-figure
red-plague
raddleman
reddleman
ruddleman
redolence
riddlings
redolency
redeliver
rudiments
redundant
Red Ensign
redingote
riding rod
radio wave
Radiohead
radiothon
radio pill
radionics
red-looked
red-polled
radio room
radiology
radiogram
radio star
red spider
redbreast
Redbridge
riderless
Red Dragon
Red Grange
radar trap
red grouse
redescend
redstreak
red mullet
rod puppet
redoubted
Red Duster
redevelop
redivivus
ruddy duck
re-examine
rheochord
re-endorse
re-elevate
rue-leaved
re-enforce
reed-grass
rye whisky
reediness
reelingly
re-edifier
reed-knife
rheologic
rheumatic
rheometer
rheumatiz
rye coffee
reed organ
rhetorise
rhetorize
reef point
re-entrant
rheotrope
rheotaxis
re-educate
reflagged
reflation
refracted
refractor
ruff-a-duff
refection
refectory
reflex arc
refreshen
refresher
rifle shot
rifle bird
reflexive

raftering
reflexion
reflected
reflecter
reflector
raffinate
raffishly
ruffianly
raffinose
refulgent
refelling
Rafflesia
refinedly
refine out
reflowing
reformade
reformado
referable
referring
refurbish
refurnish
reformism
reformist
refortify
referenda
reference
refusable
rufescent
refashion
refusenik
refutable
refutably
refitment
refitting
refounder
refluence
regrating
rigmarole
regicidal
rigidness
Rogue Male
ruggelach
rug-headed
reguerdon
regretful
rogueship
ruggedise
ruggedize
regretted
rigwiddie
roguishly
ragpicker
regulable
regal lily
regularly
reguluses
Rigoletto
regulator
regiminal
rogan josh
regionary
rigwoodie
regardant
rag-trader
regardful
regarding
régisseur
registrar
right-hand
rightward
right face!
right-bank
rightable
rightless
rightness
right side
rightsize
right wing
right-wing
right down
right-down
righteous
right away
rugby boot
rehearing
rehearsal
rehearser
rehydrate
rehousing
ruin agate
ruination
rail-borne
reimburse
rain-bound
rainbowed
raincheck
rain-cloud
reindeers
rain dance
reiterate
raise Cain
reiterant
raiseable
raised bog
Rhineodon
raise hell
Rhine wine
rained off
raised pie
re infecta
rail-fence
reinforce
rain gauge
reinhabit
Reichsrat
Reichstag
rhipidate
raininess
railingly
rhipidium
rhipidion
rainmaker
rail-motor
rhizocaul
rhizocarp
rhino bars
rhizoidal
rhinolith
rhizobium
Rhizopoda
rhinology
ruinously
reimplant
rain-print
rainproof
reinstate
reinstall
reinspect
reinspire
rain-stone
rainstorm
reinsurer
reistafel
raintight
roisterer
reinvolve
railwoman
rainwater
rejective
rejection
rajahship
rejoinder
rejoice in
rejoicing
Rajasthan
rijstafel
Rik Mayall
rakehelly
Rakaposhi
rakeshame
Release Me
roll along
roll-about
reluctate
reluctant
relieving
relief map
rillettes
relegable
religieux
religiose
religioso
religious
role model
relenting
relapsing
reliquary
reliquiae
rulership
relatable
relations
relatival
relevance
relevancy
relaxedly
relay race
ram-raider
rampaging
rampantly
remeasure
remediate
remedying
ramfeezle
ramifying
remigrate
remainder
rumminess
rompingly
rompishly
rampicked
Ramillies
remontant
roman à clé
remindful
romancing
remanence
remanency
Romany rye
reminisce
Romaniser
ruminator
Romanizer
ramrodded
Rome-penny
rime riche
remercied
Rembrandt
remarqued
rump steak
remissive
remission
remissory
remitment
remittent
remitting
remoulade
rémoulade
rum runner
rum butter
removable
removably
Romewards
ring a bell
randan gig
rangatira
ransacker
rentaller
runecraft
ring-canal
ring-cross
run across
run scared
ring dance
rangeland
rinseable
rennet-bag
run length
rendering
ranterism
run-resist
ranzelman
range pole
renversed
runners-up
ring flash
ring-fence
renegados
ring gauge
ranshakle
rancheria
rancherie
rancheros
runcinate
randiness
ranginess
rantingly
ringingly
runningly
rendition
rancidity
rantipole
renfierst
Rin Tin Tin
ringleted
ring money
ranunculi
run to seed
randomise
randomize
rancorous
ring ousel
rencontre
ring ouzel
rank-rider
runaround
ringstand
ring-shake
ring snake
rune-stave
ring-small
ringsider
renascent
run itself
run it fine
renitency
renouncer
renovator
renewable
Ringworld
rinky-dink
rhodanate
riot agent
rhodamine
rhodanise
rhodanize
rhoeadine
rhotacise
rhotacize
rhopalism
rhotacism
roof board
rhombuses
rootbound
rhonchial
root canal
root cause
Roosevelt
Rhodesian
root eater
roof guard
riot grrrl
root house
roominess
rooming-in
rhoticity
Raoul Dufy
rhodolite
rhodonite
rhodopsin
riotously
roof plate
root-prune
Rio Grande
roofscape
rootstock
rood-tower
repeating
reptation
Ripuarian
republish
repackage
repechage
rapacious
repudiate
rapidness
rapid fire
rapid-fire
rope dance
reprehend
re-present
represent
replevied
replenish
repletion
ripienist
rappelled
repressed
represser
repressor
repugnant
rope house
reprimand
replicate
replicant
rippingly
reptilian
repairman
reptiloid
reprinter
reprieval
repellant
repellent
repulsive
repelling
repulsion
rope-maker
repentant
reprobate
reprobacy
reprocess
reproving
raptorial
reprogram
reproduce
reportage
reparable
reparably
reporting
rap artist
repertory
reperusal
repercuss
repassage
reposedly
repossess
reposeful
rope-soled
repositor
repasture
reputable
reputably
reputedly
repotting
rope trick
rapturise
rapturize
rapturist
rapturous
ropeworks
repayable
repayment
Roquefort
requester
requisite
requiring
requicken
requitted
rerebrace
Rorschach
reradiate
reredorse
reredosse
raree-show
rare earth
rarefying
rerelease
rural dean
ruralness
reremouse
ra-ra skirt
Ruritania
✧rastafari
Russ Abbot
rascaldom
ressaldar
rosmarine
rascalism
rascality
rascaille
rise above
raspatory
rose apple
resnatron
restarter
raspberry
resection
rosaceous
rose cross
rosy cross
residuary
residence
residency
residuous
rose elder
rasterise
rasterize
rostering
russeting
rostellum
rostellar
res gestae
respecter
restfully
rosefinch
rosy finch
rusa grass
rush-grown
rasp-house
rest house
rusticate
riskiness
rushiness
rustiness
restively
raspingly
Russified
rusticise
rusticize
rusticial
rusticism
Rosminian
rusticity
restiform
restitute
resultant
re-soluble
resoluble
resilient
resolvent
resultful
rushlight
resulting
resumable
resembler
risk money
Rosemarie
rose noble

rosinweed
resentful
resentive
resonance
Rosinante
rus in urbe
Rising Sun
resinosis
resonator
responder
Russophil
Roscommon
Raskolnik
responsum
responser
responsor
rustproof
resurface
resorbent
resurgent
resurrect
reserpine
reservist
restraint
restringe
reservoir
rostrated
rosariums
resistant
resistent
resistive
rosa-solis
rosetting
rose topaz
rescue bid
rescuable
resources
reshuffle
rosewater
rusty-back
rusty nail
ritualise
ritualize
ritualism
retiarius
ritualist
rat-tailed
retracted
retractor
reticella
✧reticulum
reticular
reticence
reticency
rutaceous
retreaded
Rotterdam
ratherest
Rotherham
ratheripe
rattening
ratherish
ruthenium
Ruthenian
Ruth Ellis
ratifying
ruthfully
rotiferal
rotograph
retchless
ratchet up
rattiness
ritziness
retribute
retrieval
retriever
retaliate
rattlebag
rattliest
rattle off
rutilated
Rotameter®
rotundate
retentive
retention
rotundity
retinulae
retinular
retinitis
ritenutos
ritonavir
rationale
rationals
retrodden
retrocede
retroject
retrovert
retroflex
retroussé
rat-poison
rotaplane
ratepayer
retardate
retardant
retiredly
ritornell
rotor ship
retortive
retorsion
retortion
return key
rotatable
retoucher
rotavirus
Rotavator®
rotavator
Rotovator®
rotovator
retexture
Roumanian
Roumansch
rhumb line
raunchier
raunchily
rounceval
roundhand
round game
Roundhead
roundness
round fish
round clam
roundelay
roundsman
roundwood
roundworm
round down
round-down
roundarch
round trip
round-trip
round-eyed
rousement
route-step
roughcast
roughneck
rough-hewn
roughness
roughshod
rough-draw
routineer
routinely
rousingly
routinise
routinize
routinism
routinist
Rauwolfia
raucously
routously
roussette
revealing
rave about
revocable
revocably
revictual
revokable
revaluate
rivalless
ravelment
rivalship
revulsive
ravelling
revelling
revolting
revolving
rivalling
revulsion
revalenta
ravel into
rivalrous
revel-rout
revelator
Rivendell
revengive
revenging
raving mad
raven-bone
raven-duck
river sand
River Aare
River Ravi
riverbank
river-jack
river wall
River Bann
River Saar
River Yalu
reverable
River Ebro
River Eden
River Oder
River Lena
river head
riverweed
River Kemi
riverless
River Tees
reversely
revertive
riverlike
River Nile
✧riverside
river-tide
reversing
reversion
River Elbe
River Alph
river flat
River Amur
reverence
riverboat
River Towy
River Spey
River Styx
River Ouse
River Ruhr
River Avon
River Oxus
River Tyne
revisable
ravishing
rivet head
revetment
revetting
rivetting
rivet hole
revivable
revivably
rowdiness
raw sienna
rewritten
rowel-head
rowelling
rowel-spur
rowan tree
row-dow-dow
rewirable
rewardful
rewarding
rewording
reworking
Rex rabbit
Roxy Music
rix dollar
Roxburghe
Rhynchota
rhymeless
rhyme word
rhymester
rhythmise
rhythmize
rhythmics
rhythmist
Reykjavík
royal palm
royal mast
royal fern
royal fish
royal blue
royal road
ray floret
rhyolitic
royal duke
ray flower
Roy Strong
roysterer
ray fungus
Roy Fuller
Rozinante
razorback
razorable
razor edge
razor wire
razorfish
razorbill
razorclam
scarabaei
sea canary
seawardly
shamateur
sea tangle
sea margin
sea ranger
Stavanger
shanachie
sea-bather
star anise
star-anise
seafaring
✧shamanism
swarajism
shamanist
swarajist
sea-walled
spanaemia
spanaemic
sea salmon
scaraboid
swan about
star-apple
sea parrot
spadassin
stalactic
sea satyre
sea lawyer
starboard
scambling
shambling
shambolic
swag-belly
slabberer
starburst
shadberry
soapberry
Shabbatot
shadchans
starch gum
searching
stanching
stanchion
snatchily
starchily
search out
star-crost
staccatos
standgale
stand bail
stand fast
stand easy
scaldhead
stand well
staidness
St Andrews
scaldship
skaldship
stand shot
stand fire
standpipe
scaldfish
stand firm
stardrift
slam-dance
stag-dance
scaldings
stand good
stand down
stand-down
stand up in
stand upon
slanderer
standards
Ständerat
scald-crow
stander-by
stand over
Stand by Me
shade card
space band
stage hand
shape tape
shareware
space race
stage name
stalemate
Swaledale
skatepark
space walk
space-walk
state bank
shamefast
spare part
shakeable
shameable
shapeable
shareable
scare-head
snakehead
snakeweed
scale leaf
scale beam
scale fern
scaleless
scapeless
shadeless
shameless
shapeless
slakeless
spaceless
spareless
spareness
staleness
stateless
scapement
stage left
statement
scavenger
share shop
slave ship
spaceship
snakebird
scalelike
scare-line
shale mine
snakebite
snakelike
snakewise
space-time
spadelike
spare time
spare-time
stage-dive
✧stateside
statewide
shaveling
slavering
scale fish
spadefish
stapedial
Shakerism
stapedius
statelily
snakeskin
slate club
shake a leg
stage play
Seated Man
sharesman
spadesman
statesman
shame into
snakewood
statehood
share bone
Slate Cone
spade bone
scalework
slave-fork
spadework
spare room
stateroom
scale down
shake down
shakedown
stare down
stage door
scale moss
scapegoat
snakeroot
spaced out
spaceport
spade foot
stake boat
shag-eared
shade tree
seat earth
snare drum
sharecrop
scarecrow
slate-gray
slate-grey
sea nettle
sea lentil
sea-beaten
sea letter
State Duma
spadefuls
slave-hunt
snake cult
spacesuit
skate over
spare tyre
snake eyes
scaff-raff
scarfwise
scarf-ring
scarfskin
Sea of Cold
staffroom
scarf down
staff-tree
star fruit
staff duty
Sea of Azov
shanghai'd
slanguage
star grass
shaggy cap

Shangri-la
spangling
Spanglish
slangular
swan-goose
staggered
staggerer
swaggerer
slaughter
stargazer
scatheful
shashlick
Smash Hits
sea change
snaphance
sea shanty
swashwork
scaphopod
slap-happy
smasheroo
spaghetti
staghound
stash away
Swaziland
stabilate
staminate
sea girdle
stamineal
scaliness
scariness
seaminess
shadiness
shakiness
slatiness
snakiness
soapiness
staginess
suasively
sea ginger
soakingly
soaringly
sparingly
staringly
sea-fisher
slavishly
scarified
stabilise
stabilize
Stagirite
Stalinism
stasidion
scarifier
Stalinist
stability
suability
spadillio
spaniel it
Stanislaw
spatially
shamianah
stational
stationer
staminoid
staminode
staminody
stadia rod
statistic
Shah Jahan
stackyard
slack-bake
stackable
smackhead
slackness
sparkless
stalkless
starkness
sparkling
sparklies
sharkskin
spark plug
Sean Kelly
slacken up
shankbone
slack rope
spark coil
stackroom
stack arms
slack away
stalk-eyed
small-hand
small talk
snail mail
small caps
small lady
stableboy
stall-feed
sea sleeve
Stahlhelm
small beer
shawlless
smallness
stable fly
staple gun
starlight
small chop
small pica
small-time
snail-like
stamp mill
snailfish
spauld-ill
stable lad
small slam
snail-slow
stableman
scablands
scagliola
small-bore
stay loose
small-coal
small-town
scalloped
scalloper
small arms
Scarlatti
sea slater
scallawag
scallywag
swallow up
swallower
shallowly
spasmodic
swarm-cell
slammakin
staymaker
stammerer
shammosim
spasmatic
spawn cake
scannable
seannachy
stainless
stag night
sea anchor
stauncher
staunchly
stagnancy
stannator
sea potato
sea robber
shadow box
shadow-box
soap opera
Slavophil
scapolite
Slavonise
Slavonize
sea-roving
seasoning
shadowing
sialolith
statolith
Slavonian
sea rocket
scatology
sialogram
slavocrat
stay-on tab
scazontic
seabottle
sea bottom
scazontes
seaworthy
statocyst
swampland
sea spider
scalpless
sharpness
sharp-shod
stamp mill
sealpoint
sharpener
scarpines
shampooed
stamp note
star-proof
scalp lock
scamp-work
shampooer
swamp boat
stag party
scarpetti
scarpetto
scaup duck
stamp duty
sharp-eyed
sea squill
sea squirt
staircase
sea breach
stairhead
✧sea breeze
stairwell
sea dragon
sea urchin
stairwise
stairlift
sea orange
stairwork
stairfoot
Stavropol
sea grapes
Swan River
sea-island
slab-sided
sparsedly
star shell
Soay sheep
slaistery
starshine
seat-stick
slapstick
slabstone
soapstone
starstone
stag's horn
swans-down
swansdown
sea strand
smart card
swart-back
slantways
Spartacus
smartweed
scantness
shaftless
smartness
swartness
slantwise
sparteine
scantling
startling
startlish
swarthily
✧smart alec
✧smart-alec
shantyman
start in on
smarten up
smart bomb
shahtoosh
scattered
shattered
scart-free
sparterie
smart drug
scatterer
shatterer
smatterer
swart star
start over
spatulate
scapulary
status bar
statutory
✧status quo
sea turtle
statuette
star wheel
stalworth
soap-works
scaly-bark
seamy side
Stagyrite
spagyrist
subcaudal
subwarden
subjacent
sabbatine
sabbatise
sabbatize
submarine
sabbatism
Sabianism
sublation
subcavity
subfamily
subsample
subsacral
submatrix
subvassal
subcantor
suboctave
subacidly
subschema
subscribe
subaction
subscript
subocular
sebaceous
sabadilla
subeditor
subtenant
subdeacon
subgenera
submerged
sublethal
subsecive
sabrewing
subaerial
subregion
subseries
subsellia
subcellar
subdermal
subhedral
subneural
submersed
sublessee
subversal
sublessor
subjected
submental
submentum
subletter
subverter
subtenure
suboffice
subagency
subahdary
subahship
subphylum
sublimate
subniveal
subnivean
sublinear
sublimely
sobbingly
subdivide
sublimise
sublimize
subsidise
subsidize
subtilise
subtilize
subliming
sublimity
subtitles
submicron
submissly
submitted
subsist in
sob sister
submitter
sobriquet
subaltern
sibylline
subalpine
Sabellian
Sibyllist
subclimax
sibilance
sibilancy
sibilator
subclause
subimagos
subentire
subincise
subrogate
subpotent
subwoofer
subtopian
subsoiler
subnormal
subpoena'd
subdolous
subtorrid
subdorsal
subcostal
subcortex
sub specie
subapical
se-baptist
St Bernard
soberness
subursine
subbranch
subereous
subtropic
subarctic
✧sybaritic
Sebastian
subastral
substrata
substrate
substract
substylar
subatomic
substance
substruct
subjugate
sublunate
sublunary
subduable
subduedly
subbureau
sub judice
submucosa
submucous
subsultus
subsystem
sacrament
sacralgia
sacralise
sacralize
siccative
socialise
socialite
socialize
sociative
Socratise
Socratize
sectarial
sacrarium
socialism
sectarian
sociation
socialist
sacrality
sociality
sic passim
Social War
sick berth
sackcloth
sack dress
sacred ape
secretage
secretary
sacred cat
sacred cow
sachemdom
succeed in
succeeder
succès fou
secretive
sickening
socketing
secretion
Socceroos
secretory
successor
socket set
succentor
Sacred Way
suck-holer
saccharic
✧saccharum
saccharin
succinate
sacrilege
sickishly
sacrifice
sacrifide
succinite
sectility
sectional
sacciform
sacristan
siciliana
siciliane
sick leave
siciliano
sicklemia
sickleman
secularly
✧secondary
second fix
secundine
second man
sicknurse
second row
second-row
sociopath
succotash
sociolect
sectorise
sectorize
sectorial
suctorial
suctorian
sociology
sociogram
succourer
sycophant
St Cyprian
securable
secernent
securance

securitan
secession
sick-tired
secateurs
sacculate
succulent
seclusive
succubine
seclusion
succubous
succursal
sideboard
soda bread
sidebones
sideburns
side chain
seducible
seductive
seduction
side-dress
sedgeland
sedge bird
sedge wren
side issue
saddlebag
saddle bar
saddlebow
sidelight
saddle-lap
sidelined
sidelines
saddle pin
sudaminal
sodomitic
sedentary
soda nitre
St Dunstan
side plate
sudorific
siderosis
sideritic
sideswipe
soda scone
sideshoot
sidetrack
side table
seditious
Sadducean
Sadducism
sodbuster
side valve
side-wheel
sidewards
soda water
skedaddle
stewardry
scenarise
scenarize
steradian
scenarios
scenarist
Sue Barker
seek after
stewartry
shewbread
stepbairn
spec-built
speech act
speech day
speechful
stepchild
sketching
sketchily
speechify
sterculia
stenciled
seed coral
stercoral
sheldrake
speedball
steadfast
spendable
Steadicam®
speedy cut
speedwell
speedless
steadiest
speldring
steadying
seed drill
step dance
speedboat
speed trap
slenderly
speedster
shelduck
speed bump
scelerate
Stevenage
Shere Khan
Shere Hite
sieve-like
Steve Biko
shebeener
stevedore
scene dock
Steve Jobs
Steve Cram
Stevenson
sieve tube
shelf mark
seed field
Sheffield
Siegfried
shelf life
shelflike
shelfroom
sheaf toss
shelf-fuls
step fault
sleighing
Stephanie
Shechinah
see things
shechitah
sterilant
seediness
spewiness
seemingly
specified
sterilise
sterilize
sherifian
sterility
specially
specialty
St-étienne
sneak-raid
speak fair
speakeasy
speakable
sheikhdom
sleekness
speckless
sneck draw
shell-sand
steel band
steelyard
shell game
steelware
shellback
shellbark
shell-marl
smellable
spellable
spellican
Steely Dan
steelhead
steel beam
shell bean
shell heap
shell-less
smell-less
seemliest
seemlihed
seemlyhed
spellbind
shellfire
shell-like
shell lime
shellfish
shell pink
shell-pink
steel-clad
steel-blue
stellular
Snell's law
Shetlands
shell-hole
shellwork
steelwork
steel wool
spelldown
stellerid
steel drum
smell-trap
steel trap
smell a rat
steel-gray
steel-grey
stellated
shell star
shellduck
shell suit
steam bath
sperm bank
steam-haul
steamed up
sperm cell
steamship
seed money
steam coal
steam room
steamboat
steam port
steam open
spermaria
steam iron
steam trap
spermatia
spermatic
spermatid
sternward
sternfast
sternebra
Steinbeck
sternness
steenkirk
steinkirk
steinbock
sternmost
sternport
sternpost
steenbras
stegnosis
stegnotic
sternitic
steinbuck
stenopaic
stegosaur
steroidal
Suetonius
stegodont
Stenotype®
stenotypy
shemozzle
sweep hand
sheep-wash
sheepwalk
sleepwalk
sweepback
seed pearl
seed-plant
sheep scab
steeped in
sleepless
steepness
sheep meat
sheep-lice
sheeplike
sheep tick
sheepskin
sweepings
sleep on it
sheepfold
sheepcote
sleep mode
sheep-hook
sleepsuit
sleep over
sleepover
steerable
spearhead
shearlegs
sheerlegs
✧sheerness
sweirness
smear test
spear side
shearling
steerling
spearfish
spearmint
stearsman
steersman
speerings
speirings
swear-word
spearwort
shear-hulk
sheer-hulk
sheer away
seed-stalk
skeesicks
sneeshing
step stone
step short
sweat band
sweet gale
sweet-gale
sweet talk
sweet-talk
sweptback
skew-table
spectacle
sceptical
skeptical
sheet bend
sheet-feed
sheet lead
sweetmeal
scentless
sweetness
sweetmeat
sweat shop
sheathing
sweptwing
sheatfish
sweetfish
sheet film
sweet flag
sweeten up
sweetener
sweetwood
sweetcorn
sweet-wort
sweetwort
sweet upon
sweet spot
sceptered
sheltered
sweltered
sheet iron
shelterer
steatosis
steatitic
spectator
sweat suit
sweatsuit
speculate
spelunker
sleeve dog
sleeve nut
skew-whiff
sherwanis
sleazebag
sneeze box
St Francis
safranine
softcover
soft drink
softening
suffering
soft focus
soft-focus
soft fruit
safeguard
soft-grass
soft goods
safe house
safe haven
siftingly
sufficing
suffixion
safe light
siffleuse
safflower
soft-nosed
suffocate
soft pedal
soft-pedal
soft-paste
soft power
suffragan
saffroned
soft-shell
soft spile
sofa table
soft thing
safetyman
soft tommy
safety net
safety pin
soft touch
suffusive
suffusion
soft wheat
signal box
signalise
signalize
signaling
sigmatism
sigmation
signalled
signaller
signalman
signatory
sage apple
sigmatron
signature
signboard
sagebrush
sagacious
sage Derby
segregate
signeurie
segmented
segmental
suggester
sago grass
sage green
sage-green
sogginess
sighingly
signified
signifier
significs
sigillate
sigillary
sagenitic
saga novel
segholate
sigmoidal
St George's
✧signorina
signorine
signorini
signorial
✧signorino
sagapenum
sugar cane
sugarcane
sugar palm
sugar bean
sugar kelp
sugarless
sugar beet
sugar bird
sugar mite
sugar pine
sugar mill
sugarplum
sugarally
sugar snap
sugarloaf
sugar bowl
sugar soap
sugar-coat
sugar foot
sugar-free
sugar-cube
sugar bush
sugar-lump
Sigismund
sagittate
sagittary
sightable
sight-read
sightseer
sightless
sightline
sight-sing
sightsman
sight-hole
Sigourney
schiavone
schnapper
schmaltzy
schnauzer
schechita
sphacelus
scheduled
schedular
scheduler
Schreiber
scheelite
sphaerite
schlemiel
schlemihl
schnecken
schlepped
schlepper
sphygmoid
sphagnous
schlieren
schnitzel
scholiast
schilling
scholarch
scholarly
schematic
✧sphenodon
sphendone
sphincter
school age
school-age
schoolbag
schoolboy
school cap
schoolday
schoolery
schooling
schnorkel
schlocker
schoolman
school run
schnorrer

schnozzle
schmoozer
spherical
spherular
schistose
schistous
schmutter
schizopod
spiral arm
spin a yarn
spinacene
slip angle
spiralism
spiration
spiralist
spirality
Sri Lankan
stirabout
spinal tap
spiraster
spiracula
sailboard
shipboard
slip-board
spit blood
Swinburne
soil-bound
slip-coach
stir-crazy
sticcados
soil creep
snitchers
stitchery
Shih Ching
stitching
switching
switchman
ship canal
switch off
sailcloth
ski school
spiccatos
sticcatos
slip cover
spin-dried
spindling
swindling
spin drier
spindrift
skin-diver
spin dryer
spikenard
swipe card
spice cake
spice rack
slimeball
spike-nail
sliceable
swineherd
swivel-eye
spike heel
shineless
smileless
snideness
spineless
spireless
slide rest
swivel-gun
spirewise
shivering
snipefish

spikefish
swine-fish
Spigelian
snivelled
swivelled
spider leg
sniveller
Spider-Man
spiderman
sciaenoid
swinehood
seine boat
shire-moot
seize upon
stilettos
slide rule
spicebush
spike-rush
spider web
stiffware
stiff neck
stiffness
skinflick
skinflint
skilfully
stiffener
stir forth
ship fever
shin guard
skiagraph
slingback
swing-back
skin graft
stingless
swingbeat
slingshot
shingling
sniggling
swingeing
swingling
swing-wing
stingfish
sting into
swing door
swingboat
stingaree
swingtree
sniggerer
slip gauge
stingbull
stichidia
slighting
slightish
Spinhaler®
slight off
sticheron
stipitate
soi-disant
spicilege
shininess
sliminess
soiliness
spiciness
spikiness
spininess
spiritful
spirit gum
shiningly
slidingly
smilingly
swinishly

ski-kiting
spiriting
spiritism
spiritist
spirillum
spirillar
spirit off
spiniform
spiritoso
spiritous
spit it out
spiritual
spirituel
slick back
stink ball
slinkweed
stickseed
stickweed
sticky end
stinkweed
slickness
stinkbird
slinkskin
stick 'em up!
stink bomb
stinkwood
stickwork
slick down
stinkhorn
shickered
slickered
shield-arm
shield bug
shillaber
still-head
Spielberg
skill-less
stillness
skills gap
still life
still-life
shielding
ski-flying
shield ivy
spillikin
shillalah
shield law
shield-may
stillroom
stillborn
shielduck
still hunt
still-hunt
spill over
spillover
swimmable
seismical
sciamachy
skiamachy
sailmaker
ship money
Stigmaria
swimmeret
stigmatic
skinny-dip
scientise
scientize
sciential
scientism
scientist
spinnaker

seigniory
skinny-rib
seignoral
spinneret
sgian-dubh
seigneury
skibobber
sciroccos
sailor hat
slivovica
spilosite
sailoring
skijoring
Spinozism
Spinozist
spinosity
slivovitz
slivowitz
sailor-man
shipowner
spirogram
spirogyra
shimozzle
sailplane
shippable
stippling
skidproof
slippered
shippound
spit-roast
Sciuridae
shirralee
scirrhoid
scirrhous
shipshape
slip sheet
Swiss roll
skiascopy
sciosophy
scissorer
shirtband
shirt tail
shiftable
sciatical
saint's day
stiltedly
stintedly
shiftless
shirtless
skirtless
stintless
swiftness
skintight
saintship
stiltbird
saintlike
saintling
Shintoism
Shintoist
scintilla
skirtings
sainthood
shift work
saintfoin
Saint Joan
shift down
swift-foot
shirt stud
spiculate
spinulate
stimulate

stipulate
stimulant
stipulary
shibuichi
spinulose
spinulous
ski jumper
shipwreck
ship water
sojourner
sokemanry
solfatara
self-aware
sulfatase
sultanate
syllabary
sultaness
sulcalise
sulcalize
syllabise
syllabize
sylvanite
syllabism
saltation
salvation
siltation
solvation
sulcation
sulfation
syllabics
syllabify
syllabled
saliaunce
saltatory
salvatory
salvarsan
self-abuse
self-begot
self-build
self-built
salubrity
silica gel
selective
selachian
selection
salicylic
selectman
salacious
siliceous
silicious
solacious
select out
silicosis
silicotic
salicetum
solicitor
saltchuck
salad days
salad herb
solidness
solidagos
self-drive
splodgily
salad bowl
self-doubt
Silver Age
silvereye
spleenful
silver fir
silver fox
solfeggio

silverise
silverize
silvering
soldering
spleenish
solferino
Silverius
sallee-man
syllepses
syllepsis
Salientia
Silvestra
Sylvestra
sylleptic
Sylvester
saliently
self-faced
Solifugae
salifying
silk gland
salt glaze
silk-grass
silageing
sylphlike
sulphinyl
sulphonyl
sulphuric
salt horse
sulphuryl
sulphuret
sulphatic
silphiums
self-image
Sylviidae
saltiness
silkiness
silliness
sulkiness
saltishly
selfishly
sylvinite
Sylviinae
salpiform
soldier on
soldierly
soliloquy
solemness
solemnise
solemnize
solemnify
solemnity
Salomonic
Solomonic
salt-money
salt marsh
salimeter
solemn vow
shlimazel
salangane
solenodon
splendent
splintery
solonchak
splendour
selenious
selenitic
splenetic
solenette
splenitis
Sellotape®
sellotape

sulfonate
saloon bar
saloon car
salmon fly
salmon fry
syllogise
syllogize
sallowish
sulfonium
syllogism
salmonoid
salvo jure
soleplate
sale price
self-pride
solipsism
solipsist
self-pious
salopette
saltpetre
saltpeter
siliquose
solar salt
Siluridae
solar cell
salt rheum
solar year
solar wind
sclereide
solar time
salaryman
scleromas
sclerosed
sclerosal
scleroses
sclerosis
sclerotia
sclerotic
sclerotal
sclerotin
saleratus
scleritis
self-rowld
solar myth
sales talk
self-slain
Salesians
splashing
splashily
sell smoke
siltstone
salesroom
salt spoon
seldshown
sell short
splash out
Salisbury
self-study
split cane
Solutrean
split peas
spluttery
split mind
solitaire
split time
splatting
split ring
splitting
splittism
Solutrian
splittist

sola topee
self-trust
sclaunder
spleuchan
Seljukian
solo whist
self-wrong
self-worth
saltworks
saltwater
Sally Ride
sallyport
splay foot
splay-foot
Sally Army
Sally Lunn
Sam Gamgee
semiangle
sympathin
Symmachus
summarise
summarize
summative
semi-Arian
summation
simpatico
summarist
summarily
sympatric
semibreve
semi-bajan
semicolon
simpering
summering
sommelier
symmetric
symmetral
summerset
Simmental
semifinal
semifluid
semi-grand
symphonic
symphysis
symphytic
Symphytum
summiteer
summing-up
symbiosis
semeiotic
symbiotic
simulcast
semblable
semblably
simulacra
simulacre
simplices
semblance
semilunar
Simply Red
similarly
simplesse
simpliste
simulated
simpleton
simulator
simple vow
semi-metal
Simon says
semanteme
semantide
semuncial
semantics
seminally
simonious
semantron
Simon Pure
simon-pure
somnolent
symposiac
Samsonite®
Simeonite
symbolise
symbolize
sympodial
symposial
✧symbolism
sympodium
symposium
semiotics
symbolics
symbolist
symbolled
semiology
symbology
summonses
someplace
semaphore
semiplume
Samarkand
semi-rigid
Semiramis
sombreros
Samaritan
simarouba
Sam Browne
semisolid
sumpsimus
somascope
semestral
Semi-Saxon
sumptuary
✧something
sometimes
semitonic
sumptuous
sumotoris
symptosis
symptotic
semi-truck
semivowel
somewhere
somewhile
Sammy Cahn
Samoyedic
sameyness
sink-a-pace
sandarach
Santander
Sinhalese
sinuately
sennachie
sunbather
sin-eating
sensation
sinuation
San Marino
sandalled
sun parlor
suntanned
Singapore
sing along
singalong
senna pods
syngamous
sans-appel
Santa Cruz
Sun Yat-Sen
syntactic
syndactyl
synkaryon
sandblast
sand break
sand-blind
sonic bang
sand crack
songcraft
song cycle
sunscreen
sonic mine
synectics
Seneca oil
sonic boom
sine curve
sine dubio
synodical
synedrial
synedrium
synedrion
synodsman
sand dance
sand-devil
sense data
sonnetary
sentencer
singed cat
syngeneic
synoecete
synoekete
sonneteer
senseless
sincerely
sonnetise
sonnetize
synoecise
synoecize
sundering
synoecism
sanbenito
sincerity
sunbeamed
Sun Temple
Sanhedrim
Sanhedrin
sinlessly
syntectic
sunbeaten
son of a gun
songfully
sunk fence
sangfroid
sonograph
sand grain
sandglass
sand grass
synagogue
synagogal
synchrony
synchysis
syntheses
synthesis
synthetic
syndicate
sandiness
sunniness
sentiment
sinningia
singingly
sincipita
sensitise
sensitive
sensitize
sunrising
sensillum
sons-in-law
sentience
sentiency
synoicous
sun-kissed
San Miguel
sinciputs
single-cut
single-end
Sinologue
single-log
sand lance
synclinal
single-sex
single ten
singleton
single tax
sunflower
sand mason
synanthic
synangium
synonymic
syncopate
santolina
santonica
senhorina
Senhorita
syntonise
syntonize
Santorini
sensorial
sensorium
seniority
sensorily
sinuosity
sun lounge
sundowner
sun bonnet
syntonous
sinuously
syncoptic
synaptase
synapheia
sand pride
Sinophile
synopsise
synopsize
synoptist
Sinophily
sine prole
sandpaper
sandpiper
sun spurge
sentry box
sunbright
synergise
synergize
synergism
synergist
syndromic
syneresis
syncretic
send round
sonar buoy
sand-snake
sing small
Sundsvall
senescent
seneschal
songsmith
singspiel
sandstone
sandstorm
sandspout
sans serif
sinistral
sand-screw
sinusitis
sans souci
sanctuary
sand table
sunstroke
sanatoria
sanitaria
sanitiser
sunstruck
sanitizer
sensually
sunburned
singultus
synovitic
synovitis
sand wedge
sinewless
Sandy Gall
sand yacht
sand-yacht
sunny side
syncytial
syncytium
sannyasin
Sandy Lyle
St-Nazaire
synizesis
sloganeer
sporangia
stomachic
stomached
stomachal
stomacher
sloganise
sloganize
Slovakian
slob about
shopboard
snow board
snowboard
snow brake
shoeblack
shot-blast
Scooby Doo
showbread
snow-blind
snowblink
slop-built
scombroid
snow-broth
snowberry
slop basin
scorbutic
snowbound
shoe brush
showbizzy
slowcoach
stop codon
stoccados
Scotch egg
spot check
spot-check
Scotch elm
sconcheon
slop-chest
Scotch fir
slouch hat
scorching
slouching
stoically
Scotchman
stoccatas
show cause
sword-hand
sword-cane
sword-rack
swordtail
sword-bean
sword fern
swordless
sword-belt
swordlike
sword side
swordfish
swordbill
snowdrift
sword lily
spondulix
swordplay
swordsman
spot dance
sword knot
scorecard
shoreward
stonehand
stone-hard
store card
spore case
stoneware
smoke-jack
stone hawk
smoke ball
smoke-sail
stonewall
store farm
stone bass
stonecast
smokeable
shoreweed
stone-dead
stone-deaf
stone cell
scoreless
shoreless
smokeless
stoneless
smoke test
shovelful
showerful
spoken for
store ship
shovel hat
stonechat
stoneshot
shorebird
scolecite
scoreline
shoreline
shoreside
slopewise
spokewise
stone pine
stovepipe
showering
stonefish
Slovenian
stone-lily
sooterkin
shovelled
shoveller
Stokes' law
shoresman
spokesman
spokesmen
smoke bomb
scolecoid
scopeloid
smokehood
stokehold
stone-cold
smoke hole
stokehole
stonework
stone coal
smoke room
storeroom
shore boat
stoneboat
stonewort
shore crab
smoke tree
stonecrop
slope arms
score draw
smoke bush
snowflake
sootflake
snowfield
snowfleck
show fight
snowflick
snow fence
snow finch
shop floor
shop-floor
shopfront
show forth
shotfirer
snow guard
spongebag
snow goose
spongiose
slough off
sponge off
spongeous
spongious
soothfast
sloth bear
soothlich
smothered
smotherer
shochetim
slow-hound
show house
sporidesm
showiness

smokiness
snowiness
sootiness
stoniness
slopingly
Scotified
sporidial
Scoticism
sporidium
scorifier
'sbodikins
stolidity
Scotia Sea
scoliosis
scoliotic
Scotistic
storiated
storiette
spoliator
stockyard
shock wave
smock-race
stocktake
stock farm
shockable
shock-head
stockless
stock whip
stockpile
stockfish
smock mill
stocklist
stockings
stockinet
stock dove
shock jock
stocklock
stockwork
Stockholm
stockroom
stockhorn
Stockport
stonkered
stock cube
shoal mark
spoil bank
stoolball
spoil heap
shoalness
shouldest
spotlight
stoplight
shoalwise
spoilfive
spoilsman
storm sail
stormless
storm belt
stormbird
shoemaker
shotmaker
showmanly
storm cone
stormcock
storm door
slow march
slow-march
slow match
storm-stay
storm cuff
spoonways

spoonbait
spoon-feed
shot noise
spoonwise
spoonbill
stownlins
stornelli
stornello
spoonhook
spoonworm
scoundrel
snot-nosed
spoonfuls
Stornoway
scotomata
sporocarp
stomodeum
sporogeny
sporophyl
scorodite
sporozoan
sporogony
spodogram
sporocyst
showplace
snow plant
slow-paced
showpiece
scoop neck
stop press
stop-press
sloppy joe
scorpioid
shotproof
slop-pouch
scoopfuls
scorrendo
scourings
show round
snowscape
soopstake
sponsible
Scots mile
Scots pine
shoeshine
Scots pint
sponsalia
snowstorm
sloosh out
stop short
sponsored
shorthand
shortcake
short game
short sale
short wave
short-wave
slow track
shortfall
short-haul
shootable
sportable
sports car
smooth dab
short odds
short-head
short-term
shortness
sportless
spoutless
stoutness

short leet
scouthery
short-life
short time
short-time
shoutline
stop thief!
smoothing
Storthing
smoothish
show trial
short film
short list
short-list
short slip
sportsman
shoot-'em-up
sportance
shortener
short-cord
shorthold
shoot home
spout-hole
shoot down
shortgown
shorthorn
shout down
sloethorn
short-coat
stouthrie
short iron
sponte sua
shortstop
short fuse
shot tower
sport away
scopulate
shogunate
sporulate
snow under
spodumene
snob value
slow virus
snow-white
stopwatch
snow-water
Sioux City
storyline
scolytoid
storybook
storyette
sforzandi
sforzando
smorzando
sforzatos
Sephardic
Sephardim
sopranini
septarium
septarian
septation
sopranino
sopranist
sapraemia
sapraemic
sapidless
sapidness
sapodilla
septenary
supremacy
September

sapheaded
supremely
septemfid
supremity
septennia
saphenous
sapiently
septemvir
sapogenin
sapphired
sappiness
soppiness
syphilise
syphilize
septicity
syphiloma
syphiloid
septimole
septiform
sophistic
sophister
sophistry
suppliant
supplicat
supply day
sepulchre
sepulcher
supplying
sepulture
sapanwood
saponaria
supinator
siphonage
siphonate
saprolite
sepiolite
supposing
Sophocles
saprozoic
sophomore
siphon off
sapi-outan
supporter
supersafe
superwaif
superfast
supermart
supersalt
separable
superable
separably
superably
supergene
supersede
supervene
supersell
superhero
superheat
saporific
soporific
superthin
superbike
superfine
superhive
supervise
superrich
supermini
superbity
superglue
superplus
superflux

supernova
superbold
supercold
superpose
Super Bowl®
supercoil
supercool
supersoft
supertram
superbrat
superette
separatum
separator
superstar
separates
superfuse
suppurate
siphuncle
sapsucker
Sophus Lie
septuplet
sequacity
sequencer
sequestra
St-Quentin
sequester
sequently
sequinned
sarbacane
seriately
serialise
serialize
stream-ice
screaming
spreading
streaking
streaming
surfacing
serialism
Syriacism
Syrianism
Sarmatian
seriation
serration
sortation
striation
serialist
seriality
streakily
streamlet
serranoid
sorb-apple
sargassum
sargassos
sarcastic
stream-tin
surmaster
servantry
serrature
striature
scrubland
surfboard
scribable
shrubless
shrubbery
scrub bird
shrublike
scrabbing
scrubbing
strobilae
scrabbler

scribbler
strobilus
sarabande
scrub fowl
sprechery
spruce fir
strictish
spreckled
strychnia
Saracenic
strychnic
surf canoe
sericeous
sericitic
stricture
structure
sorediate
shredless
shredding
stridling
scroddled
stridence
stridency
streetage
streetboy
streetcar
surrender
surrendry
sorceress
surgeless
screenful
streetful
screecher
serrefile
serve time
screeding
screening
screeving
shrieking
surveying
surveille
surreined
sergeancy
serjeancy
serjeanty
surgeoncy
screen off
shriek-owl
surrejoin
sorcerous
surfeited
sarmentum
surfeiter
serpentry
shroffage
strifeful
sgraffiti
sgraffito
scruffily
serigraph
scragging
shrugging
spragging
sprigging
strigging
seraglios
scraggily
straggler
struggler
Saragossa
sprightly

scrog-bush
scrog-buss
Sarah Gamp
Syrphidae
Sarah Hogg
surcharge
sortilege
sarkiness
sorriness
surliness
servilely
sortilegy
surcingle
sorbitise
sorbitize
straining
surmising
surviving
surficial
servilism
Sardinian
sortition
servility
spraickle
serricorn
serpigoes
serviette
servitude
Sir A J Ayer
strokable
strike off
strike oil
stroke oar
strike out
strikeout
stroke out
strike pay
scroll bar
surpliced
serologic
scrolling
shrilling
strolling
scroll saw
strelitzi
Stralsund
scrimmage
scrummage
skrimmage
scrum half
stramaçon
scrimshaw
scramming
scrumming
shrimping
strumming
scrimpily
scrambler
shrimp net
Stromboli
scrumdown
stromatic
strumatic
strumitis
stramazon
springald
shrinkage
strongarm
Stranraer
string-bag
✧**springbok**

spring box
strongbox
serenader
Serengeti
syringeal
stringent
strongest
strangely
scrunchie
shrinking
springing
sprinting
stringing
strongish
strontium
strontian
springily
strenuity
stringily
sprinkler
strangler
strangles
springlet
strongman
Surinamer
strenuous
Stringops
string out
strung out
string pea
serinette
string tie
surf'n'turf
siren suit
strangury
strongyle
sarcomata
Sarvodaya
surrogate
sarcocarp
surrogacy
sarcomere
sermoneer
sorrowful
Sarcodina
sermonise
sermonize
sermoning
sorrowing
sartorial
sardonian
sartorian
Serbonian
sartorius
Sorbonist
sarcology
seriously
sarcoptic
Sarcoptes
scrapyard
scrippage
strap-game
strap-hang
strip mall
strappado
strip-leaf
strip cell
scrapheap
strapless
scrapegut
seraphine

strapline
strip mine
scrapping
strapping
stripling
stripping
stropping
strip mill
seraphims
seraphins
sore point
scrappily
strip club
scrapbook
strap work
strip down
strapwort
scriptory
surfperch
scrap iron
✧scripture
surprised
surprisal
surpriser
Sarasvati
strossers
stressful
seraskier
stress out
spritsail
scrutable
soritical
sort these
spriteful
strategic
stratagem
stretched
scratcher
stretcher
scratches
scrutoire
strutting
sure thing
stratonic
serotinal
serotonin
sort those
serotypic
scrutator
serrulate
stroupach
surquedry
scrounger
sprauchle
serpulite
shrouding
sprouting
strouding
surmullet
surculose
shriveled
scrivener
screw jack
screwball
screw nail
screwable
strawless
strewment
screw them
screw-pile
screw pine

shrewmice
strawlike
straw wine
scrawling
sprawling
scrawnily
shrew mole
straw vote
straw-work
straw poll
screw-worm
strawworm
screw-down
straw boss
screw bolt
straw-stem
screw over
strayling
sassarara
sussarara
Sassandra
Sassanian
sustained
sustainer
✧saskatoon
sassafras
systaltic
Sassenach
sisserary
suspended
suspender
systemise
systemize
sistering
suspenser
suspensor
sestertia
suspected
susceptor
sestettos
sostenuto
Sosigenes
suscitate
sassiness
sissiness
sustinent
sissified
suspicion
sessional
sisal hemp
sesame oil
Sisinnius
sassolite
Sisyphean
susurrate
susurrant
sasquatch
satiation
situation
St Tib's Eve
setaceous
satedness
sutteeism
setter-off
setter-out
set theory
sottishly
St Trinian
sottisier
sitzkrieg
settle-bed

set alight
satellite
suttletie
set in hand
satanical
set on edge
satin jean
satin bird
set on fire
satinwood
set on foot
satin spar
satinetta
satinette
set-top box
set to five
sit bodkin
sotto voce
set to work
sitiology
set foot in
set speech
set up shop
set square
Saturdays
saturable
satirical
satyrical
saturniid
saturnine
saturnism
Saturnian
saturnist
satyr play
suturally
saturated
saturator
so to speak
satisfied
satisfice
satisfier
shtetlach
sitatunga
situtunga
set much by
set eyes on
Soudanese
Shug Avery
squeakery
squeaking
squealing
squeamish
squeakily
Scudamore
scumbling
squibbing
squabbish
squabbler
slumbrous
slumberer
sour cream
scuncheon
scutcheon
scutching
sour-crout
soul-curer
soundcard
sound wave
soundless
soundness
sound bite

soundbite
sound film
scuddaler
soundings
sound hole
sound poem
sound poet
sound post
sound body
sourdough
spulebane
saucer eye
souteneur
sauceless
saucerful
stupefied
sautéeing
squeezing
stupefier
scutellum
scutellar
Sauternes
spulebone
sauce boat
sou'wester
studentry
smug-faced
stuffed up
scuffle up
stuff them
shuffling
snuffling
snuff-dish
snuff mill
snuff film
soulfully
stuff gown
soul-force
snuff-mull
swung dash
sluggabed
smudge box
slung shot
smuggling
squegging
stud groom
smudge pot
sour-gourd
southland
southward
Southwark
south-east
South Bend
South Seas
south-west
slush pile
South Uist
south pole
Southdown
Southroun
southmost
Southport
slughorne
stud horse
southerly
slush fund
studiedly
sauciness
sourishly
squailing
stupidity

Sauvignon
scutiform
saucisson
skunkbird
squalidly
squelcher
squalling
squillion
souvlakia
squamella
scummings
soul music
squamosal
shunnable
Sturnidae
squint-eye
squinting
squinancy
snub-nosed
stuporous
soup plate
slump test
stud poker
stump work
sculpture
squireage
square-cut
squiredom
squirrely
squirt gun
squirting
square leg
squiralty
souari-nut
squarrose
square off
scurriour
square peg
squirarch
soubrette
spur rowel
spur-royal
squash bug
spun sugar
Skupstina
squashily
soupspoon
Stuttgart
squatness
squitters
squat shop
squatting
shuttered
saunterer
sputterer
stutterer
shubunkin
spur-whang
squawk box
spur wheel
squawking
scuzzball
sovietise
sovietize
sovietism
savagedom
Sivaistic
seventeen
Seven Seas
St Vincent
seventhly

seventies
sovenance
sevenfold
severable
sovereign
severally
severalty
severance
Severinus
savourily
saw doctor
sexvalent
sexualise
sexualize
sexualism
sexualist
sexuality
sextantal
Six-Day War
sex object
sixteenth
sixteenmo
sixteener
sexlessly
saxifrage
sex change
sex-change
sixth form
sex-linked
sex kitten
sex on legs
sexennial
Saxon blue
sextoness
sex worker
six-footer
sex appeal
saxophone
saxitoxin
sextuplet
sex symbol
sixty-nine
sex typing
skyjacker
skylarker
scybalous
say-master
spymaster
styleless
stylebook
soya flour
scytheman
Smyth's Sea
stylishly
skydiving
styliform
stylistic
stylobate
stylolite
skyrocket
Styrofoam®
styrofoam
sky troops
soya sauce
styptical
sizarship
tear apart
tea garden
Trafalgar
Toamasina
thanatism

thanatist
travailed
thanatoid
thalassic
tea taster
twayblade
trancedly
thatching
tray cloth
to account
twaddling
tradename
trade sale
tragelaph
trace back
trade mark
trademark
trade-last
traceable
tradeable
traceably
traceless
tradeless
thaneship
traceried
trade wind
teaseling
trapesing
traveling
tsarevich
trapezial
trapezium
tragedian
trapezius
teaselled
travelled
tea-dealer
teaseller
traveller
tradesman
thanehood
trapezoid
trade down
to a degree
traversed
traversal
traverser
trabeated
tea kettle
travertin
toad-eater
trabecula
tea leaves
traffic in
tearfully
tear gland
toadgrass
twangling
Thargelia
Tracheata
tracheate
tracheary
teachable
teachless
trashiest
tracheide
tea things
trachinus
trashtrie
teacherly
trachytic

trachitis
twalhours
to a nicety
teasingly
traditive
✧tradition
traditors
trackball
trackable
thankless
trackless
track shoe
thankings
trackroad
track down
track-boat
Thackeray
tracksuit
trailable
trailless
trail bike
trawl-line
trawl-fish
tramlined
tramlines
thalluses
trail away
traumatic
thaumatin
trainband
trainable
trainless
train fine
train mile
train down
to a wonder
twa-lofted
traipsing
trampling
trampolin
trappings
twalpenny
Trappists
trampette
transfard
translate
trap-stair
transcend
tear shell
Tsar's Bell
tearsheet
transfect
transient
transvest
trans-ship
transship
that's that
transpire
trap stick
that's flat
transomed
transumpt
transenna
transonic
tear smoke
toadstone
transmove
transpose
toadstool
transform
transport

tear strip
transfuse
transhume
transmute
transeunt
transaxle
toast rack
tractable
tractably
traitress
toastiest
twattling
trattoria
trattorie
traitorly
tractator
teacupful
traguline
traducing
Traducian
tablature
to be brief
Toby Belch
tubicolar
tobaccoes
tubectomy
tableland
table maid
table game
tableware
✧table talk
table salt
table leaf
table beer
table wine
tablewise
table book
table-work
tubbiness
tabellion
Tubularia
tabularly
tubulated
tabulator
Tabanidae
tabbouleh
tubercled
tubercule
tabasheer
tabescent
tube skirt
tabbyhood
Toby Young
tacmahack
toccatina
Tocharish
Tocharian
tuckerbag
tuckerbox
ticket day
ticked off
tucker out
tactfully
tick fever
tackiness
techiness
tactician
tactilist
tacticity
tactility
tectiform

tacamahac
technical
technopop
technique
tycoonate
tycoonery
tectorial
tectonics
tachogram
tectrices
tucotucos
tucutucos
tacitness
tactually
tachylite
tachypnea
tachylyte
Ted Dexter
tide gauge
tidal wave
tiddliest
tidal flow
toddle off
tediosity
Tod-lowrie
tediously
Tudor rose
Tudor arch
tide table
Ted Hughes
Ted Turner
tidewater
toddy-palm
teddy bear
Teddy girl
Theravada
The Gambia
the rabble
The Warden
them and us
✧the baseej
the latest
toeragger
The Father
the rather
theralite
the Salish
therapist
tee marker
the fallen
The Tailor
The Tatler
The Tablet
✧the damned
trepanned
trepanner
Trematoda
trematoid
trehalose
trematode
thenabout
thesaurus
The Walrus
therapsid
the masses
the matter
The Cantos
tremblant
trembling
tremblier
Theobroma

trenchand
trenchard
trenchant
theocracy
theocrasy
The Scream
the screen
treachery
tiercelet
treachour
theaceous
tierceron
the Scrubs
the occult
trendiest
tweediest
treadling
treadmill
trendyism
Theodoric
The Herald
theme park
The Aeneid
themeless
thereness
thelement
The Belfry
the method
the period
Thelemite
the belief
tee-heeing
therewith
The Devils
thereinto
thereunto
✧the beyond
therefore
theme song
tregetour
these sort
The People
thereupon
therefrom
the Terror
the jet set
the depths
there it is
theme tune
thereaway
twelfthly
The Egoist
theogonic
tree heath
The Phaedo
The Chairs
the shakes
the whilst
the change
trephiner
the Shroud
the Shires
tree house
The Mikado
The Rivals
trepidant
theriacal
the cinema
the five Ks
the Virgin
thegither

the Fishes
the living
the wicked
The Miller
the gimmes
Trebizond
The Ripper
The Mirror
taeniasis
treillage
theologic
theologue
theologer
tree-lined
the old sod
trellised
The Clouds
thermical
theomachy
✧thermidor
thermally
theomania
theomancy
thermotic
treenware
tie-and-dye
the undead
'tween-deck
tweenager
The Knight
teeing-off
theandric
the potato
✧the royals
tremolant
The Hobbit
the yonder
treponema
treponeme
the Bowery
tremolite
the social
tree onion
the movies
trefoiled
the common
Theropoda
thecodont
therology
the bottle
The Vortex
teetotums
The Pogues
Theophano
theophagy
theophany
tree peony
the Spirit
theopathy
tee-square
The Squire
the squits
The Grocer
the Graces
the cradle
the grades
The Friend
the creeps
thearchic
the Archer
the Arches

theorbist
theurgist
tredrille
the crunch
tree rings
theorique
theoriser
the Arctic
theoretic
the cratur
theorizer
tree snake
tsetse fly
tzetse fly
the usages
theosophy
tressured
treasurer
tree shrew
✧thersitic
tiers état
tree stump
the attack
treatable
the sticks
twentieth
treatment
twentyish
theatrics
theotokos
theft-bote
twenty-one
theftuous
theftboot
twenty-two
the States
tree trunk
tremulate
tremulant
trebuchet
the Furies
the bullet
tremulous
the purple
the gutter
twelvemos
the Twelve
tae kwon do
Teeswater
the Lyceum
tie-dyeing
thelytoky
✧the system
tzetze fly
tufaceous
Toffeemen
tog rating
tagmemics
tegmental
tegmentum
tug-of-love
tuggingly
tigrishly
toggle off
tegularly
tegulated
tiger tail
Tiger balm®
tiger's eye
tiger team
tiger fish

✧tiger lily
tigerwood
tiger wolf
tiger moth
tiger worm
tight-lace
tightness
tight side
tighten up
tightener
tight-knit
tightrope
tight spot
tahsildar
tehsildar
Taiwanese
trivalent
trifacial
triradial
tribadism
tribalism
trisagion
tribalist
trigamist
tritanope
trigamous
tridactyl
trivalved
tailboard
trilby hat
thin-belly
twin birth
triactine
twitching
twitchier
twitchily
triecious
third-hand
third-rate
third wave
third rail
third gear
Third-Ager
twiddling
thirdsman
twice-laid
toilet bag
tail-ender
tribeless
triteness
trimethyl
tripe-shop
thio-ether
tripe-wife
tricerion
tri-weekly
tribesman
twice-told
twice-born
trimerous
trimetric
trihedral
trihedron
tricepses
toilet set
tridented
tridental
trimester
trisector
twice over
thin-faced

thieflike
thingness
thingummy
thinghood
tailgater
tritheism
tritheist
trichinae
trichinas
trichroic
thigh bone
trichrome
thigh boot
trichosis
trichitic
✧tripitaka
triticale
trilinear
twiningly
trilithic
trilithon
triticism
trivially
tuitional
trinitrin
think tank
thinkable
thickhead
thickness
trickless
trickiest
trickling
twinkling
thick film
tricksier
thick-lips
tricksily
thickskin
triskelia
triskeles
thick knee
thickener
think good
tricksome
think long
thick-sown
think upon
thicketed
trickster
trinketer
trinketry
think over
thick-eyed
trialware
trialogue
tail light
trial-fire
trialling
triallist
triploidy
triclinia
triclinic
trillions
trial trip
Triple sec
tuillette
Thin Lizzy
triumphal
triumpher
triumviri
triumvirs

triumviry
trimmings
trim marks
trip meter
triennial
triennium
triangled
triangles
trionymal
thinnings
Triandria
trilobate
trifocals
toison d'or
tailoress
Trilobita
trilobite
tailoring
trinomial
trifolium
triforium
twiforked
triformed
twiformed
✧tricolour
trigonous
tribology
thin on top
tailplane
twin plane
tailpiece
thiophene
trippiest
trig point
trierarch
tricrotic
tail rotor
tail rhyme
thirstful
thirstier
thirstily
tailstock
twin-screw
twin-track
twistable
tristichs
thirtieth
taintless
thirtyish
triathlon
triatomic
taint-worm
twist down
triptyque
trieteric
twist grip
twitterer
tristesse
tribunate
triturate
tributary
Tribunite
Tribunism
tripudium
tricuspid
triquetra
tailwheel
tridymite
trigynian
tricyclic
tricycler

trigynous
trihydric
trihybrid
take aback
take apart
take a leak
take a seat
take a hike
Tokharish
take a risk
Tokharian
take amiss
take after
take a turn
take cover
take heart
take horse
take it ill
take issue
take in tow
take leave
take-leave
tokoloshe
Takamatsu
token ring
token vote
taking-off
take order
teknonymy
take place
take pains
take shape
take sides
take steps
take stock
take short
take turns
tell a tale
tell apart
Tiliaceae
talkathon
talkative
Tullamore
talk about
tollbooth
tylectomy
telferage
taligrade
telegraph
talegalla
telegenic
telegonic
telpheric
tollhouse
talliable
talking-to
tellingly
tallithim
toluidine
tellinoid
telamones
telematic
telemeter
telemetry
teleosaur
tallow dip
tall order
tallowish
tol-lolish
teleology
teleonomy

Teleostei
talbotype
telophase
telepheme
telepoint
tulipwood
telephone
telephoto
tulip root
telephony
tulip tree
telepathy
tolerable
tolerably
talk radio
tularemia
tularemic
tolerance
tilt-rotor
tolerator
talk round
talismans
telestich
telesales
telescope
tile stone
telescopy
talk trash
tell tales
tellurate
telluride
tellurise
tellurite
tellurize
Talmudism
tellurium
tellurian
tellurion
Talmudist
tellurous
televiser
televisor
tallyshop
tally-hoed
Tom Landry
timpanist
tympanist
time about
tympanums
Tom Sawyer
timocracy
time clock
timidness
tumidness
temperate
tampering
tempering
timbering
timberman
Tim Henman
timeframe
tumefying
tomograph
Tom Sharpe
tim-whisky
Tom Finney
Tom Kitten
Tamil Nadu
tumblebug
Temple Bar
tumble car

tumble-dry
timeliest
time limit
temulence
temulency
Tom Clancy
time-lapse
temblores
timenoguy
tomentose
tomentous
Tom and Tib
tamponade
tamponage
temporary
time of day
temporise
temporize
tomboyish
tom-tommed
tambourin
timeously
timepiece
Téméraire
Tom Cruise
tamarillo
timorsome
Timisoara
timescale
timeshare
time sheet
tumescent
time slice
tombstone
tempt fate
temptable
timetable
temptress
time trial
tomatillo
Tim Burton
Timbuctoo
tamoxifen
tummy ache
tommy shop
tummy tuck
✧temazepam
tantarara
Tony Award
tantalate
Tony Adams
Tantalean
tonga-bean
tonka-bean
tantalise
tantalite
tantalize
tentative
ting-a-ling
tantalism
Tantalian
Tanzanian
tentation
Tongariro
tentacled
tantalous
tentacula
Tony Blair
tenebrism
tenebrios
tenebrist

tenebrity
tenebrose
tint block
tenebrous
Tony Cragg
tenaculum
tent cloth
tenacious
tunicated
tent dress
tinderbox
tenseless
tenseness
✧tangerine
tenderise
tenderize
tendering
tinkering
tinseling
tunneling
tinselled
tunnelled
tunneller
tunnel net
Tennessee
tunefully
Tony Greig
tanagrine
tenth-rate
tanghinin
tinniness
tintiness
tonnishly
tensility
tan pickle
tenaillon
tonsillar
tensional
tendinous
tan liquor
tin lizzie
tingliest
tangle net
tanalised
tonalitic
Tony Leung
tanalized
tant mieux
tentmaker
tonometer
tonometry
tuning key
tuning peg
tuning pin
tensorial
tentorial
tonsorial
tentorium
tenuously
tend out on
tonoplast
tin-opener
ten a penny
tenurable
Tony Roche
tenor clef
tenor drum
tungstate
tungstite
tunesmith
tinguaite

Words marked ✧ can also be spelled with one or more capital letters

Tungusian
tonguelet
tongue-tie
tank wagon
tunny fish
two-handed
two-hander
Thomasina
Thora Hird
troparion
Thomas Kyd
tropaeola
two-masted
two-parted
two-master
Thomas Tew
Trojan War
troubling
troublous
trot-cosey
Trondheim
two-headed
two-leafed
two-legged
two-decker
trowelled
troweller
those sort
twoseater
two-leaved
thoughted
thoughten
toothwash
toothache
Trochidae
trochleae
trochlear
toothless
trothless
toothiest
toothlike
trophying
troth ring
toothfish
toothpick
two shakes
trochilic
trochilus
toothcomb
toothsome
toothwort
toolhouse
two-timing
trominoes
two-lipped
Thomistic
tropistic
two-fisted
trollopee
toodle-pip
toolmaker
T-commerce
thornback
thornless
thorniest
thornbird
trouncing
thornbill
thorn moth
thorntree
thornbush

tholobate
two-forked
two-roomed
tropology
two-footed
two-bottle
thorow-wax
troopship
two a penny
Taoiseach
tool steel
trousseau
thousands
trousered
trout farm
troutless
troutling
twostroke
two-storey
two-by-four
top banana
tap-dancer
Typhaceae
topmaking
topiarian
topiarist
top hamper
top-sawyer
tapacolos
tapaculos
topically
typically
topectomy
tepidness
tape drive
tepidaria
tapaderas
tapaderos
Tipperary
Tipp-Ex out
tappet-rod
top secret
tepifying
typifying
tape grass
type genus
tip-cheese
Tupaiidae
tap cinder
tipsiness
topping-up
toppingly
tappit hen
tipsified
tephillah
tephillin
topminnow
tephigram
tip-tilted
Tipulidae
topologic
top-flight
typhlitic
typhlitis
typomania
type metal
toponymic
toponymal
tip-and-run
typhoidal
tiptoeing

tuptowing
✧typhonian
taphonomy
top-booted
tape punch
top-up loan
taperness
taperwise
tephroite
tephritic
top drawer
top-drawer
type scale
tipstaffs
tip it down
tipstaves
typewrite
tipsy cake
terramara
terramare
turn again
turnagain
termagant
Tartarean
tervalent
ternately
threatful
threadfin
tarsalgia
terza rima
tartarise
tartarize
torbanite
turn aside
terracing
terrarium
tarnation
Tartarian
threadier
throatier
throatily
tarmacked
terra alba
tarpaulin
Tarragona
Terranova
terraform
tornadoes
turn about
turnabout
Tyrian red
Tartan tax
tirra-lyra
terrazzos
terebrate
terebrant
throbless
throbbing
terebinth
Turnberry
turf drain
tiredness
teredines
three-card
three-pair
three-part
three-deck
three deep
targeteer
terseness
threeness

threepeat
terrenely
turret gun
turkey hen
torpefied
torrefied
terze rime
three-pile
Turnerian
Tortelier
target man
terpenoid
threefold
threesome
✧turkey oak
three-four
torpedoer
torpedoes
three-foot
Turkey red
tormented
tormentil
tormentum
three-star
tormenter
tormentor
terzettos
turgently
thriftier
thriftily
toruffled
turn forth
tyre gauge
torch-race
torchière
torch-lily
torchwood
torch song
terminate
turbinate
turribant
termitary
terpineol
tardiness
tarriness
tartiness
turfiness
turnip fly
tarnished
tarnisher
terrified
turbidite
Turkicise
Turkicize
terminism
terrifier
terminist
torpidity
torridity
tortility
turbidity
turgidity
tortillon
tarriance
torsional
terricole
torminous
✧territory
turnip top
torpitude
turpitude

thrillant
thralldom
thrilling
Tirol Alps
turn loose
torulosis
thrumming
thrombose
thrum-eyed
tarantara
tarantass
threnodic
tyranness
throngful
tyrannise
tyrannize
thronging
tarantism
Terentian
Tarantino
tyrannous
threnetic
✧tarantula
Turcomans
Turkomans
term of art
terrorful
tarboggin
Turcophil
terrorise
terrorize
threonine
terrorism
terrorist
turcopole
turboprop
turn-penny
Tariq Aziz
tortricid
tortrices
turn round
turnround
turf spade
Turk's head
thrust hoe
turnstile
thrashing
threshing
thrusting
thrasonic
threshold
turnstone
thrash out
turn-screw
turntable
teratogen
throttler
teratomas
teruteros
turbulent
throughly
turquoise
torturing
Tartufish
Tartufism
Tartufian
toreutics
Targumist
torturous
torquated
throw back

throwback
throw a fit
throw dirt
tire-woman
throw onto
throw down
throw-down
throw open
throwster
throw over
throw away
throwaway
taraxacum
Tisha Baav
Tishah b'Ab
Tishah B'Av
Tasman Bay
Tisha be'Ab
✧testament
Tisha Be'Av
toss aside
Toscanini
Tasmanian
testation
Tuscarora
tesla coil
testatrix
Tasman Sea
test chart
test drive
test-drive
tesseract
tasteless
tasseling
tasselled
tessellae
tessellar
taste bulb
task force
task group
Tashi Lama
tastiness
testiness
testified
testifier
testimony
tessitura
test match
tasimeter
test pilot
Tisiphone
test paper
tusk shell
tetrarchy
tête-à-tête
tetradite
titration
tetralogy
tetrapody
Titian red
✧tetragram
tête-bêche
titubancy
TFT screen
toto caelo
Tuticorin
title page
tithe barn
to the last
title deed
title leaf

titleless
to the life
to the wide
tittering
tottering
to the hilt
to the good
title role
to the bone
to the fore
title poem
tetterous
tithe-free
to the full
tête folle
tetchiest
tittivate
tattiness
totting-up
titillate
tittlebat
total heat
totalling
total up to
titularly
totaliser
totalizer
totem pole
Tuthmosis
tetroxide
tutiorism
tattooist
tutiorist
tutworker
tit for tat
tit-for-tat
titupping
totaquine
tutorship
tittuping
tittupped
tout à fait
Taufa'ahau
tout à vous
thumb mark
thumbtack
thumbnail
thumbless
thumblike
thumbling
thumb ring
thumbkins
thumb knot
thumb hole
truncheon
T-junction
truncated
tout court
true dagga
thundrous
thunderer
thunder it
truceless
Trubenise
Trubenize®
tau lepton
Tourette's
truffling
touch base
touchback
touch mark

truchmans
touchable
touchless
toughness
truthless
touchiest
touchline
truthlike
toughener
touch wood
touchwood
touch hole
Touchtone®
touchtone
tough love
touch down
touchdown
touch upon
truth drug
tough luck
touch-type
tauriform
touristic
trunk call
trunk-mail
truck-farm
trunkless
truck shop
trunk line
truckling
trunkfish
truckload
trunk road
trunk hose
trunkwork
truck stop
trunkfuls
tournedos
true north
tourneyer
Teutonise
Teutonize
Teutonism
Teutonist
tautology
tautonymy
trump card
trumped-up
truepenny
trumpeted
trumpeter
Thursdays
truss beam
trustable
trust deed
trustless
trustiest
trust fund
truculent
tovarisch
town clerk
thwacking
town crier
tow-headed
town house
townhouse
tawniness
towel-rack
towel-rail
towelling
towing net

towerless
tawdriest
thwarting
tower mill
tower over
townscape
townsfolk
tax-paying
tax farmer
toxically
taxaceous
toxocaral
taxed cart
taxidermy
tax relief
tax return
taxameter
taximeter
taxonomic
taxonomer
textorial
toxaphene
toxophily
textphone
tax credit
taxi stand
taxi track
texturise
texturize
textually
tax-exempt
thylacine
thyratron
Thysanura
toylesome
thymidine
thyristor
thyroxine
twyforked
twyformed
thymocyte
try square
Thyestean
Thyestian
tayassuid
Trygve Lie
unabashed
up against
unadapted
Ulan Bator
unaccused
unaidable
up and down
up-and-down
up-and-over
unamerced
unamended
unavenged
unashamed
unamiable
uraniscus
Upanishad
uralitise
uralitize
uraninite
unanimity
usability
unaligned
unanimous
unallayed
unalloyed

unadmired
unavoided
uvarovite
unadorned
uranology
unadopted
unapplied
unapparel
unassumed
unassured
unassayed
unactable
unaptness
upaithric
unaltered
unattired
unamusing
unadvised
unanxious
unbearded
unbraided
unbranded
upbraider
umbratile
unbearing
unbiassed
unblended
umbrella'd
unblessed
unbaffled
unbeguile
unblinded
unbridged
un-British
unbridled
unbuilt-on
unbrizzed
unbeknown
umbellate
umbilical
umbilicus
unbelieve
unbalance
umbellule
unbeloved
unbending
unbinding
unbundler
urban myth
unblooded
upbrought
unbookish
unblotted
unbaptize
unberufen
unburthen
umber-bird
upburning
unbespeak
unbashful
unbosomer
unbespoke
unbounded
upbounden
unbrushed
unbruised
unblunted
unchanged
uncharged
unceasing
uncharity

uncharmed
unclaimed
unchained
uncharnel
up-Channel
unclassed
uncharted
uncleship
✧**uncle Dick**
unchecked
uncleaned
uncleanly
uncheered
uncleared
upcheered
unclearly
uncreated
unclimbed
unclipped
uncombine
uncongeal
unconcern
unconfine
uncannily
uncanonic
unconform
uncandour
uncinated
urceolate
unclouded
uncrowded
unclogged
unclothed
uncrowned
uncropped
uncrossed
uncapable
uncertain
uncurtain
uncurable
uncurrent
up-current
uncareful
uncurling
uncordial
uncurdled
uncurious
unchrisom
uncorrupt
uncessant
uncrudded
uncouthly
uncoupled
uncrumple
uncounted
uncourtly
up-country
uncivilly
uncovered
up-draught
undrained
undebased
undecided
undecagon
undeceive
undecimal
undecayed
undreaded
undreamed
undressed
undefaced

undefiled
undefined
undignify
undyingly
undrilled
undeluded
undelight
undulancy
undiluted
undulated
undelayed
undamaged
undrowned
undercard
underhand
underlaid
underpaid
underrate
undersaye
undertake
undertane
under oath
under sail
underlain
underta'en
underpass
undercart
undercast
underpart
underfeed
underself
underdeck
under seal
underseal
undersell
underkeep
underpeep
underbear
underwear
udderless
underfelt
undervest
underwent
undershot
undergird
underbite
under fire
underfire
under-five
underline
undermine
under-ripe
underside
undertime
underking
underling
under-ring
underwing
underfish
undersign
undertint
underclub
underclad
underplot
underflow
underclay
underplay
✧**underwood**
underdone
undergone
undernote

undertone
under-roof
underfong
undersong
undercook
undertook
underwork
undercool
undersoil
undergown
underdoer
undercoat
underfoot
undermost
underbody
underbred
undergrad
underprop
under arms
underdraw
underfund
underhung
underbush
undesired
undeserve
undutiful
unduteous
undaunted
undoubted
undivided
undawning
undazzled
unexalted
unexcited
unendowed
uselessly
unelected
uneffaced
unengaged
un-English
unethical
Uredineae
uredinial
uredinium
uredinous
uterotomy
unemptied
unexpired
unexposed
unearthed
unearthly
unessence
unessayed
uneatable
unextreme
unextinct
unentered
unequable
unequally
unenvying
unenvious
use-by date
unfearful
unfraught
unfearing
unfranked
unfocused
unfadable
unfledged
unfleshed
unfleshly

unfeeling
unfuelled
unfreeman
unfretted
unfigured
unfailing
unfeigned
unfolding
upfilling
unfancied
unfrocked
unfloored
unfurnish
unfortune
unfitness
unfitting
unfounded
unguarded
ungrassed
ungodlike
ungodlily
unguessed
ungainful
unguiform
ungallant
ungenteel
ungenuine
upgrowing
ungroomed
unglossed
unghostly
ungermane
ungirthed
ungarbled
upgushing
ungrudged
unheard-of
upheaping
unhearsed
unhealthy
unheedful
unheeding
unheedily
unhelpful
upholding
upholster
Up-Helly-Aa
unhumbled
unhandily
unhandled
unhopeful
unhappily
unharness
unharmful
unhurtful
ushership
unhurried
unharming
unharbour
usherette
unhasting
unhatched
unhatting
unhaunted
univalent
urinative
✧**unitarian**
urination
uniparous
uniramous
unincited

unindexed
uniserial
universal
unisexual
Uriah Heep
unifiable
unitively
utilities
uliginose
uliginous
uninjured
un-Islamic
unillumed
uniplanar
Union Jack
Unionidae
union shop
union list
union flag
unionised
union suit
unionized
unisonant
unipotent
Uriconian
uniformed
uniformly
unicolour
unisonous
urinology
unimpeded
unit price
unimposed
uninstall
uninsured
unit trust
ubiquitin
uninvited
unjealous
unjointed
unknelled
unkindled
unknowing
unloading
unlearned
unluckily
unlocated
uplifting
ugli® fruit
unlogical
unlighted
uplighted
uplighter
unlikable
unlimited
uplinking
uplandish
unlosable
unlivable
unlovable
unlived-in
Ullswater
unmeaning
ulmaceous
unmakable
unmanacle
unmindful
unmanaged
upmanship
unmanlike
unmingled
unmanured
unmoneyed
unmarried
unmerited
unmusical
unmasking
unmatched
unmatured
unmotived
unmoulded
unmourned
unmounted
unmovable
unmovably
unmovedly
unmixedly
unmuzzled
uintahite
unneedful
urn-shaped
unnamable
unnerving
unnoticed
unnatural
upon a time
urolagnia
uroscopic
unordered
unorderly
up oneself
urodelous
urogenous
udometric
unoffered
urochrome
Urochorda
urokinase
urolithic
uxoricide
uxorially
ufologist
urologist
unopposed
ulotrichy
urography
unobvious
upon words
uropygial
uropygium
unplanked
unplained
unplanned
unpraised
unplaited
unplanted
unplagued
unpacking
unprepare
unpierced
unpledged
unprecise
unpredict
umpteenth
unpleased
unpressed
unpleated
unpliable
unpliably
unpainful
up-pricked
unpainted
unpointed
unprinted
unpoliced
unpalsied
unpolitic
unpiloted
unpennied
unprovide
unpeopled
unprovoke
unpropped
unpopular
unpapered
upper hand
upper-case
unperfect
unpervert
up-perched
unpartial
unperplex
uppermost
unpursued
unpotable
unpitiful
unpitying
up-putting
unplumbed
unplugged
unplucked
unpayable
unqualify
unquelled
unqueened
unqueenly
unquietly
unreached
unrealise
unrealize
unrealism
unreadily
unreality
unrebuked
unrebated
utricular
utriculus
unridable
unreduced
unredrest
unriddler
unruffled
unrefined
unrefuted
uprightly
Ukrainian
unrelated
unrelaxed
unrumpled
unremoved
unrenewed
uprooting
unripping
unripened
Utraquism
Utraquist
unrestful
unresting
unrosined
unreserve
unrounded
unrevoked
unrevised
unroyally
unrazored
unswaddle
unshapely
unscathed
unsparing
unstaying
upstaring
unshackle
unscanned
unstained
unstamped
unscarred
unsubject
unsubdued
unsuccess
unsickled
unsecular
unsecured
unseduced
ups-a-daisy
upsy-daisy
unsaddled
unseeable
unsued-for
unsterile
unseeming
Ulsterman
unscented
unsheathe
unslept-in
unsighing
unsighted
unsightly
unskilful
unsmiling
unsuiting
unskilled
unspilled
unstifled
unstilled
unskimmed
unskinned
unstirred
unstinted
unsmitten
unsaintly
unsalable
unsolaced
unsolidly
unsullied
unselfish
Ursulines
unsaluted
Ursa Major
Ursa Minor
unsinewed
unshocked
unstocked
unspoiled
unstopped
unstopper
unscoured
unspotted
unserious
unstriped
unshrived
unshriven
unsuspect
unsisting
unsatiate
unsatable
upsetting
upsitting
unsettled
unsourced
unsounded
unsoundly
unsnuffed
unstuffed
unstudied
unshunned
unsquared
unshutter
unsevered
unsavoury
unsayable
unscythed
unsizable
uitlander
ultra-high
unthanked
untracked
untrained
urticaria
up the wall
up the ante
up the pole
untressed
untreated
untoiling
uptrilled
untrimmed
untainted
untwisted
uptalking
untamable
untamably
untumbled
untimeous
untempted
ultimatum
untenable
untunable
untunably
untuneful
untangled
untrodden
untypable
untypical
untirable
utterable
utterless
utterness
unthrifty
unturning
upturning
utterance
uttermost
up to speed
up to snuff
untutored
upthunder
untouched
untrussed
untrusser
ululation
usucapion
unushered
usualness
usurpedly
usurp upon
unuttered
unusually
Uruguayan
unveiling
unvoicing
unvarying
unvisited
unwearied
unweeting
unwreaked
unwreathe
unweighed
unwriting
unwrinkle
unwhipped
unwritten
unwakened
unwilling
upwelling
unwelcome
unwomanly
unwinding
unwinking
unwrought
upwrought
unworldly
unworried
unwarlike
unworking
unwishful
unwasting
unwishing
unwatched
unwitting
unwittily
unwatered
unwounded
unzealous
Via Lactea
vraicking
viaticals
viability
viaticums
viatorial
via crucis
Vaal River
vibraharp
vibratile
vibrative
vibration
vibratory
vibrantly
vibracula
vibrissae
vibriosis
vacuation
vocabular
vice-chair
Vic Reeves
vaccinate
victimise
victimize
vaccinial
vaccinium
vacillate
vacillant
vocalness
vocaliser
vocalizer
vicennial
vacuolate
victoress
vectorise
vectorize
victorine
vectoring
vectorial
Victorian
viciosity
vacuously
viciously
vice-queen
vicariate
vice-regal
vicarship
vicereine
Victrola®
vicarious
vicesimal
vice squad
Vicksburg
vice versa
vide infra
videlicet
vade-mecum
Vedantism
video card
video game
videotape
video wall
videotext
videodisc
videogram
video tube
Vodaphone
vide supra
vedutista
vedutisti
vi et armis
viewiness
veeringly
vae victis
viewpoint
viewphone
Vientiane
vagueness
vogue word
vignetter
vigilance
vigilante
vaginulae
vaginules
vaginally
vaginated
vaginitis
vagarious
vigesimal
vegetable
vegetably
vegetated
vehicular
vehemence
vehemency
voilà tout
voice mail
voice-mail
voicemail
voiceless
voice vote
voice-over
vainglory
Vaishnava

voisinage
veilleuse
Vaiont Dam
veinstone
veinstuff
voiturier
vikingism
villanage
Villa Park
Vulgar era
villagery
volcanise
volcanize
vulcanise
vulcanite
vulcanize
vulgarise
vulgarize
✧volcanism
✧vulcanism
vulgarism
valuation
volcanian
✧vulcanian
vulgarian
✧volcanist
✧vulcanist
vulgarity
valuables
villa unit
villa home
viliacoes
villanous
volcanoes
villagree
valvassor
valiantly
volucrine
validness
velodrome
value date
vellenage
villenage
volte-face
vulnerate
velvet ant
vulnerary
velveteen
valve gear
valueless
valveless
velveting
vulsellae
vulsellum
value-free
Valdenses
vallecula
Vulpecula
vilifying
volageous
vellicate
voltigeur
vulpicide
vulpinite
voltinism
vulpinism
villiform
vulviform
voluminal
volumiser
voltmeter

volumeter
volumizer
voluntary
volunteer
✧valentine
Valentino
villosity
Volgograd
velarised
velarized
✧volksraad
Volkslied
veldskoen
volitient
vol-au-vent
veloutine
vulturine
vulturish
vulturism
vulturous
Valkyriur
Valkyries
Velázquez
vampirise
vampirize
vampirism
vimineous
vambraced
Vanua Levu
vandalise
vandalize
vintaging
vandalism
veniality
venial sin
Van Basten
vantbrace
vantbrass
vinaceous
vin de pays
vengeable
vengeably
vengement
Van der Hum
veneering
vindemial
vengeance
venefical
vine fruit
ventilate
vindicate
V S Naipaul
ventifact
vendition
ventiduct
ventosity
Vancouver
venerable
venerably
ventricle
ventrally
venireman
venereous
venerator
vanaspati
Venusberg
vanishing
vine-stock
vanity bag
vanity box
venatical

vingt-et-un
vin du pays
venturing
venturous
Venezuela
Violaceae
violative
violation
violently
violinist
voodooism
voodooist
vapidness
vaporware
vaporable
Viperidae
vaporific
vaporiser
vaporetti
vaporetto
vaporizer
vapouring
vapourish
vu quang ox
Verbascum
variative
verbalise
verbalize
vernalise
vernalize
versatile
verbalism
variation
verbarian
vernation
verbalist
verbality
vernality
verballed
verdantly
viricidal
virucidal
varicella
veracious
voracious
veridical
variegate
verberate
varletess
varieties
varvelled
vervelled
vermeille
vertebrae
vertebral
varifocal
verifying
viragoish
verminate
virginals
Vortigern
varnisher
versified
verbicide
vermicide
virginium
✧vorticism
Vergilian
vermilion
Virgilian
Virginian

versifier
vorticist
verticity
virginity
vorticity
versional
versioner
vorticose
vermiform
versiform
verminous
vertigoes
vertiport
verdigris
vermicule
vermifuge
vers libre
Very light
virulence
virulency
virilised
virilized
Varanidae
Varangian
✧véronique
variolate
verbosely
variolite
verbosity
varioloid
variolous
variously
verapamil
virescent
variscite
veritable
veritably
veratrine
Varityper®
virgulate
verjuiced
virtually
vargueños
Vertumnus
verrucose
verdurous
verrucous
virtuosic
virtuosos
visual aid
vassalage
vassaless
vistaless
visualise
visualize
Vespasian
visualist
visuality
vesiculae
vesicular
vasectomy
viscerate
visagiste
vestiment
vestigial
vestigium
vastidity
viscidity
vastitude
vestibule
vestiture

vasomotor
Vishnuite
Vishnuism
visionary
vis comica
visioning
visionist
viscosity
vision mix
viscounty
vis mortua
visor-mask
vestryman
visitable
visitress
vis a tergo
visitator
vasculums
vasovagal
vitiation
Vatican II
vaticinal
viticetum
Vitreosil®
Vita glass®
vetchling
vitrified
vitriolic
vitriform
vitellary
vitelline
Vitellius
vitaliser
vitalizer
Vitrolite®
vitiosity
vitascope
vetturini
Vitruvian
vetturino
Vitruvius
vouchsafe
vivianite
vivacious
vividness
vivifying
vivamente
vivandier
viverrine
vivariums
vow-fellow
vowelless
vexedness
vexillary
vox populi
vexatious
vox humana
voyeurism
vizierate
vizierial
vizirship
what a hope
what about
what cheer?
✧wyandotte
whale calf
whaleback
weasel cat
whale-head
whale line
weaseller

whale food
whalebone
weasel out
whaleboat
weaker sex
weak force
wrangling
what gives?
wrathless
weathered
weatherly
weariless
weariness
wearingly
wearisome
weak-kneed
weaponise
weaponize
weak point
wrappings
wrap round
wrapround
whatsoe'er
what's what
what's more
what's to do?
W particle
wealthily
wealth tax
Wladyslaw
webmaster
wobbegong
web offset
wobbly egg
web and pin
webfooted
web author
wych-alder
wych-hazel
wackiness
Wyclifite
wide awake
wideawake
wide-angle
Wednesday
wedge heel
wedge-like
wedgewise
wadsetter
widthways
widthwise
widow wail
widow bird
widow's man
widowhood
week about
Wiesbaden
wrenching
whencever
wieldable
wieldless
wheedling
weekender
whereness
woe betide
wherewith
whereinto
whereunto
wherefore
woebegone
whereupon

wherefrom
where it is
where away?
whey-faced
weel-faird
weel-faur'd
weel-faurt
weed-grown
weediness
weepiness
weepingly
weetingly
weedicide
weevilled
wreakless
wreck fish
wreckfish
wreck buoy
wheelbase
wheel race
wheel-less
wheelsman
wheel lock
wheelwork
wheel spin
wheel arch
weeknight
wherryman
whet-slate
whensoe'er
whetstone
wheatmeal
wheat germ
wheat bird
wrestling
wheat moth
wheatworm
wheat corn
wheat crop
wofulness
wafer cake
wafer-thin
waghalter
Wagnerite
Wagnerism
Wagnerian
Wagnerist
waggishly
W S Gilbert
wagon-lits
wagons-lit
wagonload
wagon roof
wagon lock
wagenboom
wagonette
wager boat
wage slave
wages slip
wages fund
Wahhabism
Wahabiite
Wahabiism
Wehrmacht
writative
wait about
whimberry
whinberry
whipcordy
weirdness
waiterage

whiteface
white race
white sale
whiteware
whitewash
write-back
Whitehall
whitewall
white damp
whitebass
white hass
whitebait
white salt
✧white lady
whitehead
white lead
white teak
white cell
whitebeam
white seam
white-seam
white bear
whiteness
writeress
white heat
white meat
white rent
white-shoe
white lime
white line
White Nile
white pine
white wine
waitering
whitening
whitewing
white fish
whitefish
whitelist
white flag
write-once
white gold
whitewood
white hole
white hope
white rose
white book
white coal
white worm
write down
write-down
whitecoat
white port
white iron
while away
write away
whifflery
whiffling
wait for it!
whip graft
whip-graft
whingeing
wriggling
wring bolt
weigh-bauk
weighable
weighting
weightily
weigh into
weigh down
whichever
whininess
wailingly
waitingly
whiningly
wrinklies
whisky mac
whiskered
whirligig
whirlwind
whirl bone
whirlpool
writ large
whillywha
whirl away
whinnying
whipper-in
whimperer
whisperer
whip round
wait state
whip snake
whipstaff
whipstall
whimsical
whinstone
whipstock
waistband
wristband
wait table
waist-deep
whistle up
waistless
waistbelt
wrist shot
waistline
whistling
whittling
waist-high
waistboat
waistcoat
wrist drop
whittawer
Whitworth
whizz-bang
wakeboard
Wakefield
wakefully
Wokingham
wake-robin
Will Adams
wellanear
walkathon
welfarism
welfarist
well-aimed
wall a rope
walkabout
wild about
wallboard
wellbeing
well-built
wall brown
well-borer
wild birds
wolfberry
wallchart
wall cress
wild child
Walachian
well drain
well-doing
wolverene
willemite
wolverine
wulfenite
weltering
wildering
wyliecoat
Waldenses
well-famed
well forth
well-found
waldflute
wall fruit
waldgrave
wild grape
wildgrave
Wild Geese
Weltgeist
wild goose
well-given
Welsh harp
Welshness
wild honey
Welsh hook
wolfhound
wellhouse
Welsh aunt
Walvis Bay
willingly
wolfishly
wolvishly
Will Kempe
well-known
well-lined
well-meant
wild mango
walk on air
welcomely
wild olive
walloping
wallowing
welcoming
willowish
Waltonian
well-oiled
willow tit
wall plate
wild pansy
wallpaper
Will Parry
well put on
willpower
wall space
wolf's bane
wolfsbane
well smack
Weltstadt
well-spent
Wiltshire
Will Smith
wolf's claw
wolf's foot
well-set-up
Wolfsburg
wild track
well-tried
well-timed
wolf tooth
wild thyme
Welsummer
well woman
well worth
wild water
welly-boot
wallydrag
waltz into
wambenger
wimpishly
Wimbledon
womanless
womankind
womenkind
womanlike
women's lib
womanhood
womenfolk
woman-born
Woman's Own
woman post
woman-body
womaniser
womanizer
wink-a-peep
windbreak
windblown
windborne
windburnt
wineberry
windbound
wing chair
wind chart
wind chest
wind chill
Wonderbra®
winter bud
winged elm
wonderful
winterise
winterize
wandering
wondering
Wenceslas
wonderous
Winter War
wineglass
wind gauge
win the day
wanchancy
windhover
windiness
wonkiness
wanting in
wincingly
windingly
winkingly
winningly
winkle out
window bar
window box
winsomely
wantonise
wantonize
wincopipe
windowing
winnowing
window tax
winepress
windproof
wine party
wind power
wind round
wind-shak'd
windshake
wing snail
wing shell
wind shear
windswept
wind-swift
wine-stone
windstorm
windtight
wang tooth
windthrow
wine vault
windwards
Windy City
wood avens
wood ashes
woodblock
wood-borer
woodcraft
woodchuck
wholesale
woomerang
whore's egg
wholemeal
wholeness
whole milk
wooden leg
wholefood
whole note
wholesome
whole tone
whole step
woodentop
wood fibre
wood flour
wrongness
wrong side
wrongdoer
wrong-foot
wrought-up
wood honey
woodhorse
woodhouse
woodiness
wooziness
whorishly
wholistic
woodlands
woodlouse
woodmouse
wood nymph
whosoever
wood paper
whoop it up
woodreeve
wood stamp
wood sugar
woodspite
woodstone
woodshock
woodscrew
whodunnit
who but she
woodwaxen
wipe-clean
wapper-jaw
Wuppertal
wapentake
wapenshaw
wapinshaw
warfaring
warranted
war-wasted
warrantee
warranter
warrantor
wordbreak
word-blind
workbench
✧warmblood
waribashi
wart-biter
wordbound
wire brush
word class
wart cress
wire cloth
World War I
World Bank
wiredrawn
warp drive
world line
worldwide
worldling
world-view
worseness
work ethic
wernerite
Wernerian
workerist
warden pie
war kettle
worm-eaten
✧worcester
worse luck
War Office
workfolks
worm fence
warm front
workforce
worm fever
wire guard
wire glass
wire grass
worm grass
workgroup
wire gauge
wire gauze
worthless
wormholed
workhorse
warehouse
workhouse
worriedly
wordiness
worminess
worriment
warningly
worrisome
Wurlitzer®
warble fly
workmanly
work of art
word order
warmonger
warlockry
war bonnet
workplace
workpiece
wirephoto
work party
wardrober
worksheet
wordsmith
word salad
work study
worst case
worst-case
worktable
wire wheel
worm wheel
workwoman
worrywart
worry down
worryguts
wassailer
wassailry
westabout
washboard
wash badly
washbasin
westbound
wisecrack
washcloth
wasteland
waste gate
wasteness
wasterful
waste pipe
wasterife
westering
washerman
wasserman
✧westerner
waste book
washed-out
waste away
wishfully
wistfully
wasegoose
washhouse
washiness
wispiness
washing-up
waspishly
Westmeath
Wisconsin
washstand
wasp's nest
wasps' nest
wasp-stung
West Saxon
wish to God
wasp waist
wise woman
Westworld
westwards
with a will
witwanton
with a bump
with child
withdrawn
witherite
withering
wuthering
witnesser
witlessly
watchcase
wet the bed
watchable
witchmeal
witch's hat
watch fire

witchlike
witch-wife
watch bill
witchknot
watchword
witchetty
witch hunt
withhault
watch over
wittiness
wittingly
witticism
wattmeter
wit-monger
withouten
water gage
Watergate
water gate
water rate
water wave
water-wave
water bath
water cask
watermark
waterfall
water gall
water rail
water sail
water main
water cart
water head
waterweed
water leaf
water deck
water cell
water seal
water fern
water bear
water deer
water lens
waterless
watershed
water-shot
water bird
waterline
water pipe
water rice
waterside
water vine
water mill
water sign
water lily
water-ski'd
water flea
water flag
water flow
Waterford
water core
water-core
water hole
water mole
water pore
water vole
water gong
water cock
waterwork
water-cool
waterfowl
water down
water-worn
water polo
water poet
water drop
water cure
waterbuck
water bull
water jump
water pump
water butt
withstand
withstood
withywind
with young
woundable
woundless
would that
woundwort
waulkmill
whunstane
wave aside
wavefront
waveguide
wavellite
wavemeter
wove paper
wave power
waveshape
wave train
wax tablet
wax flower
wax insect
waxworker
wax pocket
wax myrtle
way warden
waywardly
wayfaring
waylaying
wry-necked
way of life
wayzgoose
X-particle
xylograph
xyloidine
xylometer
Xylophaga
xylophage
xylophone
xylorimba
xenocryst
xenograft
xanthomas
Xanthippe
Xanthoura
xanthoxyl
xenomania
xenomenia
xenon lamp
xenophile
xenophobe
xenophoby
Xenarthra
Xiphiidae
xiphoidal
Xiphosura
xerochasy
Xyridales
xeroderma
xeromorph
xerophagy
xerophile
xerophily
xerophyte
xerostoma
yravished
year-round
year's mind
yeastlike
yobbishly
yacht race
yacht club
yachtsman
Yiddisher
yieldable
Yogi Berra
Yggdrasil
yo-heave-ho
yohimbine
Yajurveda
yoke-devil
yakety-yak
yakity-yak
yellow-boy
yellow dog
yellowfin
yellowish
Yellow Sea
yolk stalk
yammering
Yom Kippur
Yankee bet
Yankeedom
Yankeeism
Yanomamis
Yanomamos
yuppiedom
yuppie flu
yerba maté
yird-house
yersiniae
yersinias
yard of ale
Yaroslavl
Yorkshire
yardstick
Yossarian
✧yesterday
yestereve
yeshivahs
Yoshihito
yeshivoth
yes sirree
yattering
ytterbium
you name it
you beauty
young lady
youngness
youngthly
youngling
young fogy
youngster
✧young turk
young-eyed
youthhead
youth club
youthhood
youthsome
yawningly
zealotism
zealously
Z particle
zwanziger
zebrawood
zibelline
Zechariah
Zacharias
zuchettas
zuchettos
zecchinos
zucchinis
zucchetto
Zacynthus
Zechstein
Zhengzhou
zoechrome
Zhenjiang
Zrenjanin
Zeebrugge
zoetropic
zigzagged
zygaenine
zygaenoid
zygomatic
zygantrum
Zugspitze
zygophyte
zygosperm
zygospore
Zwinglian
✧zeitgeist
zoiatrics
Zeller See
zillionth
zelatrice
zelotypia
zymogenic
zymologic
zymolysis
zymolytic
zymometer
zamindari
zemindari
zamindary
zemindary
zamboorak
zumbooruk
zymoscope
✧zinfandel
zinc-bloom
Zenocrate
zinc colic
zinkenite
zante-wood
zonked out
zanthoxyl
Zanzibari
zonal axis
zanamivir
zinc oxide
Zonuridae
zinc white
zoogamete
zoogamous
zoolatria
zoomantic
zooscopic
zootechny
zooperist
zoogenous
zookeeper
zoometric
zoophobia
zoothecia
zoophagan
zootheism
zoophilia
zoophoric
zoophorus
zoophytic
zoolithic
zoobiotic
zoogloeic
zooplasty
zoologist
zoonomist
zootomist
zoogonous
zoomorphy
zoosporic
zoography
zootrophy
zoocytium
Zephaniah
Zapodidae
Ziphiidae
Zeppo Marx
zapateado
zapotilla
Zapatista
Zoroaster
Zernebock
zirconium
zero-rated
zestfully
zitherist
Zeuglodon
zeugmatic

10 – odd

asarabacca
Ava Gardner
alabandine
anax andron
alabandite
anacardium
Adam and Eve
acatalepsy
acanaceous
at a tangent
Amarasimha
Anaxagoras
anapaestic
adamantean
adamantine
amarantine
anabaptise
anabaptism
✧anabaptist
agapanthus
Amaranthus
anabaptize
a fat chance
anarchical
Adam Cooper
anandamide
academical
amazedness
à la dérobée
arabesqued
Arabesques
amateurish
amateurism
at a venture
alang-alang
amalgamate
arachnidan
anaphylaxy
anachronic
arachis oil
Araliaceae
Anaximenes
Adamitical
avaricious
Arabian Sea
Alaska Time
a hall, a hall
availingly
at all hours
at all costs
anaglyphic
anaglyptic
alablaster
anaclastic
anaplastic
alarm radio
alarm-radio
alarm clock
alarmingly
à main armée
Alain Prost
anamnestic
Alain Juppé
araeometer
araeometry
acarophily
anagogical
analogical
anatomical
Anatotitan
apagogical
anabolitic
amatorious
Amazon-like
anamorphic
asafoetida
araeostyle
anacolutha
analphabet
acarpelous
Alan Parker
anadromous
at a premium
anatropous
anacrustic
Adam's apple
ad absurdum
avant-garde
anaptyctic
amantadine
alas the day
at a stretch
apartments
anastigmat
adactylous
anastomose
anastrophe
Alan Turing
avanturine
anarthrous
Anastasius
adaptation
adaptative
acanthuses
à haute voix
adaptively
a natura rei
Arafura Sea
à la Dubarry
amanuenses
amanuensis
ayahuascos
analysable
analyzable
analytical
anadyomene
at any price
amboceptor
ambidexter
abbreviate
Albigenses
ambagitory
ambulacral
ambulacrum
arbalester
arbalister
ambulation
ambulatory
albuminoid
albumenise
albuminise
albuminate
albuminous
albumenize
albuminize
albinistic
Ambarvalia
Albert Gore
amber wheat
arbor vitae
aubergiste
amber fluid
albarellos
Albert Roux
ambassador
ambuscados
albescence

ambushment
Ambisonics®
asbestosis
ambisexual
arbitrager
arbitrable
arbitrator
ambivalent
abbey-laird
abbey-piece
Amblyopsis
Amblystoma
archaicism
archaistic
Alcibiades
arcubalist
archbishop
accubation
arch-chimic
archdeacon
accidental
accidented
accrescent
arc welding
archerfish
alchemical
accredited
alcheringa
archeology
Archenland
archegonia
ance-errand
archetypal
arch-flamen
alcoholise
alcoholism
alcoholize
ascribable
arctic char
Archimedes
alcaicería
arctic hare
auctioneer
auction off
auctionary
architrave
ascription
arctic tern
Alcelaphus
accelerant
accelerate
accultural
ascomycete
accumbency
accomplice
accomplish
accumulate
accomptant
ascendance
ascendancy
ascendable
ascendence
ascendency
as concerns
ascendible
accentless
arcaneness
accentuate
Arctogaean
Alcyonaria
Arctogaeic
anchor buoy
Anchor Boys
anchoretic
anchor-hold
arctophile
arctophily
anchoritic
anchorless
aeciospore
anchor-ring
archonship
archontate
acceptance
acceptancy
acceptable
acceptably
accept bail
acceptedly
arch-priest
arch-pirate
ancipitous
accordance
accordancy
ascariasis
accordable
accursedly
accurately
accostable
accessible
accessibly
accusement
accusingly
accustomed
access road
ancestress
access time
accusation
accusatory
accusative
asceticism
ad crumenam
accoutered
accoucheur
accoutring
account day
accountant
accounting
account for
anchylosed
anchylosis
audibility
abdication
aide-de-camp
addle-pated
Andrew Marr
Andrew Neil
André Brink
address bus
and what all
aldohexose
Andy Irvine
Andalusian
aedileship
andalusite
and all that
Andaman Sea
abdominous
aid and abet
andantinos
Andromache
andropause
Andromaque
androecial
androecium
audiometer
androgenic
audiometry
audiophile
androphore
Andronicus
and so forth
audiograph
and upwards
aldermanic
aldermanly
aldermanry
adderstone
adder's-wort
Abdus Salam
Addis Ababa
additament
additional
auditorial
audit trail
auditorium
Andy Warhol
Alexandria
alexanders
aceraceous
arenaceous
avenaceous
ametabolic
adelantado
arena stage
arefaction
acetabular
acetabulum
Azerbaijan
amerceable
amerciable
amercement
agency shop
Aberdonian
a lead towel
anecdotage
amendatory
anecdotist
aberdevine
ateleiosis
adenectomy
Aberglaube
areography
avengement
avengeress
acephalous
acetic acid
Americanos
Amerindian
ameliorate
amenity bed
amenity kit
a week today
areolation
anemometer
anemometry
anemophily
adenovirus
amenorrhea
axe to grind
anemograph
Areopagite
axe-breaker
age-bracket
a near thing
aberrantly
Averrhoism
Averrhoist
aneurismal
aneurysmal
aberration
averseness
asepticise
asepticism
asepticize
anesthesia
avertiment
azeotropic
a peg too low
a better bet
aventurine
Abel Tasman
agentivity
asexuality
adequately
adequative
à merveille
acervately
acervation
à deux mains
acetylenic
affability
affectedly
affectless
Alfred Jodl
affeerment
affricated
affrighted
affrighten
afflicting
affliction
afflictive
affiliable
at full pelt
Aufklärung
affinitive
affronting
affrontive
affirmance
affirmable
affordable
affettuoso
affluently
aggravated
Afghan coat
aggrandise
aggrandize
angwantibo
algebraist
angled deck
angleberry
angler fish
aigre-douce
angledozer
Anglepoise®
aggression
aggressive
anguifauna
Anguillula
anglistics
angel-water
Angel Falls
algolagnia
algologist
angel's hair
angelshark
angelology
Angel Clare
avgolemono
angularity
angulation
argumentum
argon laser
Argun River
at gunpoint
Algonquian
argonautic
✧anglomania
Anglo-Saxon
✧anglophobe
✧anglophile
✧anglophone
angiosperm
Anglo-Irish
algophobia
Apgar score
argyrodite
auger-shell
Angaraland
algarrobos
augustness
Augustulus
arguteness
agglutinin
ashlar-work
Athabascan
Athabaskan
adhibition
aphidicide
Ashkenazim
achievable
aphaeresis
at half-cock
anhelation
anhungered
Athanasian
Athanasius
achromatic
achromatin
aphrodisia
Athapascan
Athapaskan
athermancy
abhorrence
abhorrency
a short fuse
atheromata
Acherontic
anharmonic
aphoristic
adhesively
Achitophel
animalcula
animalcule
Anita Desai
agitatedly
animatedly
acinaceous
Animal Farm
Arimaspian
animal pole
anima mundi
animadvert
amiability
a rivederci
alineation
alimentary
abiogenist
arithmetic
Ahithophel
apitherapy
a tight spot
adipic acid
acidically
acidimeter
acidimetry
aficionado
acidifying
axiologist
Alismaceae
axiomatics
axiomatise
axiomatize
Asian Times
alienation
axinomancy
anisotropy
amino group
adiaphoron
acieration
aristocrat
Asiaticism
aristology
Aristippus
aciculated
Avicularia
Aviculidae
abiturient
apiculture
aviculture
adjectival
adjacently
abjectness
adjudicate
adjudgment
abjunction
adjunction
adjunctive
abjuration
adjuration
adjuratory
adjustable
adjustably
adjustment
awkwardish
alkyd resin
ankle-chain
ankle-biter
ankle strap
alkalinise
alkalinity
alkalinize
ankylosaur
alliaceous
allhallond
allhallown
able-bodied
all-obeying
allochiria
aplacental
allycholly
allocation
allocution
all telling
all-terrain
all-weather
alla Franca
allegeance
allegiance
allegretto
allogamous
allegorise
allegorist
allegorize
allegation
alligation
all the best
All Shook Up
all the rage
all the same
all the time
all-firedly
all-time low
allnighter
all-play-all
alla marcia
allometric
Allen screw
Allan-a-Dale
at long last
allonymous
at long stay
all and some
aplanatism
All for Love
allhollown
all-rounder
allophonic
alloparent
allopathic
allopatric
allargando
all-dreaded
allergenic
Auld Reekie
allurement
alluringly
able rating
able seaman
allosteric
arles-penny
Allosaurus
allusively
aglet babie
allotheism
ablutomane
allotropic
alliterate
all-purpose
alleviator
all-overish
almacantar
almucantar
armadillos
Armageddon
armigerous
almsgiving
armillaria
atmologist
arms-length
ammoniacal
ammoniated
ammoniacum
almond-eyed
administer
almond-tree
admonition

ammunition
admonitory
admonitive
armipotent
admiringly
admiration
admirative
admiraunce
atmosphere
admissible
admittance
admittable
admittedly
armour-clad
armourless
Anne Boleyn
Anne Brontë
anno Domini
Annie's Song
abnegation
annihilate
annuity due
annularity
annalistic
annulation
annunciate
annuntiate
abnormally
Anna Sewell
annotation
annotative
annexation
annoyingly
anonaceous
agoraphobe
aloha shirt
apocarpous
apolaustic
✧apocalypse
amoebiasis
amoebiform
avouchable
avouchment
a good thing
above-named
above water
aposematic
apodeictic
adolescent
a sore thumb
above board
above-board
apopemptic
above price
azobenzene
Adolf Meyer
alongshore
a long purse
apothecial
apothecary
apothecium
apophthegm
anopheline
apochromat
apotheoses
apotheosis
apophyseal
apophysial
abominable
abominably
atomically
abominator
atomic bomb
agonisedly
agonizedly
atomic fuel
✧aboriginal
apolitical
agonic line
atomic pile
agonistics
atomic time
a-cockhorse
Aboukir Bay
apoplectic
Apollonian
axoplasmic
à bon marché
acorn-shell
abonnement
anointment
aroint thee
apologetic
apomorphia
aeolotropy
acolouthic
acolouthos
akolouthos
aposporous
apocryphal
apotropaic
apocryphon
apotropous
apoprotein
ahorseback
acoustical
anoestrous
à l'outrance
aborticide
apostolise
apostolate
apostolize
abortional
a soft touch
apostrophe
apostatise
apostatize
abortively
acotyledon
agony uncle
appearance
appealable
appeasable
applauding
alpha decay
alphabetic
alphameric
alphametic
Alpha Romeo®
applausive
appraisive
aspectable
ampicillin
aspidistra
apple sauce
aspherical
appreciate
apple-woman
at pleasure
apprentice
arpeggione
arpeggiate
amphimacer
applicable
applicably
applicator
amphiscian
Amphineura
amphimixis
amphibious
amphibolic
amphibrach
Amphitryon
amphictyon
ampliation
ampliative
appointive
amplifying
ampelopses
ampelopsis
Alpine Club
appendices
appendixes
Alpine race
alpenstock
approvance
approvable
approaches
amphoteric
approximal
Alphonsine
apperceive
asparagine
ampere hour
aspergilla
apparelled
apparently
aspiringly
as per usual
asperities
apparition
aspiration
aspiratory
au pis aller
appositely
apposition
appositive
ampussy-and
appetising
amputation
appetition
appetitive
appetizing
asphyxiant
asphyxiate
acquainted
at question
acquirable
acquitment
acquitting
aequo animo
acroamatic
Adrian Mole
A Dream Play
air-marshal
air-passage
airmanship
abreaction
abreactive
Adriamycin®
aerobiosis
aerobiotic
acrobatics
aerobatics
acrobatism
auriculate
Africander
Africanoid
Africanise
Africanism
Africanist
Africanize
atracurium
aprication
abridgable
abridgment
arrière-ban
aero-engine
aerie light
acriflavin
air-officer
auriferous
aerography
aerogramme
aérogramme
arrogantly
arragonite
acrogenous
aeruginous
abrogation
agrégation
arrogation
abrogative
Abraham-man
arraigning
adroitness
Afrikander
air cleaner
air-bladder
aerologist
agrologist
acrylamide
acre-length
acrolithic
acromegaly
atramental
aerometric
acronychal
abranchial
aerenchyma
adrenaline
agronomial
agronomics
aeronomist
agronomist
acronymous
adrenergic
apron-stage
aeronautic
air-cooling
air hostess
Aureomycin®
abruptness
acrophobia
acrophonic
aerophobia
aerophobic
air freight
air-freight
afrormosia
airbrushed
air-grating
aerostatic
arrestable
across lots
arrestment
abrasively
aerotactic
aerotropic
acroterial
acroterion
acroterium
air station
amritattva
air-cushion
air support
air curtain
aardwolves
arrow-grass
arrhythmia
arrhythmic
assibilate
✧associated
associable
associator
answerable
answerably
answer back
abstergent
austenitic
abstemious
answerless
arsmetrick
abstersion
abstersive
abstention
assafetida
assignable
assignment
aesthetics
Anschauung
assailable
Aussiedler
abstinence
abstinency
auspicious
assailment
assoilment
abscission
adsuki bean
Ansel Adams
aes alienum
absolvitor
absolutely
absolution
absolutory
absolutism
absolutist
assemblage
assimilate
assumingly
✧assumption
assumptive
assentator
absente reo
absinthism
assentient
assonantal
absorbable
adsorbable
assertable
abstracted
abstracter
abstractly
abstractor
absorbency
assurgency
absorbedly
Australian
Australoid
Australorp
australite
assortment
austringer
absurdness
aes triplex
abstrusely
absorption
adsorption
absorptive
adsorptive
assistance
assessable
assessment
assythment
auscultate
assaultive
asseverate
assay-piece
✧astragalus
astral body
actualités
antiaditis
art gallery
attractant
attracting
attraction
attractive
actability
antebellum
antibiosis
antibiotic
antechapel
autocratic
attachable
attackable
arty-crafty
antecedent
anticlimax
anticlinal
articulacy
astacology
autecology
Articulata
articulate
altocumuli
attachment
arts centre
anticipant
anticipate
Attic order
Antichrist
artocarpus
antecessor
Antichthon
autochthon
anticivism
autodidact
antidromic
Aethelbert
at the ready
antiemetic
at the least
at the wheel
anthelices
antheridia
at the slope
antler-moth
autoerotic
at the worst
Aethelstan
anthersmut
Aethelwulf
anthemwise
artificial
antifreeze
act of grace
autography
astigmatic
autogamous
autogenics
antagonise
antagonism
antagonist
autogenous
antagonize
altogether
act the fool
act the goat
anti-heroic
art therapy
attainable
Antoinette
astringent
attainment
auto-immune
Aethiopian
astriction
attainture
astrictive
antilogous
autologous
antilopine
autumnally
automobile
attempered
antimonial
antimonide
antimonate
antimonite
ante mortem
antimerism
antimasque
antimatter
automatons
automation
automatise
automatism
automatist
astomatous
automotive
automatize
attendance
attendancy
attenuated
attenuator
ante-Nicene
attentions
actinolite
antinomian
autonomics
attendment
attunement
autonomist
antonymous
autonomous
Anton Dolin

art and part
Antony Sher
astonished
attend upon
anthomania
actionable
actionably
astrolatry
astrometry
action film
Antiochian
Antiochene
anthophore
authoriser
authorizer
astrobleme
authorless
astrologer
astronomer
astrologic
astronomic
Anthonomus
action plan
act your age!
authorship
art pottery
Art Nouveau
autophagia
autoplasty
✧antipodean
autoptical
antepenult
antiphonal
antiphoner
antiphonic
autophobia
antiproton
antipathic
antiquated
alternance
afterwards
aftersales
asteriated
alternatim
altar-rails
afterpains
alternator
aftertaste
anthracoid
anthracene
anti-racism
anti-racist
anthracite
asteridian
apterygial
Apterygota
aftershock
aftershaft
autarchist
aftershave
asteroidal
autarkical
afterpiece
altarpiece
Asteroidea
after-light
afterbirth
arthralgia
arthralgic
after blood
altar-cloth
after-image
attirement
attornment
arthromere
afterworld
anteriorly
after hours
astarboard
Arthropoda
anthropoid
aftergrass
asterisked
after a sort
Antarctica
altar-stone
alteration
alterative
after-guard
afterswarm
antistatic
attestable
antisocial
artistical
anti-Semite
altisonant
autoscopic
antisepsis
antiseptic
autostrada
antiserums
altostrati
antisexism
antisexist
antisyzygy
antitrades
antitragus
antitheses
antithesis
antithetic
antitheism
antitheist
autotheism
autotheist
autoteller
altitonant
astuteness
autotrophy
Arthur Ashe
Arthur Dent
astounding
Arthuriana
artfulness
altruistic
act curtain
active life
active list
antivenene
activeness
activities
activation
autowinder
Artaxerxes
altazimuth
Ahura Mazda
at unawares
a but and ben
aquabatics
abundantly
acute angle
aqua fortis
aquafortis
acuminated
anucleated
Adullamite
aquamanale
aquamanile
aquamarine
aquaplaner
aquaphobia
aquaphobic
aquarobics
a quarter to
Aquariuses
aqua Tofana
adulterant
adulterine
adulteress
adulterise
adulterate
adulterous
adulterize
advice-boat
arvicoline
advice note
advocation
advocatory
avvogadore
advantaged
advance man
adventitia
Adventists
Ahvenanmaa
adventurer
alveolitis
at variance
adversaria
Alvar Aalto
advertence
advertency
advertiser
advisement
advisorate
advisatory
anxiolytic
amylaceous
aryballoid
arytaenoid
asynartete
asynchrony
amygdaloid
amygdalate
anywhither
atypically
asymmetric
Asymmetron
anyone else
Amy Johnson
asymptotic
Abyssinian
asyntactic
asystolism
amyotrophy
Alzheimer's
adzuki bean
bragadisme
Bramah-lock
blancmange
branchiate
branch line
branchless
branch-work
board-wages
by and large
brandy-ball
bearded tit
brand-image
beard-grass
bladder nut
brandy snap
brandisher
beaver away
bearer bill
bearer bond
Braveheart
brazen-face
Beaker Folk
beakerfuls
beam-engine
brake-wheel
brake light
brake block
brake fluid
beaver lamb
brazenness
beaver-tree
blamefully
beaver-wood
braggingly
bear garden
braggartly
beau garçon
beach-la-mar
brachyaxis
brachydome
brachylogy
brachiopod
beachfront
brachyural
beach buggy
bear in hand
beatifical
braaivleis
Bratislava
bear in mind
beatitudes
bear in upon
brazil-wood
Beaujolais
Black Watch
blackfaced
black paper
blackwater
black magic
black Maria
black eagle
black earth
Blackbeard
blackberry
blackheart
blank verse
✧black death
black sheep
black chalk
Black Shirt
Blackshirt
blackthorn
black light
black widow
blackamoor
blacksmith
black snake
black money
✧black power
black robin
black vomit
blackboard
black house
black bread
✧black friar
black frost
black stump
Black Stone
blanketing
blanket bog
blanket box
black-bully
blackguard
by all means
beadlehood
beadleship
Brahman cow
brahmin cow
Brahmanism
Brahminism
bear market
biannually
boat-necked
brain fever
brain death
brainchild
braininess
brawniness
brain coral
brainpower
brain drain
brainstorm
brat packer
blasphemer
boat people
blanquette
boat racing
brass-faced
brass tacks
brass plate
brassiness
beadswoman
Bram Stoker
bean sprout
beam system
beast fable
beautician
blastocoel
bratticing
blastocyst
blastoderm
beat the rap
beat the air
beat the gun
beautifier
Blastoidea
blastomere
blastomata
brant goose
blastopore
beauty spot
boastfully
beatus ille
beam weapon
by any means
bradyseism
bradykinin
bob maximus
baba au rhum
Bob Paisley
baby boomer
Bible paper
Bob Newhart
baba ganouj
Bob Charles
biblically
bobbin lace
bibliology
bibliomane
bibliopegy
bibliophil
bibliopole
bibliopoly
Babbittism
baby-jumper
bubble bath
bubbly-jock
babblement
Babylonian
Babylonish
bubble over
bubble pack
bubble sort
babelesque
babblative
bibulously
bubble wrap
baby-minder
bubonocele
baby-ribbon
babiroussa
babesiasis
baby's-tears
babesiosis
baby-sitter
baby-walker
Bobby Sands
Bobby Davro
Bobby Unser
Bobby Jones
bobbysoxer
Bobby Moore
beccaficos
back boiler
back-blocks
back burner
back-burner
buck-basket
backbiting
backcombed
bucket down
bêche-de-mer
bacteremia
bacteremic
bucketfuls
bacterioid
bucketload
bucket seat
bucket shop
back-friend
backgammon
background
back garden
bacchantes
backhanded
back-hander
Bacchanale
bacchanals
buccinator
buck-jumper
buckle down
bacillemia
baculiform
backletter
bicultural
bicoloured
becomingly
Buchmanism
Buchmanite
backmarker
back margin
back number
back-office
Bucephalus
backpacker
buck-rabbit
bichromate
backspacer
back-spauld
backstairs
buck's party
bucks party
bucks' party
backsheesh
backstitch
backslider
backstreet
backstroke
bacitracin
back-to-back
backup file
backvelder
backworker
backwardly
Becky Sharp
bedraggled
body armour
bad manners
bad hair day
body colour
body carpet
body-cavity
body double
budgerigar
badderlock
bad feeling
bed-wetting
bed of nails
bed of roses
bodegueros
bedchamber
Buddhistic
Bedlington
by-drinking
bedellship
bedclothes
bidentated
bidonville
bad company
bed-hopping
body packer
body-popper
bedpresser
body search
body swerve
body-swerve
bedevilled
bed-swerver
body-warmer
bodyworker
buddy movie
Buddy Holly

buddy-buddy
beef-brewis
beefburger
beer-barrel
beer bottle
brecciated
breechless
beef cattle
bread sauce
bleed valve
breadberry
bleed white
bread knife
breadboard
breadfruit
breadcrumb
breadstick
bread study
breadstuff
beer engine
beekeeping
brevetting
by-election
beer garden
blethering
beech-drops
blepharism
breakdance
break gates
breakwater
break ranks
breakables
break of day
break sheer
break a jest
bierkeller
break cover
break point
breakpoint
Bleak House
break loose
break forth
Breakspear
break bread
break-front
break out in
beetle-eyed
beetlehead
beefmaster
beetmaster
beetmister
brewmaster
biennially
buenos dias
Brehon Laws
beer parlor
Brer Rabbit
bleary-eyed
bleariness
bienséance
breastbone
breast-deep
breastfeed
breast-high
breast-knot
bressummer
breast pump
Beer Street
breastrail
breast wall
breastwork
breathable
Brett Harte
breathless
beef tomato
brent goose
breath test
beeswinged
beef-witted
Bye Bye Baby
breezeless
breeziness
buffalo-nut
Bafta Award
buffer zone
befriender
buff-jerkin
bufflehead
bafflement
bafflingly
baffle wall
buffoonery
bifurcated
beforehand
before long
before that
beforetime
bufotenine
baggage-car
big science
big-bellied
big-hearted
bag of bones
bigamously
bigmouthed
Big Brother
bagassosis
Bagatelles
behind bars
behind-door
behindhand
behind post
behind time
behavioral
brigandage
brigandine
brigantine
blind shark
blindsight
blind alley
blind-alley
blind snake
blindingly
blind-drunk
blind trust
boil down to
baisemains
bride's-cake
bride's-maid
bridesmaid
bride price
boiler room
bridegroom
boiler suit
Bridgwater
bridgeable
bring about
bridge club
bridgehead
bling bling
bridgeless
bring under
bringing up
bring to bay
bring round
bring forth
Bridgeport
bridge roll
Bridgerama
Bridgetown
bridgework
blitheness
brightness
blithering
blithesome
brightsome
brightwork
Britishism
British gum
bailieship
bricklayer
brickmaker
brick-earth
brickfield
brickworks
brilliance
brilliancy
bridle-hand
bridlepath
bridle-road
bridle-rein
bridle-wise
Brian Bevan
Brian Moore
bairn's-part
blissed-out
blissfully
blister fly
blistering
boisterous
blitzkrieg
blizzardly
bijouterie
bejewelled
baked beans
bikini line
baking soda
Bella Abzug
Bollandist
ballabiles
bellarmine
belladonna
bellamoure
bolt-action
Bill Brandt
bell beaker
bull-beeves
bull-beggar
balibuntal
bill-broker
ball-barrow
Béla Bartók
ball-buster
bulk buying
Bill Bryson
bel-accoyle
bilocation
Bill Deedes
bulldog ant
belle laide
belle-laide
bilge-water
believable
balderdash
billet-doux
ballet-girl
billet-head
bullet-head
ballerinas
balneology
beliefless
Bill Edrich
belletrist
ballet shoe
bullet-tree
balneation
bull fiddle
ball-flower
bellflower
bald-headed
bull-headed
bellhanger
Bolshevise
Bolshevism
Bolshevist
Bolshevize
✧belshazzar
Billie Jean
bullionist
ballistics
ballistite
Bela Lugosi
bell magpie
Bill Murray
bull market
bolometric
bull-necked
Balanchine
Balenciaga
belongings
bilinguist
balconette
ball of fire
bill of fare
ballooning
balloonist
bill of sale
ball-player
billposter
bull-roarer
Balbriggan
bellringer
Belarusian
Belgravian
bell-shaped
Bell's palsy
balustered
bell-siller
ballsiness
balustrade
bell screen
Belisarius
bell the cat
Bill Tilman
Bill Tilden
belittling
bell-turret
bolstering
bolster out
balbutient
bolivianos
biliverdin
boll weevil
bellwether
belly dance
belly laugh
bellyacher
ballyhooed
Ballymoney
Billy Bones
Belize City
Bombay duck
bombardier
bump and run
bumbailiff
by my certie
bimodality
bumpkinish
bumble-foot
bimanually
bombolotti
bamboozler
bumfreezer
bimestrial
bimetallic
bomb-vessel
Bombycidae
banyan days
Bengal fire
bunya-bunya
bonkbuster
bank charge
binucleate
bank cheque
binoculars
Bing Crosby
band-clutch
bon accueil
✧benedicite
Benedictus
bent double
Bundesbank
bonded debt
bond energy
bonne femme
bank engine
bonnethead
banderilla
banker-mark
bonne grâce
Benzedrine®
Bundesrath
Bundeswehr
beneficial
beneficent
benefactor
bony fishes
benefitted
benefiting
benignancy
benighting
bone-headed
bondholder
Benthamism
Benthamite
bunchiness
bench press
bunch grass
bonnilasse
bantingism
bundle away
bandleader
Bangladesh
bunglingly
bonamiasis
benumbment
bandmaster
banana cake
banana kick
Bananaland
banana plug
banana skin
benzocaine
bandoleros
Band of Gold
Band of Hope
Ben Johnson
bongo drums
bon appetit
benzpyrene
binary code
Ben Bradlee
binary form
bankruptcy
binary star
ben trovato
boneshaker
bone spavin
bony spavin
banishment
bondswoman
band-string
bonus issue
bonesetter
bond-timber
binaurally
banqueteer
banqueting
benevolent
bandy-bandy
bandy about
Broca's area
brocatelle
brow-antler
browbeaten
browbeater
blow-by-blow
bookbinder
bioscience
bronchitic
bronchitis
bronchiole
bioecology
broad-based
broad-gauge
blood-wagon
Broad Scots
bloody-eyed
✧blond beast
bloody flux
boondoggle
broadsheet
bloody hand
broadpiece
blood-sized
blonde-lace
blood fluke
blood-plate
broadcloth
bloody Mary
broodingly
bloodiness
broodiness
blood-royal
brood-pouch
blood money
blood count
bloodhound
blood donor
blood horse
broidering
broad arrow
broadbrush
blood group
bloodstock
bloodstain
bloodstone
blood sugar
blood purge
blood-guilt
broadsword
bioreactor
broken-down
biogenesis
biogenetic
Broken Hill
broken home
biomedical
brokenness
biometrics
biodegrade
broken reed
brome-grass
buon giorno
book-holder
biochemist
biophysics
bromic acid
biotically
Brooklands
block gauge
bookkeeper
block-chain
block plane
blockboard
blockhouse
block grant
brook trout
bootlicker
bootlegger
bioplasmic
bootlessly
bookmobile
bookmaking
bootmaking
bookmarker
book-muslin
broomstick
broomstaff
brown sauce
brown paper
brown earth
browned off
Brown Betty
Brown Shirt
Brownshirt
brownfield
brown algae
brown snake
brown goods
brown jolly
brown bread
brown trout
brown study
brownstone
brown stout
brown sugar

Words marked ✧ can also be spelled with one or more capital letters

brown dwarf
Book of Amos
biopoiesis
Book of Ezra
biological
Book of Joel
Book of Life
biomorphic
Book of Ruth
biocontrol
biopolymer
biospheric
biographee
biographer
biographic
bookseller
blossoming
blossom out
boosterism
blottesque
brontosaur
Bronx cheer
booby hatch
biodynamic
booby prize
Bronze Star
bronze-wing
bipedalism
baptistery
bipolarity
bipinnaria
baphometic
bipartisan
bipetalous
bequeathal
biquintile
bergamasca
burra sahib
Barbara Pym
bureaucrat
Bernardine
Bernadette
Barnabites
barracking
bar-parlour
barcarolle
barracouta
barratrous
bursarship
barramundi
burramundi
Barnaby Day
Barbary ape
barebacked
bark-beetle
beribboned
bird-cherry
barter away
barley-bree
barrel-bulk
barley-broo
barred code
barleycorn
Berkeleian
Burmese cat
Barnet Fair
barrelfuls
Birkenhead
Barmecidal
borderland
borderline
borderless
barbellate
burnet moth
barrenness
Burne-Jones
bargeboard
barrel roll
burnet rose
burdensome
barber-shop
barbershop
barkentine
burnettise
burnettize
border upon
barley wine
barbed wire
barrenwort
barefooted
bareheaded
birthnight
birthright
birthplace
Bartholmew
barehanded
burgh court
bird-hipped
Barchester
Borchester
bur-thistle
birthstone
borghettos
bartizaned
barricados
Berlin blue
Barbie doll®
barking mad
Birmingham
Barrington
barring-out
burnishing
Barbirolli
bird impact
Barrier Act
Bar Mitsvah
Bar-Mitsvah
Barmitsvah
barbituric
Berlin Wall
Berlin wool
Bar Mitzvah
Bar-Mitzvah
Barmitzvah
barelegged
burglarise
burglarize
barometric
boringness
Barents Sea
baronetage
baronetess
Barons' Wars
bardolatry
burrow-duck
borrow hole
barrowload
Bar Council
bird of prey
barrow-tram
Bertolucci
bird-pepper
bordraging
bird-scarer
Barnstaple
barysphere
bird-spider
Burns Night
bird-skiing
Bergsonian
barasingha
Bergsonism
bird strike
Beres drops
birostrate
Barosaurus
barotrauma
burnt ochre
burnt umber
burnt cream
Bermuda rig
Berlusconi
barium meal
bird-witted
Barry White
bastard-bar
Bustard Bay
bastardise
bastardism
bastardize
byssaceous
boss around
bashawship
baseballer
base-burner
Bishen Bedi
basketball
basket case
Basse-Terre
Basseterre
basketfuls
basket-hilt
beseeching
basset horn
bespeckled
Boswellian
bushelling
Boswellise
Boswellism
Boswellize
bissextile
basketwork
bass fiddle
bush fruits
bass guitar
bus shelter
bush-harrow
bastinaded
bastinades
bestialise
bestialism
bestiality
bestialize
byssinosis
Bas Mitsvah
Bas-Mitsvah
Basmitsvah
Bas Mitzvah
Bas-Mitzvah
Basmitzvah
bush jacket
base jumper
bisulphide
basil thyme
bisulphate
basal plane
bush-lawyer
busy Lizzie
besom-rider
base-minded
bushmaster
bastnäsite
bishop-bird
Boston crab
bestowment
bassoonist
bishop's cap
bishopweed
basophilic
bescribble
bestridden
bestraddle
baserunner
bushranger
besprinkle
bestraught
busy signal
bestseller
Bass Strait
bush-shrike
besottedly
bushwalker
bisexually
bossyboots
bite and sup
batrachian
battailous
bit-mapping
Beta Crucis
Bette Davis
butter bean
butter-boat
bitter beer
butter-bake
better-ball
butterball
butter-bump
Battenberg
Battenburg
butter-bird
butterdock
butter dish
butterfish
better half
bitter-king
batteilant
bitterling
buttermilk
betterment
bettermost
betterness
bitterness
betweenity
bitter-root
bitter-spar
butlership
bothersome
butter-tree
butter-wife
bitterwood
butterwort
buttery-bar
bit of skirt
bit of stuff
bitchiness
butchering
Botticelli
bathing cap
bathing box
bathing hut
Bat Mitsvah
Bat-Mitsvah
Batmitsvah
Bat Mitzvah
Bat-Mitzvah
Batmitzvah
bottle bank
Betulaceae
bottled gas
battledoor
battledore
Betelgeuse
bottle-feed
bottlefuls
bottle-fish
batologist
bottle-head
bottle jack
battlement
bottleneck
bottle-nose
battleship
bottle shop
bottle tree
bituminise
bituminate
bituminous
bituminize
bitonality
Baton Rouge
button-back
buttonball
Battonberg
buttonbush
button cell
button-down
bathometer
buttoned up
buttoned-up
bottom fish
buttonhold
buttonhole
buttonhook
Bath Oliver
batholitic
batfowling
bottom-land
bottom line
bottomless
bottommost
bottomness
bottom upon
buttonwood
beta rhythm
bathyscape
bathymeter
bathymetry
botryoidal
bathylitic
Betty Allen
bluebreast
blue-bonnet
Bourbonism
Bourbonist
bluebottle
bounce back
blue cheese
bruschetta
bruschette
blue-collar
bounciness
bound water
B quadratum
Boulder Dam
blundering
bouldering
blue devils
Baudelaire
brute force
Blue Ensign
bluff it out
blue ground
bourgeoise
blue heeler
brushwheel
blushingly
Blue Horses
brush aside
bousingken
Bourignian
brutifying
bluejacket
bouillotte
Blue Monday
Blue Mantle
blue murder
Blue Mosque
Bruno Rossi
blue pencil
blue-pencil
brusquerie
blue riband
blue-riband
blue ribbon
blue-ribbon
blue rocket
blue-rinsed
beurre noir
bouts rimés
blue streak
blue screen
blue-screen
blues music
blue tongue
blue-tongue
bluethroat
blustering
blusterous
Blue Velvet
bivalvular
bivouacked
bowie knife
bow the knee
beweltered
bewildered
bowdlerise
bowdlerism
bowdlerize
beware lest
bow-fronted
bowerwoman
beware that
bewitching
bewitchery
bawdy-house
box-pleated
box-spanner
box profits
box Brownie®
Bay of Heats
bay the moon
boys in blue
bryologist
Bryan Adams
Bryan Ferry
beyond seas
buy and sell
bryostatin
boyishness
Buzz Aldrin
buzz phrase
bizarrerie
chaparajos
clarabella
chaparejos
Characidae
✧chamaeleon
coat-armour
Charadrius
chapatties
cravatting
charactery
chambranle
coal bunker
crabbiness
Chambertin
chambering
chamberpot
chamber-lye
chalcocite
Chalcidian
chalcedony
coal cellar
chancellor
chanceless
chanciness
Chaucerian
Chaucerism
coal-cutter
chance upon
chandlerly
chaud-mellé
Chandigarh
chandelier
chardonnay
chaudfroid
châtelaine
crane's bill
crane's-bill
cranesbill
coalescent
chapel cart
Clarenceux
crakeberry
crave after
clawed frog
Clare Short
czarevitch
✧crater lake
craterlike
coated lens
cravenness
Chaleur Bay
clawed toad
Charentais
coacervate
chauffeuse

chapfallen
chaffingly
changeable
changeably
chargeable
chargeably
Craig Raine
charge card
change down
charge down
change face
change gear
charge-hand
craigfluke
changeling
changeless
chargeless
cragginess
change over
changeover
clay-ground
clangorous
change tack
coal heaver
coach party
coach screw
cyathiform
coach-wheel
claw hammer
Clayhanger
coathanger
coach-horse
coach house
crash-proof
coach-stand
coachbuilt
cyanic acid
charitable
charitably
clarichord
clavichord
craniology
coati-mondi
cladistics
✧charioteer
craniotomy
clavicular
coati-mundi
clarifying
charity-boy
coadjacent
clamjamfry
coadjutrix
coadjutant
Clark Gable
clack valve
crack a crib
crankshaft
chank-shell
crank-sided
cracklings
crackajack
crack a joke
clankingly
chalkiness
crankiness
chalkboard
crack house
crackbrain
crack-tryst
chalkstone
chaologist
chaplaincy
chaplainry
challenged
challenger
crawlingly
crawlspace
cradle-song
✧charleston
chaulmugra
cradlewalk
claim a foul
chasmogamy
charmingly
clamminess
coalmaster
claymation
chain cable
Crab Nebula
chainwheel
channelled
channeller
channel-hop
channelise
channelize
chain-smoke
chainbrake
chauntress
chain grate
chain drive
clannishly
chain store
chatoyance
chatoyancy
coat of arms
clapometer
cyanometer
cyanogenic
Charophyta
cyanophyte
Charollais
coat of mail
clapped-out
champignon
clay pigeon
clasp knife
coal-porter
clappering
clapperboy
chairwoman
claircolle
chairborne
chairbound
chair-organ
classic car
chasse-café
chaise-cart
classicise
classicism
classicist
classicize
Chassidism
classified
classifier
coarse fish
chaiseless
classiness
coarseness
clanswoman
crab-stones
crassitude
chaussures
coastwards
✧chartreuse
chartulary
chaptalise
chaptalize
Clactonian
craft union
chasteness
chattiness
craftiness
charthouse
Chaetopoda
chattering
chatterbox
chaste tree
coaptation
craft guild
coastguard
✧chautauqua
coactivity
coagulable
coagulator
crapulence
chalumeaux
craquelure
chauvinism
chauvinist
Charybdian
chalybeate
crazy quilt
cabbage-fly
cubic metre
cubic nitre
cibachrome
cobwebbery
cuboid bone
cobalt bomb
cobalt-blue
caballeros
cabalistic
cabalettas
cabin fever
cabin class
cob cottage
cybernated
cybernetic
cyberphobe
cyberspace
cybercrime
cub-hunting
cockamamie
cock and pie
cocoa beans
cactaceous
cock a snook
cock-a-bondy
cockalorum
cockatrice
cockabully
cockchafer
Coco Chanel
cacodaemon
cicadellid
Cecidomyia
cockeye bob
cockernony
cacafuegos
cacography
cacogenics
cack-handed
cyclically
coccineous
cachinnate
cacciatora
cacciatore
cochleated
cucullated
Cochlearia
cockle boat
Cecil Sharp
cucumiform
cacuminous
cacomistle
coconut ice
coconut shy
coconut oil
cockneydom
cockneyish
cockneyism
cycloramic
cycloidian
cuckoldise
cuckoldize
cyclometer
cyclopedia
cyclopedic
cacao beans
cyclothyme
cuckoo pint
cyclograph
cyclo-cross
cuckoo-spit
cyclostyle
cyclostome
cock-paddle
cock-paidle
cacophonic
cucurbital
Ciceronian
cicisbeism
cocksiness
cocksurely
cecutiency
cicatrices
cicatrixes
cocktailed
cicatricle
cacotrophy
cacotopian
CúChulainn
cockyleeky
codicology
cudgelling
cudgel-play
caddie cart
caddis-case
cod-fishing
cod-fishery
codlin moth
caddis-worm
cuddlesome
codominant
code-number
Cader Idris
cider press
cadet corps
cadaverous
cod's-wallop
codswallop
coelacanth
coetaneous
✧cretaceous
crematoria
Caesarship
cheechalko
cheechakos
crescented
crescentic
crescendos
coercively
coercivity
crêpe paper
chevesaile
Clemenceau
✧clever dick
crewellery
crenellate
cleverness
coeternity
crêpe-soled
crève-coeur
credential
Clementina
✧clementine
clerestory
crewelwork
Cienfuegos
clergiable
clergyable
clew-garnet
Chekhovian
chevisance
chemically
creditable
creditably
credit card
chelicerae
cheliceral
chemisette
chewing gum
chemicking
credit line
credit note
cherimoyer
chemiatric
coexistent
check-taker
checklaton
cheekpiece
check digit
checkclerk
creakingly
cheekiness
creakiness
cheekpouch
checkpoint
cheektooth
Cherkesses
Chelmsford
cream-slice
creaminess
clean hands
cleansable
crew-necked
clean sheet
Caernarvon
cleromancy
chemotaxis
coelomatic
chemonasty
Ctenophora
ctenophore
coenobitic
coenosteum
coenocytic
Caerphilly
cheapskate
creepingly
creepiness
creepmouse
caespitose
cherry bean
cherry-coal
cheeriness
cherry-pick
cherry plum
Cherry Ripe
clear as mud
cherry tree
chevrotain
clearstory
cheerfully
Chelsea bun
cheesecake
clepsydrae
clepsydras
cheesed off
cheese-head
chessylite
cheesemite
cheesiness
chersonese
chessboard
cheesewood
cheesewire
crested tit
chew the fat
chew the rag
chew the cud
Cheltenham
creatinine
chestiness
creational
chest voice
cheat bread
creaturely
creatively
creativity
crenulated
chequebook
crepuscule
cheque card
cherubical
cherubimic
coequality
Che Guevara
chervonets
café au lait
caffè latte
coffee bean
coffer-fish
coffee mill
caffeinism
coffee room
coffee shop
coffee tree
café filtre
coffin bone
coffin nail
coffin ship
C S Forester
cog railway
cognisance
cognizance
cognisable
cognisably
cognizable
cognizably
cognominal
cigarillos
cogitation
cogitative
cohabitant
cohibition
cohibitive
cohune nuts
coherently
cohesively
chinaberry
chinachina
China white
climatical
cuit à point
China goose
chitarrone
chitarroni
Chinagraph®
China grass
chivalrous
China aster
cuirassier
china stone
Chimborazo
chip basket
crib-biting
coincident
✧chinchilla
child abuse
childbirth
child's play
Childermas
childproof
childishly
child-study
Clive James
Chinese red
✧chinese ink
crise de foi
crime sheet
chimerical
Cricetidae
chiselling
Clive Lloyd
Crimean War
cri de coeur
chief-baron
chiffchaff
chiffonier
ca'ing whale
cringeling
cringingly
clinginess
clingstone
chip heater
crithidial
clish-clash
Chichester
clinically
criminally
critically
criticiser
criticizer
caipirinha
chiliarchy

chiliastic
crinkliest
chick flick
click-clack
chickenpox
chicken out
chicken run
Chick Corea
click-track
clinkstone
cricketing
chillingly
chilliness
cliometric
chionodoxa
Cairngorms
clientship
chimney can
chimney pot
chimney top
chiromancy
crinoidean
ceilometer
clinometer
clinometry
crinolette
crinolined
cnidoblast
chirognomy
chilopodan
chironomer
chironomic
chironomid
chirograph
Chiroptera
crippledom
chimpanzee
chirpiness
crispiness
crispbread
crispation
crispature
chinquapin
cribriform
cribration
crio-sphinx
criss-cross
cristiform
Cristofori
clistogamy
✧chittagong
chittering
chirurgeon
chirurgery
cliquiness
cuique suum
cajolement
caking coal
coking coal
calcar avis
collatable
collar beam
collarbone
cellar-book
collar cell
collateral
collagenic
culpa levis
collarette
calcareous
cellar-flap
Collatinus
Cilla Black
collarless
collar of SS
collar stud
collar-work
celebrated
calibrator
celebrator
Colubridae
Celebes Sea
calico-bush
calyciform
culiciform
cold chisel
Calico Jack
calyculate
call centre
calico-tree
calico-wood
Caledonian
cul-de-lampe
college cap
calceiform
colleagued
collegiums
collegiate
culver-keys
calceolate
calcedonio
culvertage
Colbertine
collecting
collection
collective
calefactor
California
cold fusion
Caligulism
caliginous
calf-ground
colchicums
colchicine
Colchester
call it a day
calcinable
cultivable
collimator
cultivator
Callicarpa
calciferol
calcitonin
Celtic Park
calliature
colliquant
colliquate
colliculus
columnated
columbaria
chlamydiae
chlamydial
chlamydias
chlamydate
column inch
calumniate
calumnious
columellae
columellar
calamander
calamondin
calamancos
colemanite
calamitous
calendarer
colonnaded
Colin Davis
colonially
Colin McRae
Colin Meads
cylindroid
culinarily
cylindrite
Celtomania
colposcope
colposcopy
Cellophane®
Ciliophora
coleorhiza
cellobiose
collograph
colportage
coleoptile
call option
Coleoptera
colporteur
colloquial
calmodulin
collocutor
colloquise
colloquist
colloquium
colloquize
collotypic
Cole Porter
calyptrate
cold rubber
colorectal
caloricity
chlorodyne
chloridise
chloridate
chloridize
calorifier
chloroform
cultriform
cold-rolled
chloralism
chloralose
chloramine
chlorinise
chlorinate
chlorinity
chlorinize
celery pine
chlorophyl
chloroquin
celery salt
coloration
coloratura
colossally
calescence
call signal
calc-sinter
coltsfoots
colt's tooth
colostrous
colossuses
call to arms
call to mind
calotypist
cold turkey
colatitude
calculated
cellulated
calculable
calculably
colourable
colourably
culturable
culturally
calculator
colour code
colour-code
culture lag
colour film
colourfast
cellulitis
colluviums
colour line
colourless
cellulosic
colour-supp
calculuses
colourwash
collyriums
combatable
come-at-able
comparable
comparably
comparator
combat boot
commandeer
commandant
commanding
commandery
campaneros
campaigner
campaniles
compatible
compatibly
comparison
compatriot
come across
compass saw
compassing
compassion
compactify
compaction
compacture
campanular
campanulas
company man
companying
come before
comicality
comice pear
comic opera
comic strip
comedienne
comédienne
comedietta
cummerbund
commercial
compendium
competence
competency
campesinos
competitor
compelling
cumberless
cumberment
compearant
cumbersome
commeasure
compensate
campestral
commentary
commentate
campground
camphorate
come-hither
combinable
compilator
campimetry
commingled
Commiphora
cymbidiums
commitment
commission
commissary
commissure
committing
commixtion
commixture
comminuted
compliance
compliancy
compliable
complicacy
complected
complacent
complicant
complicate
complicity
cumuliform
camel's hair
complainer
complement
compliment
comeliness
complanate
camel-corps
camelopard
complotted
completely
completion
cumulation
completory
completist
completive
cumulative
compluvium
complexify
complexion
complexity
comanchero
camino real
commonable
compotator
campo santo
commonalty
common cold
componency
composedly
common frog
cameo-shell
commonhold
Compositae
compositor
commodious
compounder
commonness
common noun
common reed
common rail
common room
common seal
common toad
common time
comforting
composture
commonweal
cambric tea
compradore
camerlengo
comprehend
camerlingo
Camorrista
compromise
Cameronian
cembra pine
compressed
compressor
camera tube
cameration
cumbrously
camerawork
comestible
comstocker
cimetidine
camsteerie
come to heel
come to hand
cymotrichy
come to life
cometology
Camptonite
come to pass
come to rest
come to stay
come to that
comitative
communally
commutable
computable
commutator
computator
come undone
comburgess
communique
communiqué
camouflage
camoufleur
compulsion
compursion
compulsory
compulsive
combustion
combustive
cinnabaric
canvasback
connascent
convalesce
contadinas
cannabinol
contagious
cinnamonic
cantaloupe
centaurian
cantatrice
canvassing
contact man
contactual
confabular
connatural
canvas-work
cony-burrow
conscience
conacreism
cine camera
ciné camera
Canada lily
Canada rice
convenance
convex arch
conveyance
convenable
conveyable
candelabra
✧canterbury
cannel-coal
candescent
cinder cone
condescend
Concepción
canted deck
contendent
contending
confederal
✧conference
conférence
congeneric
congenetic
cankeredly
Cinderella
convexedly
convergent
converging
centesimal
congenital
candelilla
connexions
convenient
centesimos
cancelling
cannellini
cannelloni
cancellate
cancellous
conferment
centennial
concerning
convexness
cante hondo
cante jondo
cinder path
conferring
cancer root
consecrate
consensual
conversely
confessant
conversant
concession
confession
consension
conversion
condensery
condensate
concessive
concept car
conceptual
contextual
✧conventual
concentred
concentric

concertina
✧concertino
contestant
contesting
convertend
conception
confection
congestion
connection
contention
convection
✧convention
conjecture
consectary
contexture
concertise
concettism
concettist
convertite
conceitful
conceptive
congestive
connective
convective
concertize
consequent
confervoid
conservant
Cancer Ward
cankerworm
Cannery Row
coneflower
can of worms
coniferous
conchiform
conchiglie
conchoidal
conchology
cynghanedd
cinchonine
cinchonise
cinchonism
cinchonize
conchiolin
connivance
connivancy
cannibally
confinable
confidante
convincing
confiscate
confidence
confidency
connivence
connivency
continence
continency
cantilever
centimeter
considered
confiserie
centimetre
contingent
conoidical
consimilar
centiliter
concipient
conditions
consilient
centilitre
conciliary
conciliate
centillion
cantillate
Connie Mack
confirmand
confirming
consignify
cancionero
candidness
cincinnate
Cincinnati
concinnity
concinnous
centigrade
consistent
conniption
conviction
consistory
convictism
convictive
continuums
continuant
contiguity
continuate
continuity
contiguous
continuous
candle bomb
conglobate
candle-coal
canaliculi
concluding
candle-doup
confluence
candlefish
conclusion
conclusory
conclusive
candle-tree
conflation
conclavist
candlewick
candlewood
cinema-goer
cynomolgus
canonicals
canonicate
canonicity
Conan Doyle
canonistic
consonance
consonancy
condonable
consolable
cannonball
cannon bone
concordial
concordant
con sordino
condolence
canto fermo
canzonetta
canzonette
cannon-game
cannot help
cannon into
consociate
censorious
cantonment
conformist
conformity
confounded
confound it
conjointly
contour map
censorship
cannon-shot
concoction
contortion
consortism
consortium
concoctive
contortive
convoluted
Canopic jar
Canopic urn
conspectus
canophilia
cynophilia
canophobia
cynophobia
canephorus
conspiracy
conspirant
con spirito
centre-back
contraband
canary-bird
contrabass
contribute
contracted
contract in
contractor
centricity
contrecoup
contradict
congruence
congruency
centrifuge
contraflow
cancriform
centre-fire
congregant
congregate
centre-half
contrahent
centroidal
contre-jour
Central Bay
control key
controlled
controller
centreline
contraltos
control rod
centralise
centralism
centralist
centrality
centralize
centromere
contraplex
contraprop
contrarian
centre-rail
contrarily
cinerarium
canary-seed
centrosome
concretely
contritely
cineration
concretion
contrition
concretise
concretism
concretist
concretive
concretize
canorously
centre upon
contravene
controvert
canary-wood
cancrizans
Canis Major
canescence
Canis Minor
constraint
constringe
constantan
Constantia
constantly
constipate
cunctation
cunctatory
constitute
constative
cunctative
Conjugatae
cingulated
conjugated
censurable
censurably
confusable
confutable
conjugally
consumable
conjurator
conjunctly
confusedly
consumedly
conjure out
cinquefoil
conducible
confusible
consummate
cinque-pace
concurrent
concurring
conquering
conqueress
consulship
convulsant
concussion
convulsion
consubsist
concussive
convulsive
consuetude
consultant
consulting
conduction
consultory
conductive
consultive
centumviri
ciné vérité
candyfloss
condylomas
candy apple
candy store
crotalaria
chota hazri
clonazepam
Crotalidae
chocaholic
cholagogic
cholagogue
clotbuster
Coombs test
cool change
crotcheted
coomceiled
cloacaline
choiceness
choucroute
crop circle
crouch-ware
cloudscape
cloudberry
chondritic
chondritis
clog dancer
cloudiness
co-ordinate
chondromas
cropduster
cloddishly
chordotomy
cloud-built
cloudburst
close-range
close ranks
co-operator
closed book
Cronenberg
closed-door
chokeberry
choke chain
close thing
cooker hood
close shave
clove hitch
cloverleaf
choreology
closed-loop
closet play
choregraph
closed shop
close-stool
chose jugée
chopfallen
crow-flower
clogginess
cloth-eared
coolheaded
coolhunter
clodhopper
clothes-peg
clothes-pin
crocheting
cholic acid
cooling fan
cooling-off
clomiphene
choliambic
choriambic
choriambus
clofibrate
clockmaker
clock radio
crow-keeper
chock-tight
clock tower
clock speed
chockstone
clown about
choanocyte
Crown Derby
crown vetch
✧crown agent
crown-wheel
crown piece
crown glass
crown court
crown roast
crown green
crown graft
clownishly
chocolatey
chocoholic
crocoisite
choppiness
croupiness
choir organ
cross-hatch
cross-match
crosspatch
cross-ratio
cross hairs
cross-party
crossbench
cloistered
cloisterer
cross-refer
crosscheck
crosspiece
crosslight
chopsticks
cross aisle
crossfield
crossbirth
cross-slide
cross-claim
crossclaim
cross-index
crossandra
crossroads
crossbones
crossbower
cross-court
cross-armed
crossbreed
crow-shrike
cloistress
cross-dress
cross-staff
cross-stone
cross guard
caoutchouc
clostridia
clottiness
co-optation
co-optative
chorus girl
cephalagra
cephalitis
Cephalonia
cephalopod
Cap Haitian
Cape Breton
capability
capacitate
Cape doctor
cupid's dart
cupidinous
capodastro
co-presence
copresence
copperhead
copy-editor
capreolate
copper nose
copperskin
copperwork
copperworm
cup of assay
copyholder
captivance
capsizable
Capri pants
capriccios
cypripedia
copying ink
Cyprinidae
capricious
captiously
capillaire
capelletti
cipollinos
copulation
copulatory
copulative
Copenhagen
cup-and-ball
cup-and-ring
capnomancy
coprolalia
coprophagy
coprolitic
Cape pigeon
caper-sauce
copyreader
Capernaite
Cyperaceae
coparcener
Copernican
Copernicus
copartnery
capernoity
capitolian
capital sin
✧capitoline
capitulant
capitulary
capitalise
capitalism
capitalist
capitulate
capital sum
capitellum
capitalize
copy-typing
copy typist
copy taster
capotastos
capitation
cop it sweet
cappuccino
copywriter
coppy stool
coquelicot
coquetting
coquettish
coquimbite

Cortaderia
Curia Regis
coriaceous
cornaceous
curvaceous
carragheen
caryatidal
caryatides
caryatidic
curvacious
carjacking
corralling
carnallite
curtain off
carmagnole
cart around
carnassial
✧circassian
Carmarthen
currant bun
cardboardy
cornbrandy
cerebrally
cerebritis
cerebellar
cerebellic
curability
cerebellum
carabineer
carabinier
corybantes
corybantic
carabinero
care-crazed
Caricaceae
corncockle
curd cheese
card column
corn circle
card-castle
cork-cutter
corn-cutter
caricatura
caricature
corn-dealer
co-radicate
coradicate
corn dodger
Ceredigion
corn-dollie
corydaline
curselarie
cornerback
corned beef
carpet-bomb
curled dock
corselette
career girl
Carmelites
corregidor
Cordeliers
corsetière
corbelling
carpellary
carpellate
carpet-moth
cursedness
correspond
carpet plot
curled-pate
circensial
circensian
corbel step
carpet tile
cordectomy
cornettino
curvetting
correction
correption
Carpenters
correctory
cornettist
corrective
cornerwise
cornerways
cornflakes
corn-factor
cornflower
ceriferous
cerography
coregonine
Carl Gustaf
cork-heeled
card-holder
carphology
carthamine
Carchemish
cirrhipede
Cirrhopoda
Carthusian
cornhusker
cardiganed
corticated
cardinally
corrivalry
corrigenda
Cirripedia
cardiogram
corking-pin
cervicitis
corrigible
cardiology
cardialgia
cordillera
cordialise
cordiality
cordialize
carcinomas
carcinogen
carcinosis
carrier bag
carrier gas
cirrigrade
certiorari
cordierite
corbiculae
curricular
corniculum
curriculum
certifying
Carl Jacobi
corn-kister
coral berry
Carole Kidd
Carole King
Carolinian
coral snake
corylopsis
carelessly
corelation
corelative
chrome alum
ceramic hob
ceramicist
chromidium
chromogram
corn-maiden
corn-miller
caramelise
caramelize
chromomere
core memory
ceremonial
✧coromandel
ceruminous
coram nobis
chromophil
chromosome
chromatics
chromatype
chrome tape
chromotype
chrematist
chronicler
✧chronicles
chronicity
chronogram
Cerinthian
Corinthian
Carangidae
chronology
cor anglais
chronotron
coronation
caruncular
cartomancy
corporally
carbonados
corporator
cargo pants
Coriolanus
cordon bleu
Carlos Belo
carrot cake
carbon copy
carbon-copy
Carson City
cariogenic
corporeity
cartophile
cartophily
carpophore
cormophyte
corrodible
corrosible
carbonnade
cartonnage
cartoonish
cartoonist
corroboree
Carnoustie
carbon sink
carbofuran
carboxylic
coryphaeus
carapacial
corn popper
cire perdue
card reader
cornstarch
Cyrus Vance
Christabel
christener
corpse-gate
Christhood
corn spirit
cerastiums
chrysalids
Christlike
Christless
chrysolite
Chris Lloyd
Christmasy
Chris Smith
chrysophan
chrysotile
Chris Evert
carotenoid
carotinoid
cork-tipped
ceratopsid
curatorial
corn thrips
curate's egg
curateship
curatively
circulable
circularly
circulator
corrugator
carbuncled
corpuscule
circumcise
circumduce
circumduct
corpulence
corpulency
carbureter
carburetor
circumflex
circumfuse
curmudgeon
circummure
cornucopia
circumpose
curmurring
circuiteer
corruption
circuitous
corruptive
corpus vile
circumvent
Caravaggio
caravaneer
caravanned
caravanner
caravaning
corn weevil
cordwainer
cartwright
corn whisky
careworker
Carly Simon
carrying-on
cast anchor
custard pie
cistaceous
Costa Rican
cascarilla
Cossack hat
casualness
cast around
cast a spell
co-starring
casual ward
Casablanca
case-bottle
cost centre
cased glass
Cistercian
cosmetical
costean-pit
costeaning
cussedness
cashew nuts
Cisleithan
cos lettuce
cystectomy
case-harden
cuspidated
cosmically
castigator
cassia-bark
cosmic dust
cysticerci
casting-net
cash in hand
cash-in-hand
Caspian Sea
cessionary
cystinosis
Cassiopeia
cashiering
cosmic rays
cystinuria
cash-keeper
costliness
casemented
casinghead
cosentient
Cosa Nostra
cosmoramic
customable
cosmolatry
castor bean
cystoscope
cystoscopy
cestoidean
cosmogenic
cassolette
customised
customized
custom-made
cosmogonic
cosmopolis
cosmodrome
cystostomy
cismontane
cispontine
Cestracion
castration
cesarevich
cesarewich
casus belli
costus-root
cassumunar
caseworker
cottage pie
cat's-brains
catabolism
catabolite
cataclasis
cat's-cradle
catechesis
catechetic
catechiser
catechizer
catacumbal
CAT scanner
cytochrome
catechumen
city editor
cut a figure
catafalque
categorial
categories
categorise
categorist
categorize
catch-basin
catch a crab
catchpenny
catch light
catch sight
catchiness
catch-drain
cote-hardie
citric acid
cottierism
cuttle-bone
catalectic
cattle cake
cotyliform
cuttlefish
cataloguer
cattle grid
cytologist
catalogize
cataleptic
cattle prod
cattle show
cattle stop
cut flowers
catamenial
cytometric
Cotingidae
catananche
catenarian
catenation
✧cotton belt
cotton boll
cotton bush
cotton cake
Cotton Club
citronella
catholicly
Catholicoi
✧catholicon
Catholicos
cotton mill
cut corners
cottonseed
citron tree
cotton tree
cottontail
cottonweed
citron wood
cottonwood
cotton wool
cotton-worm
catapultic
cut up rough
cataphonic
cataphoric
cataphract
catoptrics
cat-cracker
catarrhine
catarrhous
coterminal
catastasis
Cat Stevens
cat-burglar
citrulline
citrus wood
cutty-stool
citizeness
citizenise
citizenize
courageful
courageous
coumarilic
crux ansata
crumbcloth
chubbiness
crumb-brush
Church Army
churchgoer
crunchiest
councilman
council tax
councillor
churchless
church-rate
church text
couscousou
churchward
churchyard
coup d'éclat
coup de main
chunderous
coup d'essai
causewayed
caulescent
chuff-chuff
chuffiness
club-footed
club-headed
crushingly
couch grass
caught up in
Cruciferae
cousinhood
Cousin Jack
cauliflory
cautionary
cousinship
cautiously
cauliculus
crucifying
chuckwalla
chuck wagon
chukka boot
Chuck Berry
chunkiness
chucker-out
couplement
churlishly
chumminess
crumminess
clubmaster
churn-drill
churn-staff
coulometer
coulometry
clumpiness
coursebook

counselled
counsellor
clumsiness
cruisewear
coursework
Count Basie
Count Paris
court-baron
crustacean
causticity
courtierly
count wheel
county hall
courtliest
crustiness
courthouse
Count Volta
counterman
counteract
court order
courtcraft
counterbid
cluster fly
clustering
counterspy
court dress
cluster-cup
countersue
county seat
courtesied
cruet-stand
crustation
county town
court guide
court sword
countryman
country-box
couturière
Cluny Abbey
Cavicornia
civic crown
cavefishes
cavil about
cavalierly
civil death
covalently
civil court
civilities
cavalryman
covenantal
covenanted
covenantee
covenanter
covenantor
covariance
covert coat
covered way
cover glass
cover point
cover price
cover drive
covetingly
cavitation
covetously
cavity wall
cowcatcher
cow-parsley
cow parsnip
cow-chervil
cowdie-pine
cowrie-pine
cowl-necked
cow college
coweringly
cowardship
cowpuncher
coxcomical
chylaceous
cryoconite
Clydesdale
clypeiform
Clydesider
cryogenics
cryometric
Ceylon moss
cryophilic
cryophorus
Cry Freedom
coyishness
cryoscopic
cryptogram
cryptogamy
crystal set
cryptology
✧cryptozoic
dramatical
draw a blank
draw a cover
diacaustic
Diana's tree
diamantine
dramaturge
dramaturgy
do away with
draw breath
drawbridge
drabbiness
dealbation
dearbought
Drawcansir
dead centre
diazeuctic
diagenesis
diagenetic
diapedesis
diapedetic
diabetical
Diadelphia
Diane Arbus
dealership
dialectics
drakestone
dead-finish
dwarfishly
dead-ground
draught-bar
draughtman
draught-net
deathmatch
deathwatch
deathwards
death adder
death metal
death-agony
death's-head
death throe
death angel
death knell
diaphanous
death-token
diachronic
death-wound
death house
death squad
diathermal
diathermic
diakinesis
draw it fine
drawing-pen
drawing pin
draw it mild
DNA library
diaskeuast
diallagoid
Dhaulagiri
deadlights
do a flanker
drawlingly
deadliness
dead-letter
dharmshala
deaf-mutism
drainpipes
drainboard
diagnostic
dead-nettle
diagonally
dragon arum
dragon boat
diamond-cut
diagometer
dragon-fish
dragonhead
deaconhood
diabolical
draconites
diaconicon
dragonlike
dragonnade
diatom ooze
dragonroot
deaconship
diacoustic
dragon-tree
Dracontium
dual-priced
dray-plough
deaspirate
diatribist
drag-racing
diagrammed
dead ringer
diarrhoeal
diarrhoeic
diagraphic
diatropism
dual school
deadstroke
draw-string
drawstring
draw stumps
diastaltic
diastemata
draftiness
draft horse
deactivate
dead-weight
dialysable
dialyzable
Dibranchia
de Beauvoir
debriefing
dabblingly
debilitate
debonnaire
debonairly
debentured
Dobson unit
debasement
debasingly
debateable
debatement
debatingly
dubitation
dubitative
debauchery
debouchure
de-blurring
declarable
declarator
declare war
declare off
declaredly
Dictaphone®
dictaphone
declaimant
declaiming
dictatress
declassify
decrassify
Doc Martens®
deck-bridge
duck-billed
docibility
Dick Butkus
decoctible
dickcissel
decadently
decreeable
decrescent
decree nisi
Dickensian
declension
Duc de Sully
duck-footed
decagramme
decigramme
decagynian
decagynous
decahedral
decahedron
deceivable
deceivably
declinable
declinator
dictionary
decollated
decollator
deckle-edge
duck-legged
decalogist
decolonise
decolonize
decolorant
dichlorvos
decolorise
decelerate
decolorate
decolorize
dochmiacal
decumbence
decumbency
Decemberly
decemviral
decimal tab
docimology
decimalise
decimalism
decimalist
decimalize
decampment
documental
decomposer
decompound
Decembrist
decompress
decamerous
dock-master
docimastic
decimation
dicynodont
decennoval
decandrian
decinormal
decandrous
diclofenac
doctor-fish
dichotomic
Dictograph®
doctorship
Doctor Slop
dice-player
decapodous
decipherer
deceptible
deceptious
decapitate
deck quoits
decurrency
dichroitic
dichromism
dichromate
decoration
decorative
decorously
decussated
decastichs
duckshover
decisively
decathlete
deck tennis
Dick Turpin
Docetistic
decoupling
decivilise
decivilize
duchy court
decryption
didactical
deductible
deducement
dedication
dedicatory
dedicative
didgeridoo
Dodie Smith
didelphian
didelphine
didelphous
didynamian
didynamous
Didunculus
didascalic
Die Walküre
die-casting
deep-browed
de-escalate
dread locks
dreadlocks
dreadfully
de-energise
de-energize
dietetical
dielectric
deep-freeze
dies feriae
deer forest
dregginess
die-sinking
dreikanter
deep litter
dreamscape
dreamwhile
dreamingly
dreaminess
Dream Songs
dream-world
dye in grain
Deep Purple
due process
drearihead
drearihood
dreariment
dreariness
deep-rooted
drearisome
deep-seated
dressmaker
dressed day
dress sense
dress shirt
deep-sinker
dress-goods
dyer's-broom
dressguard
deep throat
defeasance
defrayable
defragging
defeasible
defragment
defrayment
deflagrate
deficience
deficiency
defectible
defacement
defacingly
defecation
duffel coat
difference
differency
Def Leppard
deflection
deflective
diffidence
difficulty
defoliated
defalcator
defoliator
defilement
defamation
defamatory
defendable
defenceman
defenseman
definienda
defensible
defensibly
definement
definitude
definitely
definition
defunction
definitive
defunctive
deflowerer
daffodilly
difformity
deferrable
deformable
deformedly
deforciant
diffusedly
diffusible
degradable
dog-fancier
dog handler
dogmatical
dogmatiser
dogmatizer
digladiate
dog-parsley
dog's chance
dog's dinner
doggedness
daguerrean
degreasant
degression
digression
degressive
digressive
digger-wasp
dog's-fennel
dog biscuit
dignifying
daggle tail
degeneracy
degenerate
degenerous
digoneutic
dog-soldier
digestedly
digestible
digitiform
digitalise
digitalize
dog's-tongue
digitorium
digitately
digitation
dehydrater
dehydrator
dehumidify
dehumanise
dehumanize
dehiscence
drive shaft
drivelling
driverless
dying shift
driving-box
drink-money
drink-drive
drill-press
Deinoceras
deinothere

Djiboutian
daintiness
daisy-wheel
daisy chain
daisy-chain
dairywoman
daily dozen
Daily Sport
daily bread
dairy cream
dejectedly
dejections
dijudicate
dika-butter
dukkeripen
dyke-louper
dollar area
dollarbird
dollarless
Delia Smith
dollarship
dull-browed
deliberate
delibation
delectable
delectably
dilucidate
Dolichotis
dilacerate
delicately
dolichurus
dolcelatte
dolcemente
diligently
delegation
deligation
delightful
delphinoid
dolphin-fly
delphinium
Delhi belly
deltiology
dulciloquy
dilemmatic
delaminate
dolomitise
delimitate
dolomitize
delineavit
delineable
delineator
delinquent
dildo-glass
Dalton plan
Dalton's law
dill pickle
dilapidate
deliquesce
del credere
deliration
dolorously
dolesomely
delusional
doll's house
delustrant
delusively
dilettante
dilettanti
diluteness
dilatorily
dilatation

D H Lawrence
dull-witted
dilly-dally
delayingly
delayering
demeasnure
demobilise
demobilize
dumb blonde
democratic
Democritus
demi-cannon
damp-course
demodulate
demi-ditone
damselfish
demography
dameageable
demagogism
damagingly
Demogorgon
domoic acid
demoiselle
damping-off
dum vivimus
domain name
✧dumbledore
dimplement
demolisher
demolition
dime museum
demoniacal
demandable
Dominicans
diminuendo
dementedly
De Montfort
demonology
dominantly
demand pull
diminished
dominatrix
diminution
domination
demonetise
diminutive
dominative
demonetize
dumfounder
damson tree
Dame Pliant
demy quarto
demurrable
dimorphine
dimorphism
dimorphous
demoralise
demoralize
demureness
demirepdom
damasceene
dame-school
domestical
Damaskinos
damask plum
dumbstruck
damask rose
demoticist
dimethoate
demotivate
dumb waiter

dumpy-level
dummy whist
Donna Karan
dentaliums
Dundalk Bay
Dan Maskell
Ding an sich
dung-beetle
denudation
dance a bear
Denver boot
Dundee cake
danke schön
dancercise
Dundee City
dunderfunk
dinner-gown
dunderhead
dinner hour
dinner lady
danger line
dance floor
dinnerless
dinner-pail
donkey-pump
dunderpate
dinner-time
dance music
donkey vote
donkey-work
denigrator
Donegal Bay
denegation
dung-hunter
Dinah Craik
densimeter
densimetry
dentifrice
Dennis Tito
dynamicist
dynamogeny
denominate
dynamistic
dynamitard
✧dinanderie
dining-hall
denunciate
dining room
denervated
dendrobium
doner kebab
dendriform
dendrogram
dendroidal
dendrology
dendrophis
Danish blue
dynastical
Dane's blood
de nos jours
Dinosauria
dinosauric
denotement
dinitrogen
denaturant
denaturise
denaturize
donatistic
denotation
denotative
denouement

dénouement
Don Quixote
duniwassal
dandy-fever
dandy-horse
✧donnybrook
dandy-brush
Dan Aykroyd
denization
Deo favente
drop a brick
Dio Cassius
drop astern
Drones Club
duodecimal
duodenitis
duodecimos
do one's kind
✧diothelism
✧dyothelism
✧diothelete
✧diothelite
✧dyothelete
✧dyothelite
drop-hammer
Diophantus
✧diophysite
✧dyophysite
deoxidiser
deoxidizer
doorkeeper
Diocletian
drop-letter
drosometer
Deo volente
drosophila
deodoriser
deodorizer
deoppilate
droopingly
droop snoot
droopiness
Deo gratias
drowsihead
drossiness
drowsiness
drop serene
doomsaying
door-to-door
dioptrical
deontology
diorthosis
diorthotic
drogue bomb
depravedly
dupability
depletable
deprecable
deprecator
depredator
depreciate
dapperling
dapperness
depressant
depressing
✧depression
depressive
depth gauge
dip the flag
deprivable
duplicator

dapple-grey
depolarise
dopplerite
depolarize
depilation
depilatory
dependance
dependable
dependably
dependence
dependency
diplomatic
dipsomania
deplorable
deplorably
deployment
diprotodon
✧diplodocus
depopulate
dope pusher
do porridge
department
deportment
depuration
depuratory
depurative
departures
deposition
depositary
depository
depositive
Deputy Dawg
diphtheria
diphtheric
dipetalous
deputation
diphyodont
diphyletic
Dorian Gray
dermatitis
Dorian mode
dermatogen
dermatoses
dermatosis
durmast oak
Dermaptera
durability
direct cost
directions
direct mail
directness
deracinate
Directoire
directress
deridingly
Darjeeling
dirt-eating
dirt farmer
deregulate
deregister
derogately
derogation
derogatory
derogative
Dorchester
darning egg
Darlington
derring doe
dorsifixed
dérailleur
derailment

dorsigrade
dernier cri
durum wheat
dark matter
diremption
Duran Duran
Dermoptera
dirt-rotten
derestrict
derisively
durational
Dorothy bag
derivation
derivative
Dirty Harry
Derbyshire
dirty linen
dirty money
dirty trick
disparager
disparates
dispatcher
dispatches
diseaseful
Das Kapital
dissatisfy
déshabillé
dishabille
disbarment
disharmony
disgarnish
dismalness
discarnate
disdainful
doss around
dish aerial
despairing
despairful
dispassion
dismantler
disnatured
disability
desecrater
desiccated
desecrator
desiccator
disc camera
diseconomy
disadvance
desiderata
desiderate
desiderium
desperados
dissembler
disselboom
descendant
descendent
descending
Düsseldorf
descendeur
dissevered
disbenefit
Disneyfied
Disney film
desk editor
disherison
disheritor
disbelieve
dispelling
dispermous
discerning

disrespect
dishearten
dispersoid
distensile
dispersant
descension
dispersion
dissension
distension
dispensary
dispersive
distensive
dissecting
dissenting
disgestion
disjection
dissection
distention
disfeature
dissertate
dissective
disservice
disc floret
disc flower
designable
designator
designedly
designless
designment
dissheathe
dischuffed
dysthymiac
dysphemism
deschooler
discharger
disc harrow
dissipated
despicable
despicably
despisable
dislikable
dissipable
distinctly
dissidence
dyskinesia
despiteful
despiteous
dislikeful
dispiteous
distinguée
distichous
dissimilar
dispirited
dissilient
deskilling
discipline
distilland
distilling
distillery
distillate
distilment
discission
dismission
dismissory
dismissive
dessiatine
disc jockey
dust jacket
displeased
disyllabic
disyllable

disfluency
disulphide
disulphate
disulfiram
disclaimer
desalinise
displenish
desalinate
desalinize
disglorify
dysplastic
displosion
disclosure
desolately
desolation
desolatory
disimagine
disamenity
disembowel
disempower
disembosom
disembogue
disembroil
disimprove
disengaged
disinherit
dysenteric
disenvelop
disenthral
disinthral
disenchain
disenchant
disinhibit
disentitle
disenviron
disanalogy
disincline
disenclose
disinclose
disenslave
disanimate
disendowed
disennoble
disinvolve
disentrail
disentrain
disentwine
disco dance
dissonance
dissonancy
disloyally
disposable
disloyalty
disconcert
dispondaic
despondent
desponding
discordant
discordful
discoverer
disposedly
dishonesty
discomfort
disconfirm
discophile
Discophora
despotical
desmodiums
dispositor
dissociate
discommode
discommend
disconnect
discounsel
discounter
disjointed
disjoining
desmosomal
dishonorer
discobolus
dysmorphia
dysmorphic
discompose
discoursal
discourser
discourage
disworship
disconsent
dispossess
discontent
distortion
distortive
dissoluble
Dostoevsky
dissolvent
dissolving
disapparel
disc player
desipience
disepalous
disc plough
disappoint
disapprove
disarrange
disorganic
distribute
distracted
destructor
distractor
dispredden
disordered
deservedly
discreetly
disorderly
désorienté
disprofess
dysarthria
dispraiser
distrainee
distrainer
distrainor
desertless
desireless
descramble
distringas
disprinced
disgruntle
dysgraphia
dysgraphic
dystrophia
dystrophic
dystrophin
discrepant
descriptor
distressed
distresser
distruster
dyscrasite
dysprosium
discretely
desorption
discretion
discretive
distraught
desirously
distrouble
disprovide
destroying
desistance
desistence
disespouse
disastrous
disutility
disputable
disputably
disturbant
disturbing
disjunctor
disquieten
disquietly
discutient
disqualify
desquamate
disfurnish
disculpate
discussant
disguising
discursion
discussion
dissuasion
discursory
dissuasory
discursist
discursive
discussive
dissuasive
disburthen
disgusting
✧disruption
disgustful
disruptive
disavaunce
disownment
dishwasher
dessyatine
detracting
detraction
detractory
detractive
detachable
detectable
date coding
detachedly
detectible
detachment
✧ditheletic
do the dirty
dotted line
dotted note
dotted over
do the trick
dotted rest
ditheistic
ditchwater
Dutch metal
Dutch tiles
Dutch clock
Dutch uncle
Dutchwoman
Dutch treat
Dutch drops
Dutch lunch
detainable
ditriglyph
detainment
dithionate
data logger
datum level
datum plane
data mining
datum point
datamation
detonation
ditto marks
ditrochean
detergence
detergency
deterrence
determined
determiner
dethroning
detestable
detestably
dot-etching
detruncate
detoxicant
detoxicate
dotty about
drug addict
drupaceous
drumbledor
drug dealer
deuce court
drudgingly
dough-baked
doughfaced
Doukhobors
daughterly
dauphiness
doughiness
double axel
double back
double bill
double-bank
double bind
double bond
double-book
double bass
double chin
double-dyed
double door
double-eyed
double flat
double-gild
double-hung
double knit
double-knit
doubleness
double play
double-park
double reed
double star
Douglas fir
double salt
doubletree
double take
Double Talk
double-talk
double time
diurnalist
deutoplasm
doulocracy
drug pusher
drug-runner
doubtingly
doubtfully
diuturnity
duumvirate
Douay Bible
dive-bomber
devocalise
dove-colour
devocalize
David Mamet
David Jason
David Scott
David Niven
divide into
David Gower
David Lodge
David Bowie
dive-dapper
David Bruce
David Frost
David Steel
David Duval
David Lynch
David Byrne
divagation
devil's dung
devil's dust
divulgence
developing
devalorise
devalorize
devilishly
devolution
diving bell
✧devanagari
divineness
divineress
diving suit
divination
divinatory
divaricate
divergence
divergency
divertible
devastavit
devastator
divestible
divestment
divisional
divisively
devitalise
devitalize
devotement
devotional
devourment
devoutness
down-and-out
down at heel
down-at-heel
dawn chorus
down-easter
dew-retting
Dawn Fraser
Dawn French
downfallen
dowsing rod
dawdlingly
downlooked
dowel-joint
downmarket
✧dewar flask
dower house
downstairs
downstream
downstroke
downsizing
downturned
dewatering
downwardly
dexterwise
doxography
dextrogyre
dextrality
dextrously
day-patient
dry farming
dry canteen
dry battery
drysaltery
day-scholar
day release
day-release
day-wearied
dry measure
dry service
dry-cleaner
dry blowing
drying oils
day-boarder
dry-roasted
dry monsoon
days of yore
daydreamer
day trading
day-tripper
dry-cupping
day nursery
dazzlement
dazzlingly
dizzyingly
Elagabalus
emalangeni
epanaphora
emasculate
emancipist
emancipate
ecardinate
exacerbate
evanescent
enamelling
enamellist
elatedness
evangeliar
evangelise
evangelism
✧evangelist
evangelize
emarginate
exaggerate
Esarhaddon
edaphology
eradicated
eradicable
examinable
eradicator
examinator
emaciation
eradiation
edaciously
enablement
epaulement
eyas-musket
evaporable
elaborator
enamorados
evaporator
epagomenal
enamouring
exasperate
enarration
elasticise
elasticate
elasticity
elasticize
exactingly
enantiomer
enantiosis
exactitude
exaltation
ejaculator
evacuation
evaluation
evacuative
evaluative
emblazoner
emblazonry
eubacteria
embodiment
en badinant
emblematic
emblements
emboldener
embalmment
embolismal
embolismic
embankment
embonpoint
embroidery
embroglios
embrowning
El Brooshna
embarras de
embarkment
embargoing
ember-goose
embassador
embasement
embossment
embittered
embitterer
embouchure
embruement
elbow-chair
embowelled
embryogeny
embryology
embryulcia
embryonate
embryotomy
escharotic
enchanting
en cabochon
encyclical
escadrille
Eccles cake
excrescent
excrementa
ecclesiast
escheatage
excogitate
escribanos
encrinital
encrinitic

Words marked ✧ can also be spelled with one or more capital letters

encoignure
escritoire
exculpable
escaladoes
excellence
✧excellency
escalloped
escallonia
Esculapian
eucalyptol
eucalyptus
euchlorine
escalation
escalatory
encomienda
e e cummings
encampment
escamotage
ex concesso
ex converso
encincture
encroacher
encloister
encephalic
encephalin
encephalon
escapadoes
encopresis
exceptious
escapology
escapeless
exceptless
escapement
eccoprotic
escape road
euchred out
encircling
escarpment
eucaryotic
excerpting
excerption
excursuses
encashable
excise duty
excess fare
ecce signum
encasement
encashment
encystment
excusatory
ex cathedra
ex-cathedra
escutcheon
excitement
excitingly
excitation
excitatory
excitative
encourager
excludable
excludible
excruciate
en cavalier
excavation
ecchymosed
ecchymosis
ecchymotic
encryption
endearment
endocrinal
endocrinic
endocritic
endocarpic
endodermal
endodermic
endodermis
eudaemonia
eudaemonic
end of story
endogamous
endogenous
endemicity
eudemonism
endomorphy
Eddy Merckx
endangerer
end in smoke
eudiometer
eudiometry
endopodite
endopleura
endophytic
endermatic
endorsable
end-product
elderberry
endorse out
endermical
endorhizal
enduringly
endergonic
Endostatin®
eldest hand
endoscopic
endosmosis
endosmotic
endothelia
endothermy
end-stopped
ex dividend
eddy vortex
eye-catcher
emerald-cut
elecampane
Edenburgen
even chance
El Escorial
emendation
emendatory
epexegeses
epexegesis
epexegetic
eyelet-hole
exegetical
eye-legible
eleven-plus
eleventhly
elementary
eye-service
eye-servant
✧everglades
emergently
energetics
Erechtheum
Erechtheus
Erewhonian
even-handed
erethismic
erethistic
emetically
eremitical
eyewitness
eyeglasses
Eneolithic
ever-living
even-minded
eternalise
eternalist
eternality
eternalize
even number
eye contact
eye-opening
eye-spotted
epeirogeny
execration
execratory
execrative
eye askance
even-steven
Eleusinian
eventually
epentheses
epenthesis
epenthetic
electrical
erectility
edentulous
electrogen
electromer
electronic
electorial
electoress
electorate
exenterate
eventfully
ejectively
electively
electivity
executancy
executable
executress
enervating
enervation
enervative
emery paper
emery wheel
everything
everywhere
everyplace
emery cloth
emery board
every other
effaceable
efficacity
efficience
efficiency
effectible
effectless
effacement
enfacement
effectuate
effleurage
enfleurage
effigurate
exfoliator
effulgence
enfoldment
effeminacy
effeminise
effeminate
effeminize
enfant gâté
effloresce
effrontery
effervesce
enforcedly
effortless
enfestered
effusively
effeteness
egg capsule
ergodicity
edge effect
El Guerrouj
eagle-stone
engagement
engagingly
egg-binding
Englishman
Englishism
engulfment
ergomaniac
Eugene Aram
eigenvalue
eugenecist
eugenicist
egg-and-dart
engenderer
engineless
ergonomics
ergonomist
engine-room
engendrure
egg poacher
engrossing
ergophobia
Edgar Faure
Edgar Degas
engarrison
ergosterol
eightscore
eightpence
eight bells
eighteenmo
eightpenny
eighteenth
ergatogyne
ergotamine
eighth note
ergativity
engouement
englutting
egg custard
exhibition
exhibitory
exhibitive
ethicality
enhydritic
echoically
ethnically
ethologist
ethylamine
exhilarant
exhilarate
ethyl ether
exhalation
ephemerist
euhemerise
Euhemerism
euhemerist
ephemerous
euhemerize
exhumation
ethambutol
ethanediol
echinoderm
Echinoidea
Ethan Allen
Ethan Cohen
ethnologic
Etheostoma
echopraxia
echopraxis
ethereally
exheredate
enharmonic
euharmonic
exhaust gas
exhausting
exhaustion
exhaustive
Eric Ambler
epicardial
epicardium
ericaceous
epitaphian
epitaphist
epicanthic
epigastric
epicanthus
Enid Blyton
Eric Coates
exit charge
evincement
Emi-Scanner®
episcopacy
episcopant
episcopise
episcopate
episcopize
eviscerate
Eriocaulon
episematic
epideictic
epidendrum
epigenesis
epigenetic
epimeletic
epinephrin
epidemical
epidermoid
eviternity
eminential
epicentral
evidential
epibenthic
epibenthos
epithelial
epithelium
epithemata
epiphonema
epithermal
epiphyseal
Eli Whitney
epiphytism
Edith Evans
eliminable
eliminator
epilimnion
epidiorite
episiotomy
eximiously
epididymal
epididymis
Eric Kandel
edible crab
edibleness
epiblastic
epiplastra
epiglottal
epiglottic
epiglottis
etiolation
evil-minded
enigmatise
✧enigmatist
enigmatize
ebionitism
epicondyle
episodical
epitomical
epidotised
epidotized
epitomiser
epitomizer
editorship
epizootics
epiloguise
epiloguize
eriophorum
epispastic
epigrapher
epigraphic
emigration
emigratory
emissivity
ekistician
Erik the Red
epistolary
epistolise
epistolist
epistolize
epistemics
epistrophe
episternal
episternum
epicuticle
exiguously
Elie Wiesel
evil-worker
epicycloid
edifyingly
enjoinment
enjambment
Eskimo roll
enkephalin
eukaryotic
eolian harp
Eilean Siar
enlacement
eulogistic
Ellen Terry
Elland Road
eglandular
elliptical
enlargedly
enlistment
enlevement
enlèvement
Emma Bovary
Emmentaler
Edmund Kean
emmenology
ermine moth
ex mero motu
enmeshment
emmetropia
emmetropic
Enneandria
enneagonal
enneastyle
Edna O'Brien
Ernst Chain
Ebola virus
ecowarrior
exorbitant
exorbitate
Eton collar
exonerator
exogenetic
exoterical
egocentric
eloignment
enough said
elongation
exophagous
exothermal
exothermic
erotically
exotically
exobiology
exoticness
Eton jacket
éboulement
ecoclimate
emollition
enormously
erotomania
erotogenic
ecological
economical
economiser
economizer
exopoditic
eco-tourism
eco-tourist
ecospecies
exospheric
exosporous
étourderie
ego-tripper
egoistical
e contrario
emoluments
ego-surfing
evolutions
eloquently
evolve into
evolvement
epoxy resin
eponychium
exocytosis
exocytotic
emphatical
euphausiid
emplastron
emplastrum
expectance
expectancy
especially
expectable
expectably
expectedly
Empedocles
expedience
expediency

espadrille
expeditely
expedition
expeditate
expeditive
en plein air
expressman
expressway
express fee
expressage
expression
expressure
espressivo
expressive
expugnable
explicable
explicator
en principe
Empfindung
esprit fort
explicitly
empoisoned
expellable
empalement
expandable
expendable
expendably
expansible
expansibly
empanelled
expunction
employable
euphorbium
ecphoneses
ecphonesis
ex professo
euphonical
explosible
euphoriant
euphonious
employment
ex propriis
exprobrate
exploitage
exploitive
exportable
expurgator
ecphractic
emphractic
empiricism
empiricist
emparadise
experience
Empire gown
experiment
expertness
Euphrosyne
expiration
expiratory
exposition
expository
expositive
expatiator
empathetic
expatriate
euphuistic
empoverish
emphysemic
earbashing
Earl Beatty
Eurobabble
Eurocratic
ebracteate
Eurocheque
enrichment
Euroclydon
Eurafrican
enragement
enregiment
enregister
earthwards
earth-table
earth-shine
earth-light
euryhaline
earth-plate
earth-smoke
eard-hunger
eard-hungry
earthiness
earthwoman
earthmover
earthbound
earth-board
earth-house
earthquake
earwigging
ear-witness
earlierise
earlierize
ear-kissing
Errol Flynn
enrollment
Euromarket
errand girl
Earl of Bute
Earl of Kent
eurypterid
Eurypterus
Europhobia
enraptured
ear-trumpet
en retraite
erraticism
Eurythmics
Eurotunnel
éprouvette
ear-bussing
en revanche
Eurovision
Earl Warren
Earl Wavell
eurhythmic
ear syringe
early doors
early music
Eustachian
Eastbourne
exsiccator
easy does it
Easter dues
✧**eisteddfod**
easselgate
Easter lily
easterling
eastermost
Eastern Sea
easternise
easternism
easternize
Eastertide
Eastertime
Easter term
easselward
exsufflate
ensignship
ease-giving
enschedule
East Indian
East Indies
El Salvador
ex silentio
East London
Epsom salts
Eisenhower
eosinophil
ease nature
ensanguine
exsanguine
East of Eden
easy street
East Sussex
ensoulment
eastwardly
essayistic
euthanasia
entrancing
eutrapelia
en travesti
extraneity
extraneous
estrangelo
entrapment
extradotal
extra-solar
extra cover
extra modum
extractant
extraction
extractive
extradural
extramural
extra muros
enticeable
enticement
enticingly
ectodermal
ectodermic
entrée dish
entremesse
entreasure
entreating
entreative
ectoenzyme
ectogenous
eat the leek
eat through
extricable
entailment
entoilment
ecthlipses
ecthlipsis
entomology
entombment
extemporal
ectomorphy
estimation
estimative
extendable
extenuator
extendedly
extendible
extensible
extensions
estanciero
eat one's hat
extinction
extincture
extinctive
extinguish
Eatanswill
estipulate
Ectoprocta
Entoprocta
entophytal
ectophytic
entophytic
externally
extirpable
extirpator
enterocele
enterocyte
enterdeale
enthralled
enthraldom
enterolith
enthronise
entireness
enthronize
exteriorly
enterprise
enterotomy
estate duty
estatesman
entitative
extrudable
extrusible
enthusiasm
enthusiast
estivation
entry value
entry-level
Euthyneura
Entryphone®
entry wound
educatable
emulatress
equability
exurbanite
enunciable
enunciator
edulcorant
edulcorate
exulcerate
Ecuadorian
exuberance
exuberancy
eau de Javel
enumerable
enumerator
erubescent
erubescite
ecumenical
enuredness
egurgitate
erucic acid
elucidator
esuriently
exuviation
ebullience
ebulliency
equals sign
ebullition
equanimity
equanimous
eburnation
equiparate
equipotent
elutriator
emulsifier
equestrian
exultantly
exultingly
equational
eruptional
equatorial
equitation
eructation
exultation
eruptivity
equivocate
equivalent
envenomate
Enver Pasha
environics
Enver Hoxha
enwrapment
enwrapping
Edwin Drood
Edward Bond
Edward Coke
Edwardiana
Edward Lear
erythritic
erythritol
erysipelas
elytriform
Egyptology
enzymology
eczematous
framboesia
Fray Bentos
flabbiness
flag-basket
flamboyant
flaccidity
fianchetti
fianchetto
franchisee
franchiser
flanconade
✧**francophil**
Franciscan
flap-dragon
fraudulent
flapdoodle
fraudfully
frame-maker
Fratercula
flavescent
flake-white
flagellant
flabellate
Flagellata
flagellate
fraternise
fraternity
fraternize
frame-house
flame-grill
flameproof
flare stack
feateously
flat-footed
flagginess
frangipane
frangipani
fraughtage
flash Harry
flash about
flashlight
flash flood
flashiness
flashpoint
flashboard
flash-house
feather bed
featherbed
feathering
feather cut
fraxinella
flamingoes
Foaming Sea
Flamingant
flaminical
flagitious
flavivirus
flak jacket
frabjously
Frank Zappa
Frank Capra
Frank O'Hara
Frank Field
Frank Bruno
Frank Dyson
flail about
fearlessly
fragmental
fragmented
Fianna Fáil
flaunching
flannelled
fearnought
flavorless
flavouring
flavourful
flavorsome
flapperish
foam rubber
fratricide
flat racing
flagrantly
fragrantly
fearsomely
flat-screen
frantic-mad
fractality
flatten out
fractional
flattering
flatterous
flatulence
flatulency
featurette
flag-waving
Franz Kafka
Franz Lehár
Franz Liszt
Franz Kline
fibrescope
fibreglass
fibreboard
fibre-optic
fabricator
fibrillary
fibrillose
fibrillate
fibrillous
fibrinogen
febrifugal
fabulosity
fabulously
Fabio Chigi
fibrositis
fibroblast
fibronogen
fiberscope
fiberglass
fiberboard
fact-finder
face-fungus
face-harden
facsimiled
facsimiles
factitious
fictitious
factionary
factionist
fictionist
factiously
facileness
fickleness
focal point
fecklessly
facilities
facilitate
facinorous
factorable
factorship
factor VIII
face powder
focus group
face-saving
face to face
face-to-face
factuality
faceworker
fiducially
Fidel Ramos
fiddle-back
fiddleback
fiddlehead
fadelessly
fiddlewood
federalise
federalism
federalist
federalize
federation
federative
fuddy-duddy
free agency
flea-beetle
F Lee Bailey
freebooter
Fred Basset
flea-bitten
French bean
French cuff
French door
French heel
French hens
French horn
French kiss
flea collar
French loaf
fleeceless

fleechment
fierceness
Frenchness
French plum
French roll
French roof
flea circus
French seam
French sash
Free Church
fleece-wool
fieldwards
fieldpiece
field night
field glass
freedwoman
field notes
freedwomen
fieldworks
fieldmouse
fieldboots
field trial
fieldcraft
field train
fiendishly
fieldstone
field guide
field event
free-diving
foederatus
fremescent
free energy
frenetical
Fredericia
Free French
free flight
free-fooder
free-footed
free-for-all
free-fisher
fledgeling
freight-car
freightage
freight ton
feed-heater
flesh-eater
freshwater
freeholder
fresh blood
fresh-blown
free-handed
fleshiness
flesh wound
fresherdom
flesh-brush
flesh-broth
foeticidal
foetidness
flexi-cover
flexihours
fee-fi-fo-fum
freakiness
freakishly
freeloader
free labour
freelancer
feebleness
free-living
free-minded
flea market
free market
free-market
freemartin
feet of clay
foetoscopy
free on rail
faex populi
free pardon
fleur-de-lis
fleur-de-lys
fleeringly
Free States
free speech
free school
free-soiler
free spirit
free-select
free-spoken
freestyler
free-trader
fleetingly
Fred Titmus
free-to-view
frequenter
frequently
free-verser
fiery cross
freeze down
faff around
fifth wheel
fifty pence
fifty-fifty
figurehead
figuration
figurative
figurework
fugitation
fight it out
fugitively
Fahrenheit
Faisalabad
Frida Kahlo
fricandeau
fricasseed
fair-boding
fair befall
friability
fair dinkum
flindersia
fair enough
fringillid
fringeless
fairground
fringe tree
fair-headed
flight crew
flight deck
frightened
fair-haired
flight line
flightless
frithsoken
flight plan
flight path
frightsome
frithstool
flight test
flight-test
faithfully
fritillary
frigidness
flick-knife
friskingly
friskiness
fair-leader
fair-minded
friendlies
friendlily
friendless
friendship
frigorific
foisonless
flippantly
friar's cowl
flimsiness
fair-spoken
faint-heart
flint-heart
Flintshire
flint glass
flirtingly
feistiness
flintiness
frictional
flirtation
fairy-beads
fairy light
fairy-money
Fairyhouse
fairy-stone
fairy story
fairy-cycle
Fritz Haber
foliaceous
foliar feed
fallacious
fall across
full-bodied
fall behind
filibuster
full-bottom
full-cocked
film colour
Filicineae
filicinean
full-circle
file-cutter
felicitate
felicitous
full cousin
false jalap
fallen arch
false-faced
falderal it
filterable
filter cake
folie à deux
false pearl
false teeth
false shame
false alarm
false topaz
false tooth
false fruit
fallen star
Folkestone
false start
fillet weld
fuliginous
full-handed
filchingly
filthiness
filthy rich
falciparum
fulmineous
falling-off
falling-out
falsidical
fulfilling
fall in love
fulfilment
faldistory
follicular
falsifying
file-leader
full-length
folklorist
film-making
folk-memory
fellmonger
full-manned
full nelson
fallow-chat
fallow deer
full orders
falcon-eyed
fellow heir
follow home
full of life
fallowness
fellowship
follow suit
filopodium
filo pastry
felspathic
filariasis
full-rigged
fell-runner
filtration
folk-speech
full-sailed
full-summed
folk-singer
folksiness
file server
full sister
fill the gap
felt-tip pen
full-voiced
fell-walker
full-winged
Felix Bloch
Felix Klein
Felixstowe
filmy ferns
fimicolous
feme covert
fumigation
fumigatory
familiarly
fumblingly
family name
femaleness
familistic
family tree
feminality
femininity
femininely
femininism
femininity
feministic
femtometre
fimbriated
famishment
fumatories
fumatorium
famousness
fontanelle
fandangoes
fantastico
finicality
funiculate
fingerbowl
funded debt
fingerhold
fingerhole
fingerling
fingerless
fingermark
fingernail
fence month
fingerpick
fingerpost
finger roll
finger's-end
finger wave
fundholder
fontinalis
fungicidal
fancifully
fonticulus
final cause
fantoccini
Finno-Ugric
funereally
fan-cricket
fen-cricket
fan tracery
fund-raiser
✧fenestella
fine-spoken
fenestrate
finish with
fanaticise
fanaticism
fanaticize
fine-tuning
finiteness
functional
finite verb
fungus-gall
funny paper
fanny about
Fanny Adams
fancy woman
fancy goods
funny money
fancy bread
Fanny Price
fancy dress
funny stuff
fool around
foolbegged
footbridge
Froebelian
footballer
Froebelism
flocculent
flocculate
flosculous
foot-candle
from choice
floodwater
flooded out
floodlight
flood plain
flower-bell
florescent
flower girl
flower-head
flowerless
flower show
✧florentine
footguards
frothiness
frog-hopper
florilegia
florideous
frolicking
floridness
frolicsome
floristics
floribunda
flock-paper
foot-licker
footlights
frowningly
flown cover
from nature
foot of fine
from on high
floppy disc
floppy disk
footprints
floppiness
foot-patrol
foot-racing
floor limit
floorcloth
floorboard
floor price
flourished
flourisher
frog's-march
frowsiness
frog's-mouth
frontwards
front bench
front-bench
float plane
float glass
frost-smoke
floatingly
floutingly
frostiness
frostbound
float-board
float grass
front crawl
float-stone
floatation
food values
from whence
foot-warmer
frowziness
fore-and-aft
farrandine
ferrandine
forwarding
forsakenly
formaliter
farfalline
forfaiting
formatting
fore-advise
fire blanks
fire bucket
foreboding
fire-blight
fire-basket
forebitter
form critic
forechosen
forecasted
forecaster
forecastle
forecourse
foredamned
fer-de-lance
far-fetched
forfeuchen
fervescent
fire escape
fire engine
forge ahead
force field
fortepiano
forcedness
forkedness
forbearant
forbearing
forced sale
for certain
forgetting
forfeiture
forgettery
Formentera
fermentive
forcefully
far between
forefinger
forefather
foreground
foregather
for the best
for the chop
for the drop
forthright
fore-hammer
forehanded
forthgoing
for the rest
forcipated
ferric acid
formic acid
formicaria
farcically
forgivable
formidable
formidably
fornicator
Fortinbras
forbidding
forcing-pit
far-sighted
fertiliser
fertilizer
fernticle
foreign aid
fervidness
foreignism
fortissimo
forkit-tail
fortifying
formlessly
for all that
form letter

foraminous
fire-master
foremother
far and away
forinsecal
firing line
far and near
firing-step
fore-notice
furuncular
far and wide
foreordain
fire-office
forfoughen
for nothing
ferronière
ferro-alloy
farborough
ferrograms
ferro-print
furrow-weed
fire-policy
fire-plough
foreperson
fore-quoted
fire-raiser
forerunner
foreshadow
forest-bred
forest-born
foreshewed
foreseeing
foresheets
fire-shovel
foreshowed
fork supper
firescreen
forest-tree
first water
first cause
fernticled
ferntickle
First Reich
first thing
first-aider
fork-tailed
first light
first night
foreteller
first blood
first floor
first-floor
first-class
First World
first joint
first-fruit
first proof
forsterite
first prize
foretaught
formulable
formulator
Fortune Bay
fortuitism
fortuitist
fortuitous
fire-walker
for a wonder
fire-warden
for example
furry dance
forty-niner
forty winks
fernyticle
for my money
ferry-house
fiscal drag
fustanella
fiscal year
fussbudget
fusibility
Fassbinder
fishburger
fast bowler
fish-carver
foster-home
fosterling
Fescennine
fesse-point
Fastens-eve
fish eaters
fish finger
fish farmer
fish-gutter
fast-handed
fascinator
fossil fuel
fishing-rod
fastigiate
fastidious
fossicking
fashionist
fustianist
fustianize
fasciation
fascicular
fascicules
fisticuffs
fasciculus
fish kettle
fish-ladder
fishmonger
fish-manure
fusion bomb
fusionless
festoonery
fast stream
fish-trowel
fast worker
Fats Domino
fatherhood
fetterlock
fatherlike
fatherland
fatherless
fetterless
Father's Day
fathership
fatiguable
fit the bill
fetch a pump
Fittipaldi
fitting-out
fatalistic
fathomable
fathometer
fathom line
fathomless
fatbrained
futurology
futureless
futuristic
futurition
fatiscence
fettuccine
fitfulness
Fats Waller
fatty acids
fatty heart
foul befall
four-by-four
fourchette
four-colour
feux de joie
found money
founderous
fluid drive
foundation
fluid ounce
flugelhorn
flügelhorn
flutemouth
four-figure
fluffiness
four-footed
four-handed
four-inched
four-in-hand
fluvialist
fluxionary
fluxionist
Fourierism
Fourierist
fluviatile
flunkeydom
flunkeyish
flunkeyism
four-leafed
four-leaved
feuilleton
four-legged
fluentness
fourniture
four-o'clock
four-parted
four-poster
fluoridise
fluoridate
fluoridize
fluorinate
fluorotype
foudroyant
four-seater
foul-spoken
fourscorth
four-square
fruit salad
frustrated
fourteener
fourteenth
fault plane
fruit-knife
faultiness
fruitiness
fruitarian
fruiteress
fourth-rate
fruit sugar
fruit juice
fruitfully
fourth wall
fluoxetine
five-eighth
five-finger
fivefinger
Five Points
five-parted
fever pitch
feverishly
favoritism
five senses
five-stones
five-square
favourable
favourably
favourless
fowling-net
fowl-plague
fax machine
fixed light
fixed costs
fixed-price
fixed stars
fox terrier
foxtrotted
foxhunting
flycatcher
fly the beam
fly the flag
flypitcher
fly-fishing
fly-tipping
fly-flapper
flying-boat
flying bomb
flying camp
faying-face
flying frog
flying fish
flying leap
flying suit
flying shot
flying wing
flyposting
fly-fronted
fly-dumping
fly swatter
fly-by-night
fizzenless
fazendeiro
fuzzy logic
fizzy drink
Graham Hill
granadilla
grama grass
guaranteed
glauberite
gear-change
gearchange
glance-coal
glancingly
glauconite
glance over
grand march
granddaddy
giardiasis
grandmamma
grande dame
grand merci
grand jésus
glandiform
grandchild
grand-niece
grand piano
glandulous
grand-uncle
grand total
grand monde
Grand Hotel
guardhouse
✧grands prix
grand opera
grand prior
glanderous
grand style
grandstand
grand-ducal
grand duchy
grand juror
Grand Mufti
Guatemalan
grave-maker
grâce à Dieu
Grace Kelly
go a-begging
gravelling
graveolent
grave goods
Grace Jones
grapelouse
graded post
grapefruit
Gravettian
grapestone
gravestone
grape sugar
gracefully
gratefully
gravel-walk
graffitied
graffitist
grangerise
Grangerism
grangerize
graph paper
graphicacy
graphology
gnaphalium
graphemics
glad-hander
gnashingly
grab handle
graphitoid
graphitise
graphitize
gravimeter
gravimetry
gramineous
gramicidin
glaciology
glacialist
gratillity
gradienter
graciosity
glaciation
gladiatory
graciously
gracious me
gravity-fed
gratifying
goalkicker
goalkeeper
graplement
Graeme Hick
gnamma hole
grammarian
grammatist
granny flat
granny knot
glasnostic
Giacometti
Gramophone®
gramophone
gramophony
granophyre
Glagolitic
glamour boy
grasp after
graspingly
glass-faced
glasspaper
goatsucker
glans penis
goat's-beard
goat's-thorn
grass widow
glass fibre
goat-sallow
glass-cloth
grass cloth
gladsomely
glass snake
grass snake
glassiness
grassiness
glass-coach
glassworks
grass court
glasshouse
grass-roots
grasswrack
grass-green
grass-grown
grass style
giant panda
Grant Batty
grant-aided
graptolite
goal-tender
grant-in-aid
giant squid
ghastfully
granulater
granularly
granulator
granulitic
gradualism
gradualist
graduality
granulomas
graduation
gratuitous
Glaswegian
goat-willow
gravy train
Gobi Desert
goblet cell
Gibberella
gobble down
gabblement
gobsmacked
gobemouche
Gabon viper
go bankrupt
gubernator
gabbroitic
go-betweens
gobstopper
god's eyelid
gudgeon pin
God-fearing
gude-father
God willing
gadolinite
gadolinium
gude-mother
gadrooning
godrooning
gude-sister
go downhill
giddy-paced
Greta Garbo
Geena Davis
Grenadines
grenadilla
gregarious
grey-coated
greedy guts
greediness
glendoveer
glebe-house
Grey Friars
grey-headed
grey-haired
Greek salad
grey knight
Greek modes
Greek cross
Greek style
Greg LeMond
gleemaiden
grey mullet
grey market
grey matter
green salad
green label
✧green paper
green earth
Green Party
Greenpeace
Green Beret
✧green welly
greenheart
green thumb
greenshank
greenfinch
green light
greenfield
green algae
green gland
Glenn Close
green flash
greencloth
green snake
green pound
green goose
greenhouse
greenspeak
Greg Norman
green-drake
greenstuff
greenstone
green audit
greensward
Greco-Roman
grey parrot
grecque key

Glenrothes
greaseball
greaseband
gneissitic
greaseless
guessingly
greasiness
greisenise
greisenize
gressorial
greasewood
Great Lakes
Great Scott!
great-niece
guest-night
guestimate
great-uncle
guest-house
Great Mogul
great gross
grey-wether
Giffen good
giftedness
gaffer tape
gaff-rigged
go for broke
go-go dancer
Guggenheim
goggle-eyed
gigglesome
gag-toothed
go in and out
guitarfish
griddle car
grindingly
grindstone
Gail Devers
Gripe Water®
gripe water
✧guinea corn
guinea fowl
Ghibelline
glide slope
guilefully
✧guinea worm
griffinish
griffinism
goings-over
gain ground
going forth
gaingiving
geisha girl
grith-stool
gridlocked
grisliness
grimlooked
gaillardia
grillsteak
guillotine
grille-work
glimmering
gliomatous
grinningly
grippingly
glissandos
gainstrive
gainsaying
Gail Sayers
guilty-like
glistening
grittiness
guiltiness
glistering
glitterand
glittering
glitterati
grievingly
grievously
gain weight
glitziness
gilravager
goliardery
Galia melon
goliathise
goliathize
gallabiyah
galravitch
gilravitch
gallabiyeh
galvaniser
galvanizer
gold-beater
gold beetle
golf course
gold-digger
Golden Bear
golden bull
golden calf
gold-end-man
golden duck
golden goal
golden gram
golden girl
Golden Hind
golden hour
golden mean
golden mole
golden orfe
Golden Palm
golden rain
golden rule
gelder rose
golden rose
golden seal
Gilbertian
Gilbertine
galley-worm
galley-west
galleryite
Goldfinger
gallic acid
gallinazos
Gil Vicente
Gillingham
Goldie Hawn
galliambic
goldilocks
Gallic Wars
galimatias
Gallomania
Gallophobe
Gallophile
galloglass
gallows-lee
gold-plated
goloptious
goluptious
gold record
gillravage
Gulf States
Galashiels
Gulf Stream
gelatinoid
gelatinise
gelatinate
gelatinous
gelatinize
gold thread
Gallup poll
Galsworthy
gold-washer
gully-raker
gemmaceous
gymnasiums
gymnasiast
gimmal ring
gymnastics
game-dealer
gimlet-eyed
gombeen-man
gambit-pawn
gamekeeper
gemologist
gum elastic
gaminesque
gemination
gambolling
gymnosophy
gymnosperm
gametocyte
game theory
gametangia
game tenant
gamotropic
gum juniper
gem-cutting
game warden
genialness
genealogic
gangbuster
gynocratic
gonococcal
gonococcic
gonococcus
geniculate
gens de bien
gensdarmes
ginger beer
genderless
genteelise
genteelish
genteelism
genteelize
gander-moon
gender role
gingersnap
ginger wine
Ginkgoales
gentilesse
gunfighter
gingili oil
gingivitis
gangliated
gentlefolk
gangliform
gentlehood
ginglimoid
gunslinger
gentleness
ganglionic
Guns 'n' Roses
gynandrism
gynandrous
gyniolatry
goniometer
goniometry
✧gang of four
genophobia
gynophobia
gynophobic
Gene Pitney
genericise
genericize
gentrifier
gonorrheal
gonorrhoea
gonorrheic
generalled
Generalife
generalise
generalist
generalate
generality
generalize
gangrenous
generosity
generatrix
generation
generative
generously
gangsta rap
Genesiacal
geneticist
gens togata
Gantt chart
genethliac
genitalial
genitively
genius loci
gunrunning
genevrette
Geneva gown
Genevanism
Gene Wilder
good as gold
geoscience
Gloucester
gooneybird
Grote Reber
groceteria
gooseberry
geotechnic
geodesical
geodetical
geomedical
glove-fight
gnoseology
grovelling
gooseflesh
glove-money
goosefoots
Goose Green
geometrise
geometrist
goose-grass
geometrize
geocentric
glomerular
goose-quill
goose bumps
glomerulus
Good Friday
GoodFellas
goodfellow
good for you
good-father
Geoff Hurst
George Airy
George Byng
George Best
George Bush
George Hale
grogginess
Georg Solti
George Sand
George Town
Georgetown
geophagism
geophagist
geophagous
geophilous
geochemist
good humour
geothermal
geothermic
geophysics
gnomically
Geodimeter®
growing-bag
gnosiology
Grobianism
gloriously
glorifying
goodlihead
goodlyhead
good-liking
growlingly
goodliness
good-looker
ghoulishly
gloominess
good-morrow
good-mother
ground beef
groundbait
ground-bass
ground crew
ground-dove
groundedly
ground game
ground-hold
groundling
ground loop
groundless
ground mail
groundmass
groan under
groaningly
ground plan
ground pine
groundplot
groundprox
ground rule
ground rent
groundsman
geognostic
groundsell
groundsill
good nature
groundwork
ground wave
ground zero
geological
geoponical
gnomonical
gnotobiote
googolplex
Group of Ten
groupthink
good people
go on record
geographer
geographic
geotropism
gloss paint
good sailor
glossology
grouse moor
glossiness
glossarial
goods train
go on strike
glossarist
good-sister
growth area
Gnosticise
Gnosticism
Gnosticize
glottidean
ghost shark
glottology
gloatingly
grottiness
ghost train
growth ring
ghost-write
geostatics
ghost story
grotto-work
globularly
grooviness
go on wheels
geodynamic
goody-goody
go platinum
gypsophila
gap-toothed
gap funding
gippy tummy
gyppy tummy
German band
garlandage
gormandise
gormandism
gormandize
garbage can
garbageman
Germanicus
geriatrics
geriatrist
✧gargantuan
giro cheque
Gary Cooper
gyrocopter
garden city
garden flat
gor-bellied
garden path
garnet-rock
garden seat
garmenture
gorgeously
Girl Friday
girlfriend
garage band
garage sale
germinable
garnishing
germicidal
garnierite
girdle cake
Gerald Ford
Gerd Muller
gerundival
Gordon Bell
Gary Oldman
gorgoneion
Gordon Gray
gargoylism
garrotting
Gorgonzola
Gary Player
Gary Rhodes
gyrostatic
garishness
gyroscopic
germ theory
geratology
gyrational
Gerry Adams
gestaltism
Gestaltist
Gasherbrum
gospellise
gospellize
gasteropod
gospel side
gas chamber
Gosainthan
gashliness
gasometric
Gesundheit
gasconader
go shopping
gas-bracket
gastric flu
go straight
gastrology
gastralgia
gastronome
gastronomy
Gastropoda
Gus Grissom
gastrosoph
gastrotomy
gas turbine
gas-furnace
gas-guzzler
gut-scraper
Gothenburg
gutter pair
get weaving
go to ground
get the boot
get the bird
get the chop
get a handle
get through
get the push
Gothic arch
get hitched
Guttiferae
gatling gun
gate-keeper
gate-legged
go to market
get a move on

get one's way
get knotted!
gate of horn
get nowhere
get to sleep
get round to
get to grips
go to pieces
get spliced
get-up-and-go
get up steam
get dressed
Gethsemane
get stuck in
go to the bad
gutturally
get outside
get a wicket
glumaceous
grub around
grubbiness
gourdiness
gauge glass
gauge boson
gauffering
grudgingly
grubhunter
gauging-rod
glucosidic
glucosuria
glucosuric
grumpiness
gru-gru worm
gruesomely
Grub Street
Grubstreet
gauntleted
gaultheria
gruntingly
gluttonise
gluttonish
gluttonous
gluttonize
gaudy-night
gaudy-green
give a start
give colour
give ground
give notice
give or take
governance
governable
governante
governessy
✧government
give the air
give the lie
give the nod
give the gun
give tongue
gay-bashing
Guy Laroche
gay science
Glyn Daniel
glyphosate
gey and easy
Gay Gordons
glycogenic
glycosidic
glycosuria
glycosuric
glycolysis
glycolytic
glyptodont
glyoxaline
head-bummer
headbanger
headcheese
head-centre
heaven-bred
heaven-born
heat engine
heaven-sent
header tank
heavenward
hoar-headed
head-hugger
Heathcliff
headhunter
heathendom
heathenise
heathenish
heathenism
heathenize
heath-poult
heather ale
Headingley
hearing aid
hearing dog
head-lugged
headmaster
hyalomelan
hyalophane
hyaloplasm
headphones
headsheets
heat shield
hearse-like
hoarseness
head-stream
heatstroke
headstrong
headsquare
heartwater
health camp
healthcare
health club
heart's-ease
heartsease
heart of oak
health food
health farm
head to head
head-to-head
heart shell
heart-whole
heart-throb
hear things
heart block
heart-blood
healthless
heartening
heartiness
heart-spoon
heartbreak
heart-grief
healthsome
heart-quake
head waiter
headworker
heavy-laden
heavy water
heavy metal
heavy going
heavy horse
heavy cream
heavy-armed
heavy sugar
heavy swell
Hebraicism
Hebraistic
hubba hubba
Hebrew year
hybrid bill
hybridiser
hybridizer
Hobbianism
hobble-bush
habiliment
hobblingly
Hubble's law
habilatory
habilitate
hebdomadal
hebdomadar
hebdomader
hobjobbing
hobnobbing
hibernacle
habit-maker
habitually
habit-cloth
habitation
hebetation
habitaunce
hobby-horse
hackbuteer
Hockenheim
hockey line
hoc tempore
hectically
huckle-bone
Hock Monday
hackmatack
hackney cab
hackneyman
hectometre
hiccoughed
hectolitre
hectograph
hectorship
hectostere
hocus-pocus
huckstress
hacktivism
hacktivist
hydrazides
hydraulics
hydragogue
hod carrier
Hadley cell
hodden-grey
hiddenmost
hiddenness
hodgepodge
hydrically
Haddington
Hideki Tojo
hidalgoish
hidalgoism
hedonistic
hydromancy
hydropathy
hydromania
hydrotaxis
hydroscope
hydrometer
hydrometry
hydrotheca
hide or hair
hydrophily
hydrophane
hydrophone
hydrochore
hydrophyte
hydroplane
hydrosomal
hydropower
hydrosomes
hydrologic
hydroponic
hydropolyp
hydrospace
hydrograph
hydrolysis
hydrolytic
hoddy-doddy
hierarchal
hierarchic
heel and toe
haematinic
hiera-picra
haematosis
Hierapolis
hye-battel'd
Haemanthus
haematuria
heedlessly
hieromancy
hierolatry
hieroscopy
hyetometer
hierophant
hieroglyph
haemoconia
hierologic
hierocracy
hierograph
hyetograph
haemolysis
haemolytic
Hieronymic
haemolymph
high and low
high and dry
highbinder
Hugh Cairns
high colour
high comedy
Hugh Casson
High Church
Hughes Hall
hug-me-tight
highermost
high-flying
Hugh Greene
High German
high-heeled
hog-cholera
high-handed
highjacker
high-kilted
highlights
✧highlander
Hugh Laurie
high living
hegemonial
high-minded
hegemonism
hegemonist
high-necked
hogen-mogen
hug oneself
hagiolater
hagiolatry
hagioscope
hygroscope
hygrometer
hygrometry
hygrophobe
hygrochasy
hygrophyte
hagiologic
hagiocracy
hygrograph
high-octane
high-placed
high places
high-priced
high priest
high-reared
high-raised
high relief
high-roller
high-ranker
high season
High Sierra
high school
Higgs boson
✧high street
high-street
high-strung
high-souled
hightail it
high-tasted
high-vacuum
highwayman
higry-pigry
Heidelberg
hail-fellow
hair-pencil
hair-powder
hair-raiser
hairstreak
hair stroke
hairspring
hair-waving
hoity-toity
hiking boot
Hakenkreuz
hokey cokey
hokey-pokey
heliacally
hullabaloo
Hollandish
Holman Hunt
hellacious
hallalling
half-a-dozen
hell around
hold a brief
half-a-crown
Hal Hartley
Helianthus
hellbender
halobiotic
half-chance
half-cocked
helicoidal
Heliconian
helicopter
halocarbon
hill-digger
half-dollar
half-duplex
holodiscus
halberdier
Halle Berry
halo effect
Hildesheim
halter neck
halfe-horsy
halieutics
halleluiah
hallelujah
Heller work
holoenzyme
Holy Friday
Holy Family
half florin
Holofernes
Holy Father
Halifax Bay
holography
half guinea
Heligoland
halogenate
halogenous
holohedral
holohedron
half-hunter
half-hourly
Hillingdon
hold in hand
Holy Island
hold in play
helminthic
half-kirtle
half-length
helplessly
Helen Wills
half nelson
holing-pick
heliolater
heliotaxis
heliolatry
heliopause
helioscope
holy orders
heliometer
hollow-eyed
Holy Office
hall of fame
heliophyte
Haliotidae
hollowness
Heliopolis
Hello Dolly!
heliograph
heliotrope
heliotropy
halloysite
hollow-ware
help on with
heliotypic
holophotal
holophrase
halophytic
holophytic
hellraiser
Holy Roller
Hilary term
holosteric
hell's bells
hell's teeth
Holy Spirit
heli-skiing
✧hell's angel
holus-bolus
half-sister
hylotheism
hylotheist
hylotomous
holy terror
Holothuria
Helmut Kohl
half volley
hillwalker
Holy Willie
halfwitted
half-yearly
hylozoical
home and dry
Himyaritic
hemianopia
homoblasty
hump-backed
home-brewed
hemicrania
hemicyclic
homocyclic
homecoming
home cinema
Hemichorda
homocercal
homochromy
humidifier
humidistat
✧hamadryads
hammer away
hammer beam
homme d'état
homme d'épée
hammer-fish
hammerhead
hammer home
hammer into
hammerlock
hammerless
homoeomery
homoerotic
hammer-pond
homoeopath
homogamous
homogenise
homogenate
homogenous
homogenize
home ground
hamshackle
hemihedral
hemihedron
humming ale
humming-top
humiliator
homologise
homologate

homologous
homologize
homaloidal
humblingly
homeliness
humbleness
homiletics
homemaking
home market
human being
human chain
Hominoidea
hemangioma
homonymity
homonymous
humaneness
humanistic
humanities
hemp-nettle
homuncular
homuncules
homunculus
homeopathy
homeomeric
Home Office
homeomorph
homoousian
homoplasmy
hemipteral
hemipteran
hemiplegia
hemiplegic
homophobia
homophobic
homophonic
humgruffin
Homorelaps
humoralism
humoralist
humoristic
humoresque
humorously
hamesucken
home-signal
hemisphere
homosexual
homothally
homotonous
hemitropal
hemitropic
home-thrust
homotaxial
humbugging
humdudgeon
humbuggery
humourless
humoursome
homeworker
homozygote
hemizygous
homozygous
hansardise
hansardize
hang a right
hantavirus
hang around
hen harrier
Hans Berger
hand-barrow
hand-basket
hinderance

hendecagon
Hindenbury
hunker down
henpeckery
hanselling
hinderland
hinderlans
hinderlins
hinterland
hindermost
handedness
hinge-bound
hinge joint
henceforth
hen-hearted
hang-glider
hand gallop
henchwoman
hunting-cap
hunting-cat
huntingtin
hunting-box
hunting-cog
Huntingdon
huntiegowk
hand in hand
hand-in-hand
handicraft
handicuffs
hand lotion
hand-me-down
handmaiden
hand mating
hand puppet
hand relief
honorarium
honor-guard
handstaves
handstaffs
hony-suckle
Huntsville
handselled
handsomely
Hans Sloane
hand-screen
handspring
hand-sewing
henotheism
henotheist
hand to hand
hand-to-hand
✧honourable
honourably
honourless
honours-man
Hindustani
Hanoverian
hand-weeded
handworked
handy-dandy
Henry James
honeyeater
hanky-panky
honey-wagon
Henry Cecil
honey-chile
Henry Royce
Henry Fonda
Henry Moore
honey-mouse
honeymonth

honey-crock
honey-stalk
honey-stone
honeybunch
honey guide
Henry Every
honey-sweet
hootananny
hook and eye
Hyoscyamus
hootenanny
hookedness
hooded seal
hoodie crow
hyoplastra
hootnannie
hoots-toots
heortology
heptarchic
Hipparchos
Heptandria
Heptateuch
heptameter
Heptameron
heptachlor
heptathlon
heptachord
hop-sacking
heptagonal
heptapodic
heptatonic
hypnagogic
Hephaestus
Heptagynia
hypabyssal
hypocritic
hypocentre
hypocorism
hypodermal
hypodorian
hypodermic
hypodermis
hyphenated
hypaethral
hypaethron
happen into
happen upon
hopped-wort
hippety-hop
hypogaeous
hypogynous
hop the twig
hopping mad
hupaithric
hippiatric
hop-bitters
hypolydian
hypalgesia
hypalgesic
hopelessly
hypanthium
hippomanes
hippomania
hippocampi
hypnoidise
hypnoidize
hypsometer
hypnogenic
hypsometry
hippophobe
hypsophobe

hippophagy
hippophile
hypsophyll
hypnotiser
hypnotizer
hippogriff
hippodrome
Hippocrene
hippogryph
Hippolytus
hypoplasia
hypophyses
hypophysis
hyperbaric
hyperbatic
hypermania
hypermanic
hyperbaton
hyperacute
hyperaemia
hyperaemic
hypermedia
hop-trefoil
hyperbolas
hyperbolic
hypergolic
hypersonic
hypertonia
hypertonic
hyperspace
hyperdulia
hypostases
hypostasis
hypostatic
hypostress
hypotactic
hepatocyte
hypotheses
hypothesis
hypothetic
hepatology
hepatomata
hypotenuse
hepatitis A
hepatitis B
hoppus foot
hip-huggers
Hippurites
hippuritic
hypoxaemia
hypoxaemic
happy event
harman-beck
herbaceous
herbariums
hard as iron
hereabouts
Herbartian
hardbacked
hornblende
hard-boiled
hard-billed
herb bennet
hurlbarrow
hard-bitten
Heracleian
hard cheese
Heraclidan
Hyracoidea
Heraclitus
hirudinean

hard done by
hirudinoid
hirudinous
hereditary
hereditist
horse-faced
horse-tamer
horselaugh
horse vault
horrendous
horseleech
hartebeest
horse sense
horseshoer
horse-thief
hermetical
horse-rider
horse block
her lee-lane
horseflesh
horse-cloth
horse's neck
horse-gowan
horse-woman
horse-coper
horsepower
horse opera
horned pout
horned-pout
horse-bread
hard-earned
horse brass
harvestman
horned toad
harvest-fly
Herbert Lom
harvest bug
Herrenvolk
horn-footed
hard-fisted
hard-fought
horography
herb garden
herb Gerard
hard-gotten
hard-headed
hard-handed
hard hyphen
heroically
Harrisburg
hermit crab
heroin chic
hartie-hale
herbicidal
hermitical
heroicness
horridness
heroi-comic
heroic poem
heroic size
herniotomy
horrifying
hard labour
herald-duck
horologist
✧horologium
hare-lipped
Hartlepool
hurdle-race
hurdle rate
heraldship

harmlessly
hurtlessly
harem skirt
Harimandir
hiring fair
her indoors
Herrnhuter
haranguing
heriotable
horror film
harmonical
harmoniser
harmonizer
harmonicon
harmonious
harpooneer
harpoon-gun
harbour-bar
harbourage
Herophilus
hard palate
hard-pushed
hard rubber
herb Robert
hard-riding
horn-rimmed
heresiarch
harassedly
heresy-hunt
haruspical
haruspices
horn silver
harassment
horoscopic
hard stocks
herd's grass
hereticate
heretofore
heritrices
heritrixes
here to stay
harquebuse
harquebuss
harpy eagle
hirdy-girdy
Hardy Amies
hurryingly
hurdy-gurdy
hurly-burly
here you are
horizontal
husbandman
husbandage
histaminic
Hispaniola
hasta luego
hash browns
hysteresis
hysteretic
hysterical
Hesperides
hysteritis
hystericky
his lee-lane
hostelling
hospitaler
hospitable
hospitably
histiocyte
hostile bid
husking-bee

histiology
Hessian fly
histogenic
historical
histoblast
histologic
histolysis
histolytic
histrionic
husk-tomato
hesitantly
hash totals
hesitation
hesitatory
hesitative
hetmanship
hot desking
hot-desking
hithermost
hitherside
Hattersley
hetherward
hitherward
hit the deck
hatch beams
hitch-hiker
hotchpotch
Hatshepsut
hit the road
hit the roof
hit the sack
hatchet man
hatchet job
hot-livered
hot-blooded
hate-monger
hit-and-miss
hot-dogging
hot-cockles
hot-working
hot coppers
hothousing
hot-mouthed
Hitopadesa
heterocont
Heterocera
heterodont
heterodyne
heterodoxy
heterogamy
heterogeny
heterogony
hot-brained
heterokont
heterology
heteronomy
Heteropoda
heterotaxy
hateworthy
hitty-missy
heulandite
haunch bone
hour-circle
hounds-foot
house party
haute école
house of God
House of Fun
house agent
house white
houselling

house plant
housebound
house mouse
housecraft
house-train
house group
house-proud
house style
✧house music
house guest
Houyhnhnms
Houdini act
heuristics
haut relief
houts-touts
haunt about
haustellum
hauntingly
haustorium
have a dekko
have a heart
have a right
have a hunch
have any joy
have it made
have no idea
hoveringly
hovercraft
hovertrain
how dare you!
hawk-beaked
hawk-billed
Huw Edwards
hawser-laid
Howleglass
how do you do?
how-do-you-do
Howards End
hawksbeard
how's tricks?
hexactinal
hexaëmeron
hexagynian
hexagynous
hexahedral
hexahedron
hexamerous
hexametric
hexandrian
hexandrous
hexaplaric
hexavalent
hoydenhood
hay-de-guyes
hey-de-guyes
hay-de-guise
hey-de-guise
hazardable
in a fashion
inadaptive
Idaean vine
inaccuracy
inaccurate
Isaac Stern
in addition
image-maker
isabelline
in a measure
inadequacy
inadequate
ilang-ilang
inaugurate
imaginable
imaginably
imaginings
Italian War
Italianise
Italianism
Italianist
Italianate
Italianize
Ivan Krylov
I Pagliacci
in as much as
inasmuch as
Ivan Mauger
inamoratas
Italo Balbo
inamoratos
inapposite
inappetent
Ivan Pavlov
in absentia
inartistic
inaptitude
inactively
inactivate
inactivity
iracundity
if anything
in any event
imbibition
imbecility
in bad odour
inbreeding
inbred line
inbringing
in-bond shop
imbroccata
imbroglios
in business
imbruement
in chancery
incrassate
inch by inch
incubation
incubatory
incubative
incidental
incedingly
increscent
inclemency
incredible
incredibly
increasing
incognitos
incogitant
incoherent
inclinable
inculpable
inculpably
inculcator
incompared
income bond
incumbency
incomplete
incomposed
income unit
incantator
incunables
incunabula
incandesce
incendiary
in conflict
incinerate
inconstant
inchoately
inchoation
inchoative
incapacity
incipience
incipiency
Incaparina
incurvated
incurrable
incurrence
incoronate
incorporal
incessancy
incisiform
incasement
incisorial
incestuous
incisively
incitement
incitingly
incitation
incitative
includable
ischuretic
include out
includible
incautious
incivility
India paper
Indian corn
Indian club
Indian file
Indian fire
Indian gift
Indian hemp
India shawl
Indian meal
Indian poke
Indian pink
Indian pipe
Indian rice
Indian sign
Indian shot
inductance
indictable
indicolite
indocility
indictment
inducement
indecently
indecorous
indecision
indecisive
indication
indicatory
indicative
indwelling
indie music
indefinite
indignance
indigo bird
indigo blue
indigolite
indigently
indigenise
indigenous
indigenize
indigested
indagation
indagatory
indagative
indelicacy
in deliciis
indelicate
indulgence
indulgency
Indologist
indolently
indumentum
iodometric
Indonesian
indentures
indapamide
in deposito
indirectly
induration
indurative
indistinct
indisposed
industrial
in disgrace
indiscreet
in distress
indiscrete
inditement
individual
individuum
index rerum
indexation
inerasable
inerasably
ice dancing
Iceland-dog
ice machine
inerasible
inerasibly
in exchange
in excelsis
inesculent
inelegance
inelegancy
inefficacy
ideography
inevitable
inevitably
irenically
in evidence
ineligible
ineligibly
ice hilling
inexistant
inexistent
I believe so
ice-skating
ideologist
ideal point
idealistic
ivermectin
inexorable
inexorably
Ile d'Oléron
ice colours
inelоquent
inexpiable
inexpiably
in especial
inexplicit
inexpertly
idempotent
icebreaker
idem sonans
in extremis
identified
identifier
inextended
ideational
isentropic
ineptitude
ineducable
ineludible
ineludibly
inequality
irefulness
inequation
inflamable
inflatable
inflatedly
infeasible
infraposed
infrasonic
infrasound
infragrant
infraction
infrahuman
infibulate
infectious
infidelity
inflexible
inflexibly
inflection
inflective
infrequent
infeftment
in-fighting
infighting
infliction
inflictive
infelicity
infallible
infallibly
infiltrate
infamonise
infamonize
infamously
infanthood
infinitude
infinitely
infinitant
infinitary
infinitate
infinitive
infirmarer
infernally
inferrable
informally
inferrible
infirmness
inferiorly
infarction
infosphere
infusorial
infusorian
infatuated
influenzal
influencer
ingrateful
ingratiate
ingle-cheek
ingredient
ingression
ingressive
ingeminate
ingenerate
inglorious
in good nick
in good part
in good time
ingestible
Ishtar Gate
Ishmaelite
inhabitant
inhibition
inhibitory
inhibitive
Iphigeneia
ichthyosis
ichthyotic
inhalation
inhumanely
inhumanity
inhumation
inherently
inharmonic
inheritrix
in hot blood
iridaceous
itinerancy
iridescent
iridectomy
icing sugar
Irish dance
Irish Times
Irishwoman
Irish pound
inimically
inimitable
inimitably
initialled
initialing
initialise
initialism
initialize
initiation
initiatory
initiative
idiolectal
idiolectic
Iain M Banks
iridovirus
iridosmine
iridosmium
Inigo Jones
idiopathic
imipramine
idiot light
idiot board
idiot-proof
iniquitous
injectable
injudicial
injunction
injunctive
injury time
ink-slinger
Iskenderun
ink-stained
ill-matched
ill-natured
Illecebrum
illocution
ill-advised
ill-behaved
ill-defined
ill feeling
I'll be bound
ill bestead
illegalise
illegality
illegalize
idle-headed
Islamicise
Islamicist
Islamicize
illuminant
illuminism
illuminist
illuminate
✧illuminati
inland bill
Isle of Coll
Isle of Eigg
Isle of Iona
ill-looking
Isle of Muck
Isle of Mull
ill-founded
Isle of Skye
ill fortune
idle pulley
illipe nuts
illaqueate
illusional
illusorily
illustrate
illusively
inlet valve
illiteracy
ill-starred
illiterate
illatively
illaudable
illaudably
ill success
I'll buy that
in low water
immeasured
immobilise
immobilism
immobility
immobilize
immaculacy
immaculate
immoderacy
immoderate
immodestly
iambically
Ismailitic
immolation
immemorial
in memoriam
immune body
immunoblot
immunology
immanental
imminently
immanation
imminution
immortally
immortelle
inmarriage

immersible
immoralism
immoralist
immorality
immurement
immeritous
immiscible
immiscibly
inmeshment
immiserise
immiserize
immotility
Ismet Inönü
immaterial
immaturely
immaturity
in mourning
immoveable
immovables
Ian Paisley
ignobility
innocently
innuendoes
Ion Iliescu
Ian Fleming
innominate
innumeracy
ignimbrite
innumerate
innumerous
Ian Woosnam
ignipotent
inner child
✧inner light
ignorantly
inner woman
inner voice
Inner House
inner space
ignoration
ignes fatui
ionosphere
ionisation
innutrient
innateness
innovation
innovatory
innovative
ionization
Icosandria
isogametic
icosahedra
isopachyte
idolatress
idolatrise
idolatrous
idolatrize
Ironbridge
inosculate
inordinacy
in ordinary
inordinate
inoperable
inoperably
in one's book
isoleucine
in one's cups
isogenetic
in one's gift
inobedient
in one's road
isometrics
isoseismal
isoseismic
in one's time
in one's turn
iron-fisted
iron-glance
Ivor Gurney
isocheimal
isocheimic
iron-handed
isochronal
isothermal
isochasmic
iconically
ironically
isokinetic
isoniazide
iron-liquor
isoglossal
isoglottal
isoglottic
isoflavone
✧iron maiden
ironmonger
isoaminile
iron-mining
ironmaster
isoantigen
iconolater
iconomachy
iconomatic
iconolatry
iconoscope
iconometer
iconometry
iconoclasm
iconoclast
idoloclast
isomorphic
isosporous
isotropism
isotropous
iron ration
Isoetaceae
I don't think
isopterous
inoculable
inoculator
iron-willed
iron-worded
iron-witted
isodynamic
ivory-black
isocyanide
ivory tower
implacable
implacably
impeccancy
impeccable
impeccably
impictured
impudicity
impediment
impedingly
impudently
impeditive
impresario
impregnant
impregnate
impression
impressure
impressive
implexuous
impugnable
impugnment
imprimatur
implicit in
implicitly
impairment
impuissant
imprinting
impalpable
impalpably
impaludism
impulse buy
impalement
impolitely
impendence
impendency
impenitent
impanation
improbable
improbably
improvable
improvably
implorator
improperly
improviser
in progress
imparlance
importance
importancy
impartable
imperially
importable
imparadise
import duty
impartible
impartibly
impervious
imperilled
in parallel
impartment
impureness
impersonal
in personam
imperative
importuner
impassable
impassably
imposthume
impassible
impassibly
impossible
impossibly
imposingly
impishness
imposition
impostumed
impose upon
impatience
input block
impotently
imputation
imputative
impoundage
imprudence
impoverish
in question
inquirendo
inquilinic
inquisitor
inquietude
I A Richards
irradiance
irradiancy
irradicate
iure divino
Israelitic
irrigation
irrigative
iure humano
irreligion
irrelation
irrelative
irrelevant
irremeable
irremeably
iure mariti
irrenowned
irresolute
irrational
irritating
irritation
irritative
irreverent
Instamatic®
installant
installing
instalment
inspanning
instantial
in statu quo
insobriety
insociable
insecurely
insecurity
inside edge
inside left
inspection
inspective
insufflate
insightful
inspirable
inspirator
instigator
in stitches
instilling
lastic mode
instilment
inspissate
instituter
institutes
institutor
insolvable
insolvably
insultable
insolidity
insolvency
inselberge
insultment
insolently
insulinase
insularism
insularity
insolation
insulation
insalutary
insalivate
in sympathy
insomnious
inseminate
in some sort
insinuator
ifs and buts
insensible
insensibly
insentient
insaneness
ins and outs
insane root
insanitary
insensuous
insipidity
insipience
inseparate
insertable
instructor
insurgence
insurgency
insert mode
instrument
insurancer
in strength
insistence
insistency
insatiable
insatiably
insouciant
insoulment
it says that
in that case
intra vitam
intra vires
in training
intrazonal
intradoses
in transitu
intramural
intra muros
intubation
intactness
in the pay of
in the shade
in the chair
in the wings
in the light
in the right
intrepidly
in the first
in the clear
in the black
in the flesh
in the money
in the world
in the round
in the wrong
in the press
in the quill
in the event
integrable
integrally
integrator
integument
intuitable
intrigante
intriguant
intriguing
intolerant
intimidate
intemerate
intimately
intimation
intendance
intendancy
intendedly
intangible
intangibly
intentions
intendment
intoningly
intentness
intenerate
intinction
intonation
intent upon
iatrogenic
in two minds
in two ticks
introspect
introrsely
introducer
intercalar
interramal
internally
Interlagos
intermarry
interfaith
interregal
interceder
interferer
interreges
intervener
intermedia
interregna
interferon
intervenor
interleave
interweave
intermezzi
intermezzo
interchain
interphone
interphase
intertidal
intervital
in terminis
inter vivos
interplead
interclude
interplant
inter alios
interfluve
internment
interunion
intermodal
internodal
interpolar
interposal
interzonal
interloper
interposer
in terrorem
interiorly
interwound
intervolve
interspace
interurban
intergrade
interbreed
intertrigo
interbrain
intercross
intergrown
interested
internship
interstice
interstate
interlunar
intertwine
intertwist
intestinal
intestines
intoxicant
intoxicate
inurbanely
inurbanity
inundation
inuredness
invocation
invocatory
invigilate
invaginate
invigorant
invigorate
invaluable
invaluably
involucral
involucrum
invaliding
invalidism
invalidate
invalidity
involution
inventable
invendible
inventible
✧invincible
invincibly
inventress
inviolated
inviolable
inviolably
invariance
invariable
invariably
inveracity
in very deed
invertedly
invertible
Inverclyde
investable
invisibles
investible
investment
invitement
invitingly
inveteracy
inveterate
invitation
invitatory
inwardness
ivy-mantled
icy-pearled
in-your-face
if you ask me
Juan Carlos
Juan Fangio
Jean Fernel
Jiang Zemin
Jean Harlow
Jean Ingres
Jean Millet
Jealous Guy
Jean Piaget

Jean Racine
Jean Renoir
J H Breasted
✧jabberwock
job sharing
jubilantly
jubilation
job-hopping
Jack-a-dandy
jackanapes
jack around
Jacob sheep
Jacob Amman
Jacobinise
Jacobinism
Jacobinize
jackbooted
jackboot it
Jacobethan
Jacobitism
jack donkey
Jockey Club
jockeyship
jackhammer
Jackie Chan
Jack Lemmon
Jack London
jocularity
jaculation
jaculatory
Jack Mormon
jocundness
Jack of Lent
Jack-priest
jack rabbit
jack-rafter
Jack S Kilby
jocoseness
jackstones
Jack Straws
Jack the lad
Jacqueline
Jack Warner
judicially
judication
judicatory
judicature
judicative
Judaically
judgmental
J P Donleavy
Judenhetze
Joe Gargery
Joey Dunlop
Joe Kennedy
Joel Garner
Joe Sixpack
Joe Montana
Joe Frazier
jeely piece
joe-pye weed
jaguarondi
jaguarundi
jugged hare
jigger-mast
jaggedness
✧juggernaut
jiggety-jog
jugglingly
Jagannatha
Jugendstil
John Alcock
John a-Nokes
John Bratby
John Braine
John Buchan
John Backus
John Bright
John Bunyan
John Benbow
John Barnes
John Bruton
John Bowlby
John Cranko
John Cleese
John Calvin
John Dalton
John Denver
John Dryden
John Enders
John Evelyn
John Edrich
John Fisher
John Fowles
John Graham
John Gummer
John Gordon
John Hunter
John Huston
John Howard
John Haynes
John Kirwan
John Lennon
John McAdam
John Madden
John Milton
John Martin
John Morton
John Martyn
✧johnny-cake
Johnny Cash
Johnny Depp
John Napier
John Pilger
John Potter
John Rogers
John Rennie
John Ruskin
John Somers
Johnsonian
Johnsonese
Johnsonism
John Torrey
John Taylor
John Updike
Jehovistic
John Walter
John Wilkes
John Wallis
John Wilbye
John Wesley
J K Huysmans
join battle
jeistiecor
jointuress
joint-stock
joint-stool
jejuneness
JFK Airport
Julian year
jolie laide
jolterhead
Julie Krone
July-flower
jellied eel
Jules Verne
jolly along
Jolly Roger
jelly mould
jellygraph
Jim Hawkins
jump a claim
jam session
J B M Hertzog
jump for joy
jamahiriya
Jamaica rum
jump-jockey
jumblingly
jumble sale
jumhouriya
jimson weed
jumar clamp
Jamiroquai
Jim Crow car
Jim Crowism
James Baker
James Paget
James Mason
James Dewar
James Jeans
Jamesonite
James Joyce
James Bowie
James Tobin
James Bruce
James Braid
James Irwin
James Brown
James Ivory
James E Webb
James Dyson
jump the gun
Jimmy White
Jan van Eyck
juncaceous
Jane Austen
junk-bottle
junk-dealer
Jan Zelezny
junketings
Jan Vermeer
Jan Leeming
jinrikisha
jinricksha
junglefowl
Jane Marple
junior high
junior miss
jingoistic
junior soph
Janus-faced
Janet Baker
Janet Leigh
janitorial
janizarian
jeopardise
jeopardous
jeopardize
jippi-jappa
japan-earth
Japanesery
Japanesque
Jaquenetta
jerk around
jerked-meat
jerkinhead
jardinière
Jerome Kern
jargonelle
J R R Tolkien
jury-rudder
jury-rigged
juristical
Jerry Lewis
jerry-built
Jaruzelski
J B S Haldane
just as well
Jesse James
jus gentium
Jesse Owens
jasperware
Josef Beran
Josh Gibson
jaspideous
Jesuitical
justiciary
jus divinum
just-in-time
justifying
jostlement
J D Salinger
José Orozco
just the job
Joshua tree
jet-setting
Jethro Tull
jour de fête
jeux de mots
jeu de paume
jeune fille
jeune amour
jeu d'esprit
journal-box
journalese
journalise
journalism
journalist
journalize
journeyman
journeying
jouysaunce
jauntiness
jovialness
Javel water
javelin-man
Juvenalian
juvenilely
juvenilise
juvenility
juvenilize
JavaScript®
jovysaunce
Jew-baiting
Jews' houses
J J Williams
jewel-house
Jew's mallow
Jews' mallow
Jew's-myrtle
Jaws of Life®
jaw-breaker
jaw-crusher
Jewishness
Jewish Pale
jaw-twister
jaywalking
Joy Adamson
Jay's Treaty
joyfulness
joyousness
Jozef Glemp
knap-bottle
knave-bairn
klangfarbe
knagginess
knackiness
knackwurst
Klaus Fuchs
kraft paper
Kublai Khan
kibbutznik
kick around
kick boxing
kack-handed
kicksorter
kick up a row
Kodiak bear
kidnapping
kidney bean
kidney dish
kiddiewink
kidologist
klendusity
kieselguhr
keeperless
keepership
Kleig light
keep it dark
khediviate
keep it real
knee-length
keep posted
keep secret
Klebsiella
keep shtoom
Krebs cycle
knee-timber
keep wicket
Kafkaesque
kohanga reo
Kuiper Belt
knife pleat
knife block
knife-money
knife-point
knife-board
kaisership
Klieg light
kriegspiel
Krishnaism
knighthood
knightless
Keith Floyd
Keir Hardie
knight's fee
knick-knack
knickpoint
khidmutgar
khitmutgar
Ku Klux Klan
Kilmarnock
killer cell
kilogramme
kilometric
kill string
Kim Dae-jung
Kimball tag
kimberlite
kempery-man
kymography
ka me, ka thee
Kompong Som
Khmer Rouge
king-at-arms
king-archon
Kansas City
King Arthur
Konrad Zuse
King Creole
King Duncan
kennel-coal
Kennel Club
kennelling
kente cloth
kennelmaid
King Edward
King Farouk
kingfisher
kinchin-lay
King Henry V
Kensington
Kentish-man
Kentish rag
Kantianism
kinglihood
kindliness
kingliness
Kenilworth
kinematics
king-of-arms
King Oliver
kenspeckle
kenophobia
King's Scout
King's Bench
king's peace
king's-chair
king salmon
kind-spoken
king's-spear
kinesipath
king's brief
King's Guide
kinetic art
kenoticist
Ken Russell
kookaburra
knobbiness
know better
knot garden
kaolinitic
kaolinosis
Kuomintang
knock about
knockabout
knock-kneed
knock under
knobkerrie
knockwurst
klootchman
klootchmen
knottiness
Karmathian
kurdaitcha
kersantite
kirn-dollie
Karl Dönitz
Kerr effect
kerseymere
kerygmatic
Karageorge
kerchiefed
karmically
Karrie Webb
Karl Jansky
Karl Ludwig
Karl Malone
kerb-market
karaoke bar
karyoplasm
karyolysis
karyotypic
karyolymph
Karl Popper
Karl Rahner
Karl Renner
Khrushchev
kerb-trader
karate chop
karate-chop
keratinise
keratinous
keratinize
keratotomy
Kirsty Wark
kerb-vendor
kerb weight
Kyrgyzstan
kissing bug
Kiss Me Kate
kiss of life
kiss the rod
Kitcat Club
kith and kin
Kutab Minar
katabolism
Kate Chopin
kitten heel
kitten moth
kite-flying
kitchen-fee
kitchen tea
kitchendom
Kitakyushu
kettledrum
kettle hole
kettle-pins
kittle-pins
kite-marked
ketone body
ketonaemia
Kruger Rand
✧krugerrand
Knut Hamsun
koulibiaca
knuckle-bow
klutziness
Kevin Bacon
Kuwait City
kewpie doll
keyhole saw
keyboarder
kryptonite
Kazakhstan
lead-arming

Lhasa Apsos
lead astray
leaf beetle
leaf-bridge
leaf-cutter
leaderette
leave alone
leaderless
leadenness
leadership
leave it out!
load factor
lead glance
lead-glance
Llangollen
loan-holder
loathingly
leaf-hopper
leathering
load in bulk
leading man
loading bay
leading dog
leaf insect
leafleteer
leafletted
leafleting
leaf monkey
loadmaster
leaf mosaic
Liam Neeson
loan-office
lead pencil
leap second
leaf-sheath
leaf spring
lead the way
leastaways
lean-witted
libecchios
lob's course
libidinist
libidinous
lubber hole
Libreville
lubberlike
lubber line
librettist
lobe-footed
lubricator
lubricious
lobulation
Lubumbashi
Lebensraum
labiovelar
Liber Pater
Labor Party
liberalise
liberalism
liberalist
liberality
liberalize
Labyrinths
labor union
liberation
laboratory
liberatory
liberty cap
liberty-man
La Bastille
lobotomise
lobotomize
lobster pot
labour camp
laboursome
lackadaisy
lucubrator
loco citato
lactescent
Lycaenidae
lackey moth
locker room
lucifugous
Luciferian
luciferase
luciferous
lactic acid
locking-nut
lectionary
lock-keeper
local radio
Loch Lomond
loculament
luculently
Local Group
lackluster
lucklessly
lacklustre
locomobile
locomotion
locomotory
locomotive
laciniated
licensable
laconicism
lac insects
licentiate
licentious
Lychnapsia
lactoscope
lactometer
lactogenic
laccolitic
lectorship
lactosuria
✧lycopodium
lace-pillow
Lacertilia
lachrymals
lachrymary
lachrymose
laceration
lacerative
locust bean
locust bird
Locustidae
lockstitch
Lucy Stoner
lacustrine
locust tree
locateable
locational
lacquering
Lech Walesa
lucky charm
lucky-piece
lucky stone
Lydian mode
led captain
lady chapel
Lady Castle
ladder-back
ledger bait
Ledge Piece
ledger line
ladieswear
Ludwig Mond
lady-killer
Lydford law
lederhosen
lady's-smock
Le Douanier
Lee Iacocca
leechcraft
Lee Enfield
lie in state
lieutenant
laeotropic
Lee Kuan Yew
Leeuwarden
leery about
lherzolite
left atrium
life-estate
left-footed
left-footer
Life Guards
life-giving
left-handed
left-hander
life jacket
lifelessly
life-mortar
La Fontaine
life-rocket
life-renter
life school
life-saving
life-tenant
left-winger
leftwardly
luggage-van
leg warmers
lugubrious
legibility
legacy duty
logicality
Logie Baird
laggen-gird
loggerhead
logography
lignifying
legal eagle
legalistic
ligamental
leguminous
Lagomorpha
loganberry
lageniform
Lughnasadh
logan-stone
lignocaine
logrolling
logopedics
logopaedic
leg spinner
logorrhoea
logorrheic
lagerphone
legislator
logistical
light-faced
light water
light table
light meter
light-tight
Light blues
light-o'-love
legitimacy
legitimise
legitimism
legitimist
legitimate
legitimize
lightening
lighting-up
light-tower
light horse
lighthouse
light opera
lighterman
light-organ
light-armed
lighterage
light-proof
legateship
light lunch
light music
leg-pulling
Luis Buñuel
leishmania
Luigi Pulci
Leibnizian
Luis Somoza
leiotrichy
leisurable
leisurably
like a tansy
Lake Albert
like a charm
like blazes
Lake Baikal
likability
like billy-o
Lake Geneva
Lakshmi Bai
Lake Ladoga
likelihood
likeliness
lake-lawyer
Lake Malawi
like-minded
Lake Nasser
Lake Placid
Lake Saimaa
Lake Taimyr
Lake Taymyr
Lake Vänern
lukewarmly
lukewarmth
Lollardism
liliaceous
Lalla Rookh
lollo rosso
loll-shraub
lilly-pilly
lumbang-oil
Limnaeidae
Lammas-tide
lamp-burner
lime-burner
limaciform
limacology
limicolous
lambdacism
lambdoidal
lumber-camp
✧lambeg drum
lumberjack
lumber-mill
limpet mine
limberneck
limberness
lumber room
lumbersome
lumpectomy
lumber-yard
limb-girdle
lymphocyte
lymphogram
lymphokine
lampholder
lymph gland
lemniscate
limpidness
lamellated
lamentable
lamentably
lemon thyme
lemon shark
liminality
laminarian
laminarise
lemon grass
luminarism
luminarist
laminarize
luminosity
lamination
lumination
luminously
lampoonery
lampoonist
lumbricoid
Lemuroidea
Lamarckian
Lamarckism
lambrequin
lamb's-tails
lumpsucker
limit gauge
limited war
limitrophe
limit point
limitarian
limitation
limitative
le mot juste
limburgite
land agency
lentamente
Lancashire
landammann
longaevous
linebacker
land breeze
land bridge
lend colour
lenocinium
long corner
lancet arch
linseed oil
lancet fish
Langerhans
linked list
lanceolate
lantern fly
lanternist
lenten rose
Longfellow
laniferous
line-fisher
lanuginose
lanuginous
lanigerous
long-headed
lunch-table
long-haired
landholder
lanthanide
land-hunger
landing net
Linlithgow
lentigines
lentivirus
Long Island
lentissimo
lenticular
land-jobber
long jumper
lanzknecht
Land League
land-lubber
landlocked
long-legged
long-lining
loneliness
land-louper
landmining
link-motion
linen paper
London Clay
land office
line of fire
line of life
land-owning
London Wall
lincomycin
long primer
longprimer
long pepper
land-pirate
lansquenet
land reform
liner notes
lunar month
lunar cycle
long-staple
Landsthing
long stitch
lonesomely
land-spring
line squall
Lana Turner
long-termer
lengthsman
lengthwise
lengthways
Langue d'oïl
Langue d'oui
Lingulella
linguiform
languorous
languished
languisher
linguister
linguistic
linguistry
land-values
land-waiter
long-winded
Lenny Henry
Lenny Bruce
Lyon-at-arms
leopard cat
look and say
look-and-say
leopardess
look down on
Lionel Bart
Léo Delibes
loose cover
looyenwork
lyophilise
lyophilize
lion-hunter
looking-for
look lively!
Leo Tolstoy
look snappy
lion's share
Leon Spinks
look slippy
lion's mouth
leontiasis
Leo Szilard
lap dancing
Laplandish
lipochrome
lapidified
lepidolite
lapidarian
lapidarist
lapidation
Lope de Vega
lip-reading
lappet-head
leprechaun
leprechawn
Lippes loop
lapper-milk
lappet moth
lip service
lipography
Lippizaner
lopsidedly
Lippizzana
lipomatous
leproserie
lophophore
lap-jointed
leptosomic
Leptospira
lipophilic
Lupercalia
laparotomy
lip-syncher
Lipizzaner
loquacious
liquescent
liquefying
liquidator
liquidiser
liquidizer
liquidness
liquor laws
lardaceous

Lorna Doone
Lord Adrian
Lord Butler
lorication
Lord Cuvier
Lord Deedes
Lord Devlin
large-scale
largemouth
large order
large print
Lord Florey
Lord Fisher
lyre guitar
Lord Healey
lark-heeled
larghettos
larvicidal
Lord Irvine
Lord Joseph
Lord Kelvin
Lorelei Lee
lordliness
Lord Lister
Lord Lawson
Lord Mackay
laryngitic
laryngitis
Lord Napier
Lorentzian
lordolatry
Lord O'Neill
lord of seat
Lord Porter
Lord Raglan
Lord Reuter
Lord's table
Lord Somers
Lord Tebbit
Lord Wilson
Lord Warden
lorry-hop it
Lassa fever
les Pays Bas
lose colour
lust-dieted
listenable
listener-in
Las Meninas
lesseeship
lysigenous
lose ground
last hurrah
Leslie Ames
lascivious
lesbianism
lusciously
loss-leader
Laszlo Biro
listlessly
last-minute
Los Angeles
losing game
Lysenkoism
loss of face
lissomness
laser level
lustreless
lustration
lustrously
lustreware

Lesh states
Lysistrata
lose the way
lost tribes
Lusitanian
lose weight
lethargied
lethargise
lethargize
La Traviata
late blight
lytic cycle
letter bomb
latter-born
letter-clip
letter-card
Lotte Lenya
letterhead
Luther King
letterless
litter lout
latter-mint
lattermost
lattermath
littermate
letter-wood
latifundia
litigation
latch lever
Letchworth
latticinio
Lithistida
lithifying
Little Bear
little-ease
Little John
Little Lion
little Mary
Little Nell
littleness
Little Rock
little slam
Lutine bell
litany-desk
latent heat
Latin Union
Latin cross
lithomancy
lithomarge
litholatry
lithophane
lithophysa
lithophyse
lithophyte
lithoglyph
lithoclast
lithologic
lithotomic
Lithodomus
lithoprint
lithograph
lithotrite
lithotrity
Lythraceae
liturgical
literalise
literalism
literalist
laterality
literality
literalize

literarily
literosity
literately
literation
literature
lotus-eater
latescence
lutestring
Lotus Sutra
latitation
Lithuanian
litmus test
lauraceous
launcegaye
launch into
Launceston
laundrette
laurdalite
Laundromat®
loundering
laundryman
louver-door
laurelling
Laurentian
laureation
Laurentius
loungingly
lounge suit
Lough Neagh
leuchaemia
loudhailer
laughingly
Lough Foyle
lauric acid
louping-ill
loud-lunged
leucopenia
leucopenic
leukopenia
leukopenic
leucoderma
leukoderma
leucoblast
leucoplast
leukoblast
leukoplast
leucocytic
leukocytic
louvre-door
Louis Malle
Louis-Seize
Louisville
Louis Botha
Louis Durey
laurustine
loud-voiced
laurvikite
love affair
livebearer
livability
lovability
love-broker
live centre
love-favour
levigation
levy in mass
livelihead
lovelihead
livelihood
lavallière
liveliness

loveliness
lovelessly
love letter
lovemaking
love-monger
Living Doll
lovingness
living rock
living room
Livingston
living wage
living will
love potion
lever-watch
liver salts
lover's knot
liver fluke
lovers' lane
laver bread
laverbread
liver-grown
liverishly
leviration
liverwurst
lavishment
lavishness
lovestruck
lavatorial
lovat-green
levitation
live weight
loveworthy
lovey-dovey
lowballing
law-abiding
lawrencium
law reports
lawyer's wig
low-tension
Lawrentian
lawyer vine
law-officer
low-pitched
low-alcohol
Law Society
low-country
low spirits
lawbreaker
low profile
low-profile
lower-class
loweringly
lower house
✧lower grade
lawn tennis
lawfulness
law-burrows
lex scripta
lexicology
loxodromic
lexigraphy
Luxembourg
luxuriance
luxuriancy
lay hands on
ley-farming
lay baptism
lay a course
loyal toast
lay on hands
lay to heart

lay brother
lay store by
lizardfish
lazar house
lazarettes
lazarettos
Lazy Sunday
meandering
Miami Beach
meaningful
mealie meal
measliness
mean much to
Meal Monday
meal-monger
meat market
miasmatous
Meadowbank
miarolitic
meadow lark
meat packer
meagreness
meatscreen
meal ticket
myasthenia
myasthenic
Maastricht
measurable
measurably
measure off
measuredly
measure out
Meaux Abbey
mobocratic
mobile home
mobile shop
Mabinogion
Maccabaean
mechanical
mechanizer
Michaelmas
muck around
Mocha stone
mace-bearer
macadamise
macadamize
Macedonian
mucedinous
Mickey Finn
Michel Roux
muciferous
mock-heroic
machinable
machinator
machineman
machinegun
mackintosh
mycologist
maculation
maculature
muck-midden
mock-modest
Mt Cameroon
maconochie
Mach number
meconopses
meconopsis
microfarad
microwaves
mucronated
mock orange

✧macrozamia
macrofauna
microfauna
macrocarpa
microscale
microscope
microscopy
micrometer
Micronesia
micrometre
micrometry
microseism
macrophage
microphyll
microphone
microphyte
microfiche
microlight
microlitic
microfibre
macrobiota
macrobiote
microbiota
microskirt
microsleep
microcline
macroflora
microflora
microsomal
microtonal
micrococci
micrologic
micropolis
microtomic
macrospore
microspore
microprobe
microcrack
microprint
micrograph
macroprism
microprism
micro drive
microburst
micropylar
microcytic
macrocycle
mycoplasma
mock privet
mycorrhiza
mycorhizae
mycorhizal
muck-raking
Mucorineae
macaronics
macaronies
maceration
mica-schist
muckspread
mycetology
Mt Cotopaxi
✧mock turtle
mycetozoan
mediagenic
midday meal
mediatress
mediastina
medicalise
medicalize
medicament
medicaster

medication
medicative
medievally
midden-cock
madder-lake
madreporic
midsection
Midwestern
modifiable
Modigliani
made ground
Madagascan
Madagascar
midshipman
Madrileños
midnightly
midfielder
mudskipper
muddle away
medullated
middle-aged
Middle Ages
middlebrow
Middle East
middle game
muddle-head
middlemost
Madelenian
mudslinger
middlingly
muddlingly
middle name
modularise
modularity
modularize
modalistic
meddlesome
modulation
middle term
Middle West
madonnaish
mud volcano
mudlogging
Midlothian
mid-morning
mediocracy
mediocrity
madbrained
moderniser
modernizer
modern jazz
modernness
moderatrix
moderately
moderation
moderatism
medusiform
modishness
Midas touch
midi-system
meditation
meditative
Medjugorje
medium-term
medium-wave
myelinated
mnemonical
myeloblast
meerschaum
meet the ear
meet the eye

muffin-bell
mafficking
My Fair Lady
mefloquine
Magna Carta
migraineur
migrainous
magnetical
magnetiser
magnetizer
megagamete
magnifical
Magnificat
magpie lark
magpie moth
McGuinness
magnifying
megalosaur
megalithic
magi-marker
mega-merger
Magen David
Mogen David
meganewton
mignonette
megaphonic
megaparsec
megascopic
magistracy
magistrand
magistrate
mightiness
magnum opus
mugwumpery
Mahe Island
Mahayanist
Mainbocher
main chance
main clause
MRI scanner
main course
maiden aunt
mailed fist
✧**maidenhead**
maidenhair
maidenhood
maidenlike
maiden-meek
maiden name
maimedness
maiden over
maiden pink
maiden race
maidenweed
meiofaunal
Meiji Tenno
mainlander
mainlining
main memory
Maid Marian
meitnerium
maisonette
mainpernor
main stream
mainstream
main street
mainspring
maintained
maintainer
moisturise
moisturize
mujaheddin
major scale
major third
major piece
major-domos
majestical
majuscular
Mt Krakatoa
make amends
Mikhail Tal
make a point
make a noise
make a break
make a stand
make-belief
Mike Gibson
make little
Mt Kinabalu
make no odds
makunouchi
maker's mark
make tracks
make the cut
make-weight
melba sauce
mallanders
Malta fever
malvaceous
meliaceous
mill around
melba toast
molybdenum
molybdosis
Malabar-rat
milk bottle
malacology
melaconite
melic-grass
mile-castle
melicotton
melocotoon
maledicent
maladapted
maladdress
malodorous
mallee-bird
mallenders
Maltese dog
malleiform
mallee-fowl
mallee gate
millesimal
millefiori
malted milk
millennial
millennium
muliebrity
millet-seed
malfeasant
miller's dog
malleation
maleficial
maleficent
malefactor
My Left Foot
malignance
malignancy
malaguetta
malignment
mole hunter
Malthusian
multiparae
multiparas
multifaced
maleic acid
multi-faith
multiparty
multimeter
multimedia
millimetre
melting-pot
malling jug
Malpighian
multiphase
millilitre
mollitious
multivious
multiskill
multiplied
multiplier
multiplane
multiflora
millionary
multipolar
multivocal
multilobed
multiloquy
milliprobe
mulligrubs
multi-track
multigrade
multi-stage
multistory
multicycle
mollifying
malo-lactic
malt liquor
melomaniac
moliminous
melanocyte
malentendu
malingerer
melanaemia
melancholy
molendinar
melanomata
Melanesian
melanistic
mylonitise
mylonitize
meliorator
male orchis
mileometer
Mallophaga
mellophone
milk of lime
mellowness
millocracy
malcontent
multocular
mole plough
malapropos
malapertly
maltreater
malgré tout
male rhymes
melismatic
Miles Davis
mulishness
mild-spoken
millstream
militiaman
Militiades
militantly
militarily
militarise
militarism
militarist
mulattress
militarize
molluscoid
molluscous
malevolent
millwright
malt whisky
millworker
malaxation
Malayaalam
Molly Keane
Molly Bloom
mime artist
memberless
membership
mammectomy
mimography
mumping-day
mummifying
Mt McKinley
mamillated
mumblement
mumblingly
mumble-news
mammogenic
mammograph
mimeograph
✧**mumbo-jumbo**
memory bank
memory card
memory leak
memory lane
membranous
memorandum
memory span
memorative
Mimosaceae
mammy-wagon
mummy-wheat
mummy-cloth
manna-larch
maniacally
Monday Club
mangabeira
mental home
manzanilla
Manzanillo
mendacious
Montagnard
manna-grass
manna-croup
mandamuses
mini-budget
minibudget
montbretia
mini-buffet
manubriums
mind-bender
Manichaean
monochasia
monocratic
Manichaeus
monocyclic
Manicheism
monactinal
monoclinal
monoclinic
monoculous
menacingly
monoclonal
monocarpic
monochroic
monochrome
monochromy
manicurist
monocerous
monadiform
menu-driven
monadology
Monte Carlo
monkey boat
minced beef
Monteverdi
Montenegro
monkey-gaff
minke whale
montelimar
Montevideo
Minié rifle
monoecious
Monte Albán
mannerless
Montego Bay
montero-cap
mince words
monkey pump
mondegreen
monkey rail
monkey rope
monkey suit
manteltree
monkey tail
man's estate
manoeuvrer
manoeuvres
man-servant
munificent
munifience
man of skill
manifolder
many-folded
manifoldly
minifloppy
manifestly
manifestos
man of straw
monography
manageable
manageably
management
Montgomery
monogamist
monogamous
monogynian
monogenism
monogenist
monogenous
monogynous
managerial
manageress
Monegasque
many-headed
mind-healer
monohybrid
monohydric
month's mind
manchineel
minehunter
Manchurian
Manchester
Munchausen
mendicancy
mendicants
Monticello
Mandingoes
mansionary
Monsignore
Monsignori
Monsignors
mandibular
monticulus
mundifying
moniliasis
Monel metal®
moniliform
monologise
monologist
monologize
Manila hemp
minglement
minglingly
mantle rock
mindlessly
monolithic
monomachia
✧**minimal art**
minimalism
minimalist
monomaniac
monumental
Menominees
Montmartre
mint master
manumitted
manumitter
manometric
monometric
man-entered
meningitic
meningitis
meningioma
monandrous
monzonitic
mentorship
mangosteen
monophasic
monopodial
monopodium
monopteral
monoplegia
monoplegic
monopteron
monopteros
Montpelier
monopolise
monopolism
monopolist
manipulate
monopolize
monophobia
monophobic
monophonic
menopausal
Mina Qaboos
mind-reader
minor canon
minor scale
Man Fridays
mandragora
menarcheal
monarchial
Monarchian
menorrhoea
minor third
monarchise
monarchism
monarchist
monorchism
monarchize
monorhinal
miner's inch
minor piece
mineral tar
mineral wax
mineralogy
mineral oil
miner's lamp
mineralise
mineralist
mongrelise
mongrelism
mineralize
mongrelize
manor-house
miner's worm
monorhymed
monostable
ministeria
monastical
monistical
monoskiing
Mina Sulman
monk's cloth
monosemous
Montserrat
miniseries
minestrone
ministrant
manuscript
ministress
minuscular
meniscuses
monostylar
monstrance
man-stealer
minute-bell
minute book
monotocous
minute-drop
monothecal
minstrelsy
monotheism
monotheist
minute hand
minute-jack
minuteness
monotonous
munitioner
monitorial
monetarily
monetarism
monetarist
menstruums
menstruate
menstruous
monstruous
manducable
mensurable

monaurally
maneuverer
minauderie
man-queller
manfulness
mansuetude
minivolley
monovalent
mine worker
monoxylous
Monaxonida
moneymaker
money-taker
money wages
money talks
money-bound
money order
Muntz metal
myocardiac
myocardial
myocardium
moon around
moonflower
Maoritanga
myopically
muonic atom
Maori chief
Moominland
myoblastic
myological
moon-raised
moonraking
myographic
moonshiner
moonstruck
moonstrike
moonwalker
maple candy
map-reading
maple sugar
maple syrup
mephitical
Mt Pinatubo
map-mounter
meperidine
mopishness
maquillage
morganatic
mortal coil
mortadella
mortadelle
myrtaceous
myriadfold
margaritic
Marianists
mordacious
Mary Anning
marmarosis
mercaptide
mercantile
marcantant
Mark Antony
Maria Bueno
marc brandy
mirabilite
Myricaceae
miracidium
miraculous
Mary Cassat
meridional
marketable

Mersey beat
market-bell
marker buoy
marcescent
market-hall
Muraenidae
merceriser
mercerizer
Marseilles
marvelling
martellato
marvellous
Marie Lloyd
markedness
Merseyside
martensite
market-town
Marie Curie
Marcel wave
Marcgravia
morigerate
morigerous
marchlands
marsh-fever
morphogeny
marshalled
marshaller
Marshalsea
morphology
morphemics
marchantia
merchantry
marshiness
morphinism
marsh-robin
marshlocks
margharita
Murphy's law
march-stone
mirthfully
marginated
marginalia
Martin Amis
marginally
Martin Bell
margin call
morbidezza
martingale
marking-ink
marking-nut
Marvin Gaye
Martinique
martial law
martial art
martialism
martialist
morbillous
Marcionist
Marxianism
morbidness
Marcionite
morris-pike
Martin Pipe
Martin Rees
Martin Ryle
Morris-tube
mercifully
mortifying
Marble Arch
Mary Leakey
marble cake

moral sense
moral agent
moral fibre
mural crown
moralistic
Mark Morris
marine acid
Mare Nubium
marine glue
myringitis
Mark Napier
marine soap
Mariolater
Mariolatry
Maryolatry
Mario Lanza
mirror ball
marrow-bone
myrioscope
mirror carp
Mark O'Meera
marionette
marrowless
more or less
mirror site
Mary of Teck
mirrorwise
Mary Peters
marprelate
Mark Rothko
margravine
margravate
mare's-tails
Marc Séguin
maraschino
Mt Rushmore
Morisonian
moroseness
markswoman
meritocrat
Marita Koch
Moreton Bay
More Thomas
marathoner
moratorium
marguerite
marquisate
Mary Wigman
Mary Wesley
merrymaker
merry-night
Mostaganem
mistakable
mistakably
mustard gas
miswandred
mustard oil
muscardine
mistakenly
message box
message-boy
mustachios
muscarinic
Mrs Gaskell
mismanners
maskalonge
maskanonge
mystagogic
mess around
mystagogue
mystagogus

mascarpone
miscanthus
Mrs Danvers
mossbacked
musk beetle
misobserve
mossbunker
musicianer
music paper
musicianly
music-shell
musicology
musical box
musicality
music folio
music house
misocapnic
music drama
music stand
music stool
miseducate
mass defect
misadvised
mesodermal
Moshe Dayan
misbehaved
masked ball
muster book
missel-bird
MasterCard®
master-card
misleading
misreading
muster-file
Mister Hyde
master-hand
masterhood
mesmerical
Mustelidae
Mustelinae
mesmeriser
mesmerizer
mysterious
misbelieve
Mrs Jellyby
miscellany
mis-selling
masterless
mastermind
misdeeming
misseeming
misdeemful
master page
mussel-plum
master race
muster roll
musket-rest
mastership
musket-shot
mismeasure
Mister Toad
missel-tree
mastectomy
misfeature
misventure
masterwork
masterwort
mystery-man
mist-flower
mishguggle
misogamist

misogynist
misogynous
mischmetal
Mt St Helens
mischanter
mesohippus
masa harina
misthought
masticable
mosaically
mystically
masticator
mosaic gold
mashing-tub
mashie iron
muslin-kale
missiology
missionary
Messianism
Messianist
missionise
missionize
maskinonge
maskirovka
mystifying
mess jacket
misologist
moss-litter
Mesolithic
misallying
mass medium
musk-mallow
mass market
mass-market
mesomorphy
Miss Marple
mesomerism
misimprove
mesenteric
mesenteron
mesenchyme
mass number
mason's mark
misentreat
misandrist
misandrous
Mishnayoth
muscovados
misconceit
musk orchid
misconduct
miswording
Massoretic
Mussorgsky
Muscovitic
mess or mell
Moscow Mule
miscounsel
misjoinder
miscompute
miscorrect
misconster
misworship
Moshoeshoe
miscontent
misfortune
mastodynia
masspriest
misspelled
mysophobia
mesophytic

miscreance
miscreancy
miscreated
misarrange
miscreator
misericord
Misery Guts
mushroomer
mistrysted
mistress it
mistressly
misprision
misdrawing
mistrayned
mesoscaphe
mesosphere
moss stitch
Miss Saigon
MKSA system
Mosasaurus
mesothelia
miss the bus
miss the cut
mesitylene
mesothorax
musk turtle
muscularly
masturbate
Mussulmans
masquerade
mosquitoes
musquetoon
mosey along
mutual wall
metabolise
metabolism
metabolite
mutability
metabolize
mute button
meticulous
metacentre
metacarpal
metacarpus
Matt Dillon
mathematic
mitten-crab
mother cell
mother city
mitre wheel
mitre shell
motherhood
Matterhorn
mother lode
motherland
matterless
motherless
Metternich
mitre-joint
Methedrine®
Mitterrand
Mother's Day
mother ship
mother spot
mother-to-be
mother upon
Motherwell
motherwort
moth-flower
metagalaxy
mutagenise

mutagenize
mitigating
mitigation
mitigatory
mitigative
match-maker
matchmaker
moth-hunter
match-joint
match point
matchboard
matchstick
metrically
mythically
metri causa
matricidal
mythiciser
mythicizer
methinketh
matricliny
methionine
matrifocal
matrilocal
matriarchy
matricular
matellasse
mytiliform
metalepsis
metaleptic
mettlesome
mutilation
metallurgy
metempiric
metamerism
mating type
mutinously
motoneuron
methomania
metromania
mythomania
mutton bird
mutton chop
mutton-fist
muttonhead
matronhood
meteorital
methodical
methodiser
methodizer
meteoritic
matron-like
matrocliny
motionless
mythologer
metrologic
metronomic
✧metropolis
mythologic
mythopoeia
mythopoeic
mutton suet
matronship
metrostyle
matronymic
metronymic
metaplasia
metaplasis
metaphoric
metaphrase
metaphrast
metaphysic

Words marked ✧ can also be spelled with one or more capital letters

materially
maternally
mithridate
matureness
motorcoach
motor lodge
motor lorry
motormouth
motor areas
motor drive
maturation
maturative
motorcycle
metastases
metastasis
metastatic
mutessarif
metastable
metatheses
Metatheria
metathesis
metathetic
metatheory
metathorax
mutational
metatarsal
metatarsus
✧methuselah
Mitsubishi®
motiveless
motivation
methyldopa
matryoshka
matryoshki
Maupassant
mauvais ton
mouldiness
mouldboard
maundering
Mauretania
mouvementé
mousepiece
mouse-sight
meum et tuum
mouthparts
mouthpiece
mouth organ
moucharaby
mouth music
Mauritania
Moulinette®
moudiewart
moudiewort
maudlinism
mourningly
mournfully
mausoleums
mousseline
Mount Mayon
mountebank
moustached
moustaches
Mount Pelée
Mount Hekla
Mount Kenya
Mount Thera
Mount Thira
Mount Sinai
mountained
Mount Logan
Mount Qogir
Mousterian
mount guard
movability
movie-maker
movie house
movelessly
moving-coil
Mt Vesuvius
mavourneen
Mawlawites
mowdiewart
mowdiewort
Mexico City
Mexican War
Mexican tea
Mexican hog
mixed-media
mixed train
mixed grill
myxoedemic
✧mixolydian
maxilliped
maxillulae
myxomycete
Maximilian
maximalist
Maxim Gorky
myxomatous
mixing bowl
Max F Perutz
maxi-single
mixty-maxty
Mayologist
may blossom
mayonnaise
May-morning
mozzarella
mizzenmast
mizzensail
Mozambican
Mozambique
mezzo-piano
mezzotinto
mezzo-forte
mazarinade
near-begaun
neat-cattle
✧neandertal
neat-handed
Nias Island
near-legged
Ngaio Marsh
✧neapolitan
noble metal
noblewoman
noblewomen
nubiferous
nubigenous
Nibelungen
nibblingly
✧Nobel prize
nebulosity
nobilitate
nebulously
Nabathaean
nectareous
nyctalopes
nyctalopia
nyctalopic
Nick Bottom
nickelback
nickelling
nucleolate
nucleonics
nuclearise
nuclearize
nucleoside
nucleosome
nucleotide
nucleation
nuciferous
Nick Hornby
nyctinasty
noctilucae
necklacing
Nicol prism
necromancy
necrolater
necromania
necrolatry
nectocalyx
necroscopy
necrophobe
necrophile
necrophily
nicrosilal
necrologic
necropolis
Nicaraguan
nécessaire
Nachschlag
nicotinism
nickumpoop
nucivorous
nudibranch
nidicolous
nidderling
nudge, nudge
nidificate
nidifugous
nod through
nidulation
nodulation
nidamental
nidamentum
noematical
Noël Coward
ne'er-do-well
Noetianism
needle bank
needle-book
needle-bath
needlecord
needle-case
needlefish
needlessly
needle time
needlework
nifedipine
niffy-naffy
niggardise
niggardize
nigrescent
neglection
neglectful
neglective
negligence
negligible
negligibly
Nigel Short
nigglingly
nigromancy
negrophobe
negrophile
niger seeds
night latch
night-watch
night-raven
night-taper
negotiable
night table
negotiator
night-palsy
Night Fever
night heron
nightshade
night shift
night-chair
night-churr
night shark
nightshirt
nightpiece
nightrider
night-light
night-night
night-sight
night-blind
nightclass
night-glass
night-cloud
night-house
night-spell
nightdress
nightstick
night-steed
nightstand
night-stool
✧night nurse
negatively
negativism
negativist
negativity
nihil ad rem
Nehallenia
nihilistic
Nohon Shoki
nail-biting
Naiadaceae
nail enamel
noisemaker
noise about
nail-headed
neighborly
nail polish
Neil Sedaka
nulla-nulla
nullifying
nelumbiums
nilpotency
Nelson Mass
Nelly Sachs
nom de plume
number line
numberless
number nine
numbers man
nomography
nympholept
numskulled
nomologist
nimbleness
namelessly
nominal par
No Man's Land
no-man's-land
nominalise
nominalism
nominalist
nominalize
nominately
nomination
nominative
nomen nudum
Nemertinea
numerology
numerosity
numeration
numerously
numismatic
nematocide
nematocyst
name the day
nomothetes
nomothetic
Nematoidea
nematology
nummulated
nummulitic
nameworthy
namby-pamby
non-payment
non-factual
non-natural
non-ability
non-bearing
non-ferrous
nun's-fiddle
nonagenary
nonchalant
non-violent
non-vintage
non-fiction
nunciature
non-aligned
nonplussed
nonplusing
non-playing
non-smoking
no-nonsense
non-society
non-joinder
nincompoop
non-content
non-soluble
non-arrival
nandrolone
non-gremial
non-drinker
Nina Simone
nanisation
nineteenth
nine-to-five
non-ethical
non-utility
non-starter
non-nuclear
non-current
non-swimmer
Nancy Astor
nanny state
nanization
Neofascism
Neofascist
Neo-Kantian
neogenesis
neogenetic
noogenesis
neoterical
neorealism
neorealist
neophiliac
niobic acid
neoliberal
neoclassic
neoplastic
neological
nuptiality
napkin ring
napalm bomb
Napoleonic
nipplewort
nepenthean
nip and tuck
nephoscope
nephologic
nephograph
no par value
nephridium
nephrology
nephralgia
nephropexy
nephrotomy
naphthalic
naphthenic
nepotistic
no question
Norman arch
narratable
Norway pine
Norman Shaw
nero-antico
nerve agent
nurse-child
nurse shark
nerve fibre
nerve block
nursehound
Norbertine
nurseryman
northwards
north water
northabout
north polar
North Korea
northbound
✧northerner
nursing-bra
narcissism
narcissist
'Ndrangheta
Ndrangheta
narcomania
narrowboat
narrowband
narrowcast
narcolepsy
narrowness
narrow seas
nurturable
nystagmoid
no such luck
nosocomial
nosography
nesting box
nosologist
nasal spray
nostopathy
nostomania
nostologic
nosophobia
Nasoraeans
nose tackle
nose to tail
✧nasturtium
nitrazepam
not half bad
Nathan Hale
notability
not a chance
noticeable
noticeably
notodontid
nathelesse
nutmegging
no the wiser
natterjack
nethermore
nethermost
netherward
notifiable
notch-board
nitric acid
Nottingham
nothingism
nothing but
net-fishing
net-fishery
nutritious
nit-picking
nitwittery
nitrifying
nettle-cell
nettle-fish
nettlelike
nettle rash
nettlesome
natalitial
nettle-tree
not a little
notonectal
nationally
notionally
Nothofagus
nitrometer
note of hand
nationhood
networking
nationless
not go amiss
not for nuts
not to worry
nitro-group
nationwide
notaphilic
netiquette
notarially
not cricket
Notoryctes
nutcracker
nature cure
natural gas
natural law
naturalise
✧naturalism
naturalist
naturalize

nature-myth
naturopath
naturistic
notaryship
note-shaver
notational
nutational
natatorial
natatorium
not much of a
not much cop
not but what
native bear
native-born
native land
nativeness
native rock
nativistic
noteworthy
not exactly
neural arch
naumachiae
naumachias
naumachies
neural tube
noun clause
Nouadhibou
noumenally
neurectomy
nauseating
nauseative
nauseously
nautically
nourice-fee
neurilemma
nourishing
Niue Island
nautiluses
Nouakchott
neurocanal
neuropathy
neurogenic
neurolemma
neuroblast
neuroplasm
neurotoxic
neurotoxin
✧neuroptera
neurolysis
noun phrase
neutralino
neutralise
neutralism
neutralist
neutrality
neutralize
neutrophil
neutrettos
nourriture
novicehood
novaculite
noviceship
navigation
Nova Iguacu
Nevil Shute
naval crown
novelistic
✧never-never
Nova Scotia
news agency
newfangled
new-married
nowcasting
new economy
new-economy
newscaster
newsdealer
New Zealand
New Realism
New Kingdom
new-fledged
newsletter
newsmonger
now and then
Now, Voyager
New College
newsreader
New Orleans
New Ireland
New Britain
newishness
newsvendor
news-writer
newsworthy
next friend
nix my dolly
Nazaritism
ouananiche
opalescent
Orange Bath
orange-lily
orange peel
orange-root
orange tree
orange-wife
orange-wood
oxalic acid
On an Island
ovariotomy
Oranjestad
on all hands
on all sides
of all loves
on all fours
oratorical
on approval
Onagraceae
Omar Sharif
ox-antelope
oracularly
opaqueness
oval window
obbligatos
ombrometer
ombrophobe
ombrophile
orchardman
orcharding
orchardist
✧occidental
once-errand
orchestral
orchestics
orchestric
once for all
once-for-all
once in a way
orchideous
oscillator
oncologist
occultness
osculation
osculatory
on commando
occupation
occupative
occurrence
Oscar Wilde
occasional
occasioner
oscitantly
oscitation
ordeal bean
old-maidish
old-maidism
oldfangled
old masters
Old Scratch
old economy
old-economy
ordainable
Old Kingdom
ordainment
oedematose
oedematous
ordonnance
Oudenaarde
Old English
ordinarily
ordinately
ordination
odd-jobbing
old soldier
odd-looking
old country
old-fogyish
Oedipus Rex
order paper
order about
obdurately
obduration
orderly bin
Old Hundred
Ordovician
olde-worlde
one-man band
open access
over and out
opera seria
oleraceous
opera cloak
opera glass
overabound
opera house
one-man show
overactive
opera buffa
overbidder
overbridge
overboldly
open bundle
overburden
overbought
overcharge
open cheque
operculate
overcolour
overcommit
overcanopy
overcooked
overcaught
overdaring
overdosage
ox-eye daisy
overexcite
overexpose
overextend
operettist
overfreely
overflight
overfondly
overflowed
oleiferous
overglance
oleography
oreography
overgreedy
oleaginous
overground
overgrowth
open-hearth
open-handed
overhanded
obeliscoid
one-sidedly
overinform
one-nighter
obediently
overinsure
overleaven
overlabour
overlocker
oreologist
overlander
overlooker
open letter
ocellation
overlaunch
overlaying
open-minded
overmantel
open market
overmaster
overmatter
ocean basin
overnicely
ocean perch
oceanology
ocean-going
oceanarium
one another
overoffice
one-worlder
one's own man
overplaced
overpraise
overpriced
oleophilic
open prison
overpeople
overreckon
overridden
overriding
over-refine
oneirology
overruling
overrunner
overrashly
ore-wrought
overraught
overstayer
overslaugh
open season
overshadow
oversubtle
open secret
oversleeve
open sights
Odelsthing
open-stitch
overshower
oversupply
overspread
overstruck
overstride
overstrain
overstrike
overstrong
overstrung
overstress
open system
open sesame
over the way
over the top
over-the-top
overtimely
open-topped
overturner
overthrust
overthwart
overweight
overwinter
overworked
overwisely
off balance
officially
officiator
officialty
office-book
office girl
olfactible
offsetable
off-message
off the beam
off the bone
off the cuff
off the face
off the hook
off the mark
off the reel
off the wall
off-licence
offendedly
offenceful
offendress
off one's nut
off-roading
off spinner
Oxford bags
Oxford blue
Oxford clay
offer a knee
offer price
Oxford shoe
obfuscated
oafishness
offishness
ox-fluoride
off-putting
of few words
Olga Korbut
oogamously
organicism
organicist
organogram
organogeny
organ-point
organismal
organismic
oughtlings
ochraceous
Ophiacodon
ophicleide
ophthalmia
ophthalmic
ophiolater
ophiolatry
ophiolitic
ophiologic
ophiomorph
ochlocracy
other gates
othergates
other ranks
otherwhile
otherwhere
otherworld
other guess
otherguess
Ophiuridae
oligarchal
oligarchic
olivaceous
olive-shell
olive green
olive-green
Oliver Reed
originally
oxidisable
oxidizable
originator
opinionist
opium-eater
orientated
orientally
orientator
Orion's belt
opisometer
ovipositor
oligoclase
oligopsony
otioseness
odiousness
obituarist
Orimulsion®
object ball
object code
objectival
objectless
object-soul
objuration
objets d'art
oak leather
Ooka Shohei
oil painter
on location
oil of thyme
obligement
obligingly
obligation
obligatory
Oblomovism
Owlspiegle
owlishness
oblateness
oblational
obliterate
oil-burning
osmidrosis
osmometric
osmiridium
ommatidium
osmeterium
obnubilate
omnibus box
omnificent
omniferous
omnigenous
oenologist
ornamental
ornamenter
oenophilic
omniparity
omniparous
omnipotent
orneriness
omniscient
ornateness
ornithosis
ornithopod
omnivorous
onomastics
O's of Advent
on occasion
oboe d'amore
ozone layer
on one's case
orogenesis
orogenetic
on one's game
on one's legs
on one's mind
on one's toes
onocentaur
of one's word
omophagous
oropharynx
omophorion
opotherapy
odorimetry
orological
otological
orographic
odontocete
odontogeny
odontology
odontalgia
odontalgic
odontolite
odontomata
orotundity
oops-a-daisy
orphanhood
orpheoreon
oppression
oppressive
oppugnancy
oppilation
oppilative
oophoritis
opprobrium
opposeless
oppositely
✧opposition
oppositive
Oireachtas
o'er-drowsed

Oirishness
obsidional
oyster-bank
oyster-farm
oyster-park
obstetrics
oyster-wife
ossiferous
on schedule
obsoletely
obsoletion
obsoletism
opsomaniac
opsiometer
oesophagus
obsequious
observance
observancy
observable
observably
observator
obstructer
obstructor
oestradiol
ossivorous
outbalance
outs and ins
outlandish
ostraceous
outrageous
outbargain
out-patient
outdacious
ostracodan
outgassing
outpassion
optic nerve
optical art
octodecimo
on the latch
on the march
on the watch
on the cards
on the cadge
on the tapis
on the wagon
outgeneral
on the bench
on the level
on the verge
outperform
on the cheap
on the shelf
on the whole
on the tiles
of the clock
on the block
on the blink
on the alert
on the slate
outlet mall
on the anvil
on the money
on the ropes
on the rocks
on the house
on the loose
on the brain
on the cross
on the fritz
on the prowl
out-pension
outmeasure
on the stump
outjetting
outsetting
on the outer
on the quiet
on the buroo
out of reach
out of whack
out of shape
out of phase
Otto Frisch
out of sight
out of place
out of touch
out of joint
out of court
out of doors
out-of-doors
out of sorts
out of order
out of print
out of stock
out of synch
Otto Graham
octogenary
octogynous
octahedral
octahedron
octohedron
obtainable
outside-car
ostrich-egg
ostrichism
outfielder
outvillain
obtainment
outfitting
outwitting
on this wise
ontologist
optologist
outbluster
outclassed
outflowing
optimalise
optimality
optimalize
octamerous
optimistic
optometric
out and away
oftentimes
ostensible
ostensibly
out on a limb
octandrian
octonarian
octandrous
octonarius
octangular
orthopaedy
osteopathy
optionally
orthocaine
Orthoceras
orthogenic
orthopedia
orthopedic
osteogenic
Osteolepis
outlodging
orthophyre
osteophyte
of two minds
Ostpolitik
orthoclase
osteoblast
osteoclast
orthopnoea
orthogonal
orthotonic
orthotopic
orthodoxly
osteocolla
orthoepist
outcompete
orthodromy
outpouring
orthograph
orthotropy
orthoprism
orthopraxy
orthoptics
✧orthoptera
orthoptist
out to lunch
outspeckle
octopodous
octaploidy
octoploidy
octopusher
outbreath'd
outbreathe
otter shrew
otter shell
outer limit
otter hound
otter-board
Outer House
outer space
otter-trawl
obturation
outwrought
obtuseness
outstretch
out at elbow
outstation
optatively
obtruncate
outjutting
octavalent
Octavio Paz
ottava rima
outsweeten
out-dweller
outswinger
oculomotor
ouvirandra
or whatever
or whenever
or wherever
oxy-calcium
Ozymandias
oxygenator
oxygen debt
oxygen mask
oxygen tent
onyx marble
oxymoronic
oxy-bromide
oryctology
on your bike
on your mark
pray a tales
phalangeal
phalangist
Pharaoh ant
play around
play a prize
play-acting
play action
play-by-play
praecocial
planchette
prancingly
Planck's law
peat-caster
plat du jour
peau de soie
plauditory
Plaid Cymru
peacemaker
platelayer
platemaker
planetaria
plane table
phagedaena
peace-party
place value
prayer bead
prayer book
phagedenic
prayer flag
peace of God
placer-gold
plane chart
planetical
Peace River
plate-fleet
plate glass
plate-glass
prayerless
phanerogam
Peace Corps
plate-proof
pease-brose
pease-straw
peacefully
plateau out
playfellow
plangently
playground
peach-water
peach Melba
peach-bloom
pea shingle
poachiness
peashooter
peacherino
peach-stone
pharisaism
pratincole
play it cool
planimeter
Praxiteles
planimetry
placidness
planigraph
plagiarise
plagiarism
plagiarist
plagiarize
pianissimo
prankingly
planktonic
playleader
Pearl S Buck
phallocrat
phallicism
praeludium
pearl-shell
pearl-white
pearl diver
Pearl River
phalloidin
pearly king
pearl onion
phaelonion
pearliness
pearl-stone
plasma cell
pharmacist
plasmodial
plasmodesm
psalmodise
psalmodist
plasmodium
psalmodize
plasmogamy
plasmolyse
plasmolyze
pearmonger
praemunire
psammophil
plasmosoma
plasmosome
pragmatics
pragmatise
pragmatism
pragmatist
pragmatize
plain weave
plainchant
phaenology
plaintless
plain flour
praenomens
praenomina
plain tripe
phaenotype
planometer
Platonical
peacockery
peacock ore
peacockish
planoblast
pianoforte
piano organ
piano stool
Paavo Nurmi
phagocytic
praepostor
play possum
peat-reeker
prairie hen
prairie dog
pea-brained
pea-trainer
pear-shaped
praesidium
playschool
pear-switch
praiseless
praisingly
plastic bag
practician
practicals
Plasticine®
plastic art
plasticise
plasticity
Pratt's Club
plasticize
plastidule
play the wag
play the kip
prattlebox
plastogamy
play tricks
plastilina
platteland
phantomish
plastinate
plant-house
plant louse
praetorial
praetorian
psalterian
plastering
praetorium
psalterium
phantasmal
phantasmic
phantastic
phantasime
practisant
practising
phantastry
plantation
play truant
plaguesome
plague-spot
plague-sore
play-writer
playwright
pharyngeal
platypuses
Pobedy Peak
public bill
publishing
publicness
pebbledash
pebble-ware
puberulent
puberulous
pubescence
pick-and-mix
pochade box
pack animal
peccadillo
piccadillo
piccadilly
piccalilli
pickadillo
pickadilly
pack a punch
pace-bowler
pick-cheese
packet-boat
pocketbook
pocket-comb
picket-duty
packed file
pocket-fuls
pace-egging
pocket-hole
picket line
pocketless
pickedness
packet-note
packet-ship
pocket veto
peckerwood
pacifiable
Pacific War
Pacific Rim
pacificism
pacificist
pacificate
Pocahontas
pectinated
pectic acid
picric acid
packing box
pichiciego
picnicking
peculiarly
poculiform
peculation
pockmantie
pockmarked
pectorally
pycnometer
pictorical
picrotoxin
pycnogonid
pack or peel
pycnospore
pictograph
pycnostyle
pickpocket
pockpitted
picaresque
packsaddle
Pecos River
Picts' house
pace-setter
packthread
picture hat
picture rod
pick-up head
pachymeter
picayunish
pediatrics
podiatrist
pediculate
Pediculati
pediculous
pedicurist
padded cell
pedagogics
pedagogism
podagrical
pad the hoof
pudding bag
padding-ken
pudding-pie
paddle boat
paddlefish
pedologist
podologist
pedal point
pedal-board
pedal-organ

paddle-wood
pedal cycle
pedimental
pedimented
pedantical
peduncular
pedipalpus
pedereroes
pederastic
Podostemon
pedestrian
paddy wagon
paddymelon
paddy-whack
paddy field
paddy train
prepayable
preparator
peel-and-eat
prevalence
prevalency
phenacetin
preparedly
pied-à-terre
predaceous
presageful
prelatical
premarital
premaxilla
precarious
predacious
prepackage
prevailing
prepayment
paedagogic
pteranodon
paedagogue
precaution
poetastery
presbyopia
presbyopic
presbytery
presbytism
pierceable
preach down
prescience
prescriber
preachment
piercingly
pleochroic
pseudoacid
pseudobulb
pseudocode
pseudocarp
pseudogene
pseudology
pseudimago
pre-Adamite
pleadingly
preadapted
prevenancy
preferable
preferably
pretendant
pretendent
prebendary
precedence
precedency
preference
predevelop
predecease
prerelease
premedical
prevenient
preferment
piece goods
preferring
prehensile
prepensely
precession
prehension
presension
pre-tension
pretension
prehensory
prehensive
prepensive
preceptial
present-day
presential
paedeutics
precentrix
predestine
predestiny
presetting
prelection
prevention
preceptory
prefecture
predentate
preceptive
presentive
preventive
pledgeable
peelgarlic
psephology
poetically
predicable
plebiscite
✧presidency
pleximeter
pleximetry
pie diagram
prelingual
peeping Tom
plenishing
precipiced
precipitin
presidiums
presidiary
Plexiglass®
plexiglass
presignify
predispose
premier cru
preciosity
plesiosaur
paediatric
prediction
prefixture
prehistory
predictive
plenilunar
preciously
previously
pre-glacial
phelloderm
peerlessly
preclusion
psellismus
preclusive
pre-eminent
pleomorphy
pre-embryos
pneumatics
pre-emption
pre-emptive
pleonectic
preen gland
pregnantly
pleonastic
prednisone
pleromatic
prevocalic
preconceit
preconcert
precordial
precondemn
phenomenal
prepotence
prepotency
piezometer
phenomenon
paedophile
plerophory
premonitor
prepositor
precocious
prepollent
pie-counter
precognise
precognize
pheromonal
precompose
paedotribe
pleiotropy
phenocryst
preconsume
prepossess
Plecoptera
Piemontese
phenotypic
preppiness
preappoint
Piesporter
puerperium
prearrange
pleurodont
pietra dura
pietre dure
prefrontal
pleurotomy
peer review
pressed day
press agent
press ahead
prep school
press flesh
pleasantly
pleasingly
pressingly
pheasantry
pleasantry
presswoman
press money
pieds noirs
pleasure in
press proof
pressurise
pressurize
pretty much
prettiness
peer-to-peer
Puerto Rico
presternum
plentitude
prestation
pretty well
presumable
presumably
prepuberty
prefulgent
prejudiced
preludious
pre-qualify
presurmise
presuppose
precursory
precursive
prenuptial
pre-exilian
pterylosis
Pterygotus
puffer fish
puff pastry
pegmatitic
pugnacious
peg-tankard
pagoda-tree
pogo effect
pigmentary
pugilistic
pogonotomy
pagination
pigeonhole
pigeon pair
pigeon-post
pigeon-toed
pigeon-wing
Pegasus Bay
pig-sticker
page-turner
pygmy shrew
pohutukawa
prima facie
private law
private war
private act
philatelic
✧private eye
primatical
privatiser
privatizer
prima donna
primaquine
pliability
princified
princehood
Prince Igor
Prince John
princelike
princeling
principial
principled
principate
principium
princessly
primevally
price level
prizefight
price index
prizewoman
prime mover
prize money
prime donne
prize court
paideutics
pridefully
priggishly
Pliohippus
primiparae
primiparas
privileged
poikilitic
Philippian
philippina
✧philippine
Philippise
Philippize
Philip Roth
Philistean
Philistian
✧philistine
prick-eared
prink about
painkiller
prick-louse
prickly ash
phialiform
phillumeny
painlessly
prismoidal
poignadoes
poignantly
pliantness
philomathy
poisonable
prison bars
prison camp
prison crop
primordial
prison door
primordium
philoxenia
primogenit
poison-fang
prisonment
philologer
philosophe
philosophy
philologic
philopoena
philologue
poison pill
prison ship
psilocybin
prison yard
prioritise
prioritize
painstaker
priest hole
priesthood
priest-king
priest-like
priestling
puissantly
prissiness
puir's-hoose
puir's-house
priestship
poinsettia
puissaunce
printmaker
psittacine
painted cup
point after
point-blank
paintiness
paintworks
printworks
paintbrush
point guard
✧privy purse
Prinz Eugen
pejoration
pejorative
pukka sahib
poke bonnet
pike-keeper
Peking duck
pyknometer
poker-faced
pokerishly
pulsatance
Polyandria
paleaceous
palmaceous
pultaceous
palmatifid
Pulsatilla
palladious
pilgarlick
polyatomic
polyaxonic
Pelmatozoa
pillar-root
pellagrous
Pallas's cat
Polianthes
polyactine
polyanthus
palm branch
pall-bearer
phlebolite
palm-butter
phlebotomy
phlyctaena
Polychaeta
polychaete
polycyclic
phlyctenae
polyclinic
Polyclitus
Police Motu
polyclonal
polycrotic
Pelecypoda
palmcorder
pilocarpin
polycarpic
polychroic
polychrome
polychromy
polychrest
Pilocarpus
polycystic
policy-shop
pelycosaur
police trap
polycotton
pulp cavity
polydactyl
poll-degree
pile-driver
paludament
pole dancer
paludinous
polydipsia
pulverable
Palaeocene
pallescent
palaeogaea
Palaeogene
pulp-engine
palletiser
palletizer
pulveriser
pulverizer
palaeolith
pollenosis
Palmerston
palaestral
pollen tube
palmettoes
palaestric
palaeotype
palmer-worm
Palaeozoic
polt-footed
piliferous
polygraphy
phlegmasia
phlegmatic
palm-grease
polygamist
polygamous
polygynian
polygenism
polygenist
palagonite
polygenous
polygynous
phlegmonic
phlogopite
phlogistic
phlogiston
polyhybrid
polyhedral
polyhedric
polyhydric
polyhedron
polyhalite
Polyhymnia
polyhistor
pelvic arch
pulvinated
pollinator
pelvimeter
pulsimeter
Pulcinella
pelvimetry
pulvilised
pulvilized
pilliwinks
pulvilling
palliament
pallidness
pillionist
palliation
palliatory
palliative
pellicular
palm-kernel
palolo worm
polemicist
Pullman car
peltmonger

Words marked ✧ can also be spelled with one or more capital letters

polemonium
polymeride
polymerase
polymerise
polymerism
polymerous
polymerize
polymastia
polymastic
palimpsest
polymathic
Polyneices
palynology
polynomial
palindrome
Polynesian
Pulmonaria
Pilao Falls
pillow-beer
pillow-bere
pillowcase
pulsometer
pileorhiza
polyominos
poliovirus
pillow lace
pillow lava
pillowslip
pillow talk
polyonymic
pillorying
polyphagia
polyphasic
Polypodium
Polyphemic
polyphenol
Polyphemus
Polypterus
polyploidy
polyphonic
pill-popper
poll-parrot
pilgrimage
pilgrimise
pilgrimize
palfrenier
paltriness
pultrusion
polyrhythm
polishable
palisadoes
pilastered
polishings
polo sticks
polishment
polysemant
polysemous
Palm Sunday
palisander
poles apart
palustrian
palustrine
polystylar
politician
politicker
politicoes
politicise
polytocous
politicize
polytheism
polytheist
pilot whale
pilot light
pilot-plant
palatalise
pilot cloth
palatalize
polytunnel
politeness
palatinate
pilot house
pollutedly
pellucidly
polyvalent
palsy-walsy
pump-action
pome-citron
pummelling
pompelmous
pumie stone
pomiferous
pemphigoid
pemphigous
pump-handle
Pimpinella
pomologist
pumple-nose
Pomeranian
pineal body
panhandler
Pentandria
panjandrum
Pancake Day
pancake ice
Pentateuch
pentameter
Pentameron
pentahedra
pennaceous
pentathlon
pentachord
pentathlum
pinnatiped
pinnatifid
Puncak Jaya
pentaploid
pentagonal
pentapodic
pentapolis
pentatomic
pentatonic
pantaloons
panna cotta
pantagraph
pentagraph
pentaprism
penmanship
pentastich
pentastyle
pennatulae
pennatulas
Pentagynia
pine beauty
pine-beetle
pine-barren
pine-chafer
Punic faith
Punicaceae
pinacoidal
pink-collar
pina colada
piña colada
penicillin
paniculate
Punic apple
pine carpet
panic-grass
Pont du Gard
ponderance
ponderancy
ponderable
ponce about
pince-nezed
pangenesis
pangenetic
penteteric
Pontederia
pony engine
Pentelican
ponderment
pandermite
ponder over
✧pandemonic
Pontefract
pen-feather
pin feather
pandectist
pendentive
Pan-African
panegyrise
panegyrist
panegyrize
punch-ladle
pinchpenny
pinchingly
pinchpoint
punchboard
pantherine
punch-drunk
pantheress
pantherish
penthouses
pencil-case
Pinnipedia
ponticello
pentimenti
pentimento
Pennisetum
pontifical
pontifices
pencil-lead
pencilling
pensionnat
pension off
pensionary
pundigrion
pensieroso
panniculus
pinakoidal
pine kernel
pinakothek
panel games
penologist
penelopise
penelopize
panel truck
Panglossic
Pan-Slavism
Pan-Slavist
penalty box
penalty try
Panama City
Panamanian
pine marten
penumbrous
pond-master
penoncelle
pine needle
penannular
peninsular
punto banco
pantoscope
pantophagy
pansophism
pansophist
pantomimic
pancosmism
pontonnier
pundonores
pantograph
panton-shoe
panoptical
panopticon
panophobia
panspermia
panspermic
pancreatic
pancreatin
Pan-Arabism
ponerology
pantrymaid
pancratian
pancratist
panaritium
pancratium
pond skater
panislamic
punishable
pentstemon
pink salmon
punishment
penetrance
penetrancy
penetralia
penetrable
penetrably
punctually
penetrator
punctuator
pinstriped
Pinot Blanc
punctilios
punctulate
penitently
punctation
pandurated
pinnulated
Pinguicula
pinguidity
pincushion
penguinery
pin-buttock
pinguitude
panty-waist
penny share
penny-piece
penny-pinch
penny black
penny-plain
penny-a-line
pennyroyal
pennyworth
pennycress
penny stock
penny-stane
penny-stone
✧propaganda
propagable
proratable
propagator
prosaicism
procacious
Protagoras
protanopia
protanopic
propagulum
pro hac vice
prokaryote
Poor Clares
proscriber
proscenium
prosciutti
prosciutto
proud flesh
proud-flesh
ploddingly
Ptolemaean
provenance
promenader
phonematic
Ptolemaist
proverbial
proseuchae
Proteaceae
Provençale
proceeding
propendent
probenecid
pyogenesis
proteiform
Promethean
pronephric
pronephros
prometheum
Prometheus
promethium
phonetical
progenitor
proveditor
propellant
propellent
propelling
proteolyse
proteomics
propelment
proper name
phoneyness
properness
proper noun
proteinous
pro memoria
Proserpina
pro tempore
pioneering
processual
plover's egg
propensely
professing
procession
profession
propension
protension
propensity
protensity
propensive
protensive
propertied
protectrix
projectile
projecting
protectant
protecting
✧protestant
projection
protection
provection
projecture
protectory
pro-oestrus
projective
protective
procedural
prosecutor
protervity
proof sheet
proof-house
proffering
ploughable
plough back
ploughgate
plough-iron
plough into
ploughland
plough-team
plough-tree
plough-tail
ploughwise
pro-choicer
prothallia
prothallic
prothallus
prophesied
prophesier
prophetess
prophetism
provitamin
phonically
prodigally
profitable
profitably
providable
proximally
provincial
procidence
prominence
prominency
✧providence
proairesis
promiseful
prolicidal
prolifical
prohibiter
proficient
prosilient
provisions
prohibitor
propitiate
prodigious
prolixious
propitious
profitless
prolixness
propionate
pholidosis
promissory
promissive
probiotics
profluence
profligacy
profligate
peoplehood
proclaimer
problemist
prowlingly
proglottid
proglottis
proclivity
phorminges
proembryos
Phoenician
prognostic
prognathic
proinsulin
phoenixism
protopathy
phototaxis
promotable
proposable
provocable
provokable
provocator
photonasty
proton beam
protonemal
phonometer
photometer
phocomelia
photogenic
photometry
prolongate
photophobe
photophily
photophone
photophony
photo shoot
phonophore
photophore
Protophyta
protophyte
pronominal
prosodical
photodiode
phonolitic
photoflood
photoglyph
protoplasm
protoplast
procoelous
pronounced
pronouncer
propounder
profoundly
photonovel
protocolic
protozoans
phonograph
photograph
phototrope
phototropy
prototroph
photo-essay
protostele
protostome
proportion
photo story
promontory
Psocoptera

Words marked ✧ can also be spelled with one or more capital letters

protohuman
prolocutor
prologuise
prologuize
prototypal
protoxylem
phonotypic
photolysis
photolytic
phototypic
phosphatic
prompt book
prospector
prompt copy
prospectus
promptness
prompt-note
phosphoret
phosphoric
✧phosphorus
prosperity
prosperous
prompt side
phosphuret
promptuary
procreator
protracted
proproctor
protractor
protrudent
propraetor
proprietor
poor relief
programmed
programmer
pyorrhoeal
pyorrhoeic
procrypsis
procryptic
protreptic
Procrustes
protrusile
protrusion
protrusive
Pooh sticks
Poohsticks
poor's-house
pious fraud
prostheses
prosthesis
prosthetic
proctology
proctalgia
prostomial
prostomium
plottingly
proctorial
proctorage
proctorise
proctorize
prostatism
prostitute
procurable
procurator
procumbent
pronuncios
profundity
profulgent
promulgate
producible
pronuclear
pronucleus
propulsion
propulsory
propulsive
productile
production
productive
propylaeum
promycelia
Papiamento
poplar tree
piped music
pepper-cake
peppercorn
poppet-head
pepperidge
peppermill
peppermint
puppet play
puppet show
pepper tree
pepperwort
pupigerous
poplinette
pepsinogen
poprin pear
pipsissewa
papillated
papillitis
pipelining
papal brief
papal cross
popularise
popularity
popularize
papulation
population
populously
pipe-laying
piping crow
piping hare
pop concert
pipe-opener
Pipe Office
pupiparous
paper-faced
paper-maker
paper-gauge
paper-mâché
Piperaceae
piperidine
paper chase
paper-cigar
paper-birch
paper tiger
papyrology
paper-cloth
paperknife
paper money
paperbound
paper round
paperboard
paper route
paper trail
paper-ruler
piperazine
papistical
pop culture
papaverine
papaverous
pipe-wrench
poppy water
popsy-wopsy
Portakabin®
parramatta
permanence
permanency
portamenti
portamento
porraceous
parmacitie
permafrost
Parnassian
periastron
portal vein
parablepsy
Peru balsam
paraboloid
parabolise
parabolist
parabolize
parabemata
parabiosis
parabiotic
pork barrel
port-crayon
pericyclic
periclinal
portcullis
Paracelsus
periculous
pyracantha
port de bras
paradoctor
paradiddle
peridinian
✧peridinium
peridermal
paradisean
paradisiac
paradisial
paradisian
paradisaic
parodistic
peridotite
pyridoxine
paradoxure
paradoxist
purtenance
purveyance
parcel bomb
parcel-bawd
perdendosi
paraenesis
paraenetic
periegesis
purse-seine
parcel-gilt
permethrin
Persephone
Parmenides
paroecious
Purbeckian
parcelling
Parnellism
Parnellite
Persepolis
parcel post
purse-pride
perpetrate
purse-proud
pursership
perversely
perversion
perversity
perversive
perceptual
perfect gas
percentage
percentile
pargetting
perfecting
porpentine
perception
perfection
permeation
porrection
portentous
perceptive
perfective
permeative
persecutor
perpetuate
perpetuity
perceiving
perfervour
parpen-wall
parcelwise
paraffinic
portfolios
pore fungus
poriferous
Paraguayan
pyrography
paraglider
pyrogallol
perigonial
Port Gentil
paragonite
perigonium
perigynous
pyrogenous
paragnosis
paraglossa
pyrrhicist
parchmenty
perihelion
Pyrrhonian
Pyrrhonism
Pyrrhonist
perchloric
porphyrios
porphyrite
porphyrous
pyrrhotine
pyrrhotite
persicaria
pertinence
pertinency
parking lot
parting-cup
Portishead
parricidal
participle
Parmigiano
percipient
perficient
perfidious
pernicious
perjinkety
perjinkity
pernickety
persiflage
partialise
partialism
partialist
partiality
partial out
persifleur
partialize
parliament
Persian cat
Persian War
persiennes
Persianise
portionist
Persianize
Parkinson's
permission
permissive
permitting
persistent
persistive
particular
perviously
park-keeper
perikaryon
parakiting
parkleaves
purple-born
Pyrolaceae
paralleled
parallelly
purple fish
paralogise
paralogism
paralogize
purple-hued
paralympic
purblindly
purulently
portliness
paralipses
paralipsis
pyrolusite
perilously
purple wood
perplexing
perplexity
✧paramecium
paramedico
paramedics
pyrimidine
pyramidion
pyramidist
paramnesia
pyromaniac
pyromantic
portmantle
portmantua
Paramaribo
pyromeride
perimysium
parametral
perimetral
pari-mutuel
parametric
perimetric
pyrometric
peremptory
paramouncy
parentally
✧paronychia
pyrenocarp
parenteral
Pirandello
Pyrenaeans
parenchyma
parenthood
paranoidal
phrensical
phrenology
parentless
paronomasy
paronymous
Paraná pine
paranormal
phrenesiac
perineural
personal ad
perforated
personated
personalia
pardonable
pardonably
perforable
personable
personally
percolator
perforator
personator
portolanos
personalty
perforatus
parrot-beak
parrot-bill
parson-bird
parrot-coal
port of call
purposeful
parrot-fish
personhood
parsonical
periodical
perfoliate
Parvo virus
parvovirus
pardonless
performing
pornotopia
parlour car
pornocracy
periosteal
par contest
pernoctate
periosteum
paraphasia
paraphasic
parapodial
parapodium
peripheral
peripteral
pork-pie hat
paraplegia
paraplegic
peripheric
paraphilia
parapineal
paraphonia
paraphonic
periphonic
pyrophobia
pyrophobic
pyrophoric
✧pyrophorus
paraphrase
paraphrast
periphrase
perspirate
peripetian
peripeteia
paraphyses
paraphysis
periphyton
paraquitos
parbreaked
pure reason
pará rubber
partridges
pararthria
peroration
parastatal
porismatic
pyrostatic
perishable
perishably
Paris Pacts
phrase book
Paris, Texas
parascenia
Parisienne
parischane
Paris white
poristical
puristical
parastichy
paraselene
phraseless
peristomal
periscopic
poroscopic
Portsmouth
parish pump
parish-pump
Paris green
parasitoid
parasitise
parasitism
parasitize
peristylar
paratactic
peritectic
pyrotechny
parathesis
perithecia
perstringe
peritricha
pyretology
Port Talbot
peritoneal
puritanise
✧puritanism
peritoneum
puritanize
paratroops
per stirpes
pyrethroid
perdurance
perdurable
perdurably
permutable
Portugaise
perturbant
perturbate
parturient
percutient

Words marked ✧ can also be spelled with one or more capital letters

perjurious
pursuantly
pursuingly
porousness
percurrent
percussant
percussion
✧persuasion
percursory
persuasory
perquisite
percussive
persuasive
parquetted
pirouetter
perruquier
Portuguese
pursuivant
perovskite
periwigged
parawalker
periwinkle
peroxidase
peroxidise
peroxidize
pyroxyline
par exemple
pyroxenite
paroxysmal
peroxisome
paroxetine
paroxytone
party sales
Perry Mason
party piece
pasta maker
postal code
postal card
passageway
passamezzo
pistachios
postal note
push around
postal tube
postal vote
post-bellum
push-button
post chaise
post-chaise
postcoital
pass degree
Posidonius
poster girl
post-echoes
post-exilic
posteriors
pastellist
pesterment
pasteboard
passed pawn
Pasteurian
pas de trois
paste-grain
pasteurise
pasteurism
pasteurize
possession
possessory
possessive
pasigraphy
puschkinia
postholder
posthumous
piscifauna
pestilence
passimeter
pasticheur
pesticidal
pistillode
postillion
passiflora
pistillary
pistillate
postillate
passionary
Passionist
passionate
Post-it note®
postliminy
post letter
post-modern
post mortem
post-mortem
pass muster
past master
✧postmaster
post-Nicene
pastorales
pastorally
✧**post office**
pistol grip
pistolling
piston ring
pastorship
postocular
pistol-whip
postperson
post-partum
postpartum
pastrycook
push-stroke
PostScript®
postscript
positional
positioned
positioner
positively
positivism
positivist
positivity
postulancy
pasturable
postulator
postulatum
pasquilant
pasquinade
pasty-faced
Puseyistic
pot-wabbler
Petrarchal
Petrarchan
pot-valiant
Pythagoras
pitta bread
pâte brisée
patibulary
Pete Conrad
PET scanner
putrescent
putrescine
Pat Metheny
pathetical
pot-bellied
pettedness
patter-song
potter wasp
putrefying
pathfinder
pâte frolle
pit against
Patagonian
put the case
pitch-wheel
pitch-black
pith helmet
pitchiness
pitchwoman
put through
put-through
patchcocke
patchboard
pitcherful
pitchstone
pettichaps
patricidal
phthisical
phthisicky
patriciate
pit village
patricliny
patrialise
patrialism
patriality
Petri plate
patrialize
Patti Smith
putridness
patrifocal
patrilocal
patriarchy
petrissage
patristics
patriation
patriotism
pittie-ward
petrifying
pottle-deep
petulantly
pitilessly
potamology
patentable
potentilla
potentiary
potentiate
put on an act
put-and-take
patination
petiolated
petrolatum
pot-wobbler
petrol bomb
petrol blue
pathogenic
pythogenic
petronella
put money on
pétroleuse
put to death
petroleous
petrolhead
put to shame
patroniser
patronizer
put to sleep
patrocliny
patrolling
petrolling
potboiling
petroglyph
patronless
pathognomy
petromoney
pathologic
petrol pump
petrodrome
Petroushka
petrol tank
put to nurse
put forward
patronymic
pit-a-patted
pityriasis
paternally
Petersburg
Peter Scott
Peter-see-me
Peter Pears
Peter Debye
Peter Blake
Peter Lorre
patereroes
Peter Brook
Peter Stein
potash alum
pâte sablée
pâte sucrée
Pete Seeger
patisserie
pâtisserie
Pittsburgh
put stock in
✧**petitioner**
petit point
petits pois
potato race
petit grain
potato ring
potato trap
putatively
pot furnace
pot-hunting
put-putting
Patavinity
putty-faced
potty about
potty-chair
petty-chaps
putty-knife
potty-train
plumassier
plural vote
plum-colour
pouncet-box
pounce upon
pound scots
Paul Dombey
pound force
plunderage
plunderous
pluperfect
plume poppy
plume-grass
prudential
pausefully
Paul Eluard
plunge bath
plunge pool
pouched rat
Prudhoe Bay
pruning saw
pouring wet
✧**prusik knot**
pruriently
Paulianist
pluckiness
Paul Kruger
Paul Morphy
Paul Merton
Paul McStay
Paul M Nurse
Paul Newman
plutolatry
Paulo Rossi
plutocracy
pourparler
Paul Revere
pousse-café
plus strain
pourtraict
pourtrahed
plum tomato
poultroone
Plumularia
Paul Valéry
pave the way
pawnbroker
powder burn
powder blue
powder down
powder horn
pewter-mill
powder mill
powder puff
powder room
powder snow
power lathe
power block
power plant
power point
powerhouse
powertrain
power brake
power drill
power press
power lunch
powerfully
pawnticket
pixellated
pixillated
pixilation
phylactery
pay-per-view
psychiater
psychiatry
pay the cain
psychic bid
psychicism
psychicist
psychogram
psychogony
psychology
psychopomp
psychopath
physically
physiocrat
physicking
physiology
Phyllopoda
Phyllotria
phyllotaxy
phylloxera
pay one's way
Phytolacca
phytogenic
phytotoxic
phytotoxin
pay-as-you-go
pay station
pizzicatos
puzzle-head
puzzlement
puzzlingly
puzzle over
pozzolanic
pozzuolana
quarantine
Quai d'Orsay
Quaker-bird
quaternion
✧**quaternary**
quaternate
quaternity
quagginess
quaking ash
qualifying
quack grass
qualmishly
quaintness
quatorzain
quarriable
quadricone
quadriceps
quatrefoil
quadriform
quadriller
quarrelled
quarreller
quadrumvir
Quadrumana
quadrumane
quadrantal
quadrantes
quarrender
quadrennia
quadrangle
quadruplet
quadruplex
quadripole
quadrupole
quadrireme
quadrisect
quadratics
quadratrix
quarry tile
quadratura
quadrature
quadrivial
quadrivium
quaestuary
quantifier
quartzitic
quartz lamp
quartz-mill
quarter day
quarter-saw
quartz-rock
quarterage
quarter-ill
quartering
quarter-boy
quarteroon
quartation
quantitate
quantitive
quesadilla
quenchable
quenchless
quercitron
Queen's Club
queen-sized
Queensland
queencraft
quernstone
Queen's ware
Quezon City
quebrachos
queasiness
quersprung
questingly
questionee
questioner
queryingly
quinacrine
quinaquina
quiche dish
quinic acid
Quirinalia
quick march
quick-match
quick-sandy
quick-water
quick-hedge
quickthorn
quick-firer
quickening
quirkiness
quink-goose
quick trick
quick grass
quick-stick
quick-lunch
quill drive
quizmaster
quid pro quo
quiescence
quiescency
quit scores
quinsy-wort
quint major
quint minor
quietening
quintuplet
quietistic
quizziness
quotatious
quoad sacra
quoad omnia
Quonset hut®
rear-boiled
road bridge
reaccustom
rhabdolith
rear-dorter
readership
real estate
real-estate
reafforest

roadheader
reach after
realisable
realisably
realizable
realizably
real income
reading age
reaming-bit
reading-boy
roaring boy
reallocate
readme file
road-making
rearmament
road mender
Rhamnaceae
real number
reasonable
reasonably
reasonless
readoption
reappraise
reacquaint
road roller
roadrunner
rhapsodise
rhapsodist
rhapsodize
real school
reap-silver
reassemble
reassembly
reassuring
real tennis
reastiness
reactional
reactively
reactivate
reactivity
Rear Window
roadworthy
ready-mixed
ready money
ready-money
rubiaceous
Rebeccaism
Rebeccaite
rub-a-dub-dub
rubber band
robber crab
rubberneck
rubber room
rubber-room
rebreather
rubber tree
rubberwear
riboflavin
rubiginose
rubiginous
rub through
rubrically
rubricator
rabbitfish
rabbit hole
rubbishing
rabbinical
rib-tickler
rabbit upon
Rubik's Cube®
rebukingly
rebellious
rabblement
rabble rout
rubblework
Robyn Smith
robing room
ribbonfish
ribbon-seal
rib-roaster
ribbon-weed
ribbon worm
Robert Adam
Robert Bolt
Robert Cray
Robert Capa
Robert Dole
Robert E Lee
rebirthing
Robert Koch
Robert Kett
Robert Lynd
Robert Peel
Robert Reid
roberdsman
robertsman
roborating
ruby spinel
robustious
ruby silver
robustness
rebateable
rebuttable
rebatement
rubythroat
Richard III
Richard Roe
rectangled
rockabilly
reclaimant
rackabones
reclassify
rock-badger
rick-burner
rick-barton
rock butter
rock bottom
rock-bottom
recyclable
ricocheted
rice cooker
racecourse
recidivism
recidivist
Roche limit
recreantly
racket-tail
rickettsia
recreation
recreative
recogniser
recognizer
rock garden
Rock Hudson
rockhopper
race hatred
receivable
reclinable
recoil atom
Rockingham
recoilless
rechipping
rectifying
recallable
rick-lifter
recallment
recolonise
recolonize
recklessly
rock lizard
recommence
recompence
recumbence
recumbency
recompense
race memory
Rachmanism
Rachmanite
recompress
racemation
raconteuse
recondense
reconciler
reconsider
recontinue
ricinoleic
recentness
Racing Post
reconquest
rectoscope
raccoon-dog
rectorship
receptacle
recipience
recipiency
rock pigeon
receptible
reciprocal
recuperate
recapturer
recordable
rock-ribbed
rock rabbit
rectricial
recurrence
recurrency
recureless
rack-renter
rechristen
rock-steady
rocksteady
rock salmon
recusation
recitalist
rock temple
rock turbot
recitation
recitative
recitativi
recitativo
recoupable
recrudesce
recoupment
recruiting
rock violet
race-walker
red cabbage
ride and tie
ride and tie
red sanders
red jasmine
ride a hobby
red lattice
red-lattice
radial tyre
ride bodkin
ridability
radiciform
radicalise
Radicalism
radiculose
radicality
ridiculous
radicalize
redecorate
radication
rededicate
red admiral
redeemable
redeemably
rudderfish
ridgepiece
redeemless
rudderless
red herring
redressive
red seaweed
red-shifted
ride herd on
rodfishing
red-figured
raduliform
Rudolf Hess
riddle-like
redolently
riddlingly
red-blooded
Rudolf Otto
redelivery
rudimental
redemption
redemptory
redemptive
redundance
redundancy
riding boot
riding coat
riding crop
riding high
riding hood
rodent-like
red snapper
riding robe
riding suit
riding whip
radiopager
Radiolaria
radiopaque
radioscope
radioscopy
radiometer
radiogenic
radiometry
radiophone
radiophony
Radio Times
radio alarm
radiosonde
radiologic
radiotoxic
radiograph
radio assay
radiolysis
radiolytic
radarscope
Red Brigade
rediscover
rediscount
redissolve
redescribe
redisburse
Rod Steiger
Rod Stewart
radium bomb
redounding
redruthite
red-murrain
redcurrant
Reduviidae
redivision
Roddy Doyle
rue-bargain
Riemannian
riebeckite
re-election
re-erection
re-engineer
re-eligible
rheologist
re-enlister
rheumatics
rheumatoid
rheumatise
rheumatism
rheumatize
Rheinberry
rhetorical
re-exporter
Reet Petite
rheostatic
Rhea Silvia
Rhea Sylvia
re-entrance
re-entrancy
rheotropic
reel-to-reel
re-entering
reed-thrush
Rhesus baby
ruefulness
reflagging
refracting
refraction
refractary
refractory
refracture
refractive
raft-bridge
rifle range
refuelable
rafter-bird
refreshing
refreshful
reflexible
rifle corps
rifle green
reflecting
reflection
reflective
refringent
ruffianish
ruffianism
refillable
refulgence
refulgency
rifampicin
refundable
refinement
refundment
refine upon
reformades
referrable
reformable
reformados
Reform Club
referrible
referendum
refutation
rift valley
ragmatical
rigidified
rogue value
ragged-lady
ragged left
raggedness
ruggedness
rogue money
regression
regressive
regretting
regainable
regainment
regalement
regularise
regularity
regularize
regelation
regulation
regulatory
regulative
✧ragamuffin
regimental
Raging Bull
Regensburg
regent-bird
regeneracy
regenerate
regentship
regionally
rag-rolling
Roger Vadim
regardable
Roger Bacon
Roger Clark
regardless
Roger Moore
Roger Craig
rigorously
registered
registrant
registrary
rightwards
right about
right of way
right-of-way
right wheel
right whale
right-lined
right-field
right-click
right angle
right bower
right-drawn
rightfully
right guard
rugby shirt
Rugby fives
✧rugby union
rehearsing
rehandling
raiyatwari
reimburser
reincrease
rain-doctor
reiterance
reiterated
raise a dust
Rhineberry
raise a hand
raise a hare
Rhinegrave
✧rhinestone
rainforest
Reichsbank
Reichsland
reichsmark
Reichsrath
raising-bee
Rhipiptera
reim-kennar
reillumine
rainmaking
ruin marble
rhinolalia
rhinoscope
rhinoscopy
rhizogenic
rhinoceros
rhinocerot
rhinotheca
rhinophyma
Rhizophora
rhizophore
rhinovirus
rhizoplane
raisonneur
rhizomorph
rain-plover
reimporter
railroader
reissuable
rain shadow
reinspirit
roistering
roisterous
railwayman
reioyndure
Rajya Sabha
rejectable
rejectible
Raj Persaud
rejoindure
rejoiceful
rejoicings
rejoneador
rajpramukh
rijsttafel
rejuvenise
rejuvenate
rejuvenize
rakishness
releasable
reluctance
reluctancy
rollcollar
relocation
relievable

rollerball
rolled gold
reliefless
rolled oats
religieuse
religioner
relegation
Ralph Nader
rolling pin
rollicking
relentless
relentment
relinquish
rollocking
reliquaire
relishable
Rolls-Royce®
relational
relatively
relativise
relativism
relativist
relativity
relativize
roll-up fund
relevantly
raloxifene
relaxation
relaxative
rallyingly
rally round
rallycross
ram-raiding
rampageous
rampacious
rampallian
Ramsar site
remediable
remediably
remedially
remediless
romper suit
remigation
ramshackle
Ramphastos
rumble area
rumple-bane
ramblingly
rumblingly
rumble seat
rum blossom
rememberer
roman à clef
roman à clés
remand home
romancical
romantical
Ramón Llull
Roman snail
Ruminantia
ruminantly
remunerate
Romanistic
Romanesque
rumination
remonetise
ruminative
remonetize
Ramanavami
ramrodding
remarkable
remarkably
remorseful
remortgage
remarriage
remoralise
remoralize
Rome-runner
remark upon
remissible
remissness
remittance
remittable
remoteness
rumbullion
rumour mill
rum-running
rumpus room
rumfustian
removal van
removalist
rumpy-pumpy
ring binder
run a banker
rent-charge
ring down on
rangelands
renderable
runner bean
rannel-balk
runner duck
Ranzellaar
rinderpest
Ron Weasley
rangership
rendezvous
ring finger
röntgenise
röntgenize
renegation
Rh-negative
ranshackle
run through
run-through
ranch house
run the show
running gag
Running Man
ranging rod
running dog
Ronnie Kray
rancidness
ringleader
randle-balk
rannle-balk
rantle-balk
Ronald Ross
randle-tree
ringmaster
ring-necked
ranunculus
ransomable
run to earth
run to waste
rondoletto
randomiser
randomizer
Renzo Piano
ransomless
rencounter
randomness
Ringo Starr
random walk
randomwise
René Préval
ring-porous
run errands
rank-riding
ring roller
✧renascence
rune-singer
ring-tailed
ranivorous
renovation
renewables
Rhoeadales
rhomboidal
rhomboidei
rhomboides
rooibos tea
rhoicissus
rootedness
root-fallen
room-fellow
reorganise
reorganize
roof garden
Roodmas Day
root nodule
rhodophane
riot police
root rubber
room-ridden
root sheath
rootsiness
rood screen
root system
roots music
Rhodymenia
repealable
repeatable
repeatedly
✧republican
rope bridge
rupicoline
rupicolous
repudiable
repudiator
ripidolite
rope dancer
rappelling
rap session
repression
repressive
replevying
repugnance
repugnancy
repaginate
repairable
replicator
ripping-saw
reptilious
repair-shop
repainting
repellance
repellancy
rope ladder
repellence
repellency
ripple mark
ripplingly
ripple tank
rope-making
repentance
roping-down
repinement
repiningly
ripsnorter
reprobance
reprobater
reprovable
reprobator
reproacher
rip-roaring
repro proof
Rippon spur
rapportage
rapporteur
reproducer
repopulate
reportable
reportedly
repurchase
repertoire
reparation
reparatory
reparative
rope stitch
rupestrian
re-position
reposition
repository
Rh-positive
repose upon
repatriate
reputeless
repetition
reputation
répétiteur
repetitive
reputative
rip current
repoussage
repoussoir
rope-walker
roquelaure
requirable
requitable
requiteful
requisitor
requiescat
reredorter
rarefiable
reregulate
rare groove
reregister
Rural Rides
rere-supper
Ruritanian
resealable
researcher
rascal-like
rascallion
restaurant
rust bucket
rose beetle
risibility
rose chafer
rose colour
rose-combed
rush candle
rest centre
residually
Resedaceae
residenter
russel-cord
rose engine
Rossellini
rostellate
Russellite
restenoses
restenosis
respectant
respecting
respectful
respective
risk factor
rust fungus
rosy-footed
resignedly
resignment
rose garden
reschedule
rush holder
rosehip tea
restharrow
rusticated
respirable
rustically
respirator
rusticator
reshipment
Russian tea
Russianise
Russianism
Russianist
Russianize
rescission
rescissory
restitutor
rusticware
rusticwork
Russifying
resolvable
resilience
resiliency
resolvedly
resultless
rustlingly
rose-lipped
restlessly
resolutely
resolution
resolutive
rose laurel
rose-laurel
rose madder
resemblant
resembling
rosemaling
rose mallow
resumption
resumptive
rising damp
resentence
resinified
rosaniline
resentment
resonantly
rising tide
resinously
restorable
respondent
Russophobe
Russophile
responsory
responsive
resupinate
rose quartz
reservable
restricted
resorbence
resurgence
reservedly
restrained
restrainer
resorcinol
resorption
resorptive
✧resistance
resistible
resistibly
resistless
rose-tinted
resounding
rose window
Rathayatra
rat-catcher
retransfer
retransmit
retractile
retraction
retractive
ratability
reticulary
reticulate
reticently
✧rutherford
ruthenious
rottenness
retreatant
ratifiable
rotiferous
rate fixing
ratch about
retainable
retail bank
Rota Island
retailment
retainment
retributor
retrieving
retaliator
rattlehead
rattlepate
ruthlessly
rattletrap
ritt-master
retinacula
retinalite
rationally
ration book
ration card
retrochoir
retroviral
retrovirus
retrospect
retrograde
retrogress
retrorsely
ritardando
returnable
Rotary Club
retired pay
ritornelle
ritornelli
ritornello
Ruth Rogers
rotor plane
returnless
retardment
retirement
retiringly
rotorcraft
rotisserie
rôtisserie
rototiller
rotational
rat-hunting
✧rottweiler
rhubarbing
raunchiest
round dance
round-eared
round faced
✧round table
round-table
round about
roundabout
round angle
round dozen
round-nosed
round tower
✧round robin
roundhouse
round mouth
round brush
route march
rouseabout
Rouge Croix
Ruud Gullit
rough-hewer
roughrider
rough hound
rough house
rough-house
rough-draft
rough-grind
rough stuff
rough music
reunionism
reunionist
Rouen cross
roustabout
revealable
revealment
rove beetle
revocation
revocatory
reviewable
review body
review copy
revegetate
revokement
revolvable
revalidate
revolvency
revilement
revilingly
ravel bread
revalorise
revalorize
✧revelation
revolution
revelatory
revelative
raven's-bone

raven's-duck
revengeful
revanchism
revanchist
ravenously
rev counter
River Cauca
river water
river basin
River Marne
River Saône
River Zaire
River Tagus
riverscape
rover scout
River Adige
River Neman
River Weser
River Teifi
River Lethe
reversedly
River Seine
River Negro
River Meuse
River Benue
River Rhine
River Rhône
River Chari
River Niger
River Tiber
reversible
reversibly
revertible
River Tisza
River Clyde
River Fleet
River Glåma
River Plata
River Plate
reverencer
reverently
River Indus
River Donau
River Mosel
river novel
River Congo
River Volga
River Somme
River Boyne
River Douro
River Loire
river horse
River Forth
river mouth
River Volta
rivercraft
river drift
riverfront
River Trent
reverb unit
River Jumna
River Tweed
revestiary
ravishment
revisional
revisitant
revitalise
revitalize
rivetingly
revivified
revivalism
revivalist
revivement
revivingly
rewritable
Rawalpindi
rowing boat
rowan-berry
rewardable
rewireable
rewardless
rowdy-dowdy
Roy Laidlaw
Roy Jenkins
rhyme royal
Ray Reardon
rhythmical
rhythmless
Roy Thomson
Ray Charles
Rhyniaceae
Royal Abbey
royal icing
royal jelly
royal flush
royal burgh
royal cubit
Roy Andrews
Roy Orbison
roysterous
razzmatazz
razor shell
razor blade
razor-strop
scarabaean
sharawadgi
sharawaggi
scarabaeid
scarabaeus
sea cabbage
smaragdine
smaragdite
spatangoid
stay-at-home
sea-bathing
seamanlike
Sparagmite
stalagmite
✧scaramouch
sialagogic
swan around
sialagogue
sea vampire
sparagrass
sea passage
seamanship
sea captain
stalactite
soap bubble
swaybacked
stag beetle
soap boiler
star-bright
stabbingly
scabbiness
shabbiness
slabbiness
seam bowler
shadchanim
searchable
stanchable
swatchbook
spatchcock
starchedly
spancelled
searchless
stanchless
scarcement
scarceness
stanchness
snapdragon
scaldberry
shandygaff
stand first
scandalled
stand-alone
scandalise
scandalous
scandalize
slam dancer
stand to win
shard-borne
standpoint
stand treat
stand trial
standers-by
slanderous
stand at bay
stand still
standstill
stand guard
shandrydan
snake dance
St Adelaide
shamefaced
space cadet
state paper
state cabin
Shane Warne
stavesacre
sealed-beam
sealed book
Siamese cat
snake fence
stage fever
scavenging
scavengery
snake's-head
scape-wheel
Swadeshism
shale-miner
Snake River
stage-diver
state-aided
stage right
swage block
shade plant
spaceplane
suaveolent
share index
shame on you
searedness
spacewoman
stagecoach
scale model
skate round
spaceborne
scale board
skateboard
snake-house
stage horse
✧state house
seakeeping
sea serpent
sea leopard
space opera
state trial
space probe
scapegrace
slave trade
spacecraft
stagecraft
statecraft
shame-proof
shave-grass
sea lettuce
sea feather
scale stair
snakestone
shamefully
scaredy-cat
Sea of Japan
Sea of Waves
soap flakes
snaffle-bit
scaffolder
scaffolage
starflower
scarf-joint
staff corps
Sea of Crete
seal-fisher
staff nurse
shanghaied
shanghaier
shagged out
slang-whang
shaggy mane
slangingly
shagginess
slanginess
sparganium
staggering
swaggering
slaughtery
stargazing
stag-headed
shag-haired
stadholder
staphyloma
staphyline
scatheless
spathulate
swash plate
scathingly
smashingly
sea gherkin
sea whistle
snaphaunce
snaphaunch
shamiyanah
sialic acid
statically
sea biscuit
spadiceous
stamineous
sealing wax
Spanish fly
sea-fishing
stabiliser
stabilizer
static line
spaniolise
spaniolate
spatiality
Stanislaus
spaniolize
stationary
stationery
statistics
snap into it
spaciously
scarifying
slack water
slack-water
stark-naked
sparked out
Shackleton
slacken off
spankingly
slackening
Stan Kenton
sparkishly
small wares
snail-paced
sea blubber
spauld-bone
small-scale
stable door
Stableford
snail wheel
snail-shell
small-pipes
small-timer
stable lass
stall plate
stablemate
stallenger
stallinger
snarlingly
stableness
small goods
small hours
smallmouth
snail's pace
small craft
small fruit
small print
seamlessly
scarlet hat
scarlatina
spallation
staple town
Stan Laurel
shallowing
small sword
spasmodist
swan-maiden
starmonger
smalminess
smarminess
swarm-spore
slammerkin
stammering
Stan Musial
swan-mussel
shammashim
seannachie
sea unicorn
staunching
sea anemone
stagnantly
sharny peat
spawn brick
Stannaries
stagnation
stannotype
Sean O'Casey
seasonable
seasonably
seasonally
sea poacher
statoscope
shadowcast
sea goddess
seaborgium
Slavophobe
scatophagy
Slavophile
seasonless
shadowless
statoblast
shadow mark
shadow mask
sialogogic
stanozolol
sialogogue
shadow play
scaloppine
slavocracy
sea monster
swap option
stamp paper
sharp-edged
swamp fever
stamp hinge
stamp album
snappingly
swampiness
sharp-nosed
scampishly
snappishly
soap powder
shabracque
scabridity
shagreened
starry-eyed
staurolite
starriness
starr grass
scabrously
star-shaped
sparseness
Sears Tower
scansorial
star-struck
seamstress
stay shtoom
Stan Tracey
start-naked
stay-tackle
Spartacist
spasticity
smart phone
smartphone
start a hare
smart Aleck
smart-Aleck
smart Alick
smart-Alick
scaithless
skaithless
slantingly
smartingly
startingly
scantiness
scattiness
smart money
shaft-horse
slatternly
scattering
shattering
smattering
scatter-gun
shantytown
scapulated
shakuhachi
statutable
statutably
sea burdock
statute cap
statute law
sea surgeon
scaturient
slap-up meal
swan-upping
seaquarium
statuesque
✧starveling
starvation
sea swallow
stalwartly
spagyrical
sub-Saharan
submanager
subnascent
subtangent
Sabbath-day
sabbatical
subcabinet
subcaliber
submariner
subcalibre
subvariety
subcarrier
subnatural
suboceanic
subacidity
subscribed
subscriber
subacutely
subacetate
suboctuple
subdecanal
subtenancy
sabretache
subheading
subgeneric
subterfuge
submediant
subceiling
subsellium
subdeanery
sabretooth
subterrain
subterrane
subterrene
sable brush
subsessile
submersion
subversion
subversive
subcentral
subjectify
subfertile
subletting
subception

subjection
subreption
subsection
subvention
subjective
subreptive
subgenuses
subsequent
subofficer
sebiferous
subphrenic
subchelate
subchanter
subchapter
subcharter
subshrubby
sublimated
sublimable
subcircuit
subsidence
subsidency
sublingual
subkingdom
subliminal
subdivider
subsidiary
subdialect
submission
submissive
submitting
subsistent
subglobose
subglacial
sibilantly
subtleness
sibilation
sibilatory
subclavian
Sabinianus
subintrant
subangular
subcordate
subsoiling
subjoinder
subpoenaed
subcompact
submontane
subroutine
subspecies
subspinous
subaquatic
subaqueous
subtracter
subtractor
subprefect
subprogram
seborrhoea
subtrahend
suborbital
subordinal
sobersides
subarticle
subcranial
soberingly
subtropics
subcrustal
✧sybaritish
✧sybaritism
subarcuate
Sebastopol
substratal
substratum
substellar
subatomics
substance P
substernal
substation
substitute
subsumable
subjugator
subfuscous
subsurface
subaudible
subnuclear
subduement
submucosae
submucosal
subduction
subculture
subsultory
subsultive
subaverage
sick as a dog
social club
social evil
Sacramento
social fund
sucralfate
such as it is
socialness
social work
succedanea
societally
secretaire
succeeding
sucket fork
sacred fish
suckerfish
sacredness
secretness
sickerness
Sacre Coeur
sachemship
succession
successful
successive
sick-fallen
saccharide
saccharify
saccharoid
saccharine
saccharase
saccharise
saccharose
saccharate
saccharize
succinctly
sucking-pig
sacrificer
sectionise
sectionize
sicilianos
sicklebill
sicilienne
sickliness
secular arm
secularise
secularism
secularist
secularity
secularize
sick-listed
sick-making
second best
second-best
St Cunegund
second home
second hand
second-hand
secundines
secondment
second mark
second mate
second name
second-rate
second self
second wind
sacrosanct
socdolager
sociopathy
sociometry
St Clotilda
socdoliger
sacroiliac
socdologer
sociologic
sector scan
sycophancy
sack-posset
securiform
secernment
securement
secureness
sacerdotal
securities
securitise
Securitate
securitize
secure unit
sucks to you!
sacculated
succulence
succulency
secludedly
succursale
succussion
succussive
succubuses
sideboards
side by side
seducement
seducingly
Sadi Carnot
seductress
side effect
soddenness
suddenness
Sidney Webb
side glance
siddha yoga
Sado Island
soda jerker
saddleback
saddlebill
saddle-fast
saddleless
saddle-nose
saddle reef
saddle roof
saddleroom
saddle soap
saddle sore
saddle-sore
saddletree
sedulously
side mirror
sedan chair
Sudan grass
siderolite
siderostat
sideration
sidesaddle
sideswiper
soda-siphon
sidestream
side street
sidestroke
sedateness
sudatorium
Sadducaean
sodium lamp
sodium pump
sidewinder
Svetambara
seecatchie
skedaddler
sherardise
stewardess
sherardize
shenanigan
steganopod
she's apples
skew bridge
sueability
step by step
shea butter
sketchable
sketch book
sketchbook
Suez Crisis
stencilled
stenciller
stenciling
speechless
Spencerian
skew-corbel
stercorary
stercorate
speech-song
stench trap
speed limit
stepdancer
speediness
steadiness
speeding up
Sverdlovsk
speedfreak
slenderise
slenderize
speedfully
Steve Waugh
Steve Davis
skeletally
Swedenborg
stereobate
skene-occle
stereocard
seemelesse
shereefian
stereogram
siege piece
Steven Jobs
speleology
sieve plate
shebeening
Steve Jones
siegeworks
stereopsis
siegecraft
siege train
speleothem
stereotomy
stereotype
stereotypy
Steve Ovett
Steffi Graf
stepfather
sleigh bell
sdeignfull
stem ginger
sheng cycle
seethingly
Stephenson
Stephen Fry
stephanite
see through
see-through
scenically
speciocide
sheriffdom
specifical
steriliser
sterilizer
specialise
specialism
specialist
speciality
specialize
sterigmata
speciesism
speciesist
speciosity
speciation
speciously
specifying
shecklaton
sneak thief
steak diane
steak knife
sneakingly
speakingly
sneakiness
steakhouse
speakerine
speak a ship
sneakishly
sleekstone
spell baker
shellycoat
shellacked
stepladder
skelly-eyed
smell-feast
stellified
stelliform
seemlihead
stealth tax
shellshock
spell-check
spellcheck
stealthily
stealthing
steel plate
stellulate
Shetlander
Shetlandic
spellingly
stealingly
swellingly
seemliness
shelliness
smelliness
steeliness
shell money
steelworks
shellbound
shell mound
spellbound
swell organ
shelldrake
shellproof
stellately
spellstopt
spell it out
steam gauge
steam radio
steam navvy
spermicide
spermaceti
spermaduct
spermiduct
spermogone
sperm whale
steam chest
steamtight
steaminess
steam power
sperm count
steam organ
spermaries
spermarium
stepmother
spermatist
spermatium
stemmatous
sternwards
sternsheet
stern-chase
sternalgia
sternalgic
sternworks
sternboard
stern frame
seeing that
stenopaeic
stenotopic
skeuomorph
Stenograph®
stenograph
seed oyster
See You Then
stenotyper
sheep-faced
steeple hat
sheep's eyes
sweep-seine
sheep's-foot
sheep's-head
sleepyhead
sheepshank
sheep-biter
sheep-plant
sweepingly
sleepiness
steepiness
sleep rough
steepdowne
sheep-louse
sheeptrack
step-parent
Shepparton
sheepishly
sweepstake
seed potato
shearwater
step rocket
spear-shaft
steer clear
swear blind
sperrylite
stearsmate
steersmate
sneeringly
smeariness
shear force
shear zones
spear-point
spear grass
shear-steel
seersucker
stem stitch
Spenserian
seed shrimp
stepsister
sweet-water
sweetwater
sweet basil
spectrally
sweatpants
sheathbill
sweath-band
spectacled
spectacles
scent scale
steatocele
scepticism
skepticism
sheet metal
spectre bat
sweetie-pie
sweetheart
sheathfish
sweat-shirt
sweatshirt
scent gland
sweat gland
sweat blood
sheathless
sheet-glass
sweetening
sleetiness
sweatiness
spent force
sweet tooth
scent organ
stentorian
sweetbread
sweetbriar
sweetbrier
sheltering
sweltering
stertorous
sweet-stuff
spectatrix
sweat it out
sheet music
speculator

spelunking
sleeve fish
sleevehand
sleeveless
swerveless
seed vessel
stemwinder
sleazeball
sleaziness
sneezeweed
sneezewood
sneezewort
soft-bodied
soft-boiled
soft-billed
safe-blower
soft cheese
sufferance
sufferable
sufferably
soft-finned
soft-footed
soft fruits
soft-headed
soft hyphen
suffigance
suffisance
sufficient
sufflation
soft option
soft palate
safe period
suffragism
suffragist
Sefer Torah
safari park
safari suit
soft return
soft-spoken
soft sawder
soft sowder
safety arch
safety belt
safety bolt
safety cage
safety cell
safety film
safety fuse
safety lock
safety lamp
safety plug
safety rein
safety shot
signalling
sage cheese
segregable
signet ring
suggestion
segmentary
segmentate
suggestive
sage grouse
seguidilla
signifying
sigillarid
sign-manual
sagination
sogdolager
sogdoliger
sogdologer
sugar candy
sugar-candy
sugar daddy
sugar-baker
sugar paper
sugar basin
sugar maple
sage rabbit
sugar mimic
sugarallie
sugariness
Seger cones
sugar tongs
sugarhouse
sugar apple
sugar grass
Sagittaria
sagittally
sightlines
sign-writer
schwarzlot
schechitah
sphacelate
Schick test
sphaeridia
schlepping
Schiff base
schefflera
schlimazel
sphalerite
scholastic
schalstein
Schumacher
schematise
schematism
schematist
schematize
schemozzle
sphenogram
sphenoidal
sphinxlike
sphinx moth
Spheniscus
school-bred
school bell
school book
school dame
schooldays
schoolgirl
schoolma'am
schoolmaid
schoolmarm
schoolmate
schoolroom
school ship
schooltide
schooltime
school term
schoolward
schoolwork
school year
schipperke
scherzandi
scherzando
sphere-born
sphericity
spherocyte
spheroidal
spherelike
sphereless
spherulite
schorl-rock
schismatic
schism shop
schizocarp
schizogony
schizoidal
Schizopoda
slip a cable
spinal cord
spinaceous
stir abroad
Shivaistic
spiracular
Said Aouita
spiraculum
shibboleth
shipbroker
shin-barker
spin bowler
switchback
spitchcock
sticcadoes
switched on
switchgear
stiacciato
switch-over
sticcatoes
stitchwork
stitchwort
shidduchim
spin doctor
spin-doctor
spindle oil
skin diving
St Irenaeus
slide valve
spider crab
spinescent
swine fever
sui generis
spiceberry
shire-reeve
skin effect
spider hole
swivel-hook
Sciaenidae
spiderlike
snivelling
spider line
swivelling
stipellate
spider mite
slime mould
shire horse
spinel ruby
spinel-ruby
swine-drunk
spike grass
stilettoed
swinestone
seicentist
spitefully
spiderwork
spiderwort
sniffingly
stiffening
sniffiness
sail-flying
swingle-bar
swing-wheel
swing shift
swing-shelf
stingingly
swingingly
stinginess
sling fruit
sniggering
swing-stock
slingstone
swing-music
swing-swang
stichidium
shish kebab
ship-holder
stichology
slightness
slight over
smithereen
smithcraft
sticharion
stishovite
spirit away
suicidally
spirit-blue
spirit duck
spiritedly
spirit lamp
spiritless
stibialism
spinigrade
spirituous
skikjöring
stickybeak
sticky ends
stick shift
skip-kennel
smirkingly
stinkingly
slinkiness
stickiness
stick force
smickering
snick-a-snee
slickstone
stinkstone
still water
swirl vanes
stifle bone
stillicide
spiflicate
shield fern
smifligate
shield-hand
Shieldinch
still lifes
still video
stillbirth
spillikins
shillelagh
shieldlike
shieldling
shieldless
shield-maid
Scillonian
stiflingly
still and on
stillhouse
shield pond
sheldrake
sciolistic
ship letter
still-stand
stillatory
skillfully
shieldwall
seismicity
seismogram
sailmaking
seismology
skimmingly
swimmingly
stigmarian
shimmering
shipmaster
skirmisher
stigmatise
stigmatism
stigmatist
stigmatose
stigmatize
shinny down
scientific
skinniness
seignorage
spinnerule
seigneurie
skibobbing
spirometer
spirometry
Spiro Agnew
spirophore
sailorlike
sailorless
ski touring
spirograph
sailor suit
slit pocket
stimpmeter
skimpingly
skippingly
skimpiness
slippiness
skin-popper
slipperily
skippering
ship-rigged
stirringly
stirrup cup
spinsterly
Swiss chard
slip stitch
slip-stitch
slipsloppy
slipstream
scissor-leg
slip-string
Swiss franc
spinstress
scissor cut
spissitude
Ship's Stern
Saint-Saëns
shirtwaist
shift about
slit trench
skittle out
spittlebug
scintigram
skintights
Saint Aidan
skirt along
stintingly
shiftiness
shirtiness
stiltiness
spintronic
shirt frill
shirt front
shirt dress
scintiscan
skittishly
stimulancy
stimulable
stimulator
stipulator
ski jumping
shipwright
St John's Day
sojourning
Soka Gakkai
✧salmanazar
solfataras
✧salmanaser
solfataric
salsa verde
saltarelli
saltarello
syllabical
Salvadoran
sultanship
self-acting
self-action
salmagundi
salmagundy
self-abuser
syllabuses
sell a dummy
sell-by date
self-breath
salubrious
solubilise
salability
solubility
solubilize
self-binder
salt-butter
self-bounty
selectable
Salicaceae
self-cocker
silicified
saltcellar
salicylism
siliculose
salicylate
self-colour
solacement
selectness
salicional
salicornia
solecistic
solicitude
salicetums
solicitant
soliciting
silk cotton
solicitous
self-deceit
solidified
self-driven
salad plant
salad plate
self-denial
self-danger
solid angle
salad cream
solidarism
solidarist
solidarity
solid-state
sildenafil
silverback
silver bell
silverbill
silver-bath
sallenders
silver foil
salverform
silver fern
silverfish
silver-gilt
solfeggios
silver gate
self-exiled
solferinos
silver leaf
silverling
spleenless
sullenness
Silver Star
silverside
silverskin
salientian
silver thaw
self-esteem
silver tree
silvertail
silverweed
silverware
spleenwort
salifiable
solifidian
self-feeder
self-filler
saliferous
salt-glazed
self-glazed
selegiline
silkgrower
self-giving
sylphidine
sulfhydryl
sola helmet
sulphonate
sulphonium
sulphurise
sulphurate
sulphurous
sulphurize
self-hatred
sulphation
sulphatase
sell in bulk
salpingian
salvifical
self-inject
saltigrade
soldiering
self-killed
self-killer
self-loader
salal berry
selflessly
self-loving
solemniser
solemnizer

Words marked ✧ can also be spelled with one or more capital letters

solemn mass
Solomonian
salamander
Solomon Sea
solemnness
self-murder
self-mettle
self-motion
self-moving
shlemozzle
splent bone
splint bone
splint coal
Salina Cruz
selenodont
silent film
splanchnic
solenoidal
splendidly
silentiary
selenology
silentness
solan goose
splendrous
solonetzic
splenative
splintwood
saloon deck
salmonella
silhouette
Salmonidae
syllogiser
syllogizer
salmon leap
Selbornian
sallowness
seldomness
salmon pink
salmon-pink
seldom when
sale of work
self-praise
solipedous
self-poised
self-profit
self-parody
solo parent
salopettes
solar panel
scleriasis
scleroderm
self-regard
self-raised
self-rolled
self-ruling
solar flare
scleromata
sultriness
solar power
solar noise
solar month
self-repose
self-rising
sclerotial
sclerotomy
sclerotise
sclerotium
sclerotize
self-slayer
splashback
splash down
splashdown
self-seeder
self-seeker
sales pitch
sales clerk
salesclerk
saleswoman
splash page
silkscreen
salt spring
sales drive
self-severe
self-styled
split hairs
split-level
splutterer
split shift
splotchily
sal Atticum
split image
solutional
solitarian
split-brain
salutarily
solitarily
split trust
solstitial
salutation
salutatory
self-taught
self-unable
salbutamol
Seleucidae
Seleucidan
solivagant
Sclavonian
salivation
self-willed
silly-billy
silly mid-on
silly money
sally forth
seltzogene
somnambule
sympathies
sympathise
sympathize
semi-annual
Summar Roll
Samian ware
somebodies
semichorus
semicircle
semicirque
semi-ditone
semi-double
semi-divine
semi-drying
Sympetalae
simnel cake
Samuel Colt
simmer down
Samuel Hood
semper idem
summerlike
symmetrian
symmetrise
symmetrize
Simmenthal
summertide
summer-tree
summer time
summertime
summerwood
symphilism
symphilous
symphylous
symphonion
symphonist
Sam Shepard
symphyseal
symphysial
summitless
somniloquy
semeiotics
somniatory
somniative
semilucent
simplicity
Simplicius
simulacrum
simplified
simplifier
Simuliidae
simillimum
simpleness
semilunate
semi-liquid
similarity
simplistic
similitude
simple time
simulation
simulatory
semblative
similative
simulative
simoniacal
Simon Marks
Simon Magus
seminality
seminarial
seminarian
seminarist
semination
Simone Weil
summonable
semi-opaque
somnolence
somnolency
symbolical
symboliser
symbolizer
symposiast
semaphoric
semipostal
semiquaver
St Margaret
somersault
samariform
samarskite
sombreness
sombrerite
semestrial
sempstress
somatology
symptomise
symptomize
semiterete
somatotype
semi-uncial
somewhence
semi-weekly
somewhiles
Sammy Baugh
Sammy Davis
Santa Maria
Santa Marta
Sunday best
sunbathing
Santa Claus
syntagmata
Sunday Post
syncarpous
syndactyly
sandalwood
sandbagged
sandbagger
sand-binder
sand bunker
synecology
synecdoche
sinecurism
sinecurist
sandcastle
sand dollar
sunderance
sense datum
synaeresis
synderesis
Syngenesia
syngenesis
syngenetic
synteresis
syndetical
sinsemilla
sanbenitos
synoecious
sanderling
Sunderland
sunderment
syntenoses
syntenosis
sinke-a-pace
sense organ
Sanhedrist
sentential
sunsetting
Sinn Feiner
sonography
San Ignacio
Senegalese
sandgroper
sand grouse
Singhalese
synchronal
synchronic
synthronus
sandhopper
Sun Chariot
synthesise
synthesist
synthesize
synthetise
synthetist
synthetize
synchrysis
syndicator
syneidesis
singing-man
sincipital
sensitised
sensitiser
sensitized
sensitizer
sensibilia
Sandinismo
Sandinista
sentiently
Sandie Shaw
sun bittern
sun picture
Sangiovese
Sanskritic
single bond
single-eyed
synaloepha
single file
single-foot
Single Form
Sinologist
singlehood
single malt
singleness
singles bar
single-step
sunglasses
synclastic
singletree
Sunflowers
sand lizard
sand martin
synanthous
sans nombre
synonymise
synonymist
synonymity
synonymous
synonymize
San Antonio
synandrium
synandrous
syncopated
syncopator
San Lorenzo
Sanforized®
sensoriums
sunlounger
sun worship
synoptical
sand plough
sandpapery
sans phrase
sine qua non
Sangradoes
synergetic
✧sinarchism
sinarchist
syncretise
syncretism
syncretist
syncretize
sonorously
✧sinarquism
sinarquist
sandsucker
senescence
Sinus Medii
sinisterly
song school
sinusoidal
synostoses
Sinus Roris
synostosis
songstress
sinistrous
sand saucer
sanctified
✧sanctifier
sonata form
sanctimony
sanitarian
senatorial
sanitarily
sanitarist
song thrush
sanatorium
Sanctorius
sanitarium
sanctitude
sanctities
sanitation
singularly
sensualise
sensualism
sensualist
sensuality
sensualize
sanguinely
sanguinary
sinfulness
sanguinity
sensuously
songwriter
synaxarion
scot and lot
storage jar
sporangial
sporangium
stomachful
stomachous
sporadical
stomatitis
saouari-nut
shopaholic
shop around
slob around
stomatopod
showboater
slop bucket
shoe buckle
Scombresox
Scombridae
snowblower
spot-barred
snobbishly
snow chains
Scotch cart
Scotch hand
Scotch kale
Scotch mist
snow cannon
Scotchness
slow cooker
snow-capped
Scotch pine
Scotch rose
Scotch snap
Scotch tape®
sword dance
spot dealer
spondaical
sword-blade
spondylous
scoldingly
shoddiness
swordcraft
scowdering
swordproof
sword grass
sword-stick
scordatura
sword-guard
stone canal
shorewards
stone-eater
stonemason
shower bath
stone's-cast
scoter duck
Stonehenge
store teeth
shore leave
shovelfuls
shovelhead
scoresheet
spokeshave
smoketight
smoke-black
slovenlike
shovelling
stone-blind
stove plant
smoke alarm
showerless
stone snipe
shovelnose
stone loach
stoneborer
shore-going
scoreboard
smokeboard
smokehouse
stonehorse
storehouse
shove-groat
stonebreak
smoke-dried
stone fruit
stone-broke
storefront
smokeproof
stonebrash
stone-crazy
shower tray
smokestack
stone-still
shovelware
stolenwise
scoffingly
slow-footed
shoofly pie
spongeable
spongebags
sponge bath
sponge cake
sponge down
sponge-down
spongiform
slow-gaited
spongology
sponginess
stodginess
showground
spongewood
spongeware

soothsayer
spot height
Shoshonean
soothingly
smother-fly
smothering
stochastic
slothfully
smoking cap
smoking gun
storiology
stolidness
stobie pole
shop-in-shop
spoliation
spoliatory
spoliative
Scotifying
showjumper
smock-faced
stork's bill
storksbill
shopkeeper
stock agent
stock rider
snorkeller
stockinged
stockinger
shockingly
spookiness
stockiness
stockhorse
stock route
smock-frock
shockproof
shockstall
stock-still
shoal water
shouldered
shoplifter
spoylefull
scowlingly
spoilsport
spotlessly
snowmobile
storm beach
shoemaking
shotmaking
storm glass
storm cloud
storminess
stormbound
spot market
storm drain
stormproof
slow motion
slow-motion
stop-motion
storm surge
stormfully
slow-moving
swooningly
spoondrift
spoonerism
scornfully
spodomancy
stomodaeum
scotometer
Scotophobe
Scotophile
sporophyll
sporophore
sporophyte
scotodinia
sporogonia
sporozoite
snobocracy
scooped-out
scorpaenid
sloop-of-war
stoopingly
sloppiness
snowplough
✧scorpionic
shot-putter
smørrebrød
shoeshiner
shopsoiled
slop-seller
spouseless
Scotswoman
sponsional
sponsorial
spot stroke
shoestring
Scots Greys
smooth away
short-dated
short-range
smoothable
smooth-bore
scout about
sports coat
stotty cake
smooth calf
short score
Scotticise
Scotticism
sportscast
Scotticize
spotted dog
stop the gap
stoutherie
short metre
Scottified
short sheep
sports hall
short whist
short-lived
short sixes
shoot a line
shoutingly
snortingly
sportingly
shortening
smoothness
snootiness
snottiness
sportiness
spottiness
smooth newt
smooth over
short coats
scout's pace
smoothpate
shortbread
short order
short-order
stouthrief
scoutcraft
shoot craps
scooterist
shortcrust
smooth-shod
smooth-talk
short story
shoot it out
sportfully
sportively
sportswear
shortsword
snow-wreath
shop walker
spot-welder
shop window
shot window
Sioux Falls
snowy egret
Scolytidae
stony coral
sooty mould
storyboard
stony-broke
sforzandos
scorzonera
suprarenal
sopraninos
supralunar
suprapubic
sappanwood
suppedanea
supperless
sapperment
septennial
septennate
septennium
sapiential
suppertime
septemviri
septemvirs
sapphirine
septically
saphir d'eau
septicidal
syphilitic
septillion
septic tank
suppliance
supplicant
supplicate
sepulchral
supplejack
supplement
supplyment
supplanter
suppleness
suppletion
suppletory
suppletive
sepultural
saponified
supineness
supination
sipunculid
supposable
supposably
saprogenic
sapropelic
supposedly
saprophyte
Sophoclean
siphonogam
sophomoric
saprotroph
supporting
supporters
supporture
supportive
supersaver
supercargo
supernally
superacute
superseder
superhelix
superdense
superfecta
superheavy
supersharp
supervisal
supervisee
supertitle
supergiant
supervisor
superaltar
superclean
superfluid
superalloy
superclass
superunion
superbness
supernovae
supernovas
super-royal
superwoman
supermodel
superposed
superpower
supertough
supersonic
supertonic
superiorly
supersound
superspeed
superorder
superbrain
supergrass
supergroup
suppressed
suppressor
separatrix
separately
separation
superation
separatory
superstore
separatism
separatist
superstate
separative
superhuman
superlunar
super-duper
supernurse
supersweet
supertwist
superoxide
superexalt
Sapotaceae
Septuagint
sequacious
sequencing
sequential
sequestral
sequestrum
saquinavir
spreadable
serrasalmo
surfaceman
streamered
sarracenia
serradella
sordamente
stream-gold
Sir Ian Holm
spreaghery
Serranidae
serradilla
serrations
streamline
streamling
streamless
spread-over
serial port
surpassing
servant-man
serial time
surfactant
scrobicule
scrub rider
strobiloid
scribbling
strobiline
strobilate
scrub round
strabismal
strabismic
strabismus
surf-bather
strabotomy
spruce beer
soricident
sericteria
shriche-owl
stracchini
stracchino
sdrucciola
strychnine
Saracenism
spruceness
strictness
strychnism
spruce pine
surfcaster
structural
strictured
structured
stridelegs
stridulant
stridulate
stridulous
stridently
Stradivari
strideways
surveyance
sur le tapis
screenable
shrievalty
street cred
street-cred
screen dump
screen door
street door
strae death
streetfuls
screen grid
screech owl
shriech-owl
Serge Lifar
screenings
streetlamp
✧surrealism
surrealist
street name
serjeantry
sure enough
sure-enough
screenplay
streetroom
sorrel tree
serpentine
surfeiting
serpent god
surjection
sarmentose
screen test
screen-test
serpentise
sarmentous
serpentize
serve a writ
screen wall
streetward
streetwise
strifeless
scrofulous
surefooted
strife-torn
serigraphy
strigiform
scrag-whale
scraggling
straggling
struggling
stroganoff
scrog-apple
sprightful
soreheaded
surcharged
surcharger
Sarah Lucas
survivance
sorbic acid
surgically
surmisable
survivable
service car
serviceman
sortileger
straitened
strainedly
serving-man
straighten
straightly
straight up
serpigines
sordidness
straitness
Sir Tim Rice
servitress
strokeable
strike back
strike dumb
strike down
strike gold
strike home
strike into
strikingly
stroke play
strokeplay
strike root
strike sail
strike zone
scrollable
Struldbrug
serologist
shrillness
surplusage
strelitzes
strelitzia
scrollwork
scrollwise
scrimmager
scrummager
scrimshank
skrimshank
scrambling
scrimpness
stramonium
stromatous
shrinkable
string bean
springbuck
string band
Strindberg
string bass
spring clip
spring-cart
stringency
stringendo
strandflat
strong gale
springhaas
springhead
strong head
springhalt
stringhalt
stronghold
scrunch-dry
spring hare
springhase
syringitis
strong-knit
spring lock
shrinelike
springlike
spring line
sprinkling
strinkling
springless
stringless
strong meat
Surinamese
sereneness
strangozzi
shrinkpack
spring roll
strongroom
strong suit
spring tide
springtide
strengthen
springtail
springtime
spring upon
string vest
shrink-wrap
strandwolf

springwood
springwort
surrogatum
sarcolemma
sermonette
Sarcophaga
sarcophagi
sardonical
sermonical
Sorbonical
surnominal
sermoniser
sermonizer
sarcoplasm
sorrowless
surmounted
surmounter
Sorbonnist
seriocomic
sarcocolla
servomotor
Serbo-Croat
strappados
scrap metal
striptease
stripogram
scrapegood
scrape home
Shropshire
seraphical
strap hinge
strippings
strip light
strophiole
stripeless
scrupulous
strapontin
stripiness
strip-poker
scriptoria
strip joint
streperous
scrip issue
strepitant
strepitoso
strepitous
scriptural
✧scriptures
sororially
sororicide
surf-riding
surprising
stressless
stress mark
Strasbourg
sarus crane
stratocrat
stratified
stratiform
strategics
strategist
scratch pad
scratch-wig
scratchily
scratching
scratch out
scritch-owl
shritch-owl
struthioid
struthious
scrutineer
scrutinise
scrutinous
serotinous
scrutinize
Stratiotes
serotyping
sore throat
strathspey
suretyship
serrulated
scrounging
Serpulidae
shroud-laid
shroud line
shroudless
stravaiger
shrivelled
shriveling
Stravinsky
strivingly
scrivening
Shreveport
Shrovetide
Shrewsbury
strawberry
straw-plait
screw plate
screwiness
shrewdness
strawboard
shrewmouse
screw press
shrewishly
spray paint
spray-paint
stray field
spray-dried
spray drift
spray steel
Sassanidae
sustaining
sustenance
systematic
suspenders
St Stephen's
sisterhood
sister hook
sisterlike
sisterless
systemless
suspensoid
suspension
suspensory
suspensive
sustention
sustentate
sestertium
sestertius
suspectful
susceptive
sustentive
sostenutos
sessile oak
suscipient
suspicious
suspirious
sisal grass
sesame seed
sash weight
sash window
set dancing
satyagraha
satyagrahi
St Tibb's Eve
Sutherland
setterwort
setiferous
set against
setigerous
satchelled
set the pace
St Trinian's
Sothic year
settleable
settle down
satellites
satellitic
settlement
satin paper
satanology
set one's cap
set oneself
satin stone
set in stone
set to three
sitophobia
set up house
✧saturnalia
satyriasis
satyresque
saturation
suturation
set a sponge
satisfying
set store by
set-stitch'd
satay sauce
sausage dog
sousaphone
scuba diver
stubble-fed
stumblebum
Saul Bellow
snubbingly
stubbiness
stubbornly
slubbering
slumbering
slumberful
slumberous
squabasher
sourcebook
source code
sluicegate
suum cuique
sound radio
soundscape
sculduddry
soundcheck
sound shift
sound mixer
'sbuddikins
sound-alike
sourdeline
spudding-in
soundingly
sturdiness
squadronal
squadroned
soundboard
soundtrack
shuddering
soundproof
sound stage
squeezable
spumescent
stupendous
saucer-eyed
squeeze off
squeeze-box
saucerfuls
spuleblade
sauce-alone
saucerless
scutellate
souterrain
stupefying
snuff-paper
snuff-taker
shuffle-cap
shuffle off
snuff video
scurfiness
snuffiness
stuffiness
smut fungus
snuff movie
snuff spoon
snuff-brown
sour grapes
smudgeless
smudginess
sluggardly
sluggishly
southwards
southabout
spur-heeled
slushiness
south polar
slush money
South Korea
southbound
✧southerner
southernly
southering
studio flat
stupidness
spuriosity
spuriously
studiously
skulkingly
spunkiness
squalidity
squelching
Squaloidea
squall line
soullessly
soup meagre
stud muffin
squamiform
soup maigre
squamulose
slumminess
squamosity
squamation
squandered
squanderer
squint-eyed
squint-eyes
stunningly
sour orange
shut-out bid
stumpiness
sculptress
sculptural
sculptured
square away
squirearch
square deal
square-eyed
square eyes
squirrelly
square-face
square foot
squirehood
square inch
square knot
squirelike
squireling
scurrility
squirality
scurrilous
square meal
✧square mile
squareness
soubriquet
squirarchy
square root
sauerkraut
square-sail
squireship
square-toed
square-toes
stupration
squarewise
square yard
squashable
saussurite
soul sister
Skupshtina
squeteague
soup-ticket
scuttleful
stultified
stultifier
smuttiness
stuntwoman
shunt-wound
Scunthorpe
soup tureen
sauntering
shuttering
sputtering
stuttering
shutterbug
sluttishly
shut up shop
scurviness
spur-winged
study group
Savage Club
savageness
Savile Club
Seven Sages
seven-score
sevenpence
sevenpenny
saving game
seventh day
seventh-day
seventieth
savingness
Savonarola
seven-a-side
Seven Stars
severeness
Sevastopol
savourless
sewage farm
sow the seed
sow thistle
saw-toothed
Six Nations
sexpartite
saxicoline
saxicolous
saxicavous
sixteenmos
sexagenary
Sexagesima
sixth sense
six-shooter
sex therapy
sex-limited
sex linkage
sextillion
sexologist
Saxony blue
Saxon Shore
sex tourism
sextonship
sexlocular
saxophonic
sex-starved
sexivalent
say Kaddish
skyjacking
skylarking
sky parlour
sky marshal
skyscraper
stylesheet
scyphiform
Seychelles
scyphozoan
stylistics
stylometry
stylopised
stylopized
stylolitic
stylograph
Stymphalos
skywriting
stypticity
sky surfing
skyjumping
sizzlingly
suzerainty
tragacanth
thanatosis
thalassian
tea-tasting
tear bottle
Thai boxing
tranced-out
trancelike
thatchless
Thar Desert
trade paper
trade-falne
travelator
tradesfolk
team effort
tsarevitch
trapeziums
teaselling
travelling
trade plate
trade union
trade board
trace-horse
trade route
travelogue
trade price
tradecraft
thale cress
travel-sick
traversing
travestied
tea meeting
toad-eating
travertine
trabeation
trajection
trajectory
trabeculae
trabecular
tea service
trade cycle
traffic jam
trafficked
trafficker
traffic cop
twangingly
tracheated
Trachearia
tracheitis
trachelate
trashiness
trachytoid
tragically
tea biscuit
tragic flaw
tragic hero
traditores
tragicomic
thalictrum
tear-jerker
tracklayer
track-scout
traik after
tracker dog
thankfully
track event
trap-ladder
thalliform
tea planter
Thailander
trailingly
tea clipper
trail a pike
trawlerman
traymobile
trammelled
trammeller
trammel net
thaumasite
traumatise
traumatism
traumatize
train ferry
tea infuser
travolator
Thabo Mbeki
tramontana
tramontane

team player
tramp metal
trampoline
trappiness
tranquilly
tea trolley
tea drinker
translator
trans-fatty
transvalue
transactor
transudate
transience
transiency
transferee
transgenic
transferor
transverse
trans-shape
team spirit
transplant
transonics
transposal
transposer
trans-sonic
transposon
transeptal
transcribe
transcript
transgress
transistor
transition
transitory
transitive
translunar
transducer
transfuser
transmuter
transputer
translucid
transexual
tear the cat
tractrices
tractility
tractional
✧tractarian
trattorias
traitorism
traitorous
twaite shad
teacupfuls
traducible
traduction
traductive
tramway car
tablanette
tubicolous
table water
table d'hôte
table linen
tablecloth
table knife
table cover
table money
tablespoon
table-sport
table music
tobogganed
tobogganer
Tobagonian
tub-thumper
tubularian
tabula rasa
tabularise
tubularity
tabularize
tabulation
tubulation
tabulatory
tubulature
tibiotarsi
tabloidise
tabloidize
tuboplasty
tabernacle
Tuberaceae
tuberiform
tuberosity
Tyburn-tree
tubercular
tuberculin
tuberculum
tabescence
Tibet cloth
tibouchina
tick and toy
toccatella
Tocharian A
Tocharian B
tocher-good
ticketless
tocherless
ticker tape
ticket tout
tickety-boo
tack hammer
tactically
ticking-off
Tachinidae
tickle pink
tactlessly
ticklishly
technician
technocrat
technicals
technicise
technicism
technicist
technicize
technofear
technology
technopole
technetium
tachometer
tachometry
tacrolimus
Tycho Brahe
tachograph
to capacity
tocopherol
to cap it all
tectricial
taciturnly
tactuality
tachymeter
tachymetry
tachylitic
tachypnoea
tachygraph
tachylytic
tidal basin
tidal power
tiddlywink
tediousome
Tudoresque
Tudor-style
tidivation
tidewaiter
toddy-ladle
toddy-stick
The Bahamas
the Balance
Theravadin
The Tar Baby
The Bacchae
the hard way
the sandman
thenardite
tsesarevna
the cap fits
trepanning
The Rainbow
the Wagoner
the vapours
thenabouts
the fair sex
Therapsida
thé dansant
the Last Day
trey-antler
The Hay Wain
Theban year
trembliest
tree burial
trenchancy
theocratic
trench coat
the science
treacherer
trench feet
trench foot
Theocritus
tread water
theodicean
✧tweedledee
Tweedledum
treadwheel
theodolite
tread on air
trendiness
tweediness
The Odyssey
Theodosius
thereabout
the needful
tremendous
the Seventy
thereafter
The Bee Gees
The Seagull
The Red King
thereamong
thereunder
thereanent
there you go
the Tempter
the serpent
The Leopard
The Tempest
the year dot
The Seasons
The Beatles
trecentist
the heavies
Twelfth Day
twelfth man
theogonist
the theatre
The Shadows
the three F's
the three R's
tree-hugger
tie the knot
toe the line
the Channel
The Thinker
The Shining
trephining
tree hopper
the shivers
thetically
The Timaeus
taeniacide
the hiccups
the big cats
The Wild One
The Tin Drum
the Wise Men
taeniafuge
Trevithick
the jig is up
✧the Village
the million
the Fifteen
the jitters
treillaged
the Old Bill
treble clef
the elderly
theologian
theologise
theologist
theologate
theologize
trebleness
The Planets
thermoform
thermogram
thermology
tree mallow
thermalise
Thermalite®
thermalize
theomaniac
theomantic
thermionic
thermophil
thermopile
thermostat
thermistor
thermotics
teeing area
The Annales
the unwaged
'tweendecks
The Angelus
the sniffle
the antique
The Animals
theonomous
the unknown
the unities
the insured
tremolandi
tremolando
teetotally
The Robbers
the moodies
the Borders
treponemas
treponemes
The Hot Five
The Gorgias
the Godhead
tremolitic
The Monkees
the Rockies
tree of lead
The Hollies
tree of life
the jobless
tremorless
the boonies
Trevor Nunn
tremolo arm
the horrors
The Poetics
the Forties
the mostest
theophanic
theopneust
theophobia
theophoric
trespasser
the dreaded
tiebreaker
the Creator
theurgical
The Prelude
the Promise
the Prophet
theoretics
trekschuit
theistical
themselves
treasonous
The Osmonds
theosopher
theosophic
theotechny
twentyfold
twenty-four
twenty-five
theatrical
tree tomato
treaty port
The Eternal
tweet-tweet
The Dunciad
the ould sod
toe-curling
The Hustler
twelvefold
the evil one
twelve-note
twelve-tone
teeny-weeny
tuffaceous
tuftaffeta
tuftaffety
tufted duck
toffee-nose
tuft-hunter
tagged atom
tagliarini
taglierini
toggle iron
tegumental
tiger badge
tiger shark
tiger snake
Tiger Woods
tiger prawn
tigerishly
tight-laced
tight-lacer
tightishly
tchoukball
Trivandrum
tricameral
trilateral
trivalence
trivalency
triradiate
trifarious
tritanopia
tritanopic
✧trinacrian
tripartism
tripartite
twi-natured
twin-bedded
thimblerig
thimbleful
triactinal
thin client
twitchiest
triaconter
tail covert
third party
third-party
Third Reich
third class
third-class
third force
Third World
third order
trigeminal
trigeminus
trioecious
triternate
thimerosal
tripe-woman
tripehound
toiletries
toilet roll
toilet soap
trisectrix
Tridentine
trisection
tridentate
thief-taker
triffidian
twinflower
thingumbob
thinginess
triggerman
trigger off
trichiasis
trichocyst
trichogyne
triphthong
trichology
trip hammer
trichinise
trichinose
trichinous
trichinize
trichromat
trichromic
trithionic
trichroism
teichopsia
Triphysite
trichotomy
Trichiurus
tritically
triniscope
triliteral
toilinette
trilineate
triticeous
trilingual
twilighted
twi-nighter
trivialise
trivialism
triviality
trivialize
tuitionary
tripinnate
trinitrate
tritiation
Trinity Bay
think about
think again
think shame
tricksiest
thick-skull
triskelion
think aloud
Twickenham
thinkingly
thickening
trickiness
trick-track
thick-grown
trickishly
trinketing
think twice
triple bill
triple bond
triplicate
triplicity
triple harp
triple jump
triple-jump
triflingly
tripleness
triclinium
trial court
thill-horse
trillionth
triple play
triglyphic
triple time
triumphant
triumphing
triumphery
triumviral
trimmingly
trienniums
triandrian
triandrous
triangular
Triangulum
trilobated

trigonally
tailorbird
teinoscope
tribometer
tricoteuse
trilobitic
trifoliate
tailor-made
tailormake
trimorphic
thixotrope
thixotropy
trimonthly
tricostate
trilocular
triapsidal
thiopental
trippingly
tripperish
tribrachic
trigrammic
trierarchy
tricrotism
tricrotous
trip switch
thirstiest
thirstless
toilsomely
trio sonata
twin sister
tristearin
tristichic
thirteenth
thirtyfold
triathlete
twittingly
twist drill
twittering
tripterous
Twin Towers
thiouracil
triturator
trifurcate
trisulcate
tripudiary
tripudiate
triquetrae
triquetral
triquetrum
thievishly
thin-walled
tricycling
tricyclist
Tajikistan
take a fancy
take a dekko
take a shine
take a class
take an oath
take as read
take a brief
take advice
take breath
take charge
take effect
take flight
take fright
take it easy
take in hand
take in vain
take kindly
taken aback
taken short
takingness
token money
tokenistic
take notice
take orders
take part in
Takashi Ono
take strike
take the rap
take the air
take the rue
take the sun
take to task
take to town
take to wife
take up arms
take up rate
tillandsia
tiliaceous
Talcahuano
talebearer
telebridge
tollbridge
telechiric
telecamera
telecentre
telecasted
telecaster
tillerless
Talleyrand
tiller-rope
tellership
tilt fillet
telegraphy
telegonous
telegnosis
tilt hammer
telpherman
telpherway
telpherage
toluic acid
telling-off
Telemachus
telomerase
telematics
telemetric
talentless
talent-spot
tallow face
teleologic
teleonomic
teliospore
teleostean
tallow tree
teleostome
Teleostomi
tallow wood
tulip-eared
telophasic
telephoner
telephonic
telephotos
telepathic
telerecord
tularaemia
tularaemic
tolerantly
toleration
talismanic
telesmatic
talc schist
telescopic
telescreen
tale-teller
talk turkey
Talmudical
televiewer
televérité
televisual
television
telewriter
teleworker
talky-talky
tilly-fally
tilly-vally
tally clerk
tallywoman
tally-hoing
tally trade
tympanites
tympanitic
tympanitis
Tam Dalyell
Tammanyism
Tammanyite
Tom o' Bedlam
tamability
time-barred
timocratic
temperance
temperable
timberhead
Tom Selleck
timberland
timber line
timber-mare
timber-toes
timber tree
Tom Keating
tempestive
timber wolf
timberyard
tomography
tim-whiskey
Tom Kilburn
timekeeper
time-killer
tumble cart
tumbledung
tumbledown
tumble home
tumblehome
Tamil tiger
temulently
timeliness
tumble over
tumblerful
timelessly
tumultuary
tumultuate
tumultuous
tumbleweed
timing belt
temporally
temporalty
Tim Robbins
temporiser
temporizer
Tom Collins
tomfoolery
tom-tomming
tambourine
tumorgenic
timbrology
tamarillos
temerously
timorously
time-sharer
tumescence
time signal
time switch
time spirit
time series
time-served
timeserver
time-saving
tomatillos
temptingly
time-thrust
temptation
Timothy Yeo
time-worker
Tommy Smith
tinea pedis
tantaliser
tantalizer
tantamount
tanka boats
tennantite
tentacular
tentaculum
tenebrific
tenebrious
tenability
tankbuster
tonic water
tone colour
tonic sol-fa
tonic spasm
Tony Curtis
tented arch
Tinkerbell
tenderfeet
tenderfoot
tank engine
tenterhook
Tenrecidae
Tangerines
tenderiser
tenderizer
tunbellied
tenderloin
tinder-like
tenderling
tinselling
tunnelling
tenderness
tangential
tendential
Tinseltown
tandemwise
tank-farmer
tin whistle
Tannhäuser
tannic acid
tennis club
tensimeter
tendinitis
tonsilitis
tonsillary
tension rod
tennis shoe
tanglefoot
tanglement
tanglingly
tinklingly
tonelessly
tunelessly
tanglesome
tonalitive
tangleweed
tenemental
tenantable
tuning fork
tenantless
Tananarive
tenantship
Tin Woodman
tin soldier
Tintometer®
Tintoretto
tendonitis
ten-pointer
ten-pounder
tantony pig
tenurially
tendrillar
tendrilled
tent stitch
Toni Sailer
tonishness
tenotomist
tinctorial
Tina Turner
Tungurahua
Tantum ergo
tonguelike
tongueless
tonguester
tongue-tied
tongue-work
Thomas Arne
Thomas Cook
Thomas Edur
Thomas Gray
Thomas Gold
Thomas Hood
Thomas Lord
Thomas Mann
Thomas More
tropaeolin
tropaeolum
troubadour
troubledly
Trowbridge
trombonist
trou-de-loup
to one's cost
to one's face
Tao-te-ching
to one's hand
trowelling
to one's name
two-year-old
thoughtful
tooth fairy
toothpaste
two-wheeled
two-wheeler
toothshell
trochoidal
trophology
Trophonian
trochanter
toothiness
toothbrush
trophesial
trochiscus
trochotron
trophy wife
tropically
tropicbird
troglodyte
Trollopean
Trollopian
trolloping
trollopish
trolley car
trolley man
trolleybus
trou-madame
toolmaking
thornhedge
thorniness
thorn apple
thornproof
tropopause
tromometer
thoroughly
tropophyte
Trogonidae
tropologic
troop horse
toolpusher
two or three
trousseaus
trousseaux
thousandth
trousering
tsotsi suit
Trotskyism
Trotskyist
Trotskyite
troctolite
trout spoon
troutstone
trouvaille
two-two time
tap-dancing
tophaceous
typhaceous
topgallant
topicality
typicality
type cutter
tepidarium
tap penalty
tappet-loom
tappet-ring
top-heavily
Tupperware®
topography
typography
top the bill
type holder
topping-out
tipsifying
topologist
typologist
typhlology
tape luring
toponymics
tip one's hat
topknotted
top and tail
top-notcher
topsoiling
taphonomic
toploftily
topophilia
tape reader
tape-record
taperingly
tapestried
tapescript
typescript
typesetter
tapotement
typewriter
topi-wallah
topsy-turvy
topazolite
tarmacadam
termagancy
tartanalia
Tartan army
throatband
threadbare
thread-cell
tersanctus
threatened
threatener
terracette
tartareous
throat-full
terra firma
terrariums
tirra-lirra
threadiest
throatiest
tarmacking
thread-lace
threadlike
tarpauling
throatlash
thread mark
turn around
turnaround
terra rossa
terracotta
turn adrift
thread vein
threadworm
throatwort
Terramycin®
turnbuckle
turnbroach
tyre chains
turn colour
tirocinium
taradiddle
target area
tarte tatin
targetable
three balls
three-parts
turkey cock
target cell
torpescent
turgescent
threescore
terne metal
threepence
three bells

threepenny
terre verte
Turkey hone
three-phase
three-piece
three-piled
three-sided
three-cleft
terreplein
tortellini
terne plate
torbernite
torpedo net
three-pound
torpedoist
turret ship
torrential
tormenting
turpentine
turpentiny
torrent-bow
turkey trot
torpefying
torrefying
tortfeasor
thriftiest
tariffless
thriftless
thrift shop
tariff wall
torch-dance
torchlight
Tyrrhenian
torch-staff
turbinated
Terminalia
terminable
terminably
terminally
terminator
Torricelli
Turritella
turnip flea
turning-saw
tirling-pin
tirailleur
turnip moth
torsion bar
torpidness
torridness
turbidness
turgidness
Tardigrada
tardigrade
terminuses
tortiously
tarsia-work
terrifying
torrid zone
turtleback
turtledove
Tirolienne
Tyrolienne
✧turtleneck
tirelessly
turtle soup
Turkmenian
thromboses
thrombosis
thrombotic
tyrant bird
threnodial
threnodist
tarantella
thronged up
tyrannical
Tyrannidae
throneless
throne room
tiring-room
Turing test
Turko-Tatar
Turcophobe
Turcophile
terroriser
terrorizer
torporific
terrorless
thruppence
thruppenny
tartrazine
teres major
teres minor
thrust into
tiresomely
tyrosinase
thrust past
Torosaurus
teratogeny
teratology
throttling
teratomata
turn turtle
turbulator
turbulence
turbulency
torturedly
Tartuffian
Tartuffery
Tartuffish
Tartuffism
throughway
throughout
throughput
Targumical
Tertullian
Torquemada
Tarquinius
Turgut Ozal
tortuosity
tortuously
thriveless
thrivingly
throw about
thrown silk
throw stick
Terry Waite
Terry Jones
testaceous
Tysse Falls
tasselling
tessellate
tusser silk
tastefully
test flight
teschenite
tossicated
tosticated
testicular
testifying
test-market
taskmaster
tasimetric
taseometer
testudinal
testudines
tetrabasic
titratable
tetrarchic
Tetrandria
tetrameral
tête-à-têtes
tetrameter
tetrasemic
tetrahedra
tetrathlon
tetrachord
tetraploid
tetragonal
tetrapodic
tetrapolis
tetratomic
Tetramorph
tetraspore
tetrastich
tetrastyle
tetractine
tetraptote
tetraethyl
Tetragynia
titubation
tête-de-pont
to the death
title sheet
to the nines
to the skies
to the point
title track
Tattersall
tetchiness
tattie-claw
tithingman
tattie-shaw
titillator
tattlingly
titularity
tattletale
Tate Modern
totemistic
Titanesque
tutworkman
tetrotoxin
totipotent
tutorially
Titus Alone
Titus Groan
tittupping
tut-tutting
tatpurusha
titivation
thumb latch
thumbscrew
thumbs down
thumbs-down
thumbpiece
thumb piano
thumbikins
thumb a lift
tourbillon
thumb index
thumb-index
thumb a ride
thunbergia
thumbprint
thumbstall
truncately
truncation
trundle bed
tout de même
thuddingly
Thunder Bay
thunderegg
thundering
thunderbox
thunder god
thunderous
Truce of God
truffle pig
truffle dog
touchpaper
truth table
truth value
touch-me-not
truth serum
touch-piece
touch-plate
touch and go
touchingly
toughening
touchiness
tough going
✧touchstone
tough it out
touch rugby
touch judge
touch lucky
truthfully
touring car
trunk maker
truckle bed
truckloads
tourmaline
tournament
trunnioned
tourniquet
truantship
tauromachy
tour of duty
tautomeric
tautophony
tautologic
thump along
thumpingly
trumpeting
tauntingly
trustingly
trustiness
trust house
trust stock
trustfully
truculence
truculency
Thucydides
towel-gourd
towel-horse
towing path
towing rope
thwartedly
tower-shell
tawdry lace
tower block
toweringly
tawdriness
towardness
thwartship
thwartwise
thwartways
town's-bairn
Townsville
townswoman
tawny eagle
taxability
toxicology
toxication
Taxi Driver
taxi-driver
taxi dancer
taxidermal
taxidermic
text editor
tax shelter
taxonomist
tax holiday
toxiphobia
Texas fever
Texas wedge
Texas tower
texturally
textualism
textualist
tax evasion
trypan blue
Twyla Tharp
thysanuran
twy-natured
thymectomy
toy soldier
toy spaniel
thyrsoidal
toyishness
tryptophan
tuzzi-muzzy
tuzzy-muzzy
unawakened
unacademic
unavailing
Ural-Altaic
unanalysed
unanalyzed
unanalytic
uranalysis
unaccented
unascended
unanchored
up-and-under
up and doing
unamenable
un-American
unaffected
unarguable
unarguably
unanimated
Upanishads
unadjusted
usableness
unallotted
unadmiring
unadmitted
unarmoured
unannealed
unatonable
unavowedly
uranometry
unappeased
unapprised
unappalled
unapproved
unapparent
unaspiring
unacquaint
unabridged
unarranged
Utahraptor
unassuaged
unanswered
unassigned
unassailed
unabsolved
unassuming
unassisted
unactuated
unattached
unattended
unaltering
unattested
unartistic
unartfully
unamusable
up a gum tree
unbearable
unbearably
unbeatable
unblamable
unblamably
unbranched
upbraiding
unbeavered
unbiasedly
umbrageous
umbratical
unboastful
umbraculum
unbiblical
unbecoming
unbudgeted
unbedimmed
unbedinned
unbleached
unblenched
unbreached
unbreeched
umbrellaed
urbi et orbi
unbreathed
unbeguiled
unbegotten
unbeholden
unbailable
unbribable
upbuilding
upbringing
unblinking
unblissful
Uzbekistan
umbellated
umbilicate
unbelieved
unbeliever
umbellifer
unbalanced
unbendable
unbonneted
unbenignly
urbanology
unbundling
urbaneness
urbanistic
urbanities
umbonation
upbuoyance
unbloodied
unbrokenly
unbaptised
unbaptized
unbarbered
unburdened
unbirthday
Umberto Eco
unborrowed
upbursting
unbespoken
unbestowed
unbesought
unbetrayed
unbattered
unbettered
unbuttered
unbottomed
unbuttoned
unblushing
unbewailed
unchanging
uncharming
unchastely
unchastity
Uncle Vanya
Uncle Remus
unclerical
uncredited
uncredible
uncleansed
uncheerful
uncreating
uncoffined
uncritical
uncoloured
uncultured
uncumbered
uncommonly
uncommuted
unconfined
uncandidly
uncanonise
uncanonize
uncensored
unconsoled
unconstant
unconjugal
uncensured
unconfused
unconsumed
uncloister
uncurbable
uncerebral
uncared-for
uncarpeted
uncorseted
unchristen
ulceration
ulcerative
ulcerously
uncustomed
unclubable
unctuosity
unctuously
undramatic
undebarred

Words marked ✧ can also be spelled with one or more capital letters

undeclared
undeceived
undecimole
undoctored
undecisive
undreading
undreaming
undreamt-of
undressing
undefeated
undefended
undigested
undulately
undulating
undulation
undulatory
undelaying
undomestic
undeniable
undeniably
undrooping
undepraved
undeprived
undeplored
underjawed
underlayer
undernamed
undertaken
undertaker
under water
underwater
underearth
underpants
undervalue
undirected
underactor
underscore
underscrub
undersexed
underbelly
underlease
undersense
underneath
underagent
underwhelm
undershoot
undershirt
undershrub
underminde
underlinen
underminer
undersized
undertimed
underwired
under siege
underskirt
undercliff
underplant
underslung
underfloor
under-clerk
underclass
underglaze
undervoice
under cover
undercover
undernoted
under-power
undertoned
underbough
underworld
underborne
undergoing
under-board
underspend
undertrick
under-craft
undercroft
underdrain
underframe
under proof
underproof
under wraps
underbrush
undercrest
underdress
underprise
underwrite
underdrive
undergrove
undergrown
underprize
understock
understudy
understeer
underntime
understand
understood
understory
understate
under-tunic
underbuild
underburnt
underquote
underlying
undismayed
undesigned
undisposed
undescried
undeserved
undeserver
undesiring
undesirous
undisputed
undetected
undeterred
undoubting
undoubtful
undivulged
undiverted
undivorced
undivested
unerasable
unexamined
unexampled
unexacting
unembodied
unexcelled
unenclosed
unescorted
unexciting
unexcluded
unendeared
unendingly
uneven bars
ureteritis
unevenness
uterectomy
uneventful
unexecuted
uneffected
unenforced
urethritic
urethritis
Uredinales
unedifying
uneclipsed
Übermensch
use and wont
uneconomic
uredosorus
uredospore
uredo-stage
unexpiated
unemphatic
unexpected
unexpanded
unemployed
unexploded
unexplored
unenriched
unerringly
urea resins
unenslaved
uneasiness
unentailed
unextended
unentitled
uneducated
uneducable
useful arts
useful load
unequalled
useful life
usefulness
unenviable
unenviably
unflagging
upflashing
unfeasible
unfeatured
unfocussed
unfadingly
unfrequent
unfrighted
unfaithful
unfriended
unfriendly
unfeigning
unfairness
unfilially
unfillable
unfilleted
unfiltered
unfallible
unfellowed
unfamiliar
unfeminine
unfinished
unforsaken
unfordable
unforcedly
✧unforgiven
unforcible
unfurrowed
up for grabs
unforeseen
unforested
unforetold
unfortuned
unfastened
unfostered
unfathered
unfettered
unfatherly
unfathomed
unfoughten
unfruitful
unfavorite
upgradable
ungraceful
ungrateful
ungracious
unguentary
ungainsaid
ungenerous
ungrounded
ungarnered
ungartered
ungathered
ungrudging
ungoverned
unhealable
unheededly
unhygienic
unhelpable
unhelmeted
unholiness
unhallowed
upholstery
uphillward
unhampered
unhomelike
unhumanise
unhumanize
unhindered
unhandsome
unhonoured
unhoped-for
unhardened
unheroical
unheralded
unhurrying
unhistoric
unhouseled
unhouzzled
unhazarded
unicameral
unilateral
univalence
univalency
unimagined
univariant
unilabiate
univariate
unipartite
urinalysis
uninclosed
unindeared
uniseriate
Unigenitus
unidealism
unitedness
university
unicentral
uninflamed
uninflated
uninfected
uninforced
uninformed
unitholder
utilisable
utilizable
uniliteral
unilingual
utility man
unit-linked
uniflorous
unimmortal
Union Shona
union pipes
unisonance
unisonally
univocally
urinoscopy
urinometer
unifoliate
uniformity
univoltine
unicostate
unilobular
unilocular
unimpaired
unimplored
unimproved
unimparted
unimposing
uninspired
✧up in the air
unintended
uninuclear
ubiquinone
uniqueness
ubiquarian
ubiquitary
ubiquitous
uninvolved
uninvested
uninviting
uniaxially
unjustness
unknighted
unknightly
unkinglike
unkindness
unknowable
unleavened
unlabelled
unlaboured
unlockable
unlicensed
unladylike
unlifelike
unleisured
unlikeable
unlikeness
unlamented
unliquored
unlistened
unlessoned
unlettable
unlettered
unliterary
unliveable
unloveable
unlovingly
unlawfully
unmeasured
unmechanic
unmodified
unmeetness
unmailable
unmaidenly
unmellowed
unmolested
unmilitary
unmanacled
unmannered
unmannerly
unmanfully
unmortised
unmerciful
unmorality
unmeriting
unmissable
unmastered
unmothered
unmotherly
unmetrical
unmetalled
unmaterial
unmaternal
unmoveable
unmoveably
unmuzzling
uintathere
unnilenium
unnameable
unnumbered
unnurtured
unnoticing
unoccupied
uroscopist
unordained
unordinary
unovercome
urogenital
unobedient
unofficial
unoffended
urochordal
unoriginal
uxoricidal
unoxidised
unoxidized
utopianise
utopianism
utopianize
uxorilocal
uxoriously
upon my soul!
upon my word
uropoiesis
urological
urographic
unossified
unobserved
unobscured
upon the gad
urosthenic
urostegite
unobtained
unorthodox
Uto-Aztecan
unplayable
unpeaceful
unplausive
unpickable
unpuckered
unpacified
unprepared
unpeerable
unpoetical
unpregnant
unpleasant
unpleasing
unprizable
unprincely
unpoisoned
unprisoned
unpriestly
unpillared
unpolicied
unpillowed
unpolished
unpolitely
unpolluted
unpampered
unpanelled
unpunished
unpunctual
unprofaned
unprovable
unphonetic
unproperly
unploughed
unprofited
unpromised
unprovided
unprolific
unproposed
unprovoked
unprompted
unproduced
unpeppered
unpopulous
unpurvaide
unparadise
unpurveyed
unpurified
unparallel
upper class
upper-class
unperilous
unparental
unparented
unpardoned
unpurposed
Upper Roger
upperworks
upper house
upper crust
upper-crust
unperished
umpireship
upper story
unperfumed
unperjured
unpassable
unpossible
uppishness
unpastoral
unpastured
unpathetic
unpatented
unpowdered
unqualited
unquarried
usquebaugh
unquenched
unquotable
unreadable
unrealised
unrealized
uproarious
unreasoned
unreactive

unreceived
unrecalled
unreckoned
unrecorded
unrecuring
unrideable
unredeemed
unruffable
Ugro-Finnic
unreformed
unregarded
upright-man
unrightful
unrejoiced
unreleased
unreliable
unrelieved
unruliment
unrelentor
unruliness
unrelished
unrelative
unremedied
unromantic
unremarked
unremitted
unrendered
unransomed
unrenowned
unrepealed
unrepeated
unrepaired
unrepelled
unrepented
unrepining
unripeness
unreproved
unreported
unreposing
unrequired
unrequited
unrespited
unresolved
unresented
unrestored
unreserved
unresisted
unratified
unretarded
unreturned
unrevealed
unravelled
unraveller
unrivalled
unrevenged
unreversed
unreverted
unreverend
unreverent
unravished
unrewarded
unscalable
unshakable
unshakably
unslakable
unswayable
unscabbard
unsearched
unstanched
unstarched
upstanding
unshakenly
unshackled
unseasonal
unseasoned
unshadowed
unsublimed
unsociable
unsociably
unsocially
unseconded
upside down
upside-down
upsideowne
unsteadily
ulsterette
unspecific
unspeaking
unsleeping
unswearing
unsceptred
unsheathed
unswerving
unsoftened
unsafeness
unschooled
unseizable
unsuitable
unsuitably
unsmirched
unsmiled-on
unshingled
unspirited
unshielded
unslipping
unshifting
unstinting
unsaleable
unsellable
unsolvable
unsolidity
unsalaried
unsympathy
unsummered
unsymmetry
unseminar'd
ugsomeness
unsummoned
unsinkable
unsensible
unsensibly
unsinnowed
unsanctify
unsanitary
unscorched
unshowered
unstooping
unsmoothed
unsporting
unsupplied
unstreamed
unstriated
unsurfaced
unshrubbed
upsurgence
unscreened
unsurveyed
unstrained
unsurmised
unscramble
unstringed
unscripted
unscrupled
unstrapped
unstripped
unstressed
unsistered
unsisterly
unsatiated
unsatiable
unsettling
upsey Dutch
unsizeable
ultrabasic
ultra-rapid
untearable
unthatched
ultrashort
ultra vires
ultrafiche
unthankful
ultrasonic
ultrasound
up to a point
untrampled
untranquil
Urticaceae
untochered
untuckered
urticarial
urtication
untidiness
untrenched
up the booay
up the creek
untreasure
up the stick
untogether
unthinking
untainting
untwisting
untellable
untillable
untalked-of
untalented
ustulation
untameable
untameably
untempered
untimbered
ultimately
untuneable
untendered
untenderly
up to no good
untangible
untenanted
untroubled
ultroneous
unthorough
unthreaded
unturnable
untyreable
untiringly
ulteriorly
untortured
untasteful
untethered
up to tricks
untruthful
untrueness
untrussing
untrustful
untowardly
usucapient
usucaption
unusefully
unutilised
unutilized
usuriously
unuplifted
usurpingly
usurpation
usurpatory
usurpature
usurpative
unvaluable
unvendible
unviolated
unvariable
unveracity
unverified
unvirtuous
unvitiated
unwearable
unweakened
unweaponed
unwearying
unwedgable
unwieldily
unwifelike
unweighing
unwrinkled
unwellness
unwelcomed
unwontedly
unwinnowed
unworkable
unworthily
unwareness
unwariness
upwardness
unwiseness
unwithered
unwithheld
unwatchful
unwavering
unyielding
vibraphone
vibrations
vibraculum
vibrometer
vibrograph
vocabulary
vocabulist
vice-consul
vice-county
vociferant
vociferate
vociferous
vicegerent
vaccinator
victimhood
victimiser
victimizer
victimless
vocal score
vocal cords
vocal music
vicomtesse
vacantness
vacuolated
Victor Hugo
✧victoriana
victorious
vectograph
viceregent
vocational
vacationer
victualled
victualler
vacuum pump
vacuum tube
✧vichy water
vichyssois
video nasty
videophone
video diary
viewership
viewfinder
voetganger
view-halloo
viewlessly
✧vienna loaf
Vietnam War
Vietnamese
View of a Pig
voetstoots
vegeburger
vignettist
vigilantly
vaginismus
vigorously
vegetarian
vegetating
vegetation
vegetative
vehemently
voiceprint
Vikram Seth
Vulcanalia
Valparaiso
Valparaíso
voltameter
villanelle
volcanised
volcanized
villainage
villainess
villainous
Villanovan
Volcano Bay
Valladolid
Voltairean
Voltairian
Voltairism
volubility
velocipede
validation
vulnerable
volleyball
velvet-crab
velvet-duck
value added
Villeneuve
velvet-leaf
villeinage
velvet-pile
valleculae
vallecular
velvet worm
voluminous
volumetric
valonia oak
volente Deo
Volapükist
voluptuary
voluptuous
valorously
Volkswagen®
veldschoen
volatilise
volatility
volatilize
velutinous
volitional
volitorial
velitation
volitation
volutation
valvulitis
vampire bat
vomitorium
Von Karajan
vintage car
vine-branch
Venice gold
Venice talc
vanadinite
venae cavae
vindemiate
veneer-moth
Vanden Plas®
Vincentian
vengefully
veneficous
venography
vinegar-eel
vinegar-fly
vinegarish
ventilable
vindicable
ventilator
vindicator
vindictive
vinylidene
vinologist
vine-mildew
venomously
vinho verde
vancomycin
ventricule
ventriculi
ventricose
ventricous
ventral fin
veneration
Venus's comb
Venus-shell
vanishment
Venetianed
vanity case
Vanity Fair
venational
venatorial
vanity unit
vanquisher
Venezuelan
violaceous
violet-wood
vapulation
vaporiform
viperiform
vaporosity
vaporettos
vaporously
viperously
vapour-bath
vapour lock
vapourware
Versailles
verballing
verbal note
verbal noun
vernacular
varicocele
varicellar
varicosity
varicotomy
veridicous
variegated
verse-maker
verbena-oil
varietally
variegator
verse-smith
verge-board
Vertebrata
vertebrate
Verner's law
vergership
versed sine
verifiable
varifocals
viraginian
viraginous
voraginous
vertically
virginally
vortically
virgin-born
vermicelli
vorticella
virgin gold
varnishing
virginhood
vermicidal
vertigines
virgin knot
vermillion
versionist
vernissage
virgin soil
vermicular
vermifugal
versicular
vorticular
versifying
virologist
Verulamian
virulently
virilising
virilizing
verandahed
variolator
Vertoscope®
Very Old Man
variometer
Vireonidae
variolitic
verb phrase
Very pistol
verkrampte
virescence
varitypist
virtual pet
virtualism

virtualist
virtueless
virtuality
virtuosity
virtuously
Verey light
visual arts
viscachera
visualiser
visualizer
vasoactive
visibility
vesiculose
vesiculate
vesication
vesicatory
vesper-bell
vespertine
Visigothic
vestibular
vestibulum
vestmental
vestmented
visionally
viscometer
visiogenic
viscometry
visiophone
visionless
viscountcy
visuomotor
vest pocket
vest-pocket
vestry-room
visitorial
✧visitation
visitative
vascularly
vasculitis
vitrailled
viticolous
Vaticanism
Vaticanist
vaticinate
vitrescent
vitreosity
vitrectomy
vitiferous
vitriolise
vitriolate
vitriolize
vitellicle
vital signs
vital flame
vital force
vital spark
vitalistic
vitalising
vitalities
vital stain
vitalizing
vitaminise
vitaminize
vituperate
vita patris
veteran car
veterinary
vaudeville
vouchsafed
vauntingly
vivandière
viviparism
viviparity
viviparous
Viverridae
Viverrinae
vivisector
vowel-rhyme
vowel point
vexingness
voyageable
viziership
vizard-mask
what an idea!
wraparound
whatabouts
whale's bone
weaver bird
weasel coot
whale's food
whale shark
whale louse
wharfinger
weak-headed
weak-handed
weak-hinged
wrathiness
weather gaw
weatherman
weather map
weathering
weather bow
weather box
weatherise
weather out
weather eye
weatherize
wrathfully
whaling-gun
wearifully
weakliness
weak moment
weak-minded
weaponless
weapon-shaw
what remedy?
wrap-rascal
whatsoever
weak sister
wraithlike
what though
weak-willed
wearyingly
wobbliness
web spinner
wicket door
wicket gate
wickedness
wickerwork
Wycliffite
wacky baccy
wide-bodied
Wednesdays
Weddell Sea
wedding day
wedding bed
widershins
widespread
widescreen
widow's mite
widow's peak
wretchedly
weeldlesse
wheedle out
wieldiness
whereabout
weekending
whereafter
whewellite
whereunder
whereuntil
wheresoe'er
woe-wearied
where it's at
weeping elm
weeping ash
wreak havoc
weedkiller
wheelie bin
wheelchair
wheel clamp
wheel-clamp
wheelhorse
wheelhouse
wheel brace
whensoever
wheat berry
wrestle out
wheat sheaf
wheat midge
wheatfield
wrest block
wrest plank
wreathless
woefulness
wheezingly
wheeziness
waffle iron
wifeliness
Wife of Bath
wafer tongs
wafer irons
Wagga Wagga
wage-earner
wage freeze
wagon vault
wagon train
wage packet
wager of law
wag-at-the-wa'
Weimaraner
whidah bird
wait-a-while
wait around
white sauce
white-faced
✧white paper
white water
white-water
white magic
white eagle
white hause
white hawse
White's Club
white cedar
white metal
white meter
whitebeard
white-heart
White Teeth
white wheat
white sheet
white whale
waiterhood
whitethorn
white birch
white light
white night
white slave
whitesmith
white voice
white goods
whiteboard
Whitehorse
white horse
White House
white noise
white bread
✧white friar
white crops
white brass
white frost
white trash
writership
white stick
white stuff
white sugar
✧white dwarf
wriggle out
whiggamore
Whiggarchy
Whiggishly
wring staff
weigh-bauks
weightless
whip handle
writhingly
weighboard
weigh-house
writing pad
writing-ink
whiskified
whisky jack
whisky john
whisky sour
whirlybird
whirl-about
whirlblast
whirlingly
whillywhaw
Whit Monday
whippiness
whimpering
whispering
waitperson
whippeting
whip socket
whipstitch
Whit Sunday
Whitsunday
Whitsun ale
whimsiness
wainscoted
wristwatch
whip the cat
whistle off
whiptailed
waistcloth
written law
written off
waist apron
whitterick
whist drive
wainwright
whity-brown
whizzingly
wake a night
Wykehamist
Wake Island
wake-up call
Wallachian
walk-around
well-boring
well-beseen
wild cherry
well-chosen
wildcatter
Walt Disney
wild endive
wildebeest
Walter Hess
Wilhelm His
wilderment
Wilhelmina
Wilhelmine
wilderness
well enough
welter race
Walter Reed
well-earned
Waldegrave
Waldensian
Willemstad
wall-facing
wallflower
wild flower
well-formed
wildfowler
well-graced
wild ginger
wild garlic
well-gotten
well-heeled
Welsh uncle
Welsh onion
Welshwoman
Welsh poppy
Will Hutton
wellie-boot
wild indigo
well I never!
welding rod
✧wellington
Wilmington
Williamite
Willie Mays
Wolfianism
well-judged
well-liking
will-lessly
wall lizard
well-minded
well-marked
wild orchid
walk on eggs
Wollongong
willowherb
willow tree
willow weed
willow wren
well-placed
well-padded
wall pepper
wall rocket
wolframite
wolf's peach
wolf spider
well-sinker
well-spoken
Wall Street
wellspring
well-thewed
walk to heel
well-to-live
well-turned
wild turkey
wall-to-wall
wilfulness
walnutwood
well-willer
wallwasher
well-wished
well-wisher
walky-talky
willy-nilly
willy-willy
Willy Loman
Willy Wonka
Wim Wenders
wamblingly
wambliness
woman-hater
woman-child
woman-tired
womenfolks
woman-grown
womanishly
woman-built
womanfully
womenswear
Wemyss ware
wampum belt
wampumpeag
wonga-wonga
winebibber
wind-broken
windburned
wine bottle
wind chimes
wine cellar
wing collar
wine cooler
wind dropsy
winged bean
winged bull
winter-clad
wind energy
winceyette
Wanderjahr
winterkill
wunderkind
✧wonderland
wanderlust
winterless
Wenceslaus
wonderment
Windermere
winter moth
wontedness
wander plug
wintertide
wintertime
wanrestful
Winterthur
Wonderwall
wonderwork
wander year
windfallen
wine funnel
windflower
wing-footed
wine-grower
wanthriven
wanchancie
win through
Winchester®
✧winchester
windjammer
wentletrap
wing mirror
win and wear
wanton away
window-bole
windowless
wantonness
windowpane
window seat
windowsill
window-shop
window sash
wintriness
wondrously
wind-shaken
wind-sucker
wing sheath
wind sleeve
windshield
Wandsworth
wingspread
windscreen
windsurfer
wind tunnel
wine taster
wine vaults
wine waiter
wing-walker
win by a head
Wendy House®
wood-boring
wool-comber
woodcarver
wool-carder
woodcutter
wool church
wool-driver
wholesaler
whore's bird
whore after
wholewheat
woodenhead
whole blood
whole cloth
whole-plate
woodenness
whole bound
whorehouse
wooden pear
wholegrain
wooden type
wrong way up
wrong-timed
wool-grower
wrongdoing
woodgrouse
wrongfully
wrongously
woolly bear

woollyback
woollybutt
woodlander
woolliness
woodpecker
wool-packer
wool-picker
wood pigeon
wool staple
whomsoever
wool shears
wood spirit
wood sorrel
woolsorter
woodshrike
woodthrush
whodunitry
wool-winder
woodworker
Woody Allen
wapper-eyed
wappenshaw
wapenschaw
wapinschaw
warrandice
war machine
workaholic
Warsaw Pact
warranting
warrantise
wire bridge
workbasket
wiredrawer
World War II
worldscale
world-weary
world sheet
wired glass
world-class
wire-dancer
world power
World Court
world music
warmed-over
war-wearied
wardenship
worm-eating
workfellow
word-finder
wire-guided
worth while
worthwhile
wire-haired
worthiness
worshipped
worshipper
worshipful
Wertherian
work-harden
Wertherism
warming pan
working day
working-day
working man
Warrington
Workington
warrioress
warblingly
wordlessly
worm lizard
word memory
workmaster
war goddess
werwolfish
wirepuller
workpeople
worm powder
wordsearch
Wordsworth
ward sister
word square
wiretapper
work to rule
work-to-rule
werewolves
wire-walker
wireworker
worry beads
worryingly
washateria
wassailing
wassail cup
West Bengal
West-Banker
wash-bottle
waste paper
washeteria
Wesley Hall
westermost
westernise
westernism
westernize
wastefully
West Indian
West Indies
washing-day
wishing-cap
Washington
westlander
Wasim Akram
West Sussex
wasp-tongu'd
wasp-tongue
✧westward ho!
westwardly
wishy-washy
witgatboom
wet canteen
withdrawal
withdrawer
Wittenberg
witness box
Watteauish
watchmaker
watch paper
witch-hazel
watch after
watch chain
watch light
watch night
watch clock
witch-alder
withholden
withholder
watchglass
witchingly
watchtower
wet through
watch house
witchcraft
watchstrap
watchfully
watchguard
within call
within land
with intent
wattlebark
wattlebird
wet blanket
wattlework
wit-snapper
wet monsoon
water gauge
water table
water wagon
water maize
water about
wit-cracker
water level
water meter
water lemon
watermelon
water thief
water wheel
water thyme
water shoot
water chute
water witch
water wings
watertight
water nixie
water birth
water-skied
water-skier
water clock
water elder
water blink
water plane
water plant
water bloom
water flood
waterflood
water clerk
water glass
waterglass
water plate
watersmeet
water smoke
water snail
✧water snake
wateriness
water power
water tower
waterworks
water-borne
waterborne
water-bound
water joint
watercolor
water motor
water horse
water mouse
waterspout
water break
water gruel
watercraft
water-brain
water frame
water crane
waterfront
waterproof
water brash
water brose
watercress
waterdrive
water ouzel
✧water music
waterquake
water guard
water avens
water twist
water cycle
water nymph
with weight
woundingly
wave energy
wavelength
wave motion
wave number
waveringly
wave theory
wax and wane
wax-proofed
wax lyrical
whydah bird
way baggage
wry-mouthed
way traffic
way freight
way station
wizen-faced
xylochrome
xylography
xylogenous
xylophagan
xylophonic
xylotomous
xenobiotic
Xenocrates
xenogeneic
xenogenous
xanthomata
xantham gum
xanthan gum
xanthopsia
Xenophanes
xenophobia
xenophobic
xenarthral
xiphopagic
xiphopagus
xiphosuran
Xyridaceae
xerodermia
xerodermic
xerography
xerophytic
xerostomia
ylang-ylang
yearningly
year-on-year
yeast plant
yeastiness
ya-boo sucks
yacht-built
Yiddishism
yieldingly
yield point
Yves Tanguy
yaffingale
Yogyakarta
Yggdrasill
Yugoslavia
Yugoslavic
ythundered
yoke-fellow
Yukon River
yellowback
yellow bile
yellowbird
yellowcake
yellow card
yellow flag
yellow-girl
yellowhead
✧yellow Jack
yellowlegs
yellow line
yellowness
yellow-root
yellow rust
yellow soap
yellow snow
yellow spot
yellowtail
yellow-weed
yellow-wood
yellow-wort
yellow wash
yellow-yite
Yul Brynner
Yun-Fat Chow
Yankeefied
York Castle
yerd-hunger
yird-hunger
yird-hungry
yard-master
yard of land
Yarborough
yesterdays
yestereven
yestermorn
yesteryear
Yusuf Islam
ypsiliform
you can't win
you can talk
young adult
youngberry
young blood
young fogey
Young Italy
youth court
youthfully
you know who
you don't say!
yourselves
yours truly
Zoantharia
Zoanthidae
zoanthropy
zebra shark
zebra finch
zebra plant
zabaglione
zucchettos
zidovudine
Zeffirelli
zigzagging
zigzaggery
zygobranch
zygocactus
zygodactyl
Zygaenidae
zygomycete
zygomorphy
zygosphene
zeitgeisty
zwitterion
zelophobia
zelophobic
Zollverein
Zimbabwean
zymologist
zumbooruck
Zend-Avesta
zinc blende
zonal index
Zeno of Elea
zincograph
zincolysis
Zener cards
Zener diode
zone-ticket
zinc-worker
zoolatrous
zoophobous
zoothecial
zoothecium
zoophagous
zoophilism
zoophilist
zoophilous
zoothapses
zoothapsis
zootherapy
zoochorous
zoophytoid
zoogloeoid
zooplastic
zoological
zootomical
zoogonidia
zoomorphic
zoosporous
zoographer
zoographic
zootrophic
zootsuiter
zooculture
Zaporogian
Zaporozhye
zapateados
Zephyrinus
zephyr lily
zero option
zero-rating
zero-valent
zeuglodont

11 – odd

acatalectic
acataleptic
à la campagne
alabastrine
amaranthine
à la lanterne
Anabaptists
Alan Bullock
ad arbitrium
anarchistic
abandonedly
abandonment
abandon ship
A Tale of a Tub
academicals
academicism
academician
analemmatic
amateurship
anaphylaxis
arachnoidal
anachronism
anachronous
arachnology
anaphorical
apathetical
ad avizandum
Anaximander
arabisation
arabization
araliaceous
at a discount
amativeness
aramid fibre
anadiplosis
at a distance
as all get-out
at all points
anaplerosis
anaplerotic
acaulescent
at all events
anaemically
Alan Milburn
anagnorises
anagnorisis
against time
Apatosaurus

Ada Lovelace
araeometric
amatorially
acarologist
analogously
anamorphous
agamospermy
at a loose end
amazon-stone
anacoluthia
anacoluthic
anacoluthon
analphabete
acarpellous
a bad quarter
anaerobiont
Alan Rickman
Anacreontic
Alan Shepard
Adam's needle
Alan Shearer
anaesthesia
anaesthesis
anaesthetic
Acanthaceae
Ajanta caves
apartmental
Alastair Sim
anastomoses
anastomosis
anastomotic
abactinally
avant-propos
away with you
analyticity
Aubrey holes
abbreviator
Albigensian
albugineous
ambiguously
Amboina pine
Amboina-wood
ambilateral
albuminuria
ambrosially
Albuquerque
Albert Camus
arboraceous
Alberti bass
amber liquid
Albert Speer
arborescent
ambuscadoes
asbestiform
arbitrageur
arbitrament
arbitration
arbitrarily
arbitratrix
arbitrement
ambitiously
ambivalence
ambivalency
ambiversion
Amboyna-wood
abbey-lubber
acclamation
acclamatory
archaically
archangelic
archaeology
Arcadianism
archduchess
archdukedom
accidentals
archdiocese
accrescence
Asclepiadic
archeometry
archegonial
archegonium
ancientness
archenteron
alcohol-free
arch-heretic
acclimatise
acclimatize
acclimation
✧archipelago
Archimedean
acclivitous
Archie Moore
Arctic Ocean
architraved
Alcaic verse
accelerando
accelerator
acculturate
accompanier
accompanist
Ascomycetes
accumulator
accommodate
accomptable
A/D converter
ascensional
au contraire
al contrario
accentually
alcyonarian
arctophilia
anchor plate
anchor-stock
anchor-woman
anchovy-pear
ad captandum
acceptation
arch-prelate
acceptivity
accipitrine
accordantly
according to
accordingly
accustomary
accessorise
accessorize
accessorial
ancestorial
accessorily
ancestrally
accusatival
arch-traitor
ascetically
ascititious
accoutering
accoucheuse
accountable
accountably
accountancy
account book
arch-villain
audibleness
audaciously
Andrea Doria
addle-headed
André Agassi
André Ampère
André Breton
André Previn
addressable
address book
Andy Gregory
and then some
aid climbing
aide-mémoire
abdominally
androgenous
audiometric
audiovisual
audiologist
arduousness
audiotyping
audiotypist
androgynous
add-to system
aldopentose
aldermanity
alder-leaved
aides-de-camp
au désespoir
auditorship
auditoriums
addititious
Amelanchier
✧alexandrine
alexandrite
Alexandrian
acetate film
amenability
ametabolism
ametabolous
adelantados
acerbically
alembicated
Azerbaijani
amerciament
agency nurse
anencephaly
ahead of time
alendronate
anecdotical
anecdotally
abecedarian
Alexey Rykov
agelessness
awelessness
Alexei Sayle
atelectasis
atelectatic
at every turn
areographic
aleggeaunce
A Few Good Men
an eight days
Alex Higgins
amethystine
America's Cup
Americanise
Americanize
Americanism
Americanist
American Pie
arenicolous
ameliorator
Alexis Soyer
adenomatous
awesomeness
anemone fish
anemometric
anemophobia
axerophthol
amenorrhoea
anemography
avec plaisir
Areopagitic
averruncate
Alec Stewart
Alex Salmond
areosystile
an easy touch
amentaceous
awe-stricken
Agent Orange
acesulfame K
Aberystwyth
affranchise
anfractuous
affectation
affectively
affectingly
affectivity
affectioned
affectional
aficionado
Alfred Adler
Alfred Binet
Alfred Nobel
Alfred Polly
affricative
affrication
affrightful
affiliation
at full blast
affirmative
affirmation
affirmatory
afforcement
affirmingly
at first hand
aggravating
aggradation
aggravation
Afghan hound
Afghanistan
angwantibos
algebraical
aggregately
argie-bargie
argle-bargle
aggregative
aggregation
augmentable
Anglicanism
aiguillette
angelically
algological
angelolatry
angelophany
angels' share
alginic acid
Argentinian
✧anglomaniac
agglomerate
angiotensin
✧anglophobia
✧anglophobic
✧anglophilia
✧anglophilic
✧anglophonic
angioplasty
Anglo-Indian
Anglo-Romani
Anglo-Norman
Anglo-French
angiography
angiostatin
Auger effect
Angara River
algorithmic
Angus Calder
Angus McBean
Augustinian
Angus Wilson
August Krogh
Argathelian
angst-ridden
agglutinate
agglutinant
achievement
athleticism
achaenocarp
A Shrimp Girl
atheistical
Athole brose
Atholl brose
ashamedness
ashamed that
ashamed to do
abhominable
Aphaniptera
achromatise
achromatize
achromatism
achromatous
aphrodisiac
Aphrodisian
Atharvaveda
athermanous
abhorrently
atherogenic
Atherinidae
A Chorus Line
aphetically
animal bipes
animalcular
animalcules
animatingly
amicability
acinaciform
animatronic
acidanthera
amiableness
Alice Walker
aniseed ball
a dime a dozen
Alice Cooper
ad infinitum
Amin Gemayel
abiogenesis
abiogenetic
Anish Kapoor
a pig in a poke
aniline dyes
acidifiable
aficionados
Alick Isaacs
axiological
axillary bud
alismaceous
axiomatical
azione sacra
a hit or a miss
Adirondacks
anisocercal
anisomerous
a bit of fluff
acidophilic
acidophilus
Alison Moyet
anisotropic
a bit of rough
animo et fide
aminobutene
adiaphorism
adiaphorist
adiaphorous
aristocracy
adiathermic
at intervals
ahistorical
ami du peuple
apicultural
apiezon oils
adjectively
adjudicator
adjudgement
adjournment
awkwardness
ankle-nipper
alkalimeter
alkalimetry
alkalescent
Ankh-Morpork
asking price
acknowledge
al-Khwarizmi
allhallowen
a clean slate
a clean sweep
All About Eve
ablactation
allocheiria
allocatable
all very well
auld-farrant
allegrettos
allegorical
allegoriser
allegorizer
Allahu akbar
all-cheering
all the while
all the world
all-time high
All Right Now
all-electric
allelomorph
allelopathy
Ally Macleod
Ally McCoist
all-American
allomorphic
allineation
Allan Ramsay
aclinic line
ailanthuses

Atlanticism
Atlanticist
Allan Donald
Allan Border
aplanospore
all-powerful
at loose ends
all to pieces
All Fools' Day
All Souls' Day
all to ruffld
alloplastic
allopurinol
allopathist
ailuromania
ailurophile
ailurophobe
Aulus Celsus
alla Tedesca
a slate loose
ablutomania
all standing
ablutionary
allotropism
allotropous
ablatitious
all-building
alleviative
alleviation
alleviatory
allez-vous-en
arms control
Almack's Club
armed robber
armed forces
aimlessness
arm-chancing
Arminianism
adminicular
almond paste
ammophilous
Admiral's Cup
admiralship
atmospheric
admit to bail
armour-plate
Aonian fount
annual rings
annabergite
Anna Comnena
anno Christi
Annie Besant
annihilator
annelid worm
annunciator
Aeneolithic
Arno Penzias
Anna Pavlova
abnormalism
abnormality
acne rosacea
agnus castus
agnosticism
anno salutis
agnatically
annotatable
anniversary
amobarbital
agoraphobia
agoraphobic
aromaticity
anomalistic
avocado pear
anomalously
apogamously
apocalyptic
aposematism
adolescence
at one's elbow
a bone to pick
aponeuroses
aponeurosis
aponeurotic
above-ground
at one's worst
Adolf Hitler
a long figure
apophyllite
apotheosise
apotheosize
abomination
atomisation
atomization
atomic clock
abolishable
abolishment
agonisingly
agonizingly
apoliticism
abolitional
✧aeolian harp
Aeolian mode
aposiopeses
aposiopesis
aposiopetic
atomic power
agonistical
apodictical
apomictical
a work of time
A Doll's House
apollonicon
Apollinaire
Apollinaris
apocopation
Azotobacter
Akosombo Dam
apologetics
axonometric
agonothetes
apomorphine
azo-compound
aeolotropic
amorousness
acolouthite
Adolphe Adam
amorphously
à corps perdu
as opposed to
amor patriae
apotropaism
amour-propre
à votre santé
avoirdupois
atom-smasher
azoospermia
azoospermic
acoustician
à tout hasard
✧adoptianism
adoptianist
apostleship
à toute force
amontillado
apostolical
about-sledge
apostrophic
apostrophus
anorthosite
✧adoptionism
abortionist
adoptionist
a posteriori
à tout propos
apostatical
a colt's tooth
anovulatory
Apocynaceae
apodyterium
amoxycillin
anonymously
agony column
appeal court
appeasement
alphabetise
alphabetize
appeachment
alpha rhythm
appealingly
appeasingly
Alpha Boötis
Alpha Crucis
appraisable
aspect ratio
amphetamine
aspheterise
aspheterize
aspheterism
amplexicaul
apple-pie bed
appreciable
appreciably
appleringie
appreciator
apple-blight
apple-squire
appressoria
apple butter
amphipathic
applicative
application
applicatory
✧amphisbaena
applied arts
amphimictic
amphibolite
amphibolous
amphipodous
amphibology
amphiprotic
appointment
amphictyony
appellative
appellation
appallingly
ampullosity
approbative
approbation
approbatory
approximate
approvingly
appropinque
appropriate
aspergation
asportation
aspire after
appurtenant
appartement
appertinent
✧aspergillum
Aspergillus
apparelment
apparelling
aspersorium
apparatchik
aspirations
apparatuses
asphyxiated
asphyxiator
arquebusade
arquebusier
acquirement
acquisitive
acquisition
acquiesce in
acquiescent
acquittance
Adrian Boult
aureateness
air layering
Adrian Henri
Adriatic Sea
Afro-Asiatic
aerobraking
aerobically
acre-breadth
atrabilious
aerobiology
agrobiology
abracadabra
auricularly
auriculated
agriculture
African teak
acrocentric
Afro-centric
Afrocentric
atrociously
apricot tree
abridgeable
abridgement
aerodynamic
aeroelastic
air-mechanic
air terminal
arrhenotoky
airlessness
acriflavine
Aurignacian
Arrigo Boito
air-sickness
arraignment
aortic valve
acrylic acid
aerological
agrological
agrammatism
acromegalic
acrimonious
atramentous
air-umbrella
a prima vista
Aaron's beard
arrangeable
arrangement
abranchiate
agranulosis
agronomical
acronymania
apron-string
aeronautics
air-corridor
Ayrton Senna
agriproduct
acropetally
agrarianism
aircraftman
airbrush out
aerostation
arrestation
aerostatics
arrestingly
agriscience
agrostology
arris gutter
Airstrip One
aerotropism
agritourism
arrivederci
arrow-headed
arrow-poison
assuagement
assubjugate
associative
association
assiduities
assiduously
austereness
answerphone
abstentious
assafoetida
assignation
aesthetical
aestivation
abstinently
also known as
absolute age
assumed name
assimilable
assemblyman
assemblance
assimilator
Ars Amatoria
assentation
absenteeism
assentingly
abscondence
at short stay
assortative
abstract art
abstractive
abstraction
abstriction
assuredness
assertively
absorbingly
Australasia
Assyriology
adscription
absorptance
assassinate
assassin bug
assessorial
asses' bridge
ansate cross
Aesculapian
Aesculapius
assault boat
auscultator
assay-master
Assay Office
astraphobia
actuarially
attractable
antibilious
Antiburgher
antechamber
autochanger
anticyclone
antecedence
antecedents
attaché-case
articulable
autecologic
articulated
articulator
altocumulus
astuciously
autocephaly
anticipator
anticathode
autochthons
autochthony
at the latest
antheridial
antheridium
at the double
autoerotism
antherozoid
artlessness
authentical
Anthesteria
artefactual
anti-federal
anti-feedant
Antofagasta
antifouling
autographic
astigmatism
autogravure
acte gratuit
autogenesis
antihelices
anti-heroine
astringency
attuitively
attritional
attuitional
attainments
attaintment
attributive
attribution
✧anti-Jacobin
✧antijacobin
antijamming
autokinesis
autokinetic
artillerist
automobilia
antemundane
antimoniate
antimonious
automorphic
artemisinin
attemptable
asthmatical

automatical
antimutagen
attenuation
Aston Martin®
actinic rays
antinuclear
actinically
attendement
attentively
Anton Piller
attentional
antenniform
antinomical
autonomical
Actinomyces
antonomasia
actinometer
antenuptial
astonishing
antenatally
antineutron
anthomaniac
astronautic
artiodactyl
anteorbital
authorcraft
astrometric
action group
anthochlore
antioxidant
anthologise
anthologize
astronomise
astronomize
anthologist
astrologist
action point
action sheet
Authors' Club
Anthony Caro
Anthony Eden
anthocyanin
astrocytoma
Anthony Hope
autophagous
autophanous
autoplastic
antependium
antiphonary
antiphrasis
antipyretic
antipathist
antiquarian
antiquation
antiqueness
antiquities
alternately
altercative
alternative
arterialise
arterialize
alternating
altercation
alternation
aftermarket
anthracnose
auto ricksha
anthracosis
anthracitic
arthrodesis
attorneydom
attorneyism
after-effect
altoruffled
autarchical
antirrhinum
after-dinner
anti-roll bar
alto-rilievo
anteriority
arteriotomy
anthropical
arthropodal
arthropathy
aftergrowth
arthroscope
arthrospore
arthroscopy
afterburner
aftersupper
auto-reverse
attestative
attestation
antispastic
anti-Semitic
antistrophe
altostratus
antithalian
altitudinal
attitudinal
autotrophic
antitypical
antitussive
aetatis suae
Arthur Bliss
astoundment
Arthur Evans
Arthur Kipps
Arthur's Tomb
Arthur Wynne
Arthur Young
active birth
anteversion
antivitamin
active trust
artsy-fartsy
adumbrative
adumbration
aquaculture
aquiculture
Amundsen Sea
acute accent
amuse-bouche
amuse-gueule
aqua fontana
aquafortist
acumination
abusiveness
amusiveness
aqualeather
aquanautics
aquaplaning
aguardiente
aquarellist
acupressure
adulterator
acupuncture
ad unum omnes
advancement
advance note
adventuress
adventurism
adventurist
adventurous
adversative
adversarial
adverseness
advertently
advertising
adverbially
advertorial
advisedness
advisership
a sweet tooth
auxiliaries
auxanometer
anxiousness
amyl alcohol
asynartetic
anything but
any old thing
amyl nitrate
amyl nitrite
amyloidosis
amylopectin
alycompaine
amyotrophic
As You Like It
beat a record
Bramah-press
brabblement
bramble-bush
boat-builder
bear-baiting
bias binding
branchiopod
beam compass
branch-pilot
bean counter
branch water
bias-drawing
boardsailor
board-school
brand leader
brandy glass
Brands Hatch
Brandenburg
bladder fern
bladderworm
bladderwort
Beaverboard®
beaverboard
blaze abroad
blamelessly
Blaue Reiter
brazen-faced
brake lining
brace-and-bit
blameworthy
Beaver Scout
blaze a trail
Blade Runner
beaked whale
branfulness
Beaufort Sea
✧**braggadocio**
braggartism
brachiation
beach-master
beachcomber
Brachiopoda
brachyprism
brachyurous
bearing rein
blazing star
bearishness
black carbon
black market
blackmailer
black walnut
black cattle
blackheaded
black-fellow
black pepper
black beetle
black letter
Black Beauty
black velvet
Black Africa
blank cheque
blackbirder
blank window
black-fisher
black-figure
black clergy
black smoker
black knight
Black and Tan
black-and-tan
black powder
black Monday
black comedy
black coffee
black-boding
black-coated
black bottom
Black Friars
✧**black Friday**
brankursine
Black Prince
black bryony
black grouse
black-browed
blanket bath
blanketweed
blanket mire
black quahog
Black Muslim
black-a-vised
black-eye pea
beaumontage
Brahmanical
Brahminical
Brahman bull
brahmin bull
Brahma Samaj
Brahmo Somaj
brain damage
brainteaser
brainlessly
brainsickly
brains trust
blarney-land
Brazos River
blasphemous
brass monkey
bear's-breech
brass rubber
beam trawler
blastocoele
beat the band
bear the bell
beat the drum
beautifully
beast of prey
blastogenic
beastliness
bracteolate
beauteously
beauty queen
beauty sleep
brattishing
beauty salon
beastly-head
bear witness
bradycardia
bradypeptic
braxy mutton
Brazzaville
baby-bouncer
Bible-basher
baby-farming
baba ganoush
Bob Champion
bibliolater
bibliolatry
bibliomania
bibliomancy
bibliopegic
bibliophile
bibliophily
bibliopolic
bibliotheca
bubble-shell
bubble under
bib and brace
Bob Woodward
Bob Mortimer
Bob Cratchit
Babes in Arms
baby's breath
baby-sitting
beblubbered
Bobby Robson
back and fill
backbreaker
backbencher
back benches
back-blocker
back channel
bicycle kick
bicycle clip
bicycle polo
bicycle pump
back-country
back-draught
bacteraemia
bacteraemic
Beckenbauer
bacteria bed
bactericide
bacteriosis
bachelordom
bachelorism
bachelor pad
bucket-wheel
backfilling
Back for Good
backfitting
back-ganging
bacchanalia
buccinatory
bacciferous
backing-down
baccivorous
Bacillaceae
back-loading
bacillaemia
bucolically
bacillicide
bacilliform
buckler fern
buckle under
baculovirus
Baconianism
bicentenary
bichon frise
bicephalous
backpacking
back passage
buck passing
buck-passing
bicarbonate
bicorporate
backstabber
backscatter
bicuspidate
backsliding
backswimmer
backscratch
back stretch
back to earth
back to front
bucktoothed
Bach trumpet
backup light
buck-washing
body and soul
bad language
bad-mannered
body-builder
body-centred
baddeleyite
bad-tempered
bed of honour
body fascism
body fascist
Bodhisattva
bedside book
badging-hook
Bodhidharma
bed-blocking
bed and board
Baden-Powell
Bedford cord
body politic
body-popping
body scanner
body servant
bedevilment
bedevilling
bid a welcome
bedizenment
beef-brained
bien chaussé
breechblock
breech birth
bleach-field
breadbasket
breadthways
breadthwise
breadwinner
bleed nipple
Breeder's Cup
breadcrumbs
Bremerhaven

Biedermeier
bien entendu
boeremusiek
beer goggles
beech marten
blepharitis
blemishment
brevity code
breakdancer
break the ice
break ground
break it down
beetlebrain
beetle brows
beetle drive
Beetlejuice
Buenos Aires
bien pensant
beer parlour
bienséances
blessedness
breastplate
breast wheel
bless my soul!
breathalyse
breathalyze
breathe fire
breathiness
breeze brick
breeze block
buffalo-bird
buffalo fish
buffalo gnat
buffalo robe
buffer state
buffer stock
buff-leather
baffle-board
bifoliolate
baffle-plate
bifurcation
bifariously
befittingly
buff-tip moth
Bogdanovich
beggar's lice
beggar ticks
bag of nerves
bag of tricks
beguilement
bagging-hook
begging bowl
beguilingly
Begoniaceae
beg for a fool
Bognor Regis
bogus caller
bog asphodel
bog standard
big business
Bahia Blanca
✧bohemianism
behaviorism
behaviorist
behavioural
bridal suite
blind hookey
blind as a bat
blind-storey
blind summit
bridemaiden
bridewealth
boîte de nuit
brine shrimp
Brinell test
boilermaker
brise-soleil
boilerplate
boiled sweet
boiled shirt
brisés volés
bribery-oath
brimfulness
bridgeboard
bridge-drive
bridge-house
bring to pass
bring to heel
bring to bear
bring to life
bring to book
bridge whist
blightingly
bright spark
British warm
Britishness
bricklaying
brickmaking
brick-shaped
brilliantly
baillieship
Bridlington
Brian Barron
Brian Patten
Brian Aldiss
Brian Clough
Brian Robson
brissel-cock
bristletail
bristle-fern
brittleness
bristlebird
bristlecone
bristle worm
brittlestar
bristliness
Bristol-milk
blister card
blister pack
Baily's beads
baked Alaska
Bikini Atoll
baking sheet
biker jacket
baker's dozen
Baker Street
bald as a coot
bold as brass
baldacchino
ball-and-claw
bella figura
ballad metre
ballad opera
ballat royal
ball-bearing
bold-beating
ball-breaker
bull-baiting
ball-busting
bell-bottoms
bill-chamber
balm-cricket
Bill Clinton
bulk carrier
bulldog clip
belle-de-nuit
believingly
balderlocks
balletomane
Bellerophon
bullet point
bullet-proof
billets-doux
bullet train
bellettrist
Ballesteros
bullfighter
balefulness
bull-fronted
Bill Forsyth
bell-founder
bell-foundry
bell-heather
bell-housing
belligerent
bulbiferous
bullishness
Belgian hare
billionaire
Belgian Blue
billionfold
bellicosely
bellicosity
billiard cue
bull-mastiff
balance beam
bilingually
Bolton Abbey
✧balmorality
bill of costs
Balto-slavic
balloon-back
balloon vine
balloon tyre
ballot paper
biliousness
bulbousness
bill of sight
bellows-fish
bill of store
Belmont Park
bellringing
Belarussian
Belorussian
Bill Shankly
billsticker
bolas spider
bull session
belatedness
bull terrier
bilaterally
bolt upright
bulgur wheat
bale wrapper
below stairs
belowstairs
belly dancer
Billy the Kid
belly-timber
Billy Wilder
belaying pin
ballyhooing
Billy Boston
bully for you
Billy Wright
Billy Graham
Billy Butlin
belly button
belly putter
Billy Bunter
Bombacaceae
bombardment
bumbershoot
bombilation
bombination
bumping race
bimolecular
by my lee-lane
bimillenary
bimillennia
bumble-puppy
bums on seats
bumpsadaisy
bimetallism
bimetallist
bumptiously
bon camarade
Bandar Abbas
bank account
bankability
Bengal light
bancassurer
bone-breccia
bank balance
binocularly
Benedictine
benedictive
benediction
benedictory
banner cloud
benzene ring
bonne chance
banteringly
bonnet laird
bonne bouche
bonnet-piece
bandeirante
bonnet-rouge
banker's card
bonded store
binder twine
beneficiate
beneficiary
benefaction
beneficence
benefactory
banoffee pie
banefulness
benefitting
benignantly
benightment
bunch-backed
bench-warmer
bon chrétien
bank holiday
benchership
benthoscope
Ben Kingsley
bundle of fun
bona mobilia
bank manager
bondmanship
banana split
benzoic acid
bandoleered
Benioff zone
bandoliered
bank of issue
Bannockburn
bonbonnière
beneplacito
Bonapartean
Bonapartism
Bonapartist
binary digit
Ben Crenshaw
Benares ware
bonus shares
bondservant
bond-service
bend the knee
bang the drum
Banbury cake
benevolence
Bonaventure
bond-washing
bunny rabbit
bandy-legged
benzylidine
bunny-boiler
Bonny Dundee
bunny-hugger
blow a gasket
biocatalyst
buoyancy aid
book-account
boom and bust
biomaterial
buoyantness
browbeating
bookbindery
bookbinding
blotchiness
bronchiolar
broach-spire
boot-catcher
broadcasted
broadcaster
bloody-bones
Broad Scotch
blood vessel
bloodletter
broad-leaved
bloody-faced
✧broad church
broad-church
broadminded
blood plasma
blood-flower
Blood and Ice
Brobdingnag
blood-bought
blood doping
bloodsprent
blood sports
blood-spavin
blood orange
Broederbond
blood-frozen
bloody-sweat
bloodstream
Broadstairs
bloodsucker
blood-guilty
blood typing
biofeedback
biomedicine
broken meats
broken music
Booker Prize
broken rhyme
biochemical
brotherlike
brotherhood
biophysical
bromination
boogie board
biomimetics
booking hall
bookishness
boorishness
bromidrosis
blocked shoe
bookkeeping
block letter
Brooks's Club
blockbuster
block-system
book-learned
bootlicking
bootlace tie
bootlegging
Boodle's Club
brown George
bioengineer
Brownsville
blow one's top
Book of Hosea
book of hours
Book of Jonah
Book of Micah
Book of Nahum
biocoenoses
biocoenosis
biocoenotic
Bioko Island
Book of Tobit
book of words
bookselling
boots and all
blouson noir
Brotstudien
bloatedness
blow the gaff
blotting-pad
boot-topping
booster seat
book through
biodynamics
bronzed skin
bronze medal
Buprestidae
baptismally
bipartition
biquadratic
Barbara Ward
bureaucracy
Bernard Katz
Bernardines
Bernard Lyot
bereavement
barrage-fire
barbaresque
bur-marigold
barrack-room
bersaglieri

burial mound
bargain away
Barbados leg
barbarously
burial-place
barbastelle
birdbrained
boracic acid
Burschenism
barycentric
bird-catcher
Buridan's ass
Burseraceae
bargemaster
barley-brake
barley-break
barley-broth
Burmese Days
bordered pit
barrelhouse
barrel organ
barber's rash
burgess oath
barley sugar
barley-sugar
Barsetshire
Borsetshire
Barker's mill
barber's pole
barber's itch
barge-stones
barrel vault
barley water
barefacedly
bird-fancier
birth parent
birth weight
Bartholomew
Bert Hinkler
Berthon-boat
birth mother
Burkina Faso
Bertie Ahern
barricadoes
barking deer
burning ghat
barking iron
burling-iron
burning bush
burnishment
bar-sinister
barrier reef
barbiturate
bursiculate
bareknuckle
berylliosis
burble point
burglarious
Barclaycard
Baron Cauchy
baron bailie
Byronically
Byron Nelson
baron of beef
bird-nesting
baronetical
barbola work
burgomaster
Bardo Thodol
Barbour® coat
burrowstown
borborygmic
borborygmus
barn swallow
Boris Becker
bergschrund
Baryshnikov
barnstormer
Burns Supper
burn-the-wind
burnt sienna
baryta paper
barquentine
birdwatcher
Barry Sheene
Barry Briggs
Bessarabian
Bismarck Sea
bastard balm
bastard teak
bastard file
bastard wing
basmati rice
bespattered
baseball cap
best-beloved
bisociative
bisociation
basket chair
besiegement
Bessemer pig
busted flush
basset hound
basset-hound
bastel-house
beseemingly
besiegingly
basket-maker
Baskerville
basketweave
bushelwoman
bashfulness
bastinading
bastinadoed
Bashi-Bazouk
bastinadoes
Bastille Day
Bessie Smith
base jumping
bustle about
basilic vein
bastle-house
Basil Spence
Basil Brooke
bushmanship
bastnaesite
bi syndromes
business end
businessman
Basingstoke
Bishops' Wars
bishop's weed
base pairing
bespreading
bestridable
base station
bestselling
biscuit-root
bushwhacker
bushwalking
bisexuality
butt against
bits and bobs
battalia pie
beta-blocker
botheration
bitter aloes
bitter-apple
butter cream
bitter-cress
butter cloth
bitter-earth
butterflies
butteriness
butter icing
Bette Midler
butted joint
butter knife
bitter lemon
between-maid
betweenness
betweentime
butter plate
butter-print
butter-paper
by the squire
Bitter Sweet
bittersweet
bitter vetch
butter-woman
butcher meat
butcherbird
betting shop
bathing suit
bottle-blond
bottlebrush
bottle-chart
battledress
betel pepper
battlefield
bottle glass
batological
bottle-green
bottle-gourd
battlements
bottle-nosed
battleplane
battle-piece
bottle party
battle royal
battleships
bottle store
butyl rubber
batsmanship
Bath Mitsvah
Bath-Mitsvah
Bathmitsvah
Bath Mitzvah
Bath-Mitzvah
Bathmitzvah
botanically
baton charge
baton-charge
biting louse
biting midge
botanomancy
baton rounds
bite one's lip
bottom-glade
bottom-grass
bottom-heavy
bathophobia
betrothment
buttonholer
bottom house
batholithic
buttock-mail
button-mould
button quail
bits per inch
butyric acid
butyraceous
bat printing
bite the dust
butt welding
Betty Davies
bothy ballad
Betty Martin
bathyscaphe
bathymetric
bathylithic
bathysphere
Betty Grable
Butazolidin®
Blue Blanket
blue-blooded
bruschettas
boulder clay
blunderbuss
blue-eyed boy
Bruges group
Bruce Willis
brucellosis
bourguignon
bourgeoisie
blushlessly
brush turkey
brutishness
Bournemouth
Bruno Walter
bauson-faced
boutonnière
blue pointer
blue penguin
brusqueness
beurre manié
blue rinsers
blue-sky laws
bourtree-gun
bountifully
blunt-witted
blue thistle
bounteously
bouquetière
blue vitriol
blue whiting
bovver boots
bevel wheels
bivouacking
Bewick's swan
bow-windowed
bowline knot
bowling shoe
bewhiskered
bewildering
bowdleriser
bowdlerizer
bow and arrow
bower-anchor
bewitchment
bowstringed
boxing glove
boxer shorts
box junction
Boys' Brigade
boysenberry
Bay of Naples
Bay of Bengal
Bay of Biscay
Bay of Plenty
bay-windowed
bryological
bay platform
beyond doubt
Bryan Forbes
beyond price
B lymphocyte
Bézier curve
Byzantinism
Byzantinist
bizarreness
claw-and-ball
crag-and-tail
characinoid
chalazogamy
chamaephyte
clay-brained
cramboclink
crabbedness
charbroiled
chambermaid
✧chamberlain
clamber over
coarctation
chance-comer
chalcid wasp
chalcedonic
chalcedonyx
chancellery
chancellory
chancroidal
clam-chowder
charcuterie
chandlering
clam-diggers
Claude Monet
clandestine
Claude Simon
crapehanger
Clarencieux
coalescence
crane-necked
chameleonic
ceaselessly
clavecinist
crateriform
chaperonage
chapel royal
chapeau-bras
crape myrtle
chaff-engine
chaff-cutter
craggedness
changefully
change front
change hands
change-house
charge-house
chargrilled
chargenurse
change of air
change point
chargesheet
Cyatheaceae
cha-cha-chaed
crash-helmet
coach-office
coaching inn
crash course
crashworthy
craniectomy
clarinetist
clavigerous
chafing-gear
chafing-dish
crazing mill
craniognomy
coalitional
coalitioner
charismatic
craniometer
craniometry
clarion call
Clavicornia
cranioscopy
charity walk
charity ball
charity shop
charity-girl
coadjacency
clanjamfray
coadjutress
crankhandle
crack-halter
crackleware
crack of doom
crack willow
crackerjack
crack credit
Charlie Chan
Charlemagne
challenging
crawling peg
chaulmoogra
crawler lane
Charles Lamb
Charles Mayo
Charles Bell
Charles's law
Charlestown
Charles Ives
charlatanic
charlatanry
charm school
claims court
charmlessly
Chaim Herzog
chasmogamic
clay mineral
claim-jumper
chain harrow
chain letter
channel seam
channelling
chainplates
channel-surf
chain-smoker
chaenomeles
chain locker
chain bridge
chain armour
chain-driven
chainstitch
caa'ing whale
Chad Newsome
cracovienne

clamorously
cyanohydrin
championess
clapperclaw
champertous
crappit-head
crappit-heid
Claire Bloom
clairschach
chairperson
clair de lune
clairvoyant
class action
classically
chaise-carts
class-leader
class-fellow
classifying
chaos theory
coarse metal
chansonnier
chansonette
crapshooter
coal scuttle
coast-waiter
chanticleer
chaotically
chartaceous
coasteering
chaetognath
coal-trimmer
chastenment
Chattanooga
charter-hand
Charter Mark
chantarelle
chanterelle
chastisable
chart-buster
Chautauquan
craftswoman
coadunative
coagulative
coadunation
coagulation
coagulatory
crapulosity
coal-whipper
crazy paving
cabbage palm
cabbage rose
cabbage-moth
cabbage-worm
cabbagetown
cabbage tree
cabbalistic
cab-rank rule
Cab Calloway
cubicalness
cable-length
cablevision
cable-stitch
cabriole leg
cobalt bloom
cobblestone
cabinetwork
cybernation
cybernetics
cyberphobia
cyberphobic
cock-and-bull
cock-a-leekie
cockaleekie
cocoa butter
cycadaceous
cycle racing
cockeyed bob
cache memory
Cockermouth
cachectical
cacographic
cacographer
cacogastric
cyclicality
Cochin-China
cyclic group
coccidiosis
Cecil Beaton
Cecil Rhodes
cockleshell
coconscious
coconut palm
coconut milk
coconut crab
cyclopaedia
cyclopaedic
cuckoo clock
cyclohexane
cycloserine
cyclothymia
cyclothymic
cycloalkane
cycloplegia
cacao butter
cacophonous
cock-sparrow
cocktail bar
cicatricial
cicatricula
code-breaker
codicillary
cudgel-proof
Cyd Charisse
cod-liver oil
codling moth
caddishness
cadmium cell
co-dependant
co-dependent
code-sharing
cadet branch
cheval-glass
crémaillère
crematorial
crematorium
Caesar salad
clenbuterol
cheechakoes
clench-built
crescograph
coercimeter
crescentade
coercionist
chef d'oeuvre
Cheddar pink
crepehanger
cleverality
clever clogs
coenenchyma
crenellated
coeternally
crème brulée
crème brûlée
credentials
crêpe rubber
crepe myrtle
coefficient
clergywoman
Cheshire Cat
crepitative
clericalism
crepitation
clericalist
Chenin Blanc
Cherie Blair
Cherie Booth
chemin de fer
chelicerate
cheliferous
cherishment
credibility
credit limit
coexistence
credit union
check action
check-string
cheek by jowl
cream cheese
clean-shaven
clean-limbed
cleanliness
clean-living
clean bowled
chemotactic
ctenophoran
Coelophysis
coenobitism
chemosphere
chemotropic
coevolution
cheap labour
creophagous
clear-headed
cheerleader
cheerlessly
clear the air
clear the way
clearing-nut
cherry-stone
Chelsea ware
Chelsea clip
Chelsea boot
cheeseboard
cheesecloth
coessential
cleistogamy
cheese plant
cheesepress
cheeseparer
cheese straw
creosote oil
cheesewring
cleft palate
crestfallen
cleptomania
coextensive
coextension
✧creationism
creationist
Cleethorpes
creatorship
coeducation
crenulation
crepuscular
chemurgical
coelurosaur
credulously
chequerwise
chequerwork
café-concert
café curtain
coffee break
coffee berry
coffee house
coffee-maker
caffeinated
coffee stall
coffee table
café society
cognateness
cognitively
cognitivism
cognitivity
cognitional
cognoscible
cognoscente
cognoscenti
cognominate
cigar-shaped
cigar-holder
cohortative
coin a phrase
climatology
chiragrical
Chimaeridae
climactical
climacteric
chilblained
climbing boy
cuir-bouilli
cuir-bouilly
coincidence
coincidency
chip carving
cris de coeur
childminder
clindamycin
Chinese wall
Chinese copy
Chinese burn
crimen falsi
Chilean pine
chisel tooth
cliffhanger
chief barker
chieftaincy
chieftainry
chiffonnier
crithomancy
coinherence
coinheritor
criminalese
criminalise
criminalize
criminative
crimination
criminalist
criminality
criticality
criminal law
criminatory
criticaster
crinigerous
ceiling rose
criminology
chick-a-biddy
click beetle
chicken hawk
chickenfeed
chicken wire
chicken kiev
clickstream
chill factor
chilled meal
cliometrics
client state
chimney-nook
chimney-nuik
chiromantic
clinometric
clinochlore
Chilognatha
chiropodial
chirologist
chiropodist
chirography
chinoiserie
chiropteran
crippleware
Chippendale
chiaroscuro
chiastolite
coinsurance
chitty-faced
chitterling
chirurgical
cakes and ale
collagenase
Callanetics
collagenous
culpability
calcariform
call-at-large
collaborate
collapsable
collapsible
chloanthite
ciliary body
calibration
celebration
celebratory
colubriform
cold-blooded
Calabar-bean
call-barring
call collect
cold comfort
calycanthus
cold cathode
call cousins
calf-country
calicivirus
collembolan
collet chuck
collenchyma
colleaguing
culverineer
collegianer
calceolaria
collectable
collectible
collectedly
collectanea
collections
calefacient
calefactive
calefaction
calefactory
californium
Californian
call gapping
cologarithm
cold-hearted
cold harbour
culminate in
colligative
calcination
colligation
collimation
culmination
cultivation
Celtic cross
Celtiberian
calciferous
calcigerous
celliferous
culmiferous
calling card
calling-crab
coltishness
Calvinistic
Calvin Klein
calcicolous
call it quits
Callitriche
calligramme
calligraphy
Callistemon
colliquable
calcifugous
callipygean
callipygous
columbarium
columnarity
chlamydeous
columniated
calumniator
calamancoes
cold-moulded
Columbus Day
calendarise
calendarize
colonialism
calendarist
colonialist
calendering
colonelship
colonelling
calendrical
cylindrical
colonoscope
colonoscopy
collocation
coleorhizae
coleorrhiza
callousness
coleopteral
coleopteran
coleopteron
collocutory
colloquiums
calypsonian
calyptrogen
chloric acid
caloric test
calorimeter

chlorimeter
chlorometer
colorimeter
calorimetry
chlorimetry
chlorometry
colorimetry
chlorinator
chloroplast
chloroprene
chlorophyll
chloroquine
calisthenic
celestially
cold storage
call the tune
call to order
calculative
colour a pipe
calculating
calculation
colouration
cellularity
cultural lag
colour-blind
cultureless
Culture Club
colourfully
colour guard
colour index
collusively
colouristic
colour music
colour organ
colour phase
colourpoint
colour party
colour wheel
call waiting
cold welding
cold-without
comparative
comparatist
commandment
command line
command post
comradeship
compaginate
companiable
companioned
campaniform
campanology
compass card
compassable
compass rose
compactedly
compactness
compartment
compact disc
compact disk
campanulate
come a gutser
Campbellite
comb binding
come between
comic relief
comicalness
comedogenic
Comedy Store
commendable
commendably

compendious
commendator
compendiums
competently
Campeche Bay
competitive
competition
comme il faut
compellable
Cumbernauld
commemorate
compearance
compensable
commensally
compensator
campestrian
commentator
Comte Dunois
come forward
combinative
comminative
combination
commination
compilation
combinatory
comminatory
compilatory
commiserate
compilement
Campion Hall
commissaire
commissural
committable
comminution
camel-backed
compliantly
complacence
complacency
cumulocirri
complicated
complainant
complaisant
complaining
compliments
cumulonimbi
cameleopard
Camaldolese
Camaldolite
completable
complotting
camel's thorn
complexness
camp-meeting
camomile tea
cementation
cementatory
✧ciment fondu
cement grout
comancheros
cement mixer
coming-of-age
cement-stone
cement-water
compo ration
compotation
commonality
compotatory
common chord
Campodeidae
componental
come off best

common forms
compositely
compositive
composition
commodities
commotional
compositous
cam follower
common metre
compound eye
commonplace
common prawn
common panda
common stair
compossible
common sense
commonsense
common-shore
common stock
comfortable
comfortably
compost heap
comfortless
comportment
come out with
comportance
comfort zone
common viper
cymophanous
camaraderie
camerlengos
camerlingos
comprimario
compromiser
Cameron Diaz
Cameroonian
comprisable
compressive
compression
compressure
cyma reversa
comestibles
come to a head
come to blows
comstockery
comstockism
come to grief
come to grips
comet-finder
come to light
Comptometer®
comptroller
compte rendu
come through
come to terms
communalise
communalize
commutative
computative
communalism
commutation
computation
communalist
compunction
computerate
computerese
computerise
computerize
compurgator
come unglued
communicate

communicant
communistic
comeuppance
compulsitor
come unstuck
combustible
combustious
come what may
cinnabarine
canvas board
Conrad Black
connascence
connascency
concatenate
contango-day
consanguine
contaminate
contaminant
cinnarizine
cannabinoid
Convallaria
containable
containment
confarreate
contactable
contact lens
confabulate
cinebiology
cinébiology
cynicalness
conical buoy
consciously
cony-catcher
Canada goose
conveyancer
convenances
canceration
centenarian
congelation
candelabrum
candelabras
cinder block
canterburys
candescence
✧confederate
✧confederacy
contenement
congé d'élire
congenerous
convergence
convergency
congenially
convenience
connexional
conveniency
concealable
congealable
concealment
congealment
cancellated
conterminal
condemnable
contemnible
concernedly
concernment
concernancy
contemplate
contemplant
conferrable
consecrator
concessible

condensable
conversable
conversably
confessedly
cancer stick
conversance
conversancy
concentrate
cinder track
concert hall
Conventuals
congestible
connectable
connectible
contestable
convertible
convertibly
conceptacle
conventicle
Connecticut
conceitedly
connectedly
contentedly
conceitless
contentless
consentient
contentment
concentring
concertante
concertinos
content word
concert-goer
conceptious
connections
contentious
concentered
conjectural
conjecturer
conceptuses
consecutive
consecution
consequence
conceivable
conservable
conceivably
conservance
conservancy
conservator
cenogenesis
cinchoninic
cantharidic
cantharidal
cantharides
cannibalise
cannibalize
cannibalism
Cyndi Lauper
candidature
confiscable
convincible
condisciple
confiscator
considerate
conciseness
confineless
confinement
considering
centimetric
continental
confidently
continently

cunningness
Canning Club
contingence
contingency
canting-coin
canting arms
conciliable
confidingly
consimility
convicinity
convivially
conditioned
consilience
conditional
conditioner
concipiency
candidiasis
conciliator
confirmable
confirmator
consignable
condignness
consignment
cancioneros
centi Morgan
centigramme
consistence
consistency
configurate
continuable
continuedly
continually
continuance
continuator
canella bark
Canellaceae
candleberry
conflictive
conflicting
confliction
canalicular
canaliculus
confluently
conflagrate
conflagrant
candlelight
candle-power
candlestick
cinema-organ
CinemaScope®
canon lawyer
canonically
canine tooth
connotative
condonation
connotation
consolation
convocation
condolatory
consolatory
consolatrix
consonantal
consonantly
Canton crepe
concordance
condolences
condolement
consolement
consolidate
concomitant
consolingly

condominium
consociated
conformable
conformably
censor morum
cannon-metal
conformator
contorniate
confound him
confound you
concolorate
concolorous
cannon-proof
contour line
connoisseur
condottiere
condottieri
consortiums
convolution
convolvulus
Canopic vase
conspecific
conspicuity
conspicuous
canophilist
cynophilist
conspirator
conurbation
centreboard
centrobaric
contrabasso
contributor
contractile
contractive
contraction
centrically
contract out
contracture
contractual
contradance
contredance
congruently
centrifugal
canary-grass
congregated
central bank
control mark
controlment
central fire
Central Time
controlling
control unit
control room
centre lathe
congruously
contra pacem
centrepiece
contraption
centre punch
centripetal
contrariety
contrarious
centre round
centre stage
concrescent
contrastive
Congressman
conirostral
concrete art
contretemps
contra-tenor
cineritious
contrivable
contrivance
contravener
controverse
controversy
contrayerva
canisterise
canisterize
cenospecies
cenesthesia
cenesthesis
Conisbrough
constrained
constricted
constrictor
constellate
Constantine
Constantius
constuprate
constipated
consternate
constituent
cunctatious
constitutor
construable
constructer
constructor
confutative
conjugative
conjugating
cannulation
confutation
conjugation
conjuration
conjugality
contumacity
conjunctiva
conjunctive
conjunction
cinquecento
conjuncture
connumerate
conducement
confutement
conjurement
consumerism
consumerist
contubernal
conjure away
cantus firmi
concubinage
concubitant
concubinary
conducingly
confusingly
consumingly
connubially
centuriator
consummator
consumptive
consumption
Cinque Ports
conquerable
concurrence
concurrency
convulsible
convulsions
conductible
conductress
conductance
consultancy
condylomata
Coney Island
candy stripe
cloxacillin
clog-almanac
choice-drawn
crotcheteer
crowdedness
cloudlessly
clog dancing
co-ordinance
co-ordinator
co-ordinates
cloud-topped
chordophone
crop-dusting
crowd-puller
chord symbol
close-banded
close-handed
cholera belt
co-operative
co-operation
close-hauled
close-barred
closed-chain
closet drama
close-reefed
close tennis
close season
choreograph
clovergrass
close the gap
chokecherry
close-lipped
close-fisted
close in upon
close to hand
close-bodied
close to home
Cooper pairs
closet queen
choregraphy
Cooper's hawk
close at hand
cholesteric
cholesterol
cholesterin
cholestasis
cookery-book
cook-general
cloth of gold
clodhopping
clothes-line
clothesline
clothes-pole
clothes moth
clothes-prop
crochet hook
chorisation
chorization
cholinergic
cooling card
closing date
closing time
choking coil
Cook Islands
crocidolite
cookie-shine
crookbacked
chock-a-block
crookedness
crock of gold
Crookes tube
crown lawyer
crown octavo
crowned head
crown jewels
Crown Office
crown living
crown antler
crown colony
crown courts
crown prince
clown around
chocolatier
choroiditis
crocodilian
chorologist
chorography
Chomolungma
choirmaster
choirscreen
choir school
choirstalls
crossbanded
cross-dating
cross-garnet
crossbarred
cross action
crossed line
cross-legged
crossbearer
cross-leaved
cross-tining
cloisonnage
cross-infect
cross-border
crossbowman
cross colour
cross cousin
cross-or-pile
choose sides
cross-stitch
crosscut saw
cross swords
clostridial
clostridium
cool-tankard
Cromwellian
choux pastry
cephalalgia
cephalalgic
coplanarity
Cephalaspis
Cappah-brown
Captain Ahab
captainship
Captain Hook
cephalocele
Cephalopoda
cephalotomy
capableness
Cape buffalo
capaciously
capacitance
capodastros
copper-beech
copper-faced
copy-editing
cappelletti
cappernoity
copperplate
cypress vine
coppersmith
Cypress Hill
cypress knee
copperworks
captivating
captivation
captivaunce
capriccioso
captive time
cypripedium
cupriferous
captive bolt
Capricornus
Cyprinodont
Cape jasmine
Cape Kennedy
cupellation
capillarity
copple-crown
Cupuliferae
capillitium
copple-stone
cap and bells
coping-stone
coprolaliac
caprolactam
coprocessor
coprophagic
coprophagan
coprophilia
cupronickel
Cypro-Minoan
copiousness
coprosterol
copyreading
Capernaitic
cyperaceous
coparcenary
coparcenery
capernoited
capernoitie
caper-spurge
caparisoned
Cape sparrow
capital levy
capital ship
capitularly
capitulator
cappuccinos
copywriting
carnauba wax
carcase meat
carrageenan
carrageenin
curtal friar
cors anglais
caryatidean
carnationed
curialistic
cardan joint
curtailment
curtail-step
curtain call
curtain wall
curtain-fire
carcass meat
Carcassonne
currant cake
currant-wine
currant loaf
carnaptious
curnaptious
cerebralism
cerebration
cerebralist
curableness
cerebriform
cerebellous
cerebellums
carabiniere
carabinieri
cirl bunting
corn bunting
corybantism
carabineros
cerebroside
corn-cracker
corncob pipe
coraciiform
cork cambium
caricatural
correlative
correlation
Corfe Castle
career break
carvel-built
curlew-berry
carpet biter
cartel clock
Carley float
Carmen Jones
corneal lens
corn earworm
Curlew River
carpet snake
carpet shark
cornerstone
corbel table
correctable
correctible
corner teeth
correctness
currentness
current coil
current-cost
carpentaria
carte du pays
carte du jour
career woman
Carl Fogarty
carefulness
cerographic
Cirrhipedia
Carthusians
cornhusking
cardinalate
Cardigan Bay
carminative
cortication
corrivalled
cornice-rail
corrigendum
cornice ring
cornice-pole
cornice-hook
carbide tool
corniferous
cornigerous
corn in Egypt

cardiograph
corbie gable
carriage dog
curling pond
carding wool
carriageway
currishness
Cornish clay
certificate
certifiable
certifiably
curvilineal
curvilinear
carnificial
carrick bend
car-sickness
carrick bitt
cordialness
Corn Islands
cardiomotor
carrion crow
carcinomata
Corti's organ
carnivorous
corticolous
carcinology
carrier wave
corbie-steps
corbiculate
corniculate
curriculums
curule chair
carol singer
coralliform
corolliform
coral flower
Carolingian
coralloidal
carillonist
circle-rider
circle round
coral island
chromic acid
chromogenic
chrominance
ceremonious
coram populo
chromoplast
chromophore
chrome steel
chromosomal
chromoscope
chronically
Carl Nielsen
Cirencester
chronograph
coronagraph
coronograph
corona lucis
chronologic
chronologer
chronometer
chronometry
coronership
chronoscope
caruncculate
caruncculous
cartomancer
corporately
carbonatite
corporative
Carbonarism
corporatism
carbonation
corporation
corporatist
corporality
carbonadoes
carbon black
carbon cycle
Carnot cycle
corporeally
Corrodentia
cardophagus
cartophilic
cormophytic
cursoriness
corrosively
Carlo Blasis
Carlos Menem
corroborate
corroborant
carpogonium
carpologist
carbon paper
carpospores
cartography
caryopsides
carbon steel
curiousness
curious arts
car boot sale
cirro-strati
caryopteris
Carborundum®
cirro-cumuli
carbonylate
carbocyclic
ceroplastic
corn plaster
cerargyrite
Chris Barber
coruscating
coruscation
chrismatory
card-sharper
chrysoberyl
chrysocracy
chrysocolla
Christ-cross
Christendom
corps d'élite
christening
Christingle
caressingly
✧christiania
Christianly
chrysalides
chrysalises
chrisom-robe
Christmassy
Christopher
Christology
Christogram
chrysoprase
chrysarobin
Chris Eubank
corn shucker
corn spurrey
Cyrus R Vance
Carl Seyfert
cerotic acid
curettement
Carlton Club
ceratopsian
curatorship
circularise
circularize
circulative
circulating
carburation
circulation
corrugation
circularity
circulatory
circular saw
carbuncular
corpuscular
circumciser
carburetion
carburetted
carburetter
carburettor
corpulently
circumflect
circumfused
carousingly
corpus iuris
circumlunar
cornucopian
circumpolar
circumspect
circumsolar
corruptible
corruptibly
corruptness
circumvolve
corivalship
caravan park
caravansary
caravan site
caravanning
caravanette
cordwainery
curry favell
curry favour
curly-headed
carry weight
Carlylesque
carry the can
carry the day
carryings-on
curry powder
carry too far
curly-greens
Carey Street
carry a torch
carry it away
cash account
cost-account
custard tart
custard pies
Cossack post
cast a glance
Cistercians
cosmeticise
cosmeticize
cosmeticism
cosmetician
Castell Coch
castellated
cosmetology
caster sugar
cosignatory
case history
castigation
castigatory
cysticercus
costiveness
cassiterite
Castile soap
casting vote
cushion-tire
cushion star
cushion-tyre
cassiopeium
case in point
cashierment
Cassius Clay
casuistical
castle-guard
Castlereagh
cash machine
customarily
custom-built
cystoscopic
cosmotheism
cosmothetic
custom house
cosmopolite
cosmogonist
cosmologist
cosmosphere
cosmography
cosmocratic
castor sugar
cash payment
cash-railway
César Franck
cesarevitch
cesarewitch
Cisatlantic
costume play
cost what may
Cottage Rake
cottage loaf
cottage orné
citharistic
cutlass fish
city article
cathartical
cataclasmic
cataclastic
catechetics
catechising
catechizing
catechismal
catechistic
City Company
catachresis
catacaustic
cataclysmic
catadromous
Côte d'Ivoire
catheterism
cathedratic
catafalcoes
city fathers
cytogenesis
cytogenetic
categorical
catchweight
catchphrase
catch the sun
catch-the-ten
catching pen
catch points
cutting edge
cutting list
cutting room
cattishness
cytokinesis
catallactic
cattle guard
cytological
cataloguise
cataloguize
catalytical
city manager
city mission
cotoneaster
cut and carve
cut and cover
cut and dried
Cat in the Hat
cat-and-mouse
cut and paste
ceteosaurus
cotton candy
cathode rays
citronellal
cotton grass
cut both ways
✧catholicise
✧catholicize
✧catholicism
catholicity
cottonmouth
cotton plant
cotton press
cotton sedge
cotton waste
cytoplasmic
cataplectic
cut up didoes
catapultier
cataphonics
cat-cracking
coterminate
coterminant
Caterpillar®
caterpillar
coterminous
catercorner
cater-cousin
city slicker
catastrophe
CAT standard
cut it too fat
cat's-whisker
Cathy's Clown
catty-corner
Citizen Kane
citizenship
causatively
clubability
causational
crumbliness
church-bench
church court
churchgoing
crunchiness
church mouse
Church Times
church tower
churchwoman
churchwards
coup de grâce
coup de poing
causelessly
cauterising
cauterizing
couch potato
couch a spear
caught short
cruciverbal
cauligenous
cruciferous
✧crucifixion
cauliflower
Crucian carp
caulicolous
cauliculate
chuckle-head
Chuck Yeager
coupling-box
cruelty-free
clubmanship
coulometric
Coulommiers
chump change
cruise about
counselling
causticness
caustic lime
caustically
caustic soda
crustaceous
county court
courtierism
court tennis
coup the cran
courtliness
countrified
countenance
courteously
countermand
counterbase
counterpace
counterpane
countermark
countervail
counter-cast
counterpart
counterseal
cluster-bean
counterfect
counterfeit
cluster pine
countermine
counter-time
countersink
countersign
counter-view
counterplea
counter-plot
counterblow
counter-glow
cluster bomb
counterbond
counterbore
countermove
counter-vote
counter-work
counterwork
counterfoil

counter-roll
counterfort
counterdraw
countermure
counterbuff
countersunk
counter-turn
courtesying
country seat
countryfied
Country Life
countryside
countrywide
country club
country code
courtly love
country-folk
country rock
country-rock
country town
caveat actor
civic centre
cave-dweller
civilianise
civilianize
cavillation
cavalierish
cavalierism
✧civil rights
civil-rights
civilisable
civil-suited
civilizable
cover charge
cover shorts
cavo-rilievo
cavernously
cavernulous
civvy street
cowboy boots
coxcombical
cryobiology
Clyde Barrow
chyliferous
chymiferous
chylomicron
cry you mercy
cryophysics
cryosurgeon
cryosurgery
cryptobiont
cryptically
cryotherapy
cryptograph
Cryptogamia
cryptogamic
cryptogenic
crystal ball
crystalline
crystallise
crystallite
crystallize
crystalloid
cryptomeria
cryptorchid
clyster-pipe
cry cupboard
dead against
dead as a dodo
deaf as a post
drag and drop
drag-and-drop
Dean Acheson
dramaticism
diamagnetic
draw a covert
Diana monkey
dramaturgic
dealbreaker
dual control
dual-control
dead-clothes
diascordium
deaccession
drap-de-Berry
dram-drinker
dual-density
drape jacket
dealer brand
Diane Abbott
Diane Keaton
diadelphous
diametrical
diametrally
diatessaron
dialectical
dialectally
dwarfed tree
dead-freight
dwarf fennel
draggle-tail
draughtsman
death-marked
diaphragmal
death rattle
deathliness
diaphaneity
diachronism
diachronous
diathermacy
diathermous
diaphoresis
diaphoretic
death-stroke
death duties
deamination
drawing room
D Wayne Lukas
diagnosable
diagnostics
diamondback
diamond bird
diamond dove
diamond duck
diamond-dust
Dean of Guild
diapophyses
diapophysis
diapositive
diatonicism
dialogistic
dragonnades
dragoon-bird
diabolology
diamorphine
dragon's-head
diacoustics
dialogue box
dual pricing
dual-purpose
diagramming
diacritical
draw to a head
drastically
draw the line
draw the crow
deattribute
diastematic
draft-dodger
diastrophic
diarthrosis
✧dracunculus
debt bondage
débridement
Dublin prawn
dubiousness
debarcation
debarkation
Deborah Bull
de Bernières
debasedness
debauchedly
debauchment
debouchment
declarative
declamation
declaration
declamatory
declaratory
duck and dive
doch-an-doris
dictatorial
docibleness
decrescendo
duck-egg blue
decrepitate
decrepitude
duchesse set
Dick Francis
Dick Fosbury
Dick Gaughan
declination
dockisation
dockization
declinatory
declinature
ductileness
deceitfully
ducking-pond
declivitous
Dickin medal
decollation
décolletage
deckle-edged
decillionth
decelerator
decolourise
decolourize
Decemberish
decumbently
decemvirate
decumbiture
documentary
decomposite
decameronic
decantation
decondition
deconstruct
dichogamous
deck officer
Duc d'Orléans
dichotomise
dichotomize
dichotomist
dichotomous
dicephalous
deceptively
deck-passage
decapsulate
decurvation
decerebrate
decerebrise
decerebrize
decurrently
decorticate
decursively
dichromatic
doctrinaire
doctrinally
decarbonate
decurionate
decarbonise
decarbonize
dichroscope
decorations
decarburise
decarburize
decussately
decussation
dicotyledon
dock-warrant
dactylology
dactylogram
Dictyoptera
dedramatise
dedramatize
Dodecagynia
deductively
didacticism
Dodecandria
dodecaphony
dodecastyle
didactylous
Dudley Moore
✧duddie weans
Didelphidae
diddly-squat
dreadnaught
deep drawing
deep-drawing
dreadlessly
Dresden ware
✧dreadnought
dreadlocked
dies faustus
dredging-box
die the death
dreikanters
deep kissing
dreamlessly
dream ticket
deep-mouthed
dies nefasti
Diego Rivera
de-emphasise
de-emphasize
dress parade
dressmaking
deerstalker
dress-length
dress-reform
dress-shield
dress circle
dyer's rocket
dyer's-rocket
deep therapy
die-stamping
defeasanced
defraudment
deflagrable
deflagrator
defiantness
defibrinate
defibrinise
defibrinize
deficiently
defectively
differentia
differently
deflexional
diffidently
duffing-over
difficultly
defalcation
defiliation
defoliation
defensative
definiendum
defenceless
Defenderism
definientia
defensively
defloration
deformation
diffractive
diffraction
deforcement
deferred pay
deferential
defeudalise
defeudalize
diffuseness
diffusively
diffusivity
degradation
digladiator
deglamorise
deglamorize
dogmatology
dog's disease
daggerboard
Dogberrydom
Dogberryism
dégringoler
doggishness
dogfighting
dog's-mercury
degustation
degustatory
digestively
digitigrade
deglutinate
deglutitive
deglutition
deglutitory
doggy-paddle
dehydration
dehypnotise
dehypnotize
dehortative
dehortation
dehortatory
de haut en bas
drivability
dwindlement
Dáil Eireann
deification
driving-band
driving-gear
driving seat
driving test
driving iron
drink-driver
drill-barrow
drill-harrow
drill-master
drill-plough
drilling mud
drilling rig
drill string
Deinonychus
dripping-pan
dripping wet
deictically
deistically
drift-mining
drift-anchor
dairy cattle
Daily Record
Daisy Miller
daily double
daisy-cutter
Dukhobortsy
dak bungalow
Delta Cephei
delta rhythm
Della-Robbia
dull-brained
dolabriform
deliberator
dole-bludger
delectation
deliciously
dolefulness
delightedly
delightless
delightsome
delphically
Delphinidae
dolphinfish
dolphinaria
delphiniums
doli incapax
dollishness
doltishness
dulcifluous
delineative
delineation
Dylan Thomas
delinquency
dilapidated
dilapidator
deliriously
Dolores Haze
délassement
dull-sighted
delusionist
dilutionary
deleterious
delitescent
diluvialism
diluvialist
deliverable
delivery-man
✧deliverance
delivery-van

Delaware Bay
Dolly Varden
dolly camera
delayed drop
dolly switch
damnability
demi-bastion
democratise
democratize
democratist
domiciliate
domiciliary
dimidiation
demodulator
Damien Hirst
demyelinate
dumper truck
dumbfounder
demographic
demographer
demigration
demigoddess
demagnetise
demagnetize
demagogical
demagoguery
demagoguism
damping-down
dumbing-down
dampishness
dumpishness
demulsifier
demoniacism
demonianism
demonocracy
demand curve
diminuendos
domineering
dimensioned
dimensional
demonologic
demonolater
demonolatry
demonomania
Dominion Day
diminishing
demonstrate
dominations
demi-pension
demarcation
demarkation
dimercaprol
damascening
Demosthenic
Demosthenes
domesticate
domesticise
domesticize
domesticity
dame's-violet
damask-steel
demutualise
demutualize
dumdum fever
demiurgical
demiurgeous
demountable
dental floss
deniability
dental nurse
Don Pasquale
Donna Summer
Don McCullin
duniewassal
Daniel Boone
Daniel Defoe
dinner-dance
donkey derby
Daniell cell
Dunfermline
Daniel Malan
danger money
dance in a net
dangerously
dinner plate
danger point
dinner party
Daniel Quilp
dinner table
dinner-wagon
denigration
Don Whillans
Dennis Amiss
dentigerous
densimetric
Dennis Gabor
dancing-girl
denticulate
Don Giovanni
Donald Dewar
Don't Look Now
Donald Soper
dynamically
dynamograph
dynamometer
dynamometry
denominable
denominator
denumerable
denumerably
dining chair
denunciator
dining table
deny oneself
dendrachate
dendroglyph
dendrolatry
dendrometer
dendritical
Denis Healey
Denise Lewis
Denis Forman
dinosaurian
denitration
dinotherium
dengue fever
Danny DeVito
dandy-rigged
Danny Glover
denizenship
Dromaeosaur
drop a stitch
drop a curtsy
drop-curtain
Droseraceae
do one's block
duodecimals
do one's stuff
do one's thing
do one's worst
drop-forging
✧diotheletic
✧dyotheletic
✧dyothelitic
Diophantine
deoxidation
dronishness
dioristical
doorknocker
dromophobia
dropped arch
door-stepped
doorstepper
deobstruent
drouthiness
doomwatcher
deoxygenate
deoxygenise
deoxygenize
Dipsacaceae
depravation
depravement
depravingly
deprecative
deprecating
deprecation
depredation
deprecatory
depredatory
duplex house
depreciator
dipterocarp
depressible
depigmented
depth charge
deprivative
duplicative
duplicating
deprivation
duplication
duplicature
deprivement
duplicitous
dephlegmate
dependingly
diplomatese
dipsomaniac
diplomatise
diplomatize
deploration
diplomatics
diplomatist
deploringly
diplococcus
diprotodont
deprogramme
de profundis
depopulator
Depo-Provera®
deportation
département
diphtheroid
diphthongic
diphthongal
deplumation
depauperate
depauperise
depauperize
diphycercal
Diphysitism
dark-adapted
dermatology
durableness
Dirk Bogarde
deracialise
deracialize
direct debit
derecognise
derecognize
directivity
directional
✧directorate
directorial
directrices
dark current
dare-devilry
Darren Gough
Dermestidae
direfulness
dark glasses
Durchlaucht
dorsiferous
derring-doer
Derek Jarman
Derek Jacobi
Derek Barton
dereliction
dark lantern
derangement
durante vita
daring-hardy
dermography
dorsolumbar
Dar es Salaam
Dire Straits
derived unit
dirty old man
dirty tricks
disparately
disparaging
discalceate
✧dispatch box
dispatchful
discardable
dastardness
disbandment
discardment
discandying
dyspareunia
distaff side
dismayfully
Distalgesic®
dyspathetic
destabilise
destabilize
de-Stalinise
de-Stalinize
dismal Jimmy
disharmonic
dysharmonic
disfavourer
disgarrison
distantness
dismastment
distasteful
disobedient
disablement
disobliging
desacralise
desacralize
desiccative
desecration
desiccation
disaccustom
desideratum
desperately
desperation
desperadoes
dissembling
dismembered
descendable
descendible
disremember
dishevelled
Disneyesque
Disneyfying
disseminate
dissepiment
disseminule
disbeliever
discernible
discernibly
discernment
discerpible
discerptive
discerption
distempered
dispensable
distensible
dispensably
dispersedly
dispensator
dissectible
dyspeptical
dissentient
dessert wine
dissentious
disceptator
dissertator
disaffected
disafforest
designative
designation
designatory
desegregate
désagrément
designingly
disthronize
deschooling
dysrhythmia
dissipative
destination
dissipation
distinctive
distinction
distincture
dislikeable
dislikeness
distinguish
duskishness
dissimilate
dispiriting
dissilience
distillable
disciplinal
discipliner
dessignment
dismissible
dissimulate
destitution
displeasant
displeasing
disyllabism
disyllabify
displeasure
deselection
desilverise
desilverize
disulphuric
disulphuret
desalinator
desultorily
disillusive
disillusion
display case
disembitter
disemployed
disembodied
disimprison
disemburden
disentangle
do's and don'ts
disinterest
disinterred
disinvest in
disinfector
disenthrall
disenshroud
disenthrone
desensitise
desensitize
disinclined
desinential
disunionist
disentrance
disentrayle
disencumber
disannuller
dislocation
dissonantly
despondence
discordance
despondency
discordancy
Desmond Tutu
disbowelled
dishonestly
discomfited
dislodgment
discotheque
discothèque
discophoran
dissociable
dissociably
disposingly
dispositive
disposition
dyslogistic
despoilment
dishonorary
discoloured
dishonourer
discourtesy
discoursive
desmodromic
discography
disportment
discontinue
dissolutely
dissolutive
dissolution
dissolvable
discomycete
Dasypodidae
disc parking
disapproval

disarmament
disorganise
disorganize
describable
distribuend
desert boots
distributee
distributer
distributor
disgraceful
destructive
distractive
distracting
destruction
distraction
disgracious
disordinate
deservingly
deserpidine
disgruntled
descriptive
description
discrepance
discrepancy
disproperty
distressful
distrustful
de-stressing
distressing
disprovable
destroyable
disassemble
disassembly
dish the dirt
disputative
despumation
dismutation
disputation
disturbance
disjunctive
disjunction
dysfunction
disjuncture
disquietful
disquietive
disquieting
disquietous
disquietude
dispute over
discussable
discussible
disguisable
disguisedly
disgustedly
discus throw
disaventure
desexualise
desexualize
dusty-miller
dissyllable
dissymmetry
dusty answer
detrainment
detractress
detectivist
data capture
datacasting
✧ditheletism
do the dishes
✧dithelitism
do the rounds
dutifulness
Dutch carpet
data highway
Dutch cheese
Dutch liquid
Dutch clover
Dutch supper
detribalise
detribalize
detrimental
detritivore
dot and carry
doting-piece
duty officer
dittography
duteousness
determinate
determinant
determinacy
determinism
determinist
deteriorate
deteriorism
deteriority
detestation
dithyrambic
drum and bass
Deus avertat
drug dealing
deuteration
deuteranope
Doune Castle
deuterogamy
Deuteronomy
doughtiness
druckenness
drunkenness
drunk-driver
double agent
double bogey
double-blind
double bluff
double-check
double cream
double-click
double-cross
double-digit
double doors
double Dutch
double-ender
double-edged
double eagle
double-entry
double-faced
double first
double fault
double-fault
double helix
double-lived
double-quick
double-shade
double-space
double spare
Douglas Haig
double-sharp
doublespeak
double-stout
Douglas Hurd
Douglas Dunn
doublethink
double trill
drum machine
dourroucouli
drum printer
drug-running
Deutschmark
drug therapy
dauntlessly
doubtlessly
drusy cavity
dive-bombing
Dave Brubeck
David Bailey
David Malouf
David Mercer
David Mellor
David Seaman
David Beaton
David Wilkie
David Ginola
David Wilson
David Rizzio
David Bryant
David Storey
doveishness
devaluation
divulgation
devil's bones
devil's books
devil's dozen
devolvement
divulgement
divellicate
devil-dodger
developable
development
devil a thing
diving board
diving dress
Devon minnow
divining rod
divine right
deviousness
divorceable
divergement
divorcement
divergently
divergingly
divertingly
diversified
diverticula
devastative
devastating
devastation
divestiture
divisionary
✧divisionism
divisionist
devotedness
dovetailing
dovetail saw
devotionist
devouringly
dawn cypress
down-draught
downhearted
downlighter
Downpatrick
down payment
dawn redwood
downshifter
down-setting
down-sitting
Dawn Treader
down the wind
down the line
down-the-line
Down the Mine
down the road
down to earth
down-to-earth
downtrodden
downy mildew
doxycycline
dexterously
doxographer
doxological
dexiotropic
doxorubicin
day-labourer
day of action
dry-cleaning
day in, day out
days of grace
day hospital
epanalepses
epanalepsis
emanational
ex accidenti
emasculator
emancipator
evanescence
evangeliary
evangelical
evangeliser
evangelizer
exaggerated
exaggerator
eradicative
egalitarian
eradication
evagination
examination
exanimation
evasiveness
evanishment
enabling act
Ewan MacColl
elaborately
elaborative
evaporative
elaboration
evaporation
elaboratory
exasperator
Erastianism
elastic band
elasticness
elastically
elasticated
exaltedness
exanthemata
elastomeric
en attendant
Elastoplast®
Eoanthropus
enarthrosis
ejaculative
ejaculation
ejaculatory
embraceable
embracement
embracingly
ecblastesis
eubacterial
eubacterium
emblematise
emblematize
emblematist
emboîtement
embolectomy
embellisher
embrocation
embroiderer
en brochette
embroilment
embarcation
embarkation
embarrassed
embittering
embowelment
embowelling
elbow-grease
embowerment
embryogenic
embryologic
embryonated
exclamative
exclamation
exclamatory
Eucharistic
enchainment
eschatology
enchantedly
enchantress
enchantment
excrescence
excrescency
excremental
excrementum
exceedingly
Escherichia
ecclesiarch
escheatable
escheatment
excogitator
enchiridion
escritorial
eccrinology
encrimsoned
exculpation
exculpatory
excellently
eccaleobion
eucalyptole
encomiastic
encomendero
encumbrance
excommunion
ex concessis
eccentrical
enchondroma
euchologion
encephaline
encephaloid
encephalous
escape hatch
encapsidate
exceptional
encapsulate
escape valve
escape wheel
encarnalise
encarnalize
excarnation
excoriation
excorticate
excursively
euchromatic
euchromatin
escarmouche
excerptible
encystation
excessively
excitedness
encouraging
exclusively
exclusivism
exclusivist
exclusivity
encrustment
endearingly
eddy current
endocardiac
endocardial
endocardium
endocytosis
endocytotic
endochylous
endodontics
Eddie Lawson
eudaemonism
eudaemonics
eudaemonist
Eddie Arcaro
Eddie Irvine
endlessness
endless worm
Eddie Murphy
E M Delafield
endemically
endemiology
endomorphic
endometrial
endometrium
endomitosis
eudiometric
endoplasmic
endophagous
endoplastic
ex-directory
endorsement
elders' hours
elderliness
elderflower
elderly prim
endospermic
endoscopist
eidetically
endothelial
endothelium
endothermic
endotrophic
eremacausis
eye-catching
Emerald City
ever and anon
emerald moth
Emerald Isle
emerald type
elevational
exercisable
Everest pack
elementally
energy level

energetical
Erechtheion
elephant gun
elephantine
elephantoid
elegiacally
evening meal
evening star
✧everlasting
eternalness
exeunt omnes
eye for an eye
emetophobia
exemplarily
exemplarity
esemplastic
exemplified
exemplifier
epeirogenic
eyebrowless
even-stevens
eventualise
eventualize
eventration
eventuation
eventuality
eleutherian
Eleutherius
electric arc
electricals
electric eye
electric eel
electrified
electrician
electrifier
electricity
electric ray
ejectamenta
electroweak
electioneer
electron gun
electronica
electrolier
electronics
electrotint
electrology
electrocute
electrolyse
electrolyte
electrolyze
electrotype
electrotypy
ejector seat
electorship
electorally
executively
executioner
executorial
executrices
executrixes
Ezer Weizman
everywhence
emery powder
Evelyn Waugh
enfranchise
efficacious
efficiently
effectively
effectivity
effectually
enfleshment
Eiffel Tower
exfoliative
exfoliation
effulgently
enfant gâtée
enfeoffment
enforceable
enforcement
effortfully
enfouldered
englacially
engrailment
engrammatic
Enghalskrug
engraftment
eagle-winged
engaged tone
edge in a word
English Pale
Englishness
English bond
English rose
English horn
eugenic acid
eugenically
engineering
eigenvector
engrossment
engorgement
eager beaver
ergatocracy
eighteenmos
ergatomorph
eight-square
echo chamber
ethic dative
ethicalness
ethological
exhilarator
Ephemeridae
ephemerides
ephemerally
Echinoderma
enhancement
ethmoid bone
ethnobotany
ethnologist
ethnography
ex hypothesi
etherealise
etherealize
exhortative
exhortation
ethereality
exhortatory
etheromania
echo-sounder
exhaustible
exhaustedly
exhaustless
exhaust pipe
Elizabethan
epitaxially
epigastrium
Eric Bristow
Eric Clapton
Eric Cantona
episcopally
eviscerator
epic dialect
Eriodendron
Émile Lahoud
epipetalous
episepalous
epidendrone
epigenetics
epigenesist
epinephrine
Émile Picard
epidemicity
eviternally
evidentiary
epileptical
Edith Cavell
epicheirema
epithalamia
epithalamic
epithelioma
epiphyllous
epithymetic
epiphytical
epithetical
eliminative
edification
elicitation
elimination
edificatory
eliminatory
eligibility
Emilio Pucci
Emilio Segrè
epidiascope
Eric Liddell
epiplastral
epiplastron
enigmatical
Étienne Jouy
epicondylar
editorially
epilogistic
ex improviso
eriophorous
epitrochoid
epigraphist
evil-starred
Eric Shipton
eristically
epistle side
epic theatre
epistolical
epistilbite
existential
Emily Brontë
Emil Zatopek
enjambement
elkhorn fern
enkephaline
eclecticism
enlightener
eglandulose
ellipticity
ellipsoidal
Ellora caves
enlargement
enlarge upon
Ellery Queen
enlisted man
Ellis Island
enlivenment
Emma Goldman
en militaire
Emma Lazarus
Edmund Burke
emmenagogic
emmenagogue
Emmenthaler
Emma Tennant
enneandrian
enneandrous
enneahedral
enneahedron
ennoblement
Ernest Bevin
Enniskillen
Ernest Renan
Ernst B Chain
einsteinium
Einsteinian
ex natura rei
egomaniacal
evocatively
exorability
exorbitance
exorbitancy
Eton College
exonerative
exoneration
esotericism
exotericism
esotericist
exogenously
egocentrism
epoch-making
Enoch Powell
emotiveness
emotionable
emotionless
emotionally
egotistical
exoskeletal
exoskeleton
erotomaniac
erotogenous
econometric
erotophobia
ecofriendly
Egon Schiele
emolumental
evolutional
exonuclease
epoxy resins
explanative
explanation
explanatory
emplacement
explainable
explain away
expectative
expectation
expectantly
expectingly
expectorate
expectorant
expediently
expeditious
empiecement
euphemistic
espièglerie
en plein jour
expressible
express term
expressness
expugnation
explicative
explication
explicatory
expungement
expansively
expensively
expansivity
expansional
expenditure
empanelment
empanelling
exponential
explorative
exploration
exploratory
explosively
expromissor
expropriate
exploitable
eupepticity
en papillote
exportation
expurgation
emparlaunce
expurgatory
empirically
empiricutic
experienced
experiencer
Esperantist
en pure perte
emperorship
emperor moth
empyreumata
episcation
episcatory
exposedness
ex post facto
empassioned
expositress
expostulate
expatiative
expatiation
expatiatory
empowerment
empty-handed
empty-headed
Empty Vessel
emphyteusis
emphyteutic
empty-nester
enquiration
exquisitely
Enrico Fermi
Eurocentric
Euro-dollars
earnestness
egregiously
earthliness
earth-pillar
earth-closet
earthenware
earth mother
earthmoving
earth tremor
earth-hunger
earthquaked
ear-piercing
Errol Garner
Earl Marshal
erroneously
Earl of Derby
Earl of Essex
Europeanise
Europeanize
Europeanism
Europeanist
Eurypharynx
Eurypterida
eurypteroid
Earl Roberts
Earl Russell
Eurosceptic
Etruscology
erratically
eurythermic
eurythermal
eurhythmics
eurhythmist
early blight
enslavement
ensnarement
ens rationis
east-by-north
east-by-south
exsiccative
exsiccation
eusociality
eisteddfods
Eastern Time
Eastern bloc
easternmost
en spectacle
exstipulate
East Lothian
essentially
ensanguined
exsanguined
ease oneself
ensepulchre
elsewhither
extravagate
extravasate
extravagant
estramazone
entrance fee
estranghelo
extra virgin
extra-virgin
extradition
extrafloral
entrainment
extrapolate
extractable
extractible
ectoblastic
entablature
entablement
established
establisher
Eutychianus
extremeness
estrepement
esthesiogen
entreatable
entreatment
estreatment
ectogenesis
ectogenetic
extrication
Estrildidae
entwinement

extrinsical
extemporary
extemporise
extemporize
entomophagy
entomophily
ectomorphic
extenuative
extenuating
extenuation
extenuatory
eating apple
eating-house
extensively
extensional
eating irons
estancieros
extroverted
ectoplasmic
ectoplastic
entophytous
externalise
externalize
extirpative
externalism
extirpation
externalist
externality
entertainer
extirpatory
enterococci
enterectomy
exterminate
extorsively
extortioner
enthralment
enthralling
exteriorise
exteriorize
exteriority
enteropathy
enterpriser
enterostomy
enterotoxin
enterovirus
estate agent
entitlement
ectothermic
ectotrophic
entrustment
entry portal
equiangular
educability
educational
edutainment
equableness
equibalance
enunciative
enunciation
enunciatory
edulcorator
equidistant
enumerative
enumeration
exuberantly
erubescence
erubescency
ecumenicism
equifinally
elucidative
elucidation
elucidatory
elusiveness
enucleation
equilibrate
equilibrial
equilibrium
equilibrist
equilibrity
ebulliently
equilateral
equinoctial
elusoriness
emulousness
equipollent
elutriation
emulsionise
emulsionize
Equisetales
Equisetinae
equivocally
equivocator
equivalence
equivalency
envelopment
enviousness
Edvard Grieg
Edvard Munch
environment
Erwin Rommel
Edwin Hubble
Edward Albee
Edward Burra
Edward Elgar
Edward Heath
Edward Sapir
Edward Teach
Edward Tylor
Edward White
erythematic
erythronium
erythrocyte
erysipeloid
etymologise
etymologize
etymologist
Egyptianise
Egyptianize
Egyptian pea
Enzo Ferrari
flabbergast
flamboyance
flamboyante
flamboyancy
flaccidness
flat-chested
franc-tireur
fiançailles
✧francomania
flag-captain
✧francophile
✧francophobe
✧francophone
Franciscans
Francistown
flax-dresser
fraudulence
fraudulency
Fraserburgh
frater-house
flagellated
flagellator
fraternally
fraterniser
fraternizer
flat-earther
Fraser River
fearfulness
flash memory
feather-pate
feather palm
feather-edge
feather-head
flash-freeze
featherlike
feather star
flash around
flash-frozen
flagitation
fragileness
feasibility
franklinite
frank-pledge
Frank Smythe
Frankenfood
Frank Dobson
frankfurter
flammulated
fragmentary
flap-mouthed
Flann O'Brien
Fra Angelico
flauntingly
flannelette
flag-officer
flavourless
flavoursome
flag of truce
Frappuccino®
flapperhood
fratricidal
fiars prices
franticness
frantically
Frantz Fanon
Feast of Lots
fractionate
fractionary
fractionise
fractionize
fractionlet
fractiously
featureless
feature film
flatulently
flag-wagging
flaky pastry
Franz Mesmer
Franz Joseph
fibre optics
fabricative
fabrication
fibrillated
Fibrocement®
fibronectin
fibrocystic
facial angle
face-centred
face flannel
fact-finding
facsimilist
facultative
focal length
facilitator
fecundation
facinerious
factory farm
Factory Acts
factory ship
factory shop
facts of life
facetiously
face towards
factualness
fucoxanthin
fide et amore
fidgetiness
faddishness
fiddle about
Fidel Castro
fiddle block
fiddle-de-dee
fiddler crab
fiddlestick
fides Punica
free and easy
free-and-easy
Fred Astaire
freebootery
freebooting
French bread
French berry
French chalk
French curve
French franc
French fries
Frenchiness
French leave
free company
French pleat
French pitch
French stick
French toast
✧French white
Frenchwoman
field madder
field of view
Fields Medal
field botany
fieldworker
field hockey
field cornet
field sports
field events
fieldswoman
fremescence
feeler gauge
Fredericton
fretfulness
free-falling
freight shed
flesh-market
free-hearted
fleshliness
fleshmonger
flesh-colour
fresh breeze
fieri facias
feelingless
Flemish bond
Flemish coil
flemish down
flexibility
freeloading
freemasonic
✧freemasonry
Fresnel lens
free on board
feel oneself
feel one's way
flexography
free radical
fleurs-de-lis
fleurs-de-lys
Fleur Adcock
fleur de coin
free skating
Fleet Air Arm
freethinker
free-tongued
free-thought
fleetfooted
Fleet Prison
feedthrough
Fleet Street
Fred Trueman
Fred Whipple
freeze-frame
fifteenthly
fifth column
figured bass
figure-dance
figure of fun
fighting fit
Fehmgericht
fricandeaux
frigate bird
friableness
flinchingly
fair comment
fair-dealing
Flinders bar
fainéantise
Fair Funding
fringilline
frighteners
frightening
faith healer
faithlessly
frightfully
flightiness
faithworthy
frigidarium
fritillaria
frigid zones
flickertail
fair leather
feignedness
fairniticle
fairnyticle
flip one's lid
frigorifico
friponnerie
frivolously
Friars Minor
fair-seeming
fritto misto
fritter away
flirtatious
fair-weather
fairway wood
fairy shrimp
fairy lights
fairy-butter
foliage leaf
fallalishly
full-acorned
full-blooded
full brother
full-charged
fallen angel
false gallop
false acacia
false-bedded
fille de joie
Folketinget
falteringly
filler metal
false bottom
filter paper
false friend
fuller's-herb
fallen woman
full-fraught
full-fledged
full-frontal
full-hearted
filthy lucre
fulminating
fulmination
fulminatory
fill-in flash
falling band
falling-band
folding seat
fulling-mill
folding door
falling star
falsifiable
fallibilism
fallibilist
fallibility
falsi crimen
folliculose
folliculous
fell-lurking
filamentary
filamentous
full-mouthed
feloniously
follow-board
full of beans
fulsomeness
fallow-finch
filmography
full of years
felspathoid
fell-running
feldspathic
filmsetting
fill the bill
Falstaffian
filet mignon
fall through
fulguration
fell-walking
Felix Wankel
foley artist
fume chamber
fama clamosa
femme fatale
familiarise
familiarize
familiarity
family altar
family Bible

family baker
family coach
family court
famille rose
fomentation
Fumariaceae
fimbriation
fumaric acid
fumatoriums
Fontarabian
fundamental
fan vaulting
fanfaronade
fantastical
fantabulous
finicalness
fingerboard
funnel cloud
finger foods
fingerguard
fingerglass
finger-grass
fence-lizard
fin de siècle
Finger Lakes
fons et origo
fingerplate
finger-paint
fingerprint
fingerstall
fender-stool
finch-backed
fundholding
fungibility
fungistatic
final demand
final notice
Finn mac Cool
funambulate
funambulist
fun and games
financially
find oneself
Finno-Ugrian
fund-raising
funeral home
fines herbes
finasteride
fenestrated
fanatically
find the lady
functionate
functionary
function key
fine writing
Fanny Kemble
fancy monger
fanny around
fancy stitch
Fanny Burney
frowardness
floral dance
Flora Robson
footbreadth
footballene
footballing
footballist
Football War
flocculence
flow diagram
frondescent
flower child
florescence
flower-clock
floweriness
Flower Power
flower-stalk
froth-blower
froth-hopper
foolhardise
foolhardize
florilegium
floriferous
flowingness
foolishness
flock-master
footle about
foot-lambert
From Me to You
from nowhere
floppy drive
floorwalker
floor leader
floor timber
flooring saw
flourishing
floor turtle
frowstiness
food science
foot soldier
footslogger
footstooled
fool's errand
front-ranker
flog to death
foot the bill
frontlessly
front office
frostbitten
frontal lobe
frontolysis
floating rib
front-loaded
front-loader
foot-tapping
front-runner
from without
foppishness
fipple flute
formal cause
forward pass
forwardness
forwandered
firmamental
formational
farraginous
formalistic
fire blanket
fire brigade
fire-balloon
firebombing
Farnborough
firecracker
fire control
ferociously
foreclosure
fardel-bound
far-reaching
forgetfully
Farmer Giles
forget-me-not
forced march
forbearance
Farmers Club
farmer's lung
forfeit bail
fermentable
forfeitable
forgettable
Forrest Gump
fire-flaught
firefighter
for the birds
farthingale
forthcoming
furthcoming
furtherance
farthermore
furthermore
furthersome
farthermost
furthermost
for the worse
formicarium
forcipation
formication
fornication
formicaries
farcicality
forbiddance
forbiddenly
forgiveness
furtiveness
ferriferous
furciferous
forcing-pump
furnishment
furnishings
fortifiable
forcibility
fernitickle
foreignness
foreign bill
ferric oxide
forficulate
Ferris wheel
for a kick-off
foreknowing
ferulaceous
firelighter
for all I care
foraminifer
foraminated
fire-marshal
foremastman
farinaceous
fortnightly
firing order
firing point
firing party
firing squad
for one thing
for instance
furunculous
farm-offices
forfoughten
ferro-chrome
ferro-nickel
ferronnière
forlornness
forlorn hope
ferrography
for God's sake
furiousness
Ford Prefect
forepayment
forequarter
forereading
fore-recited
fire-raising
fire station
forestation
forestaller
Firestarter
foreseeable
foresignify
foresighted
foreshorten
fore-spurrer
form teacher
ferntickled
first school
first person
first-person
first finger
forethinker
first aid kit
forethought
first cousin
first-footer
foretopmast
for starters
first-fruits
first-attack
first strike
first-strike
first storey
first supine
fortunately
formularise
formularize
formulation
fortune-tell
fortuneless
fortune book
ferruginous
for our money
for evermore
forevermore
forevouched
firewriting
fire-walking
Fort William
fire-worship
forewarning
fire-watcher
farawayness
fernytickle
fish-bellied
fast bowling
fusidic acid
foster-child
fisheye lens
Fastern's-e'en
foster-nurse
fisherwoman
fast forward
fast-forward
fish farming
fish-gutting
festinately
fascinating
fissiparism
fascination
festination
fustigation
fustilarian
fissiparity
fissiparous
fascia-board
festiveness
fossil-fired
fishing-line
fishing-frog
fustilirian
festivities
fastigiated
fashionable
fissionable
fashionably
fushionless
fission bomb
fashionista
fasciculate
fossil water
fusillation
fusing point
fast neutron
fusion cones
fusion music
fish-packing
fast reactor
festschrift
fast-tracker
fast-talking
fish-torpedo
Fosbury flop
fetichistic
fatidically
Father Brown
fothergilla
father-in-law
fatefulness
fatigue-duty
fatiguingly
fête galante
fetch-candle
fittingness
fitting-shop
fitting-room
fata Morgana
fit to be tied
fatuousness
fatuous fire
futureproof
future shock
fetishistic
feudalistic
fauxbourdon
found object
flux density
foundations
four-foot way
four-flusher
frugiferous
frugivorous
foul-mouthed
four-pounder
fluorimeter
fluorometer
fluorescein
fluorescent
fluoroscope
fluoroscopy
fluctuating
frustrating
fluctuation
flustration
fructuation
frustration
faultlessly
fruitlessly
fault-finder
fountain pen
flusterment
Fourth World
four-wheeled
four-wheeler
five-and-dime
five-day week
fivefingers
Five Nations
favoredness
favouritism
fawningness
fixed income
fixed assets
fox and geese
foxtrotting
fly cemetery
Flying Corps
flying lemur
flying party
flying snake
flying start
flying shore
flying squad
flying squid
fly-dressing
fazendeiros
fuzzy-haired
Guadalajara
graham bread
Guadalcanal
graham flour
Graham Gooch
gradability
gradationed
gradational
Glad All Over
Graham Swift
Glauber salt
Gran Canaria
glauconitic
Graeco-Roman
glaucescent
gnatcatcher
Grand Bahama
Grande Arche
grandparent
grandfather
Grande Armée
Grand Cayman
Grand Master
grandmaster
guardedness
grandeeship
grand-nephew
grande école
Grand Vizier
grand old man
glandularly
grandiosely
grandmother
grandiosity
grand priory

grande tenue
Grande-Terre
gravel-blind
grave accent
grade school
gracelessly
graven image
grave-digger
gladfulness
Grangemouth
Glasgow City
graphicness
graphically
graphic arts
graphologic
graphomania
gnathonical
glad-handing
gravitative
gravitation
Gracie Allen
graniteware
graniferous
guaniferous
gravimetric
glaringness
graving dock
goatishness
gramicidin D
graminicide
granitiform
gladioluses
gradiometer
granivorous
gravity-feed
gravity cell
goalkicking
glaikitness
go all the way
Grallatores
Grammy Award
grammalogue
grammatical
granny bonds
Granny Smith
glasnostian
go along with
gramophonic
granophyric
granolithic
glamorously
glamour girl
glamourpuss
glass-gazing
glass-blower
Gladstonian
glassworker
grasshopper
grass-rooter
glass-cutter
grass-cutter
geanticline
granted that
giant fennel
grant of arms
ghastliness
giant-killer
giant fibres
giant slalom
graptolitic
goal-tending
Glastonbury
giant powder
gran turismo
Granth Sahib
giant stride
graft hybrid
granulative
granulation
gratulation
granularity
gratulatory
granuliform
gradualness
granulomata
granulocyte
gibberellin
gable window
goblin shark
go ballistic
gobe-mouches
gibbousness
gaboon viper
gubernation
gaberlunzie
go by the head
go by the book
goddaughter
gude-brother
God's country
godlessness
goddess-ship
God-almighty
God bless you!
god-botherer
✧god-forsaken
go down a bomb
giddy-headed
Gregarinida
guelder rose
grey economy
gleefulness
Gresham's law
Gwen Harwood
Grecian bend
Grecian nose
greeked text
Greek Church
greenmailer
green fallow
Greenmantle
green manure
greenockite
green-wellie
green-keeper
green pepper
green lentil
green cheese
Glenn Miller
green linnet
green plover
Glenn Hoddle
green monkey
greenbottle
greengrocer
green dragon
green stocks
Glenn Turner
green turtle
Gregory Peck
guerre à mort
guerrillero
grease-heels
guesstimate
grease paint
greaseproof
gressorious
greasy spoon
great octave
great schism
great-nephew
great shakes
great circle
great diesis
great mobile
guest worker
Great Sphinx
greater than
great primer
Grenzgänger
gefilte fish
gaff-topsail
gift voucher
go great guns
gegenschein
gigantesque
giganticide
Gog and Magog
gigantology
gain control
griddle-cake
guildswoman
guilelessly
✧guinea grass
gainfulness
going strong
guiding star
glimmer-gowk
gliomatosis
geitonogamy
gain-sharing
Gaius Marius
guiltlessly
gristliness
guilty party
grizzly bear
goliath frog
gallantness
gall bladder
gold-beating
Goldbergian
gull-catcher
gold-digging
goldenberry
golden bough
golden chain
golden eagle
galley-foist
Golden Globe
golden goose
golden hello
Golden Horde
gelseminine
golden oldie
galley proof
galley slave
golden share
Golden State
golden syrup
gilded spurs
Gilbertines
Gilbert Ryle
gilded youth
gallimaufry
galli-bagger
Gallicanism
galli-beggar
gullibility
gelliflowre
galliambics
galliardise
go like a bomb
gila monster
Galam butter
galantamine
galanty show
Gallowegian
gallowglass
Gallophobia
Gallovidian
gallowsness
gallows-bird
gallows-ripe
gallows-foot
gallows-free
gallows-tree
gold-plating
gold reserve
gillravitch
goldsmithry
gild the pill
gild the lily
gelatiniser
gelatinizer
gally-bagger
gally-beggar
gillyflower
gully-hunter
gamma camera
gymnasiarch
gymnastical
gamma stocks
game-chicken
gum benjamin
gammerstang
game fishing
gamogenesis
gemmiparous
gemmiferous
gummiferous
gambit-piece
gum olibanum
game licence
gemological
gum ammoniac
gaming house
gaming-table
Gymnopédies
gymnorhinal
gemmologist
gimcrackery
gambrel roof
games theory
gametangium
gamotropism
gametophyte
gemmulation
goniatitoid
gendarmerie
genealogise
genealogize
gonfalonier
genealogist
gun carriage
gangbusting
gonococcoid
geniculated
gens d'église
gens du monde
✧gingerbread
Günter Grass
ginger group
Gunn Erikson
genteelness
gander-month
gynaecomast
gynaecology
genuflexion
gone gosling
Genghis Khan
genuineness
gentilhomme
gentilitial
gentilitian
ganciclovir
gentianella
gentlemanly
gentlenesse
gentlewoman
gentlewomen
gonimoblast
gene mapping
goniometric
Gongoristic
gantry crane
generic name
generically
gonorrhoeic
gonorrhoeal
generalship
general line
generalling
general post
generations
Generation X
gangsterdom
gangsterism
gynostemium
Gene Sarazen
genetically
genetic code
gene therapy
genitivally
genouillère
Geneva Bible
Geneva bands
Geneva cross
Gene Vincent
gandy dancer
geomagnetic
geotactical
good-brother
grog-blossom
grouchiness
Groucho Marx
Groucho Club
glomeration
go overboard
good-evening
go one better
glove-shield
geotechnics
goose-winged
gloweringly
geomedicine
globeflower
goose-flower
grotesquely
grotesquery
geometrical
Geometridae
geotectonic
glomerulate
glove puppet
good feeling
Georgian Bay
Georg Kaiser
George Blake
George Boole
George Brown
George Burns
George Cross
George Carey
Georgie Best
George Eliot
George Ellis
George Green
George Gamow
George Grove
George Grosz
George Halas
George Lucas
George Medal
George Monck
George Robey
Georg Lukacs
Georg Lukács
George W Bush
George Young
good heavens
geochemical
good hunting!
geophysical
globigerina
gloria Patri
good-looking
good manners
gloom-monger
good-morning
groundburst
ground cover
ground elder
ground floor
ground frost
ground glass
ground plate
ground-robin
ground state
ground staff
groundspeed
groundswell
groundsheet
ground-sloth
ground-to-air
good-natured
ground water
good offices
geopolitics
gnotobiosis
gnotobiotic
gnomonology
grow on trees
Group of Five
group theory
groupuscule
gross margin

glossectomy
glossodynia
grossièreté
gross weight
good spirits
glossolalia
glossolalic
goods engine
gross profit
gross output
geostrategy
gnostically
glottogonic
ghostliness
glottal stop
Good Templar
geostrophic
ghost-writer
growth stock
ghostbuster
groatsworth
grow to waste
globularity
geodynamics
geosyncline
gypsiferous
gap analysis
gypsum block
gap junction
German Bight
garlandless
gormandiser
gormandizer
germaneness
Germanesque
German flute
Germanistic
German Ocean
Germanophil
German sixth
Gargantuism
Gargantuist
garbanzo pea
gyrocompass
gyre-carline
Giro d'Italia
garden-glass
Gormenghast
garden gnome
garden-house
garden leave
garget plant
garnet-paper
garden party
garden patch
Gorée Island
garter-snake
garden stuff
garmentless
germinative
germination
gurgitation
girlishness
garnishment
Garrick Club
Gordian knot
garlic press
Gary Lineker
Gerald R Ford
girdlestead
garam masala
Geraniaceae
gerontophil
gerontology
gerontocrat
Garand rifle
Gordon Banks
Gordon Brown
Gordon Craig
gird oneself
garbologist
Gordonstoun
gyrostatics
garrulously
germ warfare
gerrymander
Gustave Doré
gas gangrene
Gustav Holst
gestational
Gustav Klimt
gestatorial
gospel music
Gasteropoda
gas-fittings
gesticulate
gaseousness
gastric mill
gastrectomy
gastrologer
gastromancy
gastronomic
gastronomer
gastroscope
gastrostomy
gastrosophy
gas-guzzling
gutta-percha
gutta serena
gatecrasher
gutter board
gutterblood
go the rounds
gutter press
gutlessness
guttersnipe
get the elbow
get the goods
get the heave
get physical
guttiferous
Gothic novel
go to lengths
go-to-meeting
get one's oats
get one's wind
get together
get-together
get cracking
get it across
go to the wall
go to the wars
go to the dogs
gutturalise
gutturalize
get even with
glutathione
glutaminase
grumblingly
gauge theory
gauze-winged
gouvernante
grudge fight
grudge match
glumiferous
Glumiflorae
glutinously
go up in smoke
gruellingly
gourmandise
gourmandism
grummet-hole
glufosinate
glue-sniffer
give and take
give it welly
give leg bail
give offence
governorate
give the wire
give the slip
give the push
go with a bang
gay deceiver
glyphograph
glycosylate
glyptotheca
gazing-stock
Gezhouba Dam
headbanging
heat barrier
headborough
heave the log
heaven knows
Heaven's Gate
heavenwards
haaf-fishing
headhunting
heathenesse
heather bell
hyacinthine
hyalomelane
head of state
head-station
headscarves
hearse-cloth
heat-seeking
head teacher
heart-easing
heart's-blood
hearth-brush
heartlessly
heart of palm
healthfully
heart-shaped
healthiness
hearth-money
heart cockle
hearth-penny
heart urchin
heartbroken
health stamp
health salts
hearthstone
heart attack
heart-strike
heart-string
heart-strook
heart-struck
heart murmur
heavy-handed
hoary marmot
heavy-headed
heavyweight
Hebraically
hobbledehoy
habiliments
hobble skirt
habilitator
hebdomadary
hobgoblinry
hebephrenia
hebephrenic
haberdasher
hibernation
hibernacula
✧hibernicise
✧hibernicize
Hibernicism
Hubert Parry
habituation
habitudinal
heckelphone
hockey stick
hic sepultus
hectic fever
hacking coat
huckleberry
hiccoughing
hectogramme
hickory tree
hucksterage
hucksteress
hic et ubique
Hock Tuesday
Hedda Gabler
hide-and-seek
hydra-headed
hydrated ion
hydrargyral
hydrargyrum
Hudibrastic
hedge-parson
hedge-school
hedge-priest
hedge-writer
hedgecutter
hedge-hyssop
hedging-bill
hedonomania
hiding-place
hide nor hair
hydrocarbon
hydropathic
Hydnocarpus
hydromantic
hydrotactic
hydrogenase
hydrogenate
hydrometeor
hydrogenise
hydrogenize
hydrogen ion
hydrogenous
hydrometric
hydromedusa
hydrophobia
hydrophobic
Hydrophidae
hydrophilic
hydrochoric
Hydrocharis
hydrothorax
hydrophytic
hydrophyton
hydrosomata
hydroponics
hydrologist
hydrosphere
hydrobromic
hydrotropic
hydrography
Hudson River
hideousness
hydrostatic
hydrolysate
hydroxylate
hydrocyanic
hydroxyurea
hierarchise
hierarchize
hierarchism
haemangioma
haematocele
haematology
haematocrit
heedfulness
Haeckel's law
hierophobia
hierophobic
haemophilia
haemophilic
haemoglobin
hierologist
haemorrhage
haemorrhoid
hierography
hyetography
hierocratic
haemoptysis
haemostasis
haemostatic
Hieronymite
Hieronymian
haemocyanin
hierurgical
huffishness
high as a kite
haggardness
Haggadistic
high admiral
Hagia Sophia
high bailiff
highblooded
highbrowism
high-battled
high command
high-density
Higher grade
high feather
high-feeding
highfalutin
high fashion
Hugo Grotius
high-hearted
high hurdles
hog-shouther
hoggishness
highjacking
Hegelianism
highlighted
highlighter
Highlandman
highly tried
Hugh Latimer
hegemonical
high-mettled
hogen-mogens
hog in armour
hagioscopic
hygroscopic
high old time
hygrometric
hygrophytic
hagiologist
Hagiographa
hagiography
hugeousness
hog's pudding
high polymer
high profile
high-profile
high-pitched
high-powered
high-rolling
high-ranking
high society
high sheriff
high-stepper
high-sighted
high spirits
high treason
high-tension
high-voltage
High Wycombe
Hugh Walpole
High Windows
highwrought
Highway Code
hair-brained
hairbreadth
hairdresser
hoisin sauce
heinousness
hair-raising
hairstylist
hair trigger
hair-trigger
hairy woubit
hold against
hill and dale
half-and-half
Hollands gin
holoblastic
hall-bedroom
holobenthic
half-binding
half-blooded
half-brother
halobiontic
half-baptise
half-baptize
half-checked
helicograph
half-century
✧helichrysum
holocaustic
holocaustal
holiday camp
helve-hammer
halfendeale
Hellenistic
hälleflinta
helleborine
helmet-shell
helper T cell

Heldentenor
helpfulness
holographic
hellgramite
hylogenesis
half-hearted
holohedrism
half-holiday
hold in check
helping hand
Helsingborg
hellishness
half-integer
helminthoid
helminthous
half-leather
half-landing
half measure
hylomorphic
Helen Mirren
helioscopic
help oneself
hold one's jaw
hold one's own
heliometric
heliophobic
heliochrome
heliochromy
heliosphere
heliotropic
heliotropin
heliography
hylophagous
halophilous
halfpennies
haloperidol
half past one
half past two
hill-pasture
hylopathism
hylopathist
half-pounder
holophytism
Holy-rood Day
hilariously
hill station
Halbstarker
half-starved
helispheric
Holy Sonnets
hold the belt
half the time
hold the line
hold the ring
hold the road
hold the fort
holothurian
hallucinate
hillwalking
halcyon days
Holly Hunter
hylozoistic
home-and-home
home-and-away
hemianopsia
hemianoptic
homoblastic
home banking
humectation
homocentric
home-crofter
home circuit
home-defence
Hampden Park
hamadryades
hammer-brace
hammercloth
hammer drill
homme de bien
Homo erectus
homoeomeric
homoeomorph
homoerotism
homoeopathy
Hammersmith
hammer throw
hempen widow
homogametic
homogeneity
homogeneous
homogeniser
homogenesis
homogenetic
homogenizer
Homo habilis
hemihydrate
hemihedrism
Humphry Davy
Humming-Bird
hummingbird
homoiousian
home-keeping
humiliative
humiliating
humiliation
humiliatory
homological
Hamiltonian
homiletical
hemimorphic
homomorphic
human nature
Human League
human shield
human rights
Hymenoptera
human dynamo
homeopathic
homeomerous
hymnologist
homeomorphy
hymnography
homeostasis
homeostatic
homoplastic
hemipterous
homopterous
homopolymer
homophonous
humgruffian
humeral veil
hemeralopia
hemeralopic
homesteader
hemispheric
hemistichal
homosporous
Homo sapiens
home stretch
homothallic
homothermic
homothermal
hamstringed
hemitropous
humbuggable
homeworking
homozygosis
homozygotic
hand and foot
hangability
Handa Island
Hans Buchner
handbreadth
handbagging
handcrafted
Hang-Chow Bay
hunt counter
hunt-counter
Hans Driesch
hanker after
hinderingly
hinderlands
hinderlings
hunger march
hunter's moon
hand-feeding
Hans Fischer
handfasting
hand grenade
hang-gliding
hunchbacked
henchperson
Hans Holbein
handicapped
handicapper
Hanni Wanzel
hunting-mass
hunting-seat
hunting-whip
hunting-tide
hand in glove
hunting-song
hunting horn
Hunting Dogs
Huntington's
hunting-crop
Henrik Ibsen
Henri Breuil
hang in there
Henri Fuseli
hand-knitted
handkercher
hand-me-downs
hand of glory
Hondo Island
hand-painted
hand-promise
Hans Richter
hundredfold
honorifical
hand-running
honorariums
handshaking
honest Injun
handselling
honest-to-God
hunt-the-gowk
hand to mouth
hand-to-mouth
hung up about
honour-bound
honour-point
honours easy
honours list
handwriting
handwritten
handwrought
honey-waggon
honey badger
Henry Pelham
Henry Miller
honeycombed
Henry Morgan
honeymoon in
honeymooner
Henry Cooper
honey possum
Henry Cotton
honey locust
Henry Briggs
Henry Irving
Henry Ireton
honey fungus
honey-suckle
honeysuckle
honey-sucker
Henry Hudson
hootanannie
Hoorah Henry
Hooray Henry
hyoscyamine
hook-climber
hooliganism
hyoplastral
hyoplastron
haphazardly
heptarchist
heptandrous
heptamerous
heptahedron
hypoaeolian
heptagynous
hypoblastic
hypocycloid
hypocorisma
hyphenation
haplessness
hippeastrum
hopefulness
hypoglossal
hypogastric
hippiatrics
hippiatrist
hypallactic
hypolimnion
Hepplewhite
hop-o'-my-thumb
hyponitrite
hypnopaedia
hippodamist
hippodamous
hippocampal
hippocampus
hypnogenous
hypsometric
hippophobia
hypsophobia
hypnotistic
haptoglobin
hippopotami
hippologist
hoplologist
hypnopompic
hippodromic
haptotropic
haplography
hypsography
Hippocratic
Hippocrates
hypoplastic
hypophyseal
hypophysial
hypermarket
hypergamous
hyperdactyl
hyperactive
hyperacusis
hyperphagia
hypercharge
hyperplasia
hyperemesis
hyperemetic
hypermnesia
hyperinosis
hyperinotic
hyperborean
hyperbolise
hyperbolize
hyperbolism
hyperdorian
hypersonics
hypersomnia
hyperboloid
hypercolour
hypertrophy
hypercritic
hypersthene
hyperstress
hyperextend
hyperlydian
hypostasise
hypostasize
hypostatise
hypostatize
hypospadias
hypesthesia
hypesthesic
hypostrophe
hepatectomy
hypothecate
hypothecary
hypothesise
hypothesize
hypothetise
hypothetize
hypothermia
hypothermal
hypothenuse
hypotensive
hypotension
hypotyposis
hepatoscopy
hepatotoxic
hypothyroid
happy medium
happy-clappy
Hardacanute
hard and fast
hard-and-fast
hortatively
Hermann Weyl
hard as nails
hortatorily
hard as stone
her ladyship
hare-brained
hornblendic
horn balance
Hirobumi Ito
hard bestead
Heracleidan
Heraclitean
haricot bean
hors d'oeuvre
hard drinker
hereditable
horse marine
horse-racing
horseradish
horned cairn
horse-dealer
hermeneutic
horned horse
hurley-house
horse-riding
hermeticity
horse pistol
horse-litter
Herzegovina
horse-collar
herpetology
horse-couper
horse-doctor
horned poppy
horse-drench
horse around
harness race
harness-cask
Harvey Smith
harness-room
harvest lady
harvest mite
harvest tick
harvest lord
harvest home
harvest moon
✧horse guards
horse mussel
horned viper
herpes virus
harmfulness
hurtfulness
hark forward
horographer
hard-grained
hard-hearted
hard-hitting
hurricanoes
hereinafter
Hardicanute
hurriedness
herring pond
herringbone
herring gull
herring-buss
horripilate
horripilant
horrisonant
herbivorous
horrisonous
Harris tweed
Harris tweed®
heroic verse
Hare Krishna
hurtleberry

Harold C Urey
Harold Evans
horological
Harold Kroto
Harold Lloyd
hard landing
hurdle-racer
harum-scarum
horn-madness
horn mercury
hardmouthed
hariolation
hercogamous
harp on about
horror comic
her lordship
hircocervus
herb-of-grace
harrowingly
harmoniphon
harmonistic
horror novel
harmonogram
harbour seal
harbourless
harbour dues
horror story
Harmony Mass
hard pressed
hard-pressed
hard put to it
harpsichord
haruspicate
harassingly
hard science
hart's tongue
hornswoggle
horoscopist
heresiology
heretically
heritresses
herb-trinity
Horatio Ross
Herculaneum
hirsuteness
hard-visaged
hard-wearing
hero-worship
hardworking
hardwareman
horny-handed
Harry Vardon
Harry Lauder
hurly-hacket
Harry Warren
hurry-scurry
hurry-skurry
hardy annual
Harry Hopman
Harry Potter
hasta mañana
husbandland
husbandless
husbandlike
histaminase
✧hispanicise
✧hispanicize
hispanicism
Hesychastic
hysteresial
Hesperiidae
hesperidium
hysteroidal
hysterogeny
hysterotomy
hostess-ship
hospitalise
hospitalize
hospitality
hospitaller
HMS Pinafore
histiocytic
hostilities
Hessian boot
his lordship
historicise
historicize
historicism
historicist
historicity
historiated
historiette
histologist
history play
Hush Puppies®
hush puppies
histrionism
histrionics
hasty-witted
hetaerismic
hot-tempered
hatlessness
hot-melt glue
hitherwards
hatefulness
hitch-hiking
hit the trail
hatchettite
hatti-sherif
hetairismic
hotel-keeper
hot-spirited
heteroclite
heterocercy
heteroecism
heterograft
Heteroptera
heteropolar
hot property
hot cross bun
heteroscian
heterospory
heterostyly
heterotroph
heterotopia
heterotopic
heterotypic
heterotaxis
✧heterousian
hounds-berry
hound's-tooth
houseparent
house-father
house martin
house-factor
housemaster
housekeeper
house of call
House of Keys
house church
housewifely
housewifery
house lights
householder
house-mother
haute époque
house arrest
house-broken
house-hunter
haughtiness
hour of cause
haustellate
have at heart
have a load on
hevea rubber
have designs
have had a few
have had that
have it in for
have it in one
have it large
have kittens
have no right
have nothing
have no truck
have one's way
HIV positive
have the hots
have with you
have you done?
Howling Wolf
hawkishness
Howard Hawks
Hexham Abbey
hexadecimal
hexagonally
hexahedrons
hexametrise
hexametrize
hexametrist
hexaplarian
hexastichal
hexateuchal
hazel grouse
hazardously
in a large way
in a bad light
inadaptable
Isaac Newton
Isaac Pitman
Isaac Asimov
inaugurator
inanimately
imaginative
imagination
inanimation
imaginarily
Iran-Iraq War
inalienable
inalienably
Italian iron
in a small way
in arm's reach
in a good hour
isapostolic
itacolumite
inappetence
inappetency
in abstracto
in at the kill
inauthentic
inattentive
inattention
inalterable
inalterably
in altissimo
I'm a Dutchman
in a nutshell
inadvertent
inadvisable
imbricately
imbrication
in by the week
in character
incrassated
incremation
incoercible
incremental
inclemently
increasable
increaseful
incredulity
incredulous
incognisant
incognizant
incogitable
incogitancy
incoherence
incoherency
inclination
inclinatory
incriminate
inculcative
inculcation
inculpation
inculcatory
inculpatory
in cold blood
incalescent
in commendam
incompetent
incumbently
income group
in committee
incompliant
incomposite
incommodity
incantation
incensation
incantatory
incunabulum
incunabular
inconscient
inconscious
incensement
incense-boat
incontinent
incentivise
incentivize
in condition
incendivity
inconsonant
incongruent
incongruity
incongruous
incinerator
inconstancy
incrossbred
incapacious
incipiently
incapsulate
incarnadine
✧incarnation
incurvation
incertainty
incurvature
incarcerate
incorrectly
incardinate
incarvillea
incertitude
incoronated
incorporate
incorporall
incorporeal
incuriosity
incuriously
incorruptly
incessantly
incest taboo
inclusively
itchy-palmed
Indian agent
Indian bread
Indian berry
Indian bison
Indian cress
Indian giver
Indian Ocean
India proofs
India rubber
india-rubber
indubitable
indubitably
indeciduate
indeciduous
Indo-Chinese
inductively
inductility
inductivity
inductional
in due course
in deep water
indifferent
indefinable
indefinably
indignation
indignantly
indigo finch
indignified
indigo snake
indigestive
indigestion
indehiscent
Indo-Iranian
indulgently
indemnified
indemnifier
indumentums
indomitable
indomitably
indentation
Indo-Pacific
in duplicate
induplicate
✧independent
indirection
indirect tax
indesignate
industrials
industrious
individuate
individable
indivisible
indivisibly
indexterity
index-finger
index-linked
index fossil
index number
Iceland moss
Iceland spar
iteratively
inelaborate
inenarrable
inexactness
ipecacuanha
inescapable
inescapably
inexcusable
inexcusably
inexcitable
Iles du Salut
Iles d'Hyères
inelegantly
inexecrable
inexecution
inefficient
ineffective
ineffectual
ideographic
inexhausted
itemisation
itemization
inedibility
inexistence
ideological
iteroparity
iteroparous
ineloquence
ideopraxist
inexpectant
inexpedient
inexpensive
idempotency
icebreaking
inebriation
inessential
identically
identic note
identifying
inestimable
inestimably
inextension
ineluctable
inequitable
ineluctably
inequitably
infrangible
infrangibly
inflatingly
inflammable
inflammably
infracostal
in flagrante
infectively
infecundity
inflexional
infrequence
infrequency
inflictable
inflict upon
in full blast
infiltrator
in full swing
infomercial

infanticide
infantilism
infantility
infundibula
infantryman
infantrymen
infangthief
infinite set
infinitival
informative
infuriating
infirmarian
information
infuriation
informatics
infernality
informality
informatory
infertility
inferential
inferiority
infestation
infatuation
infeudation
influential
infructuous
ingratitude
in great part
ingeniously
ingenuously
in good faith
in good heart
in good order
in good odour
in good shape
in good voice
ingurgitate
✧**ingathering**
inhabitable
inhibitedly
inhabitress
inhabitance
inhabitancy
ichthyosaur
ichthyoidal
ichthyolite
ichthyornis
ichthyology
ichthyopsid
ichnography
ithyphallic
✧**ithyphallus**
in her wisdom
inheritable
inheritress
inheritance
in his wisdom
imitatively
imitability
idioblastic
itineration
itinerantly
iridescence
idiographic
idioglossia
Irish setter
Irish coffee
Irish bridge
Irish Guards
iridisation
iridization
inimicality
initial caps
initial cell
initialling
Iain MacLeod
idiomorphic
Iris Murdoch
idiomatical
Ilie Nastase
iridologist
idiot savant
idiotically
injudicious
injuriously
ink-blot test
inking-table
irksomeness
inkhorn-mate
ill-mannered
ill-favoured
illiberally
illicitness
Isla Cozumel
ill-tempered
ill-versed in
ill-affected
illogically
ill-disposed
illuminable
illuminance
illuminator
illimitable
illimitably
ill-informed
Island of Rab
in-line skate
Isle of Arran
Isle of Barra
Isle of Islay
Isle of Tiree
Isle of Wight
illiquation
illaqueable
illiquidity
ill-equipped
ill breeding
ill-wresting
illusionary
illusionism
illusionist
ill-assorted
✧**illustrious**
illustrated
illustrator
ill-humoured
illuviation
illy whacker
immobiliser
immobilizer
in microcosm
immediately
immediatism
in medias res
immedicable
in midstream
immigration
immomentous
immunoassay
in miniature
immenseness
immunogenic
immunologic
immanentism
immanentist
immunotoxic
immunotoxin
immortalise
immortalize
immortality
immarginate
in mothballs
immitigable
immitigably
immoveables
ignobleness
Ionic school
Ian McKellen
innocuously
Ian Chappell
innominable
ignominious
innumerable
innumerably
Inns of Court
innervation
Inner Temple
inner planet
ignoramuses
Ignorantine
ignis fatuus
ionospheric
innutrition
I'm Not in Love
ignition key
innavigable
innavigably
ion-exchange
innoxiously
icosandrian
icosandrous
icosahedral
icosahedron
isolability
isomagnetic
✧**iron curtain**
in order that
inoperative
in one's blood
isolecithal
inobedience
in one's light
isometrical
in one's sleep
in one's shirt
isogeotherm
inofficious
inoffensive
iron-founder
iron-foundry
inorganised
inorganized
iron-hearted
isochronise
isochronize
isochronism
isochronous
isorhythmic
idolisation
idolization
isodiaphere
isoelectric
ironmongery
isoantibody
Ivor Novello
isotonicity
iconologist
inodorously
isomorphism
isomorphous
iconography
iconostases
iconostasis
iron pyrites
inopportune
isoxsuprine
inobservant
inobtrusive
inoculative
inoculation
inoculatory
idoxuridine
isobutylene
I Got You Babe
implacental
impeachable
impeachment
implausible
implausibly
impractical
impecunious
impedimenta
imprecation
impresarios
imprecatory
implemental
implementer
imprecisely
imprecision
impregnable
impregnably
impressible
impressment
impugnation
impignorate
implicative
implication
implicature
in principle
in principio
impuissance
impulsively
impolitical
impoliticly
impingement
il penseroso
imponderous
impinge upon
impenetrate
impenitence
impenitency
imploration
improbation
imploratory
improvement
improve upon
improvisate
improvident
imploringly
improvingly
impropriate
impropriety
impiousness
impermanent
imperialise
imperialize
imperialism
imparkation
impartation
importation
imperialist
imperiality
importantly
imperceable
impermeable
impermeably
imperfectly
imperviable
impertinent
impartially
imperilment
imperilling
imperforate
impersonate
imperiously
imperatival
importunate
importunacy
importunely
importuning
importunity
impastation
imposthumed
impassively
impassivity
impassioned
impostumate
impetrative
impetration
impetratory
it pitieth me
input device
impatiently
impetigines
impetuosity
impetuously
input/output
impoundable
impoundment
imprudently
inquination
inquiration
inquirendos
inquire into
inquiringly
inquisitive
inquilinism
✧**inquisition**
inquilinity
inquilinous
irreceptive
iure coronae
irrecusable
irrecusably
irradiative
irradiation
irreducible
irreducibly
irreduction
✧**irredentism**
✧**irredentist**
Israelitish
irreflexive
irreflexion
irrefutable
irrefutably
irregularly
Imre Kertész
irreligious
irrelevance
irrelevancy
irremissive
irremission
irremovable
irremovably
irruptively
irreparable
irreparably
irresoluble
irresolubly
irretentive
irretention
ipratropium
irritatedly
irrevocable
irrevocably
irreverence
instatement
instability
installment
instaurator
instantiate
in substance
insectarium
insectaries
insecticide
Insectivora
insectivore
insectiform
insectifuge
insectology
insidiously
inside right
inside track
insufflator
inspirative
instigative
inspiration
instigation
inspiratory
instinctive
instinctual
inspiringly
inspiriting
institorial
inspissated
inspissator
institutive
institution
institutist
insalubrity
insultingly
ipselateral
ipsilateral
inseminator
insensately
insinuative
insinuating
insinuation
insinuatory
insincerely
insincerity
insensitive
insentience
insentiency
insipidness

insipiently
inseparable
insuperable
inseparably
insuperably
instreaming
inscribable
instructive
instruction
insertional
inscriptive
inscription
inscrutable
inscrutably
insistently
insessorial
insatiately
insouciance
insculpture
inseverable
Issey Miyake
intradermal
intravenous
intrasexual
intrathecal
intractable
intractably
in the saddle
in the face of
in the making
in the market
in the manner
intrenchant
in the secret
in the offing
in the throes
in the middle
intrepidity
in the clutch
in the clouds
in the groove
intreatfull
integrative
integration
integrality
intagliated
intricately
intuitively
intuitivism
intuitional
intrinsical
intriguante
intellected
intelligent
intolerable
intolerably
intolerance
intimidator
intemperate
intemperant
intumescent
intensative
intenseness
intensively
intensified
intensitive
intensifier
intentioned
intensional
intentional
Il Trovatore
introverted
Istiophorus
intromitted
intromitter
intercalate
intercalary
interjacent
intertangle
internalise
internalize
interfacing
interfacial
interracial
interradial
interradius
internality
intervallic
intervallum
interrailer
intertarsal
inter partes
interactant
interactive
interscribe
interaction
interocular
interrelate
interbedded
intermeddle
interdepend
intercedent
internecine
internecive
interfering
intervening
intermedial
intermedium
interleukin
interdealer
interregnum
interneural
interneuron
intercensal
intercessor
interdental
interseptal
intersertal
intercepter
interceptor
interjector
interventor
intersexual
interleaves
intermezzos
interchange
inturbidate
interlinear
✧interlingua
intermingle
interlining
intermitted
interdictor
interviewee
interviewer
interfluent
interallied
interfluous
Interglossa
interpolate
interrogate
interrogant
internodial
interiority
interlocker
intercooled
intercooler
intercourse
intercostal
inter pocula
interspinal
intersperse
intertribal
intertrigos
intercrural
interpreter
intergrowth
interosseal
interesting
interatomic
icteritious
interlunary
internuncio
interludial
interfusion
interrupted
interrupter
interruptor
into the blue
into thin air
intrusively
Intoximeter®
intoximeter
Iguaçu Falls
inusitation
inutterable
inviability
invidiously
invigilator
invigorator
involucrate
invalidness
invalidhood
involvement
involuntary
inventively
inventorial
inviolately
invert sugar
investigate
investitive
investiture
investments
it would seem
idyllically
if you please
Jean Anouilh
Jean Buridan
Jean Borotra
Jean Cocteau
Jean de Meung
Jiang Jieshi
Joan Hammond
Jean Jacques
Jean Lafitte
Jean Lamarck
Juan-les-Pins
jealousness
jealoushood
jabberingly
joblessness
✧jabberwocky
jubilee clip
job rotation
Jack Brabham
Jacob Marley
Jacob Schick
Jacobinical
Jacob's staff
Jacobitical
Jack Dawkins
jockey strap
jactitation
Jack Kerouac
Jack-pudding
Jack Russell
jocoserious
Jacqueminot
Jacques Tati
Jocky Wilson
judiciarily
judiciously
judgemental
Jodie Foster
Judges' Rules
Judy Garland
Judaisation
Judaization
Judgment Day
✧judas window
Judas Priest
Judit Polgar
Joe DiMaggio
Jaffa orange
Jeff Bridges
Jeff Thomson
jagging-iron
J K Galbraith
John Ashbery
John-a-dreams
John a-Stiles
John a-Styles
John Bullism
John Boorman
John Bircher
John Barclay
John Barbour
John Bartram
John Charles
John Cadbury
John Cleland
John Collins
John Company
John Citizen
John Dowland
John Fairfax
John F Enders
John Gielgud
John Grisham
John Habgood
John Hancock
John Hawkins
John Hawkyns
John Kendrew
John Lubbock
John Le Carré
John Lydgate
John Lambert
John McEnroe
John Montagu
John Manners
John Marston
Johnny Bench
Johnny Carey
Johannes Rau
John Nevison
John Osborne
John of Gaunt
John o'dreams
John Pullman
John Profumo
John Rackham
John Redmond
John Redwood
John Russell
John Skelton
John Smeaton
John Simpson
Johnsoniana
John Surtees
John Sotheby
John Tenniel
John Toshack
John Tavener
John Vorster
John Webster
John Wyndham
joie de vivre
joint tenant
join the club
Jakob Boehme
joking apart
joking aside
Julian Bream
Jules Bordet
Jilly Cooper
jam sandwich
Jim Bergerac
Jamie Oliver
Jimi Hendrix
Jamaica bark
Jamaica plum
jumping hare
jumping jack
jumping gene
jumping bean
jumping deer
jam tomorrow
jam roly-poly
James Taylor
James Cagney
James Watson
James Galway
James Kelman
James Tissot
James Hilton
jimpson weed
James Howell
James Monroe
James Coburn
James Bridie
James Ussher
James Stuart
James Tyrone
Jim Sullivan
Jimmy Carter
Jimmy Riddle
Jane Fairfax
Jane Grigson
jinrickshaw
jungle fever
jungle-green
jungle juice
jungle music
Jana Novotna
Jonjo O'Neill
Jan Gossaert
Jane Russell
Janis Joplin
Jane Seymour
junction box
janitorship
Jan Purkinje
Jenny Pitman
jenny donkey
J B Priestley
Japan tallow
Japan laurel
Japanophile
juridically
J P R Williams
Jeremy Irons
jargonistic
jury-process
jury service
jerrymander
jus naturale
Jesse window
juste milieu
Jasper Johns
Josh Gifford
justiceship
justiciable
justifiable
justifiably
Jesuits' bark
Joseph Banks
Joseph Beuys
Joseph Henry
Joseph Haydn
josephinite
Joseph Lyons
Joseph Losey
Joseph Smith
Jesus Christ
just the same
Joshua Nkomo
jusqu'au bout
jitteriness
jeux d'esprit
journey-work
jaunting car
juvenescent
Java sparrow
jaws of death
jaw-breaking
jaw-dropping
joylessness
Joy Division
Kuala Lumpur
kwashiorkor
knavishness
Krasnoyarsk
Keanu Reeves
kibble-chain
kachina doll
kick oneself
kick the beam
kick up a fuss
kick up a dust
kidney stone
kidney vetch
keep an eye on
keep a secret
keep company
knee-capping

kneecapping
keep counsel
keelhauling
keep in check
keeping-room
keep in sight
Kierkegaard
Klein bottle
keep on about
keep one's bed
kleptocracy
keep the ring
knee-tribute
kleptomania
Kagera River
kohanga reos
knife-switch
kriegsspiel
Keith Joseph
Kris Kringle
knick-knacky
knickerless
Keizo Obuchi
kokum butter
kikuyu grass
kilocalorie
killer whale
killing time
killikinick
Kilimanjaro
Kaliningrad
✧kalashnikov
Kulturkreis
Kulturkampf
Kelly Holmes
Kim Basinger
Kommersbuch
kymographic
kamelaukion
Kimeridgian
Kendal green
kangaroo dog
kangaroo-hop
kangaroo paw
kangaroo rat
Kenzaburo Oë
Ken Scotland
kingdomless
kingdom come
kinderspiel
kind-hearted
kinchin-cove
kinchin-mort
King Henry VI
King Henry IV
Kentish fire
kinnikinick
kinematical
king of birds
Ken Rosewall
✧king of kings
king penguin
kindredness
kindredship
kinesiatric
king's-yellow
kinesthesia
kinesthesis
kinesthetic
king's bounty
kinesiology
King's Speech
kinesipathy
kinetically
kinetochore
kinetograph
kinetoplast
kinetoscope
king-vulture
know by sight
knowing card
knowingness
knock-rating
knocked-down
knock on wood
knock for six
knock around
know-nothing
klootchmans
know who's who
Kepler's laws
kerb-crawler
Kirk Douglas
kernicterus
Karl Jaspers
Karen Blixen
Karen Briggs
karbovanets
Kurt Russell
kirk session
keratometer
keratophyre
Kerry Packer
Korky the Cat
✧kiss and tell
kiss-and-tell
kissing gate
kiss-me-quick
Kashmir goat
kiss of death
kiss of peace
kiss the book
kite-balloon
katabothron
kitschiness
katadromous
kitten heels
kittenishly
kitchen-maid
kitchenware
kitchen-sink
kitchen unit
kitchenette
katavothron
Kate Winslet
knuckleball
knuckle-head
knuckle-bone
knuckle down
Kevin Keegan
Kevin Spacey
Kavir Desert
Kiwanis Club
key industry
keyboardist
keystroking
Kazakhstani
Kazantzakis
lead acetate
load-bearing
leaf-climber
lean cuisine
leaf-cushion
leaf-cutting
lo and behold
Leander Club
leave-taking
leaderboard
leader-cable
leave behind
leave unsaid
leaseholder
leapfrogged
loathedness
loathliness
loathsomely
leatherback
leather-head
leatherneck
leatherwood
leather-coat
Leatherette®
leach-trough
leading card
leading case
leading lady
leading edge
leaving-shop
leaping-time
leading note
loading coil
leafletting
learnedness
loan-society
loadsamoney
load the dice
leaf through
league match
leaguer-lass
leaguer-lady
league table
labia majora
librational
labia minora
Labrador dog
labradorite
Labrador Sea
Labrador tea
libidinally
lubber fiend
lubber's line
lubber's hole
labefaction
lubricative
lubrication
lubritorium
lubricously
Lobeliaceae
libellously
Laban system
labiodental
loblolly bay
loblolly-boy
libertarian
libertinage
liberticide
libertinism
liberalness
liberal arts
labyrinthic
labyrinthal
laboriously
✧liberty hall
liberty ship
liberty-boat
lobster moth
labour force
Labour Party
Lubavitcher
lobby-member
lobby system
lactalbumin
Lochaber axe
Lucian Freud
lucratively
lactational
lucubration
loco disease
laced mutton
luckenbooth
lactescence
luckengowan
lickerishly
lichenology
lecherously
Lecher wires
lock forward
lactiferous
lactifluous
Locrian mode
Loch Katrine
loculicidal
local action
Lucille Ball
local search
local colour
local option
localisable
localizable
locum tenens
laciniation
laconically
lycanthrope
lycanthropy
lychnoscope
laccolithic
lactoflavin
lick-platter
Lycopodinae
lacertilian
lachrymator
Loch Rannoch
Locarno Pact
locorestive
Le Corbusier
lickspittle
Lacus Mortis
locus standi
locust-years
lick the dust
lecithinase
locutionary
lectureship
lacquerware
lacquer tree
lucky strike
Lydian stone
ludicrously
lodge-keeper
Led Zeppelin
lodging turn
laddishness
Lady Jackson
La Dolce Vita
Lady Macbeth
Lady Provost
lady's-mantle
lady's finger
lady-trifles
Lee Van Cleef
lie hard upon
Lee Hartwell
lie detector
Lee De Forest
lie in the way
leesome-lane
Leeds Castle
lieutenancy
lues venerea
lift a finger
life annuity
lifeboatman
luffer-board
Laffer curve
lofted house
life history
lifemanship
life peerage
life peeress
life-rentrix
laggardness
loggan-stone
legibleness
logicalness
logodaedaly
leglessness
leg-of-mutton
logographic
logographer
lignivorous
legal tender
logomachist
ligamentary
ligamentous
Leguminosae
lagomorphic
Loganiaceae
legendarily
legionnaire
logopaedics
Ligurian Sea
legerdemain
logorrhoeic
logarithmic
legislative
legislation
legislature
logistician
Lagos rubber
light-handed
light-headed
light-legged
lightweight
light-heeled
light-minded
light-winged
light engine
lightsomely
light source
light-footed
light breeze
legatissimo
Light My Fire
leg-business
lignum-swamp
lignum-scrub
lignum vitae
Luis Alvarez
loiteringly
Luing cattle
lying-in ward
leishmaniae
leishmanias
laicisation
laicization
Leisler's bat
Leibnitzian
leisurewear
leisure suit
Like a Virgin
likeability
like a streak
likableness
Lake Balaton
like billy-oh
Lake Chapala
lake-dweller
Lakshmi-puja
lokshen soup
lake herring
Lake Lucerne
Lake of Death
Lake Ontario
Lake Scutari
like the wind
Lake Turkana
Lake Torrens
like winking
lukewarmish
Lillian Gish
lollipop man
✧lilliputian
lily-livered
lalapalooza
lily-trotter
lumbaginous
lamebrained
lamp chimney
Lyme disease
lammergeier
lammergeyer
Lambeth Walk
lymphoblast
lymphangial
lumpishness
limelighted
lamplighter
lamelliform
lamellicorn
lamentation
lemon-yellow
lemon cheese
lamentingly
lemon squash
laminar flow
luminescent
Lamborghini®
limnologist
Lumbricidae
lumbricalis
lamprophyre
lamb's tongue
limitedness
limited-over
limitlessly
limp-wristed

Limp Watches
longanimity
longanimous
landaulette
linear motor
line abreast
Lancastrian
Long Barnaby
long-clothes
linocutting
line drawing
line dancing
linseed-cake
linseed-meal
lance pesade
Len Deighton
lingeringly
lanceolated
lantern jaws
lance-knecht
lance-knight
lantern fish
Linzertorte
linked verse
landfilling
line-fishing
landgravate
land-grabber
landgravine
landholding
long hundred
luncheon-bar
lancinating
lancination
landing-beam
landing gear
landing-ship
lunging whip
landing flap
lentiginose
lentiginous
Line Islands
longinquity
Lanai Island
land-jobbing
long jumping
lonely heart
lonely-heart
landlordism
land-measure
long measure
line manager
linen-scroll
linen-draper
lingonberry
Londonderry
line of force
lingoa geral
Lennox Lewis
London pride
line of sight
langoustine
long-playing
long paddock
line printer
long-purples
lunar theory
long-running
Lanarkshire
land-spaniel
landscapist
land-steward
long-sighted
landsknecht
line-shooter
Lynn Seymour
Link trainer
lengthiness
long-tongued
languidness
languescent
languishing
linguistics
long-visaged
longwearing
long weekend
long-waisted
leopard-wood
leopard moth
look askance
Leon Brittan
Leoncavallo
Lloyd Webber
Lloyd-George
look daggers
loose cannon
loose change
loose-limbed
loose-bodied
loosestrife
look forward
Léon Gaumont
lion-hearted
L Ron Hubbard
lionisation
lionization
Leos Janácek
loop of Henle
look the part
loop the loop
Leon Trotsky
lapidifying
Lepidoptera
Lepidosteus
lapidescent
Lepidosiren
lap of honour
lap of luxury
lipogenesis
Leptis Magna
lap dissolve
Lippizzaner
lapilliform
lip-smacking
lipomatosis
leprosarium
leptodactyl
leptocercal
lip-rounding
leptorrhine
lophobranch
lipoprotein
Lupercalian
La Périchole
laparoscope
laparoscopy
lapis lazuli
liposuction
liquescence
liquescency
liquefiable
Liquidambar
liquidation
liquid lunch
Lord Bullock
Lord Cowdrey
Lord Denning
large-handed
large-minded
larcenously
Lord Erskine
Lord Fairfax
Lord Grimond
Lord Harlech
larviparous
larrikinism
Lord Jenkins
Lord marcher
Lorin Maazel
laryngismus
laryngology
laryngotomy
Lord of hosts
Lord Olivier
Lord Provost
Lord Robbins
Lord Renfrew
Lord Russell
Lord Scarman
Lord's Prayer
Lord's Supper
Lord Thomson
Lord Wrangel
Lord Winston
Larry Holmes
listeners-in
listening-in
listeriosis
Las Hermanas
lesser panda
lister ridge
Lester Young
lustfulness
lysigenetic
last honours
lastingness
luskishness
Lossiemouth
Lesbian rule
Lise Meitner
lese-majesté
lese-majesty
lose oneself
lissomeness
lose one's rag
lose one's way
last offices
Laserpicium
Laserpitium
lose the plot
lethargical
littérateur
Lutheranise
Lutheranize
Lutheranism
letter-board
letterboxed
letterpress
letter-stamp
latifundium
let off steam
litigiously
latchstring
lattice-leaf
latticework
lethiferous
letting down
Little Horse
little woman
Little Women
littleworth
Latin Church
latent image
Latin Empire
Latin Square
litany-stool
litholapaxy
lithogenous
lithochromy
lithophysae
lithophytic
latrocinium
lithologist
lithotomist
lithodomous
lithotomous
lithosphere
lithography
lithotripsy
lithotritic
lithotritor
lythraceous
laterigrade
literalness
lateral line
literaliser
literalizer
literaryism
latirostral
lateritious
literatured
Lotus-eaters
lotus-eating
latus rectum
latiseptate
latitudinal
litmus paper
Laura Davies
Laura Riding
laudability
leucaemogen
leukaemogen
Laura Knight
Laura Ashley
launderette
laundry-maid
laundry list
louver-board
laurel-water
lounge music
laughing gas
Lough Corrib
laughworthy
loutishness
loudmouthed
leucodermia
leukodermia
leucodermic
leukodermic
leucodermal
leukodermal
leucoplakia
leukoplakia
leucorrhoea
leukorrhoea
leucocratic
leukocratic
Lou Costello
louvre-board
loudspeaker
Louis Leakey
Louis B Mayer
Louis Jouvet
Louis Aragon
Louis-Treize
Louis-Quinze
loup-the-dyke
laurustinus
liveability
loveability
live-bearing
lovableness
live circuit
love handles
love-in-a-mist
level-headed
level-pegged
living death
Livingstone
liver-colour
leviratical
Lévi-Strauss
levitically
live through
law-merchant
lawlessness
law of nature
low-spirited
lawbreaking
low-pressure
lower eyelid
Lewis Namier
lawn sleeves
lex talionis
loxodromics
lexigraphic
luxulianite
luxulyanite
luxuriation
luxuriantly
luxury goods
luxuriously
lixiviation
lay about one
lay the table
lay the venue
loyalty card
leze-liberty
leze-majesty
lazy painter
Me and My Girl
meaningless
Mt Annapurna
meadow-brown
Mt Aconcagua
meadow-grass
meadow mouse
meadow pipit
meadowsweet
meat packing
Mean Streets
measureless
measurement
mobile phone
mobilisable
mobilizable
Möbius strip
mechanicals
mechanician
mechanistic
Michael J Fox
Michael Foot
Michael Owen
much about it
Machaerodus
Machairodus
mechatronic
mycodomatia
mackerel sky
Mickey Mouse
mock-heroics
machination
machine-made
machineable
machine head
machine-shop
machine code
machine-work
machine tool
mockingbird
machicolate
Machiavelli
mycological
macula lutea
Mechlin lace
mock-modesty
micromanage
macrogamete
microgamete
macrodactyl
macroscopic
microscopic
microneedle
microreader
microcephal
Micronesian
microkernel
microsecond
micrometric
microphonic
microphytic
microlithic
microfiches
microfiling
macrobiotic
microfloppy
microinject
micrococcal
micrococcus
micrologist
microtomist
macrocosmic
microcosmic
microporous
macrofossil
microfossil
microcredit
microgroove
micrography
microwriter
microtubule
microswitch
macrocyclic
mycophagist
mycoplasmas
McCarthyite

McCarthyism
mycorrhizae
mycorrhizal
maceranduba
macassar oil
mock saffron
Mack Sennett
mycotrophic
Machu Picchu
Michurinism
micturition
Micawberish
Micawberism
mediateness
mediatorial
mediatrices
median strip
mediastinal
mediastinum
mediaevally
medico-legal
medicinable
Medicine Hat
medicinally
medicine man
medievalism
medievalist
maddeningly
madreporite
medley relay
middenstead
madefaction
midshipmate
Madeira cake
madrigalian
madrigalist
midwife toad
midnight sun
midlittoral
muddle along
middle class
middle-class
mode-locking
middle eight
✧middle-earth
Middle Latin
Middlemarch
mudslinging
middle price
modularised
modularized
middle-sized
middle-world
middle watch
madonnawise
Madonna-lily
mud engineer
made of money
modern dance
modernistic
Modern Latin
Madara Rider
moderations
mid-Atlantic
mad staggers
made to order
medium-dated
mediumistic
medium waves
Muddy Waters
muddy-headed
middy blouse
Maeve Binchy
meet halfway
Moeso-gothic
muffin-fight
muffin-worry
muffler shop
Magdalenian
Magna Charta
magnanimity
migrational
magnanimous
Magic Marker®
magic marker
magic carpet
magic circle
magic sphere
magic square
magic number
magic bullet
Magherafelt
magnetic dip
magnetic ink
magnetician
Maglemosian
magnesstone
Miguel Torga
magnifiable
magnificent
magnificoes
Maggie Smith
megaloblast
megalomania
megalopolis
megalosauri
megalosaurs
Meghnad Saha
maggotorium
magisterial
magisterium
magistratic
Megatherium
megatonnage
megaton bomb
might as well
magnum bonum
Magnus force
megavitamin
magazine-gun
mahua butter
Mahabharata
Muhammad Ali
Muhammad Zia
Mohammed Ali
Mohenjo-daro
Maharashtra
Moira Stuart
mail-carrier
mail-catcher
moiré effect
mailing list
maisonnette
Meissen ware
maidservant
meiotically
maintenance
maintopsail
maintopmast
maisterdome
moisturiser
moisturizer
McIntosh red
Maja Clothed
major planet
major orders
majoritaire
majoretting
make a dinner
make a figure
make a hole in
make a go of it
make believe
make-believe
make cheeses
make contact
make certain
make friends
Mike Gatting
make history
Mekhitarist
make no doubt
McKinley Sea
Mekong River
make or break
make-or-break
make one's bow
make one's way
Mt Karisimbi
Mt Kosciusko
make the pace
make the most
make unready
make whoopee
multangular
multanimous
Malibu board
molybdenite
Malacca-cane
Molucca bean
mole cricket
molecularly
maliciously
malacophily
molecatcher
mole drainer
maledictive
malediction
melodically
maledictory
Melody Maker
melodiously
maladroitly
maladaptive
maladjusted
millenarism
millenarian
millet-grass
mille fleurs
millefleurs
millenniums
mal del pinto
mulberry fig
malfeasance
mallee scrub
malt-extract
malefaction
malefically
maleficence
malefactory
malignantly
multivalent
multiracial
multiparity
multiparous
multiscreen
multi-access
multiserial
Mulciberian
millisecond
melliferous
meltingness
milking-time
multilineal
multilinear
multi-vision
multifidous
mellifluent
multiplying
mellifluous
multiplexer
multiplexor
milliampere
millionaire
millionfold
multilobate
multisonant
multipotent
multinomial
multicolour
mellivorous
multispiral
milligramme
multistrike
multiethnic
multistorey
multijugate
multi-author
multijugous
multicuspid
Milt Jackson
milk-kinship
malakatoone
milk-livered
melon baller
malonic acid
melanochroi
melanterite
melancholia
melancholic
molendinary
melanophore
meliorative
melioration
malposition
melioristic
Milton Obote
mellowspeak
meliphagous
milk pudding
malapropism
malpractice
malariology
molestation
Milos Forman
milk thistle
malfunction
mal du siècle
✧milquetoast
malevolence
malt vinegar
Melvyn Bragg
mollycoddle
mammalogist
mammee apple
mimographer
mammiferous
mumpishness
mammillaria
mamillation
mamilliform
momentarily
memento mori
momentously
mammoth-tree
mammonistic
mammoplasty
mammography
✧mumbo-jumbos
Memorial Day
memorialise
memorialize
memorialist
memory board
✧memorabilia
membraneous
memorandums
memorisable
memory trace
memorizable
mimosaceous
mimetically
mum's the word
mental block
man-watching
mansard-roof
mundaneness
mandarinate
manna-lichen
mentalistic
Montanistic
mandatorily
manna-groats
mangalsutra
miniaturise
miniaturize
miniaturist
monoblepsis
mind-bending
mind-blowing
monochasial
Manichaeism
monochasium
minicabbing
monoclinous
monocularly
monoculture
mine-captain
municipally
monocardian
monochromic
monochromat
monocarpous
Monica Seles
Monocotylae
Monaco-Ville
monocrystal
monodactyly
Monadelphia
Monodelphia
monodelphic
mont-de-piété
Manuel Azaña
monkey about
monkey board
monkey bread
monkey block
mantel clock
mendelevium
Montenegrin
monkey-gland
monkey-grass
Monseigneur
Minnesinger
manneristic
montes pubis
mantelpiece
Minneapolis
mantelshelf
monkey shine
Mendelssohn
men-servants
monkey wheel
munificence
manufactory
manufacture
mindfulness
manifestoes
monographic
monographer
monogrammed
managed fund
✧montgolfier
monogenesis
monogenetic
managership
mind-healing
Munchhausen
monohydrate
men-children
mentholated
monchiquite
Munchausen's
monthly rose
mancipation
mancipatory
manniferous
mannishness
monkishness
Mendip Hills
man-milliner
mentionable
monticolous
mandibulate
monticulate
monticulous
muntjac deer
Manilla hemp
monological
monologuise
monologuize
monologuist
monolingual
monolatrist
monolatrous
monomyarian
minimum wage
monomorphic
manumission
manumitting
mononuclear
Minenwerfer
meningiomas
mind-numbing
meningocele
ma non troppo

Munro-bagger
Mennonitism
mandolinist
mentonnière
Mantoux test
monophagous
manipulable
Montpellier
monopoliser
manipulator
monopolizer
monopsonist
monophthong
✧monophysite
menaquinone
mind-reading
monarchical
menorrhagia
mineral well
minor planet
mineral coal
mineral wool
mineraliser
mineralizer
minor orders
miner's right
minoritaire
ministering
ministerial
monasterial
ministerium
menispermum
minesweeper
monasticism
minus strain
Monotremata
✧monothelete
✧monothelite
✧monothelism
monothecous
minute-glass
many-tongued
munitioneer
monstrosity
monstrously
monitorship
mine-thrower
minute steak
minute-while
Minute Waltz
minute-watch
mensurative
manducation
mensuration
manducatory
mantua-maker
monovalence
monovalency
mons veneris
moneymaking
money market
moneylender
money for jam
money to burn
money spider
money broker
mind your eye
money supply
money's-worth
Monty Python
monozygotic

myocarditis
moor-band pan
moorbuzzard
meo periculo
moon goddess
mooring mast
Moorish Idol
myoelectric
moonlighter
moon-madness
myographist
Mt Pichincha
map-measurer
meprobamate
Mt Paricutin
maquiladora
Maria Callas
mortarboard
Mariah Carey
more and more
Murrayfield
marram grass
Morgan le Fay
Murray River
mornay sauce
Maria Mutola
meroblastic
moribundity
more by token
Marc Chagall
Mark Chapman
mare clausum
miracle rice
miracle play
Mare Crisium
mariculture
mercenarism
mercenarily
marmem alloy
marcescible
marcescence
market cross
Marcel Carné
Marcel Dupré
Marie-Jeanne
market-house
Marie Bichat
merveilleux
Marie Claire
Marcellinus
market maker
market overt
Marie Louise
myrmecology
murderously
Mar del Plata
marketplace
market-price
market share
Muriel Spark
morgenstern
martensitic
Mersey sound
Marie Stopes
market-value
market-woman
mirifically
merogenesis
merogenetic
marshlander
marsh-mallow

marshmallow
mirthlessly
morphogenic
Marshallese
morphologic
marshalship
marshalling
Mare Humorum
merchant bar
merchandise
merchandize
merchanting
Myra Hindley
merchantman
merchantmen
marchioness
Murphy's game
morphotropy
marginalise
marginalize
marginalism
margination
marginalist
marginality
Marginal Sea
Martin Buber
Mare Imbrium
Morris chair
Martin Crowe
morris dance
martinetish
martinetism
mortice lock
mortise lock
morbiferous
mortiferous
mortise bolt
mercilessly
morning-land
marriage-bed
morningtide
morning gift
Mare Ingenii
morning roll
morning room
morning gown
morsing-horn
morning coat
✧morning star
margin index
martialness
martial arts
myrmidonian
Martin Opitz
merdivorous
Martin Sheen
marlinspike
mare liberum
moral defeat
marble-edged
mural circle
moral rights
marble-paper
Meryl Streep
Mark McGwire
more majorum
Marantaceae
Moringaceae
moronically
myringotomy
marine snail

merino sheep
marine store
marrow-bones
marionberry
Markov chain
marmoreally
mirror glass
mirror image
marconigram
Marion Jones
Mariologist
Morton's fork
Mary Poppins
Mary Renault
margraviate
Mary Seacole
Mary Shelley
maraschinos
Mare Spumans
Mare Smythii
meritocracy
Marston Moor
Marathonian
meritorious
moratoriums
mercuration
murmuration
Marcus Allen
Mare Undarum
murmuringly
Marsupialia
mercurially
murmurously
marquessate
marquisette
marqueterie
murmur vowel
Moravianism
Merovingian
Mare Vaporum
marivaudage
merrymaking
mercy flight
Martyn Lewis
merry-andrew
marry come up
martyrology
Mervyn Peake
massasauger
Mrs Malaprop
Mustard-seed
mustard tree
Mesoamerica
message-girl
message unit
mustachioed
maskallonge
mishallowed
Mrs Dalloway
moshav ovdim
muscatorium
miscarriage
mismarriage
mesoblastic
mossbluiter
music master
music-seller
moss-cheeper
music centre
masochistic
musical sand

musicalness
music holder
mesocephaly
misidentify
misrelation
master-class
misdescribe
misperceive
Mister Chips
master-clock
miscegenate
misremember
miscegenist
misdemeanor
masterfully
mesmerising
mesmerizing
misbeliever
master-joint
miscellanea
muskellunge
master mason
misbecoming
misdevotion
Musée d'Orsay
misbegotten
mise en place
masterpiece
musket-proof
mistempered
mispersuade
mussel-scalp
mussel-scaup
mise en scène
mussel-shell
misfeasance
misfeatured
misbestowal
master-wheel
mystery ship
mystery play
mystery tour
mesogastria
mesogastric
missheathed
Mischa Elman
mischievous
Muschelkalk
misshapenly
mastication
mussitation
masticatory
massiveness
masking tape
Mistinguett
missing link
misdiagnose
missishness
Messiahship
miscibility
Mystic River
Mississippi
mispleading
muscle-bound
mésalliance
misalliance
misclassify
muscle sense
mass meeting
mesomorphic
mush-mouthed

mesonic atom
mesenterial
mesenchymal
misanthrope
misanthropy
misoneistic
misinformer
misinstruct
misdoubtful
misconceive
mastoid bone
mastoiditis
miss oneself
misgovernor
miss one's tip
Mrs Robinson
museologist
mastodontic
misconstrue
misfortuned
muscovy duck
mesopelagic
misspelling
misoprostol
mass-produce
miscreative
mistreading
miscreation
miscreaunce
miserablist
misericorde
misery index
miserliness
Mastroianni
Mt Stromboli
mistrustful
Moses basket
mesospheric
misestimate
mesothelial
mesothelium
miss the boat
Mesut Yilmaz
musk thistle
mosstrooper
musculation
muscularity
musculature
masturbator
misguidedly
misguidance
misjudgment
meshuggenah
meshuggeneh
masculinely
masculinise
masculinize
masculinist
masculinity
mesquinerie
museum piece
masquerader
mosquito net
Mussulwoman
mutual funds
mutualistic
mitrailleur
mitral valve
mutableness
Mutabilitie
metacentric

Words marked ✧ can also be spelled with one or more capital letters

metachrosis
mathematise
mathematize
mutteration
mathematics
motherboard
mothercraft
mutteringly
mother-in-law
mother-naked
Mother of God
Matteo Ricci
mother-right
mother's mark
mother's help
mothers-to-be
mother's ruin
mothers' ruin
mother water
metafiction
metagenesis
mutagenesis
metagenetic
mitogenetic
matchmaking
matchlessly
metrication
matrilineal
matrilinear
methicillin
matriclinic
matrimonial
matriarchal
metri gratia
Mathias Rust
matriculate
mottled calf
metaldehyde
mottle-faced
metalliding
metalloidal
metallogeny
metalworker
metallurgic
metempirics
metamorphic
Mt Tongariro
matinée idol
matinée coat
metonymical
mythomaniac
mutton cloth
meteoritics
Methodistic
matroclinic
meteoroidal
meteorolite
mythologise
mythologize
mythologian
Mythologies
metrologist
mythologist
mythopoeist
meteorology
methodology
meteorogram
mythopoetic
mythography
meteor swarm
meteor storm

metaplastic
metaphorist
motu proprio
metaphrasis
metoposcopy
metapsychic
metaphysics
motor-bandit
materialise
materialize
motor racing
materialism
maternalism
materialist
materiality
motor-launch
✧mithradatic
✧mithridatic
Mithridates
Mithraicism
motor-driven
metastasise
metastasize
metasilicic
metasomatic
metasequoia
mitotically
metathesise
metathesize
metatherian
mutationist
Matsuo Basho
motive power
methylamine
methylation
methyl group
mauvais goût
mould-candle
mould-facing
maundy money
Mauretanian
mouse potato
mouse-colour
mouth-honour
mouth-friend
Mauritanian
Mauritshuis
Mount Sangay
Mountbatten
moustachial
Mount Egmont
mountain ash
mountain cat
mountain dew
mountaineer
mountainous
mountain tea
mountain-top
Mount Elbert
Mount Elbrus
mountenance
Mount Ararat
Mount Hudson
moveability
movableness
mawkishness
Max Mallowan
moxibustion
Mexican wave
mixed number
Max Delbrück

Max de Winter
Max Beerbohm
maxillipede
maximum card
maxim-monger
maximaphily
myxomatosis
mixing valve
Max von Sydow
Myxophyceae
mixotrophic
Maya Angelou
May-meetings
maysterdome
Mozambiquan
Mezz Mezzrow
Mezzogiorno
mezzotinter
mezzotintos
Noam Chomsky
✧neanderthal
near-sighted
near the wind
near the bone
Nyamuragira
Noah Webster
nobody's fool
noble savage
noble-minded
nubbing-cove
neck and neck
neck and crop
nectar-guide
nyctanthous
nociceptive
niche market
nickel-bloom
nucleic acid
neckerchief
nucleolated
nickelodeon
nickel-ochre
nucleoplasm
nuclear fuel
nickel steel
neck-herring
noctivagant
nictitation
noctivagous
nyctinastic
nyctitropic
noctilucent
noctilucous
Nico Ladenis
Nicole Farhi
Nicol's prism
Nicolas Cage
Nicolas Roeg
Nicene Creed
necromancer
necromantic
necroscopic
necrophobia
nyctophobia
necrophobic
necrophilia
necrophilic
nicrosilial
necrobiosis
necrobiotic
necropoleis

necrologist
nocuousness
necessarian
necessaries
necessarily
necessitate
necessitied
necessitous
nocturnally
nudicaudate
nudicaulous
nodding duck
nuée ardente
needcessity
needfulness
needlecraft
needle-furze
needlepoint
needle paper
needlestick
needle valve
needlewoman
Niersteiner
Niels Finsen
Nietzschean
nefariously
no fewer than
nigrescence
neglectable
negligeable
negligently
Nigel Lawson
Negro pepper
negrophobia
nightfaring
night-waking
nightmarish
negotiation
night-walker
negotiatrix
night school
night-cellar
night terror
night-season
night letter
night-shriek
night vision
night sister
night-flying
night-flower
nightingale
negationist
night-worker
night-porter
night-attire
night-hunter
nihil obstat
Neil Diamond
noise abroad
noiselessly
neighboring
neighbourly
Neil Jenkins
Neil Kinnock
noisomeness
nail varnish
naked ladies
Nikkei index
Nikola Pasic
Nikola Tesla
nikethamide

null and void
nulliparity
nulliparous
nullifidian
Nellie Melba
Namib Desert
name-calling
nomadically
name-dropper
number eight
number plate
numbers game
numbers pool
nom de guerre
nomographic
nomographer
Nymphalidae
nympholepsy
nymphomania
nomological
nomenclator
nominatival
nimbostrati
numerically
numismatics
numismatist
nematoblast
nematodirus
nematophore
nummulation
Nanga Parbat
non-Catholic
non-harmonic
non-marrying
non-partisan
non-naturals
non-abrasive
non obstante
non-academic
non-economic
non-negative
non-metallic
nondescript
non-resident
non-delivery
non-believer
nonsensical
non-feasance
non-sequence
non sequitur
nonagesimal
nonchalance
nunnishness
non-dividing
non-violence
non-elective
non-election
non-electric
non-allergic
nonylphenol
nonillionth
non-flam film
non-clinical
nonplussing
nanomachine
non-invasive
non-unionist
non-volatile
non-specific
non-priority
non-provided

none-sparing
non-issuable
none the less
nonetheless
non-standard
nuncupative
nuncupation
nuncupatory
nun's-veiling
non-existent
ninny-hammer
Nancy Friday
Nancy-pretty
neopaganise
neopaganize
neopaganism
Neo-Catholic
neonatology
neovitalism
neovitalist
Naomi Uemura
Neoplatonic
neologistic
neocortical
Neotropical
nook-shotten
neostigmine
Neoptolemus
nephelinite
Napier's rods
nuptial Mass
napoleonite
Napoleonism
nip in the bud
nephologist
nephrectomy
nephrolepis
nephropathy
nephritical
naphthalane
naphthalene
naphthalise
naphthalize
ne plus ultra
Norman cross
Normanesque
narratively
normatively
Norway maple
no reason but
Norman Stone
nurse-tender
nervelessly
nerve centre
nerve ending
Norbertines
nurserymaid
northlander
northwardly
North Dakota
north-easter
North Sea gas
North Sea oil
north-wester
Northampton
northernise
northernize
northernism
northermost
North Island
North Utsire

Words marked ✧ can also be spelled with one or more capital letters

north-by-east
north-by-west
nursing home
narcissuses
narcoleptic
narrow gauge
narrow-gauge
nervousness
nervuration
Narayanganj
no such thing
Naseem Hamed
nasofrontal
nosographic
nosographer
nasogastric
nosological
nose-nippers
no-score draw
nasopharynx
nostradamic
Nostradamus
✧nosey parker
not bat an eye
nitraniline
not harm a fly
notableness
not a bit of it
noticeboard
notochordal
net register
netherlings
netherstock
netherworld
netherwards
not give a fig
nutrimental
nothingness
Notting Hill
nothing-gift
nothing in it
Nat King Cole
nothing to it
net dividend
nutritively
nutritional
nitric oxide
nattier blue
nettle-cloth
Natalie Wood
natale solum
no time at all
notungulate
national air
nationalise
nationalize
nitrosamine
nationalism
nitrosation
nationalist
notionalist
nationality
Nationalrat
nitrogenase
nitrogenise
nitrogenize
nitrogenous
nitrometric
nitrocotton
nation state
nitrous acid

notaphilism
notaphilist
not a problem
not up to much
not a patch on
nutcrackers
net practice
natural year
naturalness
natural-born
notoriously
naturopathy
nature strip
nature study
nature trail
not a sausage
Nototherium
natatoriums
not much chop
native title
nitty-gritty
Natty Bumppo
neural plate
nautch-girls
naughtiness
naughty pack
nourishable
nourishment
Nautiloidea
naupliiform
neuropathic
neuroleptic
neuroticism
neurofibril
neurologist
neurotomist
neurotropic
neurotrophy
neuropteran
neutral zone
neutraliser
neutral axis
neutralizer
neutron bomb
neutron star
Navratilova
navel-gazing
Nevill F Mott
navel orange
navel-string
novelettish
novelettist
✧never say die
never-fading
never-ending
Novosibirsk
Novatianism
Novatianist
newscasting
nowhere near
New Year's Day
New Year's Eve
New Learning
news fiction
New Age music
New Plymouth
now and again
New Romantic
New York City
news-theatre
Nawaz Sharif

next biggest
next dearest
noxiousness
Ouagadougou
ob-and-soller
Öland Island
opalescence
Osage orange
on aggregate
orange-grass
Orange Prize
orange pekoe
Orange River
orange stick
orange-tawny
orang-outang
oral hygiene
oral history
Oxalidaceae
ovariectomy
Omar Khayyám
Oda Nobunaga
onagraceous
ora pro nobis
Olaus Roemer
ora et labora
oracularity
oraculously
orbiculares
orbicularis
orbicularly
ombrogenous
orbital road
Orbitsville
orchestrate
orchestrina
orchestrion
oncogenesis
Orchidaceae
orchiectomy
orchid-house
orchidology
oscillative
oscillating
occultation
oscillation
oscillatory
oncological
oscillogram
oecumenical
Occam's razor
on condition
on cloud nine
once or twice
occipitally
odds and ends
old-maidhood
odds and sods
Old Catholic
old bachelor
old identity
Old Believer
ondansetron
ordinary ray
old-womanish
old-fogeyish
Old Dominion
Old Trafford
orderliness
order around
Old Prussian

orderly room
Ordos Desert
opera-dancer
overarching
open-and-shut
over and over
one-way glass
overachieve
operatively
opera singer
operability
operational
one-day match
opera bouffe
opéra bouffe
over-anxiety
over-anxious
overbearing
overblanket
overbidding
over-breathe
overbrimmed
overbalance
overburthen
open borstal
overcoating
operculated
overcrowded
overcorrect
overcareful
open circuit
overcasting
overdraught
over-drowsed
opeidoscope
overdevelop
opere citato
open economy
overearnest
omelette pan
on every hand
overfraught
overfreedom
overfreight
overfulness
overfunding
overflowing
overforward
oleographic
oreographic
overgrazing
overgrainer
overgarment
overheating
open-hearted
overhandled
open harmony
overhastily
overindulge
opening time
olefiant gas
obediential
overleather
overlocking
oreological
overmeasure
open-mouthed
overnighter
one in the eye
oceanariums
ocean-stream

operoseness
one-worldism
onerousness
overpicture
overprepare
over-precise
open primary
overproduce
overpitched
overpayment
overreached
oneirodynia
oneiromancy
overrunning
oneiroscopy
open slather
overstrooke
overstretch
overtrading
overtedious
open the ball
over the odds
over the left
over the hill
over the moon
open the door
over the hump
overthrower
overviolent
open verdict
overweather
overweening
overwrestle
overwrought
over-zealous
offhandedly
officialdom
officialese
officialism
officiation
officiality
office block
office hours
officinally
olfactology
officiously
offscouring
off the hooks
off the rails
off the shelf
off-the-shelf
off the track
off the wagon
offenceless
offensively
off one's case
off one's face
off one's game
off one's oats
off one's feed
off one's head
offload onto
off-coloured
off-Broadway
Oxford cloth
Oxfordshire
obfuscation
obfuscatory
organic vein
organ-screen
organically

organisable
organistrum
organizable
ophicalcite
ophidiarium
ophthalmist
ochlophobia
ophiophobia
ochlophobic
ophiologist
ochlocratic
otherwhiles
Ophiuroidea
oxidational
oviparously
oeil-de-boeuf
obiter dicta
Oliver Hardy
Origenistic
olive branch
Oliver Stone
Oliver's Army
Oliver Twist
Oliver Tambo
originative
origination
oxidization
originality
original sin
olivine-rock
opinion poll
opinionated
opinionator
oriel-window
opium-smoker
orientalise
orientalize
Orientalism
orientation
Orientalist
orientality
oligomerous
Oligochaeta
oligochaete
oligochrome
oviposition
oligopolist
oligotrophy
ominousness
Otis Redding
opisthosoma
object-glass
objectivate
objectively
objectivise
objectivize
objectivism
objectivist
objectivity
objurgative
objurgation
objurgatory
objet trouvé
Oak-apple Day
oil painting
oilseed rape
oil of cloves
oil platform
olla-podrida
obliquation
oblique case

obliqueness
obliquitous
obliterated
obliterator
obliviously
Ormeli Falls
Osmundaceae
of many words
osmotically
ommatophore
obmutescent
on no account
omnibus book
of necessity
omnificence
omniformity
omnifarious
oenological
ornamentist
omnipresent
oenophilist
omnipatient
omnipotence
omnipotency
owner-driver
omniscience
Ornithogaea
ornithosaur
Ornithopoda
ornithology
ornithopter
obnoxiously
odonatology
onomasticon
on one's guard
on one's hands
on one's plate
or otherwise
ozonisation
ozonization
odoriferous
ozoniferous
ozonosphere
odorousness
odontoblast
odontograph
odontogenic
odontoid peg
odontologic
odontophore
oppignerate
oppignorate
on principle
Oppenheimer
opprobrious
opportunely
opportunism
opportunist
opportunity
oarsmanship
Ossianesque
obsecration
obsidionary
obsceneness
oyster-field
oyster-knife
oyster plant
oyster-patty
obstetrical
oyster-shell
oyster-tongs
oyster-woman
oyster-wench
obsignation
obsignatory
obstinately
obstipation
on shipboard
od's pitikins
obsolescent
Orson Welles
od's bodikins
oesophageal
observative
observation
observatory
observantly
obstructive
obstriction
obstruction
oestrogenic
observingly
obsess about
obsessively
on suspicion
obsessional
obscuration
obscureness
obscurement
out-paramour
outwardness
ostracoderm
ostracodous
outmarriage
on that score
optical disk
octachordal
octodecimos
on the parish
on the market
on the way out
on the carpet
on the batter
on the razzle
ostreaceous
on the record
on the agenda
on the fiddle
on the tiddly
ostreophage
ostreophagy
on the square
on the ground
on the stocks
on the street
on the stroke
on the button
out of favour
out of action
out of temper
out of season
Out of Africa
out of the Ark
out of the way
out-of-the-way
out of kilter
out of pocket
out-of-pocket
out of bounds
out of course
out of breath
out of humour
octagonally
ontogenesis
ontogenetic
octahedrite
octahedrons
outside half
outside edge
outside left
ostrich-farm
ostrich-like
outdistance
ontological
octillionth
obtemperate
optometrist
ostentation
out and about
Otto Nicolai
octonocular
octingenary
ostensively
octennially
out-and-outer
orthopaedic
osteopathic
optionality
out for blood
orthoscopic
orthogenics
orthopedics
orthopedist
osteodermic
osteodermal
osteogenous
orthocentre
orthophyric
osteophytic
osteoclasis
osteoplasty
orthoborate
Ostrogothic
osteologist
ortho-cousin
orthodontia
orthodontic
orthoepical
outsourcing
orthodromic
orthotropic
orthography
osteography
orthopraxis
orthostichy
orthopteran
orthopteron
orthostatic
octuplicate
outspokenly
outer bailey
outbreeding
outer limits
outer planet
outcrossing
obtuse angle
obtestation
octastichon
outstanding
obtrusively
outbuilding
outquarters
octave-flute
outswinging
Otto Warburg
Ottawa River
obumbration
ovuliferous
opus musivum
Orust Island
obviousness
Oswald Avery
oxygenation
onychomancy
oxyrhynchus
oxy-chloride
onychophagy
Onychophora
oxycompound
Olympic Flag
on your marks
oxy-hydrogen
Platanaceae
play a part in
planar diode
Pharaoh's ant
placability
phalanstery
play-actress
Peasants' War
Peasblossom
plaice-mouth
praecordial
peat-casting
peacemaking
planetarium
plate-basket
plate-warmer
phagedaenic
peace-parted
place before
peacekeeper
plateresque
prayerfully
place-kicker
plane figure
planetoidal
placeholder
plate-powder
peace-monger
place-monger
Phanerozoic
planetology
player piano
plate armour
prayer shawl
Placentalia
place-hunter
prayer wheel
playfulness
play footsie
play for time
platforming
play for love
peach brandy
pharisaical
play it by ear
plagioclase
Praxitelean
phariseeism
planimetric
playing-card
✧platinotype
planisphere
psaligraphy
pianissimos
plagiostome
Plagiostomi
placket-hole
Pearl Harbor
pearl barley
pearly gates
pearl-fisher
pearl millet
pearl-powder
pearly queen
pearlescent
pearl mussel
pearl button
pearl oyster
psalmodical
plasmodesma
plasmalemma
plasmolysis
plasmolytic
plasminogen
psammophile
psammophyte
plasmosomes
plasmatical
pragmatical
Phasmatodea
Phasmatidae
pragmatiser
pragmatizer
plain pastry
plain dealer
phaenogamic
Phaenogamae
plaintively
phaenomenon
plain-spoken
plainstanes
plainstones
planogamete
piano-school
play one's ace
phagophobia
Platonicism
peacock-like
peacock-fish
peacock-blue
piano-player
piano nobile
pianofortes
plano-convex
Prado Museum
phagocytism
phagocytose
prairie wolf
prairie fowl
PlayStation®
plantocracy
practicable
practicably
plastic clay
practically
plastic bomb
plastic wood
plastic wrap
plasticiser
plasticizer
play the game
play therapy
prattlement
play the fool
play the goat
plantigrade
Plantagenet
phantom pain
phantom limb
phantomatic
Phaethontic
planta pedis
plaster cast
praetorship
plasterwork
plaster over
phantasiast
plantcutter
plantswoman
piacularity
planuliform
pharyngitic
pharyngitis
platyrrhine
publication
✧public enemy
public funds
publishable
publishment
public house
public image
public lands
public purse
public woman
public wrong
public works
pebble-stone
Pablo Casals
Pablo Neruda
pack and peel
pick-and-pick
package deal
package tour
peccability
peccadillos
Pico Bolívar
pace-bowling
pococurante
picket fence
picket-guard
pocket-glass
pickelhaube
pocket knife
packed lunch
pocket money
pocket mouse
pocket-piece
pocketphone
pocket-sized
Pacific Time
pacifically
pacificator
pick holes in
pectinately
pectination
pectisation
pectization
packing case
peckishness
pichiciegos
picnic races
peculiarise
peculiarize
peculiarity

pecuniarily
pace oneself
pick one's way
pictorially
Pycnogonida
pycnogonoid
pictography
pock-pudding
picture card
picture rail
picture-wire
picture-play
picture cord
picture book
picture-goer
picturesque
picture tube
pactum nudum
pick-up truck
Pickwickian
pachysandra
pachydactyl
pachydermia
pachydermic
pachydermal
pick-your-own
pudibundity
pedicellate
Pedicularis
pediculosis
pediculated
pedder-coffe
pedagogical
pedagoguery
pedagoguish
pedagoguism
pudding-pipe
pudding-time
pudding bowl
pudding-bowl
Pedaliaceae
piddle about
paddle-board
pedal-action
pedological
pad-elephant
paddle-staff
paddle-shaft
paddle wheel
pedanticise
pedanticize
pedanticism
pedantocrat
Podsnappery
pedunculate
Pedipalpida
Podophyllum
podophyllin
pedestalled
pedetentous
preparative
preparation
preparatory
Precambrian
presanctify
presagement
prelateship
prevalently
prevaricate
premaxillae
prepackaged
prevailment
prevail upon
prevail over
prefatorial
predatorily
prefatorily
prêt-à-porter
phenanthene
precautions
precautious
prematurely
prematurity
presbycusis
plea bargain
plea-bargain
presbyteral
presciently
preachiness
prescindent
preschooler
pleochroism
prescission
preoccupate
preoccupant
preoccupied
preacquaint
pseudograph
pseudologia
pseudologue
pre-adamical
pseudomonad
pseudomonas
pseudomorph
pre-adamitic
preadmonish
pseudopodia
preadaptive
pseudoscope
plead guilty
plebeianise
plebeianize
plebeianism
pretendedly
predeceased
predecessor
precedented
preselector
precedently
piece of cake
piece of work
preterhuman
premedicate
premeditate
preteritive
preterition
prevenience
prerecorded
preferrable
Pherecratic
prehensible
presentable
preventable
preventible
presentably
precentress
preceptress
presentness
presentient
presentment
prefectship
pretentious
prefectoral
prefectural
present arms
preservable
pre-ignition
plethorical
predicament
predicative
predication
prelibation
predicatory
preliterate
preciseness
pleximetric
predilected
preside over
peevishness
Pterichthys
precipitate
precipitant
preliminary
previsional
precipitous
Premium Bond
plenipotent
pteridology
premiership
predictable
predictably
pietistical
paediatrics
paediatrist
prehistoric
prefigurate
peelie-wally
pre-election
preclinical
pre-emphasis
piedmontite
pre-eminence
pneumonitis
pleomorphic
pre-emptible
pneumatical
pneumathode
preambulate
preambulary
pie in the sky
plein-airist
preannounce
prerogative
Pterosauria
pterodactyl
pteroic acid
preconceive
premovement
phenomenise
phenomenize
phenomenism
phenomenist
pleiomerous
paedophilia
paedophilic
plerophoria
predominate
prenominate
predominant
premonitive
prepositive
premonition
pre-position
preposition
premonitory
prepollence
prepollency
precognosce
precolonial
paedologist
phenologist
paedodontic
pre-conquest
pleiotropic
paedotrophy
pyelography
precontract
puerperally
Pierre Bayle
Pierre Curie
pleurodynia
Pierre Laval
preprandial
pleuritical
precritical
press of sail
press office
please it you
plessimeter
plessimetry
Pleistocene
Piers Morgan
pleasurable
pleasurably
pleasureful
pieds-à-terre
press button
press-button
pre-stressed
plentifully
prestigious
Prestonpans
plenteously
Plectoptera
Pretty Polly
Puerto Rican
phentermine
Prester John
peep-through
prestissimo
Pretty Woman
prepunctual
presume upon
prepubertal
prejudgment
prejudicate
prejudicant
prelusively
presumingly
pre-judicial
prejudicial
preaudience
prelusorily
presumptive
presumption
pied wagtail
pre-existent
pigheadedly
pig-ignorant
piggishness
pig's knuckle
pignoration
pigeon-berry
pigeon chest
pigeon-flier
pigeon-flyer
pigeonholer
pigeonholes
pigeon-house
pigeon's milk
pig-sticking
pig's whisper
philanderer
private bank
privateness
primateship
private life
private bill
philatelist
private view
primariness
privatively
prima donnas
primatology
psi particle
primaevally
primary care
primary cell
primary coil
pliableness
Phil Bennett
pair-bonding
pain barrier
Priscianist
Phil Collins
principally
prince royal
Princess Ida
pricelessly
prime of life
price-fixing
prize-winner
pride and joy
Phileas Fogg
prime number
painfulness
philhellene
primiparity
primiparous
primigenial
Philip Glass
pairing-time
priming-wire
priming-iron
primitively
✧primitivism
primitivist
poikilocyte
Philippines
prickleback
prickliness
painkilling
prickly pear
prickly heat
phillipsite
prismatical
Psilotaceae
philomathic
psilomelane
primogenial
poison-gland
Psilophyton
prison house
philosophic
philosopher
philologian
philologist
poisonously
pair of stays
pair of steps
poison sumac
Philoctetes
philogynist
philogynous
primrose way
painstaking
priestcraft
priest's hole
point d'appui
psittacosis
painted lady
pointedness
pointed arch
point-device
point-devise
print-seller
pointlessly
point of sale
point-of-sale
point of view
✧pointillism
pointillist
Pointe-Noire
printing ink
point toward
paint roller
point source
Point-a-Pitre
paint-bridge
printer's ink
printer's pie
Primulaceae
primus stove
pyjama party
poke mullock
poking-stick
polyandrous
palmatisect
palpability
pilgarlicky
polyamorous
polka-dotted
pillar-saint
polyactinal
phlyctaenae
palm-cabbage
police burgh
police-court
police force
palace guard
police-judge
polyculture
Polacanthus
pelican-fish
polycentric
polycrotism
pilocarpine
polychroism
polychromic
polycarpous
police state
policewoman
polycrystal
polydactyly
pile-driving
Piltdown man

pulveration
pallescence
pollen count
pollen grain
poltergeist
pilferingly
Palaearctic
pullet-sperm
palaeotypic
pulverulent
pulp fiction
polygraphic
palsgravine
Pelagianism
polygonally
polygenesis
polygenetic
polygonatum
phlegmonoid
phlegmonous
polyglottic
polyglottal
pale-hearted
polyhedrons
polyhydroxy
pulchritude
polyhistory
palpitation
pollination
pillion-seat
pilniewinks
polemically
polymorphic
polymastism
palingenesy
palindromic
pillow-block
poliorcetic
pillow-fight
palm off upon
pulmobranch
Pelton wheel
polyonymous
polyphagous
Polyphemian
polyphonist
polypeptide
polar circle
polar lights
pilgrimager
polarimeter
polarimetry
polar forces
poltroonery
pelargonium
polariscope
Polystichum
Palestinian
Palus Somnii
Palm Springs
pull strings
polystyrene
pilot jacket
pilot scheme
politicking
politically
polytechnic
pelotherapy
Polytrichum
pilot engine
pull through

pull-through
Politbureau
pilot burner
pullulation
pellucidity
pale-visaged
pole-vaulter
palmyra wood
palmyra nuts
pollyannish
polyzoarial
polyzoarium
pampas grass
Pemba Island
pomiculture
pumice-stone
Pompeian red
pommel horse
pampelmoose
pompelmoose
pampelmouse
pompelmouse
pomegranate
pamphleteer
pumpkinseed
pomological
pompousness
pump-priming
Pomfret cake
Pandanaceae
pentavalent
pan-galactic
pentadactyl
pentandrian
pentandrous
panjandarum
pancake race
pancake bell
pentamerism
pentamerous
pentahedral
pentahedron
pantaletted
pantalettes
pineal gland
pentangular
pentathlete
pinnatisect
pentamidine
pentaploidy
pentazocine
pantalooned
Pentacrinus
Punta Arenas
pentastichs
pennant flag
pentactinal
pennant rock
pendant-post
pennant grit
pentagynian
pentacyclic
pentagynous
punicaceous
penicillate
Penicillium
paniculated
panic-monger
panic attack
pinacotheca
pinocytosis

panic-struck
panic-buying
panic button
ponderation
Pinteresque
ponderingly
✧**panhellenic**
✧**pandemoniac**
✧**pandemonium**
✧**pandemonian**
ponderosity
ponderously
Pentecostal
penteconter
pony express
ponce around
punt-fishing
panegyrical
panegyricon
punched card
punched tape
pinch effect
pantheistic
pinch-hitter
penthemimer
Panchen Lama
punching-bag
Punchinello
pantheology
Pancho Villa
pencil-cedar
pensileness
pensiveness
ponticellos
pinking iron
pinkishness
punkishness
Pondicherry
pontificate
pontificals
pensionable
pensionless
pension fund
pantisocrat
pencil skirt
pencil-stone
panel beater
penological
penultimate
pentlandite
panel doctor
Panglossian
Pan-Slavonic
Pont-l'Évêque
penalty rate
penalty shot
penalty line
penalty kick
penalty goal
penalty spot
penalty area
panel system
Panama Canal
panomphaean
Pan-American
panentheism
panentheist
Pan-Anglican
peninsulate
Pandora's box
pennoncelle

pantoscopic
pantophobia
pansophical
pantothenic
pantothenol
pantomimist
pantography
punto dritto
Pantocrator
Pink Panther
panspermism
panspermist
penuriously
pancratiast
panislamism
panislamist
panpsychism
panpsychist
panesthesia
punishingly
penetrative
punctuative
penetrating
penetralian
penetration
punctuation
punctualist
punctuality
puncto banco
Panathenaea
Panathenaic
punctilious
punctulated
penitential
panduriform
penguin suit
pan-European
pendulosity
pendulously
pennyweight
panty girdle
penny-wisdom
pennywinkle
pinnywinkle
penny-a-liner
penny loafer
penny arcade
propagative
profanation
propagation
profanatory
prosaicness
prosaically
pros and cons
protandrous
profaneness
prolateness
probate duty
probabilism
probabilist
probability
probational
probationer
protanomaly
protagonist
prosauropod
prokaryotic
prosciuttos
proud-minded
proterandry
proletarian

proletariat
proper chant
proteaceous
prosenchyma
projet de loi
proceedings
procerebral
procerebrum
proper-false
procephalic
phonemicise
phonemicize
phoneticise
phoneticize
progenitive
phoneticism
phonetician
phonemicist
phoneticist
provenience
proveditore
progenitrix
progeniture
Procellaria
proteolysis
proteolytic
proteinuria
prolegomena
Proterozoic
proterogyny
prose-writer
professedly
proleptical
protectress
projectment
progestogen
property man
protectoral
property tax
prosecution
prosecutrix
proselytise
proselytize
proselytism
proofreader
proof-charge
proof spirit
prop forward
proof-puller
prong-horned
ploughshare
plough-staff
plough-stilt
ptochocracy
prochain ami
prochein ami
prochain amy
prochein amy
prothallial
prothallium
prothalamia
prothalloid
prophylaxis
prothrombin
prochronism
prothoracic
prothoraces
prothoraxes
prophesying
prophetical
prophetship

prophethood
proximately
prodigalise
prodigalize
proximation
prodigality
prodigal son
promiscuity
promiscuous
proliferate
promiseless
profiterole
proliferous
prominently
providently
prolificacy
propitiable
promisingly
prohibitive
✧**prohibition**
prolificity
proficience
✧**provisional**
proficiency
prosiliency
prohibitory
propitiator
provisorily
propinquity
Provins rose
profit-taker
poodle-faker
proclaimant
problem page
problem play
problematic
people mover
people power
pro indiviso
prognathism
prognathous
protogalaxy
provocateur
protopathic
provocative
prorogation
provocation
provocatory
photonastic
phototactic
protomartyr
Proboscidea
proboscides
photoactive
proboscises
protonemata
provokement
photoperiod
photo-relief
photoresist
photometric
prolongable
photo-ageing
phonophobia
photophobia
photophobic
photophilic
photophonic
photochromy
Prototheria
protophytic

Words marked ✧ can also be spelled with one or more capital letters

phonofiddle
provokingly
protolithic
photo finish
proposition
proso millet
promotional
photoglyphy
pronouncing
photomosaic
protonotary
protococcal
Protococcus
prosopopeia
protocolise
protocolize
photocopier
phonologist
protocolist
protocolled
photosphere
phototropic
phonography
photography
prototrophy
proconsular
provostship
proportions
prolocution
prolocutrix
phonotypist
protogynous
phosphatase
phosphatide
phosphatise
phosphatize
prospective
prospecting
prospection
promptitude
phosphorate
phosphorise
phosphorite
phosphorize
phosphonium
phosphorism
phosphorous
procreative
procreation
protractile
protractive
protraction
protrudable
proprietary
proprieties
proprietrix
programming
✧propranolol
protrusible
Procrustean
✧progressive
progressism
progression
progressist
prostration
proctodaeal
proctodaeum
prosthetics
prosthetist
proctorship
proctoscope
proctoscopy
prostitutor
prostatitis
procuration
procuratory
protuberate
protuberant
profuseness
procurement
producement
producer gas
promulgator
propylamine
proxy-wedded
promycelium
propylitise
propylitize
Procyonidae
pappardelle
pop-lacrosse
pop-fastener
pipe-cleaner
pipe-dreamer
papier collé
peppercorny
pepper grass
pepperiness
papier-mâché
pop festival
poppet-valve
puppet-valve
pipe fitting
peptisation
peptization
peptide bond
peptic ulcer
pupillarity
pipe-lighter
papilliform
populariser
popularizer
Papal States
papillulate
pipe one's eye
pipe of peace
paperhanger
paper-making
paper-sailor
papyraceous
piperaceous
paper-feeder
paperweight
paper-office
paper-enamel
paper-folder
paper-credit
paper-pusher
paper-muslin
paper-cutter
pipe-stapple
pipe-stopple
pipistrelle
papovavirus
puppy-walker
puppy-headed
park-and-ride
permanently
permanganic
Port Augusta
pervasively
purgatively
parvanimity
portability
Parma violet
port admiral
purgatorial
purgatorian
parablepsis
parableptic
parabolical
parabolanus
pyroballogy
parabematic
pure-blooded
parabaptism
pork-butcher
port charges
pericranial
pericranium
pyroclastic
periclitate
parochially
Paracelsian
pure culture
part company
pericentric
pericentral
paracrostic
pericardiac
pericardial
pericarpial
pericardium
pericardian
Port Cartier
paracetamol
parachutist
perichylous
peridiniums
peridesmium
paradoxical
Paradoxides
purse-taking
partenariat
perseverate
perseverant
persevering
purse-seiner
purse-bearer
porter-house
porterhouse
parheliacal
permeameter
perpetrable
perpetrator
porte-crayon
parcel shelf
porters' knot
parpen-stone
parcels post
perfect game
perceptible
perfectible
pervertible
perceptibly
perfect year
perfectness
parrel truck
perpetuable
persecutive
persecution
perpetually
perpetuance
persecutory
perpetuator
perceivable
perceivably
purificator
paraffinoid
paraffin oil
paraffin wax
Phrygian cap
paragraphia
paragraphic
paragrapher
periglacial
Paraguay tea
pyrogravure
paragogical
peregrinate
paragliding
peregrinity
paragenesia
paragenesis
perigenesis
paragenetic
pyrogenetic
paraglossae
paraglossal
pyrognostic
Perigordian
Périgord pie
perigastric
parchedness
perchlorate
perihepatic
porphyritic
purchasable
purchase out
purchase tax
pereira bark
pertinacity
pervicacity
pertinently
parting shot
purging flax
participate
participant
partitively
participial
partibility
percipience
partitioner
percipiency
porriginous
Persian lamb
Persian Wars
portionless
Persian Gulf
parti-coated
permissible
permissibly
permittance
persistence
persistency
particulate
pyrokinesis
parallactic
parallelise
parallelize
paralleling
parallelism
parallelist
paraldehyde
purple finch
✧purple heart
paraleipses
paraleipsis
purple laver
paralympics
Portland Bay
Portlandian
purple patch
perplexedly
parsley fern
parsley pert
paramedical
pyramidical
paramedicos
pyramidally
portmanteau
paramorphic
perimorphic
Port Moresby
paramastoid
perambulate
paramountcy
paramountly
perennation
parentcraft
paronychial
paranthelia
parentheses
parenthesis
parenthetic
perennially
phrenologic
paronomasia
paranephric
perinephric
paranephros
partnership
phrenetical
per incuriam
perineurium
perforative
personalise
personalize
personative
personating
personalism
percolation
perforation
personation
personalist
personality
persona muta
period drama
purposeless
purpose-like
port of entry
park-officer
parrot fever
personified
pyrrolidine
personifier
periodicity
periodic law
Porto Alegre
performable
performance
parrot mouth
pornotopian
periodontia
periodontal
period piece
personpower
parlour-maid
parlour game
parlour pink
pornography
Port of Spain
parson's nose
purportedly
purportless
periostitic
periostitis
perlocution
perspective
perspicuity
perspicuous
paraphiliac
paripinnate
parapenting
pyrophorous
perspirable
paraphrenia
paraphraser
paraparesis
periphrases
periphrasis
paraparetic
paraphraxia
paraphraxis
peripeteian
peripatetic
part-payment
parapsychic
portraitist
portraiture
purpresture
pyrargyrite
peristalith
perishables
peristalsis
peristaltic
parish clerk
peristerite
parascenium
perispermic
perispermal
ports de bras
paresthesia
perishingly
parasuicide
parasailing
parascience
pure science
parishioner
phrasal verb
paraselenae
phrasemaker
part-singing
peristomial
perissology
phraseology
phraseogram
perestroika
parasitical
parasitosis
parity check
piratically
pyrotechnic
parotiditis
port the helm
perithecial

perithecium
pyritohedra
puritanical
peritonaeal
peritonaeum
peritonitic
peritonitis
paratrooper
paratyphoid
parathyroid
perduration
permutation
perturbable
perturbedly
perturbance
perturbator
perfunctory
persuadable
perfumeless
parturition
perduellion
persulphate
persuasible
perquisitor
perlustrate
pyruvic acid
periwigging
part-writing
party animal
party-pooper
party popper
party-coated
party spirit
passacaglia
post and pair
passage hawk
passage beds
passagework
passage-boat
postal meter
postal order
piscatorial
pass a motion
pissasphalt
pass airside
postal union
push-bicycle
post captain
pass current
past dispute
pas de basque
poster child
pesteringly
post-exilian
posteriorly
pas redoublé
poster paint
pester power
✧pasteurella
pasteuriser
pasteurizer
possessable
pas de quatre
pushfulness
post-forming
pasigraphic
post-glacial
paschal lamb
paschal moon
Puss in Boots
passiveness

pestiferous
pestilently
passing bell
passing shot
passing note
passing tone
possibilism
possibilist
passibility
possibility
pessimistic
postillator
✧Passion week
passionless
Passiontide
passion play
Poseidonian
piscicolous
piscivorous
posological
post-lingual
post-nuptial
posing pouch
pastoralism
pastoralist
post-orbital
push-over try
pestologist
pastourelle
post-primary
postponence
past perfect
pastry board
pastry brush
Pasir Gudang
postscenium
pass the mark
pass the buck
post-tension
positronium
pass through
push through
postulation
pustulation
postulatory
pasture-land
pastureless
pastures new
pasquinader
post-vocalic
post village
post-vintage
pussy willow
pussyfooter
Petrarchise
Petrarchize
Petrarchism
Petrarchian
Petrarchist
pot-walloner
pot-walloper
Pythagorean
Pythagorism
pot-valorous
potter along
putrescible
putrescence
patter flash
putrefiable
potteringly
pattern race

pattern-shop
Pat Jennings
pitifulness
put the arm on
pitched roof
pitchperson
pitch circle
pitchblende
pitch and pay
pitch and run
pitch-roofed
patch pocket
Pitti Palace
putrid fever
potting shed
pettishness
patrilineal
patrilinear
patricianly
phthiriasis
patriclinic
pettifogger
patrimonial
petticoated
patriarchal
patristical
patelliform
petalomania
potamogeton
patent agent
put on weight
put on the dog
put on the map
potentially
potentiated
patent right
patent rolls
poting-stick
patent still
put to ransom
pathogenous
Pythonesque
pathophobia
put to rights
patronising
patronizing
put to flight
patroclinic
petroglyphy
pots of money
patroonship
pathologist
petrologist
petropounds
pittosporum
Petrodromus
pathography
petrography
piteousness
patron saint
patrol-wagon
patrolwoman
pit-a-patting
'pataphysics
pataphysics
paternalism
Peter Pindar
Peter Lilley
Peter Alliss
✧paternoster
Peter Porter

Peter's pence
Peter Grimes
pattress box
Peter O'Toole
Pete Sampras
pâte-sur-pâte
potash water
potass water
potato apple
petit maître
potato bogle
potato chips
put it across
put it mildly
petitionary
petitioning
petitionist
potato salad
potato scone
Petite Sirah
pet aversion
pit-dwelling
putty-powder
petty spurge
plug-and-play
Paul A M Dirac
pluralistic
Paul Boateng
plumbic acid
plum-blossom
plumber-work
Paul Cézanne
pound-master
pound weight
pound-keeper
Paul Delvaux
pauselessly
poule de luxe
plume-pluckt
Paul Ehrlich
prudentials
pause button
Paul Gauguin
pluriserial
plumigerous
pruning bill
pruning hook
prudishness
pruriginous
Paulinistic
pluviometer
✧prusik sling
Paul Keating
plus or minus
plutologist
plutonomist
plutocratic
plum-pudding
pourparlers
Paul Robeson
Prussianise
Prussianize
Prussianism
prussic acid
Paul Theroux
Paul Tillich
poultry yard
poultry-farm
plumularian
paving-stone
poverty line

poverty trap
pivot bridge
pawnbroking
P G Wodehouse
powder flask
power factor
power series
powerlessly
power shovel
power-diving
power broker
power-driven
pixillation
pax vobiscum
phylacteric
payment card
psychiatric
psychically
psychodrama
psychedelia
psychodelia
psychedelic
psychodelic
psychograph
psychagogue
psychogenic
psychologic
psychometer
psychomotor
psychometry
psychonomic
psychophily
pay the piper
psychopathy
psychotoxic
physicalism
physicalist
physicality
physiocracy
physiognomy
physitheism
physicianer
physiciancy
physiologic
physiologus
physiolater
physiolatry
physiatrics
phylloclade
ptyalagogic
ptyalagogue
phyllomania
phyllotaxis
pay envelope
paying guest
pay one's dues
phycophaein
phytophagic
phytochrome
phytoalexin
phycologist
phytologist
phytotomist
phytography
Plymouthite
Plymouthism
Plymouthist
phytosterol
phycomycete
phycocyanin
quandong-nut

quaveringly
quaternion'd
quaternions
qualitative
qualifiable
qualifiedly
quality time
quacksalver
quarrel-pane
quarrelling
quadrillion
quarrelsome
quarrellous
quadrennial
quadrennium
quarrington
quadrupedal
quadraphony
quadrophony
quadratical
quarry-water
quaestorial
quartz clock
quartz glass
quantum leap
Quantometer®
quantometer
quantum jump
quarterback
quarter-jack
quarter-rail
quarter-sawn
quarter past
quarterdeck
quarter-seal
quarter-wind
quarter-road
quarter note
quarter-tone
quarter hour
quarter bred
quarter-evil
quartz watch
queene-apple
Queen's Bench
queen-regent
Queen's Guide
queenliness
queen mother
queen's peace
Queen's Scout
queen-stitch
Queer Street
queer cuffin
questionary
questioning
questionist
question tag
querulously
queez-maddam
quibblingly
quitch grass
Quincy Jones
quincuncial
quiveringly
Quiberon Bay
quick-change
quick-firing
quick-witted
quicksilver
quicken-tree

 Words marked ✧ can also be spelled with one or more capital letters

quick-freeze
quick-frozen
quick assets
quick-sticks
quill-driver
quinquereme
quinquennia
quinsy-berry
quiescently
quintillion
quilting bee
quizzically
Qinhuangdao
quota sample
quotability
quota-hopper
quo warranto
quota system
quoteworthy
quodlibetic
real account
reawakening
readability
rhagadiform
rear admiral
Reaganomics
reascension
rhabdomancy
rhabdomyoma
Rhabdophora
reamendment
reach-me-down
road-hoggish
roadholding
realisation
realization
reanimation
reading-lamp
reading-desk
reading-book
reaping-hook
reading-room
realignment
reallotment
road manager
road-mending
readmission
rhamnaceous
real numbers
reappraisal
reappraiser
Rhamphastos
road pricing
realpolitik
reapportion
rear-roasted
rhapsodical
reassertion
reassurance
road scraper
reattribute
roasting pan
reactionary
reactionism
reactionist
readvertise
ready-witted
ready-monied
ready to drop
rib-vaulting
Rebecca West
rubicundity
rubber check
rubber-cored
rubber goods
rubberiness
rabbet-joint
rubber plant
rubber stamp
rubber-stamp
Robber Synod
riboflavine
rubefacient
rubefaction
rubrication
Robbie Burns
rabbit fever
rubbing post
rubbish heap
rabbit hutch
rib-tickling
rabbit punch
rebukefully
Rebekah Wade
Rabelaisian
rabble-rouse
rubble stone
rebroadcast
Ribbon Falls
ribbon-grass
rib-roasting
rebarbative
Robert Blake
Robert Brown
Robert Burns
Robert Bruce
Robert Boyle
Robert Cecil
Robert Cohan
Robert Clive
Robert Ensor
Robert Frost
Robert Hooke
Robert Remak
Ribesiaceae
Robespierre
rabattement
ruby wedding
reclamation
Richards Bay
Richard Gere
Richard Long
rock and roll
rack and ruin
Richard Kuhn
Richard Axel
rectangular
Rechabitism
racialistic
rechallenge
reclaimable
reclaimably
rock breaker
rice biscuit
ricocheting
ricochetted
rock climber
rock crystal
racket about
racket-court
rocker cover
recremental
Rock English
ricketiness
rocket motor
rocket plane
racket-press
rocker panel
rocket range
rickettsiae
rickettsial
rickettsias
rock-forming
recognitive
recognition
recognitory
Rockhampton
reclination
receivables
rectipetaly
rectiserial
rocking tool
recriminate
rectifiable
rectilineal
rectilinear
rock leather
rock lobster
recollected
recalescent
recalculate
recommender
race meeting
recompenser
recumbently
recombinant
recommittal
Rachmaninov
recantation
reconditely
recondition
reconfigure
rock'n'roller
reconnoitre
reconnoiter
reconstruct
receptacula
rice pudding
receptively
receptivity
reciprocate
reciprocant
reciprocity
recuperable
recuperator
recordation
recurvature
recurrently
rack railway
recirculate
rock sparrow
recessively
race suicide
recessional
rock the boat
recitatives
recitativos
recluseness
racquetball
recruitable
recountment
recruitment
recoverable
rock wallaby
race-walking
radiata pine
radial drill
red valerian
radiational
radiant heat
reductively
redactional
radicalness
radical chic
radical sign
radicellose
radical axis
redactorial
Rodney Marsh
redressable
Ridley Scott
Rediffusion®
red river hog
redding-kame
redding-comb
reddishness
Rudolf Kempe
riddle-me-ree
redeliverer
rodomontade
rudimentary
redemptible
redundantly
riding cloak
riding glove
riding habit
riding horse
rodenticide
riding light
riding-rhyme
riding skirt
rodent ulcer
radio galaxy
radiocarbon
radiopaging
radiolarian
radioactive
radioscopic
radio beacon
radiometric
radiophonic
radiologist
red-hot poker
radiography
radiolucent
reduplicate
red squirrel
redirection
radar beacon
Red Crescent
Rudesheimer
Rüdesheimer
rediscovery
ride shotgun
ride the beam
ride the rods
redetermine
redoubtable
redoubtably
re-enactment
reef-builder
reed bunting
re-encourage
reed-drawing
re-endowment
re-elevation
re-emergence
Riefenstahl
Rhenish wine
re-existence
rheological
rheumatical
rheumaticky
rheumateese
rhetorician
re-emphasise
re-emphasize
re-expansion
reed-sparrow
re-establish
rheotropism
Rhett Butler
re-education
reed warbler
refrangible
refractable
refectioner
refocillate
rifacimenti
rifacimento
refectorian
reflex angle
refreshment
refreshener
reflexively
reflexivity
refuellable
reflex light
reflexology
reflectance
refrigerate
refrigerant
refringency
raffishness
ruffianlike
refulgently
refinedness
refinancing
reflowering
reformative
re-formation
✧reformation
reformadoes
reformatory
Reform flask
referendary
referential
referendums
reformulate
refuse stays
Rifat Ozbeck
reggae music
Ragman Rolls
raggamuffin
rigidifying
regretfully
regredience
rogues' Latin
rogue's march
rogues' march
ragged Robin
ragged right
ragged staff
regrettable
regrettably
rigging loft
rigging-tree
roguishness
Reggie White
regimentals
regenerable
regenerator
regionalise
regionalize
regionalism
regionalist
regardfully
regurgitate
regurgitant
Roger Corman
rigor mortis
register ton
registrable
right-handed
right-hander
rightwardly
right-of-ways
right of feud
right of drip
right-minded
right-winger
rights issue
right-angled
right enough
right-to-life
righteously
right-footed
rights-of-way
right as rain
right atrium
regium donum
Rugby School
✧rugby league
rugby jersey
rehydration
rail against
roi fainéant
rhizanthous
rain-chamber
reincarnate
Reindeer Age
reiterative
reiteration
raised beach
raise a siege
raise a stink
reinflation
reification
reificatory
rhizomatous
rhizocarpic
rhinoscopic
raison d'être
raison d'état
rhinocerote
rhizogenous
rhinoplasty
rhinologist
rhizosphere
rhinorrhoea
ruinousness
railroad car
reinstation
reinsertion
reinsurance
Reil's island

reintegrate
reintroduce
reinterment
reinterpret
reinvention
Railway Club
rejoicement
rejoicingly
rejoneadora
Rijksmuseum
Rajiv Gandhi
rejuvenesce
rejuvenator
releasement
reliability
reluctation
reluctantly
relict organ
relic-monger
Rollerblade®
rollerblade
rollerblind
roller derby
roller skate
roller-skate
rallentandi
rallentando
roller towel
religionary
religionise
religionize
religionism
religionist
religiosity
religiously
Ralph Lauren
rolling news
rolling mill
rule of faith
rule of three
rule of thumb
rule-of-thumb
role-playing
relatedness
relationism
relationist
rallying-cry
rummage sale
remediation
remigration
rumti-iddity
rompishness
Ramakrishna
rumble strip
✧remembrance
Roman candle
roman à clefs
Roman cement
Roman nettle
Raman effect
romanticise
romanticize
✧romanticism
romanticist
roman fleuve
Roman Empire
Roman sorrel
Romano Prodi
remunerable
remunerator
reminiscent

remonstrate
✧remonstrant
roman à thèse
Ram Mohan Roy
Rambouillet
RBMK reactor
remorseless
Rumer Godden
remissively
remittently
romp through
rumgumption
ramgunshoch
rumbustical
rumbustious
removedness
rank and file
rentability
ring binding
ring-carrier
ring circuit
Ranger Guide
rangefinder
rannell-balk
ringed snake
ring-fencing
röntgen rays
renegotiate
run the guard
rinthereout
running hand
running mate
running back
running head
running gear
running text
running fire
running time
running high
running knot
ranging pole
ringing tone
running sore
✧renaissance
Ronald Biggs
Rene Lacoste
René Laënnec
randle-perch
Ring Lardner
run into debt
run one's face
ring network
run together
Runyonesque
rondolettos
rancorously
run to ground
rinforzando
run up a score
renormalise
renormalize
ring spanner
ring stopper
ring-straked
ring the bell
ring the shed
renewedness
ring-winding
Randy Newman
Rhopalocera
rhombohedra

rhomboideus
root climber
room-divider
Rhode Island
roofing felt
rhodium-wood
reorientate
Rhodian laws
rhododaphne
rhododendra
riotousness
root-pruning
rood-steeple
room service
replaceable
replacement
raptatorial
republisher
rapscallion
rapaciously
repudiative
repudiation
reprehender
repleteness
representee
representer
representor
repleviable
replenished
replenisher
repressible
repressibly
repugnantly
replicative
reprivatise
reprivatize
replication
reptilianly
repellantly
repellently
repulsively
repellingly
rope machine
repentantly
repentingly
ripsnorting
reprobative
reprobation
reprobatory
reproachful
reprovingly
reprogramme
reprography
reportingly
repartition
reportorial
report stage
Rupert's drop
reparations
reposedness
rapeseed oil
repossessor
ropes of sand
reposefully
reputed pint
repatriator
repetitious
raptureless
rupturewort
rapturously
rope-walking

request note
request stop
Raquel Welch
requiteless
requirement
requitement
requisitely
requisition
requisitory
Requiem Mass
Rory Bremner
reradiation
ruridecanal
rarefactive
rarefaction
Ras Tafarian
✧rastafarian
researchful
restatement
rascalliest
rush bearing
rosy-bosomed
rose-cheeked
rosy-cheeked
resectional
rose campion
risk capital
Rosicrucian
rose diamond
residential
russet apple
resveratrol
risperidone
respectable
respectably
respectless
restfulness
resignation
Rosh Hashana
respiration
rustication
respiratory
rescindable
rescindment
respite care
restiveness
Russianness
Russian vine
Russian doll
restitutive
restitution
restitutory
resultative
reselection
resiliently
resplendent
resemblance
resinifying
resentfully
resentingly
Rosencrantz
restorative
✧restoration
respondence
respondency
Russophobia
Russophobic
Rostov-on-Don
responsible
responsibly
responsions

resipiscent
reservation
reservatory
restrictive
restriction
restructure
reserve bank
resurrector
restraining
restringent
resuscitate
resuscitant
resistively
resistingly
resistivity
Rose Tremain
resourceful
rescue-grass
res judicata
rosewood oil
res extincta
ritual abuse
rat-catching
ritual choir
retraceable
rat-kangaroo
rateability
ritualistic
retranslate
retractable
retractible
reticularly
reticulated
rate-capping
rate-cutting
rotten apple
rother-beast
rottenstone
retreatment
rotogravure
ratchet down
retributive
retribution
retributory
retrievable
retrievably
retaliative
retaliation
retaliatory
rattlebrain
rattle-pated
rattlesnake
retinaculum
retinacular
retentively
retentivity
retinispora
retinospora
retinoscope
retinoscopy
rationalise
rationalize
rationalism
rationalist
rationality
retroactive
retroaction
retrocedent
retroverted
retrolental
retrophilia

ratiocinate
retrofitted
retroflexed
ration money
retro-rocket
retroussage
retrobulbar
ritardandos
retardative
Rotarianism
retardation
retardatory
retiredness
retired list
ritornellos
rotary index
return match
Ruth Rendell
return order
rotary press
return shock
ratatouille
ritournelle
rhumb course
raunchiness
round-backed
roundedness
round-headed
round-leaved
round window
round-winged
roundarched
Rouge Dragon
rouge-et-noir
rough-handle
rough-legged
reupholster
rough collie
rough-coated
rough-footed
rough-spoken
rough string
rouping-wife
Ruud Lubbers
raucousness
revealingly
revaccinate
rival-hating
revaluation
revoltingly
Revelations
revengeless
revengement
revendicate
revindicate
revengingly
River Paraná
River Pahang
River Salado
River Gambia
River Ganges
River Yamuna
River Danube
River Ubangi
reverberate
reverse pass
reverberant
River Severn
reverse gear
reverseless
River Seyhan

River Mersey
River Jhelum
River Thames
River Chenab
River Ribble
River Liffey
rover ticket
reversional
reversioner
River Tigris
River Kistna
River Vltava
River Clutha
River Amazon
reverential
River Dnestr
River Jordan
River Tornio
river bottom
riverworthy
River Kolyma
river-dragon
river-driver
River Irtysh
River Escaut
River Humber
River Sutlej
river mussel
Ravi Shankar
ravishingly
revisionary
revisionism
revisionist
rivet hearth
revivifying
revivescent
reviviscent
raw material
Rex Harrison
Rex Williams
Roy Campbell
rhynchocoel
rhynchodont
rhyme scheme
rhyme letter
rhythmicity
royal octavo
royal tennis
Roy Eldridge
royal assent
royal purple
royal quarto
Royal Lytham
Raymond Dart
Ray Bradbury
razzamatazz
scarabaeist
scarabaeoid
sea lavender
seakale beet
svarabhakti
scalability
scalariform
shamanistic
sparagmatic
stalagmitic
Stabat Mater
✧scaramouche
spanakopita
sham Abraham
sea passport
stalactical
stalactitic
stalactited
stalactital
scabbedness
scamblingly
soap boiling
shad-bellied
swag-bellied
star billing
Scarborough
seam bowling
✧star chamber
snatch block
starch-grain
search image
starchiness
searchingly
snatchingly
stanchioned
searchlight
Sean Connery
star-crossed
starch paper
snatch-purse
search party
sea scorpion
snatch squad
snatch-thief
span-counter
standpatter
shard beetle
standoffish
scandaliser
scandalizer
standing bed
slam dancing
stand to gain
standardise
standardize
stand at ease
stage-manage
spade mashie
spacefaring
sharefarmer
slave labour
stake a claim
state school
Space Oddity
slate pencil
shamelessly
shapelessly
statemented
space heater
stage effect
state of play
sea hedgehog
space charge
stave-church
snake lizard
shapeliness
stateliness
slaveringly
stage rights
sharemilker
snake-hipped
shared logic
stage flower
stage-player
statesmanly
scale insect
shame on them
shareholder
slaveholder
stakeholder
scaremonger
state-monger
shameworthy
Shakespeare
spacer plate
share option
slave-trader
stage fright
scale armour
state prison
slate-writer
space writer
skate around
space travel
slave-driver
slave states
stage-struck
share-pusher
spade guinea
scaberulous
stateswoman
Sean Edwards
stately home
stagflation
snaffle-rein
Sea of Nectar
staff of life
scaffoldage
scaffolding
Sea of Clouds
Sea of Crises
seal-fishing
staff-system
shanghaiing
shaggedness
shagge-eared
spang-cockle
swagger cane
swagger coat
St Augustine
slaughtered
slaughterer
spathaceous
spathic iron
staphylitis
swan-hopping
slasher film
spaghettini
suasiveness
scapigerous
seaming lace
staging base
sparingness
skating rink
shaving-soap
staging post
staging area
searing-iron
Spanish walk
Spanish-walk
Spanish Main
slavishness
snakishness
Spanish rice
stadia hairs
Spanish fowl
Spanish Town
Spanish soap
Spanish moss
stabilisers
stabilizers
seasickness
sea milkwort
sea-milkwort
spaniel-like
stadia lines
stadium rock
station hand
staminodium
stasimorphy
statistical
slack-handed
shark patrol
shackle-bone
shackle-bolt
sparklessly
sparklingly
sharksucker
stack system
span loading
Stahlianism
snail darter
stallmaster
small octave
small screen
small-screen
Stahlhelmer
small letter
small change
small circle
small-minded
small claims
snail flower
stalling-ken
smallholder
small wonder
stallholder
shawl collar
small cornet
sea elephant
scarlet bean
staple towns
small quarto
swallowtail
shallowness
swallow-dive
swallow hole
swallow-wort
spasmodical
spasmolytic
Shalmaneser
spasmatical
stannic acid
shawnee-wood
stainlessly
staunchable
staunchless
staunchness
spawning-bed
skaines mate
St Agnes's Eve
seasonality
Star of David
sea rosemary
sea colewort
shadow fight
shadow forth
sharon fruit
shadowgraph
sea longworm
shadowiness
Slavonicise
Slavonicize
shadow price
sialorrhoea
sialography
Sharon Stone
snap out of it
sea dotterel
stamp office
scalpriform
sharp-witted
sharp-ground
staircasing
stair carpet
staurolitic
Starry Night
seal rookery
stauroscope
sparrowhawk
sparrow-bill
snapshooter
seamstressy
star-studded
smarty-boots
spastically
Shasta daisy
stay the pace
scant-o'-grace
swarthiness
startlingly
smart-ticket
star thistle
smart-alecky
Shatt al-Arab
stactometer
staktometer
starting gun
stadtholder
smartypants
shatter-pate
spatterdash
scatterable
scatteredly
scattershot
scatterling
scattergood
starter home
spatterdock
spatterwork
scatter rugs
sea furbelow
statute mile
statute book
statutorily
sea purslane
sea cucumber
seam welding
✧sabbatarian
subpanation
subparallel
subcardinal
subbasement
subcategory
sublanguage
submarginal
Sabbathless
subtacksman
subharmonic
subcapsular
sebacic acid
subacidness
subscribing
subeconomic
subscapular
sabre-rattle
subdeaconry
submergible
submergence
subdelirium
subaerially
subregional
subcellular
subterminal
submersible
subsensible
subvertical
subjectless
subjectship
subsequence
subservient
subaffluent
subchloride
sublimation
subdiaconal
sublimeness
subdivisive
subdivision
subvitreous
submissible
submissness
subdistrict
subsistence
sublittoral
subglobular
suballiance
subclinical
subimaginal
subimagines
subumbrella
subindicate
subincision
Sabine's gull
Subungulata
subungulate
subindustry
subvocalise
subvocalize
subrogation
submolecule
subdominant
subcontract
subcontrary
subcortical
subspecific
suburbanise
suburbanite
suburbanize
suburbanism
saburration
subarration
subornation
suburbanity
subtreasury
suberic acid
subtractive
subtraction
subfreezing
seborrhoeic
subirrigate

subordinate
subordinacy
subordinary
sober-minded
subarboreal
subprioress
subtropical
subcritical
✧sybaritical
sober-suited
subassemble
subassembly
substrative
substractor
substandard
substantive
substantial
subitaneous
substituent
substituted
subjugation
subluxation
subjunctive
subjunction
subduedness
subaudition
submunition
subsumptive
subsumption
submultiple
subcultural
subaxillary
such-and-such
sacramental
sociability
socialistic
social whale
sick benefit
sick chamber
sockdolager
sockdoliger
sockdologer
succedaneum
secret agent
secretarial
secretariat
Sacred Heart
secretively
sickeningly
secretional
sycee silver
sacred music
sucker-punch
successless
sucket spoon
Sacher torte
Sachertorte
saccharated
succinctory
sacrilegist
sacring bell
sucking fish
sickishness
sacrificial
section mark
sectionally
suction stop
suction pump
secular hymn
sycomore fig
Socinianise
Socinianize
Socinianism
secondarily
second class
second-class
second floor
second-floor
second-guess
second joint
sicknursing
Second Reich
second-rater
seconds hand
second sight
Second World
sociopathic
sociometric
sociologese
sociologism
sociologist
sacrocostal
succourable
succourless
sycophantic
sycophantry
secessional
sick to death
sacculation
succulently
sacculiform
soda cracker
seductively
side cutting
sudden death
Sudden Light
Sidney Nolan
Sydneysider
Sydney Smith
sedigitated
saddlecloth
saddle-girth
saddle horse
saddle-nosed
sedimentary
sodomitical
sedentarily
sidereal day
siderophile
sideropenia
sedes vacans
sidestepper
seditionary
seditiously
sodium amide
Sadduceeism
sede vacante
St David's Day
side-wheeler
stewardship
shenanigans
see daylight
spelaeothem
spelaeology
steganogram
stepbrother
speechcraft
speech-crier
sketchiness
speechifier
stencilling
speechmaker
seed capital
speed camera
steadfastly
steady-going
spendthrift
speedometer
stepdancing
spend a penny
slenderness
steady state
siege basket
Steve Martin
Steve Paxton
stereoblind
stereobatic
scène à faire
stereograph
stevengraph
stereometer
stereometry
skeleton bob
skeletonise
skeletonize
skeleton key
stereoptics
stereophony
stereosonic
stereoscope
stereoscopy
stereotypic
stereotyped
stereotyper
stereotaxia
stereotaxic
stereotaxis
shelftalker
sleigh bells
sledge-chair
Spenglerian
sdeignfully
Spergularia
see the light
Stephen King
Stephen Gray
stephanotis
shepherdess
stethoscope
stethoscopy
sheriffship
sheriffalty
sheriffhood
seemingness
specificate
specifiable
specificity
specialness
specialogue
special area
specialised
specialiser
specialized
specializer
Stevie Smith
sleek-headed
speakership
sneck drawer
shell jacket
shell parrot
shellacking
swelled head
steel-headed
swell-headed
stellifying
shed light on
spellbinder
steel-plated
spelling bee
stellionate
steelworker
steel collar
stelleridan
stellar wind
shell-crater
stellarator
sperm candle
steam jacket
steam packet
steam hammer
steam launch
spermicidal
steam vessel
spermogonia
spermogones
steam shovel
steam engine
steam boiler
steam-roller
spermophile
spermaphyte
spermophyte
steamer clam
steamer duck
steam-driven
St Elmo's fire
spermatical
spermatheca
spermatozoa
Steinberger
sternsheets
stern-chaser
seeing stone
sternotribe
sternutator
✧sweeney todd
stenocardia
stenohaline
✧stegosaurus
sceuophylax
stenochrome
stenochromy
see you later
stenotropic
scenography
stenography
stenotypist
sweep-washer
sleepwalker
sheep-farmer
sheep-master
suet pudding
steepedowne
steeplejack
steeple fair
sleeplessly
steeplebush
sheep-biting
sheep-silver
sleeping bag
sleeping car
Steppenwolf
sleep apnoea
sleep around
sweepstakes
stearic acid
steerage way
Sierra Leone
sherris-sack
SPET scanner
spessartine
spessartite
spectrality
stentmaster
sweet pastry
spectacular
sceptically
skeptically
sheath dress
sheet-feeder
sceptreless
sweetie-wife
sweet fennel
sweet pepper
spectre crab
sweet sherry
sleuth-hound
sweet cicely
sweet willow
sheath knife
sheet anchor
sweet potato
spectrology
sheet copper
spectrogram
scent bottle
steatopygia
scepterless
shelterless
shelter belt
shelter tent
steatorrhea
sweater-girl
sweet orange
spectatress
sheet rubber
sweet sultan
speculative
speculation
speculatist
speculatory
speculatrix
sleeve board
sleaved silk
sleeve notes
see eye to eye
safe-breaker
safe-blowing
soft chancre
safe-cracker
soft-centred
safe-conduct
safe-deposit
soft-hearted
suffixation
sufficience
sufficiency
safekeeping
soft landing
suffocative
suffocating
suffocation
suffragette
saffron cake
so far so good
soft-shelled
soft science
safety catch
safety glass
safety light
safety match
safety paper
sift through
safety razor
safety valve
suffumigate
sagaciously
segregative
segregation
suggestible
segmentally
significate
significant
signifiable
sigillarian
sigillation
sigmoidally
sago pudding
sign-painter
sugar of lead
sugar sifter
sugar glider
sugaring off
sugar-coated
Sagittarian
Sagittarius
sight screen
sight-reader
sightseeing
sightlessly
sightliness
sight-singer
sagittiform
sight-player
sight unseen
sightworthy
sign-writing
sphragistic
schwärmerei
Schwann cell
sphacelated
schecklaton
Schick's test
schreech-owl
Schlesinger
sphaeridium
schrecklich
Schiff's base
sphagnology
sphygmology
sphygmogram
scholiastic
schillerise
schillerize
so help me God
scholarship
scholar-like
schematical
sphingosine
sphincteric
sphincteral
school board
schoolcraft
schoolchild
schoolgoing
school house

Words marked ✧ can also be spelled with one or more capital letters

schoolhouse
Schrödinger
school nurse
school point
school shark
schoolwards
scherzandos
spherically
Scharnhorst
spheroidise
spheroidize
spherulitic
spherometer
schorlomite
schismatise
schismatize
schism house
schistosity
Schistosoma
schistosome
schottische
schizogenic
schizanthus
schizopodal
Schizophyta
schizophyte
spiral bound
spinal canal
spinal chord
spic and span
spinach beet
Scitamineae
spina bifida
suitability
spiraliform
spiraculate
sailboarder
swim bladder
ship-breaker
shipbuilder
stilbestrol
ship biscuit
spin bowling
switchboard
switchblade
stitchcraft
scincoidian
switch-plant
spindle-legs
spindle side
spindle hole
spindle tree
spine-basher
scire facias
swivelblock
swivel-chair
swine's cress
spinescence
stipendiate
stipendiary
spinelessly
shiveringly
shigellosis
spider plant
stilettoing
slime fungus
slide guitar
spider wheel
stiff-necked
spifflicate
skilfulness
swing-handle
swingle-hand
swingletree
sling the bat
swingeingly
swing-plough
swingometer
swing bridge
slightingly
stichometry
smithsonite
smithereens
suicide pact
spiniferous
spinigerous
sliding keel
ship it green
shiningness
smilingness
sliding seat
sailing ship
sailing boat
sliding-rule
swinishness
spiritistic
spirillosis
spirit level
suicidology
spirit rally
spirituelle
spiritually
spiritualty
spirit world
stickhandle
stickleback
stickleader
stick insect
slickenside
snickersnee
snick or snee
stick or snee
stick around
skillcentre
skilligalee
skilligolee
Scilly Isles
stifle-joint
still and all
still and end
spill-stream
still-hunter
seismic wave
seismically
skimmed milk
slimmed-down
seismograph
seismologic
seismometer
seismometry
seismonasty
skimmington
shimmy-shake
skirmishing
seismoscope
stigmatical
science park
scientistic
skinny latte
spinning top
seigniorage
seigniorial
Scientology
Scientology®
spinnerette
seigneurial
spirometric
spirochaete
Spinozistic
Shimon Peres
spirography
shinplaster
slipped disc
skin-popping
slipper bath
slippery elm
slipperwort
ship railway
stirrup bone
stirrup dram
stirrup iron
stirrup pump
ship's papers
spinsterdom
spinsterish
spinsterial
spinsterian
soil science
shin splints
Swiss fondue
scissor case
scissortail
scissorwise
scissor kick
scissorbill
scissor hold
Swiss Guards
stilt-walker
saintpaulia
Saint-Paulin
Sainte-Beuve
sciatically
stiltedness
stintedness
stilted arch
skittle-ball
ship the oars
Saint Helena
shiftlessly
shittah tree
saintliness
swift-winged
scintillate
scintillant
shirtsleeve
stilt-plover
shittim wood
spintronics
shift worker
swift-footed
skirt around
skim through
skip through
shinty-stick
shirt button
stimulative
stimulating
stimulation
stipulation
stimulatory
stipulatory
Switzerland
St John's wort
sojournment
St Kunigunde
Sal Paradise
syllabarium
sallal berry
salvageable
saltarellos
soldatesque
self-affairs
syllabicate
saleability
salvability
solvability
syllabicity
sulfadoxine
saltatorial
Salvadorian
self-assumed
self-assured
salableness
self-blinded
self-basting
self-charity
silicic acid
self-cocking
salicaceous
self-created
selectively
selectivity
self-culture
self-command
self-concern
self-conceit
self-concept
self-content
silicon chip
self-centred
self-control
self-closing
selectorial
salaciously
self-covered
solid matter
solidifying
self-defence
splodginess
self-delight
self-damning
self-denying
solid-hoofed
solid colour
self-despair
salad burnet
self-devoted
self-example
silver birch
self-excited
self-elected
silver-grain
silveriness
self-evident
Silver Latin
silver medal
self-evolved
silver plate
self-express
silverpoint
silver paper
sallee-rover
silversides
silver steel
silversmith
silver-stick
Silverstone
spleenstone
sylleptical
silvestrian
sylvestrian
silver white
silver-white
self-feeding
self-feeling
self-figured
self-fertile
solifluxion
salt glazing
selaginella
self-healing
self-harming
sulphureous
sulphur-root
sulphurwort
sulphureted
sulphurator
sulphur tuft
sulphhydryl
sillimanite
solmisation
solmization
saltimbocca
saltimbanco
self-induced
saltirewise
selling race
salpingitic
salpingitis
saltishness
selfishness
Sylvia Plath
self-imposed
soldiership
soldierlike
soldier crab
self-invited
self-knowing
self-loading
self-locking
self-limited
soliloquise
soliloquize
soliloquist
self-mockery
sal ammoniac
self-mastery
self-misused
selenic acid
solanaceous
splenectomy
splinter bar
selenograph
self-neglect
splendidous
salinometer
splendorous
splenetical
sal volatile
sulfonamide
sulfonation
salmonberry
salmon coble
self-opening
salmonellae
salmonellas
self-offence
self-opinion
syllogistic
saloon rifle
salmon spear
seldom-times
sallow-thorn
salmon trout
self-planted
solipsistic
self-pitying
self-pruning
self-powered
sclerocauly
scleroderma
self-raising
self-reliant
self-relying
solar plexus
sclerometer
solarimeter
sal prunella
sal prunelle
solar energy
self-reproof
sclerophyll
self-respect
sclerotioid
sclerotitis
solar system
self-sealing
Silas Marner
self-starter
splashboard
self-subdued
self-sterile
self-seeking
salesperson
splashproof
self-support
self-service
self-serving
self-trained
split screen
split-screen
sell the pass
spluttering
split second
split-second
self-tempted
solutionist
solution set
self-tapping
self-torment
self-torture
sell through
sell-through
silk-thrower
sclate-stane
salsuginous
Silbury Hill
Salk vaccine
self-winding
silkworm-gut
self-worship
silly season
silly mid-off
splay-footed
somnambulic
somnambular

Samian earth
sympathique
sympathiser
sympathetic
sympathizer
summariness
summational
semi-annular
Samian stone
semi-aquatic
semicircled
semi-diurnal
symmetalism
symmetallic
sympetalous
simnel bread
semper eadem
summerhouse
simperingly
semi-ellipse
Samuel Morse
Samuel Pepys
symmetrical
summer stock
summersault
sempervivum
summer wheat
symphonious
sempiternal
sempiternum
somniferous
summit-level
summit talks
semi-jubilee
semelparity
semelparous
simpliciter
simulacrums
simplifying
Simple Minds
sembling box
sampler-work
sample space
semi-monthly
Simon Rattle
Simon Schama
Simon Legree
semanticist
same numeric
Simon Hughes
someone else
somnolently
symbol group
semiotician
sympodially
symposiarch
symbolistic
semiologist
symbolology
Sam Torrance
Samson's post
semipalmate
sempstering
semi-skilled
semi-skimmed
semasiology
semi-trailer
semi-tubular
somatic cell
somatically
somatogenic

so mote I thee
somatologic
somatomedin
symptomatic
semi-tropics
sumptuosity
sumptuously
somatoplasm
somatotonia
somatotonic
summum bonum
summum genus
somewhither
Sennacherib
sensational
San Pablo Bay
Sunday lunch
syntagmatic
Singaporean
Sunday punch
Sunday saint
sandal shoon
Sunday Sport
syntactical
San Salvador
sandblaster
sandbox tree
synecologic
sansculotte
synecdochic
sand-casting
sang-de-boeuf
synodically
Sandemanian
sincereness
senselessly
sansevieria
synoeciosis
syndesmoses
syndesmosis
syndesmotic
synoecology
sinlessness
sunlessness
sanderswood
syntectical
sententious
son of a bitch
sin-offering
Sinn Feinism
songfulness
sonographer
synagogical
synchromesh
synchronise
synchronize
synchronism
synchronous
synchrotron
sancho-pedro
synchoresis
synthesiser
synthesizer
synthetical
synthetiser
synthetizer
syndicalism
syndication
syndicalist
Sanni Abacha

sentinelled
sentimental
singing sand
singing-bird
sinking fund
sensitively
sensibility
sensitivity
Sanskritist
single-blind
single cream
single-cross
single-digit
single-ended
single-entry
Sinological
single house
synclinoria
single-phase
singlestick
singles club
single-soled
Syngman Rhee
synanthesis
synanthetic
synonymical
synonymicon
synonymatic
syngnathous
syncopation
sensorially
sinfonietta
Song of my Cid
Sandown Park
sindonology
sinuousness
Song of Songs
send packing
Sinophilism
synoptistic
sinupallial
synergistic
sundrenched
song sparrow
sinisterity
sand-skipper
Sinus Iridum
sinistrally
sinistrorse
sand spurrey
sanctuarise
sanctuarize
Sino-Tibetan
send to dorse
sanctifying
senate-house
sanctioneer
senatorship
sanatoriums
sanitariums
sand-thrower
sanctus bell
singularise
singularize
singularism
singularist
singularity
sensualness
sanguineous
sanguinaria
Sensurround®

Sanguisorba
sandwich man
sandwich tin
sinews of war
sunny side up
Sonny Liston
sandy blight
Sandy Koufax
syndyasmian
show-and-tell
sporangiola
sporangiole
stomachache
stomachical
stomachless
stomach pump
stomachfuls
sloganising
sloganizing
stomatology
snowboarder
snowblading
snobbocracy
shopbreaker
snow bunting
Scotch broth
Scotch cuddy
Scotch catch
scorchingly
Scotch-Irish
stoicalness
Scotchwoman
sword-bearer
sword-shaped
spondulicks
spondylosis
spondylitic
spondylitis
swordplayer
sword-dollar
snow-dropper
stone falcon
stonewashed
stonewaller
stone hammer
store farmer
store cattle
stone marten
shovelboard
smokescreen
smoke helmet
storekeeper
smokelessly
shore effect
stone circle
showeriness
smoke signal
scoleciform
stone plover
stove enamel
stone-colour
showerproof
stoneground
stone's-throw
snowed under
stone curlew
smoke tunnel
stonecutter
spokeswoman
spokeswomen
sponge cloth

snow-goggles
smörgåsbord
soothsaying
soothfastly
smother mate
scoriaceous
scoring card
smoking room
spolia opima
showjumping
stock saddle
stocktaking
stock market
stock-farmer
Stockhausen
shock-headed
stock-feeder
shopkeeping
stockpiling
snorkelling
stocking cap
stock in horn
stockinette
stockjobber
stockholder
shock horror
shock-horror
stockbroker
shock troops
shoe leather
shoulder bag
shouldering
smouldering
shoulder pad
shoplifting
stool pigeon
Scotlandite
snow leopard
spoilt paper
shoe latchet
slot machine
storm cellar
storm petrel
storm centre
storm-beaten
storm window
storm signal
showmanship
storm collar
storm-tossed
storm troops
storm-stayed
scoundrelly
slow neutron
scopolamine
scotomatous
spodomantic
scolopendra
sporogenous
scopophobia
Scotophobia
Scotophobic
scopophilia
Scotophilia
scopophilic
Scotophilic
show of hands
sporophoric
sporophytic
sporogonium
snobography

sporocystic
scorpaenoid
shopping bag
stopping-out
scorpion fly
slow-release
Stourbridge
shop steward
slow-sighted
stoss and lee
show-stopper
sponsorship
snowsurfing
Scots Guards
short-handed
scoutmaster
sportcaster
short pastry
smooth-bored
short-acting
spottedness
spotted dick
stop the show
scouthering
show the flag
short-termer
short tennis
snout beetle
smooth-faced
Scottifying
short shrift
short-change
shoot the sun
smooth hound
short-winded
shorten sail
shooting box
spontaneity
spontaneous
snotty-nosed
shooting war
shortcoming
Scott Joplin
short corner
smooth-paced
short-spoken
short-priced
scout around
smooth snake
sports shirt
short-staple
sportswoman
sporulation
storyteller
smoky quartz
supracostal
sapucaia-nut
suppedaneum
supremacism
✧suprematism
septenarius
supremacist
✧suprematist
Septembrist
supper cloth
supremeness
supper party
saplessness
so please you
septentrial
septentrion

septicaemia
septicaemic
septiferous
Sophia Loren
syphilology
septifragal
sophistical
suppliantly
supply chain
supply curve
supplicavit
sepulchrous
supply-sider
saponaceous
saponifying
sipunculoid
sapropelite
saprolegnia
saprogenous
saprophytic
suppositive
supposition
suppository
saprobiotic
siphonogamy
supportable
supportably
supportless
supportress
supportment
sepiostaire
supportance
support hose
support area
supernatant
superjacent
supersafety
superlative
superfamily
supertanker
supermarket
superdainty
superfatted
supernature
superabound
superoctave
superscreen
superactive
superscribe
superscript
superscalar
superfetate
supersedere
supersedeas
superrefine
superweapon
superheater
supersedure
superphylum
supercharge
supercherie
superficial
supervision
superficies
supervisory
superfluity
superfluous
supersleuth
superimpose
superintend
superinfect
superinduce
superioress
supersonics
superiority
supercoiled
supernormal
supervolute
superbright
superpraise
suppressant
suppressive
suppression
superstrong
superstruct
superlunary
superfusion
supersubtle
sapotaceous
suppurative
suppuration
sequestrate
sequestrant
sequestered
serrasalmos
surtarbrand
Sir Lancelot
surface mail
surbasement
spread eagle
spread-eagle
surface wind
streakiness
streaminess
screamingly
spreadingly
streamingly
streamlined
surpassable
spreadsheet
Sargasso Sea
servant-maid
servant-lass
servantless
servantship
servant-girl
serratulate
scrobicular
scribacious
shrubberied
shrubbiness
strabometer
stroboscope
surf-bathing
scrub turkey
scrub typhus
sericterium
sericulture
Saracenical
seroconvert
surfcasting
Straduarius
suraddition
stridulator
stride piano
Sergey Bubka
screencraft
street cries
sarcenchyme
surrenderee
surrenderer
surrenderor
screech-hawk
Sir Bedivere
shriekingly
Sergey Kirov
surveillant
streetlight
Serge Blanco
street-level
surgeonship
surgeonfish
streetscape
streetsmart
sarsen-stone
screen saver
street style
serpentlike
serpentinic
serpent-star
surrebuttal
surrebutter
street value
screen-wiper
streetwards
series-wound
scruffiness
serigraphic
serigrapher
scragginess
Sir J G Frazer
sprightless
survival bag
survivalism
survivalist
service mark
Servile Wars
serviceable
serviceably
serviceless
service line
service pipe
service wire
service flat
service road
service book
service room
service area
service tree
strain gauge
straight-arm
straight-cut
straightish
straight-jet
straight man
straight off
straight out
straight-out
straight tip
straightway
serpiginous
strait-laced
servitorial
surmistress
strike a pose
strikebound
strike force
strike fault
strike hands
stroke index
strike plate
strike price
scroll chuck
serological
Sir J M Barrie
scrimshoner
scrimshandy
scrimpiness
stramineous
shrimp plant
scrumptious
spring a leak
spring a mine
string along
springboard
stringboard
spring-clean
strong drink
strangeness
stringently
Springfield
strong flour
strong force
spring fever
springhouse
springiness
stringiness
stringing up
shrinkingly
serendipity
Surinam toad
spring onion
strenuosity
syringotomy
strenuously
string piece
strong point
strongpoint
shrink-proof
spring scale
Springsteen
strengthful
strangulate
spring wheat
strong wheat
springwater
stringy-bark
strongyloid
surrogation
sarcomatous
sarcoidosis
sarcolemmal
sorrowfully
sarcophagal
sarcophagus
Sir Robin Day
sardonicism
sartorially
Sorbonnical
surmounting
surrounding
Sir John Ross
seriousness
sorbo rubber
sarcocystis
strap-hanger
scrape along
striped bass
strip search
strip-search
strep throat
strap-shaped
scrappiness
Soroptimist
scriptorial
scriptorium
scripophile
scripophily
scrapepenny
scraper ring
scripturism
scripturist
surprisedly
stressed out
stressed-out
stratocracy
serotherapy
stratifying
strategical
strategetic
scratchcard
scratchback
scratchless
stretchless
scratch test
stretch limo
scratch blue
scratch-work
scratch coat
stretch over
struttingly
Struthiones
serotine bat
scrutiniser
scrutinizer
stratopause
serrulation
sertularian
surturbrand
scriveboard
shrivelling
screwballer
screw-capped
strawweight
screw thread
scrawniness
scrawlingly
straw flower
strawflower
screwing die
straw-colour
screw-topped
screw-wrench
screwdriver
straw-cutter
spray drying
syssarcoses
syssarcosis
sustainable
sustainedly
sustainment
systematise
systematize
systematism
systematics
systematist
Susie Salmon
system-built
sister-in-law
system-maker
Susie Orbach
suspensible
suspenseful
susceptible
suspectable
susceptibly
suspectedly
suspectless
susceptance
sustentator
suscitation
suspiration
sessile-eyed
sessionally
sesame grass
Susan Faludi
Susan Sontag
susurration
sesquialter
sesquioxide
sesquipedal
Sissy Spacek
satiability
sat sapienti
situational
Satyajit Ray
Sitka spruce
setter-forth
set the scene
Sothic cycle
sitting room
sitting duck
sottishness
set little by
settledness
satellitise
satellitize
satellitium
settling day
satanically
satin finish
satin flower
set in motion
Satan monkey
satanophany
set one's hand
set one's seal
set one's mind
satin stitch
sitiophobia
set to rights
saturnalian
satirically
saturninely
soteriology
Saturn's tree
satisfiable
satisficing
set at naught
set at nought
Satsuma ware
sausage meat
sausage roll
sausage tree
squeakiness
squeakingly
squeamishly
scuba diving
shunamitism
stubble rake
stumblingly
soul brother
slumbrously
slumberland
slumberless
slumbersome

spud-bashing
scutch grass
sculduddery
skulduddery
slum-dweller
soundlessly
sculduggery
skulduggery
sound shadow
spudding bit
sounding out
sounding rod
shuddersome
sound system
spumescence
stupendious
squeeze play
squeeze home
sauce-crayon
souter's clod
studentship
snuff-taking
soul-fearing
soufflé dish
shufflingly
snuff-dipper
soulfulness
stuffing box
snuff-colour
spur gearing
stun grenade
slumgullion
sluggardise
sluggardize
southlander
southwardly
South Dakota
sought after
south-easter
south-wester
South Africa
Southampton
southernise
southernize
southernism
southermost
Southern Sea
South Island
South Utsire
south-by-east
south-by-west
saurischian
studio couch
studiedness
Saudi Arabia
soul-killing
soup kitchen
spur leather
squalidness
Skull Island
squandering
squintingly
sauropodous
sauropsidan
stump speech
scuppernong
stump orator
sculpturing
squirearchy
square-built
square dance
square-dance
square metre
squarsonage
squirarchal
sauerbraten
Studs Terkel
soul-sleeper
squashiness
saussuritic
stuntedness
scuttle cask
Sturt Desert
shuttlewise
shuttlecock
scuttlebutt
stultifying
squat thrust
squattiness
shutterless
scurvy grass
savableness
savoir-faire
savoir-vivre
seven-league
seventeenth
saving grace
savings bank
sovereignly
sovereignty
severalfold
save the mark
Sivatherium
savouriness
saw palmetto
sewage works
sow the seeds
sexual abuse
sex-reversal
sixpenny bit
sixteenthly
sexlessness
sex offender
sexagesimal
sixth-former
sexological
sexennially
sextodecimo
sex-positive
sex hormones
saxophonist
scyphistoma
scythe-stone
stylisation
stylization
styliferous
stylishness
Stygian oath
sky-blue pink
spy in the cab
stylopodium
sky-coloured
stylography
Seymour Cray
sky-aspiring
Skye terrier
Suzanne Vega
tear and wear
tea canister
travail pang
travail pain
thanatology
thanatopsis
thalassemia
thalassemic
tracasserie
tharborough
thatch-board
Thatcherite
Thatcherism
trance music
travel agent
trademarked
trade-fallen
trade school
tea ceremony
trade secret
tracelessly
tragedienne
tragédienne
trapeziform
trapeziuses
trapezoidal
trace fossil
traversable
tracer shell
travestying
trabeculate
trades union
tradeswoman
trafficless
trafficking
traffic cone
trafficator
tearfulness
tear-falling
twanglingly
trachearian
teach school
teaching aid
Trachinidae
tracheotomy
teacherless
teachership
teacher's pet
trading post
traditional
traditioner
tragic irony
tragicomedy
thalidomide
that is to say
tear-jerking
tracklaying
track-walker
tracklement
track record
thanklessly
tracklessly
thanksgiver
thankworthy
trackerball
track events
trailbaston
trailblazer
Thallophyta
thallophyte
trailer park
trammelling
Thai massage
thaumatrope
thaumaturge
thaumaturgy
traumatised
traumatized
traineeship
train-bearer
trample upon
trampoliner
twalpennies
teaspoonful
Trappistine
tea equipage
tranquilize
tranquility
transpadane
transmanche
transcalent
transparent
translative
transmarine
translation
tear-stained
translatory
transvaluer
transaction
transection
transferase
transgender
transfer day
transfer fee
transgenics
transdermal
transfer RNA
transferred
transferral
transferrin
transferrer
transversal
transvestic
transiently
trans-sexual
transsexual
transceiver
transfinite
transfixion
transhipper
transpierce
transmitted
toad spittle
transmittal
transmitter
transfigure
transilient
transalpine
that's an idea
transandean
transandine
translocate
transponder
that's done it
transposing
trans-sonics
transformed
transformer
that's torn it!
toad-spotted
transported
transportal
transporter
trapshooter
transeptate
transcriber
transuranic
transit camp
transitable
transit visa
transit duty
transhumant
translunary
translucent
transfusive
transfusion
transductor
tea-strainer
toastmaster
tractor feed
traitorship
traitorhood
traducement
traducingly
to advantage
tear webbing
Tracy Austin
Toby Crackit
tobacco pipe
tobacconist
table-dancer
table napkin
tables d'hôte
table tennis
table-topped
tabefaction
tubiflorous
tobogganing
tobogganist
tub-thumping
tabular spar
tibiotarsus
taboparesis
tabernacled
tuberaceous
tuberculate
tuberculise
tuberculize
tuberculoma
tuberculose
tuberculous
ticket agent
tacheometer
tacheometry
tschernosem
ticket punch
tickettyboo
tactfulness
tucking-mill
tectibranch
tickle-brain
tickled pink
tickler file
technocracy
Technicolor®
technically
technomania
technomusic
technophile
technopolis
technophobe
technospeak
tachometric
tachophobia
tichorrhine
tick-tack-toe
tick-tack-too
tick trefoil
taciturnity
tack-welding
tachycardia
tachymetric
tachyphasia
tachygraphy
Ted Williams
toddlerhood
tiddlywinks
tediousness
Tudorbethan
Tudor flower
the Nazarene
trepanation
The Pardoner
tsesarevich
tsesarewich
the game is up
therapeutic
Therapeutae
the Waggoner
The Talisman
Tremadog Bay
The Man of Law
thesauruses
the Bay State
the last gasp
the last cast
✧**the faithful**
the last word
tree bicycle
tremblement
The Observer
tremblingly
theobromine
✧**the absolute**
trenchantly
treacle tart
trencher cap
trencher-fed
trencherman
treachetour
treacherous
tree creeper
the scaffold
thenceforth
trench fever
Theocritean
treacliness
trench knife
trench mouth
theocentric
The Eclogues
the Scorpion
tree diagram
trendle-tail
trendsetter
theodolitic
tread on eggs
Theodorakis
the departed
teeter-board
thereabouts
The Merchant
the Red Cross
therebeside
the Redeemer
the deceased
therewithal
therewithin
The Germania

Words marked ✧ can also be spelled with one or more capital letters

there you are
theretofore
The Red Queen
The Retreate
The Peasants
The Red Shoes
The Republic
the New World
the very idea
Twelfth cake
Twelfthtide
The Agricola
theogonical
The Phaedrus
tree-hugging
the whole kit
the shallows
The Third Man
trepidation
trepidatory
the Big Apple
The Wild Wood
The Wild Duck
the biter bit
the size of it
The Firebird
The Hireling
the five wits
the fine arts
the dingbats
The King and I
The Big Issue
The Sick Rose
theriolatry
theriomorph
The Lion King
thesis novel
The Big Sleep
✧the big smoke
The Gleaners
the black dog
treble-dated
the old enemy
The Sluggard
theological
theologiser
theologizer
the Almighty
the Classics
trellis work
the Old World
thermobaric
thermocline
theomachist
thermically
thermoduric
thermograph
thermogenic
thermolysis
thermolytic
thermometer
thermometry
thermonasty
thermionics
thermophile
theomorphic
thermoscope
thermotical
thesmothete
thermotaxic
thermotaxis
the sniffles
theanthropy
the Anointed
The Analects
The Universe
tremolandos
teetotalism
teetotaller
The Sorceror
The Woodlark
the Good Book
The Gold Rush
treponemata
the homeless
The Rose Bowl
the long robe
the nobility
the noble art
trefoil arch
The Dormouse
the Colonies
Theromorpha
the Conquest
the four seas
The Hot Seven
the Boat Race
the Holy City
theophagous
theopneusty
theophobiac
theophobist
trespassing
the greatest
the Preacher
✧the Creation
the creature
The Crucible
The Graduate
theory-laden
theorematic
✧the trenches
The Franklin
The Prioress
the prophets
theoretical
the Writings
the Troubles
tree sparrow
treasonable
treasonably
theosophise
theosophize
theosophism
theosophist
tree surgeon
tree surgery
treasury tag
✧thersitical
theotechnic
the other day
the other man
trestlework
theatre-goer
trestletree
theatricals
theatricise
theatricize
theatricism
treaty money
theftuously
twenty pence
Trent Bridge
the munchies
the Auld Kirk
the Dukeries
the business
The Fugitive
The Music Man
The Summoner
The European
tremulously
The Guardian
The Outsider
the Quatorze
The Evil Dead
twelvemonth
twelve-penny
twelve score
tree worship
The Exorcist
The Exstasie
thelytokous
teeny-bopper
tweezer case
Tiffany lamp
toffee apple
toffee-nosed
tuft-hunting
toffishness
tufftaffeta
tufftaffety
Tegucigalpa
tigrishness
tagliatelle
Tugela Falls
toggle joint
tegumentary
tiger beetle
tiger shrimp
tiger flower
tiger-footed
tight-lacing
tight-lipped
tight-fisted
tightly-knit
tag question
toga virilis
tiggywinkle
Tchaikovsky
thioalcohol
this and that
tribalistic
tritagonist
trivalvular
thimble case
thimbleweed
thimblefuls
twin brother
thiocyanate
twitch grass
Trincomalee
twin crystal
Third market
trindle-tail
third degree
third person
third estate
third stream
third-stream
this day week
third eyelid
triceratops
tripetalous
twin-etching
toilet cloth
toilet cover
toilet glass
twin-engined
tripe-visag'd
toilet paper
trimetrical
Trimetrogon
tailed rhyme
tripersonal
toilet table
trimestrial
tribeswoman
toilet water
tail feather
thingliness
thingamybob
thingumabob
thingamyjig
thingumajig
triggerfish
triphibious
t'ai chi ch'uan
tritheistic
triphyllous
trichomonad
trichomonal
Trichomonas
trichinella
trichinosis
trichinotic
trithionate
trichronous
Trichoptera
thitherward
Trinidadian
Trinitarian
trivialness
this instant
Trinity Hall
Trinity term
thickheaded
trickle-down
twinkletoes
thick-ribbed
tricksiness
thick-lipped
thick-witted
thick-coming
triple crown
triple event
triple point
Trial by Jury
triumph over
triumvirate
trimming tab
thigmotaxis
triennially
triangulate
tridominium
tribologist
tricoloured
trimorphism
trimorphous
thixotropic
tailor's tack
thiopentone
twin paradox
thin red line
trierarchal
thirstiness
thin-skinned
tristichous
triatic stay
twisted pair
Tainted Love
thistledown
taintlessly
twitter-bone
thirty-twomo
tribulation
trituration
tributarily
trifurcated
tribute band
tribuneship
tribunicial
tribunitial
tribunician
tribunitian
trisulphide
triquetrous
tributyltin
trisyllabic
trisyllable
take a gander
take against
take a wicket
take by force
take by storm
take captive
take courage
Takada Kenzo
take delight
take-home pay
take it out on
take on board
take one's way
take offence
teknonymous
take pride in
take pot luck
take revenge
take stock in
take to court
take the cake
take the veil
take the road
take the word
take to heart
take time off
take time out
take trouble
take thought
take up about
take umbrage
take up short
Tallahassee
telearchics
talkatively
talkability
Taliacotian
talebearing
telebanking
telecommand
telecommute
telocentric
telecontrol
telecasting
telecottage
tiller-chain
téléférique
telegraphic
telegrapher
telegrammic
telegnostic
telpherline
talking head
talking shop
talking book
telekinesis
telekinetic
Telemessage®
talent scout
Tall Nettles
Teleosaurus
tallow catch
tallow-faced
teleologism
teleologist
teleprinter
tulipomania
telephonist
tulip poplar
telepathise
telepathize
telepathist
Telesphorus
telesthesia
telesthetic
telescience
teleselling
Telescopium
telescopist
telestrator
tell the time
tale-telling
talk through
tolbutamide
telluretted
Talmudistic
televiewing
teleworking
talk-you-down
tally system
tameability
tympaniform
Tammany Hall
tamableness
time bargain
time charter
tame cheater
time capsule
time deposit
temperament
temperately
temperative
temperature
timber hitch
tamper-proof
time-expired
tempestuous
tempest-tost
tumefacient
tumefaction
tomographic
Tammie Norie
timekeeping
time-killing
tumble-drier
tumble-dryer

Temple Mount
tumbling box
tumblerfuls
time machine
Tom and Jerry
tempolabile
temporaries
temporality
temporarily
tomboyishly
temporising
temporizing
time-pleaser
tumorigenic
time-release
timbromania
Tempranillo
timbrophily
temerarious
time-sharing
Tam O'Shanter
tumescently
time-service
time-serving
tomatilloes
Tom Stoppard
tomato sauce
temptatious
tempus fugit
Tommy Walker
Tommy Lawton
Tommy Cooper
Tommy Dorsey
Tommy Atkins
tummy button
Tin Pan Alley
Tyne and Wear
tentatively
tantalising
tantalizing
Tony Allcock
tentaculate
Tantalus-cup
tentaculite
tentaculoid
tenableness
tunableness
Tony Bennett
tenebrosity
tankbusting
tonic accent
tone control
tenaciously
tone cluster
tendencious
tender-dying
tunnel diode
tenderfoots
Ten Years' War
tangentally
tendentious
tunnel vault
tunefulness
tank furnace
tank-farming
Tony Hancock
tennis elbow
tensile test
tonnishness
tangibility
tensibility
tentiginous
tonsillitic
tonsillitis
tensiometer
tensiometry
tensionless
tensionally
tonsilotomy
Tony Jacklin
tenementary
tenant right
toning table
Tony O'Reilly
tan-coloured
tenuousness
tantony bell
tone picture
tent-pegging
tenorrhaphy
tendrillous
tenure track
Tiny Rowland
tonetically
tin-streamer
tonquin-bean
Thomas Blood
Thomas Brown
two-handedly
Trojan horse
Thomas Hardy
Thomas Lodge
Thomas Moore
Thomas Nashe
thoracotomy
tropaeolums
Thomas Otway
Thomas Pride
Thomas Wyatt
Trojan Women
Thomas Young
trombiculid
troublesome
trouble-town
trouble spot
troublefree
troublously
T-Bone Walker
twopenny bit
two-penn'orth
to one's taste
trough fault
trough shell
thought wave
thoughtcast
thoughtless
thought-sick
trophoblast
tooth-picker
Trochilidae
trothplight
trochometer
tooth powder
toothsomely
trophoplasm
trochophore
tooth-drawer
trophotaxis
trophozoite
Thomistical
Teotihuacán
troglodytic
Troglodytes
troll-my-dame
thorny devil
thornproofs
twofoldness
tromometric
thoroughpin
thoroughwax
tropophytic
troposphere
tropomyosin
trompe l'oeil
Thompson gun
trous-de-loup
trouserings
trouser suit
trout basket
two-storeyed
trout stream
typicalness
typecasting
topped crude
taphephobia
toplessness
tepefaction
type founder
type foundry
typographia
topographic
typographic
topographer
typographer
tip the scale
topping lift
topological
typological
tape measure
tape machine
toponymical
top one's part
taphophobia
taphonomist
toploftical
tephromancy
tap-dressing
top dressing
type species
tapestrying
typesetting
typewriting
typewritten
turn against
termagantly
threatening
terra ignota
tarradiddle
threadiness
throatiness
throatlatch
threadmaker
targa-topped
thread-paper
tartar steak
throatstrap
tartar sauce
terraqueous
ternary form
terebration
terebratula
throbbingly
three-handed
terfenadine
three-masted
three-parted
three-master
turkey brown
torpescence
turgescence
turgescency
turret clock
three-leafed
three-legged
three-decker
Turneresque
three-leaved
three cheers
Three Rivers
torpedinous
Turbellaria
turret lathe
terremotive
three-nooked
torpedo boom
three-colour
torpedo boat
three-bottle
three-volume
torpedo tube
Turner Prize
three-square
Turkey stone
turkey-shoot
tormentedly
terrestrial
torrentuous
Terme Museum
three-suited
thriftiness
thrift store
tirage à part
tyroglyphid
torchbearer
torch singer
torchon lace
torch-staves
terminate in
terminative
termitarium
termination
turbination
terminatory
terrigenous
turbine pump
torsiograph
turfing iron
Turkish bath
tarnishable
Turkish lira
terribility
torsibility
tertium quid
torsionally
territoried
✧territorial
Torridonian
torticollis
terricolous
terminology
turriculate
turtle doves
thrillingly
turtleshell
turtle-stone
thrummed hat
thrummingly
thrombocyte
tiring-glass
tiring-house
tyrannicide
Tironensian
Tyronensian
tyrannosaur
tyrannously
threnetical
tiring-woman
turbo-ram-jet
turnover tax
Turcophobia
turbocharge
terroristic
terror novel
turcopolier
turn of speed
turn out well
term of years
turnpike man
Tortricidae
Terpsichore
thrash metal
thrasonical
thrust plane
thrust stage
turn traitor
turntablist
turn the wind
teratogenic
teratologic
taratantara
turn to stone
turn towards
torturesome
turbulently
Tartufferie
throughfare
through ball
throughgaun
through pass
through bolt
torturingly
Targumistic
torque meter
tire-valiant
throw weight
throw around
tardy-gaited
Terry-Thomas
tarry breeks
tessaraglot
toss and turn
testamental
testamentar
tussac grass
testability
Tessa Jowell
tastelessly
tassell-gent
tessellated
tostication
testificate
testimonial
testiculate
tussock moth
test pattern
testudinary
tissue paper
tetravalent
tetradactyl
tetrarchate
tetrandrian
tetrandrous
tetramerism
tetramerous
Titianesque
tetrahedral
tetrahedron
tetratheism
tetraplegia
tetraplegic
tetraploidy
tetragonous
tetrapodous
tetrasporic
tetradrachm
tetractinal
tetrapteran
tetradymite
tetragynian
tetracyclic
tetragynous
Tate Britain
tithe-paying
to the marrow
to the letter
titteringly
totteringly
title-holder
Tattersall's
Tattersalls
Tate Gallery
tittivation
tattie-bogle
tattiebogle
to think of it
tutti-frutti
titillative
titillating
titillation
total recall
totalisator
totalizator
titanic acid
tetanically
✧titanically
titanic iron
Tut'ankhamun
Titanomachy
totipalmate
totipotency
têtes-à-têtes
tau particle
thumb-marked
tourbillion
truncheoned
truncheoner
trundle-tail
tour de force
Thunderball
thunder-dart
thunderhead
thunder peal
thunderless
thunderbird
thunderlike
thunderclap

thunderbolt
tout de suite
true-devoted
tau neutrino
Tsung-Dao Lee
true-hearted
touch screen
touch-screen
truth-teller
touchy-feely
tough-minded
touch-in-goal
touch bottom
touch rugger
touch-typing
touch-typist
thuriferous
truck-farmer
trunksleeve
truck system
tout le monde
tous-les-mois
tautomerism
tautometric
tautophonic
tautochrone
Teutonicism
tautologise
tautologize
taurobolium
tautologism
tautologist
tautologous
tautonymous
trump marine
thump around
trumpet call
trumpetfish
trumpet wood
trumpet tone
trumpet tree
true-seeming
trusteeship
trustworthy
trust estate
trustbuster
truculently
town and gown
town council
town dweller
town meeting
towing-bitts
tow-coloured
town planner
Tower of Pisa
thwartingly
thwartships
townscaping
townspeople
tax gatherer
textbookish
toxicogenic
toxicologic
toxicomania
taxidermise
taxidermize
taxidermist
text message
taxonomical
toxoplasmic
toxiphagous
toxophilite
toxiphobiac
Texas hold 'em
textureless
trypanocide
trypanosome
thysanurous
trying plane
try one's hand
try one's luck
thyroiditis
thyrotropin
Thyrostraca
T-lymphocyte
trypsinogen
Tayassuidae
trysting-day
tryptophane
unawareness
unawakening
unavailable
unavailably
up against it
unadaptable
unambiguous
unambitious
unaccusable
unaccusably
unaddressed
up and coming
up-and-coming
unamendable
unavertable
unavertible
unaffecting
unaugmented
unashamedly
unalienable
unalienably
unanimously
unallowable
unannotated
unannounced
Uranoscopus
unavoidable
unavoidably
unabolished
uranoplasty
uranography
unapostolic
unappealing
unappointed
unapproving
unaspirated
unagreeable
unabrogated
unassertive
unassisting
unauthentic
unattainted
unattempted
unattentive
unattending
unalterable
unalterably
unamusingly
unadvisable
unadvisably
unadvisedly
unblameable
unblameably
umbratilous
unbiassedly
unbeautiful
umbraculate
unblenching
unblemished
unbreakable
umbrella-ant
umbrella fir
unbreathing
unbefitting
unbeginning
unblindfold
umbriferous
unbeknownst
umbellately
unballasted
unbelieving
urban legend
unbeneficed
unbenefited
unbenignant
unbenighted
unbendingly
unbrotherly
unburthened
unbarricade
unburnished
unbeseeming
unboundedly
unceasingly
unclassical
unchastened
unchartered
unchastised
unchastized
uncuckolded
uncheckable
uncleanness
unclearness
unclimbable
unchildlike
urchin-shows
uncalled-for
uncollected
uncompanied
uncompacted
uncommended
uncompelled
uncommitted
uncompliant
uncomplying
uncompleted
uncomforted
uncomatable
unconscious
uncongenial
unconcealed
unconcerned
uncontemned
unconfessed
unconcerted
unconnected
uncontested
unconverted
unconceived
unconvinced
uncanniness
unconfident
unconniving
unconfirmed
unconvicted
uncanonical
uncanonised
uncanonized
unconcocted
uncontrived
unconquered
uncrossable
uncurtailed
uncurtained
uncertainly
uncertainty
uncorrected
uncertified
unchristian
uncorrupted
upcast-shaft
unclubbable
uncrushable
uncouthness
uncountable
uncourteous
uncluttered
uncivilised
uncivilized
undrainable
undiagnosed
undebauched
undecidable
undecidedly
undeclining
undecorated
undreamed-of
undefinable
undignified
undriveable
undyingness
undrinkable
undelegated
undelighted
undelivered
undemanding
undepressed
undepending
underhanded
undertaking
undermanned
underdamper
undermasted
undervaluer
under canvas
under-sawyer
underaction
under a cloud
under-school
undertenant
underweight
underseller
under-report
underkeeper
underbearer
underletter
under the lee
underthings
undershapen
undercharge
undershorts
underthirst
under the sun
underthrust
underbidder
undermining
underwiring
undersigned
underbitten
underviewer
undersleeve
underclothe
underinsure
undercovert
underhonest
underlooker
underworker
under-bonnet
underbreath
underpriced
underbridge
under arrest
underpraise
underwriter
underground
under-driven
undergrowth
under-espial
understrata
understorey
understated
under duress
underfulfil
underbudget
undersupply
underexpose
undescended
undiscerned
undispensed
undesigning
undistilled
undisclosed
undespoiled
undistorted
undissolved
undescribed
undesirable
undesirably
undeserving
undestroyed
undisturbed
undiscussed
undisguised
undutifully
undauntable
undoubtable
undauntedly
undoubtedly
undeviating
undividable
undividedly
undeveloped
undiverting
unelaborate
unenchanted
unescapable
unexcitable
unexclusive
unexcavated
unendurable
unendurably
unexercised
uselessness
unelectable
un-English
unexhausted
unevidenced
urediospore
unenjoyable
unemotioned
unemotional
unexplained
unexpectant
unexpressed
unexpensive
unexploited
unexperient
unenquiring
unessential
unequitable
unequivocal
unfearfully
unfeathered
unflavoured
unflappable
unflappably
unfeelingly
unflinching
unfailingly
unfeignedly
unfaltering
unfulfilled
unfiltrable
unfinishing
Ulf von Euler
unformatted
unfermented
unforfeited
unforbidden
unfurnished
unfortified
unforgiving
unforeknown
unforgotten
unfortunate
unfashioned
unfittingly
unfeudalise
unfeudalize
unfoundedly
unfructuous
unflustered
unfavourite
unfixedness
upgradation
unguardedly
upgradeable
ungratified
ungrammatic
unglamorous
ungraspable
ungodliness
unguerdoned
unguiculate
ungallantly
unguligrade
ungenteelly
ungentility
ungenitured
ungarmented
ungarnished
unget-at-able
ungetatable
ungazed upon
unhealthful
unhealthily
unhabitable

unhackneyed
unhidebound
unheedfully
unheedingly
upholstress
upholsterer
unhingement
unhandiness
unhopefully
unhappiness
unharnessed
unharvested
unharmfully
unhurtfully
unhurriedly
unharboured
unhusbanded
unhazardous
univalvular
uninchanted
uniserially
unigeniture
unicellular
universally
unipersonal
unisexually
uninflected
uninforming
uninhabited
uninhibited
unification
unitisation
unitization
utilisation
utilitarian
utilization
uriniparous
uriniferous
uninitiated
unidiomatic
utility pole
utility room
unillumined
unipolarity
uniformness
unicorn-moth
unicolorate
unicolorous
unicoloured
unimpeached
unimpededly
unimpressed
unit-pricing
unimportant
uninquiring
uninspiring
uninsulated
uninscribed
uninsurable
uninucleate
uninvidious
uninventive
unjustified
unjaundiced
unknowing or
unknowingly
unknownness
unlearnedly
unlaborious
unliberated
unlabouring
unluckiness
upliftingly
unlightened
unlightsome
unleisurely
unlimitedly
unlooked-for
unliquefied
unlistening
unloverlike
unluxuriant
unluxurious
unmeaningly
unmechanise
unmechanize
unmodulated
unmeditated
unmoistened
unmalicious
unmelodious
unmalleable
unmemorable
unmindfully
unmanliness
unmentioned
unmercenary
unmortgaged
unmarriable
unmortified
unmoralised
unmoralized
unmeritable
unmeritedly
unmurmuring
unmusically
unmasculine
unmitigable
unmitigably
unmitigated
unmatchable
unmutilated
unmotivated
unnecessary
unneedfully
unniloctium
unnilhexium
unnaturally
unnourished
unnavigable
unnavigated
unoperative
unofficious
unofficered
unoffensive
unoffending
unorganised
unorganized
Urochordata
urochordate
unoriginate
utopianiser
utopianizer
unobnoxious
ulotrichous
unobservant
unobserving
upon the shun
upon the wing
unorthodoxy
unobtrusive
urodynamics
unpeaceable
unplausible
unplausibly
unpractical
unplastered
unpractised
unpublished
unpedigreed
unpreaching
unpreferred
unprevented
unpresuming
unpaintable
unprintable
unpolarised
unpolarized
unpalatable
unpalatably
unpolitical
upping-block
unpensioned
upping-stone
upping-stock
unprocessed
unprofessed
unprojected
unprotected
unprotested
unprophetic
unprovident
unprofiting
unpromising
unprovoking
unpopularly
unpopulated
upper school
unperfected
unperverted
unperfectly
unperceived
unparagoned
unpurchased
upper circle
unportioned
unperplexed
unpardoning
unperformed
unperishing
upper storey
unperturbed
unpersuaded
upper eyelid
unpossessed
unpassioned
unpatterned
unpitifully
unpityingly
unpatriotic
unpathwayed
unqualified
unqualitied
unquantised
unquantized
unqueenlike
unquickened
unquietness
unreachable
unreadiness
unrealistic
unreasoning
unreclaimed
Ulrich Boner
unrectified
unreceipted
unrecalling
utricularia
unreceptive
unrecounted
unrecovered
unreducible
unredressed
unrefracted
unrefreshed
unreflected
unregulated
unregarding
uprightness
unrighteous
unrehearsed
unrejoicing
unreluctant
unreligious
unrelenting
unremaining
unromanised
unromanized
unremittent
unremitting
unremovable
unrooted out
unrepugnant
unreprieved
unrepentant
unrepenting
unreproving
unreposeful
unrequisite
unrespected
unrescinded
unrestingly
unresentful
unresenting
unrestraint
unresisting
unretentive
unreturning
unretouched
unrevealing
unravelment
unravelling
unrewarding
unstaidness
unshakeable
unslakeable
unshakeably
unsparingly
unswallowed
unstainable
unstaunched
unseaworthy
unsharpened
unsubscribe
unsubmerged
unsubjected
unsubduable
unsocialism
unsectarian
unsociality
unsucceeded
unsuccoured
unsteadfast
unspecified
unspeakable
unspeakably
unsweetened
unsheltered
Ulsterwoman
unsoftening
unsighed-for
unsegmented
unscheduled
unscholarly
unskilfully
unsmilingly
unspiritual
unscissored
unsyllabled
unselective
unsolicited
unselfishly
unsoldierly
unsandalled
ups and downs
unsentenced
unsensitive
unshockable
unstoppable
unstoppably
unsupported
unseparable
unseparated
unsurpassed
unshrinking
unsprinkled
unsurprised
unscratched
unsustained
unsuspended
unsuspected
unsuspicion
unsatiating
unsettledly
unsatirical
unsaturated
unsatisfied
unslumbrous
unsoundable
unsoundness
unshunnable
unsavourily
upsey Friese
ultramarine
untraceable
untravelled
untraversed
unteachable
ultraviolet
ultrafilter
ultrasonics
untractable
urticaceous
untechnical
urticarious
untrembling
untreatable
untremulous
up to high doh
unthinkable
unthickened
untaintedly
untamedness
untempering
untimeously
ultima ratio
ultima Thule
untunefully
untinctured
unthought-of
untormented
unthriftily
untarnished
unterrified
up to scratch
up to the mark
up to the hilt
up to the eyes
untouchable
usucaptible
unutterable
unutterably
unusualness
unvocalised
unvocalized
unvulgarise
unvulgarize
upvaluation
unvenerable
unveracious
unvarnished
unvisitable
unvitrified
unweathered
unweariable
unweariably
unweariedly
unwedgeable
unweetingly
unwillingly
unwelcomely
unwelcoming
unwandering
unwinkingly
unwholesome
unwarranted
unwished-for
unwithering
unwitnessed
unwatchable
unwittingly
unwithstood
unwoundable
Vladivostok
via dolorosa
vibratility
vibrational
vice anglais
Vaclav Havel
vice-admiral
vociferance
vociferator
vicegerency
vaccination
vaccinatory
victimology
vacillating
vacillation
vacillatory
vice-marshal
vacuolation
Victoria Day
vectorially
vacuousness
viciousness
vectorscope

victoryless
victory ship
victory roll
Vicar of Bray
vicar-choral
vicar-forane
vicariously
viceroyship
viceroyalty
vicissitude
vacationist
vacuum brake
vacuum-clean
vacuum flask
vacuum gauge
victuallage
victualless
victualling
vichyssoise
video camera
video sender
videosender
video signal
video jockey
vedette-boat
view askance
vienna steak
View of Delft
vagabondage
vagabondise
vagabondize
vagabondish
vagabondism
vigilantism
vegetal pole
Vehmgericht
voix céleste
vaivodeship
voivodeship
voltaic cell
voltaic pile
village cart
volcanic ash
volcanicity
vulcanicity
volcanic mud
valuational
Vulgar Latin
volcanology
vulcanology
villanously
volt-amperes
volubleness
velocimeter
velocimetry
velocipeder
valediction
valedictory
vulneration
valley fever
velvet glove
velvetiness
valve bounce
velvet-paper
valleculate
vellication
villication
Vallisneria
volumometer
Valoniaceae
voluntative
voluntarism
voluntarist
voluntarily
Valentinian
vale of years
valeric acid
Volkskammer
Volkslieder
volitionary
vulture fund
vomeronasal
vintage year
vantageless
vintage port
vandalistic
Venice glass
viniculture
Venn diagram
vine-dresser
vine-disease
Vendémiaire
venefically
veneficious
vinificator
vine-fretter
venographic
vinegarette
ventilative
vindicative
venditation
ventilation
vindication
ventilatory
vindicatory
vendibility
vincibility
vinaigrette
vinyl resins
vinblastine
Van Morrison
ventricular
ventricules
ventriculus
ventral tank
ventriloquy
venereology
vincristine
Vanessa Bell
venesection
venisection
vanishingly
Venetian red
venatically
vanity plate
vanity table
venturesome
venturingly
✧venturi tube
venturously
vanguardism
viola d'amore
violinistic
Voodoo Chile
violoncello
voodooistic
✧voortrekker
viper's grass
vaporimeter
vaporisable
vaporizable
vapouringly
vapour trail
vernal grass
versatilely
variability
versability
versatility
variational
Vargas Llosa
verd-antique
varicelloid
varicellous
veraciously
voraciously
veridically
viridescent
Verbenaceae
verse-making
variegation
verberation
verde-antico
verse-monger
vertebrally
vertebrated
variety meat
variety show
Variety Club
vertical fin
vermination
verticality
✧virgin birth
verbigerate
vorticellae
virgin honey
varnish tree
vertiginous
vortiginous
vermivorous
vermiculate
vermiculite
vermiculous
verslibrist
virological
virilescent
verumontana
variolation
verboseness
varsovienne
variousness
verisimilar
verdureless
verruciform
vertue-proof
virtue-proof
visual field
Vesta Tilley
visual noise
visibleness
vesiculated
vasodilator
vas deferens
vespertinal
vestimental
vis inertiae
Vasco da Gama
viscometric
vision mixer
viscountess
viscousness
viscous flow
vision thing
vasopressin
vasopressor
vestry-clerk
visiting-day
vascularise
vascularize
vascularity
vasculature
vasculiform
vesuvianite
vote against
vitraillist
viticulture
Vatican City
vaticinator
vitrescible
vitrescence
vitrifiable
vital organs
vituperable
vituperator
Veterans Day
Vitus Bering
vouchsafing
vivaciously
vivacissimo
Vivien Leigh
Vivekananda
vivisective
vivisection
vexillation
vexillology
vox angelica
vexatiously
voyeuristic
wear and tear
weasand-pipe
wearability
what a plague
weasel-faced
weaver finch
whale-fisher
weasel round
weaver's knot
weasel words
wranglesome
weak-hearted
weather gage
weather vane
weather gall
weatherable
weather-fend
weather beam
weather helm
weather ship
weather side
weather-wise
weathergirl
weather sign
weathercock
weather roll
weather-worn
weathermost
what have you
wearilessly
whaling-port
wearisomely
weak-kneedly
weapon-schaw
weapon salve
wrapped up in
weak-sighted
whatsomever
what the hell
wealthiness
wear through
Weary Willie
web designer
web-fingered
wobble board
W A B Coolidge
Woburn Abbey
Wabash River
widechapped
wedge-tailed
wedge-shaped
Weddell seal
widdershins
wedding band
wedding cake
wedding ring
wide-ranging
wade through
Widow Wadman
widow's bench
widow's cruse
widowerhood
wide-watered
widow's weeds
whenceforth
wheedlesome
wheedlingly
whereabouts
wherewithal
where you are
wheresoever
wienerwurst
whet forward
whether or no
weeping-ripe
weeding-fork
weeding-hook
weeping rock
wheyishness
wreckmaster
wheelbarrow
wheel of life
wheel window
wheel plough
wheel animal
wheelwright
wheel-cutter
when pigs fly
wheat mildew
wag-'n-bietjie
Wagneresque
wage-earning
waggishness
waggle dance
wagonwright
wage slavery
whip and spur
Waitangi Day
Whitby Abbey
White Rabbit
white-handed
whitewasher
white radish
white-tailed
white-haired
white matter
white-headed
white pepper
whitethroat
Whitechapel
white-winged
white finger
white-billed
white-listed
white flight
White Plains
white clover
white slaver
white knight
White Ensign
white coffee
✧whiteboyism
white-collar
white bonnet
white copper
white bottle
white spirit
white squall
white squire
White Friars
white bryony
white-rumped
white hunter
whiffletree
whingeingly
wringing wet
wring staves
weightiness
weigh anchor
whichsoever
whitherward
weighbridge
weight-train
waiting-maid
writing case
Wailing Wall
writing desk
whiting-time
waiting list
writing-book
waiting room
whiting pout
whitishness
whisky-liver
whiskerando
whisky toddy
whiskeyfied
whiskey sour
whitleather
whitlow-wort
whigmaleery
Weismannism
whippletree
whipping boy
whipping-top
waitressing
whimsically
Whitsun week
Whitsuntide
wainscoting
wainscotted
whistleable
whistle fish
whittle down
whistle stop
whistle-stop
whistle away
whittle away
whistlingly

waistcloths
whist-player
waist anchor
wakefulness
waking hours
Willa Cather
well and good
welfare work
Wild at Heart
wild animals
weldability
welfaristic
walk all over
well-advised
will be along
well-behaved
well-beloved
wallcreeper
wallclimber
wild chicory
Will Carling
well-coupled
well-covered
well-dressed
well-defined
well-derived
well-desired
Walter Baade
well-endowed
Walter Hagen
Wilhelm Wien
Walter Mitty
Walter Scott
well-entered
well-founded
wildfowling
waldgravine
well-groomed
Welsh rabbit
walking-cane
walking case
walking race
walking bass
walking part
walking lady
walking leaf
walking-beam
walking fern
willingness
walking fish
walking toad
walking-song
walking boot
walking twig
William Lamb
William Laud
William Hare
William Tell
William Penn
William Kent
William Kidd
William Pitt
William Byrd
welwitschia
well-judging
well-looking
well-meaning
wall mustard
wild mustard
walk Matilda
wall of death
well-ordered
welcomeness
walk off with
welcomingly
Weltpolitik
Wilfred Owen
well-rounded
walk Spanish
well-stacked
Will Scarlet
✧waldsterben
Weltschmerz
well-sinking
wild service
Wilms' tumour
Wole Soyinka
well-trodden
walk-through
well-thumbed
walnut juice
Wilbur Smith
Walt Whitman
wolf whistle
wolf-whistle
will-worship
well-wishing
Willy Brandt
wimpishness
womb-leasing
woman-vested
womanliness
Women in Love
Woman's Realm
wine and dine
wing-and-wing
winnability
winebibbing
Windbreaker®
windbaggery
wine biscuit
windcheater
want-catcher
wonder about
winter apple
winter-bloom
winterberry
winter cress
wonderfully
wintergreen
Winged Horse
wanderingly
wonderingly
Wanderjahre
winter melon
Winterreise
winter's bark
winter-sweet
winter wheat
winged words
windfall tax
wing forward
wind furnace
wine-growing
winningness
winning post
want jam on it
wing loading
windlestrae
windlestraw
Wensleydale
wine measure
wind machine
Winona Ryder
window blind
window-barne
winsomeness
wend one's way
window frame
window glass
window ledge
wind-sucking
Windsor Park
windsurfing
Windsor knot
Windsor soap
wind turbine
wine tasting
wine vinegar
wing-walking
wood alcohol
wood anemone
wool-bearing
woodcreeper
wool-combing
woodcarving
wool-carding
woodcutting
whoremaster
whole-length
wooden horse
wholesomely
whole-hoofed
whole-hogger
whoremonger
whole-souled
whole-footed
whosesoever
wooden spoon
wholestitch
whole number
wooden wedge
wooden walls
wood-fretter
wrong-headed
wrong-minded
wool-growing
wrought iron
wrought-iron
wrong number
whorishness
woolly aphis
woollen mill
wholly-owned
wood naphtha
whooper swan
Woodruff key
wool-stapler
wood swallow
wood sanicle
whodunnitry
wood vinegar
wood warbler
Woody Herman
woody-tongue
wapper-jawed
wappenschaw
work against
workability
workaholism
warrant card
warrant sale
warrantable
warrantably
wire binding
warm-blooded
worlds apart
wiredrawing
world-famous
World Series
world record
world-beater
worldliness
wire-dancing
worldly-wise
war memorial
war neurosis
Warren Spahn
war of nerves
word for word
worm gearing
warm-hearted
worthlessly
worshipable
worshipless
worshipping
warehousing
warlikeness
working face
working edge
working week
working-beam
working girl
working-over
wordishness
worrisomely
workmanship
workmanlike
War and Peace
wire netting
ward of court
word-of-mouth
word picture
word-painter
wirepulling
word-perfect
word-puzzler
war criminal
work-sharing
workstation
words fail me
warts and all
wire service
worsted-work
wiretapping
work through
werewolfery
werewolfish
werewolfism
work wonders
wireworking
workwatcher
wash-and-wear
washability
wassail bowl
wassail bout
west-by-north
west-by-south
wisecracker
West Country
wash drawing
Wesleyanism
waste basket
wastel bread
washer-drier
washer-dryer
wasterfully
Western Wall
western roll
westernmost
waste ground
washerwoman
wishfulness
wistfulness
wash-gilding
wise-hearted
wishing well
washing line
washing-blue
washing-soda
wishing-bone
wishing tree
waspishness
wash its face
wash leather
West Lothian
Westminster
wisdom tooth
Westphalian
wishtonwish
wasp-waisted
with a wanion
witwanton it
witheringly
witlessness
withershins
wither-wrung
watchmaking
witch-ridden
witch-finder
watch pocket
witch doctor
watchspring
witches' meat
witches' brew
within cooee
within reach
within sight
with knobs on
witenagemot
wet one's clay
without fail
without book
without-door
with profits
water jacket
water bailie
water hammer
water cannon
water vapour
water barrel
watered-down
water meadow
water cement
water pepper
Water Bearer
water beetle
water-heater
water of life
water thrush
water-finder
Water Lilies
water violet
water pistol
water-skiing
water blinks
water closet
watering can
watering-cap
water engine
watering pot
water souchy
waterlogged
water bouget
water monkey
water-cooled
water cooler
watercolour
watercourse
water bottle
water doctor
water splash
water spider
water sprite
water spring
water sports
water spirit
water tunnel
water purpie
water supply
withstander
with the best
Wounded Knee
wound tissue
wauking-song
wax painting
wax-chandler
waywardness
Wayne's World
Weymouth Bay
X-ray therapy
X-generation
X-chromosome
xylocarpous
xylographic
xylographer
xylophagous
xylophilous
xylophonist
xenodochium
xenogenesis
xenogenetic
xenoglossia
xanthic acid
Xanthochroi
xanthophyll
xenomorphic
xenoplastic
xiphopagous
xyridaceous
xerographic
xeromorphic
xeranthemum
xerophilous
xerothermic
xerotripsis
XYY syndrome
yeard-hunger
year of grace
yeast powder
yackety-yack
yachtswoman
Yves Montand
yogic flying
Yugoslavian
Y-chromosome

Words marked ✧ can also be spelled with one or more capital letters

yah-boo sucks
yellow alert
yellow-ammer
yellow-belly
yellow earth
yellow fever
Yellowknife
yellow metal
yellow ox-eye
✧yellow press
Yellow Pages®
Yellow River
Yam Kinneret
yince-errand
yerba de maté
Yuri Gagarin
yersiniosis
Yardie squad
York Minster
yesternight
yatteringly
yttriferous
yttrocerite
you can't talk
young person
young fustic
youth leader
youth hostel
youth credit
you-know-what
you and yours
Yousuf Karsh
Yevtushenko
zealousness
Ziaur Rahman
Zsa Zsa Gabor
zoantharian
zoanthropic
zebra spider
zygocardiac
Zygomycetes
zygomorphic
zygopleural
Zygophyllum
Zaheer Abbas
zwischenzug
Zimmer® frame
zum Beispiel
zymological
zymosimeter
zymotically
zymotechnic
zinciferous
zinkiferous
zincography
zone therapy
Zonotrichia
Zen Buddhism
zoomagnetic
zoodendrium
zootechnics
zoocephalic
zootheistic
zoochemical
zoophytical
zeolitiform
zooplankton
zoogonidium
zoomorphism
zoospermium
zoografting
zoographist
zip fastener
Zoroastrian
zero-grazing
zestfulness

12 – odd

anacatharsis
anacathartic
anapaestical
Amarantaceae
anabaptistic
à la hauteur de
anarchically
Aladdin's cave
Aladdin's lamp
apage Satanas
academically
amateurishly
Academy Award
amalgamation
amalgamative
agathodaimon
anaphylactic
anathematise
anathematize
arachnophobe
azathioprine
avariciously
Arabian camel
acaridomatia
availability
an all-time low
Alan L Hodgkin
an arm of flesh
at arm's length
agalmatolite
Alain Resnais
agamogenesis
anagogically
analogically
anatomically
apagogically
acarodomatia
anamorphoses
anamorphosis
araeosystyle
analphabetic
anaerobiosis
anaerobiotic
anagrammatic
anaesthetics
anaesthetise
anaesthetist
anaesthetize
Alan Sillitoe
Adam's flannel
avant-gardism
avant-gardist
acanthaceous
Acanthamoeba
adaptability
alas the while
anastigmatic
abaft the beam
avant-courier
anarthrously
adaptiveness
analytically
ambidextrous
abbreviation
abbreviatory
abbreviature
ambient noise
Albigensians
ambulanceman
album Graecum
Albany herald
amber gambler
Albert Claude
Albert Finney
Auberon Waugh
Alberto Tomba
arborescence
arborisation
Albert Square
arborization
ambassadress
as best one can
ambitionless
ambivalently
Abbey Theatre
abbey-counter
acciaccatura
archaeometry
archdeaconry
accidentally
archdiocesan
aecidiospore
Asclepiadean
Archer Martin
archegoniate
ancien régime
ancient Greek
archetypally
archetypical
acclimatiser
acclimatizer
Arctic Circle
archipelagic
archipelagos
architecture
Archie Fisher
Archilochian
acceleration
acceleratory
accelerative
accompanyist
ascomycetous
accomplished
accomplisher
accumulation
accumulative
accommodable
accommodator
aichmophobia
as concerning
Ascension Day
Ascension-day
accentuality
accentuation
anchoretical
arctophilist
anchoritical
anchor string
accursedness
ascorbic acid
accordionist
accurateness
access charge
access course
arcus senilis
arco saltando
accustrement
accusatorial
accusatively
accouterment
accouchement
accoutrement
at death's door
addictedness
André Malraux
André Masséna
Andrew Irvine
Andrei Markov
Andrew Motion
Andrea Pisano
addle-brained
and that's that
Andro Ferrara
audiometrist
androcentric
and no mistake
audiological
androsterone
aldermanlike
aldermanship
alder-liefest
adder's-tongue
at discretion
additionally
additive-free
Aldous Huxley
andouillette
Andrzej Wajda
acetaldehyde
age hardening
acetate rayon
amenableness
alembication
Azerbaijanis
anencephalia
anencephalic
Aberdeen City
Ade Edmondson
anecdotalist
ayeremaining
A Severed Head
age of consent
Alex Ferguson
Alec Guinness
American aloe
Adelina Patti
American plan
Alexis Carrel
aperiodicity
alexipharmic
amelioration
ameliorative
Abel Magwitch
awe-inspiring
anemophilous
anemographic
atemporality
averruncator
Aneurin Bevan
aberrational
A Sea Symphony
area sampling
agent-general
amentiferous
ave atque vale
agentive noun
adequateness
affectedness
affectionate
aficionados
Alfred Austin
Alfred Deller
Alfred Kinsey
arfvedsonite
Alfred Sisley
affrightened
affrightedly
affrightment
apfel strudel
Alfonso Reyes
affinity card
affrontingly
afforestable
at first sight
at first blush
affluentness
argue the toss
angle bracket
angle grinder
aggressively
augmentation
augmentative
Angling Times
anguilliform
argillaceous
Angela Carter
angelica-tree
Angelo Dundee
Angela Rippon
Argentinidae
angiosarcoma
as good as gold
angiocarpous
agglomerated
angiogenesis
Anglocentric
✧anglophobiac
Angiospermae
angiospermal
angiostomous
Auguste Rodin
Auguste Comte
Angus Deayton
Augustinians
Augustus John
agglutinated
agglutinable
agglutinogen
achlamydeous
athlete's foot
athletically
Ash Wednesday
Achilles' heel
Alhambresque
atheological
athrocytoses
athrocytosis
atheromatous
ashes to ashes
adhesiveness
animalculism
animalculist
animated film
avitaminoses
avitaminosis
amicableness
Anita Roddick
animal rights
animatronics
animadverter
axis cylinder
a piece of cake
a mile a minute
alive and well
Alice Springs
alimentation
alimentative
a king's ransom
a tight corner
arithmetical
arithmomania
arithmometer
axioma medium
alienability
amitotically
à l'improviste
amissibility
aristocratic
aristolochia
Aristophanes
Aristophanic
Aristotelean
Aristotelian
Aristotelism
amicus curiae
apiculturist
A View to a Kill
adjectivally
adjudication
adjudicative
adjunctively
adjutant bird
au jour le jour
awkward squad
at knife-point
alkali metals
alkalescence
alkalescency
Ankylosauria
Ankylosaurus
All Saints' Day
Aulic Council
alla cappella
all edges gilt

all-pervading
all of a doodah
all of a dither
all of a sudden
Auld Lang Syne
all-important
all-embracing
aplanogamete
Atlantic City
Atlantic seal
Atlantic Time
all-inclusive
all and sundry
all-roundness
all-up service
All or Nothing
all-or-nothing
ailurophilia
ailurophilic
ailurophobia
ailurophobic
able seawoman
A Glass of Beer
alla stoccata
allusiveness
alliteration
alliterative
ailourophobe
ailourophile
all over again
allowability
all systems go
Ahmed Sukarno
armamentaria
adminiculate
Armand Hammer
admonishment
administrant
administrate
Admiralty Bay
arm wrestling
atmospherics
Armistice Day
armour-bearer
armour-plated
Ann Radcliffe
annual nettle
annual report
Anne Bancroft
Anna Christie
annihilation
annihilative
Anna Ivanovna
annuity share
Arne Jacobsen
Anna Karenina
Arnold Palmer
Arnold Wesker
✧annunciation
annunciative
Anne of Cleves
abnormal load
Arne Tiselius
announcement
aromatherapy
aromatically
adorableness
avowableness
Avogadro's law
a good innings
apodeictical
above measure
above the line
above-the-line
above the salt
aforethought
above oneself
apogeotropic
A Song to David
A Song to Celia
apothegmatic
apochromatic
another place
anotherguess
atomic energy
aboriginally
apolitically
abolitionary
abolitionism
abolitionist
atomic number
a rod in pickle
atomic second
atomic theory
atomic volume
atomic weight
an oaken towel
apoplectical
a fool's errand
Apollinarian
apologetical
apocryphally
acoustically
acoustic lens
à contre coeur
amontillados
apostolic see
apostolicism
apostolicity
as often as not
apostrophise
apostrophize
abortion pill
amortisement
amortisation
abortiveness
amortizement
amortization
apocynaceous
applaudingly
alphabetical
alphamerical
alphabet soup
alpha-blocker
Alpha Doradus
appraisement
appraisingly
appeals court
applausively
appraisively
alphanumeric
apprehension
apprehensive
apple of Sodom
apple-cheeked
appreciation
appreciatory
appreciative
apple-blossom
apple-knocker
appressorium
apple strudel
arpeggiation
appoggiatura
appoggiature
amphigastria
amphisbaenae
amphisbaenas
amphisbaenic
amphitheatre
amphibiously
amphibrachic
amphitropous
au poids de l'or
appointments
amphistomous
amphictyonic
Appalachians
ampelography
appendectomy
appendicitis
appendicular
Alpine skiing
approachable
approach road
approach shot
appropriator
appertaining
appurtenance
apperception
apperceptive
asparaginase
asparagus pea
aspartic acid
appercipient
aspergillums
apparentness
aspiringness
apparent time
apparatchiki
apparatchiks
apparitional
aspirational
appositeness
appositional
appetisement
appetisingly
appetizingly
asphyxiation
acquaintance
acquiescence
acroamatical
Afro-American
agribusiness
agrobusiness
acrocyanosis
agrichemical
agrochemical
agricultural
Afrocentrism
aerodynamics
aeroembolism
agreeability
arrière-garde
Adrienne Rich
air-sea rescue
ad referendum
agroforestry
acrogenously
Abraham Darby
agroindustry
Afrikanerdom
agrimonetary
air ambulance
acronychally
adrenal gland
Aaron Copland
à grands frais
aeronautical
aeroneurosis
air-force blue
air-condition
air pollution
air-commodore
aeroplankton
acrophonetic
air-breathing
aircraftsman
auroral zones
air-propeller
aerostatical
aerosiderite
arrester gear
arrester hook
acrostically
aoristically
across the way
à bras ouverts
abrasiveness
aerating root
a broth of a boy
a pretty penny
assibilation
associations
at second hand
assuefaction
abstemiously
Austen Layard
arsphenamine
aesthesiogen
aesthetician
aestheticise
✧aestheticism
aestheticist
aestheticize
Austin canons
Arshile Gorky
Austin friars
abscisic acid
adscititious
auspiciously
absciss layer
absoluteness
absolute zero
assembly hall
assembly line
assembly room
assembly shop
assimilation
assimilatory
assimilative
assemblaunce
assuming that
assentaneous
absinthiated
absent-minded
Arsène Wenger
as sure as a gun
Assurbanipal
abstractedly
abstractness
absorbed dose
alstroemeria
assortedness
Australia Day
Australasian
Austronesian
abstruseness
absorptivity
assassinator
assessorship
absit invidia
absquatulate
auscultation
auscultatory
auscultative
asseverating
asseveration
Art Garfunkel
anti-abortion
anti-aircraft
autoantibody
attractingly
attractively
antibacchius
antibarbarus
anticyclonic
antecedently
anticlerical
autocritique
astacologist
articulately
articulation
articulatory
anticipation
anticipatory
anticipative
autocatalyse
autocatalyze
antichthones
autochthones
anticatholic
Aztec two-step
autodidactic
antediluvial
antediluvian
autodestruct
antidiuretic
Astley Cooper
Althea Gibson
anthelmintic
antherozooid
autoexposure
authenticate
authenticity
at the outside
artificially
antifriction
anti-Gallican
antagonistic
autogenously
antigropelos
antihalation
autohypnosis
autohypnotic
astringently
auto-immunity
attributable
artilleryman
✧antilegomena
altaltissimo
automobilism
automobilist
autumn crocus
antimacassar
antimnemonic
anti-magnetic
antimalarial
antemeridian
ante meridiem
automorphism
antimetabole
automaticity
altimetrical
Antoni Artaud
actinic glass
Anton Chekhov
Antony Hewish
actinomorphy
autonomously
antoninianus
Antananarivo
Antonine Wall
Antonio Gaudí
Attenborough
astonishment
anti-national
antineutrino
anthocarpous
astronautics
anthoxanthin
Artiodactyla
astrogeology
anthophilous
astrophysics
authorisable
authorizable
aetiological
astrological
astronomical
astrocompass
action-packed
action radius
action replay
author's proof
action-taking
Anthony Blunt
astrocytomas
Anthony Quinn
anteprandial
anti-predator
autoptically
antiphonally
antiphonical
antiparticle
antiparallel
antiperiodic
antiphrastic
antipathetic
antipetalous
antipruritic
arterial road
alterability
antirachitic
auto rickshaw
autorickshaw
attorneyship
after the fact
antarthritic
afterthought
alto-rilievos
aethrioscope
afternoon tea
arthroplasty
anthropogeny
anthropogony

anthropoidal
anthropology
anthropotomy
arthroscopic
after its kind
afterburning
antisocially
antasthmatic
artistically
autistically
anti-Semitism
antisepalous
antistrophic
antistrophon
artist's proof
attitudinise
altitudinous
attitudinize
antithetical
antitheistic
autotrophism
antithrombin
Arthur Cayley
Artful Dodger
astoundingly
Arthur Harris
Arthur Miller
Arthur Porter
active matrix
autoxidation
autoxidative
Arundhati Roy
amuse-bouches
amuse-gueules
a quarter past
A Suitable Boy
à quatre mains
ayuntamiento
a quattr'occhi
adulteration
adulterously
advantageous
advance guard
adventitious
alveolar arch
adverbialise
adverbialize
advisability
Aswan High Dam
Anwar el-Sadat
asynchronism
asynchronous
amygdaloidal
✧anything goes
asymmetrical
asymptomatic
asymptotical
Bhagavad Gita
beat a retreat
Beata Beatrix
bearableness
blamableness
Blatant Beast
blah-blah-blah
bramble-berry
bramble-finch
beanbag chair
blabbermouth
blanc-de-Chine
Branchiopoda
boardsailing

brandy butter
brandy-bottle
bearded wheat
branded goods
board-measure
board meeting
✧board of trade
boarding card
branding-iron
boarding-pike
boarding pass
brand loyalty
brandy-pawnee
bladder senna
bladderwrack
blandishment
bear down upon
blamefulness
✧braggadocios
brachycephal
brachydactyl
brachygraphy
beachcombing
by a short head
blatherskite
bearing cloth
beatifically
Brazilian wax
Black Sabbath
Black Hawk War
blackballing
black salsify
Black Panther
black economy
black-hearted
black-visaged
blackbirding
black-fishing
black diamond
blacklisting
black-figured
black-and-blue
Black on Black
Black English
Black Country
black treacle
black draught
brackishness
bracket clock
blanket spray
bracket-creep
black pudding
black-quarter
blackguardly
blackcurrant
Black Russian
black mustard
black-eye bean
black-eyed pea
Bramley apple
beaumontague
Beaumarchais
brain-damaged
brainwashing
Blaenau Gwent
by a long chalk
beacon school
beat socks off
beam splitter
brass monkeys
brass-bounder

brassfounder
Blaise Pascal
brass rubbing
beam trawling
beat the pants
beat the clock
blastulation
blastosphere
beat to sticks
blast furnace
boastfulness
beaux esprits
baby-batterer
baby carriage
Bible-bashing
Bible-thumper
Bible-pounder
baba ghanouzh
bibliography
bibliologist
bibliomaniac
bibliopegist
bibliopolist
bibliophobia
bibble-babble
bubble-headed
bubble memory
bibulousness
babingtonite
baby-snatcher
bobby-dazzler
Bobby Fischer
baccalaurean
back and forth
buccaneering
buccaneerish
backbreaking
backboneless
by cock and pie
bicycle chain
back-crossing
bactericidal
bacteriology
bacteriostat
bachelor flat
bachelor girl
bachelorhood
bachelorship
Becher's Brook
Becket Thomas
bacchanalian
backing track
backing group
backing store
buckle-beggar
back-lighting
becomingness
bicameralism
bicameralist
back-mutation
bicentennial
bacon-and-eggs
back pressure
backstabbing
backspace key
back-slapping
backstarting
backswordman
back straight
backtracking
back to basics

back to nature
back-to-nature
backwoodsman
backwardness
back-wounding
body-building
body-checking
bodice-ripper
bad behaviour
badger-legged
by definition
bed of justice
bedside table
bedding plant
body language
Bedfordshire
bide one's time
body piercing
body snatcher
body stocking
badly-behaved
badly-dressed
bedazzlement
Buenaventura
buenas noches
buenas tardes
breeches-buoy
breeches part
breeches role
breech-loader
bread-chipper
Brendan Behan
bleeding edge
bleeding-edge
bread pudding
Baedeker raid
brewer's yeast
brewer's droop
bletherskate
bletheration
brevipennate
breakdancing
breakfast-set
break wedlock
break service
break the bank
break through
breakthrough
break a record
break-promise
break a strike
beetle-browed
beetleheaded
blennorrhoea
Byelorussian
breast cancer
bless the mark
breastplough
breastsummer
breaststroke
Breathalyser®
breathalyser
breathalyzer
breathe again
breathlessly
beesting lips
beestung lips
breathtaking
Bye Bye Birdie
breezeblocks
breeze up sale

buffalo-berry
buffalo chips
Buffalo wings
buffalo-grass
buffing-wheel
Baffin Island
before Christ
beggar belief
baggage-train
beggarliness
beggar's ticks
bog pimpernel
Buggins's turn
Bignoniaceae
begrudgingly
Bohemian ruby
by her lee-lane
by his lee-lane
behaviorally
behaviourism
behaviourist
brigade major
bridal wreath
building line
blind tooling
Blind Freddie
build a sconce
blind-stamped
Bailey bridge
bride-chamber
brimfullness
bring a charge
bridging loan
bring to terms
bring to a head
bring to light
bring forward
bring up short
bridge the gap
Bridget Riley
Bridget Jones
Brigham Young
Brighton Rock
Blithe Spirit
blithesomely
boiling point
British plate
brinkmanship
brickfielder
brick-nogging
brilliantine
brilliant-cut
Brian De Palma
Brian Perkins
blimpishness
blissfulness
brittle bones
bristle-grass
Bristol board
Bristol-brick
blister-steel
boisterously
baking powder
Bakewell tart
Balaam-basket
ball and chain
ballade royal
Balaamitical
balladmonger
balsam of Peru
balsam of Tolu

balsam poplar
ballanwrasse
biliary fever
bilharziasis
bilharziosis
Bill Beaumont
ball-breaking
bell-bottomed
bulk discount
belle passion
ballet-dancer
bullet-headed
balletically
balneologist
ballet-master
balletomania
belletristic
Balmer series
bullfighting
Bologna phial
Bologna stone
bulghur wheat
belligerence
belligerency
billingsgate
bolting cloth
bolting-hutch
Belgian franc
billiard ball
balanced flue
balance sheet
balance wheel
balanced pair
balancing act
belonephobia
bilingualism
Bilbo Baggins
ballon d'essai
balm of Gilead
bill of health
bill of lading
balloon whisk
✧bill of rights
bull-of-the-bog
ballpoint pen
belittlement
bilateralism
below the line
below-the-line
below the salt
belly landing
Billy McNeill
Billy Bremner
Billy Crystal
bombacaceous
bump and grind
bomb disposal
Bomber Harris
bomber jacket
bimillennium
bamboo shoots
Bonham-Carter
benzaldehyde
benjamin-tree
bantamweight
Benedictines
bene decessit
✧bunsen burner
bunker buster
bonnes grâces
bonne vivante

banderillero
bonnet monkey
bandersnatch
banker's order
banker's draft
beneficially
beneficently
benefactress
benightening
bench-warrant
bunch of fives
Bonfire night
Ben Nicholson
Bonnie Parker
bank interest
banalisation
banalization
benumbedness
banana-bender
Bananalander
banana liquid
Bonin Islands
bunko-steerer
benzoquinone
bona peritura
bank pass book
binary number
binary pulsar
bank reserves
binary system
binary weapon
bend-sinister
bend the elbow
Benito Juárez
bang to rights
bona vacantia
benevolently
bonny-clabber
Benny Goodman
biosatellite
biomagnetics
broncobuster
bioscientist
bronchoscope
bronchoscopy
blood packing
blood sausage
broadcasting
Blood Wedding
broad pennant
bloodletting
bloodthirsty
blood blister
blonde moment
bloody-minded
blood and iron
blood brother
bloodstained
blood pudding
bloodsucking
broken-backed
broker-dealer
biogeography
biomechanics
Bromeliaceae
biometrician
bioterrorism
bioterrorist
broken-winded
be off with you
bromhidrosis
biochemistry
brother-in-law
biophysicist
biorhythmics
bromide paper
biodiversity
booking clerk
boogie-woogie
block capital
blocked style
block release
block of flats
block diagram
blockbusting
book-learning
broiler house
bootlessness
bioflavonoid
Bloemfontein
blow-moulding
brownie point
Brownie Guide
brown mustard
Book of Baruch
Book of Daniel
blow one's mind
Book of Exodus
Book of Esther
Book of Haggai
Book of Isaiah
biologically
Book of Judges
Book of Judith
Book of Joshua
biocoenology
Book of Psalms
Book of Sirach
boomps-a-daisy
biographical
Books of Kings
book-scorpion
blow the coals
brontophobia
✧brontosaurus
bioturbation
bioavailable
biosynthesis
biosynthetic
bipropellant
bequeathable
bequeathment
bureaucratic
Bernard Levin
burial ground
Barranquilla
barratrously
Barbary sheep
Barbary coast
Barnaby Rudge
bare-breached
bird-catching
barodynamics
bored to tears
burn daylight
burseraceous
Border collie
border effect
Burmese glass
barber-monger
Barcelona nut
barge-couples
barber's block
Barnes Wallis
birefringent
Berufsverbot
Boraginaceae
birthday-book
birthday cake
birthday suit
Bertholletia
birthing pool
birth control
burn in effigy
Berbice chair
birding-piece
burying place
burning-glass
burning-point
burning-house
burning issue
bar billiards
bertillonage
barrier layer
barrier cream
Born in the USA
barristerial
bareknuckled
burglar alarm
barometrical
Baron Scarman
baron-officer
Baron Holberg
Baroness Hogg
bardolatrous
borrowed time
burrowing-owl
baryon number
borlotti bean
bird of wonder
baroreceptor
Burt Reynolds
Boris Karloff
Boris Yeltsin
bird's-nesting
borosilicate
barnstorming
Boris Johnson
Boris Godunov
Boris Spassky
bird's-eye view
burn to a crisp
born to be wild
burn the water
burst binding
burnt almonds
Bermuda grass
borough-reeve
borough court
birdwatching
Barry Sanders
barmy-brained
Barry St Leger
bastard title
bastard types
bass clarinet
✧basic English
basic process
basidiospore
basket clause
Bessemer iron
beseechingly
Buster Keaton
basket-making
basket-stitch
bespectacled
Besserwisser
Bosch process
base hospital
bastinadoing
basking shark
basal ganglia
beso las manos
baselessness
base-levelled
business card
businesslike
business plan
business park
business suit
bus conductor
bust one's butt
basso-relievo
basso-rilievo
bishop sleeve
bishop's court
bush sickness
base-spirited
besottedness
bushwhacking
by transverse
bate-breeding
betacarotene
butter-cooler
butter curler
battered baby
buttered eggs
battered wife
butterfly net
butterfly-bow
butterfly nut
battering-ram
butter muslin
between-decks
between times
betweentimes
between us two
bitter orange
butterscotch
buttery-hatch
butcher's hook
butcher's meat
bathing belle
bathing dress
Bettino Craxi
bottle-blonde
battleground
bottle-holder
butyl alcohol
battlemented
bottle-opener
Battle of Jena
Battle of Loos
Battle of Zama
bottle-slider
bottle-washer
bit on the side
butanoic acid
bet one's boots
bottom drawer
buttoned-down
bottom feeder
bottom fisher
bathochromic
battological
button scurvy
bottom-sawyer
buttress-root
bite the thumb
Bat Out of Hell
bathypelagic
butty-collier
Betty Friedan
blue asbestos
bougainvilia
Bougainville
bouncy castle
bound-bailiff
Bourdon gauge
blunderingly
boulevardier
Bruce McLaren
blue-eyed soul
Bruce Chatwin
Brunelleschi
bourgeoisify
brush strokes
Blue Mountain
boudoir grand
blue pipe-tree
blue quandong
Brussels lace
bluestocking
bounty hunter
blusteringly
Blut und Eisen
brutum fulmen
bouquet garni
blue water gas
Bavarian Alps
beverage room
Beverly Hills
bowling alley
bowling green
bewilderment
bow and scrape
bow-compasses
bewitchingly
box jellyfish
boy-meets-girl
Boyana Church
beyond number
beyond recall
bayonet joint
boy in buttons
buyer's market
buyers' market
Bayes' theorem
bay at the moon
buzzard-clock
chalazogamic
Charadriidae
character set
characterise
characterism
characterful
characterize
coadaptation
crambo-jingle
chamber organ
chamber-stick
chamber music
charcoal grey
chalcography
chalcogenide
Chalcolithic
chance-medley
chalcanthite
chalcopyrite
Chandragupta
claudication
Coanda effect
Claddagh ring
chauds-mellés
crapehanging
clare-obscure
chapel master
chapel of ease
Clare College
chapeaux-bras
coacervation
change colour
changelessly
change of life
clangorously
change the leg
crash-landing
crash barrier
crash-matting
cha-cha-chaing
coachbuilder
clavicembalo
clarinettist
coalitionism
coalitionist
coaxial cable
coaxial pairs
cranial nerve
craniologist
cranial index
chalicothere
clamjamphrie
crack a bottle
cracked wheat
crack the whip
chalk and talk
crackbrained
Charlie Sheen
chaplainship
Chaplinesque
Charles Dance
Charles Hallé
Charles Barry
Charles Reade
Charles Rolls
Charles Forte
Charles's Wain
cradle-scythe
charlatanism
charley horse
Coal Measures
claiming race
coal merchant
claymore mine
chain reactor
chain-gearing
Chaunticleer
charnel house
channel stane
channel stone
chain-breaker
chain printer
clannishness
cladogenesis
cladogenetic
cyanogenesis

Cyanophyceae
chamomile tea
cladosporium
championship
clapperboard
chairmanship
clair-obscure
clairvoyance
clairvoyancy
Claire Rayner
clairaudient
classic races
classicalism
classicalist
classicality
chassé-croisé
classifiable
Crassulaceae
chaise-longue
crassamentum
chat-show host
claustration
coat-trailing
claptrappery
craftmanship
chaetiferous
chartography
chattel house
chattels-real
coast-to-coast
craftspeople
craftsperson
charter mayor
charter party
charterparty
charter-chest
clatteringly
chapterhouse
Charterhouse
craft brother
chastisement
chastity belt
coal titmouse
chart-busting
chauvinistic
cabbage-white
cable railway
cable release
cable's-length
cable tramway
cobalt glance
cobbler's pegs
cabalistical
cabin cruiser
cabinetmaker
cubistically
cyclandelate
cockfighting
cack-handedly
cocking piece
cucking stool
coccidiostat
cockieleekie
cachinnation
cachinnatory
cucumber tree
Cicindelidae
cichoraceous
cuckold-maker
cyclodextrin
cuckoo flower
cyclonically
cecropia moth
cuckoo pintle
cyclosporin A
cuckoo-roller
cyclographic
cyclopropane
cuckoo shrike
Cyclostomata
cyclostomous
cacophonical
cacophonious
cocksureness
Cocos Islands
cicatrichule
cockthrowing
cactus dahlia
Cactus People
code-breaking
cedrelaceous
codification
co-dependency
coelacanthic
cremationist
cheval mirror
crematoriums
coerciveness
crème caramel
crepehanging
Clemence Dane
clever-clever
crème de cacao
crepe-de-chine
crêpe-de-chine
crenellation
crème fraîche
Clément Marot
Coelenterata
coelenterate
Clement Freud
crêpe suzette
Czechoslovak
chemical bond
chemical cosh
Chemical Mace
chemical wood
credibleness
caesium clock
credit rating
Cheviot Hills
credit titles
creditworthy
checkweigher
clerk of works
checking-room
checkerberry
checkerboard
creolisation
creolization
cream cracker
clean and jerk
cleaning lady
Chen Ning Yang
caenogenesis
cue someone in
Cherokee rose
chemotherapy
coenobitical
coenospecies
chemotropism
creepy-crawly
cherry brandy
clear-obscure
cherry bounce
clear felling
clear-sighted
cherry laurel
clearing bank
chevron board
clearing sale
cherry picker
cherry-pepper
clear as a bell
cheerishness
cherry tomato
cheerfulness
cheeseburger
cheesecutter
cheesehopper
cheesemonger
cleistogamic
chefs d'oeuvre
cheeseparing
cheese-rennet
cheese slicer
cheesetaster
chest of viols
chest freezer
chesterfield
creatureship
chestnut tree
creativeness
crepusculous
cherubically
cheluviation
chequerboard
cresylic acid
café-chantant
coffin-dodger
cognitive map
cigarette end
cohabitation
cohesibility
cohesiveness
china cabinet
climatically
chivalrously
climbing boot
climbing iron
climbing wall
coincidental
coincidently
clincher-work
Cain-coloured
child benefit
child welfare
child-bearing
childbearing
childcrowing
childishness
child support
Chinese paper
Chinese walls
crise de nerfs
Chinese white
Chinese block
Chinese boxes
Chinese goose
chimerically
crime fiction
cliffhanging
chieftainess
✧chief of staff
Cliff Richard
Chief Bromden
clip-fastener
chief justice
cringe-making
cringeworthy
cliché-ridden
critical mass
criticalness
chiliahedron
criticisable
criticizable
criminogenic
chick-a-diddle
click-through
clinker-block
clinker-built
cricket table
chill cabinet
chilli powder
cairn terrier
Chiantishire
client-server
chimney shaft
chimney piece
chimneyboard
chimney stack
chimney stalk
chimney-sweep
chimney swift
Chimonanthus
coin-operated
cainogenesis
Chirotherium
Chironomidae
chiropractic
chiropractor
chirographer
chirographic
chiropterous
crimping-iron
chiaroscuros
cuisse-madame
cristobalite
chitterlings
Chinua Achebe
chiquichiqui
chirurgeonly
cliquishness
collaterally
collared dove
culpableness
collaborator
Celia Johnson
Calvary cross
calabash tree
celibatarian
Calyciflorae
calico-flower
calycoideous
calycanthemy
cell division
Colley Cibber
collegialism
collegiality
calceamentum
culvertailed
collectorate
collectively
collectivise
collectivism
collectivist
collectivity
collectivize
Cologne water
caliginosity
cultivatable
collinearity
Celtic fringe
calling birds
calcium oxide
calligrapher
calligraphic
callisthenic
call into play
colliquation
colliquative
Culm Measures
calumniation
columniation
calumniatory
calumniously
cell membrane
calamitously
cold moulding
Colin Jackson
calendar-line
calendar year
Colin Renfrew
cylinder head
cylinder hole
cylinder lock
cylinder seal
Colonel Blimp
Colin Cowdrey
cylindricity
cylindriform
colonisation
colonization
Collop Monday
call of nature
coleorrhizae
coleopterist
coleopterous
colloquially
coloquintida
chloroformer
calorimetric
chlorimetric
chlorometric
colorimetric
chlorambucil
chlorination
chloroplasts
calorescence
chlorous acid
Celesteville
calisthenics
cold shoulder
cold-shoulder
colostomy bag
colossus-wise
call the shots
cole titmouse
culture shock
colour filter
colourlessly
colour scheme
colour screen
colluctation
collywobbles
command paper
commandingly
compare notes
companionway
companion set
companionate
combat jacket
compatriotic
come a cropper
compass plane
compass plant
Campanularia
company union
come-by-chance
camp-drafting
come down with
commercially
commencement
commendation
commendatory
cumber-ground
compellingly
compellation
compellative
commemorable
commemorator
commensalism
commensality
commensurate
compensation
compensatory
compensative
commentation
camp-follower
combinations
commiserable
commiserator
commissioned
commissioner
commissarial
commissariat
come it strong
committeeman
come into play
camiknickers
complacently
cumulocirrus
complication
complicative
Camille Corot
complaisance
complemental
complimental
complimenter
cumulonimbus
complanation
Camaldolites
Camillo Golgi
cumulostrata
completeness
cumulatively
complexional
complexioned
cement-copper
cementitious
Cominformist
common as muck
common debtor
campodeiform
Come on Eileen
composedness

componential
come off worst
common gender
common ground
common ink cap
commorientes
commodiously
common millet
common mallow
compos mentis
✧common market
compoundable
compound leaf
compound time
Common People
common-riding
common school
common scoter
come on stream
common sorrel
common shrimp
come on strong
comfortingly
comfort woman
common vestry
commonwealth
camp-preacher
camera lucida
comprimarios
compressible
Combretaceae
cumbrousness
camp-shedding
camp-sheeting
cometography
cymotrichous
come to naught
Camptosaurus
compunctious
commuter belt
computer code
computer game
commune bonum
come ungummed
compurgation
compurgatory
communicable
communicably
communicator
communitaire
communion cup
compulsorily
compulsatory
compulsative
compulsively
come up trumps
cinnabar moth
Canaan Banana
connate water
contabescent
convalescent
cinnamic acid
contaminable
contaminator
contagionist
contagiously
cantankerous
containerise
containerize
cinnamon bear
Cantabrigian
contact sport
contact print
contact-print
connaturally
confabulator
cane-bottomed
conic section
conscientise
conscientize
conscription
conscionable
conscionably
Cynocephalus
Canada balsam
conidiophore
conidiospore
conveyancing
canterburies
contend about
conférencier
conferencing
congenerical
cankeredness
concelebrant
concelebrate
conferential
centesimally
congenitally
congeniality
conveniently
conseil d'état
cancellarial
cancellarian
cancellation
conterminant
conterminate
conterminous
condemnation
condemnatory
conveyor belt
contemplable
contemplator
contemptible
contemptibly
cancerphobia
contemporary
contemporise
contemporize
contemptuous
consecration
consecratory
consecrative
consensually
confessional
confessoress
condensation
conversation
conversative
conceptually
contextually
concentrator
concert party
concert waltz
conventicler
consentience
concentrical
concert pitch
concertinaed
consentingly
contestingly
conceptional
connectional
convectional
conventional
confectioner
conventioner
concentering
concert grand
contentation
contestation
connectively
connectivity
consequences
consequently
conservatrix
conservation
conservatory
✧conservatism
✧conservative
conchiferous
conchologist
cantharidian
cantharidine
convincement
candid camera
convincingly
confiscation
confiscatory
considerance
considerable
considerably
cantilevered
confidential
canting-wheel
contingently
conning-tower
convivialist
conviviality
conditioning
conditionate
conciliation
conciliatory
conciliative
centillionth
cantillation
cantillatory
confirmation
confirmatory
confirmative
consignation
contignation
consignatory
consistently
consistorial
consistorian
continuation
continuative
contiguously
continuously
conglobulate
conglobation
canaliculate
candle-holder
conglomerate
conclamation
candle-paring
canalisation
conclusively
conglutinant
conglutinate
candle-waster
canalization
cinematheque
cinemathèque
cinéma vérité
canon regular
canon secular
canine letter
canonisation
canonization
concordantly
console table
cannon fodder
concomitance
concomitancy
consolidated
consolidator
consociation
censoriously
conformation
confoundedly
conjoint will
concorporate
contortional
convolutedly
conspectuity
conspiracist
conspiringly
conspiration
centre around
contrabbasso
contribution
contributary
contributory
contributive
contractable
contractedly
centroclinal
contractible
contractural
contradictor
congregation
control panel
controllable
controllably
control lever
central angle
control total
central force
control tower
central conic
central dogma
control board
control freak
control group
control stick
control event
contra mundum
concremation
confrontment
contranatant
centre of mass
contrapuntal
contrapposto
contrariness
contrariwise
concrescence
centrosphere
centre spread
congratulant
congratulate
concreteness
contriteness
contriturate
canorousness
contrivement
canary yellow
Canis Majoris
canister shot
Canis Minoris
constabulary
constringent
constriction
constrictive
constipation
constituency
constatation
constitution
constitutive
construction
constructure
constructive
contumacious
conjunctivae
conjunctival
conjunctivas
contumelious
contubernyal
confusedness
cantus firmus
concubitancy
concupiscent
connubiality
Confucianism
Confucianist
centuriation
centuplicate
conduplicate
consummately
consummation
consummatory
consummative
concurrently
conqueringly
conquistador
convulsional
convulsively
consultation
consultatory
consultative
conductively
conductivity
centumvirate
century plant
candy-striped
cloud-seeding
cloud ceiling
cloud chamber
chondriosome
cloud-kissing
crowd-pleaser
co-ordinately
co-ordination
co-ordinative
chondroblast
chondrostian
chordophonic
cloddishness
close harmony
cloven-footed
choreography
close the door
cloven-hoofed
cholerically
close-fitting
choreologist
close-tongued
close borough
close-coupled
close company
close-mouthed
close-grained
close-cropped
closed season
cloth of state
Cool Hand Luke
clothes-sense
clothes-horse
clothes-brush
clothes-press
cookie-cutter
cooking-range
cooling tower
cooking apple
closing price
chorioid coat
chorizontist
cookie-pusher
clomipramine
clock-watcher
Crookes glass
crown witness
clownishness
chocolate-box
chocolate log
chorological
chorographer
chorographic
crop rotation
crossbanding
cross-lateral
crossbencher
cross bedding
cross-selling
cross-section
cross-lighted
cross-linking
cross-ply tyre
crossing over
cross-and-pile
cross-country
cross-grained
cross-dresser
cross-purpose
cross-current
cross-buttock
crosscutting
cross-examine
clotted cream
clouted cream
cook the books
chorus master
Cappagh-brown
cuprammonium
Captain Flint
cephalometry
capabilities
Cape Coloured
capacitation
copper-bottom
copper-fasten
copper-glance
copper-nickel
cypress swamp
cap of liberty

Cape hyacinth
cupping-glass
copying press
capriciously
Capricornian
captiousness
capillaceous
cupuliferous
co-polymerise
co-polymerize
copulatively
coprophagist
coprophagous
coprophilous
cupboard-love
Cape primrose
capercaillie
capercailzie
cypermethrin
capital gains
capital goods
capital cross
capitalistic
capitulation
capitulatory
capstan lathe
capstan table
caput mortuum
coquettishly
carragheenin
carbamic acid
carnal-minded
curtain-sider
circassienne
Cordaitaceae
currant-jelly
carpal tunnel
currant bread
Caribbee bark
Caribbean Sea
cerebrotonia
cerebrotonic
corn-chandler
card-carrying
caricaturist
correlatable
carpet beetle
carpetbagger
corn exchange
Carmen Callil
currency note
carte des vins
curietherapy
Cartesianism
carpet-knight
carte blanche
corneal graft
carpetmonger
Correr Museum
carpet python
correctional
correctioner
carpenter-bee
carpenter-ant
correctitude
correctively
cerographist
cardinal-bird
curvicaudate
corrivalling
cardinalship
corrivalship
corrie-fisted
cardiography
carriageable
carriage bolt
carriage-free
carriage line
carving knife
curling tongs
corning house
carriage-paid
curling irons
curling-stone
Cornish pasty
certificated
carriwitchet
cardiologist
cardiomegaly
corni inglesi
carcinogenic
curvifoliate
curvirostral
curvicostate
corridor work
curliewurlie
corallaceous
corollaceous
circle around
Carl Linnaeus
Carolina pink
carillonneur
circle-riding
carelessness
coram paribus
card mechanic
ceramic oxide
ceramography
ceremonially
chromophilic
chromophoric
corn marigold
corn-merchant
chromosphere
chrome spinel
chromaticism
chromaticity
chromatogram
chromatopsia
chrematistic
chrome yellow
chronography
chronologise
chronologist
chronologize
chronometric
carbonaceous
corpora vilia
corporalship
Corporal Trim
corpora lutea
carbon dating
curl one's lips
corporealise
corporealism
corporealist
corporeality
corporealize
carbon fibres
carpophagous
cartophilist
carbolic acid
carbonic acid
Carlovingian
carbolic soap
corno inglese
corroborable
corroborator
carpological
cartological
carton-pierre
cartographer
cartographic
cirro-stratus
corn on the cob
cargo cultist
cirro-cumulus
carbohydrate
ceroplastics
cartridge pen
corpse candle
Christ Church
Christchurch
Christian era
Christianise
Christianism
Christianity
Christianize
Christliness
chrisom child
chrisom-cloth
Christmas Day
Christmas box
Christmas eve
Carl Sandburg
chrestomathy
Christolatry
corespondent
christophany
christophene
christophine
Christ's-thorn
corn-shucking
Ceratosaurus
circular file
circular note
circumcentre
✧circumcision
circumfusile
circumfusion
circumfluent
circumfluous
curmudgeonly
circumgyrate
circumjacent
circumlocute
corpus luteum
cor pulmonale
cerium metals
circumnutate
corduroy road
circumstance
circumscribe
circuit rider
circuit board
circuit judge
circuitously
caravansarai
caravanserai
Carl Wernicke
caraway seeds
carry the flag
carry through
carry one's bat
carry your bat
carry forward
carry-forward
cash and carry
cash-and-carry
custard slice
custard apple
Cascade Range
Cusparia bark
Cossack boots
casual labour
casualty ward
cashew apples
caster action
cosmetically
castellation
costermonger
cassette deck
Cosí Fan Tutte
così fan tutte
casting couch
cushion-plant
coscinomancy
cosmic string
Casino Royale
cosmonautics
castor action
cosmoplastic
cost of living
cosmogonical
cosmological
✧cosmopolitan
cosmopolitic
cosmographer
cosmographic
customs union
customs house
custom-shrunk
cash register
cash-strapped
cost the earth
CNS stimulant
costume piece
costume drama
cestui que use
Casey Stengel
cottage piano
Citlaltépetl
Citeaux Abbey
catechetical
catachrestic
catacoustics
catadioptric
cathetometer
citification
cityfication
cytogenetics
categorially
cut the cackle
cutting grass
citriculture
catallactics
cotyledonary
cotyledonous
cattle-lifter
cetyl alcohol
cattle market
Catilinarian
cattle-plague
catamountain
cat o' mountain
cetane number
catena patrum
cetane rating
cut one's teeth
cut one's stick
cutinisation
cut one's lucky
cut and thrust
cut-and-thrust
cutinization
catholically
Catholic King
Catholicoses
Cotton Mather
cut boon whids
cottonocracy
cathodograph
city of refuge
city planning
cataphoresis
cataphractic
cataphysical
cataphyllary
caterwauling
cetera desunt
cytoskeletal
cytoskeleton
catastrophic
Côtes du Rhône
cytotoxicity
citrus fruits
Cotswold lion
Cathy Freeman
Citizens' Band
causa causans
courageously
causationism
causationist
clubbability
Churchillian
churchianity
councilmanic
council of war
council-board
council house
churchpeople
church-parade
church school
churchwarden
coup de foudre
coup de maître
cause célèbre
crush barrier
cough mixture
cough lozenge
cousin-german
caution money
cautiousness
chuckie-stane
chuckie-stone
caulking-iron
churlishness
coulombmeter
crumple zones
counsellable
club sandwich
court martial
court-martial
caustic curve
courtierlike
Courtney Pine
county family
club together
count the cost
court plaster
countenancer
counting room
Count Tolstoy
county-people
countermarch
counter-paled
counter-gauge
counter-tally
counter-parry
Count Dracula
counterscarp
counter-weigh
counter-tenor
counterpoise
counter-sense
counteroffer
counter-agent
countercheck
counter-wheel
countershaft
countercharm
counterlight
counterplead
counterbluff
counterclaim
counter-flory
counterblast
counter-force
counterpoint
counter-round
counterpoise
counterbrace
cluster graft
counter-drain
counterproof
court-dresser
counterstain
counter-stand
counter-punch
counter-guard
County school
country dance
country party
countrywoman
country house
country music
caveat emptor
civil defence
civil service
civil servant
civil liberty
covalent bond
civilisation
cavalry twill
civilization
Covent Garden
cavendo tutus
Coventry blue
covered wagon
coversed sine
cover version
cover the feet
covetousness
covetiveness
cow blackbird
Cawdor Castle

Cowardly Lion
cowardliness
Clytemnestra
cryoglobulin
crymotherapy
chymotrypsin
cry roast-meat
cryopreserve
cryptobiosis
cryptobiotic
cryptochrome
cryptography
cryptogamian
cryptogamist
cryptogamous
crystal-gazer
cryptologist
crystallitis
crystal clear
cryptomnesia
cryptomnesic
cryptanalyst
cryptonymous
cry quittance
dead-and-alive
drama therapy
dramatically
dramatisable
dramatizable
dead as mutton
diamagnetism
deaf alphabet
dramaturgist
dead-ball line
deambulatory
de-alcoholise
de-alcoholize
diadem spider
dialectician
dialecticism
dialectology
diageotropic
dwarfishness
draughtiness
draught-hooks
draughtboard
draught horse
draught-house
draught-proof
death warrant
death penalty
death-dealing
diaphanously
diachronical
diathermancy
death futures
drawing paper
drawing-table
doating-piece
drawing-knife
drawing board
drawing-frame
dialling code
drawlingness
dialling tone
dead language
deaf language
dual monarchy
Dean Moriarty
drainage-tube
Dean of Arches
diatomaceous
diamond-wheel
diamond-hitch
diamond-field
diamond snake
diamond-drill
drag one's feet
diapophysial
diabolically
diatonically
dragon lizard
dragon's teeth
dragon's blood
dracontiasis
deaspiration
DNA profiling
diagrammatic
Dead Sea apple
Dead Sea fruit
draw to a close
dearticulate
draw the table
draw the teeth
draw the cloth
draw the board
draft-dodging
diastrophism
draw-top table
deactivation
Dibranchiata
dibranchiate
debilitating
debilitation
debilitative
debonairness
debt of honour
debt of nature
dubitatively
doch-an-dorach
dictatorship
decrescendos
decrepitness
duchesse lace
decreasingly
declensional
decaffeinate
ducking-stool
declinometer
dock-labourer
decalcomania
deceleration
decoloration
decalescence
decommission
decimal point
decomposable
decompressor
deconsecrate
decongestant
decongestion
decongestive
decentralise
decentralize
Doctor Jekyll
Doctor Moreau
doctor's stuff
Doctor Watson
da capo al fine
decipherable
decipherment
decapitalise
decapitalize
decapitation
dicarpellary
dichromatism
doctrinarian
dichrooscope
dichroscopic
decoratively
decorousness
decasyllabic
decasyllable
decisiveness
decitizenise
decitizenize
decrustation
dactylically
dactyliology
dactyloscopy
dictyopteran
deducibility
dodecagynian
dodecagynous
dodecahedral
dodecahedron
didactically
dodecandrous
dodecaphonic
dedicational
dedicatorial
Didelphyidae
Dieu avec nous
dietary fibre
de-escalation
diencephalic
diencephalon
Dresden china
deep-discount
dreadfulness
diesel engine
dietetically
deep-fat fryer
diethylamine
diethyl ether
dreamcatcher
dye in the wool
deed of saying
dies profesti
deerstalking
dressing-case
dressing-down
dress uniform
dressing-gown
dressing-room
dressing-sack
deepwaterman
deepwatermen
defraudation
deflationary
deflationist
deflagration
defectionist
differentiae
differential
deflectional
difficulties
defamatorily
definability
definiteness
definitional
definitively
deformedness
deforciation
diffrangible
diffusedness
diffusionism
diffusionist
Dufourspitze
dogmatically
digladiation
degree Kelvin
dagger of lath
digressional
digressively
dégringolade
digging stick
degenerately
degenerating
degeneration
degenerative
dig oneself in
dogtooth-spar
digital watch
digital radio
digital clock
digital socks
digitisation
digitization
dehumidifier
driveability
drivethrough
Dwight L Moody
driving range
driving wheel
driving shaft
drinking bout
drinking-horn
drink-driving
drilling pipe
de-ionisation
de-ionization
deinotherium
do-it-yourself
Daily Express
dejectedness
dijudication
Dr John Watson
Duke of Omnium
dollarocracy
Della-Cruscan
dolman sleeve
deliberately
deliberation
deliberative
dilucidation
dilaceration
delicateness
delicatessen
dulce de leche
delightfully
dolphinarium
deltiologist
delamination
delimitation
delimitative
delinquently
dilapidation
deliquescent
doloriferous
dolorousness
delusiveness
dilettantish
dilettantism
dilatability
dilatoriness
delitescence
delivery note
delivery-pipe
delivery-tube
dolly mixture
damnableness
democratical
demi-culverin
demodulation
dame d'honneur
demi-distance
Dombey and Son
dimmer switch
demographics
demagnetiser
demagnetizer
demilitarise
demilitarize
demi-mondaine
Dame Myra Hess
demoniacally
demand-driven
diminuendoes
domino effect
dementedness
domineer over
demonologist
demineralise
demineralize
diminishable
diminishment
demonstrable
demonstrably
demonstrator
domino theory
diminutively
damson cheese
dumortierite
demoralising
demoralizing
dimerisation
dimerization
Domesday book
domesticated
domesticable
domestically
domesticator
dumb terminal
demotivation
De Maupassant
denuclearise
denuclearize
✧danse macabre
donkey-engine
dance of death
dunderheaded
dinner jacket
donkey jacket
Daniel Mannix
Daniel Ortega
danseur noble
donkey's years
Donnerwetter
Denzil Davies
Dancing Brave
Dancing Queen
Denbighshire
Dennis Hopper
dentilingual
Dennis Lillee
Dennis Nilsen
densitometer
densitometry
dentirostral
denticulated
dunniewassal
Donald Coggan
dingle-dangle
Donald Michie
Donald Sinden
Donald Wolfit
dynamic range
dynamometric
denomination
denominative
denunciation
denunciatory
Dantophilist
dendrologist
dendrologous
dynastically
Denis Diderot
Denis Compton
Danish pastry
Denis Burkitt
do-nothingism
denaturalise
denaturalize
donatistical
denotatively
denouncement
drop a clanger
droseraceous
duodecennial
duodenectomy
do one's head in
drongo-cuckoo
drongo-shrike
droughtiness
✧dyotheletism
drop-in centre
droplock loan
doom-merchant
dropped scone
deoppilation
deoppilative
dropping fire
dropping-well
Doomsday book
doorstepping
droit des gens
deontologist
doomwatching
depravedness
depredations
doppelganger
doppelgänger
depreciation
depreciatory
depreciative
depressingly
depressurise
depressurize
depth of field
depth of focus
depth sounder
diprionidian
dephlegmator
dipole moment
depolymerise

depolymerize
Doppler shift
depoliticise
depoliticize
diplomatical
diplogenesis
Diplock court
diploblastic
depopulation
dipyridamole
departmental
depositional
deposit money
depositation
diphtheritic
diphtheritis
diphthongise
diphthongize
dermatophyte
dermabrasion
dorsal suture
direct access
direct action
direct labour
directly that
direct method
direct motion
deracination
direct object
directorship
director's cut
direct speech
Derwent Water
dormer window
deregulation
derogatorily
derogatively
dorsiventral
Darling Range
Darling River
Darlingtonia
dorsiflexion
dormitory-car
Derek Malcolm
Derek Walcott
duraluminium
dorsolateral
dorsoventral
derepression
dark reaction
Doris Lessing
derisiveness
derivational
derivatively
dirty laundry
dirty weekend
Darby and Joan
Darryl Zanuck
dispatch-boat
dispatch case
distanceless
discandering
diseasedness
dismayedness
dissatisfied
destabiliser
destabilizer
disharmonise
disharmonize
disdainfully
dispauperise
dispauperize
despairingly
disobedience
disaccharide
disaccordant
disk capacity
disadvantage
disadventure
desideration
desiderative
disregardful
dissemblance
disseverance
dysteleology
dishevelling
dishevelment
disseverment
disseminator
disrelishing
dysmenorrhea
discerptible
distemperate
disheartened
descensional
dispensation
dispensatory
dispensative
dispense with
dissected map
dysaesthesia
dysaesthetic
dissentingly
dessertspoon
dissenterish
dissenterism
disceptation
dissertation
dissertative
disreputable
disreputably
disaffection
disaffiliate
disagreeable
disagreeably
designer drug
disagreement
disaggregate
Das Rheingold
dysphemistic
dissipatedly
distinctness
despisedness
despitefully
dispiteously
des richesses
dissimilarly
dispiritedly
dispiritment
disciplinant
disciplinary
discipleship
distillation
distillatory
dissimulator
displeasance
displeasedly
displaceable
displacement
desulphurise
desulphurate
desulphurize
disclamation
desalination
disallowance
disallowable
desolateness
disembarrass
disembellish
disambiguate
disembrangle
disinherison
disinterment
disinterring
disintegrate
disinfectant
disinfection
disincentive
disingenuity
disingenuous
disenchanted
disenchanter
desensitiser
desensitizer
disanalogous
disinflation
disendowment
disintricate
disannulling
disannulment
dislocatedly
despondently
despondingly
discordantly
discoverable
disbowelling
discoverture
Discomedusae
discomedusan
Discovery Bay
discomfiting
discomfiture
disgorgement
dislodgement
discophorous
despotically
disco biscuit
dissocialise
dissociality
dissocialize
despoliation
dissociation
dissociative
discommodity
discommunity
discountable
disconnected
disjointedly
discount rate
disconnexion
dishonorable
dishonorably
despotocracy
discorporate
discomposure
discourteise
discourteous
discouraging
discographer
disconsolate
dispossessed
dispossessor
discontented
distortional
Discomycetes
disappointed
disoperation
disapproving
dasyphyllous
disorganised
disorganized
desirability
distribution
distributary
distributive
distractedly
destructible
distractible
disgradation
deservedness
discreetness
disorientate
disgregation
distrainable
desert island
distrainment
discriminant
discriminate
disfranchise
Desert Orchid
dispropriate
distrustless
discreteness
discretional
discretively
desirousness
disprivacied
disprivilege
disestablish
disaster area
disassembler
disaster film
disassociate
disastrously
desaturation
disputatious
disturbative
dispute about
disquietness
disauthorise
disauthorize
disqualified
disqualifier
desquamation
desquamatory
desquamative
disguiseless
disbursement
disguisement
disquisition
disquisitory
disquisitive
discursively
dissuasively
disgustingly
disgustfully
disruptively
disaventrous
dissymmetric
detractingly
detractively
detachedness
detectophone
dotted around
✧ditheletical
do the honours
dotted rhythm
ditheistical
Dutch bargain
Dutch clinker
Dutch elm tree
Dutch concert
Dutch comfort
Dutch courage
Dutch auction
ditriglyphic
detumescence
dating agency
determinable
determinably
determinedly
dethronement
detruncation
detoxication
dithyrambist
Dougal Haston
deuteranopia
deuteranopic
douse the glim
deuteroscopy
deuteroplasm
Deuteronomic
daughterling
dough-kneaded
deuch-an-doris
doughnutting
drunk-driving
drunk as a lord
double-acting
double-bubble
double boiler
double bridle
double-banked
double-biting
double-bottom
double-charge
double-dealer
double-decked
double-decker
double dagger
double-figure
double florin
double-formed
double-glazed
double-headed
double-header
double-handed
double-locked
double-manned
double-minded
doubling time
double obelus
Douglas Bader
Douglas Adams
double-storey
double spread
double-tongue
double vision
double whammy
deutoplasmic
Deutsche Mark
drug smuggler
doubtfulness
Deus vobiscum
deviationism
deviationist
device driver
David Barclay
David Daiches
David Campese
David Garrick
David L Clarke
divided skirt
David Beckham
David Bellamy
David Ricardo
David Hilbert
David Hockney
David Trimble
David Starkey
David Duckham
devil-may-care
devil of a mess
Devil's Island
devil-in-a-bush
devil-worship
devilishness
devil's tattoo
diving beetle
diving petrel
divinity calf
divinity hall
divinatorial
divarication
divertimenti
divertimento
diversionary
diversionist
diverticular
diverticulum
diversifying
Dover's powder
divisibility
division bell
divisiveness
dovetail into
devotionally
down-and-dirty
down-and-outer
dowager's hump
downloadable
downshifting
down the hatch
down the drain
downwardness
Dexter Gordon
dextrocardia
dextrogyrate
dextrousness
daylight lamp
day-blindness
dry-stane dyke
Elaeagnaceae
exalbuminous
emasculation
emasculatory
emancipation
emancipatory
exacerbation
evanescently
evangelicism
evangelistic
emargination
exaggeration
exaggeratory
exaggerative

examinership
Erasistratus
edaciousness
enabling bill
elasmobranch
Ewan McGregor
evaporimeter
evaporometer
evaporograph
Eratosthenes
epanorthoses
epanorthosis
exasperating
exasperation
exasperative
Epacridaceae
elastic limit
exanthematic
exactingness
enantiopathy
enantiomeric
enantiomorph
enantiotropy
enantiostyly
enarthrodial
ex abundantia
embranchment
emblazonment
emblematical
embolisation
embolization
embarrassing
embarquement
embitterment
embattlement
embourgeoise
embryologist
embryophytes
embezzlement
exchangeable
exchangeably
exchange rate
eschatologic
enchantingly
✧encyclopedia
encyclopedic
ecclesiology
Ecclesiastes
ecclesiastic
encheiridion
excogitation
excogitative
enclitically
excel oneself
eucalyptuses
encumberment
encomenderos
encumbrancer
eccentricity
encroachment
enchondromas
encephalitic
encephalitis
escape clause
encipherment
escapologist
escort agency
excursionise
excursionist
excursionize
encirclement
excess demand
eschscholzia
excess supply
excitability
escutcheoned
excitingness
exclusionary
exclusionism
exclusionist
excruciating
excruciation
Encounter Bay
encrustation
endocarditic
endocarditis
Eddie Cochran
endless screw
endless chain
end of the line
endogenously
endamagement
endometritis
endonuclease
endangerment
endoparasite
endophyllous
endarteritis
endoskeletal
endoskeleton
endosymbiont
endosmometer
emerald green
epencephalic
epencephalon
exercise bike
exercise book
exercitation
epexegetical
exegetically
eleventh hour
eleventh-hour
elementalism
elementarily
evergreen oak
elephant cord
even-handedly
elephant seal
elephant's-ear
etepimeletic
evening class
evening dress
eleemosynary
Eleonora Duse
Eleanor Rigby
Eleanor Cross
eternisation
eternity ring
eternization
exemplifying
exempt rating
execratively
electability
eventide home
eleutherarch
electrically
electric blue
electric fire
electric hare
electric seal
electrifying
even-tempered
electron beam
electroscope
electrometer
electrogenic
electromeric
electrometry
electroshock
electrophile
event horizon
electron lens
electroplate
electropolar
electrosonde
electrotonic
electromotor
electrotonus
electron pair
electro-optic
electrograph
ejection seat
electron tube
electronvolt
electrolyser
electrotyper
electrolysis
electrolytic
electrotypic
electorially
exenteration
eventfulness
executive toy
executorship
Eyes Wide Shut
every man Jack
everydayness
every few days
everywhither
every so often
effectuality
effectuation
enfeeblement
effiguration
effeminately
enfant trouvé
efflorescent
effervescent
effortlessly
effusiometer
effusiveness
eggs-and-bacon
engraftation
eggs Benedict
egg separator
eagle-sighted
engagingness
English flute
Englishwoman
English sweat
Elgin marbles
egg-and-anchor
Eugène Dubois
engine-driver
engenderment
engine-fitter
Eugenio Barba
Eugene Onegin
Eugene O'Neill
egg-and-tongue
engine-turned
egg apparatus
Edgard Varèse
eighteen-hole
eighteenthly
ergative case
ephebophilia
exhibitioner
exhibitively
echo location
ethyl acetate
ethyl alcohol
exhilarating
exhilaration
exhilaratory
exhilarative
ephemeridian
ephemerality
euhemeristic
Echinocactus
echinococcus
echinodermal
ethanoic acid
ethnoscience
ethnocentric
ethnobotanic
ethnological
ethnographer
ethnographic
etheostomine
enhypostasia
enhypostatic
ethereal oils
exheredation
etheromaniac
enharmonical
etherisation
etherization
echo-sounding
exhaust valve
exhaustingly
exhaust steam
exhaustively
ethoxyethane
Elizabeth Fry
episcopalian
episcopalism
episcopise it
episcopize it
evisceration
epideictical
epidemically
epidemiology
evidentially
evil-favoured
Edith Wharton
Edith Sitwell
epithalamion
epithalamium
epitheliomas
epiphenomena
Édith Cresson
elixir of life
epididymides
evil-mindedly
episodically
editorialise
editorialist
editorialize
epirrhematic
epigrammatic
epigraphical
emigrational
Elias Canetti
evil-speaking
epistolarian
epistolatory
evil-tempered
epistemology
Epicureanism
Elihu Thomson
epicuticular
exiguousness
Emily Davison
epicycloidal
enjoyability
enjoy oneself
eclectically
eulogistical
enlightening
Ealing comedy
elliptically
ellipsograph
enlargedness
eflornithine
Edmé Mariotte
Edmond Halley
Edmund Rubbra
Edmund Waller
Edmund Wilson
Esmeralda Dam
Emma Thompson
Eunice Barber
eunuchoidism
E Annie Proulx
Ernst Haeckel
Edouard Manet
eco-labelling
exorbitantly
esoterically
exoterically
ecoterrorism
ecoterrorist
epoch-marking
exophthalmia
exophthalmic
exophthalmos
exophthalmus
exothermally
exotic dancer
exobiologist
emotionalise
emotionalism
emotionalist
emotionality
emotionalize
emollescence
enormousness
Evonne Cawley
econometrics
econometrist
ecologically
economically
economic rent
economic zone
economy-class
exospherical
egoistically
emolumentary
elocutionary
evolutionary
elocutionist
evolutionism
evolutionist
Eton wall game
emphatically
Euphausiacea
Euphausiidae
explantation
expectations
expectorator
expediential
expeditation
express rifle
empressement
expressional
express train
expressively
expressivity
espagnolette
esprit follet
explicitness
empoisonment
expanded type
expansionary
expansionism
expansionist
en pantoufles
euphorically
expromission
euphoniously
expropriable
expropriator
exprobration
exprobratory
exprobrative
exploitation
exploitative
experiential
experimental
experimented
experimenter
esparto grass
export reject
expert system
empyreumatic
empassionate
expositional
expositively
expostulator
empathically
expatriation
Euro-American
Enrico Caruso
ebracteolate
Earl Campbell
Eurocentrism
Eurocurrency
ear defenders
earnest-penny
earnest-money
earth science
earthshaking
earth-created
earthquaking
Earl Jellicoe
Earl of Surrey
European plan
ear-splitting
earl palatine
Europassport
error message
Earl Stanhope
Eero Saarinen
Eurosterling
erratic block

eurythermous
euroterminal
early-warning
eurhythmical
early-closing
Early English
Early-English
early and late
enswathement
ecstatically
eustatically
East Ayrshire
East China Sea
Easter cactus
eisteddfodau
eisteddfodic
Easter Island
easterliness
Easter Monday
Easter Sunday
ensheathment
exsufflicate
exsufflation
East Germanic
East-Indiaman
East Kilbride
essentialism
essentialist
essentiality
Eisen und Blut
eosinophilia
eosinophilic
exsanguinate
exsanguinity
exsanguinous
easy on the ear
easy on the eye
enstructured
ex-serviceman
enshrinement
extravagance
extravagancy
extravaganza
extramarital
euthanasiast
entrancement
entrancingly
extraversion
extrasensory
extraversive
extra-regular
extraneously
estrangement
extraditable
extralimital
entraînement
extrapolator
extra-special
extractor fan
extra-uterine
extramurally
extramundane
extranuclear
entrenchment
extreme sport
extremophile
entrepreneur
entreatingly
entomologise
entomologist
entomologize

entomophobia
Entomostraca
extended-play
extensimeter
extensionist
entanglement
extensometer
eat one's terms
eat one's words
extinguisher
extroversion
extroversive
eutrophicate
entropically
entoplastral
entoplastron
ectypography
ectoparasite
entertaining
enterococcus
enteric fever
exteroceptor
enterchaunge
exterminable
exterminator
extortionary
extortionist
extortionate
entertissued
enthrallment
Enteromorpha
enthronement
enteropneust
enteroptosis
enterprising
estate agency
eat humble pie
enthusiastic
educationist
edulcoration
exulceration
edulcorative
equidistance
eau de Javelle
ecumenically
eau de Cologne
equifinality
equilibrator
ebullioscope
ebullioscopy
equalisation
equalitarian
equalization
equimultiple
equanimously
equipollence
equipollency
equiprobable
equiparation
emulsifiable
equestrienne
Equisetaceae
equisetiform
equitability
equatorially
eruptiveness
elucubration
equivocality
equivocation
equivocatory
equivalently

enviableness
envenomation
envisagement
eavesdropped
eavesdropper
Elvis Presley
Edwin Forrest
Edwin Lutyens
Edward Alleyn
Edward A Doisy
Edward B Lewis
Edward De Bono
Edward Forbes
Edward Gibbon
Edward German
Edward Hulton
Edwardianism
Edward Jenner
Edward Teller
Edward Thomas
Edward Vernon
Edward Wilson
Ely Cathedral
erythematous
erythropenia
erythroblast
erythrocytic
erythromycin
etymological
etymologicon
etymologicum
elytrigerous
Egyptologist
enzymologist
feal and divot
flatbed lorry
flatbed truck
flat-bed press
flamboyantly
Franco Baresi
François Rude
✧francophobia
fiat currency
Francis Maude
Francis Baily
Francis Bacon
Francis Crick
Francis Drake
fraudulently
Frauendienst
flame-thrower
Fraser Island
flabelliform
flagelliform
flabellation
flagellation
flagellatory
frame-breaker
flame-grilled
frangibility
flash forward
flash-forward
featheriness
feather-brain
feather-grass
flagitiously
feasibleness
Frank Sedgman
Frank Kermode
Frank Whittle
Frank Sinatra

frankalmoign
frankincense
Frankenstein
Frank Loesser
flank forward
Frank Buchman
fearlessness
flammability
flammiferous
flammulation
flannelboard
flannelgraph
Fear of Flying
flavoprotein
foam plastics
fragrantness
Feast of Weeks
Feast of Herod
Feast of Fools
Feast of Asses
fractography
fractionally
fractionator
flatteringly
flatterously
Franz Klammer
febrifacient
fibrillation
fibrinolysin
fibrinolysis
fabulousness
Febronianism
fibroblastic
facsimileing
factitiously
fictitiously
factionalise
factionalism
factionalist
fictionalise
fictionality
factionalize
fictionalize
factiousness
fecklessness
focalisation
facilitation
facilitative
focalization
factory floor
face painting
face the music
fiddle around
fiddle-faddle
fiddlesticks
fiddle-string
fide non armis
federal court
fidus Achates
fidus et audax
fuel assembly
feel bad about
French fennel
free climbing
French letter
French polish
French-polish
French sorrel
French window
field walking
field marshal

Freudian slip
field battery
fielded panel
Freddie Laker
field geology
field meeting
Freddie Starr
field officer
field kitchen
field glasses
field colours
field-spaniel
fiendishness
frenetically
Frederikstad
free-floating
Freightliner®
freight-train
freshmanship
flesh-pottery
fresh as paint
feeding point
fuel-injected
fuel injector
flexible disk
flexibleness
freakishness
feeble-minded
Fresnel zones
feeing-market
feed one's face
feel one's feet
feel one's legs
feel one's oats
flexographic
free-standing
free-swimming
free-selector
Floot paroons
fleet admiral
feel the pinch
freethinking
Fleetwood Mac
frequentness
freewheeling
freeze-drying
freezing-down
fugie-warrant
figurability
figure-caster
figure skater
figuratively
fighting cock
fighting fish
fighting talk
fugitiveness
figgy pudding
Fehmgerichte
fait accompli
fricasseeing
fringe effect
Fringillidae
✧faith healing
faithfulness
flick through
flickeringly
flicker noise
feigned issue
friendly fire
friendly lead
friendliness

fairnitickle
fairnytickle
frigorificos
flippantness
friar's balsam
Friese-Greene
faint-hearted
flint-hearted
flint-knapper
fail to notice
frictionless
friction tape
flitter-mouse
faintishness
fairy penguin
foliage plant
fallaciously
fall back upon
filibusterer
full-bottomed
felicitation
felicitously
false pareira
false saffron
false vampire
filter coffee
false bedding
folie de doute
false-hearted
filter-feeder
false colours
filter-passer
✧fuller's earth
filter-tipped
filbert brush
fuliginosity
fuliginously
folding money
falling stone
fulminic acid
fall into line
folliculated
Falklands War
falcon-gentil
falcon-gentle
fellow member
follow the sea
filtrability
feldspathoid
full-throated
filius populi
filius terrae
fully-fledged
fume cupboard
femme savante
femme du monde
family credit
female condom
✧family circle
family doctor
famille jaune
famille verte
famille noire
family jewels
female thread
feminineness
feminisation
feminization
Finlay Calder
finnan haddie
finback whale

fantasticoes
fantasticism
fantasticate
finger-and-toe
finger buffet
fender bender
fence-mending
fennel-flower
fingerlickin'
fan the flames
Fantin-Latour
fancifulness
fenfluramine
fent-merchant
funambulator
finance house
financialist
find one's feet
find one's legs
findon haddie
fenestration
functionally
functionless
function word
fancy oneself
Fanny Cradock
foot-and-mouth
fromage frais
football boot
flocculation
foot-dragging
Floyd Bennett
frondiferous
floodlighted
frondescence
from day to day
flower delice
flower-delice
flower deluce
flower-de-luce
flower-deluce
flower-garden
frozen mitten
flower of Jove
flowerpecker
✧flower people
flowers of tan
from fordonne
foolish-witty
Frobisher Bay
frolicsomely
floriculture
footle around
Frodo Baggins
footplateman
footplatemen
floor manager
flour dredger
fool's parsley
frog's lettuce
from sun to sun
footslogging
front-bencher
frontiersman
front of house
front-of-house
float chamber
floating debt
floating dock
front-end load
foot-ton force
floating vote
front-loading
from top to toe
frontispiece
front-running
Fernand Léger
fore-and-after
formaldehyde
forward price
fire and sword
forsakenness
forfaultable
fore-admonish
forebodement
forebodingly
foreclosable
forecarriage
Fort-de-France
faradisation
faradization
force majeure
ferae naturae
ferret-badger
firmer chisel
force-feeding
for pete's sake
force the pace
fortepianist
forced labour
force and fear
Fortean Times
forbearingly
Faroe Islands
Furness Abbey
forset-seller
forgettingly
fermentation
fermentative
forcefulness
firefighting
foregoneness
for the asking
for the better
forthrightly
farthingland
farthingless
for the record
for the taking
forth-putting
fornicatress
forbiddingly
forcing-house
forcibleness
foreign draft
foreign-built
furniture van
ferricyanide
forejudgment
foreknowable
farm labourer
fork luncheon
formlessness
Foraminifera
fireman's lift
forensically
Ferenc Puskas
for one's pains
furunculosis
ferrocyanide
fire practice
fireproofing
forequarters
forestalling
forestalment
farm steading
foreseeingly
foresightful
Forest Marble
first reading
first refusal
first-nighter
foretokening
first and last
first-footing
furfuraceous
ferrugineous
fortuitously
forswornness
fire-watching
fish and chips
fast-and-loose
fusible metal
foster-father
foster-mother
foster-parent
fosset-seller
foster-sister
fish-hatchery
festina lente
fissilingual
fastidiously
fascioliasis
fustillirian
fashion plate
fashion house
fissirostral
fissicostate
fasciculated
fashiousness
fusion energy
festoon blind
fish-salesman
fish-strainer
father figure
fatherliness
father-lasher
fathers-in-law
fit of the face
fatigue-party
fatigue-dress
futilitarian
futtock-plate
futurologist
fit as a fiddle
feu d'artifice
fluidisation
foundational
foundationer
fluidized bed
fluidization
four-eyed fish
faute de mieux
frumentation
fourfoldness
four-four time
Fourieristic
fourpenny one
Four Quartets
fluorochrome
fluorocarbon
fluoridation
fluorography
fluorimetric
fluorometric
fluorination
fluorescence
fluoroscopic
fluorouracil
fruit machine
fourteenthly
fourth estate
fructiferous
fault-finding
fountainhead
fountainless
fruiting body
Fourth of July
fruitfulness
fructivorous
Five Articles
five-line whip
fever therapy
feverishness
favouredness
fowling-piece
fixed capital
fixed-penalty
fixed charges
flying bridge
flying column
flying dragon
flying doctor
fly-on-the-wall
flying lizard
fry in one's fat
flying saucer
guaraná bread
Grahame Clark
Graham Greene
guaranteeing
goat-antelope
Glauber's salt
glaucomatous
glaucescence
grand larceny
Grand Marnier®
guardianship
Grande Comore
grande entrée
glandiferous
Grand Signior
glandulously
grande marque
grand amateur
grand touring
Grandisonian
grand atelier
✧grand guignol
grand duchess
grapeseed-oil
grave-clothes
Grateful Dead
gracefulness
gratefulness
gravel-voiced
Gradgrindery
graphics card
graphic novel
graphologist
graph plotter
graphophobia
graminaceous
Glamis Castle
gratis dictum
Gracie Fields
glaciologist
gravitometer
gladiatorial
gladiatorian
graciousness
gravity waves
gratifyingly
grallatorial
Graeme Garden
gram-molecule
grammaticise
grammaticism
grammaticize
grammatology
granny annexe
grain leather
✧gram-negative
grain alcohol
gramophonist
granodiorite
Giacomo Manzú
grapple-plant
graspingness
Gram-positive
glass ceiling
glassyheaded
grass widower
glass-blowing
gladsomeness
Gladstone bag
glass cockpit
glass-cutting
Glass Pyramid
geanticlinal
Giant Despair
graft chimera
giant-killing
giant's-kettle
giant's stride
granulations
gradualistic
granulocytic
graduateship
gratuitously
Gladys Knight
Gibraltarian
Gabriel Fauré
Goblin Market
gobbledegook
gobbledygook
gibble-gabble
gubernacular
gubernaculum
gobar numeral
go by the board
go by the worse
G K Chesterton
Gideon Bibles
✧god-forgotten
Godfrey Hardy
Godfrey Evans
go down a treat
go down a storm
go downstream
gregarianism
gregariously
Greg Chappell
grey eminence
geese a-laying
Gaelic coffee
Greek pattern
grey-lag goose
Gherman Titov
Greenland Sea
Green Wellies
Guernsey lily
green fingers
green vitriol
Green Goddess
Green College
greengrocery
greenishness
Gregorian wig
guerrilleros
Greg Rusedski
grease monkey
grey squirrel
Great Eastern
Great Malvern
Glen T Seaborg
great-bellied
great-hearted
Great Western
guest-chamber
great omentum
great oneyers
Great Britain
great hundred
great mullein
Great Pyramid
grex venalium
go fifty-fifty
gefüllte fish
go for nothing
gagging order
gigantically
gigantomachy
glioblastoma
grit blasting
Guildenstern
grind to a halt
guild-brother
Guinea-Bissau
griseofulvin
guilefulness
going concern
guiding light
gliding plane
gainlessness
guillotining
glimmeringly
Guido d'Arezzo
Geissler pump
Geissler tube
Gainsborough
go into detail
go into hiding
guilt complex
glisteringly
glitteringly
go into the red
grievousness
galvanically
galvanic belt
galvanic cell
galvanoscope
galvanometer
galvanometry
galactagogue
galactic halo

galactometer
golden bowler
Gilles de Rais
golden fleece
Golden Friday
Golden Legend
Golden Miller
golden number
golden oriole
golden plover
golden salmon
Golden Sonata
Gilbert White
Golden Temple
Galveston Bay
golden wattle
goldfish bowl
gallinaceous
galligaskins
go like a dream
galilee porch
gallows-maker
gallows frame
gold standard
gall-sickness
gallsickness
goldsmithery
gelatination
gum sandarach
Gamgee tissue®
gamgee tissue
Gemeinschaft
gambling hell
gem-engraving
gymnosophist
gemmological
game preserve
gamopetalous
gamophyllous
gamesmanship
gamesomeness
game-show host
gamosepalous
Gunnar Myrdal
genealogical
geniculately
geniculation
gens de guerre
gynodioecism
gonadotropic
gonadotropin
gender bender
Günter Blobel
gander-mooner
gynaecomasty
gynaecologic
gynaecocracy
gender person
Ginger Rogers
Gunter's scale
Gunter's chain
genuflection
gingivectomy
gentilitious
Gentianaceae
gentle breeze
gentle reader
general issue
general staff
General Synod
generatrices
generational
generousness
gangster film
gangsterland
gang switches
gene splicing
genetic drift
gang-there-out
genethliacal
genethliacon
genotypicity
Gondwanaland
geomagnetism
geomagnetist
global search
good breeding
gaol delivery
Globe Theatre
geotechnical
globe thistle
geodetically
geodesic dome
geodesic line
geodetic line
goose-pimples
go one's own way
grotesquerie
geometrician
globetrotter
go over the top
geocentrical
geotectonics
goose-stepped
Geoffrey Hill
Geoffrey Howe
go off the boil
go off at score
good gracious
George Beadle
George Crabbe
George C Scott
George Colman
George Cayley
George Devine
Georg Bednorz
George Graham
George Gallup
György Ligeti
George Orwell
George Palade
George Patton
Georges Bizet
George Stokes
Giorgi system
George Stubbs
Georges Auric
George Thomas
Georg Büchner
geochemistry
good-humoured
geophysicist
gnomic aorist
globigerinae
growing pains
growing-point
Goodison Park
Grolieresque
gloriousness
glockenspiel
ghoulishness
ground annual
ground-beetle
ground-cuckoo
ground cherry
groan beneath
ground effect
ground-feeder
Groundhog Day
groundhopper
groundlessly
ground-pigeon
geognostical
ground storey
ground stroke
ground tackle
geologically
gnomonically
geopolitical
gnotobiology
gnotobiotics
group calling
group-captain
Group of Seven
Group of Eight
group therapy
group trading
good riddance
Geographe Bay
geographical
glossography
glossologist
grossularite
gross tonnage
glossarially
geostrategic
go on the shout
growth factor
grow together
good-tempered
growth market
Ghostbusters
geodynamical
geosynclinal
go pear-shaped
gormandising
gormandizing
Germanically
Germanophobe
Germanophile
geriatrician
German silver
girder bridge
garden centre
garret-master
Garden of Eden
garden suburb
garter-stitch
gorgeousness
garrison town
Geraint Evans
Gerald Scarfe
gyromagnetic
gerontophobe
gerontophile
gerontocracy
Gordon Childe
Gordon Ramsay
Gordon setter
Gerard Debreu
Gerard Kuiper
Gastarbeiter
Gaspard Monge
Gustav Mahler
Gesneriaceae
gas-permeable
gasification
gossip column
gossip-monger
gesticulator
gossip-writer
Gesellschaft
gasometrical
gas-condenser
gastric fever
gastrocnemii
gastric juice
gastrulation
gastronomics
gastronomist
gastropodous
gastrosopher
gather breath
gather ground
gathering-cry
go to extremes
get a guernsey
get the finger
get the hang of
get the mitten
get the needle
get the wind up
get-rich-quick
Gottlob Frege
gateleg table
get undressed
get one's cards
get one's books
get one's lumps
get one's eye in
gate of silver
gut-wrenching
gates of death
get stuck into
go to the walls
go to the devil
go to the world
get itchy feet
get a wiggle on
glutamic acid
Glubbdubdrib
Gough Whitlam
go up in flames
go up in the air
glucoprotein
glue-sniffing
gruesomeness
go up the flume
gluttonously
give a meeting
give in charge
give it laldie
give it wellie
give on a plate
give one's word
give points to
governess car
governmental
governorship
give the heave
give the elbow
give the alarm
Guys and Dolls
gay deceivers
glyphography
glycogenesis
glycogenetic
glycoprotein
glyptography
gazetteerish
heat-apoplexy
heat capacity
heaven-fallen
heaven forbid
heaven-gifted
heave the lead
heavenly city
heavenly host
heavenliness
heave in sight
heavens above
heater-shield
head foremost
Huang He River
Huang Ho River
heathenishly
heather-bleat
headmistress
headquarters
head register
heads or tails
headshrinker
heart failure
heartwarming
health centre
heart-rending
heart-service
heart disease
heart and hand
heart and soul
heart-to-heart
heartbreaker
health resort
heart-strings
heartburning
hiatus hernia
heavy-hearted
heavy petting
habeas corpus
Hebraistical
Hobbesianism
hybridisable
hybridizable
hybrid vigour
hubble-bubble
habilitation
hebdomadally
Hobson-Jobson
hobgoblinism
hebephreniac
haberdashery
hibernaculum
Hibernically
Hibernianism
Haber process
Hubert Walter
habitualness
habitability
hebetudinous
habit-forming
habitational
hoc genus omne
huckle-backed
hackney coach
hectocotylus
hectographic
hydrargyrism
hydraulic ram
hydraulicked
Hudibrastics
hedge warbler
hidden agenda
hedge-parsley
hedge sparrow
hedge-creeper
hedge trimmer
Huddersfield
hodge-pudding
hedge-mustard
Hadrian's Wall
hydropathist
hydrogenated
hydrogen bomb
hydrogen bond
hide one's head
hydrogeology
Hydromedusae
hydromedusan
hydrophobous
hydrophilite
hydrophilous
hydrophanous
hydrochloric
hydrothermal
hydrotherapy
hydrophytous
hydrozincite
hydrokinetic
hydrobiology
hydronium ion
hydrofluoric
hydroelastic
hydrological
hydrocolloid
hydrographer
hydrographic
hydrotropism
hydrostatics
hydroquinone
hydrodynamic
hydatidiform
hierarchical
haematemesis
haematoblast
haematolysis
haematoxylin
Haematoxylon
heedlessness
haemophiliac
hierophantic
hieroglyphic
haemopoiesis
hierological
haemorrhagic
hierogrammat
haemorrhoids
hierographer
hierographic
hyetographic
heeby-jeebies
Hafez al-Assad
high-coloured
hygienically
hugger-mugger
high fidelity
high-fidelity

highfaluting
high-five-sign
High Holidays
High Holy Days
highly geared
higgle-haggle
highly-strung
hygrophilous
hygrochastic
hagiological
hagiographer
hagiographic
hygrographic
hog-constable
high-pressure
high-priestly
high-reaching
high-seasoned
high-stepping
high-spirited
high-sticking
high-sounding
highty-tighty
high-velocity
Hainan Island
heir apparent
heir-by-custom
hairdressing
height of land
hairlessness
Heinrich Böll
hair restorer
hair-splitter
hair's-breadth
hail the dules
hojatoleslam
hojatolislam
Helmand River
Holy Alliance
hallan-shaker
Helianthemum
half after one
half after two
helicoid cyme
holidaymaker
helmet flower
halter-necked
Hildebrandic
Halley's Comet
Heldentenöre
Heldentenors
Hell-fire Club
hellgrammite
half-integral
helplessness
half measures
hylomorphism
half-marathon
half-mourning
Hélène Cixous
H W Longfellow
Helen Sharman
Heliogabalus
heliolatrous
heliocentric
hollow-ground
holy of holies
heliophilous
heliochromic
heliotherapy
heliospheric
heliographer
heliographic
heliotropism
heliogravure
holoplankton
holophrastic
half-seas-over
hold sway over
holistically
Holy Saturday
hold the field
hold the floor
hold together
half-timbered
hold to ransom
Holy Thursday
hallucinogen
hallucinosis
Helmut Newton
helium speech
halfway house
Hollywoodise
Hollywoodize
hemp agrimony
Hemichordata
home-crofting
homochromous
homocysteine
home counties
hummel bonnet
hempen caudle
homme sérieux
homme d'esprit
hammer-headed
homoeomorphy
homoeomerous
homoeopathic
homoeostasis
homoeostatic
homme du monde
humification
home from home
Homage to Clio
homoiomerous
hummle bonnet
homologumena
homologation
homelessness
hemimorphism
homomorphism
hemimorphite
homomorphous
human capital
humane killer
homonymously
human bowling
hymenopteran
humanisation
humanitarian
humanization
homeopathist
Hammond Innes
Hammond organ®
Humboldt's Sea
homeothermal
homeothermic
homeomorphic
hymnographer
homopolarity
home-produced
hemiparasite
Hemerocallis
hamarthritis
hamartiology
humorousness
homesickness
homesteading
hemispheroid
home shopping
home straight
homothallism
✧humpty-dumpty
hump the bluey
homothermous
Hamburg steak
hand and glove
Hungary water
handbag music
hendecagonal
hunger-bitten
hunter-killer
henceforward
hunger strike
hunger-strike
hindforemost
Henri Matisse
hang in effigy
hunting-field
hunting-knife
hunting-lodge
hunting-sword
Henri Giffard
handkerchief
hand on a plate
hand over fist
hand over head
hang one's head
hand over hand
Hindoostanee
hindquarters
honoris causa
huntsmanship
honest broker
hunt saboteur
handsomeness
hand's breadth
henotheistic
hang together
Honduras bark
honour bright
honours of war
honour system
Hans von Bülow
Henry Raeburn
Henry Mancini
Henry Vaughan
Henry Segrave
honeycombing
honey-tongued
honey-mouthed
honey creeper
Henry Grattan
Henry Purcell
honey buzzard
Hookey Walker
hooping cough
hooping-cough
hoodman-blind
hood-moulding
heortologist
heptateuchal
hypocritical
hypocalcemia
hypochlorite
hypochondria
hypocoristic
happenstance
hypoeutectic
hypaesthesia
hypaesthesic
hypognathism
hypognathous
hypogastrium
hypoglycemia
hypoglycemic
hopelessness
hypnogenesis
hypnogenetic
hippocentaur
hippophagist
hippophagous
hypnotherapy
hypnotically
hypnotisable
hypnotizable
hippopotamic
hippopotamus
hippocrepian
haptotropism
Hippocratise
Hippocratism
Hippocratize
hypoplastron
hypophrygian
hypersarcoma
hyperdactyly
Hypericaceae
hyperacidity
hyperidrosis
hypersensual
hypertension
hypertensive
hyperthermal
hyperthermia
hyperthyroid
hyperkinesia
hyperkinesis
hyperkinetic
hyperlipemia
hyperalgesia
hyperalgesic
hyperplastic
Hyperboreans
hyperbolical
hypercorrect
hypertrophic
hypersthenia
hypersthenic
hyperpyretic
hyperpyrexia
hypostatical
hyposulphate
hyposulphite
hypothalamic
hypothalamus
hepaticology
hypothecator
hypothetical
hephthemimer
hepatologist
hepatomegaly
hypotrochoid
hepatisation
hepatization
happy-go-lucky
happy as Larry
Hernán Cortés
here and there
Hermann Maier
Hermann Hesse
Hermann Bondi
Heracleitean
hors concours
hard currency
hors de combat
hors d'oeuvres
Herod Agrippa
Herod Antipas
hors de saison
hereditament
hereditarian
hereditarily
horsemanship
horrendously
horse-dealing
hermeneutics
hermeneutist
horseshoe bat
horseshoeing
hermetically
Harvey Keitel
horned lizard
horse-knacker
herpetofauna
horse soldier
herpetologic
horse-courser
horse-breaker
horse-trading
horse-trainer
harness-maker
Harley Street
harvest-feast
harvest-field
Herbert Boyer
harvest-goose
harvest louse
harvest mouse
harvest queen
harlequinade
herpes zoster
hard-featured
hard feelings
hard-favoured
Hermitage Bay
heroicalness
hereinbefore
horrifically
horribleness
Harrison Ford
heroi-comical
heroic remedy
herd instinct
hormic theory
hermit thrush
horticulture
horrifyingly
heraldically
Harold Pinter
hurdle-racing
harmlessness
hurtlessness
Harold Varmus
Harold Wilson
hard measures
horometrical
hart of grease
harmonically
harmoniphone
harmonichord
harmonic mean
harmoniumist
harmoniously
harmonic wave
harmonometer
harmonograph
horn of plenty
harbour-light
Harrow School
horror-struck
hire-purchase
hard-standing
hard-sectored
hard swearing
heresy-hunter
hard shoulder
heritability
Horatio Gates
Hercules' club
hortus siccus
Harry Secombe
Harry Enfield
Harry S Truman
horizontally
hasta la vista
his name is mud
Hispanically
✧hispaniolise
✧hispaniolize
Hispanophile
host computer
His Reverence
hysterectomy
hysterically
hysteromania
hysterogenic
hospital pass
hospital ship
Histiophorus
Hosni Mubarak
histogenesis
histogenetic
histochemist
historically
historic cost
historiology
histological
History Today
histrionical
hesitatingly
hasty pudding
hot favourite
hit a bad patch
hither and yon
Hottentot fig
Hottentot god
hit the bottle
hot chocolate
hitch and kick
hitching post
hatchet-faced
hôtel de ville
hatelessness
hot gospeller
Hattons Grace

heteroblasty
heterocyclic
heteroclitic
Heterocontae
heterocercal
heterochrony
heterodactyl
heteroduplex
heteroecious
heterogamous
heterogonous
heterokontan
heterologous
heteromorphy
heteromerous
heteronomous
✧heteroousian
heteroplasia
heteroplasty
heteropteran
heterophylly
Heterosomata
heterosexual
heterosexism
heterosexist
heterostyled
heterothally
heterotactic
heterotrophy
heterauxesis
heterozygote
heterozygous
hound's-tongue
house-warming
housekeeping
house of cards
House of Peers
house officer
House of Lords
housey-housey
house-sitting
house-to-house
haute couture
house sparrow
housebreaker
house-trained
house-steward
house-husband
house surgeon
haute cuisine
house-hunting
housing joint
haussmannise
haussmannize
have an affair
have a nice day
have a flutter
have bought it
have it coming
have no use for
have one's fill
have one's will
have on the hip
have recourse
hover between
have the law of
have the law on
have the heart
have the mount
have the worse
have two faces
howler monkey
hawthorn tree
how squares go
Howard Carter
Howard Florey
Howard Hughes
Hawk Roosting
hexadactylic
hexametrical
hazard lights
Isaiah Berlin
Itala version
in a family way
inadaptation
irascibility
Isaac Dineson
Isaac Albéniz
inaccurately
inaccessible
inaccessibly
inaudibility
Isabel Archer
in an evil hour
image-worship
image breaker
image printer
inadequately
inauguration
inauguratory
Italian sixth
in all but name
inadmissible
inadmissibly
Italo Calvino
in a good light
in a cold sweat
itaconic acid
inappeasable
inapplicable
inapplicably
inappellable
inappositely
inabstinence
inauspicious
in actual fact
inarticulacy
inarticulate
in at the death
inartificial
Ivan Turgenev
inactivation
iracundulous
inadvertence
inadvertency
imbibitional
in banco regis
incharitable
incrassation
incrassative
incoagulable
incidentally
incident room
increasingly
incognisance
incognizance
incognisable
incognizable
incogitative
incoherently
inclinometer
incalescence
incalculable
incalculably
incomparable
incomparably
incompatible
incompatibly
incompetence
incompetency
in commission
incompliance
incompletely
incompletion
incomunicado
incommodious
incommutable
incommutably
incomputable
incunabulist
incandescent
in conference
inconvenient
inconversant
inconsequent
in confidence
incontinence
incontinency
inconcinnity
inconcinnous
incendiarism
inconsistent
incontiguous
in conclusion
inconclusion
inconclusive
inconsonance
inconsolable
inconsolably
incongruence
incineration
inconstantly
inconsumable
inconsumably
inco-ordinate
incoordinate
incrossbreed
inchoateness
incapability
incapacitant
incapacitate
incurability
incarcerator
incorrigible
incorrigibly
incoronation
incorporated
incorporator
incorporeity
incorrodible
incorrosible
incorruption
incorruptive
incestuously
incisiveness
incatenation
incautiously
incrustation
incivilities
India Pale Ale
Indianapolis
Indian giving
Indian millet
Indian mallow
Indian runner
Indian summer
Indian turnip
indebtedness
indeclinable
indeclinably
indoctrinate
indecorously
indecisively
indicatively
Indo-European
in deep waters
indefeasible
indefeasibly
indefectible
indifference
indifferency
indefensible
indefensibly
indefinitely
indignifying
indigenously
Indo-Germanic
indigestible
indigestibly
indehiscence
indelibility
indelicately
indemnifying
indomethacin
indoor relief
induplicated
independence
✧independency
indirectness
Indira Gandhi
indistinctly
indiscipline
indissoluble
indissolubly
industrially
indiscreetly
indiscretely
indiscretion
indisputable
indisputably
indetectable
indetectible
indetermined
individually
indivertible
index mineral
index-linking
index locorum
Iceland poppy
ineradicable
ineradicably
inelasticity
inexactitude
inescutcheon
inexecutable
ineffability
ineffaceable
ineffaceably
inefficiency
inexhaustive
ideal crystal
idealisation
idealization
ineloquently
inexpectancy
inexpedience
inexpediency
inexpressive
inexpugnable
inexpugnably
inexplicable
inexplicably
inexplicitly
inexpansible
inexpungible
inexperience
inexpertness
ice-cream soda
inerrability
identifiable
identifiably
inextricable
inextricably
inextensible
ideationally
inextirpable
identity card
identity disc
inequipotent
inflationary
inflationism
inflationist
inflammation
inflammatory
infraorbital
infibulation
infectiously
inflectional
infrequently
infringement
infringe upon
infelicitous
infiltration
infiltrative
infanticidal
infundibular
infundibulum
infant school
infinite loop
infiniteness
infinitively
informidable
infusibility
infotainment
ingravescent
ingratiating
ingratiation
in great price
ingemination
ingloriously
Ishmaelitish
inhabitation
ichneumon fly
ichthyolatry
ichthyophagy
ichthyolitic
ichthyologic
ichthyocolla
Ichthyopsida
inhalatorium
ichnographic
inharmonical
inharmonious
inhospitable
inhospitably
in his buttons
in hot pursuit
I should cocoa
I should worry!
imitableness
Irina Rodnina
iridescently
icing syringe
Irish terrier
inimicalness
inimicitious
Idiom Neutral
idiorhythmic
iris scanning
idiosyncrasy
idiothermous
iniquitously
injudicially
injunctively
inking-roller
ill-naturedly
illiberalise
illiberality
illiberalize
ill-advisedly
Isla de Pascua
ill-beseeming
illegibility
illogicality
illegitimacy
illegitimate
illuminating
illumination
illuminative
Islamisation
illimitation
Islamization
Island of Elba
Island of Maui
Island of Oahu
illaqueation
ill-treatment
illusoriness
illustration
illustratory
illustrative
illusiveness
illiterately
immeasurable
immeasurably
immaculately
immoderately
immoderation
immemorially
Immanuel Kant
immunoglobin
immunologist
immune system
immunisation
immensurable
immunization
iambographer
immersionism
immersionist
immiseration
immutability
immethodical
immaterially
immatureness
immovability
it may be added

Ian McGeechan
Ionic dialect
Innocents' Day
ion implanter
innominables
Ion Antonescu
ionophoresis
Ignorantines
Ian Trethowan
ignitability
ignitibility
innutritious
ignition coil
innovational
icosahedrons
isolationism
isolationist
isolator tent
idolatrously
inosculation
inoccupation
inordinately
inordination
inoperculate
isoperimeter
isoperimetry
inobediently
in one's own way
in one's pocket
in one's senses
in one's tracks
isocheimenal
isochromatic
isochronally
isothermally
in other words
isobilateral
ironing-board
iconic memory
isodiametric
isodimorphic
I wouldn't know
iconomachist
iconophilism
iconophilist
isotopically
isotopic spin
iconoclastic
iconological
iconographer
iconographic
isoprenaline
isotretinoin
Igor Sikorsky
inobservance
inobservable
isosthenuria
isostemonous
ivory-towered
implantation
impedimental
impierceable
impregnation
impressional
impressively
implicitness
imprisonable
imprisonment
impulse buyer
impoliteness
imponderable
imponderably
iopanoic acid
impenetrable
impenetrably
impenitently
improvisator
improvidence
in proportion
impropriator
imperial city
impermanence
impermanency
imperial yard
imperfection
imperceptive
imperfective
impertinence
impertinency
impercipient
impartiality
impersistent
in particular
imperviously
imperforated
imperforable
impersonally
impersonator
imperishable
imperishably
imperatorial
imperatively
imposthumate
impassionate
imposingness
imputability
it pitieth you
impetiginous
input routine
input program
imputatively
inquire after
inquisitress
irrealisable
irrealizable
irrebuttable
irreconciled
irreciprocal
irredeemable
irredeemably
irrefragable
irrefragably
irreflection
irreflective
irreformable
irreformably
irregularity
irrigational
irrelatively
irrelevantly
irremediable
irremediably
irremissible
irremissibly
irrepealable
irrepealably
irrepairable
irreprovable
irreprovably
irrespective
irrespirable
irresolvable
irresolvably
irresolutely
irresolution
irresponsive
irresistance
irresistible
irresistibly
irritability
irrationally
irritatingly
irreversible
irreversibly
irreverently
it's early days
installation
instar omnium
instauration
insubjection
insectariums
in succession
insecticidal
insect powder
inspectingly
inspectional
inspectorial
inspectorate
insufferable
insufferably
insufficient
insufflation
issuing house
instillation
inspissation
insalubrious
insolubilise
insolubility
insolubilize
insulin shock
insalivation
insomuch that
insemination
insomnolence
insanitation
in short order
inseparables
insurability
instructible
instructions
instructress
insurrection
instrumental
instrumented
insusceptive
insouciantly
intracardiac
intracranial
intrapreneur
intransigent
intransitive
intrauterine
intramurally
intramundane
Ixtaccihuatl
in the balance
in the fashion
intrenchment
in the thick of
in the picture
in the long run
in the running
in the twinkle
in the extreme
in the by-going
integumental
intuitionism
intuitionist
in triplicate
in this regard
intrinsicate
intriguingly
intellectual
intellection
intellective
intelligence
I'm telling you
intelligible
intelligibly
intolerantly
intoleration
intimidating
intimidation
intimidatory
intemperance
intempestive
intemerately
intumescence
intensifying
inteneration
intonational
introversion
introversive
introjection
introvertive
iatrochemist
intromission
intromissive
intromittent
intromitting
introducible
introduction
introductory
introductive
intercalated
interjacency
interlaminar
internalised
internalized
intermaxilla
interoceanic
inter-science
interoceptor
interrelated
Internet café
intermeddler
interbedding
interference
intermediacy
intervenient
intermediary
intermediate
interpellant
interpellate
interregnums
interfemoral
interneurone
intercession
intercessory
intertextual
interfertile
interception
interjection
intersection
intervention
interjectory
intertexture
interceptive
interservice
interchanger
interchapter
interminable
interminably
interkinesis
interlingual
interdigital
intercipient
intertissued
intermission
intermissive
intermittent
intermitting
interdiction
interdictory
intermixture
interdictive
interpleader
interglacial
interfluence
interclusion
interpleural
interfluvial
interpolater
interrogatee
intervocalic
interpolable
interrogable
interpolator
interrogator
interfoliate
interlocking
intercolline
intercommune
interconnect
intermontane
interlobular
interlocutor
interconvert
interspinous
interspersal
interspatial
interwreathe
intertraffic
interorbital
interfrontal
intercropped
interfretted
interpretess
interpretate
interpretive
interwrought
interestedly
interosseous
interest-free
interest rate
interstadial
interstellar
interstitial
internuncial
internuncios
intermundane
intercurrent
interruption
interruptive
intertwining
intussuscept
intrusionist
intoxicating
intoxication
invigilation
invagination
invigorating
invigoration
inveiglement
invalidation
invulnerable
invulnerably
involutional
invultuation
Irving Berlin
inverted arch
inverse ratio
Invertebrata
invertebrate
inverted snob
inverted turn
invisible ink
invisibility
investigable
investigator
invitingness
inveterately
in weal and woe
in with a shout
in your dreams
Joan Crawford
Jean Chrétien
Jean Dubuffet
Joan Fontaine
Joachim Murat
Joanna Lumley
Jeanne Moreau
Jean Sibelius
Jean Tinguely
Jubilate Agno
Jack-a-lantern
Jacobean lily
Jacob's ladder
Jacob Epstein
Jack Charlton
jacket potato
Jack Harkness
✧jack-in-office
✧jack-in-the-box
Jack Nicklaus
✧jack-o'-lantern
Jack Sheppard
Jacksonville
Jacquard loom
Jacques Monod
Jeddart staff
judgement-day
judgmentally
jodhpur boots
Joe Millerism
Jeffersonian
Jeff Goldblum
Juglandaceae
jigsaw puzzle
John Burgoyne
John Berryman
John Betjeman
John Charnley
John Chinaman
John Coltrane
John Comnenus

Words marked ✧ can also be spelled with one or more capital letters

John Christie
John Ericsson
John Francome
John Franklin
John Fletcher
John F Kennedy
John Falstaff
John Galliano
John Humphrys
John Herschel
John Jarndyce
John Lilburne
John McCarthy
John Marshall
John Mortimer
Johnny B Goode
Johann Cruyff
Johannesburg
Johnny Hodges
Johannisberg
Jahangir Khan
Johann Tetzel
John Newcombe
John of Leyden
John Prescott
John Richmond
John Suckling
John Sessions
John Travolta
John the Blind
John Vanbrugh
John W Mauchly
John Wycliffe
John Whitgift
John Williams
jail delivery
joint account
joint tenancy
joint venture
jointing-rule
jointer plane
Julian Barnes
Julian Huxley
Julia Roberts
Julie Walters
jolies laides
Julie Andrews
Jules Mazarin
Jules Maigret
Julius Caesar
jumper cables
Jamaica ebony
Jamaica cedar
jumping mouse
Jomo Kenyatta
jump one's bail
James Mancham
James Baldwin
James Cameron
James Madison
James Earl Ray
James Nasmyth
James Weddell
James Thomson
James Thurber
James Clavell
James Boswell
James Bradley
James Stewart
jump the besom
jump the queue

Jammu-Kashmir
Jimmy Tarbuck
✧jimmy-o'goblin
Jimmy Woodser
Jimmy Connors
Jimmy Greaves
Jan Tinbergen
jingle-jangle
Joni Mitchell
junior optime
junior school
Jonas Savimbi
je ne sais quoi
Janet Jackson
jenny-spinner
jeopardously
Japan varnish
Japan lacquer
japonaiserie
Japanese tosa
Japan Current
✧jordan almond
Jorge Sampaio
Jeremy Isaacs
Jeremy Paxman
Jeremy Thorpe
juristically
Jurassic Park
jurisdiction
jurisdictive
jurisconsult
jurisprudent
Jerry Falwell
jerry-builder
jus sanguinis
jus canonicum
José Carreras
Jesse Jackson
Jasper Conran
Jusuf Habibie
Just Fontaine
Jessica Lange
jesting-stock
Jesuitically
justificator
✧justicialism
Justin Martyr
just like that
Joseph Butler
Joseph Conrad
Joseph Heller
Joseph Lister
Joseph Paxton
Joseph Stalin
Joseph Wright
Jesus College
José Saramago
jet-propelled
jeune premier
journalistic
journey-bated
Javed Miandad
Javelle water
javelin throw
juvenileness
juvenilities
juvenescence
Jews' leavings
Jayne Torvill
Jazz Warriors
Kwame Nkrumah

knacker's yard
Keble College
kicking strap
kickie-wickie
kick up a stink
kick upstairs
kidney-potato
kiddiewinkie
keep a lookout
keep a quarter
knee-breeches
knee-crooking
Kielder Water
keep good time
keeking-glass
Kremlinology
keep one's cool
keep one's head
keep one's word
kleptocratic
knee-trembler
keep the peace
keep the field
keep the house
kleptomaniac
Kaffe Fassett
kaisar-i-Hindi
Klinefelter's
Keiren Fallon
knife through
knife-and-fork
knife-grinder
Keith Jarrett
knight errant
knightliness
knick-knacket
kainogenesis
klipspringer
Kriss Kringle
Kristiansand
kakistocracy
kill by inches
kill-courtesy
Kylie Minogue
Kilkenny cats
Kelvin effect
killing field
kaleidoscope
kaleidophone
kilfud-yoking
kilowatt hour
Kimball O'Hara
Komodo dragon
Komodo Island
Kimmeridgian
Kemal Jumblat
kimono sleeve
Konrad Lorenz
kangaroo vine
kindergarten
Kenneth Baker
Kenneth Clark
Kenneth Brown
kinaesthesia
kinaesthesis
kinaesthetic
Kanchenjunga
Kentish glory
kindly tenant
king of beasts
king of metals

kinesiatrics
Kingsley Amis
✧king's highway
king's English
King's College
King's Counsel
kinesipathic
✧king's proctor
king's-cushion
Kenny Roberts
Kenny Everett
knowableness
knocking copy
knocking shop
knocking-shop
knowledgable
knowledgably
knowledge box
Kwok's disease
know the score
know the ropes
know what it is
kupfernickel
kerb-crawling
kirschwasser
Kyrie eleison
kurchatovium
Karelia Suite
Kuril Islands
kerb-merchant
karyokinesis
karyotypical
Karl Schiller
keratogenous
Kiri Te Kanawa
keratoplasty
keraunograph
Kurt Vonnegut
Kurt Waldheim
Kosrae Island
kissing-crust
kissogram man
katharevousa
katharometer
Kitab al-Aqdas
kitten-heeled
katzenjammer
kitchen-range
kitchen table
kitchen-wench
kitchen chair
kitchen-knave
kitchen-stuff
kitchen Dutch
Kota Kinabalu
kittle cattle
kettle-holder
kettlestitch
Katerina Witt
Kitty Godfree
knur and spell
Kyushu Island
knuckle under
knuckle-bones
knuckle joint
Kevin Costner
Klyuchevskoy
Keynesianism
key signature
Lualaba River
lean concrete

leave the room
leave one cold
leave for dead
leader-writer
leapfrogging
Luang Prabang
leathercloth
leather-knife
leathergoods
loathfulness
leasing-maker
loading gauge
leaving party
leading reins
leading light
leaping-house
lead-in groove
lead in prayer
lead monoxide
learnability
leaf-nosed bat
learn by heart
loan sharking
load shedding
leads and lags
lead the field
libidinosity
libidinously
l'Abbé Prévost
lubriciously
labelled atom
labanotation
loblolly pine
loblolly tree
liberticidal
Liberal Party
liberalistic
labyrinthian
labyrinthine
liberty horse
labour of love
labour-saving
Luciano Berio
Lucretia Mott
lickety-split
lucifer-match
lock-hospital
Lachlan River
lucklessness
localisation
localization
locomobility
locum tenency
locomotivity
Lucinda Green
lacing course
license block
license plate
lycanthropic
licentiously
lick one's lips
lactoprotein
Lycopodiales
Lycopodineae
lachrymal urn
lachrymosely
lachrymosity
lachrymation
lachrymatory
lick-trencher
lick the birse

Lichtenstein
Lucky Luciano
ledger tackle
Ludwig Erhard
lodging house
Ludwigshafen
Lady Jane Grey
ladylikeness
Ludlow Castle
lady's-thistle
lady's fingers
lady's-slipper
lady's tresses
lady's-cushion
Lady Thatcher
Lady Williams
lie heavy upon
lie of the land
Lee Strasberg
lieutenantry
life-and-death
left-handedly
luffing crane
life instinct
life-interest
lifelikeness
lifelessness
left-of-centre
lift one's hand
life sciences
life sentence
lift the elbow
lugubriously
legacy-hunter
logic circuit
logic diagram
logodaedalic
logodaedalus
loggerheaded
ligniperdous
logging-stone
Liguliflorae
liguliforal
legal fiction
legal holiday
legalisation
legalization
lagomorphous
legionnaire's
legionnaires'
lager loutery
legislatress
logistically
light railway
light-hearted
light therapy
lightning rod
lightning bug
legitimately
legitimation
Loghtan sheep
Loghtyn sheep
Luís de Camões
Leif Eriksson
Luigi Galvani
Li-ion battery
laisser-faire
laisser-aller
laissez-faire
laissez-aller
leiotrichous

Lajos Kossuth
likeableness
like anything
Lake Balkhash
lake dwelling
Lake District
like gold dust
like hey-go-mad
Lake Issyk Kul
Lake Michigan
Lake Maggiore
Lake of Dreams
like old boots
Lake Superior
Lake Tiberias
like the devil
Lake Tonlé Sap
Lake Titicaca
Lake Victoria
like wildfire
Lake Winnipeg
lukewarmness
lallapalooza
lollapalooza
lollipop lady
Lilliputians
Lillibullero
Lilliburlero
Lalique glass
lampadedromy
lampadomancy
limacologist
lumberjacket
Lamberto Dini
lymphography
lymphangitis
Lemnian earth
limbic system
lomentaceous
Lamentations
lemon verbena
luminiferous
Lymantriidae
luminescence
luminous flux
luminousness
limnophilous
limnological
lumbriciform
lamprophyric
lamp-standard
lamb's lettuce
lamb's quarter
Limbus patrum
Lancasterian
line breeding
long-breathed
lino blocking
Lynn Chadwick
long-drawn-out
Lonsdale belt
long-distance
long division
long-day plant
line-engraver
lanceolately
lantern-jawed
lantern wheel
lantern slide
lance prisade
lance prisado

lancet window
land-grabbing
landgraviate
lunch voucher
luncheonette
luncheon meat
longicaudate
lenticellate
longipennate
line-item veto
landing field
landing-place
landing-speed
landing craft
landing stage
landing strip
lenticularly
longitudinal
longleaf pine
land-lubberly
linoleic acid
landlessness
line of beauty
line of battle
line of credit
Land o' the Leal
London Museum
Lincolnshire
Lincoln green
line of vision
lunar caustic
Land Registry
long-standing
Linus Pauling
line scanning
Linz Symphony
lonesomeness
longshoreman
land-surveyor
land set-aside
length of days
langue de chat
Languedocian
lingua franca
languageless
languorously
linguistical
languishment
long vacation
long-windedly
land-yachting
leopard's-bane
leopard shark
Leonard Nimoy
Leonard Cohen
Lloyd Bridges
loop diuretic
Lionel Jospin
loose-jointed
loose housing
loose forward
Lionel Richie
Léon Goossens
Leonine rhyme
Laodiceanism
looking-glass
Leonid Kuchma
Leopold Bloom
lookout tower
lapidicolous
lepidomelane

lepidopteran
lapidescence
lappered-milk
lopsidedness
leptocephali
lophophorate
lepton number
leptosomatic
laparoscopic
lapsus calami
loquaciously
liquefacient
liquefaction
liquefactive
liqueur glass
liquid assets
liquid helium
liquid storax
larva migrans
Lord Advocate
Lyra Belacqua
Lord Bentinck
Lord Cheshire
Lyric Theatre
Lorne sausage
larder beetle
large-hearted
larder fridge
Lord Gardiner
lurking-place
larking-glass
Lord Ironside
Lord Jeffreys
Lord knows who
Lord Macaulay
Lord Morrison
laryngectomy
laryngoscope
laryngoscopy
laryngophony
laryngospasm
Lorentz force
Lord Ordinary
liriodendron
Lord Rees-Mogg
Lord Shinwell
lord-superior
Lord Tennyson
Larry Winters
lorry-hopping
lost-and-found
loss adjuster
Los Caprichos
lust-breathed
List D schools
Lesser Bairam
listenership
lesser litany
lasagne verde
lese-humanity
lasciviously
lusciousness
listlessness
losing hazard
lose one's cool
lose one's head
lose one's hair
lose one's seat
lysergic acid
laser printer
lustrousness

lusus naturae
lose the place
Les Sylphides
Lethal Weapon
laticiferous
litter basket
letterboxing
Lotte Lehmann
let well alone
Letter of Jude
Letter of Paul
lit de justice
letter-writer
letter-weight
late in the day
Little Dipper
Little Dorrit
Little-endian
little finger
little Hitler
little office
little people
little wonder
Latin Kingdom
Latin America
latent period
let oneself go
Latinisation
Latin Quarter
Latinization
litholatrous
lithophagous
lithophilous
lithological
lithotomical
lithospheric
lithospermum
lithographer
lithotripter
lithographic
lithotriptic
lithotriptor
lithotritise
lithotritist
lithotritize
lite pendente
liturgically
liturgiology
lateral shift
literalistic
Lateran Pacts
literariness
latirostrate
laterisation
laterization
lath-splitter
lots to blanks
latitudinous
laudableness
launching-pad
launch window
laundrywoman
Lauren Bacall
laureateship
louver-window
lounge lizard
laughing gear
laugh to scorn
Loughborough
leucoplastid
leukoplastid

leucopoiesis
leukopoiesis
leucocytosis
leucocytotic
leukocytosis
leukocytotic
louvre-window
Louis Pasteur
Louis Agassiz
Louis Blériot
live and learn
loveableness
levée en masse
live-feathers
live in clover
level pegging
levelling-rod
lovelornness
lovelessness
living fossil
living memory
liver sausage
livery stable
liverishness
levorotatory
Liverpudlian
lovesickness
love-stricken
live together
low watermark
low-water mark
law of nations
law of octaves
law of the land
Low-Churchman
Low-Churchism
low-thoughted
laws of honour
laws of motion
lower regions
lower the flag
lower chamber
lower mordent
low frequency
lower-bracket
Lewis Wallace
Lewis Carroll
Lewis Binford
law-stationer
lexicography
lexicologist
loxodromical
luxullianite
Luxembourger
laxativeness
lay a finger on
lay on the line
lay communion
lay it on thick
Lizzie Borden
Liza Minnelli
Luzon Islands
lizard-hipped
lizard orchid
meat and drink
Mtarazi Falls
mean business
mean free path
Moabite stone
meaningfully
meat-offering

meadow fescue
mean sea level
mean-spirited
meat-salesman
Maarten Tromp
measuring-rod
measuring cup
measuring jug
mealy-mouthed
mobile police
mobilisation
mobilization
mechanically
Michael Palin
Michael Caine
Michael Foale
Michael Grade
Michael Frayn
Michael Buerk
machairodont
mechatronics
mycobacteria
macaberesque
macadamia nut
mycodomatium
Michelangelo
Michel Fokine
Mickey Mantle
Mickey Rooney
mickey-taking
Mackenzie Bay
mock-heroical
machinations
Mt Chimborazo
machine screw
machine proof
machine-ruler
Mechitharist
Macmillanite
machicolated
mucilaginous
Macclesfield
my conscience
microbalance
microwavable
microhabitat
microcapsule
macrodactyly
microscooter
microscopist
Microscopium
microneedles
macrocephaly
microcephaly
microseismic
microphagous
microphysics
microfilaria
microcircuit
micropipette
microbiology
macrobiotics
microclimate
microanatomy
microtonally
Macropodidae
micrological
microtomical
microcopying
microprogram
microprinted

microgranite
micrographer
micrographic
microgravity
microbrewery
macropterous
micropterous
microsurgeon
microsurgery
microtubular
mycoplasmata
mucopurulent
muckspreader
Mack the Knife
Machtpolitik
mockumentary
McCoy Airport
Midway Island
mediatorship
mediatresses
mediaevalism
mediaevalist
medicamental
medicine ball
madreporitic
Midwesterner
modification
modificatory
modificative
midnight blue
Midnight Mass
mid-Victorian
medullary ray
modulability
middle ground
muddle-headed
middle-income
Middle States
middle school
meddlesomely
Middle Temple
middleweight
Madame Bovary
✧mademoiselle
mud in your eye
Modern Greats
mud wrestling
maderisation
moderate gale
moderateness
maderization
mad as a hatter
modus vivendi
meditate upon
meditatively
Midsummer day
midsummer-men
medium quarto
medium sherry
muddy-mettled
meeting-house
mnemotechnic
mnemonically
mifepristone
migrationist
magic lantern
magic realism
magic realist
Magic Johnson
magic pyramid
magnetically
magnetisable
magnetizable
magnetic card
magnetic core
magnetic disc
magnetic disk
magnetic drum
magnetic flux
magnetic lens
magnetic mine
magnetic tape
magnetometer
magnetometry
magnetograph
magnet school
Maggie Cheung
magnifically
magnificence
Magnitogorsk
magniloquent
megalomaniac
megalosaurus
Muggletonian
me generation
Magnoliaceae
magistrature
might and main
magnum bonums
Magnus effect
mail-carriage
maiden assize
moiré pattern
maiden battle
maiden castle
maidenliness
moire antique
maiden stakes
maiden speech
maiden voyage
maid of honour
Mail on Sunday
maître d'hôtel
Meissen china
main sequence
maintainable
moistureless
majolicaware
Major Barbara
major-general
major premise
majority rule
majestically
majesticness
make a day of it
make-and-break
make a beeline
make an errand
make a killing
make a pig's ear
make a long arm
make a wry face
make as though
make ends meet
make good time
Mike Hailwood
Mika Häkkinen
make it snappy
Mike Oldfield
make old bones
make one's mark
make one's name
makeover show
Miklós Horthy
make question
make the grade
make up leeway
milk-and-water
milk and honey
molybdenosis
molybdic acid
malacologist
molecularity
malocclusion
Malacostraca
melodramatic
melodic minor
malleability
millefeuille
✧maltese cross
millesimally
miller's thumb
malversation
Moll Flanders
mulligatawny
multilateral
multivalence
multivalency
multifaceted
multivariate
multifarious
multivarious
multitasking
multicauline
multicasting
multipartite
multiscience
multiseriate
multiversity
multicentral
multicentric
multidentate
multiseptate
malting floor
melting-point
milling grade
milking stool
multichannel
multivitamin
multilingual
multicipital
millisievert
multipliable
multiplicand
multiplicate
multiplicity
mellifluence
multiply into
multiflorous
multiple star
multiple shop
multinominal
multifoliate
multiformity
multivoltine
multicostate
multilobular
multilocular
multiloquent
multiloquous
multipresent
multigravida
multisulcate
multinuclear
multipurpose
mill-mountain
Milindapanha
melanochroic
Melanie Klein
melancholiac
melancholiae
Milanese silk
melanotropin
Milan Kundera
mallophagous
Milton Keynes
Malcolm Lowry
malformation
Melbourne Cup
malnourished
malcontented
milk porridge
malapertness
maltreatment
milk sickness
Mills-and-Boon
mill-sixpence
military band
militaristic
molluscicide
Molluscoidea
multungulate
malnutrition
malevolently
Molly Maguire
mammalogical
mammary gland
mammee-sapota
mammillarias
momentaneous
miminy-piminy
memorability
membrane bone
memorisation
memorization
manganic acid
mandarin duck
mandarin neck
mendaciously
mind-altering
Montague Tigg
mind-boggling
man-about-town
Manicheanism
monocultural
many-coloured
mono-compound
minicomputer
municipalise
municipalism
municipality
municipalize
monochromasy
monochromist
monochromate
monodramatic
monodelphian
monadelphous
monodelphous
monodisperse
mine detector
monkey around
mince matters
monkey engine
Monterey Jack
monkey flower
monkey hammer
monte di pietà
monkey jacket
Munsell scale
mannerliness
mangetout pea
monkey puzzle
Montessorian
monkey tricks
manoeuvrable
monkey wrench
mangel-wurzel
man-of-war bird
man-of-war's-man
munificently
minification
manufactural
manufacturer
man of letters
monofilament
manifoldness
manifestable
manifestible
manifestness
monographist
monogramming
ménage à trois
monogamously
monogenistic
managerially
monthly nurse
monticellite
monti di pietà
mansion-house
mantis shrimp
mandibulated
mini-lacrosse
mingle-mangle
monolinguist
mindlessness
manslaughter
monomaniacal
monumentally
many moons ago
monomorphism
monomorphous
minimisation
manometrical
monometrical
monometallic
mini-motorway
men's movement
minimization
Manon Lescaut
man in the moon
meningiomata
meningococci
Munro-bagging
mend one's pace
mend one's ways
Mongoloid eye
monopodially
monopolistic
manipulation
manipulatory
manipulative
monopetalous
monophyodont
monophyletic
✧monophysitic
monorchidism
monarchise it
monarchistic
monarchize it
mineral water
mineral jelly
mineralogise
mineralogist
mineralogize
mineral pitch
minor planets
minor premise
monts-de-piété
minesweeping
ministership
meniscectomy
monk's rhubarb
monastically
monostichous
monosyllabic
monosyllable
Mont-St-Michel
monosepalous
monostrophic
ministration
ministrative
monothalamic
monstre sacré
✧monotheletic
monotheistic
monotonously
munitionette
monitorially
monetary unit
monetisation
monstruosity
menstruation
monetization
maneuverable
moneylending
moneychanger
money-spinner
money-grubber
moonlighting
myographical
moon-stricken
mariage blanc
Margaret Mead
Maria Theresa
margaric acid
marcatissimo
mordaciously
Mare Australe
mercantilism
mercantilist
Murray Walker
mirabile visu
miracle berry
miracle fruit
miraculously
Morecambe Bay
meridionally
Marie Rambert
Morte d'Arthur
Mercedes-Benz®
Marie Celeste
Mircea Eliade
Merlene Ottey
market forces
market garden

market-garden
Marie biscuit
marketing mix
market leader
Marseillaise
merveilleuse
marvellously
market-making
Myrmecophaga
myrmecophile
myrmecophily
myrmecologic
marvel of Peru
Marcel Proust
market square
marked with a T
Mare Frigoris
mortgageable
mortgage rate
morigeration
marsh warbler
marsh-harrier
Marsh of Decay
Marsh of Mists
Marsh of Sleep
Martha Graham
morphography
morphallaxes
morphallaxis
morphologist
merchantable
merchant bank
merchandiser
merchandizer
merchant iron
merchantlike
merchant navy
merchant ship
march-treason
morphotropic
mirthfulness
marginal cost
marginal firm
marginal land
marginal seat
marginal-unit
marginal ward
morris dancer
Marsileaceae
marline-spike
morning watch
marking gauge
marriageable
marriage-bone
Martin Guerre
morning glory
marriage-ring
morning dress
Martini-Henry
morbilliform
Martin Luther
Marcionitism
Mercian Hymns
mercifulness
mortifyingly
moral faculty
marble-cutter
marbled-white
moral victory
moral courage
moralisation
morality play
moral support
moralization
Mary McAleese
marimbaphone
Mary McCarthy
Mare Marginis
marine boiler
Mare Nectaris
Myron Scholes
marine engine
Marino Marini
myringoscope
marine stores
murine typhus
Marina Warner
Mariolatrous
Marlon Brando
mirror finish
marrowfat pea
marconigraph
mereological
Marcobrunner
marrow-squash
Mariotte's law
mirror writer
Mary Pickford
Mark Phillips
mariposa lily
Mary Robinson
Morarji Desai
marksmanship
meristematic
myristic acid
meritocratic
Marattiaceae
meretricious
Marcus Garvey
mercurialise
mercurialism
mercurialist
mercuriality
mercurialize
Marius Petipa
merry dancers
Marty Feldman
merrythought
mercy killing
merry England
merry-go-round
merry as a grig
massaranduba
miscalculate
mismatchment
✧mesoamerican
mistakenness
message board
message-stick
mystagogical
musicianship
music teacher
music theatre
music therapy
musicologist
musical flame
mesocephalic
miseducation
misadventure
misadvisedly
master-at-arms
masseranduba
misbehaviour
Mister Bumble
misleadingly
miscegenator
misdemeanant
misdemeanour
Messeigneurs
messenger RNA
mesmerically
mysteriously
misbelieving
misreckoning
masterliness
miscellanist
muster-master
mashed potato
mesne profits
misrepresent
Mrs Henry Wood
master-switch
mastersinger
masterstroke
mussel shrimp
misfeaturing
missel-thrush
misventurous
Mister Wopsle
misogynistic
mesogastrium
moschiferous
mischallenge
mischanceful
Miss Havisham
mysticalness
misdirection
misdiagnosis
mission creep
missionarise
missionarize
Mastigophora
mystifyingly
misplacement
misalignment
misallotment
mistle-thrush
mesomorphous
misinterpret
misanthropic
misanthropos
misinformant
misknowledge
misconceiver
mosbolletjie
misformation
museological
misconstruct
miscontented
Muscovy glass
mass-produced
mass producer
misapprehend
mistreatment
mistranslate
mispronounce
mushroom pink
Mistress Ford
mistressless
mistrustless
Mistress Page
mistress-ship
Most Reverend
mesothelioma
mesothoracic
mosstrooping
misstatement
museum beetle
masturbation
masturbatory
mispunctuate
misjudgement
missummation
mosquito fish
mosquito hawk
misquotation
mutual friend
mitrailleuse
methanometer
methaqualone
meticulously
mitochondria
metachronism
mathematical
mathematised
mathematized
mother church
Mittel-Europa
Mitteleuropa
mother figure
motherliness
mother liquor
motley-minded
matter-of-fact
mothers-in-law
mother tongue
Mother Teresa
metagnathous
metagalactic
mutagenicity
Matthew Paris
Matthew Prior
matriclinous
matriarchate
metric system
matriculator
metal fatigue
metallically
metallic bond
metalanguage
metallogenic
metallophone
metalworking
metaleptical
metallurgist
metempirical
metamorphism
metamorphist
metamorphose
Metonic cycle
Mt Tungurahua
mutinousness
method acting
meteor crater
mythogenesis
muttonheaded
meteorically
methodically
meteoritical
meteoric iron
matroclinous
motionlessly
mute of malice
metrological
metropolitan
mythological
metropolises
mythologiser
mythologizer
meteorologic
meteorograph
metrorrhagia
mythographer
methotrexate
meteor shower
metaphorical
moto perpetui
moto perpetuo
metaphrastic
metoposcopic
metapsychics
metaphysical
motor caravan
material fact
Material Girl
materialness
motor scooter
mithridatise
mithridatism
mithridatize
motor neurone
motor-bicycle
motorbicycle
motor-tractor
motorisation
maturational
motorcycling
motorcyclist
motorization
mutessarifat
metasilicate
metasomatism
mitotic index
metathetical
mutato nomine
metathoracic
mutationally
mutation mink
mutation rate
mutation stop
motivelessly
motivated art
motivational
methyl violet
mauvais sujet
Mound Builder
mound-builder
mouse-milking
mouse-buttock
mouth-filling
mouth-to-mouth
mouthbreeder
mouthbrooder
Maurice Ravel
mourning band
mourning dove
mourning ring
mournfulness
Mauvoisin Dam
mousquetaire
Mount Rainier
mountebank it
moustache cup
mount of Venus
Mount Kilauea
mountain bike
mountain blue
mountain cork
mountain flax
mountain goat
mountain-high
mountain hare
mountain lion
mountain meal
mountain soap
mountainside
Mountain Time
mountain wood
Mount Olympus
mountenaunce
Mount Snowdon
Mount Roraima
Mount Stanley
Mount Ruapehu
Mount Everest
moveableness
movable feast
movie theatre
movelessness
mixobarbaric
mixed farming
mixed-ability
mixed economy
mixed chalice
myxedematous
mixed doubles
mixed crystal
mixter-maxter
mixtie-maxtie
maximisation
maximization
mizzencourse
muzzle-loader
mezzo-relievo
mezzo-rilievo
mezzo-soprano
mazarine dish
mazarine hood
Mazarin Bible
Niagara Falls
near as a touch
near as dammit
✧neandertaler
neat's leather
neat's-foot oil
Nubian Desert
noble science
nubbing-cheat
nebulisation
nobilitation
nebulousness
nebulization
noctambulism
noctambulist
nucleocapsid
nucleophilic
nuclear waste
nuclear power
nickel silver
necking party
nyctitropism
noctilucence
Nicole Kidman
Nicola Pisano
neck-moulding
Nicholas Rowe

Words marked ✧ can also be spelled with one or more capital letters

nectocalyces
necrophagous
necrophiliac
necrophilism
necrophilous
necrophorous
necrological
necropolises
necrographer
necktie party
nychthemeral
nychthemeron
nicotinamide
nidification
niddle-noddle
noematically
needlessness
nielsbohrium
neglectingly
neglectfully
Nigel Mansell
Nigel Kennedy
negrophilism
negrophilist
negotiatress
night terrors
Night of Power
night fighter
night-fishery
nightclubber
nightclothes
nugatoriness
night-brawler
night crawler
negativeness
negative pole
negative sign
negativistic
noise control
nail-head-spar
neighborhood
neighborless
neighbouring
nail scissors
Nikolai Gogol
nolens volens
Nelson Piquet
name and shame
name-dropping
nomadisation
nomadization
numberlessly
number system
number theory
Nymphaeaceae
nympholeptic
nymphomaniac
nimble-footed
namelessness
nimble-witted
nominal value
nominalistic
nomenclature
nomenklatura
nomenclative
niminy-piminy
nominatively
numinousness
nimbostratus
numerability
numerologist
numerousness
nematocystic
nomothetical
nematologist
Nematomorpha
namby-pambies
non-fattening
non-objective
non-absorbent
non-scheduled
non-admission
non-addictive
✧nunc dimittis
non-renewable
non-technical
non-residence
non-resistant
non-resisting
nonsense word
non-sectarian
non-effective
non-efficient
nonagenarian
non-Christian
nonchalantly
non-divisible
non-fictional
non-alignment
non-flammable
non-alcoholic
non-flowering
nonanoic acid
non-intrusion
non-combining
non-combatant
non-conductor
non-communion
non-committal
non-complying
non-corrosive
non-poisonous
nanoplankton
non-breakable
non-essential
none-so-pretty
none the wiser
none the worse
nineteenthly
non-attention
non-nucleated
non-Euclidean
non-automatic
non-custodial
non-executive
non-existence
Nancy Mitford
Neo-Darwinian
Neo-Darwinism
Neo-Darwinist
Neoceratodus
neoterically
Neohellenism
neorealistic
Neo-Christian
noodle farfel
neon lighting
neoclassical
Neoplatonism
Neoplatonist
neologically
neonomianism
nephelometer
nephelometry
Napier's bones
Naples yellow
nuptialities
nipple-shield
Nepenthaceae
nephological
nephrologist
nephroptosis
Norman French
Norman Foster
Norman Fowler
Norman Lamont
Norman Mailer
normal school
Norway spruce
Norman Tebbit
Norman Wisdom
noradrenalin
nerve-racking
nurse-tending
Norwegian Sea
nerve impulse
nursery rhyme
nursery class
nursery nurse
North Pacific
north-eastern
north-seeking
north-western
Northumbrian
North America
Northrop Frye
north-country
northern fern
northernmost
nursing chair
Nordic skiing
narcissistic
narrow escape
normotensive
narcotherapy
narcotically
Norfolk capon
narrow-minded
Norton Priory
nervous wreck
narrow squeak
Narasimha Rao
nosebleeding
no sae Hieland
nesting-place
nasolacrymal
nasalisation
nasalization
Nestorianism
nostological
nose-painting
nuts and bolts
not have a clue
Notodontidae
Notre Dame Bay
nutmeg grater
Netherlander
Netherlandic
notification
not give a damn
not give a toss
nothing if not
nothing to say
nothing doing
nothing loath
nothingarian
nutritionist
nutritiously
natal therapy
Notonectidae
national bank
national code
national call
National Club
national debt
national grid
✧national hunt
national park
nitromethane
not to mention
nitrobenzene
nitrophilous
not for Joseph
nitroaniline
nitroso-group
nitrotoluene
nitrous oxide
Nat Lofthouse
natural magic
natural scale
natural death
natural light
natural order
naturalistic
notary public
naturopathic
notoungulate
not turn a hair
nativity play
noteworthily
neurasthenia
neurasthenic
nauseatingly
nouveau riche
nouveau-riche
nauseousness
nouveau roman
nautical mile
nourishingly
neuropathist
neuroscience
neurogenesis
neuropeptide
neurotically
neurobiology
neurofibroma
neuroanatomy
neurological
neurohormone
neurotrophic
neurotrophin
neuropterans
neuropterist
neuropterous
neurosurgeon
neurosurgery
neutralistic
neutrophilic
neurypnology
navigability
navigational
naval officer
Naval Brigade
novelisation
novelization
Novum Organum
never-failing
nevertheless
neverthemore
✧never country
Novorossiysk
Novaya Zemlya
Newgate frill
newfangledly
New Mangalore
new-fashioned
New Hampshire
New Scientist
New Zealander
new year party
New Jersey tea
New Testament
New Jerusalem
new dimension
news magazine
newsmagazine
No Woman No Cry
New Amsterdam
New Englander
New Model Army
Newtownabbey
Newfoundland
Newton's rings
newspaperman
newspaperdom
newspaperism
New Brunswick
new criticism
New Statesman
Nixon in China
next Saturday
Nazification
on and on and on
on an even keel
orange-flower
orange roughy
orange squash
ovariotomist
on a knife-edge
oratorically
oracularness
orbicularity
on bended knee
ombrophobous
ombrophilous
once-accented
once and again
orchard-house
orchard-grass
occidentally
orchestra pit
orchestrally
orchestrator
oncogenicity
orchidaceous
once in a while
orchidectomy
orchidomania
oscilloscope
oscillograph
obcompressed
occupational
oncornavirus
Oncorhynchus
occasionally
occasioned by
old-maidishly
Old Catholics
Old Fashioned
old-fashioned
old man's beard
old school tie
Old Testament
old wives' tale
ordinariness
odd-come-short
old moustache
Old Mortality
✧order of merit
Old Pretender
obdurateness
Old Hundredth
over and above
over-and-under
overachiever
operatically
operationism
operationist
opera glasses
one-way mirror
opéra comique
open adoption
overactivity
overabundant
Open Brethren
over-cannoped
overcanopied
overcrowding
overcapacity
one's cup of tea
overcautious
open diapason
overdo things
overexertion
overemphasis
overexposure
overestimate
overfullness
Owen Falls Dam
overfamiliar
overfineness
overfondness
overfinished
overflourish
open-handedly
overhand knot
overinclined
one-sidedness
opening night
obedientiary
overkindness
open learning
overlordship
overmultiply
open-mindedly
open marriage
overniceness
oceanic crust
oceanography
overnight bag
oceanologist
one-and-thirty
over one's head
one for his nob
one's own woman

one-horse race
Ode to Evening
one-upmanship
overprepared
overpressure
overpopulate
overpersuade
Oreopithecus
overpowering
open question
overreaction
oneirocritic
oneiromancer
overrun brake
overripeness
overrashness
oleoresinous
oversubtlety
overschutcht
oversimplify
open sentence
open sandwich
overstrained
overscutched
open to debate
over the score
overwhelming
over-weighted
official list
office-bearer
office-holder
office-hunter
office junior
olfactometer
olfactometry
olfactronics
office-seeker
offscourings
off-reckoning
off the ground
off the hinges
off the record
off-the-record
off one's hands
off one's chump
off one's onion
off one's guard
on firm ground
Oxford groups
offers to bail
off-puttingly
oughly-headed
organ-gallery
organicistic
orgone energy
organ of Corti
organography
organoleptic
organ-grinder
organismally
organisation
organ-builder
organizer-bag
organization
orgasmically
orgastically
ophthalmitis
ophiolatrous
ochroleucous
ochlophobiac
ophiophagous
ophiophilist
Ophioglossum
ophiological
ophiomorphic
otherworldly
Ohinamatsuri
oligarchical
Oliver de Bois
obiter dictum
orichalceous
opinionately
opinionative
Oriel College
Oriental Club
oriental ruby
orienteering
oligopeptide
oligospermia
oligotrophic
oeils-de-boeuf
omissiveness
opisthotonic
opisthodomos
opisthotonos
opisthograph
object finder
object lesson
objet de vertu
Ockham's razor
only begetter
oil of rhodium
oil of mirbane
oil of vitriol
obligingness
obligational
obligatorily
Oklahoma City
oil the wheels
oil immersion
oblanceolate
obliteration
obliterative
obliviscence
Of Mice and Men
obmutescence
obnubilation
omnibus train
ornamentally
omnipresence
omnipotently
owner's equity
omnisciently
Ornithischia
ornithomancy
ornithogalum
ornithoscopy
ornithophily
Ornithomimus
ornithomorph
omnivorously
onomasiology
onomatopoeia
onomatopoeic
otosclerosis
otosclerotic
oboe di caccia
orogenic belt
on one's person
on one's uppers
oxonium salts
ororotundity
orographical
odontography
odontologist
odontomatous
odontophoral
odontophoran
odontophobia
Odontophorus
orphan-asylum
omphalomancy
oppressively
Orphic Cubism
oophorectomy
opposability
oppositeness
oppositional
on reflection
ourang-outang
obreptitious
on Shanks's nag
obstacle race
obstetrician
ossification
on sufferance
obsolescence
obsoleteness
obsequiously
Observantine
obstropalous
obstropulous
obstreperate
obstreperous
obsessionist
of set purpose
obscurantism
obscurantist
Outward Bound®
outward-bound
outlandishly
outdatedness
outrageously
outfangthief
optoacoustic
outmanoeuvre
oath-breaking
optical maser
optical fibre
on the wallaby
on the rampage
on the warpath
on the decline
on the rebound
on the improve
on the knocker
on the one hand
on the instant
on the bow hand
on the horizon
on the lookout
on the port bow
on the up and up
of the order of
of the essence
out-pensioner
on the streets
on the qui vive
out of fashion
out of warrant
out of service
out-of-the-body
out of the blue
out of the loop
out of thin air
out of the road
out of the wood
out of all cess
out of all nick
out of nowhere
out of context
out of spirits
out of drawing
octogenarian
ontogenetics
out the window
outside right
outside novel
outmigration
outplacement
optimisation
optometrical
Otto Meyerhof
optimization
ostentatious
octane number
out on one's ear
octane rating
osteomalacia
osteomalacic
osteosarcoma
orthopaedics
orthopaedist
osteopathist
option clause
orthogenesis
orthogenetic
osteogenesis
osteogenetic
orthopedical
osteodermous
outmodedness
orthorhombic
osteoblastic
osteoclastic
osteoplastic
orthognathic
orthogonally
orthotonesis
osteological
osteoporosis
osteoporotic
orthomorphic
orthodontics
orthodontist
orthodromics
orthographer
orthographic
orthotropism
orthotropous
orthopteroid
orthopterist
orthopterous
outspreading
octopetalous
out from under
otter-hunting
obtuse-angled
octastichous
octostichous
octosyllabic
octosyllable
Otto Skorzeny
octosepalous
octastrophic
outstretched
ocular muscle
opus operatum
onus probandi
Oswald Mosley
oxyacetylene
onychophoran
Olympic games
Olympic flame
Olympic torch
platanaceous
placableness
platanna frog
Phalaenopsis
Peasant Dance
play at waster
plane sailing
pease-bannock
peace-warrant
praseodymium
planetesimal
peacekeeping
plate-leather
place setting
peace officer
pia desideria
prayerlessly
pease-blossom
prayer-monger
Phanerogamae
Phanerogamia
phanerogamic
phanerophyte
peace-breaker
peace process
planet-struck
Plateosaurus
Placentia Bay
placentiform
placentology
placentation
pease pudding
peacefulness
Prader-Willi's
platform game
platform heel
platform sole
peach-yellows
peach blossom
playing field
praxinoscope
planispheric
plagiotropic
platinum disc
platinum lamp
Pearl Harbour
pearl-tapioca
phallocratic
pearl-sheller
pearl disease
pearl-fishing
pearl-fishery
pralltriller
Pearl Islands
pearl-essence
pharmacology
pharmaceutic
phasmophobia
psammophytic
plasmosomata
plasma screen
plain sailing
plain dealing
plain-dealing
plain-hearted
phaenogamous
Plains Indian
plainclothes
plain cookery
prawn cracker
Piano Fantasy
phaeomelanin
Phaeophyceae
platonically
Platonic year
peacock's tail
peacock-stone
plano-concave
plano-conical
planographic
phagocytical
phagocytosis
prairie value
plausibility
praiseworthy
practicalism
practicalist
practicality
plastic force
plastic money
play the devil
play the field
play the woman
Plattdeutsch
plantain lily
plastination
plaster saint
plasteriness
plasterboard
plasterstone
phantasmally
phantasmical
practise upon
practitioner
peanut butter
play with fire
pharyngology
pharyngotomy
public domain
public-domain
public health
public orator
public sector
public school
public-school
pebble-powder
Pablo Picasso
peccadilloes
piccadilloes
pickadilloes
pickerel-weed
pocket gopher
pocket-pistol
Pacific Ocean
pacification
pacificatory
pectinaceous
packing-paper
packing-sheet
pecking order
packing-press

pectoral fins
Pechora River
picrocarmine
pictorically
pectoriloquy
pictographic
picornavirus
Picardy third
Pecksniffian
pick to pieces
picture ratio
Picturephone®
picture house
picture frame
pichurim bean
pick up the tab
pachycarpous
Pachydermata
pachydermous
pedicellaria
pediculicide
pediculation
podoconiosis
pudding-faced
pudding basin
pudding-basin
pudding-plate
pudding mould
pudding-stone
pedal-clavier
pedal pushers
pedantically
pedantocracy
pedunculated
paddock-stool
pedestal desk
Paddy Ashdown
precancerous
preparedness
prelatically
prevaricator
premaxillary
precariously
prevailingly
prefabricate
prelapsarian
precautional
poetastering
presbyacusis
presbycousis
presbyterial
presbyterian
presbyterate
pre-eclampsia
preachership
prescription
prescriptive
piercingness
preoccupancy
pseudocyesis
pseudography
pseudo-Gothic
pseudomonads
pseudomartyr
pleading diet
pseudonymity
pseudonymous
pseudopodium
pseudorandom
pretenceless
pretendingly
predetermine
precedential
preferential
preselection
piece of eight
piece of goods
premeditated
preheminence
predesignate
pretermitted
prenegotiate
Pherecratean
prehensility
precessional
pre-tensioned
pre-tensioner
pretensioner
prehensorial
premenstrual
presentially
present value
presenteeism
presentiment
predestinate
preceptorial
prefectorial
presentation
presentative
preventative
preventively
prerequisite
preservation
preservatory
preservative
phengophobia
pre-Christian
prechristian
psephologist
plebiscitary
presidential
predigestion
predilection
presidentess
precipitance
precipitancy
precipitator
precisianism
precisianist
precisionist
pteridomania
plenipotence
plenipotency
Pteridophyta
pteridophyte
pteridosperm
predisposing
prehistorian
predictively
preciousness
previousness
prefloration
preclassical
peerlessness
preclusively
✧poet laureate
pneumococcus
pneumocystis
preamplifier
pre-eminently
Piet Mondrian
pleomorphism
pleomorphous
pre-embryonic
pneumaticity
pneumatology
pneumothorax
pleonastical
prednisolone
Peep-o'-day Boys
prerogatived
pterosaurian
pterodactyle
paedobaptism
paedobaptist
preponderant
preponderate
precondition
phenomenally
paedogenesis
paedogenetic
paedophiliac
pleiochasium
predominance
predominancy
prefoliation
precociously
preformation
preformative
precognisant
precognition
precognitive
precognizant
paedological
phenological
pteropod ooze
paedomorphic
paedodontics
pleiotropism
preconscious
preconstruct
Premonstrant
prepossessed
plecopterous
preposterous
pre-Columbian
phenotypical
peer pressure
preoperative
Pierre Boulez
Pierre Cardin
preordinance
Pierre Lescot
Pleuronectes
Poetry Review
pleurisy-root
Pre-Dravidian
press gallery
pre-establish
pressed glass
press release
press officer
press against
press charges
Piers Plowman
plessimetric
pleasantness
pleasingness
pleasantries
pheasant's-eye
press council
press forward
pleasure boat
pressure-cook
pressure into
pleasureless
pressure suit
pressure sore
pleasure trip
preassurance
press cutting
Puerto Cortes
'prenticeship
prenticeship
Plectognathi
prestigiator
prestriction
pretty nearly
pretty-pretty
prestissimos
pretty-spoken
prepubescent
prejudgement
presumptuous
plenum system
pregustation
pre-existence
phenylalanin
puftaloonies
pufftaloonas
pugnaciously
pagoda sleeve
pigmentation
pugilistical
pigs might fly
Pagan temples
pigeon breast
pigeon-flying
pigeon's-blood
privat-docent
privat-dozent
private parts
private means
Private Lives
private hotel
private house
Philadelphia
Philadelphia®
✧philadelphus
privateering
private wrong
private press
philanthrope
philanthropy
psilanthropy
primary phase
Prince Albert
prince-bishop
princeliness
Prince Naseem
principal boy
✧principality
Prince Rupert
Princess Anne
prince's metal
princess line
primeval atom
Phi Beta Kappa
pride of place
price of money
prizefighter
prize-winning
pride oneself
price control
pridefulness
price support
price current
price-cutting
Prix Goncourt
priggishness
philhellenic
psi phenomena
philharmonic
Philip Larkin
poikilotherm
primigravida
Philip Sidney
Philistinise
✧philistinism
Philistinize
prickly poppy
phillumenist
Phillip Sharp
painlessness
Paisley shawl
primordially
✧philodendron
primogenital
primogenitor
philosophess
philosophise
philosophism
philosophist
philosophize
philological
poison sumach
Philo Judaeus
primrose path
Plimsoll line
Plimsoll mark
priestliness
priest-ridden
printability
painted cloth
painted snipe
painted woman
painted grass
point of order
pointy-headed
paint the lily
print-through
pointillisme
pointilliste
printing-head
point-to-point
printer's mark
printer's ream
Paint It Black
primulaceous
primum mobile
privy chamber
✧privy council
Prizzi's Honor
pyjama jacket
pejoratively
poke one's head
poke one's nose
poker machine
Pallas Athene
pull a fast one
pillar-box red
Polyadelphia
palma Christi
Palladianism
pull a flanker
palpableness
pull a wry face
polyanthuses
Pelham Warner
phlebography
phlebotomise
phlebotomist
phlebotomize
policyholder
police-manure
pelican's-foot
police office
Pelycosauria
paludicolous
pile-dwelling
polydemonism
paludamentum
pollen basket
palaeobotany
polyembryony
palaeography
polyethylene
pulverisable
pulverizable
Palaeo-Indian
pulvering day
palaebiology
Palaeolithic
palaestrical
pulverulence
palification
phlegmatical
phlegmagogic
phlegmagogue
Polygalaceae
polygamously
Polygonaceae
polyglottous
polyhistoric
pollice verso
polling booth
pelvic girdle
palmitic acid
pulvilliform
pillion-rider
polyisoprene
pulp magazine
polymyositis
polymorphism
polymorphous
palingeneses
palingenesia
palingenesis
palynologist
palindromist
Polonisation
polyneuritis
pulp novelist
Polonization
poliorcetics
polypharmacy
pole position
polypetalous
polyphyodont
polyphyletic
polyphyllous
polarography
pilgrim's sign
pilgrimise it
polarimetric
pilgrimize it

polarisation
polyrhythmic
polarization
polysyllabic
polysyllable
polysulphide
polysiloxane
polysyndeton
polysepalous
poles asunder
pilot balloon
palatability
politicaster
pull the wires
palette knife
polytheistic
pilot officer
pull together
polytonality
pull to pieces
pilot project
polyurethane
pollutedness
pellucidness
Palau Islands
pull up stakes
pollyannaish
pollyannaism
palazzo pants
pamperedness
pumpernickel
pompholygous
pandanaceous
pentadactyle
pentadactyly
pentateuchal
Ponta Delgada
pentahedrons
pinealectomy
pons asinorum
✧pandaemonium
pentagonally
pentapolitan
pantaloonery
pentacrinoid
pantagrapher
pennant stone
paniculately
pony carriage
pantechnicon
panhellenion
Panhellenism
Panhellenist
panhellenium
Pan-Germanism
Pandean pipes
Pentecostals
pen-feathered
pin-feathered
panaesthesia
pendente lite
pansexualism
pansexualist
pansexuality
panification
Penghu Island
Punch and Judy
Punchinellos
panchromatic
pinchcommons
panpharmacon
Panchatantra
pontifically
pantisocracy
pencil-pusher
pencil-sketch
pinniewinkle
panel beating
panel heating
panel working
penalisation
penalty bench
penalization
Penang-lawyer
punto reverso
pantophagist
pantophagous
punto riverso
pantomimical
pantographer
pantographic
panspermatic
pancreatitis
panarthritis
panorama head
pancreozymin
Pennsylvania
Panathenaean
pony-trekking
punctulation
penitent form
penitentials
penitentiary
penetrometer
puncturation
penny-wedding
penny whistle
propagandise
propagandism
propagandist
propagandize
propaedeutic
Probate Court
procathedral
probationary
pro-marketeer
protagonists
phonasthenia
protactinium
proscription
proscriptive
proud-hearted
proletariate
proverbially
Provence-rose
pro-celebrity
proteoglycan
promethazine
phonemically
phonetically
progenitress
procellarian
propeller fan
proper motion
prove oneself
prolegomenon
process block
propenseness
processional
professional
processioner
professorial
professoress
professorate
property band
protectingly
protestingly
projectional
prosectorial
protectorial
progesterone
property room
✧protectorate
protestation
protectively
projectivity
prosecutable
procès-verbal
proselytiser
proselytizer
Ptolemy Soter
proofreading
proof-correct
plough-jogger
Plough Monday
ploughwright
prophylactic
prothalamion
prothalamium
prothonotary
propheticism
provincially
profit centre
province rose
promised land
profiteroles
profiteering
provided that
providential
prolifically
proficiently
provisionary
prolificness
prodigiosity
propitiation
propitiatory
propitiative
prodigiously
propitiously
profitlessly
profit margin
phonic method
proditorious
promissorily
profit-taking
protistology
profligately
problem child
problem novel
problematics
proclamation
proclamatory
problematise
problematize
people person
People's Party
people's front
proglottides
pro-and-conned
photocathode
phonocamptic
phonotactics
proboscidean
proboscidian
Paolo Uccello
protonematal
photogeology
photorealism
photosetting
prolongation
photophilous
photochemist
photochromic
prototherian
phototherapy
Paolo Di Canio
pronominally
prosodically
photokinesis
photobiology
photofission
proto-history
photoglyphic
protoplasmal
photoelastic
protoplasmic
protoplastic
probouleutic
pronouncedly
profoundness
prosopopeial
phonological
protozoology
protocolling
prosopopoeia
protomorphic
photomontage
photovoltaic
photopolymer
photocopying
photospheric
photo-process
phonographer
photographer
phonographic
photographic
phototrophic
prototrophic
phototropism
photogravure
proconsulate
photo-etching
proportional
proportioned
Photostatted
provost guard
photocurrent
photodynamic
phonotypical
prototypical
phosphaturia
prospectuses
phosphoresce
phospholipid
prosperously
protractedly
protractible
progradation
proprietress
poor relation
programmatic
programmable
protreptical
Pyotr Wrangel
protrusively
poor-spirited
pious opinion
prostacyclin
proctologist
prostanthera
proctorially
prostitution
promuscidate
protuberance
promulgation
propugnation
productional
productively
productivity
prosyllogism
progymnasium
pipe and tabor
Popocatepetl
pepper-caster
pepper-castor
peppered moth
Pepper's ghost
pepper-shrike
pupilability
pupil teacher
papuliferous
Papilionidae
popular front
populousness
pop one's clogs
paper-marbler
paper-washing
papyrologist
pipers piping
paper profits
paper-stainer
papistically
pope's knights
Papaveraceae
Port Adelaide
pergameneous
permanent way
permanent set
permanganate
Parian marble
phreatophyte
Port-au-Prince
portal system
permaculture
paraboloidal
paracyanogen
perichaetial
pyroclastics
perichaetium
pyrochemical
paroccipital
parochialise
parochialism
parochiality
parochialize
paracentesis
pericynthion
perichoresis
pericarditis
parachronism
peradventure
paradigmatic
parade ground
paradisiacal
paradise fish
paradisaical
Paradise Lost
paradoxidian
paradoxology
paradoxurine
parietal lobe
porcelainise
porcelainous
porcelainize
permeability
part-exchange
perseverance
perseverator
paraenetical
pyro-electric
purse-sharing
paroemiology
Purbeck stone
porcellanise
porcellanite
porcellanous
porcellanize
porte-cochère
porte-bonheur
porte-monnaie
perpetration
perverseness
porter's lodge
paraesthesia
perfect tense
perfect pitch
purse strings
perfect fifth
perfect fluid
perceptional
perfectation
portentously
perfectively
perceptivity
perpetualism
perpetuallst
perpetuality
porteous roll
perpetuation
perfervidity
purification
purificatory
purificative
paraffin test
paragnathism
paragraphist
paragnathous
Phrygian mode
peregrinator
paraglossate
pyrognostics
Parthian shot
perched block
parchmentise
parchmentize
Port Harcourt
pertinacious
pervicacious
pareira brava
partisanship
partie carrée
parking meter
parking-light
parking place
participable
participator

Porfirio Díaz
partitionist
perfidiously
perniciously
Purkinje cell
particle size
Persian berry
Persian wheel
parsimonious
Perrier water
Parkinsonism
permissively
persistently
persistingly
permittivity
particularly
perviousness
purple airway
parallel bars
parallel port
parallel turn
parallelwise
pyroligneous
Portland Club
purblindness
Portland sago
paralanguage
paralipomena
perilousness
perplexingly
parsley piert
pyramidology
paramagnetic
paramilitary
pyromaniacal
portmanteaus
portmanteaux
paramorphism
pyromorphite
perimorphous
parametrical
perimetrical
pyrometrical
peremptorily
perambulator
paring chisel
parenterally
Pirandellian
paranthelion
paranthropus
parenthesise
parenthesize
perenniality
phrontistery
phrenologise
phrenologist
phrenologize
paronomastic
perinephrium
partner whist
perinatology
perineuritis
persona grata
purpose-built
purposefully
Person Friday
periodic acid
periodically
perfoliation
periodic wind
personifying
performative
periodontics
periodontist
pornographer
pornographic
part of speech
periostracum
pernoctation
parrot-wrasse
perionychium
perspicacity
perspectival
peripherical
paraphimosis
parapophyses
parapophysis
paraphrastic
periphrastic
perspiration
perspiratory
parapsychism
pyrophyllite
paraquadrate
portrait-bust
porismatical
parish church
parascending
peristeronic
parasphenoid
puristically
parisyllabic
pyrosulphate
periselenium
phrasemonger
parasyntheta
peristomatic
perispomenon
phraseologic
phraseograph
parish priest
peristrephic
parasiticide
parasitaemia
parasitology
paratactical
pyrotechnics
pyrotechnist
parotid gland
pyritiferous
pyritohedral
pyritohedron
peritrichous
pyrithiamine
parathormone
pyrotartaric
pyrotartrate
percutaneous
porous alloys
perturbation
perturbatory
perturbative
perfusionist
percussional
perquisition
percussively
persuasively
pursuit plane
Peruvian bark
Port Victoria
periwig-pated
port-wine mark
peroxidation
party machine
party-capital
party-verdict
party selling
Porgy and Bess
Percy Lubbock
postal ballot
postage meter
passage-money
passage grave
postage stamp
passableness
Pestalozzian
postal system
postal worker
postdoctoral
post-diluvial
post-diluvian
passe-partout
post exchange
passemeasure
posteriority
passed master
pas de bourrée
poster paints
✧pasteurellae
✧pasteurellas
pusser's sneer
possessional
possessioned
pusser's logic
possessively
postfeminism
postfeminist
postgraduate
posthumously
post-hypnotic
pestilential
passibleness
postillation
passion fruit
passionately
Passion-music
pisciculture
postliminary
postliminous
postmeridian
post meridiem
postmistress
past one's best
push one's luck
pass one's word
pestological
postprandial
postponement
postposition
postpositive
pastry cutter
pass sentence
post-synching
postsurgical
Post-Tertiary
positiveness
positive pole
positive rays
positive sign
positivistic
posture-maker
pasqueflower
passy-measure
Puseyistical
pâte à savarin
pitiableness
pot-walloping
potichomania
put a damper on
putrefacient
putrefaction
putrefactive
patience-dock
Petter engine
pathetically
pattern-maker
pattern-wheel
pitter-patter
potter's wheel
potter's field
put a finger on
put the acid on
put the boot in
put the bite on
patch through
put the make on
pitch and putt
pitching tool
pitch-and-toss
pitcher plant
put the wind up
Patripassian
petrifaction
petrifactive
petting party
putting-cleek
putting green
putting-stone
patrilineage
Patrick Henry
Patrick White
Patrick Moore
patriclinous
Pythian games
Pythian verse
pettifogging
pettifoggery
patriarchism
patriarchate
patristicism
pottle-bodied
patellectomy
petaliferous
pitilessness
Potomac River
potamologist
pat on the back
put in the boot
put on the foil
put on the line
✧put on the ritz
potentialise
potentiality
potentialize
patent inside
potentiation
put on one side
Patent Office
put one's oar in
put one's bib in
pathogenesis
pathogenetic
petrogenesis
petrogenetic
petrol engine
put money into
put to the horn
petrophysics
patroclinous
petroglyphic
put down roots
put to one side
pathological
petrological
petrodollars
pythonomorph
pot companion
petrographer
petrographic
pater patriae
Peter Gabriel
Peter Abelard
Peter Ackroyd
Peter Medawar
Peter Sellers
Peter Behrens
Peter Shaffer
Peter Shilton
Peter Sissons
Peter Fleming
Peter Lombard
Peterborough
Peter Fricker
Peter Ustinov
pityrosporum
Peter Cushing
put a sock in it
Pott's disease
potato blight
potato crisps
Pitt the Elder
potato finger
potato masher
potato spirit
petty larceny
petty officer
petty treason
plumbiferous
plumbaginous
plumber-block
plum curculio
pound of flesh
pound foolish
pound-foolish
poules de luxe
Paule Régnier
prudentially
Paul Elvström
plunging fold
pouched mouse
pluriseriate
pruning knife
pluriliteral
pluviometric
plurilocular
pauciloquent
Paul Langevin
plummer-block
plum-porridge
✧prussian blue
Prussian carp
Prussianiser
Prussianizer
Paul Scofield
Paul Tournier
plumulaceous
Paul Verlaine
pavilion-roof
paving debate
powder closet
powdering-tub
powder monkey
powder-skiing
power take-off
power-sharing
powerlifting
power-dressed
power station
powerfulness
Payne Stewart
psychiatrist
psychoactive
psychobabble
psychic force
psychography
psychologise
psychologism
psychologist
psychologize
psychometric
psychonomics
psychrometer
psychrometry
psychopathic
psychosocial
psychosexual
psychoticism
psychotropic
physiocratic
physiography
physiognomic
physic garden
physiologist
phyllotactic
phytonadione
phycoxanthin
phylogenesis
phylogenetic
phytogenesis
phytogenetic
phytobenthos
phytophagous
phycological
phytological
phytohormone
phytographer
phytographic
Plymouth Rock
Phycomycetes
pay-as-you-earn
pay attention
puzzle-headed
puzzle-monkey
Quaker-colour
quare impedit
quaking-grass
qualificator
quacksalving
qualmishness
quadriennial
quadriennium
quadragenary
Quadragesima
quadrumanous
quarrymaster
quadrinomial

quadrangular
quadraplegia
quadriplegia
quadriplegic
quadraphonic
quadrophonic
quadrivalent
quaestionary
quaestorship
quantifiable
quantum yield
quantum state
quattrocento
quarter-sawed
quarter after
quarter-final
quarter-miler
quarterlight
quartern loaf
quarter-blood
quarter-plate
quarter-bound
quarter-pound
quarter-round
quarter-horse
quarterstaff
quarter-guard
quartz-schist
quantisation
quantitative
quantitively
quantivalent
quantization
quaquaversal
quenchlessly
queue-jumping
querimonious
queen's bounty
queen regnant
queen-regnant
Queen of Sheba
Queenslander
queen dowager
queen consort
Queen's Speech
queen's yellow
quelque chose
questionable
questionably
questionless
question mark
question time
quidditative
quinine water
quick-scented
quick-selling
quick-sighted
quicksilvery
quill-feather
quill-driving
quixotically
quinquenniad
quinquennial
quinquennium
quintessence
quizzicality
quotableness
quota-hopping
quota quickie
Rhadamanthus
Rhadamanthys
readableness
readaptation
rhabdomancer
rhabdomyomas
rhabdosphere
reach-me-downs
Real Huntsman
roaring drunk
reality check
readjustment
reallocation
readmittance
reannexation
reappearance
real presence
real property
rhamphotheca
reassignment
reassemblage
reassumption
road surveyor
reassuringly
reabsorption
reassessment
reattachment
roasting jack
reaction time
re-alteration
reactiveness
reactivation
ready-moneyed
Rebecca riots
ruby-coloured
rubber bullet
rubber cheque
rubber cement
rabbeting-saw
Rube Goldberg
rub shoulders
rubbing stone
rabbinically
rabbit-sucker
rabbit warren
R M Ballantyne
rebelliously
ribble-rabble
rabble-rouser
ribonuclease
Robin Cousins
rub one's hands
Roberta Flack
Robert Altman
Robert Browne
Robert De Niro
Robert Fulton
Robert Graves
Robert Greene
Robert Lowell
Robert Mugabe
Roberto Duran
Robert Palmer
Robert Raikes
Robert Runcie
Robert Wilson
robustiously
ribosomal RNA
rubythroated
Rubeus Hagrid
Richard Scott
Richard Adams
Richard Meade
Richard Nixon
Richard Lower
Richard Pryor
Richard Stone
rechargeable
ricochetting
rock climbing
rice crispies
recidivistic
Rachel Carson
rocket engine
racketeering
racket-ground
Rochelle-salt
rocker switch
racket-tailed
recreational
recognisance
recognizance
recognisable
recognisably
recognizable
recognizably
Richie Benaud
rachischisis
receivership
rocking chair
rocking horse
rocking stone
recriminator
receiving-set
rectirostral
Rice Krispies®
recollection
recollective
recalcitrant
recalcitrate
recalescence
recklessness
recommitment
recommission
recomforture
racemisation
racemization
reconveyance
raconteuring
reconsecrate
reconversion
reconnection
reconcilable
reconcilably
reconnoitrer
reconstitute
raccoon-berry
receptacular
receptaculum
receptionist
reciprocally
reciprocator
recuperation
recuperatory
recuperative
recapitalise
recapitulate
recapitalize
recordership
Record Office
record player
record sleeve
recessed arch
recessionary
rock scorpion
reciting-note
Richter scale
recrudescent
rockumentary
recovery time
ride at anchor
radial artery
radial engine
Redwall Abbey
reducibility
radicicolous
reductionism
reductionist
ridiculously
redecoration
radicivorous
Red Leicester
Red Delicious
rudder pedals
radiesthesia
radiesthetic
redefinition
ride for a fall
Rudolf Carnap
Rudolf Diesel
rodomontader
redemptioner
Redemptorist
redemptively
redintegrate
rodenticidal
riding master
riding school
radiochemist
radiophonics
radiophonist
radiotherapy
radio-thorium
radiomimetic
radiobiology
radioelement
radio amateur
radiological
radio compass
red corpuscle
radiographer
radiographic
radioisotope
radio station
radionuclide
redeployment
Rider Haggard
rediscoverer
redistribute
ride to hounds
red quebracho
redoublement
radius vector
re-embodiment
reefer jacket
re-engagement
re-enlistment
rheometrical
rheumatology
rheumatismal
rien ne va plus
rhetorically
reed-pheasant
Rhesus factor
roebuck-berry
rhesus monkey
reflationary
refractional
refractorily
refractively
refractivity
rifleman bird
reflex camera
ruffed grouse
refreshments
refreshingly
refreshfully
rifle grenade
reflectogram
reflectingly
reflectively
reflectivity
refrigerator
raffle-ticket
referred pain
reform school
refoundation
Ragnar Frisch
ragged school
regressively
regressivity
raggle-taggle
regulatively
regimentally
Reginald Kray
Reginald Pole
regeneration
regeneratory
regenerative
Roger McGough
Roger Penrose
Roger Chaffee
Roger Clemens
regardlessly
rigorousness
registration
right-hand man
right of entry
right the helm
right-and-left
Rogation Days
right-to-lifer
Rogation Week
rags-to-riches
rightfulness
rehabilitate
reimbursable
reimbattell'd
rainbow trout
Rainbow Guide
reindeer moss
reiteratedly
raise the ante
raise the roof
raise the wind
raise one's hat
raise money on
raised pastry
Rhinegravine
Rhipidoptera
rhizocarpous
rhizogenetic
Rhizocephala
rhinocerical
rhinoceroses
rhinocerotes
rhinocerotic
rhizophagous
rhizophilous
rhinoplastic
rhinological
rhinorrhagia
rhinorrhoeal
reimpression
reimposition
reinstalment
reinspection
rail-splitter
roisterously
reinvigorate
reinvestment
rejectamenta
rejectionist
rejoneadores
rejuvenation
reliance loss
reliableness
rollerblader
Relief Church
roller hockey
roller-skater
rallentandos
religionless
Rolf Hochhuth
Ralph Fiennes
rolling hitch
rolling stock
rolling stone
roll in the hay
relentlessly
role reversal
rule the roast
rule the roost
relationally
relationless
relationship
relativeness
relativistic
relativities
relativitist
remedilessly
ramjet engine
ramification
remainder-man
rumble-tumble
rumblethumps
rememberable
rememberably
remembrancer
remembrances
remand centre
romantically
✧Roman holiday
remineralise
remineralize
remuneration
remuneratory
remunerative
reminiscence
Romanisation
remonstrance
remonstrator
ruminatingly
ruminatively
Romanization
Rome, Open City
Ramapithecus

remorsefully
Rembrandtish
Rembrandtism
remote access
rumpti-iddity
rambunctious
removability
removal terms
ring-armature
ring-compound
ring-dropping
ring dotterel
rangefinding
range oneself
ringed plover
renversement
rendezvoused
rendezvouses
run-of-the-mill
röntgenogram
röntgenology
renegotiable
Ronnie Browne
Ronnie Barker
renminbi yuan
run-time error
running water
running belay
running fight
running title
running board
running costs
René Just Haüy
Ronald Fisher
Ronald Reagan
Ronald Searle
René Magritte
renunciation
renunciatory
renunciative
ranunculuses
random access
Randolph Stow
random sample
run up against
Ron Greenwood
Renfrewshire
ringside seat
ringside view
ring-streaked
run its course
renounceable
renouncement
renewability
rhopaloceral
Room at the Top
rhombohedral
rhombohedron
reoccupation
reordination
Rio de Janeiro
Rhodes Boyson
Rhodesian man
rooming house
rooflessness
rootlessness
rhododendron
Rhodophyceae
rhodomontade
root pressure
root parasite
root tubercle
replantation
Rip Van Winkle
rope-drilling
reprehension
reprehensory
reprehensive
representant
replevisable
repressively
repagination
repairable by
ripple effect
ripple-marked
reproachable
reproachless
reprocessing
rip-roaringly
reprographer
reprographic
reproducible
reproduction
reproductive
reparability
Rupert Brooke
Rupert's drops
repercussion
repercussive
repossession
reputed quart
reputed owner
repatriation
repetitional
repetitively
reputatively
requiem shark
reregulation
ruralisation
ruralization
risk analysis
researchable
rise and shine
restauration
restaurateur
rush-bottomed
rose-coloured
rosy-coloured
rust-coloured
ruse de guerre
residentiary
residentship
Russell Crowe
Rosie Boycott
respectfully
respectively
rosy-fingered
resignedness
rose geranium
rescheduling
Rosh Hashanah
resting place
resting spore
resting stage
Rosminianism
Russian salad
Russian boots
respirometer
re-solubility
resolubility
resolvedness
Rosalyn Yalow
resplendence
resplendency
restlessness
resoluteness
✧resolutioner
Rose Macaulay
Rosemary West
resumptively
resiniferous
resonance-box
respondentia
Russocentric
Russophobist
Russophilism
Russophilist
rose of Sharon
responseless
responsorial
response time
responsively
resupination
rustproofing
resipiscence
resipiscency
restrictedly
reserve ratio
reserved list
reservedness
reserve price
reserve grade
✧resurrection
resurrective
reserved word
restrainable
restrainedly
✧risorgimento
resuscitable
resuscitator
resistlessly
Rosetta stone
resettlement
resourceless
resoundingly
rescue remedy
rushy-fringed
ritual murder
retractility
retractation
retractively
ratable value
reticulocyte
reticulately
reticulation
retrenchment
ratification
ratchet-wheel
Rita Hayworth
ratbite fever
retainership
retaining fee
retail outlet
retrievement
rattle-headed
ruthlessness
retina camera
retinoic acid
retentionist
rationaliser
rationalizer
retrocession
retroversion
retrocessive
retrojection
retrophiliac
ratiocinator
retromingent
retrofitting
retroflected
retroflexion
retrogradely
retropulsion
retropulsive
return crease
rotary engine
retiringness
return of post
return ticket
rotor-station
rhumb-sailing
roundaboutly
round the bend
round-mouthed
rough hawkbit
rough passage
rough-perfect
rough diamond
rough-grained
rough-wrought
rough grazing
rough justice
reunionistic
revocability
revegetation
revalidation
revulsionary
revelational
revolutional
revolutioner
revengefully
ravenousness
River Marañón
River Zambezi
River Madeira
River Maritsa
River Waikato
River Narmada
River Garonne
River Salween
River Schelde
River Acheron
River Ucayali
reverberator
River Sénégal
River Selenga
River Yenisei
river-terrace
reverse swing
River Phoenix
River Shannon
reversionary
River Limpopo
River Vistula
River Alpheus
River Glommen
River Dnieper
river dolphin
River Uruguay
River Orinoco
revisitation
revivability
revivalistic
revivescence
revivescency
reviviscence
reviviscency
Rhynchonella
Rhynchophora
Rayleigh disc
Rayleigh wave
rhyme to death
rhythmically
rhythm method
rhythmometer
rhythmopoeia
rhytidectomy
rhyming slang
Royal Marines
royal warrant
Royal Academy
Royal Doulton
Raymond Barre
Raymond Floyd
razzle-dazzle
scarabaeuses
shamateurism
scalableness
stalactiform
star-blasting
scabbard fish
scabbardless
search engine
starchedness
standpattism
St Andrew's Day
staddle stone
stand-off half
stand the pace
scandal sheet
scandalously
standing crop
standing joke
standing-room
Scandinavian
standing wave
stand-up comic
✧standardbred
standard cost
standardiser
standardizer
standard lamp
standard time
slanderously
standard wing
stage manager
shamefacedly
share capital
scapegallows
sharefarming
space capsule
scare tactics
space lattice
scare-heading
space vehicle
stapedectomy
space-heating
statementing
Siamese twins
state of siege
scavenge pump
scavengering
snake-charmer
stage whisper
space shuttle
Staten Island
space blanket
shareholding
slaveholding
sealed orders
skateboarder
scapegoating
statesperson
slave traffic
state trooper
share cropper
sharecropper
slate-writing
space station
shamefulness
Sea of Galilee
Sea of Marmara
Sea of Vapours
staff officer
Sea of Showers
snaffling-lay
Sea of Okhotsk
staff college
span-farthing
snap-fastener
staff surgeon
snaggleteeth
snaggletooth
slang-whanger
shaggy ink-cap
staggeringly
swaggeringly
swagger stick
slaughterman
slaughterous
stargazey pie
scaphoid bone
slash fiction
slash-and-burn
smash-and-grab
St Athanasius
stakhanovism
stakhanovite
staghorn fern
staghorn moss
slasher movie
swashbuckler
seaside grape
shaking palsy
staying power
shaving-brush
shaving-stick
Spanish sheep
Spanish chalk
Spanish white
Spanish onion
Spanish topaz
Spanish broom
Spanish cress
Spanish grass
Spanish Steps
Spanish juice
scarificator
stabilisator
stabilizator
Stanislavsky
static memory
station wagon
station house
statistician
spaciousness

stack against
spark chamber
sparking-plug
slack in stays
snack counter
small calorie
shawl pattern
Stahlhelmist
small letters
small-clothes
snarling-iron
snarling-tool
smallholding
scallop shell
smallest room
scarlet fever
scarlet woman
Stanley Falls
Stanley knife®
stammeringly
stained glass
stanniferous
scanning-disc
swainishness
shadow-boxing
sea porcupine
shadow effect
shadow figure
scatophagous
seasoning-tub
scazon iambus
scatological
season ticket
sharpshooter
sharp-sighted
stamping mill
scalping-tuft
sharp-tongued
sharp-looking
sharp-pointed
sharp-toothed
scampishness
snappishness
swamp cypress
stauroscopic
scabrousness
sparrow grass
sparrow-grass
star-spangled
Stars and Bars
snapshooting
star sapphire
smart missile
starting gate
starting hole
starting post
slantingways
St Anthony pig
scatteringly
shatteringly
smatteringly
scattermouch
starter motor
scatterbrain
shatter-brain
shatterproof
Seamus Heaney
scapulimancy
sea buckthorn
Seamus Mallon
scapulomancy
statutory law
Statue of Zeus
status symbol
statuesquely
sea butterfly
stalwartness
submarine pen
submaxillary
✧sublapsarian
subfactorial
subhastation
subabdominal
subscribable
suboccipital
subscription
subscriptive
subeditorial
subfeudation
subfeudatory
subreference
subcelestial
submergement
subdelirious
subtemperate
subterranean
subvertebral
subfertility
subjectively
subjectivise
subjectivism
subjectivist
subjectivity
subjectivize
subsequently
subservience
subserviency
subaggregate
subthreshold
subdiaconate
sublineation
subdirectory
subliminally
subcivilised
subcivilized
subdivisible
subsidiarily
subsidiarity
subminiature
sublibrarian
submissively
subglacially
subalternant
subalternate
subalternity
soboliferous
Sabellianism
subumbrellar
subantarctic
Sabin vaccine
subinfeudate
subinspector
subintroduce
St Benet's Hall
subnormality
subcommunity
subcommittee
subconscious
subcontinent
subopercular
suboperculum
subapostolic
subtreasurer
subarachnoid
subarrhation
subprincipal
suberisation
subarcuation
suberization
Sebastian Coe
substraction
substantival
substantiate
substitution
substitutive
substruction
substructure
subcutaneous
subauricular
subduplicate
subsultorily
✧social credit
sick and tired
sacramentary
social graces
saccadically
Socratically
sectarianise
sectarianism
sectarianize
sociableness
social worker
sack-doudling
succedaneous
secretariate
secretagogue
sacred beetle
socket chisel
secret police
successantly
successional
success story
successfully
successively
socket wrench
sick headache
saccharoidal
saccharinity
succinctness
sacrilegious
sucking louse
succinic acid
sectionalise
sectionalism
sectionalist
sectionalize
secular games
secularistic
sickle-shaped
sycamore tree
Second Advent
second ballot
second banana
Second Coming
second cousin
second degree
second fiddle
second growth
second nature
second person
second storey
second supine
second strike
second-strike
second string
second-to-none
secundum quid
sociometrist
sociobiology
sacroiliitis
sociological
sycophantise
sycophantish
sycophantize
sacerdotally
security risk
secessionism
secessionist
seclusionist
succussation
sedge warbler
Sidney Altman
Sidney Bechet
Sydney Carton
sodden-witted
se defendendo
soda fountain
saddlebacked
saddle hackle
saddle pillar
saddle-shaped
saddle stitch
saddle-stitch
saddle spring
sedulousness
sidereal time
sidereal year
sudoriferous
siderophilic
sudoriparous
sadistically
Sodium Amytal®
side whiskers
Stefan Edberg
Sue MacGregor
steganograph
step aerobics
stencil plate
speechlessly
speechmaking
stercoranism
stercoranist
Spencer Tracy
speechwriter
speedballing
speed reading
speed skating
speedboating
Speedwriting®
stepdaughter
Steve Backley
scene-painter
stereoacuity
stereocamera
siege economy
stereochrome
stereochromy
Steve McQueen
Steve McCurry
stereography
scene-shifter
stereoisomer
speleologist
stereometric
Steven Norris
skeleton suit
Steve Fossett
stereopticon
stereophonic
stereoscopic
stereotactic
stereotropic
stereotyping
step function
sledgehammer
see the last of
Stephen Hales
Stephen Benét
Stephen Crane
shepherdling
shepherdless
shepherd's pie
shepherd's rod
stethoscopic
specimen page
sheriff clerk
sheriff court
sheriff's post
specifically
specific heat
specific name
special needs
special offer
special trust
specialise in
specialistic
special issue
specialize in
speciousness
Stevie Wonder
steak tartare
speckledness
specksioneer
specktioneer
speaking tube
speak volumes
speakerphone
sneak preview
sneck-drawing
sneakishness
she'll be right
stelliferous
shellshocked
spellchecker
stealthiness
steal the show
spellbinding
sterling area
spelling book
shealing-hill
sheeling-hill
Stellenbosch
Shetland pony
Shetland wool
steelworking
shell company
swell-mobsman
steel erector
shell program
stellar month
spermogonium
steam whistle
St Edmund Hall
spermaphytic
spermophytic
Skelmersdale
spermatocele
spermatocyte
spermathecal
stepmotherly
spermatogeny
spermatozoal
spermatozoan
spermatozoic
spermatozoid
spermatozoon
steam turbine
Sheena Easton
stern-wheeler
sternutation
sternutatory
sternutative
stegocarpous
stegosaurian
stegophilist
stenothermal
skeuomorphic
stenographer
scenographic
stenographic
step on the gas
sleepwalking
sheep-scoring
steeplechase
steeple house
steeple-crown
sheep's fescue
sheepshearer
✧sleepy hollow
sweepingness
sleeping pill
sleeping-suit
sleeper shark
sheepishness
sheep's sorrel
sheep-stealer
sheep station
spear carrier
smear tactics
spear-thrower
spear thistle
steering gear
shearing shed
Sierra Nevada
spear-running
spear pyrites
speiss cobalt
sneeshin-mull
spectral type
sweet-scented
spectre lemur
sweet william
sweet alyssum
steatomatous
sweet-and-sour
spectroscope
spectroscopy
spectrometer
spectrometry
sweet sorghum
sweat cooling
spectrograph
sweet-toothed
steatopygous
steatorrhoea
stertorously

sweetishness
spectatorial
sheath-winged
specular iron
safe and sound
safe as houses
safe-breaking
safe-cracking
soft currency
sufficiently
softly-softly
safflower oil
Suffolk punch
safari jacket
safari supper
suffruticose
soft-sectored
safety factor
segmentation
suggestively
significance
significancy
significator
Sigrid Undset
sign language
sigmoid colon
St George's Day
sugar-refiner
sugar the pill
sugar snap pea
sight-reading
sight-singing
sight-playing
sage-thrasher
Sigmund Freud
Schiaparelli
sphragistics
sphacelation
Schneiderian
sphygmoscope
sphygmometer
sphygmophone
sphygmograph
Schéhérazade
sphairistike
schiller spar
scholar's mate
scholastical
sphincterial
schindylesis
schindyletic
schoolboyish
school doctor
school-divine
school-friend
schoolfellow
school-leaver
schoolmaster
school phobia
school-taught
schorlaceous
sphericality
Sahara Desert
schismatical
Scheuermann's
schizocarpic
Schizaeaceae
schizogonous
schizomycete
schizopodous
schizophrene
schizophytic
schizothymia
schizothymic
spinal column
spiral galaxy
scitamineous
suitableness
spinal marrow
slip a mooring
sailboarding
stilboestrol
shipbuilding
ship chandler
switch hitter
slip-carriage
swindle-sheet
spindle shell
spindle whorl
spine-bashing
spider beetle
swine-keeping
spider flower
spine-chiller
seine fishing
spider-legged
spider monkey
spider stitch
spire-steeple
stiletto heel
spitefulness
spider wrench
spit feathers
stiff-hearted
swing the lead
spiegeleisen
swinging-boom
sting and ling
swinging-post
sniggeringly
stichometric
stichomythia
stichomythic
suicide watch
spiritedness
sliding scale
spiritlessly
spirit master
spirit of salt
spirit of wine
spirit rapper
spiritualise
spiritualism
✧spiritualist
spirituality
spiritualize
spirituosity
skipjack tuna
stickability
stickler-like
stick the pace
slickensided
spick and span
snick and snee
snicker-snack
slink butcher
sticky wicket
shield-bearer
spill a bibful
spiflication
shielded line
shielded pair
still-peering
still-piecing
shield-maiden
still and anon
spilling line
shillingless
shilling mark
Stirling Moss
skillion roof
shield-shaped
shilly-shally
skillfulness
still hunting
Shirley poppy
seismic shock
seismic array
seismography
skin magazine
seismologist
seismometric
swimming-bell
swimming-bath
swimmingness
swimming-pond
swimming-pool
seismonastic
shimmeringly
seismoscopic
skinny-dipper
scientifical
spinning-mill
spinning mule
seignioralty
seigniorship
suit one's book
slip one's ways
slip of the pen
skipping-rope
slipper satin
slipperiness
slipper socks
snippetiness
stirrup pants
Sciuropterus
stirrup strap
spinsterhood
spinstership
ship's biscuit
scissiparity
scissors hold
scissors kick
scissor blade
scissor-tooth
ship's husband
skirt-dancing
Saint Laurent
shirtwaister
sciatic nerve
slip the cable
skittle-alley
spittle-house
Saint George's
scintigraphy
scintillator
shirtsleeved
skip-tooth saw
shift working
snifter-valve
Saint Francis
skittishness
Saint-Exupéry
stipulaceous
spinulescent
spiny lobster
suit yourself
swizzle-stick
✧St John's bread
self-analysis
Salaam Bombay!
salvage-corps
self-affected
self-adhesive
syllabically
saltationism
saltationist
Salvationism
Salvationist
sulfadiazine
saleableness
Salvador Dali
saltatorious
self-anointed
self-applause
self-approval
self-assembly
self-absorbed
self-activity
sella turcica
Silva Eusebio
self-advocacy
soluble glass
self-begotten
salubriously
self-betrayal
silicicolous
self-cleaning
self-creation
siliciferous
self-critical
selectionist
salicylamide
self-coloured
self-contempt
self-consumed
solecistical
self-catering
solicitation
solicitously
select vestry
self-deceived
self-deceiver
solidifiable
self-delusion
salad spinner
self-directed
self-director
self-disliked
self-destruct
self-distrust
self-devotion
silver-beater
self-exciting
self-endeared
silver dollar
self-electing
self-election
self-exertion
self-elective
self-effacing
silver-glance
silver iodide
self-evidence
self-existent
silver lining
silver-plated
self-employed
salver-shaped
silver salmon
silver screen
silver surfer
solvent abuse
Sylvestrines
self-educated
silver-voiced
self-flattery
self-focusing
salification
solifluction
self-gracious
self-glorious
sulphonamide
sulphonation
Solzhenitsyn
self-hypnosis
sulphuretted
sulphureting
sulphuration
sulphite pulp
saltimbancos
self-identity
selling plate
selling-price
salvifically
Salviniaceae
salpiglossis
self-interest
silviculture
sylviculture
self-involved
self-lighting
Salt Lake City
self-luminous
sal alembroth
self-limiting
soliloquiser
soliloquizer
selflessness
salamandrian
salamandroid
salamandrine
Solomon's seal
self-murderer
splint armour
splenic fever
splinter bone
selenography
solenoidally
splendidious
splendidness
selenologist
splenomegaly
Silent Spring
solonisation
splenisation
selenium cell
solonization
splenization
salsolaceous
salmon-colour
self-occupied
self-ordained
salmon-fisher
sulfonic acid
saloon-keeper
sallow kitten
salmon ladder
saloon pistol
sale or return
salt of sorrel
salt of tartar
salt of wisdom
self-prepared
self-pleasing
self-produced
self-portrait
saltpetreman
solar battery
solar eclipse
sclerodermia
sclerodermic
solar heating
self-rigorous
self-righting
self-reliance
sclerometric
sclerenchyma
solar-powered
self-reproach
sclerophylly
solarisation
solar furnace
self-reverent
solarization
self-standing
salesmanship
self-schooled
self-sameness
solitudinous
splatter film
splatterpunk
split leather
sell the dummy
salutiferous
splotchiness
split the vote
self-thinking
split on a rock
splat cooling
salutariness
solitariness
solstitially
salutational
salutatorian
salutatorily
self-violence
splay-mouthed
Sally Gunnell
somnambulant
somnambulary
somnambulism
somnambulist
somnambulate
semi-Arianism
Samian letter
semi-annually
semi-attached
semicylinder
semicomatose
semicircular
semi-diameter
Samudragupta
semideponent
semi-detached
symmetallism

Samuel Butler
Samuel Cunard
Sam Peckinpah
Samuel Lister
Samuel Phelps
Samuel Palmer
summer season
summer school
summer savory
Simmenthaler
summer-weight
Samuel Weller
semifinalist
semi-finished
semiglobular
sumphishness
somnifacient
semi-imbecile
sempiternity
somniloquise
somniloquism
somniloquist
somniloquize
semeiotician
simultaneity
simultaneous
simple-minded
semiliteracy
semiliterate
simoniacally
Simon Langham
seminiferous
semantically
seminal fluid
Simón Bolívar
Simon Kuznets
someone taped
somnolescent
semi-official
symbol grocer
semiotically
symbolically
symbololatry
semiological
semi-precious
semipalmated
Semi-Pelagian
semipellucid
semiparasite
Samaritanism
symptomatise
symptomatize
semi-tropical
somatopleure
sumpter horse
somatostatin
Semitisation
somatotensic
somatotropic
somatotropin
Semitization
semiwater gas
Santa Barbara
santalaceous
Sunday driver
sensationism
sensationist
singableness
Sunday Mirror
syntagmatite
senza sordino
sunray pleats
Sunda Islands
Sunday school
syndactylism
syndactylous
sandblasting
sonic barrier
synectically
synecologist
sansculottic
synecdochism
synodic month
synadelphite
San Sebastian
syngenesious
syndetically
sententially
synaesthesia
synaesthetic
sandfly fever
sunshine roof
synchroscope
synchronical
synchroniser
synchronizer
synchroflash
synthesis gas
syntheticism
sentinel crab
sentinelling
singing hinny
singing flame
sensibleness
sensible note
sensitometer
single-acting
single-action
single combat
single-decker
single-figure
single-handed
single-minded
single market
synclinorium
single-priced
single parent
single-seater
single-wicket
Sinanthropus
synantherous
synonymously
sun-and-planet
Syngnathidae
San Jose scale
sensorimotor
senior moment
sindonophany
Santo Domingo
senior optime
synoptically
sand painting
sinupalliate
synarthroses
synarthrosis
San Francisco
syncretistic
sonorousness
sinisterness
Sinus Aestuum
sinisterwise
sinusoidally
sinistrality
sinistrorsal
sinistrously
sanctifiable
sanctifiedly
sanctionable
senatorially
sanitariness
sanitary ware
sanitisation
son et lumière
sanitization
sanguiferous
sensualistic
sanguinolent
sanguineness
sanguinarily
sensuousness
sanguivorous
sandwich tern
sun-expelling
sand-yachting
Sonny Rollins
sloganeering
sporangioles
sporangiolum
sporadically
stomatodaeum
snowboarding
shot-blasting
shopbreaking
snowball tree
show business
slobbishness
snobbishness
Scotch bonnet
Scotch barley
Scotch draper
Scotch fiddle
slouch-hatted
stoechiology
stoichiology
slop-clothing
Scotch pebble
sword-bayonet
scold's bridle
spondoolicks
snowdrop tree
sword-breaker
shove ha'penny
stonewalling
stonemasonry
stone parsley
storekeeping
score through
stovepipe hat
smoke signals
slovenliness
Stoke-on-Trent
stone boiling
spokespeople
spokesperson
stone-breaker
stone bramble
stone dresser
stonecutting
stooge around
spongicolous
sponge finger
sponge fisher
spongologist
sponge rubber
snow-gatherer
slow handclap
smotheringly
smotheriness
slothfulness
scoring board
storiologist
snow-in-summer
stock car race
stock-raising
shock tactics
shockability
shock therapy
stocking-foot
stock and horn
stockingless
stocking mask
shockingness
shocking pink
stock-in-trade
stocking-sole
slockdolager
stockjobbing
stockjobbery
slockdoliger
slockdologer
stock company
stockbreeder
stockbroking
stockpunisht
shoulder arms
shoulder belt
shoulder bone
shoulder-high
shoulder knot
shoulder mark
shoulder note
shoulder slip
Scotland Yard
spotlessness
spoils system
storm warning
storm lantern
storm shutter
stormy petrel
storm trooper
storm trysail
stormfulness
scoundrelism
Sloane Ranger
scornfulness
scolopaceous
scolopendrid
sporogenesis
show one's face
show one's head
show one's hand
scopophiliac
sporophorous
snobographer
stoop-gallant
stoppage time
scoop the pool
shopping list
shopping mall
stoop and roop
stoup and roup
scorpion fish
snooperscope
scouring rush
scouring-rush
snowshoe hare
show-stopping
sportability
smooth-browed
smooth-coated
sportscaster
spotted fever
spotted hyena
short selling
short-termism
short-termist
stout-hearted
short measure
sports ground
shoot the crow
short-changer
shout the odds
shoot through
short circuit
short-circuit
short-sighted
sports injury
sports jacket
Shostakovich
smooth-leaved
short clothes
smooth muscle
shooting iron
shooting star
sport one's oak
short commons
scoptophilia
scoptophobia
sportsperson
Scottishness
smooth-spoken
short-staffed
smooth-talker
short subject
sportfulness
sportiveness
sportswriter
storytelling
stony-hearted
snooze button
supraciliary
supraorbital
supracrustal
supramundane
Septembriser
Septembrizer
Septemberish
Supreme Being
Supreme Court
septennially
sapientially
septentrions
septemvirate
sapphire blue
sapphire-wing
septilateral
Sopwith Camel
septillionth
sophisticate
supplicating
supplication
supplicatory
sepulchrally
supplemental
supplementer
sapindaceous
saponifiable
Siphonaptera
saprophagous
saprophytism
suppositious
siphonophore
sophomorical
siphonostele
saprotrophic
support level
support group
supercargoes
superpatriot
supermassive
supernacular
supernatural
supernaculum
separability
superteacher
supersedence
superrefined
supervenient
superrealism
superrealist
superheroine
supersensual
supersession
supersensory
supervention
soporiferous
supercharger
superhighway
superficials
superciliary
supercilious
superglacial
supercluster
superplastic
supereminent
superimposed
superannuate
superposable
superconduct
superiorship
superpolymer
superspecies
superorganic
supererogant
supererogate
superordinal
superfrontal
supergravity
suppressedly
suppressible
superstratum
separatrices
separateness
superstardom
superstition
superhumanly
supermundane
superhumeral
superluminal
supersubtile
superevident
superovulate
St Petersburg
St Peter's fish
St Peter's wort
Septuagintal

septuagenary
Septuagesima
sequaciously
sequentially
sequestrable
sequestrator
stream anchor
sarsaparilla
spread a plate
Sir Max Aitken
Sir Marcus Fox
Syrian Desert
surface water
surface plate
surface-to-air
surface noise
surface-craft
Sir Nathaniel
Sir David Lean
serial killer
Sir Jack Hobbs
Sir Paul Nurse
serial number
Sir Carol Reed
surpassingly
Sirhan Sirhan
Sir Hans Krebs
servants' hall
Sir Matt Busby
surfboarding
scrobiculate
strobiliform
scribblement
scribblingly
strobilation
strabismical
stroboscopic
Sir Scudamour
sprachgefühl
sprechgesang
sericultural
strychninism
sprechstimme
structurally
straddleback
stridelegged
stridulantly
stridulation
stridulatory
Stradivarius
sorbefacient
Sir Peter Buck
sir-reverence
Sir Peter Hall
scrieveboard
street hockey
serve the turn
streetkeeper
surveillance
surrealistic
sergeant fish
surgeon's knot
sergeantship
serjeantship
surrejoinder
surveyorship
street-raking
Sir Henry Tate
Sir Henry Vane
Sir Henry Wood
street smarts

Sir Jesse Boot
streets ahead
streets apart
serpent-eater
serpentiform
serpentinely
serpentining
serpentinise
serpentinite
serpentinous
serpentinize
screen turtle
serpent-stone
screenwriter
streetwalker
surefootedly
scraggedness
Strigiformes
stragglingly
strugglingly
sprightfully
Sarah Vaughan
Sarah Egerton
Sarah Siddons
surgical boot
surgical mask
surgical neck
strain a point
surgical shoe
service hatch
serviceberry
service metre
servicewoman
service court
Sergio Garcia
straight away
straightaway
straightener
straightedge
skreigh of day
straight gear
straight line
straightness
straight play
straight talk
straightways
straitjacket
servitorship
survivorship
strain viewer
Sir J J Thomson
strike a match
strike a chord
strike a light!
strike it rich
strikingness
stroke of luck
shrill-gorged
Sir Elton John
Sir Alf Ramsay
shrill-voiced
scrimshander
skrimshanker
serum therapy
scramblingly
serum albumin
stromatolite
spring-bladed
spring beauty
spring beetle
strong breeze

string course
strange quark
string figure
seronegative
spring-heeled
springing cow
strontianite
springkeeper
spring-loaded
stranglehold
stranglement
strangle-weed
strong-minded
spring peeper
sprung rhythm
strengthener
string theory
strengthless
strangulated
strongylosis
sarcomatosis
sarcophagous
sardonically
Sertoli cells
sarcoplasmic
surmountable
surroundings
Sir John Mills
Sir John Soane
Sir John Junor
seriocomical
servocontrol
Sir Roy Strong
Sir Toby Belch
strophanthin
strip cartoon
strophanthus
script doctor
stripped atom
stripped-down
strippergram
seraphically
strophiolate
script kiddie
scrupulosity
scrupulously
Streptoneura
streptococci
streptosolen
streptomycin
seropurulent
scraperboard
seropositive
strepitation
scrophularia
scripturally
scriptwriter
Sir Fred Hoyle
Sir Arnold Bax
surprise into
surprisingly
Sir W S Gilbert
seraskierate
stratocratic
straticulate
Seretse Khama
sprat-weather
stratigraphy
stretch marks
scratchingly
scratchiness

scratchboard
stretcher off
scratch brush
scratchbuild
scratchbuilt
scrutinising
scrutinously
scrutinizing
stratosphere
stratotanker
serotaxonomy
Sir Hugh Munro
sarrusophone
shriving-time
screw-worm fly
straw-breadth
shrewishness
screw steamer
Saskatchewan
sassafras oil
sassafras nut
systematical
systematiser
systematizer
sisterliness
system-monger
sisters-in-law
suspensorial
suspensorium
suspensively
sustentation
sustentative
susceptivity
suspiciously
session-clerk
session-house
sesamoid bone
Susannah York
sesquialtera
sesquitertia
situatedness
situationism
situationist
Satchel Paige
Sothic period
settle a score
Sittlichkeit
settling pond
satanic abuse
satanophobia
set one's teeth
sit down under
saturability
satirisation
saturated fat
satirization
satisfaction
satisfactory
satisfyingly
set by the ears
squeaky clean
stubble field
stubble goose
snubbing post
slumber party
slubberingly
slumberingly
stubbornness
slumberously
sound ranging
sound barrier

sound-carrier
sound effects
sound therapy
sounding lead
sounding line
studding-sail
studdingsail
shudderingly
sound as a bell
saucepan-fish
stupefacient
stupefaction
stupefactive
stupendously
scutellation
sauve qui peut
stuffed shirt
shuffleboard
snuff-dipping
snuffbox bean
spurge laurel
sluggishness
South Pacific
south-eastern
south-seeking
South Georgia
south-western
South African
South Shields
South America
soughing-tile
Southcottian
Southern Alps
Southern blot
Southern Fish
southernmost
southernwood
Scutigeridae
Saudi Arabian
spuriousness
studiousness
skunk cabbage
scullery-maid
soullessness
skullduggery
shut one's eyes
slumpflation
stump oratory
sculpturally
squirearchal
Stuart Blanch
squirrel away
squirrel cage
squirrel fish
squirrel-tail
scurrilously
square matrix
square number
square-rigged
square-rigger
slurry tanker
soul-stirring
squash tennis
spurtle-blade
shunt-winding
squattocracy
squat lobster
skutterudite
saunteringly
sputteringly
stutteringly

sluttishness
spur valerian
Seven Samurai
saving clause
savings ratio
seventy-eight
save one's face
save one's neck
save one's skin
Sivapithecus
severance pay
Savoy Theatre
sexual abuser
sexual system
sexcentenary
six of the best
sexagenarian
sex therapist
six-eight time
sextillionth
sexton beetle
sextodecimos
styracaceous
Scythian lamb
scyphistomae
scyphistomas
sky-tinctured
say one's piece
stylographic
tralaticious
tralatitious
thanatomania
thalassaemia
thalassaemic
thatched roof
travel agency
tragelaphine
trade barrier
tracer bullet
traceability
tradescantia
trade edition
trade deficit
trace element
trapezohedra
trade journal
traded option
tradespeople
travel-soiled
travesty role
trabeculated
Tracey Ullman
trash talking
trash farming
teachability
teach a lesson
trachomatous
tracheoscopy
tracheophyte
tracheostomy
trachypterus
tragicalness
tracing paper
trading stamp
traditionary
traditionist
tragicomical
thank heavens
✧thanksgiving
tracking shot
thank-you-ma'am

thankfulness
trailblazing
trailing edge
to all intents
thallophytic
trailer truck
trailer trash
trauma centre
thaumatogeny
thaumatology
traumatology
thaumaturgic
thaumaturgus
traumatising
traumatizing
trainability
training ship
training shoe
trainspotter
trainer pants
tear one's hair
tear-off strip
tramp element
trampolining
trampolinist
teaspoonfuls
tramp steamer
tranquilizer
tranquillise
tranquillity
tranquillize
tranquilness
translatable
transcalency
transparence
transparency
transpacific
transoceanic
transudation
transudatory
transferable
transfer book
transcendent
transference
transgenesis
transfer list
transferring
transversely
transversion
transleithan
transfection
transvestism
transvestist
transvestite
that's the idea
transshipper
transpirable
transhipment
transhipping
transmigrant
transmigrate
transmission
transmissive
transmitting
transpicuous
transiliency
transplanter
transaminase
transumption
transumptive
transposable
transforming
transformism
transformist
transmogrify
transmontane
transpontine
transporting
trapshooting
transportive
transuranian
transuranium
transgressor
that's as may be
transitional
transit trade
transitorily
transitively
transitivity
transhumance
transfusable
transmutable
transmutably
transmundane
translucence
translucency
transfusible
transduction
team teaching
tractability
toasting fork
toasting iron
traction load
tear to pieces
tractoration
traitorously
tear to shreds
Traducianism
Traducianist
Tubuai Island
tobacco-heart
tobacco plant
tobacco pouch
table-dancing
table manners
table-rapping
table licence
table-turning
tab character
tabulae rasae
Tubuliflorae
tubulifloral
tubular bells
tubeless tire
tubeless tyre
tabernacular
tuberiferous
Tyburn-ticket
Tyburn-tippet
tuberculated
tuberculosed
tuberculosis
tuberous root
Tibet Plateau
ticket-holder
tacheometric
ticket office
ticket porter
ticket writer
ticket window
tactlessness
ticklishness
technobabble
technocratic
technicality
technicolour
technography
technojunkie
technologist
technomaniac
technophilia
technophilic
technophobia
technophobic
technostress
tectonically
to crown it all
tachyphrasia
tachygrapher
tachygraphic
tiddledywink
Todor Zhivkov
The March Hare
the hand of God
then and there
the hard stuff
The Caretaker
tsesarevitch
tsesarewitch
therapeutics
therapeutist
The Mad Hatter
thematically
the Caribbean
The Valkyries
the Wallabies
The Carpenter
The Waste Land
the last enemy
the last trump
theocratical
trench mortar
The Economist
The Scapegoat
trench plough
The Scarecrow
the Adversary
trendsetting
the Admiralty
thés dansants
Theodor Heuss
there's a thing
The Beach Boys
tremendously
the Seven Seas
thereagainst
therethrough
the Peninsula
The Red Knight
the real McCoy
the real thing
thereinafter
there and then
The Second Sex
the Red Planet
The Searchers
the bee's knees
teeter-totter
the very thing
Twelfth Night
teething ring
trephination
the chosen few
Theriodontia
The Windhover
The Wild Bunch
the time of day
The Nightmare
the die is cast
The Visionary
The Pink Paper
the wicked one
The Hill-Shade
taedium vitae
Theriomorpha
Themistocles
the bitter end
The City of God
tree kangaroo
the Old Bailey
treble chance
The Old Devils
theologaster
The Alchemist
treelessness
thermic lance
thermocouple
Thermidorian
thermography
thermohaline
thermolabile
thermal shock
thermal noise
thermometric
thermophilic
Thesmophoria
theomorphism
The Umbrellas
thermostatic
thermostable
thermosphere
Thermos® flask
thermoscopic
thermosiphon
thermotactic
thermotropic
the underhand
teeing ground
theanthropic
the knowledge
Trevor Bailey
the Word of God
The Golden Ass
the done thing
The Go-Between
The Boy Friend
The Godfather
tree of heaven
Trevor Howard
the world over
the world's end
the morn's morn
the boondocks
The Moonstone
the Conqueror
the Household
tree of silver
The Mousetrap
the Forty-five
The Lost World
The Spectator
theopneustic
The Apartment
Theophrastus
Theopaschite
theopathetic
theophylline
the squitters
the Great Bear
the treatment
theorematist
The Grand Duke
the wrong shop
The Troop Ship
theorisation
theoretician
theorization
the estimates
Thessaloníki
theosophical
Treasury bill
Treasury bond
treasure-city
treasure hunt
treasury note
teensy-weensy
trestle table
Theatre Royal
theatre organ
the other side
twenty-fourmo
theatrically
theatromania
theatrophone
Treaty of Rome
the story goes
twenty-twenty
The Dubliners
the full monty
The Huguenots
The Lucy Poems
the jury is out
Twelve Tables
The Symposium
Tiffany glass
Tagliacotian
toggle switch
tiger country
tag wrestling
tigerishness
togetherness
trilaterally
trinacriform
tridactylous
tripartitely
tripartition
thiobacillus
thin blue line
third reading
thiodiglycol
triadelphous
Third-Worlder
thirdborough
tripe de roche
trimethylene
tricephalous
tribespeople
tricentenary
toilet tissue
thief-catcher
thingummyjig
thingummybob
trigger-happy
trigger point
triphthongal
trichologist
trichiniasis
trichinellae
trichinellas
Trichinopoly
trichromatic
trichopteran
trichophyton
thitherwards
trichotomise
trichotomous
trichotomize
Trichiuridae
triticalness
twining plant
twilight zone
Trinity House
think through
thick-sighted
thick-skulled
thick-skinned
thick and fast
thick-and-thin
trick or treat
trickishness
trickstering
trick cyclist
trial balance
trial balloon
triglyceride
triplication
triple-headed
triple-jumper
triflingness
triple-tongue
triple-turned
triple whammy
Triplex® glass
Trismegistus
triumphalism
triumphalist
triumphantly
thigmotactic
thigmotropic
triangularly
trinomialism
trinomialist
trigonometer
trigonometry
tricorporate
tailor's chalk
tail of the eye
trip recorder
trigrammatic
thiosulphate
toilsomeness
thirteenthly
twitteringly
twitter-boned
thirty-two-bit
thirty-twomos
trifurcation
trituberculy
tribute money
Tribune Group
tripudiation
tricuspidate
thieves' Latin
thievishness
take a scunner
take a telling

Words marked ✧ can also be spelled with one or more capital letters

take a beating
take a dim view
take a pride in
take a grinder
take charge of
take down a peg
take for a ride
take it from me
take it kindly
take measures
take no notice
take occasion
take one's ease
take one's hook
take one's seat
take one's time
take one's turn
take prisoner
take shipping
take the reins
take the wheel
take the chair
take the field
take the Fifth
take the floor
take to flight
take to pieces
take unawares
telecommuter
till doomsday
telaesthesia
telaesthetic
talkee-talkee
tilley-valley
telegraphese
telegraphist
toll-gatherer
Talking Heads
talking point
telemedicine
teleosaurian
tallow candle
teleological
teleostomous
telepresence
téléphérique
telephone box
Teleprompter®
tolerability
telergically
talismanical
telesmatical
telesoftware
telescopical
teleshopping
teleservices
tell the truth
telluric acid
tellurometer
teleutospore
Telautograph®
talcum powder
televisually
televisional
Tel Aviv-Jaffa
Telly Savalas
time and again
time and a half
tameableness
time-bewasted
timocratical
time constant
timed-release
time dilation
temperalitie
time exposure
time-honoured
Tampico fibre
Temple of Hera
timely-parted
tumbler-drier
tumbler-dryer
tamelessness
timelessness
tumultuation
tumultuously
Time Magazine
timing pulley
temporaneous
temporal lobe
temporalness
temporal peer
Tom Hopkinson
tambourinist
Tamaricaceae
timbrologist
timbromaniac
timorousness
temptability
temptingness
Timothy Spall
timothy grass
Tommy Handley
Tonya Harding
tantalic acid
Tinian Island
ten-gallon hat
Tennant Creek
tantalum lamp
tone dialling
tone-deafness
tender-hefted
Tintern Abbey
tenpenny nail
tunnel of love
tandem roller
tangentially
tonneau cover
tunnel vision
tonsilectomy
tangibleness
tonsillotomy
tintinnabula
tenuirostral
tangle-netter
tone language
tangle-picker
tonelessness
tunelessness
Toni Morrison
tenant at will
tenant-at-will
tenant farmer
tuning hammer
tanto uberior
tungsten lamp
tungstic acid
tin-streaming
tongue-tacked
Thomas Browne
Thomas Cubitt
Thomas Dekker
Thomas Hobbes
Thomas Hughes
thoracic duct
Two Fat Ladies
Thomas Morley
Thomas Murner
two-way mirror
thoracoscope
thoracostomy
Thomas Savery
Thomas Waller
Thomas Wolsey
Thomas Willis
Thomas Warton
troublemaker
troubleshoot
trouble-mirth
trouble-world
trouble-house
trouble-state
tromba marina
thoughtfully
trocheameter
trophobiosis
trophobiotic
trophic level
toothed whale
trophallaxis
trochanteric
tooth and nail
tooth-drawing
trochosphere
trophotactic
trophotropic
tropical year
toorie bonnet
two-sidedness
troglodytism
trolling-bait
troll-my-dames
trolley table
trolley wheel
trolley dolly
troposcatter
two-toed sloth
✧thoroughbred
thorough bass
thoroughfare
thoroughness
tropophilous
two pound coin
tropological
tropospheric
two-horse race
troop carrier
two-speed gear
trompe l'oeils
troisième âge
thousandfold
thousand-legs
thousand-year
tootsy-wootsy
Trout Quintet
two-eyed steak
tapsalteerie
type cylinder
tappet-motion
top-heaviness
typification
top of the pops
tip off liquor
type founding
typographist
tip the scales
topside-turvy
tapsieteerie
type locality
typhoid fever
taphonomical
toploftiness
tape recorder
to perfection
type specimen
tape streamer
tapestry moth
topsy-turvily
tartare sauce
tartar emetic
turn a deaf ear
terrace house
terrae filius
tartaric acid
thread of life
terraforming
Tyrian purple
terra nullius
terebratulae
terebratulas
terebinthine
turacoverdin
turn down cold
threeha'porth
Tarpeian Rock
torrefaction
Turkey carpet
three-went way
three-centred
tercel-gentle
three-wheeler
Three Witches
Torpedinidae
tercel-jerkin
turbellarian
three-pounder
Tardenoisian
three-monthly
three-pricker
three estates
torrentially
tormentingly
tercentenary
three-quarter
thriftlessly
Tariff Reform
torch-thistle
torchon paper
turbinacious
terminal unit
Torricellian
tergiversate
turning lathe
turnip greens
turning point
Turkish manna
Turkish towel
terrifically
turbidimeter
terribleness
torsion meter
turriculated
terminus a quo
tirlie-wirlie
terrifyingly
turtle-necked
tirelessness
Turkmenistan
thrombolytic
taramasalata
Tironian sign
Terence Stamp
tyrannically
tyrannicidal
Te Rangi Hiroa
turn one's back
turn one's coat
turn of events
turn one's head
turn one's hand
Turcophilism
turbocharged
turbocharger
turn of phrase
terror-struck
turnpike road
Turk's cap lily
terms of trade
throstle-cock
tiresomeness
turn the screw
turn the scale
throttle back
throttle down
teratologist
throttle pipe
teratomatous
through-going
through train
through-other
through-stane
through-stone
turn up trumps
tortuousness
torque wrench
thrivingness
throw light on
throw a wobbly
Terry Gilliam
testamentary
tassel-gentle
tessellation
tastefulness
testificator
tussie mussie
testiculated
taskmistress
tussock grass
testosterone
task swapping
test-tube baby
test the water
testudineous
tissue-typing
tetradactyly
tetrarchical
to that effect
tetrahedrons
tetrahedrite
tetrachordal
tetrachotomy
tetragonally
tetrapolitan
tetramorphic
tetrasporous
tetrastichal
tetrastichic
tetrapterous
Tetradynamia
tetracycline
tithe-proctor
to the purpose
Tet Offensive
total eclipse
total theatre
totalisation
totalitarian
tittle-tattle
total quality
totalization
titaniferous
tetanisation
Titanosaurus
tetanization
tetrodotoxin
Truman Capote
thumb through
Thurberesque
Tour de France
tour d'horizon
thunder sheet
thunder-plump
thunderflash
thundercloud
thunderingly
thunder-drive
thunderstone
thunderstorm
thunderously
truce-breaker
tout ensemble
truth-telling
touch therapy
touchingness
truthfulness
tourist class
tourist route
truck-farming
true-love knot
tauromachian
tour operator
Teutonically
tautological
trumpet major
trumpet shell
tours de force
trust account
trustee stock
trustafarian
trustingness
trust company
true-type font
trustfulness
tu-whit tu-whoo
town planning
Tower Hamlets
Tower of Babel
towardliness
toxicologist
toxicophobia
toxocariasis
tax threshold
tax-sheltered
tax allowance
taxing master
tax collector

toxophilitic
Texas Rangers
Texas Stadium
tax avoidance
trypaflavine
trypanocidal
trypanosomal
trypanosomic
Thysanoptera
thyroid gland
thyrotrophin
trysting-tree
unanalysable
unanalyzable
unanalytical
unaccredited
unascendable
unascendible
unacceptance
unacceptable
unaccustomed
up and running
unaffectedly
unaffiliated
unachievable
unanimated by
unamiability
uranium glass
unadmonished
unapologetic
uranographer
uranographic
unappealable
unappeasable
unapplausive
unapplicable
unapproached
unapparelled
unaspiringly
unappetising
unappetizing
unacquainted
unacquaint in
unassociated
unanswerable
unanswerably
unassignable
unassailable
unauspicious
unassumingly
unassistedly
unattractive
unarticulate
unartificial
unattainable
unattainably
unattributed
unauthorised
unauthorized
unartistlike
unadulterate
unadventrous
unadvertised
unbiasedness
umbrageously
unbecoming in
unbecomingly
unbreachable
umbrella bird
umbrella pine
umbrella tree
unbreathable
unbreathed-on
unbefriended
unblinkingly
umbilication
unbelievable
unbelievably
Umbelliferae
urban renewal
unbeneficial
urbanologist
urbanisation
urbanization
unbrokenness
unbetterable
unbottomed in
unblushingly
unchaperoned
unchangeable
unchangeably
unchangingly
uncharitable
uncharitably
unchallenged
unclassified
unchasteness
uncreditable
uncheerfully
unchivalrous
uncritically
uncelebrated
uncultivated
uncultivable
uncalculated
uncomeatable
uncommercial
uncomeliness
uncomposable
uncompounded
uncommonness
unconcealing
unconcerning
unconsecrate
unconversant
unconsenting
unconfinable
unconvincing
unconsidered
unconfinedly
uncandidness
unconclusive
uncensorious
unconforming
unconformity
uncinariasis
uncontrolled
unconstraint
unconfusedly
uncloistered
uncapsizable
uncoquettish
unchronicled
unchristened
ulcerousness
uncatalogued
uncounselled
unctuousness
uncovenanted
undeceivable
undocumented
undecomposed
undeliberate
undelectable
undelightful
undulatingly
undemocratic
undiminished
undependable
undiplomatic
undertakable
under hatches
under-hangman
undergarment
underpayment
underpassion
underachieve
undertenancy
underdevelop
underperform
undersealing
undermeaning
underpeopled
underbearing
underletting
under the heel
under-sheriff
undersheriff
under the rose
under the wire
underkingdom
underpinning
underskinker
underblanket
underclothed
underclothes
under-and-over
under one's hat
underinsured
underpowered
under-workman
underproduce
underdressed
underwriting
under protest
underwrought
underdrawing
understratum
understaffed
underutilise
underutilize
understanded
understander
underfunding
undersurface
underbuilder
under-turnkey
underrunning
undercurrent
undispatched
undespairing
undismantled
undissembled
undiscerning
undesignedly
undischarged
undiscipline
undiscordant
undiscording
undiscovered
undisposed-of
undissolving
undistracted
undisordered
undeservedly
undisturbing
undisputedly
undetectable
undetermined
undoubtingly
undivestedly
unelaborated
unembittered
unencumbered
unendangered
unendingness
uneventfully
user-friendly
urethroscope
urethroscopy
uneconomical
unexpectedly
unexpressive
unexpugnable
unemployable
unemployment
unexpurgated
unerringness
unextenuated
unenthralled
unfranchised
unflaggingly
unflattering
unfadingness
unfrequented
unfrequently
unfrightened
unfaithfully
unfriendlily
unfriendship
unfilterable
unfamiliarly
unformalised
unformalized
unforeboding
unforgivable
unformidable
unfertilised
unfertilized
unforeseeing
unformulated
unforewarned
unfossilised
unfossilized
unfastidious
unfittedness
unfathomable
unfathomably
unfruitfully
unfavourable
unfavourably
ungracefully
ungratefully
ungraciously
unguentarium
ungainliness
unguiculated
ungentleness
ungenerously
ungrounded in
ungroundedly
ungrudgingly
ungovernable
ungovernably
unhabituated
unhandselled
unhandsomely
unhyphenated
unheroically
unharmonious
unhospitable
unhistorical
unhesitating
unilaterally
unimaginable
unimaginably
✧unitarianism
unincumbered
uniseriately
unidealistic
United States
universal set
universalise
Universalism
Universalist
universality
universalize
unidentified
unisexuality
uninfluenced
unified scale
unified field
utility truck
unionisation
unionization
urinogenital
unimolecular
unifoliolate
unicorn-shell
unicorn-whale
unimpressive
unimpugnable
unimprisoned
unimportance
unimportuned
uninstructed
unintegrated
unintroduced
uninterested
ubiquitarian
ubiquitously
unity element
unkindliness
unlibidinous
ugly customer
ugly duckling
uillean pipes
uglification
unlikelihood
unlikeliness
upland cotton
unlooked into
unliquidated
unlistenable
unlistened-to
unliveliness
unloveliness
unlovingness
unlawfulness
unmeasurable
unmeasurably
unmechanical
unmechanised
unmechanized
unmodifiable
unmodernised
unmodernized
unmaintained
unmanageable
unmanageably
unmunitioned
unmiraculous
unmarketable
unmercifully
unmoralising
unmoralizing
unmistakable
unmistakably
unmethodical
unmethodised
unmethodized
Uintatherium
unnilpentium
unnilseptium
unnilquadium
unnoticeable
unnaturalise
unnaturalize
unnourishing
upon a thought
up one's sleeve
up one's street
unoverthrown
unofficially
urolithiasis
unoriginated
uxoriousness
upon my honour
unornamental
unornamented
upon one's legs
unoppressive
Ulotrichales
unobservance
unobservable
unobstructed
unobservedly
upon the whole
upon the alert
upon the anvil
unobtainable
unorthodoxly
unpeacefully
unpreparedly
unprelatical
unprevailing
unprescribed
unpretending
unpoetically
unpleasantly
unpleasingly
unpleasantry
unprettiness
unprejudiced
unprincipled
unprivileged
unpolishable
unpoliteness
unpunishable
unpunishably
unpunctuated
unpropertied
unprotesting
unprocedural
unprofitable
unprofitably

unprovidedly
unprohibited
unpropitious
unproclaimed
unprovokedly
unpronounced
unprosperous
unprocurable
unproductive
unpopularity
upper regions
unperfection
unperceptive
unpersecuted
upper chamber
unparalleled
upper classes
unperforated
unpardonable
unpardonably
upper mordent
unperforming
upper-bracket
unperishable
unpersuasive
unpossessing
unpassionate
unpatronised
unpatronized
unpavilioned
unquantified
unquenchable
unquenchably
unquestioned
unrealisable
unrealizable
uproariously
unreasonable
unreasonably
unroadworthy
unrecognised
unrecognized
unrecallable
unreconciled
unreckonable
unredeemable
unriddleable
unrefreshing
unreflecting
unreflective
unreformable
unregimented
unregeneracy
unregenerate
unregistered
upright piano
unrightfully
unrelievable
unrelievedly
unremembered
unromantical
unremarkable
unremorseful
unremittedly
unrepealable
unrepeatable
unrepairable
unrepulsable
unrepentance
unrepiningly
unreprovable
unreproached
unreportable
unrequitedly
unrespective
unresolvable
unresponsive
unrestricted
unreservedly
unrestrained
unresistible
unreturnable
unrevealable
unrevengeful
unrewardedly
unrhythmical
unsearchable
unsearchably
unstanchable
unstableness
unseasonable
unseasonably
unshadowable
unstatutable
unstatutably
unsubscribed
unsublimated
unsubsidised
unsubsidized
unsubmissive
unsubmitting
unsocialised
unsocialized
unsuccessful
unsuccessive
unsteadiness
unsterilised
unsterilized
unseemliness
unspectacled
unswervingly
unsufferable
unsufficient
unsegregated
unscientific
unstimulated
unsalability
unsolicitous
unseminaried
unsensitised
unsensitized
unsanctified
unsanctioned
unsensualise
unsensualize
unstockinged
unscottified
unsepulchred
unsuppleness
unsupposable
unsupervised
unsuppressed
unstructured
unshrinkable
unscrupulous
unscriptural
unsurprising
unstratified
unsustaining
unsystematic
unsuspecting
unsuspicious
unsettlement
unsaturation
unsatisfying
unslumbering
unsculptured
upsey English
ultrasensual
unthankfully
untrammelled
ultramontane
untranslated
untransmuted
ultramundane
untremendous
unthinkingly
Ustilagineae
ustilaginous
untimeliness
untumultuous
ultimate load
untenability
untenantable
untroubledly
up to one's neck
ultroneously
unthoughtful
unthreatened
Ust'-Urt Desert
unthriftyhed
unterminated
unterrifying
Uttar Pradesh
untruthfully
untrustiness
untowardness
unusefulness
Ujung Pandang
Ulugh Muztagh
usuriousness
usus loquendi
usufructuary
unutterables
unvaccinated
unvulnerable
unventilated
unvanquished
unvariegated
unverifiable
unvirtuously
unvoyageable
unwearyingly
unwieldiness
unwontedness
unworthiness
unworshipped
unworshipful
unwithholden
unwatchfully
unwaveringly
unyieldingly
vibraphonist
vibratiuncle
vibracularia
vocabularian
vocabularied
vice-chairman
vocicultural
vociferosity
vociferation
vociferously
vice-governor
Vacciniaceae
vocalisation
vocalization
Victoria Nile
Victorianism
Victoria Peak
✧victoria plum
victoriously
Victoria Wood
vicar-general
vocationally
vacationless
vacuum-packed
veggie-burger
vaginicoline
vaginicolous
vigorousness
vegetable wax
vegetable oil
vegetational
vegetatively
Vehmgerichte
voicefulness
vainglorious
voiding-lobby
Volga-Baltaic
village idiot
Villahermosa
volcanically
vulcanisable
vulcanizable
volcanic bomb
volcanic dust
volcanic sand
valuableness
villainously
Vulcan's badge
vulgar tongue
velocipedean
velocipedian
velocipedist
velociraptor
velvet-guards
velvet-scoter
vilification
voluminosity
voluminously
volumetrical
voluntaryism
voluntaryist
volunteerism
Valenciennes
Velloziaceae
Valpolicella
vulvo-uterine
voluptuosity
voluptuously
valorisation
velarisation
valorization
velarization
valet parking
valetudinary
valet de place
volatileness
volatile oils
volitionally
volitionless
volitational
velouté sauce
Volsungasaga
valium picnic
vomiturition
vantage point
vinicultural
Vannevar Bush
Vincent D'Indy
Vincent Price
vengefulness
vinification
veneficously
vinegar-plant
vindicatress
vendibleness
vindictively
vinyl acetate
venom'd-mouth'd
venomousness
Vinson Massif
venepuncture
venipuncture
ventre à terre
venire facias
vin ordinaire
ventriloqual
ventripotent
Venus's girdle
Venus flytrap
Venetian mast
vanity mirror
✧vanitory unit
Venture Scout
vanquishable
vanquishment
Vandyke beard
vandyke brown
viola da gamba
violent storm
violin spider
violoncellos
vaporisation
vaporousness
vaporization
vu quang bovid
variationist
variable gear
variableness
variable star
vernacularly
Vera Brittain
varicoloured
veridicality
viridescence
verbenaceous
vervet monkey
vertebration
vortex street
vortex theory
verification
verificatory
verticalness
versificator
Virginia Leng
verticillate
verticillium
Virginia reel
Virginia Wade
vermin-killer
✧vernis martin
virgin's-bower
vermiculated
vermiculture
verslibriste
virilescence
virilisation
virilization
verumontanum
virgo intacta
Very Reverend
virus disease
verisimility
verisimilous
virtual image
virtual focus
virtuosoship
virtuousness
visual acuity
visual purple
vestal virgin
visible means
visibilities
vesiculation
vesica piscis
vasodilation
vasodilatory
viscerotonia
viscerotonic
vestimentary
vestibulitis
viscose rayon
viscosimeter
viscosimetry
viscoelastic
Viscount Hood
viscountship
viscous water
visiting-book
visiting card
visitors' book
visitational
visitatorial
viticultural
vaticination
vitreousness
vitrifaction
vitrifacture
vitriolation
vitalisation
vitilitigate
vitalization
voting rights
vitro-di-trina
vituperation
vituperatory
vituperative
veterinarian
vote straight
vitativeness
votive tablet
vaudevillean
vaudevillian
vaudevillist
vaunt-courier
vivification
viviparously
vox caelestis
weal-balanced
whale of a time
whale-fishing
whale-fishery
weaver's hitch
weaker vessel
wranglership

weather gauge
weather chart
weather gleam
weather along
weather glass
weathercloth
weather-bound
weatherboard
weather house
weatherproof
weather stain
weather strip
wrathfulness
weaning brash
Whatman paper®
weak-mindedly
what's-her-name
what's the odds?
what's with you?
weak-spirited
what's-his-name
what's cooking?
what's-its-name
what the devil
web authoring
wicketkeeper
Wycliffe Hall
wedding march
wedding cards
wedding dower
wedding dress
wide receiver
wide-spectrum
Wedgwood blue
Wedgwood ware
wretchedness
whencesoever
whereagainst
wherethrough
whether or not
weeping birch
weeding-tongs
Weeping Cross
weeping-cross
wheel and axle
wheel and deal
wheel forward
wife-swapping
Wagnerianism
wagger-pagger
wiggle-waggle
wages council
wag-at-the-wall
wag-by-the-wall
whip-and-derry
waif and stray
white rabbits
white pareira
white campion
white admiral
white-bellied
white-bearded
white herring
white feather
white leather
white settler
white-livered
white vitriol
white slavery
white-knuckle
white arsenic
white-fronted
white-crested
write protect
write-protect
white-crowned
writer's block
writer's cramp
white pudding
White Russian
white mustard
white pyrites
whip-grafting
Whiggishness
weightlifter
weightlessly
whitherwards
which is which?
writing paper
writing table
waiting-woman
whisky-frisky
Whisky Galore!
whiskerandos
whitlow grass
whigmaleerie
whipping-post
whippoorwill
whimperingly
whisperingly
whisperously
whimsicality
Weil's disease
whip scorpion
wainscotting
whistle-drunk
whiptail hake
waistcoateer
waistcoating
wakeboarding
wake the night
walk away with
well and truly
Wallace's line
welfare state
well-affected
wollastonite
well-becoming
well-breathed
well-balanced
wallcovering
well dressing
well-directed
well-disposed
well-deserved
Walter Cannon
walleyed pike
walled garden
Wilhelm Kühne
Walter Payton
welter stakes
Walter S Adams
well-educated
welterweight
Wolffian body
Wolffian duct
well-favoured
well-grounded
Welsh rarebit
wild hyacinth
Welsh terrier
Waltham Abbey
Wild Huntsman
Welsh dresser
Willie Carson
well, I declare!
well-informed
walking reins
walking on air
✧wellingtonia
willing horse
walking frame
walking straw
walking stick
walking-stick
walking-staff
William Carey
William James
William Paley
William Lawry
William Hague
Williamsburg
William Beebe
William Cecil
William Perry
William Bligh
William Blake
William Clark
William Smith
William Boyce
William Booth
William Bragg
William Prout
William Osler
William Burke
William Wyler
walkie-talkie
williewaught
Will Ladislaw
wildlife park
will-lessness
well-mannered
Wilton carpet
Waldorf salad
willow grouse
will-o'-the-wisp
wallop in a tow
well-pleasing
well-plighted
wall painting
well putten on
Wall-Streeter
walk the wards
walk the chalk
walk the plank
well-tempered
well-timbered
Wilbur Wright
wild Williams
Wild-West Show
Wally Schirra
wallydraigle
Willy Russell
waltz Matilda
Wembley Arena
women's libber
woman to woman
women's rights
womanishness
woman-queller
Woman's Weekly
wind-changing
wine-coloured
winter-beaten
winterbourne
winter cherry
winter clover
Wankel engine
winter-ground
winter garden
✧wandering Jew
wunderkinder
wondermonger
winter sports
wonder-struck
winter-weight
wonder-worker
wineglassful
Wyndham Lewis
winding sheet
winding stair
Winslow Homer
wine merchant
win in a canter
win one's spurs
wind of change
winnowing-fan
window screen
wondrousness
wing shooting
Windsor chair
Winston-Salem
Winston Smith
woodburytype
wholehearted
wood engraver
woodenheaded
wooden kimono
whole-skinned
wooden tongue
wrong side out
wrongfulness
wood hyacinth
wood hedgehog
woolly-headed
woolly-haired
woolly-minded
woodlessness
wood mushroom
wood-offering
whooping swan
woodshedding
whortleberry
Woody Guthrie
work a flanker
workableness
word-building
worm conveyor
word deafness
world-wearied
world-beating
world-shaking
World Wide Web
Warren Beatty
Werner Herzog
worker priest
work function
worshipfully
warehouseman
working paper
working party
working class
working-class
working woman
working model
working hours
working house
working lunch
Warwickshire
wordlessness
workmistress
work one's will
warmongering
word of honour
word-painting
ware potatoes
wire-stitched
wordsmithery
works council
wire-stringed
wirestripper
worm's eye view
word wrapping
West Bromwich
wisecracking
West End Girls
westerliness
Western Samoa
Western Front
Western Isles
western swing
waste product
wastefulness
West Germanic
Washington DC
✧washingtonia
washing-board
washing-house
wasting asset
wishing stone
West Midlands
West Virginia
with a thought
with a witness
with bad grace
withdrawment
with dispatch
witheredness
witness stand
Wittgenstein
watchability
watch officer
withholdment
witching hour
watch and ward
watch crystal
witches' broom
watchfulness
wetting agent
within limits
within reason
wattle and dab
Withnail and I
with open arms
with one voice
Watton Priory
without tears
without doubt
without doors
without price
water bailiff
water ballast
Water Carrier
watermanship
water parsnip
water wagtail
water-parting
water battery
water reactor
water hemlock
water bellows
water measure
water-channel
water biscuit
water-gilding
water milfoil
water diviner
water blister
water-flowing
water flowers
watering-call
watering hole
water soldier
water-cooling
water boatman
water torture
water-soluble
water spaniel
water opossum
water-drinker
watercresses
waterishness
water strider
water turbine
water buffalo
water culture
would you mind?
W Eugene Smith
Woulfe bottle
waulking-song
wave equation
wave function
wave offering
wave property
waveringness
waxed leather
ways and means
way passenger
Wayne Shorter
Wayne Gretzky
X-ray spectrum
xylobalsamum
xanthochroia
xanthochroic
xanthochroid
xanthomatous
xanthopterin
xiphisternum
xerodermatic
xeromorphous
yada yada yada
yieldingness
yoghurt maker
Yukio Mishima
yellowhammer
yellow jacket
yellow jersey
yellow poplar
yellow pepper
yellow ribbon
yellow rocket
yellow rattle
yellow streak
yellow-yowley
Yom Kippur War
Yamoussoukro

Words marked ✧ can also be spelled with one or more capital letters

Yankee-Doodle
Yangtze River
Yuri Andropov
yard-long bean
Yorkshire fog
Yasser Arafat
Yitzhak Rabin
you're welcome
you never know
Young America
Young England
Young modulus
young fogyish
Young Ireland
Young Britain
youthfulness
youth custody
your ladyship
your lordship
Zeeman effect
zigzag stitch
zygodactylic
zygomycetous
zygomorphism
zygomorphous
zygapophyses
zygapophysis
Zwinglianism
Zwinglianist
zwitterionic
Zeitvertreib
Zoltán Kodály
zalambdodont
Zola Pieterse
zymotechnics
Zinzan Brooke
✧zantedeschia
Zante currant
zonal defence
Zeno of Citium
zinc ointment
zincographer
zincographic
zone refining
Zandra Rhodes
zenith sector
zoopathology
zoomagnetism
zoogeography
zoochemistry
zoophytology
zoologically
zootomically
zoospermatic
zoographical
Zarathustric
Zeuglodontia
Zsuzsa Polgar

13 – odd

Atacama Desert
acatamathesia
Alan Ayckbourn
Anacardiaceae
Amaranthaceae
amarantaceous
Alan Bleasdale
a hard row to hoe
academicalism
a capful of wind
away from it all
anaphylactoid
anathematical
Alashan Desert
arachnoiditis
arachnophobia
arachnophobic
anaphrodisiac
anachronistic
arachnologist
anachronously
anaphorically
apathetically
Arabian Desert
Arabian Nights
acaridomatium
atavistically
Alan Jay Lerner
availableness
à la Florentine
again and again
Alain-Fournier
against nature
araeometrical
Anatole France
Anatoli Karpov
à la bonne heure
acarodomatium
analogousness
à la Portugaise
Anatoly Karpov
anaerobically
a hair of the dog
anagrammatise
anagrammatize
anagrammatism
anagrammatist
anal retentive
Alan Sainsbury
avant-gardiste
adaptableness
anastigmatism
A Taste of Honey
avant-couriers
a matter of form
analysis situs
ambidexterity
ambidexterous
Albrecht Dürer
ambiguousness
Ambrose Bierce
arboriculture
Akbar the Great
Albert Herring
Albert Métraux
Alberto Ascari
ambassadorial
arbitrariness
ambitiousness
archaeometric
archaeologist
archaeopteryx
archbishopric
accidentalism
accidentality
accident-prone
accreditation
Archegoniatae
Arc de Triomphe
ancient lights
alcoholometer
alcoholometry
acclimatation
archimandrite
archipelagoes
architectonic
architectural
archidiaconal
auctioneer off
auction bridge
Alcaic strophe
accelerometer
acculturation
accompaniment
accommodative
accommodating
accommodation
Ascensiontide
acceptability
acceptilation
ascertainable
ascertainment
accessibility
accessory shoe
accouterments
accoutrements
accoustrement
audaciousness
Andrea Dworkin
Andrea Ferrara
Andrew Ferrara
Andrei Gromyko
Audrey Hepburn
André Michelin
Andrew Jackson
Andrew Johnson
Andrew Marvell
Andreas Baader
Addressograph®
Andrés Segovia
Andrei Tupolev
ardentia verba
adding machine
ardent spirits
audio cassette
androdioecism
audiovisually
audio-engineer
audio-location
Anders Celsius
Andhra Pradesh
additionality
audita querela
auditory canal
auditory nerve
audax et cautus
Alexander Haig
Alexander Blok
Alexander Pope
acetaminophen
Aberdeen Angus
Aberdeenshire
a new departure
Alexei Kosygin
American bison
American bowls
American cloth
American eagle
American organ
American robin
American Samoa
American tiger
Amelia Earhart
acetification
Alec Issigonis
a week on Friday
a means to an end
adenoidectomy
anemometrical
averruncation
Aleksei Leonov
a kettle of fish
agents-general
acetylcholine
anfractuosity
Alfred Dreyfus
affreightment
Alfred Wallace
affaire d'amour
affenpinscher
affinity group
affirmatively
affordability
afforestation
as far as it goes
aggravatingly
Aegean Islands
algebraically
angle of attack
anglicisation
anglicization
Argyll and Bute
Angelic Doctor
algologically
Angelina Jolie
angel-food-cake
angular motion
argumentative
argumentation
argentiferous
Anglo-Catholic
Anglo-Saxondom
agglomerative
agglomeration
Anglo-American
aggiornamento
angiospermous
Auger electron
argus pheasant
Augustus Pugin
agglutinative
agglutination
angry young man
atheistically
apheliotropic
athematically
Athenaeum Club
aphanipterous
achromaticity
achromatopsia
aphrodisiacal
atherogenesis
arhythmically
a shot in the arm
animalisation
animalization
animal implume
animal kingdom
avis au lecteur
Anita Brookner
animal spirits
Akira Kurosawa
animadversion
animal-worship
adiabatically
A Kind of Loving
acid-free paper
A Bigger Splash
arithmetician
arithmophobia
acidification
Alicia Markova
axiologically
axial skeleton
axiomatically
Asian elephant
adipose tissue
anisophyllous
a bit on the side
adiaphoristic
ad inquirendum
amitryptyline
aristocratism
adiathermancy
Alistair Cooke
ariston metron
Aviculariidae
adjustability
alkaline earth
Arkansas River
ask for trouble
All-hallowmass
All Hallows Day
All-hallowtide
allochthonous
at loggerheads
allegorically
alligator pear
alligator clip
all-time record
as likely as not
allelomorphic
Atlantic Ocean
Allen Ginsberg
Atlantosaurus
all in good time
a fly on the wall
all for the best
as large as life
ailes de pigeon
ailourophobia
ailourophobic
ailourophilia
ailourophilic
allowableness
Arms and the Boy
Arms and the Man
admeasurement
Ahmed Ben Bella
armed services
armed bullhead
a small fortune
armamentarium
almond-blossom
administrable
administrator
admirableness
Admiralty Arch
atmospherical
admissibility
armour of proof
armour-plating
Anna Akhmatova
Ann Widdecombe
Alnwick Castle
Arnold Bennett
Arnold Toynbee
amniocenteses
amniocentesis
amniotic fluid
Agnes MacPhail
Aung San Suu Kyi
annexationist
apocatastasis
aromatisation
aromatization
anomalistical
anomalousness
Avogadro's rule
Apocalypse Now
apocalyptical
at one's command
above reproach
at one's leisure
above one's head
apogeotropism
at one's wit's end
at one's wits' end
Adolf Eichmann
alongshoreman
apophlegmatic
apothegmatise
apothegmatize
apothegmatist
apochromatism
aboriginalism
✧aboriginality
apoliticality
agonistically
apodictically
apomictically
atomistically
atomic warfare
Apollo Theatre
acorn-barnacle
Adolphe Thiers
amorphousness
amour courtois
Apostles' Creed
apostle spoons
abortifacient
apostolically

about one's ears
acotyledonous
a copy of verses
anonymousness
alpha particle
alphabetarian
alphabetiform
Alpha Centauri
appealingness
alpha and omega
Aspects of Love
apprehensible
apple of the eye
apple-pie order
apple polisher
Appleton layer
apple turnover
apple dumpling
appoggiaturas
applicability
amphigastrium
amphitheatric
amphitheatral
amplification
amphiprostyle
at point of sale
appellatively
appellational
appel au peuple
appendiculate
Alpine orogeny
approximately
approximative
approximation
appropinquate
appropinquity
appropriately
appropriative
appropriation
Alphonse Mucha
appertainment
appertainance
asparagus bean
asparagus fern
aspergillosis
apportionable
apportionment
aspirant after
appeteezement
acquirability
acquired taste
acquisitively
acquiescently
acquiescingly
airs and graces
aerial railway
aerial ropeway
aerobiologist
agrobiologist
acrobatically
agriculturist
✧african violet
atrociousness
Afro-Caribbean
aerodynamical
agreeableness
arrière-pensée
agree to differ
agroecosystem
air letter form
aerogenerator
at right angles
Abraham's bosom
air lieutenant
acrylic resins
acrylaldehyde
acrylonitrile
April Fools' Day
aural speculum
aerolithology
acrimoniously
aurum potabile
adrenal glands
adrenal cortex
Air Force Cross
Air Force Medal
air loadmaster
air-compressor
airworthiness
aura popularis
à propos de rien
aircraftwoman
agrostologist
aerated waters
associateship
associability
associativity
associational
assiduousness
answerability
abstentionism
abstentionist
aesthetically
Austin hermits
absolutely not
absolute music
absolute pitch
absolute ruler
absolute units
absolute value
assemblywoman
Assumptionist
absence of mind
absent healing
assentiveness
arsenopyrites
at short notice
Austrian blind
absorbability
adsorbability
Austroasiatic
abstractively
abstractional
abstract verse
assertiveness
Australianism
assert oneself
Assyriologist
assistantship
assisted place
assassination
asset-stripper
assault course
actualisation
actualization
astrapophobia
astral spirits
antiasthmatic
antiarthritic
antibacterial
antiballistic
autobiography
anticoagulant
articles of war
anticlimactic
anticlinorium
astacological
autecological
anticlockwise
autocephalous
anticorrosive
antichristian
Azteca Stadium
autocatalysis
autocatalytic
autochthonism
autochthonous
auto-digestion
antidesiccant
at the same time
at the earliest
at the sharp end
anthelminthic
autoeroticism
at the coalface
asthenosphere
authentically
authenticator
act of oblivion
artificialise
artificialize
artificiality
artifical life
autograph book
antigenically
antigropeloes
antihistamine
attainability
attributively
antilogarithm
antimicrobial
anti-modernist
anti-marketeer
asthmatically
automatically
attendant upon
actinobacilli
Antony Gormley
attentiveness
antenniferous
attention line
attention span
antinomianism
autonomically
actinomycosis
actinomorphic
Antonin Artaud
Antoninus Pius
Antonín Dvořák
Antonio Canova
Anton Mosimann
Antony of Padua
antinephritic
Anton Bruckner
astonishingly
actinotherapy
astronautical
astrometrical
Antiochianism
anthophyllite
astrophysical
authoritative
authorisation
authoritarian
authorization
astrodynamics
astrocytomata
Anthony Dowell
Anthony Powell
Anthony Island
Anthony Quayle
anti-personnel
antipsychotic
antiquitarian
alternate host
alternatively
attorney at law
after a fashion
alterum tantum
arteriovenous
arteriography
anthropogenic
anthropolatry
anthropomorph
anthropometry
anthropophagi
anthropophagy
anthropopathy
anthropophyte
anthroposophy
anthraquinone
autoresponder
artesian basin
antispasmodic
antisubmarine
antisocialism
antisocialist
antisociality
autoschediaze
autoschediasm
acta sanctorum
antiscorbutic
antisepticise
antisepticize
antisepticism
attitude angle
attitudiniser
attitudinizer
a stitch in time
antiterrorist
Arthur Balfour
Arthur C Clarke
Arthur Rackham
Arthur Rimbaud
Arthur Ransome
active service
adumbratively
ab urbe condita
aqua caelestis
Arundel Castle
arundinaceous
amusement park
Aquifoliaceae
aluminiferous
aqua mirabilis
Aquinas Thomas
aqueous humour
a quarter after
a vuestra salud
ayuntamientos
acupuncturist
Arval Brethren
advantageable
advantage rule
advanced guard
✧advanced level
adventure game
adventure film
adventuresome
adventuristic
adventurously
alveolar ridge
advertisement
advertizement
advisableness
auxiliary verb
Aix-en-Provence
amygdalaceous
anythingarian
anybody's guess
Abyssinian cat
abyssopelagic
at your service
Bharata Natyam
Blanche Du Bois
blanchisseuse
branch officer
bearded lizard
bearded collie
bearded dragon
boarding house
boarding party
bladder cherry
blandishments
blameableness
blamelessness
✧brave new world
blaze the trail
Beaufort scale
brachycephaly
brachydactyly
✧brachiosaurus
brachypterous
beati pacifici
beatification
Brazilian ruby
blackberrying
black bindweed
black diamonds
blacktip shark
black skipjack
black and white
blankety-blank
blanket finish
blanket stitch
bracket fungus
blackguardism
black-eyed bean
by all accounts
braille-writer
brainlessness
brainchildren
brainsickness
brainstorming
blasphemously
by appointment
boatswain-bird
brass farthing
Brass in Pocket
brassfounding
brattice-cloth
beauty contest
beat the record
beat the bounds
beast of burden
blastogenesis
beasts of chase
beauteousness
beauty parlour
blast-freezing
beauty therapy
baby-battering
Bible-thumping
Bible-pounding
bibliographic
bibliographer
bibliological
bibliolatrist
bibliolatrous
bibliophagist
bibliophilism
bibliophilist
bibliopolical
bibliothecary
Babbitt's metal
bubble chamber
babbling brook
bubonic plague
baby-snatching
Bobby Charlton
bob's your uncle
baccalaureate
béchamel sauce
back-calculate
bacteriolysin
bacteriolysis
bacteriolytic
bacteriophage
bachelor party
bachelor's hall
bachelor's wife
back-formation
Buckfast Abbey
backhoe loader
bacillophobia
biculturalism
become unglued
back-pedalling
Bactrian camel
bicuspid valve
backscratcher
backwardation
Becky Thatcher
bad scran to you
body carpeting
body corporate
budget account
badger-baiting
badger-drawing
Buddhist cross
bedside manner
bidding-prayer
body mass index
bad conscience
bidirectional
Breeches Bible
breech-loading
breach of trust
bleed like a pig
bleeding heart
blepharospasm
breakfast-room
breakableness
break the balls
breaking point
break one's mind

break one's word
break one's duck
breakdown gang
break your duck
beetlebrained
beetle-crusher
Blessed Virgin
Beefsteak Club
breastfeeding
breast the tape
brent barnacle
breathe easily
breathe freely
breathing-time
breathing hole
breeze through
before the fact
before the mast
before the beam
before the wind
baggage-animal
Big Bang theory
big White Chief
begging letter
bag and baggage
beginner's luck
beginningless
bignoniaceous
bigarade sauce
Big Brotherism
Bohemian topaz
Behind the Line
behaviourally
bait and switch
blindman's buff
building-board
building block
building paper
blind stamping
Brinell number
Bridgwater Bay
bridge-builder
bring into line
bring into play
bring to naught
bridge of boats
bridge passage
British Legion
British Museum
brinksmanship
brilliantness
Brian Hanrahan
Briançon manna
Brian Horrocks
Brian Mulroney
blister beetle
blister copper
ballad concert
belt-and-braces
Balsaminaceae
Balkanisation
Balkanization
balsamiferous
ballast-heaver
beleaguerment
ball cartridge
ballet-dancing
belle peinture
bulletin board
belles-lettres
balneum Mariae
balneotherapy
belligerently
Billie Holiday
billionairess
billiard cloth
billiard table
ball lightning
balance of mind
Balanoglossus
bullock's-heart
Balto-slavonic
ballot-rigging
bellows to mend
ballroom dance
Belisha beacon
Bildungsroman
bulrush millet
Bollywood film
Billy Connolly
bombastically
bumper sticker
bimillenniums
bamboo curtain
bamboozlement
bumptiousness
Benjamin Baker
bancassurance
benedictional
banderilleros
bungee jumping
bonheur-du-jour
beneficiation
beneficential
benthopelagic
Bendigeidfran
banking engine
binding energy
binary fission
bank statement
bank switching
bone turquoise
bone-turquoise
Benazir Bhutto
boot and saddle
bioscientific
bronchiolitis
bronchial tube
book-canvasser
bronchoscopic
bronchography
bioaccumulate
broad daylight
blood relative
blood relation
bloodlessness
broadmindedly
blood donation
blood-boltered
broad-spectrum
blood pressure
Blood Brothers
bloodcurdling
biogenetic law
biogeographer
broken-hearted
biotechnology
bromeliaceous
biodegradable
blow great guns
biochemically
brother-german
brotherliness
brothers-in-law
booking office
block printing
Bloomsburyite
browntail moth
brownie points
Brownie Guider
brown seaweeds
bioenergetics
Book of Changes
Book of Ezekiel
blow one's stack
Book of Genesis
Book of Malachi
Book of Numbers
Book of Obadiah
biocompatible
bioconversion
biopsychology
Books of Samuel
Books of Esdras
blow the lid off
blotting-paper
biosystematic
baptism of fire
baptismal name
baptismal vows
Barbara Castle
bureaucratise
bureaucratize
bureaucratist
bord and pillar
Bernard Lovell
barbarisation
barbarization
barrack square
barnacle-goose
bargain-hunter
Barbados earth
Barbados pride
barbarousness
burial society
Barnaby Bright
Baruch Spinoza
barrel-chested
Berkeleianism
Berberidaceae
burden of proof
barber-surgeon
barter trading
Burnett salmon
Barnett Newman
Border terrier
barbecue sauce
barrel-vaulted
barefacedness
birefringence
boraginaceous
birthday party
burgh of barony
Berthe Morisot
Birminghamise
Birminghamize
burying beetle
burning-mirror
burying ground
bernicle-goose
Birgit Nilsson
barrier method
barristership
born in wedlock
Bertie Wooster
barfly jumping
Burt Lancaster
bareland croft
burbling point
burglariously
Berenice's Hair
burn one's boats
barcode reader
borrowing days
bird of passage
Barbour® jacket
Burton Richter
borrow trouble
Bertolt Brecht
Barnstaple Bay
bird's-nest soup
barnsbreaking
bird's-eye maple
burnt-offering
Burnt by the Sun
Bermuda shorts
Bermuda rigged
Burgundy pitch
borough-monger
Barry McGuigan
Barry Richards
Barry Cunliffe
Basic Instinct
beside oneself
beside the mark
basset-hornist
beseemingness
Bassenthwaite
Bashir Gemayel
Basil the Great
Basil Ringrose
business class
business cycle
business hours
businesswoman
basso profondo
basso profundo
bespottedness
Bosworth Field
Boston terrier
bestsellerdom
bush telegraph
bascule bridge
Busby Berkeley
be that as it may
bits and pieces
Batman Forever
Batman Returns
butter-and-eggs
butter-biscuit
battered child
butterfingers
butterfly weed
butterfly fish
butterfly kiss
butterfly clip
butterfly bush
betweenwhiles
better oneself
butler's pantry
butcher's broom
bathing beauty
batwing sleeve
battle against
bottle-coaster
battle-cruiser
bottle-feeding
battle fatigue
Battle of Anzio
Battle of Crécy
Battle of Issus
Battle of Liège
Battle of Maipó
Battle of Maipú
Battle of Mylae
Battle of Pavia
Battle of Sedan
Battle of Sluys
Battle of Valmy
Battle of Varna
Battle of Ypres
battle-scarred
batement light
botanic garden
baton-sinister
bite one's thumb
buttock planes
bottomless pit
button-through
button your lip
bits per second
beta particles
bite the bullet
bathymetrical
Buteyko method
brutalisation
brutalization
bougainvillea
Blueberry Hill
boundlessness
boundary layer
boundary rider
blue-eyed grass
Bruce Oldfield
brush kangaroo
brush quandong
boutique hotel
bouillabaisse
Blue Mountains
bountifulness
boulting cloth
boulting-hutch
boustrophedon
bounteousness
bowling crease
bewilderingly
bowel movement
by word of mouth
bowstring-hemp
box the compass
Bay of Rainbows
beyond compare
beyond dispute
beyond measure
beyond one's ken
beyond the pale
bayonet socket
Chagas' disease
Clara Peggotty
chaparral cock
character part
characterless
character code
cranberry tree
cranberry bush
chalcographic
chalcographer
chance one's arm
Claude Bernard
Claude Chabrol
Claude Debussy
Claude Dornier
Claudio Abbado
clandestinely
clandestinity
chase rainbows
chameleon-like
✧chateaubriand
charge account
changeability
Changi Airport
charge-capping
charge carrier
charge density
changefulness
charge machine
changing-piece
change oneself
change of heart
change of state
change of venue
change-ringing
crash recorder
coachwhip-bird
Cyathophyllum
coachbuilding
clavicembalos
clarification
craniological
clay-ironstone
cranioscopist
charity-school
coadjutorship
cracker-barrel
Charlie Parker
Charlie Bucket
challengeable
challengingly
Charles Mackay
Charles Darwin
Charles the Fat
Charles Mingus
Charles Morgan
Charles Gounod
Charlottetown
Charlotte Gray
charlatanical
Chaim Weizmann
chammy leather
charm bracelet
chain reaction
chain of office
channel-hopper
channel-surfer
chain moulding
cyanoacrylate
Chagos Islands
clamorousness
Champs Elysées
clapperclawer
clapperboards
clapper bridge
champ at the bit
clairvoyantly
clairaudience
classicalness

classlessness
coarse fishing
coarse-grained
crassulaceous
class interval
claustrophobe
classes aisées
class struggle
Chantilly lace
craftsmanship
charter member
coagulability
cabbalistical
cubic zirconia
cable-moulding
cable-drilling
cobelligerent
cobaltiferous
cobbler's punch
cabin altitude
cabinetmaking
Cabernet Franc
cyberneticist
cyberslacking
cybersquatter
cyberstalking
Cyclanthaceae
cocker spaniel
cacographical
cocainisation
cocainization
cochleariform
Cecil Day-Lewis
cockle-brained
coconut butter
cycloparaffin
cyclodialysis
cyclospermous
cuckoo-spittle
cock of the walk
cock-of-the-rock
cock of the loft
Cucurbitaceae
Ciceronianism
cockspur grass
cicatrisation
cicatrization
cocktail dress
cocktail mixer
cocktail party
cocktail stick
cock-thrappled
cock-throppled
co-counselling
codeclination
codicological
cadmium yellow
code of conduct
cheval-de-frise
Chesapeake Bay
✧caesaropapism
Caesar's Palace
coenaesthesia
coenaesthesis
coercive force
chef de cuisine
credence shelf
credence table
crème de cassis
crème de menthe
Clement Attlee
Czech Republic
chemical abuse
credit account
creditability
credit balance
coeliac plexus
Ctesiphon arch
chemisorption
credit scoring
credit squeeze
checked square
checkweigh man
Czeslaw Milosz
cream of tartar
cream-coloured
clean-timbered
cleaning woman
chemoreceptor
creeping Jenny
creeping Jesus
cheap and nasty
clear-headedly
cheerlessness
clear the decks
clearance sale
clearing house
cherry-picking
clear-starcher
cleistogamous
cheese skipper
creosote plant
chest register
Chester Nimitz
cheque account
coeducational
credulousness
chequered flag
cleavableness
coffee disease
coffee essence
coffee grinder
coffee grounds
coffee-housing
coffee klatsch
coffee morning
coffee service
cognate object
cognomination
cigarette card
cigarette case
cigarette butt
cogito, ergo sum
climatologist
climatography
climactically
climacterical
cribbage-board
climbing-frame
climbing perch
clincher-built
childbed fever
childlessness
child guidance
Chinese radish
Chinese leaves
Chinese puzzle
Clive Sinclair
chieftainship
Clifford Odets
clishmaclaver
coinheritance
critical angle
criminal court
clinical death
critical point
critical state
clinical trial
criminologist
criminousness
coin-in-the-slot
criniculture
chicken-hazard
chicken breast
chinkerinchee
clickety-clack
clickety-click
cliometrician
Chien-Shiung Wu
Chiang Kai-Shek
chimney-pot hat
chimney-corner
chimneybreast
chiromantical
clinopinacoid
clinopinakoid
clinodiagonal
Caicos Islands
Chinook Jargon
Chinook salmon
chirographist
clinopyroxene
criss-cross-row
Clint Eastwood
Caister Castle
Chiltern Hills
cold as charity
collaterality
calcariferous
collaborative
collaboration
collar of esses
call attention
caliature-wood
cold-bloodedly
colobus monkey
College of Arms
colleagueship
Culver's physic
collectedness
collecting box
collectorship
call for trumps
cold-heartedly
calcification
Calvinistical
calligraphist
collieshangie
callisthenics
chlamydomonas
chlamydospore
Columbia River
colonial goose
colon bacillus
calendar month
Colin Campbell
cylinder block
cylinder press
cylindrically
cylindraceous
colposcopical
Call of the Wild
colloquialism
colloquialist
chlorobromide
caloric theory
chlorocruorin
Colorado River
chlorhexidine
calorifically
chloroformist
Chloromycetin®
chlorine water
chloroplastal
Chlorophyceae
chlorargyrite
chloritic marl
call to account
calculatingly
calculational
cellular radio
cultural shock
culture medium
cultured pearl
colourfulness
colour hearing
colourisation
colourization
celluliferous
colour masking
colour-process
colour therapy
comparatively
comparability
comma bacillus
command module
commandership
comrade-in-arms
combat fatigue
compagination
combativeness
compatibility
companionable
companionably
companionless
companionship
companionhood
companion star
campanologist
compatriotism
compass timber
compass window
compass signal
compassionate
compact camera
compactedness
compartmental
Campanulaceae
company doctor
Coma Berenices
Comte Lagrange
commercial art
commercialese
commercialise
commercialize
commercialism
commercialist
commerciality
campeachy wood
compendiously
Comte de Barras
Comte Bertrand
Comte de Buffon
Commelinaceae
competitively
commemorative
commemoration
commemoratory
commeasurable
commensurable
commensurably
camshaft cover
camphoraceous
combinability
combinational
combinatorial
combinatorics
commiserative
commiseration
cummingtonite
combining form
Campion Edmund
commit oneself
commit suicide
committeeship
complicatedly
complications
Camille Jordan
complaisantly
complainingly
complementary
complimentary
cumulostratus
complexedness
complex number
common burdock
common carrier
common caustic
compositeness
composing room
compositional
common lobster
common-law wife
common measure
compound ratio
compound umbel
Cambridge ring
Cambridge blue
comprehensive
comprehension
cum grano salis
camera obscura
compressed air
compressional
cum privilegio
comprovincial
camp-sheathing
Compsognathus
come to nothing
come to oneself
comptes rendus
come to the boil
come up against
commutatively
commutability
computability
computational
communalistic
communautaire
computer crime
computer fraud
computer virus
communicative
communication
communitarian
communicatory
Communism Peak
communion card
communion rail
community card
community care
community home
community work
Campus Martius
compulsionist
campylobacter
canvas-climber
concatenation
contabescence
convalescence
convalescency
consanguinity
contaminative
contamination
cannabis resin
container ship
container port
concavo-convex
cinnamon stone
confarreation
contact lenses
contact flight
contact poison
connaturalise
connaturalize
confabulation
confabulatory
conscientious
canicular days
canicular year
consciousness
Canadian canoe
Canadian River
Canada thistle
condescending
condescension
confederative
confederation
consenescence
consenescency
cancellariate
concernedness
cancerophobia
convexo-convex
contemplative
contemplation
contemplatist
condensed milk
condensed type
concessionary
confessionary
concessionist
confessorship
conversazione
conversazioni
✧conceptual art
concentrative
conceptualise
conceptualize
contextualise
contextualize
conceptualism
concentration
conceptualist
concertmaster
convent school

conceitedness
contentedness
concentricity
confetti money
concertinaing
consentaneity
consectaneous
consentaneous
connecting rod
confectionary
conventionary
Conception Bay
conventioneer
confectionery
connectionism
Conceptionist
conventionist
contentiously
convertiplane
conjecturable
conjecturally
consecutively
consequential
conservatoire
conchological
cinchonaceous
canthaxanthin
candidateship
cannibalistic
considerately
considerative
consideration
consideringly
consimilarity
confidingness
consimilitude
conditionally
condition code
conniption fit
configuration
continuedness
continuity man
canaliculated
candle-dipping
conflagration
candle-lighter
conglomeratic
candle-snuffer
conglutinator
cinematically
cinematograph
convocational
consolidative
cantonisation
cantonization
consolidation
concomitantly
confoundingly
contortionate
contortionism
contortionist
convolutional
convolvuluses
conspicuously
cine projector
ciné projector
conspurcation
conspiratress
contra account
contrabandism
contrabandist
contrabassoon
contributable
canary-creeper
contractility
contractional
centricalness
centre console
contraceptive
contraception
contractually
contradictive
contradiction
contradictory
centrifugally
centrifugence
contrafagotto
centre-forward
contragestive
contragestion
Canary Islands
Central Pahari
Central Powers
control column
contralateral
confrontation
congruousness
contrapuntist
contrappostos
centripetally
contrariously
contristation
congressional
Congresswoman
congratulable
congratulator
concrete music
concrete mixer
concretionary
contraterrene
confraternity
concrete steel
contrate-wheel
Congreve-match
contravention
controversial
controvertist
Canes Venatici
Coniston Water
constrainable
constrainedly
constableship
constablewick
constringency
constellation
constellatory
Constance Spry
Constantinian
constupration
consternation
constructable
constructible
conjugate foci
confusability
conjugational
conjunctively
conjunctional
connumeration
consumer goods
consul general
concupiscible
concupiscence
confusibility
consumptively
consumptivity
conquistadors
convulsionary
convulsionist
cinque-spotted
conducted tour
conductor rail
conductorship
concyclically
condylomatous
chop and change
Choral Fantasy
choral prelude
choral society
Coomassie Blue®
crotchetiness
clouded yellow
clouded agaric
co-operatively
close a bargain
closed circuit
closed couplet
choreographic
choreographer
chorepiscopal
chose in action
close one's eyes
Close Brethren
close quarters
cholecystitis
clothe in words
clothes-basket
clothes-screen
cook-housemaid
clock-watching
crook the elbow
cloak-and-sword
Crowland Abbey
Crohn's disease
crown of thorns
crown imperial
crown princess
Crown attorney
chocolate cake
choroid plexus
cool one's heels
crocodile bird
crocodile clip
choropleth map
chopping-board
chopping-block
chopping-knife
cross-hatching
cross-matching
cross-vaulting
cross-magnetic
cross-gartered
crossed cheque
cloister-garth
cross the floor
cross-division
cross-platform
cross compiler
cross-springer
crossbreeding
cross-training
cross-dressing
cross-crosslet
cross-purposes
cross-quarters
cross-question
cross-cultural
crossover vote
cross-examiner
✧croix de guerre
copia verborum
Capparidaceae
cephalisation
cephalization
cephalic index
captain's chair
Captain Cooker
cephalothorax
cephalosporin
capuchin cross
Cape Canaveral
capaciousness
copper-captain
copper pyrites
copper trumpet
captivatingly
copying pencil
caprification
capillary tube
copple-crowned
capellmeister
ciprofloxacin
cupboard faith
copyrightable
copartnership
capital assets
capital murder
capitation fee
Cuquenán Falls
carbamazepine
coriander seed
curtain-raiser
curtain speech
care assistant
Carmarthen Bay
care attendant
Carrantuohill
cerebral death
cardboard city
cerebral palsy
cerebrospinal
Carl Bernstein
corn-chandlery
card catalogue
correlatively
correlativity
correlational
cornet-à-piston
carpet beating
carpet-bedding
carpet-bombing
carte-de-visite
cartelisation
cartelization
correspondent
corresponsive
corresponding
carpet-sweeper
carpet-slipper
current assets
coreferential
cerographical
cardinalatial
carnivalesque
cardinalitial
cartilaginous
cardinal point
cervical smear
Carmina Burana
cardiac arrest
cardiac muscle
cardiographer
carriage clock
carriage-drive
carriage horse
carriage trade
Cornish chough
carnification
certification
cornification
certificatory
certified milk
curvilineally
corrigibility
Carrickfergus
cardiological
carrion beetle
carrion-flower
carcinomatous
carcinologist
carnivorously
cervicography
corridor-train
carrier pigeon
carrier rocket
coreligionist
coralliferous
coralligenous
Coralline Crag
Corolliflorae
corollifloral
Carole Lombard
Carol Ann Duffy
Cyril Tourneur
ceruloplasmin
chrome leather
ceremonialism
ceremonialist
ceremoniously
chrome plating
chromospheric
chromatically
chromotherapy
chromatograph
chrome tanning
chromatophore
chrematistics
chromium steel
chronobiology
chronicle play
chronographer
corinthianise
corinthianize
chronological
coronal suture
coroner's court
Caryocaraceae
corporateness
corporate bond
corporativism
corporativist
Cordoba Mosque
carbon dioxide
cordocentesis
carbonisation
carbonization
corrosiveness
✧carboniferous
cercopithecid
corrosibility
corroborative
corroboration
corroboratory
carbon process
Carlos Santana
carbonylation
cartridge-belt
cartridge clip
corps de ballet
Christ in Glory
Christian name
Christianness
Christianlike
Christian Dior
Christianiser
Christianizer
Christminster
Christmas card
Christmas cake
Christmas-tide
Christmas-time
Christmas rose
Christmas tree
chrysanthemum
chrestomathic
Christologist
Chris Boardman
chrysophilite
carotid artery
Corythosaurus
circumambient
circumambages
Corpus Christi
circumduction
circumductory
corpus delicti
circumflexion
circumference
circumfluence
carburisation
carburization
Curculionidae
circumjacency
circumstances
circumspectly
circumscriber
corruptionist
circumvallate
circumventive
circumvention
carry the torch
carrying value
carry to excess
Corazon Aquino
cast a nativity
cascara amarga
casual clothes
custard powder
custard coffin
costardmonger
Casuarinaceae
casualisation
casualization
cash dispenser
cosmeceutical
cost-efficient
cost-effective

cosmetologist
case-hardening
cessio bonorum
cysticercosis
casting-weight
casuistically
casement cloth
customariness
cosmochemical
cosmothetical
customisation
customization
custodianship
cosmopolitism
cosmopolitics
Cesar Milstein
case-sensitive
casus foederis
cottage cheese
cathartically
Cate Blanchett
Cuthbert's duck
cytochemistry
catechistical
catecholamine
catechumenate
catechumenism
cytodiagnosis
Catherine Parr
Catherine pear
categorically
categorematic
catchment area
cut the mustard
catch on the hip
catch at straws
co-trimoxazole
Cetti's warbler
cytologically
cattle-lifting
catalytically
cat-o'-nine-tails
cut one's throat
cut one's losses
City of Bristol
citronella oil
cut to the chase
cut to the quick
Catholic Times
cut down to size
cathodography
cotton-picking
cotton stainer
cotton spinner
cotton thistle
catapult fruit
cytopathology
coterminously
catercornered
catastrophism
catastrophist
catty-cornered
Chulalongkorn
Church in Wales
council school
councilorship
council estate
churchmanship
church officer
church service
coup de bonheur
crux decussata
coup de théâtre
causelessness
cause of action
cauterisation
cauterization
couleur de rose
coureur de bois
cough medicine
crush syndrome
cousins-german
chuck-farthing
chuckle-headed
chuckie-stanes
crux medicorum
cruise control
counsel-keeper
counselorship
cruise missile
coursing-joint
cruiserweight
count palatine
court martials
county borough
county cricket
caustic potash
county council
court reporter
Courtney Walsh
court of record
Court of Honour
Court of Appeal
Court of Arches
court circular
courts martial
counting frame
counting house
court-bouillon
courteousness
counter-parole
counter-caster
counteractive
counteraction
counter-weight
counterfeiter
counterfeitly
counterchange
countercharge
counterbidder
counter-signal
counter-fleury
countermotion
counter-poison
counterspying
counter-attack
counterstroke
counter-jumper
courtesy light
courtesy title
court cupboard
country cousin
C Auguste Dupin
civil marriage
civil engineer
civil aviation
civil twilight
covert coating
cover one's back
cevitamic acid
Cowper's glands
coxcombically
cryobiologist
Clyde Tombaugh
chylification
chymification
cry blue murder
cayenne pepper
cry for the moon
cryptographic
cryptographer
Crystal Palace
crystal-gazing
cryptological
crystallinity
crystal violet
cryptanalysis
cryptanalytic
cryptesthesia
cryptozoology
draw a veil over
diacatholicon
dramatisation
dramatization
dramatic irony
draw attention
dramaturgical
drawbar outfit
dead-colouring
dead-cat bounce
diabetologist
diametrically
dialectically
diageotropism
dwarf antelope
draggle-tailed
draught-screen
draught-engine
draught animal
draughtswoman
diaphragmatic
diaphragm pump
deathlessness
Death in Venice
diaphanometer
diachronistic
diathermanous
diaphototropy
drawing-master
drawing-pencil
dualistically
draw-leaf table
dead-letter box
dramma giocoso
dead-men's bells
dead man's pedal
dead men's shoes
drainage basin
draining board
diagnostician
diagonal scale
Diamond Sculls
diamond-beetle
diamond-powder
diamond python
drag one's heels
Dean of Faculty
dialogistical
drag-parachute
deacquisition
dead-reckoning
draftsmanship
dialypetalous
Debatable Land
debauchedness
declaratively
declamatorily
declaratorily
dictatorially
deciduousness
decrepitation
duchesse cover
decaffeinated
deceivability
deceitfulness
decriminalise
decriminalize
dichlamydeous
decelerometer
decimal places
decimal system
documentarise
documentarize
documentation
documentalist
documentarist
documentarily
decomposition
decompressive
decompression
decontaminate
decontaminant
Doctor Crippen
Doctor Faustus
dichotomously
Doctor Proudie
Doctor Zhivago
da capo al segno
deceptiveness
deceptibility
deck passenger
decerebration
decortication
dichromic acid
doctrinairism
decarbonation
dichrooscopic
decarboxylase
Decoration Day
decision table
Dicotyledones
dice with death
dactyliomancy
dactylography
Dido and Aeneas
deducibleness
deductibility
dodecaphonism
dodecaphonist
daddy-long-legs
Drew Barrymore
dreadlessness
dieselisation
dieselization
dieffenbachia
dies infaustus
dyed-in-the-wool
Die Fledermaus
dwelling-house
dwelling-place
dreamlessness
Die Another Day
Diego Maradona
dree one's weird
dressed to kill
dress-improver
dressing-table
deep structure
Dieu vous garde
defeasibility
diffarreation
defibrination
defibrillator
deficientness
defectiveness
defectibility
differentiate
defencelessly
defensibility
deformability
defervescence
defervescency
deferentially
deforestation
diffusiveness
diffusibility
diffusion-tube
dog's breakfast
degree Celsius
dog-periwinkle
daguerreotype
daguerreotypy
dignification
digestibility
dog's-tail grass
digital camera
digital design
digitizing pad
deglutination
dihedral angle
dehydrogenase
dehydrogenate
Dr Henry Jekyll
driving-mirror
drinkableness
drink-offering
drill-sergeant
drilling lathe
deipnosophist
dripping roast
dribs and drabs
daily parallax
dairy products
Duke Ellington
Duke Frederick
Duke of Bedford
Duke of Grafton
Duke Vincentio
dollarisation
dollarization
delectability
Dolichosauria
Dolichosaurus
dolichocephal
deliciousness
delightedness
dolphinariums
dulcification
deltoid muscle
Daltons Weekly
dilapidations
deliquescence
delirifacient
deliriousness
dilettanteism
deleteriously
Dr Livingstone
Delaware River
delayed action
Daley Thompson
Dame Clara Butt
democrat wagon
domiciliation
demi-caractère
Dame Diana Rigg
Dame Eva Turner
demyelination
damageability
damage control
damage feasant
damnification
dim-wittedness
Dame Judi Dench
demolishments
demolitionist
demand deposit
demand feeding
dimensionless
dimension work
demonological
Dominique Pire
diminishingly
demonstrative
demonstration
demonstratory
Dome of the Rock
demeritorious
domestication
domesticities
Damascus blade
Damascus steel
Dame Thora Hird
demythologise
demythologize
dematerialise
dematerialize
dimethylamine
demiurgically
Duncan Edwards
dental formula
dental hygiene
dental surgeon
Daniel arap Moi
Daniel Auteuil
Daniel Deronda
dunderheadism
Daniel Nathans
dangerousness
dangerous drug
dinner service
Dandie Dinmont
dancing-master
densitometric
Dennis Skinner
denticulation
Donald A Glaser
Donald Bradman
Donald Maclean
dynamic memory
dynamogenesis
don't mention it
Dendrocalamus
dendrological
Dunstable road
do-nothingness
denationalise

denationalize
dinoturbation
Dunster Castle
Don't You Want Me
Dioscoreaceae
drophead coupé
✧diotheletical
✧dyotheletical
✧dyothelitical
deoch-an-doruis
deoxidisation
deoxidization
dioristically
drowned valley
Dionne Warwick
deodorisation
deodorization
deontological
deprecatingly
deprecatorily
dipleidoscope
depressed area
diphenylamine
dipping-needle
dephlegmation
Doppler effect
dependability
diplomatic bag
deplorability
diplomatology
Diprotodontia
diprotodontid
dephosphorise
dephosphorize
depersonalise
depersonalize
diphthongally
dermatophytic
dermatoplasty
dermatologist
dermatography
Dorcas society
direct current
direct damages
derecognition
directionless
Dark Continent
direct selling
Darcey Bussell
Dornford Yates
Darwin College
darning-needle
dormitory town
dereligionise
dereligionize
derequisition
Der Freischütz
derestriction
Doris Humphrey
Dorothea Beale
Dorothea Lange
Dorothy Jordan
Darius Milhaud
derived demand
derivationist
disparateness
disparagement
discapacitate
disparagingly
dispatch rider

dastardliness
dishabilitate
disharmonious
dispassionate
dismantlement
distastefully
distant-signal
disnaturalise
disnaturalize
disobediently
disobligation
disobligatory
disobligement
désobligeante
disobligingly
disadvantaged
desperateness
dissemblingly
dismemberment
disseveration
disseminative
dissemination
dissepimental
disfellowship
dysmenorrheic
dysmenorrheal
dysmenorrhoea
disrespectful
dust explosion
disheartening
dispersedness
disperse phase
dyspeptically
disceptatious
disreputation
disaffectedly
disaffirmance
desegregation
disagreeables
designer label
Design for Life
discharge lamp
dischargeable
discharge tube
despicability
distinctively
distinguished
distinguisher
dusting powder
Dustin Hoffman
dissimilation
dissimilarity
dispiritingly
dissimilitude
disciplinable
dissimulative
disfiguration
dissimulation
disfigurement
displeasingly
desulphuriser
desulphurizer
displantation
desultoriness
disilluminate
disillusioned
disembarkment
disemployment
disembodiment
disengagement
disentailment

disinterested
disintegrable
disintegrator
disinvestment
disinhibition
disinhibitory
disinvigorate
disposability
disconcerting
disconcertion
Desmond Haynes
Desmond Morris
discovery well
disconformity
dispositively
dispositioned
dispositional
discommodious
discommission
disconnection
discount house
discount store
discoloration
dishonourable
dishonourably
disgospelling
dispossession
distortedness
discontiguity
discontiguous
discontentful
discontenting
discontinuity
discontinuous
dissoluteness
dissolubility
discomycetous
disappearance
disappointing
disequilibria
desirableness
distributable
district court
disgracefully
destructively
distractively
distractingly
destructivist
destructivity
destructional
district judge
district nurse
discreditable
discreditably
disordinately
desertisation
desertization
deservingness
dispraisingly
disarticulate
discriminable
discriminator
descriptively
descriptivism
disproportion
distressfully
distrustfully
distressingly
desert the diet
discretionary
desert varnish

disuse atrophy
disaster movie
disestimation
disassimilate
disputatively
disputability
disjunctively
dysfunctional
disquietingly
disqualifying
disguisedness
disgustedness
dispurveyance
detachability
do the business
Dutchman's pipe
detail drawing
detrimentally
dithionic acid
determinately
determinative
determination
deterministic
deteriorative
deterioration
detestability
dataveillance
data warehouse
deuteragonist
deus ex machina
deuterogamist
deuteroscopic
Deuteronomist
daughter board
daughter-in-law
drunk as a piper
double-banking
double bar line
double bassoon
double coconut
double-chinned
double-concave
double-crosser
double-dealing
double digging
doubly dentate
double-density
double feature
double figures
double-fronted
double-founted
double-glazing
double Gloster
double-hearted
double-jointed
double-meaning
double-mouthed
double-natured
double obelisk
double or quits
double-or-quits
double spacing
Douglas Gordon
double-shotted
double-shuffle
double-tongued
double wedding
drum majorette
Drummond light
drug smuggling
dauntlessness

David Sheppard
David Dimbleby
David Blunkett
devil's boletus
developmental
devolutionary
devolutionist
divertisement
diverging lens
diversifiable
divertibility
diverticulate
devastatingly
divisibleness
devisal of arms
divisionalise
divisionalize
division lobby
devotionalist
devotionality
downcast-shaft
Downing Street
downrightness
Down's syndrome
down to the wire
dexterousness
dexamfetamine
dexamethasone
dextrocardiac
dextro tempore
day care centre
drying-up cloth
epanadiploses
epanadiplosis
evangeliarium
evangeliarion
evangelically
evangelistary
exaggeratedly
edaphic factor
examinability
examinational
elaborateness
elaborate upon
evaporability
exasperatedly
États-Généraux
exact sciences
elastic tissue
exanthematous
enantiomorphy
enantiodromia
enantiodromic
enantiotropic
Emanuel Lasker
Emanuel Ungaro
embranglement
embracingness
Eubacteriales
embrittlement
embellishment
embarrassedly
embarrassment
embourgeoised
elbow macaroni
embryogenesis
embryological
embryonically
embryotically
exclamational
exchange blows

exchange words
Eucharistical
eschatologist
✧encyclopaedia
encyclopedism
encyclopedian
encyclopedist
excrescential
ecclesiolater
ecclesiolatry
exchequer bill
etching needle
etching ground
encompassment
encomiastical
excommunicate
excommunicant
ex consequenti
eccentrically
encroachingly
enchondromata
enclosed order
enclosure wall
Encephalartos
encephalocele
encephalotomy
encephalogram
encapsidation
exceptionable
exceptionably
exceptionally
encapsulation
escort carrier
excortication
excursiveness
excursion fare
excusableness
excess baggage
eschscholtzia
excessiveness
excess luggage
excuse-me dance
excuse oneself
excess postage
excitableness
encouragement
encouragingly
exclusiveness
exclusive zone
exclusion zone
encaustic tile
endearingness
endeavourment
endocrinology
Eddie the Eagle
eudaemonistic
endometriosis
eudiometrical
endoparasitic
endurableness
Elder brethren
endosymbiosis
endosymbiotic
endosmometric
eye-catchingly
emerald-copper
even-Christian
exercise price
Exeter College
Ebenezer Cooke
emergency room

emergency exit
energetically
elephant folio
elephant grass
elephantiasis
elephant's-ears
elephant's-foot
elephant shrew
everlastingly
exemplariness
exemplifiable
exempli gratia
execrableness
epeirogenesis
epeirogenetic
eventlessness
electrisation
electrization
electric chair
electric field
electric fence
electrifiable
electric motor
electric organ
electric piano
electric shock
electric storm
electrovalent
electromagnet
electroscopic
electrocement
electromerism
electrometric
electioneerer
electrophilic
electrochemic
electrophorus
electrothermy
electronic tag
electroplated
electroplater
electromotive
electro-optics
electron probe
electrography
electron shell
electrostatic
electrocution
electrotypist
electoral vote
electoral roll
every few hours
Evelyn Glennie
every which way
efficaciously
efficiency bar
effective rate
effectiveness
efface oneself
effectualness
enfants perdus
efflorescence
effervescible
effervescence
effervescency
efferent nerve
en grande tenue
eagle-flighted
engaged signal
Eugène Ionesco
Eugène Labiche

ergonomically
Eugene of Savoy
engine-turning
eigenfunction
Edgar Mitchell
Edgar Allan Poe
eighteen-pence
eighteen-penny
ergatomorphic
Eight and a Half
eightsome reel
exhibitionism
exhibitionist
ethical dative
ethologically
ephemeralness
Ephemeroptera
ephemeris time
Echinodermata
ethanolamines
ethnocentrism
ethnolinguist
ethnobotanist
ethnographica
enhypostatise
enhypostatize
Elizabeth Ryan
epinastically
Edinburgh rock
Eriocaulaceae
éminence grise
epigeneticist
evidentiality
eminent domain
et id genus omne
epithalamiums
epitheliomata
epiphenomenal
epiphenomenon
Erich Honecker
epithetically
édition de luxe
Eric Linklater
Eric Morecambe
enigmatically
epicondylitis
epidotisation
epidotization
epitomisation
epitomization
Eric Partridge
epitrachelion
epigrammatise
epigrammatize
epigrammatist
emigrationist
epistemically
existentially
eviction order
Eric Wieschaus
epicyclic gear
enjoyableness
✧enlightenment
Emlyn Williams
elliptic space
e pluribus unum
Ellesmere Port
enlisted woman
Éamon de Valera
Edmund Hillary
Edmund Husserl

Edmontosaurus
Edmond Rostand
Edmund Spenser
Emma Woodhouse
Ernesto Geisel
Ernst Cassirer
ex natura rerum
Ernst Lubitsch
Edouard Lartet
evocativeness
erogenous zone
egocentricity
exothermicity
epoxide resins
eroticisation
eroticization
exobiological
emotionlessly
egotistically
econometrical
economisation
economization
ecotoxicology
evolutionally
Ebony Concerto
explanatorily
euphausiacean
expectorative
expectoration
expeditionary
expeditiously
express parcel
express packet
express letter
express agency
✧expressionism
✧expressionist
esprit de corps
expandability
expendability
expanded metal
expansiveness
expensiveness
expansibility
expansion card
expansion slot
expansion bolt
exponentially
employability
explorational
Euphorbiaceae
explosiveness
explosive bolt
exploding star
explosion shot
expropriation
ex proprio motu
exportability
expurgatorial
empire-builder
experimentist
empyreumatise
empyreumatize
expose oneself
exposure meter
expostulative
expostulation
expostulatory
emphysematous
exquisiteness

Earl Alexander
Enrico Dandolo
Eurocommunism
Eurocommunist
egregiousness
earth-chestnut
earthing tyres
earth-movement
earth-motherly
earthly-minded
Earl Kitchener
Earl Marischal
erroneousness
Earl of Asquith
Earl of Halifax
Earl of Snowdon
Earl of Warwick
European bison
European Union
Europocentric
Etruscologist
easy as winking
Eastern Pahari
Eastern Church
East India Club
easy listening
easy-listening
Epsom and Ewell
essentialness
essential oils
eosinophilous
east-north-east
exsanguineous
ensanguinated
eusporangiate
ensorcellment
east-south-east
extravagation
extravasation
extragalactic
extravagantly
extravascular
extracellular
extrametrical
estrangedness
extra-physical
extralimitary
extrapolative
extrapolation
extrapolatory
extraposition
extraordinary
extratropical
extrajudicial
extra-axillary
✧establishment
eutectic point
entrepreneuse
extrinsically
entomological
extemporarily
entomophagist
entomophagous
entomophilous
entomostracan
extenuatingly
extendability
extensiveness
extendibility
extensibility
extension lead

extensionally
extension tube
extinguishant
eat boiled crow
ectoparasitic
entertainment
external store
Ettore Bugatti
enteric-coated
exteroceptive
exteroception
enter the lists
exterminative
extermination
exterminatory
exterritorial
exterior angle
Enteropneusta
enter a protest
estate-bottled
entry corridor
educatability
Educating Rita
educationally
equidifferent
equidistantly
eau des creoles
ecumenicalism
eau de toilette
equilibration
ebullioscopic
equinoctially
equiponderate
equiponderant
equipotential
Eduard Buchner
emulsion paint
equestrianism
equisetaceous
equitableness
equity finance
Equatoguinean
equivocalness
environmental
Elvis Costello
eavesdropping
Edwin Landseer
Erwin Panofsky
Erwin Chargaff
Erwin Piscator
Edward Kennedy
Edward R Murrow
Edward Whymper
erythrophobia
erysipelatous
Elysian fields
Egyptological
enzymological
franchisement
Francis Galton
Francis Joseph
Francis Horner
Flanders poppy
flagellomania
flagellantism
flame-coloured
flash flooding
flash in the pan
feather-headed
featherweight
feather-bonnet

feather stitch
feather duster
flasher switch
Franjo Tudjman
frank-tenement
Frank Wedekind
Frankie Howerd
Frank Williams
Frankeniaceae
Frank Auerbach
fragmentation
fragmentarily
Flammenwerfer
fear no colours
flannel-flower
flapping track
fractocumulus
fractionalise
fractionalize
fractionalism
fractionation
fractionalist
fractiousness
fractostratus
feature-length
Franz Schubert
fibrovascular
facial mapping
fictionalised
fictionalized
fiction writer
facultatively
focal distance
façon de parler
factorability
factorisation
factorization
focusing cloth
facetiousness
fide et fiducia
fidei defensor
fiddle-faddler
fiddle pattern
fiddle-pattern
fiddler's green
fiddler's money
fed to the teeth
feel-bad factor
French cricket
French kissing
free companion
French morocco
French mustard
field capacity
field of vision
field of honour
field emission
field wood rush
field hospital
field cow-wheat
field preacher
field strength
field mushroom
Frederick Jane
Frederick West
Frederikshavn
flesh and blood
flesh-coloured
flesh-pressing
fresh as a daisy
feeding bottle

Words marked ✧ can also be spelled with one or more capital letters

feeding frenzy
Flemish school
Flemish stitch
fuel injection
flexible drive
free-marketeer
free-selection
frequentative
frequentation
freezing point
fifth interval
Fogg Art Museum
fugaciousness
figure-casting
figure-hugging
figure of eight
figure of merit
figure skating
figure-weaving
fighting drunk
fighting words
fair-and-square
Flinders grass
faites vos jeux
fringe benefit
fringe-dweller
fridge-freezer
fringilliform
fringe theatre
frighteningly
faithlessness
flight-feather
frightfulness
flight of fancy
frilled lizard
frivolousness
frit porcelain
Friar Laurence
friar's lantern
fail to mention
flint-knapping
flirtatiously
Fritz Kreisler
filibustering
filibusterism
filibusterous
felicitations
false calabash
filterability
false relation
filter-feeding
fille d'honneur
file extension
false quantity
Fallen Warrior
folk etymology
fall from grace
full-fashioned
falsification
fall into place
filing cabinet
feloniousness
fellow citizen
fellow feeling
full of oneself
fellow servant
follow through
follow-through
filipendulous
film projector
fill someone in
felt-tipped pen
filius nullius
familiarities
family butcher
family therapy
feminine rhyme
femoral artery
F O Matthiessen
fundamentally
finnan haddock
Fontainebleau
fantastically
fine Champagne
fine chemicals
Fontenay Abbey
Finnegans Wake
finger-breadth
finger-pointer
fine gentleman
Fonthill Abbey
fencing-master
final approach
funambulation
funambulatory
financial year
find one's level
findon haddock
finishing post
find someone in
functionalism
functionalist
functionality
fine-tooth comb
fonctionnaire
funny peculiar
funny business
floral diagram
flotation tank
flora and fauna
Froebel system
floccillation
flow cytometry
floodlighting
Florence flask
flower-de-leuce
flower essence
flowering rush
flowers of zinc
flower-service
foolhardiness
floristically
floricultural
foot-land-raker
food poisoning
food processor
foot passenger
flourishingly
fool's paradise
from the word go
frontogenesis
floating crane
floating grass
floating light
floutingstock
floating voter
forward market
formalisation
formalization
formal verdict
form criticism
ferociousness
furaciousness
for mercy's sake
force de frappe
forgetfulness
farmer general
force the issue
forced landing
forget oneself
Farmers Weekly
fermentitious
forefeelingly
for the account
for the present
for that matter
farmhouse loaf
Ferdinand Foch
Ferdinand Cohn
formidability
ferrimagnetic
fertilisation
fertilization
fortification
fortified wine
fertility drug
fertility cult
forcible entry
✧foreign legion
Foreign Office
fire insurance
fortississimo
fortitudinous
ferricyanogen
forejudgement
foreknowingly
foreknowledge
fork-lift truck
for altogether
for all you care
Ford Madox Ford
foramen magnum
foraminiferal
forementioned
forensicality
ferromagnetic
for good and all
ferro-chromium
ferroelectric
ferroconcrete
ferrosoferric
forgottenness
ferrocyanogen
furor poeticus
furor loquendi
fire-resistant
fire-resisting
foreshadowing
foresightless
first-day cover
first meridian
first-begotten
first offender
First Minister
fortunateness
formularistic
fortune-teller
fortune cookie
fortune-hunter
for ever and aye
firework party
foster-brother
fisherman's pie
fissiparously
fishing-tackle
fishing ground
fossilisation
fossilization
fossiliferous
fashion victim
fission fungus
fasciculation
fusion cooking
fusion reactor
fusion welding
fits and starts
fête champêtre
Fettes College
fitness walker
fatigableness
fetch a compass
fetch a circuit
fetch and carry
fit like a glove
futurological
future perfect
future studies
Fêtes Galantes
feudalisation
feudalization
fauna and flora
founder member
feux d'artifice
foundation-net
flugelhornist
flügelhornist
frumentaceous
frumentarious
fluvioglacial
Fourier series
feuilletonism
feuilletonist
frustratingly
fruit pastille
faultlessness
fruitlessness
fruit cocktail
Faust Symphony
favorableness
favours to come
fowls of warren
foxtail millet
fixed-interest
flying colours
flying machine
flying officer
flying pickets
Graham Chapman
gradationally
grabbing crane
glance through
✧guardian angel
granddaughter
grandfatherly
Grand National
granddad shirt
grande cocotte
grand seigneur
Grand Seignior
guard of honour
grandiloquent
grandiloquous
grandmotherly
grande passion
grande vedette
Guatemala City
Graves' disease
gracelessness
grade crossing
grape hyacinth
graphic design
graphic artist
graphological
graphemically
gnathonically
gravitational
Grazia Deledda
gravimetrical
grading system
granitisation
granitization
gratification
graminivorous
Glacial Period
glaciological
glaziers' putty
gladiatorship
graticulation
Graeme Pollock
grammar school
Graeme Souness
grammatically
granny dumping
granny glasses
grain amaranth
Gianni Versace
glamorisation
glamorization
grappling-hook
grappling-iron
grasp at a straw
grasp at straws
glass-painting
grass sickness
glans clitoris
glass-grinding
grass staggers
giant hockweed
giant tortoise
granuliferous
granulomatous
Graf von Moltke
Gladys Aylward
go-as-you-please
Gabriel hounds
gubernatorial
Gödel's theorem
Gideon Mantell
go down the tube
Glenda Jackson
grey-goose wing
greyhound race
Greville Wynne
Greek valerian
Greek alphabet
Greenland seal
green manuring
green seaweeds
green-fingered
Greenwich Time
green with envy
green sickness
Green Room Club
greenhouse gas
grey reef shark
Great Yarmouth
Great Salt Lake
ghetto-blaster
Great Bear Lake
guest of honour
Great White Way
Great Zimbabwe
greetings card
Greater Bairam
gift of tongues
gigantomachia
grin and bear it
Geiger counter
guilelessness
guided missile
grief-stricken
going for a song
Gaidhealtachd
geitonogamous
grid reference
Gaius Lucilius
guiltlessness
go into reverse
Gilgamesh Epic
goliath beetle
galvanisation
galvanization
galvanometric
galvanoplasty
galactic plane
galactosaemia
galactorrhoea
Gilded Chamber
golden-crested
golden goodbye
golden jubilee
golden section
golden wedding
gillie-wetfoot
Galina Ulanova
Galeopithecus
gallows humour
gamma globulin
gymnastically
gumple-foisted
gambling house
gymnospermous
game preserver
gum up the works
gum tragacanth
gametogenesis
Gemütlichkeit
gunwales under
gens de lettres
gynodioecious
gonadotrophic
gonadotrophin
genre painting
gender-bending
ginger cordial
gynaecomastia
gynaecologist
gynaecocratic
gene frequency
gentianaceous
gentian violet
gentilshommes
gentle-hearted
gentlemanship
gentlemanlike
gentlemanhood

gentlewomanly
gynomonoecism
gynandromorph
goniometrical
General Patton
general legacy
general ledger
general degree
general effect
generalisable
generalissimo
generalizable
generation gap
generationism
Generation Xer
genetic spiral
gene therapist
genethlialogy
genotypically
genetotrophic
genito-urinary
globalisation
globalization
geotactically
good afternoon
global village
global warming
geoscientific
Giordano Bruno
glow discharge
goose-barnacle
geotechnology
grotesqueness
geometric mean
geometrically
globetrotting
go over the edge
geocentricism
goose-stepping
go off the rails
George Alagiah
Georgia O'Keefe
George Bentham
George Chapman
George Cadbury
George Canning
George Clooney
George Eastham
George Eastman
George Foreman
George Gissing
George Herbert
Georg Simon Ohm
George Michael
George Macbeth
George Mallory
Giorgio Vasari
Giorgio Armani
Georges Danton
George S Patton
Georges Seurat
Georges Claude
Georges Braque
George Thomson
George Wickham
George Wishart
Giorgiy Zhukov
geochemically
geochronology
glorification
Grotian theory
Gloria Swanson
Gloria Steinem
good-King-Henry
grow like Topsy
goodman's croft
ground-angling
ground control
groin-centring
ground moraine
groaning board
ground-officer
goodness of fit
good-naturedly
grown-junction
geopolitician
geomorphogeny
geomorphology
group marriage
group practice
group dynamics
geotropically
gross earnings
grouse-disease
gross register
glossographer
glossological
good Samaritan
go out of the way
growth hormone
geostationary
globuliferous
Gerhard Berger
Gerhard Domagk
Germanisation
Germanization
Garda Siochana
German measles
Germaine Greer
Germanophilia
German Requiem
garnetiferous
garden village
garden warbler
garnisheement
garlic mustard
Gerald Durrell
Gerald Kaufman
girdle of Venus
gyromagnetism
gerund-grinder
gerontophobia
gerontophilia
gerontologist
gerontocratic
Gardner Murphy
Gordon Bennett
Girton College
Gareth Edwards
garrulousness
gerrymanderer
Gerry Rafferty
Garry Kasparov
Gerry Mulligan
Gustave Eiffel
Gustaf Fröding
gasteropodous
gas centrifuge
gesticulative
gesticulation
gesticulatory
go someone's way
gas and gaiters
gastrocnemius
gastroenteric
gastrological
gastronomical
go to any length
go the whole hog
go the whole way
gathering-peat
gathering-coal
go the distance
gather to a head
get the heave-ho
get the message
get the picture
Gothic Revival
Getúlio Vargas
get in on the act
get on one's bike
get into the act
get one's hand in
get one's kit off
get one's own way
gate of justice
get it together
ghubar numeral
Grumbletonian
Giuseppe Peano
Giuseppe Verdi
glutinousness
gluconeogenic
glucosinolate
goutte à goutte
gauntlet-guard
Gavin Hastings
governability
governess cart
Gavarnie Falls
governing body
give the needle
give the bucket
give to the dogs
give utterance
Gawain Douglas
go with the flow
Guy of Gisborne
glyphographic
glyphographer
gay liberation
glycosylation
glyptographic
glyptal resins
Gay-Lussac's law
heat exchanger
heave-offering
heaven forfend
heave the gorge
heave-shoulder
heaven-kissing
Heath-Robinson
hyalinisation
hyalinization
head over heels
headquartered
head restraint
heat-resistant
heads will roll
hear the last of
heartlessness
heat treatment
heart of hearts
healthfulness
heartsickness
heartbreaking
health service
heart-stricken
heart-stirring
health visitor
head-up display
heavy particle
heavy industry
heavy breather
heavy hydrogen
hybridisation
hybridization
hubristically
Hobson's choice
Hubert de Burgh
hibernisation
hibernization
habitableness
habitat module
hobby-horsical
heck and manger
hacking jacket
Ho Chi Minh City
Hector Berlioz
hide-and-go-seek
Hydrangeaceae
hydraulic jack
hydraulic belt
hydraulicking
hydraulically
hydrazoic acid
hydrarthrosis
hedge-marriage
hedge-accentor
hidden economy
hydropathical
hydromagnetic
hydrogenation
hydrocephalic
hydrocephalus
hydrometrical
hydromedusoid
hydrochloride
hydrokinetics
hydro-airplane
hydroelectric
hydrosomatous
hydrocracking
hydrostatical
hydrosulphide
hydrosulphite
hydroxylamine
hydrodynamics
haematogenous
haematologist
heebie-jeebies
haemodialysis
hieroglyphics
hieroglyphist
hierogrammate
haemorrhoidal
heels o'er gowdy
heels over head
high and mighty
High Constable
High-Churchism
High-Churchman
high explosive
high-explosive
high frequency
Hugh Gaitskell
Hugh Kingsmill
Highland dress
Highland dance
Highland fling
Highland Games
high-muck-a-muck
hygroscopical
hygrometrical
hagiographist
high priestess
high-stomached
high-water mark
high-watermark
highway patrol
Haile Selassie
H Rider Haggard
hair extension
height to paper
heir-portioner
Heinrich Barth
Heinrich Heine
Heinrich Hertz
hair-splitting
Heinz Sielmann
Heinz Holliger
hale and hearty
hole-and-corner
Holy Communion
Halicarnassus
holiday season
half-evergreen
Hollerith code
Hellenistical
Hildebrandism
helter-skelter
half-heartedly
Hilaire Belloc
holding ground
Holy Innocents
hole in the wall
hole-in-the-wall
helminthiasis
helminthology
holometabolic
Helena Kennedy
hold one's peace
heliometrical
hollow-hearted
heliotropical
Holyrood Abbey
helispherical
Holy Sepulchre
half-sovereign
hold to account
half the battle
Holothuroidea
hallucinative
hallucination
hallucinatory
Helmut Schmidt
humpback whale
hemicellulose
homochromatic
Hammerklavier
homoeomorphic
homoeroticism
home economics
home economist
homoeopathist
homoeothermic
homoeothermal
homogenetical
homoiothermal
homologically
homologoumena
humble-mouthed
Hamilton Smith
homiletically
homomorphosis
hemimetabolic
Hymenomycetes
human interest
hymenopterous
humane society
homeoteleuton
homeothermous
hemlock spruce
homeomorphism
homeomorphous
hemiparasitic
Hemerobaptist
Home Secretary
hemispherical
Homes and Ideas
homosexualism
homosexualist
homosexuality
homeward-bound
handbrake turn
hang by a thread
hang by the wall
hunger-marcher
hunger-striker
Henri Barbusse
hanging garden
hanging valley
hanging matter
Huntingdonian
hunting spider
hunting-ground
Henri Rousseau
hang in the wind
handkerchiefs
hanuman monkey
hundredweight
Honoré Daumier
honorifically
honorary canon
honoris gratia
Handsel Monday
Hang Seng index
hunt the letter
hang up one's hat
Henry Maudslay
honeydew melon
Henry Bessemer
Henry Beaufort
Henry Sidgwick
Henry Fielding
honeycomb-moth
Henry Steinway
Hook of Holland
heortological
haphazardness
heptasyllabic
hypocycloidal
hypocalcaemia
hypochondriac
hypochondrium
hyphenisation

hyphenization
hypoglycaemia
hypoglycaemic
hypomenorrhea
hypsophyllary
hypnotisation
hypnotization
hypno-analysis
hippopotamian
hypophosphite
hyperparasite
hypercalcemia
hypersarcosis
hyperactivity
hypervelocity
hypermetrical
hypermetropia
hypermetropic
hyperphysical
hyperphrygian
hyperlipaemia
hyperhidrosis
hyperglycemia
hypertrophied
hypertrophous
hypercritical
hyperesthesia
hyperesthetic
hypersthenite
hypereutectic
hyposulphuric
hypothecation
happy families
happy dispatch
here and yonder
hare and hounds
hermaphrodite
Herod the Great
hard disk drive
horse mackerel
horsehair worm
horseman's word
Harvey Cushing
hermeneutical
horsefeathers
Harlech Castle
horseshoe crab
horseshoe arch
horse chestnut
hermetic books
horse-sickness
horse-milliner
horseflesh ore
horse-and-buggy
Horse and Hound
herpetophobia
herpetologist
horse-wrangler
harness racing
herpes simplex
harden the neck
Herbert Hoover
harvest spider
harvest supper
horse mushroom
harlequin duck
Herefordshire
Hertfordshire
hard-heartedly
hurricane lamp
hurricane deck
heroic couplet
Herbie Hancock
horrification
horripilation
herniorrhaphy
Harriet Harman
Harriet Tubman
horticultural
hard-luck story
Harold Clurman
Harold Larwood
Harold Robbins
Harold Shipman
hard of hearing
harmonisation
harmonization
herborisation
herborization
harmonic minor
harmonic range
harmonic triad
harbour master
Harlow Shapley
hard radiation
hardshell clam
haruspication
heresiologist
heresiography
Horatio Nelson
her number is up
Hercule Poirot
Horyuji Temple
Haroun Tazieff
here we go again
Hertzian waves
horizontal bar
horizontality
Hassan al-Banna
hysteranthous
Hester Chapone
hospital trust
Hastings Banda
His Girl Friday
histiophoroid
histochemical
histrionicism
his number is up
hither and yond
Hottentot's god
hit the big time
hit the ceiling
hit the jackpot
Hutchinsonian
Hitchcock film
hatch coamings
hot-air balloon
Hattie Jacques
hot on the heels
hit one's stride
hit rock bottom
hot gospelling
heteroblastic
heteroclitous
heterochronic
heterocarpous
heterogametic
heterogeneity
heterogeneous
heterogenesis
heterogenetic
heteromorphic
heteroplastic
heteropterous
heterosporous
heterostrophy
heterostylism
heterostylous
heterothallic
heterothermal
heterotrophic
hound-trailing
house of refuge
house of prayer
House of States
housewifeship
housewifeskep
housemistress
household word
household gods
housebreaking
housing scheme
housing estate
heuristically
have a basinful
have a thin skin
have a time of it
have a big mouth
have a good mind
have a good time
have first call
have had its day
have half a mind
have itchy feet
have it one's way
have no time for
have one's eye on
have the wind up
have the jump on
Hawley Crippen
Hawaiian goose
howling monkey
Howard Hodgkin
hexactinellid
hexadactylous
Heysel Stadium
hazardousness
inaudibleness
image orthicon
image printing
inanimateness
imaginariness
imaginatively
Itatinga Falls
italicisation
italicization
Italian garden
Italian millet
Italian sonnet
Italic version
in all fairness
in a cleft stick
Isadora Duncan
inappreciable
inappreciably
inappropriate
inattentively
inadvertently
in anyone's book
incrementally
incredibility
incredulously
inclinational
inclinatorium
inclined plane
itching powder
incriminating
incrimination
incriminatory
incompatibles
incompetently
in competition
incommiscible
incompossible
incomes policy
income support
incommunicado
incombustible
incombustibly
incantational
inconsciently
incandescence
inconvenience
incondensable
inconversable
incontestable
inconvertible
incontestably
inconvertibly
inconsecutive
in consequence
inconsequence
incense-burner
inconceivable
inconceivably
inconvincible
inconsiderate
incontinently
inconsistence
inconsistency
inconsonantly
inconspicuous
incongruently
incongruously
inconstruable
in contumaciam
in conjunction
incurableness
incarceration
incorrectness
incardination
incorporative
incorporating
incorporation
incorporeally
incuriousness
in circulation
incorruptible
incorruptibly
incorruptness
incessantness
inclusiveness
in countenance
Indian buffalo
Indianisation
Indianization
Indian tobacco
inductiveness
induction coil
induction port
indoctrinator
indifferently
indefatigable
indefatigably
indigo bunting
indigo carmine
indelibleness
indentureship
induplication
independently
indiscernible
indiscernibly
indispensable
indispensably
indistinctive
indistinction
indisciplined
indissociable
indisposition
indissolvable
industrialise
industrialize
industrialism
industrialist
indescribable
indescribably
industriously
indissuadable
indissuadably
indeterminate
indeterminacy
indeterminism
indeterminist
individualise
individualize
individualism
individuation
individualist
individuality
index verborum
index learning
index-tracking
index auctorum
Iceland falcon
inegalitarian
inelaborately
ineffableness
inefficacious
inefficiently
ineffectively
ineffectually
ideographical
Isenheim Altar
inexhaustible
inexhaustibly
inevitability
ineligibility
ideologically
inexorability
inexplainable
inexpectation
inexpediently
inexpressible
inexpressibly
inexpensively
inexperienced
inerrableness
identic action
identicalness
ineducability
ineludibility
infeasibility
infraposition
infraspecific
in facie curiae
infectiveness
inflexibility
inflexionless
inflexionally
in full feather
infill housing
infallibilism
infallibilist
infallibility
infima species
infundibulate
infinite canon
infinitesimal
infinitivally
inflorescence
informatively
infuriatingly
informatician
informational
inferentially
influx control
influenceable
influentially
infructuously
infix notation
Ingmar Bergman
ingravescence
in gremio legis
in great demand
Ingrid Bergman
ingeniousness
ingenuousness
ingurgitation
Ichthyosauria
ichthyosaurus
ichthyologist
ichthyopsidan
inhomogeneity
inhomogeneous
in honour bound
inharmonicity
inhospitality
imitativeness
iris diaphragm
inimitability
idiomatically
idiorrhythmic
in its entirety
idiosyncratic
injudiciously
injury benefit
injuriousness
ink-jet printer
ill-favouredly
Illecebraceae
Isla Contadora
illocutionary
ill-temperedly
illegibleness
illogicalness
illuminations
island-hopping
Island of Kauai
✧inland revenue
in-line skating
ill-considered
Isles of Scilly
illusionistic
illustriously
illustrissimo
inlet manifold

ill-humouredly
immediateness
Immelmann turn
in malam partem
immunifacient
immunological
immunotherapy
immarcescible
immersion lens
immersion foot
immiscibility
immutableness
ismaticalness
immaterialise
immaterialize
immaterialism
immaterialist
immateriality
immovableness
Ionian Islands
innocuousness
Iannis Xenakis
ignominiously
iontophoresis
iontophoretic
Inner Hebrides
inner-directed
innovationist
innoxiousness
isobarometric
inoperability
Isobel Baillie
in one's element
isomerisation
isomerization
in one's own time
isometric line
isometrically
isogeothermic
isogeothermal
inofficiously
inoffensively
isoagglutinin
inorganically
isochronously
isodimorphism
isodimorphous
isoelectronic
iconomaticism
inodorousness
inopportunely
inopportunity
inobservation
in on the secret
isostatically
inobtrusively
inoculability
isocyanic acid
implacability
impracticable
impracticably
impractically
impeccability
impacted tooth
impecuniosity
impecuniously
impact printer
impreciseness
✧impressionism
✧impressionist
imprest system
impignoration
implicatively
implicational
in point of fact
impalpability
impulse buying
impulsiveness
impoliticness
impolitically
imponderables
impenetration
improbability
improvability
improvisation
improvisatory
improvisatrix
improvidently
impropriation
impermanently
imperialistic
imperial pound
imperseverant
imperceptible
imperfectible
imperceptibly
imperfectness
impertinently
impartibility
impercipience
impartialness
impermissible
impermissibly
import licence
impersonalise
impersonalize
imperforation
impersonation
impersonality
imperiousness
in perspective
imparipinnate
impurity level
importunately
imperturbable
imperturbably
impassability
impassiveness
impossibilism
impossibilist
impassibility
impossibility
impassionedly
imposing stone
imposing table
impostumation
imputableness
it pitieth them
impetuousness
inquisitively
inquisitional
inquisitorial
irreclaimable
irreclaimably
irrecognition
irreciprocity
irrecoverable
irrecoverably
irredeemables
Israel in Egypt
irrefrangible
irrefrangibly
irreligionist
irreligiously
irreplaceable
irreplaceably
irrepleviable
irrepressible
irrepressibly
in rerum natura
iure sanguinis
irresponsible
irresponsibly
irritableness
irretrievable
irretrievably
irrationalise
irrationalize
irrationalism
irrationalist
irrationality
irreverential
instant camera
instantiation
instant replay
instantaneity
instantaneous
insubordinate
insubstantial
insociability
insectivorous
insectologist
insidiousness
inspectorship
insufficience
insufficiency
insignificant
instigatingly
inspirational
instinctively
instinctivity
instinctually
inspiritingly
institutively
institutional
insolvability
insolubleness
in some measure
in so many words
insensateness
insinuate into
insinuatingly
insensitively
insensibility
insensitivity
It's Now or Never
in short supply
It's Not Unusual
insupportable
insupportably
instructively
instructional
inscriptively
inscriptional
insusceptible
insusceptibly
insatiateness
insatiability
intravasation
intravascular
intracavitary
intranational
intraparietal
intracapsular
intrapetiolar
intracellular
intravenously
intrathecally
intraspecific
intra-arterial
intransigeant
intransigence
intransigency
intramuscular
in the same boat
in the majority
in the fast lane
in the nature of
in the abstract
in the short run
in the wind's eye
in the pipeline
in the smallest
in the wrong box
integrability
integumentary
intricateness
intuitiveness
intrinsically
intellectuals
intelligencer
intelligently
Isthmian Games
intemperately
intensive care
intensiveness
intangibility
intensionally
intentionally
iatrogenicity
introversible
iatrochemical
introspective
introspection
introgression
intercalative
intercalation
intergalactic
interlacement
interlanguage
interlaminate
interracially
interradially
✧international
interparietal
interrail pass
intermarriage
internal rhyme
interjaculate
interactively
interactivity
interactional
interoceptive
interscapular
interrelation
intermetallic
interferingly
interpetiolar
intermediator
intercellular
interpellator
interferogram
interpersonal
interdentally
interjectural
interpilaster
intersidereal
interdigitate
intermittence
intermittency
interior angle
interpolative
interrogative
interlocation
interpolation
interrogation
interrogatory
interior grate
interposition
intercommunal
intercolonial
intercostally
interlocution
intercolumnar
interlocutory
interlocutrix
interspecific
interoperable
interspersion
interbreeding
intertropical
intercropping
interpretable
interpretress
interproximal
interest group
interestingly
interosculate
interosculant
interstratify
interstellary
interlunation
interpunction
intercurrence
interruptible
interruptedly
Into the Groove
into the ground
intrusiveness
intown multure
in utroque iure
invidiousness
involucellate
involuntarily
inventiveness
invendibility
invincibility
inventorially
in vino veritas
inviolateness
inviolability
invariability
inverted pleat
invertibility
invisibleness
investigative
investigation
investigatory
Ilya Prigogine
if you don't mind
Itzhak Perlman
Jean Fragonard
Jean Froissart
Jean-Luc Godard
Juan Luis Vivés
Jean Paul Getty
Jean Paul Marat
Job's comforter
job evaluation
Jacobinically
Jacob Sprenger
jack-crosstree
Jackie Stewart
Jack Nicholson
Jack Teagarden
Jack the Ripper
Jacques Necker
Jacques Chirac
Jacques Copeau
judiciousness
judge advocate
judgement-hall
judgement-debt
judgement-seat
judgementally
Judaistically
Judas-coloured
Judas Iscariot
Jedburgh Abbey
jee one's ginger
Jefferson City
Jeffrey Archer
juglandaceous
jogger's nipple
jiggery-pokery
John Broadwood
John Bessarion
John Constable
John Churchill
John de Balliol
John Dillinger
John Dankworth
John Dos Passos
Johne's disease
John Flamsteed
John H Northrop
John Jacob Abel
John Lee Hooker
John McCormack
John Malkovich
John Masefield
Johnny H Mercer
Johann Strauss
John Steinbeck
Johnsonianism
Jailhouse Rock
jointed cactus
jointing plane
Jekyll and Hyde
Julie Burchill
jellification
jollification
Jules Laforgue
Jules Massenet
Jules Michelet
Jules Poincaré
Julius Axelrod
Julius Nyerere
Jamaica pepper
jumping spider
Jim Crow school
James Naughtie
James Hanratty
James Melville
James Chadwick
James Christie

Words marked ✧ can also be spelled with one or more capital letters

James Mirrlees
James Knox Polk
James Bond film
Jamestown weed
James Brindley
James Stanhope
James Stirling
James Buchanan
Jemmy Twitcher
Jennifer Lopez
junk jewellery
jingling match
Jan Ingen-Housz
junior college
junior service
Jonathan Swift
June Whitfield
jenny-long-legs
janizary music
Japanese cedar
Japanese maple
Japanese paper
Jupiter's beard
jequirity bean
juridical days
Jeremy Bentham
Jeremy Guscott
Jerome K Jerome
jargonisation
jargonization
jury of matrons
Jaroslav Hasek
Jerusalem sage
Jerusalem pony
jurisprudence
Jerry Rawlings
Jerry Lee Lewis
Jerry Seinfeld
jerry-building
Jasper Carrott
Jascha Heifetz
justificative
justification
justificatory
Joseph Andrews
Joseph Addison
Joseph Brodsky
Joseph Chaikin
Joseph Rotblat
Josip Broz Tito
Joseph Surface
Just So Stories
Just Seventeen
just think of it
jet propulsion
jeune première
jeunesse dorée
journal intime
journal proper
journey-weight
juvenile court
Jewel Mountain
jow one's ginger
jaw-breakingly
jaw-droppingly
juxtaposition
khaki election
kick one's heels
kick the bucket
kick up a shindy
Kodiak Islands
kidney machine
Kidderminster
keen as mustard
keep good hours
keep one's end up
keep one's eye in
keep one's eye on
keep open house
keep to oneself
✧kletterschuhe
keep your end up
Kailasa Temple
knight marshal
Knight of Malta
knights errant
knight service
knick-knackery
✧knickerbocker
Kaieteur Falls
Ku Klux Klanner
Killiecrankie
kaleidoscopic
Kenyapithecus
kangaroo-apple
kangaroo court
kangaroo grass
kangaroo mouse
kangaroo-thorn
Ken Barrington
Kangchenjunga
kindergärtner
Kenneth Kaunda
Kenneth Clarke
Kennelly layer
kind-heartedly
King Henry VIII
kindly-natured
kinematically
kinematograph
King of Navarre
✧king of terrors
kinesiologist
kinesipathist
kinesitherapy
King's evidence
kinetic theory
kinetic energy
Kentucky Derby
Kenny Dalglish
know inside out
knock sideways
knock-on effect
knock together
knock spots off
knockout drops
knowledge base
knowledgeable
knowledgeably
know one's place
know one's stuff
know what's what
kapellmeister
Kirkcudbright
Kornelia Ender
kermes mineral
Kirkintilloch
Kara Kum Desert
Karl Lagerfeld
Karl von Frisch
kiss and make up
kiss-and-make-up
kissing-comfit
kissing cousin
kiss-in-the-ring
kist o' whistles
kissogram girl
kittenishness
Kate Greenaway
kitchen garden
kitchen Kaffir
kitchen scales
kitchen physic
kitchen midden
kitchen police
kittly-benders
kettledrummer
kitty-cornered
Kyung-Wha Chung
knuckleballer
knuckle-headed
knuckleduster
Knud Rasmussen
keyhole limpet
Kazuo Ishiguro
lead by the nose
leave one's mark
Leaves of Grass
leave it at that
Loaghtan sheep
loathsomeness
leatherjacket
leather-winged
leather-lunged
leasing-making
Leamington Spa
leap in the dark
learning curve
lead-out groove
lead poisoning
labialisation
labialization
librarianship
labefactation
La Belle Hélène
la Belle Époque
labor improbus
labyrinthical
labyrinth fish
labyrinthitis
laboriousness
liberationism
liberationist
liberty bodice
lackadaisical
Leclanché cell
lucrativeness
lickerishness
lichenologist
lecherousness
lectisternium
lick into shape
local variable
local preacher
locum tenentes
Licence to Kill
lycanthropist
licentia vatum
lactobacillus
lick one's chops
lactoglobulin
lacrosse stick
Lycopodiaceae
lachrymal vase
lachrymal duct
Lecythidaceae
Lyceum Theatre
✧lady bountiful
ludicrousness
ladies dancing
ladies' fingers
ladies' gallery
lodgepole pine
ladies' tresses
lady-in-waiting
Lady of Shalott
Lady's bedstraw
laesa majestas
Liebfraumilch
Liechtenstein
lie on one's oars
lied ohne worte
laevorotation
laevorotatory
lie by the heels
life assurance
left-hand drive
left-handiness
lifting-bridge
life insurance
life-preserver
life-rendering
life scientist
lift the lid off
left ventricle
la Grande Armée
le Grand Siècle
lag of the tides
logographical
lignification
legal capacity
Legion of Merit
logarithmical
legislatively
legislatorial
light-headedly
light of nature
light-fingered
lightning-tube
light emission
light infantry
light industry
lightsomeness
light horseman
lighthouseman
light-spirited
Leicester plan
leishmaniases
leishmaniasis
leishmanioses
leishmaniosis
Leibnizianism
laissez-passer
leisure centre
leisureliness
Leipzig option
Lake Constance
like clockwork
like grim death
Lake Maracaibo
Lake Nicaragua
Lake Neuchâtel
Lillie Langtry
lollipop woman
lily of the Nile
Lombard Street
lampadephoria
lemmatisation
lemmatization
Lambeth degree
lymphadenitis
lymphatically
lymphotrophic
Lemnian ruddle
Lamellicornia
lamellibranch
lemon geranium
lemon-coloured
lemon squeezer
luminous paint
Lamarckianism
Le Misanthrope
limitlessness
linearisation
linearization
longcase clock
long-descended
Lansdowne Club
lance sergeant
line-engraving
lantern pinion
lance corporal
linsey-woolsey
line-fisherman
Lonnie Donegan
landing-ground
linolenic acid
land-measuring
line of country
lend oneself to
land-ownership
long-suffering
long-sightedly
lunisolar year
land-surveying
lunatic fringe
lunatic asylum
Long Tall Sally
lingue franche
lingua francas
languishingly
linguistician
linguistic map
loosehead prop
Lionel Hampton
Lionel Robbins
Leonhard Euler
look in the face
lion's provider
Lepidodendron
lepidopterist
lepidopterous
Lepidostrobus
lipogrammatic
lip microphone
leptocephalic
leptocephalus
leptophyllous
leptospirosis
lupus vulgaris
liposculpture
lapsus linguae
liquid crystal
liquidus curve
liquorice-vine
liquorishness
Lord Beveridge
Lord Callaghan
Lord Churchill
large bindweed
Lord Grenville
Lord knows what
Lord Kitchener
Lord Macdonald
laryngectomee
laryngoscopic
laryngologist
Lord of Misrule
Lord of Session
Lord President
Lord Privy Seal
Lord Parkinson
Lord Robertson
Lords Temporal
Lord Sainsbury
lords a-leaping
Lords Ordinary
Lord Voldemort
Lord Zuckerman
Last Christmas
listenability
listed company
listening post
Lester Piggott
Les Miserables
Les Misérables
Leslie Edwards
Leslie Scarman
Lasiocampidae
lose one's nerve
lose one's place
lose one's shirt
lissotrichous
les grands vins
lethargically
Lytham St Anne's
Luther Burbank
letter-carrier
letter-founder
letter-heading
letter missive
lithesomeness
Letter of James
letter of peace
letter-perfect
letter quality
letter-quality
letters patent
Letters of John
litigiousness
latchkey child
latch follower
lattice-girder
lattice window
lattice energy
lattice-bridge
lithification
luteinisation
luteinization
Little Bighorn
little masters
little penguin
Little Richard
Little Russian
little theatre
Latin American

lithotriptist
lithontriptic
lithontriptor
Lateran Treaty
literary agent
lotus position
latitudinally
leucaemogenic
leukaemogenic
launching-ways
launch vehicle
Laurent Fabius
laughableness
laughing hyena
laughing stock
leucitohedron
leuco-compound
leuko-compound
Louis MacNeice
Louis Daguerre
Louis-Philippe
Louis Sullivan
Louis-Quatorze
lauryl alcohol
Live and Let Die
Livia Drusilla
live cartridge
live like a lord
level crossing
lavender water
Levant morocco
livery company
lever de rideau
liver-coloured
lever arch file
livery-servant
lavatory paper
Lawrence Bragg
Lawrence Oates
low level waste
low technology
low-technology
law of identity
law of averages
low-mindedness
low side window
Law Commission
lawn-sprinkler
lexicographic
lexicographer
lexicological
lexigraphical
lex non scripta
luxuriousness
lay in lavender
lay on the table
lay down the law
lay by the heels
lozenge-shaped
meaninglessly
moaning minnie
mealie pudding
meadow foxtail
meadow saffron
mean solar time
meals on wheels
measurability
measured block
measure swords
measuring-tape
measuring-worm

mobile library
mechanisation
mechanization
Michael Gambon
Michael Manley
Michael Ramsay
Michael of Kent
Michael Bishop
Michael Clarke
Michael Howard
Michael Jordan
Michael Powell
Michael Doohan
mycobacterium
Michela Figini
mackerel guide
mackerel midge
mackerel shark
machinability
machine-pistol
machine-tooled
machinegunned
machine-gunner
mockingthrush
machicolation
Machiavellism
Machiavellian
microwaveable
microwave oven
microcassette
macrodactylic
macroeconomic
microeconomic
microscopical
microdetector
macrocephalic
microcephalic
micrometrical
microfelsitic
microphyllous
microphysical
microfilament
microfilariae
macropinakoid
micropipettes
macrodiagonal
microlighting
macroglobulin
microclimatic
microanalysis
microtonality
macromolecule
microcosmical
microporosity
microcomputer
micro-organism
microcracking
microprinting
microgranitic
microsurgical
macronutrient
micronutrient
macaronically
muckspreading
Mick the Miller
Much the Miller
mycotoxicosis
mediatisation
mediatization
mediatorially
mid-ocean ridge

medicamentary
medicine chest
medicine woman
Medieval Latin
medieval modes
mid-life crisis
midnight feast
Middle America
middle article
middle-bracket
muddle-brained
middlebreaker
Middle England
Middle English
Middle-Eastern
Middle Kingdom
middle passage
Middlesbrough
muddle through
Middle Western
Madame de Staël
mad cow disease
Modern English
modernisation
modernization
moderate a call
moderatorship
Madison Avenue
modus operandi
made to measure
✧mediterranean
meditate about
Madhur Jaffrey
Midsummer's Day
midsummer moon
Madhya Pradesh
mnemotechnics
mnemotechnist
meet one's maker
Magdalene Mary
magnanimously
migrant worker
magna cum laude
megacephalous
magic mushroom
magic cylinder
magnetisation
magnetization
magnetic board
magnetic chuck
magnetic field
magnetic fluid
magnetic media
magnetic north
magnetic poles
magnetic storm
magnetomotive
magnetosphere
magneto-optics
megaherbivore
magnification
magnificently
magniloquence
megalopolitan
megalosaurian
Maginot-minded
magnoliaceous
magisterially
megasporangia
megastructure
might-have-been

magazine-rifle
Muhammad Iqbal
Muhammad's Tomb
maiden century
maiden herring
maiden-tongued
maiden-widowed
maid of all work
maid-of-all-work
maison de ville
meibomian cyst
maids a-milking
mainstreaming
mainstreeting
Meistersinger
Major Mitchell
Major Dick Hern
major interval
major prophets
make a fast buck
make an issue of
Mikhail Glinka
Mikhail Suslov
make a good meal
make a good fist
make a long nose
make a monkey of
make a wry mouth
make first base
make foul water
Mike Hawthorne
Mike Hazelwood
make it strange
Mt Kilimanjaro
make mincemeat
make merry over
make no bones of
make one's lucky
make sparks fly
make the rounds
make things hum
malabsorption
malacological
milk chocolate
maliciousness
malacophilous
malacostracan
melodramatise
melodramatize
melodramatics
melodramatist
maladminister
milk-dentition
melodiousness
maladroitness
maladaptation
maladjustment
mallemaroking
malleableness
millefeuilles
Miller indices
maldeployment
millennianism
millenniarism
millennialist
millennium bug
mulberry-faced
Malthusianism
multicamerate
multicapitate

multiramified
multiracially
multinational
multipartyism
multicellular
milling cutter
Malpighiaceae
multifilament
mellification
mollification
multilinguist
multidigitate
multivibrator
multiskilling
multiplicable
multiplicator
mellifluently
multiple fruit
mellifluously
multiple store
multiply words
millionairess
multipolarity
multicoloured
multilobulate
multiloculate
multiloquence
multipresence
multigravidae
multigravidas
multi-authored
multitudinary
multitudinous
multinucleate
multicultural
male menopause
melanochroous
melancholious
Mull of Kintyre
Malcolm Morley
Malcolm Fraser
milk of sulphur
Mildred Pierce
malariologist
Milesian tales
Melastomaceae
✧millstone grit
Myles Standish
military cross
military medal
molluscicidal
multum in parvo
Milovan Djilas
mammaliferous
mummification
momentariness
momentousness
moment of truth
memorableness
membrum virile
memory manager
memory mapping
membranaceous
man-management
mental cruelty
manganese spar
manganiferous
mental patient
Mt Nyamuragira
mind-blowingly
Manichaeanism

Menachem Begin
mint condition
monochromatic
monochromator
monocotyledon
monodactylous
mine detection
Mandelbrot set
minced collops
Manuel de Falla
mind-expanding
Montepulciano
montes veneris
Man of La Mancha
manufacturing
Mansfield Park
man of the cloth
man of the match
man of the world
man of his hands
manifold-paper
manifestative
manifestation
man of business
mini flyweight
monographical
manageability
monogrammatic
managerialism
managerialist
Man with a Glove
mundificative
mundification
monomolecular
minimum weight
monumentality
monometallism
monometallist
mononucleosis
meningococcic
meningococcal
meningococcus
mangold-wurzel
Mindoro Island
Monmouthshire
Monopoly money
manipulatable
monopsonistic
monophthongal
✧monophysitism
miner's anaemia
Monarchianism
monarchically
mineral tallow
mineralogical
mineral alkali
mineral spring
minor interval
minor prophets
minority group
mini-submarine
many-sidedness
ministerially
monosyllabism
monosymmetric
monostrophics
monothalamous
monotrematous
✧monotheletism
✧monothelitism
monotelephone

monstrousness
monitor lizard
mensurability
Manny Shinwell
money-spinning
money-grubbing
moon blindness
Maori side-step
moonlight flit
mops and brooms
map projection
marmalade plum
marmalade tree
Maria Walliser
mermaid's glove
mermaid's purse
Margaret Court
Margaret Tudor
Morgan Freeman
Mercalli scale
mortal-staring
mercantile law
mirabile dictu
miracle-monger
meridionality
mercenariness
marketability
Marcel Duchamp
Marie de Médici
market economy
Marie de France
marketisation
marketization
mercerisation
mercerization
martello tower
Marcel Marceau
murder mystery
myrmecologist
murderousness
market profile
murder will out
marsh marigold
marsh-samphire
mirthlessness
morphographer
morphogenesis
morphogenetic
morphological
morphemically
merchandising
merchandizing
morphinomania
morphophoneme
Merthyr Tydfil
morbid anatomy
Martina Hingis
Martin Bormann
Martin Brundle
morris dancing
mercilessness
marriage-lines
morning prayer
mortification
martial artist
morbillivirus
marsipobranch
Marek's disease
mural painting
moral majority
morale-booster
marble-hearted
moral theology
Marilyn Monroe
morello cherry
Myrtle Simpson
Mary Lou Retton
Mary Magdalene
marine trumpet
Merton College
Margot Fonteyn
Mare Orientale
mirror machine
Mario Andretti
marrons glacés
mirror writing
mariposa tulip
Myristicaceae
Morisonianism
Moreton Bay fig
meritoriously
Moritz Schlick
marquee player
mercurialness
marsupial mole
Mercurochrome®
Marquis de Sade
Marquis Curzon
mercury switch
martyrisation
martyrization
martyrologist
mismanagement
mescal buttons
Massachusetts
✧missa solemnis
moshav shitufi
misobservance
music mistress
musicological
musical chairs
musical comedy
mesocephalism
mesocephalous
musicotherapy
misadvertence
misadventured
misadventurer
master aircrew
master-builder
masked battery
misperception
miscegenation
masterfulness
messenger-wire
mesmerisation
mesmerization
Mister Jaggers
miscellaneous
Master McGrath
master-mariner
master-passion
mispersuasion
Messerschmitt
masters-at-arms
Mister Wemmick
mystery-monger
mischief-maker
mischievously
misshapenness
mosaic disease
Missing the Sea
mystification
mashie-niblick
Mission Indian
mastigophoric
mastigophoran
Mississippian
muscle-reading
misemployment
mass-marketing
mesencephalic
mesencephalon
misunderstand
misunderstood
misanthropist
misconception
misgovernment
misconjecture
miscomprehend
mess of pottage
miscorrection
Missouri River
misappreciate
miserableness
mushroom cloud
misproportion
mistrustfully
mistrustingly
Moses and Aaron
mesaticephaly
muscular sense
masculineness
mutualisation
mutualization
mutual mistake
methanoic acid
metabolically
metabolisable
metabolizable
metacognition
mitochondrial
mitochondrion
metachromatic
Mother and Baby
mathematicise
mathematicize
mathematicism
mathematician
mother country
Mother Hubbard
mother-of-pearl
Mother Shipton
metafictional
metagrabolise
metagrabolize
metagrobolise
metagrobolize
matched sample
matchlessness
matchboarding
Matthew Parker
Matthew Arnold
metrification
matrilineally
matrifocality
matrilocality
matrimonially
matrix printer
matriculation
matriculatory
Matti Nykaenen
metal detector
metallisation
metallization
metalliferous
metallography
metallurgical
metempiricism
metempiricist
metamerically
✧metamorphoses
✧metamorphosis
matinée jacket
metonymically
mutton-dummies
metronidazole
meteoriticist
Methodistical
meteorologist
methodologist
motion picture
meteor streams
mutton-thumper
metaphosphate
metoposcopist
metapsychical
metaphysician
material cause
materia medica
materfamilias
material issue
materialistic
maternalistic
mater dolorosa
motor-traction
mature student
metastability
methyl alcohol
methylene blue
mauvaise honte
mauvais moment
moulding board
mouse-eared bat
mouse-coloured
mouthwatering
mouthbreather
Maurice Béjart
Maurice Herzog
Maurice Allais
Maurice Greene
Mauritius hemp
maurikigusari
mourning-bride
mourning coach
mourning cloak
mourning piece
mourning-stuff
Mount Cameroon
mountebankery
mountebanking
mountebankism
Mount McKinley
Mount Vesuvius
Mount Kinabalu
mountain avens
Mount Pinatubo
mountain biker
mountain chain
mountain devil
mountain range
mountain sheep
mountains-high
mounting block
Mount Cotopaxi
Mount Krakatoa
Mount St Helens
Mount Rushmore
movement chart
moving average
moving walkway
mowing machine
mixed language
mixed marriage
mixed metaphor
mixed blessing
mixed foursome
mixed fraction
myxoedematous
Maxwell's demon
maxillofacial
Max Horkheimer
Mayotte Island
Mazo De La Roche
muzzle-loading
mezzo-relievos
mezzo-rilievos
mezzo-sopranos
Mazarine Bible
mazarine plate
✧neanderthaler
Neapolitan ice
near-sightedly
noble crayfish
Nobel laureate
Nyctaginaceae
nectariferous
no-claims bonus
nickel-and-dime
nickeliferous
nucleon number
nickel-plating
nucleoprotein
nuclear family
nuclear sexing
nuclear weapon
nuclear charge
nuclear winter
nuclear energy
nuclear poison
nuclear fusion
Nick Farr-Jones
noctivagation
Nicolaus Steno
nick-nackatory
Nicholas Scott
necromantical
Nicholas Udall
necroscopical
neck or nothing
necessariness
necessitarian
necessitation
necessitously
nicotinic acid
nicotine patch
Nadia Comaneci
nodding donkey
node of Ranvier
needle-pointed
nefariousness
niggardliness
neglectedness
no great shakes
negligibility
Naguib Mahfouz
Nigella Lawson
night-warbling
night-watchman
nightmarishly
negotiability
Night of Ascent
nightclubbing
night-tripping
negative angle
no holds barred
no-holds-barred
nuisance value
Neil Armstrong
naive painting
noiselessness
neighbourless
neighbourhood
Nikkei average
nalidixic acid
nolle prosequi
nulli secundus
nullification
noli me tangere
noli-me-tangere
Nelson Mandela
Nelson's Column
numbers racket
nomographical
nymphaeaceous
nomenclatural
Naming of Parts
nominatively
numeric keypad
numerological
numismatology
nemathelminth
namby-pambical
namby-pambyish
namby-pambyism
non-parametric
non-carbonated
non-pathogenic
non-observance
non-accessible
non-scientific
non-acceptance
non-accidental
non-regardance
nondescriptly
non-resistance
non-negotiable
non-democratic
nonsensically
non-persistent
nonsense verse
non-returnable
non-aggression
non-biological
non-figurative
non-classified
non-infectious
non-concurrent
non-conclusive
non-conducting
non-forfeiting
nonconforming
✧nonconformist
nonconformity
non-collegiate
nannoplankton

non-commercial
non-cognizable
non-homologous
non-compliance
non-compounder
non-consenting
non-contagious
non-specialist
non-appearance
ninepenny marl
non-productive
non-production
non-proficient
non-attendance
nineteenth man
non-functional
non-fulfilment
non-judgmental
Nancy Kerrigan
Neo-Lamarckism
Neo-Lamarckian
Neo-Kantianism
Neo-Melanesian
neoliberalism
no oil painting
✧neoclassicism
Neo-Plasticism
neoplasticism
neoclassicist
neologistical
neogrammarian
nephelometric
nephrological
naphthylamine
Norman Borlaug
Norman Douglas
Norway haddock
normalisation
normalization
normativeness
Norway lobster
Norman Lockyer
Norman MacCaig
noradrenaline
nervelessness
Norwegian nest
Norwegian oven
nerve-wracking
Norbert Wiener
nursery cannon
nursery school
nursery slopes
nursery stakes
North Carolina
north-eastward
north-easterly
North Germanic
north-westward
north-westerly
North and South
North Somerset
Northern Crown
northerliness
North Atlantic
North Ayrshire
nursing-father
narrowcasting
narcotisation
narcotization
Norfolk jacket
Norfolk Island
Norfolk turkey
narcoanalysis
nervous system
narcohypnosis
nostalgically
Nasser Hussain
nose heaviness
nutraceutical
Netherlandish
not before time
nether regions
nothing patent
netting-needle
nitrification
nitwittedness
not on one's life
not on your life
nitroparaffin
National Front
National Guard
nationalistic
nitrobacteria
National Trust
not good enough
nitrogen cycle
nitro-compound
not worth a damn
nutcracker man
natural magnet
natural causes
natural resins
natural person
natural number
natural system
notoriousness
nature reserve
nature-worship
net asset value
native speaker
not by any means
neuraminidase
neural network
neurastheniac
Nouvelle Vague
nautical table
neurovascular
neuropathical
neurolinguist
neurofibromas
neuroblastoma
neurotoxicity
neurocomputer
neuroethology
neuromuscular
neurosurgical
neutral monism
neutron source
neutron poison
neutron number
navicular bone
novocentenary
Nevado del Ruiz
navigableness
navigation bar
never the wiser
Newgate fringe
newfangleness
new world order
Newton's cradle
New South Wales
New Grub Street
Newstead Abbey
new Australian
next to nothing
on a large scale
orange blossom
on a shoestring
oral hygienist
on a small scale
on approbation
oraculousness
Olbers' paradox
Osbert Sitwell
orbis terrarum
orbital engine
once and for all
occidentalise
occidentalize
Occidentalism
Occidentalist
orchesography
orchestration
orchestralist
orchidomaniac
orchidologist
oscilloscopic
oscillography
occipital bone
occipital lobe
Oscar Peterson
Oscar Niemeyer
occasionalism
occasionalist
occasionality
occluded front
once upon a time
ordnance datum
old campaigner
old age pension
old-age pension
Old Vic Theatre
old clothesman
ordinal number
Ordinary grade
Ordinary level
odd-come-shorts
✧old boy network
order of battle
order of the day
✧ondes Martenot
old as the hills
overambitious
operativeness
operating room
operationally
overabounding
overabundance
over-anxiously
overbearingly
over-breathing
overcredulity
overcredulous
over-confident
overdramatise
overdramatize
overdependent
overelaborate
overexcitable
open-endedness
over-emotional
overemphasise
overemphasize
over-exquisite
overflowingly
oreographical
overhead costs
open-heartedly
overhastiness
overindulgent
opening gambit
one-night stand
overinsurance
overmultitude
oleomargarine
Ocean of Storms
oceanographic
oceanographer
overnight case
oceanological
one's name is mud
one in a million
one's other half
one for the road
open-plan house
overqualified
oneiroscopist
overstatement
oversubscribe
oversensitive
over the wicket
overvaluation
overweeningly
offhandedness
olfactologist
officiousness
Office of Works
✧officer of arms
off-reckonings
offensiveness
off one's rocker
off one's stroke
off one's own bat
Oxford English
offer document
orgiastically
organogenesis
organotherapy
of good warrant
ophthalmology
ophiomorphous
ochlocratical
on her beam-ends
other-directed
otherworldish
olivary bodies
Oliver Mellors
Oliver Martext
Oliver Plunket
Olivia Manning
opinionatedly
orientational
oriental topaz
oligopolistic
on its last legs
opisthobranch
opisthography
on-job training
objectivation
objectiveness
objective test
objectivistic
objectionable
objectionably
object of virtu
object program
objets de vertu
objets trouvés
Orkney Islands
oil of lavender
oblique motion
oblique speech
Only the Lonely
obliviousness
omnibus clause
omnicompetent
on no condition
omnifariously
ornamentalism
ornamentation
ornamentalist
owner-occupied
owner-occupier
ornithischian
ornithichnite
ornithomantic
Ornitholestes
ornithophobia
ornithologist
obnoxiousness
Orobanchaceae
odonatologist
onomatopoesis
onomatopoetic
onomastically
Ojos del Salado
ozone-depleter
on one's own hook
ozone-friendly
odoriferously
ovoviviparity
ovoviviparous
omoplatoscopy
opossum shrimp
odontoglossum
odontological
odontophorous
odontornithes
Oh, Pretty Woman
oppignoration
opprobriously
opportuneness
opportunities
opportunistic
oppositionist
on Shanks's mare
on Shanks's pony
on shaky ground
obsecration by
oyster-catcher
oyster-fishery
obstetrically
obstinateness
observational
obstructively
obstructional
oestrous cycle
obsessiveness
obsessionally
optic thalamus
optical centre
octocentenary
on the pavement
on the face of it
of the same mind
on the safe side
ostreiculture
on the increase
on the long side
on the contrary
on the port beam
ostreophagous
outsettlement
on the strength
outrecuidance
outlet village
out of harm's way
out of the woods
out of one's head
out of one's mind
out of one's road
out of one's tree
out of training
out of question
ontogenically
obtainability
outside chance
out like a light
Otto Klemperer
ontologically
on tenterhooks
outing flannel
ostensiveness
ostensibility
out on one's feet
osteomalacial
orthopaedical
orthogenesist
osteopetrosis
orthopinakoid
orthodiagonal
orthosilicate
orthognathism
orthognathous
orthogonality
ortho-compound
outdoor relief
orthographist
orthostichous
osteomyelitis
Otto Preminger
outspokenness
outer garments
Outer Hebrides
otter-trawling
obtuse-angular
out at the elbow
outstandingly
obtrusiveness
octave coupler
opus operantis
Orville Wright
On Wenlock Edge
onychophagist
Ogygian deluge
o' my conscience
plagal cadence
phalansterism
phalansterian
phalansterist
play at wasters
planetary gear
peaceableness
peacelessness
peace offering
prayerfulness

peace dividend
prayer meeting
phanerogamous
placebo effect
planetologist
pease-porridge
plate-printing
play for safety
peach-coloured
play hard to get
pharisaically
plagiocephaly
planimetrical
praying mantis
praying insect
planing bottom
platiniferous
Plagiostomata
plagiostomous
pianississimo
pianistically
plagiotropism
plagiotropous
platinum black
platinum-blond
platitudinise
platitudinize
platitudinous
platinum metal
phallocentric
pearl-shelling
Praslin Island
pharmacognosy
pharmacopoeia
pharmaceutics
pharmaceutist
plasmodesmata
psammophilous
pragmatically
plain language
plaintiveness
prawn cocktail
plain speaking
play one's hunch
play one's prize
Platonic solid
Peacock Throne
peacock-flower
peacock copper
prairie grouse
prairie turnip
prairie oyster
plausibleness
practicalness
practical joke
practical arts
plastic bullet
play the wanton
plantie-cruive
plantain-eater
plant hormones
planter's punch
phantasmalian
phantasmality
platycephalic
platyhelminth
pharyngoscope
pharyngoscopy
platyrrhinian
public company
public holiday
public inquiry
public lecture
public opinion
public records
public servant
✧public trustee
public utility
pebble-glasses
Pablo Sarasate
pick and choose
pococurantism
pococurantist
pocket borough
pocket-picking
packet sniffer
packing-needle
pucciniaceous
pycnidiospore
pickle-herring
pectoral cross
pycnoconidium
pocas palabras
picture palace
picture window
picturesquely
pedicellariae
pedagogically
pidgin English
pudding-headed
pudding-sleeve
pidginisation
pidginization
paddle steamer
pedantocratic
podsolisation
podsolization
podzolisation
podzolization
Podostemaceae
pedestrianise
pedestrianize
pedestrianism
Paddy's lantern
preparatively
preparatorily
premandibular
prepared piano
Pre-Raphaelite
Pre-Raphaelism
prevarication
predatoriness
prefatorially
prefabricated
prefabricator
precautionary
prematureness
plenary powers
presbyacousis
presbytership
Pierce Brosnan
phencyclidine
prescientific
prescriptible
preoccupation
pseudo-archaic
plead the Fifth
preadolescent
pseudomonades
pseudomorphic
pre-adamitical
preadmonition
preadaptation
preferability
prefer charges
Pieter de Hooch
pretendership
predeterminer
premeditative
premedication
premeditation
preteriteness
predefinition
pretermission
pretermitting
preternatural
piece together
preterperfect
presentiality
predestinator
pretentiously
precentorship
preceptorship
preserving-pan
psephological
plethorically
predicate upon
predicamental
predicatively
predicability
presidentship
precipitately
precipitative
plebification
precipitation
preliminaries
preliminarily
precipitantly
precipitously
poetic justice
poetic licence
premillennial
pteridologist
plesiosaurian
paediatrician
prehistorical
prefigurative
prefiguration
prefigurement
plenitudinous
precious stone
phellogenetic
phelloplastic
pneumogastric
pneumonectomy
pneumatically
pneumatic tyre
pneumatolysis
pneumatolytic
pneumatometer
pneumatophore
pre-emptive bid
preambulatory
pre-engagement
pre-industrial
phenobarbital
prerogatively
piezomagnetic
preconception
preponderance
preponderancy
phenomenalise
phenomenalize
phenomenalism
phenomenalist
phenomenality
phenomenology
phenothiazine
preconisation
preconization
predomination
predominantly
premonishment
prepositively
prepositional
Piero di Cosimo
premonitorily
phenolic resin
piezoelectric
paedomorphism
prepossessing
prepossession
precopulatory
Pietro Aretino
preordainment
Pierre Balmain
Pierre Bonnard
preproduction
preprogrammed
preordination
Pierre Laplace
piecrust table
Pierre Trudeau
Pierre Vernier
press fastener
press of canvas
press the flesh
pressure cabin
pressure group
pleasure house
pressure point
pressure ridge
plentifulness
plectognathic
plenteousness
plectopterous
plenum chamber
prejudicative
prejudication
presuming that
prejudicially
presumptively
phenylalanine
phenylbenzene
pterygoid bone
pterylography
pigheadedness
pigeon-chested
pigeon-fancier
pigeon-hearted
pigeon-livered
Paget's disease
Peggy Ashcroft
private pay bed
private school
private sector
private income
Philadelphian
private treaty
privateersman
privatisation
privatization
plica Polonica
primatologist
peirastically
primal therapy
philanthropic
psilanthropic
primary school
primary planet
primary stress
prince consort
Prince Maurice
Prince of Peace
Prince of Wales
principalness
principalship
principal axis
princess dress
Princess Grace
princess royal
prices current
prime meridian
pricelessness
prime vertical
prizefighting
prime minister
paired reading
philhellenism
philhellenist
priming-powder
primitiveness
Philip Marlowe
poikilothermy
Philippine Sea
Philippe Sella
primigravidae
primigravidas
pain in the neck
Philip the Arab
prick-me-dainty
prick-the-louse
Phillips curve
Phillips screw®
Paisley design
prismatically
philomathical
prison-breaker
pair of bellows
pair of colours
primordialism
primordiality
primogenitary
primogenitive
primogenitrix
primogeniture
prisoner of war
prisoner's base
prisoners' base
Psilophytales
prison officer
philosophical
philosophiser
philosophizer
poisonousness
prison visitor
poisson d'avril
Poisson's ratio
pointlessness
point of honour
point-and-click
printing error
printing house
printing press
printing paper
pointing-stock
point-and-shoot
point for point
painter's colic
printer's devil
painters' putty
point mutation
pyjama cricket
piked position
poke one's bib in
polyadelphous
pulsating star
palpable-gross
pull a long face
pull a wry mouth
pelican-flower
police officer
polychromatic
polycarbonate
police station
polycythaemia
polecat-ferret
Palace Theatre
polycotyledon
polydactylism
polydactylous
polydaemonism
palaeobiology
palaeobotanic
polyembryonic
palaeoclimate
palaeocurrent
palaeocrystic
palaeoecology
pulselessness
palaeographic
palaeographer
palletisation
palletization
pelletisation
pelletization
pulverisation
pulverization
pulse dialling
palaeontology
Palaeotherium
palaeozoology
polygalaceous
polygonaceous
phlogisticate
Phlegethontic
polyhistorian
palmification
pollicitation
polliniferous
pile it on thick
Peltier effect
palm-kernel oil
Polemoniaceae
palingenesist
palynological
polynomialism
palindromical
poliomyelitis
Polypodiaceae
polyphloisbic
Peloponnesian
polyprotodont
polypropylene
polarographic
polar distance

pilgrim-bottle
pilgrim's shell
polar equation
Palestine soup
polysyllabism
polysyllogism
polysynthesis
polysynthetic
polythalamous
palatableness
polytechnical
pull the plug on
Pulitzer Prize
Palawan Island
pumped storage
pompier-ladder
Pamela Andrews
Pembrokeshire
pembroke table
pentadactylic
pancake make-up
pentadelphous
Pinball Wizard
panharmonicon
pentanoic acid
pineapple weed
Pineapple Poll
Pantagruelism
Pantagruelian
Pantagruelion
Pantagruelist
pentastichous
pentasyllabic
penicillinase
penicilliform
panic-stricken
panic stations
ponderability
panleucopenia
pink elephants
✧pandemoniacal
ponderousness
panaesthetism
Pan-Africanism
pinafore dress
pinafore skirt
panegyrically
pantheistical
penthemimeral
Punchinelloes
panchromatism
pantheologist
pencil-compass
pennilessness
pinking shears
pontificality
pantisocratic
Pontius Pilate
pandiculation
penalty corner
peninsularity
Peninsular War
pentobarbital
pinhole camera
pontoon bridge
panspermatism
panspermatist
panophthalmia
pendragonship
pangrammatist
penuriousness
punishability
panpsychistic
Pennsylvanian
penetratively
penetratingly
penetrability
pine-tree money
punctiliously
punctum caecum
penitentially
pendulousness
penny-farthing
penny-pinching
penny dreadful
prosaicalness
pro'd and conned
propaedeutics
probabilities
probabilistic
probable cause
probable error
protanomalous
propanoic acid
proparoxytone
phonautograph
proterandrous
promenade deck
proverbialise
proverbialize
proverbialism
proverbialist
proteoclastic
probe scissors
phonendoscope
phonetisation
phonetization
progenitorial
propeller-head
proteinaceous
propenoic acid
prolegomenary
prolegomenous
proterogynous
process-server
processionary
processioning
pooper-scooper
professoriate
professorship
proleptically
Protestantise
Protestantize
Protestantism
protectionism
projectionist
protectionist
protectorless
prosectorship
protectorship
profectitious
prosecutorial
prosecutrices
prosecutrixes
procès-verbaux
plough through
pro-chancellor
prophetically
prophet of doom
profitability
provincialise
provincialize
provincialism
provincialist
provinciality
promiscuously
proliferative
proliferation
Providence Bay
proliferously
promise-breach
proving flight
proving ground
prolification
providing that
prohibitively
provisionally
proximity fuse
propionic acid
profit-sharing
plonking great
people carrier
People in a Wind
problematical
People's Friend
pro-and-conning
prognosticate
protolanguage
provocatively
promotability
prosopagnosia
phonocamptics
protoactinium
photonegative
photoreceptor
photoperiodic
Paolo Veronese
photochemical
photochromism
photochromics
Protochordata
protochordate
photophoresis
propositional
proto-historic
photoelectric
photoelectron
photo-emission
pronounceable
pronouncement
protonotarial
protonotariat
Protococcales
photocopiable
photopositive
prosopopoeial
prosopography
photovoltaics
protospataire
phonographist
photographist
proconsulship
Prokop the Bald
proportionate
proportioning
Photostatting
prospect-glass
prospectively
prompt neutron
phosphoretted
phospholipase
phosphorylase
phosphorylate
phosphuretted
procreational
propraetorial
proprietorial
propraetorian
program trader
proprioceptor
procrastinate
progressively
progressivism
progressivist
progressional
prostaglandin
plotting-paper
prosthodontia
prostatectomy
prostate gland
procuratorial
pronunciation
protuberation
protuberantly
producer goods
producibility
production car
propyl alcohol
pepper-and-salt
poppering pear
peppermint tea
puppet theatre
popping crease
popping-crease
peptidoglycan
papilliferous
Papilionaceae
papillomatous
pipeless organ
Pepin the Short
peptonisation
peptonization
papaprelatist
paperhangings
paper nautilus
paper fastener
paper the house
paper mulberry
popeseye steak
papaveraceous
part and parcel
Pär Lagerkvist
per fas et nefas
permanent wave
pervasiveness
phreatophytic
Parnassianism
part brass rags
parabolically
parabolic arch
perichondrial
perichondrium
perscrutation
paradigm shift
paradoxically
parietal bones
parietal cells
porcelain clay
porcelaineous
perpendicular
perseveration
perseveringly
Port Elizabeth
pyrheliometer
Purbeck marble
porcellaneous
purse-snatcher
perfect market
perfect metals
perfect insect
perfectionate
perfectionism
✧perfectionist
perfect fourth
perfect square
perfect number
perfervidness
paraffin-scale
par of exchange
paragraph mark
paragraphical
peregrination
peregrinatory
perigastritis
parchment bark
perching birds
parthenocarpy
perihepatitis
purchase money
Per Lindstrand
parking ticket
porridge-stick
participative
participating
participation
participatory
participantly
participially
partition wall
perditionable
partitionment
parliamentary
parliamenting
parliament-man
Persian carpet
Persian blinds
Persian powder
parti-coloured
Parkinson's law
particularise
particularize
particularism
particularist
particularity
parallactical
purple boletus
parallelistic
parallel lines
parallelogram
purple emperor
parallel ruler
purple-in-grain
paraleipomena
Portland sheep
Portland stone
paralipomenon
paralysis time
perplexedness
pyramidically
paramagnetism
paramenstruum
pyrimethamine
perambulation
perambulatory
paramyxovirus
parental leave
parent company
parencephalon
parenthetical
perennibranch
phrenological
Pyrenomycetes
perinephritis
phrenetically
personal chair
personalistic
personal space
parrot disease
purposelessly
parrot-fashion
periodisation
periodization
periodicalist
purposiveness
periodic month
periodic table
period of grace
periodontitis
parlour tricks
perspicacious
perspectively
perspectivism
perspectivist
perspicuously
peripherality
paraphernalia
pyrophosphate
parapophysial
peripatetical
parapsychical
parapsychosis
partridge-wood
perishability
parish council
pyrosulphuric
parasynthesis
parasynthetic
parasyntheton
perissodactyl
phraseologist
parasitically
pyrotechnical
puritanically
perityphlitis
pyretotherapy
perttaunt like
Portulacaceae
portulan chart
perdurability
permutability
permutational
perfunctorily
porcupine fish
porcupine wood
porous plaster
percussion cap
percussionist
perlustration
parquet circle
perivitelline
port-wine stain
par excellence
party politics
party-coloured
party-spirited
Percy Grainger

passage of arms
postal service
push-button war
postclassical
Passchendaele
post-communion
poster colours
poste restante
passementerie
passenger-mile
posterisation
posterization
Passeriformes
post-existence
pusser's dagger
possessionate
possessionary
possessorship
poster session
pasigraphical
puss-gentleman
paschal candle
paschal flower
pestiferously
possibilities
pessimistical
passion flower
Passion Sunday
piscicultural
pass judgement
Pushkin Museum
pusillanimity
pusillanimous
postliminiary
postliminious
✧post-modernism
post-modernist
postman's knock
postmenstrual
pastoral staff
post-operative
post-office box
push-pull train
passport photo
post-traumatic
pass the parcel
push the bottle
post-tensioned
position paper
position ratio
push to the wall
positive angle
positive organ
postulational
posture-master
post-war credit
pe-tsai cabbage
phthalocyanin
put a cheat upon
put behind bars
potbellied pig
put a foot wrong
pitch-farthing
put the brake on
put the black on
pitched battle
pitched-roofed
put the lid on it
put the moves on
pitching wedge
patch together
put the skids on
pituitary body
petrification
patrilineally
Patrick Manson
Patrick Rafter
Patrick Meehan
Patrick Devlin
Patrick Swayze
patrifocality
patrimonially
patriotically
potamological
pit and gallows
put in the shade
put on the screw
put in the wrong
potential well
potentiometer
potentiometry
patent leather
put into effect
patent outside
put one's face on
put one's feet up
put one's mind to
pathogenicity
petroleum coke
put to the blush
petrochemical
petrophysical
put to the sword
put to the torch
put to the worse
petroliferous
patronisingly
patronizingly
petrol lighter
pathognomonic
Pythonomorpha
petrol station
petrocurrency
put a premium on
put upon points
put up one's hair
paterfamilias
paternalistic
paternity test
paternity suit
Pott's fracture
potato disease
petit déjeuner
put it together
potato pancake
put out of court
put out of sight
put out to grass
put out to nurse
Petty Sessions
putty-coloured
potty-training
pluralisation
pluralization
plural society
plumber's snake
plumbisolvent
plumbosolvent
pauperisation
pauperization
prudentialism
prudentialist
prudentiality
Paul Gascoigne
Paul Hindemith
pruning shears
pluripresence
Paul McCartney
Paul Tortelier
Paul Whitehead
pavement light
Peveril Castle
powder compact
powdered sugar
powdering-room
powdering-gown
powdery mildew
powered glider
powerlessness
power politics
power dressing
power-assisted
power steering
payback period
phylacterical
pay television
psychoanalyse
psychoanalyze
psychoanalyst
psychiatrical
psychobiology
psychodynamic
psychographic
psychogenesis
psychogenetic
psychohistory
psychokinesis
psychokinetic
psychological
psychometrics
psychometrist
psychrometric
psychrophilic
psychopathist
psychophysics
physharmonica
psychasthenia
psychosomatic
psychosurgery
psychotherapy
physical force
physical jerks
physiographic
physiographer
physiognomist
physitheistic
physicianship
physiological
physiotherapy
phyllophagous
phylloquinone
pay and display
pay-and-display
phylogenetics
phytochemical
payroll giving
phytoplankton
phytotoxicity
phycoerythrin
phytoestrogen
physostigmine
peyote buttons
quatch-buttock
Quaker-buttons
quaternionist
qualitatively
qualificative
qualification
qualificatory
quasi-contract
quality factor
quality of life
quality circle
quadricipital
quadrifoliate
quadrifarious
quatrefeuille
quadrigeminal
quadragesimal
quadrilocular
quadrillionth
quadrilingual
quarrelsomely
quadrilateral
quadriliteral
quadrumvirate
quadringenary
quadrennially
quadruple time
quadruplicate
quadruplicity
quadraphonics
quadrophonics
quadripartite
quadrisection
quadratic mean
quadrivalence
quartz crystal
quartodeciman
quartier latin
quartziferous
quantum meruit
quantum theory
quantum number
quant analysis
quartermaster
quarterdecker
quarter dollar
quarter-hourly
quarter-gunner
quantivalence
quenched spark
Queen's College
Queens' College
Queen's Counsel
queen's English
Queen of Heaven
Queen of the May
Queen's highway
Queensland nut
Queen Anne's War
queen's pudding
✧queen's proctor
queer the pitch
Quentin Massys
questioningly
questionnaire
question of law
querulousness
query language
quincentenary
quincuncially
quingentenary
quick-scenting
quick-tempered
quicksilvered
quick and dirty
quick-answered
quinquagenary
Quinquagesima
quinquevalent
quinquivalent
quintillionth
quilting-frame
quilting party
quintuplicate
Quintus Ennius
quizzing-glass
quota sampling
quotation mark
quoted company
quodlibetical
Rhadamanthine
reacclimatise
reacclimatize
rhabdomantist
Roald Amundsen
rhabdomyomata
Reader's Digest
reaffirmation
real gymnasium
realisability
realizability
reading matter
realistically
read like a book
road-metalling
RSA encryption
read oneself in
reapplication
reappointment
realpolitiker
reappropriate
rearrangement
rhapsodically
reattribution
reactionarism
reactionarist
Rhaeto-Romanic
Rhaeto-Romance
read-write head
ready reckoner
ready, steady, go
rebecca-eureka
robe-de-chambre
Robber Council
rub of the green
rabble-rousing
robin's-egg blue
rub on the green
Robin Williams
Robin Hood's Bay
Robert Aldrich
Robert Bridges
Robert Barclay
Robert Catesby
Robert Herrick
Robert Muldoon
Robert Mitchum
Robert Maxwell
Roberto Baggio
Robert Redford
Robert Simpson
Robert Southey
Robert Thomson
Robert Walpole
Robert Winston
ruby silver ore
Ribston pippin
rack and manger
Richard Hadlee
Richard Wagner
Richard Hannay
Richard Harris
Richard Martin
Richard Baxter
Richard Deacon
Richard Seddon
Richard Leakey
Richard E Grant
rack and pinion
Richard M Nixon
Richard Cobden
Richard Rogers
Richard Hooker
rock and roller
Richard Bright
Richard Wright
Richard Steele
Richard Butler
Richard Burton
Richard Avedon
rectangularly
recycled paper
rocket science
Rickettsiales
receivability
rectipetality
recriminative
recrimination
rectification
recriminatory
rectilineally
rectilinearly
receiving-ship
receiving line
receiving-room
recoil nucleus
rectitudinous
recollectedly
recalcitrance
recommendable
recommendably
recompensable
recumbent fold
recombination
recomposition
recomfortless
recompression
reconditeness
reconcilement
reconsolidate
reconnoiterer
reconstituent
reconstructor
receptiveness
receptibility
reception room
reciprocative
reciprocation
reciprocality
race relations
recessiveness
recitationist
recrudescence
recrudescency

recovery stock
Rocky Marciano
recrystallise
recrystallize
red sandalwood
radialisation
radialization
redback spider
radial-ply tyre
ride at the ring
radiant energy
reducibleness
reductiveness
reducing agent
reducing flame
redeemability
red-legged crow
Rodney R Porter
radiesthesist
radii vectores
redding-straik
red kidney bean
Rodrigo Borgia
Rudolf Nureyev
Rudolf Steiner
redeliverance
rudimentarily
Redemptionist
riding clothes
rodent officer
riding the fair
radiolabelled
radioactively
radio-actinium
radioactivity
radiotelegram
radioteletype
radiochemical
radiolocation
radio spectrum
radioisotopic
red spider mite
reduplicative
reduplication
redissolution
redevelopment
ruddy shelduck
re-examination
Rievaulx Abbey
re-embarkation
re-endorsement
Roedean School
re-enforcement
re-engineering
reefing-jacket
re-edification
re-eligibility
roe-blackberry
rheumatically
re-exportation
re-entry window
refractometer
refractometry
refocillation
reflexiveness
reflexibility
reflexologist
reflectograph
reflectometer
refrigerative
refrigeration
refrigeratory
Rafflesiaceae
riffle through
reformability
reformational
refurbishment
Reform Judaism
reference-mark
reference book
referentially
reforestation
refashionment
rogues' gallery
ruggedisation
ruggedization
Reggie Jackson
regulating rod
regimentation
rag-and-bone-man
regardfulness
regurgitation
Roger Williams
Roger Staubach
Register House
register-plate
registrarship
right-handedly
Right Reverend
right of search
right-of-centre
right of common
right-thinking
righteousness
right triangle
rehabilitator
reimbursement
rainbow-chaser
rainbow-tinted
reincarnation
raise the alarm
raise the devil
raise one's hand
reinforcement
Raining Stones
Reign of Terror
rhinoscleroma
rhizomorphous
reimportation
reinstatement
raid the market
reintegration
reinterrogate
railway bridge
railway-stitch
rejuvenescent
roller bearing
rollerblading
roller bandage
rollercoaster
relieve nature
relieving arch
rolled into one
roller-skating
religiousness
Ralph Cudworth
rolling launch
rolling strike
Rila Monastery
Rila Mountains
Roland Barthes
roll-on roll-off
rule of the road
rallying-point
remeasurement
rumlegumption
ramshorn snail
Romain Rolland
ram-air turbine
rumbledethump
rumelgumption
Roman Catholic
Roman de la Rose
romanticality
Roman alphabet
Roman Polanski
reminiscently
remonstrative
remonstration
remonstratory
remonstrantly
roman à tiroirs
Roman numerals
ramapithecine
remorselessly
remissibility
remittance man
remote control
remote sensing
rumbustiously
rental library
rent-collector
runic alphabet
ranz-des-vaches
René Descartes
röntgenoscopy
renegotiation
Ronnie Corbett
run-time system
running battle
running lights
run rings round
running stitch
running buffet
run in the blood
Ranunculaceae
randomisation
randomization
rensselaerite
run a tight ship
ringtailed cat
run out of steam
root-and-branch
rhotacisation
rhotacization
rhopalocerous
rhombohedrons
rhombporphyry
root directory
reorientation
Rhodian school
rhododendrons
rhodochrosite
root vegetable
repeatability
repeating coil
repeat oneself
Republican era
republicanise
republicanize
republicanism
republication
rapaciousness
reprehensible
reprehensibly
representable
representment
representamen
replenishment
reptiliferous
repulsiveness
ripsnortingly
reproachfully
rapprochement
Rupert Murdoch
reportorially
report program
repetitionary
repetitiously
rapturousness
requisiteness
Rorschach test
Rory Underwood
restaurant car
raspberry bush
rosebay laurel
residual value
residentially
Russification
✧russia leather
Russian Museum
resolvability
re-solubleness
resolubleness
resplendently
resolutionist
Rosa Luxemburg
resentfulness
resynchronise
resynchronize
restoratively
Risso's dolphin
Russocentrism
Russocentrist
rose of Jericho
restrictively
restructuring
risorgimentos
reservoir rock
Reservoir Dogs
rust-resistant
resistance box
resuscitative
resuscitation
resistibility
rise to the bait
resourcefully
rusty-coloured
ritualisation
ritualization
rateable value
retranslation
rated capacity
rated altitude
rite de passage
rotten borough
rutherfordium
retaining wall
retail therapy
retributively
rattle-brained
Rathlin Island
rattle the cage
retentiveness
retinoscopist
rational dress
rationalistic
retroactively
retroactivity
ratiocinative
ratiocination
ratiocinatory
retromingency
retroflection
retrospective
retrospection
rite of passage
retrogressive
retrogression
Rett's syndrome
round the clock
round-the-clock
round the twist
rounding error
round brackets
roundtripping
rough shooting
rough-and-ready
reunification
routinisation
routinization
Réunion Island
revocableness
revaccination
ravelled bread
revolving door
revolving fund
revolutionary
revolutionise
revolutionize
revolutionism
revelationist
revolutionist
revenue tariff
revenue cutter
revendication
revindication
River Paraguay
River Achelous
reverberative
reverberation
reverberatory
reverberantly
reversibility
reversionally
River Okavango
River Dniester
reverentially
River Dordogne
River Eridanus
River Tunguska
Rowan Williams
rowing machine
Rowan Atkinson
rhyparography
Roy Hattersley
rhyme or reason
ray of sunshine
rhythm section
Roy Williamson
Royal Pavilion
royal marriage
Royal Red Cross
Royal Peculiar
Royal Air Force
Royal Birkdale
royal standard
Raymond Carver
Roy Greenslade
Reye's syndrome
slap and tickle
Seanad Eireann
seam allowance
stalagmometer
stalagmometry
stalagmitical
scalar product
scalar segment
stalactitical
stalactitious
shabby-genteel
scambling-days
starch blocker
searchingness
Stan Collymore
starch-reduced
star catalogue
staccatissimo
search warrant
stand off and on
swaddling-band
scandal-bearer
scandalmonger
standing order
standing rules
stand one's hand
standing stone
standing to sue
standing waves
stand together
stand to reason
standard bread
standard error
Standard grade
standard gauge
Spandau Ballet
shamefastness
space medicine
state religion
shamelessness
shapelessness
statelessness
state of repair
state of the art
state-of-the-art
state of events
seal-engraving
States General
scavenger hunt
space platform
statesmanship
statesmanlike
Space Invaders®
scale and platt
shake one's head
stagecoaching
stagecoachman
scalenohedron
slate-coloured
skateboarding
Shakespearean
Shakespearian
state prisoner
✧swanee whistle
Sea of Serenity
staff sergeant

Sea of Geniuses
snaffle-bridle
staff notation
Sea of Moisture
Stanford Moore
Staffordshire
shaggy milk cap
slanging match
shaggy parasol
slaughterable
scaphocephaly
scathefulness
staphylococci
Stanhope press
spathiphyllum
staghorn coral
swashbuckling
scaling ladder
Spanish dagger
Spanish guitar
scarification
stabilisation
stabilization
staminiferous
spadicifloral
stationmaster
statistically
slap in the face
stab in the back
spacious times
sparkling wine
shark's manners
stalking-horse
smack one's lips
small capitals
small-mindedly
small bindweed
stable isotope
small-and early
small potatoes
scarlet letter
Scarlett O'Hara
scarlet runner
swallowtailed
spasmodically
shammy leather
slamming stile
stainlessness
Shannon Miller
star-nosed mole
seasonability
shadow cabinet
shadowcasting
Svatopluk Cech
shadow of death
sea gooseberry
slap on the back
seaworthiness
sharpshooting
sharp-wittedly
scalpelliform
scalping-knife
sharp practice
sharp's the word
Sharron Davies
stay stitching
stag the market
stay the course
starting block
starting price
starting point

St Anthony's nut
statute labour
statute-barred
scapulimantic
scapulomantic
statutory rape
status quo ante
shalwar-kameez
slaty cleavage
scaly anteater
star-ypointing
sublanceolate
submandibular
Sabbath school
submachine-gun
subscriber set
sebaceous cyst
subeditorship
sabre-rattling
subdeaconship
sable antelope
subternatural
sable-coloured
subterraneous
subversionary
subject matter
subject-object
subventionary
subreptitious
subsequential
subserviently
subtilisation
subtilization
subdivisional
subsistential
sublieutenant
suballocation
subclavicular
subindicative
subindication
subinvolution
St Bonaventure
subcommission
subcontractor
sub-postmaster
sub-postoffice
subcontiguous
subcontinuous
subpopulation
subspeciality
subappearance
subequatorial
St Bernard's dog
subtriangular
subprefecture
subordinately
subordinative
subirrigation
subordination
suburbicarian
subtropically
subtriplicate
Siberut Island
substantively
substantivise
substantivize
substantivity
substantially
substitutable
substructural
subjunctively

sick as a parrot
Social Chapter
social charter
social climber
social compact
social dumping
social disease
sacramentally
sacralisation
sacralization
socialisation
socialization
Socratic irony
social realism
social science
social service
social studies
secretary hand
secretaryship
secretary bird
secretary type
Sacred College
succès d'estime
sockeye salmon
secretiveness
socket spanner
secret society
successlessly
successionist
successorship
✧secret service
sick-feathered
saccharic acid
Saccharomyces
saccharimeter
saccharometer
saccharimetry
succinctorium
sucking bottle
sacrificially
suctional stop
section-cutter
St Crispin's Day
sickle feather
secondariness
secondary cell
secondary coil
second chamber
second officer
second reading
second-sighted
secundum artem
sacrosanctity
sectorisation
sectorization
sociolinguist
sociologistic
sycophantical
sacerdotalise
sacerdotalize
sacerdotalism
sacerdotalist
security guard
suck the monkey
sick-thoughted
Saddam Hussein
seductiveness
Sydney Brenner
Sidney Poitier
Sydney Pollack
side-impact bar

saddle blanket
saddle feather
sedimentation
sedimentology
sadomasochism
sadomasochist
sodomitically
sedentariness
sedentary soil
sidereal month
side-splitting
sedes impedita
seditiousness
sodium nitrate
scenarisation
scenarization
spelaeologist
steganopodous
steganography
Stewart Island
sketchability
Sketches By Boz
speechfulness
speech reading
Spencerianism
stercoraceous
stercorarious
speech therapy
steadfastness
speedy cutting
speed merchant
speed dialling
spending money
Swedenborgian
Steve Redgrave
Siege of Tobruk
stereographic
scene-shifting
speleological
skeletogenous
Steve Donoghue
stereoscopist
stereotropism
stereotypical
sleight of hand
sleight-of-hand
Stephen Hendry
Stephen Frears
shepherd check
Shepherd kings
shepherd plaid
shepherd's club
stethoscopist
specimen glass
sheriff depute
sheriff clerks
specification
sterilisation
sterilization
special school
Special Branch
scenic railway
scenic reserve
speckled trout
sneak-thievery
speaking clock
speak one's mind
speaking-voice
spell backward
swelled-headed
Stella Gibbons

stealth bomber
steal a march on
Shetland sheep
smelling salts
stellio lizard
shell ornament
steam governor
spermatoblast
spermatic cord
spermatogenic
spermatophore
Spermatophyta
spermatophyte
spermatorrhea
spermatotheca
spermatozoids
seek-no-further
stern-foremost
sue one's livery
Stegocephalia
stenophyllous
skeuomorphism
stenographist
step out of line
steeplechaser
sleep learning
sleeplessness
sheepshearing
sweep the board
sleep like a log
sleep like a top
sleeping berth
sleeping coach
Sleeping Gypsy
stepping-stone
sleep together
step-parenting
sheep-stealing
Sherpa Tenzing
smear campaign
sherry-cobbler
swear the peace
Sierra Leonean
steering wheel
sweet-savoured
spectacularly
sweated labour
spectre shrimp
spectre insect
sweet-tempered
sweetheart ivy
Scent of a Woman
sweet chestnut
smelting-house
spectinomycin
smelting-works
spectroscopic
sweet woodruff
spectrometric
sweet nothings
spectrography
spectatorship
speculatively
specular stone
speculum metal
sufficingness
suffocatingly
soft radiation
suffraganship
suffragettism
suffrutescent

soft-sectoring
soft sculpture
safety bicycle
safety curtain
safety-deposit
safety officer
suffumigation
software house
signal letters
signal peptide
signature tune
sagaciousness
segregational
segmental arch
suggestionise
suggestionize
suggestionism
suggestionist
significative
signification
significatory
significantly
sigmoidectomy
sigmoidoscope
sigmoidoscopy
sugar-refinery
sugar-refining
sugar charcoal
sugar diabetes
Sagittariuses
sign the pledge
sightlessness
schwärmerisch
schadenfreude
Scheele's green
Schwenkfelder
Schlemm's canal
sphagnicolous
sphagnologist
sphygmography
Schilling test
scholarliness
scholasticism
schematically
Schindler's Ark
sphingomyelin
Sihanoukville
schoolgirlish
school-leaving
schoolmarmish
schoolteacher
school-trained
sphericalness
spherocytosis
spheroidicity
spheristerion
Schottky noise
Schutzstaffel
schlumbergera
schizocarpous
schizaeaceous
schizogenesis
schizogenetic
schizomycetic
Schizomycetes
schizophrenia
schizophrenic
Schizophyceae
spiral binding
spit and polish
Stig Blomqvist

Seven Sleepers
save one's bacon
save reverence
St Vitus's dance
sewing machine
sexual athlete
sexualisation
sexualization
sexual therapy
sixteenth note
sixpenny piece
Saxifragaceae
sexagesimally
sixth interval
sex chromosome
sextile aspect
sexploitation
sex intergrade
Styracosaurus
styrene resins
Seyfert galaxy
stylistically
styptic pencil
Thalamiflorae
thalamifloral
thanatophobia
thanatography
thalassocracy
Trajan's Column
thalattocracy
tear a strip off
tram conductor
traceableness
tracer element
trade-weighted
trapeze artist
trade-off study
trade discount
travelling rug
traveller's joy
tradesmanlike
trade unionism
trade unionist
trapezohedral
trapezohedron
travel-stained
travel-tainted
travel writing
traffic warden
traffic circle
traffic lights
traffic police
traffic island
teachableness
trading estate
tragic heroine
traditionless
traditionally
toad in the hole
toad-in-the-hole
thanklessness
tracklessness
thank-offering
track and field
track-and-field
thank goodness
thankworthily
tea plantation
trail one's coat
traumatically
thaumatolatry
traumatonasty
thaumaturgism
thaumaturgics
thaumaturgist
training pants
✧trainspotting
tear off a strip
tranquilliser
tranquillizer
translate into
transparently
translational
transnational
translatorial
transactinide
transactional
transcendence
transcendency
transgendered
transfer paper
transferrable
transferrible
transversally
transpersonal
transientness
transshipment
transshipping
that's the stuff!
transpiration
transpiratory
transliterate
that's big of him
transmigrator
transmissible
transmittable
transmittible
transmittance
transplanting
transom window
translocation
transpositive
transposition
transformable
that's your sort
transport café
transportable
transportedly
transport ship
transportance
transcribable
transcriptase
transcriptive
transcription
transgressive
transgression
transisthmian
transistorise
transistorize
transatlantic
transit circle
transitionary
transit lounge
transmutative
transmutation
translucently
transfusively
translucidity
transexualism
transexuality
tractableness
toastmistress
Tractarianism
tractive force
to beat the band
tobaccanalian
table skittles
Table Mountain
table football
tablespoonful
tableau vivant
tubuliflorous
tubal ligation
tuberculation
tabes dorsalis
ticket of leave
ticket-writing
tachistoscope
tickle a th' sere
tickly-benders
tickle to death
technicalness
technical foul
technical area
technological
technopolitan
to conjure with
tachometrical
tectonic plate
tic douloureux
To Catch a Thief
tachymetrical
tachyphylaxis
tachygraphist
tiddledywinks
tadpole shrimp
The Pajama Game
the paranormal
The Jabberwock
The Dam Busters
The Watchtower
The Naked Lunch
the latest word
The Magic Flute
The Mabinogion
the main chance
The Fairy Queen
très au sérieux
the Kaiser's war
the party's over
✧the Last Supper
The Last Tycoon
The Jazz Singer
Theobald Boehm
Theobald Smith
treacherously
thenceforward
trench warfare
tread a measure
Theodor Adorno
Theodor Boveri
The Odessa File
Thérèse Raquin
the here and now
the devil to pay
the real Mackay
the yellow leaf
The Terminator
the penny drops
thereinbefore
The Jew of Malta
The Sex Pistols
the Reproaches
the Depression
The Deer Hunter
the Lesser Wain
the whole shoot
the whole world
the chances are
The Shangri-las
the ghost walks
The White Devil
The Wife of Bath
The Virginians
the king's peace
The Right Stuff
✧the high street
The Night Watch
theriomorphic
Trevi Fountain
The Winslow Boy
The Dirty Dozen
the Little Bear
The Tin Woodman
✧the black death
The Albert Hall
theologically
theologoumena
the altogether
trellis window
the old serpent
the cloven hoof
thermo-balance
thermochemist
thermodynamic
thermographic
thermographer
thermogenesis
thermogenetic
thermonuclear
thermoplastic
thermophilous
thermosetting
thermotherapy
thermotropism
The Underworld
theanthropism
theanthropist
the unemployed
The Knot Garden
the inevitable
The Moody Blues
The Gondoliers
The Golden Bowl
The Homecoming
Thelonius Monk
The Bookseller
The Book of Thel
The Mock Turtle
the common weal
the common good
the morn's nicht
the noes have it
the boys in blue
The Bostonians
The Spice Girls
Theopaschitic
The Crying Game
the grim reaper
theorematical
The Art of Fugue
theoretically
The Pretenders
treason felony
Treasury bench
treasure-chest
treasure-house
treasurership
treasure-trove
The Stranglers
theatre of fact
theatre sister
The Other Place
trestle bridge
the other woman
the other world
theatricalise
theatricalize
theatricalism
theatricality
treaty Indians
Treaty of Dover
Treaty of Ghent
the eternities
The Story of Art
The Nutcracker
The Jungle Book
the public weal
tremulousness
The Eurythmics
twelve-note row
twelve-tone row
The Awkward Age
the ayes have it
toggle between
to good purpose
toga praetexta
tight-head prop
tight junction
tricarboxylic
trisaccharide
trilateralism
trilateration
trilateralist
tricarpellary
thimblerigged
thimblerigger
thiocarbamide
twiddling-line
third interval
Third-Worldism
toilet service
thing-in-itself
trigger finger
tritheistical
trichological
trichromatism
trichopterist
trichopterous
triliteralism
trilingualism
twilight sleep
Trinity Sunday
trickle-charge
thick-wittedly
thick-pleached
trial marriage
triploblastic
triple-crowned
Triple Entente
trial of the pyx
triple glazing
trial by record
triumphal arch
thigmotropism
triangulately
triangulation
triangularity
trim one's sails
triboelectric
trigonometric
tricorporated
trisoctahedra
twist the knife
triatomically
twistor theory
triethylamine
tributariness
tritubercular
triquetrously
trisyllabical
take a back seat
take communion
take exception
take it in snuff
take its toll on
take its course
take liberties
take lying down
Tokelau Island
take me with you
take one's leave
take one's lumps
take one's place
take-off rocket
take the mickey
take the lid off
take the pledge
take the plunge
take to one's bed
take to the bent
take to the road
take up the word
talkativeness
tilt at the ring
telecommuting
teleconverter
telecottaging
teledildonics
telefacsimile
telegraph wire
telegraph pole
telegrammatic
tulchan bishop
tilting fillet
talk like a book
tell me another
tell me about it!
telemarketing
telencephalic
telencephalon
talent spotter
tell one's beads
talk out of turn
telephone book
telephoto lens
teleportation
tolerableness
telerecording
tolerance dose
tolerationism
tolerationist
telescopiform
telautography
tellurous acid
televangelism

televangelist
televisionary
television set
time after time
time-beguiling
time-bettering
time-consuming
temperateness
temperamental
temperability
tamper-evident
Tim Berners-Lee
tempest-beaten
tempest-tossed
tempestuously
tumbler-switch
Timon of Athens
temporariness
temporalities
temporisation
temporization
tomboyishness
temporisingly
temporizingly
time out of mind
tumorgenicity
tumorigenesis
timbrophilist
temerariously
time signature
temptableness
time-trialling
Tommy Hilfiger
Tommy Docherty
tantalisation
tantalization
tentativeness
tantalisingly
tantalizingly
Tenebrionidae
tenaciousness
tenpence piece
tender-hearted
tenpenny piece
tangentiality
tendentiously
tenpin bowling
Tenzing Norgay
tonsillectomy
tintinnabulum
tintinnabular
ten-minute rule
tenement house
tenant-in-chief
tune one's pipes
tent-preaching
tungsten steel
tenosynovitis
tongue-doubtie
tongue in cheek
tongue-in-cheek
tongue-lashing
tongue-twister
tenovaginitis
Thomas Addison
Thomas à Becket
Thomas à Kempis
Thomas Arundel
Thomas Beecham
Thomas Cranmer
Thomas Creevey
Thomas Campion
Thomas Carlyle
thoracentesis
Thomas Fairfax
Thomas Linacre
two-ball putter
Thomas Müntzer
Thomás Masaryk
Tropaeolaceae
thoracoplasty
Thomas Peachum
Thomas Pynchon
Thomas Sopwith
Thomas Telford
Trombiculidae
troublesomely
troublousness
two pence piece
twopenceworth
twopenny piece
two pennyworth
two-pennyworth
thought-reader
thoughtlessly
trophoblastic
toothache tree
trophallactic
trothplighted
toothsomeness
tooth-ornament
trophotropism
Thor Heyerdahl
tropical month
tropical sprue
Trofim Lysenko
troglodytical
trolling-spoon
thoroughbrace
thoroughgoing
thorough-paced
Thomson effect
thousand-pound
trout-coloured
topic sentence
top dead centre
topographical
typographical
tip the balance
topside-turvey
topologically
tippling-house
tape recording
tape-recording
taphrogenesis
tape transport
topsy-turvydom
terra-japonica
terraced house
threateningly
Tarka the Otter
tartarisation
tartarization
Tartarian lamb
turn a blind eye
toreador pants
term assurance
Turnbull's blue
three-jaw chuck
three-day event
three-farthing
turkey buzzard
three-per-cents
threepenny bit
threepenn'orth
three-line whip
turmeric paper
threefoldness
three-cornered
three-four time
torrentiality
terrestrially
tercentennial
three quarters
turkey vulture
tariffication
Tyrrhenian Sea
terminatively
terminability
terminational
turnip cabbage
turbine engine
tergiversator
turning circle
Turkish carpet
Turkish coffee
turnip lantern
territorially
terminologist
tertius gaudet
turnkey system
thrillingness
thrill through
thremmatology
thrombophilia
thrombokinase
Tironian notes
Terence O'Neill
Terence Conran
tar and feather
Tyrone Guthrie
Turing machine
tyrannosaurus
turbocharging
terrorisation
terrorization
turbo-electric
tortoise plant
tortoiseshell
turn of the year
turn on the heat
turnpike stair
thrust bearing
terpsichoreal
terpsichorean
thresher-shark
thresher whale
thrashing-mill
threshing mill
throstle frame
thrasonically
Teresa of Avila
threshold dose
thrust through
turn to account
turn the tables
turn the corner
teratogenesis
teratological
throttle lever
throttle valve
turbulent flow
through the day
through ticket
through bridge
turquoise-blue
torque spanner
Torquato Tasso
throwing stick
throwing table
throw together
Terry Eagleton
tarry-fingered
Tasmanian wolf
test-ban treaty
tastelessness
Tyssetrengane
Testicardines
testing clause
testification
testificatory
to some purpose
task switching
test the waters
tissue culture
to say the least
tetrabasicity
tetrahedrally
tetrachloride
Tetrabranchia
tetrastichous
tetradynamous
tetrasyllabic
tetrasyllable
totidem verbis
tithe-gatherer
to the backbone
to the contrary
toties quoties
tattie-howking
tattie-lifting
titillatingly
total football
titular bishop
tittle-tattler
Titanotherium
titanium white
totipalmation
tetartohedral
thumb one's nose
thunder-darter
thunder-master
thunder-bearer
thundershower
thunderstrike
thunder-stroke
thunderstruck
true-disposing
touchableness
truthlessness
touch football
truth function
thurification
Trucial States
touristically
Tourist Trophy
trunk dialling
trunk breeches
true-love grass
tautometrical
tautophonical
tautochronism
tautochronous
Teutonisation
Teutonization
tautologously
tauromorphous
trumpet marine
trumpet agaric
trumpet-shaped
trumpet flower
trumpeter swan
tsutsugamushi
tours d'horizon
trustlessness
trust hospital
trustworthily
Tower of London
toxicological
toxicophagous
tax-deductible
text messaging
taxonomically
toxoplasmosis
Texas scramble
Texas longhorn
Thymelaeaceae
thyroidectomy
trysting-place
trysting-stile
unabbreviated
unambiguously
unambitiously
unaccompanied
unaccentuated
unascertained
unaccountable
unaccountably
un-Americanise
un-Americanize
unamiableness
uralitisation
uralitization
Ural Mountains
uranographist
unadopted road
unapostolical
unapprehended
unappreciated
unapprovingly
unappropriate
unassuageable
unassimilable
unassimilated
unarticulated
unanticipated
unadulterated
unadventurous
unadvisedness
unbiassedness
umbraculiform
umbrella group
umbrella plant
umbrella stand
unblessedness
unbridledness
umbilical cord
unbelievingly
umbelliferous
unbendingness
urban district
unbrotherlike
Umberto Nobile
unbeseemingly
unboundedness
unchallenging
unchastisable
unchastizable
uncleanliness
uncreatedness
urchin-snouted
uncalculating
uncompanioned
uncommendable
uncommendably
uncompetitive
uncompensated
uncomplicated
uncomplaisant
uncomplaining
uncomfortable
uncomfortably
uncontainable
unconsciously
unconcealable
unconcernedly
unconcernment
unconsecrated
unconversable
uncontestable
unconvertible
uncontentious
unconjectured
unconceivable
unconceivably
unconsidering
unconditioned
unconditional
unconformable
unconformably
unconstrained
unconjunctive
unconsummated
unconquerable
unconquerably
uncloudedness
unco-ordinated
uncoordinated
unco-operative
uncooperative
uncrowned king
uncertainness
unceremonious
unchristianly
uncircumcised
uncourtliness
undifferenced
undulant fever
undulationist
undeliverable
undomesticate
undepreciated
underhandedly
underpainting
undercarriage
underachiever
under the eye of
under the knife
under-shepherd
under the table
underniceness
underfinished
Under Milk Wood
underclassman
underclothing
underemployed

under one's hand
under one's belt
under one's nose
undergraduate
underprepared
under pressure
underestimate
understrapper
underutilised
underutilized
understanding
underexposure
undescendable
undescendible
undiscernible
undiscernibly
undiscernedly
undistempered
undistinctive
undisciplined
undiscomfited
undissociated
undishonoured
undiscouraged
undescribable
undistributed
undistracting
undeservingly
undisturbedly
undiscussable
undiscussible
undisguisable
undisguisedly
undutifulness
undeterminate
undauntedness
undeviatingly
undividedness
undiversified
unevangelical
unexaggerated
unembellished
unembarrassed
unexceptional
unexclusively
unexemplified
unelectrified
unenforceable
urethroscopic
urediniospore
user interface
unenlightened
unemotionally
unexplainable
unexpressible
unexpensively
unexperienced
unearthliness
uberrima fides
uneatableness
unestablished
unentertained
unequivocally
unfeelingness
unflinchingly
unfeignedness
unfalteringly
unfamiliarity
unforced error
unforgettable
unforgettably
unforthcoming
unforgiveness
unforeseeable
unforeskinned
unfortunately
unfashionable
unfashionably
Uffizi Gallery
upgradability
unguardedness
ungrammatical
ungainsayable
ungenuineness
ungentlemanly
unhealthfully
unhealthiness
unhurtfulness
unicameralism
unilateralism
unicameralist
unilateralist
unilaterality
uninaugurated
unimaginative
United Kingdom
United Nations
universal beam
universalness
universal time
uninflammable
uninformative
uninforceable
unit furniture
uninfluential
uninhabitable
utility player
unilluminated
unillustrated
union language
unit of account
uti possidetis
unimpeachable
unit-packaging
unimpregnated
unimpressible
unimpassioned
uninquisitive
uninstructive
unintelligent
unintentional
unintermitted
uninteresting
uninterrupted
unjustifiable
unjustifiably
unknowingness
unlearnedness
uilleann pipes
unlimitedness
unmeaningness
unmacadamised
unmacadamized
unmedicinable
unmindfulness
unmentionable
unministerial
unmurmuringly
unmistakeable
unmistakeably
unmistrustful
unmitigatedly
unnecessarily
unneighboured
unneighbourly
unnaturalness
unnaturalised
unnaturalized
unoriginality
unobstructive
unobtrusively
unpracticable
unpractically
unpreoccupied
unprecedented
unpresentable
unpreventable
unpretentious
unpredictable
unpredictably
unpleasurable
unpleasurably
unphilosophic
unpolarisable
unpolarizable
unpunctuality
unprophetical
unprovided-for
unpromisingly
unprovisioned
unprovocative
unprogressive
unperpetrated
unperfectness
unperceivable
unperceivably
unperceivedly
unpurchasable
unpersuadable
unpasteurised
unpasteurized
unpitifulness
unputdownable
unqualifiable
unqualifiedly
unquestioning
unreasoningly
unreclaimable
unreclaimably
unrecognising
unrecognizing
unrecollected
unrecommended
unrecompensed
unrecoverable
unrecoverably
unregenerated
unrighteously
uprighteously
unreliability
unrelentingly
unremembering
unremorseless
unremittently
unremittingly
unreplaceable
unrepresented
unreplenished
unreprimanded
unreprievable
unrepentingly
unreproachful
unreproaching
unrestfulness
unrestingness
unresistingly
unreturningly
unscavengered
unsparingness
unstaunchable
unsubstantial
unsociability
unstercorated
unsteadfastly
unspecialised
unspecialized
unspectacular
unspeculative
unsightliness
unscholarlike
unsuitability
unskilfulness
unspiritually
unstigmatised
unstigmatized
unsaintliness
Ursula Andress
unsalvageable
unsaleability
unselfishness
unsoldierlike
unsympathetic
unsymmetrical
unsymmetrised
unsymmetrized
unsensational
unsentimental
unsmotherable
unspottedness
unsupportable
unsupportedly
unsuperfluous
unsurpassable
unsurpassably
unserviceable
unshrinkingly
unscrutinised
unscrutinized
unsustainable
unsusceptible
unsuspectedly
unsettledness
unsatisfiable
unsavouriness
unsewn binding
untraversable
ultrafiltrate
ultra-distance
ultra-virtuous
ultra-tropical
untransparent
untransmitted
untransformed
untremblingly
untheological
untrespassing
untaintedness
Ustilaginales
ustilagineous
untamableness
ultimus haeres
untenableness
untunableness
untunefulness
Upton Sinclair
utterableness
unterrestrial
unthriftiness
unthriftyhead
up to the minute
up-to-the-minute
up to the elbows
up to the moment
up-to-the-moment
untrustworthy
unvitrifiable
unwhistleable
unwillingness
unwelcomeness
unwomanliness
unwholesomely
unwarrantable
unwarrantably
unwarrantedly
unworldliness
unworkmanlike
unwithdrawing
unwithholding
unwittingness
Ulysses S Grant
Vladimir Putin
vraisemblance
vibrationless
vibracularium
vice-admiralty
vice-consulate
victimisation
victimization
Vaccinioideae
vaccinologist
victimologist
vacillatingly
vacuolisation
vacuolization
vectorisation
vectorization
Victoria Cross
Victoria Falls
victor ludorum
vector product
vicious circle
vice-president
vice-principal
Vicar of Christ
vicariousness
vocationalism
vacuum cleaner
vacuum forming
Veduggio Sound
video cassette
video recorder
video-on-demand
vegetarianism
voice response
voicelessness
Volcán El Misti
volcanic ashes
villagisation
villagization
volcanisation
volcanization
vulcanisation
vulcanization
vulgarisation
vulgarization
volcanic glass
valuation roll
volcanic rocks
volcanologist
vulcanologist
villanousness
Voltaireanism
Voltairianism
valedictorian
vulnerability
value-added tax
value received
velvet-fiddler
villeggiatura
volumenometer
velt-mareschal
voluntariness
voluntaristic
Valerianaceae
volatilisable
volatilizable
vantage ground
Vanuatu Island
viniculturist
vena contracta
Venice treacle
Vince Lombardi
Vincent O'Brien
Vincent de Paul
veneficiously
venographical
vindicability
vindicatorily
Von Ribbentrop
von Richthofen
Vansittartism
Van Allen belts
vinyl chloride
vinyl plastics
venerableness
ventriloquise
ventriloquize
ventriloquial
ventriloquism
ventriloquist
ventriloquous
venereologist
Venus's flytrap
Venus Williams
Venetian blind
Venetian glass
venturesomely
venturousness
Vandyke collar
viola da spalla
viol-de-gamboys
violoncellist
viper's bugloss
vapour density
vapourishness
vernal equinox
verbalisation
verbalization
vernalisation
vernalization
versatileness
variable costs
variable-sweep
vernacularise
vernacularize
vernacularism

vernacularist
vernacularity
voraciousness
Vera Cáslavská
varicose ulcer
vers d'occasion
vers de société
verifiability
verbigeration
varnishing-day
verbification
versification
Virginia Beach
Virgin Islands
verticillated
virginiamycin
vertiginously
Virginia stock
Virginia Woolf
virgin neutron
versicoloured
vermiculation
virulent phage
verumontanums
verisimilarly
veritableness
virtual memory
Vassar College
visualisation
visualization
Visible Church
visible speech
visceroptosis
Vasily Smyslov
visionariness
viscometrical
viscosimetric
Viscount Astor
visiting hours
Visayan Island
viticulturist
vitrification
vitrified fort
vital capacity
vitelligenous
Vitaly Scherbo
voting machine
vote-splitting
votive picture
vouchsafement
vaulting-horse
vaulting-house
vivaciousness
vivisectional
vivisectorium
vivisepulture
vowel mutation
vexed question
vexillologist
vexatiousness
Vézelay Church
what ails him at?
what do you know?
Wrangel Island
weather-headed
weather report
weather-beaten
weather window
weatherliness
weather-bitten
weatherometer
weather anchor
weathercock it
weather a point
weather-driven
weather symbol
whaling-master
wearing course
wearisomeness
weaponisation
weaponization
wrapping paper
what the plague
wide-awakeness
Wadham College
wedding favour
wedding finger
wide of the mark
wide-stretched
widow's chamber
wheech through
whereinsoever
weeding-chisel
weeping willow
weeping spring
week in, week out
wheel carriage
wheeler-dealer
Wig and Pen Club
wager of battle
white-favoured
white sapphire
White Hart lane
white pipe-tree
whitetip shark
white elephant
White Squadron
white-breasted
weightlifting
weight of metal
whithersoever
weight-watcher
waiting-vassal
writing-master
writing-school
whip into shape
whiskerandoed
whirling-table
whirlpool bath
writ of inquiry
whipping cream
whipping-cheer
whimsicalness
wainscot chair
whistled-drunk
whistle-blower
wristlet watch
whistling-shop
whistling swan
Willard F Libby
wild and woolly
welfare worker
Wiliam Gilbert
well-appointed
well-beseeming
well-connected
well-conducted
well-developed
Walter Bagehot
Walter Gilbert
Walter Gropius
Wolverhampton
Wilhelm Keitel
Walter Mondale
Wilhelm Freund
Walter Matthau
Walter Raleigh
Walter Sickert
wild gladiolus
Wolfgang Pauli
Waltham Forest
Walther Nernst
Welsh Assembly
Willie Brennan
Wilkie Collins
walking papers
walking-ticket
walking-orders
William Baffin
William Warham
William Barnes
William Ramsay
William Walton
William Harvey
William Temple
William of Tyre
William Empson
William Cowper
William Morris
William Dorrit
William Godwin
William Dunbar
William Hudson
Willie Renshaw
Willie Waddell
wild liquorice
Wolf Mankowitz
will-o'-the-wisps
Wilson Pickett
willow pattern
willow warbler
well-preserved
Wilfred Rhodes
well-regulated
well-respected
Wolf-Rayet star
walls have ears
wills-o'-the-wisp
well-thought-of
well-warranted
well-worked-out
waltzing mouse
wamble-cropped
women-children
Woman's Journal✧
women's studies
woman-suffrage
wing commander
wind dispersal
winter aconite
wonderfulness
✧winter gardens
winterisation
winterization
winter jasmine
wonder-working
wonder-wounded
winning hazard
winding engine
winding-strips
Winnie-the-Pooh
winkle-pickers
window curtain
window-dresser
window-shopper
Wings of Desire
winds of change
Windsor Castle
Winston Graham
wind up and down
woodcock's-head
woodchip board
woodchip paper
whoremasterly
wood engraving
whoremistress
wholesomeness
whole-coloured
wrong way round
wrong-headedly
wood germander
wool-gathering
woolly milk cap
woollen-draper
whooping crane
whooping cough
Woodrow Wilson
wood sandpiper
wood-wool slabs
wappenshawing
word blindness
world language
wired wireless
worldly-minded
War Department
warm-heartedly
worthlessness
worth one's salt
work-hardening
warehouse club
working memory
Warwick Castle
Wernicke's area
war to the knife
word processor
wardrobe trunk
work shadowing
word-splitting
Wordsworthian
work the oracle
West Berkshire
wastepaper bin
wasterfulness
Western Sahara
Western Pahari
western saddle
Western schism
Western Church
Western Empire
washhand basin
washhand stand
washing liquid
washing powder
washing-bottle
waspish-headed
West Nile virus
west-north-west
wash one's hands
West Side Story
west-south-west
West Yorkshire
with a bad grace
with a siserary
Watteau bodice
with good grace
witch of Agnesi
watch the clock
watching brief
watch one's back
watch one's step
witches' butter
witchetty grub
Watling Street
within measure
wattle and daub
with one accord
without a doubt
without frills
without number
water-vascular
water sapphire
water-carriage
water scorpion
water measurer
water chestnut
water witching
water plantain
waterflooding
watering-house
watering place
water moccasin
watercolorist
water tortoise
water softener
water-sprinkle
water-breather
waterproofing
water dropwort
with respect to
water-standing
water starwort
water purslane
water hyacinth
with the manner
with whole skin
wave mechanics
wayfaring tree
Way of the Cross
X-ray astronomy
X-ray telescope
xylographical
X-inactivation
xanthochroism
xanthochromia
xanthochroous
xanthopterine
xiphiplastral
xiphiplastron
xiphophyllous
xerodermatous
xerophthalmia
Xavier Francis
ylang-ylang oil
year in, year out
yachtsmanship
yieldableness
yield strength
Yves St Laurent
Yehudi Menuhin
Yohji Yamamoto
Yekaterinburg
yakitori sauce
yellow-bellied
yellow bunting
yellow berries
yellowishness
yellow yorling
yeoman service
yuppification
Yaren District
Yorkshire grit
yesterevening
yestermorning
Yosemite Falls
Yitzhak Shamir
young offender
Young's modulus
young fogeyish
Your Reverence
zebra parakeet
zebra crossing
Zachary Taylor
zodiacal light
Zoë Fairbairns
zygodactylism
zygodactylous
zygomatic bone
zygomatic arch
zygapophyseal
zygapophysial
zygotic number
Zuleika Dobson
Zöllner's lines
zymotechnical
Zinjanthropus
Zingiberaceae
zincification
zinkification
zenana mission
zona pellucida
zoogeographic
zoogeographer
zoophysiology
zoon politikon
zoosporangium
zoopsychology
Zorba the Greek
zero tolerance
Zarathustrism
Zarathustrian

anacardiaceous
at a rate of knots
amaranthaceous
A Hard Day's Night
Alan Dershowitz
A Handful of Dust
à la belle étoile
Anaheim Stadium
an ace in the hole
A Rake's Progress
amateurishness
Agatha Christie
anachronically
arachnological
Arabic alphabet
acarine disease
avariciousness
Arabic numerals
Arab-Israeli War
a warm reception
anamnestically
against the head
against the hair
against the wool
a majori ad minus
anamorphic lens
anacoustic zone
analogue signal
anagrammatical
Alan Rusbridger
apartment house
Alastair Burnet
Acanthocephala
anarthrousness
Anastas Mikoyan
Amaryllidaceae
ambidextrously
Albigensianism
ambulancewoman
Arbroath smokie
Albert Calmette
arboricultural
Albert Einstein
Albert Memorial
Alberto Moravia
Albert Reynolds
Albert the Great
ambassadorship
asbestos cement
Archaebacteria
archaeometrist
Archaeornithes
archaeological
archaeozoology
Archbishop Tutu
Asclepiadaceae
ancient history
archetypically
archgenethliac
alcoholisation
alcoholization
acclimatisable
acclimatizable
architectonics
archiepiscopal
accomplishable
accomplishment

accumulator bet
accumulatively
ascending aorta
Arctostaphylos
acceptableness
accepting house
accustomedness
accountability
accountantship
Aldabra Islands
Andrew Bonar Law
Andrew Carnegie
Andrea del Sarto
Andrea Mantegna
André Courrèges
Andrea Palladio
addressability
Andrei Sakharov
at daggers drawn
and all that jazz
androcephalous
andromedotoxin
audiometrician
androdioecious
andromonoecism
audio-frequency
Andorra la Vella
alder-buckthorn
audit committee
Aldwych Theatre
Adela Pankhurst
Alexandre Dumas
Alexandr Oparin
Alexander Balus
Alexander Korda
Alexander Monro
average costing
ahead of the game
Amedeo Avogadro
avenger of blood
Aretha Franklin
American Beauty
American blight
American Indian
American-Indian
American Legion
alexipharmakon
a week of Sundays
adenocarcinoma
Adelphi Theatre
anesthesiology
a certain person
affectionately
affectlessness
Alfred de Musset
Alfred Munnings
Alfred Marshall
auf Wiedersehen
affaire de coeur
affair of honour
at full throttle
affine geometry
as far as I can see
as fit as a fiddle
au grand sérieux
aggrandisement
aggrandizement

algae poisoning
aggressiveness
argumenti causa
argent comptant
angina pectoris
angiostomatous
Algernon Sidney
Auguste Piccard
Auguste Blanqui
Auguste Lumière
Augustinianism
angustifoliate
August Weismann
à chacun son goût
achievement age
Achille Bazaine
Achilles' tendon
apheliotropism
achondroplasia
achromatically
A Shropshire Lad
aphoristically
a shot in the dark
apical meristem
animal risibile
animadvert upon
a wise thing to do
alimentiveness
arithmetically
arithmetic mean
acid-house party
a will of one's own
at it like knives
alignment chart
azione teatrale
a bit of all right
anisodactylous
azidothymidine
a minori ad majus
axis of symmetry
aristocratical
Aristide Briand
adiathermanous
aviation spirit
Anjelica Huston
abjure the realm
acknowledgment
a flea in one's ear
a place in the sun
all-terrain bike
allegorisation
allegorization
alligator apple
alloiostrophos
Adlai Stevenson
allelomorphism
all in a day's work
all-round camera
a fly on the wheel
allopathically
Atlas Mountains
alliteratively
all over the shop
all-overishness
Almeida Theatre
armamentariums
administratrix

administration
administrative
armes parlantes
admissibleness
annual accounts
as near as dammit
annual parallax
Anne Bradstreet
Annie Leibovitz
Anna Howard Shaw
annular eclipse
amniotic cavity
annus mirabilis
aromatherapist
anomalous water
a touch of the sun
avoidable costs
apodeictically
at one's disposal
at one fell swoop
above-mentioned
aforementioned
alopecia areata
above and beyond
above suspicion
Adolf von Baeyer
Adolf Butenandt
apothegmatical
apophthegmatic
abominableness
atomic mass unit
apolipoprotein
atomic radiator
apoplectically
A Room of One's Own
A Room with a View
A Town Like Alice
apologetically
acoustic guitar
Alois Alzheimer
a sop to Cerberus
apostolic vicar
a foot in the door
a host in himself
alpha radiation
alpha particles
alphabetically
alphamerically
appraisal wells
alphanumerical
apples and pears
apprehensively
apple of discord
apple charlotte
appreciatively
apprenticehood
apprenticement
apprenticeship
applied physics
amphibiousness
amphibological
appendicectomy
Appendicularia
approach stroke
approved school
asparagus-stone

aerobiotically
aerobiological
agrobiological
agriculturally
Africanisation
Africanization
aerodynamicist
aeroelastician
aeroelasticity
aerohydroplane
Abraham Hayward
Abraham Lincoln
agroindustrial
air vice-marshal
Afrikander Bond
airing cupboard
aerenchymatous
arrondissement
aeronautically
air-conditioned
air-conditioner
airport fiction
a prophetic week
✧Aurora Borealis
aircraftswoman
aerospace-plane
agrostological
across-the-table
across the board
across-the-board
arrhythmically
associationism
answer back code
abstemiousness
aesthesiogenic
Aussichtspunkt
adscititiously
auspiciousness
at someone's beck
arsenic hydride
absent-mindedly
abstractedness
abstractionism
abstractionist
absorbefacient
Australian Alps
absorptiometer
absorptiometry
absorptiveness
asset-stripping
Afsluitdijk Dam
absquatulation
asseveratingly
antiarrhythmic
attractiveness
a stab in the dark
autobiographer
autobiographic
autocratically
article of virtu
articulateness
anticonvulsant
anticonvulsive
autocoprophagy
anticapitalist
anticipatorily
anticipatively

Words marked ✧ can also be spelled with one or more capital letters

antediluvially
antidepressant
as the case may be
as the crow flies
authentication
artificialness
artificial silk
anti-federalism
anti-federalist
Act of Indemnity
a stiff upper lip
autograph album
astigmatically
antagonisation
antagonization
attainableness
Antoine Barnave
Antoine Watteau
Antoine Arnauld
Altai Mountains
auto-intoxicant
anti-Jacobinism
artillery-plant
altum silentium
antimonarchist
antimetabolite
attemptability
automatic pilot
automatic drive
altimetrically
antimetathesis
actinobacillus
actinide series
attention value
Antonio Salieri
Antonio Vivaldi
Antonio Corelli
Anton von Webern
astrogeologist
a strong stomach
astrochemistry
astrophysicist
aetiologically
astrologically
astronomically
antiodontalgic
action painting
action stations
Acts of Sederunt
action spectrum
Anthony Perkins
Anthony of Padua
Anthony Hopkins
Anthony Burgess
antipodal cells
antiphlogistic
antiphonically
antaphrodisiac
antiperspirant
antiperistasis
antiphrastical
antipathetical
antiquarianism
autoradiograph
attorney in fact
after-mentioned
anthropography
anthropologist
anthropometric
anthropophobia
anthropophobic
anthropopathic
anthropophuism
Antarctic Ocean
auto-suggestion
auto-suggestive
antiseptically
antiscriptural
altitudinarian
attitudinarian
attitudinising
attitudinizing
antithetically
autotypography
Arthur Griffith
Arthur Honegger
Arthur Koestler
Arthur Kornberg
Artium Magister
altruistically
Arthur Sullivan
active immunity
abundance ratio
aquifoliaceous
advocate-depute
anvil secateurs
advantage court
advantageously
advance factory
Advanced Higher
advancing years
adventitiously
as who should say
auxiliary nurse
asynchronously
asymmetrically
asymmetric bars
asymptotically
bear-animalcule
beatae memoriae
Bravais lattice
bearded vulture
beardless wheat
boarding school
bladder campion
brand awareness
brake parachute
bearer security
beat generation
brachial artery
brachycephalic
brachydiagonal
brachydactylic
brachypinakoid
brachium civile
beatific vision
black-hat hacker
black-marketeer
blank cartridge
black in the face
black horehound
Blackpool Tower
blankety-blanky
black guillemot
black-eyed Susan
be-all and end-all
Brahms and Liszt
brain-fever bird
✧béarnaise sauce
beat one's brains
beat one's breast
boa constrictor
blaxploitation
Beatrice Lillie
boatswain's call
boatswain's mate
boatswain's pipe
beauté du diable
beat the retreat
Bran the Blessed
beautification
beasts of warren
bibliomaniacal
Bob Fitzsimmons
babbling thrush
Babinski effect
Babes in Toyland
bicycle ricksha
bucket and spade
bacteriologist
bacteriophobia
bacteriostasis
bacteriostatic
Bachelor of Arts
backing storage
Buckley's chance
back-projection
back-seat driver
backscratching
bid/offer spread
Bedrich Smetana
bedsitting-room
bodily function
breech delivery
bleaching green
bread-and-butter
breeding ground
breeder reactor
Blenheim Palace
bletheranskate
blepharoplasty
breakfast-table
break new ground
break the record
break one's heart
breaking stress
breakbone fever
breakdown truck
break no squares
beetle-crushers
bremsstrahlung
breathing-while
breathing space
breathlessness
breathtakingly
beef Wellington
breeze concrete
buffer solution
before one's time
baggage reclaim
beg the question
big girl's blouse
Big Bill Broonzy
behind schedule
behind the times
Bahasa Malaysia
Britannia metal
Brief Encounter
bridge-building
bringings forth
Bringing Up Baby
bring to account
bring to justice
bring up the rear
bright and early
Bright's disease
blithesomeness
British cholera
British disease
British bulldog
Brigitte Bardot
Brillat-Savarin
Bristol fashion
Bristol-diamond
blistered-steel
blister-plaster
boisterousness
balsam of Gilead
belladonna lily
Baluchitherium
bill-discounter
Belted Galloway
ballet-mistress
belletristical
belle assemblée
Bologna sausage
bull-headedness
Billings method
Billie Jean King
Balliol College
billiard-marker
bulimia nervosa
Belém Monastery
balance of power
balance of trade
Balmoral Castle
bill of exchange
balloon barrage
bill of oblivion
ballpeen hammer
ballpark figure
bells of Ireland
belt-tightening
Bamburgh Castle
Benjamin Jowett
Beniamino Gigli
Benedict Arnold
Benedetto Croce
banner headline
bonne compagnie
beneficialness
benefit society
benefit tourism
benefit tourist
Bonnie and Clyde
bundle of laughs
bundle of nerves
bene merentibus
banana-fingered
banana republic
banana solution
benzodiazepine
band-pass filter
binary munition
binary notation
bang-tail muster
binaural effect
banqueting-hall
biomathematics
buoyant density
bronchiectasis
bronchodilator
blood-sacrifice
blood-bespotted
bloodthirstily
broad in the beam
✧brobdingnagian
blood corpuscle
blood-consuming
blood poisoning
biogeochemical
biometeorology
by one's lonesome
Boolean algebra
biodegradation
Broughty Castle
brought forward
brothel creeper
Brother Cadfael
blow hot and cold
blockade-runner
blocking motion
Brocken spectre
block and tackle
Brooks Robinson
bootlace fungus
bioelectricity
bioclimatology
book-mindedness
Brownian motion
bioengineering
bioinformatics
Book of Habakkuk
Book of Jeremiah
Book of Nehemiah
Book of Proverbs
biographically
blow the whistle
bioluminescent
biosystematics
by prescription
baptism of blood
bipartisanship
Barbara Jackson
Barbara Dickson
Bernard Malamud
Bernard Manning
Bernard Haitink
bureau de change
Bernard Hinault
barrage-balloon
bargaining chip
bargain and sale
bargain-counter
Barbados cherry
Burschenschaft
berberidaceous
Bargello Museum
Barney Oldfield
Barberton daisy
barefoot doctor
bertha army worm
Bernhard Langer
Borghese Museum
birth-strangled
Barbican Centre
burling-machine
Barbizon School
barrier nursing
barrister-at-law
barbituric acid
barometrically
Baron Haussmann
Baron de Fourier
Baron Shawcross

barcode scanner
burn one's faggot
Bartolomeu Diaz
bird of paradise
Boris Pasternak
Birds of America
birds of one wing
bury the hatchet
borough-English
bastard saffron
bastardisation
bastardization
busman's holiday
best-before date
Basidiomycetes
beside the point
beseechingness
Bashi-Bazoukery
Basil D'Oliveira
businessperson
Bustopher Jones
basso profundos
batrachophobia
batrachophobic
by the same token
Battenberg cake
Battenburg cake
butterfingered
butterfly valve
butterfly screw
butterfly knife
by the holy poker
Batten's disease
Betsey Trotwood
battery of tests
buttery fingers
bathing machine
bathing costume
beta interferon
battle-axe block
botulinum toxin
Battle of Amiens
Battle of Arnhem
Battle of Actium
Battle of Cannae
Battle of Harlaw
Battle of Kosovo
Battle of Lützen
Battle of Mycale
Battle of Midway
Battle of Mohács
Battle of Naseby
Battle of Pinkie
Battle of Quebec
Battle of Shiloh
Battle of Towton
Battle of Verdun
Battle of Wagram
bituminisation
bituminous coal
bituminization
Battonberg cake
button mushroom
buttress-thread
Betty Boothroyd
bathygraphical
bougainvillaea
blueback salmon
Bourbon biscuit
Bluecoat School
bouleversement

blue ear disease
blue-green algae
brush discharge
Bruno of Cologne
Blue Ribbon Army
Blue Suede Shoes
Brussels carpet
✧brussels sprout
bowdlerisation
bowdlerization
Bix Beiderbecke
Boxer Rebellion
beyond reproach
bayonet fitting
boys will be boys
character actor
characterology
characteristic
✧chamber of trade
chamber concert
chamber counsel
chamber council
cranberry sauce
clap by the heels
charcoal burner
chalcographist
chancellorship
chance one's luck
Chancery Office
Chandler wobble
chalet bungalow
Clarence Darrow
chase the dragon
château bottled
changeableness
chargeableness
changelessness
change one's mind
change one's tune
clash-ma-clavers
claw-hammer-coat
Chatham Islands
charitableness
coaling station
Chariots of Fire
clavicytherium
Charlie Chaplin
chaulmoogra oil
Charlton Heston
Charles Babbage
cradle-snatcher
Charles Laveran
Charles Haughey
Charles Causley
Charles Kennedy
Charles the Bald
Charles Dickens
Charles Nicolle
Charles Bourbon
Charles Bronson
Charles Surface
Charlotte Yonge
Charlotte Green
charlotte russe
Charley-pitcher
claims assessor
charm offensive
chain of command
chain lightning
channel seaming
channel-hopping

Channel Islands
channel-surfing
cyanobacterium
cyanoacetylene
cyanocobalamin
chamois leather
Clairvaux Abbey
classical Latin
classical music
classification
classificatory
Claes Oldenburg
chanson de geste
class-conscious
claustrophobia
claustrophobic
chaises-longues
chassés-croisés
Chaetodontidae
chaptalisation
chaptalization
coastguardsman
chacun à son goût
cabbage-lettuce
cabbage-root fly
cabbage-tree hat
cubic saltpetre
Cybill Shepherd
cobble together
cabin passenger
cabinet-edition
cabinet picture
Cabinet Council
cabinet pudding
cyberterrorism
cyberterrorist
cybersquatting
cock-a-doodle-doo
cyclanthaceous
cycle per second
cack-handedness
cyclic compound
Cecil Parkinson
Cicely Wedgwood
coconut matting
cyclobarbitone
cyclopentolate
cucurbitaceous
cocktail lounge
cocktail shaker
Cadmean letters
Cadmean victory
code of practice
Cider with Rosie
cadaverousness
coelanaglyphic
chelating agent
chevaux-de-frise
crème de la crème
crêpes suzettes
clergyman's knee
Cheshire cheese
clerical collar
chemical closet
creditableness
chemical toilet
coeliac disease
credibility gap
credit standing
credit transfer
cleansing-cream

clean up one's act
chemoreceptive
chemotherapist
Chenopodiaceae
coevolutionary
chemoautotroph
chemosynthesis
clear-sightedly
clearance cairn
cheer to the echo
clear-starching
coessentiality
chest of drawers
chest protector
cigarette paper
climate control
climatological
chivalrousness
coincidentally
chincherinchee
child-resistant
Children's Panel
children's court
children's nurse
child allowance
child endowment
Cuisenaire rods
Chile saltpetre
Chinese cabbage
Chinese lantern
Chinese New Year
Chinese cracker
Chief Constable
chief executive
criminal lawyer
cuisine minceur
criminological
crinkle-crankle
chickling vetch
crinkum-crankum
chicken-hearted
chicken-livered
chilli con carne
coign of vantage
cairngorm-stone
chimney-sweeper
chimney swallow
clitoridectomy
Chilon of Sparta
chirographical
caisson disease
chittagong wood
clitter-clatter
calcareous tufa
collapsability
collapsibility
calabash nutmeg
Calycanthaceae
calico-printing
Chladni figures
Caledonian Club
cold dark matter
college pudding
Colles' fracture
collector's item
called to the bar
collective farm
collective noun
collectivistic
Calvin Coolidge
calliper splint

calcium carbide
calcium blocker
call in question
calligraphical
colliquescence
columella auris
Coleman Hawkins
calamine lotion
calamine powder
calamitousness
Colonial Office
colonial system
Colin Blakemore
colonel-in-chief
Calippic Period
Colorado beetle
chloride of lime
✧calorie counter
calorific value
calorification
chloral hydrate
chlorophyllous
chlorpromazine
chlorothiazide
chlorite-schist
chloritisation
chloritization
celestial globe
celestial poles
calf's-foot jelly
cultural cringe
calculated risk
colour contrast
coloured pencil
culture vulture
colour fastness
colour magazine
colour reversal
Colour Symphony
colour-sergeant
comparableness
command economy
commandantship
comrades-in-arms
compatibleness
companion hatch
campanological
compassionable
combat trousers
campanulaceous
comma butterfly
Comédie humaine
comedy of menace
commercial bank
commercial room
comme çi, comme ça
commensurately
commensuration
compensational
commentatorial
come full circle
come from behind
camphorated oil
commissionaire
commissaryship
come into effect
committeewoman
committee stage
commit to memory
Camilo José Cela
Camelopardalis

cumulative dose
cumulativeness
cumulative vote
complexionless
Common Entrance
common fraction
composite class
composing stick
commodiousness
common multiple
compound engine
compound number
common-or-garden
common plantain
common puffball
common recovery
compossibility
commonsensical
Common Serjeant
common toadflax
come on the scene
comfort station
Cambridgeshire
comprehensible
comprehensibly
Combretastatin®
comitia tributa
comitia curiata
come to one's hand
come to the front
compunctiously
computer dating
come unfastened
compurgatorial
communications
communion table
communion cloth
community radio
community chest
community nurse
compulsoriness
combustibility
cum multis aliis
campylotropous
consanguineous
contagiousness
cantankerously
container crane
concavo-concave
contact tracing
contact process
connaturalness
conscienceless
conscriptional
canicular cycle
Canadian dollar
Canadian French
centenarianism
Canterbury bell
Canterbury lamb
condescendence
condescend upon
conference call
concelebration
conterminously
canteen culture
convexo-concave
contemporanean
contemporarily
contemperation
contemperature
contemptuously
condensability
concessionaire
concession road
contesseration
conversational
conversaziones
convertibility
concerti grossi
concerto grosso
concentrically
conventionally
conceivability
conservational
conservatorium
conservatively
cinchonisation
cinchonization
canthaxanthine
confidentially
continental day
continentalism
continentalist
contingent upon
conditional fee
conditionality
conciliatorily
cuneiform bones
continuity girl
contiguousness
continuousness
continuous wave
conglobulation
canellini beans
conglomeration
conclusiveness
conglutination
conglutinative
Cinema Paradiso
cinematography
canine appetite
canonical hours
canon of the mass
convocationist
cannot be helped
cannonball-tree
consociational
censoriousness
conformability
conformational
conjoined twins
contour farming
Convolvulaceae
conspiratorial
Can't Pay? Won't Pay!
contract bridge
contracyclical
contractedness
contractionary
contradictable
contradictious
centrifugalise
centrifugalize
centrifugation
contrafagottos
✧congregational
contraindicant
contraindicate
control account
controlled drug
controllership
central heating
central incisor
central locking
centralisation
Central Station
control surface
centralization
contrapuntally
contraposition
contrapositive
centripetalism
contrary motion
contrast medium
Congressperson
contrat de vente
concrete jungle
congratulation
congratulatory
congratulative
concrete poetry
concretisation
concretization
controvertible
controvertibly
con espressione
Constantinople
constitutional
constitutively
construability
constructional
construct state
constructively
✧constructivism
constructivist
conjugate angle
contumaciously
censurableness
conjugal rights
conjunctivitis
contumeliously
centuplication
conquistadores
consubstantial
consuls general
convulsiveness
conductibility
consuetudinary
consulting room
clonal deletion
chorale prelude
Choral Symphony
Crouched-friars
clouded leopard
chordamesoderm
co-ordinateness
chondromatosis
chondrogenesis
chondrophorine
chondrocranium
close the record
cholelithiasis
close encounter
close to the bone
closed syllable
Cooley's anaemia
cholecystotomy
Coolgardie safe
cloth-yard shaft
cholinesterase
cloak and dagger
Crockford's Club
crown and anchor
crocodile tears
choronographic
chorographical
cross-marketing
crossbar switch
cross batteries
cross-reference
cross-fertilise
cross-fertilize
cross-sectional
cross-fingering
cross-infection
cross one's heart
crossing-warden
cross-pollinate
cross-correlate
Crossopterygii
cross assembler
crossover voter
clotting factor
croque-monsieur
Cho Oyu Mountain
capparidaceous
Captain Marryat
captain-general
Captain W E Johns
Captain Corelli
capuchin monkey
copper-bottomed
copper sulphate
Cape Finisterre
Cape gooseberry
capriciousness
Caprifoliaceae
capillary joint
cup-and-ring mark
cyproheptadine
Cape of Good Hope
capital account
capital offence
capitalisation
capitalization
coquettishness
curtate annuity
curtain walling
curtain lecture
certain annuity
cerebral cortex
Caribbean Times
core curriculum
cornet-à-pistons
cartes blanches
carpetbag steak
career diplomat
cartes-de-visite
correligionist
Cartesian devil
Cartesian diver
Cornelius Nepos
correspondence
correspondency
careers adviser
careers officer
currente calamo
current account
current bedding
current density
current affairs
cardinal beetle
cardinal-bishop
cardinal-deacon
corrida de toros
cardinal flower
cardinal number
Cardinal Newman
cardinal-priest
cardinal virtue
cardiac failure
cardiac massage
carline thistle
carriage return
certified check
curvilinearity
cardiomyopathy
carcinomatosis
carcinogenesis
carcinological
corticotrophin
corticosteroid
corticosterone
Cartier-Bresson
cardiothoracic
curricula vitae
cardiovascular
care killed a cat
Cyril Ramaphosa
corolliflorous
Carolina Nairne
Curtley Ambrose
caramelisation
caramelization
Coromandel wood
Coromandel work
chromatic scale
chromatography
chromatosphere
Corona Borealis
chronometrical
coronary artery
coronary bypass
corpora callosa
carrot and stick
corporate state
corporation tax
corpora striata
Coriolis effect
cercopithecoid
carbon monoxide
Cerro Incahuasi
cartographical
carboxylic acid
cartridge-paper
Cyrus McCormick
Christ-cross-row
Christian de Wet
Christmas daisy
Christmas party
chrysanthemums
Christocentric
Christoph Gluck
Christopher Lee
Christopher Sly
Christopher Fry
Chris Bonington
Christological
Chrysostom John
Christ's College
circumambience
circumambiency
circumambulate
corrugated iron

circular letter
circumbendibus
corpus callosum
corpuscularian
corpuscularity
carburetted gas
circumforanean
circumferentor
circumgyration
circumgyratory
circumlocution
circumlocutory
circumlittoral
circumnutation
circumnutatory
circumnavigate
circumposition
circumstantial
circumspection
circumspective
circumscissile
corpus striatum
corruptibility
circuit breaker
circuitousness
circumvolution
corkwing wrasse
carry one's point
cascara sagrada
cost-accountant
cost-accounting
cascarilla bark
casual labourer
cast a horoscope
Castanospermum
cast a spell upon
cast aspersions
cosmeceuticals
cost efficiency
cassette player
cassette single
cosmic constant
cystic fibrosis
castle-building
castles in Spain
Cosimo de' Medici
casement window
cash on delivery
cash-on-delivery
cosmochemistry
cystolithiasis
cosmopolitical
castor-oil plant
cosmographical
castrametation
cast to the winds
costus arabicus
cestui que trust
Cuthbert's beads
catechetically
catachrestical
catechumenical
catechumenship
catadioptrical
Catherine-wheel
cytogeneticist
category killer
categorisation
categorization
catchment basin
Catchment board
catch one's death
cuttlefish bone
City Livery Club
cotemporaneous
cathode-ray tube
Catholic Herald
cathodographer
cataphorically
cytophotometer
cytophotometry
ceteris paribus
citizen's arrest
courageousness
clumber spaniel
Church Assembly
clutch at straws
Crutched-friars
crux criticorum
Churchill Falls
Churchill Downs
Council of State
council chamber
councillorship
church militant
Church Slavonic
causes célèbres
cruciverbalism
cruciverbalist
cauliflower ear
counsel-keeping
counsellorship
caustic ammonia
caustic surface
Court of Session
court holy water
county palatine
counterbalance
counter-salient
counter-passant
counterfactual
counter-battery
countermeasure
counterfeiting
countershading
counterchanged
cluster physics
counter-riposte
counter-skipper
counter-opening
counter-trading
counter-wrought
counter-subject
counter-current
counterculture
country dancing
country bumpkin
civil liberties
civil commotion
cover the buckle
cover the ground
covering letter
✧coxsackie virus
coxcombicality
cryobiological
Clyde W Tombaugh
cry one's eyes out
cryptococcosis
cryptaesthesia
cryptaesthetic
cryptographist
crystal healing
crystal therapy
crystallisable
crystallizable
crystal indices
crystallomancy
cryptorchidism
cryptosporidia
cry out to be done
cry out to be used
dead as a herring
diamantiferous
diaheliotropic
dialectologist
Drang nach Osten
draughtsperson
death's-head moth
Death on the Nile
diaphanousness
diachronically
diathermaneity
death-practised
diaphototropic
dead in the water
Dear John letter
dead-letter drop
dead man's handle
Dial M for Murder
diagnosability
diamond wedding
diamondiferous
diamond jubilee
diazonium salts
dragon-standard
Dead Sea Scrolls
dead set against
draw the long bow
draw the curtain
dead to the world
Dublin Bay prawn
Debateable Land
declaratory act
Decca Flight Log
dicta probantia
decubitus ulcer
De Clerambault's
decree absolute
Duc de Richelieu
deceivableness
Decline and Fall
decolonisation
decolonization
decolorisation
decolorization
ductless glands
decompensation
decommissioner
decimalisation
decimalization
document reader
decompoundable
decontaminator
deconsecration
deconstruction
Doctors' Commons
dechristianise
dechristianize
Decorated style
decorative arts
decorativeness
decision theory
decus et tutamen
dicotyledonous
dactyliography
deducted spaces
dodecanoic acid
dodecasyllabic
dodecasyllable
dodge the column
diesel-electric
Dieu et mon droit
die in one's shoes
die in one's boots
deed of covenant
Diego Velázquez
Diego de Almagro
Dnepropetrovsk
dress-rehearsal
dressing-jacket
dyer's-greenweed
defoaming agent
defeasibleness
daffadowndilly
deflagrability
defibrillation
defective virus
difference tone
differentiable
differentially
differentiator
defenestration
definitive host
definitiveness
diffractometer
deferred credit
deferred shares
diffusion plant
daguerreotyper
digressiveness
dog in the manger
dig in one's heels
degenerateness
dig one's heels in
dogtooth violet
digestive tract
digital plotter
digitalisation
digitalization
dog's-tooth grass
drive to the wall
driver's license
driving licence
drip irrigation
drink like a fish
drinking-up time
drill-husbandry
do-it-yourselfer
Dakin's solution
Duke of Hamilton
Duke of Portland
Dilwara temples
deliberateness
deliberatively
delectableness
dolichocephaly
dolce far niente
delightfulness
dolomitisation
dolomitization
deliverability
delayed neutron
demobilisation
demobilization
democratically
Dame Edith Evans
Dame Ellen Terry
Dame Janet Baker
D F Malan Airport
Dame Ngaio Marsh
dementia precox
demonetisation
diminutiveness
demonetization
demoralisation
demoralization
dames de la halle
demisemiquaver
Dunbartonshire
Dunvegan Castle
Daniel Day-Lewis
Dante Alighieri
Danielle Steele
danseurs nobles
dinoflagellate
don't get me wrong
Dennis Bergkamp
Donald Campbell
Donald Johanson
dynamic geology
dynamic routing
dynamo-electric
dynamometrical
denominational
denominatively
Donato Bramante
denitrificator
dinitrobenzene
denazification
Dvorak keyboard
dioscoreaceous
do one's business
do oneself wrong
do one's homework
do one's own thing
drop handlebars
drop one's bundle
droit au travail
depletion layer
depreciatingly
dipterocarpous
dip of the needle
depigmentation
duplicate ratio
depolarisation
depolarization
Daphnis et Chloé
diplomatically
deplorableness
diplostemonous
departmentally
deposit account
deposit-receipt
dark adaptation
dermatoplastic
dermatological
dermatographia
dermatographic
Dirac's constant
direct drilling
directed number
directionality
direct mailshot
director circle
director's chair

deregistration
derogatoriness
durchkomponirt
Durchmusterung
dérailleur gear
dernier ressort
darkling beetle
Der Blaue Reiter
Dorothea Brooke
Dorothy Hodgkin
Dorothy L Sayers
Derbyshire neck
Derbyshire spar
disdainfulness
distant healing
disacknowledge
disaccommodate
disadventurous
disregardfully
dysteleologist
Disneyfication
dysmenorrhoeal
dysmenorrhoeic
discerpibility
disrespectable
distemperature
dispensability
distensibility
dispensational
dispensatorily
dispensatively
dessert-service
disjecta membra
dissertational
disceptatorial
dose equivalent
disserviceable
disaffiliation
disaffirmation
design engineer
disaggregation
despicableness
despitefulness
dispiteousness
distinguishing
dispiritedness
distilled water
disciplinarian
disciplinarium
displeasedness
desulphuration
displenishment
desalinisation
desalinization
disillusionary
disillusionise
disillusionize
display cabinet
disembarkation
disimpassioned
disambiguation
do someone right
disembowelment
do someone wrong
do someone proud
disembogue into
disemboguement
disincarcerate
disengagedness
disinteresting
disinheritance
disintegration
disintegrative
disinfestation
disinvestiture
disingenuously
disenthralment
disenchantment
disenchantress
disinclination
disinformation
disincorporate
disentrainment
disenfranchise
disencumbrance
disposableness
discombobulate
discomboberate
disconcertment
discodermolide
dispose towards
discomfortable
disconformable
despoticalness
dissociability
discommendable
discount-broker
disconnectedly
discountenance
disjointedness
discount market
discolouration
discourteously
discouragement
discouragingly
disconsolately
disconsolation
discontinuance
discontentedly
discontentment
dissolutionism
dissolutionist
dissolubleness
dissolvability
disapplication
disappointment
disapprobation
disapprobatory
disapprobative
disappropriate
disapprovingly
disequilibrate
disequilibrium
disarrangement
distributional
distributively
distractedness
destructionist
disorderliness
disorientation
discriminately
discriminating
discrimination
discriminatory
discriminative
disgruntlement
desert pavement
distressed area
distress signal
discretionally
Disasters of War
disassociation
disattribution
disputatiously
disputableness
disqualifiable
disfurnishment
disquisitional
discursiveness
disgustingness
disgustfulness
dissymmetrical
detached retina
detective story
data processing
data protection
determinedness
detestableness
detoxification
deuterium oxide
Deuteronomical
daughterliness
daughters-in-law
Deuxième Bureau
double-breasted
double-barreled
double concerto
double-declutch
double exposure
double entendre
double-flowered
double jeopardy
double majority
double negation
double negative
double rollover
Douglas Jardine
double standard
double-stopping
double saucepan
double-tonguing
drug resistance
Doubting-Castle
doubting Thomas
David Fabricius
David Baltimore
divided highway
David Ben-Gurion
David Berkowitz
dividing-engine
David Coulthard
devil's advocate
devil's food cake
devil-on-the-neck
development aid
devalorisation
devalorization
devil's snuff-box
Divina Commedia
davenport-trick
divertissement
diverticulated
diverticulitis
diverticulosis
Davis apparatus
devitalisation
devitalization
devotionalness
Downing College
down in the mouth
down in the dumps
down on one's luck
dexamphetamine
dextrorotation
dextrorotatory
Day of Atonement
Day of Judgement
daylight-saving
dizygotic twins
dazzle-painting
Dizzy Gillespie
exacerbescence
evangelicalism
evangelisation
evangelization
egalitarianism
examine-in-chief
Évariste Galois
Elasmobranchii
evaporated milk
exasperatingly
enantiomorphic
enantiostylous
emblematically
embellishingly
embolismic year
embarrassingly
embourgeoising
embryo transfer
eschatological
exclaustration
encyclopedical
Encyclopédiste
excrementitial
ecclesiologist
ecclesiastical
Ecclesiasticus
escalier dérobé
excommunicable
excommunicator
encephalopathy
encephalograph
exceptionalism
exceptionality
escape sequence
escape velocity
excursion train
excess capacity
excuse my French
excision repair
exclusion order
excruciatingly
encounter group
endless gearing
Eudemian Ethics
endoradiosonde
endarterectomy
elderberry wine
elder statesman
✧elder statesmen
endoscopically
endosmotically
Ebenezer Howard
epexegetically
elementariness
emerging market
emergency light
Elephanta caves
even-handedness
elegiac stanzas
eternalisation
eternalization
exempt supplies
Electra complex
eleutheromania
electric guitar
electric heater
electric window
electrifyingly
electrovalence
electrovalency
electron camera
electrogenesis
electrotechnic
electioneering
electrochemist
electrothermal
electrothermic
electrotherapy
electronically
electronic book
electrogilding
electrokinetic
electrobiology
electronic mail
electrowinning
electroplating
electromotance
electroforming
electron optics
electro-optical
electro-osmosis
electro-osmotic
electrostatics
electroculture
electrodynamic
electromyogram
electrolytical
execution error
every second day
enemy at the door
enemy at the gate
efficient cause
effeminateness
enfant terrible
enforceability
effervescingly
effortlessness
ergocalciferol
engagement ring
English terrier
English disease
English mustard
engineer's chain
Eugene Goossens
Eugenio Montale
eigen-frequency
Eighty Years' War
et hoc genus omne
echocardiogram
ethnic minority
ethylene glycol
Ethel Rosenberg
exhilaratingly
ethnobotanical
ethnologically
ethnographical
etherification
enharmonically
exhaustibility
exhaustiveness
Elizabeth David
Elizabeth Kenny
Elisabethville
Elizabethanism

Elizabeth Bowen
Elizabeth Arden
Elizabeth Frink
Elizabeth Grant
Eliza Doolittle
epigenetically
epidemiologist
Emile Clapeyron
Epidermophyton
Emiliano Zapata
editio princeps
edible dormouse
evil-mindedness
enigmatography
Elinor Dashwood
epicontinental
epigrammatical
epigraphically
emission theory
epistolography
epistemologist
existentialism
existentialist
Emil von Behring
Emily Dickinson
Ella Fitzgerald
eulogistically
eclipse plumage
enlisted person
El Misti Volcano
Ernest Starling
Edouard Beneden
Eroica Symphony
egocentrically
enough is enough
exothermically
emotionalistic
econometrician
economy of scale
evolutionarily
evolutionistic
emphaticalness
expediently
express oneself
expressionless
expression mark
express company
expression stop
express volumes
expressiveness
espagnole sauce
expense account
expanding metal
expansion joint
expansion board
expansionistic
explorationist
euphorbiaceous
explosive rivet
empire-building
experienceable
experienceless
experientially
experimentally
emperor penguin
Emperor Akihito
empyreumatical
empathetically
euphuistically
Eurocentricity
earth satellite
earthshakingly
Egremont Castle
Earl of Aberdeen
Earl of Cardigan
edriophthalmic
Earl of Rosebery
Earl of Sandwich
Euro-Parliament
Euroscepticism
erratic boulder
early day motion
early-Victorian
Eustachian tube
East Coast fever
et sic de ceteris
ens per accidens
Easter Saturday
Elsinore Castle
exsanguination
ex-servicewoman
extramaritally
extra marmalade
extra-parochial
extracanonical
extravehicular
extraneousness
extraforaneous
extra-condensed
extracorporeal
extraordinaire
extractability
Estuary English
extreme unction
extrinsicality
extemporaneity
extemporaneous
entomostracous
extended credit
extended family
extended memory
extensionalism
extensionality
eat one's head off
extinguishable
extinguishment
eutrophication
external degree
entertainingly
enterocentesis
esterification
Enter the Dragon
extortionately
enthronisation
enthronization
enteropneustal
enterprisingly
enterprise zone
Ettore Sottsass
Estates General
enthusiastical
enthymematical
equiangularity
educationalist
eburnification
equiponderance
ex utraque parte
emulsification
equation of time
en ventre sa mère
Edward de Baliol
Edward John Eyre
Edward M Kennedy
Edward Molyneux
Edward Steichen
Edward the Elder
Edward Woodward
erythroblastic
erythropoiesis
erythropoietic
erythropoietin
etymologically
fray at the edges
foam at the mouth
flatbed scanner
flamboyant-tree
Françoise Sagan
François Guizot
François Villon
Francis of Sales
Francis Picabia
Francis Kilvert
Francis Poulenc
Francis Quarles
flame-retardant
flagelliferous
flagellomaniac
fraternisation
fraternization
foamed plastics
flat-footedness
flaughter-spade
flash blindness
featherbedding
feather-brained
flagitiousness
foam insulation
Frank Tarkenton
Frankie Dettori
Frank Churchill
Franklin Pierce
flag-lieutenant
flag of distress
flagrante bello
fabric softener
fibrocartilage
factitiousness
focal infection
facile princeps
facinorousness
factor analysis
factory farming
fiduciary issue
fiddle-faddling
federalisation
federalization
fides implicita
French-Canadian
French dressing
French knickers
French marigold
French-polisher
French vermouth
Freddie Mercury
field allowance
freedom fighter
field ambulance
field preaching
field artillery
Frédéric Chopin
Frederick Soddy
Frederick Loewe
Frederick Twort
free enterprise
feel-good factor
free-handedness
feeble-mindedly
free-spokenness
feel the draught
Fifth Amendment
fifth columnist
figure of speech
figurativeness
fight windmills
fighting chance
Fighting French
Friedrich Krupp
Flinders Petrie
Flinders Ranges
fringillaceous
fringe medicine
flight engineer
flight envelope
flight-recorder
Frisian Islands
friendlessness
faint-heartedly
fair to middling
Fridtjof Nansen
fairy godmother
Fritz Schaudinn
fallaciousness
felicitousness
full-court press
fille de chambre
false pregnancy
false pretences
folding-machine
filling station
falsifiability
Feliks Topolski
fellow creature
fellow-commoner
fall on deaf ears
Fallopian tubes
filiopietistic
follow-my-leader
fall on one's feet
follow one's nose
fellow townsman
Felipe González
Filippino Lippi
full steam ahead
film supporting
full to bursting
fully-fashioned
femme de chambre
family grouping
family planning
feminine ending
Fontana Magiore
Finlandisation
Finlandization
✧fundamentalism
fundamentalist
fundamentality
fantasticality
fantastication
fantasy cricket
finger-alphabet
fence the tables
finger-painting
finger-pointing
fingerprinting
finders keepers
fingers-breadth
Finn mac Cumhail
Fenimore Cooper
finance company
Financial Times
Fanconi anaemia
funeral parlour
finishing touch
fenestra ovalis
functional food
functus officio
fancy dress ball
flog a dead horse
from bad to worse
from bank to bank
food-controller
Florence fennel
frozen shoulder
Florentine iris
flowery-kirtled
froth flotation
frolicsomeness
foot-in-the-mouth
floriculturist
flock wallpaper
footplatewoman
footplatewomen
foot-pound force
floor exercises
frontierswoman
from time to time
floating beacon
floating bridge
floating charge
floating island
floating kidney
front-end loaded
floating policy
front-end system
Fernando Alonso
Fernando de Soto
fore-and-aft sail
forward-looking
forward pricing
fire department
force force pump
former prophets
fermentability
fermentescible
for heaven's sake
for the duration
for the high jump
for the hell of it
forthrightness
for the life of me
for the love of it
for the most part
farthingsworth
further outlook
Ferdinand Braun
formidableness
ferrimagnetism
forbiddingness
forbidden fruit
far-sightedness
fortifications
forcible feeble
forbid the banns
for all it's worth
for all the world

Words marked ✧ can also be spelled with one or more capital letters

Ford Madox Brown
foraminiferous
for one's own hand
ferro-manganese
ferromagnesian
ferromagnetism
for good measure
foreordination
ferroprussiate
furor scribendi
forisfamiliate
foreseeability
fire salamander
foreshortening
first-class mail
first-class post
forethoughtful
fore-topgallant
furfuraldehyde
fortune-telling
Fergus Slattery
fortuitousness
fire-worshipper
fast and furious
foster-daughter
fisherman's luck
fisherman's ring
Fastens Tuesday
fastidiousness
fashionability
fission reactor
fashionmonging
fatherlessness
Fathers and Sons
fatiguableness
fitting-out dock
futtock-shrouds
four-centre arch
fluid mechanics
founding father
founders' shares
foundation-stop
fluff one's lines
four-leaf clover
four-letter word
fructification
Fountains Abbey
fourth interval
fault tolerance
fourth official
four-wheel drive
four-wheel-drive
fovea centralis
Five Easy Pieces
fivepence piece
fives-and-threes
favourableness
fixed satellite
Flyfishers' Club
Feynman diagram
flying bedstead
flying buttress
Flying Dutchman
flying squirrel
graham crackers
granadilla tree
Guardian Angels
granddad collar
grand serjeanty
goal difference
glanduliferous

grandiloquence
glandular fever
Grand St Bernard
grande toilette
Grand Jury Prize
graveyard shift
Gräfenberg spot
grace-and-favour
gram-equivalent
graffiti artist
grangerisation
grangerization
Gnathobdellida
graphic formula
graphic granite
graphics tablet
graphitisation
graphitization
gracious living
grammaticality
grammaticaster
go along with you
Glagolitic Mass
Giacomo Puccini
grasp the nettle
glass harmonica
grass someone up
Giant's Causeway
Glastonbury Tor
graduate school
gratuitousness
Granville Hicks
Gibraltar board®
Gabriel's hounds
God save the mark
God's own country
go down the drain
go down the tubes
gregariousness
gleg at the uptak
Greyfriars Hall
Gielgud Theatre
grey-goose shaft
grey-goose quill
Gaea hypothesis
Greyhound Derby
Gaelic football
gleg in the uptak
grey literature
Greenland whale
green labelling
Green Cross Code
Gregorian chant
Gregorian modes
Gregorian tones
Gregory of Tours
Gregory of Nyssa
Gregory's powder
grecque meander
Giessbach Falls
greisenisation
greisenization
ghetto fabulous
great white hope
Great Slave Lake
great prolation
Great Attractor
Grenville Davey
greywacke-slate
go for the doctor
Guild Socialism

Griff Rhys Jones
griffon vulture
going-away dress
Gaia hypothesis
Guillermo Vilas
Guillaume Farel
Guillaume Dufay
grist to the mill
galvanized iron
galvanoplastic
galactophorous
galactopoietic
golden pheasant
Golden Pavilion
Gilbert Sheldon
Gilbert Islands
Gillian Wearing
Golgi apparatus
go like hot cakes
Galileo Galilei
galeopithecoid
galeopithecine
gold-of-pleasure
gelatinisation
gelatinization
gamma radiation
Gamaliel Pickle
gaming contract
genealogically
Gennady Yanayev
gingerbread man
gynaecological
gender-specific
gone for a Burton
gentleman-cadet
gentleman usher
genomic library
gynomonoecious
gynandromorphy
genericisation
genericization
gentrification
general damages
general paresis
general reserve
general meeting
general servant
general officer
general council
general journal
generalissimos
generalisation
general-purpose
generalization
genetic parents
genethliacally
genethlialogic
Geneva movement
global exchange
Giovanni Pisano
global variable
good conscience
gooseberry-bush
gooseberry-fool
gooseberry-moth
gooseberry-wine
globe artichoke
geometrisation
geometrization
glove-stretcher
geocentrically

Geoffrey Bolton
Geoffrey Fisher
good fellowship
goodfellowship
good-for-nothing
George A Akerlof
Georgian planet
George Buchanan
George Berkeley
Georgi Dimitrov
George Gershwin
George H Whipple
George Harrison
George Knightly
George Lansbury
George Meredith
Georges Simenon
Georgette Heyer
good-humouredly
geothermometer
geolinguistics
groundbreaking
good neighbours
groundlessness
geognostically
ground squirrel
geological time
geopolitically
geomorphogenic
geomorphologic
group selection
group insurance
geoarchaeology
geographically
glossy magazine
goods for own use
glossy starling
geostrategical
growth industry
growth promoter
Giosuè Carducci
Good Vibrations
geosynchronous
glory of the snow
German shepherd
gardening leave
garnishee order
Garrick Theatre
Garfield Sobers
Gerald Gardiner
Gerald M Edelman
gerontological
Gordon Richards
garboard strake
gyrostabiliser
gyrostabilizer
gyroscopically
Gareth of Orkney
Garry Winogrand
Gustave Courbet
Gestalt therapy
Gasteromycetes
go to all lengths
gated community
gutter-merchant
go the extra mile
get off one's bike
get the breeze up
get the best of it
get the better of
get jiggy with it

Gatwick Airport
get one's fairing
get one's jollies
get one's own back
get someone at it
get to first base
go to the country
get it in the neck
glutaraldehyde
glutaminic acid
Giuseppe Giusti
gluteus maximus
grudge a thought
go up in the world
glucocorticoid
give a hammering
Gavrilo Princip
governmentally
give someone gyp
give the meeting
give the heave-ho
give up the ghost
Gewürztraminer
go with the worse
Gwyneth Paltrow
Hoare-Laval Pact
heaven-directed
heat exhaustion
heavenly bodies
heavenly-minded
heathenishness
heather mixture
heather-bleater
heather-bluiter
heather-blutter
Heaviside layer
heavier-than-air
headmastership
heads and thraws
heart-searching
heart-heaviness
healthlessness
hyaluronic acid
heavy chemicals
heavy breathing
Hebraistically
Hebrew alphabet
hybrid computer
Hubble constant
hobbledehoydom
hobbledehoyish
hobbledehoyism
hebetudinosity
habit and repute
hickery-pickery
huckleberrying
hack someone off
hydraulic brake
hydraulic press
hidden treasure
hydromagnetics
hydrocephalous
hydromechanics
hydronephrosis
hydronephrotic
hydrogeologist
hydrocellulose
hydro-aeroplane
hydrophobicity
hydrobiologist
hydropneumatic

hydrocoralline
hydrologically
hydroponically
hydrocortisone
hydrographical
Hydropterideae
hydrosulphuric
hydroextractor
hydrodynamical
hydroxyapatite
hydatid disease
hierarchically
haemagglutinin
haematogenesis
haematophagous
haematopoiesis
haematopoietic
heel of Achilles
hieroglyphical
Hierosolymitan
hierogrammatic
hierographical
hyetographical
haemocytometer
Hogwarts School
High Commission
Hague Agreement
high-handedness
Highland cattle
highly-seasoned
high-level waste
Hugh MacDiarmid
high-mindedness
hygroscopicity
hagiographical
hygrographical
high-principled
high-priesthood
high-resolution
high-speed steel
high technology
Heinrich Olbers
Heinrich Rohrer
heliacal rising
hold all the aces
half-a-sovereign
Holy Cross Abbey
Halldór Laxness
holier-than-thou
hell for leather
hold in contempt
holding pattern
holding company
hole in the heart
helminthologic
holometabolism
holometabolous
heliosciophyte
hold one's breath
hold one's ground
hold one's tongue
hold one's whisht
heliographical
halfpennyworth
Haloragidaceae
hallucinogenic
hold up one's head
half-wellington
Holly Golightly
hold your horses
humpback bridge
humidification
Home Department
hammer and tongs
homme d'affaires
homme de lettres
homoeomorphism
homoeomorphous
homoeothermous
homoeoteleuton
Humbert Humbert
homogenisation
homogenization
Humphrey Bogart
Humphry Clinker
Hemel Hempstead
Hamamelidaceae
hemimetabolous
human resources
human guinea pig
Hamersley Range
hemispheroidal
Hamish MacInnes
humoursomeness
hunter-gatherer
Henley-on-Thames
Hansen's disease
Henri Becquerel
Hanging Gardens
hunting leopard
hunting-leopard
handicraftsman
Henrietta Maria
Henri Dutrochet
handkerchieves
hen-and-chickens
Honoré de Balzac
hundred-per-cent
huntsman spider
hunt-the-slipper
honourableness
Henry Cavendish
Henry the Fowler
Henry VI Part One
Henry VI Part Two
Henry Kissinger
honeycomb tripe
Henry John Heinz
Henry Armstrong
Henry IV Part One
Henry IV Part Two
H Gobind Khorana
hooly and fairly
hypoallergenic
hypocritically
hypochondriasm
hypochondriast
hypocoristical
hypodermically
hip replacement
hippety-hoppety
hop, skip and jump
hypomenorrhoea
hypomixolydian
hypnotherapist
hippopotamuses
haplostemonous
hypophysectomy
hypercatalexis
hypercalcaemia
hyperbatically
hypernatraemia
hyperacuteness
hyperkeratosis
hypersensitise
hypersensitive
hypersensitize
hyperaesthesia
hyperaesthesic
hyperaesthetic
hyperventilate
hyperlipidemia
hyperglycaemia
hyperinflation
hyperbolically
hyperconscious
hypertrophical
hypercriticise
hypercriticism
hypercriticize
hyperextension
hypostatically
hepaticologist
hypothetically
hephthemimeral
hop, step and jump
hypothyroidism
hapax legomenon
Hernando de Soto
hermaphroditic
herbal medicine
Herman Melville
Hermann Goering
hereditability
hereditariness
horse latitudes
horae canonicae
horrendousness
Harley Davidson®
horse-godmother
herpetological
horse artillery
Herbert Marcuse
Herbert Spencer
Horse Lying Down
Harefoot Harold
Hurlingham Club
herring-fishery
Heraion of Samos
horticulturist
Harold D Babcock
Harold Nicolson
Herald's College
harmonic motion
harmonic pencil
harmonic series
harmoniousness
horror-stricken
harpsichordist
heresiographer
heritage centre
Hercules beetle
Hercules' choice
harrying of hell
his cake is dough
hysterectomise
hysterectomize
Hesketh Pearson
hostess trolley
hospital corner
hospital doctor
hospitableness
hostile witness
histopathology
histogenically
histochemistry
historical cost
historiography
histoplasmosis
histologically
histolytically
histrionically
hesitation form
hot-water bottle
hot and bothered
hit one in the eye
heterochromous
heterochronism
heterochronous
heteromorphism
heteromorphous
heterophyllous
heterospecific
heterosomatous
heterostrophic
heterothallism
heterozygosity
housemaid's knee
house of ill fame
House of Commons
house of worship
house physician
House and Garden
haute politique
have an edge over
have a thick skin
have a tile loose
have a roving eye
have a great mind
have been around
have clean hands
have come to stay
have everything
have had a gutful
have had one's day
have it both ways
have no words for
have one too many
have one's own way
have the jitters
have the goods on
how the wind lies
Hawaiian guitar
Hexactinellida
hexagonal chess
Isaac Rosenberg
inaccurateness
Isabelita Perón
Isabelle Adjani
image converter
image processor
inadequateness
imaginableness
inalienability
Italianisation
Italianization
I'm all right, Jack
Ioannis Metaxas
in another world
inapprehension
inapprehensive
inappreciation
inappreciative
inapproachable
inapproachably
inappositeness
inauspiciously
inarticulately
inarticulation
inauthenticity
inartificially
inalterability
inartistically
in a state of flux
inadvisability
incidentalness
incident centre
incident office
incredibleness
Increase Mather
incogitability
inclinableness
income drawdown
incommensurate
incompleteness
incommodiously
incompressible
incommunicable
incommunicably
inconscionable
incandescently
inconveniently
inconversant in
inconsequently
inconsiderable
inconsiderably
incendiary bomb
inconsistently
incontiguously
inconclusively
incontrollable
incontrollably
inco-ordination
incoordination
incapacitation
incorporeality
incestuousness
incautiousness
Indian Civil War
Indian elephant
Indian medicine
Indian Uprising
indubitability
induced current
induction lamps
induction valve
induction motor
indecomposable
indecipherable
indecipherably
indoctrination
indecorousness
indecisiveness
indifferentism
indifferentist
indefiniteness
indigenisation
indigenousness
indigenization
indemonstrable
indemonstrably
indomitability
indoor firework
indirect object
indirect speech

indiscerptible
indistinctness
indiscoverable
indisposedness
industrial park
indescribables
indestructible
indestructibly
indiscreetness
indiscriminate
indiscreteness
indeterminable
indeterminably
indivisibility
inexcusability
iceberg lettuce
ineffectuality
inevitableness
idealistically
Irek Mukhamedov
inexorableness
inexpiableness
inexpressibles
inexpressively
inexplicitness
inertia selling
identical rhyme
identical twins
identification
inestimability
identity crisis
identity parade
ineluctability
I beg your pardon?
inframaxillary
Infralapsarian
infrangibility
infeasibleness
inflation-proof
inflammability
infrastructure
infectiousness
inflexibleness
inflectionally
inflectionless
infelicitously
infimae species
infopreneurial
ingratiatingly
ingloriousness
inhabitability
inhabitiveness
ichthyosaurian
ichthyolatrous
ichthyophagist
ichthyophagous
ichthyological
ichnographical
Ithuriel's spear
inharmoniously
inheritability
inherited error
inheritance tax
imitation pearl
icing on the cake
Irish wolfhound
inimitableness
initialisation
initialization
initiation rite
initiator codon
idiopathically
iniquitousness
ill-naturedness
in loco parentis
illegitimately
illegitimation
Islamicisation
Islamicization
illuminatingly
illimitability
ill-intentioned
Island of Staffa
island universe
Isle of Anglesey
Isle of Colonsay
ill-conditioned
illustrational
illustratively
illiterateness
in living memory
immobilisation
immobilization
immaculateness
immoderateness
Ismail Merchant
immunochemical
immunogenicity
immunogenetics
immunoglobulin
immunophoresis
immune response
immunosuppress
immiserisation
immiserization
immitigability
immethodically
innominate bone
innominate vein
innumerability
Inns of Chancery
inner-direction
isolated replay
inordinateness
inoperableness
in one's born days
in one fell swoop
in one's mind's eye
in one's own right
inorganisation
inorganization
isothiocyanate
isodiametrical
isotopic number
iconographical
Ironside Edmund
Igor Stravinsky
I don't believe so
ivory-porcelain
implacableness
in plain English
implausibility
impracticality
impact adhesive
impacted faeces
implementation
impregnability
impressibility
impressionable
impressiveness
imponderabilia
in penny numbers
improvableness
improvvisatore
imperial bushel
imperial gallon
imperial octavo
Imperial Palace
imperial weight
imparidigitate
impermeability
imperceptively
imperfectively
imperviability
impercipiently
imperviousness
imparisyllabic
imperative mood
imperativeness
imperturbation
impassableness
imposthumation
impassibleness
impoverishment
inquisiturient
irrecognisable
irrecognizable
irreconcilable
irreconcilably
irreducibility
irrefutability
irrelativeness
irremovability
irreplevisable
irreproachable
irreproachably
irreproducible
irreparability
irrespectively
irresolubility
irresoluteness
irresponsively
irrestrainable
irresuscitable
irresuscitably
in round figures
in round numbers
irrevocability
instalment plan
in sober sadness
insider dealing
insider trading
Inside the Whale
Inspector Rebus
Inspector Morse
insufficiently
insignificance
insignificancy
inspirationism
inspirationist
institutionary
insalubriously
insulating tape
in someone's debt
insensibleness
insanitariness
it's your funeral
inseparability
insuperability
insuppressible
insuppressibly
instructorship
insurrectional
instrumentally
insurmountable
insurmountably
inscrutability
it's a small world
insusceptively
ipsissima verba
insatiableness
intrafallopian
intra-abdominal
intramercurial
intramedullary
intramolecular
intra-articular
intransigeance
intransigeancy
intransigently
intransitively
intransitivity
intransmutable
intractability
in the same canoe
in the family way
in the aggregate
in the big league
in the slightest
in the top flight
in the ascendant
integrationist
intuitionalism
intuitionalist
intrinsicality
intellectually
intelligential
intelligentsia
intelligentzia
intolerability
intempestively
intempestivity
intangibleness
intentionality
iatrochemistry
introductorily
internal energy
intermaxillary
Internationale
internal memory
internal market
intervalometer
interactionism
interactionist
interdependent
interpenetrant
interpenetrate
interferential
intermediately
intermediation
intermediatory
interpellation
interferometer
interferometry
intercessional
intercessorial
intervertebral
interjectional
intersectional
interventional
intersexuality
interchange fee
interlineation
interlingually
intermigration
intermittently
interplanetary
interambulacra
interior design
intermolecular
intercommunion
intercommunity
interconnector
interconnexion
interior-sprung
interlocutrice
interlocutress
interspatially
intergradation
interpretation
interpretative
interpretively
interestedness
interstitially
interpunctuate
interruptively
intertwinement
intertwiningly
intussuscepted
into the bargain
intrusive sheet
intoxicatingly
in usum Delphini
invigoratingly
invaluableness
invincibleness
Irving Langmuir
inviolableness
invariableness
inverted commas
inversion layer
investment bank
investment bond
investment club
inveterateness
in working order
Ieyasu Tokugawa
Jean de Florette
Jean Henri Fabre
Jean-Luc Dehaene
Joan Littlewood
Jean Mari Roland
Joanna Trollope
Jean-Paul Sartre
Joan Sutherland
job description
jobs for the boys
jackboot around
Jacob Bronowski
✧jack-by-the-hedge
Jack Cunningham
Jackie Robinson
Jack-in-the-green
Jackson Pollock
Jacques Derrida
Jeddart justice
judicial combat
judicial factor
judicial murder
judicial review
Jude the Obscure
jogging bottoms
John Barleycorn
John Barbirolli
John Boyd Dunlop

John Couch Adams
John Duns Scotus
John Galsworthy
John Jacob Astor
John Logie Baird
John McLaughlin
Johann Agricola
Johannes Brahms
Johannes Fugger
Johannes Kepler
Johannisberger
John of the Cross
John Rutherford
John Stuart Mill
John the Baptist
John Von Neumann
juice extractor
join the colours
joint-stock bank
Julian calendar
jalapeño pepper
July Revolution
Julius Dedekind
Julius von Sachs
Jamie Lee Curtis
James Mackenzie
James Parkinson
James Callaghan
James Clark Ross
James A Michener
Jimmy Johnstone
jingling Johnny
jingoistically
Japanese beetle
Japanese garden
Japanese medlar
Japanese vellum
Japanese War God
Jürgen Habermas
Jeremiah Clarke
Jaroslav Drobny
J Presper Eckert
jurisdictional
Jerusalem cross
Jerry Abershawe
Jerzy Grotowski
José Capablanca
Joschka Fischer
justifiability
just intonation
José María Aznar
Joseph Goebbels
Joseph Grimaldi
Josephine Baker
Joseph P Kennedy
Joseph Pulitzer
Joseph Rowntree
José Ramos-Horta
Joshua Reynolds
jusqu'auboutist
joukery-pawkery
journalisation
journalization
jeweller's rouge
jewellers' putty
Jayne Mansfield
Józef Pilsudski
Krapp's Last Tape
knapping-hammer
kick in the pants
kick in the teeth
keep a calm sough
keep a tight rein
keep a good house
kneading-trough
keep early hours
Kremlinologist
keep one's chin up
keep one's hair on
keep one's hand in
keep one's mind on
keep one's wool on
keep quiet about
keep under wraps
Kegel exercises
knight bachelor
knight-bachelor
knight banneret
knight errantry
Knight of St John
Knights Templar
Knights of Labor
knickerbockers
knitting needle
Kailyard school
Ku Klux Klansman
Kilmarnock cowl
Kalahari Desert
Kellogg College
Konrad Adenauer
kindergartener
Kenneth Grahame
Kenneth Branagh
Ken Livingstone
King James Bible
King Philip's War
Kingsley Martin
king's messenger
kinesiological
kinetheodolite
know a move or two
Knotenschiefer
knock on the head
knowledge-based
know-nothingism
know one's onions
knotted spurrey
Kupferschiefer
Kipp's apparatus
Kaposi's sarcoma
Karma Chameleon
karaoke machine
Kirkstall Abbey
Kurt Schwitters
karstification
keratinisation
keratinization
kissing disease
kissing-strings
kitchen cabinet
Kathleen Turner
Kathy Whitworth
keyhole surgery
keystone effect
Kyzyl Kum Desert
Kazan Cathedral
lead apes in hell
loan collection
leave well alone
leave of absence
leave no effects
loaded question
leaden-stepping
leather-mouthed
leathery turtle
leading counsel
leading article
leading strings
liaison officer
lead tetraethyl
lead to the altar
lead up the aisle
labradorescent
library edition
library binding
libidinousness
Lubbock Airport
libertarianism
liberalisation
liberalization
labyrinthodont
lobar pneumonia
liberated woman
lobotomisation
lobotomization
Labour Exchange
lucid intervals
local authority
LA Confidential
licentiateship
licentiousness
lector benevole
lick one's wounds
lachrymal gland
Lucas van Leyden
locus classicus
Lacus Somniorum
lecythidaceous
Lucius Apuleius
Leda and the Swan
lady of the night
Ludovic Kennedy
Leeward Islands
lie on one's hands
lieutenantship
Lee Buck Trevino
life expectancy
left-handedness
Lofoten Islands
Le Grand Macabre
luggage-carrier
lugubriousness
logical atomism
legalistically
lignocellulose
Legion of Honour
legislatorship
light-heartedly
lightning chess
light flyweight
legitimisation
legitimateness
legitimization
light intensity
lighting-up time
light pollution
lighter-than-air
Leicestershire
Leibnitzianism
like a dying duck
lokshen pudding
like it or lump it
like-mindedness
Lake Okeechobee
Lake Stymphalos
Lake Tanganyika
Lake Windermere
Lombardy poplar
lumbar puncture
lambda particle
Lemuel Gulliver
lumbersomeness
lymphoid tissue
lymphangiogram
lamellirostral
laminated glass
luminous energy
Le Morte d'Arthur
limited edition
limited company
limited express
Limbus infantum
linear equation
Linacre College
landed interest
long-headedness
lanthanum glass
luncheon-basket
longhorn beetle
lending library
long in the tooth
longitudinally
Long John Silver
Langmuir trough
line management
Lenin Mausoleum
Lyndon B Johnson
Lennox Berkeley
line one's pocket
London Marathon
Lincoln Airport
Lincoln College
Long Parliament
lunar distances
longs and shorts
longshore drift
Langston Hughes
languorousness
linguistically
longwall system
long-windedness
Leonard Woolley
Lloyd Honeyghan
Lionel Trilling
look for trouble
lyophilisation
lyophilization
Leonhard Hutter
Leonid Brezhnev
Léonide Massine
Leonid Kravchuk
Lyon King of arms
Lhotse Mountain
lepidodendroid
lapidification
lipogrammatism
lipogrammatist
leptodactylous
leptocephalous
lapsus memoriae
loquaciousness
liquidity ratio
liquid paraffin
liquorice-vetch
Lord Chancellor
Lyrical Ballads
Lord Carrington
large intestine
larger than life
larger-than-life
Lord Elwyn-Jones
lyriform organs
Lord Hattersley
Lord Howe Island
Lord John Fisher
Lord Lieutenant
Lorenzo Da Ponte
laryngoscopist
laryngological
Lord of the Rings
Lord of the Flies
Lord Rutherford
lords in waiting
lords and ladies
Lords Spiritual
La Resurrezione
lares et penates
listed building
listen to reason
lost generation
lasciviousness
Les Fleurs du Mal
lose one's tongue
laser-light show
Lothar Matthaus
Latter-day Saint
letter of credit
letter-of-marque
latter prophets
Letters of peace
Letters of Peter
Lëtzebuergesch
Luther Vandross
let the side down
Little and Large
little by little
little green men
little magazine
let someone know
lithochromatic
lithologically
lithographical
Lytton Strachey
lithontriptist
lithonthryptic
lettre de change
lettre de cachet
lettre de marque
liturgiologist
lateral incisor
lateralisation
lateralization
Literary Review
literary source
latitudinarian
Launcelot Gobbo
Launcelot du Lac
Laurel and Hardy
Laurence Binyon
Laurence Eusden
Laurence Sterne
louping-on-stane
leucocythaemia
leukocythaemia
leucocytopenia

leucocytopenic
leukocytopenia
leukocytopenic
leucocytolysis
leukocytolysis
Louis Chevrolet
Louis Althusser
Louis Armstrong
live and let live
live and breathe
live by one's wits
love-in-idleness
levelling screw
levelling-staff
lavender cotton
loving kindness
livery cupboard
Love Songs in Age
law-abidingness
law of parsimony
law of the jungle
low-alcohol beer
lower criticism
lowest of the low
lexicographist
lexical meaning
loxodromic line
Leyland cypress
Loyalty Islands
lay it on the line
mean lethal dose
Muammar Gaddafi
meadow mushroom
Maarten Schmidt
measurableness
measuring-wheel
measuring spoon
Mobutu Seze Seko
mechanicalness
mechanized Sikh
moccasin flower
Michael Faraday
Michael Jackson
Michaelmas term
Michael Meacher
Michael Denness
Michael Bentine
Michael Tippett
Michael Holding
Michael Hordern
Michael Douglas
Michael Collins
Michael Johnson
Michael Holroyd
Michael Brunson
macadamisation
macadamization
mackerel breeze
Michele Platini
Michel Foucault
Mickey Spillane
Mackenzie Range
Mackenzie River
mock-heroically
machinegunning
Macmillan nurse
macro-marketing
micromarketing
microbarograph
macrodactylous
macroeconomics
microeconomics
micrometeorite
microdetection
macrocephalous
microcephalous
micropegmatite
microaerophile
microseismical
microchemistry
microcircuitry
microminiature
microbiologist
microinjection
macromolecular
micrologically
microcomponent
microcomputing
macrosporangia
microsporangia
microprocessor
microstructure
macroevolution
microevolution
macaroni cheese
mocks the pauses
mock turtle soup
mucous membrane
mucoviscidosis
medical officer
medicalisation
medicalization
medicamentally
medicine bottle
medicinal leech
mode dispersion
Midnight Cowboy
Middle-American
middle distance
middle-distance
muddle-headedly
modularisation
modularization
meddlesomeness
modal auxiliary
Modern Painters
moderate breeze
meditativeness
muddy the waters
meeting of minds
Mies van der Rohe
magical realism
magical realist
Miguel Asturias
magnetic bottle
magnetic curves
Miguel Indurain
magnetic moment
magnetic mirror
magnetic needle
magnetic stripe
magneto-elastic
magnetospheric
magneto-optical
magniloquently
Maggie Tulliver
megalomaniacal
Magister Artium
megasporangium
megasporophyll
megatechnology
Magnus Albertus
megavertebrate
Mohamed al-Fayed
Mohammed Aideed
Mohammed Neguib
Mahamuni Pagoda
Mohandas Gandhi
Mahayana Sutras
maiden fortress
maidenhair-tree
mailing machine
maître de ballet
Meissner effect
Mt Ixtaccihuatl
maintenance-man
Meistersingers
major-generalcy
majesticalness
make a night of it
Mikhail Kalinin
Mikhail Bakunin
make a song about
make a poor mouth
Mt Kanchenjunga
McKenzie Friend
make rings round
make so free as to
make the running
make up one's mind
multarticulate
male chauvinism
male chauvinist
molecular sieve
malice prepense
Malacopterygii
malacostracous
malodorousness
millenarianism
multilaterally
multiracialism
multifariously
multifactorial
milking machine
milling machine
milking parlour
multithreading
multiple cinema
multiple-choice
multiplication
multiplicative
multiflora rose
multifoliolate
multiprocessor
melt in the mouth
multinucleated
multicuspidate
multi-ownership
melamine resins
Multnomah Falls
mylonitisation
mylonitization
Milton Friedman
Miltonic sonnet
Malcolm Sargent
milk of magnesia
Malcolm Rifkind
malnourishment
malcontentedly
malappropriate
mole salamander
miles gloriosus
melastomaceous
military police
militarisation
militarization
malfunctioning
multum non multa
moment of a force
memorandum-book
memory-resident
Mr Mistoffelees
Mindanao Island
manual alphabet
manual exercise
manganese steel
mental hospital
mandarin collar
man-eating shark
mandarin orange
mind-bogglingly
Monochlamydeae
municipal court
monocarpellary
monochromatism
monkey business
monkey's wedding
manufacturable
man of the moment
manifold-writer
manageableness
McNaghten rules
manriding train
monolingualism
man in the street
mind-numblingly
men in grey suits
Man and Superman
Monroe doctrine
mend one's fences
Man Booker Prize
Monoplacophora
monoprionidian
manipulability
monopolisation
manipulatively
monopolization
monopropellant
monophthongise
monophthongize
mineral kingdom
mineral spirits
mineralisation
mongrelisation
mineralization
mongrelization
miner's phthisis
minority waiter
monosaccharide
ministerialist
Menispermaceae
Manx shearwater
✧**monotheletical**
monotheistical
monotonousness
munition-worker
minotaur beetle
menstrual cycle
money-scrivener
money of account
myocardiopathy
Mephistopheles
Mephistophelic
Mephistophilis
Mephostophilus
Mt Popocatepetl
morganatically
Maria Edgeworth
Mermaid Theatre
Margaret Atwood
Margaret DuPont
Margaret Fuller
Margaret Sanger
Murray Gell-Mann
margaritic acid
miraculousness
morocco leather
meridian circle
marketableness
market-gardener
murdering-piece
marvellousness
myrmecophagous
myrmecophilous
myrmecological
market research
morceau de salon
Marcgraviaceae
Marc Girardelli
Martha Gellhorn
merchandisable
merchandizable
Marchantiaceae
morphinomaniac
marching orders
merchant prince
merchant tailor
marsh woundwort
morphophonemic
marriage-broker
marriage bureau
marriage-favour
morning prayers
Martin Scorsese
Martin Van Buren
marble-breasted
marble-constant
moral necessity
moral certainty
moralistically
Marco Van Basten
Mario Chipolini
Marjorie Proops
mirror nuclides
Marco Polo sheep
mirror symmetry
mark of the Beast
mark/space ratio
meretriciously
Marcus Aurelius
Marcus Antonius
Marburg disease
morbus gallicus
marsupial mouse
martyrological
miscalculation
mustard plaster
massage parlour
mistake one's man
mistake one's way
musicians' cramp
misacceptation
music therapist
musical glasses
misadventurous

misadvisedness
misdescription
mysteriousness
miscellanarian
master of hounds
Mesdemoiselles
master sergeant
mismeasurement
misogynistical
mischief-making
Mrs Tiggy-Winkle
mastigophorous
mose in the chine
Miss Jean Brodie
Miss Jane Marple
Musala Mountain
misimprovement
misinterpreter
misanthropical
Mason-Dixon Line
misinformation
misinstruction
mastoid process
misgovernaunce
miscomputation
miscontentment
misapplication
mass production
misappropriate
misarrangement
mistranslation
mushroom-anchor
Musgrave Ranges
mesa transistor
mesaticephalic
mispunctuation
masculine rhyme
mosquito canopy
mutual inductor
Matra Mountains
meticulousness
metachromatism
mathematically
mathematicised
mathematicized
Mittel-European
Mitteleuropean
matresfamilias
motte and bailey
matter-of-factly
mothers' meeting
mother superior
Matthew Boulton
Matthew Bramble
mythical theory
matriarchalism
metalinguistic
metallogenetic
metal composite
metallographer
metallographic
metalloprotein
mettlesomeness
metempsychoses
metempsychosis
methodicalness
meteoric shower
meteoric stones
matron of honour
mythologically
metropolitical
meteorological
methodological
motion sickness
metaphorically
metaphosphoric
metoposcopical
metapsychology
metaphysically
motor generator
maternity leave
motivelessness
motivationally
methyl chloride
matryoshka doll
Maundy Thursday
Maurice Wilkins
Maurice Utrillo
mourning border
Mount Karisimbi
Mount Paricutin
Mount Aconcagua
mountain beaver
mountain biking
mountaineering
Mount Pichincha
mountain laurel
mountain marrow
mountain stream
mountain sorrel
mountain tallow
Mount Annapurna
Mount Kosciusko
Mount Tongariro
Mount Stromboli
moving pictures
moving pavement
mover and shaker
maxima cum laude
may it please you
mezzanine floor
muzzle velocity
✧neanderthal man
✧neanderthaloid
near the knuckle
✧nebuchadnezzar
noblesse oblige
noctambulation
nectareousness
nyctaginaceous
Nicobar Islands
niche marketing
nuclear warfare
nuclear reactor
nuclear physics
nuclear fission
nuclear-powered
nuclearisation
nuclearization
Nicolas Fouquet
Nicolas Poussin
Nicholas Ridley
neck of the woods
necessarianism
necessary place
necessary house
neck-sweetbread
Nadia Boulanger
Nudibranchiata
nudibranchiate
Nadine Gordimer
nievie-nick-nack
needle exchange
Nietzscheanism
neglectfulness
Nigel Hawthorne
Negro spiritual
Nightmare Abbey
night-blindness
night-flowering
night-foundered
night-fossicker
negative equity
negative number
negative proton
no hard feelings
noise pollution
neighborliness
naked-light mine
Nikolai Vavilov
nolo contendere
nolo episcopari
nil desperandum
null-modem cable
number-cruncher
numberlessness
nymphomaniacal
nimble-fingered
nominal account
nominalisation
nomenclatorial
nominalization
numerus clausus
numismatically
nematodiriasis
namby-pambiness
nine days' wonder
non-penetrative
non-performance
non-residential
non-belligerent
Nansen passport
nonsensicality
non-restrictive
non-destructive
non-chromosomal
nondisjunction
non-electrolyte
nine men's morris
Ninon de Lenclos
non-inflammable
non-involvement
non-concurrence
non-comedogenic
non-conformance
non-communicant
non-committally
non-compearance
non-co-operation
non-cooperation
non-competitive
non-contentious
non-operational
nanotechnology
nineteenth hole
non-judgemental
Naomi Mitchison
neocolonialism
neocolonialist
Neopythagorean
Napoleonic Wars
Norman Conquest
Norman Hartnell
normal solution
north-eastwards
north-westwards
Northumberland
North Yorkshire
north-north-east
north-north-west
northern lights
nursing officer
narcocatharsis
narcoterrorism
narrow-mindedly
nervous tension
nervous impulse
narcosynthesis
norepinephrine
norm-referenced
norethisterone
Nathaniel Bliss
not be having any
not the full quid
not a happy bunny
nothing special
nutritiousness
not lift a finger
not unnaturally
not any the wiser
national anthem
national church
national income
notional income
national school
nitrocellulose
nitroglycerine
not for the world
not worth shucks
natural wastage
natural science
natural therapy
natural virtues
natural history
naturalisation
natural numbers
naturalization
natura naturans
natura naturata
nature printing
Native American
Native-American
Native Canadian
Native-Canadian
native language
noteworthiness
not by a long shot
neural computer
neuraminic acid
nouveaux riches
neuropathology
neuroradiology
neuroscientist
neurobiologist
neurofibrillar
neurofibromata
neuroblastomas
neuroendocrine
neuroanatomist
neurologically
neurocomputing
Neuropteroidea
neurohypnology
neutral spirits
neutralisation
neutralization
Nevil Maskelyne
naval architect
✧never-never land
newfangledness
news conference
New Zealand flax
Newnham College
News of the World
newspaperwoman
newsworthiness
Newry and Mourne
orange-coloured
orange-squeezer
Ozark Mountains
oncogeneticist
oscillographic
occult sciences
oecumenicalism
onchocerciasis
occupationally
Ordnance Survey
old man of the sea
Oddfellows Club
old-gentlemanly
Old Deuteronomy
ordinary degree
ordinary seaman
ordinary shares
odd-come-shortly
Oedipus complex
Order of the Bath
order in council
orderly officer
old-established
ondes musicales
operative words
operating table
operationalism
operationalist
over-absorption
overburdensome
one's better half
overcompensate
overcommitment
over-confidence
overcapitalise
overcapitalize
overcorrection
overdependence
over-determined
overestimation
overeat oneself
one of these days
one of a thousand
oleaginousness
one's gorge rises
open-handedness
overindulgence
one-dimensional
one with another
one's jaw dropped
over my dead body
open-mindedness
oceanic islands
ocean-greyhound
one in a thousand
overprotective
overproduction
overpopulation

Words marked ✧ can also be spelled with one or more capital letters

overpoweringly
oneirocritical
one-armed bandit
over-refinement
overspecialise
overspecialize
overscrupulous
over-the-counter
open to question
✧open university
overwhelmingly
official family
offset printing
off-off-Broadway
off the back foot
off the shoulder
off one's trolley
off-job training
✧Oxford movement
of great article
organ-harmonium
organic disease
organ-pipe coral
organometallic
organisability
organismically
organisational
organizability
organized crime
organizer-purse
organizational
ophthalmoscope
ophthalmoscopy
ophthalmometer
ophthalmometry
oligarchically
Oliver Cromwell
Oliver Plunkett
opinionatively
Olivier Theatre
Oriental Region
oligopsonistic
oligocythaemia
Oki Archipelago
obiit sine prole
opisthoglossal
opisthocoelian
opisthocoelous
opisthographic
object language
oak-leaf cluster
Oskar Kokoschka
obligatoriness
oil-filled cable
Orlando Gibbons
Orlando Furioso
oil-control ring
oblate spheroid
osmoregulation
osmoregulatory
omnibenevolent
omnibus edition
omnicompetence
of no fixed abode
Ornette Coleman
Ornithodelphia
ornithodelphic
ornithophilous
ornithological
ornithomorphic
omnium-gatherum

omnivorousness
orobanchaceous
onomatopoiesis
otolaryngology
on one's beam-ends
on one's deathbed
on one's doorstep
ozone-depleting
ozone depletion
on one's head be it
on one's lonesome
on one's last legs
orographically
on prescription
oppressiveness
oophorectomise
oophorectomize
opposite number
opposite prompt
on special offer
oyster mushroom
on someone's tail
oesophagoscope
obsequiousness
observation car
observableness
obstructionism
obstructionist
obstreperously
outward-sainted
outlandishness
outrageousness
optical pumping
optoelectronic
on the off chance
on the off-chance
on the offchance
outperformance
on the shop floor
on the short side
on the windy side
ottrelite-slate
on the high ropes
on the right tack
on the breadline
on the wrong tack
on the other hand
out of character
out of this world
out of the window
out of one's depth
out of one's skull
out of condition
ostrich-feather
Otto Lilienthal
optimalisation
optimalization
optimistically
ostentatiously
octingentenary
orthopedically
osteodermatous
orthochromatic
orthophosphate
Osteoglossidae
Orthodox Church
osteologically
osteoarthritic
osteoarthritis
osteoarthrosis
orthographical

out for the count
orthopterology
opus latericium
Osvaldo Ardiles
Oswald Spengler
oxyhaemoglobin
oxygen cylinder
Peasant Wedding
Peasants' Revolt
Phaedra complex
plate tectonics
place of worship
Peace of Utrecht
prayerlessness
plane-polarised
plane-polarized
planet-stricken
planing-machine
Plácido Domingo
platinum blonde
platinum sponge
phallocentrism
pearly nautilus
pharmacologist
pharmacopoeial
pharmacopoeian
pharmacopolist
pharmaceutical
plasma membrane
plasmapheresis
pragmaticality
pragmatisation
pragmatization
planned economy
plain chocolate
planning blight
plains wanderer
piano accordion
prairie chicken
Praeraphaelite
praiseworthily
practicability
practical units
practical joker
plastic surgeon
plastic surgery
Plantaginaceae
phantom circuit
plant-formation
praetorian gate
plaster of Paris
phantasmagoria
phantasmagoric
plantation song
Prague Symphony
plague-stricken
platycephalous
public attorney
public document
public defender
Public Image Ltd
public nuisance
public spending
public speaking
public-spirited
pickaback plant
package holiday
pococuranteism
pocket an insult
peculiar motion
Peculiar People

pickled herring
pectoral girdle
picture gallery
picture-writing
pachydactylous
pachydermatous
Pedro Almodovar
podophthalmous
pedestrian deck
precariousness
predaciousness
prevailing wind
prefabrication
plea bargaining
presbyterially
preaching-house
preaching friar
preaching-cross
prescriptively
prescriptivism
prescriptivist
pseudo-archaism
pseudaesthesia
preadolescence
pseudomembrane
pseudomorphism
pseudomorphous
pseudonymously
plead not guilty
pseudepigrapha
pseudepigraphy
pseudosolution
pseudosymmetry
pseudoscorpion
Pieter Breughel
Pieter Brueghel
presence of mind
prebendal stall
predeterminism
predeterminate
predevelopment
preferentially
premeditatedly
preterite tense
predesignation
predesignatory
pièce d'occasion
prenegotiation
pre-Reformation
presentability
preventability
presentimental
predestinarian
predestination
predestinative
presentational
presentiveness
preventiveness
preservability
psephoanalysis
plethysmograph
precipitinogen
premillenarian
plenipotential
pteridophilist
predisposition
premier danseur
predictability
precious metals
Pier Luigi Nervi
phelloplastics

pneumoconiosis
pneumoconiotic
pneumodynamics
pneumokoniosis
pneumatologist
pleonastically
phenobarbitone
piezomagnetism
preconcertedly
preponderantly
pyelonephritic
pyelonephritis
piezochemistry
phenolic resins
precociousness
paedomorphosis
precompetitive
preconsonantal
peer of the realm
preposterously
puerperal mania
puerperal fever
preoperational
prearrangement
Pietro Annigoni
Pietro Badoglio
Pierre de Fermat
poetry in motion
Pietro Mascagni
Pleuronectidae
pleurapophyses
pleurapophysis
pleased as Punch
press the button
pressure cooker
pleasure ground
pleasure-giving
pressure helmet
pleasure-seeker
pressurisation
pressure vessel
pressurization
please yourself
prettification
plectognathous
pretty-pretties
presupposition
presumptuously
preux chevalier
phenylbutazone
pterygoid plate
pterylographic
puffin crossing
pugnaciousness
pageboy haircut
pugilistically
pig-in-the-middle
pigeon-breasted
pigeon-fancying
piggyback plant
prima ballerina
pain au chocolat
private patient
private baptism
private company
philanthropist
psilanthropism
psilanthropist
primary battery
primary colours
primary process

pribble-prabble
Prince Charming
prince-imperial
Prince of Orange
principal parts
principal focus
principalities
prince's feather
Philip Augustus
poikilothermal
poikilothermic
Philippe Pétain
prick-the-garter
Paisley pattern
prison-breaking
primordial soup
Philo Remington
philosopheress
philosophaster
philosophistic
philologically
pair of snuffers
pair production
Primrose League
prioritisation
prioritization
printed circuit
prittle-prattle
pointing device
printing office
point-to-pointer
painter-stainer
pyjama trousers
palmatipartite
polyacrylamide
Pillars of Islam
pollen analysis
palaeobiologic
palaeobotanist
polyembryonate
palaeoclimatic
palaeoecologic
palaeographist
pulse diagnosis
palaebiologist
palaeanthropic
Palaeanthropus
palaeopedology
Palaeosiberian
phlegmatically
palagonite-tuff
polling station
palliative care
polemoniaceous
polymerisation
polymerization
polynucleotide
palingenetical
polynorbornene
pulmonary valve
pull one's weight
pillow-fighting
pile on the agony
Polyplacophora
polar wandering
Pilgrim Fathers
pelargonic acid
polysaccharide
palisade tissue
polishers' putty
Palus Nebularum
polishing-paste
polishing-slate
polysyllabical
polysynthetism
Polish notation
palato-alveolar
political verse
pull technology
politicisation
politicization
pull the long bow
polytheistical
pull the strings
palatalisation
palatalization
pile up the agony
pamphleteering
pentadactylism
pentadactylous
pins and needles
Pancake Tuesday
pinnatipartite
pennatulaceous
panzer division
Pontederiaceae
Panhellenistic
pincer movement
Pentecostalism
Pentecostalist
Pontefract cake
Pancho Gonzales
pontifical mass
penal servitude
Penelope Lively
Pan-Americanism
pin one's faith on
pin one's hopes on
peninsular unit
pentobarbitone
pinhole glasses
pantomime horse
pantomimically
pantopragmatic
pantographical
pancreatectomy
panoramic sight
punctuationist
penetrableness
pin it on someone
penny-a-linerism
penny-in-the-slot
pennystone-cast
propagandistic
propaedeutical
probabiliorism
probabiliorist
proscriptively
proscenium arch
proud-stomached
Protevangelium
phonematically
proletarianise
proletarianism
proletarianize
prosencephalic
prosencephalon
proceleusmatic
proper fraction
progenitorship
properispomena
propeller shaft
propeller-blade
pioneer species
professionally
process control
professorially
protected state
proventriculus
property master
projectisation
protectiveness
projective test
projectization
plough the sands
prothonotarial
prothonotariat
proximate cause
profitableness
provincial rose
promise-keeping
promise-breaker
promise-crammed
provided school
providentially
prohibitionary
prohibitionism
prohibitionist
propitiatorily
prodigiousness
propitiousness
proximity talks
promissory note
protistologist
prognosticator
Phoenix Theatre
Phoenix Islands
photocatalysis
photocatalytic
phototelegraph
photoperiodism
photorealistic
photosensitise
photosensitive
photosensitize
photochemistry
photobiologist
photoelectrode
photoflood lamp
protoplasmatic
photo-engraving
protozoologist
pro bono publico
protospathaire
Prototracheata
photogrammetry
photographical
provost marshal
proportionable
proportionably
proportionally
proportionless
proportionment
photoluminesce
prolocutorship
photosynthesis
photosynthetic
phosphor bronze
phosphorescent
phosphonic acid
phosphoric acid
phosphoprotein
Prosper Mérimée
prosperousness
proprietorship
programme music
program trading
proprioceptive
procryptically
Pyotr Kropotkin
progress chaser
procrastinator
progressionary
progressionism
progressionist
pro aris et focis
protrusiveness
prosthodontics
prosthodontist
procuratorship
pronunciamento
producers' goods
productibility
production line
productiveness
poor white trash
Papua New Guinea
peppermint-drop
pop the question
papilionaceous
popularisation
popularization
paper tape punch
purdah carriage
pyro-acetic acid
permanent teeth
permanent press
Pergamum Museum
parochial board
paradigmatical
Père David's deer
Parmesan cheese
parhelic circle
paroemiography
pyrheliometric
purse-snatching
perfect cadence
perfectibilian
perfectibilism
perfectibilist
perceptibility
perfectibility
perfect binding
percentile rank
portentousness
perceptiveness
perpetual screw
perpetual check
paragrammatist
pyrogallic acid
Port Georgetown
Pyrrhic victory
parchment paper
parthenocarpic
porphyrogenite
purchase system
pertinaciously
permis de séjour
perfidiousness
perniciousness
pernicketiness
partial product
parliament-cake
parliament-heel
Persian morocco
parsimoniously
permissibility
permissiveness
particularness
Port Jackson Bay
purple-coloured
parallel cousin
parallelepiped
parallel motion
parallelopiped
parallel planes
parallel rulers
parallel slalom
parallel-veined
paraleipomenon
Portland cement
paralinguistic
pyramid selling
pyramidologist
per impossibile
pyrometallurgy
peremptoriness
paramount chief
parenchymatous
pyrenomycetous
paronomastical
personal column
personal estate
pardonableness
personableness
personal rights
personal remark
personal stereo
purposefulness
Periophthalmus
periodic system
pardon my French
performing arts
performance art
person of honour
periodontology
parlour-boarder
person-to-person
perlocutionary
peripheral unit
Port Phillip Bay
pyrophotograph
pyrophosphoric
paraphrastical
periphrastical
peripateticism
parapsychology
partridgeberry
pararosaniline
perishableness
parish minister
Perissodactyla
phraseological
parish register
parasitologist
paratactically
pyrotechnician
peritoneoscopy
percutaneously
perturbational
porcupine grass
persuasibility
percussion-fuse
percussion-lock
persuasiveness

party-political
Past and Present
posse comitatus
Pasteurelloses
Pasteurellosis
pasteurisation
pasteurization
possessiveness
postindustrial
passive smoking
pestilentially
Passifloraceae
passionateness
pisciculturist
post-millennial
postmenopausal
postmastership
pastoral charge
pastoral letter
post-production
past participle
postpositional
postpositively
push technology
push the boat out
positive action
positive number
Petrarchianism
Petrarchianist
Pythagoreanism
phthalocyanine
put a call on hold
pâté de foie gras
patresfamilias
pattern therapy
Patagonian hare
put a good face on
put the brakes on
put the change on
put the finger on
put the kibosh on
patchwork quilt
put the screws on
put the tin hat on
put the tin lid on
put the whammy on
pituitary gland
putting the shot
potting compost
patrialisation
patrialization
petticoat-tails
patria potestas
patriarchalism
patellar reflex
put on the market
potentiometric
patent medicine
put in mothballs
put on a pedestal
put one's shirt on
petroleum jelly
petroleum ether
put someone wise
petrochemistry
petrophysicist
Petko Slaveykov
pathologically
petrologically
petrographical
Peter Pan collar
Peter Mandelson
Peter Scudamore
paternity leave
Paterson's curse
Peter Greenaway
Peter principle
Peter Sutcliffe
petit battement
Pitt the Younger
petit bourgeois
pit bull terrier
put out to tender
pattypan squash
petty serjeanty
petty bourgeois
petty constable
Paula Radcliffe
Plumbaginaceae
plumbisolvency
plumbosolvency
Paul Henri Spaak
Pauline Letters
pluviometrical
pluck up courage
pluto-democracy
Prussification
Paul Whitehouse
Pavel Cherenkov
pavement artist
powder magazine
powder one's nose
power of the keys
power-amplifier
power breakfast
power structure
psychoanalysis
psychoanalytic
psychochemical
psychodramatic
psychodynamics
psychographics
psychogenetics
psycholinguist
psychometrical
psychoneuroses
psychoneurosis
psychoneurotic
psychophysical
psychosomatics
psychotechnics
physiognomical
psyllid yellows
phyllotactical
Phytolaccaceae
phytopathology
phytogenetical
phytogeography
phytochemistry
quarantine flag
quality control
quadrigeminate
quadrigeminous
quadragenarian
quadrangularly
quadrisyllabic
quadrisyllable
quantification
quantum gravity
quart and tierce
quattrocentism
quattrocentist
quartz-porphyry
quarter-gallery
quarter section
quarter-binding
quarter-pounder
quantity theory
quantitatively
quaquaversally
querimoniously
Queen's evidence
Queensland blue
Queen Elizabeth
Queen Anne's dead
Queen Anne's lace
queen substance
qwerty keyboard
question master
question of fact
quincentennial
quite something
quicksilvering
quicksilverish
quick on the draw
quinquagesimal
quinquevalence
quinquefarious
quinquennially
quinquefoliate
quinquecostate
quilting-cotton
quintessential
quizzification
quota immigrant
quodlibetarian
reading-machine
reaping machine
roaring forties
reasonableness
read only memory
reappraisement
reacquaintance
Rhapsody in Blue
roast-beef plant
read the riot act
rear-view mirror
rear-wheel drive
roadworthiness
rabbeting-plane
rubber solution
rub the wrong way
Robbie Coltrane
rubbing alcohol
rabbit-squirrel
Robbie Williams
Rabelaisianism
rebelliousness
ribonucleotide
robin redbreast
Robinson Crusoe
ribbon building
Robert Bakewell
Robert Browning
Robert Chambers
Robert Delaunay
Robert Devereux
Robert F Kennedy
Robert Guiscard
Robert Helpmann
Robert Henryson
Robert Koldewey
Robert Pitcairn
Robert Robinson
Robert Schumann
Roberts Airport
Robert the Bruce
robes-de-chambre
robustiousness
robotic dancing
Richard Dawkins
Richard Hakluyt
Richard Ellmann
Richard Ingrams
Richard Roberts
Richard Hoggart
Richard Rodgers
Richard Woolley
Richard Branson
Richard Strauss
Richard Burbage
rectangularity
recrementitial
Rochelle-powder
rocket launcher
roche moutonnée
Rickettsia body
Rickettsiaceae
recreation room
receivableness
received wisdom
rectilinearity
receiving-house
receiving order
recollectively
recalcitration
recolonisation
recolonization
recommencement
recommendation
recommendatory
recombinant DNA
reconnaissance
reconsecration
recondensation
reconciliation
reconciliatory
ricinoleic acid
reconstitution
✧reconstruction
reconstructive
rack one's brains
reception class
reception order
rice polishings
recapitulation
recapitulatory
recapitulative
recording angel
recurvirostral
rich tea biscuit
recitation-room
rich text format
recoverability
Rocky Mountains
Rudyard Kipling
radiation belts
radial symmetry
radial velocity
reduction works
reductionistic
radicalisation
ridiculousness
radicalization
redeemableness
red-bloodedness
Rudolf von Laban
Redemptionists
riding breeches
redintegration
redintegrative
riding-interest
riding the stang
radio telescope
radiotelemeter
radiotelephone
radiotelephony
radiotelegraph
radioresistant
radiometric age
radiosensitise
radiosensitive
radiosensitize
radiochemistry
radiotherapist
radiobiologist
radio altimeter
radiologically
radio frequency
radio astronomy
radio-strontium
radioautograph
Roderick Random
radar altimeter
Redcross Knight
radar astronomy
Riders to the Sea
redistillation
ride someone off
redistrib›arution
redistrib›arutive
Roehampton Club
Rhemish version
reed instrument
rheumatic fever
rheumatologist
ruff and honours
refrangib›arility
refractometric
refractoriness
refectory table
reflexological
reflectography
reflectionless
Rafferty's rules
reflectiveness
reformationist
regressiveness
regularisation
regularization
regulatory gene
Reginald Jeeves
regeneratively
Roger Bannister
regardlessness
registered post
register office
registry office
right-hand drive
right about face
right about face!
right ventricle
right off the bat
Rogation flower
Rogation Sunday

right ascension
right as a trivet
rehabilitation
rehabilitative
rainbow therapy
rhinencephalic
rhinencephalon
raise the market
raise one's glass
raise an eyebrow
reinforcements
rhinoceros bird
Rhinocerotidae
Rhizophoraceae
reimplantation
Reims Cathedral
reintroduction
reinvigoration
Rajendra Prasad
rejuvenescence
Rikki-Tikki-Tavi
relief printing
relentlessness
relinquishment
rule out of court
relapsing fever
Ralf Schumacher
relativisation
relativization
rampageousness
remedilessness
rummelgumption
Rimsky-Korsakov
rumbledethumps
rumblegumption
rummlegumption
Romulus Francis
romantic comedy
reminiscential
remonetisation
remonetization
Romeo and Juliet
Rump Parliament
remarkableness
remorsefulness
remoralisation
remoralization
Rembrandtesque
rime suffisante
remittent fever
remote job entry
rambunctiously
rangatiratanga
Renée Zellweger
run off one's feet
röntgenography
run the gauntlet
run their course
running balance
run rings around
running banquet
running repairs
ringing chamber
running rigging
running footman
Renaissance man
Ranulph Fiennes
run in the family
ranunculaceous
run for one's life
Random Sketches

random variable
ring the changes
rhombenporphyr
reopener clause
Rhode Island red
reorganisation
reorganization
root mean square
repudiationist
reprehensively
representation
representative
repressiveness
Ripon Cathedral
reprogrammable
reproductively
reproductivity
reported speech
reported verses
Ripstone pippin
repetitiveness
requisitionary
requisitionist
Rastafarianism
risk assessment
ruse contre ruse
Rosicrucianism
respectabilise
respectability
respectabilize
respectfulness
respectiveness
rustic capitals
Russian thistle
Russianisation
Russianization
restitutionism
restitutionist
resolving power
resultlessness
resinification
restorationism
restorationist
restorableness
rush one's fences
rest on one's oars
responsibility
responsiveness
Russo-Byzantine
restricted area
restrictedness
restrictionist
rostrocarinate
resurrectional
restrainedness
risorius muscle
resistance coil
resistlessness
roses all the way
rosette disease
retransmission
retaliationist
retinoblastoma
rational number
rate of exchange
ratio decidendi
retroreflector
retrocognition
retro-operative
retrogradation
retirement home

rites de passage
rites of passage
roundaboutedly
roundaboutness
round the corner
round the wicket
rough-and-tumble
rough breathing
revolving stage
revalorisation
revalorization
revengefulness
river-jack viper
reverse printer
reverse osmosis
reversing layer
reversing light
river blindness
Reverend Mother
River Irrawaddy
River Euphrates
Revised Version
revitalisation
revitalization
revivification
rewardableness
rhyparographer
rhyparographic
rhynchophorous
rhythm and blues
Royal Worcester
Reynolds number
stalactitiform
Staubbach Falls
Svalbard Island
starch hyacinth
star connection
St Andrew's cross
stand the racket
scandalisation
scandalousness
scandalization
stand in the gate
standing orders
stand confessed
stand upon terms
standard-bearer
standard candle
slanderousness
shamefacedness
state of affairs
Staten-Generaal
stage direction
stare in the face
skate on thin ice
shake one's sides
scaremongering
state socialism
states of matter
Shakespeariana
space traveller
scale staircase
stagflationary
Sea of Fertility
Stamford Bridge
Stafford Cripps
shaggy-dog story
snaggle-toothed
slaughterhouse
slaughterously
scaphocephalic

scaphocephalus
staphylococcal
staphylococcus
staphyloplasty
spaghetti strap
scaling circuit
Spanish bayonet
Spanish needles
Spanish customs
sea gillyflower
station-manager
Stationers' Hall
stationariness
stationary wave
static pressure
spatiotemporal
shark repellent
sparkling water
stacking system
shawl waistcoat
small intestine
small-tooth comb
swallow-shrikes
Stanley Baldwin
Stanley Spencer
Stanley Kubrick
stainless steel
spawning-ground
scanning speech
Stannary Courts
St Agnes's flower
St Anne's College
shalom aleichem
seasonableness
seal of approval
Slavonic Dances
seat-of-the-pants
star-of-the-earth
slap on the wrist
stamping-ground
snapping-turtle
stamp collector
Spasskaya Tower
swans a-swimming
smart sanctions
startle colours
starting blocks
starting handle
slantendicular
slantindicular
starting pistol
starting stalls
St Anthony's fire
scatter diagram
slatternliness
scatterbrained
shatter-brained
Shaquille O'Neal
statuesqueness
Sabbatarianism
Sabbath-breaker
sabbatical year
sebaceous gland
subgenerically
submergibility
subterrestrial
submersibility
subject heading
subjectiveness
subjectivistic
subaggregation

subminiaturise
subminiaturize
submicroscopic
submissiveness
Sybille Bedford
subalternation
Sybil Thorndike
Sibylline Books
subinfeudation
subinfeudatory
subinsinuation
subconsciously
subcontrariety
subcontracting
subcontinental
subarborescent
Sebastian Cabot
subassociation
substance abuse
substantivally
substantialise
substantialism
substantialist
substantiality
substantialize
substantiation
subatmospheric
substitutional
substitutively
substitutivity
subcutaneously
subduction zone
social climbing
social contract
✧social democrat
social engineer
sacramentalise
sacramentalism
sacramentalist
sacramentality
sacramentalize
sacrament house
sacramentarian
Socratic method
social mobility
social security
social services
société anonyme
sacred mushroom
Secrets and Lies
successionally
succession duty
successionless
successfulness
successiveness
Society of Jesus
Society Islands
saccharic ester
sacchariferous
saccharisation
saccharization
sacrilegiously
sectionisation
sectionization
secularisation
secularization
secondary radar
second interval
second mortgage
second thoughts
second wrangler

sacrosanctness
sociobiologist
sacrococcygeal
St Cross College
sycophantishly
security camera
securitisation
securitization
St Dabeoc's heath
Sudeck's atrophy
side horse vault
sidereal period
sodium benzoate
sodium chloride
sodium chlorate
spelaeological
steganographer
steganographic
Sherborne Abbey
speechlessness
speech-training
speedway racing
Sheldon Glashow
siege mentality
Siege of Antwerp
stereoisomeric
stereometrical
skeleton shrimp
siege-artillery
stereospecific
stereoscopical
stereotactical
Steven Weinberg
shelf-catalogue
Sheffield plate
Stephen Langton
Stephen Hawking
Stephen Decatur
Stephen Dedalus
Stephen Dorrell
Stephen Spender
shepherd's check
shepherd's plaid
shepherd's glass
shepherd's cress
shepherd's-purse
shepherd tartan
Sheridan Le Fanu
sheriff deputes
sheriff officer
Swedish massage
specific charge
specific legacy
special damages
special verdict
special effects
special licence
specialisation
specialization
speak in tongues
speak out of turn
speak by the card
shell parrakeet
Sherlock Holmes
smell of the lamp
stealth fighter
shell-limestone
Stella Kowalski
steal a marriage
smelling bottle
steel engraving
Steller's sea-cow
steamed pudding
steaming lights
spermiogenesis
spermatogenous
spermatogonium
spermatophytic
spermatorrhoea
spermatothecal
stegocephalian
stegocephalous
sceuophylacium
scenographical
step on the juice
steeplechasing
steeple-crowned
sheep-whistling
sleepy staggers
sheep's scabious
sleepy sickness
steering column
spectacularity
sheet lightning
sweating system
sweet-and-twenty
spectroscopist
spectrological
spectrographic
sweet horsemint
stertorousness
spectator sport
soft-conscienc'd
sufferableness
suffice it to say
saffron milk cap
soft underbelly
Sagrada Familia
sigma particles
signal sequence
segregationist
suggestibility
suggestiveness
sigmoid flexure
sigmoidoscopic
St George's cross
sign of the cross
sagittal suture
Sigmund Romberg
schedule tribes
Schwenkfeldian
sphaerocrystal
Schafer's method
Schiff's reagent
sphygmographic
St Hugh's College
Schmitt trigger
schola cantorum
scholastically
schematisation
schematization
Schindler's List
school-divinity
schooner-rigged
schoolmasterly
schoolmistress
schoolteaching
spherical angle
schismatically
Schottky defect
Schottky effect
schizognathous
schizomycetous
schizophyceous
spit and sawdust
skimble-skamble
spindle-shanked
spindle moulder
swindge-buckler
sliver building
slide projector
stiletto-heeled
swingling-stock
sting in the tail
stinging nettle
stichometrical
Sailing Tonight
spiritlessness
spirit-stirring
spiritualistic
spirituousness
sticky-fingered
stinking badger
stick one's oar in
stick one's bib in
stick at nothing
Stirling Castle
Stirling engine
shillingsworth
Stillson wrench®
shilly-shallier
Seidlitz powder
seismometrical
swimming trunks
stigmatiferous
stigmatophilia
stigmatisation
stigmatization
science fiction
scientifically
stir one's stumps
spirochaetosis
spironolactone
snipper-snapper
stirrup leather
ship's carpenter
snip-snap-snorum
Swiss army knife
Saint Valentide
spinthariscope
Saint Magnus Bay
Saint Kentigern
scintillascope
scintilloscope
scintillometer
shifting-boards
Saint-John Perse
Saint Bride's Bay
St John's College
St Justin Martyr
Sakhalin Island
Selman A Waksman
self-accusation
self-accusatory
self-affrighted
self-admiration
self-abnegation
self-assumption
self-absorption
self-assessment
self-advertiser
salubriousness
solubilisation
solubilization
silicification
self-compatible
self-comparison
self-commitment
self-complacent
silicon carbide
self-condemning
self-consequent
self-confidence
self-consistent
self-conviction
self-controlled
self-correcting
solecistically
solicitousness
solidification
self-dependence
self-discipline
self-displeased
self-destroying
self-determined
self-developing
self-effacement
self-effacingly
self-explaining
silver pheasant
self-expression
self-expressive
self-employment
silver quandong
self-enrichment
silversmithing
self-flattering
self-fulfilling
self-fulfilment
self-generating
self-government
sulphacetamide
sulphadimidine
sulphanilamide
sulphur dioxide
sulphurisation
sulphurous acid
sulphurization
sulphathiazole
self-heterodyne
self-inductance
self-indulgence
self-immolation
Sylvian fissure
self-importance
self-interested
self-justifying
salamander-like
self-management
Solomon Islands
salami strategy
self-mutilation
self-motivating
self-motivation
Selina Hastings
silentium altum
silent majority
salmon-coloured
saloon carriage
salt of the earth
salt of wormwood
self-preserving
self-pollinated
self-punishment
self-propelling
self-protecting
self-protection
self-protective
self-proclaimed
self-propulsion
self-possession
saltpetre-paper
self-rectifying
self-regulating
self-regulation
self-regulatory
self-repression
self-repugnance
sclerophyllous
self-respecting
self-respectful
self-restrained
sclerotisation
sclerotization
self-revelation
self-revelatory
self-sufficient
self-suggestion
self-supporting
self-sustaining
self-sustenance
sales assistant
self-satisfying
sales executive
solitudinarian
solitaire board
splitting image
split one's sides
split one's votes
self-tormenting
splat quenching
Sulawesi Island
Sully Prudhomme
Solly Zuckerman
somnambulistic
somnambulation
sympathy strike
sympathetic ink
summary offence
semi-centennial
semiconducting
semicarbazones
semicircularly
semicrystallic
Samuel L Jackson
semi-elliptical
Samuel Pickwick
symmetrophobia
symmetrisation
symmetrization
summer solstice
simultaneously
simple fraction
simple fracture
simplification
simplificative
simple interest
simple-mindedly
simplistically
simple sentence
simulated pearl
Simon Bar Kokhba
Simon the Zealot
semantic memory
Simone Signoret

semi-occasional
someone or other
semi-officially
symbolicalness
semaphorically
simaroubaceous
semasiological
sempstress-ship
something like a
symptomatology
sensationalise
sensationalism
sensationalist
sensationalize
Singapore Sling
Sunday painters
Sonia O'Sullivan
synectics group
sansculotterie
sansculottides
sonnet sequence
Sant Fateh Singh
synchronically
synthetic resin
sentimentalise
sentimentalism
sentimentalist
sentimentality
sentimentalize
singing-gallery
Santiago de Cuba
sensitive flame
sensitive plant
single-breasted
single currency
senile dementia
single-handedly
single-mindedly
synonymousness
Song of Hiawatha
senior wrangler
synaposematism
Songs of degrees
Songs of ascents
sinistrorsally
send to Coventry
sanctification
sanitary cordon
sanitary napkin
senatus consult
sanguification
sensualisation
sensualization
sanguinariness
sanguinivorous
sandwich boards
sandwich course
Sandwich Island
Sunny Afternoon
stoma-care nurse
storage battery
sporangiophore
sporangiospore
stoma therapist
stomachfulness
stomatogastric
Scombresocidae
Scotch attorney
Scotch bluebell
stoicheiometry
stoechiometric
stoichiometric
Scotch woodcock
sword-swallower
Stokesay Castle
shove-halfpenny
smoke abatement
Stone of Destiny
score an own goal
stone-cold sober
smoke-room story
score points off
Smokey Robinson
spongy platinum
São Tiago Island
smoking concert
stock car racing
stocking filler
stocking stitch
Stockton-on-Tees
shock treatment
shouldered arch
shoulder girdle
shoulder-height
storm in a teacup
sporotrichosis
stoope-gallaunt
shopping basket
shopping centre
scorpion spider
swoop-stake-like
swoopstake-like
snowshoe rabbit
stouth and routh
stout-heartedly
Scottification
shoot the breeze
smoothing plane
short-sightedly
sports medicine
sporting chance
shooting jacket
shooting script
Scottish Office
Supralapsarian
suprasegmental
supramolecular
sapphire-quartz
sophistication
supplicatingly
supplementally
saponification
supposititious
suppositionary
supercargoship
supersaturated
supernaturally
superabundance
superabsorbent
superscription
supercelestial
superterranean
supersensitive
soporiferously
superphosphate
superficialise
superficiality
superficialize
superciliously
supervisorship
superelevation
super flyweight
superambitious
supereminently
superimportant
superintendent
superintending
superinfection
superincumbent
superannuation
superinduction
superconductor
superconfident
supersonically
supersonic boom
supernormality
supercontinent
superfoetation
supererogation
supererogatory
supererogative
superessential
suppressor cell
suppressor grid
separate school
Separate Tables
superstruction
superstructure
superstructive
superovulation
superexcellent
septuagenarian
sequaciousness
Sir Max Beerbohm
surface tension
spread-eagleism
Sarraceniaceae
striated muscle
screaming farce
serratirostral
Sir Basil Spence
Sir David Wilkie
Sir Jack Brabham
Sir Ian McKellen
Sir Max Mallowan
serial monogamy
Sir Harold Kroto
Sir Harry Lauder
surpassingness
Sir Walter Scott
scrubbing-board
scrubbing-brush
strobe lighting
scribbling-book
strobilisation
strobilization
strabismometer
seroconversion
sericitisation
sericitization
structural gene
Sir Edward Heath
Sir Edward Elgar
Sir Edward Tylor
Sir Adrian Boult
straddle-legged
street-credible
surrender value
Sir Derek Barton
Sir Derek Jacobi
Sir Rex Harrison
Sir Cecil Beaton
Sir Denis Forman
Sir Nevill F Mott
Sir Lewis Namier
Sergei Ilyushin
Sergei Korolyov
sergeant-at-arms
serjeant-at-arms
surgeon general
Sir Sean Connery
Sir Bernard Katz
Sir Leon Brittan
screen printing
Sir Henry Cotton
Sir George Robey
Sir George Grove
Sir Henry Irving
Sir Henry Morgan
serpentiningly
serpent goddess
serpent-worship
surefootedness
Sir P G Wodehouse
sprightfulness
Sarah Bernhardt
Sir Thomas Pride
Sir Thomas Wyatt
Sir Charles Bell
surgical spirit
strain courtesy
serviceability
service ceiling
service station
straight as a die
straightjacket
straight ticket
Sir Dirk Bogarde
Sir Sidney Nolan
strike a balance
strike a bargain
strikebreaking
striking circle
stroke of genius
seral community
serum hepatitis
spring-cleaning
spring-carriage
Strange Meeting
seronegativity
Sir Anthony Caro
Sir Anthony Eden
spring ligament
strong language
spring mattress
strand-scouring
Sir Angus Wilson
Serena Williams
Sir Bobby Robson
Sir Joseph Banks
servomechanism
Sir Joseph Lyons
Sir Robert Ensor
Sir John Hawkins
Sir John Hawkyns
Sir John Kendrew
Sir John Tenniel
Sir John Gielgud
Sir John Lubbock
seriocomically
Sartor Resartus
Sir Tom Stoppard
Sarepta mustard
Seraphic Doctor
Seraphic Father
strepsipterous
scrupulousness
Syrophoenician
seropositivity
scrape together
Sir Arthur Bliss
Sir Arthur Evans
Sir Ernst B Chain
surprisingness
Sir Isaac Newton
Sir Isaac Pitman
stress fracture
stratification
stratigraphist
stretching-bond
stretching iron
scratchbuilder
scrutin de liste
scrutinisingly
strut one's stuff
scrutinisation
scrutinizingly
scrutinization
Sir Hubert Parry
Sir Hugh Walpole
serous membrane
Sir Humphry Davy
strawberry leaf
strawberry mark
strawberry roan
strawberry tree
straw in the wind
screw propeller
screw-propeller
stray radiation
sustainability
sustained yield
systematically
system building
suspend payment
system operator
suspensibility
sisters of mercy
systems analyst
systems program
susceptibility
susceptiveness
Sistine Madonna
suspiciousness
Susumu Tonegawa
sesquipedalian
sesquipedality
sesquisulphide
set a game to five
satellite state
satem languages
sit on the splice
sit on one's hands
set on a pedestal
set one's heart on
sit in judgement
soteriological
satisfactorily
set-aside scheme
sausage machine
sausage bassoon
stumbling-block
soul-confirming
sounding rocket
squadron leader

soul-destroying
stupendousness
sauce espagnole
slug-foot-second
sluggardliness
south-eastwards
south-westwards
South Yorkshire
south-south-east
south-south-west
southern lights
South Australia
Sauvignon Blanc
skunk-blackbird
Sturmabteilung
sauropterygian
squirearchical
square brackets
squirrel monkey
scurrilousness
square shooting
squash racquets
shuttle service
stultification
✧sovietological
savanna-sparrow
savant syndrome
save one's breath
saxifragaceous
sex-and-shopping
skylight filter
Suzanne Lenglen
Sézary syndrome
thalassography
trapdoor spider
trade paperback
travelling folk
Travellers Club
traveller's tree
traveller's tale
trapezohedrons
travel sickness
traffic manager
traffic-calming
traffic pattern
traffic returns
traffic signals
Tuatha dé Danaan
teaching fellow
Trachypteridae
traditionalism
traditionalist
traditionality
traditionarily
tragicomically
That'll Be the Day
trailing vortex
that'll teach him
that'll teach you
thaumatography
thaumaturgical
traumatisation
traumatization
Training Agency
training wheels
tea and sympathy
✧transcaucasian
Transvaal daisy
transvaluation
transcendental
transcendently
transferential
transversality
transverse wave
transfer ticket
transvestitism
transsexualism
transsexuality
that's the ticket
transliterator
transmigration
transmigratory
transmigrative
transmissional
transmissively
transmissivity
transpicuously
transplantable
transamination
transformistic
transformation
transformative
transmogrified
transport rider
transportingly
transportation
transitionally
transitoriness
transitiveness
transcutaneous
transfusionist
toasted teacake
traction engine
traitorousness
Traducianistic
Tobias Smollett
tobacco-stopper
tablespoonfuls
tabularisation
tabularization
tabloidisation
tabloidization
tabernacle-work
Tibetan terrier
tacheometrical
tactical voting
tachistoscopic
tickled a th' sere
technical hitch
technicoloured
technology park
tachygraphical
tidewaitership
The Card Players
The Garden Party
The Water-Babies
The Gates of Hell
The Da Vinci Code
The Cat in the Hat
The Mask of Zorro
the cat's pyjamas
The Last Emperor
the Earthshaker
The Ladykillers
theocratically
trencher-friend
trencher-knight
treacle mustard
tread the boards
Theodor Schwann
Theodor Mommsen
tremendousness
the general weal
The Seventh Seal
The Selfish Gene
The Netherlands
the devil and all
The Feel of Hands
there's no saying
The Temptations
the Year of Grace
The Secret Agent
the gentle craft
The New York Post
The Age of Bronze
The Age of Reason
The Ship of Death
The White Rabbit
the Six Counties
The Time Machine
The Life of Jesus
the life of Riley
The Life of Brian
the life and soul
the Virgin Queen
The Rights of Man
The Divine Image
theriomorphism
theriomorphous
therianthropic
The First Circle
the little woman
The Winter's Tale
the clean potato
the Black Prince
theologoumenon
The Elephant Man
the flowery land
The Ambassadors
thermochemical
thermodynamics
thermoelectric
thermal barrier
thermal reactor
thermal neutron
thermal imaging
thermal springs
thermal printer
thermalisation
thermalization
thermometrical
thermionic tube
thermophyllous
thermotolerant
The Independent
the unconscious
the Inquisition
The Coral Island
Trevor Chappell
The Woodlanders
The Golden Bough
the Lord's tokens
The Rokeby Venus
The Lovely Bones
The Long Goodbye
the world to come
the worm may turn
Trevor McDonald
the common touch
The Commitments
The Country Wife
the boy next door
The Four Seasons
the roaring game
the four hundred
The Forsyte Saga
The Lost Weekend
The Boston Globe
The Lotus-Eaters
Theopaschitism
the Great Beyond
The Great Escape
The Great Gatsby
the Crucifixion
The Prodigal Son
Tierra del Fuego
The Kraken Wakes
theosophically
Treasure Island
theatre weapons
twenty-four hour
theatricalness
Treaty of Amiens
the Eternal City
The Human Comedy
the Hundred Days
The Sunday Times
The Music Lovers
The Turkish Bath
the sum of things
✧the everlasting
tree worshipper
the Oxford group
tug the forelock
trifacial nerve
thimblerigging
thiocyanic acid
third dimension
third-programme
tail-end Charlie
trimethylamine
tripersonalism
tripersonalist
tripersonality
toilet training
toing and froing
trichobacteria
trichomoniasis
triphenylamine
trichinisation
trichinization
trithionic acid
trichophytosis
trichotomously
Trinitarianism
tridimensional
trivialisation
Trivial Pursuit®
trivialization
trinitrophenol
trinitrotoluol
Trinity College
trickle charger
trinkum-trankum
think nothing of
Triple Alliance
twin-lens reflex
triple-tonguing
twinned crystal
triconsonantal
triconsonantic
trisoctahedron
Tristram Shandy
Tristan da Cunha
'twixt sun and sun
Thirty Years' War
trituberculism
trituberculate
tricuspid valve
thieves' kitchen
take a hammering
take a raincheck
take by surprise
take for granted
take it on the lam
take one's breath
take one's chance
take one's choice
take personally
take the edge off
take the biscuit
take the liberty
take the michael
take the trouble
take to one's toes
take to the boats
take up a quarrel
take up the reins
teleconference
talk-down system
telegraph cable
telegraph plant
telegraph board
talking machine
tell it like it is
tell its own tale
telejournalism
telejournalist
telangiectasia
telangiectasis
telangiectatic
tallow chandler
teleologically
talk of the devil
telephone kiosk
telephone booth
teleprocessing
telephonically
telephotograph
telepathically
teleradium unit
telesmatically
telescopically
Teletypesetter®
teletypewriter
telautographic
televangelical
television tube
temperate phage
temperate zones
temperamentful
Tom, Dick, or Harry
time immemorial
tumbling barrel
Temple of Athena
Temple of Apollo
Temple of Amon-Ra
Temple of Heaven
Templeton Prize
tumultuousness
tomfoolishness
Tomb of Mausolus
tumorigenicity
Timothy Severin
Tintagel Castle

Words marked ✧ can also be spelled with one or more capital letters

Tennessee River
tinsel-slipper'd
tintinnabulant
tintinnabulary
tintinnabulate
tintinnabulous
tenants' charter
tendovaginitis
Tunbridge Wells
tuner amplifier
Thomas Chalmers
Thomas Cromwell
Thomas Keneally
Thomas Macaulay
Thomas Newcomen
Thomas Shadwell
Thomas Sydenham
Thomas Traherne
troubleshooter
thought-reading
thought process
thoughtfulness
trochlear nerve
Trochelminthes
trophoneurosis
two-dimensional
✧tropic of Cancer
Thornton Wilder
thoroughbraced
two for his heels
two-for-his-heels
tropologically
two-pot screamer
two-start thread
top of the league
topsy-turviness
Tequila Sunrise
thread and thrum
threadbareness
Tyrian cynosure
turf accountant
terra sigillata
terra incognita
three-card monte
three-card trick
three-halfpence
three-halfpenny
three-farthings
turpeth mineral
three-mile limit
target language
Turkey merchant
three-toed sloth
three-point turn
three-bottle man
target practice
three-speed gear
turpentine tree
thriftlessness
tariff reformer
terminableness
terminal market
tergiversation
tergiversatory
turbine steamer
Turkish delight
Torvill and Dean
torsion balance
territorialise
territorialism
territorialist
territoriality
territorialize
terminological
tertiary amines
tertius gaudens
terminus ad quem
Terek sandpiper
turnkey package
thrilled to bits
turtle graphics
thromboplastin
tyrannicalness
tarantula juice
turbofan engine
turn one's back on
turbogenerator
turn on one's heel
tortoise beetle
terror-stricken
thrashing-floor
threshing floor
Turks and Caicos
terotechnology
turn the air blue
turn the stomach
through-ganging
through the nose
through traffic
turquoise-green
turn up one's toes
throw the book at
throw in one's lot
throw oneself on
throw to the dogs
throw up one's cap
throw overboard
terry towelling
Terry Pratchett
Tessa Sanderson
testamentarily
Tasmanian devil
Tasmanian tiger
testimonialise
testimonialize
tetradactylous
tetrachotomous
Tatra Mountains
✧tetragrammaton
tetraethyl lead
tatterdemalion
total abstainer
total depravity
tittle-tattling
toucan crossing
thunderousness
truth condition
true-lover's knot
tautologically
trumpet-tongued
trustee account
trust territory
town councillor
text processing
textus receptus
thysanopterous
thymelaeaceous
try conclusions
thyrotoxicosis
unavailability
unaccomplished
unaccommodated
unaccounted-for
unaffectedness
Uralian emerald
unacknowledged
unavoidability
uranographical
unapprehensive
unappreciative
unapproachable
unapproachably
unappropriated
unaspiringness
unacquaintance
unacquainted in
unassumingness
unattractively
unauthenticity
unartificially
unalterability
unbearableness
umbrageousness
unbecomingness
urban guerrilla
unbusinesslike
unclassifiable
Uncle Tom's Cabin
uncheerfulness
Un Chien Andalou
uncultivatable
uncomprehended
uncompromising
uncommunicated
uncommunicable
uncontaminated
unconscionable
unconscionably
unconfederated
uncongeniality
uncontemplated
unconventional
unconciliatory
unconsolidated
uncontradicted
uncontrollable
uncontrollably
uncontrolledly
uncontroverted
uncrowned queen
uncertain about
uncertificated
uncorroborated
unchristianise
unchristianize
uncircumcision
uncrystallised
uncrystallized
undecomposable
undecipherable
undue influence
undiminishable
undemonstrable
undomesticated
undeniableness
under bare poles
undersaturated
undervaluation
under penalty of
underdeveloped
under-secretary
undermentioned
under the hammer
under-clerkship
underemphasise
underemphasize
under one's thumb
undernourished
under-constable
underpopulated
undergraduette
understrapping
understandable
understandings
understatement
under suspicion
undespairingly
undesignedness
undiscoverable
undiscoverably
undesirability
undistractedly
undeservedness
undeterminable
uterogestation
unexpectedness
unearned income
unextinguished
unentertaining
unenterprising
unenthusiastic
unflappability
unflatteringly
unfaithfulness
unfriendedness
unfriendliness
unforeknowable
unfruitfulness
upgradeability
ungracefulness
ungratefulness
ungraciousness
ungroundedness
unhandsomeness
Uther Pendragon
unhesitatingly
Urim and Thummim
unincorporated
United Brethren
United Irishmen
universal joint
universal donor
universalistic
universitarian
unidentifiable
utilitarianise
utilitarianism
utilitarianize
unidirectional
utility vehicle
utility program
unilluminating
union catalogue
union territory
uniformitarian
unintellectual
unintelligible
unintelligibly
unintermitting
unintoxicating
uninvestigated
unknightliness
unknowableness
unmaintainable
unmalleability
unmannerliness
unmanufactured
unmentionables
unmerchantable
unmarriageable
unmercifulness
unmathematical
unmatriculated
unmetaphorical
unmetaphysical
unmaterialised
unmaterialized
Ummayyad Mosque
upon conscience
unostentatious
uropygial gland
unpraiseworthy
unpracticality
unpreparedness
unpretendingly
unpremeditated
unpremeditable
unpoeticalness
unprepossessed
unpleasantness
unpresumptuous
unprofessional
unpropitiously
unproportioned
unprosperously
unproductively
unproductivity
unpurchaseable
unpassableness
usque ad nauseam
unquestionable
unquestionably
Urquhart Castle
unreadableness
uproariousness
unrecognisable
unrecognisably
unrecognizable
unrecognizably
unreconcilable
unreconcilably
unreciprocated
unrecapturable
unreflectingly
unrightfulness
unreliableness
unromantically
unremunerative
unremorsefully
unreproducible
unresolvedness
unresponsively
unrestrictedly
unreservedness
unrestrainable
unrestrainedly
unrhythmically
unsectarianism
unsociableness
unsuccessfully
upside-down cake
unsuitableness
unspiritualise
unspiritualize
unsplinterable

Words marked ✧ can also be spelled with one or more capital letters

unsympathising
unsympathizing
unsophisticate
unstrengthened
unsurmountable
unscrupulously
unscripturally
unsystematical
unsystematised
unsystematized
unsisterliness
unsuspectingly
unsuspiciously
unsaturated fat
unsatisfaction
unsatisfactory
ultramicrotome
ultramicrotomy
unthankfulness
ultrasonically
✧ultramontanism
ultramontanist
ultracrepidate
untranslatable
untranslatably
untransferable
untransmutable
ultrastructure
unthinkability
unthinkingness
Ustilaginaceae
untameableness
ultimogeniture
up to one's ears in
up to one's tricks
ultroneousness
unthoughtfully
utter barrister
up to the knocker
untruthfulness
untowardliness
unvanquishable
upwardly mobile
upward mobility
unwatchfulness
unyieldingness
vibroflotation
vice-chancellor
vice-consulship
vociferousness
Victor Emmanuel
vectorgraphics
Victoria Island
Victoria sponge
victoriousness
Victor/Victoria
Victor Vasarely
vice-presidency
vicar-apostolic
vicesimo-quarto
vacuum cleaning
vacuum concrete
videotelephone
video digitizer
video frequency
Vidkun Quisling
Vreni Schneider
View on the Stour
vigesimo-quarto
vegetable sheep
vegetable mould
vegetable ivory
vegetativeness
Voice of America
voice synthesis
vaingloriously
Viktor Korchnoi
voltage divider
village college
vulgar fraction
villainousness
volcanological
vulcanological
vulnerableness
value judgement
vulpine opossum
voluminousness
volumetrically
voluntary chain
voluptuousness
valerianaceous
valerianic acid
valetudinarian
valet de chambre
volatile alkali
volatile memory
volatilisation
volatilization
Vincent Van Gogh
Vincent's angina
vending machine
vindictiveness
venereological
vanishing point
vanishing cream
Venetian mosaic
venture capital
viola da braccio
vapour pressure
variable region
verse-mongering
vertical angles
vertical circle
verticillaster
viral marketing
viral hepatitis
verisimilitude
virtute officii
virtual reality
virtuous circle
Vaslav Nijinsky
visible imports
visible horizon
visible exports
vasa deferentia
vasodilatation
vasodilatatory
vested interest
vespertilionid
Viscount Nelson
viscous damping
visitor general
vascular bundle
vascular plants
vascular tissue
Vaticanologist
Vatican Council
Vatican Museums
vitrescibility
vitreous enamel
vitreous humour
vitriolisation
vitriolization
vital principle
vitalistically
vitilitigation
vital functions
Viti Levu Island
Vittorio De Sica
vituperatively
vouch to warrant
Viviana Durante
Vivian Richards
viviparousness
vivisectionist
vowel gradation
vexata quaestio
what a vengeance
wear another hat
weak at the knees
what-d'you-call-'em
what-d'you-call-it
what do you say to?
weather prophet
weather station
wearing-apparel
What Maisie Knew
weak-mindedness
what's eating you?
what's the damage?
what's biting you
what the dickens
wedding garment
weeding-forceps
wheel of fortune
wheeler-dealing
woe worth the day
wheat-ear stitch
wreathed string
wreath filament
wigs on the green
Weimar Republic
wait attendance
white-hat hacker
white-headed boy
✧white Christmas
white blood cell
white horehound
white corpuscle
white quebracho
white supremacy
weightlessness
weighing-bottle
weigh to the beam
weight-training
weight-watching
whiplash injury
Whitley Council
Whitney Houston
whispering dome
whippersnapper
waifs and strays
whittie-whattie
whistle-blowing
Wallace Stevens
walk a tightrope
well-acquainted
Weltanschauung
Walter Cronkite
Walter De La Mare
Willesden paper
Walter Lippmann
Wilhelm Dilthey
Wilhelmstrasse
Walter Ulbricht
wild-goose chase
willing-hearted
wellington boot
walking wounded
William Barclay
William MacEwen
William Bateson
William Barentz
William Wallace
William Hazlitt
William Dampier
William H Bonney
William Nevison
William Thomson
William Shatner
William Gilbert
William Vickrey
William Siemens
William Hogarth
William Cobbett
William Golding
William Ireland
William Huggins
William Russell
William Wyndham
William Tyndale
Willie Whitelaw
walk one's chalks
Wilson Kipketer
Wilson's disease
Wilfred Mannion
Wilfred O'Reilly
Wells Cathedral
Wolfson College
walk the streets
well-thought-out
Walpurgis night
Wembley Stadium
woman of letters
woman of the town
✧women's movement
women's suffrage
wandering nerve
Winter Olympics
winter quarters
winter solstice
wonder-stricken
Winifred Atwell
Winifred Holtby
win the exchange
Winchester disk
winning-gallery
wind instrument
win one's worship
window-dressing
window envelope
Wynton Marsalis
window-shopping
wholemeal bread
wholeheartedly
wooden overcoat
whole-tone scale
wrong in the head
woolly-hand crab
woollen-drapery
wood nightshade
whoopee cushion
Whoopi Goldberg
warrant officer
world-weariness
worker director
Warren G Harding
Warren Mitchell
work experience
Worcester sauce
worcesterberry
Worcester china
Worcestershire
War of Secession
war of attrition
worth one's while
worshipfulness
warehouse party
ward in Chancery
working capital
working classes
working drawing
Wars of Religion
Wars of the Roses
word processing
wardrobe master
works committee
Wormwood Scrubs
western hemlock
westernisation
westernization
wish fulfilment
washing machine
Westman Islands
with a vengeance
with an ill grace
with a good grace
withering-floor
watchman's clock
watch the birdie
watch like a hawk
withholding tax
watch one's mouth
Watch Committee
witches' Sabbath
witches' thimble
within an inch of
wet-and-dry paper
wet one's whistle
with one consent
with one's tail up
without reserve
without measure
without dispute
without more ado
without compare
water barometer
water-repellent
water-resistant
watertightness
water pimpernel
water on the knee
watering-trough
water horehound
water potential
watercolourist
Waterloo Sunset
water-breathing
water privilege
would to God that
Wayland's Smithy
xylopyrography
xylotypography
xanthomelanous
xenotransplant

xiphihumeralis
xiphoid process
Yukon Territory
yellow centaury
yellow yoldring
Yale University
yeoman's service
yttro-tantalite
yttro-columbite
you're telling me
Young Pretender
youth hosteller
yours sincerely
yours to command
Yoweri Museveni
Zygobranchiata
zygobranchiate
zygomatic fossa
Zygophyllaceae
Zinedine Zidane
zingiberaceous
zinziberaceous
zinckification
zincographical
Zeno's paradoxes
zenith distance
Zhores I Alferov
zoophytologist
zeolite process
zoological park
Zoroastrianism
zero-coupon bond
zero fuel weight
zero-zero option

15 – odd

à la maître d'hôtel
as a matter of fact
anarchistically
a hard nut to crack
A Farewell to Arms
arachidonic acid
Aravinda Da Silva
Arabian numerals
Alaskan malamute
Alaskan malemute
available market
against the clock
against the grain
at a loss for words
anacreontically
A Passage to India
anaesthesiology
anaesthetically
a nasty bit of work
Alastair Dunnett
acanthocephalan
a matter of course
Anastasio Somoza
analytical logic
amaryllidaceous
Aubrey Beardsley
ambulance-chaser
ambulance broker
ambrosia beetles
Albert Chevalier
arboriculturist
Albertina Museum
Albert Nile River
Alberto Fujimori
Albus Dumbledore
abbot of unreason
Alcide de Gasperi
Accademia Museum
Aachen Cathedral
asclepiadaceous
ancient monument
Archibald Garrod
acclimatisation
acclimatization
architecturally
Archichlamydeae
archiepiscopate
archiepiscopacy
accelerator card
accommodatingly
Ascension Island
ascend the throne
at close quarters
at cross purposes
accordion pleats
ancestor-worship
accountableness
Andrew Aguecheek
Andreas Vesalius
Andrei Vyshinsky
Andy Goldsworthy
Abdullah Ibrahim
Andromeda galaxy
Andromeda nebula
audiometrically
audiovisual aids
andromonoecious
Anderson shelter
Addison's disease
Audit Commission
addition product
Alexander Calder
Alexander Nevski
Alexander Gibson
Alexander Irvine
Alexander Dubcek
average adjuster
avec acharnement
agency secretary
Aberdeen terrier
ahead of one's time
amende honorable
Alec D'Urberville
Alec Douglas-Home
age of discretion
Americanisation
Americanization
Amerigo Vespucci
Alexius Comnenus
a week on Saturday
a new lease of life
adenocarcinomas
adenohypophyses
adenohypophysis
Aleister Crowley
Aleksandr Tairov
Alessandro Volta
aversion therapy
Aleutian Islands
affranchisement
Alfred Hitchcock
Alfred Stieglitz
Alfred Whitehead
affaire d'honneur
affluent society
angular velocity
angular momentum
argumentatively
argumentum ad rem
algorithmically
Auguste Mariette
angustirostrate
Augusto Pinochet
a sheet in the wind
a sheet to the wind
A Christmas Carol
al-hallown summer
A Child of our Time
Athena Promachos
achondroplastic
achromatisation
achromatization
Ashmolean Museum
anharmonic ratio
atherosclerosis
atherosclerotic
adhesive binding
a thousand and one
animated cartoon
animal husbandry
amicable numbers
animal magnetism
animal rationale
Ariadne auf Naxos
alive and kicking
alimentary canal
abiogenetically
a finger in the pie
a fish out of water
axial tomography
Amiens Cathedral
a widow bewitched
amino-acetic acid
axis of incidence
anisotropically
acid soil complex
Alistair Darling
Alistair Maclean
Aristotelianism
Arjuna Ranatunga
adjutant-general
ankylostomiasis
acknowledgeable
acknowledgeably
acknowledgement
all-changing-word
all along the line
as long as one's arm
Atlantic Charter
Allan Quatermain
All Souls College
a slap on the wrist
aplastic anaemia
allotriomorphic
all over the place
Army and Navy Club
armed to the teeth
armillary sphere
ammonium nitrate
Admiral Graf Spee
admiralty anchor
atmospherically
ad misericordiam
Anne Bracegirdle
Annie Macpherson
Annie Get Your Gun
annihilationism
Arnold Dolmetsch
Arnolfini Museum
Arnold of Brescia
Annunciation Day
annus horribilis
anomalistic year
anomalistically
apocalyptically
above the weather
anorexia nervosa
a hole in one's coat
along the lines of
apophthegmatize
apophthegmatist
another cup of tea
aeolian deposits
atomic structure
a bowl of cherries
Apollinarianism
Aloys Senefelder
acoustic coupler
acousto-electric
about one's person
a month of Sundays
à tort et à travers
appearance money
alphabetisation
alphabetization
alpha-chloralose
amphitheatrical
appointment book
appendicularian
approachability
approved schools
appropinquation
appropriateness
apparent horizon
acquisitiveness
Adrian Edmondson
Adriano Olivetti
aerial surveying
atrabiliousness
arrectis auribus
agriculturalist
African marigold
African mahogany
African elephant
African-American
Airedale terrier
aerodynamically
air-chief-marshal
airtime provider
acrimoniousness
acromion process
Aaron Temkin Beck
agranulocytosis
air-conditioning
a crook in one's lot
abruptly pinnate
a drop in the ocean
à propos de bottes
✧Aurora Australis
aircraft-carrier
aerospike nozzle
across the tracks
aerated concrete
arrow-poison frog
association copy
Aussichtspunkte
abscission layer
absolute alcohol
absolute address
absolute ceiling
assimilationist
abstract of title
absorbent cotton
Australian crane
Australian rules
absorption bands
absorptiometric
absorption lines
assisted take-off
as sound as a roach
anticlericalism
articles of faith
attachment order
anticholinergic
autocorrelation
antichristianly
autodidacticism
at the first blush
autrefois acquit
at the drop of a hat
act of parliament
act of contrition
antiglare switch
autographically
anti-Gallicanism
act the giddy goat
as thick as a plank
attributiveness
autumnal equinox
antimonarchical
automorphically
automatic teller
antenatal clinic
Anton Rubinstein
astronavigation
Acts of Adjournal
astronautically
action committee
authoritatively
Astronomer Royal
action potential
astrodynamicist
Anthony Trollope
antepenultimate
antiperistalsis

antiperistaltic
alternate energy
arterialisation
arterialization
alternative vote
alternative host
alternative fuel
autoradiography
Attorney-General
a storm in a teacup
alternis vicibus
anterior chamber
anthropobiology
anthropocentric
anthropogenesis
anthropological
anthropomorphic
anthropophagite
anthropophagous
anthropopathism
anthropopsychic
anthroposophist
Antarctic Circle
Arturo Toscanini
Artur Rubinstein
antistatic agent
antistatic fluid
autoschediastic
autotransformer
antitheft device
Arts Theatre Club
antitrinitarian
Arthur Eddington
Arthur Pendennis
Arthur Wellesley
activity holiday
antivivisection
Artaxerxes Ochus
amusement arcade
acute rheumatism
aluminium bronze
Aquila and Prisca
advance workings
adventurousness
brandy Alexander
Brandenburg Gate
bear down towards
brake horsepower
blameworthiness
bear heavily upon
brachycephalous
brachydactylous
brachiocephalic
brachistochrone
blackwater fever
black-tailed deer
Bracknell Forest
black rhinoceros
black nightshade
Black Forest cake
Blackfriars Hall
blanket coverage
Beaumaris Castle
boatswain's chair
beat someone to it
brass someone off
blast-furnaceman
Baby Doc Duvalier
baby-doll pyjamas
bibliographical
bubble and squeak

Baby One More Time
bicycle rickshaw
back-calculation
bacteriological
background queue
background tasks
bacchanalianism
Buckinghamshire
back on one's heels
back translation
back to square one
Back to the Future
backward-looking
body-line bowling
bodyline bowling
bed and breakfast
bed-and-breakfast
beer and skittles
bleaching powder
breach of promise
Blenheim spaniel
beefsteak fungus
breast screening
breathe one's last
before-mentioned
Begin the Beguine
bigeneric hybrid
behind the scenes
by hook or by crook
Bahasa Indonesia
building society
Brinell hardness
bring and buy sale
bright as a button
Brighton and Hove
British Columbia
bricks-and-mortar
bristlecone pine
Bakewell pudding
Balearic Islands
balsamic vinegar
✧balaclava helmet
Belvedere Museum
Baltimore oriole
balance of nature
Bel and the Dragon
bill of adventure
bill of mortality
balloon catheter
ballroom dancing
below one's breath
belly-button ring
bomb calorimeter
bimetallic strip
beneath contempt
Benjamin Britten
binocular vision
bunker mentality
banker's envelope
bonded warehouse
benefit of clergy
Bankim Chatterji
binomial theorem
bankruptcy order
Benito Mussolini
banqueting-house
bronchiodilator
bronchoscopical
bioaccumulation
blonde bombshell
broad-leaved dock

broadmindedness
blood-and-thunder
bloodcurdlingly
blood-guiltiness
biogeochemistry
biogeographical
broken-heartedly
biotechnologist
biodestructible
brothel-creepers
Blowin' in the Wind
Bloomsbury Group
Brown University
biological clock
Book of Leviticus
Book of Zechariah
Book of Zephaniah
biopsychosocial
boots and saddles
bioastronautics
biostratigraphy
bioluminescence
bioavailability
baptism by desire
biquadratic root
Barbara Cartland
Barbara Hepworth
Bernabau Stadium
Barbara Stanwyck
bargain-basement
Border Leicester
burnet saxifrage
Bordeaux mixture
birthday honours
burgh of regality
Bornholm disease
Bartholomew Fair
Bartholomew-tide
Bernhard Leopold
Bernhard Riemann
Barbican Theatre
burning mountain
burning question
burr in the throat
born in the purple
Burkitt lymphoma
Beryl Bainbridge
Berengar of Tours
Baroness Kennedy
burn one's bridges
burn one's fingers
Barrow-in-Furness
Burton-upon-Trent
Bertrand Russell
Barbra Streisand
birds of a feather
bore the pants off
burnt to a frazzle
Bermuda Triangle
Burgundy mixture
by small and small
basidiomycetous
Bessemer process
basal metabolism
butterfly effect
butterfly flower
butterfly orchid
butterfly orchis
butterfly stroke
by the short hairs
between you and me

between two fires
by the strong hand
buttery-fingered
batch processing
batch production
by trial and error
Battle of Britain
Battle of Bull Run
Battle of Colenso
Battle of Cambrai
Battle of Corunna
Battle of Cassino
Battle of Cowpens
Battle of Dresden
Battle of Dunkirk
Battle of Flodden
Battle of Iwo Jima
Battle of Jutland
Battle of Leipzig
Battle of Lepanto
Battle of Leuctra
Battle of Marengo
Battle of Okinawa
Battle of Plassey
Battle of Salamis
Battle of Salerno
Battle of Thapsus
Battle of the Neva
Battle of the Nile
botanical garden
butanedioic acid
button accordion
bite on the bridle
bite on the bullet
bathroom cabinet
Batesian mimicry
blue-footed booby
brushtail possum
Brussels griffon
blunt instrument
bowl a maiden over
Bay of Heligoland
beyond suspicion
Byzantine Church
Byzantine Empire
character sketch
chamberlainship
chamber practice
chalcographical
Chandler's wobble
clandestineness
Claudius Dornier
chapelle ardente
charged particle
chargé-d'affaires
change of address
crashworthiness
Chavín de Huantar
Clarissa Harlowe
chalking the door
cradle-snatching
Charles James Fox
Charles Laughton
Charles Yanofsky
Charles de Gaulle
Charles Kingsley
Charles Goodyear
Charlotte Amalie
Charlotte Corday
Charlotte Sophia
Charlotte Brontë

Charlottesville
coat-of-mail shell
Ciampino Airport
Classical Greats
coastline effect
chattel mortgage
chapter and verse
coal-tar creosote
cabbage palmetto
cubic centimetre
cable television
cabinet minister
cache controller
cochineal insect
coccidiomycosis
Cecil James Sharp
coconsciousness
cockneyfication
cocculus indicus
co-determination
Caesalpiniaceae
Cleve-Garth Falls
Clemens Brentano
Czechoslovakian
chemical element
chemical warfare
credit insurance
clerk of the court
clerk of the works
checking account
Clermont-Ferrand
clean as a whistle
chenopodiaceous
chemopsychiatry
chemoattractant
creeping thistle
clear one's throat
Chelsea Arts Club
crease-resistant
crease-resisting
crested screamer
cheat the gallows
creation science
Chester-le-Street
creature of habit
chestnut boletus
creative therapy
coeducationally
coffee-table book
cigarette holder
climax community
child-safety seat
Children's Corner
crime passionnel
Chinese layering
Chinese pavilion
Chinese checkers
Chinese chequers
Chinese whispers
crime prevention
chief technician
clinical baptism
clinical convert
critical damping
criminalisation
criminalization
clinical lecture
clinical surgery
clicks and mortar
crimping-machine
chipping sparrow

coinstantaneity
coinstantaneous
collaboratively
cold-bloodedness
Cold Comfort Farm
collenchymatous
calves'-foot jelly
collegial church
collector's piece
collective fruit
Californian bees
California poppy
cold-heartedness
collision course
calcium chloride
calcium sulphate
Callippic Period
Callitrichaceae
colonial animals
calendarisation
calendarization
colonels-in-chief
colposcopically
colloidal system
Colorado Springs
chloramphenicol
Celestial Empire
celestial sphere
cellular therapy
colour blindness
colour threshold
command language
campaign against
companion ladder
companion-in-arms
compassionately
compartmentally
company promoter
comedy of humours
comedy of manners
commercial break
Commercial Court
commercial paper
commendableness
compendiousness
Comte de Mirabeau
competitiveness
come home to roost
combination lock
combination room
combination oven
commission agent
commissary court
come into one's own
Camille Pissarro
complementation
complementarily
complementarity
complete annuity
complex sentence
compotationship
common chickweed
composite school
commodification
common in the soil
commodity market
common knowledge
common logarithm
compound animals
compound larceny
Commodore Keppel
common of pasture
commonplaceness
commonplace book
common spadefoot
common stinkhorn
comfortableness
comfortlessness
Commonwealth Day
Cambridge roller
comprehensively
comprehensivise
comprehensivize
come rain or shine
camera-ready copy
compressibility
come someone's way
come the raw prawn
comity of nations
communalisation
communalization
computer hacking
computerisation
computerization
computer science
computer-to-plate
communicatively
communicability
communi consensu
communibus annis
community school
community health
community centre
community charge
community worker
community spirit
combustibleness
come up to scratch
cineangiography
canvas-stretcher
conscience money
conscience-proof
conscientiously
conscriptionist
canicular period
conic projection
candelabrum tree
Canterbury Tales
condescendingly
Cinderella dance
convergence zone
convenience food
congealableness
cannellini beans
contemplatively
contemptibility
contempt of court
contemporaneity
contemporaneous
consecratedness
confessionalism
confessionalist
concessionnaire
conversationism
conversationist
conceptualistic
consenting adult
consentaneously
conventionalise
conventionalize
conventionalism
conventionalist
conventionality
contentiousness
concert overture
consecutiveness
consequentially
conceivableness
conservationist
conservation law
conservatorship
cannibalisation
cannibalization
considerateness
consideratively
confidence trick
centinel private
confidentiality
confident person
configurational
continuation-day
Candle in the Wind
cinemicrography
cinematographic
cinematographer
canine distemper
consolation race
cannot choose but
contour feathers
connoisseurship
convolvulaceous
conspicuousness
Centre Beaubourg
contraband of war
contractability
contractibility
contradictively
contradictorily
centrifugal pump
controllability
control register
centrally-heated
confrontational
centre of gravity
centre of inertia
contrapropeller
Congratulations
contravallation
controversially
canisterisation
canisterization
conus arteriosus
Constant Lambert
constitutionist
constructionism
constructionist
conjugate angles
conjunctiveness
conjunctive mood
conjunctionally
consumer society
centum languages
consumptiveness
conquerableness
consubstantiate
conduct disorder
cingulum Veneris
cool as a cucumber
cholangiography
clonal selection
chondrification
co-ordinate bonds
cloud-compelling
Cloudcuckooland
cloud-cuckoo-land
cholecalciferol
co-operativeness
cooked breakfast
closed community
close to the chest
cholesterolemia
cholecystectomy
cholecystokinin
cholecystostomy
cloth-lined board
choriocarcinoma
Crown prosecutor
clown's woundwort
chocolate éclair
Crocodile Dundee
cross-laterality
Cloisters Museum
Cross of St George
cross the Rubicon
chops and changes
crossing-sweeper
crossword puzzle
crossopterygian
cross-curricular
clootie dumpling
Captain MacHeath
Captain Absolute
captain's biscuit
cephalochordate
capacity for heat
Cepheid variable
copper engraving
caprifoliaceous
capillary action
Cape nightingale
Capernaitically
capital gains tax
capitation grant
carnal knowledge
carnassial tooth
Carmarthenshire
cerebrovascular
coracoid process
correlativeness
curse of Scotland
Cornelis Drebbel
cornelian cherry
Cornelius Jansen
correspondently
correspondingly
correcting fluid
correction fluid
Cardinal Mazarin
Cardiff Arms Park
carriage and pair
carriage driving
carriage-forward
corbie messenger
carcinogenicity
carnivorousness
cardiopulmonary
curriculum vitae
Coral Sea Islands
Coralline Oolite
Carolus Linnaeus
Careless Whisper
coromandel ebony
ceremoniousness
coram domino rege
chromatographic
chromoxylograph
Corona Australis
Corynebacterium
Corinthian brass
chronologically
corporate raider
carbon anhydride
corporation sole
carpometacarpus
Caryophyllaceae
carbonic-acid gas
corno di bassetto
corporification
Carson McCullers
cordon sanitaire
Christadelphian
Christ in Majesty
Christian de Duve
Christian Slater
Christmas cactus
Christmas beetle
Christmas flower
Christmas Island
cards on the table
chrestomathical
Christopher Dean
Christopher Wren
Christy minstrel
core temperature
circumambagious
corrugated paper
circularisation
circularization
circular measure
circumferential
circumforaneous
circumincession
circuminsession
circumnavigable
circumnavigator
circumstantiate
circumstantials
circumspectness
circumscribable
circumscriptive
circumscription
corruptibleness
circuit training
circumvallation
carry off the bell
carry into effect
carry conviction
Cosmas and Damian
Caspar Bartholin
castanospermine
cask-conditioned
cosmetic surgery
cosignificative
cosmic abundance
Cushing's disease
casting director
cash in one's chips
cosmic radiation
case-insensitive
castles in the air
casement curtain
cosmopolitanism
custos rotulorum
cost someone dear
cottage industry

cottage hospital
cataclysmically
catted and fished
catheterisation
catheterization
Catherine Howard
cytogenetically
categoricalness
category mistake
catch one's breath
catch-as-catch-can
citric acid cycle
catallactically
cytomegalovirus
cut and come again
cut one's eye teeth
City of Edinburgh
citronella grass
✧catholicisation
✧catholicization
Citizen's Charter
causa sine qua non
Council of States
Council of Europe
Church of England
couldn't care less
caught and bowled
Crucible Theatre
Cautionary Tales
chuck-will's-widow
churrigueresque
court-martialled
courts-bouillons
Count Leo Tolstoy
Court of Requests
countermandable
countervailable
counteractively
clustered column
counterfesaunce
counterfeisance
counter-security
counter-flowered
countermovement
counter-approach
counter-irritant
counter-proposal
counter-pressure
counter-evidence
covenant of grace
covenant of works
Coventry Patmore
cover one's tracks
cavity radiation
cowboy and Indian
cry one's heart out
cryoprecipitate
crypto-communist
crypto-Christian
crystallisation
crystallization
crystalline lens
crystallography
cry stinking fish
cryptosporidium
dead as a doornail
diamagnetically
dual carriageway
diaheliotropism
dialectological
Django Reinhardt
draughtsmanship
draught-proofing
diaphragmatitis
diaphototropism
draw in one's horns
dead men's fingers
dramma per musica
drawn-thread work
diamondback moth
do a roaring trade
dual personality
dead tree edition
dear to one's heart
diastereoisomer
Debrett's Peerage
Deccan Mountains
decree of nullity
decalcification
decolourisation
decolourization
decommissioning
decimal notation
decimal fraction
decimal currency
decomposability
decontaminative
decontamination
decontextualise
decontextualize
decipherability
doctrinarianism
decarbonisation
decarbonization
decarboxylation
decarburisation
decarburization
diesel-hydraulic
deed of accession
due process of law
dyer's-yellowweed
dressing station
deficit spending
differentiation
defencelessness
deferred annuity
deferred payment
diffrangibility
Dog Day Afternoon
Dag Hammarskjöld
degree of freedom
daguerreotypist
degenerationist
dig one's own grave
digital computer
dog's-tooth violet
digitizing board
digitizing table
dehypnotisation
dehypnotization
Dr Hawley Crippen
deindustrialise
deindustrialize
drilling machine
drift transistor
Duke of Newcastle
dollar diplomacy
dolichocephalic
dulcified spirit
Dolores Ibárruri
delirium tremens
deleteriousness
deliver the goods
Dame Barbara Ward
democratisation
democratization
democratifiable
Dame Flora Robson
demagnetisation
demagnetization
Dame Iris Murdoch
Dame Joan Hammond
demulsification
demolition derby
Dame Laura Knight
Dame Maggie Smith
Dame Muriel Spark
dominical letter
dementia praecox
Dame Nellie Melba
Dominion Theatre
demonstratively
demonstrability
damp-proof course
Dame Rebecca West
domestic economy
demystification
domestic science
demutualisation
demutualization
dimethylaniline
dental hygienist
Donmar Warehouse
Daniel Barenboim
Daniel Bernoulli
dance attendance
Dunsinane Castle
Donald Pleasence
don't make me laugh
denitrification
do one's damnedest
do one's endeavour
do one's level best
drown someone out
drop one's aitches
Diodorus Siculus
Deo Optimo Maximo
doorstep selling
droit du seigneur
drogue parachute
duplex apartment
depleted uranium
dip of the horizon
depth psychology
duplicate bridge
doppio movimento
dephlogisticate
Daphne Du Maurier
dependent clause
Daphnis and Chloe
diplomatic corps
diplomatic pouch
Diprotodontidae
departmentalise
departmentalize
departmentalism
department store
departure lounge
Durham Cathedral
dermatoglyphics
dermatomyositis
direct discourse
direct injection
direction-finder
direct marketing
director-general
durchkomponiert
dorsiventrality
darning mushroom
dormitory suburb
dorsibranchiate
dissatisfaction
dissatisfactory
destabilization
de-Stalinisation
de-Stalinization
dishabilitation
disharmoniously
dispassionately
distastefulness
disobligingness
desacralisation
desacralization
disadvantageous
dysteleological
disrespectfully
dishearteningly
dispensableness
dispersal prison
dissecting table
dessertspoonful
disreputability
disaffectedness
disaffectionate
disafforestment
disagreeability
discharging arch
distinctiveness
distinguishable
distinguishably
distinguishment
Dashiell Hammett
displeasingness
displaced person
displacement ton
desilverisation
desilverization
disillusionment
do someone reason
disimprisonment
disentanglement
disinterestedly
disenthrallment
desensitisation
desensitization
disinflationary
disentrancement
discovered check
disconfirmation
dissociableness
dyslogistically
discommodiously
discommendation
dysmorphophobia
discontinuation
discontinuously
dissolvableness
dissolving views
disappointingly
disorganisation
disorganization
district council
disgracefulness
district heating
destructiveness
destructibility
distractibility
district visitor
disorderly house
desertification
disarticulation
descriptiveness
disproportional
distressfulness
distrustfulness
discretionarily
destroying angel
disassimilative
disassimilation
disputativeness
disquisitionary
desexualisation
desexualization
data compression
Do the Right Thing
Dutch admiral pea
Dutch elm disease
detribalisation
detribalization
detention centre
determinateness
determinability
dithyrambically
druidical circle
Dzungaria Desert
drumhead cabbage
douche écossaise
double-barrelled
double-facedness
double indemnity
double pneumonia
double standards
diurnal parallax
Deutsches Museum
dividend warrant
David Cronenberg
devil-worshipper
developmentally
development area
Devonshire cream
diversification
Divisional Court
devitrification
Dow-Jones average
down to the ground
day-neutral plant
daylight robbery
dry distillation
dry construction
emancipationist
evangelicalness
evangelistarion
enantiomorphism
enantiomorphous
emblic myrobalan
embryologically
exclamation mark
Exchange and Mart
exchangeability
exchange control
exchange student
exchange teacher
excrementitious
Escherichia coli
ecclesiological

ecclesiasticism
escalator clause
encomiastically
excommunicative
excommunication
excommunicatory
encephalisation
encephalization
encephalography
escape character
escape mechanism
excursion ticket
exclusion clause
endocrinologist
Eudoxus of Cnidus
exercise bicycle
Exeter Cathedral
Ebenezer Scrooge
elegiac couplets
evening primrose
Evening Standard
everlastingness
eternal triangle
Eleanor Rathbone
esemplastically
exemplificative
exemplification
exemption clause
eleutherodactyl
eleutherophobia
eleutherophobic
eleutherococcus
electrical storm
electric blanket
electric battery
electric current
electric furnace
electrification
electromagnetic
electron capture
electroacoustic
electronegative
electrotechnics
electrometrical
electrochemical
electrothermics
electrophoresis
electrophoretic
electronic brain
electrokinetics
electronic flash
electronic music
electronic organ
electronic piano
electroanalysis
electropositive
electrodynamics
electromyograph
every second week
Emelyan Pugachev
every now and then
every mother's son
enfranchisement
efficaciousness
enforcement work
en grand seigneur
English Civil War
English sickness
English ryegrass
eggs in moonshine
Eugène Delacroix
egg-and-spoon race
engrossing a deed
ergatandromorph
Ephraim Chambers
exhibitionistic
ethical genitive
echocardiograph
ethnic cleansing
ephemeris second
echinodermatous
ethnocentricity
ethnolinguistic
Ethiopian region
Ethiopian pepper
ethnomusicology
etherealisation
etherealization
exhaust manifold
Elizabeth Taylor
Elizabeth Bennet
Elizabeth Bishop
Edinburgh Castle
episcopalianism
Eriocaulonaceae
epidemiological
epitheliomatous
elixir of vitriol
Elie Metchnikoff
emission current
epistolary novel
epistemological
éclaircissement
Erlenmeyer flask
Ellesmere Island
Emmanuel College
Ernest Hemingway
Ernst Walter Mayr
Edouard Daladier
Édouard Daladier
Evonne Goolagong
ecological niche
economic migrant
ecotoxicologist
economic refugee
Expectation Week
expeditiousness
euphemistically
express delivery
expressionistic
expressis verbis
expenses account
emperick qutique
experientialism
experientialist
experimentalise
experimentalize
experimentative
experimentalism
experimentation
experimentalist
Emperor Concerto
earthshattering
Earl Mountbatten
Earl of Godolphin
edriophthalmian
edriophthalmous
Earl of Lichfield
Earl of Liverpool
Earl of Rochester
Earl of Shelburne
Earl of Strafford
European Council
Europeanisation
Europeanization
Eustachian valve
Easter offerings
Easter Rebellion
Easter sepulchre
Elsie Stephenson
Erskine Caldwell
Erskine Childers
essential organs
East Siberian Sea
extracellularly
extra-illustrate
extraordinaries
extraordinarily
extra-provincial
extrajudicially
extra-curricular
extreme fighting
entrepreneurial
entrepreneurism
entomologically
extemporariness
extemporisation
extemporization
entente cordiale
extensification
extensivization
eat one's heart out
externalisation
externalization
external storage
external student
exteroceptivity
exteriorisation
exteriorization
ebullioscopical
equalitarianism
equilateral arch
equinoctial year
equinoctial line
equine distemper
equiprobability
Eduardo Paolozzi
envelope stuffer
environmentally
Edward G Robinson
Edward the Martyr
Edward V Appleton
Egyptianisation
Egyptianization
Erziehungsroman
Flaubert's Parrot
flamboyante-tree
François Boucher
franchise player
François Fénelon
François Mauriac
Francis Palgrave
Francis Beaufort
Francis Beaumont
Francis of Assisi
Francisco de Goya
Francisco Franco
Franciscus Vieta
fraternity house
flash photolysis
feathered friend
feather one's nest
feather-boarding
Fra Filippo Lippi
Flavius Josephus
franking-machine
Frankfurt am Main
fragmentariness
Fraunhofer lines
flavor of the week
flavour enhancer
feast of trumpets
fractionisation
fractionization
Fibonacci series
facts and figures
Federico Fellini
federal theology
fides et justitia
free association
Frenchification
French Polynesia
French-polishing
field naturalist
field-sequential
Frederick Sanger
Frederick Delius
Frederick Temple
Frederick Blanda
Frederick Treves
Frederick Ashton
Frédéric Mistral
Frederic Raphael
freshwater snail
free-heartedness
feel in one's bones
fuelling machine
flehmen reaction
flex one's muscles
freezing mixture
fifth generation
fifth-generation
Fifth-monarchism
Fifth-monarchist
fifty pence piece
Figure and Clouds
figurate numbers
fight one's corner
fight to the ropes
flibbertigibbet
Friedrich Bessel
Friedrich Engels
fling to the winds
flight attendant
Flight into Egypt
faithworthiness
Frick Collection
friendly numbers
friendly society
Friars Preachers
friction welding
full-bottomed wig
full-dress debate
filterable virus
folie de grandeur
folded mountains
false conception
fulminating gold
falling sickness
full-line forcing
Falkland Islands
Full Metal Jacket
full motion video
full-motion video
fall over oneself
fellow traveller
fall to the ground
femme incomprise
family allowance
family fruit tree
feminine caesura
fundamental unit
fantasticalness
fantasy football
funnel-web spider
fencing mistress
fungistatically
find one's account
Fanconi's anaemia
funeral director
finishing school
finishing stroke
fenestra rotunda
functional group
fine-toothed comb
fancy dress party
Fyodor Chaliapin
foot-pound-second
from stem to stern
from the shoulder
front of the house
front-wheel drive
floating battery
floating capital
front-end loading
Fernando Arrabal
forward delivery
forward contract
fire-crested wren
forked lightning
for the life of him
for the life of her
for the time being
Ferdinand Marcos
forbidden planet
forbidden ground
fertile material
fortiter et recte
Fertile Crescent
foreign exchange
fire in one's belly
furniture beetle
for old sake's sake
for old time's sake
forensic science
for goodness sake
ferro-molybdenum
For Your Eyes Only
ferrous sulphate
first generation
first degree burn
first lieutenant
first in, first out
first principles
formularisation
formularization
Ferruccio Busoni
ferruginous duck
forswear oneself
fissiparousness
Festival Theatre
fashionableness
fission spectrum
fossil turquoise
fish skin disease

fishskin disease
Father Christmas
fitting-out basin
Fatal Attraction
Fatima Whitbread
fits of the mother
Foucault current
four-dimensional
foundation-stone
flux-gate compass
Flushing Meadows
Fourier analysis
foul-mouthedness
fluorescent tube
four-stroke cycle
fourth dimension
flutter-tonguing
fivepenny morris
fly off the handle
flying phalanger
G Marconi Airport
grande amoureuse
Grand Pensionary
grandiloquently
Grand Inquisitor
grade separation
graphic designer
graphics plotter
graphite reactor
gravitationally
granitification
glacial deposits
gravity platform
gramophonically
Giacomo Leopardi
Giacomo Agostini
grass characters
grasscloth plant
Gladstone sherry
grasshopper mind
grant-maintained
Ggantija temples
Giant Clothespin
granulated sugar
granulitisation
granulitization
Graf von Zeppelin
gibberellic acid
Gabriela Mistral
God Save the Queen
God's honest truth
God bless the mark
Glencoe Massacre
Gleichschaltung
Greyfriars Bobby
greyhound-racing
green accounting
green revolution
green woodpecker
greenery-yallery
Gregory the Great
Gregory's mixture
guerre à outrance
guerrilla strike
grease the wheels
great white shark
Great Bitter Lake
greeting meeting
greater plantain
great-grandchild
go for the jugular
go-faster stripes
gris-amber-steam'd
grind the faces of
going-away outfit
Guiana Highlands
go into committee
galvanic battery
gold-beater's skin
gold certificate
Golden Delicious
golden handcuffs
golden handshake
golden parachute
gold export point
golden rectangle
golden retriever
golden saxifrage
Gillian Shephard
gold import point
gillie-white-foot
goldsmith beetle
Gulf War syndrome
gamma securities
gemstone therapy
gens de condition
ginger beer plant
genteel business
gentleman farmer
gentlemanliness
gentlemen ushers
Gentleman-at-arms
Gene Myron Amdahl
gynandromorphic
goniometrically
general warranty
General Galtieri
general retainer
General Belgrano
general delivery
General Pinochet
general election
general epistles
general practice
General Assembly
Geneva mechanism
Genevan theology
Gone with the Wind
Giovanni Agnelli
Giovanni Bellini
Giovanni Cassini
Giovanni Gentile
Giovanni Tiepolo
good-conditioned
Gloucestershire
Grover Cleveland
gooseberry-stone
geodemographics
geometrical mean
Geoffrey Boycott
Geoffrey Chaucer
go off the deep end
good for anything
go off at half cock
go off at a tangent
George Du Maurier
George Grenville
George Grossmith
Georgi Plekhanov
Georges Lemaître
George Santayana
Georges Pompidou
George von Hevesy
George Vancouver
Giorgiy Malenkov
geochronologist
globigerina ooze
Glorious Twelfth
good-naturedness
gnotobiological
gnotobiotically
geomorphogenist
geomorphologist
group discussion
glossographical
gross investment
goods on approval
go out of business
go out like a light
growth substance
globular cluster
German Catholics
Gerhard Schröder
German police dog
Girolamo Cardano
germ-line therapy
Gordon Greenidge
Gérard Depardieu
gird up one's loins
Gustave Flaubert
gossip columnist
gastroenteritis
gesture politics
Götterdämmerung
gathering-ground
Gottfried Keller
Gottfried Semper
get off one's chest
get the drop on one
get the finger out
get the worst of it
Gottlieb Daimler
get on one's nerves
get one's dander up
get one's bearings
get one's shirt out
get one's skates on
get one's rocks off
get one's monkey up
go to one's account
get someone's goat
go to rack and ruin
get out of one's way
gaudeamus igitur
Gaucher's disease
Giulio Andreotti
gluconeogenesis
give it some welly
give it to someone
give oneself airs
give oneself away
government paper
government stock
governor-general
give someone hell
give someone best
give someone five
give someone rope
give the game away
give the show away
Gewürztraminer
go without saying
Guy de Maupassant
gazetted officer
head-down display
heaven of heavens
Heathrow Airport
heath fritillary
hearing-impaired
hyaloid membrane
heat of formation
health-conscious
Hoagy Carmichael
hobbledehoyhood
Hubble's constant
Huckleberry Finn
hackney carriage
hackney-coachman
hydraulic cement
hydraulic mining
Hodgkin's disease
hydropathically
hydrometallurgy
hydrogen cyanide
hydrobiological
Hydrocorallinae
hydrostatically
hydrodynamicist
hydrocyanic acid
hyetometrograph
haemoglobinuria
hierogrammatist
Hieronymus Bosch
Haffner Symphony
Hoggar Mountains
higher criticism
higher education
Hugh Esmor Huxley
high-gravel-blind
Highland costume
high-maintenance
hygroscopic salt
heir presumptive
Haleakala Crater
heliacal setting
hold all the cards
Holocaust Museum
holocrystalline
Holden Caulfield
Hellenistically
half-heartedness
helminthologist
Helena Blavatsky
Helen Wills Moody
heliotropically
hall of residence
Holy Roman Empire
humpbacked whale
homochlamydeous
homecoming queen
hemicrystalline
hamadryas baboon
✧hammer and sickle
hammerhead shark
homogeneousness
humanitarianism
homeopathically
Homeric laughter
Homeric question
humoral immunity
Homerton College
Hamish Henderson
Homes and Gardens
Hansel and Gretel
hendecasyllabic
hendecasyllable
Hunter S Thompson
Hanseatic league
Henri van de Velde
hanging buttress
hand it to someone
hen on a hot girdle
Hundred Years' War
Hans Reichenbach
Hendrik Verwoerd
Henry Cabot Lodge
honeycomb stitch
hope against hope
hypnagogic image
hypochondriacal
hypochondriasis
hypomagnesaemia
hyponitrous acid
hypnotisability
hypnotizability
hip joint disease
hypnogogic image
Hippocratic face
Hippocratic oath
Hippocratic look
hypopituitarism
hypercatalectic
hyperadrenalism
hyperthyroidism
hyperlipidaemia
hypercorrection
hypercritically
hepaticological
hoppus cubic foot
hypoventilation
hard-and-fastness
Herman Hollerith
hermaphroditism
hard act to follow
herb Christopher
hereditarianism
hereditarianist
horseradish tree
hermeneutically
horse-shoe magnet
horse and hattock
Harvey Smith wave
Harpers and Queen
harvest festival
Hertford College
hard-heartedness
Hermitage Museum
Hermione Granger
Harold Macmillan
harrowing of hell
harp on one string
harbour of refuge
harbour porpoise
hard-rock geology
horns of a dilemma
horns of the altar
Hereward the Wake
horizontal scrub
hospitalisation
hospitalization
historical novel
historiographic
historiographer
historic pricing
hesitation waltz

hither and yonder
hit below the belt
hot-melt adhesive
Hottentot's bread
hit the headlines
hit the high spots
Hotel California
hot foil stamping
heterocercality
heterochromatic
heterochromatin
heterodactylous
heteroduplex DNA
heterogeneously
heterosexuality
House of Assembly
household troops
haud one's wheesht
have a way with one
have a screw loose
have by the throat
have itching ears
have one's end away
have one's knife in
have one's marbles
Haversian canals
have seen service
have someone's ear
have the edge over
have the best of it
have two left feet
have what it takes
Hawthorne effect
how the wind blows
Hawaiian Islands
how goes the enemy?
hawksbill turtle
hexachlorophane
hexachlorophene
hexagonal system
Hay-Herran Treaty
inaccessibility
Isabelle Huppert
image processing
imaginativeness
imaginary number
Italian vermouth
Italian Concerto
Italian ryegrass
in all conscience
inadmissibility
inapprehensible
inapplicability
inappropriately
Ivan the Terrible
inauthentically
inattentiveness
inalterableness
inadvisableness
in black and white
in between whiles
incidental music
Ilchester cheese
incredulousness
incalculability
incomparability
incompatibility
incommensurable
incommensurably
incomprehensive
incomprehension
incommutability
incommunicative
inconsecutively
inconsequential
inconsiderately
inconsideration
incentivisation
incentivization
inconsolability
inconspicuously
incongruousness
incapaciousness
incorrigibility
inclusion bodies
Indian liquorice
Indian rope-trick
India rubber tree
Indian wrestling
indubitableness
inducible enzyme
induced abortion
induction course
indecent assault
indefeasibility
indefinableness
indefensibility
indigestibility
indemnification
indomitableness
Independence Day
indirect address
indirect damages
indistinctively
indisciplinable
indissolubility
indistributable
industriousness
indisputability
indeterminately
indetermination
indeterministic
individualistic
indivisibleness
inexcusableness
ineffaceability
inefficaciously
ineffectiveness
ineffectualness
ideographically
ideal transducer
ice contact slope
inexpugnability
inexplicability
inexpensiveness
inextricability
inestimableness
inextensibility
identity element
inequitableness
infrangibleness
infra dignitatem
inflammableness
infrastructural
infundibuliform
infant mortality
infinitesimally
in forma pauperis
informativeness
infernal machine
inferior planets
infusorial earth
Ingemar Stenmark
ichthyodorulite
ichthyodorylite
Ichthyopterygia
I Shot the Sheriff
Isidor Isaac Rabi
iris recognition
idiosyncratical
injection string
injudiciousness
ill-favouredness
illimitableness
Island of Molokai
I'll trouble you to
illustriousness
immunochemistry
immunocompetent
immunologically
immunopathology
immensurability
immortalisation
immortalization
immersion heater
immaterial issue
ion implantation
ignominiousness
innumerableness
inner dead centre
isomagnetic line
inoperativeness
isoperimetrical
in one's right mind
inofficiousness
inoffensiveness
icositetrahedra
isoimmunisation
isoimmunization
inopportuneness
inobtrusiveness
implausibleness
impracticalness
impecuniousness
impact parameter
imprescriptible
impressionistic
imponderability
impenetrability
improvisational
improvisatorial
improvvisatrice
imperial measure
impermeableness
imperfect flower
imperfect fungus
imperviableness
imperishability
importunateness
impassionedness
inquisitiveness
inquisitorially
irreconcilement
irreducibleness
irreductibility
irredeemability
irrefragability
irrefutableness
irreligiousness
irremissibility
irremovableness
irrepealability
irreprehensible
irreprehensibly
irreparableness
irresolvability
irresistibility
irretentiveness
irrationalistic
irrevocableness
irreversibility
installment plan
instantaneously
insubordinately
insubordination
insubstantially
insect repellent
it's a free country
insignificative
insignificantly
insight learning
inspirationally
institutionally
insulin reaction
insulating board
in someone's power
in someone's teeth
insensitiveness
inseparableness
insuperableness
instructiveness
insurrectionary
insurrectionism
insurrectionist
instrumentalism
instrumentation
instrumentalist
instrumentality
instrument board
instrument panel
inscrutableness
in seventh heaven
intrapreneurial
intransigentism
intransigentist
intransmissible
intractableness
intramuscularly
in the same breath
in the last resort
in the melting-pot
in the nick of time
in the first flush
in the first place
in this day and age
intrinsic factor
intrinsicalness
intellectualise
intellectualize
intellectualism
intellectualist
intellectuality
intelligibility
intolerableness
intemperateness
isthmus of fauces
I stand corrected
intensification
intention tremor
introspectively
introsusception
interfascicular
intertanglement
interlamination
internalisation
internalization
internationally
internal student
interjaculatory
interscholastic
interference fit
interdependence
interdependency
interpenetrable
interferometric
interpersonally
intertextualise
intertextualize
intertextuality
intertentacular
interjectionary
interventionism
interventionist
interchangeable
interchangeably
interchangement
interdigitation
interim accounts
interim dividend
interambulacral
interambulacrum
interrogatively
interrogational
intercollegiate
interconnection
intercolonially
intermodulation
interconversion
interpretership
interprovincial
interestingness
interosculation
interstratified
intersubjective
intertwistingly
intestinal flora
intussusceptive
intussusception
in totidem verbis
invulnerability
involuntariness
inverted mordent
investigational
investment trust
Joan Armatrading
Jean Claude Killy
Joachim du Bellay
Juan José Arreola
Jean-Michel Jarre
Jeannette Rankin
Jacobus Arminius
Jack-in-the-pulpit
✧jack-of-all-trades
Jacqueline du Pré
Jacques Cousteau
Jacquetta Hawkes
judicial trustee
jodhpur breeches
Judas Maccabaeus
jeepers creepers
Joe Willie Namath
John Bennet Lawes
John Henry Newman
John Harvey-Jones
Johannes Eckhart

Johannes V Jensen
Johnny-head-in-air
Johann Pachelbel
John Philip Sousa
John Quincy Adams
John Schlesinger
Johnston Islands
John Wilkes Booth
Juilliard School
J Pierpont Morgan
join the majority
joint resolution
Julian of Norwich
Juliette Binoche
Julius Rosenberg
Julius Streicher
Jelly Roll Morton
jumping-off place
Jumpin' Jack Flash
Jungermanniales
Jonah Barrington
Jan Smuts Airport
junior flyweight
Jonathan Edwards
japanned leather
Japanese lantern
Jupiter Symphony
Jurgen Klinsmann
Jorge Luis Borges
Jérôme Bonaparte
Jaroslav Seifert
jurisprudential
jerry-come-tumble
Josiah Bounderby
José Enrique Rodó
justices' justice
justifiableness
Joseph Guillotin
Joseph Nollekens
Joseph Priestley
Joseph Whitworth
jus primae noctis
Jesus of Nazareth
Joshua Lederberg
jusqu'auboutisme
jusqu'auboutiste
Justus von Liebig
juvenile hormone
Jawaharlal Nehru
jewel in the crown
juxtapositional
Koch's postulates
kick up one's heels
keep a low profile
keep good quarter
keep one's shirt on
keep one's thumb on
Keith Waterhouse
knight of the whip
knight of the road
knights bachelor
Knights Templars
knight's progress
knick-knackatory
knitting machine
kilogram-calorie
Killing Me Softly
Kelvin Mackenzie
Kalamazoo® system
kangaroo closure
kangaroo justice
Kenneth Williams
kind-heartedness
Kentish ragstone
king of the castle
king of the forest
kinesitherapist
King William's War
know a thing or two
knock all of a heap
knockout auction
knowledgability
known better days
know one's own mind
know what's o'clock
Kiribati Islands
Karl Guthe Jansky
kerbstone-broker
Kirsten Flagstad
Kurt Vonnegut, Jnr
Kasbah of Algiers
Kasimir Malevich
Kossuth Overture
Katherine Graham
kitchen gardener
Kathleen Ferrier
katathermometer
knuckle sandwich
Kawasaki disease
loaves and fishes
leather on willow
leading business
leading question
learning support
La Aurora Airport
loan translation
League of Nations
labradorescence
lubricated water
Lob-lie-by-the-fire
Liberal Democrat
labour-intensive
lackadaisically
Luca della Robbia
La Cage aux Folles
Luchino Visconti
local government
locomotor ataxia
Loch Ness monster
lactovegetarian
lachryma Christi
ladies' companion
Ludwig Boltzmann
Ludwig Feuerbach
Ludwig von Köchel
Lady Margaret Jay
Ludovico Ariosto
Lee Harvey Oswald
Liechtensteiner
Liebig condenser
lie in one's throat
Life is Beautiful
luffing-jib crane
logical designer
logical elements
logical analysis
leg before wicket
logographically
legal separation
logarithmic sine
logarithmically
logistics vessel
light-headedness
light-mindedness
light literature
lightning strike
legitimate drama
lying-in hospital
Luigi Pirandello
laissez-faireism
like a house afire
like a dog's dinner
like gangbusters
like the clappers
Leland H Hartwell
lily of the valley
Lombardic script
lymphadenopathy
lymphatic system
lamellirostrate
luminance signal
lumbrical muscle
limited monarchy
Limburger cheese
Lantern Festival
luncheon voucher
landing-carriage
Linford Christie
line one's pockets
line of flotation
Lincoln Memorial
London Palladium
line of scrimmage
Leni Riefenstahl
landscape-marble
long-sufferingly
long-sightedness
linguistic atlas
longwall working
Le Nozze di Figaro
Leonardo da Vinci
Leonard Cheshire
Leonard Hobhouse
Look Back in Anger
Lionel Barrymore
Leopold von Ranke
Leonor Michaelis
look the other way
look who's talking
✧lapsang souchong
lepidopterology
lophobranchiate
lapis lazuli ware
lapis lazuli blue
lipstick lesbian
Lord Beaverbrook
Lord Baden-Powell
Lord Chamberlain
Lord Collingwood
Lord George-Brown
Lord High Admiral
Lord High Steward
Lord Hore-Belisha
Lord James Mackay
Lord Lieutenants
Lorenzo Ghiberti
Lord Peter Wimsey
Lords Lieutenant
Le Rouge et le Noir
Lissajous figure
last but not least
lesser celandine
lissencephalous
lesser prolation
lesser spearwort
Leslie Charteris
lose one's marbles
laser disc player
laser disk player
lose the exchange
lethal injection
letter of comfort
letters-of-marque
letters rogatory
little Englander
Little Nell Trent
let one's hair down
lithochromatics
liturgiological
lateral thinking
Lateran Councils
let it all hang out
leucaemogenesis
leukaemogenesis
Laurence Olivier
laugh like a drain
laughing jackass
laugh and lie down
laugh and lay down
Louise Bourgeois
Louisa May Alcott
live cell therapy
Love is all Around
Lives of the Poets
Love without Hope
Lawrence Durrell
law of mass action
low-spiritedness
lower one's sights
lexicographical
lexicologically
lexical analysis
loxodromic curve
laying-on of hands
lay one's finger on
lay down one's arms
lay great store by
lazy daisy stitch
meat and potatoes
meaninglessness
meadow-saxifrage
measure strength
mechanistically
Michaelmas-daisy
Michail Saltykov
Michael Redgrave
Michael Ondaatje
MacFarlane's buat
Michael Portillo
Michael Atherton
mechanoreceptor
mechanomorphism
machine language
machine-washable
machine-readable
micromanagement
much of a muchness
macroscopically
microscopically
micrometer gauge
microtechnology
micropegmatitic
microaerophilic
Microchiroptera
microphotograph
microbiological
micromillimetre
microfilm reader
micromicrocurie
micromicrofarad
microdissection
microelectronic
microanalytical
microcosmic salt
macrocosmically
macrosporangium
microsporangium
microsporophyll
microprocessing
microtunnelling
mucosanguineous
Macquarie Island
medicine cabinet
medicine-dropper
madreporic plate
middle-age spread
medullary sheath
Middle Englander
Middle-Easterner
middle-of-the-road
middle-stitching
Middle Westerner
Madama Butterfly
Madame Butterfly
Madonna del Prato
Madonna and Child
moderate in a call
meditate the muse
medium frequency
Meet Me in St Louis
Magdalen College
Magna est Veritas
Megacheiroptera
magnetic battery
magnetic compass
magnetic equator
magnetic forming
magnetic pyrites
magnetic therapy
magneto-electric
magnifying glass
magisterialness
Magnus Magnusson
Mohamed V Airport
Meindert Hobbema
main purpose rule
maintainability
majority carrier
majority verdict
make a difference
make a clean break
make a clean sweep
Mikhail Bulgakov
make a good dinner
make common cause
make fair weather
make inroads into
Mt Kangchenjunga
make one's excuses
make one's manners
make out one's case
make someone's day
make someone tick
make short work of
Millard Fillmore

Words marked ✧ can also be spelled with one or more capital letters

molecular weight
malacopterygian
Malmesbury Abbey
mole-electronics
millefiori glass
Mulberry harbour
milage allowance
multilateralism
multilateralist
maleic hydrazide
multilingualism
mellifluousness
multilocational
multiprocessing
multiarticulate
maldistribution
multitudinously
multinucleolate
multiculturally
Melanie Griffith
melancholically
malconformation
Malcolm Campbell
Malcolm Bradbury
malpractitioner
malpresentation
malassimilation
military academy
military honours
military two-step
milites gloriosi
Molotov cocktail
moment of inertia
memoria technica
memorial service
manganese nodule
manganese bronze
mandarin palette
Manhattan Island
Montagu's harrier
miniaturisation
miniaturization
Munich Agreement
manic-depressive
monochlamydeous
Monocotyledones
monocrystalline
Monte Carlo rally
Ménière's disease
manneristically
manoeuvrability
managed currency
management buy-in
Montgomery Clift
many-headed beast
Monsieur de Paris
montmorillonite
Minamata disease
minimizing glass
Manon des Sources
manhood suffrage
mind one's p's and q's
Manfred Symphony
Monarchianistic
mineralogically
minority carrier
menispermaceous
Minister of State
monosymmetrical
Ministry of Works
maneuverability

monounsaturated
money for old rope
Moog synthesizer®
Mephistophelean
Mephistophelian
mortar and pestle
Margaret Beckett
Margaret Drabble
Margaret Forster
Margaret of Anjou
margaritiferous
meroblastically
mirabelle brandy
mari complaisant
Maracana Stadium
meridian passage
Mordecai Richler
Marlene Dietrich
market-gardening
Marie Antoinette
Merce Cunningham
marsh-cinquefoil
morphologically
marshalling yard
Marshall Islands
merchant of death
merchant service
Marghanita Laski
morphophonemics
Martha's Vineyard
Marchese Marconi
marginalisation
marginalization
marginal revenue
marginal tax rate
married quarters
Martínez de Perón
mortiferousness
Mortimer Wheeler
Martin Frobisher
Marriage à la Mode
marriageability
morning sickness
marriage-licence
marriage-portion
marriage partner
Martin Heidegger
Marxism-Leninism
Martin Niemöller
Marsipobranchii
Morrison shelter
Moral Rearmament
moral philosophy
Mare Moscoviense
marine insurance
Mariner's Compass
meristem culture
myristicivorous
Mare Serenitatis
meritoriousness
Marquês de Pombal
Marquis of Granby
Meriwether Lewis
mustard and cress
Mössbauer effect
masochistically
musical director
music to one's ears
Mister Fezziwigg
messenger-at-arms
miscellaneously

misbecomingness
Mister Wonderful
mischievousness
misintelligence
Mason Locke Weems
mesonephric duct
mass observation
misconstruction
misappreciative
misappreciation
misapprehensive
misapprehension
musique concrète
mass radiography
misproportioned
mistrustfulness
Mistress Quickly
Moses Maimonides
mesaticephalous
masculine ending
masculinisation
masculinization
musculoskeletal
Museum of Mankind
mosquito curtain
methamphetamine
mathematisation
mathematization
Mothering Sunday
mother of vinegar
Matthew Meselson
Matthew Flinders
matric potential
metalinguistics
metallurgically
Mr Tambourine Man
metempsychosist
metamathematics
Methodistically
metropolitanate
metropolitanise
metropolitanize
metropolitanism
mythologisation
mythologization
material fallacy
materialisation
materialization
materfamiliases
materialistical
motorway madness
maternity rights
Mstislav Keldysh
metastable state
metasilicic acid
mutatis mutandis
mutuus consensus
Mathurin Régnier
methylphenidate
Maureen Connolly
Maurice Johnston
Mourne Mountains
mousseline sauce
Mount Chimborazo
mountain bramble
mountain bicycle
mountain leather
mountain railway
mountain ringlet
Mount Tungurahua
movement therapy

moving staircase
Mexican standoff
mezzanine window
near as ninepence
Neath Port Talbot
Neapolitan sixth
near-sightedness
near to one's heart
Nubian monuments
nobody's business
noble-mindedness
nuclear membrane
nuclear reaction
nuclear medicine
nuclear umbrella
nuclear-free zone
nucleosynthesis
necromantically
Nicholas Wiseman
Niccolò Paganini
necessary truths
necessitousness
nick translation
nodding mandarin
Niels Henrik Abel
Nuffield College
nightmarishness
night starvation
neighbourliness
Nikhanj Kapil Dev
Nikolai Bulganin
Nikolaus Pevsner
Nikolay Bukharin
number-crunching
numbered account
nomographically
numismatologist
nemathelminthic
Nemathelminthes
nondescriptness
non-belligerency
nonsensicalness
non-disciplinary
non-fiction novel
non-intervention
non-intrusionist
non-governmental
non-commissioned
non compos mentis
non-contributory
non-conventional
ninepenny morris
non-professional
non-profit-making
non-prescription
Ninette de Valois
non-attributable
non-attributably
non-judgmentally
Nantucket Island
Neo-Christianity
neoconservative
neoconservatism
nepheline-basalt
neptunium series
Norway saltpetre
Norodom Sihanouk
north-eastwardly
north-east-by-east
north-westwardly
north-west-by-west

Northanger Abbey
north-countryman
Norroy and Ulster
Norfolk dumpling
norm-referencing
nasogastric tube
no spring chicken
Nathanael Greene
Nathan Söderblom
not the word for it
nitric anhydride
Nottinghamshire
nothing less than
nothing for it but
nothingarianism
notwithstanding
not on one's nellie
not to have a ghost
National Gallery
nationalisation
nationalization
National Lottery
National Society
national service
National Theatre
nitrogen dioxide
nitro-derivative
nitrogenisation
nitrogenization
nitrogen mustard
network computer
nitrous bacteria
nature knowledge
natural language
natural religion
natural theology
natural immunity
natural cycle IVF
not much the wiser
not much to look at
native companion
neural computing
nouvelle cuisine
naughty nineties
Nautical Almanac
neurophysiology
neurolinguistic
neurobiological
neurofibrillary
neuroblastomata
neuroanatomical
neuropsychiatry
neuropsychology
neurohypophyses
neurohypophysis
navigation light
Nevsky Alexander
Newgate Calendar
New Scotland Yard
New Red Sandstone
New-Age Traveller
now there's a thing
New England aster
New English Bible
New York Marathon
new-Commonwealth
now you're talking
Nizhniy Novgorod
on another planet
Osborne Reynolds
Osbert Lancaster

orbital motorway
occidental topaz
orchestral music
orchestra stalls
once in a blue moon
osculating orbit
occupation level
occasional cause
occasional table
Old Red Sandstone
old-age pensioner
oyer and terminer
one-parent family
overachievement
operating system
open aestivation
overbearingness
Owen Chamberlain
overdevelopment
overfamiliarity
overflow meeting
overforwardness
oreographically
over God's forbode
over head and ears
overhead charges
open-heartedness
overleap oneself
Ode on Melancholy
oceanographical
one's native heath
overpreparation
oneirocriticism
overthrust fault
one's true colours
one hundred hours
overuse syndrome
one over the eight
overweeningness
offhand grinding
officer of the day
Orfeo ed Euridice
organophosphate
ophthalmoscopic
ophthalmophobia
ophthalmoplegia
ophthalmoplegic
ophthalmologist
Ophioglossaceae
ochlocratically
oxidative stress
Oliver Goldsmith
Oliver Heaviside
opinionatedness
Olivier Messiaen
oriental emerald
oriented towards
oligosaccharide
oligonucleotide
opisthognathous
Opisthobranchia
objective danger
objectification
objectivisation
objectivization
oil of turpentine
oil someone's palm
osmotic pressure
omnibenevolence
of no consequence
omnidirectional
omnifariousness
owner-occupation
ornithodelphian
ornithodelphous
ornithorhynchus
onomasiological
on one's high horse
of one's own making
of one's own accord
on one's own ground
on one's pantables
odoriferousness
odontoid process
odontostomatous
opprobriousness
opportunity shop
opportunity cost
Our Mutual Friend
on speaking terms
observationally
observation post
obstructiveness
obstructionally
optical activity
optical illusion
optical spectrum
optical splitter
On the Waterfront
on the danger list
on the back burner
on the barrelhead
ostreiculturist
on the never-never
optoelectronics
on the right track
of the first water
on the wrong track
out of whole cloth
out of the running
out of all measure
out of one's senses
out of commission
out of proportion
ontogenetically
orthopaedically
osteopathically
orthokeratology
osteochondroses
osteochondrosis
orthophosphoric
orthodontically
orthopsychiatry
on top of the world
outer dead centre
Otto von Bismarck
opus reticulatum
oxy-calcium light
oxytetracycline
onychocryptosis
Pharaoh's serpent
Planck's constant
planetary nebula
place of business
Prayer of Azariah
peasecod-bellied
peasecod-cuirass
phase modulation
play first fiddle
pharisaicalness
plagiostomatous
platitudinarian
pharmacognosist
pharmacognostic
pharmacokinetic
pharmacotherapy
pragmaticalness
peacock-pheasant
prairie schooner
practicableness
practical reason
plantaginaceous
phantom material
praetorian guard
plasterers' putty
phantasmagorial
plant succession
peak viewing time
Platyhelminthes
public ownership
public relations
public-relations
public transport
public utilities
pocket an affront
pocket one's pride
packet switching
pycnodysostosis
picaresque novel
picture restorer
picture moulding
picture postcard
picture-postcard
picturesqueness
pactum illicitum
pick up the pieces
pedagoguishness
Pedro de Valdivia
Pedro de Alvarado
prenatal therapy
Pre-Raphaelitish
Pre-Raphaelitism
Pre-Raphaelistic
phenakistoscope
✧presbyterianise
✧presbyterianize
✧presbyterianism
preacquaintance
pseudoephedrine
pseudopregnancy
pseudepigraphic
presence chamber
predeterminable
preferentialism
preferentialist
piece of one's mind
preregistration
preternaturally
preferred shares
presentableness
prefect of police
pretentiousness
presentationism
presentationist
preservationist
President Marcos
precipitousness
plenipotentiary
predictableness
prehistorically
pneumonia blouse
pneumatic trough
pneumatological
pre-emption right
phenomenalistic
phenomenologist
prepositionally
preformationism
preformationist
phenolphthalein
preconstruction
prepossessingly
Pierre Corneille
Pierre de Ronsard
Pierre d'Aubusson
pleuropneumonia
press conference
pleasurableness
pleasure-seeking
pressure therapy
prestidigitator
phenylketonuria
phenylketonuric
pigs and whistles
pygmy chimpanzee
prima ballerinas
Philadelphaceae
private practice
private attorney
prima inter pares
philanthropical
primary meristem
primary election
primary assembly
principal dancer
principal clause
principal mobile
price leadership
Price Commission
plight one's troth
primitive streak
prick up one's ears
prismatic powder
psionic medicine
pair of compasses
poisoned chalice
philosophically
pair of virginals
point of no return
paint the town red
printing machine
✧privy counsellor
✧privy councillor
pyknodysostosis
Palma de Mallorca
police constable
police inspector
polychlorinated
polychloroprene
pelican crossing
palace of culture
polycrystalline
palaeoanthropic
Palaeoanthropus
palaeobiologist
palaeobotanical
palaeoethnology
palaeoecologist
polyelectrolyte
palaeographical
palaeogeography
palaeolimnology
palaeomagnetism
palaeontologist
palaeontography
pulse modulation
palaeopathology
palaeophytology
Pulver Wednesday
palaeozoologist
pulchritudinous
pull in one's horns
pull one's punches
pulmobranchiate
pillow-structure
pullorum disease
polyphloesboean
Polyprotodontia
polarity therapy
polishing-powder
polysyllabicism
pull someone's leg
polysynthetical
Palus Putredinis
political animal
political asylum
political status
palm-tree justice
pull the forelock
pull up one's socks
polyunsaturated
Pembroke College
pin back one's ears
pantechnicon-van
penlight battery
pencil moustache
pencil-sharpener
penal settlement
penalty shoot-out
pin on one's sleeve
Pentothal sodium
pantopragmatics
panophthalmitis
pancreatic juice
panoramic camera
Pan-Presbyterian
penetrativeness
punctuation mark
punctiliousness
punitive damages
Pindus Mountains
prolate spheroid
probationership
phonautographic
Ptolemaic system
prosenchymatous
Prometheus Bound
phonemicisation
phonemicization
phoneticisation
phoneticization
properispomenon
professionalise
professionalize
professionalism
processionalist
protection money
proof of identity
proof of purchase
proof-correcting
proof correction
ploughman's lunch
ploughshare bone
proximate object
Proxima Centauri

proxime accessit
prohibitiveness
problematically
People's Republic
People's Congress
People's Assembly
poor man of mutton
prognosticative
prognostication
phonocardiogram
provocativeness
photomacrograph
proboscis monkey
phototelegraphy
photomechanical
photorefractive
photodegradable
photosensitiser
photosensitizer
photozincograph
photolithograph
photomicrograph
photomicroscope
photoelasticity
photoconductive
photoconducting
photoionization
protozoological
photojournalism
photojournalist
protospatharius
photogrammetric
phototransistor
provost-sergeant
proportionately
proportionality
photomultiplier
phototypesetter
photoxylography
photosynthesize
prospectiveness
phosphorescence
phosphorous acid
phosphocreatine
phosphorylation
procreativeness
proprietorially
programmability
programme trader
procrastinative
procrastinating
procrastination
procrastinatory
progressiveness
progressive rock
pronunciamentos
propylene glycol
propylitisation
propylitization
Papua New Guinean
pipped at the post
peppermint cream
papillary muscle
Papal knighthood
paper tape reader
permanent magnet
pergamentaceous
permanent deacon
Père Armand David
parabiotic twins
parachute troops
paradoxicalness
porcelain cement
perpendicularly
pyro-electricity
paroemiographer
perfect interval
perfectionistic
perpetual motion
perpetual curate
perpetuum mobile
paragraphically
paragogic future
peregrine falcon
Peregrine Pickle
paraheliotropic
parthenogenesis
parthenogenetic
Perth and Kinross
particle physics
partial fraction
partial pressure
parliamentarism
parliamentarian
parliamentarily
Parliament clock
parliament-hinge
parliament-house
permissible dose
particularistic
parallelepipeda
parallel imports
purple gallinule
paralinguistics
purple of Cassius
purple of Cassuis
perfluorocarbon
Pyramid of Cheops
Pyramid of the Sun
Pyramids of Egypt
portmanteau word
parametral plane
pure mathematics
pyrometric cones
parenthetically
perennial nettle
phrenologically
personal effects
personalisation
personalization
personality cult
persona non grata
personal pronoun
personal shopper
personal service
personal trainer
purposelessness
personification
performance test
performance poet
performing right
par for the course
perspicaciously
perspicuousness
periphery camera
pyrophotography
portrait-gallery
portrait-painter
per ardua ad astra
peristaltically
parasol mushroom
parasympathetic
perissodactylic
perissosyllabic
pork scratchings
parasiticalness
Parasaurolophus
pyrotechnically
perfunctoriness
Portuguese shark
party-government
Pascal's triangle
postconsonantal
passenger-pigeon
possession order
postfix notation
posigrade rocket
Pasch of the Cross
paschal full moon
Piscis Austrinus
passive resister
passive immunity
pessimistically
puss in the corner
pusillanimously
post-millenarian
pastoral address
Pastoral Letters
push one's fortune
post-Reformation
pass round the hat
post-synchronise
post-synchronize
push the envelope
positive vetting
postulationally
put back the clock
Pitcairn Islands
put a brave face on
Pithecanthropus
pathetic fallacy
pot-bellied stove
Patient Griselda
put a fast one over
put the clock back
put the mockers on
pitching niblick
put the squeeze on
Patripassianism
putting the stone
put on a brave face
put in the picture
potential energy
put into practice
put one's back into
put one's finger on
put one's foot in it
put one's foot down
pathophysiology
paterfamiliases
Peter Paul Rubens
Peter and the Wolf
potassium iodide
Petition of Right
put out to pasture
plumbaginaceous
pour cold water on
prunes and prisms
paulo-post-future
Paul Pierre Broca
poulters' measure
poverty-stricken
powdering-closet
power of attorney
power-on self-test
pay off old scores
psychobiologist
psychobiography
psychochemistry
psychographical
psychogenetical
psychogeriatric
psychohistorian
psychologically
psychometrician
psychrometrical
psychopathology
psychophysicist
psychosomimetic
psychosynthesis
psychotherapist
psychotomimetic
physiographical
physiologically
physicochemical
physiotherapist
phytogeographic
phytogeographer
phytoestrogenic
Plymouth Brother
puzzle-prize book
quatercentenary
qualis ab incepto
qualifying round
Quatorze Juillet
quarrelsomeness
quadruplication
quadripartition
quantum sufficit
quarter-sessions
quartermistress
queen of puddings
queen's messenger
questionability
question-begging
quick off the mark
quick-wittedness
quick-conceiving
quinquagenarian
quintuplication
road fund licence
reafforestation
rear its ugly head
Rhamphorhynchus
reappropriation
reapportionment
reaction turbine
readvertisement
read-write memory
rub salt in a wound
Rebecca de Winter
ribonucleic acid
Robinson College
Robin Goodfellow
ribbon parachute
ribwort plantain
Robert A Millikan
Robert Henry Dick
Robert Jenkinson
Roberto Clemente
Robert Southwell
Robert S Mulliken
Richard Hamilton
Richard P Feynman
Richard Dimbleby
Richard Lovelace
Richard Crossman
Richard Dreyfuss
Richard Dunwoody
recrementitious
roche moutonnéed
rocket scientist
Rachel Whiteread
recognisability
recognizability
Received English
receiver general
receiving-office
recollectedness
Recumbent Figure
Richmal Crompton
reconvalescence
racing certainty
reconcilability
reconsideration
reconsolidation
reconstitutable
reconstructable
reconstructible
reception centre
reception theory
reciprocal cross
reciprocity rule
recoverableness
recovered memory
Rodrigues Island
rudimentariness
redemption yield
riding committee
radiolarian ooze
radioscopically
radiotelegraphy
radiometrically
radio microphone
radiogoniometer
radio-gramophone
redetermination
radium emanation
Radovan Karadzic
Riemannian space
rheumatological
re-establishment
re-entry corridor
re-education camp
refrangibleness
refractive index
Refection Sunday
refreshment-room
refortification
Rift Valley fever
regaliamantling
regular customer
regional council
regionalisation
regionalization
Roger de Coverley
right-handedness
right off the reel
right-mindedness
Right Honourable
Roget's Thesaurus
regius professor
rainbow-coloured
rainbow dressing
rain cats and dogs

reindustrialise
reindustrialize
raise one's dander
raise one's sights
raise to the bench
✧reichian therapy
reinterrogation
railway carriage
railway crossing
reliability test
Ralph Abercromby
Ralph Richardson
roly-poly pudding
Rollright Stones
relative address
relative density
relatively prime
Ramsay MacDonald
romanticisation
romanticization
Romantic Revival
remonstratingly
remorselessness
rumbustiousness
Randall Davidson
Ringelmann chart
Ringer's solution
röntgenotherapy
running headline
running ornament
run one's eyes over
run someone close
renormalisation
renormalization
rent restriction
ring-tailed lemur
run a temperature
renewable energy
rhombencephalon
rhombenporphyry
reopening clause
rooting compound
room temperature
room to swing a cat
reprivatisation
reprivatization
replication fork
reproachfulness
repetitiousness
residential area
respectableness
Russian Civil War
Russian roulette
Russian dressing
Rosamond Lehmann
rosin rosin plant
Russo-Finnish War
responsibleness
res ipsa loquitur
restrictiveness
resurrectionary
resurrectionise
resurrectionize
resurrectionism
resurrectionist
resurrection man
resurrection pie
reserve currency
risus sardonicus
resourcefulness
ritualistically

retrievableness
rational horizon
rationalisation
rationalization
retroreflective
retrospectively
retrotransposon
retrogressively
retrogressional
Return of the Jedi
roundaboutation
roundaboutility
round-shouldered
rouche moutonnée
rough puff-pastry
Rev Obadiah Slope
revolving credit
reverse takeover
reverse genetics
reverse yield gap
River Shenandoah
riverworthiness
Raynaud's disease
Rhynchobdellida
Rhynchocephalia
Roy Lichtenstein
Royal Albert Hall
✧royal commission
Raymond Chandler
Raymond Williams
Raymond Poincaré
stalagmitically
stalactitically
shabby-gentility
standoffishness
stand and deliver!
stand on ceremony
standing ovation
standing-off dose
standing rigging
stand one's corner
stand one's ground
stand to one's guns
stand upon points
standard English
standardisation
standardization
state capitalism
State Department
scalene triangle
snake in the grass
shape one's course
shared ownership
slave-trafficker
space travelling
staff-tree family
scaphocephalous
swathling-clouts
staphylorrhaphy
swathing-clothes
Spanish mackerel
Spanish chestnut
Spanish windlass
Spanish Civil War
Spanish omelette
smack on the wrist
stable companion
small-mindedness
stapling machine
scarlet geranium
Stanley Matthews

Stanley Kowalski
Spasmodic School
stagnation point
star of Bethlehem
snap one's fingers
shadow pantomime
stamp of approval
sharp-wittedness
stamping machine
stamp collecting
sparring partner
slapstick comedy
Stars and Stripes
Svante Arrhenius
St Antony of Padua
St Anthony's cross
scatter cushions
Statue of Liberty
✧sealyham terrier
Sabbath-breaking
submarine canyon
submarine effect
Sublapsarianism
subterraneously
subject-superior
subcivilisation
subcivilization
subsistence wage
subintellection
subintelligence
subintelligitur
subcommissioner
sub-postmistress
subspecifically
St Barbara's cress
suburbanisation
suburbanization
subordinateness
sober-mindedness
Sebastian Faulks
substratosphere
substantiveness
substantialness
substitutionary
social cleansing
social democracy
social exclusion
Sacramento River
social insurance
socialistically
social ownership
social secretary
sacral vertebrae
succculent-house
socket head screw
successlessness
succession house
succinylcholine
Sicilian Vespers
sickle-cell trait
second-adventist
secondary causes
secondary action
secondary school
secondary picket
secondary modern
secondary colour
second-class mail
second-class post
second childhood
second honeymoon

second-in-command
secundogeniture
sickness benefit
seconds pendulum
secundum naturam
secundum ordinem
secundum regulam
sociolinguistic
sociobiological
sycophantically
security blanket
Security Council
Secession Church
St Cuthbert's duck
saddle-bill stork
saddler-sergeant
saddler-corporal
sedimentologist
sadomasochistic
Sydenham's chorea
sodium ascorbate
sodium carbonate
sodium hydroxide
stewards' enquiry
saeva indignatio
steganographist
Stefan Wyszynski
speech community
speechification
speech pathology
Spencer Perceval
speech synthesis
speech therapist
spend one's breath
stereochemistry
Speyer Cathedral
stereoisomerism
Steven Spielberg
Stephen Jay Gould
Stephen Sondheim
shepherd's tartan
shepherd's needle
shepherd's myrtle
see what one can do
specific gravity
specific impulse
special warranty
special retainer
special delivery
special pleading
special hospital
speak to the heart
Stella McCartney
Shetland Islands
smelling of roses
Sheila Rowbotham
stemless thistle
steam locomotive
spermatoblastic
spermatic artery
spermatogenesis
spermatogenetic
see someone right
sweep second hand
sleeping draught
sleeping partner
sweet Fanny Adams
sheathe the sword
smelting-furnace
spectroscopical
speculativeness

sleeve waistcoat
soft commodities
soft furnishings
softly-sprighted
soft-rock geology
significatively
Sugar Ray Leonard
Sigourney Weaver
scheduled castes
Schrecklichkeit
sphaerosiderite
St Hilda's College
schillerisation
schillerization
Sphenisciformes
school inspector
schoolmastering
schoolmasterish
schoolmistressy
Schiphol Airport
spheroidisation
spheroidization
schistosomiasis
schizo-affective
schizophrenetic
spiral staircase
Skiddaw Mountain
shiver my timbers
stiff-neckedness
spirit of ammonia
Shikibu Murasaki
stick in one's craw
sticking-plaster
stinking parasol
spick and span new
stick to one's guns
stickit minister
shilling shocker
shilly-shallying
Shirley MacLaine
Shirley Williams
seismographical
seismologically
swimming costume
slimmers' disease
stigmatophilist
sail near the wind
St Ignatius's bean
spirochaetaemia
ship of the desert
slip of the tongue
stilpnosiderite
Saint George's Bay
scintillatingly
shifting spanner
shift one's ground
shift for oneself
St Kitts and Nevis
self-abandonment
self-affirmation
syllabification
Salvador Allende
self-approbation
self-approvingly
self-advancement
sell by the candle
select committee
selective mating
self-complacence
self-consciously
self-consequence

self-considering
self-confidently
self-consistency
self-centredness
self-constituted
self-capacitance
self-certificate
self-documenting
self-degradation
self-deprecating
solid propellant
self-disciplined
self-destructive
self-destruction
self-determining
solid-state light
self-development
self-examination
silver birch tree
self-explanatory
self-explication
self-forgetfully
self-fertilizing
self-humiliation
sulphinpyrazone
sulphur bacteria
sulphureousness
sulphur trioxide
self-indulgently
Sylvia Pankhurst
self-improvement
self-importantly
self-liquidating
salami technique
selenographical
splendide mendax
self-opinionated
syllogistically
self-observation
self-preparation
solipsistically
self-pollination
self-propagating
self-propagation
self-portraiture
self-questioning
self-realisation
self-realization
sclerodermatous
self-referential
self-registering
self-righteously
solar microscope
self-reproachful
solar prominence
self-resemblance
self-slaughtered
self-substantial
self-sacrificing
sales resistance
self-sufficiency
self-sustainment
self-sovereignty
split-level house
split-level trust
split infinitive
Seleucus Nicator
self-vindication
St Lawrence River
Süleyman Demirel
sympathomimetic
sympathetically
Sam Jackson Snead
semicylindrical
so much the better
semicrystalline
semidocumentary
Samuel Hahnemann
symmetricalness
semi-independent
semi-logarithmic
semilunar valves
semi-latus rectum
semimanufacture
Simon de Montfort
sum and substance
Summoned by Bells
sympodial growth
Semi-Pelagianism
Somerset Maugham
St Martin's summer
semisubmersible
semesterisation
semesterization
semitransparent
somatic mutation
symptomological
symptomatically
song-and-dance act
sensation-monger
sing another song
sing another tune
Sunday Telegraph
synecologically
synecdochically
Sunset Boulevard
sense perception
sententiousness
senega snakeroot
synchronisation
synchronization
synchronistical
synchronousness
synchro swimming
synthetic resins
syndical chamber
sunrise industry
singing telegram
Singin' in the Rain
sensible horizon
single-heartedly
single use camera
San Joaquin River
Synoptic Gospels
synarthrodially
synergistically
San Francisco Bay
send round the hat
sonorous figures
Sangster Airport
sinistrodextral
Sans Souci Museum
sanctimoniously
singularisation
singularization
storage capacity
stomach staggers
spot advertising
scotched collops
stoicheiometric
stoechiological
stoichiological
sword-and-buckler
sword-and-sorcery
smoke and mirrors
stop-frame camera
swothling-clouts
smoking carriage
stocks and stones
stocking stuffer
stockbroker belt
shoulder-clapper
shoulder-slipped
shoulder-shotten
spoilt for choice
spoiling tactics
scolopendriform
slog one's guts out
show one's ivories
shopping-bag lady
Saorstát Eireann
slotted aerofoil
short-term memory
short sharp shock
shoot tip culture
Scott Fitzgerald
shout blue murder
shooting gallery
slotting-machine
spontaneousness
shoot from the hip
Scottish Borders
Scottish terrier
September people
septentrionally
supplementation
supplementarily
saprophytically
suppositionally
supportableness
supercalendered
superlativeness
superpatriotism
supernaturalise
supernaturalize
supernaturalism
supersaturation
supernaturalist
superabundantly
superadditional
superheterodyne
superficialness
superfluousness
superplasticity
superimposition
superintendence
superintendency
superincumbence
superincumbency
superinducement
superconductive
superconfidence
superior planets
superordination
suppressor T-cell
superstitiously
superstructural
superexcellence
superexaltation
St Patrick's cross
St Peter's College
surface activity
spread-eaglewise
sarraceniaceous
Sir David Barclay
screaming abdabs
screaming meemie
Sir Barnes Wallis
Sir Jacob Epstein
spread one's wings
Sir Patrick Moore
serial technique
Sir Ian Trethowan
Sir Samuel Cunard
scribaciousness
scribbling-paper
sericiculturist
structural steel
Sir Edward German
Sir Edward Hulton
Sir Edwin Lutyens
straddle carrier
Sir Geraint Evans
sarcenchymatous
Sergei Diaghilev
Sir Peter Medawar
Sir Seretse Khama
Sir Peter Ustinov
Sir Jeremy Isaacs
street furniture
Sir Pelham Warner
Sir Hermann Bondi
sergeant-drummer
Sergei Prokofiev
Sir George Cayley
Sir George Thomas
Sir George Stokes
Sir Henry Raeburn
Sir Henry Segrave
serpentine verse
surreptitiously
Sir Rhodes Boyson
Sir Philip Sidney
Sir Thomas Browne
Sir Charles Barry
Sir Charles Hallé
serviceableness
service industry
service contract
service provider
Sir Michael Caine
straightforward
strain hardening
Sir Richard Stone
Sir Richard Scott
straight shooter
straight talking
straight-talking
Sir William Bragg
Sir William Osler
straitwaistcoat
strike a bad patch
strike-slip fault
Sir Alec Guinness
Sir Cliff Richard
strolling player
Sir Clement Freud
Sir Alan L Hodgkin
Sir Alex Ferguson
scrumptiousness
strombuliferous
springer spaniel
shrinking violet
serendipitously
sprinkler system
string orchestra
shrink-resistant
Sir Donald Sinden
Sir Ronald Fisher
Sir Donald Wolfit
surrogate mother
Sir Joseph Paxton
servomechanical
Sir Douglas Bader
Sir Tom Hopkinson
Sir Norman Fowler
Sir Norman Foster
Sir John Vanbrugh
Sir John Falstaff
Sir John Marshall
Sir John Betjeman
Sir John Herschel
Sir John Charnley
Sir John Mortimer
Sir John Franklin
Sir John Suckling
strephosymbolia
scrape the barrel
scripture-reader
Sir Freddie Laker
Sir Arthur Harris
Sir Francis Drake
Sir Frank Whittle
Sir Oswald Mosley
Sir Isaiah Berlin
Sir Astley Cooper
stress of weather
stratigraphical
strategic metals
stretching frame
stretch one's legs
stretcher-bearer
scratchbuilding
Sir Julian Huxley
Sir Austen Layard
scrivener's palsy
screwball comedy
strawberry shrub
screwing machine
sustaining pedal
systematisation
systematization
St Stephen's House
suspense account
systems analysis
systems software
susceptibleness
session musician
sesquicentenary
sesquicarbonate
situation comedy
situation ethics
Sutherland Falls
set a game to three
settle old scores
set one's sights on
St Thomas Aquinas
Sutton Coldfield
set great store by
saturation point
South Bank Centre
south-eastwardly
south-east-by-east
South Seas Island
south-westwardly

south-west-by-west
South Uist Island
Southern Comfort®
spur of the moment
slumpflationary
square kilometre
square leg umpire
Squire Trelawney
squish lip system
Sturt's desert pea
shutter priority
save appearances
St Valentine's Day
seven deadly sins
seventeen-hunder
seventh interval
saving reverence
Shwe Dagon Pagoda
sow one's wild oats
Shwezigon Pagoda
sexual selection
sexual therapist
sixty-fourth note
say the magic word
thanatognomonic
thalassographic
thalassographer
thalassotherapy
thatched cottage
trapezius muscle
Thales of Miletus
teaching machine
teacher-governor
traditional jazz
Thanksgiving Day
tracking station
thankworthiness
trailing arbutus
traumatological
training college
tear one's hair out
tranquilization
tranquilizingly
translatability
transparentness
translationally
transubstantial
transactionally
transferability
transfer machine
transfer payment
transverse colon
transverse flute
transliteration
✧transfiguration
transfigurement
transplantation
transilluminate
transposability
that's more like it
transpositional
transmogrifying
transportedness
transcriptively
transcriptional
transgressively
transgressional
transistor radio
transition metal
transition point
transmutability
transmutational
Thatta monuments
tableau curtains
tableaux vivants
tuberculisation
tuberculization
ticket collector
Tectibranchiata
tectibranchiate
technical writer
technologically
technostructure
Tadpole and Taper
the fatal sisters
The Dance of Death
The Garden of Eden
The Garden of Love
The Rape of Europa
the same old story
therapeutically
the hale hypothec
the Paris Commune
the back of beyond
The Faerie Queene
the cat's whiskers
the Mansion House
The Raft of Medusa
the Last Judgment
The Marx Brothers
the lady vanishes
trembling poplar
treacle wormseed
treacherousness
The Iceman Cometh
Theodor Billroth
Theodore Roethke
Theodor Svedberg
The Female Eunuch
The Dead Kennedys
the feudal system
The Beggar's Opera
the devil's tattoo
the weaker vessel
there's no telling
The Second Coming
The Pearl Fishers
the merry monarch
the Weird Sisters
The Secret Garden
The Death of Marat
The New York Times
The African Queen
The Age of Anxiety
The Three Sisters
the Three Wise Men
The Three Witches
The Charnel House
the chosen people
the bitch goddess
the big enchilada
The Rite of Spring
the nine worthies
The Divine Comedy
theriomorphosis
therianthropism
The Little Prince
The Littlest Hobo
the gift of the gab
The Birth of Venus
the silver screen
The Bicycle Thief
the sky's the limit
The Sleepwalkers
The Flagellation
theolinguistics
the plot thickens
the gloves are off
The Old Wives' Tale
Thelma and Louise
thermobaric bomb
thermochemistry
thermodynamical
thermal capacity
thermionic valve
The Invisible Man
the end of the line
the end of the road
The Annunciation
the how and the why
The Cowardly Lion
The Woman in White
The Potato Eaters
the Low Countries
the Good Shepherd
The Tower of Babel
the powers that be
the noble science
the common people
the morn's morning
the morning after
The Sound of Music
the fourth estate
the Four Freedoms
The Sorrow of Love
the worse for wear
the coast is clear
The Boston Herald
the Greek calends
The Artful Dodger
the bright lights
theorematically
the Principality
the crescent moon
The Grauballe Man
The Essays of Elia
The Isle of Avalon
treasonableness
theosophistical
Treaties of Paris
twenty-four-seven
the Supreme Being
twelve-hour clock
The Eve of St Agnes
Tigran Petrosian
tighten the screw
tighten one's belt
tightrope walker
thiobarbiturate
third-rail system
third-generation
third degree burn
trigeminal nerve
trine to the cheat
trichloroethane
trinitrobenzene
trinitrotoluene
Trinity Brethren
thickheadedness
thick-wittedness
think on one's feet
think twice about
trial of strength
twirl one's thumbs
Triumph of Caesar
triangular prism
trigonometrical
thin on the ground
trisoctahedrons
thin-skinnedness
thirtysomething
trisyllabically
take a name in vain
take at advantage
take advantage of
take French leave
take it from there
take it lying down
take it or leave it
take it on the chin
take into account
take no prisoners
take one's cue from
take some beating
take someone up on
take the shilling
take the chill off
take the shine off
take their course
take the wraps off
take to one's heart
take to one's heels
take upon oneself
talk against time
talk a blue streak
tilt at windmills
telegraphically
talk like a pen-gun
tell one's own tale
telephone number
telephotography
telestereoscope
telescopic shaft
telescopic sight
telethermoscope
temperance hotel
temperamentally
tamper-resistant
tempestuousness
Tom, Dick, and Harry
Temple of Artemis
Temple of Hathoor
Temple of Solomon
Temple of Somnath
Tim Brooke-Taylor
tempt providence
time-zone disease
time-zone fatigue
Tantallon Castle
tentaculiferous
tent caterpillar
tender-heartedly
tendentiousness
tensile strength
tan someone's hide
Ten Commandments
tungsten carbide
tong-test ammeter
tongue-and-groove
Thomas Babington
Thomas De Quincey
Thomas Gradgrind
Thomas Jefferson
Thomas Middleton
thoracocentesis
two-pair-of-stairs
troubleshooting
troublesomeness
to one's knowledge
thoughtlessness
thought disorder
Thojib N J Suharto
thorn in the flesh
too good to be true
thoroughgoingly
Toots Thielemans
Thomson's gazelle
two hundred hours
too much too young
tip of the iceberg
topographically
typographically
Tarzan of the Apes
Tarzan the Ape Man
three-day eventer
threepenceworth
three-legged race
Three Men in a Boat
threepenny piece
threepennyworth
three times three
three-ring circus
terminal illness
turn in one's grave
Territorial Army
turn in on oneself
tertiary college
tertiary colours
thromboembolism
Terence Rattigan
Toronto blessing
tarsometatarsal
tarsometatarsus
turn one's stomach
threshold lights
thrust to the wall
turntable ladder
torque converter
through the night
through-composed
throw in the cards
throw in the towel
throw in one's hand
throw to the winds
throw up the cards
testament-dative
Tasmanian myrtle
Tess Durbeyfield
tossing the caber
to someone's teeth
tetrasporangium
Tetrabranchiata
tetrabranchiate
Tetractinellida
tetrasyllabical
to the manner born
tatterdemallion
to the effect that
To the Lighthouse
Tattersall check
total body burden
totalitarianism
titanium dioxide
Titus Andronicus
tout au contraire

thumbnail sketch
truncation error
thunderstricken
true-heartedness
tough-mindedness
tough as old boots
Teutonic Knights
Toulouse-Lautrec
trustworthiness
Taurus Mountains
tower of strength
toxicologically
Tay-Sachs disease
trypanosomiasis
unavailableness
unaccommodating
unascertainable
unavoidableness
unapostolically
unapprehensible
unauthenticated
unauthoritative
unalterableness
unadvisableness
Umberto Boccioni
unchangeability
unchallengeable
unchallengeably
Unchained Melody
uncompanionable
uncompassionate
uncomplaisantly
uncomplainingly
uncomplimentary
uncomprehensive
uncomprehending
uncommunicative
unconscientious
unconsciousness
unconcernedness
unconsentaneous
unconditionally
uncanonicalness
uncontroversial
unconstrainable
unconstrainedly
unco-operatively
uncooperatively
unceremoniously
unchristianlike
uncircumscribed
undemonstrative
underhandedness
under-the-counter
Under the Volcano
under the weather
under plain cover
underemployment
under one's breath
under lock and key
under correction
underproduction
underprivileged
underestimation
understandingly
undersubscribed
undistinguished
undisciplinable
undisappointing
undesirableness
undetermination

unexceptionable
unexceptionably
unexceptionally
unforgivingness
unfortunateness
unfossiliferous
ungrammatically
ungentlemanlike
unhealthfulness
unimaginatively
unitary taxation
United Provinces
unidiomatically
utility function
unintentionally
unintermittedly
uninterpretable
uninterestingly
uninterruptedly
unknown quantity
unleavened bread
unnecessariness
Utopia Unlimited
unobjectionable
unobjectionably
unobtrusiveness
unpeaceableness
unpractisedness
unprecedentedly
unpremeditation
unprepossessing
unphilosophical
unprotectedness
unprotestantise
unprotestantize
unprofitability
unpronounceable
unproportionate
unprogressively
unparliamentary
upper atmosphere
unpatriotically
unqualifiedness
unrecommendable
unreconciliable
unreconstructed
unrighteousness
unrelentingness
unremittingness
unstatesmanlike
unseaworthiness
unsubstantiated
unsteadfastness
unspeakableness
unselfconscious
unsymmetrically
unsportsmanlike
unsophisticated
unsuspectedness
unsatisfiedness
ultracentrifuge
unteachableness
ultra-high vacuum
ultraviolet star
ultramicroscope
ultramicroscopy
ultrafiltration
ultrasonography
untransferrable
untransmigrated
untransmissible

untractableness
up to the eyeballs
up to the eyebrows
untrustworthily
unverifiability
unwholesomeness
Vladimir Nabokov
vice-chamberlain
Victorien Sardou
vicissitudinous
victualling-yard
victualling-ship
victualling-bill
videoconference
vegetable marrow
vegetable butter
vegetable oyster
vulcanized fibre
Valiant-for-Truth
value in exchange
Völkerwanderung
voluntary school
voluntary muscle
Vale of Glamorgan
volutin granules
Vincenzo Bellini
vindicativeness
venereal disease
ventriloquially
ventriloquistic
Vanessa Redgrave
Venture Sea Scout
Venture Air Scout
venturesomeness
Violeta Chamorro
violinistically
variae lectiones
very approximate
vertebral column
vertical take-off
vermis cerebelli
Virginia creeper
vertiginousness
virgin parchment
verdigris agaric
visible spectrum
vasoconstrictor
vested interests
Vosges Mountains
vestibular nerve
viscosimetrical
viscoelasticity
Viscount Allenby
Viscount Camrose
Viscount Haldane
visiting fireman
vascular disease
vascularisation
vascularization
vital statistics
vitamin B complex
Vaughan Williams
vouch to warranty
vox populi vox Dei
weather the storm
weather notation
weather forecast
weatherboarding
what is he for a man?
weak interaction
what's the big idea?

what's your poison?
wear several hats
wear the breeches
wear the trousers
Wladyslaw Anders
Wackford Squeers
wide area network
wedge-heeled shoe
wield the sceptre
Where Eagles Dare
Wiener schnitzel
When I Fall In Love
wheelbarrow race
wheel animalcule
Weedon Grossmith
wages-fund theory
white sandalwood
white man's burden
white rhinoceros
Whitechapel cart
whited sepulchre
whiter than white
wringing-machine
weighted average
weighing-machine
Waiting for Godot
whirligig beetle
whirling dervish
whirling-machine
writ of execution
writ of privilege
whistle for a wind
whistle-stop tour
whistling kettle
Wilt Chamberlain
well-conditioned
Willem De Kooning
Willem Einthoven
Walter Greenwood
Wilhelm Steinitz
wallflower brown
wall gillyflower
Walther Rathenau
Walther Flemming
Wallis and Futuna
walking dragline
William Davenant
William Langland
William Hamilton
William Faulkner
William Marshall
William J Brennan
William McKinley
William Herschel
William Rees-Mogg
William Beaumont
William of Ockham
William Christie
William Chambers
William Whitelaw
William Congreve
William Friedkin
William Kunstler
Wilkins Micawber
Willie Shoemaker
well-intentioned
walk on eggshells
wallop in a tether
Wilfred Thesiger
well-upholstered
walrus moustache

well-woman clinic
woman of the world
Women's Institute
wind-chill factor
wandering sailor
Wendell M Stanley
wondermongering
windfall profits
Winchester rifle®
window gardening
wind synthesizer
windscreen-wiper
Windward Islands
win by a short head
wrong-headedness
woody nightshade
word association
warrantableness
warm-bloodedness
world-shattering
world without end
world-without-end
work double tides
War of Jenkins' Ear
War of Devolution
War of the Pacific
warm-heartedness
worth the whistle
Wernher von Braun
working majority
warning triangle
wireless station
work one's guts out
work one's passage
Wars of the Vendée
western blotting
waste one's breath
wishful thinking
Wassily Leontief
Wasily Kandinsky
Wisdom of Solomon
Weston-super-Mare
wish someone well
with a wild wanion
with a difference
with bated breath
with compliments
with closed doors
withdrawing-room
wet the baby's head
within arm's reach
wetting-out agent
without ceremony
without recourse
water on the brain
Waterloo cracker
water equivalent
water tube boiler
X-ray diffraction
X-ray micrography
xylotypographic
xeroradiography
yadda yadda yadda
yield up the ghost
yellow archangel
yellow brick road
yellow-eyed grass
yellow pimpernel
Yellow Submarine
Yamabe no Akahito
Yorkshire Ripper

you've got me there
Young Vic Theatre
yours faithfully
Ziegler catalyst
Zagros Mountains
zygophyllaceous
Zöllner's pattern
zoogeographical
zoophysiologist
zoophytological
zero-point energy

Words Arranged According to Even Letters

For Words Arranged According to Odd Letters see p1085

4 – even

baba
caba
✧cama
capa
Cara
casa
Cava
Dada
Dana
data
fa la
fa-la
Gaea
gaga
Gaia
gala
Gaza
ha-ha
haka
Java
Java®
Kaba
kaka
✧kama
kana
kara
kata
kava
Lada®
la-la
lama
lana
Lara
lava
Maia
mama
mana
mara
masa
✧maya
nada
naga
Naha
Naia
Naja
nala
✧nana
napa
Nara
NASA
paca
✧papa
Pará
para
paua
pawa
raca
raga
raja
Rama
✧rana
rata
Raza
Saba
saga
sama
San'a

Sara
sa sa
taha
taka
tala
tana
tapa
tara
ta-ta
tava
tawa
taxa
vara
✧vasa
waka
Yama
Zara
Badb
✧barb
carb
daub
gamb
garb
iamb
jamb
✧lamb
Saab®
banc
laic
Macc
marc
narc
saic
talc
Waac
bald
✧band
✧bard
baud
bawd
card
Dard
daud
dawd
eard
Fahd
fand
fard
gaid
gaud
gawd
hand
hard
haud
kaid
laid
✧land
lard
laud
maid
mand
mard
✧maud
nard
paid
pand
pard

rag'd
raid
✧rand
said
sand
✧sard
wadd
Wafd
waid
wald
wan'd
wand
ward
yald
✧yard
yaud
✧babe
bade
bake
bale
bane
bare
base
bate
baye
cade
cafe
café
cage
cake
came
cane
✧cape
care
case
cate
cave
dace
dale
dame
Dane
dare
date
Dave
daze
eale
ease
face
fade
fake
fame
fane
fare
fate
fave
Faye
faze
gade
gage
✧gale
game
gane
gape
gare
gate
gave
Gaye

gaze
hade
hake
hale
hame
hare
hate
have
haze
jade
✧jake
✧jane
jape
kade
kaie
kale
kame
Kate
Kaye
lace
lade
lake
lame
lamé
lane
lare
lase
late
lave
laze
Mace®
mace
made
mage
make
Malé
male
mane
mare
mase
mate
maté
maze
✧name
nape
nare
nave
naze
✧pace
✧page
pale
pane
pape
pare
pate
pâté
pave
pavé
race
rade
rage
rake
rale
râle
rape
rare
rase

rate
rave
raze
✧sade
safe
sage
sake
saké
sale
same
sane
sate
save
✧saxe
tace
take
tale
tame
ta'ne
tane
tape
tare
✧tate
vade
vale
vane
vare
vase
wade
wage
wake
wale
wame
wane
ware
wase
wate
wave
wawe
Yale®
yale
yare
yate
baff
barf
caff
calf
cauf
daff
faff
gaff
haaf
haff
half
kaif
lauf
naff
naif
naïf
raff
Taff
Waaf
waff
waif
✧wakf
✧waqf
yaff

zarf
bang
cang
dang
darg
fang
gang
hagg
hang
kang
✧lang
magg
mang
marg
pang
ragg
rang
saag
sang
T'ang
✧tang
vang
wang
✧yang
✧bach
bagh
bash
✧bath
✧cash
dash
each
eath
fash
gash
gath
hash
hath
kaph
Kath
lakh
lash
lath
mash
math
nach
Nash
oath
pash
path
rach
rash
rath
sash
tach
tanh
tash
tath
wash
Zach
Babi
Bali
bani
Bari
cadi
Cali
capi
✧dali

✧dari
Gabi
gadi
haji
Hani
Hari
Iasi
Jawi
kadi
kaki
✧kali
kami
kati
kazi
lari
lati
✧magi
✧mali
mani
Maui
maxi
Nazi
Pali
qadi
rabi
ragi
raki
rami
rani
Ravi
Safi
✧saki
Sami
sari
sati
tabi
taki
tali
Tati
taxi
vagi
vali
wadi
wali
Yagi
zati
hadj
hajj
back
balk
bank
bark
bask
bauk
calk
cark
cask
cauk
cawk
dank
dark
dawk
faik
fank
gawk
hack
haik

✧hank
hark
hask
hawk
✧jack
jark
kark
lack
laik
lank
lark
lawk
mack
maik
✧mark
mask
mawk
nabk
naik
nark
pack
paik
✧park
pawk
rack
raik
rank
sack
sank
✧sark
tack
talk
tank
task
wack
walk
wark
wauk
yack
✧yank
✧zack
Baal
bael
bail
ball
bawl
call
✧carl
caul
daal
✧dahl
Dáil
earl
fail
fall
farl
Gael
Gail
✧gall
gaol
Gaul
hail
hall
harl
haul
jail
jarl

kail
Karl
mail
mall
marl
maul
nail
pail
pall
✧paul
pawl
rail
sail
✧saul
Taal
tael
tail
tall
vail
wail
wall
waul
wawl
y'all
yawl
balm
barm
calm
caum
farm
gaum
haem
halm
harm
hawm
kaim
ma'am
maim
malm
marm
naam
palm
Saam
saim
warm
barn
bawn
Caen
✧cain
cann
damn
darn
✧dawn
eaon
earn
fain
faun
fawn
gain
gaun
hain
harn
lain
Jain
jann
kain
kaon

lain
larn
lawn
main
Mann
maun
naan
nain
paan
pain
pawn
rain
raun
rawn
sain
sawn
ta'en
tarn
vain
✧wain
warn
yarn
yawn
capo
Caro
dado
fado
faro
gajo
gapó
halo
haro
Iago
jato
kago
Kano
kayo
lazo
mako
mano
✧mayo
Nato
paco
Pavo
sago
taco
taro
Waco
barp
calp
camp
carp
caup
damp
gamp
gasp
gaup
gawp
harp
hasp
jasp
jaup
lamp
Lapp
palp
parp
ramp

rasp
salp
samp
tamp
tarp
vamp
warp
✧wasp
yapp
yaup
yawp
Marq
baur
bawr
carr
daur
fair
gair
gaur
haar
✧hair
laer
lair
maar
mair
mawr
Nair
pair
parr
sair
tahr
vair
waur
yarr
baas
Babs
bags
bars
bass
bats
bays
cans
Cass
Cats
dabs
dags
dais
daks
dams
✧days
eats
Hals
jass
✧jaws
kans
lags
Laos
lass
lats
mags
Mars
✧mass
nabs
naos
oafs
Oaks
oats

pads
pais
pass
pays
rads
rags
Rams
rats
sans
sass
says
tags
taps
tass
taws
wats
ways
yaws
baft
baht
bait
Balt
bant
Bart
bast
batt
bayt
can't
cant
cart
cast
daft
dalt
dant
d'art
dart
daut
dawt
✧east
fact
fast
gait
gant
gart
gast
haet
haft
ha'it
halt
ha'n't
hart
hast
haut
✧kant
kart
lant
last
Maat
malt
mart
mast
✧matt
oast
pact
pant
part
past

Words marked ✧ can also be spelled with one or more capital letters

raft
rait
rant
rapt
rast
salt
✧sant
saut
tact
tait
tart
tatt
taut
tawt
vant
vast
vaut
wadt
waft
wait
Walt
want
wart
wast
watt
babu
baju
Baku
balu
bapu
Danu
hapu
kagu
Manú
masu
Oahu
Rahu
raku
ratu
tabu
tapu
tatu
vatu
Zanu
Zapu
Maev
calx
faix
falx
faux
lanx
Manx
Marx
baby
cagy
caky
cany
cavy
Davy
easy
fady
gaby
gamy
Gary
gazy
hazy
jasy
jazy
Katy
lacy
lady

laky
lazy
many
✧mary
maty
mazy
nary
✧navy
oaky
oary
oaty
pacy
paly
racy
sagy
taky
vary
wady
waly
wany
wary
wavy
waxy
yawy
zany
jazz
razz
✧**abba**
obia
Abib
abac
abed
abid
'zbud
abbé
able
abye
oboe
pbuh
Abel
obol
ebon
Oban
Obon
tbsp
Aber
CBer
mbar
T-bar
à **bas**
Abos
ibis
Ibos
obos
abet
a bit
abut
obit
ybet
ibex
Abby
ably
Ibby
obey
acta
octa
scab
AC/DC
acid
ecad
ecod

iced
scad
✧scud
ache
acme
acne
acre
ecce
eche
oche
scye
scag
scog
scug
Acol
acyl
Icel
kcal
scul
scam
scum
icon
scan
ecco
✧echo
scop
scup
acer
icer
scar
scur
acct
echt
scat
✧scot
scut
ecru
CCTV
scaw
scow
Ickx
achy
icky
scry
Edda
Edna
idea
odea
odic
a **due**
adze
edge
Edie
idée
idle
Odie
Adil
Edel
idol
idyl
odal
odyl
udal
Adam
Edam
idem
Aden
Eden
Odin
udon
eddo

odso
Adar
odor
Ades
ados
Gdns
✧ides
odds
Odes
udos
adit
edit
adaw
CD-RW
Addy
adry
D-day
✧eddy
edgy
Edwy
g'day
idly
V-day
bema
beta
ceca
deva
feta
gena
geta
Hera
keta
Leda
Lena
leva
mega
mela
mesa
Meta
peba
pela
sena
sera
seta
tela
Tema
Veda
✧vega
✧vela
vena
Vera
weka
weta
Xema
Zena
zeta
Beeb
herb
kemb
kerb
Medb
Serb
verb
wemb
aesc
merc
Oeic
bead
bend
dead
deed

deid
fee'd
feed
fend
feod
feud
geed
geld
head
heed
heid
held
hend
herd
lead
lend
lewd
mead
meed
meld
mend
need
nerd
pend
read
redd
reed
regd
rend
retd
Revd
seed
seld
send
tea'd
tead
tee'd
teed
teld
tend
veld
vend
weed
weid
weld
✧wend
yead
yeed
yeld
yerd
Zend
✧**bede**
bene
bere
bete
bête
cede
cere
cete
deke
dele
deme
dene
dere
feme
fere
fete
fête
gene
gêne
gere

✧hebe
he-he
hele
heme
here
hete
jeté
leke
leme
lere
lese
leve
leze
Mede
meme
mene
mere
mese
mete
meve
meze
mézé
nene
nete
névé
peke
✧pele
pene
père
Pete
rede
reke
Rene
René
rete
sele
semé
sene
sere
sese
tele
teme
tene
tête
vele
we're
were
we've
wexe
yede
yeve
zeze
beef
deaf
delf
✧jeff
kerf
leaf
neif
pelf
reef
reif
seif
self
serf
teff
terf
berg
leng
meng
peag

tegg
yegg
beth
eech
hech
heth
kesh
Leah
lech
mesh
nesh
pech
pegh
resh
sech
sesh
Seth
tech
teth
yeah
yech
beni
cedi
Ceri
deli
Devi
Dewi
feni
kepi
Levi
meri
nevi
peni
peri
semi
yeti
benj
beak
beck
berk
deck
deek
desk
feck
geck
geek
heck
jerk
keck
keek
leak
leek
meek
merk
neck
nerk
neuk
peak
peck
peek
penk
perk
reak
reck
reek
reik
seek
seik
serk
teak
weak

week
welk
yelk
yerk
yesk
yeuk
bell
ceil
cell
✧deal
deil
dell
feal
feel
fell
geal
Genl
heal
heel
heil!
he'll
✧hell
herl
jeel
jell
keel
kell
leal
meal
mell
merl
mewl
✧neal
Neil
Nell
peal
peel
pell
Perl
real
reel
seal
seel
seil
sell
teal
teel
teil
tell
veal
veil
vell
weal
weel
weil
we'll
✧well
yell
zeal
beam
berm
deem
derm
Fehm
ferm
germ
geum
helm
herm
leam
neem

neum
perm
ream
seam
seem
Sejm
team
teem
term
Vehm
weem
yelm
aeon
bean
been
bein
Benn
Bern
dean
deen
dern
eev'n
eevn
fern
gean
hern
hewn
jean
keen
kern
✧lean
León
mean
mein
nemn
neon
pean
peen
pein
peon
pern
rean
reen
rein
✧sean
seen
sewn
Tean
teen
tein
tern
vein
wean
ween
yean
zein
aero
bego
cero
✧deco
demo
Devo
✧hero
keno
kero
Lego®
leno
Leto
memo
meno
Nero

pepo
peso
redo
rego
Reno
repo
seco
sego
veto
zero
beep
deep
geep
heap
Help!
help
hemp
hesp
Jeep®
keep
kelp
kemp
leap
leep
lerp
neap
neep
peep
perp
reap
repp
seep
temp
veep
weep
yelp
Seaq
bear
beer
dear
deer
fear
feer
gear
hear
heir
Herr
jeer
keir
✧lear
leer
lehr
leir
✧meer
near
ne'er
pear
peer
rear
sear
seer
seir
serr
tear
teer
tehr
veer
wear
weir
year
bees

Bess
ceas
cens
cess
deus
fegs
feis
fess
Gems
gens
geos
Gers
hers
Hess
✧jess
keks
Keys
lees
lens
Leos
'less
less
✧mess
mews
ne is
ness
nets
news
peas
Pécs
pecs
Reds
reis
reps
sens
seps
sess
tems
Tess
vers
yes's
Zeus
beat
beet
belt
bent
Bert
✧best
✧celt
cent
cert
debt
deet
deft
delt
dent
✧dept
feat
feet
felt
fent
fest
fett
geat
geit
gelt
✧gent
Gert
gest
heat
heft

hent
hept
hest
jeat
jest
✧kelt
✧kent
kept
kest
leat
leet
left
✧lent
lest
Lett
meat
meet
melt
ment
neat
nest
nett
newt
next
peat
pelt
pent
pert
pest
Rect
reft
✧rent
rest
Seat®
seat
sect
✧sekt
sent
sept
sett
sext
teat
telt
tent
test
text
vent
vert
vest
vext
weet
weft
✧welt
went
wept
wert
✧west
yelt
yest
yett
zest
beau
Bedu
Cebu
genu
Jehu
Jesu
menu
Pegu
Peru
tegu

zebu
deev
derv
perv
deaw
meow
Leix
aery
bevy
defy
demy
deny
dewy
eely
eery
hery
levy
rely
reny
Secy
sexy
tedy
very
Geëz
Jeez
Metz
Afra
Efta
Offa
Efik
✧**afro**
afar
Ifor
✧**ufos**
E-fit®
a few
Sfax
affy
iffy
offy
agha
agma
Agra
egma
Ogma
aged
egad
igad
agee
ague
ogee
ogle
ogre
ygoe
agog
Agni
Ugli®
egal
ogam
agen
agin
agon
Egon
agio
Igbo
agar
eger
ages
egis
Ogpu
Aggy

eggy
ugly
✧**rhea**
shea
Shia
shwa
Thea
whoa
Ahab
chub
✧**chic**
choc
✧**chad**
chid
khud
shad
she'd
shed
shod
thud
whid
who'd
Chae
ghee
shoe
thae
thee
whee
chaf
chef
khaf
chug
shag
shog
thig
thug
✧whig
phoh
shah
uh-uh
bhai
chai
dhai
Shri
Thai
chik
dhak
bhel
chal
dhal
dhol
Phil
Phyl
Rhyl
shul
ahem
✧cham
chum
sham
Shem
shim
them
Wham!
wham
whim
whom
chin
chon
khan
phon
Rhun

✧shan
shin
'shun
shun
than
then
thin
thon
Thun
when
whin
Ohio
shmo
shoo
Theo
thro
thro'
chap
chip
chop
Shep
ship
✧shop
whap
whip
whop
whup
char
✧cher
khor
shir
thar
thir
Thor
whe'r
whir
mhos
rhos
rhus
Rhys
she's
shes
this
thus
who's
chat
chit
chut
ghat
khat
phat
phot
phut
shat
shet
shot
shut
that
what
whet
✧whit
whot
chou
thou
thru
chiv
shiv
chaw
chew
✧chow
dhow

phew
✧shaw
shew
show
thaw
thew
whew
whow
ahoy
✧chay
shay
they
whey
chez
chiz
phiz
whiz
✧**aida**
biga
Bixa
Ciba
dika
disa
dita
diva
giga
gila
Gina
Gita
hila
hiya
Jima
kina
kiva
✧lima
Lina
lipa
lira
Lisa
Liza
mica
✧mina
Mira
Nina
✧nipa
Nita
Oita
✧pica
pika
pila
piña
pipa
Pisa
pita
Riga
rima
Rita
riva
riza
sida
sika
sima
Sita
Siva
tika
Tina
vina
visa
✧vita
viva
zila

dieb
limb
nimb
sibb
zimb
C-in-C
disc
fisc
zinc
bind
bird
died
eild
find
gied
gild
gird
hied
hild
hind
jird
kild
kind
lied
lind
mild
mind
pied
rind
sild
sind
tied
tind
vied
vild
✧wild
wind
yird
aide
aîné
bice
bide
bike
bile
bine
bise
bite
cide
cine
ciné
ciré
cite
cive
dice
dike
dime
dine
dire
dite
dive
eine
fife
fike
file
fine
fire
five
gibe
Gide
gite
gîte

give
hide
hike
hire
hive
jibe
jive
kibe
kine
kipe
kite
lice
Lide
life
like
lime
✧line
lire
Lise
lite
live
mice
✧mike
mile
mime
mine
mire
mise
mite
nice
nide
nife
Nike
✧nine
nite
pice
pike
pile
pine
pipe
pisé
pize
rice
ride
rife
rile
rime
rine
ripe
rise
rite
rive
sice
side
sike
sile
Síne
sine
sipe
sire
site
size
tice
tide
tige
tike
tile
✧time
tine
tire
tite

vibe
✧vice
vide
vile
vine
vire
vise
visé
vite
vive
wice
wide
wife
wile
wine
wipe
wire
✧wise
wite
wive
yike
yite
zine
zite
biff
fief
jiff
lief
miff
nief
niff
Piaf
riff
tiff
ziff
bigg
bing
biog
ding
Eigg
ging
hing
king
ling
✧ming
ping
rigg
ring
sing
ting
wing
zing
bish
dich
dish
✧fish
high
hish
kish
kith
lich
lith
nigh
pish
pith
rich
sich
sigh
Sikh
sinh
sith

✧tich
wich
wish
with
bidi
Cixi
Didi
Dili
divi
dixi
Fiji
fini
Gigi
✧hi-fi
hili
Jixi
kiwi
✧midi
Mini®
mini
miri
nidi
nisi
pili
pipi
simi
✧siri
tiki
tipi
titi
wili
ziti
bilk
bink
birk
bisk
✧dick
dink
dirk
disk
fink
firk
fisk
gink
hick
jink
kick
kink
kirk
lick
link
lirk
lisk
✧mick
milk
mink
mirk
✧nick
oink
pick
pink
✧rick
rink
risk
sick
silk
sink
tick
tink
✧wick
wink

yirk
✧**bill**
birl
ciel
cill
cirl
dial
dill
diol
dirl
fill
gill
girl
hill
jill
Kiel
kill
lill
mill
n'ill
nill
nirl
pill
pirl
rial
riel
rill
sial
sill
till
tirl
vial
vill
viol
virl
wiel
will
yill
film
firm
gism
jism
Liam
pium
riem
Sium
airn
bien
cion
Dian
Finn
firn
gien
ginn
girn
his'n
hisn
jinn
kiln
kirn
Lian
lien
limn
linn
✧lion
mien
pion
pirn
Sian
sien
sign

Sion
Siôn
tian
Wien
winn
Xian
Zion
Biko
Biro®
bito
ciao
cito
✧dido
dino
fico
Fido
✧figo
filo
fino
✧giro
jiao
✧kilo
kino
lido
Lilo®
limo
lino
mico
milo
mino
Miró
miso
rivo
sijo
silo
Tico
tiro
Tito
Vigo
vino
vivo
wino
Zibo
Zico
gimp
jimp
kilp
✧kipp
limp
✧lisp
pimp
ripp
risp
simp
wimp
wisp
bier
birr
Dior
fiar
girr
kier
liar
lier
pier
tiar
tier
tirr
vier
AIDS
airs

bias
bins
bios
cits
dibs
dies
digs
diss
fils
gios
hiss
✧kiss
Lias
mips
mirs
✧miss
nibs
oils
pics
Pils
Pius
Riss
Sids
siss
tits
vibs
wits
yips
ain't
airt
bint
Birt
bitt
cist
dict
✧diet
dint
dirt
ditt
Fiat®
fiat
fist
fitt
gift
gilt
girt
gist
hilt
hint
hipt
hist
jilt
kilt
kist
lift
lilt
lint
'list
list
milt
mint
mist
mitt
mixt
oint
Pict
piet
pint
Pitt
rift
riot

ript
ritt
sift
silt
sist
tift
tilt
tint
tipt
vint
wilt
win't
wist
Zift
Ainu
aitu
Dieu
Gifu
lieu
rimu
✧**kiev**
mirv
✧**view**
jinx
minx
airy
✧city
dixy
fiky
lily
limy
liny
Livy
miny
miry
mity
mixy
nixy
oily
piny
pioy
pipy
pity
pixy
ricy
rimy
sizy
tidy
tiny
viny
vizy
wily
winy
wiry
ditz
fizz
gizz
hizz
Linz
mizz
Ritz
tizz
zizz
ajee
ajar
Ajax
ekka
okra
okta
skua
OKed

ski'd
skid
akee
Skye
skag
skeg
skug
skol
skim
akin
ikon
skin
skeo
skio
skep
skip
sker
skyr
skis
ikat
skat
skit
skaw
skew
okay
skry
alfa
alga
✧alma
Elba
Ella
Elma
Elva
flea
glia
ilea
ilia
ilka
Olea
Olga
olla
plea
ulna
ulva
blab
bleb
blob
blub
club
flab
flub
glib
glob
pleb
slab
slob
slub
✧alec
bloc
flic
floc
Aled
alod
blad
bled
clad
clod
fled
glad
gled
glid

olid
pled
plod
sled
'slid
slid
alae
albe
alee
alme
aloe
blae
blee
blue
clue
Elle
else
flee
floe
flue
glee
glue
Klee
olpe
plié
slae
slee
sloe
slue
ylke
alef
alif
clef
Olaf
blag
clag
cleg
clog
flag
fleg
flog
gleg
glug
plug
slag
slog
slug
Alph
blah
glei
vlei
flak
El Al
Elul
alum
clam
✧clem
flam
glam
glim
glom
glum
plim
plum
slam
✧slim
slum
ylem
Alan
Alun
blin

clan
élan
flan
✧glen
Glyn
Klan
plan
aloo
also
alto
Cleo
Clio
oleo
olio
alap
blip
clap
clip
clop
flap
flip
flop
glop
plap
plop
slap
slip
slop
Alar®
alar
✧blur
flor
slur
alas
alls
alms
Alps
elks
Glis
olds
plus
alit
blat
blet
blit
blot
Blut
clat
clot
Elat
flat
flit
glit
glut
plat
plot
slat
slit
slot
slut
clou
Olav
Slav
alew
alow
blew
blow
claw
clew
clow
flaw

flew
flow
glow
plow
slaw
slew
slow
Alex
flax
flex
flix
flux
ilex
ulex
alay
Algy
alky
✧ally
blay
bley
clay
cloy
elmy
flay
fley
Floy
gley
illy
oldy
play
ploy
slay
sley
amla
✧emma
umma
YMCA
amid
amie
✧smee
ympe
smog
smug
amah
umph
impi
amok
Omsk
amyl
✧imam
amen
Amin
G-man
Oman
omen
ambo
ammo
imho
umbo
amir
emir
Omar
✧omer
smir
smur
Umar
amis
Amos
emys
Xmas
amn't

emit
omit
smit
smut
ympt
emeu
ombu
ombú
smew
Amex
Emmy
✧anna
anoa
anta
Inca
Inga
inia
knob
knub
snab
sneb
snib
snob
snub
Enid
sned
snod
ance
Anne
ante
Inge
in re
in se
knee
once
snee
snye
unbe
unce
unde
undé
knag
snag
snig
snog
✧snug
ankh
inch
anti
inti
unci
anal
anil
anan
anon
in on
an mo
anno
info
ingo
inro
into
onto
unco
undo
Unio
unto
knap
knop
snap
snip

gnar
knar
knur
oner
snar
ana's
anas
anis
anus
gnus
Ines
ings
inns
mnas
onus
gnat
in it
knit
knot
✧knut
onst
snit
snot
✧unit
unau
anew
anow
enew
enow
gnaw
knew
know
snow
Knox
onyx
Pnyx
Unix
Andy
Angy
envy
inby
Indy
inky
inly
only
Inez
boba
boma
bona
bora
coca
coda
✧cola
coma
Cora
coxa
Doha
Doña
dona
dopa
Dora
fora
Goya
hora
Hova
hoya
Iona
iota
Iowa
jota
koka

✧kola
kora
Kota
Lola
loma
lota
mola
✧mona
mora
mowa
moxa
moya
Nola
noma
Nona
Nora
nova
✧roma
Rona
Rosa
✧rota
soca
soda
sofa
soja
sola
Soma®
✧soma
sora
soya
toea
toga
tola
tosa
vola
Xosa
yoga
zoea
Zola
zona
boab
bomb
boob
cobb
comb
doab
doob
forb
✧sorb
tomb
womb
Zorb®
douc
torc
zoic
bold
bond
bord
coed
cold
con'd
cond
cord
dowd
foid
fold
fond
food
Ford®
✧ford
foud

goad
gold
good
gowd
hoed
hold
hond
'hood
hood
kond
load
loid
✧lord
loud
✧mold
mood
MOT'd
✧pond
pood
road
roed
rood
sold
sord
toad
toed
told
void
woad
wold
wood
✧word
yold
yond
you'd
a one
bode
boke
bole
bone
bore
bote
code
C of E
Coke®
✧coke
cole
come
cone
cope
core
cose
cote
cove
coze
doge
dole
dome
done
dope
Doré
dose
dote
✧dove
doze
fone
fore
gole
gone
gore
hoke

hole
home
hone
hope
hore
hose
hote
✧hove
howe
jobe
joke
jole
Jove
Kobe
✧kore
lobe
lode
loge
loke
Lomé
lome
lone
lope
lore
lose
lote
love
lowe
mode
moke
✧mole
mome
mope
More!
more
mose
mote
moue
move
moze
node
nole
nome
none
nope
nose
n'ote
no'te
note
oose
ooze
poke
✧pole
pome
pone
✧pope
pore
pose
posé
pote
'robe
robe
rode
roke
role
rôle
Rome
rone
rope
rore
rose

rosé
rote
roué
rove
soke
sole
some
sone
sore
to-be
toge
toke
tole
tome
tone
tope
tore
tose
tote
toze
vole
vote
woke
wore
wove
yode
yoke
yore
yowe
zone
boff
coff
coif
conf
coof
corf
doff
dowf
goaf
goff
✧golf
goof
gowf
hoof
houf
howf
koff
loaf
loof
poof
pouf
Rolf
roof
sowf
toff
wolf
woof
wowf
yoof
bong
Borg
boyg
dong
Doug
gong
hogg
hong
long
'mong
mong
Moog®

nogg
nong
pong
rong
✧song
tong
booh
bosh
both
coch
cosh
coth
dosh
doth
gosh
Goth
hogh
✧josh
koph
loch
losh
loth
moch
mosh
✧moth
Noah
nosh
✧pooh
posh
qoph
roch
Roth
soph
Toc H
tosh
yodh
yogh
C of I
coni
foci
gobi
hoki
Holi
Hopi
Jodi
Joni
lobi
loci
lo-fi
Logi
Loki
loti
modi
moki
mooi
nodi
nori
not-I
roji
roti
Sofi
soli
sori
Toni
topi
tori
yogi
yoni
zori
boak
bock

bonk
✧book
bosk
bouk
cock
conk
cook
✧cork
dock
doek
dook
dork
folk
fork
Gonk®
gonk
gouk
gowk
hock
hoik
honk
✧hook
howk
✧jock
jook
jouk
konk
kook
lock
look
mock
monk
mook
nock
nook
pock
polk
ponk
pook
pork
pouk
✧rock
rook
soak
sock
sook
souk
tock
tonk
took
touk
volk
wock
wonk
work
yock
yolk
✧york
youk
zonk
zouk
boil
Böll
boll
bool
bowl
coal
coil
✧coll
cool
cowl

doll
dool
dowl
eorl
foal
foil
fool
foul
fowl
goal
goel
Gogl
gool
gowl
howl
Joel
joll
jowl
koel
✧kohl
loll
moil
✧moll
mool
moyl
✧noel
✧noël
noil
noll
noul
nowl
✧poll
pool
roil
roll
rotl
roul
soil
✧soul
sowl
toil
toll
tool
wool
yowl
boom
Colm
coom
corm
doom
dorm
foam
form
gorm
holm
loam
loom
Noam
norm
poem
roam
room
roum
soom
soum
sowm
toom
worm
zoom
Bonn
boon

born
bo's'n
bos'n
boun
coin
conn
coon
corn
doen
do in
do-in
✧down
eoan
Eoin
foen
föhn
foin
Goan
go in
go on
goon
gown
hoon
✧horn
Joan
✧john
join
koan
Köln
loan
loin
loon
lorn
loun
lown
moan
✧moon
morn
mown
noon
Norn
noun
nown
poon
porn
pown
roan
roin
roon
soon
sorn
sown
toon
torn
toun
town
woon
worn
zoon
boho
boko
bolo
Boro
boyo
bozo
coco
coho
Como
Cono
dodo
dojo

gobo
go-go
gogo
Gozo
hobo
✧homo
joco
jomo
kobo
kolo
koto
lobo
loco
logo
loto
Moho
✧mojo
moko
mono
Moro
no go
no-no
poco
pogo
polo
po-mo
Romo
ro-ro
so-ho
soho
solo
so so
so-so
toco
to-do
Togo
to go
toho
Tojo
toko
topo
Toto
yo-ho
yo-yo
zobo
comp
co-op
coop
coup
cowp
dorp
do up
doup
dowp
golp
goop
gorp
go up
holp
hoop
loop
loup
moop
Mopp
moup
noop
noup
pomp
poop
romp
roop

roup
soap
soop
soup
sowp
yomp
yoop
boar
Boer
boor
bowr
coir
cour
doer
door
dorr
dour
four
goer
goor
hoar
hoer
hour
jour
loir
loor
lour
mohr
✧moor
poor
pour
roar
soar
soor
✧sour
torr
tour
voar
your
bobs
Bors
boss
bots
bows
boys
C of S
coms
coss
cows
dods
does
dogs
dohs
Dons
doss
dows
foes
foss
God's
gods
goes
Goss
goys
hoas
hohs
hols
Homs
hops
hors
hoss
joes

✧joss
koss
logs
Lois
loos
loss
löss
lots
✧mods
Mons
✧moss
noes
nous
oons
oops
pons
pops
poss
pots
Ross
soss
sous
togs
tons
tops
toss
Voss
woes
wots
boat
✧bolt
boot
bort
bott
bout
coat
coft
coit
Colt®
colt
coot
Copt
cost
cott
doat
doit
dolt
don't
dort
dost
dout
dowt
font
✧foot
fort
go at
✧goat
go it
gout
goût
holt
hoot
✧host
hout
jolt
loft
✧loot
lost
lout
lowt
moat

moit
molt
moot
mort
most
mott
nott
nout
nowt
oont
poet
polt
pont
poot
port
post
pott
pout
ront
root
rort
rost
rout
rowt
soft
soot
sort
sout
to a T
toft
tolt
toot
tort
tost
tout
towt
volt
won't
wont
woo't
woot
wort
wost
yont
Lomu
✧motu
non-U
tofu
✧tolu
zobu
co-ax
coax
hoax
roux
body
bogy
bony
boxy
coky
coly
cony
copy
cosy
coxy
cozy
do by
dogy
domy
dopy
dory
doty

doxy
dozy
fogy
foxy
fozy
go by
go-by
goby
goey
gory
holy
homy
Jody
✧joey
joky
Jozy
logy
lory
moly
mony
mopy
nosy
nowy
oofy
oosy
oozy
poky
poly
pony
pory
posy
poxy
roky
ropy
✧rory
rosy
Soay
✧toby
tody
toey
✧tony
Tory
towy
Lódz
mozz
pozz
Apia
epha
epic
spec
apod
op-ed
sped
spod
spud
apse
épée
spae
spie
spue
Ipoh
opah
spek
opal
Spam®
spam
J-pen
open
span
spin
spun

upon
Apso
oppo
upgo
spar
spur
Apis
Apus
epos
opus
upas
spat
✧spet
spit
spot
spiv
spaw
spew
✧apex
apay
spay
spry
upby
upsy
spaz
aqua
arba
area
aria
arna
Irma
orca
orra
proa
urea
Ursa
urva
Arab
✧crab
crib
drab
drib
drub
frab
grab
grub
krab
prob
croc
✧eric
uric
ared
arid
brad
bred
brod
cred
crud
drad
Fred
grad
✧grid
irid
prad
✧prod
trad
trod
arle
brae
bree
Brie

✧cree
crue
dree
erne
Erse
frae
free
froe
gree
grue
orfe
orle
pree
Prue
tree
trie
✧true
trye
urdé
urge
Graf
prof
tref
areg
brag
brig
brog
crag
drag
dreg
drug
frag
✧frog
grig
grog
prig
prog
trig
trog
trug
arch
argh
pruh
arak
brak
drek
Erik
trek
Uruk
aril
aryl
Eryl
oral
Ural
vril
arum
Bram
brim
Brum
✧cram
crim
dram
drum
from
gram
grim
grum
pram
prim
prom
tram

trim
Aran
Arun
✧bran
✧bren
Bryn
cran
Erin
gran
gren
grin
Iran
iron
Oran
trin
tron
✧wren
arco
Argo
arvo
brio
Brno
broo
Dr No
ergo
Kroo
or so
orzo
proo
trio
urao
crap
crop
drap
drip
drop
frap
grip
prep
prop
trap
trip
tryp
wrap
Iraq
arar
brer
brrr
Ards
Ares
aris
arms
bras
crus
ergs
Eris
Eros
fris
gris
Grus
iris
kris
orts
pros
prys
très
urus
aret
brat
✧brit
brut

crit
drat
erst
fret
frit
grat
grit
grot
prat
trat
tret
✧trot
writ
erhu
✧frau
prau
Urdu
eruv
arew
a-row
arow
braw
brew
brow
craw
crew
✧crow
draw
✧drew
drow
frow
grew
grow
prow
trew
trow
vrow
✧crux
oryx
prex
T Rex
Trix
army
'Arry
arsy
arty
bray
dray
drey
fray
Frey
gray
grey
orby
orgy
pray
prey
tray
trey
✧troy
urdy
X-ray
✧xray
Druz
friz
Graz
trez
Asia
Asma
Esda
Isla

ossa
used
esne
esse
isle
as if!
as of
Esth
asci
Asti
Ossi
Tshi
Oslo
asap
åsar
ksar
tsar
user
USSR
as is
Isis
uses
✧asst
isn't
psst
Esau
ashy
Esky®
espy
I say!
I-spy
✧etna
stoa
stab
stob
stub
atoc
otic
sted
stud
ethe
stie
stye
stag
etch
itch
Ptah
Utah
étui
atok
et al
it'll
atom
Atum
item
stem
stum
Aten
eten
Eton
✧sten
stun
Otho
✧otto
atap
atop
Q-Tip®
stap
step
stop
star

Words marked ✧ can also be spelled with one or more capital letters

stir
utas
Utes
utis
at it
état
stat
stet
stot
staw
stew
stow
Styx
Atty
stay
stey
aula
aura
buba
buna
Cuba
✧duma
dura
guga
gula
huia
hula
huma
juba
juga
✧jura
kula
kuna
Lüda
luma
✧luna
Musa
ouma
oupa
puja
pula
puma
puna
pupa
rusa
Ruta
sura
Susa
Suva
tuba
tufa
Tula
tuna
yuca
yuga
zupa
bulb
burb

curb
dumb
numb
fusc
auld
✧bund
burd
cued
curd
duad
fund
guid
hued
Kurd
Lund
muid
nurd
ould
✧quad
quid
quod
rudd
rued
rund
sudd
sued
suid
surd
tund
aune
buke
✧bute
cube
cure
curé
cute
duce
dude
duke
dule
dune
dupe
dure
euge
fume
fuse
fuze
gude
gule
huge
hule
iure
jube
Jude
juke
Jule
June
jure

✧jute
juve
lube
luce
luge
✧luke
lune
lure
lute
luxe
mule
mure
✧muse
mute
nude
nuke
Nupe
puce
puke
pule
pure
rube
rude
rule
rume
rune
✧ruse
rusé
Suke
supe
sure
✧tube
tule
tune
yuke
✧yule
buff
bumf
cuff
cuif
duff
fuff
guff
✧gulf
huff
humf
luff
muff
nuff
puff
ruff
surf
tuff
turf
zurf
bung
burg
dung

fung
hung
Jung
lung
quag
rung
✧sung
bush
cush
dush
eugh
gush
Hugh
hush
Lugh
lush
much
mush
ouch
ouph
pugh
push
rukh
✧rush
✧ruth
such
sukh
tush
Audi®
euoi
fuci
Fuji
Fuji®
kuri
muti
puli
puri
Pu Yi
Sufi
suni
Tupi
Tupí
Wuxi
Zuni
Zuñi
buck
buik
bulk
bunk
burk
busk
cusk
duck
dunk
dusk
funk
guck
gunk

huck
hulk
hunk
husk
junk
luck
lunk
lurk
lusk
✧muck
murk
musk
oulk
✧puck
pulk
punk
ruck
rusk
suck
sulk
sunk
tuck
Turk
tusk
yuck
buhl
✧bull
burl
cull
curl
dual
duel
✧dull
fuel
full
furl
gull
gurl
✧hull
hurl
lull
muil
✧mull
murl
null
nurl
pull
purl
wull
culm
Guam
mumm
turm
Würm
burn
curn
duan
durn

Euan
guan
gurn
muon
ourn
quin
ruin
sunn
tuan
turn
vuln
yuan
auto
✧bubo
budo
bufo
duro
euro
Hugo
huso
judo
Juno
ludo
muso
ouzo
sumo
Yugo®
yuko
bump
burp
cusp
dump
gulp
gump
hump
jump
lump
mump
✧pulp
pump
quep
quip
quop
✧rump
rurp
sump
tump
yump
burr
curr
duar
furr
guar
huer
✧junr
muir
nurr
puer

puir
purr
suer
buns
buss
cuss
dubs
duds
dues
duos
fuss
guts
huis
huss
jugs
lues
muss
nuts
ours
outs
puls
puss
runs
Russ
subs
suds
suss
tuts
wuss
✧aunt
buat
bunt
bust
butt
cuit
cult
curt
duct
duet
dunt
dust
fust
gust
hunt
hurt
just
Kurt
luit
lunt
lust
munt
must
mutt
oust
punt
putt
quat
quit

runt
rust
suet
suit
Supt
tuft
yuft
yurt
fugu
guru
Hutu
ju-ju
juju
kudu
kuku
kuru
kuzu
luau
✧lulu
Oulu
pudu
puku
pulu
ruru
✧sulu
✧susu
✧tutu
Wuhu
✧zulu
yunx
buoy
✧bury
busy
Dufy
duly
duty
fumy
✧fury
guly
Huey
hugy
✧judy
July
jury
Lucy
ou ay
puky
puly
pumy
puny
quay
quey
ruby
ruly
Suky
sumy
Susy
Suzy

tuny
yuky
buzz
fuzz
Günz
lutz
muzz
putz
quiz
Suez
tuzz
uvea
avid
ivy'd
Ovid
Evie
evoe
aval
evil
oval
vvll
ovum
Evan
even
Ivan
Ivon
oven
aver
ever
Ivor
over
Aves
avos
Yves
evet
Lvov
avow
YWCA
swab
swob
awed
owed
swad
owre
swee
twae
twee
swag
swig
twig
lwei
awdl
AWOL
hwyl
twal
dwam
swam
swim

swum
Ewan
Ewen
Gwen
Gwyn
Owen
swan
twin
swap
swop
ewer
ower
iwis
Owls
'twas
ywis
swat
swot
twit
away
awny
awry
I-way
M-way
owly
sway
swey
tway
swiz
ixia
exec
axle
axel
axil
exul
exam
axon
exon
oxen
Oxon
expo
oxer
axes
axis
exes
✧exit
cyma
eyra
hyla
Lyra
myna
Myra
sync
dyad
dyed
eyed
fyrd
kynd

rynd
synd
tyn'd
tynd
wynd
ayre
byke
byre
byte
cyme
cyte
dyke
dyne
eyne
eyre
fyke
fyle
gybe
gyre
gyte
gyve
hyke
hyle
hype
kyle
kyne
kype
kyte
Lyle
✧lyme
lyne
lyre
lyse
lyte
pyne
pyre
Ryde
ryfe
ryke
rype
syce
syke
syne
sype
tyde
tyke
✧tyne
type
tyre
tyte
wyte
zyme
ayah
myth
wych
Dyak
gyal
myal

ryal
lyam
ayin
cyan
hyen
hymn
Lynn
Lyon
Ryan
syen
wynn
gyro
hypo
pyro
sybo
typo
tyro
gymp
tymp
dyer
Györ
Iyar
oyer
byes
eyas
eyes
nyas
oyes
cyst
eyot
kyat
pyat
pyet
pyot
ryot
xyst
lynx
✧jynx
✧lynx
eyry
gyny
oyez
Ezra
Azed
mzee
azym
azan
dzho
czar
tzar
Ozzy

5 – even

Baha'i
Bahai
✧bajan
Bajau
balas
banal
Banat
basal
basan

Bayan
bazar
cabal
cabas
cacao
caman
camas
canal
carap

carat
Cavan
Dakar
daman
damar
Danae
daraf
datal
Davao

Dayak
dayan
falaj
fanal
farad
Farah
Fatah
fatal
galah

Gamal
gamay
gayal
gazal
gazar
hadal
Hagar
hakam
halal

hamal
Hamas
hanap
haram
Hasan
hazan
jalap
Jamal
✧japan

Javan
jawan
kabab
kahal
kaiak
Kamal
Kanak
Karaj
karat

katal
Kauai
kayak
Kazak
Kazan
Laban
lagan
lahar
✧lanai

La Paz
lavas
lazar
Macao
macaw
✧madam
Makah
makar
malar

malax
Malay
manat
marae
marah
Marat
Masai
Masan
matai

Mayan
✧nahal
naiad
Naias
naras
nasal
✧natal
naval
nawab

Nayar
paean
pagan
palae
palas
Palau
palay
panax
papal
papaw
pavan
pawaw
Qajar
qanat
Qatar
✧rabat
radar
rajah
ramal
rasae
ratan
rayah
Sabal
Sagan
Sakai
salad
salal
saman
Sana'a
sapan
Sarah
Saran®
Satan
satay
sawah
✧tacan
talak
talaq
talar
talas
tamal
Tamar
tapas
tasar
Tatar
tavah
vagal
vakas
varan
vasal
watap
zakat
zaman
Balbo
Bambi
barbe
bar-b-q
barbs
Caaba
cabby
carby
daube
dauby
fabby
gabba
✧gabby
Galba
gamba
gambo
garbe
✧garbo
iambi
jambe
jambo
jambu
Kaaba
lay by
lay-by
mamba
mambo
mauby
maybe
Nabby
✧rabbi
samba
sambo
sauba
tabby
taube
warby
yabby
zambo
bacca
bacco
baccy
banco
barca
batch
caeca
casco
catch
Dacca
dance
dancy
darcy
fancy
farce
farci
farcy
fasci
ganch
gaucy
gawcy
haick
hance
hanch
hatch
lance
lanch
larch
latch
lauch
✧march
match
Nancy
narco
narcs
natch
pance
Parca
parch
Pasch
patch
rance
ranch
ratch
saice
saick
sauce
sauch
saucy
talcy
watch
yacca
baddy
baldy
banda
B and B
Bände
bandh
bands
bandy
bardo
bards
bardy
bawdy
caddy
c and b
C and G
can do
can-do
Candu
C and W
✧candy
cardi
cards
cardy
daddy
Dagda
D and C
dandy
faddy
G and S
✧g and t
garda
Gaudí
gaudy
Haida
h and c
hands
handy
hards
✧hardy
Haydn
Iai-do
I-and-I
✧kandy
labda
laldy
lande
Lando
lardy
Lauda
lauds
Magda
Mahdi
Mande
Mandy
mardy
Maude
Mazda®
N and Q
nandu
✧paddy
panda
P and O
p and p
pandy
pardi
pardy
ragde
R and A
R and B
R and R
rands
✧randy
saddo
sands
✧sandy
Saudi
tardy
V and A
vardy
waddy
waide
✧waldo
Wanda
Babee
✧babel
Baden
bagel
baked
baken
baker
baler
based
basen
bases
caber
cadee
cadet
caged
cagey
cakey
camel
cameo
caneh
caner
caper
capex
carer
caret
carex
cater
cates
cavel
caver
daker
Dalek
dalet
dared
dares
dated
Datel®
dater
daven
dazed
dazer
eager
eared
easel
easer
eaten
eater
eaves
faced
facer
facet
fader
faker
fakes
famed
farer
fated
Fates
✧favel
fazed
galea
Galen
gamer
games
gamey
gaper
gapes
gases
gated
gavel
gayer
gazer
hacek
Hades
haler
Haley
harem
hater
Havel
haven
haver
haves
✧hazel
hazer
jaded
jäger
jakes
✧james
Janet
japer
Jared
jasey
javel
jawed
Kamet
kaneh
Karen
Kayes
label
laced
lacet
lacey
laded
laden
lager
laker
lamed
lapel
lares
laser
lated
laten
later
latex
✧laver
layer
Mabel
macer
✧maker
mamee
mamey
maned
maneh
✧manes
✧manet
maser
mater
matey
maven
mazer
naked
naker
named
namer
nares
nates
navel
navew
oaken
oaker
oared
oases
oaten
oater
oaves
paced
pacer
pacey
pager
pages
palea
Pales
palet
paned
panel
paper
pareo
parer
pareu
paseo
pated
paten
pater
paved
paven
paver
payed
payee
payer
racer
races
ragee
rager
rakee
raker
ramee
ramen
ramet
ranee
raper
rased
rated
ratel
rater
rates
✧ravel
raven
raver
rayed
razed
razee
saber
saker
Salem
salep
salet
samel
samen
samey
sared
saree
sated
saved
saver
savey
sawed
sawer
sayer
tabes
tacet
taken
taker
talea
taler
tales
tamer
tapen
taper
tapet
Taser®
taser
tater
Tavel
taver
tawer
taxed
taxer
taxes
vales
valet
vaned
varec
wader
wafer
waged
wager
wages
waked
waken
waker
wakes
✧waler
wales
wamed
waned
waney
wares
water
waved
waver
waves
wavey
waxed
waxen
waxer
yager
yamen
yawey
zazen
baffy
Banff
calfs
ca' off
daffy
gaffe
Haifa
halfa
halfs
✧jaffa
Naafi
nakfa
samfu
✧taffy
waefu'
waift
wauff
yarfa
aargh
badge
baggy
bangs
barge
cadge
cadgy
cargo
dagga
daggy
darga
fadge
fango
Fargo
faugh
gadge
gauge
hangi
haugh
jaggy
✧kanga
kaugh
laigh
large
largo
laugh
✧madge
maggs
manga
mange
mango
mangy
marge
Margo
naggy
Paige
panga
parge
radge
ragga
raggy
range
rangy
saggy
saiga
sarge
sargo
saugh
Taegu
taggy
taiga
✧tanga
tangi
✧tango
tangy
targe
✧waugh
basho
bathe
baths
cache
Cathy
dacha
eathe
hashy
kacha
kasha
Kathy
lathe
lathi
laths
lathy
Macha
macho
mashy
maths
nache
nacho
nashi
oaths
pacha
pasha
pashm
paths
rache
Radha
raphe
raphé
ratha
rathe
Sacha
sadhe
sadhu
Sasha
tache
tacho
takhi
washy
yacht
✧bania
baric
✧basic
✧basij
✧basil
basin
basis
batik
bavin
cabin
cadie
Cádiz
calid
calif
calix
camis
canid
Canis
can it
capiz
Carib
cavie
cavil
Dalit
danio
daric
Datin
David
Davie
davit
eat in
facia
Fagin
fakie
fakir
Farid
gamic
gamin
Gavin
habit
hafiz
hakim
harim
Hasid
jagir
Jamie
Jamil
Janis
kalif
kamik
kamis
Karin
Kasim
Katie
labia
labis
Ladin
lakin
lamia
lam it
Laois
lapis
laris
Latin
lawin
lay in
madid
✧mafia
mafic
magic
malic
malik
Malin
Mamie
mania
manic
Manis
✧maria
marid
Marie
✧matin
mavin
✧mavis
✧maxim
Nabis
Nadia
nadir
Nasik
nazir
Oasis®
✧oasis
panic
panim
Paris
patin
patio
Pavia
pavid
pavin
pavis
pay in
Qasim
rabic
rabid
Rabin
radii
radio
radix
Rajiv
ramie
ramin
rapid
ratio
ravin
sabin
Sadie
sahib
sakia
✧salic
Salim
salix
Samit
sapid
sarin
sasin
Satie
satin
savin
sayid
tabid
tacit
tafia
Tajik
takin
Talib
Tamil
tamin
tamis
Tania
tap-in
tapir
tapis
Tariq
tatie
tawie
taxis
vakil
valid
Vanir
vapid
varix
vatic
Walid
Wasim
wazir
x-axis
y-axis
zamia
z-axis
zayin
banjo
Baoji
gadje
ganja
gauje
hadji
hajji
kanji
lapje
zanja
balk'd
balky
Banks
barky
daiko
darky
gawky
Haikh

haiku
hanky
hawks
jacks
Kafka
✧laika
lanky
larky
latke
lawks
maiko
manky
marka
mawky
narks
narky
pakka
palki
parka
parki
parky
pawky
ranke
ranks
sanko
sarky
tacky
taiko
talks
talky
✧tanka
tanky
wacke
wacko
wacky
walks
yakka
badly
balls
bally
Basle
baulk
bayle
cable
calla
caple
Carla
Carly
cauld
caulk
daily
dalle
dally
dault
eagle
early
easle
fable
farle
fatly
fault
gable
gaily
Galle
gally
gault
Gavle
Gayle
hable
haily
Halle
Hallé
hallo
haply
hauld
haulm
hault
hayle
Kahlo
kails
Karla
kayle
ladle
Lalla
Lally
laxly
Layla
macle
madly
maile
manly
maple
marle
marls
marly
matlo
nabla
nalla
padle
pagle
palla
pally
paoli
paolo
parle
parly
patly
Paula
raile
rails
rally
rawly
rayle
sable
sadly
Sails
salle
✧sally
saola
sault
tabla
table
tails
tally
tauld
vails
vault
walla
walls
✧wally
wanle
wanly
waulk
yauld
balmy
barmy
calms
calmy
damme
gamma
gamme
gammy
gaumy
halma
hammy
✧haoma
Jaime
jammy
kaama
kamme
karma
lammy
magma
Malmo
Malmö
mamma
mammy
Naomi
✧padma
Palma
palmy
Parma
rammy
Saame
Sabme
Sabmi
salmi
Salmo
Sammy
tagma
talma
✧tammy
ba'ing
banns
canna
canny
carny
daine
daint
Danny
daunt
daynt
faine
fains
faint
✧fanny
✧fauna
fayne
garni
gaunt
hadn't
Hanno
harns
hasn't
haunt
Jaina
jaunt
kaons
Larne
laund
lawny
Maine
mains
Mainz
manna
Manny
maund
mayn't
✧nanna
nanny
naunt
pains
paint
panne
Patna
✧raine
rains
rainy
Rajni
rayne
saine
saint
sauna
saunt
Sawny
sayne
Taino
'taint
taint
tanna
taunt
tawny
✧varna
vaunt
wanna
Warne
wasn't
Wayne
yawny
Aaron
baboo
✧bacon
Bagot
✧baloo
Balor
baron
bason
baton
bayou
bazoo
cabob
caboc
Cabot
cagot
canoe
Canon®
canon
cañon
capon
capos
capot
carob
✧carol
carom
caxon
dados
Dagon
Damon
Davos
fados
fagot
fanon
favor
Gabon
gajos
galop
gapós
gator
gazon
gazoo
halo'd
halon
halos
Hanoi
havoc
jabot
Jacob
Jason
jatos
kabob
kagos
kapok
✧karoo
kayos
kazoo
labor
Lagos
lay on
Mâcon
macon
Madoc
ma foi
Magog
magot
mahoe
✧major
makos
manor
manos
maron
maror
Marot
mason
Mayon
mayor
nabob
nagor
napoo
Naxos
pacos
paeon
pagod
parol
Paros
racon
radon
rat on
ratoo
rayon
razoo
razor
sabot
sajou
✧salon
salop
Samoa
Samos
sapor
sarod
saros
savor
✧savoy
Saxon
sayon
taboo
tabor
tacos
talon
taroc
tarok
taros
tarot
tatou
Taxol®
taxon
taxor
valor
vapor
✧wagon
wahoo
ya-boo
✧yahoo
yakow
yapok
yapon
calpa
campo
campy
carpi
dampy
gappy
gaspy
happy
harpy
jaspe
jaspé
kalpa
kappa
Nampo
nappa
nappe
nappy
palpi
pampa
pappy
paspy
Ralph
raspy
salpa
sampi
sappy
✧talpa
Tampa
tappa
taupe
waspy
yappy
zappy
Zarqa
bairn
bajra
bajri
Barra
barre
barré
Barry
Basra
cabré
cadre
caird
cairn
Cairo
Capri
Carré
carry
dairy
darre
eagre
fa'ard
faery
fairy
faurd
Fauré
fayre
garre
Garry
Gauri
hairy
✧harry
Hatra
karri
kauri
laari
labra
laird
lairy
Larry
✧laura
lavra
macro
Máire
maire
Màiri
Maori
marri
marry
Maura
nacre
naira
narre
Nauru
padre
pagri
paire
pairs
parry
raird
sabra
sabre
sacra
saury
taira
tarre
tarry
tayra
vairé
vairy
warre
zabra
Zahra
zaire
zaïre
bags I
baisa
balsa
basse
bassi
basso
bassy
caese
canst
carse
causa
'cause
cause
daisy
earst
false
farse
Farsi
fatso
Faust
gadso
gassy
Gatso®
gauss
gawsy
hadst
halse
Hansa
Hanse
harsh
Hausa
hause
hawse
karst
karsy
laksa
lapse
lassi
lasso
lassu
maise
manse
✧marsh
massa
massé
massy
mayst
paisa
palsy
pansy
parse
Parsi
passé
✧patsy
pause
paysd
raise
rasse
saist
salsa
salse
sansa
sasse
sassy
says I
say-so
sayst
taish
tansy
tarsi
tasse
Tasso
tawse
Vaasa
valse
waist
warst
Aalto
BAFTA
balti
Balto
✧bantu
Bart's
basta
baste
basto
batta
batts
battu
batty
cacti
canto
canty
carta
carte
caste
catty
Dante
darts
✧earth
faith
Fanti
fasti
fatty
gaita
gaitt
garth
haith
Haiti
hasta
haste
hasty
Hatty
haute
janty
jarta
Kanta
katti
laith
✧laity
latte
Malta
malty
✧manta
manto
manty
masty
matte
Matty
Nantz
nasty
natty
panto
pants
panty
parti
parts
party
pasta
paste
pasty
patte
patté
✧patty
pay TV
raita
✧rasta
✧ratty
saith
Sakta
Sakti
salto
salts
salty
sauté
tanti
tanto
tarty
taste
tasty
Tatts
tatty
vasty
vaute
vawte
waite
waits
walty
waltz
wants
wanty
warty
waste
yarta
yarto
zante
babul
Babur
bahut
balun
✧cajun
Calum
✧camus
capul
caput
Datuk
datum
eat up
FA Cup
Fagus
Faruq
favus
Gadus
✧galut
gamut
garum
Hague
Harun
Janus
jarul
Kabul
kaput
Laius
lap up
larum
Larus
lay up
lay-up
✧magus
mahua
manul
manus
maqui
mazut
Nahum
Namur
oakum
Padua
pay up
rag up
ramus
rap up
sagum
salue
sarus
✧tabun
tabus
taluk
talus
tap up
Taxus
vacua
Vaduz
vague
vagus
value
varus
wamus
wax up
Yakut
zap up
calve
carve
carvy
Fauve
halva
halve
larva
lavvy
Maeve
malva
mal vu
mauve
naeve
naevi
naive
naïve
navvy
Saiva
salve
✧salvo
savvy
valve
varve
waive
Yahve
fatwa
mahwa
Yahwe
banya
barye
calyx
Carys
Katya
many a
nary a
satyr
Tanya
baiza
baize
Bazza
darzi
gauze
gauzy
Gazza
✧hamza
jazzy
kanzu
karzy
Lanza
Lao Zi
lazzi
lazzo
maize
matza
matzo
sadza
tazza
tazze
wanze
zanze
Abd-al
abeam
abear
✧abram
abray
E-boat
H-beam
I-beam

obeah
Q-boat
U-boat
abaca
abaci
aback
abide
abode
a'body
X-body
abbey
abcee
abies
abled
abler
ablet
absey
Ibsen
objet
abaft
aboil
abrim
abrin
absit
Eblis
Iblis
obiit
Abuja
Mbeki
abele
Ebola
obeli
oboli
U-bolt
A-bomb
H-bomb
aband
abuna
abune
ebony
obang
T-bone
U-bend
Z-bend
abbot
abhor
ablow
e-book
ebook
Ibrox
abord
abore
abort
mbira
ybore
abase
abash
abask
abuse
abysm
abyss
obese
abate
kbyte
mbyte
Abdul
about
Abrus
above
ab ovo
abaya
ob-gyn
abuzz
Ibiza
achar
éclat
ictal
occam
ocean
octad
octal
sceat
Sclav
scrab
scrae
scrag
scram
scran
scrap
scrat
scraw
scray
yclad
scuba
acock
acidy
scads
scudi
scudo
scuds
ackee
acned
acred
acres
C clef
F-clef
G-clef
icker
ocher
✧ocker
ocrea
octet
scree
screw
ycled
scaff
sci-fi
scoff
scuff
scuft
acrid
actin
ictic
scail
sclim
scrim
scrip
V-chip
acold
B cell
E coli
icily
oculi
P-Celt
Q-Celt
scala
scald
scale
scall
scalp
scaly
scold
sculk
scull
sculp
T-cell
scamp
schmo
acini
Iceni
icing
scand
scant
scena
'scend
scend
scene
scent
scone
ycond
accoy
act on
acton
actor
ichor
scion
scoog
✧scoop
scoot
scrod
scrog
scrow
scapa
'scape
scape
scapi
scopa
✧scope
Scops
acari
Accra
acerb
Acorn®
acorn
ochre
ochry
scare
scarf
scarp
✧scart
scary
score
scorn
scurf
T-cart
'scuse
scuse
acute
scath
scatt
Scots
Scott
scuta
scute
act up
actus
ice up
ictus
occur
scaud
scaup
scaur
schul
scoug
scoup
scour
scout
scrub
scrum
schwa
scowl
scowp
scuzz
addax
ad-man
adman
Adnan
adrad
Edgar
idea'd
ideal
ydrad
adobe
edict
educe
educt
adder
Adeel
adeem
adieu
adred
ad rem
advew
edged
edger
Edred
idler
udder
ydred
edify
adage
Idaho
Addie
add-in
addio
ad lib
ad-lib
adlib
admin
admit
admix
Eddic
Eddie
Edwin
Idris
sdein
addle
Adela
Adèle
adult
edile
✧idola
idyll
Ndola
oddly
odyle
Adams
à demi
edema
Adana
Adeni
adunc
idant
ident
Idunn
OD'ing
add-on
ad hoc
adiós
CD-ROM
idiom
idiot
odeon
adapt
adept
adopt
L-dopa
adore
adorn
hdqrs
adust
id est
Idist
odism
odist
add to
Aditi
adyta
Edith
add up
à deux
adsum
odeum
odium
odour
adown
adays
sdayn
bedad
begad
began
begar
begat
Behar
bekah
belah
belay
bemad
bepat
beray
cecal
cedar
César
debag
debar
decad
decal
decay
dedal
defat
✧degas
delay
deman
denar
denay
deray
dewan
dewar
fecal
femal
feral
fetal
feuar
genal
gerah
getas
get at
geyan
Hecat
hejab
hemal
he-man
hepar
hexad
Ieuan
jehad
jelab
kebab
kenaf
✧kesar
Kevan
leear
legal
leman
medal
Medan
Medau
Megan
Merak
mesal
metal
ne has
Neman
Nepal
ne was
pecan
pedal
pekan
penal
perai
Pesah
petal
petar
re-bar
recal
recap
redan
regal
Regan
regar
rehab
✧relax
relay
reman
remap
renal
renay
repay
resat
resay
rewax
Sebat
sedan
segar
selah
sepad
sepal
serac
sérac
serai
seral
setae
setal
Teian
telae
tepal
terai
teras
Texan
✧texas
Vedas
VE day
✧vegan
velar
venae
venal
Vesak
Wesak
ceiba
✧debby
✧derby
gerbe
get by
herby
kembo
let be
melba
o'erby
✧rebbe
set by
webby
yerba
beach
beech
belch
bench
cerci
Decca®
de-ice
deuce
fence
fetch
hence
heuch
keech
ketch
leach
leccy
leech
Leica®
letch
leuch
Mecca
✧mercy
peace
peach
peece
pence
Perca
perce
perch
Percy
reach
react
recce
recco
reccy
reech
Reich
retch
secco
teach
telco
tench
terce
teuch
vetch
✧welch
wench
beads
beady
beedi
bendy
deedy
fendy
geode
Gerda
heads
heady
heedy
Heidi
Jedda
kendo
leads
leady
Leeds
Lendl
Mehdi
mends
✧neddy
needs
needy
nerdy
Penda
perdu
perdy
ready
reddy
reede
reedy
seedy
teade
teddy
Vedda
veldt
Verdi
weeds
weedy
Wendy
Yezdi
Zelda
zerda
aedes
bedel
bedew
begem
beget
belee
Belém
benet
beret
besee
beset
betel
bevel
bever
bewet
bezel
celeb
Ceres
debel
defer
Deneb
denet
Derek
desex
deter
devel
eeven
feces
fever
fezes
gemel
✧genet
heben
heder
Hefei
Hegel
Helen
hevea
hewed
hewer
jebel
jewel
kevel
keyed
leger
lemel
lenes
leper
levee
level
lever
Lewes
Medea
Médée
mêlée
mered
merel
mesel
meted
meter
nebek
nebel
neper
nevel
never
newel
pedes
Pelée
penes
✧peter
pewee
rebec
rebel
refel
refer
rekey
relet
remen
remex
Renée
renew
reney
repel
reset
revel
revet
Reye's
Seder
sedes
Sefer
Seles
semée
semen
senes
sesey
seven
sever
sewed
sewel
sewen
sewer
sexed
sexer
seyen
teaed
Tebet
te-hee
telex
temed
tenet
tepee
terek
teres
Tevet
tewel
Texel
veney
vexed
vexer
weber
xebec
Xeres
Yemen
yeses
yeven
yewen
zebec
beefs
beefy
be off
deify
delfs
delft
feoff
Geoff
leafy
neafe
reify
selfs
serfs
terfe
beige
belga
benga
cerge
deign
feign
get-go
hedge
hedgy
heigh
Helga
henge
heugh
hewgh
kedge
kedgy
ledge
ledgy
legge
leggy
Leigh
let go
leugh
menge
merge
neigh
✧peggy
reggo
reign
renga
sedge
sedgy
Senga
serge
Sergt
tenge
terga
teugh
venge
verge
wedge
wedgy
weigh
Delhi
fecht
hecht
Lethe
meshy
meths
Pecht
Peght
techy
wecht
aecia
Aegir
aegis
aerie
aesir
bedim
befit
✧begin
belie
Benin
besit
betid
Bevin
bewig
Cecil
cedis
Celia
Celie
ceria
ceric
debit
Delia
demic
demit
denim
Denis
derig
✧devil
eejit
eerie
fecit
felid
Felis
Felix
fetid
gelid
genic
genie
genii
genip
geoid
get in
get it?
✧helix

hem in
jerid
kefir
kelim
Kevin
key in
Le Cid
leg it
legit
Lenin
lenis
lepid
let in
levin
Levis®
Lewie
✧lewis
lexis
media
✧medic
Melia
melic
melik
meril
merit
mesic
metic
✧metif
Metis
✧métis
nelis
nepit
newie
penie
penis
peril
petit
pewit
rebid
récit
redia
redid
redip
refit
régie
re-jig
rejig
relic
relie
remit
remix
renig
renin
resin
resit
retia
retie
revie
see in
Selim
semie
semis
sepia
✧seric
serif
serin
set in
sewin
telia
telic
tenia

tepid
tewit
Vedic
vegie
venin
vezir
xenia
xeric
Zenic
Meiji
beaky
becke
Becky
decko
dekko
fenks
gecko
geeky
jerky
kecks
leaky
nerka
Neski
Peake
peaky
pecke
perky
pesky
reaks
reeky
reiki
weeke
weeks
welke
welkt
be-all
Bella
✧belle
bells
belly
ceili
cella
’cello
cello
dealt
Della
fella
felly
ferly
gelly
gerle
heald
Hekla
Hello!
hello
Henle
jeely
jello
jelly
✧kelly
Leila
meal’d
mealy
medle
merle
Neale
neeld
neele
✧nelly
newly
realm

realo
reals
redly
reels
repla
reply
seeld
seely
sella
selle
sells
teals
tell’d
telly
tesla
veale
vealy
veily
✧weald
Weil’s
Wells
✧welly
wetly
yealm
beamy
derma
Fehme
femme
fermi
✧gemma
gemmy
heame
herma
herms
Jemma
jemmy
keema
kerma
lemma
neemb
neume
pelma
reame
reams
reamy
regma
Reims
seame
seamy
terms
Vehme
weamb
Yerma
beano
beans
being
benne
benni
✧benny
Berne
cerne
Denny
feint
fenny
ferny
gerne
Heine
henna
henny
jeans
Jenna

✧jenny
jeune
Kenna
ken-no
Kenny
kerne
leant
leany
Lemna
Lenny
Leona
leone
Lerna
Lerne
meane
means
meant
meany
Meena
meint
meiny
mesne
meynt
penna
penne
penny
peony
reins
renne
segno
seine
✧senna
teend
teene
teens
teeny
teind
teins
Temne
tenné
tenno
tenny
terne
veena
veiny
weeny
wenny
Aesop
bebop
befog
begot
below
berob
besom
besot
béton
celom
decor
décor
decoy
Delos
demob
demon
demos
depot
detox
Devon
dévot
felon
fetor
gemot

✧genoa
genom
get on
helot
Herod
heron
jeton
kebob
lemon
lenos
Leroy
let on
mebos
Médoc
melon
Melos
memos
meson
metol
me-too
peeoy
pekoe
pepos
Perón
pesos
redox
rejón
repos
repot
segol
segos
Ségou
sekos
✧señor
sepoy
seron
serow
set on
seton
teloi
telos
tenon
tenor
venom
xenon
Xerox®
zeros
delph
dempt
heaps
heapy
hempy
kelpy
kemps
kempt
kempy
leapt
nempt
peepe
peppy
seepy
Serps
Tempe
tempi
tempo
’tempt
tempt
Vespa®
vespa
weepy
beard

beare
beery
Beira
berry
ceorl
deare
dearn
deary
Debra
decry
deere
✧derry
feare
feart
ferry
geare
genre
Genro
Gerry
heard
heare
heart
hejra
Henri
✧henry
herry
✧jerry
Jewry
Kerry
leare
learn
leary
leery
lepra
mear’d
meare
merry
metre
✧metro
✧métro
✧negro
Nehru
peare
pearl
peart
✧pedro
peery
✧perry
Petra
petre
rearm
rears
reird
repro
✧retro
retry
seare
sehri
serra
serre
serry
teary
terra
terry
tetra
tetri
veery
verry
weary
weird
yeard

yearn
years
zebra
✧beast
Bessy
Betsy
cease
cense
cesse
deism
deist
dense
desse
feast
feese
fesse
geese
geist
gesse
gesso
heast
heist
herse
Hesse
Jesse
Jessy
Kelso
lease
leash
least
leese
leish
mease
Mensa
mense
mensh
merse
messy
meuse
neese
neist
Nessa
newsy
pease
peise
Pepsi®
per se
perse
perst
peyse
reast
reest
reist
reuse
sease
seise
seism
sensa
sense
sessa
tease
temse
tense
terse
Tessa
verse
verso
verst
weise
✧welsh
wersh

Wessi
yeast
beath
benty
berth
✧betty
cento
cents
certy
death
✧deity
✧delta
depth
derth
felty
festa
Feste
fetta
Geeta
gents
genty
geste
✧heath
hefte
hefty
hertz
Hetty
jetty
Keats
Keith
kelty
kente
lefte
lefty
Leith
lenti
lento
lepta
Letty
✧meath
meaty
meith
melty
mento
mesto
’neath
neath
Nesta
Netta
✧netty
peaty
pelta
Perth
pesto
petty
reata
reate
recta
recti
recto
rente
resty
Rett’s
rewth
seity
sente
senti
septa
set-to
teeth
tenth

tenty
terts
testa
teste
testy
texts
vertu
✧vesta
weete
wefte
Yeats
yenta
yesty
zesty
beaus
beaut
beaux
begum
begun
bemud
bevue
Cebus
cecum
Cetus
debug
debur
debus
debut
début
degum
demur
fed up
femur
fetus
gebur
gee up
gen up
genus
get up
get-up
het up
Jesus
jésus
key up
ledum
lemur
Lepus
let up
let-up
Lexus®
✧negus
nevus
nexus
pep up
rebus
rebut
recur
redux
regur
Remus
rerun
revue
rev up
sebum
sedum
segue
Seoul
serum
set up
set-up
sew up

tee up
tenue
velum
venue
✧venus
zebub
bevvy
deave
deeve
delve
heave
heavy
helve
keeve
kerve
leave
leavy
neive
Nerva
nerve
nervy
peavy
peeve
perve
pervy
reave
reeve
reive
selva
senvy
serve
servo
verve
weave
deawy
fetwa
Benxi
bedye
beryl
cetyl
Debye
Denys
herye
hexyl
Kenya
Meryl
Nerys
Pepys
ceaze
feeze
heeze
Jeeze
Kenzo
leaze
leeze
mezze
mezzo
neeze
peaze
peize
Penza
seaze
seize
senza
teaze
weize
afear
aflaj
B flat
iftar
offal

oflag
Ofwat
after
offer
Ofgem
of new
Oftel
often
of age
affix
Afric
afrit
Effie
offie
off it
of kin
afald
of old
à fond
afoot
Ffion
Ofcom
’sfoot
afara
afire
afore
yfere
of use
Éfaté
afoul
eggar
ogham
agger
aglee
aglet
agley
Agnes
Agnew
agree
agued
egger
egret
ngwee
ogee’d
ogeed
ogler
ugged
agoge
à go-go
à gogo
again
Aggie
agrin
✧ngaio
oggin
ogmic
Ugric
agila
agile
Agama
agami
Agana
Agene®
agene
agent
aging
agone
agony
ngana
Ngoni
Nguni

agios
aglow
agood
egg on
igloo
agape
Egypt
igapó
aggri
aggro
aggry
agora
agast
agist
egest
a'gate
agate
aguti
agave
ogive
agaze
ahead
aheap
Ahmad
Ahvaz
cheap
cheat
Chian
chiao
ihram
phial
Rhian
sheaf
sheal
shear
Shiah
Shoah
shoal
shoat
thrae
thraw
uhlan
wheal
whear
wheat
Chiba
Chubb®
dhobi
Sheba
thebe
chace
chack
chaco
check
chica
chich
chick
chico
chock
choco
chuck
✧phoca
shack
shock
shuck
thack
theca
thick
whack
Which?
which
chide
chode
khadi
kheda
Rhoda
rhody
shade
shady
Zhu De
Ahmed
cheek
cheep
cheer
chief
chiel
Khmer
pheer
sheel
sheen
sheep
sheer
sheet
shied
shiel
shier
shies
shlep
shmek
shoed
shoer
shoes
shred
Shrek
shrew
shyer
theek
thief
three
threw
wheel
wheen
chafe
chaff
chaft
chufa
chuff
shaft
shift
theft
thoft
wheft
whiff
whift
ahigh
phage
shogi
thagi
thegn
the go
thigh
shchi
Chaim
chain
chair
choir
Chris
ohmic
Ohrid
Rheia
sheik
thaim
theic
their
thrid
bhaji
khoja
shoji
thuja
✧cheka
choke
choko
choky
Dhaka
khaki
shake
shako
shakt
shaky
ahold
ahull
✧chalk
chela
child
✧chile
chili
chill
choli
chyle
dhole
dholl
f-hole
ghyll
jhala
phyla
phyle
shale
shall
shalm
shalt
shaly
shelf
she'll
shell
shill
shily
shola
Shula
shule
shuln
shuls
shyly
thali
thelf
thilk
thill
thole
tholi
Thule
✧whale
whelk
whelm
whelp
while
whilk
whole
who'll
champ
Chams
chemo
chimb
chime
chimo
chimp
chomp
chump
chyme
rhime
rhomb
rhumb
rhyme
shama
shame
Shema
thema
theme
thumb
thump
thyme
thymi
thymy
zhomo
ahent
ahind
ahint
bhang
bhuna
chana
chank
chant
✧china
chine
chiné
chink
chino
chunk
chynd
Ghana
Ghent
ohone
phang
phene
'phone
phone
phony
✧rhine
rhino
Rhona
rhone
rhyne
shand
Shane
Shang
Shani
shank
sha'n't
shan't
shend
shent
shine
shiny
Shona
shone
shunt
thana
thane
thang
thank
thine
thing
think
thong
whang
whine
whiny
chaos
Chios
Chloe
choof
chook
✧choom
oh boy!
pheon
✧phlox
✧she'ol
✧sheol
shook
shool
shoon
shoot
shrow
theow
thiol
throb
throe
throw
whoop
whoot
chape
✧chaps
chips
chops
shape
shaps
shope
whipt
chara
chard
chare
chark
charm
charr
chars
chart
chary
✧chère
chert
chirk
chirl
chirm
chirp
chirr
chirt
chiru
chord
chore
churl
churn
churr
mhorr
phare
shar'd
shard
share
shark
sharn
sharp
sherd
shere
shire
shirk
shirr
shirt
shore
shorn
short
shura
Thera
there
therm
Thira
third
thirl
Thora
thorn
thorp
uhuru
whare
wharf
where
whirl
whirr
whore
whorl
whort
chase
chasm
chess
chest
chose
chuse
ghast
ghest
ghost
Lhasa
phase
phese
shash
shush
these
thesp
those
whish
whisk
whiss
whist
whose
whoso
why, so
Xhosa
cheth
Chita
chota
chott
chute
dhoti
Ghats
photo
rhyta
shote
shott
shute
theta
thete
Thoth
✧white
✧whity
chout
choux
ghaut
ghoul
H-hour
Khnum
khoum
✧rheum
Shaun
shiur
✧shout
shrub
shrug
shtum
thou'd
thous
thrum
uh-huh
whaup
whaur
chave
chevy
chive
chivy
shave
sheva
✧shiva
shive
shove
who've
chewy
shawl
shawm
Shawn
shewn
shown
showy
thawy
thews
thewy
thowl
chaya
ghayn
khaya
shaya
shoyu
they'd
thuya
chizz
ghazi
khazi
whizz
Aidan
bigae
Bihar
✧cigar
cimar
cital
Dinah
dinar
Dipak
diram
dital
divan
diwan
Eilat
filar
final
hi-hat
hijab
hilar
jihad
Jinan
kiaat
Kiran
kisan
ligan
lilac
limax
linac
lipas
liras
litai
litas
Micah
micas
Midas
Milan
minae
minar
minas
nicad
Nicam
nidal
nikau
Nisan
nival
✧nizam
pi-jaw
pilaf
pilau
pilaw
pipal
pirai
rimae
rival
riyal
Sican
Silas
simar
Sirah
sisal
sitar
Sivan
sizar
tical
tidal
Tikal
tilak
✧titan
vicar
Vidar
Vijay
Vilas
vinal
Vinay
viral
vitae
vital
vitas
vivat
✧wigan
witan
zigan
Bibby
bilbo
bilby
bimbo
dibbs
himbo
jibba
kimbo
Libby
lie by
✧limbi
✧limbo
nimbi
Nimby
Niobe
ribby
sit by
Tibby
timbó
zimbi
aitch
biccy
Binca®
birch
bitch
cinch
cinct
circa
Circe
circs
cisco
diact
disco
ditch
filch
finch
fitch
hilch
hitch
linch
milch
mince
misca'
mitch
niece
piccy
piece
pièce
pilch
pinch
pitch
since
ticca
tinct
✧titch
vinca
✧wicca
wilco
wince
winch
witch
yince
zilch
zinco
zincy
✧biddy
bindi
Cindy
diddy
dildo
diode
giddy
Hilda
Hindi
Hindu
kiddo
kiddy
kinda
kindy
Linda
Lindy
Middx
middy
misdo
rindy
Sindi
Sindy
tiddy
Tilda
tilde
vifda
vilde
vivda
widdy
Wilde
wilds
winds
windy
aided
Aiden
aider
aînée
airer
bided
bidet
biker
biped
biter
Bizet
cider
cimex
citer
civet
diced
dicer
dicey
diker
dimer
diner
dived
diver
Dives
dizen
eider
Eiger
eisel
fiber
✧fides
fifer
filed
filer
filet
finer
fines
fired
firer
fiver
fives
fixed
fixer
gibel
giber
Giles
gilet
gimel
given
giver
hider
hiker
hired
hirer
hi-res
hi-tec
hiver
hives
✧hizen
jiber
jiver
jivey
kidel
kiley
libel
liber
lifer
liger
liken
liker
limen
limes
limey
lined
linen
liner
lines
liney
liter
lived
liven
liver
lives
miler
✧miles
mimer
miner
miser
miter
mixed
mixen
mixer
mizen
Nigel
✧niger
Nîmes
nisei
niter
nixer
nixes
oiled
oiler
Picea
piked
piker
pilea
pilei
piler
piles
piney
piped
✧piper
pipes
pixel
Ribes
ricer
ricey
rider
Rigel
Riley®
riley
rimed
rimer
ripen
riper
risen
riser
rived
rivel
riven
river
rivet
Sicel

Words marked ✧ can also be spelled with one or more capital letters

sided
sider
Sikel
✧silen
siler
silex
sinew
✧siren
siver
sixer
sized
sizel
sizer
Tibet
tiger
tiled
tiler
timed
timer
✧times
✧tinea
tined
tired
Tiree
titer
vibes
vibex
video
viner
vinew
viper
vireo
vires
vitex
viver
vives
vixen
widen
wiles
winey
wiper
✧wired
wirer
wires
wives
wizen
yikes
zibet
zineb
zizel
jiffy
miffy
niffy
biggy
bilge
bilgy
binge
bingo
bingy
biogs
ciggy
dinge
dingo
dingy
dirge
fidge
Giggs
hinge
✧jingo
jirga
kidge
Kings
Liège
liege
ligge
linga
lingo
lingy
midge
midgy
mingy
misgo
✧piggy
pingo
ridge
ridgy
rings
siege
singe
tinge
virga
virge
Virgo
wilga
winge
✧wings
wingy
zingy
Aisha
bigha
bight
dicht
dight
dishy
eight
fiche
fichu
fight
fishy
hight
hithe
kight
kithe
lichi
licht
light
lithe
litho
miche
might
niche
night
pight
pithy
richt
right
rishi
sidha
sight
sithe
tichy
tight
tithe
vichy
✧wight
withe
withy
Ailie
bid in
bifid
bikie
ci-gît
cilia
civic
civil
dig in
digit
Dilip
dinic
dip in
dixie
finis
fit in
hit it
Jilin
kilim
kinin
licit
lie in
lie-in
likin
limit
linin
lipid
Livia
livid
milia
mimic
Mimir
minim
mirin
mix-in
mix it
nihil
nip in
nitid
nixie
oidia
Oisin
pig it
pipit
pixie
ricin
rigid
Rigil
sigil
Sinic
sirih
sit in
sit-in
tibia
tie-in
Tilia
timid
tip in
tiyin
vigia
vigil
virid
visie
visit
Vitis
vivid
vizir
wifie
zip-in
✧ninja
Rioja
wilja
✧dicky
Dinky®
dinky
dirke
finks
kinky
licks
links
✧micky
milko
milky
minke
Nicky
picky
pinko
pinky
pisky
Ricky
risky
sicko
silky
sinky
ticky
tikka
wicky
zinke
zinky
aioli
aïoli
aisle
aizle
✧bible
bield
billy
birle
dilli
dilly
dimly
field
fille
filly
fitly
gilly
girly
hillo
hilly
Lille
lisle
mille
mirly
Mitla
Niall
nirly
piel'd
pills
qibla
rifle
rille
sidle
sield
sigla
silly
✧tilly
title
✧villa
villi
✧viola
viold
wield
wills
✧willy
yield
biome
disme
films
filmy
Fiume
gimme
gismo
gizmo
hiems
✧jimmy
limma
Miami
Niamh
pigmy
sigma
Timmy
Wilma
biont
Diana
Diane
diene
dinna
eigne
fiend
fient
finny
Fiona
Fionn
giant
✧ginny
hiant
hinny
jinni
jinns
Jinny
kiang
✧liana
liane
liang
ligne
linny
ninny
piani
✧piano
piend
✧pinna
pinny
pions
piony
riant
Siena
sient
signs
tinny
'tisn't
viand
visne
winna
zirna
aidos
bidon
bigot
bijou
bipod
Biros
bisom
bison
bitos
cibol
Cimon
dicot
didos
Dijon
divot
eikon
ficos
figos
finos
gigot
Gijon
giron
giros
hit on
jigot
kid on
kid-on
kikoi
kilos
kinos
Kirov
Libor
lidos
limos
livor
miaow
micos
mid-on
milor
milos
✧minor
✧minos
misos
✧nicol
nidor
Nikon®
Nilot
ninon
niton
Nixon
picot
pi-dog
pilot
pilow
piñon
✧pinot
pirog
piton
pivot
rigol
rigor
Ripon
Sidon
silo'd
silos
Simon
siroc
sit on
Ticos
tigon
✧timon
Timor
✧tiros
vigor
vinos
vison
visor
vizor
✧widow
winos
zip-on
cippi
dippy
gilpy
gimpy
hippo
hippy
jimpy
kippa
Kipps
lippy
✧nippy
Pippa
pippy
timps
tippy
wimpy
wispy
yippy
✧zippo
zippy
aiery
Ciara
Cipro®
cirri
diary
fiars
fibre
fibro
fiere
fiery
fiord
firry
hijra
Kiera
kirri
liard
liart
✧libra
litre
livre
micra
micro
mikra
mitre
nitre
nitro
nitry
picra
Piers
piert
Sitra
tiara
Tisri
titre
Ailsa
birse
birsy
bitsy
✧cissy
didst
dipso
ditsy
first
gipsy
giust
kiosk
miasm
'midst
midst
mimsy
Minsk
✧missa
missy
nisse
rinse
sissy
tipsy
biota
birth
bitte
bitts
bitty
dicta
dicty
diota
dirty
ditto
ditty
✧fifth
fifty
filth
firth
fisty
fitte
gilts
girth
hilts
kilty
✧kitty
linty
lists
mifty
miltz
minty
mirth
misty
Mitty
nifty
ninth
nitty
pieta
✧pietà
piety
✧pinta
pinto
piste
✧pitta
riata
rifte
rifty
sieth
silty
Sitta
sixte
sixth
sixty
tilth
tinty
titty
virtu
vista
visto
vitta
width
witty
bid up
big up
dig up
dip up
ficus
fig up
fit up
fit-up
fix up
gibus
gigue
hilum
hilus
kitul
kit up
lie up
Linus
Linux
lit up
miaul
Mimus
minus
mix up
mix-up
nidus
nisus
picul
Picus
pikul
pilum
pilus
pin-up
pious
pipul
pique
piqué
rig up
rip up
risus
simul
sinus
Sioux
sirup
sit up
sit-up
situs
tie up
tie-up
Timur
tip-up
titup
Titus
virus
Vitus
zip up
bivvy
civvy
divvy
kieve
lieve
mieve
nieve
rieve
sieve
silva
Kitwe
viewy
Dilys
Libya
pioye
✧sibyl
Sigyn
vinyl
bizzy
diazo
ditzy
dizzy
fizzy
Liszt
Mirza
piezo
Pinza
pizza
ritzy
tizzy
winze
ajwan
VJ day
eject
ojime
djinn
fjord
Njord
akkas
skean
skear
skoal
skran
Skoda®
skeer
skeet
skied
Skien
skier
skies
skiey
skyer
skyey
skiff
skoff
skegg
skail
skein
sklim
skrik
Akela
P-Kelt
Q-Kelt
skald
skelf
skell
skelm
skelp
skill
skulk
skull
Nkomo
skimp
akene
OK'ing
OKing
skank
skene
skink
skint
skunk
I know
skeos
skios
okapi
skart
skirl
skirr
skirt
skyre
ukase
akita
skate
skatt
skite
skyte
Aksum
ek dum
skive
skivy
okays
alaap
Alban
✧algae
algal
alias
Allah
Allan
allay
almah
altar
alway
bleak
blear
bleat
bloat
clean
clear
cleat
cloak
cloam
Elgar
eliad
Elian
Elsan®
elvan
fleam
float
fly at
gleam
glean
glial
gloat
ileac
ileal
✧iliac
Iliad
Ilian
ollav
plead
pleat
ploat
sloan
ulnae
ulnar
Ulsan
Ultan
alibi
all-be
clubs
fly-by
glebe
gleby
globe
globy
plebe
plebs
slubb
alack
Aleck
Alice
✧black
block
clack
cleck
click
✧clock
cluck
elect
flack

dogie
dolia
Doric
Doris
dovie
dowie
Eolic
eosin
folia
folie
folio
foxie
god it
gonia
gopik
goyim
hog it
homie
Hopis
hop it
iodic
Ionia
✧ionic
Jodie
Josie
logia
logic
logie
log in
log-in
login
loric
loris
lotic
Louie
✧louis
mob it
modii
✧moria
motif
movie
moxie
nomic
noria
no-win
oobit
oorie
ootid
podia
pokie
polio
polis
posit
potin
powin
robin
Rodin
Romic
ronin
roric
rorid
rorie
Rosie
rosin
rosit
rotis
rozit
sodic
Sofia
Sofis
solid
Sonia
sonic
Tobit
toe-in
tonic
topic
toric
torii
to wit
toxic
toxin
tozie
vogie
vomit
yogic
yogin
yowie
zooid
zoril
zoris
✧zowie
h**o**d**j**a
kopje
polje
pooja
b**o**o**k**s
booky
bosky
cocky
conky
cooky
corky
docks
dorky
folks
forky
Gorky
hokku
honky
hooka
hooky
jocko
kooky
Korky
Locke
locks
looks
mocks
nooky
poaka
poake
pocky
polka
pooka
porky
✧pouke
rocks
✧rocky
rooky
socko
socks
vodka
wonky
works
yolky
yonks
zooks
b**o**d**l**e
bogle
boule
boult
bowls
Boyle
coaly
coble
colly
cooly
could
coyly
do-all
doilt
doily
dolly
doole
doula
dowle
doyly
fogle
folly
fonly
foulé
fowls
foyle
goals
godly
golly
goold
gooly
goyle
holla
hollo
holly
hooly
hotly
Joely
jolly
Jools
joule
jowly
koala
lolly
lowly
moble
molla
✧molly
moola
mooli
mools
mooly
mould
Mouli®
mouli
mouls
moult
✧moyle
noble
nobly
Noele
noils
n’ould
nould
noule
poilu
✧polly
Poole
pools
poule
poulp
poult
Roald
roble
roily
Rolls
rotls
roule
socle
soily
Solly
soole
sowle
soyle
toile
toils
tools
voilà
voile
voulu
wolly
woold
world
would
yodle
you’ll
b**o**o**m**y
comma
commo
comms
commy
coomb
coomy
Cosmo
dogma
dolma
dooms
doomy
dormy
douma
foamy
forme
gormy
homme
horme
korma
loamy
momma
mommy
✧norma
pommy
rooms
roomy
rowme
Somme
✧tommy
✧worms
wormy
B**o**a**n**n
boing
boink
bonne
bonny
borne
borné
bound
bowne
conne
corni
corno
cornu
corny
count
doing
Donna
✧donne
donné
doona
downa
Down’s
✧downs
downy
found
fount
foyne
going
gonna
horny
hound
joint
✧koine
KOing
loins
loons
loony
Lorna
Lorne
lound
lownd
lowne
moony
Morna
morne
morné
mound
✧mount
no end
’noint
noint
nonny
no one
no-one
Norna
Norns
nouns
nouny
poind
point
Poona
porno
✧pound
pownd
powny
poynt
ronne
round
rownd
royne
sonne
sonny
sound
sownd
sowne
tonne
towny
wound
xoana
young
zoons
b**o**b**o**l
bohos
bokos
bolos
boron
bosom
boson
Botox®
boyos
bozos
Cobol
cocoa
cocos
codon
cohoe
cohog
cohos
colog
Colón
colon
color
Conor
Corot
dodos
do for
dojos
dolor
domoi
donor
fogou
gobos
hobos
Hohot
homos
✧honor
hoo-oo
jokol
kolos
Koror
kotos
kotow
locos
log on
log-on
logon
✧logos
lolog
lotos
mojos
mokos
monos
moron
Moros
motor
nohow
no joy
nomoi
nomos
no-no’s
no-nos
not on
polos
potoo
robot
ro-ros
rotor
Sodom
Solon
solos
sopor
tocos
to-dos
tokos
topoi
topos
toyon
Wolof
c**o**a**p**t
compo
compt
co-opt
coopt
coppy
corps
coupe
coupé
coypu
go ape
golpe
gompa
goopy
Hoops
hoppy
koppa
loipe
loopy
loupe
moppy
morph
oomph
poppa
poppy
poupe
poupt
roopy
roupy
soapy
soppy
soupy
zoppa
zoppo
b**o**a**r**d
boart
boord
Bosra
bourd
bourg
bourn
coarb
cobra
copra
courb
courd
coure
court
cowry
dobra
Dobro®
doorn
doura
dowry
fours
goary
go dry
✧goura
gourd
hoard
hoary
hoord
houri
hours
howre
kokra
koori
loord
lorry
loure
loury
Lowry
Moera
Moira
moire
moiré
moory
morra
morro
mourn
mowra
Moyra
poori
poort
powre
roary
soare
sopra
sorra
sorry
Tours
worry
you’re
yourn
yours
yourt
zorro
b**o**a**s**t
Boise
boose
boost
bossy
bouse
bousy
bowse
✧coast
coost
copse
copsy
corse
corso
doest
dorsa
dorse
douse
dowse
foist
✧fossa
fosse
godso
goest
goose
goosy
gorse
gorsy
gosse
hoast
hoise
hoist
Holst
hoosh
horse
horst
horsy
✧house
how so?
howso
joist
joust
loast
loess
loose
lossy
louse
lousy
lowse
moist
moose
mopsy
✧morse
mosso
mossy
mouse
moust
mousy
noise
noisy
noose
Norse
poesy
poise
popsy
posse
poyse
roast
roist
roosa
roose
roost
Rossi
rouse
roust
royst
sonse
sonsy
souse
sowse
toast
toise
Tomsk
Topsy
torse
torsi
torsk
✧torso
tossy
touse
tousy
towse
towsy
woosh
worse
worst
youse
zoism
zoist
a**o**r**t**a
Aosta
bolts
booth
boots
booty
botte
botty
boxty
coate
coati
conte
✧conté
conto
costa
coste
costs
cotta
couth
doeth
dorts
dorty
dotty
foots
footy
forte
✧forth
✧forty
fouth
fowth
goats
goaty
goeth
goety
gotta
gouty
hoots
hosta
how-to
jolty
jonty
kofta
loath
lofty
los’te
lotto
Louth
molto
monte
month
monty
Mopti
motte
motto
motty
mouth
✧north
ponty
porta
Porte
porty
potto
Pott’s
potty
pouty
roate
ronte
✧roots
rooty
rorty
rösti
route
routh
rowth
softa
softs
softy
Solti
soote
sooth
sooty
✧south
sowth
tooth
tools
torte
totty
volta
volte
wootz
worth
youth
b**o**b **u**p
bogus
bolus
bonus
bo’sun
bosun
box up
cogue
Colum
✧comus
conus
Donus
donut
do out
focus
fog up
✧forum
go out
hocus
ho-hum
hokum
hop up
Horus
hot up
jorum
✧jotun
kokum
lobus
locum
locus
logum
✧lotus
modus
✧mogul
mohur
Momus
mop up
mop-up
mopus
Morus
Mosul
✧motus
nodus
notum
not up
Notus
novum
pop-up
pot up
rogue
roguy
roque
sohur
solum
solus
sop up
sorus
Soyuz
togue
tog up
ton-up
tonus
top up
top-up
toque
Torun
torus
tot up
✧vogue

woful
yokul
convo
hoove
loave
moove
poove
poovy
Soave
solve
volva
volve
Volvo®
wolve
you've
Conwy
mol wt
dohyo
gonys
Konya
polyp
polys
Powys
Robyn
Sonya
Tokyo
Tonys
bonza
bonze
booze
boozy
cobza
colza
doozy
gonzo
Monza
motza
Pozzo
pozzy
toaze
touze
touzy
towze
towzy
woozy
apeak
apian
appal
appay
ephah
Oprah
speak
speal
spean
spear
speat
spial
splat
splay
sprad
sprag
sprat
spray
spyal
uplay
uptak
apace
epact
epoch
space
spacy
speck
specs
✧spica
spice
spick
spicy
apode
epode
spade
spado
spide
✧spode
apeek
apnea
appel
après
mpret
opter
spaer
✧speed
speel
speer
spied
spiel
spies
spred
spree
sprew
upjet
upled
upped
upper
upsee
upset
upsey
Ypres
spiff
apage
spahi
apaid
aphid
aphis
April
apsis
épris
op cit
opsin
Optic®
optic
opt in
✧spain
speir
✧split
spoil
sprig
sprit
uptie
spake
Speke
spike
spiky
spoke
✧apple
apply
aptly
spald
spale
spall
spalt
speld
spelk
spell
spelt
spile
spill
spilt
spule
spume
spumy
Epona
opine
spane
spang
spank
spend
spent
spina
spine
spink
spiny
spunk
up-end
upend
apiol
apoop
apron
ephod
ephor
Epsom
ippon
oppos
speos
spoof
spook
spool
spoom
spoon
spoor
spoot
sprod
sprog
upbow
up for
up top
epopt
opepe
apart
apert
apery
Aphra
aport
appro
✧op art
opera
spard
spare
spark
spart
sperm
spero
spire
spirt
spiry
spore
sport
spurn
Spurs
spurt
spyre
apish
apism
spasm
sposh
spate
spite
✧spitz
spots
sputa
appui
appuy
opium
spaul
spout
sprue
sprug
uprun
spawl
spawn
spewy
epoxy
apayd
spayd
upbye
spazz
equal
squab
squad
squat
Aqaba
squeg
equid
equip
squib
squid
squit
squiz
Equus
Ardas
aread
areal
arear
argal
argan
Arian
A-road
arrah
Arran
✧arras
array
artal
arval
Aryan
braai
bread
break
bream
Brian
briar
broad
Bryan
creak
cream
croak
Croat
dread
dream
drear
dryad
freak
friar
graal
great
groan
groat
kraal
oread
organ
orval
praam
prial
Priam
pro-am
tread
treat
✧triad
✧trial
Trias
troad
troat
✧urban
ureal
urial
urman
urnal
wreak
araba
Araby
aroba
bribe
crabs
grebe
grebo
oribi
probe
tribe
urubu
areca
Arica
brace
brach
brack
bract
brick
broch
brock
Bruce
crack
crick
crock
cruck
Draco
dreck
drice
erect
✧erica
erick
Eruca
eruct
frack
fract
frock
✧grace
grece
grice
gryce
orach
oracy
price
prick
pricy
Pruce
trace
track
tract
Tracy
treck
trice
trick
trock
truce
truck
wrack
wreck
wrick
aredd
arede
Breda
brede
✧bride
✧credo
crude
crudy
erode
Freda
grade
gride
grody
gryde
irade
predy
pride
Prodi
prude
trade
tride
trode
Trudy
uredo
arced
Ardea
ardeb
✧ariel
Arien
Aries
✧arles
armed
armet
arrêt
artel
Artex®
breed
breem
breer
brief
brier
✧creed
✧creek
creel
creep
Crees
cried
crier
cries
cruel
cruet
dried
drier
dries
dryer
erred
erven
freed
freer
freet
fried
frier
fries
fryer
greed
Greek
✧green
grees
greet
grief
Grieg
gruel
orbed
✧order
or e'er
oriel
ormer
preen
pried
prief
prier
proem
pryer
treed
treen
Trees
tried
✧trier
tryer
urdee
urdée
urger
urned
wrier
wryer
yrneh
arefy
craft
croft
draff
draft
drift
graff
graft
griff
grift
grufe
gruff
kraft
trefa
triff
Bragi
brogh
dregs
Frigg
grège
grego
tragi
Archy
ortho
prahu
argil
armil
aroid
arris
arsis
artic
braid
brail
brain
broil
Bruin
bruit
craic
✧craig
drail
drain
droil
droit
✧druid
erbia
Ernie
frail
fraim
freit
fruit
grail
grain
graip
grein
groin
krait
Mr Big
orbit
orcin
orgia
orgic
ornis
orpin
orris
Praia
preif
proin
traik
T-rail
trail
train
trait
treif
Troic
ureic
vraic
brake
braky
broke
crake
✧drake
grike
gryke
iroko
proke
trike
troke
wroke
Arkle
brill
brûlé
drill
drily
drôle
droll
dryly
frill
grill
krill
prill
prole
proll
tra-la
trild
trill
troll
trull
truly
urali
Urals
wryly
arame
aroma
brame
breme
brume
crame
cramp
creme
crème
crême
crime
crimp
cromb
crome
crumb
crump
drama
drome
frame
fremd
Frome
frump
grama
grame
grime
grimy
groma
grume
grump
premy
✧prima
prime
primo
primp
primy
promo
tramp
trema
tromp
trump
arena
aren't
Aruna
brand
brank
✧brent
brine
bring
brink
briny
Brona
brond
Bronx
Bruno
brunt
crane
crank
crena
crine
crone
cronk
crony
drank
drant
drent
D-ring
drink
drone
drony
drunk
franc
✧frank
frena
frond
front
grana
grand
✧grant
grind
grone
grunt
Irena
Irene
irons
irony
krang
krans
kranz
kreng
krona
króna
krone
orang
orant
O-ring
prana
prang
prank
prent
prink
print
prone
prong
pronk
prune
prunt
trant
trend
Trina
trine
trona
tronc
trone
trunk
urena
urent
urine
wring
wrong
wrung
yrent
arbor
ardor
argol
argon
Argos
argot
ariot
armor
Arnor
arrow
arson
arvos
brood
✧brook
brool
broom
Creon
crook
croon
cruor
droob
droog
drook
drool
droop
ergon
ergot
Errol
error
Freon®
griot
groof
groom
Kreon
kroon
M-roof
Orion
Orlon®
orlop
Orson
Orton
Oryol
preon
prion
prior
proof
trior
trios
Troon
troop
try on
try-on
urson
vroom
wroot
crape
craps
crapy
crepe
crêpe
crept
crepy
crêpy
crypt
drape
drops
drupe
erupt
grape
graph
Grapo
grapy
gripe
grips
grope
grype
grypt
props
trape
traps
tripe
tripy
trope
wraps
wrapt
yrapt
Iraqi
ard-ri

ardri
arere
brere
crare
crore
crura
drere
frère
frore
frorn
frory
or ere
prore
Truro
urari
arise
arish
arose
artsy
brash
brass
brast
Brest
brisé
brisk
brose
brush
brust
crash
crass
cress
crest
crise
crisp
✧cross
crost
cruse
crush
crust
crusy
dress
drest
dross
✧druse
drusy
erase
Ernst
erose
frass
fresh
frisk
frist
✧frost
frush
frust
grasp
grass
grese
grise
grist
grisy
gross
grosz
Irish
prase
presa
prese
✧press
prest
prise
prism

prose
proso
prosy
pryse
trash
trass
tress
trest
Trish
trist
truss
trust
tryst
wrast
wrest
wrist
Areta
arête
arett
Arita
Brett
broth
brute
crate
Crete
crith
crwth
Erato
frate
frati
frith
fritz
froth
grate
Greta
grith
grits
irate
orate
prate
pratt
praty
Proto®
tratt
trite
troth
truth
urate
urite
wrate
wrath
write
wrote
wroth
arcus
argue
✧argus
Århus
Arius
arnut
croup
crout
cry up
drouk
dry up
fraud
Freud
fry-up
grouf
group
grout

Orcus
orgue
proud
proul
trout
Ursus
vrouw
brava
brave
bravi
✧bravo
breve
crave
cruve
drave
✧drive
drove
grave
gravy
greve
✧grove
preve
privy
prove
Provo
trave
trove
yrivd
brawl
brawn
braws
brown
crawl
✧crewe
crowd
✧crown
Crows
drawl
drawn
drown
frown
frowy
growl
grown
prawn
prowl
trawl
trews
Urawa
wrawl
braxy
druxy
prexy
proxy
Trixy
Freya
Oriya
Priya
proyn
braze
brize
craze
crazy
croze
Druze
frize
frizz
froze
graze
grize
Oryza

prize
Asian
Aslan
assai
Assam
assay
Aswan
as was
asway
CS gas
eskar
essay
Isaac
Isiac
Islam
Islay
Oscan
Oscar®
✧oscar
oshac
pshaw
psoas
usual
dsobo
tsuba
psych
A-side
aside
B-side
tsadi
ashen
Asher
✧ashes
ashet
asker
askew
✧aspen
as per
asper
asses
asset
aster
as yet
as-yet
esker
Essen
Essex
ester
Isbel
islet
issei
osier
usher
usnea
Osage
Tsuga
usage
V-sign
as why
Asdic
aspic
astir
aswim
Essie
g-suit
osmic
ossia
Ossie
Ossis
✧ostia
Q-ship

Osaka
esile
Isold
istle
psalm
at sea
dsomo
ysame
asana
usen't
✧ascot
as for
as how
as now
assot
escot
estoc
estop
f-stop
psion
psyop
estro
psora
Q-sort
usure
usurp
usury
ascus
astun
issue
pseud
use up
Estyn
Isuzu®
at bat
at-bat
✧atlas
atman
at par
attap
attar
ethal
ottar
stead
steak
steal
steam
stean
stear
stoae
stoai
stoas
stoat
strad
strae
strag
strak
strap
straw
stray
U-trap
Stubb
stubs
U-tube
stack
Stacy
stich
stick
stock
stuck
Utica
étude

stade
stedd
stede
study
Ethel
ether
etwee
other
Otley
otter
steed
steek
✧steel
steem
steen
steep
steer
stied
sties
stoep
strep
strew
styed
styes
utter
staff
stiff
stuff
étage
stage
stagy
stogy
itchy
atria
atrip
✧attic
Attis
ethic
ettin
staid
staig
stain
stair
steil
stein
✧stoic
stoit
stria
strig
strim
strip
atoke
otaku
stake
stoke
at all
atilt
atoll
ettle
Itala
Italy
stal'd
stale
stalk
stall
stela
stele
stell
stilb
stile

still
stilt
stole
stoln
stull
stulm
style
styli
stylo
utile
atimy
atomy
etyma
stamp
steme
stime
stimy
stoma
stomp
stumm
stump
styme
at one
atone
atony
ctene
Ethna
Ethne
Etons
stand
stane
stang
stank
stend
steno
stent
sting
stink
stint
stond
stone
stong
stonk
stonn
stony
stung
stunk
stunt
Athos
ethos
stood
stook
stool
stoop
stoor
strop
strow
stroy
atopy
étape
Mt Apo
n-type
p-type
staph
steps
stept
stipa
stipe
stope
stupa
stupe

otary
stare
stark
starn
starr
stars
start
stere
stern
stire
stirk
stirp
store
stork
storm
story
sture
sturt
styre
uteri
U-turn
Mt Usu
stash
Stasi
stoss
ytost
state
styte
stoun
stoup
stour
stout
strum
strut
stave
Steve
stive
stivy
stove
stews
stewy
stown
ataxy
Ethyl®
ethyl
stays
aurae
aural
aurar
auras
bubal
buran
Busan
Cuban
curat
Dubai
ducal
ducat
dural
eupad
fugal
fural
furan
gulag
gular
human
Judah
✧judas
jugal
jumar
jural

jurat
kulak
kulan
Kumar
kunar
Lucan
Lucas
lumas
lunar
Murad
mural
Musak
Muzak®
muzak
nugae
pumas
pupae
pupal
pupas
Pusan
quean
quoad
Qur'an
Quran
rubai
rudas
rumal
Ruman
rural
subah
Sudan
sugar
sumac
surah
sural
✧surat
Susan
tubae
tubal
tubar
tubas
tunas
Wuhan
yulan
zupan
bubby
bumbo
busby
cubby
✧dumbo
fubby
✧gumbo
hubby
jumbo
jumby
nubby
outby
put by
rugby
rumba
rumbo
run by
subby
tubby
turbo
Buick®
bunce
bunch
bunco
✧butch
culch

curch
cutch
Cuzco
dunce
dunch
✧dutch
guaco
gulch
hunch
hutch
juice
juicy
junco
kutch
lunch
lurch
mulch
mulct
✧munch
Musca
Musci
mutch
ounce
punce
✧punch
quack
quich
quick
runch
succi
sulci
Turco
yucca
buddy
bundu
Bundy®
cuddy
cundy
curdy
duddy
fundi
funds
fundy
✧guide
gundy
hurds
Lundy
muddy
Munda
Murdo
Nuada
nuddy
Oujda
oundy
outdo
puddy
quids
ruddy
rueda
suede
suède
Auden
auger
aurei
buret
buses
Butea
buteo
buyer
cubeb
culet

culex
cumec
cupel
curer
curet
cusec
cutey
cuvée
duper
Dürer
duvet
fumes
fumet
fusee
fuzee
gules
gulet
julep
luces
Luger®
luger
lumen
Lurex®
luter
luxes
muley
murex
mused
muser
muset
muted
numen
Nupes
ousel
outed
outer
ouzel
pubes
puker
pukey
puler
Pulex
puree
purée
Purex
puzel
✧queen
queer
quiet
ruler
✧rules
rumen
Rumex
runed
rupee
suber
sujee
super
tubed
✧tuber
tuned
tuner
tupek
tutee
buffa
buffe
buffi
buffo
buffs
cuffo
fuffy

gulfy
huffy
kulfi
luffa
puffy
quaff
quiff
ruffe
sulfa
sulfo
surfy
tuffe
turfs
turfy
budge
buggy
bulge
bulgy
bungy
burgh
dungy
Durga
durgy
fudge
fuggy
fungi
fungo
gunge
gungy
gurge
judge
lunge
lungi
✧lurgi
lurgy
mudge
muggy
mulga
✧mungo
nudge
outgo
pudge
pudgy
puggy
punga
purge
ruggy
surge
surgy
vuggy
vulgo
aught
buchu
✧bushy
cushy
Dubhe
duchy
gushy
hushy
lushy
musha
mushy
nucha
oucht
ought
ouphe
pushy
qui-hi
ruche
rushy
sushi
tushy
✧wu shu
✧wushu
audio
audit
aulic
aumil
auric
auxin
bunia
burin
buy in
buy-in
cubic
cubit
Cufic
cumin
✧cupid
curia
curie
curio
cutie
cut in
cut-in
cutin
cutis
cut it
dulia
fugie
fusil
Fuxin
humic
humid
hutia
Judie
Julia
Julie
Kufic
Lucia
lucid
ludic
lug in
lupin
lurid
mucid
mucin
mudir
mujik
music
musit
nubia
nudie
oubit
ourie
pubic
pubis
pudic
pugil
pumie
Punic
pupil
Purim
purin
putid
Putin
put in
put-in
quail
quair
qubit
quoif
quoin
quoit
Rubia
Rubik
rub in
rubin
rudie
runic
run in
run-in
rupia
rutin
Sufic
Sufis
Sukie
Sunil
Susie
tulip
tumid
tunic
Tunis
tupik
Turin
Yupik
zuzim
bunje
bunjy
Ouija®
ouija
Bubka
bucko
bucku
bulky
bunko
burka
burke
busky
ducks
ducky
dumka
dumky
dusky
funky
gucky
hulky
hunks
hunky
husks
husky
junky
✧lucky
mucky
murky
musky
pucka
pukka
pulka
punka
punky
quake
quaky
sucks!
sulks
sulky
Tunku
Turki
Turku
tusky
yucky
yukky
bugle
build
built
✧bulla
bully
burly
cully
curly
Duala
dully
duple
duply
fugle
fully
Guelf
guild
guile
guilt
gully
gurly
gusla
gusle
gusli
guyle
hullo
hully
hurly
murly
Nuala
nulla
pusle
quale
qualm
quell
quill
quilt
quoll
ruble
rumly
sully
surly
tulle
tuple
Burma
dummy
duomi
duomo
guimp
gumma
gummy
Kurma
lumme
lummy
mummy
pulmo
queme
rummy
rusma
summa
Suomi
tummy
turme
yummy
✧bunny
Burns
burnt
cuing
curny
Duane
dunno
dunny
funny
guana
guano
gunny
Husni
Lubna
ouens
quant
quena
quina
quine
quint
quonk
ruana
ruing
ruins
runny
suing
suint
Sunna
Sunni
sunny
tui na
tuina
tunny
zurna
auloi
aulos
autos
budos
buroo
buxom
Dukou
duros
duroy
euros
eusol
furol
furor
futon
guyot
humor
Huron
husos
jupon
juror
kudos
ludos
Luton
Luxor
Luzon
mucor
musos
muton
ouzos
pudor
put on
put-on
rumor
run on
run-on
sudor
sumos
sutor
Suwon
Tudor
tumor
tutor
Yukon
yupon
bumph
bumps
bumpy
buppy
cuppa
dumps
dumpy
duppy
gulph
guppy
✧humph
humpy
jumps
jumpy
lumpy
mumps
pulpy
puppy
purpy
quipo
quipu
rumpy
sumph
tumpy
turps
✧yuppy
burqa
burro
burry
curry
durra
fuero
furry
guard
guiro
gurry
Huari
hurra
hurry
kukri
kurre
lucre
lurry
mucro
mudra
Munro
murra
murre
murry
outré
quare
quark
quart
quern
query
quire
quirk
quirt
Quorn®
Rudra
sucre
Sudra
Sun Ra
supra
surra
sutra
tuart
tugra
buist
bulse
bursa
burse
burst
bussu
cuish
curse
curst
dulse
dunsh
durst
fubsy
fussy
guess
guest
guise
gutsy
guyse
✧hurst
hussy
Kursk
muist
mulse
mulsh
mumsy
musse
mussy
✧nurse
pudsy
pulse
purse
pursy
pussy
quash
quasi
quest
quist
qursh
sudsy
tuism
Tulsa
Tutsi
wurst
wussy
aunty
✧bunty
busty
butte
butty
culty
cutto
cutty
due to
duets
duett
dusty
furth
fusty
gusto
gusty
gutta
gutty
junta
junto
jutty
kurta
lusty
✧mufti
muntu
Muntz
musth
musty
nutty
punto
punty
purty
putti
putto
putty
quite
Quito
quits
quota
quote
quoth
quyte
runty
ruoti
rusty
rutty
suety
Suita
suite
tuath
tufty
tutti
tutty
augur
butut
buy up
cusum
cut up
cut-up
durum
Eurus
fucus
fugue
Fusus
Gueux
gum up
humus
jugum
kurus
✧lupus
mucus
mug up
put up
put-up
queue
rub up
Rubus
Rufus
run up
run-up
suhur
sum up
sunup
tuque
curve
curvy
guava
lurve
luvvy
murva
suave
vulva
bunya
butyl
Kuo-yü
quayd
queyn
Surya
buaze
buzzy
furze
furzy
fuzzy
huzza
huzzy
kudzu
muzzy
avgas
avian
uveal
evict
evade
ivied
evohe
avail
avoid
Avril
ovdim
ovoid
Svein
evoke
avale
Ávila
mvule
ovoli
ovolo
ovule
uvula
avant
Avena
avens
avine
evens
event
Ivana
ovine
avion
evhoe
avert
evert
every
ivory
ovary
overt
avast
avise
aviso
kvass
ovist
Evita
evite
ovate
Ovett
avize
avyze
dwaal
sweal
swear
sweat
tweak
swabs
swack
twice
✧swede
a-week
aweel
awned
awner
dweeb
owler
owlet
owner
owsen
sweel
sweep
sweer
sweet
tweed
tweel
'tween
tweer
tweet
twier
twoer
twyer
✧swift
swage
owche
await
owrie
swain
sweir
✧twain
awake
awoke
Iwaki
Kwok's
dwale
dwalm
dwell
dwelt
dwile
kwela
Pwyll
swale
swaly
swell
swelt
swill
swoln
'twill
twill
twilt
✧swami
swamp
a-wing
bwana
Dwane
dwang
dwine
owing
swang
swank
swine
✧swing
swink
swung
twang
twank
twine
twink
✧twins
twiny
ewhow
swoon
swoop
swapt
swept
swipe
swopt
award
aware
awarn
awmry
awork
dwarf
sward
sware
swarf
swarm
swart
swerf
swire
swirl
sword
swore
sworn
'twere
twerp
twire
twirl
twirp
✧awash
ewest
swash
swish
Swiss
twist
aweto
swath
swats
swith
swits
twite
awful
dwaum
own up
swoun
swy-up
two-up
awave
swive
'twixt
aways
swayl
Sweyn
bwazi
Swazi
axial
axman
exeat
expat
Oxfam
Uxmal
VX gas
exact
exode
exude
oxide
excel
exeem
exies
expel
oxter
axoid
ex div
ex-div
oxlip
axile
exalt
✧exile
exult
ixtle
exeme
oxime

exine
axiom
axion
expos
extol
Ixion
ox-bot
ox-bow
exert
extra
exurb
exist
ox-eye
by far
bylaw
byway
cycad
cymae
cymar
cymas
Dylan
gynae
gyral
✧hyrax
lyyar
my hat!
Mylar®
mynah
My Way
pygal
pyral
rybat
symar
✧syrah
typal
tyran
Zyban®
zygal
sybbe
lynch
synch
Byrds
Hyads
hynde
kynde
Lynda
tynde
cyder
dyker
hyleg
✧hymen
hyper
Hywel
lycée
Myles
Pyrex®
ryper
sycee
syker
syren
syver
tyler
tyned
tyred
xylem
nyaff
Aysha
hypha
hythe
kythe
lythe
sythe
Tyche
Typha
tythe
ayrie
by air
cylix
✧cynic
Cyril
eyrie
eyrir
Eytie
gynie
hylic
hyoid
✧kylie
kylin
kylix
Kyrie
Lydia
lyric
lysin
lysis
lytic
myoid
pyoid
✧pyxis
✧sybil
Syria
typic
xylic
Xyris
zymic
ayelp
cycle
cyclo
gyeld
myall
nyala
myoma
pygmy
rymme
ayont
by-end
dying
eying
gynny
hyena
hying
kyang
lying
Lynne
Lyons
Myrna
nying
tying
vying
Wynne
Byron
Cynon
cyton
Dyson
gyron
hypos
hyson
kyloe
lysol
My God!
Myron
nylon
pylon
syboe
sybow
synod
sysop
typos
tyros
Tyson
xylol
zygon
lymph
myope
myops
nymph
sylph
aygre
Cymry
✧hydra
hydro
lyart
Lycra®
myrrh
gypsy
kydst
lyase
lyssa
nyssa
Eyeti
fytte
Kyoto
lytta
synth
typto
xysti
Cyrus
eye up
gyrus
Pyrus
syrup
sylva
my eye
tyiyn
xylyl
izzat
Czech
azide
tzade
Aztec
Uzbeg
Uzbek
azygy
azoic
Izmir
Ozzie
ozeki
azole
azyme
azine
e-zine
ozone
ZZ Top
Azeri
azure
azurn
azury
izard
azote
azoth
pzazz

6 – even

bahada
Bahasa
bajada
balata
banana
baraza
batata
cabala
cabana
Canada
cañada
casaba
dagaba
fa la la
halala
Havana
jacana
jaçana
✧jataka
kabaka
kabala
kabaya
kamala
✧kanaka
karaka
katana
Malaga
Málaga
Manama
mañana
maraca
masala
Nacala
nagana
Narada
palama
panada
✧panama
papaya
pataca
Ravana
Sahara
✧samara
satara
taiaha
✧tamara
Tarawa
✧zapata
✧bayard
cafard
canard
farand
Harald
hazard
maraud
mazard
nasard
navaid
tabard
tarand
vaward
Banate
canapé
carafe
damage
eatage
facade
✧façade
galage
garage
gavage
hamate
Harare
karate
Lalage
Lamaze
lanate
lavage
✧madame
malate
manage
oarage
palace
palate
✧parade
parage
pavage
pavane
rafale
ramate
ravage
salade
sarape
savage
savate
takahe
tamale
vacate
wakame
zarape
lalang
Malang
✧padang
parang
satang
zamang
calash
camash
gamash
Kazakh
lavash
paraph
Tanach
calami
dalasi
Danaoi
Hawaii
jawari
karahi
Malawi
manati
marari
nagari
Pahari
palagi
Qatari
Rajani
safari
salami
tamari
tatami
uakari
Vasari
Wahabi
waragi
wasabi
carack
damask
Lanark
padauk
saxaul
Balaam
napalm
salaam
Canaan
Danaan
Gawain
papain
samaan
wabain
babaco
Bamako
catalo
da capo
galago
kakapo
lavabo
macaco
Malabo
Nagano
Navaho
Navajo
paramo
rabato
bazaar
badass
Calais
camass
cavass
harass
kababs
kavass
madams
Manaus
Masais
✧naiads
palais
basalt
basant
caract
galant
karait
naiant
natant
savant
talant
vacant
gagaku
Kakadu
Makalu
tamanu
Xanadu
canary
datary
✧galaxy
malady
panary
papacy
salary
Tatary
vagary
bazazz
pazazz
balboa
cambia
lambda
Zambia
baobab
earbob
iambic
Malbec
tambac
barbed
dabbed
✧day bed
gabbed
nabbed
pay bed
tabbed
tan bed
Babbie
babble
Barbie®
barbie
bauble
bawbee
bawble
cabbie
dabble
faible
gabble
gamble
garble
hamble
jabble
jambee
lambie
lay-bye
marble
rabble
ramble
wabble
wamble
warble
yabbie
gasbag
✧may bug
ragbag
ratbag
sag bag
casbah
✧kasbah
jambok
✧zambuk
barbel
gambol
jambul
sambal
carbon
far ben
Harbin
kanban
rabbin
bamboo
gabbro
yah-boo
barber
camber
dabber
dauber
gabber
gambir
harbor
jabber
jamber
lamber
nabber
raw bar
sambar
sambur
tamber
yabber
garbos
iambus
Jambos
lay-bys
mambos
rabbis
sambos
zambos
Babbit
barbet
gag-bit
gambet
gambit
hagbut
rabbet
✧rabbit
sabbat
Talbot®
talbot
wabbit
Tambov
hatbox
haybox
jawbox
pay-box
tar box
babbly
carboy
dawbry
day-boy
fanboy
marbly
tarboy
wambly
fascia
Garcia
kaccha
Lancia®
Marcia
calcic
calced
rancid
raucid
talced
eatche
gauche
gaucie
✧jaycee
manche
mascle
Parcae
raucle
Ranchi
sancai
t'ai chi
caecal
cancel
faecal
faucal
laical
✧marcel
parcel
✧pascal
rancel
rascal
tarcel
caecum
talcum
cancan
earcon
falcon
farcin
garçon
✧gascon
Marcan
mascon
fascio
gaucho
rancho
sancho
ear-cap
gas cap
madcap
calcar
✧cancer
dancer
lancer
lascar
Nascar®
rancor
saucer
calces
cascos
caucus
darcys
faeces
falces
fasces
fauces
Jancis
lances
mancus
Marcos
Marcus
narcos
saccos
catcht
fat cat
fat-cat
faucet
✧lancet
mascot
ramcat
waucht
Manchu
catchy
dancey
far cry
patchy
talcky
✧war cry
Candia
Kandla
Sandra
bardic
Dardic
banded
barded
candid
caudad
fanded
gadded

handed
landed
padded
parded
sanded
wadded
warded
baddie
baldie
caddie
candie
candle
caudle
daddle
daidle
dandle
dawdle
faddle
haddie
handle
lac-dye
laddie
laldie
paddle
paidle
pardie
raddle
randie
saddhe
saddie
saddle
taddie
vat dye
waddie
waddle
wandle
Yardie
bandog
gay dog
lapdog
wardog
Bao **Dai**
Gandhi
gardai
sandhi
haiduk
zaddik
caudal
daedal
fardel
Handel
Jandal®
pardal
Randal
sandal
sardel
✧vandal
fandom
mandom
randem
random
Saddam
tandem
Camden
Cardin
Dardan
farden
garden
hadden
hagden
hagdon
Handan
hand-in
harden
Hayden
Haydon
lardon
madden
maidan
✧maiden
pardon
pardon?
randan
randon
sadden
Walden
warden
nandoo
nardoo
vaudoo
wandoo
hard-up
laid up
land up
paid-up
badder
Balder
bandar
candor
carder
dander
gadder
gander
gaydar
hander
ladder
Länder
lander
larder
lauder
madder
mandir
padder
pandar
pander
raider
sadder
sander
sardar
sawder
wander
warder
zander
caddis
Sardis
Tardis
waldos
bandit
Bardot
pandit
saidst
landau
saddhu
May-**dew**
caudex
baldly
bawdry
hardly
laidly
law-day
lay-day
man-day
May Day
✧mayday
pay day
rag day
tag day
tawdry
bauera
camera
catena
favela
galena
Ganesa
kamela
Karena
lagena
mabela
pakeha
Pamela
patera
tapeta
valeta
Walesa
zabeta
zareba
maleic
fag end
Fareed
hareld
lag-end
salewd
taberd
tag end
wax end
barege
barège
camese
✧carême
facete
galère
gamete
kabele
La Tène
manège
Na-Dene
paleae
raceme
sagene
sapele
taleae
taxeme
valete
care of
make of
daleth
Ganesh
Gareth
lamedh
Rajesh
samech
samekh
varech
Baresi
tapeti
✧**baseej**
✧**favell**
rameal
vakeel
hareem
Saleem
baleen
cage in
careen
casein
casern
cave in
cave-in
cavern
fade in
fade-in
have in
have on
have-on
lateen
rake in
Ramean
Sabean
sateen
take in
take-in
take on
tavern
wade in
gazebo
Maceio
make do
make-do
sapego
Sasebo
ease up
fade up
fade-up
have up
lace up
lace-up
made up
make up
make-up
rake up
rave-up
save up
take up
take-up
wake up
wake-up
career
fadeur
laveer
paneer
pasear
cameos
caress
halers
havers
jabers
kamees
manehs
Marek's
Paget's
papers
tavers
waders
waters
cadent
caveat
gayest
have it
haven't
jacent
lament
latent
latest
make it
manent
mayest
parent
patent
sayest
take it
talent
tavert
bateau
cadeau
gateau
gâteau
haleru
Maseru
bakery
barely
basely
calefy
eatery
fakery
gaiety
gamely
gamesy
jadery
japery
lamely
lately
madefy
namely
napery
palely
papery
rakery
rarefy
rarely
safely
safety
sagely
samely
sanely
tabefy
tamely
tawery
Valéry
wafery
watery
wavery
yarely
kameez
Jaffna
✧maffia
raffia
taffia
baffle
Caffre
gaufre
raffle
waffle
yaffle
zaffre
bagful
barful
canful
capful
earful
hatful
jarful
lapful
lawful
manful
panful
sapful
vatful
waeful
halfen
samfoo
gaffer
gaufer
zaffer
farfet
haffet
haffit
carfax
carfox
barfly
day-fly
gadfly
mayfly
naffly
pan-fry
sawfly
waffly
Bangla
kangha
Pangea
sangha
bagged
banged
fagged
fanged
gagged
hagged
hanged
jagged
lagged
nagged
ragged
sagged
tagged
tanged
wagged
war god
zagged
bangle
bargee
cangle
cangue
daggle
dangle
dargle
fangle
gadgie
gaggle
gangue
gargle
haggle
jangle
langue
✧maggie
maigre
mal gré
malgre
malgré
mangle
maugre
paigle
raggee
raggle
taggee
taigle
tangie
tangle
waggle
wangle
dargah
Bangui
Haggai
mangal
mangel
Targum
bangin'
bang on
gas gun
Gaugin
hang in
hang on
jargon
laggen
laggin
largen
margin
pangen
ray gun
Saigon
Sargon
tangun
waggon
wangan
wangun
Yangon
Baggio
Day-Glo
dayglo
Fangio
bang up
bang-up
gang up
hang up
hang-up
✧**badger**
banger
Bangor
cadger
dagger
danger
gagger
ganger
gauger
hangar
hanger
Jaeger®
jaeger
jagger
Kalgar
laager
lagger
Langer
langur
manger
nagger
✧ranger
saggar
sagger
sangar
sauger
tagger
yagger
fangos
haggis
largos
mangos
sargos
sargus
tangos
valgus
Vargas
war gas
baggit
catgut
caught
faggot
gadget
garget
haught
maggot
naught
parget
raught
target
taught
waught
pang-fu'
dangly
gangly
jangly
laughy
mangey
margay
Sangay
tangly
waggly
mashua
✧raphia
pathic
mashed
washed
Cathie
daphne
Kathie
lathee
mashie
mazhbi
Nan Hai
✧**kathak**
pachak
Cathal
Gadhel
Rachel
Warhol
fathom
mayhem
pashim
sachem
Aachen
bash on
cash in
fat hen
lathen
machan
Nathan
Pathan
Sathan
sazhen
washen
wash-in
Pakhto
Pashto
carhop
cash up
lash-up
mayhap
wash up
wash-up
basher
bather
Cathar
✧dasher
✧father
gather
Hathor
jaghir
Jashar
Jasher
lasher
lather
macher
Madhur
masher
rasher
rather
washer
Aarhus
bathos
hachis
Jan Hus
laches
machos
nachos
Paphos
pathos
rachis
raphis
tachos
bach it
cachet
sachet
cachou
Pakhtu
Pashtu
bashaw
cashaw
cashew
haw-haw
Cathay
eathly
gashly
rashly
sashay
cafila
calima
capita
Carica
✧carina
Dalila
Davina
fajita
farina
Fatima
Hamina
Jamila
Janina
kafila
kamila
Karina
la-di-da
Lalita
lamina
La Niña
Latina
✧manila
✧marina
maxima
Nabila
patina
qasida

Sabina
sahiba
salina
saliva
tahina
vagina
zariba
maniac
manioc
panisc
babied
ravin'd
taxied
varied
barite
camise
canine
caribe
dacite
Danite
dative
facile
famine
gamine
habile
halide
halite
Hamite
Janice
Janine
karite
labile
larine
malice
marine
Maxine
maxixe
Nadine
nanite
narine
native
patine
pavise
Racine
ranine
rapine
ratine
ratiné
ratite
ravine
Sabine
saline
samite
sasine
satire
sative
savine
tajine
tamine
tamise
vagile
vahine
valine
valise
wahine
walise
tariff
baaing
baking
basing
bating
caging
caking
caning
caring
casing
caving
cawing
Daqing
daring
dating
Ealing
earing
eating
facing
fading
gaming
gaping
gating
having
haying
hazing
japing
jawing
lacing
lading
lasing
lawing
laying
making
maying
naming
paging
paling
paring
paving
paying
racing
raging
raking
raping
raring
rating
raving
rawing
saring
saving
sawing
saying
taking
taming
taring
tawing
taxing
wading
waking
waning
waving
waxing
banish
barish
caliph
Danish
dawish
eadish
famish
garish
Hadith
Hamish
harish
jadish
lakish
lamish
Lapith
latish
lavish
marish
oafish
palish
papish
pariah
parish
radish
rakish
ravish
rawish
sakieh
Salish
vanish
Cabiri
Kafiri
panini
ragini
samiti
tahini
Tahiti
wakiki
wapiti
Danisk
panick
panisk
Daniel
facial
garial
gavial
labial
narial
parial
racial
radial
samiel
Babism
barium
favism
kalium
labium
Lariam®
laxism
magism
malism
Maoism
nanism
Nazism
papism
racism
radium
Ramism
sadism
Sapium
Taoism
Valium®
✧**banian**
camion
cation
Dalian
Damian
Damien
Darién
Fabian
fanion
gabion
Janian
kalian
kation
Latian
magian
Malian
malign
Marian
Marion
nasion
nation
Parian
radian
ration
Sabian
Salian
Samian
talion
Walian
wanion
Zabian
calico
caligo
casino
katipo
✧ladino
Latino
manito
matico
magilp
cahier
caviar
cavier
matier
Napier
pavior
racier
rapier
varier
Xavier
basics
capias
caries
danios
Darius
facies
ladies
ladies'
✧matins
patios
rabies
radios
radius
rapids
ratios
sanies
taxies
Babist
galiot
lariat
laxist
malist
Maoist
Marist
papist
racist
Ramist
rapist
sadist
Samiot
tanist
Taoist
tapist
jabiru
cagily
cavity
easily
family
gasify
hazily
lacily
ladify
laxity
lazily
matily
mazily
Nazify
pacify
parity
racily
ramify
rarity
ratify
salify
sanify
sanity
satiny
vanity
warily
wavily
waxily
masjid
sanjak
Tadjik
Banjul
gaijin
garjan
Taejon
gas jar
hanjar
jamjar
banjos
kanjis
matjes
fan-jet
gas jet
ramjet
banjax
Sanjay
backra
markka
sabkha
Saskia
✧tankia
backed
hawked
marked
masked
narked
racked
ranked
tacked
tanked
vacked
bakkie
cackle
darkle
fankle
hackee
hackle
hankie
hawkie
mackle
palkee
parkee
parkie
rankle
tackle
talkie
wankle
✧yankee
yankie
Makkah
haikai
kaikai
Naskhi
saikei
jackal
Balkan
barkan
barken
calkin
catkin
daikon
darken
gaskin
Haakon
harken
jack in
Larkin
malkin
mawkin
nankin
napkin
parkin
Rankin
talk-in
walk-in
walk-on
back up
back-up
backup
bank up
jack up
jack-up
mark up
mark-up
pack up
rack up
talk up
tank up
walk-up
backer
balker
banker
barker
calker
canker
cauker
cawker
dacker
daiker
gawker
hacker
hanker
hawker
janker
lacker
laiker
larker
marker
masker
packer
parker
racker
ranker
sacker
tacker
talker
tanker
tasker
wacker
✧walker
wauker
yacker
yakker
yanker
Barkis
daikos
faikes
haikus
maikos
sakkos
sankos
taikos
tankas
wackos
backet
banket
basket
casket
gasket
hawkit
jacket
kark it
lasket
market
nacket
nark it!
packet
racket
Rajkat
tacket
walk it
darkey
darkly
hackly
hawkey
jacksy
lackey
lankly
parkly
rankly
tab key
dahlia
halloa
Kahlúa®
paella
pallia
lablab
Gaelic
✧gallic
garlic
ballad
balled
callid
fabled
failed
gabled
macled
maelid
mailed
marled
nailed
palled
pallid
pat-lid
sailed
sallad
tabled
tailed
walled
bailee
bailie
caille
Carlie
faille
Lallie
mallee
pallae
rallye
sallee
saulge
saulie
taille
tailye
✧wallie
bablah
nallah
pallah
wallah
bailli
mallei
maulvi
fallal
hallal
sallal
Baalim
Caelum
Callum
Harlem
mallam
vallum
ballan
ballon
callan
call in
call on
caplin
Caslon
Fablon®
fail in
fallen
fall in
fall-in
gallon
hallan
kaolin
lallan
mail-in
marlin
Marlon
maslin
raglan
ratlin
Callao
Gallio
halloo
bail up
ball up
ballup
callop
call up
call-up
cat-lap
dallop
earlap
gallop
haul up
nail up
oar-lap
wallop
wall up
bailer
bailor
batler
bawler
caller
fabler
faller
gaoler
hailer
hauler
jailer
jailor
Mahler
✧mailer
nailer
pallor
parlor
railer
sailer
sailor
samlor
tailor
tatler
vallar
wailer
waller
Callas
callus
caules
caulis
Dallas
dalles
Eagles
gallus
hallos
Laclos
✧majlis
matlos
Nablus
Naples
Pallas
Rallus
sables
tables
ballat
ballet
ballot
batlet
cablet
callet
camlet
caplet
carlot
eaglet
gablet
gallet
gaslit
haglet
✧hamlet
harlot
haslet
haulst
mallet
pallet
raylet

Words marked ✧ can also be spelled with one or more capital letters

sallet
samlet
tablet
tallat
tallet
tallot
taslet
varlet
wallet
maglev
ballow
callow
Carlow
fallow
gallow
hallow
Harlow
lay low
mallow
matlow
sallow
tallow
wallow
hallux
bailey
ballsy
barley
bawley
call by
Canley
faulty
galley
Harley®
Hayley
parlay
parley
railly
valley
vaulty
waylay
Y-alloy
kalmia
caimac
haemic
karmic
Tarmac®
tarmac
bammed
calmed
dammed
jammed
Mahmud
maimed
palmed
rammed
✧talmud
warmed
lammie
mammae
mammee
Palmae
palmie
Tammie
lad mag
malmag
warmth
Kalmyk
Carmel
haemal
hammal
harmel
mahmal
mammal
wadmal
wadmol
Dammam
hammam
badman
bagman
barman
✧batman
cabman
caiman
carman
Carmen
cayman
daemon
daimen
daimon
farm-in
gagman
gammon
gasman
haemin
harman
harmin
Jarman
law-man
lawman
layman
madman
✧mammon
Paxman
ragman
salmon
taxman
✧vatman
warman
Yasmin
daimio
warm up
warm-up
bammer
dammar
dammer
farmer
gammer
hammer
jammer
lammer
mammer
palmar
palmer
rammer
tammar
warmer
yammer
Cadmus
lacmus
Lammas
magmas
Patmos
salmis
wammus
dammit
mammet
marmot
maumet
mawmet
haymow
Mad Max
calmly
warmly
Tammuz
Jamnia
kainga
Kaunda
maunna
Narnia
pa'anga
taenia
taonga
Zainab
Zaynab
tannic
zarnec
banned
canned
damned
darned
hained
lawned
maenad
manned
pained
panned
tanned
vanned
cannae
faunae
jaunce
jaunse
✧launce
paunce
pawnce
✧pawnee
raunge
sannie
sarnie
vaunce
pad-nag
gaunch
hainch
Hannah
haunch
Jabneh
launch
paunch
raunch
tannah
fains I
cannel
carnal
darnel
fannel
faunal
tarnal
wannel
magnum
painim
paynim
bainin
cannon
magnon
rain in
Saanen
Tainan
tannin
bagnio
catnap
catnep
catnip
gain-up
sannup
banner
canner
darner
dauner
dawner
earner
Fafnir
fanner
fawner
gainer
garner
Gaynor
lanner
mainor
manner
pawner
tanner
vanner
Wagner
warner
yawner
Barnes
Cannes
faints
faunas
Faunus
Kaunas
magnes
Magnus
pannus
Saints
Tainos
Vannes
bag-net
Bannat
✧barnet
basnet
cannot
carnet
'gainst
gainst
gannet
garnet
magnet
oak-nut
walnut
larnax
Magnox®
magnox
✧**barney**
Cagney
carney
dainty
fainly
fainty
gainly
jaunty
larney
mainly
maundy
maungy
painty
sarney
✧sawney
Tannoy®
tannoy
tawney
vainly
vaunty
canola
Carola
dagoba
Dakota
Lakota
Latona
macoya
Masora
Nagoya
pagoda
pakora
Paloma
payola
samosa
sapota
Tacoma
Vanora
yaqona
haboob
dadoed
day-old
gadoid
ganoid
haloed
haloid
Harold
kayoed
laroid
Samoed
cajole
camote
✧capote
Carole
day one
favose
galore
hamose
Lahore
lanose
matoke
parole
pavone
radome
ramose
Salome
Salote
Savoie
vadose
vamose
day off
eat off
far-off
lay off
lay-off
pay off
pay-off
zap off
barong
Datong
kalong
sarong
galosh
caroli
maloti
satori
barock
Farouk
padouk
paiock
pajock
yapock
cagoul
gas oil
jarool
ja wohl
kagool
kagoul
waboom
baboon
batoon
cacoon
ca' down
Eamonn
gaboon
ganoin
gazoon
Haroun
lagoon
Mahoun
maroon
racoon
ratoon
sagoin
saloon
Samoan
Barolo
manoao
palolo
saloop
favour
✧labour
savour
tabour
valour
vapour
cabobs
dadoes
famous
Faroes
favous
haloes
hamous
kabobs
kaross
kayoes
majors
patois
ramous
taboos
tarots
Yahoos
cahoot
cavort
dacoit
dakoit
day out
eat out
fan out
far-out
galoot
Lamont
lam out
lavolt
lay out
layout
mahout
map out
mazout
pan out
pay out
pay-out
rag out
rag-out
ragout
way-out
barony
✧calory
canopy
jalopy
paeony
parody
savory
saxony
yarpha
calpac
capped
happed
lampad
lapped
mapped
napped
rapped
sapped
tapped
wapped
warped
cample
dapple
lappie
magpie
rappee
salpae
sample
sapple
taupie
tawpie
wampee
waspie
yappie
hatpeg
T'aipei
kalpak
carpal
carpel
lappel
palpal
rappel
wampum
dampen
happen
hatpin
jampan
map-pin
parpen
rappen
sampan
sanpan
sappan
taipan
tampon
tarpan
tarpon
yaupon
Sappho
camp up
ramp up
camper
capper
carper
Caspar
damper
dapper
gapper
gasper
gauper
gawper
hamper
harper
Jaipur
jasper
Kanpur
Kaspar
lapper
mapper
Nagpur
napper
pamper
pauper
Raipur
ramper
rapper
rasper
✧sapper
tamper
tapper
vamper
wapper
warper
yapper
yawper
zapper
✧**campos**
campus
carpus
gaupus
gawpus
jaspis
kalpis
lampas
mawpus
palpus
pampas
pappus
salpas
wampus
bampot
carpet
jampot
lappet
Rajput
rat-pit
sawpit
tan pit
tappet
tappit
tar pit
Karpov
pawpaw
camply
damply
barque
✧basque
caique
caïque
calque
casque
haique
Jacque
lasque
manqué
marque
masque
sacque
saique
yanqui
Banquo
garrya
latria
✧varroa
Zagreb
capric
fabric
matric
tanrec
tauric
barred
caprid
darred
garred
haired
hatred
jarred
labrid
Madrid
manred
marred
nacred
paired
ramrod
sacred
tarred
warred
waured
wax-red
bajree
cabrie
Carrie
faerie
Laurie
Lawrie
tagrag
jarrah
Matrah
barrel
carrel
labral
✧laurel
parral
parrel
patrol
sacral
saurel
Bairam
bay rum
labrum
marram
marrum
sacrum
vagrom
barren
Dacron®
Darren
farren
garran
garron
hadron
latron
Lauren
macron
marron
matron
napron
natron
patron
rat run
warran

warren
barrio
cabrio
hairdo
✧karroo
larrup
satrap
Cairns
Capris
Harris
Labrus
labrys
Laurus
macros
madras
Maoris
nairas
narras
tarras
Taurus
walrus
barrat
barret
cabrit
carrat
carrot
✧garret
garrot
hairst
labret
parrot
tabret
waurst
barrow
farrow
harrow
Jarrow
marrow
narrow
tarrow
yarrow
matrix
fairly
Man Ray
warray
warrey
Tabriz
✧**cassia**
fatsia
Marsha
✧nausea
tarsia
Vaisya
yaksha
Barsac
parsec
capsid
gassed
halsed
Hassid
lapsed
passed
Bassae
Cassie
dassie
hassle
laesie
laisse
✧lassie
Maisie
Parsee
passée
says he
✧tassie
warsle
massif
taisch
sansei
causal
damsel
eassel
eassil
Faisal
Faysal
hansel
haysel
Kassel
pausal
ransel
tahsil
tarsal
tarsel
tassel
varsal
vassal
balsam
hansom
passim
ransom
Carson
causen
damson
Datsun®
Hassan
Jansen
kamsin
Lawson
parson
pass on
raisin
ramson
Samson
Samsun
sarsen
Tamsin
camsho
Cassio
catsup
pass up
✧**caesar**
causer
falser
gasser
halser
hassar
hawser
✧kaiser
mahsir
Mauser
Nasser
parser
passer
pauser
raiser
bassos
cassis
fatsos
Kansas
lapsus
lassos
masses
passus
Ramses
✧tarsus
basset
saw set
tasset
wadset
Nassau
samshu
padsaw
Warsaw
carsey
causey
gansey
jansky
karsey
marshy
naysay
pass by
Bastia
caltha
Eartha
kantha
maltha
mantra
✧mantua
Martha
Raetia
sastra
✧tantra
yautia
✧**baltic**
haptic
lastic
lactic
mantic
mastic
nastic
nautic
tactic
Zantac®
batted
canted
casted
fantad
fantod
fatted
hatted
malted
mantid
masted
matted
parted
patted
raited
ratted
salted
tasted
vatted
wafted
want ad
wanted
warted
wasted
bastle
battle
battue
cantle
castle
cattle
daftie
dartle
dartre
dautie
dawtie
Fantee
hantle
Hattie
jantee
mantle
✧mattie
pattée
Pattie
pattle
✧rattle
saithe
Sartre
tattie
tattle
tawtie
wattle
Xanthe
ragtag
tautog
zaftig
nautch
canthi
Mai Tai
Bartók
baetyl
battel
Cantal
cartel
cautel
dactyl
hartal
mantel
martel
pastel
pastil
santal
Tactel®
wastel
bantam
factum
fantom
lactam
pactum
partim
santim
tam-tam
barton
batten
caftan
canton
captan
carton
cast on
Caxton
dalton
✧danton
Dayton
fan-tan
fasten
fatten
Halton
hapten
harten
hasten
kaftan
kanten
latten
marten
✧martin
Martyn
panton
pantun
partan
parton
patten
rattan
ratten
ratton
santon
Tartan®
tartan
tauten
wait on
wait-on
want in
wanton
Castro
tattoo
cast up
gas tap
laptop
ragtop
tart up
wait up
want up
baiter
banter
barter
baster
batter
baxter
cantar
canter
cantor
captor
✧carter
caster
✧castor
cauter
daftar
darter
✧easter
factor
faitor
falter
faster
fatter
fautor
gaiter
✧garter
gas-tar
gaster
halter
hatter
kantar
karter
laster
latter
martyr
✧master
matter
natter
palter
panter
parter
paster
pastor
patter
✧rafter
ranter
raptor
raster
ratter
saeter
salter
santir
santur
sartor
✧tartar
taster
tatter
vatter
wafter
waiter
Walter
wanter
waster
yatter
bastos
cactus
cantos
cantus
factis
mantes
mantis
mantos
Nantes
pantos
pastis
saltos
saltus
Santos
sautés
wastes
Bastet
past it
rat-tat
tautit
Baotou
Lao-tzu
tattow
daftly
earthy
fast by
fastly
gantry
lastly
paltry
pantry
partly
pastry
raptly
rattly
saltly
tartly
tautly
vastly
wastry
bacula
canula
Cayuga
datura
facula
✧garuda
Kaluga
lacuna
Laputa
macula
manuka
masula
mazuma
natura
papula
radula
ranula
tabula
taluka
valuta
Varuna
yakuza
caduac
salued
tabued
valued
Canute
cayuse
lagune
Mabuse
macule
manure
mature
nasute
✧nature
papule
parure
rasure
razure
salute
Ranulf
Baluch
Baruch
✧galuth
Batumi
hamuli
kabuki
kaluki
lazuli
ramuli
saluki
Watusi
Canuck
Kanuck
✧**casual**
manual
Raquel
Samuel
vacuum
Eamunn
Paduan
Papuan
saguin
Saturn
taguan
baguio
basuco
Basuto
Caruso
lanugo
Majuro
Maputo
gazump
faquir
Jaguar®
jaguar
valuer
Jaques
✧maquis
values
kaputt
yaourt
Basutu
maguey
raguly
Latvia
salvia
carved
valved
varved
garvie
jarvie
larvae
halvah
Jahveh
Yahveh
Narvik
carvel
larval
marvel
valval
varvel
Calvin
carven
Marvin
mauvin
calver
ca' over
carver
halver
marver
salver
salvor
taiver
valvar
waiver
calves
canvas
cauves
halves
Jarvis
naeves
naevus
parvis
✧salvos
tan vat
Harvey
jarvey
savvey
fatwa'd
bagwig
earwig
talweg
fatwah
wah-wah
Yahweh
qawwal
Darwen
Darwin
Taiwan
Daewoo®
earwax
paxwax
Galway
calxes
baryta
satyra
Dafydd
sayyid
haüyne
Kabyle
papyri
✧**banyan**
baryon
canyon
karyon
lawyer
✧magyar
sawyer
Satyrs
Pamyat
raiyat
gay-you
larynx
ladyfy
razzia
Balzac
dazzle
razzle
Danzig
hamzah
matzah
matzoh
banzai
ranzel
hazzan
kaizen
Tarzan
jazz up
jazzer
mahzor
mamzer
panzer
patzer
baizas
matzas
matzos
Taizés
tazzas
matzot
aboard
abraid
ablate
ablaze
abrade
oblate
obtain
Abbado
abrazo
abdabs
ablaut
oblast
abbacy
Ibibio
obeche
abacus
ibices
abided
ibidem
Abadan
Ibadan
Ibadat
obtend
abrégé
abseil
abbess
abbeys
objets
obsess
abject
ablest
absent
object
obtect
obtest

obvert
yblent
ybrent
ubiety
oblige
B B King
abeigh
obeism
obiism
obsign
ablins
oboist
abelia
abolla
abulia
obelus
obolus
obi-man
Abomey
ubuntu
Abroma
absorb
abroad
'sblood
oblong
abloom
abvolt
ubique
aborne
sbirri
aboral
Oberon
sbirro
iberis
aburst
uberty
abased
Ubasti
W boson
Z boson
abuser
ibises
ebitda
abated
obital
abator
abitur
obiter
abatis
abattu
abound
absurd
obtund
ybound
abduce
abjure
obdure
objure
obtuse
ablush
abouts
abduct
abrupt
ibexes
obeyer
scramb
PC card
achage
✧ice age
ice axe
octane
octave
sclate
sclave
scrape
scraye
sclaff
ack-ack
acrawl
scrawl
scrawm
octavo
éclair
Octans
actant
octant
sceatt
X-craft
occamy
C-cubed
ice bag
icebox
scabby
acacia
icicle
icecap
acedia
acidic
acidly
eczema
schema
sclera
accend
screed
accede
Achebe
achene
ocreae
scheme
sclere
screak
schelm
scream
screen
access
ackers
uckers
accent
accept
octett
scient
yclept
ochery
screwy
Ecofin
act for
Scogan
scried
accite
acmite
active
scribe
scrike
scrine
scrive
scliff
aching
acting
I Ching
scaith
tchick
Actium
echium
schism
action
schizo
scrimp
ickier
schist
script
acuity
acajou
achkan
scilla
scolia
Scylla
scaled
scalae
sculle
ocelli
schlep
ocular
scalar
scaler
oculus
✧scales
sculls
ocelot
sculpt
scolex
accloy
scally
schmoe
scampi
scamel
acumen
ice man
ecomap
scummy
iconic
scenic
sconce
scunge
acanth
acinus
econut
acknew
acknow
scanty
scungy
echoic
accord
echoed
ecbole
eclose
ochone
scrobe
J-cloth®
scoosh
T-cloth
octopi
o'clock
accoil
school
schorl
scroll
scrowl
scroop
echoer
across
echoes
scrows
T-cross
Y-cross
accost
act out
ice out
schout
echoey
ectopy
scopae
scyphi
ice pan
scapes
scapus
✧scopas
Icaria
ochrea
scarpa
scoria
scarab
sciroc
acarid
scared
scarr'd
accrue
écarté
écurie
J-curve
scarce
scarre
scerne
scorse
scarph
scarth
scorch
octroi
ice run
scarer
scorer
acarus
Acorus
Icarus
scarfs
Scarus
scores
accrew
ochrey
scarey
scarry
scurfy
scurry
scurvy
O'Casey
ice tea
✧scotia
acetic
Scotic
scathe
scythe
scatch
✧scotch
scutch
schtik
acetal
acetyl
scutal
✧scutum
acater
scoter
acates
scatty
Scotty
accuse
acture
✧scouse
scruze
scruff
scouth
actual
schuln
scruto
scrump
octuor
schuls
schuss
scours
✧scrubs
acquit
occult
schuit
schuyt
scrunt
occupy
scaury
scowth
ectype
scryde
scryne
scryer
scazon
scuzzy
Eddaic
adland
adward
Edward
ID card
ideaed
adnate
adware
ideate
'sdeath
ad-mass
admass
edible
adnexa
adverb
addend
adread
adhere
advene
Edberg
addeem
Idaean
adieus
✧advent
advert
adieux
Eddery
adagio
Edwina
eddied
admire
advice
advise
sdaine
edging
eddish
Edrich
oddish
Adrian
sdeign
add-ins
addict
adrift
Idoist
edgily
oddity
odd-job
Adella
addled
✧idolum
✧idolon
odd lot
Adamic
odd-man
Adonia
Gdynia
AD and C
Adonic
Edenic
Odense
Adonai
Gdansk
Adonis
adsorb
Ed Koch
addoom
adjoin
adnoun
add-ons
adoors
eddoes
odeons
odious
adroit
idiocy
adipic
adored
adorer
Odessa
Edison
odds-on
Odette
adytum
editor
Edmund
adduce
adjure
adduct
adjust
befana
gelada
Gemara
Kerala
medaka
Megara
Nevada
petara
Renata
retama
terata
zenana
bedaub
decarb
aefald
belaud
demand
Gerald
Gerard
herald
petard
regard
relaid
remand
repaid
repand
retard
reward
sex aid
Weland
wesand
weyard
wezand
aerate
became
bedaze
behave
bejade
belace
belate
bename
berate
betake
beware
cerate
cetane
debase
debate
decade
decane
decare
deface
defame
dégagé
delate
derate
female
Hecabe
Hecate
hexane
legate
let-a-be
menace
menage
ménage
metage
metate
negate
✧new age
✧new-age
pedate
pelage
pesade
rebate
redate
reface
regale
✧relate
remade
remake
rename
resale
retake
sea ape
sebate
sedate
✧senate
serape
sesame
sewage
tenace
velate
behalf
decaff
Hegang
Penang
rehang
serang
bedash
detach
Pesach
rehash
rewash
seraph
teraph
decani
Dewali
dewani
gelati
Nepali
debark
demark
Newark
reback
re-mark
remark
repack
becall
befall
bemaul
bewail
derail
detail
devall
jezail
mesail
mezail
recall
rerail
retail
serail
tenail
becalm
cedarn
demain
detain
regain
remain
retain
gelato
legato
melano
pedalo
rebato
decamp
revamp
bel air
repair
sea air
dedans
kebabs
Le Mans
lemans
megass
metals
repass
bejant
bezant
decant
defast
depart
desalt
hexact
✧levant
nefast
pedant
pesant
pezant
recant
recast
redact
red ant
repast
secant
sejant
tenant
tewart
zelant
déjà vu
belamy
denary
fegary
legacy
petary
senary
telary
tetany
bezazz
cembra
jerboa
Serbia
wet bob
lesbic
terbic
herbed
nebbed
redbud
seabed
tebbad
verbid
webbed
Debbie
feeble
Herbie
kebbie
leg bye
newbie
pebble
remble
Seabee
semble
bedbug
tea bag
teabag
lebbek
nebbuk
reebok
gerbil
herbal
jerbil
verbal
Reuben
sea bun
Berber
herbar
member
wet bar
Lesbos
hen-bit
sea bat
Tebbit
yes-but
dew-bow
✧bembex
✧bembix
pegbox
red box
tee box

feebly
pebbly
sea boy
betcha
sea cob
deuced
fenced
peacod
recced
✧deccie
fescue
rescue
seiche
cercal
mescal
pencel
pencil
Tencel®
tercel
webcam
beacon
deacon
leucin
percen
re-echo
tercio
Velcro®
Mencap
redcap
sea cap
teacup
de-icer
fencer
mercer
Redcar
cercus
recces
reccos
seccos
telcos
hep-cat
mercat
Rex cat
sea cat
tercet
sea cow
beachy
descry
leachy
peachy
reechy
tetchy
vetchy
serdab
geodic
herdic
Wendic
beaded
bedded
bended
gelded
headed
leaded
reeded
seeded
sended
tedded
tended
wedded
weeded
wended

beadle
beedie
bendee
cendré
Deidre
heddle
meddle
Neddie
need-be
needle
peddle
perdie
perdue
reddle
✧teddie
tendre
vendee
vendue
red dog
red-dog
sea dog
Jeddah
keddah
Sendai
zendik
feodal
feudal
Kendal
sendal
beldam
seldom
deaden
dead on
dead-on
Devdan
head-on
herden
leaden
lead in
lead-in
lead on
ledden
Leiden
Leyden
read in
read-in
redden
reeden
send in
send on
tendon
verdin
feed up
head up
lead up
lead-up
read up
redd up
send up
send-up
bedder
bender
deader
deodar
feeder
fender
gelder
gender
header
herder
leader

lender
melder
mender
needer
pedder
reader
redder
reeder
render
seeder
sender
tedder
tender
Veadar
vender
vendor
wedder
weeder
welder
weldor
vendis
geddit
re-edit
verdet
verdit
meadow
deadly
Hendry
heyday
lewdly
needly
pet-day
verdoy
genera
✧geneva
Hedera
Helena
meseta
nepeta
never a
oedema
pereia
peseta
pesewa
✧reseda
réséda
semeia
Seneca
senega
Serena
telega
terefa
Teresa
veleta
zereba
reverb
befeld
behead
beheld
defend
depend
deseed
jereed
legend
✧nereid
remead
remeid
reread
seméed
tele-ad
bemete

delete
hexene
kebele
ketene
lexeme
re-cede
recede
red-eye
remede
renege
retene
✧revere
secede
Selene
Semele
sememe
✧serene
severe
temene
terete
vegete
venewe
hereof
sea egg
Benesh
secesh
Tebeth
seseli
Yemeni
bedeck
nebeck
rebeck
zebeck
bedell
befell
cereal
merell
newell
redeal
reheel
✧repeal
reseal
resell
retell
reveal
sea eel
beseem
beteem
redeem
Te Deum
telesm
Aegean
bemean
Berean
beseen
decern
demean
devein
hele in
herein
hereon
Nemean
secern
serein
Verein
✧wedeln
Herero
hereto
hetero
teredo
beweep

meneer
meteor
rehear
rêveur
sea ear
veneer
Aeneas
cereus
heders
Jewess
Kegels
merels
Nereus
Peleus
recess
revels
revers
sevens
behest
bepelt
bereft
bewept
cement
deceit
decent
defeat
defect
deject
dement
desert
detect
detent
detest
devest
Gelert
gerent
hereat
merest
✧recent
recept
refect
regent
regest
reheat
reject
relent
repeat
repent
reseat
resect
resent
revert
revest
sedent
select
weren't
détenu
réseau
teledu
Telegu
celery
hereby
heresy
Jeremy
merely
remedy
revery
severy
tepefy
venery
deific

leafed
reffed
sexfid
web-fed
neaffe
Newfie
sea fog
keffel
netful
penful
pepful
deafen
perfin
sea fan
beef up
heifer
reefer
sea fir
telfer
perfet
see fit
Ceefax®
red fox
sea fox
bee fly
belfry
deafly
deffly
let fly
medfly
perfay
wet-fly
zeugma
Belgic
´begged
ledged
legged
menged
pegged
sea god
sedged
wedged
beagle
dengue
feague
gee-gee
league
meagre
reggae
Reggie
teagle
Teague
veggie
wedgie
beegah
length
beigel
Bengal
tergal
red gum
tergum
✧bergen
Keegan
pen-gun
Reagan
reagin
Reggio
beggar
hedger
kedger
ledger

legger
leiger
lenger
Megger®
merger
seggar
venger
verger
Fergus
tenges
Verges
height
keight
weight
Bengpu
Tengku
geegaw
gewgaw
peshwa
tephra
Meshed
method
lechwe
lethee
rechie
techie
tee-hee
seahog
bethel
lethal
methyl
seghol
derham
Ken Hom
Newham
✧pelham
peahen
sephen
Jethro
techno
gee hup
rechip
reship
aether
Ben-Hur
hether
kephir
lecher
menhir
nether
pether
✧senhor
tether
wether
✧zephyr
Tethys
red hat
red-hot
tewhit
heehaw
nephew
Aegina
Celina
De Sica
hegira
hejira
hemina
✧jemima
✧medina
Nerita
Peziza

✧regina
retina
Selina
vesica
zeriba
celiac
heliac
begild
begird
behind
belied
defied
denied
Hesiod
levied
period
rebind
relied
remind
renied
revied
rewind
aedile
bedide
belike
belive
Belize
bemire
beside
betide
betime
bêtise
cerise
cerite
debile
decide
decile
décime
de fide
defile
define
delice
demise
Denise
deride
derive
desine
desire
device
devise
Felice
feline
ferine
✧levite
mediae
Medise
Medize
mesite
nerine
nerite
pelite
penile
petite
rebite
Recife
recipe
recite
rediae
refine
regime
régime

regive
rehire
relide
reline
relive
remise
repine
reside
resile
re-site
retile
retime
retire
revile
revise
revive
rewire
Rexine®
sea ice
sedile
Semite
senile
serine
Venice
venire
venite
vérité
belief
relief
besing
feeing
geeing
hewing
hexing
Peking
seeing
sewing
teaing
teeing
vexing
besigh
ceriph
delish
fetich
fetish
Jewish
nebish
newish
perish
relish
seriph
zenith
✧gemini
periti
seniti
Yezidi
medick
melick
aerial
Belial
denial
fecial
ferial
fetial
genial
medial
menial
Meriel
mesial
penial
redial

refill
retial
serial
telial
venial
xenial
aecium
cerium
cesium
helium
Medism
medium
merism
Nerium
sepium
sexism
tedium
telium
Vedism
verism
xenium
benign
Delian
design
Fenian
Gefion
legion
lesion
✧median
mesian
region
re-sign
resign
De Niro
medico
merino
Mexico
pepino
megilp
belier
defier
denier
métier
relier
senior
verier
bekiss
cecils
Delius
demies
demiss
denims
✧genius
Helios
medius
merils
merits
nelies
regius
relics
remiss
series
begift
begirt
delict
demist
depict
desist
dewitt
heriot
legist
Nesiot
oecist
relict
remint
resist
sexist
Vedist
verist
Zenist
re-view
review
meninx
bepity
Cecily
cecity
dewily
eerily
ferity
geminy
lenify
lenity
levity
sexily
verify
verily
✧verity
feijoa
Benjie
Seljuk
deejay
vee-jay
veejay
beaked
decked
necked
peaked
recked
deckle
heckle
keckle
reekie
reskue
seckle
selkie
Neskhi
seckel
teckel
beckon
jerkin
meeken
merkin
perkin
reckan
reckon
weaken
weak in
welkin
perk up
beaker
Becker
decker
jerker
keeker
leaker
lekker
pecker
✧seeker
Wesker
deckos
dekkos
geckos
✧becket
perk it
reskew
bed-key
Del key
feckly
kecksy
meekly
weakly
weekly
realia
Aeolic
Belloc
belled
ceiled
celled
gelled
heeled
keeled
new lad
peeled
sealed
veiled
wealk'd
cellae
felloe
jeelie
keelie
Leslie
mealie
✧nellie
rellie
wellie
jet lag
peg leg
redleg
reflag
verlig
Beulah
fellah
health
keblah
sealch
sealgh
wealth
bedlam
beflum
peplum
replum
vellum
✧berlin
Ceylon
Declan
feel in
heel in
Hellen
leglan
leglen
leglin
merlin
merlon
replan
sell in
sell-in
sell on
Teflon®
tellen
tellin
vellon
well in
dewlap
feel up
sell up
well up
cellar
dealer
de-blur
feeler
feller
healer
heeler
heller
keeler
Kevlar®
mealer
medlar
pedlar
peeler
reeler
sealer
seller
tellar
teller
vealer
Aeolus
cellos
Hellas
hellos
✧mejlis
peplos
peplus
reales
realos
✧tellus
leglet
Merlot
pellet
reflet
reglet
vellet
✧zealot
✧bellow
✧fellow
mellow
reflow
sea law
yellow
deflex
reflex
reflux
berley
Bexley
deploy
fealty
Healey
Henley
leally
lealty
Lesley
medley
mellay
o'erlay
re-ally
really
realty
replay
Wesley
Hermia
dermic
Fehmic
Vehmic
deemed
desmid
gemmed
helmed
hemmed
Hermod
red-mad
red mud
teamed
teemed
gemmae
hermae
meemie
sepmag
dermal
vermal
vermil
desman
fenman
gemman
gemmen
✧german
germen
germin
Henman
hetman
key man
leg-man
merman
met man
Newman
✧new man
penman
red man
✧seaman
sermon
tegmen
vermin
yeoman
yeomen
yes-man
team up
beamer
reamer
seamer
seemer
teamer
teemer
termer
termor
Weimar
dermis
Geomys
Hermes
Jeames
kermes
kermis
lemmas
Seamas
Seamus
Seumas
Termes
✧vermes
vermis
besmut
cermet
Dermot
Fermat
fewmet
Heimat
helmet
hermit
Mehmet
pelmet
permit
sea mat
semmit
sea maw
sea mew
Tex-Mex
seemly
termly
Deanna
hernia
Leonia
neb-neb
fennec
neanic
kenned
leaned
Leonid
penned
Pernod®
Seanad
veined
beanie
Bernie
Deanne
heinie
Jeanie
Jennie
Kennie
Leanne
Lennie
Leonie
meanie
meinie
peenge
pennae
séance
Teenie
weenie
Seonag
beenah
mehndi
fennel
gennel
kennel
kernel
pennal
regnal
ternal
vennel
vernal
weanel
hennin
lean on
Lennon
Memnon
peen in
pennon
rein in
rennin
Vernon
lean-to
rein up
deaner
henner
keener
kenner
penner
seiner
tenner
weaner
beanos
Dennis
feints
Keynes
Lemnos
Meknès
Rennes
segnos
Temnes
tennis
tennos
bennet
ben-nut
dennet
gennet
jennet
kennet
Nernst
peanut
peinct
rennet
sennet
sennit
✧telnet
begnaw
dernly
Heaney
keenly
leanly
meanly
meiney
teensy
teenty
✧fedora
femora
hebona
Pecora
pelota
redowa
remora
✧señora
serosa
Verona
xeroma
desorb
resorb
heroic
behold
✧beyond
devoid
keloid
new-old
peloid
record
reload
remoud
reword
second
zeroed
aerobe
become
before
begone
behote
behove
Belone
belove
cenote
decode
decoke
delope
démodé
demote
denote
depone
depose
dévoré
devote
dévote
Eeyore
genome
hexose
Jerome
ketone
ketose
merome
metope
perone
peyote
rebore
recode
redone
remote
remove
repone
repose
resole
revoke
rezone
setose
veloce
venose
beg off
behoof
get off
let off
let-off
re-roof
see off
set off
set-off
tee off
tee-off
belong
debosh
zeroth
neroli
perogi
bemock
betook
retook
rework
befool
befoul
behowl
bemoil
ben-oil
betoil
defoul
reboil
recoil
retool
sea owl
befoam
deform
deworm
megohm
re-form
reform
bemoan
besoin
ceroon
dehorn
heroin
heroon
reborn
recoin
rejoin
✧renown
seroon
zero in
de novo
rebozo
zeloso
recoup
bezoar
detour
devoir
devour
memoir
Renoir
retour
tenour
velour
betoss
cerous
deboss
heroes
kebobs
Merops
Pelops
serous
venous
vetoes
bed out
Benoît
besort
decoct
dégoût
dehort
deport
detort
devout
get out
get-out
let out
let-out
Mel Ott
peg out
reboot
red out
refoot
report
repost
resort
retort
revolt
see out
set out
set-out
veg out
wet out
betony
felony
gelosy
gemony
lemony
melody
memory
pelory
leipoa
besped

Words marked ✧ can also be spelled with one or more capital letters

heaped
helped
keypad
leaped
lepped
neaped
peapod
repped
deepie
kelpie
kemple
pee-pee
people
sea pie
semple
sempre
teepee
✧temple
weepie
sea-pig
tempeh
Deepak
keypal
peepul
pen pal
bedpan
deepen
hempen
hen-pen
keep in
keep on
reopen
sea pen
tenpin
weapon
keep up
beeper
helper
Hesper
keeper
✧kelper
kemper
Keuper
leaper
peeper
pepper
reaper
semper
temper
✧vesper
weeper
yelper
delphs
herpes
tempos
bespat
bespit
bespot
despot
keppit
set pot
sexpot
teapot
deeply
teapoy
jerque
✧**kerria**
Cedric
ferric
metric
tenrec
Aelred
bedrid
betrod
feared
geared
get rid
Hebrid
meered
metred
retrod
seared
see red
tetrad
beurre
beurré
dearie
dear me
decree
degree
féerie
George
Gerrie
hearie
hearse
Leerie
✧pearce
peerie
retree
reurge
searce
serrae
terrae
defrag
lea-rig
red rag
dearth
hearth
search
bedral
ferrel
neural
petrel
petrol
retral
tetryl
verrel
betrim
megrim
Red Rum
retrim
feerin
Hebron
hen run
Herren
keiren
keirin
neuron
perron
serran
Tehran
Terran
wear on
Nearco
weirdo
bear up
bedrop
beer-up
de trop
gear up
let rip
rear up
rewrap
tear up
bearer
hearer
jeerer
nearer
rearer
tearer
✧terror
wearer
cerris
debris
débris
degras
derris
des res
✧hearts
henrys
✧métros
nebris
pearls
repros
retros
serras
Sèvres
terras
Weirds
Beirut
berret
ferret
Heorot
learnt
Meerut
pearst
red rot
regret
searat
secret
Seurat
terret
territ
wet rot
Henry V
decrew
Hebrew
redraw
bear by
betray
bewray
dearly
defray
Delroy
Georgy
hearsy
hearty
near by
nearby
nearly
pearly
rearly
verrey
yearly
geisha
Red Sea
felsic
Persic
hersed
jessed
new-sad
seised
sensed
temsed
versed
Bessie
heaste
✧jessie
keksye
lessee
measle
Nessie
pensée
persue
mensch
jet ski
jet-ski
meishi
sensei
deasil
mensal
new sol
pensel
pensil
teasel
tehsil
versal
vessel
weasel
jetsam
jetsom
pensum
semsem
sensum
Besson
geason
jetson
kelson
lessen
lesson
Mersin
messan
mess in
✧nelson
peason
pepsin
person
reason
season
seisin
telson
tenson
Velsen
ven'son
versin
fess up
mess up
mess-up
censer
censor
cesser
geyser
✧keasar
leaser
lesser
lessor
Mensur
sensor
teaser
tensor
verser
census
lenses
menses
Messrs
mewses
Nessus
senses
sepses
sepsis
versos
versus
Wessis
yesses
bedsit
eel-set
pet-sit
tea set
verset
leasow
seesaw
Wessex
feisty
✧jersey
kersey
measly
reasty
reesty
yeasty
✧**bertha**
centra
Hestia
✧kentia
tertia
Celtic
gestic
hectic
lentic
Lettic
pectic
peptic
septic
belted
bestad
bested
bestud
betted
debted
heated
heptad
jetted
letted
melted
netted
pentad
petted
retted
seated
teated
tented
vented
vested
vetted
wetted
✧**beetle**
berthe
Bertie
centre
debtee
fettle
feutre
gentle
Gertie
jestee
keltie
kettle
leetle
leftie
Lettie
lettre
meathe
mentee
mestee
mettle
nestle
Nettie
nettle
pestle
pettle
seethe
settee
settle
tee-tee
teethe
tentie
testae
testee
ventre
vertue
Westie
der Tag
centai
cestui
cental
dental
dentel
dentil
festal
lentil
meatal
mental
pentyl
rectal
rental
septal
ventil
✧vestal
centum
mentum
rectum
restem
septum
tectum
beaten
dentin
deuton
jetton
lectin
✧lenten
leptin
lepton
melton
Merton
neaten
nekton
newton
pecten
pectin
seiten
seston
sextan
sexton
teston
Teuton
weeten
✧**gentoo**
beat up
beat-up
belt up
meet up
peg-top
pent-up
red-top
redtop
beater
belter
bestar
bestir
better
bettor
center
debtor
✧dexter
felter
fester
fetter
fewter
getter
heater
✧hector
Hester
jester
kelter
lector
lentor
Lester
letter
melter
mentor
nectar
nester
Nestor
neuter
pelter
pester
petter
pewter
rector
reiter
renter
rester
seater
sector
setter
teeter
tenter
tester
tetter
texter
vector
venter
welter
✧wester
wetter
yester
zester
centas
centos
certes
cestos
cestus
gentes
lentos
meatus
mentos
rectos
rectus
rentes
set-to's
set-tos
testes
testis
vestas
beat it
dectet
septet
sestet
sextet
bestow
dentex
meat-ax
Pentax®
Semtex®
tettix
vertex
Beatty
centry
deathy
deftly
featly
gently
gentry
heathy
meetly
neatly
nettly
nextly
peltry
pertly
sentry
vestry
beluga
Betula
cedula
cesura
fecula
✧ferula
Hecuba
✧medusa
mezuza
nebula
Neruda
Petula
regula
remuda
tegula
veduta
benumb
defus'd
fecund
gerund
Pequod
re-fund
refund
retund
secund
segued
aemule
Beaune
bemuse
cerule
ceruse
cesure
deduce
defuse
defuze
de jure
deluce
delude
deluge
de luxe
demure
denude
depute
detune
ferule
heaume
jejune
legume
nebule
nebulé
peruke
peruse
rebuke
recule
recure
recuse
reduce
refuge
refuse
refute
relume
repure
repute
resume
résumé
retune
retuse
secure
seduce
setule
tenure
vedute
velure
venule
bepuff
rebuff
returf
bebung
bedung
besung
reguli
Senusi
tenuti
beduck
begunk
debunk
becurl
refuel
sequel
sexual
✧**beduin**
beguin
béguin
leguan
repugn
re-turn
return
sequin
tea urn
Regulo®
regulo
tenuto
repulp
femurs
lemurs
serums
tenues
tenuis

bedust
deduct
degust
Jesuit
penult
reduit
reluct
requit
result
Telugu
beauty
decury
deputy
nebuly
penury
rebury
Dervla
pelvic
cervid
fervid
heaved
leaved
nerved
peeved
reeved
revved
weaved
keavie
oeuvre
renvoi
devvel
nerval
serval
vervel
weevil
Yeovil
✧**heaven**
Hesvan
✧kelvin
leaven
Leuven
Melvin
Melvyn
Mervyn
verven
beaver
delver
Denver
fervor
heaver
leaver
nerver
peever
reaver
reiver
server
weaver
weever
beeves
delves
heaves
Jervis
leaves
nerves
pelves
pelvis
selvas
selves
servos
velvet
vervet

cervix
Hervey
lenvoy
peavey
renvoy
red-wud
deawie
peewee
wee-wee
meawes
peewit
keyway
leeway
Medway
seaway
deixis
Xerxes
bedyed
bedyde
desyne
menyie
re-type
Delyth
Deryck
Geryon
Kenyan
Nedyet
see you
fezzed
bezzle
heezie
teazle
Herzog
benzal
benzil
benzol
benzyl
Denzil
meazel
teazel
seizin
tenzon
weazen
beezer
geezer
seizer
fezzes
mezzos
afeard
afraid
aflame
efface
of late
affair
off-air
Offaly
offcut
off-day
afield
offend
effere
effete
afresh
affear
affeer
effeir
afters
affect
afreet
effect
eftest

✧**afghan**
Africa
affied
affine
office
offing
offish
Uffizi
affirm
iffier
effigy
off-job
off-key
afflux
efflux
if only
afford
of note
of yore
afloat
afront
effort
Eftpos
off pat
offput
affrap
of arms
affret
affray
effray
offset
Ofsted
effuse
Q-fever
afawld
affyde
Aglaia
iguana
agname
agnate
O grade
O-grade
agnail
ignaro
aghast
egg box
egg-box
eggcup
Agadic
Agadah
Agadir
agreed
agrégé
agleam
egress
ogress
Egbert
eggery
agogic
agnise
agnize
agrise
agrize
aguise
aguize
ignite
ageing
a-going
agoing
ogling
aguish

ogrish
ageism
egoism
Ugrian
ngaios
Ogmios
ageist
egoist
egoity
uglify
uglily
eggler
egally
agamic
ogamic
agamid
agenda
mganga
Uganda
agonic
egence
eggnog
Ngunis
agency
egency
age-old
ogdoad
ignore
ugsome
T-group
ignomy
agapae
agapes
Egeria
agaric
agorae
agoras
agorot
Ugarit
egesta
Agassi
Agatha
kgotla
Agatho
agutis
agouta
agouti
agouty
ogival
agryze
agazed
choana
ohmage
phrase
sheave
theave
the axe
thrave
wheare
thrang
sheath
thrash
chiack
chyack
shrank
thwack
thrall
chiasm
thrawn
cheapo
chiaus

shears
'sheart
thwart
cheapy
phrasy
sheafy
shoaly
wheaty
phobia
phobic
Ghebre
thible
shibah
rhebok
chibol
Theban
Gheber
Thebes
Shebat
✧thibet
the box
chubby
shabby
cha-cha
chacma
chicha
Thecla
chicle
phocae
thecae
chi-chi
chichi
shtchi
thecal
chicon
the can
chocho
chocko
shacko
thicko
whacko
chucks
phocas
shucks
checky
chicly
choccy
thicky
whacky
khodja
Chadic
rhodic
chided
shaded
Phèdre
rhodie
shaduf
whidah
whydah
chadar
chador
cheder
chider
shader
shoder
Rhodes
✧shades
shadow
chuddy
shoddy
the day

✧the dry
chaeta
Sheela
Sheena
phaeic
chield
shield
shrewd
the end
thread
three-D
cheese
pheere
pheese
pheeze
✧phoebe
thieve
threne
wheeze
thresh
wheech
wheesh
phreak
shreek
shreik
shtetl
phlegm
Phleum
sheepo
threap
threep
oh dear!
cheers!
sheers
sheets
wheels
shiest
shyest
threat
cheeky
cheery
cheesy
✧sheeny
sheepy
sheety
wheely
wheezy
shufti
chafer
shofar
chafts
the few
chaffy
chuffy
shifty
shufty
The Fly
whiffy
bhagee
chigoe
chigre
chagan
shogun
thuggo
shaggy
eh whow
Shaiva
✧sheila
chaîné
chaise
choice

Shiite
shrike
shrine
shrive
theine
thrice
thrive
thyine
shying
shaikh
sheikh
shyish
shriek
shrink
shtick
shrill
thrill
chrism
Shiism
thairm
theism
shairn
shrimp
chains
Rheims
theirs
thrips
Christ
shrift
theist
thrift
thrist
bhajee
bhajan
shojis
chakra
chokra
chukka
Shakta
shiksa
choked
shaked
shikse
bhakti
chokri
Shakti
shekel
shaken
chikor
choker
chukar
chukor
✧shaker
shikar
chokos
shakes
shakos
Phuket
chokey
cholla
Khalka
Khalsa
Khulna
Shelta
Thalia
Thelma
thulia
cholic
Khalid
whelk'd
chelae

childe
chylde
shelve
the lie
khalif
the leg
Shiloh
chilli
phalli
shalli
thalli
tholoi
khilim
Philem
phylum
shalom
sholom
whilom
chalan
phyllo
Philip
choler
thaler
whaler
chiles
chilis
✧pholas
Thales
thalis
tholos
tholus
whiles
chalet
châlet
khalat
khilat
shalot
the lot
whilst
the law
chalky
chilly
Philby
shelfy
shelly
shelty
shelvy
whally
whelky
whilly
wholly
ahimsa
rhumba
shamba
✧**the mob**
chemic
thymic
rhymed
shamed
themed
Phemie
rhombi
thymol
shaman
whammo
chimer
rhymer
shamer
Shamir
chimes
✧shamus

Thames
Themis
Thomas
thymus
chammy
chemmy
chummy
shammy
shamoy
shimmy
thumby
whammy
whimmy
whimsy
khanga
Rhonda
thanna
whenua
phenic
phonic
shined
chance
change
Chinee
shinne
thence
whence
whinge
chinch
thanah
bhindi
Chanel
phenol
phenyl
phonal
rhinal
khanum
phenom
phonon
thin'un
Shinto
chin up
shin up
chenar
chinar
phoner
shiner
thenar
whiner
chinks
chinos
'phones
phones
rhinos
thanks
things
whenas
chenet
the Net
why-not
Chonju
nhandu
whanau
the now
chenix
chancy
chanty
chunky
phoney
shandy
shanny

shanty
shindy
shinny
shinty
shonky
thingy
thinly
whingy
whinny
chintz
bhoona
chroma
✧shroud
shrowd
choose
chrome
shoole
✧shrove
the one
throne
throve
throwe
shroff
shy off
the off
throng
phwoah
whoosh
dhooti
she-oak
shlock
shmock
shtook
phloem
shtoom
shoo-in
thrown
chromo
phwoar
Cheops
shmoes
whoops
throat
choosy
dhooly
phooey
theory
chapka
shaped
chypre
rhaphe
Bhopal
chapel
chip in
chop in
✧chopin
shapen
whip in
shippo
chop up
whip up
shaper
chappy
chippy
choppy
shoppy
whippy
cheque
chequy
charka
charta

chorda
chorea
choria
dharma
dharna
dhurra
khurta
✧sharia
✧sheria
✧sherpa
shirra
Theria
thoria
cherub
Chirac
choric
chared
shared
ahorse
charge
chargé
Cherie
chirre
choree
✧thorpe
thyrse
wharve
kharif
✧sharif
sherif
church
Thorah
gharri
thyrsi
bharal
chiral
choral
Sheryl
the Ram
thiram
Charon
Chiron
Sharon
shoran
thoron
✧chi-rho
gherao
Thurso
cherup
sharer
shorer
charas
Charis
charms
charts
chorus
pharos
sharps
shores
shorts
therms
wharfs
Bharat
charet
thirst
the raw
thorax
charry
cherry
cherty
chirpy

gharry
sharny
✧sherry
shirty
shorty
thirty
thorny
wherry
whirly
whirry
Shiraz
Phasma
The Sea
phasic
physic
Chasid
phased
chasse
chassé
chaste
ghesse
Thisbe
bhisti
Shashi
chesil
chisel
chosen
the Son
The Sun
Xhosan
physio
chaser
phasis
rhesus
theses
thesis
whisht
the sex
chasmy
chesty
ghosty
whisky
chatta
whatna
phatic
photic
rhotic
thetic
shotte
what if
photog
chetah
thatch
thetch
chatti
chital
rhythm
Bhutan
chaton
chitin
chiton
photon
phyton
rhyton
shut in
shut-in
whaten
whiten
ghetto
what ho
whatso

chat up
shut up
rhetor
photos
whites
chatty
chitty
Whitby
✧whitey
should
chaufe
chouse
chauff
chough
sheuch
sheugh
shough
though
thrush
wheugh
shmuck
shrunk
shtuck
shtumm
rheums
chaunt
thrust
rheumy
shouty
shaved
chèvre
shavie
shivah
shovel
thivel
bhavan
cheven
chevin
shaven
shivoo
shaver
shiver
shover
chives
shives
chevet
Shevat
chivvy
shewed
showed
thewed
chewie
chowri
shewel
thowel
show in
✧the who
chew up
show up
chewer
shower
thawer
thewes
chewet
chowry
the Way
The Wiz
rhexis
they're
they've
they'll

wheyey
rhizic
phizog
ghazal
ghazel
chazan
whizzo
whizzy
Bimana
cicada
cicala
gitana
jicama
piñata
piraña
piraya
Pitaka
pitara
sifaka
tinaja
Tirana
vihara
Vijaya
vimana
Vinaya
bicarb
ligand
✧lizard
ribald
riband
ribaud
rizard
visaed
vizard
wisard
wizard
binate
cicale
dilate
finale
fixate
hidage
hirage
kinase
libate
ligase
ligate
linage
lipase
micate
mid-age
milage
mirage
Pilate
pipage
pirate
rivage
silage
silane
tirade
tisane
vidame
visage
vivace
Zidane
pilaff
Riyadh
Sirach
✧siwash
Bihari
ditali

Divali
Diwali
Kigali
miladi
eirack
hijack
limail
air-arm
disarm
misaim
dizain
sixain
gitano
mikado
Pisano
virago
midair
dirams
finals
Titans
aidant
dicast
dikast
libant
Timaru
bigamy
binary
digamy
Hilary
litany
milady
piracy
vicary
vivary
bizazz
pizazz
limbec
limbic
niobic
air-bed
big-bud
dibbed
disbud
fibbed
gibbed
jibbed
limbed
nibbed
nimbed
pig-bed
ribbed
diable
dibble
dimble
fimble
jirble
kibble
liable
nibble
nimble
Tibbie
timbre
viable
wibble
wimble
airbag
big bug
bin-bag
kitbag
Liebig
jibbah

kirbeh
gimbal
timbal
Big Ben
gibbon
Lisbon
ribbon
sin bin
sin-bin
Bilbao
bibber
dibber
disbar
fibber
Finbar
gibber
jibber
libber
limber
mimbar
minbar
timber
Airbus®
bilbos
bimbos
himbos
✧limbos
✧limbus
nimbus
timbós
gibbet
Lisbet
tidbit
titbit
nimbly
Riccia
kincob
diacid
minced
viscid
zinced
circle
fiacre
fitché
miscue
kimchi
litchi
discal
fiscal
tincal
nincom
nincum
sitcom
✧viscum
niacin
oilcan
piecen
siccan
tin can
viscin
wiccan
zircon
gilcup
hiccup
oil-cup
air car
circar
kit-car
mincer
piecer
pincer

siccar
sircar
wincer
circus
ciscos
discos
✧discus
Pisces
viscus
zincos
big cat
gib-cat
✧kit-cat
Tib-cat
tipcat
Biscay
bitchy
fitchy
hitchy
pitchy
titchy
wincey
witchy
zincky
siddha
windac
gilded
girded
kidded
lidded
minded
misdid
ridded
rinded
tinded
winded
Biddie
birdie
diddle
dièdre
dildoe
dindle
fiddle
girdle
kiddle
kindie
kindle
✧middle
piddle
riddle
tiddle
tie-dye
widdle
windle
pie-dog
Jiddah
bindhi
✧siddhi
Sindhi
dik-dik
Mindel
tindal
air dam
diadem
dirdam
dirdum
✧wisdom
bidden
Diodon
gilden
hidden

linden
midden
milden
ridden
sindon
Hindoo
giddap
giddup
wind up
wind-up
bidder
binder
birder
cinder
didder
finder
gilder
girder
hidder
hinder
kidder
kinder
lieder
minder
Pindar
pinder
qindar
ridder
siddur
sirdar
tinder
wilder
winder
dildos
kiddos
windas
mildew
✧window
air-dry
fiddly
kindly
midday
mildly
six-day
tiddly
vildly
wildly
cinema
kinema
pineta
Ribena®
Rijeka
big end
bin-end
Sinéad
tineid
viséed
bigeye
bireme
give me
misère
Nicene
picene
pinene
silene
kilerg
Li Peng
hi tech
Himeji
✧sileni
ripeck

Words marked ✧ can also be spelled with one or more capital letters

cineol
eisell
lineal
pineal
tineal
pileum
Aileen
bite in
Eileen
Gideon
live in
live-in
pigeon
pile in
pipe in
ride in
ride on
side-on
Simeon
wigeon
wire in
wivern
cicero
libero
fire up
give up
hike up
hive up
line up
line-up
mike up
pile up
pile-up
pipe up
ride up
rile up
rise up
size up
wipe up
wire up
wise up
diseur
fineer
linear
biceps
citess
cizers
divers
Fifers
five Ks
Hibees
oilers
pileus
Sirens
videos
vireos
vivers
bident
bisect
digest
direct
divert
divest
eident
piment
rident
silent
Tibert
tide it
virent
wisent
✧cicely
cidery
fikery
finely
finery
likely
live by
lively
livery
✧misery
nicely
nicety
ninety
nitery
oilery
pinery
rifely
ripely
rivery
sinewy
tigery
tilery
timely
titely
vilely
vinery
vively
widely
wifely
winery
wisely
miffed
misfed
piaffe
piffle
riffle
siffle
aidful
bibful
dinful
Eiffel
fitful
sinful
tinful
wilful
biffin
tiffin
differ
liefer
niffer
pilfer
titfer
filfot
misfit
kid-fox
lingua
Viagra®
digged
dinged
figged
gigged
hinged
jigged
minged
pigged
ridged
rigged
ringed
singed
tigged
tin god
wigged
winged
zigged
biggie
bingle
ciggie
dingle
gidgee
giggle
gilgie
gingle
higgle
jiggle
jilgie
jingle
kidgie
kingle
lingle
midgie
mingle
niggle
piggie
pingle
single
tingle
widgie
wiggle
fisgig
fizgig
✧binghi
gilgai
nilgai
Fingal
gingal
jingal
lingel
ridgel
ridgil
Virgil
zingel
lingam
air-gun
biggin
big gun
biogen
fingan
mingin'
pidgin
piggin
ring in
six-gun
✧virgin
zip gun
gingko
Ningbo
airgap
ring up
bigger
binger
digger
dinger
finger
✧ginger
jigger
lidger
lieger
ligger
linger
minger
Pinger®
pinger
ridger
rigger
ringer
sieger
singer
Tigger
virger
winger
zinger
air-gas
bilges
biogas
dinges
dingus
Hingis
oil-gas
pingos
Virgos
fidget
giggit
king it
lingot
midget
mid-gut
nidget
Piaget
widget
wing it
witgat
nilgau
dingey
dinghy
giggly
jiggly
jingly
kingly
niggly
singly
tingly
wiggly
Eithna
lithia
Mishna
Mithra
lithic
dished
niched
pished
tithed
Eithne
kishke
lichee
Richie
eighth
highth
mishmi
pithoi
Tishri
Nichol
withal
dirham
dirhem
lichen
nigh on
richen
siphon
sithen
within
Yichun
righto
bishop
dish up
high-up
hip-hop
mishap
bichir
cipher
cither
dither
either
✧fisher
✧higher
hither
lither
micher
mither
nicher
sigher
tither
wisher
wither
zither
dishes
eights
✧fishes
lights
lithos
nights
pithos
riches
rights
sithes
tights
wishes
mishit
tin hat
with it
with-it
Vishnu
eighty
highly
linhay
mighty
nighly
nighty
richly
minima
silica
lilied
pitied
tidied
cilice
dirige
divide
divine
finite
fixive
liaise
lipide
Milice
picine
pinite
ribibe
simile
tibiae
virile
visile
visite
visive
aiding
ailing
airing
biding
biking
biting
dicing
diving
filing
fining
firing
fixing
giving
hiding
hieing
hiring
kiting
liking
liming
lining
living
mining
niding
pieing
piling
piping
✧riding
rising
siding
siring
sizing
tiling
timing
tiring
✧viking
wiping
wiring
Xining
Eilidh
Fifish
fikish
finish
Lilith
linish
minish
nicish
Oirish
widish
bikini
miriti
Rimini
tisick
filial
finial
simial
tibial
bivium
cilium
civism
Lilium
milium
minium
Miriam
oidium
sizism
bilian
Eirian
Fijian
Lilian
minion
Ninian
pinion
simian
Sirian
✧titian
virion
vision
Vivian
Vivien
aikido
Himiko
libido
virino
cimier
pitier
tidier
tinier
visier
vizier
wizier
civics
filius
Lilias
Sirius
tibias
tinies
tiyins
oikist
qiviut
sizist
timist
vibist
milieu
Titipu
airily
citify
dimity
fixity
jiminy
minify
nidify
oilily
Sicily
tidily
tinily
vilify
vivify
wilily
wirily
kibitz
gidjee
jigjig
jig-jog
jimjam
finjan
✧ninjas
picked
pinked
ticked
wicked
wiz kid
zinked
bickie
birkie
✧dickie
fickle
kie-kie
kinkle
mickle
pickle
✧pinkie
rickle
sickie
sickle
silkie
tickle
tinkle
Wilkie
winkle
Kirkuk
Wim Kok
nickel
dinkum
nickum
Sikkim
birken
Dicken
Dickon
firkin
girkin
kick in
kirkin'
libken
milken
misken
pick on
pipkin
sicken
silken
simkin
sink in
Sir Ken
siskin
ticken
wicken
ginkgo
dikkop
kick-up
link up
link-up
pick up
pick-up
sick up
bicker
bilker
dicker
jinker
kicker
licker
linker
milker
nickar
nicker
picker
ricker
risker
sicker
sinker
sirkar
ticker
tinker
wicker
winker
yicker
yikker
Yizkor
pinkos
sickos
picket
ricket
ticket
wicket
wisket
dickey
dickty
hickey
Kirkby
✧mickey
miskey
rickey
rickly
sickly
tickey
tickly
tinkly
Lib-Lab
sialic
aisled
billed
dialed
hilled
milled
misled
nilled
nirled
rilled
titled
willed
✧billie
diploe
gillie
girlie
Killie
Lillee
Millie
nirlie
vielle
Willie
dialog
mid-leg
pin-leg
kiblah
zillah
nielli
Hillel
billon
diplon
fill in
fill-in
Hielan'
riglin
rivlin
sialon
tiglon
villan
Villon
violin
billy-o
niello
Rialto
will do
dial-up
fillip
fill up
fill-up
kill up
birler
filler
Hitler
killer
✧miller
pillar
rifler
siller
tiller
titler
villar

violer
willer
Eirlys
killas
rifles
titles
villus
aiglet
billet
diglot
fillet
firlot
giblet
giglet
giglot
gillet
gimlet
jillet
kidlet
killut
✧millet
nirlit
oillet
✧piglet
piolet
riblet
rillet
violet
willet
Kisleu
pillau
Kislev
billow
lie low
pillow
willow
diplex
bieldy
Finlay
Finley
Lilley
mislay
Ridley
Sisley
wieldy
willey
mia-mia
filmic
Micmac
dimmed
nimmed
rimmed
Jimmie
Timmie
diamyl
dismal
gimmal
hiemal
airman
binman
disman
firman
gigman
hitman
Kirman
min min
oilman
pieman
pig-man
pin-man
pitman
'simmon
tinman
wimmin
Xiamen
miombo
bitmap
firm up
bismar
dimmer
firmer
gimmer
gimmor
kimmer
limmer
nimmer
simmer
Zimmer®
gimmes
gismos
gizmos
litmus
✧**kismet**
dismay
firmly
Niamey
Bianca
Lianna
sienna
Vienna
zinnia
bionic
finnac
Finnic
picnic
pionic
binned
dinned
finned
ginned
nid-nod
pinned
pioned
sinned
tinned
Dianne
dinnae
dinnle
Dionne
fiancé
girnie
jinnee
Lianne
✧minnie
nix-nie
pinnae
pinnie
pirnie
tinnie
wienie
Winnie
winnle
Dipnoi
dirndl
ginnel
girnel
lienal
✧lionel
signal
simnel
lignum
finnan
lignin
mignon
sign in
sign on
kidnap
sign up
dinner
finner
ginner
girner
limner
pinner
pioner
signer
✧signor
sinner
tinner
wiener
winner
pianos
viands
Widnes
dip-net
linnet
lionet
oilnut
pig-nut
pignut
pinnet
pirnit
signet
sinnet
SI unit
minnow
winnow
Disney
Finney
jitney
kidney
linney
lionly
pioney
riancy
Sidney
aikona
eidola
Finola
Ginola
kia-ora
lipoma
mimosa
Nicola
Winona
fi donc!
bifold
lipoid
milord
siloed
viroid
bizone
citole
dipole
ditone
filose
kinone
Nicole
Nilote
Nivôse
picoté
pilose
pinole
ribose
rimose
Simone
virose
aim off
die off
hit off
mid-off
nip off
rip off
rip-off
tip off
tip-off
zip-off
qi gong
qigong
simorg
Viborg
kibosh
Biloxi
pirogi
tifosi
titoki
nim-oil
rigoll
til oil
biform
simoom
Aizoon
bicorn
disown
Minoan
simoon
gigolo
kimono
tifoso
vigoro
giaour
rigour
vigour
didoes
limous
minors
Nilots
pilous
rimous
timous
tiroes
vinous
virous
die out
dig out
dim out
dim-out
fig out
fit out
fit-out
hit out
kit out
lip out
pig out
pip out
rig out
rig-out
rip out
sit out
wig out
win out
bijoux
dipody
disomy
Kid Ory
simony
biopic
hippic
dipped
hipped
hispid
limpid
lipped
nipped
pipped
ripped
sipped
tipped
zipped
Dieppe
dimple
disple
fipple
hippie
hirple
lippie
Nippie
nipple
pimple
ripple
simple
sipple
tipple
wimple
yippee
yippie
simpai
Biopol®
dispel
hippen
hippin
kirpan
lippen
Nippon
oil pan
pigpen
pippin
Rippon
tiepin
wippen
diaper
diapir
✧dipper
hipper
kipper
lisper
✧nipper
Nippur
ripper
simper
sipper
tipper
yipper
zipper
cippus
hippos
hippus
big pot
limpet
pit-pat
sippet
tinpot
tippet
piupiu
Tipp-Ex®
Tippex
biopsy
dimply
gilpey
jimply
limply
pimply
ripply
simply
bisque
cinque
cirque
risque
risqué
✧**sierra**
midrib
mihrab
citric
nitric
picric
ric-rac
vitric
fibred
kinred
Nimrod
pierid
sirred
tiara'd
tiered
tie rod
cierge
fierce
kierie
lierne
✧pierce
Pierre
sirree
tierce
tiercé
ti tree
oil rig
diarch
hijrah
sirrah
Sifrei
citral
fibril
mitral
nitryl
Vibram®
Vikram
Ciaran
citrin
citron
fibrin
fiorin
Kieran
Kieron
Libran
micron
mikron
vibrio
rip-rap
riprap
sitrep
mirror
cirrus
✧citrus
fibros
micros
miurus
Pieris
vivres
pierst
pig-rat
tirrit
fin-ray
fiesta
miasma
mid-sea
siesta
vizsla
air-sac
biased
birsle
Cissie
fissle
hirsle
kiss-me
missee
tissue
kirsch
kitsch
diesel
hirsel
kissel
missal
missel
tinsel
dim sum
jissom
lissom
bisson
gipsen
Nissan®
Pilsen
fiasco
finsko
giusto
sissoo
bitser
kisser
rinser
cissus
dieses
diesis
✧dipsas
dipsos
lisses
miasms
miosis
Misses
✧missis
missus
nisses
misset
Bissau
jigsaw
pit-saw
ripsaw
Kirsty
linsey
mid-sky
milsey
mimsey
missay
pigsny
pigsty
tinsey
winsey
sistra
wiltja
biotic
cistic
fistic
miotic
Mixtec
tic-tac
tietac
bitted
cisted
ditted
fitted
gifted
kilted
listed
pioted
pitted
tilted
tinted
vista'd
witted
big toe
bistre
bittie
filtre
histie
kiltie
kirtle
Kittie
kittle
lintie
little
mistle
pintle
Sittwe
tiptoe
tittle
virtue
vittae
vittle
wintle
distal
distil
hiatal
kittul
lintel
listel
pistil
✧pistol
rictal
vistal
wittol
diatom
dictum
victim
biotin
bitten
Fintan
kirtan
kitten
listen
Liston
litten
Milton
Minton
mitten
piston
pitten
Wilton
bistro
Giotto
big top
lift up
mist up
silt up
tiptop
tittup
ziptop
bister
bitter
bittor
bittur
dieter
fictor
filter
fitter
hitter
jitter
kilter
lictor
lifter
linter
✧lister
litter
milter
minter
✧mister
nipter
Pictor
Pinter
pitter
qintar
rioter
ritter
sifter
sinter
sister
sittar
sitter
tilter
tinter
titter
viator
✧victor
winter
witter
cistus
dittos
hiatus
pintos
rictus
Sixtus
vistos
diktat
dittit
sin tax
dittay
filthy
kittly
riotry
vintry
wintry
wistly
cicuta
fibula
ligula
pilula
situla
tipula
vicuna
vicuña
liquid
dilute

Words marked ✧ can also be spelled with one or more capital letters

disuse
figure
fixure
ligule
ligure
minute
misuse
pilule
titule
Vimule®
simurg
kiaugh
pituri
lifull
ritual
vidual
visual
Siouan
liquor
lituus
si quis
diquat
fiaunt
kidult
minuet
misust
✧piquet
✧kikuyu
titupy
Silvia
kidvid
silvae
mikvah
mikveh
silvan
liever
riever
silver
Milvus
silvas
bigwig
tie-wig
wigwag
wigwam
did won
Dilwyn
viewer
tiswas
tizwas
dimwit
nitwit
airway
midway
rid way
viewly
jinxed
biaxal
diaxon
dioxan
dioxin
pinxit
Libyan
minyan
Pinyin
cityfy
piazza
fizzed
fizzle
Lizzie
mizzle
pizzle

sizzle
vizzie
zigzag
fizzen
gizzen
mizzen
fizzer
rizzar
rizzer
rizzor
diazos
mizzly
Ojibwa
djebel
ejecta
ujamaa
djembe
djinni
ajowan
A J Ayer
sklate
skeary
skibob
ski bum
akedah
Ski-doo®
skidoo
ekuele
skreen
sklent
skeely
skeery
skliff
skiing
skying
skaith
skeigh
skyish
skrimp
skolia
✧skylab
skelum
skills
skelly
skilly
skolly
skyman
akimbo
skimpy
Skanda
skin up
skanky
skinny
Akmola
skoosh
eke out
Skopje
okapis
skip it!
skippy
skarth
ski run
Skiros
skerry
skurry
sketch
skater
ski tow
skrump
skivie
skiver

skivvy
skewed
skewer
skyway
okayed
ukiyo-e
skryer
albata
alpaca
cloaca
Alcaic
Altaic
Eluard
algate
alkane
alnage
cleave
eluate
fluate
gleave
old age
oleate
please
sleave
sleaze
Sloane
ullage
ulnare
bleach
fleadh
fly ash
ollamh
pleach
Alhagi
alkali
✧almain
El Paso
Altair
always
floats
eluant
olfact
pliant
Albany
Almany
bleaky
bleary
floaty
gleamy
sleazy
globed
à l'abri
global
globin
flub up
all but
blobby
clubby
flabby
glibly
globby
old boy
plebby
slabby
slobby
slubby
Alicia
placed
placid
cleché
cliché

cloche
flèche
plicae
eltchi
flocci
glycol
plical
flacon
glycin
ulicon
Alecto
elf cup
placer
slicer
blacks
blocks
flicks
flocks
glacis
ilices
slacks
elicit
placet
placit
blocky
clucky
plucky
Elodea
alidad
bladed
sleded
slided
bludge
bludie
fledge
gledge
kludge
pledge
sledge
sludge
aludel
blader
eluder
glider
slider
blades
Gladys
all-day
cloddy
clodly
fledgy
gladly
sludgy
alteza
alkene
allege
allele
cleeve
fleece
sleeve
fleech
sleech
aldern
alpeen
altern
clue in
albedo
Cluedo®
alleys
Elaeis
pliers

albeit
✧albert
client
eldest
eluent
fluent
oldest
sliest
slyest
almery
bluely
bluesy
fleecy
gleety
sleeky
sleepy
sleety
sleezy
olefin
cliffy
clifty
fluffy
pluffy
alogia
alegge
blague
plague
flugel
flügel
Glagol
plagal
flagon
plug in
plug-in
slogan
clog up
alegar
alight
blight
elegit
flight
ill-got
plight
'slight
slight
bluggy
claggy
cloggy
flaggy
plaguy
slaggy
✧althea
all-hid
elchee
Elohim
Oldham
elshin
old-hat
El Gîza
Eloisa
Elvira
Ulrica
ultima
allied
illiad
Pleiad
albite
Aldine
al fine
allice
✧alpine

alsike
alvine
✧blaise
blaize
Claire
Elaine
Eloise
glaive
gloire
illipe
illite
plaice
sluice
bluing
elding
flying
gluing
plying
slairg
ulling
bluish
elfish
elvish
gluish
oldish
sleigh
slyish
Alpini
allium
Albion
eloign
ultion
albino
Alnico®
Alpino
El Niño
ultimo
gluier
allies
glaiks
✧plains
plaint
bluidy
glairy
ploidy
sluicy
Elijah
sloken
ulikon
Alt key
blokey
flukey
alalia
alulae
slalom
alulas
alumna
blamed
flamed
plumed
clambe
flambé
alumni
Altman
flamen
flyman
old man
old-man
clam up
glam up
clamor

flamer
glamor
clumps
glumps
slimes
flemit
slum it
climax
blimey
clammy
clumpy
clumsy
flimsy
glammy
glumly
glumpy
plummy
plumpy
slimly
slimsy
slummy
slumpy
Glenda
planta
clinic
clonic
Eluned
plongd
blende
Blonde®
blonde
blunge
elance
flange
flense
glance
plonge
plunge
✧blanch
blench
clench
clinch
clunch
elench
flanch
flench
flinch
planch
plinth
à l'envi
clinal
clonal
plenum
Alonso
blanco
Elinor
planar
planer
blinis
blinks
clints
clonus
Glenys
Glynis
llanos
Olenus
slangs
elanet
planet
blenny
Clancy

clingy
clunky
flinty
flunky
plenty
plonky
slangy
slinky
blintz
glioma
algoid
almond
alcove
aldose
Al Gore
all one
cleome
Old One
ill off
ill-off
klooch
sloosh
Alboin
alsoon
allons
almous
Cloots
ellops
floods
all out
all-out
almost
fly out
bloody
bloomy
floosy
floozy
gloomy
gloopy
sloomy
aliped
elapse
clypei
clip-on
slip-on
Aleppo
clap up
slap-up
slip up
slip-up
eloper
Elspet
klepht
flappy
floppy
slippy
sloppy
claque
clique
cloqué
plaque
cliquy
✧gloria
Alaric
cleric
Alfred
all-red
florid
fly rod
alerce
florae

floral
plural
alarum
aldrin
florin
claros
clarts
flares
floras
Flores
Glires
claret
floret
blurry
clarty
clergy
flirty
flurry
slurpy
slurry
Alaska
alisma
clusia
Elisha
glossa
plasma
closed
plused
plaste
plissé
✧flysch
Alison
closer
flaser
clasts
pluses
ulosis
closet
blashy
classy
flashy
fleshy
flisky
flossy
flushy
glassy
glossy
I'll say!
plashy
plushy
sloshy
slushy
elytra
Flotta
clitic
alated
elated
fluted
plated
slated
blithe
clothe
blotch
clatch
clutch
fletch
flitch
glitch
klatch
slatch
glutei

flotel
Old Tom
Cloten
gluten
platan
platen
pluton
slot in
blotto
Clotho
elater
elutor
fluter
plater
slater
✧ulster
cloths
flatus
plates
ulitis
zlotys
blotty
clotty
flatly
flatty
glitzy
klutzy
plotty
pleura
allude
allure
almuce
blouse
Claude
clause
flaune
flouse
illude
illume
ill-use
cleuch
cleugh
clough
floush
pleuch
pleugh
✧plough
sleuth
slouch
✧slough
illupi
Alcuin
albugo
albums
flaunt
cloudy
fleury
floury
glaury
clivia
Flavia
Olivia
Old Vic
Slavic
gloved
slived
clavie
Slovak
A level
A-level
O level
O-level
Y-level
alevin
cloven
eleven
elevon
flavin
sliven
sloven
claver
clever
clover
flavor
glover
Oliver!
✧oliver
plover
slaver
sliver
claves
clavis
clevis
cloves
Clovis
olivet
slavey
blowed
clawed
flawed
flewed
flowed
slewed
blowie
blow me
blowse
blowze
blow in
blow-in
flow-on
blow up
✧blow-up
clew up
slow up
slow-up
blower
flower
glower
blow it
blowsy
blowzy
flyway
slowly
✧**alexia**
alexic
Alexei
Alexej
alexin
flaxen
✧klaxon
elixir
flexor
plexor
Alexis
ilexes
plexus
clayed
cloyed
flayed
gleyed
played
slayed
alkyne
Olwyne
aliyah
play on
play up
E-layer
F-layer
flayer
player
slayer
play at
play it
clayey
blazed
glazed
blazon
glazen
blazar
blazer
glazer
blazes
impala
ambage
embace
embale
embase
empale
empare
imbase
immane
impale
impave
em dash
smeath
embank
embark
imbark
immask
impark
embail
emball
emparl
imparl
embalm
impawn
impair
empart
impact
impart
umlaut
smeary
amebic
Amabel
Amicus
imidic
smudge
Amidol®
emydes
amidst
amadou
smiddy
smudgy
amoeba
impend
ampere
ampère
impede
emmesh
immesh
smeech
smeeth
Amiens
embers
ambery
empery
umbery
smegma
émigré
Imogen
imager
amigos
Images
imagos
smight
smoggy
smugly
amrita
✧**empire**
imbibe
smoile
umpire
impish
omnium
amnion
Emmies
impies
omnify
smoked
smokie
smoker
smokos
✧**amelia**
Emilia
Imelda
emblic
Amélie
emulge
smalti
amylum
emblem
smalto
ambler
smiler
smalls
umbles
amulet
omelet
smilet
implex
smilax
employ
smalmy
smelly
smiley
amomum
amtman
Amanda
amenta
omenta
omened
amende
Amun-Re
emunge
Imbolc
amoove
emmove
impone
impose
smooch
smooth
imbosk
emboil
emboss
imboss
embost
import
impost
embody
emboly
imbody
omerta
omertà
Smyrna
amerce
amorce
embrue
emerge
emerse
imbrue
umbrae
smirch
Amtrak
amoral
umbral
umbrel
umbril
am-dram
embryo
umbras
amoret
imaret
improv
imbrex
smarmy
smarty
smirky
smirry
smurry
amused
omasal
omasum
K-meson
amuser
emesis
tmeses
tmesis
emetic
smatch
smutch
amatol
Amytal®
emetin
emoter
smiter
Smiths
smithy
smutty
✧**empusa**
ampule
émeute
empuse
em rule
immune
immure
impure
impute
smeuse
smouse
ambush
smouch
impugn
amours
amount
embusy
B-movie
smoyle
✧**amazon**
Ankara
Annaba
antara
indaba
inyala
enjamb
in banc
enlard
in hand
inlaid
inland
inward
on hand
onward
unhand
unlaid
unmard
unpaid
unsaid
anlace
anlage
ansate
encage
encase
encave
en face
enface
engage
engagé
enlace
ennage
enrace
enrage
enragé
ensate
entame
incage
in care
in case
incase
incave
infame
infare
ingate
inhale
inlace
inmate
in name
innate
in pace
insane
intake
invade
on sale
unbare
uncage
uncape
uncase
uncate
undate
unease
Uniate
unlace
unlade
unmade
unmake
unrake
unsafe
untame
unware
in calf
in-calf
An Wang
unhang
aneath
encash
en dash
in cash
on oath
sneath
uneath
unlash
incavi
enrank
unbark
unmask
unpack
untack
and all
end-all
engaol
entail
enwall
infall
inhaul
in tail
inwall
on bail
on call
onfall
unnail
unvail
encalm
in vain
ungain
enhalo
incavo
Ungaro
encamp
unhasp
en l'air
unfair
unhair
annals
in-laws
in mass
endart
enfant
enrapt
indart
in fact
infant
in part
intact
uncart
unfact
unlast
angary
infamy
sneaky
uneasy
unwary
enable
snebbe
snubbe
unable
ink-bag
anabas
Anubis
knobby
knubby
snobby
snubby
onycha
ink-cap
Cnicus
knicks
anicut
Sno-cat
ant cow
knacky
anodic
cnidae
on edge
snudge
unedge
anodal
enodal
anadem
snod up
any day
one day
one-day
snidey
Angela
Anneka
entera
injera
ennead
in deed
indeed
intend
on-lend
unbend
undead
unfeed
unhead
unlead
unread
annexe
en fête
enlevé
entêté
incede
indene
in fere
infere
inhere
sneeze
unhele
undeaf
unself
enmesh
in mesh
inmesh
sneesh
undeck
unmeek
anneal
enseal
unheal
unleal
unreal
unreel
unseal
unseel
unveil
unweal
unwell
Anselm
enseam
inseam
inseem
unhelm
unseam
unteam
Andean
intern
undern
unhewn
unrein
unseen
unsewn
Angelo
ante up
endear
ensear
unbear
undear
ungear
Engels
unless
inbent
incept
incest
indent
infect
infeft
infelt
infest
ingest
in heat
inject
insect
insert
intent
invent
invert
invest
on heat
unbelt
unbent
unfelt
unkent
unkept
unmeet
unnest
unpent
unrent
unrest
unseat
unsent
untent
unwept
en beau
ingénu
Annecy
sneery
sneezy
unredy
unific
knifer
sniffy
snifty
snuffy
✧**enigma**
Onagra
Onegin
onager
anight

Words marked ✧ can also be spelled with one or more capital letters

knight
knaggy
snaggy
snugly
Anthea
inched
unshed
unshod
unshoe
anthem
Anshan
Inchon
inship
unship
anchor
Anghar
anther
inches
in that
unshot
unshut
and how!
anyhow
on show
unthaw
angina
Annika
Indira
in rixa
intima
Oneida
engild
engird
envied
enwind
in bird
in kind
invis'd
inwind
unbind
ungild
ungird
unkind
untied
unwind
ancile
Andine
endite
endive
enfire
engine
ensile
entice
entire
incise
incite
indite
ingine
in line
in-line
inside
in time
intime
intine
intire
invite
in wine
Kneipe
ondine
on file
on fire

on hire
on-line
online
onside
on-site
on time
undine
unfine
unhive
unlike
unlime
unline
unlive
unripe
untile
unwire
unwise
unwive
anting
ending
enring
inning
onding
unking
enrich
inwith
on high
unlich
unwish
uncini
antick
enlink
in milk
inwick
on tick
unlink
unpick
infill
O'Neill
uncial
unwill
indium
infirm
unfirm
ensign
enzian
Indian
indign
angico
indigo
in vivo
antiar
envier
inkier
inlier
antics
gneiss
in fits
on-dits
'snails
unbias
undies
unkiss
anoint
engirt
enlist
indict
insist
unbitt
ungilt
ungirt

unwist
in situ
in view
on view
enmity
entity
snaily
unmiry
untidy
ink-jet
INS key
✧**antlia**
en bloc
angled
ankled
unclad
unglad
unglue
analog
unclog
unplug
anelli
inulin
inclip
angler
antler
Anglos
anklet
englut
inflow
onflow
unclew
influx
anally
in play
on a lay
snelly
anemia
anemic
anomic
gnomic
mnemic
anomie
gnomae
animal
enamel
end man
gnomon
mnemon
one-man
enamor
animus
enemas
gnomes
ynambu
inanga
ananke
anonym
unsnap
ananas
unknit
unknot
Ancona
ancora
✧angola
✧angora
Annona
entomb
enwomb
intomb
untomb

any old
enfold
in-bond
infold
inroad
in-toed
intoed
in word
on hold
uncord
unfold
ungord
unhood
unload
unlord
unsold
untold
ancome
Ankole
any one
anyone
encode
encore
engobe
engore
enmove
enrobe
enzone
income
indole
Indore
in-joke
in love
insole
intone
invoke
inwove
oncome
one-one
snooze
unbone
uncope
undone
unlove
unpope
unrobe
unrope
unyoke
one-off
unroof
on song
inkosi
enlock
in dock
in hock
inlock
inwork
uncock
uncork
undock
unhook
unlock
unwork
enroll
ensoul
entoil
in foal
in-foal
insoul
uncoil
uncool

uncowl
unfool
unroll
unsoul
enform
inform
unform
enjoin
inborn
intown
inworn
on loan
unborn
ungown
unmown
unsown
untorn
unworn
in toto
inhoop
unhoop
indoor
undoer
unmoor
endoss
ingoes
snooks
enroot
inmost
in sort
oncost
on foot
unbolt
unboot
uncolt
unlost
unroot
unsoft
unwont
Antony
incony
oniony
✧snoopy
snooty
snoozy
unholy
on spec
inkpad
uniped
unipod
unsped
unspi'd
inspan
unspun
snap up
sniper
unspar
snipes
inkpot
snappy
snippy
unique
Andrea
anuria
oniric
inbred
Ingrid
unbred
untrod
enerve
enfree

entrée
unfree
untrue
anarch
enarch
inarch
anorak
antral
Antrim
antrum
engram
ingram
ingrum
untrim
endrin
intron
entrap
enwrap
inwrap
unprop
unwrap
snarer
snorer
Andros
in arms
indris
Ingres
intros
in a rut
Andrew
in a row
undraw
anergy
anerly
energy
gnarly
in-tray
knurly
snarly
snorty
unpray
entrez
ink-sac
unused
enisle
in esse
inisle
snaste
unison
enoses
enosis
gnoses
gnosis
unisex
angsty
anatta
anetic
✧**united**
snathe
knitch
snatch
snitch
instal
instil
unital
Gnetum
anatto
one-two
in step
instep
unstep

unstop
instar
uniter
unstow
knotty
snotty
Anoura
induna
infula
insula
pneuma
ungula
ensued
endure
end use
ennuyé
en rule
ensure
incuse
induce
infuse
inhume
injure
insure
in tune
intuse
unrude
unrule
unsure
untune
engulf
ingulf
unturf
unhung
unsung
anough
enough
inrush
onrush
annuli
incubi
unhusk
untuck
annual
in full
uncurl
unfurl
ungual
in turn
unturn
enduro
Anguis
ungues
unguis
incult
induct
indult
Innuit
insult
intuit
unhurt
unjust
unsuit
anbury
injury
on duty
snouty
unbury
unbusy
unduly
unruly

snivel
uneven
knives
gnawed
unawed
unowed
knawel
snow up
answer
gnawer
knower
anyway
in a way
one-way
anoxia
anoxic
in sync
undyed
uneyed
enzyme
oneyre
ungyve
oneyer
encyst
snazzy
Douala
posada
Roxana
somata
sonata
Soraya
torana
totara
Toyama
yojana
comarb
✧**mosaic**
Romaic
sodaic
✧**coward**
Donald
dotard
Godard
go hard
Howard
Poland
Roland
Ronald
togaed
to hand
toward
woman'd
bocage
borage
borane
borate
bovate
co-mate
comate
cowage
dog-ape
dogate
donate
dosage
dotage
douane
folate
forage
forane
for aye
homage

Horace
iodate
lobate
locale
locate
lorate
lovage
mopane
morale
nocake
nomade
nonage
nonane
notate
novate
noyade
pomace
pomade
potage
potale
romage
rosace
rotate
Roxane
socage
solace
sorage
to date
togate
to-name
towage
volage
Volare
voyage
zonate
Zouave
go bang
gobang
go hang
kobang
bodach
fogash
pot-ash
potash
bon ami
jowari
mopani
romaji
Romani
Somali
souari
go back
✧mohawk
Polack
for all
go bail
monaul
morall
no-ball
to-fall
you-all
domain
sodain
✧**dorado**
kokako
Monaco
pomato
potato
robalo
Romano
solano

Tobago
tomato
vorago
wo ha ho
hot air
hot-air
mohair
no fair
corals
Iolaus
morals
morass
noways
potass
✧royals
sowans
vocals
Volans
Bogart
cobalt
comart
dopant
dotant
go-cart
go-kart
Hobart
monact
Mozart
✧pop art
sonant
tonant
tooart
volant
vorant
nogaku
boyaux
✧**botany**
covary
donary
go easy
goramy
gowany
horary
nomady
nonary
notary
oogamy
Romany
rosary
✧rotary
so many
volary
votary
zonary
tombac
tombic
tomboc
bobbed
bombed
box-bed
combed
dobbed
forbad
forbid
gobbed
hotbed
jobbed
lobbed
mobbed
morbid
not bad
robbed
sobbed
too bad
wombed
Bobbie
bobble
cobble
comble
corbie
doable
dobbie
dog-bee
double
foible
forbye
gobble
hobble
hombre
mobbie
mobble
nobble
Robbie
rouble
sombre
wobble
✧zombie
dor-bug
sow bug
bosbok
tombak
corbel
bobbin
bonbon
corban
✧dobbin
booboo
gombro
bobber
bomber
cobber
comber
dobber
goober
jobber
robber
roo bar
somber
tow bar
bombos
combos
Forbes
Hobbes
morbus
sorbus
yobbos
combat
fox-bat
gobbet
hobbit
nobbut
sorbet
wombat
woobut
woubit
you bet
boubou
fog-bow
bombax
Bombyx
bobbly
Bombay
boo-boy
bow-boy
cowboy
doubly
lowboy
potboy
tomboy
Tor Bay
Torbay
toy boy
wobbly
concha
gotcha
lorcha
morcha
wotcha
coccid
forced
roscid
voiced
✧**bosche**
bouche
bouché
bouclé
conche
couché
douche
louche
potche
rotche
touché
coccal
coucal
low-cal
dot-com
dotcom
non-com
rom-com
romcom
Lorcan
mod con
non-con
toucan
honcho
poncho
mob cap
toecap
boxcar
concur
forcer
soccer
voicer
coccos
coccus
conchs
Dorcas
forces
hoicks
yoicks
zoccos
bobcat
doocot
doucet
forçat
low-cut
tomcat
Top Cat
cou-cou
roucou
moo-cow
Moscow
coccyx
botchy
coachy
conchy
notchy
poachy
poncey
pouchy
touchy
bonduc
Nordic
aoudad
bonded
codded
corded
dodded
doodad
fonded
fordid
godded
hooded
✧loaded
nodded
podded
rodded
sordid
voided
woaded
wooded
worded
boddle
boodie
boodle
coddle
coldie
condie
doddle
doodle
fondle
fondue
foodie
Goldie
✧hoddle
hoodie
howdie
noddle
noodle
poodle
poudre
roadie
toddle
voidee
woodie
fog-dog
hopdog
hot dog
hot-dog
top dog
toy dog
doodah
good-oh
houdah
howdah
pondok
bordel
Goidel
ooidal
rondel
condom
goddam
hold 'em
bolden
cordon
fold in
god-den
godden
golden
Gordon
hodden
hoiden
holden
hold in
hold on
houdan
hoyden
✧jordan
loaden
London
louden
sodden
soldan
sold on
wooden
doo-doo
hoodoo
koodoo
voodoo
fold up
hold up
hold-up
road up
wood up
bonder
bordar
border
codder
conder
condor
dodder
donder
fodder
folder
Gondor
holder
loader
moider
Mordor
nodder
polder
ponder
pouder
powder
solder
voider
wonder
yonder
condos
rondos
tondos
hold it!
lord it
voudou
row-dow
boldly
box-day
coldly
fondly
god day
goodly
hobday
hold by
lordly
loudly
Monday
woodsy
bodega
modena
monera
novena
Rowena
solera
Topeka
womera
dog-end
token'd
to-rend
cohere
Docete
Eocene
foveae
Göreme
Jolene
pop-eye
toneme
cosech
✧joseph
Molech
moneth
no-tech
boleti
soneri
copeck
kopeck
to seek
✧**boreal**
do well
foveal
go well
Howell
lozell
✧nowell
roseal
sorell
to sell
zooeal
boreen
come in
come on
come-on
done in
Doreen
govern
home in
Joleen
Korean
love-in
✧modern
moreen
move in
no mean
Noreen
nosean
poleyn
poteen
rope in
solein
solemn
tone in
voteen
vote in
Boléro
bolero
comedo
forego
korero
non-ego
pomelo
Soweto
Toledo
torero
bo-peep
come up
hoke up
hole up
move up
nose up
tone up
tote up
coheir
dog-ear
howe'er
no fear
poseur
to-tear
voyeur
bogeys
Boreas
bowels
coleus
covers
dozens
fogeys
moneys
no less
novels
pokeys
powers
rodeos
Romeos
soleus
sowens
volens
vowels
vowess
cogent
come it
covent
covert
docent
dolent
domett
foment
forest
go west
honest
loment
lowest
Model T
modest
molest
moment
motett
nocent
ponent
potent
Robert
rodent
so be it
sobeit
to-rent
coteau
Roseau
poleax
✧**bowery**
come by
comedy
comely
foreby
homely
lonely
lovely
lowery
moiety
mopery
oogeny
popery
ropery
rosery
rosety
solely
sorely
towery
volery
gowf-ba'
confab
coffed
hoofed
poufed
roofed
sol-fa'd
woofed
bouffe
coffee
coffle
poffle
pouffe
Roofie
toffee
loofah
boxful
joyful
potful
woeful
Corfam®
boffin
bowfin
coffin
goof up
wolf up
coffer
confer
doffer
doofer
goffer
golfer
gowfer
hoofer
loafer
✧rolfer
roofer
wolfer
woofer
doofus
comfit
confit
hoof it
konfyt
low-fat
non-fat
soffit
confix
dogfox
forfex
bob-fly
botfly
dor-fly
hop-fly
Borgia
gorgia
loggia
cogged
dogged
fogged
gorged
hogged
jogged
logged
nogged
pongid
sogged
togged
bodgie
boggle
bon gré
boogie
bougie
coggie
coggle
coigne
congee
doggie
dongle
goggle
google
hoagie
joggle
loggie
moggie
morgue
pongee
poogye
porgie
soigné
soogee
soogie
toggle
tongue
woggle
congii
Mowgli
Dougal
googol
✧mongol
sol-gel
solgel
Cow Gum®
Dodgem®
✧**gorgon**
hoggin
longan
moggan
Morgan
Morgan®
morgen
noggin
popgun
potgun
Tongan
Top Gun
gorgio
sorgho
bodger
codger
cogger
conger
cougar

Words marked ✧ can also be spelled with one or more capital letters

dodger
✧dogger
fogger
forger
hogger
jogger
lodger
logger
longer
monger
sodger
bongos
Borges
borgos
corgis
mongos
pongos
sorgos
bouget
bought
bowget
dought
forgat
forget
forgot
fought
gorget
hogget
loggat
'mongst
mought
nougat
nought
rotgut
rought
sought
congou
coggly
doughy
goggly
googly
longly
morgay
roughy
boshta
Joshua
kochia
lochia
Sophia
✧**gothic**
Sothic
mothed
bothie
mochie
Sophie
towhee
hoo-hah
boohai
kowhai
nochel
Bochum
Botham
bothan
Cochin
eothen
Goshen
lochan
Roshan
so then
boo-hoo
forhoo
Rothko
yoo-hoo
dog-hep
dog-hip
no chop
nosh-up
posh up
bother
cosher
fother
✧gopher
josher
kosher
mosher
mother
nosher
pother
rother
tocher
tosher
t'other
tother
tophus
go phut
log-hut
pot hat
rochet
so that
so what?
top hat
top-hat
Tophet
moshav
forhow
no-show
po'chay
pochay
poshly
coaita
conima
copita
✧dolina
Konica®
Lolita
lorica
Louisa
Monica
nomina
Robina
Rosina
vomica
oomiac
zodiac
bodied
copied
do bird
gobiid
Gobind
Govind
honied
monied
bodice
bolide
boride
bovine
comice
conine
cosine
cotise
docile
doline
dorise
dorize
do time
go live
iodide
iodine
iodise
iodize
iolite
✧ionise
✧ionize
Kosice
Louise
✧mobile
moline
motile
motive
no dice
norite
no-side
notice
no time
novice
nowise
✧oolite
podite
✧police
polite
solive
somite
sopite
tonite
votive
boding
Boeing
boning
boring
bowing
boxing
coding
✧coming
cooing
coping
coving
doning
doping
doting
dozing
foxing
goring
hoeing
holing
homing
joying
lobing
loping
loring
losing
loving
lowing
moving
mowing
nosing
poking
poling
posing
robing
roding
roping
roving
rowing
sowing
toeing
toling
toning
towing
toying
Woking
woning
wooing
yoking
zoning
boyish
cowish
coyish
dotish
dovish
eolith
goyish
Josiah
lowish
modish
mopish
morish
oolith
✧polish
popish
Romish
tonish
toyish
Kojiki
solidi
yogini
Kodiak
Morisk
oomiak
Yorick
✧**jovial**
monial
Novial
oorial
podial
social
tomial
bonism
corium
dolium
Dorism
eonism
folium
holism
iodism
Ionism
ionium
lolium
monism
nomism
podium
porism
sodium
Sofism
tomium
yogism
Aonian
Dorian
Eolian
gonion
Ionian
Jovian
logion
Lorien
lotion
morion
motion
notion
Popian
potion
solion
bonito
Comino
domino
dosi-do
Lobito
loligo
solito
vomito
zorino
copier
cosier
cozier
foliar
gooier
gorier
hosier
ropier
rosier
bodies
bogies
conics
fogies
folios
gobies
golias
gopiks
Möbius
modius
monies
movies
pokies
polios
solids
sonics
Tobias
to bits
Tonies
aorist
bonist
codist
forint
holist
Ionist
loriot
modist
monist
✧soviet
bodily
codify
comity
cosily
dopily
gorily
holily
homily
hominy
jokily
modify
mopily
moyity
nosily
notify
novity
oozily
policy
polity
ropily
rosily
rosiny
Torify
hobjob
conjee
poojah
moujik
log jam
donjon
popjoy
soojey
cocked
corked
forked
hooked
pocked
soaked
worked
yolked
zonked
bookie
cockle
cookie
folkie
honkie
kookie
rookie
✧yorkie
hookah
bodkin
book in
docken
dodkin
joskin
lock in
lock-in
lock on
look in
look-in
morkin
soaken
work in
work-in
work on
cock up
cock-up
cook up
cork up
fork up
hook up
hook-up
lock up
lock-up
look up
lookup
mock-up
soak up
work up
booker
bosker
✧cocker
conker
cooker
corker
corkir
docker
Fokker
forker
hocker
honker
hooker
howker
korkir
locker
looker
mocker
porker
✧rocker
soaker
tonker
worker
yonker
yorker
jockos
bosket
cocket
docket
dooket
hook it
locket
nocket
pocket
pookit
poukit
rocket
socket
booksy
cocksy
donkey
folksy
hockey
hookey
horkey
hot key
jockey
low-key
monkey
holloa
bolled
bowled
cowled
doiled
foiled
howled
jolled
jowled
mobled
polled
pot-lid
rolled
soiled
souled
toiled
boulle
collie
coolie
coulée
doolie
dowlne
goalie
goolie
Joelle
mollie
Noelle
noulde
poulpe
voulge
bow leg
dogleg
log-log
loglog
coolth
koolah
mollah
moolah
tol-lol
coelom
Gollum
Moslem
bollen
codlin
goblin
gollan
gowlan
koulan
moulin
norlan'
pollan
pollen
poplin
roll in
roll on
roll-on
Toulon
woolen
collop
dollop
doll up
foul up
foul-up
gollop
lollop
roll up
roll-up
tool up
boiler
bowler
coaler
collar
cooler
dollar
✧fowler
gollar
goller
holler
howler
joller
jowler
loller
moiler
poller
poplar
✧roller
sollar
soller
toiler
toller
tooler
yodler
boules
coulis
dowlas
hollos
moulds
oodles
poules
collet
cool it
goblet
goglet
goslet
howlet
job lot
toilet
tonlet
follow
go slow
go-slow
hollow
mob law
bollix
pollex
Pollux
Bowlby
Colley
coolly
doyley
foully
gooley
hooley
jolley
Mosley
motley
mouldy
podley
Sorley
volley
woolly
yowley
Boulez
cosmea
holmia
Nouméa
cosmic
formic
holmic
doomed
formed
roomed
tommed
wormed
commie
coombe
dormie
roomie
Bokmål
cormel
formal
formol
formyl
normal
pommel
Rommel
bogman
bowman
common
con man
cowman
dodman
dolman
dolmen
foeman
foemen
fogman
Forman
hodman
log-man
Mormon
✧norman
potman
rodman
Rouman

socman
to a man
topman
towmon
toyman
zoom in
boomer
Colmar
commer
Donmar
dormer
former
roamer
roemer
roomer
wormer
commis
commos
cormus
Cosmas
cosmos
dolmas
Holmes
houmus
kosmos
bon mot
commit
commot
format
mommet
motmot
commix
Bosnia
cornea
cornua
goanna
goonda
✧joanna
hobnob
round B
✧**cognac**
poonac
zoonic
conned
corned
donned
downed
Gounod
gowned
horned
mooned
morned
wonned
✧**bonnie**
bounce
Connie
donnée
Donnie
Downie®
Hornie
Joanie
Joanne
jounce
loanee
loonie
lounge
Moonie
pointe
poonce
pounce
pownie

rounce
toonie
townee
townie
tonnag
cornel
nounal
zoonal
horn in
join in
Poznan
xoanon
Borneo
go into
coinop
join up
coiner
conner
Connor
corner
Donner
downer
Hoenir
horner
joiner
loaner
moaner
mooner
nooner
sooner
sorner
bounds
doings
donnés
points
pounds
sounds
zounds
bonnet
cobnut
coin it
cornet
donnat
donnot
hognut
hornet
non-net
posnet
sonnet
tow net
for now
how now?
Fornax
fornix
bouncy
✧bounty
coonty
county
gooney
Johnny
mornay
Mounty
pointy
powney
Rodney
rouncy
townly
woundy
Bogotá
corona
Dodoma

Honora
jojoba
korora
lobola
Pomona
Toyota
Toyota®
Yo-Yo Ma
Eozoic
conoid
go cold
go gold
kobold
locoed
no good
no-good
toroid
toxoid
zonoid
bog ore
botoné
comose
coyote
for one
go home
ionone
jocose
lobose
mopoke
morose
nodose
no-hope
no joke
no more
nosode
porose
sobole
to come
tofore
torose
cop off
fob off
hop-off
job off
log off
log-off
logoff
nod off
pop off
top off
bogong
go long
oolong
so long
so long!
so-long
cohosh
golosh
lo moth
✧moloch
colobi
Moroni
Potosí
somoni
bogoak
mocock
Mohock
cocoon
cohorn
cojoin
do down

Eozoon
go down
go-down
godown
Motown®
bonobo
comodo
corozo
lobolo
✧rococo
rotolo
yo-ho-ho
bow-oar
colour
dolour
✧honour
notour
bosoms
cohoes
colons
comous
dodoes
goboes
hoboes
iodous
joyous
locoes
mojoes
nodous
no-noes
noyous
porous
torous
bow out
cohort
co-host
cop out
cop-out
go soft
job out
log out
log-out
logout
not out
to boot
tog out
top out
volost
gomoku
bosomy
colony
corody
gobony
monody
monosy
motory
nobody
oology
polony
sodomy
cowpea
hoop-la
copped
couped
hopped
joypad
looped
lopped
mopped
pooped
popped

sopped
topped
torpid
wopped
copple
corpse
coupee
couple
doppie
hoopoe
hopple
koppie
popple
soapie
souple
topple
toupee
✧woopie
oompah
compel
gospel
vorpal
pom-pom
pompom
coppin
coupon
gowpen
hog-pen
holpen
loipen
loupen
pompon
tompon
eo ipso
morpho
poo-poo
coop up
joypop
soup up
vox pop
bopper
comper
cooper
copper
couper
✧dopper
hooper
hopper
looper
lopper
mopper
✧popper
romper
soaper
souper
topper
torpor
compos
corpus
coypus
bowpot
compot
cowpat
forpet
forpit
hotpot
loupit
moppet
Pol Pot
poppet
poppit

roopit
roupit
toupet
cowpox
comply
✧pompey
popply
mosque
torque
boorka
moorva
cobric
Conrad
con-rod
forrad
horrid
hot rod
Modred
Socred
torrid
boorde
bo tree
bourne
✧bourse
coarse
coerce
corrie
course
cowrie
Dorrie
gourde
hoarse
loerie
lourie
Lowrie
Moerae
pourie
roarie
soirée
source
sourse
toorie
tourie
bodrag
toerag
tow-rag
fourth
hoorah
Howrah
Moirai
Tobruk
borrel
Bovril®
corral
sorrel
worral
worrel
fogram
pogrom
Conran
forren
poprin
sovran
gooroo
hooroo
journo
horror
pourer
roarer
soarer
tourer

boards
gourds
kouros
Morris®
morris
morros
zorros
forrit
hog-rat
Poirot
torret
worrit
borrow
morrow
sorrow
dourly
forray
gourdy
hooray
hourly
Norroy
pomroy
poorly
Rob Roy
sourly
foussa
poisha
gossib
corsac
bossed
fossed
hoised
Mossad
poised
soused
tossed
bowsie
cossie
donsie
fo'c'sle
fossae
mossie
mousie
mousle
mousmé
mousse
nousle
possie
pousse
sonsie
Sousse
sowsse
tousle
Monsig
borsch
bonsai
roesti
consul
dorsal
dorsel
dossal
dossel
dossil
fossil
housel
morsal
morsel
norsel
podsol
tolsel
tonsil

torsel
woosel
dorsum
'possum
Possum®
possum
Boyson
coosen
coosin
cousin
foison
godson
gossan
horson
loosen
poison
poyson
Roisin
tocsin
toison
tossen
worsen
gossip
toss up
toss-up
✧**bowser**
cooser
dorser
dosser
douser
dowser
fossor
josser
louser
moiser
motser
mouser
poiser
posser
rosser
rouser
tonsor
tosser
✧touser
✧towser
worser
wowser
Consus
corsos
gooses
horses
houses
louses
noesis
noises
souses
torsos
Comsat®
corset
cosset
doesn't
Dorset
dowset
lowsit
posset
Honshu
sou-sou
bowsaw
log-saw
bolshy
forsay

fousty
goosey
gousty
horsey
housey
mousey
toasty
tolsey
Wolsey
contra
footra
foutra
✧noctua
Nootka
Portia
rostra
hot tub
Yom Tob
aortic
Coptic
goetic
noetic
nostoc
poetic
✧pontic
Toltec
zoetic
booted
costed
cotted
cottid
doited
dotted
foetid
footed
hotted
jotted
lofted
lotted
moated
motto'd
potted
rooted
rotted
routed
sorted
sotted
totted
wonted
wotted
boatie
bootee
bootie
Bootle
bottle
bow tie
coatee
cootie
costae
Dottie
dottle
footie
footle
foutre
goatee
Goethe
goitre
goutte
hogtie
hottie
jostle

Words marked ✧ can also be spelled with one or more capital letters

loathe
Lottie
montre
mottle
pontie
pootle
postie
pottle
rootle
softie
soothe
sortie
to a tee
toetoe
tootle
tottie
toutie
wortle
sort of
dog tag
sontag
zoftig
hootch
toitoi
aortal
boatel
coital
costal
coutil
foetal
fontal
hostel
mortal
pontal
pontil
portal
postal
postil
bottom
montem
tom-tom
Bolton
bolt-on
bon ton
✧boston
bouton
coltan
cotton
gotten
looten
molten
moutan
mouton
ponton
rottan
rotten
soften
soft on
torten
won ton
too too
too-too
boot up
pop-top
post-op
post up
root up
boater
bolter
coater
colter

copter
co-star
coster
cottar
cotter
couter
doater
doctor
dorter
douter
foetor
footer
✧foster
fouter
goiter
hooter
hotter
jolter
jotter
lofter
loiter
looter
low-tar
mooter
mortar
mouter
✧pooter
✧porter
poster
potter
pouter
powter
rooter
rorter
roster
rotter
router
sorter
soutar
souter
sowter
tolter
tooter
totter
touter
zoster
Boötes
coitus
contos
Cortes
Cortés
costus
cottus
foetus
fortes
fortis
lottos
mottos
mouths
nostos
pontes
portas
pottos
sortes
tortes
youths
boat it
doitit
foot it
Post-it®
tomtit

kowtow
cortex
vortex
costly
couthy
forthy
hostry
loathy
mostly
mouthy
poetry
portly
rootsy
softly
toothy
tootsy
worthy
youthy
copula
gopura
koruna
morula
motuca
Podura
rosula
rotula
torula
Yoruba
zonula
toluic
jocund
rotund
cohune
colure
conure
lobule
locule
module
nodule
solute
vocule
volume
volute
zonule
zonure
coburg
go bung
go bush
so much
gomuti
lobuli
loculi
moduli
toruli
bohunk
mocuck
Podunk
toluol
column
✧jötunn
to burn
colugo
gomuto
modulo
roguer
voguer
forums
locums
moguls
coquet
go bust

locust
loquat
robust
roquet
yogurt
Mobutu
voguey
corvid
corvée
✧louvre
coeval
box van
hooven
Morven
bovver
do over
go over
Hoover®
✧hoover
louvar
louver
soever
solver
wolver
corves
✧corvus
hooves
loaves
looves
wolves
corvet
convex
volvox
convey
convoy
✧cobweb
bobwig
cotwal
kotwal
doo-wop
Cod War
hot war
godwit
wou-wou
bowwow
powwaw
powwow
wow-wow
for why
forwhy
Norway
bonxie
coaxer
hoaxer
coryza
corymb
cotyle
covyne
oocyte
polype
polypi
Jolyon
ronyon
cosy up
pony up
bowyer
polyps
nor yet
oocyst
Toryfy
boozed

foozle
mozzie
mozzle
nozzle
sozzle
touzle
borzoi
donzel
podzol
gozzan
zoozoo
bonzer
boozer
momzer
nozzer
rozzer
howzat
boozey
sozzly
tolzey
appaid
appayd
spraid
uphand
uphaud
upland
upward
L-plate
opiate
P-plate
T-plate
update
upgaze
upmake
uprate
uptake
sprang
upgang
uphang
splash
sprack
uptalk
sprawl
sprain
appair
sphaer
optant
upcast
upwaft
yplast
apiary
speary
epocha
ipecac
spaced
spiced
✧apache
specie
spicae
apical
epical
spycam
spacer
spicer
apices
specks
spicas
spacey
speccy
specky
epodic

apodal
apedom
spader
spider
spados
spadix
spuddy
append
spread
spredd
upheld
uplead
upsend
a piece
apiece
ephebe
sphene
sphere
speech
ephebi
appeal
upwell
spleen
uplean
speedo
upheap
upkeep
upleap
appear
sphear
upbear
uprear
uptear
splent
sprent
up-beat
upbeat
uprest
speedy
sphery
spiffy
spoffy
apogee
✧epigon
spight
spigot
ypight
spahee
op shop
upshot
✧epeira
optima
upbind
uphild
up-wind
upwind
aplite
éprise
épuisé
✧ophite
optime
splice
spline
sprite
Updike
up-line
uprise
upside
uptime
spliff
spaing

✧spring
spying
upping
splish
uppish
uplink
upfill
uphill
up-till
Ophism
option
aphids
optics
speiss
splits
spoils
à point
splint
spoilt
sprint
uplift
uprist
uptilt
✧sphinx
uppity
spritz
spiked
spoked
spoken
spikes
opaled
spalle
spulye
epilog
spilth
✧apollo
apples
epulis
opulus
applet
upblow
upflow
apeman
epimer
spammy
spined
spence
sponge
spunge
spinal
spinel
eponym
spinto
open up
opener
spinar
spinet
upknit
C P Snow
openly
spinny
spongy
spunky
apnoea
aplomb
opioid
uphold
upload
appose
aptote
opcode

oppose
splore
upcome
uprose
sprong
splosh
uplock
uplook
upboil
upcoil
uproll
uptorn
up town
uptown
uproar
apport
opt out
opt-out
sprout
spy out
upmost
uproot
aphony
spooky
spoony
epopee
apepsy
opaque
aporia
Sparta
spirea
spiric
sparid
spired
a-per-se
sparge
sparke
sparre
sparse
sperre
sperse
spurge
spurne
uphroe
updrag
Aphrah
eparch
sparth
spiral
operon
Oporto
upwrap
sparer
sparks
sports
sperst
✧spirit
aperçu
éperdu
updraw
upgrew
upgrow
approx
sparky
sparry
sporty
spurry
upbray
eposes
opuses
sposhy

aphtha
spathe
spetch
spital
sputum
spot-on
spit up
apathy
spotty
upstay
spauld
epaule
spouse
spruce
sprung
sprush
upgush
uprush
spruik
upcurl
upfurl
uphurl
oppugn
upturn
spruit
spouty
spavie
spavin
up-over
spivvy
spewer
spawny
upsway
a pox on
apexes
spayad
spryer
upryst
spryly
epizoa
apozem
squama
equate
squame
square
squash
squawk
squail
squall
equant
squeak
squeal
Aquila
equine
équipe
squire
squiff
squish
squill
squirm
squier
squirr
squids
squint
squirt
✧equity
squiny
Sqn Ldr
arcana
argala
armada

errata
organa
Oriana
argand
✧briard
errand
friand
Ormazd
arcade
arcane
breare
crease
create
dreare
ergate
✧grease
greave
ornate
preace
prease
triage
troade
urbane
areach
Armagh
breach
breath
broach
creach
creagh
eriach
preach
wreath
wroath
argali
Armani
arrack
cry aim
orgasm
ordain
preamp
broads
dreads
✧dryads
Greats
groats
✧oreads
trials
Arnaut
arrant
breast
creant
criant
dreamt
errant
triact
truant
Arcady
ariary
creaky
creamy
creasy
croaky
dreamy
dreary
freaky
friary
greasy
treaty
ersatz
dry bob

Arabic
arable
criblé
treble
tribal
arabin
graben
briber
prober
arabis
Erebus
grebos
Probus
probit
Irn-Bru®
crabby
drabby
drably
grabby
grubby
Kru-boy
pre-buy
trebly
Tricia
graced
priced
broché
Brücke
✧crèche
croche
Gracie
orache
Oracle®
oracle
troche
uracil
drachm
bracer
gricer
grocer
pricer
tracer
tricar
trocar
arccos
braces
crocus
cruces
fracas
Graces
grices
preces
précis
traces
tracks
Brecht
fricht
precut
tricot
Cracow
bricky
cricky
drecky
pricey
Tracey
tricky
uredia
iridic
eroded
traded
bridge

✧bridie
bridle
cradle
dredge
drudge
fridge
grudge
trudge
bridal
credal
iridal
Dryden
gradin
Grodno
crud up
grader
trader
✧credos
gradus
irides
trades
credit
aridly
cruddy
Freddy
Friday
Proddy
fraena
Frieda
freez'd
friend
breese
breeze
creese
freeze
frieze
Graeae
Graeme
✧greece
greese
greete
griece
grieve
kreese
preeve
priefe
prieve
triene
breech
creesh
ordeal
Orwell
orcein
free up
arrear
breeks
briefs
Creeks
cruels
✧greens
orders
uraeus
ardent
argent
arpent
arrect
arrest
driest
Ernest
freest
orgeat

✧orient
priest
urgent
urtext
wriest
wryest
artery
breezy
briery
creeky
creepy
freely
freety
greedy
greeny
griesy
gryesy
ornery
orrery
troely
prefab
trifid
griffe
trifle
trofie
armful
artful
ireful
urnful
Gräfin
gryfon
prefer
drafts
Arafat
profit
orifex
prefix
crafty
draffy
drafty
drifty
dry-fly
bregma
tragic
Brigid
frigid
brigue
brogue
Brugge
dragée
drogue
Prague
Progne
grigri
frugal
Aragon
brogan
drag on
✧dragon
grog-on
Oregon
origan
Origen
origin
orogen
trigon
trogon
Trygon
drag up
grog-up
droger

fragor
Bruges
gregos
tragus
troggs
aright
bright
Brigit
fright
frigot
wright
gru-gru
bragly
craggy
drag by
draggy
dreggy
druggy
✧froggy
groggy
trigly
Brahma
Orphic
arched
Mr Chad
orchid
Archie
Brahmi
archil
orchel
orchil
Arnhem
Graham
archon
arghan
arshin
brehon
orphan
urchin
✧archer
Arthur
✧arches
Brahms
Crohn's
✧orchis
orthos
orchat
archly
arnica
orbita
pruina
✧troika
urtica
braird
araise
Argive
arkite
arride
arrive
arsine
braide
braise
braize
bruise
cruise
cruive
dry ice
ermine
fraise
froise
Graiae

graile
graine
greige
Irvine
orcine
oreide
oroide
orpine
praise
preife
proine
pruine
ureide
ursine
arcing
crying
drying
erring
frying
prying
trying
urging
urning
arrish
dreich
droich
dryish
graith
wraith
erbium
truism
Arrian
proign
Orsino
brails
brains
fruits
grains
orgies
aroint
'Arriet
artist
fruict
brainy
freity
fruity
grainy
orbity
prajna
frijol
Trajan
Trojan
tri-jet
arcked
grakle
broken
kraken
Wrekin
wroken
broker
proker
irokos
Kraków
trek-ox
crikey
aralia
arolla
brolga
frolic
Uralic
grille

grilse
or else
Tralee
proleg
✧prolog
arilli
prelim
Dralon®
trillo
Dr Slop
proler
frills
armlet
pre-let
prolix
brolly
drolly
frilly
orally
✧trilby
trolly
gramma
premia
uremia
bromic
dromic
eremic
uremic
framed
premed
gramme
premie
tremie
trémie
trompe
grumph
dromoi
Urumqi
brumal
primal
Bremen
crimen
crumen
dromon
Kru-man
Truman
crambo
Crimbo
Dromio
drum up
Mrs Mop
cremor
framer
primer
tremor
trimer
Aramis
cramps
crumbs
dromos
Grimes
grumps
primos
Primus®
primus
promos
fremit
gromet
Gromit
prompt
premix

trimix
brumby
crampy
crimpy
crumby
crummy
crumpy
drumly
frumpy
Grammy
grimly
grumly
grumpy
primly
trimly
Aranea
Brenda
crania
Grania
Granta
Granya
Urania
irenic
ironic
uranic
branle
brenne
Brontë
bronze
cringe
France
frenne
fringe
Fronde
grande
grange
grunge
✧orange
prance
✧prince
trance
transe
branch
brunch
cranch
crunch
drench
✧french
Granth
trench
wrench
Brunei
pranck
Brunel
crenel
crinal
trinal
uranyl
urinal
crinum
frenum
granum
iron-on
kronen
uranin
Brando
bronco
drongo
eringo
eryngo
franco

gringo
pronto
Trento
pre-nup
ironer
kroner
kronor
krónur
pruner
branks
crants
Cronus
Erinys
Kronos
prunus
trunks
Uranus
Brandt
brunet
cronet
ere now
erenow
brandy
branky
branny
bronzy
cranky
cranny
franzy
frenzy
fringy
granny
grungy
Orkney
pranky
tranny
trendy
krantz
areola
arroba
Arnold
areole
arkose
Brooke
broose
✧creole
croove
droome
groove
orgone
oriole
triode
triose
cry off
dry off
brooch
ariosi
krooni
arioso
arroyo
arbour
ardour
armour
arrows
kroons
proofs
troops
cry out
dry out
pry out
try out

try-out
ormolu
argosy
armory
arrowy
✧briony
broody
broomy
✧bryony
✧droopy
grooly
groovy
priory
grappa
tropic
draped
trepid
tripod
uropod
craple
frappé
graple
griple
grippe
triple
trophi
drupel
propel
propyl
crepon
drop in
drop-in
fripon
trapan
trepan
wrap in
crypto
troppo
crop up
prop up
trip up
wrap up
draper
griper
groper
proper
cripes
Cripps
drapes
gripes
trapes
tripos
armpit
drapet
crepey
croppy
drappy
drippy
drop by
dropsy
grapey
grippy
prepay
preppy
trappy
tripey
triply
trippy
trophy
Griqua
Braque

frorne
crural
dry run
froren
dry rot
arista
Crispa
crissa
crista
crusta
friska
frusta
Orissa
Prisca
Trisha
erased
irised
crosse
crusie
frisée
graste
grosze
grysie
triste
wrasse
dry ski
✧**prusik**
cresol
trisul
arcsin
arisen
grison
orison
prison
aristo
fresco
Fresno
presto
eraser
groser
priser
proser
crases
crasis
crises
crisis
crisps
irises
krises
preses
prisms
uresis
urosis
uruses
cruset
groset
preset
prosit
Brasov
brashy
brassy
brisky
brushy
crispy
Crosby
crusty
dressy
drosky
drossy
frisky
frosty

grassy
grisly
groszy
prismy
prissy
trashy
tressy
trusty
wristy
Aretha
protea
✧**arctic**
✧cretic
critic
erotic
iritic
uretic
grated
X-rated
pratie
wrethe
writhe
cratch
crotch
crutch
fratch
grutch
wretch
brutal
crotal
protyl
trotyl
pro tem
arctan
✧breton
Briton
craton
Cretan
cretin
croton
erg-ten
gratin
Proton®
proton
✧triton
grotto
bruter
✧crater
cratur
frater
grater
krater
orator
prater
pretor
ureter
writer
Brutus
gratis
iritis
frutex
pre-tax
bratty
fratry
fretty
frothy
gritty
grotty
pretty
truthy
wrathy

trauma
Ursula
around
ground
Ormuzd
arbute
argute
armure
arouse
brouze
croupe
crouse
croûte
grouse
ordure
triune
troule
troupe
trouse
brough
crouch
drouth
grouch
grough
trough
arguli
arguer
trouts
draunt
irrupt
Proust
argufy
croupy
groupy
grouty
trouty
hryvna
trivia
graved
gravid
proved
prevue
drivel
frivol
gravel
grovel
travel
craven
driven
graven
proven
à **ravir**
craver
driver
drover
graver
or ever
prover
Trevor
trover
bravos
Graves'
✧graves
travis
Treves
trevis
brevet
cravat
grivet
grovet
privet

trivet
crowed
browse
drawee
drowse
frowie
prawle
growth
crewel
trowel
draw in
draw on
prewyn
brew up
brew-up
draw up
grow up
brewer
drawer
grower
pre-war
brewis
browst
frowst
brawly
brawny
browny
browsy
crawly
drowsy
frowsy
frowzy
growly
Trixie
wraxle
cruxes
orexis
praxis
Freyja
prayed
arayse
argyle
grayle
groyne
proyne
trayne
Cruyff
Argyll
crayon
Troyan
brayer
crayer
prayer
aroynt
greyly
Prozac®
crazed
prized
✧**brazil**
drazel
frazil
brazen
frozen
Arezzo
grazer
prizer
frizzy
Grozny
Asmara
Astana
espada

Iswara
Tswana
Asgard
island
Oswald
usward
ashake
ashame
aslake
astare
escape
estate
osmate
V-shape
askari
assail
Ismail
Israel
aswarm
escarp
askant
aslant
assart
astart
as many
usable
✧**isabel**
Ishbel
Isobel
ash-bin
isobar
usably
psocid
✧**psyche**
ash-can
✧**psycho**
Isodia
Ashdod
used in
used-up
usedn't
ascend
Ostend
yshend
Essene
as hell
as well
osteal
esteem
astern
ossein
asleep
asmear
assess
assets
ascent
aspect
assent
assert
astert
Osbert
ostent
ashery
astely
esnecy
osiery
useful
isogon
usager
usages
asthma

ischia
isohel
as then
eschar
Escher
Esther
eschew
espied
ashine
aspine
aspire
assize
essive
oscine
aswing
Isaiah
aspick
Ostiak
aswirl
espial
ostial
osmium
ostium
ascian
assign
Ossian
ustion
Eskimo
assist
T-shirt
aseity
ossify
ash-key
esc key
Isolda
psylla
Isolde
a salti
asylum
as also
ashlar
ashler
ostler
Psalms
Ashley
tsamba
Ostmen
isomer
Asimov
usance
Usenet
Esmond
ashore
aslope
astone
osmose
assoil
aswoon
esloin
essoin
astoop
osmous
ask out
asport
aspout
assort
assott
escort
astony
isopod
ash-pan

ash-pit
Ostrea
escroc
psoric
Astrid
user ID
Ashraf
astral
escrol
asarum
as from
ashram
T-strap
usurer
Esdras
estrus
Osiris
tsuris
astrut
esprit
escrow
Astrex
astray
estray
osprey
Osasco
tsetse
tsotsi
isatin
Ishtar
Isatis
Ashura
oscula
osmund
assume
assure
astute
oscule
as much
as such
escudo
pseudo
issuer
asquat
Iseult
psywar
Ostyak
ottava
Ottawa
strata
at hand
steard
strand
Utgard
at ease
at gaze
ethane
steale
steane
steare
strafe
strake
straff
attach
strath
attack
attask
strack
straik
Y-track
atlatl

Mt Taal
St Paul
attain
atwain
Q-train
strain
strawn
St Malo
Strabo
Strato
stramp
it says
strass
strays
at last
stealt
strait
Stuart
steady
steamy
strawy
stable
atabeg
atabek
atabal
Stubbs
stably
stubby
atocia
stacte
stucco
sticks
stocks
Stacey
sticky
stocky
stadda
stadia
stedde
stodge
studio
at odds
Études
steddy
stodgy
studly
Athena
Strega®
attend
steeld
Athene
ethene
St Bede
steeve
stieve
strene
itself
streak
streek
atweel
streel
stream
atween
Etnean
strewn
Stheno
Athens
Atreus
steels
stress
at best

at rest
attent
attest
ita est
✧street
steedy
steely
steepy
steery
Staffa
stifle
staffs
stiffy
stuffy
stigma
staged
stigme
stogie
stager
stag it
stagey
stogey
stuggy
etcher
at that
Attila
striga
attire
étoile
striae
stride
strife
strike
Strine
stripe
strive
a'thing
string
stying
k'thibh
staith
strich
at risk
at-risk
atrial
at will
It Girl
atrium
Mt Sion
Mt Zion
Ethiop
étrier
Atkins
ethics
stairs
atwixt
strict
strift
stripy
stoked
atokal
stoker
stakes
stokes
Stella
✧**italic**
stoled
stolid
Attlee
stelae
stalag
etalon
Stalin
stolen
stolon
Otello
stalko
stelar
stylar
stalls
Still's
stylos
stylus
stilet
stylet
otalgy
stalky
stilly
stilty
stemma
✧**atomic**
etymic
stemme
stimie
stymie
stomal
ataman
etymon
stamen
a tempo
stumer
stumps
stumpy
stanza
atonic
ethnic
stoned
at once
stance
stanze
stonne
stanch
stench
stanck
atonal
stuns'l
stonen
stanzo
stingo
stinko
atoner
stoner
stenos
stinks
stingy
stinky
stinty
Atropa
stroma
stromb
Atwood
strond
✧stroud
at home
at-home
attone
otiose
stooge
stoope
strobe
strode
stroke
strove
strong
Mt Cook
strook
stroll
stroam
attorn
St John
strown
stroup
stools
at most
strout
utmost
✧**utopia**
atopic
etypic
stupid
staple
steppe
stipel
step in
step-in
step on
stop in
stop-go
step up
step-up
stop up
stupor
stapes
stipes
stop by
pteria
sterna
stirra
yttria
athrob
steric
yttric
à terre
eterne
starve
Sterne
sterve
stirre
storge
starch
sterol
iterum
pterin
stereo
Sterno®
attrap
stir up
starer
storer
Pteris
stirps
stores
uterus
attrit
storax
styrax
starry
storey
stormy
sturdy
Mt Ossa
ptisan
ptoses
ptosis
stasis
Mt Etna
statua
static
at stud
stated
statue
stitch
statal
statim
statin
stotin
stater
stator
otitis
✧states
status
stithy
stotty
struma
stound
attune
strung
stoush
stouth
Mt Fuji
struck
at outs
strunt
stoury
staved
stived
Stevie
Ativan®
✧steven
stiver
stover
staves
St Ives
stawed
stewed
stownd
stowre
stewer
stower
ataxia
ataxic
ptyxis
stayed
ethyne
stayne
stayre
stay in
stay up
stayer
curara
Guyana
Judaea
kumara
Lusaka
Purana
Tucana
Tupaia
yukata
Judaic
Dugald
aubade
aurate
butane
cubage
curare
curate
fumage
furane
humane
jubate
jugate
lunate
luxate
mucate
Mugabe
murage
mutate
nutate
outage
pupate
rugate
sudate
tubage
tubate
musang
queach
sumach
curari
gurami
jupati
✧kumari
ourali
ourari
rubati
Eubank
out-ask
aumail
eucain
fusain
Husain
supawn
bumalo
fugato
fumado
Lugano
rubato
turaco
au pair
Suhair
oubaas
au fait
durant
jumart
jurant
Kuwait
mutant
nutant
subact
Subaru®
Tuvalu
curacy
eutaxy
lunacy
lunary
muzaky
punany
queasy
queazy
sudary
sugary
Puebla
hubbub
✧**quebec**
bulbed
cubbed
cue bid
dubbed
gubbed
numbed
outbid
rubbed
rum bud
subbed
sunbed
surbed
turbid
bubble
bum-bee
✧bumble
burble
fumble
Guebre
humble
jumbie
jumble
mumble
nubble
outbye
rubble
rumble
suable
subbie
tumble
bum bag
bumbag
humbug
gubbah
jubbah
bulbel
bulbil
bulbul
jumbal
dubbin
Durban
nubbin
tulban
turban
✧**pueblo**
bulbar
busbar
cumber
durbar
Gueber
Humber
lubber
lumbar
lumber
number
outbar
rubber
tubber
bumbos
gumbos
jumbos
rumbos
turbos
burbot
numbat
rubbet
rubbit
surbet
turbit
turbot
sunbow
out-box
outbox
aumbry
bubbly
busboy
dumbly
humbly
jumbly
nubbly
numbly
rubbly
rumbly
suably
cutcha
fulcra
kuccha
kutcha
Murcia
puncta
juiced
muscid
Dulcie
muscle
nuncle
quiche
tusche
succah
buccal
furcal
sulcal
Duncan
Tuscan
✧vulcan
nuncio
puncto
hub-cap
juicer
succor
buncos
cuscus
guacos
juncos
juncus
ruscus
succès
succus
sulcus
Turcos
dulcet
mudcat
✧muscat
dun-cow
bunchy
muscly
outcry
punchy
✧**buddha**
sundra
tundra
mundic
budded
funded
rudded
buddle
bundle
burdie
cuddie
cuddle
Culdee
curdle
duddie
Dundee
fuddle
fundie
guddle
huddle
hurdle
muddle
nurdle
puddle
ruddle
rundle
subdue
sundae
gun dog
pug dog
sundog
numdah
purdah
sundri
dum-dum
dumdum
durdum
quidam
burden
cudden
cuddin
guidon
gulden
hudden
hurden
lurdan
lurden
Mukden
pudden
sudden
tundun
huddup
dudder
dunder
funder
furder
✧guider
judder
mudder
murder
pudder
rudder
sudder
sunder
fundus
Turdus
pundit
subdew
sundew
cuddly
muddly
puddly
Purdey®
run dry
Sunday
sundry
eureka
muleta
murena
superb
but-end
butene
Eugene
quaere
Sûreté
tuyère
super G
humeri
ourebi
puteli
Lübeck
rule OK
cuneal
luteal
puteal
museum
Augean
dudeen
Humean
Judean
lucern
lutein
luzern
tune in
tureen
pukeko
pumelo
tupelo
tuxedo
dude up
tune up
tune-up
auteur
fureur
auceps
aureus
buteos
duress
duvets
fumets
lumens
Queens
Rubens
rumens
duke it
funest
Hubert
humect
lucent
outeat
ouvert
pudent
queest
Rupert
bureau
Juneau
cutely
cutesy
dukery
dupery
hugely
humefy
mutely
nudely
purely
queeny
rubefy
rudely
rudery
surely
surety
tumefy
puffed
ruffed
turfed
cuffle
duffle
guffie
muffle

Words marked ✧ can also be spelled with one or more capital letters

purfle
ruffle
surfie
cupful
dueful
duffel
fulfil
gutful
jugful
mugful
rueful
tubful
cuffin
muffin
nuffin
puffin
ruffin
turfen
duff up
puff up
buffer
duffer
fun fur
furfur
puffer
suffer
sulfur
surfer
buffet
outfit
tuffet
subfeu
curfew
guffaw
outfox
suffix
outfly
purfly
quagga
bugged
fulgid
hugged
jugged
lugged
lunged
mugged
rugged
sun-god
tugged
turgid
budgie
bungee
bungie
bungle
burgee
burgle
Duggie
guggle
gurgle
juggle
jungle
luggie
lungie
muggee
puggie
puggle
jungli
cudgel
fungal
subgum
buggan

buggin
durgan
✧kurgan
outgun
burgoo
gung-ho
hung up
budger
Bulgar
bulger
bulgur
burger
fulgor
hunger
lugger
mudger
mugger
nudger
nuggar
purger
rugger
sungar
tugger
turgor
vulgar
Burgos
fungus
Judges
mungos
outgas
Tungus
vulgus
✧budget
nugget
quight
kung fu
bungey
hungry
jungly
quaggy
tughra
bushed
hushed
pushed
ruched
euchre
Hughie
nuchae
qui-hye
rushee
tushie
nurhag
quahog
muzhik
burhel
bushel
muchel
Mughal
nuchal
Durham
✧fulham
humhum
Buchan
eughen
euphon
Fushun
Kuchen
mud hen
Pushan
push on
rushen

tuchun
Pushto
tu-whoo
Wu Chao
hush up
push-up
author
gusher
husher
lusher
Luther
musher
Nuphar
outher
pusher
rusher
wuther
Hughes
rushes
cushat
lum hat
outhit
sunhat
Fuzhou
Pushtu
Suzhou
Xuzhou
cushaw
cushty
lushly
muchly
oughly
Auriga
cubica
Judica
Lucina
lumina
numina
Punica
Rubina
✧rumina
guaiac
buried
busied
dutied
rubied
audile
augite
dugite
dunite
Eunice
fusile
futile
gunite
humite
kumite
Lucite®
lumine
lupine
munite
murine
musive
mutine
nubile
pumice
purine
rubine
rusine
rutile
supine
sutile

busing
buying
cueing
during
luging
luting
musing
outing
puling
rueing
ruling
tubing
tuning
dudish
Judith
Jutish
mulish
Munich
punish
quaich
quaigh
rudish
rupiah
Zurich
buriti
audial
Auriel
Auriol
burial
curial
Muriel
autism
✧cubism
curium
dudism
Humism
mutism
nudism
✧purism
Sufism
bunion
dupion
durian
durion
fusion
Humian
Julian
Lucian
Tupian
turion
Zunian
Zuñian
subito
✧junior
punier
tunier
audios
curios
Furies
Julius
kumiss
Lucius
quoits
rubies
aurist
cubist
cueist
curiet
Humist
✧juliet
jurist

lutist
nudist
purist
quaint
queint
quoist
aurify
bulimy
busily
humify
munify
mutiny
nudity
punily
purify
purity
rubify
nutjob
Punjab
bunjee
bunjie
jug-jug
gurjun
outjet
outjut
buckra
funkia
Gurkha
pulkha
quokka
Turkic
busked
husked
musked
sucked
tusked
buckie
buckle
huckle
junkie
luckie
muckle
muskle
puckle
ruckle
runkle
suckle
sunkie
muskeg
punkah
sukkah
bunkum
bumkin
buskin
dusken
lucken
muck in
rumkin
Ruskin
sucken
suck in
suck-in
sunken
tuck in
tuck-in
cuckoo
buck up
bulk up
bunk-up
muck up
muck-up

ruck up
suck up
tuck up
bucker
bulker
bunker
busker
ducker
duiker
✧dunker
duyker
hunker
husker
✧junker
kunkar
kunkur
lunker
lurker
✧mucker
pucker
✧quaker
sucker
tucker
Tunker
tuskar
tusker
yucker
bubkes
bunkos
ruckus
turkis
bucket
busket
busk it
junket
musket
sucket
Sukkot
sunket
tucket
musk ox
duskly
turkey
Huelva
qualia
quelea
mucluc
public
curled
Euclid
guiled
mulled
bullae
humlie
ouglie
outlie
ruelle
tuille
putlog
Guelph
Gullah
mullah
nullah
quelch
nuclei
mukluk
suslik
fullam
Muslim
dualin
Dublin

dunlin
fullan
full-on
Lublin
muflon
murlan
murlin
muslin
pull in
pull-in
pull-on
purlin
sullen
duello
burlap
curl up
Dunlop
full up
pull up
pull-up
bugler
buller
burler
butler
culler
curler
cutler
fuller
guiler
guller
guslar
guyler
hurler
muller
outler
puller
purler
sutler
cullis
hullos
auklet
buglet
bullet
cullet
cutlet
duplet
gullet
Gullit
gurlet
juglet
mullet
nutlet
outlet
pullet
runlet
sublet
sunlit
curlew
Ludlow
outlaw
run low
duplex
Ku Klux
suplex
burley
dually
Dudley
guilty
gulley
hurley
mulley

outlay
pulley
qualmy
wurley
mummia
Suomic
bummed
gummed
hummed
mummed
summed
bummle
summae
nutmeg
bummel
hummel
kümmel
mulmul
pummel
hummum
Burman
busman
culmen
cummin
cupman
gunman
musmon
outman
subman
summon
tutman
bummer
cummer
fulmar
hummer
mummer
murmur
rummer
summar
summer
duomos
hummus
submit
summat
summit
muu-muu
lummox
bunnia
duenna
✧guinea
Luanda
quanta
quinoa
quinta
Hunnic
muonic
quinic
burned
dunned
gunned
punned
ruined
sunned
tunned
turned
vulned
Bunnie
duende
nuance
✧quince
quinie

quinte
quinze
numnah
quench
Sunnah
nudnik
funnel
gunnel
quinol
runnel
✧tunnel
burn in
burn-in
guenon
turn in
turn-in
turn on
turn-on
guango
quango
burn up
burn-up
turnip
turn up
turn-up
burner
cunner
gunner
punner
ruiner
runner
✧turner
wunner
guanos
burnet
gumnut
gurnet
punnet
runnet
Tuanku
curney
gurney
quinsy
✧aurora
cupola
Euboea
Europa
judoka
mucosa
rucola
au fond
cuboid
fucoid
lupoid
mucoid
Aurore
dumose
Europe
furole
furore
quooke
rugose
buy off
cut off
cut-off
fub off
put off
put-off
rub off
Rudolf
run off

run-off
bugong
dugong
oulong
judogi
zufoli
nut oil
suborn
zufolo
Euro-MP
humour
huzoor
rumour
tumour
aurous
buboes
dumous
fumous
humous
lupous
mucous
putois
rufous
rugous
bug out
bug-out
buy out
buyout
cut out
cut-out
dugout
jut out
put out
rub out
rubout
run out
run-out
eulogy
sulpha
cupped
cusped
cuspid
humped
pumped
pupped
supped
tupped
burpee
dumple
mud pie
purpie
purple
rumple
supple
✧yumpie
✧yuppie
huppah
curpel
dump on
✧humpen
jump on
lumpen
luppen
bump up
jump-up
pump up
bumper
cupper
dumper
gulper
humper
jumper
lumper
mumper
pulper
pumper
Rumper
supper
Puppis
quipos
rumpus
Vulpes
muppet
output
pulpit
puppet
put-put
sumpit
Quapaw
furphy
humpty
murphy
numpty
purply
rumply
supply
tumphy
pulque
murrha
nutria
cupric
lubric
rubric
furred
outred
putrid
currie
durrie
quar'le
quarte
✧**runrig**
Tuareg
tugrug
gurrah
hurrah
tugrik
burrel
musrol
murram
quorum
fun run
Gudrun
murren
murrin
outrun
cuerpo
quarto
querpo
bum rap
Tubruq
Führer
burros
Durres
fueros
guards
guiros
hubris
mucros
Munros
Gujrat
gutrot
rug rat
turret
burrow
furrow
tutrix
Aubrey
Audrey
hurray
✧murray
murrey
quarry
quirky
sunray
surrey
quartz
cuesta
✧russia
subsea
cursed
cussed
gutsed
pulsed
sussed
Aussie
bursae
cuisse
✧gussie
nursle
puisne
pursue
tussle
hussif
Bursch
putsch
tussah
tusseh
bukshi
muesli
munshi
Russki
bursal
cursal
gunsel
mussel
pussel
russel
tussal
outsum
✧**bunsen**
Hudson
Hun Sen
Tucson
tutsan
muss up
bursar
curser
cursor
cusser
fusser
guiser
gutser
hussar
nurser
pulsar
purser
pusser
quasar
sudser
tusser
busses
cursus
tussis
gusset
outset
outsit
russet
subset
sunset
pursew
gun-shy
pudsey
puisny
Russky
lustra
quite a
quotha
cultic
fustic
fustoc
luetic
rustic
bunted
busted
gutted
hunted
hutted
jutted
nutted
putted
quited
runted
rusted
rutted
suited
tufted
tutted
✧**auntie**
bustee
bustle
buttle
cup-tie
cuttle
cuttoe
gustie
guttae
guttle
hurtle
hustle
justle
lustre
mustee
puntee
puttee
puttie
quethe
rustle
rustre
✧subtle
suttee
suttle
turtle
cultch
quatch
quetch
quitch
duetti
tuk tuk
buntal
curtal
subtil
custom
multum
qui tam
quotum
tum-tum
Austen
Austin
Austin®
bun tin
✧burton
butt in
button
Buxton
Dustin
Justin
luiten
lutten
Multan
muntin
mutton
pultan
pulton
pultun
putten
sultan
suntan
Sutton
duetto
just so
bust up
bust-up
dust-up
hunt up
outtop
aunter
Auster
✧bunter
✧buster
butter
cuiter
culter
cutter
duster
guitar
gunter
gutter
hunter
hurter
Kultur
luster
muster
mutter
nutter
ouster
punter
putter
quoter
rutter
suitor
tufter
cultus
✧custos
duetts
juntos
Muftis
puntos
quotas
quotes
tuttis
fustet
Muftat
mustn't
tut-tut
Gustav
surtax
auntly
curtly
curtsy
justly
subtly
suetty
sultry
suttly
aucuba
lucuma
lunula
Luzula
mutuca
suburb
queued
cupule
curule
euouae
future
jujube
lunule
mutule
nucule
puture
suture
tubule
fu yung
Duluth
eunuch
cumuli
tumuli
Nubuck
Buñuel
mutual
mutuel
mutuum
auburn
autumn
lucumo
queuer
bututs
✧**august**
tumult
augury
humusy
luxury
curved
fulvid
Humvee®
luvvie
outvie
pulvil
vulval
culver
pulver
quaver
quiver
vulvar
curves
turves
curvet
survew
kurvey
purvey
survey
suivez
outwin
pulwar
tulwar
outwit
runway
subway
Jun Xie
lunyie
gunyah
yum-yum
Bunyan
bunyip
buoy up
huzza'd
fuzzle
guzzle
muzzle
nuzzle
puzzle
wuzzle
puzzel
zuzzim
buzzer
guizer
gutzer
nuzzer
putzes
aviate
TV game
aviary
ovibos
avocet
Evadne
Avedon
avidin
evader
avidly
Oviedo
Evreux
Aveira
availe
avails
evejar
evoker
avulse
évolué
evolve
evulse
svelte
uvulae
Avalon
Evelyn
ovular
uvular
Aviles
uvulas
evilly
ovally
avenge
✧avenue
evince
Evonne
Yvonne
avanti
even so
even up
avenir
evener
evenly
evzone
uveous
Evipan®
Avarua
Svarga
averse
Averil
DVD-ROM
ever so
overdo
overgo
overby
overly
Avesta
ovisac
avised
Kvasir
avisos
avoset
ivy-tod
Yvette
kvetch
avital
avatar
ovator
avoure
avouch
avaunt
evovae
avowed
avowal
avower
avowry
avoyer
sweard
awhape
awrack
sweats
aweary
sweaty
two-bit
swabby
kwacha
owl-car
twicer
Sweden
swaddy
a'where
tweeze
twyere
awheel
a wheen
sweets
tweeds
sweert
owlery
sweeny
sweepy
✧sweety
tweedy
tweely
tweeny
swag it
twight
twiggy
ewghen
awhile
twaite
awning
aweigh
owlish
sweirt
awaked
awaken
awoken
✧**twelve**
twilit
owelty
twilly
swampy
swimmy
Gwenda
kwanza
Rwanda
twined
swinge
twinge
swan in
swan up
twiner
swink't
swanky
swanny
swingy
twangy
twenty
awsome
ywroke
awrong
swoosh
awmous
swiper
swipes
swipey
two-ply
Swarga
Swerga
awmrie
swarve
swerve
swarth
swaraj
dwarfs
swords
owerby
qwerty
swardy
swarty
swirly
twirly
swashy
swishy
twisty
swathe
awatch
swatch
Switch®
switch
twitch
awetos
ewftes
swathy
swatty
swotty
swound
'twould
swoune
swivel
sweven
swivet
swownd
swowne
two-way
swayed
sway up
swayer
awayes
excamb

expand
oxland
exhale
oxgate
oxgang
oxtail
extant
extasy
Exocet®
exedra
exodic
✧exodus
exceed
expend
extend
oxhead
extern
excess
except
expect
expert
exsect
exsert
extent
exogen
oxygen
ox-bird
excide
excise
excite
expire
extine
extirp
expiry
axilla
exilic
oxalic
oxslip
oxalis
oxymel
axeman
examen
exomis
exempt
axenic
exonic
ex ante
axonal
exonym
extold
✧oxford
expose
exposé
ex dono
ex voto
Exmoor
exhort
export
extort
exopod
exequy
exarch
exergy
axises
exotic
Exeter
excuse
exhume
expugn
exeunt
ox-eyed
Aymara
by hand
aye aye
aye-aye
by-lane
by-name
byname
cytase
gyrate
hypate
lynage
lyrate
mygale
my lane
zymase
by half
pygarg
bypath
dynamo
bypass
by-past
byzant
dynast
gyrant
Tybalt
tyrant
my lady
bye-bye
dyable
nybble
dybbuk
cymbal
gymbal
symbol
tymbal
fynbos
Syncom
eye-cup
dyadic
syndic
kynded
pye-dog
gylden
Hyades
syndet
hyaena
Cybele
Cyrene
pyrene
xylene
myself
rypeck
✧lyceum
wyvern
zydeco
hype up
eyeful
fylfot
kyogen
myogen
syngas
Kyrgyz
Pythia
mythic
Pythic
hyphae
lychee
hyphal
zythum
by then
hyphen
✧python
syphon
✧typhon
cypher
sypher
mythos
mythus
sythes
typhus
Myrica
Syriac
eyliad
myriad
byline
bylive
by-time
lysine
pyrite
zymite
dyeing
eyeing
pyeing
typing
tykish
cytisi
hylism
lyrism
Myriam
Syrism
Lydian
Syrian
Tyrian
Vyvian
Zyrian
Cynips
lyrics
hylist
lyrist
typist
✧syrinx
typify
ryokan
cyclic
eyelid
syrlye
cyclin
hyalin
myelin
myelon
Syalon®
cycler
Byblos
cyclos
cyclus
nyalas
by-plot
eyalet
eyelet
by-blow
bye-law
byrlaw
by-play
pyemia
gymmal
Nyanja
nyanza
cyanic
gymnic
hymnic
hypnic
pycnic
pyknic
hymned
byrnie
hymnal
hypnum
cyanin
pycnon
pyoner
Cygnus
Hypnos
cygnet
gynney
Sydney
Lycosa
myxoma
Pyrola
Wynona
xyloma
zygoma
Ty Cobb
ayword
byroad
byword
cymoid
cytoid
hypoid
jymold
My Lord
my word
xyloid
zymoid
bygone
by Jove
by rote
cymose
cytode
dynode
gyrose
Mysore
pyrope
tylote
Tyrone
xylose
zygose
zygote
zymome
cyborg
Nyborg
kybosh
by-work
by-form
byroom
tycoon
dyvour
cymous
gyrous
pylons
syboes
sybows
tyroes
my foot!
Dympna
myopia
myopic
gypped
tympan
Nymphs
eye-pit
sylphy
hydria
pyuria
Cymric
hydric
synroc
cybrid
cyprid
hybrid
rya rug
Pyrrho
cy pres
cypris
✧cyprus
hybris
hydros
Hydrus
Ayesha
byssal
gypsum
myosin
hyssop
byssus
cyeses
cyesis
Hyksos
myosis
Lynsey
cystic
mystic
cystid
Eyetie
✧myrtle
tystie
xystoi
hyetal
✧system
syntan
oyster
xyster
Myrtus
syrtes
syrtis
xystos
xystus
syntax
lyfull
Tyburn
dysury
syrupy
✧sylvia
sylvae
sylvan
sylvas
lynxes
hydyne
Vyvyan
tyiyns
syzygy
izzard
Azrael
azo dye
tzaddi
ozaena
Szeged
azygos
Tz'u Hsi
Uzziah
Szekel
azalea
azolla
Ozalid®
Azania
Nzinga
azonic
ozonic
azonal
mzungu
azione
czapka
dzeren
Azores
azotic
tzetse
tzetze

7 – even

Bahamas
bananas
baracan
Calabar
Canajan
carabao
caracal
Caracas
caravan
caraway
Cataian
Catalan
catapan
Catayan
Daya Bay
eat away
✧faraday
faraway
Galahad
Halakah
halalas
halavah
jacamar
jai alai
jamadar
Java man
kahawai
kajawah
lay away
layaway
macadam
Malayan
maracas
Maracay
nacarat
pajamas
palamae
palatal
Palauan
Palawan
Pan-Arab
patamar
qabalah
Ramadan
rat-a-tat
Sabaean
Sabahan
sagaman
Saharan
sarafan
Satanas
tamarao
tamarau
tanadar
waratah
yatagan
caramba
catawba
Garamba
✧balance
balancé
Jamaica
navarch
Tabasco®
vacance
vacancy
valance
Bacardi®
calando
kabaddi
mafalde
tamandu
Banares
cabaret
cadaver
camaïeu
caramel
caravel
damages
data set
falafel
galabea
✧galatea
garagey
hanaper
Janácek
Java Sea
Kara Sea
kayaker
lazaret
manager
manatee
naiades
palaver
panacea
Papaver
parader
parapet
para-red
Pasajes
ravager
Saracen
tabaret
tanager
Wahabee
Falange
galanga
sarangi
calathi
earache
Falasha
ganache
Halacha
Karachi
Malachi
Maratha
Marathi
Natasha
navarho
panache
paratha
sagathy
samadhi
tamasha
baladin
canakin
cap-a-pie
cap-à-pie
carabid
carabin
Catania
dalasis
dataria
fanatic
faradic
Gagarin
galabia
gazania
hadarim
jalapic
jalapin
Latakia
malacia
malaria
manakin
Mazarin
nagapie
Nasalis
Natalia
Natalie
navarin
paladin
Panagia
Paradip
patagia
Patarin
ramakin
ratafia
✧salamis
Samaria
Sarapic
Sarapis
satanic
savarin
tabanid
talaria
tamarin
Tataric
vanadic
karaoke
malarky
banally
batable
capable
capably
cavalla
cavally
datable
eatable
fadable
fatally
hatable
makable
manacle
Manaslu
namable
nasally
pacable
papable
papally
parable
parafle
payable
ratable
ratably
salable
salably
savable
sayable
takable
tamable
taxable
taxably
✧vatable
wadable
✧mahatma
paracme
salaams
ca' canny
caranna
carauna
Danaans
Gawayne
lasagna
lasagne
rabanna
savanna
talaunt
Badajoz
camaron
caracol
Caradoc
catalog
catalos
galagos
gasahol
kakapos
lavabos
laxator
Layamon
macacos
magalog
marabou
matador

Navahos
Navajos
pakapoo
Panadol®
Papa Doc
parador
parados
paradox
paragon
paramos
parasol
✧parazoa
sabaton
sabayon
sacaton
salamon
sapajou
Saratov
Tagalog
Tagálog
talayot
catalpa
bagarre
catarrh
cavalry
macabre
palabra
✧tanagra
waza-ari
zamarra
zamarro
babassu
bagasse
Bahaism
Bahaist
Dadaism
Dadaist
fadaise
karaism
Lamaism
Lamaist
malaise
Sabaism
Bahaite
canasta
catasta
Jakarta
Karaite
Maranta
namaste
rabatte
Sabaoth
savante
Taranto
Bahadur
Balanus
✧calamus
Calanus
✧caracul
Damasus
databus
✧karakul
labarum
ladanum
Lazarus
macaque
mamaguy
Managua
pará nut
Tabanus
vacatur
Varanus
paranym
palazzi
palazzo
cambial
catboat
dayboat
Gambian
jambeau
pap-boat
Zambian
rag baby
war baby
fatback
hawbuck
iambics
layback
pay back
payback
sambuca
sawbuck
Tarbuck
way back
✧zambuck
Barbuda
carbide
fat body
gambado
lambada
man-body
naebody
babbler
bas-bleu
bawbees
cambrel
dabbler
darbies
gabbler
gambier
gambler
gamboes
gambrel
garbled
garbler
has-been
jambier
mad-bred
marbled
marbler
marbles
rabbler
rambler
tabbied
wabbler
warbler
Babbage
cabbage
cabbagy
camboge
gamboge
garbage
cambric
far be it
garboil
lambkin
parboil
barbell
barbola
barbule
cabbala
falbala
fan belt
hagbolt
kabbala
lamb-ale
lap belt
patball
pay-bill
ragbolt
sawbill
tambala
tap bolt
waxbill
waybill
car bomb
car-bomb
bambini
bambino
canbank
carbene
carbine
dabbing
daubing
ear-bone
gabbing
hatband
hayband
jambone
jawbone
lambent
lambing
nabbing
rabbins
rabboni
rawbone
Ray-Bans®
sabbing
salband
tabbing
Zamboni®
can buoy
dambrod
dan buoy
day book
gabbros
gas-buoy
jambool
law-book
rag-book
Aalborg
Banbury
Barbara
Barbary
catbird
daubery
gabbard
gabbart
garbure
halberd
halbert
Hamburg
hauberk
lambert
lay bare
Marburg
Max Born
may-bird
tambura
tanbark
cambism
cambist
earbash
fan base
gambist
had best
iambist
lambast
rag-bush
tarbush
Babbit's
✧babbitt
barbate
dabbity
hay-bote
Lambeth
Macbeth
rabbits
rabbity
✧sabbath
Barbour®
cambium
harbour
jambeux
tambour
jambiya
lamboys
Zambezi
Bacchae
barchan
Calchas
car-coat
day-coal
fascial
faucial
gas-coal
Marceau
Marcian
panchax
✧paschal
pascual
bawcock
dawcock
Hancock
haycock
barcode
cascade
falcade
saccade
sarcode
catched
catchen
catcher
darcies
fancied
fancier
farcied
hatchel
hatcher
hatchet
larchen
latchet
manchet
Märchen
marcher
✧marches
mascled
matched
matcher
✧nancies
narceen
Natchez
parched
patched
patcher
ranched
rancher
raschel
ratchet
satchel
saucier
talcked
Tancred
watcher
watches
watchet
calcify
farcify
✧bacchic
bacchii
batch it
catch it
macchie
pay cain
sarcoid
watch in
watch it!
carcake
gas-coke
oatcake
pancake
bascule
bauchle
calculi
catcall
falcula
law-calf
Malcolm
mancala
masculy
Pascale
saccule
sacculi
saucily
vascula
catch me
fat camp
sarcoma
Satchmo
balcony
calcine
dancing
farcing
fascine
larceny
Mancini
✧marconi
nascent
talcing
vaccine
cas crom
catch on
eat crow
fauchon
gauchos
halcyon
Laocoon
Manchoo
pak choi
raccoon
ranchos
salchow
sanchos
baccara
baccare
cascara
d'accord
day care
✧lancers
mascara
tax cart
cap-case
carcase
carcass
✧fascism
✧fascist
laicise
Marcuse
Pat Cash
pay cash
sarcasm
talcose
baccate
calcite
falcate
✧fat city
laicity
marcato
paucity
saccate
Bacchus
calcium
catch up
catchup
fan club
farceur
jacchus
matchup
patch up
patch-up
rancour
raucous
sanctum
Sanctus
sarcous
talcous
watch up
laicize
bandeau
band-saw
Caddoan
cardiac
handbag
handcar
handjar
handsaw
hard hat
hard man
hard pad
hard-pan
land law
landman
land-rat
Landtag
land tax
Mazdean
Pandean
sandbag
sand bar
sand dab
sandman
Wardian
yardman
bad debt
habdabs
caddice
Candace
Candice
candock
cardecu
daddock
haddock
maddock
paddock
pandect
candida
Candide
bandied
candied
candies
candler
dandler
dawdler
handier
handled
handler
handsel
handset
hard-set
Hay diet
ländler
mandrel
paddler
pardner
raddled
randier
saddler
sand bed
sand eel
tardier
waddler
Cardiff
dandify
Gaddafi
hand-off
laid off
Macduff
ward off
bandage
faldage
fardage
yardage
baldric
Baldwin
Band-aid®
band-aid
baudric
bawdkin
gaudgie
hard hit
hard-hit
mandril
maudlin
sandpit
Vaudois
hardoke
may-duke
✧vandyke
zaddiks
bawdily
candela
dandily
Gandalf
gaudily
handily
hardily
mandala
Mandela
mandola
pardale
rag doll
Randall
randily
Randolf
sandfly
tardily
wax doll
balding
bandana
banding
Bandung
candent
carding
farding
gadding
gardant
✧gardens
jamdani
landing
madding
nandine
padding
pardine
sanding
sardana
sardine
wadding
warding
yardang
band-box
bandook
bandrol
Caedmon
caldron
cardoon
card row
cat door
caudron
eardrop
hands-on
hard bop
hard-got
hard roe
hardtop
hard-won
laid low
lardoon
mandioc
Pandion
pandoor
pan drop
sandbox
sandboy
sandhog
tandoor
wardrop
bandora
bandore
bandura
caldera
eat dirt
gaudery
Ian Dury
laddery
mandira
mandora
✧pandora
pandore
pandura
pay dirt
sanders
yardarm
baddest
baddish
baldish
bardash
caddish
caddyss
faddish
faddism
faddist
hardish
Kaddish
laddish
laddism
maddest
Mahdism
Mahdist
maidish
maidism
pay-desk
Qaddish
rag-dust
RAM disk
saddest
saddish
saidest
sawdust
tax disc
bandits
caudate
✧mandate
candour
carduus
eardrum
handful
handgun
hand out
hand-out
handout
hands up
hard-run
pandour
sardius
taedium
vaudoux
war drum
tardive
hagdown
lay down
lay-down
pay down
Sandown
handaxe
man-days
baseman
café bar
camerae
cameral
cameras
cane rat
case law
caseman
catenae
catenas
cateran
caveman
✧danelaw
faceman

Fareham
game bag
gamelan
gametal
gateman
gateway
have way
kamerad
lace-man
Lake Van
laneway
lateral
Lateran
made man
make hay
make war
make way
name day
pace car
paterae
raceway
rare gas
rate-cap
Sazerac®
Taleban
tame cat
tapetal
wage war
wakeman
zareeba
cadence
cadency
faience
faïence
fayence
ha'pence
latence
latency
patency
valence
valency
van Eyck
calends
fazenda
kalends
base fee
capelet
caperer
caterer
cat-eyed
faceted
gateleg
gate net
havened
haverel
lakelet
lameter
latexes
layered
paperer
racemed
Rameses
ravener
safe sex
sage tea
sakeret
same-sex
tagetes
take ten
tapered
taperer
Tasered
Tavener
wagerer
wakened
wakener
watered
waterer
wavelet
waverer
ease off
face off
face-off
have off
make off
rake-off
take off
take-off
wave off
Fabergé
have a go
have-a-go
Marengo
pace egg
pace-egg
parerga
Raleigh
Raleigh®
saw-edge
catechu
Ganesha
Babesia
cake tin
camelid
capelin
casemix
eaterie
Galenic
gametic
hare-lip
javelin
malefic
paresis
paretic
racemic
ramekin
rape oil
rarebit
ravelin
tabetic
take aim
take air
Valerie
basenji
cadelle
canella
Capella
dazedly
eagerly
fadedly
gabelle
gazelle
hazelly
jadedly
labella
lamella
mace-ale
nacelle
nakedly
padella
pale ale
parella
parelle
✧patella
sabella
sacella
save-all
zanella
maremma
maremme
Palermo
caserne
✧cayenne
ha'penny
Karenni
pageant
Ravenna
Salerno
taverna
cabezon
✧camelot
Cape Cod
catelog
Game Boy®
gazebos
have got
have-not
Jane Doe
make for
mamelon
matelot
name-son
pageboy
paletot
saveloy
save you
waveson
Mazeppa
Cabeiri
camelry
cave art
Madeira
pareira
Far East
make use
✧vanessa
vareuse
cavetti
cavetto
G-agents
galeate
galette
gaseity
✧gazette
jadeite
Janeite
Janetta
Janette
Lacerta
ladette
layette
magenta
majesty
maleate
Nanette
navette
palette
paneity
Papeete
ramenta
V-agents
Valetta
baleful
bale out
baneful
base out
bateaux
cadeaux
cage-cup
cajeput
careful
caseous
dareful
easeful
face out
fade out
fade-out
fateful
gaseous
gateaus
gâteaux
gazeful
hateful
haveour
have out
Iapetus
lace bug
make out
mazeful
pace out
race-cup
rageful
rameous
take out
takeout
taleful
tapetum
wakeful
wameful
Max Euwe
cadenza
cat-flap
earflap
half-cap
half-day
half pay
half-pay
halfway
saffian
fat-face
maffick
baffler
fat-free
gauffer
haaf-net
maffled
palfrey
raffler
Raffles
rat-flea
tax-free
waffler
naff off
caffein
hafflin
halflin
half-pie
halfwit
mafflin
Mayfair
parfait
rag-fair
bagfuls
caffila
canfuls
capfuls
fanfold
hatfuls
jarfuls
jawfall
naff all
panfuls
vatfuls
war film
daffing
gaffing
half-one
naffing
pakfong
payfone
ratfink
damfool
jaw-foot
saffron
half-ape
bad form
carfare
fanfare
gas fire
hayfork
oak fern
salfern
Salford
warfare
Watford
wayfare
batfish
catfish
gabfest
garfish
hagfish
oar fish
raffish
ratfish
sawfish
waifish
taffeta
taffety
half-cut
gang saw
gangway
hangman
langsam
laugh at
pangram
tangram
Vaughan
Haggada
raggedy
baggies
bangled
cargoes
dangler
fangled
gangrel
haggler
jangler
langrel
langued
languet
laugher
Maigret
mangler
mangoes
Pangaea
rangier
✧tangier
tangled
tangler
tangoed
waggler
wangler
bang off
hang off
baggage
Van Gogh
langaha
bargain
barge in
ganglia
Gauguin
languid
large it
sangria
tanghin
baggily
largely
mangily
mangold
nargile
nargily
oak gall
rangoli
tangelo
May-game
pangamy
sangoma
Targums
war game
bagging
banging
fagging
far gone
gagging
ganging
gauging
gay gene
hanging
jagging
lagging
margent
nagging
pangene
panging
pargana
ragging
sagging
Sargent
tagging
tangent
wagging
waygone
zagging
Bangkok
hangdog
jargoon
languor
Rangoon
Calgary
day-girl
faggery
haggard
jaggery
laggard
Margery
raggery
saggard
Sat Guru
taggers
waggery
bargest
haggish
largess
largish
margosa
waggish
gadgety
gangsta
gargety
haughty
maggoty
Margate
naughty
paughty
saw gate
Targets
bang out
hang out
hangout
valgous
gang-bye
Yangtze
Baghdad
bath mat
bathyal
cathead
each way
each-way
fathead
Lachlan
lashkar
Mashhad
mashlam
mashman
mash-vat
nashgab
Paphian
pathway
rachial
rawhead
saphead
warhead
washday
washrag
yakhdan
yashmak
Wahhabi
cachaça
cathode
kathode
raphide
rawhide
cashier
dasheen
machree
Maghreb
Rachael
Raphael
tar heel
yachter
dash off
kachcha
naphtha
bashlik
bathmic
Daphnia
daphnid
Daphnis
✧kashmir
machair
Maghrib
mashlim
mashlin
Samhain
yachtie
dasheki
dashiki
cathole
ear-hole
Ian Holm
jawhole
lapheld
manhole
rathole
fathoms
Iachimo
nathemo
pay home
sashimi
bashing
dashing
Hamhung
hashing
kachina
lashing
lathing
machine
manhunt
mashing
Mashona
nap hand
sadhana
saphena
washing
cash-box
cash cow
cathood
dashpot
fashion
machzor
manhood
tachyon
washpot
wanhope
bathers
Cathari
Cathars
fashery
fathers
gathers
hachure
jaghire
kacheri
lathery
saxhorn
washers
washery
Zachary
hashish
pachisi
rathest
tachism
tachist
Japheth
machete
bashful
Bath bun
bathtub
Bauhaus
dash out
gashful
hash out
✧kashrus
✧kashrut
lash out
man-hour
mashlum
mash-tub
mash-tun
Pakhtun
Pashtun
wash out
wash-out
washout
washtub
war hawk
cachexy
Kathryn
basilar
Caliban
Canidae
capital
capitan
Cariban
carinae
carinas
caritas
Dalilah
datival
fajitas
Gadidae
habitat
Halifax
Harijan
janizar
laminae
laminar
Laridae
latitat
magical
Mahican
marital
matinal
maximal
paginal
✧radical
Ranidae
Ratitae
sahibah
salival
Taliban
talipat
taxicab
taximan
taxiway
vaginae
vaginal
vaginas
vanitas
Vatican
wanigan
marimba
paxiuba
✧carioca
da Vinci
tapioca
Cabinda
Matilda
may I add

basinet
✧cabinet
caliber
calices
calipee
caliver
carices
✧galilee
Galileo
habited
lamiger
lamiter
latices
Latiner
Malines
mariner
matinee
matinée
patined
radicel
radices
ravined
sakiyeh
salices
salicet
samisen
satinet
tabinet
taliped
talipes
varices
Dario Fo
satisfy
facings
havings
makings
savings
takings
babiche
caliche
kamichi
Lapiths
malicho
Tabitha
taniwha
Tarim He
basidia
Cabiric
canikin
davidia
Fatimid
Hamitic
Hasidic
Hasidim
Kalinin
lacinia
Lavinia
manikin
maximin
Namibia
✧pacific
Palikir
Palilia
paninis
✧papilio
Ramilie
salicin
satiric
Tamilic
Malinke
panicky
bacilli
barilla
calicle
Camilla
cariole
Daniela
dariole
lapilli
mamilla
manilla
manille
maniple
maxilla
panicle
papilla
patible
rabidly
radiale
radicle
rapidly
ravioli
sanicle
tacitly
validly
vanilla
vapidly
variola
variole
cariama
radium A
radium B
A A Milne
Mariana
nations
patient
radiant
rations
Sabians
salient
sapient
taxiing
valiant
variant
bar-iron
calicos
cami-top
Capitol
caribou
casinos
galipot
halidom
halimot
haricot
janitor
✧ladinos
lay it on
✧madison
malison
manihoc
Manihot
manitou
maticos
parison
paritor
sadiron
saligot
talipot
warison
calibre
cariere
caviare
laniard
laniary
Savitri
Babiism
harissa
✧mafiosi
✧mafioso
matiest
Matisse
may I ask
Naziism
raciest
balista
barista
batiste
eat into
Jacinta
jacinth
labiate
lam into
lay into
Marists
✧radiata
radiate
✧sagitta
Samiote
satiate
satiety
tap into
variate
variety
badious
cacique
Calicut
carious
cazique
fatigue
garigue
habitué
habitus
halibut
halitus
haviour
La Digue
Latinus
Manipur
Marinus
maximum
Panicum
paviour
Salique
sanious
✧saviour
Tacitus
vagitus
various
zap it up
Marilyn
San Juan
Panjabi
carjack
man jack
man-jack
manjack
banjoes
Mas-John
mah-jong
Nanjing
Marjory
zanjero
San José
back pay
backsaw
barkhan
Gaekwar
Gaikwar
hacksaw
jackdaw
jackman
✧jack tar
jarkman
markkaa
markkas
markman
packman
pack-rat
packway
parkway
sabkhah
sabkhat
tank car
taskbar
Walkman®
walkway
pack ice
tap kick
backset
backsey
bark-bed
cackler
fankled
hackler
hackles
hacklet
✧hackney
✧jackeen
mankier
mawkier
nankeen
tackier
tackies
tackled
tackler
talkies
Zadkiel
back off
jack off
mark off
pack off
rack off
walk off
package
sackage
tankage
✧banksia
hawkbit
Jacklin
jacksie
talk big
lack-all
lankily
pawkily
sarkily
tackily
wackily
back-end
backing
balking
banking
✧barking
carking
gaskins
hacking
✧hawking
lacking
mankind
marking
Nanking
packing
parking
racking
Rankine
ranking
sacking
sarking
tacking
talking
tanking
tankini
tasking
vacking
walking
yanking
backhoe
backlog
backlot
back row
back-row
hack-log
I ask you!
jackpot
Jackson
markhor
tank top
backare
cankery
Falkirk
hackery
jankers
Sankara
saw kerf
tankard
dankish
darkish
hawkish
jackass
larkish
mawkish
parkish
rackets
rackett
rackety
tackety
back out
hackbut
mark out
sackbut
sackful
talk out
tankful
walk out
walkout
hawk owl
lackeys
Sankhya
bay leaf
Caelian
carload
eat lead
fabliau
hallian
hallway
kail-pat
mailbag
mail-car
mailman
mailvan
mall rat
oak-leaf
pallial
pan loaf
Paulian
payload
railcar
railman
railway
tableau
tael bar
tall hat
war loan
earlobe
wallaba
wallaby
bad luck
carlock
daglock
earlock
fallacy
Gallice
laylock
Matlock
oarlock
padlock
raploch
warlock
bag lady
ballade
May-lady
Baalbek
caulker
dailies
dallied
dallier
earlier
earlies
gaulter
haulier
manlier
nail-bed
nail set
railbed
rallied
rallier
sallied
tablier
tailles
tallied
tallier
tallies
tall men
vaulted
vaulter
wallies
waulker
bailiff
call off
fall off
fall-off
gas lift
haul off
hayloft
tail off
hac lege
haulage
railage
tallage
tally-ho
baillie
haploid
mail-gig
marl-pit
racloir
São Luis
tabloid
tail fin
taillie
tailzie
tall oil
waylaid
catlike
had like
lac-lake
man-like
saclike
sawlike
warlike
Carlyle
day lily
gallfly
hallali
may-lily
tail fly
caulome
gas lamp
gas-lime
Kallima
oak lump
ballant
balling
bar line
bawling
bay-line
cabling
callant
calling
calluna
carline
✧carling
catling
cauline
darling
daylong
eanling
fabling
failing
falling
fatling
gadling
gallant
galling
garland
halling
haplont
harling
kaoline
Karling
Lallans
lalling
lawland
madling
mailing
Marlene
marline
marling
Maulana
nailing
Oakland
oakling
palling
pallone
Paulina
Pauline
railing
ralline
ratline
ratling
sailing
sapling
tabling
tag line
tail end
tailing
tallent
Tallinn
tanling
wailing
walling
warling
wauling
wawling
Wayland
ball-boy
balloon
call-box
call-boy
earldom
early on
fall for
Gaeldom
galleon
Gallios
galliot
galloon
hallion
hallyon
kail-pot
mailbox
maillot
nail-rod
paillon
tallboy
Walloon
fahlerz
fahlore
failure
gallery
Law Lord
mallard
maulers
maulgre
May-lord
nailery
Paul Pry
sail arm
tailard
vallary
warlord
Baalism
bagless
ballast
carlish
Carlism
Carlist
earless
gallise
Gaulish
hapless
hatless
jawless
lawless
law-list
manless
mapless
napless
oarless
paylist
rayless
sacless
Sallust
sapless
tagless
tallish
taplash
taxless
tax loss
wayless
Baalite
fat-lute
gallate
Hazlitt
La Plata
tallith
bail out
bail-out
bailout
ballium
bawl out
callous
call out
call-out
fall guy
fall out
fall-out
fallout
gallium
gallnut
mail-out
malleus
nail gun
pailful
pallium
parlour
parlous
railbus
wailful
wall rue
baclava
baklava
Pahlavi
✧pavlova
gallows
Marlowe
matlows
Mawlawi
May laws
sallowy
tallowy
valleys
walleye
gallize
bar meal
Cadmean
nagmaal
oatmeal
palm cat
pap-meat
wadmaal

Words marked ✧ can also be spelled with one or more capital letters

Calmuck
gammock
hammock
Kalmuck
mammock
man-made
Daimler®
larmier
malmsey
palmiet
palm off
Balmain
barmaid
barmkin
fan mail
gas main
palm oil
palm-oil
balmily
hammily
harmala
sawmill
wadmoll
tagmeme
bamming
caimans
calmant
carmine
catmint
caymans
damming
farming
garment
haemony
harmans
harmine
harmony
✧jamming
jasmine
lamming
maiming
payment
ragment
raiment
ramming
Raymond
salmons
salmony
sarment
Tammany
varment
varmint
warming
wayment
barmpot
daimios
Marmion
palmtop
daymark
earmark
farmery
Hammers
mammary
May-morn
palmary
palmyra
saimiri
waymark
badmash
farmost
gas mask

harmost
marmose
oak mast
palmist
rammish
warmish
magmata
mammate
mammoth
Marmite®
marmite
palmate
tagmata
wax moth
cadmium
farm out
harmful
palmful
nae mows
balneal
dawn-man
gainsay
harn-pan
Launfal
Rain Man
taeniae
taenias
Barnaby
wannabe
bannock
cannach
jannock
Larnaca
pannick
zarnich
Kannada
Maenads
cain-hen
carnies
daunder
daunter
fainted
had need
haunted
haunter
jauntee
Laender
launder
maunder
nainsel'
nannied
nannies
painted
painter
pannier
Pawnees
✧rainier
sainted
saunter
tainted
taunter
vaunted
vaunter
carnify
damnify
magnify
sawn-off
warn off
carnage
pannage
tannage

wainage
paunchy
raunchy
jauntie
cannily
cannula
damn all
faintly
fannell
gauntly
paenula
Parnell
saintly
day name
magnums
banning
bar none
✧canning
cannons
damning
darning
dawning
earning
fawning
haining
manning
Nanning
panning
tanning
vanning
warning
yawning
bagnios
daunton
La Union
maintop
✧rainbow
Taunton
wannion
cannery
gauntry
laundry
manners
tannery
badness
carnose
earnest
farness
fatness
faunist
gabnash
garnish
gayness
harness
Jainism
Jainist
laxness
madness
mannish
mannose
pannose
patness
rawness
sadness
tannish
tarnish
varnish
waeness
wanness
wannish
bainite

Cainite
gahnite
kainite
magnate
magneto
mannite
Samnite
tannate
war note
Dawn Run
earn out
gainful
hafnium
hahnium
mainour
painful
bad news
barn owl
carneys
caporal
Dakotas
majorat
man-o'-war
Masorah
mayoral
samosas
samovar
tatouay
j'adoube
barocco
capouch
Majorca
patonce
La Ronde
lay odds
baconer
baloney
baronet
bayonet
cacolet
cajoler
calomel
caloyer
caromel
damosel
damozel
fan oven
favored
favorer
gas oven
halogen
Hanover
haroset
jaconet
lay open
layover
Mahomet
parolee
Rasores
Samoyed
tabooed
taborer
taboret
taloned
valonea
✧wagoner
Zapotec
Zatopek
katorga
basoche
Basotho

caroche
galoche
karoshi
panocha
Aaronic
caloric
✧calorie
camogie
canonic
Canopic
carotid
carotin
fasolia
galopin
✧jacobin
Japonic
✧laconic
lanolin
mahonia
major in
masonic
paeonic
parodic
parotic
parotid
parotis
sagouin
saponin
saronic
Saxonic
taborin
✧valonia
bazooka
bazouki
gazooka
kalooki
matooke
paiocke
pajocke
palooka
talooka
cagoule
kagoule
majorly
panoply
tabouli
baronne
dadoing
façonné
ganoine
kayoing
Madonna
Mahound
gasohol
manoaos
Nabokov
nanobot
palolos
cacoepy
jaloppy
✧camorra
✧canonry
favours
Jan Oort
masonry
savoury
vapours
vapoury
baboosh
Barotse
caboose

carouse
jalouse
papoose
vamoose
zamouse
calotte
dacoity
dakoiti
fagotti
fagotto
garotte
gavotte
hap'orth
haporth
Lacoste
lavolta
✧baroque
Canopus
carolus
jacobus
madoqua
cacodyl
Carolyn
kakodyl
paronym
tan ooze
pampean
salpian
Sampras
calpack
daypack
earpick
manpack
rampick
ratpack
Tampico
tappice
ba'spiel
camp-bed
Dampier
dappled
day-peep
Harpies
lamprey
Magpies
nappies
sampler
sapples
rampage
warpage
dauphin
lamplit
nauplii
✧sapphic
Tarpeia
garpike
lampuka
lampuki
rampike
fan palm
happily
Kampala
lamp-fly
maypole
sappily
tadpole
Walpole
wax palm
campana
camping
capping

carping
damping
gasping
happing
jampani
kampong
lamping
lapping
mapping
napping
parpane
parpend
parpent
rampant
ramping
rapping
rasping
salpinx
sapping
T'ai-p'ing
tamping
tapping
vamping
wappend
wapping
warping
zampone
zamponi
camphor
campion
car pool
car-pool
harpoon
lampion
lampoon
marplot
Rajpoot
rampion
tampion
bagpipe
gas pipe
bal paré
Campari
campery
car park
carport
jaspery
lampern
lampers
mappery
pampero
rampart
rampire
rapport
sampire
Sapporo
vampire
Bagpuss
dampish
gampish
harpist
Lappish
mappist
pappose
Rappist
vampish
wampish
waspish
waypost
palpate
Rappite

warpath
camp out
earplug
gasp out
pappous
banquet
basqued
Jacques
lacquer
lacquey
marquee
masquer
parquet
racquet
marquis
Pasquil
Pasquin
Tarquin
fair-day
fairway
Hadrian
Mauriac
Nauruan
pairial
pair-oar
patrial
saurian
✧taurean
Zairean
Nairobi
saprobe
barrace
barrack
barrico
caprice
cap rock
carrack
carract
carrect
farruca
hatrack
hayrick
matrice
Maurice
parrock
✧patrick
patrico
rat race
tarrock
hag-ride
hayride
tan ride
barrier
cairned
carried
carrier
farrier
Gabriel
hair-eel
hair gel
hairnet
harried
harrier
Harriet
Laertes
married
marrier
Maureen
parried
tarried
tarrier

vaurien
caprify
pair off
sacrify
barrage
farrago
lairage
Bahrain
caproic
carry it
darrain
gag-rein
hair oil
hairpin
labroid
Lacroix
ram-raid
sauroid
naartje
hayrake
paprika
bairnly
caerule
carrell
fairily
favrile
jam roll
laurels
marrels
payroll
rag-roll
safrole
hadrome
macramé
macrami
San Remo
barrens
barring
cab-rank
cadrans
Cairene
caprine
earring
fairing
farrand
farrant
gas ring
jarring
Katrina
Katrine
ladrone
latrant
latrine
madroña
madrone
madroño
manrent
Marrano
marring
padrone
padroni
pairing
Sabrina
sacring
tacrine
tarring
taurine
vagrant
warrand
warrant
warring

wauring
barrios
bar-room
carrion
carry on
carry-on
day room
fair do's
gadroon
hairdos
maormor
patriot
patroon
taproom
taproot
warrior
manrope
satrapy
Cabrera
Macrura
tabrere
fairish
Ian Rush
labrose
lairise
madrasa
matrass
matross
Maurist
sacrist
caprate
carroty
garrote
nacrite
narrate
parroty
Babrius
carry up
haircut
Malraux
marry up
nacrous
natrium
sabreur
marrowy
narrow a
narrows
darrayn
lairize
bass-bar
batsman
Capsian
capstan
cat's-ear
cat's-paw
darshan
daysman
daystar
gadsman
Harstad
magsman
marshal
Marsyas
oarsman
Pan-Slav
passman
rakshas
ramstam
tapsman
tar seal
tar-seal
cassaba
sassaby
car-sick
cassock
daysack
hassock
lassock
ransack
sad sack
Matsudo
passade
passado
wayside
banshee
dabster
daisied
Dansker
falsies
fatsoes
gagster
hag-seed
hamster
harshen
harslet
hayseed
kamseen
lassoed
lassoer
lassoes
laus Deo
mahseer
maister
mawseed
mayster
✧paisley
palsied
pansied
parsley
parsnep
passkey
sarsden
sarsnet
tapster
tarsier
wabster
waisted
waister
yapster
falsafa
falsify
hats off
pass off
salsify
massage
passage
paysage
sapsago
sausage
catskin
catsuit
caustic
karstic
lawsuit
Mao-suit
parsnip
payslip
vassail
warship
wassail
Baisaki
bansela
bay salt
capsule
falsely
harshly
Mansell
Marsala
raw silk
sassily
tassell
Walsall
balsamy
gaysome
Lakshmi
satsuma
waesome
bausond
cassino
cassone
dapsone
gassing
Hansen's
✧lapsang
paisano
parsing
passant
passing
pausing
raising
raisiny
ramsons
tar sand
war song
bad shot
bad show
bassoon
caisson
earshot
mansion
✧passion
samshoo
Sassoon
says you
tab stop
tap shoe
tar spot
caesura
Hansard
Hans Arp
Kayseri
maestri
maestro
maistry
mansard
Massora
matsuri
samsara
San Siro
tapstry
bassist
falsish
falsism
Parsism
cassata
falsity
gap site
passata
varsity
wadsett
caesium
caestus
Cassius
danseur
hassium
masseur
pas seul
pass out
passout
saksaul
cassava
massive
passive
Cat's-eye®
cat's-eye
janskys
Vaishya
capsize
man-size
caltrap
cartway
castral
Dantean
dart-sac
factual
fast-day
gas trap
Haitian
haut pas
Kantian
lacteal
Laotian
last man
maltman
manteau
mantram
mantrap
Mantuan
✧martial
Martian
partial
part way
part-way
Raetian
raftman
✧rat trap
saltcat
salt-fat
salt pan
tactual
tag team
Watteau
xantham
xanthan
zaptiah
cattabu
mastaba
bar tack
Caltech
cantico
castock
factice
haptics
hattock
Lactuca
lattice
mastich
mattock
nautics
tactics
zaitech
bastide
fantads
fantods
Barthes
battler
canteen
cantlet
cantred
cantref
castled
earthen
East Sea
fanteeg
farthel
farther
fartlek
Fastnet
gantlet
Gautier
maatjes
maître d'
malt tea
manteel
mantlet
mantoes
martlet
mast-fed
Matthew
mauther
mawther
may tree
✧narthex
oak tree
pad-tree
panther
panties
pantler
✧partlet
partner
pasties
ratteen
rattier
rattler
salt eel
saltier
saltoed
sautéed
tartier
tartlet
tastier
tattier
tattler
waltzer
wastrel
wattled
wattles
wax tree
zabtieh
zaptieh
caitiff
cart off
cast off
cast-off
laithfu'
mastiff
part-off
Santa Fe
Tartufe
tartufo
wait off
cartage
lastage
vantage
waftage
wantage
wastage
wattage
bad trip
bartsia
Caitlín
cantrip
captain
day trip
eastlin
factoid
fantail
gastric
gastrin
mastoid
mattoid
nartjie
rat-tail
rattlin
salt pit
sautoir
tag tail
tant pis
✧tantric
wagtail
want-wit
xanthic
xanthin
partake
battels
battill
cantala
cattalo
cattily
daytale
earthly
hartely
hastily
kantela
kantele
Kartell
nastily
nattily
nautili
pantile
pastels
rattily
saltily
tactile
tastily
tattily
daytime
laytime
Maytime
pastime
ragtime
Sao Tomé
São Tomé
wartime
baiting
banteng
banting
basting
Batten's
batting
bay-tine
cantina
canting
Cantona
cantons
casting
darting
Daytona
East End
easting
Fastens
fasting
fatting
gas tank
Gatting
halting
hatting
karting
lactone
Lagting
lantana
lasting
malting
Martina
Martine
Martini®
✧martini
matting
mattins
paktong
pantine
panting
Pantone®
parting
pasting
patting
rafting
raiting
ranting
ratting
saltant
saltine
salting
Santana
tantony
tartana
tartane
tartine
tasting
tatting
vatting
wafting
waiting
wanting
wasting
bastion
caltrop
cantdog
cantion
caption
cartoon
caution
faction
Gasthof
hautboy
haut ton
paction
partook
saltbox
santoor
taction
wart hog
warthog
Zantiot
bastard
battero
battery
capture
castory
cattery
cautery
dastard
✧eastern
factory
facture
jam tart
laetare
lantern
martyry
mastery
mattery
nattery
parture
pastern
pasture
pattern
rafters
rapture
rattery
saltern
saltire
tantara
✧tartare
Tartary
tatters
tattery
wafture
wastery
baptise
baptism
✧baptist
cattish
Dantist
fantasm
fantast
fantasy
fastish
fattest
fattish
fattism
fattist
Kantism
Kantist
lactase
lactose
maltase
Maltese
maltose
Nastase
Pap test
rattish
Saktism
saltish
tactism
tartish
battuta
cantata
cantate
hastate
lactate
partita
partite
saltate
saltato
vastity
cab-tout
canthus
cartful
cast out
earth up
faitour
hauteur
last out
Malthus
mastful
pantoum
paste-up
Pasteur
rastrum
salt out
santour
tactful
tantrum
want out
caitive
captive
factive
tantivy
Fastext
martext
baptize
canulae
canulas
fabular
faculae
facular
hamular
✧hanuman
lacunae
lacunal
lacunar
Laputan
maculae
macular
Madurai
natural
pabular
paludal
papulae
papular
radulae
radular
ramular
samurai
tabulae
tabular
calumba
macumba
Nabucco
Yaoundé
cacumen
caducei
calumet
Capulet
manumea
manurer
natured
papules
raguled
saluter
taluses
babuche
Baluchi
capuche
Bakunin
manumit
pagurid
paludic
parulis

patulin
raoulia
Tamulic
mazurka
yamulka
zakuska
zakuski
casuals
Max Uhle
vacuole
vaguely
vacuums
calumny
tabuing
babudom
baguios
lanugos
lay upon
tax upon
galumph
Ranulph
capuera
daquiri
January
saburra
saguaro
saouari
vaquero
babuism
casuist
vacuist
Watutsi
faculty
fatuity
Nahuatl
vacuate
vacuity
valuate
Vanuatu
baculum
cajuput
famulus
fatuous
hamulus
pabulum
ramulus
vacuous
Jacuzzi®
jacuzzi
maruzze
Latvian
garvock
vaivode
waivode
navvied
salvoes
salvage
mauvais
mauvein
naevoid
Marvell
naively
naïvely
valvula
valvule
Calvino
carving
mauvine
parvenu
salving
calvary
carvery
halvers
Malvern
taivert
canvass
Fauvism
Fauvist
harvest
Jahvism
Jahvist
naivist
parvise
Saivism
Yahvist
larvate
naiveté
naïveté
naivety
naïvety
Parvati
Saivite
salvete
valvate
carve up
carve-up
daywear
narwhal
Gatwick
Harwich
Warwick
waiwode
waywode
hag-weed
man-week
matweed
mayweed
oarweed
ragweed
rag week
say when
tarweed
lay wait
catwalk
gadwall
gas well
jaywalk
✧maxwell
oak wilt
qawwali
warwolf
batwing
lapwing
lauwine
waxwing
barwood
camwood
dagwood
oak-wood
rag-wool
sapwood
catworm
day-work
hayward
haywire
lapwork
madwort
maw-worm
nayward
nayword
ragwork
ragworm
ragwort
saw-wort
vanward
war-worn
waxwork
wayward
wayworn
bagwash
car-wash
fanwise
Far West
Mae West
mapwise
Yahwist
faux pas
Manx cat
Manxman
Marxian
faux ami
Marxism
Marxist
bauxite
gap year
Lady Day
Lady Jay
man-year
satyral
Taiyuan
barytes
calyces
calyxes
Lady Lee
lazy-bed
baby oil
baby-sit
barytic
katydid
ladykin
satyric
satyrid
calycle
Dalyell
ladyfly
babying
taxying
varying
Baby Doc
Babylon
baryton
dasypod
ladycow
Babygro®
dasyure
halyard
lanyard
tanyard
babyish
calypso
easy-osy
ladyish
ladyism
zanyism
manyata
Dasypus
ladybug
marybud
papyrus
lazy eye
jazzman
wazzock
dazzler
jazz age
matzahs
Tadzhik
jazzily
calzone
calzoni
canzona
canzone
canzoni
fanzine
jazz-pop
Lanzhou
madzoon
matzoon
mamzers
mazzard
matzoth
bazzazz
pazzazz
Abraham
✧abraxas
ebb away
Abbasid
CB radio
Ibrahim
ablator
abrazos
Absalom
Mbabane
Ibibios
abscind
abscond
obscene
abactor
obscure
abscess
abscise
absciss
a bad hat
Abidjan
Obadiah
abide by
abidden
a bad egg
abiding
Abaddon
a bad job
a bad lot
abreact
absence
ableism
ableist
abreast
obverse
W B Yeats
obsequy
observe
✧abigail
abthane
E B White
R B Kitaj
obligee
obliger
abridge
obligor
ebriose
absinth
ebriate
ebriety
obviate
oblique
obvious
abalone
obelion
Abelard
obolary
abolish
ebbless
obelise
obelisk
Tbilisi
ability
obelize
Abu Mena
abomasa
abomasi
Ebonics
abandon
ab intra
ebonise
ebonist
ebonite
ebonize
abroach
abdomen
abiosis
abiotic
obconic
abrooke
abjoint
obloquy
absolve
Aberfan
Iberian
obtrude
abortee
uberous
abysmal
abyssal
abashed
abusage
NBC suit
abusion
obesity
Ibn Saud
abusive
abettal
abuttal
obitual
ebb-tide
abetted
abetter
abutted
abutter
a bit off
abattis
abstain
abettor
abature
abjurer
abought
ébauche
Aboukir
aboulia
obovoid
obovate
abaxial
ab extra
abeyant
Achaean
Achaian
octaval
scraich
scranch
✧scratch
scrauch
Achates
ectases
scraper
scraggy
scraigh
scraugh
acrasia
acratic
ectasis
Oceania
oceanic
✧oceanid
octadic
Octavia
sciarid
sciatic
scrapie
accablé
actable
octapla
scrawly
acharné
scranny
scrawny
Actaeon
Ecuador
ichabod
octagon
octavos
échappé
schappe
scrappy
O C Marsh
schanse
Oceanus
acharya
schanze
iceboat
ice beer
scabbed
scabies
scabrid
iceball
ice-belt
scabble
scybala
iceberg
ice-blue
acacias
ice cube
ecocide
acyclic
scuchin
ice-calk
ice-cold
Acadian
act dido
iced gem
iced tea
ich dien
scudded
scudder
scudler
acidify
scedule
scuddle
academe
academy
act drop
acidity
acid dye
à cheval
Acre Bay
schemas
scleral
✧science
screech
screich
acceder
schemer
screwed
screwer
ycleped
acreage
screigh
icteric
icterid
screw in
screaky
écuelle
Uccello
ack emma
Acheron
echelon
ycleap'd
ycleepe
Acmeism
Acmeist
accents
ocreate
octette
icterus
screw up
screw-up
screeve
scherzi
scherzo
scoff at
ice-free
scoffer
scaffie
ice fall
Scafell
scuffle
ice floe
ice-foot
aciform
ice fern
ice fish
scaglia
Scoggin
ice hill
ecthyma
Acrilan®
actinal
Occitan
scribal
scriech
scritch
ActiveX
scriber
accinge
accidie
aclinic
acridin
actinia
actinic
acridly
schisma
echidna
scriene
actinon
schizos
scrimpy
Echiura
✧eclipse
ickiest
echinus
Ictinus
occiput
achieve
scrieve
ocellar
schlich
schlock
occlude
scalade
scalado
scalder
scalled
scalpel
scalper
scolder
sculler
ecology
acclaim
oceloid
P-Celtic
Q-Celtic
scaldic
sculpin
Iceland
scalene
scaleni
scaling
scallop
scolion
scollop
acaleph
schlepp
oculist
schloss
acolyte
acolyth
oculate
aculeus
ocellus
scale up
scumbag
schmeck
schmock
schmuck
scammer
scamper
schmoes
Scomber
scumber
scummed
scummer
scamble
schmelz
scumble
schmooz
à compte
scandal
scanned
scanner
scented
scunner
iconify
acantha
acanthi
Scandic
scantle
scantly
schnell
economy
McEnroe
schnook
schnaps
e contra
scenary
scenery
schnorr
acinose
iciness
iconise
aconite
ichnite
acinous
acknown
iconize
Acrobat®
acrobat
scholar
scrotal
accoied
accoyed
acrogen
acroter
ice over
October
scooped
scooper
scooter
scroggy
✧scrooge
scrouge
acromia
ecbolic
ectopia
ectopic
octofid
scholia
accoyld
actorly
schoole
schools
scrowle
scroyle
account
echoing
ectozoa
octopod
accompt
accourt
accoast
echoise
echoism
echoist
sciolto
eclogue
octopus
scrotum
acronym
echoize
icepack
ice pick
scepter
scupper

acapnia
scepsis
✧sceptic
scapple
scapula
scopula
✧sceptre
sceptry
scopate
scyphus
acarian
accrual
Icarian
ochreae
scoriac
scoriae
Acarida
acorned
scarfed
scarlet
scarped
scarper
scarred
scarves
scorner
scorper
scorser
scarify
scorify
écorché
acaroid
acerbic
ochroid
Scorpio
scurril
scarily
Acarina
acarine
eccrine
ice rink
ocarina
scoring
acerose
actress
accrete
acerate
acerous
ochrous
scare up
scarf up
Scirpus
ice spar
scissel
scissil
acushla
ice show
scissor
Scotian
schtick
schtuck
Scotice
scatted
scatter
scutter
scythed
scyther
acetify
Scotify
scutage
Scotchy
ichthic

Scottie
acutely
scatole
scuttle
scytale
scotoma
scotomy
acetone
Achtung
ecotone
schtook
schtoom
ecotype
acetose
✧ecstasy
Scotism
Scotist
acetate
scutate
acatour
acetous
ichthys
acaudal
accusal
scrubby
scrunch
accused
accuser
ictuses
scauper
scourer
Scouser
scouter
scruffy
scourge
acouchi
acouchy
scourie
octuple
scruple
scrummy
scrutos
scrumpy
acquire
actuary
accurse
accurst
acquest
acquist
scourse
acquite
actuate
scrunty
scrub up
scavage
scowder
scowler
scowrer
scowrie
ice worm
ectypal
acrylic
ecdysis
scrying
icky poo
scazons
advance
Odoacer
P D James
Idi Amin
ideally

adharma
ad manum
od's bobs
edibles
oddball
edictal
eductor
edacity
educate
adnexal
adrenal
addenda
adherer
odd-even
uddered
adverse
idlesse
edge out
edifice
edified
edifier
odd fish
adagios
admiral
ad finem
ad litem
admirer
advices
advised
adviser
CD video
L-driver
adhibit
Adriana
sdeigne
advisor
ad vivum
odd jobs
Idalian
odaller
udaller
od's life
odd legs
idyllic
odd-like
idolise
idolism
idolist
odalisk
odylism
adulate
idolize
Adamnan
adamant
oddment
Adamite
edental
adenoid
identic
odontic
adenoma
adenine
adonise
oddness
Odinism
Odinist
Odonata
adonize
idiotcy
od-force
Ed Moses

idiotic
odzooks
adjoint
ad court
adjourn
à droite
ad modum
adapted
adapter
adopted
adoptee
adopter
edaphic
adeptly
adaptor
adipose
adermin
adoring
odorant
address
addrest
adpress
odorate
odorous
oddsman
✧odyssey
ad astra
edition
edit out
adjunct
adducer
odoured
adjudge
add up to
adaxial
Edexcel
eddying
ceramal
decadal
decanal
get away
getaway
jemadar
megabar
megarad
peg away
tetanal
welaway
debauch
hexarch
medacca
mesarch
penance
recatch
rematch
tenancy
xerarch
regards
veranda
aerated
bedazed
behaved
belated
belayed
bemazed
benamed
Benares
betaken
cedared
cerated
debased

debaser
debater
decayed
defacer
delayed
delayer
dewater
fedayee
felafel
H E Bates
legatee
medaled
medalet
menacer
metaled
metamer
métayer
✧new ager
pedaled
penates
rebater
related
relater
relaxed
relayed
remanet
renayed
repaper
retaken
retaker
rewater
velamen
velated
deraign
derange
melange
mélange
rebadge
relâche
seraphs
Bedawin
ceramic
cerasin
Cesario
denarii
fedarie
gelatin
heparin
hepatic
hexadic
keramic
keratin
megabit
melanic
Melanie
melanin
nematic
Nepalis
pelagic
regalia
relaxin
remanié
sebacic
sematic
senarii
serafin
Serapic
Serapis
Tel Aviv
tetanic
vedalia

veganic
velaria
velaric
venatic
xerafin
xerasia
aefauld
cenacle
debacle
débâcle
default
hexapla
legally
mesally
metally
penally
regally
Renault®
retable
seeable
tenable
venally
bepaint
besaint
betaine
Cézanne
delaine
demaine
demayne
depaint
dewanny
Geraint
pesaunt
remains
repaint
aerator
belabor
celadon
decagon
decapod
delator
hexagon
hexapod
Lebanon
legator
legatos
levator
megafog
megaron
megaton
melanos
✧metazoa
negator
pedalos
peraeon
relator
senator
telamon
venator
zelator
genappe
hetaera
hetaira
Le Carré
Le Havre
Megaera
remarry
bécasse
because
degauss
delapse

megasse
relapse
de facto
defaste
meranti
penalty
pesante
regatta
Vedanta
Belarus
devalue
✧pegasus
petasus
renague
revalue
tetanus
jet boat
lee beam
✧lesbian
membral
remblai
sea bean
sea bear
sea-beat
sea boat
Serbian
get back
kebbock
kebbuck
nebbich
peg back
redback
set back
setback
wetback
red beds
herblet
herb tea
keg beer
pebbled
Peebles
sea beet
verbify
herbage
leg bail
wet bike
bee balm
cembali
cembalo
netball
sea belt
tea ball
verbals
sex bomb
geebung
henbane
seabank
verbena
webbing
red book
temblor
Berbera
gerbera
herbary
Herbert
newborn
Newbury
redbird
seabird
sea-born
herbist

herbose
nebbish
sea bass
verbose
bedbath
herbous
sea-blue
terbium
Beecham
berceau
dewclaw
pea coat
pea-crab
red clay
redcoat
Red Crag
sea coal
Sercial
teuchat
meacock
✧peacock
percoct
petcock
red cock
seacock
deicide
beached
beechen
belcher
bencher
fetcher
geechee
leechee
leuchen
Meacher
merchet
peacher
perched
percher
reached
reacher
recceed
reccied
rescued
rescuer
teacher
welcher
wencher
mercify
Netcafé
deictic
helcoid
percoid
reechie
teachie
teach-in
teacake
descale
key-cold
percale
red cell
re-scale
rescale
sea calf
sex cell
wet cell
leucoma
newcome
o'ercome
welcome
Aeschna

descant
descend
descent
fencing
leucine
Meccano®
peccant
per cent
percine
red cent
rescind
hen-coop
peach on
reactor
sea cook
sea crow
tercios
percept
keycard
mercery
✧mercury
net cord
peccary
red card
red-card
rescore
sea card
metcast
pen-case
percase
percuss
tea cosy
tea-cosy
webcast
leucite
fetch up
ketchup
Mencius
mesclum
mesclun
new chum
reoccur
peccavi
red-cowl
beadman
deadpan
dead-pay
headcap
headman
headway
herdman
jet d'eau
✧new deal
seed-lac
Vendean
lewdsby
geoduck
heyduck
sea dace
sea duck
vendace
verdict
wet dock
Ken Dodd
bendlet
dead men
Dead Sea
dead set
dead-set
head sea
headset

Words marked ✧ can also be spelled with one or more capital letters

leidger
meddler
needler
peddler
per diem
readied
readier
readies
red deer
reedbed
reedier
seedbed
feed off
head off
lead off
lead-off
read off
re-edify
send off
send-off
Bendigo
headage
vendage
wendigo
dead air
headrig
Hendrix
readmit
seedlip
seed-oil
tendril
Veddoid
deedily
headily
needily
readily
reedily
seedily
beldame
beading
bedding
bending
dead end
dead-end
deodand
feeding
feuding
gelding
heading
leading
lending
mending
pendant
pendent
pending
reading
redding
reeding
seeding
sending
tedding
tendenz
verdant
wedding
weeding
welding
dendron
dewdrop
feedlot
head boy
herdboy
leg drop
let drop
seedbox
send for
tendron
readapt
readopt
feodary
feudary
Jeddart
leaders
perdure
verdure
weedery
berdash
feudist
geodesy
herdess
key-desk
nerdish
reddest
reddish
sea dust
tea dish
vendiss
Wendish
deodate
feu-duty
Perdita
verdite
deedful
heads-up
heedful
lead out
lead-out
needful
read out
read-out
send out
weed out
sea dove
bed down
get down
let down
let-down
meadowy
peg down
set down
set-down
deadeye
Mendoza
bedeman
bederal
bemedal
federal
general
Genevan
hederal
medevac
Peneian
peregal
pesewas
Rebekah
renewal
Senecan
Senegal
several
Teheran
telefax
terefah
vegetal
veteran
Yerevan
beseech
decency
defence
Rebecca
recency
regence
✧regency
remercy
Terence
delenda
✧nereids
bejewel
Celebes
Demeter
fevered
geneses
Jezebel
leveret
meseled
✧nemeses
referee
reneger
renewer
reverer
seceder
teletex
venerer
demerge
deterge
remerge
revenge
reweigh
telergy
dépêche
bedevil
benefic
benefit
ceresin
demerit
generic
✧genesis
genetic
heretic
memetic
nemesia
✧nemesis
pedesis
pedetic
revel in
reverie
Seferis
selenic
senecio
telesis
venefic
Venetia
zetetic
beseeke
deleble
de règle
Fenella
levelly
merells
vexedly
beteeme
dejeune
demeane
demesne
Gehenna
sejeant
develop
Fénelon
hebenon
Hereros
heteros
pereion
reredos
semeion
telecom
temenos
teredos
benempt
receipt
bebeeru
bepearl
cerebra
jewelry
pereira
relearn
revelry
✧terebra
decease
defense
demerse
never so
recense
release
reverse
reversi
reverso
rêveuse
teleost
beneath
celesta
celeste
dejecta
démenti
détente
genette
memento
perenty
seventh
✧seventy
vedette
aeneous
Benelux
cereous
deke out
détenue
gerenuk
level up
mete out
Peredur
renegue
réseaus
réseaux
revenue
Severus
sexed-up
bereave
deceive
deserve
receive
re-serve
reserve
Relenza®
reseize
beef-ham
leaf fat
✧red flag
sea foam
A-effect
geofact
perfect
red face
perfidy
beef tea
deified
deifier
feoffee
feoffer
Jeffrey
leaflet
reified
reifier
sea fret
self-fed
set free
Wee Free
leafage
serfage
deaf aid
jeofail
jetfoil
set fair
sexfoil
beefalo
dewfall
dewfull
let fall
menfolk
merfolk
penfold
seafolk
tenfold
perfume
perfumy
beffana
leafing
reefing
reffing
self-end
selfing
feoffor
seafood
self-sow
serfdom
ten-foot
webfoot
Bedford
deiform
eelfare
fee-farm
fen-fire
leafery
perform
sea-fire
set fire
Telford
welfare
Wexford
bedfast
Belfast
gemfish
jewfish
net-fish
perfuse
redfish
sea fish
selfish
selfism
selfist
serfish
wet fish
leafbud
peafowl
seafowl
Belgian
Bergman
Sea Goat
verglas
yeggman
beagler
beignet
feigned
gee-gees
✧leaguer
leughen
Neogaea
veggies
weighed
weigher
lee gage
heigh-ho
lengthy
key grip
penguin
weigh in
weigh-in
Bengali
bergylt
pergola
seagull
weigela
wergild
bergama
Bergamo
net game
red game
begging
Ben Gunn
geogeny
geogony
hedging
legging
Neogene
o'ergang
pegging
reagent
V-engine
wedging
Peugeot®
beggary
belgard
bergère
sea-girt
leggism
lengest
Newgate
Reigate
sea gate
tergite
weights
weighty
bee-glue
Belgium
Sergius
weigh up
sea gown
tea gown
Heshvan
lethean
Lew Hoad
recheat
redhead
red heat
sea haar
recheck
Methody
beshrew
fechter
lethied
Sekhmet
techier
tee-heed
meshuga
Jephtha
Beth Din
Mechlin
nephric
technic
Bexhill
get hold
keyhole
New Hall
techily
beshame
bethumb
bethump
beshine
beshone
Bethany
bethink
meshing
methane
methink
red hand
rethink
nephron
reshoot
perhaps
reshape
becharm
beghard
be there
bewhore
Jethart
lechery
✧leghorn
rechart
sea hare
✧senhora
Peshito
pet hate
rechate
Cepheus
beehive
yeshiva
seahawk
Cebidae
decimal
Delilah
devisal
Felidae
Felinae
feminal
fenitar
genipap
genital
genizah
geoidal
helical
helipad
jemidar
lexical
medical
metical
Mexican
Oedipal
pedicab
pelican
pemican
recital
reginal
retinae
retinal
retinas
retiral
revisal
revival
seminal
seminar
semitar
vesicae
vesical
Xenical®
Let It Be
bewitch
dehisce
mediacy
menisci
Belinda
periods
bedizen
bemired
besides
betided
betimes
decibel
decided
decider
defiler
definer
Delibes
deliver
demirep
demi-sec
denizen
derider
Désirée
desirer
deviled
devilet
devisee
deviser
Devizes
femiter
helices
helixes
Mérimée
netizen
pedicel
penises
perigee
recipes
reciter
refined
refiner
regimen
reliver
remiges
repiner
resider
resiner
retired
retiree
retirer
reviler
reviser
reviver
semiped
veliger
vetiver
Yezidee
Zezidee
besiege
seringa
bedight
behight
benight
betight
ceviche
delight
fetiche
Jericho
relight
aecidia
Cecilia
cecitis
deficit
delimit
deliria
✧felicia
Geminid
Geminis
legitim
Letitia
levitic
lewisia
neritic
pelitic
periwig
revisit
sebific
sedilia
Semitic
sericin
tenioid
betitle
cedilla
delible
gelidly
hemiola
legible
legibly
Melilla
Neville
pedicle
petiole
reticle
retitle
Seville
tepidly
vehicle
vesicle
vexilla
mediums
melisma
seriema
verismo
beginne
defiant
deviant
hemione
lenient

mediant
Reliant®
reliant
resiant
benison
debitor
demigod
devisor
genitor
get in on
get it on
helicon
heritor
leg-iron
lexicon
medicos
melilot
merinos
pea-iron
pericon
peridot
perigon
retinol
revisor
revivor
semi-log
sericon
venison
periapt
deciare
devilry
Félibre
Kenitra
retiary
semi-pro
hérissé
Melissa
✧métisse
Nerissa
pelisse
periost
sepiost
veriest
deviate
genista
let into
mediate
rebirth
seriate
bezique
decidua
dedimus
detinue
devious
Lepidus
Oedipus
perique
peritus
relique
repique
residua
residue
retinue
serious
tedious
believe
relieve
relievo
C E M Joad
Hey Jude
Mes-John
Beijing
perjink
perjure
perjury
Beckham
weekday
peekabo
deckled
geckoes
heckler
necklet
vetkoek
leakage
necktie
deskill
jerkily
perkily
peskily
reskill
seakale
serkali
decking
desking
Jenkins
jerking
lekking
necking
peaking
pecking
reeking
sea king
weekend
desktop
peckish
weakish
Beckett
bee-kite
deck out
jerk out
leak out
peak out
seek out
✧aeolian
bell jar
bellman
feel-bad
feelbad
heelbar
heeltap
hellcat
keelman
meal-man
realgar
red lead
reelman
refloat
sealwax
tea lead
tea leaf
jellaba
deflect
fetlock
genlock
hemlock
neglect
pellach
pellack
pellock
re-elect
reflect
replace
replica
sea lace
sea loch
wedlock
Wenlock
yelloch
ceilidh
seclude
tea lady
Belleek
bellied
Cellnet®
hellier
jellied
mealies
re-alter
replied
replier
Wealden
well-fed
✧wellies
well met
well-set
hell of a
jellify
New Left
peel off
reel off
seal off
see life
sell off
sell-off
tell off
well off
well-off
geology
keelage
negligé
néglígé
neology
realign
sea legs
fellahs
healthy
wealthy
declaim
new-laid
reallie
realtie
reclaim
eel-like
sea-like
web-like
cellule
heal-all
real ale
sea lily
deplume
réclame
reclimb
Tellima
beeline
bell end
Bellini
Bellona
berline
ceiling
dealing
decline
deplane
devling
DEW line
feeling
Fellini
fenland
Geelong
gelling
healing
heeling
Hellene
hemline
her lane
herling
keeling
keyline
lee-lane
ley line
merling
peeling
recline
Red Lane
red line
red-line
reeling
replant
sea lane
sealant
sealine
sealing
sea lung
seeling
setline
telling
veiling
Weiland
welling
wetland
yelling
Zealand
zealant
begloom
bell-boy
bellhop
Berlioz
ceòl mór
hell-box
hellion
keelson
new look
reallot
Realtor®
realtor
rebloom
sea lion
well now
well-won
wet-look
yealdon
dewlapt
declare
De Klerk
deplore
meal-ark
pedlary
sea lark
sealery
✧sea lord
'cellist
cellist
cellose
declass
get lost!
hellish
keyless
legless
realise
✧realism
realist
reclose
recluse
rellish
sexless
deflate
deplete
mellite
neolith
Peelite
perlite
reality
reflate
replete
zeolite
becloud
gealous
jealous
kellaut
perlous
sell out
sell-out
well out
zealful
zealous
beslave
hellova
helluva
Mevlevi
Pehlevi
replevy
bellows
mellowy
yellows
yellowy
realize
besmear
Permian
red meat
term day
vermian
Bermuda
new-made
beamlet
beam sea
Heimweh
jemmied
meemies
reamier
seamset
Vermeer
dermoid
desmoid
germain
mermaid
seamaid
vermeil
red moki
beamily
gemmule
sea mell
sea mile
vermell
vermily
beaming
desmine
Desmond
ferment
gemming
geomant
germane
Germans
Germany
hemming
hetmans
lemming
reamend
reaming
seeming
segment
teaming
teeming
tegmina
termini
verminy
Vermont
fermion
new moon
Denmark
gemmery
seamark
beamish
sea moss
bee-moth
fermata
fermate
fewmets
gemmate
lemmata
permute
regmata
termite
fermium
teemful
new-mown
aeonian
Aetnean
beanbag
hernial
Lemnian
Leonian
lernean
her nibs
Bernice
Kennick
redneck
re-enact
Kennedy
beinked
dernier
hennaed
Leander
Leontes
meander
pennied
pennies
reannex
re-enter
reinter
veinlet
vernier
reunify
peonage
teenage
deontic
Jeannie
kennels
mean ill
pennill
Reynold
pen name
pet name
Bernini
eevning
ferning
keening
kenning
kerning
leaning
✧leonine
meaning
pennant
pennine
penning
regnant
remnant
renning
seining
veining
vernant
lean bow
lean-tos
re-endow
reunion
ternion
beanery
Bernard
deanery
fernery
hennery
Jean Arp
Leonard
Leonora
re-entry
rein-arm
✧reynard
ternary
fennish
fewness
kernish
newness
peonism
redness
setness
teentsy
wennish
wetness
Zennist
Bennett
Kenneth
kernite
keynote
neonate
peanuts
pennate
reunite
ternate
dernful
heinous
mean sun
veinous
beknave
beknown
fern-owl
neo-Nazi
Deborah
deposal
femoral
Jehovah
Kerouac
✧menorah
men-o'-war
nemoral
removal
repoman
reposal
Seconal®
serosae
serosal
serosas
Seroxat®
Veronal®
veronal
xeromas
redoubt
debouch
deforce
devoice
heroics
Menorca
rejoice
retouch
seconde
secondi
secondo
seconds
aerogel
begored
✧beloved
besomed
betoken
decoder
demoded
deposer
devoted
devotee
get over
Helodea
kerogen
meioses
oenomel
re-cover
recover
recower
rejoneo
rejones
remodel
removed
remover
reposed
revoker
see over
tenoner
venomed
xerotes
regorge
Lesotho
Sesotho
aerobic
✧bedouin
begonia
celosia
demonic
✧demotic
deposit
Feronia
genomic
hedonic
henotic
kenosis
kenotic
ketonic
ketosis
ketotic
meconic
meconin
meiosis
meiotic
melodic
mesonic
Metonic
metopic
nepotic
Neronic
Pelopid
peloria
peloric
reposit
Segovia
xerosis
xerotic
Zenobia
Men Only
recoyle
remould
Berowne
demount
heroine
reboant
rebound
re-count
recount
redound
refound
remount
repoint
re-sound
resound
rewound
W E Johns
zeroing
aerobot
aerosol
decolor
Mesozoa
metopon
peloton
rebozos
begorra
Ben Okri
demonry
devoirs
felonry
helotry
heronry
memoirs
recoure
rejourn
velours
zedoary
delouse
Genoese
Heloise
heroise
heroism
rehouse
remorse
bemouth
Menotti

Words marked ✧ can also be spelled with one or more capital letters

reroute
velouté
Aerobus®
decorum
defocus
pelorus
refocus
seropus
Xenopus
zero-sum
behoove
devolve
resolve
revolve
benomyl
meronym
metonym
heroize
bespeak
leap day
net-play
respeak
respray
Tempean
✧templar
bespice
henpeck
new pice
✧respect
wet pack
bespeed
deep-fet
deep-sea
deep-set
jeepney
keepnet
peoples
perplex
telpher
templed
templet
✧tempter
keep off
seepage
serpigo
✧web page
deep-six
✧delphic
delphin
despair
despoil
keep fit
keep-fit
Leipzig
Memphis
vespoid
bespake
bespoke
sea pike
seppuku
leg-pull
Leopold
pep pill
reapply
redpoll
respell
weepily
despond
dew-pond
heaping
helping

keeping
kemping
leaping
perpend
perpent
red pine
repping
respond
sea pink
Serpens
✧serpent
tenpins
terpene
vespine
weeping
yelping
new poor
peep-toe
jet pipe
besport
deep-fry
jeepers
jeopard
lempira
leopard
Newport
peppery
respire
seaport
sexpert
tempera
tempore
tempura
vespers
bedpost
despise
hey pass
new peso
sea pass
tempest
bespate
despite
respite
bespout
eelpout
helpful
help out
keep mum
keep out
Newquay
jerquer
mesquin
mesquit
re-equip
bearcat
beer-mat
betread
cerrial
decrial
Feargal
get real
hearsay
meercat
meerkat
Meg Ryan
✧ne'erday
retread
re-treat
retreat
retrial
sea road

tear bag
tear gas
tear-gas
bedrock
defrock
✧derrick
detract
metrics
new rich
rebrace
re-erect
refract
retrace
retract
secrecy
terrace
tetract
verruca
débride
degrade
Derrida
detrude
let ride
regrade
regrede
tetrode
bearded
berried
debrief
decreed
decreet
decried
decrier
deerlet
ferried
hearken
hearted
hearten
henries
learned
learner
merrier
✧negroes
pearled
pearler
Perrier®
perrier
refried
regreet
reorder
retried
sea reed
serried
terreen
terrier
wearied
yearner
petrify
redraft
tear off
terrify
wear off
beerage
ferrugo
peerage
sevruga
verruga
beardie
bear pit
detrain
Detroit

Geordie
Georgia
georgic
Georgie
Hebraic
Henry IV
✧negroid
pearlin
pedrail
recruit
refrain
retrain
retrait
tear pit
terrain
terroir
weirdie
zebroid
heureka
bedroll
Cedrela
dearnly
deer fly
febrile
ferrule
heartly
merrily
peartly
wearily
weirdly
zebrula
zebrule
begrime
deary me
megrims
neuroma
reframe
reprime
bearing
cedrine
feering
gearing
hearing
herring
jeering
key ring
leering
neurine
neurone
pébrine
Petrine
pew-rent
rear-end
rebrand
regrant
regrind
reprint
searing
tearing
terrane
terrene
terrine
veering
wearing
year-end
zebrina
zebrine
bedroom
gearbox
heirdom
legroom

Reardon
rear-dos
redroot
reproof
sea room
tea room
weirdos
bedropt
Cecrops
decrypt
Kekrops
Deirdre
Ferrara
Ferrari®
pedrero
petrary
Terrors
bearish
bed-rest
beprose
dearest
defrost
depress
heiress
heurism
leg-rest
leprose
leprosy
metrist
nearest
necrose
neurism
New Ross
peeress
rearise
recross
re-dress
redress
Red Rose
refresh
regress
re-press
repress
reprise
seeress
tea rose
wearish
zebrass
bedrite
betroth
cedrate
Debrett
ferrate
ferrety
ferrite
Negrito
neurite
Penrith
regrate
regrets
retrate
rewrite
rewrote
secreta
secrete
secrets
serrate
bear hug
bear out
beer gut
defraud

fearful
ferrous
hear out
leprous
near cut
petrous
regroup
tearful
wear out
deprave
deprive
Henry VI
redrive
reprive
reprove
repryve
decrown
reprize
beeswax
censual
deiseal
felspar
geishas
✧hessian
Jersian
Jew's-ear
key-seat
lensman
mensual
✧messiah
✧messias
Newsday
newsman
new star
Persian
redsear
sea star
seismal
sensual
Tees Bay
Telstar
Jessica
persico
seasick
Versace
bedside
depside
lee side
leg side
legside
seaside
bee-skep
Deus det
feaster
gessoes
heister
hepster
keister
leisler
leister
measled
measles
Meissen
meister
mens rea
messier
oersted
Perspex®
Pevsner
red seed
✧webster

welsher
densify
versify
message
beastie
cesspit
deasoil
deistic
hership
leg slip
leg spin
leg-spin
let slip
mess kit
mess-tin
Perseid
seismic
set sail
verse in
vessail
wet suit
netsuke
beastly
densely
hersall
herself
messily
pensile
sea salt
sensile
sessile
tensely
tensile
tersely
beesome
jessamy
pessima
ceasing
jessant
leasing
Messina
peasant
pepsine
persant
persona
persons
retsina
sea sand
sensing
teasing
temsing
versant
versine
versing
weasand
Beeston
cession
gemsbok
get shot
leg-show
mersion
neuston
newsboy
peascod
pension
red snow
session
sex shop
tea shop
tee shot
tension

tersion
✧version
wet-shod
bedsore
berserk
censure
dessert
leasure
leisure
measure
pessary
seasure
sensory
seysure
tessera
Persism
✧persist
sensism
sensist
density
felsite
sensate
tensity
versute
✧web site
web-site
website
Celsius
deasiul
pea soup
Perseus
Persius
reissue
sea slug
pensiv'd
pensive
tensive
zemstva
zemstvo
leasowe
peishwa
Jew's eye
belt bag
beltman
beltway
Bentham
Bertram
bestead
bestial
best man
central
dextral
dextran
gentian
kept man
meat-man
neutral
oestral
peat-hag
peatman
rent-day
rest day
tea tray
tertial
tertian
test ban
text-man
textual
Vectian
ventral
vestral

bedtick
bestick
bestuck
Lettice
lettuce
pentact
pentice
peptics
restock
testacy
Cestoda
cestode
lee tide
pentode
peptide
red tide
✧testudo
Bentley®
bestrew
centner
centred
de Staël
feather
felt pen
fettler
genteel
heathen
heather
hen-toed
jettied
kestrel
leather
meatier
meat-tea
mettled
neither
peat bed
rentier
reutter
seethed
seether
seltzer
settled
settler
tea tree
tent bed
tent peg
test bed
testier
vent-peg
weather
web-toed
Werther
yew tree
beatify
beat off
certify
left-off
rectify
restaff
restiff
testify
centage
lentigo
nest egg
restage
tentage
tentigo
ventage
ventige
✧vertigo

vestige
weftage
gertcha
beatnik
Beatrix
benthic
bestain
bestrid
centric
certain
cestoid
deltaic
deltoid
dentoid
Deutzia
dextrin
fee tail
felt tip
Leitrim
lentoid
meat pie
penthia
pertain
rectrix
Septrin®
tectrix
tent pin
testril
ventail
westlin
Yeltsin
De Stijl
hei-tiki
pertake
beet-fly
bestill
centile
deathly
fertile
✧gentile
✧gestalt
heftily
meat-fly
meatily
pep talk
pettily
reptile
restyle
Seattle
sectile
sextile
tent-fly
tenthly
test-fly
testily
textile
beats me
bedtime
centime
centimo
leptome
meltemi
rectums
septime
teatime
beating
Beltane
belting
best end
Bettina
betting

bettong
bez-tine
dentine
destine
destiny
felting
gestant
getting
heating
heptane
jesting
jetting
Keating
leptons
letting
meeting
melting
neoteny
Neptune
nesting
netting
pelting
pentane
pentene
peptone
petting
reptant
resting
retting
seating
sestina
sestine
setting
✧sextans
✧sextant
tenting
testing
texting
ventana
venting
vesting
vetting
weeting
West End
westing
wetting
beatbox
benthos
best boy
destroy
festoon
Hertzog
keitloa
lection
menthol
mention
nest box
neutron
peat bog
rection
section
septuor
settlor
sextuor
testoon
Ventnor
✧gestapo
peg-tops
red tape
red-tape
bestorm

betters
centare
century
dentary
denture
feature
fetters
gesture
hectare
lectern
lecture
lecturn
leotard
lettern
letters
nectary
peatary
peatery
perturb
rectory
✧restart
restore
rettery
sea term
sea turn
sectary
testern
texture
venture
✧venturi
vesture
vettura
✧western
yestern
dentist
Kentish
leftish
leftism
leftist
lentisc
lentisk
Lettish
pectise
pectose
peltast
pentise
pentose
peptise
pertuse
pettish
Ventôse
ventose
wettest
wettish
dentate
gestate
meltith
peltate
pentiti
pentito
restate
septate
sestett
sextett
tektite
testate
beat out
belt out
best buy
centaur
centrum

featous
jestful
lentous
meat-tub
Nerthus
nestful
oestrum
oestrus
Pentium®
pestful
restful
tentful
tent-guy
tertius
zestful
centavo
festive
restive
new town
meat-axe
Nepthys
mestiza
mestizo
pectize
peptize
cesural
decuman
jejunal
Ketubah
leguaan
medusae
medusan
medusas
menu-bar
mezuzah
nebulae
nebular
nebulas
perusal
refusal
refutal
regulae
regular
secular
tegulae
tegular
nelumbo
defunct
felucca
sebundy
beaufet
bemused
cerumen
deluded
deluder
genuses
✧lemures
peruked
peruser
rebuker
rebuses
reduced
reducer
refugee
refuser
refuter
reputed
✧requiem
securer
seducer
tenured

rejudge
remuage
resurge
penuche
penuchi
beaufin
decuria
legumin
Lemuria
Perugia
✧petunia
refugia
repunit
Senusis
sequoia
beguile
decuple
medulla
rebuild
recuile
sequela
setuale
tequila
beguine
béguine
genuine
returns
sequent
set upon
tenutos
requere
require
beauish
bequest
Debussy
✧repulse
request
Senussi
Jesuits
requite
requote
tenuity
jejunum
Réaumur
✧regulus
remueur
seculum
Telugus
tenuous
Xenurus
Zebulun
decurve
recurve
seruewe
Servian
leave be
service
pervade
bevvied
heavier
oeuvres
sea view
leave go
selvage
heave ho!
heave-ho
delve in
vervain
heavily
nervily
nervule

servile
weevily
cervine
fervent
heavens
heaving
leaving
nervine
revving
servant
serving
weaving
beavery
nervure
peevers
pervert
servery
✧dervish
Gervase
peevish
nervate
Servite
velvety
fervour
nervous
serve up
servewe
legwear
Keswick
Lerwick
between
seaweed
wee-weed
hen-wife
seawife
gee whiz
reawake
Beowulf
sea wall
sea wolf
sea-wolf
setwall
werwolf
red wine
redwing
sea wind
sea wing
seewing
red-wood
✧redwood
bedward
bedwarf
bed-work
dew worm
eelworm
felwort
keyword
leeward
legwork
network
o'erword
seaward
seaware
seaworm
sea-worn
webworm
wetware
weyward
sea wasp
lee wave
✧new wave

✧new-wave
sea wave
betwixt
Zeuxian
re-exist
zeuxite
levy war
New Year
recycle
kerygma
belying
defying
denying
levying
relying
renying
revying
New York
very own
Merzbau
benzoic
benzoin
Neozoic
benzole
leeze me
benzene
benzine
mezzani
seizing
Tenzing
weazand
seizure
seize up
benzoyl
bezzazz
effacer
affable
affably
effable
affaire
affairs
off beam
off-beam
offbeat
off base
off-come
Q factor
X-factor
off duty
off-duty
offence
effendi
offeree
offerer
offeror
affear'd
affeard
affeare
offense
effects
offer up
off-fore
afghani
offhand
affinal
African
affined
officer
offices
affiche
affiant

iffiest
offload
afflict
ufology
off line
off-line
offline
of a mind
aftmost
sfumato
of an age
pfennig
afforce
efforce
affoord
of no use
of sorts
Y-fronts
off-peak
offpeak
off-plan
off-road
of price
sferics
off-ramp
affront
a far cry
offside
off spin
off-spin
of a sort
off-site
offscum
of a size
offtake
a fat lot
effulge
a few bob
off-ward
affying
iguanas
agnamed
agraffe
agrapha
agnatic
agravic
iguanid
oghamic
Igraine
ignaros
agraste
egg-bird
egg cell
agaçant
egg case
egg-cosy
ague-fit
Egreria
M G Lewis
Agnelli
H G Wells
ogreish
igneous
egg-flip
Ogygian
agogics
egghead
agrised
igniter
Agrippa
against

Aga Khan
agilely
age-long
agelong
agelast
ageless
eggless
egoless
agility
egality
agamoid
eggmass
agamous
Ugandan
aginner
agonise
agonist
agonize
agnomen
ignorer
agnosia
ignoble
ignobly
aground
egg plum
aggrace
C G Bruce
W G Grace
aggrade
Agartha
igarapé
aggress
aggrate
agister
Aga saga
agistor
ego-trip
egotise
egotism
egotist
agitate
agitato
egotize
à gauche
agoutis
Iguvine
eggwash
ugly man
Iggy Pop
choanae
pheazar
phrasal
shy away
cheapen
cheater
phraser
sheared
shearer
sheaved
sheaves
theater
wheaten
sheathe
sheaths
sheathy
cheapie
thiamin
Cheadle
cheaply
chiasma
chiasmi

chiasms
whoa-hoa
Zhdanov
phratry
theatre
shiatsu
Chianti
shmaltz
thwaite
pH value
thiasus
chlamys
shiatzu
chobdar
Shabbat
shebeen
the Big C
Chablis
Thebaic
Thebaid
shabble
The Bell
the Bill
the Bull
the bomb
shebang
Chabrol
rhabdom
✧the book
rhubarb
the Bard
phobism
phobist
chabouk
chibouk
rhabdus
choc-bar
✧choctaw
the clap
the Crab
choc-ice
shy-cock
Chechen
checked
checker
chicken
chocker
shicker
shochet
shocked
shocker
shucker
thicken
thicket
whacked
whacker
whicker
Chicago
chéchia
check in
check-in
chuckie
chuck in
chuck it
phacoid
rhachis
thickie
chuckle
shackle
thickly
chicana
chicane
✧chicano
chochos
the chop
thickos
whackos
the Cape
chicory
The Cure
shicksa
the case
thecate
✧the city
check up
check-up
chuck up
shack up
thick'un
chaddar
Chadian
Cheddar
chuddah
chuddar
khaddar
Phidias
Rhodian
the dead
the dods
chidden
shedded
shedder
shidder
shudder
thudded
whidded
whidder
shadily
chiding
shading
chaddor
shadoof
cheders
rhodora
the dust
rhodium
rhodous
khediva
✧khedive
shadowy
chaetae
cheetah
shreddy
threads
thready
cheeper
cheerer
cheesed
chiefer
sheeted
shoe peg
shtetel
thieves
wheeled
wheeler
wheezer
whoever
whyever
wheenge
wheesht
cheerio
choenix
phoenix
phocine
phrenic
Rhaetia
Rhaetic
shoe tie
wheelie
cheerly
chiefly
sheerly
shtetls
wheedle
wheeple
wheezle
phlegmy
shoeing
chaebol
phaeton
sheepos
threnos
Wheeson
chiefry
Phaedra
phaeism
phrensy
the East
bheesty
thretty
cheer up
Phoebus
threave
the flat
The Face
chaffer
chuffed
shafted
shafter
shifted
shifter
whiffer
whiffet
the fair
shuffle
The Fall
whiffle
chiffon
The Fool
shofars
the form
shift up
Bhagwan
Chogyal
the Goat
the gods
chigger
shagged
shogged
thigger
thuggee
whigged
chagrin
the grip
thiggit
Chagall
shoggle
shoggly
the Gulf
the game
chignon
the good
thuggos
shahada
the hell
shahdom
the Horn
shehita
T H White
shih tzu
Ahriman
Khoisan
✧shaitan
shrinal
shriech
shritch
chained
Shriner
shrived
shrivel
shriven
shriver
thrived
thriven
thriver
aheight
sheikha
shright
x-height
Shiitic
shrilly
thrilly
whaisle
whaizle
chrisom
shrimpy
thrimsa
Christo
✧christy
thrifty
thristy
chain up
shrieve
Choisya
the Klan
the kick
shakudo
chukker
shakoes
shakily
shekels
chi kung
shaking
Chekhov
chikhor
chikara
Shakers
shikari
chekist
The Kiss
choke up
shake up
shake-up
challah
challan
Chilean
chiliad
Chilian
ghilgai
shalwar
shellac
thalian
chalice
Shylock
The Lady
Chaldee
chalder
Chelsea
childed
childer
chilies
chilled
chiller
phellem
philter
shelled
sheller
Shelley
✧shelter
shelver
shelves
thalweg
thiller
whelked
chylify
khalifa
Shelagh
Khalkha
chalcid
challie
challis
cheloid
chillis
ghillie
phallic
phallin
Phillip
Phyllis
sheltie
shilpit
thallic
the like
childly
thalami
the Lamb
the lump
chalone
chelone
cholent
choline
phalanx
✧the line
whaling
shallon
shallop
shallot
✧shallow
Shilton
the Lion
cholera
choltry
philtre
whalery
whilere
thylose
wholism
wholist
chalutz
chelate
thulite
chalk up
chillum
✧phallus
thallus
thulium
chalaza
champac
champak
shimaal
chamade
chamber
chamfer
chamlet
chimley
chimney
chumley
chummed
shammed
shammer
shammes
shimmer
shimmey
thumbed
thumper
whammed
whimmed
whimper
whimsey
chymify
whim off
Thimphu
chamois
chime in
khamsin
rhombic
Thummim
Chomsky
shamble
shambly
shemale
thimble
whample
whemmle
whimple
whomble
whommle
whummle
shamans
the Manx
the many
thymine
rhomboi
rhombos
shampoo
shim rod
chambré
✧chimera
chimere
the morn
chamise
chamiso
chemise
chemism
chemist
Rhemish
Rhemist
rhymist
Thomism
Thomist
chametz
chometz
Shemite
themata
chymous
Rhamnus
rhombus
Thammuz
Shimizu
Chantal
chinwag
dhansak
khanjar
Shankar
shin pad
thannah
whangam
phonics
Chengdu
Rhondda
the nude
chancel
chancer
chances
chancey
changer
✧channel
channer
chanter
chantey
chunder
✧chunnel
chunner
chunter
shanked
shantey
shoneen
shunned
shunner
shunter
thankee
thanker
thinker
thinned
thinner
thonder
thonged
thunder
whangee
whene'er
whinger
thanage
Chungho
rhonchi
chantie
✧chindit
phone-in
shank it
shindig
think-in
shingle
shingly
shinily
phoneme
shining
the Nine
whining
chanson
chantor
✧chinook
Khonsou
phantom
Shannon
ahungry
bhangra
chancre
Chandra
chantry
chondre
chondri
shandry
✧chinese
Rhenish
shiness
shyness
Cheng-tu
khanate
phenate
phonate
rhenium
think up
thin out
chanoyu
chintzy
chloral
The Oval
theorbo
thrombi
shrouds
shroudy
chooser
choosey
chromel
phloxes
shooter
theorem
throned
thrower
whoopee
whooper
through
chaotic
chloric
chookie
chromic
chronic
✧phlomis
shoogie
theoric
throw in
throw-in
The Oaks
shoofly
shoogle
shoogly
chromos
chronon
shmoose
throaty
shoot up
throw up
whoobub
thionyl
shmooze
shmoozy
chapeau
chapman
chappal
chip hat
chuppah
shiplap
✧shipman
shipway
shophar
shopman
whipcat
whipsaw
chaplet
chapped
chapter
chipped
chipper
chipset
chopped
chopper
shipmen
shipped
shippen
shipper
shopped
shopper
whapped
whipped
whipper
whippet
whopped
whopper
whupped
chip off
Chaplin
chappie
chippie
rhaphis
Thepsis
shapely
the pill
chopine
shaping
ship boy
shippon
shop boy
whip-top
the pips
chapess
the push
chapati
chupati
the pits
shape up
shape-up
shipful
shopful
whip out
chequer
The Quip
chordae
chordal
chorial
gharial
Phar Lap
Shari'ah
✧shariat
Shergar
✧sheriat
✧sherpas
thereat
theriac
therian
thermae
thermal
Thoreau
whereas
whereat
cherubs
thereby
the robe
whereby
charact
the Rock
charade

charged
charger
charges
Charles
✧charley
charmed
charmer
charnel
charred
charter
chirper
chordee
sharded
sharker
Shar-Pei
sharpen
sharper
sherbet
shereef
shirker
Shirley
shirred
shorten
thorned
thyrses
wharves
where'er
wherret
whirler
whirred
whirret
whorled
Sharifa
sheriff
thurify
charkha
churchy
✧charlie
charpie
chervil
choreic
choroid
dhurrie
gherkin
sharpie
sherris
shortie
therein
thermic
Thermit®
theroid
thyroid
wharfie
wherein
charily
chorale
chortle
sharply
shortly
thirdly
whirtle
the Rump
charing
chorine
pharynx
sharing
shoring
the Rand
The Ring
the runs
chariot

charpoy
cheroot
chorion
gheraos
Kharkov
Kherson
✧pharaoh
thereof
thereon
Thermos®
whereof
whereon
therapy
the rope
charism
cherish
chorism
chorist
Theresa
whereso
whorish
Bharati
charity
thereto
thirsty
thorite
whereto
charqui
chirrup
choreus
churn up
churrus
shore up
thorium
thyrsus
chorizo
chasmal
Chesvan
Ohm's law
The Star
thus far
physics
the sack
bhistee
chasmed
chasten
chessel
chesses
chested
Chester
Chislev
ghessed
shaster
shyster
whisker
whisket
✧whiskey
whisper
✧who's who
chasmic
Chassid
chassis
phase in
phasmid
ghastly
ghostly
thistle
thistly
thyself
whistle
the same

chasing
phasing
physios
the Shop
shastra
the sere
chesnut
Theseus
chateau
château
khotbah
khutbah
shittah
the Taal
Whitman
whittaw
photics
photo CD
chatted
chattel
chatter
chitter
chutney
khotbeh
shatter
shotted
shotten
shutter
thether
thither
thother
whate'er
whatten
whether
whetted
whetter
whither
whitret
whitter
shut off
shut-off
thatcht
chetnik
shittim
whatsis
whatsit
shottle
shuttle
whitely
whittle
the tomb
rhatany
rhytina
the tane
whiting
ghettos
photo op
what not
whatnot
what now?
whitlow
the tops
chutist
photism
whitish
chetrum
Photius
shotgun
shot put
shut out
shutout

what's up?
Whitsun
shut-eye
shout at
thruway
shrubby
chaunce
thrutch
Chaucer
chaufer
chaumer
rheumed
shouter
W H Auden
chaunge
theurgy
thought
chauvin
shiurim
thrummy
H H Munro
Shavian
Dhivehi
I have it
the void
shaving
Cheviot
chevron
Shavuot
shivery
showman
chowder
shawley
Shawnee
the weed
show off
show-off
showghe
shawlie
show biz
showbiz
the Wain
showily
✧the wall
chewink
showing
thawing
showbox
showery
the Word
the West
chew out
show out
thaw out
the year
they say
the yips
the Yard
thrymsa
wheyish
chayote
whey tub
whizzed
whizzer
rhizoid
whiz kid
rhizome
rhizine
bimanal
cicadae
cicadas

cicalas
didakai
die away
die-away
Mica Dam
Nicaean
picamar
pit-a-pat
pitapat
pitarah
Sinaean
timarau
aidance
finance
Miranda
Rivaldo
viranda
virando
Vivaldi
citadel
didakei
dilated
dilater
filabeg
filacer
filazer
fixated
hicatee
Kilauea
lie-abed
limacel
limaces
minaret
Pilates
vilayet
visaged
giraffe
hidalga
hidalgo
hibachi
piranha
✧cidaris
dibasic
Di Canio
dika-oil
✧filaria
jigajig
Kiwanis
piratic
Ritalin®
tilapia
Titania
✧titanic
✧titanis
Vinalia
vis-à-vis
vitamin
vivaria
zizania
bidarka
ziganka
citable
disable
disally
finable
finagle
finally
fixable
hirable
likable
likably

livable
minable
mirable
miracle
misally
mixable
ridable
sizable
sizably
tidally
vitally
digamma
gisarme
sixaine
dilator
disavow
girasol
gitanos
jigajog
limaçon
mikados
mirador
picador
tinamou
viragos
bizarre
rivalry
simarre
Sinatra
filasse
Picasso
Sivaism
tirasse
vinasse
ailanto
di salto
picante
Sivaite
Cimabué
Hilarus
Piraeus
piragua
vivamus
bivalve
airboat
Big Beat
kit-boat
Niobean
pigboat
Siobhán
tie beam
die back
dieback
finback
hit back
lie back
limbeck
sit back
tieback
bilboes
dibbler
kimboed
nibbler
nibbles
timbrel
wimbrel
yibbles
fimbria
air-bell
diabolo
gimbals

hip-belt
oil-belt
piebald
pinball
pit bull
timbale
big band
big-band
✧big bang
dibbing
disband
fibbing
gibbing
hip bone
jibbing
mirbane
nibbing
ribband
ribbing
rib bone
ribbons
ribbony
jib boom
pit brow
disbark
fibbery
fig-bird
filberd
filbert
Finbarr
✧gilbert
libbard
limbers
Lisburn
misborn
oilbird
✧tilbury
timbers
airbase
diabase
gibbose
air-bath
hip bath
kibbutz
limbate
Lisbeth
Lizbeth
niobate
niobite
oil bath
six bits
Big Blue
gibbous
limbous
niobium
niobous
Rimbaud
Circean
Piscean
pit-coal
bibcock
biocide
discide
zincode
zip code
aircrew
biccies
birchen
Bircher
Circaea
circled

circler
circlet
ciscoes
discoed
discoer
ditcher
filcher
finched
fitchée
fitchet
fitchew
hitcher
kitchen
linchet
piccies
pilcher
pinched
pincher
pitched
pitcher
tinchel
wincher
witchen
zincked
zincify
discage
ribcage
biochip
birchir
biscuit
circlip
circuit
discoid
kinchin
lit crit
pitch in
tie clip
winch in
zincoid
oil-cake
air-cell
Lincoln
miscall
piccolo
vincula
Zincala
Zincali
Zincalo
discant
fir cone
hircine
mincing
Miocene
piscina
piscine
Vincent
wincing
zincing
air-cool
✧jim crow
pilcrow
discept
hiccups
hiccupy
miscopy
bin card
discard
discern
discerp
discord
discure

pilcorn
pincers
pin curl
piscary
ripcord
SIM card
sincere
tip-cart
viscera
circusy
die-cast
diocese
discase
discuss
giocoso
miscast
pincase
viscose
big cats
siccity
zincite
bitch up
hitch up
linctus
minceur
piece up
pitch up
viscous
winch up
zincous
big deal
birdman
diedral
findram
Lindsay
misdeal
misdial
misdraw
wildcat
wild man
wild oat
windbag
wind gap
piddock
viaduct
windock
diddler
dildoes
fiddler
fiddley
girdled
girdler
hindleg
kiddier
kiddies
kindler
kindred
Lindsey
lip-deep
middle C
Mildred
mindset
misdeed
misdeem
misdiet
misdoer
piddler
pig-deer
riddler
tiddled
tiddler

Words marked ✧ can also be spelled with one or more capital letters

tiddley
tie-dyed
Windies
windage
wind egg
windigo
Airdrie
disdain
giddily
mild ale
Mindelo
windily
bidding
binding
birding
eilding
finding
gilding
girding
hilding
kidding
lindane
minding
misdone
ridding
wilding
winding
airdrop
bird-dog
diadrom
jib-door
mind you
wild dog
windrow
Windsor
bindery
cindery
Kildare
pindari
tindery
windore
kiddush
middest
piedish
pin-dust
wild ass
wildish
Yiddish
Zip® disk
zip disk
biodata
misdate
find out
giddy-up
hind-gut
mindful
mind out
oil drum
windgun
wind out
die down
kip down
lie down
lie-down
mildewy
pin down
pindown
sit down
sit-down
tie down
tip down

Windows®
windows
bikeway
bipedal
dime bag
fire-bar
fireman
firepan
five-bar
give ear
give way
hire car
✧liberal
like mad
lineman
literal
live oak
mineral
pikeman
pile-cap
pine tar
side-bar
sidebar
✧sidecar
sideman
sideral
Tibetan
tideway
tile hat
time lag
time was
vinegar
virelay
wide-gab
wine bag
wine bar
wine fat
Winesap
wine-sap
wine vat
wire bar
wireman
wiretap
wireway
wise man
licence
silence
vivency
limeade
videnda
bigener
bi-level
cinerea
dimeter
fibered
fine leg
fire-new
hive bee
Lineker
livener
minever
Nineveh
pie-eyed
pig-eyed
pikelet
pin-eyed
pipe-key
ridered
rivered
riveret
riveted

riveter
sidemen
sinewed
tile-red
videoed
vinewed
widener
wizened
Ximenes
dine off
file off
fire off
give off
hive off
hive-off
live off
ride off
wipe off
disedge
diverge
hireage
kitenge
lineage
mileage
cimelia
cinerin
dimeric
Dioecia
eidetic
eirenic
Fidelio
fivepin
give aim
kinesis
kinetic
Liberia
limelit
limepit
lipemia
lived-in
mimesis
mimetic
Nigeria
ninepin
niterie
piperic
silesia
sine die
sirenic
tide rip
viremia
cineole
firefly
fixedly
Giselle
micella
micelle
mineola
miserly
mixedly
nigella
sitella
tigerly
tiredly
vitelli
vixenly
Viyella®
dilemma
pip emma
fire ant
aileron

bibelot
dice-box
Diderot
filemot
firebox
firedog
firepot
liberos
live-box
livelod
Niterói
pi-meson
River Ob
side box
Simenon
viceroy
vine-rod
viretot
wide boy
wine box
dirempt
River Po
fine art
firearm
linear A
linear B
sidearm
✧viverra
cineast
dis-ease
disease
diseuse
diverse
fideism
fideist
fineish
finesse
jive-ass
license
Mideast
misease
niceish
sizeism
sizeist
Vitebsk
ailette
biretta
Bizerta
dinette
liberty
lineate
Linette
lisente
Lisette
minette
Ninette
pileate
pimento
pipette
vidette
ciseaux
dine out
direful
firebug
fire out
give out
hideous
hideout
hire out
lifeful
like fun

line-out
live out
Miletus
mixed-up
niveous
piceous
pileous
pile out
pine nut
pinetum
pipeful
piteous
ride out
✧silenus
time gun
timeous
✧time out
wileful
wine gum
wipe out
wipeout
wired up
wise guy
Minerva
Vicenza
bigfeet
biofuel
misfeed
piaffer
piffler
pigfeed
riffler
Wilfred
miff off
airfoil
bid fair
milfoil
tinfoil
Wilfrid
kinfolk
miffily
misfall
misfell
misfile
pinfold
pitfall
sixfold
tinfuls
disfame
✧tiffany
tiffing
airflow
✧bigfoot
fiefdom
finfoot
six-foot
difform
disform
misfare
misfire
misform
piffero
pilfery
pin-fire
rim-fire
big fish
diffuse
liefest
pig-fish
pinfish
sitfast

tin fish
Big Four
ziffius
gin fizz
diagram
dingbat
gingham
lingual
ringman
ring taw
ringway
Virgoan
Biggles
dingoes
giggler
giggles
higgler
jingler
jinglet
jingoes
kinglet
lingoes
mingier
mingler
niggler
piggies
pingler
pingoes
ringlet
singles
singlet
tingler
wiggler
wing-led
winglet
ring off
diagrid
king-hit
kingpin
Kirghiz
nilgais
pilgrim
pinguid
pinguin
ringbit
ringgit
cingula
gingall
gingili
Lingala
✧lingula
riggald
singult
virgule
big game
die game
big guns
biogeny
digging
figging
gigging
hinging
jigging
ligging
minging
misgone
pigging
ridging
rigging
ringent
ringing

singing
sirgang
tigging
tinging
wigging
Xingang
zigging
Zingana
Zingano
airglow
hinge on
kingdom
King Log
king mob
king-rod
pidgeon
ring rot
widgeon
figgery
fingers
gingery
Midgard
niggard
piggery
wiggery
Zingara
Zingare
Zingari
Zingaro
biggest
biggish
disgest
disgust
jiggish
piggish
riggish
fidgets
fidgety
Niigata
Piggott
virgate
hip-gout
kingcup
nilgaus
ring out
sing out
vingt-un
wing nut
misgave
misgive
disgown
airhead
bighead
dishrag
fish-day
fish-fag
fish-way
high bar
high day
high-hat
highman
highway
lichway
mishear
Mishnah
Mithras
pinhead
pithead
pith hat
Xiphias
Bishkek

fighter
fish-net
high-fed
high-key
highmen
high-set
high tea
kishkes
lighted
lighten
lighter
lithoed
Michael
mishmee
nighted
righten
righter
sighted
sighter
tighten
fishify
lithify
big hair
cichlid
fishgig
fish-oil
lithoid
Mishnic
nightie
xiphoid
airhole
dishelm
lichtly
lightly
lithely
Nichola
nightly
pightle
pinhole
pithily
rightly
sightly
Sinhala
tightly
wightly
Wilhelm
dishome
diphone
dishing
fishing
high-end
Li Ching
miching
mightn't
nithing
sighing
sithens
Tim Hunt
tithing
wishing
fish-god
highboy
high-low
high-top
light on
pisheog
right-oh
right on
right-on
mishapt
bichord

bighorn
cithara
cithern
dichord
✧die hard
diehard
dishorn
dithery
fishery
kithara
lie hard
pig-herd
Richard
tinhorn
withers
zithern
highest
highish
mightst
Sikhism
lithate
lithite
Wichita
dishful
dish out
fishful
fish out
light up
lithium
mid-hour
pithful
sighful
wishful
without
Ziphius
eightvo
lich-owl
fisheye
bifilar
digicam
digital
finical
liminal
militar
mimical
minibar
minicab
minicam
mini-car
minimal
minimax
minivan
similar
simitar
sinical
tiki bar
vicinal
Viminal
bilimbi
viliaco
cimices
citizen
divider
diviner
filibeg
Filices
limited
limiter
limites
Minitel
miniver

minivet
similes
vibices
visitee
visiter
filings
finings
fixings
linings
tidings
viliago
rikishi
bidie-in
divisim
finikin
militia
minikin
mirific
silicic
Sinitic
vivific
finicky
hijinks
kibitka
civilly
licitly
lividly
ribible
rigidly
risible
risibly
silicle
timidly
visible
visibly
vividly
biriani
ripieni
ripieno
didicoi
didicoy
divisor
kirimon
liaison
libidos
midiron
Nitinol
pig iron
pin it on
silicon
similor
Sir Ivor
Vidicon®
visitor
biliary
ciliary
miliary
mimicry
riviera
rivière
tidiest
tiniest
ciliate
din into
dip into
filiate
miniate
nimiety
rip into
viciate
vitiate

bilious
bivious
fidibus
hit it up
milieus
milieux
minibus
minimum
minimus
mini-sub
nimious
pilinut
pitiful
Ricinus
siliqua
silique
simious
vicious
vidimus
rilievi
rilievo
disject
disjoin
misjoin
jinjili
jimjams
pig-jump
disjune
link man
linkman
milk bar
milk cap
milkman
milk pan
pickmaw
sick bag
sick bay
silk hat
silk-man
miskick
dinky-di
bickies
dinkies
fin keel
milk leg
pickeer
pickled
pickler
pickles
pinkoes
riskier
sickbed
sickled
tickler
tinkler
winkler
kick off
kick-off
pick off
pickoff
tick off
zinkify
linkage
sinkage
ricksha
pink gin
kinkily
milkily
riskily
silkily
✧dickens

dicking
kicking
kirking
licking
milking
picking
pinking
Rifkind
sinking
ticking
winking
zinking
hip-knob
kirkton
linkboy
milk-cow
milksop
misknow
Wicklow
einkorn
hickory
mickery
pickery
Sickert
winkers
air kiss
air-kiss
kick-ass
pinkish
sickish
Miskito
rickets
rickety
kick out
milk run
pick out
riskful
sick-out
tick out
wickiup
pickaxe
pink-eye
billman
disleaf
disleal
disload
fig leaf
Gillian
Hillman®
Jillian
Kiel Bay
Killian
Lillian
Lillias
milldam
Millian
mislead
pig-lead
William
airlock
dialect
hillock
hip-lock
killick
killock
misluck
niblick
pillock
rim lock
sillock
ziplock

billies
dialled
dialler
fielded
fielder
fitlier
gill net
hillmen
killdee
vialled
wielder
willies
yielder
airlift
kill off
biology
pillage
tillage
✧village
diploid
Millais
mislaid
sialoid
sirloin
villain
villein
dislike
liplike
mislike
riblike
siclike
wiglike
gill ale
pig-lily
sillily
diploma
dislimb
dislimn
millime
aiblins
air-lane
airline
✧aisling
billing
biplane
birling
birlinn
cieling
dialing
dilling
diplont
dislink
filling
Finland
Gin Lane
girlond
hidling
hidlins
Hieland
Hielant
hirling
his lane
kidling
killing
Kipling
kitling
✧midland
mid-Lent
milling
pigling
pilling

rifling
rigling
rivlins
sibling
tie line
tilling
titling
Villans
villany
violent
violone
willing
witling
billion
billy-oh
gillion
hilltop
jillion
killcow
killjoy
million
Niel Gow
niellos
pillbox
pillion
witloof
zillion
diglyph
Hillary
pillars
pillory
Sillery
titlark
aidless
aimless
airless
biblist
bitless
dialist
dialyse
finless
girlish
hit list
kinless
lidless
lipless
oil-less
pipless
ribless
rimless
sinless
tieless
tipless
villose
violist
wigless
willest
witless
giblets
tillite
violate
fill out
Gielgud
millrun
pill bug
vialful
villous
willful
mislive
billowy
pillowy

willowy
mill-eye
dialyze
film fan
pigmean
pigmeat
gimmick
mimmick
titmice
Diomede
mismade
film set
filmset
airmail
pigmoid
riempie
sigmoid
mismake
air mile
✧dismals
gig mill
oil mill
ailment
diamine
diamond
dimming
dinmont
figment
fitment
pigment
siamang
siemens
filmdom
miombos
pismire
pit-mirk
air mass
air miss
biomass
dimmest
dimmish
dismask
dismast
dismiss
filmish
kirmess
midmost
✧siamese
titmose
bismuth
mismate
sigmate
mim-mou'd
dismayd
dismayl
mizmaze
siameze
dipnoan
Linnean
his nabs
his nibs
bionics
finnack
finnock
Kinnock
minnick
minnock
pinnace
pinnock
tie-neck

winnock
zip-neck
Dionaea
fiancée
Fiennes
Limnaea
lioncel
pinnoed
pioneer
pionies
tinnier
dignify
lignify
signify
sign off
lignage
signage
lianoid
Tianjin
finnsko
giantly
Pianola®
pinnula
pinnule
tinnily
big name
misname
sirname
visnomy
binning
dinning
finning
ginning
limning
pianino
pinning
pioning
signing
sinning
tinning
winning
midnoon
✧signior
diandry
giantry
ginnery
kiln-dry
signary
✧signora
✧signore
signori
signors
signory
bigness
dimness
disnest
Finnish
fitness
hipness
lignose
lioness
lionise
lionism
pianism
pianist
Sienese
witness
Zionism
Zionist
big-note
dignity

lignite
pinnate
SI units
lion-cub
signeur
sign out
Vilnius
lionize
bifocal
bilobar
bimodal
bipolar
bitonal
bivouac
bizonal
Diconal®
digonal
dipolar
Filofax®
mimosae
mimosas
Nicolas
pivotal
divorce
divorcé
Minorca
sirocco
zimocca
bigoted
bilobed
disobey
lie over
Limoges
litotes
mitogen
mitoses
Nilotes
picotee
pivoted
pivoter
Siporex®
visored
vizored
widower
win over
tip-offs
nihonga
✧timothy
ciboria
cipolin
digoxin
disomic
gironic
kilobit
limosis
minor in
mitosis
mitotic
Nicosia
Nilotic
nimonic
pilotis
Sidonie
sinopia
sinopis
virosis
Vitoria
binocle
girolle
pinocle
bicorne

Livorno
bicolor
eidolon
gigolos
girosol
kiloton
kimonos
Mikonos
dimorph
bigotry
Titoism
Titoist
Minolta®
ricotta
ridotto
riposte
risotto
vicomte
linocut
pirogue
air play
display
disprad
misplay
dispace
nit-pick
six-pack
dimpled
diopter
dispred
hippies
pimpled
rippier
rippler
ripples
ripplet
simpler
simplex
tippler
kippage
limpkin
silphia
✧simpkin
nippily
oil palm
Tiepolo
wispily
Air Pump
air-pump
oil pump
dipping
dispend
dispone
hipping
limping
lipping
lisping
lispund
nipping
pimping
pipping
pit pony
ripping
sipping
timpani
timpano
tipping
zipping
airprox
biophor
pitprop

Words marked ✧ can also be spelled with one or more capital letters

dip-pipe
airport
bit-part
dioptre
dispark
dispart
disport
nippers
diapase
dispose
dispost
hippest
hippish
wimpish
dispute
Tirpitz
wimp out
picquet
diarial
diarian
diurnal
lip-read
misread
Nitrian
Pierian
sierran
disrobe
microbe
oil-rich
pibroch
rimrock
Tim Rice
vitrics
nitride
Citroen®
pierced
piercer
tiaraed
tierced
tiercel
tiercet
midriff
nigrify
nitrify
vitrify
air rage
pierage
pierogi
vitrage
diarchy
air-raid
air-rail
fibroid
fibroin
Giardia
ligroin
milreis
tigroid
vitrail
vitrain
fierily
fig roll
misrule
nitrile
diorama
fibroma
citrine
disrank
firring
microns
migrant
mikrons
sirring
tigrine
vibrant
Vitrina
vitrine
disroot
hip-roof
✧pierrot
vibrios
vitriol
digraph
disrupt
library
Bifrost
cirrose
citrusy
diarise
diarist
digress
diorism
fibrose
Midrash
nitroso
piarist
tigress
tigrish
vin rosé
bit-rate
cirrate
citrate
diorite
disrate
librate
migrate
misrate
nitrate
nitrite
picrate
picrite
titrate
vibrate
vibrato
cirrous
citrous
fibrous
Librium®
nitrous
vitraux
vitreum
diarize
disseat
kinsman
miasmal
miasmas
oil seal
Rigsdag
Riksdag
Riksmål
Rissian
airsick
dissect
pig sick
pig-sick
airside
biassed
diaster
fibster
hipster
linseed
minster
misseem
misstep
oilseed
pigsney
✧pilsner
til seed
tipsier
tipster
kiss off
kiss-off
tipsify
air sign
kitschy
airship
cirsoid
cissoid
diascia
hirstie
jib sail
kidskin
kinship
kipskin
Kirstie
Kirstin
Liassic
miasmic
midship
missaid
missuit
niks-nie
oilskin
pigskin
pigsnie
pissoir
sibship
firstly
fissile
himself
hisself
mis-sell
missile
oil silk
rissole
tipsily
lissome
winsome
biasing
cissing
Diasone®
dissent
ginseng
hissing
linsang
lip-sync
missend
missent
missing
oil sand
rinsing
sinsyne
air shot
airshow
airstop
big shot
dies non
fiascos
fission
ginshop
hip-shot
mission
pie-shop
pit stop
ribston
rim-shot
ripstop
Winston
dissert
fissure
piastre
missish
hirsute
bias-cut
miss out
fissive
missive
Tib's Eve
midsize
air-trap
dip-trap
fist-law
gin trap
lift-man
mint-man
mistral
victual
Vietnam
virtual
biotech
bittock
diptych
distich
mistico
pin tuck
Riot Act
tietack
tintack
viatica
pintado
riptide
Aintree
big tree
bistred
dirt-bed
dirtied
dittoed
✧fifteen
fifties
fig tree
fin-toed
fir tree
kirtled
mintier
mint-new
mista'en
mistier
mist net
mist-net
oil-tree
sixteen
sixties
tiptoed
vintner
vistaed
vittles
distaff
lift off
lift-off
mintage
vintage
dirt-pie
distain
Gift Aid
histoid
histrio
liatris
littlin
pigtail
pintail
Pistoia
victrix
mistake
dirtily
distill
distyle
fictile
fifthly
fistula
mistell
mistily
mistold
niftily
ninthly
pistole
sixthly
wittily
airtime
big time
big-time
mistime
biltong
bitting
dietine
distant
distend
distent
distune
dittany
fitting
histone
hitting
kitteny
listing
misting
mistune
mittens
pitting
rioting
sifting
Sistine
sittine
sitting
tilting
tinting
witting
bistros
cistron
diction
fiction
lift-boy
miction
mistook
mixtion
pint-pot
biotope
biotype
tintype
tittupy
bistort
bittern
bitters
cistern
cittern
dietary
✧diptera
distort
disturb
fixture
gittern
history
jitters
jittery
linters
littery
midterm
misterm
mistery
mixture
picture
sintery
✧victory
wintery
dietist
fittest
Pictish
pietism
pietist
Pittism
riotise
biotite
dictate
Hittite
listeth
nictate
✧pittite
via tuta
vittate
wistiti
bittour
fistful
giltcup
listful
mistful
riotous
sistrum
wistful
fictive
midtown
Miltown®
air taxi
diethyl
riotize
fibular
figural
ligular
pilular
simular
situlae
titular
vitular
bitumed
bitumen
dilutee
diluter
disused
figured
minutes
misuser
piculet
rivulet
sinuses
tituped
liquefy
divulge
liturgy
simurgh
viduage
Virunga
hirudin
minutia
silurid
piously
vihuela
visuals
diluent
minuend
piquant
Tijuana
dilutor
fie upon
hit upon
kikumon
lie upon
sit upon
sit-upon
win upon
sinuose
liquate
pituita
pituite
sinuate
situate
viduity
limulus
liqueur
mimulus
sinuous
viduous
dibutyl
Kiev Dam
Rigveda
civvies
divvied
milvine
✧nirvana
Silvana
sievert
silvern
silver Y
silvery
lievest
divvy up
vis viva
Midwich
✧mid-week
misween
pigweed
midwife
oil well
witwall
miswend
miswent
viewing
firwood
airward
die-work
figwort
misword
pinworm
ribwork
ribwort
tinware
fig wasp
Midwest
pigwash
airwave
midwive
airways
biaxial
dioxide
Pinxter
dioxane
city man
lily pad
mid-year
pixy-led
Digynia
sibylic
Tiny Tim
disyoke
misyoke
bicycle
Sibylla
biryani
minyans
pitying
tidying
jipyapa
mitzvah
diazoes
dizzied
ritzier
sizzler
fizzgig
dizzily
ritzily
Cinzano®
fizzing
FitzRoy
Jinzhou
Liuzhou
dizzard
gizzard
rizzart
bizzazz
pizzazz
djibbah
Ojibwas
Ajaccio
ejector
ijtihad
Mjölnir
à jamais
Djemila
sjambok
ajutage
akrasia
akvavit
skiable
Ukraine
sky-bred
ikebana
skyborn
sky blue
sky-blue
skyclad
Ski Club
Skiddaw
skid pad
skid pan
skidpan
skidded
skidder
skudler
skid lid
skid row
skydive
skeeter
skreigh
skiffle
skegger
sky-high
skyhook
Akihito
skriech
skriegh
skyjack
ski jump
skelder
skelter
skilled
skillet
skulker
ski lift
skaldic
skellie
skollie
skulpin
ukelele
ukulele
skyline
skolion
skylark
skyless
skellum
skilful
skimmed
skimmer
skummer
skim off
skimmia
okimono
skinker
skinned
skinner
skin-pop
skinful
Okinawa
skepped
skipped
skipper
skippet
skepsis
✧skeptic
ski pole
skepful
skirret
skirted
skirter
sky sign
ekistic
skysail
C K Stead
skitter
sketchy
skatole
skittle
skuttle
skating
skiving
ekpwele
skyward
skew-put
sky wave
Okayama
okaying
alcázar
almanac

cloacae
cloacal
flea-bag
flyaway
ilkaday
Alcaics
Fleance
pliancy
alcaide
alcalde
alcayde
El Mahdi
Al-Fayed
algates
Alhazen
aliases
alkanet
allayer
alnager
bleared
bleater
bloated
bloater
cleaner
clearer
cleaved
cleaver
floatel
floater
gleaner
gloater
pleaded
pleader
pleased
pleaser
pleated
pleater
sleaved
Sloaney
alfalfa
Albania
alkalic
alkalis
Alsatia
cloak in
Eleatic
ellagic
fleapit
gliadin
olearia
ulnaria
bleakly
cleanly
clearly
flyable
pliable
pliably
Almaine
Oleanna
Eleanor
cleanse
illapse
Alma-Ata
al pasto
alfaquí
clean up
clean-up
clear up
clear-up
El Aaiún
iliacus
club-law
clubman
flyboat
old bean
plebean
flyback
slob ice
blabbed
blabber
blubbed
blubber
clabber
clobber
clubbed
clubber
flubbed
ill-bred
slabbed
slabber
slobber
slubbed
slubber
plebify
Aly Bain
globoid
elf-bolt
flybelt
globule
Old Bill
Alabama
flybane
flyblow
flybook
old boot
old bird
ale-bush
globose
globate
glebous
globous
clachan
glacial
old chap
placcat
placebo
blacken
blocked
blocker
Blücher
blucher
clacker
cliché'd
clicker
clicket
clocked
clocker
elected
flacker
flacket
flecked
flecker
flicker
glacéed
glacier
placket
plucked
plucker
slacken
slacker
slicken
slicker
slocken
block in
clock in
flaccid
placoid
blackly
slackly
slickly
alicant
glucina
glycine
placing
slicing
clock on
✧elector
olycook
ulichon
Electra
electro
placard
plectra
plectre
alecost
glucose
glycose
elocute
placate
placita
plicate
clock up
floccus
pluck up
slack up
alodial
old dear
alidade
cladode
bladder
bludger
cladder
clodded
fledged
gladded
gladden
glidder
pledgee
pledger
pledget
plodded
plodder
sledded
sledger
slidden
slidder
Aladdin
cludgie
gladdie
all done
gliding
sladang
sliding
gladdon
pledgor
Old Dart
cladism
cladist
alodium
gladful
gladius
glad eye
blue bag
bluecap
blue jay
gleeman
glue ear
illegal
fluence
fluency
Iliescu
Allende
already
alférez
aliened
alienee
✧alleged
alleger
alleyed
all eyes
altered
bleeder
bleeper
cleeked
fleeced
fleecer
fleerer
Kleenex®
sleeken
sleeker
sleeper
sleeved
sleever
ulcered
albergo
alledge
allegge
allergy
sleechy
Algeria
algesia
algesis
allelic
Almeria
aloetic
bluefin
blue tit
cleekit
Elzevir
sleekit
sleep in
sloe gin
blue-sky
alveole
alveoli
elderly
fleetly
Floella
sleekly
al segno
alterne
blueing
fleeing
albedos
alienor
blue box
blue fox
blue-rot
glue-pot
sleep on
algebra
all ears
Allegra
allegro
alveary
sleepry
altesse
blueish
Alberta
al dente
bluette
blue gum
clued-up
gleeful
blue-eye
altezza
fly-flap
old face
bluffer
cliffed
clifted
flaffer
old fogy
bluffly
ill fame
olefine
plafond
aliform
fly-fish
fluff up
elegiac
✧flag day
flagman
plug-hat
blagger
clagged
clogged
clogger
flagged
flogged
flogger
glugged
plaguey
plugged
plugger
slagged
slogged
slogger
slugger
slag off
old gold
elegant
old gang
all-good
clog box
Aligarh
old girl
elegise
elegist
elogist
oligist
ologist
blighty
flighty
elogium
plagium
elegize
allheal
althaea
flehmen
fly high
Alfheim
all-hail
fly half
alchemy
alchymy
Althing
old hand
ale-hoof
elfhood
alchera
Alphard
alphorn
althorn
Elohist
Alphito
Alpheus
Alcidae
almirah
fluidal
Pléiade
Pleiads
Alcides
claimer
eloiner
glaiket
glaived
plaided
plaited
plaiter
sleided
alright
sleight
albinic
albitic
alginic
fluidic
glaikit
glairin
ileitis
illicit
plainly
albinos
Allison
cloison
Algiers
ellipse
gluiest
slàinte
fly-kick
olykoek
flukily
Elektra
flokati
flyleaf
ill luck
old lady
elfland
fly line
old-line
ululant
ululate
alumnae
alameda
alamode
à la mode
clamber
clammed
clamper
climbed
climber
clumber
clumper
flamfew
glimmer
glommed
glummer
plumber
plummet
plumpen
plumper
slammed
slammer
slimmed
slimmer
slumber
slummer
plumage
à la main
Alamgir
alembic
old maid
Olympia
Olympic
plumbic
plumb in
plumpie
slammin'
plumply
plumula
plumule
slimily
aliment
alimony
alumina
clamant
✧clement
element
flaming
Fleming
flummox
old moon
plumcot
alamort
plumery
slumbry
alumish
blemish
✧flemish
glimpse
plumist
plumose
climate
plumate
alumium
alumnus
clamour
✧glamour
Olympus
Olympus®
plumbum
plumous
alannah
Clannad
Cluniac
plantar
Old Nick
Al Unser
blanket
blended
blender
blinded
blinder
blinked
blinker
Blondel
blunder
blunger
blunker
clanger
clinger
clinker
clunker
flanged
flanker
flannel
flannen
flinder
flinger
flunkey
glandes
klinker
planned
planner
planter
plonker
plunder
plunger
plunker
slander
slanger
slanted
slender
slenter
slinger
slinker
slinter
Blanche
elenchi
Blondie
flan tin
glenoid
glonoin
Plantin
Tlingit
alonely
blandly
blankly
blindly
bluntly
planula
slantly
alanine
clangor
Clinton
plenipo
llanero
planury
plenary
allness
alongst
illness
oldness
planish
plenish
plenist
slyness
alength
alunite
planxty
flâneur
blintze
Alcoran
Alkoran
also-ran
gliomas
klootch
all over
all-over
allowed
almoner
blooded
bloomer
blooper
flooded
floored
floorer
fly open
flyover
oleo leg
allonge
Clootie
floosie
floozie
fluoric
gliosis
illogic
plookie
alforja
aloofly
bloosme
alsoone
alcohol
alcopop
pleopod
almonry
Alfonso
al conto
allonym
alcorza
clypeal
klipdas
slipway
clapnet
clapped
clapper
clip-fed
clipped
clipper
flapped
flapper
flipper
plopped
slapped
slapper
slipped
slipper
slopped
slip off
à la page
clippie
clupeid
glyphic
glyptic
ale-pole
alepine
clip-ons
sloping
flip-dog
flip-top
clipart
ill part
flypast
Elspeth
clypeus
flip out
slop out
cliquey
aliquot

Words marked ✧ can also be spelled with one or more capital letters

Floréal
floreat
glareal
glory be
Clarice
cleruch
El Greco
Florida
alarmed
Al Green
✧blarney
blurred
claroes
gloried
slurper
slurred
clarify
glorify
clarain
clarkia
Florrie
floruit
fly rail
glory in
alertly
clerkly
pleroma
plerome
clarini
clarino
flaring
glaring
alerion
clarion
clerisy
florist
old rose
oloroso
clarity
flare up
flare-up
all-star
alms-man
Elysian
fly swat
glossal
close by
Alister
allseed
all-seer
alms-fee
blasted
blaster
blessed
blister
blusher
blushet
bluster
clasher
clasper
classed
cluster
clyster
flasher
flasket
fleshed
flesher
flushed
flusher
fluster
glassen
glasses
glisten
glister
glosser
ill seen
oldster
plashet
plaster
plushes
plussed
plusses
slashed
slasher
sloshed
Ulysses
plusage
classic
classis
clastic
close in
close-in
elastic
elastin
Flossie
fly slip
Glossic
plasmic
plasmid
plasmin
plastic
plastid
pliskie
closely
fleshly
old salt
bless me!
all's one
closing
old song
plusing
blesbok
blossom
close on
elf-shot
elision
elusion
fly-slow
Glasgow
plasmon
plessor
plosion
closure
elusory
Flustra
close to
alyssum
close up
close-up
Elysium
flush up
slush up
elusive
plosive
all that
elytral
flat cap
flatcar
flotsam
flytrap
glottal
gluteal
plateau
pluteal
Blu-Tack®
klatsch
blather
blatted
blatter
blether
bletted
blither
blitter
blitzed
Blitzen
blotted
blotter
clatter
clitter
clothed
clothes
clotted
clotter
clutter
flatbed
flatlet
flatted
flatten
flatter
flitted
flitter
flutter
glitter
glutaei
glutted
platted
platter
plotted
plotter
slather
slatted
slatter
slither
slitter
slotted
slotter
flotage
blotchy
alethic
glottic
glottis
plottie
all told
old talk
old-talk
all-time
old-time
blatant
flotant
flutina
fluting
flyting
platane
platina
plating
Platini
slating
elation
elution
elytron
fletton
glutton
platoon
a latere
cloture
ill turn
olitory
elitism
élitism
elitist
élitist
flutist
blot out
clotbur
elytrum
flat out
gluteus
plotful
pluteus
elative
clausal
pleurae
pleural
flaunch
flounce
flouncy
aliunde
albumen
allurer
clouded
clouted
clouter
fleuret
ileuses
ill-used
plouter
claucht
claught
flaught
slouchy
sloughi
sloughy
albumin
Alcudia
alluvia
Claudia
Claudio
plaudit
ploukie
albugos
aleuron
blaubok
bloubok
blouson
fleuron
fly upon
pleuron
flaunty
Glaucus
eluvial
Flavian
fluvial
pluvial
clavier
flivver
klavier
Olivier
Slavify
Plovdiv
elevens
flavine
flavone
gloving
olivine
Slovene
Slavdom
clivers
clovery
olivary
plovery
slavery
slavish
Slavism
clavate
elevate
eluvium
flavour
Clew Bay
Alnwick
blowsed
blowzed
clowder
plowter
alewife
blow off
blow-off
claw off
old wife
flowage
blowfly
ill-will
blowing
ellwand
flowing
glowing
slowing
elmwood
plywood
all-work
blawort
blewart
blow-dry
flowers
flowery
slowish
Alawite
blewits
blowgun
blow out
blow-out
flexile
flexion
fluxion
flexure
plexure
Alexius
fluxive
ally-taw
claypan
play-day
play-way
play-act
playlet
playpen
play off
play-off
clay-pit
play kip
Alcyone
allying
cloying
flaying
playing
ally-tor
play-box
✧playboy
Play-Doh®
play hob
clayish
Playbus®
playful
play out
al-Azhar
glazier
klezmer
blazing
glazing
glozing
alizari
blaze up
impalas
ambatch
ambages
embased
empaler
empanel
impaler
impanel
ommatea
smearer
embargo
embathe
empathy
imbathe
Amharic
impavid
amiable
amiably
embayld
impaint
empaire
empayre
ambassy
amearst
ampassy
embassy
impasse
embaste
impaste
impasto
BMX bike
amabile
smacker
smicker
smicket
smectic
smickly
emicant
omicron
emicate
smidgen
smudger
smidgin
Amadeus
smeddum
amoebae
amoebas
empeach
emperce
impeach
ambered
ammeter
umbered
immerge
amnesia
amnesic
amoebic
imperia
imperil
emperor
impearl
immense
immerse
amnesty
omneity
Umberto
impetus
amygdal
imagoes
smugger
smuggle
✧imagine
imaging
imagery
✧imagism
imagist
umwhile
amphora
ammiral
e-mailer
imbiber
impinge
empight
à moitié
empiric
omnific
ambient
omniana
ambitty
amniote
impiety
omniety
impious
omnibus
a majori
smoke-ho
smokily
smoking
amakosi
amalgam
amildar
implead
emplace
implode
implied
smelled
smeller
smelter
smolder
ymolten
amplify
amyloid
emulsin
emblema
emplume
ambling
amylene
emplane
implant
smiling
embloom
emulsor
smaltos
implore
amylase
amylose
emulate
implate
implete
emulous
emblaze
imamate
amental
omental
um and ah
amender
Emanuel
emonges
amenage
R months
amentia
emanant
eminent
a minori
amongst
emongst
amanita
amenity
emanate
amentum
omentum
ominous
ammonal
immoral
umbonal
ambones
embowed
embowel
embower
empower
imbower
Imhotep
imposer
imposex
umbones
smoochy
ammonia
embolic
emporia
ampoule
embound
impound
embosom
imbosom
embogue
embolus
embread
Umbrian
America
amtrack
embrace
emerods
emersed
smarten
smirker
impregn
smaragd
umbrage
ambroid
embraid
embroil
smartie
emerald
smartly
amarant
Amerind
amorant
amorini
amorino
imprint
a mark on
embryon
embryos
Emerson
umbrere
Ambrose
amorism
amorist
amorosa
amoroso
empress
emprise
imbrast
impresa
imprese
impress
imprest
umbrose
embrute
emeriti
emirate
Emirati
imbrute
amorous
umbrous
embrave
improve
embrewe
embrown
imbrown
Ameslan
Amistad
ambs-ace
ames-ace
smashed
smasher
I myself
amusing
amosite
smash-up
amusive
emitted
emitter
emptied
emptier
empties
omitted
omitter
smatter
smitten
smother
smutted
umpteen
empty in
S-matrix
smytrie
emptily
smittle
emetine
imitant
amation
emotion
emption
amatory
imitate
amateur
amative
emotive
amputee

imputer
smouser
ampulla
imburse
impulse
emu wren
Omayyad
Umayyad
empyema
amazing
endarch
enhance
in banco
infancy
infarct
unlatch
en garde
innards
inwards
onwards
unhandy
unhardy
anlagen
anlages
Annabel
annates
ansated
Antares
engaged
✧engager
enraged
inhaler
inlayer
invader
kneader
on paper
sneaked
sneaker
unbaked
unbated
uncaged
undated
uneared
uneaten
unfaded
unfamed
unfazed
ungazed
unjaded
unladen
unmated
unnamed
unpaced
unpaged
unpanel
unpaper
unpared
unpaved
unraced
unraked
unrated
unravel
unsated
unsaved
untaken
untamed
untaped
untaxed
unwaged
unwaked
unwares
unwater
unwayed
enlarge
enrange
Inkatha
antacid
entasis
inhabit
insanie
in vadio
invalid
Ontario
unwarie
entayle
envault
in fault
unhable
unmanly
unvaile
infauna
uncanny
unpaint
unsaint
unhappy
ondatra
unmarry
en masse
infaust
inhaust
andante
annatta
annatto
inearth
infanta
infante
in waste
on earth
unearth
unfaith
unhasty
unlaste
in vacuo
sneak-up
antbear
anybody
in a body
enabler
knobbed
knobber
snubbed
snubber
knobble
knobbly
knubble
knubbly
snabble
ink-blot
antbird
Anobium
Unicode
knacker
knicker
knocker
snicker
snicket
unacted
unscrew
V-necked
gnocchi
onychia
inocula
insculp
knuckle
knuckly
unscale
enactor
knock on
knock-on
inscape
✧unicorn
unscary
unicity
knock up
knock-up
sneck up
snick up
unidea'd
unideal
snodded
snoddit
snidely
anodyne
anodise
anodize
in a daze
enteral
indexal
knee-cap
kneecap
knee-pad
knee-pan
Entebbe
inherce
in peace
unperch
unteach
underdo
unheedy
unready
unweldy
anoeses
end even
enterer
entêtée
indexer
indexes
ingener
integer
invexed
kneeled
kneeler
one-eyed
sneerer
sneezer
unbeget
unfeued
unmeted
unsewed
unsexed
unvexed
enfeoff
undeify
ant-eggs
inveigh
undergo
anaemia
anaemic
angelic
Angevin
annelid
anoesis
anoetic
antefix
endemic
enteric
inherit
✧interim
invenit
angerly
en règle
injelly
innerly
undealt
in terms
on terms
antenna
inbeing
✧inferno
interne
unbeing
unmeant
angekok
Angelou
enderon
enfelon
enteron
envelop
envenom
unbegot
unkempt
in tears
Integra®
unheard
unheart
unlearn
unweary
incense
intense
inter se
inverse
unherst
unleash
unsense
Annette
entente
in depth
in-depth
ingesta
in petto
Insecta
unneath
untenty
angelus
Anterus
ingénue
knees-up
unbegun
innerve
inweave
unnerve
unreave
unreeve
unweave
en effet
ink-feed
on offer
sniffer
snifter
snuffer
unified
unifier
unoften
snuff it
onefold
snaffle
sniffle
sniffly
snuffle
snuffly
knifing
✧uniform
ink-fish
anagram
snagged
snigger
snugged
snugger
anagoge
anagogy
sniggle
snuggle
✧endgame
endgate
anthrax
enthral
inthral
uncheck
encheer
enwheel
in chief
enchafe
on the go
anthoid
enchain
inchpin
on the in
unchain
ant-hill
enshell
inshell
unchild
unshale
unshell
Anthony
enchant
unshent
unshun'd
unthink
unshoot
in shape
unshape
unwhipt
on the QT
anchors
encharm
inkhorn
inshore
in short
on shore
on-shore
onshore
uncharm
unchary
unshorn
anchusa
enchase
enthuse
inchase
inkhosi
in phase
inphase
enrheum
inch out
on the up
unshout
anchovy
unshewn
unshown
anginal
antigay
antiwar
indican
infimae
inqilab
intimae
intimal
unvital
Antioch
unhitch
unwitch
unfilde
Antibes
antigen
enfiled
engined
enginer
enliven
enriven
enticer
incised
inciter
indices
inditer
infidel
insider
insides
insinew
invitee
inviter
knaidel
kneidel
on-liner
onliner
unaided
unaimed
unaired
uncited
unfiled
unfired
unfixed
unhired
unlimed
unlined
unmixed
unoiled
unrimed
unrisen
unriven
unrivet
unsinew
unsized
untiled
untired
unwiped
unwived
innings
on wings
unhinge
enlight
in sight
insight
on sight
undight
unright
unsight
incipit
incivil
indicia
inhibit
insipid
oneiric
snail it
uncivil
anticke
unpinkt
Anfield
Enfield
entitle
en ville
infield
unfitly
angioma
ancient
antient
anziani
Indiana
insigne
andiron
angicos
antilog
endiron
environ
incisor
indigos
unvisor
in fieri
in vitro
inkiest
onliest
anxiety
ungirth
unwitty
annicut
Antigua
antique
anxious
envious
infimum
invious
uncinus
snakily
in a kind
unaking
unskan'd
snakish
Anglian
antliae
unclean
unclear
uncloak
englobe
inglobe
anelace
✧anglice
inflect
inflict
in place
unblock
unplace
include
on sleep
unglued
anglify
analogy
en clair
unplait
unslain
unalike
enflame
inflame
unplumb
unplume
angling
aniline
anklong
anklung
endlang
endlong
enplane
incline
inkling
in pleno
unblent
unblind
unsling
unslung
antlion
engloom
in blood
unclipt
analyse
analyst
anglist
enclasp
enclose
endless
enflesh
English
inclasp
inclose
in flesh
inulase
unalist
unbless
unblest
unclasp
unclose
unflesh
unflush
anility
inflate
encloud
uncloud
enclave
enslave
unalive
unglove
unblown
analyze
cnemial
E number
f-number
anomaly
in small
anemone
any more
unsmart
animism
animist
endmost
gnomish
gnomist
animate
animato
enemata
enomoty
unsmote
enamour
onymous
Ananias
unsneck
in-kneed
in-and-in
in antis
inanely
anonyma
on and on
ensnare
ensnarl
insnare
unsnarl
onanism
onanist
oneness
endnote
inanity
unknown
Angolan
Anjouan
in no way
insofar
unmoral
unroyal
unvocal
unwoman
in doubt
enforce
in force
inforce
in touch
in voice
invoice
unvoice
ancones
annoyed
annoyer
CN Tower
encoder
endogen
endowed
endower
enjoyer
incomer
in holes
in power
intoner
invoker
inwoven
oncogen
snooded
snooker
snooper
snoozer
unbowed
uncover
ungored
unhoped
unloved
unmoved
unnoted
unposed
untoned
unwooed
unwoven
unyoked
unzoned
uncomfy
engorge

Words marked ✧ can also be spelled with one or more capital letters

enrough
ungorg'd
unrough
anionic
Antonia
Antonio
encomia
entomic
entopic
entotic
inconie
Indocid®
in folio
in for it
inkosis
unsolid
ennoble
snoozle
ungodly
unmould
unnoble
enround
inbound
inconnu
ingoing
injoint
in point
on-going
ongoing
unbound
undoing
unfound
unjoint
unmount
unround
unsound
unwound
endozoa
entozoa
unbosom
Andorra
inboard
indoors
on board
on-board
onboard
unhoard
endorse
indorse
in-house
in posse
on toast
unhorse
unhouse
unloose
unroost
unsonsy
en poste
en route
insooth
oncosts
uncouth
unsoote
unworth
in focus
involve
antonym
indoxyl
endplay
unspeak
inspect

unspide
knapped
knapper
snapped
snapper
snipped
snipper
snippet
unspied
unspoke
inaptly
ineptly
knapple
unaptly
unspell
unspilt
sniping
unspent
inspire
on appro
anapest
in spate
in spite
snap out
unequal
anyroad
entreat
inbreak
intreat
on trial
untread
engrace
infract
unbrace
unfrock
untrace
intrada
intrude
untride
enarmed
gnarled
gnarred
inbreed
in brief
in order
knarred
knurled
on order
snarled
snarler
snorkel
snorter
unarmed
undried
unfreed
ungreen
unorder
untried
unurged
engraff
engraft
indraft
ingraft
anarchy
android
anergia
anergic
aneroid
energic
energid
engrail

engrain
entrail
en train
entrain
inertia
in fruit
in grain
ingrain
in train
introit
unbroke
angrily
entrall
entrold
inertly
introld
on a roll
snirtle
untruly
enframe
Andrina
enprint
entrant
inbring
in drink
in front
in print
intrant
snaring
snoring
undrunk
unwrung
encrypt
entropy
ancress
encrust
engrasp
engross
en prise
entrism
entrist
entrust
incross
incrust
ingress
in gross
ingross
in trust
intrust
on trust
uncross
undress
untruss
untrust
encraty
ingrate
in truth
uncrate
untruth
unwrite
anurous
ingroup
onerous
snarl up
snarl-up
engrave
on drive
on-drive
indrawn
ingrown
uncrown

ungrown
anorexy
unusual
aniseed
✧gnasher
in a stew
Knesset
one-step
unasked
inn sign
anosmia
anosmic
endship
E Nesbit
✧gnostic
Onassis
Anushka
one self
oneself
and so on
in a spot
inkspot
one-shot
one-stop
in a sort
Oniscus
one's own
and that
gnathal
initial
instead
onstead
snotrag
unstrap
D-Notice
in stock
unstack
unstick
unstock
unstuck
A N Other
another
ensteep
knitted
knitter
knotted
knotter
snotter
unsteel
unstuft
on stage
on-stage
snatchy
gnathic
snottie
unstaid
unstrip
enstyle
install
instill
in style
inutile
knittle
anatomy
anytime
enstamp
on a time
one-time
instant
uniting
anattos

enation
unction
unition
in store
in-store
in utero
unitard
unitary
anatase
unitise
instate
unstate
unitive
in stays
unitize
angular
annular
infulae
inhuman
insulae
insular
ungulae
unhuman
end up by
enounce
injunct
in funds
annulet
endurer
end-user
ennuied
ennuyed
ensurer
incudes
inducer
infuser
inhumer
injurer
inquiet
insured
insurer
snouted
uncured
unfumed
unguled
unqueen
unquiet
unruled
unsured
untuned
unruffe
indulge
✧aneurin
indulin
indusia
insulin
unlucky
Anouilh
in-built
unbuild
unbuilt
anguine
ensuing
unburnt
unfunny
unguent
unsunny
engulph
ingulph
enguard
enquire

enquiry
inquere
inquire
inquiry
on guard
unguard
anguish
inburst
inquest
insulse
uncurse
unfussy
unpurse
annuity
en suite
unquote
annulus
en queue
incubus
incurve
una voce
andvile
knevell
en avant
knavery
knavish
snowcap
snowman
unswear
snow-ice
anywhen
ensweep
snow-fed
snow pea
unowned
unsweet
in twain
unswai'd
indwell
indwelt
inkwell
know-all
snowily
entwine
gnawing
inswing
intwine
knowing
untwine
know-how
knowhow
snow box
Snowdon
snow job
unswept
Antwerp
in a word
unaware
unsworn
anywise
endwise
entwist
intwist
snowish
untwist
snow gun
anyways
endways
anaxial
inexact
Indy car

in synch
ungyved
enzymic
envying
inlying
undying
untying
only too
innyard
snuzzle
endzone
gonadal
Mozarab
oolakan
sola hat
tokamak
copaiba
Lobamba
joyance
monarch
nomarch
noyance
polacca
✧romance
sonance
sonancy
tobacco
to match
toparch
monarda
no can do
notanda
Ronaldo
towards
Yolanda
dowager
forager
foramen
forayer
gowaned
homager
kokanee
nodated
nonaged
not a few
po-faced
potager
Romanes
Rosabel
rosacea
rosaker
royalet
socager
sofa bed
togated
voyager
zonated
botargo
gouache
Bobadil
bonamia
boracic
botanic
cohabit
conaria
domatia
folacin
Goiânia
gonadic
Horatio
kohanim

komatik
Koranic
logania
monacid
monadic
Moravia
nomadic
not a bit
novalia
Novalis
podalic
Polaris
potamic
Romania
Romanic
rosalia
Rosalie
✧rosaria
Rosario
solatia
Somalia
somatic
sosatie
Sotadic
vocalic
volatic
woman it
romaika
coracle
coralla
dowable
focally
locally
losable
lovable
loyally
modally
morally
movable
movably
nodally
no-fault
notable
notably
potable
ropable
rowable
royally
tonally
totally
towable
vocable
vocally
volable
womanly
wooable
Cocagne
cocaine
hoc anno
hosanna
Johanna
moraine
no' canny
posaune
romaine
romaunt
Rosanna
Roxanne
sodaine
borazon
donator

dorados
dos-à-dos
hob-a-nob
kokakos
locator
Mogadon®
monaxon
nonagon
polaron
robalos
rotator
soda pop
solanos
Bonaire
conacre
Conakry
podagra
polacre
sowarry
Molasse
morassy
Mosaism
potassa
Romansh
soda ash
Zolaism
coranto
dopatta
go Fanti
Hogarth
Jocasta
loyalty
royalty
volante
bonasus
conatus
notaeum
pomatum
popadum
Romanus
solanum
totanus
Volapük
copaiva
✧royal we
sokaiya
bonanza
bogbean
box beam
corbeau
forbear
Goa bean
Hobbian
rowboat
Sorbian
soy bean
tow boat
hogback
roebuck
sowback
forbade
forbode
bobbles
bomblet
cobbler
doobrey
doubler
doubles
doublet
double-u
doubted

doubter
gobbler
gombeen
hobbler
lobbyer
low-bred
nobbler
nombles
wobbler
yobboes
zombify
con brio
corbeil
doobrie
Holbein
howbeit
nombril
cowbell
dog-belt
dogbolt
fog-bell
loobily
low-bell
nobbily
tombola
tombolo
bobbing
bombing
bowbent
boy band
combine
cowbane
dobbing
dogbane
fog bank
gobbing
hopbind
hopbine
jobbing
lobbing
mobbing
pot bank
robbing
sobbing
sorbent
Zorbing
boobook
Joe Blow
logbook
lowbrow
top boot
bobbery
bombard
bombora
Colbert
cowbird
forbore
Hofburg
Homburg
jobbery
Lombard
low-born
mowburn
poe-bird
poy-bird
robbery
Roobarb
wosbird
yobbery
bobbish
bombast

combust
hobbish
Hobbism
Hobbist
mobbish
Mombasa
Sorbish
soubise
yobbish
yobbism
bobbitt
Cobbett
combats
Corbett
Moabite
sorbate
sorbite
bomb out
comb out
comb-out
go about
Joe Baxi
box-coat
conceal
conchae
conchal
dog-crab
Joycean
morceau
ponceau
Roscian
topcoat
concoct
gorcock
concede
concedo
botcher
bouchée
Boucher
coachee
coacher
conches
concrew
couchee
couchée
moocher
moucher
notched
notchel
notcher
poacher
potcher
pouched
roached
torcher
touched
toucher
vouchee
voucher
wotcher
boscage
soccage
coccoid
conceit
conchie
log-chip
Noachic
rotchie
toeclip
hoe-cake
box-calf

cow-calf
doucely
to scale
zoccolo
coxcomb
how come?
non-come
concent
doucine
porcine
porcini
voicing
volcano
bok choy
gorcrow
honchos
ponchos
torchon
touch on
concept
concupy
forceps
concern
concert
✧concord
dogcart
popcorn
sorcery
concise
concuss
corcass
cot case
low-cost
✧boycott
doucets
toccata
botch up
douceur
Jobclub
job club
notch up
Roscius
touch up
touch-up
concave
bondman
cold war
cordial
good-day
✧goodman
Gordian
hoodman
mondial
roadman
road map
road tax
roadway
rondeau
Rood Day
woodman
woodrat
wood tar
woodwax
cordoba
✧córdoba
conduce
conduct
hordock
top deck
howdy-do
soldado

boodied
coddler
doodler
fondler
food web
good-den
good-e'en
goodies
hog-deer
moodier
roadbed
roe deer
soldier
toadied
toddler
wondred
hold off
bondage
condign
cordage
good egg
pondage
sondage
wordage
boudoir
cold pig
conduit
foudrie
good oil
hordein
Lord Jim
lordkin
mondain
Mordvin
non-drip
wood oil
woodsia
wood tin
condole
condyle
dowdily
gondola
holdall
Mondale
moodily
rowdily
sondeli
wordily
condemn
goddamn
bonding
codding
condone
cording
cow-dung
folding
fondant
fordone
gold ink
holding
loading
Londony
lording
mordant
mordent
nodding
podding
road end
roading
rodding
rondino

sordini
sordino
tondini
tondino
voiding
wood ant
wording
bold bow
good-now
good-son
Lord Coe
road hog
tordion
wood lot
hold-ups
borders
bordure
doddard
doddery
goldarn
moidore
powdery
rondure
coldish
foodism
goddess
goldish
goodish
loudish
wood ash
wordish
cordate
cordite
hot date
foldout
foodful
gold-bug
goldcup
Gordius
hold out
holdout
hoodlum
Hordeum
woodcut
Moldova
bog down
hoedown
low-down
mow down
top-down
wood owl
dog days
goldeye
goodbye
Mondays
Docetae
Donegal
forecar
fore-day
forelay
foreman
forepaw
foreran
foresaw
foresay
gomeral
hoseman
lose way
love-day
love rat
Mohegan

mole rat
nosebag
nosegay
nose rag
note-pad
polecat
rodeway
rokelay
ropeway
rosebay
sokeman
someday
someway
tonepad
tote bag
cogence
cogency
Ionesco
Moresco
potence
potencé
potency
Hodeida
morendo
bone-bed
boneset
cogener
coherer
covelet
covered
coveted
cozener
doe-eyed
dovelet
foreleg
foremen
foresee
for ever
forever
Gore-Tex®
honeyed
hose-net
hoveled
however
lobelet
✧lorelei
lovered
modeled
modeler
moneyed
moneyer
nose-led
notelet
pop-eyed
powered
rose-red
some few
toweled
towered
come off
come-off
cone off
doze off
zone off
foreign
lozenge
lozengy
somewhy
bone-oil
cole tit
comedic

cometic
coterie
cover in
Docetic
dovekie
forelie
fox-evil
Gobelin
godetia
go-devil
gomeril
Goneril
Homeric
Homerid
Jocelin
lobelia
polemic
poperin
roper-in
rosehip
rose oil
soredia
tonemic
tonetic
totemic
toxemia
toxemic
zooecia
corella
foveola
foveole
loverly
modelli
modello
morello
Moselle
notedly
novella
novelle
rosella
roselle
roseola
rozelle
soberly
vowelly
toc emma
codeine
doyenne
fore-end
moderne
Mole End
someone
boleros
boredom
Comecon
comedos
come for
come low
copepod
dovecot
foretop
holesom
homeboy
koreros
moneron
none too
nose job
note row
pomelos
pomeroy
popedom

Robeson
somehow
sorehon
toheroa
Toledos
tone row
toreros
vote for
bone-dry
forearm
tone arm
bone ash
Couéism
Couéist
Donetsk
doveish
moreish
nor'-east
poseuse
codetta
Colette
dogeate
dozenth
fouetté
foveate
honesty
Josette
lomenta
Loretta
lorette
modesty
mofette
momenta
mozetta
nonette
nonetti
nonetto
novelty
podestà
polenta
poverty
Roberta
roseate
Rosetta
rosette
rosetty
to death
tomenta
bodeful
✧boletus
coked-up
come out
coteaux
cover up
cover-up
doleful
dole out
foregut
forerun
hole out
home run
✧hopeful
lose out
loved up
mole out
more suo
move out
nose out
pokeful
poke fun
power up

rosebud
rose bug
rose-cut
sober up
vote out
poleaxe
homelyn
Jocelyn
Lorenzo
for fear
golf bag
Wolfian
wolfram
confect
confide
coffret
coiffed
comfrey
for free
Godfrey
hop-flea
pomfret
pouffed
sol-faed
Toffees
Torfaen
woofter
goof off
solfège
forfair
forfeit
loaf tin
wolfkin
box file
boxfuls
cot-folk
goofily
Norfolk
potfuls
souffle
soufflé
topfull
confine
forfend
golfing
loafing
✧rolfing
roofing
wolfing
Corfiot
hoofrot
hotfoot
mouflon
rooftop
tomfool
wolf dog
wolf-dog
bonfire
comfort
confirm
conform
foxfire
zoeform
box-fish
codfish
confess
confest
confuse
cowfish
dogfish
hogfish

toffish
wolfish
confute
conflux
hot flue
loofful
✧wolf cub
congeal
couguar
Dong Hai
Douglas
Gorgias
loggias
low gear
low-gear
Morglay
songman
Songnam
top gear
Vosgean
Vosgian
torgoch
fougade
boggler
boogied
congree
cougher
doggrel
goggled
goggler
goggles
joggled
long leg
long ten
mongrel
pongoes
poogyee
roughen
rougher
soignée
tongued
toughen
wongied
long off
foggage
long-ago
dot gain
long-oil
long pig
long sin
roughie
rough in
rough it
toughie
coagula
foggily
roughly
soggily
toughly
con game
Dodgems®
zoogamy
co-agent
cogging
dodging
dogging
doggone
forging
forgone
Gorgons
hogging

jogging
kongoni
lodging
logging
longing
nogging
sogging
togging
zoogeny
zoogony
for good
gorgios
longbow
long hop
✧long Tom
long ton
lorgnon
sorghos
boggard
boggart
boy-girl
cowgirl
dodgery
doggery
forgery
gougère
hoggery
joggers
long arm
mongery
Rodgers
toggery
congest
doggess
doggish
hoggish
longest
longish
doughty
foughty
loggats
zorgite
bon goût
congius
congrue
cough up
rough up
songful
sorghum
forgave
forgive
bodhran
bodhrán
bowhead
dog-head
go ahead
go-ahead
✧godhead
hophead
hothead
lochial
log-head
Loghtan
Lothian
mophead
moth-eat
Pooh-Bah
pot-head
pothead
tow-head
Gothick

ootheca
toshach
Toshack
cowhide
boshter
cochlea
cowheel
moshvei
mothier
potheen
cowhage
co-chair
Lothair
mosh pit
pochoir
to a hair
bothole
doghole
foxhole
mochell
not half
pothole
toehold
top-hole
bow-hand
cowhand
forhent
fox hunt
moshing
nothing
boyhood
cosh boy
godhood
hoghood
pothook
Bob Hope
coehorn
coshery
cothurn
cowherb
cowherd
foghorn
go short
mothery
non-hero
noshery
nowhere
pochard
pot herb
pothery
so there
yoghurt
dobhash
sophism
sophist
göthite
go white
oophyte
box-haul
Jodhpur
dorhawk
goshawk
Loghtyn
✧bolivar
Bovidae
comical
comital
conical
corival
cotidal
domical

holiday
logical
loricae
✧mohican
nodical
nominal
Novi Sad
rooikat
somital
topical
toxical
zooidal
cowitch
goyisch
✧morisco
oomiack
to-pinch
codices
conifer
dominee
Dorigen
folioed
fomites
ioniser
ionizer
lobiped
lorimer
loriner
Mogilev
molimen
molinet
moniker
no-fines
nominee
porifer
posited
rosined
rotifer
soliped
sorites
vomited
borings
cotinga
Domingo
foliage
Moringa
mowings
moriche
potiche
tonight
bodikin
Bolivia
codicil
cohibit
colitis
comitia
conidia
domicil
Dominic
dominie
gobioid
gonidia
gonidic
hominid
monilia
motivic
notitia
oolitic
politic
positif
robinia

solicit
somitic
soritic
colicky
kopiyka
bouilli
codilla
codille
docible
foliole
gorilla
Modiola
modioli
mouillé
Moviola®
rouille
solidly
zorilla
zorille
zorillo
woe is me
coniine
Corinna
Corinne
motions
notions
totient
bog iron
bonitos
box-iron
co-pilot
copilot
dominos
dosi-dos
Honiton
horizon
kopiyok
monitor
non-iron
norimon
positon
soliton
tow-iron
zorinos
colibri
goliard
Honiara
Honiari
hosiery
Molière
poniard
rosiere
topiary
foliose
go first
gooiest
goriest
ropiest
rosiest
Corinth
Corinto
foliate
Goliath
modiste
sociate
society
comique
copious
corious
holibut
modicum

noxious
solidum
solidus
vomitus
Zosimus
dopiaza
Don Juan
conject
Don John
conjoin
Pohjola
toe jump
goujons
conjure
conjury
non-jury
bonjour
Bon Jovi
bookman
cork mat
cork oak
folkway
Hock-day
Lockean
Lockian
lockjaw
lockman
lockram
mooktar
rocklay
rock tar
workbag
workday
workman
yolk sac
cockade
mockado
booklet
cockled
✧cockney
Hockney
✧jockney
look-see
mockney
polkaed
porkies
rockier
Rockies
Tolkien
cook off
work off
boskage
corkage
dockage
lockage
mockage
soakage
cockshy
workshy
booksie
cockpit
hook-pin
hook-tip
pockpit
pork pie
rock oil
rokkaku
cockily
kookily
Rockall
rock elm

rockily
wonkily
bonking
bookend
booking
corking
docking
Don King
Dorking
god-king
honking
mocking
rocking
soaking
socking
Tom King
working
bowknot
cooktop
kolkhoz
look you
rock cod
topknot
workbox
worktop
you know
bonkers
conkers
cookery
folk art
jookery
joukery
mockery
monkery
pockard
rock art
rockery
rookery
Yonkers
bookish
dockise
dorkish
jockish
Lockist
lookism
monkish
rookish
Yorkish
Yorkist
box kite
bookful
book out
conk out
cookout
forkful
fork out
lockful
locknut
lock out
lockout
look out
lookout
mock sun
soukous
workful
work out
workout
cockeye
donkeys
monkeys
sockeye

dockize
Boolean
coal gas
coalman
coal tar
cobloaf
coeliac
cool bag
pollman
poll tax
poll-tax
rollbar
rouleau
souldan
toll bar
tollman
tollway
toolbag
toolbar
toolman
woolfat
woolman
Zoilean
could be
would-be
collect
cowlick
dorlach
hoc loco
hoolock
✧pollack
pollicy
✧pollock
porlock
potlach
pot luck
rollick
rollock
rowlock
collide
collude
roulade
✧boulder
boulter
bowlder
coal-bed
✧colleen
collier
coulter
dollied
dollier
dowlney
Follies
foulder
godlier
goolies
holloes
jollyer
moulder
moulten
poulder
poulter
woolded
woolder
woolled
woollen
woolsey
worlded
boil off
cool off
doll off

for life
jollify
low life
low-life
mollify
roll-off
collage
college
moulage
noology
soilage
tollage
zoology
holla-ho!
coal oil
coalpit
coal tit
colloid
couloir
douleia
toolkit
wool oil
godlike
rodlike
toylike
godlily
jollily
lowlily
worldly
coelome
coulomb
fog lamp
to blame
bogland
boiling
bowline
bowling
Coblenz
codling
colling
✧collins
coolant
cotland
couldn't
cowling
foiling
fooling
fopling
forlana
forlend
forlent
fowling
go blank
godling
golland
gosling
Gotland
gowland
hog-line
holland
hot line
hotline
howling
jolling
Koblenz
logline
lowland
morling
norland
oodlins
pollent

polling
rolling
Rowland
soiling
toiling
tolling
tooling
topline
towline
Toyland
yowling
coal-box
coal pot
cool box
dolldom
Kowloon
moellon
rollmop
roll-top
toe loop
toolbox
toylsom
boilery
bollard
collard
foolery
forlorn
foulard
Lollard
pollard
poulard
pouldre
poultry
soilure
coalise
coolish
coxless
dollish
fogless
foolish
godless
goulash
jobless
joyless
mollusc
mollusk
rodless
sonless
topless
toyless
wouldst
Zoilism
Zoilist
Coalite®
collate
hoplite
jollity
pollute
zoolite
zoolith
bowlful
bowl out
doll out
jolly up
rollout
soulful
toilful
poll-axe
pollaxe
volleys
coalize

goombah
holm-oak
Wormian
dormice
Formica®
hommock
too much
commode
commodo
boomlet
roomier
foamily
formula
hot melt
pommelé
roomily
booming
Bormann
coaming
command
commend
comment
✧commons
commune
dooming
dormant
foaming
formant
forming
gormand
hog-mane
hormone
Normans
noumena
roaming
Rommany
rouming
souming
tomming
torment
tormina
towmond
towmont
boombox
hoummos
mormaor
Mormops
Coimbra
commère
foumart
fox-mark
Kommers
woomera
wormery
bog moss
cosmism
cosmist
koumiss
Low Mass
topmast
topmost
commote
commute
con moto
formate
cormous
doomful
holmium
roomful
worm out
zoom out

commove
Bosnian
cooncan
corneal
corn law
cornual
corn van
gownman
horn-mad
John Gay
Johnian
John Ray
moineau
moon rat
noonday
point at
poundal
somnial
tonneau
town gas
connect
cornice
dornick
Bob Nudd
downa-do
poinado
tornade
✧tornado
boonies
bouncer
bounded
bounden
bounder
corn-fed
counsel
counted
counter
données
down-bed
founder
go under
hornlet
joannes
John Dee
joinder
jointed
jointer
lounder
lounger
loungey
Moonies
moonlet
moonset
mounted
mounter
poinder
pointed
pointel
pointer
pointes
pounced
pouncet
pounder
rounded
roundel
rounder
sounder
wounder
younger
younker
coinage

cornage
tonnage
coontie
corn bin
corn oil
corn pit
corn rig
council
count in
hobnail
Johnnie
moonlit
Mountie
poon-oil
toenail
Roanoke
bonnily
cornfly
cornily
jointly
roundle
roundly
soundly
tonnell
youngly
zoonomy
coining
conning
donning
fornent
horning
joining
loaning
looning
morning
nooning
poynant
ronning
sorning
town end
wonning
coin box
coondog
corncob
corn dog
cornrow
count on
downbow
going on
gownboy
John Doe
John Hop
Johnson
moonbow
moon god
round on
Bonnard
Connors
country
donnard
donnart
donnerd
donnert
foundry
joinery
cognise
Cornish
cornist
coyness
donnish
donnism

Goanese
hognose
hornish
hornist
hotness
lowness
moonish
nowness
roinish
roynish
so-and-so
soonest
Souness
tonnish
townish
bornite
bound to
cognate
connate
connote
cornett
cornute
cornuto
Hornets
hornito
Sonnite
youngth
zoonite
bound up
hornbug
hornful
horn-nut
moanful
mount up
point up
round up
round-up
worn-out
wound up
connive
horn owl
John Pym
mooneye
romneya
cognize
cocopan
cocoyam
Comoran
coronae
coronal
coronas
Donovan
go to war
locoman
Molokai
Potomac
soroban
sororal
so to say
Colombo
no doubt
for once
morocco
boloney
bosomed
cojones
colonel
colones
coroner
coronet
coyotes

Dolores
fog over
go to bed
go to sea
ionomer
monomer
no-hoper
popover
poroses
Rolodex®
row over
soboles
vocoder
borough
Dorothy
soroche
Boeotia
bolo tie
boronia
colobid
colonic
coronis
dog on it
do to wit
go for it
monodic
monofil
monosis
moronic
oogonia
Polonia
polonie
porosis
robotic
rosolio
sorosis
monoski
corolla
monocle
Bologna
✧cologne
go round
pogoing
to point
to-torne
to-worne
bonobos
Comoros
corozos
Cotonou
go to pot
hobodom
homolog
Molotov
monocot
Monodon
monolog
monopod
potoroo
Robocop
rococos
rotolos
Solomon
colours
coloury
honours
sojourn
colossi
hoboism
hop-oast
molossi

poloist
soloist
cocotte
Toronto
coconut
colobus
homonym
toponym
compear
Gosplan
compact
coppice
hospice
torpedo
torpids
compeer
complex
compter
coupler
couplet
hopples
kouprey
morphew
pompier
poppied
toupeed
torpefy
compage
Solpuga
✧complin
✧dolphin
low-paid
morphia
morphic
Pompeii
cowpoke
toe poke
compile
Coppola
Gospels
hop-pole
pompelo
soapily
soppily
compand
company
compend
comping
componé
compony
dopping
forpine
gowpens
hopping
looping
lopping
mopping
pompano
popping
sooping
sopping
topping
volpino
Volpone
wopping
complot
morphos
pompion
pompoon
soapbox
soupçon

tompion
cob pipe
compare
compart
compère
comport
coopery
coppery
corpora
coupure
foppery
go spare
Gosport
oospore
poppers
rompers
row port
to spare
zoopery
compass
compast
compose
compost
foppish
hoop-ash
lompish
poppish
porpess
rompish
compete
compote
compute
Morpeth
towpath
hog-plum
nonplus
pompous
poop out
roup out
soup run
coequal
rorqual
Torquay
bosquet
bouquet
conquer
docquet
rocquet
torqued
jonquil
Torquil
Boer War
Boorman
Bourgas
bourlaw
courlan
doorman
doormat
doorway
for real
four-oar
journal
Locrian
moorman
moor-pan
poor law
poor-law
sour gas
to-break
Tournai
correct

morrice
nourice
porrect
sourock
touraco
comrade
corrade
corrida
corrode
corrody
joyride
boarder
bourder
bourrée
coarsen
Courbet
courier
courser
courses
fourses
gourmet
hoarder
hoarsen
journey
log-reel
Lou Reed
moorhen
mourner
poursew
sorrier
to order
tourney
worried
worrier
horrify
torrefy
courage
moorage
porrigo
bourkha
Goorkha
Boursin
do or die
do-or-die
to-brake
borrell
courtly
four-ale
hoarily
logroll
loo roll
lorrell
moorill
noursle
sorrily
woorali
wourali
gourami
no-trump
courant
dourine
do wrong
for rent
Goering
go wrong
horrent
louring
low-rent
mooring
pouring
roaring

Words marked ✧ can also be spelled with one or more capital letters

soaring
soprani
soprano
souring
toe ring
torrent
touring
✧bourbon
bourdon
boxroom
fourgon
go crook
godroon
journos
moorlog
morrion
poor box
poor-oot
soursop
you're on!
corrupt
tow rope
fou rire
Moorery
woorara
boarish
boorish
dog rose
low-rise
Mooress
✧moorish
noir-ish
noirish
nourish
poorish
sourish
to-brusd
tourism
tourist
votress
co-write
board up
bohrium
morrhua
pour out
pour-out
poursue
zoarium
do brown
go crazy
borstal
box seat
coastal
cob-swan
dog's-ear
Dog Star
✧foss way
hot seat
Housman
Joe Soap
mobsman
moss hag
pop star
Potsdam
rodsman
Sod's law
topsman
Corsica
Cossack
dog-sick
fossick

hop-sack
hopsack
nonsuch
popsock
pot-sick
toisech
bow-side
go aside
✧gorsedd
topside
torsade
boasted
boaster
bobsled
bolster
booster
✧coaster
conster
corslet
corsned
cowshed
dogsled
dossier
foister
hoister
holster
jouster
lobster
lokshen
mobster
moisten
monster
mossier
mousier
mousmee
roaster
rodster
roister
rooster
Ross Sea
rouster
royster
toasted
toaster
tousled
Vorster
worsted
consign
corsage
dog's age
borscht
Porsche®
bolshie
bonsoir
conseil
corsair
cowslip
doeskin
dogship
dogskin
donship
foxship
godship
god's lid
hog-skin
horse it
loessic
non-skid
non-slip
nonsuit
✧poussin

sonship
souslik
sow-skin
toastie
topsail
topsoil
topspin
toustie
✧worship
forsake
mousaka
bossily
console
consols
consult
fossula
loosely
lousily
moistly
mousily
noisily
nousell
tossily
woosell
consume
noisome
noysome
toysome
woesome
bousing
consent
godsend
horsing
housing
lousing
mousing
pop song
Rossini
rousant
rousing
sossing
sousing
tossing
tousing
bowshot
copshop
for show
forsloe
forslow
forsook
God slot
gorsoon
gossoon
hoosgow
hot shoe
hotshot
hot spot
Houston
Jon Snow
monsoon
non-stop
poisson
pop-shop
potshop
pot shot
Tolstoy
torsion
tosspot
toyshop
God's ape
gossipy

consort
for sure
goosery
morsure
mousery
Ronsard
tonsure
bossism
consist
possess
dowsets
zoisite
conspue
Hotspur
louse up
toss out
corsive
God save
torsive
boatman
Comtian
contrat
costean
don't say
footbar
foot-jaw
footman
footpad
footway
for that
Fortran
fox-trap
Godthab
koftgar
lost wax
mootman
Noetian
not that
Pontiac®
Pontian
portman
portray
postbag
post day
postman
post-tax
post-war
root cap
rostral
voetsak
low toby
bortsch
contact
conteck
dog-tick
low tech
low-tech
mortice
poetics
portico
Rostock
boutade
low tide
tostada
bootleg
bottled
bottle-o
bottler
bow-tied
box-tree
costrel

cottier
cowtree
dottled
dottrel
fontlet
footmen
✧forties
fortlet
goateed
goitred
hop-tree
hostler
loathed
loather
moither
mottled
mottoed
mottoes
mouther
norther
now then!
poitrel
Portree
posteen
pouther
pout net
✧röntgen
rootier
rootlet
sonties
soother
souther
Southey
toothed
fortify
mortify
pontiff
pontify
post off
bottega
cortège
cottage
footage
hostage
montage
pontage
portage
postage
pottage
rootage
voltage
bobtail
contain
cottoid
couthie
doitkin
Footsie
fox-tail
goat-fig
hoatzin
mouth it
noctuid
nostril
postfix
routhie
✧tootsie
tortrix
voltaic
worth it
boat-fly
coctile

cortile
cortili
goutfly
hostile
loathly
loftily
monthly
noctule
pontile
soothly
sootily
tortile
youthly
bottoms
contemn
costume
zootomy
Boateng
boating
bolting
bottine
bottony
box tent
coating
contend
content
contund
cottony
doating
dotting
Fontina
footing
Fortuna
✧fortune
hosting
hotting
houting
jotting
Løgting
looting
lotting
Montana
montane
montant
mooting
norteña
norteño
pontine
portend
portent
posting
potting
pouting
rooting
rorting
rotting
routine
routing
sorting
sotting
soutane
tontine
tortoni
totting
wotting
boot boy
coction
coition
control
dogtrot
footboy

foot rot
foot-ton
fox-trot
✧foxtrot
goat-god
hot trod
hot-trod
jogtrot
pontoon
✧porthos
portion
postbox
post boy
postdoc
post hoc
soft roe
soft rot
soft top
soft-top
soft you
Tom-trot
zootype
contort
✧costard
couture
doctors
hooters
lottery
montero
monture
nocturn
non-term
postern
posture
pottery
soft art
to a turn
torture
tottery
voiture
Zostera
coltish
Comtism
Comtist
contest
contuse
cottise
doltish
goatish
hostess
hottest
hottish
loutish
mortise
MOT test
ooftish
poetess
poetise
portess
softish
sottish
wottest
costate
portate
wotteth
bootcut
boot out
contour
dortour
nostrum
portous

postbus
root out
rostrum
routous
rout out
sort out
costive
Poltava
tortive
cottown
dogtown
context
zootaxy
bostryx
Fonteyn
poetize
copulae
copular
copulas
gopuram
jocular
lobular
locular
modular
morulae
morular
morulas
nodular
popular
rotulae
rotulas
torulae
vocular
zonular
Columba
go Dutch
rotunda
Volundr
boluses
columel
focused
focuses
hocused
ioduret
lobules
locules
moguled
noduled
non-user
volumed
voluted
zonulet
tohunga
botulin
torulin
volubil
volutin
nonuple
soluble
voluble
volubly
wofully
coquina
Corunna
roguing
toluene
voguing
colugos
do out of
gomutos
✧völuspa

goburra
roguery
roguish
voguish
coquito
✧locusta
robusta
toluate
woe unto
lobulus
loculus
modulus
nocuous
Romulus
torulus
nouveau
Vouvray
convect
convict
couvade
voivode
bouvier
louvred
for vain
Louvain
convoke
✧lowveld
Torvill
convene
convent
corvine
dogvane
hop-vine
solvent
wolving
bosvark
convert
couvert
✧j'ouvert
not very
poovery
wolvish
solvate
volvate
convive
no sweat
Norwich
woiwode
cow-weed
hogweed
pop-weed
you wait!
Boswell
cob wall
hot wall
hot well
forwent
morwong
boxwood
dogwood
logwood
boo-word
forward
forwarn
forworn
godward
hogward
hot-wire
lobworm
nor'ward
norward

woe-worn
hogwash
nor'-west
sou'-west
bow wave
coaxial
coexist
body bag
bogyman
copycat
cotylae
holydam
holy day
holy war
polygam
polyact
cotyles
gory dew
Holy See
loxygen
polymer
polypes
Rosy Lee
Corypha
coryphe
polynia
holy-ale
ko cycle
polyoma
bodying
bowyang
copying
foo yong
foo yung
Holy One
polyene
Corydon
fogydom
holy Joe
polygon
polypod
Polyzoa
hop-yard
bogyism
copyism
copyist
fogyish
fogyism
Toryish
Toryism
corylus
polypus
✧toby-jug
polynya
Wozzeck
foozler
sozzled
boozily
Gonzalo
woozily
boozing
Boyzone
momzers
non-zero
forzato
booze-up
aplanat
apparat
apsaras
splatch
upcatch
upwards
apparel
opiated
P-plater
speaker
speared
sprayed
sprayer
sprayey
upmaker
splashy
aphagia
aphasia
aphasic
aplasia
apraxia
apraxic
sprawly
spraint
spray-on
sphaere
upraise
appalti
appalto
speak up
upvalue
spa bath
✧apician
epochal
spacial
special
epicede
épicier
species
specter
specify
epacrid
epacris
speckle
specula
spicily
spicula
spicule
upscale
epicene
spacing
apocope
epicarp
epicure
spectra
spectre
spicery
epicism
epicist
C P Scott
opacity
spicate
opacous
spice up
spadger
spadoes
apadana
Spiders
spidery
epidote
apodous
spodium
apteral
spaeman
spheral
appeach
spredde
ephebes
speeded
speeder
speeler
sphered
spieler
spreagh
aphelia
aphesis
aphetic
apperil
apteria
ephebic
ephelis
Ophelia
sphenic
spheric
splenic
spleeny
ephebos
speedos
up-tempo
ephedra
spheare
appease
épéeist
aplenty
ephebus
Ephesus
speed up
speed-up
upheave
apteryx
spreaze
spreeze
spy film
spiff up
apogeal
apogean
epigeal
epigean
epigram
spignel
apagoge
epagoge
apogamy
epigene
✧epigone
✧epigoni
✧epigons
epigyny
spag bol
upchuck
upcheer
spyhole
apehood
upshoot
upthrow
upwhirl
apsidal
oppidan
optical
optimal
uprisal
aphides
apsides
épuisée
splicer
spoiled
spoiler
uppiled
uprisen
upriver
upsides
spairge
spriggy
springe
springy
spright
upright
uptight
yplight
epeirid
Ophidia
✧ophitic
upfield
Options
apricot
epsilon
upsilon
ypsilon
a priori
ophiura
à pointe
optimum
split up
split-up
spikily
upskill
Spokane
spikery
spelean
applied
applier
spalted
spelder
spelled
speller
spelter
spilled
spiller
apology
speldin
spulyie
spulzie
upclimb
apolune
opaline
opulent
spiling
up-along
upflung
apollos
epulary
upclose
epilate
spilite
Spoleto
applaud
upblown
apomict
ipomoea
spammed
spammer
spumone
spumoni
spumous
open day
open-jaw
sponsal
spinach
spinode
open sea
spancel
Spandex®
spandex
spaniel
spanker
spanned
spanner
span new
✧spencer
spender
Spenser
spinner
spinnet
spinney
spondee
sponger
spin off
spin-off
apanage
spinage
open-air
open-mic
opuntia
spongin
spunkie
spangle
spangly
spindle
spindly
spinule
open-end
opening
open-top
opinion
sponson
sponsor
spin-dry
spun-dry
aptness
Spanish
spinose
spinate
open out
spinous
spin out
spinout
spunk up
spun-out
spondyl
Spinoza
splotch
apposer
opposer
speoses
spoofer
spooler
spooney
spoorer
splodge
splodgy
aphonia
aphonic
aphotic
aptotic
opsonic
opsonin
appoint
upbound
upgoing
upwound
apropos
uphoard
uphoord
upcoast
uphoist
uprouse
apports
upspeak
upspear
apoplex
apepsia
upspake
upspoke
spa pool
a pip out
✧spartan
sporran
spuriae
spurway
upbreak
oporice
upgrade
à portée
sparger
sparred
sparrer
spersed
spiraea
sporter
spurner
spurred
spurrer
spurrey
eparchy
sparthe
sperthe
Ephraim
sparkie
sparoid
spermic
spiroid
sport it
upbraid
up-train
uptrain
sparely
sparkle
sparkly
spirtle
sporule
spurtle
spireme
epergne
operand
operant
sparing
spirant
upbring
up front
up-front
upfront
uptrend
approof
sparrow
appress
apprise
operose
oppress
upbrast
epurate
operate
spirits
spirity
éperdue
Spurius
approve
updrawn
upgrown
apprize
episode
✧opus Dei
apostil
spasmic
spastic
apishly
✧apostle
✧epistle
opuscle
Uppsala
episome
opossum
aphthae
spatial
apothem
epithem
epithet
spathed
spattee
spatter
spitted
spitten
spitter
spotted
spotter
sputter
up a tree
upstage
Epstein
spathic
sputnik
upstair
apetaly
spatula
spatule
spittle
epitome
épatant
upstand
spit box
upstood
✧epitaph
epitope
upstare
upstart
apatite
upstate
spit out
spot out
spa town
epitaxy
spousal
appuied
epaulet
spouter
splurge
splurgy
upsurge
upbuild
appulse
upburst
Ipswich
spawner
upsweep
upswell
upswing
upswept
spyware
up-swarm
epaxial
epoxide
epoxied
aphylly
uplying
spryest
epizoan
epizoic
epizoon
spaz out
squamae
squabby
squacco
squaddy
aquafer
square B
squared
squarer
squashy
aquafit
aquaria
aquatic
aquavit
squalid
squawky
equable
equably
equally
squails
squally
equator
squalor
à quatre
squatty
squelch
squeaky
equerry
aqueous
✧squeeze
squeezy
Equidae
equinal
squinch
squitch
aquifer
aquiver
equites
squiffy
squidge
squidgy
squishy
equinia
squilla
squills
squirmy
squinny
✧aquilon
equinox
Iquitos
squinty
Iquique
areaway
Arrabal
arrayal
orra man
creance
errancy
Mr Darcy
triarch
truancy
errands
friande
organdy
Orlando
arcaded
arrased
arrayer
breaded
breaker
briared
broaden
creamer
creaser
croaker
dreaded
dreader
dreamed
dreamer
dryades
ergates
greaser
greaten
greater
✧greaves
groaner
oreades
treader
treater
wreaked
wreaker
arraign
arrange
great go
breathe
breathy
preachy
wreathe
wreaths
wreathy
Arcadia
break in
break-in
creatic
creatin
Croatia
erratic
organic
✧priapic
triacid
triadic
triatic
broadly
dreadly
errable
friable
friarly
greatly
treacle
treacly
treadle
triable
Ariadne
✧creator
dream on
Eriador

Words marked ✧ can also be spelled with one or more capital letters

organon
treason
triaxon
preasse
breadth
arcanum
Arnaout
break up
break-up
dream up
erratum
organum
Priapus
treague
organza
Arabian
drybeat
grab-bag
Grobian
urd bean
crybaby
arabica
try back
ore body
tribade
tribady
crabbed
crabber
cribbed
cribber
crubeen
drabber
drabbet
drabler
dribber
driblet
drubbed
dry beer
grabbed
grabber
grubbed
grubber
problem
triblet
crabbit
crab-oil
frabbit
brabble
cribble
drabble
dribble
dribbly
fribble
grabble
gribble
grubble
prabble
pribble
proball
tribble
wrybill
armband
prebend
proband
probang
pro bono
tri-band
tribune
bribery
preborn
arabise

Arabism
Arabist
probate
probity
tribute
Art Brut
crab-nut
arabize
Araceae
brecham
brochan
crucial
crucian
fractal
✧grecian
proctal
trochal
trucial
Wroclaw
brocade
precede
brachet
bracken
bracket
bricken
brocked
brocket
cracked
cracker
cricket
crickey
crochet
crocked
crocket
drucken
erected
erecter
fracted
frocked
fructed
pricier
pricker
pricket
proceed
trachea
tracked
tracker
tricker
trochee
trocken
trucker
wracked
wrecked
wrecker
crucify
brocage
trucage
arachis
braccia
braccio
brachia
breccia
brickie
brockit
bruchid
crack it
cricoid
crocein
ericoid
orectic
practic

prick in
truckie
brickle
bricole
bruckle
crackle
crackly
Dracula
dry-cell
erectly
freckle
freckly
gracile
grackle
grockle
prickle
prickly
trickle
trickly
truckle
drachma
Arachne
bracing
brucine
Dracone®
dracone
gricing
iracund
tracing
crack on
erector
precook
precool
proctor
Procyon
tractor
Aricept®
precept
triceps
brocard
dry-cure
grocery
procure
tracery
tricorn
Grecism
Iricism
precast
precess
precise
process
tricksy
uricase
brucite
crack up
crackup
crock up
grecque
prick up
Proclus
track up
tractus
✧trochus
urachus
precava
cracowe
Grecize
Bradman
graddan
gradual
Irideae

irideal
iridial
iridian
predial
pridian
triduan
Trudeau
Art Deco
dry dock
dry-dock
predict
produce
product
traduce
Bridget
bridled
bridler
brodded
dredger
drudger
gridder
grodier
prodded
prodder
trodden
trudgen
trudger
prodigy
sraddha
bride it
brodkin
Freddie
Fredrik
Proddie
Prydain
trade in
trade-in
cruddle
crudely
gradely
griddle
treddle
Urodela
urodele
credent
erodent
gradine
grading
gradini
gradino
mridang
prudent
trading
✧trident
uredine
uridine
bridoon
predoom
trade on
prudery
tridarn
iridise
prudish
aridity
credits
crudity
erudite
gradate
predate
erodium
iridium

prodrug
trade up
triduum
uredium
bradawl
cry down
predawn
Fridays
iridize
arsenal
creedal
freeman
freeway
trueman
ardency
oriency
urgence
urgency
arreede
Arieses
breeder
briered
creeper
dry-eyed
freebee
freemen
freezer
friezed
greener
greeted
greeter
grieced
griever
orderer
praeses
creeshy
pre-echo
Armenia
arsenic
Artemis
creepie
ermelin
freebie
freesia
Friesic
greenie
griesie
preemie
troelie
true rib
uraemia
uraemic
briefly
cruells
cruelly
greenly
griesly
gryesly
orderly
freeing
orleans
treeing
freedom
praetor
treetop
pre-empt
arrears
free-arm
arietta
ariette
cruelty

greenth
Trieste
Croesus
fraenum
orifice
preface
prefect
proface
prefade
crofter
draftee
drafter
drifter
grafter
grifter
grufted
proffer
trifler
griffin
traffic
trefoil
triffic
triffid
armfuls
gruffly
profile
trifoly
truffle
urnfuls
Profumo
profane
draft ox
dry-foot
griffon
art form
prefard
preform
triform
dry-fist
profess
profuse
drag-bar
drag-man
frogman
grogram
program
trigram
Uruguay
brigade
tragedy
bragged
brogged
cragged
dragged
dragnet
drogher
droguet
drugged
drugger
drugget
fragged
frigger
frogged
froglet
prigged
prigger
trigged
trigger
trogged
Brighid
druggie

frogbit
grigris
arugula
draggle
fragile
gregale
tragule
wriggle
wriggly
origami
trigamy
brigand
oregano
origane
orogeny
progeny
dragoon
E-region
triglot
Gregory
a-rights
brights
frigate
drag out
trig out
Archean
archway
Brahman
Orphean
orthian
preheat
archlet
arsheen
orphrey
bruhaha
archaic
Brahmin
armhole
dry hole
trehala
Grahame
arshine
errhine
prehend
arch-foe
orthros
archery
orchard
Orphism
✧archeus
Orpheus
archive
arrival
artisan
orbital
ordinal
ordinar
arbiter
armiger
arsines
braided
brained
broider
broiler
bruiser
cruiser
drainer
dreidel
dry-iced
ermined
fruited

fruiter
grained
grainer
greisen
groined
orbiter
ordinee
praiser
trailer
trained
trainee
trainer
arriage
droichy
freight
Mr Right
cruisie
druidic
prairie
traikit
armilla
article
Braille
frailly
greisly
treille
orcinol
traitor
try it on
arriéré
arriero
orgiast
traipse
artiste
frailty
Orvieto
Troilus
Ursinus
project
traject
frijole
prejink
trekked
trekker
brokage
Prakrit
arcking
broking
erl-king
brokery
Fraktur
Grallae
Oral Law
Trullan
Uralian
trilobe
armlock
prelacy
prelect
prelude
preludi
Aral Sea
cruller
driller
grilled
griller
Grolier
kruller
proller
trilled
troller

trolley
pro-life
orology
trilogy
urology
brulyie
brulzie
trellis
arc-lamp
prelims
dry land
ere long
erelong
Ireland
praline
proline
prolong
Trilene®
try-line
trollop
arblast
armless
artless
braless
oralism
oralist
orality
prelate
prelaty
prolate
trilith
uralite
urolith
arillus
Krilium®
trilbys
frampal
grammar
gremial
tramcar
tramway
trimtab
trumeau
Grimsby
cromack
grimace
primacy
bromide
Bramley
brimmed
brimmer
Bromley
brommer
brummer
crammed
crammer
cramped
crampet
crimmer
crimped
crimper
crombec
crumpet
drummed
drummer
grimmer
grommet
grummet
krimmer
premier
primmed

primmer
prommer
trammed
trammel
tramper
trampet
trimmed
trimmer
trommel
trumpet
from off
primage
Aramaic
Brummie
crampit
cremsin
Crombie®
drum kit
drumlin
gremlin
✧kremlin
primsie
bramble
brambly
crimple
crumble
crumbly
crumple
crumply
drumble
frumple
grimily
grumble
grumbly
primely
primula
trample
tremble
trembly
tremolo
Trimble
Art Monk
briming
bromine
Cremona
crimina
crimine
crimini
dromond
framing
primine
priming
tromino
crampon
crimson
Mrs Mopp
gramary
✧primary
primero
uromere
Arimasp
bromism
cramesy
dry Mass
gramash
grumose
premise
premiss
✧promise
bromate
cremate

eremite
primate
promote
brimful
brumous
drum out
frame-up
from out
grampus
grumous
premium
primeur
trump up
premove
Grammys
Araneae
Brendan
brinjal
cranial
frontal
grandad
grandam
grannam
Iranian
iron man
iron-pan
trangam
trental
truncal
✧uranian
Bronach
irenics
tranect
wryneck
Granada
Grenada
grenade
uranide
branded
brander
bran-new
Branwen
brinded
bringer
Bronwen
bronzed
bronzen
bronzer
Cranmer
cringer
drinker
drunken
Erinyes
Frances
fringed
fronded
fronted
grandee
granfer
granger
granted
grantee
granter
Grendel
grinded
grinder
grinned
grinner
grunter
iron-red
orangey

✧prancer
prince's
printer
pronged
prunted
tranced
trancey
tranter
trinket
trunked
trunnel
wringed
wringer
wronger
Bronagh
cranage
Iron Age
branchy
bronchi
broncho
crunchy
Frenchy
Granthi
tranche
araneid
bran-pie
bring in
crinoid
drink in
Francie
Francis
Frankie
frantic
grannie
prank it
prenzie
trannie
Transit®
transit
trenail
wren tit
prancke
brangle
bransle
brantle
brindle
Brundle
crankle
cringle
crinkle
crinkly
crunkle
frankly
frenula
grandly
granola
granule
gruntle
prankle
pronely
trangle
trindle
tringle
trundle
wrangle
wrinkle
wrinkly
wrongly
grandma
erg-nine
ironing

pruning
urinant
Branson
bring on
broncos
Bronson
crannog
drone on
drongos
eryngos
franion
fronton
grantor
gringos
grunion
princox
pronaoi
pronaos
transom
Trenton
grandpa
Granary®
granary
iron ore
trinary
urinary
brinish
crinose
dronish
dryness
ironise
ironist
trenise
uranism
urinose
wryness
crenate
crinate
crinite
drink to
e re nata
erinite
granita
granite
pronate
pronota
✧trinity
uranite
urinate
bran tub
✧bren gun
bring up
cranium
crank up
drink up
iron out
prink up
proneur
pronoun
trankum
trinkum
uranium
uranous
urinous
wrong'un
Orkneys
ironize
areolae
areolar
areolas
Kroo-man

ortolan
preoral
arboret
arrowed
brooder
crooked
crooner
cruores
cryogen
grooved
groover
triolet
triones
trooper
brioche
arborio
Armoric
cryonic
drookit
ergodic
prootic
troolie
criollo
croodle
ariosos
arroyos
Bryozoa
creosol
Kroo-boy
armoire
armoury
Ariosto
arnotto
trionym
crop-ear
cryptal
prepack
prepuce
tropics
tripody
crapped
Crippen
cropped
cropper
crupper
drapier
dripped
droplet
drop-net
dropped
dropper
frapped
frappée
fripper
grapnel
gripped
gripper
prepped
✧prophet
prop-jet
propped
trapped
trapper
triplet
triplex
tripped
tripper
trippet
wrapped
wrapper
drop off

drop-off
propage
Arapaho
crappie
cryptic
drappie
drip-tip
erepsin
graphic
Graphis
krypsis
prepaid
tripsis
trophic
trypsin
tryptic
aripple
cripple
dropfly
dropple
grapple
gripple
propale
propyla
✧tripoli
tripple
griping
groping
prepone
propane
propend
propene
propine
propone
trepang
crop top
crypton
cryptos
✧gryphon
krypton
trip hop
drapery
drip-dry
grapery
gropers
prepare
tripery
Tripura
oropesa
prepose
propose
tropism
tropist
crap out
cropful
crop out
drop out
dropout
trap-cut
trip out
trapeze
Iraq War
briquet
croquet
prequel
croquis
orarian
araroba
ard-righ
ardrigh
prurigo

trireme
Brer Fox
orarion
prerupt
armrest
pro rata
prorate
orarium
aristae
artsman
Brassaï
cristae
crusian
crustae
crustal
crustas
crystal
Drusian
Frisian
Grisham
trishaw
Tristan
trisect
crusade
crusado
drostdy
preside
prosody
brasier
brasset
brisken
brisket
brushed
brusher
cresset
crested
crisper
crosier
crossed
crosser
crushed
crusher
Dresden
dressed
dresser
freshen
fresher
freshet
fresnel
Frisbee®
frisker
frisket
frosted
grasper
grasser
grisled
Irisher
Orestes
pressed
presser
Prestel®
prosper
trashed
tressed
tressel
trussed
trusser
trusses
trustee
truster
tryster

wrester
prosify
presage
prisage
brassie
Brescia
✧crispin
drastic
dry suit
eristic
griskin
pressie
prosaic
prussic
trysail
droshky
brashly
briskly
bristle
bristly
crassly
crisply
crossly
dry-salt
freshly
grisely
gristle
gristly
grossly
grysely
pre-sell
prosily
trestle
trisula
wrestle
irksome
presume
prosoma
triseme
trisome
trisomy
urosome
art-song
Krishna
present
prosing
aristos
Bristol
creston
dry-shod
erasion
erosion
frescos
frisson
grysbok
press on
pressor
Preston
prestos
brasero
brisure
drosera
erasure
frisure
grosert
Irishry
irisate
brush up
brush-up
brusque
crissum

dress up
Erasmus
friseur
frustum
grassum
grass up
gross up
press-up
pre-stun
trismus
erosive
fretsaw
Grotian
✧protean
urethan
erotica
protect
tritide
Britten
brothel
brother
critter
dratted
erathem
Eritrea
fretted
fritted
fritter
gritter
grutten
pre-teen
pretzel
prithee
pr'ythee
prythee
trotted
trotter
writhen
written
wrythen
brutify
frutify
gratify
protégé
fratchy
arctiid
arctoid
crottin
oratrix
proteid
protein
write in
write-in
britska
britzka
Trotsky
brattle
brittle
brittly
crotala
crottle
fritfly
irately
prattle
protyle
tritely
erotema
eroteme
Tritoma
bruting
gratiné

Words marked ✧ can also be spelled with one or more capital letters

grating
orotund
prating
pretend
protend
tritone
Tritons
writing
Britpop
Brython
grottos
krytron
oration
Britart
fratery
friture
✧oratory
preterm
protore
urethra
British
brutish
cretism
erotism
pretest
protest
protist
crathur
crittur
fretful
✧proteus
protium
tritium
trot out
write up
write-up
pretext
prothyl
arousal
traumas
braunch
craunch
frounce
graunch
praunce
trounce
grounds
✧arguses
arouser
crouper
graupel
grouper
grouser
grouter
prouler
trouper
trouser
trouses
trouter
brought
draught
drought
drouthy
fraught
froughy
grouchy
wrought
droukit
groupie
proudly
trouble
croupon
croûton
Triumph®
triumph
Irkutsk
arcuate
arbutus
arduous
argulus
gravlax
trivial
drive-by
crevice
privacy
bravado
privado
provide
bravoes
brevier
preview
drive-in
prevail
travail
travois
provoke
bravely
drevill
gravely
privily
travels
craving
crivens
driving
droving
graving
prevene
prevent
provand
provant
provend
provine
proving
bravery
bravura
gravure
preverb
proverb
previse
proviso
provost
treviss
breveté
brevity
gravity
pravity
private
privity
trivium
hryvnya
crewman
crowbar
drawbar
grow-bag
brawler
brawned
browser
crawler
Crawley
crowded
crowder
crowned
crowner
crownet
drawler
draw-net
drowner
growler
oreweed
prowler
trawler
draw off
brewage
Brownie®
✧brownie
crowdie
prawlin
crewels
cry wolf
drywall
grow old
brewing
drawing
growing
crow-toe
draw-boy
draw hoe
Erewhon
frown on
artwork
brewers'
brewery
drawers
froward
prewarm
prewarn
dry-wash
pre-wash
prowess
frowsty
brewpub
crew bus
crew cut
draw out
grown-up
Wrexham
proximo
bruxism
drayman
grey-lag
greyhen
drayage
argyria
traybit
treybit
grayfly
army ant
fraying
greying
praying
Croydon
Gruyère
prayers
'Arryish
greyish
Dreyfus
grey-out
preyful
trayful
grey owl
cruzado
brazier
crazier
crazies
crozier
Frazier
frizzed
grazier
Prizren
wrizled
prezzie
crazily
drizzle
drizzly
frazzle
frizzle
frizzly
grizzle
grizzly
Arizona
crazing
grazing
trizone
assagai
Isfahan
Isiacal
Tswanas
askance
ashamed
assayer
escapee
escaper
essayed
essayer
T-shaped
U-shaped
V-shaped
yslaked
ascarid
ascaris
Asianic
Asiatic
askaris
Aspasia
astatic
Islamic
ismatic
astatki
assault
astable
Ismaili
Israeli
Osmanli
usually
ascaunt
escalop
Astaire
Ashanti
Astarte
esparto
Tsabian
isobare
isobase
isobath
asocial
psychic
isochor
psychos
usucapt
psych up
psych-up
asudden
tsaddik
tsaddiq
isodoma
isodont
Isadora
Isadore
Isidora
Isidore
Isodore
Ashdown
assegai
isleman
essence
AS level
assever
Essenes
isoetes
osiered
osselet
osseter
asperge
ascesis
ascetic
askesis
astelic
asteria
asterid
C S Lewis
osteoid
usher in
Estella
Estelle
osteoma
asperse
asteism
osseous
as of now
Ashford
Asa Gray
isogram
isagoge
Isegrim
isogamy
isogeny
tsigane
ash-heap
escheat
ischial
oscheal
isohyet
ash-hole
asphalt
pschent
asthore
esthete
ischium
isthmus
asphyxy
estival
astilbe
ascites
ashiver
assizer
assizes
Oscines
assiege
ascidia
ascitic
aspidia
aspirin
ossific
ossicle
ostiole
assigns
Eskimos
ostiary
osmiate
ostiate
osmious
Esbjerg
isokont
✧psalter
psyllid
asylums
asklent
isoline
T S Eliot
useless
isolate
Ishmael
isomere
Ostmark
asinico
asunder
isonomy
tsunami
asinine
p's and q's
Asmoday
escolar
a sconce
asconce
ask over
estover
Estonia
osmosis
osmotic
psionic
estoile
astound
esloyne
essoyne
Osborne
L S Lowry
espouse
isopach
Isopoda
asepses
asepsis
aseptic
aspread
csárdás
estreat
Osirian
ascribe
escribe
astrict
estrich
ostraca
ostrich
astride
estrade
usurped
usurper
astroid
ostraka
as a rule
escroll
ashrama
astrand
c-spring
eserine
G-string
tsarina
usuring
tsardom
estrepe
tsarism
tsarist
usuress
asprout
usurous
asprawl
as usual
isospin
ashtray
isatine
isotone
isotron
isotope
isotopy
isotype
esotery
oscular
osmunda
assumed
assured
assurer
assuage
escuage
tsouris
asquint
issuant
escudos
Eskuara
✧esquire
estuary
ossuary
T-square
osculum
asswage
asexual
astylar
espying
A S Byatt
isozyme
ethanal
stratal
attacca
atlases
B Traven
steaded
stealed
stealer
steamed
steamer
strawed
strawen
strayed
strayer
at large
strange
attaché
Athalia
ptyalin
steamie
stearic
stearin
attaskt
at fault
at table
attaint
straint
athanor
attaboy
ethanol
Mt Mayon
strap-on
strappy
Strauss
Atlanta
stealth
straits
steam up
stratum
stratus
stibial
stabbed
stabber
stabler
stables
stubbed
atabrin
atebrin
stabile
stibble
stubble
stubbly
stibine
at a blow
stibium
stub out
stick by
e-ticket
stacked
stacker
stacket
sticked
sticker
stocker
atactic
stichic
stick in
stick it
stickit
stickle
Atacama
stichoi
stichos
stucco'd
stuccos
etacism
itacism
otocyst
stack up
stick up
stick-up
stock up
stuck-up
stachys
stadial
stodger
studded
studden
studied
studier
studies
St Edwin
stiddie
staddle
studdle
student
studios
stadium
at peace
stretch
Mt Pelée
steeled
steepen
steeper
steerer
St Leger
strewed
strewer
utterer
Utrecht
atresia
etaerio
etheric
St Denis
steekit
sthenic
streaky
Mt Hekla
Othello
steeple
steeply
utterly
it seems
streamy
étrenne
attempt
at heart
atheise
atheism
atheist
at least
steep-to
streety
stretta
strette
stretti
stretto
strewth
atheous
steed up
steepup
Mt Kenya
atheize
staffer
stiffen
stifled
stifler
stuffed
stuffer
stiffie
stuff it
stiffly
ataghan
stigmas
Stygian
stagger
stage it
stagily
staging
étagère
stagery
itchier
etchant
etching
Mt Thera
Mt Thira
ethical
Mt Sinai
St Aidan
stoical
strigae

St Kilda
at times
e-tailer
stained
stainer
Staines
staired
Steiner
stoiter
strider
strides
Striges
striker
striped
stripes
stripey
strived
striven
striver
strings
stringy
at sight
staithe
strigil
strip in
a trifle
staidly
utricle
Utrillo
atriums
stridor
ethiops
at first
athirst
striate
atokous
stoke up
Italian
stellar
italics
atelier
Ctrl key
stalked
stalker
stalled
stelled
stiller
stilted
stilter
stollen
étalage
otology
otalgia
styloid
stalely
Ptolemy
stelene
Italiot
Stilton®
at a loss
stylise
stylish
stylist
utilise
athleta
athlete
otolith
stylate
stylite
utility
atalaya

stylize
utilize
stomach
stammel
stammer
stamper
stemlet
stemmed
stemmer
stempel
stomper
stummed
stummel
stumped
stumper
stymied
ethmoid
stemple
stimuli
stumble
stumbly
atamans
etymons
stamens
stamina
stamnoi
stamnos
stembok
stemson
atomise
atomism
atomist
itemise
stomata
stem cup
stump up
atomize
itemize
Etonian
stengah
stand by
stand-by
FT Index
standee
standen
stander
staniel
Stanley
stannel
stanyel
stinged
✧stinger
stinker
stinted
stinter
stonied
stonker
stunned
stunner
stunted
at one go
stenchy
ctenoid
stand in
stand-in
stannic
stencil
utensil
atingle
stonily
stone me!

at an end
stoning
stand on
stanzos
stentor
stingos
stonern
ut infra
stand-to
stand up
stand-up
✧sten gun
stun gun
Mt Logan
✧ottoman
attonce
attones
stooden
stooker
stooped
stooper
stroken
stroker
strowed
strower
atrophy
strophe
atropia
atropin
etiolin
Mt Qogir
Otto Dix
St Louis
stookie
stoolie
strobic
strooke
strodle
at point
St John's
Atropos
stroppy
at worst
stopgap
✧utopian
stapler
Stephen
stepney
stepped
stepper
stopped
stopper
stop off
stop-off
stopoff
stupefy
stop hit
stypsis
styptic
stapple
stipple
stipule
stopple
stipend
stoping
stupent
stepson
at a push
utopism
utopist
step-cut

step out
stop out
stop-out
✧eternal
Starman
star map
sternal
stirrah
attract
at grade
otaries
starken
star-led
starlet
starred
starter
starved
sterlet
stirpes
stirred
stirrer
storied
stories
stormer
✧sturmer
storage
starchy
ptarmic
starlit
starnie
start in
steroid
athrill
pteryla
starkly
startle
startly
sterile
sternly
iterant
otarine
staring
styrene
uterine
pterion
stardom
start on
stereos
starers
stir-fry
at press
attrist
attrite
iterate
starets
staretz
start up
start-up
sternum
stir out
stirrup
sturnus
yttrium
ataraxy
storeys
etesian
stashie
stishie
stushie
stasima
a-tishoo

atishoo
at issue
statice
statics
statued
stetted
stotter
stutter
stottie
at stake
stately
à tâtons
statant
station
Stetson®
Atatürk
stature
statism
statist
statute
stative
strumae
staunch
étourdi
stouten
strudel
Etruria
St Lucia
stoutly
attuent
ut supra
attuite
strunts
stovies
stave in
stoving
atavism
stew-can
stewpan
at twice
stowage
stewing
stowing
stewpot
at a word
athwart
steward
Stewart
St Cyril
stay out
stay put
✧curaçao
cutaway
Gujarat
Judaean
Mubarak
nunatak
oulakan
Puranas
put away
rub away
run away
runaway
subadar
durance
Judaica
surance
bucardo
mutanda
aurated
duramen

lunated
Musales
mutagen
putamen
subarea
sudamen
sugared
lumache
nuraghe
nuraghi
queachy
bubalis
cumarin
Eurasia
Fumaria
lunatic
puparia
Puranic
run a rig
rusa oil
subacid
subarid
Sudanic
suramin
turacin
tutania
autarky
rusalka
aurally
buyable
curable
ducally
dupable
durable
durably
fugally
humanly
jurally
mutable
mutably
rulable
rurally
sueable
tunable
tunably
eucaine
lucarne
✧muraena
Susanna
bugaboo
butanol
curaçoa
curator
Euratom
fugatos
fumados
fusarol
rubatos
run amok
subatom
turacos
✧sumatra
dumaist
Judaise
Judaism
Judaist
dupatta
Kuwaiti
mulatta
mulatto
Bubalus

buy a pup
Nunavut
punalua
sub-aqua
subaqua
Surayya
Judaize
bugbear
bum-boat
cudbear
gunboat
Jumblat
mud-boat
outbrag
sunbeam
sun bear
sunbeat
tugboat
rum baba
buy-back
cut back
cutback
jumbuck
outback
Purbeck
put back
runback
bubbler
Bubbles
bumbler
burbler
fumbler
humbles
jumbler
mumbler
numbles
outbred
rumbler
tubbier
tumbler
tumbrel
lumbago
Cumbria
gumboil
ouabain
quiblin
tumbril
sunbake
bulb fly
cue ball
quibble
Sun Belt
✧sunbelt
bugbane
cubbing
cui bono?
cumbent
dubbing
gubbing
gubbins
husband
jug band
lumbang
numbing
pubbing
rubbing
subbing
tubbing
turband
turbant
turbine

turbond
gumboot
nun buoy
✧pueblos
Bunbury
dun-bird
fubbery
Humbert
lubbard
✧numbers
outburn
rubbers
rubbery
Sudbury
sunbird
sunburn
turbary
cubbish
dumb-ass
furbish
kurbash
rubbish
subbase
surbase
tubbish
mudbath
sunbath
surbate
turbith
bulbous
bumbaze
humbuzz
dulcian
Dunciad
Funchal
nuoc mam
sun-clad
surcoat
tulchan
succuba
succubi
succade
suicide
bunched
bunches
butcher
futchel
guichet
gutcher
juncoes
luncher
lurcher
mulcted
muncher
muscled
puncher
putcher
quacker
quicken
succeed
dulcify
culchie
muscoid
quickie
cupcake
furcula
juicily
out cold
Purcell
quackle
quickly

sun cult
curcuma
outcome
succumb
buccina
mud-cone
muscone
Puccini
Vulcano
functor
nuncios
outcrop
puccoon
punctos
subcool
duncery
Euscara
Runcorn
succory
dulcose
muscose
nutcase
outcast
put case
success
succise
succose
succuss
dulcite
furcate
Guscott
juncate
Succoth
sulcate
fulcrum
fuscous
hunch up
juice up
punch-up
punctum
putchuk
Quechua
Quichua
succour
succous
Muscovy
cut dead
quadrat
subdean
subdual
suidian
sundial
burdock
gun deck
Murdoch
puddock
ruddock
subduce
subduct
sun deck
sundeck
bundler
Culdees
curdler
fuddled
fuddler
huddled
hundred
hurdies
hurdler
hurdles

Words marked ✧ can also be spelled with one or more capital letters

muddied
muddier
muddler
puddler
ruddied
ruddier
rundled
rundlet
subdued
subduer
mundify
guidage
mueddin
quadric
quiddit
quids in
quodlin
turdoid
Dundalk
muddily
quiddle
ruddily
rundale
ducdame
quidams
budding
burdens
duodena
funding
✧guiding
lurdane
mundane
nundine
pudding
turdine
bundook
cut drop
gumdrop
outdoor
puldron
turdion
duddery
juddery
Kundera
outdare
outdure
sundari
burdash
Kurdish
Luddism
sun disc
sun disk
tun-dish
due date
Luddite
outdate
surdity
buddy up
humdrum
sub divo
cut down
cut-down
gun down
put down
put-down
rub down
rubdown
run down
run-down
rundown
sundown
Sundays
funeral
gudeman
humeral
Jude Law
✧juvenal
Luce Bay
lumenal
✧mudéjar
numeral
nu-metal
puberal
ruderal
subedar
tutelar
tutenag
rudesby
lucency
pudency
quiesce
tumesce
pudenda
bug-eyed
cupeled
murexes
Nureyev
quieten
quieter
auberge
outedge
queechy
aurelia
auxesis
auxetic
Dunedin
✧eugenia
eugenic
Eugenie
Eugénie
Eusebio
eutexia
numeric
✧queenie
queen it
subedit
suberic
suberin
Zuleika
aureola
aureole
cure-all
jumelle
nucelli
✧pucelle
queenly
queerly
quietly
rubella
rubeola
Judezmo
museums
✧lucerne
lugeing
Auberon
dukedom
eugenol
fuse box
gude-son
jukebox
mu-meson
pukekos
rude boy
rules OK
tupelos
tuxedos
Yule log
Euterpe
Auxerre
funèbre
jug-ears
duresse
eupepsy
rulesse
aureate
aureity
au reste
burette
buvette
cuneate
cunette
curette
cuvette
fumette
fumetti
fumetto
lunette
musette
ouverte
puberty
bureaus
bureaux
dureful
duteous
hugeous
humerus
June bug
luteous
museful
quietus
rule out
tubeful
tuneful
tune out
duvetyn
Gulf War
huff-cap
mudflap
mudflat
ruffian
runflat
surfman
turfman
turf war
outface
suffect
suffice
surface
sulfide
muffled
muffler
purfled
quaffer
ruffled
ruffler
turfier
funfair
furfair
huffkin
surfeit
buffalo
cupfuls
fulfill
huffily
jugfuls
mugfuls
outfall
puffily
Suffolk
tubfuls
zuffoli
zuffolo
buffing
duffing
puffing
sulfone
surfing
turfing
buffoon
mudflow
outflow
outfoot
puff-box
gunfire
puffery
dun-fish
huffish
lubfish
mudfish
muffish
outfish
pupfish
subfusc
subfusk
suffuse
sunfast
sunfish
tubfast
tubfish
suffete
sulfate
sulfite
turfite
turf out
burghal
burglar
Jungian
subgoal
aufgabe
bungler
✧burgher
fungoes
juggler
jungled
muggier
outgoer
outgoes
puggled
puggree
burgage
luggage
fungoid
tung oil
cupgall
dung-fly
nutgall
buggane
bugging
bulgine
bulging
fulgent
hugging
Huygens
jugging
juggins
lugging
lunging
mugging
muggins
outgone
pugging
pungent
purging
rugging
sugging
surgent
surging
tugging
turgent
burgeon
dudgeon
dungeon
gudgeon
Guignol
murgeon
outgrow
sunglow
surgeon
budgero
busgirl
Hungary
puggery
surgery
burgess
muggish
outgush
puggish
suggest
nuggety
outgate
✧vulgate
budge up
bulghur
burghul
fulgour
fungous
gunge up
lungful
outgive
rug gown
bush-cat
✧bushman
cuphead
jughead
lum-head
mukhtar
subhead
tushkar
hushaby
bushido
bush tea
cushier
dudheen
euchred
Euphues
Fuehrer
luthier
mushier
tushker
push off
push-off
Buphaga
nurhags
run high
kuchcha
bush pig
bushtit
du choix
fuchsia
fuchsin
hush kit
push fit
Pushkin
pushpin
pushpit
Rushdie
tughrik
bush-fly
lughole
muchell
mudhole
mushily
out-half
Duchamp
bushing
euphony
gushing
Kuching
pushing
ruching
Ruthene
bush dog
cubhood
cushion
euphroe
fushion
mudhook
nunhood
nut-hook
pushrod
Pushtoo
Wu Zhaov
Bukhara
euphory
futhark
futhorc
futhork
Kuh-horn
Kushiro
luthern
outhire
outhyre
run hard
tushery
duchess
Cushite
Kushite
Kurhaus
outhaul
pushful
push out
push-out
push-tug
Pushtun
quahaug
ruthful
cubical
cubital
Guri Dam
Huainan
kufiyah
luminal
Muridae
musical
pupilar
✧puritan
rufiyaa
Surinam
Lucinda
culices
jubilee
juniper
Jupiter
✧lucifer
lucigen
mucigen
murices
pubises
quoiter
tubifex
bubinga
rupiahs
augitic
bulimia
bulimic
culicid
cutikin
juridic
mudiria
tunicin
Tunisia
audible
audibly
auricle
cubicle
cuticle
funicle
fusible
fusilli
humidly
lucidly
Lucilla
Lucille
luridly
tumidly
tunicle
audient
Juliana
Luciana
auditor
humidor
musimon
put it on
✧rubicon
Lumière
curiosa
furioso
ju-jitsu
puniest
tuniest
buy into
dubiety
muriate
run into
au mieux
bulimus
cubitus
curious
dubious
dutiful
euripus
furious
lulibub
rubious
Punjabi
subject
subjoin
outjump
quo jure?
suo jure
outjest
sub Jove
buckram
bucksaw
junkman
musk-bag
musk-cat
muskrat
musk-sac
Turkman
buckeen
buckler
buckoes
bunk bed
muckier
muskier
suckler
turkies
Turkmen
bunk off
Turkify
bulkily
cuckold
duskily
huskily
luckily
murkily
muskily
suck'ole
sulkily
bucking
busking
duck-ant
ducking
hulking
husking
lurking
muskone
quaking
sucking
tusking
bucksom
duck-coy
Lucknow
musk-cod
musk-pod
tuck box
Dunkard
Dunkirk
Euskera
hunkers
ouakari
puckery
Quakers
buckish
duskish
luskish
murkish
puckish
punkish
Turkess
Turkish
Sukkoth
sunkets
bulk-buy
bulk out
duck out
luck out
muck out
tuck-out
buckeye
bullbat
hurlbat
nucleal
nuclear
outleap
Pullman
pull-tab
quillai
Tullian
lullaby
bullace
bullock
gunlock
mullock
putlock
rullock
suo loco
nuclide
our Lady
builded
builder
bullied
bull pen
cullied
curlier
duelled
dueller
fuelled
fueller
full-fed
guilder
gullied
gullies
outlier
purlieu
queller
quilled
quillet
quilted
quilter
sullied
wurlies
nullify
pull off
qualify
fullage
sullage
build in
built-in
fuel oil
Guelfic
mullein
murlain
nuclein
purloin
ruellia
surloin
tuilyie
tuilzie
nutlike
sunlike
surlily
mud-lump
sublime
sunlamp
bull ant
bulling
bus lane

eyebolt
pyebald
symbole
eye bank
myrbane
eyebrow
symbion
eyebath
lyncean
lyncher
lynchet
hyacine
syncope
rye corn
syncarp
synchro
Wyndham
hylding
eye-drop
lyddite
synd out
byreman
Hygeian
hymenal
Lyme Bay
Mycenae
typebar
✧mycetes
typeset
synergy
Ayeesha
hymenia
mycelia
pyaemia
pyaemic
pyretic
pyrexia
pyrexic
synesis
K-Y® jelly
lyceums
by means
hyperon
xylenol
bynempt
by heart
Lynette
my certy
hyped up
hyped-up
eye-flap
synfuel
myogram
nylghau
syngamy
Pytheas
Pythian
by the by
mynheer
Lychnic
lychnis
typhoid
eyehole
wych-elm
by-thing
eyehook
typhoon
mythise
mythism
mythist
tychism
Lythrum
pythium
typhous
mythize
cynical
Lycidas
lyrical
symitar
typical
by times
cylices
lymiter
pyrites
pyxides
myringa
✧syringa
syringe
by right
pyritic
pyxidia
Sybilla
hygiene
lyricon
xylitol
Syriasm
cytisus
Dyticus
Hyginus
Mytilus
wysiwyg
eyeliad
syllabi
byplace
byrlady
dyslogy
myology
sylloge
cycloid
hyaloid
myalgia
myalgic
myeloid
myeloma
cycling
cyclone
dyeline
hyaline
✧cyclops
cyclist
eyelash
eyeless
myalism
hyalite
pygmean
pygmoid
Wyoming
Ayamará
Lyomeri
Hyundai®
Myanmar
Nyanjas
by and by
by-and-by
cyanide
hymnody
Lymnaea
hypnoid
lying-in
dyingly
lyingly
vyingly
cyanine
hymning
hypnone
gymnura
hymnary
by a nose
cyanise
gymnast
hymnist
kyanise
cyanate
cyanite
kyanite
pycnite
syenite
cyanize
kyanize
gyrocar
Sycorax
synodal
xylomas
zygomas
bycoket
bygones
bywoner
hypogea
mycoses
pyrogen
tyloses
tyrones
xylogen
zymogen
Byronic
dysodil
gyronic
hypoxia
hypoxic
mycosis
mycotic
pyloric
pyrosis
sybotic
sycosis
synodic
synovia
tylosis
xylonic
Xylopia
zygosis
zygotic
zymosis
zymotic
by-going
Cy Young
gyronny
cytosol
lycopod
mylodon
tylopod
dyvoury
hyloist
Nynorsk
pylorus
pyropus
hyponym
synonym
lymphad
nymphae
nymphal
ryepeck
dyspnea
nymphet
lyophil
nymphic
sylphid
syrphid
nymphly
gypping
tympana
tympani
tympano
tympany
nymphos
symptom
Syrphus
✧cyprian
hydride
dyarchy
hydroid
myrrhic
✧pyrrhic
pyrrole
rye-roll
cyprine
hydrant
Cypriot
myrrhol
Nyerere
cypress
gytrash
hydrate
hydrous
Pyrrhus
hydroxy
Ayeshah
dyester
byssoid
gym slip
cypsela
byssine
eyeshot
eye-spot
gym shoe
eyesore
myosote
myotube
Cyathea
mystify
syntagm
cyathia
Cynthia
cystoid
systole
systyle
myotome
cystine
syntony
synthon
mystery
cyathus
hypural
zymurgy
dysuria
dysuric
by turns
Sylvian
hyrvnia
sylvine
sylvite
rye wolf
Tynwald
eye-wink
dyewood
dye-work
eyewash
Czechic
tzaddik
tzaddiq
Izhevsk
tzigany
azygous
Ezekiel
Szekler
Szekely
Azilian
azulejo
tzimmes
azimuth
✧azymite
azymous
Azanian
ozonide
ozonise
ozonize
Azariah
azurean
czardas
azurine
czarina
czardom
czarism
czarist
azurite
azotise
azotous
azotize

8 – even

caracara
caragana
jararaca
jararaka
katakana
kawakawa
lava-lava
maharaja
Mahayana
matamata
Nataraja
pacarana
Ramayana
sasarara
takamaka
faradaic
✧la-la land
Nagaland
saraband
carapace
catalase
database
malaxage
malaxate
palamate
paravane
vanadate
parasang
calabash
Malagash
calamari
Ganapati
Kalahari
Kawasaki
maharani
Mata Hari
Nagasaki
Varanasi
databank
tamarack
paravail
pay a call
Fanagalo
galapago
lava lamp
cataract
paravant
calamary
Malagasy
harambee
tapas bar
Barabbas
balanced
valanced
Jamaican
Masaccio
balancer
Damascus
navarchy
tamandua
kalamdan
qalamdan
malander
marauder
hazardry
habanera
✧kamadeva
karateka
lavatera
Mahadeva
parabema
Pasadena
Sama-Veda
Samaveda
tapadera
bayadère
Canarese
Fagaceae
Gadarene
Japanese
Javanese
Kanarese
Macanese
Nazarene
paramese
paranete
Taxaceae
lay an egg
galabeah
Nazareth
maravedi
kaka beak
Vanaheim
fava bean
Nazarean
panacean
tara fern
habanero
habañero
jalapeño
Sarajevo
tapadero
lazarets
law agent
malapert
parakeet
parament
camaïeux
Japanesy
lamasery
savagely
savagery
paraffle
paraffin
carangid
canaigre
harangue
galangal
radar gun
Jahangir
barathea
calathea
Halachic
kazachoc
Halachah
Halakhah
marathon
matachin
Ramadhan
yataghan
rajaship
cataphor
tabashir
Caiaphas
calathus
cavatina
salaried
tamarind
baladine
banalise
banalize
basanite
calamine
calamite
canalise
canalize
carabine
catamite
faradise
faradize
fayalite
Japanise
Japanize
kamacite
laxative
lay aside
macarise
macarize
magazine
mala fide
man alive
mazarine
nasalise
nasalize
Nazarite
paganise
paganize
✧palatine
papalise
papalize
✧paradise
parasite
Patarine
rabatine
sanative
saxatile
taxative
Wahabite
zaratite
damaging
garaging
kayaking
managing
maraging
salading
dahabieh
galabiah
paganish
Tanalith®
vagarish
hara-kiri
Paganini
tarakihi
tamarisk
kaka bill
malarial
palatial
patagial
cabalism
caladium
faradism
fatalism
macarism
navalism
paganism
papalism
paradigm
patagium
ranarium
samarium
satanism
savagism
vanadium
Wahabism
Bahamian
Batavian
Canadian

Words marked ✧ can also be spelled with one or more capital letters

halation
Hawaiian
lavation
malarian
Malawian
natation
pacation
par avion
ranarian
Tatarian
taxation
vacation
palamino
✧**cavalier**
gasalier
canaries
Makarios
vagaries
cabalist
calamint
Fanariot
fatalist
garagist
Lazarist
papalist
safarist
salariat
satanist
banality
calamity
capacity
fatality
Macavity
nasality
natality
rapacity
sagacity
salacity
satanity
Habakkuk
damaskin
namaskar
malarkey
caballed
halalled
canaille
parallel
Java plum
macallum
Mazatlan
rataplan
caballer
dataller
eatables
data flow
parallax
Macaulay
marasmic
marasmus
japanned
✧**savannah**
Manannan
japanner
Casanova
maha yoga
Maradona
matadora
parabola
paranoea
paranoia
raja yoga
Saratoga
catacomb
paranoic
Garamond
paranoid
vagabond
caracole
matadore
parabole
paragoge
sagamore
zabaione
tag along
zap along
macaroni
carap-oil
parafoil
salad oil
lavaform
macaroon
parazoan
parazoon
talapoin
cacafogo
tapacolo
paramour
tamanoir
vavasour
cataloes
lavaboes
rabatoes
vanadous
day about
gad about
gadabout
layabout
mad about
marabout
racahout
tacahout
catatony
lavatory
natatory
paradoxy
paralogy
sanatory
vavasory
bad apple
mad-apple
may apple
oak apple
Jabalpur
Taganrog
datagram
paragram
paradrop
zamarras
zamarros
Malaysia
banausic
badassed
harassed
Tanaiste
Manasseh
damassin
harasser
macassar
Makassar
hamartia
Marattia
Samantha
basaltic
galactic
tac-au-tac
cadastre
calanthe
lamantin
canaster
varactor
tarantas
vacantly
macahuba
Maja Nude
malamute
tapaculo
catapult
Paraquat®
Paraguay
gaga over
rara avis
Japan wax
catalyse
catalyze
paralyse
paralyze
catalyst
kazatzka
Karadzic
kala-azar
Matanzas
damboard
garboard
lap-board
larboard
pax-board
wayboard
sawblade
vambrace
gas black
madbrain
sauba ant
jambeaux
Ian Brady
barbecue
barbicel
barbican
tabby cat
Cambodia
Barbados
gambados
day by day
nan bread
waybread
pax-brede
bad break
daybreak
parbreak
tax break
has-beens
lamb's fry
gambogic
barbwire
Darbyite
lamb-like
war bride
babbling
baubling
dabbling
gabbling
gambling
garbling
lambling
marbling
rabbling
rambling
saibling
tabbying
wambling
warbling
Cambrian
Habbakuk
lambskin
Marbella
carbolic
kabbalah
jambolan
tambalas
tan balls
zambomba
carbonic
✧rabbinic
rawboned
carbonyl
galbanum
garbanzo
bambinos
sawbones
tabbinet
lambency
gabbroic
bad blood
gabbroid
lambdoid
tarboosh
may bloom
gambroon
lamb down
barbeque
Canberra
barbaric
jamboree
Hamburgh
carbaryl
tamburin
Van Buren
harborer
jabberer
carburet
barberry
bayberry
hagberry
tayberry
waxberry
gambusia
lambaste
gambeson
barbasco
iambuses
gambetta
sabbatic
barbated
rabbeted
barbette
barbital
rabbit on
rambutan
rabbiter
Babbitt's
Daibutsu
zaibatsu
Babbitry
rabbitry
tamboura
mawbound
faubourg
hatbrush
tarboush
tar brush
Vanbrugh
cambiums
carboxyl
jambiyah
Barbizon
barchane
calceate
fasciate
Nanchang
catch-all
lay claim
Marciano
bacchant
bar chart
farcy-bud
cascabel
matchbox
patch box
saucebox
watchbox
fascicle
farcical
watch cap
saccadic
sarcodic
barcoded
watchdog
Fancy Dan
Sarcodes
marchesa
calcrete
marchese
pasch-egg
marchesi
parchesi
lay clerk
pancheon
manchego
ranchero
Gaucher's
pancreas
sauciest
war chest
hatchery
hatchety
patchery
calcific
fanciful
watchful
catchfly
lancegay
catch him
bacchiac
man-child
cancrine
narceine
war crime
batching
catching
fancying
Fasching
hatching
matching
patching
ranching
talcking
watching
dabchick
✧**bacchian**
falchion
fauchion
panchion
sanction
bacchius
patchily
sanctify
sanctity
carcajou
latchkey
watch key
marcella
cancelli
saeculum
vasculum
parcel up
calcular
saccular
vascular
calculus
saccules
sacculus
lancelet
Lancelot
rascally
fancy man
marchman
ranchman
watchman
sarcomas
calcanea
garcinia
vaccinia
nascence
calcanei
vaccinal
mancando
falconer
larcener
parcener
Maecenas
balconet
carcanet
falconet
sarcenet
sarconet
falconry
nascency
fasciola
cancroid
war cloud
fasciole
Halcyone
parclose
pad-cloth
waxcloth
tau cross
catch out
watch out
watch-out
manciple
saucepan
calcspar
catch-pit
calcaria
Sancerre
carceral
caschrom
mascaron
baccarat
Fascista
rascasse
saucisse
Fascisti
narcissi
Fascismo
✧**fascists**
mancuses
narcoses
narcosis
Calcutta
pancetta
calcitic
narcotic
falcated
lanceted
dancette
dancetté
caecitis
dancetty
calc-tufa
farceuse
calc-tuff
Taichung
lawcourt
pay court
hatchway
handmaid
hard card
landward
yardland
yardwand
baldpate
baud rate
cardcase
card game
handmade
hardbake
hard case
hardface
hardware
laid bare
landrace
maid-pale
mandrake
yard sale
hard cash
sand bath
aardvark
hardback
hardhack
hardtack
laid-back
land bank
landmark
sandbank
sand-lark
band-call
handball
handrail
hardball
landfall
land-haul
landrail
sand wasp
waldrapp
candy-ass
land laws
landmass

Words marked ✧ can also be spelled with one or more capital letters

handcart
handfast
sand-cast
sand-dart
bandeaux
landlady
laudable
mandible
laudably
cardecue
caudicle
raddocke
Sadducee
handicap
panda car
caudices
Pandects
hard edge
lah-di-dah
candidal
candidly
gaudy-day
bald-head
hand-held
handheld
hardhead
land-herd
sand leek
handbell
hard sell
bad dream
daydream
hardbeam
hand-sewn
hard-fern
Mandaean
San Diego
saddle up
sandheap
sand-peep
Landseer
Landwehr
baldness
handless
hardness
landless
maidless
paddlers
wardress
handiest
hard left
randiest
tardiest
saddlery
cardigan
hay-de-guy
sandshoe
dandy-hen
bardship
hardship
land-ship
wardship
Kandahar
landwind
yardbird
card file
hand line
hard line
hardline
hard time
land-line
landmine
landside
sand-like
sand pipe
dandriff
bandying
bardling
daidling
handling
Maudling
paddling
sandling
waddling
bandfish
dandyish
land-fish
✧sandwich
sandyish
baldrick
baudrick
hand-pick
hard disk
handbill
hand-mill
landfill
land girl
mandrill
sandhill
dandyism
Gandhism
Mahdiism
Mazdaism
Mazdeism
Paddyism
Gandhian
tawdrier
Gandhist
handlist
Mahdiist
Mazdaist
tawdrily
vandyked
zaddikim
baudekin
landskip
Baedeker
sand flea
daedalic
Vandalic
hard-a-lee
sardelle
sand-flag
Bardolph
Habdalah
Havdalah
Randolph
✧magdalen
mandolin
caudillo
gardyloo
handclap
landslip
candelas
Daedalus
pardalis
bandelet
sand blow
caudally
handplay
Mandalay
pandemia
pandemic
Landsmål
cardamom
cardamum
bandsman
bandyman
candyman
cardamon
handyman
landsman
mal de mer
mandamus
randomly
bandanna
✧gardenia
Sardinia
sardonic
hardened
fan dance
lap dance
pardon me
tap-dance
war dance
✧cardinal
eau de Nil
labdanum
laudanum
fandango
Mandingo
gardener
hardener
pardoner
Pandanus
sardines
hand-knit
handknit
sardonyx
maidenly
wardenry
mandioca
cardioid
handhold
hardwood
landlord
maidhood
card-vote
handsome
hard core
hard-core
sand mole
sand sole
wardmote
wardrobe
aardwolf
hands off
hands-off
tandoori
handbook
handwork
hard rock
laid work
hard coal
land-roll
hand-loom
landform
sandworm
wardroom
bawd-born
hand down
hand-horn
waldhorn
wardcorn
hard soap
land-poor
✧baudrons
eardrops
bald-coot
hand-post
sandwort
hard copy
hard-copy
caldaria
mandorla
land crab
P A M Dirac
sandarac
laddered
wandered
banderol
falderal
fal de rol
✧mandarin
wanderoo
handgrip
sand trap
larderer
✧wanderer
landdros
Pandarus
land-army
panderly
Banda Sea
sawdusty
faldetta
caudated
banditti
bandster
mandator
sand-star
carditis
hard at it
banditry
sand-dune
dandruff
handcuff
hard luck
Baudouin
sandpump
handfuls
eau de vie
hand over
handover
sandiver
Maldives
pandowdy
caudexes
Kalevala
Lake Tana
baseband
baselard
care card
face card
✧lakeland
racecard
saleyard
savegard
waveband
bakeware
base rate
caretake
careware
casemate
catenane
catenate
date rape
lacerate
latewake
macerate
makebate
namesake
nametape
paleface
racemate
rape cake
take care
tapenade
waterage
Danelagh
racepath
bareback
baresark
cakewalk
face mask
face pack
have back
lacebark
take back
baseball
game ball
game call
hate mail
make sail
race-ball
date palm
base pair
game laws
Rabelais
Cape cart
jazerant
lacerant
name part
take part
catenary
water boa
make a bed
naked bed
water bed
dateable
hateable
Lake Abbé
makeable
nameable
rateable
saleable
takeable
tameable
tapeable
wadeable
water bag
water bug
water bus
take a bow
water box
paperboy
rateably
saleably
Valencia
cadenced
face-ache
tape echo
water cow
Kate Adie
water dog
babeldom
calendar
calender
kalendar
lavender
taberdar
take odds
Baker day
calendry
paper-day
danegeld
gapeseed
pale-dead
rapeseed
take heed
waxed end
naked eye
same here
lace-leaf
tape deck
farewell
harebell
rakehell
cameleon
gate-vein
male-fern
Pareoean
paderero
paterero
bateleur
cameleer
Cape Fear
cave-bear
hare's-ear
bareness
baseless
baseness
bateless
careless
materess
dateless
easeless
faceless
fadeless
fameless
gameness
gateless
haleness
hateless
lameness
lateness
makeless
maleness
maneless
mateless
nameless
paleness
rareness
safeness
sageness
sameness
saneness
sateless
tameless
tameness
tapeless
vaneless
wageless
wakeless
wareless
waveless
bakemeat
basement
batement
casement
danegelt
easement
fakement
gazement
haterent
lavement
mazement
pavement
safe seat
care a fig
have a fit
James Fox
water fly
saw-edged
water god
parergon
water gun
Lavengro
Taleggio
water gap
oak egger
water gas
Lake Chad
catechol
Dagenham
catechin
hazel hen
waterhen
mageship
mateship
take ship
canephor
case-shot
same that
Take That
game show
Katerina
Lake Biwa
cage-bird
game bird
rare bird
rarefied
tape-tied
Bakelite®
bale-fire
baregine
baseline
cameline
capeline
date line
dateline
facetiae
face time
galenite
gate-fine
lakeside
laterite
Madeline
maderise
maderize
made wine
make like
make time
malefice
palewise
racemise
racemize

rare-ripe
sagenite
take fire
take five
take rise
tapelike
tapeline
tax exile
Vaseline®
wakerife
water ice
wavelike
base ring
cageling
catering
Havering
lacewing
layering
make wing
papering
ravening
salering
take wing
tapering
valeting
wakening
watering
wavering
babelish
camelish
cavefish
game fish
hamewith
made dish
waterish
✧**maverick**
take silk
cane-mill
material
materiel
matériel
Babeeism
babelism
Galenism
racemism
Jamesian
Naperian
Sahelian
Salesian
✧valerian
gaselier
Galerius
facelift
Galenist
maledict
race riot
Lake Kivu
Have Pity!
take pity
water-jet
kabeljou
capeskin
water key
camellia
labelled
Lake Bled
lapelled
panelled
ravelled
lamellae
patellae

saxe blue
wage plug
waterlog
date plum
labellum
sacellum
game plan
Waterloo
make a lip
tape slap
wage slip
gabeller
labeller
lamellar
patellar
patellas
satelles
capellet
water lot
Bareilly
gameplay
make play
Waverley
dalesman
dayes-man
gavelman
salesman
talesman
waterman
caverned
cayenned
maternal
paternal
lace into
wade into
taverner
base unit
Cabernet
hazelnut
Max Ernst
wale knot
base-load
cameloid
cane-toad
case-load
catenoid
galenoid
gatefold
harewood
late wood
made road
make bold
make good
pagehood
take hold
barebone
cake hole
dane-hole
gamesome
have done
have to be
matelote
racemose
take note
sawed-off
taper off
bale-dock
cagework
capework
Cape York
casebook

casework
gamecock
gavelock
havelock
laverock
sage cock
wage work
Yale lock
garefowl
case-worm
gapeworm
saleroom
tapeworm
waveform
baseborn
base coin
Cameroon
Cape Horn
Cape Town
careworn
face down
fade down
fade-down
make down
pare down
take down
take-down
wave down
kakemono
Lake Como
tape loop
café noir
racegoer
gazeboes
have-nots
ravenous
waverous
banewort
bareboat
barefoot
Danewort
gatepost
hanepoot
hare-foot
lace-boot
ravel out
take root
category
laser pen
panel pin
taper pin
have a pop
take a pop
water pot
waterpox
Palenque
Balearic
carefree
date tree
Lake Erie
water rug
water ram
name-drop
take arms
water rat
Zane Grey
vanessid
water-ski
cavesson
Ramesses
panel saw

balestra
caper-tea
palestra
maieutic
majestic
galeated
gazetted
lamented
talented
patentee
parental
ramentum
water tap
gamester
man-eater
patentor
mazel tov
mazeltov
sales tax
latently
patently
tapestry
wage fund
make sure
malemute
Mameluke
tape-lure
Babe Ruth
Kate Bush
lame duck
palebuck
ramequin
mameluco
base jump
panel van
make over
makeover
maneuver
rave over
take over
takeover
fade-away
make away
take away
takeaway
waterway
pale-eyed
Jane Eyre
Lake Eyre
water yam
make eyes
panegyry
saufgard
half-face
halfpace
saw frame
half-calf
halfback
half mark
gaff sail
half-ball
taffrail
half mast
half-mast
half a bar
fat-faced
daffodil
canfield
Garfield
gasfield
half-dead

hayfield
jalfrezi
halfbeak
half-term
waffle on
half-year
calfless
naffness
half-text
cat-fight
caffeine
calf-time
half-life
half-pike
half-pipe
half-size
half-tide
half-time
waiflike
baffling
halfling
maffling
waffling
bad faith
calflick
caffeism
halflins
half-pint
half-tint
calfskin
farfalla
farfalle
half-blue
matfelon
lawfully
manfully
half anna
half-inch
hawfinch
calf-love
half-done
half-hose
half-note
half-sole
half-tone
half loaf
half-loaf
half-cock
half-moon
half-door
half-hour
half-boot
saffrony
gas-fired
half-bred
far-forth
tafferel
fanfaron
warfarin
warfarer
wayfarer
car ferry
half step
taffetas
far-flung
Dan Fouts
half-butt
hay fever
kaffiyeh
gangland
hatguard

rat-guard
vanguard
langrage
language
margrave
langlauf
bar graph
hang back
bang-tail
hangnail
Sangraal
Sangrail
malgrado
Sangrado
Gang Days
matgrass
oat grass
sawgrass
hangable
tangible
mangabey
tangibly
Haggadic
Haggadah
jaggedly
raggedly
bargeese
cargeese
gangrene
Sangreal
sap-green
vargueño
fangless
pangless
barghest
hangnest
rangiest
tangiest
laughful
Langshan
Tangshan
Hangzhou
hangbird
hang fire
hangfire
narghile
sanguine
dangling
gaggling
gangling
jangling
laughing
tangling
tangoing
wangling
way-going
Dalglish
languish
gang mill
ganglion
gangliar
sanglier
tangoist
narghily
sanguify
gang plug
nargileh
pangolin
bargello
tangelos
Caughley

nargilly
pangamic
Targumic
bargeman
gangsman
war-gamer
manganic
margined
Wanganui
mangonel
marginal
Manganin®
hang onto
✧**waggoner**
daggings
hangings
garganey
tangency
bargoose
cargoose
gas-globe
mangrove
waygoose
laugh off
rap group
bang goes
langspel
margaric
sangaree
hanger-on
margarin
kangaroo
Margaret
badgerly
largesse
sargasso
pargeted
targeted
targa top
bangster
daughter
gangster
laughter
pargeter
gadgetry
pang-full
hang over
hangover
lawgiver
gargoyle
lang syne
cash card
washland
pathname
wash sale
MacHeath
Naphtali
cashback
hashmark
washball
cashable
oathable
warhable
washable
Wahhabis
bad habit
cachucha
cathedra
cathodic
cathodal
washed-up

Words marked ✧ can also be spelled with one or more capital letters

rachides
raphides
Bagheera
cashmere
hasheesh
cash desk
wash well
Kathleen
Tashtego
bashless
cashless
nathless
pathless
rashness
Tashkent
Panhagia
pathogen
kachahri
naphthol
pashmina
lathlike
rathripe
washwipe
yachting
Kashmiri
bathmism
taghairm
Cathaian
wash-dirt
Mathilda
parhelia
rachilla
Valhalla
Walhalla
✧catholic
Gadhelic
pachalic
parhelic
pashalik
Van Halen
bachelor
cachalot
cacholot
cash flow
sachemic
Baphomet
bauhinia
raphania
tachinid
pachinko
lashings
Raphanus
Sathanas
washings
sash cord
bathrobe
mashloch
cash-book
washbowl
bathroom
washroom
cash down
Pakhtoon
wash down
fashions
fashious
sash bolt
cachepot
bathorse
pad-horse
sawhorse
warhorse
Mathurin
vacherin
cash crop
gatherer
lathyrus
Bathurst
fatherly
cathisma
tachisme
tachiste
machismo
Lachesis
mathesis
rachises
bathetic
Japhetic
pathetic
rachitic
catheter
cathetus
rachitis
Daihatsu®
bathcube
cathouse
madhouse
taphouse
✧kashruth
man-hours
Pakhtuns
Pashtuns
tax haven
wash away
wash-away
cachexia
cathexes
cathexis
Cathayan
calisaya
marinara
Camisard
radicand
badinage
camisade
capitate
carinate
cavitate
fatigate
kamikaze
Karitane
laminate
lapidate
Latinate
marinade
marinate
maritage
navigate
paginate
palisade
radicate
saginate
salivate
sanitate
vaginate
validate
Varidase®
calipash
capitani
hari-kari
mahi-mahi
taxi rank
mani wall
capitayn
camisado
capitano
palisado
habitans
harigals
habitant
latitant
radicant
vaginant
janizary
laminary
lapidary
salivary
sanitary
satiable
variable
cabin-boy
panic-buy
variably
mariachi
maniacal
cariacou
havildar
zamindar
samizdat
variedly
marinera
saliceta
Balinese
casimere
magic eye
variceal
Galilean
caginess
calipers
easiness
gaminess
haziness
laciness
laziness
matiness
maziness
raciness
wariness
waviness
waxiness
zaniness
Kabinett
manifest
navicert
wariment
facilely
natively
basinful
radio fix
Faringee
Maxim-gun
daring-do
malinger
Salinger
caringly
daringly
gapingly
Haringey
ragingly
ravingly
savingly
takingly
famished
Lapithae
Manichee
Pasiphae
padishah
caliphal
radio ham
parishen
Salishan
papisher
ravisher
vanisher
Laoighis
garishly
lavishly
oafishly
rakishly
basilica
cavitied
ladified
ramified
ratified
salified
Catiline
kalinite
laciniae
Latinise
Latinize
maritime
maximise
maximize
Nazirite
salicine
sanidine
sanitise
sanitize
satirise
satirize
vaticide
basilisk
basidial
familial
basidium
fakirism
✧familism
Hasidism
Latinism
Marinism
nativism
pacifism
Basilian
Cabirian
Galician
magician
Maximian
Namibian
Parisian
pavilion
Tahitian
Tamilian
familiar
gasifier
pacifier
ratifier
canities
papilios
Ramilies
Familist
had-I-wist
Hasidist
Latinist
Marinist
maximist
nativist
pacifist
satirist
basicity
calidity
caninity
facility
lability
Ladinity
lapidify
Latinity
✧nativity
rabidity
rapidity
salinity
sapidity
vagility
validity
vapidity
magicked
panicked
Daniella
radialia
Cadillac®
cavilled
panicled
Danielle
mamillae
maxillae
papillae
Ramillie
panislam
carillon
papillon
vanillin
bacillar
caviller
mamillar
papillar
variolar
✧bacillus
Salic law
facially
labially
racially
radially
✧kakiemon
talisman
hacienda
Panionic
talionic
gabioned
patience
radiance
salience
sapience
valiance
variance
✧national
rational
maligner
malignly
radiancy
saliency
valiancy
Manitoba
mariposa
manifold
marigold
tapiroid
baritone
camisole
farinose
halicore
halimote
laminose
palinode
varicose
yakitori
gasiform
Janiform
maniform
napiform
natiform
paliform
ramiform
raniform
variform
vasiform
cavicorn
naricorn
makimono
yakimono
calicoes
caribous
halitous
Califont®
palimony
palinody
Vanitory®
vanitory
calibred
caviarie
taxiarch
marigram
variorum
janitrix
tap issue
Taliesin
radiuses
Jacintha
papistic
sadistic
Taoistic
radiated
Jacinthe
Labiatae
parietal
sagittal
varietal
Calixtin
Hamilton
Pakistan
sapi-utan
banister
canister
ganister
magister
radiator
varistor
Calixtus
✧haliotis
papistry
tanistry
babirusa
Caligula
Canicula
capitula
Kaliyuga
navicula
vaginula
fatigued
habitude
latitude
manicure
radicule
vaginule
habitual
taciturn
fatigues
maximums
Wahiguru
carjacou
banjoist
lap joint
mah-jongg
Marjorie
marjoram
zanjeros
backband
backhand
backland
backward
backyard
bank card
lackland
parkland
parkward
back-date
back lane
bank rate
Jack Cade
sack race
backlash
backwash
backpack
back talk
hark back
hark-back
talk back
talkback
backfall
rack rail
talk tall
walk tall
tank farm
bank barn
hacksawn
back-hair
back pass
darkmans
backcast
jack easy
bankable
sackable
talkable
walkable
Hawke Bay
backache
back edge
tacked-on
tanked up
lackaday
markedly
backveld
hawkweed
tack-weld
back-heel
hawkbell
jack bean
backless
barkless

dankness
darkness
lankness
nankeens
rankness
sackless
saikless
tankless
backbeat
back rest
dark meat
mankiest
mawkiest
rack-rent
tackiest
talkfest
packaged
packager
Dark Ages
talk shop
backchat
bank shot
talk show
talkshow
backbite
backfile
backfire
backside
back time
balkline
hawklike
hay knife
jack pine
mark time
Parklife
parklike
sacklike
talktime
waukrife
darkling
tackling
bank-high
jackfish
jack-high
backfill
back-lill
bank-bill
walk-mill
walkmill
waukmill
bank giro
backlift
back-lilt
backlist
jack plug
backflip
banksman
marksman
tacksman
Häkkinen
back onto
hack into
jack into
talk into
walk into
markings
mackinaw
back-comb
backbond
back-load
backword
Mark Todd
pack-load
backbone
back-rope
banknote
darksome
lack-love
packfong
hawk moth
backwork
bank book
hackwork
rackwork
taskwork
bankroll
Jack-fool
back room
backroom
darkroom
tack room
back down
backdown
bank down
bank loan
mark down
mark-down
talk down
back door
backdoor
backmost
hackbolt
jackboot
backspin
larkspur
cankered
jack-tree
sack tree
Valkyrie
Walkyrie
mackerel
walker-on
jackaroo
jackeroo
backdrop
tank trap
bankerly
jacketed
hackette
pack it in
backstop
pack it up
dark star
marketer
racketer
basketry
racketry
packmule
sackfuls
tankfuls
bankrupt
talk over
walk over
walkover
hark away
walk away
walk-away
walk awry
hawk-eyed
Macleaya
fahlband
gaillard
galliard
halliard
kailyard
palliard
railcard
sail-yard
tailband
ball game
fail safe
fail-safe
malleate
palliate
tailgate
tail male
tailrace
talliate
vaultage
wall game
wayleave
Earl Haig
kaoliang
caillach
Paul Nash
Cagliari
ball park
ballpark
call back
call-back
fall back
fall-back
hallmark
mailsack
tailback
wall walk
pall-mall
Galliano
Galliano®
gall wasp
tail lamp
Karl Baer
galleass
galliass
wall bars
wall pass
jailbait
mail-cart
fabliaux
Karl Marx
tableaux
✧hail Mary
gallabea
gallabia
Karlsbad
bailable
fallible
mailable
sailable
fallibly
Table Bay
caulicle
Gallican
mallecho
cable-car
ballocks
halluces
table-cut
garlicky
palladia
palladic
Rallidae
balladin
Palladio
balled-up
Ballades
balladry
pallidly
gable end
nail-head
railhead
✧wallsend
banlieue
eagle eye
Paul Berg
carl-hemp
tailleur
gall-less
nailless
railless
sailless
tailless
tallness
wall-less
bailment
earliest
manliest
wall newt
raillery
Karl Benz
faultful
ladleful
tableful
lallygag
l'allegro
daylight
fanlight
gaslight
wax light
tally-ho'd
faulchin
ballyhoo
tall ship
tally-hos
hailshot
mailshot
call-bird
gaolbird
jailbird
tail wind
calltime
fall line
nail file
tail-like
tailpipe
wall tile
caulking
dallying
rallying
sallying
tallying
vaulting
fallfish
sailfish
wallfish
ball-girl
ball mill
call-girl
Gaullism
call sign
Harleian
Gaultier
Gaullist
rallyist
faultily
haploidy
tabloidy
tailskid
mail-clad
Paul Klee
Rawlplug®
hallaloo
fall flat
ballclay
gallumph
bailsman
Lac Léman
Paul's-man
sally-man
tallyman
table mat
vallonia
kaolinic
parlance
bar lunch
parlando
Faulkner
badlands
garlands
railings
tail ends
tailings
ballonet
wall knot
wall unit
mail bomb
nail bomb
bailbond
Hailwood
railroad
✧calliope
call-note
Earl Howe
nail-hole
tail rope
badly off
Carl Cori
taglioni
bail-dock
ballcock
eagle-owl
ballroom
Karl Böhm
mailroom
sailroom
tail boom
ball-gown
call down
call-loan
nail down
hall-door
wall moss
hall-moot
ladle out
mail-boat
sailboat
sail loft
tail coat
wallwort
tall copy
call upon
fall upon
tailspin
calliper
galloper
walloper
gallipot
galleria
caller ID
tailored
hall tree
Mallarmé
wall tree
Carl Orff
ballyrag
mail-drag
mailgram
cauldron
pauldron
taileron
wallaroo
fall-trap
mail drop
eagle-ray
Earl Grey
sailorly
ballista
Carlisle
galluses
Wallasey
Valletta
balletic
balloted
galleted
palleted
ballotee
Paulette
raclette
law Latin
tarlatan
varletto
table top
talliths
harlotry
varletry
Carl Jung
halloumi
gall duct
kail-runt
day-level
call over
fall over
jaw lever
gallivat
hallowed
wallowed
wallower
Mawlawis
cableway
call away
fall away
Galloway
tail away
walleyed
fail-dyke
waylayer
Paolozzi
farm hand
farmyard
barm cake
Naum Gabo
farmable
caimacam
naumachy
gammadia
Talmudic
warmed-up
Palme d'Or
farm team
calmness
gaumless
harmless
warmness
mammifer
earmuffs
lammiger
Taj Mahal
Parma ham
MacMahon
palmchat
dalmahoy
palm wine
wagmoire
kaimakam
haymaker
lawmaker
way-maker
Mammalia
mammilla
yarmulka
yarmulke
harmalin
palm-play
Mamma Mia
Mamma Mia!
tagmemic
sarmenta
Tasmania
daemonic
daimonic
harmonic
salmonid
farm into
gammoner
salmonet
rag-money
calm down
farm-toun
warm down
warm-down
warm boot
warm-boot
palmiped
qaimaqam
Mad Maria
palm tree
balmoral
hammer in
Palmerin
hammerer
gamma ray
rap music
Parmesan
marmoset
harmosty
Dalmatia
gammatia
kaumatua
Sarmatia
dalmatic
haematic
magmatic
Sarmatic
Halmstad
palmated
palmette
haematin

palmitin
palmetto
gas meter
gas-motor
mammetry
maumetry
mawmetry
razmataz
fat mouse
badmouth
Falmouth
panmixia
panmixis
Jan Mayen
barnyard
dawn raid
gainsaid
mainland
mainyard
rainband
raindate
taeniate
vauntage
manna-ash
rainwash
sannyasi
mainsail
rainfall
maintain
gainsays
fainéant
mainmast
balneary
cannabic
damnable
gainable
tannable
✧wannabee
cannibal
cannabin
Barnabas
cannabis
paintbox
damnably
Garnacha
barnacle
pannicle
wainscot
maenadic
saintdom
manna-dew
main-deck
nainsell
Mannheim
rainwear
fainness
gainless
painless
rainless
saintess
vainness
darndest
rainiest
vauntery
magnific
vauntful
carnifex
nannygai
pawnshop
launcher
rainbird
gain time
jaundice
main line
mainline
daunting
fainting
haunting
jaunting
nannying
painting
taunting
vauncing
vaunting
faintish
nannyish
saintish
Sam Neill
saintism
Laingian
daintily
jauntily
paint job
Mauna Kea
pannikel
cannikin
mannikin
pannikin
larnakes
magnolia
Mauna Loa
cannulae
cannular
cannulas
gauntlet
Barnsley
carnally
tarnally
paynimry
earnings
fannings
gainings
cannonry
taenioid
nainsook
tawny owl
mainboom
sainfoin
barn door
maindoor
carneous
raincoat
rainbowy
lagnappe
fawn upon
gain upon
banner ad
bannered
mannered
gauntree
rain tree
main drag
Far North
Ragnarok
Ragnarök
bannerol
raindrop
Barnard's
banneret
lanneret
mannerly
magnesia
vainesse
farnesol
magnetic
mannitol
magneton
magnetar
fainites
magnetos
samnitis
gannetry
mainstay
carnauba
painture
tainture
Raynaud's
carnival
Hannover
warn away
yarn-dyed
caponata
panorama
sayonara
Vadodara
✧savoyard
baronage
cabotage
Hakodate
malonate
sabotage
wagonage
Zakopane
Takoradi
Yanomami
sago palm
marocain
gado-gado
mako-mako
Pago Pago
Yanomamo
mahogany
wagon bed
mason bee
wagon box
Daboecia
babouche
barouche
farouche
pabouche
Majorcan
baroccos
razor cut
razor-cut
caboodle
canoodle
Ganoidei
Saxondom
Bay of Dew
Labor Day
carotene
Gabonese
gasogene
gasolene
gazogene
La Bohème
Masorete
Taxotere®
haroseth
Masoreth
nanotech
Carolean
Jacobean
✧napoleon
caboceer
saboteur
baroness
bayonets
canoness
mayoress
cajolery
barometz
wagonful
man of God
Laforgue
baton gun
taboggan
Calor Gas®
caboched
caboshed
pahoehoe
basophil
cabochon
parochin
Basothos
Zalophus
capoeira
Carolina
japonica
maiolica
majolica
Salonica
Salonika
canopied
parodied
camomile
canonise
canonize
caponise
caponize
Caroline
DA-Notice
datolite
favorite
gasoline
Jacobite
jarosite
Katowice
lanoline
Majorite
Maronite
Masonite®
pavonine
saponite
Saxonise
saxonite
Saxonize
Taborite
taconite
valorise
valorize
vaporise
vaporize
canoeing
fagoting
tabooing
Pasolini
baronial
cacomixl
manorial
rasorial
laconism
Majorism
Saxonism
Taxodium
Baconian
Bajocian
Catonian
Favonian
Jacobian
Laconian
Maeonian
Maronian
pavonian
Racovian
✧salopian
Saxonian
palomino
caponier
gasolier
sabotier
calorist
canoeist
canonist
parodist
Saxonist
majority
saponify
✧mason jar
havocked
kalookie
major key
carolled
masoolah
caroller
Parolles
wagon-lit
canon law
man of law
paroemia
Calormen
lagoonal
marooner
ratooner
jato unit
Gaborone
naloxone
malodour
canorous
saporous
savorous
valorous
vaporous
batology
cacodoxy
cacology
Mayology
taxonomy
vagotomy
magot-pie
favoured
laboured
savoured
vapoured
barogram
tabourin
favourer
labourer
vapourer
tabouret
savourly
parousia
jalousie
Larousse
carousal
✧carousel
damoisel
man of sin
carouser
galowses
famously
panoptic
capotted
garotted
garotter
barostat
La Coruna
nanotube
maroquin
paroquet
man-of-war
calotype
kalotype
paroxysm
paronymy
camphane
vamplate
warplane
gas-plant
hat plant
hat-plant
wax plant
mappable
palpable
tappable
palpably
salpicon
gazpacho
Talpidae
pappadom
Sarpedon
San Pedro
camphene
earpiece
say-piece
harp seal
campness
dampness
lampreys
waspnest
samplery
campagna
zampogna
rampager
camp-shot
campfire
camphine
camphire
campsite
dauphine
samphire
sapphire
wasp-like
sampling
✧sapphism
campaign
Tarpeian
nauplius
✧sapphics
Hay Point
parpoint
sapphist
tax point
war paint
way point
gas poker
paspalum
pamphlet
rampsman
jampanee
sarpanch
harpings
raspings
rampancy
Pamplona
car phone
earphone
lamphole
pappoose
payphone
ratproof
war-proof
Haiphong
lamp-room
damp down
tamp down
lamp-hour
lamppost
bagpiper
cap-paper
rag paper
tar paper
wax paper
bagpipes
Pan-pipes
Walpurga
vampiric
rampired
camporee
rapparee
pamperer
tamperer
pamperos
Kasparov
dapperly
lampasse
campuses
carpeted
lappeted
Rasputin
camp it up
hampster
rampauge
São Paulo
camp oven
manpower
taxpayer
La Spezia
✧jacquard
Pasquale
May queen
lacqueys
marquess
basquine
marquise
vanquish
daiquiri
narquois
hairband
caproate
carriage
fair game
hair-wave
laureate
marriage
pair case
patriate

Hal Roach
Max Roach
carry-all
carryall
fair fall
hair-ball
hair-tail
hauriant
Maori bug
Patricia
capricci
barracan
barracks
barricos
Caprices
matrices
carrycot
sabre-cut
Capridae
Labridae
Oak Ridge
fairydom
Maoridom
harridan
car radio
laired up
Labrador
manrider
sacredly
fair-lead
hairbell
hair seal
barriers
fairness
hairless
haurient
✧yahrzeit
farriery
caprifig
garrigue
warragle
madrigal
warragal
warragul
warrigal
kauri gum
larrigan
tarragon
farragos
Maori hen
darraine
hairlike
hairline
pairwise
carrying
dairying
harrying
marrying
parrying
tarrying
Bahraini
fairyism
darraign
larrikin
caprylic
barrulet
fair play
RAC Rally
harrumph
haeremai
lacrimal
lacrymal
dairyman
yarraman
barranca
Tauranga
hadronic
Caprinae
Laurence
Lawrence
patronne
matronal
patronal
safronal
Saarinen
safranin
barranco
warrener
madroños
Marranos
matronly
vagrancy
warranty
Catriona
pair-bond
cabriole
capriole
carriole
carry off
marry off
hair-work
gairfowl
hairworm
nacreous
carry out
carry-out
Barr body
fair copy
macropod
pauropod
sauropod
sapropel
satrapal
sacraria
Saururae
macrural
hair grip
hairgrip
Carreras
Laurasia
madrassa
Fair Isle
Fair-Isle
lacrosse
madrasah
garrison
sarrasin
warrison
Tauruses
sacristy
cabretta
Lauretta
Mahratta
Sabratha
garreted
garroted
parroted
barrette
garrotte
Magritte
carritch
parritch
barrator
narrator
parroter
parrot it
barratry
Hanratty
parrotry
pay round
Bayreuth
carraway
narrowly
matrixes
rat-rhyme
sarrazin
rakshasa
cab-stand
ham stand
hatstand
pass band
camstane
nauseate
palstave
Ramsgate
ratsbane
rat snake
Sam Spade
Falstaff
palstaff
tau staff
haystack
pass-back
sawshark
cat's-tail
laystall
rat's-tail
pass laws
camshaft
layshaft
naissant
nauseant
lapsable
passable
passible
raisable
waist bag
False Bay
passably
passibly
Nausicaa
massacre
capsicum
Tay-Sachs
waesucks
massicot
hassocky
Hassidic
passados
lay siege
mansuete
sans gêne
ear-shell
gas shell
mass-bell
Pap smear
passless
cat's-meat
far-spent
passment
pay-sheet
rap sheet
Parsifal
pauseful
dal segno
massager
marsh-gas
sapsagos
day-sight
raise hob
false hem
Faustina
bar slide
bassline
batswing
lassoing
Ian Smith
canstick
cat-stick
malstick
mapstick
panstick
bass viol
Parsiism
✧**faustian**
✧gaussian
marshier
day shift
manshift
karstify
Baisakhi
baasskap
Marsilea
Marsilia
mausolea
tasseled
mamselle
bass clef
false leg
sassolin
capsular
Rasselas
causally
tasselly
vassalry
balsamic
marsh-man
ransomer
parsonic
Sassanid
Lausanne
raisonné
Ram Singh
Bassanio
cassinos
paisanos
bassinet
sarsenet
mansonry
massoola
basswood
password
tarsioid
camstone
capstone
gas stove
lad's love
lapstone
ragstone
camshoch
fat stock
fatstock
mass-book
passbook
tap stock
bar stool
bass horn
lasslorn
mansworn
Mass-John
mass noun
pap-spoon
pass down
ram's-horn
maestoso
caesious
mansions
nauseous
cat's-foot
marsport
passport
tarsiped
pass upon
Tarsipes
pansophy
false rib
Gaiseric
samsaric
caesurae
causerie
sanserif
Massorah
caesural
bass drum
Hans Gram
kaiserin
caesuras
maestros
Passeres
Sanscrit
Sanskrit
hausfrau
cap screw
passer-by
say sorry
cassette
falsetto
masseter
passatas
marsh tit
bass tuba
danseuse
masseuse
Far South
Jan Smuts
Passover
pass over
causeway
pass away
causeyed
naysayer
man-sized
capsizal
gastraea
Santa Ana
eastland
eastward
Carthage
castrate
fast lane
last name
rag trade
salt cake
salt lake
tartrate
xanthate
salt bath
canthari
castrati
Haft Wadi
pastrami
cast back
fastback
fast-talk
cant-rail
fastball
way train
castrato
Santiago
last-gasp
daft days
Gasthaus
manteaus
manteaux
taste bud
vartabed
pantable
partible
tastable
wastable
earth-bag
waste bin
wait-a-bit
✧**canticle**
particle
pastiche
pasticci
nautical
tactical
canticum
canticos
masticot
canticoy
salty dog
mastodon
tarted-up
day-to-day
cattleya
masthead
wartweed
xanthene
Galtieri
Hartnell
mast cell
paste-eel
✧**pantheon**
xanthein
last heir
daftness
fastness
fattrels
gastness
hartbees
mastless
Matthews
mattress
partners
pattress
saltless
saltness
tactless
tartness
tautness
vastness
waitress
wartless
wastness
farthest
maltreat
rattiest
tartiest
tastiest
tattiest
battle ax
battle-ax
Bartlemy
lactific
earth-fed
pantofle
✧tartuffe
✧**faithful**
tasteful
wasteful
tartufos
Mantegna
fantigue
martagon
Rattigan
gas-tight
earth-hog
East Side
gantline
ianthine
part-time
rattline
salt-mine
wartlike
wastrife
xanthine
car-thief
bantling
eastling
farthing
Lagthing
mantling
naething
rattling
sautéing
tattling
waltzing
wattling
baitfish
saltfish
hat trick
paitrick
salt lick
malt-mill
wanthill
war trial
Ba'athism
Baathism
casteism
partyism
Tantrism
Xanthium
Bactrian
malt-kiln
Parthian
Sartrian
Xanthian
rattlier
Castries
eastlins
Matthias
Ba'athist
Baathist
Tantrist

wait list
wait-list
earthily
paltrily
Lattakia
partaken
lantskip
partaker
kantikoy
battalia
mantilla
dactylic
✧tantalic
pantiled
✧**bastille**
pastille
salt plug
nastalik
tantalum
pantalon
santalin
martello
nasta'liq
batteler
dactylar
daytaler
Wat Tyler
cattalos
Dactylis
nautilus
naythles
✧tantalus
mantelet
salt flat
wastelot
earthman
man to man
party man
raftsman
✧rastaman
ragtimer
tautomer
Gay Times
caatinga
Castanea
galtonia
cantoned
pattened
tartaned
laitance
pastance
cantonal
tautonym
santonin
saltando
fastener
fattener
hastener
✧**hastings**
saw-tones
castanet
earth-nut
Martenot
martinet
tartanry
wantonly
xanthoma
cartload
cartroad
Dartford
fast food
Hartford
last word
tattooed
gantlope
raft-rope
salt-cote
salt dome
Zantiote
malt loaf
part-song
dart-moth
fantoosh
gag-tooth
jaw-tooth
sawtooth
canthook
partwork
maltworm
cast down
hawthorn
lanthorn
salt down
want down
tattooer
watt-hour
caltrops
captious
cast lots
cautious
dartrous
factious
fastuous
hautbois
lacteous
xanthous
eastmost
faltboat
last post
raft-port
salt-foot
saltwort
wartwort
earth-pea
Xantippe
Zantippe
pattypan
wait upon
hag-taper
bacteria
Cantoria
Hatteria
martyria
Santeria
bacteric
✧tartaric
battered
gaitered
nattered
raftered
raptured
tattered
batterie
parterre
Sauterne
Tartarie
Haftorah
pastoral
pastural
Santarém
cast iron
cast-iron
factor in
hapteron
calthrop
banterer
barterer
batterer
capturer
natterer
palterer
patterer
cantoris
halteres
Jam tarts
Raptores
Tartarus
master it
bastardy
dastardy
easterly
latterly
✧manta ray
masterly
pastorly
✧tartarly
Earthsea
fantasia
mantissa
bartisan
partisan
Baptists
cactuses
Hattusas
mantises
saltuses
hastated
factotum
maltster
Partitur
mastitis
partitas
gastrula
sastruga
Xanthura
zastruga
cartouch
saltbush
sastrugi
zastrugi
salt-junk
fauteuil
gastfull
wastfull
cartfuls
malt-dust
pantsuit
tastevin
earthwax
cast away
castaway
salt away
bartizan
partizan
sapucaia
carucage
carucate
hamulate
jaculate
lacunate
maculate
maturate
radulate
saturate
tabulate
vapulate
lacunars
saturant
lacunary
salutary
valuable
raw umber
valuably
caruncle
capuccio
faburden
gazunder
lay under
talukdar
Saturday
caducean
caduceus
maturely
babushka
✧**capuchin**
La Guaira
baculine
baculite
daturine
fabulise
fabulize
lazulite
lazurite
matutine
paludine
sabuline
manuring
naturing
manurial
masurium
naturism
paludism
Laputian
pagurian
fabulist
naturist
caducity
maturity
Hanukkah
vacuolar
casually
casualty
manually
Saturnia
saturnic
laburnum
lacunose
maculose
paludose
papulose
ramulose
sabulose
Januform
caducous
fabulous
pabulous
paludous
papulous
patulous
ramulous
sabulous
kalumpit
haruspex
manubria
taqueria
saburral
calutron
saguaros
vaqueros
paduasoy
baguette
maquette
haqueton
baluster
valuator
Sarum use
salvable
lay vicar
Salvador
Calvados
salvific
aasvogel
salvager
Las Vegas
mauvaise
mauveine
navvying
par value
valvulae
Malvolio
valvular
valvules
valvelet
Salvinia
galvanic
halve-net
valve off
carve out
calvaria
calvered
A Alvarez
malvasia
malvesie
larvated
fauvette
war-weary
war widow
cam-wheel
fan wheel
ragwheel
man-weeks
earwiggy
tarwhine
batwoman
day-woman
laywoman
madwoman
rag-woman
war whoop
✧**tamworth**
wanworth
catworks
gasworks
waxworks
wanwordy
lay waste
radwaste
waywiser
gas-water
tap water
tar water
faux-naïf
Vauxhall®
banxring
bauxitic
capybara
Maryland
navy yard
baby face
easy-care
easy game
Mary Jane
baby talk
easy mark
lazy jack
Davy lamp
man-years
Mary Daly
Wavy Navy
Caryocar
Mary Eddy
Mary Read
Ganymede
baby beef
Baby Bell
lady fern
lady-help
cagyness
gamyness
satyress
easy meat
laryngal
larynges
ladyship
ladybird
ladyfied
calycine
ladylike
satyrisk
navy list
calycled
baby blue
navy blue
lady's man
Lady Anne
Baryonyx
baby bond
babyfood
babyhood
calycoid
ladyhood
manyfold
Baby Love
barytone
lady-love
Mary Rose
baby doll
baby boom
baby corn
easy-goer
many-root
Lady Grey
lawyerly
calypsos
calyptra
kalyptra
manyatta
caryatic
caryatid
karyotin
calycule
Lady Muck
easy over
larynxes
many-eyed
Zanzibar
zarzuela
dazzling
manzello
Tanzania
calzones
canzonas
canzonet
jazz-rock
gadzooks
marzipan
mahzorim
mamzerim
Salzburg
jazz-funk
abradant
Abbaside
ablative
abrasive
abbatial
obeahism
ablation
abrasion
oblation
Abram-man
obtainer
oblatory
obscurer
abscissa
abscisse
abscisin
abacuses
Abu Dhabi
obedient
abidance
a bad turn
abnegate
Abderite
Ibsenite
Ibsenism
Abderian
Ibsenian
obtemper
obtected
absentee
objector
à bientôt
abjectly
absently
obsequie
observer
ibogaine
abdicate
obligate
obligati
obligato
abdicant
obeisant
obligant
aboideau
aboiteau
abridger
obliging
oblivion
obsidian
abricock
ebriated
absinthe
obliquid
abampere
abomasal
abomasum

abomasus
T-bandage
abundant
Abu Nidal
ébéniste
ob and sol
ab initio
ebenezer
abrogate
absonant
absorbed
absorber
obsolete
ebionise
Ebionite
ebionize
ebionism
abnormal
abhorred
✧abhorrer
✧absolute
obvolute
absolver
ubiquity
mbaqanga
aberrate
aberrant
obtruder
Aberdeen
eburnean
aborigen
aborigin
abortive
aborning
abortion
T-bar lift
a best bet
abessive
ubi supra
abuttals
abstract
obituary
abatable
obstacle
abetment
abutment
abetting
abutting
abstrict
abutilon
abat-jour
abattoir
abat-voix
absterge
a battuta
abstruse
a bit much
obstruct
obdurate
obturate
obduracy
ybounden
absurdly
abducent
obtusely
ablution
obtusity
abductee
abductor
abruptly
above all

above par
Ebbw Vale
obi-woman
abeyance
abeyancy
oceanaut
scrabbed
Scrabble®
scrabble
scramble
scratchy
scrag-end
scrape up
écraseur
scragged
scraggly
sciatica
scraping
Occamism
Accadian
occasion
Oceanian
✧oceanids
Occamist
scramjet
scrawler
scrammed
scrap-man
sciaenid
scrannel
octaroon
octapody
scrapped
scrapple
scrapper
eclampsy
ice apron
schapska
schantze
scrattle
octantal
sceattas
McCarthy
scabbard
scablike
iceblink
scybalum
ice block
scabious
scabrous
icebound
ice craft
ice cream
scuchion
acicular
acid rain
acid salt
acid jazz
acid-head
acidness
acid test
scudding
academia
academic
ice dance
acid rock
acid drop
acidosis
schemata
acierage
acierate

scienced
screw cap
screechy
screeder
sclerema
sclereid
screw eye
acoemeti
icterine
sclerite
scheming
screwing
achenial
achenium
✧ockerism
schellum
screamer
Achernar
screener
scleroma
scleroid
sclerose
ecce homo
ocherous
sclerous
acre-foot
eclectic
accepted
screw tap
screwtop
accentor
accepter
acceptor
scienter
schedule
screever
screw you
scherzos
icefield
ecofreak
scoffing
scuffler
scofflaw
scaffold
ice front
ice house
Schizaea
activate
echinate
scribble
scribbly
schiedam
accident
✧occident
actively
scriggle
achingly
scriggly
acridine
actiniae
actinide
scribing
actinism
actinium
activism
scribism
actinian
actinias
activist
acridity
activity

achillea
schiller
Achilles
W C Fields
schimmel
actioner
actinoid
echinoid
schizoid
ochidore
Echinops
schizont
acrimony
scrimped
scrimply
echiuran
scoinson
ecliptic
scripted
scrimure
achiever
Acajutla
aculeate
ocellate
scalable
eco-label
scalably
scolecid
scoleces
scolices
scilicet
schlocky
ice-ledge
occluder
scalades
scalados
scullery
ecologic
schläger
scalding
scalping
scolding
sculling
scaldini
scallion
scullion
scaldino
scalpins
scaly-leg
ice lolly
scalenus
scolioma
Acalepha
acalephe
schleppy
Scalaria
scalprum
scelerat
ocularly
ecclesia
occlusal
occlusor
sculpsit
oculated
scolytid
sculptor
Scolytus
scalawag
scamping
scumming
scampish

scomfish
scumfish
scambler
schmaltz
ecumenic
schmooze
scammony
schmoozy
scombrid
scimitar
scent bag
scent box
scene bay
schnecke
scenical
scandent
scentful
acanthin
acanthus
scanning
scenting
scandium
Scandian
scansion
scontion
scanties
scantily
scantity
economic
sceneman
scincoid
schnapps
scenario
aconitic
aconitum
acknowne
ectosarc
accolade
accorage
octonary
scrowdge
accorder
ectoderm
acrolein
echoless
ectogeny
scoopful
act of God
scroggie
scroggin
scrouger
eclogite
scooping
acrolith
actorish
acromial
acrotism
scholium
sciolism
acromion
eclosion
scholion
sciolist
schooled
scrolled
schoolie
scrounge
schooner
accounts
scoop net
Ochotona

Octopoda
ectozoic
octopoid
acrosome
ectozoan
ectozoon
octoroon
ichorous
sciolous
echogram
acrostic
accoutre
accouter
scrofula
octopush
scuppaug
ice plant
ice-plant
scuppers
ice point
scopelid
scapulae
Acapulco
scapular
scapulas
Scopelus
scaphoid
sceptred
sceptral
acerbate
acervate
ochreate
Scarface
scordato
scarabee
scirocco
acorn-cup
Scaridae
acaridan
Schröder
accredit
Scorsese
scarless
Scarlett
scarcely
scornful
scorched
scorcher
scirrhus
scurrile
scarfing
scarping
scarring
scorning
scarfish
Scorpian
✧scorpion
scurrier
Scorpios
Scorpius
acerbity
scarcity
scurvily
achromat
scarmoge
score off
acarpous
ochreous
scarious
scorious
scarf out

score out
ectropic
scarf-pin
eccrisis
actressy
eccritic
ecostate
ice skate
ice-skate
ice shelf
acescent
ice sheet
scissile
acosmism
scission
acosmist
icestone
ice storm
scissors
scissure
Scotland
ice track
Scotican
scattery
Scots fir
scutiger
scutcher
Scottice
scathing
scatting
Scottish
Scythian
scattily
Scottify
scutella
ocotillo
scuttler
scotomia
Scotsman
scotomas
acutance
scotopia
scotopic
scot-free
ecstasis
ecstatic
ecotoxic
ichthyic
acaudate
accurate
ecaudate
occupate
Schumann
occupant
accuracy
scrubbed
scrubber
scout car
scrunchy
I could go
à couvert
Schubert
McGuffin
scourger
acquight
scouther
occupied
acauline
sciurine
accusing
scouring

scouting
occupier
acquaint
scrutiny
scrupler
scruples
octuplet
scout law
actually
scrummed
sciuroid
acaulose
scrumple
scrumpox
acquired
occurred
actus rei
acquiral
accursed
à coup sûr
acoustic
occulted
accustom
actuator
occultly
scavager
scavenge
scowther
scawtite
scowling
Schwerin
ice water
ice yacht
ecdysone
scuzzbag
advanced
N'Djamena
idealess
adjacent
ideal gas
idealise
idealize
ideative
idealism
adnation
ideation
idealist
ideality
ad patres
Adiantum
a dab hand
I declare!
idocrase
educable
educible
eduction
adscript
edacious
educated
educator
edge rail
edgeways
ad verbum
addendum
edgeless
idleness
adherent
udderful
adhesive
edgewise
idée fixe

idle time
adhesion
idlehood
edgebone
edge coal
edge tool
addebted
Q D Leavis
edifying
odograph
ad-libber
edginess
additive
admiring
advising
addition
Adrianne
Adrienne
Addison's
advisory
Adriatic
addicted
admitted
Id al-Adha
Adalbert
adultery
Adelaide
bdellium
idyllian
Id al-Fitr
idyllist
odalique
adularia
ad clerum
idoliser
adulator
idolater
idolator
idolatry
idolizer
Adam's ale
Adamical
Adam Bede
a dim view
Idomeneo
oddments
Adamitic
odometer
udometer
odometry
idem quod
Edentata
aduncate
edentate
adenoids
odontist
aduncity
identify
identity
adynamia
adynamic
adenomas
odontoma
odontoid
aduncous
adenitis
ad unguem
od's nouns
✧advocate
advocaat
advocacy

idiot box
idiolect
ad hocery
admonish
idiotish
idiotism
ideology
ideogram
idiogram
addorsed
advowson
odiously
Edmonton
adroitly
advoutry
adaptive
adoptive
adaption
adoption
adequate
adequacy
adorable
adorably
I dare say
I daresay
à dessein
Odyssean
Odysseus
adessive
adespota
editable
editress
Ode to Joy
adjutage
adjutant
adjuvant
ad eundem
adducent
adjuring
ad summum
adductor
adjuster
adjustor
Eddy Shah
metadata
vena cava
mesaraic
legal aid
beta wave
De La Mare
Delaware
métayage
separate
seladang
Semarang
beta rays
megawatt
relaxant
set apart
legatary
bedabble
pedal bin
démarche
menarche
revanche
Besançon
heraldic
retarded
veranda'd
rehandle
verandah

demander
Menander
regarder
retarder
rewarder
sea adder
heraldry
De Valera
rewarewa
get ahead
Lebanese
legalese
metamere
Nepalese
HeLa cell
Serapeum
Cesarean
cetacean
fedayeen
Pegasean
bejabers
beta test
beta-test
decadent
red alert
remanent
pedately
sedately
Pelasgic
deranged
bedaggle
red algae
redargue
resalgar
seraphic
detached
seraphim
teraphim
seraphin
xeraphin
metaphor
regather
Hepatica
velamina
ceramide
déraciné
gelatine
get a life
get a line
hematite
hepatise
hepatite
hepatize
ketamine
legalise
legalize
legatine
melamine
melanite
metafile
metalize
negative
penalise
penalize
petaline
relative
sedative
sepaline
serafile
set aside
set-aside

tetanise
tetanize
velarise
velarize
debasing
defaming
delaying
derating
medaling
menacing
metaling
pedaling
relaxing
renaying
repaying
retaking
megalith
terakihi
geraniol
betacism
geranium
legalism
melanism
petalism
regalism
teratism
veganism
velarium
aeration
✧dedalian
delation
deration
gelation
legation
negation
✧pelagian
regalian
relation
sedation
venation
vexation
Zelanian
behavior
pedalier
ceramics
denarius
Gelasius
Pelagius
senarius
ceramist
legalist
medalist
metalist
regalist
denazify
femality
feracity
legality
megacity
regality
tenacity
venality
veracity
remarked
bedarken
remarker
medallic
metallic
bewailed
detailed
Heraclid

medalled
metalled
pedalled
petalled
De Gaulle
tenaille
befallen
seraglio
megaflop
petaflop
teraflop
derailer
hexaplar
pedaller
retailer
Heracles
metaplot
becalmed
demanned
detainee
relaunch
per annum
detainer
regainer
retainer
cedar-nut
pecan nut
Decapoda
hepatoma
Hexapoda
lecanora
melanoma
Metabola
metanoia
Nematoda
teratoma
hecatomb
metazoic
ceratoid
get a load
keratoid
melanoid
nematoid
petaloid
sepaloid
sesamoid
teratoid
tetanoid
keratose
let alone
let-alone
megadose
megapode
nematode
see a wolf
get along
hexafoil
metazoan
metazoon
sea acorn
belabour
melanous
pedaloes
petalous
rebatoes
sepalous
get about
megavolt
see about
set about
dekalogy

demagogy
hexapody
negatory
pedagogy
petalody
sepalody
vexatory
behappen
pétanque
remarque
gematria
hetairia
debarred
hetaerae
métairie
hetairai
decagram
hexagram
veratrum
betatron
bevatron
negatron
veratrin
repairer
hetaeras
hetairas
zelatrix
Veracruz
relapsed
relapser
xeransis
wet assay
semantra
gelastic
pedantic
semantic
Vedantic
xerantic
behatted
defatted
repartee
decanter
departer
✧levanter
megastar
recanter
recaptor
redactor
remaster
sea aster
cerastes
pedantry
secantly
tenantry
tenacula
velatura
denature
peracute
resalute
megabuck
megabyte
megadyne
terabyte
bedazzle
keyboard
lee-board
pegboard
Redbeard
seaboard
teaboard
membrane

verbiage
sea beach
jet-black
pea-brain
neoblast
sea beast
semblant
Derby dog
red biddy
bee-bread
tea bread
leg break
tea break
sea bream
herb-beer
herbless
verbless
herbaged
keybugle
kerbside
seablite
sea brief
pebbling
feeblish
red brick
redbrick
herb mill
gerbille
cembalos
herbelet
redbelly
verbally
reabsorb
let blood
new blood
pembroke
new broom
new-blown
sea boots
temblors
herbaria
membered
seaborne
new birth
berberis
Cerberus
dewberry
fen-berry
peaberry
sea-berry
teaberry
nebbishe
Nembutal®
verbatim
verboten
deuce-ace
leachate
bescrawl
pew-chair
merchant
penchant
pencraft
perceant
reactant
sea chart
seacoast
seacraft
berceaux
petchary
fencible
peccable
beach bum
beach boy
peacocky
Percidae
deicidal
leechdom
red cedar
Mercedes
Mercedes®
deucedly
tea caddy
heuchera
New Crete
bescreen
nescient
sea chest
tea chest
perchery
merciful
peaceful
beach hut
heich-how
descried
merchild
describe
descrive
perceive
reactive
zecchine
kerchief
sea cliff
fetching
leaching
letching
perching
reaching
recceing
reccying
rescuing
teaching
zecchini
pea-chick
reaction
Reichian
Teucrian
zecchino
tetchier
rescript
tetchily
Leucojum
mea culpa
teocalli
aesculin
mescalin
pencil in
percolin
Aesculus
Hercules
tercelet
Newcombe
henchman
newcomer
welcomer
Newcomes
Meccania
peacenik
medcinal
bel canto
seicento
percents
beechnut
deaconry
peccancy
seacunny
fetch off
tea cloth
beech-oil
deschool
leachour
Red Cross
fetch out
cercopid
per caput
cercaria
mercuric
red coral
geocarpy
leucosin
Mercosur
leachtub
leucitic
seecatch
Mercutio
Mercator
teuchter
berceuse
selcouth
hen-court
reoccupy
Perceval
Percival
bedcover
peccavis
dead hand
headband
headland
reed-band
reed-rand
headcase
headrace
reed-mace
seedcake
seedcase
red dwarf
headbang
feedback
headmark
seed bank
dead-fall
dead-wall
headrail
headsail
deuddarn
headlamp
dead-cart
headfast
beddable
beddy-bye
bendable
feedable
lendable
mendable
readable
sendable
vendible
weldable
readably
Teddy boy
vendibly
berdache
headache
pendicle
headachy
dead-head
deadhead
feed-head
beady eye
seed leaf
Weldmesh®
dead-deal
meddle in
seed fern
seldseen
headgear
deadness
deedless
headless
heedless
leadless
lewdness
needless
seedless
seedness
weedless
weldless
dead-beat
deadbeat
dead cert
dead heat
dead-heat
dead-meat
head rent
headrest
needment
readiest
reediest
weldment
red dagga
hey-de-guy
headship
feldsher
dead shot
headshot
rendzina
dead-wind
headwind
reed-bird
bendwise
dead-fire
deadline
dendrite
feed-line
feed-pipe
headline
head-tire
lead-line
lead time
let drive
needfire
readvise
reed pipe
seedlike
seed time
sex drive
der-doing
headring
meddling
peddling
readying
reedling
seedling
yeldring
seed-fish
herdwick
head girl
dead-lift
New Delhi
pendulum
verdelho
pendular
seed plot
feudally
hebdomad
beadsman
headsman
✧herdsman
leadsman
seedsman
✧mesdames
ready-mix
reddenda
tea dance
tendance
tendence
vendange
perdendo
read into
reddendo
deadener
new dinar
leadenly
pendency
read-only
tendency
verdancy
dead load
dead wood
dead-wood
dendroid
head cold
headword
reed-rond
send word
dead-rope
headnote
headrope
seadrome
seed-lobe
headlong
dead-lock
deadlock
dead-work
headlock
headwork
herd-book
yeldrock
bead-roll
deed poll
head-boom
headroom
dead-born
seed corn
send down
dead loss
tendrons
dead-bolt
headmost
leadwort
seed coat
tend upon
feldspar
dead spit
gendered
verdured
gendarme
lead-free
lead tree
reed-wren
renderer
tenderer
verderer
verderor
feldgrau
tenderly
geodesic
vendetta
geodetic
seedy-toe
Redditch
reed stop
lewdster
verditer
vendeuse
dead duck
reedbuck
dead-pull
feed-pump
head-butt
headhunt
readjust
sea devil
demerara
serenata
metewand
meteyard
rereward
bel étage
beverage
defecate
delegate
federate
generale
generate
hebetate
leverage
regelate
relegate
renegade
renegate
selenate
serenade
serenate
sewerage
telesale
vegelate
vegetate
venerate
ceterach
telepath
Leo Esaki
gene bank
telemark
femerall
renegado
Menelaus
benefact
generant
hebetant
pederast
relevant
revenant
se-tenant
telecast
vegetant
delegacy
federacy
federary
femetary
resemble
December
remember
jewel box
defenced
Seleucid
Seleucus
defended
deseeded
beheadal
rebeldom
tenendum
defender
degender
nereides
legendry
seven-day
repetend
✧reverend
Genevese
teleseme
terebene
venereal
mezereum
mezereon
venerean
pederero
hereness
redeless
cerement
decedent
deferent
deselect
referent
reselect
reverent
Serevent®
teletext
tenement
vehement
cemetery
serenely
severely
bedeafen
feverfew
telergic
merengue
red eagle
sea eagle
demerger
Meleager
revenger
revenges
sewer gas
petechia
telethon
secesher
telechir
Teresina
celeriac
Genesiac
jeremiad
remedied
weregild
benefice
Berenice
ceresine
deletive

reillume
well-hung
bell push
bell pull
bell buoy
gealousy
jealousy
belle vue
Keflavik
sea level
replevin
beslaver
keel over
well over
Mevlevis
newly-wed
Nell Gwyn
beflower
bellower
deflower
reflower
fellowly
mellowly
well away
wellaway
deflexed
reflexed
reflexes
reflexly
Wesleyan
Vellozia
realizer
permease
permeate
team game
teammate
re-embark
Heimdall
neomycin
pemmican
gemma-cup
new-model
Bermudan
Bermudas
germ cell
beamless
helmless
seamless
seemless
teemless
termless
reamiest
✧**germaine**
germ line
teamwise
term-time
jemmying
seemlier
bedmaker
helmsman
tegmenta
Germanic
sermonic
vermined
helminth
✧**renminbi**
✧**germinal**
terminal
Leo Minor
sermoner
terminer

beam-ends
per minas
✧terminus
sermonet
geomancy
key money
seamanly
yeomanly
yeomanry
geomyoid
Hermione
reimpose
teamwork
teem down
gemmeous
reimport
re-embody
Belmopan
Vehmique
mesmeric
beam tree
neem tree
re-emerge
sea marge
seamfree
besmirch
kermesse
let me see
dermatic
hermetic
pelmatic
helmeted
besmutch
deemster
geometer
seamster
teamster
wet meter
fermatas
new maths
geometry
sea mouse
vermouth
Weymouth
seamount
fern land
rein-hand
re-engage
rein back
neon lamp
penny-bun
vernicle
Les Noces
penny-dog
genned up
Leonidas
fern-seed
Seinfeld
meunière
penneech
penneeck
mean well
lernaean
Sean Penn
reindeer
beinness
keenness
leanness
meanders
meanness
reinless

reinsert
reinvent
reinvest
penny fee
penny-fee
Jennifer
teenaged
nennigai
teenager
hen night
se'nnight
sennight
deanship
Jean Rhys
fernshaw
hernshaw
fernbird
mean time
meantime
bean-king
weanling
yeanling
deontics
re-enlist
Léon Blum
Reynolds
fernally
kernelly
vernally
sea nymph
reinsman
pennoned
Pennines
seine net
pernancy
beanpole
mean-tone
Jean Rook
reinform
mean-born
cernuous
penny-pig
gesneria
bean tree
wet nurse
wet-nurse
penn'orth
Leonardo
Tennyson
senna tea
✧**jeanette**
reinette
neonatal
Leinster
bean curd
reinfund
ceinture
reinfuse
reinsure
Dean Rusk
lean-burn
Jean Muir
peen over
Ben Nevis
reanswer
xeromata
Legoland
decorate
denotate
derogate
desolate

detonate
helotage
lemonade
meconate
pejorate
perorate
relocate
renovate
resonate
segolate
zero-rate
✧**cenotaph**
reposall
mesocarp
debonair
aerodart
aeronaut
resonant
xenogamy
demobbed
redouble
débouché
heroical
penoncel
resorcin
rejoicer
tenor cor
heroicly
lemon dab
secondee
keloidal
beholden
beholder
bepowder
New Order
✧recorder
seconder
secondly
felo de se
Genovese
kerosene
telomere
Veronese
peroneal
mesoderm
De Lorean®
melodeon
zero-zero
set one up
demoness
peroneus
deforest
deponent
redolent
reforest
behovely
recovery
remotely
belonger
besought
xenophya
oenophil
Xenophon
heroship
geropiga
melodica
semolina
✧señorita
✧veronica
demoniac
aerolite

cenobite
deionise
deionize
demonise
demonize
genocide
kerosine
leporine
meionite
melodise
melodize
memorise
memorize
mesolite
pemoline
peroxide
serotine
tenorite
xenotime
becoming
beloving
besoming
aerolith
demolish
regolith
xenolith
Menomini
memorial
demonism
hedonism
helotism
meconium
metopism
nepotism
pelorism
Peronism
peyotism
besonian
bezonian
demonian
demotion
Devonian
devotion
melodion
Neronian
red onion
remotion
sea onion
Senonian
Geronimo
pecorino
Aerobics®
aerobics
✧bedouins
genomics
hedonics
melodics
perogies
demonist
demotist
hedonist
Jehovist
melodist
nepotist
Peronist
peyotist
tenorist
detoxify
ferocity
remodify
serosity

velocity
venosity
besouled
recoiler
récollet
lemon law
deformed
re-formed
✧reformed
bepommel
deformer
dewormer
✧reformer
recommit
reformat
renowned
denounce
renounce
zero in on
besognio
bemoaner
dehorner
renowner
levodopa
aerobomb
Cenozoic
Mesozoic
aerotone
menopome
merosome
aerofoil
✧**jeroboam**
rehoboam
tenoroon
decolour
zero hour
decorous
felonous
nemorous
venomous
besom out
secodont
aerology
aeronomy
cetology
demology
gemology
menology
merogony
oecology
oenology
pedology
pelology
penology
serology
sexology
tenotomy
decouple
bebopper
below par
recourse
resource
begorrah
metopryl
aerogram
venogram
mesotron
devourer
✧**democrat**
reborrow
repoussé

Senoussi
heronsew
tenon saw
lemon tea
gerontic
besotted
retorted
revolted
deportee
begotten
dehorter
reporter
resorter
retorter
revolter
sea otter
aerostat
devoutly
reposure
resolute
revolute
resolved
resolver
revolver
reconvey
men-of-war
aerodyne
cerotype
genotype
serotype
meronymy
metonymy
deep-laid
bedplate
helpmate
jet plane
jetplane
keep cave
keep pace
keepsake
key plate
seaplane
template
wet plate
keep back
keep dark
hemp-palm
keep calm
keep warm
neoplasm
keep tabs
pea-plant
tea plant
geophagy
keepsaky
vespiary
helpable
keepable
respects
hen-padle
Vespidae
bespread
deep-read
hempseed
resplend
bel paese
neoprene
sea piece
set piece
set-piece
helpdesk

leap year
reappear
deepness
helpless
besprent
deepfelt
helpmeet
neopagan
despight
peepshow
helpline
keep time
Memphite
mesprise
mesprize
neophile
semplice
tempting
✧delphian
Memphian
deep kiss
her paiks
dewpoint
set point
bespoken
serpulid
Deep Blue
✧zeppelin
red panda
Responsa
geoponic
weaponed
response
tenpence
key punch
keypunch
reopener
new penny
sea pansy
tenpenny
weaponry
keep hold
geophone
neophobe
peephole
weephole
deep down
keep down
leaprous
deepmost
hesperid
tempered
sea purse
leapfrog
sea perch
Leopardi
temporal
vesperal
pepperer
temperer
Hesperis
Hesperus
hen party
jeopardy
tea party
despisal
despiser
despotic
herpetic
despatch
keep step
dempster
sempster
despotat
keep at it
ten-pound
sea power
keep away
deep-dyed
geophyte
neophyte
seaquake
verquere
mesquine
mesquite
verquire
jerquing
bear hard
bearward
near-hand
rearward
decrease
degrease
ferriage
gear-case
near gale
recreate
pearl ash
reproach
deer-park
rear-rank
beerhall
near-gaun
pearmain
reordain
rear lamp
deer-hair
Near East
recreant
retroact
segreant
February
get ready
bearable
tearable
terrible
wearable
berry bug
sea robin
bearably
terribly
terraced
tetracid
verrucae
metrical
heart cam
jerrican
jerrycan
terraces
verrucas
tear a cat
tetradic
degraded
begrudge
perradii
Hebrides
bear-lead
befriend
dearie me
defreeze
derrière
pearl-eye
refreeze
repreeve
repriefe
reprieve
retrieve
deer-neck
ne'er-weel
bear's ear
bear's-ear
hear, hear!
near beer
dearness
✧fearless
gearless
heirless
nearness
peerless
regreets
searness
tearless
merriest
rearrest
reorient
febrific
petrific
terrific
pea-rifle
dearnful
weariful
yearn for
retrofit
tetragon
verrugas
bedright
New Right
search me
wear thin
heirship
searcher
Georgina
bearbine
bepraise
Hebraise
Hebraize
nearside
pearlite
rearmice
retraite
berrying
dearling
decrying
ferrying
learning
pearling
retrying
wearying
yearling
yearning
deer lick
near-silk
Hebraism
Georgian
Georgics
hearties
near miss
pearlies
pearlins
weirdies
Hebraist
retraict
retraitt
heartily
bearskin
deerskin
terrella
petrolic
Negrillo
heartlet
neurally
retrally
ferryman
merryman
✧merry men
neuromas
neuronic
serranid
befringe
refringe
Terrance
bedrench
retrench
neuronal
petronel
tetronal
tear into
bearings
Serranus
zebrinny
fearsome
yearlong
yearbook
Beerbohm
heirloom
bear down
Dearborn
deer horn
deer-horn
gear down
tear down
wear down
ferreous
hen roost
rearmost
weary out
weird out
cecropia
heartpea
tetrapla
tetrapod
Henry Pye
neuropil
bear upon
cecropin
Terrapin®
terrapin
decrepit
necropsy
détraqué
perruque
terraria
pear-tree
retrorse
Petrarch
rear-arch
tetrarch
wear iron
pear drop
tear drop
bear arms
heart-rot
Nebraska
petrosal
reprisal
new-risen
detrusor
necrosis
neuroses
neurosis
Letraset®
ferritic
heuretic
Nearctic
necrotic
neuritic
neurotic
ferreted
serrated
decretal
detrital
ferritin
secretin
ferreter
regrater
regrator
secretor
detritus
metritis
Negritos
neuritis
serratus
aegrotat
keiretsu
secretly
get round
see round
rearouse
red route
pear-push
beer pump
tear duct
depraved
deprived
deprival
reproval
sea raven
Red River
reprover
Retrovir®
sea rover
regrowth
bear away
tear away
tearaway
wear away
tetraxon
defrayed
✧betrayal
defrayal
betrayer
defrayer
Peer Gynt
terrazzo
key stage
messmate
messuage
Netscape®
persuade
perswade
redshare
seascape
sea snake
Teasmade®
bed-staff
newshawk
red shank
redshank
sea snail
jew's harp
✧jew's-harp
✧jews'-harp
see stars
newscast
redstart
feasible
leasable
reusable
sensible
tensible
feasibly
sensibly
peasecod
versicle
bedsocks
persicot
versed in
Messidor
feast-day
bedstead
reascend
kenspeck
mess deck
Netspeak
news desk
✧newspeak
Newsweek
✧seaspeak
deisheal
newsreel
seashell
peesweep
REM sleep
eel-spear
menswear
mess gear
newsless
reassess
bed-sheet
messiest
reascent
reassert
feastful
menseful
senseful
messages
memsahib
less than
fess-wise
let slide
newswire
perspire
redshire
sea snipe
sea swine
Teesside
beeswing
feasting
Mel Smith
sea stick
newsgirl
seismism
reassign
jet-skier
measlier
red shift
Red Shirt
tee shirt
beastily
feistily
perseity
sensilla
tessella
teaseled
mersalyl
teaseler
weaseler
verselet
weaselly
pessimal
pessimum
verse-man
Welshman
Bessemer
yersinia
reasoned
seasoned
personae
teosinte
Helsinki
personal
seasonal
reasoner
seasoner
personas
peasanty
keeshond
lens hood
felstone
gemstone
keystone
lee shore
pea-stone
seashore
ten-score
penstock
cesspool
sesspool
mess-room
newsroom
sea storm
gemshorn
Mess-John
teaspoon
velskoen
sensuous
sessions
redshort
Sea Scout
tease out
herstory
menstrua
sensoria
sea shrub
lease-rod
leisured
measured
tesserae
mensural
tesseral
Mensuren
measurer
measures
bedstraw
pea-straw
setscrew
felsitic

reassume
reassure
Deus vult
persaunt
pea-soupy
zemstvos
peishwah
feast-won
Gershwin
New Style
yea-sayer
best maid
left-hand
leftward
Lettland
peatland
test card
text-hand
westland
westward
berthage
centiare
heat wave
left face!
meat safe
test case
peat-hagg
reattach
Left Bank
left-bank
meat rack
peat bank
West Bank
best-ball
meatball
reattain
restrain
rest mass
best part
bestiary
✧tertiary
textuary
vestiary
vertebra
deathbed
beatable
bed-table
gettable
lettable
meltable
rentable
tea table
testable
wettable
Petty Bag
bento box
denticle
lenticle
pentacle
tentacle
testicle
hectical
lenticel
vertical
verticil
death cap
death cup
Test Acts
vertices
Kentucky
pentadic

bestadde
keftedes
testudos
pettedly
septleva
meathead
neat-herd
aesthete
get there
bestreak
peat-reek
Lent term
bestrewn
leathern
settle in
yestreen
settle up
deftness
de-stress
feetless
heathens
leathers
lectress
meatless
meetness
neatness
nextness
Pentheus
pertness
rectress
restless
seatless
tentless
textless
ventless
weetless
meatiest
next best
peetweet
seat belt
seat rent
sentient
testiest
vestment
feathery
heathery
leathery
beatific
pettifog
deathful
vestigia
heptagon
✧pentagon
vertigos
heath-hen
peatship
Beatrice
bestride
dextrine
gentrice
lectrice
nestlike
perthite
tentwise
ventaile
vent-pipe
West Side
beetling
centring
fettling
left wing

left-wing
nestling
restring
seething
settling
teething
ventring
meet with
heat sink
best girl
oestriol
testrill
centrism
Hertzian
neutrino
destrier
fewtrils
westlins
centoist
centrist
restrict
gentrify
lent lily
dentalia
Reptilia
gentilic
Pentelic
dentelle
vent-plug
Ventolin®
sextolet
festally
mentally
rectally
pentomic
septimal
beat-'em-up
testamur
centimos
leptonic
neotenic
Newtonic
tectonic
Teutonic
sentence
meet in wi'
centinel
centonel
fentanyl
pectinal
pentanol
sentinel
lentando
centones
pectines
bentwood
centroid
Hertford
Westwood
bestrode
centrode
dextrose
oestrone
peat-hole
rest home
ten to one
tent pole
tent rope
vent-hole
meat loaf
pentroof

jestbook
tent-work
textbook
benthoal
rent roll
sept-foil
rest room
beat down
bestrown
melt down
meltdown
pelt down
next door
next-door
peat moor
dextrous
feateous
featuous
oestrous
peat moss
vent'rous
ventrous
vertuous
beetroot
sea trout
tent coat
westmost
centuple
septuple
sextuple
Zentippe
beat up on
gestapos
heatspot
L'Estaque
dentaria
septaria
tentoria
neoteric
bettered
lettered
nectared
textured
vestured
meat-free
rent-free
sesterce
heptarch
pentarch
gestural
pectoral
rectoral
sectoral
textural
vestural
deuteron
setter-on
welter in
setter-up
hectorer
lecturer
letterer
pesterer
pewterer
restorer
venturer
vesturer
dentures
features
set terms
death row

Heathrow
death ray
delta ray
hectorly
westerly
pertused
jettison
pentosan
centeses
centesis
meatuses
rectitic
dentated
septette
sestette
sextette
teetotal
teetotum
testatum
sestetto
set to two
rest stop
sectator
testator
rectitis
Gertrude
rest cure
test tube
heat pump
Centaurs
centrums
destruct
centaury
aestival
festival
leftover
centavos
bestowal
tea towel
debt swap
bestower
melt away
neotoxin
geotaxis
vertexes
ventayle
sentry-go
mestizas
mestizos
denudate
depurate
peculate
regulate
bequeath
Beauvais
mezuzahs
debutant
débutant
depurant
petulant
recusant
penumbra
benumbed
renumber
nelumbos
zerumbet
semuncia
peduncle
befuddle
bemuddle
secundum

refunder
secundly
beau-pere
cerulean
cerulein
teru-tero
feculent
relucent
tegument
temulent
demurely
jejunely
securely
bemuffle
gefuffle
kefuffle
beauffet
debugger
requight
penuchle
✧nenuphar
reduviid
beauxite
cerusite
delusive
deputise
deputize
Jebusite
lemurine
me judice
nebulise
nebulize
reguline
regulise
regulize
relumine
resupine
xenurine
reducing
reputing
seducing
segueing
reburial
tenurial
nebulium
peculium
refugium
decurion
delusion
lemurian
Peruvian
refusion
Venusian
Venutian
✧vesuvian
Perugino
✧peculiar
beauties
Merulius
Vesuvius
beautify
jejunity
repurify
security
sedulity
debunker
tequilla
republic
medullae
sequelae
beguiler

medullar
medullas
sexually
remurmur
resubmit
sequined
returnee
sequence
refusnik
returnik
returner
lemuroid
medusoid
levulose
setulose
jelutong
mezuzoth
beau jour
nebulous
sedulous
setulous
tenuious
delusory
demurred
recurred
required
demurral
delubrum
demurrer
requirer
debussed
merum sal
Senussis
Jesuitic
besuited
rebutted
requited
petuntse
petuntze
rebuttal
requital
rebutton
result in
rebutter
requiter
seductor
Jesuitry
decurved
recurved
resurvey
teguexin
requoyle
perviate
cervical
cervices
services
selvedge
revved-up
Fervidor
fervidly
nerve end
heaviest
servient
selvaged
selvagee
nerve gas
serve its
weeviled
venville
Benvolio
nervular

Words marked ✧ can also be spelled with one or more capital letters

cervelat
nervelet
weevilly
pea-viner
leavings
servants
nerve net
fervency
heavenly
leave off
heavy oil
pervious
leave out
serve out
beavered
perverse
renverse
renverst
velveret
heavy sea
pelvises
Helvetic
velveted
servitor
heavy wet
cervixes
sei whale
eelwrack
sea wrack
see where
webwheel
red wheat
tea wagon
reawaken
dey-woman
leg-woman
✧new woman
penwoman
seawoman
get wrong
pen-wiper
New World
bedwards
seawards
redwater
seawater
re-expand
re-export
very same
cetywall
hexylene
Terylene®
me myself
very well
demyship
Lecythis
lecythus
lekythos
merycism
Pepysian
beryllia
very good
Kenyatta
desyatin
set you up
dewy-eyed
benzoate
Weizmann
seizable
Lenz's law
Penzance
terzetta
terzetti
terzetto
off and on
off-and-on
off-board
off break
afebrile
off-comer
off drive
after all
offended
offender
aftereye
afferent
efferent
effetely
offering
affeered
of secret
aftersun
affected
affecter
effecter
effector
after-tax
CFA franc
CFP franc
off guard
efficacy
iffiness
of nights
offishly
official
effigies
affinity
affirmer
affiance
effierce
off-label
affluent
effluent
afflated
afflatus
effluvia
sfumatos
of a night
pfenning
Afro-jazz
afforest
Afro-rock
of course
of a piece
offprint
off-piste
sforzati
sforzato
affright
effraide
affronté
affrayed
off-shake
off-stage
off-shakt
offsider
off-sales
offshore
eftsoons
offshoot
off-sorts
offtimes
of a truth
effulged
effusive
affusion
effusion
aflutter
off-white
off-wards
aguacate
eglatere
agraphia
agraphic
agraphon
agnation
agrarian
Ignatian
yglaunst
ignaroes
Agra Fort
egg-apple
Eggboard
egg-bound
agaçante
agacerie
agedness
egg dance
ague-cake
agrémens
agrément
agreeing
agrestic
agrestal
eggfruit
egg glass
age group
ego ideal
ugliness
aguishly
ignition
aglimmer
Agricola
agrimony
ignitron
egoistic
aglitter
age limit
agalloch
ngultrum
Agamidae
egomania
agentive
agential
Aganippe
agonised
agonized
agiotage
ignorant
a good bet
a good buy
a good few
ignominy
a good job
agrology
agronomy
agnostic
eggplant
Egyptian
egg purse
Agapetus
aggraced
aggrieve
agar-agar
Ygdrasil
ageratum
J G Frazer
eggshell
egestive
egg slice
egestion
egg spoon
egg timer
egg tooth
✧agit-prop
✧agitprop
agitated
agitator
✧agnus dei
agouties
egg white
egg whisk
thraward
the Alamo
pheasant
thrawart
thearchy
shraddha
thraldom
Theaceae
wheat eel
wheat ear
wheatear
cheaters
cheatery
wheat fly
sheathed
shear-hog
thrasher
the Ashes
Theatine
thiamine
thiazide
thiazine
cheating
phrasing
sheading
shealing
shearing
shoaling
cheapish
thwacker
phialled
shearleg
shearman
chiasmas
chiasmus
shrapnel
Rhiannon
the above
thiazole
whoa-ho-ho
the Apple
thrapple
shear pin
theatric
shea tree
theatral
chiastic
thwarted
Rh-factor
thwarter
shmaltzy
thwartly
shea nuts
shabrack
The Beano
the brass
the Beast
the Backs
Chibchan
the blind
thebaine
chubbily
shabbily
the briny
the balks
the bends
rhabdoid
Shabuoth
The Bronx
Ghiberti
The Birds
rhubarby
✧the basij
who but he
✧the blues
The Boxer
the Boyne
cha-chaed
the chase
The Clash
the Chalk
the crack
chechako
the chair
check box
Phocidae
shock dog
Chichewa
Phocaena
the Creed
The Clerk
thick ear
checkers
thickety
shechita
shocking
Shu Ching
shucking
whacking
thickish
chuckies
check-key
✧phacelia
chuckler
shackles
chick lit
chaconne
chicaner
chicanas
✧chicanos
check off
check-off
chuck off
shuck off
the cloth
thickoes
check out
check-out
checkout
chuck out
chiccory
chickpea
the curse
checksum
thickset
the cough
Chaco War
shedhand
The Dream
Thaddeus
shuddery
The Dagda
shadchan
cheddite
shedding
thudding
whidding
the drink
chuddies
shoddily
the Deity
shadblow
Ghadamès
rhodanic
whodunit
The Dandy
shedload
shaddock
The Doors
chadarim
The Derby
Rhodites
shadbush
shidduch
khedival
shadower
the Downs
the downy
shoelace
shoe nail
wheel-cut
shredded
shrewdie
sheepdog
chiefdom
threaden
Whieldon
sheep-dip
shielder
shredder
threader
shrewdly
Phoebean
chiefess
shoeless
cheese it
chiefest
the elect
chiefery
the enemy
thievery
cheerful
The Eagle
chee-chee
threshel
Phaethon
shoe shop
thresher
bheesite
cheering
sheeting
shieling
thieving
wheeling
wheezing
sheepish
shrewish
thievish
cheewink
shlemiel
shoebill
phrenism
Rhaetian
cheerios
cheekily
cheerily
wheezily
sheep ked
sheerleg
wheedler
phlegmon
three-man
wheelman
threnode
sheer off
shoehorn
chaebols
wheel out
threnody
shred-pie
sheep-pen
shlepper
threapit
threepit
sheep-pox
three-ply
shoetree
sheep run
Phaedrus
sheep-rot
phreatic
bheestie
sheet tin
threaten
Thyestes
three-way
The Field
the Fleet
chaffery
Shafiite
chaffing
shafting
shifting
whiffing
The Friar
The Flies
shiftily
the fritz
shift key
whiffled
the filth
shuffler
whiffler
the fancy
the Flood
the F-word
shofroth
chiffons
The Frogs
chaffron
the Forty
the Fates
the grape
shagbark
rhagades

libatory
minatory
didapper
disapply
misapply
disagree
filagree
binaural
cicatrix
disarray
misarray
Limassol
bioassay
final say
dicastic
didactic
gigantic
Silastic®
silastic
Sinaitic
didactyl
cilantro
disaster
pilaster
pinaster
ailantos
Gigantes
Rifaites
simaruba
disabuse
filature
fixature
ligature
picayune
nip a bung
bimanual
Pinatubo
pirarucu
gigabyte
vin blanc
✧big board
pinboard
air-brake
rim brake
midbrain
bioblast
Zimbabwe
bit by bit
big bucks
timbrel'd
Tibb's Eve
tie-break
limbmeal
wibble on
limbless
diablery
misbegot
gibbsite
nibbling
air-brick
fimbrial
nimbyism
witblits
air-built
Timbuktu
diabolic
cimbalom
diabolos
timbales
disbench
air-bends
jibbings
ribbonry
wig block
Jim Brown
timbered
airborne
disburse
Gisborne
misbirth
Simbirsk
limber up
jig borer
Filberts
airburst
bilberry
Kimberly
nisberry
diabasic
nimbused
bimbashi
disbosom
nimbuses
ciabatta
diabetic
bimbette
ciabatte
diabetes
airbrush
lip brush
disbowel
pilchard
jib crane
gimcrack
Jim Clark
jimcrack
disclaim
tie clasp
aircraft
pie chart
miscible
vincible
biscacha
bizcacha
viscacha
vizcacha
milch-cow
ditch-dog
biocidal
miscreed
discrete
witch-elm
Circaean
pinchers
discreet
bitchery
witchery
birch fly
miscegen
pinchgut
pinch-hit
diactine
mischief
bitching
cinching
circling
discoing
filching
pinching
pitching
witching
zincking
dipchick
biscuity
bitchily
circuity
hitchily
zinckify
vinculum
circular
discolor
miscolor
piacular
piccolos
fiscally
zircaloy
Zircoloy®
pitchman
winchman
Piacenza
zirconia
zirconic
piscinae
Visconti
diaconal
piecener
Circinus
piscinas
discinct
discandy
pince-nez
cinchona
disclose
oilcloth
discrown
disclost
piece out
hiccuped
disciple
mince pie
linchpin
sinciput
birch rod
visceral
miscarry
diocesan
circussy
hiccatee
biscotti
biscotto
circiter
✧piscator
cincture
discoure
lincture
tincture
hiccough
discount
miscount
piecrust
✧viscount
air-cover
discover
Biscayan
hindward
wild card
wildland
wind band
windward
birdcage
wild mare
birdbath
wind park
birdcall
windfall
windgall
windsail
wind farm
air-drain
airdrawn
wind harp
wild oats
windlass
misdealt
zindabad
biddable
findable
diadochi
diddicoy
big Daddy
bindweed
birdseed
hindhead
misdread
bindi-eye
bird's-eye
mind's eye
mild beer
kindless
kindness
mildness
mindless
piedness
rindless
vildness
wildness
windless
Wild West
misdight
lindy hop
windship
birdshot
bird-lice
bird-life
birdlike
bird-lime
Hinduise
Hinduize
wildfire
wildlife
wild rice
windpipe
wind side
Zip® drive
birdwing
fiddling
hindwing
kindling
middling
misdoing
piddling
riddling
windring
wild silk
windmill
Hinduism
tiddlier
kindlily
vindaloo
windblow
diademed
misdempt
misdonne
riddance
findings
sindings
hiddenly
jim-dandy
wildwood
airdrome
wind cone
wind-rode
wind rose
birdsong
Windhoek
wind rock
windsock
wildfowl
lindworm
wild-born
wind down
wind-down
pied noir
wild boar
fiddious
bird-bolt
hindfoot
hindmost
piedmont
wild goat
mind-body
qindarka
Pindaric
wildered
pindaree
siddur-im
siddurim
wild arum
hinderer
wild iris
mind-cure
windsurf
Firdausi
wild duck
wild-duck
windburn
wind pump
misdoubt
Wild Hunt
bind over
mildewed
windowed
bird-eyed
wild-eyed
wild type
Cinerama®
cider-and
hiveward
pipe band
sideband
sideward
tideland
timecard
vineyard
wideband
Airedale
filename
fire sale
Liberace
liberate
likewake
literate
liveware
pipe-case
rice cake
siderate
sine wave
tide gate
tide race
tidewave
wine lake
limewash
sidepath
digerati
literati
bite back
fireback
firemark
fire-walk
jive talk
Kite mark
Kitemark
kite-mark
likewalk
pipe rack
sidewalk
tidemark
wine cask
wine rack
fife rail
Fine Gael
fireball
firewall
give bail
live-rail
sidewall
time ball
vine-gall
wire nail
wine palm
riverain
literato
fire damp
firedamp
time warp
fixed air
wire-hair
Gil Evans
sideways
ci-devant
life raft
live bait
cinerary
fine lady
literacy
literary
siserary
vicenary
vinegary
mixed bud
river bed
citeable
fineable
hireable
likeable
liveable
mineable
rideable
sizeable
wipeable
mixed bag
likeably
sizeably
silenced
wiseacre
libeccio
cider-cup
ricercar
silencer
civet cat
tiger cat
Givenchy
Birendra
fire-edge
Tineidae
videndum
River Don
give odds
disendow
fireweed
line feed
pike-head
✧miserere
River Exe
tiger eye
vine-leaf
cinereal
like hell
live well
live-well
sidereal
wire-heel
give rein
nineteen
vice-dean
wire-sewn
ciseleur
life peer
rice beer
direness
fineless
fineness
fireless
hiveless
lifeless
likeness
niceness
pipeless
rifeness
ripeness
riteless
River Ems
tideless
timeless
tireless
viceless
vileness
wideness
wifeless
wireless
wiseness
witeless
give vent
hive-nest
lifebelt
life-rent
side meat
virement
videofit
river god
hired gun
pile shoe
river-hog
dimethyl
fireship
like that
sideshow

fire-bird
liveried
ricebird
side wind
wire bird
bitesize
dimerise
dimerize
fireside
give line
give rise
hivelike
lifelike
lifeline
life-size
lifetime
likewise
live wire
mimetite
nine-mile
pipelike
pipeline
piperine
pipe-wine
riverine
sideline
siderite
sidewise
sirenise
sirenize
timeline
vicelike
viperine
wifelike
wire line
wise-like
zibeline
hireling
libeling
nidering
riveting
sideling
tireling
vice-king
vice ring
videoing
wiseling
filefish
line-fish
liverish
pipefish
side dish
tigerish
tilefish
viperish
vixenish
fire-risk
limerick
rice milk
sidekick
biserial
tidemill
time bill
cine film
dimerism
dioecism
tigerism
fire sign
Liberian
limekiln
Milesian
Nigerian
Nigerien
River Inn
Sicelian
Sikelian
sirenian
Rivelino
timelier
fivepins
kinesics
kinetics
Liberius
niceties
ninepins
nineties
Sibelius
Tiberias
Tiberius
Tiresias
Siceliot
Sikeliot
wine list
side view
fidelity
livelily
ciderkin
wineskin
bi-weekly
libelled
rivelled
vine-clad
libellee
live a lie
Nile blue
rice glue
fire-flag
fireplug
vitellin
sideslip
libeller
micellar
vitellus
time slot
fire-plow
cineplex
dice-play
fire clay
lineally
pipeclay
linesman
riverman
sidesman
tidesman
nine-inch
hibernal
dive into
give into
pile into
wire into
Zigeuner
tiger nut
time unit
pigeonry
dive-bomb
fine comb
firebomb
pipe bomb
side comb
time bomb
firewood
fivefold
lifehold
lime-wood
live load
livelood
Mike Todd
ninefold
pinewood
sideroad
wifehood
wivehood
cicerone
fire-bote
fire hose
lifesome
literose
nine-hole
pine cone
sidenote
side tone
time code
time zone
tiresome
wire rope
wirewove
dire wolf
lifelong
livelong
sidelong
ciceroni
fire-hook
firelock
firework
life-work
pilework
pipework
sidelock
tide lock
time-work
wirework
dice-coal
niger oil
pine-wool
Pipe Roll
rice bowl
wire wool
fireworm
pile-worm
wireworm
fine down
live-born
live down
pipe down
ride down
time loan
time-worn
tire down
rice soup
fire door
side door
dimerous
viperous
diner-out
lifeboat
milepost
nine-foot
pilewort
pipewort
rise to it
side-foot
side post
wiped out
mirepoix
file copy
widebody
fire opal
finespun
give upon
lifespan
ride upon
wide open
wide-open
dimetric
viverrid
lime-tree
pine tree
pipe-tree
dihedral
disenrol
mire-drum
side drum
dihedron
firetrap
vine-prop
fine arts
firearms
give arms
pile arms
sidearms
firebrat
liver rot
river-rat
fine-draw
wiredraw
bi-yearly
linearly
diseased
licensed
cineaste
cinéaste
licensee
finesser
licenser
licensor
diversly
dicentra
lineated
pileated
rivetted
digestif
bidental
line item
pipe-stem
pile it on
fire-step
give it up
live it up
mixer tap
sidestep
bisector
digester
director
mimester
sin-eater
pimentos
videotex
directly
misentry
River Tay
silently
ciselure
fine-tune
fire-tube
sinecure
time fuse
Nibelung
tile-hung
bisexual
ritenuto
mine dump
pipefuls
lifebuoy
like fury
River Váh
give over
tide over
River Wye
lime-twig
fire away
give away
giveaway
hideaway
riverway
wile away
wipe away
wire away
live axle
fire-eyed
wide-eyed
nine-eyes
airframe
giff-gaff
niffnaff
riff-raff
hip flask
pia fraus
diffract
Jiffy bag®
pig-faced
airfield
midfield
misfield
oilfield
disflesh
siffleur
Hilfiger
piffling
misfaith
misfeign
misfalne
fitfully
sinfully
wilfully
sinfonia
disfrock
air frost
zip-front
oil-fired
✧air force
air-force
pilferer
pifferos
diffused
diffuser
disfavor
oil gland
disgrace
disgrade
wing case
misgraff
jingbang
airgraph
biograph
diagraph
pie graph
ring back
ring-bark
ring mark
ring walk
wing back
ring-tail
ringtail
ring wall
ring main
king pair
dingbats
nit-grass
rib-grass
ringhals
misgraft
diggable
singable
zingiber
liegedom
wingedly
Sieg Heil
King Lear
kingless
ringless
ringlets
wingless
mingiest
wingbeat
pinguefy
siege-gun
kingship
wing shot
wing-shot
kingbird
disguise
kinglike
king-size
linguine
misguide
ringside
ring-time
ringwise
winglike
giggling
higgling
kingling
mingling
niggling
pingling
ridgling
singeing
singling
sing-sing
tingeing
tingling
wingding
jingoish
kingfish
tinglish
Yinglish
linguini
ring dial
jingoism
tinglier
jingoist
linguist
cingulum
kingklip
lingular
singular
gingelly
Kingsley
king's-man
liegeman
Virginia
biogenic
Diogenic
diagonal
virginal
diggings
virgin it
virginly
kinghood
kingwood
ring road
diagnose
kid glove
ringbone
ringdove
ringtone
ding-dong
King Kong
Ping-Pong®
singsong
ringwork
ringworm
ding doun
King John
ring down
gingkoes
lip gloss
kingbolt
kingpost
ringbolt
ring fort
wingspan
king crab
fingered
jiggered
disgorge
lingerie
ring true
ginger up
jigger up
lingerer
ziggurat
king-crow
gingerly
diegesis
fidgeted
Kingston
lingster
ringster
oil gauge
ring pull
disgavel
gingival
misgiven
wingover
ridgeway
ring dyke
diaglyph
ginglymi
Mithraea
Mishnaic
Mithraic
high hand
✧highland
misheard
nigh-hand
fish cake

lichgate
lichwake
night-ape
with calf
mishmash
wish-wash
fish-hawk
highjack
fishball
fishtail
highball
hightail
pithball
fish farm
right arm
Eichmann
high camp
light air
night air
High Mass
Sikh Wars
tight ass
lie heavy
dishable
fishable
tithable
dishabit
Tisha Bov
light box
dithecal
nightcap
night-dog
eight-day
Michaela
tight end
withheld
high tech
high-tech
fishmeal
eighteen
fish-weir
high gear
high-gear
✧**highness**
high seas
nighness
pithless
richness
high-test
mightest
rich-left
night-foe
lightful
mightful
rightful
night-fly
pishogue
Michigan
high shoe
night-hag
with this
with that
aich whow
eighthly
withwind
fish-dive
fishwife
high five
high-five
high life
high-rise

high tide
high time
high wire
pithlike
Vichyite
fighting
lighting
lithoing
righting
sighting
lightish
rightish
tightish
high kick
high-risk
ditheism
rightism
high sign
eighties
ditheist
rightist
wish list
mightily
nightjar
fishskin
fish-glue
Michelle
Nicholas
night-man
siphonic
lichened
sithence
biphenyl
diphenyl
siphonal
lichenin
dishonor
lichanos
Tithonus
siphonet
Kishinev
dichroic
cichloid
fish pond
highroad
Richmond
withhold
fish-bone
high-lone
Nichrome®
wishbone
fight off
right off
fish-hook
night owl
with foal
high-born
✧high noon
eight-oar
highmost
light out
night out
right out
high toby
high spec
tithe-pig
light pen
high spot
high-bred
withered
dishorse

litharge
pilhorse
pith-tree
pichurim
hitherto
higher-up
ditherer
Richards
disherit
highbrow
withdraw
withdrew
litherly
dichasia
biphasic
richesse
sightsee
lithosol
fight shy
dichotic
fish-stew
air-house
big house
dishouse
ginhouse
high jump
fish-guts
Highbury
dishevel
eightvos
tightwad
digitate
litigate
militate
mitigate
sibilate
silicate
tidivate
titivate
vicinage
vizirate
biriyani
Kiribati
dividant
litigant
✧militant
minimart
mitigant
sibilant
vigilant
✧visitant
limitary
military
vivipary
pitiable
vitiable
cicisbei
sigisbei
cicisbeo
sigisbeo
pitiably
✧**hibiscus**
viliacos
civil day
dividend
vilipend
bilinear
airiness
dividers
liminess
miriness

oiliness
pitiless
siziness
tidiness
tininess
wiliness
wiriness
diligent
dirigent
diriment
liniment
miniment
vivisect
divinely
finitely
gibingly
finished
finish up
finisher
linisher
pixie hat
Filipina
Libitina
oiticica
Sigiriya
MiniDisc®
citified
vilified
ciminite
civilise
civilize
digitise
digitize
divinise
divinize
divisive
filicide
liripipe
minibike
minimise
minimize
miticide
rigidise
rigidize
silicide
similise
similize
sinicise
sinicize
viricide
viridite
viticide
dividing
limiting
visiting
diminish
minidish
dividivi
piri-piri
minidisk
lixivial
minipill
vizirial
dirigism
lixivium
minimism
✧nihilism
silicium
Sinicism
virilism
civilian

division
Milicien
Sicilian
viridian
Filipino
Pilipino
vitiligo
vilifier
vivifier
Licinius
Siricius
Vigilius
civilist
minimist
nihilist
civility
divinify
divinity
lividity
nihility
rigidify
rigidity
silicify
timidity
vicinity
viridity
virility
vividity
mimicked
mimicker
mini-skis
visibles
air inlet
civil law
filially
visioned
visional
pimiento
visioner
cicinnus
ripienos
lie in one
silicone
hit it off
Visigoth
filiform
piliform
pisiform
liripoop
sibilous
midi-coat
Hiri Motu
filioque
miliaria
Winifred
filigree
siriasis
Nijinsky
disinter
minister
sinister
vitiator
ministry
silicula
disinure
finitude
ridicule
silicule
dividual
minimums
civil war

kibitzer
hic jacet
misjudge
disjoint
hip joint
Sid James
disjunct
jiu-jitsu
ninjitsu
ninjutsu
kirkward
kirkyard
milkmaid
rickyard
Milk Race
nickname
disk pack
kick back
kickback
milk-walk
nick-nack
pickback
rick-rack
tick-tack
hickwall
kickball
Kirkwall
silktail
milk-warm
Nicklaus
rinkhals
Pink Lady
kickable
linkable
sinkable
dinky-die
wickedly
milk-weed
silkweed
pick-me-up
diskless
milkless
pinkness
sickness
riskiest
tick shop
kickshaw
rickshaw
sicklied
tick bird
disk file
milklike
silk-like
tickling
tinkling
milkfish
ticklish
tick-tick
Kip Keino
sick list
sicklily
jickajog
kinkajou
nickelic
nickeled
sick flag
pink slip
pink-slip
Kirkaldy
pick'n'mix
sickener

pickings
jirkinet
sink unit
Kilkenny
milkwood
Mirkwood
sick note
sink hole
sinkhole
milk loaf
linkwork
picklock
silky oak
tick-tock
sickroom
silkworm
kickdown
kirk town
tick down
rink polo
ginkgoes
kink-host
milkwort
pinkroot
wickered
milk-tree
pickerel
bick-iron
licker-in
picker-up
tinkerer
zikkurat
sickerly
picketed
diskette
nicky-tam
linkster
picketer
Pinkster
ricketty
kick turn
pick over
tick over
tick-over
Milky Way
tick away
pink-eyed
kielbasa
billiard
millhand
milliard
willyard
diallage
disleave
milliare
millrace
rillmark
milltail
villiaco
villiago
willyart
milliary
sillabub
field bed
millable
tillable
violable
willable
dilly bag
fillibeg
millibar

title bar
billyboy
violably
pirlicue
biblical
billy-can
hillocky
dislodge
villadom
killadar
silladar
field-dew
field day
billhead
mill-head
pillhead
millième
misleeke
Mill Reef
Will Self
Niflheim
gill beer
killdeer
will-less
fitliest
diplegia
dialogic
dialogue
killogie
diplogen
field gun
villagio
pillager
villager
mislight
silly-how
millrind
field ice
hillside
kill line
kill time
kill-time
dialling
fielding
yielding
billfish
Kill Bill
mill girl
disloign
niellist
diploidy
villainy
disliken
Jim Laker
misliker
hielaman
rifleman
gig-lamps
diplomat
violence
airliner
bin-liner
cislunar
lip liner
milliner
fillings
hidlings
✧midlands
billfold
girlhood
millpond
nielloed
dial tone
billbook
billhook
hillfolk
millwork
pillworm
billions
millions
hill-fort
pillwort
diplopia
diplopod
filliped
milleped
milliped
Lilliput
rifle pit
gill arch
millirem
dieldrin
gillaroo
jillaroo
killcrop
dialyser
biolysis
dialyses
dialysis
✧dielytra
dialytic
villatic
billeted
filleted
misletoe
Villette
ciclaton
mirliton
pig Latin
violater
violator
gillyvor
mill over
billowed
pillowed
willowed
williwaw
disloyal
diplozoa
dialyzer
filmland
firmware
Kismaayo
filmable
gimme cap
gimmicky
via media
dismoded
Diomedes
pigmaean
firmless
firmness
giambeux
gimme hat
vis major
pin-maker
wig-maker
dismally
diamanté
big money
pin money
firm down
filmgoer
film noir
Tia Maria®
biomorph
Bismarck
mismarry
più mosso
sigmatic
mismated
mismetre
mismatch
diameter
film star
pia mater
viameter
biometry
titmouse
bigmouth
dismount
Zionward
Biennale
Lion Gate
kirn-baby
winnable
cinnabar
binnacle
pinnacle
picnicky
dianodal
limnaeid
Siennese
Viennese
Linnaean
Sinn Fein
signieur
giantess
Linnaeus
signless
tinniest
lientery
midnight
dianthus
bien-aimé
big noise
lionlike
fiendish
kirn-milk
biennial
giantism
signaled
signaler
Mirna Loy
signally
bionomic
cinnamic
fisnomie
visnomie
cinnamon
misnomer
bignonia
mignonne
Tir nan-Og
Tir-na-nOg
pianinos
winnings
minneola
kiln-hole
dipnoous
ligneous
signpost
pinniped
Winnipeg
Diandria
signoria
vigneron
sinner it
Dionysia
pianiste
finnesko
lioniser
Dionysus
lignitic
limnetic
pinnated
signeted
bien-être
pianette
vignette
tinnitus
biannual
sign over
winnowed
winnower
sign away
Disneyfy
lionizer
lipomata
bilobate
pilotage
pinotage
siloxane
dinosaur
Minotaur
bifocals
kilowatt
misogamy
disorbed
oil of ben
divorcee
divorcée
divorcer
siroccos
Girondin
disorder
misorder
limonene
Timorese
Tirolese
virogene
linoleum
mid-ocean
Tirolean
timoneer
Minoress
vinolent
Lilongwe
pinochle
piroshki
pirozhki
Sinophil
finochio
Pinochet
ricochet
simoniac
cimolite
licorice
limonite
lino tile
Minorite
nicotine
picotite
pisolite
sinopite
Timonise
Timonize
pivoting
vigorish
binomial
ciborium
rigorism
Timonism
nicotian
Tironian
Hirohito
pirogies
risorius
rigorist
simonist
Timonist
minority
pilosity
vinosity
pilot jet
minor key
pilotman
pivot-man
widowman
ritornel
disowner
Dinornis
kilopond
kimonoed
liposome
ribosome
Dino Zoff
vigoroso
bicolour
ditokous
nidorous
rigorous
timorous
vigorous
kilovolt
kidology
misology
Sinology
sitology
vinology
virology
Titograd
kilogram
lipogram
kilogray
Timor Sea
Sikorski
Limousin
✧sikorsky
timously
ridottos
risottos
risoluto
biconvex
kilobyte
Linotype®
ribozyme
misogyny
airplane
dioptase
dispeace
displace
misplace
pie plate
tinplate
bioplasm
air-plant
bioplast
displant
pie-plant
tippable
hippydom
limpidly
dispread
misplead
jimpness
limpness
oil press
bid price
diopside
disprize
misprise
misprize
rippling
simpling
pinprick
✧silphium
simplism
his paiks
mid-point
midpoint
mispoint
misprint
oil paint
pinpoint
simplist
simplify
Hispanic
diapente
dispence
dispense
disponee
disponge
dispunge
fippence
sixpence
disponer
rispings
sixpenny
misproud
biophore
diaphone
displode
disprove
disproof
oil paper
diapiric
dioptric
hippuric
zippered
disperse
dispurse
hipparch
kipperer
simperer
Hippuris
dispirit
lie perdu
disposed
disposal
diapason
disposer
tippy-toe
dispatch
rispetti
rispetto
disputer
dispathy
lispound
diapause
displume
air-power
cinquain
disquiet
misquote
litreage
rib-roast
microbic
microbar
microbus
mitre box
didrachm
microcar
wirricow
Pieridae
Pierides
microdot
pierhead
Disraeli
hirrient
fiercely
air rifle
nitrogen
diarrhea
diarchic
diarchal
libraire
migraine
piercing
Biarritz
fibrilla
Fiorello!
dioramic
fibromas
gin rummy
Tigrinya
vibronic
citrange
vibrancy
citreous
vitreous
cirriped
mirrored
hierarch
Micrurus
hierurgy
micrurgy
vibrissa
nitrosyl
nigrosin
diereses
dieresis
diuresis
fibrosis
hidrosis
citrussy
dicrotic
dioritic
diuretic
fibrotic
hidrotic
hieratic
aigrette
libretti
libretto
migrator
vibrator

vibratos
win round
misroute
vin rouge
tirrivee
tirrivie
nitroxyl
Kinshasa
miasmata
piassaba
piassava
first aid
airspace
diastase
dissuade
misshape
misstate
oil shale
tipstaff
pig's-wash
airshaft
kissable
missable
rinsable
rinsible
Dipsacus
dipsades
first-day
diastema
airspeed
misspend
Ginsberg
misspeak
misspell
Einstein
Kirsteen
hipsters
jib sheet
misspelt
misspent
tipsiest
hissy fit
first fix
dissight
pinscher
bit-slice
disseise
disseize
miss fire
biassing
gin sling
Riesling
sissyish
tinsmith
big stick
dipstick
lipstick
oil slick
pig swill
pigswill
midships
tinsnips
tipsy key
tinseled
dissolve
lipsalve
missilry
tinselly
tinselry
lissomly
lip-synch
✧pilsener
rinsings
✧diaspora
misshood
bioscope
diascope
diaspore
diastole
dip-slope
misspoke
oilstone
ribstone
sixscore
tinstone
die-stock
kinsfolk
linstock
fiascoes
miasmous
Air Scout
rinse out
fissiped
Giuseppe
fissured
dies irae
disserve
minstrel
Pissarro
airstrip
diestrus
airscrew
hit squad
dip snuff
Dioscuri
Missouri
kiss-curl
minshuku
dissever
missives
jigsawed
diastyle
fistiana
tilt yard
filtrate
misteach
liftback
mint mark
distrail
gilt-tail
cistvaen
distrain
kistvaen
air-to-air
victuals
distract
distrait
bistable
liftable
listable
pintable
tiltable
ditty bag
ditty box
bittacle
fistical
viaticum
tic-tac-to
distichs
misticos
dirty dog
birthdom
pintados
birthday
giftedly
gilt-head
lintseed
disthene
fistmele
fiftieth
sixtieth
little go
Little Mo
riot gear
distress
listless
✧mistress
riftless
tintless
victress
mintiest
mistiest
mistreat
ointment
mirthful
histogen
vintager
airtight
sit tight
giftshop
via trita
diatribe
dirt bike
girtline
pint-size
uintaite
birthing
dirtying
dittoing
littling
Dietrich
fiftyish
misthink
lift-girl
mistrial
riot girl
histrion
histrios
district
filthily
wintrily
mistaken
sittella
fistulae
biathlon
fistular
fistulas
pistolet
distally
wittolly
diatomic
mistimed
mittimus
miltonia
diatonic
Miltonic
mittened
distance
pittance
listen in
Nintendo®
listen up
listener
fittings
listings
siftings
distinct
virtuosa
dirt road
giltwood
histioid
virtuose
Viet Cong
Vietcong
virtuosi
gift-book
tint tool
lift down
virtuoso
dirt-poor
virtuous
tilt-boat
tittuped
pitty-pat
cisterna
listeria
✧victoria
Vittoria
wistaria
wisteria
historic
littered
wintered
tin terne
dipteral
littoral
pictural
riot grrl
dipteran
sitter-in
witter on
gift-wrap
titterer
winterer
dipteros
pictures
bitterly
sisterly
winterly
distaste
cistuses
hiatuses
rictuses
dietetic
mistitle
dictator
lift pump
distrust
mistrust
bistoury
mist over
mistryst
disusage
figurate
ligulate
misusage
simulate
titubate
figurant
simulant
titubant
titulary
liquable
lie under
sit under
liquidus
liquidly
virulent
minutely
liturgic
disunite
figuline
figurine
minutiae
virucide
vituline
tituping
diluvial
fiducial
diluvium
simulium
dilution
diluvian
diluvion
disunion
Siculian
Silurian
figurist
✧silurist
piou-piou
disunity
vieux jeu
aiguille
piquillo
Tibullus
ritually
visually
viburnum
piquancy
liguloid
siluroid
sinusoid
bibulous
bicuspid
titupped
liquored
liquor up
liquesce
sinuated
situated
sinuitis
nieveful
divvying
disvalue
sirvente
Giovanni
Silvanus
pit viper
silverly
disvouch
viewdata
fin whale
viewable
big wheel
pinwheel
viewless
midwifed
miswrite
airwoman
pig-woman
bijwoner
airwards
tin works
Hiawatha
midwived
midwives
view away
city hall
city farm
mixy-maxy
city desk
tityre-tu
Sisyphus
zizyphus
cityfied
Vinylite
pixy-ring
didymium
digynian
bicyclic
dicyclic
sibyllic
minyanim
pityroid
hidy-hole
didymous
digynous
dizygous
dihydric
dihybrid
sitz-bath
mitzvahs
ritziest
zigzaggy
dizzying
mizzling
sizzling
piazzian
diazinon
mitzvoth
diazepam
pizzeria
Djibouti
ejective
ejection
Sjögren's
Djakarta
djellaba
Mjöllnir
tjanting
A J Cronin
Fjorgynn
skean-dhu
Skiathos
Akkadian
Oklahoma
Oklahoma!
skiagram
skiatron
Sky blues
skidding
skid road
skydiver
skeechan
Skegness
skijorer
skokiaan
skullcap
skilless
skillful
skylight
skelping
skilling
skulking
skillion
skelloch
skeletal
skeleton
skimming
skimping
skim milk
skimpily
skim over
skincare
skin game
skene-dhu
skinhead
skin-deep
skinless
skin test
skin-like
skanking
skinking
skinning
skinfood
skin wool
akinesia
akinesis
akinetic
eklogite
skiplane
skipjack
skepping
skipping
sky pilot
ski pants
skip zone
skip over
skirling
skirting
skirmish
skerrick
akaryote
skyscape
ski stick
ekistics
ski slope
sketcher
skittish
skittles
skivvies
skive off
skewbald
skewback
skewness
ekpweles
skew arch
skywards
okey-doke
illawara
altarage
clearage
cleavage
flea-bane
floatage
floatant
pleasant
Alhambra
cloak-bag
altar boy
clean-cut
clear-cut
oleander
Oleaceae
Ulmaceae
pleaseth
cleavers

Words marked ✧ can also be spelled with one or more capital letters

alcahest
alkahest
Almagest
please it
bleacher
pleather
Altamira
alkaline
alkalise
alkalize
allanite
allative
elvanite
flea-bite
fly a kite
gliadine
illative
aliasing
allaying
bleating
bloating
cleaning
clearing
cleaving
floating
gleaming
gleaning
gloaming
pleading
pleasing
Aldaniti
Albanian
✧alsatian
illation
Al Pacino
alkalies
alkalify
blearily
sleazily
algaroba
alta moda
alkaloid
albacore
Al Capone
Eleanore
fleasome
clear off
all along
Ullapool
clean out
clean-out
clear out
clear-out
fleawort
aleatory
alcatras
elf-arrow
all at sea
cleanser
oleaster
pliantly
pleasure
clearway
clubland
slobland
club-face
glabrate
club-haul
clubable
clubhead
glibness

blubbery
glibbery
slabbery
slobbery
club-line
blabbing
blubbing
clubbing
flubbing
ill-being
slubbing
clubbish
slobbish
clubbism
plebeian
clubbist
flabbily
glabella
globulin
globular
globulet
globally
alebench
olibanum
club soda
ill blood
clubroom
flyblown
club moss
glabrous
slyboots
club foot
clubroot
ale-berry
globated
clubrush
clochard
blockade
blockage
glaciate
placcate
black art
flock-bed
placable
black bun
placebos
black box
clackbox
blackboy
placably
black cap
blackcap
black-cat
✧**black dog**
placidly
clichéed
black eye
all-clear
black-fox
black fly
glucagon
glycogen
elf-child
black ice
elective
blacking
blocking
clecking
clicking
clocking
glacéing

slicking
blackish
blockish
election
flection
alacrity
pluckily
slack jaw
glycolic
blackleg
placeman
placemen
place mat
placenta
glyconic
Alicante
glucinum
floccose
clock off
pluck off
slack off
black out
blackout
block out
clock out
glyceria
electric
glyceric
Black Rod
à la carte
glycerol
glyceryl
electrum
plectrum
electron
glycerin
plectron
electros
black rat
black rot
electret
Black Sea
glucosic
glycosyl
glacises
black tea
plicated
black tie
placitum
block-tin
blacktop
elicitor
flichter
floccule
flocculi
glad hand
glad-hand
clodpate
gladiate
glad rags
eludible
slidable
bludgeon
pledgeor
gladness
bladdery
gliddery
sliddery
fly-drive
cladding
clodding

gladding
plodding
sledding
sledging
cloddish
Vladimir
clodpole
gladiole
gladsome
gladioli
clodpoll
alienage
alienate
blue hare
ulcerate
blueback
glueball
blue laws
alterant
blue baby
alleycat
✧**aloe vera**
blueweed
bluebell
sleeveen
alter ego
blueness
clueless
sleepery
alder-fly
allergic
alberghi
allergen
elder-gun
blue-chip
bluebird
✧**algerine**
blue line
Blue Nile
elsewise
flue pipe
ilmenite
bleeding
bluewing
fleering
fleeting
sleeking
sleeping
sleeving
bluefish
bluegill
alienism
blue film
Algerian
allerion
ulterior
alienist
alterity
sleepily
Allen key
glee club
blue flag
Fluellen
fluellin
alveolar
alveolus
alderman
aldermen
Algernon
alternat
Alderney

✧**bluenose**
blue note
gleesome
sleep off
blue book
fluework
bluegown
blue john
alley-oop
ulcerous
bleep out
bluecoat
sleep out
sleepout
allegory
sloetree
allegros
blue-grey
alveated
cliental
fluent in
flue stop
alley-tor
Al Oerter
Alcestis
alley-taw
fluently
alleluia
flue-cure
sloebush
bluebuck
blue duck
blue funk
blue ruin
alleyway
sloe-eyed
aldehyde
olefiant
bluff bow
ill-faced
old fogey
gliffing
cly-faker
olefinic
Clifford
fly front
all-fired
ill-faste
Blefuscu
ill-fated
all found
ill-faurd
all-fours
old fruit
all-fives
old guard
sluggard
flag rank
elegiacs
elegiast
flagrant
plagiary
slug-a-bed
eligible
eligibly
alogical
slag heap
blagueur
slugfest
plug-ugly
flagship

clagging
flagging
flogging
glugging
plugging
slagging
slogging
sluggish
plaguily
flagella
oligomer
elegance
elegancy
flagpole
plughole
slag wool
flag-worm
flag down
slughorn
Old Glory
aligarta
oliguria
oliguric
oligarch
flag iris
alighted
blighted
flighted
plighted
blighter
plighter
slightly
all-giver
plug away
alphabet
✧**glühwein**
blah-blah
alchemic
Old Harry
elkhound
alehouse
although
ultimata
alginate
alligate
ultimate
all in all
plein-air
claimant
plainant
ultimacy
plain bob
Pleiades
Klaipeda
albiness
alaiment
plainful
sleigher
✧**almighty**
albitise
albitize
algicide
Blairite
fluidise
fluidize
plaiding
plaining
plaiting
plainish
albinism
alpinism

Blairism
illinium
illision
fluidics
alpinist
algidity
fluidify
fluidity
plaidman
alliance
eloigner
cleidoic
albicore
all in one
all-in-one
Elsinore
Illinois
ellipses
ellipsis
elliptic
cloister
plaister
slaister
illiquid
altitude
blokedom
blokeish
flake out
Tlalocan
elflocks
Old Light
slalomer
old-liner
clambake
plumbate
plum-cake
slam-bang
✧**plumbago**
plumb bob
blamable
blamably
flambéed
all my eye
Alcmaeon
glumness
slimness
slumbers
glummest
slimmest
flambeau
flummery
glimmery
plumbery
slumbery
blameful
plumaged
flame gun
✧**olympiad**
Alemaine
plumbite
slimline
blimbing
clamming
climbing
clumping
glomming
plumbing
slamming
slimming
slumming
blimpish

ampullae
Omdurman
impugner
empurple
impurple
embusqué
embussed
empyreal
empyrean
empyemic
empyesis
amazedly
Amazonia
endamage
indagate
inhalant
unbarbed
unhatch'd
en garçon
sneak-cup
enhancer
unbanded
uncandid
unwarded
unsaddle
in tandem
inlander
Anzac Day
inwardly
onwardly
in camera
on camera
unnaneld
sneakeup
unmade-up
innately
insanely
unsafely
unsafety
unwarely
unwatery
unlawful
enlarged
ungauged
unhanged
unpanged
entangle
untangle
enlargen
endanger
enlarger
in danger
on target
uncaught
untaught
unbathed
uncashed
undashed
unpathed
unsashed
unwashed
unwashen
ingather
uneathes
unvaried
annalise
annalize
in capite
indamine
infamise
infamize
innative
invasive
unnative
engaging
inlaying
sneaking
sneaping
uncaring
unfading
unlading
unmaking
unsating
enravish
sneakish
uniaxial
invasion
uno animo
annalist
insanity
sneakily
uneasily
unwarily
unbacked
unbanked
unbarked
unhacked
unmarked
unmasked
unpacked
unracked
untackle
unmasker
unpacker
uncalled
unfabled
ungalled
unhailed
unmailed
unsailed
untailed
unwalled
unfallen
intaglio
entailer
inhauler
enwallow
unhallow
unfaulty
undammed
unharmed
unmaimed
unwarmed
✧encaenia
undamned
unearned
unfanned
unmanned
unpained
unsained
untanned
unwarned
enraunge
infaunal
unpannel
ungainly
Anna Ford
Ansafone®
in favour
infamous
uncapped
undamped
unmapped
unsapped
untapped
unwarped
ensample
en rappel
encarpus
unbarred
unhaired
unmarred
unpaired
untarred
unfairly
intarsia
uncaused
unhalsed
unraised
envassal
Inmarsat
sneaksby
unbaited
unhatted
unsalted
untasted
unwanted
unwasted
Ondaatje
unmantle
unfasten
one-acter
annattos
infantry
unvalued
Antabuse®
undazzle
anabaena
anableps
snobbery
enabling
snobling
snubbing
snobbish
snubbish
snobbism
anabolic
one by one
snub nose
inkberry
anabasis
anabatic
unabated
snub cube
unobeyed
snack bar
unicycle
Anacreon
on-screen
knackers
knickers
knockers
inscient
knackery
enactive
inactive
inscribe
onychite
unactive
enacting
knocking
unaching
knackish
onychium
enaction
inaction
unscaled
inoculum
unicolor
insculpt
anaconda
aniconic
ensconce
insconce
anechoic
anecdote
knock off
inscroll
knock out
knockout
una corda
Anicetus
enacture
inedible
unadored
inedited
unedited
in demand
on demand
on remand
unrepaid
antedate
enterate
under age
under-age
antenati
in detail
underarm
unrepair
antepast
interact
underact
untenant
underbid
unwebbed
enfeeble
ensemble
inner bar
under-boy
underbuy
unfenced
intercom
intercut
undercut
enneadic
intended
unbedded
unbended
undeeded
underdid
unheeded
unleaded
unneeded
unseeded
untended
unwedded
unweeded
underdog
unfeudal
unseldom
engender
entender
Enzedder
intender
untender
antecede
undelete
knee-jerk
unbeseem
inhere in
Angeleno
knee-deep
inner ear
interess
antevert
indecent
inherent
interest
unbereft
undecent
undesert
underfed
underfur
unbegged
unhedged
enveigle
in league
inveagle
inveigle
enneagon
in weight
sneeshan
sneeshin
untether
unnethes
✧angelica
Angelina
Annelida
antefixa
undefied
andesine
andesite
ankerite
anserine
en vérité
inferiae
undefide
unbelief
entering
indexing
sneering
sneezing
unseeing
knee-high
endemial
in denial
ungenial
endemism
ingenium
annexion
inhesion
unbenign
anterior
inferior
interior
in series
unsexist
under-jaw
invecked
undecked
unrecked
angekkok
enter key
unfelled
unhealed
unpeeled
unsealed
unveiled
underlie
unhealth
underlap
underlip
annealer
unveiler
entellus
underlet
interlay
underlay
unreally
endermic
unhelmed
unseamed
inner man
underman
intermit
intermix
unseemly
unkenned
unpenned
unreined
unweaned
unweened
unyeaned
antennae
enceinte
internee
antennal
enkernel
infernal
internal
unkennel
antennas
infernos
inter nos
✧internet
unheroic
on record
anaerobe
antelope
envelope
kneehole
once more
knee sock
anteroom
ante-post
undevout
unhelped
unreaped
unpeople
Interpol
underpin
unheppen
unweapon
under par
untemper
underpay
endeared
inferred
interred
unfeared
ungeared
unpeered
enhearse
inhearse
unhearse
anhedral
integral
integrin
underrun
an-heires
in secret
unlearnt
unsecret
interrex
undersea
unleased
unsensed
unversed
Andersen
Anderson
in person
in reason
in season
unperson
unreason
unseason
incenser
incensor
Intelsat
underset
intersex
undersay
undersky
enfested
indebted
indented
infefted
inserted
invected
inverted
unbelted
unheated
unmelted
unnetted
unseated
untented
untested
unvented
unvetted
unwetted
incentre
intertie
in ventre
ungentle
unsettle
insectan
invertin
invest in
unbeaten
knee-stop
ancestor
anteater
enfetter
inceptor
indenter
indentor
infector
injector
inserter
insetter
inventor
inverter
invertor
investor
onsetter
unfetter
under tow

undertow
ancestry
intently
ungently
unmeetly
infecund
annexure
insecure
underuse
unsexual
in return
unnerved
interval
endeavor
once-over
on velvet
interwar
underwit
under way
underway
endeixis
unseized
unafraid
knife-box
snuffbox
knife-boy
one flesh
snifters
snuffers
in effect
sniffing
snuffing
unifying
sniffily
sniffler
snuffler
unifilar
sniffles
snuffles
knife-man
snuff out
snugness
snuggest
snuggery
anagogic
snagging
snugging
sniggler
knightly
anaglyph
inchoate
inch-tape
ensheath
enthrall
in thrall
inthrall
in the air
on the air
in the bag
on the bit
on the bot
in the can
unshaded
on the dot
unshadow
on the ebb
enshield
in the end
unthread
inchmeal
on the fly

on the hop
enshrine
inshrine
unthrift
on the job
on-the-job
on the jar
unshaked
unshaken
anthelia
on the lam
anthelix
enthalpy
anthemia
anthemic
unrhymed
unshamed
on the map
on the mat
on the nod
unchancy
enshroud
unshroud
enthrone
unthrone
in shtook
inch-worm
unshaped
unshapen
in the poo
enchoric
Angharad
in the red
unshared
encharge
in charge
one-horse
uncharge
on the rag
unchurch
on the run
in chorus
anchoret
in the raw
in a hurry
enchased
unchaste
unchosen
Anchises
anthesis
on the sly
enthetic
unthatch
unshrubd
unshaved
unshaven
unchewed
unthawed
in the way
on the way
Anthozoa
intifada
unvizard
anti-fade
enfilade
ensilage
envisage
indicate
intimate
uncinate
antimask

anti-tank
incitant
indicant
intimacy
unribbed
enviable
inviable
unviable
unlimber
enviably
encircle
anti-icer
in pieces
ungilded
ungirded
unlidded
unminded
engirdle
enkindle
in kindle
unriddle
unwisdom
unbidden
unhidden
unridden
unkindly
antisera
one-idea'd
antimere
indigene
inficete
unlineal
anti-hero
engineer
inkiness
incident
indigent
indigest
indirect
enginery
entirely
entirety
snailery
unlikely
unlively
untimely
unwifely
unwisely
unwilful
enridged
unhinged
unrigged
unringed
untinged
unwigged
unwinged
unkingly
unfished
unwished
antiphon
anti-chip
antiship
unbishop
encipher
uncipher
antithet
unpitied
anticize
incisive
infinite
in limine

undivine
enticing
inviting
on liking
ungiving
unliving
untiring
✧india ink
indicial
unfilial
incivism
indicium
intimism
oncidium
undinism
envision
incision
antiriot
intimist
infinity
intimity
unfixity
untidily
anticked
antiskid
unlicked
unlinked
unmilked
unpicked
unpinked
unsicker
unfilled
unmilled
unrifled
untilled
untitled
unwilled
unwieldy
undimmed
unfilmed
Indiaman
Indiamen
angiomas
infirmly
insignia
unpinned
unsigned
untinned
in bianco
ancients
until now
ensigncy
indigoid
antidote
Antigone
Antilope
antinode
✧antipode
antipole
antipope
Annigoni
anti-lock
anti-roll
ensiform
unciform
anticous
environs
indigoes
antibody
antilogy
antimony

antinomy
incisory
undipped
unripped
enfierce
encierro
gneissic
unbiased
unkissed
unmissed
Anointed
unbitted
undinted
unfitted
ungifted
unlisted
unsifted
indictee
in little
on tiptoe
unvirtue
enlist in
anointer
enlister
indicter
antistat
incisure
intitule
in liquor
antirust
unviewed
antitype
Ann Jones
snake eel
snake fly
snake-oil
snake-pit
angklung
antliate
enallage
unpliant
unilobed
angle bar
unilobar
analecta
unplaced
unsliced
Anglican
analects
included
influent
angle for
analogic
analogue
analogon
in-flight
unallied
analcime
analcite
unsluice
unslaked
analemma
inflamed
unblamed
inflamer
inclined
unclench
incliner
one-liner
in plenty
unbloody

antlered
unclosed
Uncle Sam
analyser
encloser
incloser
analyses
analysis
enclisis
Anglesey
unclassy
analytic
enclitic
inflated
unelated
enclothe
unclothe
unclutch
Uncle Tom
inflater
inflator
inflatus
uncloudy
enslaved
ungloved
uncloven
enslaver
unblowed
unflawed
enflower
inflexed
unplayed
unglazed
analyzer
inimical
unsmoked
animalic
animally
gnomonic
mnemonic
unsmooth
Antmusic
unamused
animatic
animated
animater
animator
unimbued
unamazed
Onondaga
inundate
inundant
unknight
unanchor
unenvied
unending
unaneled
on and off
on-and-off
Anonioni
uninured
endosarc
un-Mosaic
untoward
annotate
innovate
insolate
intonate
infobahn
intonaco
endocarp

endogamy
uncombed
unforbid
untombed
undouble
unforced
unvoiced
enforcer
unfolded
unhooded
unloaded
unlorded
unwooded
unworded
unsodden
inholder
unfolder
unloader
unsolder
unlordly
oncogene
infotech
endoderm
entoderm
unsolemn
enforest
indolent
✧innocent
insolent
unhonest
endogeny
ontogeny
uncomely
unhomely
unlovely
unroofed
snootful
unjoyful
onion fly
engorged
unforged
ungorged
unrouged
end organ
unbought
unforgot
unfought
unsought
unbodied
unmonied
indocile
in no wise
unionise
unionize
unpolite
annoying
incoming
intoning
oncoming
unboding
unloving
unmoving
unmodish
unpolish
unsocial
encomium
✧unionism
encomion
in Domino
✧unionist
snootily

unholily
unbooked
uncooked
undocked
unlocked
unlooked
unworked
onlooker
in pocket
unsocket
engouled
enrolled
uncowled
unpolled
unsoiled
unsouled
enrollee
enroller
informed
undoomed
unformed
unwormed
informal
unformal
in common
uncommon
informer
✧**insomnia**
uncoined
uncoyned
ungowned
unmoaned
announce
en pointe
inconnue
enjoiner
ongoings
unbonnet
endozoic
entozoic
one-on-one
entozoal
endozoon
entozoon
encolour
unjoyous
Indology
oncology
oncotomy
ontology
unlopped
unsoaped
incorpse
uncouple
unholpen
unsoured
in course
Andorran
endorsed
enmossed
unhoused
unpoised
unroused
endorsee
unloosen
unpoison
endorser
endorsor
entoptic
enzootic
unpoetic
intorted
unbolted
uncoated
unfooted
unposted
unrooted
unrotted
unsorted
unwonted
ungotten
unrotten
one or two
uncostly
unworthy
unco guid
encolure
involute
insomuch
involved
unsolved
endodyne
antonymy
anaphase
anyplace
knapsack
ink plant
in specie
knapscal
in spades
knapweed
ensphere
insphere
one-piece
unsphere
snap bean
anapaest
snippety
snipe fly
snapshot
knapping
snapping
snipping
snappish
snap-link
unspoilt
snappily
unspoken
unipolar
unopened
snip-snap
anaphora
snap roll
endpaper
inspired
unspared
ens per se
snap-brim
inspirer
inspirit
Anoplura
unsprung
uniquely
inequity
✧iniquity
encrease
enervate
ens reale
increase
increate
inornate
inurbane
uncreate
encroach
unpreach
inerrant
undreamt
entreaty
inarable
Enard Bay
unbraced
ungraced
unpriced
untraced
entr'acte
ungraded
untraded
encradle
unbridle
infra dig
intruder
intrados
unfriend
enfreeze
engrieve
unfreeze
unbreech
unpriest
entry fee
unartful
intrigue
androgen
inert gas
anarchic
anorthic
enarched
anarchal
enargite
energise
energize
unpraise
knurling
snarling
snorting
unerring
inertial
entryism
untruism
gnarlier
entrails
entryist
enormity
unbroken
engramma
unframed
unprimed
in gremio
entremes
intromit
encrinic
unironed
unpruned
en prince
entrance
infringe
intrince
entrench
indrench
intrench
encrinal
intranet
engroove
ingroove
enormous
inermous
entropic
✧**intrepid**
undraped
unproper
entrepot
entrepôt
Andropov
infrared
antrorse
introrse
unbrused
en brosse
unbraste
entresol
enfrosen
unarisen
unprison
anuresis
enuresis
undrossy
untrusty
anoretic
enuretic
Andretti
unpretty
unargued
unground
en croupe
en croûte
engraved
unproved
engraven
undriven
unproven
engraver
ungravly
ingrowth
anorexia
anorexic
ungrazed
unprized
unfrozen
inkstand
unusable
unusably
one-sided
one's self
gnashers
unuseful
ants'-eggs
unespied
inessive
gnashing
inustion
in a sense
unisonal
oniscoid
inkstone
anasarca
angstrom
Ångström
anestrus
anisette
inositol
and stuff
inasmuch
one's turn
initiate
one-track
unsteady
instable
unstable
unitedly
anathema
knotweed
in itself
unit cell
on stream
on-stream
knitwear
instress
knotless
snottery
unstuffy
snatcher
snitcher
gnathite
on strike
anything
gnatling
knitting
knotting
unstring
knottily
snottily
Gnetales
knittles
anatomic
unatoned
instance
instants
instinct
instancy
knothole
one-to-one
knotwork
unctuous
unit cost
anatropy
unstarch
unstated
unstitch
unstrung
unstruck
instruct
unstayed
Annulata
angulate
annulate
inaurate
incubate
indurate
inhumane
inhumate
insulate
intubate
undulate
ungulate
insurant
undulant
uncurbed
undubbed
unrubbed
unturbid
encumber
incumber
in lumber
unbudded
unfunded
unguided
unbundle
unburden
unsued-to
in sunder
unmuffle
unruffle
unpurged
enhunger
indulger
unvulgar
an hungry
an-hungry
unburied
enlumine
induciae
induline
induviae
infusive
enduring
ennuying
indusial
induvial
aneurism
indusium
infusion
unsucked
untucked
unbuckle
insucken
Anguilla
in public
annulled
unculled
uncurled
undulled
unpulled
annually
unguilty
ungummed
unsummed
unburned
unsunned
unturned
inguinal
innuendo
annulose
undulose
anourous
incubous
undulous
infusory
anguiped
unsupple
incurred
unfurred
en cuerpo
in cuerpo
in querpo
enquirer
inquirer
unburrow
intuited
unhunted
unquoted
unsuited
inductee
unsubtle
unbutton
enaunter
inductor
inputter
insulter
industry
unjustly
incurved
uncurved
aneurysm
unmuzzle
univocal
univalve
snivelly
unevenly
universe
DNA virus
unavowed
snowpack
✧**snowball**
snowfall
snow-capt
knowable
snowed in
snowed up
anywhere
snowless
snowshoe
snowbird
snowlike
snowline
snow flea
snowslip
one-woman
snow cone
snow-hole
snowy owl
snowboot
Answer Me
answer to
snowdrop
answerer
unawares
enswathe
inswathe
unswathe
snow bush
snowbush
unswayed
snow-eyes
in excess
inexpert
Endymion
encyclic
on my word
ankylose
enhydros
encysted
endzones
rotavate
soda-lake
coranach
bonamani
tomahawk
not at all
bonamano
nowadays
donatary
focaccia
Comanche
Monarcho
polar cap
romancer
tobaccos
monarchy

Words marked ✧ can also be spelled with one or more capital letters

nomarchy
toparchy
mokaddam
notandum
colander
Polander
pomander
solander
cowardly
cowardry
monandry
solar day
towardly
to camera
Moraceae
nota bene
Rosaceae
vocalese
soda jerk
moray eel
not a bean
Sotadean
soya bean
not a peep
voyageur
votaress
covalent
god-awful
pot-au-feu
coxalgia
Cocaigne
coraggio
botargos
podargus
do-naught
monachal
Jonathan
Jonathon
Monaghan
borachio
Monachus
pot ashes
pot-ashes
foramina
Mona Lisa
sonatina
Tomasina
Rosalind
bona fide
boracite
botanise
botanize
conative
coramine
donative
dopamine
focalise
focalize
for a time
go native
localise
localize
locative
monazite
moralise
moralize
nodalise
nodalize
nomadise
nomadize
notarise
notarize
polarise
polarize
Romanise
Romanize
Rosaline
rotative
royalise
royalize
soda lime
sodalite
sodamide
solanine
solarise
solarize
tonalite
topazine
totalise
totalize
vocalise
vocalize
vocative
volatile
womanise
womanize
Romanish
tovarich
tovarish
womanish
soya milk
conarial
domanial
gonadial
monaxial
notarial
conarium
domatium
donatism
iotacism
localism
loyalism
modalism
monadism
moralism
nomadism
Romanism
rosarium
royalism
solarism
solarium
solatium
somatism
vocalism
conation
donation
dotation
Horatian
jobation
Kolarian
lobation
location
Moravian
nodation
notation
Novatian
novation
Polabian
potation
rogation
Romanian
rosarian
Rotarian
rotation
solation
vocalion
vocation
zonation
douanier
botanist
Donatist
localist
✧loyalist
modalist
moralist
Romanist
✧royalist
solarist
somatist
vocalist
votarist
Iowa City
locality
modality
molality
molarity
morality
nodality
polarity
sodality
tonality
totality
vocality
voracity
cop a plea
so-called
totalled
rocaille
corallum
moraller
notables
Bonar Law
moral law
Roman law
tomalley
toxaemia
toxaemic
Mohammed
morainic
domainal
morainal
johannes
bona-roba
Coca-Cola®
Rosa Mota
coracoid
homaloid
Polaroid®
Rosamond
comatose
con amore
Copaxone®
not a hope
Vodafone®
jog along
sola topi
Royal Oak
oogamous
pomatoes
potatoes
tomatoes
voragoes
donatory
moratory
potatory
rogatory
rotatory
tomatoey
bob-apple
zoiatria
podagric
sowarree
Coral Rag
monaural
podagral
doxapram
Moharram
Coral Sea
potassic
Romansch
Polanski
mocassin
bonassus
molasses
cobaltic
doxastic
monastic
romantic
do battle
Iolanthe
cofactor
no matter
corantos
Rosamund
Zola Budd
coq au vin
go halves
total war
boxboard
logboard
mopboard
Joe Blake
hot-brain
top brass
hot blast
zooblast
bombycid
Don Budge
morbidly
sowbread
Corbiere
sombrero
cobble up
double up
gobble up
cobblers
combless
Goebbels
tombless
no object
cobblery
sombrely
morbific
doubtful
bombsite
combwise
womblike
cobbling
doubling
doubting
hobbling
lobbying
not-being
wobbling
boobyish
boobyism
hobbyism
zombiism
hobbyist
lobbyist
gorblimy
corbeled
morbilli
tombolos
gor-belly
pot-belly
combined
Sorbonne
combings
bobbinet
go abroad
tolbooth
doubloon
Joe Brown
sombrous
bobby pin
sorbaria
bombarde
forborne
row barge
zomboruk
dobber-in
mowburnt
cowberry
✧dogberry
foxberry
sorbuses
sorbitic
combated
sorbitol
Hobbiton
hobbitry
fogbound
pot-bound
boob tube
doublure
fox-brush
comb over
combover
mouchard
conchate
conclave
non-claim
couchant
morceaux
ponceaux
forcible
boschbok
log cabin
coach box
touch-box
voice box
forcibly
cow cocky
✧coccidia
Coccidae
coachdog
conceder
roncador
forcedly
concrete
torchère
dog-cheap
botchery
louchely
force-fed
forceful
pouchful
voiceful
coccyges
colchica
godchild
coactive
conceive
botching
coaching
couching
notching
poaching
torching
touching
dobchick
coaction
Noachian
torchier
touchier
conceity
touchily
Roccella
Joscelin
concolor
torcular
Cocculus
zoccolos
coachman
Golconda
volcanic
joncanoe
log-canoe
col canto
toucanet
conchoid
honchoed
zoochore
touch off
souchong
box-cloth
mouchoir
poaceous
zoochory
touch pad
concepti
forcipes
hotchpot
Concorde
concerti
concerto
sorcerer
moccasin
zoocytia
concetti
concetto
concause
conclude
concours
Foucault
coach-way
hoactzin
Gondwana
bondmaid
food-card
gold card
hold hard
hold hard!
woodland
woodward
woodyard
boldface
cold wave
gold lace
good-dame
road game
road race
road rage
wood sage
woodwale
wordgame
cot death
cold pack
good-lack
hold back
holdback
woodlark
Toad Hall
cordwain
gold-wasp
moldwarp
wood wasp
holdfast
Bordeaux
rondeaux
foldable
fordable
voidable
wood ibis
Boadicea
Boudicca
wood acid
rondache
conducti
Mordecai
pond scum
toddy cat
soldados
rowdedow
rowdydow
Lord's Day
sordidly
cold-weld
pondweed
gold leaf
gold-leaf
word-deaf
woodmeal
rood beam
Sondheim
how-d'ye-do
toodle-oo
goodyear
boldness
coldness
cordless
fondness
foodless
goldless
goodness
hoodless
lordless
loudness
roadless
top-dress
voidness
woodless
woodness
wordless
cold feet
moodiest

road test
road-test
soldiery
bondager
woodshed
lordship
woodchip
woodchat
good show
roadshow
gold disc
woodbind
woodwind
gold mine
goldsize
gold wire
goodsire
goodtime
✧goodwife
load line
lordlike
mondaine
pond-life
roadside
✧woodbine
woodlice
wood mite
woodpile
word bite
boodying
fondling
fordoing
lordling
toadying
toddling
yoldring
cold fish
dowdyish
food-fish
goldfish
rowdyish
toadfish
toadyish
hoodwink
wood tick
goodwill
road kill
dowdyism
rowdyism
toadyism
Mondrian
road sign
goodlier
Mordvins
Lord Birt
dog-daisy
non-dairy
pond lily
woodskin
Cordelia
Goidelic
Bob Dylan
bordello
jordeloo
condylar
cold slaw
toadflax
gondelay
hold play
wordplay
moody-mad
bondsman
goadsman
roadsman
woodsman
condense
Joe Dante
toe dance
toe-dance
voidance
goad into
cold snap
cordiner
Londoner
gold-ends
holdings
lordings
rondinos
tondinos
voidings
goldenly
mordancy
woodenly
cordwood
hold good
hoodooed
cold sore
gold note
Lord Home
Lord Howe
woodhole
woodnote
woodwose
wordlore
woodroof
cold work
cold-work
goldwork
good folk
road book
roadwork
woodcock
woodwork
wordbook
gold foil
wood coal
wood wool
good form
woodworm
hold down
wood-born
wondrous
cold boot
cold-boot
foldboat
rood loft
wood opal
toad spit
Borduria
bordered
doddered
powdered
wondered
bouderie
foedarie
rood-tree
folderol
ponderal
Honduran
wood wren
word wrap
borderer
dodderer
fodderer
ponderer
solderer
wonderer
Honduras
corduroy
yonderly
lordosis
lordotic
Low Dutch
goadster
loadstar
roadster
Lord Hurd
woodruff
gold rush
toadrush
woodrush
cold duck
Lord Muck
sow-drunk
wood duck
good turn
road hump
wood pulp
cold cuts
doldrums
gold dust
Lord Hunt
rondavel
wood-evil
cordovan
good-even
Moldovan
hold over
holdover
Joe Davis
Lord Owen
foldaway
hold sway
hobdayed
Lord Lyon
boneyard
Copeland
forehand
foreland
foresaid
foreward
foreyard
hole card
homeland
homeward
lone hand
noseband
Romeward
Roseland
bone-cave
bone-lace
codename
copemate
coverage
cozenage
foredate
forename
home base
home-made
home page
lose face
love game
Lovelace
moderate
notecase
somegate
tolerate
toleware
yoke-mate
rose rash
come back
comeback
fore-rank
mopehawk
rope-walk
coverall
dovetail
foresail
Rosewall
home farm
forewarn
rope yarn
moderato
power-amp
lone pair
someways
cosecant
cotenant
covenant
forecast
foremast
forepart
forepast
honey ant
molecast
tolerant
cometary
monetary
novenary
rosemary
hover-bed
honey bee
loveable
moveable
poseable
ropeable
honey-bag
money bag
honeybun
✧november
homeobox
money box
moveably
bone-ache
novercal
power cut
Rome-scot
bone-idle
comeddle
fore-edge
fogeydom
noveldom
Poseidon
box elder
toreador
honeydew
nose-herb
bonehead
cokehead
coleseed
forehead
forelend
foreread
pokeweed
rope's end
rope's-end
sorehead
novelese
pope's eye
somedele
nose-leaf
rose leaf
tone-deaf
foredeck
forepeak
bone meal
forefeel
foretell
hose reel
somedeal
foremean
foreseen
Love Me Do
home help
forebear
boneless
coreless
doneness
goneness
homeless
hopeless
lobeless
loneness
loveless
moveless
noseless
noteless
roseless
soleness
soreness
toneless
voteless
zoneless
bodement
coherent
coregent
dome tent
forefeet
forefelt
forehent
forelent
forewent
homefelt
love-feat
love nest
love seat
movement
non-elect
non-event
no remedy
powerful
cover for
hoverfly
lozenged
somewhen
dogeship
foreship
popeship
comether
together
somewhat
foreshew
foreshow
forelimb
forewind
home bird
lovebird
cohesive
coteline
covetise
dolerite
dovelike
foreside
foretime
home-fire
home-life
homelike
home time
hosepipe
Joceline
lobeline
lose time
lovebite
love life
monetise
monetize
nosedive
noselite
novelise
novelize
polemise
polemize
ronepipe
rope-ripe
roselike
soberise
soberize
solecise
solecize
sometime
somewise
vomerine
vowelise
vowelize
covering
forcking
forewing
honeying
hoteling
lowering
modeling
nose-ring
popeling
sobering
toweling
towering
bonefish
come high
fogeyish
novelish
pokerish
rosefish
yokelish
homesick
lovesick
Roderick
rose-pink
bone-mill
homegirl
molehill
mote-hill
soredial
soterial
bogeyism
Docetism
fogeyism
nobelium
novelism
solecism
soredium
tokenism
totemism
Wodenism
zooecium
✧bohemian
cohesion
comedian
Rogerian
comelier
hotelier
hôtelier
motelier
Gobelins
polemics
Docetist
forebitt
forelift
Nobelist
novelist
noverint
polemist
solecist
totemist
homelily
lovelily
foreskin
moleskin
Honecker
bowelled
coverlid
hovelled
modelled
rowelled
towelled
vowelled
novellae
foreplan
lower lip
hoveller
modeller
roseolar
yodeller
modellos
morellos
coverlet
Bode's law
coleslaw
foreslow
role-play
bogeyman
Doberman
lodesman
moneyman
Roseanna
Roseanne
come into
power nap
governor
cokernut
home unit
love-knot
rose knot
foreknow
modernly
solemnly
Copepoda
rose comb

codeword
foretold
foreword
go beyond
popehood
rosewood
solenoid
yoke-toed
borecole
borehole
come home
dolesome
dovecote
forebode
foregone
holesome
home zone
jokesome
lonesome
lovesome
nose cone
rotenone
some hope
wobegone
lone wolf
love-song
codebook
forehock
forelock
homework
lovelock
morepork
notebook
ropework
rosebowl
foredoom
tone poem
come down
comedown
forenoon
home-born
home loan
home town
lovelorn
Pope Joan
tone down
vote down
foregoer
covetous
colewort
forefoot
foremost
home port
honewort
lobe-foot
roseroot
fore-body
home body
somebody
so help me
bone up on
come upon
dote upon
dowel-pin
homespun
pore upon
honeypot
Moresque
dog-eared
dowel-rod
home-bred
lop-eared
come true
rose tree
love-drug
fox-earth
rose drop
foie gras
home-brew
dove grey
Rose Gray
forensic
honey-sac
Bodensee
coleuses
homeosis
power set
✧somerset
power tea
Rodentia
domestic
homeotic
toreutic
forested
rosetted
forestal
go mental
lomentum
momentum
tomentum
fomenter
✧forester
go better
go-getter
lodestar
molester
Pole Star
nonettos
cogently
Coventry
covertly
forestay
forestry
honestly
modestly
momently
nocently
non-entry
potently
rose-hued
✧**home rule**
molecule
to be sure
nonesuch
rosebush
core dump
bone-dust
love-suit
mole hunt
come over
moreover
move over
pore over
rove-over
come away
doze away
zone axis
dove-eyed
mole-eyed
golfiana
box-frame
conflate
hog-frame
loaf-cake
hot flash
hoof-mark
roof rack
wolf pack
golf ball
goofball
korfball
bouffant
golf cart
dog-faced
confocal
confider
boofhead
confrère
coiffeur
dowfness
hoofless
roofless
hoofbeat
solfeggi
dogfight
rooflike
roof tile
wolflike
coiffing
sol-faing
wolfling
wolffish
sol-faism
forfairn
Wolffian
forfeits
conflict
sol-faist
wolfskin
golf club
gonfalon
moufflon
joyfully
woefully
confined
gonfanon
confiner
confines
Corfiote
wolf note
soffioni
wolf down
con fuoco
soy flour
confront
conferva
coffered
conferee
rooftree
confused
not fussy
confetti
non-fatal
confound
coiffure
hot flush
forfault
to a fault
longhand
bongrace
fox-grape
long face
long-wave
Lough Awe
roughage
long mark
long haul
long-haul
long-tail
longwall
poignado
long-hair
congrats
cowgrass
dog-grass
log-glass
longways
lopgrass
rotgrass
poignant
zoograft
congiary
doggy-bag
doughboy
rough cut
long odds
doggedly
rough-dry
long-head
Congoese
Congreve
ronggeng
long-term
jongleur
longueur
✧**congress**
long-legs
longness
songless
congreet
lodgment
songfest
tongue it
tough guy
longship
long shot
rough-hew
yongthly
songbird
long-life
long-line
long-nine
long side
long-time
longwise
songlike
coughing
forgoing
goggling
joggling
tonguing
wongiing
roughish
toughish
long-firm
Hodgkin's
longlist
long view
Mongolia
Mongolic
coagulum
boogaloo
long slip
forgeman
Gorgonia
congenic
zoogenic
doggoned
congener
lodgings
Longinus
doughnut
co-agency
zoogloea
Longford
conglobe
foxglove
long home
long robe
longsome
mongoose
Hong Kong
songbook
song form
longhorn
mongcorn
pop group
gorgeous
long moss
long-togs
longboat
rough out
rough-out
tough out
long-spun
longspur
boughpot
Congo red
Novgorod
doggerel
hoggerel
gorgerin
longeron
long iron
fougasse
nox gases
Golgotha
boughten
foughten
Loaghtan
long stop
long-stop
gongster
songster
tongster
forget it
long-stay
long jump
long suit
longeval
forgiven
God-given
forgiver
cowheard
Rochdale
Noah's ark
mothball
Loch Earn
top-heavy
to the bad
oothecae
cochleae
poshteen
cochlear
Loch Ness
poshness
mothiest
dochmiac
forhaile
po'chaise
dochmius
do the job
Rochelle
potholer
bonhomie
bothyman
non-human
no chance
nowhence
to the nth
Tom Hanks
forhooie
pooh-pooh
sopheric
cothurni
sopherim
oophoron
Lothario
cosherer
cothurns
go shares
motherly
pochette
hot hatch
hot-hatch
foxhound
cot-house
cowhouse
doghouse
hothouse
log-house
pothouse
row house
lothfull
jodhpurs
yoghourt
moshavim
Bob Hawke
✧**boniface**
cogitate
dominate
loricate
motivate
nominate
rosinate
solidare
solidate
volitate
komitaji
solidago
holidays
dominant
toxicant
volitant
docimasy
poticary
solidary
solitary
sociable
sociably
zodiacal
✧**moriscos**
to pieces
Gobiidae
louis-d'or
fog index
Doris Day
Robin Day
lonicera
Porifera
Rotifera
bonibell
✧**coliseum**
domineer
bodiless
boniness
boxiness
cosiness
coxiness
dopiness
doziness
foxiness
foziness
gooiness
goriness
✧holiness
jokiness
mopiness
nosiness
ooziness
poriness
ropiness
rosiness
lorikeet
moniment
bovinely
politely
to die for
foliaged
jowing-in
boringly
cooingly
dotingly
hopingly
jokingly
losingly
lovingly
mopingly
movingly
posingly
rovingly
wooingly
✧**eolithic**
polished
polish up
polisher
✧**dolichos**
boyishly
coyishly
modishly
mopishly
popishly
tonishly
toyishly
Dominica
codified
modified
notified
cotinine
domicile
eolipile
homicide
lonicise
lonicize
logicise
logicize
mobilise

monopoly
monosomy
monotony
nomology
nosology
podology
pomology
posology
tocology
tokology
topology
no-go area
✧coloured
honoured
coco-tree
honouree
Gomorrah
hologram
logogram
monogram
nomogram
sonogram
tomogram
colour in
colour up
colourer
honourer
mobocrat
monocrat
to borrow
tomorrow
colossal
Son of Sam
colossus
molossus
Colonsay
joyously
holoptic
Holostei
Joe Orton
solo stop
yokozuna
monohull
Honolulu
sonobuoy
motorway
gonocyte
holotype
homodyne
homotype
logotype
monocyte
Monotype®
monotype
topotype
homonymy
homotypy
monogyny
toponymy
Zoophaga
soapland
hotplate
towplane
volplane
soapbark
soap-ball
complain
cow-plant
pot plant
zoophagy
compadre
poppadum
Don Pedro
gooped up
hopped-up
souped-up
gospodar
hospodar
torpedos
Pompidou
Poppy Day
torpidly
codpiece
complete
morpheme
oosphere
toe-piece
poop deck
morphean
compress
hot press
hot-press
Morpheus
soapless
box-pleat
compleat
complect
soap test
solpugid
compages
complied
complice
✧compline
comprise
co-optive
loop-line
morphine
porpoise
Tom Paine
zoophile
coupling
morphing
complish
soap dish
co-option
Pompeian
sorption
complier
comprint
zoophily
Coppélia
compulse
compiler
nonpolar
pompelos
cow-pilot
hot pants
jog pants
jogpants
pompanos
toppings
volpinos
top-proud
loophole
romp home
poppy-oil
Woop Woop
soaproot
soapwort
soap tree
corporal
zooperal
copperas
corporas
non-party
composed
compesce
porpesse
Tok Pisin
composer
hospitia
not-pated
compital
hospital
computer
zoopathy
compound
soapsuds
Porphyra
Zoophyta
zoophyte
✧porphyry
torquate
top quark
cotquean
✧conquest
mosquito
non-quota
door-yard
gourmand
hour hand
moor-band
moorland
poor hand
doorcase
poor rate
kourbash
sour mash
four-pack
doornail
four-ball
poor laws
four-part
pot roast
pot-roast
horrible
pourable
poor's-box
horribly
boy racer
touracos
worricow
worrycow
porridge
corridor
forrader
joyrider
court-day
horridly
torridly
hoarhead
hog-reeve
four-leaf
yourself
doorbell
bourgeon
fourteen
dourness
journeys
poorness
sourness
sorriest
coarsely
courtesy
hoarsely
sobriety
horrific
mournful
non-rigid
Morrigan
porrigos
lorry-hop
fourthly
coercive
Lorraine
sourdine
to-bruise
voir dire
boarding
coursing
courting
hoarding
mourning
sourcing
worrying
boarfish
coarsish
poortith
sorryish
door-sill
poorwill
coercion
boursier
courtier
four bits
to-broken
no frills
no-frills
courtlet
doors-man
doorsman
no-trumps
doorknob
courante
couronne
Sobranje
Sobranye
Torrance
moorings
sopranos
Courtney
sovranly
sovranty
botryoid
fourfold
sour-cold
sourwood
botryose
foursome
hourlong
moorcock
moorfowl
poor-John
board out
doorpost
four-foot
moor-poot
moor-pout
worry out
boortree
bourtree
pourtray
coprosma
touristy
Socratic
doorstep
doorstop
co-writer
botritis
Botrytis
Socrates
go-around
tournure
boerbull
moorburn
sourpuss
poursuit
Monrovia
Don Revie
corrival
co-driver
borrowed
sorrowed
borrower
sorrower
soaraway
sour-eyed
bob royal
four-eyes
Botswana
moussaka
mossland
potshard
bob skate
constate
dog'sbane
for shame
job share
job-share
jobshare
log-slate
potshare
Rosslare
moss hagg
toiseach
cow shark
forslack
foxshark
hog's-back
mossback
borstall
coxswain
Torshavn
Tórshavn
bobstays
Constans
constant
forswatt
Konstanz
Lok Sabha
possible
horse bot
house bat
horse box
loose box
horse-boy
houseboy
possibly
God's acre
Popsicle®
goose cap
horsecar
loose-cut
lopsided
house-dog
mouse-dun
consider
topsides
monstera
forspend
✧godspeed
hogshead
loose end
potsherd
top-shelf
goose-egg
forspeak
Godspell
top-shell
zoosperm
Holstein
dogsleep
forswear
✧monsieur
mouse-ear
Job's news
dog's-meat
forspent
mossiest
mousiest
Rousseau
boastful
houseful
noiseful
horsefly
housefly
goosegob
goosegog
hoosegow
horse hoe
sous-chef
boss shot
how's that
cowslip'd
conspire
dog's life
God's life
mosslike
solstice
top-slice
boasting
coasting
hoisting
housling
roasting
roisting
roysting
toasting
god-smith
cow's lick
forswink
joystick
mopstick
non-stick
pot stick
bonspiel
loessial
pot still
pot-still
Volscian
toastier
God's gift
moistify
forsaken
mousekin
forsaker
bonsella
consulta
podsolic
fossulae
consoler
consular
Koestler
corselet
moss-flow
boy's play
dorsally
Wolseley®
consommé
Comsomol
Komsomol
hoastman
hoistman
horseman
houseman
Norseman
consumer
gossamer
consumpt
mousemat
nonsense
loosen up
loosener
poisoner
housings
Volsungs
cousinly
cousinry
Cotswold
boy's love
dog's-nose
fog-smoke
forswore
hog-score
moss rose
potstone
roestone
rot-stone
top stone
zoospore
worse off
forsooth
doss down
forsworn
Joe Slovo
voussoir
bons mots
couscous
kouskous
Boy Scout
for short
God's foot
hot-short
Job's post
dog's-body
dogsbody
sob story
Toy Story
zooscopy
gossiped
mousepad
gossypol
gossipry
house red
tonsured
conserve
construe

coistrel
coistril
coystrel
coystril
moss-crop
bowsprit
house-sit
tousy tea
fossette
noisette
housetop
house-tax
corsetry
God squad
moisture
soy sauce
hot stuff
sob stuff
low-slung
forswunk
✧**fosse way**
hoistway
horseway
powsowdy
toss away
boss-eyed
postcava
Godthaab
coat-card
✧portland
Port Said
postcard
post-paid
✧**boat race**
bootlace
boot sale
contrate
font name
footpace
footpage
foot-race
moot case
mortgage
mort-safe
postdate
postface
rostrate
rout-cake
software
voutsafe
footbath
footpath
koftgari
postnati
boot-jack
coatrack
footmark
postmark
softback
soft mark
boattail
contrail
football
footfall
footwall
moot hall
root ball
softball
mortmain
boot camp
contrair
root hair
bootlast
contract
contrast
portlast
portrait
root-fast
contrary
costmary
go steady
mortuary
noctuary
bootable
loo-table
mootable
portable
sortable
top table
bontebok
cottabus
kottabos
post-obit
monticle
postiche
soutache
cortical
poetical
vortical
Toltecan
post-echo
morticer
cortices
porticos
vortices
Cottidae
hotted-up
rootedly
bolthead
goatherd
goatweed
goutweed
jolthead
mort-head
nowt-herd
softhead
Southend
portière
bottle-oh
fortieth
boat deck
boat neck
footwell
Montreal
mortbell
soft sell
soft-sell
✧**northern**
✧southern
bottle up
footgear
footwear
root beer
bootless
coatless
doctress
footless
fortress
fostress
Poitiers
portress
rootless
soft lens
softness
sootless
wontless
bottle it
footrest
rootiest
rout-seat
soft meat
sortment
top tweet
Montreux
mortific
pontific
loathful
mouthful
soothful
toothful
worthful
youthful
pontifex
cottaged
Montague
portague
portigue
Portugee
Portugal
cottager
cottagey
boat shoe
soft-shoe
poetship
post ship
mostwhat
Port-Vila
Coctaine
contline
contrite
contrive
doctrine
goethite
port-fire
portoise
port wine
post time
rootlike
soft line
tortoise
Voltaire
footling
goatling
jostling
loathing
mortling
mottling
non-thing
northing
routeing
softling
soothing
southing
tottring
Worthing
fortyish
goatfish
monteith
bootlick
con trick
dog-trick
forthink
boatbill
foothill
moot-hill
post mill
voltaism
mouthier
toothier
poetries
worthies
contrist
fortuity
port-winy
toothily
worthily
bootikin
cootikin
goatskin
Montilla
tortilla
coutille
footslog
tortelli
portolan
portulan
noctilio
Portaloo®
Portillo
hosteler
cost plus
cost-plus
soft-slow
hostelry
mortally
postally
zootomic
bottomed
costumed
Northman
routeman
bottom-up
costumer
contempt
bottomry
continua
fortuned
boutonné
continue
fontange
Oostende
portance
sortance
bostangi
fontanel
cotton on
contango
continuo
montanto
soften up
softener
tontiner
contents
norteñas
norteños
Portunus
root-knot
don't-know
moltenly
rottenly
boatload
coltwood
foothold
post road
roothold
softwood
bolthole
bolt rope
boothose
contrôlé
footnote
foot-rope
footsore
Montrose
porthole
postcode
post hole
postpone
postpose
soft-core
soft sore
zoetrope
zoothome
zootrope
mouth off
boat-song
dogtooth
goat-moth
boathook
boot-hook
footwork
koftwork
soft rock
controul
lost soul
soft-boil
Postcomm
boxthorn
footworn
poltroon
post horn
post town
soft loan
Nostromo
soft soap
soft-soap
goitrous
porteous
porthors
tortious
tortuous
footpost
goutwort
hoot-toot
hout-tout
poltfoot
soft copy
zootypic
soft spot
southpaw
boutique
montaria
dog-tired
postgrad
tortured
tottered
boot-tree
cost-free
goat's-rue
✧nocturne
post-free
doctoral
dotterel
postoral
postural
soft iron
✧southron
contorno
root crop
fosterer
loiterer
mouterer
posturer
potterer
torturer
totterer
monteros
doctorly
porterly
souterly
contessa
North Sea
South Sea
portesse
cortisol
mortiser
not to say
soothsay
southsay
costated
toe to toe
toe-to-toe
footstep
aortitis
Tom Thumb
Dortmund
footrule
postlude
footmuff
cost push
Portrush
tow truck
footpump
zoot suit
post over
kowtower
non-toxic
zootoxin
cortexes
vortexes
copulate
lobulate
loculate
modulate
populace
populate
rosulate
Columbia
conurbia
columbic
Columban
conurban
Columbus
homuncle
Moluccas
corundum
mocuddum
Rogun Dam
pop-under
jocundly
rotundly
document
monument
to ruffl'd
go hungry
so much so
co-author
roburite
solutive
volumise
volumize
focusing
hocusing
vogueing
botulism
populism
locution
non-union
solution
volution
roturier
populist
volumist
coquilla
toquilla
go public
coquille
nonuplet
columned
columnal
columnar
volutoid
nodulose
torulose
docusoap
nodulous
populous
tohu bohu
locutory
colubrid
focussed
hocussed
mofussil
coquette
locustae
moquette
roquette
loquitur
coquitos
coquetry
robustly
To Autumn
souvlaki
solvable
Corvidae
convolve
convulse
nouvelle
tog value
volvulus
coevally
convince
Corvinae
convener
convenor
souvenir
solvency
louvered
converge
converse
poxvirus
pop-visit
corvette
non-voter
convexed
convexly
conveyal

conveyer
conveyor
cow whale
top whack
dog-weary
forweary
cobwebby
dog-whelk
bobwheel
cogwheel
joy-wheel
cow-wheat
dog-wheat
box-wagon
bobwhite
non-white
Tom Waits
Tom Wolfe
con woman
toywoman
Morwenna
low wines
woe worth
forwards
godwards
forwaste
dogwatch
fob-watch
hot water
low water
pomwater
Norweyan
coextend
to excess
polygala
Holy Land
holydame
polymath
ponytail
Polycarp
corybant
polygamy
polypary
polyacid
molybdic
copy-edit
copyread
Holyhead
hony-seed
polygene
polyseme
polytene
Holy Week
Holywell
Tony Benn
Holy Year
Body Heat
polygeny
polymery
polysemy
coryphee
coryphée
polyphon
body shop
to my mind
bodyline
bony pike
iodyrite
polypide
polypine
polypite

Moby Dick
Polybius
holy city
ponyskin
✧**polyglot**
body blow
Polymnia
Rohypnol
Rohypnol®
polyonym
bowyangs
polyzoic
copyhold
cotyloid
holy-rood
polypoid
polysome
bodywork
copybook
Tony Lock
cony-wool
polyzoan
polyzoon
polypous
holy coat
hoky-poky
polygony
polypody
polysomy
roly-poly
polyuria
polyarch
body wrap
rosy drop
✧**holy writ**
bodysurf
bodysuit
polyaxon
polygyny
foozling
Gonzales
forzando
colzaoil
douzeper
momzerim
mozzetta
bozzetti
bozzetto
bouzouki
appanage
uplander
upwardly
a piacere
apparent
spragged
sprangle
spear gun
spray gun
upcaught
splasher
upgather
aphasiac
aphanite
optative
speaking
upmaking
apiarian
apiarist
sprackle
upmarket
appalled

sprawler
spearman
sphagnum
spraints
sprauncy
speak out
speakout
upraised
aplastic
apractic
sprattle
splatter
epiblast
space age
space-age
speciate
spectate
Special K
spiccato
space bar
spice box
epicycle
epicedia
epicedes
specific
apocrine
speckled
speculum
spiculum
specular
spicular
epicalyx
apically
epically
spaceman
specimen
spicknel
Apocynum
spacious
specious
space out
spectral
spectrum
Epicurus
spicated
epicotyl
spadices
spadeful
spudding
upadaisy
spadille
spadillo
epidemic
spademan
spadones
spadroon
epidural
apodosis
epidotic
speed-cop
uppercut
splendid
splendor
spreader
appendix
ephemera
appetent
speedful
speed gun
aphetise
aphetize

appetise
appetite
appetize
spaewife
speeding
apperill
splenial
apterism
apterium
splenium
aphelian
aphelion
Ephesian
spherics
splenius
speedily
appellee
upper lip
sphenoid
spheroid
apterous
upreared
appearer
apres-ski
après-ski
appeaser
spreathe
spreethe
upper ten
upsetter
appestat
spherule
upheaval
speedway
epifocal
opificer
spiffing
spoffish
epifauna
apograph
epigraph
spyglass
apogaeic
epigaeal
epigaean
apagogic
epagogic
Spigelia
apogamic
epigamic
✧**epigones**
epigeous
spageric
spagiric
spagyric
upcheard
upthrust
apricate
oppilate
optimate
speisade
spoilage
opsimath
split cap
split end
spritely
spoilful
sphingid
sprigged
springed
springle

springal
spring on
springer
sphinges
uppishly
aphicide
optimise
optimize
uprising
Aprilish
Ophitism
optimism
aphidian
Aprilian
ophidian
optician
optimist
sprinkle
Iphicles
optional
split-new
ypsiloid
split-off
apricock
split pea
split pin
ophiurid
ophiuran
splitted
uplifted
uptilted
splinter
splitter
sprinter
uplifter
aptitude
sphinxes
spuilzie
spritzig
spritzer
Spike Lee
spikelet
spike oil
spekboom
spillage
spoliate
spalpeen
spelaean
spellful
apologia
epilogic
apologue
epilogue
Apolline
applying
spalling
spelding
spelling
spilling
epyllion
spilikin
Apple Mac®
opulence
spell out
apple-pie
epilepsy
appliqué
speldrin
opalised
epulotic
spilitic

epilator
applause
spillway
Apollyon
opalized
spamming
spumante
spy-money
epimeric
apomixis
spondaic
Spaniard
upon oath
spendall
spunyarn
open-cast
openable
opinable
opinicus
epanodos
open-reel
openness
spanless
spinneys
spin-text
spintext
spinnery
spinifex
apanaged
open shop
up-anchor
spanghew
open mind
open fire
open-mike
open side
spanking
spanning
spending
spinning
sponsing
spun silk
sponsion
spinnies
spongily
spangled
open-plan
spangler
spanglet
eponymic
spongoid
open note
span roof
span-long
open book
openwork
open town
spontoon
open door
open-door
spunk out
spandrel
spandril
up in arms
epinosic
Upanisad
epinasty
spinette
spinster
spansule
ependyma

open-eyed
ephorate
up to date
up-to-date
splotchy
upholder
opponent
spoofery
spookery
spoon-fed
spoonfed
apronful
spoonful
aphorise
aphorize
apposite
epsomite
opposite
opsonise
opsonize
up to time
opposing
spooming
upcoming
spookish
aphorism
opsonium
aphorist
spookily
spoonily
uplocked
sprocket
upfollow
apron-man
uptowner
Epyornis
up so down
aphonous
optology
sprouted
uprootal
uprooter
spy plane
upsprang
✧**epiphany**
epopoeia
apoplexy
upspring
epipolic
opopanax
epiploic
epiploon
upsprung
apophyge
epiphyte
opaquely
approach
spar-hawk
spur-gall
spermary
operable
sparable
spiracle
sporidia
sporadic
upgrader
spar deck
spur gear
spurless
aperient
sparsely

 Words marked ✧ can also be spelled with one or more capital letters

sportful
spark gap
opera hat
appraise
sportive
sparling
sparring
sperling
spirling
sporting
spurling
spurning
spurring
sparkish
spur-rial
spurrier
sparsity
sportily
spirilla
sparkler
sporular
sparklet
spirally
spark off
sperm oil
spermous
spurious
spark out
spare rib
appriser
operetta
apyretic
operatic
spirated
spirited
aperitif
apéritif
operator
spiritus
opercula
Spergula
aperture
approval
approver
upgrowth
apyrexia
sparaxis
spur-ryal
Sporozoa
apprizer
apostate
apostasy
episodic
episodal
episperm
epistler
episemon
episcope
epispore
apospory
episcopy
upas-tree
apositia
apositic
opuscula
opuscule
epistyle
spot cash
spatfall
up sticks
epithema

spot-weld
✧spätlese
apothegm
upstream
epithems
spotless
sputtery
spiteful
spitcher
epitrite
✧spitfire
spitting
spotting
spot kick
upstairs
spottily
spatular
epitomic
epitonic
✧spetsnaz
✧spetznaz
spathose
upstroke
spittoon
aphthous
epitases
epitasis
apatetic
spit curl
spousage
spousals
opium den
uphudden
spruce up
sprucely
appuying
spouting
opiumism
spruiker
upturned
oppugner
à peu près
aplustre
splutter
upcurved
spivvery
spavined
spawning
a pox take
epoxying
spryness
sphygmic
sphygmus
epizoite
Squamata
aquacade
squamate
squabash
aquanaut
squabble
squad car
squaccos
squaddie
squander
squalene
square up
squarely
squasher
equalise
equalize
equative

squaring
squarish
squarial
aquarium
✧aquarian
equation
Aquarius
aquatics
aquarist
aquatint
equality
squawker
equalled
squailer
squaller
squawman
squaloid
squamose
squamous
squab pie
squadron
squarson
squatted
squattle
squatter
aqua pura
squamula
squamule
aqualung
squelchy
squeegee
squegger
squeaker
squealer
aqueduct
squeezer
equipage
squirage
equitant
squireen
squiress
squirely
squiffer
squiggle
squilgee
squiggly
aquiline
equities
equinity
equivoke
equipped
equipper
squirrel
squinter
squirter
a quoi bon?
Equuleus
breakage
great ape
great auk
try a fall
preadapt
preamble
bread bin
cream bun
triarchy
organdie
Great Dog
Ertan Dam
broad day
trial-day

arrasene
Briarean
Priapean
Brian Eno
crease up
arbalest
armament
greatest
ornament
R R Marett
arcanely
creamery
dreamery
ornately
urbanely
great fee
dreadful
dreamful
freakful
groanful
wreakful
triangle
great gun
arranger
arraught
breathed
wreathed
wreathen
preach up
breather
broacher
or rather
✧preacher
treacher
wreather
Arianise
Arianize
Armalite®
Aryanise
Aryanize
creatine
creative
ergative
kreatine
organise
organize
treatise
triazine
urbanise
urbanite
urbanize
arcading
breaking
croaking
dreaming
drearing
groaning
treading
treating
broadish
freakish
triaxial
Arianism
ordalium
organism
priapism
trialism
urbanism
Arcadian
✧creation
Croatian

Graafian
Orcadian
ordalian
creakier
creamier
croakier
greasies
arbalist
arcanist
organist
triadist
trialist
urbanist
creakily
creamily
croakily
dreamily
drearily
greasily
organity
triality
urbanity
cream jug
break-jaw
breaskit
trialled
treadler
orgasmic
Armagnac
ordainer
breadnut
cream-nut
ergatoid
area code
creasote
kreasote
triazole
break off
breakoff
cream off
break out
breakout
freak out
freak-out
trial run
creatrix
Great Sea
Triassic
triapsal
Dr Watson
Arkansas
cream tea
orgastic
breasted
art autre
great toe
great tit
arrantly
errantly
errantry
truantry
armature
creature
treasure
✧treasury
break-vow
Great War
✧broadway
cribbage
cribrate
trabeate

tribrach
crab-yaws
bribable
dry-bible
probable
probably
tribadic
drabness
grub shop
crablike
crabwise
crabbing
cribbing
drubbing
grabbing
grubbing
drabbish
grub kick
crabbier
crabbily
grubbily
Arabella
cribella
cribbled
drabbler
dribbler
fribbler
grabbler
dribblet
tribally
tribunal
crab-wood
cribrose
cribwork
cribrous
frabjous
crab tree
tribasic
drabette
tributer
Fribourg
à rebours
crab-nuts
orichalc
trochaic
braccate
brockage
croceate
cruciate
eructate
trackage
tractate
truckage
wreckage
crachach
proclaim
armchair
fructans
trackbed
✧crucible
brickbat
uric acid
tricycle
grace cup
brocaded
Eric Idle
fricadel
Dracaena
tracheid
preceese
tracheae

bracteal
tracheal
dry-clean
crackers
proceeds
priciest
crockery
trickery
graceful
wrackful
wreckful
crucifer
crucifix
trichina
crocoite
erectile
erective
fructive
practice
practise
practive
procaine
proclive
tractile
tractive
trichite
trochite
bricking
cracking
fracking
frocking
pricking
tracking
tricking
trucking
wrecking
brackish
trickish
practick
trochisk
brachial
brachium
erection
fraction
friction
traction
trickier
practics
fructify
trickily
crackjaw
trochlea
freckled
Bruce Lee
oracular
tricolor
truckler
bracelet
bractlet
tricklet
drachmae
drachmai
trackman
truchman
truchmen
truckman
drachmas
✧draconic
arachnid
brick-nog
cracknel

trecento
areca-nut
precinct
procinct
trachoma
trichoid
trichord
trochoid
urochord
fructose
orecrowe
trichome
broccoli
gracioso
araceous
croceous
gracious
precious
tractors
prick out
trick out
crackpot
precepit
tric-trac
brick-red
track rod
precurse
tre corde
tricorne
brockram
procurer
tractrix
précised
dricksie
crocuses
brick-tea
cricetid
price tag
brocatel
brochure
fracture
preclude
price war
trackway
trachyte
graduand
bride-ale
eradiate
graduate
trad jazz
bride-bed
credible
erodible
gradable
tradable
credibly
tridacna
producer
traducer
Bridgend
trudgeon
dredge up
aridness
gradient
grodiest
drudgery
prideful
tradeful
prodigal
trade gap
Bradshaw
fredaine
bridging
brodding
cradling
grudging
prodding
trudging
drudgism
Brad Pitt
brodekin
predella
tredille
gridelin
urodelan
brideman
credenda
credenza
mridanga
uredinia
credence
prudence
Eridanus
uredines
Bradford
arid zone
prodnose
prodrome
trade off
trade-off
prodromi
gridlock
crude oil
grade out
Frederic
Frederik
gridiron
gradatim
creditor
predator
proditor
traditor
crudités
Bradbury
praecava
free hand
freehand
arsenate
freebase
freeware
tree calf
free fall
free-fall
treenail
tree farm
artefact
brief-bag
green-bag
green ban
friended
Greekdom
friendly
free reed
free-reed
armed eye
greeneye
Praesepe
tree fern
breeze up
freeze-up
freeness
treeless
trueness
praefect
pre-elect
greenery
grieful
greenfly
Greek god
arpeggio
breeched
triethyl
treeship
breeches
free-shot
urge that
arsenide
arsenite
free ride
Graecise
Graecize
treelike
tree line
true time
breeding
briefing
creeping
freezing
✧greeking
greening
greesing
greeting
grueling
ordering
Friesish
Greekish
greenish
free kick
arterial
free will
free-will
praedial
proemial
true bill
Graecism
Armenian
✧artesian
Friesian
creepier
greenies
Ortelius
free gift
free list
pre-exist
prie-dieu
breezily
creepily
free-city
greedily
tree lily
Greek key
orsellic
orielled
orseille
true blue
true-blue
crueller
urceolus
greenlet
freedman
freedmen
green man
triennia
Armenoid
freehold
freeload
tree toad
argemone
Freefone®
free love
free vote
gruesome
truelove
Greenock
free-soil
free-form
freeborn
Freetown
true-born
grievous
tree moss
free-cost
Freeport
free port
Freepost®
true-bred
greegree
tree frog
free drop
green ray
cruet set
green tea
oriented
arrestee
✧oriental
free atom
arrester
arrestor
Argestes
ardently
priestly
urgently
F R Leavis
Greek way
green way
Dr Jekyll
driftage
Truffaut
draft-bar
trifecta
trifocal
urnfield
drift ice
crofting
grafting
trifling
draffish
gruffish
graffiti
graffito
craftier
greffier
craftily
triffidy
truffled
profiler
artfully
irefully
profaner
drift net
Graf Spee
driftpin
pro forma
pro-forma
triforia
profuser
profiter
profound
drift-way
bregmata
drag race
prograde
trigraph
braggart
cragfast
fragrant
pregnant
tragical
frigidly
Drogheda
preggers
progress
trigness
fragment
frog test
froggery
groggery
priggery
grog-shop
drag-shot
dragline
bragging
briguing
brogging
dragging
drugging
fragging
frogging
frogling
prigging
trigging
trogging
broguish
frogfish
priggish
priggism
craggier
proggins
drag lift
druggist
Erdgeist
groggily
wriggler
brigalow
frugally
cragsman
dragoman
dragsman
Braganza
Trigynia
erogenic
orogenic
trigonic
dragonné
original
trigonal
origanum
oreganos
dragonet
prog rock
prig down
dry goods
oragious
tragopan
frog-spit
Fragaria
progeria
erigeron
gregatim
brighten
Brighton
frighten
dragster
brightly
armgaunt
drag hunt
triglyph
Brahmana
Orpheans
prohibit
orthicon
✧orthodox
Archaean
✧archaeus
archness
orthoepy
archaise
archaize
archwise
prehnite
archaism
archaist
orchella
orchilla
prehuman
arch-mock
arch-poet
orthopod
trahison
orchesis
orthoses
orthosis
orchitic
orthotic
orchitis
archduke
archlute
arthouse
try house
archival
archives
ordinand
drainage
fruitage
grainage
irrigate
irritate
ordinate
urticate
arm in arm
arrivals
artifact
irritant
ordinant
urticant
ordinary
fruit-bud
fruit bat
brainbox
draisene
armigero
froideur
artiness
✧druidess
Ernie Els
trainers
orpiment
broidery
fruitery
brain fag
fruitful
fruit fly
erringly
pryingly
tryingly
ornithic
graithly
brainiac
prairied
arginine
artifice
draisine
fruitive
troilite
braiding
bruising
fruiting
graining
groining
praising
trailing
training
brainish
frailish
Prairial
Braidism
✧druidism
troilism
Arminian
fruition
irrision
Arminius
Orbilius
troilist
vraicker
articled
brailler
articles
fruitlet
trail mix
trail-net
Arvicola
arvicole
pruinose
trail off
train-oil
irrisory
brain-pan
brainpan
arbitral
arrieros
fruit tea
artistic
truistic
frailtee
Orvietan
orlistat
artistry
bruilzie
prejudge
Trujillo
frijoles
Praktica®
trekking
brakeman
broken-in
brokenly

brake pad
Krakatoa
brake van
arillate
grillade
grillage
arillary
trilobed
drill bit
preludio
trolleys
drollery
prolific
pro-lifer
urologic
prologue
arc-light
dry light
Araldite®
drilling
drolling
frilling
grilling
trilling
trolling
drollish
trillium
orillion
trillion
frillies
trilbies
trollies
trollius
trilemma
prolamin
Sri Lanka
prolonge
arilloid
arillode
Trollope
gralloch
trilloes
trollopy
prolapse
grill pan
breloque
drill rig
prelatic
uralitic
prolixly
drammach
crummack
Drum Mass
trumeaux
gramoche
dromical
grimacer
bromidic
premedic
drumhead
premiere
première
cromlech
Cromwell
from hell
gromwell
Aramaean
primless
grimness
grumness
primness
trammels
trimness
drumbeat
erumpent
grimmest
primmest
trumpery
crimeful
grumphie
dram-shop
Brumaire
drumfire
Frimaire
grimoire
tramline
trim size
brimming
cramming
cramping
drumming
primming
tramming
tramping
trimming
trumping
drumfish
frumpish
trampish
Aramaism
crimpier
crumbier
crummier
Grammies
arum lily
cramoisy
grumpily
bromelia
Tremella
crumpled
promulge
Grimaldi
bromelin
frampler
grumbler
premolar
trampler
trembler
trembles
tremolos
primally
Bramante
criminal
crumenal
trominos
fromenty
frumenty
frampold
tramroad
Mrs Moore
primrose
trombone
crummock
drammock
drummock
drum roll
crumhorn
krumhorn
cramboes
primrosy
cromorna
krameria
trimeric
cremorne
cromorne
gramarye
premorse
Trimurti
trimaran
Cromarty
gramercy
premised
promisee
cremosin
promiser
promisor
premises
frame-saw
kromesky
from A to B
aromatic
dramatic
eremitic
primatic
trematic
eremital
primatal
prometal
gram-atom
tram-stop
cremator
promoter
promotor
prompter
trimeter
fremitus
Primates
promptly
from A to Z
Drambuie®
drymouth
brim-full
cramfull
premiums
primeval
brim over
Craniata
brancard
drunkard
iron hand
iron-sand
brandade
craniate
frondage
frontage
grandame
ironware
truncate
bran-mash
ironbark
iron-mail
transact
Grenoble
Grenache
irenical
ironical
irenicon
grand cru
granddad
Trinidad
front-end
frondeur
grandeur
Irenaeus
princess
frondent
prince it
transect
transept
grindery
orangery
princely
printery
frank-fee
prankful
trunkful
wrongful
transfer
transfix
cranefly
drone fly
Srinagar
branchia
bronchia
branched
prong-hoe
Grantham
tranship
brancher
cruncher
drencher
trencher
bronchos
bronchus
Trenches
Bronx hat
tranchet
Araneida
brandied
crannied
frenzied
brandise
bronzite
Cronkite
Francine
ironlike
iron-mine
Ironside
'prentice
prentice
Príncipe
transire
bringing
bronzing
cringing
drinking
grinding
grinning
grunting
prancing
pranking
printing
pronking
trunking
wringing
brandish
Frankish
orangish
prankish
✧brindisi
iron-sick
prandial
cronyism
eryngium
francium
Orangism
Bruneian
trunnion
crankier
frontier
trendier
bronzify
crankily
trendily
Brunella
✧prunella
uranylic
brindled
gruntled
iron-clad
wrinkled
crenelle
prunelle
frenulum
✧franklin
prunello
granular
trundler
wrangler
frontlet
iron-clay
grand mal
brinkman
front man
frontman
transmit
transmew
ordnance
brand-new
Cranford
ironwood
Francome
frondose
iron-mole
bring off
drink off
wring off
ironwork
princock
frontoon
araneous
drongoes
eryngoes
wrongous
bring out
grind out
print out
printout
wring out
brine-pan
crank pin
brine-pit
Arenaria
dry-nurse
print run
front row
iron-gray
iron-grey
prenasal
grandson
frenetic
granitic
uranitic
crenated
crinated
brunette
prenatal
pronotal
pronotum
pronator
urinator
Iron Duke
transude
transume
iron lung
Brancusi
tranquil
Trinculo
craniums
areolate
arrogate
priorate
✧argonaut
arrogant
preorder
Arbor Day
arboreta
arboreal
armozeen
✧prioress
Dr Moreau
cryogeny
armozine
arsonite
brookite
cryolite
ergotise
ergotize
erionite
trioxide
brooding
crooning
drooking
proofing
droogish
armorial
troopial
ergotism
creolian
Triodion
cryonics
arborist
armorist
arsonist
creolist
errorist
broodily
droopily
groovily
priority
Brooklyn
criollos
brooklet
pre-owned
creosote
kreosote
Oroonoko
arborous
creodont
arcology
bryology
oreology
arboured
armoured
ergogram
cryotron
groo-groo
armourer
brood-sac
cryostat
cropland
dry-plate
griptape
prophage
prophase
triplane
triptane
wrappage
kreplach
drop tank
gripsack
trapball
trapfall
frappant
proppant
trippant
tropical
tripedal
tripodal
drip-feed
drop dead
drop-dead
grapheme
drop-leaf
trappean
drop test
frippery
prophecy
prophesy
trippery
trophesy
Arapahos
drop-shot
arapaima
dropsied
trophied
drop-ripe
dropwise
eruptive
graphite
traplike
trapline
trephine
tripwire
crapping
cropping
dripping
dropping
frapping
gripping
prepping
propping
trapping
tripling
tripping
wrapping
cropsick
drop kick
drop-kick
graphium
eruption
trippier
graphics
dry-point
pre-print
Trappist
grape ivy

preppily
propylic
crippled
propylon
crippler
grappler
trippler
propolis
drupelet
tripe-man
araponga
arapunga
crepance
prepense
propense
propanol
propenal
trapunto
triploid
drop zone
triphone
triptote
drop lock
traprock
trip-hook
drop goal
drop down
drop-down
trapdoor
dropwort
prop-root
crêpe pan
art paper
troparia
prepared
creperie
preparer
properly
property
proposal
proposer
crepitus
propound
cropfull
cropfuls
wrapover
drop away
triptych
prophyll
trapezia
trapezii
truquage
truqueur
frequent
cry quits
Iroquois
Arbroath
dry-roast
prurient
prorogue
prurigos
dry riser
pruritic
pruritus
Ark Royal
brassard
aristate
arms race
Brisbane
crispate
cristate

crustate
dressage
frescade
ore-stare
pristane
prostate
✧**frascati**
trespass
brassart
grossart
press bed
erasable
cross bun
crossbar
crush bar
crossbow
grass box
press box
trashcan
Irish car
crosscut
presidia
prosodic
presidio
crusader
Crusades
crusados
Oresteia
cross-eye
Grasmere
triskele
urostege
grosbeak
Irish elk
ark-shell
dry steam
drisheen
Prospero
Brussels
trossers
crescent
✧prospect
Prospekt
trashery
friskful
pressful
tristful
trustful
pressfat
presager
✧**groschen**
brass hat
crush hat
brassica
Cressida
Kristina
Pristina
prescind
crescive
prestige
pristine
brisling
brushing
crashing
cresting
crossing
crushing
dressing
frisking
frosting
grasping

grassing
gressing
pressing
trussing
trusting
briskish
crossish
freshish
tristich
crostini
grissini
urushiol
Irishism
prosaism
Crispian
Erastian
pression
Prussian
grissino
crispier
crustier
trashier
trustier
prosaist
brassily
crustily
friskily
frostily
prissily
Prussify
trashily
trustily
prusiked
Brasília
Griselda
Arts Club
cresylic
bristled
wrestler
crosslet
wristlet
trisemic
trisomic
Prosimii
Erysimum
freshman
Irishman
pressman
prose-man
proseman
trashman
presumer
crash-mat
presence
prisoner
presents
fresh-new
bresaola
frescoed
prismoid
crustose
dry-stone
dry-stove
iriscope
brass off
brush off
brush-off
grass-oil
frescoer
bristols
frescoes

griseous
crash out
gross out
gross-out
Prescott
uroscopy
urostomy
crashpad
prosopon
wrest pin
wrist pin
cross-rib
preserve
Tristram
fresh-run
braseros
gris-gris
grisgris
cross-row
cross sea
Irish Sea
crosstie
dress tie
frisette
grisette
frustule
pressure
tressure
frustums
crossway
Criseyde
presbyte
prostyle
urostyle
frittata
protease
tritiate
urethane
brat pack
brat-pack
bratpack
pratfall
protract
writable
critical
erotical
protocol
tritical
Triticum
frutices
erythema
Eritrean
brothers
druthers
fretless
oratress
pre-teens
trotters
grittest
frothery
crateful
grateful
trothful
truthful
wrathful
froth-fly
protégée
Hrothgar
crotched
crutched
wretched

britches
cratches
bratchet
crotchet
brattice
brettice
trotline
bratling
fretting
fritting
trotting
writhing
brattish
erethism
pretties
frothily
gratuity
grittily
prettify
prettily
wrathily
writhled
crotalum
prattler
Crotalus
brutally
prytanea
tritonia
cratonic
protonic
cretonne
gratinée
pretence
pretense
protense
pro tanto
writings
grottoed
proteome
proteose
proto-ore
write off
write-off
fretwork
grattoir
trottoir
grottoes
write out
trot-cozy
critique
pratique
criteria
Pretoria
ureteric
urethrae
ureteral
urethral
brethren
oratorio
Arcturus
urethras
preterit
writerly
britzska
Protista
bretesse
erotesis
protases
protasis
erotetic
protatic

Art Tatum
Arethusa
protrude
prothyle
pretty up
✧**protozoa**
brouhaha
traumata
croupade
frautage
groupage
arguable
arquebus
arguably
trouncer
grounded
grounden
grounder
trouvère
✧**fräulein**
trouveur
groupers
trousers
argument
argutely
crousely
fraudful
proudful
troutful
trauchle
Breughel
brougham
Proudhon
draughts
draughty
droughty
braunite
Ursuline
drouking
grouping
grouting
trouting
proudish
troupial
art union
Freudian
argufier
croupier
groupist
triunity
troubled
troubler
grouplet
troutlet
croupous
ordurous
orgulous
fraus pia
trout rod
frou-frou
arcuated
triumvir
creutzer
kreutzer
breviate
proviant
breviary
drivable
provable
provably
provided

provedor
provider
providor
bravados
privados
crivvens
travails
provoker
groveled
traveled
trivalve
travelog
groveler
traveler
gravelly
trevally
gravamen
province
cravenly
previous
traverse
proviral
Proverbs
provirus
crevasse
provisor
provisos
travesty
breveted
crevette
graviton
gravitas
privates
grave-wax
driveway
browband
brown ale
grow pale
draw back
drawback
drawable
growable
brown-bag
crown cap
prowl car
Brown Cow
drownded
crew neck
a raw deal
draw-well
draw rein
draw-gear
draw near
browless
trowsers
browbeat
growlery
brown fat
brow-tine
erewhile
brawling
✧browning
browsing
crawling
crowning
drowning
frowning
growling
prowling
trawling
brownish

crawfish
grow rich
crow-bill
Brownism
Brownian
crawlier
Brownist
drowsily
crownlet
trewsman
grow into
drawings
trawl-net
✧brown owl
drawdown
draw lots
brownout
crow boot
crowd out
crowfoot
draw upon
frowards
brown rat
brown rot
crown rot
crown saw
brewster
frowster
draw-tube
draw cuts
crow over
prix fixe
wraxling
proximal
Fraxinus
grey mare
grey seal
greyness
argyrite
trey-tine
grayling
crayfish
grey-fish
army list
X-ray unit
Gray code
grey wolf
army worm
grey-coat
prey upon
grey area
tray-trip
X-ray tube
Grey nuns
trayfuls
grey-eyed
prizable
cruzados
craziest
cruzeiro
Krazy Kat
Grizelda
grizzled
brazilin
grizzler
prizeman
Trizonia
Brezonek
trizonal
Brezhnev
brazenly
brazenry
grazioso
frizette
escalade
escalate
escapade
estacade
escalado
escapado
Istanbul
estancia
Islandia
Aswan Dam
islander
Assamese
Esha Ness
escargot
Issachar
astatine
Islamise
Islamite
Islamize
ashaming
assaying
essaying
essayish
escapism
Islamism
ossarium
escalier
espalier
ascarids
escapist
essayist
Islamist
escallop
assailer
escalope
escarole
ask along
Istabraq
assassin
espartos
osnaburg
✧isabella
ash-blond
isobront
isobaric
isochasm
isocracy
Psocidae
isocheim
isochime
isocline
psychism
C-section
psychics
psychist
psychoid
isochore
psych out
isocryme
isodicon
isodomum
isodomon
asperate
esterase
assegaai
osier-bed
assemble
assemblé
✧assembly
Essencia
ascender
usheress
osteogen
asperger
asperges
ushering
asterisk
especial
ascetism
asterism
Essenism
Asterias
asperity
esterify
aspermia
esteemed
Essex Man
islesman
asteroid
asperous
assessor
asbestic
assenter
assentor
asserter
assertor
asbestos
osteitis
Oswestry
usefully
ask for it
usufruct
Ashgabat
isagogic
isogamic
isogenic
isogonic
isogonal
isogloss
asphodel
isthmian
eschalot
ischemia
ischemic
R S Thomas
asthenia
asthenic
ischuria
aspheric
esthesia
esthetic
as though
eschewal
eschewer
asphyxia
aspirate
estimate
estivate
oscitate
ostinato
Ustilago
aspirant
oscitant
espiègle
ossified
oscinine
aspiring
ascidium
aspidium
ascidian
astigmia
aseismic
Ossianic
assignee
assiento
assigner
assignor
assignat
assisted
assist in
assister
Ishiguro
ash-leach
isolable
psilocin
✧psaltery
isologue
Ashleigh
psellism
psyllium
✧psalmist
psalmody
psilosis
psilotic
isolated
Psilotum
isolator
psammite
isomeric
isomorph
isometry
asyndeta
Asunción
isonomic
as one man
Isengrim
asynergy
assonate
assonant
ascorbic
Asmodeus
astonied
essonite
astonish
Estonian
psionics
US dollar
essoiner
A S Hornby
astomous
estopped
estoppel
espousal
espouser
assorted
assotted
assorter
assolute
aseptate
ash-plant
isopodan
Isoptera
isoprene
isopleth
psephite
psephism
username
ostracod
ostracon
estridge
esurient
astragal
estrogen
ostreger
usurping
ostrakon
psoralen
astringe
estrange
usurious
espresso
tsaritsa
tsarevna
ash-stand
isostasy
tsessebe
asystole
isospory
USA Today
as it were
isothere
isotherm
ashtanga
isotonic
isotropy
isotopic
esoteric
tsutsumu
osculate
osculant
issuable
issuably
esculent
astutely
pseudery
assuming
pseudish
Asturias
astucity
Esquimau
issuance
espumoso
esquisse
as a whole
Assyrian
ashy-grey
stearage
stearate
Strabane
stravaig
stramash
athanasy
steam car
straicht
straucht
stranded
straddle
à travers
St James's
atrament
strategy
straggle
strangle
étranger
stranger
straight
straught
Mt Sangay
straggly
attached
straw-hat
Strachey
steadied
atrazine
Ottamite
ptyalise
ptyalize
stearine
steatite
steading
stealing
steaming
steaning
straying
attagirl
ptyalism
strabism
ottavino
steadier
St David's
stradiot
steadily
steamily
stratify
attacker
St Gallen
strammel
straw man
strained
straunge
strainer
steatoma
stratose
strap-oil
stratous
strapped
strapper
steapsin
Atlantic
straiten
Atlantes
Atlantis
stealthy
straitly
steady on!
stub-nail
stibnite
stabbing
stabling
stubbing
stablish
stubbled
stibbler
stubborn
stoccata
stockade
staccato
sticcado
sticcato
stoccado
stock car
stickful
stacking
sticking
stocking
stiction
stickies
stockist
stickily
stockily
stickjaw
stickler
stockman
stuccoed
stuccoer
stocious
stick out
stick pin
stockpot
Stockton
studfarm
stedfast
studding
studying
stodgily
studenty
studbook
studwork
studious
stud bolt
St Edmund
stadiums
steerage
strewage
ytterbia
atremble
steenbok
steelbow
attercop
ethercap
ettercap
stretchy
attendee
attender
et cetera
etcetera
St Helena
et ceteri
ethereal
steepeup
St Helens
strepent
utterest
steevely
stievely
streigne
at length
strength
streight
Strephon
atherine
athetise
athetize
etherise
etherize
atheling
steeling
steening
steering
steeving
strewing
uttering
steepish
etherial
etherism
Athenian
etherion
St Helier
etaerios
etherist
etherify
strelitz
streaked

streaker
steepled
steelman
steelmen
streamer
étrennes
Ethernet
atheroma
athetoid
St Jerome
steel pan
attemper
Ethelred
stressed
streusel
stressor
attested
streeted
Atherton
attester
attestor
attentat
Strepyan
staffage
stiff-arm
stiff bit
stifling
stuffing
stiffish
stuffily
Stafford
stuff you
stigmata
staggard
stagnate
stagnant
stegodon
staggers
staghorn
Mt Egmont
stag hunt
at the bar
itchweed
atchieve
itchiest
At the Hop
itch-mite
Stahlism
Stahlian
Otchipwe
strigate
steinbok
striddle
stridden
strike in
strike-on
strike up
strident
at livery
stringed
string up
stringer
Atticise
Atticize
ethicise
ethicize
strigine
attiring
e-tailing
staining
steining
striking
striping
striving
Atticism
ethicism
stoicism
ethicist
strickle
strinkle
stricken
strip map
Strimmer®
strigose
strip off
Strigops
strip out
Ethiopia
Ethiopic
stripped
stripper
stair rod
striated
striatum
ut dictum
atwitter
strictly
attitude
utriculi
stairway
Steinway
stake net
stake off
stake out
stake-out
stallage
stellate
stillage
St Albans
stalwart
stolidly
stilbene
Mt Elbert
stall-fed
stalagma
stulchak
stelline
stilbite
stalking
stalling
stilling
stilting
stiltish
stallion
stellion
stillion
stellify
stultify
stallman
Atalanta
Italiote
stall off
stalkoes
Mt Elbrus
utiliser
ptilosis
styluses
athletic
stiletto
I tell you
utilizer
stemmata
stemware
stumpage
Stamp Act
atomical
stomachy
stampede
stem cell
stampedo
stemless
ptomaine
stamping
stemming
stumming
stumpily
stumbler
stimulus
stamened
staminal
atom bomb
Stamford
stem form
stamp out
stump out
atomiser
itemiser
stomatic
stomatal
stembuck
stem turn
atomizer
itemizer
stanzaic
Standard®
standard
stinkard
stunkard
stannate
Stone Age
✧stone-age
stone axe
stunsail
✧stannary
stink bug
ethnical
ctenidia
St Anselm
Stan Getz
stonefly
stanchel
Stendhal
at anchor
stancher
stanchly
stannite
standing
stinging
stinking
stinting
stonking
stunning
standish
Stundism
Stundist
stingily
stand low
atonally
stone-mad
stuntman
at an inch
stanhope
stand off
stand-off
standoff
stenlock
stand oil
stentour
stannous
stanzoes
stand out
standout
stink out
stand pad
stand pat
stink pot
stinkpot
stone pit
stonerag
ethnarch
Eton crop
stoneraw
stingray
stenosed
stand sam
stenoses
stenosis
stone saw
stenotic
Eton suit
stromata
etiolate
strombus
stroddle
at rovers
otiosely
strongyl
stronger
strongly
atrophic
strophic
stooshie
strobila
atropine
Ottoline
Ottomite
strobile
stooping
strobing
stroking
strowing
strobili
atropism
atrocity
otiosity
St Moritz
strooken
stroll on!
stroller
Eteocles
at points
attorney
Otto John
atropous
atmology
ethology
etiology
stropped
stroupan
strontia
at bottom
atmolyse
atmolyze
Stoppard
stepdame
stephane
stoppage
stuprate
stop bath
stopbank
Stephano
utopiast
atypical
etypical
stapedes
stupidly
stopless
at a price
stepwise
stepping
stopping
at a point
stapelia
stippled
stipuled
stippler
stipular
at a pinch
step into
step on it
Stepford
stopcock
step down
step-down
stop down
stop-loss
stipites
stop over
stopover
star-pav'd
star-gaze
sternage
ITAR-Tass
✧star wars
storable
star-read
sturgeon
starkers
starless
starters
stirless
startful
stormful
pterygia
sterigma
staragen
starched
starship
starcher
sturdied
eternise
eternize
starlike
sternite
sturnine
starling
starring
starting
starving
✧sterling
Stirling
stirring
storming
Storting
storying
starfish
startish
star sign
eternity
starrily
stormily
sturdily
storm jib
startled
pterylae
startler
storeman
iterance
sturnoid
stereome
yttrious
stare out
start out
starwort
pteropod
starspot
St-Tropez
star trap
Stari Ras
Mt Ararat
starosta
sternson
starosty
uteritis
Starbuck
star turn
star jump
sternums
stardust
star ruby
sternway
ataraxia
ataraxic
storeyed
it is said
St Oswald
stasimon
otoscope
statuary
statable
statical
statedly
stitched
stitch up
stitch-up
stitcher
stetting
stotinka
stotinki
stotious
statured
étatisme
étatiste
statuses
Etruscan
étourdie
struggle
strung up
stoutish
Etrurian
St Julien
strucken
strummed
strummel
strummer
strumose
strumous
strumpet
Mt Hudson
strutted
strutter
stived-up
stovaine
stave off
stowlins
stewpond
stowdown
stow away
stowaway
ethylate
stay lace
stay tape
staysail
ethylene
stayless
stay bolt
stay upon
stay over
stayaway
rutabaga
Surabaya
pupa-case
runagate
cut a dash
Gujarati
Bulawayo
nunataks
lunanaut
subabbot
Judaical
autarchy
hum and ha
muqaddam
mutandum
subaudio
subahdar
bucardos
Turandot
Guyanese
Musaceae
Rutaceae
Sudanese
cut a deal
Budapest
subagent
humanely
sugar gum
nuraghic
quoad hoc
eulachan
eulachon
oulachon
putamina
sudamina
bubaline
curarine
curarise
curarize
curative
durative
eutaxite
humanise
humanize
mutative
put aside
putative
run a mile

Words marked ✧ can also be spelled with one or more capital letters

ruralise
ruralize
sugaring
tuna fish
bucatini
run a risk
puparial
humanism
puparium
ruralism
sudarium
aularian
duration
Eurasian
lunarian
lunation
Lusatian
luxation
mutation
nudation
nutarian
nutation
pupation
Rumanian
sudation
Turanian
Eulalius
humanist
lunarist
lutanist
muralist
ruralist
audacity
fugacity
furacity
humanity
queasily
rurality
autarkic
Muhammad
aux armes
Susannah
Aura-Soma
autacoid
humanoid
fumarole
fusarole
cut along
rub along
run along
luna moth
bumaloti
ducatoon
hula hoop
fumadoes
put about
runabout
curatory
fumatory
juratory
mutatory
nugatory
sudatory
sugar pea
eupatrid
subacrid
subaural
Muharram
Muharrem
Sumatran
curatrix

Jurassic
Rumansch
Judaiser
curassow
put a stop
run after
mulattos
cunabula
hula-hula
cubature
Quaalude®
subacute
Guyaquil
punaluan
Tuvaluan
subadult
eucaryon
eukaryon
eucalypt
eucaryot
eukaryot
✧rubaiyat
Judaizer
cupboard
funboard
outboard
dumb-cane
hub-brake
outbrave
sunbeamy
curbable
tubbable
hubbuboo
Quebecer
turbo car
turbocar
turbidly
outbreed
subbreed
outbreak
dumb-bell
tumble in
tumble up
curbless
dumbness
numbness
tubbiest
turbofan
lumbagos
surbahar
dumbshow
purblind
sun-blind
sunblind
curbside
jumboise
jumboize
bumbling
burbling
humbling
mumbling
rumbling
tumbling
sun-blink
jumbo jet
turbojet
sunbaked
quibbler
furbelow
rumbelow
tunbelly

turbaned
turbined
turbinal
turbines
curb-roof
sunblock
dumb down
nut-brown
cumbrous
cumbered
cumberer
lumberer
numberer
outburst
sunburnt
sunburst
Burberry®
lubberly
lumberly
mulberry
sunberry
surbased
subbasal
rubbishy
surbated
sunbathe
Subbuteo®
outbound
dulciana
Furcraea
fulcrate
punctate
purchase
surcease
sun crack
pub-crawl
subclaim
guacharo
lug-chair
outclass
subclass
run chart
nunchaku
runcible
succubae
punch-bag
Mulciber
succubas
succubus
lunch box
Dutch cap
Muscidae
muscadel
suicidal
duncedom
muscadin
juiced up
Muscadet
mud-clerk
sun cream
hurcheon
luncheon
muscle in
nuncheon
puncheon
putcheon
butcher's
butchery
cutchery
quackery
quick-fix

Dutch hoe
subchief
bunching
butching
muscling
quackish
zucchini
function
junction
munchies
munchkin
mutchkin
curculio
furcular
muscular
surculus
buncombe
curcumin
Dutchman
Turcoman
dulcimer
Dulcinea
Puccinia
succinic
✧vulcanic
succinyl
Buccinum
succinct
subchord
run close
bum-clock
putchock
luscious
outcross
punch out
sun-cured
cup coral
subcosta
outcaste
subcaste
quickset
furcated
sulcated
dulcitol
muscatel
juncture
punctule
puncture
punctual
Quechuan
Quichuan
fulcrums
subcrust
Dutch War
Guicowar
gurdwara
quadrate
quadrans
quadrant
quiddany
fundable
guidable
Fundy Bay
guide dog
buddleia
outdwell
bundle up
huddle up
muddle up
fundless
hundreds

sundress
muddiest
ruddiest
Buddy Guy
purdahed
quadriga
sun-dried
outdrive
quad bike
quod vide
bundling
fuddling
hurdling
muddying
puddling
ruddying
outdrink
Buddhism
sundries
Buddhist
quiddity
quiddler
guidance
outdance
sun dance
duodenal
nundinal
duodenum
pundonor
puddings
puddingy
suddenly
suddenty
quadroon
outdoors
sundrops
subduple
sundered
murderee
subdural
murderer
sunderer
cul-de-sac
outdated
suedette
punditry
quidnunc
dun-diver
superadd
sure card
fuselage
gude-dame
numerate
pucelage
suberate
superate
tutelage
rugelach
Gujerati
lukewarm
suzerain
numerals
funerary
numeracy
numerary
tutelary
queen bee
tuneable
superbug
outer bar
auger-bit

superbly
tubercle
Lupercal
pudendal
Nurek Dam
pudendum
queendom
juve lead
funereal
tube well
superego
mule deer
muleteer
cureless
cuteness
hugeness
muteness
nudeness
pureness
rudeness
ruleless
sureness
tubeless
tuneless
suberect
superfit
supergun
dukeship
tumefied
duvetine
euxenite
fuse wire
gudesire
gudewife
juvenile
Puseyite
quae vide
queenite
quietive
suberise
suberize
sure-fire
tubelike
✧yuletide
cupeling
dukeling
queening
quieting
queerish
luderick
eugenism
eumerism
lutecium
lutetium
Puseyism
quietism
aurelian
Eusebian
Lutetian
Sumerian
superior
Aurelius
eugenics
Eugenius
Eusebius
eugenist
lutenist
quietist
queerity
superjet
aureoled

cupelled
luteolin
rubellan
superloo
nucellar
bucellas
duxelles
nucellus
queenlet
Du Bellay
Queen Mab
Süleyman
superman
supermax
supernal
au second
fume hood
fumerole
suberose
tubenose
tuberose
fumed oak
fusel-oil
tube worm
au revoir
cute hoor
numerous
suberous
tuberous
tuxedoes
cube root
tube foot
pure-bred
dule-tree
funebral
June drop
eupepsia
suversed
Rusedski
superspy
cuneatic
eupeptic
eutectic
pubertal
Nuneaton
quaestor
supertax
nubecula
quietude
Queequeg
subequal
tubefuls
rule over
mute swan
duvetyne
subframe
sufflate
suffrage
outflash
outflank
puffball
pug-faced
surfaced
sufficer
surfacer
puffed up
gulfweed
outfield
subfield
turfiest
bun fight

gunfight
outfight
puffbird
surfbird
outfling
purfling
ruffling
surffish
cuff link
Dumfries
gunflint
Turf Club
turf-clad
ruefully
cup final
sulfinyl
sulfonyl
outfrown
subfloor
buff-coat
surf boat
buffered
put forth
furfural
furfurol
furfuran
sufferer
run for it
dumfound
bumfluff
puff-puff
outflush
surf duck
duff over
suffixal
mudguard
outguard
burgrave
outglare
subgrade
cut glass
cutglass
nut-grass
sunglass
dung-cart
burglary
fungible
huggable
luggable
fungo bat
surgical
Gunga Din
ruggedly
turgidly
dungmere
sungrebe
hung-beef
mung bean
dungheap
lungless
outguess
rungless
bung-vent
judgment
muggiest
jugglery
surgeful
quagmire
bungling
juggling
lungeing
outgoing
lungfish
dunghill
junglist
hungrily
quagmiry
bungalow
pungence
subgenre
subgenus
burganet
burgonet
Turgenev
✧**burgundy**
fulgency
pungency
bunghole
mungoose
dung-fork
lung-book
lungworm
mungcorn
subgroup
outgross
lungwort
Bulgaria
Bulgaric
budgeree
dungaree
puggaree
tung tree
fulgural
budgeros
Jungfrau
budgerow
hungerly
vulgarly
Tungusic
funguses
Tunguses
budgeted
tungsten
hung jury
hung over
gurgoyle
sungazer
bushwalk
push-ball
push-cart
bushbaby
euphrasy
euphobia
Dukhobor
muchacha
muchacho
bushveld
lushness
much less
muchness
ruthless
suchness
bushmeat
cushiest
Cuthbert
mushiest
such that
bushfire
euphuise
euphuize
fuchsine
fuchsite
pushbike
rushlike
such like
suchlike
suchwise
rush ring
✧**euphuism**
euphuist
Euphemia
subhumid
subhuman
euphonia
euphonic
ruthenic
Duchenne
Dushanbe
Cushing's
bush-rope
mushroom
rush hour
rush-hour
hush-boat
cushiony
euphoria
Eutheria
euphoric
out-Herod
Lutheran
eucharis
duchesse
fughetta
zuchetta
Cushitic
Kushitic
nuthatch
zuchetto
bughouse
gunhouse
mug-house
Mulhouse
nuthouse
Our House
outhouse
hush-hush
bushbuck
push-pull
Pushtuns
pushover
Tunicata
audit ale
dubitate
fumigate
✧jubilate
mucilage
muricate
musicale
mutilate
pumicate
pupil age
pupilage
ruminate
supinate
suricate
Suriname
tunicate
sukiyaki
nudicaul
subimago
fumigant
jubilant
luminant
ruminant
rutilant
tulipant
culinary
luminary
pupilary
dutiable
music box
guaiacum
Gurinder
Rupinder
fusileer
mutineer
business
puniness
muniment
rudiment
futilely
supinely
Tübingen
musingly
pulingly
Ruaidhri
punisher
mulishly
Curitiba
mutinied
purified
rubified
auditive
culicine
cutinise
cutinize
fugitive
pulicide
punitive
subitise
subitize
quailing
quoining
mudirieh
Ruairidh
judicial
pugilism
rubidium
audition
munition
musician
punition
Tunisian
auxiliar
fusilier
purifier
nudities
burinist
luminist
pugilist
cupidity
futility
humidify
humidity
humility
lucidity
nubility
pudicity
tumidity
tunicked
musicker
auricled
pupillar
audience
julienne
tubicole
auriform
cubiform
fusiform
muriform
nubiform
tubiform
luminous
mucinous
muticous
mutinous
nubilous
numinous
cut it out
auditory
fumitory
punitory
cutie-pie
music pen
Tubigrip®
Hudibras
furiosos
Julia set
autistic
cubistic
juristic
muriatic
puristic
Sufistic
muriated
quaintly
✧**auricula**
furibund
pudibund
rubicund
Punjabee
Nur Jahan
sui juris
cunjevoi
Auckland
junkyard
buckrake
muck-rake
suck face
buck-wash
Gurkhali
duck-hawk
rucksack
duck-tail
junk mail
musk-ball
duck's ass
Turkmans
musk-cavy
lucky bag
Turk's cap
lucky dip
bulkhead
duckweed
lunkhead
buckbean
muckheap
buik-lear
musk deer
musk pear
Buckley's
duskness
luckless
sucklers
Turkmens
tuskless
muckiest
muskiest
ruckseat
buckshee
tuckahoe
junk shop
tuck shop
buckshot
duck-shot
buckling
duckling
junk-ring
suckling
duckbill
tuck-mill
puckfist
Lucky Jim
buckskin
musk-plum
Turkoman
buskined
junkanoo
luck into
tuck into
suckener
duck-pond
junk bond
junk food
duckmole
funkhole
murksome
musk rose
suck-hole
duck hook
punk rock
muck-worm
buckhorn
duck soup
luck upon
bunkered
suckered
buckaroo
buckeroo
pucker up
Quakerly
junketed
huckster
junketer
musketry
muckluck
musk duck
buckayro
Quillaia
Quillaja
dual band
full hand
full-face
full name
full-page
nuclease
nucleate
sublease
bull-calf
full back
pull back
pullback
pull rank
full sail
outlearn
bullbars
pull caps
Dunleary
gullable
gullible
bully boy
bully-boy
curlicue
purlicue
publican
bullocky
publicly
Culloden
bullhead
Bullseye
bull's-eye
bull-beef
fuel cell
full beam
bull kelp
dullness
fullness
nullness
purlieus
curliest
full pelt
full-pelt
guileful
full-aged
duologue
mulligan
sunlight
bullwhip
bullshot
bullgine
full time
full-time
nucleide
suilline
building
bullring
bullying
cullying
duelling
fuelling
gull-wing
outlying
qualming
quilling
quilting
sullying
qualmish
bullyism
cullyism
duellist
full tilt
full-tilt
guiltily
sublimed
fugleman
quillman
quill-nib
muslined
bull into
sublunar
outlands
muslinet
sullenly
bulldoze
bullnose
cut loose
duelsome

Words marked ✧ can also be spelled with one or more capital letters

full-bore
nucleole
bull-hoof
bully off
bully-off
nucleoli
full-cock
bullhorn
full moon
hull-down
pull down
pull-down
full toss
quill-pen
bullfrog
bullyrag
mullarky
burletta
bulletin
full stop
cum laude
furlough
turlough
bulldust
buplever
mull over
pull over
pullover
mulloway
outlawry
pull away
duplexer
Ku Kluxer
dull-eyed
full-eyed
gunlayer
guimbard
hummable
hummocky
outmoded
rummager
nutmeggy
mummying
duumviri
duumvirs
Gurmukhi
gunmaker
nummular
pulmonic
lux mundi
Murmansk
summoner
pulmones
furmenty
turmeric
bummaree
submerge
submerse
outmarch
dummy run
dummerer
murmurer
summerly
surmisal
surmiser
gummosis
outmatch
gunmetal
summital
Durmitor
luxmeter
Pulmotor®
summitry
surmount
quandang
turn back
turn-back
turnback
turn tail
quintain
quandary
ruinable
runnable
guanacos
huanacos
burned up
Nürnberg
sunn hemp
burnt-ear
quintett
runniest
aulnager
outnight
bunny hug
bunny-hug
Huang Hai
bunny hop
quencher
quinsied
burnside
Burnsite
cut no ice
Huon pine
quantise
quantize
quintile
turnpike
Burnsian
quantify
quantity
dunnakin
turnskin
quinella
tunneled
burn blue
quenelle
tunneler
euonymin
funny man
euonymus
turn into
turnings
turnsole
quandong
quantong
turncock
burn down
turn down
turn-down
turncoat
turn upon
turnspit
runner-up
Juan Gris
pug-nosed
turn it in
turn it up
Muenster
burnouse
turn Turk
buln-buln
quincunx
turn over
turnover
turn away
automata
cupolaed
Euroland
autocade
auto-da-fé
automate
autosave
Lucozade®
subovate
tutorage
Autobahn
autocarp
autoharp
Euromart
autogamy
out of cry
dupondii
cuboidal
fucoidal
suborder
humoresk
aurorean
European
tutoress
Euroseat
autogeny
rugosely
rub off on
Kuroshio
eulogise
eulogize
put on ice
suboxide
tutorise
tutorize
tutoring
eusocial
sutorial
tutorial
eulogium
europium
tutorism
Ausonian
Huronian
Junonian
sutorian
autogiro
eulogies
eulogist
humorist
dumosity
fumosity
gulosity
mucosity
rugosity
out of key
Jugo-Slav
Jugoslav
Yugo-Slav
Yugoslav
suborner
Dubonnet
Eurobond
autosome
Eurozone
sumotori
humorous
rumorous
sudorous
tumorous
bunodont
Europort
autology
autonomy
autotomy
ourology
euro area
humoured
rumourer
autocrat
Eurocrat
autopsia
Rumonsch
autoptic
run out on
culottes
Furostat
out of use
tucotuco
tug-of-war
autodyne
autolyse
autolyze
autotype
autogyro
outplace
sulphate
sur place
gulp back
hump-back
humpback
jump bail
jump ball
suppeago
supplant
culpable
jumpable
culpably
auspices
puppy-dog
cuspidal
puppodum
puppydom
jumped-up
cuspidor
subpoena
jump lead
pump-head
pump-well
rumpless
suppress
jump seat
tumpiest
supplely
puppy fat
jump ship
jump shot
supplied
cut-price
outprice
outprize
sulphide
sulphite
surplice
surprise
tumpline
dumpling
lumpfish
puppyish
purplish
quippish
sumphish
pulpmill
supplial
puppyism
gumphion
gumption
subprior
supplier
murphies
supplies
gunpoint
outpoint
sun print
lumpy jaw
subpolar
suspence
suspense
tuppence
rum punch
bump into
lumpenly
tuppenny
pulpwood
pumphood
jump rope
rump bone
sulphone
sunproof
pump room
gulp down
jump to it!
rump-post
mudpuppy
purpuric
cutpurse
pump iron
purpurin
Humphrey
purposed
supposed
supposal
supposer
purposes
supposes
pulpited
pulpitum
sumpitan
dumpster
pulpiter
quipster
pulpitry
puppetry
jump-turn
jump suit
sulphury
outpower
musquash
huaquero
surquedy
guardage
outreach
guardant
surrebut
curricle
huarache
lubrical
rubrical
guard dog
guéridon
outrider
putridly
aubrieta
ouvrière
quartern
quarters
nutrient
quartett
furriery
outright
Guernica
quarried
murrhine
quartile
currying
hurrying
querying
quirkish
Ruaraidh
guardian
outreign
quarrier
quartier
quirkily
guerilla
murrelet
supremum
outremer
supremos
outrance
outrange
Quirinal
guaranis
mucrones
Quirinus
curranty
currency
guaranty
cupreous
muir-poot
muir-pout
eutropic
outroper
quart-pot
eutrophy
gum resin
currasow
bulrushy
✧guernsey
aubretia
Lucretia
eucritic
turreted
au gratin
burritos
Quirites
surround
muirburn
outrival
sur-reyn'd
surroyal
outstand
bud-scale
outstare
purslane
substage
substate
sunshade
fuss-ball
purslain
suss laws
Tuesdays
outsmart
puissant
pursuant
questant
suasible
pussy-cat
tussocky
pulsidge
outsider
outsides
cursedly
cussedly
outspeed
outspend
outspeak
nutshell
outswell
outsleep
bum steer
outswear
bumsters
mumsiest
outspent
pulsific
purseful
gunsight
outsight
Burschen
mudslide
outshine
sunshine
guessing
nursling
outswing
pursuing
questing
quisling
gunsmith
ouistiti
gunstick
Russniak
question
dum spiro
Luis Figo
huissier
sunshiny
pulsejet
pulsojet
vulsella
russulae
subsolar
Huis Clos
russulas
subsonic
nuisance
purse-net
cussword
outscold
gunstone
mudstone
outscore
rubstone
sunstone
puss-moth
gunstock
outscorn
Cub Scout
cut short
outshoot
outsport

run short
rum shrub
subshrub
subserve
humstrum
outstrip
cursores
cursitor
pulsator
bursitis
Augsburg
Duisburg
numskull
cum-savvy
substyle
outsized
subsizar
purtraid
purtrayd
australe
cultrate
duct tape
lustrate
must-have
suitcase
dust-bath
dust-ball
hunt ball
quatrain
nuptials
dustcart
subtract
put to bed
gustable
quotable
suitable
quotably
suitably
mustache
rustical
justicer
buttocks
subtidal
custodes
butthead
cut teeth
rustle up
buttress
curtness
ductless
dustless
huntress
hurtless
justness
lustless
rustless
suitress
furthest
guttiest
mustiest
quit-rent
quotient
✧rust belt
rust-belt
rustiest
subtlety
multifid
multifil
hurt a fly
multigym
cultigen
bust a gut
dust-shot
buntline
lustrine
subtribe
wurtzite
bustling
duetting
hustling
lustring
puttying
quitting
rustling
turtling
outthink
cult film
Austrian
duettino
duettist
subtrist
multeity
sultrily
cuitikin
outtaken
pustular
curtalax
Funtumia
customed
buttyman
huntsman
puntsman
customer
subtonic
sultanic
subtense
button up
hustings
suitings
dust-hole
punt-pole
gust-lock
✧dust bowl
hunt down
lustrous
ructions
dustcoat
out to out
subtopia
multiped
multiple
multi-ply
multiply
lustique
Suctoria
cultured
✧quatorze
cultural
guttural
nurtural
muster in
putter-on
butter up
muster up
multurer
musterer
mutterer
nurturer
put to sea
kurtosis
eustatic
guttated
subtitle
surtitle
subtotal
sum total
rum-ti-tum
pultrude
subtrude
tub-thump
lustrums
cultivar
Gustavus
huntaway
Fukuyama
cumulate
cupulate
jugulate
lunulate
subulate
tubulate
tumulary
suburbia
suburban
cucumber
cucurbit
furuncle
luculent
muculent
purulent
Dubuffet
guruship
autunite
Eugubine
lupuline
zulu time
queueing
augur ill
✧futurism
futurist
luxurist
futurity
put-up job
Lucullic
Lucullan
mutually
Musulman
autumnal
Huguenot
cumulose
rugulose
tubulous
tu quoque
susurrus
Augustan
Augustus
augustly
subucula
durukuli
tucutuco
sucurujú
surucucu
subvocal
quo vadis?
curviest
outvoice
outvalue
pulville
pulvilli
pulvilio
suivante
outvenom
pulvinar
pulvinus
quivered
subverse
subviral
culverin
sub verbo
quaverer
subverst
nuevo sol
sun visor
curvated
curveted
curvital
outvoter
vulvitis
survival
survivor
surveyal
kurveyor
purveyor
surveyor
outweary
outwrest
outweigh
Dunwoody
outworth
outwards
outworks
sunwards
outwatch
cutwater
quixotic
quixotry
duty-paid
butyrate
ruby-tail
jurymast
butylene
busyness
✧eurythmy
Eurydice
quayside
eucyclic
buoyance
buoyancy
busywork
jury room
ruby port
busybody
duty-free
jury duty
zugzwang
fuzz-ball
buzzbait
buzz term
muzziest
quizzery
quiz show
huzzaing
puzzling
quizzing
quizzify
subzonal
buzz bomb
buzz word
buzzword
pulza-oil
Würzburg
aviation
aviarist
aviatrix
evacuate
evacuant
evocable
avocados
evection
eviction
Avicenna
evocator
evadable
oviducal
avidness
evidence
avadavat
Aviemore
avifauna
A V Kidder
availful
availing
avoision
TV dinner
evaluate
evulgate
ovo-lacto
evilness
ovalness
evolvent
Ovaltine®
avulsion
evulsion
à volonté
evil-doer
uvularly
uvulitis
evil-eyed
ave Maria
even date
ovenware
Svengali
aventail
evenfall
Evans Bay
evenness
evangely
eventful
ovenbird
Aventine
eventide
evincive
avenging
eventing
evenings
ovenwood
evensong
even-down
evanesce
aventure
eventual
even-even
avionics
Eva Perón
oviposit
overhand
overlaid
overland
overlard
overhale
overlade
overname
overpage
overrake
over rate
overrate
overtake
overgang
overhang
overrash
overwash
overrack
overrank
overtalk
overtask
overcall
overfall
overgall
overhaul
oversail
overlain
overhair
overpass
overcast
overmast
overpart
overpast
overt act
every bit
everyday
overfeed
overhead
overlend
overread
overleaf
oversell
overveil
overteem
overkeen
overseen
overween
overkeep
overleap
overbear
overhear
overpeer
overseer
overwear
overyear
over seas
overseas
averment
overbeat
overheat
overhent
overkest
overlent
overneat
overwent
aversely
over-shoe
overshoe
overshot
overkind
overwind
aversive
overbite
overfine
overgive
overlive
overnice
override
overripe
over side
overside
oversize
overtime
overtire
overwise
averring
overking
overwing
overfish
overfill
overkill
aversion
eversion
overlier
overview
overskip
overclub
overclad
overslip
overalls
overplus
overblow
overflow
overcloy
overplay
✧everyman
oversman
overknee
ivory-nut
overbold
overfold
overfond
overhold
overload
✧overlord
overloud
oversold
overword
evermore
everyone
ovariole
overcome
overdone
overdose
overrode
overtone
overwore
overlong
overbook
overcook
overlock
overlook
overwork
overboil
over-cool
oversoul
overtoil
overworn
overdoer
Averroës
ovarious
overcoat
overdo it
overpost
overspin
overfree
overarch
overbrim
overcrop
overtrip
overwrap
overbrow
overcraw

overcrow
overdraw
overgrow
overstep
ovaritis
overstay
overfund
overrule
overture
overruff
overhung
overmuch
overbulk
overfull
overburn
overturn
overjump
overdust
overbusy
overswim
everyway
oversway
overhype
overtype
evasible
svastika
evitable
kvetcher
avoutrer
avowable
avowedly
a-weather
awearied
swealing
swearing
sweating
tweaking
swear off
own-brand
swabbers
swabbing
two bells
two by two
twichild
twoccing
two-digit
swaddler
twaddler
twiddler
Swadeshi
sweet ale
tweenage
zwieback
sweet bay
tweeness
tweezers
two-edged
sweet gum
sweet gas
sweeping
sweeting
sweetish
tweedier
tweedily
tweedler
sweep-net
owreword
owrecome
sweet-oil
sweet pea
E W Benson
sweetsop
sweep-saw
two-faced
swift fox
Swiftian
swiftlet
Owl-glass
Ewigkeit
swagshop
swagging
swigging
twigging
swagsman
twigsome
two-horse
owlishly
swaining
swainish
Kwakiutl
own-label
swell box
swelldom
twelvemo
owl-light
twilight
swelchie
dwelling
swelling
swilling
swellish
swell-mob
swill out
swill-tub
swimwear
swamp gas
swimming
swamp oak
swimsuit
Swan Lake
swan-mark
swingbin
swanherd
Rwandese
swan neck
twin-lens
swannery
twi-night
twinship
swan-shot
swan dive
swanlike
awanting
swanking
swanning
swinging
twanging
twinling
twinning
Swan Hill
swingism
twenties
swan-skin
swanskin
swindler
twinkler
swan song
swansong
Gwen John
twin-born
twin town
swankpot
swine-pox
swine-sty
twin axis
swooning
two-phase
two-piece
swap meet
swap-shop
swap file
swap line
swapping
swopping
swaption
two pence
twopence
twopenny
two pound
sword-arm
sword-cut
swarming
swerving
dwarfish
dwarfism
sword-law
swordman
owerloup
two-sided
swastika
swashing
swishing
swissing
twisting
two-score
twist-off
owl-train
twittery
switchel
switch on
switcher
twitcher
swatting
swotting
twitting
twattler
two-timer
swayback
swayling
excavate
exhalant
ox-warble
expanded
expander
expandor
ox-halide
ex tacito
axiality
execrate
exocrine
exacting
exaction
executer
executor
executry
oxidiser
oxidizer
ex re nata
extended
expender
extender
exoergic
expedite
exterior
oxpecker
excelled
expelled
expellee
expeller
external
externat
excerpta
axle-tree
exhedrae
extensor
excesses
expenses
expected
exserted
expert in
exceptor
expecter
expertly
exigeant
exigible
exiguity
exogamic
exigence
exigency
exiguous
exegesis
exegetic
exchange
excitant
expirant
expiable
exciting
expiring
excision
ex nihilo
ex libris
ex-libris
expiator
exultant
axillary
explicit
excluded
exploded
excludee
excluder
exploder
✧explorer
exemplum
examplar
exemplar
examinee
examiner
eximious
oxymoron
oximeter
exanthem
exponent
ox-tongue
ox-iodide
extolled
extoller
axiology
exhorter
exporter
extorter
exposure
axoplasm
exoplasm
exophagy
exequial
exequies
exorable
Oxbridge
extruder
extrados
exarchal
exercise
exertive
exorcise
exorcize
exordial
exorcism
exordium
exertion
exorcist
extra jam
extremer
extremes
extranet
uxorious
extrorse
expresso
ex gratia
excretal
excreter
exergual
existent
axe-stone
exosmose
exospore
oxytocic
oxytocin
oxytonic
exitance
exit poll
exoteric
exotoxic
exotoxin
exhumate
excubant
excuse me
excuse-me
expunger
excusive
excursus
exuviate
Ayia Napa
pyjamaed
cynanche
synarchy
bylander
Lysander
gynandry
Myra Hess
hypalgia
synaphea
myna bird
dynamise
dynamite
dynamize
lyra-wise
✧sybarite
sycamine
tyramine
lyra viol
lyra-viol
cymatium
dynamism
gyration
cymatics
dynamics
✧pyramids
dynamist
tyrannic
lycaenid
zygaenid
tyrannis
hydatoid
hyracoid
sycamore
gyratory
dynatron
synapses
synapsis
dynastic
synaptic
synanthy
synastry
Syracuse
by halves
eye-black
myoblast
cymbidia
ryebread
Ayub Khan
symbolic
cymbalos
symbiont
syncline
lynching
lynch-law
lynch mob
hyacinth
eye candy
syncopic
syncopal
lynchpin
dyschroa
syncarpy
syncytia
syndical
syndings
syndrome
eye-drops
pyoderma
syndesis
syndetic
Syldavia
Cyrenaic
lykewake
type case
typeface
gybe mark
lykewalk
typecast
myxedema
hymeneal
hymenean
Pyrenean
Pyrenees
tyreless
synergic
synergid
by weight
synechia
lyrebird
type-high
hymenial
mycelial
pyrexial
gynecium
hymenium
mycelium
by design
Hyperion
hypernym
mycetoma
pyrenoid
type-body
type spec
cyberpet
synedria
cybersex
synectic
my certie
Cynewulf
by return
ryeflour
myograph
syngraph
eyeglass
nylghaus
rye grass
syngamic
dysgenic
myogenic
pyogenic
lychgate
by the bye
mythical
Typhoean
Typhoeus
by choice
syphilis
hyphenic
pythonic
Tychonic
✧typhonic
hyphened
by chance
kyphosis
kyphotic
dye-house
by the way
symitare
dytiscid
Dytiscus
myriadth
cylinder
syringes
by rights
typified
cytidine
cytisine
pyridine
pyritise
pyritize
pygidial
cynicism
hylicism
lyricism
pygidium
pyxidium
typifier
hylicist
lyricist
Cyrillic
kyrielle
hygienic
mytiloid
lyriform
pyriform

pyritous
myriapod
myriopod
Syriarch
myristic
syrinxes
gymkhana
syllabub
syllabic
syllable
syllabus
cyclical
Cyclades
Hyblaean
byrlakin
cyclamen
myelomas
cyclonic
myelinic
eyeliner
cyclopic
✧cyclopes
cycloses
cyclosis
kyllosis
pyelitic
myelitis
pyelitis
eye level
eye-level
wye-level
cycleway
dyslexia
dyslexic
✧myrmidon
pygmaean
dysmelia
dysmelic
myomancy
symmetry
pyinkado
pyengadu
hyena dog
cyanogen
by inches
ayenbite
Myrna Loy
pyonings
hymn-book
cyanuret
gymnasia
gymnasic
cyanosed
lyings-in
cyanosis
hypnosis
pycnosis
cyanotic
hypnotic
kyanitic
syenitic
hypnotee
hypogaea
myxomata
xylomata
zygomata
hylobate
xylocarp
gyroidal
xyloidin
eye of day
hypogene
lycopene
pyroxene
Tyrolese
zygotene
hypogeal
hypoderm
hypogeum
hypogean
Tyrolean
lysogeny
hypothec
by-motive
cytokine
cytosine
dysodile
gyrolite
mylonite
tyrosine
Xylonite®
xylonite
zylonite
synovial
Byronism
sybotism
syconium
hypocist
by-corner
Pyrosoma
Tylopoda
cytosome
hypobole
lysosome
pyrosome
sycomore
mylodont
zygodont
cytology
mycology
typology
xylology
zymology
kymogram
synopses
synopsis
synoptic
gyrostat
pyrostat
cynosure
dysodyle
gyrodyne
lysozyme
pyrolyse
pyrolyze
pyroxyle
hypogyny
hyponymy
synonymy
Nymphaea
symplast
dysphagy
sympodia
dyspneic
eyepiece
by-speech
dyspneal
nymphean
lyophile
sylphide
sylphine
symphile
nymphish
sylphish
symphily
tympanic
tympanal
tympanum
dyspnoea
lymphoma
lymphoid
lyophobe
symploce
symphony
dyspepsy
symposia
dyspathy
myopathy
sympathy
Symphyla
cyprides
✧ayurveda
Tyrrhene
hydrogel
hydrogen
myrrhine
hydremia
hydromel
Hydromys
cyprinid
hydranth
Cypriote
pyrrhous
hydropic
hydropsy
hydroski
hydroxyl
eye-rhyme
✧hydrozoa
eyeshade
eyestalk
gypsydom
eyesight
Ayrshire
hyoscine
gypsyism
cypselae
eye-salve
eyes down
gypseous
rye-straw
syssitia
myositis
myosotis
dyestuff
ryotwari
dystocia
mystical
eye to eye
by itself
Tyrtaean
by-street
syntagma
syntagms
cysteine
oystrige
cyathium
systolic
systemic
systemed
dystonia
myotonia
dystonic
gym tunic
myotonic
syntonic
syntonin
eye tooth
dystopia
mystique
✧hysteria
hysteric
nystatin
cystitis
syntexis
pyruvate
Lycurgus
sylviine
Sylvania
✧sylvaner
sylvatic
dye-works
eye-water
lynx-eyed
by my will
syzygial
syzygies
Ozacling®
izvestia
azulejos
Dzongkha
ozoniser
ozonizer
czaritsa
czarevna
tzatziki
azoturia
Szczecin

9 – even

Canada Day
catamaran
maharajah
Malayalam
Nabataean
panama hat
tacamahac
Maracaibo
calamanco
calavance
caravance
catafalco
jacaranda
sarabande
caravaned
caravaner
maharanee
Mahajanga
camanachd
maranatha
banana oil
Barataria
catabasis
katabasis
katabatic
macadamia
Pan-Arabic
parabasis
paralalia
parataxis
balalaika
Caracalla
palatable
palatably
man-at-arms
paravaunt
Galápagos
galapagos
malaxator
Canada Dry®
Navaratra
Navaratri
Takamatsu
paramatta
Paranagua
taraxacum
paparazzi
paparazzo
canal-boat
carambola
carambole
gaga about
salad bowl
cavalcade
canal-cell
✧damascene
kalanchoe
Naval Club
parasceve
hazard pay
bavardage
calandria
farandole
farandine
gabardine
marauding
cat-and-dog
man and boy
man-and-dog
malanders
hazardous
salad days
hazardize
dahabeeah
lamaserai
palace-car
paralegal
tapaderas
casarecci
zapateado
Japaneses
palaverer
parameter
parapeted
taxameter
cadaveric
catalexis
catamenia
✧hamamelis
paralexia
paramecia
paramedic
Saracenic
bagatelle
panatella
savagedom
tapaderos
catalepsy
karateist
cabaletta
cabalette
Canaletto
lazarette
lazaretto
fabaceous
fagaceous
sagapenum
taxaceous
paraffine
paraffiny
Varangian
harangued
haranguer
carangoid
Sarah Gamp
salangane
had as good
✧falangism
✧falangist
Walachian
panachaea
tabasheer
Sarah Hogg
cataphyll
pararhyme
catarhine
matachina
matachini
Malathion®
parathion
cataphora
salad herb
malachite
parachute
barathrum
Carabidae
dahabiyah
fanatical
galabiyah
paradisal
Samaritan
satanical
Tabanidae
Varanidae
carabiner
dahabiyeh
karabiner
tanalised
tanalized
barasinga
maharishi
Narasimha
balanitis
Nazaritic
paradisic
parasitic
zanamivir
camarilla
sabadilla
tamarillo
caladiums
capacitor
caparison
lavaliere
Wahabiism
garagiste
palafitte
Wahabiite
Zapatista
capacious
malarious
rapacious
sagacious
salacious
vagarious
Nagarjuna
damaskeen
palankeen
Samarkand
kalamkari
ra-ra skirt
had as lief
lazar-like
Dalai Lama
caballine
caballing
halalling
caballero
cataclasm
cataclysm
cataplasm
✧paraclete
✧balaclava
dataglove
cataplexy
rabatment
Balaam-box
Balaamite
Marasmius
japanning
carap-nuts
Jagannath
parabolas
paradoxal
paranoiac
cataloger
paradores
paradoxer
saga novel
Rakaposhi
baragouin
catabolic
catatonia
catatonic
macaronic
macaronis
madarosis

natatoria
parabolic
paragogic
paralogia
paranoeic
parapodia
paratonic
sanatoria
datacomms
bat around
catamount
paramount
cacafogos
tapacolos
paramorph
lay aboard
calaboose
Saragossa
babacoote
Pavarotti
catalogue
paragogue
macaw-palm
palampore
vanaspati
damasquin
palanquin
catarrhal
hamadryad
hamadryas
balas ruby
maladroit
parabrake
tanagrine
paragraph
calabrese
gala-dress
gama grass
pará grass
bara brith
banausian
camass-rat
Malaysian
Dadaistic
lamaistic
rajahship
tayassuid
harassing
palaestra
Carausius
cadastral
radar trap
Rajasthan
bay-antler
macaw-tree
Max Aitken
kadaitcha
tarantula
hay asthma
galantine
abatting
Tarantino
tarantara
galactose
ap artist
arantass
arantism
cacafuego
paracusis
malagueña
apaculos

Kama Sutra
Kamasutra
Famagusta
marabunta
paraquito
Sarasvati
may as well
carap-wood
sapanwood
salaryman
catalyser
catalyzer
paralyser
paralyzer
catalysis
catalytic
kanamycin
paralysis
paralytic
paranymph
vambraced
parbuckle
sarbacane
carbachol
Barbadian
Cambodian
Barbadoes
gambadoes
✧may beetle
warble fly
lamb's ears
Lamb of God
cambiform
lay before
gambogian
Lambegger
tarboggin
tabbyhood
Banbridge
Cambridge
gambolled
garbology
jambolana
Cat Ballou
cabbalism
cabbalist
jambalaya
carbamide
car-bomber
carbamate
carbon tax
carbonade
carbonado
carbineer
carbinier
harbinger
wambenger
war bonnet
carbuncle
lambently
jawboning
carbanion
garbanzos
carbonara
carbon arc
Carbonari
carbonise
rabbinism
rabbinist
carbonate
rabbinate

rabbinite
sanbenito
carbonize
bamboo rat
zamboorak
bamboozle
Sam Browne
barbarian
gas-burner
hamburger
Pat Barker
harborage
cambering
jabbering
barbarise
barbarism
carburise
barbarity
carburate
barbarous
barbarize
carburize
barbastel
earbasher
Van Basten
barbascos
cambistry
Ian Botham
had better
gas-bottle
barbitone
barbotine
rabbeting
sabbatine
jawbation
talbotype
Babbittry
sabbatise
sabbatism
lambitive
sabbatize
Lambrusco
harbourer
tabbouleh
tambourin
lamb'swool
Cambazola
Cambozola®
carbazole
✧bacchanal
catch away
Dance Away
panchayat
fat chance
wanchancy
calceated
fasciated
pancratic
saccharic
saccharin
Kamchatka
catchable
danceable
fanciable
matchable
patchable
watchable
bacchante
bacchants
✧saccharum
hatch boat

Maccabean
sauce boat
hatchback
Maccabees
March beer
fancy ball
latch bolt
watch bill
dance band
matchbook
fascicled
fascicles
fancy cake
calcicole
catch cold
ear-cockle
fascicule
fasciculi
catch-crop
match-cord
sarcocarp
watchcase
march-dike
march-dyke
calcedony
Sarcodina
cascadura
rancidity
dance drug
cauchemar
gauchesco
gaucherie
rancheria
rancherie
tax credit
parchedly
rancheros
Parcheesi®
haecceity
ratchet up
fancy-free
calcifuge
fancy fair
batch file
bacciform
catch fire
falciform
lanciform
sacciform
watch fire
catch hold
dance hall
✧March hare
raccahout
fasciitis
rascaille
fat client
Gascoigne
lancejack
batch loaf
caecilian
matchlock
canceleer
cancelier
cancelled
canceller
marcelled
parcelled
sarcology
vasculums
Barcelona

hatchling
masculine
cancelbot
rascaldom
calculary
calculose
fanciless
matchless
rascalism
sauceless
calculate
falculate
laccolite
laccolith
rascality
sacculate
calculous
cancel out
Marcellus
parcel out
calcimine
catchment
hatchment
parchment
parcimony
sarcomere
sarcomata
calcaneal
calcanean
Mancunian
vaccinial
gasconade
balconied
tap cinder
carcinoma
falconine
day centre
law centre
parcenary
gasconism
larcenist
sauciness
fascinate
lancinate
vaccinate
calcaneum
calcaneus
larcenous
vaccinium
lanceolar
Marc Bolan
gas cooker
gas-cooled
watch over
patchocke
patchouli
patchouly
match play
matchplay
Sarcoptes
sarcoptic
catchpole
catchpoll
Marco Polo
marchpane
march past
mancipate
Cancerian
camcorder
barcarole
calcarine

gas-carbon
calcarate
cancerate
cancerous
rancorous
saucerful
saucer eye
Caucasian
fancy-sick
Lancaster
Caucasoid
fascistic
pancosmic
sarcastic
Marcus Fox
saucisson
bad cess to
marcasite
narcissus
fancy that
dancettee
dance tune
narcotine
falcation
narcotise
narcotism
narcotist
patch test
narcotize
Vancouver
raucously
sanctuary
catchweed
lancewood
matchwood
catchword
fancywork
patchwork
watchword
cardiacal
dandiacal
hard sauce
sand dance
sand lance
landwards
bald-faced
baldpated
hand-paper
hard-faced
laid paper
sandpaper
cardialgy
land-yacht
sand yacht
sand-yacht
bald eagle
card-table
sand table
landdamne
bandwagon
galdragon
sand mason
paediatry
hard facts
hardparts
hard-paste
gaudeamus
land-value
Nandi bear
bandy-ball
Magdeburg

paddy-bird
bandobast
Laodicean
pas de chat
Sadducean
dandy-cock
hand-screw
sand-screw
baldachin
land-scrip
lardy-cake
baldicoot
bandicoot
mad-doctor
saw doctor
landscape
dandy-cart
labdacism
Sadducism
manducate
candidacy
candidate
pas de deux
Nanda Devi
hands down
caddie car
Candlemas
handlebar
hard-metal
raddleman
saddlebag
saddle bar
saddle-lap
sand wedge
saddle pin
sand-devil
candle-end
paddle-box
saddlebow
candlenut
caudle cup
land-reeve
dandified
hands-free
yard of ale
dandyfunk
✧land of Nod
Mardi Gras
Sandy Gall
land agent
bald wheat
hardihead
hard wheat
band-wheel
handshake
bandshell
hardshell
maid-child
cardphone
hardihood
card-sharp
land-shark
bandeiras
cab-driver
hardliner
hard lines
Hard Times
hard-wired
sandpiper
hard right
baudricke

land-pilot
Gandhi-ism
tawdriest
bandwidth
Hardaknut
✧daedalian
fardel-bag
landslide
bandelier
bandoleer
bandolier
sandalled
paedology
Sandy Lyle
bandoline
Bardolino
land-plane
✧magdalene
mandoline
sand-blind
bandoleon
caudillos
dandelion
land-flood
Mandelson
✧mandilion
✧mandylion
bandalore
bandolero
handclasp
hand glass
sandblast
sandglass
vandalise
vandalism
lardalite
waldflute
vandalize
landamman
Landsmaal
pandemian
Candomble
Candomblé
cardamine
hardiment
randomise
randomize
Dardanian
Sardinian
sardonian
card index
card-index
lap dancer
tap-dancer
Valdenses
Waldenses
harden off
land snail
randan gig
warden pie
Kandinsky
sand-snake
fandangle
MacDonald
maddingly
gardening
hardening
maddening
pardoning
bandoneon
bandonion

fandangos
Mandingos
bawdiness
faddiness
gaudiness
handiness
hardiness
maidenish
randiness
sandiness
tardiness
landforce
mandiocca
hard words
baldmoney
handtowel
hardcover
hard money
hardnosed
land-loper
landloper
Land Rover®
wardrober
cardboard
hardboard
hard court
eard-house
dandiprat
dandyprat
handspike
sandspout
mal du pays
baldaquin
ealdorman
hand organ
sand break
garderobe
sandarach
sand crack
sand pride
pas d'armes
bard-craft
handcraft
sand grain
bandbrake
handbrake
banderole
dandy-roll
handprint
land grant
mandarine
wandering
handgrips
ganderism
hand-press
hardgrass
landdrost
paederast
panderess
panderism
sand grass
pandurate
caldarium
panderous
Van der Hum
hard drive
landgrave
waldgrave
hard-drawn
caddis fly
caddishly

pas de seul
yardstick
candytuft
handstaff
hard stuff
bandstand
band-stone
handstand
Landsting
Maidstone
sandstone
faldstool
laudation
pandation
hand's turn
handsturn
Landsturm
laudatory
mandatary
mandatory
sandstorm
laudative
Hasdrubal
cardpunch
hard-cured
hard-ruled
landaulet
handcuffs
paedeutic
paideutic
Maldivian
landowner
card swipe
handiwork
handywork
cameraman
Lake Garda
barefaced
camerated
care label
caretaker
casemaker
casemated
cave canem
face-saver
lace-paper
lacerated
make faces
make water
make waves
name names
pacemaker
ratepayer
safe haven
Cape dagga
camera-shy
have had it
lake-basin
Late Latin
lacerable
laterally
talegalla
face paint
take pains
Lake Patos
Lake Tahoe
macerator
Lake Taupo
have cause
matelasse
matelassé

cave-earth
make haste
rare earth
face value
saleratus
gate valve
wager boat
water bear
camelback
make a back
paperback
take aback
waterbuck
lager beer
Barenboim
have a ball
water bull
make a bomb
James Bond
Palembang
raven-bone
wagenboom
Camembert
paperbark
water bird
caper-bush
have a bash
water bath
water butt
calembour
care about
rave about
naked boys
mareschal
paper-coal
water cock
male screw
paper clip
layer cake
wafer cake
water cell
canescent
latescent
tabescent
James Cook
water-cool
gas escape
have a care
laser card
make a card
taxed cart
water cart
water core
water-core
water cure
paper-case
water cask
patercove
have ideas
James Dean
raven-duck
water deck
calendrer
water deer
calendric
eavesdrip
calendula
gaberdine
haberdine
eavesdrop
water drop

Pat Eddery
cavendish
laser disc
laser disk
water down
base metal
sage Derby
make peace
make-peace
Cape Verde
make ready
make-ready
base-level
gate fever
wavemeter
cafeteria
dare-devil
papeterie
parenesis
rakehelly
make terms
madeleine
lay eyes on
pademelon
patereros
tax-exempt
baneberry
make merry
naseberry
take heart
make sense
vade-mecum
take leave
take-leave
water flag
make a face
maleffect
make after
name after
take after
water flea
Lagerfeld
paper-file
waterfall
wages fund
hare's-foot
water flow
water fern
Waterford
make a fuss
waterfowl
water gage
galengale
water gall
panel game
gas engine
malengine
water gong
habergeon
papergirl
Watergate
water gate
Gateshead
water head
namecheck
mane-sheet
page three
page-three
makeshift
James Hogg
camel hair

cane-chair
Lake Ohrid
take a hike
date-shell
name-child
water hole
rakeshame
James Hunt
James Hook
game chips
take shape
waveshape
canephora
canephore
take short
catechise
catechism
catechist
catechize
Camelidae
Galenical
cane piece
baseliner
caregiver
take sides
haverings
have right
make light
safe light
lateritic
sagenitic
Masefield
materials
Wakefield
Salesians
cafetière
ravel into
facetious
parecious
water jump
kabeljouw
gavelkind
Sabellian
take a leak
water leaf
have place
take place
naked lady
Dave Allen
labelloid
lamelloid
water lily
bake blind
canellini
capelline
hare along
James Lind
labelling
Mayerling
panelling
ravelling
water lens
waterline
tabellion
case glass
lace glass
lamellose
panellist
paperless
waterless
baseplate

facecloth
faceplate
faveolate
lamellate
nameplate
patellate
satellite
wavellite
lager lout
wage slave
make a meal
water main
Cape smoke
paper mill
water mill
water mole
ravelment
watermark
take amiss
labelmate
make a move
Falernian
case-knife
careenage
Lake Onega
have in tow
take in tow
pageantry
cageyness
eagerness
fadedness
gameyness
jadedness
mare's-nest
mateyness
nakedness
sameyness
satedness
taperness
maternity
paternity
cavernous
made woman
have words
Jane Fonda
bare bones
gate-money
gate-tower
latecomer
make money
paper over
take cover
wave power
Malebolge
categoric
Macedonia
paregoric
wake-robin
case-bound
game point
gaze-hound
have round
macédoine
racegoing
kakemonos
Lake Poopó
bakeboard
baseboard
base-court
wakeboard
bakehouse

gatehouse
panegoism
racehorse
safe house
take horse
warehouse
wasegoose
Lake poets
Lake Volta
make a play
water poet
bakeapple
paper-pulp
sage apple
water polo
water pump
water pipe
cameo-part
davenport
palempore
take apart
water pore
make a pass
face cream
make or mar
racetrack
sale price
water rice
care order
jade green
male order
paper-reed
sage green
sage-green
take order
canefruit
lamebrain
water rail
wave train
canebrake
cameo-role
hate crime
lace-frame
have wrong
Janet Reno
name brand
navel ring
wavefront
page-proof
salesroom
cane grass
cane-trash
careerism
careerist
gatecrash
sagebrush
take a risk
tape grass
Cape Wrath
water rate
tape drive
have a stab
oakenshaw
take a seat
wapenshaw
water seal
haversack
waterside
wave aside
watershed
water sign
cadetship
camel spin
wages slip
water sail
water-ski'd
caressing
haversine
have a shot
raree-show
water-shot
take issue
caressive
cadential
lacertian
maieutics
take stock
case-study
gazetteer
fare stage
parentage
hare's-tail
have-at-him
mare's-tail
paper-thin
wafer-thin
wapentake
sales talk
take it ill
date-stamp
vasectomy
bakestone
gazetting
hare-stane
lacertine
lamenting
man-eating
Palestine
panettone
panettoni
parenting
✧valentine
Valentino
balection
caseation
patent log
paper tape
take steps
calenture
take a turn
caber toss
have it out
Maxentius
Jamestown
cane sugar
date-sugar
Cape Dutch
tape punch
waveguide
balefully
banefully
carefully
fatefully
hatefully
wakefully
take turns
Lake Huron
make fun of
mamelucos
face-guard
safeguard
water vole
water vine
basen wide
waterweed
cameo ware
laserwort
navelwort
paperware
paperwork
waterwork
water-worn
paper wasp
taperwise
James Watt
caterwaul
water wave
water-wave
safetyman
yakety-yak
safety net
panegyric
safety pin
rarefying
Lake Nyasa
Taufa'ahau
half-hardy
half-baked
half-faced
half-caste
faff about
mafficker
half-adder
bafflegab
halfpence
palfreyed
parfleche
Rafflesia
ramfeezle
halfpenny
carfuffle
lay-figure
half-cheek
half-shift
calf whale
half-shell
half-rhyme
Man Friday
half hitch
half-miler
half-timer
halflings
half-light
half-title
lawful day
gas-filled
jaw-fallen
half-blind
half-blood
half-close
half-plate
Baffin Bay
Garfunkel
raffinose
raffinate
ray fungus
half-royal
calfdozer
dayflower
half-dozen
✧mayflower
oar-footed
ray floret
ray flower
safflower
saffroned
wax flower
far from it
calf-bound
half-bound
half-pound
half-round
half board
half groat
half-price
half-track
fanfarade
half-breed
malformed
tax farmer
half-frame
fanfarona
warfaring
wayfaring
half-truth
half-crown
ham-fisted
raffishly
gas-fitter
hamfatter
half-sword
languaged
pay gravel
gaugeable
laughable
laughably
barghaist
Langobard
hang about
Largactil®
cargo cult
Fay Godwin
Haggadist
fagged out
Maggie May
tangle net
Margrethe
Langue d'oc
malgré moi
vargueños
languette
larghetto
malgré lui
MacGuffin
bargainer
langridge
tanghinin
languidly
narghilly
ganglions
barge into
gangliate
hang-glide
hang a left
gangplank
rangeland
bargellos
Bangalore
Sam Gamgee
Targumist
bargander
jargoneer
laggingly
bagginess
jargonise
jargonist
largeness
manganese
manginess
ranginess
manganate
manganite
marginate
Gargantua
manganous
jargonize
hang tough
baignoire
gangboard
hang loose
wang tooth
langspiel
bargepole
range pole
danger man
Pan-German
sangfroid
haggardly
laggardly
bangsring
margarine
✧tangerine
badger-dog
✧kangaroos
gargarise
gargarism
✧margarita
margarite
dangerous
gargarize
mangostan
haggishly
waggishly
laughsome
Langesund
sargassos
pargasite
sargassum
target man
Jay Gatsby
gadgeteer
pargetted
pargetter
targeteer
maggot-pie
haughtily
naughtily
faggoting
pargeting
largition
rangatira
mangetout
gang-punch
langouste
mangouste
lawgiving
parge-work
Haphtarah
Kathmandu
fan heater
fat-headed
gas heater
sapheaded
cash ratio
washbasin
wash badly
bath salts
Bath Abbey
Wahhabism
bathybius
cachectic
cathectic
yacht club
cathedral
rachidial
rachidian
Sanhedrim
Sanhedrin
pachyderm
washed-out
cashierer
machmeter
cachaemia
cachaemic
tachogram
pathogeny
Bathsheba
bath sheet
dash-wheel
✧bath chair
dachshund
naphthene
eachwhere
bakhshish
cash limit
Nashville
Kaohsiung
das heisst
✧kathakali
mashallah
gas helmet
gasholder
waghalter
pathology
Tashi Lama
cacholong
lay hold on
parhelion
natheless
batholite
batholith
bathylite
bathylith
tachylite
tachylyte
washcloth
nachtmaal
cat-hammed
sachemdom
nathemore
Bathonian
ham-handed
Nathanael
Nathaniel
dashingly
manhandle
panhandle
taphonomy
machinery
machinist
washiness
machinate
saphenous
washing-up
Haphtorah
bath-towel
fashioner
machzorim
Cashpoint®
cashpoint
Pakhtoons
dashboard
washboard
bath-house
bathhouse
washhouse
tachypnea
parhypate
gather way
jaghirdar
washerman
Zacharias
bacharach
bath-brick
yacht race
catharses
catharsis
cathartic
katharsis
Catharine
Catherina
Catherine
gathering
Katharina
Katharine
Katherine
Mathurine
Mathurins
ratheripe
catharise
Catharism
Catharist
lathyrism
ratherest
ratherish
catharize
yachtsman
Ian Hislop
cache-sexe
Manhattan
pathetics
each other
Mad Hatter
Bath stone
washstand
bashfully
bashawism
cashew nut
lachrymal
hatha yoga
haphazard
Kariba Dam
latitancy
✧garibaldi
harigalds
camisades
carinated
kahikatea
laminated
palisades
patinated
radicated
vaginated
waribashi
Laminaria
palilalia
sanitaria

Words marked ✧ can also be spelled with one or more capital letters

razorback
razorbill
Saxon blue
razorclam
capocchia
man-orchid
baroscope
paroicous
major-domo
baronetcy
paloverde
barometer
bayoneted
can-opener
gasometer
manometer
razor edge
Masoretic
Samoyedic
sapogenin
cacodemon
barometry
gasometry
manometry
nanometre
majorette
salopette
vaporetti
vaporetto
wagonette
pay-office
War Office
camouflet
razorfish
parochial
halophobe
Damon Hill
halophile
halophily
Max Ophuls
Kagoshima
cacophony
halothane
parochine
saxophone
mako shark
masochism
masochist
halophyte
Aaronical
canonical
laconical
parodical
Zapodidae
Maeonides
parotides
tamoxifen
vaporiser
vaporizer
barotitis
calorific
Jacobinic
Jacobitic
parotitis
saporific
vaporific
sapodilla
zapotilla
halobiont
palominos
caponiere
laborious
havocking
Man of Kent
Damoclean
lay on load
wagonload
wagon lock
panoplied
way of life
carolling
favorless
wagon-lits
Yaroslavl
paroemiac
paroemial
major mode
saloon bar
saloon car
marooning
baboonery
baboonish
taxonomer
cacotopia
Salomonic
taxonomic
paso doble
vasomotor
lagomorph
Bay of Pigs
Labour Day
Carol Reed
masonried
savourily
vapouring
wagon roof
barograph
Camorrism
Camorrist
labourism
labourist
sago grass
vapourish
favourite
Labourite
manor-seat
jalousied
majorship
major suit
mayorship
panoistic
wagons-lit
Aaron's rod
Vaiont Dam
cacoethes
dacoitage
catoptric
capotting
garotting
major tone
major term
fagottist
raconteur
caroluses
jacobuses
manoeuvre
razor wire
vaporware
mason wasp
cacodylic
canopying
parodying
Max Planck
campeador
wasp waist
palpebral
jam-packed
Kampuchea
pay packet
ragpicker
rampicked
wax pocket
carpaccio
tan pickle
gazpachos
jaspidean
carpe diem
campodeid
lampadary
lampadist
Lampedusa
dapple-bay
camp-fever
raspberry
paupiette
salpiform
Malpighia
rampaging
lampshade
camp-chair
harp-shell
lamp-shell
Hampshire
happy hour
sapphired
lamplight
nauplioid
rat-poison
Las Palmas
Jan Palach
lampblack
rappelled
carpology
lamp-glass
mappemond
Harpo Marx
tamponade
carpenter
tamponage
campanile
campanili
campanula
carpingly
gaspingly
rampantly
raspingly
happening
campanero
carpentry
campanist
gaspiness
happiness
nappiness
sappiness
wasp's nest
wasps' nest
car-pooler
harpooner
lampooner
camphoric
panphobia
rasp-house
bagpiping
damp squib
camper van
gaspereau
wapper-jaw
Harper Lee
campcraft
tampering
barperson
damp-proof
layperson
jasperise
nappy rash
pauperess
pauperise
pauperism
vampirise
vampirism
Max Perutz
jasperous
warp drive
jasperize
pauperize
vampirize
waspishly
campesino
cap pistol
carpetbag
carpet-bed
tappit hen
carpeting
palpitant
wasp-stung
camp-stool
carpet-rod
Kárpathos
palpation
tappet-rod
raspatory
palpitate
carpet bug
tarpaulin
tax-paying
sasquatch
Dan Quayle
Marquesan
banqueted
banqueter
lacquerer
parqueted
✧jacquerie
hacqueton
marquetry
parquetry
banquette
harquebus
marquises
pasquiler
carry away
fair catch
matriarch
patriarch
tarriance
fair-faced
hair-waver
lay reader
map-reader
macro-axis
Fairbanks
macrobian
carry back
carry-back
Larry Bird
Lauraceae
✧patrician
barracuda
barricade
barricado
macrocode
matricide
parricide
patricide
barracker
barricoes
patricoes
✧batrachia
capriccio
fairy cake
matricula
fabricant
latrociny
barracoon
lay rector
macrocopy
Capricorn
macrocosm
fabricate
macrocyte
Patroclus
Dalradian
sacred cat
Sacred Way
hag-ridden
ramrodded
macrodome
manriding
sacred cow
sacred ape
Laura Dern
Laurie Lee
parrhesia
sapraemia
sapraemic
Gabrielle
sacrifice
sacrifide
Pat Rafter
caprifoil
fair's fair
barrefull
caprifole
capriform
dairy farm
tauriform
carrageen
cat-rigged
farragoes
fairy gold
iatrogeny
Tarragona
cairngorm
gay rights
Harrogate
Harry Hill
fairyhood
hair shirt
hairpiece
ram-raider
fair field
darraigne
marry into
Barry John
parrakeet
Marrakesh
caerulean
patrol car
patrolman
hair slide
barrelled
bas-relief
lap-roller
laurelled
patrolled
patroller
tax relief
barrelage
macrology
patrology
sacrilege
sacralgia
bairnlike
fairylike
✧fairyland
madrilène
Madrileño
Maoriland
matriliny
patriliny
sacralise
caprylate
garrulity
haircloth
natrolite
sacrality
saprolite
barrelful
garrulous
sacralize
dairymaid
matrimony
patrimony
sacrament
hairy Mary
lacrimary
lacrymary
fairy moss
lacrimoso
lagrimoso
carronade
cab-runner
dak runner
warranted
warrantee
warranter
matronage
patronage
Garrincha
carron oil
Ian Rankin
jarringly
safranine
barrancos
warrantor
hairiness
la trenise
matronise
patroness
patronise
tarriness
matronize
patronize
pair-royal
fair words
cabriolet
carry over
carry-over
gadrooned
garryowen
Maori oven
patriotic
dayr'house
pair-horse
hairspray
hair space
Pauropoda
Cal Ripken
kauri-pine
madrepore
parroquet
fair trade
fair-trade
hairdrier
hairdryer
fairy ring
hairbrush
hair-grass
macrurous
sacrarium
Laurasian
madrassah
sacristan
barrister
lairdship
patristic
hadrosaur
bairn-team
barret-cap
Mauritian
parrot-jaw
barretter
garreteer
garrotted
garrotter
had rather
hairst-rig
carrot fly
carrytale
fairy tale
fairytale
hairstyle
bairn-time
garroting
parroting
latration
narration
day return
fairy tern
gas-retort
narratory
parrot-cry
tax return
Mauritius
narrative
carrousel
Harrovian
galravage
marrowfat
fairy wren
marrow-men
marrowsky
harrowing
narrowing
sabrewing
barrow boy
Maori Wars

marrowish
saprozoic
marshalcy
fan-shaped
man-slayer
pass water
Hans Sachs
Pan-Slavic
Haystacks
raiseable
ranshakle
camstairy
waistboat
waistbelt
hause-bane
waistband
waistcoat
cassocked
ransacker
sapsucker
raise Cain
capsicums
false card
false-card
passadoes
waist-deep
raised pie
pad-saddle
raised bog
Hassidism
capsid bug
false dawn
camsheugh
Hans Bethe
mass media
sans serif
haustella
panspermy
far-seeing
raw sienna
camsteary
baksheesh
Parseeism
cap sleeve
sassafras
false face
falsified
falsifier
marsh fern
Days of Awe
massagist
paysagist
pass-check
waist-high
hawsehole
raise hell
day school
falsehood
marsh hawk
daysailer
Pan's pipes
wassailer
capsaicin
Catskills
Mansfield
mal soigné
bad sailor
daysailor
wassailry
marshiest
Ian St John

mausolean
tahsildar
hause-lock
cat-silver
hanselled
tasselled
vassalage
causalgia
tarsalgia
damselfly
marshland
tasseling
waistline
capsulary
capsulise
causeless
cause list
pauseless
vassaless
waistless
capsulate
causality
sassolite
mausoleum
capsulize
hansom-cab
baisemain
balsam fir
facsimile
Balsamina
Kalsomine®
Lakshmana
parsimony
passament
passement
cassimere
massymore
false move
Pausanias
Sassanian
Sassenach
cassonade
passenger
parsonage
cassingle
pausingly
Cassandra
Sassandra
falseness
gassiness
harshness
Jansenism
Jansenist
massiness
parsonish
sassiness
Samsonite®
Vaishnava
batswoman
oarswoman
passional
sans souci
passioned
Naas Botha
haustoria
pass round
maestosos
marsupial
bar supper
passepied
sans-appel

pansophic
hawsepipe
marsupium
Caesarean
Caesarian
lapstreak
lat spread
wasserman
Hans Krebs
passers-by
cassareep
lapstrake
casserole
dayspring
hamstring
hamstrung
maistring
passerine
kaiserdom
cassaripe
mag-stripe
sassarara
Caesarism
Caesarist
kaiserism
lapse rate
Massorete
palsgrave
false step
lay sister
lassitude
wadsetter
cassation
causation
falsettos
causative
cassoulet
far-sought
marsquake
massively
passively
passivism
passivist
passivate
passivity
balsawood
cassowary
falsework
marshwort
pansexual
naysaying
✧balthasar
✧balthazar
Matthaean
waste away
eastwards
castrated
cast water
day trader
rag-trader
saltwater
cantharid
cantharis
martially
partially
tactually
wait table
castratos
Matt Damon
salt marsh
cantharus

gastraeum
lanthanum
earth-bred
wax tablet
cantabile
taste bulb
cantabank
waste book
earthborn
earth-bath
cast about
eastabout
wait about
Cactaceae
tactician
Baltic Sea
✧canticles
pastiches
pasticcio
party-call
latticini
latticino
faith cure
manticora
manticore
facticity
masticate
tacticity
Santa Cruz
canticoys
vastidity
paste-down
Castlebar
cattleman
Martlemas
rattlebag
Bartlemew
saltpeter
wattmeter
rattle off
Eastleigh
eat the air
sautéeing
panthenol
Parthenon
battle-cry
saltpetre
gastnesse
hartlesse
pantheism
pantheist
battlebus
castle nut
battle axe
battle-axe
earthflax
Tartufian
earthfall
pantoffle
cactiform
✧rastafari
earthfast
Tartufish
Tartufism
cartogram
D'Artagnan
partygoer
pantagamy
Cartagena
castigate
waste gate

fastigium
saltchuck
cartwheel
fact sheet
last thing
hartshorn
pantihose
pantyhose
salt rheum
mastoidal
captaincy
last-ditch
East River
fantailed
fat-tailed
last rites
part-timer
rat-tailed
wart-biter
cartridge
eastlings
partridge
cast light
Fantaisie
gastritis
East Timor
Xanthippe
captain RN
captainry
rattliest
waltz into
tant mieux
party-jury
partake in
Gaitskell
partaking
kantikoys
Kartikeya
Castalian
castellan
Castilian
Tantalean
Tantalian
cattaloes
martelled
battology
cartilage
cartology
tautology
nautiloid
cantilena
earthling
maltalent
pantiling
panty line
party line
santolina
wasteland
battalion
malt-floor
martellos
pantaleon
✧pantaloon
cartulary
cartelise
cartelism
cartelist
casteless
dactylist
faithless
tactilist

tantalise
tantalism
tasteless
pantalets
tactility
tantalate
tantalite
cantaloup
castellum
cautelous
tantalous
cartelize
salt glaze
tantalize
Jan Timman
bad temper
pantomime
battement
Baltimore
caste-mark
mattamore
Daltonian
Martinmas
Tartan tax
Waltonian
santonica
bastinade
bastinado
bartender
East-ender
Fasten-e'en
Santander
cartonage
wanting in
cantingly
dartingly
haltingly
lastingly
pantingly
rantingly
waitingly
tautonymy
battening
cantoning
fastening
fattening
rattening
cantiness
Cantonese
cantonise
cattiness
✧daltonism
fattiness
hastiness
nastiness
nattiness
pastiness
rattiness
saltiness
tartiness
tastiness
tattiness
wantonise
wasteness
castanets
cast an eye
cantonize
wantonize
factional
pactional
xanthomas

fast foods
haut monde
bastioned
cautioner
salt-money
danthonia
wait for it!
saltworks
fatty oils
eastbound
Hawthorne
gastropod
cant-board
cautionry
dartboard
Xanthoura
cart-horse
cart-house
cast loose
malt-horse
malt-house
masthouse
oast house
salt horse
tattooist
gastropub
xanthoxyl
zanthoxyl
parti pris
rantipole
salt spoon
waste pipe
bacterial
bacterian
cantorial
Easter Day
factorial
lactarian
latter-day
Pasternak
raptorial
sartorial
sartorian
Tartarean
Tartarian
cart-track
fast track
fast-track
vantbrace
✧easterner
master-key
panta rhei
patterned
Sauternes
wasterife
Easter egg
factorage
pasturage
waiterage
bacteroid
castor oil
latter-wit
dastardly
pastorale
pastorali
bantering
cauterant
factoring
faltering
Hart Crane
latter end

ideograph
idiograph
advoutrer
idiot tape
adaptable
adipocere
adoptious
adeptness
adiposity
Adar Sheni
adornment
adoringly
addressed
addressee
addresser
addresses
adpressed
addressor
adoration
odorously
Adis Abeba
Eduskunta
Edith Piaf
editorial
adjutancy
adjuvancy
adjunctly
adducible
odourless
adduction
adductive
iddy-umpty
megafarad
separates
metabasis
metabatic
verapamil
debatable
get-at-able
rebatable
relatable
reparable
reparably
repayable
separable
separably
megafauna
separator
metacarpi
megagauss
separatum
pedal-bone
cedar-bird
cevapcici
penal code
bepatched
debauched
debauchee
debaucher
decalcify
renascent
sea anchor
megascope
defaecate
defalcate
demarcate
demand-led
Decandria
Hexandria
web and pin
celandine
demandant
demanding
Geraldine
pen-and-ink
regardant
regarding
retardant
rewarding
decaudate
retardate
nefandous
regardful
rewardful
beta decay
✧temazepam
decadence
decadency
Hexateuch
melaleuca
recalesce
remanence
remanency
Mesa Verde
hexameter
metapelet
Melanesia
menagerie
metameric
sesame oil
belatedly
relaxedly
cesarevna
ten a penny
Decameron
decametre
hexahedra
secateurs
✧**new ageism**
megadeath
megahertz
revalenta
cepaceous
ceraceous
cetaceous
debateful
sebaceous
setaceous
Pelasgian
debagging
Metal Guru
decay heat
selachian
seraphims
megaphone
seraphine
seraphins
decathlon
refashion
decachord
hexachord
melaphyre
semaphore
metaphase
Hepaticae
hepatical
relatival
venatical
feralised
feralized
velarised
velarized
set alight
ceratitis
hepatitis
keratitis
pedatifid
cebadilla
cevadilla
menadione
relations
Beta fibre
decalitre
reradiate
retaliate
behaviour
feracious
nefarious
tenacious
veracious
vexatious
seraskier
repackage
Heraclean
defaulter
hexaploid
metalloid
regal lily
befalling
bewailing
delay line
medalling
metalline
metalling
pedalling
Heraklion
médaillon
medallion
seraglios
tenaillon
megaflora
Jena glass
medallist
metallise
metallist
metaplasm
Heraclius
penal laws
metallize
debarment
recalment
repayment
besainted
remainder
demanning
degarnish
decagonal
decapodal
decapodan
hepatomas
hexagonal
hexapodal
melanomas
teratomas
keratoses
telamones
teratogen
demagogic
keratosis
melanosis
melanotic
melatonin
metabolic
pedagogic
megajoule
get around
peraeopod
belamoure
ceratodus
✧decalogue
demagogue
pedagogue
medal play
medalplay
sex appeal
melampode
megaspore
remarqued
Velázquez
repairman
relay race
zelatrice
Delacroix
debarring
mepacrine
petaurine
veratrine
debarrass
Dekabrist
get across
hetaerism
hetaerist
hetairism
hetairist
petaurist
repassage
relapsing
delapsion
net assets
Sebastian
decastich
hexastich
semantics
semantide
bez-antler
pecan tree
demantoid
oenanthic
decastyle
hexastyle
semanteme
defatting
departing
desalting
✧levantine
recaption
redaction
semantron
web author
decastere
departure
depasture
megastore
recapture
repasture
Xenarthra
pedantise
pedantism
rebaptise
rebaptism
se-baptist
Vedantism
decantate
devastate
cerastium
pedantize
rebaptize
megacurie
melanuria
melanuric
megabucks
devaluate
revaluate
tenaculum
cedarwood
medaewart
metalware
metalwork
legal year
Decagynia
Hexagynia
megacycle
get any joy
bedazzled
semblance
keyboards
Rembrandt
sea-beaten
herb Paris
semblable
semblably
herbicide
verbicide
Benbecula
sea breach
herb Peter
redbreast
✧**sea breeze**
leg before
Redbridge
Herb Ritts
Hezbollah
herbal tea
verballed
cembalist
herbalism
herbalist
verbalise
verbalism
verbalist
verbality
verbalize
meibomian
yerba maté
Serbonian
temblores
merbromin
Mel Brooks
cerberean
cerberian
herbarian
verbarian
herb-grace
kerb drill
berberine
herborise
herborist
perborate
verberate
herbarium
herborize
eel-basket
nebbisher
verbosely
verbosity
Verbascum
sea-bather
rebbetzin
bed-bottle
seabottle
kerbstone
sea bottom
Zeebrugge
Melbourne
herbivora
herbivore
herbivory
Leibovitz
perchance
reactance
Neuchâtel
sea change
sex change
sex-change
merciable
peaceable
peaceably
perceable
reachable
rescuable
teachable
beach-ball
peach-blow
leuco-base
beccaccia
peace camp
leucocyte
peace drug
nescience
leucaemia
leucaemic
rescue bid
teacherly
percheron
new-create
beccafico
mercifide
bench fees
beech fern
perciform
hercogamy
beachhead
bench-hole
describer
perceiver
new critic
zecchinos
tetchiest
✧**herculean**
d'escalier
pencilled
penciller
mescaline
percaline
vetchling
Deucalion
pencil-ore
fenceless
merciless
mescalism
peaceless
reachless
retchless
teachless
percolate
Neocomian
welcomely
welcoming
benchmark
beech mast
Hercynian
percental
descended
descender
new candle
peccantly
mercenary
per contra
rencontre
sea canary
deaconess
hercynite
bed-closet
mercy on us
mercaptan
peace pill
peach-palm
peace pipe
per capita
beach plum
teacupful
cercariae
cercarian
✧mercurial
per curiam
Descartes
neocortex
red carpet
red-carpet
geocarpic
L'Escargot
mercerise
mercurise
mercurate
mercurous
mercerize
mercurize
bench seat
mercy-seat
Reichsrat
Reichstag
Wenceslas
Leicester
percussed
peace sign
Newcastle
percussor
Leuciscus
beech tree
bescatter
leg-cutter
peach-tree
leucotome
leucotomy
peacetime
bench test
bench-test
New Church
reacquire
reactuate
beachwear
beechwood
peach-wood
descrying
Aeschylus
dead march
readvance

Words marked ✧ can also be spelled with one or more capital letters

dead-water
feed-water
headwater
tea-dealer
lead-paint
pendragon
Red Dragon
sea dragon
hendiadys
teddy bear
beddy-byes
weedicide
pendicler
mendicant
headscarf
mendacity
mendicity
re-educate
reddleman
headpeace
headreach
beady-eyed
dead-level
red diesel
needle-tin
Leadbelly
beadledom
seed pearl
headlease
lend-lease
needleful
needle-gun
heddle-eye
re-edifier
Heidegger
verdigris
Teddy girl
dead thraw
deid-thraw
headchair
headshake
head-rhyme
headphone
lend a hand
needy-hood
seldshown
headpiece
dendrimer
headliner
headlines
hen-driver
jet-driven
Mendaites
pen-driver
deadlight
headlight
dendritic
seed-field
head first
feu de joie
veldskoen
Mendelian
new dollar
pendulums
penduline
seed-plant
feudalise
feudalism
feudalist
lead glass
Mendelism

feudality
headcloth
pendulate
pendulous
read aloud
dead-alive
feudalize
ready meal
ready-made
Desdemona
needs must
jeu de mots
neodymium
lend an ear
Leyden jar
reed-knife
bendingly
pendently
verdantly
deadening
Ferdinand
reddendos
headiness
heediness
neediness
readiness
reediness
seediness
weediness
reddendum
redding-up
tendinous
head-woman
seed coral
head voice
head money
seed money
lead colic
Dead Souls
dead-doing
dead point
head count
send round
headboard
bead-house
deadhouse
dead's part
feldspath
reed organ
gendarmes
seed drill
headframe
dead drunk
deodorant
leaderene
rendering
tendering
bead-proof
herd-groom
deodorise
head-crash
headdress
herd grass
readdress
reed-grass
tenderise
verdurous
weed-grown
deodorize
tenderize
Red Duster

geodesist
deadstock
feedstock
geodetics
headstick
headstock
feedstuff
headstall
seed-stalk
headstone
perdition
rendition
vendition
feudatory
head start
heedfully
needfully
tend out on
Red Devils
Les Dawson
ready-wash
meadow-rue
Ted Dexter
deadly sin
relevance
relevancy
severance
hederated
leveraged
serenader
telesales
vegetated
telepathy
federarie
generalia
Seneca oil
telematic
deferable
delegable
generable
generally
referable
relegable
renewable
reverable
severable
severally
vegetable
vegetably
venerable
venerably
defecator
generator
renegados
revelator
venerator
Téméraire
pederasty
severalty
peter-boat
Peter Buck
resembler
leger bait
hereabout
seneschal
beseeched
beseecher
decencies
remercied
level-coil
redescend

senescent
Peter Cook
telescope
telescopy
jewel case
repercuss
beheading
defendant
dependant
dependent
depending
✧defenders
legendary
legendist
level down
deference
reference
reverence
vehemence
vehemency
referenda
delete key
telemeter
tête-bêche
telegenic
cerebella
Gene Kelly
pedereros
redevelop
set eyes on
here we are
telemetry
rerelease
venereous
hereafter
sevenfold
jewelfish
bevel gear
beleaguer
detergent
jet engine
revenging
Serengeti
Betelgeux
revengive
fever-heat
petechiae
petechial
Peterhead
repechage
Pele's hair
Peter Hall
telepheme
telephone
telephony
telephoto
generical
genetical
heretical
venefical
benefit by
beneficed
benefited
redeliver
televiser
teredines
benedight
Genesitic
selenitic
jerepigos
televisor

remediate
terebinth
selenious
Severinus
Genevieve
reaedifye
genealogy
mereology
teleology
peneplain
rebel-like
bevelling
debelling
jewelling
leger line
levelling
✧never land
peneplane
rebelling
refelling
repellant
repellent
repelling
revealing
revelling
rebellion
jewellery
cerealist
cerecloth
meter maid
beseeming
besetment
bevelment
deferment
determent
determine
never mind
redeeming
revetment
nevermore
decennial
perennial
sexennial
Aegean Sea
hereunder
teleonomy
secernent
decennary
levelness
vexedness
belemnite
perennate
perennity
decennium
demeanour
developed
developer
✧pele-tower
bene vobis
hegemonic
heterosis
heterotic
peperomia
semeiotic
telegonic
tête folle
telepoint
heterodox
heteropod
pereiopod
développé

bête noire
✧pele-house
reredorse
reredosse
reremouse
gene locus
heteronym
bel esprit
reserpine
newel post
rehearsal
rerebrace
rehearser
redecraft
meteoroid
cerebrums
bebeerine
celebrant
deferring
deterrent
deterring
Dexedrine®
gemel-ring
penetrant
peregrine
referring
rehearing
terebrant
veneering
tenebrios
telegraph
derepress
meteorism
meteorist
tenebrism
tenebrist
tenebrose
celebrate
celebrity
cerebrate
desecrate
meteorite
penetrate
tenebrity
terebrate
Demetrius
meteorous
revel-rout
tenebrous
petersham
Seven Seas
Teleostei
Red Ensign
bedelship
reversely
Release Me
reversing
decession
demersion
detersion
Peter Snow
recension
recession
reversion
secession
necessary
remeasure
necessity
teleosaur
defensive
detersive

recessive
celestial
desert rat
fenestral
nemertean
nemertian
selectman
semestral
Terentian
metestick
telestich
desert pea
fever tree
mementoes
Nepenthes
seventeen
seventies
seventhly
begetting
besetting
✧celestine
denetting
Heseltine
merestone
nemertine
relenting
repeating
repentant
revetting
deception
defection
dejection
desertion
detection
detention
reception
refection
rejection
resection
retention
selection
debenture
deceptory
defeature
dejectory
mesentery
refectory
repertory
retexture
sedentary
defeatism
defeatist
celestite
cementite
dementate
Nefertiti
tête-à-tête
cement gun
deceitful
resentful
select out
deceptive
defective
detective
receptive
rejective
resentive
retentive
revertive
selective
reperusal

Venezuela
reservoir
deserving
receiving
decemviri
decemvirs
reservist
jewel-weed
mere swine
remedying
pelecypod
beefeater
self-faced
self-abuse
perfecter
perfectly
perfector
perfectos
leaf-metal
leafleted
leaf cells
self-begot
renfierst
kerfuffle
red-figure
leaf miner
pen friend
self-pious
beefaloes
new-fallen
self-slain
bedfellow
gerfalcon
jerfalcon
pew-fellow
beef olive
self-image
feoffment
perfumery
newfangle
deafening
leafiness
self-doubt
bee-flower
leaf-nosed
webfooted
set foot in
leaf mould
self-rowld
reef point
self-worth
leaf trace
self-pride
leaf-green
performer
telferage
perfervid
new for old
perforans
perforant
seafaring
self-wrong
Jefferson
perfervor
self-trust
welfarism
welfarist
beef broth
perforate
self-drive
sea-fisher

selfishly
perfusion
perfusate
perfusive
beefsteak
self-study
leaf-stalk
self-build
self-built
Delftware
self-aware
fee-faw-fum
sergeancy
vengeance
pea gravel
sea grapes
Red Grange
geography
dei gratia
zeugmatic
vengeable
vengeably
weighable
hedgebill
Mel Gibson
hedge-born
sedge bird
hedge-bote
neighbour
weigh-bauk
berg-adder
weigh down
berg-cedar
feignedly
seigneury
hedge fund
lengthman
wedge heel
lengthily
Leigh Hunt
lengthful
New Guinea
penguinry
seigniory
weigh into
Vergilian
wedge-like
bengaline
sedgeland
Bengalese
vengement
✧bergamask
✧bergomask
pergunnah
bergander
merganser
sea ginger
beggingly
legginess
Reaganism
Reaganite
seignoral
geognosis
Zeuglodon
red grouse
beggar-man
tea garden
sea girdle
beggardom
res gestae
Neo-Gothic

weightily
weighting
sedge wren
wedgewise
déchéance
red-headed
nephralgy
Rechabite
methadone
pethidine
methodise
Methodism
✧methodist
Methodius
methodize
Bethlehem
red-heeled
tee-heeing
rechlesse
reshuffle
meshugaas
nephogram
tephigram
Ted Hughes
metheglin
technical
red-haired
nephritic
nephritis
tephritic
technique
tephillah
Aethelred
penholder
pew-holder
nephology
tephillin
methylene
nepheline
nephalism
nephalist
netheless
cephalate
lethality
methylate
nephelite
segholate
cephalous
bethumbed
Zephaniah
mechanics
redhanded
bethankit
mechanise
mechanism
mechanist
techiness
mechanize
dethroner
nephrosis
nephrotic
technopop
tephroite
Zechariah
De Chirico
recharter
recherché
lethargic
Sephardic
Sephardim
senhorina

Senhorita
lecherous
methystic
Zechstein
Len Hutton
mephitism
réchauffé
bethought
methought
yeshivahs
let have it
yeshivoth
perinatal
semi-bajan
demi-lance
hesitance
hesitancy
Mélisande
dedicated
dedicatee
medicated
meditated
Mehitabel
devil a bit
genitalia
genitalic
Lewis acid
Semiramis
tepidaria
decidable
decimally
definable
definably
demisable
derivable
derivably
desirable
desirably
devisable
Géricault
helically
heritable
heritably
levigable
lexically
medicable
medically
recitable
revisable
revivable
revivably
rewirable
seminally
veritable
veritably
devil a one
decimator
dedicator
depilator
hesitator
levitator
meditator
mesic atom
Semi-Saxon
Pedipalpi
demitasse
perinaeum
✧peripatus
perikarya
Lewis base
devil-crab

Meliaceae
periscian
meniscoid
dehiscent
desiccant
heliscoop
periscope
debit card
desiccate
Pekin duck
zemindari
zemindary
periodise
periodate
remindful
periodize
mediaeval
semi-metal
venireman
desinence
penitence
penitency
renitency
residence
residency
reticence
reticency
bedizened
decimeter
deliverer
perimeter
demi-deify
demi-devil
peripetia
decidedly
deliverly
refinedly
reticella
retiredly
decimetre
hemihedry
perimetry
delineate
femineity
serinette
deviceful
refine out
sericeous
penis envy
relief map
devilfish
petit four
Hemingway
meningeal
Peking man
Bering Sea
Feringhee
teeing-off
besieging
Lexington
Pekingese
redingote
benighted
benighten
benighter
delighted
delight in
perishing
set in hand
periphery
fetichise

fetichism
fetichist
fetishise
fetishism
fetishist
fetichize
fetishize
feticidal
genitival
Helicidae
levitical
medicinal
Neritidae
regicidal
regiminal
semifinal
veridical
reminisce
deciliter
delimiter
feliciter
mediciner
felicific
peridinia
retinitis
semi-rigid
sericitic
derisible
deliriums
deficient
definiens
deliriant
desipient
recipient
resilient
decilitre
religiose
religioso
delicious
delirious
demipique
Leviticus
redivivus
religieux
religious
seditious
petit jury
heli-skier
Cecil King
periaktos
Periclean
aetiology
heliology
semiology
megillahs
hemialgia
semifluid
venial sin
petiolule
semiplume
devilling
pericline
perilling
pétillant
sea-island
decillion
penillion
vexillary
aerialist
genialise
periblast

periclase
periplast
serialise
serialism
serialist
aeriality
feuilleté
geniality
legislate
megilloth
petiolate
sepiolite
seriality
veniality
genialize
serialize
Media Mail
bedimming
depigment
devilment
refitment
remitment
melismata
Periander
defiantly
leniently
semiangle
beginning
benignant
designing
legionary
regionary
Fenianism
fetidness
gelidness
tepidness
benignity
debit note
designate
gelignite
designful
Meliboean
demi-monde
pericones
semivowel
demi-gorge
peridotic
resinosis
semisolid
semitonic
heliborne
periboloi
peribolos
semicolon
perimorph
Demi Moore
demi-volte
peribolus
Lenin Peak
Menippean
hemispace
hemiopsia
petit pain
petit pois
perisperm
semi-Arian
periproct
peritrack
peritrich
semi-truck
pedigreed

denitrify
devitrify
Félibrige
demiurgic
peridrome
pericrany
semi-grand
hemitrope
serigraph
heritress
meliorism
meliorist
denigrate
denitrate
meliorate
meliority
remigrate
seniority
demiurgus
retiarius
semibreve
heliostat
devil's-bit
devilship
✧peninsula
demission
remission
remissory
tediosity
régisseur
demissive
remissive
devil's own
✧leviathan
registrar
revictual
hemistich
semiotics
rebirther
Genistein®
geriatric
mediatrix
mediately
peristyle
seriately
peristome
befitting
besitting
penistone
refitting
remittent
remitting
resistant
resistent
depiction
deviation
mediation
seriation
heliotype
heliotypy
decistere
depicture
deviatory
Hemiptera
mediatory
periptery
mediatise
helictite
Aegisthus
depictive
mediative

resistive
mediatize
pedicular
reliquiae
reticular
retinulae
retinular
semilunar
vehicular
vesiculae
vesicular
deviously
seriously
tediously
reliquary
residuary
deciduate
deciduous
deliquium
de rigueur
✧pediculus
residuous
✧reticulum
believe in
believing
relieving
hemicycle
pericycle
tepifying
verifying
perilymph
heliozoan
heliozoic
serjeancy
serjeanty
bed-jacket
pea jacket
verjuiced
Seljukian
Ben Jonson
New Jersey
perjurous
jerkwater
deck-cargo
Reykjavík
leuko-base
week about
leukocyte
peaked cap
beekeeper
leukaemia
leukaemic
neckverse
seek after
herkogamy
deckchair
Berkshire
neckpiece
weeknight
neckcloth
berkelium
Peckinpah
weak-kneed
weekender
reckoning
jerkiness
leakiness
perkiness
weak force
desk-bound
deskbound

weak point
deckhouse
peck order
weaker sex
beakerful
sex kitten
tea kettle
leukotome
leukotomy
hellwards
hell-hated
real wages
tea leaves
tell tales
well-famed
bellyache
belle amie
weel-faird
weel-faur'd
weel-faurt
jelly bean
jelly baby
beslobber
beslubber
bellibone
belly-band
welly-boot
hellebore
New Labour
deflected
fetlocked
neglecter
reflected
reflecter
tesla coil
replicant
deflector
reblochon
reflector
bellicose
replicate
vellicate
bell-metal
mealie pap
refluence
Nellie Kim
real terms
wellbeing
well-meant
veilleuse
Beelzebub
well-set-up
feel after
belly flop
belly-flop
jelliform
jellyfish
geologian
neologian
jet-lagged
red-legged
reflagged
pellagrin
negligent
geologise
geologist
neologise
neologism
neologist
geologize
neologize

feel cheap
wealth tax
fellaheen
healthily
wealthily
cellphone
sell short
healthful
heel-piece
declaimer
reclaimer
well-aimed
well-given
well-lined
well-oiled
well-timed
hell-black
celluloid
✧celluloid®
get laldie
bell-glass
cellulase
cellulose
realmless
cellulite
well smack
real image
sell smoke
feel small
belle-mère
bedlamism
bedlamite
beglamour
wellanear
ceilinged
sex-linked
vellenage
leylandii
red lentil
sea lentil
tellinoid
feelingly
healingly
reelingly
tellingly
declinant
reclining
red-lining
Ceylonese
✧hellenise
Hellenism
Hellenist
jeely nose
mealiness
replenish
ceylanite
ceylonite
declinate
reclinate
well-known
✧hellenize
hell to pay
well woman
bell tower
✧peel-tower
red-looked
well-borer
hellhound
Neil Young
sealpoint
well-doing

well-found
✧peel-house
wellhouse
well forth
well worth
dewlapped
aeolipile
aeolipyle
well-spent
tell apart
cellarman
Keplerian
tellurian
real price
telluride
beglerbeg
de-blurred
well-tried
Zeller See
cellarage
well drain
bell crank
declarant
tellurion
cellarist
tellurise
deflorate
hell-broth
tellurate
tellurite
cellarous
tellurium
tellurous
tellurize
beplaster
déclassée
realistic
hellishly
reclusely
sexlessly
realising
reblossom
reclusion
seclusion
reclusory
reclusive
seclusive
red-letter
sea letter
pelletify
Bellatrix
Neolithic
tell a tale
belly tank
deflation
depletion
Mellotron®
reflation
repletion
Sellotape®
sellotape
depletory
pellitory
pelletise
zealotism
reality TV
depletive
pelletize
bell-punch
jealously
well-built

zealously
well put on
replevied
keelivine
keelyvine
declivity
re-elevate
declivous
fellow man
sea lawyer
Yellow Sea
yellowfin
reflowing
yellow-boy
yellow dog
yellowish
mellow out
deflexion
defluxion
reflexion
deflexure
reflex arc
reflexive
cell cycle
realizing
permeance
germ layer
permeable
permeably
set much by
germicide
vermicide
vermicule
Bermudian
desmodium
vermifuge
term of art
vermiform
termagant
Geomyidae
Des Moines
mermaiden
seemlihed
vermeille
seemliest
Lee Miller
red mullet
gemmology
reimplant
permalloy
vermilion
germ plasm
hermandad
segmental
tegmental
Germanice
fermented
fermenter
geomancer
germander
per mensem
segmented
sermoneer
Fermanagh
geomantic
beamingly
germanely
seemingly
germinant
permanent
sermoning

fermentor
beaminess
Germanise
Germanish
Germanism
Germanist
jemminess
✧pelmanism
seaminess
sermonise
terminism
terminist
deaminate
germinate
hetmanate
terminate
verminate
germanium
tegmentum
verminous
Germanize
sermonize
jemmy open
✧newmarket
tee marker
sea margin
mesmerise
mesmerism
mesmerist
beam trawl
mesmerize
kermes oak
seamy side
bee-master
webmaster
dermestid
desmosome
kermesite
hermetics
besmutted
den mother
permitted
permitter
hermitage
dermatoid
geometric
geometrid
dermatome
gemmation
termitary
hermitess
lemmatise
pegmatite
permutate
gemmative
lemmatize
reimburse
New Mexico
seemlyhed
bean caper
herniated
lean-faced
seannachy
reinhabit
Jean Patou
Léon Bakst
penny ante
penny-ante
seine boat
Zernebock
penny-bank

Lemnaceae
sennachie
Jean Genet
Jennie Lee
meandered
Sean Kelly
de integro
neon tetra
reindeers
beanfeast
Jeannette
re infecta
penniform
penny gaff
Benny Hill
meanwhile
bean shoot
neon light
fernticle
kennelman
kennelled
Jenny Lind
pennyland
Penny Lane
mesne lord
beingless
Jean Alesi
pennalism
penniless
vernalise
vernality
vernalize
neonomian
penny mail
reanimate
Memnonian
Fernandel
pennoncel
meaningly
teknonymy
Cernunnos
beingness
Mennonite
penninite
genning up
re-enforce
reinforce
Jean Bodin
re-endorse
reinvolve
reinspect
senna pods
reinspire
penny-post
meandrian
Wernerian
Deinornis
penny-rent
re-entrant
wernerite
meandrous
Keynesian
Wednesday
benne-seed
benni-seed
Tennessee
be oneself
deinosaur
rennet-bag
veinstuff
Bernstein

peanut oil
beanstalk
pennatula
reinstall
sea nettle
ternately
jenneting
veinstone
resnatron
vernation
means test
means-test
reinstate
ceanothus
Pernettya
reinsurer
heinously
jenny-wren
pennywort
penny wise
neo-Nazism
aeromancy
belomancy
ceromancy
oenomancy
resonance
memoranda
decorated
desolater
zero-rated
sea orange
aerobatic
aerotaxis
demomania
melomania
melomanic
oenomania
xenomania
denotable
deposable
memorable
memorably
removable
removably
revocable
revocably
revokable
meiofauna
decorator
desolator
detonator
renovator
resonator
Sea of Azov
menopause
mesopause
redoubted
lemon balm
demobbing
recombine
resorbent
retoucher
tenor clef
heroic age
bee-orchis
rejoice in
Genoa cake
reconcile
Sea of Cold
rejoicing
fetoscopy

lemon curd
second man
decoy-duck
second fix
beholding
beyond one
recording
rewording
lemon drop
second row
second-row
✧secondary
recordist
recondite
tenor drum
bed of down
redolence
redolency
aerometer
decoherer
mekometer
oenometer
pedometer
pew-opener
recoveree
recoverer
set on edge
hecogenin
ketonemia
pedogenic
xenomenia
devotedly
reposedly
xeroderma
recoveror
aerometry
behoveful
reposeful
Met Office
web offset
set on foot
recomfort
reconfirm
set on fire
lemonfish
decongest
besom-head
aerophobe
xenophobe
xenophoby
aerophagy
oesophagi
xerophagy
aeroshell
mesophyll
nemophila
oenophile
oenophily
xenophile
xerophile
xerophily
aerophone
Oenothera
telophase
xerochasy
aerophyte
mesophyte
xerophyte
Belonidae
denominal
genocidal

meloxicam
Meropidae
meropidan
serotinal
memoriser
memoriter
memorizer
✧menominee
menomines
pelorised
pelorized
aerolitic
neroli oil
memorials
Peronismo
aerobiont
defoliant
devotions
négociant
negotiant
depositor
repositor
defoliate
negotiate
Peronista
felonious
ferocious
melodious
✧véronique
sex object
reworking
re-collect
recollect
remoulade
rémoulade
mesogloea
sex on legs
xenon lamp
aeroplane
mesoblast
decollate
décolleté
reformade
reformado
recommend
reformism
reformist
Aerosmith
deformity
recountal
reconnect
denouncer
refounder
rejoinder
renouncer
recoinage
bemoaning
besognios
recognise
recognize
oecologic
serologic
serotonin
aeromotor
melocoton
mesomorph
xeromorph
meno mosso
merozoite
Herodotus
melon-pear

aerospace
recompact
decomplex
lemon peel
decoupage
découpage
aerospike
devonport
decompose
recompose
reconquer
✧democracy
menorrhea
resources
xenograft
be your age!
aerotrain
bezoardic
aerobrake
aerodrome
melodrama
melodrame
velodrome
devouring
aerograph
cerograph
memoirism
memoirist
xenocryst
democraty
Zenocrate
A E Housman
heronshaw
bemonster
meroistic
perovskia
lemon sole
debossing
rehousing
detorsion
retorsion
repossess
lemon tree
refortify
reportage
xerostoma
befortune
besotting
detox tank
remontant
reporting
repotting
revolting
veloutine
decoction
decontrol
detortion
reboation
retortion
decocture
lemon tart
Mecoptera
decoctive
retortive
ketonuria
re-soluble
resoluble
désoeuvré
reconvene
resolvent
revolving

reconvert
lemon-weed
lemonwood
genotypic
metonymic
serotypic
zelotypia
keep watch
net-player
reapparel
neoplasia
temptable
keep faith
red-plague
henpecked
respecter
bespeckle
hen-paddle
Temple Bar
telpheric
hey presto
peep of day
tempt fate
Perpignan
serpigoes
despoiler
keep sight
peep sight
delphinia
geophilic
Memphitic
neophilia
deep field
hen-paidle
Delphinus
pemphigus
leg-puller
red-polled
neopilina
serpulite
Melpomene
Zeppo Marx
despumate
geoponics
keep an act
keep under
responder
responser
terpenoid
bespangle
weepingly
responsor
terpineol
serpentry
weaponise
weepiness
responsum
weaponize
deep-toned
geophones
neophobia
neophobic
merpeople
keep count
reappoint
keep house
Deep South
deep space
red pepper
Hesperian
keep track

desperado
jeoparder
peppering
pepperoni
tempering
pepper box
pepper pot
sea parrot
temporary
temporise
temptress
desperate
temperate
deiparous
leaperous
leaporous
deep-drawn
temporize
Vespasian
Herpestes
pen-pusher
heapstead
keep at bay
perpetual
bespatter
bespotted
herpetoid
keep a term
cespitose
despotism
despotate
sea potato
keep quiet
keepy-uppy
Deepavali
geophytic
neophytic
becquerel
terra alba
recreance
recreancy
retreaded
rearrange
heartache
Wehrmacht
gear ratio
learnable
✧lehrjahre
✧béarnaise
ferry-boat
heartbeat
reprobacy
sea robber
Rex rabbit
heart-bond
red riband
red ribbon
heartburn
reprobate
retribute
Kerry blue
metrician
retrocede
refracted
retracted
sea rocket
neurochip
Petruchio
febricula
febricule
terricole

ferrocene
terracing
detractor
metric ton
refractor
retractor
negro-corn
serricorn
metricise
metricist
reprocess
verrucose
deprecate
febricity
metricate
verrucous
metricize
heart-dear
Hebridean
Hebridian
perradial
reproduce
bedridden
betrodden
retrodden
degrading
✧petri dish
depredate
tetradite
perradius
degree day
reprieval
retrieval
deer fence
gear-lever
hearkener
pearl-eyed
retriever
pearl-edge
beer belly
learnedly
decreeing
George Fox
bearberry
deerberry
georgette
Henrietta
heart-free
metrifier
petrified
retroflex
terrified
terrifier
febrifuge
heartfelt
serrefile
bear's-foot
Henry Ford
terraform
deprogram
neurogram
pearl-gray
petrogram
reprogram
✧tetragram
defragger
pearl-grey
neuroglia
bedraggle
segregate
hearth-tax
negrohead
Beersheba
gearwheel
tearsheet
gearshift
tear shell
bear a hand
deprehend
reprehend
searching
near-white
hearth rug
search out
Hebraical
negroidal
recruital
debruised
Hebraiser
Hebraizer
pearlised
pearlized
recruiter
pearlings
rear light
heartikin
pearlitic
Georgiana
retroject
neural net
petrolled
metrology
necrology
neurology
petrolage
petrology
tetralogy
neuralgia
neuralgic
heartland
heartling
tear gland
Negrillos
beardless
heartless
weariless
febrility
neurility
serrulate
petroleum
pétroleur
cetrimide
merry-make
tear smoke
decrement
detriment
herriment
herryment
merriment
recrement
reprimand
year's mind
Henry More
terramara
terramare
neuromata
derring do
derring-do
derringer
herringer
L'Étranger
reprinter
sea ranger
serranoid
jeeringly
leeringly
terrenely
veeringly
wearingly
metronome
beeriness
merriness
Petrinism
weariness
weirdness
Terranova
dear knows
near touch
beer money
deerhound
near point
year-round
beer house
deer mouse
rear-dorse
rearhorse
rearmouse
tetrapody
bedropped
metroplex
necrophil
negrophil
tear apart
neuropath
détraquée
Jerry Rice
tetrarchy
bear fruit
gear train
deergrass
terrorise
terrorism
terrorist
peer group
terrarium
terrorful
terrorize
pearl-spar
redressal
heartsick
Beardsley
defroster
depressed
heartseed
medresseh
redresser
refreshen
refresher
repressed
represser
pearl-sago
heuristic
peirastic
bearishly
heartsome
wearisome
heartsink
re-present
represent
depressor
detrusion
jerry-shop
repressor
heart-sore
leprosery
leprosity
betrothal
heir-at-law
Nemrut Dag
gear-stick
negritude
betrothed
regretted
rewritten
secretage
tear strip
✧decretals
red rattle
necrotomy
neurotomy
ferreting
regrating
detrition
neuration
secretion
serration
ferrotype
decretory
secretary
secretory
serrature
✧territory
decretist
necrotise
Henry Tate
regretful
decretive
secretive
necrotize
rearousal
defrauder
fearfully
tearfully
rearguard
retroussé
Henry VIII
Henry Vane
reproving
sea-roving
retrovert
depravity
Henry Wilt
heartwood
Henry Wood
zebrawood
pearlwort
Hebrewess
Hebrewism
tetroxide
nearly man
defraying
terrazzos
newspaper
persuader
reistafel
sea slater
Teeswater
geostatic
✧messianic
sensually
feiseanna
Welsh aunt
sea shanty
news-value
leaseback
lease-band
Jesse Boot
mess about
fen-sucked
Persicise
persecute
Persicize
sense data
set speech
gens de peu
Deusdedit
Menshevik
persienne
gens de loi
penstemon
✧messieurs
neesberry
sea sleeve
densifier
versified
versifier
ceasefire
versiform
messaging
newsagent
news-sheet
leasehold
beasthood
Welsh hook
geosphere
Jews' thorn
Welsh harp
deistical
seismical
hemstitch
Jew's-pitch
red spider
sea spider
beastings
beestings
vers libre
measliest
ressaldar
tehsildar
tessellae
tessellar
weasel cat
teaselled
teaseller
weaseller
beastlike
yeastlike
lease-lend
Messalina
perseline
teaseling
red salmon
sea salmon
ceaseless
menseless
newsflash
senseless
tenseless
pensility
tensility
per saltum
sensillum
weasel out
pease-meal
Welsummer
fee simple
gelsemine
gessamine
jessamine
persimmon
sex symbol
pessimism
pessimist
gelsemium
yersiniae
yersinias
messenger
personnel
personify
personage
personals
teasingly
lessoning
reasoning
seasoning
peasantry
denseness
messiness
newsiness
personise
tenseness
terseness
Welshness
hessonite
pepsinate
personate
bel sangue
personize
newswoman
sessional
tensional
versional
pensioner
versioner
newshound
bedspread
censorial
censorian
jet stream
jetstream
menstrual
redstreak
sensorial
tensorial
tesseract
newstrade
berserker
yes sirree
keystroke
berserkly
leisurely
sensorily
✧jew's-trump
✧jews'-trump
cee-spring
gee-string
jesserant
measuring
newsprint
sea strand
feast-rite
geyserite
measure up
menstruum
newsgroup
sensorium
persist in
pease-soup
celsitude
bed-settee
bedsitter
jet-setter
pet-sitter
red setter
versatile
Jew's-stone
news-stand
cessation
sensation
sea satyre
tessitura
sensitise
sensitive
sensitize
pea-souper
reassurer
sea squill
sea squirt
set square
tee-square
pensively
persevere
peaseweep
fesse-wise
leastwise
leastways
bestead by
test match
Bert Hardy
leftwards
westwards
besteaded
meat-eater
melt-water
tentmaker
test paper
c'est la vie
centrally
dextrally
neutrally
textually
ventrally
restraint
meat wagon
West Saxon
meat paste
seat earth
vertebrae
vertebral
death-bell
heath bell
vestibule
depth bomb
deathblow
Celtiberi
heathbird
Betty Blue
westabout
petticoat
heathcock
menticide
pesticide
Celtic Sea
tentacled
geotactic
death cell
rectocele

Words marked ✧ can also be spelled with one or more capital letters

shrewmice
shrew mole
threonine
✧sheerness
threeness
phaenogam
threnodic
chaetodon
chaetopod
The Egoist
threepeat
three-pair
three-pile
three-part
wheel race
shoe brush
sheep scab
three-star
wheelsman
chiefship
sheepskin
wheel spin
threesome
Thyestean
Thyestian
phrentick
sheep tick
chieftain
threatful
sheepwalk
wheelwork
sheep-wash
shiftable
theftboot
theft-bote
shift down
chafferer
chaffinch
Sheffield
The Friend
the fallen
shuffling
whiffling
whifflery
shaftless
shiftless
the Furies
the Fishes
The Father
theftuous
the five Ks
shift work
shag-eared
the Graces
the grades
thigh bone
thigh boot
phagocyte
phagedena
chagrined
the gimmes
The Gambia
shogunate
The Grocer
thegither
the gutter
Shug Avery
shaggy cap
Shah Jahan
chihuahua
The Hobbit
Shih Ching
phthalein
phthalate
chthonian
shahtoosh
The Herald
shlimazel
ohmically
chain bolt
à huis clos
chain down
chairdays
shriveled
choiceful
chain-gear
chain gang
choirgirl
sheikhdom
cheilitis
shrinkage
shrieking
shrinking
shriek-owl
chairlift
choir loft
shrilling
thrillant
thrilling
chainless
chain mail
chain pier
shrimp net
chain pump
shrimping
chain rule
chainshot
Christian
Christmas
thriftier
thriftily
Christina
Christine
chainwork
the jet set
shake a leg
shakeable
choke back
chokebore
chokecoil
chokedamp
choke down
shake down
shakedown
choke-full
The Knight
Chaka Khan
choke line
shakiness
choke-pear
Shakerism
Chekovian
Chaldaean
shillalah
while away
chiliarch
phillabeg
shillaber
chiliagon
Chaldaism
chalybean
shell bean
whaleboat
shellback
whaleback
whalebone
shellbark
chalybite
tholobate
whale calf
thylacine
chelicera
child care
cholecyst
the Lyceum
shelduck
shellduck
sheltered
shelterer
challenge
cholaemia
cholaemic
chalkface
shelf-fuls
whale food
wholefood
cheliform
shellfire
shellfish
khalifate
shell game
philogyny
phylogeny
shell heap
whale-head
shell-hole
childhood
cheloidal
phillibeg
chilli dog
child lock
shelf life
philology
chilblain
chalklike
childlike
shelflike
shell-like
shell lime
whale line
childless
shell-less
cholelith
chalumeau
wholemeal
Philomela
whole milk
Philomene
shale mine
thelement
shelf mark
shell-marl
philomath
Thelemite
chelonian
phalangal
phalanger
phalanges
phalanxes
✧philander
phalangid
phelonion
childness
chillness
wholeness
whole note
chalcogen
phellogen
shallowly
phyllopod
philhorse
✧philippic
Chile pine
philopena
shell pink
shell-pink
phylarchy
choleraic
sheldrake
shelfroom
phalarope
shell star
Philister
whole step
chelaship
shell suit
thalassic
wholistic
wholesale
wholesome
shell-sand
thelytoky
chalk talk
philately
whole tone
chelation
the latest
phalluses
thalluses
the living
child-wife
shellwork
Phillyrea
whillywha
chilly bin
chalazion
shamianah
champaign
shameable
champagne
chime bars
chemicked
thymocyte
thymidine
chambered
chamberer
chamfered
whimperer
whimberry
champerty
shamefast
rhamphoid
thumb hole
whimsical
shame into
Chomskian
Chomskyan
The Mikado
thumbkins
thumb knot
The Miller
thumblike
rhumb line
shambling
thumbling
✧chameleon
rhymeless
shameless
themeless
thumbless
champlevé
chamomile
thumb mark
thumbnail
✧shamanism
shamanist
them and us
shampooed
shampooer
shambolic
shammosim
theme park
chamfrain
chemurgic
thumb ring
The Mirror
chimerism
chemostat
rhymester
the masses
Thomas Tew
Thomistic
theme song
Thomasina
chemistry
chymistry
Thomas Kyd
thumbtack
the matter
theme tune
the method
chemitype
chemitypy
shamateur
rhombuses
the movies
rhyme word
shemozzle
shimozzle
khansamah
thin-faced
chincapin
chinkapin
phantasim
shunnable
thinkable
phantasma
shankbone
china bark
rhino bars
thenabout
china clay
Phenician
Phonic Ear®
shanachie
phone call
phenocopy
phonecard
phenacite
Changchun
ahungered
channeler
phonmeter
thunderer
whencever
thunder it
chandelle
thin-belly
whingeing
chunder on
chunner on
chunter on
whinberry
chanteuse
chanceful
changeful
phonogram
think good
rhonchial
shanghai'd
thanehood
thinghood
Rhynchota
chinch bug
phansigar
phengites
thankings
thinnings
Chantilly
Zhenjiang
Thin Lizzy
China jute
Chanukkah
Chungking
phenakism
phenakite
phenol red
phenology
phonology
rhinology
shingling
think long
chandlery
shineless
thankless
phenolate
phonolite
rhinolith
phonemics
phenomena
shiningly
whiningly
thin on top
phoniness
shininess
thingness
whininess
think over
whensoe'er
chincough
phantosme
Rhineodon
Shintoism
Shintoist
phonopore
Chongqing
chondrify
chancroid
chondroid
chondrule
Shangri-la
chinaroot
Phanariot
chantress
China rose
chondrite
chancrous
thundrous
thaneship
chinstrap
phenetics
phonetics
china tree
thanatoid
think tank
whinstone
whunstane
phonation
phenotype
phonotype
phonotypy
phonatory
phonetise
phonetism
phonetist
thanatism
thanatist
Chinatown
phonetize
thingummy
think upon
shin guard
chinovnik
Rhine wine
chinaware
shantyman
whinnying
Zhengzhou
throw away
throwaway
theomancy
chromakey
theomachy
theopathy
chromatic
chromatid
chromatin
chronaxie
rheotaxis
theomania
throw a fit
shootable
chloracne
throw back
throwback
throbbing
theorbist
thrombose
the occult
chlordane
shrouding
the old sod
throw dirt
shoot down
throw down
throw-down
rheometer
theoretic
chlorella
shoot-'em-up
shroffage
cheongsam
throughly
thronging
throngful
theophagy
shoot home

Theophano
theophany
thiophene
Oh So Sharp
rheochord
chronical
Ohio River
theoriser
theorizer
chloritic
chromidia
rhyolitic
chronicle
theorique
whoop it up
throbless
chromogen
theologer
throw open
throw over
theosophy
chlorosis
chlorotic
rheologic
Theodoric
theogonic
theologic
theotokos
throw onto
theologue
Phnom Penh
theocracy
Theobroma
rheotrope
theocrasy
throwster
thio-ether
throatier
throttler
throatily
ship canal
The Phaedo
chip-based
ship water
shapeable
shippable
chaprassi
chaprassy
chuprassy
chipochia
rhipidion
rhipidate
rhipidium
chapleted
ship fever
whipper-in
The Pogues
shipshape
rhaphides
shop floor
shop-floor
chapeless
rhopalism
shapeless
chipolata
rhapontic
whip snake
whipcordy
ship money
chop logic
choplogic
rhapsodic
chopsocky
The People
shippound
whip-round
chipboard
shipboard
shopboard
chop-house
chophouse
chaparral
shipwreck
whip graft
whip-graft
the purple
chaperone
shopfront
the period
chapstick
chopstick
whipstock
chapaties
whipstaff
chapattis
whipstall
shape tape
the potato
shipowner
chequered
charlatan
thereaway
theriacal
where away?
whirl away
shirralee
Third-Ager
sherwanis
shareable
thermally
Charmaine
shore boat
thornback
Charybdis
the rabble
thornbill
cherubims
char-à-banc
charabanc
share bone
shirtband
whirl bone
shorebird
thornbird
thornbush
Characeae
shore crab
short-coat
character
shortcake
sharecrop
short-cord
churidars
Thursdays
charge-cap
charge-man
chartered
charterer
sharpener
sharp-eyed
shortener
Thargelia
Chernenko
Charleroi
charnecos
charmeuse
chargeful
sherifian
shortfall
short film
therefrom
wherefrom
therefore
wherefore
short fuse
third gear
chiragric
short game
shortgown
churchman
churchway
short-head
church key
cherchef't
church-ale
Churchill
shorthold
churching
shorthand
third-hand
shorthorn
Thora Hird
churchism
Shere Hite
short-haul
Charminar
thermical
there it is
✧thersitic
where it is
whirligig
short iron
✧thermidor
thorniest
thereinto
thirtieth
whereinto
Shere Khan
short leet
short-life
chirology
chorology
therology
Charolais
shoreline
charmless
chartless
choralist
shirtless
shoreless
short list
short-list
thornless
cheralite
chirality
theralite
churnmilk
pheromone
shire-moot
thorn moth
cherimoya
chirimoya
pharyngal
pharynges
pharynxes
chironomy
charangos
chariness
sharpness
shortness
thereness
whereness
charwoman
short odds
chernozem
chorionic
pharaonic
thermotic
chermoula
Cherbourg
✧charlotte
Chernobyl
chiropody
Theropoda
The Ripper
therapsid
whirlpool
therapist
charbroil
third rail
chargrill
chart-room
third-rate
sharesman
shoresman
thirdsman
shoreside
cherished
chorister
whore's egg
pharisaic
sharkskin
short slip
dharmsala
short sale
whorishly
chorusing
share shop
sharp-shod
shortstop
thyristor
charoseth
shirt stud
charities
the rather
thirstier
thorntree
shirt tail
thirstily
short time
short-time
thyratron
short-term
thirstful
thereupon
whereupon
thereunto
whereunto
Theravada
The Rivals
charivari
thorow-wax
shoreweed
whirlwind
churr-worm
shareware
shoreward
therewith
wherewith
short wave
short-wave
third wave
thyroxine
wherryman
cherryade
cherry red
cherry-pie
cherry-pit
✧the royals
cherry-bob
thirtyish
chorizont
the shakes
the States
Ghislaine
Lhasa Apso
physician
the social
physicked
physicals
physicism
physicist
physic nut
Chasidism
chastened
chastener
whiskered
whisperer
whosoever
chassepot
ghastfull
phosphide
phosphene
phosphine
phosphate
phosphite
Phasmidae
chastiser
the Shires
Chassidic
the Spirit
the sticks
shashlick
chiselled
chiseller
ghostlike
whistling
phaseless
the Salish
whistle up
ghost moth
Thysanura
ghastness
chest-note
phaseolin
chaseport
The Scream
the Scrubs
the screen
the Shroud
✧the system
these sort
those sort
chest tone
ghost town
The Squire
the squits
thesaurus
ghost word
phossy jaw
whisky mac
Shetlands
Chet Baker
shotmaker
whittawer
whitebeam
white bear
The Tablet
whitebait
white book
whitebass
what about
white coal
whitecoat
photo call
photocell
white cell
photocopy
rhotacise
rhotacism
rhoticity
rhotacize
white damp
chatterer
shattered
shatterer
shuttered
the Twelve
that's flat
white flag
whiteface
white fish
whitefish
photogram
white gold
photogene
photogeny
phytogeny
whitehead
white heat
what cheer?
Whitehall
white hole
thatching
what a hope
white hope
white hass
shotfirer
what gives?
chitlings
The Tailor
white iron
white lead
✧white lady
phytology
châtelain
white lime
white line
whittling
photolyse
shot-blast
whitelist
whet-slate
white meat
rhythmics
what's more
rhythmise
rhythmist
rhythmize
photonics
chitinoid
White Nile
whitening
Bhutanese
whiteness
chitinous
shot tower
whatsoe'er
ghettoise
shot noise
Whitworth
ghettoize
photophil
photopsia
white pine
white port
white race
white rent
shotproof
the Terror
rhetorise
white rose
rhetorize
Photostat®
white seam
white-seam
white sale
white salt
white-shoe
that's that
white teak
phototube
what's to do?
The Tatler
phytotomy
whetstone
phytotron
phototype
phototypy
what's what
whitewall
white wine
whitewing
whitewood
whiteware
white worm
whitewash
chatoyant
thousands
the usages
rheumatic
rheumatiz
thaumatin
shrubbery
Chu'un Ch'iu
the undead
shouldest
shout down
thrum-eyed
chauffeur
shrugging
theurgist
thoughted
thoughten
shrublike
shoutline
shrubless

thrumming
thrusting
thrust hoe
chevrette
shovel hat
chevalier
shovelled
shoveller
chivalric
shaveling
chevelure
shovelful
chavender
Chevrolet®
chevroned
The Vortex
the Virgin
shivering
showmanly
chawbacon
show cause
the wicked
chowkidar
showpiece
show fight
the whilst
showbizzy
showplace
shawlless
The Walrus
chewiness
showiness
show round
show house
show forth
shewbread
showbread
show trial
The Warden
showering
showerful
whey-faced
chrysalid
chrysalis
chrysanth
chiyogami
the yonder
phlyctena
whizz-bang
rhizobium
rhizocarp
rhizocaul
rhizoidal
Rhizopoda
Himalayan
Himalayas
dilatancy
jigamaree
Sir A J Ayer
Eid al-Adha
dilatable
dilatator
Nicaragua
Digambara
financial
financier
disanchor
vitascope
disaccord
cigar case
Ricardian
pin and web
ribaudred
vivandier
girandola
girandole
filanders
hit-and-run
tip-and-run
tie-and-dye
bicameral
bilateral
bivalence
bivalency
divalency
minareted
vis a tergo
mirabelle
Pisanello
silageing
cigarette
gigahertz
vivamente
filaceous
limaceous
micaceous
vinaceous
disaffect
giraffoid
giraffine
tidal flow
disaffirm
Eid al-Fitr
Kisangani
lilangeni
sisal hemp
lie at host
piratical
misavised
vitaliser
vitalizer
mirabilia
✧mirabilis
miracidia
cigarillo
vivariums
bivariant
bilabiate
bivariate
vicariate
visagiste
bibacious
bifarious
dicacious
hilarious
minacious
vicarious
vivacious
hijacking
misallied
misallege
rivalling
rivalless
Vita glass®
mica-slate
piña-cloth
disarming
misaunter
disavowal
simarouba
disavouch
pinafored
disanoint
viragoish
disappear
nikau palm
cisalpine
dika-bread
pita bread
cicatrice
bizarrely
cicatrise
rivalrous
cicatrize
Midas's ear
misassign
rivalship
Sivaistic
sizarship
vicarship
Dinantian
gigantean
didactics
cigar tree
digastric
disattune
dicastery
disattire
gigantism
bipartite
ribattuta
ailanthus
sitatunga
hibakusha
misadvise
tidal wave
disbranch
air-bubble
misbecome
Timbuctoo
disbodied
sit bodkin
diablerie
oil beetle
Wimbledon
nimblesse
Kirbigrip®
kirbigrip
kirby grip
misbehave
air-bridge
fimbriate
Hizbollah
Hizbullah
disbelief
misbelief
diabology
diabolise
diabolism
diabolist
liability
viability
diabolize
Gibbonian
Ribbon-man
Ribbonism
disbursal
timberman
disburden
disburser
Kimberley
Limburger
oil-burner
Big Bertha
timbering
Tim Burton
gibberish
misbeseem
misbestow
gibbosity
ciabattas
kibbutzim
hit bottom
Die Brücke
gibbously
Jim Baxter
mischance
mischancy
discharge
mischarge
pinchbeck
aitchbone
pitch bend
birchbark
Hitchcock
pinchcock
pitch camp
circadian
piccadell
piccadill
diacodion
pitch-dark
viscidity
diacodium
kitchener
discredit
miscredit
miscreant
big cheese
nipcheese
tip-cheese
fiochetti
miscreate
witchetty
pisciform
pitchfork
pinchfist
miscegene
miscegine
disc wheel
hitch-hike
witch hunt
zinc white
diactinal
discoidal
diacritic
diactinic
circuitry
pitch into
hitch kick
witchknot
discalced
witchlike
zinc-bloom
pieceless
circulate
niccolite
discolour
miscolour
oil colour
mincemeat
piecemeal
witchmeal
vis comica
discumber
discomfit
discommon
discandie
Wisconsin
mincingly
wincingly
circinate
diaconate
cincinnus
zirconium
air-cooled
cinchonic
zinc colic
Discworld
pitch-pole
pitch-poll
hiccuping
pitchpine
pitchpipe
wincopipe
sincipita
sinciputs
discerner
Jim Carrey
disc brake
dip-circle
sincerely
diachrony
Kit Carson
piece rate
sincerity
viscerate
discursus
witch's hat
discusser
hircosity
viscosity
birch tree
pitch-tree
piscatrix
piscatory
siccative
dischurch
cinctured
linctuses
via crucis
pitch upon
discourse
lincrusta
viscounty
piacevole
discovert
✧discovery
air-cavity
witch-wife
piecework
zinc oxide
diachylon
diachylum
hindrance
windwards
wild water
wild mango
wind gauge
bird table
find fault
find-fault
wild pansy
wild about
vindicate
Windy City
middle ear
middleman
biodiesel
misdeemed
Lindbergh
middle-age
tie-dyeing
fiddle-bow
Middleton
hindberry
Wild Geese
birdsfoot
wind shear
hind-wheel
wind-shak'd
windshake
wild child
wind chill
wild thyme
windthrow
wind chart
wind chest
wild birds
disdained
pied piper
middlings
riddlings
hindsight
windtight
tiddliest
Hindu Kush
Mindelian
rix-dollar
bird-alane
bird-alone
wild olive
windblown
misdemean
vindemial
kiddingly
windingly
bird's-nest
giddiness
windiness
hiddenite
bird-lover
Eindhoven
wild honey
windhover
wind power
windborne
windbound
wind round
bird-house
bird-louse
wild goose
yird-house
✧big dipper
vin de pays
vin du pays
windbreak
misdirect
wild track
birdbrain
hindbrain
kilderkin
hinder-end
niddering
wildering
tinderbox
windproof
wild grape
Pindarise
Pindarism
Pindarist
wildgrave
Pindarize
Yiddisher
misdesert
mild steel
windstorm
mind-curer
mindfully
windburnt
window bar
window tax
wind-swift
kiddywink
windowing
window box
windswept
Six-Day War
line dance
hivewards
sidewards
di penates
fire-eater
firewater
life-saver
like water
limewater
minelayer
pipe-layer
rice paper
rice water
tidewater
tide gauge
wire gauge
cinematic
cineramic
cineraria
kinematic
literatim
disenable
liberally
life table
literally
live tally
miserable
miserably
side table
tide table
timetable
wine vault
cinerator
fife-major
liberator
literator
pipe major
River Avon
River Alph
River Aare
give pause
time-lapse
wine party
literatus
River Amur
side valve
wire gauze
riverboat
give a back

disembody
Tiger balm®
Nigel Benn
riverbank
River Bann
disembark
like a bird
time about
rise above
libecchio
timescale
virescent
libeccios
kinescope
ninescore
ricercare
video card
ricercata
Big-endian
eider duck
Rivendell
videodisc
eiderdown
fine metal
vice-regal
River Elbe
fivepence
line-fence
ninepence
pike-perch
diaereses
River Eden
Mike Leigh
bigeneric
diaeresis
fivepenny
ninepenny
vicereine
life-weary
nine-metre
River Ebro
wineberry
vice versa
cinereous
river flat
time of day
linen-fold
tiger fish
videogram
disengage
video game
air-engine
divergent
diverging
oil engine
line ahead
river head
rivet head
bioethics
side-wheel
time sheet
wire wheel
side chain
vice-chair
cinephile
hidey-hole
live shell
rivet hole
sideshoot
firethorn
timeshare

give chase
wirephoto
kinetical
mimetical
vicesimal
vigesimal
Viperidae
pine-finch
timepiece
fixed idea
life-sized
sidelined
sidelines
videlicet
firefight
firelight
limelight
pipe-light
rime riche
sidelight
sideritic
time limit
minefield
rice field
eirenicon
timeliest
give birth
live birth
ninetieth
dioecious
river-jack
give a knee
River Kemi
firefloat
wipe-clean
fireplace
give place
line block
time clock
time slice
kite-flyer
like flies
riverlike
✧tiger lily
divellent
libellant
libelling
niderling
River Lena
vitelline
zibelline
lifeblood
fire alarm
vitellary
fiberless
fire-blast
life class
riderless
riverless
sinewless
wineglass
wire glass
lineality
lineolate
side plate
wire cloth
libellous
rice flour
Vitellius
pineal eye
like smoke

lineament
give a miss
tiger moth
Hibernian
vicennial
live under
pigeon pea
live in sin
live on air
pipe snake
River Nile
wide-angle
given name
mire-snipe
vide infra
fixedness
givenness
hibernise
mixedness
tiredness
Gibeonite
hibernate
Simeonite
hibernize
firewoman
piperonal
tire-woman
wise woman
give voice
life-force
fixed odds
cicerones
dime novel
firepower
fire-robed
hive-honey
nineholes
River Oder
sidebones
Ciceronic
siderosis
fireworks
fixed oils
hidebound
lime-hound
sideboard
firehouse
pine-house
River Ouse
give forth
River Oxus
timenoguy
Didelphia
didelphic
didelphid
Didelphis
pineapple
disemploy
Liverpool
misemploy
Didelphys
vice squad
firebreak
pipe dream
pipe organ
time trial
firebrick
fire truck
pipe-track
sidetrack
wisecrack

lime green
lime-green
Nile green
River Ruhr
fire trail
rice grain
vine fruit
firedrake
fire drill
sine prole
timeframe
fine print
firebrand
fire irons
viverrine
fire-arrow
fireproof
bide tryst
firecrest
linearise
rice grass
side-dress
winepress
wire brush
wire grass
biserrate
fire-grate
fixed-rate
linearity
bite or sup
line-grove
River Ravi
fine-drawn
wiredrawn
like crazy
linearize
River Saar
five-a-side
✧riverside
River Spey
diversify
fideistic
siren suit
diversely
finessing
river sand
dimension
diversion
like a shot
liver spot
licensure
diversity
hideosity
side issue
River Styx
tiger's eye
direct tax
live steam
tiger team
video tube
fire-stick
livestock
vine-stock
dipeptide
river-tide
disesteem
liberties
misesteem
River Tees
pikestaff
give it a go

directrix
disentail
tiger tail
lifestyle
disentomb
lipectomy
diverting
eigentone
firestone
libertine
like stink
limestone
milestone
minestone
pipestone
River Tyne
rivetting
sin-eating
tile stone
wine-stone
bijection
bisection
digestion
direction
lineation
videotape
dime store
✧directory
divesture
fire-storm
life story
line-storm
bidentate
dioestrus
bijective
digestive
directive
divertive
River Towy
videotext
lime juice
vice-queen
line judge
mixed up in
sine dubio
direfully
hideously
piteously
timeously
sideburns
dine out on
ritenutos
fireguard
lifeguard
vide supra
wire guard
bile ducts
sine curve
Minervois
binervate
mine owner
riverweed
wide awake
wideawake
river wall
tiger wolf
video wall
liverwing
tigerwood
sideswipe
liverwort

tiger worm
liveryman
life cycle
River Yalu
livery pot
Mike Tyson
niff-naffy
misfeasor
difficile
difficult
diffident
siffleuse
disfigure
air filter
misfallen
oil filter
pie funnel
✧zinfandel
miffiness
fin-footed
six-footer
tit for tat
tit-for-tat
pilferage
hit for six
different
misfaring
pilfering
Mia Farrow
pifferari
pifferaro
disforest
diffusely
diffusion
diffusive
diffluent
disfluent
disfavour
ring-canal
ring dance
Rio Grande
disgracer
kingmaker
ring gauge
biography
lingually
qinghaosu
tinguaite
piggyback
ridgeback
ring a bell
piggy bank
ridge bone
singed cat
disgodded
winged elm
Dingle Bay
single tax
ring-fence
ringleted
single-sex
single ten
king's evil
single-end
single-log
singleton
single-cut
vingt-et-un
misguggle
wing chair
ring-shake

bingo hall
wing shell
king's-hood
air guitar
Diaghilev
disguised
disguiser
king-sized
misguided
misguider
pilgrimer
ringsider
tingliest
bilge keel
Virgilian
ding-a-ling
King's Lynn
sing along
singalong
ting-a-ling
liege-lord
Cingalese
liegeless
ring flash
cingulate
lingulate
virgulate
singultus
ring-small
sing small
jiggumbob
Virginian
wing snail
king snake
ring snake
ringingly
singingly
virginals
dinginess
minginess
virginity
biogenous
virginium
diagnoses
kingdomed
ring money
diagnosis
Ringworld
king cobra
misgrowth
singspiel
king-apple
ridgepole
bilge-pump
Singapore
King Priam
gingerade
Siegfried
kingcraft
fingertip
ginger ale
hip-girdle
niggardly
finger-end
fingering
jingo-ring
lingering
ginger pop
ridge rope
finger-dry
ring-cross

ginger nut
gingerous
king prawn
disgusted
piggishly
misgotten
ridge tile
fidgeting
ringstand
King Stork
Kingstown
ring ousel
ring ouzel
misgiving
misgovern
ginglymus
right away
Highlands
bigheaded
dish-faced
dishwater
high-taper
high water
mid-heaven
pigheaded
lithiasis
Lithuania
fightable
fish eagle
high table
rightable
sightable
withhault
Mithraism
Mithraist
fish-garth
Mithraeum
Tisha Baav
Tisha be'Ab
Tisha Be'Av
fight back
fightback
fishyback
light-ball
light bulb
night-bell
with a bump
right-bank
nightbird
tithe barn
fish-scrap
Night Café
pithecoid
night-crow
night-cart
lithocyst
dithecous
nightclub
light-dues
Nithsdale
night duty
right down
right-down
high-level
tightener
lighten up
righteous
tighten up
right face!
lithified
tithe-free
eightfoil
eightfold
nightfall
eight-foot
light-foot
nightfire
light-fast
night-fowl
mishegaas
nightgear
dichogamy
nightgown
Tishah b'Ab
Tishah B'Av
highchair
sight-hole
with child
rich rhyme
diphthong
right-hand
eight-hour
nighthawk
Cichlidae
lithoidal
Xiphiidae
xiphoidal
Ziphiidae
high-viced
highlight
high jinks
Lichfield
eightieth
light into
tight-knit
high altar
fish slice
high-place
tight-lace
✧high-flier
✧high-flyer
Michel Ney
Richelieu
nightlife
lithology
night-line
nightlong
sightline
dishallow
✧dithelism
high-blest
high-class
lightless
nightless
rightless
sightless
Sinhalese
dishcloth
✧dithelete
fishplate
dish-clout
high-blown
high-flown
light-mill
nightmare
nightmary
dishumour
Tim Henman
mishanter
fish knife
siphon off
siphonage
Pichincha
lichenoid
mishandle
sighingly
siphuncle
lightning
dishonest
fishiness
lichenism
lichenist
lichenose
lightness
litheness
pithiness
rightness
tightness
siphonate
dishonour
lichenous
dichromat
fish-woman
high words
dish-cover
dishtowel
high-toned
pinhooker
dichromic
fish-joint
high point
with young
wish to God
high court
dichroism
fish louse
high horse
dichroite
fish-spear
high-speed
mishappen
bishopric
lithopone
bishopdom
bishopess
either way
fisherman
sight-read
night-robe
high-grade
cipher key
fish-creel
high-dried
✧bilharzia
night-rail
Richardia
Richard II
night-rule
dithyramb
ciphering
withering
high-proof
tightrope
citharist
high cross
night-rest
zitherist
witherite
high-grown
withdrawn
dichasial
eightsman
sightsman
nightside
right side
tight side
sightseer
night safe
lightship
lithistid
night-soil
eightsome
lightsome
lithesome
sight-sing
light show
nightspot
tight spot
Xiphosura
✧diphysite
dichasium
lights out
rightsize
light trap
fish stick
night-tide
big hitter
dichotomy
light time
lithotome
lithotomy
night-time
withstand
withstood
dish it out
High Dutch
withouten
wishfully
fish-guano
light upon
Fishguard
Vishnuism
Vishnuite
nightwear
night-walk
with a will
right wing
right-wing
withywind
nightward
night-work
rightward
light-year
biohazard
militancy
sibilance
sibilancy
vigilance
Niki Lauda
digitated
Filicales
pixilated
silica gel
digitalin
digitalis
militaria
civically
dividable
finically
limitable
litigable
minimally
mitigable
similarly
visitable
divinator
litigator
mitigator
sibilator
visitator
vigilante
Minié ball
bilimbing
Liliaceae
Tiliaceae
viliacoes
miniscule
Dixie Dean
tip it down
biliteral
diligence
niaiserie
dividedly
limitedly
citizenry
midinette
siliceous
vimineous
viticetum
disinfect
misinform
disinfest
bilingual
dining-car
mining bee
firing pin
fining-pot
piping hot
riding rod
vikingism
Rising Sun
finish off
disinhume
finishing
linishing
Tisiphone
pixie hood
bicipital
Cimicidae
Filipinas
libidinal
mirifical
miticidal
viricidal
civilised
civiliser
civilized
civilizer
digitiser
digitizer
minimiser
minimizer
virilised
virilized
dirigible
divisible
divisibly
dirigisme
Miliciens
siciliana
siciliane
siciliano
Filipinos
dimidiate
dirigiste
lixiviate
cilicious
litigious
lixivious
silicious
finicking
mimicking
midi-skirt
miniskirt
finickety
disillude
sitiology
Dixieland
sigillary
civil list
limitless
ciliolate
sigillate
titillate
Sigismund
disimmure
Titian red
vision mix
visioning
pimientos
visionary
lividness
rigidness
ripienist
timidness
visionist
vividness
bipinnate
vivianite
Sisinnius
silicosis
silicotic
Timisoara
pin it onto
minibreak
vizierial
Minitrack®
citigrade
filigreed
filigrain
kiwi fruit
filigrane
minidress
minim rest
visitress
vizierate
nisi prius
vizirship
Kim Il-sung
dimissory
viciosity
vitiosity
sinistral
air-intake
civil time
misintend
filiation
miniation
vitiation
miniature
minirugby
Ricinulei
ridiculer
bilirubin
biliously
pitifully
viciously
siliquose
dividuous
disinvent
disinvest
disinvite
lie in wait
civil year
vilifying
vivifying
air-jacket
Kim Jong Il
disjaskit
Kirkcaldy
Nick Faldo
kirkyaird
pick oakum
pickaback
Dicky Bird
dicky-bird
Vicksburg
kick about
ticked off
pickadell
pickadill
rinky-dink
sickleman
milk vetch
milk fever
Nickie-ben
pickeerer
tick fever
sicklemia
lickpenny
sick berth
winkle out
sick leave
milk shake
pick-thank
milk-white
kickshaws
sick-tired
Kinkakuji
kick pleat
milk float
nickelled
milk-gland
nickeline
nickeling
silk gland
milk glass
nickelise
nickelous
Pink Floyd
nickelize
Dick Emery
milken-way
milk snake
winkingly
sickening
kinkiness
milkiness
pinkiness
riskiness
silkiness
zinkenite
milk-molar
kick boxer
risk money
kink-cough
Dicksonia

milk round
nickpoint
pink pound
milk-house
pink noise
milk tooth
pick-tooth
pickapack
sink-a-pace
wink-a-peep
milk train
tinkering
✧pinkerton
lickerish
silk-grass
disk drive
milk gravy
sickishly
ticket day
nickstick
rickstick
Rick Stein
ricketily
kickstand
Minkstone
picketing
rickstand
disk store
kick-start
milk stout
picket out
milk sugar
milk punch
pick-purse
sicknurse
dickey bow
billiards
Bill Gates
Bill Haley
dill-water
misleader
misleared
niellated
diallagic
wieldable
yieldable
Will Parry
Billy Budd
Niels Bohr
Bible belt
Mills bomb
billabong
field book
rifle bird
mill about
dialectal
millocrat
Violaceae
billycock
pillicock
Via Lactea
dialectic
millscale
Millicent
biblicism
biblicist
dislocate
field club
Girl Scout
title deed
Bill Oddie
Will Adams
birlieman
Will Kempe
killdeers
fieldfare
villiform
killifish
billy goat
field goal
field gray
milligram
sialogram
field grey
mirligoes
villagree
dialog box
villagery
biologist
dialogise
dialogist
dialogite
dialogize
millwheel
villa home
field hand
Bill Sikes
fill light
hillbilly
Billy Joel
misliking
Billy Liar
title leaf
field lark
gillflirt
jillflirt
titleless
wieldless
dial-plate
gill slits
sialolith
diplomacy
millimole
field mark
diplomate
willemite
Will Smith
Finlander
midlander
uitlander
villanage
villenage
diplontic
Finlandia
millennia
killingly
violently
willingly
millenary
millinery
diclinism
hilliness
silliness
violinist
oil length
diclinous
villanous
Bill Cosby
gill pouch
gill cover
girl power
willpower
nielloing
billboard
millboard
fill-horse
gill-house
mill-horse
billionth
millionth
mill-tooth
zillionth
Diplopoda
millepede
millipede
fillipeen
mislippen
title poem
title page
filliping
millepore
Villa Park
filler cap
Millerian
Killarney
pilloried
title role
filler rod
pillar box
Hitlerism
Hitlerist
pillarist
pillorise
Hitlerite
millerite
Girl Crazy
pillorize
fieldsman
fillister
diglossia
aimlessly
girlishly
sinlessly
witlessly
rifle shot
dislustre
villosity
air letter
rillettes
field trip
billeting
diplotene
filleting
millstone
violation
field test
field-test
ciclatoun
violative
Girl Guide
villa unit
fieldvole
Jim Lovell
mill owner
willow tit
billowing
fieldward
fieldwork
willowish
pillow-cup
tin lizzie
diplozoon
film-maker
film badge
gimmickry
diamagnet
sigmoidal
pin-making
bismillah
dismal day
gimmalled
gismology
gizmology
dismality
dismember
firmament
pigmental
Simmental
air-minded
diamonded
pigmented
wit-monger
mismanage
dismantle
biomining
filminess
gigmanity
bit-mapped
Cimmerian
biomarker
rigmarole
vis mortua
dismissal
midmashie
diametral
biometric
diametric
filmstrip
sigmation
sigmatron
sigmatism
migmatite
Rik Mayall
dismaying
dismayful
lion-tamer
picnicked
picnicker
pinnacled
finnochio
Diana Dors
dianoetic
lienteric
lioncelle
lion-heart
significs
dignified
lignified
signified
signifier
ligniform
Minnehaha
gianthood
Vientiane
signalman
lign-aloes
lignaloes
signalled
signaller
limnology
fiendlike
signaling
signal box
pianolist
signalise
pinnulate
bien élevé
signalize
bionomics
sinningia
winningly
tinniness
signboard
pinnipede
✧kidnapped
kidnapper
Giant Pope
Kilner jar®
signorial
giant rude
dinner set
kiln-dried
Diana Rigg
piano roll
✧signorina
signorine
signorini
✧signorino
Diana Ross
pignerate
pignorate
diandrous
Dionysiac
Dionysian
giant star
witnesser
giantship
pianistic
Minnesang
Minnesota
Dionysius
Dianetics®
vignetter
pinnately
dignitary
signatory
signature
signeurie
winnowing
piano wire
kidney ore
Fibonacci
dinomania
minor axis
ritonavir
pivotally
lidocaine
Tirol Alps
milo maize
pilot-boat
widow bird
Aizoaceae
oil of cade
finocchio
Pinocchio
biconcave
divorcive
Girondism
Girondist
Dinoceras
milometer
Nilometer
tin-opener
Milosevic
mitogenic
filoselle
kilometre
misoneism
misoneist
kilohertz
linoleate
Nicolette
pirouette
Rigoletto
Nicodemus
pilot flag
pilot fish
Sinophile
Sinophily
Hiroshima
widowhood
dinothere
binominal
Dipodidae
Minorites
nicotined
pisoliths
limonitic
minoxidil
nicotinic
pisolitic
disorient
nicotiana
kilolitre
bifoliate
filovirus
simonious
pilot jack
disoblige
filoplume
pilot lamp
cipollino
misoclere
pilotless
minor mode
hit-or-miss
visor-mask
ginormous
Pinot Noir
ritornell
liposomal
ribosomal
bicolored
filopodia
kilojoule
kilotonne
Sinologue
minor poet
dimorphic
nicompoop
Simon Pure
simon-pure
timocracy
giro order
Sigourney
eidograph
bicoastal
widow's man
minorship
minor suit
timorsome
limousine
Simon says
Pitot tube
bimonthly
minor tone
minor term
bilobular
bilocular
binocular
widow wail
Dicotylae
lipolysis
kilocycle
bit player
displayed
displayer
cisplatin
hippiatry
dispraise
mispraise
hippocras
air-pocket
fig-pecker
hip pocket
mispickel
nit-picker
hippodame
cispadane
hispidity
limpidity
diapyesis
diapyetic
bisphenol
hippiedom
simpleton
simple vow
displease
misplease
simplesse
Kim Philby
misprised
simplices
silphiums
disprison
simpliste
gin palace
dispelled
hippology
Hippolyta
dispensed
dispenser
dispondee
limpingly
lispingly
nippingly
rippingly
lippening
Hispanist
nippiness
Nipponese
timpanist
wispiness
disproval
disproved
disproven
rib-plough
disprofit
dispeople
disproove
dispersal
air-piracy
biopiracy
dioptrics
hit parade
disperser
dispurvey

Words marked ✧ can also be spelled with one or more capital letters

Amy Lowell
implexion
Emile Zola
Emin Pasha
amino acid
amendable
emendable
emendator
Amen glass
amendment
eminently
Amenhotep
amenities
emanation
emunction
emanatory
emunctory
emanatist
emanative
amenaunce
ominously
immorally
immovable
immovably
imposable
immolator
emboscata
impotence
impotency
immodesty
smooth dab
smoothing
smoothish
impolitic
emporiums
impounder
E M Forster
embossing
J M Coetzee
✧immortals
impostume
important
importune
imposture
embodying
omophagia
omophagic
âme perdue
smorzando
✧smart alec
✧smart-alec
embreathe
smart bomb
improbity
Americana
Americano
embracing
embraceor
embracery
smart card
imprecise
embrocate
imbricate
imprecate
americium
embracive
imprudent
smart drug
emergence
emergency
smarten up

embroglio
imbroglio
amorphism
amorphous
embroider
amornings
umbrella'd
amaryllid
amaryllis
amoralism
amoralist
amorality
impromptu
amarantin
Amerindic
embrangle
imbrangle
smartness
Amarantus
embryonal
embryo-sac
embryonic
embryotic
ombrophil
ambrosial
✧ambrosian
Amerasian
embrasure
impresari
amorosity
embrittle
umbratile
amarettos
ambrotype
amorously
improving
improvise
smartweed
a merry pin
embrazure
amassable
smasheroo
Smash Hits
amissible
omissible
amassment
amusement
amusingly
impsonite
omittance
Ametabola
smatterer
smothered
smotherer
umpteenth
emptiness
emotional
emptional
amatorial
amatorian
Amsterdam
J M W Turner
Smyth's Sea
imitation
imitative
emotively
emotivism
emotivist
emotivity
ambulance
immutable

immutably
imputable
imputably
ambulator
amputator
ambulacra
ambuscade
ambuscado
impundulu
impudence
amourette
ambush bug
immuniser
immunizer
immunogen
amaurosis
amaurotic
✧ombudsman
✧ombudsmen
embussing
impulsion
impulsive
empyreuma
Ambystoma
amazement
Amazonian
amazingly
amazon ant
amazonite
on balance
unbalance
undamaged
unmanaged
en caballo
incapable
incapably
kneadable
uncapable
uneatable
unfadable
unmakable
unmanacle
unnamable
unpayable
unsalable
unsatable
unsayable
untamable
untamably
indagator
inhalator
ungarbled
unharbour
unfancied
unhatched
unmatched
unwatched
Antarctic
enranckle
enhancive
Inland Sea
unhandled
unsaddled
one and all
unhandily
uncandour
unpapered
unwakened
unwatered
Annabella
Annabelle

uncareful
unbaffled
untangled
in fashion
unbashful
inhabiter
en famille
invalidly
in-patient
invariant
inhabitor
insatiate
insatiety
unsatiate
unmasking
unpacking
unmanlike
unwarlike
engarland
unfailing
ungallant
intaglios
in ballast
inharmony
inpayment
unharming
unharmful
undaunted
unhaunted
unpainted
untainted
uncannily
unsaintly
undawning
in earnest
in harness
unharness
incarnate
ungainful
unpainful
endamoeba
entamoeba
unrazored
Annapolis
uncanonic
any amount
unsavoury
in cahoots
unhappily
en rapport
in bad part
unmarried
sneak-raid
Anna Freud
unpalsied
encaustic
en passant
in passing
unpartial
unearthed
encanthis
infantile
unearthly
andantino
infantine
unhasting
unhatting
unwasting
incaution
enrapture
in tatters

unbaptize
unnatural
unmanured
unmatured
unsaluted
infatuate
unvarying
undazzled
anabranch
snob value
in a bad way
in a big way
Anobiidae
inebriant
inebriate
inebriety
inebrious
unobvious
anabolism
anabolite
inability
snub-nosed
anabiosis
anabiotic
Enobarbus
unabashed
knobstick
ink-bottle
✧anacharis
enactable
unactable
knock back
knock-back
knock cold
knock copy
sneck draw
knock down
knock-down
inscience
knackered
knickered
anucleate
enucleate
Anacletus
knocker-up
inscriber
anaclitic
onychitis
knock-knee
Anschluss
inoculate
unicolour
enactment
unscanned
unscented
aniconism
aniconist
anecdotal
on account
unscarred
unscathed
unscythed
anacruses
unaccused
unscoured
anacrusis
knock wood
in advance
unadmired
unadvised
snideness

unadapted
unadopted
cnidarian
unadorned
inodorous
antenatal
ink-eraser
undebased
undecayed
undefaced
undelayed
unrebated
unrelated
unrelaxed
inter alia
enterable
in default
inferable
intenable
on default
unseeable
untenable
under arms
endecagon
undecagon
underbear
underbody
interbred
underbred
interbank
inselberg
underbush
underbite
underclad
underclay
undercoat
intercede
unreached
endeictic
angel cake
unwelcome
intercrop
undercook
undercool
intercept
undercard
undercart
index case
undercast
inner city
inner-city
Intercity®
intercity
underclub
interdeal
underdraw
interdict
underdeck
underdoer
unheedily
unreadily
intendant
interdine
unbending
underdone
unheeding
engendure
angel dust
interdash
unheedful
unneedful

in general
in several
indecency
inference
inherence
inherency
enfevered
unrenewed
unsevered
entelechy
Angelenos
sneeze box
interesse
undeceive
undeserve
unreserve
interface
in-yer-face
unperfect
underfeed
interfile
interfold
underfelt
index fund
underfong
underfund
interflow
underflow
underfoot
interfere
under fire
underfire
angelfish
interfuse
underfish
unselfish
under-five
enneagram
undergrad
inveigler
unfeigned
unweighed
once again
undergone
intergrow
undergird
undergown
angel hair
antechoir
sneeshing
underhand
underhung
angelhood
angelical
annelidan
antefixal
endemical
indexical
undecimal
antefixes
endenizen
undecided
undefiled
undefined
undesired
unmerited
unrefined
unrevised
undelight
andesitic
enteritis

indelible
indelibly
intenible
inheritor
enter into
ingenious
unserious
unbelieve
interject
interjoin
underkeep
interknit
underking
interleaf
intellect
interlace
interlock
interlude
unhealthy
underlaid
underlain
annealing
index-link
interline
interlink
underline
underling
unfeeling
unveiling
interlope
interlard
angerless
indexless
unrealise
unrealism
in reality
unreality
unjealous
unzealous
unrealize
envermeil
annexment
interment
undermine
ungermane
unseeming
intermure
innermost
undermost
internode
unpennied
indemnify
antennule
internals
unmeaning
antennary
innerness
internist
Inverness
indemnity
undernote
unbeknown
knee-cords
enveloped
envenomed
unbeloved
unremoved
unrevoked
anaerobic
anhedonia
anhedonic
knee-holly
Anne Bonny
knee joint
under oath
indecorum
interplay
unbespeak
underplay
interpret
underpeep
unpeopled
unperplex
untempted
interpage
underpaid
unbespoke
in keeping
interpone
underplot
underprop
inner part
underpart
Intelpost
interpose
underpass
unhelpful
enhearten
unbearded
unhearsed
unlearned
unwearied
interrail
knee-drill
Anne Frank
endearing
inferring
integrand
integrant
interring
unbearing
under-ring
unfearing
under-roof
unheard-of
interrupt
under-ripe
unredrest
integrate
integrity
underrate
unfearful
under seal
underseal
intersect
underside
intensify
on-message
undersign
under sail
undersoil
intensely
inversely
underself
undersell
incessant
unceasing
uncessant
undersong
angel shot
en pension
in session
intension
inversion
undershot
incensory
intersert
insensate
intensate
intensity
intensive
inversive
undersaye
ancestral
inner tube
intestacy
insect net
underta'en
ungenteel
unsettled
entertain
incertain
uncertain
entertake
undertake
infertile
insectile
undertime
annectent
insetting
intestine
onsetting
undertane
undertint
undertone
unresting
unweeting
inception
indention
infection
ingestion
injection
insection
insertion
intention
invention
undertook
Intertype®
indenture
in pectore
insectary
inventory
invertase
intestate
anoestrum
anoestrus
unrestful
incentive
inceptive
infective
ingestive
injective
intentive
invective
inventive
intertext
antelucan
unsecular
ante lucem
unberufen
undeluded
unrebuked
unreduced
unrefuted
unsecured
unseduced
unbeguile
ungenuine
enter upon
on request
ingenuity
ingenuous
in service
in-service
interview
intervein
intervale
intervene
unnerving
unpervert
undervest
innervate
✧endeavour
innerwear
underwear
in-between
inner wall
knee-swell
interwind
underwent
underwing
✧underwood
inner ward
interwork
underwork
Anne Tyler
interzone
uneffaced
ineffable
ineffably
unifiable
snuff-dish
unoffered
knife-edge
snuff film
knife into
knifelike
snuffling
knifeless
snuff mill
snuff-mull
uniformed
uniformly
end for end
knife-rest
enigmatic
sniggerer
sniggling
knightage
Anaglypta®
ensheathe
insheathe
unsheathe
anthracic
encheason
on the beam
on the beat
on the bias
in the buff
on the boil
on the ball
on the bone
on the broo
on the bash
anthocyan
unchecked
unshocked
on the cuff
unshackle
anthocarp
in the cart
in the club
on the club
in the dock
on the dole
in the dark
uncheered
on the edge
on the game
on the hoof
on the hour
unchained
unshrived
unshriven
unchrisom
unthrifty
in the know
inshallah
enchilada
enshelter
inkholder
inshelter
anthology
in the lump
on the line
anthelion
in the loop
anchylose
in the mean
in the main
on the make
enthymeme
on the mend
anthemion
in the mass
on the move
on thin ice
enchanted
enchanter
one-handed
unchanged
unshunned
unthanked
on the nail
on the nose
anthropic
unwhipped
on the pill
on the pull
unshapely
in the pink
anchor man
anchor-man
enchorial
in the road
✧on the road
anchor-ice
on the rack
anchor leg
uncharged
uncharmed
uncharnel
uncharted
✧anchorage
anchoress
on the rise
anchorite
uncharity
anthurium
on the side
in the swim
unghostly
on the spot
on-the-spot
in the scud
in the soup
unshutter
on the take
on the trot
on the turn
✧on the town
enrheumed
in thought
anchoveta
in the wind
on the wing
in the zone
antipapal
uncinated
antipathy
indinavir
inaidable
unaidable
unlikable
unlivable
unridable
unsizable
untirable
✧indicator
antipasti
antipasto
antiscian
insincere
Antiochus
enkindled
unkindled
unriddler
unbinding
unwinding
unmindful
engine-man
Gneisenau
inside-car
incidence
indigence
indigency
on-licence
enlivener
unripened
unsinewed
antigenic
antihelix
antimeric
antivenin
unlived-in
unmixedly
antisense
On Liberty
antiserum
inside out
untimeous
snailfish
angiogram
unmingled
in disgust
enlighten
in high leg
unlighted
unsighted
antitheft
Annie Hall
unsightly
antiphony
unsighing
unwishing
antichlor
unwishful
ancipital
antiviral
inhibited
inhibiter
undivided
unlimited
unvisited
anticivic
insipidly
invisible
invisibly
uncivilly
incipient
insipient
inhibitor
intimiste
antivirus
insidious
invidious
unpitiful
unsickled
anticking
unwinking
inviolacy
knaidloch
kneidlach
infielder
snail-like
anticline
infilling
unwilling
ancillary
anti-flash
inviolate
snail mail
infirmary
angiomata
infirmity
Indian War
antiknock
Indian red
indignify
undignify
Indian fig
anciently
✧indian ink
indignant
ancientry
Indianise
Indianist
unfitness
indignity
Indianize
antidotal
antinodal
✧antipodal
anti-novel
✧antipodes
indigo red
unpiloted

antimonic
antinomic
antitoxic
antitoxin
indigotin
antinoise
Antigonus
on display
unripping
antispast
indispose
in dispute
antitrade
unpierced
antitragi
encierros
antitrust
unbiassed
gneissoid
snail-slow
gneissose
ungirthed
unwittily
insistent
unfitting
unsisting
unwitting
indiction
undiluted
unfigured
indirubin
antiquely
anxiously
enviously
antiquark
antiquary
antiquate
antiquity
insinuate
antitypal
antitypic
unpitying
ink-jerker
snakebird
snakebite
snake cult
innkeeper
snake eyes
snakehead
Inuktitut
unskilled
snakelike
unskilful
unskimmed
unskinned
snakiness
snakeroot
snakeskin
snakeweed
snakewood
snakewise
unallayed
uncleaned
uncleared
unpleased
unpleated
uncleanly
unclearly
unpliable
unpliably
ankle-boot

englacial
inflicter
unelected
unplucked
analectic
inflictor
anglicise
anglicism
anglicist
anglicize
✧uncle Dick
unfledged
unpledged
include in
including
influence
unaltered
analgesia
analgesic
influenza
Englified
one-legged
unaligned
unclogged
unplagued
unplugged
inelegant
analogise
analogist
analogous
analogize
unclaimed
unplained
unplaited
angle iron
ankle-jack
unclimbed
unplumbed
inclement
Englander
unblended
unblinded
unblunted
unplanked
unplanned
unplanted
inclining
inglenook
ingleneuk
unalloyed
unblooded
unfloored
unclipped
analeptic
✧anglophil
unslept-in
Snell's law
ankle sock
ingle-side
Englisher
unblessed
unclassed
unfleshed
unglossed
inelastic
uncleship
endlessly
unfleshly
analysand
angle shot
inclusion

enclosure
Englishry
inclosure
anglesite
inclusive
englutted
unblotted
unclothed
inflation
inflative
unclouded
unillumed
onslaught
ingluvial
ingluvies
inflowing
angleworm
anglewise
inflexion
influxion
inflexure
unamiable
anamneses
unimpeded
anamnesis
anemogram
enamelled
enameller
anemology
unsmiling
animalise
animalism
animalist
animality
anomalous
animalize
gnomonics
mnemonics
in a manner
unamended
mnemonist
unimposed
enamorado
unamerced
enumerate
inamorata
inamorato
inumbrate
animistic
onomastic
Mnemosyne
unamusing
animosity
unemptied
unsmitten
animating
animation
animatism
enamoured
on impulse
unengaged
Anonaceae
in any case
unentered
unindexed
unsnuffed
enanthema
in any hand
ananthous
unincited
uninvited

enunciate
unanxious
unenvious
unknelled
un-English
anonymise
anonymity
inanimate
unanimity
anonymous
unanimous
anonymize
inaneness
unendowed
anandrous
in one's way
on one's way
onanistic
on one's own
uninstall
inanition
inunction
one-nation
uninjured
uninsured
unknowing
in one word
in any wise
unenvying
Angora cat
in so far as
annoyance
unlocated
unsolaced
endogamic
infomania
enjoyable
enjoyably
unlosable
unlovable
unmovable
unmovably
unpotable
unroyally
unwomanly
annotator
innovator
intonator
undoubted
uncombine
untouched
ensorcell
unvoicing
endoscope
endoscopy
in concert
unconcern
uncordial
onion dome
infolding
unfolding
unloading
any old how
incondite
income tax
indolence
indolency
innocence
innocency
insolence
oncometer

onion-eyed
uncovered
unmoneyed
endogenic
Indonesia
oncogenic
ontogenic
unmovedly
anno regni
unhopeful
union flag
unconfine
unconform
uncongeal
endophagy
angophora
endotherm
endophyte
entophyte
on holiday
Unionidae
unlogical
unionised
unionized
unmotived
unnoticed
unpoliced
unrosined
endomixis
unpolitic
indocible
unsolidly
encomiums
encomiast
Antoninus
innoxious
Union Jack
inworking
onlooking
unworking
unbookish
unmoulded
ungodlike
ungodlily
unworldly
ennobling
enrolling
untoiling
endoblast
endoplasm
entoblast
union list
incommode
endowment
engoûment
enjoyment
enrolment
informant
endosmose
insomniac
announcer
encounter
unbounded
uncounted
unfounded
unjointed
unmounted
unpointed
unrounded
unsounded
unwounded

in council
unsoundly
incognito
unbosomer
ontologic
endomorph
OncoMouse®
uncoupled
endorphin
in company
in-company
encolpion
endosperm
endospore
encompass
encolpium
Indo-Aryan
entoproct
incorrect
unmourned
unsourced
unworried
encourage
entourage
uncourtly
endocrine
inpouring
incorrupt
uncorrupt
envoyship
onion-skin
union suit
intorsion
union shop
in consort
endosteal
En-Tout-Cas®
en tout cas
oncostman
entoptics
uncouthly
infortune
unfortune
intortion
Angostura
endosteum
in context
unpopular
anno mundi
involucel
involuted
unfocused
insoluble
insolubly
involucre
innocuity
innocuous
insolvent
antonymic
oncolysis
oncolytic
endolymph
uniplanar
snaphance
unapparel
anaplasty
in special
knapscull
inspector
anopheles
insphear'd

snipefish
unspoiled
knapskull
unapplied
unspilled
inspanned
ink pencil
inaptness
ineptness
unaptness
inopinate
unopposed
anaphoric
kniphofia
inspiring
unsparing
one-person
in spirits
uniparous
unspotted
in epitome
unipotent
anaptyxis
unsquared
inequable
unequable
unequally
inerrancy
end-reader
increaser
uncreated
undreaded
undreamed
untreated
unwreaked
enwreathe
inbreathe
inwreathe
unwreathe
inorganic
inerrable
inerrably
anorectal
entrechat
intricacy
Antrycide®
Androcles
infracted
unfrocked
untracked
anorectic
infractor
unprecise
entrecôte
intricate
introduce
unpredict
unbridged
unbridled
uncrudded
ungrudged
untrodden
andradite
inerudite
snare drum
unfreeman
unordered
androecia
energetic
unorderly
enfreedom

in arrears
entry form
André Gide
intriguer
androgyne
androgyny
intrigant
anarchial
anarchise
anarchism
anarchist
anorthite
anarchize
energizer
engrained
engrainer
ingrained
ingrainer
unbraided
unbruised
undrained
unpraised
untrained
en arrière
gnarliest
introitus
introject
entralles
undrilled
andrology
✧andromeda
entrammel
untrimmed
uncrumple
enurement
increment
inurement
encrimson
entremets
incremate
en primeur
uniramous
infringer
unbranded
unfranked
unprinted
engrenage
in transit
intrinsic
unwrinkle
angriness
inertness
encrinite
entre nous
ungroomed
Andreotti
encrypted
entrapper
uncropped
unpropped
entropion
unprepare
entropium
András Fay
engrossed
engrosser
unbrushed
uncrossed
undressed
ungrassed
unpressed
untressed
untrussed
untrusser
end result
intrusion
intrusive
unfretted
unwritten
ingrately
unwriting
incretion
Encratism
un-British
Encratite
energumen
inbrought
indraught
inwrought
on draught
unfraught
unwrought
in trouble
onerously
unprovide
unprovoke
engraving
engravery
introvert
in private
uncrowded
uncrowned
undrowned
in drawing
ingrowing
energy gap
unbrizzed
in as far as
unashamed
unassayed
unessayed
Anastasia
anastasis
anastatic
anosmatic
un-Islamic
unusually
in essence
unessence
unushered
anisogamy
gnostical
unisonant
unisonous
uniserial
Innsbruck
on a string
inusitate
unassumed
unassured
unisexual
gnateater
initialed
initially
initiator
Gnetaceae
unstocked
unstudied
anathemas
unuttered
and twenty
unstifled
unstuffed
instigate
Anita Hill
snatchily
snitchers
unethical
unattired
unstained
unstriped
and things
Anatolian
installed
installer
instilled
unstilled
inutility
unstamped
anatomise
anatomist
anatomize
on stand-by
instanter
unstinted
instantly
snot-nosed
gnathonic
inotropic
unstopped
unstopper
✧unitarian
unit price
unstirred
unsterile
ant thrush
knotgrass
unit trust
enstatite
institute
unitively
unstaying
endurance
insurance
undulancy
angulated
annulated
indurated
input area
undulated
pneumatic
angularly
endurable
endurably
incunable
incurable
incurably
inhumanly
insularly
insurable
uncurable
untunable
untunably
incubator
insulator
unhumbled
untumbled
incumbent
in numbers
unsuccess
inculcate
infuscate
unbundler
uncurdled
unsubdued
unsued-for
intumesce
unqueened
inquietly
unqueenly
unquietly
indumenta
unduteous
untuneful
unruffled
anguiform
unguiform
anhungred
indulge in
indulgent
insurgent
endungeon
inrushing
Inguri Dam
unmusical
inaudible
inaudibly
inducible
infusible
indusiate
induviate
infuriate
incurious
indubious
injurious
uncurious
undutiful
unsubject
unluckily
unfuelled
unquelled
unsullied
unqualify
aneuploid
in full fig
in full rig
annulling
inquiline
uncurling
unbuilt-on
in full cry
annualise
annualize
annulment
inburning
unturning
innuendos
unfurnish
inquinate
untutored
✧infusoria
pneumonia
pneumonic
unsuspect
anguipede
unrumpled
on purpose
inculpate
unguarded
unhurried
incurrent
incurring
inquiring
uncurrent
inquorate
anguished
unguessed
unpursued
incursion
insulsity
incursive
injustice
unburthen
encurtain
uncurtain
inductile
annuitant
inputting
insultant
insulting
unsuiting
induction
intuition
unhurtful
inductive
intuitive
inaugural
incubuses
incurvate
incurvity
unmuzzled
unavoided
snivelled
sniveller
anovulant
univalent
an even bet
unavenged
universal
on average
I never did!
knaveship
knavishly
snow-water
snowscape
unswaddle
snow fence
anywheres
knowledge
snowberry
snow-white
snow finch
snowfield
snowfleck
snowflick
indweller
snowflake
snow-blind
snowblink
snow plant
inswinger
snow under
knowingly
snowiness
snowbound
snow board
snowboard
snow goose
snowdrift
snow brake
answer for
snow-broth
untwisted
in two twos
snowstorm
snow guard
inexactly
in extenso
unextinct
unexcited
unexpired
unexalted
unexposed
unextreme
enzymatic
untypable
engyscope
untypical
undyingly
in my voice
ankylosed
ankylosis
anhydride
anhydrite
enhydrite
anhydrous
enhydrous
go bananas
soya sauce
soda water
for a laugh
cobalamin
Mozarabic
polar axis
zonal axis
locatable
roman à clé
rotatable
sofa table
copataine
Rotavator®
rotavator
Dolayatra
polar bear
polar body
woman-body
Iona Abbey
rocambole
sonar buoy
woman-born
royal blue
monarchal
Mosaic Law
mosaic map
not a scrap
Comanches
tobaccoes
Holarctic
monarchic
local call
solar cell
romancing
soda scone
somascope
mosaicism
mosaicist
non-access
cowardice
cowardree
Rob Andrew
Monandria
Tom and Tib
royal duke
Box and Cox
hob-and-nob
hot-and-hot
go hard but
forage cap
lorazepam
covalency
God-a-mercy
Rotameter®
copacetic
copasetic
kopasetic
logaoedic
Donatello
pomace-fly
how are you?
dogaressa
moraceous
pomaceous
rosaceous
volageous
coral fern
royal fern
coral-fish
royal fish
botargoes
cotangent
total heat
notaphily
not at home
not a thing
toxaphene
Vodaphone
borachios
womanhood
Local Hero
monachism
monachist
Fomalhaut
botanical
foraminal
monadical
tovarisch
bona fides
cohabitee
cohabiter
localiser
localizer
moraliser
moralizer
polarised
polariser
polarized
polarizer
Romaniser
Romanizer
totaliser
totalizer
vocaliser
vocalizer
womaniser
womanizer
Loya Jirga
logarithm
Mogadishu
notabilia
tonalitic
tomatillo
rosariums
covariant
soda nitre
bodacious
rotavirus
solacious

loaf-bread
✧comforter
conferred
conferrer
confirmed
confirmee
confirmer
conformer
God forbid
goffering
hoofprint
solferino
confirmor
not for Joe
loaferish
Nosferatu
cod-fisher
confessed
not fussed
rodfisher
confestly
wolfishly
confusing
confessor
confusion
confiseur
godfather
✧confiteor
comfiture
confiture
solfatara
loaf sugar
confluent
roof guard
poignancy
long-dated
long-eared
long-faced
long-range
zoography
forgeable
tonga-bean
Golgi body
hobgoblin
dodgeball
doughball
Bob Gibson
Longobard
longicorn
roughcast
Doug Scott
rough-draw
cough drop
Lough Derg
bongo drum
conga drum
cough down
longaeval
Long Beach
tonguelet
toughener
toggle off
tongue-tie
mongrelly
boogieing
Joe Greene
goggle-box
long metre
longueurs
borghetto
lorgnette
God-gifted
Fongafale
Volgograd
lodge-gate
long sheep
long-chain
Lou Gehrig
Longchamp
dough hook
longshore
long whist
rough-hewn
long since
long-liner
long-lived
long sixes
long-sixes
long field
go against
Mongolian
tough luck
✧mongoloid
coagulant
coagulase
Congolese
Mongolise
✧mongolism
coagulate
longcloth
tough love
Mongolize
lodgement
songsmith
zoogamete
zoogamous
congenial
gorgonian
roughneck
gorgoneia
longingly
bogginess
dogginess
fogginess
gorgonise
podginess
roughness
sogginess
toughness
morganite
zoogenous
zoogonous
gorgonize
long dozen
mongooses
zoogloeic
long johns
longhouse
long-coats
lodgepole
doggerman
Low German
box girder
conger-eel
congeries
hop-garden
songcraft
rodgersia
long drink
mongering
Tongariro
Gongorism
Gongorist
congested
Moygashel®
doggishly
hoggishly
roughshod
gong-stick
longitude
forgather
forgetter
forgotten
doughtily
forgetful
forgetive
songfully
congruent
congruity
congruous
forgiving
longevity
longevous
longe whip
song cycle
hog heaven
hotheaded
mop-headed
moth-eaten
not-headed
tow-headed
to the bone
doohickey
no chicken
Sophocles
pothecary
gothicise
Gothicism
Gothicist
gothicize
lophodont
Loch Leven
cochleare
cochleate
lothefull
to the full
to the fore
to the good
to the hilt
Yoshihito
Kozhikode
pot holder
to the life
potholing
to the last
Lon Halévy
top hamper
bonhommie
Ho Chi Minh
vox humana
sophomore
Gothamist
Gothamite
bonhomous
cochineal
Lochinvar
foxhunter
mob-handed
pot-hanger
pot-hunter
mochiness
Loch Morar
go through
go the pace
Rotherham
Tocharian
Tokharian
mother hen
mother wit
coshering
mothering
Lotharios
mothproof
Tocharish
Tokharish
cothurnus
mother lye
Rochester
sophister
sophistic
Sophus Lie
go whistle
sophistry
bodhi tree
no whither
nowhither
go the vole
to the wide
doli capax
dominance
dominancy
jouisance
boric acid
folic acid
comitadji
cogitable
comically
conically
ionisable
ionizable
logically
nominable
nominally
topically
toxically
cogitator
dominator
motivator
nominator
solidagos
corivalry
solitaire
bonilasse
Rosinante
Rozinante
comitatus
logic bomb
ionic bond
sonic bang
yohimbine
comic book
sonic boom
Politburo
dowitcher
✧moriscoes
Robin Cook
koniscope
Bo Diddley
go wilding
policeman
poriferal
poriferan
rotiferal
dosimeter
focimeter
konimeter
Polixenes
Sosigenes
homiletic
police dog
dosimetry
Yogi Berra
nobilesse
politesse
Donizetti
Cominform
Kominform
Boxing Day
coping-saw
moving map
sociogram
Wokingham
moviegoer
towing net
comings-in
loving cup
holing-axe
polish off
Robin Hood
do without
go without
dominical
Dominican
Dorididae
homicidal
Hominidae
political
soritical
domiciled
mobiliser
mobilizer
politicly
boliviano
dominions
Louisiana
volitient
politicos
solicitor
nobiliary
noviciate
novitiate
politique
gorillian
Social War
sociolect
moniplies
dosiology
koniology
sociology
gorilloid
gorilline
movieland
cotillion
modillion
nonillion
foliolose
socialise
socialism
socialist
foliolate
joviality
socialite
sociality
socialize
sonic mine
motion-man
coriander
Ionian Sea
motionist
notionist
solidness
polianite
soliloquy
sociopath
hodiernal
topiarian
posigrade
goliardic
colicroot
monitress
topiarist
movie star
go airside
go missing
solipsism
solipsist
logistics
covin-tree
foliation
sociation
Comintern
foliature
Komintern
sovietise
sovietism
goniatite
joliotium
sociative
sovietize
coticular
lodiculae
Solifugae
copiously
noxiously
rosinweed
codifying
modifying
notifying
hobjobber
Poujadism
Poujadist
conjugant
conjugate
conjoined
conjuring
nonjuring
conjure up
forjaskit
forjeskit
cockmatch
folk dance
rock candy
bookmaker
rockwater
rock-basin
pockmanky
cock-padle
workmanly
worktable
cocklaird
work party
book value
tonka-bean
corkscrew
cock's-comb
cockscomb
Jock Scott
cocked hat
mockadoes
booked-out
hooked rug
zonked out
cockle hat
cockleman
rock perch
workbench
boxkeeper
jockteleg
Rock fever
zookeeper
cockneyfy
Monk Lewis
rock melon
cocklebur
folk-weave
look after
Book of Job
cocksfoot
work of art
fork-chuck
worksheet
rockshaft
lock-chain
bookshelf
cook-chill
cock-a-hoop
cock-shoot
monkshood
look sharp
look where
Yorkshire
workpiece
cockfight
folk-right
rock pipit
Cockaigne
book block
workplace
Volkslied
lookalike
rock plant
bookplate
rock flour
look alive
look small
look smart
locksmith
dog-kennel
rock snake
mockingly
soakingly
boskiness
cockiness
corkiness
forkiness
kookiness
rockiness
wonkiness
moskonfyt
workwoman
cockroach
workforce
book token
corkborer
hook-nosed
kolkhozes
rock borer

Words marked ✧ can also be spelled with one or more capital letters

folkloric
rock-solid
rock socks
workfolks
lock horns
look-round
rock-bound
Doukhobor
corkboard
booklouse
cockhorse
cookhouse
lockhouse
rock house
workhorse
workhouse
Yom Kippur
✧volksraad
book price
book trade
rock brake
rock drill
rock'n'roll
lookers-on
rock tripe
rocker arm
dock-cress
rock cress
workerist
cock-broth
mockernut
workgroup
Hooke's law
monk's seam
monkishly
cocky's joy
jock strap
jockstrap
work study
cockateel
cockatiel
rocketeer
socket set
Tom Kitten
forky-tail
Jock Stein
work ethic
bookstall
yolk stalk
bookstand
docketing
Folketing
honky-tonk
pocketing
socketing
bookstore
folk story
Cook's tour
pocketful
Cookstown
fork lunch
folk music
rock music
rock guano
cockswain
donkey-man
jockey cap
monkey bag
monkey jar
monkey pod
monkey pot
jockeyism
monkeyish
monkeyism
monkey nut
monkey run
foolhardy
low-loader
toolmaker
mouldable
✧pollyanna
fool-happy
colleague
coulibiac
jollyboat
koala bear
World Bank
colly bird
dolly bird
roll-about
hoolachan
collected
colliculi
collector
collocate
Roald Dahl
collodion
coolie hat
poulterer
no flies on
mollified
mollifier
poultfoot
holly-fern
collegial
collegian
bow-legged
doglegged
fool's gold
dolly girl
collagist
zoologist
colligate
lowlights
collegium
jollyhead
lowlihead
hollyhock
loll-shrob
Coulthard
colloidal
coal-fired
coalminer
coalfield
mouldiest
not likely
coal-black
mould-loft
hoplology
bowl along
coal plant
roll along
world line
worldling
tol-lolish
coal-plate
mould-made
jolliment
Collymore
Moslemism
Coelomata
coelomate
collimate
fool's mate
mollymawk
collinear
non-linear
pollen sac
Hollander
✧lowlander
lollingly
Tom Landry
dolliness
godliness
jolliness
lowliness
nobleness
soiliness
pollinate
pollinium
noble opal
soul-force
Joel Cohen
poll-money
foilborne
soil-bound
coalhouse
coal mouse
coolhouse
dollhouse
tollhouse
toolhouse
goalmouth
tollbooth
collapsar
lolloping
lollipops
non liquet
colloquia
pot liquor
bowler hat
bowler-hat
dollar gap
soil creep
forlornly
foolproof
foul-brood
Lollardry
coal-brass
dollarise
goslarite
collyrium
dollarize
Boyle's law
coelostat
molluscan
molluskan
coulisses
foolishly
godlessly
joylessly
toylesome
collision
collusion
dolly-shop
dolly shot
pollusion
collusive
non-lethal
popliteal
toilet bag
would that
dog letter
holly tree
mollities
toilet set
tool steel
cowl-staff
bolletrie
zoolatria
zoolithic
Collatine
pollutant
coalition
collation
pollution
collotype
voilà tout
collative
pollutive
soul-curer
soul music
soulfully
colluvial
colluvies
world-view
boulevard
colluvium
worldwide
coal owner
Tod-lowrie
following
Bollywood
Hollywood
holloware
mouldwarp
World War I
follow out
hollow out
jolleying
no-fly zone
doomwatch
doom-laden
doomsayer
worm-eaten
loom large
Dormobile®
cosmocrat
formicant
formicary
formicate
commodify
commodore
commodity
cormidium
worm fence
worm fever
form genus
cosmogeny
cosmogony
worm wheel
topmaking
Joe Miller
pommelled
sommelier
cosmology
formulaic
boomslang
Commelina
Cosmo Lang
formulary
foam glass
formalise
formalism
formalist
form class
formulise
formulism
formulist
normalise
formality
formulate
normality
formalize
formulize
normalize
non-member
commendam
commensal
common law
Rosminian
Roumanian
Roumansch
commander
commenter
low-minded
tormented
tormenter
commonage
Normandie
rooming-in
tormentil
zoomantic
commingle
foamingly
commoning
communing
commandos
commentor
communion
hodmandod
topminnow
tormentor
Common Era
✧communard
communise
✧communism
✧communist
foaminess
loaminess
Mormonism
Normanise
Normanism
roominess
worminess
comminate
comminute
community
Mormonite
cosmonaut
tormentum
torminous
communize
Normanize
wormholed
form horse
for my part
Bob Marley
Joe Mercer
bon marché
zoomorphy
bog myrtle
cosmorama
boomerang
commorant
cormorant
coumarone
rosmarine
woomerang
worm grass
commissar
Holmesian
Hormisdas
job-master
Toamasina
tommy shop
committal
commutual
cosmetics
dogmatics
committed
committee
committer
formatted
formatter
godmother
dot matrix
zoometric
coemption
commotion
cosmotron
dormition
formation
dogmatory
dormitory
dogmatise
dogmatism
dogmatist
commutate
dormitive
formative
normative
dogmatize
form tutor
corn-salad
roundarch
downwards
horn-maker
moon-faced
✧moonraker
bonne amie
countable
mountable
woundable
John Wayne
John Cabot
John Canoe
John Kanoo
John Major
John Mayow
moon daisy
loon-pants
connubial
moong bean
countback
sound body
bonnibell
mound-bird
coenobite
sound bite
soundbite
coenobium
moon about
Cornaceae
round clam
connected
connecter
low-necked
pound coin
pound cake
downscale
connector
cornichon
Mount Cook
moonscape
townscape
soundcard
coenocyte
fornicate
to a nicety
connect up
poinadoes
tornadoes
John Adams
point duty
count down
countdown
horned owl
round down
round-down
lounge-bar
pounce bag
rounceval
roundelay
John Dewey
round-eyed
young-eyed
John Keble
pointedly
Mount Etna
counselor
pounce box
pounce pot
John Henry
John Keats
John Reith
bounteous
John Rebus
young fogy
Mount Fuji
sound film
townsfolk
corniform
Joan of Arc
houndfish
round fish
born-again
round game
John Ogdon
hornyhead
Roundhead
corn shuck
downshift
joint heir
sound hole
moonshine
moonshiny
pounching
roundhand
downthrow
John O'Hara
loan shark
moonphase
downriver
downsizer
hobnailed
John Piper

soft-paste
Port Salut
log tables
cost a bomb
South Bend
port a beul
mortician
foeticide
hot ticket
porticoed
porticoes
corticoid
monticule
poeticule
forthcome
toothcomb
conticent
zootechny
contactor
poeticise
poeticism
✧vorticism
vorticist
vorticose
corticate
vorticity
posticous
youth club
poeticize
contadina
contadine
contadini
contadino
North Down
Southdown
bottle gas
soft pedal
soft-pedal
voltmeter
bottle off
pontlevis
zoothecia
northerly
southerly
bottle-imp
pottle-pot
hostlesse
north-east
poetresse
south-east
zootheism
bottleful
bottle out
portreeve
pontifice
volte-face
fortified
fortifier
for toffee
mortified
mortifier
mouthfeel
tout à fait
mouthfuls
coltsfoot
soothfast
toothfish
✧forty-five
Portuguee
contagion
Vortigern
contagium
voltigeur
soft wheat
youthhead
goat's-hair
soft-shell
soft thing
youthhood
mouth harp
sort these
sort those
doctrinal
Noctuidae
postviral
bobtailed
container
contrived
contriver
postrider
tortrices
no strings
no-strings
footlight
fortnight
tortricid
foothills
Montaigne
Port Limon
mouthiest
toothiest
boot virus
rostellar
bootblack
fortalice
noctiluca
portulaca
soothlich
hosteller
postiller
Tortelier
fortilage
nostology
sortilege
sortilegy
costalgia
nostalgia
nostalgic
sootflake
toothlike
hostilely
go it alone
Mont Blanc
monthling
northland
portolani
portolano
postulant
southland
noctilios
postilion
tortillon
mortalise
mouthless
toothless
worthless
footcloth
footplate
hostility
mortality
mortcloth
postulate
tortility
Oort cloud
rostellum
Fortaleza
mortalize
contumacy
mouth-made
contemner
contemper
costumier
tom-tommed
contumely
bottom end
contemnor
northmost
southmost
zootomist
bottom out
bottoms up
continual
montan wax
pottingar
cottonade
boutonnée
contender
contented
continued
continuer
molten sea
pontoneer
pontonier
pottinger
routineer
cotton gin
Hortensio
joltingly
poutingly
routinely
✧continent
most an end
softening
contangos
continuos
✧hottentot
post-entry
dottiness
goutiness
loftiness
Montanism
Montanist
pottiness
routinise
routinism
routinist
sootiness
voltinism
fortunate
sostenuto
continuum
cotton bud
souteneur
totting-up
Boston ivy
Porto Novo
fortunize
routinize
postwoman
soft touch
soft goods
pontooner
portioned
portioner
postponer
softcover
soft-nosed
soft power
zootrophy
portfolio
Port Louis
zoetropic
most noble
soft tommy
foot-pound
moot point
rootbound
non troppo
footboard
moot court
tout court
boathouse
footloose
Lofthouse
moot house
porthouse
posthorse
posthouse
root house
Fort Worth
soft focus
soft-focus
toothpick
dottipoll
north pole
soft spile
south pole
mouthpart
Southport
coeternal
doctorial
nocturnal
Rotterdam
coat-frock
Costa Rica
cost price
contorted
co-starred
couturier
Monterrey
Nocturnes
voiturier
fosterage
porterage
boat train
cotter-pin
soft fruit
sooterkin
footbrake
doctorand
footprint
fostering
loitering
pottering
root-prune
rostering
soft drink
torturing
tottering
contornos
foster-son
poster boy
posterior
coat-dress
doctoress
Pooterish
Pooterism
porteress
posturist
soft-grass
doctorate
posterity
Southroun
torturous
contessas
North Star
South Seas
contested
contester
poetaster
route-step
sottisier
coltishly
doltishly
goatishly
loutishly
sottishly
don't ask me!
loathsome
toothsome
youthsome
cortisone
contusion
poetastry
contusive
bootstrap
rootstock
fortitude
coat-style
footstalk
foot-stall
portatile
coatstand
font-stone
mort-stone
footstool
hortation
hot to trot
sortation
sortition
footsteps
hortatory
hortative
portative
Port Sudan
contoured
routously
North Uist
South Uist
sotto voce
costively
tout à vous
boatswain
howtowdie
northward
southward
Southwark
toothwort
mouthwash
north-west
south-west
toothwash
forthwith
post-synch
Montezuma
lobulated
nodulated
non-usager
jocularly
popularly
joculator
modulator
Columbian
✧columbine
columbary
columbate
columbite
columbium
homuncles
homuncule
homunculi
coruscant
coruscate
loquacity
toluidine
jocundity
rotundate
rotundity
conundrum
volumeter
cohune oil
columella
toruffled
Roquefort
Jotunheim
novus homo
voluminal
Zonuridae
volumiser
volumizer
top-up loan
coquilles
Lotus-land
locuplete
Rogue Male
columnist
wofulness
torulosis
colubriad
Solutrean
Solutrian
docudrama
colubrine
volucrine
rogueship
roguishly
focussing
hocussing
coquetted
volunteer
coculture
voluntary
nocuously
cocuswood
vogue word
Norueyses
souvlakia
convector
convocate
coevality
convolute
pot valour
convincer
dog violet
Hoover Dam
non-verbal
converser
converter
go over big
polverine
wolverene
wolverine
bovver boy
convertor
wolvishly
non-voting
solvation
convivial
bon vivant
bon viveur
convexity
bon voyage
Norwegian
porwiggle
boxwallah
pot-waller
Colwyn Bay
forwander
to a wonder
bow window
forwarder
forwardly
nor'-wester
nor'wester
sou'wester
Norway rat
coaxially
coaxingly
cony-catch
holy water
polywater
polymathy
corydalis
polybasic
Polygamia
polygamic
corybants
polymasty
corymbose
Tony Adams
molybdate
molybdous
Toby Belch
polygenic
polymeric
polylemma
Tony Leung
cotyledon
polyhedra
body-check
coryphaei
Soay sheep
polyphagy
bodyshell
coryphene
polyphone
polyphony
polythene
Holy Ghost
polyphase
rosy finch
Polynices
copyright
Holyfield
Polyfilla®
polypidom
polyvinyl

body clock
monyplies
polyploid
Tony Blair
cosy along
polyglott
polyamide
polyimide
body image
polyomino
polyamory
polyonymy
Houyhnhnm
polyandry
polygonal
polytonal
polyzonal
Tony Roche
polyconic
polyposis
polyzooid
body count
Toby Young
polymorph
body board
polyzoary
body forth
polygonum
Polyporus
cohyponym
holy-cruel
Tony Cragg
polyarchy
✧holy grail
Tony Greig
polygraph
holy grass
rosy cross
polyester
polyptych
polystyle
holystone
body-curer
Roxy Music
bodyguard
Tony Award
polyaxial
Polygynia
polymyxin
polytypic
pozzolana
booziness
wooziness
monzonite
douzepers
appanaged
apsarases
aplanatic
speakable
ups-a-daisy
apparatus
spraickle
sprauchle
uplandish
apparency
speakeasy
sphacelus
speak fair
splay foot
splay-foot
spearfish
spragging
spearhead
splashily
splashing
splash out
apparitor
uptalking
appalling
sprawling
spearmint
sphagnous
Appaloosa
sphaerite
spear side
upmanship
L P Hartley
splatting
Apgar test
a plague on
spearwort
opobalsam
specially
spectacle
spectator
spiccatos
specialty
space band
spicebush
epicyclic
spice cake
epicedial
epicedian
epicedium
spaced out
epicleses
epiclesis
specified
epicritic
spicilege
spaceless
speckless
apiculate
speculate
spiculate
epicenter
epicentre
spiciness
spaceport
apocopate
✧epicurean
space race
spice rack
epicardia
epicormic
epic drama
epicurise
epicurism
epicurize
spaceship
spacesuit
space-time
spec-built
space walk
space-walk
✧apocrypha
spade bone
apodictic
spadefuls
spade foot
spadefish
spodogram
spadillio
spadelike
opodeldoc
spodumene
epedaphic
epidermal
Spider-Man
spiderman
spider leg
spider web
epidermic
epidermis
spadesman
spadassin
epidosite
Epidaurus
spadework
speedboat
speedball
speed bump
Spielberg
spleuchan
up-perched
upper-case
après coup
appendage
appendant
sphendone
splendent
spreading
splendour
ephemerae
ephemeral
ephemeras
appetence
appetency
apheresis
epaenetic
ephemerid
ephemeris
splenetic
ephemeron
a peepe out
après-goût
speech day
speech act
speechify
upper hand
sprechery
speechful
spherical
appetiser
appetizer
ephelides
speerings
ipse dixit
splenitis
appetible
spreckled
Up-Helly-Aa
appealing
appellant
upwelling
speedless
appellate
uppermost
spleenish
spleenful
✧sphenodon
upheaping
ephedrine
speedster
appeasing
speed trap
a pretty go
appertain
upsetting
spherular
speedwell
apteryxes
speedy cut
apoenzyme
epifaunal
epigraphy
spaghetti
epigaeous
up against
Spigelian
apogamous
epigynous
spagyrist
up the ante
upcheered
up-Channel
upthunder
up the pole
up the wall
optimates
opsimathy
optic axis
optically
optimally
spoil bank
sphincter
split cane
Ophiuchus
iprindole
optic disc
epainetic
spriteful
April fool
April-fish
spoilfive
springlet
springald
springily
sprigging
springing
✧springbok
spring box
spoil heap
uplighted
uplighter
upaithric
sprightly
uprightly
Epeiridae
optimiser
optimizer
speirings
apsidiole
aphidious
sprinkler
uplinking
optic lobe
ephialtes
ophiology
upfilling
ophiolite
split mind
split peas
ophiuroid
split ring
apriorism
apriorist
apriority
spoilsman
spritsail
optic tube
split time
splitting
sprinting
uplifting
upsitting
splintery
splittism
splittist
spikefish
spike heel
spike-nail
spoken for
spikenard
spikiness
spike-rush
spokesman
spokesmen
spokewise
appliance
appliable
spellable
spoliator
spellbind
spulebane
spulebone
epilobium
applicant
apple-cart
applicate
spelldown
apologise
apologist
epilogise
epilogist
apologize
epilogize
spellican
spillikin
apple-jack
apple-John
opal glass
epilimnia
spelunker
opulently
spill over
spillover
epileptic
speldring
spilosite
apple tree
epilithic
epilation
epulation
apple-tart
applauder
apple-wife
apomictic
epimerise
epimerism
epimerize
spymaster
epimysium
Spinhaler®
spinnaker
sponsalia
spendable
epinician
spinacene
epinicion
open score
up and down
up-and-down
spongebag
spinneret
sponge off
spanaemia
spanaemic
spaniel it
spongeous
sponte sua
open-weave
spiniform
open-chain
Apennines
open-field
sponsible
spongiose
spongious
epinikian
open skies
epinikion
spinal tap
spangling
spindling
Spanglish
spineless
spinulose
spinulate
spinulous
eponymous
open-ended
spininess
upon words
opinioned
sponsored
up-and-over
open court
open house
open-armed
open order
spin-dried
spin drier
spin dryer
spindrift
Upanishad
epinastic
up oneself
spinosity
open-steek
open stage
upon a time
epineural
spun sugar
spondulix
ependymal
spin a yarn
Spinozism
Spinozist
opsomania
opposable
epeolatry
ephoralty
ipso facto
spoonbait
spoonbill
upholding
opponency
optometer
optometry
spoon-feed
spoonfuls
splodgily
optophone
spoonhook
aphoriser
aphorizer
appointed
appointee
appointer
upbounden
up to snuff
appointor
up-country
up to speed
upholster
opportune
sprouting
uprooting
apportion
spoonworm
spoonwise
spoonways
apophasis
apophatic
epiphanic
epipolism
apiphobia
apoptosis
apoptotic
epiphragm
epiphytal
apophyses
epiphyses
apophysis
epiphysis
epiphytic
sport away
sportance
spermaria
spermatia
spermatic
spermatid
sportable
Spartacus
Aphra Behn
sperm bank
approbate
up-pricked
spark coil
sperm cell
spiracula
sporocarp
spore case
sporocyst
sporidial
sporidesm
Aphrodite
sporidium
sparterie
sparsedly
sparteine
spirogram
sporogeny
sporogony
spirogyra
spur wheel

archstone
orthotone
archetype
architype
orthotist
archducal
archduchy
archivolt
archivist
artisanal
trail away
arrivance
arrivancy
irritancy
ordinance
urticaria
drainable
irrigable
irritable
irritably
trailable
trainable
Craigavon
irrigator
irritator
ordinaire
fruit body
fruit beer
trail bike
trainband
fruit cage
fruitcake
braincase
brain-dead
train down
armigeral
cruiseway
praiseach
broiderer
fruiterer
Praise You
praiseful
train fine
frying-pan
Orpington
Irvingism
Irvingite
freighter
ornithoid
artichoke
fraîcheur
druidical
✧artificer
arrivisme
arriviste
vraicking
treillage
armillary
arpillera
artillery
Braillist
brainless
fruitless
trailless
trainless
argillite
orgillous
train mile
frailness
traitorly
drainpipe
arbitrage
arris rail
orris-root
arbitrary
arbitress
traitress
arbitrate
arbitrium
Artie Shaw
brainsick
grain side
brainstem
orgiastic
croissant
traipsing
drain-trap
armistice
fruit tree
arris tile
drain-tile
fruit tart
articular
orbicular
irriguous
fruitwood
brainwash
Ernie Wise
brainwave
a rainy day
projector
prejudice
prejudize
Trojan War
Prajapati
frikkadel
Erik Satie
brake drum
brake-fade
Prokofiev
Erika Hess
Prakritic
brakeless
Broken Bay
broken man
urokinase
brake pads
brokerage
prokaryon
prokaryot
brakesman
brake shoe
krakowiak
arillated
pre-loaded
trilobate
Trilobita
trilobite
prolicide
frolicked
prolactin
prelector
preludial
urolagnia
orologist
prologise
urologist
prologize
drillhole
trellised
brilliant
trillions
prolamine
Sri Lankan
trilinear
prolonger
dry lining
drollness
trollopee
prolepses
prolepsis
proleptic
prolapsus
Brylcreem®
grill room
arblaster
drillship
artlessly
prolusion
prelusory
prolusory
prelusive
prelatial
trilithic
urolithic
prolately
prelation
prolation
trilithon
prelature
proletary
prelatess
prelatise
prelatish
prelatism
prelatist
uralitise
prolative
prelatize
uralitize
grillwork
prolixity
trilby hat
✧brummagem
grammatic
trim marks
crammable
drum table
drum-major
cramp ball
cramp-bone
crampbark
promachos
cremocarp
trump card
prime cost
dromedare
dromedary
primaeval
trumpeted
trumpeter
drum-belly
trampette
trumped-up
bromoform
cramp-fish
Cro-Magnon
krummholz
from where
krummhorn
tramlined
tramlines
trimmings
Grampians
cramp-iron
crimpiest
crumbiest
crummiest
bromeliad
crumblies
tremblier
bromelain
grimalkin
brambling
Crimplene®
crumpling
grumbling
primuline
trampling
tremblant
trembling
tremolant
tremulant
crimeless
gremolata
primality
tremolite
tremulate
tremulous
Primo Levi
Dramamine®
Gramineae
promenade
Preminger
trominoes
Fremantle
prominent
brominism
griminess
premonish
primeness
criminate
criminous
primrosed
trampolin
primipara
drum brake
primarily
cramp-ring
prime rate
trimerous
Grimm's law
cremaster
trimester
premosaic
promuscis
promising
promissor
crumb-tray
primatial
primitiae
primitial
primitias
dramatics
drumstick
Trematoda
trematode
trematoid
trimetric
prime time
prime-time
brimstone
brimstony
prompting
cremation
premotion
promotion
prompt box
crematory
dramaturg
premature
prompture
aromatise
dramatise
dramatist
eremitism
✧primitive
promotive
trimethyl
aromatize
dramatize
prom queen
✧primavera
framework
crime wave
grind away
grandaddy
frontager
iron-cased
truncated
Zrenjanin
cranially
drinkable
grantable
printable
transaxle
grand-aunt
brinjarry
Franz Boas
prongbuck
prenubile
wring bolt
Franz Bopp
cranachan
wry-necked
trunk call
transcend
crankcase
irenicism
grand coup
Grenadian
grenadier
wrongdoer
grand duke
✧grenadine
front door
bring down
grind down
Orangeman
Prince Hal
cranreuch
orangeade
brandered
princelet
trinketer
Bronze Age
Frankenia
orange-tip
princekin
drunkenly
trancedly
transenna
transeunt
princedom
Princeton
cranberry
trinketry
Orangeism
princesse
transfect
gronefull
trunkfuls
wrong-foot
Frankfort
Frankfurt
transfard
transform
transfuse
trunkfish
branchiae
branchial
bronchial
Frenchman
grindhval
printhead
branchlet
crunchier
branch off
Frenchify
drink-hail
Trondheim
crunchily
Frans Hals
bring home
transhume
branching
trenchand
trenchant
wrenching
French pox
truncheon
branchery
French fry
pronghorn
trenchard
franchise
trunk hose
branch out
Araneidae
crinoidal
frenzical
principal
Brunhilde
Crinoidea
iron-miner
iron-sided
Ironsides
Arondight
principia
frangible
franticly
principle
transient
brand-iron
frontiers
crankiest
grandiose
trendiest
grand jury
crenelled
crinklier
wrinklies
irenology
uranology
urinology
✧franglais
granuloma
brandling
brangling
crinoline
front line
front-line
trunk line
wrangling
prunellos
granulary
frontless
granulose
printless
trunkless
crenelate
crenulate
granulate
granulite
translate
granulous
grand luxe
trinomial
grund mail
trunk-mail
grandmama
Franz Marc
ironsmith
transmute
transmove
Brunonian
Groningen
pronuncio
droningly
brand name
brininess
crankness
frankness
grandness
proneness
wrongness
uraninite
bring over
transomed
francolin
Prontosil®
transonic
ironworks
iron mould
iron-bound
iron horse
front-page
✧grand prix
drone-pipe
grandpapa
transpire
transport
transpose
trunk road
Mrs Norris
front-rank
Iron Cross
brandreth
Iron Crown
grand slam
wrong side
prankster
trans-ship
transship
dronishly
pranksome
print shop

grandsire
uraniscus
prenotify
granitoid
trinitrin
ironstone
arenation
crenation
prenotion
pronation
urination
crenature
Grand Turk
granitise
granitite
Grand Tour
urinative
granitize
orang-utan
pronounce
transumpt
granivore
transvest
Brunswick
frontward
grunt work
trunkwork
frontwise
frontways
iron oxide
pranayama
brondyron
Grundyism
trendyism
arrogance
areolated
ergomania
Argonauts
Areopagus
crookback
broomball
proof coin
cryoscope
cryoscopy
preoccupy
broom-corn
Arnold Bax
orlop deck
preordain
areometer
cryometer
ergometer
eriometer
kryometer
cryogenic
crookedly
orgone box
arboreous
arboretum
erroneous
o're-office
arrowhead
Bryophyta
bryophyte
Armorican
Oriolidae
arbovirus
brooklime
errorless
proofless
prooemion
proof-mark
prooemium
Dr Johnson
droop nose
brood over
drool over
ergonomic
proofread
cryoprobe
arrowroot
broomrape
ergograph
groomsman
arrow-slit
priorship
troopship
arrow-shot
areostyle
preoption
proof text
preocular
Ernö Rubik
brookweed
arrowwood
arrowworm
trionymal
orepearch
crop-eared
cryptadia
crop-marks
drape coat
prepacked
drop-scene
drop scone
trepidant
propodeon
propodeum
tripudium
fripperer
Triple sec
trip meter
graphemic
prophetic
tropaeola
gruppetti
gruppetto
uropygial
propagule
propagate
uropygium
prop shaft
crapshoot
cryptical
dropsical
graphical
trephiner
droppings
trappings
wrappings
graphitic
graphicly
trippiest
propriety
Trappists
prepollex
propelled
propeller
propylaea
tropology
crapulent
crepoline
crippling
propylene
propulsor
grapeless
propylite
crapulous
trepanned
trepanner
gripingly
gropingly
treponema
treponeme
propanone
proponent
crepiness
drepanium
cryptogam
triploidy
drop-forge
proptosis
cropbound
wrap round
wrapround
cryptonym
draperied
draperies
properdin
drop-drill
troparion
drop-press
grapeseed
gripe's egg
drape suit
tropistic
crêpe sole
crepuscle
trapesing
grapeshot
prepostor
tripe-shop
preputial
trap stick
grapetree
pro patria
trap-stair
✧tripitaka
crepitant
dripstone
dropstone
prepotent
crepitate
grapevine
tripe-wife
trophying
triptyque
trapezial
trapezoid
trapezium
trapezius
croquante
frequence
frequency
triquetra
briquette
croquette
Iroquoian
prorector
prerecord
triradial
prurience
pruriency
prorogate
drerihead
Drury Lane
pro re nata
propylite
Dr Crippen
ore-rested
prerosion
ororotund
proration
ore-raught
Dr Proudie
brush away
Ernst Abbe
Aristarch
Crustacea
crustated
urn-shaped
prismatic
prostatic
crushable
graspable
trustable
Cresta Run
crush a cup
crossbeam
truss beam
crossbuck
crossbred
cross bill
crossbill
brass band
crossband
wristband
press book
grassbird
Pressburg
crossbite
frostbite
dress coat
arcsecond
prosector
trisector
grass carp
prosecute
presidial
prosodial
prosodian
trust deed
president
presidios
wrist drop
prosodist
presidium
crash dive
crash-dive
dress down
crescendo
crosiered
cross-eyed
freshener
triskeles
brasserie
triskelia
dry sherry
tristesse
crossette
freshen up
cross-fade
crossfall
trust fund
brush fire
crossfire
dress form
crossfish
press gang
press-gang
trisagion
crosshead
grasshook
preschool
eristical
prosaical
Aristides
tristichs
grisaille
irascible
irascibly
Priscilla
crescioni
dry skiing
prescient
brassiere
brassière
crispiest
crustiest
trashiest
trustiest
prussiate
prescious
crossjack
cross-kick
prusiking
preselect
drysalter
frostlike
grass-like
bristling
crash-land
cross-link
frost line
grassland
grass line
wrestling
crestless
crustless
frostless
graspless
grassless
gross loss
trustless
proselyte
Prosimiae
prosimian
Ernst Mach
frusemide
gris-amber
dressmake
grist-mill
Irish mile
irksomely
erasement
presuming
pressmark
Irish moss
grass moth
prison van
brass neck
presentee
presenter
frost-nail
pre-senile
presently
brashness
briskness
crassness
crispness
crossness
freshness
grossness
Irishness
prosiness
prisonous
erosional
crossover
uroscopic
Aristotle
frescoing
Gros Morne
gros point
frescoist
prose poem
grass-plot
grassquit
crossroad
prescribe
proscribe
preserver
preserves
cross-ruff
Ernst Röhm
grosgrain
grass-rake
pre-shrink
crush room
pressroom
grass rope
prescript
proscript
erostrate
frustrate
prostrate
Irish stew
dress suit
cross-sill
Irish Scot
wrist shot
press stud
crosstree
grass tree
trashtrie
cross-talk
irisation
crash-test
prosateur
crosstown
grossular
orestunck
Ernst Udet
pressures
tressured
proseucha
proseuche
brusquely
press upon
try square
prescutum
brisé volé
Prestwick
crosswalk
crosswind
brushwood
brassware
brushwork
crossword
crosswort
frostwork
presswork
crosswise
crossways
presbyter
presbytic
presbyope
presbyopy
write away
Bretwalda
writ large
Brittania
Brittanic
protoavis
prothalli
write-back
frithborh
protected
britschka
graticule
triticale
arctic fox
✧protector
Briticise
Briticism
criticise
criticism
eroticise
eroticism
eroticist
fruticose
triticism
Briticize
criticize
eroticize
truth drug
write down
write-down
erythemal
fritterer
prothesis
prothetic
brotherly
tritheism
tritheist
brute fact
brutified
gratified
gratifier
cratefuls
froth-fomy
Arctogaea
frithgild
protogine
protogyny
dratchell
erstwhile
fratching
crotchety
fratchety
Pratchett
Arctiidae
erethitic
proteinic
Bratsk Dam
erotology
brutelike
truthlike
brittlely

brattling
crotaline
Fritz Lang
gratulant
brutalise
brutalism
brutalist
crotalism
frothless
trothless
truthless
wrathless
brutality
gratulate
brutalize
protamine
Britomart
Aretinian
✧breton hat
pretended
pretender
arytenoid
Britannia
Britannic
cretinoid
croton oil
gratingly
pratingly
protonema
protanope
tritanope
protandry
Britoness
bruteness
cretinise
cretinism
irateness
triteness
gratinate
B rotundum
cretinous
Croton bug
prytaneum
cretinize
prothorax
write-once
trot-cosey
Brittonic
Brythonic
trattoria
trattorie
fretboard
frat house
arctophil
fraternal
oratorial
✧oratorian
pretermit
erythrina
troth ring
criterion
oratorios
erythrism
preterist
writeress
erythrite
preterite
triturate
craterous
protostar
Britisher
✧protester
bretasche
protistic
brutishly
✧protestor
grotesque
✧proto team
gratitude
gritstone
prototype
writative
proteuses
fretfully
grate upon
bratwurst
protoxide
prettyish
prettyism
protozoal
protozoan
protozoic
protozoon
✧araucaria
traumatic
groupable
grauncher
trouncing
groundman
ground oak
ground ice
groundsel
groundage
grounding
groundhog
ground-ash
groundnut
ground run
ground ivy
ground-ivy
Argus-eyed
trousered
trout farm
draughter
grouchily
draught ox
wrought-up
Ursulines
troubling
troutling
troutless
troublous
proudness
triumphal
proud-pied
triumpher
fraudsman
trousseau
fraudster
Proustian
croustade
arcuation
irruption
proustite
irruptive
arduously
triumviri
triumvirs
triumviry
groupware
group work
groupwork
driveable
proveable
proveably
trivially
gravy boat
drive belt
provocant
Dravidian
gravadlax
bravadoes
privadoes
provident
providing
provedore
gravidity
drive home
travailed
prevail on
provoking
drivelled
driveller
gravelled
grovelled
groveller
travelled
traveller
trivalved
privilege
gravel-pit
groveling
prevalent
provolone
traveling
trivalent
graveless
frivolity
frivolous
brevi manu
gravamina
Provençal
preventer
provender
provinces
graveness
drove road
preverbal
pre-vernal
traversal
traversed
traverser
Mr Average
travertin
driver ant
✧privy seal
graveside
provisoes
yravished
Gravesend
prevision
provision
provisory
provostry
gravy-soup
brevetted
cravatted
privateer
privately
drive time
breveting
gravitron
privation
privatise
gravitate
privative
privatize
graveyard
browsable
draw-table
brown bear
draw a bead
brown bill
crow's-bill
crown-bark
brown Bess
brown coal
crown cork
draw level
tri-weekly
crowberry
crow's-feet
crow's-foot
trawl-fish
crown gall
crown-head
draw-sheet
growthist
drowsihed
grow tired
crawliest
dry-waller
trowelled
troweller
brown lung
crown land
draw blank
trawl-line
crewelist
crownless
draw-plate
grow angry
brownness
crow's-nest
draw poker
brow-bound
grewhound
brew-house
crowfoots
crown-post
brown rice
frowardly
brown spar
prowessed
crowd sail
crow-steps
crow-quill
frown upon
crownwork
drawn work
Brix scale
proxemics
proximate
proximity
argy-bargy
graywacke
greywacke
arty-farty
greyscale
greybeard
arsy-versy
arhythmia
arhythmic
grey whale
tray cloth
pray in aid
prayingly
grey mould
greyhound
army corps
dray-horse
grey goose
✧grey friar
prayer mat
prayerful
prayer rug
greystone
frizzante
crazy bone
prize crew
cruzadoes
crazy golf
cruzeiros
Brazilian
brazilein
brazeless
prize list
Brazil nut
prozymite
craziness
prize ring
Islamabad
assayable
escapable
escalator
asparagus
estate car
escape key
escabeche
ashamedly
essayette
estafette
Ascaridae
ismatical
ascarides
estaminet
Islamitic
Ismailian
assaulter
assailant
establish
Ismailism
Israelite
Ismailiya
espagnole
usualness
Asian pear
V S Naipaul
Osnabrück
Kshatriya
aspartame
ash-bucket
use-by date
usability
ash-blonde
isobathic
isocratic
isocyclic
isochimal
isoclinal
psychical
isoclinic
psychogas
as accords
psychoses
isochoric
psychosis
psychotic
usucapion
isochrone
isocrymal
isodomous
isodontal
Isidorian
esperance
as regards
Esperanto
assembler
assez bien
ascendant
ascendent
ascending
osteoderm
osmeteria
usherette
Isle of Man
Isle of Rum
ashen-grey
aspergill
osteogeny
Asperger's
Essex Girl
ascetical
osteology
aspen-like
osteopath
aspersoir
ushership
✧ascension
aspersion
aspersory
ostensory
ascensive
aspersive
ostensive
aspectual
essential
ascertain
osteotome
osteotomy
asbestine
assertion
assertory
asbestous
assentive
assertive
isoenzyme
asafetida
isagogics
isogamete
isogamous
isogenous
asthmatic
ischiadic
ischiatic
escheator
isohyetal
ischaemia
ischaemic
asphalter
asphaltic
asphaltum
Esthonian
asphyxial
oscitancy
osmic acid
estimable
estimably
aspirator
estimator
ostinatos
W S Gilbert
Islington
astichous
ascitical
aspidioid
oscillate
ostiolate
espionage
assientos
Issigonis
Eskimo dog
ossifraga
ossifrage
assistant
ossicular
assiduity
assiduous
ossifying
Ashkhabad
Isokontae
isokontan
Ashkenazi
Ashkenazy
psalm-book
psalteria
isologous
Psyllidae
esplanade
esclandre
asplenium
isallobar
psalmodic
asclepiad
asclepias
Asclepios
Asclepius
ashlaring
ashlering
ostleress
psaltress
uselessly
as all that
psalm-tune
isolation
isolative
asymmetry
psammitic
esemplasy
isomerase
isomerise
isomerism
isomerous
isomerize
isometric
asymptote
isoniazid
asyndetic
asyndeton
isinglass
isonomous
asininely
asininity
asynergia
isenergic
as and when
assonance

Oshogatsu
ascorbate
osmometer
osmometry
escopette
Escoffier
associate
asmoulder
assoilzie
astounded
estoppage
estopping
ascospore
espousals
escortage
iso-octane
osso bucco
as you were
esophagus
isopycnic
isopodous
isopteran
psephitic
isopolity
asepalous
isopropyl
psoriasis
psoriatic
Tsar's Bell
escribano
ostracean
Ostracoda
Ostracion
ostracise
ostracism
astrocyte
ostracize
astraddle
astrodome
esurience
esuriency
usurpedly
astrofell
astragali
astragals
Ostrogoth
astrakhan
astrolabe
astrology
estrildid
ashramite
astringer
estranged
estranger
astrantia
astronomy
astronaut
estrapade
astrophel
espressos
AstroTurf®
usurp upon
tsarevich
isostatic
isosceles
isosteric
isosmotic
Psittacus
isotactic
isotheral
tsetse fly
as it comes
isotropic
esoterica
Esztergom
esoterism
Ashtaroth
Ashtoreth
assurance
pseudaxis
assumable
assumably
assurable
assumedly
assuredly
assuaging
assurgent
astucious
Esquiline
issueless
Esquimaux
espumosos
pseudopod
pseudonym
assumpsit
estuarial
estuarian
estuarine
esquiress
assuasive
assuetude
asexually
stratagem
stramaçon
stramazon
St-Nazaire
steamboat
straw boss
steam bath
steam coal
strategic
steamed up
steadfast
straggler
strangler
strangles
strangely
strap-game
étrangère
strangury
strap-hang
steam-haul
Steadicam®
steatitic
ottavinos
steam iron
steadiest
strawlike
strapline
strayling
strapless
strawless
attainder
Mt Rainier
straining
steam open
steatosis
stratonic
strappado
straw poll
strapping
steam port
Stranraer
steam room
stearsman
straw-stem
steamship
Stralsund
Atlantean
steam trap
Utraquism
Utraquist
straw vote
straw wine
strap work
strapwort
straw-work
strawworm
steadying
stable lad
stableman
stable fly
stableboy
stabilise
stabilate
stability
stabilize
stoccatas
stackable
stack arms
staccatos
sticcados
sticcatos
stoccados
stock cube
stock dove
sticheron
stick 'em up!
stock farm
stockfish
Stockholm
stockhorn
stockinet
stockings
stichidia
stocklock
stockless
stocklist
atacamite
CT scanner
stockpile
Stockport
stackroom
stockroom
stickseed
stocktake
stickweed
stock whip
stickwork
stockwork
sticky end
stackyard
stockyard
stadia rod
studiedly
studentry
stud poker
stud horse
stud groom
utterance
athematic
steerable
utterable
Athenaeum
steel beam
steenbras
steel band
Ethelbert
steel-blue
ytterbium
steel-clad
stretched
stretcher
attendant
steel drum
etceteras
athetesis
steeped in
ethereous
steel-gray
steel-grey
steelhead
etherical
strelitzi
streakily
streaking
steenkirk
atheology
steerling
utterless
stream-ice
streamlet
stream-tin
streaming
strewment
uttermost
St Bernard
otherness
steepness
utterness
atheromas
athetosic
athetosis
athetotic
attempter
St George's
Athelstan
steersman
atheistic
at leisure
stressful
stress out
steel trap
streetcar
streetage
it beats me
attention
streetboy
streetful
attentive
attenuant
attenuate
strenuity
strenuous
Ethelwulf
steel wool
steelware
steelwork
otherwise
Steely Dan
steelyard
staff duty
stiffener
stuffed up
stuff gown
stiff neck
stiffness
staffroom
staff-tree
stuff them
stiffware
at a glance
stag-dance
stagnancy
Stigmaria
stigmatic
stag party
stegodont
stage door
stage-dive
staggered
staggerer
stage hand
stag's horn
stag night
stage left
stage name
staginess
stegnosis
stegnotic
staghound
stage play
Stagirite
Stagyrite
stegosaur
Atahualpa
at the full
at the fore
Stahlhelm
at the most
itchiness
at the time
Mt Kilauea
ethically
stoically
Steinbeck
steinbock
steinbuck
strip cell
St Vincent
staircase
strip club
strip down
strike pay
stridence
stridency
strike off
strike oil
at liberty
strifeful
strike out
strikeout
stairfoot
string-bag
string pea
string tie
stringily
strigging
stringent
stringing
Stringops
string out
stairhead
a thick ear
steinkirk
strip-leaf
stairlift
stridling
stripling
stainless
strip mall
strip mill
strip mine
staidness
Ethiopian
stripping
Attic salt
St Tib's Eve
a thin time
striation
striature
stricture
strictish
Itaipu Dam
utricular
utriculus
stairwell
stairwork
stairwise
stake boat
stokehold
stokehole
Stokes' law
stellated
stylebook
stillborn
stiltbird
stylobate
stalactic
italicise
Italicism
italicize
stolidity
stalk-eyed
stellerid
stiltedly
stall-feed
styliform
otologist
still-head
still hunt
still-hunt
still life
still-life
stalkless
styleless
stylolite
Ptolemaic
stalemate
Mt Olympus
staleness
Stalinism
Stalinist
stillness
stalworth
stillroom
stylistic
stylishly
athletics
utilities
otolithic
stilettos
stellular
at a low ebb
stomachal
stomached
stomacher
stomachic
atomicity
stamp duty
stomodeum
stammerer
ethmoidal
etymology
stimulant
stimulate
stamp mill
stamineal
staminode
staminody
staminoid
staminate
stamp note
atemporal
atomistic
stump work
standards
stingaree
stannator
stoneboat
stand bail
stingbull
stink ball
Stand by Me
stink bomb
stinkbird
stone bass
stonechat
stone coal
ethnocide
stone cell
stone-cold
stonecrop
at any cost
ethnicism
stonecast
atonicity
ethnicity
stone-dead
stone-deaf
ctenidium
stand down
stand-down
Ständerat
stander-by
stonkered
stintedly
stand easy
cteniform
stand fire
stand firm
stand fast
stingfish
stonefish
standgale
stand good
at any hand
stanching
stonehand
stanchion
stinkhorn
stone-hard
stone hawk
stenciled
sting into
ethnology
stone-lily

auric acid
Lusitania
mucic acid
puritanic
Ruritania
cubically
dubitable
dubitably
judicable
ludically
musically
fumigator
judicator
mutilator
ruminator
subimagos
supinator
luminaire
audio book
Rubiaceae
quail-call
auriscope
music case
subincise
music-demy
audio disc
audio disk
Judi Dench
luminesce
luciferin
rubicelle
A Universe
muniments
rudiments
pumiceous
rubineous
cut it fine
run it fine
cubic foot
audiogram
tuning key
tuning peg
tuning pin
music hall
music-hall
audiphone
punishing
Munichism
Culicidae
juridical
lunitidal
municipal
Pulicidae
cubic inch
Euripides
humiliant
munitions
auxiliary
judiciary
humiliate
judicious
musicking
fusillade
audiology
pupillage
pupillary
curialism
curialist
eudialyte
pupillate
put in mind
audiencia
fusionism
fusionist
humidness
lucidness
luridness
tumidness
lunisolar
tubicolar
auditoria
Tuticorin
audiophil
Lucia Popp
quail-pipe
music rack
music roll
music room
tulip root
auditress
duricrust
tutiorism
tutiorist
juniority
ludicrous
pupilship
run itself
Cupid's bow
curiosity
dubiosity
furiosity
juliet cap
tulip tree
audiotape
auricular
cuticular
funicular
rus in urbe
curiously
dubiously
dutifully
furiously
funiculus
tulipwood
Punic Wars
Mutiny Act
mutinying
purifying
rubifying
cubic yard
nutjobber
outjockey
subjected
subjacent
sub judice
subjugate
Punjaubee
buck naked
muck-raker
bulk cargo
bulk large
buck-wagon
Puck-hairy
huckaback
buckyball
muck about
Turkicise
Buck's Club
Turkicize
hunky-dory
luckie-dad
sunk fence
buck fever
luck-penny
musk melon
busk after
duck's-foot
✧buck's fizz
buckwheat
Turk's head
musk-sheep
musk shrew
tusk shell
buck's-horn
buckthorn
buckshish
duckshove
buckskins
cuckoldly
musk gland
musk-plant
cuckoldom
cuckoldry
duck's-meat
muck-a-muck
Turkomans
Burkinabé
muckender
quakingly
bulkiness
duskiness
funkiness
huskiness
junkiness
luckiness
muckiness
murkiness
muskiness
punkiness
quakiness
sulkiness
musk-pouch
cuckoo bee
suck-holer
cuckoo fly
buckhound
buckboard
duck-board
bunkhouse
bucktooth
cuckoo-bud
Euskarian
tuckerbag
Junkerdom
Quakerdom
tuckerbox
Junkerism
Quakeress
Quakerish
Quakerism
Quaker gun
tucker out
sun-kissed
buckishly
duskishly
buckytube
junketeer
musketeer
bucketing
junketing
musketoon
huckstery
bucketful
mucksweat
✧turkey oak
turkey hen
Turkey red
buckayros
bull-dance
curlpaper
cut-leaved
full-faced
nucleated
pull baker
pull faces
rue-leaved
fuel gauge
full marks
nucleator
bully-beef
bugle-band
pull about
public bar
public law
public act
cup lichen
public-key
bugle-call
full-scale
duplicand
full score
public art
publicise
publicist
duplicate
duplicity
publicity
publicize
Euclidean
pull devil
guillemot
oubliette
tuillette
pull a face
nullified
nullifier
qualified
qualifier
Guildford
mudlogger
pull ahead
bullwhack
full whack
bull whale
guildhall
gully-hole
bugle-horn
bull shark
bullfinch
full pitch
full-timer
purloiner
bullfight
Kubla Khan
full blues
full fling
full-blood
full blast
full-blast
guileless
guiltless
qualmless
pullulate
full-blown
sublimely
subliming
Tullamore
Muslimism
sublimise
sublimate
sublimity
sublimize
Dublin Bay
outlinear
sublinear
full and by
Ausländer
cullender
outlander
euglenoid
puy lentil
bull snake
Dubliners
sublunary
burliness
curliness
surliness
run length
sublunate
nucleolar
bulldozer
bull-nosed
mullioned
guilloche
cullionly
bull point
full-bound
full point
pull round
bull-board
full board
full house
nucleolus
full-speed
full split
full-split
nullipara
nullipore
pull apart
full-cream
full organ
full-orbed
butlerage
fullerene
full-front
bully-rook
full dress
full-dress
bull trout
full-grown
guildsman
publisher
sublessee
dualistic
bullishly
gutlessly
sublessor
outlustre
burlesque
sublethal
bully-tree
qualitied
qualities
subletter
Wurlitzer®
bulletrie
guilt trip
sublation
outlaunce
outlaunch
sun lounge
bugle-weed
bull's wool
quillwort
tummy ache
hummocked
submicron
mummy-case
submucosa
submucous
mummified
mummiform
nutmegged
duumviral
hummeller
pummelled
surmullet
nummuline
nummulary
bummaloti
nummulite
submental
augmented
augmenter
summonses
Augmentin®
outmantle
culminant
fulminant
augmentor
mud minnow
pulmonary
dumminess
gumminess
rumminess
culminate
fulminate
Pulmonata
pulmonate
fulminous
submentum
summing-up
Mummerset
submerged
submersed
summerset
summarily
murmuring
submarine
summering
summarise
summarist
jus mariti
murmurous
summarize
surmaster
submissly
surmising
gummosity
tummy tuck
submitted
submitter
summiteer
submatrix
summation
gummatous
summative
guinea hen
guinea pig
turntable
funny bone
turn about
turnabout
turn-screw
burnt cork
burnt-cork
pugnacity
quinidine
burned out
turn-penny
Juan Perón
Turnberry
quintette
quintetti
quintetto
funny farm
tunny fish
turn again
turnagain
✧bunny girl
Funny Girl
ruin agate
funny ha-ha
quenching
quantical
quinoidal
funnelled
funnel-net
funnel-web
tunnelled
tunneller
tunnel net
quinoline
quinolone
tunneling
outnumber
quand même
buonamani
buonamano
furniment
quinonoid
burningly
cunningly
punningly
runningly
funniness
sunniness
turn round
turnround
turn loose
turn forth
turnip fly
turnip top
subnormal
Turnerian
nunneries
quintroon
vulnerary
vulnerate
runners-up
burnt sack
sunny side
turn aside
burnisher
furnished
furnisher
buona sera

Words marked ✧ can also be spelled with one or more capital letters

turnstile
turnstone
nunnation
ruination
furniture
subneural
quintuple
quintuply
ruinously
quinquina
subniveal
subnivean
Guinevere
guanazolo
Tudor arch
automated
cupolated
Hugo Capet
Mucorales
autogamic
automatic
aurorally
humorally
automaton
autolatry
put on airs
out-of-body
autoscopy
mutoscope
ouroscopy
out of curl
out of cash
autos-da-fé
out-of-door
out of date
out-of-date
dupondius
auxometer
autogenic
autotelic
autoreply
suboffice
humongous
Putonghua
autophoby
Europhobe
autophagy
Europhile
Lusophile
autophony
out of hand
bucolical
autotimer
sudorific
eulogiums
autogiros
autopilot
autopista
out of line
autoflare
humorless
autoclave
ug-of-love
out of mind
buxomness
autosomal
autonomic
autotoxic
autotoxin
umotoris
utopoint

ouroboros
Eurocorps
Europoort
autoroute
autofocus
Eurospeak
out of play
autocracy
dulocracy
Eurocracy
autograft
autocrime
au courant
autograph
autotroph
auxotroph
autocross
Tudor rose
put on side
out of step
put on sail
tutorship
out of sync
Junoesque
out of time
out of tune
put option
out of true
suboctave
out-of-town
subocular
autoguide
tucotucos
out of work
out-of-work
autolysis
autolytic
autocycle
autogyros
Autolycus
outplacer
pump-water
sulphatic
vulpicide
nutpecker
suspected
Vulpecula
suspicion
auspicate
cuspidore
cuspidate
subpoena'd
jump leads
yuppie flu
yuppiedom
dub poetry
puppyhood
supplicat
surprisal
surpliced
surprised
surpriser
suppliant
bumptious
gumptious
mumpsimus
sumpsimus
sulphinyl
bumpology
culpa lata
puppy love

suspended
suspender
suspenser
suspensor
bumpiness
dumpiness
jumpiness
lumpiness
pulpiness
vulpinism
vulpinite
pulp novel
pulpboard
sulphonyl
bumper car
purpureal
Wuppertal
dump truck
out-porter
supporter
sun parlor
out-parish
suppurate
dumpishly
lumpishly
mumpishly
purposely
supposing
purposive
rump steak
turpitude
pulpiteer
puppeteer
put-putted
pulpstone
subpotent
bump-start
culpatory
jump-start
lump sugar
outpourer
sulphuret
sulphuric
sumptuary
sumptuous
sulphuryl
gunpowder
Bud Powell
supply day
supplying
Humpty Doo
subphylum
surquedry
turquoise
guardable
turribant
guard-book
rubrician
curricula
guard cell
currycomb
✧hurricane
hurricano
lubricant
lubricate
lubricity
rubricate
lubricous
outredden
putridity
puerperal

quartered
aubrietia
quercetin
guardedly
hurriedly
quarterly
quartette
quartetti
quartetto
quercetum
putrefied
surrogacy
outrigger
subregion
subrogate
surrogate
guard hair
murrained
surreined
guerrilla
Muirfield
outraigne
Guarnieri
surrejoin
currajong
kurrajong
curry-leaf
outrelief
guardless
puerilism
puerility
querulous
supremacy
au premier
au fromage
supremely
nutriment
querimony
supremity
fun runner
guaranies
guarantee
gunrunner
outrunner
quarenden
quarender
rum runner
surrender
currently
purringly
guarantor
surrendry
furriness
mucronate
outrooper
eucryphia
eutrophic
eutrapely
eutropous
guardrail
guard ring
guardroom
guardsman
guard's van
quirister
buprestid
Buprestis
guard-ship
guardship
hubristic
currishly

sunrising
run-resist
Cupressus
buhrstone
burrstone
nutrition
Lucretius
turret gun
lucrative
nutritive
Dubrovnik
burrawang
currawong
quarryman
quarry-sap
quarrying
quartzose
quartzite
Huascarán
puissance
pursuance
substance
run scared
Dunstable
guessable
pursuable
puissaunt
guest beer
Russ Abbot
nuts about
subsacral
subsecive
outside in
outsiders
subsidise
subsidize
sub specie
Russified
pussyfoot
bursiform
subschema
putschist
Mutsuhito
subsoiler
gumshield
outskirts
Zugspitze
Mussulman
vulsellae
Kunstlied
musselled
Mussulmen
ourselves
subsellia
nurselike
Mussolini
nurseling
nun's-flesh
pulseless
subsultus
vulsellum
Quasimodo
nursemaid
fulsomely
subsample
Hudson Bay
cuisinier
nuisancer
cursenary
out-sentry
curstness

fussiness
gutsiness
mussiness
pursiness
outspoken
Russophil
bursarial
cursorial
outspread
subscribe
substract
substruct
sunstruck
subseries
sunscreen
outstrain
outstrike
sunstroke
cursorily
outspring
guest-room
guest rope
subscript
cursorary
sussarara
questrist
pulse-rate
substrata
substrate
subsystem
subsist in
pulsatile
gusseting
nurse-tend
russeting
pulsation
cursitory
pulsatory
Hussitism
mussitate
guts it out
pulsative
outsource
sun spurge
cursively
suasively
guesswork
guestwise
pulse-wave
substylar
quittance
australes
cultrated
outtravel
quetzales
quite a few
Luftwaffe
Australia
Aunt Sally
rusty-back
just about
justiciar
rusticial
mustaches
mustachio
rusticise
rusticism
rusticate
rusticity
rusticize
custodial

custodian
ducted fan
quotidian
custodier
must needs
furtherer
murtherer
dust devil
suttletie
Kurt Weill
sutteeism
hunt after
justified
justifier
lust after
multifoil
dusty-foot
multiform
butty-gang
fustigate
Muz Tag Ata
lustihead
dustsheet
butt-shaft
multihull
lustihood
Dusty Hare
curtailer
sustained
sustainer
butt hinge
duettinos
curtain up
curtilage
fustilugs
quitclaim
musteline
pustulant
pultaloon
subtilise
ductility
pustulate
pustulous
curtalaxe
subtilize
multimode
Guatemala
Sun Temple
customary
custumary
customise
customize
Huttonian
Justinian
mutton ham
suntanned
rusty nail
cuttingly
juttingly
subtenant
sustinent
subtenure
dustiness
fustiness
gustiness
lustiness
mustiness
nuttiness
rustiness
sultaness
austenite

sultanate
outtongue
Suetonius
tuitional
dust cover
Kurt Gödel
subtropic
Bunthorne
Kurt Jooss
subtopian
multipack
multipede
multiplet
multiplex
multipara
juxtapose
auctorial
butterfat
butter pat
cut-throat
gutter-man
Hunterian
suctorial
suctorian
butter oil
subtorrid
austerely
butterfly
mud turtle
multirole
butterine
dust-brand
guttering
muttering
nurturant
vulturine
butter-box
dustproof
rustproof
culturist
dust-brush
guitarist
vulturish
vulturism
austerity
butterbur
buttercup
butternut
muster out
putter-out
vulturous
run to seed
Cutty Sark
cutty-sark
out to stud
multitude
subtitles
curtation
gustation
guttation
luctation
quotation
quotition
ructation
dust storm
gustatory
multitask
gustative
quotative
multiuser
hurtfully
lustfully
dust bunny
furtively
cultivate
multi-wall
tuptowing
Guru Nanak
cumulated
lunulated
tubulated
Tubularia
suturally
Bujumbura
Burundian
purulence
purulency
humungous
eunuchoid
eunuchise
eunuchism
eunuchize
lupulinic
luxuriant
luxuriate
luxurious
queue-jump
Lucullean
Lucullian
Nuku'alofa
mutualise
mutualism
mutualist
cucullate
mutuality
mutualize
vu quang ox
lucumones
susurrant
lucubrate
susurrate
augurship
subursine
Augustine
tucutucos
augur well
curveball
luvviedom
curviform
vulviform
surveille
pulvillar
pulvilled
pulvillio
pulvillus
nux vomica
pulvinule
curviness
pulvinate
subversal
culver-key
subverter
pulverine
quavering
quivering
pulverise
quiverish
pulverous
quiverful
pulverize
subvassal
curvesome
curvetted
curveting
curvation
curvature
curvative
surviving
surveying
nut-wrench
nut-weevil
jut-window
subwoofer
outworker
subwarden
tutworker
outwardly
outwitted
out with it!
quixotism
Eumycetes
Eutychian
eurytherm
ruby glass
jurywoman
jurywomen
eurytopic
duty-bound
Guayaquil
Sun Yat-Sen
pumy stone
muzzle-bag
puzzle-peg
puzzledom
puzzle out
quizzical
puzzolana
buzzingly
fuzziness
muzziness
Eve Arnold
aviatress
ovibovine
evacuator
Avicebrón
avocation
evocation
evocatory
evocative
oviductal
evidently
oviferous
avifaunal
evaginate
ovigerous
evagation
avoidance
available
availably
avoidable
avoidably
ivy-leaved
evolvable
evaluator
Ivy League
ovo-lactos
avalanche
evil-doing
evolution
ovulation
ovulatory
evolutive
ovalbumin
aventaile
Ivan Lendl
oven-ready
evangelic
avengeful
avant-goût
evincible
evincibly
eventless
oven glove
événement
even money
oven-roast
eventrate
evanition
avuncular
Ivan Bunin
eventuate
avoparcin
evaporate
evaporite
oviparity
oviparous
overcatch
overmatch
overwatch
overdated
overladen
overtaken
overwater
avertable
overhaile
overpaint
overhappy
overcarry
overhaste
overhasty
overvalue
everybody
overscore
overpedal
overperch
overreach
overreact
overheads
oversexed
overweigh
avertedly
overmerry
overweary
over again
averagely
ivory gate
overcheck
overshade
over-shoes
overwhelm
overshine
overshoot
overthrow
overshirt
every inch
overpitch
overrider
overripen
oversized
overtimer
overdight
overnight
oversight
avertible
eversible
overskirt
✧everglade
overalled
oversleep
avirulent
overgloom
every last
overclass
overflush
overplast
overcloud
overblown
overflown
overglaze
overinked
overcover
overjoyed
overpower
overtones
overtower
overgorge
overbound
overcount
overgoing
overmount
overwound
over to you!
overboard
Averroism
Averroist
overpoise
overroast
ivory-palm
overspill
overspend
overspent
oviraptor
overgreat
overprice
overtrick
overtrade
evergreen
overgreen
overdraft
overgrain
overtrain
overtrump
overprint
over proof
overproof
overdress
overgrass
overpress
overtrust
overwrest
overwrite
overproud
overdrive
overcrowd
overgrown
overgraze
overprize
Evaristus
overissue
overstock
overstudy
ivory-tree
oversteer
overstrew
overstaff
overstuff
overstain
overstand
overstink
overstunk
overstare
overstate
overruler
overtures
ever such a
overbuild
overlusty
uvarovite
overswear
everywhen
every whit
overswell
over-exact
overexert
overlying
a vast many
avisement
avisandum
avascular
evasively
ovational
eviternal
Eva Turner
ovotestes
ovotestis
evitation
avouterer
avizefull
avizandum
sweat band
two a penny
E W Maunder
sweat suit
sweatsuit
sweat shop
swear-word
two-by-four
two-bottle
twice-born
ewe-cheese
twice-laid
twice over
twice-told
two-decker
twaddling
twiddling
tweenager
sweepback
sweetcorn
'tween-deck
sweetener
sweeten up
sweet flag
sweetfish
sweet gale
sweet-gale
sweep hand
sweepings
tweediest
F W de Klerk
Owle-glass
ownerless
sweetmeal
sweetmeat
sweetness
ownership
sweet spot
sweet talk
sweet-talk
sweet upon
sweetwood
sweet-wort
sweetwort
swift-foot
swiftness
two-footed
twiforked
twiformed
two-forked
twyforked
twyformed
two-fisted
swaggerer
swag-belly
two-headed
two-handed
two-hander
sweirness
awakening
two-leafed
two-leaved
Swaledale
sweltered
twalpenny
twelvemos
twa-lofted
two-legged
swallower
twalhours
swallow up
two-lipped
twelfthly
swimmable
swamp boat
swimmeret
swampland
two-masted
two-master
swingbeat
swingboat
swing-back
swan about
ewe-necked
twin-screw
swing door
swung dash
swans-down
swansdown
swingeing
swine-fish
swinehood
swineherd
Swan River
zwanziger
twentieth
twin birth
Zwinglian
swindling
swingling
twangling
twinkling
twin plane
twiningly
Gwendolen
swan-goose
twin-track
swinishly

Words marked ✧ can also be spelled with one or more capital letters

swingtree
Swinburne
swing-wing
twenty-one
twentyish
twenty-two
sweptback
swipe card
two-parted
owl-parrot
sweptwing
sword-bean
swart-back
sword-belt
swordbill
swarm-cell
sword-cane
sword fern
swordfish
swarthily
sword-hand
swarajism
swarajist
sword knot
swordlike
sword lily
swordless
awareness
swartness
two-roomed
swordplay
sword-rack
swart star
swordsman
sword side
aware that
swordtail
twoseater
two shakes
twistable
twist down
twist grip
awesomely
two-storey
awe-struck
awe-strike
twostroke
Swiss roll
swashwork
twitterer
switchman
twitchier
switch off
twitchily
switching
twitching
twattling
two-timing
awfulness
swivelled
swivel-gun
swivel-eye
awkwardly
twayblade
away you go!
Swaziland
exhalable
excavator
excambion
excambium
excaudate

expatiate
Excalibur
excarnate
exhausted
exhauster
expansile
expansion
expansive
exuberant
exuberate
exactable
execrable
execrably
exactment
exactness
exactress
executrix
executant
execution
executory
executive
ixodiasis
exodermal
exodermis
exudation
oxidation
exudative
oxidative
exceeding
extendant
expediter
expedient
expeditor
exteriors
ex delicto
excellent
excelling
expellant
expellent
expelling
extermine
externals
excerptor
extempore
excerptum
extensile
✧excelsior
extension
extensity
excessive
expensive
extensive
excentric
exsertile
exceptant
excepting
expectant
expecting
exception
exsection
exsertion
expertise
exceptive
expertize
axle-guard
extenuate
ex-service
exoenzyme
ex officio
exigeante
exogamous

exigently
oxygenise
oxygenate
exogenous
oxygenous
oxygenize
exegetics
exegetist
exchanger
✧exchequer
excitancy
excisable
excitable
excitably
expirable
extincted
exsiccant
episcate
exsiccate
excise law
exciseman
excise tax
excitedly
exhibiter
excipient
exhibitor
extirpate
ex-librism
ex-librist
Axminster
expiation
expiatory
exultance
exultancy
explicate
excluding
exaltedly
explainer
exploiter
exilement
exploring
exclusion
explosion
exclosure
exclusory
exclusive
explosive
expletory
expletive
exemplify
exemplary
examinant
examining
examinate
exemption
exanthema
exanthems
exanimate
exonerate
axiomatic
exposable
Oxfordian
exponible
exfoliant
expositor
excoriate
exfoliate
extolling
extolment
expounder
extorsive

extortion
exposture
extortive
exopodite
exequatur
uxorially
uxoricide
extractor
extricate
extradite
exarchist
exarchate
exerciser
exercises
exorciser
exorcizer
exordiums
extremely
excrement
extremest
extremism
extremist
extremity
extrinsic
exergonic
extrapose
extrorsal
expresser
expressly
extrusile
extrusion
extrusory
extrusive
extra time
exaration
excretion
exoration
excretory
excretive
extraught
extravert
extrovert
existence
exosphere
exosporal
exostoses
exosmosis
exosmotic
exostosis
exit value
exoticism
exit wound
excusable
excusably
exsuccous
expurgate
exculpate
excurrent
excursion
expulsion
exquisite
excursive
expulsive
pyracanth
mynah bird
gynaecoid
gynaeceum
gynaecium
rybaudrye
cyma recta
synangium

hydathode
synapheia
dynamical
Pyralidae
pyramidal
dynamiter
pyramides
pyramises
pyramidic
✧sybaritic
pyramidon
hypallage
zygaenoid
zygaenine
tyranness
tyrannise
tyrannous
tyrannize
synagogal
dynamotor
synagogue
cymagraph
by-passage
synanthic
Byzantine
synaptase
Byzantium
zygantrum
cymbidium
cymbiform
eyebright
symbolics
cymbaloes
symbolled
symbology
Cymbeline
cymbalist
symbolise
✧symbolism
symbolist
symbolize
symbiosis
symbiotic
dyscrasia
syncretic
rye coffee
synclinal
syncoptic
syncopate
dyschroia
myocardia
synchrony
syncytial
syncytium
synchysis
syndicate
syndactyl
syndromic
Hyderabad
hymenaeal
hymenaean
Mycenaean
Pyrenaean
tyre gauge
by default
hyperbola
hyperbole
Aylesbury
hypercube
cybercafé
type scale

type metal
cynegetic
hyperemia
hyperemic
myxedemic
syneresis
hymeneals
Pyreneans
pyreneite
type genus
hyperfine
lysergide
hypergamy
synergise
synergism
synergist
synergize
pyrethrin
✧pyrethrum
Hyaenidae
✧hypericum
hyperlink
my lee-lane
hypermart
hypernymy
cybernate
cybernaut
byrewoman
hyperopia
lyme-hound
Mycetozoa
cyberpunk
synedrial
by degrees
synedrion
lyme-grass
typewrite
synedrium
synectics
tylectomy
dysentery
hypertext
Lymeswold®
dyke swarm
myofibril
gyrfalcon
eye-glance
myography
syngamous
dysgenics
syngeneic
myoglobin
ayahuasco
wych-hazel
by the book
Typhaceae
mythicise
mythicism
mythicist
mythicize
typhoidal
typhlitic
typhlitis
wych-alder
mythology
syphiloid
syphiloma
syphilise
syphilize
mythomane
✧typhonian

hyphenise
hyphenism
✧pythoness
hyphenate
hyphenize
mythopoet
Cytherean
by the yard
Xyridales
cynically
lyrically
lytically
typically
wyliecoat
Syriacism
cylindric
lysimeter
lysigenic
synizesis
syringeal
Lymington
Cynipidae
Mytilidae
pyritical
hygienics
Tyrian red
hygienist
Syrianism
pyridoxal
hypinosis
pyridoxin
Myriapoda
myriorama
Myristica
by mistake
typifying
synkaryon
syllabics
syllabled
syllabify
syllabary
syllabise
syllabism
syllabize
dyslectic
cyclic AMP
cyclicism
cyclicity
Wyclifite
pyelogram
myologist
syllogise
syllogism
syllogize
cycloidal
cycle lane
cyclolith
cyclamate
myelomata
hyalonema
hyalinise
cyclonite
hyalinize
cyclopean
cyclopian
Cyclopses
syllepses
syllepsis
sylleptic
cyclepath
cycle race

cyclorama
eyeleteer
cyclotron
eye lotion
byrlaw-man
cyclizine
myrmecoid
Symmachus
Myrmidons
Pygmalion
myomantic
lyam-hound
lyomerous
eye muscle
symmetral
symmetric
✧lyonnaise
cyaniding
hymnodist
pycnidium
hypnogeny
hypnoidal
Ryan Giggs
hymnology
hypnology
cyanamide
dyingness
Lyon Court
✧wyandotte
gymnasial
gymnasien
gymnastic
by oneself
pyknosome
gymnosoph
gymnasium
hypnotoid
cyanotype
hypnotise
hypnotism
hypnotist
hypnotize
Pyongyang
hypogaeal
hypogaean
myrobalan
gyromancy
pyromancy
Hylobates
pyrolater
cynomania
hypomania
hypomanic
hypotaxis
pyromania
typomania
zygomatic
pyrolatry
hypocaust
hyponasty
gyrovague
hypogaeum
gyroscope
pyroscope
zymoscope
synoecise
synoecism
synoecete
gynoecium
synoicous
synoecize
myxoedema
xyloidine
cytometer
eye-opener
pyrometer
xylometer
zymometer
cytopenia
hypoxemia
hypoxemic
pyrogenic
pyroxenic
zymogenic
hypoderma
by no means
cytometry
pyrometry
hypogeous
mycophagy
Xylophaga
xylophage
cymophane
pyrophone
sycophant
xylophone
gynophore
hylophyte
zygophyte
mycorhiza
Lycosidae
synodical
xylorimba
cytokinin
mylonitic
synovitic
synovitis
myxovirus
synoekete
gyroplane
cytoplasm
hypoblast
pyroclast
tycoonery
bytownite
tycoonate
lysosomal
cynomolgi
cytotoxic
cytotoxin
hypotonia
hypotonic
mycologic
mycotoxin
zymologic
hylozoism
hylozoist
hypocotyl
zygosperm
zygospore
gynocracy
cymograph
kymograph
xylograph
hypocrisy
hypocrite
synodsman
hyson-skin
synopsise
synopsize
hypostyle
pygostyle
synoptist
cytolysis
cytolytic
mylohyoid
pyrolysis
pyrolytic
pyroxylic
pyroxylin
synonymic
zymolysis
zymolytic
dysphagia
dysphagic
dysphasia
dysplasia
dyspraxia
lymphatic
nymphalid
nymphaeum
sympodial
sympodium
nymphette
nymphical
Syrphidae
lyophilic
nymphlike
sylphlike
lymph node
tympanums
tympanist
dyspnoeal
dysphonia
dysphonic
dysphoria
dysphoric
dyspnoeic
lyophobic
symphonic
symptosis
symptotic
dyspepsia
dyspeptic
symposiac
symposial
symposium
sympathin
sympatric
symphysis
symphytic
Symphytum
mydriasis
mydriatic
hydrocele
by-product
hygrodeik
hybridoma
hybridise
hybridism
hybridity
hybridous
hybridize
✧ayurvedic
hydraemia
hydrofoil
pyorrhoea
by-ordinar
hydrology
hygrology
hydrolase
hydrolyse
hydrolyte
hydrolyze
hydrangea
cyprinoid
hydronaut
hydriodic
Pyrrhonic
hydroptic
hygrophil
hydropult
hydrostat
hygrostat
hydrosoma
hydrosome
hygristor
hydration
hydraulic
hydrovane
dyer's-weed
dyer's-weld
hydroxide
hydrozoan
hydrazine
hydrozoon
eyeshadow
eye socket
eye splice
gypsy moth
eyestrain
eye-string
gypsywort
Myrtaceae
dystectic
syntactic
syntectic
cystocele
cystocarp
mysticism
cystidean
myrtle-wax
syntheses
dysthesia
dysthetic
synthesis
synthetic
bye the bye
mystified
mystifier
cystiform
mystagogy
nystagmic
nystagmus
Ayutthaya
Cystoidea
✧ayatollah
hyetology
systaltic
nyctalops
cystolith
Eye Temple
systemise
systemize
bystander
syntonise
syntonous
syntonize
dystrophy
dystopian
hysterics
mysteries
oyster-bed
hysteroid
cystotomy
dysthymia
dysthymic
by numbers
Sylviidae
Sylviinae
sylvanite
sylvinite
Sylvester
Sylvestra
rye whisky
by my certy
Ezra Pound
Azobacter
ozocerite
izvestiya
dziggetai
azygously
ozokerite
azimuthal
ozone hole
ozonation
azeotrope
czarevich
tzetse fly
tzetze fly
Aziz Nesin

10 – even

Bananaland
banana cake
Ramanavami
catananche
Madagascan
Madagascar
calamancos
calamander
salamander
Naiadaceae
caravaneer
Caravaggio
masa harina
Canada rice
macadamise
macadamize
palatalise
palatalize
Paraná pine
Tananarive
caravaning
banana kick
carapacial
Pan-Arabism
datamation
malaxation
Panamanian
Paramaribo
Mahayanist
Canada lily
Panama City
banana skin
parawalker
banana plug
Malayaalam
caravanned
caravanner
baba ganouj
catafalque
Malabar-rat
paratactic
maladapted
cacao beans
papal brief
salal berry
damasceene
salad cream
Balanchine
Lamarckism
Lamarckian
maraschino
JavaScript®
parascenia
naval crown
papal cross
Jamaica rum
wax and wane
hazardable
far and near
maladdress
far and wide
far and away
parabemata
garage band
garage sale
damageable
manageable
manageably
zapateados
paraselene
manageress
savageness
management
Japanesery
karate chop
karate-chop
caramelise
caramelize
papaverine
catamenial
managerial
✧paramecium
Saracenism
paramedico
paramedics
Savage Club
Bagatelles
cadaverous
papaverous
Japanesque
parametric
Karageorge
japan-earth
parametral
Paracelsus
catalectic
cataleptic
cabalettas
lazarettes
lazarettos
malapertly
paraffinic
Carangidae
haranguing
paraphrase
cataphract
paraphrast
Nabathaean
Galashiels
paraphilia
paraphonia
cataphonic
paraphonic
marathoner
Takashi Ono
cataphoric
paraphasia
paraphasic
paraphyses
paraphysis
parathesis
Kazakhstan
lazar house
paradisaic
capacitate
mazarinade
palatinate
safari park
paradiddle
taradiddle
parapineal
paradisean
carabinero
carabineer
barasingha
damagingly
jamahiriya
paradisiac
fanaticise
fanaticize
parasitise
parasitize
vanadinite
data mining
law-abiding
parakiting
natalitial
paradisial
fanaticism
Nazaritism
panaritium
parasitism
paradisian
carabinier

capability
Patavinity
ratability
salability
tamability
taxability
tamarillos
vacationer
parasitoid
samariform
calamitous
cavalierly
parabiosis
paralipses
paralipsis
cabalistic
fatalistic
parabiotic
canaliculi
safari suit
karaoke bar
damask plum
Damaskinos
Dan Aykroyd
damask rose
Sarah Lucas
paraglider
lavallière
paraplegia
paraplegic
paralleled
parallelly
Casablanca
zabaglione
parablepsy
caballeros
paraglossa
cataclasis
napalm bomb
paramnesia
paraenesis
paragnosis
Jagannatha
paraenetic
palaeogaea
paranoidal
calamondin
Palaeocene
Palaeogene
data logger
catabolite
catalogize
palagonite
parabolise
parabolize
paragonite
paralogise
paralogize
palaeolith
lavatorial
natatorial
parapodial
katabolism
catabolism
natatorium
paralogism
parapodium
sanatorium
patagonian
macaronics
macaronies

parabolist
paradoxist
paranormal
paramouncy
Palaeozoic
paraboloid
laparotomy
malacology
satanology
lay a course
paradoctor
paradoxure
cataloguer
palaeotype
basal plane
salad plate
salad plant
Rawalpindi
✧hamadryads
Pan-African
catarrhine
cavalryman
catarrhous
paratroops
malapropos
harassedly
harassment
samarskite
Eatanswill
radarscope
palaestric
palaestral
nasal spray
bagassosis
satay sauce
sal Atticum
parastichy
wag-at-the-wa'
vacantness
tarantella
La Bastille
San Antonio
pararthria
catastasis
parastatal
catacumbal
pará rubber
✧ragamuffin
cacafuegos
baba au rhum
Lana Turner
malaguetta
catapultic
paraquitos
Paraguayan
canary-seed
canary-bird
canary-wood
paralympic
pay-as-you-go
day-boarder
babblative
lambdacism
gas-bracket
fatbrained
madbrained
iambically
barbed wire
marble cake
babblement
gabblement

rabblement
parbreaked
jaw-breaker
lawbreaker
Barbie doll®
rabble rout
Marble Arch
lambrequin
carbofuran
way baggage
garbage can
cabbage-fly
garbageman
✧lambeg drum
wambliness
Balbriggan
dabblingly
ramblingly
wamblingly
warblingly
cambric tea
barbellate
gambolling
carbonnade
rabbinical
carbonados
carbon sink
carbuncled
carbon copy
carbon-copy
sanbenitos
lambdoidal
lay brother
bamboozler
may blossom
gabbroitic
lay baptism
namby-pamby
Barbary ape
barber-shop
barbershop
halberdier
Barbirolli
cat-burglar
✧jabberwock
law-burrows
Barbara Pym
carbureter
carburetor
farborough
Yarborough
earbashing
ear-bussing
gay-bashing
gambit-pawn
sabbatical
Sabbath-day
far between
balbutient
rabbitfish
Babbittism
lamb's-tails
salbutamol
rabbit hole
rabbit upon
barbituric
harbourage
harbour-bar
tambourine
carboxylic
Bacchanale

saccharase
saccharate
bacchanals
gas chamber
wanchancie
dance a bear
saccharide
saccharine
saccharise
saccharize
pancratium
fasciation
pancratian
pancratist
saccharify
cat-cracker
Ray Charles
cacciatora
saccharoid
cacciatore
saccharose
sauce-alone
ratch about
catch a crab
marchantia
Nancy Astor
watch after
bacchantes
matchboard
patchboard
hatch beams
fancy bread
Maccabaean
catch-basin
watch chain
patchcocke
talc schist
sarcocolla
fascicular
fascicules
fasciculus
farcically
watch clock
catch-drain
fancy dress
rancidness
calcedonio
Carchemish
hatchet job
satchelled
hatchet man
pancreatic
pancreatin
Barchester
Manchester
Marc Séguin
fancifully
watchfully
dance floor
calciferol
watchguard
watchglass
fancy goods
Talcahuano
ranch house
watch house
cancrizans
manchineel
catchiness
sanctified
✧sanctifier

sanctities
fan-cricket
calceiform
cancriform
sanctimony
calc-sinter
sanctitude
match-joint
Pancake Day
pancake ice
parcel-bawd
cancellate
Marcel wave
calculable
calculably
catch light
watch light
parcelwise
rascal-like
cancelling
parcelling
rascallion
parcel-gilt
sarcolemma
marchlands
parcel bomb
cancellous
parcel post
narcolepsy
vascularly
calculuses
laccolitic
calculated
sacculated
calculator
vasculitis
latch lever
bad company
vancomycin
match-maker
matchmaker
watchmaker
narcomania
parchmenty
dance music
marcantant
calcinable
gasconader
malcontent
par contest
carcinogen
watch night
carcinomas
carcinosis
balconette
fascinator
vaccinator
falcon-eyed
calceolate
lanceolate
raccoon-dog
cancionero
Marcionite
Sanctorius
Marcionist
Sarcophaga
sarcophagi
sarcoplasm
match point
catchpenny
watch paper

falciparum
Cancer Ward
saucerless
dancercise
cascarilla
barcarolle
marc brandy
mascarpone
calcareous
cancer root
saucerfuls
Marcgravia
calcar avis
saucer-eyed
marcescent
catch sight
Lancashire
matchstick
narcissism
pancosmism
narcissist
march-stone
watchstrap
rat-catcher
lancet fish
calcitonin
lancet arch
watchtower
Bar Council
jaw-crusher
Manchurian
lascivious
fancy woman
hard palate
sand saucer
hard-handed
handmaiden
sandpapery
cardialgia
sandbagged
sandbagger
hand mating
Maid Marian
Hardy Amies
hardbacked
hand-basket
hand gallop
hard-earned
mandragora
hard labour
bandy about
candy apple
paediatric
hand-barrow
card-castle
sandcastle
sand martin
bandmaster
land-waiter
yard-master
land-values
mandibular
bandy-bandy
dandy-brush
handicraft
manducable
hand-screen
Sadducaean
handicuffs
pandectist
lardaceous

padded cell
candidness
handedness
handy-dandy
randle-balk
saddleback
caddie cart
saddle-fast
bald-headed
hand-weeded
hard-headed
bandleader
card reader
saddle reef
saddleless
Land League
Sandie Shaw
hand relief
hand-sewing
candlefish
paddlefish
candlewick
saddlebill
handselled
daydreamer
candle bomb
candlewood
paddle-wood
saddle-nose
saddle sore
saddle-sore
saddle roof
candle-coal
land reform
saddleroom
hand-me-down
candle-doup
saddle soap
paddle boat
candle-tree
randle-tree
saddletree
yard of land
paddy field
land office
Band of Gold
Band of Hope
candyfloss
dandy-fever
Tardigrada
tardigrade
Waldegrave
gaudy-green
paedagogic
paedagogue
hay-de-guise
cardiganed
land agency
hay-de-guyes
hard cheese
dandy-horse
bawdy-house
sand lizard
land-pirate
sand-binder
tawdriness
dawdlingly
hard-riding
landmining
maudlinism
hard-billed

hard-fisted
hard-bitten
ward sister
eau de Javel
candelabra
Tam Dalyell
Baudelaire
candelilla
sandalwood
bandoleros
band-clutch
bardolatry
sand plough
random walk
landammann
randomness
randomwise
tandemwise
paddymelon
✧pandemonic
randomiser
mandamuses
randomizer
hand in hand
hand-in-hand
maiden name
maiden race
garden path
maidenhair
pardonable
pardonably
sardonical
✧maidenhead
maidenweed
jardinière
maiden-meek
pardonless
garden seat
gaudy-night
wardenship
maidenlike
lap dancing
tap-dancing
maiden pink
Waldensian
garden city
padding-ken
Vanden Plas®
garden flat
cardinally
landing net
maidenhood
fandangoes
Mandingoes
Sandinista
Sandinismo
Haddington
maiden aunt
maiden over
hand to hand
hand-to-hand
land-jobber
card-holder
landholder
handsomely
hard done by
hard-fought
Said Aouita
hand lotion
handworked
landlocked
hard-boiled
sand dollar
nandrolone
cardiology
land-louper
sandhopper
cardiogram
cardboardy
hard-gotten
card column
aardwolves
paedophile
handspring
land-spring
madder-lake
balderdash
ladder-back
Wanderjahr
land bridge
land breeze
wander year
pandermite
sanderling
banderilla
wander plug
falderal it
badderlock
gander-moon
sandgroper
pandurated
sand grouse
wanderlust
caddis-case
candescent
candy store
caddis-worm
faldistory
hard as iron
paddy train
hard stocks
handstaffs
paedotribe
band-string
Landsthing
pas de trois
handstaves
hard rubber
land-lubber
eard-hunger
land-hunger
eard-hungry
hard-pushed
paedeutics
paideutics
sand bunker
sandsucker
hand puppet
vaudeville
paddy-whack
paddy wagon
land-owning
Wandsworth
tawdry lace
hard hyphen
Lake Malawi
taken aback
sage rabbit
barehanded
case-harden
face-harden
game warden
Lake Vänern
water avens
gametangia
ka me, ka thee
lacerative
face-saving
cameration
catenarian
catenation
laceration
maceration
racemation
tax evasion
laterality
barebacked
Lake Baikal
race-walker
wage packet
pâte sablée
baseballer
Lake Saimaa
Lake Taimyr
Lake Taymyr
wage-earner
Lake Ladoga
camerawork
water about
Jane Marple
race hatred
Lake Nasser
take part in
calefactor
malefactor
camera tube
ease nature
lake-lawyer
James Braid
paperboard
water brash
water-brain
baked beans
laver bread
laverbread
ravel bread
make a break
water break
take a brief
water blink
James Baker
Janet Baker
Dane's blood
water brose
water bloom
James Brown
water-borne
waterborne
paper-birch
water birth
paperbound
water-bound
James Bruce
James Bowie
Balenciaga
paper chase
water crane
take a class
watercraft
maleic acid
water cycle
sales clerk
salesclerk
water clerk
watercress
paper-cigar
tapescript
watercolor
calescence
canescence
latescence
tabescence
paper-cloth
water clock
dame-school
paleaceous
cadet corps
camel-corps
water chute
parenchyma
sales drive
take advice
waterdrive
fazendeiro
have a dekko
take a dekko
calendarer
James Dyson
sacerdotal
Magen David
James Dewar
game tenant
bareheaded
tape reader
water elder
Lake Geneva
James E Webb
barelegged
gate-legged
wavelength
make-weight
safe period
make-belief
Madelenian
game-dealer
tale-teller
tape-record
patereroes
race memory
par exemple
gamekeeper
gate-keeper
babelesque
mace-bearer
talebearer
carelessly
fadelessly
namelessly
casemented
pace-setter
water frame
paper-faced
take effect
take a fancy
water flood
waterflood
sale of work
gate of horn
waterfront
water guard
cased glass
water glass
waterglass
pace-egging
panel games
paper-gauge
water gauge
water gruel
take the air
have a heart
make the cut
name the day
sage cheese
catechumen
male rhymes
have a hunch
game theory
wave theory
Kate Chopin
take charge
take the rue
water horse
take the rap
canephorus
take the sun
catechiser
catechesis
catechetic
pave the way
catechizer
rarefiable
base-minded
take kindly
Cape pigeon
wateriness
maledicent
maleficent
taperingly
waveringly
cavefishes
ease-giving
rate fixing
maleficial
lace-pillow
materially
javelin-man
lageniform
wafer irons
James Ivory
hare-lipped
Cader Idris
babesiasis
babesiosis
café filtre
make little
James Irwin
James Jeans
water joint
James Joyce
sauerkraut
Hakenkreuz
paperknife
Dame Pliant
Lake Placid
Lake Albert
late blight
take flight
Janet Leigh
water lemon
camerlengo
camerlingo
matellasse
satellitic
lamellated
capelletti
satellites
laser level
water level
safe-blower
paper-mâché
water maize
paper-maker
watermelon
make amends
paper money
✧water music
James Mason
taseometer
water meter
water motor
water mouse
take in hand
take an oath
take in vain
tabernacle
wake a night
Capernaite
make a noise
capernoity
have any joy
maternally
paternally
water nymph
wave energy
water nixie
camelopard
face to face
face-to-face
take to task
have no idea
face powder
make no odds
Tate Modern
malevolent
hate-monger
categorise
categorize
Jamesonite
take notice
take to wife
date coding
categorial
Caledonian
Cameronian
Macedonian
wave motion
categories
categorist
careworker
caseworker
faceworker
pace-bowler
wager of law
take to town
racecourse
ravenously
barefooted
case-bottle
Cape doctor
hateworthy
nameworthy
gametocyte
water ouzel
take-up rate
water plane
water plate
wake-up call
water plant
James Paget
make a point
lagerphone
waterproof
take up arms
sales pitch
water power
waterquake
take breath
make tracks
wage freeze
take orders
have a right
take fright
male orchis
career girl
pâte frolle
paper-ruler
rare groove
pâte brisée
Cape Breton
made ground
paper round
paper route
sage grouse
care-crazed
Mahe Island
make a stand
Wake Island
✧water snake
maker's mark
water snail
camel's hair
take as read
cameo-shell
watersmeet
wapenschaw
water-skied
take a shine
water-skier
harem skirt
raven's-bone
water smoke
taken short
water shoot
waterspout
caper-sauce
raven's-duck
have it made
paper trail
take it easy
lamentable
patentable
water table
James Tobin
lamentably
majestical
parentless
talentless
latent heat
paper tiger
watertight
tapestried
take strike
water thief
mare's-tails
water twist
Lacertilia
parentally

wafer tongs
malentendu
parenthood
talent-spot
man-entered
parenteral
Barents Sea
panel truck
water tower
water thyme
café au lait
wave number
face-fungus
tape luring
Mare Nubium
hamesucken
base-burner
baserunner
page-turner
base jumper
pâte sucrée
Jane Austen
maneuverer
water wheel
water wagon
saleswoman
water wings
waterworks
water witch
Javel water
safety cage
safety lamp
safety cell
safety rein
safety belt
safety shot
panegyrise
panegyrize
safety film
panegyrist
safety plug
safety lock
safety bolt
safety arch
safety fuse
malfeasant
mafficking
half-a-crown
daffodilly
half-a-dozen
baffle wall
bafflement
half-length
way freight
bad feeling
gauffering
Ian Fleming
balfrenier
waffle iron
half-yearly
half nelson
Max F Perutz
half-chance
halfe-horsy
Man Fridays
gaff-rigged
bafflingly
caffeinism
halfwitted
half-kirtle
half-sister
lawfulness
manfulness
farfalline
half florin
caffè latte
yaffingale
gap funding
half-cocked
half-dollar
half volley
half-hourly
gaffer tape
gas-furnace
calf-ground
faff around
Sanforized®
far-fetched
half-duplex
half guinea
half-hunter
batfowling
margravate
Bangladesh
margharita
margravine
Sangradoes
bargeboard
mangabeira
gauge boson
ragged-lady
jaggedness
raggedness
war goddess
ragged left
tagged atom
daggle-tail
tangleweed
tanglement
marguerite
tanglesome
Langue d'oui
Langue d'oïl
gangrenous
malgré tout
tanglefoot
larghettos
✧gang of four
gauge glass
baggage-car
sanguinary
sanguinely
laughingly
tanglingly
languished
languisher
sanguinity
ganglionic
gangliform
gangliated
hang-glider
rangelands
Targumical
largemouth
margin call
laggen-gird
tangential
marginalia
jargonelle
marginally
gauging-rod
ranging rod
pangenesis
pangenetic
marginated
✧gargantuan
large order
Sangiovese
languorous
Panglossic
large print
cargo pants
Langerhans
hang a right
rangership
danger line
Tangerines
Gay Gordons
margaritic
hang around
large-scale
mangosteen
targetable
target cell
pargetting
caught up in
target area
gangsta rap
daughterly
gangbuster
Wagga Wagga
gargoylism
gas-guzzler
Rachmanite
Rachmanism
yacht-built
Nachschlag
Sanhedrist
sash weight
cashiering
cash-keeper
mashie iron
tachograph
tachygraph
pathogenic
pathognomy
naphthalic
naphthenic
pathfinder
sash window
bad hair day
gashliness
Cap Haitian
Catholicoi
✧catholicon
Catholicos
catholicly
tax holiday
pathologic
nathelesse
batholitic
bathylitic
tachylitic
tachylytic
Bath Oliver
fathomable
fathomless
sachemship
fathom line
baphometic
mathematic
bathometer
bathymeter
fathometer
pachymeter
tachometer
tachymeter
bathymetry
tachometry
tachymetry
cash in hand
cash-in-hand
cachinnate
Nathan Hale
machinable
bathing box
bathing cap
Tachinidae
washing-day
machinegun
bathing hut
rat-hunting
panhandler
taphonomic
machineman
lay hands on
mashing-tub
Washington
machinator
hash totals
fashionist
wash-bottle
tachypnoea
fatherland
Father's Day
fatherless
saphir d'eau
fathership
fatherlike
Hal Hartley
fatherhood
Gasherbrum
hash browns
bathyscape
pathetical
washateria
washeteria
Mach number
bashawship
cashew nuts
lachrymals
lachrymary
lachrymose
Rathayatra
radio alarm
Halifax Bay
taxi dancer
Harimandir
palisander
Caricaceae
Salicaceae
Manila hemp
capitalise
capitalize
laminarise
laminarize
radicalise
radicalize
capitalism
Radicalism
sanitarium
Vaticanism
capitation
cavitation
habitation
janizarian
laminarian
lamination
lapidarian
lapidation
latitation
nanisation
nanization
navigation
pagination
patination
radication
sagination
salivation
sanitarian
sanitation
validation
galimatias
capitalist
lapidarist
maximalist
sanitarist
Vaticanist
radicality
sanitarily
magi-marker
habitaunce
Sadi Carnot
Marita Koch
palisadoes
saxicavous
cavil about
habilatory
Wasim Akram
Salina Cruz
capital sum
capital sin
radio assay
caricatura
caricature
Maria Bueno
David Byrne
David Bruce
David Bowie
parischane
cabin class
hagiocracy
Fabio Chigi
maniacally
fatiscence
habit-cloth
Latin cross
Marie Curie
palindrome
David Duval
native land
marine acid
native bear
facileness
nativeness
Savile Club
marine glue
capitellum
varicellar
taxidermic
taxidermal
native rock
native-born
marine soap
laniferous
lanigerous
saliferous
gaminesque
tasimetric
manifestos
manifestly
salicetums
tariff wall
tariffless
satisfying
David Frost
cabin fever
faying-face
saving game
radiograph
panic-grass
casinghead
Paris green
savingness
takingness
cariogenic
radiogenic
baking soda
caking coal
Racing Post
malingerer
Maxim Gorky
variegated
variegator
Raging Bull
David Gower
mating type
Manichaean
garishness
lavishness
Manichaeus
oafishness
rakishness
banishment
famishment
lavishment
ravishment
vanishment
Manicheism
Danish blue
I A Richards
parish pump
parish-pump
facilitate
habilitate
pacificate
vaticinate
pacifiable
ratifiable
salifiable
habiliment
maxi-single
lapidified
pacificism
Maximilian
facilities
pacificist
vaginismus
Parisienne
salicional
Sabinianus
radiciform
caliginous
Pacific Rim
familiarly
familistic
nativistic
laciniated
Tajikistan
Pacific War
David Jason
David Lodge
hagiologic
radiologic
capillaire
maxillulae
bacillemia
panislamic
Mario Lanza
David Lynch
Marie Lloyd
maxilliped
Radiolaria
radiolysis
radiolytic
variolitic
mamillated
papillated
hagiolater
Mariolater
variolator
papillitis
hagiolatry
Mariolatry
radial tyre
barium meal
Canis Major
habit-maker
Galia melon
David Mamet
talismanic
Papiamento
Canis Minor
radium bomb
radiometer
variometer
radiometry
ration card
Samian ware
San Ignacio
nationless
malignment
nationwide
sapiential
salientian
nationally
rationally
malignance
malignancy
nationhood
ration book
Marianists
marionette
David Niven
Calico Jack
varifocals
manifolder
manifoldly
varicocele
camino real
✧capitoline
saxicoline
janitorial
capitolian
Mabinogion
varicosity
California

Laurentius
matronymic
patronymic
matronhood
barrenwort
barring-out
patroniser
Barrington
Warrington
fair enough
patronizer
capreolate
hair-powder
warrioress
matryoshka
matryoshki
fair-boding
gadrooning
patriotism
macrophage
hairspring
macroprism
fair-spoken
sapropelic
Capri pants
madreporic
law reports
saprophyte
fairground
bairn's-part
wanrestful
laurustine
patristics
sacrosanct
fairy-stone
macrospore
fairy story
Harrisburg
carrot cake
narratable
sabretache
hairstreak
parrot-beak
garrotting
parrot-fish
parrot-bill
Maoritanga
Mauretania
Mauritania
hair stroke
sabretooth
saprotroph
parrot-coal
barratrous
La Traviata
galravitch
narrowband
narrowcast
marrowless
narrowness
narrow seas
Barry White
dairywoman
barrowload
marrow-bone
narrowboat
barrow-tram
✧macrozamia
raise a hand
raise a hare
cassia-bark
false alarm
nauseative
nauseating
Pan-Slavism
pay station
way station
Pan-Slavist
hamshackle
ramshackle
ranshackle
mass market
mass-market
marshalled
Fats Waller
marshaller
CAT scanner
tarsia-work
waist apron
Marshalsea
raise a dust
daisy chain
daisy-chain
Law Society
waistcloth
passed pawn
falsidical
Sam Shepard
Cat Stevens
mass defect
Hans Berger
mass medium
haustellum
man-stealer
panspermia
panspermic
camsteerie
pass degree
Hatshepsut
tax shelter
mansuetude
false-faced
Jaws of Life®
falsifying
pausefully
passiflora
days of yore
false fruit
Lassa fever
marsh-fever
sausage dog
far-sighted
passageway
sans phrase
day-scholar
wassail cup
bass fiddle
Fassbinder
marshiness
wassailing
causticity
Marseilles
gay science
caespitose
false jalap
easselward
easselgate
Hans Sloane
Faisalabad
marshlocks
hanselling
tasselling
damselfish
cassolette
mausoleums
ransomable
Lakshmi Bai
ransomless
baisemains
facsimiled
facsimiles
cassumunar
passimeter
passamezzo
raising-bee
parsonical
Sassanidae
raisonneur
parson-bird
Carson City
damson tree
maisonette
passionate
mansionary
passionary
sans nombre
Cassiopeia
lay store by
haustorium
Fats Domino
bassoonist
Passionist
nauseously
Galsworthy
false pearl
pansophism
pansophist
hawser-laid
man-servant
Jay's Treaty
marsh-robin
Maastricht
cat's cradle
masspriest
Caesarship
kaisership
hansardise
hansardize
Ramsar site
cat's-brains
ear syringe
Massoretic
Sanskritic
false shame
man's estate
false start
jam session
rap session
Kansas City
Bass Strait
false teeth
false tooth
basset horn
false topaz
Basse-Terre
Basseterre
mass number
saussurite
lansquenet
bass guitar
pass muster
salsa verde
Warsaw Pact
daisy-wheel
palsy-walsy
causewayed
capsizable
Bafta Award
martial art
fast-handed
eastwardly
fan tracery
way traffic
gastralgia
xantham gum
xanthan gum
bastnäsite
carthamine
lanthanide
partialise
partialize
tartrazine
day trading
Watteauish
Kantianism
martialism
partialism
castration
fatty acids
martialist
partialist
factuality
partiality
tactuality
martial law
partial out
past master
earth-board
pasteboard
hartebeest
earthbound
Santa Claus
Gantt chart
masticable
lactic acid
pasticheur
Tao-te-ching
fantoccini
particular
nautically
tactically
latticinio
lastic mode
cactaceous
mastectomy
participle
masticator
canted deck
malted milk
mastodynia
fastidious
cattle cake
hartie-hale
rattlepate
tattletale
rantle-balk
wattlebark
pay the cain
rattlehead
eat the leek
pantheress
battlement
battleship
cattle show
tattie-shaw
wattlebird
pantherine
haut relief
pantherish
saltcellar
tattie-claw
battledore
haute école
pad the hoof
mantle rock
wattlework
Hartlepool
bay the moon
battledoor
cattle grid
cattle prod
rattletrap
waitperson
tactlessly
cattle stop
maltreater
pasty-faced
East of Eden
Tartuffery
Tartuffish
Tartuffism
Tartuffian
faithfully
tastefully
wastefully
canto fermo
Malta fever
fastigiate
saltigrade
pantagraph
pantograph
paste-grain
lactogenic
castigator
fatty heart
lay to heart
cante hondo
malt whisky
earth-house
batteilant
fact-finder
earthiness
paltriness
gastric flu
partridges
tattlingly
Matt Dillon
Walt Disney
battailous
day-tripper
jaw-twister
last-minute
malt liquor
cante jondo
cantillate
martellato
hasta luego
tautologic
earth-light
pastellist
pantaloons
manteltree
tantaliser
nautiluses
cantaloupe
cantilever
salt-glazed
tantalizer
pasta maker
pantomimic
cartomancy
Santa Maria
Santa Marta
tautomeric
Tantum ergo
lactometer
tantamount
earthmover
cartonnage
martingale
parting-cup
bastinaded
bastinades
Fastens-eve
Battenberg
Battonberg
Martin Bell
Martin Rees
wantonness
cantonment
panton-shoe
cast anchor
martensite
Martin Pipe
bantingism
East Indian
East Indies
tartanalia
Dalton plan
Dalton's law
Martin Amis
casting-net
tantony pig
Martinique
Tartan army
Battenburg
wanton away
Martin Ryle
xanthomata
cautionary
factionary
East London
gag-toothed
gap-toothed
saw-toothed
cartoonish
cartoonist
factionist
fast worker
fast bowler
Bartholmew
Gastropoda
gastronome
gastrosoph
gastrology
gastronomy
gastrotomy
Eastbourne
xanthopsia
captiously
cautiously
factiously
earth-plate
pantophagy
party piece
cartophile
salt spring
cartophily
tautophony
waste paper
earthquake
MasterCard®
master-card
master-hand
master page
master race
masturbate
lattermath
natterjack
Tattersall
factorable
pasturable
bastard-bar
raft-bridge
Walter Reed
halter neck
Easter term
castor bean
masterless
matterless
Walter Hess
parturient
lantern fly
cartwright
factorship
mastership
pastorship
mastermind
rafter-bird
bastardise
bastardize
easternise
easternize
Eastertide
Eastertime
gas turbine
easterling
factor VIII
bastardism
easternism
✧nasturtium
lanternist
latter-mint
Easter lily
saltarelli
saltarello
pastorales
Hattersley
pastorally
bacteremia
bacteremic
bacterioid
masterhood
waiterhood
patter-song
masterwork
latter-born
Matterhorn
tartareous
eastermost
lattermost
masterwort
gasteropod
Eastern Sea
cart around
cast around
wait around

eat through
Easter dues
✧canterbury
wanthriven
barter away
Maltese dog
cast a spell
lactescent
baptistery
earth-shine
Patti Smith
fantastico
party sales
earth-smoke
lactoscope
pantoscope
lactosuria
earth-table
fast stream
cantatrice
factitious
tarte tatin
pasteurise
pasteurize
pasteurism
Carthusian
Malthusian
Pasteurian
ear-trumpet
last hurrah
East Sussex
salt-butter
captivance
hantavirus
wait-a-while
panty-waist
earthwoman
earthwards
pantrymaid
pastrycook
bartizaned
tabula rasa
value added
paludament
natural gas
maturative
naturalise
naturalize
tabularise
tabularize
naturalism
jaculation
maculation
maturation
papulation
salutation
saturation
tabulation
vapulation
naturalist
salutarily
natural law
jaculatory
salutatory
tabulatory
maculature
casus belli
sarus crane
manuscript
caruncular
majuscular
ranunculus
caoutchouc
matureness
Jaruzelski
nature cure
nature-myth
Janus-faced
lanuginose
baculiform
raduliform
cacuminous
lanuginous
paludinous
naturistic
manumitted
manumitter
casual ward
maquillage
casualness
Samuel Hood
Samuel Colt
vacuolated
datum level
vacuum tube
vacuum pump
calumniate
✧saturnalia
calumnious
Jaquenetta
saquinavir
naturopath
makunouchi
fabulosity
fabulously
datum plane
haruspical
haruspices
datum point
daguerrean
jaguarondi
jaguarundi
saouari-nut
salubrious
manubriums
balustrade
lacustrine
palustrine
palustrian
balustered
larvicidal
malvaceous
Salvadoran
salvifical
mauvais ton
marvelling
marvellous
valvulitis
Marvin Gaye
Paavo Nurmi
galvaniser
Jan van Eyck
galvanizer
Jan Vermeer
salverform
canvasback
harvest bug
harvest-fly
canvassing
harvestman
canvas-work
Parvo virus
parvovirus
day-wearied
war-wearied
earwigging
jaywalking
Ian Woosnam
ear-witness
Marxianism
faex populi
baby-walker
Mary Cassat
Lady Castle
many-headed
Mary Peters
Mary Leakey
Mary Wesley
satyresque
Mary of Teck
satyagraha
satyagrahi
laryngitic
laryngitis
Gary Rhodes
lady chapel
baby-ribbon
baby-minder
lady-killer
Mary Wigman
calyciform
satyriasis
baby-sitter
Labyrinths
karyolymph
Gary Oldman
karyolysis
Maryolatry
Gary Player
banyan days
Mary Anning
many-folded
Babylonish
Babylonian
baby boomer
palynology
papyrology
Gary Cooper
easy does it
karyoplasm
barysphere
lawyer vine
lawyer's wig
Rajya Sabha
lady's-smock
calyptrate
raiyatwari
baby's-tears
caryatidic
caryatidal
caryatides
easy street
karyotypic
calyculate
Lazy Sunday
baby-jumper
razzmatazz
dazzlement
dazzlingly
Ranzellaar
Jan Zelezny
lanzknecht
manzanilla
Manzanillo
canzonetta
canzonette
Laszlo Biro
Abraham-man
abranchial
oblateness
abrasively
oblational
obtainable
obtainment
ebracteate
abscission
obediently
'sbuddikins
able rating
abnegation
oboe d'amore
abreactive
abreaction
able seaman
abbey-laird
able-bodied
abbey-piece
objets d'art
object ball
abjectness
objectless
object code
object-soul
absente reo
objectival
obsequious
observable
observably
observance
observancy
observator
J B S Haldane
J B M Hertzog
abdication
obligation
obligatory
obliterate
obligement
abridgable
abridgment
obligingly
obsidional
absinthism
Abel Tasman
I believe so
obbligatos
ebullition
ebullience
ebulliency
obeliscoid
Ebola virus
abominable
abominably
abominator
à bon marché
abundantly
abonnement
abrogative
abrogation
absorbable
absorbedly
absorbency
obsoletely
obsoletism
obsoletion
abiogenist
ebionitism
abdominous
abnormally
Oblomovism
absorptive
absorption
abhorrence
abhorrency
absolutely
absolutism
absolution
absolutist
absolutory
absolvitor
ubiquarian
ubiquitary
ubiquinone
ubiquitous
aberration
eburnation
aberrantly
aberdevine
Übermensch
✧aboriginal
abortively
aborticide
abortional
Aberglaube
obtruncate
Aberdonian
abbreviate
Abyssinian
obituarist
abstracted
abstracter
abstractor
abstractly
a better bet
abstemious
a but and ben
abstention
abstinence
abstinency
abiturient
abstergent
abstersive
abstersion
obstetrics
abstrusely
obstructer
obstructor
obdurately
abjuration
obduration
objuration
obturation
abjunction
obfuscated
absurdness
obtuseness
éboulement
obnubilate
Aboukir Bay
ablutomane
Abdus Salam
abruptness
above board
above-board
above-named
above price
above water
octavalent
oceanarium
scrambling
ocean basin
scratching
scratchily
scratch out
scratch pad
scratch-wig
octandrian
octandrous
scrapegood
scrape home
octamerous
octahedral
octahedron
ocean-going
scraggling
octangular
actability
occasional
occasioner
Octavio Paz
octaploidy
scrap metal
Sciaenidae
Ecuadorian
Sclavonian
oceanology
ocean perch
schalstein
scrag-whale
scuba diver
icebreaker
scabbiness
scabridity
scabrously
a-cockhorse
ecoclimate
aciculated
ice colours
act curtain
acidically
acidifying
academical
acidimeter
acidimetry
ice dancing
schematise
schematize
schematism
acieration
schematist
eczematous
screech owl
accelerate
accelerant
acre-length
schefflera
schechitah
screwiness
ecce signum
scleriasis
screen wall
screenable
screen test
screen-test
screenplay
screenings
screen door
screen grid
screen dump
scleromata
scleroderm
sclerotise
sclerotize
sclerotial
sclerotium
sclerotomy
Acherontic
schemozzle
screw plate
screw press
accessible
accessibly
access time
access road
accentuate
accept bail
acceptable
acceptably
acceptedly
accentless
scientific
acceptance
acceptancy
scherzandi
scherzando
scoffingly
scaffolage
scaffolder
ecphractic
ecthlipses
ecthlipsis
ice hilling
ecchymosed
ecchymosis
ecchymotic
ecphoneses
ecphonesis
activation
scribbling
scritch-owl
activeness
active life
scrivening
active list
accidented
accidental
✧occidental
Schiff base
scaithless
activities
scrip issue
Schick test
acriflavin
scrimmager
schism shop
schismatic
actionable
actionably
action film
action plan
schizocarp
Echinoidea
schizoidal
echinoderm
Achitophel
actinolite
Schizopoda

schizogony
scrimpness
schipperke
scrimshank
scriptoria
scriptural
✧scriptures
achievable
ocellation
scale board
scaldberry
ochlocracy
ecological
scoldingly
scale model
oculomotor
schlimazel
Iceland-dog
Scillonian
scaloppine
schlepping
Eccles cake
scale stair
ecclesiast
Scolytidae
sculptress
sculptured
sculptural
sculduddry
acolouthic
acolouthos
ice machine
scampishly
ecumenical
acuminated
Scombridae
Scombresox
scandalise
scandalize
scandalled
scandalous
iconoclasm
iconoclast
iconically
scenically
acanaceous
acinaceous
scent gland
Scunthorpe
acanthuses
scintiscan
scantiness
scintigram
iconolater
iconolatry
economical
iconomachy
economiser
iconomatic
iconometer
iconometry
economizer
scent organ
scansorial
e contrario
scent scale
icing sugar
iconoscope
acrobatism
octonarian
acrobatics
octonarius
scrog-apple
scholastic
accoucheur
echoically
accordable
accordance
accordancy
acromegaly
octogenary
acroterial
acroterium
acroterion
octodecimo
scooterist
ectodermic
ectodermal
acrogenous
ectogenous
scooped-out
octohedron
act of grace
acrophobia
acrophonic
ectophytic
acrolithic
sciolistic
scrobicule
tchoukball
schoolmaid
schoolward
school dame
schoolmate
schoolma'am
schoolmarm
schooldays
scrollable
school bell
school term
school year
school ship
schooltide
schooltime
scrollwise
schoolgirl
octoploidy
school book
schoolwork
schorl-rock
scrollwork
schoolroom
school-bred
acroamatic
accountant
account day
account for
accounting
scrounging
ectoenzyme
octopodous
ectomorphy
accomptant
accomplice
accomplish
Ectoprocta
eccoprotic
echopraxia
echopraxis
across lots
accostable
accoutring
accoutered
octopusher
scrofulous
acronychal
acronymous
octogynous
icy-pearled
acephalous
scapegrace
scepticism
scyphiform
scapulated
scyphozoan
scape-wheel
acervately
scarlatina
acervation
scorpaenid
scordatura
scoreboard
scarabaeid
scarabaean
scarabaeus
aceraceous
ochraceous
scaredy-cat
accredited
scarceness
scarcement
scarlet hat
acarpelous
scarifying
scornfully
ecardinate
scurfiness
scurviness
scurrility
✧scorpionic
scurrilous
scarf-joint
achromatic
achromatin
✧scaramouch
scorzonera
acarophily
acorn-shell
accrescent
scoresheet
ice-skating
ecospecies
icosahedra
Icosandria
scissor cut
scissor-leg
acute angle
acetabulum
acetabular
acetic acid
scotodinia
scatheless
scatter-gun
scattering
act the fool
act the goat
Scotifying
Scots Greys
Scotch hand
Scotch kale
Scotch tape®
Scotch cart
Scotchness
Scotch pine
Scotch mist
Scotch snap
Scotch rose
scattiness
scathingly
Scottified
Scotticise
Scotticize
Scotticism
scutellate
acotyledon
scuttleful
acetylenic
acatalepsy
scotometer
scot and lot
scatophagy
Scotophile
Scotophobe
scaturient
scoter duck
eco-tourism
eco-tourist
Scotswoman
ichthyosis
ichthyotic
accurately
Schumacher
accusative
occupative
accubation
accusation
occupation
scout about
accusatory
accumbency
scoutcraft
scrunch-dry
accusement
scrutineer
accusingly
scrutinise
scrutinize
scrutinous
acquainted
actualités
scrummager
McGuinness
acquirable
scrub rider
occurrence
scrub round
scout's pace
accursedly
acoustical
occultness
acquitment
acquitting
accustomed
accultural
accumulate
scrupulous
scavengery
scavenging
scowdering
scowlingly
ecowarrior
schwarzlot
acrylamide
act your age!
Edna O'Brien
advance man
Edwardiana
Edward Lear
Edgar Degas
Edward Bond
Edward Coke
adjacently
Edgar Faure
'Ndrangheta
Ndrangheta
adiaphoron
J D Salinger
ideational
idealistic
ideal point
advantaged
edibleness
edible crab
ad absurdum
edaciously
educatable
adactylous
adrenaline
idle-headed
adrenergic
edge effect
adhesively
A Dream Play
Idaean vine
adderstone
adder's-wort
adversaria
advertence
advertency
adventurer
advertiser
Adventists
adventitia
adjectival
idle pulley
edifyingly
Addis Ababa
additament
admirative
admiration
admiraunce
advisatory
Edwin Drood
advisement
advice note
advice-boat
admiringly
adhibition
additional
administer
Adriamycin®
Adrian Mole
sdeignfull
advisorate
admissible
admittable
admittedly
admittance
odd-jobbing
Adullamite
idoloclast
adulterate
adulterant
adulteress
adulterine
adulterise
adulterize
adulterous
Adolf Meyer
adelantado
edulcorate
edulcorant
odd-looking
addle-pated
adolescent
idolatress
idolatrise
idolatrize
Odelsthing
idolatrous
Adam's apple
Adam and Eve
adamantean
adamantine
idem sonans
idempotent
Adam Cooper
Adamitical
odontalgia
odontalgic
adenectomy
identified
identifier
odontomata
odontocete
odontogeny
odontolite
odontology
I don't think
Edenburgen
edentulous
adenovirus
idiopathic
advocation
advocatory
idiot board
adsorbable
idiolectic
idiolectal
admonitive
admonition
admonitory
idiot light
ideologist
adsorptive
adsorption
idiot-proof
ideography
odiousness
adroitness
adaptative
adaptation
adipic acid
adaptively
edaphology
adequately
adequative
ad crumenam
odorimetry
address bus
Edith Evans
editorship
adjuration
adjuratory
adjunctive
adjunction
sdrucciola
Edmund Kean
adjudgment
adjudicate
adsuki bean
adzuki bean
à deux mains
adjustable
adjustably
adjustment
Eddy Merckx
eddy vortex
✧devanagari
metagalaxy
get a handle
megagamete
hexavalent
separately
relaxative
reparative
separative
separatism
defamation
relaxation
reparation
separation
separatist
melanaemia
set against
defamatory
reparatory
separatory
metacarpal
metacarpus
separatrix
megaparsec
metatarsal
metatarsus
Béla Bartók
pedal-board
sedan chair
pedal cycle
menarcheal
debauchery
revanchism
revanchist
✧renascence
melancholy
megascopic
defalcator
venae cavae
bel-accoyle
gey and easy
demandable
regardable
rewardable
regardless
rewardless
retardment
verandahed
heraldship
rehandling
decandrian
hexandrian
Gerald Ford
remand home
decandrous
hexandrous
herald-duck
demand pull
sewage farm

sexagenary
debateable
rebateable
sesame seed
femaleness
sedateness
beware lest
debasement
debatement
defacement
rebatement
regalement
legal eagle
mega-merger
legateship
beware that
Sexagesima
delayering
dewatering
cesarevich
cesarewich
metamerism
Melanesian
sea anemone
decamerous
hexamerous
hexametric
decahedral
hexahedral
decahedron
hexahedron
metalepsis
metaleptic
metacentre
meganewton
decadently
✧dewar flask
Texas fever
hemangioma
metaphrase
metaphrast
detachable
seraphical
detachedly
decathlete
detachment
megaphonic
metatheory
Metatheria
metaphoric
semaphoric
metathorax
metaphysic
metatheses
metathesis
metathetic
beta rhythm
decapitate
delaminate
deracinate
desalinate
gelatinate
repaginate
revalidate
negatively
relatively
debasingly
debatingly
defacingly
delayingly
menacingly
ceramic hob
megalithic
hepatitis A
hepatitis B
desalinise
desalinize
gelatinise
gelatinize
keratinise
keratinize
relativise
relativize
negativism
relativism
ceramicist
negativist
relativist
negativity
relativity
tenability
get a wicket
relational
venational
aes alienum
gelatinoid
gelatinous
keratinous
behavioral
legalistic
melanistic
retaliator
remarkable
remarkably
remark upon
retail bank
recallable
Heraclidan
dérailleur
derailment
recallment
retailment
Heracleian
Nehallenia
hexaplaric
metallurgy
metaplasia
metaplasis
Heraclitus
red admiral
hexaëmeron
detainable
regainable
retainable
detainment
regainment
retainment
repainting
penannular
hepatomata
melanomata
teratomata
megalosaur
Nematoidea
get a move on
teratogeny
pedal-organ
devalorise
devalorize
melaconite
metabolise
metabolite
metabolize
nematocide
revalorise
revalorize
senatorial
venatorial
demagogism
metabolism
pedagogism
pedagogics
decalogist
decapodous
geratology
hepatology
keratotomy
nematology
teratology
ceratopsid
hepatocyte
melanocyte
nematocyst
decampment
pedal point
set a sponge
remarriage
repatriate
repairable
Beta Crucis
repair-shop
decagramme
metastable
tenantable
penalty box
pedantical
decastichs
tenantless
department
tenantship
hexactinal
Sebastopol
Sevastopol
xenarthral
recapturer
departures
metastases
metastasis
metastatic
devastator
penalty try
cerastiums
devastavit
Texas tower
denaturant
Pegasus Bay
denaturise
denaturize
Belarusian
Bela Lugosi
Texas wedge
decagynian
hexagynian
decagynous
hexagynous
legacy duty
herb garden
keyboarder
cembra pine
semblative
lesbianism
kerb-market
wet blanket
Ben Bradlee
pea-brained
membranous
herbicidal
herbaceous
Serbo-Croat
herb Gerard
pebble-ware
pebbledash
kerb-vendor
feebleness
kerb weight
herb bennet
verb phrase
Red Brigade
New Britain
Jew-baiting
Leibnizian
verballing
verbal note
verbal noun
verbena-oil
red-blooded
herb Robert
kerb-trader
memberless
membership
seaborgium
Herbartian
Selbornian
Herbert Lom
sea burdock
herbariums
Derbyshire
melba sauce
sea biscuit
tea biscuit
melba toast
sea-bathing
sea blubber
descramble
bedchamber
leuchaemia
neoclassic
reach after
merchantry
fetch a pump
red cabbage
sea cabbage
leucoblast
beach buggy
peach-bloom
leechcraft
peacockery
peacockish
peacock ore
Peace Corps
leucocytic
deuce court
peccadillo
beech-drops
leucoderma
del credere
teschenite
peacherino
geochemist
Seychelles
reschedule
beccaficos
mercifully
peacefully
beachfront
henceforth
deactivate
reactivate
bescribble
tetchiness
reactively
kerchiefed
perceiving
reactivity
fen-cricket
reactional
tea clipper
descriptor
pencil-case
pencil-lead
New College
pencilling
beach-la-mar
perchloric
percolator
peacemaker
peach Melba
fence month
percentage
descendant
wet canteen
descendeur
descendent
deaconship
Fescennine
mercantile
percentile
descending
descension
seicentist
deaconhood
geocentric
peace of God
bedclothes
deschooler
teichopsia
led captain
sea captain
leucoplast
bench press
percipient
mercaptide
perceptive
perception
leucopenia
leucopenic
peace-party
perceptual
teacupfuls
redcurrant
percurrent
percursory
merceriser
Peace River
mercerizer
Reichsland
Reichsrath
Reichsbank
reichsmark
Wenceslaus
percussant
percussive
percussion
rescission
peach-stone
rescissory
percutient
seecatchie
gem-cutting
reacquaint
reaccustom
rencounter
rev counter
henchwoman
Letchworth
peach-water
headbanger
headmaster
head waiter
hendecagon
mendicants
mendicancy
veldschoen
mendacious
needle-case
needle-bath
needle bank
lead pencil
dead-weight
beadleship
needle time
readme file
needlefish
beadlehood
needlecord
meddlesome
needle-book
needlework
get dressed
seed vessel
heedlessly
needlessly
dead centre
dead-nettle
head-centre
dead-letter
feed-heater
herd's grass
hey-de-guise
hey-de-guyes
headcheese
headsheets
seed shrimp
headphones
Wendy House®
reed-thrush
lead the way
deadliness
dead ringer
deadlights
dead-finish
tea drinker
tendrilled
tendrillar
weedkiller
dendriform
Léo Delibes
Heidelberg
fer-de-lance
lead glance
lead-glance
Weddell Sea
hebdomadal
hebdomadar
hebdomader
seldomness
seldom when
ready money
ready-money
Geodimeter®
ready-mixed
reading age
wedding bed
reading-boy
leading dog
wedding day
leadenness
pendentive
set dancing
tendential
Headingley
geodynamic
leading man
perdendosi
welding rod
tendinitis
tendonitis
seed potato
dendroidal
head to head
head-to-head
dendrophis
dendrobium
headworker
lend colour
dendrology
dendrogram
o'er-drowsed
readoption
jeu de paume
headsquare
header tank
perdurable
renderable
perdurably
genderless
leaderless
tenderness
tenderfeet
leadership
readership
lead-arming
tenderling
perdurance
gelder rose
gender role
tenderloin
tenderfoot
deodoriser
tenderiser
leaderette
dead-ground
deodorizer
tenderizer
geodesical
jeu d'esprit
lead astray
geodetical
head-stream
deadstroke
headstrong
head-lugged
head-hugger
yerd-hunger
Gerd Muller
head-bummer
headhunter

Zend-Avesta
Meadowbank
meadow lark
beadswoman
seed oyster
rendezvous
generalate
veteran car
telecamera
Resedaceae
Senegalese
telepathic
Telemachus
federalise
federalize
federative
Generalife
generalise
generalize
generative
revelative
seven-a-side
vegetative
vegetating
federalism
Genevanism
defecation
delegation
denegation
federation
generation
hebetation
regelation
relegation
renegation
✧revelation
vegetarian
vegetation
veneration
telematics
federalist
generalist
generality
generalled
renewables
oedematose
Geneva gown
oedematous
revelatory
generatrix
pederastic
telecasted
benefactor
telecaster
relevantly
Peter Blake
resemblant
resembling
Decembrist
reverb unit
Peter Brook
rememberer
Decemberly
hereabouts
Seleucidae
Seleucidan
telescreen
Rebeccaite
redescribe
beseeching
Rebeccaism

defenceman
senescence
Seger cones
telescopic
Zener cards
aerenchyma
mesenchyme
defendable
dependable
Peter Debye
dependably
dependance
dependence
dependency
Zener diode
Beres drops
decelerate
degenerate
regenerate
revegetate
degeneracy
regeneracy
reverencer
referendum
sereneness
severeness
Pete Seeger
televérité
cerebellic
bejewelled
cerebellum
cerebellar
telerecord
degenerous
pedereroes
tête-de-pont
telemetric
Celebes Sea
telecentre
tenemental
reverently
vehemently
Lee Enfield
revengeful
detergence
detergency
Betelgeuse
genethliac
telephonic
telephoner
telechiric
lederhosen
telephotos
jewel-house
hereticate
rededicate
hereditary
veterinary
remediable
remediably
Genesiacal
Gene Wilder
répétiteur
remediless
beneficent
redelivery
feverishly
✧benedicite
genericise
genericize
meperidine

repetitive
selegiline
benefiting
beneficial
Ceredigion
repetition
television
geneticist
hereditist
bedevilled
remedially
Venetianed
Gene Pitney
veneficous
heresiarch
benefitted
deregister
reregister
Benedictus
televisual
televiewer
repealable
resealable
revealable
revealment
genealogic
teleologic
Verey light
bedellship
repellance
repellence
repellancy
repellency
rebellious
Peter Lorre
redeemable
redeemably
redeemless
teres major
determined
determiner
teres minor
telesmatic
secernment
teleonomic
telegnosis
decennoval
✧never-never
here you are
redecorate
heterogamy
heterotaxy
Heterocera
benevolent
feme covert
heterogeny
penelopise
penelopize
developing
ceremonial
hegemonial
hegemonism
semeiotics
hegemonist
generosity
teleworker
Heteropoda
heretofore
telegonous
heterocont
heterodont

heterokont
selenodont
heterodoxy
heterogony
heterology
heteronomy
new economy
new-economy
selenology
Pete Conrad
generously
temerously
reredorter
here to stay
werewolves
heterodyne
Peter Pears
redemptive
redemption
sevenpence
sevenpenny
peremptory
redemptory
metempiric
fever pitch
deferrable
penetrable
referrable
referrible
penetrably
telebridge
tenebrific
researcher
rehearsing
penetralia
cerebrally
deterrence
penetrance
penetrancy
veneer-moth
tenebrious
telegraphy
meteoritic
celebrated
genevrette
meteorital
celebrator
desecrater
desecrator
penetrator
telewriter
cerebritis
René Préval
Lebensraum
Seven Stars
defeasible
defensible
releasable
reversible
defensibly
reversibly
reversedly
Peter-see-me
Peter Stein
teleostean
Seven Sages
nécessaire
defenseman
defeasance
seven-score
teleostome

Teleostomi
Peter Scott
demeasnure
Petersburg
Regensburg
fenestrate
revestiary
deceptible
defectible
delectable
detectable
detectible
detestable
receptible
rejectable
rejectible
repeatable
revertible
selectable
delectably
detestably
receptacle
dejectedly
dementedly
repeatedly
seventh day
seventh-day
seventieth
nepenthean
desertless
recentness
relentless
selectness
relentment
resentment
regentship
regent-bird
repertoire
semestrial
pedestrian
derestrict
✧fenestella
Nemertinea
repentance
resentence
deceptious
dejections
mesenteric
beweltered
debentured
Sefer Torah
mesenteron
tête-à-têtes
deregulate
reregulate
vegeburger
Venezuelan
de Beauvoir
rere-supper
deceivable
receivable
reservable
deceivably
deservedly
reservedly
decemviral
denervated
Helen Wills
lever-watch
celery salt
celery pine

Pelecypoda
heresy-hunt
self-danger
self-taught
pen-feather
sea feather
self-parody
self-hatred
self-raised
beef cattle
beefmaster
self-abuser
perficient
perfect gas
perfective
perfecting
self-acting
perfection
self-action
perfidious
self-regard
self-feeder
self-seeder
self-severe
leafleteer
self-deceit
new-fledged
leafleting
self-denial
self-seeker
self-repose
selflessly
leafletted
leaf beetle
self-mettle
fee-fi-fo-fum
red-figured
leaf-sheath
Geoff Hurst
self-binder
self-giving
self-rising
self-killed
self-willed
self-filler
self-killer
beef-witted
perfoliate
self-slayer
self-glazed
self-unable
leaf insect
self-inject
newfangled
leaf mosaic
beef tomato
self-loader
reafforest
self-loving
self-moving
self-motion
self-cocker
leaf monkey
self-rolled
self-bounty
self-colour
leaf-hopper
self-poised
leaf spring
self-breath
perforable

leaf-bridge
self-profit
self-praise
ley-farming
performing
Zeffirelli
perfervour
perforated
perforator
perforatus
self-driven
beef-brewis
self-esteem
net-fishery
net-fishing
sea-fishing
Neofascism
Neofascist
self-styled
self-murder
beefburger
self-ruling
deaf-mutism
leaf-cutter
Deo favente
self-exiled
geographic
geographer
Belgravian
Deo gratias
verge-board
weighboard
neighborly
weigh-bauks
sea goddess
meagreness
sea gherkin
seigneurie
vengefully
lengthways
lengthwise
lengthsman
weigh-house
penguinery
Serge Lifar
Bengal fire
bergamasca
neogenesis
neogenetic
seignorage
Bergsonism
Bergsonian
zeuglodont
geognostic
Ledge Piece
ledger bait
vergership
ledger line
weightless
Lech Walesa
nephralgia
hen-hearted
déshabillé
Delhi belly
methodical
Methedrine®
bêche-de-mer
methodiser
methodizer
Gethsemane
technetium

Words marked ✧ can also be spelled with one or more capital letters

Hephaestus
nephograph
technicals
technicise
technicize
nephridium
technicism
technician
technicist
rechristen
Aethelbert
cephalagra
nephologic
Cephalonia
methyldopa
cephalopod
keyhole saw
Aethelstan
cephalitis
Aethelwulf
methomania
mechanical
methinketh
mechanizer
technofear
nephropexy
methionine
dethroning
Aethiopian
technopole
nephrology
nephrotomy
technology
technocrat
Jethro Tull
reshipment
bed-hopping
rechipping
hetherward
netherward
lethargied
lethargise
lethargize
red herring
hen harrier
zephyr lily
Zephyrinus
nethermore
nethermost
✧methuselah
nephoscope
mephitical
get hitched
Lesh states
medicament
sexivalent
delicately
Mexican hog
decimalise
decimalize
dedicative
derivative
devitalise
devitalize
hesitative
medicalise
medicalize
medicative
meditative
recitative
retinalite
revitalise
revitalize
recitativi
genitalial
seminarial
decimalism
revivalism
tepidarium
decimation
dedication
delibation
deligation
deliration
denization
depilation
derivation
gemination
hesitation
levigation
leviration
levitation
medication
meditation
recitation
remigation
seminarian
semination
velitation
vesication
recitativo
Belisarius
decimalist
recitalist
revivalist
seminarist
feminality
seminality
demi-cannon
dedicatory
depilatory
hesitatory
vesicatory
pedipalpus
Mexican tea
decimal tab
medicaster
hesitantly
retinacula
Mexican War
perikaryon
Kevin Bacon
beribboned
Felix Bloch
redisburse
mediocracy
Lee Iacocca
bewitchery
bewitching
mediocrity
heliacally
seriocomic
dehiscence
meliaceous
periscopic
meniscuses
desiccated
desiccator
rediscount
rediscover
behindhand
behind bars
periodical
behind time
behind-door
her indoors
behind post
bewildered
desiderata
Venice talc
New Ireland
deliberate
desiderate
delineable
rewireable
demirepdom
peripeteia
semiterete
desireless
defilement
definement
refinement
repinement
retirement
revilement
revivement
aedileship
desiderium
perihelion
peripetian
Belize City
semi-weekly
peridermal
Venice gold
ceriferous
sebiferous
setiferous
setigerous
refine upon
retired pay
perimetric
hemihedral
perimetral
perineural
hemihedron
peritectic
pedimented
pedimental
regimental
delineator
residenter
penitently
reticently
delineavit
beliefless
reliefless
tea infuser
heliograph
petit grain
melic-grass
vexingness
seeing that
mediagenic
meningioma
teeing area
periegesis
meningitic
meningitis
Peking duck
Jewish Pale
periphrase
perishable
relishable
perishably
perithecia
Jewishness
newishness
delightful
benighting
periphonic
Hemichorda
peripheric
peripheral
decipherer
semichorus
periphyton
debilitate
delimitate
felicitate
legitimate
revisitant
legitimacy
verifiable
semicircle
decisively
definitely
derisively
femininely
genitively
periwigged
deridingly
repiningly
retiringly
revilingly
revivingly
devilishly
resinified
revivified
decivilise
decivilize
definitive
legitimise
legitimize
semi-divine
femininism
legitimism
✧peridinium
recidivism
definition
peridinian
redivision
legitimist
recidivist
feminility
femininity
legibility
periwinkle
penicillin
definienda
deficience
desipience
recipience
resilience
meridional
revisional
✧petitioner
religioner
deficiency
recipiency
resiliency
demi-ditone
semi-ditone
felicitous
veridicous
semicirque
feministic
semi-liquid
definitude
religieuse
Felix Klein
heli-skiing
refillable
genialness
hemiplegia
hemiplegic
aerie light
serial time
periclinal
serial port
petiolated
feuilleton
heliolater
legislator
heliolatry
medium-wave
medium-term
melismatic
heliometer
designable
designedly
resignedly
designless
designment
resignment
Helianthus
semi-uncial
regionally
benignancy
hemianopia
designator
semi-annual
Heligoland
semi-double
helicoidal
peritoneal
peritoneum
lepidolite
peridotite
perigonial
perigonium
Heliconian
Mexico City
decinormal
lexicology
meritocrat
desirously
perilously
resinously
semipostal
melicotton
helicopter
Cecidomyia
hemisphere
petit point
Heliopolis
semi-opaque
heliopause
heliophyte
delinquent
relinquish
peritricha
reciprocal
heritrices
semi-drying
decigramme
hemicrania
hemitropic
hemitropal
lexigraphy
serigraphy
denigrator
meliorator
heritrixes
Cecil Sharp
remissible
periosteal
periosteum
remissness
mediastina
Delia Smith
redissolve
peninsular
aeciospore
Felixstowe
helioscope
set in stone
teliospore
genius loci
petits pois
periastron
Nevil Shute
devil's dung
devil's dust
registrant
registrary
heriotable
remittable
resistible
resistibly
mediatress
resistless
belittling
rebirthing
Cerinthian
geriatrics
pediatrics
geriatrist
peristylar
peristomal
desistance
desistence
remittance
✧resistance
heliotrope
heliotropy
heliotypic
sericteria
registered
hemipteral
peripteral
hemipteran
heliotaxis
geniculate
pediculate
reticulate
semilunate
vesiculate
Pediculati
reticulary
semilucent
reliquaire
pedicurist
residually
tediousome
vesiculose
meticulous
pediculous
periculous
Oedipus Rex
deliquesce
netiquette
semiquaver
believable
relievable
medievally
reviewable
review body
review copy
Kenilworth
mesitylene
perimysium
hemicyclic
pericyclic
hemizygous
perigynous
serjeantry
Medjugorje
Ben Johnson
perjinkety
perjinkity
perjurious
red jasmine
Meiji Tenno
weak-handed
necklacing
verkrampte
Lee Kuan Yew
leukoblast
leukocytic
jerked-meat
leukoderma
desk editor
weak-headed
deckle-edge
beekeeping
seakeeping
deck tennis
fecklessly
recklessly
weak-minded
weakliness
weak-hinged
weak-willed
weak sister
deskilling
Berkeleian
New Kingdom
jerkinhead
weekending
Neo-Kantian
weak moment
get knotted!
leukoplast
leukopenia
leukopenic
deck-bridge
peckerwood
Beaker Folk
jerk around
beakerfuls
Becky Sharp
deck quoits
well-padded
✧hell's angel
bellhanger
bellyacher
dealbation

egocentric
egg capsule
egg custard
Yggdrasill
agrégation
aglet babie
ignes fatui
ignimbrite
Ngaio Marsh
ignipotent
egoistical
agglutinin
agonic line
agentivity
agonisedly
agonistics
agony uncle
agency shop
agonizedly
ignoration
ignorantly
ugsomeness
ignobility
Ugro-Finnic
agronomial
agronomics
agrologist
agronomist
a good thing
egg poacher
agapanthus
Egyptology
egurgitate
aggrandise
aggrandize
agoraphobe
aggressive
aggression
aggravated
ego-surfing
ego-tripper
agitatedly
pheasantry
cheat bread
wheat berry
phraseless
phrase book
wheatfield
shear force
The Angelus
sheathless
sheathfish
sheathbill
The Animals
phialiform
Rhea Silvia
wheat midge
The Annales
choanocyte
theatrical
D H Lawrence
cheapskate
wheat sheaf
shear-steel
thwartways
thwartedly
thwartship
thwartwise
the antique
shea butter
shearwater
shoal water
chlamydate
chlamydiae
chlamydial
chlamydias
Rhea Sylvia
shear zones
The Beatles
shabracque
The Bacchae
The Bee Gees
shebeening
the big cats
The Bahamas
chubbiness
shabbiness
Ghibelline
the Balance
Thabo Mbeki
Theban year
shibboleth
rhabdolith
the boonies
the Borders
rhubarbing
the Channel
Chuck Berry
checkclerk
Chick Corea
Thucydides
check digit
thickening
chicken out
chucker-out
chickenpox
chicken run
Chichester
the Creator
chick flick
thick-grown
chocaholic
chocoholic
shockingly
checklaton
Shackleton
shecklaton
chocolatey
phocomelia
the cap fits
checkpoint
shockproof
shockstall
chockstone
thick-skull
chock-tight
check-taker
chuck wagon
chuckwalla
the dreaded
shuddering
whidah bird
whydah bird
shadchanim
shoddiness
thuddingly
Rhodymenia
thé dansant
The Dunciad
whodunitry
rhodophane
shade plant
khidmutgar
shidduchim
khediviate
shadow mark
shadow mask
shadowcast
shadowless
shadow play
Rh-negative
shoemaking
chrematist
Ahvenanmaa
wheel brace
three balls
three bells
chief-baron
sheep-biter
wheel clamp
wheel-clamp
wheelchair
three-cleft
shield-hand
shield-maid
shieldrake
threadbare
thread-lace
thread mark
shieldwall
thread-cell
shield fern
thread vein
shieldless
shrewdness
threadiest
shieldlike
threadlike
shieldling
Rhoeadales
Shieldinch
shield pond
threadworm
the elderly
cheesecake
cheese-head
phrenesiac
cheesemite
cheesewire
The Eternal
cheesewood
cheesed off
Shreveport
sheep-faced
cheerfully
sheet-glass
cheechakos
cheechalko
shoeshiner
wheelhorse
wheelhouse
wheelie bin
cheekiness
cheeriness
cheesiness
wheeziness
wheezingly
sheepishly
shrewishly
thievishly
phoenixism
Phoenician
the evil one
wheedle out
sheep-louse
phlegmonic
phlegmasia
sheet music
phlegmatic
sheet metal
shrewmouse
phlebolite
threnodial
phaelonion
threnodist
Chaetopoda
phaenology
phlebotomy
phrenology
phaenotype
shlemozzle
three-phase
sheep-plant
cheekpiece
three-piece
three-piled
threepence
threepenny
three-parts
three-pound
cheekpouch
Khmer Rouge
sheepshank
phrensical
three-sided
sheep's-head
threescore
sheep's-foot
Shrewsbury
sheep's eyes
sheeptrack
shoestring
thief-taker
threatened
threatener
cheektooth
shoe buckle
shift about
chiffchaff
chuff-chuff
the Fifteen
shaft-horse
chuffiness
shiftiness
chaffingly
the fair sex
shuffle-cap
shuffle off
chiffonier
the Forties
Whiggarchy
whiggamore
shag-haired
phagocytic
phagedaena
the Godhead
phagedenic
Che Guevara
shagreened
shagged out
shagginess
Whiggishly
The Gorgias
shaggy mane
the heavies
the hiccups
The Hollies
the horrors
the hard way
phthisical
phthisicky
The Hustler
The Hot Five
The Hay Wain
Thailander
chainbrake
chairborne
Rheinberry
chairbound
chain cable
shriech-owl
shritch-owl
chain drive
chaise-cart
chaiseless
choiceness
thriveless
Chris Evert
shrinelike
shriveling
shrivelled
chain grate
shriche-owl
thrivingly
rhoicissus
shrinkpack
shrinkable
shrink-wrap
shrillness
Chris Lloyd
chair-organ
choir organ
Thai boxing
Chris Smith
chain-smoke
chain store
the insured
Christmasy
Christabel
theistical
Christless
thriftless
thriftiest
thrift shop
Christlike
christener
Christhood
shrievalty
chainwheel
chairwoman
the jobless
the jig is up
the jitters
chukka boot
chokeberry
choke chain
shakuhachi
Chekhovian
a hall, a hall
choliambic
chiliarchy
shellacked
chiliastic
child abuse
chalkboard
chalybeate
whole blood
childbirth
shellbound
whole bound
cholic acid
thale cress
phylactery
whole cloth
chylaceous
chelicerae
cheliceral
thalictrum
shelldrake
pholidosis
shillelagh
Chelsea bun
challenged
challenger
Cheltenham
sheltering
Childermas
chalcedony
wholegrain
cholagogic
cholagogue
thill-horse
chalkiness
chilliness
shelliness
chillingly
childishly
phallicism
Chalcidian
thalliform
philologic
philologue
philologer
whale louse
chalumeaux
shale-miner
shell money
philomathy
shell mound
phalangeal
whaling-gun
phalangist
The Leopard
phyllotaxy
phalloidin
phylloxera
phelloderm
chalcocite
shallowing
Phyllopoda
Phyllotria
phallocrat
whole-plate
chilopodan
philopoena
philippina
✧philippine
Philippise
Philippize
Philippian
childproof
shellproof
Philip Roth
whale shark
the Last Day
Philistean
✧philistine
Philistian
thalassian
wholesaler
child's play
Chelmsford
whale's food
chalkstone
whale's bone
shellshock
philosophe
philosophy
child-study
philatelic
Chaleur Bay
phillumeny
wholewheat
philoxenia
whillywhaw
shellycoat
Rhamnaceae
shammashim
thumb a ride
thumb a lift
thump along
chemiatric
chimpanzee
chemicking
chemically
thymectomy
chimney can
✧chamaeleon
chambering
shimmering
whimpering
chamber-lye
chamberpot
chimney pot
Chambertin
chimney top
themselves
shamefaced
shamefully
thumb index
thumb-index
chumminess
whimsiness
thumpingly
thumbikins
champignon
thimbleful
the million
thimblerig
thumb latch
The Monkees
chemonasty
Chimborazo
rhomboidei
rhomboidal
rhomboides
the moodies
whomsoever
shame on you
thumb piano
thumbpiece
thumbprint
shame-proof
chimerical
chambranle
thimerosal
rhyme royal

 Words marked ✧ can also be spelled with one or more capital letters

thumbstall
Thomas Mann
Thomas Edur
the mostest
Thomas Gold
Thomas Hood
Thomas Lord
Thomas More
Thomas Cook
thumbs down
thumbs-down
Thomas Arne
thumbscrew
Thomas Gray
chemisette
chemotaxis
shamiyanah
think again
Rhyniaceae
phantasime
shin-barker
thin-walled
phantasmic
phantasmal
think aloud
think about
phantastic
China aster
phantastry
chinaberry
Rhineberry
thenabouts
sheng cycle
chinachina
phonically
rhinoceros
rhinocerot
phenacetin
phenocryst
change face
change tack
changeable
thunderbox
changeably
Thunder Bay
thunderegg
change gear
chanceless
changeless
the needful
thunbergia
thunder god
channel-hop
channelise
channelize
changeling
thundering
chandelier
channelled
chancellor
channeller
change down
thunderous
thunderous
chance upon
change over
changeover
hankfully
Rhinegrave
Chinagraph®
phonograph
China grass
China goose
shanghaied
shanghaier
✧chinchilla
Chandigarh
chanciness
chunkiness
thinginess
thinkingly
thin client
rhinolalia
chandlerly
phonolitic
phenomenal
phenomenon
phonematic
phonometer
shenanigan
phantomish
whensoever
phonophore
rhinophyma
shandrydan
phanerogam
thenardite
chondromas
chondritic
chondritis
think shame
chank-shell
✧chinese ink
china stone
✧rhinestone
rhinoscope
rhinoscopy
Chinese red
phonetical
rhinotheca
think twice
phenotypic
phonotypic
thanatosis
thingumbob
chinquapin
rhinovirus
China white
Shane Warne
shunt-wound
shandygaff
phoneyness
shantytown
shinny down
theomaniac
chloramine
shoot a line
chloralism
chromatics
chloralose
throw about
theomantic
chromatype
thromboses
thrombosis
thrombotic
shoot craps
shroud-laid
shroudless
shroud line
the Old Bill
chrome tape
throneless
theotechny
Shrovetide
theoretics
chrome alum
throne room
thiopental
thronged up
throughout
throughput
throughway
theophobia
theophanic
theophoric
chloridate
chlorinate
theodicean
chloridise
chloridize
chlorinise
chlorinize
Rh-positive
chromidium
chlorinity
chronicity
chronicler
✧chronicles
shoot it out
phlogistic
phlogiston
shoofly pie
the ould sod
The Osmonds
thrown silk
theopneust
theologate
chromomere
theosophic
chlorophyl
chromophil
theosopher
phlogopite
theodolite
theologise
theologize
theologian
Theodosius
chaologist
rheologist
theogonist
theologist
chionodoxa
chromosome
chloroform
theonomous
chronology
chromogram
chronogram
chronotron
chloroquin
chlorodyne
chromotype
thiouracil
rheotropic
theocratic
Theocritus
Shropshire
throw stick
throatband
throatlash
throatiest
throttling
throatwort
rheostatic
throat-full
The Odyssey
whip handle
The Planets
chaptalise
chaptalize
shop walker
chip basket
whiptailed
chapfallen
chopfallen
chaplaincy
chaplainry
Shepparton
shipmaster
whippeting
The Poetics
shopkeeper
chip heater
ship letter
The Prelude
whip the cat
shopaholic
shop window
choppiness
whippiness
ship-rigged
shoplifter
chapel cart
shop-in-shop
ship-holder
the Prophet
rhapsodise
rhapsodize
the Promise
rhapsodist
whip socket
shopsoiled
Rhipiptera
shipwright
chaparajos
chaparejos
shipbroker
shop around
Ship's Stern
chopsticks
chapatties
whipstitch
cheque card
chequebook
choriambic
choriambus
thereanent
thermalise
Thermalite®
thermalize
pharmacist
thereamong
thereabout
whereabout
whirl-about
thorn apple
J H Breasted
thereafter
whereafter
whore after
whirlblast
cherubical
shortbread
The Robbers
Charybdian
cherubimic
shard-borne
short coats
third class
third-class
Characidae
charactery
the Rockies
shortcrust
shirt dress
The Red King
churn-drill
Charadrius
short-dated
charge card
charge-hand
ahorseback
chargeable
chargeably
chargeless
Thar Desert
sharp-edged
shortening
shereefian
thirteenth
charge down
Cherkesses
✧charleston
sheriffdom
shirt frill
shirt front
third force
chirograph
choregraph
shore-going
chirognomy
churchward
churchyard
church-rate
thornhedge
churchless
church text
churchgoer
shire horse
Church Army
charthouse
whorehouse
The Rainbow
share index
chirpiness
shirtiness
thorniness
wharfinger
phorminges
charmingly
whirlingly
churlishly
thermionic
where it's at
thermistor
shore leave
Charollais
short-lived
pheromonal
chiromancy
short metre
cherimoyer
Ahura Mazda
Charentais
pharyngeal
chironomic
chironomid
chironomer
sharp-nosed
Pharaoh ant
thyrsoidal
short order
short-order
third order
chersonese
✧charioteer
chervonets
thermophil
lherzolite
thermopile
thermotics
chardonnay
thermoform
chordotomy
choreology
thermology
thermogram
thermostat
Chiroptera
Therapsida
thornproof
third party
third-party
Charophyta
shire-reeve
chirurgeon
chirurgery
sherardise
sherardize
Third Reich
short-range
✧chartreuse
dharmshala
churn-staff
short sheep
wheresoe'er
whore's bird
chorus girl
pharisaism
shortsword
short score
short story
short sixes
charitable
charitably
charity-boy
thirstless
thirstiest
chartulary
thereunder
whereunder
thoroughly
whereuntil
Theravadin
sharawadgi
sharawaggi
shirtwaist
short whist
Third World
shorewards
cherry bean
sharny peat
whirlybird
Cherry Ripe
cherry-pick
cherry plum
thirtyfold
cherry-coal
cherry tree
there you go
The Seasons
The Shadows
Lhasa Apsos
The Seagull
chessboard
physicking
physically
whist drive
chasse-café
chasteness
whispering
chaste tree
ghastfully
phosphoric
✧phosphorus
phosphoret
phosphuret
phosphatic
chestiness
the shivers
the sniffle
whiskified
The Shining
Chassidism
the science
chose jugée
shish kebab
chiselling
whistle off
the sandman
thysanuran
chasmogamy
Shoshonean
physiology
physiocrat
she's apples
the serpent
ghost shark
Rhesus baby
ghost story
ghost train
chest voice
the Seventy
ghost-write
whisky jack
chessylite
whisky john
whisky sour
Shetlandic
Shetlander
shotmaking
✧chittagong
whitebeard
whiteboard
white brass
white bread
whity-brown
white birch
whatabouts
white cedar
thetically
white crops
✧white dwarf
photodiode
shutterbug

chatterbox
what remedy?
white eagle
chattering
chittering
shattering
shuttering
whitterick
photo-essay
the theatre
white-faced
✧white friar
photoflood
white frost
photograph
photogenic
phytogenic
white goods
photoglyph
white-heart
thatchless
Whitehorse
white horse
white hause
White House
what though
white hawse
chota hazri
shot window
chattiness
The Thinker
Phytolacca
white light
châtelaine
photolysis
photolytic
rhythmical
rhythmless
The Timaeus
The Tempest
white magic
white metal
photometer
the Tempter
white meter
photometry
what an idea!
white night
white noise
The Tin Drum
photonasty
photonovel
Whit Monday
Ahithophel
whatsoever
shut up shop
photophily
photophobe
photophone
photophore
photophony
✧white paper
The Tar Baby
rhetorical
the three F's
the three R's
chitarrone
chitarroni
white slave
white sheet
white sugar

whitesmith
white stick
White's Club
photo shoot
photo story
white sauce
white stuff
white trash
White Teeth
phototrope
whitethorn
phototropy
phototypic
phytotoxic
phytotoxin
phototaxis
Whitsun ale
shut-out bid
Whit Sunday
Whitsunday
khitmutgar
shot-putter
white voice
white whale
white wheat
white water
white-water
chatoyance
chatoyancy
thousandth
rheumatise
rheumatize
thaumasite
Dhaulagiri
rheumatism
rheumatics
rheumatoid
✧chautauqua
shouldered
Chaucerism
Chaucerian
à haute voix
chaudfroid
chauffeuse
theurgical
thoughtful
Khrushchev
shoutingly
ghoulishly
chauvinism
the unities
chauvinist
the unknown
chaulmugra
chaud-mellé
thruppence
thruppenny
choucroute
chaussures
thrust past
chauntress
thrust into
the unwaged
shave-grass
shove-groat
Shivaistic
shovelware
✧the Village
shovelhead
shovelling
shovelnose

chivalrous
shovelfuls
chevrotain
the vapours
chevesaile
chevisance
the Wagoner
chew the cud
chew the fat
chew the rag
whewellite
The Wild One
chewing gum
showboater
shower bath
showerless
shower tray
showground
the Wise Men
showjumper
thixotrope
thixotropy
the year dot
chrysalids
chrysophan
chrysolite
chrysotile
phlyctaena
phlyctenae
rhizogenic
whizzingly
rhizomorph
rhizoplane
Rhizophora
rhizophore
dilatation
divagation
disavaunce
pit against
Mina Qaboos
disanalogy
vita patris
pit-a-patted
Nicaraguan
tidal basin
Dinah Craik
✧sinarchism
mica-schist
sinarchist
didascalic
final cause
vizard-mask
aid and abet
vivandière
win and wear
lizardfish
hit-and-miss
misandrist
Pirandello
ritardando
misandrous
✧dinanderie
minauderie
nip and tuck
dilacerate
disamenity
cicadellid
picaresque
Titanesque
ligamental
nidamental

nidamentum
vital flame
Pilao Falls
vital force
sisal grass
hidalgoish
hidalgoism
cibachrome
dilapidate
disanimate
divaricate
mirabilite
vitaminise
vitaminize
vitalising
vitalizing
miracidium
viraginian
vitalities
disability
likability
livability
ridability
cigarillos
Nina Simone
limaciform
viraginous
filariasis
vitalistic
tirailleur
misallying
pina colada
piña colada
pinacoidal
pinakoidal
pinakothek
dilatorily
limacology
bigamously
rifampicin
disappoint
disapprove
disapparel
tidal power
✧sinarquism
sinarquist
cicatricle
cicatrices
binaurally
disarrange
misarrange
bizarrerie
cicatrixes
vital spark
vital stain
vital signs
didactical
disastrous
pilastered
bipartisan
Midas touch
picayunish
bimanually
Mina Sulman
Tina Turner
miraculous
dika-butter
bivalvular
disadvance
misadvised
litany-desk

Hilary term
binary code
binary form
Kitakyushu
binary star
air-bladder
win by a head
Zimbabwean
niobic acid
riebeckite
nimbleness
tiebreaker
misbehaved
limb-girdle
nibblingly
fimbriated
diabolical
disbelieve
misbelieve
big-bellied
Kimball tag
ribbon-weed
ribbon-seal
disbenefit
ribbonfish
ribbon worm
Big Brother
timbrology
timberland
timberyard
timber-mare
timberhead
limberneck
limberness
disbarment
disburthen
Gilbertine
kimberlite
limburgite
timber line
oil-burning
Gilbertian
Gibberella
timber wolf
timber-toes
timber tree
diabetical
kibbutznik
pin-buttock
airbrushed
witch-alder
disc camera
discharger
wit-cracker
disclaimer
disc harrow
mischanter
pitch-black
discobolus
witchcraft
viscachera
minced beef
piccadillo
piccadilly
disco dance
discrepant
kitchendom
discretely
kitchen-fee
pitcherful
discretive

Diocletian
discretion
biochemist
miscreance
air cleaner
miscreancy
kitchen tea
miscreated
miscreator
Winchester®
✧winchester
discreetly
piscifauna
zincograph
piece goods
hitch-hiker
witch-hazel
circuiteer
bitchiness
pitchiness
filchingly
pinchingly
witchingly
kinchin-lay
circuitous
disculpate
miscellany
circulable
fiscal year
piccalilli
zinc blende
fiscal drag
disc floret
circularly
zincolysis
circulator
disc plough
disc flower
disc player
lincomycin
discommend
circumvent
circumcise
circumflex
circumpose
discommode
discompose
nincompoop
discomfort
Giacometti
mischmetal
viscometer
viscometry
circumduce
circumfuse
circummure
miscompute
circumduct
cincinnate
Cincinnati
diaconicon
disconcert
disconnect
disconsent
discontent
misconceit
miscontent
miscanthus
circensial
disconfirm
circensian

Vincentian
biocontrol
misconster
misconduct
pince-nezed
Jim Crow car
cinchonine
cinchonise
cinchonize
air-cooling
tinctorial
cinchonism
Jim Crowism
zinc-worker
disc jockey
disclosure
discipline
discophile
pinchpoint
pinchpenny
Discophora
sincipital
discarnate
air curtain
discordant
miscorrect
rip current
discordful
discursive
discerning
discursion
discursist
diachronic
discursory
discussant
discussive
die-casting
air-cushion
✧circassian
discission
discussion
pincushion
Dio Cassius
pitchstone
discutient
Kitcat Club
discourage
dischuffed
hiccoughed
discounsel
discoursal
miscounsel
discourser
diacaustic
diacoustic
discounter
pie-counter
viscountcy
discoverer
pitch-wheel
pitchwoman
mince words
ditchwater
winceyette
misdrawing
wild garlic
windfallen
windjammer
siddha yoga
pie diagram
wildcatter

wildebeest
vindicable
windscreen
vindictive
bird-scarer
vindicator
girdle cake
middle game
middle name
fiddle-back
fiddleback
Middle East
mind-bender
mind-reader
fiddlehead
middle term
Middle West
misdeemful
middle aged
Middle Ages
riddle-like
misdeeming
kiddiewink
mind-healer
fiddlewood
middlemost
bird-pepper
middlebrow
mindlessly
Kim Dae-jung
bird of prey
biodegrade
dildo-glass
hirdy-girdy
windshield
wind-shaken
wind chimes
bird-cherry
wild cherry
kindliness
disdainful
wild ginger
middlingly
riddlingly
bird-hipped
bird-witted
bird-skiing
wind sleeve
Diadelphia
wild flower
windflower
vindemiate
bird impact
hiddenness
sildenafil
wild endive
wild indigo
pieds noirs
biodynamic
midden-cock
hiddenmost
wind energy
Hindenbury
wildfowler
giddy-paced
bird-spider
kind-spoken
mild-spoken
hinderland
cinder path
hinderlans
Windermere
wilderness
rinderpest
wilderment
wild orchid
tinder-like
nidderling
hinderlins
wind-broken
Cinderella
hinderance
cinder cone
hindermost
wind dropsy
Hindustani
Hildesheim
Yiddishism
bird strike
pied-à-terre
windsurfer
yird-hunger
yird-hungry
wind-sucker
wild turkey
windburned
wind tunnel
windowpane
window sash
windowless
window seat
window-shop
windowsill
window-bole
midday meal
tiddlywink
wire-dancer
sidesaddle
fire-warden
cine camera
ciné camera
Piperaceae
vinegar-eel
literately
vinegar-fly
liberalise
liberalize
literalise
literalize
mineralise
mineralize
piperazine
River Adige
life-saving
pipe-laying
time-saving
vinegarish
bipedalism
cinerarium
liberalism
literalism
cineration
liberation
literation
sideration
kinematics
liberalist
literalist
mineralist
liberality
literality
literarily
kite-marked
fire-walker
linebacker
wire-walker
fire-basket
life jacket
bimetallic
wine vaults
mineral oil
cinema-goer
bipetalous
dipetalous
disepalous
liberatory
mineralogy
dive-dapper
wiretapper
pine carpet
time-barred
wire-haired
pine-barren
fire-raiser
five-parted
mile-castle
pine marten
fire-master
mineral tar
tidewaiter
wine taster
wine waiter
literature
mineral wax
fiberboard
tiger badge
disembogue
River Benue
disembroil
disembosom
river basin
disembowel
River Boyne
River Chari
like a charm
disenchain
disenchant
rivercraft
firescreen
widescreen
libecchios
virescence
River Congo
disenclose
Tibet cloth
life school
fixed costs
Oireachtas
River Cauca
River Clyde
video diary
river drift
River Donau
River Douro
Miles Davis
disendowed
aide-de-camp
life-tenant
cire perdue
pine needle
ride herd on
file-leader
vicegerent
viceregent
live weight
ciné vérité
time series
wine cellar
nineteenth
pine kernel
pike-keeper
timekeeper
livebearer
five senses
lifelessly
timelessly
tirelessly
live centre
pine-beetle
life-renter
pine beauty
time-served
file server
timeserver
Wife of Bath
wizen-faced
River Fleet
side effect
fire-office
line of fire
line of life
Pipe Office
riverfront
River Forth
liver fluke
River Glåma
mimeograph
fiberglass
wired glass
disengaged
mixed grill
divergence
divergency
liver-grown
dimethoate
give the air
ride a hobby
pine-chafer
give the gun
give the lie
give the nod
river horse
time-sharer
time-thrust
fire-shovel
Eisenhower
kinesipath
kinetic art
winebibber
like-minded
sidewinder
River Indus
vine-mildew
livelihead
likeliness
liveliness
timeliness
wifeliness
five-finger
fivefinger
rivetingly
five-eighth
line-fisher
liverishly
tigerishly
cimetidine
nifedipine
piperidine
life-giving
pipelining
like billy-o
time-killer
time signal
likelihood
livelihood
misericord
viperiform
Hideki Tojo
side mirror
Mike Gibson
River Jumna
vitellicle
fire blight
fixed light
River Loire
kite-flying
side glance
fire blanks
pineal body
pixellated
River Lethe
fire-plough
dice-player
like blazes
mixed-media
River Marne
piped music
River Mosel
dilemmatic
mileometer
River Meuse
river mouth
pigeon pair
disennoble
hibernacle
Vireonidae
River Negro
River Niger
fire engine
pigeon-wing
Eilean Siar
River Neman
pigeon-toed
pigeonhole
pigeon-post
bite and sup
video nasty
ride and tie
ride-and-tie
liner notes
river novel
dive-bomber
tiresomely
give tongue
wide-bodied
give notice
nine-to-five
siderolite
Ciceronian
fire-policy
literosity
ride bodkin
mine worker
rice cooker
time-worker
wireworker
life-rocket
wine cooler
Five Points
vice-county
give colour
bioecology
diseconomy
sideboards
vice-consul
viperously
wine bottle
life-mortar
siderostat
River Plata
River Plate
tiger prawn
tinea pedis
widespread
cider press
didelphine
fixed-price
didelphian
diremption
fine-spoken
pipe-opener
videophone
didelphous
linen paper
time spirit
Liber Pater
disespouse
disempower
five-square
line squall
give or take
hide or hair
Viverridae
wire bridge
pileorhiza
River Rhine
mime artist
Fidel Ramos
Viverrinae
pipe-wrench
vine-branch
River Rhône
give ground
pile-driver
wine-grower
wiredrawer
Niue Island
disenslave
fire escape
life-estate
riverscape
tiger snake
tiger shark
miner's lamp
fixed stars
give a start
licensable
niger seeds
diseaseful
River Seine
widershins
liver salts
River Somme
miner's inch
fiberscope
River Saône
miner's worm
Nigel Short
licentiate
direct mail
disentrail
disentrain
mixed train
silentiary
digestible
divertible
divestible
River Tiber
liberty cap
digestedly
River Tweed
sidestream
directness
directress
silentness
divestment
misentreat
River Trent
side street
River Tagus
Directoire
disentwine
River Teifi
bimestrial
silent film
liberty-man
dilettante
dilettanti
five-stones
like a tansy
minestrone
sidestroke
directions
licentious
direct cost
disenthral
River Tisza
bidentated
disentitle
miseducate
wire-guided
dime museum
Nibelungen
fine-tuning
sinecurism
sinecurist
fire bucket
wirepuller
bisexually
wine funnel
sine qua non
lime-burner
Life Guards
file-cutter
minehunter
River Volga
River Volta
eigenvalue
disenvelop
disenviron
Tiger Woods
sideswiper
liverwurst
River Weser
time switch
river water
side by side

dispersive
dispersion
dispersoid
dispermous
hippuritic
dispirited
disparates
Hippurites
air-passage
disposable
disposedly
dispossess
dispassion
Lippes loop
dispositor
disputable
disputably
hippety-hop
dispatcher
dispatches
limpet mine
gippy tummy
nilpotency
dispiteous
✧diophysite
biophysics
Lippizzana
Lippizaner
disqualify
cinque-pace
cinquefoil
disquieten
disquietly
lip-reading
misreading
rip-roaring
diurnalist
bioreactor
rib-roaster
fibreboard
fibroblast
Tim Robbins
microbiota
microburst
microcrack
hierocracy
citric acid
nitric acid
picric acid
micrococci
ditrochean
microcline
vibraculum
fiery cross
vitrectomy
jinricksha
microcytic
micro drive
aigre-douce
pierceable
fierceness
bierkeller
microfibre
microfiche
nitrifying
microflora
microfarad
microfauna
cirrigrade
hierograph
micrograph
vibrograph
fibreglass
nitro-group
ditriglyph
hieroglyph
diarrhoeic
diarrhoeal
diorthosis
diorthotic
cirrhipede
migraineur
piercingly
vitrailled
migrainous
giardiasis
mitre-joint
jinrikisha
fibrillate
fibrillary
hierologic
micrologic
microlight
citrulline
fibrillose
fibrillous
tirra-lirra
miarolitic
microlitic
hierolatry
Vikram Seth
hieromancy
nigromancy
micrometre
micrometer
nitrometer
vibrometer
micrometry
fibrinogen
fibronogen
Dibranchia
citronella
Hieronymic
citron wood
citron tree
Micronesia
vitriolate
vitriolise
vitriolize
vitreosity
Cirrhopoda
fibre-optic
hierophant
hiera-picra
Cirripedia
higry-pigry
disruptive
microprism
✧disruption
microprint
micropylar
Hierapolis
micropolis
microphone
microprobe
vibraphone
microphyte
microphyll
mirror ball
mirror carp
hierarchic
hierarchal
mirror site
mirrorwise
microscale
mitre shell
microsleep
disrespect
nigrescent
vitrescent
digressive
microseism
digression
microskirt
nicrosilal
microsomal
citrus wood
fibrescope
microscope
microspore
hieroscopy
microscopy
fibrositis
titratable
diprotodon
librettist
microtomic
microtonal
vibrations
picrotoxin
gilravager
Libreville
gilravitch
mitre wheel
microwaves
nitrazepam
first-aider
Miss Saigon
dissuasive
air station
dissuasion
miasmatous
dissuasory
Miss Marple
wit-snapper
diastaltic
first blood
Mitsubishi®
dissociate
first-class
dissective
dissecting
dissection
midsection
first cause
dissidence
diastemata
Kiss Me Kate
diaskeuast
dies feriae
misseeming
misspelled
linseed oil
dissheathe
kiss of life
tipsifying
first floor
first-floor
first-fruit
miss the bus
miss the cut
biospheric
kiss the rod
pig-sticker
midshipman
big science
bioscience
first joint
dissoluble
dissilient
dissolvent
first light
missel-bird
dissolving
mis-selling
tinselling
tin soldier
disselboom
Tinseltown
missel-tree
kieselguhr
lissomness
sinsemilla
dissembler
dissimilar
dipsomania
kissing bug
jimson weed
first night
lip-syncher
die-sinking
dissenting
dissension
dissonance
dissonancy
missionary
missionise
missionize
missiology
Piesporter
ripsnorter
six-shooter
dissipable
first prize
first proof
air support
dissipated
dissertate
disservice
lip service
First Reich
minstrelsy
pinstriped
Nias Island
pipsissewa
rijsttafel
first thing
dissatisfy
dissevered
First World
first water
bissextile
Kirsty Wark
Vietnamese
distraught
dirt-eating
virtualism
filtration
virtualist
virtuality
victualled
victualler
rift valley
dirt farmer
tilt hammer
mistrayned
distrainee
distrainer
distrainor
virtual pet
distracted
distractor
mint master
ritt-master
pietra dura
Vietnam War
histoblast
pitta bread
Pittsburgh
fisticuffs
pistachios
rib-tickler
biotically
cistaceous
distichous
giftedness
✧eisteddfod
pittie-ward
little-ease
hit the sack
little Mary
✧diothelete
hit the deck
Little Nell
Little Bear
littleness
virtueless
✧diothelite
fit the bill
✧diothelism
Little Lion
kittle-pins
dip the flag
little slam
diathermic
diathermal
sixteenmos
tie the knot
hit the road
hit the roof
Little Rock
Little John
distressed
distresser
mistress it
listlessly
mistressly
pietre dure
fifty-fifty
mirthfully
Dictograph®
pictograph
vintage car
histogenic
Dirty Harry
Picts' house
filthiness
wintriness
distringas
diatribist
tilt fillet
histrionic
distribute
mistakable
mistakably
mistakenly
distilland
distillate
pistillate
pistillary
distilment
distillery
histologic
pistol-whip
distilling
pistolling
dirty linen
pistillode
pistol grip
histolysis
histolytic
mist-flower
victimless
Sir Tim Rice
histaminic
dirty money
victimhood
diatom ooze
ditto marks
victimiser
hitty-missy
Tintometer®
mixty-maxty
victimizer
listenable
Wittenberg
kitten heel
birthnight
distensile
distensive
piston ring
distension
distention
kitten moth
fitting-out
mitten-crab
listener-in
distinctly
distinguée
dictionary
distrouble
misthought
riot police
diatropism
fictionist
virtuosity
histiology
virtuously
dirt-rotten
histiocyte
birthplace
tittupping
Fittipaldi
fifty pence
Dictaphone®
dictaphone
✧victoriana
hinterland
Mitterrand
filter cake
littermate
disturbant
filterable
historical
pictorical
bitter beer
bitterness
sisterless
winterless
birthright
Winterthur
picture hat
distortive
sisterlike
wintertide
wintertime
bitter-king
bitterling
disturbing
winterkill
Cistercian
distortion
diuturnity
winter-clad
bitterwood
Mister Toad
sisterhood
winter moth
sister hook
victorious
bitter-root
litter lout
bitter-spar
picture rod
Tintoretto
win through
Victor Hugo
Mister Hyde
sixth sense
birthstone
dietetical
uintathere
dictatress
dirty trick
fictitious
distruster
fifth wheel
filthy rich
mistrysted
figurative
simulative
figuration
nidulation
simulation
titubation
titularity
Titus Alone
simulatory
simulacrum
sipunculid
minuscular
Didunculus
bifurcated
liquidness
liquidiser
liquidator
liquidizer
minute hand
vituperate
minute-jack
lieutenant
figurehead
minute-bell
diluteness
minuteness
figurework
minute book

minute-drop
virulently
pious fraud
liquefying
Sioux Falls
disulfiram
liturgical
divulgence
Titus Groan
bituminate
dijudicate
dilucidate
Simuliidae
hirudinean
bituminise
bituminize
disutility
fiducially
hirudinoid
bituminous
hirudinous
binucleate
visual arts
visualiser
visualizer
Sinus Medii
visuomotor
biquintile
sinusoidal
bibulously
bisulphate
disulphate
bisulphide
disulphide
liquor laws
Sinus Roris
liquescent
bicultural
Gil Vicente
pit village
misventure
sieve plate
silver gate
silverware
silver-bath
silverback
silvertail
silverweed
silver leaf
silver bell
silver fern
silver thaw
silverside
silverling
silverfish
silverbill
silver-gilt
silverskin
silver foil
silver tree
Silver Star
view-halloo
viewlessly
View of a Pig
viewfinder
tim-whiskey
tin whistle
Die Walküre
Wim Wenders
miswandred
Tin Woodman
disworship
misworship
viewership
miswording
Midwestern
nitwittery
didynamian
didynamous
city editor
vinylidene
pityriasis
disyllabic
disyllable
dicynodont
Himyaritic
pizzicatos
fizzy drink
zigzaggery
zigzagging
dizzyingly
sizzlingly
piezometer
mizzensail
mizzenmast
fizzenless
diazeuctic
Djiboutian
ejectively
ejaculator
J J Williams
MKSA system
skibobbing
skedaddler
skaithless
skrimshank
skyjacking
ski jumping
skyjumping
skikjöring
skillfully
skulkingly
skylarking
skeletally
akolouthos
skelly-eyed
skimpiness
skimmingly
skimpingly
sky marshal
skin effect
skinniness
skintights
skin diving
skene-occle
skin-popper
skippering
skip-kennel
Skupshtina
skippingly
skepticism
sky parlour
skirt along
skirmisher
ekistician
sky surfing
skyscraper
skateboard
sketchable
sketch book
sketchbook
skittishly
skittle out
skate round
ski touring
skeuomorph
J K Huysmans
skywriting
skew-corbel
skew bridge
Allan-a-Dale
alla marcia
cloacaline
floatation
flea market
Alvar Aalto
clear as mud
almacantar
pleasantly
pleasantry
float-board
altar-cloth
alcaicería
illaudable
illaudably
Elland Road
all and some
sleazeball
albarellos
flea-beetle
float glass
float grass
allargando
clean hands
Bleak House
flea circus
bleariness
sleaziness
illatively
floatingly
gloatingly
pleadingly
pleasingly
alkalinise
alkalinize
alkalinity
pliability
oleaginous
flea-bitten
altazimuth
Olga Korbut
flea collar
float plane
altarpiece
algarrobos
altar-rails
alla Franca
cleansable
clean sheet
altar-stone
float-stone
clearstory
olfactible
pliantness
a lead towel
illaqueate
pleasure in
El Salvador
ill-advised
bleary-eyed
alablaster
clubmaster
I'll be bound
club-headed
slubbering
glebe-house
ill-behaved
flabbiness
slabbiness
Klebsiella
flabellate
globularly
fly-by-night
alabandine
alabandite
club-footed
elaborator
slob around
ill bestead
plebiscite
I'll buy that
glaciation
glacialist
blackamoor
Blackbeard
blackboard
blockboard
black bread
black-bully
blackberry
black chalk
click-clack
block-chain
✧black death
placidness
elucidator
black eagle
slackening
slacken off
black earth
blackfaced
✧black friar
black frost
blackguard
block grant
glycogenic
block gauge
blackheart
black house
blockhouse
pluckiness
electively
electivity
flaccidity
flick-knife
black light
glycolysis
glycolytic
elecampane
black magic
clockmaker
black money
black Maria
electorate
electoress
electorial
Clactonian
glaciology
block plane
Plecoptera
black paper
flock-paper
✧black power
black robin
electrical
clock radio
electrogen
electromer
electronic
placer-gold
black snake
glucosidic
glycosidic
clock speed
black sheep
blacksmith
Black Shirt
Blackshirt
Black Stone
slickstone
glucosuria
glycosuria
glucosuric
glycosuric
black stump
click-track
flycatcher
blackthorn
clock tower
flocculate
flocculent
old country
clack valve
place value
black vomit
black widow
Black Watch
blackwater
slack water
slack-water
glad-hander
gladiatory
à la Dubarry
pledgeable
all-dreaded
fledgeling
bladder nut
ill-defined
ploddingly
cloddishly
Ile d'Oléron
fly-dumping
gladsomely
clodhopper
à la dérobée
Clydesdale
Clydesider
cladistics
glide slope
slide valve
gleemaiden
Alcelaphus
alterative
illegalise
illegalize
ulcerative
alienation
allegation
alteration
ulceration
illegality
bluejacket
F Lee Bailey
Blue Mantle
elderberry
blue screen
blue-screen
albescence
sleevehand
blue pencil
blue-pencil
fleeceless
sleeveless
sleeve fish
blue devils
blue heeler
allegeance
fleece-wool
Illecebrum
Blue Velvet
Old English
allergenic
blue cheese
fleechment
bluethroat
blue riband
blue-riband
blue ribbon
blue-ribbon
sleepiness
sleetiness
fleeringly
fleetingly
allegiance
ulteriorly
blue-rinsed
Elie Wiesel
alleviator
Klieg light
alveolitis
aldermanic
aldermanly
aldermanry
blues music
Blue Ensign
alternance
alternatim
alternator
Blue Monday
blue tongue
blue-tongue
allegorise
allegorize
allegorist
blue rocket
olde-worlde
blue-collar
blue-bonnet
old economy
old-economy
Blue Mosque
Blue Horses
ulcerously
bluebottle
bluebreast
algebraist
allegretto
blue ground
sleep rough
sleekstone
alpenstock
Allen screw
eldest hand
blue streak
fluentness
clientship
Albert Gore
Albert Roux
Ellen Terry
blue murder
bleed valve
bleed white
sleepyhead
fly-flapper
clofibrate
ill feeling
old-fogyish
fluffiness
bluff it out
oldfangled
fly-fronted
all-firedly
All for Love
ill fortune
fly-fishing
ill-founded
clog dancer
sluggardly
plagiarise
plagiarize
flag-waving
plagiarism
plagiarist
flag-basket
flagrantly
Elagabalus
oligoclase
plaguesome
plague-sore
plague-spot
clogginess
flagginess
sluggishly
Flagellata
flagellate
flagellant
flugelhorn
flügelhorn
Glagolitic
oligopsony
oligarchic
oligarchal
flight path
flight deck
flightless
slightness
flight test
flight-test
flight line
flight plan
flagitious
flight crew
slight over
alphabetic
alpha decay
Alzheimer's
allhallond
allhallown
allhollown
alchemical
alphameric
alphametic
Alphonsine
Old Hundred
Alpha Romeo®
alcheringa
aloha shirt

ultimately
alligation
claim a foul
flail about
plainchant
claircolle
Plaid Cymru
alliaceous
fluid drive
alliterate
Alpine race
illiterate
sluicegate
illiteracy
Alpine Club
oleiferous
Albigenses
illipe nuts
plain flour
flying camp
flying leap
flying shot
flying wing
flying fish
flying bomb
flying-boat
flying frog
flying suit
sleigh bell
Alcibiades
albinistic
Alain Juppé
Kleig light
eloignment
altisonant
altitonant
fluid ounce
Alain Prost
elliptical
cloistress
plaintless
plain tripe
pleiotropy
cloistered
cloisterer
plain weave
flak jacket
Old Kingdom
flake-white
ill-looking
slam dancer
clamjamfry
glumaceous
slumberful
glimmering
slumbering
slammerkin
slumberous
blamefully
plume-grass
flame-grill
clamminess
clumpiness
clumsiness
flimsiness
slumminess
old-maidish
old-maidism
Plumularia
slime mould
Flamingant
alimentary
elementary
eliminable
flaminical
Clemenceau
Clementina
✧clementine
flamingoes
eliminator
plum tomato
flamboyant
plum-colour
clomiphene
flameproof
plume poppy
glomerular
glomerulus
old masters
plumassier
climatical
ill-matched
glamour boy
alang-alang
Cluny Abbey
Glyn Daniel
alineation
elongation
plantation
Alan Parker
blind alley
blind-alley
✧blond beast
planoblast
bling bling
plane chart
clinically
Glenn Close
blind-drunk
blonde-lace
plunderage
plunge bath
blanket bog
blanket box
flunkeydom
slenderise
slenderize
blanketing
blundering
flunkeyish
flunkeyism
flannelled
glance-coal
plunge pool
glanderous
plunderous
slanderous
flindersia
plangently
glance over
klangfarbe
sling fruit
planigraph
flint glass
allnighter
flint-heart
planchette
plant-house
ilang-ilang
clinginess
flintiness
slanginess
slinkiness
blindingly
clankingly
glancingly
slangingly
slantingly
clannishly
glandiform
plentitude
Planck's law
plenilunar
plant louse
blancmange
clinometer
planimeter
planometer
clinometry
planimetry
flanconade
glendoveer
Glenrothes
Llangollen
clangorous
glans penis
a long purse
blind snake
blind shark
blindsight
Flintshire
plenishing
alongshore
clingstone
clinkstone
slingstone
plane table
planetical
planktonic
planetaria
ill-natured
blind trust
Alan Turing
klendusity
glandulous
blanquette
blank verse
slang-whang
clanswoman
ylang-ylang
clonazepam
alloparent
allopathic
glyoxaline
allocation
algolagnia
allogamous
gliomatous
allopatric
Allosaurus
pleonastic
floorboard
elbow-chair
klootchman
klootchmen
floorcloth
blood count
blood donor
almond-tree
almond-eyed
altogether
fluoxetine
all-obeying
all-overish
aldohexose
flooded out
allometric
cliometric
pleonectic
blood fluke
blood-guilt
blood group
algophobia
allotheism
oleophilic
allophonic
pleochroic
allochiria
blood horse
bloodhound
fluoridate
fluorinate
bloodiness
gloominess
fluoridise
fluoridize
Pliohippus
floodlight
floor limit
blood money
alcoholise
alcoholize
alcoholism
algologist
pleomorphy
sloop-of-war
fluorotype
blood-plate
flood plain
floor price
blood purge
Algonquian
allotropic
oleography
blood-royal
bloodstain
blood sugar
bloodstone
bloodstock
blood-sized
altostrati
allosteric
allocution
illocution
altocumuli
blood-wagon
floodwater
bloody hand
bloody Mary
bloody flux
allonymous
bloody-eyed
all-play-all
blepharism
flippantly
slip a cable
clapperboy
clappering
flapperish
slipperily
slop-seller
clapped-out
floppiness
slippiness
sloppiness
clypeiform
slipsloppy
clapometer
glyphosate
flapdoodle
glyptodont
slap-up meal
pluperfect
flap-dragon
all-purpose
flyposting
slipstream
flypitcher
slip-string
slip stitch
slip-stitch
slop bucket
floppy disc
floppy disk
clepsydrae
clepsydras
eloquently
cliquiness
flirtation
clarabella
floribunda
ultrabasic
clarichord
alarm clock
oleraceous
floridness
Alfred Jodl
florideous
ultrafiche
clarifying
glorifying
Clark Gable
clergiable
alarmingly
flirtingly
altruistic
florilegia
plural vote
cleromancy
pleromatic
Clarenceux
✧florentine
ultroneous
El Brooshna
gloriously
plerophory
alarm radio
alarm-radio
ultra-rapid
flare stack
florescent
floristics
ultrasonic
Clare Short
ultrashort
clerestory
ultrasound
all-rounder
ultra vires
clergyable
glissandos
Alismaceae
plasma cell
Alaska Time
glossarial
glossarist
flash about
ill-starred
fly swatter
flashboard
flesh-broth
flesh-brush
clish-clash
glass-coach
ill success
glass-cloth
closed shop
closed book
closed-loop
closed-door
cluster-cup
blister fly
cluster fly
blistering
blustering
clustering
glistening
glistering
plastering
Glaswegian
blusterous
blissed-out
flesh-eater
glass fibre
glass-faced
blissfully
flash flood
alas the day
blasphemer
flash Harry
flash-house
glasshouse
elasticate
plastinate
plastic art
plastic bag
classic car
classiness
flashiness
fleshiness
glassiness
glossiness
slushiness
blushingly
plastilina
classified
classicise
classicize
elasticise
elasticize
Plasticine®
plasticise
plasticize
almsgiving
classicism
classifier
classicist
elasticity
plasticity
plastidule
clasp knife
flashlight
old soldier
slush money
blastomata
plesiosaur
clistogamy
plasmogamy
plastogamy
Blastoidea
blastomere
blastoderm
plasmodesm
blossoming
El Escorial
plasmodial
plasmodium
All Shook Up
plasmosoma
blastopore
plasmosome
blastocoel
blossom out
glossology
glasnostic
plasmolyse
plasmolyze
blastocyst
flashpoint
gloss paint
glasspaper
clostridia
close-range
close ranks
Old Scratch
close shave
glass snake
close-stool
plus strain
close thing
closet play
flosculous
glassworks
flesh wound
flat racing
plateau out
plutocracy
flat-screen
elatedness
glitterand
platteland
all the rage
all the same
glitterati
fly the beam
blitheness
all the best
all the time
blethering
blithering
flattering
glittering
fly the flag
slatternly
blithesome
flatterous
flatten out
clothes-peg
clothes-pin
blottesque
cloth-eared
plate-fleet
slothfully
plate glass
plate-glass
glottidean
clottiness

Words marked ✧ can also be spelled with one or more capital letters

glitziness
klutziness
plottingly
sluttishly
elytriform
elutriator
blitzkrieg
all-telling
flatulence
flatulency
plutolatry
platelayer
platemaker
all-time low
flutemouth
Platonical
gluttonise
gluttonize
gluttonish
slit pocket
gluttonous
glottology
flat-footed
fly-tipping
plate-proof
platypuses
all-terrain
slit trench
ulsterette
plat du jour
clotbuster
almucantar
cloud-built
cloudburst
cloudberry
flaunching
fleur-de-lis
fleur-de-lys
allurement
albumenise
albumenize
glauberite
Gloucester
Klaus Fuchs
ploughland
ploughgate
plough back
plough-tail
ploughable
plough-team
slaughtery
ploughwise
plough into
plough-tree
plough-iron
albuminate
illuminate
illuminati
illuminant
cloudiness
allusively
illusively
alluringly
floutingly
flourished
flourisher
albuminise
albuminize
illuminism
Eleusinian
illuminist

illusional
albuminoid
albuminous
plauditory
glauconite
illusorily
pleurodont
pleurotomy
à l'outrance
El Guerrouj
cloudscape
illustrate
fluviatile
fluvialist
slavocracy
clavicular
clavichord
olivaceous
glove-fight
olive green
olive-green
clove hitch
Clive James
Clive Lloyd
glove-money
eleventhly
slovenlike
eleven-plus
Slavophile
Slavophobe
Oliver Reed
cloverleaf
plover's egg
cleverness
flavorless
✧clever dick
flavorsome
olive-shell
flavescent
slave trade
flavourful
flavouring
flavivirus
all-weather
claw hammer
clew-garnet
clown about
slow-gaited
flown cover
clawed toad
clawed frog
clownishly
Eli Whitney
slow-moving
slow motion
slow-motion
slow cooker
slow-footed
flower-head
flower-bell
flowerless
flower show
flower girl
blow-by-blow
flexi-cover
Plexiglass®
plexiglass
flexihours
pleximeter
pleximetry
alexanders

Alexandria
fluxionary
fluxionist
Clayhanger
claymation
play-acting
play action
playschool
playleader
playfellow
play the kip
allycholly
play the wag
clay pigeon
Alcyonaria
play possum
play a prize
play truant
play tricks
playwright
alkyd resin
play-writer
clay-ground
play around
playground
play it cool
play-by-play
blizzardly
emparadise
imparadise
immanation
impanation
embasement
empalement
impalement
immaterial
empanelled
immanental
embargoing
empathetic
smeariness
ommatidium
amiability
impatience
ambagitory
embankment
embarkment
imparlance
embalmment
Emma Bovary
impalpable
impalpably
impairment
embarras de
impassable
impassible
impassably
impassibly
ambassador
embassador
impartable
impartible
impartibly
impartment
immaculate
immaculacy
immaturely
impaludism
immaturity
Ambarvalia
emaciation

smickering
smock-faced
smock-frock
smudgeless
smudginess
imperative
impeccable
impeccably
impeccancy
impendence
impendency
ampere hour
amber fluid
ember-goose
impediment
impenitent
impedingly
impeditive
imbecility
imperilled
imperially
amoebiform
immeritous
amoebiasis
umbellifer
umbellated
immemorial
Empedocles
emmenology
ampelopses
ampelopsis
emmetropia
emmetropic
immersible
impersonal
immeasured
Umberto Eco
Emmentaler
impervious
amber wheat
smifligate
Empfindung
amygdalate
emigration
amygdaloid
emigratory
image-maker
imaginable
imaginably
imaginings
emphractic
amphibrach
amphibolic
amphibious
amphictyon
amphimacer
amphimixis
Amphineura
amphiscian
emphysemic
emphatical
amphoteric
Amphitryon
ambivalent
omniparity
à main armée
omniparous
amritattva
immiscible
immiscibly
omniscient

umpireship
immiserise
immiserize
Empire gown
omniferous
omnigenous
ambidexter
imminently
ambisexual
impishness
umbilicate
omnificent
empiricism
imbibition
empiricist
ampicillin
omnipotent
Ambisonics®
omnivorous
embittered
impictured
embitterer
omnibus box
imminution
Amy Johnson
smoke alarm
smokeboard
smoke-black
smoke-dried
smokehouse
smoking cap
smoking gun
smokeproof
smokestack
smoketight
amalgamate
ampliative
ampliation
small craft
implacable
implacably
amylaceous
implicit in
implicitly
smell-feast
amplifying
small fruit
small goods
small hours
smalminess
smelliness
emollition
emulsifier
emblements
emoluments
emblematic
smallmouth
emalangeni
ameliorate
Amblyopsis
small print
small-pipes
imploratorsmall-scale
Amblystoma
small sword
emplastrum
emplastron
emulatress
small-timer
small wares

implexuous
employable
employment
emblazoner
emblazonry
amantadine
emendation
amendatory
emendatory
amanuenses
amanuensis
amino group
emancipate
emancipist
eminential
amenorrhea
amenity bed
amenity kit
immoralism
immolation
umbonation
immoralist
immorality
immovables
embouchure
emboldener
immoderate
immoderacy
immoveable
empoverish
impoverish
embowelled
impose upon
amboceptor
immodestly
impotently
smoothpate
smooth calf
smooth-talk
smoothable
smoothness
smooth newt
smooth-shod
smooth-bore
smooth over
smooth away
ammoniacal
ammoniacum
embodiment
impolitely
imposingly
immobilise
immobilize
immobilism
imposition
immobility
immotility
embolismic
embolismal
ammoniated
impoundage
embonpoint
amyotrophy
impossible
impossibly
embossment
empoisoned
importable
immortelle
immortally
impostumed

importance
importuner
importancy
imposthume
import duty
imipramine
omophagous
omophorion
smart Aleck
smart-Aleck
smart Alick
smart-Alick
emery board
improbable
improbably
imbroccata
umbraculum
Americanos
emery cloth
imprudence
amerceable
amercement
embruement
imbruement
à merveille
smørrebrød
emergently
impregnate
impregnant
smaragdine
smaragdite
embroglios
imbroglios
umbrageous
Omar Sharif
emarginate
amerciable
smarminess
embroidery
smartingly
smirkingly
umbrellaed
emerald-cut
smart money
imprimatur
ombrometer
Amaranthus
amarantine
imprinting
Amerindian
embryonate
embryogeny
embryology
embryotomy
ombrophile
ombrophobe
smart phone
smartphone
emery paper
improperly
impressive
impression
Amarasimha
impresario
impressure
umbratical
embryulcia
improvable
improvably
improviser
emery wheel

embrowning
Emi-Scanner®
smashingly
emissivity
emasculate
ametabolic
smithcraft
emetically
smithereen
smother-fly
smattering
smothering
smuttiness
amatorious
smut fungus
amateurish
amateurism
imputative
ambulation
amputation
imputation
ambulatory
ambulacral
ambulacrum
ambuscados
impureness
immurement
immune body
impudently
ambushment
ammunition
impudicity
impugnable
impugnment
immunoblot
immunology
ampussy-and
impuissant
impulse buy
amazedness
Amazon-like
Angaraland
unbalanced
unhazarded
Incaparina
unsalaried
indagative
indapamide
unparadise
indagation
inhalation
en cavalier
incapacity
unmanacled
in parallel
unparallel
indagatory
Andaman Sea
enjambment
unbarbered
unwatchful
Antarctica
infarction
unsanctify
uncandidly
inwardness
inland bill
unhardened
unpardoned
unmaidenly
unhandsome

incandesce
ins and outs
unnameable
unsaleable
untameable
untameably
Anna Sewell
innateness
insaneness
unsafeness
unwareness
encasement
enfacement
engagement
enlacement
enragement
incasement
uncared-for
unwavering
unmaterial
unlabelled
unpanelled
unravelled
unraveller
unmaternal
insane root
unlamented
unparented
unpatented
untalented
unparental
unlawfully
unmanfully
intangible
untangible
intangibly
enlargedly
ensanguine
endangerer
encashable
encashment
unfathomed
unfathered
ungathered
unfatherly
unpathetic
insalivate
invaginate
invalidate
en badinant
inhabitant
insanitary
unsanitary
insatiable
invariable
unsatiable
unvariable
insatiably
invariably
sneakiness
uneasiness
unwariness
engagingly
sneakingly
unfadingly
unravished
sneakishly
unpacified
unratified
invaliding
invalidism

unfamiliar
invalidity
uniaxially
invariance
annalistic
unsatiated
untalked-of
infallible
unbailable
unfallible
unmailable
infallibly
entailment
and all that
unhallowed
anharmonic
enharmonic
inharmonic
ungainsaid
untainting
ungarnered
unmannered
unmannerly
en cabochon
one another
antagonise
antagonize
infamonise
infamonize
uncanonise
uncanonize
unfavorite
antagonism
antagonist
in bad odour
unlaboured
infamously
encampment
unhampered
unpampered
uncarpeted
inmarriage
unfairness
engarrison
unpassable
unransomed
enfant gâté
intactness
unfaithful
untasteful
sneak thief
a near thing
unfastened
andantinos
infanthood
incautious
enraptured
unbattered
ungartered
unmastered
unpastured
unpastoral
unbaptised
incantator
unbaptized
insalutary
invaluable
unvaluable
invaluably
andalusite
Andalusian

infatuated
unladylike
unobtained
snobocracy
unobscured
inobedient
unobedient
enablement
knobkerrie
in absentia
unobserved
knobbiness
unabridged
snubbingly
snobbishly
anabolitic
unabsolved
anabaptise
anabaptize
anabaptism
✧anabaptist
unscramble
on occasion
snick-a-snee
knock about
knockabout
anaclastic
Anschauung
unscabbard
unacademic
unscreened
anucleated
unaccented
enschedule
on schedule
inactivate
knackiness
inactively
inactivity
uneclipsed
unscripted
knick-knack
knock-kneed
inoculable
unscalable
knuckle-bow
anacolutha
inoculator
unicameral
onocentaur
uneconomic
unicentral
anecdotage
anecdotist
unschooled
knickpoint
unsceptred
unscorched
anacardium
anachronic
unicostate
inaccurate
inaccuracy
knock under
unoccupied
unacquaint
unscrupled
anacrustic
unactuated
knackwurst
knockwurst

unidealism
cnidoblast
ineducable
uneducable
uneducated
unedifying
unadmiring
in addition
unadmitted
Enid Blyton
anadyomene
anadromous
inadaptive
inadequate
inadequacy
unadjusted
inseparate
Ansel Adams
en revanche
unheralded
unregarded
unretarded
unrewarded
underagent
unrelative
undelaying
anhelation
annexation
indexation
inter alios
inveracity
unveracity
unremarked
unbewailed
unmetalled
unrecalled
undebarred
unrepaired
untenanted
underactor
under-board
interbrain
interbreed
underbuild
underbelly
inselberge
underborne
underburnt
underbough
underbrush
Angel Clare
interchain
underclass
under-craft
interceder
under-clerk
undercrest
unmerciful
unpeaceful
inner child
undescried
unreactive
undercliff
intercalar
unwelcomed
intercross
undercroft
interclude
under cover
undercover
Inverclyde

enterdeale
underdrain
incendiary
invendible
unbendable
unreadable
unvendible
intendedly
unheededly
underdress
intendment
underdrive
intendance
intendancy
unrendered
untendered
engenderer
untenderly
engendrure
ingenerate
intemerate
intenerate
inveterate
inveteracy
undefended
sneezeweed
unreverend
antecedent
enlevement
enlèvement
unreverent
unrevenged
knee-length
unremedied
unrepealed
unrepelled
unrevealed
antebellum
unredeemed
sneezewood
ungenerous
sneezewort
undeterred
underearth
uncerebral
unreleased
unreversed
antecessor
interested
undefeated
undetected
unrepeated
unrepented
unresented
unreverted
unrelentor
indecently
inherently
antepenult
undeceived
undeserved
unreceived
unreserved
undeserver
underframe
interfaith
Angel Falls
unperfumed
underfloor
interferon
interferer

interfluve
intergrade
underglaze
unwedgable
undergoing
unfeigning
unweighing
endergonic
enneagonal
undergrove
intergrown
undergrown
enmeshment
inmeshment
encephalic
encephalin
encephalon
enkephalin
unmechanic
antechapel
untethered
Inner House
Enver Hoxha
unseminar'd
indelicate
ingeminate
inseminate
indelicacy
undeniable
unreliable
knee-timber
undeniably
ante-Nicene
enregiment
incedingly
sneeringly
unperished
unrelished
unverified
indecisive
indefinite
undecisive
unfeminine
undesiring
unmeriting
unrepining
indecision
in deliciis
endemicity
infelicity
unbedimmed
unbedinned
undesigned
unbenignly
undecimole
undesirous
unperilous
inheritrix
anteriorly
inferiorly
interiorly
unremitted
unresisted
enregister
unbelieved
unrelieved
unbeliever
unperjured
underjawed
unreckoned
unweakened

interleave
underlease
unhealable
unsellable
untellable
unwellness
Interlagos
✧inner light
underlying
underlinen
interlunar
interloper
undeclared
undeplored
unrealised
unfellowed
unmellowed
underlayer
unrealized
endermical
intermedia
intermodal
underminde
underminer
in terminis
intermarry
endermatic
unhelmeted
intermezzi
intermezzo
underneath
internodal
internment
internship
underntime
infernally
internally
undernamed
Enneandria
undernoted
once in a way
envenomate
once for all
once-for-all
unrejoiced
unheroical
unrecorded
unseconded
unbeholden
enterocele
Anne Boleyn
unbesought
unbecoming
unreposing
enterolith
in memoriam
in deposito
unreformed
unrenowned
indecorous
angelology
enterotomy
unreported
ante mortem
unbegotten
unresolved
enterocyte
interphase
interplant
underplant
unhelpable
interplead
enterprise
underprise
underprize
unbespoken
interpolar
unweaponed
underpants
interphone
under proof
underproof
unpeppered
untempered
Enver Pasha
interposal
interposer
unrespited
under-power
underquote
ance-errand
once-errand
inferrable
inferrible
integrable
unbearable
unpeerable
untearable
unwearable
unbearably
unmetrical
endearment
interregna
interregal
interreges
unsearched
en retraite
unwearying
integrally
interramal
Anne Brontë
index rerum
in terrorem
integrator
undepraved
undeprived
unreproved
unbetrayed
understand
inner space
interspace
interstate
understate
angelshark
angel's hair
infeasible
insensible
unfeasible
unsensible
insensibly
unsensibly
underspend
under siege
understeer
interstice
undershirt
underskirt
unlessoned
unreasoned
unseasoned
undersense
unseasonal
in personam
incessancy
understood
underscore
understock
insensuous
undershoot
understory
underscrub
undershrub
uncensored
uncensured
unleisured
unmeasured
underslung
understudy
undersexed
enneastyle
undersized
ingestible
injectable
insertable
inventable
inventible
invertible
investable
investible
unbeatable
unlettable
intertidal
invertedly
ancestress
intentness
inventress
unmeetness
infeftment
insentient
investment
intertwine
unsettling
undertrick
intertrigo
intertwist
undertaken
undertaker
undertimed
under-tunic
undertoned
intestinal
intestines
insert mode
anoestrous
incestuous
infectious
intentions
intent upon
enfestered
unbettered
unfeatured
unfettered
unlettered
unrestored
indentures
unbestowed
interurban
integument
insecurely
unrecuring
interunion
insecurity
unbeguiled
unreturned
unrequired
unrequited
inner voice
undervoice
inlet valve
intervolve
undervalue
unleavened
intervener
intervenor
unbeavered
intervital
inter vivos
interweave
under wraps
underwhelm
underwrite
inner woman
underwired
underworld
angel-water
under water
underwater
interwound
in very deed
unseizable
interzonal
knife-board
knife block
snuff-brown
unoffended
unaffected
uneffected
inefficacy
sniffiness
snuffiness
sniffingly
unofficial
unifoliate
snaffle-bit
knife-money
snuff movie
uniflorous
knife pleat
knife-point
snuff-paper
uniformity
in a fashion
snuff spoon
snuff-taker
snuff video
Onagraceae
enigmatise
enigmatize
✧enigmatist
sniggering
anagogical
knagginess
Inigo Jones
Unigenitus
knightless
knight's fee
knighthood
anaglyphic
anaglyptic
enthraldom
anthracene
on the alert
inchoately
unsheathed
anthracite
inchoative
inchoation
enthralled
anthracoid
on the anvil
in the black
on the brain
on the blink
on the bench
on the block
on the buroo
in the chair
on the cadge
on the cheap
in the clear
unshackled
on the cross
on the cards
unshadowed
unshielded
unthreaded
in the event
uncheerful
in the flesh
unshifting
on the fritz
in the first
on the house
unchristen
unshakable
unshakably
unshakenly
anthelices
in the light
on the loose
anchylosed
anchylosis
on the latch
on the level
anthemwise
anthomania
in the money
on the money
on the march
in chancery
unthankful
enchanting
unchanging
unthinking
unshingled
Anthonomus
unphonetic
enthronise
enthronize
anthropoid
on the outer
in the press
anthophore
on the prowl
in the pay of
in the quill
on the quiet
on the rocks
antheridia
anchorless
in the right
anchor-ring
uncharming
anthersmut
anchor-hold
Anchor Boys
on the ropes
anchoretic
anchoritic
in the round
unthorough
anchor buoy
in the shade
on the slate
enthusiasm
enthusiast
on the shelf
unchastely
on this wise
unchastity
on the stump
in that case
unthatched
on the tiles
on the tapis
unshrubbed
on the verge
on the wagon
in the wings
on the whole
in the wrong
in the world
unshowered
on the watch
inch by inch
intimately
antipathic
entitative
incitative
indicative
anti-racism
incitation
indication
intimation
invitation
anti-racist
unrivalled
indicatory
invitatory
antimasque
antimatter
untimbered
✧invincible
invincibly
Antiochene
indiscrete
indiscreet
encircling
Antiochian
intinction
encincture
unkindness
unhindered
antiaditis
incinerate
unliterary
enticeable
unlikeable
unliveable
unrideable
unsizeable
inside edge
antivenene
engineless
entireness
unlikeness
unripeness
unwiseness
enticement
incitement
inditement
inside left
invitement
anti-Semite
indigenise
indigenize
unlifelike
unwifelike
antimerism
antisexism
unnilenium
antisexist
infidelity
anti-heroic
engine-room
indigenous
unlicensed
antisepsis
antiseptic
indigested
undigested
undirected
undiverted
undivested
incidental
indigently
indirectly
antiserums
in disgrace
unkinglike
unwithheld
enrichment
insightful
unrightful
Antichthon
in-fighting
infighting
antitheism
Antichrist
antitheist
antiphonic
antiphonal
antiphoner
unwithered
antitheses
antithesis
antithetic
annihilate
anticipate
infinitate
intimidate
invigilate
anticipant
infinitant
infinitary
unmilitary
untidiness
incisively
infinitely
enticingly
incitingly
invitingly
untiringly
unfinished
infinitive
inhibitive
anticivism

Words marked ✧ can also be spelled with one or more capital letters

moral agent
to capacity
Soka Gakkai
roman à clef
roman à clés
sonata form
Mosasaurus
Joy Adamson
Douay Bible
Mozambican
woman-built
Mozambique
royal burgh
coral berry
loganberry
rowan-berry
royal cubit
romancical
bon accueil
comanchero
low-alcohol
woman-child
monarchise
monarchize
monarchial
monarchism
Monarchian
monarchist
mosaically
coparcener
mosaic gold
Nouakchott
vocal cords
Nova Scotia
top and tail
Howards End
Roy Andrews
towardness
now and then
cowardship
monandrous
Ronald Ross
Conan Doyle
nonagenary
locateable
voyageable
solacement
soda jerker
sola helmet
Romanesque
covalently
solar flare
moral fibre
womanfully
royal flush
cor anglais
Nova Iguacu
lovat-green
Los Angeles
solan goose
woman-grown
Local Group
kohanga reo
Nouadhibou
Ooka Shohei
notaphilic
potash alum
not a chance
woman-hater
co-radicate
coradicate
to cap it all
cohabitant
zonal index
soda-siphon
womanishly
rosaniline
tonalitive
volatilise
volatilize
royal icing
lovability
movability
non-ability
notability
volatility
tomatillos
notarially
non-aligned
covariance
locational
notational
rotational
vocational
monadiform
foraminous
voraginous
bonamiasis
donatistic
modalistic
moralistic
Romanistic
not a little
colatitude
royal jelly
go bankrupt
for all that
solar month
vocal music
domain name
coram nobis
Gosainthan
solar noise
potato race
homaloidal
for a wonder
Monaxonida
topazolite
potato ring
moratorium
Tobagonian
monadology
potamology
somatology
potato trap
oogamously
Cosa Nostra
Pocahontas
somatotype
focal point
solar panel
bon appetit
solar power
podagrical
local radio
conacreism
monaurally
non-arrival
No Man's Land
no-man's-land
Rota Island
coral snake
Roman snail
moral sense
logan-stone
vocal score
loyal toast
monastical
romantical
copartnery
cobalt-blue
monactinal
cobalt bomb
woman-tired
vocabulary
novaculite
vocabulist
Volapükist
no par value
notaryship
Rotary Club
forbearant
forbearing
non-bearing
Hobbianism
hot-brained
sorbic acid
Bombycidae
corbiculae
morbidness
forbidding
Bobby Davro
morbidezza
double take
double back
double-bank
double-park
Double Talk
double-talk
double bass
double salt
double reed
doubleness
sombreness
double chin
double bind
double-gild
double time
sombrerite
double bill
double flat
double play
gombeen-man
double knit
double-knit
double bond
double-book
gobble down
double door
doubletree
bomb-vessel
double star
double-hung
hobble-bush
double axel
double-dyed
double-eyed
doubtfully
go a-begging
hobby-horse
booby hatch
wobbliness
doubtingly
hobblingly
potboiling
soubriquet
Bobby Jones
gor-bellied
pot-bellied
corbelling
lowballing
morbillous
bombolotti
corbel step
Bobby Moore
bobbin lace
combinable
Sorbonical
Sorbonnist
hot-blooded
box Brownie®
booby prize
comburgess
Colbertine
Norbertine
torbernite
bombardier
robber crab
combustive
combustion
Bobby Sands
dog biscuit
bobbysoxer
combatable
hop-bitters
not but what
combat boot
Bobby Unser
Bombay duck
nonchalant
moucharaby
touch and go
conclavist
Bob Charles
ponce about
notch-board
coachbuilt
concoctive
concoction
hot-cockles
forced sale
forcedness
torch-dance
concretely
concretise
concretive
concretize
concretism
concretion
concretist
pouched rat
Borchester
Colchester
Dorchester
cow-chervil
force field
forcefully
couch grass
coach-horse
coach house
poachiness
touchiness
conceitful
touchingly
colchicine
coactivity
not cricket
conchiglie
conchiolin
conchiform
colchicums
touch judge
conciliate
conciliary
touch lucky
cow college
torchlight
Tom Collins
dolcelatte
pop culture
zooculture
coxcomical
dolcemente
touch-me-not
you can talk
Volcano Bay
non-content
pop concert
concinnity
coccineous
concinnous
forcing-pit
concentric
concentred
volcanised
you can't win
volcanized
conchoidal
hog-cholera
zoochorous
conchology
touch-plate
concept car
touch-piece
hot coppers
concipient
conceptive
Concepción
conception
voiceprint
touchpaper
coach party
forcipated
hotchpotch
conceptual
coacervate
for certain
concordant
concurrent
non-current
touch rugby
concertina
concertise
concertize
concerning
concurring
toe-curling
concordial
✧concertino
hod carrier
coach-stand
torch-staff
vouchsafed
concessive
concussive
nowcasting
concession
concussion
✧touchstone
coach screw
cob cottage
cowcatcher
concettism
concettist
toccatella
conclusive
concluding
conclusion
conclusory
low-country
coach-wheel
Moscow Mule
Lord Warden
woodlander
Roodmas Day
coadjacent
gold-washer
good-father
cordialise
cordialize
bordraging
road-making
toad-eating
Lord Napier
cordiality
Lord Mackay
Lord Raglan
Woody Allen
good sailor
loudhailer
cordwainer
Lord Lawson
load factor
loadmaster
pond-master
good nature
food values
woodcarver
hold a brief
conducible
rood screen
conductive
conduction
mordacious
cordectomy
hoddy-doddy
hooded seal
sordidness
bonded debt
Lord Adrian
rowdy-dowdy
Roddy Doyle
Goldie Hawn
moudiewart
mowdiewart
Lord Tebbit
roadheader
road mender
Lord Deedes
bowdlerise
bowdlerize
cordierite
cowdie-pine
soldiering
bowdlerism
woodpecker
Lord Devlin
GoodFellas
goodfellow
Lord Healey
gold record
moudiewort
mowdiewort
word memory
good people
wordsearch
hoodie crow
wordlessly
gold beetle
gold-beater
Lord Reuter
Lord Kelvin
lord of seat
mondegreen
hot-dogging
goody-goody
gold thread
woodshrike
cold chisel
woodthrush
bond-timber
word-finder
goodlihead
wood pigeon
goodliness
lordliness
gold-digger
Goldfinger
Lord Fisher
good-liking
non-drinker
Lord Wilson
good-sister
Lord Lister
pond skater
goldilocks
toddy-ladle
cordillera
Cordeliers
socdolager
socdoliger
socdologer
sogdolager
sogdoliger
sogdologer
condylomas
condolence
Lord Florey
gold-plated
rondoletto
lordolatry
sordamente
hold in hand
condensate
golden calf
London Wall
Golden Palm
golden rain
Houdini act
condonable
loading bay
woodenhead
golden seal
Gordon Bell
golden mean
Golden Bear
wooden pear

soddenness
woodenness
condensery
Golden Hind
golden girl
Lord O'Neill
cordon bleu
hold in play
London Clay
gold-end-man
hoydenhood
golden mole
golden rose
golden goal
golden hour
golden orfe
golden gram
bond energy
Gordon Gray
hodden-grey
you don't say!
golden rule
golden duck
load in bulk
golden bull
wooden type
foudroyant
loud-voiced
bondholder
Lord Joseph
Lord Somers
good-mother
wood-boring
good-looker
woodworker
cold-rolled
road roller
wood sorrel
good-morrow
wondrously
Lord Porter
roadworthy
good for you
wood spirit
nom de plume
word square
borderland
wonderland
Wonderwall
ponderable
road bridge
Good Friday
borderless
ponderment
wonderment
borderline
Lord Irvine
powder mill
powder blue
ponderance
powder snow
ponderancy
wonderwork
powder room
powder down
powder horn
border upon
foederatus
woodgrouse
powder puff
powder burn
ponder over
how dare you!
condescend
hot desking
hot-desking
toddy-stick
good as gold
goods train
Lord's table
conditions
coadjutant
cold rubber
loud-lunged
cold fusion
Lord Cuvier
cold turkey
Lord Butler
roadrunner
good humour
coadjutrix
woodcutter
bondswoman
Wordsworth
goodlyhead
Monday Club
how do you do?
how-do-you-do
poles apart
Donegal Bay
pole dancer
rope dancer
forehanded
cote-hardie
rose garden
rope ladder
rose madder
moderately
foretaught
forefather
foregather
colemanite
corelative
homemaking
lovemaking
rope-making
rosemaling
moderatism
monetarism
corelation
moderation
Pomeranian
toleration
monetarist
monetarily
nose tackle
rope-walker
home market
rose mallow
fore-hammer
foredamned
mosey along
love-favour
for example
Monegasque
rose laurel
rose-laurel
moderatrix
covenanted
forecasted
covenantee
forecastle
covenantal
covenanter
covenantor
forecaster
not exactly
tolerantly
power brake
Roger Bacon
honeybunch
power block
tower block
Josef Beran
money-bound
Roger Craig
Roger Clark
lower-class
hovercraft
honey-chile
dot-etching
hokey cokey
honey-crock
come across
Rouen cross
cover drive
fore-advise
power drill
roberdsman
molendinar
Mogen David
lovey-dovey
bone-headed
soreheaded
Lope de Vega
lose weight
foreseeing
Lorelei Lee
foreteller
yoke-fellow
come before
core memory
foreperson
hopelessly
lovelessly
movelessly
tonelessly
rose beetle
rove beetle
bonesetter
honeyeater
love letter
coherently
covered way
note of hand
love affair
poker-faced
Home Office
womenfolks
powerfully
foreign aid
✧lower grade
cover glass
Jozef Glemp
honey guide
foreignism
towel-gourd
non-ethical
foreshadow
foresheets
rose chafer
Copenhagen
boneshaker
somewhiles
More Thomas
somewhence
sore throat
towel-horse
forechosen
dower house
lower house
powerhouse
home-thrust
note-shaver
foreshewed
foreshowed
lose the way
rose window
home cinema
lovelihead
comeliness
homeliness
loneliness
loveliness
cohesively
forefinger
covetingly
coweringly
hoveringly
loweringly
soberingly
toweringly
come-hither
pokerishly
polemicist
zone-ticket
comedienne
comédienne
home-signal
rose-lipped
pome-citron
comedietta
rosehip tea
Docetistic
novelistic
solecistic
tokenistic
totemistic
rose-tinted
forebitter
dowel-joint
doner kebab
power lunch
power lathe
mole plough
coneflower
hogen-mogen
moneymaker
honeymonth
coterminal
token money
Roger Moore
homeomeric
homeomorph
Monel metal®
honey-mouse
solemn mass
fore-and-aft
modern jazz
governable
Copernican
Copernicus
nomen nudum
home and dry
modernness
solemnness
✧government
rose engine
governance
governante
come undone
moderniser
solemniser
governessy
modernizer
solemnizer
come to hand
nose to tail
come to pass
rose-combed
Moreton Bay
gobemouche
solenoidal
money order
come to heel
come to rest
dolesomely
lonesomely
love-monger
foremother
come to that
come to life
coregonine
fore-notice
foreboding
homecoming
polemonium
love potion
somebodies
homeworker
poke bonnet
dove-colour
lose colour
rose colour
tone colour
cometology
ponerology
forecourse
covetously
lobe-footed
Cole Porter
come to stay
loveworthy
noteworthy
power plant
Coleoptera
power press
coleoptile
cover price
✧Nobel prize
cover point
power point
vowel point
hokey-pokey
homeopathy
bone spavin
foreordain
rope bridge
more or less
coleorhiza
love-broker
foreground
home ground
lose ground
home-brewed
vowel-rhyme
José Orozco
lovers' lane
honey-stalk
sobersides
tower-shell
womenswear
honey-sweet
lover's knot
honey-stone
rover scout
somersault
Robert Capa
potentiate
hovertrain
powertrain
potentiary
come-at-able
comestible
domestical
Robert Adam
volente Deo
Robert Reid
Robert Peel
cosentient
Robert Kett
rodent-like
Lorentzian
money-taker
potentilla
Robert E Lee
money talks
robertsman
Robert Dole
Robert Koch
forest-born
covert coat
Robert Bolt
forest-bred
forest-tree
Robert Cray
rope stitch
lovestruck
Robert Lynd
code-number
pore fungus
dope pusher
forerunner
Rome-runner
bodegueros
rose quartz
fore-quoted
mole hunter
Roger Vadim
go-betweens
honey-wagon
money wages
bowerwoman
Pobedy Peak
roof garden
wolframite
God-fearing
Wolfianism
conflation
Joe Frazier
do a flanker
confabular
confection
non-fiction
non-factual
confidante
confidence
confidency
confederal
coffee bean
coffee shop
coffee mill
toffee-nose
coffee room
coffee tree
solfeggios
forfaiting
forfeiture
joyfulness
woefulness
coffin nail
confinable
coffin ship
dog-fancier
coffin bone
tomfoolery
golf course
bow-fronted
wolf's peach
wolf spider
confirmand
pot furnace
conferment
comforting
conferring
confirming
coffer-fish
conformist
conformity
✧conference
conférence
solferinos
confervoid
non-ferrous
not for nuts
confiscate
confessant
confusable
confusible
confusedly
cod-fishery
cod-fishing
rodfishing
confession
confiserie
confutable
solfataric
solfataras
confounded
confound it
forfeuchen
forfoughen
confluence
forge ahead
Douglas fir
zoographic
zoographer
not go amiss
poignadoes
long-haired
poignantly
dough-baked
song school
Rouge Croix
rough-draft
doggedness
bongo drums

congregate
congregant
long-headed
tongueless
long-legged
tongue-tied
mongrelise
mongrelize
tonguelike
toughening
non-gremial
mongrelism
Longfellow
long-termer
tongue-work
longaevous
long pepper
toggle iron
tonguester
borghettos
goggle-eyed
doughfaced
Lough Foyle
rough-grind
tough going
rough hound
rough house
rough-house
song thrush
rough-hewer
long-winded
doughiness
long-lining
tough it out
topgallant
coagulable
googolplex
coagulator
rough music
Lough Neagh
zoogonidia
gorgoneion
Gorgonzola
congeneric
noogenesis
congenetic
morganatic
congenital
conglobate
long corner
zoogloeoid
gorgeously
hodgepodge
roughrider
loggerhead
Joe Gargery
long primer
longprimer
songwriter
Long Island
congestive
congestion
rough stuff
songstress
forgettery
forgetting
long-staple
long stitch
congruence
congruency
long jumper
forgivable
wonga-wonga
top-heavily
Joshua tree
Sophoclean
Sothic year
tophaceous
Gothic arch
to the death
pochade box
do the dirty
Moshe Dayan
Moshoeshoe
Cochlearia
cochleated
Nothofagus
dochmiacal
Josh Gibson
not half bad
Roche limit
moth-flower
sophomoric
nothing but
foxhunting
pot-hunting
nothingism
dog handler
to the nines
Gothenburg
Loch Lomond
go shopping
job-hopping
to the point
lophophore
Tocharian A
Tocharian B
motherland
Mother's Day
mother cell
Motherwell
motherless
tocherless
mother ship
mother city
motherhood
tocher-good
bothersome
mother lode
mother-to-be
motherwort
mother upon
mother spot
oophoritis
to the skies
Mocha stone
Pooh sticks
Poohsticks
do the trick
hothousing
moth-hunter
no the wiser
solivagant
folie à deux
nominately
solid angle
cogitative
comitative
dominative
nominalise
nominalize
nominative
nominalism
solidarism
cogitation
domination
ionisation
ionization
lorication
motivation
nomination
solitarian
toxication
volitation
nominalist
solidarist
comicality
logicality
solidarity
solitarily
topicality
topi-wallah
Toni Sailer
nominal par
dominatrix
docimastic
dominantly
Logie Baird
Louis Botha
coriaceous
foliaceous
Louis Durey
Colin Davis
morigerate
vociferate
vociferant
noticeable
noticeably
comice pear
motiveless
politeness
Gobi Desert
mobile shop
noviceship
homiletics
novicehood
mobile home
coniferous
morigerous
pomiferous
poriferous
rotiferous
solipedous
vociferous
Police Motu
police trap
losing game
towing path
Cotingidae
boringness
lovingness
holing-pick
towing rope
coking coal
moving-coil
robing room
roping-down
rowing boat
toxiphobia
polishable
boyishness
coyishness
modishness
mopishness
tonishness
toyishness
polishment
polishings
dolichurus
Dolichotis
movie house
nobilitate
Dominicans
solicitant
modifiable
notifiable
soricident
positively
solidified
cohibitive
politicise
politicize
soliciting
positivism
cohibition
politician
solifidian
positivist
docibility
positivity
politicker
positioned
positional
volitional
positioner
bolivianos
moniliform
moliminous
politicoes
solicitous
moniliasis
Ion Iliescu
solicitude
Kodiak bear
bowie knife
Modigliani
jovialness
socialness
sociologic
jolie laide
social club
Coriolanus
social work
bouillotte
social fund
social evil
sodium lamp
Colin Meads
movie-maker
Louis Malle
Colin McRae
porismatic
goniometer
goniometry
sociometry
sodium pump
eolian harp
motionless
Polianthes
notionally
Dorian mode
Dorian Gray
Hominoidea
comic opera
totipotent
eosinophil
monitorial
volitorial
vomitorium
Morisonian
Posidonius
codicology
docimology
toxicology
rooibos tea
horizontal
sociopathy
foliar feed
goliardery
solid-state
tonic spasm
forinsecal
cop it sweet
Louis-Seize
Dodie Smith
tonic sol-fa
rotisserie
rôtisserie
comic strip
logistical
monistical
poristical
goliathise
goliathize
Corinthian
podiatrist
societally
Louisville
poliovirus
tonic water
policy-shop
hobjobbing
conjecture
conjugally
conjugated
Conjugatae
non-joinder
conjointly
Roy Jenkins
conjunctly
conjure out
conjurator
rock rabbit
cock-paddle
cock-paidle
rock garden
work-harden
rock-badger
bookmaking
Tom Keating
pockmarked
bookmarker
workbasket
cocktailed
fork-tailed
rock salmon
pork barrel
pockmantie
York Castle
dock-master
workmaster
cockabully
rockabilly
cock-a-bondy
kookaburra
monk's cloth
forkedness
hookedness
cockneydom
cockneyish
cockneyism
cork-heeled
bookseller
workfellow
mock-heroic
cockle boat
folk-memory
rock temple
workpeople
bookkeeper
lock-keeper
Book of Life
Book of Amos
Book of Joel
Book of Ruth
Book of Ezra
cockchafer
workaholic
rock lizard
rock-ribbed
bookbinder
rock pigeon
cocksiness
folksiness
look lively!
folk-singer
pork-pie hat
rock violet
cork-tipped
pockpitted
cockyleeky
look slippy
cockalorum
poikilitic
Tom Kilburn
cockamamie
working day
working-day
hook and eye
Hockenheim
Joe Kennedy
looking-for
Rockingham
working man
locking-nut
cock and pie
corking-pin
look snappy
look and say
look-and-say
Workington
book-holder
Hock Monday
mock-modest
bookmobile
folklorist
look down on
Doukhobors
rockhopper
topknotted
rock bottom
rock-bottom
work to rule
work-to-rule
you-know-who
folk-speech
Von Karajan
mock orange
cooker hood
locker room
cockernony
mock privet
Folkestone
cock a snook
forkit-tail
rock-steady
rocksteady
pocket veto
pocketless
cockatrice
pocket-comb
pocket-hole
pocketbook
lockstitch
pocket-fuls
rock turbot
cocksurely
book-muslin
fork supper
Rock Hudson
✧mock turtle
bonkbuster
cork-cutter
rock butter
Volkswagen®
monkey-gaff
monkey rail
monkey tail
cockeye bob
jockeyship
hockey line
Jockey Club
donkey vote
monkey rope
donkey-work
monkey boat
donkey-pump
monkey pump
monkey suit
wool-carder
toolmaking
wool-packer
Joel Garner
jolly along
poll-parrot
coalmaster
colleagued
koulibiaca
mouldboard
Molly Bloom
world-class
doulocracy
collective
collecting
rollicking
rollocking
collection
follicular
colliculus
coelacanth
collocutor
World Court
rolled oats
rolled gold
foul befall
coolheaded
Boulder Dam

goal-tender
Zollverein
foolbegged
bouldering
cowl-necked
coal cellar
goalkeeper
poll-degree
soullessly
boll weevil
coal heaver
mollifying
toploftily
collegiate
collograph
Howleglass
zoological
college cap
collagenic
collegiums
loll-shraub
wool shears
cool change
wool church
doll's house
wool-winder
mouldiness
woolliness
goalkicker
wool-picker
Roy Laidlaw
soul sister
Molly Keane
fowl-plague
world music
coelomatic
noble metal
collimator
coulometer
coulometry
cooling fan
Hollandish
Bollandist
fowling-net
cooling-off
Wollongong
codlin moth
rolling pin
pollenosis
Moulinette®
poplinette
toilinette
pollinator
pollen tube
Noël Coward
wool-comber
toilsomely
rollcollar
boil down to
coal-porter
woolsorter
foul-spoken
roll-up fund
world power
colliquate
colliquant
colloquise
colloquize
colloquial
colloquium
colloquist
rollerball
tollbridge
collar cell
collar beam
collarless
dollarless
collar of SS
Jolly Roger
dollarship
dollarbird
Lollardism
collarbone
poultroone
collar-work
boiler room
dollar area
poplar tree
lollo rosso
collar stud
collarette
fool around
collyriums
boiler suit
wool-driver
wool-grower
Rolls-Royce®
worldscale
coalescent
world sheet
molluscoid
molluscous
collatable
pollutedly
goblet cell
toiletries
go platinum
Collatinus
toilet roll
toilet soap
mollitious
zoolatrous
collotypic
wool staple
collateral
cos lettuce
toolpusher
coal bunker
coal-cutter
coolhunter
hot-livered
colluviums
hollow-ware
world-weary
hollowness
noblewoman
noblewomen
follow home
World War II
follow suit
hollow-eyed
woollyback
volleyball
woolly bear
woollybutt
doomsaying
worm-eating
commeasure
cosmic rays
formic acid
not much cop
cosmically
not much of a
formicaria
cosmic dust
formidable
formidably
cosmodrome
commodious
homme d'épée
homme d'état
coomceiled
room-fellow
formlessly
form letter
cosmogenic
cosmogonic
worm lizard
room-ridden
formulable
formaliter
formulator
cosmolatry
for my money
Joe Montana
Moominland
commentate
common rail
commandant
commentary
commonable
Formentera
common reed
common seal
commonweal
commandeer
commonness
commandery
Norman Shaw
common time
gormandise
gormandize
commanding
tormenting
gormandism
commingled
commonalty
communally
noumenally
common cold
commonhold
common toad
common room
common noun
communique
communiqué
common frog
Norman arch
Foaming Sea
comminuted
Holman Hunt
worm powder
cosmopolis
Commiphora
cormophyte
Doc Martens®
zoomorphic
commercial
coumarilic
cosmoramic
form critic
commissary
Coombs test
Tommy Smith
commission
commissure
commutable
cosmetical
dogmatical
noematical
commitment
committing
formatting
dogmatiser
commutator
dogmatizer
foam rubber
hot-mouthed
commixtion
bob maximus
commixture
corn-maiden
John Madden
downwardly
round angle
somniative
sound-alike
moonraking
foundation
John Napier
moonwalker
John Backus
downmarket
downfallen
John Taylor
John Wallis
mountained
John Barnes
John Haynes
round about
roundabout
somniatory
moon-raised
join battle
John Dalton
John Martin
John Martyn
corn-factor
down-easter
John Walter
point after
young adult
John Calvin
soundboard
point-blank
hobnobbing
town's-bairn
young blood
✧donnybrook
youngberry
Count Basie
coenobitic
round brush
pornocracy
John McAdam
soundcheck
non-nuclear
connective
connection
corniculum
cornaceous
cornucopia
coenocytic
fornicator
corned beef
John Edrich
round dance
horned toad
Lorna Doone
horned pout
horned-pout
round dozen
bounce back
Connie Mack
mountebank
counteract
counterbid
John Benbow
pouncet-box
loundering
counselled
corn-dealer
counsellor
John Wesley
counterman
John Rennie
John Lennon
go on record
founderous
pounce upon
round-eared
Ronnie Kray
countersue
counterspy
poinsettia
lounge suit
corn weevil
John Denver
round-faced
young fogey
loan-office
bonne femme
pound force
going forth
mount guard
point guard
bonne grâce
noun phrase
Zoanthidae
go on wheels
corn thrips
Mount Hekla
moonshiner
zoanthropy
Zoantharia
corn whisky
roundhouse
Young Italy
John Wilbye
corn circle
bounciness
coincident
John Pilger
loungingly
soundingly
woundingly
John Fisher
downsizing
John Wilkes
corn-miller
councillor
horn-rimmed
councilman
John Milton
corn-kister
council tax
horn silver
John Kirwan
Mount Kenya
Donna Karan
John Cleese
Mount Logan
cornflakes
hornblende
somnolence
somnolency
John Alcock
somniloquy
bonnilasse
noun clause
cornflower
moonflower
cognominal
found money
somnambule
round mouth
sound mixer
Mount Mayon
John Enders
John a-Nokes
down-and-out
go in and out
round-nosed
John Howard
John Gordon
loan-holder
Johnsonese
John Rogers
John Somers
boondoggle
corn dodger
Johnsonism
Johnsonian
downlooked
corncockle
corn-dollie
John Fowles
John Bowlby
corn popper
John Torrey
horn-footed
John Morton
John Potter
John Updike
conniption
Mount Pelée
soundproof
Count Paris
corn spirit
Mount Qogir
cornerback
cornerways
✧round robin
country-box
John Dryden
sound radio
John Bright
John Graham
cornerwise
John Braine
countryman
John Cranko
cornbrandy
John Bruton
John Bratby
moon around
to one's hand
soundscape
sound stage
to one's face
to one's name
cognisable
cognisably
coenosteum
connascent
do one's kind
sound shift
cognisance
Mount Sinai
joint-stock
joint-stool
pound scots
hounds-foot
to one's cost
goings-over
soundtrack
✧round table
round-table
Mount Thera
bonnethead
down at heel
down-at-heel
downstream
top-notcher
Mount Thira
go on strike
moonstrike
for nothing
cornettino
downstairs
cornettist
downstroke
pornotopia
cornstarch
connatural
non-natural
moonstruck
round tower
jointuress
John Buchan
John Ruskin
cornhusker
John Gummer
downturned
John Huston
corn-cutter
John Hunter
John Bunyan
Count Volta
Townsville
John Evelyn
connivance
connivence
connivancy
connivency
Bob Newhart
count wheel
townswoman
bound water
connexions
✧johnny-cake
Johnny Cash
county hall
Johnny Depp
county seat
gooneybird
county town

continuous
portentous
Boston crab
cotton tree
Fortinbras
sostenutos
cotton bush
continuums
postholder
soft sowder
post-modern
controvert
Montgomery
mouth organ
zootrophic
soft-bodied
portfolios
portionist
tortuosity
control key
controlled
soft-boiled
controller
control rod
Roy Thomson
tortiously
tortuously
foxtrotted
polt-footed
soft-footed
postcoital
post mortem
post-mortem
root nodule
fortepiano
mouthpiece
soft option
soft-spoken
north polar
south polar
mouthparts
toothpaste
nostopathy
souterrain
potter wasp
lost tribes
Costa Rican
montero-cap
footbridge
torturedly
jolterhead
couturière
forthright
doctorship
contortive
co-starring
fosterling
doctor-fish
poster girl
contortion
fox terrier
soft fruits
coeternity
Doctor Slop
bouts rimés
footprints
foster-home
coat-armour
posteriors
montbretia
nod through
port-crayon
contestant
Portishead
toothshell
poetastery
month's mind
contesting
fortissimo
costus-root
foetoscopy
soothsayer
potty-train
hoity-toity
Post-it note®
colt's tooth
goat's-thorn
hoots-toots
voetstoots
houts-touts
Pont du Gard
root rubber
goatsucker
portcullis
contour map
posthumous
footguards
zootsuiter
Montevideo
Monteverdi
worth while
worthwhile
forty winks
northwards
southwards
not to worry
north water
post-exilic
contexture
contextual
soft hyphen
root system
loculament
copulative
modularise
modularize
popularise
popularize
copulation
lobulation
modulation
nodulation
population
volutation
jocularity
modularity
popularity
copulatory
holus-bolus
columbaria
toluic acid
homuncular
homuncules
homunculus
loquacious
jocundness
columellae
columellar
volumetric
documental
monumental
lotus-eater
cohune nuts
focus group
no such luck
solubilise
solubilize
non-utility
solubility
volubility
solutional
poculiform
voluminous
bonus issue
coquelicot
roquelaure
coquimbite
rogue money
column inch
columnated
populously
hocus-pocus
Colubridae
no question
Lotus Sutra
voluptuary
Locustidae
locust bean
robustness
locust bird
coquetting
coquettish
goluptious
robustious
voluptuous
locust tree
pohutukawa
rogue value
convective
convictive
convictism
convection
conviction
louvre-door
convulsant
pot-valiant
convulsive
convulsion
convalesce
convoluted
mouvementé
non-vintage
convenable
convenient
convincing
✧convention
convenance
✧conventual
non-violent
conversant
convertend
convergent
conversely
convertite
converging
conversion
louver-door
convexedly
convexness
convex arch
conveyable
Now, Voyager
conveyance
woe-wearied
Ron Weasley
cobwebbery
pot-wabbler
pot-wobbler
Boswellise
Boswellize
God willing
Boswellism
Boswellian
forwarding
hot-working
Norway pine
do away with
coexistent
polyvalent
polymathic
Holy Father
corydaline
polyhalite
polygamist
body-cavity
Holy Family
body packer
body-warmer
jouysaunce
jovysaunce
polygamous
polycarpic
body carpet
polymastia
corybantic
polymastic
polydactyl
copy taster
corybantes
polyactine
molybdenum
molybdosis
copy-editor
polymerase
polysemant
Polyneices
copyreader
polymeride
polymerise
polymerize
polygenism
polymerism
Polynesian
polygenist
polygenous
polymerous
polysemous
polyhedric
body search
polyhedral
polyhedron
holy terror
Holy Office
Polychaeta
polychaete
coryphaeus
polychrest
polyphagia
polytheism
polytheist
Polyphemic
Polyphemus
polyphonic
polyphenol
polychroic
polychrome
polychromy
polyphasic
polyrhythm
bony fishes
Holy Willie
cotyliform
polydipsia
polyhistor
Yogyakarta
polyploidy
polyclinic
polyclonal
Polyclitus
polyominos
polyanthus
pony engine
copying ink
polyonymic
Houyhnhnms
looyenwork
Polyandria
body double
copyholder
polynomial
Polypodium
bodyworker
Holy Roller
body colour
polytocous
body-popper
corylopsis
rosy-footed
polycotton
Holy Spirit
bony spavin
Holy Friday
holy orders
body armour
polygraphy
polycrotic
copywriter
Holy Island
Robyn Smith
polystylar
polyatomic
Polypterus
hony-suckle
Joey Dunlop
polytunnel
cony-burrow
Tony Curtis
body swerve
body-swerve
polyaxonic
copy-typing
polygynian
copy typist
polycyclic
Polyhymnia
polygynous
polyhydric
polyhybrid
polycystic
pozzolanic
monzonitic
pozzuolana
mozzarella
speak a ship
aplanatism
splanchnic
upwardness
spray-dried
spray drift
sphacelate
speakerine
sphalerite
apparelled
aplacental
apparently
spear grass
splash page
splashback
splash down
splashdown
optatively
speakingly
apparition
spear-point
spray paint
spray-paint
sphaeridia
aphaeresis
spear-shaft
spray steel
Apgar score
epiblastic
epibenthic
epibenthos
specialise
specialize
specialism
speciation
specialist
speciality
spectacled
spectacles
spectatrix
spaceborne
spiceberry
spacecraft
space cadet
epicycloid
speciesism
speciesist
specifical
specifying
✧apocalypse
speculator
apiculture
epicanthic
epicanthus
epicentral
epicondyle
space opera
speciocide
speciosity
spaciously
speciously
spaceplane
space probe
spectre bat
epicardial
epicardium
spectrally
apochromat
apocarpous
epicuticle
spacewoman
apocryphal
apocryphon
spadiceous
epididymal
epididymis
spudding-in
apodeictic
epideictic
epidemical
spodomancy
epidendrum
epidiorite
spiderlike
spider line
spider mite
epidermoid
spider hole
spiderwork
spiderwort
spider crab
epidotised
epidotized
splenative
upper class
upper-class
apperceive
upper crust
upper-crust
spreadable
appendices
splendidly
splendrous
upsey Dutch
spread-over
appendixes
sphereless
spherelike
ephemerist
sphere-born
ephemerous
speedfreak
speedfully
spreaghery
speechless
speech-song
upper house
Spheniscus
speediness
speeding up
appetitive
appetising
appetizing
appetition
sphericity
appealable
speed limit
spleenless
spleenwort
sphenoidal
spheroidal
sphenogram
spherocyte
Upper Roger
appearance
appeasable
upper story
splent bone
spherulite
upperworks
apterygial
Apterygota
spiflicate
epigraphic

epigrapher
apagogical
I Pagliacci
epagomenal
up a gum tree
epigenesis
epigenetic
a peg too low
epiglottic
epiglottal
epiglottis
spagyrical
epigastric
up the booay
up the creek
up the stick
optical art
oppilative
optimalise
optimalize
aprication
oppilation
optimality
split-brain
Ophiacodon
Iphigeneia
upside down
upside-down
upsideowne
spring hare
springhase
springtail
springhaas
spring-cart
springhalt
springhead
springless
springlike
spring line
spring tide
springtide
springtime
spring clip
springwood
spring lock
spring roll
springwort
spring upon
springbuck
uppishness
sprightful
split hairs
upright-man
split image
aphidicide
ypsiliform
optimistic
sprinkling
uphillward
ophiologic
ophicleide
ophiolitic
ophiolater
ophiolatry
split-level
ophiomorph
opsiometer
optionally
optic nerve
epeirogeny
Ophiuridae
split shift
spoilsport
splintwood
splint bone
splint coal
split trust
sphinxlike
sphinx moth
spike grass
spokeshave
spoliative
spallation
spoliation
spoliatory
spuleblade
spell baker
spellbound
applicable
applicably
spell-check
spellcheck
applicator
epiloguise
epiloguize
apologetic
spellingly
spillikins
spell it out
epilimnion
spelunking
speleothem
Apollonian
speleology
opalescent
upflashing
spellstopt
apple sauce
apolitical
applausive
applauding
apolaustic
apple-woman
epimeletic
apomorphia
spumescent
spondaical
open-handed
open market
open access
eponychium
spinaceous
up and doing
open sesame
sponge cake
spongeware
sponge bath
spongebags
spongeable
Spencerian
Spenserian
spancelled
spongewood
sponge down
sponge-down
open-hearth
open secret
open season
open letter
spinnerule
spent force
spinigrade
✧up in the air
upon the gad
open cheque
epentheses
epenthesis
epenthetic
open-minded
sponginess
spunkiness
spankingly
open sights
sponsional
spongiform
spinal cord
spindle oil
spinel ruby
spinel-ruby
spaniolate
spaniolise
spaniolize
sponsorial
opinionist
spin bowler
spongology
open-topped
spin doctor
spin-doctor
epanaphora
epinephrin
spintronic
open prison
Upanishads
spinescent
Spanish fly
spinstress
spinsterly
open-stitch
open bundle
up-and-under
upon my word
upon my soul!
spondylous
open system
opsomaniac
splotchily
spoondrift
opposeless
spoonerism
optometric
up for grabs
spookiness
appositely
oppositely
appositive
oppositive
apposition
✧opposition
aphoristic
J P Donleavy
appointive
optologist
up to no good
up to a point
up to tricks
uproarious
apron-stage
upholstery
Epsom salts
éprouvette
epiplastra
apoplectic
apopemptic
epiphonema
apoprotein
apophthegm
apophyseal
epiphyseal
apophysial
epiphytism
opaqueness
spermaceti
approaches
sparganium
spermarium
spermatium
spermaries
Spartacist
spermatist
Spiro Agnew
spermaduct
opera buffa
opprobrium
appreciate
spiraculum
spiracular
opera cloak
sperm count
upgradable
sporadical
aphrodisia
sparseness
spur-heeled
sparked out
sportfully
spirograph
opera glass
sparagrass
Sparagmite
sporogonia
opera house
sportiness
sportively
spur-winged
sportingly
sparkishly
appraisive
spermicide
upbraiding
spermiduct
apartments
spirometer
spirometry
apprentice
upbringing
sporangial
sporangium
spuriosity
spermogone
spuriously
spirophore
sporophore
sporophyte
sporophyll
sports hall
sportscast
sportswear
oppressive
oppression
sports coat
opera seria
spirit lamp
spiritedly
spiritless
operettist
spirit-blue
spirituous
spirit duck
spirit away
operculate
approvable
approvance
sperm whale
approximal
sperrylite
sporozoite
apostatise
apostatize
epispastic
episodical
epistemics
episternal
episternum
spasticity
spissitude
aposematic
episematic
opisometer
apostolate
episcopate
episcopant
episcopacy
epistolary
apostolise
apostolize
episcopise
episcopize
epistolise
epistolize
epistolist
spasmodist
aposporous
episiotomy
apostrophe
epistrophe
spatiality
spot market
ophthalmia
ophthalmic
spot-barred
epithemata
apitherapy
apothecary
opotherapy
spotted dog
spot-welder
spot height
sputtering
apothecial
epithelial
apothecium
epithelium
spot dealer
epithermal
apotheoses
apotheosis
spotlessly
spitefully
spatchcock
spitchcock
spottiness
spittlebug
epitomical
epitomiser
epitomizer
upstanding
spatangoid
apotropaic
apotropous
epitaphian
epitaphist
spot stroke
spathulate
spauld-bone
spruce beer
spouseless
spruceness
epaulement
spruce pine
opium-eater
upsurgence
upbuilding
oppugnancy
upbursting
splutterer
upbuoyance
spawn brick
epexegeses
epexegesis
epexegetic
epoxy resin
spoyleful1
epizootics
aquamanale
squabasher
aquamanile
aquamarine
squamation
aquabatics
squandered
squanderer
square yard
square-face
square-sail
square deal
square meal
squareness
✧square mile
squarewise
square inch
square knot
square-toed
square-toes
square foot
square root
square away
square-eyed
square eyes
aquaphobia
aquaphobic
squashable
equability
equanimity
squalidity
equational
squamiform
equanimous
Aquariuses
squall line
aquaplaner
aqua Tofana
Squaloidea
equatorial
aquarobics
squamosity
aqua fortis
aquafortis
squadroned
squadronal
B quadratum
equals sign
a quarter to
squamulose
squelching
squeteague
equestrian
squeezable
squeeze-box
squeeze off
equiparate
squirarchy
equivalent
equitation
squirality
squireship
squirelike
squireling
squirehood
squirearch
equivocate
equipotent
squirrelly
squint-eyed
squint-eyes
Bryan Adams
break a jest
pre-Adamite
breakables
broad arrow
preadapted
breadboard
break bread
breadberry
broad-based
broadbrush
Brian Bevan
broadcloth
breadcrumb
trial court
break cover
art and part
errand girl
triandrian
breakdance
triandrous
greaseband
greaseball
Armageddon
arcaneness
greaseless
ornateness
urbaneness
urea resins
greasewood
ornamental
arbalester
ornamenter
Artaxerxes
dreadfully
break-front
break forth
Bryan Ferry
breadfruit
arraigning
Triangulum
triangular

truncately
iron ration
truncation
bring about
prink about
ironmaster
transactor
front bench
front-bench
Grant Batty
Frank Bruno
front crawl
Bronx cheer
pronuclear
pronucleus
grandchild
transcribe
✧trinacrian
transcript
irenically
ironically
arenaceous
Frank Capra
grand-ducal
transducer
grand duchy
granddaddy
drink-drive
wrongdoing
granadilla
grenadilla
Grenadines
Frank Dyson
grande dame
Orange Bath
orange peel
fringeless
Prinz Eugen
Prince Igor
grangerise
grangerize
orange-wife
princelike
trancelike
bronze-wing
cringeling
princeling
trinketing
Grangerism
orange-lily
orange-wood
princehood
Prince John
orange-root
tranced-out
fringe tree
orange tree
princessly
Oranjestad
transeptal
Bronze Star
transexual
Frank Field
wrongfully
transferee
bring forth
transferor
transfuser
trans-fatty
transgress
transgenic
brant goose
brent goose
branchiate
French sash
French heel
French seam
French bean
branchless
French hens
Frenchness
crunchiest
trench feet
branch line
French kiss
French plum
trenchancy
bronchiole
French loaf
French roof
branch-work
French roll
French horn
French door
trench coat
trench foot
franchisee
franchiser
bronchitic
Grand Hotel
bronchitis
French cuff
grant-in-aid
brand-image
frangipane
principate
frangipani
Franciscan
crinoidean
crankiness
trendiness
bringing up
cringingly
grindingly
grinningly
gruntingly
prancingly
prankingly
brandisher
princified
transitive
iron-mining
principial
principium
transition
fringillid
iron-willed
principled
frantic-mad
trunnioned
transience
transiency
transitory
iron-fisted
iron-witted
transistor
iron-liquor
grand juror
grand jésus
Franz Kafka
Franz Kline
crenellate
trundle bed
translucid
crinkliest
Franz Lehár
granulomas
crinolined
iron-glance
translunar
granularly
uranalysis
urinalysis
Franz Liszt
granulitic
crenulated
crinolette
granulater
granulator
translator
Grand Mufti
printmaker
trunk maker
grandmamma
grand monde
pronominal
drink-money
grand march
grand merci
transmuter
urinometer
uranometry
grand-niece
Cronenberg
pronuncios
pruning saw
Frank O'Hara
brontosaur
iron-worded
grand opera
ironmonger
✧francophil
transonics
craniology
craniotomy
wrongously
grand piano
transplant
prenuptial
grand prior
pronephric
pronephros
transposal
transposon
transposer
transputer
granophyre
Ironbridge
Bruno Rossi
bring round
grandstand
arena stage
trans-shape
wring staff
crankshaft
crank-sided
crane's bill
crane's-bill
cranesbill
Drones Club
trans-sonic
grindstone
triniscope
urinoscopy
✧grands prix
grand style
trinitrate
bring to bay
Trinity Bay
frenetical
wrong-timed
grand total
transudate
pronounced
grand-uncle
pronouncer
bring under
Art Nouveau
tranquilly
transvalue
transverse
frontwards
printworks
wrong way up
brandy-ball
granny flat
brandy snap
granny knot
Frank Zappa
ergomaniac
Areopagite
ergotamine
areolation
arrogation
Eriocaulon
artocarpus
argonautic
arrogantly
trioecious
cryoscopic
cryogenics
cryometric
Errol Flynn
arrow-grass
ergophobia
cryophilic
troop horse
eriophorum
cryophorus
proof-house
broodiness
droopiness
grooviness
broodingly
droopingly
prioritise
prioritize
Ordovician
ergodicity
Brooklands
argon laser
ordonnance
trio sonata
cryoconite
ergonomics
bryologist
ergonomist
oreologist
crio-sphinx
brood-pouch
armourless
armour-clad
areography
oreography
broomstaff
Orion's belt
proof sheet
broomstick
droop snoot
pro-oestrus
brook trout
ergosterol
bryostatin
arbor vitae
wrap-rascal
trap-ladder
drop-hammer
trip hammer
propraetor
oropharynx
drop a brick
prepuberty
prepackage
tropicbird
tropically
prep school
drupaceous
tripudiate
tripudiary
triple harp
drop serene
prophetess
tripleness
graplement
prophesied
triple time
tripperish
triple bill
trophesial
prophetism
prophesier
graphemics
tropaeolum
tropaeolin
triple play
triple bond
tripterous
drop-letter
triple jump
triple-jump
grapefruit
propagable
propagulum
✧propaganda
propagator
tripehound
triplicate
graphicacy
crop circle
preppiness
trappiness
grippingly
trippingly
graphitise
graphitize
trephining
eruptivity
triplicity
eruptional
graphitoid
uropoiesis
proprietor
propellant
crippledom
propylaeum
prepollent
propellent
propelment
tropologic
propulsive
propelling
propulsion
crapulence
propulsory
grapelouse
tripinnate
propendent
prepensely
propensely
prepensive
propensive
trepanning
propension
propensity
trypan blue
treponemas
treponemes
propionate
cryptogamy
tryptophan
graptolite
kryptonite
Trophonian
✧cryptozoic
cryptology
graphology
trophology
cryptogram
proproctor
crêpe paper
graph paper
tropopause
tropophyte
proper name
preparedly
properness
propertied
tripartite
tripartism
proportion
proper noun
preparator
wraparound
proposable
drop astern
prepossess
grape sugar
crêpe-soled
grapestone
prepositor
crepuscule
propitiate
art pottery
prepotence
prepotency
triphthong
propitious
propounder
cropduster
tripe-woman
trip switch
Gripe Water®
gripe water
prepayable
prepayment
Triphysite
trophy wife
trapeziums
pre-qualify
triquetrae
triquetral
triquetrum
frequenter
frequently
craquelure
Brer Rabbit
dry-roasted
triradiate
pruriently
prerelease
proratable
crossandra
press ahead
crustacean
press agent
brush aside
prostatism
crispation
crustation
prestation
cross-armed
MRI scanner
cross aisle
trespasser
crystal set
grasp after
crispature
crispbread
crossbreed
crossbench
crossbones
fresh blood
wrest block
fresh-blown
crossbirth
frostbound
crossbower
cross-claim
crossclaim
Ernst Chain
crosscheck
trisection
grass cloth
criss-cross
trisectrix
prosecutor
cross-court
grass court
presidiary
prosodical
cross-dress
crise de foi
Irish dance
✧presidency
presidiums
fresherdom
crescendos
dressed day
pressed day
arms-length
urostegite
proscenium
triskelion
prosperity
presternum
prosperous
tristearin

crescentic
crescented
arts centre
prospector
prospectus
crested tit
brass-faced
crossfield
press flesh
trustfully
cross guard
dressguard
grass-green
presageful
presignify
grass-grown
dress-goods
cross hairs
urosthenic
prostheses
prosthesis
bruschetta
prosthetic
bruschette
cross-hatch
trust house
cross-index
brassiness
crispiness
crustiness
drossiness
friskiness
frostiness
grassiness
grisliness
prissiness
trashiness
trustiness
crushingly
friskingly
graspingly
pressingly
trustingly
tristichic
prosaicism
prescience
cristiform
Aristippus
prosciutti
prosciutto
crassitude
prostitute
✧prusik knot
trisulcate
prosilient
drysaltery
crosslight
wrestle out
presumable
presumably
dressmaker
press money
cross-match
drosometer
prison yard
prison camp
prison bars
present-day
prisonment
prison ship
presentive
presential
Krishnaism
presension
prison door
prison crop
prismoidal
gressorial
prostomial
prostomium
uroscopist
Cristofori
aristology
aristocrat
brass plate
wrest plank
crosspiece
drosophila
erysipelas
presuppose
crash-proof
press proof
cross-party
crosspatch
Irish pound
crossroads
prescriber
proscriber
cross-refer
Proserpina
dry service
presurmise
grass-roots
frustrated
cross-ratio
grass snake
cross-staff
cross-slide
dress shirt
dress sense
cross-stone
frost-smoke
trust stock
grass style
brass tacks
presetting
Irish Times
proseuchae
pressurise
pressurize
bressummer
brusquerie
grasswrack
grass widow
brushwheel
Irishwoman
presswoman
wristwatch
freshwater
presbytery
presbytism
presbyopia
presbyopic
Proteaceae
tritiation
brat packer
prothallia
prothallic
prothallus
protracted
protractor
arctic hare
protectant
arctic tern
arctic char
protective
protecting
protection
protocolic
critically
erotically
tritically
✧cretaceous
triticeous
protectory
protectrix
criticiser
criticizer
art therapy
written law
arytaenoid
written off
protreptic
brutifying
gratifying
gratefully
truthfully
wrathfully
brute force
Arctogaeic
Arctogaean
erotogenic
Greta Garbo
Protagoras
Fritz Haber
wretchedly
protohuman
Brett Harte
crotcheted
frothiness
grittiness
grottiness
prettiness
wrathiness
writhingly
fratricide
bratticing
crithidial
erethismic
trithionic
proteiform
gratuitous
proteinous
erethistic
Trotskyite
Trotskyism
Trotskyist
fritillary
prattlebox
Crotalidae
J R R Tolkien
gratillity
crotalaria
erotomania
pro tempore
arithmetic
pretendant
proton beam
pretendent
protensive
writing-ink
pre-tension
pretension
protension
orotundity
protensity
protonemal
pratincole
protanopia
tritanopia
protanopic
tritanopic
writing pad
proteomics
trattorias
grotto-work
proteolyse
protoplasm
protoplast
arctophile
arctophily
protopathy
Protophyta
protophyte
✧crater lake
triternate
Grote Reber
oratorical
writership
craterlike
fraternise
fraternize
fraternity
protervity
erythritic
urethritic
erythritol
triturator
ureteritis
urethritis
Fratercula
Bratislava
✧protestant
protostele
British gum
Britishism
frithsoken
Pratt's Club
protostome
frithstool
grith-stool
truth serum
truth table
prototroph
prototypal
protrudent
protrusile
protrusive
protrusion
truth value
protoxylem
pretty well
pretty much
protozoans
trou-madame
traumatise
traumatize
traumatism
arcubalist
trouvaille
troubadour
ground game
ground wave
ground mail
ground-bass
groundmass
groundbait
groundedly
ground beef
groundsell
ground zero
groundless
ground rent
ground pine
groundling
groundsill
ground plan
groundplot
groundsman
ground-hold
ground-dove
groundwork
ground loop
ground crew
groundprox
ground rule
arguteness
trousering
trou-de-loup
grouse moor
argumentum
proud flesh
proud-flesh
fraudfully
crouch-ware
fraughtage
draught-bar
draughtman
draught-net
croupiness
troubledly
Group of Ten
triumphant
triumphery
triumphing
Argun River
trousseaus
trousseaux
troutstone
trout spoon
groupthink
fraudulent
triumviral
trivialise
trivialize
trivialism
triviality
crave after
provocable
crève-coeur
provection
prevocalic
provocator
providable
✧providence
a rivederci
proveditor
grave goods
Braveheart
prevailing
provokable
gravel-walk
privileged
travelogue
drivelling
gravelling
grovelling
travelling
travel-sick
prevalence
trivalence
prevalency
trivalency
travelator
travolator
grave-maker
gravimeter
gravimetry
Provençale
driving-box
cravenness
prevenient
preventive
provincial
prevention
provenance
prevenancy
Trivandrum
graveolent
previously
✧privy purse
driverless
travertine
traversing
proverbial
Trevor Nunn
drive shaft
travestied
gravestone
provisions
gravy train
private act
✧private eye
gravity-fed
brevetting
cravatting
Trevithick
Gravettian
private law
provitamin
privatiser
private war
privatizer
✧crown agent
brown algae
Drawcansir
brewmaster
draw a blank
brown bread
Brown Betty
crown court
draw a cover
brown dwarf
Crown Derby
crew-necked
trawlerman
browned off
crow-keeper
brown earth
browbeaten
browbeater
brownfield
crown glass
crown graft
crown green
brown goods
crow-shrike
growth ring
growth area
drowsihead
brawniness
drowsiness
frowsiness
frowziness
crawlingly
drawlingly
frowningly
growlingly
prowlingly
brown jolly
crewellery
arc welding
trowelling
crewelwork
crow-flower
growing-bag
brow-antler
drawing-pen
drawing pin
ore-wrought
Erewhonian
crown piece
brown paper
draw breath
crown roast
drawbridge
Trowbridge
brown snake
crawlspace
brown sugar
Brown Shirt
Brownshirt
brownstone
brown stout
brown sauce
brown study
draw it mild
draw it fine
draw-string
drawstring
draw stumps
brown trout
crown vetch
crown-wheel
proximally
crux ansata
fraxinella
Praxiteles
grey market
grey-haired
grey parrot
grey matter
grey-headed
grey-wether
Fray Bentos
dray-plough
grey knight
trey-antler
argyrodite
traymobile
grey-coated
Grey Friars
prayer bead
prayerless
arty-crafty
prayer flag
prayer book

rum blossom
cumbrously
zumbooruck
lumber-yard
rubber band
lumberjack
outbargain
rue-bargain
lumber-camp
rubberneck
rubberwear
cumberless
numberless
cumberment
lubberlike
lubber line
number line
number nine
lumber-mill
numbers man
cumbersome
lubber hole
lumbersome
lumber room
rubber room
rubber-room
rubber tree
rubbishing
rugby shirt
sun bittern
sunbathing
dumbstruck
✧rugby union
outbluster
Yul Brynner
bubbly-jock
surcharged
surcharger
cunctative
subcranial
cunctation
punctation
subclavian
Sun Chariot
nutcracker
cunctatory
outclassed
Munchausen
subchanter
subchapter
subcharter
nunciature
punchboard
subcabinet
succubuses
Dutch clock
juncaceous
suicidally
succedanea
Dutch drops
punch-drunk
subchelate
butchering
quickening
succeeding
quiche dish
zucchettos
quick-firer
bunch grass
quack grass
quick grass
quick-hedge
bunchiness
subceiling
punctilios
functional
Puncak Jaya
puschkinia
auscultate
subcalibre
subcaliber
punch-ladle
succulence
Dutch lunch
quick-lunch
succulency
dulciloquy
muscularly
subculture
subcompact
outcompete
quick march
quick-match
Dutch metal
Pulcinella
Vulcanalia
subcentral
buccinator
succinctly
lusciously
suscipient
susceptive
Turcophile
subception
Turcophobe
subcordate
succursale
cut corners
muscardine
subcarrier
muscarinic
subcircuit
successful
successive
succussive
quick-stick
succession
succussion
quick-sandy
lunch-table
Dutch treat
quick trick
Dutch tiles
quickthorn
punctulate
Dutch uncle
punctually
subcrustal
punctuator
muscovados
Muscovitic
Dutchwoman
quick-water
subdialect
subdeanery
quadrangle
quadratics
quadratrix
fund-raiser
quadrantal
quadrantes
quadratura
quadrature
buddy-buddy
subduction
duodecimal
duodecimos
subdecanal
outdacious
fuddy-duddy
humdudgeon
funded debt
Dundee cake
hurdle-race
hurdle rate
muddle-head
subduement
Dundee City
Auld Reekie
out-dweller
quadrennia
cuddlesome
bundle away
muddle away
mundifying
pundigrion
hurdy-gurdy
curd cheese
Buddy Holly
kurdaitcha
quadrireme
quadriceps
quadrisect
muddlingly
quadrivial
quadrivium
quadriller
quadricone
quadripole
quadriform
Buddhistic
Dundalk Bay
cul-de-lampe
buddy movie
pudding bag
suddenness
burdensome
pudding-pie
pundonores
duodenitis
fundholder
Sunderland
dunderpate
dunderhead
rudderless
sunderment
wunderkind
rudderfish
sunderance
quid pro quo
dunderfunk
Bundesrath
Bundesbank
Bundeswehr
Duc de Sully
Quadrumana
quadrumane
quadruplet
Ruud Gullit
quadruplex
quadrupole
quadrumvir
subdivider
jus divinum
Sunday best
Sunday Post
Tuberaceae
gude-father
iure mariti
Juvenalian
numeration
superation
superalloy
lukewarmth
lukewarmly
suzerainty
Oudenaarde
gum elastic
superaltar
superacute
superbrain
superbness
Luxembourg
superclass
queencraft
superclean
Lupercalia
tuberculum
tuberculin
tubercular
pubescence
quiescence
tumescence
quiescency
supercargo
superdense
super-duper
Jugendstil
superexalt
euhemerise
euhemerize
quietening
Euhemerism
eugenecist
euhemerist
funereally
Eugene Aram
pure reason
tunelessly
superfecta
superfluid
supergrass
supergiant
supergroup
aubergiste
superheavy
Bucephalus
superhelix
superhuman
Judenhetze
Outer House
juvenilely
rune-singer
juvenilise
juvenilize
iure divino
eugenicist
juvenility
tuberiform
mucedinous
superiorly
Puseyistic
quietistic
gude-sister
outer limit
superlunar
Aureomycin®
supermodel
supernally
supernurse
gubernator
sure enough
sure-enough
supernovae
supernovas
superorder
gude-mother
superoxide
eudemonism
numerosity
tuberosity
autecology
numerology
numerously
surefooted
superposed
superpower
run errands
super-royal
Queensland
outer space
Queen's ware
superstate
supersharp
superseder
superspeed
auger-shell
supersweet
Queen's Club
supersonic
superstore
mutessarif
supersound
supersaver
queen-sized
quaestuary
lutestring
rupestrian
supertwist
supertonic
supertitle
supertough
iure humano
puberulent
superunion
puberulous
bureaucrat
mute button
Jules Verne
supervisee
supervisal
supervisor
superwoman
Huw Edwards
suretyship
surf-bather
ruffianish
ruffianism
suffragism
sufflation
suffragist
surfcaster
puff pastry
surfactant
sufficient
surfaceman
tuffaceous
outfielder
bufflehead
buff-jerkin
bumfreezer
suffigance
gunfighter
surfeiting
surf-riding
ruefulness
fulfilment
fulfilling
buffalo-nut
duffel coat
muffin-bell
cut flowers
Sunflowers
buffoonery
outflowing
put forward
sufferable
sufferably
subfertile
puffer fish
sufferance
buffer zone
rumfustian
suffisance
subfuscous
Gulf Stream
Yun-Fat Chow
outfitting
Gulf States
dumfounder
sulfhydryl
burglarise
burglarize
subglacial
sunglasses
fungicidal
surgically
burgh court
jugged hare
ruggedness
turgidness
junglefowl
dung-beetle
judgmental
luggage-van
quagginess
bunglingly
jugglingly
Gus Grissom
cudgelling
cudgel-play
nudge, nudge
Guggenheim
jus gentium
subgeneric
outgeneral
sui generis
subgenuses
subglobose
gudgeon pin
Luigi Pulci
✧juggernaut
budgerigar
Tungurahua
fungus-gall
turgescent
suggestive
outgassing
suggestion
Turgut Ozal
humgruffin
dung-hunter
Lughnasadh
rush candle
bushranger
Buchmanite
subheading
Buchmanism
bushwalker
bush jacket
Hugh Laurie
Hugh Cairns
bush-harrow
Hugh Casson
bushmaster
bush-lawyer
duchy court
euchred out
ruthlessly
bush-shrike
euphuistic
bushelling
CúChulainn
oughtlings
euphonical
cub-hunting
euphonious
ruthenious
euthanasia
Euthyneura
rush holder
Ruth Rogers
euchlorine
mushroomer
Euphrosyne
Sutherland
euphoriant
Hugh Greene
authorless
authorship
Luther King
euphorbium
bush fruits
✧rutherford
authoriser
push around
authorizer
Hughes Hall
such as it is
eurhythmic
push-stroke
jumhouriya
euphausiid
push-button
musical box
ouvirandra
Punicaceae
Surinamese
dubitative
judicative
puritanise
puritanize
ruminative
luminarism
✧puritanism
dubitation
fugitation

fumigation
jubilation
judication
lumination
Lusitanian
mutilation
rumination
Ruritanian
supination
luminarist
culinarily
musicality
au pis aller
pupiparous
fumigatory
judicatory
Punic apple
duniwassal
Ruminantia
jubilantly
ruminantly
judicature
muliebrity
rubiaceous
music drama
luciferase
Lutine bell
supineness
Luciferian
auriferous
luciferous
muciferous
nubiferous
nubigenous
nuciferous
pupigerous
tulip-eared
rudimental
Punic faith
music folio
audiograph
Turing test
tuning fork
punishable
mulishness
punishment
music house
munificent
fugitively
humidifier
audibility
fusibility
judicially
munifience
munitioner
musicianer
musicianly
rubiginose
culiciform
cupidinous
fuliginous
rubiginous
pugilistic
humiliator
humidistat
Julie Krone
numismatic
cubic metre
audiometer
eudiometer
audiometry
eudiometry
Julian year
fusionless
fusion bomb
cubic nitre
rupicoline
auditorial
auditorium
luminosity
nucivorous
rupicolous
tubicolous
musicology
luminously
mutinously
Quai d'Orsay
audiophile
music paper
Curia Regis
junior high
junior miss
nudibranch
junior soph
music stand
cupid's dart
music-shell
pumie stone
music stool
Rubik's Cube®
audit trail
subintrant
juristical
puristical
quaintness
auriculate
funiculate
lucifugous
subjective
subjection
surjection
subjectify
subjugator
subjoinder
gum juniper
outjetting
outjutting
buck-rabbit
muck-raking
buck-basket
musk-mallow
Aufklärung
lucky charm
duck-legged
Turkmenian
junk-dealer
huckle-bone
buckle down
lucklessly
musk beetle
duckshover
muck-midden
duck-billed
cuckoldise
cuckoldize
quaking ash
husking-bee
subkingdom
sucking-pig
husk-tomato
cuckoo pint
cuckoo-spit
duck-footed
junk-bottle
muckspread
lucky-piece
buck's party
bucks party
bucks' party
musk orchid
Quaker-bird
suckerfish
hunker down
dukkeripen
muck around
pukka sahib
lucky stone
huckstress
bucket seat
musket-rest
bucket shop
musket-shot
junketings
bucketload
sucket fork
bucket down
Turko-Tatar
bucketfuls
sucks to you!
bulk buying
buck-jumper
musk turtle
Turkey hone
turkey cock
turkey trot
Pullman car
full-handed
nuclearise
nuclearize
nucleation
bull market
full-sailed
full-manned
hurlbarrow
hullabaloo
hurly-burly
publicness
public bill
dual school
duplicator
curled-pate
quill drive
outlodging
curled dock
bull-headed
full-length
bull-beggar
bull-necked
full nelson
bull-beeves
full of life
nullifying
qualifying
guilefully
mudlogging
mulligrubs
full-circle
bull fiddle
guiltiness
full-rigged
full-winged
Kublai Khan
qualmishly
dull-witted
full sister
sublimable
subliminal
sublimated
muslin-kale
sullenness
outlandish
nulla-nulla
sublingual
nucleolate
bulldog ant
full-voiced
full-bodied
guillotine
nucleoside
nucleotide
nucleonics
bullionist
full-cocked
nucleosome
bull-roarer
full cousin
full-bottom
dual-priced
Guy Laroche
full orders
butlership
gully-raker
dull-browed
publishing
outlet mall
bullet-head
subletting
sur le tapis
bullet-tree
sunlounger
full-summed
Ku Klux Klan
guilty-like
outmeasure
mummy-cloth
submucosae
submucosal
submediant
curmudgeon
mummifying
nutmegging
duumvirate
pummelling
nummulitic
nummulated
humming ale
submontane
Kuomintang
summonable
submanager
fulmineous
Pulmonaria
humming-top
put money on
summerlike
summertide
summer time
summertime
curmurring
submersion
submariner
summerwood
Summar Roll
summer-tree
cummerbund
surmisable
Burmese cat
submissive
submission
durmast oak
summitless
hug-me-tight
submitting
suum cuique
surmounted
surmounter
mummy-wheat
dummy whist
ruin marble
Juan Fangio
Juan Carlos
guinea fowl
✧guinea worm
✧guinea corn
quinic acid
burnt cream
subnuclear
quinacrine
pugnacious
muonic atom
turn adrift
Quonset hut®
quink-goose
quenchable
quenchless
quantitate
quantitive
quantifier
buon giorno
Burne-Jones
tunnelling
quint major
surnominal
quint minor
funny money
ouananiche
running dog
running gag
Burns Night
Running Man
turning-saw
burnt ochre
turn colour
turnip flea
turnip moth
funny paper
quinaquina
turnbroach
vulnerable
runner bean
turn around
turnaround
runner duck
subnascent
burnishing
buenos dias
funny stuff
burnettise
burnettize
burnet rose
burnet moth
subnatural
burnt umber
turnbuckle
quintuplet
turn turtle
quinsy-wort
put on an act
Eurobabble
out on a limb
automatise
automatize
automatism
humoralism
automation
automatist
humoralist
Euromarket
autogamous
automatons
cup of assay
suborbital
autoscopic
out of court
subordinal
cuboid bone
out of doors
out-of-doors
hug oneself
bufotenine
autogenics
autoteller
suboceanic
autogenous
humoresque
Tudoresque
subofficer
Rudolf Hess
Rudolf Otto
tumorgenic
autophobia
Europhobia
autophagia
autochthon
autotheism
autotheist
Eurocheque
autodidact
autowinder
Mucorineae
Eurovision
tutorially
eulogistic
humoristic
out of joint
Euroclydon
autoplasty
tuboplasty
Yugoslavia
Yugoslavic
auto-immune
out of order
bubonocele
automobile
automotive
autonomics
autonomist
autologous
autonomous
humorously
out of phase
out of place
out of print
out of reach
humourless
rumour mill
humoursome
autography
autotrophy
autocratic
autoerotic
Eurocratic
Yukon River
out of shape
out of sight
out of synch
out of stock
out of sorts
Tudor-style
autostrada
autoptical
suboctuple
out of touch
Eurotunnel
out of whack
sulphatase
pump-handle
sulphation
pulp cavity
hump-backed
supplanter
jump a claim
suspectful
pump-action
auspicious
suspicious
lumpectomy
sun picture
suppedanea
cuspidated
subpoenaed
rumple-bane
supplejack
suppleness
subprefect
supplement
suppletive
purple fish
suppletion
purple wood
pumple-nose
purple-born
suppletory
suppressed
suppressor
purple-hued
jump the gun
supplicate
supplicant
surprising
bumpkinish
suppliance
dumpy-level
culpa levis
mumping-day
suspenders
pulp-engine
suspensive
turpentine
out-pension
suspension
turpentiny
suspensoid
suspensory
bump and run
sulphonate
due process

sulphonium
jump for joy
jump-jockey
subprogram
rumpy-pumpy
Tupperware®
supperless
supporters
Kuiper Belt
suppertime
supportive
supporting
subphrenic
outperform
suspirious
supporture
supposable
supposably
supposedly
purposeful
surpassing
outpassion
rumpus room
out-patient
puppet show
put-putting
puppet play
sulphurate
surplusage
sulphurise
sulphurize
outpouring
lumpsucker
sulphurous
supplyment
Murphy's law
musquetoon
cuique suum
✧surrealism
quartation
surrealist
curriculum
curricular
rubrically
lubricious
lubricator
rubricator
putridness
furry dance
quarterage
quarter-boy
quarrender
quarter day
quartering
quarter-ill
puerperium
quarrelled
quarreller
quarteroon
quarter-saw
putrefying
outrageous
surrogatum
puir's-hoose
guardhouse
puir's-house
quarriable
quirkiness
hurryingly
queryingly
quercitron
sucralfate
supralunar
burramundi
currant bun
guaranteed
quarantine
gunrunning
rum-running
Quirinalia
mucronated
Puerto Rico
suprapubic
subreptive
subreption
eutrapelia
quersprung
suprarenal
putrescent
burra sahib
putrescine
cuirassier
quernstone
turret ship
Turritella
nutritious
subroutine
furrow-weed
burrow-duck
quarry tile
quartz lamp
quartz-mill
quartz-rock
quartzitic
substance P
Russianise
Russianize
Russianism
outstation
substation
Russianist
puissaunce
Russian tea
puissantly
pursuantly
nurse-child
subsection
subsidiary
outside-car
cursedness
cussedness
quesadilla
subsidence
subsidency
subspecies
outspeckle
Aussiedler
substellar
substernal
outsweeten
bus shelter
Russifying
sub-Saharan
nursehound
guest-house
guestimate
pursuivant
nun's-fiddle
gunslinger
mudslinger
outswinger
guessingly
pursuingly
questingly
subsoiling
questionee
questioner
subspinous
mudskipper
substitute
Mussulmans
Russellite
subsultive
subsellium
mussel-plum
russel-cord
Düsseldorf
subsultory
curselarie
subsumable
pulsimeter
pulsometer
nursing-bra
guest-night
outs and ins
put stock in
Luis Somoza
purse-pride
Russophile
purse-proud
Russophobe
subsequent
subsurface
subscribed
subscriber
subshrubby
bursarship
pursership
tusser silk
nurseryman
gut-scraper
Guns 'n' Roses
Mussorgsky
outstretch
substratal
substratum
nurse shark
subsistent
purse-seine
subsessile
outsetting
sunsetting
Pulsatilla
pulsatance
fussbudget
numskulled
Luis Buñuel
subtrahend
australite
fustianize
Australian
lustration
fustianist
nuptiality
dust jacket
Australoid
Australorp
subtracter
subtractor
punto banco
rusticware
justiciary
multicycle
Eustachian
mustachios
multocular
rustically
rusticwork
pultaceous
quit scores
rusticated
rusticator
put to death
tufted duck
lustreware
put the case
turtleback
✧turtleneck
lustreless
subtleness
run the show
cuttlefish
cuttle-bone
turtledove
huntiegowk
quatrefoil
turtle soup
run to earth
hurtlessly
multifaced
putty-faced
tuftaffeta
tuftaffety
justifying
multi-faith
multiflora
Guttiferae
multigrade
just the job
sultriness
austringer
rustlingly
sustaining
curtain off
cultriform
lust-dieted
bur-thistle
putty-knife
multilobed
Mustelidae
Mustelinae
out to lunch
multiloquy
custom-made
customable
multimedia
Guatemalan
customised
Muntz metal
multimeter
customized
sustentate
button-back
buttonball
hunting-box
hunting-cog
hunting-cap
hunting-cat
Huntingdon
buttoned up
buttoned-up
muttonhead
button cell
subtangent
mutton chop
sultanship
mutton bird
just-in-time
sustentive
sustention
mutton-fist
fustanella
purtenance
sustenance
subtenancy
buttonhold
buttonwood
buttonhole
buttonhook
button-down
put to nurse
austenitic
huntingtin
buttonbush
mutton suet
auctionary
tuitionary
auctioneer
subtropics
auction off
lustrously
multiphase
multiplane
multiplied
multiplier
cuit à point
multipolar
multiparae
multiparas
multiparty
butter-bake
quaternate
subterrane
butterball
quatorzain
subterrain
gutter pair
✧quaternary
culturable
nurturable
buttery-bar
Bustard Bay
subterrene
butter bean
mustard gas
butter-bird
butter-wife
muster-file
butter dish
butterfish
guitarfish
buttermilk
quaternion
quaternity
culture lag
culturally
gutturally
butterdock
muster book
mustard oil
muster roll
butter-boat
butterwort
custard pie
butter-tree
subterfuge
put through
put-through
rub through
run through
run-through
butter-bump
multi-stage
put to shame
just as well
put to sleep
multiskill
cutty-stool
multistory
multi-track
tut-tutting
quotatious
rust fungus
pultrusion
rust bucket
tub-thumper
tuft-hunter
cultivable
multivocal
Huntsville
multivious
cultivator
run to waste
cumulative
cumulation
suturation
tubularian
tubulation
tubularity
tubulature
Lubumbashi
cucurbital
furuncular
futureless
luculently
purulently
futurition
Yusuf Islam
luxuriance
luxuriancy
cucumiform
cumuliform
futuristic
mutual wall
cucullated
autumnally
futurology
lugubrious
lucubrator
cut up rough
tumultuate
tumultuary
augustness
Augustulus
tumultuous
durum wheat
curvaceous
curvacious
outvillain
mud volcano
pulvilling
pulvilised
pulvilized
subvention
pulvinated
suaveolent
culvertage
pulverable
culver-keys
subvariety
subversive
subversion
pulveriser
pulverizer
curvetting
survivable
dum vivimus
survivance
purveyance
surveyance
Ludwig Mond
mugwumpery
outwrought
sun worship
tutworkman
outwitting
euryhaline
bunya-bunya
Eurythmics
rubythroat
jury-rigged
busy signal
ruby silver
busy Lizzie
July-flower
ruby spinel
Lucy Stoner
eurypterid
Eurypterus
jury-rudder
quizmaster
puzzle-head
puzzlement
puzzle over
buzz phrase
quizziness
puzzlingly
fuzzy logic
Buzz Aldrin
tuzzi-muzzy
tuzzy-muzzy
Quezon City
Suez Crisis
evacuative
evacuation
Aviculidae
Avicularia
aviculture
evidential
Ava Gardner
availingly
evaluative
evaluation
evolvement
evolve into
evil-minded
oval window
evil-worker
evolutions
ivy-mantled
even-handed
Ivan Mauger
Ivan Pavlov
avenaceous
avengeress
avengement
evincement

evangelise
evangelize
evangelism
evangeliar
✧evangelist
eventfully
avant-garde
even chance
even-minded
Ivan Krylov
evanescent
even-steven
even number
avanturine
aventurine
eventually
avvogadore
avgolemono
evaporable
evaporator
ovipositor
overhanded
overlander
overcaught
overraught
overrashly
overdaring
overlaying
overlaunch
overlabour
overcanopy
overmantel
overmaster
overmatter
ivory-black
overabound
overactive
avaricious
averseness
overweight
over-refine
overreckon
overpeople
ivermectin
overleaven
overoffice
overthwart
overshadow
Averrhoism
Averrhoist
overcharge
over the top
over-the-top
overthrust
overshower
over the way
overridden
overbidder
avertiment
overnicely
overtimely
overwisely
ever-living
overriding
overwinter
overplaced
everglades
oversleeve
overflight
overglance
overslaugh
Sverdlovsk
overflowed
overinform
over and out
overinsure
overdosage
overboldly
overfondly
overbought
every other
overcooked
overworked
overlocker
overlooker
overcommit
overcolour
ovariotomy
everyplace
overspread
overpriced
overbridge
overfreely
overgreedy
overpraise
overground
overgrowth
overstrain
overstress
overstride
overstrike
everything
overstrong
overstrung
overstruck
ivory tower
overstayer
overburden
overruling
overrunner
overturner
Ivor Gurney
oversupply
oversubtle
everywhere
overextend
overexcite
overexpose
Yves Tanguy
eviscerate
Svetambara
eviternity
avouchable
avouchment
swear blind
sweat blood
sweat gland
sweath-band
sweatiness
sweat it out
sweatpants
sweat-shirt
sweatshirt
Twickenham
Swedenborg
Swadeshism
sweetbread
sweetbriar
sweetbrier
sweet basil
'tweendecks
sweetening
sweetheart
tweediness
sweepingly
sweetie-pie
✧tweedledee
Tweedledum
sweepstake
sweep-seine
sweet-stuff
a week today
tweet-tweet
sweet tooth
sweet-water
sweetwater
swage block
swaggering
twaite shad
owlishness
sweltering
twelvefold
twelve-note
twelve-tone
twilighted
swellingly
swell organ
Twyla Tharp
Twelfth Day
twelfth man
swamp fever
swampiness
swimmingly
swan-maiden
swine-drunk
twin-bedded
swine fever
twi-nighter
swingingly
twangingly
twin sister
swingle-bar
twinflower
swing-music
Twin Towers
swan-upping
swan around
swing-swang
swing-shelf
swing shift
swinestone
swing-stock
twi-natured
twy-natured
swan-mussel
swing-wheel
twenty-five
twentyfold
twenty-four
swooningly
two or three
swap option
sword-blade
swordcraft
sword dance
swerveless
sword-guard
sword grass
dwarfishly
swordproof
sword-stick
swarm-spore
swirl vanes
Swiss chard
twist drill
Swiss franc
Owlspiegle
swash plate
twittering
zwitterion
switchback
switched on
switchgear
twitchiest
swatchbook
switch-over
twittingly
two-two time
swivelling
swivel-hook
two-wheeled
two-wheeler
awkwardish
swaybacked
two-year-old
excavation
exhalation
expandable
exsanguine
ex cathedra
ex-cathedra
expatiator
expatriate
expansible
expansibly
exhaust gas
exhaustive
exhausting
exhaustion
axe-breaker
oxy-bromide
exobiology
exuberance
exuberancy
execrative
execration
execratory
exactingly
exactitude
oxy-calcium
exacerbate
executable
executress
executancy
exocytosis
exocytotic
oxidisable
oxidizable
expendable
extendable
extendible
expendably
extendedly
exheredate
expeditate
experiment
expeditely
expeditive
expedition
expedience
experience
expediency
exteriorly
expellable
excellence
✧excellency
externally
ex mero motu
excerpting
excerption
extemporal
excess fare
extensible
extensions
expectable
expectably
expectedly
exceptless
expertness
expectance
expectancy
exceptious
extenuator
exaggerate
oxygen mask
oxygen debt
oxygen tent
exogenetic
oxygenator
exiguously
exegetical
exhilarate
exhilarant
excitative
excitation
expiration
excitatory
expiratory
extinctive
extinction
exsiccator
extincture
excitement
ex silentio
excise duty
extinguish
ex dividend
excitingly
exhibitive
exhibition
exhibitory
extirpable
extirpator
exaltation
exultation
exultantly
explicable
oxalic acid
explicator
explicitly
excludable
excludible
exulcerate
exploitage
exultingly
exploitive
ox-fluoride
explosible
examinable
examinator
eximiously
oxymoronic
exenterate
ox-antelope
axinomancy
exonerator
axiomatise
axiomatize
axiomatics
ex concesso
Oxford bags
Oxford shoe
Oxford blue
Oxford clay
excogitate
expositive
exposition
expository
exfoliator
axiologist
exportable
ex converso
axoplasmic
exophagous
exopoditic
exurbanite
exprobrate
excruciate
extractant
extricable
uxoricidal
extractive
extraction
extra cover
extrudable
extradural
extradotal
ex professo
exorbitate
exorbitant
uxorilocal
extra modum
excrementa
extramural
extra muros
extraneity
extraneous
uxoriously
ex propriis
expressage
extrusible
excrescent
express fee
expressive
expression
extra-solar
expressman
expressure
expressway
exasperate
exospheric
exosporous
exoticness
exotically
exothermic
exothermal
axe to grind
exit charge
exoterical
exhumation
excusatory
expunction
exsufflate
expurgator
expugnable
exculpable
excursuses
exuviation
ox-eye daisy
synaxarion
pyracantha
gynandrism
synandrium
gynandrous
synandrous
hypalgesia
hypalgesic
dynamitard
✧sybaritish
✧sybaritism
pyramidion
dynamicist
pyramidist
gyrational
dynamistic
eye askance
tyrannical
Lycaenidae
Tyrannidae
Zygaenidae
Hyracoidea
dynamogeny
synaloepha
My Fair Lady
synaeresis
dynastical
tyrant bird
hypanthium
synanthous
dysarthria
hypaethral
hypaethron
hypabyssal
myoblastic
cymbidiums
Bye Bye Baby
symbolical
symboliser
symbolizer
hye-battel'd
dyscrasite
synclastic
syncretise
syncretize
syncretism
syncretist
eye contact
syncopated
syncopator
myocardiac
myocardial
myocardium
synchronic
synchronal
syncarpous
synchrysis
eye-catcher
syndicator
syndactyly
synderesis
syndetical
Pyrenaeans
Cyperaceae
Wykehamist
hyperaemia
hyperaemic
hyperacute

hyperbolic
hyperbolas
hyperbaric
hyperbatic
hyperbaton
cybercrime
typescript
synecdoche
hyperdulia
syneidesis
typesetter
hypergolic
synergetic
tyre chains
pyrethroid
Lysenkoism
hypermedia
hypermania
hypermanic
cybernetic
cybernated
pyrenocarp
type holder
mycetozoan
mycetology
pyretology
synecology
dyke-louper
cyberphobe
typewriter
cyberspace
hyperspace
hypersonic
hypertonia
hypertonic
My Left Foot
dysenteric
lyre guitar
type cutter
Lydford law
cynghanedd
dysgraphia
dysgraphic
myographic
eyeglasses
Syngenesia
pyogenesis
syngenesis
syngenetic
Kyrgyzstan
ayahuascos
Lythraceae
Lychnapsia
Tycho Brahe
mythically
typhaceous
mythiciser
mythicizer

pythogenic
Pythagoras
mythologic
mythologer
syphilitic
mythomania
hyphenated
typhlology
mythopoeia
mythopoeic
Myricaceae
Xyridaceae
typicality
lytic cycle
cylindrite
cylindroid
myriadfold
lysigenous
dye in grain
myringitis
syringitis
pyrimidine
mytiliform
gyniolatry
Lydian mode
pyridoxine
myrioscope
Lysistrata
dyskinesia
myeloblast
syllabical
syllabuses
by-election
cyclically
cyclo-cross
Wycliffite
cyclograph
eye-legible
myological
syllogiser
syllogizer
cycloidian
by all means
hyalomelan
cyclometer
myelinated
hyalophane
hyaloplasm
cyclopedia
cyclopedic
cycloramic
cyclostome
cyclostyle
eyelet-hole
cyclothyme
dysmorphia
dysmorphic
pygmy shrew

symmetrise
symmetrize
symmetrian
cyanic acid
hypnagogic
cyanogenic
hypnogenic
pycnogonid
hypnoidise
hypnoidize
by and large
by any means
cyanometer
pycnometer
pyknometer
cyanophyte
gymnasiast
gymnosperm
gymnastics
dying shift
pycnospore
gymnosophy
gymnasiums
pycnostyle
Lyon-at-arms
hypnotiser
hypnotizer
Pyrolaceae
pyromaniac
pyrogallol
hypoxaemia
hypoxaemic
hypogaeous
myxomatous
hypotactic
pyromantic
zygodactyl
zygocactus
synoecious
gyroscopic
myxoedemic
pyrotechny
pyromeride
pyroxenite
eye-opening
hypodermic
hypodermal
hypodermis
pyrogenous
xylogenous
cytometric
pyrometric
hypocentre
hypotenuse
cynophobia
gynophobia
mysophobia
pyrophobia

gynophobic
pyrophobic
xylophagan
hylotheism
hylotheist
cynophilia
xylophonic
sycophancy
cytochrome
xylochrome
pyrophoric
✧pyrophorus
hypophyses
hypophysis
hypotheses
hypothesis
hypothetic
mycorhizae
mycorhizal
tyrosinase
mylonitise
mylonitize
Tyrolienne
hypoplasia
mycoplasma
hylozoical
cynomolgus
hypocorism
✧lycopodium
hypodorian
cytologist
mycologist
typologist
zymologist
hylotomous
xylotomous
zygomorphy
gyrocopter
zygosphene
cymotrichy
mycorrhiza
zygobranch
kymography
pyrography
typography
xylography
gynocratic
hypocritic
synoptical
hypostress
hypostases
hypostasis
synostoses
synostosis
gyrostatic
hypostatic
pyrostatic
pyrolusite

myxomycete
zygomycete
pyroxyline
synonymise
synonymize
hypolydian
synonymist
synonymity
hypogynous
synonymous
hyoplastra
dysplastic
myopically
dysphemism
lymph gland
lyophilise
lyophilize
sylphidine
symphilism
symphilous
tympanitic
tympanites
tympanitis
nympholept
lymphokine
symptomise
symptomize
dysprosium
symphonion
symphonist
lymphogram
lymphocyte
symposiast
sympathise
sympathize
sympathies
Sympetalae
gyppy tummy
symphyseal
✧dyophysite
symphysial
symphylous
dyer's-broom
hygrochasy
hydrically
hydrochore
hybrid bill
hybridiser
hybridizer
Tyrrhenian
hydrograph
hygrograph
hydragogue
pyorrhoeic
pyorrhoeal
pyrrhicist
hydrologic
hydrolysis

hydrolytic
hydromania
hydromancy
hydrometer
hygrometer
hydrometry
hygrometry
Cyprinidae
by-drinking
pyrrhotine
pyrrhotite
Pyrrhonism
Pyrrhonian
Pyrrhonist
hydrophane
hydroplane
cypripedia
hydrophily
hydropolyp
hydroponic
hydrophone
hygrophobe
hydropathy
hydropower
hydrophyte
hygrophyte
hydrospace
hydrosomal
hydrosomes
hydroscope
hygroscope
hydrotheca
hydrotaxis
hydraulics
hydrazides
byssaceous
Tysse Falls
myasthenia
myasthenic
hypsometer
hypsometry
byssinosis
eye-spotted
gypsophila
hypsophobe
hypsophyll
eye-servant
eye-service
eyas-musket
Hyoscyamus
mystically
myrtaceous
cystectomy
cysticerci
✧dyothelete
✧dyothelite
synthesise
synthesize

synthetise
synthetize
✧dyothelism
synthesist
synthetist
mystifying
syntagmata
hyetograph
mystagogic
mystagogue
mystagogus
nystagmoid
cyathiform
nyctalopia
nyctalopic
nyctalopes
systemless
systematic
hyetometer
cystinuria
cystinosis
syntenoses
syntenosis
nyctinasty
dystrophia
dystrophic
dystrophin
oyster-bank
oyster-park
oyster-farm
hysterical
hystericky
oyster-wife
mystery-man
synthronus
mysterious
hysteresis
synteresis
hysteretic
hysteritis
cystoscope
cystoscopy
cystostomy
dysthymiac
Tyburn-tree
Cyrus Vance
eyewitness
by my certie
azobenzene
Uzbekistan
Ozymandias
ozone layer
azeotropic
Azerbaijan
czarevitch

11 – even

Panama Canal
Calabar-bean
calamancoes
catafalcoes
Palaearctic
camaraderie
paraparesis
paraparetic

caravanette
Takada Kenzo
Narayanganj
Maharashtra
Madara Rider
parasailing
caravanning
farawayness

malakatoone
baba ganoush
Canada goose
lalapalooza
banana split
caravan park
catacaustic
caravansary

caravan site
paramastoid
datacasting
data capture
taratantara
parabaptism
maladaptive
gap analysis

radar beacon
salad burnet
cacao butter
Galam butter
balance beam
Jamaica bark
Malacca-cane
parascience

maraschinos
damascening
parascenium
Jamaica plum
War and Peace
cap and bells
paraldehyde
Garand rifle

Camaldolese
Camaldolite
cat-and-mouse
hazardously
parabematic
paracetamol
paraselenae
paragenesia
paragenesis
paragenetic
Raman effect
managed fund
paranephric
paranephros
Pan-American
paramedical
Saracenical
paramedicos
natale solum
paraleipses
paraleipsis
Paracelsian
managership
parapenting
palace guard
paraffin wax
paraffinoid
paraffin oil
Pan-Anglican
paraphraser
paraphraxia
paraphraxis
catachresis
paraphrenia
Wabash River
✧kalashnikov
paraphiliac
Marathonian
cataphonics
Panathenaea
Panathenaic
parathyroid
Mahabharata
'pataphysics
pataphysics
Kazakhstani
parachutist
capacitance
fanatically
satanically
carabineros
magazine-gun
data highway
parasitical
carabiniere
carabinieri
malariology
Lanai Island
vacationist
caparisoned
parasitosis
cavalierish
cavalierism
canalicular
capaciously
rapaciously
sagaciously
salaciously
canaliculus
Natalie Wood
maladjusted
Lanarkshire
damask-steel
catallactic
cataplectic
parallactic
paragliding
paralleling
parallelise
parallelism
parallelist
parallelize
fama clamosa
capableness
salableness
savableness
tamableness
parablepsis
parableptic
paraglossae
paraglossal
cataclasmic
cataclastic
cataclysmic
Maja Clothed
Japan laurel
sal ammoniac
Satan monkey
garam masala
Maya Angelou
parabolanus
laparoscope
laparoscopy
vagabondage
vagabondise
vagabondish
vagabondism
vagabondize
fata Morgana
Japanophile
malacophily
satanophany
katabothron
katavothron
parabolical
paradoxical
paragogical
Paradoxides
ratatouille
natatoriums
sanatoriums
paramountcy
paramountly
Jana Novotna
paramorphic
lay about one
cataloguise
cataloguize
palaeotypic
Oak-apple Day
Java sparrow
hamadryades
maladroitly
catadromous
katadromous
paratrooper
paragrapher
paragraphia
paragraphic
malapropism
paracrostic
Ramakrishna
Papal States
Nawaz Sharif
parapsychic
Tayassuidae
harassingly
macassar oil
Laban system
Kazantzakis
Marantaceae
paranthelia
Japan tallow
galantamine
rabattement
catastrophe
galanty show
parasuicide
catapultier
Paraguay tea
paratyphoid
catalytical
paralympics
canary-grass
Ray Bradbury
carbocyclic
Barbados leg
carbide tool
marble-paper
Max Beerbohm
marble-edged
jaw-breaking
lawbreaking
rabble-rouse
gambrel roof
cabbage-moth
cabbage palm
cabbage rose
cabbage tree
cabbagetown
cabbage-worm
garbologist
cabbalistic
barbola work
carbon paper
dak bungalow
carbonadoes
carbon black
carbonylate
garbanzo pea
Carbonarism
carbon steel
carbonation
carbonatite
carbuncular
carbon cycle
car boot sale
yah-boo sucks
Banbury cake
Lamborghini®
barber's itch
jabberingly
Carborundum®
✧jabberwocky
barber's pole
barber's rash
barbaresque
carburetted
carburetter
carburation
carburetion
carburettor
barbarously
Barbara Ward
barbastelle
rabbit fever
gambit-piece
Sabbathless
lamb's tongue
rabbet-joint
✧sabbatarian
Halbstarker
barbiturate
rabbit hutch
rabbit punch
Lambeth Walk
Barbour® coat
harbour dues
Rambouillet
harbourless
harbour seal
karbovanets
saccharated
bacchanalia
Barclaycard
wax-chandler
pancratiast
cat-cracking
paschal lamb
paschal moon
fascia-board
Ian Chappell
sauce-crayon
farcicality
fasciculate
calcicolous
ganciclovir
sarcocystis
Vasco da Gama
ratchet down
Panchen Lama
parchedness
Haeckel's law
hatchettite
calcifugous
Nancy Friday
bacciferous
calciferous
calcigerous
Marc Chagall
dance in a net
catching pen
t'ai chi ch'uan
war criminal
sanctioneer
marchioness
sarcoidosis
sanctifying
pancake bell
lance-knecht
lance-knight
pancake race
cancellated
Marcel Carné
sacculiform
vasculiform
parcel shelf
rascalliest
Marcellinus
sarcolemmal
masculinely
masculinise
masculinist
masculinity
masculinize
Cab Calloway
narcoleptic
parcels post
vascularise
vascularity
vascularize
matchlessly
laccolithic
calculating
calculation
sacculation
vasculature
calculative
tan-coloured
Marcel Dupré
matchmaking
watchmaking
fancy monger
sarcomatous
marconigram
dancing-girl
sarcenchyme
carcinology
carcinomata
fascinating
lancinating
calcination
fascination
lancination
vaccination
vaccinatory
larcenously
lanceolated
calceolaria
halcyon days
cancioneros
sancho-pedro
W A B Coolidge
Pancho Villa
sarcophagal
sarcophagus
patch pocket
watch pocket
Nancy-pretty
catch points
catchphrase
lance pesade
mancipation
mancipatory
calcariform
cancer stick
canceration
rancorously
marcescence
fancy stitch
marcescible
Marcus Allen
carcase meat
carcass meat
Carcassonne
Lancastrian
latchstring
watchspring
laicisation
bancassurer
narcissuses
catch-the-ten
catch the sun
rat-catching
sanctus bell
raucousness
sanctuarise
sanctuarize
baccivorous
catchweight
laicization
Saudi Arabia
hard landing
hardwareman
handbagging
hardy annual
hand-painted
paediatrics
paediatrist
handfasting
sand-casting
sandy blight
laudability
mandibulate
pas de basque
hard science
Sadduceeism
baldacchino
gay deceiver
Hardacanute
Hardicanute
handicapped
handicapper
landscapist
manducation
manducatory
candidiasis
gandy dancer
paedodontic
candidature
handkercher
hand-feeding
randle-perch
candleberry
paddle wheel
paddle-shaft
candlelight
saddle-girth
handselling
saddlecloth
candle-power
saddle-nosed
hand-me-downs
paddle-board
saddle horse
Yardie squad
hard-hearted
hard-wearing
tap-dressing
land-measure
hard bestead
candlestick
paddle-staff
maidservant
hand of glory
ward of court
vas deferens
tardy-gaited
Cardigan Bay
handshaking
sand-thrower
card-sharper
hard-visaged
bandeirante
sandwich man
sandwich tin

Handa Island
landfilling
hard-hitting
landsknecht
sand-skipper
Sandy Koufax
candelabras
candelabrum
bandoleered
bandoliered
bandy-legged
paedologist
sandal shoon
mal del pinto
Mar del Plata
Magdalenian
mandolinist
fardel-bound
Max Delbrück
sandblaster
vandalistic
baddeleyite
✧pandemoniac
✧pandemonian
Sandemanian
✧pandemonium
garden patch
garden party
landing-beam
Pandanaceae
sardonicism
garden leave
landing flap
hand and foot
hard and fast
hard-and-fast
landing gear
garden-glass
cardinalate
hand in glove
maddeningly
garden gnome
cardan joint
garden-house
landing-ship
hand-knitted
garden stuff
Randy Newman
carding wool
land-jobbing
landholding
landlordism
hardworking
cardiomotor
hand to mouth
hand-to-mouth
jaw-dropping
cardiograph
hardmouthed
sandbox tree
cardophagus
paedophilia
paedophilic
land-spaniel
sand spurrey
pas de quatre
Wanderjahre
handbreadth
Bandar Abbas
land-grabber
handcrafted

panduriform
dandy-rigged
hard-grained
hand-promise
hand grenade
hard drinker
wanderingly
mandarinate
balderlocks
gander-month
hard pressed
hard-pressed
Pandora's box
handwritten
handwriting
handwrought
landgravine
waldgravine
landgravate
sanderswood
hard as nails
bald as a coot
candescence
mal du siècle
caddishness
faddishness
laddishness
lap dissolve
candy stripe
hard as stone
paedotrophy
Bardo Thodol
✧waldsterben
mandatorily
land-steward
landaulette
hand-running
hard put to it
Max de Winter
Sandown Park
have had a few
baked Alaska
Lake Balaton
maceranduba
cakes and ale
barefacedly
gametangium
tape machine
Kagera River
calefacient
race-walking
kamelaukion
baseball cap
lateral line
name-calling
Tate Gallery
Cape jasmine
wage-earning
Mare Vaporum
rate-capping
Jane Fairfax
base pairing
Rabelaisian
have had that
calefaction
labefaction
madefaction
malefaction
rarefaction
tabefaction
calefactory

malefactory
calefactive
rarefactive
take captive
cadet branch
eager beaver
panel beater
sauerbraten
Water Bearer
camel-backed
water beetle
Karen Blixen
Karen Briggs
James Bridie
water bailie
water blinks
rateability
saleability
tameability
water barrel
water bottle
water bouget
James Coburn
paper-credit
James Cagney
watercolour
water cement
water cannon
water closet
water-cooled
water cooler
catercorner
paper-cutter
Lake Scutari
cater-cousin
watercourse
panel doctor
water doctor
calendrical
fazendeiros
make a dinner
calendering
calendarise
calendarist
calendarize
haberdasher
paper-enamel
rapeseed oil
watered-down
take revenge
water engine
pad-elephant
take delight
have designs
dare-devilry
make believe
make-believe
tale-telling
Jane Seymour
Cape Kennedy
safe-deposit
safekeeping
cameleopard
pale-hearted
lake herring
talebearing
tape measure
face-centred
make certain
race meeting
take offence

paper-feeder
vale of years
Lake of Death
make a figure
paper-folder
water-finder
made of money
take against
James Galway
take a gander
make a go of it
hazel grouse
navel-gazing
tame cheater
water-heater
game-chicken
take the cake
make cheeses
have the hots
make a hole in
James Hilton
water hammer
save the mark
make the most
paperhanger
make whoopee
wade through
make the pace
Lake Chapala
take the road
catechismal
catechistic
catechising
catechetics
take thought
take the veil
James Howell
take the word
catechizing
pale-visaged
valeric acid
malefically
Babes in Arms
game licence
maleficence
take time off
mare liberum
take time out
watering can
watering-cap
watering pot
La Périchole
game fishing
have with you
lateritious
materialise
materialism
materialist
materiality
materialize
laterigrade
Kate Winslet
have kittens
malediction
valediction
case history
make history
maledictory
valedictory
maledictive
facetiously

water jacket
James Kelman
have a load on
canella bark
Canellaceae
lamellicorn
naked ladies
lamelliform
patelliform
waterlogged
Water Lilies
face flannel
gaberlunzie
camerlengos
camerlingos
satellitise
satellitium
satellitize
mare clausum
wage slavery
safe-blowing
Naseem Hamed
water meadow
paper-making
water monkey
James Monroe
take umbrage
Mare Imbrium
paper-muslin
Mare Smythii
laced mutton
Lake Ontario
Mare Undarum
tabernacled
bareknuckle
make unready
Mare Ingenii
capernoited
Capernaitic
capernoitie
maternalism
paternalism
cavernulous
case in point
take on board
have one's way
make one's way
take one's way
✧paternoster
ease oneself
pace oneself
make one's bow
cavernously
face towards
navel orange
café-concert
Cameron Diaz
safe-conduct
have you done?
take-home pay
malevolence
take to heart
paper-office
have nothing
gametophyte
categorical
have no right
café society
take pot luck
water of life
pace-bowling

Cameroonian
make no doubt
take to court
have no truck
made to order
take courage
Lake Torrens
warehousing
make contact
take up about
Laserpicium
take up short
Caterpillar®
caterpillar
Mare Spumans
water pepper
water purpie
Cape sparrow
salesperson
paper-pusher
water pistol
Laserpitium
Baden-Powell
safe-breaker
Zaheer Abbas
Dave Brubeck
safe-cracker
Madeira cake
take pride in
make friends
Jane Grigson
hare-brained
lamebrained
career woman
pan-European
bale wrapper
name-dropper
career break
make or break
make-or-break
gatecrasher
Hare Krishna
Mare Crisium
Tate Britain
take trouble
Vanessa Bell
camel's thorn
water spider
water spirit
water-skiing
paper-sailor
Dar es Salaam
water splash
caressingly
baker's dozen
water sports
water supply
Baker Street
Carey Street
navel-string
water spring
water sprite
panel system
caper-spurge
water souchy
James Stuart
have it large
take stock in
caveat actor
talent scout
parentheses

Words marked ✧ can also be spelled with one or more capital letters

panesthesia
parenthesis
parenthetic
paresthesia
games theory
have at heart
panentheism
panentheist
patent agent
patent right
lacertilian
latent image
Palestinian
Valentinian
water tunnel
lamentingly
have it in one
have it in for
patent rolls
parentcraft
James Tyrone
water thrush
James Tissot
patent still
base station
lamentation
take it out on
tapestrying
James Taylor
race suicide
same numeric
Lake Lucerne
Cape buffalo
Lake Turkana
balefulness
banefulness
carefulness
fatefulness
gaseousness
hatefulness
wakefulness
Mare Humorum
base jumping
pâte-sur-pâte
James Ussher
Jane Russell
café curtain
rate-cutting
pay envelope
dame's-violet
water violet
water vapour
take a wicket
paperweight
cave-dweller
lake-dweller
James Watson
safety catch
safety match
safety paper
safety razor
safety valve
panegyrical
safety light
panegyricon
safety glass
take by force
take by storm
malfeasance
half-landing
half past one
half-baptise
half past two
half-baptize
baffle-plate
halfpennies
baffle-board
half-hearted
half measure
half-leather
half-century
half-checked
half the time
caffeinated
half-binding
haaf-fishing
cam follower
half-blooded
half-integer
halfendeale
half-and-half
malfunction
Jaffa orange
saffron cake
half-holiday
half-pounder
calf-country
gaff-topsail
fanfaronade
half-brother
Laffer curve
raffishness
gas-fittings
half-starved
vanguardism
margraviate
hangability
tangibility
ragged right
ragged Robin
Haggadistic
ragged staff
waggle dance
languescent
Maggie Smith
sang-de-boeuf
rangefinder
bang the drum
large-handed
Hang-Chow Bay
bargain away
sanguinaria
sanguineous
laughing gas
languishing
languidness
Sanguisorba
pan-galactic
hang-gliding
mangalsutra
raggamuffin
large-minded
bargemaster
Targumistic
tangentally
ramgunshoch
badging-hook
bagging-hook
hang in there
jagging-iron
Marginal Sea
marginalise
marginalism
marginalist
marginality
marginalize
margin index
ranging pole
gas gangrene
jargonistic
margination
Gargantuism
Gargantuist
Panglossian
Nanga Parbat
haggardness
laggardness
kangaroo paw
kangaroo rat
danger money
danger point
kangaroo dog
kangaroo-hop
daggerboard
Ranger Guide
dangerously
Jan Gossaert
Vargas Llosa
waggishness
barge-stones
Sargasso Sea
tax gatherer
gauge theory
caught short
garget plant
haughtiness
naughtiness
naughty pack
targa-topped
gangsterdom
gangsterism
maggotorium
gangbusting
langoustine
laughworthy
gas-guzzling
Machiavelli
cash machine
Rachmaninov
cash-railway
cash payment
Mathias Rust
washability
Bashi-Bazouk
cachectical
machicolate
cash account
tachycardia
cathedratic
pachydactyl
pachydermal
pachydermia
pachydermic
cathode rays
cashierment
Machaerodus
wash leather
pathography
tachygraphy
pathogenous
naphthalane
naphthalene
naphthalise
naphthalize
wash-gilding
Kashmir goat
Machairodus
Bath Mitsvah
Bath-Mitsvah
Bathmitsvah
Bath Mitzvah
Bath-Mitzvah
Bathmitzvah
parheliacal
✧catholicise
✧catholicism
catholicity
✧catholicize
✧panhellenic
pathologist
bachelor pad
bachelordom
bachelorism
batholithic
bathylithic
cache memory
mathematics
bathymetric
tachometric
tachymetric
mathematise
mathematize
machineable
washing-blue
machine code
kachina doll
machine head
washing line
machine-made
taphonomist
washing-soda
bathing suit
machine-shop
machination
machine tool
wash-and-wear
machine-work
fashionable
fashionably
tacheometer
tacheometry
fashionista
tachyphasia
Machu Picchu
bathophobia
pathophobia
tachophobia
taphephobia
taphophobia
Las Hermanas
Magherafelt
cathartical
Bach trumpet
father-in-law
washerwoman
Sacher torte
Sachertorte
washer-drier
washer-dryer
Father Brown
wash drawing
bathyscaphe
bathysphere
day hospital
Cathy's Clown
pachysandra
yachtswoman
wash its face
catheterism
bashfulness
lachrymator
haphazardly
radical axis
radical chic
Vatican City
marivaudage
farinaceous
salicaceous
laminar flow
maximaphily
sanitariums
capital levy
radicalness
radical sign
capital ship
panic attack
radioactive
caricatural
Bahia Blanca
David Beaton
radio beacon
Marie Bichat
David Bailey
magic bullet
satiability
variability
Basil Brooke
panic button
David Bryant
panic-buying
Marie Claire
Maria Callas
ratiocinate
magic carpet
magic circle
radiocarbon
Taliacotian
Latin Church
labiodental
palindromic
Kavir Desert
Namib Desert
day in, day out
matinée coat
lapidescent
Sabine's gull
native title
matinée idol
facinerious
varicelloid
radicellose
varicellous
taxidermise
taxidermist
taxidermize
marine snail
canine tooth
Latin Empire
manifestoes
marine store
latiseptate
cabinetwork
satisfiable
satisficing
satin finish
satin flower
daring-hardy
Hagiographa
hagiography
radiography
gaming-table
savings bank
Pasir Gudang
baking sheet
caa'ing whale
radio galaxy
Rajiv Gandhi
David Ginola
palingenesy
waking hours
eating-house
gaming house
eating apple
saving grace
eating irons
gazing-stock
Basingstoke
paving-stone
variegation
paying guest
Mariah Carey
Manichaeism
parish clerk
Ravi Shankar
ravishingly
vanishingly
parishioner
fatidically
pacifically
satirically
facilitator
habilitator
pacificator
vaticinator
habiliments
Kaliningrad
calicivirus
paripinnate
familiarise
familiarity
familiarize
Pacific Time
laciniation
maliciously
basilic vein
lapidifying
Marie-Jeanne
Janis Joplin
Daniel Malan
Bacillaceae
bacillicide
Daniell cell
radiolucent
bacillaemia
Daniel Defoe
bacilliform
lapilliform
mamilliform
papilliform
hagiologist
Mariologist
radiologist
Manilla hemp
papillulate
panislamism
panislamist

ochlocratic
scoleciform
scale insect
acclamation
acclimation
acclamatory
acclimatise
acclimatize
Iceland moss
Iceland spar
scolopendra
ochlophobia
ochlophobic
scalariform
scalpriform
ecclesiarch
ecblastesis
Schlesinger
a colt's tooth
sculpturing
sculduddery
sculduggery
acolouthite
acclivitous
Scilly Isles
scamblingly
ecumenicism
acumination
scène à faire
scandaliser
scandalizer
scent bottle
acinaciform
ichnography
iconography
scenography
Acanthaceae
scintillant
scintillate
iconologist
econometric
scincoidian
McIntosh red
scant-o'-grace
iconostases
iconostasis
acknowledge
scholar-like
scholarship
accoucheuse
accordantly
accordingly
according to
acromegalic
acropetally
ectogenesis
ectogenetic
octodecimos
acrocentric
echo chamber
ectothermic
scholiastic
scrobicular
schoolwards
scroll chuck
schoolchild
school shark
schorlomite
schoolgoing
school point
school board
school house
schoolhouse
schoolcraft
ectoblastic
ectoplasmic
ectoplastic
school nurse
accommodate
accountancy
accountable
accountably
account book
echo-sounder
ectomorphic
octonocular
accomptable
accompanier
accompanist
ectotrophic
accoutering
schottische
A Chorus Line
acronymania
scepterless
scuppernong
acupressure
scapigerous
sceptically
scyphistoma
scopolamine
acupuncture
scopophilia
scopophilic
scopophobia
sceptreless
scoriaceous
scorpaenoid
scarabaeoid
scarabaeist
schrecklich
Schrödinger
scarlet bean
schreech-owl
acarpellous
scire facias
scorchingly
acerbically
scorpion fly
acarologist
scaremonger
X-chromosome
Y-chromosome
achromatise
achromatism
achromatous
achromatize
✧scaramouche
scoring card
eccrinology
Scarborough
accrescence
à corps perdu
scurvy grass
icosahedral
icosahedron
acesulfame K
icosandrian
icosandrous
scissorbill
scissor case
scissor hold
scissor kick
scissortail
scissorwise
acute accent
Scotlandite
scatterable
scatteredly
scattergood
scatterling
scatter rugs
scattershot
scythe-stone
Scots Guards
Scotch catch
Scotchwoman
Scotch-Irish
scutch grass
Scotch broth
Scotch cuddy
Scottifying
Scott Joplin
scuttlebutt
acatalectic
scuttle cask
acataleptic
Scitamineae
scotomatous
Scotophilia
Scotophilic
Scotophobia
Scotophobic
acetate film
ichthyoidal
ichthyology
ichthyolite
ichthyopsid
ichthyornis
ichthyosaur
accusatival
scout around
scoundrelly
acquiesce in
acaulescent
acquiescent
scruffiness
scouthering
scrutiniser
scrutinizer
octuplicate
scoutmaster
scrumptious
sceuophylax
actuarially
acquirement
acquisition
acquisitive
acquittance
acoustician
accustomary
scrub typhus
scrub turkey
acculturate
occultation
accumulator
Schwann cell
schwärmerei
acrylic acid
advancement
advance note
Edward Sapir
Edward Teach
Edward Heath
Edward White
Edward Elgar
Edward Albee
Edvard Grieg
Edvard Munch
Edward Burra
Edward Tylor
adiathermic
adiaphorism
adiaphorist
adiaphorous
ad captandum
od's bodikins
educability
adscription
educational
adverbially
edge in a word
adverseness
adversarial
adversative
advertently
advertorial
adventuress
adventurism
adventurist
adventurous
advertising
adjectively
edification
edificatory
Eddie Arcaro
admiralship
Admiral's Cup
advisedness
advisership
Edwin Hubble
addititious
adminicular
Eddie Irvine
Eddie Lawson
Eddie Murphy
Adrian Henri
Adrian Boult
sdeignfully
admit to bail
Adriatic Sea
adulterator
Adolphe Adam
addle-headed
Adolf Hitler
idyllically
adelantados
edulcorator
adolescence
A Doll's House
idolisation
Ada Lovelace
idolization
a dime a dozen
Adam's needle
idempotency
adumbration
adumbrative
Oda Nobunaga
identically
ad infinitum
identic note
identifying
ad unum omnes
adenomatous
odontoid peg
odontogenic
odontophore
odontoblast
odontologic
odontograph
odonatology
idiomatical
idiotically
idioblastic
idioglossia
ideological
idiomorphic
adjournment
ideographic
idiographic
ideopraxist
idiot savant
A/D converter
✧adoptianism
adoptianist
✧adoptionism
adoptionist
od's pitikins
odoriferous
ad arbitrium
Adirondacks
addressable
address book
odorousness
odds and ends
odds and sods
Edith Cavell
edutainment
editorially
add-to system
Edmund Burke
adjudgement
adjudicator
ad avizandum
idoxuridine
eddy current
Delaware Bay
reparations
pedal-action
perambulate
decarbonise
decarbonate
decarbonize
decarburise
decarburize
rebarbative
debauchedly
recalculate
debauchment
revaccinate
melancholia
melancholic
debarcation
defalcation
demarcation
Gerald R Ford
metaldehyde
bed and board
retardation
retardatory
retardative
regardfully
demand curve
hexateuchal
recalescent
delayed drop
metagenesis
metagenetic
hexadecimal
sexagesimal
cesarevitch
cesarewitch
belatedness
debasedness
relatedness
decameronic
sewage works
senate-house
hexahedrons
hexametrise
hexametrist
sesame grass
hexametrize
pet aversion
metacentric
hepatectomy
metasequoia
New Age music
Benares ware
César Franck
derangement
pelargonium
cerargyrite
metaphrasis
Texas hold 'em
metachrosis
metatherian
metaphorist
Megatherium
metaphysics
metathesise
metathesize
megavitamin
sebacic acid
tetanically
venatically
desalinator
Geraniaceae
Pedaliaceae
selaginella
belaying pin
gelatiniser
gelatinizer
metasilicic
semasiology
deracialise
deracialize
negationist
Pelagianism
relationism
relationist
behaviorism
behaviorist
aetatis suae
legatissimo
metafiction
reradiation
retaliation
retaliatory
retaliative
behavioural
nefariously
tenaciously
veraciously
vexatiously

debarkation
demarkation
mésalliance
beta-blocker
metalliding
metallogeny
Heracleidan
metalloidal
tenableness
hexaplarian
metallurgic
metaplastic
Heraclitean
demagnetise
demagnetize
set at naught
set at nought
megalomania
metasomatic
petalomania
hexagonally
megalosauri
megalosaurs
megaton bomb
hepatoscopy
keratometer
teratogenic
melanochroi
keratophyre
melanophore
nematophore
demagogical
pedagogical
nematodirus
megaloblast
nematoblast
megatonnage
hepatotoxic
megalopolis
teratologic
metamorphic
ceratopsian
senatorship
demagoguery
pedagoguery
demagoguism
pedagoguish
pedagoguism
depauperise
depauperate
depauperize
repatriator
desacralise
desacralize
désagrément
hetaerismic
hetairismic
✧renaissance
metapsychic
decapsulate
délassement
penalty area
hexastichal
pedantocrat
pedanticise
pedanticism
semanticist
pedanticize
xeranthemum
penalty goal
tenant right
penalty kick
penalty line
département
de haut en bas
legal tender
redactional
redactorial
melanterite
penalty rate
penalty shot
penalty spot
metastasise
metastasize
devastating
decantation
devastation
recantation
repartition
devastative
menaquinone
Belarussian
devaluation
revaluation
metalworker
keyboardist
membraneous
Lesbian rule
Zen Buddhism
yerba de maté
pebble-stone
herb-of-grace
verbigerate
sembling box
Pemba Island
Leibnitzian
Verbenaceae
bed-blocking
herb-trinity
verberation
kerb-crawler
leg-business
verboseness
deobstruent
herbivorous
merchandise
merchandize
get cracking
merchant bar
merchantman
merchantmen
merchanting
peach brandy
peccability
leucocratic
peacock-blue
peacock-fish
peacock-like
beachcomber
sea cucumber
fetch-candle
peccadillos
leucodermal
leucodermia
leucodermic
Red Crescent
geochemical
teacherless
leucaemogen
rescue-grass
Ben Crenshaw
teacher's pet
benchership
teachership
deaccession
mercy flight
hercogamous
deictically
describable
perceivable
perceivably
men-children
teaching aid
reactionary
reactionism
reactionist
description
descriptive
peacekeeper
pencil-cedar
pencil skirt
Herculaneum
Aesculapian
Aesculapius
perchlorate
mercilessly
pencil-stone
percolation
sea colewort
fence-lizard
reach-me-down
peacemaking
peace-monger
welcomingly
welcomeness
beech marten
beach-master
descendable
rescindable
descendible
rescindment
mercenarily
mercenarism
tea canister
deschooling
leucoplakia
percipience
percipiency
perceptible
perceptibly
peace-parted
henchperson
mercurially
leucorrhoea
neocortical
tea ceremony
mercuration
teach school
leach-trough
Neo-Catholic
bench-warmer
reed warbler
headbanging
dendrachate
seed capital
send packing
verde-antico
readability
vendibility
weldability
headscarves
Leeds Castle
re-education
lead acetate
needle paper
needle valve
head teacher
perduellion
needlewoman
needlepoint
needlecraft
needcessity
needlestick
readvertise
needle-furze
Lee De Forest
head of state
Hedda Gabler
dead against
bend the knee
feedthrough
Len Deighton
dendritical
tendrillous
readmission
Kendal green
Weddell seal
Mendelssohn
feudalistic
pendulosity
dead-clothes
pendulously
mendelevium
Vendémiaire
hebdomadary
seldom-times
ready-monied
wedding band
reading-book
wedding cake
redding-comb
leading card
leading case
reading-desk
leading edge
Heldentenor
weeding-fork
weeding-hook
tendencious
tendentious
verd-antique
redding-kame
leading lady
reading-lamp
geodynamics
leading note
pendant-post
wedding ring
reading-room
wend one's way
dendrolatry
dendrometer
dendroglyph
headborough
send to dorse
Mendip Hills
reed-sparrow
feldspathic
leader-cable
gendarmerie
dead-freight
verdureless
pedder-coffe
leaderboard
tenderfoots
fender-stool
perduration
reed-drawing
tender-dying
dead as a dodo
web designer
reddishness
ready to drop
sea dotterel
head-station
venditation
heedfulness
needfulness
headhunting
reed bunting
net dividend
merdivorous
meadow pipit
meadow mouse
meadow-grass
meadow-brown
ready-witted
meadowsweet
see daylight
Geneva bands
Gene Sarazen
fête galante
sede vacante
têtes-à-têtes
lese-majesté
lese-majesty
leze-majesty
severalfold
telepathise
telepathist
telepathize
Geneva Bible
generations
Generation X
Revelations
temerarious
telebanking
general line
generalling
Peter Alliss
René Laënnec
hemeralopia
hemeralopic
Rene Lacoste
Pete Sampras
vegetal pole
gene mapping
general post
Geneva cross
Veterans Day
generalship
telecasting
benefaction
tepefaction
benefactory
Rebekah Wade
✧remembrance
resemblance
reverberant
Derek Barton
Decemberish
reverberate
telescience
defenceless
telescopist
Telescopium
Rebecca West
mesenchymal
revendicate
defeudalise
defeudalize
legerdemain
dependingly
serendipity
legendarily
Defenderism
regenerable
decelerator
regenerator
referendums
never-ending
referendary
sea elephant
deleterious
téléférique
venereology
cerebellums
teleselling
cerebellous
redetermine
renewedness
see eye to eye
decerebrise
decerebrate
decerebrize
Telemessage®
deferential
referential
reverential
deselection
reselection
venesection
tenementary
pedetentous
get even with
never-fading
Peter Grimes
revengeless
revengement
revengingly
level-headed
hebephrenia
hebephrenic
telephonist
gene therapy
selenic acid
generically
genetically
hereditable
heretically
venefically
genetic code
Gene Vincent
beneficence
redeliverer
telekinesis
telekinetic
leze-liberty
beneficiary
beneficiate
repetitious
veneficious
heresiology
bedevilling
bedevilment
Venetian red

ne plus ultra
hellishness
leglessness
recluseness
sexlessness
perlustrate
realisation
well-stacked
zeolitiform
set little by
belly-timber
repleteness
deglutinate
aeolotropic
belletrist
deglutition
deglutitory
deglutitive
real numbers
well-judging
jealoushood
fell-lurking
fell-running
jealousness
zealousness
repleviable
sea lavender
mellivorous
re-elevation
declivitous
Yellow Pages®
yellow earth
yellow metal
yellow fever
yellow-belly
bellows-fish
Yellow River
yellow alert
yellow-ammer
Yellowknife
mellowspeak
reflowering
✧yellow press
yellow ox-eye
reflex light
reflexology
reflex angle
deflexional
reflexively
reflexivity
medley relay
Wesleyanism
realization
permeameter
germ warfare
vermiculate
vermiculite
vermiculous
geomedicine
desmodromic
seam welding
Fehmgericht
Vehmgericht
term of years
gemmiferous
femme fatale
dermography
geomagnetic
termagantly
de-emphasise
re-emphasise
de-emphasize
re-emphasize
gemmologist
gemmulation
sea milkwort
sea-milkwort
Terme Museum
permanganic
fermentable
segmentally
German Ocean
helminthoid
helminthous
German Bight
German sixth
seaming lace
terminology
German flute
reamendment
permanently
germaneness
seemingness
Germanophil
Belmont Park
Germanistic
Germanesque
terminate in
deamination
germination
termination
vermination
terminatory
Desmond Tutu
germinative
terminative
hermeneutic
Hermann Weyl
seam bowling
beam compass
gemmiparous
re-emergence
mesmerising
beam trawler
mesmerizing
Dermestidae
permissible
permissibly
permittance
hermeticity
seamstressy
helmet-shell
geometrical
Geometridae
dermatology
termitarium
permutation
Seymour Cray
Weymouth Bay
vermivorous
Jean Lamarck
Leoncavallo
penny arcade
penny-a-liner
Jean Lafitte
Léon Gaumont
reincarnate
Jean Jacques
teeny-bopper
Sennacherib
Dean Acheson
kernicterus
re-enactment
Sean Edwards
jenny donkey
Leander Club
Jean de Meung
reinterment
reinterpret
Reindeer Age
reintegrate
✧neanderthal
reinsertion
reinvention
Dean of Guild
Venn diagram
ferntickled
geanticline
penny loafer
vernal grass
reinflation
Me and My Girl
reanimation
Deinonychus
pennoncelle
pennant flag
pennant grit
meaningless
teknonymous
pennant rock
Mennonitism
Jean Anouilh
re-endowment
bean counter
Sean Connery
Jean Borotra
re-encourage
Jean Cocteau
Jenny Pitman
reintroduce
Keanu Reeves
ternary form
Bernardines
Bernard Katz
Bernard Lyot
Werner Arber
Leon Brittan
Leon Trotsky
Dennis Gabor
tennis elbow
Dennis Amiss
fernitickle
fernytickle
Mean Streets
neonatology
reinstation
reinsurance
Jean Buridan
heinousness
lean cuisine
pennyweight
pennywinkle
penny-wisdom
Lennox Lewis
Deborah Bull
memorandums
✧memorabilia
decorations
aeronautics
mesogastria
mesogastric
redoubtable
redoubtably
melon baller
recombinant
Le Corbusier
heroic verse
lemon cheese
Sea of Crises
debouchment
deforcement
rejoicement
rejoicingly
Sea of Clouds
second-rater
Second Reich
seconds hand
second sight
second floor
second-floor
second class
second-class
beyond doubt
Second World
second joint
beyond price
secondarily
reconditely
decondition
recondition
recordation
second-guess
mesopelagic
recoverable
wet one's clay
rejoneadora
cenogenesis
merogenesis
merogenetic
xenogenesis
xenogenetic
mesocephaly
set one's hand
set one's mind
devotedness
removedness
reposedness
get one's oats
set one's seal
telocentric
reposefully
get one's wind
reconfigure
sex offender
let off steam
Yegor Gaidar
Mekong River
oesophageal
mesothelial
oenophilist
mesothelium
xerophilous
bed of honour
xerothermic
pelotherapy
serotherapy
cerotic acid
aerobically
denominable
meiotically
melodically
memorisable
memorizable
denominator
mesonic atom
Begoniaceae
demoniacism
serotine bat
velocimeter
velocipeder
velocimetry
Merovingian
Memorial Day
aerobiology
genouillère
memorialise
memorialist
refocillate
memorialize
demonianism
devotionist
negotiatrix
defoliation
negotiation
feloniously
ferociously
melodiously
recollected
aeroelastic
ceroplastic
meroblastic
mesoblastic
xenoglossia
xenoplastic
décolletage
decollation
reformadoes
Reform flask
renormalise
reformulate
renormalize
recommender
Devon minnow
Mesoamerica
recommittal
deformation
leg-of-mutton
re-formation
✧reformation
reformatory
reformative
demountable
Sea of Nectar
reconnoiter
reconnoitre
recountment
recognition
recognitory
recognitive
demonolater
demonomania
hedonomania
demonolatry
metoposcopy
xenodochium
aerological
gemological
oenological
pedological
penological
serological
sexological
demonologic
mesomorphic
xenomorphic
xeromorphic
demonocracy
decolourise
decolourize
hero-worship
seroconvert
cenospecies
mesospheric
recompenser
decomposite
tenorrhaphy
menorrhagia
resourceful
aerobraking
devouringly
seborrhoeic
demographer
cerographic
demographic
venographic
xerographic
xerotripsis
aerotropism
democratise
democratist
democratize
Depo-Provera®
zero-grazing
below stairs
belowstairs
remorseless
deconstruct
reconstruct
✧remonstrant
demonstrate
remonstrate
repossessor
lemon squash
gerontocrat
decorticate
Demosthenes
Demosthenic
gerontology
reportingly
revoltingly
gerontophil
reportorial
aerostatics
report stage
aerostation
dehortation
deportation
dehortatory
dehortative
demodulator
depopulator
Belorussian
devolvement
Melody Maker
aerodynamic
metonymical
lemon-yellow
memory board
memory trace
Tempranillo
temptatious
Neoplatonic
net practice
respectable
respectably
respectless

bespreading
resplendent
perplexedly
Hepplewhite
telpherline
people mover
people power
Temple Mount
neopaganise
neopaganism
serpiginous
neopaganize
peep-through
keep the ring
deep therapy
delphically
Terpsichore
Delphinidae
delphiniums
despoilment
deep kissing
tempolabile
geopolitics
despumation
weapon salve
keep on about
weapon-schaw
despondence
despondency
respondence
respondency
keep in check
helping hand
reaping-hook
keep in sight
serpentinic
responsible
responsibly
responsions
hempen widow
serpentlike
weeping rock
keeping-room
weeping-ripe
serpent-star
keep one's bed
help oneself
leaping-time
keep an eye on
Neoptolemus
keep counsel
keep company
reupholster
deep-mouthed
reapportion
semper eadem
helper T cell
meo periculo
desperadoes
hesperidium
leapfrogged
Hesperiidae
reappraisal
vespertinal
reappraiser
sempervivum
sea purslane
temporality
temperament
leopard moth
pepperiness
peppercorny
temporaries
temporarily
pepper grass
temporising
desperately
temperately
desperation
respiration
respiratory
temperature
temperative
deep drawing
deep-drawing
leopard-wood
temporizing
keep a secret
herpes virus
sea passport
tempest-tost
sex-positive
tempus fugit
tempestuous
perpetuance
perpetrable
perpetuable
perpetually
perpetrator
perpetuator
respite care
bespattered
herpetology
sempiternal
sempstering
sempiternum
helpfulness
geophysical
get physical
New Plymouth
sesquipedal
mesquinerie
perquisitor
sesquialter
sesquioxide
rebroadcast
merry-andrew
reproachful
tear-falling
beer parlour
retreatment
heart attack
bear-baiting
retroaction
retroactive
bear's-breech
Henri Breuil
Henry Briggs
retrobulbar
detribalise
terribility
wearability
detribalize
meprobamate
heartbroken
necrobiosis
necrobiotic
pearl barley
pearl button
reprobation
retribution
reprobatory
retributory
reprobative
retributive
refractable
retraceable
retractable
depreciator
tetracyclic
heart cockle
retrocedent
verruciform
tetractinal
retractible
terricolous
Henry Cooper
ferro-chrome
detractress
deprecating
deprecation
Henry Cotton
metrication
deprecatory
deprecative
ferric oxide
tetradrachm
tetradactyl
regredience
rear admiral
débridement
tetradymite
Petrodromus
degradation
depredation
depredatory
George Halas
George Carey
beurre manié
retrievable
retrievably
George Gamow
tear webbing
George W Bush
pearlescent
George Medal
tear-jerking
George Ellis
George Blake
George Eliot
hearse-cloth
learnedness
George Monck
George Robey
George Boole
George Young
George Green
George Cross
George Grosz
George Grove
George Brown
heart-easing
reorientate
George Lucas
George Burns
neurofibril
retroflexed
de profundis
year of grace
ferriferous
pearl-fisher
Henri Fuseli
retrofitted
ferrography
petrography
reprography
metri gratia
deprogramme
reprogramme
tetragynian
ferruginous
terrigenous
tetragonous
tetragynous
refrigerant
refrigerate
net register
segregation
segregative
petroglyphy
search party
bear the bell
near the bone
tetrahedral
Henry Hudson
tetrahedron
hearth-penny
searchlight
search image
reprehender
yeard-hunger
searchingly
hearth-money
wear through
Pearl Harbor
hearth-brush
hearthstone
near the wind
Hebraically
recruitable
Georgie Best
Henry Ireton
near-sighted
detrainment
recruitment
Georgian Bay
bear witness
terra ignota
Henry Irving
Henrik Ibsen
Georg Kaiser
metrologist
necrologist
neurologist
petrologist
Georg Lukacs
Georg Lukács
neural plate
retrolental
neuroleptic
heartlessly
wearilessly
serrulation
merrymaking
Henry Miller
pearl millet
detrimental
recremental
gerrymander
jerrymander
necromancer
necromantic
New Romantic
recriminate
Henry Morgan
tetramerism
heart murmur
tetramerous
pearl mussel
dedramatise
terremotive
dedramatize
herringbone
herring-buss
ferro-nickel
derring-doer
refringency
herring gull
refrangible
searing-iron
ferronnière
retranslate
dégringoler
herring pond
tetrandrian
bearing rein
tetrandrous
wear and tear
tear and wear
beer goggles
heart of palm
pearl oyster
rear-roasted
Kerry Packer
tetrapodous
neuropteran
tetrapteran
tetraplegia
tetraplegic
necrophilia
necrophilic
retrophilia
Henry Pelham
necropoleis
tetraploidy
necrophobia
necrophobic
negrophobia
Negro pepper
decrepitude
neuropathic
decrepitate
petropounds
pearl-powder
terraqueous
retro-rocket
Petrarchian
Petrarchise
Petrarchism
Petrarchist
tetrarchate
Petrarchize
terror novel
terroristic
heart-shaped
redressable
decrescendo
refreshener
Ferris wheel
zebra spider
depressible
repressible
repressibly
heart's-blood
serrasalmos
wearisomely
refreshment
sea rosemary
representee
representer
representor
bearishness
necroscopic
tetrasporic
terrestrial
heart-struck
heart-strike
heart-string
heart-strook
leprosarium
Ken Rosewall
regrettable
regrettably
neuroticism
tetratheism
secret agent
tear-stained
deerstalker
serratulate
betrothment
neurotomist
secretional
Terry-Thomas
neurotrophy
neurotropic
secretarial
secretariat
✧territorial
territoried
regretfully
secretively
detritivore
heart urchin
defraudment
fearfulness
tearfulness
retroussage
tetravalent
depravement
deprivement
depravingly
reprovingly
sex-reversal
retroverted
red river hog
depravation
deprivation
reprivatise
deprivative
reprivatize
Weary Willie
pearly gates
pearly queen
Leos Janácek
persuadable
Hessian boot
Persian Gulf
felspathoid
persuasible
Persian lamb
re-establish
sensualness
Weismannism
Messiahship
newscasting
Persian Wars

feasibility
sensibility
tensibility
versability
seasickness
persecution
persecutory
persecutive
bedside book
Wensleydale
gens d'église
Bessie Smith
Leisler's bat
reascension
reassertion
perspective
Meissen ware
message-girl
bersaglieri
dessignment
message unit
news-theatre
leaseholder
deistically
perspirable
seismically
neostigmine
verslibrist
news fiction
perspicuity
perspicuous
seismic wave
Tessa Jowell
tessellated
weasel-faced
sessile-eyed
beastly-head
persulphate
beastliness
pensileness
weasel words
weasel round
ceaselessly
senselessly
Peasblossom
tensile test
verse-making
leesome-lane
leishmaniae
leishmanias
verse-monger
gelseminine
Bessemer pig
pessimistic
densimetric
Helsingborg
personified
personifier
geosyncline
personalise
personalism
personalist
personality
seasonality
personalize
persona muta
personpower
yersiniosis
weasand-pipe
Peasants' War
personating
personation
personative
pensionable
sessionally
tensionally
seismonasty
seismoscope
seismometer
tensiometer
seismometry
tensiometry
pension fund
Ken Scotland
pensionless
tensionless
Feast of Lots
teaspoonful
seismologic
beast of prey
sea scorpion
seismograph
yeast powder
lesser panda
sensorially
men-servants
Bessarabian
Welsh rabbit
tessaraglot
tea-strainer
keystroking
measureless
measurement
Sensurround®
censor morum
geostrophic
leisure suit
geostrategy
mensuration
mensurative
leisurewear
dessert wine
persistence
persistency
versatilely
versatility
sensational
sensitively
sensitivity
reassurance
gens du monde
red squirrel
pensiveness
Deus avertat
perseverant
persevering
perseverate
Jesse window
Mersey sound
neutral axis
central bank
pentlandite
gentianella
meet halfway
central fire
neutraliser
neutralizer
meat packing
restraining
heat barrier
Central Time
peat-casting
ventral tank
test pattern
neutral zone
tectibranch
vertebrated
vertebrally
destabilise
rentability
testability
destabilize
Celtiberian
petticoated
depth charge
pentacyclic
hectic fever
septicaemia
septicaemic
geotactical
pentactinal
Pentacrinus
peptic ulcer
tentaculoid
vertical fin
denticulate
gesticulate
tentaculate
tentaculite
testiculate
verticality
Deutschmark
Weltschmerz
geotechnics
penteconter
geotectonic
Delta Cephei
leptocercal
festschrift
Celtic cross
Pentecostal
peptide bond
sextodecimo
leptodactyl
pentadactyl
testudinary
death duties
Betty Davies
centre lathe
gentlemanly
weatherable
weather beam
leatherback
heather bell
leather-coat
weathercock
set the scene
feather-edge
gentlenesse
heathenesse
Leatherette®
get the heave
weather-fend
weather gage
weather gall
tent-pegging
weathergirl
feather-head
leather-head
weather helm
Bertie Ahern
aesthetical
centrepiece
penthemimer
see the light
heat-seeking
featherlike
bestselling
get the elbow
nettle-cloth
weathermost
leatherneck
genteelness
settledness
gentlewoman
get the goods
best-beloved
gentlewomen
centre round
centreboard
feather palm
feather-pate
beetlebrain
weather roll
vertue-proof
next dearest
beetle drive
beetle brows
feather star
weather side
text message
weather sign
weather ship
de-stressing
centre stage
Beetlejuice
centre punch
weather vane
leatherwood
weather-worn
weather-wise
septifragal
certifiable
certifiably
rectifiable
certificate
testificate
pettifogger
pestiferous
septiferous
Betty Grable
centigramme
hectogramme
pentagynian
lentiginose
heptagynous
lentiginous
pentagynous
tentiginous
vertiginous
dentigerous
get together
get-together
Teotihuacán
beat the band
pentahedral
heptahedron
pentahedron
beat the drum
Westphalian
bestridable
centrically
centripetal
settling day
restringent
next biggest
Bert Hinkler
ventriloquy
Westminster
restriction
restrictive
centrifugal
ventricular
ventricules
ventriculus
Keith Joseph
reptilianly
pestologist
mental block
dental floss
rectilineal
rectilinear
pestilently
deathliness
de-Stalinise
de-Stalinize
lex talionis
gentilhomme
sertularian
mentalistic
gentilitial
gentilitian
ventilation
ventilatory
ventilative
dental nurse
Bette Midler
pentamidine
sentimental
testamental
testamentar
testimonial
vestimental
centi Morgan
death-marked
Betty Martin
pentamerism
Septembrist
heptamerous
pentamerous
centimetric
Teutonicism
pertinacity
letting down
geitonogamy
Pelton wheel
mentonnière
sententious
sentinelled
pertinently
meltingness
centenarian
pentandrian
septentrial
septentrion
heptandrous
pentandrous
septenarius
betting shop
festinately
pectinately
destination
festination
pectination
pentangular
rectangular
mentholated
centrobaric
destroyable
mentionable
sectionally
Berthon-boat
neutron bomb
benthoscope
debt bondage
oestrogenic
West Lothian
Neotropical
Weltpolitik
textbookish
section mark
West Country
neutron star
pentaploidy
rectipetaly
perturbance
perturbable
vectorially
centuriator
perturbator
deattribute
reattribute
vectorscope
beat a record
perturbedly
feature film
deuterogamy
set to rights
leptorrhine
heptarchist
yesternight
featureless
textureless
westernmost
pesteringly
venturingly
Deuteronomy
deuteranope
letterboxed
pester power
Lester Young
letter-board
teeter-board
setter-forth
western roll
letterpress
lectureship
venturesome
✧venturi tube
death rattle
letter-stamp
deuteration
reiteration
✧restoration
reiterative
restorative
nectar-guide
dexterously
venturously
Western Wall
delta rhythm
Leptis Magna
Yevtushenko
Kentish fire
pentastichs
pettishness

rectiserial
death-stroke
pectisation
peptisation
petty spurge
teetotaller
Vesta Tilley
teetotalism
pentathlete
restatement
gestational
gestatorial
destitution
restitution
restitutory
restitutive
tentatively
restfulness
zestfulness
tertium quid
destruction
restructure
destructive
pentavalent
festiveness
restiveness
festivities
aestivation
vestry-clerk
west-by-north
west-by-south
pentazocine
pectization
peptization
ferulaceous
secular hymn
decumbently
recumbently
decumbiture
denunciator
pedunculate
Jesus Christ
sepulchrous
resuscitant
resuscitate
redundantly
fecundation
denumerable
denumerably
recuperable
remunerable
recuperator
rejuvenator
remunerator
rejuvenesce
oecumenical
Requiem Mass
reputed pint
tenure track
tegumentary
refuse stays
beauteously
rebukefully
refulgently
regurgitant
regurgitate
Tegucigalpa
delusionist
decurionate
vesuvianite
Leguminosae
pecuniarily
peculiarise
peculiarity
peculiarize
repudiation
repudiative
beautifully
penuriously
refuellable
sexual abuse
reduplicate
beguilement
beguilingly
republisher
genuflexion
return match
return shock
repugnantly
genuineness
return order
Beaufort Sea
beaumontage
verumontana
resurrector
requirement
decurrently
recurrently
sequestered
demulsifier
request note
sequestrant
sequestrate
request stop
decussately
requisitely
decussation
requisition
requisitory
decursively
repulsively
Jesuits' bark
requiteless
requitement
penultimate
reluctantly
desultorily
degustation
reluctation
degustatory
resultative
deductively
reductively
seductively
demutualise
demutualize
tenuousness
decurvation
recurvature
beauty salon
Mesut Yilmaz
beauty sleep
beauty queen
leave behind
service area
serviceable
serviceably
service book
pervicacity
service flat
service line
serviceless
service mark
nerve centre
service pipe
service road
service room
service tree
service wire
nerve ending
heavy-headed
helve-hammer
heavy-handed
merveilleux
red valerian
nervelessly
Servile Wars
heavenwards
Mervyn Peake
servant-girl
Heaven's Gate
Lee Van Cleef
servant-lass
servantless
servant-maid
heaven knows
Melvyn Bragg
servantship
leaving-shop
Beaver Scout
weaver finch
pervertible
weaver's knot
Beaverboard®
beaverboard
nervuration
resveratrol
peevishness
pervasively
velvet-paper
heave the log
leave-taking
neovitalism
neovitalist
velvet glove
velvetiness
servitorial
nervousness
leave unsaid
heavyweight
between-maid
betweenness
betweentime
reawakening
Rex Williams
Ted Williams
welwitschia
re-expansion
deoxidation
jeux d'esprit
deoxygenise
deoxygenate
deoxygenize
re-existence
New Year's Day
Ten Years' War
New Year's Eve
Hesychastic
demyelinate
beryllíosis
deny oneself
dehypnotise
dehypnotize
New York City
dehydration
rehydration
Meryl Streep
see you later
Kenzaburo Oë
Mezz Mezzrow
Mezzogiorno
Herzegovina
benzoic acid
benzylidine
benzene ring
Keizo Obuchi
Led Zeppelin
mezzotinter
mezzotintos
of many words
off-Broadway
off-coloured
aficionados
afterburner
offenceless
after-dinner
after-effect
of necessity
aftergrowth
aftermarket
aftersupper
offensively
effectually
affectingly
affectional
affectioned
affectation
affectively
effectively
affectivity
effectivity
offhandedly
Afghan hound
Afghanistan
efficacious
African teak
office block
office hours
officinally
officialdom
officialese
officialism
officiality
afficionado
efficiently
affiliation
officiation
officiously
affirmingly
affirmation
affirmatory
affirmative
offload onto
afforcement
off one's case
off one's face
off one's feed
off one's game
off one's head
off one's oats
Afro-centric
Afrocentric
if you please
Afro-Asiatic
effortfully
affrication
affricative
affrightful
affranchise
offscouring
off the rails
off the wagon
off the shelf
off-the-shelf
off the hooks
off the track
effulgently
A Few Good Men
aguardiente
eglandulose
agnatically
agrarianism
agrammatism
Iguaçu Falls
agranulosis
egocentrism
egregiously
agriscience
ignis fatuus
ignition key
agritourism
agriproduct
against time
agriculture
agglomerate
agelessness
agglutinant
agglutinate
egalitarian
egomaniacal
agamospermy
Egon Schiele
agony column
Agent Orange
X-generation
agonistical
agonisingly
agonothetes
agency nurse
agonizingly
Ignorantine
ignoramuses
P G Wodehouse
ignominious
agrobiology
ignobleness
agrological
agronomical
agnosticism
agrostology
Egyptian pea
Egyptianise
Egyptianize
aggradation
aggregately
aggregation
aggregative
agoraphobia
agoraphobic
aggravating
aggravation
I Got You Babe
egotistical
agnus castus
The Analects
phrasal verb
phrasemaker
phraseogram
phraseology
thrash metal
sheath knife
sheath dress
cheap labour
the Auld Kirk
the Almighty
wheat mildew
chiaroscuro
thrasonical
the Anointed
ahead of time
The Agricola
theatricals
theatricise
theatricism
theatricize
theatre-goer
✧the absolute
thwartships
chiastolite
thwartingly
theanthropy
chlamydeous
the black dog
the Boat Race
The Big Sleep
✧the big smoke
the Big Apple
The Big Issue
rhabdomancy
Rhabdophora
rhabdomyoma
the business
the biter bit
the Bay State
cha-cha-chaed
chick-a-biddy
chock-a-block
the Classics
check action
phycocyanin
thick-coming
chickenfeed
chicken hawk
chicken kiev
✧the Creation
the creature
chicken wire
shock-headed
thickheaded
shock horror
shock-horror
shackle-bolt
shackle-bone
phycologist
chuckle-head
the Colonies
thick-lipped
chocolatier
phycomycete
the Conquest
phycophaein
thick-ribbed
whichsoever
check-string
shock troops
The Crucible

thick-witted
Chuck Yeager
Rhodian laws
Cheddar pink
the deceased
rhododendra
rhododaphne
shad-bellied
Chad Newsome
shuddersome
shed light on
Rhode Island
the Dukeries
the dingbats
whodunnitry
the departed
The Dormouse
rhodium-wood
shadow fight
shadowiness
shadow forth
shadow price
shadowgraph
shoe latchet
sheet anchor
wheel animal
cheek by jowl
chief barker
wheelbarrow
three-bottle
sheep-biting
three cheers
three-colour
sheet copper
wheel-cutter
threadmaker
thread-paper
three-decker
threadiness
cheeseparer
phrenetical
threnetical
cheese plant
cheesecloth
cheeseboard
cheesewring
cheesepress
cheese straw
shoe leather
sheet-feeder
sheep-farmer
cheechakoes
three-handed
Phaethontic
The Evil Dead
cheerleader
three-leafed
three-leaved
The Eclogues
three-legged
wheedlingly
cheerlessly
wheedlesome
phlegmonoid
phlegmonous
sheep-master
three-masted
three-master
three-nooked
Phaenogamae
phaenogamic
The Exorcist
chaenomeles
phaenomenon
wheel of life
chaetognath
phrenologic
wheel plough
three-parted
sheet rubber
The European
Three Rivers
The Exstasie
three-suited
sheep-silver
three-square
chieftaincy
chieftainry
threatening
three-volume
wheelwright
wheel window
The Franklin
chaff-cutter
chaff-engine
The Fugitive
✧the faithful
shufflingly
shiftlessly
whiffletree
the fine arts
chafing-dish
chafing-gear
chiffonnier
chef d'oeuvre
The Firebird
the four seas
theftuously
the five wits
shift worker
The Guardian
whigmaleery
The Graduate
phagocytism
phagocytose
phagedaenic
rhagadiform
shagge-eared
The Gleaners
shaggedness
the greatest
shigellosis
The Gold Rush
the game is up
thigmotaxis
the Good Book
phagophobia
The Germania
the Holy City
the homeless
phthiriasis
The Hireling
The Hot Seven
chain armour
Thai massage
chain bridge
Chris Barber
chain-driven
chaise-carts
Chris Eubank
shrivelling
choice-drawn
Chaim Herzog
chain harrow
shriekingly
shrinkingly
shrink-proof
chain locker
thrillingly
chain letter
choirmaster
chrismatory
chrisom-robe
chainplates
shrimp plant
chairperson
choirstalls
choir school
chainstitch
chain-smoker
choirscreen
✧christiania
Christianly
Christmassy
Christogram
Christology
Christingle
christening
Christendom
thriftiness
Christopher
Christ-cross
thrift store
chokecherry
The King and I
choking coil
Shakespeare
Shalmaneser
Phileas Fogg
shellacking
Chilean pine
shell-crater
Philoctetes
phylacteric
chelicerate
thalidomide
shelter belt
Chelsea boot
Chelsea clip
challenging
philhellene
shelterless
chilled meal
Phil Bennett
chalcedonic
chalcedonyx
shelter tent
Chelsea ware
chill factor
whole-footed
cheliferous
chyliferous
whale-fisher
Chilognatha
philogynist
philogynous
whole-hogger
whole-hoofed
phillipsite
chalcid wasp
shell jacket
philologian
philologist
chilblained
whole-length
chylomicron
childminder
philomathic
philanderer
whole number
whaling-port
the long robe
cholinergic
phalanstery
phyllomania
phyllotaxis
Thallophyta
thallophyte
The Lion King
phylloclade
Phil Collins
shallowness
Philippines
Philip Glass
shell parrot
cholera belt
cholestasis
the last cast
cholesteric
cholesterin
thalassemia
thalassemic
cholesterol
the last gasp
wholestitch
wholesomely
philosopher
philosophic
whole-souled
the last word
thelytokous
shelftalker
philatelist
wholly-owned
chalazogamy
rhamnaceous
thump around
sham Abraham
chump change
rhumb course
chamaephyte
Chimaeridae
✧chamberlain
chambermaid
chimney-nuik
chimney-nook
champertous
chymiferous
Rhamphastos
whimsically
championess
thimble case
thimblefuls
Chomolungma
chameleonic
shamelessly
rhyme letter
thimbleweed
thumb-marked
chemin de fer
Shimon Peres
The Man of Law
the munchies
shamanistic
rhomboideus
rhombohedra
shame on them
The Merchant
chemurgical
Thomas Hardy
Thomas Nashe
The Music Man
rhyme scheme
chemosphere
Thomistical
Thomas Blood
Thompson gun
Thomas Lodge
Thomas Young
Thomas Moore
Thomas Pride
Thomas Brown
Thomas Otway
Thomas Wyatt
chemotactic
chemotropic
shameworthy
shimmy-shake
chantarelle
phantasiast
thingamyjig
thingamybob
the noble art
the nobility
rhinocerote
change hands
Thunderball
thunderbolt
thunderbird
thunderclap
thunder-dart
chanterelle
change of air
thunderhead
thunderlike
channelling
thin red line
chancellery
chancellory
thunderless
phentermine
whingeingly
chance-comer
change point
change-house
thenceforth
whenceforth
thunder peal
change front
channel seam
channel-surf
changefully
phonofiddle
phonography
rhynchocoel
rhynchodont
shanghaiing
chinoiserie
chanticleer
when pigs fly
thin-skinned
phenologist
phonologist
rhinologist
thingliness
chandlering
shinplaster
thanklessly
phonemicise
phonemicist
phonemicize
phenomenise
phenomenism
phenomenist
phenomenize
shunamitism
shenanigans
phenanthene
Chenin Blanc
shiningness
phantomatic
chansonette
phantom limb
chansonnier
phantom pain
rhinoplasty
shin splints
phonophobia
rhinorrhoea
chancroidal
Phanerozoic
Chinese burn
Chinese copy
thanksgiver
rhinoscopic
Chinese wall
Rhenish wine
phonetician
phoneticise
phoneticism
phoneticist
phoneticize
thanatology
thanatopsis
phonotypist
thingumajig
thingumabob
the New World
thankworthy
shinty-stick
the Nazarene
theomachist
throw around
thrombocyte
throbbingly
the old enemy
the Old World
theorematic
theotechnic
theoretical
choose sides
whooper swan
chrome steel
theocentric
thiopentone
through ball
through bolt
throughfare
throughgaun
through pass
theophobiac
theophobist
theophagous
the other day
the other man
chrominance

chloric acid
chromic acid
chaotically
chronically
chlorinator
chlorimeter
chlorimetry
shooting war
shooting box
thioalcohol
chloanthite
theopneusty
Theodorakis
chromoscope
chronoscope
chlorometer
chronometer
chromogenic
chlorometry
chronometry
chlorophyll
chromophore
theosophise
theosophism
theosophist
theosophize
rheological
theogonical
theological
theologiser
theologizer
theodolitic
chloroplast
chromoplast
chromosomal
chronologer
chronologic
theomorphic
chloroprene
chronograph
chloroquine
theobromine
rheotropism
Theocritean
The Observer
throatlatch
chaos theory
shoot the sun
The Outsider
throatiness
throatstrap
throw weight
theory-laden
thiocyanate
The Peasants
chapeau-bras
The Phaedrus
ship railway
ship carving
the Preacher
Chippendale
shepherdess
shopkeeping
ship the oars
ship biscuit
shopping bag
whipping boy
whipping-top
the Prioress
shoplifting
Rhopalocera
shapeliness
chapel royal
shapelessly
whippletree
whip and spur
the prophets
rhapsodical
ship's papers
ship-breaker
shopbreaker
chaperonage
The Pardoner
ship it green
shop steward
shipbuilder
the Quatorze
chequerwork
chequerwise
charlatanic
charlatanry
chartaceous
thereabouts
whereabouts
short-acting
shard beetle
therebeside
chart-buster
shirt button
short-change
Pherecratic
shortcoming
characinoid
short corner
thoracotomy
the Redeemer
third degree
The Red Shoes
shared logic
the Red Cross
The Red Queen
Charlemagne
Charles Bell
third eyelid
shore effect
chargesheet
charter-hand
Charles Ives
Cherie Blair
Charles Lamb
Charter Mark
Charles Mayo
charge-house
Cherie Booth
Charles's law
shorten sail
third estate
Charlestown
chargenurse
sheriffalty
sheriffhood
sharefarmer
thuriferous
sheriffship
chirography
choregraphy
chorography
chiragrical
sharp-ground
churchwards
church-bench
Church Times
shareholder
short-handed
churchwoman
church tower
churchgoing
church court
church mouse
thermically
Charlie Chan
✧thersitical
choroiditis
thyroiditis
thermionics
sherris-sack
chirologist
chorologist
charmlessly
sharemilker
whoremonger
chiromantic
Third market
Theromorpha
whoremaster
pharyngitic
pharyngitis
sharon fruit
Sharon Stone
thermobaric
thermotaxic
thermotaxis
theriolatry
thermonasty
thermoscope
thermometer
thermogenic
thermometry
thermophile
chordophone
thermotical
thermocline
tharborough
theriomorph
choreograph
thermograph
Pharaoh's ant
share option
thermoduric
thermolysis
thermolytic
The Republic
chiropodial
chiropodist
chiropteran
short-priced
thornproofs
third person
share-pusher
short pastry
shark patrol
Therapeutae
therapeutic
chirurgical
charbroiled
chargrilled
charismatic
short-staple
The Rose Bowl
sharksucker
wheresoever
phariseeism
shirtsleeve
charm school
pharisaical
cherishment
chord symbol
whorishness
short-spoken
third stream
third-stream
Thyrostraca
short shrift
chorisation
charity ball
The Retreate
theretofore
charity-girl
short tennis
thirstiness
thyrotropin
short-termer
charity shop
charity walk
charcuterie
thoroughwax
thoroughpin
short-winded
therewithal
wherewithal
sharp-witted
therewithin
thorny devil
cherry-stone
there you are
where you are
thirty-twomo
chorization
Shasta daisy
the scaffold
Phasmatidae
the shallows
Phasmatodea
physiatrics
this day week
ghostbuster
physiciancy
physicianer
physicalism
physicalist
physicality
The Sick Rose
whiskerando
whiskeyfied
chastenment
whiskey sour
phosphonium
phosphorise
phosphorism
phosphorate
phosphorite
phosphorous
phosphorize
phosphatide
phosphatase
phosphatise
phosphatize
chastisable
Cheshire Cat
the sniffles
whistle away
whistleable
thistledown
whistle fish
whistlingly
ghastliness
ghostliness
chisel tooth
whistle stop
whistle-stop
The Summoner
thysanurous
this and that
this instant
physiolater
chasmogamic
physiolatry
thesmothete
ahistorical
physiognomy
physiologic
physiologus
the Scorpion
physiocracy
whist-player
The Sorceror
whosesoever
thesis novel
physitheism
The Sluggard
thesauruses
ghost-writer
whisky-liver
whisky toddy
the size of it
Shatt al-Arab
phytoalexin
photo-ageing
what have you
that's an idea
Chattanooga
shittah tree
photoactive
white-billed
white bonnet
Rhett Butler
white bottle
white bryony
✧whiteboyism
Whitechapel
white coffee
white-collar
white clover
photocopier
white copper
photochromy
phytochrome
that's done it
✧the trenches
chitterling
shutterless
whether or no
shatter-pate
White Ensign
whitleather
thitherward
whitherward
white flight
White Friars
white finger
photo finish
photography
phytography
photoglyphy
white-headed
what the hell
white-haired
white-handed
white hunter
thatch-board
Thatcherism
Thatcherite
The Third Man
shittim wood
white knight
whittle away
shuttlecock
whittle down
phytologist
The Talisman
white-listed
shuttlewise
rhythmicity
photomosaic
white matter
photometric
whiting pout
photonastic
whiting-time
the Troubles
whatsomever
whet forward
whitlow-wort
phytophagic
White Plains
what a plague
photophilic
photophobia
photophobic
photophonic
white pepper
photoperiod
White Rabbit
rhetorician
white radish
photo-relief
white-rumped
a hit or a miss
photoresist
white slaver
phytosterol
photosphere
white spirit
whitishness
that is to say
white squall
white squire
phototactic
white-tailed
phytotomist
phototropic
whitethroat
that's torn it!
Whitsuntide
Whitsun week
white-winged
whitewasher
chitty-faced
Whitby Abbey
rheumateese
rheumatical
rheumaticky
Chautauquan
thaumatrope
thaumaturge
thaumaturgy

shrubbiness
shrubberied
shoulder bag
shoulder pad
shouldering
thoughtcast
thoughtless
thought-sick
thought wave
The Universe
thrummed hat
thrummingly
chaulmoogra
choux pastry
thrust plane
thrust stage
cheval-glass
shovelboard
shaving-soap
the very idea
shiveringly
showmanship
shawl collar
shawnee-wood
show of hands
the Waggoner
show the flag
the Writings
The Wild Duck
The Wild Wood
show-and-tell
the whole kit
The Woodlark
showeriness
showerproof
show-stopper
showjumping
thixotropic
chrysalides
chrysalises
chrysarobin
Phrygian cap
chrysoberyl
chrysocolla
chrysocracy
chrysoprase
wheyishness
phlyctaenae
rhizocarpic
rhizogenous
rhizomatous
rhizanthous
rhizosphere
pit-a-patting
bicarbonate
Micawberish
Micawberism
financially
vicar-choral
disaccustom
final demand
ritardandos
bib and brace
bilaterally
bid a welcome
tirage à part
disaventure
filamentary
ligamentary
filamentous
ligamentous

disaffected
vicar-forane
disafforest
vinaigrette
cigar-holder
Sivatherium
rival-hating
dilapidated
titanic acid
piratically
✧titanically
dilapidator
Kiwanis Club
rifacimenti
rifacimento
titanic iron
vivacissimo
bifariously
hilariously
vicariously
vivaciously
misalliance
disablement
Cisatlantic
mid-Atlantic
likableness
miracle play
miracle rice
disarmament
Silas Marner
disannuller
final notice
Titanomachy
Vicar of Bray
Rifat Ozbeck
vital organs
pinacotheca
gila monster
disapproval
cicatricial
cicatricula
bizarreness
cigar-shaped
disassemble
disassembly
giganticide
didacticism
gigantology
didactylous
finasteride
misanthrope
misanthropy
gigantesque
bipartition
ailanthuses
binary digit
litany-stool
vinblastine
misbecoming
Sir Bedivere
kibble-chain
misbegotten
fimbriation
disbeliever
misbeliever
diabolology
Ribbon Falls
disbandment
ribbon-grass
timbromania
timbrophily

Jim Bergerac
Silbury Hill
timber hitch
Gilbertines
gibberellin
Wilbur Smith
Gilbert Ryle
Kim Basinger
big business
misbestowal
nimbostrati
airbrush out
gibbousness
disbowelled
pitch and pay
pitch and run
disc parking
gimcrackery
Mischa Elman
misclassify
aircraftman
finch-backed
pitchblende
miscibility
vincibility
piscicolous
pitch circle
hircocervus
witch doctor
discrepance
discrepancy
witches' brew
kitchenette
pinch effect
biochemical
circle-rider
witches' meat
kitchen-maid
biocoenoses
biocoenosis
biocoenotic
circle round
yince-errand
pitched roof
kitchen-sink
miscreation
miscreative
miscreaunce
kitchen unit
kitchenware
witch-finder
zinciferous
discography
zincography
miscegenist
miscegenate
hitch-hiking
pinch-hitter
aid climbing
kinchin-cove
diacritical
kinchin-mort
biscuit-root
vincristine
mischievous
miscellanea
discalceate
circular saw
circularise
circularity
piacularity

circularize
circulating
circulation
circulatory
circulative
discoloured
discomycete
circumciser
discomfited
circumflect
circumpolar
circumsolar
circumvolve
circumspect
viscometric
circumlunar
circumfused
misconceive
discontinue
misconstrue
discandying
piece of cake
cinchoninic
piece of work
disceptator
disciplinal
discipliner
discophoran
pitchperson
discordance
discordancy
discardable
witch-ridden
miscarriage
discernible
discernibly
discerpible
air-corridor
discardment
discernment
diachronism
sincereness
diachronous
pitch-roofed
discerption
discerptive
discussable
discus throw
discussible
discotheque
discothèque
biocatalyst
piscatorial
viscous flow
hiccoughing
viscousness
discoursive
diacoustics
discourtesy
viscountess
piscivorous
bird-catcher
bird-fancier
birdwatcher
pieds-à-terre
windbaggery
wind machine
windfall tax
misdiagnose
pied wagtail
middy blouse

vindication
vindicatory
vindicative
gilded youth
gilded spurs
Middlemarch
middle watch
Middle Latin
✧middle-earth
fiddle about
piddle about
fiddler crab
mind-bending
mind-reading
fiddle-de-dee
riddle-me-ree
middle-sized
middle eight
fiddle block
mind-healing
pit-dwelling
middle class
middle-class
kindredness
middle-world
middle price
kind-hearted
kindredship
girdlestead
windlestrae
windlestraw
fiddlestick
bird-nesting
wild service
giddy-headed
windcheater
wild chicory
find the lady
gild the lily
gild the pill
diadelphous
via dolorosa
mind-blowing
misdemeanor
wisdom tooth
sindonology
biodynamics
wild animals
find oneself
gird oneself
middenstead
Windsor knot
wildfowling
Windsor Park
mind your eye
Windsor soap
piedmontite
hinderlands
Windbreaker®
Biedermeier
widdershins
birdbrained
hinderlings
cinder block
hinderingly
kinderspiel
cinder track
binder twine
fin de siècle
misdescribe
lie detector

Wild at Heart
mind-numbing
wind turbine
windsurfing
wind-sucking
wind furnace
mindfulness
wild mustard
misdoubtful
misdevotion
window-barne
window ledge
window blind
window glass
window frame
tiddlywinks
diddly-squat
Vivekananda
line manager
River Amazon
liberal arts
mineral coal
fire-watcher
line dancing
wire-dancing
CinemaScope®
wide-watered
witenagemot
vinegarette
piperaceous
time bargain
wide-ranging
time machine
kinematical
literaliser
literalizer
mineraliser
mineralizer
Five Nations
tire-valiant
fire-walking
fire-balloon
kite-balloon
bimetallism
bimetallist
miserablist
liberalness
literalness
wiretapping
cinema-organ
fire-marshal
vice-marshal
lifemanship
time capsule
fire-raising
fixed assets
mine-captain
Mike Gatting
wine tasting
literatured
five-day week
mineral well
mineral wool
literaryism
disembodied
tiger beetle
line abreast
likeability
liveability
disemburden
disembitter

river bottom
River Chenab
liver-colour
disencumber
video camera
dimercaprol
Cirencester
Fidel Castro
River Clutha
linen-draper
river-dragon
aides-de-camp
River Dnestr
vice-admiral
river-driver
River Danube
give leg bail
River Escaut
vicegerency
time-release
sidereal day
time deposit
aide-mémoire
timekeeping
Nicene Creed
wise-hearted
life peerage
live-bearing
life peeress
wine measure
Lise Meitner
life-rentrix
wire netting
time-service
wire service
time-serving
give offence
pipe of peace
line of sight
line of force
tiger flower
tiger-footed
River Gambia
divergement
bioengineer
River Ganges
divergently
divergingly
rivet hearth
ride the beam
bite the dust
side-wheeler
bicephalous
dicephalous
nikethamide
River Humber
line-shooter
mine-thrower
ive through
widechapped
give the push
ide the rods
ines herbes
ime charter
ime-sharing
give the slip
ide shotgun
ike the wind
give the wire
inesipathy
idetically

kinetically
mimetically
winebibbing
Ribesiaceae
live circuit
rice biscuit
wine biscuit
fixed income
wire binding
wine vinegar
vine-disease
Kimeridgian
fivefingers
firefighter
firelighter
limelighted
pipe-lighter
line-fishing
cineritious
like winking
cinebiology
cinébiology
kinesiology
time-killing
like billy-oh
misericorde
kinesiatric
pipe fitting
life history
River Irtysh
biker jacket
video jockey
River Jhelum
River Jordan
River Kolyma
River Kistna
pipe-cleaner
time-pleaser
divellicate
River Liffey
pineal gland
fire blanket
miserliness
fire-flaught
libellously
Nigel Lawson
filet mignon
River Mersey
river mussel
hibernacula
mise en scène
✧hibernicise
Hibernicism
✧hibernicize
five-and-dime
wine and dine
pigeon-berry
pigeon chest
mise en place
pigeon-flier
pigeon-flyer
vice anglais
mixed number
pigeon's milk
pigeonholer
pigeonholes
pigeon-house
hide-and-seek
bite one's lip
pipe one's eye
give and take

hibernation
life annuity
viceroyalty
dive-bombing
firebombing
kinetoscope
sideropenia
hide nor hair
siderophile
kinetochore
wireworking
kinetoplast
kinetograph
fire-worship
viceroyship
lifeboatman
fire control
River Pahang
Didelphidae
fides Punica
disemployed
River Paraná
pipe-dreamer
River Ribble
firecracker
wisecracker
fire brigade
line printer
linear motor
vine-dresser
vine-fretter
fine writing
firewriting
pile-driving
line drawing
wine-growing
wiredrawing
Line Islands
sinews of war
diversified
video signal
miner's right
River Salado
video sender
videosender
dimensional
dimensioned
like a streak
linen-scroll
tiger shrimp
viper's grass
disenshroud
River Sutlej
River Severn
River Seyhan
disentrance
River Thames
disentrayle
Dire Straits
liberty-boat
liberticide
diverticula
direct debit
kinesthesia
kinesthesis
kinesthetic
give it welly
River Tigris
✧liberty hall
directrices
fide et amore

misestimate
libertinage
disentangle
divertingly
bicentenary
libertinism
directional
✧ciment fondu
sidestepper
pipe-stapple
pipe-stopple
directorial
libertarian
Firestarter
River Tornio
disenthrall
disenthrone
✧directorate
liberty ship
fire station
divestiture
digestively
directivity
River Ubangi
rice pudding
hic et ubique
wirepulling
bisexuality
direfulness
hideousness
piteousness
side cutting
eigenvector
Like a Virgin
River Vltava
minesweeper
Minenwerfer
riverworthy
time-expired
River Yamuna
misery index
misfeasance
diffraction
diffractive
misfeatured
difficultly
diffidently
biofeedback
Wilfred Owen
Eiffel Tower
sinfonietta
Tiffany lamp
Riefenstahl
rinforzando
differentia
differently
pilferingly
misfortuned
zip fastener
diffuseness
diffusively
diffusivity
disfavourer
Ring Lardner
lingoa geral
disgraceful
disgracious
wing-walking
diagramming
ring-carrier
siege basket

king's bounty
ringed snake
winged words
Winged Horse
ring-fencing
singles club
king penguin
single-phase
single-digit
single-blind
single-ended
single-entry
single-soled
single house
single cream
King Henry IV
single-cross
King Henry VI
singlestick
ring network
king of birds
✧king of kings
ring the bell
ring the shed
misguidance
pilgrimager
disguisable
ring circuit
ring binding
ring-winding
disguisedly
misguidedly
linguistics
singularise
singularism
singularist
singularity
singularize
singing-bird
lingonberry
✧virgin birth
rigging loft
virgin honey
singing sand
rigging-tree
ringing tone
wing-and-wing
diagnosable
kingdom come
wing loading
kingdomless
diagnostics
wing forward
ring spanner
Singaporean
Finger Lakes
finger-paint
pilgarlicky
disgarrison
fingerglass
fingerplate
lingeringly
finger foods
fingerboard
✧gingerbread
fingerprint
finger-grass
ginger group
fingerstall
fingerguard
Diego Rivera

King's Speech
disgustedly
piggishness
ring-straked
fidgetiness
ring stopper
disgruntled
king-vulture
misgovernor
tiggywinkle
king's-yellow
✧mithradatic
Highway Code
Mithraicism
Highlandman
pigheadedly
Qinhuangdao
right-angled
high fashion
fish-packing
highjacking
high-ranking
high bailiff
fish farming
right as rain
right atrium
high-battled
night-attire
highfalutin
might as well
light breeze
pichiciegos
night-cellar
diphycercal
lithochromy
high admiral
lithodomous
high-feeding
Michael Foot
light engine
Michael J Fox
fish-bellied
eighteenmos
Michael Owen
right enough
high-hearted
high-tension
high-density
high feather
high-mettled
righteously
light-footed
night-flower
right-footed
nightfaring
tight-fisted
night-flying
lithography
dichogamous
lithogenous
light-headed
with the best
dish the dirt
light-heeled
diphthongal
light-handed
night-hunter
right-handed
right-hander
diphthongic
high sheriff

ultrasonics
pluriserial
ultraviolet
Il Trovatore
clergywoman
all standing
plasmalemma
alismaceous
close at hand
plasmatical
flash around
Alastair Sim
class action
close-bodied
close-banded
glass-blower
close-barred
flesh-colour
glass-cutter
closed-chain
cluster-bean
cluster bomb
blister card
plaster cast
slasher film
flusterment
blessedness
plaster over
blister pack
cluster pine
clyster-pipe
glossectomy
plasterwork
flash-freeze
class-fellow
flash-frozen
close-fisted
glass-gazing
Iles d'Hyères
blasphemous
close-handed
close-hauled
elasticated
classically
elastically
plastic bomb
elastic band
plastic clay
plessimeter
plessimetry
plasticiser
plasticizer
elasticness
plasminogen
close in upon
plastic wrap
plastic wood
classifying
class-leader
fleshliness
close-lipped
blushlessly
flash memory
fleshmonger
flesh-market
bless my soul!
closing date
Alison Moyet
closing time
glossolalia
glossolalic
Glastonbury
Glasgow City
blastogenic
elastomeric
plasmodesma
Elastoplast®
plasmosomes
blastocoele
glasnostian
glossodynia
plasmolysis
plasmolytic
clostridial
clostridium
close-reefed
plus or minus
elusoriness
flustration
close season
close the gap
close to home
close to hand
close tennis
closet drama
closet queen
Iles du Salut
All Souls' Day
elusiveness
glassworker
Old Trafford
slot machine
plate armour
glottal stop
flat-earther
plate-basket
plutocratic
all the while
clothes-line
clothesline
clothes moth
all the world
clothes-pole
clothes-prop
blotchiness
flat-chested
blotting-pad
ulotrichous
elutriation
plutologist
flatulently
ill-tempered
all-time high
glutaminase
Platanaceae
Platonicism
plutonomist
✧platinotype
glutinously
cloth of gold
plethorical
platforming
glottogonic
all to pieces
slate pencil
plate-powder
all to ruffld
platyrrhine
Ulsterwoman
plateresque
glutathione
slate-writer
plate-warmer
Fleur Adcock
fleur de coin
glaucescent
Claude Simon
Claude Monet
Glauber salt
slaughtered
slaughterer
ploughshare
sleuth-hound
eleutherian
Eleutherius
plough-staff
plough-stilt
illuminance
illuminable
illuminator
albugineous
flourishing
pleuritical
illusionary
illusionism
illusionist
illuviation
albuminuria
cloudlessly
glauconitic
blouson noir
pleurodynia
Olaus Roemer
Blaue Reiter
fleurs-de-lis
fleurs-de-lys
illustrated
illustrator
✧illustrious
flauntingly
cloud-topped
Albuquerque
olive branch
clavecinist
Clavicornia
slave-driver
clavigerous
slaveholder
slave labour
Slavonicise
Slavonicize
olivine-rock
Ulf von Euler
pluviometer
glove puppet
Oliver Tambo
Oliver Hardy
Oliver's Army
ill-versed in
clever clogs
cleverality
slaveringly
clovergrass
Oliver Stone
all very well
Oliver Twist
slave states
glove-shield
slavishness
slave-trader
elevational
flavourless
flavoursome
clown around
slow-release
ill-wresting
slow neutron
blow a gasket
blow the gaff
flow diagram
slow-sighted
old-womanish
claw-and-ball
flowingness
blow one's top
flower child
flower-clock
gloweringly
floweriness
Flower Power
flower-stalk
Alex Salmond
flexibility
cloxacillin
flux density
flexography
Alexei Sayle
Alex Higgins
pleximetric
Alexandrian
✧alexandrine
alexandrite
flax-dresser
Alexis Soyer
Alexey Rykov
Ally Macleod
Ally McCoist
play-actress
Lloyd-George
illy whacker
play the fool
play the goat
play the game
play therapy
clay mineral
playing-card
alcyonarian
play one's ace
play for love
play footsie
play for time
play a part in
clay-brained
player piano
PlayStation®
play it by ear
playfulness
Lloyd Webber
blaze abroad
blaze a trail
Elizabethan
blazing star
Emma Lazarus
embarcation
empanelling
empanelment
Emma Tennant
immanentism
immanentist
immarginate
impatiently
embarkation
imparkation
amiableness
emparlaunce
Emma Goldman
ommatophore
embarrassed
empassioned
impassioned
impassively
impassivity
impartially
impartation
impastation
amobarbital
amicability
ami du peuple
I'm a Dutchman
imperatival
E M Delafield
emmenagogic
emmenagogue
impeachable
imperceable
impeachment
impenetrate
Imre Kertész
imperfectly
imperforate
immedicable
impenitence
impenitency
impedimenta
impetigines
imperilling
imperialise
imperialism
imperialist
imperiality
imperialize
imperilment
immediately
immediatism
imperiously
amber liquid
embellisher
umbellately
impermeable
impermeably
impermanent
emperor moth
emperorship
impetration
impetratory
impetrative
immenseness
impersonate
Emmenthaler
impertinent
impecunious
impetuosity
impetuously
imperviable
imaginarily
imagination
imaginative
amphibology
amphibolite
amphibolous
amphictyony
amphimictic
amphipodous
amphiprotic
amphipathic
✧amphisbaena
amphetamine
emphyteusis
emphyteutic
ambilateral
ambivalence
ambivalency
omnipatient
omnifarious
omniscience
empiecement
ambiversion
impingement
impinge upon
empirically
immitigable
immitigably
omnificence
empiricutic
ambitiously
impignorate
omnipotence
omnipotency
omniformity
omnipresent
immigration
embittering
omnibus book
impiousness
ambiguously
smoke helmet
smokelessly
smoking room
smoky quartz
smoke signal
smokescreen
smoke tunnel
Emil Zatopek
Emily Brontë
small change
small claims
emplacement
implacental
small cornet
small circle
implication
implicature
implicative
smallholder
emulsionise
emulsionize
amyloidosis
amyl nitrate
amyl nitrite
Émile Lahoud
amyl alcohol
small letter
emolumental
implemental
implementer
small-minded
emblematise
emblematist
emblematize
Amelanchier
smilingness
ameliorator
Emilio Segrè
small octave
Emilio Pucci
amylopectin

 Words marked ✧ can also be spelled with one or more capital letters

Émile Picard
small quarto
imploringly
imploration
imploratory
small screen
small-screen
omelette pan
implausible
implausibly
emulousness
small wonder
amplexicaul
amentaceous
amenability
aminobutene
Amin Gemayel
emancipator
amontillado
amenorrhoea
Amundsen Sea
emanational
ominousness
imponderous
immoveables
embowelling
embowelment
embowerment
empowerment
embolectomy
immomentous
smooth-faced
smooth-paced
ammophilous
smooth snake
smooth-bored
smooth hound
impolitical
immobiliser
immobilizer
impoliticly
I'm Not in Love
impoundable
impoundment
Amboina pine
Amboina-wood
Amboyna-wood
amyotrophic
immortalise
immortality
immortalize
emboîtement
impostumate
importunacy
importantly
importunely
importuning
importunate
importunity
importation
imposthumed
HMS Pinafore
smörgåsbord
smart-alecky
amor patriae
improbation
embraceable
impractical
umbraculate
embracement
American Pie
embracingly
Americanise
Americanism
Americanist
Americanize
imprecisely
imprecision
America's Cup
imbricately
embrocation
imbrication
imprecation
imprecatory
imprudently
umbriferous
impregnable
impregnably
ombrogenous
amorphously
Omar Khayyám
embroiderer
amerciament
embroilment
umbrella fir
umbrella-ant
Emerald City
Emerald Isle
emerald moth
emerald type
amaranthine
embryonated
embryogenic
embryologic
impropriate
impropriety
emery powder
ambrosially
impressible
impressment
impresarios
smart-ticket
umbratilous
amorousness
improvident
improvement
improvingly
improvisate
improve upon
smartypants
smarty-boots
amuse-bouche
amuse-gueule
emasculator
amusiveness
ametabolism
imitability
ametabolous
smithereens
smother mate
empty-headed
empty-handed
empty-nester
emotionable
emotionally
emotionless
emetophobia
amatorially
smithsonite
imitatively
amateurship
amativeness
emotiveness
Empty Vessel
amethystine
ambuscadoes
smouldering
ampullosity
impugnation
immunogenic
immunologic
immunotoxic
immunotoxin
immunoassay
amour-propre
impuissance
impulsively
amoxycillin
empyreumata
amazon-stone
unpalatable
unpalatably
unhazardous
Angara River
incapacious
Anna Pavlova
unparagoned
enjambement
unharboured
unmatchable
unwatchable
unmasculine
enhancement
incarcerate
unsandalled
unpardoning
unhandiness
incardinate
unwandering
incalescent
annabergite
unravelling
unravelment
untamedness
ansate cross
engaged tone
ungazed upon
infangthief
ensanguined
enlargement
enlarge upon
unpathwayed
unfashioned
✧ingathering
inhabitance
inhabitancy
unnavigated
inhabitable
innavigable
innavigably
unhabitable
unnavigable
unsatisfied
invalidhood
unsatirical
unmalicious
en papillote
invalidness
inhabitress
insatiately
unsatiating
unhackneyed
intagliated
unmalleable
uncalled-for
entablement
unfailingly
ungallantly
unmanliness
unballasted
entablature
ungarmented
unharmfully
undauntable
unpaintable
incarnadine
undauntedly
untaintedly
unjaundiced
encarnalise
encarnalize
uncanniness
ungarnished
unharnessed
untarnished
unvarnished
✧incarnation
uncanonical
uncanonised
uncanonized
unlaborious
Anna Comnena
unsavourily
unlabouring
unfavourite
unhappiness
unmarriable
unbarricade
unwarranted
unpatriotic
encapsidate
encapsulate
incapsulate
unpassioned
ondansetron
enfant gâtée
infanticide
infantilism
infantility
unpatterned
unfaltering
incantation
incantatory
infantryman
infantrymen
unsaturated
unnaturally
insalubrity
infatuation
incarvillea
unharvested
an easy touch
inobedience
in a bad light
inobservant
unobservant
unobserving
snobography
enabling act
inebriation
unabolished
unabrogated
unobnoxious
snobbocracy
ink-blot test
Anabaptists
inobtrusive
unobtrusive
in abstracto
unscratched
knock around
sneck drawer
knocked-down
knickerless
Anacreontic
snickersnee
enucleation
unscheduled
knock for six
inscribable
inscription
inscriptive
knick-knacky
knuckleball
knuckle-bone
knuckle down
knuckle-head
unicolorate
unicolorous
anacoluthia
anacoluthic
anacoluthon
inoculation
inoculatory
insculpture
inoculative
unicellular
unicoloured
onychomancy
anecdotally
unscholarly
onychophagy
Onychophora
anecdotical
snick or snee
knock on wood
Enoch Powell
unicorn-moth
anachronism
anachronous
knock-rating
unscissored
inscrutable
inscrutably
unaccusable
unaccusably
inedibility
inadvertent
inadvisable
unadvisable
unadvisably
unadvisedly
unidiomatic
inadaptable
unadaptable
anadiplosis
unaddressed
inodorously
one-day match
unseparated
antenatally
inseparable
inseparably
unget-at-able
ungetatable
unseparable
undebauched
undemanding
unregarding
unrewarding
unveracious
interallied
unrecalling
under a cloud
unremaining
interatomic
knee-capping
kneecapping
under arrest
interactant
interaction
underaction
interactive
underbearer
interbedded
underbidder
underbudget
underbreath
underbridge
under-bonnet
underbitten
interchange
undercharge
unpeaceable
unreachable
unteachable
intercedent
undescribed
unperceived
intercalary
intercalate
unwelcomely
unwelcoming
intercensal
under canvas
undescended
unrescinded
unmercenary
intercooled
intercooler
underclothe
intercepter
interceptor
intercostal
intercessor
intercrural
intercourse
undercovert
interdealer
interdictor
under-driven
unfeudalise
unfeudalize
underdamper
interdental
unbendingly
unheedingly
unreadiness
interdepend
under duress
infeudation
unheedfully
unneedfully
incendivity
undelegated
inseverable

uncongenial
unforgotten
incongruent
incongruity
incongruous
unforgiving
in mothballs
into the blue
endophagous
anno Christi
endothelial
endochylous
endothelium
into thin air
Indo-Chinese
endothermic
entophytous
incogitancy
unmotivated
incogitable
indomitable
indomitably
innominable
Intoximeter®
intoximeter
unpolitical
unsolicited
unsocialism
unsociality
endomitosis
encomiastic
innoxiously
unlooked-for
uncollected
enfouldered
ennoblement
ungodliness
endoplasmic
endoplastic
incommodity
informality
in commendam
uncommended
untormented
informatics
in committee
uncommitted
unformatted
information
informatory
informative
uncountable
unsoundable
unwoundable
unconnected
unboundedly
unfoundedly
unsoundness
incognisant
unconniving
incognizant
incoronated
antonomasia
entomophagy
entomophily
oncological
ontological
endomorphic
endodontics
uncompacted
uncompleted
incompliant
uncompliant
Anton Piller
uncompelled
uncompanied
incorporeal
endospermic
incorporall
incorporate
incomposite
incompetent
uncomplying
unconquered
on your marks
uncorrected
incorrectly
uncourteous
encouraging
incoercible
Indo-Iranian
uncorrupted
endotrophic
incorruptly
unnourished
inconstancy
unmoistened
inconscient
inconscious
unconscious
endorsement
inconsonant
unpossessed
unmortgaged
unrooted out
unfortified
unmortified
uncontrived
uncontemned
incontinent
unsoftening
uncouthness
unfortunate
unportioned
uncontested
unmodulated
unpopulated
unpopularly
involucrate
involuntary
innocuously
unconvicted
involvement
unconvinced
unconverted
endocytosis
endocytotic
unspeakable
unspeakably
en spectacle
unspecified
inappetence
inappetency
unappealing
anaplerosis
anaplerotic
snapshooter
unsprinkled
unipolarity
anaphorical
unappointed
inopportune
inspiringly
unsparingly
unipersonal
unspiritual
inspiriting
inspiration
inspiratory
inoperative
inspirative
unoperative
unapproving
inspissated
inspissator
unapostolic
snap out of it
anaphylaxis
inequitable
inequitably
unequitable
unequivocal
entreatable
increasable
unbreakable
untreatable
André Agassi
undreamed-of
increaseful
intreatfull
unbreathing
unpreaching
inorganised
inorganized
unorganised
unorganized
entreatment
Andrea Doria
André Ampère
in great part
André Breton
intractable
intractably
untraceable
untractable
en brochette
unpractical
unpractised
infracostal
unprocessed
intricately
anfractuous
infructuous
unfructuous
incredulity
incredulous
intradermal
energetical
snorkelling
in order that
engraftment
unpreferred
unprofessed
unprofiting
intriguante
unoriginate
androgenous
androgynous
unorthodoxy
enarthrosis
anarchistic
anorthosite
undrainable
engrailment
entrainment
unprojected
engrammatic
ungrammatic
untrembling
untremulous
incremental
incriminate
encrimsoned
unpromising
intromitted
intromitter
incremation
undrinkable
unprintable
entrance fee
intrenchant
enfranchise
intrinsical
in principio
infrangible
infrangibly
in principle
on principle
intrepidity
André Previn
unprophetic
entry portal
infrequence
infrequency
incrassated
uncrossable
uncrushable
ungraspable
incrossbred
in arm's reach
encrustment
engrossment
entrustment
unpresuming
intrusively
intrasexual
unprotected
intrathecal
unbrotherly
ungratified
ens rationis
unprotested
ingratitude
onerousness
undriveable
unprovident
unprovoking
untravelled
unprevented
intravenous
introverted
untraversed
energy level
inescapable
inescapably
unescapable
unashamedly
in a small way
unusualness
anisocercal
aniseed ball
inessential
unessential
unassertive
Inns of Court
unaspirated
gnostically
inestimable
inestimably
unassisting
Anish Kapoor
anisomerous
anastomoses
anastomosis
anastomotic
uniserially
angst-ridden
anisotropic
inusitation
unisexually
gnatcatcher
initial cell
initial caps
unsteadfast
initialling
unattainted
instability
gnotobiosis
gnotobiotic
inutterable
unutterable
unutterably
en attendant
unattending
instreaming
unattempted
and then some
inattention
inattentive
unattentive
instigation
instigative
snatch-thief
in at the kill
snatch block
snatchingly
snatch squad
snatch-purse
unstainable
anything but
unstaidness
installment
instantiate
instinctual
instinctive
gnathonical
unstoppable
unstoppably
unit-pricing
unitisation
instatement
institorial
institution
institutist
institutive
instaurator
unstaunched
instruction
instructive
snotty-nosed
unitization
pneumathode
pneumatical
incunabular
incunabulum
encumbrance
inturbidate
snout beetle
unhusbanded
incumbently
unpurchased
annunciator
unquickened
unsucceeded
Angus Calder
unguiculate
inculcation
inculcatory
inculcative
unsuccoured
in due course
unsubduable
infundibula
input device
innumerable
innumerably
insuperable
insuperably
intumescent
en pure perte
unqueenlike
unquietness
indumentums
untunefully
insufflator
unfulfilled
indulgently
unvulgarise
unvulgarize
ingurgitate
inauthentic
unauthentic
unmutilated
indubitable
indubitably
unmusically
injudicious
unguligrade
incuriosity
infuriating
infuriation
incuriously
injuriously
undutifully
unsubjected
uncuckolded
unluckiness
in duplicate
induplicate
unqualified
annual rings
in full blast
inquilinism
inquilinity
inquilinous
unpublished
unqualitied
in full swing
Angus McBean
unaugmented
unsubmerged
unmurmuring
unquantised
unquantized
unburnished
unfurnished

inquination
pneumonitis
input/output
unsuspected
on suspicion
unsuspicion
unsurprised
unsuspended
unsupported
unsurpassed
inculpation
inculpatory
unguardedly
unhurriedly
inquire into
inquiringly
inquirendos
unguerdoned
enquiration
innutrition
inquiration
in substance
unsubscribe
inquisition
inquisitive
unburthened
unjustified
uncurtailed
uncurtained
unsustained
industrials
industrious
inductility
insultingly
inductional
intuitional
unhurtfully
inductively
intuitively
intuitivism
inductivity
inaugurator
unluxuriant
unluxurious
incurvation
incurvature
Angus Wilson
unevidenced
unavailable
unavailably
unavoidable
unavoidably
unovulatory
univalvular
unavertable
universally
on every hand
unavertible
knavishness
snowed under
unsweetened
snow leopard
know who's who
unawakening
snowblading
unswallowed
knowing card
angwantibos
intwinement
knowingness
snow-goggles

know-nothing
snowboarder
one-worldism
answerphone
unawareness
snow-dropper
snowsurfing
snow bunting
know by sight
one-way glass
unexcavated
inexhausted
unexhausted
inexecrable
inexactness
inexecution
inexpedient
unexperient
inextension
inexpensive
unexpensive
inexpectant
unexpectant
inexcitable
unexcitable
unexplained
unexploited
unexclusive
Anaximander
unexercised
unexpressed
inexistence
inexcusable
inexcusably
in by the week
unsyllabled
undyingness
Andy Gregory
encystation
not a patch on
non-academic
solanaceous
roman à thèse
roman à clefs
not a sausage
royal assent
Bonapartean
local action
Bonapartism
Bonapartist
Polacanthus
Mozambiquan
comancheros
monarchical
local colour
Roman cement
Roman candle
coparcenary
coparcenery
tobacconist
tobacco pipe
polar circle
Howard Hawks
Gog and Magog
dot and carry
Donald Dewar
Tom and Jerry
fox and geese
moral defeat
now and again
Ronald Biggs

Donald Soper
you and yours
do's and don'ts
bow and arrow
solar energy
nonagesimal
Monadelphia
Roman Empire
Bonaventure
roman fleuve
coral flower
polar forces
vox angelica
kohanga reos
potash water
notaphilism
notaphilist
foraminated
boracic acid
botanically
localisable
localizable
nomadically
somatically
totalisator
totalizator
Loganiaceae
somatic cell
polariscope
polarimeter
solarimeter
polarimetry
coraciiform
logarithmic
foraminifer
toga virilis
for a kick-off
tomatilloes
coral island
Moravianism
Novatianism
Novatianist
Rotarianism
not a bit of it
Horatio Ross
voraciously
for all I care
coralliform
polar lights
coralloidal
lovableness
movableness
notableness
womanliness
focal length
non-allergic
go ballistic
Royal Lytham
Mohammed Ali
God-almighty
Locarno Pact
Johannes Rau
Roman nettle
potato salad
botanomancy
tomato sauce
potato scone
somatogenic
somatomedin
potamogeton
potato chips

bona mobilia
Monaco-Ville
moratoriums
somatoplasm
somatologic
somatotonia
somatotonic
potato bogle
potato apple
Romano Prodi
local option
royal octavo
solar plexus
bog asphodel
coram populo
royal purple
royal quarto
not a problem
soda cracker
total recall
dolabriform
moral rights
non-abrasive
local search
potass water
Woman's Realm
so far so good
bolas spider
Roman sorrel
solar system
loyalty card
monasticism
romanticise
✧romanticism
romanticist
romanticize
cobalt bloom
royal tennis
monasterial
woman-vested
rotary index
rotary press
forbearance
Bombacaceae
corbiculate
forbiddance
forbiddenly
double-faced
corbie gable
double eagle
double fault
double-fault
double-edged
double helix
hobbledehoy
double agent
double-check
double-shade
doublethink
double-sharp
double-lived
double-digit
double first
hobble skirt
double-click
double bluff
double-blind
double-ender
double-entry
double bogey
double doors

wobble board
doublespeak
double-space
double spare
double cream
double trill
double-cross
womb-leasing
God bless you!
cobblestone
corbie-steps
double-stout
double Dutch
double-quick
Robbie Burns
morbiferous
comb binding
corbel table
non-believer
doubtlessly
bombilation
lobby-member
Sorbonnical
bonbonnière
bombination
combination
combinatory
combinative
sorbo rubber
Bobby Robson
Fosbury flop
borborygmic
borborygmus
Norbertines
bombardment
Dogberrydom
Robber Synod
Dogberryism
combustible
combustious
lobby system
god-botherer
tolbutamide
not bat an eye
cowboy boots
tomboyishly
nonchalance
concealable
Bob Cratchit
concealment
ponce around
couch a spear
Bob Champion
torchbearer
forcibility
concubinage
concubinary
concubitant
touch bottom
forced march
coccidiosis
concrescent
concrete art
zoochemical
conceivable
conceivably
conceitedly
touch-in-goal
coaching inn
non-clinical
conceitless

monchiquite
conciliable
conciliator
concolorate
concolorous
tow-coloured
Roy Campbell
coxcombical
bon camarade
concomitant
volcanic ash
volcanicity
volcanic mud
concentered
volcanology
forcing-pump
concentring
concentrate
you can't talk
coach-office
torchon lace
hot cross bun
zoocephalic
conceptacle
concipiency
conceptious
forcipation
couch potato
conceptuses
concernancy
concordance
concertante
no-score draw
concurrence
concurrency
concernedly
concert-goer
touch rugger
concert hall
concertinos
concernment
bon chrétien
torch-staves
Lou Costello
vouchsafing
concessible
torch singer
conciseness
touch screen
touch-screen
concatenate
non-Catholic
touch-typing
touch-typist
touchy-feely
road manager
wood warbler
cold harbour
Lord marcher
coadjacency
cold cathode
wood naphtha
bond-washing
wood sanicle
Gordian knot
Lord Harlech
word-painter
cordwainery
good manners
cordialness
loadsamoney

Lord Fairfax
bondmanship
to advantage
good-natured
woodcarving
conductance
road scraper
food science
Pondicherry
conductible
conducement
conducingly
Lord Scarman
conductress
coeducation
bonded store
poodle-faker
soldier crab
Boodle's Club
cold welding
road-mending
gold reserve
word-perfect
Lord Renfrew
Goldbergian
goods engine
toddlerhood
bowdleriser
bowdlerizer
Lord Jenkins
soldierlike
good feeling
Lord Denning
Good Templar
cold-hearted
load-bearing
soldiership
top dressing
bold-beating
gold-beating
bond-service
bondservant
good heavens
good offices
words fail me
Lord of hosts
word-of-mouth
nom de guerre
hold against
condignness
hold the belt
load the dice
hold the fort
hold the line
Lord Thomson
hold the road
Woody Herman
hold the ring
wood vinegar
gold-digging
cold-without
Hondo Island
Lord Winston
word picture
condolement
condylomata
condolences
cold-blooded
wood alcohol
gold-plating
rondolettos
condolatory
Lord Olivier
non-delivery
condemnable
Joe DiMaggio
condominium
goldsmithry
Gordon Banks
condensable
golden eagle
wooden walls
loading coil
nodding duck
folding door
wooden wedge
golden hello
goldenberry
Londonderry
hold in check
golden chain
golden share
Golden Globe
golden oldie
wood anemone
Golden Horde
golden bough
golden goose
wooden horse
wooden spoon
✧London pride
Gordon Craig
zoodendrium
Gordon Brown
folding seat
hold one's jaw
hold one's own
coadunation
condonation
Golden State
Gordonstoun
coadunative
Bogdanovich
golden syrup
Lord Robbins
Lord Cowdrey
roadholding
cold comfort
road-hoggish
Voodoo Chile
good-looking
cold-moulded
good-morning
voodooistic
loudmouthed
word for word
Lord's Prayer
loudspeaker
good spirits
toad-spotted
toad spittle
wonder about
road pricing
bordered pit
woodcreeper
Ford Prefect
Lord Erskine
powder flask
Lord Grimond
Lord Wrangel
ponderingly
wonderingly
ponderosity
good-brother
wood-fretter
ponderation
ponderously
wonderfully
Lord Provost
condisciple
wordishness
Lord's Supper
nondescript
bold as brass
goddess-ship
rood-steeple
condottiere
condottieri
woody-tongue
conditional
conditioned
conditioner
cold storage
soldatesque
Woodruff key
goddaughter
Lord Bullock
coadjutress
Lord Russell
good hunting!
woodcutting
word-puzzler
non-dividing
good-evening
Joy Division
wood swallow
molecatcher
bower-anchor
love handles
Dodecandria
dodecaphony
rope machine
moderations
home banking
rope-walking
dovetail saw
pole-vaulter
dovetailing
forepayment
forewarning
more majorum
rose campion
foremastman
dodecastyle
foley artist
Dodecagynia
honey badger
loveability
moveability
money broker
power broker
Moses basket
cover charge
ion-exchange
nomenclator
Rosencrantz
honeycombed
Roger Corman
power-driven
Roy Eldridge
Poseidonian
molendinary
power-diving
foreseeable
co-dependant
co-dependent
forereading
home-defence
lower eyelid
sovereignly
sovereignty
fore-recited
joie de vivre
for evermore
forevermore
home-keeping
no fewer than
non-electric
non-election
novelettish
novelettist
non-elective
come between
come off best
power factor
comet-finder
honey fungus
money for jam
foreign bill
vote against
foreignness
come a gutser
Joseph Haydn
Joseph Banks
rose-cheeked
Joseph Henry
Joseph Beuys
none the less
nonetheless
Joseph Smith
forethinker
josephinite
Joseph Losey
come through
lose the plot
foreshorten
code-sharing
zone therapy
come what may
somewhither
forethought
Joseph Lyons
polemically
tonetically
Lobeliaceae
home circuit
foresighted
soteriology
Coney Island
Gorée Island
Women in Love
rose diamond
foresignify
✧bohemianism
Côte d'Ivoire
nose-nippers
non-existent
tone picture
Mohenjo-daro
hotel-keeper
honey locust
dole-bludger
moneylender
tone cluster
powerlessly
foreclosure
role-playing
hogen-mogens
moneymaking
sober-minded
coterminant
coterminate
coterminous
honeymooner
honeymoon in
money market
homeomorphy
homeomerous
home-and-away
modern dance
Modern Latin
someone else
home-and-home
come unglued
more and more
love-in-a-mist
governorate
lose one's rag
lose one's way
modernistic
lose oneself
come unstuck
foreknowing
vomeronasal
forevouched
gobe-mouches
rosewood oil
comedogenic
come to terms
come to a head
come to light
Wole Soyinka
homeworking
mode-locking
gone gosling
come to blows
foretopmast
non-economic
Tower of Pisa
come to grief
come to grips
ropes of sand
tone control
come forward
comeuppance
coleopteral
coleopteran
coleopteron
so help me God
Robespierre
fore-spurrer
✧nosey parker
none-sparing
honey possum
homeopathic
code-breaker
mole cricket
bone-breccia
home-crofter
coleorrhiza
coleorhizae
mole drainer
Rose Tremain
pomegranate
voyeuristic
homeostasis
homeostatic
honey-sucker
honey-suckle
honeysuckle
money spider
sober-suited
doveishness
no reason but
power shovel
boxer shorts
cover shorts
money's-worth
money supply
power series
homesteader
potentiated
potentially
comestibles
money to burn
rodenticide
rover ticket
domesticise
domesticate
domesticity
domesticize
Robert Remak
home stretch
Robert Cecil
forestaller
rodent ulcer
Robert Blake
poverty line
Robert Clive
Robert Ensor
honest Injun
Robert Cohan
Robert Hooke
Robert Boyle
honest-to-God
Robert Bruce
momentarily
Robert Frost
Robert Brown
poverty trap
fomentation
forestation
molestation
momentously
Robert Burns
molecularly
poke mullock
dolefulness
hopefulness
forequarter
come out with
honey-waggon
lonely heart
lonely-heart
more by token
Comedy Store
non-feasance
non-flam film
conflagrant
conflagrate
confabulate
forficulate
Corfe Castle
confidently
confidingly
✧confederacy

✧confederate
coffee-maker
coffee table
Pomfret cake
coffee berry
toffee-nosed
coffee house
toffee apple
coffee break
coffee stall
configurate
dogfighting
wolf whistle
wolf-whistle
forfeitable
forfeit bail
roi fainéant
coefficient
conflicting
confliction
conflictive
soufflé dish
gonfalonier
roofing felt
confineless
confinement
god-forsaken
comfortable
comfortably
conferrable
confirmable
conformable
conformably
confirmator
conformator
confarreate
comfortless
comfort zone
confiscable
confiscator
pop-fastener
confessedly
pop festival
confusingly
offishness
confutement
confutation
confutative
confound him
confound you
forfoughten
confluently
congealable
long paddock
Douglas Dunn
Douglas Haig
Douglas Hurd
oographist
ongealment
ong Barnaby
ong-waisted
oografting
obgoblinry
ough-coated
ough collie
ough Corrib
ouge Dragon
ongé d'élire
r God's sake
ongregated
ng weekend

rouge-et-noir
toggle joint
boogie board
longwearing
Congressman
long measure
rough-footed
Song of Songs
Song of my Cid
rough-handle
long-visaged
long-sighted
lodge-keeper
rough-legged
long-clothes
coagulation
congelation
coagulatory
coagulative
long-playing
tough-minded
congenially
zoogonidium
Morgan le Fay
longanimity
longanimous
congenerous
loggan-stone
lodging turn
morgenstern
longinquity
Don Giovanni
long-tongued
doggy-paddle
song sparrow
Gongoristic
congestible
doggishness
hoggishness
rough-spoken
rough string
forgettable
forget-me-not
sought after
doughtiness
forgetfully
long hundred
congruently
long-running
songfulness
long-purples
long jumping
congruously
not give a fig
forgiveness
Rosh Hashana
Joshua Nkomo
Loch Rannoch
Sophia Loren
Loch Katrine
lophobranch
bothy ballad
Lochaber axe
Gothic novel
Sothic cycle
Bodhidharma
do the dishes
Noah Webster
Josh Gifford
to the letter
to the marrow

nothing-gift
Cochin-China
nothing in it
nothingness
doch-an-doris
to think of it
nothing to it
mother-naked
mother water
not harm a fly
rother-beast
Mother of God
mother's help
mother-right
fothergilla
mother's mark
mother-in-law
nowhere near
non-harmonic
motherboard
mothercraft
mother's ruin
mothers' ruin
mothers-to-be
botheration
do the rounds
go the rounds
sophistical
Bodhisattva
moshav ovdim
Louis Aragon
conical buoy
holiday camp
tonic accent
Monica Seles
nominatival
dominations
totipalmate
hog in armour
comicalness
logicalness
corivalship
Louis B Mayer
Boris Becker
sociability
Conisbrough
Politbureau
solid colour
vociferance
vociferator
go like a bomb
mobile phone
homiletical
policewoman
police force
motive power
noticeboard
police-court
domineering
no time at all
police state
nociceptive
police burgh
police-judge
Jodie Foster
yogic flying
toning table
Moringaceae
coming-of-age
doting-piece
towing-bitts

foliage leaf
boxing glove
posing pouch
joking apart
joking aside
poking-stick
poting-stick
coping-stone
toxiphobiac
go with a bang
toxiphagous
solid-hoofed
mobilisable
mobilizable
politically
domiciliary
domiciliate
politicking
codicillary
Dominion Day
volitionary
Socinianise
Socinianism
Socinianize
solidifying
Louis Jouvet
Louis Leakey
sociologese
sociologism
sociologist
social whale
docibleness
nonillionth
socialistic
solifluxion
Lorin Maazel
sodium amide
solid matter
goniometric
sociometric
doli incapax
notionalist
Aonian fount
cosignatory
toxicomania
totipotency
toxicogenic
gonimoblast
toxicologic
monitorship
conirostral
soliloquise
soliloquist
soliloquize
sociopathic
Louis-Quinze
Rosicrucian
poliorcetic
comic relief
positronium
for instance
non-issuable
Ionic school
solipsistic
Möbius strip
logistician
Louis-Treize
goliath frog
goniatitoid
moribundity
copiousness

noxiousness
moxibustion
pomiculture
non-invasive
conjectural
conjecturer
conjugality
conjugating
conjugation
conjugative
box junction
conjunction
conjuncture
conjunctiva
conjunctive
Jonjo O'Neill
conjure away
conjurement
conjuration
cork cambium
workwatcher
mock saffron
look daggers
cocktail bar
rock wallaby
workmanlike
Rockhampton
dock-warrant
workmanship
workability
book-account
polka-dotted
cook-general
cockleshell
cookie-shine
bookselling
mock-heroics
bookkeeping
book-learned
rock leather
Book of Nahum
Book of Micah
Book of Jonah
book of words
Book of Hosea
Book of Tobit
book of hours
work against
rock the boat
workaholism
book through
work through
look the part
work-sharing
nook-shotten
bookbinding
bookbindery
York Minster
Volkskammer
poikilocyte
Volkslieder
cock-a-leekie
cockaleekie
hook-climber
rock climber
working-beam
cock-and-bull
mockingbird
working edge
working face
working girl

booking hall
Rock English
working-over
rock and roll
rocking tool
working week
sockdolager
work wonders
mock-modesty
sockdoliger
rock-forming
sockdologer
rock lobster
you-know-what
lock forward
look forward
cock-sparrow
rock sparrow
rock breaker
rocker panel
cookery-book
rock'n'roller
rocker cover
Cockermouth
Booker Prize
rock crystal
look askance
Cook Islands
bookishness
monkishness
dockisation
rocket range
Korky the Cat
pocketphone
pocket-piece
pocket-sized
rocket plane
pocket-glass
Folketinget
pocket knife
pocket money
rocket motor
pocket mouse
workstation
pork-butcher
pock-pudding
Hock Tuesday
Jocky Wilson
monkey about
cockeyed bob
donkey derby
monkey wheel
monkey shine
monkey block
monkey-gland
monkey board
monkey bread
monkey-grass
jockey strap
hockey stick
dockization
wool-carding
foolhardise
foolhardize
so please you
cool-tankard
pollyannish
colleaguing
world-beater
collaborate
collectanea

collectable
mollycoddle
soil science
collectedly
collectible
collections
folliculose
folliculous
dolly camera
mould-candle
pop-lacrosse
coal scuttle
collocation
collocutory
boiled shirt
poule de luxe
boiled sweet
boulder clay
goal-tending
woollen mill
fool's errand
soul-fearing
wool-bearing
mould-facing
toplofticel
world-famous
collegianer
collagenase
hooliganism
collagenous
colligation
colligative
Holly Hunter
coal-whipper
goalkicking
soul-killing
soul-sleeper
hoplologist
worldliness
worldly-wise
loblolly bay
loblolly-boy
Coulommiers
noble-minded
collembolan
coulometric
collimation
cooling card
collenchyma
goblin shark
bowline knot
rolling mill
codling moth
rolling news
pollen count
pollen grain
coplanarity
Hollands gin
bowling shoe
pollination
Howling Wolf
go along with
wool-combing
foul-mouthed
collapsable
collapsible
lollipop man
Coelophysis
colliquable
colloquiums
boilermaker
world record
roller derby
poultry-farm
forlorn hope
roller skate
roller-skate
Rollerblade®
rollerblade
rollerblind
boilerplate
coal-trimmer
forlornness
roller towel
coelurosaur
soul brother
wool-growing
poultry yard
coalescence
dolly switch
dollishness
foolishness
godlessness
joblessness
joylessness
toplessness
worlds apart
World Series
noble savage
collusively
toilet paper
toilet water
toilet table
go all the way
collet chuck
toilet glass
toilet cloth
coalitional
coalitioner
toilet cover
wool-stapler
soulfulness
Dolly Varden
cod-liver oil
follow-board
woolly aphis
doomwatcher
Tommy Atkins
cosmocratic
not much chop
Don McCullin
Tommy Cooper
formicaries
formicarium
formication
homme de bien
Tommy Dorsey
commodities
form teacher
worm gearing
room service
cosmography
zoomagnetic
cosmogonist
Noam Chomsky
comme il faut
room-divider
formal cause
cosmologist
hot-melt glue
pommel horse
formularise
formularize
formalistic
formulation
Tommy Lawton
commemorate
common panda
commendable
commendably
commensally
commendator
commentator
boom and bust
communicant
communicate
tormentedly
common metre
common sense
commonsense
common chord
common-shore
Gormenghast
common viper
gormandiser
gormandizer
commonplace
command line
communalise
communalism
communalist
commonality
communalize
commandment
common forms
command post
Norman cross
common prawn
communistic
Normanesque
common stock
common stair
Norman Stone
commination
comminution
comminatory
comminative
cosmopolite
cormophytic
Kommersbuch
zoomorphism
Bob Mortimer
non-marrying
commissaire
cosmosphere
commiserate
solmisation
commissural
committable
cosmetician
cosmeticise
cosmeticism
cosmeticize
cosmothetic
cosmotheism
cosmetology
dogmatology
non-metallic
commotional
formational
commutation
commutative
normatively
Tommy Walker
solmization
Mount Ararat
horn balance
John Cadbury
John Lambert
John Barbour
John Barclay
John Hancock
roundarched
John Tavener
John Habgood
foundations
Point-a-Pitre
John Rackham
John Hawkins
John Hawkyns
corneal lens
down payment
Joan Hammond
mountain cat
fountain pen
mountain dew
mountaineer
mountain tea
mountain-top
John Manners
horn-madness
moon-madness
mountain ash
mountainous
John Fairfax
Downpatrick
John Marston
John Bartram
corn earworm
connubially
round-backed
lo and behold
go one better
Mountbatten
coenobitism
bonne bouche
bonne chance
connectable
connectedly
cornice-hook
connectible
connections
Connecticut
corniculate
John McEnroe
cornucopian
cornice-pole
townscaping
cornice-rail
cornice ring
Doune Castle
fornication
horned cairn
John-a-dreams
John o'dreams
horned viper
Bonny Dundee
horned poppy
horned horse
point d'appui
point-device
point-devise
countenance
mountenance
pointed arch
John Le Carré
counterbuff
counterbond
counterblow
counterbore
Mount Elbert
counterbase
Mount Elbrus
horn mercury
counter-cast
counterdraw
John Kendrew
John F Enders
coinherence
counterfect
counterfeit
counterfoil
counterfort
counter-glow
coinheritor
John Nevison
Wounded Knee
counselling
countermand
countermine
John Redmond
Mount Egmont
countermark
countermure
countermove
John Tenniel
pointedness
roundedness
Pointe-Noire
counterpace
counterplea
counterpane
counter-plot
counterpart
downhearted
counter-roll
counterseal
John Webster
countersign
countersink
countersunk
counter-time
down-setting
town meeting
counter-turn
lounge music
bounteously
counter-view
countervail
counter-vote
John Redwood
counter-work
counterwork
John of Gaunt
corniferous
somniferous
young fustic
pornography
cornigerous
non-negative
round headed
corn shucker
join the club
Mount Hudson
downshifter
down the line
down-the-line
Down the Mine
horny-handed
zoanthropic
Eoanthropus
down the road
zoantharian
John Charles
down the wind
John Bircher
coincidence
coincidency
sounding rod
sounding out
downlighter
moonlighter
John Citizen
✧pointillism
pointillist
John Gielgud
John Simpson
connoisseur
down-sitting
bountifully
pound-keeper
John Skelton
round-leaved
John Cleland
town planner
hornblendic
somnolently
corn plaster
pointlessly
soundlessly
Sonny Liston
John Smeaton
downy mildew
cognominate
connumerate
pound-master
somnambular
somnambulic
morning coat
morning gift
corn in Egypt
morning gown
town and gown
coenenchyma
morning-land
morning roll
morning room
✧morning star
morningtide
down to earth
down-to-earth
moon goddess
John Sotheby
John Toshack
Johnsoniana
loan-society
found object
John Collins
John Dowland
town council
John Company
corncob pipe
John Boorman
John Vorster
point of sale
point-of-sale

John Montagu
point of view
townspeople
corn spurrey
young person
coin a phrase
country code
corn-cracker
country club
downtrodden
Bognor Regis
corner teeth
countrified
countryfied
country-folk
John Profumo
Country Life
country rock
country-rock
country seat
John Grisham
countryside
cornerstone
country town
down-draught
countrywide
Corn Islands
sound shadow
to one's taste
John Ashbery
Cornish clay
connascence
connascency
hounds-berry
cognoscente
cognoscenti
do one's thing
John a-Stiles
cognoscible
do one's block
Donna Summer
Mount Sangay
onnishness
ohn Osborne
lo one's worst
ound's-tooth
going strong
ound system
lo one's stuff
oint source
ohn a-Styles
onnet laird
onnet-piece
oint tenant
ognateness
ognitional
onnet-rouge
ornotopian
on-naturals
ound tissue
onnotation
onnotative
ognitively
ognitivism
ognitivity
oint toward
oinsurance
hn Lubbock
ornhusking
hn Pullman
hn Bullism
John Russell
John Surtees
corn bunting
hornswoggle
pound weight
town dweller
round-winged
round window
connexional
mornay sauce
Rodney Marsh
John Wyndham
Johnny Bench
John Lydgate
county court
monocardian
logopaedics
logodaedaly
monovalence
monovalency
homogametic
logomachist
son of a bitch
cologarithm
Homo habilis
honorariums
Homo sapiens
monocarpous
coronagraph
monolatrist
monolatrous
holocaustal
holocaustic
monodactyly
corona lucis
motor-bandit
cocoa butter
horoscopist
motor-driven
homogenesis
homogenetic
monogenesis
monogenetic
homogeneity
homogeneous
go to lengths
for one thing
Dolores Haze
homogeniser
homogenizer
jocoserious
colonelling
Monodelphia
monodelphic
top one's part
holohedrism
cotoneaster
colonelship
coronership
so mote I thee
holobenthic
homocentric
go-to-meeting
locorestive
tobogganing
tobogganist
monothecous
go to the dogs
monophagous
monophthong
homothallic
podophyllin
✧monothelism
✧monothelete
✧monothelite
toxophilite
Podophyllum
homophonous
monochromat
monochromic
holothurian
homothermal
notochordal
homothermic
Nototherium
monochasial
✧monophysite
monochasium
holophytism
go to the wall
go to the wars
moronically
colorimeter
colorimetry
loco disease
monolingual
honorifical
sodomitical
Novosibirsk
colonialism
colonialist
notoriously
corolliform
monoclinous
monoblepsis
holoblastic
homoblastic
homoplastic
toxoplasmic
motor-launch
go down a bomb
homoeopathy
gonococcoid
colonoscope
colonoscopy
homoeomeric
doxological
homological
horological
monological
nomological
nosological
pomological
posological
topological
monopoliser
monopolizer
homoeomorph
homomorphic
monomorphic
coronograph
homoiousian
rodomontade
monologuise
monologuist
monologuize
Monocotylae
homopolymer
ionospheric
homosporous
colour party
Zonotrichia
motor racing
Homo erectus
honours easy
colour wheel
colour phase
colour-blind
honours list
loxodromics
monogrammed
sojournment
Monotremata
colour index
gonorrhoeal
for our money
gonorrhoeic
logorrhoeic
colourpoint
honour-bound
honour-point
doxographer
horographer
logographer
monographer
nomographer
nosographer
sonographer
topographer
holographic
logographic
monographic
nomographic
nosographic
tomographic
topographic
colour a pipe
colour organ
monocrystal
colouristic
colouration
homoerotism
colour music
colourfully
colour guard
rotogravure
non obstante
coconscious
monopsonist
Zoroastrian
Soroptimist
homopterous
cohortative
monocularly
pococurante
coconut crab
doxorubicin
mononuclear
coconut milk
coconut palm
monoculture
nobody's fool
hop-o'-my-thumb
toponymical
homozygosis
homozygotic
monozygotic
monomyarian
monohydrate
compearance
complacence
complacency
zooplankton
complainant
complaining
complaisant
compact disc
compact disk
compactedly
compactness
torpedo boat
torpedo boom
corps d'élite
torpedinous
topped crude
torpedo tube
completable
compte rendu
complexness
coup de poing
coup de grâce
copple-crown
compression
compressure
low-pressure
compressive
copple-stone
loop of Henle
compaginate
coup the cran
loup-the-dyke
loop the loop
romp through
complicated
comprimario
dolphinaria
comprisable
soup kitchen
compliments
dolphinfish
coupling-box
Pompeian red
compliantly
non-priority
compellable
compulsitor
compilement
corpulently
pompelmoose
pompelmouse
compilation
compilatory
gospel music
companiable
compensable
compensator
compendiums
compendious
topping lift
go up in smoke
componental
companioned
compunction
rouping-wife
Comptometer®
morphogenic
hot property
compromiser
non-provided
soap boiling
morphologic
morphotropy
complotting
comportance
copper-faced
corporeally
compurgator
Cooper pairs
copper-beech
Cooper's hawk
non-partisan
comptroller
copperplate
corporality
compartment
comportment
coppersmith
copperworks
corporately
compo ration
co-operation
corporation
comparatist
corporatism
corporatist
comparative
co-operative
corporative
compassable
compass card
torpescence
compost heap
compossible
foppishness
rompishness
compass rose
compositely
composition
compositous
compositive
corpuscular
corpus iuris
Don Pasquale
poppet-valve
hospitaller
hospitalise
hospitality
hospitalize
competently
computerese
computerise
computerate
computerize
competition
compotation
computation
compotatory
competitive
computative
compound eye
pompousness
nonplussing
zoophytical
porphyritic
conquerable
torque meter
bouquetière
tonquin-bean
mosquito net
moor-band pan
gourmandise
gourmandism
go great guns
pourparlers

progenitive
dragoon-bird
Troglodytes
troglodytic
frigorifico
Gregarinida
Gregory Peck
progestogen
Bruges group
frigate bird
frightening
frighteners
bright spark
frightfully
drug-running
frugivorous
Brahma Samaj
Brahman bull
Brahmanical
orthoborate
✧prohibition
prohibitory
prohibitive
orthocentre
ortho-cousin
Orchidaceae
orchidology
orthodontia
orthodontic
orthodromic
orchid-house
arch-heretic
orthoepical
archaeology
Archie Moore
orchiectomy
orthography
archegonial
orthogenics
archegonium
archaically
brahmin bull
archdiocese
Brahminical
arch-villain
Archimedean
graham flour
Graham Gooch
graham bread
Graham Swift
archangelic
archenteron
urchin-shows
prehensible
arrhenotoky
arthropathy
arthroscope
arthroscopy
arthrodesis
archeometry
arthropodal
Brahmo Somaj
arthrospore
orthopraxis
orthopedics
orthopedist
orthopteran
orthopaedic
orthopteron
✧archipelago
orthophyric
arch-traitor
Arthur Kipps
Arthur Bliss
arch-prelate
Arthur Young
Arthur's Tomb
Arthur Evans
Arthur Wynne
orthostatic
orthostichy
orthoscopic
prehistoric
orchestrina
orchestrion
orchestrate
architraved
orthotropic
archdukedom
archduchess
irritatedly
urticaceous
urticarious
orbital road
dreikanters
ordinary ray
trailblazer
train-bearer
argie-bargie
trailbaston
artiodactyl
brain damage
pro indiviso
cruise about
arrivederci
trailer park
traineeship
trying plane
arris gutter
Ornithogaea
ornithology
Ornithopoda
ornithopter
freight shed
ornithosaur
prairie fowl
Arminianism
prairie wolf
artillerist
brainlessly
fruitlessly
pre-ignition
traitorhood
Arrigo Boito
traitorship
arbitrageur
Erwin Rommel
arbitrament
arbitrement
arbitrarily
arbitratrix
arbitration
brainsickly
Orbitsville
brains trust
brainteaser
articulated
orbiculares
orbicularis
articulable
orbicularly
articulator
projectment
pre-judicial
prejudicial
prejudicant
prejudicate
prejudgment
Trojan Women
Trojan horse
projet de loi
brake lining
broken meats
broken rhyme
broken music
prokaryotic
araliaceous
Grallatores
argle-bargle
drill-barrow
prelibation
prolocutrix
prolocution
prolificacy
prolificity
proliferate
proliferous
prolegomena
drill-harrow
drilling rig
drilling mud
brilliantly
oral history
trellis work
troll-my-dame
preliminary
drill-master
prolongable
proleptical
drill-plough
artlessness
prelusorily
drill string
prelusively
prolateness
proletarian
proletariat
preliterate
prelateship
oral hygiene
drum machine
grammatical
grammalogue
crème brulée
crème brûlée
gramicidin D
promycelium
eremacausis
premedicate
Tremadog Bay
aramid fibre
prima donnas
bromidrosis
premeditate
primaevally
trumpet call
trumpetfish
grummet-hole
Cromwellian
trammelling
trompe l'oeil
From Me to You
premiership
Dromaeosaur
trumpet tree
trumpet tone
trumpet wood
primigenial
primogenial
Bramah-press
trimming tab
from without
crémaillère
trombiculid
promulgator
bramble-bush
Primulaceae
tremblement
grumblingly
tremblingly
tremolandos
crumbliness
Mrs Malaprop
tremulously
trample upon
trump marine
tromometric
crimen falsi
drum and bass
graminicide
priming-iron
criminal law
criminology
criminalese
criminalise
criminalist
criminality
criminalize
prime number
prominently
bromination
crimination
premonition
criminatory
premonitory
criminative
premonitive
priming-wire
primrose way
from nowhere
trampoliner
prime of life
cramboclink
dromophobia
gramophonic
primiparity
primiparous
Bremerhaven
primary coil
primary cell
primary care
trimorphism
trimorphous
dram-drinker
drum printer
primariness
fremescence
promiseless
promisingly
trimestrial
primus stove
promiscuity
promiscuous
dramaticism
aromaticity
trimetrical
primatology
promotional
Trimetrogon
crematorial
dramaturgic
prematurely
prematurity
crematorium
primateship
promptitude
primitively
✧primitivism
primitivist
Premium Bond
brimfulness
premovement
premaxillae
Grammy Award
Gran Canaria
transandean
transandine
frontal lobe
transalpine
transaction
Grand Bahama
Trent Bridge
transceiver
transcriber
transcalent
arenicolous
Grand Cayman
Frank Dobson
transductor
Trinidadian
drink-driver
drunk-driver
transdermal
orange-tawny
Brandenburg
grande école
frondescent
bronze medal
orange pekoe
Grande-Terre
grande tenue
Frankenfood
Orange River
drunkenness
prince royal
Grangemouth
Grande Armée
iron-hearted
Grande Arche
orange-grass
Orange Prize
Princess Ida
bronzed skin
grandeeship
printer's pie
printer's ink
granted that
orange stick
craniectomy
transection
transeptate
trance music
transfigure
transfinite
transfer day
transferral
frankfurter
transfer fee
transferred
transferrer
transformed
transformer
transferrin
transfer RNA
transferase
graniferous
uriniferous
transfusion
transfusive
grandfather
transfixion
uranography
transgenics
Grenzgänger
transgender
crinigerous
branch water
wrong-headed
Granth Sahib
trench fever
French berry
French leave
French chalk
✧French white
French pitch
branch-pilot
French pleat
transhumant
trench knife
crankhandle
trenchantly
crunchiness
Frenchiness
bronchiolar
Frenchwoman
truncheoned
truncheoner
branchiopod
French toast
trench mouth
transhipper
French bread
trencher cap
trencherman
French fries
prong-horned
trencher-fed
French franc
French stick
French curve
frantically
principally
transitable
transit camp
Franciscans
transit duty
wringing wet
printing ink
transilient
fringilline
transiently
franticness
grandiosely
grandiosity
Francistown
transit visa

Franz Joseph
brand leader
crenellated
front-loaded
front-loader
translucent
granulocyte
translocate
granuliform
granulomata
translunary
franklinite
granularity
frontlessly
wranglesome
granolithic
trendle-tail
trindle-tail
trundle-tail
crenulation
granulation
translation
translatory
Brinell test
granulative
translative
wrong-minded
transmanche
prenominate
transmarine
Franz Mesmer
Grand Master
grandmaster
transmittal
grandmother
transmitted
transmitter
pruning bill
crane-necked
pruning hook
wrong number
grand-nephew
Trincomalee
francomania
grant of arms
cranioscopy
grand old man
craniometer
craniometry
front office
ironmongery
francophobe
francophile
francophone
iron-founder
craniognomy
iron-foundry
orang-outang
frontolysis
uranoplasty
transpadane
transpierce
frank-pledge
grand priory
ransponder
ransportal
ransported
ransporter
grandparent
ransparent
uriniparous

transposing
granophyric
front-ranker
front-runner
Iran-Iraq War
Brands Hatch
wring staves
trunksleeve
print-seller
trans-sonics
dronishness
Uranoscopus
brine shrimp
trendsetter
trans-sexual
transsexual
Frank Smythe
bring to bear
bring to book
granitiform
bring to heel
Trinity Hall
bring to life
bring to pass
Trinitarian
franc-tireur
Trinity term
graniteware
transuranic
L Ron Hubbard
pronouncing
gran turismo
tranquility
tranquilize
branfulness
brankursine
✧iron curtain
transvaluer
transversal
granivorous
transvestic
Grand Vizier
Bruno Walter
iron pyrites
brandy glass
Granny Smith
granny bonds
Frantz Fanon
arboraceous
Areopagitic
crookbacked
proof-charge
preoccupied
preoccupant
preoccupate
Ordos Desert
arborescent
Eriodendron
try one's hand
try one's luck
crookedness
Crookes tube
erroneously
Arno Penzias
Errol Garner
arrow-headed
creophagous
cryotherapy
eriophorous
cryophysics
cryobiology

creosote oil
bryological
oreological
arrow-poison
proof-puller
proofreader
armour-plate
areographic
oreographic
Brooks's Club
proof spirit
cryosurgeon
cryosurgery
Orson Welles
areosystile
preprandial
✧propranolol
prepubertal
prepackaged
drop a curtsy
trepidation
trepidatory
dropped arch
drap-de-Berry
prophethood
prophetical
tropaeolums
triple point
triple crown
prophetship
wrapped up in
triple event
prophesying
propagation
propagative
crapehanger
crepehanger
crapshooter
trapshooter
cryptically
graphically
graphic arts
dripping-pan
dripping wet
crappit-head
crappit-heid
triphibious
graphicness
trypsinogen
proprieties
proprietrix
Trappistine
proprietary
drape jacket
prepollence
prepollency
propylamine
crapulosity
propylitise
propylitize
crippleware
tropomyosin
crape myrtle
crepe myrtle
trypanocide
friponnerie
treponemata
trypanosome
prepunctual
trepanation
propinquity

Cryptogamia
cryptogamic
graphomania
trophotaxis
cryptorchid
cryptogenic
cryptomeria
drop-forging
tryptophane
graptolitic
cryptobiont
trophoblast
trophoplasm
graphologic
ora pro nobis
trophozoite
cryptograph
prop forward
tropophytic
proper-false
crêpe rubber
proper chant
proportions
tripersonal
preparation
preparatory
preparative
property man
property tax
troposphere
drop a stitch
pre-position
preposition
proposition
prepositive
crepuscular
propitiable
propitiator
tripetalous
crepitation
crepitative
Frappuccino®
drop-curtain
crop-dusting
tripe-visag'd
prophylaxis
triphyllous
trapeziform
trapezoidal
trapeziuses
triquetrous
Mrs Robinson
prerecorded
pruriginous
prorogation
prerogative
crystal ball
crustaceous
prismatical
prostatitis
crystalloid
crystalline
crystallise
crystallite
crystallize
Gresham's law
trespassing
cross action
crossbearer
fresh breeze
Ernst B Chain

Irish bridge
crossbanded
crossbarred
cross-border
trustbuster
frostbitten
press button
press-button
crossbowman
Irish coffee
cross colour
dress circle
crosscut saw
grass-cutter
prosecutrix
prosecution
cross cousin
crash course
drusy cavity
preside over
cross-dating
brissel-cock
Prester John
crossed line
Fresnel lens
cris de coeur
trusteeship
crescentade
prospecting
prospection
trust estate
prospective
Dresden ware
crestfallen
artsy-fartsy
Irish Guards
presagement
cross-garnet
crash-helmet
preschooler
grasshopper
bruschettas
prosthetics
prosthetist
prussic acid
drastically
eristically
prosaically
prescindent
cross-infect
trysting-day
tristichous
prestigious
Orust Island
presciently
Erastianism
Priscianist
prosaicness
Prussianise
Prussianism
Prussianize
grossièreté
prestissimo
prescission
prosciuttos
prostitutor
✧prusik sling
cross-leaved
trisyllabic
trisyllable
bristlebird

bristlecone
preselector
prosiliency
bristle-fern
cross-legged
trisulphide
bristliness
gristliness
dress-length
trestletree
bristletail
proselytise
proselytism
proselytize
bristle worm
trestlework
dressmaking
proso millet
brass monkey
presumingly
irksomeness
gross margin
presumption
presumptive
presume upon
presentable
presentably
present arms
pros and cons
prosenchyma
presentient
presentment
presentness
prison house
presanctify
Krasnoyarsk
press office
gressorious
Bristol-milk
cross-or-pile
Prestonpans
aristocracy
crescograph
press of sail
arms control
gross output
erysipeloid
gross profit
prosopopeia
dress parade
preservable
brass rubber
Droseraceae
dress-reform
Fraser River
Kris Kringle
grass-rooter
pre-stressed
frustrating
frustration
prostration
Fraserburgh
cross-stitch
dress-shield
brise-soleil
cross swords
brisés volés
Irish setter
cross-tining
brush turkey
Iris Murdoch

stereoblind
stereosonic
sternotribe
stereograph
stereoptics
stereotyped
stereotyper
stereotypic
iteroparity
iteroparous
storm petrel
star-crossed
storm-stayed
sternsheets
storm signal
Pterosauria
star-studded
storyteller
attritional
storm troops
storm-tossed
iteratively
sternutator
stirrup bone
stirrup dram
stirrup iron
stirrup pump
storm window
Starry Night
stoss and lee
Otis Redding
stasimorphy
stitchcraft
stately home
stateliness
statemented
state-monger
Mt Stromboli
stethoscope
stethoscopy
station hand
state of play
state prison
statesmanly
state school
statistical
stateswoman
statute book
statute mile
statutorily
Stourbridge
staunchable
Etruscology
staunchless
staunchness
à toute force
Struthiones
à tout hasard
St Kunigunde
at full blast
stauroscope
staurolitic
à tout propos
struttingly
attuitional
attuitively
St Augustine
stave-church
stove enamel
Stevie Smith
Steve Martin
stevengraph
Steve Paxton
at every turn
stewardship
ithyphallic
✧ithyphallus
stay the pace
funambulist
funambulate
subarboreal
sugar-coated
autarchical
mural circle
fun and games
cut and paste
cut and carve
out and about
human dynamo
cut and cover
cut and dried
subaudition
suraddition
out-and-outer
mutagenesis
Susan Faludi
subaffluent
sugar glider
fumaric acid
Fumariaceae
Lubavitcher
sugaring off
Mutabilitie
subaxillary
mutationist
subacidness
audaciously
Tut'ankhamun
suballiance
Human League
curableness
durableness
mutableness
tunableness
Muhammad Zia
Muhammad Ali
gum ammoniac
eudaemonics
eudaemonism
eudaemonist
human nature
Suzanne Vega
auxanometer
Butazolidin®
fumatoriums
sugar of lead
curatorship
Judas Priest
subaerially
human rights
subarration
sugar sifter
human shield
subassemble
subassembly
Susan Sontag
Judaisation
lunar theory
eubacterial
eubacterium
durante vita
✧judas window
eucalyptole
Judaization
turbocharge
outbreeding
tumblerfuls
bubble-shell
bubble under
burble point
tumble-drier
tumble-dryer
rumble strip
rubble stone
bumble-puppy
bulbiferous
humbuggable
lumbaginous
lumbricalis
outbuilding
tumbling box
Lumbricidae
zum Beispiel
✧mumbo-jumbos
rugby jersey
Turbellaria
✧rugby league
quibblingly
turbulently
gum benjamin
nubbing-cove
dumbing-down
husbandlike
husbandland
husbandless
turbine pump
rubbing post
turbination
dumbfounder
Cumbernauld
numbers game
rubber check
lubber's hole
bumbershoot
number eight
lubber fiend
lubber's line
rubber plant
number plate
turbo-ram-jet
Quiberon Bay
rubberiness
rubber goods
rubber-cored
numbers pool
rubber stamp
rubber-stamp
mulberry fig
rubbish heap
Rugby School
rumbustical
rumbustious
subbasement
surbasement
cut both ways
bulbousness
purchasable
purchase tax
purchase out
cunctatious
nutcrackers
Munchausen's
quick assets
bunch-backed
hunchbacked
Mulciberian
quick-change
Dutch cheese
Dutch clover
Dutch carpet
suicidology
succedaneum
suicide pact
butcherbird
punched card
muscle sense
Muschelkalk
butcher meat
luncheon-bar
muscle-bound
quicken-tree
punched tape
quick-freeze
quick-frozen
quick-firing
furciferous
dulcifluous
Munchhausen
Punchinello
punching-bag
subclinical
subcritical
punctilious
function key
junction box
functionary
functionate
auscultator
succulently
Dutch liquid
subchloride
muscularity
musculation
musculature
subcellular
subcultural
Durchlaucht
vulcanicity
vulcanology
subcontract
subcontrary
buccinatory
succinctory
puncto banco
outcrossing
susceptance
susceptible
susceptibly
turcopolier
Turcophobia
nuncupation
nuncupatory
nuncupative
subcapsular
subcardinal
subcortical
gun carriage
pulchritude
quick-sticks
quacksalver
quicksilver
successless
Dutch supper
subcategory
muscatorium
suscitation
punctulated
succourable
punctualist
succourless
punctuality
punctuation
punctuative
muscovy duck
quick-witted
quadraphony
quadratical
subdiaconal
subdeaconry
auld-farrant
fund-raising
duodecimals
hurdle-racer
sundrenched
✧duddie weans
hundredfold
bundle of fun
muddle along
quadrennial
subduedness
quadrennium
muddy-headed
quodlibetic
quadrillion
Guadalcanal
Guadalajara
subdelirium
dumdum fever
fundamental
subdominant
pudding bowl
pudding-bowl
sudden death
Sudden Light
mundaneness
pudding-pipe
guiding star
pudding-time
fundholding
quadrophony
Duc d'Orléans
murderously
outdistance
subdistrict
Ruud Lubbers
quadrupedal
subdivision
subdivisive
Muddy Waters
Sunday saint
Sunday Sport
Sunday lunch
Sunday punch
Tugela Falls
tuberaceous
funeral home
rubefacient
tumefacient
lukewarmish
superabound
rubefaction
tumefaction
superactive
humeral veil
outer bailey
superbright
Jules Bordet
supercharge
pure science
supercherie
queer cuffin
supercoiled
Lupercalian
tuberculoma
tuberculise
tuberculose
tuberculate
tuberculous
tuberculize
quiescently
tumescently
superdainty
Musée d'Orsay
juvenescent
Auger effect
au désespoir
queene-apple
rule of faith
superficial
superficies
rule of three
rule of thumb
rule-of-thumb
superfamily
superfusion
superfatted
superfetate
superfluity
superfluous
Rumer Godden
mud engineer
superheater
Rudesheimer
Rüdesheimer
fume chamber
eugenic acid
suberic acid
eugenically
numerically
superinduce
superinfect
superimpose
superioress
superiority
superintend
superjacent
museologist
outer limits
superlunary
queenliness
pure-blooded
cupellation
superlative
queez-maddam
museum piece
supermarket
queen mother
supernormal
supernatant
gubernation
supernature
iure coronae
autecologic
subeconomic
superoctave
outer planet

superpraise
superphylum
nuée ardente
superrefine
queen-regent
gude-brother
superscalar
supersubtle
Queen's Scout
supersedeas
supersedere
supersedure
Queen's Bench
queen's peace
supersleuth
supersafety
queen-stitch
supersonics
superscribe
superstruct
Queer Street
superscreen
superstrong
superscript
Queen's Guide
Hubert Parry
eupepticity
Rupert's drop
curettement
supertanker
aureateness
quaestorial
humectation
duteousness
hugeousness
tunefulness
bureaucracy
pure culture
supervolute
supervision
supervisory
superweapon
suffragette
tufftaffeta
tufftaffety
surf-bathing
ruffianlike
surfcasting
sufficience
sufficiency
surface mail
suffocating
suffocation
suffocative
surface wind
sulfadoxine
muffler shop
buff-leather
subfreezing
buff-tip moth
buffalo-bird
buffalo fish
buffalo gnat
buffalo robe
suffumigate
muffin-fight
turfing iron
sulfonamide
duffing-over
muffin-worry
sulfonation
Dunfermline
out for blood
luffer-board
buffer stock
buffer state
huffishness
suffixation
burglarious
fungibility
Ouagadougou
jungle fever
jungle-green
Judgment Day
jungle juice
jungle music
cudgel-proof
judgemental
burgomaster
rumgumption
purging flax
lunging whip
surgeonfish
surgeonship
subglobular
hung up about
hunger march
Vulgar Latin
bulgur wheat
fulguration
fungistatic
turgescence
turgescency
suggestible
burgess oath
Judges' Rules
purgatorial
purgatorian
gurgitation
purgatively
humgruffian
Hugh Latimer
bushwalking
Hugh Walpole
bushmanship
Dukhobortsy
much about it
Ruth Rendell
rush bearing
bushwhacker
push through
push-bicycle
euchologion
bushelwoman
euphemistic
authentical
such-and-such
euchromatic
euchromatin
fushionless
cushion star
mush-mouthed
cushion-tire
cushion-tyre
Authors' Club
Lutheranise
Lutheranism
Lutheranize
subharmonic
authorcraft
Eucharistic
duchesse set
eurhythmics
eurhythmist
pushfulness
Hush Puppies®
hush puppies
push-over try
Yuri Gagarin
nudicaudate
punicaceous
subitaneous
puritanical
subimaginal
subimagines
nudicaulous
cubicalness
musicalness
put it across
musical sand
Buridan's ass
Surinam toad
music centre
subincision
subindicate
subindustry
ruridecanal
jubilee clip
luminescent
businessman
business end
pumice-stone
rudimentary
fusing point
music holder
punishingly
fusidic acid
juridically
municipally
purificator
munificence
munitioneer
auxiliaries
judiciarily
humiliating
humiliation
humiliatory
humiliative
judiciously
Lucille Ball
audiologist
burial-place
audibleness
burial mound
Muriel Spark
pupillarity
tubiflorous
curialistic
fusillation
put it mildly
music master
numismatics
audiometric
eudiometric
numismatist
Aurignacian
fusion cones
Julian Bream
Lucian Freud
fusion music
tulipomania
Susie Orbach
auditoriums
auditorship
Judit Polgar
tulip poplar
subirrigate
Hudibrastic
ludicrously
music-seller
Susie Salmon
run into debt
cut it too fat
audiotyping
audiotypist
auriculated
auricularly
curious arts
pudibundity
rubicundity
curiousness
dubiousness
dutifulness
furiousness
audiovisual
duniewassal
subjectless
subjectship
subjugation
subjunction
subjunctive
buck-washing
bulk carrier
buck passing
buck-passing
huckleberry
buckler fern
buckle under
duck-egg blue
musk thistle
muskellunge
duck and dive
Burkina Faso
sucking fish
tucking-mill
luckengowan
luckenbooth
ducking-pond
cuckoo clock
bucktoothed
sucker-punch
Turkish bath
Turkish lira
duskishness
luskishness
punkishness
lucky strike
bucket-wheel
sucket spoon
hucksterage
musket-proof
hucksteress
turkey-shoot
turkey brown
Turkey stone
gull-catcher
nuclear fuel
bull-mastiff
bull-baiting
gullibility
public lands
public image
✧public enemy
public woman
public works
public house
full-acorned
public wrong
duplicating
duplication
publication
duplicature
duplicitous
duplicative
public funds
public purse
quill-driver
bull terrier
full-hearted
guelder rose
bull session
dual-density
qualifiable
nullifidian
qualifiedly
full of beans
full of years
bully for you
curly-greens
curly-headed
hurly-hacket
gully-hunter
pull through
pull-through
full-charged
nucleic acid
quilting bee
bullfighter
dull-sighted
full-fledged
Kuala Lumpur
full-blooded
guilelessly
guiltlessly
pullulation
sublimeness
sublimation
burling-iron
fulling-mill
curling pond
Dublin prawn
sublanguage
null and void
nucleolated
bulldog clip
nucleoplasm
full-mouthed
dual control
dual-control
nulliparity
nulliparous
dual pricing
fuller's-herb
dull-brained
full-frontal
bull-fronted
full brother
full-fraught
publishable
cutlass fish
publishment
bullishness
gutlessness
sunlessness
guildswoman
pull strings
sublittoral
bullet point
pullet-sperm
bullet train
bullet-proof
quality time
qualitative
dual-purpose
curlew-berry
Curlew River
duplex house
subluxation
guilty party
Dudley Moore
hurley-house
pulmobranch
tummy button
culmiferous
gummiferous
rummage sale
submolecule
submultiple
nummulation
summum genus
summum bonum
augmentable
Humming-Bird
hummingbird
culminate in
fulminating
culmination
fulmination
submunition
fulminatory
summersault
submergence
bur-marigold
summer wheat
submarginal
outmarriage
submergible
submersible
murmuringly
summariness
murmur vowel
summerhouse
summer stock
murmuration
murmurously
Burmese Days
submissible
submissness
surmistress
summit talks
summit-level
summational
surmounting
turntablist
✧guinea grass
bunny-boiler
Luing cattle
Juan-les-Pins
turn of speed
guaniferous
turn against
bunny-hugger
burn-the-wind
turn the wind
turnpike man
quintillion

tunnel vault
tunnel diode
funnel cloud
running back
burning bush
running fire
burning ghat
running gear
running head
running high
running hand
running knot
running mate
cunningness
running sore
running time
running text
turn towards
Quantometer®
quantometer
quandong-nut
turn to stone
curnaptious
bunny rabbit
turn traitor
Gunn Erikson
Turner Prize
Turneresque
vulneration
sunny side up
burnt sienna
Buenos Aires
furnishings
burnishment
furnishment
nunnishness
Burns Supper
jus naturale
quincuncial
quantum jump
quantum leap
quinquennia
ruinousness
quinquereme
turn out well
turnover tax
quinsy-berry
Quincy Jones
automatical
Out of Africa
fucoxanthin
out of action
out of breath
Tudorbethan
out of bounds
Eurosceptic
out of course
subordinacy
subordinary
subordinate
autogenesis
auto-reverse
run one's face
autocephaly
Europeanise
Europeanism
Europeanist
Europeanize
Eurocentric
Rudolf Kempe
Tudor flower
out of favour
autophagous
autochthons
autochthony
out of humour
autochanger
autophanous
bucolically
gum olibanum
autokinesis
autokinetic
tumorigenic
auto ricksha
eusociality
out of kilter
autoplastic
Yugoslavian
subornation
autonomical
automobilia
Euro-dollars
automorphic
out of pocket
out-of-pocket
autographic
autotrophic
autoerotism
Hugo Grotius
autogravure
out of season
au contraire
out of the way
out-of-the-way
put on the map
put on the dog
out of the Ark
out of temper
put on weight
bumpsadaisy
culpability
suspectable
suspectedly
suspectless
suppedaneum
purple patch
purple laver
✧purple heart
purple finch
suppressant
suppression
suppressive
purpresture
puppy-headed
sulphhydryl
supplicavit
surprisedly
suppliantly
subprioress
pumpkinseed
pulp fiction
bumptiously
jumping bean
jumping deer
suspenseful
jumping gene
jumping hare
suspensible
jumping jack
bumping race
subpanation
supportance
support area
supportable
supportably
supper party
Humphry Davy
purportedly
support hose
subparallel
purportless
supportless
supper cloth
pump-priming
supportment
out-paramour
dumper truck
supportress
suppuration
suspiration
suppurative
surpassable
purpose-like
purposeless
dumpishness
lumpishness
mumpishness
supposition
suppository
suppositive
puppet-valve
sulphurator
sulphureted
sulphureous
sulphur-root
sumptuosity
sulphur tuft
sumptuously
sulphurwort
puppy-walker
Murphy's game
supply chain
supply-sider
supply curve
jusqu'au bout
outquarters
Munro-bagger
surrebuttal
surrebutter
curriculums
turriculate
hurricanoes
supracostal
lubrication
rubrication
lubricative
lubricously
putrid fever
puerperally
quarterback
quarter-bred
quarterdeck
quarter-evil
quarter hour
quarter-jack
quarrelling
quarrellous
guerre à mort
guardedness
hurriedness
quarter note
quarrel-pane
quarter past
quarter-road
quarter-rail
quarter-seal
quarrelsome
quarter-sawn
quarter-tone
quarter-wind
putrefiable
cupriferous
curry favell
curry favour
subregional
subrogation
surrogation
quarrington
guerrillero
querulously
supremacism
supremacist
nutrimental
supremeness
✧suprematism
✧suprematist
cupronickel
current coil
currant cake
current-cost
surrenderee
surrenderer
surrenderor
currant loaf
currentness
currant-wine
Puerto Rican
cuir-bouilli
cuir-bouilly
curry powder
putrescence
Buprestidae
putrescible
currishness
hurry-scurry
hurry-skurry
turret lathe
turret clock
nutritional
lubritorium
lucratively
nutritively
surrounding
burrowstown
quarry-water
Murray River
Murrayfield
Aubrey holes
quartz watch
quartz clock
quartz glass
Russian doll
outstanding
substandard
Russianness
substantial
substantive
subscapular
Russian vine
purse-bearer
bursiculate
tussock moth
tussac grass
outside edge
outside half
outside left
lues venerea
subspecific
nun's-veiling
pussyfooter
Burschenism
mum's the word
mudslinging
outswinging
question tag
questioning
questionary
questionist
substituted
substituent
Luis Alvarez
mussel-scalp
mussel-scaup
mussel-shell
Mussulwoman
fulsomeness
subsumption
subsumptive
bums on seats
nursing home
Hudson River
subsensible
Puss in Boots
outspokenly
Russophobia
Russophobic
subsequence
subscribing
Burseraceae
substractor
subservient
nurserymaid
cursoriness
substrative
subsistence
purse-seiner
purse-taking
guesstimate
nurse-tender
russet apple
mussitation
outsourcing
suasiveness
pussy willow
guest worker
Australasia
multi-access
muntjac deer
Punta Arenas
nuptial Mass
dusty answer
multi-author
subtraction
subtractive
quotability
suitability
justiciable
mustachioed
multicolour
buttock-mail
furthcoming
subtacksman
justiceship
multicuspid
rustication
punto dritto
busted flush
butted joint
furtherance
bustle about
butt welding
hurtleberry
multiethnic
turtleshell
furthermore
furthermost
turtle doves
put the arm on
furthersome
subtreasury
turtle-stone
run the guard
justifiable
justifiably
multifidous
put to flight
guttiferous
tutti-frutti
butt against
run to ground
run together
fustigation
hunt-the-gowk
quota-hopper
quitch grass
just the same
sustainable
curtain call
rumti-iddity
sustainedly
curtain-fire
punt-fishing
curtailment
sustainment
curtail-step
curtain wall
multijugate
multijugous
multilobate
multilineal
multilinear
ductileness
curtal friar
fustilarian
fustilirian
pustulation
dusty-miller
juste milieu
custom house
customarily
custom-built
sustentator
hunting-crop
Hunting Dogs
cutting edge
hunting-horn
cutting list
mutton cloth
multinomial
hunting-mass
multanimous
buttonholer
button-mould
cutting room
hunting-seat
hunting-song

hunting-tide
Huntington's
multangular
button quail
hunting-whip
subtropical
hunt counter
hunt-counter
suction pump
suction stop
multiplexer
multiplexor
gutta-percha
multiparity
multiparous
multipotent
putty-powder
multiplying
butter-paper
Kulturkampf
multiracial
butter icing
Culture Club
vulture fund
put to rights
subterminal
quaternion'd
quaternions
cultural lag
butterflies
gutterblood
cultureless
gutturalise
butter cloth
outter plate
gutturalize
iunter's moon
outter knife
nutteringly
out to ransom
guttersnipe
usterenes
outteriness
outter-woman
gutter board
ustard pies
utter cream
ulturkreis
utter-print
urtarbrand
urturbrand
Günter Grass
utter press
Mustard-seed
ustard tree
utteration
ustard tart
upturewort
ultispiral
uota sample
ultisonant
ultistorey
ultiserial
ultiscreen
ultistrike
utta serena
uota system
et pudding
rtfulness
stfulness
b-thumping

Kurt Russell
tuft-hunting
Gustave Doré
Gustav Klimt
multivalent
furtiveness
Gustav Holst
multi-vision
cultivation
quoteworthy
run up a score
subumbrella
suburbanise
suburbanism
suburbanite
suburbanity
suburbanize
Aulus Celsus
furunculous
cut up didoes
future shock
curule chair
futureproof
Subungulata
subungulate
Cupuliferae
luxuriantly
luxulianite
luxuriation
luxuriously
mutualistic
mutual funds
cumulonimbi
cumulocirri
lucubration
susurration
Augustinian
August Krogh
luxulyanite
luxury goods
subvocalise
subvocalize
surveillant
curvilineal
curvilinear
subvertical
pulverulent
culverineer
quaveringly
quiveringly
pulveration
subvitreous
survival bag
survivalism
survivalist
quo warranto
outwardness
butyraceous
Judy Garland
ruby wedding
jury service
duty officer
Eutychianus
eurythermal
eurythermic
Eurypharynx
butyric acid
buoyantness
Runyonesque
buoyancy aid
butyl rubber

jury-process
Eurypterida
eurypteroid
fuzzy-haired
quizzically
avocado pear
avec plaisir
evocatively
evidentiary
evagination
avoirdupois
ovuliferous
Evelyn Waugh
evolutional
evil-starred
evangelical
evangeliser
evangelizer
evangeliary
evening meal
evening star
avant-propos
eventration
evanescence
evanishment
even-stevens
eventualise
eventuality
eventualize
eventuation
evaporation
evaporative
oviparously
oviposition
overbalance
overhandled
overcareful
overgarment
overpayment
overearnest
overhastily
✧everlasting
overcasting
svarabhakti
overachieve
overreached
overdevelop
overtedious
over-zealous
overweening
overbearing
overmeasure
overleather
overweather
ovariectomy
overheating
over the hill
over the hump
over the left
over the moon
over the odds
overthrower
overpitched
overbidding
overnighter
overviolent
overpicture
overblanket
overflowing
ever and anon
over-anxiety

over-anxious
over and over
overindulge
Ivor Novello
overlocking
overcorrect
overcoating
overforward
over-breathe
over-precise
overproduce
overtrading
overfreedom
overarching
overgrainer
overfreight
overbrimmed
overprepare
overwrestle
overdraught
overfraught
overwrought
overcrowded
over-drowsed
overgrazing
Everest pack
overstretch
overstrooke
averruncate
overfunding
overrunning
overfulness
overburthen
everywhence
eviscerator
Yves Montand
evasiveness
à votre santé
eviternally
sweater-girl
sweet cicely
owner-driver
tweezer case
✧sweeney todd
sweet fennel
sweetie-wife
sweet orange
sweet pepper
sweet pastry
sweet potato
sweepstakes
sweet sherry
sweet sultan
sweet willow
sweep-washer
swift-footed
twofoldness
swift-winged
swagger coat
swagger cane
swag-bellied
two-handedly
twelve score
twelve-penny
swelled head
twalpennies
twelvemonth
swell-headed
swallow-dive
swallow hole
swallowtail

swallow-wort
awelessness
Twelfth cake
Twelfthtide
swim bladder
twin paradox
Ewan MacColl
Gwen Harwood
swing bridge
swingeingly
swing-handle
swingle-hand
dwindlement
twanglingly
swingletree
twinkletoes
twin-engined
swingometer
swan-hopping
swing-plough
twin crystal
twin brother
swinishness
swine's cress
twin-etching
twenty pence
two-penn'orth
twopenny bit
sword-bearer
sword-dollar
dwarfed tree
dwarf fennel
swarthiness
a work of time
swordplayer
sword-shaped
twisted pair
Swiss fondue
Swiss Guards
zwischenzug
kwashiorkor
awesomeness
two-storeyed
awe-stricken
twitter-bone
Switzerland
switchblade
switch-plant
switchboard
twitch grass
swivel-chair
swivelblock
awkwardness
D Wayne Lukas
away with you
exsanguined
expatiation
expatiatory
expatiative
excarnation
exhaustedly
exhaustible
exhaustless
expansional
exhaust pipe
expansively
expansivity
ex natura rei
exuberantly
ex accidenti
oxy-chloride

oxycompound
executrices
executrixes
executioner
executorial
executively
oxidational
oxidization
exceedingly
expenditure
expeditious
experienced
experiencer
expediently
exteriorise
exteriority
exteriorize
excellently
exterminate
externalise
externalism
externalist
externality
externalize
excerptible
extemporary
extemporise
extemporize
extensional
excessively
expensively
extensively
expectantly
expectingly
exceptional
expectorant
expectorate
expectation
expectative
extenuating
extenuation
extenuatory
extenuative
exaggerated
exaggerator
oxygenation
exogenously
oxy-hydrogen
exhilarator
expiscation
exsiccation
expiscatory
exsiccative
excitedness
ex-directory
extirpation
extirpatory
extirpative
axillary bud
explication
explicatory
explicative
Oxalidaceae
exaltedness
explain away
explainable
exploitable
exclamation
exclamatory
exclamative
explanation

explanatory
explanative
exploration
exploratory
explorative
exclusively
explosively
exclusivism
exclusivist
exclusivity
exemplified
exemplifier
exemplarily
exemplarity
examination
ex improviso
exonuclease
exanthemata
axonometric
exanimation
exoneration
exonerative
axiomatical
ex concessis
Oxfordshire
Oxford cloth
exposedness
exponential
excogitator
expositress
excoriation
exfoliation
exfoliative
excommunion
axiological
extorsively
ex post facto
excorticate
expostulate
extortioner
exhortation
exportation
exhortatory
exhortative
exorability
extractable
extractible
extrication
extradition
extrafloral
exorbitance
exorbitancy
exercisable
excremental
extremeness
excrementum
expromissor
extrinsical
expropriate
extrapolate
axerophthol
excrescence
excrescency
expressible
expressness
express term
extravagant
extravagate
extroverted
extra virgin
extra-virgin
extravasate
oxyrhynchus
exasperator
exoskeletal
exoskeleton
existential
exstipulate
exotericism
expungement
expurgation
expurgatory
expugnation
exculpation
exculpatory
exquisitely
excursively
exeunt omnes
ex hypothesi
pyjama party
cycadaceous
gynaecology
gynaecomast
cyma reversa
pyrargyrite
dynamically
pyramidally
Myra Hindley
pyramidical
✧sybaritical
hypallactic
tyrannicide
tyrannosaur
tyrannously
dynamometer
dynamometry
synagogical
dynamograph
synanthesis
synanthetic
Byzantinism
Byzantinist
Dylan Thomas
lycanthrope
lycanthropy
symbolology
symbol group
symbolistic
eyebrowless
Cyd Charisse
synclinoria
hyacinthine
synchoresis
syncopation
myocarditis
synchromesh
synchronise
synchronism
synchronous
synchronize
synchrotron
eye-catching
syndyasmian
syndicalism
syndicalist
syndication
Cyndi Lauper
syndesmoses
syndesmosis
syndesmotic
cyperaceous
gyre-carline
typecasting
hyperactive
hyperacusis
hyperboloid
hyperbolise
hyperbolism
hyperbolize
hyperborean
hypercharge
hypercritic
hypercolour
synecdochic
hyperdactyl
hyperdorian
hyperemesis
hyperemetic
myoelectric
hyperextend
typesetting
hypergamous
synergistic
Lyme disease
hyperinosis
hyperinotic
hyperlydian
hypermnesia
hypermarket
cybernetics
cybernation
Tyne and Wear
type founder
type foundry
synecologic
Hymenoptera
hyperphagia
hyperplasia
type species
cyberphobia
cyberphobic
typewritten
typewriting
hypersthene
sycee silver
hypersomnia
hypersonics
hyperstress
hypesthesia
hypesthesic
hypertrophy
dysfunction
eye for an eye
myographist
syngnathous
Syngman Rhee
lythraceous
mythography
Pythagorean
Pythagorism
mythologian
Mythologies
mythologise
mythologist
mythologize
syphilology
mythomaniac
Pythonesque
hyphenation
lychnoscope
mythopoetic
mythopoeist
dysharmonic
by the squire
xyridaceous
cynicalness
typicalness
cylindrical
lysigenetic
myringotomy
syringotomy
Lydian stone
pyritohedra
cycloalkane
syllabicate
syllabicity
syllabarium
cyclicality
cyclic group
pyelography
dyslogistic
syllogistic
cyclohexane
hyalomelane
cyclopaedia
cyclopaedic
cycloplegia
sylleptical
cycle racing
cycloserine
cyclothymia
cyclothymic
myrmecology
myrmidonian
Nyamuragira
symmetrical
symmetallic
symmetalism
Hydnocarpus
Lynn Seymour
hymnography
Pycnogonida
pycnogonoid
hypnogenous
cyanohydrin
lying-in ward
hymnologist
Gymnopédies
hypnopaedia
hypnopompic
gymnorhinal
gymnasiarch
gymnastical
hypnotistic
Sydneysider
Sydney Smith
zygocardiac
hylopathism
hylopathist
pyroballogy
myxomatosis
xylocarpous
hypogastric
synoecology
synoeciosis
cytogenesis
cytogenetic
hylogenesis
pyrogenetic
pyrotechnic
zymotechnic
hypoaeolian
Tyronensian
hypotension
hypotensive
Myxophyceae
hypothecary
hypothecate
mycophagist
hylophagous
xylophagous
cynophilist
xylophilous
Zygophyllum
sycophantic
sycophantry
hypothenuse
xylophonist
cymophanous
hypothermal
hypothermia
hypothyroid
pyrophorous
hypophyseal
hypophysial
hypothesise
hypothesize
hypothetise
hypothetize
Byronically
synodically
zymotically
zymosimeter
cytokinesis
pyrokinesis
hypolimnion
hyponitrite
tyroglyphid
hypoglossal
mycoplasmas
cytoplasmic
hypoblastic
hypoplastic
pyroclastic
zygopleural
Byron Nelson
pyrognostic
mycodomatia
sycomore fig
cytological
Lycopodinae
mycological
typological
zymological
hypocorisma
hylomorphic
zygomorphic
gyrocompass
hylozoistic
hypospadias
mycorrhizae
mycorrhizal
typographer
xylographer
kymographic
mycotrophic
typographia
typographic
xylographic
pyrogravure
gynostemium
hypostrophe
synoptistic
hypostasise
hypostasize
gyrostatics
hypostatise
hypostatize
synonymatic
Zygomycetes
synonymical
synonymicon
hypocycloid
hypotyposis
lymphangial
Nymphalidae
hyoplastral
hyoplastron
sympodially
tympaniform
nymphomania
symptomatic
nympholepsy
symphonious
lymphoblast
dyspeptical
dyspareunia
symposiarch
dyspathetic
sympathetic
sympathiser
sympathizer
sympathique
sympetalous
hydrobromic
Hydrocharis
hydrocyanic
hydrochoric
hydrocarbon
hydrography
hydrogen ion
hydrogenase
hydrogenise
hydrogenate
hydrogenous
hydrogenize
hydra-headed
pyrrolidine
hydrologist
hydrolysate
hydromedusa
Cypro-Minoan
hydromantic
hydrometric
hygrometric
hydrometeor
Cyprinodont
cypripedium
Hydrophidae
hydrophilic
hydroponics
hydrophobia
hydrophobic
hydropathic
hydrophytic
hygrophytic
hydrophyton
dyer's rocket
dyer's-rocket
hydrargyral
hydrargyrum
hydrostatic
Cypress Hill
hydrosphere
cypress knee
hydrosomata

hygroscopic
cypress vine
hydrotactic
hydrated ion
hydrothorax
hydrotropic
hydroxylate
hydroxyurea
dysrhythmia
gypsiferous
hypsography
gypsum block
hypsometric
XYY syndrome
hypsophobia
syssarcoses
syssarcosis
hyoscyamine
syntactical
syntectical
Mystic River
cysticercus
Cyatheaceae
✧dyotheletic
synthetical
synthesiser
synthesizer
synthetiser
synthetizer
✧dyothelitic
hyetography
syntagmatic
system-maker
systematics
systematise
systematism
systematist
systematize
system-built
Ayrton Senna
nyctanthous
nyctinastic
nyctophobia
oyster-patty
oyster-wench
hysterogeny
oyster-shell
hysteroidal
oyster-field
oyster plant
oyster-knife
oyster-woman
oyster-tongs
mystery play
hysteresial
mystery ship
hysterotomy
mystery tour
cystoscopic
nyctitropic
pyruvic acid
Cyrus R Vance
Sylvia Plath
sylvestrian
by my lee-lane
azo-compound
ozoniferous
ozonosphere
ozonisation
ozonization
azione sacra
azoospermia
azoospermic
Azerbaijani
Ezer Weizman
Azotobacter

12 – even

taramasalata
yada yada yada
Bananalander
Canada balsam
mad as a hatter
salamandrine
salamandrian
salamandroid
banana-bender
Sahara Desert
paralanguage
calabash tree
palatability
macadamia nut
banana liquid
paramagnetic
caraway seeds
caravansarai
caravanserai
paratactical
Naval Brigade
zalambdodont
palaebiology
Jamaica cedar
balanced pair
balanced flue
amaica ebony
balancing act
parascending
apan Current
balance sheet
balance wheel
hazard lights
Camaldolites
Papaveraceae
al alembroth
apanese tosa
macaberesque
arah Egerton
managerially
Madame Bovary
parametrical
parade ground
malapertness
aracentesis
araffin test
asal ganglia
ahangir Khan
ataphractic
araphrastic
atachrestic
ataphyllary
araphimosis
anathenaean
baba ghanouzh
parachronism
parathormone
cataphoresis
cataphysical
Zarathustric
paradisaical
Tamaricaceae
Samaritanism
banalisation
banalization
canalisation
canalization
capacitation
faradisation
faradization
nasalisation
nasalization
safari jacket
parasitaemia
satanic abuse
Mazarin Bible
laxativeness
mazarine dish
paradise fish
mazarine hood
Paradise Lost
lay a finger on
Ramapithecus
Narasimha Rao
paramilitary
paradisiacal
parasiticide
capabilities
Palau Islands
paradigmatic
vacationless
Bavarian Alps
paralipomena
parasitology
calamitously
catadioptric
cabalistical
canaliculate
safari supper
catallactics
Japan lacquer
parallel bars
parallelwise
parallel port
parallel turn
paraglossate
ratable value
tax allowance
Balaam-basket
Salaam Bombay!
Balaamitical
Canaan Banana
paraenetical
paragnathism
paragnathous
lasagne verde
labanotation
laparoscopic
tax avoidance
naval officer
satanophobia
parapophyses
parapophysis
Palaeolithic
paradoxidian
da capo al fine
catamountain
Palaeo-Indian
palaeobotany
paraboloidal
malacologist
paradoxology
paramorphism
palaeography
catacoustics
Malacostraca
man-about-town
paradoxurine
parasphenoid
paragraphist
cavalry twill
parapsychism
Sarah Siddons
panaesthesia
paraesthesia
salad spinner
palaestrical
Marattiaceae
galactic halo
wag-at-the-wall
natal therapy
paranthelion
bay at the moon
galactagogue
Pagan temples
galactometer
pay attention
catastrophic
hamartiology
paranthropus
hamarthritis
panarthritis
paraquadrate
Japan varnish
Sarah Vaughan
canary yellow
paracyanogen
parasyntheta
pay-as-you-earn
palazzo pants
Darby and Joan
rabble-rouser
marble-cutter
marbled-white
iambographer
cabbage-white
carbohydrate
bad behaviour
day-blindness
gambling hell
carbolic acid
carbolic soap
bar billiards
lamb's lettuce
carbamic acid
carbon dating
carbonic acid
rabbinically
carbonaceous
carbon fibres
rambunctious
bamboo shoots
l'Abbé Prévost
namby-pambies
lamb's quarter
barber's block
Barbary coast
barber-monger
Lamberto Dini
Hamburg steak
Barbary sheep
rabbit warren
wag-by-the-wall
ratbite fever
rabbeting-saw
rabbit-sucker
tambourinist
harbour-light
bacchanalian
Panchatantra
tab character
watch and ward
calceamentum
saccharinity
watchability
saccharoidal
Marcobrunner
fasciculated
watch crystal
saccadically
Cascade Range
hatchet-faced
Macclesfield
Kanchenjunga
Satchel Paige
pancreatitis
ratchet-wheel
pancreozymin
fancifulness
watchfulness
sanctifiable
sanctifiedly
sanctionable
cancellarial
cancellarian
cancellation
tax collector
Malcolm Lowry
Barcelona nut
pauciloquent
Marcel Proust
baccalaurean
parchmentise
parchmentize
talcum powder
Nancy Mitford
sarcomatosis
lay communion
Vacciniaceae
Dancing Brave
gas-condenser
malcontented
falcon-gentle
falcon-gentil
marconigraph
carcinogenic
Dancing Queen
lanceolately
raccoon-berry
dance of death
fancy oneself
watch officer
Marcionitism
fascioliasis
sarcoplasmic
sarcophagous
lance prisade
lance prisado
saucepan-fish
cancerphobia
panchromatic
Marcus Garvey
Lancasterian
narcissistic
narcotically
narcotherapy
march-treason
lancet window
patch through
marcatissimo
calcium oxide
lasciviously
Saudi Arabian
Zandra Rhodes
land-yachting
sand-yachting
Paddy Ashdown
handbag music
sand painting
hard-favoured
Pandean pipes
card-carrying
hand's breadth
laudableness
mandibulated
paedobaptism
paedobaptist
pas de bourrée
Laodiceanism
gay deceivers
eau de Cologne
paddock-stool
candid camera
paedodontics
land set-aside
candle-paring
saddlebacked
saddle hackle
candle-waster
handkerchief
card mechanic
saddle-shaped
saddle pillar
Land Registry
hard feelings
candle-holder
✧pandaemonium
saddle spring
landlessness
hard measures
hard-featured
hard-sectored
saddle stitch
saddle-stitch

call into play
Darling Range
Marlon Brando
ballanwrasse
Darling River
marline-spike
falling stone
Darlingtonia
Mail on Sunday
wallcovering
ballpoint pen
fail to notice
sailboarding
Paul Tournier
balloon whisk
mallophagous
Pablo Picasso
rail-splitter
lallapalooza
wallop in a tow
harlequinade
ball-breaking
tailor's chalk
Paule Régnier
cable railway
cable release
table-rapping
cable's-length
Naples yellow
eagle-sighted
callisthenic
Wally Schirra
Pallas Athene
ballet-dancer
ballet-master
cable tramway
balletically
Wall-Streeter
balletomania
Earl Stanhope
table-turning
Paolo Uccello
Carlovingian
tallow candle
gallows frame
sallow kitten
gallows-maker
early-warning
Halley's Comet
walleyed pike
Bailey bridge
Harley Street
farm labourer
barmy-brained
palma Christi
mammee-sapota
harmlessness
balm of Gilead
Ian McGeechan
Jammu-Kashmir
Macmillanite
mammillarias
mammalogical
salmon ladder
Carmen Callil
Raymond Barre
harmonic wave
harmonic mean
harmonically
harmonichord
warmongering
Raymond Floyd
harmonograph
salmon-fisher
Hammond Innes
harmonometer
Hammond organ®
salmon-colour
harmoniously
harmoniphone
harmoniumist
haemophiliac
haemopoiesis
hammer-headed
Balmer series
mammary gland
haemorrhagic
haemorrhoids
farm steading
haematoblast
palmitic acid
haematolysis
haematemesis
haematoxylin
Haematoxylon
maintainable
damnableness
Barnaby Rudge
Gainsborough
Fanny Cradock
wainscotting
vaunt-courier
painted cloth
painted grass
saunteringly
E Annie Proulx
gainlessness
painlessness
painted snipe
Saint-Exupéry
main sequence
painted woman
Saint Francis
magnifically
magnificence
Wayne Gretzky
caenogenesis
cainogenesis
kainogenesis
Saint George's
faint-hearted
launch window
launching-pad
Paint It Black
faintishness
Magnoliaceae
carnal-minded
magniloquent
vainglorious
Saint Laurent
magnum bonums
cannon fodder
Hainan Island
Rainbow Guide
balneologist
Cain-coloured
rainbow trout
Wagnerianism
mannerliness
Ragnar Frisch
laundrywoman
Barnes Wallis
Payne Stewart
Magnus effect
harness-maker
earnest-money
Wayne Shorter
earnest-penny
magnetic card
magnetic tape
magnetic lens
magnetic disc
magnetic mine
magnetic disk
magnetic flux
magnetically
magnetic core
magnet school
magnetic drum
paint the lily
magnetograph
Magnitogorsk
malnutrition
magnetometer
magnetometry
barnstorming
Jayne Torvill
magnetisable
magnetizable
malnourished
Vannevar Bush
panorama head
bacon-and-eggs
pagoda sleeve
nasolacrymal
japonaiserie
Major Barbara
Aaron Copland
paroccipital
malocclusion
Harold Varmus
Harold Wilson
Harold Pinter
gamopetalous
gamosepalous
calorescence
baroreceptor
bayonet joint
Jacobean lily
say one's piece
barometrical
gasometrical
manometrical
Jacob Epstein
Baroness Hogg
eat one's terms
eat one's words
major-general
parochialise
parochialize
parochialism
parochiality
Baron Holberg
gamophyllous
cacophonical
cacophonious
majolicaware
Carolina pink
canonisation
canonization
valorisation
valorization
vaporisation
vaporization
vasodilation
vasodilatory
calorimetric
parotid gland
saponifiable
Faroe Islands
majority rule
Lajos Kossuth
cap of liberty
nanoplankton
Manon Lescaut
man of letters
paroemiology
saloon-keeper
saloon pistol
law of nations
paronomastic
baron-officer
cat o' mountain
lagomorphous
canorousness
vaporousness
law of octaves
major premise
labour-saving
favouredness
labour of love
canon regular
Jacob's ladder
Baron Scarman
canon secular
Yamoussoukro
law of the land
pat on the back
lay on the line
Savoy Theatre
Bat Out of Hell
raconteuring
manoeuvrable
man-of-war bird
man-of-war's-man
barodynamics
happy as Larry
panpharmacon
palpableness
Tampico fibre
Sam Peckinpah
lampadedromy
campodeiform
lampadomancy
Ralph Fiennes
Cappagh-brown
happy-go-lucky
salpiglossis
camp-shedding
camp-sheeting
sapphire-wing
sapphire blue
Tarpeian Rock
Valpolicella
carpological
carpal tunnel
carpenter-ant
carpenter-bee
Campanularia
happenstance
Camptosaurus
lamprophyric
camp-follower
carpophagous
camp-preacher
pamperedness
lappered-milk
gas-permeable
camp-drafting
Gaspard Monge
Jasper Conran
way passenger
carpetbagger
carpet beetle
lamp-standard
carpet-knight
carpetmonger
tappet-motion
carpet python
Jacquard loom
pasqueflower
Jacques Monod
vanquishable
vanquishment
matriarchate
patriarchate
patriarchism
carriage-paid
carriageable
marriageable
laureateship
carriage line
marriage-ring
marriage-bone
carriage bolt
carriage-free
Hadrian's Wall
hair's-breadth
macrobiotics
iatrochemist
Patrick Henry
matriclinous
matroclinous
patriclinous
patroclinous
matriculator
Patrick Moore
capriciously
macrocephaly
Capricornian
Maurice Ravel
Patrick White
macrodactyly
sacred beetle
barrier cream
Harry Enfield
Gabriel Fauré
barrier layer
Das Rheingold
hairlessness
Maarten Tromp
hair restorer
carry forward
carry-forward
carragheenin
fairnitickle
sacroiliitis
Darryl Zanuck
sacrilegious
patrilineage
tauromachian
sacramentary
Lauren Bacall
Warren Beatty
Barranquilla
carry one's bat
saprophagous
Macropodidae
macropterous
hair-splitter
fairy penguin
madreporitic
Patripassian
saprophytism
hairdressing
Harry Secombe
barristerial
patristicism
Barry St Leger
Barry Sanders
Harrison Ford
garrison town
sarrusophone
Harry S Truman
garret-master
carry the flag
saprotrophic
barratrously
cairn terrier
parrot-wrasse
carry through
marrowfat pea
Harrow School
narrow-minded
Larry Winters
marrow-squash
narrow squeak
narrow escape
carriwitchet
fairnytickle
carry your bat
manslaughter
nauseatingly
law-stationer
capstan lathe
capstan table
false bedding
passableness
passibleness
San Sebastian
waistcoateer
waistcoating
cause célèbre
false colours
causa causans
passed master
raised pastry
laisser-aller
laissez-aller
tapsieteerie
laisser-faire
laissez-faire
panspermatic
parsley piert
Paisley shawl
pass sentence
tax-sheltered
sassafras nut
sassafras oil
laws of motion
laws of honour
passage grave
passage-money
false-hearted
marsh-harrier
caustic curve

Marseillaise
Marsileaceae
salsolaceous
tapsalteerie
tassel-gentle
bass clarinet
ear-splitting
passemeasure
passy-measure
✧danse macabre
balsam of Peru
balsam of Tolu
facsimileing
haussmannise
haussmannize
parsimonious
raise money on
balsam poplar
damson cheese
ways and means
pass one's word
passionately
Hans von Bülow
Marsh of Decay
raise one's hat
passion fruit
mansion-house
rags-to-riches
Passion-music
Marsh of Mists
Marsh of Sleep
nauseousness
false pareira
sarsaparilla
passe-partout
mass-produced
mass producer
kaisar-i-Hindi
basso-relievo
basso-rilievo
massaranduba
masseranduba
Yasser Arafat
lapsus calami
false saffron
cassette deck
aise the wind
aise the ante
aise the roof
causationism
causationist
caesium clock
danseur noble
ansculottic
alse vampire
narsh warbler
pansexualism
pansexualist
pansexuality
Valtham Abbey
alt Lake City
antharidine
antharidian
Martha Graham
arte blanche
Cantabrigian
anta Barbara
article size
arth-created
aute cuisine
autical mile

particularly
pantechnicon
fait accompli
participable
party-capital
participator
Zante currant
haute couture
faute de mieux
Santo Domingo
fastidiously
✧zantedeschia
carte des vins
cattle market
partie carrée
rattle-headed
battlemented
Battle of Zama
Battle of Jena
Battle of Loos
maître d'hôtel
Ian Trethowan
cattle-lifter
cattle-plague
fan the flames
East Germanic
wattle and dab
Matthew Prior
Matthew Paris
saltpetreman
battleground
tactlessness
maltreatment
partner whist
salt of tartar
salt of wisdom
faithfulness
tastefulness
wastefulness
Marty Feldman
salt of sorrel
part of speech
hart of grease
cartographic
pantographic
cartographer
pantagrapher
pantographer
vantage point
Mastigophora
✧faith healing
East China Sea
East Kilbride
Captain Flint
gastric fever
farthingland
farthingless
cartridge pen
gastric juice
Parthian shot
cantillation
castellation
cantillatory
tantalic acid
dactylically
santalaceous
battological
cartological
tautological
tantalum lamp
pantaloonery

dactyliology
dactyloscopy
cantilevered
hasta la vista
saltimbancos
party machine
bantamweight
pantomimical
waltz Matilda
Fantin-Latour
wasting asset
casting couch
bastinadoing
Jan Tinbergen
cantankerous
malting floor
Hattons Grace
Martini-Henry
East-Indiaman
carton-pierre
fast-and-loose
Watton Priory
past one's best
Martin Luther
Martin Guerre
canting-wheel
waiting-woman
factionalise
factionalize
factionalism
factionalist
xanthomatous
xanthochroia
xanthochroic
xanthochroid
caution money
gastrocnemii
hawthorn tree
gastrosopher
gastronomics
gastronomist
gastropodous
captiousness
cautiousness
factiousness
xanthopterin
pantophagist
pantophagous
hasty pudding
cartophilist
Dantophilist
lactoprotein
waste product
earthquaking
Walter S Adams
masturbation
Walter Cannon
masturbatory
Walter Payton
Easter cactus
tartaric acid
bactericidal
caster action
castor action
battered baby
battered wife
halter-necked
Gastarbeiter
matter-of-fact
factory floor
easterliness

masterliness
mastersinger
lantern-jawed
pattern-maker
tartar emetic
battering-ram
Easter Monday
bacteriology
bacteriostat
Easter Island
lantern slide
tax threshold
tartare sauce
masterstroke
bastard types
master-at-arms
bastard title
garter-stitch
Easter Sunday
canterburies
lantern wheel
pattern-wheel
master-switch
earthshaking
Cartesianism
cactus dahlia
pantisocracy
✧maltese cross
Cactus People
mantis shrimp
fantasticate
fantasticism
cantus firmus
earth science
fantasticoes
party selling
partisanship
haptotropism
saltationism
partitionist
saltationist
factitiously
saltatorious
gastrulation
tanto uberior
✧pasteurellae
✧pasteurellas
party-verdict
part-exchange
East Ayrshire
pastry cutter
natural death
saturated fat
paludamentum
salutariness
saturability
maturational
salutational
naturalistic
natural light
natural magic
natural order
salutatorian
salutatorily
tabulae rasae
natural scale
manufactural
manufacturer
valuableness
ranunculuses
papuliferous

salutiferous
paludicolous
Samuel Palmer
casual labour
Samuel Weller
Samuel Phelps
Samuel Lister
Samuel Cunard
Samuel Butler
casualty ward
vacuum-packed
caput mortuum
calumniation
calumniatory
calumniously
naturopathic
fabulousness
Samudragupta
salubriously
Salvador Dali
salvifically
salvage-corps
Mauvoisin Dam
mauvais sujet
marvel of Peru
marvellously
larva migrans
Salviniaceae
galvanic cell
galvanic belt
galvanically
carving knife
galvanometer
galvanometry
galvanoscope
sauve qui peut
malversation
Calvary cross
salver-shaped
harvest-feast
harvest-field
harvest-goose
harvest louse
harvest mouse
Galveston Bay
harvest queen
Salvationism
Salvationist
Harvey Keitel
Warwickshire
tag wrestling
Lady Jane Grey
baby carriage
calycanthemy
baby-batterer
Mary McCarthy
Mary McAleese
lady's-cushion
lady's fingers
laryngectomy
laryngophony
laryngospasm
laryngoscope
laryngoscopy
dasyphyllous
Lady Thatcher
ladylikeness
Mary Pickford
Lady Williams
Calyciflorae
labyrinthine

labyrinthian
karyokinesis
easy on the eye
easy on the ear
baby-snatcher
baryon number
calycoideous
Mary Robinson
many moons ago
palynologist
papyrologist
many-coloured
lady's-slipper
lady's tresses
lady's-thistle
karyotypical
Jazz Warriors
razzle-dazzle
katzenjammer
Abraham Darby
oblanceolate
abrasiveness
à bras ouverts
ebracteolate
obscurantism
obscurantist
abscisic acid
absciss layer
obedientiary
abbey-counter
objet de vertu
able seawoman
oboe di caccia
obsessionist
object lesson
Abbey Theatre
absent-minded
object finder
obreptitious
obsequiously
Observantine
abaft the beam
obligational
obligatorily
obliterative
obliteration
obliviscence
obligingness
absit invidia
absinthiated
Abel Magwitch
ebullioscope
ebullioscopy
abolitionary
abolitionism
abolitionist
absorbed dose
obsolescence
obsoleteness
a broth of a boy
abnormal load
obcompressed
absorptivity
absolute zero
absoluteness
absquatulate
ubiquitarian
ubiquitously
aberrational
Aberdeen City
aboriginally

abortiveness
abortion pill
abbreviation
abbreviatory
abbreviature
abstractedly
abstractness
obstacle race
obstreperate
obstreperous
abstemiously
obstropalous
obstropulous
obiter dictum
obstetrician
abstruseness
obdurateness
obmutescence
obtuse-angled
obnubilation
above measure
above oneself
above the salt
above the line
above-the-line
scramblingly
scratchboard
scratchbuild
scratchbuilt
scratch brush
scratchiness
scratchingly
octane rating
scraperboard
octane number
scraggedness
oceanic crust
occasioned by
occasionally
sciatic nerve
oceanologist
oceanography
octastichous
octastrophic
scabbardless
scabbard fish
scabrousness
ice-cream soda
Academy Award
academically
Schéhérazade
accelerative
acceleration
acceleratory
sclerenchyma
Scheuermann's
screenwriter
screen turtle
scleroderma
sclerodermic
sclerometric
sclerophylly
screw steamer
access charge
access course
accentuation
accentuality
eclectically
scientifical
eccentricity
screw-worm fly

Ockham's razor
Schizaeaceae
scribblement
scribblingly
acciaccatura
schindylesis
schindyletic
active matrix
accidentally
occidentally
actinic glass
schiller spar
Achilles' heel
schismatical
action-taking
action radius
action-packed
action replay
schizocarpic
Echinocactus
echinodermal
schizophrene
schizothymia
schizothymic
schizophytic
echinococcus
schizogonous
schizopodous
actinomorphy
schizomycete
Schiaparelli
scrimshander
script kiddie
script doctor
scripturally
scriptwriter
scrieveboard
scalableness
eco-labelling
scullery-maid
ecologically
scalping-tuft
achlamydeous
acclimatiser
acclimatizer
Iceland poppy
scallop shell
scolopaceous
scolopendrid
ochlophobiac
ocular muscle
ecclesiastic
Ecclesiastes
ecclesiology
scold's bridle
sculpturally
scampishness
ecumenically
scandalously
scandal sheet
iconoclastic
iconic memory
ichnographic
iconographic
scenographic
iconographer
acanthaceous
Acanthamoeba
Scandinavian
Schneiderian
scanning-disc

scintillator
scintigraphy
iconological
economy-class
economic rent
iconomachist
economically
economic zone
econometrics
econometrist
iconophilism
iconophilist
scene-painter
à contre coeur
scene-shifter
icing syringe
ichneumon fly
ectoparasite
McCoy Airport
scholar's mate
scholastical
accouchement
accordionist
octogenarian
octopetalous
octosepalous
acrogenously
scrophularia
acrophonetic
scrobiculate
school-taught
schoolmaster
schorlaceous
schoolfellow
school-leaver
school phobia
school-divine
schoolboyish
school doctor
school-friend
accommodable
accommodator
acroamatical
echo location
echo-sounding
accomplished
accomplisher
accompanyist
across the way
acrostically
octostichous
accoutrement
scoop the pool
accouterment
acronychally
octosyllabic
octosyllable
acrocyanosis
scapegoating
scapegallows
scyphistomae
scyphistomas
scapulimancy
scapulomancy
scaphoid bone
scoptophobia
scoptophilia
scopophiliac
scarabaeuses
acaridomatia
acarodomatia

scarlet fever
scarlet woman
scarificator
scornfulness
scare-heading
scorpion fish
scurrilously
ochroleucous
scoring board
scare tactics
score through
icosahedrons
scissiparity
scissor blade
scissors kick
scissors hold
scissor-tooth
Scotland Yard
scatterbrain
scatteringly
scattermouch
Scutigeridae
Scotch barley
Scotch pebble
Scotch fiddle
Scotch bonnet
Scotch draper
Scottishness
Scythian lamb
scutellation
acetaldehyde
scatological
scitamineous
scatophagous
ecoterrorism
ecoterrorist
ecstatically
acetate rayon
ichthyocolla
ichthyologic
ichthyolitic
ichthyolatry
ichthyophagy
Ichthyopsida
accurateness
accusatively
occupational
accusatorial
scoundrelism
acquiescence
scouring rush
scouring-rush
scrutinising
scrutinizing
scrutinously
acquaintance
Sciuropterus
accursedness
acoustic lens
acoustically
accustrement
accumulative
accumulation
scrupulosity
scrupulously
scavengering
scavenge pump
ectypography
scazon iambus
advance guard
ideal crystal

Edgard Varèse
Edwardianism
Edward A Doisy
Edward Teller
Edward German
Edward Vernon
Edward Jenner
Edward De Bono
Edward Thomas
Edward Gibbon
Edward Wilson
Edward Alleyn
Edward B Lewis
Edward Forbes
Edward Hulton
idealisation
idealization
ideationally
advantageous
odd-come-short
edaciousness
educationist
adscititious
adrenal gland
Edmé Mariotte
adverbialise
adverbialize
ad referendum
adhesiveness
Ade Edmondson
adder's-tongue
adventitious
adjectivally
advisability
Admiralty Bay
Eddie Cochran
Edwin Forrest
additive-free
additionally
administrate
administrant
adminiculate
Edwin Lutyens
Adrienne Rich
addictedness
addle-brained
adulteration
adulterously
Adelina Patti
edulcorative
edulcoration
idolatrously
Adam's flannel
identifiable
identifiably
identity card
identity disc
odontomatous
odontophobia
odontophoral
odontophoran
Odontophorus
odontologist
odontography
Edmond Halley
idiothermous
idiorhythmic
admonishment
Idiom Neutral
idiosyncrasy
adaptability

adaptiveness
adequateness
adorableness
Édith Cresson
Ode to Evening
editorialise
editorialize
editorialist
Edith Sitwell
Edith Wharton
adjutant bird
adjunctively
Edmund Waller
Edmund Wilson
Edmund Rubbra
adjudicative
adjudication
Edouard Manet
metagalactic
separateness
metalanguage
reparability
separability
betacarotene
defamatorily
separatrices
hexadactylic
perambulator
pedal-clavier
decalcomania
melancholiac
melancholiae
recalcitrate
recalcitrant
heraldically
Gerald Scarfe
Gerard Debreu
regardlessly
remand centre
demand-driven
Gerard Kuiper
cetane rating
sexagenarian
decalescence
recalescence
female thread
female condom
hexametrical
metaleptical
ménage à trois
cetane number
legal fiction
decaffeinate
metal fatigue
Penang-lawyer
Te Rangi Hiroa
metaphrastic
seraphically
detachedness
legal holiday
metachronism
metathoracic
metaphorical
metaphysical
metathetical
decapitalise
decapitalize
recapitalise
recapitalize
decapitation
delamination

deracination
desalination
gelatination
hepatisation
hepatization
legalisation
legalization
penalisation
penalization
repagination
revalidation
tetanisation
tetanization
velarisation
velarization
negativeness
relativeness
negative sign
negative pole
petaliferous
get a wiggle on
aerating root
metasilicate
rehabilitate
relativities
relativitist
negativistic
relativistic
Tel Aviv-Jaffa
Melanie Klein
relationless
relationship
relationally
ceramic oxide
hepaticology
behaviorally
recapitulate
behaviourism
behaviourist
Kemal Jumblat
seraskierate
metallically
metallic bond
metallogenic
Heracleitean
metallophone
metallurgist
retail outlet
Geraint Evans
remainder-man
keraunograph
retaining fee
retainership
metagnathous
ferae naturae
demagnetiser
demagnetizer
megalomaniac
metasomatism
teratomatous
Ceratosaurus
megalosaurus
sesamoid bone
hepatomegaly
keratogenous
melanochroic
senatorially
keratoplasty
hepatologist
nematologist
teratologist

Nematomorpha
metamorphism
metamorphist
metamorphose
melanotropin
ceramography
nematocystic
De Maupassant
pedal pushers
repatriation
repairable by
Texas Rangers
Vera Brittain
Texas Stadium
metapsychics
New Amsterdam
telaesthesia
telaesthetic
Sebastian Coe
tenant farmer
penalty bench
pedantocracy
pedantically
semantically
departmental
Telautograph®
web authoring
tenant at will
tenant-at-will
denaturalise
denaturalize
desaturation
get a guernsey
peradventure
metalworking
decasyllabic
decasyllable
legacy-hunter
bedazzlement
Rembrandtish
Rembrandtism
membrane bone
Berbice chair
sea buckthorn
Wembley Arena
kerb-merchant
feeble-minded
pebble-powder
Denbighshire
heeby-jeebies
verbenaceous
reabsorption
Herbert Boyer
kerb-crawling
set by the ears
sea butterfly
Melbourne Cup
New Brunswick
deuch-an-doris
merchandiser
merchandizer
teach a lesson
Mercian Hymns
teachability
neoclassical
merchant bank
merchant navy
merchantable
merchant ship
merchantlike
merchant iron

peace-breaker
peach blossom
beachcombing
peacock's tail
peacock-stone
leucocytosis
leucocytotic
peccadilloes
Mercedes-Benz®
perched block
rescue remedy
geochemistry
rescheduling
mercifulness
peacefulness
henceforward
deactivation
reactivation
reactiveness
new criticism
reaction time
peacekeeping
mercy killing
Percy Lubbock
tercel-jerkin
tercel-gentle
pencil-sketch
Hercules' club
pencil-pusher
reach-me-downs
fence-mending
beacon school
sexcentenary
tercentenary
mercantilism
mercantilist
descensional
geocentrical
peace officer
leucoplastid
perceptivity
perceptional
leucopoiesis
peace process
mercurialise
mercurialize
mercurialism
mercurialist
mercuriality
Neo-Christian
Neoceratodus
red corpuscle
percussively
percussional
percutaneous
reoccupation
bench-warrant
peace-warrant
peach-yellows
leads and lags
dead language
dead-ball line
readableness
vendibleness
hendecagonal
mendaciously
Dead Sea apple
Dead Sea fruit
head register
meddlesomely
heedlessness

needlessness
deed of saying
reed-pheasant
bend the elbow
lead the field
headshrinker
bend-sinister
headmistress
readmittance
Red Delicious
hebdomadally
new dimension
ready-moneyed
dead-and-alive
wedding cards
wedding dress
wedding dower
pendente lite
Heldentenöre
Heldentenors
leading light
geodynamical
wedding march
bedding plant
feeding point
leading reins
lead-in groove
lead in prayer
feed one's face
mend one's pace
mend one's ways
weeding-tongs
herd instinct
head foremost
lead monoxide
dendrologist
dendrologous
heads or tails
readaptation
feldspathoid
fender bender
gender bender
gender person
tender-hefted
feu d'artifice
Neo-Darwinism
Neo-Darwinian
Neo-Darwinist
leader-writer
Jeddart staff
geodesic line
geodesic dome
dead as mutton
geodetic line
geodetically
headquarters
readjustment
meadow fescue
rendezvoused
rendezvouses
severance pay
federal court
Peter Abelard
beverage room
cetera desunt
vegetatively
renewability
generational
revelational
vegetational
general issue

Peter Ackroyd
vegetable oil
vegetable wax
generatrices
René Magritte
general staff
General Synod
je ne sais quoi
benefactress
heterauxesis
remembrancer
remembrances
Peter Behrens
rememberable
rememberably
reverberator
Peterborough
beseechingly
telescopical
Rebecca riots
Terence Stamp
repercussive
Peter Cushing
repercussion
Ferenc Puskas
✧never country
degenerately
degenerative
regenerative
degenerating
deceleration
degeneration
me generation
regeneration
revegetation
regeneratory
se defendendo
bene decessit
telemedicine
Hélène Cixous
levée en masse
teleservices
Peter Fleming
never-failing
Peter Fricker
New Englander
gem-engraving
Peter Gabriel
telergically
revengefully
hebephreniac
genethliacal
genethliacon
telephone box
teleshopping
téléphérique
hereditament
hereditarian
veterinarian
hereditarily
genetic drift
remedilessly
beneficently
feverishness
repetitively
redefinition
beneficially
repetitional
televisional
selenium cell
Venetian mast

veneficously
terebinthine
Benedictines
televisually
Gesellschaft
genealogical
mereological
teleological
Beverly Hills
Peter Lombard
levelling-rod
rebelliously
redeployment
Peter Medawar
Derek Malcolm
determinable
determinably
determinedly
telesmatical
perenniality
Gemeinschaft
hereinbefore
here and there
redecoration
Hemerocallis
heterogamous
heterotactic
heterodactyl
heteroecious
heterocercal
heterosexism
heterosexist
heteromerous
benevolently
heterosexual
heterophylly
heterothally
heterochrony
renegotiable
semeiotician
ceremonially
heteroplasia
heteroblasty
heteroplasty
heteroclitic
telecommuter
Heterosomata
selenologist
heterogonous
heterologous
heteronomous
heteromorphy
Heterocontae
heterokontan
heterotrophy
selenography
generousness
telesoftware
heterostyled
heteropteran
✧heteroousian
heteroduplex
heterocyclic
heterozygote
heterozygous
level pegging
redemptively
gene splicing
redemptioner
Redemptorist
peremptorily

depoliticize
depositional
melodic minor
deposit money
devotionally
negotiatress
bed of justice
recollective
recollection
aeroplankton
ceroplastics
reform school
deformedness
aeroembolism
Sea of Marmara
✧mesoamerican
decommission
recommission
recommitment
refoundation
reconnection
renounceable
denouncement
renouncement
resoundingly
reconnoitrer
recognisable
recognisably
recognisance
recognizable
recognizably
recognizance
decoloration
levorotatory
metoposcopic
Sea of Okhotsk
seropositive
demonologist
mesomorphous
xeromorphous
decorousness
venomousness
decompressor
decomposable
leiotrichous
resourceless
melodramatic
demographics
cerographist
democratical
deconsecrate
reconsecrate
remorsefully
reconstitute
Sea of Showers
demonstrable
demonstrably
remonstrance
demonstrator
remonstrator
repossession
gerontocracy
besottedness
below the salt
below the line
below-the-line
gerontophile
gerontophobe
velouté sauce
aerostatical
demodulation

depopulation
resoluteness
re-solubility
resolubility
revolutional
✧resolutioner
revolutioner
seropurulent
resolvedness
Sea of Vapours
lemon verbena
reconversion
reconveyance
aerodynamics
depolymerise
depolymerize
genotypicity
deepwaterman
deepwatermen
deep-fat fryer
temptability
Neoplatonism
Neoplatonist
bespectacled
respectfully
respectively
Peep-o'-day Boys
resplendence
resplendency
people person
Temple of Hera
people's front
perplexingly
People's Party
reappearance
helplessness
hemp agrimony
keep the field
keep the house
keep the peace
deoppilative
deoppilation
deep-discount
temptingness
despairingly
despoliation
Leopold Bloom
keep a lookout
geopolitical
hempen caudle
weeping birch
Weeping Cross
weeping-cross
responseless
response time
respondentia
serpent-eater
despondently
leaping-house
responsively
serpentinely
despondingly
serpentinise
serpentinite
serpentinize
serpentining
serpentiform
serpentinous
responsorial
keep one's head
keep one's word

serpent-stone
keep one's cool
tenpenny nail
keep good time
jet-propelled
keep a quarter
pepper-caster
pepper-castor
peppered moth
leapfrogging
Pepper's ghost
pepper-shrike
temporal peer
temporalness
temporal lobe
temperalitie
respirometer
temporaneous
jeopardously
leopard's-bane
leopard shark
sea porcupine
despisedness
herpes zoster
perpetualism
perpetration
perpetuation
perpetualist
perpetuality
despotocracy
despotically
despitefully
herpetofauna
herpetologic
sempiternity
geophysicist
desquamative
desquamation
desquamatory
red quebracho
sesquitertia
perquisition
sesquialtera
neuroanatomy
merry as a grig
heart and hand
heart and soul
reproachable
reproachless
decreasingly
learnability
recreational
neorealistic
Georg Büchner
Georg Bednorz
bearableness
terribleness
heartbreaker
learn by heart
jerry-builder
neurobiology
heartburning
depreciative
ferricyanide
ferrocyanide
depreciation
retractation
depreciatory
tetracycline
des richesses
terrace house

detractively
refractively
retractively
detractingly
refractivity
retractility
refractional
tetrachordal
refractorily
tetrachotomy
get-rich-quick
retrocessive
reprocessing
retrocession
metric system
reproducible
reproductive
reproduction
tetradactyly
begrudgingly
petrodollars
merry dancers
Tetradynamia
heart disease
pearl disease
recrudescent
depredations
tetrodotoxin
George Palade
George Gallup
George Cayley
Georges Auric
George Patton
Georges Bizet
George Beadle
retrievement
George Devine
degree Kelvin
merry England
George Thomas
terrae filius
George Colman
George Crabbe
George Orwell
George Graham
fearlessness
peerlessness
pearl-essence
George C Scott
George Stubbs
George Stokes
bearded wheat
Perrier water
neurofibroma
febrifacient
petrifactive
petrifaction
terrifically
retroflexion
retroflected
terrifyingly
heart failure
Jerry Falwell
Fear of Flying
terraforming
pearl-fishery
pearl-fishing
tear-off strip
retrofitting
retrogradely
petrographic

reprographic
necrographer
petrographer
reprographer
Henry Grattan
Henri Giffard
Terry Gilliam
tetragonally
ferrugineous
neurogenesis
petrogenesis
petrogenetic
refrigerator
merry-go-round
petroglyphic
tetrahedrite
tetrahedrons
reprehensive
search engine
reprehension
reprehensory
neurohormone
Pearl Harbour
reordination
Pearl Islands
Hebraistical
dearticulate
retrojection
cedrelaceous
metrological
necrological
neurological
petrological
petrol engine
retromingent
Henry Mancini
recriminator
tetramorphic
Henri Matisse
Febronianism
detruncation
Keiren Fallon
bearing cloth
retrenchment
terra nullius
dégringolade
tear one's hair
tear to shreds
tear to pieces
bear down upon
heortologist
heir apparent
cecropia moth
necrophagous
neuropterans
neuropterist
neuropterous
tetrapterous
necrophiliac
retrophiliac
necrophilism
negrophilism
negrophilist
necrophilous
retropulsive
retropulsion
metropolises
necropolises
metropolitan
tetrapolitan
necrophorous

neurypnology
neuropeptide
Henry Purcell
decrepitness
neuropathist
petrophysics
Henry Raeburn
tetrarchical
metrorrhagia
heart-rending
peer pressure
terror-struck
decrustation
near as dammit
decrescendos
pearl-sheller
refreshfully
Henry Segrave
neurasthenia
neurasthenic
regressively
repressively
depressingly
refreshingly
tetrastichic
tetrastichal
regressivity
neuroscience
refreshments
representant
tetrasporous
neurosurgeon
neurosurgery
heart-service
heart-strings
near as a touch
depressurise
depressurize
ferret-badger
neurotically
secretagogue
heart-to-heart
deerstalking
merrythought
neurotrophic
neurotrophin
secret police
pearl-tapioca
secretariate
defraudation
depravedness
retroversion
Henry Vaughan
heartwarming
heir-by-custom
news magazine
newsmagazine
geese a-laying
de-escalation
Persian berry
newspaperdom
newspaperism
newspaperman
New Statesman
persuasively
sensualistic
Persian wheel
feasibleness
sensibleness
sensible note
pease-bannock

pease-blossom
Jessica Lange
Welsh dresser
seaside grape
bedside table
reassemblage
Meissen china
reassessment
perspectival
gens de guerre
Jews' leavings
versificator
key signature
message board
message-stick
deaspiration
perspiration
perspicacity
perspiratory
seismic array
beesting lips
reassignment
New Scientist
Messeigneurs
verslibriste
seismic shock
Jesse Jackson
tessellation
Les Sylphides
Geissler tube
Geissler pump
Bessemer iron
Peasant Dance
messenger RNA
personifying
persona grata
season ticket
Nelson Piquet
geosynclinal
leasing-maker
seasoning-tub
Person Friday
Feast of Asses
seismonastic
session-clerk
seismoscopic
men's movement
seismometric
Feast of Fools
Feast of Herod
session-house
Deus vobiscum
teaspoonfuls
seismologist
seismography
sensuousness
Feast of Weeks
pease pudding
menstruation
Lesser Bairam
lesser litany
Besserwisser
sensorimotor
measuring cup
measuring jug
measuring-rod
censoriously
Welsh rarebit
Lee Strasberg
dessertspoon
geostrategic

persistently
persistingly
densitometer
sensitometer
densitometry
sensationism
sensationist
Welsh terrier
beestung lips
reassuringly
get stuck into
reassumption
perseverance
perseverator
Gentianaceae
central angle
heat capacity
central conic
left-handedly
central dogma
septuagenary
Septuagesima
meat-salesman
central force
reattachment
neutralistic
Septuagintal
restrainable
restrainedly
next Saturday
vertebration
Beata Beatrix
destabiliser
vestibulitis
destabilizer
Deutsche Mark
pentacrinoid
lenticellate
verticillate
nectocalyces
verticalness
verticillium
lenticularly
denticulated
testiculated
gesticulator
geotechnical
geotectonics
leptocephali
Celtic fringe
Pentecostals
hectocotylus
death-dealing
sextodecimos
pentadactyle
pentadactyly
testudineous
get the hang of
sex therapist
weather along
see the last of
weatherboard
feather-brain
heather-bleat
weather-bound
fent-merchant
weather chart
leathercloth
weathercloth
beetleheaded
get the needle

gentle reader
centre of mass
feather-grass
weather glass
weather gleam
leathergoods
weather gauge
weather house
get the wind up
featheriness
aesthesiogen
get the finger
heathenishly
aestheticise
aestheticize
✧aestheticism
aesthetician
aestheticist
get the mitten
leather-knife
West Germanic
kettle-holder
centre spread
weatherproof
gentle breeze
centre around
beetle-browed
weather stain
restlessness
settle a score
weather strip
Zeitvertreib
ventre à terre
kettlestitch
debt of nature
beatifically
certificated
testificator
meat-offering
left-of-centre
pettifoggery
pettifogging
Betty Friedan
neat's-foot oil
debt of honour
death futures
hectographic
pentagonally
beat the clock
pentahedrons
beat the pants
test the water
teething ring
West Virginia
settling pond
West Midlands
ventripotent
ventriloqual
restrictedly
cestui que use
Keith Jarrett
neat's leather
Sertoli cells
pestological
vestal virgin
centillionth
septillionth
sextillionth
pestilential
dentilingual
bertillonage

petty larceny
gentilitious
septilateral
Pestalozzian
Septemberish
centumvirate
septemvirate
testamentary
vestimentary
Septembriser
Septembrizer
wetting agent
Bettino Craxi
tectonically
Teutonically
pectinaceous
pertinacious
meat and drink
sexton beetle
West End Girls
meeting-house
sententially
septennially
sentinelling
festina lente
sentinel crab
nesting-place
resting place
melting-point
petting party
Newton's rings
septentrions
resting stage
resting spore
jesting-stock
lepton number
dextrocardia
sectionalise
sectionalize
sectionalism
sectionalist
festoon blind
petty officer
depth of focus
depth of field
neutrophilic
beat socks off
centroclinal
Bertholletia
deltiologist
centrosphere
dextrousness
beat to sticks
dextrogyrate
deutoplasmic
centuplicate
pentapolitan
death penalty
heat-apoplexy
perturbative
sectarianise
sectarianize
Nestorianism
sectarianism
centuriation
perturbation
perturbatory
neoterically
letter-weight
welterweight
Letter of Paul

Western Front
Letter of Jude
heater-shield
westerliness
Western Isles
pectoral fins
pectoriloquy
West Bromwich
Petter engine
Deuteronomic
deuteranopia
deuteranopic
Dexter Gordon
letterboxing
teeter-totter
deuteroplasm
century plant
letter-writer
western swing
Western Samoa
Venture Scout
deuteroscopy
dentirostral
rectirostral
reiteratedly
beat a retreat
welter stakes
New Testament
testosterone
Kentish glory
centesimally
leptosomatic
depth sounder
petty treason
heptateuchal
pentateuchal
restaurateur
restauration
test-tube baby
destructible
Newtownabbey
death warrant
serum albumin
Beaumarchais
secular games
bequeathable
bequeathment
regulatively
reputatively
secularistic
benumbedness
renunciative
denunciation
renunciation
denunciatory
renunciatory
Jesus College
pedunculated
sequaciously
sepulchrally
resuscitable
resuscitator
get undressed
secundum quid
recuperative
remunerative
recuperation
rejuvenation
remuneration
recuperatory
remuneratory

detumescence
reputed owner
beaux esprits
reputed quart
requiem shark
Venus flytrap
nebulisation
nebulization
resupination
delusiveness
dehumidifier
deducibility
reducibility
Peruvian bark
security risk
denuclearise
denuclearize
sexual abuser
genuflection
gefüllte fish
medullary ray
sexual system
return of post
return ticket
sequentially
return crease
nebulousness
sedulousness
beaumontague
verumontanum
resumptively
desulphurate
desulphurise
desulphurize
resurrective
✧resurrection
tenuirostral
Berufsverbot
Venus's girdle
revulsionary
sequestrable
sequestrator
Jesuitically
serum therapy
reductionism
reductionist
serviceberry
pervicacious
service court
service hatch
pelvic girdle
service metre
servocontrol
servicewoman
leave for dead
heavy-hearted
merveilleuse
nerve impulse
heave in sight
heaven-fallen
heavens above
Kelvin effect
heavenliness
heaven-gifted
heaven forbid
leaving party
servants' hall
heavenly city
heavenly host
leave one cold
perviousness

Words marked ✧ can also be spelled with one or more capital letters

white pudding
photophilous
photopolymer
photo-process
white pareira
white pyrites
photorealism
white rabbits
rhetorically
White Russian
white slavery
Photostatted
photospheric
photosetting
white settler
phototherapy
that's the idea
what's the odds?
phototrophic
phototropism
photovoltaic
white vitriol
what's with you?
thousand-year
thousand-legs
thousandfold
rheumatismal
thaumatogeny
rheumatology
thaumatology
thaumaturgic
thaumaturgus
The Umbrellas
the underhand
shoulder mark
shoulder belt
shoulder-high
shoulder slip
shoulder knot
shoulder bone
shoulder note
shoulder arms
thoughtfully
ghoulishness
chauvinistic
chauds-mellés
Chaunticleer
shout the odds
shove ha'penny
cheval mirror
chivalrously
The Valkyries
shaving-brush
shaving-stick
chevron board
Cheviot Hills
the very thing
The Visionary
the wicked one
the Wallabies
The Wild Bunch
The Windhover
show one's hand
show one's face
show one's head
the wrong shop
shawl pattern
the world's end
the world over
the Word of God
The Waste Land
show-stopping
show business
Phrygian mode
Rhizocephala
rhizocarpous
rhizogenetic
rhizophagous
rhizophilous
Kitab al-Aqdas
fit as a fiddle
dilatability
Mika Häkkinen
bioavailable
disanalogous
hit a bad patch
Rita Hayworth
disambiguate
air ambulance
disaccharide
financialist
finance house
disaccordant
lizard-hipped
Pirandellian
lizard orchid
Picardy third
bicameralism
bilateralism
dilaceration
bicameralist
Milanese silk
cigarette end
disaventrous
Sir Alf Ramsay
disaffection
disaffiliate
disaggregate
vicar-general
dilapidation
divarication
vitalisation
vitalization
vitativeness
mirabile visu
titaniferous
Sivapithecus
misalignment
Liza Minnelli
Milan Kundera
miracle berry
miracle fruit
misallotment
disallowable
disallowance
Sir Arnold Bax
disannulment
disannulling
Titanosaurus
dilatoriness
limacologist
misapprehend
disappointed
dicarpellary
disapproving
cicatrichule
disagreeable
disagreeably
disagreement
disassociate
kinaesthesia
kinaesthesis
kinaesthetic
disassembler
didactically
gigantically
gigantomachy
disauthorise
disauthorize
disastrously
disaster film
misanthropic
misanthropos
Sinanthropus
disaster area
miraculously
disadvantage
disadventure
misadventure
misadvisedly
binary weapon
binary number
binary pulsar
binary system
Bilbo Baggins
finback whale
limbic system
bibble-babble
gibble-gabble
ribble-rabble
nimble-witted
nimble-footed
air-breathing
misbehaviour
diabolically
misbelieving
Kimball O'Hara
timbromaniac
timbrologist
filbert brush
disbursement
Wilbur Wright
Gilbert White
Limbus patrum
nimbostratus
disbowelling
disclamation
mischanceful
hitch and kick
pitch-and-toss
pitch and putt
Mircea Eliade
mischallenge
aircraftsman
disco biscuit
pisciculture
pinchcommons
piccadilloes
viscoelastic
witches' broom
kitchen chair
kitchen Dutch
discreteness
discretively
circle-riding
discretional
biochemistry
kitchen-knave
biocoenology
pitcher plant
kitchen-range
circle around
kitchen-stuff
kitchen table
discreetness
kitchen-wench
zincographic
discographer
zincographer
miscegenator
circuit board
pitching tool
witching hour
hitching post
discriminate
discriminant
circuit judge
circuitously
circuit rider
zinc ointment
miscellanist
Lincoln green
circular file
circular note
Lincolnshire
miscalculate
circumjacent
circumscribe
Discomycetes
Discomedusae
discomedusan
circumcentre
discomfiting
✧circumcision
discomfiture
circumfluent
circumfluous
Giacomo Manzú
discommodity
air-commodore
circumlocute
discomposure
mince matters
circumstance
circumnutate
circumfusile
circumfusion
discommunity
circumgyrate
Vincent D'Indy
discandering
disconnexion
disconnected
discontented
miscontented
misconceiver
air-condition
disconsolate
Vincent Price
misconstruct
piece of eight
piece of goods
disceptation
discipleship
disciplinant
disciplinary
discophorous
discordantly
discursively
Sir Carol Reed
diachronical
discorporate
discerptible
viscerotonia
viscerotonic
circassienne
viscosimeter
viscosimetry
viscose rayon
discouraging
discount rate
discountable
viscountship
discourteise
Viscount Hood
discourteous
viscous water
discoverable
Discovery Bay
discoverture
bird-catching
birdwatching
misdiagnosis
Hildebrandic
vindictively
vindicatress
fiddle-faddle
middle school
middleweight
bird's-eye view
Middle Temple
kiddiewinkie
middle-income
niddle-noddle
fiddle around
middle ground
mindlessness
fiddlesticks
Wild-West Show
fiddle-string
Middle States
tiddledywink
wind of change
bird of wonder
wind-changing
wildlife park
disdainfully
wild Williams
Rio de Janeiro
lit de justice
mind-altering
misdemeanant
misdemeanour
diadem spider
findon haddie
hidden agenda
sindonophany
birding-piece
winding stair
find one's legs
find one's feet
winding sheet
bird's-nesting
Windsor chair
hindforemost
mind-boggling
Hindoostanee
kindergarten
misdirection
girder bridge
pia desideria
hindquarters
Wild Huntsman
Sir David Lean
biodiversity
window screen
sit down under
wild hyacinth
kindly tenant
Time Magazine
fire-watching
cinéma vérité
cinematheque
cinemathèque
River Acheron
literariness
mixed-ability
liberalistic
literalistic
mineral jelly
Mike Hailwood
mineralogise
mineralogize
mineralogist
vinegar-plant
River Alpheus
Liberal Party
mineral pitch
fireman's lift
mineral water
disembrangle
likeableness
disembellish
disembarrass
fixed charges
mixed chalice
disenchanted
disenchanter
life sciences
line scanning
fixed capital
tiger country
mixed crystal
River Dnieper
river dolphin
mixed doubles
disendowment
time-bewasted
wine merchant
lite pendente
mine detector
wide receiver
like hey-go-mad
sidereal year
sidereal time
nineteenthly
mixed economy
lifelessness
timelessness
tirelessness
live-feathers
life sentence
line of battle
line of beauty
line of vision
line of credit
mixed farming
River Glommen
River Garonne
six-eight time
give the alarm
like the devil
give the elbow
Rider Haggard
give the heave
vice-chairman

side whiskers
bite the thumb
kinesipathic
dimerisation
dimerization
time dilation
like wildfire
lifelikeness
five-line whip
liverishness
tigerishness
firefighting
kinesiatrics
Nigel Kennedy
like old boots
pinealectomy
Mike Oldfield
River Limpopo
wineglassful
River Madeira
give a meeting
Nigel Mansell
River Marañón
River Maritsa
time and a half
time and again
Hibernianism
pigeon's-blood
hibernaculum
Hibernically
life-and-death
life-interest
give in charge
Gideon Bibles
live and learn
pigeon-flying
live in clover
give on a plate
River Narmada
pigeon breast
line-engraver
hide one's head
bide one's time
rise and shine
fire and sword
give one's word
pipe and tabor
like anything
life instinct
ride for a fall
fide non armis
like gold dust
tiresomeness
live together
vice-governor
siderophilic
River Orinoco
give points to
ride to hounds
time-honoured
wine-coloured
time constant
Tibet Plateau
wide-spectrum
Liverpudlian
fixed-penalty
River Phoenix
Didelphyidae
fire practice
wisecracking
line breeding

Five Articles
timed-release
birefringent
fireproofing
rice crispies
Rice Krispies®
mifepristone
River Shannon
license block
diseasedness
diversifying
River Schelde
pipers piping
River Salween
River Selenga
River Sénégal
diversionary
diversionist
license plate
liver sausage
give it laldie
direct labour
direct object
disestablish
liberticidal
direct access
direct action
diverticulum
diverticular
direct method
give it wellie
liberty horse
wire-stringed
wirestripper
line-item veto
divertimenti
divertimento
ride at anchor
dilettantish
bicentennial
dilettantism
Sir Elton John
direct motion
licentiously
direct speech
Silent Spring
river-terrace
director's cut
directorship
wire-stitched
directly that
River Ucayali
Citeaux Abbey
miseducation
hire-purchase
Eisen und Blut
River Uruguay
River Vistula
minesweeping
River Waikato
pile-dwelling
wife-swapping
time exposure
timely-parted
River Yenisei
livery stable
River Zambezi
disfranchise
diffrangible
pin-feathered
bioflavonoid

misfeaturing
difficulties
kilfud-yoking
Sir Fred Hoyle
Tiffany glass
misformation
air-force blue
differentiae
differential
diffusedness
diffusionism
diffusionist
disgradation
biographical
diagrammatic
lingua franca
singableness
King's College
king's-cushion
King's Counsel
ringed plover
single-handed
single parent
dingle-dangle
higgle-haggle
jingle-jangle
mingle-mangle
wiggle-waggle
disgregation
single market
single-acting
single-action
single-decker
single-seater
king's English
single-minded
single-wicket
single-figure
single combat
siege economy
single-priced
king of metals
king of beasts
✧king's highway
wing shooting
disguiseless
disguisement
ringside seat
ringside view
pilgrimise it
pilgrimize it
pilgrim's sign
virgo intacta
linguistical
Kingsley Amis
Virginia Wade
Virginia Leng
Virginia reel
virgin's-bower
singing flame
singing hinny
digging stick
ring-compound
diageotropic
biogeography
ring dotterel
figgy pudding
✧king's proctor
ring-armature
disgorgement
Niagara Falls

fingerlickin'
finger-and-toe
Ginger Rogers
ring-dropping
finger buffet
disgustfully
disgustingly
ring-streaked
gingivectomy
fish-hatchery
might and main
right-and-left
fish-salesman
with bad grace
Withnail and I
disheartened
highfaluting
lie heavy upon
night-brawler
night crawler
nightclothes
nightclubber
Michael Buerk
Michael Caine
high-reaching
Richie Benaud
Michael Foale
Michael Frayn
Michael Grade
eighteenthly
eighteen-hole
high-velocity
Michael Palin
Richter scale
Lichtenstein
high-seasoned
night fighter
rightfulness
night-fishery
lithographic
lithographer
Sir Hugh Munro
light-hearted
diphthongise
diphthongize
right-hand man
diphtheritic
diphtheritis
mithridatise
mithridatize
mithridatism
high-five-sign
high fidelity
high-fidelity
fighting talk
fighting fish
fighting cock
with dispatch
ditheistical
lithological
Wilhelm Kühne
Michelangelo
Michel Fokine
Nicholas Rowe
✧ditheletical
litholatrous
fish and chips
within reason
Sirhan Sirhan
within limits
Sir Hans Krebs

lightning bug
lightning rod
Siphonaptera
siphonophore
dishonorable
dishonorably
siphonostele
wishing stone
with one voice
Sir Henry Tate
Sir Henry Vane
Sir Henry Wood
dichromatism
dichroscopic
withholdment
right of entry
aichmophobia
High Holidays
high-sounding
high-coloured
Night of Power
dichrooscope
High Holy Days
sight-playing
lithophagous
bishop's court
lithophilous
bishop sleeve
with open arms
tithe-proctor
high-spirited
Richard Adams
sight-reading
cichoraceous
witheredness
high-priestly
bilharziasis
bilharziosis
light railway
Richard Lower
Richard Meade
pichurim bean
dithyrambist
Richard Nixon
hither and yon
disharmonise
disharmonize
Richard Pryor
Richard Stone
Richard Scott
high-pressure
withdrawment
lithospermum
xiphisternum
lithospheric
sight-singing
fish-strainer
high-sticking
light therapy
right the helm
lithotritise
lithotritize
lithotritist
lithotriptic
lithotripter
lithotriptor
right-to-lifer
lithotomical
with a thought
high-stepping
night terrors

without doors
without doubt
without price
without tears
dishevelment
dishevelling
with a witness
highly geared
highty-tighty
highly-strung
win in a canter
digital clock
visitational
militaristic
divinatorial
visitatorial
viviparously
digital radio
mini-lacrosse
digital socks
digital watch
military band
pitiableness
disincentive
civil defence
Cicindelidae
liriodendron
Milindapanha
Kiri Te Kanawa
viridescence
virilescence
Citizens' Band
pitilessness
divided skirt
disinflation
disinfectant
disinfection
misinformant
bilingualism
riding master
riding school
living memory
diving petrel
diving beetle
disingenuity
disingenuous
living fossil
timing pulley
disinherison
citification
civilisation
civilization
digitisation
digitization
minification
minimisation
minimization
nidification
vilification
vinification
virilisation
virilization
vivification
divisiveness
siliciferous
visiting card
visiting-book
diminishable
diminishment
vitilitigate
visibilities

divisibility
division bell
libidinosity
silicicolous
libidinously
divinity calf
divinity hall
civil liberty
visible means
bimillennium
oil immersion
Tinian Island
mini-motorway
minicomputer
visitors' book
biliary fever
filius terrae
filius populi
civil servant
civil service
ministrative
ministration
sinistrality
disintegrate
disintricate
sinistrorsal
sinistrously
sinisterness
disinterment
ministership
sinisterwise
disinterring
misinterpret
diminutively
diminuendoes
ridiculously
vinicultural
viticultural
filibusterer
miminy-piminy
niminy-piminy
Sir Jack Hobbs
misjudgement
Sir John Junor
Sir John Mills
Sir John Soane
disjointedly
Sir Jesse Boot
Sir J J Thomson
disk capacity
pickadilloes
sick headache
sickle-shaped
kickie-wickie
lick the birse
ticklishness
milk sickness
nickel silver
milk and honey
risk analysis
lick one's lips
milking stool
kicking strap
sick and tired
milk-and-water
Kilkenny cats
pick to pieces
misknowledge
milk porridge
pick up the tab
kick up a stink
kick upstairs
pickerel-weed
lick-trencher
wicketkeeper
ticket office
ticket window
ticket-holder
ticket porter
ticket writer
lickety-split
mickey-taking
Mickey Mantle
Mickey Rooney
William Blake
William Bragg
William Beebe
William Bligh
William Booth
William Burke
William Boyce
William Clark
William Cecil
William Carey
billiard ball
Mills-and-Boon
William Hague
misleadingly
Will Ladislaw
William James
William Lawry
William Osler
William Paley
William Prout
uillean pipes
William Perry
William Smith
Williamsburg
William Wyler
diploblastic
Billy Bremner
nielsbohrium
Lillibullero
Lilliburlero
Bible-bashing
field battery
Diplock court
dialecticism
dialectician
field colours
dialectology
dislocatedly
Billy Crystal
digladiation
dislodgement
viola da gamba
williewaught
Willie Carson
tirlie-wirlie
fielded panel
will-lessness
Bill Beaumont
Kielder Water
bill of lading
bill of health
✧bill of rights
millefeuille
field glasses
biologically
rifle grenade
village idiot
diplogenesis
field geology
Villahermosa
yieldingness
dialling code
dialling tone
villainously
mill-sixpence
field kitchen
Citlaltépetl
field meeting
rifleman bird
Billy McNeill
field marshal
diplomatical
violoncellos
killing field
milling grade
willing horse
violin spider
billingsgate
violent storm
bibliomaniac
bibliopegist
field officer
bibliophobia
till doomsday
mill-mountain
bibliologist
bibliopolist
pillion-rider
kill-courtesy
bibliography
Lilliputians
Bible-pounder
pillar-box red
Willy Russell
miller's thumb
field-spaniel
Gilles de Rais
millisievert
millesimally
Miklós Horthy
will-o'-the-wisp
Bible-thumper
field walking
willow grouse
Finlay Calder
tilley-valley
kill by inches
biomechanics
Jimmy Connors
diamagnetism
biomagnetics
Jimmy Greaves
sigmoid colon
pigmentation
diamond-drill
diamond-field
Sigmund Freud
Simmenthaler
diamond-hitch
diamond snake
diamond-wheel
✧jimmy-o'goblin
Kimmeridgian
firmer chisel
Sir Marcus Fox
dimmer switch
Siamese twins
Sir Matt Busby
mismatchment
biometrician
Jimmy Tarbuck
Jimmy Woodser
Sir Max Aitken
dismayedness
sign language
cinnabar moth
Giant Despair
rien ne va plus
diencephalic
diencephalon
pinniewinkle
significance
significancy
significator
Piano Fantasy
Midnight Mass
midnight blue
fiendishness
giant-killing
limnological
Lionel Richie
Lionel Jospin
cinnamic acid
his name is mud
cinnamon bear
finnan haddie
Bignoniaceae
limnophilous
ligniperdous
dinner jacket
giant's-kettle
witness stand
giant's stride
Sir Nathaniel
winnowing-fan
Sidney Bechet
Sidney Altman
kidney-potato
mixobarbaric
Nikolai Gogol
Nicola Pisano
kilowatt hour
pilot balloon
Simón Bolívar
Li-ion battery
vin ordinaire
disoperation
linoleic acid
dig oneself in
Nicole Kidman
disobedience
dipole moment
win one's spurs
tip off liquor
✧risorgimento
disorganised
disorganized
timothy grass
mitochondria
Timothy Spall
ricochetting
nicotinamide
Nixon in China
simoniacally
mitotic index
disorientate
Tironian sign
Simon Kuznets
lino blocking
Simon Langham
oil of mirbane
picornavirus
ribosomal RNA
pilot officer
kimono sleeve
rigorousness
timorousness
vigorousness
minor planets
minor premise
pilot project
oil of rhodium
ailourophile
ailourophobe
timocratical
lie of the land
fit of the face
six of the best
bit on the side
ribonuclease
oil of vitriol
misogynistic
displaceable
displacement
misplacement
diaphanously
Hippocratise
Hippocratize
Hippocratism
hippocrepian
hippocentaur
ripple-marked
ripple effect
nipple-shield
simple-minded
displeasedly
displeasance
disprivacied
disprivilege
air pollution
dispensative
dispensation
dispensatory
Hispanically
dispense with
✧hispaniolise
✧hispaniolize
Hispanophile
mispunctuate
air-propeller
mispronounce
dispropriate
hippophagist
hippophagous
hippopotamic
hippopotamus
diapophysial
dispiritedly
dispiritment
dispossessed
dispossessor
dispute about
dispatch case
dispatch-boat
dispiteously
Sir Peter Hall
Sir Peter Buck
disputatious
dispauperise
dispauperize
Sir Paul Nurse
biophysicist
disqualified
disqualifier
disquisitive
disquisition
disquisitory
disquietness
misquotation
microanatomy
Sierra Nevada
rip-roaringly
nitroaniline
fibroblastic
microbrewery
microbalance
nitrobenzene
microbiology
microclimate
vibracularia
citriculture
cirro-cumulus
misreckoning
microcephaly
microcopying
microcapsule
picrocarmine
microcircuit
Sigrid Undset
vitro-di-trina
Pierre Cardin
Pierre Lescot
Pierre Boulez
vitrifaction
vitrifacture
microfilaria
hierographic
micrographic
hierographer
micrographer
microgranite
microgravity
hierogrammat
disregardful
ditriglyphic
hieroglyphic
microhabitat
piercingness
mitrailleuse
Giorgi system
fibrillation
Gibraltarian
hierological
micrological
disrelishing
nitromethane
microneedles
Dibranchiata
dibranchiate
fibrinolysin
fibrinolysis
vitriolation
diprionidian
vitreousness
microphagous
hierophantic
misrepresent
micropterous
disruptively
nitrophilous
microprinted
bipropellant

vibraphonist
Piers Plowman
microprogram
micropipette
disreputable
disreputably
microphysics
hierarchical
mirror finish
mirror writer
nitroso-group
digressively
microseismic
digressional
Microscopium
microscopist
microscooter
microsurgeon
microsurgery
citrus fruits
cirro-stratus
microtubular
nitrotoluene
microtomical
microtonally
migrationist
vibratiuncle
nitrous oxide
His Reverence
sir-reverence
microwavable
biorhythmics
Sir Roy Strong
first and last
air-sea rescue
misstatement
dissuasively
Miss Havisham
dissocialise
dissocialize
dissociative
dissociation
dissociality
dissected map
fissicostate
tissue-typing
first-footing
kissogram man
kirschwasser
pigs might fly
bioscientist
missel-thrush
diesel engine
fissilingual
missummation
Midsummer day
midsummer-men
dissymmetric
dissemblance
dissimilarly
dissimulator
disseminator
Vinson Massif
kissing-crust
dissenterish
dissenterism
first-nighter
biosynthesis
biosynthetic
dissentingly
missionarise
missionarize
mission creep
Winslow Homer
Winston Smith
Winston-Salem
dissipatedly
dissertative
first reading
tin-streaming
dissertation
dies profesti
first refusal
diastrophism
fissirostral
biosatellite
dissatisfied
Sir Scudamour
disseverment
disseverance
jigsaw puzzle
virtual focus
virtual image
filtrability
distrainable
distrainment
mistranslate
distractible
distractedly
Sir Toby Belch
histochemist
birth control
eisteddfodic
eisteddfodau
birthday cake
birthday-book
birthday suit
kittle cattle
mixtie-maxtie
tittle-tattle
tip the scales
little people
little office
oil the wheels
mistle-thrush
little finger
little Hitler
Little Dipper
diathermancy
Little-endian
little wonder
Little Dorrit
hit the bottle
Mistress Page
Wittgenstein
listlessness
mistressless
mistress-ship
Mistress Ford
mistreatment
mirthfulness
pictographic
Kitty Godfree
histogenesis
histogenetic
lift the elbow
Pitt the Elder
birthing pool
Sittlichkeit
histrionical
distributary
distributive
distribution
mistakenness
distillation
distillatory
histological
dirty laundry
Mittel-Europa
Mitteleuropa
diatomaceous
distemperate
Wilton carpet
tintinnabula
diatonically
distanceless
kitten-heeled
Milton Keynes
listenership
lift one's hand
distinctness
fictionalise
fictionalize
fictionality
Piet Mondrian
Histiophorus
virtuosoship
virtuousness
dictyopteran
Tintern Abbey
winter garden
Victoria Peak
disturbative
Victoria Nile
Victorianism
bioturbation
litter basket
✧victoria plum
Victoria Wood
filter-passer
mixter-maxter
pitter-patter
historically
pictorically
historic cost
filter-feeder
winter-weight
winter-beaten
picture frame
dietary fibre
winter cherry
picture house
sisterliness
sisters-in-law
distortional
filter-tipped
winter clover
filter coffee
bioterrorism
bioterrorist
historiology
winterbourne
Mister Wopsle
victoriously
Picturephone®
winter sports
bitter orange
picture ratio
winter-ground
History Today
Mister Bumble
hiatus hernia
List D schools
dietetically
Uintatherium
fictitiously
dictatorship
fiat currency
distrustless
mistrustless
dirty weekend
diethylamine
diethyl ether
fidus Achates
figuratively
figurability
sinupalliate
Sinus Aestuum
liquid helium
virus disease
liquid assets
liquid storax
fidus et audax
vituperative
vituperation
vituperatory
figure-caster
lieutenantry
figure skater
liquefacient
liquefactive
liquefaction
liturgically
liturgiology
dijudication
dilucidation
Liguliflorae
liguliforal
visual acuity
ritual murder
visual purple
sinusoidally
ailurophobia
ailurophobic
ailurophilia
ailurophilic
pious opinion
bibulousness
Linus Pauling
situatedness
simultaneity
simultaneous
situationism
situationist
liqueur glass
Dieu avec nous
silviculture
mid-Victorian
Silva Eusebio
Rip Van Winkle
misventurous
silver salmon
silver screen
silver-beater
silver lining
silver-glance
silver-plated
silver-voiced
silver iodide
silver dollar
silver surfer
Sir W S Gilbert
Midwesterner
Midway Island
vinyl acetate
city of refuge
cityfication
dipyridamole
bicycle chain
city planning
pityrosporum
Yitzhak Rabin
Lizzie Borden
zigzag stitch
mizzencourse
Zinzan Brooke
Linz Symphony
ejection seat
Ujung Pandang
Oklahoma City
skreigh of day
G K Chesterton
skrimshanker
skullduggery
Skelmersdale
skillfulness
skillion roof
skeleton suit
skin magazine
skunk cabbage
a king's ransom
skinny-dipper
skipjack tuna
skipping-rope
skip-tooth saw
skirt-dancing
skateboarder
skutterudite
skittishness
skittle-alley
sky-tinctured
skeuomorphic
clear as a bell
clean and jerk
alla cappella
pleasantness
pleasantries
Alhambresque
float chamber
Elias Canetti
all and sundry
Sloane Ranger
alkalescence
alkalescency
clear felling
alkali metals
clearing sale
clearing bank
cleaning lady
pleasingness
floating debt
pleading diet
floating vote
floating dock
Eleanor Cross
Eleanor Rigby
clear-obscure
clear-sighted
alla stoccata
olfactometer
olfactometry
olfactronics
altaltissimo
illaqueation
pleasureless
pleasure boat
pleasure trip
ill-advisedly
Albany herald
club sandwich
clubbability
Glubbdubdrib
slubberingly
blabbermouth
globigerinae
slobbishness
flabellation
global search
flabelliform
club together
ill-beseeming
plebiscitary
Globe Theatre
globe thistle
globetrotter
black-and-blue
electability
elucubration
placableness
blackballing
blackbirding
blockbusting
block capital
blackcurrant
Black Country
black draught
black diamond
block diagram
slockdolager
slockdoliger
slockdologer
black-eye bean
black-eyed pea
Black English
cliché-ridden
flickeringly
flicker noise
black economy
slickensided
glockenspiel
blocked style
black-figured
black-fishing
blackguardly
glycogenesis
glycogenetic
black-hearted
Black Hawk War
slack in stays
blacklisting
black mustard
placentation
Placentia Bay
placentiform
placentology
Black on Black
block of flats
electorially
Plectognathi
glaciologist
black pudding
plecopterous
Black Panther
glucoprotein
glycoprotein
black-quarter

electric hare
electric seal
electric fire
electric blue
electrically
electrifying
electrograph
electrogenic
block release
electrolyser
electrolysis
electrolytic
electromeric
electrometer
electromotor
electrometry
electron pair
electron beam
electron lens
electronvolt
electron tube
electro-optic
electroplate
electrophile
electropolar
Black Russian
electrosonde
electroscope
electroshock
electrotonic
electrotonus
electrotypic
electrotyper
Black Sabbath
black salsify
Alice Springs
place setting
black treacle
Ely Cathedral
elocutionary
Old Catholics
elocutionist
click-through
flick through
flocculation
Alec Guinness
black-visaged
clock-watcher
Claddagh ring
gladiatorial
gladiatorian
sledgehammer
bladder senna
bladderwrack
cladogenesis
cladogenetic
cloddishness
Aladdin's cave
Aladdin's lamp
gliding plane
sliding scale
gladsomeness
Gladys Knight
cladosporium
Gladstone bag
blue water gas
Blaenau Gwent
alienability
alterability
fleet admiral
all-embracing
sleeper shark
Bloemfontein
Elaeagnaceae
all edges gilt
blue pipe-tree
bleeding edge
bleeding-edge
sleeping pill
sleeping-suit
illegitimate
illegitimacy
illegibility
alder-liefest
alveolar arch
aldermanship
aldermanlike
glue-sniffing
Blue Mountain
ulcerousness
eleemosynary
Fleet parsons
blue asbestos
bluestocking
client-server
Albert Finney
Albert Claude
Albert Square
Alberto Tomba
blue quandong
sleepwalking
Fleetwood Mac
blue-eyed soul
✧sleepy hollow
cliffhanging
Cliff Richard
Old Fashioned
old-fashioned
sluggishness
flagellation
flagellatory
flagelliform
Ulugh Muztagh
sloganeering
plagiotropic
oligopeptide
oligarchical
oligospermia
oligotrophic
flagitiously
Althea Gibson
alpha-blocker
alphabetical
alphabet soup
Alpha Doradus
blah-blah-blah
alphamerical
alphanumeric
Old Hundredth
Elihu Thomson
à la hauteur de
clairaudient
ultimate load
pleiochasium
plain cookery
plainclothes
all-inclusive
plain dealing
plain-dealing
Blaise Pascal
illiterately
alliterative
illiberalise
illiberalize
alliteration
illiberality
Claire Rayner
Alpine skiing
altimetrical
Albigensians
flying saucer
flying lizard
flying doctor
flying column
flying bridge
flying dragon
plain-hearted
fluidisation
fluidization
illimitation
fluidized bed
claiming race
Elgin marbles
clair-obscure
Elvis Presley
all-important
Alain Resnais
ellipsograph
plain sailing
Plains Indian
elliptically
cleistogamic
pleiotropism
altitudinous
clairvoyance
clairvoyancy
flammability
plumbaginous
clamjamphrie
blamableness
plumber-block
plummer-block
glimmeringly
slumberingly
slumberously
slumber party
slumpflation
blamefulness
flame-grilled
alembication
flammiferous
plumbiferous
Olympic flame
climbing wall
Olympic games
climbing boot
climbing iron
blimpishness
old-maidishly
Olympic torch
plumulaceous
alimentative
elementalism
alimentation
elementarily
old man's beard
Clemence Dane
Clement Freud
Clément Marot
flamboyantly
Plimsoll mark
Plimsoll line
plum-porridge
clomipramine
Old Mortality
à l'improviste
Glamis Castle
climatically
flame-thrower
flammulation
plum curculio
Plymouth Rock
old moustache
plantain lily
slink butcher
plano-concave
plano-conical
blanc-de-Chine
flannelboard
clinker-built
clinker-block
flannelgraph
blunderingly
blonde moment
slanderously
blanket spray
Blind Freddie
Klinefelter's
flank forward
planographic
flint-hearted
Alan L Hodgkin
clincher-work
glandiferous
slantingways
plunging fold
clannishness
blandishment
Alan Sillitoe
flint-knapper
plenum system
clangorously
blennorrhoea
plenipotence
plenipotency
Glen T Seaborg
blind-stamped
planispheric
plane sailing
blind tooling
ill-naturedly
planetesimal
planet-struck
glandulously
slang-whanger
blood and iron
all of a dither
allowability
all of a doodah
pleonastical
all of a sudden
blood blister
blood brother
all over again
fluorescence
oleoresinous
fluoridation
fluorination
illogicality
fluorimetric
alto-rilievos
floodlighted
glioblastoma
bloodletting
floor manager
All or Nothing
all-or-nothing
fluorocarbon
Eleonora Duse
fluoroscopic
fluorometric
fluorochrome
pleomorphism
pleomorphous
fluorouracil
fluorography
blood packing
blood pudding
bloodstained
bloodsucking
Alfonso Reyes
blood sausage
Aldous Huxley
fly-on-the-wall
bloodthirsty
Blood Wedding
bloody-minded
slip-carriage
elephant seal
elephant's-ear
flippantness
clip-fastener
elephant cord
clapperboard
Old Pretender
slipperiness
slipper socks
slipper satin
slip of the pen
slip the cable
slop-clothing
slip a mooring
slip one's ways
kleptomaniac
glyphography
glyptography
kleptocratic
klipspringer
all-pervading
claptrappery
cliquishness
Clare College
floriculture
Alfred Deller
Alfred Sisley
Alfred Kinsey
Alfred Austin
plurilocular
pluriliteral
ultramontane
ultramundane
ultroneously
clarinettist
gloriousness
clare-obscure
clerk of works
ultrasensual
pluriseriate
all-roundness
slurry tanker
plasma screen
slash-and-burn
glossarially
glass-blowing
close borough
glass cockpit
glass ceiling
close company
close-cropped
glass-cutting
close-coupled
closed season
plasterboard
cluster graft
plasteriness
blusteringly
glisteringly
slasher movie
blister-steel
plaster saint
plasterstone
slash fiction
blissfulness
flash forward
flash-forward
blast furnace
close-fitting
close-grained
old school tie
close harmony
alas the while
classicalism
plastination
classicalist
classicality
plessimetric
plastic force
classifiable
elastic limit
plastic money
classic races
All Saints' Day
close-mouthed
closing price
plasmosomata
glossologist
blastosphere
elasmobranch
glossography
Glass Pyramid
flesh-pottery
all systems go
bless the mark
close the door
close-tongued
blastulation
glassyheaded
Plattdeutsch
bletheration
clothes-brush
clotted cream
clothes-horse
clatteringly
flatteringly
glitteringly
flatbed lorry
flitter-mouse
blithesomely
flatterously
clothes-press
flat-bed press
Blithe Spirit
bletherskate
blatherskite
clothes-sense
ill-treatment

 Words marked ✧ can also be spelled with one or more capital letters

flatbed truck
slothfulness
elytrigerous
sluttishness
Ulotrichales
plate-leather
glutamic acid
Clytemnestra
platanna frog
Blatant Beast
Platonic year
platonically
platanaceous
Blut und Eisen
platinum lamp
platinum disc
Plateosaurus
platform game
platform heel
platform sole
alstroemeria
gluttonously
cloth of state
Old Testament
slate-writing
cloud chamber
cloud ceiling
flour dredger
clouted cream
glaucescence
Glauber's salt
album Graecum
slouch-hatted
slaughterman
slaughterous
Plough Monday
plough-jogger
ploughwright
eleutherarch
Klyuchevskoy
illuminative
illuminating
claudication
illumination
allusiveness
illusiveness
plausibility
pleurisy-root
cloud-kissing
glaucomatous
Pleuronectes
illusoriness
cloud-seeding
all-up service
illustrative
claustration
illustration
illustratory
alive and well
clavicembalo
slaveholding
eleventh hour
eleventh-hour
slovenliness
cloven-hoofed
cloven-footed
pluviometric
flavoprotein
Oliver de Bois
clever-clever
slave traffic
slow handclap
blow the coals
clownishness
blow one's mind
blow-moulding
flower-garden
flower delice
flower-delice
flowerpecker
✧flower people
flower deluce
flower-de-luce
flower-deluce
flower of Jove
flowers of tan
old wives' tale
flexibleness
flexible disk
Alex Ferguson
flexographic
alexipharmic
elixir of life
Alexis Carrel
Lloyd Bridges
Floyd Bennett
play the devil
play the field
play the woman
play with fire
playing field
claymore mine
play at waster
Elizabeth Fry
immaterially
empathically
Emma Thompson
R M Ballantyne
embarquement
embarrassing
ambassadress
empassionate
impassionate
impartiality
smear tactics
embattlement
immaculately
immatureness
Immanuel Kant
amicableness
amicus curiae
imperatively
imperatorial
impercipient
imperceptive
impenetrable
impenetrably
imperfective
imperfection
imperforable
imperforated
amber gambler
immethodical
impedimental
impenitently
imperishable
imperishably
impetiginous
imperial yard
imperial city
Umbelliferae
I'm telling you
impermanence
impermanency
immemorially
ampelography
impersonally
impersonator
immersionism
immersionist
immeasurable
immensurable
immeasurably
impersistent
impertinence
impertinency
imperviously
embezzlement
emigrational
amygdaloidal
image breaker
image printer
image-worship
amphibrachic
amphibiously
amphictyonic
amphigastria
omphalomancy
amphisbaenic
amphisbaenae
amphisbaenas
amphistomous
emphatically
amphitheatre
amphitropous
ambivalently
omnisciently
immiseration
ambidextrous
umbilication
imbibitional
ambitionless
ambient noise
omnipotently
omnivorously
impierceable
omnipresence
embitterment
omnibus train
smoke signals
amalgamative
amalgamation
a mile a minute
small calorie
small-clothes
implicitness
Emily Davison
emollescence
smallest room
smallholding
emulsifiable
small letters
emolumentary
emblematical
implantation
ameliorative
amelioration
emblazonment
amenableness
emancipation
emancipatory
amentiferous
amontillados
immovability
imponderable
imponderably
immoderately
immoderation
smooth-talker
smooth-leaved
smooth-coated
smooth-spoken
smooth-browed
smooth muscle
embolisation
embolization
impoliteness
imposingness
embourgeoise
empoisonment
imposthumate
American aloe
American plan
impregnation
umbrageously
amortisation
amortization
emargination
amortisement
amortizement
umbrella bird
umbrella pine
umbrella tree
emerald green
smart missile
Amarantaceae
embranchment
embryophytes
embryologist
ombrophilous
impropriator
ombrophobous
empressement
impressively
impressional
imprisonable
imprisonment
improvidence
improvisator
smash-and-grab
amuse-bouches
amuse-gueules
omissiveness
amissibility
emasculation
emasculatory
imitableness
smotheriness
smatteringly
smotheringly
emotionalise
emotionalize
emotionalism
emotionalist
emotionality
amitotically
amateurishly
ambulanceman
imputatively
immutability
imputability
immune system
immunisation
immunization
immunoglobin
immunologist
impulse buyer
empyreumatic
Antananarivo
unmanageable
unmanageably
endamagement
Anna Karenina
incapacitate
incapacitant
incapability
unsalability
unparalleled
inhalatorium
uncatalogued
unwatchfully
unsanctified
unsanctioned
incalculable
incalculably
uncalculated
unvaccinated
in banco regis
incarcerator
uncandidness
unhandselled
one-and-thirty
unpardonable
unpardonably
unhandsomely
incandescent
incatenation
incalescence
unwaveringly
Anwar el-Sadat
an oaken towel
unlawfulness
enlargedness
entanglement
endangerment
Anna Christie
unfathomable
unfathomably
inhabitation
insalivation
insanitation
invagination
invalidation
unsatisfying
engagingness
unfadingness
unvariegated
sneakishness
unpavilioned
unfamiliarly
unhabituated
unmarketable
enharmonical
inharmonical
inharmonious
unharmonious
unmaintained
ungainliness
antagonistic
unfavourable
unfavourably
sneak preview
unvanquished
unpatronised
unpatronized
unpassionate
uncapsizable
infanticidal
in particular
infant school
unfastidious
unfaithfully
antasthmatic
incautiously
antarthritic
endarteritis
enfant trouvé
en pantoufles
unnaturalise
unnaturalize
unsaturation
insalubrious
Anna Ivanovna
unobtainable
inobediently
inobservable
unobservable
unobservedly
inobservance
unobservance
snobographer
enabling bill
snubbing post
snobbishness
anabaptistic
inabstinence
unobstructed
snick and snee
snack counter
sneck-drawing
knacker's yard
snicker-snack
inaccessible
inaccessibly
unacceptable
unscientific
unacceptance
inactivation
knocking shop
knocking-shop
knocking copy
unscriptural
unachievable
knick-knacket
knuckle-bones
knuckle joint
in a cold sweat
unsculptured
knuckle under
uneconomical
anecdotalist
onychophoran
unaccredited
unicorn-shell
unicorn-whale
anacatharsis
anacathartic
unscottified
inaccurately
inoccupation
unacquainted
unacquaint in
in actual fact
unaccustomed
unscrupulous
unidealistic

homelessness
hopelessness
lovelessness
movelessness
tonelessness
non-executive
covered wagon
non-efficient
non-effective
to perfection
rose of Sharon
powerfulness
come off worst
foreign-built
foreign draft
money-grubber
Joseph Paxton
Joseph Heller
Joseph Lister
Tower Hamlets
Joseph Conrad
lose the place
home shopping
togetherness
Joseph Wright
Joseph Stalin
Joseph Butler
none the worse
none the wiser
monetisation
monetization
novelisation
novelization
cohesiveness
covetiveness
foresightful
cohesibility
homesickness
lovesickness
tone dialling
cole titmouse
Bohemian ruby
solecistical
non-existence
nomenklatura
pope's knights
nosebleeding
powerlifting
son et lumière
moneylending
foreclosable
poker machine
Roger McGough
lower mordent
homeomorphic
honey-mouthed
fore-and-after
governmental
Come on Eileen
come into play
Modern Greats
governorship
lose one's hair
governess car
lose one's head
poke one's head
lose one's seat
poke one's nose
lose one's cool
come on stream
come on strong
someone taped
come ungummed
foreknowable
come to naught
Tower of Babel
solenoidally
foregoneness
lonesomeness
forebodement
foretokening
forebodingly
pole position
lovelornness
come down with
home counties
rose-coloured
cometography
none-so-pretty
covetousness
noteworthily
coleopterist
coleopterous
corespondent
Rome, Open City
Roger Penrose
come up trumps
homeopathist
code-breaking
home-produced
home-crofting
lower regions
go pear-shaped
coleorrhizae
rope-drilling
home from home
power-sharing
power station
forensically
coversed sine
women's libber
women's rights
money-spinner
non-essential
Dover's powder
nolens volens
Forest Marble
Covent Garden
home straight
vote straight
potentialise
potentialize
homesteading
potentiation
potentiality
Robert Raikes
Robert Palmer
domesticable
rodenticidal
domestically
lomentaceous
domesticated
domesticator
Roberto Duran
cover the feet
Robert De Niro
lower the flag
homeothermic
homeothermal
Roberta Flack
Lorentz force
love-stricken
Robert Wilson
power take-off
forestalment
forestalling
Robert Altman
momentaneous
honey-tongued
Robert Lowell
Robert Greene
honest broker
Robert Graves
Robert Browne
Rosetta stone
bored to tears
come it strong
Robert Mugabe
Robert Runcie
Robert Fulton
Coventry blue
molecularity
forejudgment
forequarters
cover version
come-by-chance
non-flammable
go off at score
confabulator
Confucianism
Confucianist
non-fictional
confectioner
confidential
Godfrey Evans
Godfrey Hardy
rooflessness
low frequency
Wolffian body
Wolffian duct
Norfolk capon
coffin-dodger
non-flowering
Rolf Hochhuth
confrontment
confirmative
confirmation
conformation
confirmatory
comfortingly
Bonfire night
conferencing
conferential
conférencier
not for Joseph
Porfirio Díaz
✧god-forgotten
comfort woman
confiscation
confiscatory
confusedness
confessional
confessoress
non-fattening
go off the boil
confoundedly
forfaultable
hot favourite
Douglas Adams
long vacation
Douglas Bader
Porgy and Bess
zoographical
long-day plant
congratulate
congratulant
hobgoblinism
Volga-Baltaic
Loughborough
longicaudate
rough diamond
congregation
tongue-tacked
longleaf pine
Ron Greenwood
boogie-woogie
toggle switch
rough grazing
rough-grained
longshoreman
rough hawkbit
long-windedly
soughing-tile
long division
long-distance
bougainvilia
Bougainville
rough justice
dough-kneaded
Dougal Haston
Mongoloid eye
cough lozenge
cough mixture
congeniality
lodging house
congenerical
hoc genus omne
logging-stone
doughnutting
congenitally
conglobation
conglomerate
zoogeography
gorgeousness
conglobulate
hodge-pudding
longipennate
rough-perfect
rough passage
long-breathed
loggerheaded
long-drawn-out
hot gospeller
Jorge Sampaio
longitudinal
forgettingly
long-standing
conglutinate
conglutinant
not give a damn
not give a toss
Gough Whitlam
rough-wrought
Rosh Hashanah
top-heaviness
Loghtan sheep
Sothic period
do the honours
Rochelle-salt
Bonham-Carter
sophomorical
nothingarian
nothing doing
nothing if not
nothing loath
doch-an-dorach
nothing to say
Tom Hopkinson
lophophorate
to the purpose
oophorectomy
Mother Teresa
mother church
motherliness
mothers-in-law
mother figure
mother liquor
yoghurt maker
mother tongue
sophisticate
to that effect
jodhpur boots
not have a clue
Loghtyn sheep
Louis Agassiz
motivated art
solitariness
nominatively
motivational
volitational
nominalistic
holidaymaker
Cosí Fan Tutte
così fan tutte
nominal value
sociableness
Louis Blériot
sociobiology
sonic barrier
boy in buttons
Rosie Boycott
logic circuit
Robin Cousins
Colin Cowdrey
Ionic dialect
logic diagram
folie de doute
morigeration
vociferation
votive tablet
police-manure
go like a dream
motivelessly
police office
bodice-ripper
mobile police
vociferosity
vociferously
domineer over
Cominformist
losing hazard
Boris Godunov
voting rights
foliage plant
potichomania
modificative
codification
mobilisation
mobilization
modification
nobilitation
notification
solicitation
modificatory
politicaster
Joni Mitchell
positive rays
positiveness
positive sign
positive pole
solidifiable
positivistic
Bonin Islands
volitionless
volitionally
solicitously
conidiophore
conidiospore
Colin Jackson
Boris Johnson
Boris Karloff
solifluction
sociological
social worker
social graces
✧social credit
Doris Lessing
Sodium Amytal®
porismatical
sociometrist
motionlessly
domino effect
toxicophobia
eosinophilia
eosinophilic
domino theory
monitorially
toxicologist
Toni Morrison
horizontally
soliloquiser
soliloquizer
ion implanter
Louis Pasteur
poliorcetics
Colin Renfrew
jolies laides
Boris Spassky
conic section
aoristically
holistically
logistically
movie theatre
go fifty-fifty
non-intrusion
vomiturition
solitudinous
vocicultural
Boris Yeltsin
policyholder
conjoint will
box jellyfish
conjunctivae
conjunctival
conjunctivas
dock-labourer
workableness
book-scorpion
rock scorpion
works council
cockieleekie
mock-heroical
book-learning
cookie-pusher
cookie-cutter
Book of Haggai

Book of Daniel
work a flanker
Book of Baruch
Book of Sirach
Book of Joshua
Book of Esther
Book of Isaiah
Book of Psalms
Book of Judges
Book of Judith
Book of Exodus
cook the books
cockthrowing
Yorkshire fog
cockfighting
workmistress
rock climbing
poikilotherm
mockumentary
rockumentary
cooking apple
rocking chair
working class
working-class
booking clerk
looking-glass
rocking horse
working house
working hours
working lunch
working model
cocking piece
working paper
working party
cooking-range
work one's will
rocking stone
working woman
Books of Kings
lock-hospital
Yom Kippur War
worker priest
monk's rhubarb
rocker switch
socket chisel
pocket-pistol
rocket engine
pocket gopher
socket wrench
fork luncheon
work function
cocksureness
lookout tower
Hookey Walker
donkey jacket
monkey jacket
monkey hammer
monkey flower
donkey-engine
monkey engine
monkey tricks
monkey wrench
monkey around
monkey puzzle
donkey's years
Cool Hand Luke
toll-gatherer
pollyannaish
pollyannaism
world-beating
collaborator

colluctation
collectively
collectivise
collectivize
collectivism
collectivist
collectivity
folliculated
coelacanthic
collectorate
pollice verso
coal merchant
Woulfe bottle
soullessness
Coal Measures
toploftiness
collegialism
collegiality
zoologically
coal titmouse
to all intents
Moll Flanders
loblolly pine
loblolly tree
Molly Maguire
coulombmeter
dolly mixture
collinearity
Goblin Market
pollen basket
bowling alley
polling booth
Coelenterata
coelenterate
bowling green
roll in the hay
rolling hitch
fowling-piece
boiling point
rolling stone
rolling stock
cooling tower
toilsomeness
lollapalooza
Collop Monday
lollipop lady
fool's parsley
colliquative
colliquation
colloquially
dollarocracy
collared dove
roller-skater
rollerblader
howler monkey
roller hockey
world-shaking
poules de luxe
molluscicide
noble science
Molluscoidea
wollastonite
foolish-witty
pollutedness
borlotti bean
toilet tissue
coalitionism
coalitionist
soul-stirring
collaterally
boulevardier

world-wearied
collywobbles
World Wide Web
follow the sea
Hollywoodise
Hollywoodize
hollow-ground
woolly-haired
woolly-headed
Colley Cibber
motley-minded
woolly-minded
would you mind?
doomwatching
hormic theory
cosmic string
homme du monde
commodiously
homme d'esprit
Doomsday book
doom-merchant
worm's eye view
formlessness
boy-meets-girl
cosmographic
cosmographer
zoomagnetism
cosmogonical
Tommy Handley
normal school
Joe Millerism
formaldehyde
cosmological
foam plastics
commemorable
commemorator
commensalism
Rosminianism
commendation
commentation
commensality
✧common market
Norman Mailer
common mallow
Norman Lamont
commendatory
commune bonum
communicable
communicably
common school
common scoter
communicator
Norman Tebbit
common gender
commencement
commonwealth
Common People
common debtor
common vestry
common shrimp
rooming house
Norman Wisdom
commandingly
tormentingly
common-riding
gormandising
gormandizing
common millet
dolman sleeve
common ink cap

communion cup
Norman Fowler
common sorrel
Norman Foster
command paper
Norman French
common ground
common as muck
communitaire
commensurate
cosmonautics
worm conveyor
cosmoplastic
cosmopolitic
✧cosmopolitan
commorientes
dormer window
commercially
commissarial
commissariat
boomps-a-daisy
commissioned
commissioner
commiserable
homme sérieux
commiserator
cosmetically
dogmatically
noematically
committeeman
Room at the Top
normotensive
dormitory-car
commuter belt
sound as a bell
John Vanbrugh
joint account
tonneau cover
downwardness
Young America
Coanda effect
corneal graft
foundational
foundationer
corn marigold
John Galliano
mountain hare
fountainhead
mountain meal
fountainless
mountain bike
mountainside
Mountain Time
mountain-high
mountain lion
mountain blue
mountain flax
mountain wood
mountain cork
mountain soap
mountain goat
John Jarndyce
roundaboutly
John Falstaff
John Marshall
Joanna Lumley
connubiality
Young Britain
Mound Builder
mound-builder
bound-bailiff

sound barrier
coenobitical
bonny-clabber
John McCarthy
non-nucleated
connectively
connectivity
connectional
going concern
sound-carrier
fornicatress
Count Dracula
horned lizard
countenancer
counter-agent
Bonnie Parker
Ronnie Barker
mountebank it
mountenaunce
counterbrace
counterblast
counterbluff
countercharm
counterclaim
corn-merchant
countercheck
John Newcombe
counter-drain
Mount Everest
sound effects
counter-flory
counter-force
counter-guard
Young England
counter-gauge
lounge lizard
John Betjeman
counsellable
counterlight
countermarch
counteroffer
jointer plane
counterplead
counterpeise
counterpoise
counterpoint
counter-paled
counter-punch
counterproof
counter-parry
John Berryman
counter-round
Ronnie Browne
counter-stand
counterstain
counterscarp
countershaft
John Herschel
counter-sense
John Sessions
counter-tally
counter-tenor
counter-wheel
counter-weigh
somnifacient
John of Leyden
young fogyish
horn of plenty
pound foolish
pound-foolish
pornographic

pornographer
John the Blind
corn-shucking
down the drain
downshifting
down the hatch
John Christie
corn-chandler
John Chinaman
loan sharking
John Charnley
go on the shout
John Whitgift
council-board
John Lilburne
Young Ireland
coincidental
coincidently
sounding lead
corno inglese
corni inglesi
sounding line
counting room
jointing-rule
moonlighting
John Richmond
council house
John Williams
pointillisme
pointilliste
councilmanic
council of war
Mount Kilauea
John F Kennedy
town planning
somniloquise
somniloquize
somniloquism
somniloquist
somnolescent
John Fletcher
Hosni Mubarak
Young modulus
somnambulate
somnambulant
somnambulary
round-mouthed
John W Mauchly
somnambulism
somnambulist
morning dress
down-and-dirty
morning glory
corn on the cob
Born in the USA
corning house
down-and-outer
conning-tower
morning watch
downloadable
go into detail
born to be wild
pound of flesh
go into the red
go into hiding
John Comnenus
point of order
John Coltrane
Joan Fontaine
John Mortimer
mount of Venus

polyrhythmic
go by the worse
rosy-fingered
polysiloxane
body piercing
polyhistoric
Holy Alliance
polyglottous
polyembryony
polyanthuses
copying press
body snatcher
Polygonaceae
polytonality
rosy-coloured
polymorphism
polymorphous
pony-trekking
polyurethane
polyisoprene
body stocking
polyethylene
body-building
polysulphide
polysyndeton
polysyllabic
polysyllable
polymyositis
Solzhenitsyn
apparatchiki
apparatchiks
Appalachians
splat cooling
spear carrier
upland cotton
sphacelation
speakerphone
apparentness
apparent time
sprachgefühl
speaking tube
apparitional
splay-mouthed
aplanogamete
spear pyrites
spear-running
sphairistike
spear thistle
splatter film
splatterpunk
spear-thrower
speak volumes
sprat-weather
spick and span
specialise in
specialize in
special issue
specialistic
special needs
special offer
spectatorial
special trust
space blanket
epicycloidal
space capsule
specific name
specific heat
specifically
space-heating
Epacridaceae
speckledness
specular iron
space lattice
apiculturist
specimen page
epoch-marking
apocynaceous
spaciousness
speciousness
Epicureanism
spectrograph
spectre lemur
spectral type
apochromatic
spectrometer
spectrometry
spectroscope
spectroscopy
space station
specksioneer
space shuttle
epicuticular
specktioneer
space vehicle
apocryphally
epididymides
apodeictical
epideictical
epidemically
epidemiology
spider-legged
spider beetle
spider flower
spider monkey
spider wrench
spider stitch
speedboating
upper-bracket
speedballing
upper chamber
upper classes
appercipient
apperceptive
apperception
appendicular
appendectomy
appendicitis
splendidness
splendidious
spread a plate
ephemerality
spiegeleisen
a piece of cake
upsey English
ephemeridian
speechmaking
sprechgesang
speechlessly
speechwriter
sprechstimme
splenisation
splenization
sphericality
appetisement
splenic fever
appetisingly
appetizingly
appeals court
upper mordent
splenomegaly
ephebophilia
speed reading
upper regions
speed skating
apfel strudel
appertaining
a pretty penny
Speedwriting®
spiflication
epigraphical
epigrammatic
apagogically
apogeotropic
apage Satanas
optical fibre
optical maser
sphincterial
spring-heeled
springkeeper
spring peeper
spring beetle
spring beauty
spring-bladed
springing cow
spring-loaded
Ophioglossum
sprightfully
upright piano
optimisation
optimization
split leather
ophiological
ophiolatrous
ophiomorphic
option clause
split on a rock
ophiophagous
ophiophilist
speiss cobalt
spoils system
split the vote
splinter bone
splint armour
spokespeople
spokesperson
spill a bibful
spellbinding
apple-blossom
apple-cheeked
spellchecker
apologetical
Apollinarian
spilling line
spelling book
apple-knocker
speleologist
apple of Sodom
apple strudel
apolitically
applausively
applaudingly
open-handedly
open sandwich
open marriage
span-farthing
spine-bashing
spine-chiller
open adoption
epencephalic
epencephalon
sponge finger
sponge fisher
open learning
Spencer Tracy
open sentence
sponge rubber
upon the alert
upon the anvil
upon the whole
open-mindedly
spinning-mill
spinning mule
spongicolous
open diapason
spinal marrow
spiny lobster
spinal column
spindle shell
spinulescent
spindle whorl
opening night
upon one's legs
opinionately
opinionative
open to debate
spondoolicks
spongologist
epanorthoses
epanorthosis
up and running
Open Brethren
Spanish broom
Spanish chalk
Spanish cress
Spanish grass
Spanish juice
up one's sleeve
Spanish onion
Spanish sheep
Spanish Steps
up one's street
Spanish topaz
Spanish white
upon a thought
spinstership
spinsterhood
open question
upon my honour
opposability
splotchiness
optoacoustic
optometrical
appoggiatura
appoggiature
appositeness
oppositeness
appositional
oppositional
appointments
up to one's neck
uproariously
epiphenomena
apoplectical
spur valerian
approachable
spermathecal
approach shot
approach road
spermaphytic
sportability
spermatocele
spermatogeny
spermatozoic
spermatozoid
spermatozoal
spermatozoan
spermatozoon
spermatocyte
spark chamber
appreciative
appreciation
appreciatory
opéra comique
sporadically
spurge laurel
sportfulness
opera glasses
sporogenesis
sphragistics
epirrhematic
apprehensive
apprehension
sportiveness
appraisement
sparking-plug
appraisively
appraisingly
spiral galaxy
spurtle-blade
sporangiolum
sporangioles
sport one's oak
sparrow grass
sparrow-grass
spermophytic
aperiodicity
spermogonium
spuriousness
appropriator
sporophorous
sports jacket
sportscaster
spire-steeple
sportsperson
oppressively
sports injury
appressorium
sportswriter
sports ground
spiritualise
spiritualize
spiritualism
✧spiritualist
spirituality
spirit rapper
spirit master
operatically
spiritedness
spiritlessly
spirit of salt
spirit of wine
operationism
operationist
spirituosity
episodically
epistemology
opisthodomos
opisthograph
opisthotonic
opisthotonos
episcopalism
episcopalian
epistolarian
epistolatory
episcopise it
episcopize it
apostolicism
apostolicity
apostolic see
opus operatum
apostrophise
apostrophize
epithalamium
epithalamion
ophthalmitis
spotted fever
spotted hyena
sputteringly
epitheliomas
apothegmatic
spotlessness
spit feathers
spitefulness
spittle-house
sprung rhythm
appurtenance
epexegetical
sphygmograph
sphygmometer
sphygmophone
sphygmoscope
square matrix
square-rigged
square-rigger
square number
squash tennis
equalisation
equalitarian
equalization
equanimously
squat lobster
equatorially
à quatre mains
squattocracy
a quattr'occhi
a quarter past
squeaky clean
equestrienne
equiparation
equivalently
equitability
Equisetaceae
equisetiform
squirearchal
equifinality
equilibrator
equidistance
equivocation
equivocality
equivocatory
equipollence
equipollency
equiprobable
squirrel cage
squirrel-tail
squirrel fish
squirrel away
equimultiple
break a record
area sampling
break a strike
Great Britain
organ-builder
great-bellied
trial balance
trial balloon

Words marked ✧ can also be spelled with one or more capital letters

groan beneath
cream cracker
bread-chipper
broadcasting
dreamcatcher
Armand Hammer
breakdancing
pro-and-conned
Brian De Palma
grease monkey
triadelphous
Great Eastern
ornamentally
armamentaria
dreadfulness
breakfast-set
organ-grinder
organ-gallery
triangularly
breathe again
breathtaking
great-hearted
breathlessly
Breathalyser®
breathalyser
breathalyzer
great hundred
preachership
organisation
organization
urbanisation
urbanization
erratic block
ergative case
organizer-bag
creativeness
freakishness
organicistic
organismally
irrationally
orgasmically
Great Malvern
great mullein
organ of Corti
great oneyers
organoleptic
great omentum
urbanologist
organography
bread pudding
preamplifier
broad pennant
break-promise
Brian Perkins
Great Pyramid
urban renewal
friar's balsam
break service
oreassurance
oreast cancer
orgastically
oreak the bank
oreastplough
oreak through
oreakthrough
oreaststroke
oreastsummer
creatureship
reasure-city
reasure hunt
reasury bill
Treasury bond
treasury note
break wedlock
Great Western
Treaty of Rome
Arabian camel
trabeculated
problematise
problematize
problematics
problem child
treble chance
problem novel
Tribune Group
Frobisher Bay
tribespeople
proboscidean
proboscidian
Probate Court
tribute money
probationary
probouleutic
proclamation
proclamatory
orichalceous
traceability
tractability
crack a bottle
preclassical
trochanteric
crackbrained
truce-breaker
Bruce Chatwin
trick cyclist
price control
precociously
price current
price-cutting
precedential
bracket-creep
bracket clock
trace element
Gracie Fields
trocheameter
tracheophyte
tracheoscopy
tracheostomy
cricket table
cracked wheat
brickfielder
gracefulness
truck-farming
precognisant
precognizant
precognitive
precognition
practicalism
practicalist
practicality
trichinellae
trichinellas
fructiferous
practise upon
tracking shot
brackishness
trickishness
practitioner
trichiniasis
friction tape
frictionless
fractionally
traction load
fractionator
fructivorous
Trichinopoly
Trichiuridae
procellarian
pro-celebrity
pre-Columbian
prickly poppy
oracularness
Bruce McLaren
preconscious
tricentenary
precancerous
brick-nogging
precondition
dracontiasis
arachnophobe
tracing paper
preconstruct
proconsulate
iracundulous
tractoration
trachomatous
trichophyton
proctorially
price of money
trichotomise
trichotomize
proctologist
trichologist
trichotomous
trochosphere
fractography
graciousness
preciousness
trick or treat
trichopteran
tricephalous
preceptorial
precipitance
precipitancy
precipitator
trichromatic
tricorporate
precariously
pre-Christian
prechristian
tracer bullet
precisianism
precisianist
process block
procès-verbal
fricasseeing
trickstering
tricuspidate
precessional
processional
processioner
precisionist
price support
crack the whip
procathedral
preclusively
precautional
brachydactyl
brachycephal
Tracey Ullman
brachygraphy
trachypterus
graduateship
Pre-Dravidian
gradualistic
credibleness
Frodo Baggins
trade barrier
bride-chamber
Traducianism
Traducianist
predictively
productively
productivity
productional
tridactylous
trade deficit
traded option
cradle-scythe
bridge the gap
trade edition
Bridget Jones
Bridget Riley
pridefulness
prodigiosity
prodigiously
predigestion
bridging loan
Freddie Laker
prednisolone
Freddie Starr
trade journal
predilection
bridal wreath
predominance
predominancy
a rod in pickle
prudentially
trading stamp
pride oneself
pride of place
Prader-Willi's
Frederikstad
Gradgrindery
tradescantia
tradespeople
iridescently
predesignate
predestinate
predisposing
credit rating
credit titles
traditionary
traditionist
creditworthy
predetermine
proditorious
tree kangaroo
irrelatively
Arne Jacobsen
irrepairable
pre-embryonic
Green College
Oriel College
friendliness
friendly lead
friendly fire
Graeme Garden
irrelevantly
Arsène Wenger
free-selector
irreverently
irremediable
irremediably
irrepealable
irrepealably
breezeblocks
irredeemable
irredeemably
breeze up sale
Friese-Greene
freeze-drying
irreversible
irreversibly
treelessness
tree of heaven
tree of silver
green fingers
arpeggiation
Green Goddess
greengrocery
freewheeling
freethinking
breech-loader
breeches part
breeches role
breeches-buoy
Arne Tiselius
pre-eminently
freezing-down
greenishness
arterial road
irreciprocal
irremissible
irremissibly
irresistible
irresistibly
irresistance
pre-existence
free-floating
irreflective
irreflection
free climbing
pre-eclampsia
Greenland Sea
irrealisable
irrealizable
irreconciled
gruesomeness
true-love knot
irreformable
irreformably
✧order of merit
grievousness
irresolutely
irresolution
irresolvable
irresolvably
irrespective
irresponsive
irrespirable
Greek pattern
irrefragable
irrefragably
irreprovable
irreprovably
araeosystyle
pre-establish
orienteering
priest-ridden
priestliness
Oriental Club
oriental ruby
Argentinidae
free-standing
arrester gear
arrester hook
irregularity
irrebuttable
green vitriol
Green Wellies
free-swimming
true-type font
creepy-crawly
prefabricate
craft brother
proficiently
graft chimera
prefectorial
draft-dodging
profligately
triflingness
prefoliation
Artful Dodger
craftmanship
prefloration
preformative
preformation
trifurcation
preferential
craftspeople
craftsperson
professional
professorate
professoress
professorial
profit margin
profit-taking
profiteering
profitlessly
profit centre
profiteroles
profoundness
progradation
orographical
programmable
programmatic
trigrammatic
✧braggadocios
fragrantness
Brigham Young
tragicalness
tragicomical
brigade major
trigger-happy
trigger point
Greg Chappell
priggishness
tragelaphine
frog's lettuce
progymnasium
drug smuggler
dragon's blood
orogenic belt
dragon lizard
trigonometer
trigonometry
drag one's feet
dragon's teeth
progenitress
proglottides
troglodytism
gregarianism
Gregorian wig
frigorificos
gregariously

Art Garfunkel
pregustation
progesterone
Brighton Rock
Greg Rusedski
triglyceride
Orphic Cubism
orchidaceous
orchidectomy
orchidomania
orthodontics
orthodontist
orthodromics
archdeaconry
Archie Fisher
archaeometry
orthognathic
orthographic
orthographer
archegoniate
orthogonally
orthogenesis
orthogenetic
archdiocesan
Archilochian
Arshile Gorky
Grahame Clark
preheminence
Graham Greene
orthomorphic
prehensility
prehensorial
orphan-asylum
Mrs Henry Wood
arthroscopic
arthroplasty
orthopedical
orthopaedics
orthopaedist
orthopterist
orthopteroid
orthopterous
archipelagic
archipelagos
Arthur Cayley
Arthur Harris
Archer Martin
orchard-grass
orchard-house
Arthur Miller
orthorhombic
Arthur Porter
prehistorian
orchestrally
orchestra pit
orchestrator
architecture
orthotonesis
orthotropism
orthotropous
archetypical
archetypally
grain alcohol
drainage-tube
ordinariness
irritatingly
irritability
trainability
irrigational
trailblazing
Artiodactyla
brain-damaged
droit des gens
broiler house
praiseworthy
trainer pants
trailer trash
trailer truck
fruitfulness
Irving Berlin
ornithogalum
Freightliner®
Ornithomimus
ornithomancy
ornithomorph
ornithophily
Ornithischia
ornithoscopy
freight-train
trailing edge
training shoe
training ship
fruiting body
artificially
troisième âge
prairie value
grain leather
argillaceous
artilleryman
fruit machine
fry in one's fat
traitorously
arrière-garde
trainspotter
Armistice Day
artistically
artist's proof
articulately
articulation
orbicularity
articulatory
brainwashing
projectivity
projectional
prejudgement
broken-backed
broken-winded
broker-dealer
grallatorial
frolicsomely
trolley dolly
Grolieresque
trolley table
trolley wheel
prolificness
prolifically
prolegomenon
trolling-bait
drilling pipe
brilliant-cut
brilliantine
troll-my-dames
prolongation
prelapsarian
prelatically
tralaticious
pralltriller
urolithiasis
proletariate
trilaterally
tralatitious
tromba marina
grammaticise
grammaticize
grammaticism
grammatology
from day to day
frame-breaker
crème caramel
crème de cacao
bromide paper
premeditated
✧gram-negative
Bramley apple
tramp element
trumpet major
trompe l'oeils
trumpet shell
crème fraîche
crime fiction
primigravida
fromage frais
primogenital
primogenitor
crimping-iron
Kremlinology
bromhidrosis
Bromeliaceae
promulgation
bramble-berry
primulaceous
bramble-finch
crumple zones
primum mobile
frumentation
Truman Capote
graminaceous
criminogenic
tremendously
Premonstrant
premenstrual
from fordonne
primrose path
gram-molecule
crambo-jingle
Gram-positive
trampolining
trampolinist
from top to toe
gramophonist
pro-marketeer
primordially
primary phase
promised land
tramp steamer
promuscidate
promissorily
promethazine
aromatically
dramatically
aromatherapy
crymotherapy
drama therapy
cremationist
dramaturgist
crematoriums
dramatisable
trimethylene
dramatizable
brimfullness
from sun to sun
primeval atom
premaxillary
grand amateur
drunk as a lord
Brendan Behan
grand atelier
bring a charge
transaminase
cranial index
printability
frankalmoign
cranial nerve
Frank Buchman
front-bencher
trinacriform
transcalency
transcendent
grand duchess
transduction
drink-driving
drunk-driving
granodiorite
Prince Naseem
cringe-making
grande marque
frondescence
front-end load
fringe effect
branded goods
princeliness
prince-bishop
Prince Albert
orange-flower
prince's metal
grande entrée
orange roughy
Grande Comore
cringeworthy
orange squash
printer's mark
printer's ream
Frankenstein
princess line
Princess Anne
Prince Rupert
transfection
wrongfulness
bring forward
transferable
transferring
transforming
transformism
transfer list
transformist
transference
transfer book
transfusable
transfusible
uranographic
uranographer
transgressor
✧grand guignol
transgenesis
urinogenital
prenegotiate
French fennel
French letter
French window
trench plough
transhumance
French polish
French-polish
Branchiopoda
French sorrel
trench mortar
transhipment
transhipping
bronchoscope
bronchoscopy
Arundhati Roy
principal boy
✧principality
Francis Bacon
Francis Baily
Francis Crick
frankincense
Francis Drake
'prenticeship
prenticeship
frondiferous
printing-head
drinking-horn
drinking bout
branding-iron
transitively
frangibility
transitivity
transitional
transiliency
Fringillidae
Francis Maude
Grandisonian
transitorily
frontispiece
frontiersman
transit trade
Franz Klammer
Frank Kermode
front-loading
crenellation
translucence
translucency
granulocytic
Brunelleschi
Frank Loesser
transleithan
grand larceny
wranglership
translatable
granulations
brand loyalty
trinomialism
trinomialist
transmigrate
transmigrant
transmogrify
transmontane
transmundane
brinkmanship
pronominally
Grand Marnier®
transmissive
transmission
transmutable
transmutably
transmitting
ironing-board
pruning knife
Franco Baresi
✧brontosaurus
transoceanic
brontophobia
✧francophobia
drongo-shrike
front of house
front-of-house
craniologist
François Rude
drongo-cuckoo
broncobuster
transplanter
transpacific
transpicuous
transpontine
transpirable
transportive
transporting
transparence
transparency
transposable
Irina Rodnina
front-running
Frank Sedgman
wrong side out
Grand Signior
transshipper
Frank Sinatra
trendsetting
grind to a halt
bring to a head
frenetically
Trinity House
bring to light
print-through
bring to terms
grand touring
transuranium
transudation
transuranian
transudatory
pronouncedly
uranium glass
tranquilness
tranquillise
tranquillize
tranquillity
tranquilizer
transumptive
transumption
bring up short
transversely
transversion
transvestite
transvestism
transvestist
Frank Whittle
brandy-pawnee
granny annexe
brandy-bottle
brandy butter
arco saltando
preoccupancy
proof-correct
troop carrier
Arnold Palmer
Arnold Wesker
preordinance
preoperative
arborescence
Crookes glass
orgone energy
arborisation
arborization
creolisation
creolization

Oreopithecus
cryoglobulin
error message
Dr John Watson
proofreading
armour-bearer
armour-plated
cryopreserve
cryptanalyst
trophallaxis
prepubescent
drop a clanger
tropical year
tripudiation
crepe-de-chine
crêpe-de-chine
tripe de roche
arsphenamine
triple headed
propaedeutic
Triplex® glass
triple whammy
ropheticism
rip recorder
riple-tongue
ropped scone
riple-turned
riple-jumper
ypaflavine
ropugnation
ropagandise
ropagandize
ropagandism
ropagandist
rapehanging
repehanging
rapshooting
rephination
iplication
ruptiveness
ropping-well
ropping fire
ophic level
raphic novel
raphics card
roprietress
ropeller fan
opological
rapple-plant
ypanocidal
reponderate
eponderant
openseness
op-in centre
panosomic
panosomal
op rotation
yptogamian
yptogamist
yptogamous
photactic
aphophobia
yptochrome
yptobiosis
phobiosis
yptobiotic
phobiotic
plock loan
ptomnesia
ptomnesic
ptologist
graphologist
trophotropic
cryptography
cryptonymous
tropophilous
graph plotter
preparedness
tripartitely
tripartition
proportioned
proportional
proper motion
property band
property room
troposcatter
grapeseed-oil
preposterous
prepossessed
tropospheric
crepusculous
crêpe suzette
propitiative
propitiation
propitiatory
triphthongal
propitiously
prophylactic
trapezohedra
frequentness
cry quittance
cry roast-meat
prerogatived
prerequisite
ororotundity
trustafarian
press against
crystal clear
trust account
cross-and-pile
crassamentum
dry-stane dyke
crystal-gazer
crystallitis
fresh as paint
prostanthera
prostacyclin
cross bedding
crossbencher
crossbanding
crash barrier
crush barrier
cross-buttock
brass-bounder
press charges
trust company
iris scanning
prosectorial
cross-current
prosecutable
crosscutting
press cutting
press council
cross-country
prosodically
cross-dresser
presidentess
presidential
crise de nerfs
cross-examine
Dresden china
pressed glass
Trismegistus
prosperously
Brussels lace
trustee stock
prospectuses
Fresnel zones
trustfulness
press forward
trash farming
brassfounder
cross-grained
press gallery
Ernst Haeckel
dressing-case
dressing-sack
graspingness
trustingness
dressing-room
dressing-down
dressing-gown
trysting-tree
crossing over
irascibility
prestigiator
Kristiansand
Prussian carp
✧prussian blue
Prussianiser
Prussianizer
prestissimos
prostitution
Kriss Kringle
cresylic acid
preselection
bristle-grass
cross-lighted
crash-landing
cross-linking
prosyllogism
trestle table
cross-lateral
proselytiser
proselytizer
brass monkeys
freshmanship
crash-matting
presumptuous
presentative
presentation
presenteeism
presentiment
presentially
present value
cristobalite
Bristol board
Bristol-brick
Aristotelean
Aristotelism
Aristotelian
press officer
Aristophanic
Aristophanes
aristolochia
aristocratic
griseofulvin
praseodymium
prosopopoeia
prosopopeial
cross-purpose
cross-ply tyre
preservative
preservation
preservatory
brass rubbing
prestriction
droseraceous
press release
prescriptive
proscriptive
prescription
proscription
Fraser Island
cross-section
cross-selling
brush strokes
Erasistratus
trash talking
gross tonnage
Irish terrier
Crassulaceae
grossularite
pressure into
pressure sore
pressure-cook
pressure suit
dress uniform
grass widower
presbyacusis
presbyterate
presbyterial
✧presbyterian
presbycousis
prothalamium
prothalamion
protractible
protractedly
protuberance
trituberculy
Arctic Circle
protectively
protectingly
protactinium
critical mass
criticalness
triticalness
protocolling
✧protectorate
protectorial
criticisable
criticizable
erythematous
brother-in-law
protreptical
gratifyingly
Grateful Dead
gratefulness
truthfulness
wrathfulness
protagonists
wretchedness
proto-history
gratuitously
brittle bones
grit blasting
arithmomania
arithmometer
protomorphic
arithmetical
brutum fulmen
pretenceless
pretendingly
pre-tensioned
pre-tensioner
pretensioner
protonematal
writing paper
writing table
proteoglycan
prothonotary
protoplasmic
protoplasmal
protoplastic
arctophilist
write protect
write-protect
erythroblast
writer's block
writer's cramp
oratorically
erythrocytic
pretermitted
erythromycin
erythropenia
urethroscope
urethroscopy
protestation
Eratosthenes
protestingly
gratis dictum
protistology
British plate
grotesquerie
prototherian
truth-telling
prototrophic
prototypical
protrusively
pretty nearly
pretty-spoken
pretty-pretty
protozoology
trauma centre
traumatising
traumatizing
traumatology
group calling
group-captain
ground tackle
ground-feeder
groundlessly
ground-beetle
ground effect
ground cherry
ground-pigeon
ground annual
Groundhog Day
groundhopper
ground stroke
ground storey
ground-cuckoo
proud-hearted
draughtboard
draught-hooks
draught horse
draught-house
draughtiness
droughtiness
draught-proof
Freudian slip
trouble-house
troublemaker
trouble-mirth
trouble-state
troubleshoot
trouble-world
Frauendienst
Group of Eight
Group of Seven
triumphalism
triumphalist
triumphantly
Trout Quintet
arcus senilis
group trading
group therapy
argue the toss
fraudulently
driveability
privy chamber
grave-clothes
✧privy council
provided that
providential
arfvedsonite
prevailingly
travel agency
gravel-voiced
travel-soiled
preventative
Provence-rose
province rose
preventively
provincially
driving range
driving shaft
driving wheel
prove oneself
previousness
brevipennate
Trevor Bailey
prevaricator
proverbially
Trevor Howard
provost guard
provisionary
travesty role
privateering
private hotel
private house
Private Lives
private means
gravitometer
privat-docent
privat-dozent
private press
private parts
drivethrough
private wrong
gravity waves
prawn cracker
arm wrestling
growth market
growth factor
draw the board
draw the cloth
draw the table
draw the teeth
drawlingness
Brownie Guide
brownie point
brown mustard
drawing board
drawing-frame
drawing-knife

growing pains
growing-point
drawing paper
drawing-table
draw to a close
grow together
draw-top table
crowd-pleaser
brewer's droop
brewer's yeast
crown witness
grex venalium
praxinoscope
Prix Goncourt
grey-lag goose
grey eminence
X-ray spectrum
grey squirrel
prayerlessly
prayer-monger
prizefighter
Prizzi's Honor
Brazilian wax
frozen mitten
prize-winning
Isaac Albéniz
asparaginase
asparagus pea
Island of Maui
Island of Oahu
Island of Elba
Isaac Dineson
Oswald Mosley
Isla de Pascua
estate agency
escape clause
Aswan High Dam
Islamisation
Islamization
espagnolette
astacologist
escapologist
assassinator
aspartic acid
esparto grass
A Sea Symphony
Isabel Archer
isobilateral
isocheimenal
psychic force
psychiatrist
psychobabble
psychopathic
psychoactive
psychometric
psychosexual
psychoticism
psychologise
psychologize
psychosocial
psychologism
psychonomics
psychologist
psychotropic
psychography
isochromatic
psychrometer
psychrometry
isochronally
isodiametric
isodimorphic

Esmeralda Dam
assemblaunce
osteoblastic
assembly hall
assembly shop
assembly line
assembly room
osteoclastic
osteodermous
asseverating
asseveration
aspergillums
osteogenesis
osteogenetic
osteological
osteomalacia
osteomalacic
osteoplastic
osteoporosis
osteoporotic
osteopathist
Ascension Day
Ascension-day
assessorship
osteosarcoma
ashes to ashes
essentialism
essentialist
essentiality
as best one can
assentaneous
ostentatious
as often as not
usufructuary
eschscholzia
eschatologic
asphyxiation
Ustilagineae
aspirational
ustilaginous
A Suitable Boy
Isaiah Berlin
assimilative
assibilation
assimilation
ossification
assimilatory
aspiringness
oscillograph
oscilloscope
psilanthropy
Asclepiadean
isolationism
isolationist
isolator tent
Astley Cooper
Ishmaelitish
asymmetrical
psammophytic
asymptomatic
asymptotical
asynchronism
asynchronous
A Song to Celia
A Song to David
ascorbic acid
as concerning
as good as gold
astonishment
associations
I should cocoa

I should worry!
astoundingly
assortedness
escort agency
ascomycetous
isoprenaline
psi phenomena
psephologist
isoperimeter
isoperimetry
astrocompass
astrocytomas
astrogeology
astrological
estrangement
astringently
astronomical
astronautics
usuriousness
astrophysics
user-friendly
esprit follet
isostemonous
isosthenuria
usus loquendi
tsesarevitch
tsesarewitch
isotretinoin
isothermally
isotopically
isotopic spin
esoterically
Assurbanipal
escutcheoned
as sure as a gun
assuefaction
assuming that
issuing house
pseudorandom
pseudomartyr
pseudomonads
pseudo-Gothic
pseudopodium
pseudography
pseudonymity
pseudonymous
pseudocyesis
Ust'-Urt Desert
A Severed Head
Ash Wednesday
Zsuzsa Polgar
it may be added
straw-breadth
straddleback
strangle-weed
stranglement
stranglehold
stragglingly
strangulated
strange quark
straight talk
straightways
straightedge
straight gear
straightness
straight line
straight play
straightener
straight away
straightaway
Stradivarius

strabismical
stratigraphy
straticulate
strain viewer
strain a point
stratotanker
steatomatous
ethanoic acid
stratosphere
steatorrhoea
stratocratic
steatopygous
Uttar Pradesh
straitjacket
Atlantic seal
Atlantic Time
Atlantic City
steal the show
stealthiness
Stuart Blanch
steak tartare
steam turbine
steam whistle
stubble field
stubble goose
stabilisator
stabilizator
stubbornness
stack against
stock and horn
stickability
stockbreeder
stockbroking
stock company
stock car race
stocking mask
stockingless
stocking-sole
stocking-foot
stock-in-trade
stockjobbery
stockjobbing
stickler-like
itaconic acid
stichometric
stichomythia
stichomythic
stockpunisht
stock-raising
stick the pace
sticky wicket
studding-sail
studdingsail
staddle stone
studiousness
St Edmund Hall
Attenborough
stretcher off
stretch marks
steel erector
ethereal oils
St Benet's Hall
St Peter's fish
St Peter's wort
St Petersburg
strengthless
strengthener
otter-hunting
stoechiology
etherisation
etherization

strepitation
steering gear
steeplechase
steeple-crown
atheological
steeple house
stream anchor
etheromaniac
atheromatous
at second hand
St George's Day
it's early days
etheostomine
streets apart
streets ahead
street-raking
streetwalker
streptococci
streetkeeper
streptomycin
street smarts
Streptoneura
street hockey
streptosolen
at death's door
otherworldly
steelworking
staff college
stuffed shirt
stiff-hearted
Stefan Edberg
staff officer
staff surgeon
stegocarpous
staggeringly
stage manager
steganograph
staghorn fern
staghorn moss
stegophilist
stegosaurian
a tight corner
stage whisper
Stahlhelmist
Mt Chimborazo
at the outside
at discretion
strip cartoon
strike a chord
stridelegged
stained glass
strike a light!
strike a match
strike it rich
string theory
string figure
string course
stoichiology
strikingness
Strigiformes
it pitieth you
stripped-down
stripped atom
strippergram
at first blush
at first sight
stridulation
stridulatory
stridulantly
attitudinise
attitudinize

stakhanovite
stakhanovism
Stoke-on-Trent
still and anon
stellar month
Italian sixth
stalwartness
stalactiform
Italo Calvino
Stellenbosch
stylographic
still hunting
stelliferous
Ptolemy Soter
stilboestrol
still-peering
still-piecing
athletically
stiletto heel
athlete's foot
utility truck
Itala version
atomic weight
atomic second
atomic theory
atomic energy
atomic volume
atomic number
stammeringly
stamping mill
etymological
etymologicum
etymologicon
atemporality
stump oratory
stomatodaeum
standard lamp
standard time
standard wing
sting and ling
standard cost
✧standardbred
standardiser
standardizer
Eton wall game
stone bramble
stone-breaker
stone boiling
ethnobotanic
ethnocentric
stonecutting
stone dresser
Stanley Falls
Stanley knife®
at knife-point
ethnographic
stenographic
ethnographer
stenographer
stony-hearted
St Anthony pig
stanniferous
standing wave
standing joke
standing-room
standing crop
stencil plate
ethnological
stonemasonry
stand-off half
stone parsley

Words marked ✧ can also be spelled with one or more capital letters

standpattism
St Andrew's Day
Stanislavsky
ethnoscience
stand the pace
stenothermal
stand-up comic
stonewalling
stoop and roop
stromatolite
Otto Meyerhof
stroke of luck
stooge around
strong-minded
stoop-gallant
strongylosis
strong breeze
strophanthin
strophanthus
strophiolate
strobilation
strobiliform
Otto Skorzeny
St John's bread
attorneyship
stroboscopic
atmospherics
strontianite
ethoxyethane
stoppage time
stepdaughter
stapedectomy
Stephen Benét
Stephen Crane
Stephen Hales
tep aerobics
tupefacient
tupefactive
tupefaction
tipulaceous
tepimeletic
tep on the gas
tupendously
tepmotherly
tep function
tars and Bars
targazey pie
tar sapphire
ttributable
yracaceous
ttractively
ttractingly
throcytoses
hrocytosis
terodactyle
teridomania
teridophyta
teridophyte
teridosperm
arter motor
ormfulness
archedness
ernisation
ernization
arting gate
arting hole
rling Moss
arting post
erling area
ernity ring
orekeeping
storm lantern
star-blasting
stereocamera
stercoranism
stercoranist
stereotactic
stereoacuity
stereoscopic
stereometric
stereophonic
stereochrome
stereochromy
storiologist
stertorously
stereotropic
stereography
stereoisomer
stereopticon
stereotyping
pteropod ooze
star-spangled
at arm's length
pterosaurian
storm shutter
storytelling
storm trooper
storm trysail
sternutative
sternutation
sternutatory
stirrup pants
stirrup strap
stern-wheeler
storm warning
stormy petrel
Mtarazi Falls
otosclerosis
otosclerotic
St Athanasius
static memory
Statue of Zeus
stutteringly
statuesquely
statementing
Staten Island
stethoscopic
station house
state of siege
station wagon
statesperson
statistician
status symbol
state trooper
statutory law
stoup and roup
strugglingly
Mt Tungurahua
stout-hearted
stauroscopic
structurally
Steve Backley
Stevie Wonder
Steve Fossett
Steve McCurry
Steve McQueen
Steven Norris
stovepipe hat
ethyl alcohol
ethyl acetate
strychninism
staying power
subarachnoid
put a damper on
funambulator
human bowling
subarcuation
human capital
lunar caustic
cut and thrust
cut-and-thrust
sun-and-planet
subabdominal
mutagenicity
humane killer
subaggregate
ourang-outang
humanisation
humanitarian
humanization
ruralisation
ruralization
put a finger on
mutation rate
mutation mink
mutationally
mutation stop
Susannah York
butanoic acid
turacoverdin
nugatoriness
put a sock in it
mutato nomine
subapostolic
subarrhation
subauricular
sugar-refiner
sugar snap pea
Jurassic Park
sugar the pill
subalternate
subalternant
subalternity
subantarctic
duraluminium
eucalyptuses
cupboard-love
turbocharged
turbocharger
Purbeck stone
turbidimeter
tumbler-drier
tumbler-dryer
bubble-headed
bubble memory
rumblethumps
dumb terminal
hubble-bubble
rumble-tumble
purblindness
lumbriciform
turbellarian
Humboldt's Sea
nubbing-cheat
turbinacious
rubbing stone
cumbrousness
cut boon whids
lumberjacket
rubber cement
numberlessly
number theory
rubber cheque
cumber-ground
rubber bullet
number system
Dutch auction
Punch and Judy
kurchatovium
Dutch bargain
Dutch clinker
Dutch comfort
Dutch concert
Dutch courage
dulce de leche
succedaneous
suicide watch
Dutch elm tree
luncheon meat
luncheonette
butcher's meat
butcher's hook
Punchinellos
✧nunc dimittis
functionless
functionally
function word
auscultative
auscultation
auscultatory
subcelestial
subcommittee
subcommunity
Vulcan's badge
succinic acid
subconscious
buccaneering
buccaneerish
subcontinent
jus canonicum
vulcanisable
succinctness
bus conductor
vulcanizable
bunch of fives
lusciousness
Turcophilism
susceptivity
succussation
successantly
quick-scented
successfully
quick-sighted
successively
successional
quicksilvery
quacksalving
quick-selling
success story
subcutaneous
punctulation
puncturation
Muscovy glass
subcivilised
subcivilized
lunch voucher
quadragenary
Quadragesima
quadrangular
Auld Lang Syne
quadraphonic
quadraplegia
subdiaconate
duodecennial
Guido d'Arezzo
hurdle-racing
muddle-headed
quadrivalent
quidditative
quadriplegia
quadriplegic
Sunda Islands
quadriennial
quadriennium
quadrinomial
subdelirious
muddy-mettled
pudding basin
pudding-basin
duodenectomy
pudding-faced
guiding light
pudding mould
pudding-plate
pudding-stone
quadrophonic
subduplicate
subdirectory
rudder pedals
dunderheaded
Huddersfield
wunderkinder
outdatedness
quadrumanous
subdivisible
put down roots
Sunday school
Sunday Mirror
Sunday driver
numerability
lukewarmness
superannuate
Luxembourger
supercharger
superciliary
supercilious
tuberculosed
tuberculosis
tuberculated
queen consort
superconduct
supercargoes
supercluster
queen dowager
juvenescence
supereminent
superevident
euhemeristic
Eugene Onegin
Eugene O'Neill
supererogate
supererogant
tunelessness
tubeless tire
tubeless tyre
Eugène Dubois
ruse de guerre
mute of malice
superficials
Duke of Omnium
superfrontal
superglacial
supergravity
superhighway
superhumanly
superhumeral
rule the roast
superheroine
rule the roost
suberisation
suberization
Eugenio Barba
juvenileness
tuberiferous
juvenilities
subeditorial
superimposed
superiorship
Puseyistical
museological
superluminal
museum beetle
Jules Maigret
supermundane
supermassive
Jules Mazarin
gubernaculum
supernaculum
gubernacular
supernacular
supernatural
Rube Goldberg
superordinal
superorganic
numerologist
Queen of Sheba
numerousness
tuberous root
surefootedly
superovulate
Auberon Waugh
superplastic
sun-expelling
superpolymer
superposable
superpatriot
superrealism
superrealist
superrefined
queen regnant
queen-regnant
superstardom
Queenslander
buyer's market
buyers' market
Rubeus Hagrid
supersubtile
supersedence
superspecies
queen's yellow
superstition
supersensory
supersensual
queen's bounty
Queen's Speech
mutessarifat
superstratum
supersession
superteacher
Hubert Walter
Rupert's drops
quaestionary
quaestorship
Rupert Brooke
fume cupboard
bureaucratic

supervenient
supervention
pufftaloonas
surface-craft
sufficiently
surface noise
subfactorial
surface plate
surface-to-air
surface water
sulfadiazine
ruffed grouse
buffalo-berry
buffalo chips
buffalo-grass
Suffolk punch
Buffalo wings
luffing crane
sulfonic acid
outfangthief
buffing-wheel
surfboarding
out from under
furfuraceous
subfertility
kupfernickel
subfeudation
subfeudatory
suffruticose
burglar alarm
subglacially
surgical mask
surgical neck
surgical shoe
surgical boot
Muggletonian
judgmentally
Luigi Galvani
judgement-day
Buggins's turn
surgeon's knot
hunger-bitten
vulgar tongue
hunger strike
hunger-strike
hugger-mugger
Hungary water
suggestively
tungstic acid
tungsten lamp
bulghur wheat
ruthlessness
rushy-fringed
bushwhacking
bush sickness
authenticate
authenticity
euphoniously
euthanasiast
push one's luck
mushroom pink
cushion-plant
rush-bottomed
euphorically
author's proof
authorisable
authorizable
subhastation
duchesse lace
eurhythmical
tu-whit tu-whoo
Euphausiacea
Euphausiidae
oughly-headed
Julie Andrews
Jubilate Agno
musical flame
dubitatively
ruminatively
ruminatingly
pupilability
mucilaginous
jurisconsult
Aulic Council
jurisdictive
jurisdiction
Lucinda Green
Eunice Barber
luminescence
lucifer-match
business card
business park
businesslike
business plan
business suit
murine typhus
subinfeudate
tuning hammer
municipalise
municipalize
purificative
municipalism
cutinisation
cutinization
futilitarian
humification
purification
municipality
purificatory
fugitiveness
luminiferous
munificently
Kuril Islands
musicianship
munitionette
fuliginosity
fuliginously
pugilistical
audiological
fusible metal
burial ground
Yukio Mishima
audiometrist
Julian Barnes
Luciano Berio
Nubian Desert
fusion energy
Yuri Andropov
Julian Huxley
musicologist
luminousness
mutinousness
numinousness
luminous flux
jurisprudent
Julia Roberts
junior school
junior optime
Hudibrastics
Julius Caesar
subinspector
run its course
music teacher
pupil teacher
autistically
cubistically
juristically
puristically
curietherapy
music therapy
put in the boot
music theatre
subintroduce
Julie Walters
fugie-warrant
mud in your eye
subjectively
subjectivise
subjectivize
subjectivism
subjectivist
subjectivity
Turk's cap lily
huckle-backed
buckle-beggar
Turkmenistan
lucklessness
bulk discount
Lucky Luciano
cuckold-maker
Purkinje cell
quaking-grass
sucking louse
lurking-place
cucking stool
ducking-stool
cuckoo shrike
cuckoo pintle
cuckoo flower
cuckoo-roller
muckspreader
Quaker-colour
bunker buster
bunko-steerer
Turkish manna
Turkish towel
Turkey carpet
build a sconce
nuclear power
nuclear waste
sublibrarian
guild-brother
Lualaba River
public school
public-school
public health
public sector
guilt complex
public domain
public-domain
public orator
quill-driving
Guildenstern
curliewurlie
quill-feather
pull a flanker
qualificator
fully-fledged
bull-of-the-bog
guilefulness
pull a fast one
mulligatawny
full-throated
pull the wires
building line
qualmishness
bullfighting
subliminally
Juglandaceae
sublineation
fuel-injected
fuel injector
outlandishly
curling irons
curl one's lips
curling-stone
curling tongs
dual monarchy
nucleocapsid
pull together
nucleophilic
pull to pieces
guillotining
full-bottomed
✧sublapsarian
pull up stakes
✧fuller's earth
fuel assembly
bullet-headed
quelque chose
Ludlow Castle
pull a wry face
Sue MacGregor
outmodedness
curmudgeonly
hummle bonnet
Culm Measures
outmigration
nutmeg grater
hummel bonnet
augmentative
augmentation
subminiature
fulminic acid
outmanoeuvre
put money into
summer savory
summer school
submergement
summer-weight
summer season
submarine pen
Burmese glass
submissively
surmountable
submaxillary
Guinea-Bissau
burn daylight
burnt almonds
pugnaciously
turn a deaf ear
dunniewassal
quintessence
turn of phrase
turn of events
quenchlessly
Huang He River
Huang Ho River
turn the scale
turn the screw
burn the water
quantivalent
quantitative
quantisation
quantization
turnpike road
quantifiable
quantitively
tunnel of love
tunnel vision
running board
running belay
running costs
running fight
burn in effigy
burning-glass
burning-house
burning issue
turning lathe
burning-point
turning point
turn one's hand
turn one's back
turn one's head
turn one's coat
running title
quinine water
running water
burn to a crisp
turn down cold
Luang Prabang
turnip greens
turn up trumps
subnormality
Gunnar Myrdal
Furness Abbey
buenas tardes
buenas noches
furniture van
quinquenniad
quinquennial
quinquennium
quantum state
quantum yield
Buenaventura
autocatalyse
autocatalyze
automaticity
out of all cess
out of all nick
Europassport
auroral zones
out of context
suboccipital
out of drawing
au poids de l'or
put one's bib in
suboperculum
subopercular
rub one's hands
cut one's lucky
euroterminal
European plan
put one's oar in
autogenously
cut one's stick
cut one's teeth
Eurocentrism
autodestruct
Rudolf Carnap
Rudolf Diesel
out of fashion
autochthones
autoxidative
autoxidation
sudoriparous
autodidactic
sudoriferous
auto rickshaw
autorickshaw
Luzon Islands
eulogistical
Euro-American
auto-immunity
autoantibody
out of nowhere
out on one's ear
put on one side
automobilism
automobilist
autonomously
automorphism
humorousness
au jour le jour
autotrophism
Dufourspitze
autocritique
out of spirits
out of service
autoptically
dumortierite
put on the line
run-of-the-mill
✧put on the ritz
out of the blue
out of the road
out of the wood
put on the foil
out of the loop
out-of-the-body
out of thin air
Eurosterling
Eurocurrency
mucopurulent
out of warrant
autoexposure
autohypnosis
autohypnotic
pulp magazine
outplacement
culpableness
auspiciously
suspiciously
supplemental
supplementer
sumpter horse
purple airway
suppressible
suppressedly
jump the besom
hump the bluey
jump the queue
supplicating
supplication
supplicatory
subprincipal
rumpti-iddity
surprise into
sulphite pulp
sumphishness
surprisingly
cupping-glass
bump and grind
suspensively
out-pensioner
jumping mouse

suspensorial
suspensorium
jump one's bail
sulphonamide
sulphonation
pulp novelist
Cusparia bark
jumper cables
support group
pumpernickel
support level
purpose-built
purposefully
surpassingly
suppositious
sulphuration
sulphureting
sulphuretted
humpty dumpty
quaquaversal
surrealistic
Munro-bagging
supraciliary
urriculated
ubriciously
upracrustal
uarter after
uarter-blood
uarter-bound
uarter-final
uarter-guard
uarter-horse
uarterlight
uarter-miler
uartern loaf
uarter-plate
uarter-pound
uarter-round
uarterstaff
uarter-sawed
utrefacient
utrefactive
utrefaction
ubreference
utrageously
uerrilleros
uardianship
uare impedit
rrejoinder
upreme Being
upreme Court
pramundane
uerimonious
prammonium
rrant bread
araná bread
aranteeing
rrant-jelly
rrency note
praorbital
erto Cortes
trophicate
ernsey lily
cretia Mott
tritionist
tritiously
rroundings
rrowing-owl
urray Walker
arrymaster
nray pleats

quartz-schist
Russian boots
Russian salad
substantiate
substantival
burst binding
guest-chamber
tussock grass
Russocentric
subsidiarily
subsidiarity
outside novel
outside right
cuisse-madame
Luís de Camães
tussie mussie
sunshine roof
question mark
questionable
questionably
questionless
question time
pursuit plane
substitutive
substitution
Russell Crowe
mussel shrimp
subsultorily
Munsell scale
cue someone in
gum sandarach
nuts and bolts
nursing chair
Guys and Dolls
✧bunsen burner
jus sanguinis
rub shoulders
Russophilism
Russophilist
Russophobist
subsequently
outspreading
subscribable
nursery class
substraction
substruction
burseraceous
substructure
subservience
subserviency
pusser's logic
nursery nurse
subscriptive
subscription
nursery rhyme
pusser's sneer
outstretched
purse-sharing
purse strings
nurse-tending
Australasian
Kurt Waldheim
Australia Day
nuptialities
hunt saboteur
quotableness
suitableness
✧justicialism
multichannel
butty-collier
multicentric

multicentral
futtock-plate
multicipital
multicostate
multicasting
multicauline
multidentate
put the make on
cut the cackle
put the acid on
turtle-necked
put the wind up
out the window
put the bite on
Burt Reynolds
put the boot in
hurtlessness
buttress-root
subtreasurer
multifaceted
justificator
multifoliate
multiflorous
multiformity
multifarious
multigravida
quota-hopping
just like that
curtain-sider
multilobular
multilocular
fustillirian
multilingual
puftaloonies
multiloquent
multiloquous
multilateral
subtemperate
run-time error
customs house
custom-shrunk
huntsmanship
customs union
Austen Layard
sustentative
sustentation
Austin canons
Justin Martyr
putting-cleek
multinuclear
button scurvy
buttoned-down
muttonheaded
hunting-field
cutting grass
putting green
hunting-knife
hunting-lodge
multinominal
Austin friars
hunting-sword
putting-stone
suit one's book
bust one's butt
multungulate
put to one side
Austronesian
Kurt Vonnegut
rust-coloured
suit yourself
lustrousness

Just Fontaine
multipresent
multiple shop
multiple star
multiplicand
multiplicate
multipliable
multiplicity
multipartite
multipurpose
multiply into
quota quickie
subterranean
lust-breathed
custard apple
muster-master
Gunter's chain
quattrocento
butterscotch
buttered eggs
Buster Keaton
buttery-hatch
hunter-killer
Günter Blobel
butterfly-bow
butterfly net
butterfly nut
rustproofing
butter-cooler
Gunter's scale
custard slice
subthreshold
culture shock
butter muslin
butter curler
punto reverso
punto riverso
multiscience
multisulcate
multiseptate
multiseriate
eustatically
put to the horn
multitasking
Gustav Mahler
multivoltine
multivalence
multivalency
multivariate
multiversity
multivarious
cultivatable
multivitamin
run up against
tubular bells
cumulatively
subumbrellar
cucumber tree
furunculosis
Jusuf Habibie
eunuchoidism
cupuliferous
Tubuliflorae
tubulifloral
Tubuai Island
queue-jumping
luxullianite
mutual friend
vu quang bovid
autumn crocus
lusus naturae

cumulonimbus
cumulocirrus
futurologist
cumulostrata
lugubriously
tumultuation
Auguste Comte
Augustinians
tumultuously
Auguste Rodin
Augustus John
curvicostate
curvicaudate
curvifoliate
surveillance
pulvilliform
culvertailed
subvertebral
pulverulence
pulvering day
pulverisable
curvirostral
pulverizable
vulvo-uterine
survivorship
surveyorship
gut-wrenching
mud wrestling
Ludwigshafen
Ludwig Erhard
Outward Bound®
outward-bound
quixotically
butyl alcohol
rubythroated
eurythermous
burying place
ruby-coloured
puzzle-headed
muzzle-loader
puzzle-monkey
quizzicality
buzzard-clock
ave atque vale
evidentially
A View to a Kill
Avogadro's law
availability
evil-favoured
evil-tempered
evil-mindedly
evil-speaking
evolutionary
evolutionism
evolutionist
even-handedly
avant-courier
Evonne Cawley
evangelicism
evangelistic
even-tempered
eventfulness
avant-gardism
avant-gardist
event horizon
eventide home
evening class
evening dress
evanescently
Ivan Turgenev
evaporograph

evaporimeter
evaporometer
overcapacity
overhand knot
overrashness
overfamiliar
over-cannoped
overcanopied
overcautious
overabundant
overactivity
overachiever
avariciously
overscutched
overschutcht
everydayness
overreaction
over-weighted
overpersuade
every few days
overwhelming
over the score
overkindness
overfineness
overniceness
overripeness
overnight bag
overfinished
oversimplify
overflourish
overemphasis
every man Jack
over and above
overinclined
over one's head
over-and-under
overfondness
overlordship
overpowering
overdo things
ovariotomist
overpopulate
evergreen oak
overprepared
overpressure
overcrowding
overestimate
every so often
overstrained
ivory-towered
overrun brake
averruncator
overfullness
oversubtlety
overmultiply
everywhither
overexposure
overexertion
evisceration
avitaminoses
avitaminosis
avowableness
sweat cooling
sweet-and-sour
sweet alyssum
two-eyed steak
sweepingness
sweetishness
sweet-scented
owner's equity
sweet sorghum

sweet-toothed
sweet william
Two Fat Ladies
swaggeringly
swagger stick
Dwight L Moody
two-horse race
swainishness
awe-inspiring
Kwok's disease
Twelve Tables
twilight zone
swell-mobsman
Twelfth Night
swamp cypress
swimming-bath
swimming-bell
swimmingness
swimming-pond
swimming-pool
Kwame Nkrumah
Owen Falls Dam
Ewan McGregor
swinging-boom
swinging-post
swine-keeping
Zwinglianism
Zwinglianist
swindle-sheet
twining plant
swing the lead
twenty-fourmo
twenty-twenty
H W Longfellow
two pound coin
sword-breaker
sword-bayonet
dwarfishness
swashbuckler
two-sidedness
two-speed gear
twitter-boned
twitteringly
zwitterionic
two-toed sloth
switch hitter
I wouldn't know
awkward squad
two-way mirror
swizzle-stick
Ixtaccihuatl
expanded type
oxyacetylene
exsanguinate
exsanguinity
exsanguinous
expatriation
exhaustively
exhaustingly
expansionary
expansionism
expansionist
exhaust steam
exhaust valve
ex abundantia
exobiologist
execratively
exactingness
exacerbation
executorship
executive toy
extended-play
exheredation
expeditation
experimented
experimental
experimenter
expediential
experiential
exterminable
exterminator
excel oneself
exteroceptor
excess demand
extensimeter
extensometer
extensionist
excess supply
expectorator
expectations
expert system
ex-serviceman
exaggerative
exaggeration
exaggeratory
exiguousness
exegetically
exchange rate
exchangeable
exchangeably
exhilarative
exhilarating
exhilaration
exhilaratory
excitability
extinguisher
excitingness
exhibitively
exhibitioner
explicitness
exulceration
exploitative
exploitation
explantation
exclusionary
exclusionism
exclusionist
exalbuminous
exemplifying
examinership
exempt rating
exenteration
exanthematic
oxonium salts
axioma medium
Oxford groups
excogitative
excogitation
expositively
expositional
export reject
expostulator
extortionate
extortionary
extortionist
exophthalmia
exophthalmic
exophthalmos
exophthalmus
exprobrative
exprobration
exprobratory
excruciating
excruciation
extractor fan
extraditable
exercitation
exorbitantly
exercise bike
exercise book
extralimital
extramundane
extremophile
extramurally
extramarital
expromission
extreme sport
extranuclear
extraneously
uxoriousness
expropriable
expropriator
extrapolator
extra-regular
extra-special
expressively
expressivity
expressional
extrasensory
express rifle
express train
extra-uterine
extravaganza
extravagance
extravagancy
extraversive
extroversive
extraversion
extroversion
exasperative
exasperating
exasperation
exospherical
axis cylinder
exotic dancer
exothermally
exoterically
exsufflation
exsufflicate
excursionise
excursionize
excursionist
pyjama jacket
gynaecocracy
gynaecologic
gynaecomasty
Lyra Belacqua
synadelphite
hydatidiform
pyramidology
dynamic range
tyrannicidal
tyrannically
dynamometric
sycamore tree
zygapophyses
zygapophysis
dysaesthesia
hypaesthesia
synaesthesia
hypaesthesic
dysaesthetic
synaesthetic
dynastically
synantherous
Lymantriidae
lycanthropic
synarthroses
synarthrosis
Bye Bye Birdie
symbolically
symbololatry
symbol grocer
syncretistic
synclinorium
synchroflash
synchronical
synchroniser
synchronizer
synchroscope
Wyndham Lewis
syndactylism
syndactylous
syndetically
hyperalgesia
hyperalgesic
hyperacidity
hyperbolical
Hyperboreans
hypercorrect
synecdochism
hyperdactyly
myxedematous
lysergic acid
Hypericaceae
by definition
hyperidrosis
hyperkinesia
hyperkinesis
hyperkinetic
by her lee-lane
hyperlipemia
cypermethrin
type locality
type founding
synecologist
hymenopteran
hyperplastic
type specimen
hyperpyretic
hyperpyrexia
hypersthenia
hypersthenic
hypersensual
hypersarcoma
synectically
hyperthermia
hyperthermal
hypertensive
hypertension
hypertrophic
hyperthyroid
type cylinder
myographical
Syngnathidae
syngenesious
Pythian games
Pythian verse
mythographer
mythogenesis
nychthemeral
nychthemeron
typhoid fever
mythological
mythologiser
mythologizer
pythonomorph
cylindricity
cylindriform
cylinder head
cylinder seal
cylinder hole
cylinder lock
Kyrie eleison
myringoscope
pyrithiamine
typification
pyritiferous
by his lee-lane
Kylie Minogue
hygienically
Syrian Desert
Tyrian purple
pyritohedral
pyritohedron
myristic acid
dye in the wool
Lyric Theatre
syllabically
cyclodextrin
Wycliffe Hall
cyclographic
by a long chalk
cyclonically
cyclandelate
cyclopropane
Byelorussian
Cyclostomata
cyclosporin A
cyclostomous
myrmecologic
Myrmecophaga
myrmecophile
myrmecophily
dysmenorrhea
symmetallism
ayuntamiento
hymnographer
cyanogenesis
hypnogenesis
hypnogenetic
Lynn Chadwick
Cyanophyceae
gymnosophist
hypnotically
hypnotherapy
hypnotisable
hypnotizable
Sydney Carton
hypocalcemia
pyromaniacal
gyromagnetic
xylobalsamum
pyrotartrate
hypogastrium
zygodactylic
mycobacteria
pyrotartaric
cytogenetics
pyrotechnics
zymotechnics
pyrotechnist
Cynocephalus
pyrometrical
hypothecator
pyrophyllite
hypothalamic
hypothalamus
pyrochemical
sycophantise
sycophantize
sycophantish
hypochondria
hypochlorite
hypothetical
hypophrygian
gynodioecism
synodic month
pyroligneous
cytoskeletal
cytoskeleton
by cock and pie
hypoglycemia
hypoglycemic
pyro-electric
mycoplasmata
pyroclastics
hypoplastron
pyrognostics
hypognathism
hypognathous
mycodomatium
Lycopodineae
cytotoxicity
Lycopodiales
hypocoristic
pyromorphite
hylomorphism
zygomorphism
zygomorphous
hypotrochoid
cymotrichous
typographist
hypocritical
Myron Scholes
my conscience
synoptically
hypostatical
hypoeutectic
hyposulphate
pyrosulphate
hyposulphite
zygomycetous
synonymously
Nymphaeaceae
lymphangitis
dysphemistic
nymphomaniac
symptomatise
symptomatize
nympholeptic
lymphography
hydrobiology
hygrochastic
hydrocolloid
hydrochloric
hybrid vigour
hydrodynamic
hybridisable
hybridizable
hydroelastic
hydrofluoric
hydrographic
hygrographic
hydrographer
hydrogen bomb

hydrogen bond
hydrogenated
hydrogeology
hydrokinetic
hydrological
Hydromedusae
hydromedusan
ayeremaining
hydronium ion
by transverse
hydrophanous
hydrophilite
hydrophilous
hygrophilous
hydrophobous
hydropathist
hydrophytous
hydroquinone
hydrargyrism
hydrostatics
cypress swamp
hydrotherapy
hydrothermal
hydrotropism
hydraulicked
hydraulic ram
György Ligeti
hydrozincite
Eyes Wide Shut
by a short head
Kyushu Island
mysticalness
✧dyotheletism
synthesis gas
syntheticism
mystifyingly
hyetographic
syntagmatite
mystagogical
dysteleology
system-monger
systematical
systematiser
systematizer
hysterically
hysterectomy
hysterogenic
hysteromania
mysteriously
nyctitropism
Pyotr Wrangel
Tyburn-ticket
Tyburn-tippet
sylviculture
Sylvestrines
Czechoslovak
Aztec two-step
Azerbaijanis
azathioprine

13 – even

data warehouse
Canada thistle
Palawan Island
palatableness
paramagnetism
maladaptation
Lamarckianism
balance of mind
amaica pepper
Damascus blade
Damascus steel
ag and baggage
as and gaiters
alad dressing
ar and feather
ay and display
ay-and-display
ag-and-bone-man
azardousness
apaveraceous
amageability
nanageability
panese paper
panese maple
panese cedar
amage feasant
Madame de Staël
alace Theatre
anagerialism
anagerialist
lade niçoise
taveillance
amage control
raleipomena
ramenstruum
racen's-stone
raffin-scale
raphernalia
rathustrian
rathustrism
tanicalness
ami tactics
agazine-rifle
azarine Bible
azarine plate
napithecine
rasitically
lariologist
radigm shift
nadian canoe
nadian River
waiian goose
ralipomenon
anic school
naliculated
aciousness
rapaciousness
sagaciousness
salaciousness
maladjustment
parallactical
parallelogram
parallel lines
parallelistic
parallel ruler
Van Allen belts
salaam aleikum
maladminister
Gavarnie Falls
savanna flower
savanna-forest
Gawain Douglas
savanna-wattle
Saratoga trunk
palaeoecology
malacophilous
Palaeotherium
parapophysial
parabolic arch
macaronically
parabolically
paradoxically
palaeobiology
da capo al segno
palaeoclimate
Balanoglossus
palaeobotanic
malacological
palaeozoology
palaeographer
palaeographic
palaeocrystic
malacostracan
palaeontology
palaeocurrent
lavatory paper
Pan-Africanism
maladroitness
papaprelatist
paragraphical
paragraph mark
ram-air turbine
parapsychical
parapsychosis
panaesthetism
malabsorption
galactic plane
catastrophism
catastrophist
galactorrhoea
galactosaemia
Kara Kum Desert
catapult fruit
catalytically
paralysis time
paramyxovirus
canary-creeper
Canary Islands
parasynthesis
parasynthetic
parasyntheton
barbecue sauce
payback period
Barbados earth
Barbados pride
marble-hearted
jaw-breakingly
rabble-rousing
wamble-cropped
eat boiled crow
Cambridge blue
gambling house
Cambridge ring
babbling brook
cabbalistical
carbamazepine
✧carboniferous
carbon dioxide
carbonylation
carbon process
carbonisation
carbonization
bamboozlement
bamboo curtain
namby-pambical
namby-pambyish
namby-pambyism
Barbara Castle
barbarisation
carburisation
barber-surgeon
barbarousness
barbarization
carburization
Lambeth degree
lay by the heels
Babbitt's metal
Sabbath school
Barbour® jacket
harbour master
narcoanalysis
paschal candle
Jascha Heifetz
paschal flower
saccharic acid
saccharimeter
saccharimetry
saccharometer
Saccharomyces
catch at straws
matchboarding
hatch coamings
fasciculation
lance corporal
barcode reader
matched sample
calcification
latch follower
narcohypnosis
watching brief
sanctimonious
sanctifyingly
pancake make-up
Nancy Kerrigan
latchkey child
Marcel Marceau
cancellariate
bascule bridge
Malcolm Fraser
Malcolm Morley
masculineness
matchlessness
calculatingly
calculational
baccalaureate
Marcel Duchamp
Law Commission
catchment area
parchment bark
bad conscience
carcinologist
vaccinologist
dancing-master
carcinomatous
Vaccinioideae
gas centrifuge
watch one's back
watch one's step
catch on the hip
sarcophaguses
cascara amarga
day care centre
calcariferous
panchromatism
cancerophobia
sarcastically
lance sergeant
Caicos Islands
bancassurance
watch the clock
patch together
narcotisation
narcotization
mad cow disease
Darcey Bussell
card catalogue
cardiac arrest
maids a-milking
hard radiation
cardiac muscle
paediatrician
pandiculation
tax-deductible
candidateship
handkerchiefs
saddle feather
candle-lighter
Dandie Dinmont
candle-dipping
Gaidhealtachd
saddle blanket
Handsel Monday
Gardner Murphy
candle-snuffer
hard-heartedly
land-measuring
paddle steamer
hard of hearing
maid of all work
maid-of-all-work
hardshell clam
raid the market
hard disk drive
Vandyke collar
daddy-long-legs
Magdalene Mary
Mandelbrot set
sandy-laverock
✧pandemoniacal
paedomorphism
randomisation
Saddam Hussein
randomization
garden warbler
maiden herring
maiden century
landing-ground
harden the neck
garden village
maiden-widowed
cardinal point
cardinalatial
cardinalitial
maiden-tongued
wardrobe trunk
cardiological
jaw-droppingly
cardboard city
cardiographer
maldeployment
War Department
sandarac resin
sandarach tree
handbrake turn
banderilleros
Paddy's lantern
Garda Siochana
eau des creoles
eau de toilette
hard-luck story
land-surveying
land-ownership
lay down the law
Lake Maracaibo
Cape Canaveral
sale-catalogue
camera obscura
case-hardening
bareland croft
barefacedness
have half a mind
have had its day
Pamela Andrews
Lateran Treaty
rated altitude
labefactation
James Buchanan
take a back seat
rateable value
water-breather
have a big mouth
James Brindley
James Bond film
have a basinful
James Chadwick
water chestnut
par excellence
watercolorist
parencephalon
rated capacity
catercornered
water-carriage
James Christie
mater dolorosa
eavesdropping
water dropwort
lavender water
tabes dorsalis
calendar month
kaleidoscopic
Yaren District
sacerdotalise
sacerdotalism
sacerdotalist
sacerdotalize
race relations

earth-chestnut
lattice-girder
nautical table
particularise
particularism
particularist
particularity
particularize
parti-coloured
party-coloured
participially
participantly
participating
participation
participatory
participative
catty-cornered
tautochronism
tautochronous
lattice window
carte-de-visite
battle fatigue
Matthew Arnold
Hattie Jacques
battle-scarred
Battle of Pavia
Battle of Valmy
Battle of Varna
Battle of Maipó
Battle of Maipú
Battle of Sedan
Battle of Liège
Battle of Sluys
Battle of Anzio
Battle of Ypres
Battle of Crécy
Battle of Issus
Battle of Mylae
battle against
rattle the cage
cattle-lifting
tattie-lifting
pantheologist
wattle and daub
Walther Nernst
parthenocarpy
tattie-howking
Matthew Parker
battle-cruiser
rattle-brained
pantheistical
salt of vitriol
vantage ground
lactoglobulin
mastigophoran
mastigophoric
Pantagruelian
Pantagruelion
Pantagruelism
Pantagruelist
Last Christmas
Captain Cooker
cartridge-belt
cartridge clip
waltzing mouse
partridge-wood
earthing tyres
Bactrian camel
captain's chair
dactylography
cartilaginous

tautologously
earthly-minded
dactyliomancy
martello tower
tantalisingly
faithlessness
tastelessness
cartelisation
tantalisation
pay television
tantalizingly
cartelization
tantalization
earth-motherly
tautometrical
earth-movement
Martina Hingis
East India Club
Matti Nykaenen
Martin Bormann
part and parcel
Martin Brundle
Hastings Banda
bait and switch
cantonisation
cast a nativity
waiting-vassal
Daltons Weekly
casting-weight
cantonization
xanthochromia
xanthochroism
xanthochroous
gastroenteric
gastrocnemius
gastrological
gastronomical
salts of sorrel
east-north-east
east-south-east
xanthopterine
party politics
tautophonical
wastepaper bin
masters-at-arms
Walter Raleigh
Walter Bagehot
master-mariner
Tartarian lamb
master-passion
Walter Matthau
factorability
Master McGrath
Eastern Church
battered child
Walter Gilbert
master aircrew
Walter Sickert
martyrologist
dastardliness
pastoral staff
Walter Mondale
bacteriophage
bacteriolysin
bacteriolysis
bacteriolytic
gasteropodous
Eastern Pahari
lantern pinion
barter trading
Walter Gropius

part brass rags
cauterisation
factorisation
martyrisation
tartarisation
master-builder
masterfulness
rapturousness
wasterfulness
cauterization
factorization
martyrization
tartarization
baptismal name
Balto-slavonic
baptismal vows
pantisocratic
fantastically
party-spirited
baptism of fire
faites vos jeux
war to the knife
partitionment
partition wall
Malthusianism
captivatingly
natural causes
value-added tax
natural magnet
hanuman monkey
natural number
natural person
natural resins
natural system
manufacturing
Naguib Mahfouz
Ranunculaceae
nature reserve
nature-worship
mature student
casus foederis
capuchin cross
Baruch Spinoza
Kazuo Ishiguro
Samuel Langley
Gaius Lucilius
Manuel de Falla
Samuel Beckett
Samuel Slumkey
casual clothes
Samuel Goldwyn
Samuel Johnson
casualisation
vacuolisation
casualization
vacuolization
vacuum cleaner
vacuum forming
haruspication
value received
daguerreotype
daguerreotypy
Casuarinaceae
casuistically
Vanuatu Island
valuation roll
facultatively
Salvador Luria
mauvaise honte
mauvais moment
salviniaceous

galvanometric
galvanoplasty
Calvinistical
galvanisation
galvanization
naive painting
laevorotation
laevorotatory
canvas-climber
harvest spider
harvest supper
Salvation Army
Harvey Cushing
Warwick Castle
Maxwell's demon
Darwin College
batwing sleeve
Man with a Glove
Mary Magdalene
baby-battering
Lady's bedstraw
Caryocaraceae
Lady of Shalott
laryngectomee
laryngologist
laryngoscopic
many-sidedness
labyrinth fish
labyrinthical
labyrinthitis
easy listening
easy-listening
lady-in-waiting
baby-snatching
✧lady bountiful
palynological
Mary Lou Retton
easy as winking
ranz-des-vaches
Abraham's bosom
obtainability
absence of mind
obsecration by
objets de vertu
obsessionally
objets trouvés
obsessiveness
absent healing
object of virtu
objectionable
objectionably
object program
objectiveness
objectivistic
objectivation
objective test
observational
A Bigger Splash
obliviousness
oblique motion
oblique speech
ebullioscopic
Ebony Concerto
Ebenezer Cooke
absorbability
obnoxiousness
absolute value
absolute pitch
absolute units
absolute ruler
absolute music

absolutely not
Aberdeenshire
Aberdeen Angus
ab urbe condita
aboriginalism
✧aboriginality
uberrima fides
abortifacient
obtrusiveness
Abyssinian cat
abyssopelagic
abstract verse
abstractional
abstractively
a bit on the side
abstentionism
abstentionist
obstinateness
obstetrically
obstructional
obstructively
obtuse-angular
about one's ears
above one's head
above reproach
acta sanctorum
scrambled eggs
schadenfreude
scrape through
octave coupler
occasionalism
occasionalist
occasionality
scrap merchant
oceanological
oceanographer
oceanographic
Ocean of Storms
acidification
academicalism
acid-free paper
schematically
screech-martin
Science Museum
screech-thrush
accelerometer
Scheele's green
screening test
screen process
screenwriting
scleromalacia
sclerocaulous
sclerodermite
sclerodermous
sclerotic coat
scleroprotein
accessibility
accessory shoe
acceptability
scientificity
eccentrically
Scientologist
acceptilation
schizaeaceous
scribbling-pad
Schindler's Ark
scrivenership
active service
accidentalism
occidentalise
Occidentalism

Occidentalist
accidentality
occidentalize
accident-prone
occipital bone
occipital lobe
Schilling test
scrimmage line
actinobacilli
schizocarpous
schizogenesis
schizogenetic
Echinodermata
Schizophyceae
schizophrenia
schizophrenic
scripophilist
actinotherapy
acrimoniously
actinomorphic
Schizomycetes
schizomycetic
actinomycosis
scripturalism
scripturalist
scriptwriting
scale and platt
scaly anteater
ochlocratical
Scoleciformia
occluded front
scalpelliform
scalping-knife
schlumbergera
Schlemm's canal
acclimatation
Iceland falcon
scalenohedron
scaling ladder
scolopendrine
scolopendrium
scalar segment
scalar product
ecclesiolater
ecclesiolatry
sculpturesque
scambling-days
ecumenicalism
scandal-bearer
scandalmonger
scenic railway
scenic reserve
scintiscanner
scintilliscan
scintillating
scintillation
scintigraphic
economisation
iconomaticism
econometrical
economization
Scent of a Woman
scenarisation
scenarization
scene-shifting
ectoparasitic
acrobatically
scholarliness
scholasticism
octocentenary
scrobiculated

schoolmarmish
schoolteacher
school-leaving
schoolgirlish
school-trained
accommodating
accommodation
accommodative
act of oblivion
accompaniment
accoustrement
accoutrements
accouterments
Schottky noise
scapulimantic
scapulomantic
acupuncturist
scaphocephaly
a copy of verses
a capful of wind
acorn-barnacle
acaridomatium
acarodomatium
accreditation
scarlet letter
scarlet runner
Scarlett O'Hara
scarification
scorification
scorchingness
scorpion grass
achromaticity
achromatopsia
scorbutically
Scotney Castle
scathefulness
acetification
Scotification
Scotch pancake
Scotch verdict
Scotch terrier
Scotch thistle
Scotch collops
Scotch curlies
acotyledonous
acetylcholine
acetaminophen
acatamathesia
ecotoxicology
ichthyologist
ichthyopsidan
Ichthyosauria
ichthyosaurus
acquiescently
acquiescingly
scouring stick
actualisation
actualization
scrumptiously
acquirability
acquired taste
acquisitively
acculturation
Schutzstaffel
scavenger hunt
Schwenkfelder
schwärmerisch
acrylaldehyde
acrylic resins
acrylonitrile
adiabatically

Edgar Allan Poe
✧advanced level
advanced guard
Edward Kennedy
Edward Whymper
Edward R Murrow
Eduard Buchner
adiathermancy
adiaphoristic
Edgar Mitchell
advantageable
advantage rule
odd-come-shorts
educatability
Educating Rita
educationally
adrenal cortex
adrenal glands
admeasurement
adventure film
adventure game
adventuristic
adventuresome
adventurously
advertisement
advertizement
admirableness
advisableness
Admiralty Arch
adding machine
additionality
administrable
administrator
Edwin Landseer
admissibility
Eddie the Eagle
Adolf Eichmann
Adolphe Thiers
adumbratively
identicalness
identic action
adenoidectomy
odontophorous
odontoglossum
odontornithes
odontological
odonatologist
Edinburgh rock
ad inquirendum
idiomatically
adsorbability
Edmond Rostand
ideologically
ideographical
idiorrhythmic
Edmontosaurus
idiosyncratic
adaptableness
edaphic factor
adipose tissue
odoriferously
Addressograph®
édition de luxe
Edmund Hillary
Edmund Spenser
Edmund Husserl
Edouard Lartet
adjustability
Delaware River
set a game to two
separationism

separationist
zenana mission
Debatable Land
separableness
Vera Cáslavská
beta particles
hexadactylous
perambulation
perambulatory
decarbonation
decarboxylase
debauchedness
revaccination
melancholious
legal capacity
recalcitrance
Gerald Kaufman
demand feeding
demand deposit
metal detector
regardfulness
Gerald Durrell
delayed action
megaherbivore
megacephalous
dexamethasone
metamerically
sexagesimally
Yekaterinburg
dematerialise
dematerialize
sebaceous cyst
aerated waters
decaffeinated
dexamfetamine
detachability
Seraphic Order
nemathelminth
Menachem Begin
metachromatic
refashionment
metaphysician
metaphosphate
Benazir Bhutto
mesaticephaly
negative angle
rehabilitator
semasiologist
denationalise
denationalize
metafictional
behaviourally
nefariousness
tenaciousness
vexatiousness
metalliferous
metallography
retail therapy
Texas longhorn
metallurgical
detail drawing
metallisation
metallization
Cesar Milstein
retaining wall
megalosaurian
teratogenesis
Nevado del Ruiz
melanochroous
metabolically
metabolisable

metabolizable
pedagogically
metacognition
megalopolitan
teratological
✧metamorphoses
✧metamorphosis
vena contracta
megasporangia
metagrabolise
metagrobolise
metagrabolize
metagrobolize
metapsychical
new Australian
Texas scramble
net asset value
metastability
pedantocratic
penalty corner
semantic error
telautography
tetartohedral
Melastomaceae
tenant-in-chief
hexactinellid
Levant morocco
devastatingly
megastructure
membranaceous
Serbo-Croatian
redback spider
Herbie Hancock
heebie-jeebies
pebble-glasses
verbification
verbigeration
Leibnizianism
verbalisation
verbalization
meibomian cyst
pembroke table
Pembrokeshire
Berberidaceae
Jedburgh Abbey
Herbert Hoover
Ken Barrington
herborisation
herborization
set by the heels
membrum virile
fetch and carry
deoch-an-doruis
merchandising
merchandizing
fetch a circuit
peaceableness
teachableness
fetch a compass
✧neoclassicism
neoclassicist
peacock copper
peacock-flower
peach-coloured
leuco-compound
Peacock Throne
peace dividend
geochemically
leucaemogenic
Percy Grainger
perching birds

reactionarism
reactionarist
descriptively
descriptivism
Mercalli scale
reacclimatise
reacclimatize
pencil-compass
Hercule Poirot
mercilessness
peacelessness
mescal buttons
tercentennial
mercantile law
fencing-master
geocentricism
mercenariness
peace offering
cercopithecid
mercurialness
Mercurochrome®
sex chromosome
geochronology
mercury switch
mercerisation
mercerization
Leicester plan
percussion cap
percussionist
leucitohedron
deacquisition
dead-cat bounce
pendragonship
dead man's pedal
dead-reckoning
needle-pointed
dead-men's bells
dead men's shoes
head restraint
dead-letter box
re-edification
Bendigeidfran
read like a book
feudalisation
pendulousness
feudalization
feeding bottle
weeding-chisel
feeding frenzy
wedding finger
wedding favour
tendentiously
reading matter
Ferdinand Cohn
Ferdinand Foch
read oneself in
lend oneself to
redding-straik
Dendrocalamus
send to the dogs
dendrological
dead-colouring
lead poisoning
head-up display
perdurability
ready reckoner
Reader's Digest
gender-bending
tender-hearted
deodorisation
read-write head

deodorization
ready, steady, go
perditionable
lead-out groove
headquartered
head over heels
meadow saffron
heads will roll
meadow foxtail
lead by the nose
lever arch file
Vézelay Church
general degree
general effect
Helena Kennedy
Teresa of Avila
televangelism
televangelist
generalisable
generalizable
generation gap
Generation Xer
generationism
revelationist
vegetarianism
generalissimo
temerariously
telemarketing
general ledger
general legacy
venerableness
General Patton
telefacsimile
reverberantly
reverberation
reverberatory
reverberative
seneschalship
Terence Conran
rebecca-eureka
defencelessly
Terence O'Neill
level crossing
mesencephalic
telencephalic
mesencephalon
telencephalon
telescopiform
dependability
revendication
serendipitist
serendipitous
lever de rideau
reference book
reference-mark
René Descartes
deleteriously
venereologist
telerecording
decelerometer
here we go again
redevelopment
decerebration
deferentially
referentially
reverentially
tenement house
beleaguerment
Fêtes Galantes
genethlialogy
fête champêtre

telephone book
gene therapist
telephoto lens
Peveril Castle
teledildonics
redeliverance
Berenice's Hair
beneficential
heresiography
television set
repetitionary
televisionary
dereligionise
dereligionize
beneficiation
repetitiously
veneficiously
heresiologist
Venetian blind
Venetian glass
demeritorious
sedes impedita
deterioration
deteriorative
genetic spiral
benedictional
selenious acid
redeemability
beseemingness
deterministic
determinately
determination
determinative
Jewel Mountain
perennibranch
Aegean Islands
here and yonder
heterogametic
heterocarpous
Hemerobaptist
Herefordshire
heterogenesis
heterogenetic
heterogeneity
heterogeneous
heterothallic
heterochronic
heterothermal
semeiotically
ceremonialism
ceremonialist
renegotiation
ceremoniously
heteroblastic
heteroplastic
heteroclitous
developmental
telecommuting
derecognition
selenological
heteromorphic
heterosporous
selenographer
genetotrophic
heterotrophic
selenographic
telecottaging
heterostylism
heterostylous
heterostrophy
heteropterous
teleportation
teleconverter
Redemptionist
metempiricism
metempiricist
vexed question
penetrability
desegregation
cerebral palsy
cerebral death
meteorologist
telegrammatic
peregrination
peregrinatory
Tenebrionidae
telegraph pole
telegraph wire
gene frequency
cerebrospinal
meteoriticist
meteor streams
penetratingly
penetratively
defeasibility
defensibility
reversibility
Seven Sleepers
depersonalise
depersonalize
Reye's syndrome
reversionally
remeasurement
necessariness
necessitarian
necessitation
necessitously
recessiveness
desert varnish
deceptibility
defectibility
delectability
detestability
receptibility
repeatability
never the wiser
seventeenthly
seventh heaven
desert the diet
pedestrianise
pedestrianism
pedestrianize
derestriction
repeating coil
repeat oneself
reception room
sedentariness
sedentary soil
desertisation
deceitfulness
resentfulness
deceptiveness
defectiveness
receptiveness
retentiveness
selectiveness
desertization
revenue cutter
derequisition
revenue tariff
deceivability
receivability
Reservoir Dogs
reservoir rock
receiving line
deservingness
receiving-room
receiving-ship
defervescence
defervescency
seven-year itch
Seven Years' War
Jeremy Bentham
Jeremy Guscott
self-balancing
self-satisfied
self-sacrifice
self-abasement
perfect fourth
perfectionism
✧perfectionist
perfectionate
perfect insect
perfect market
perfect metals
perfect number
perfect square
self-education
self-addressed
selfe-despight
self-adjusting
Jeffrey Archer
self-regarding
self-dependent
self-reverence
self-levelling
self-revealing
self-referring
self-defensive
self-defeating
self-repeating
self-deception
self deceitful
self-reliantly
self-recording
self-reproving
Der Freischütz
self-restraint
self-centredly
self-fertility
self-repugnant
self-denyingly
self-shielding
self-financing
self-discharge
self-direction
self-righteous
reaffirmation
self-dispraise
self-pityingly
self-slaughter
self-important
self-annealing
self-infection
self-injection
reefing-jacket
self-inflicted
newfangleness
self-enjoyment
perfunctorily
self-insurance
self-indulgent
self-induction
self-inductive
self-knowledge
self-conceited
self-condemned
self-governing
self-confident
self-confiding
self-confessed
self-forgetful
self-motivated
self-conjugate
self-collected
self-pollution
self-communion
self-tormentor
self-conscious
self-consuming
self-possessed
self-contained
self-convicted
self-opinioned
self-appointed
self-operating
self-approving
self-treatment
self-professed
Seyfert galaxy
perfervidness
Jefferson City
self-propelled
self-criticism
welfare worker
self-asserting
self-assertion
self-assertive
per fas et nefas
self-assurance
self-assuredly
Beefsteak Club
self-sterility
self-murdering
self-sufficing
self-judgement
self-publicist
self-publicity
self-supported
self-surrender
self-sustained
self-surviving
self-evidently
self-awareness
self-executing
self-existence
self-hypnotism
hedge-accentor
les grands vins
Peggy Ashcroft
neogrammarian
Sergeant Baker
sergeant-major
neighbourhood
neighbourless
Reggie Jackson
Sergei Aksakov
Sergei Korolev
hedge-marriage
begging letter
sea gooseberry
Reign of Terror
Geiger counter
weight-watcher
weight of metal
Newgate fringe
weightlifting
height to paper
New Grub Street
tergiversator
methodologist
Methodistical
Seth Pecksniff
dephlegmation
technical area
technical foul
technicalness
cephalic index
keyhole limpet
methyl alcohol
nephelometric
methylene blue
cephalosporin
cephalisation
cephalothorax
cephalization
béchamel sauce
methanoic acid
mechanisation
mechanization
nephrological
technological
technopolitan
Netherlandish
Gerhard Berger
Gerhard Domagk
nether regions
lethargically
lecherousness
dephosphorise
dephosphorize
be that as it may
hemiparasitic
semiparasitic
Semipalatinsk
demi-caractère
semi-barbarian
semi-barbarism
semicarbazide
meditate about
peripatetical
medicamentary
pelican-flower
cevitamic acid
derivationist
recitationist
semi-sagittate
desirableness
veritableness
semipalmation
devisal of arms
decimal places
decimal system
perigastritis
Le Misanthrope
semiochemical
periodic table
periodicalist
periodic month
revindication
period of grace
Behind the Line
petit déjeuner
periodontitis
bewilderingly
periodisation
Cecil Day-Lewis
periodization
perihepatitis
hemimetabolic
derived demand
perinephritis
beside the mark
semiperimeter
hemicellulose
pedicellariae
semipermeable
semi-permanent
beside oneself
Venice treacle
✧mediterranean
semimenstrual
penitentially
residentially
sedimentology
regimentation
sedimentation
sewing machine
meningococcal
meningococcic
meningococcus
Belisha beacon
perishability
delightedness
perichondrial
perichondrium
peripherality
delirifacient
felicitations
verifiability
reminiscently
feminine rhyme
medicine chest
perivitelline
medicine woman
verisimilarly
penicilliform
penicillinase
decision table
meridionality
deficientness
deliciousness
deliriousness
religiousness
seditiousness
sericiculture
aerial railway
vexillologist
Seville orange
aerial ropeway
serialisation
feuilletonism
feuilletonist
legislatorial
legislatively
serialization
heliometrical
Legion of Merit
beginningless
Design for Life
designer label
beginner's luck
semiporcelain
retinoscopist
semiconductor
Lepidodendron

 Words marked ✧ can also be spelled with one or more capital letters

meritoriously
lexicological
genito-urinary
lexicographer
lexicographic
semiconscious
get in on the act
Lepidostrobus
lepidopterist
lepidopterous
helispherical
hemispherical
reciprocality
reciprocation
reciprocative
senior service
demiurgically
senior citizen
defibrillator
defibrination
lexigraphical
remissibility
perissodactyl
series winding
Peninsular War
peninsularity
redissolution
devil's boletus
registrarship
resistibility
Pepin the Short
get it together
remittance man
resistance box
heliotropical
mediatorially
register-plate
Register House
sex intergrade
mediatisation
get into the act
mediatization
residual value
semi-automatic
deliquescence
sericulturist
deciduousness
Medieval Latin
medieval modes
relieving arch
relieve nature
semioviparous
semi-evergreen
perityphlitis
serjeant-at-law
Benjamin Baker
deck passenger
leuko-compound
red kidney bean
leukaemogenic
Berkeleianism
week in, week out
Neo-Kantianism
neck and manger
seek-no-further
neck or nothing
Becky Thatcher
feel-bad factor
well-warranted
neoliberalism
neglectedness
reflectometer
reflectograph
hemlock spruce
tell me about it!
Leslie Scarman
Leslie Edwards
well-beseeming
well-developed
tell me another
well-respected
well-regulated
mealie pudding
jellification
mellification
mellifluently
mellifluously
negligibility
re-eligibility
red-legged crow
belligerently
neologistical
health service
health visitor
well-thought-of
healthfulness
celluliferous
cellular radio
Neo-Lamarckian
Neo-Lamarckism
declamatorily
Leclanché cell
selling-plater
seal-engraving
tell one's beads
Hellenistical
replenishment
Per Lindstrand
well-conducted
heels over head
realpolitiker
well-worked-out
well-connected
heels o'er gowdy
meals on wheels
belle peinture
well-appointed
deplorability
seller's market
sellers' market
well-preserved
Neil Armstrong
declaratorily
declaratively
tellurous acid
realisability
belles-lettres
realistically
perlustration
deglutination
pelletisation
pelletization
yellow-bellied
fellow feeling
yellow berries
fellow servant
fellow citizen
yellow yorling
yellowishness
bellows to mend
yellow bunting
reflexibility
reflexologist
reflexiveness
real gymnasium
realizability
re-embarkation
vermiculation
Bermuda rigged
Bermuda shorts
Germaine Greer
mermaid's glove
mermaid's purse
Selma Lagerlöf
Neo-Melanesian
seam allowance
segmental arch
Selman Waksman
terminability
German measles
German Requiem
yeoman service
helminthiasis
helminthology
Desmond Haynes
fermentitious
terminologist
Desmond Morris
permanent wave
Germanophilia
Germanisation
Leamington Spa
terminational
ten-minute rule
terminatively
hermeneutical
Germanization
reimportation
hermaphrodite
geomorphogeny
geomorphology
mesmerisation
mesmerization
kermes mineral
Les Miserables
Les Misérables
term assurance
permutability
Helmut Schmidt
hermetic books
dermatography
geometrically
Jemmy Twitcher
geometric mean
dermatologist
dermatoplasty
dermatophytic
lemmatisation
permutational
lemmatization
reimbursement
Leonhard Euler
Jean Paul Marat
Jean Paul Getty
reincarnation
Lemnian ruddle
Wernicke's area
bernicle-goose
vernacularise
vernacularism
vernacularist
vernacularity
vernacularize
penny dreadful
Seanad Eireann
Kenny Dalglish
reinterrogate
reintegration
✧neanderthaler
Dean of Faculty
reunification
penny-farthing
Jennifer Lopez
Heinz Holliger
re-engineering
Heinrich Barth
Heinrich Heine
Heinrich Hertz
jenny-long-legs
vernal equinox
pennilessness
vernalisation
Kennelly layer
vernalization
her number is up
lex non scripta
meaninglessly
mean solar time
re-enforcement
reinforcement
Réunion Island
deontological
herniorrhaphy
re-endorsement
jeune première
penny-pinching
Semnopithecus
Jean Fragonard
Jean Froissart
Bernard Lovell
re-entry window
Heinz Sielmann
jeunesse dorée
Dennis Skinner
seine-shooting
keen as mustard
Kenneth Clarke
Kenneth Kaunda
reinstatement
Jean-Luc Godard
Pennsylvanian
femoral artery
tenovaginitis
Decoration Day
Setonaikai Sea
memorableness
revocableness
recombination
reconcilement
lemon-coloured
heroic couplet
second reading
beyond measure
second officer
second chamber
beyond the pale
second-sighted
beyond dispute
beyond one's ken
beyond compare
secondary coil
secondary cell
secondariness
reconditeness
set one's back up
aerogenerator
remote sensing
jee one's ginger
before the beam
before the fact
mesocephalism
mesocephalous
before the mast
get one's hand in
before the wind
Jerome K Jerome
get one's kit off
set one's mind on
xerodermatous
become unglued
get one's own way
remote control
set one's seal on
deforestation
reforestation
peyote buttons
recovery stock
recomfortless
Sea of Geniuses
lemon geranium
xerophthalmia
negotiability
demolishments
aerolithology
demolitionist
aerobiologist
refocillation
devotionalist
devotionality
feloniousness
ferociousness
melodiousness
recollectedly
désobligeante
recoil nucleus
deformability
reformability
Sea of Moisture
recommendable
recommendably
reformational
Reform Judaism
reconnoiterer
metoposcopist
zero tolerance
get on one's bike
serologically
Peloponnesian
demonological
seroconverted
decompression
recompression
decompressive
recompensable
decomposition
recomposition
resourcefully
melodramatics
melodramatise
melodramatist
melodramatize
cerographical
venographical
democrat wagon
reconstituent
reconsolidate
remorselessly
reconstructor
remonstrantly
Sea of Serenity
demonstration
remonstration
demonstratory
remonstratory
demonstrative
remonstrative
lemon squeezer
gerontocratic
decortication
Herod the Great
gerontologist
decontaminant
decontaminate
gerontophilia
gerontophobia
reportorially
report program
devolutionary
revolutionary
devolutionist
resolutionist
revolutionise
revolutionism
revolutionist
revolutionize
re-solubleness
resolubleness
resolvability
revolving door
revolving fund
memory manager
aerodynamical
memory mapping
genotypically
metonymically
tenosynovitis
temptableness
Neo-Plasticism
neoplasticism
tea plantation
despicability
people carrier
resplendently
perplexedness
People's Friend
People in a Wind
terpsichoreal
terpsichorean
Leipzig option
reapplication
geopolitician
Neapolitan ice
Serpent Bearer
tenpence piece
leap in the dark
perpendicular
serpent-lizard
tenpin bowling
keep one's end up
weeping spring
weaponisation
keep one's eye in
keep one's eye on
weeping willow
tenpenny piece
weaponization

chemical abuse
The Mock Turtle
chimneybreast
chimney-corner
chimney-pot hat
chymification
shamefastness
The Magic Flute
whimsicalness
the main chance
Thymelaeaceae
chameleon-like
thimblerigged
thimblerigger
shamelessness
Thomson effect
thumb one's nose
rhombohedrons
rhyme or reason
The Moody Blues
rhombporphyry
chemoreceptor
the morn's nicht
Thomás Masaryk
Thomas Carlyle
Thomas Campion
Thomas Fairfax
Thomas à Becket
Thomas Addison
Thomas Beecham
Thomas Peachum
Thomas Telford
Thomas Linacre
Thomas à Kempis
Champs Elysées
Thomas Sopwith
Thomas Creevey
Thomas Arundel
Thomas Cranmer
chemisorption
Thomas Müntzer
Thomas Pynchon
chammy leather
shammy leather
phantasmalian
phantasmality
phenobarbital
phonocamptics
thunder-bearer
changeability
thunder-darter
change of heart
change of venue
change of state
channel-hopper
the noes have it
chinkerinchee
change-ringing
thunder-master
change oneself
chance one's arm
thenceforward
thundershower
thunderstruck
channel-surfer
thunderstrike
thunder-stroke
changefulness
phonographist
thank goodness
The Night Watch
changing-piece
Changi Airport
thing-in-itself
Chantilly lace
The Naked Lunch
phenolic resin
phenylbenzene
phenylalanine
shingle-roofed
thanklessness
phenomenology
phenomenalise
phenomenalism
phenomenalist
phenomenality
phenomenalize
phonendoscope
thank-offering
Chinook Jargon
Shannon Miller
Chinook salmon
phanerogamous
Chinese leaves
rhinoscleroma
Chinese puzzle
Chinese radish
thanatography
phenothiazine
thanatophobia
The Nutcracker
phonetisation
phonetization
phonautograph
thankworthily
phencyclidine
thiocarbamide
Theopaschitic
Theobald Smith
Theobald Boehm
chlorargyrite
chromatically
chromatophore
chromatograph
thrombokinase
thrombophilia
the old serpent
theorematical
chrome tanning
chrome leather
theoretically
chrome plating
The Odessa File
Shrove Tuesday
through bridge
through ticket
through the day
The Other Place
the other woman
the other world
chlorhexidine
chlorine water
shooting range
throwing table
shooting lodge
whooping cough
shooting board
shooting brake
whooping crane
shooting stick
throwing stick
chloritic marl
chronicle play
chromium steel
phlogisticate
Theodor Adorno
Theodor Boveri
Chlorophyceae
chromotherapy
theologically
chronobiology
chloroplastal
chronological
theologoumena
chloroformist
chromospheric
chlorobromide
chlorocruorin
chronographer
Chloromycetin®
throttle valve
throttle lever
shoot the works
throstle frame
throw together
ship carpenter
the public weal
ship's chandler
shepherd's club
shepherd check
Shepherd kings
shepherd plaid
The Pretenders
ship of the line
ship chandlery
shipping agent
whipping-cheer
chopping-block
shipping clerk
chopping-knife
chopping-board
whipping cream
The Pajama Game
rhopalocerous
shapelessness
chop and change
whip into shape
the penny drops
rhapsodically
chaparral cock
rhyparography
ship's register
the paranormal
the party's over
shop assistant
cheque account
chequered flag
charlatanical
short and sweet
pharmaceutics
pharmaceutist
Sherpa Tenzing
the real Mackay
pharmacognosy
pharmacopoeia
charm bracelet
character code
characterless
character part
thoracentesis
thoracoplasty
short covering
short division
short-day plant
charge machine
charge-capping
charge carrier
Shirley Bassey
charge account
Charles Darwin
Thor Heyerdahl
charge density
Charles Gounod
Charles Mackay
charter member
Charles Mingus
Charles Morgan
Charles the Fat
Shirley Temple
sheriff clerks
thurification
sheriff depute
chirographist
The Right Stuff
churchmanship
church service
church officer
Church in Wales
Charlie Bucket
thereinbefore
thyroidectomy
whirling-table
choroid plexus
Charlie Parker
whereinsoever
third interval
Choral Fantasy
choral society
choral prelude
chiromantical
whoremasterly
whoremistress
pharyngoscope
pharyngoscopy
thermo-balance
Sharron Davies
thermogenesis
thermogenetic
thermosetting
thermophilous
thermochemist
thermotherapy
thermoplastic
theriomorphic
choreographer
thermographer
choreographic
thermographic
thermotropism
Charlotte Gray
Charlottetown
thermonuclear
thermodynamic
sharp practice
choropleth map
whirlpool bath
the Reproaches
chorepiscopal
a hard row to hoe
shark's manners
sharp's the word
pharisaically
sharpshooting
Thérèse Raquin
short-tempered
Bharata Natyam
charity-school
Oh, Pretty Woman
thorough-paced
thoroughgoing
thoroughbrace
Third-Worldism
sharp-wittedly
cherry-picking
sherry-cobbler
The Shangri-las
physharmonica
physicianship
physical jerks
physical force
whiskerandoed
Chester Nimitz
phospholipase
phosphorylase
phosphorylate
phosphoretted
phosphuretted
chose in action
The Spice Girls
whistle-blower
whistled-drunk
whistling swan
whistling-shop
physiotherapy
physiognomist
physiological
physiographer
physiographic
The Story of Art
Chesapeake Bay
chest register
chase rainbows
The Stranglers
physostigmine
physitheistic
The Sex Pistols
✧chateaubriand
Shetland sheep
white-breasted
that's big of him
photochemical
phytochemical
photocopiable
photochromics
photochromism
rhotacisation
rhotacization
white elephant
photoelectric
photoelectron
photo-emission
whithersoever
phytoestrogen
white-favoured
photographist
what the plague
White Hart lane
what ails him at?
rhythm section
photonegative
The Tin Woodman
ghetto-blaster
shot to nothing
what do you know?
phytoplankton
photophoresis
white pipe-tree
photoperiodic
photopositive
photoreceptor
The Terminator
Photostatting
white sapphire
White Squadron
that's the stuff!
whitetip shark
phytotoxicity
photovoltaics
that's your sort
thousand-pound
rheumatically
thaumatolatry
thaumaturgics
thaumaturgism
thaumaturgist
shoulder blade
shoulder plane
The Underworld
shoulder joint
shoulder strap
the unemployed
thoughtlessly
thought-reader
shouting match
thrust bearing
thrust through
cheval-de-frise
The Virginians
shove the queer
The Wife of Bath
The White Devil
The Winslow Boy
show one's cards
show one's paces
the whole shoot
the whole world
shower curtain
The Watchtower
chrysanthemum
the yellow leaf
chrysophilite
rhizomorphous
bigarade sauce
Visayan Island
final approach
financial year
bioaccumulate
vital capacity
pit and gallows
Wig and Pen Club
cigarette butt
cigarette card
cigarette case
disaffectedly
disaffirmance
dilapidations
mirabile dictu
titanium white
vicariousness
vivaciousness
miracle-monger
Rila Monastery
Vicar of Christ
pinafore skirt
pinafore dress
Die Another Day

Titanotherium
Sihanoukville
Rila Mountains
disappearance
misappreciate
disappointing
Hilaire Belloc
disagreeables
cicatrisation
cicatrization
disassimilate
disarticulate
gigantomachia
Sir Antony Sher
disaster movie
misanthropist
X-inactivation
simarubaceous
disadvantaged
misadventured
misadventurer
misadvertence
Vitaly Scherbo
binary fission
Siobhan Davies
Pinball Wizard
Big Bang theory
timbrophilist
Big Brotherism
Tim Berners-Lee
Liebfraumilch
lie by the heels
liabetologist
lischargeable
lischarge lamp
lischarge tube
inclair Lewis
ircraftwoman
litchcock film
iscicultural
ninced collops
vitches' butter
itched battle
itchen garden
iochemically
iscreditable
iscreditably
iscretionary
itchen Kaffir
itchen midden
itchen police
itchen physic
itched-roofed
itchen scales
itchetty grub
incification
itch-farthing
iscegenation
ischief-maker
itching wedge
iscriminable
iscriminator
ischievously
iscellaneous
ince Lombardi
r Colin Davis
scoloration
rcumjacency
ocompatible
rcumvallate
rcumscriber

discomycetous
circumference
circumvention
circumventive
discommission
circumfluence
circumflexion
circumambages
circumambient
discommodious
circumspectly
miscomprehend
air-compressor
viscometrical
circumstances
circumduction
circumductory
Vincent de Paul
bioconversion
disconcerting
discontenting
disconcertion
disconnection
misconception
misconjecture
discontentful
discontiguity
discontinuity
discontiguous
discontinuous
disconformity
Vincent O'Brien
cinchonaceous
witch of Agnesi
Jim Crow school
disceptatious
discapacitate
disciplinable
miscorrection
diachronistic
visceroptosis
viscosimetric
piece together
Liechtenstein
diacatholicon
piecrust table
discount house
Viscount Astor
discount store
discovery well
Hildebrandism
vindicability
vindicatorily
Gilded Chamber
fiddle-faddler
middle passage
fiddle pattern
fiddle-pattern
Middle-Eastern
Middlesbrough
bird's-eye maple
Middle Western
girdle of Venus
Middle Kingdom
Middle America
Middle England
Middle English
Mildred Pierce
middlebreaker
middle-bracket
kind-heartedly

middle article
fiddler's money
fiddler's green
tiddledywinks
bird of passage
biodegradable
lied ohne worte
wind dispersal
wild liquorice
wild gladiolus
mind-blowingly
findon haddock
hidden economy
binding energy
winding engine
sindonologist
bidding-prayer
find one's level
Bildungsroman
winding-strips
bird's-nest soup
wild and woolly
winds of change
Windsor Castle
find someone in
wind up and down
kindergärtner
Mindoro Island
Kidderminster
tic douloureux
Sir David Bruce
Sir David Frost
window-shopper
window-dresser
window curtain
mind-expanding
kindly-natured
mineral alkali
Mike Hazelwood
River Achelous
cinematically
kinematically
liberationism
liberationist
miserableness
mineralogical
cinematograph
kinematograph
mineral spring
live cartridge
mineral tallow
Mike Hawthorne
literary agent
disembodiment
mixed blessing
disembarkment
life scientist
liver-coloured
video cassette
Licence to Kill
fidei defensor
vice-admiralty
River Dniester
ailes de pigeon
River Dordogne
rite de passage
life-rendering
mine detection
bioenergetics
River Eridanus
fire-resistant

fire-resisting
sidereal month
nineteenth man
ninepenny marl
pipeless organ
fine gentleman
time-bettering
time-beguiling
rite of passage
mixed fraction
time after time
wide of the mark
eigenfunction
line of country
mixed foursome
disengagement
diverging lens
give the bucket
bite the bullet
dimethylamine
fine Champagne
fine chemicals
give the needle
kinesipathist
kinetic energy
live like a lord
dice with death
line-fisherman
kinesitherapy
kinesiologist
Milesian tales
time signature
kinetic theory
fixed-interest
like clockwork
vitelligenous
Nigella Lawson
mixed language
side-impact bar
mixed marriage
mixed metaphor
pigeon-fancier
Gideon Mantell
pigeon-hearted
hide-and-go-seek
pigeon-chested
pigeon-livered
Live and Let Die
Siméon Poisson
line-engraving
bite one's thumb
hibernisation
Sir Ernst Chain
fire insurance
life insurance
hibernization
River Okavango
video-on-demand
rise to the bait
give to the dogs
Ciceronianism
firework party
vice-consulate
time-consuming
fine-tooth comb
side-splitting
Pineapple Poll
pineapple weed
Aix-en-Provence
disemployment
misemployment

River Paraguay
piked position
time-trialling
video recorder
pine-tree money
cine projector
ciné projector
dihedral angle
like grim death
birefringence
vice-principal
vice-president
life-preserver
linearisation
linearization
diversifiable
miner's anaemia
dimensionless
dimension work
life assurance
viper's bugloss
direct damages
licentia vatum
silent partner
liberty bodice
digestibility
divertibility
diverticulate
give utterance
wide-stretched
direct selling
ride at the ring
disentailment
fide et fiducia
disestimation
dilettanteism
pile it on thick
River Tunguska
directionless
divertisement
direct current
Siberut Island
disequilibria
time out of mind
wide-awakeness
Sir Edward Coke
wired wireless
file extension
livery-servant
livery company
Sir Frank Dyson
dieffenbachia
Die Fledermaus
riffle through
Wilfred Rhodes
disfigurement
disfiguration
disfellowship
Air Force Medal
Air Force Cross
diffarreation
differentiate
diffusibility
diffusion-tube
diffusiveness
disgracefully
ringtailed cat
lingua francas
Zingiberaceae
single-hearted
single-chamber

King's evidence
single figures
single soldier
single pricing
lingue franche
King Henry VIII
King of Navarre
✧king of terrors
pilgrim-bottle
disguisedness
jingling match
pilgrim's shell
linguistician
linguistic map
Diego Maradona
Gilgamesh Epic
Virginia Beach
Virginia Woolf
Virginia stock
virginiamycin
virgin neutron
diagonal scale
singing master
pidgin English
Virgin Islands
pidginisation
biogenetic law
pidginization
Wings of Desire
Sir George Airy
Sir Georg Solti
wing commander
biogeographer
diageotropism
Siege of Tobruk
diagnostician
Singer Sargent
His Girl Friday
niggardliness
ginger cordial
finger-pointer
jiggery-pokery
finger-breadth
disgospelling
disgustedness
Birgit Nilsson
misgovernment
Highland dance
Highland Games
Eight and a Half
Highland fling
Highland dress
high-water mark
high-watermark
pigheadedness
highway patrol
disheartening
dichlamydeous
with a bad grace
dishabilitate
nightclubbing
Michael Bishop
Michael Clarke
Michael Doohan
Michael Gambon
Michael Howard
light emission
Michael Jordan
Michael Manley
eighteen-pence
eighteen-penny

Michael of Kent
with respect to
Michael Powell
Michael Ramsay
righteousness
lithification
light-fingered
Sir Hugh Casson
Sir Hugh Greene
tithe-gatherer
light-headedly
tight-head prop
with whole skin
with the manner
diphthongally
right-handedly
light horseman
High-Churchman
High-Churchism
lighthouseman
might-have-been
light industry
light infantry
Mikhail Glinka
fighting words
fighting drunk
Mikhail Suslov
tight junction
pinhole camera
Wilhelm Freund
Michela Figini
Wilhelm Keitel
Nicholas Scott
Nicholas Udall
sightlessness
nightmarishly
with one accord
within measure
fishing ground
lichenologist
diphenylamine
high and mighty
lightning-tube
siphonapteran
lithontriptic
lithontriptor
Sir Hans Sloane
fishing-tackle
dishonourable
dishonourably
Sir Henry Royce
Night of Ascent
right of common
right-of-centre
with good grace
dichromic acid
dithionic acid
light of nature
right of search
High Constable
dichrooscopic
xiphiplastral
xiphiplastron
xiphophyllous
Richard Avedon
fisherman's pie
Richard Bright
Richard Burton
Richard Butler
Richard Baxter
Richard Cobden
Richard Deacon
Richard E Grant
high priestess
Richard Hadlee
Richard Hannay
Richard Hooker
Richard Harris
Richard Leakey
Richard M Nixon
Richard Martin
hither and yond
disharmonious
high frequency
Richard Rogers
Richard Seddon
Richard Steele
Right Reverend
Richard Wagner
Richard Wright
Sir Hardy Amies
light-spirited
lightsomeness
lithesomeness
eightsome reel
with a siserary
right-thinking
right triangle
night-tripping
lithotriptist
high-stomached
dichotomously
without a doubt
without frills
high-muck-a-muck
without number
night-warbling
night-watchman
high explosive
high-explosive
digital camera
digital design
civil aviation
similar motion
military medal
military cross
Livia Drusilla
filipendulous
civil engineer
bidirectional
vivisectional
vivisectorium
vivisepulture
filing cabinet
riding the fair
riding clothes
disinhibition
disinhibitory
finishing post
visiting hours
diminishingly
digitizing pad
divisibleness
divisionalise
divisionalize
division lobby
litigiousness
Visible Church
disilluminate
bimillenniums
visible speech
limitlessness
disillusioned
titillatingly
mini flyweight
Wiliam Gilbert
civil marriage
visionariness
silicon valley
filius nullius
disintegrable
disintegrator
civil twilight
sinistrorsely
ministerially
disinterested
vicious circle
mini-submarine
filibustering
filibusterism
viniculturist
viticulturist
filibusterous
minimum weight
disinvigorate
disinvestment
Sir John Alcock
Sir James Paget
Sir James Dewar
Sir James Jeans
Zinjanthropus
disjunctively
nick-nackatory
Nick Farr-Jones
pickle-herring
sickle feather
winkle-pickers
tickle to death
Wilkie Collins
sick-feathered
tickle a th' sere
milk-dentition
zinkification
milk of sulphur
kick the bucket
milk chocolate
Mick the Miller
silk-throwster
sick-thoughted
Nikkei average
nickeliferous
nickel-plating
nickel-and-dime
pink elephants
pick and choose
Kirkintilloch
lick into shape
kick one's heels
pinking shears
lick one's chops
kick up a shindy
Sir Karl Popper
lickerishness
sick as a parrot
ticket of leave
ticket-writing
Rickettsiales
Kirkcudbright
tickly-benders
William Baffin
William Barnes
William Cowper
billiard table
billiard cloth
William Dunbar
William Dorrit
William Empson
William Godwin
William Hudson
William Harvey
yieldableness
William Morris
air loadmaster
uilleann pipes
William of Tyre
William Ramsay
William Temple
William Walton
William Warham
dialectically
Billy Connolly
field capacity
field cow-wheat
fille d'honneur
viola da spalla
viol-de-gamboys
Willie Waddell
Lillie Langtry
gillie-wetfoot
Willie Renshaw
field emission
Billie Holiday
Willie Brennan
Killiecrankie
air lieutenant
mid-life crisis
millefeuilles
villeggiatura
dialogistical
villagisation
villagization
field hospital
dipleidoscope
fit like a glove
field mushroom
diplomatic bag
diplomatology
milling cutter
violoncellist
millennialist
millennium bug
millennianism
millenniarism
villanousness
bibliolatrist
billionairess
millionairess
bibliolatrous
fill someone in
bibliothecary
bibliophagist
bibliophilism
bibliophilist
field of honour
wills-o'-the-wisp
bibliological
bibliopolical
bibliographer
bibliographic
field of vision
field preacher
dialypetalous
Bible-pounding
Willard F Libby
Miller indices
field strength
yield strength
air letter form
will-o'-the-wisps
✧millstone grit
Bible-thumping
willow warbler
willow pattern
field wood rush
lip microphone
sigmoidectomy
sigmoidoscope
sigmoidoscopy
dismemberment
diamond-beetle
mismanagement
Birminghamise
Birminghamize
dismantlement
diamond python
diamond-powder
Diamond Sculls
Sir Martin Rees
Sir Martin Ryle
film projector
diametrically
Dionne Warwick
Sir Noël Coward
Winnie-the-Pooh
significantly
dignification
lignification
signification
significatory
significative
Finnegans Wake
midnight feast
giant hockweed
sign the pledge
Gianni Versace
Lionel Hampton
signal peptide
signal letters
Lionel Robbins
his number is up
cinnamon stone
finnan haddock
bignoniaceous
winning hazard
lion's provider
dinner service
pianistically
pianississimo
fitness walker
disnaturalise
disnaturalize
giant tortoise
signature tune
kidney machine
Sidney Poitier
Milovan Djilas
Nicolaus Steno
liposculpture
disordinately
Simone Martini
linolenic acid
disobediently
mid-ocean ridge
hit one's stride
risorgimentos
mitochondrial
mitochondrion
nicotine patch
nicotinic acid
Tironian notes
minor interval
minority group
disobligement
disobligingly
disobligation
disobligatory
oil of lavender
Dido and Aeneas
Timon of Athens
lie on one's oars
minor prophets
lipogrammatic
ailourophilia
ailourophilic
ailourophobia
ailourophobic
widow's chamber
misobservance
sit on the fence
dinoturbation
Dicotyledones
diaphanometer
dispraisingly
displantation
simple larceny
simple-hearted
displeasingly
tippling-house
simplificator
dipping-needle
sixpenny piece
Simpson Desert
diaphototropy
disproportion
misproportion
hippopotamian
dispurveyance
disperse phase
dispersedness
misperception
diaphragmatic
disparagement
disparagingly
diaphragm pump
dispiritingly
disparateness
mispersuasion
disposability
dispossession
dispassionate
dispositional
dispositioned
dispositively
disputability
dispatch rider
Sir Peter Scott
Sir Peter Pears
disputatively
Sir Paul M Nurse
biopsychology
disqualifying
cinque-spotted
disquietingly
microanalysis
Sierra Leonean
Giordano Bruno

nitrobacteria
Sir Robert Peel
microcracking
hit rock bottom
microclimatic
vibracularium
nitro-compound
microcomputer
microcephalic
microcassette
microcosmical
Piero di Cosimo
microdetector
Pierre Laplace
Pierre Balmain
Pierre Vernier
Pierre Bonnard
microeconomic
Pierre Trudeau
Pierce Brosnan
nitrification
vitrification
vitrified fort
microfelsitic
microfilament
microfilariae
ciprofloxacin
microgranitic
hierogrammate
nitrogen cycle
hieroglyphics
ieroglyphist
iorgio Armani
iorgio Vasari
iorgiy Zhukov
nicrolighting
nicrometrical
itronella oil
ir Ronald Ross
nicronutrient
nigrant worker
nicro-organism
nicroprinting
nicropipettes
itroparaffin
icroporosity
isreputation
icrophysical
icrophyllous
irror machine
brarianship
irror writing
isrespectful
ioristically
icroscopical
icrosurgical
iprotodontia
protodontid
icrotonality
brationless
rovascular
icrowaveable
icrowave oven
isshapenness
st-begotten
st-day cover
ts per second
sue culture
ssogram girl
oscientific
ssolubility

dieselisation
dissoluteness
dieselization
midsummer moon
Midsummer's Day
dissemblingly
dissimilarity
dissimilitude
dissimilation
dissimulation
dissimulative
First Minister
dissemination
disseminative
first meridian
dies infaustus
kissing-comfit
kissing cousin
airs and graces
kiss-in-the-ring
Wilson Pickett
kiss and make up
kiss-and-make-up
bits and pieces
fits and starts
Missing the Sea
Dioscoreaceae
first offender
fission fungus
Winston Graham
Mission Indian
Ribston pippin
ripsnortingly
Giuseppe Verdi
Giuseppe Peano
dissepimental
fissiparously
biosystematic
Mississippian
✧missa solemnis
Risso's dolphin
lissotrichous
Missouri River
disseveration
linsey-woolsey
virtual memory
distractingly
distractively
histochemical
biotechnology
kitty-cornered
listed company
birthday party
tip the balance
hit the jackpot
tittle-tattler
little masters
little penguin
✧diotheletical
hit the ceiling
little theatre
Little Bighorn
Little Richard
hit the big time
diathermanous
distressingly
distressfully
sixteenth note
Little Russian
gift of tongues
lift the lid off

histrionicism
district court
fifth interval
sixth interval
district judge
district nurse
distributable
mirthlessness
victimologist
victimisation
victimization
tintinnabular
tintinnabulum
lifting-bridge
listenability
Sistine Chapel
tilting fillet
listening post
Girton College
sitting pretty
distant-signal
kittenishness
sitting tenant
sitting target
distinctively
distinguished
distinguisher
fictionalised
fictionalized
Sir Thomas More
mint condition
histiophoroid
Pietro Aretino
fiction writer
Victoria Falls
✧winter gardens
Mister Jaggers
winter jasmine
Victoria Cross
filterability
winter aconite
filter-feeding
Mister Wemmick
distortedness
Pieter de Hooch
picture palace
winterisation
picturesquely
victor ludorum
picture window
winterization
distastefully
tilt at the ring
dictatorially
mistrustingly
distrustfully
mistrustfully
kist o' whistles
kittly-benders
titular bishop
liquid crystal
misunderstand
misunderstood
liquidus curve
figure-casting
figure-weaving
figure of merit
figure of eight
figure skating
virulent phage
disuse atrophy

figure-hugging
ritualisation
visualisation
ritualization
visualization
Dieu vous garde
bicuspid valve
liquorice-vine
liquorishness
situationally
pituitary body
biculturalism
silver wedding
silver service
silver nitrate
silver-tongued
silver-mounted
silver jubilee
Rievaulx Abbey
big White Chief
airworthiness
dim-wittedness
nitwittedness
vinyl chloride
lily of the Nile
City of Bristol
vinyl plastics
Yitzhak Shamir
piezoelectric
piezomagnetic
Ojos del Salado
Akbar the Great
skulking-place
skeletogenous
A Kind of Loving
skinny-dipping
skirting-board
skirl-in-the-pan
Akira Kurosawa
skateboarding
sketchability
Sketches By Boz
skittle-ground
a kettle of fish
skeuomorphism
clearance sale
cloak-and-sword
cleavableness
Alcaic strophe
old age pension
old-age pension
clear-headedly
alkaline earth
floating light
cleaning woman
floating voter
clearing house
floating crane
floating grass
Ilya Prigogine
clear-starcher
clear the decks
old as the hills
plead the Fifth
olfactologist
clean-timbered
pleasure house
plebification
global warming
globuliferous
global village

globalisation
globalization
à la bonne heure
elaborateness
elaborate upon
globetrotting
✧old boy network
Alicia Markova
black and white
Glacial Period
placebo effect
black bindweed
blackberrying
black diamonds
black-eyed bean
clickety-clack
clickety-click
blackguardism
floccillation
electioneerer
old campaigner
ill-considered
gluconeogenic
electoral roll
electoral vote
old-clothesman
plectognathic
glaciological
plectopterous
block printing
plica Polonica
electric fence
electrochemic
electric shock
electric chair
electric field
electric piano
electrocement
electric motor
electric organ
electrocution
electric storm
electrifiable
electrography
electromagnet
electromerism
electrometric
electromotive
electronic tag
electron shell
electron probe
electro-optics
electroplated
electroplater
electrophilic
electrophorus
electrostatic
electroscopic
electrisation
electrothermy
electrotypist
electrovalent
electrization
black skipjack
Alec Issigonis
glycosylation
glucosinolate
blacktip shark
clock-watching
gladiatorship
bladder cherry

slide fastener
Vladimir Putin
Gladys Aylward
Clyde Tombaugh
slide trombone
Elder brethren
Illecebraceae
Blueberry Hill
Allen Ginsberg
bleeding heart
sleeping berth
sleeping coach
Sleeping Gypsy
illegibleness
sleep learning
bleed like a pig
sleep like a log
sleep like a top
alveolar ridge
sleeplessness
Ellesmere Port
alternate host
alternatively
allegorically
Blue Mountains
allelomorphic
algebraically
Olbers' paradox
Alberto Ascari
Albert Herring
Albert Métraux
sleep together
alterum tantum
blue-eyed grass
Clifford Odets
à la Florentine
all for the best
ill-favouredly
plagal cadence
flagellantism
flagellomania
flugelhornist
flügelhornist
plagiocephaly
plagiotropism
plagiotropous
Plagiostomata
plagiostomous
oligopolistic
flight-feather
flight of fancy
alpha and omega
alphabetiform
alphabetarian
Alpha Centauri
All-hallowmass
All Hallows Day
All-hallowtide
ill-humouredly
Alphonse Mucha
alpha particle
clairaudience
alligator clip
alligator pear
Elvis Costello
Alpine orogeny
Alain-Fournier
flying machine
flying officer
flying pickets
flying colours

all in good time
sleight of hand
sleight-of-hand
plain language
plain speaking
elliptic space
cleistogamous
cloister-garth
plaintiveness
ultimus haeres
clairvoyantly
Aleksei Leonov
blameableness
climacterical
climactically
flame-coloured
plumber's snake
Flammenwerfer
climbing perch
climbing-frame
slamming stile
plumbisolvent
blamelessness
Clement Attlee
aluminiferous
plumbosolvent
glamorisation
clamorousness
glamorization
Flemish school
Flemish stitch
climatography
climatologist
Glenda Jackson
Alan Jay Lerner
plantain-eater
Alan Sainsbury
slingback shoe
glans clitoris
clinical death
clinical trial
clinodiagonal
blanket finish
flannel-flower
glance through
blanket stitch
Flanders poppy
Flinders grass
planter's punch
Clint Eastwood
clandestinely
clandestinity
plenteousness
blankety-blank
Blanche Du Bois
plant hormones
clincher-built
blanchisseuse
plantie-cruive
slanging match
plonking great
blandishments
plentifulness
flint-knapping
Alan Bleasdale
plenum chamber
blindman's buff
planimetrical
planing bottom
sling one's hook
clinopinacoid
clinopinakoid
clinopyroxene
plenary powers
blind stamping
alongshoreman
plenitudinous
planetologist
planetary gear
ylang-ylang oil
Alan Ayckbourn
oleomargarine
allowableness
blood-boltered
Blood Brothers
bloodcurdling
almond-blossom
blood donation
cliometrician
allochthonous
illogicalness
floodlighting
bloodlessness
elbow macaroni
algologically
alcoholometer
alcoholometry
blood pressure
blood relation
blood relative
Bloomsburyite
illocutionary
blepharospasm
glyptal resins
elephantiasis
elephant's-ears
elephant's-foot
elephant shrew
elephant folio
elephant grass
clapperboards
clapper bridge
clapperclawer
slipper limpet
slipper orchid
flapping track
slap on the back
slap in the face
slap and tickle
slipform paver
glyphographer
glyphographic
glyptographic
à la Portugaise
flora and fauna
flirtatiously
Gloria Steinem
Gloria Swanson
floricultural
Albrecht Dürer
Alfred Wallace
Alfred Dreyfus
ultra-distance
clarification
glorification
ultrafiltrate
floral diagram
plural society
pluralisation
pluralization
Florence flask
pluripresence
Clara Peggotty
floristically
ultra-tropical
ultra-virtuous
slurry sprayer
close a bargain
flesh and blood
Alashan Desert
Elysian fields
Alistair Cooke
Close Brethren
flesh-coloured
closed circuit
closed couplet
classes aisées
blister beetle
blister copper
flasher switch
Ulysses S Grant
Blessed Virgin
blast-freezing
flash flooding
glass-grinding
blasphemously
classicalness
plastic bullet
flash in the pan
class interval
elastic tissue
classlessness
clishmaclaver
plesiosaurian
close one's eyes
blastogenesis
plasmodesmata
glossological
glossographer
flesh-pressing
glass-painting
close quarters
class struggle
slot-car racing
slaty cleavage
slate-coloured
platycephalic
clothes-basket
clothe in words
✧kletterschuhe
clothes-screen
platyhelminth
blotting-paper
plotting-paper
ill-temperedly
all-time record
Platonic solid
platiniferous
platinum metal
platinum black
platinum-blond
glutinousness
plethorically
plate-printing
platyrrhinian
platitudinise
platitudinous
platitudinize
flotation tank
clouded agaric
Claude Bernard
Claude Debussy
Claude Chabrol
Claude Dornier
clouded yellow
slaughterable
plough through
Claudio Abbado
illuminations
floutingstock
flourishingly
plausibleness
illusionistic
illustrissimo
illustriously
claustrophobe
Olivia Manning
Old Vic Theatre
clavicembalos
fluvioglacial
Oliver Martext
olivary bodies
Oliver Mellors
Oliver Plunket
Clive Sinclair
Alnwick Castle
blow the lid off
glow discharge
blow one's stack
blow great guns
flower-de-leuce
flower-service
flowering rush
flowers of zinc
flower essence
flow cytometry
flexible drive
Alexei Kosygin
Alexander Blok
Alexander Haig
Alexander Pope
play hard to get
play the wanton
play one's prize
play one's hunch
play for safety
clay-ironstone
play at wasters
Elizabeth Ryan
glaziers' putty
blaze the trail
smear campaign
immarcescible
immaterialise
immaterialism
immaterialist
immateriality
immaterialize
imparipinnate
Emma Woodhouse
impalpability
embarrassedly
embarrassment
impassability
impassibility
ambassadorial
impassionedly
a means to an end
impassiveness
impartialness
impartibility
impacted tooth
impact printer
o' my conscience
smack one's lips
impeccability
impercipience
imperceptible
imperceptibly
impenetration
imperfectible
imperfectness
imperforation
imperial pound
imperialistic
immediateness
imperiousness
umbelliferous
embellishment
impermanently
Immelmann turn
impermissible
impermissibly
impersonalise
impersonality
impersonalize
impersonation
immersion foot
immersion lens
imperseverant
Umberto Nobile
impertinently
imperturbable
imperturbably
impecuniosity
impecuniously
impetuousness
amygdalaceous
emigrationist
imaginariness
imaginatively
image orthicon
image printing
amphigastrium
amphiprostyle
emphysematous
amphitheatral
amphitheatric
omnifariously
immiscibility
amniocenteses
amniocentesis
ambidexterity
ambidexterous
empire-builder
umbilical cord
ambitiousness
impignoration
omnicompetent
amniotic fluid
omnibus clause
ambiguousness
smoke-consumer
smoke detector
smokeless fuel
smokelessness
smokeless zone
smoking jacket
Amelia Earhart
small-and-early
small bindweed
implacability
small capitals
implicational
implicatively
amplification
smelling salts
smelting-works
smelting-house
emulsion paint
small-mindedly
small potatoes
employability
Smiley's People
Emanuel Lasker
Emanuel Ungaro
eminent domain
éminence grise
immovableness
imponderables
smooth-talking
smooth-chinned
smooth-dittied
smoothing iron
smooth-tongued
imposing table
imposing stone
impolitically
impoliticness
embourgeoised
impossibilism
impossibilist
impossibility
import licence
impostumation
importunately
omoplatoscopy
improbability
impracticable
impracticably
impractically
umbraculiform
American eagle
American Samoa
American tiger
American bison
American cloth
embracingness
American robin
American bowls
American organ
impreciseness
emergency exit
emergency room
amorphousness
umbrella plant
umbrella group
umbrella stand
emerald-copper
amarantaceous
Amaranthaceae
embranglement
embryogenesis
embryonically
embryotically
embryological
impropriation
Ambrose Bierce
✧impressionism
✧impressionist
imprest system
embrittlement
improvability
improvidently
improvisatrix

Words marked ✧ can also be spelled with one or more capital letters

improvisation
improvisatory
amusement park
smothered mate
a matter of form
emotionlessly
imitativeness
amitryptyline
immutableness
imputableness
amour courtois
smoulderingly
immunifacient
impurity level
immunotherapy
immunological
impulse buying
impulsiveness
empyreumatise
empyreumatize
Emlyn Williams
unmacadamised
unmacadamized
uneatableness
untamableness
in malam partem
uncalculating
ncarceration
nland revenue
ncardination
ncandescence
nsaleability
ngaged signal
ntangibility
nsanguinated
nfashionable
nfashionably
nsatiability
nvariability
n facie curiae
nsatisfiable
nfamiliarity
satiateness
nna Akhmatova
fallibilism
fallibilist
fallibility
harmonicity
ngainsayable
ndauntedness
ntaintedness
nsaintliness
nsavouriness
nwarrantable
nwarrantably
nwarrantedly
capsidation
caustic tile
capsulation
eak-thievery
earthliness
fants perdus
falteringly
cantational
pasteurised
pasteurized
naturalised
naturalized
naturalness
salvageable
ybody's guess
inobservation
inobtrusively
unobtrusively
unabbreviated
unobstructive
✧knickerbocker
unaccentuated
in a cleft stick
inscriptional
inscriptively
knick-knackery
knuckleballer
inoculability
knuckleduster
knuckle-headed
unicameralism
unicameralist
unscholarlike
knock on effect
onychophagist
unaccountable
unaccountably
unaccompanied
knockout drops
Anacardiaceae
anachronistic
anachronously
knock sideways
knock spots off
knock together
unscrutinised
unscrutinized
unscavengered
Knud Rasmussen
ineducability
inadvertently
unadventurous
unadvisedness
unadulterated
unadopted road
inodorousness
index auctorum
underachiever
indefatigable
indefatigably
annexationist
untenableness
enter a protest
interactional
interactively
interactivity
on her beam-ends
interbreeding
underclassman
indescribable
indescribably
undescribable
unperceivable
unperceivably
unperceivedly
intercolumnar
intercolonial
intercalation
intercalative
intercellular
unwelcomeness
intercommunal
undescendable
undescendible
underclothing
intercropping
intercurrence
undercarriage
intercostally
invendibility
interdigitate
interdentally
unbendingness
inner-directed
unremembering
independently
unregenerated
indeterminacy
unbeseemingly
indeterminism
indeterminist
indeterminate
undeterminate
unceremonious
underemployed
underexposure
unnecessarily
inferentially
underestimate
interestingly
unrelentingly
unrepentingly
interest group
undeservingly
unperfectness
underfinished
angel-food-cake
interferogram
interferingly
unselfishness
undergraduate
unneighboured
unneighbourly
unfeignedness
intergalactic
Inner Hebrides
encephalocele
encephalogram
Encephalartos
encephalotomy
underhandedly
Angelina Jolie
unreliability
enteric-coated
Angelic Doctor
undeliverable
unmedicinable
indelibleness
interior angle
interior grate
undeviatingly
unremittently
unremittingly
unresistingly
ingeniousness
unbelievingly
interjaculate
interjectural
index learning
unreplaceable
On Wenlock Edge
interlacement
interlocutrix
interlocation
interlocution
interlocutory
intellectuals
intelligencer
intelligently
unhealthiness
unhealthfully
unreclaimable
unreclaimably
interlaminate
unfeelingness
unreplenished
interlunation
interlanguage
intermediator
Under Milk Wood
inlet manifold
✧ondes Martenot
intermarriage
intermittence
intermittency
intermetallic
underniceness
once and for all
antenniferous
unsewn binding
internal rhyme
unmeaningness
✧international
interosculant
interosculate
interoperable
unrecoverable
unrecoverably
under one's belt
under one's hand
under one's nose
interoceptive
anaerobically
unrecollected
unrecommended
unrecognising
Enteropneusta
unrecognizing
unrecompensed
unremorseless
underprepared
interpretable
interpretress
under pressure
underpainting
interpellator
interpilaster
interpolation
interpolative
once upon a time
interpunction
interproximal
interparietal
interpersonal
intemperately
interposition
unperpetrated
interpetiolar
unreproaching
unreproachful
integrability
undepreciated
interracially
interradially
unreprievable
unlearnedness
interrogation
interrogatory
interrogative
interrail pass
interrelation
unreprimanded
endearingness
interruptedly
interruptible
unrepresented
unterrestrial
unpersuadable
understanding
interscapular
infeasibility
insensibility
incense-burner
intersidereal
under-shepherd
interspecific
interstellary
interspersion
Anders Celsius
in perspective
unreasoningly
incessantness
intensionally
understrapper
interstratify
insensateness
unsensational
insensitively
insensitivity
intensive care
intensiveness
index-tracking
invertibility
inverted pleat
under the table
ungentlemanly
enter the lists
under the knife
unsettledness
under the eye of
investigation
investigatory
investigative
entertainment
uncertainness
insectologist
unsentimental
unrestingness
intentionally
unmentionable
intertropical
inventorially
on tenterhooks
indentureship
unrestfulness
infectiveness
inventiveness
insectivorous
integumentary
underutilised
underutilized
unreturningly
ungenuineness
in rerum natura
ingenuousness
unserviceable
index verborum
endeavourment
ineffableness
snuff-coloured
inoffensively
ineffectually
ineffectively
inefficacious
snifting-valve
inefficiently
inofficiously
snaffle-bridle
one for the road
enigmatically
anagrammatise
anagrammatism
anagrammatist
anagrammatize
inegalitarian
knight marshal
knights errant
knight service
Knight of Malta
Andhra Pradesh
in the abstract
anthraquinone
on the contrary
on the face of it
in the fast lane
on the increase
unshrinkingly
unchristianly
unthriftyhead
unthriftiness
on shaky ground
unchallenging
anthelminthic
on the long side
unwholesomely
unphilosophic
in the majority
Anthony Dowell
Anthony Island
Anthony Powell
Anthony Quayle
enchondromata
on Shanks's mare
on Shanks's pony
in the nature of
anthropopathy
anthropolatry
anthropogenic
anthropometry
anthropophagi
anthropophagy
anthropophyte
untheological
anthroposophy
anthropomorph
in the pipeline
on the port beam
on the pavement
anthophyllite
in short supply
in the smallest
on the safe side
unchastisable
unchastizable
unwhistleable
in the same boat
in the short run
on the strength
in the wind's eye
in the wrong box

force the issue
concatenation
concavo-convex
coachwhip-bird
good Samaritan
top dead centre
wood sandpiper
Lord Macdonald
lords a-leaping
Lord Parkinson
Lord Callaghan
Lord Sainsbury
Ford Madox Ford
Roedean School
goodman's croft
good-naturedly
Cordoba Mosque
conducted tour
cordocentesis
conductor rail
conductorship
coeducational
road-metalling
Lord Beveridge
soldierliness
wood germander
cold-heartedly
goodness of fit
good afternoon
Lord of Session
Lord of Misrule
woodchip paper
woodchip board
Lord Churchill
Lord Kitchener
good-King-Henry
condylomatous
word blindness
cold-bloodedly
non-democratic
nodding donkey
golden wedding
condensed milk
Gordon Bennett
golden section
condensed type
holding ground
toad in the hole
toad-in-the-hole
golden goodbye
bord and pillar
golden-crested
wood engraving
hold one's peace
golden jubilee
Lord knows what
hold to account
Lord Voldemort
Lords Ordinary
Lord Robertson
woodcock's-head
wood-wool slabs
food poisoning
Woodrow Wilson
word-splitting
ponderability
food processor
word processor
powdered sugar
Border terrier
powdery mildew
powdering-gown
Lord Grenville
soldering iron
powdering-room
wonder-working
wonder-wounded
powder compact
Lord President
ponderousness
wonderfulness
Lord Privy Seal
condescending
condescension
cold as charity
nondescriptly
Lords Temporal
conditionally
condition code
Lord Zuckerman
coadjutorship
Wordsworthian
tolerance dose
Moses and Aaron
Homes and Ideas
homeward-bound
moderate a call
polecat-ferret
dodecaphonism
dodecaphonist
Tokelau Island
tolerationism
tolerationist
tolerableness
rosebay laurel
moderatorship
power-assisted
job evaluation
nomenclatural
women-children
honeycomb-moth
home economics
home economist
power dressing
toreador pants
honeydew melon
for ever and aye
coreferential
popeseye steak
powered glider
robe-de-chambre
forefeelingly
Home Secretary
movement chart
forementioned
nose heaviness
node of Ranvier
rose of Jericho
Dome of the Rock
code of conduct
✧foreign legion
Foreign Office
lozenge-shaped
money-grubbing
Joseph Addison
foreshadowing
Joseph Chaikin
something else
something is up
something like
Joseph Andrews
Joseph Rotblat
Joseph Brodsky
Joseph Surface
Yosemite Falls
Some Like It Hot
foresightless
coreligionist
Bohemian topaz
morello cherry
cobelligerent
codeclination
powerlessness
Nobel laureate
coterminously
homeomorphism
homeomorphous
vowel mutation
bowel movement
governability
hole-and-corner
hole in the wall
hole-in-the-wall
governing body
Modern English
governess cart
lose one's nerve
lose one's shirt
poke one's bib in
lose one's place
modernisation
solemnisation
foreknowledge
foreknowingly
modernization
solemnization
Moreton Bay fig
cover one's back
come to the boil
Polemoniaceae
Tower of London
come to oneself
come to nothing
come up against
vote-splitting
power politics
Roger Staubach
forensicality
power steering
Gödel's theorem
money-spinning
women's studies
Robert Barclay
Robert Catesby
Robert Walpole
potential well
Robert Maxwell
Roberto Baggio
domesticities
domestication
Robert Redford
homeothermous
Robert Herrick
rodent officer
moment of truth
to beat the band
Robert Thomson
Robert Mitchum
Robert Simpson
Robert Winston
Robert Aldrich
homeoteleuton
potentiometer
potentiometry
Robert Southey
covert coating
Robert Bridges
momentariness
Robert Muldoon
momentousness
forejudgement
bone turquoise
bone-turquoise
Roger Williams
confraternity
Wolf-Rayet star
Wolfgang Pauli
Wolf Mankowitz
conflagration
confabulation
confabulatory
confectionary
confectionery
confidingness
confederation
confederative
coffee service
coffee disease
coffee klatsch
coffee morning
coffee-housing
coffee grinder
coffee grounds
coffee essence
configuration
non-figurative
Zoë Fairbairns
Norfolk Island
non-fulfilment
Norfolk jacket
Norfolk turkey
non-functional
confrontation
non-forfeiting
confarreation
confusability
confusibility
confessionary
confessorship
go off the rails
confetti money
confoundingly
rough-and-ready
longcase clock
Douglas Gordon
Long Tall Sally
congratulable
congratulator
tongue-lashing
long-descended
Congreve-match
toggle between
tongue in cheek
tongue-in-cheek
Roy Greenslade
tongue-doubtie
congressional
Congresswoman
tongue-twister
Song of Solomon
long-sightedly
bougainvillea
coagulability
cough medicine
Morgan Freeman
for good and all
conglomeratic
not good enough
zoogeographer
zoogeographic
lodgepole pine
Fogg Art Museum
jogger's nipple
hot gospelling
rough shooting
forgottenness
Loaghtan sheep
forget oneself
forgetfulness
long-suffering
conglutinator
congruousness
Song by Isbrand
to the backbone
do the business
Gothic Revival
to the contrary
go the distance
cochleariform
Sophie Grigson
non-homologous
Ho Chi Minh City
nothing patent
mother-of-pearl
Mother Shipton
Mother and Baby
mother country
Mother Hubbard
sophisticated
sophistically
sophisticator
Roy Hattersley
bonheur-du-jour
moshav shitufi
go the whole way
go the whole hog
nominatively
totipalmation
solitaire ring
holiday season
Josip Broz Tito
zodiacal light
Colin Campbell
Louis Daguerre
noli me tangere
noli-me-tangere
police officer
homiletically
mobile library
votive picture
police station
totidem verbis
non-infectious
mowing machine
rowing machine
voting machine
moving walkway
moving average
dolichocephal
go with the flow
Doris Humphrey
Robin Hood's Bay
Dolichosauria
Dolichosaurus
positive angle
positive organ
solifidianism
domiciliation
position paper
position ratio
solicitorship
Dominique Pire
Kodiak Islands
bouillabaisse
social science
social realism
social service
sociologistic
Social Chapter
social charter
social disease
social climber
sociolinguist
social compact
socialisation
social studies
social dumping
socialization
Louis MacNeice
poliomyelitis
sodium nitrate
goniometrical
coriander seed
motion picture
Ionian Islands
toxicophagous
eosinophilous
Morisonianism
monitor lizard
codicological
toxicological
cogito, ergo sum
horizontal bar
horizontality
Louis-Philippe
no oil painting
Louis-Quatorze
robin's-egg blue
Louis Sullivan
solid solution
topic sentence
toties quoties
goliath beetle
corinthianise
corinthianize
✧sovietologist
Coniston Water
solidungulate
solidungulous
copia verborum
Robin Williams
Moritz Schlick
conjecturable
conjecturally
non-judgmental
conjugate foci
conjugational
conjunctional
conjunctively
Yohji Yamamoto
work-hardening
cocktail party
cocktail mixer
cocktail dress
cocktail stick
book-canvasser

cockle-brained
Book of Malachi
Book of Obadiah
Book of Genesis
cock of the loft
Book of Changes
cock-of-the-rock
cock of the walk
Hook of Holland
Book of Numbers
Book of Ezekiel
cock-thrappled
work shadowing
work the oracle
cock-throppled
Yorkshire grit
fork-lift truck
poikilothermy
Rocky Marciano
look in the face
working memory
booking office
rock and roller
mockingthrush
Books of Esdras
Books of Samuel
cook-housemaid
cockspur grass
cocker spaniel
rocket science
pocket-picking
olk etymology
ocket borough
ocket spanner
ockeye salmon
oolhardiness
vool-gathering
oeliac plexus
Roald Amundsen
olleagueship
ollaboration
ollaborative
oble crayfish
ollectedness
ollecting box
ollectorship
ollicitation
olled into one
oollen-draper
oil mechanics
ollieshangie
oul-searching
öllner's lines
llification
ollification
ollege of Arms
oulting cloth
oulding board
oulting-hutch
o-claims bonus
orldly-minded
orld language
owling crease
olliniferous
lling launch
wling monkey
l-on roll-off
ol one's heels
lling strike
wls of warren
lle prosequi

lollipop woman
fool's paradise
colloquialism
colloquialist
roller bandage
roller bearing
collar of esses
roller-skating
rollerblading
rollercoaster
dollarisation
Hollerith code
dollarization
molluscicidal
toilet service
collaterality
couleur de rose
low level waste
hollow-hearted
follow through
follow-through
Bollywood film
Sorley MacLean
woolly milk cap
commeasurable
comma bacillus
cosmochemical
cosmeceutical
formidability
Tommy Docherty
Tommy Hilfiger
formal verdict
Commelinaceae
formularistic
formalisation
normalisation
formalization
normalization
commemoration
commemoratory
commemorative
Norman MacCaig
common carrier
common caustic
common-law wife
communication
communicatory
communicative
low-mindedness
commandership
common measure
communalistic
command module
communion card
Norman Douglas
Norman Lockyer
Norman Borlaug
communion rail
common lobster
Communism Peak
community card
community care
community home
communitarian
community work
commensurable
commensurably
communautaire
common burdock
cosmopolitics
cosmopolitism

commercial art
commercialese
commercialise
commercialism
commercialist
commerciality
commercialize
form criticism
for mercy's sake
Coomassie Blue®
commiseration
commiserative
commutability
cosmothetical
committeeship
cosmetologist
commit oneself
dormitory town
commutatively
commit suicide
normativeness
Monmouthshire
point-and-shoot
point-and-click
John Masefield
foundation-net
John Dankworth
John Malkovich
mountain range
mountain devil
mountain sheep
mountains-high
mountain chain
mountain biker
mountain avens
John Jacob Abel
downcast-shaft
boundary layer
boundary rider
sound boarding
round brackets
connecting rod
connectionism
Mount Cameroon
John McCormack
Mount Cotopaxi
mountebanking
mountebankery
mountebankism
John de Balliol
counter-attack
counteraction
counteractive
counterbidder
counterchange
countercharge
jointed cactus
counter-caster
counter-fleury
counterfeiter
counterfeitly
sound engineer
John Lee Hooker
coinheritance
counter-jumper
counsel-keeper
founder member
countermotion
Ronnie Corbett
Lonnie Donegan
counselorship

counter-poison
counter-parole
counter-signal
counterstroke
John Bessarion
counterspying
coenaesthesia
coenaesthesis
bounteousness
counter-weight
cornification
young fogeyish
point for point
going for a song
non-negotiable
corn-chandlery
John Churchill
council estate
mounting block
jointing plane
sounding board
counting house
counting frame
rounding error
pointing-stock
moonlight flit
downrightness
John Dillinger
councilorship
council school
bountifulness
Mount Krakatoa
Mount Kinabalu
Kornelia Ender
John Flamsteed
moon blindness
somniloquence
boundlessness
pointlessness
Mount McKinley
cognomination
connumeration
point mutation
somnambulance
somnambulator
born in wedlock
coin-in-the-slot
moaning minnie
morning prayer
John H Northrop
Downing Street
Dornford Yates
go into reverse
sound off about
young offender
point of honour
down to the wire
zoon politikon
Johnsonianism
John Dos Passos
John Constable
conniption fit
count palatine
Mount Pinatubo
soundproofing
John Broadwood
country cousin
sooner or later
Mount Rushmore
Cornish chough
Mount St Helens

Johne's disease
Down's syndrome
Young's modulus
hound-trailing
round the clock
round-the-clock
sound the alarm
round the twist
John Steinbeck
roundtripping
cognate object
cornet-à-piston
connaturalise
connaturalize
Mount Vesuvius
Johnny H Mercer
county council
county borough
Rodney R Porter
county cricket
Sonoran Desert
Colorado River
coronal suture
monodactylous
honorary canon
colon bacillus
no holds barred
no-holds-barred
to good purpose
monometallism
monometallist
Honoré Daumier
holometabolic
monotelephone
homogenetical
jow one's ginger
go someone's way
coroner's court
novocentenary
homosexualism
homosexualist
homosexuality
to some purpose
borough-monger
Dorothea Lange
Dorothea Beale
monophthongal
Dorothy Jordan
monothalamous
✧monotheletism
✧monothelitism
do-nothingness
homochromatic
monochromatic
monochromator
Holothuroidea
✧monophysitism
honoris gratia
honorifically
sodomitically
colonial goose
notoriousness
to conjure with
Corolliflorae
corollifloral
toxoplasmosis
co-counselling
go down the tube
go to any length
Solon of Athens
homoeopathist

not on one's life
monomolecular
homoeothermal
homoiothermal
homoeothermic
homologically
topologically
homologoumena
homoeomorphic
homomorphosis
monocotyledon
Monopoly money
colour masking
colour hearing
colour therapy
monogrammatic
monotrematous
logographical
monographical
nomographical
topographical
colour-process
colourisation
homoeroticism
colourfulness
colourization
porous plaster
monopsonistic
non-observance
motor-traction
son of the manse
hot on the heels
Podostemaceae
monostrophics
pococurantism
pococurantist
coconut butter
mononucleosis
colobus monkey
monosyllabism
monosymmetric
not on your life
complainingly
complaisantly
compact camera
compactedness
corps de ballet
Doppler effect
complexedness
comprehension
comprehensive
complementary
coup de théâtre
morphemically
pompier-ladder
complex number
coup de bonheur
comptes rendus
copple-crowned
compressed air
compressional
compagination
complicatedly
dolphinariums
complications
complimentary
morphinomania
compulsionist
popping crease
popping-crease
company doctor

compendiously
companionable
companionably
companionhood
companionless
companion star
companionship
morphogenesis
morphogenetic
morphophoneme
comprovincial
non-proficient
Compsognathus
morphological
morphographer
non-production
non-productive
copper-captain
comparability
pooper-scooper
Cowper's glands
non-persistent
compartmental
non-parametric
poppering pear
copper trumpet
corporate bond
corporateness
comparatively
co-operatively
corporativism
corporativist
dog-periwinkle
copper pyrites
corpus delicti
Corpus Christi
compassionate
composing room
colposcopical
compass signal
compass timber
compositeness
compositional
compass window
compatibility
computability
compatriotism
hospital trust
non-pathogenic
computer virus
computer crime
computer fraud
computational
competitively
compound ratio
compound umbel
zoopsychology
zoophysiology
Torquato Tasso
torque spanner
conquistadors
journal intime
journal proper
no great shakes
Von Ribbentrop
corroboration
corroboratory
corroborative
court-bouillon
court cupboard
court circular
von Richthofen
porridge-stick
comrade-in-arms
tours d'horizon
corridor-train
Your Reverence
coarse fishing
coarse-grained
Fourier series
courteousness
journey-weight
courtesy light
courtesy title
horrification
corrigibility
Rodrigo Borgia
non-regardance
coercive force
boarding party
mourning piece
mourning cloak
mourning coach
coursing-joint
boarding house
mourning-bride
mourning-stuff
correlational
correlatively
correlativity
court martials
co-trimoxazole
torrentiality
Courtney Walsh
Court of Arches
Court of Appeal
Court of Honour
court of record
corruptionist
horripilation
court reporter
morris dancing
courts martial
corrosibility
touristically
correspondent
corresponding
corresponsive
non-resistance
Tourist Trophy
corrosiveness
Socratic irony
non-returnable
coureur de bois
borrowing days
borrow trouble
sorrowfulness
Constance Spry
Horse and Hound
horse-and-buggy
dog's-tail grass
constableship
constablewick
Constantinian
housebreaking
possibilities
goose-barnacle
consectaneous
horse chestnut
mouse-coloured
consecutively
consideringly
considerately
consideration
considerative
topside-turvey
low side window
non-specialist
constellation
constellatory
consternation
mouse-eared bat
horsefeathers
horseflesh ore
sons of bitches
loosehead prop
Rorschach test
horsehair worm
household gods
household word
conspiratress
non-scientific
conscientious
consciousness
conspicuously
consolidation
consolidative
consul general
tonsillectomy
fossiliferous
noiselessness
fossilisation
podsolisation
fossilization
podsolization
horse mackerel
horse-milliner
consimilarity
consimilitude
horseman's word
consumer goods
horse mushroom
housemistress
toastmistress
consumptively
consumptivity
consentaneity
consentaneous
mops and brooms
Hobson's choice
nonsense verse
housing estate
cousins-german
nonsensically
Sons and Lovers
consenescence
consenescency
housing scheme
poisonousness
consanguinity
zoosporangium
poisson d'avril
Job's comforter
house of prayer
go-as-you-please
house of refuge
bob's your uncle
House of States
Poisson's ratio
consequential
dog's breakfast
conservatoire
constructable
constructible
constrainable
constrainedly
constringency
bowstring-hemp
boustrophedon
monstrousness
horse-sickness
goose-stepping
possessionary
possessionate
horseshoe arch
horseshoe crab
possessorship
topsy-turvydom
conspurcation
constupration
horse-wrangler
housewifeskep
housewifeship
contrabandism
contrabandist
contralateral
contrafagotto
contrabassoon
post-war credit
contra account
foot-land-raker
Portland sheep
North and South
Portland stone
contrate-wheel
software house
contraterrene
contraception
contragestion
contravention
contraceptive
contragestive
toothache tree
contradiction
soft radiation
contradictory
contradictive
contrariously
North Atlantic
South Atlantic
for that matter
contrappostos
North Ayrshire
South Ayrshire
postman's knock
foot passenger
contractually
contractility
contractional
contrapuntist
mouthbreather
Comte Bertrand
contabescence
contact flight
South China Sea
poetic licence
contact lenses
soft sculpture
horticultural
low technology
low-technology
contact poison
North Carolina
South Carolina
poetic justice
Comte de Buffon
Comte de Barras
for the account
Southend-on-Sea
root vegetable
bottle-feeding
goutte à goutte
northerliness
southerliness
Southern Ocean
Southern Cross
Northern Crown
Southern Crown
röntgenoscopy
box the compass
bottle-coaster
for the present
north-easterly
south-easterly
post-tensioned
postmenstrual
north-eastward
south-eastward
don't mention it
soft-sectoring
Pott's fracture
pontificality
fortification
mortification
cost-effective
fortified wine
post-office box
cost-efficient
soothfastness
cottage cheese
North Germanic
doctrinairism
tortoiseshell
Fontainebleau
tortoise plant
Voltaireanism
container port
container ship
port-wine stain
root directory
postliminiary
postliminious
Voltairianism
Fonthill Abbey
foxtail millet
contristation
contributable
Portulacaceae
postal service
Comte Lagrange
nostalgically
portulan chart
postclassical
worthlessness
postulational
mortal-staring
Port Elizabeth
bottomless pit
contemplation
contemplatist
contemplative
contamination
contaminative
root-and-branch
fortune cookie
contentedness
continuedness
Boston terrier
fortune-hunter
cotton thistle
cotton-picking
contentiously
continuity man
sorting office
rotten borough
Hottentot's god
cotton spinner
boot and saddle
routinisation
cotton stainer
fortune-teller
fortunateness
Fontenay Abbey
routinization
pontoon bridge
control column
✧post-modernism
post-modernist
controversial
worth one's salt
controvertist
post-communion
tooth-ornament
Don't You Want Me
Montepulciano
iontophoresis
iontophoretic
post-operative
boutique hotel
Doctor Faustus
poster session
Doctor Zhivago
contortionism
contortionist
contortionate
costardmonger
posture-master
poster colours
Doctor Crippen
foster-brother
Doctor Proudie
poste restante
posterisation
post-traumatic
posterization
montes veneris
fortississimo
loathsomeness
toothsomeness
North Somerset
potty-training
fortitudinous
Pontius Pilate
noctivagation
boatswain-bird
north-westerly
south-westerly
north-westward
south-westward
mouthwatering
post-existence
contextualise
contextualize
Columbia River
volumenometer

documentalist
monumentality
documentarily
documentarise
documentarist
documentarize
documentation
focusing cloth
modus operandi
go out of the way
lotus position
rogues' gallery
locum tenentes
voluntariness
voluntaristic
convocational
Nouvelle Vague
convulsionary
convulsionist
convalescence
convalescency
convolutional
convolvuluses
conventioneer
conventionary
conventionist
convent school
conversazione
conversazioni
Wolverhampton
go over the edge
convertiplane
convexo-convex
Solvay process
Norwegian nest
Norwegian oven
Roy Williamson
not worth a damn
Bosworth Field
orward market
Norway haddock
Norway lobster
olygalaceous
olycarbonate
olydaemonism
ody carpeting
ody mass index
olydactylism
olydactylous
olyadelphous
olytechnical
Holy Sepulchre
olythalamous
olychromatic
olyphloisbic
Corythosaurus
opyrightable
olyhistorian
Horyuji Temple
olyembryonic
ory Underwood
Holy Innocents
opying pencil
olygonaceous
Holyrood Abbey
olypodiaceae
olynomialism
oly Communion
ody corporate
olycotyledon
olypropylene

polyprotodont
polycythaemia
polysyllabism
polysyllogism
polysynthesis
polysynthetic
podzolisation
podzolization
splanchnocele
splanchnology
speaking clock
speaking-voice
aphanipterous
sphagnicolous
sphagnologist
speak one's mind
spray-painting
splatter movie
Special Branch
spectatorship
special school
spectacularly
epicyclic gear
specification
spectinomycin
Space Invaders®
speckled trout
speculum metal
Apocalypse Now
apocalyptical
specular stone
speculatively
space medicine
specimen glass
epicondylitis
spacious times
space platform
spectrography
spectre insect
spectrometric
apochromatism
spectroscopic
spectre shrimp
apocatastasis
spadicifloral
apodictically
spider phaeton
spider spanner
epidotisation
epidotization
appel au peuple
speed dialling
appendiculate
spread betting
splendiferous
ephemeralness
splenetically
ephemeris time
Ephemeroptera
appeteezement
speech reading
speech therapy
speechfulness
sphericalness
apheliotropic
spheristerion
appealingness
appellational
appellatively
speed merchant
spheroidicity

spherocytosis
appertainance
appertainment
speedy cutting
spifflication
epigrammatise
epigrammatist
epigrammatize
epigeneticist
apogeotropism
optical centre
split decision
spoiler signal
April Fools' Day
spring balance
spring chicken
spring-cleaner
sphingomyelin
spring equinox
uprighteously
sprightliness
ophiomorphous
oppignoration
epeirogenesis
epeirogenetic
split one's vote
optic thalamus
splinter party
splinter-proof
splinter group
spike lavender
Spike Milligan
spokespersons
spell backward
applicability
apple dumpling
spelaeologist
spill one's guts
Apollo Theatre
speleological
apple of the eye
apple-pie order
apple polisher
apoliticality
spill the beans
Appleton layer
apple turnover
apomictically
Spandau Ballet
spontaneously
spiny anteater
spine-chilling
epanadiploses
epanadiplosis
sponge fishing
Spencerianism
open-heartedly
sponge pudding
spin the bottle
spin-the-bottle
spinning jenny
spinning-wheel
spending money
spinning-house
sponging-house
spunging-house
spinuliferous
spindle-legged
open-plan house
spindle-shaped
spindle-shanks

spinelessness
open-endedness
opening gambit
opinionatedly
sponsored walk
Spanish dagger
Spanish guitar
epinastically
spine-tingling
spondylolysis
Epsom and Ewell
appoggiaturas
up to the elbows
up to the moment
up-to-the-moment
up to the minute
up-to-the-minute
oppositionist
sprocket wheel
à propos de rien
Upton Sinclair
opportuneness
opportunistic
opportunities
apportionable
apportionment
epiphenomenal
epiphenomenon
apophlegmatic
spermatic cord
spermatogenic
spermatotheca
spermatophore
Spermatophyta
spermatophyte
spermatoblast
spermatozoids
spermatorrhea
opprobriously
upgradability
aphrodisiacal
apprehensible
sporting house
spiral binding
sparkling wine
appropriately
appropriation
appropriative
appropinquate
appropinquity
sportsmanlike
sportsmanship
sportswriting
spiritualiser
spiritualizer
spiritualness
spirit varnish
spiritual peer
spirit-rapping
operating room
operationally
spirits of salt
spirits of wine
spiritus lenis
spiritus asper
spiritousness
operativeness
approximately
approximation
approximative
epistemically

opisthobranch
opisthography
apostle spoons
Apostles' Creed
apostolically
spasmodically
opus operantis
opossum shrimp
epithalamiums
epitrachelion
ophthalmology
apathetically
epithetically
epitheliomata
apothegmatise
apothegmatist
apothegmatize
spitting image
spathiphyllum
spittle insect
epitomisation
epitomization
spit and polish
spruce budworm
e pluribus unum
splutteringly
epoxide resins
sphygmography
aqua caelestis
squandermania
squanderingly
square-dancing
square-bashing
square measure
square shooter
square-pierced
square bracket
squash rackets
aqua mirabilis
Equatoguinean
a quarter after
squeak through
squeamishness
equestrianism
aqueous humour
squeezability
squeeze bottle
squeezy bottle
squirarchical
squinancy wort
equitableness
Aquinas Thomas
equisetaceous
squire of dames
equidifferent
equilibration
equidistantly
equivocalness
equiponderant
equiponderate
equipotential
Aquifoliaceae
equinoctially
squirrel shrew
equity finance
tread a measure
pre-adamitical
breakableness
preadaptation
Great Bear Lake
Arval Brethren

preambulatory
trial by record
cream-coloured
Briançon manna
pro-and-conning
urban district
breakdown gang
broad daylight
Greater Bairam
ornamentalism
ornamentalist
armamentarium
ornamentation
breakfast-room
triangularity
triangulately
triangulation
breathe easily
breathe freely
breach of trust
Brian Hanrahan
breathing hole
breathing-time
Brian Horrocks
treacherously
breaking point
groaning board
irrationalise
irrationalism
irrationalist
irrationality
irrationalize
dreadlessness
dreamlessness
Friar Laurence
Brian Mulroney
broadmindedly
preadmonition
trial marriage
preadolescent
break one's duck
organogenesis
break one's mind
break one's word
treason felony
organotherapy
triatomically
ergatomorphic
trial of the pyx
cream of tartar
friar's lantern
broad-spectrum
Great Salt Lake
Arkansas River
break the balls
breastfeeding
breast the tape
treasure-chest
treasure-house
treasure-trove
treasurership
Treasury bench
Great White Way
Treaty of Ghent
Treaty of Dover
treaty Indians
Great Yarmouth
break your duck
Great Zimbabwe
dribs and drabs
Arabian Desert

cribbage-board
Arabian Nights
probable cause
probable error
probabilistic
probabilities
problematical
triboelectric
grabbing crane
Orobanchaceae
probe scissors
tributariness
cry blue murder
pro-chancellor
track and field
track-and-field
Tractarianism
traceableness
tractableness
Trucial States
Eric Partridge
procrastinate
crocodile bird
crocodile clip
cracker-barrel
bracket fungus
procreational
Erich Honecker
practical arts
practical joke
practicalness
tractive force
Eric Linklater
fractionalise
fractionalism
fractionalist
fractionalize
fractionation
Eric Wieschaus
✧brachiosaurus
fractiousness
trickle-charge
gracelessness
pricelessness
tracklessness
oraculousness
prick-me-dainty
preconception
arachnoiditis
arachnologist
precentorship
arachnophobia
arachnophobic
preconisation
proconsulship
preconization
Bruce Oldfield
Eric Morecambe
trichological
precious stone
fractostratus
trichopterist
trichopterous
fractocumulus
precopulatory
preceptorship
precipitantly
precipitately
precipitation
precipitative
precipitously

tricarpellary
tracer element
trichromatism
tricorporated
tricarboxylic
procuratorial
procès-verbaux
processioning
processionary
process-server
prices current
prick-the-louse
precautionary
brachydactyly
brachycephaly
brachypterous
predicability
producibility
production car
predicamental
grade crossing
producer goods
predicate upon
predicatively
trade discount
bridge passage
grid reference
bridge of boats
fridge-freezer
bridge-builder
predefinition
credulousness
predominantly
predomination
pro'd and conned
credence table
credence shelf
trading estate
prudentialism
prudentialist
prudentiality
urediniospore
grading system
trade-off study
H Rider Haggard
Frederick Jane
Frederick West
Frederikshavn
tradesmanlike
predestinator
credit balance
creditability
credit account
credit scoring
Arc de Triomphe
gradationally
traditionally
traditionless
credit squeeze
predeterminer
predatoriness
trade unionism
trade unionist
trade-weighted
Bridgwater Bay
free-marketeer
Greek alphabet
armed bullhead
irreverential
free-selection
breeze through

irredeemables
Graeme Pollock
Graeme Souness
Froebel system
green-fingered
pre-engagement
triethylamine
breech-loading
Breeches Bible
greenhouse gas
arteriography
greetings card
creeping Jenny
creeping Jesus
freezing point
irreligionist
irreligiously
artesian basin
true-disposing
irreciprocity
arteriovenous
irreplaceable
irreplaceably
irreclaimable
irreclaimably
Greenland seal
irrepleviable
green manuring
araeometrical
dree one's weird
order of battle
irrecoverable
irrecoverably
true-love grass
irrecognition
free companion
order of the day
arsenopyrites
pre-emptive bid
irresponsible
irresponsibly
irretrievable
irretrievably
Dr Henry Jekyll
irrefrangible
irrefrangibly
Green Room Club
irrepressible
irrepressibly
green seaweeds
green sickness
grief-stricken
armed services
ardentia verba
argentiferous
Ernesto Geisel
oriental topaz
ardent spirits
orientational
Greek valerian
Greenwich Time
green with envy
prefabricated
prefabricator
profectitious
prefigurement
prefiguration
prefigurative
traffic circle
traffic island
traffic lights

traffic police
traffic warden
Trofim Lysenko
Graf von Moltke
preferability
cry for the moon
prefer charges
craftsmanship
draftsmanship
professoriate
professorship
profitability
profit-sharing
prefatorially
drag-parachute
pragmatically
program trader
tragic heroine
trigger finger
progressional
progressively
progressivism
progressivist
fragmentarily
fragmentation
draggle-tailed
drug smuggling
trigonometric
drag one's heels
progenitorial
erogenous zone
prognosticate
troglodytical
frighteningly
frightfulness
prohibitively
ortho-compound
archidiaconal
orthodiagonal
orchidologist
orchidomaniac
archaeologist
archaeometric
archaeopteryx
orthognathism
orthographist
orthognathous
Archegoniatae
orthogonality
orthogenesist
archbishopric
Graham Chapman
archimandrite
urchin-snouted
orthopaedical
archipelagoes
orthopinakoid
Arthur Balfour
Arthur Rackham
Arthur Ransome
Arthur C Clarke
Arthur Rimbaud
orchesography
Crohn's disease
orthostichous
orthosilicate
prehistorical
orchestralist
orchestration
architectonic
architectural

grain amaranth
drainage basin
orbital engine
irritableness
ordinal number
Ordinary level
Ordinary grade
Erwin Chargaff
fruit cocktail
brainchildren
groin-centring
✧croix de guerre
pre-industrial
vraisemblance
cruise missile
cruise control
cruiserweight
drying-up cloth
ornithichnite
ornithologist
Ornitholestes
ornithomantic
ornithophobia
ornithischian
artifical life
training pants
draining board
prairie grouse
Dr Livingstone
artificialise
artificiality
artificialize
prairie oyster
prairie turnip
articles of war
brainlessness
fruitlessness
braille-writer
Orville Wright
trail one's coat
Erwin Panofsky
Erwin Piscator
fruit pastille
arrière-pensée
arbitrariness
brainsickness
orgiastically
brainstorming
✧trainspotting
orbis terrarum
projectionist
prejudicially
prejudication
prejudicative
Trajan's Column
broken-hearted
Prokop the Bald
frilled lizard
prolification
proliferation
proliferative
proliferously
prolegomenary
prolegomenous
drilling lathe
trolling-spoon
brilliantness
trellis window
preliminaries
preliminarily
trilingualism

Ural Mountains
proleptically
drill-sergeant
trilateralism
trilateralist
triliteralism
trilateration
uralitisation
uralitization
oral hygienist
grammatically
dramma giocoso
drum majorette
grammar school
crème de cassis
premedication
crème de menthe
premeditation
premeditative
trumpet agaric
trumpeter swan
trumpet flower
trumpet marine
trumpet-shaped
primigravidae
primigravidas
primogenitrix
primogenitary
primogeniture
primogenitive
from the word go
Trombiculidae
bromeliaceous
premillennial
primal therapy
Grumbletonian
tremulousness
prime minister
prime meridian
frumentaceous
frumentarious
promenade deck
premandibular
criminologist
criminal court
priming-powder
trim one's sails
premonishment
premonitorily
criminousness
graminivorous
tram conductor
Drummond light
primordialism
primordiality
primary planet
primary school
primary stress
promise-breach
promiscuously
promotability
dramatic irony
prompt neutron
primatologist
dramaturgical
prematureness
aromatisation
dramatisation
primitiveness
aromatization
dramatization

Words marked ✧ can also be spelled with one or more capital letters

prime vertical
drunk as a piper
Frank Auerbach
transatlantic
drinkableness
transactinide
transactional
trunk breeches
brent barnacle
transcribable
transcription
transcriptase
transcriptive
crinicultural
transcendence
transcendency
trunk dialling
granddad shirt
granddaughter
Prince Maurice
grande passion
Arundel Castle
fringe benefit
grande vedette
Prince of Wales
Prince of Peace
fringe theatre
Frankeniaceae
Wrangel Island
orange blossom
grande cocotte
rince consort
ranberry bush
ranberry tree
rinter's devil
rincess royal
Princess Grace
rincess dress
ransexualism
ransexuality
ringe-dweller
ransfer paper
ransferrable
ransformable
ransferrible
ransfusively
randfatherly
ranographist
ransgression
ransgressive
ansgendered
rong-headedly
ench warfare
ronchial tube
ranch officer
ronchography
rench kissing
ronchiolitis
ench morocco
rench cricket
anchisement
ronchoscopic
ench mustard
rincipal axis
undinaceous
incipalness
incipalship
ansit circle
inting paper
ancis Galton
inting house

printing error
printing press
Francis Horner
Frankie Howerd
transitionary
Francis Joseph
fringilliform
transit lounge
transientness
grandiloquent
grandiloquous
bring into line
transisthmian
bring into play
transistorise
transistorize
translucidity
translucently
translocation
granuliferous
granulomatous
Brinell number
translate into
translational
translatorial
transliterate
transmigrator
transmissible
transmittance
transmittable
grandmotherly
transmittible
transmutation
transmutative
grin and bear it
ordnance datum
pronunciation
pruning shears
Grand National
transnational
cranioscopist
frontogenesis
drink-offering
craniological
Franjo Tudjman
transom window
transplanting
transportance
transportable
transport café
transportedly
transparently
transpersonal
transport ship
transpiration
transpiratory
transposition
transpositive
brinksmanship
Franz Schubert
transshipment
Grand Seignior
grand seigneur
transshipping
frank-tenement
bring to naught
Trinity Sunday
granitisation
granitization
pronounceable
pronouncement

tranquilliser
tranquillizer
transversally
Frank Wedekind
Frank Williams
wrong way round
granny glasses
Orkney Islands
granny dumping
Eriocaulaceae
preoccupation
Arnold Bennett
preordainment
preordination
Arnold Toynbee
erroneousness
cryobiologist
arboriculture
creosote plant
ergonomically
armour of proof
armour-plating
oreographical
crook the elbow
cryptanalysis
cryptanalytic
trophallactic
propraetorial
propraetorian
tropical month
tropical sprue
drophead coupé
propaedeutics
graphemically
prophetically
Tropaeolaceae
triple glazing
Triple Entente
prophet of doom
triple-crowned
cryptesthesia
grape hyacinth
graphic artist
proprioceptor
graphic design
wrapping paper
dripping roast
proprietorial
propeller-head
propyl alcohol
grappling-hook
grappling-iron
preponderance
preponderancy
propanoic acid
propenoic acid
propionic acid
triploblastic
trophoblastic
cryptological
graphological
cryptozoology
preprogrammed
cryptographer
cryptographic
trophotropism
preproduction
prepared piano
proportioning
proportionate
preparatorily

preparatively
proparoxytone
prepossessing
prepossession
prepositional
propositional
prepositively
trapeze artist
trapezohedral
trapezohedron
triquetrously
frequentation
frequentative
prerogatively
Pre-Raphaelism
Pre-Raphaelite
fresh as a daisy
grasp at a straw
prostate gland
prostatectomy
crystal-gazing
prismatically
prostaglandin
crystallinity
Crystal Palace
grasp at straws
crystal violet
crossbreeding
trisoctahedra
trisaccharide
cross-cultural
cross compiler
cross-crosslet
prosectorship
criss-cross-row
Ernst Cassirer
prosecutrices
prosecutrixes
prosecutorial
cross-dressing
presidentship
cross-division
cross-examiner
crossed cheque
gross earnings
dressed to kill
prospect-glass
prospectively
brass farthing
press fastener
brassfounding
cross-gartered
prosthodontia
trust hospital
cross-hatching
prosaicalness
dressing-table
trysting-place
trysting-stile
Praslin Island
prescientific
Brass in Pocket
dress-improver
iris diaphragm
brush kangaroo
trisyllabical
trestle bridge
Ernst Lubitsch
trustlessness
wristlet watch
cross-magnetic

presuming that
cross-matching
presumptively
prison officer
prison visitor
presentiality
prison-breaker
prisoner's base
prisoners' base
prisoner of war
Arms and the Man
Arms and the Boy
press of canvas
crossover vote
ariston metron
aristocratism
cross-platform
prosopography
prosopagnosia
erysipelatous
prosopopoeial
cross-purposes
brush quandong
cross-quarters
cross-question
crash recorder
gross register
preserving-pan
prescriptible
frustratingly
grass staggers
grass sickness
crush syndrome
cross-springer
cross-training
cross the floor
press the flesh
crassulaceous
pressure cabin
pressure ridge
très au sérieux
pressure point
pressure group
cross-vaulting
trustworthily
presbyacousis
presbytership
Grotian theory
protoactinium
protuberantly
protuberation
tritubercular
Protococcales
protectionism
protectionist
critical angle
critical point
graticulation
critical state
Protochordata
protochordate
protectorless
protectorship
eroticisation
eroticization
brother-german
brotherliness
tritheistical
brothers-in-law
gratification
truth function

writ of inquiry
proto-historic
crotchetiness
proteinaceous
brattice-cloth
Fritz Kreisler
protolanguage
truthlessness
brutalisation
brutalization
arithmophobia
arithmetician
pretendership
pretentiously
protanomalous
writing-master
writing-school
protonotarial
protonotariat
frit porcelain
proteoclastic
trothplighted
preternatural
preterperfect
proterogynous
pretermission
pretermitting
proterandrous
erythrophobia
urethroscopic
preteriteness
protospataire
Protestantise
Protestantism
Protestantize
British Legion
British Museum
grotesqueness
traumatically
Ursula Andress
traumatonasty
trout-coloured
ground-officer
ground-angling
group dynamics
ground moraine
ground control
grouse-disease
argumentation
argumentative
draught animal
draught-engine
draughtswoman
draught-screen
troublesomely
troublousness
group marriage
triumphal arch
group practice
argus pheasant
provocatively
Providence Bay
providing that
Trevi Fountain
travel-tainted
traveller's joy
Greville Wynne
travelling rug
travel writing
travel-stained
frivolousness

pull a long face
guilelessness
guiltlessness
juglandaceous
sublanceolate
fuel injection
nucleon number
nucleoprotein
butler's pantry
nulli secundus
dualistically
sur les pointes
quality circle
quality factor
outlet village
bulletin board
quality of life
qualitatively
pull a wry mouth
Ku Klux Klanner
submachine-gun
summa cum laude
mummification
submandibular
cummingtonite
turmeric paper
summer-seeming
Summer Holiday
summer pudding
summer cypress
summit meeting
quant analysis
turn a blind eye
funny business
Burnt by the Sun
turnkey system
quincentenary
quingentenary
turn of the year
turn the corner
quenched spark
turn the tables
quantivalence
turnpike stair
quintillionth
Quentin Massys
running buffet
running battle
turning circle
turn on the heat
running lights
burning-mirror
running stitch
burn one's boats
turn to account
burnt-offering
turnip cabbage
turnip lantern
funny peculiar
vulnerability
Burnett salmon
quincuncially
Quintus Ennius
quinquagenary
Quinquagesima
Turnbull's blue
quintuplicate
quantum meruit
quantum number
Juan Luis Vivés
quantum theory
quinquevalent
quinquivalent
autocatalysis
autocatalytic
automatically
autoschediasm
autoschediaze
subordinately
subordination
subordinative
put one's face on
put one's feet up
autocephalous
cut one's losses
sue one's livery
put one's mind to
European bison
European Union
autoresponder
cut one's throat
Rudolf Steiner
Rudolf Nureyev
tumorgenicity
Guy of Gisborne
autochthonism
autochthonous
out of harm's way
tumorigenesis
auto-digestion
autobiography
bubonic plague
furor loquendi
out on one's feet
out of one's head
out of one's mind
out of one's road
out of one's tree
Europocentric
autonomically
Eurocommunism
Eurocommunist
furor poeticus
out of question
autograph book
autoeroticism
out of training
put on the screw
out of the woods
rub of the green
rub on the green
put out of sight
put out of court
run out of steam
put out to grass
put out to nurse
sulphadiazine
humpback whale
supplantation
suspectedness
suspicionless
pumped storage
subprefecture
supplementary
purple emperor
purple-in-grain
purple boletus
gumple-foisted
yuppification
cum privilegio
bumptiousness
suspender-belt
sul ponticello
jumping spider
sulphonic acid
sulphonylurea
subpopulation
supporting act
eusporangiate
suspercollate
bumper sticker
support tights
support worker
purposelessly
sub-postmaster
sub-postoffice
suppositional
purposiveness
puppet theatre
sulphur-bottom
sulphuretting
sulphureously
sulphuric acid
sulphur sponge
sumptuousness
turquoise-blue
supra-axillary
outrecuidance
suprachiasmic
hurricane deck
hurricane lamp
nutraceutical
quarterdecker
quarter dollar
quarter-gunner
quarter-hourly
quartermaster
quarrelsomely
surrogateship
✧guardian angel
quartier latin
query language
querulousness
supramolecule
Supreme Soviet
current assets
run rings round
supranational
quartodeciman
guard of honour
subreptitious
surreptitious
hubristically
bulrush millet
suprasensible
supratemporal
lucrativeness
surround sound
Audrey Hepburn
quartziferous
quartz crystal
outstandingly
✧russia leather
Dunstable road
Russian Museum
substantially
substantively
substantivise
substantivity
substantivize
quasi-contract
Russocentrism
Russocentrist
pulse dialling
outside chance
Dunster Castle
subspeciality
puss-gentleman
Russification
questionnaire
question of law
questioningly
substitutable
pulselessness
nuisance value
nursing-father
outspokenness
guest of honour
subsequential
subscriber set
nursery cannon
substructural
pusser's dagger
subserviently
nursery stakes
nursery school
nursery slopes
purse-snatcher
subsistential
outsettlement
pulsating star
Sussex spaniel
gum tragacanth
Burt Lancaster
Australianism
multi-authored
multicellular
multicultural
multicoloured
putty-coloured
rusty-coloured
multicamerate
buttock planes
multicapitate
custodianship
multidigitate
quoted company
quatrefeuille
Just Seventeen
Surtsey Island
put the lid on it
rust-resistant
put the skids on
put the black on
put the moves on
put the brake on
cut the mustard
justification
justificatory
justificative
multifilament
Gustaf Fröding
multigravidae
multigravidas
hunt the letter
just think of it
quatch-buttock
subtriplicate
Austrian blind
subtriangular
curtain-raiser
curtain speech
multilobulate
multiloculate
multilinguist
multiloquence
subtilisation
subtilization
Guatemala City
multum in parvo
customariness
run-time system
customisation
customization
sustentacular
sustentaculum
multinucleate
Huntingdonian
Austin hermits
hunting-ground
mutton-thumper
button-through
Burton Richter
Dustin Hoffman
button your lip
dusting powder
hunting spider
multinational
mutton-dummies
suctional stop
auction bridge
auctioneer off
subtropically
Austroasiatic
Just So Stories
multipresence
multiple fruit
multiple store
multiplicable
multiplicator
multipolarity
multipartyism
juxtaposition
multiply words
subterraneous
subternatural
multiracially
custard coffin
cultured pearl
butter-biscuit
butterfingers
quaternionist
butterfly bush
butterfly clip
butterfly fish
cultural shock
butterfly kiss
butterfly weed
culture medium
multiramified
butter-and-eggs
custard powder
multiskilling
quota sampling
multitudinary
multitudinous
cut to the chase
put to the blush
put to the torch
put to the worse
cut to the quick
put to the sword
quotation mark
multivibrator
Gustave Eiffel
dust explosion
suburbicarian
Cucurbitaceae
future perfect
future studies
tubuliflorous
luxuriousness
mutual mistake
mutualisation
mutualization
Cuquenán Falls
put up one's hair
futurological
put upon points
cumulostratus
aurum potabile
gum up the works
Augustus Pugin
lupus vulgaris
curvilineally
subventionary
subversionary
Culver's physic
pulverisation
pulverization
suovetaurilia
survivability
survival curve
gunwales under
sun worshipper
sunworshipper
jury of matrons
ruby silver ore
burying beetle
burying ground
muzzle-loading
quizzing-glass
eviction order
Aviculariidae
evocativeness
evidentiality
a vuestra salud
Avogadro's rule
availableness
Evelyn Glennie
evolutionally
avant-couriers
evangelically
evangeliarion
evangeliarium
evangelistary
avant-gardiste
even-Christian
eventlessness
evaporability
everlastingly
overhastiness
overvaluation
overabundance
overabounding
overhead costs
overdependent
overweeningly
overbearingly
oversensitive
every few hours
over the wicket
overnight case
overelaborate
overflowingly
overemphasise

overemphasize
overambitious
over-emotional
over-anxiously
overinsurance
overindulgent
over-confident
over-breathing
overcredulity
overcredulous
overdramatise
overdramatize
overstatement
averruncation
overqualified
oversubscribe
overmultitude
every which way
overexcitable
over-exquisite
Yves St Laurent
avis au lecteur
Svatopluk Cech
ovoviviparity
ovoviviparous
sweated labour
swear the peace
two-ball putter
swaddling-band
swiddling-line
Swedenborgian
sweet chestnut
sweetheart ivy
sweet nothings
owner-occupied
owner-occupier
week on Friday
sweet-savoured
sweep the board
sweet-tempered
sweet woodruff
swelled-headed
swollen-headed
twelve-note row
twelve-tone row
twilight sleep
dwelling-place
dwelling-house
swallowtailed
swimming-baths
swanee whistle
swinge-buckler
swinging-block
swine's succory
two pence piece
twopenceworth
twopenny piece
two pennyworth
two-pennyworth
dwarf antelope
swordsmanship
swashbuckling
twistor theory
twist the knife
switch selling
away from it all
expandability
expanded metal
exsanguineous
expansibility
axial skeleton
expansion bolt
expansion card
expansion slot
expansiveness
ex natura rerum
exobiological
execrableness
exact sciences
expendability
extendability
extendibility
experimentist
expeditionary
expeditiously
exterior angle
extermination
exterminatory
exterminative
external store
exteroception
exteroceptive
extemporarily
exterritorial
excess baggage
extensibility
extensionally
extension lead
extension tube
excess postage
excess luggage
excessiveness
expensiveness
extensiveness
exceptionable
exceptionably
exceptionally
expectoration
expectorative
extenuatingly
exaggeratedly
exchange blows
exchange words
exchequer bill
excitableness
extinguishant
exhibitionism
exhibitionist
exploding star
exclamational
explanatorily
explorational
explosion shot
exclusion zone
explosive bolt
exclusiveness
explosiveness
exclusive zone
exemplifiable
exempli gratia
exemplariness
examinability
examinational
exanthematous
axiomatically
Oxford English
expose oneself
exponentially
excommunicant
excommunicate
axiologically
ex consequenti
exportability
excortication
expostulation
expostulatory
expostulative
exposure meter
extra-axillary
extracellular
extragalactic
exercise price
extrajudicial
extralimitary
extrametrical
extrinsically
extraordinary
ex proprio motu
expropriation
extrapolation
extrapolatory
extrapolative
extraposition
extra-physical
express agency
excrescential
✧expressionism
✧expressionist
express letter
express packet
express parcel
extratropical
extravagantly
extravagation
extravasation
extravascular
exasperatedly
existentially
exothermicity
Exeter College
excusableness
excuse-me dance
excuse oneself
expurgatorial
excursion fare
exquisiteness
excursiveness
pyjama cricket
gynaecocratic
gynaecologist
gynaecomastia
gynandromorph
pyramidically
dynamic memory
synallagmatic
tyrannosaurus
synaposematic
dynamogenesis
zygapophyseal
zygapophysial
synarthrodial
lycanthropist
symbolic logic
symbolography
symbolistical
symbolisation
symbolization
symbiotically
synchondroses
synchondrosis
synchronicity
synchronology
synchronistic
synchronously
eye-catchingly
syndical union
syndicalistic
dyed-in-the-wool
hyperactivity
hypercritical
hypercalcemia
synecdochical
hypereutectic
hyperesthesia
hyperesthetic
hyperglycemia
hyperhidrosis
hyperlipaemia
Lyceum Theatre
hypermetrical
hypermetropia
hypermetropic
cyberneticist
pyretotherapy
synecological
hymenopterous
Hymenomycetes
Pyrenomycetes
synecphonesis
hyperphrygian
hyperparasite
hyperphysical
Myles Standish
cyberslacking
cyberstalking
hypersthenite
hypersarcosis
cybersquatter
hypertrophied
hypertrophous
hypervelocity
dysfunctional
syphilologist
pyrheliometer
syphilophobia
syphilisation
syphilization
Lytham St Anne's
Pythonomorpha
hyphenisation
hyphenization
cylindraceous
cylindrically
cylinder block
cylinder press
pyrimethamine
syringomyelia
Myristicaceae
Cyril Tourneur
by all accounts
syllabic metre
syllabic verse
syllabication
cyclodialysis
syllogistical
syllogisation
syllogization
Cyclanthaceae
hyalinisation
hyalinization
sylleptically
cycloparaffin
cyclospermous
myrmecologist
dysmenorrheal
dysmenorrhoea
dysmenorrheic
symmetrically
hypno-analysis
ayuntamientos
cyanoacrylate
pycnoconidium
pycnidiospore
gymnospermous
gymnastically
hypnotisation
hypnotization
Kyung-Wha Chung
Sydney Pollack
Sydney Brenner
hypocalcaemia
cytopathology
zygomatic arch
zygomatic bone
gyromagnetism
zygodactylism
zygodactylous
mycobacterium
by word of mouth
myxoedematous
pyrotechnical
zymotechnical
hypomenorrhea
Tyrone Guthrie
hypothecation
Syrophoenicia
cytochemistry
sycophantical
hypochondriac
hypochondrium
hypophosphite
pyrophosphate
gynodioecious
cytodiagnosis
zygotic number
synodic period
hypoglycaemia
hypoglycaemic
cytologically
Lycopodiaceae
mycotoxicosis
gynomonoecism
typographical
xylographical
hyposulphuric
pyrosulphuric
hypocycloidal
nymphaeaceous
lymphadenitis
lymphatically
sympiesometer
symptomatical
symphonic poem
by appointment
lymphotrophic
dyspeptically
sympathetical
sympathectomy
sympatholytic
symphyseotomy
symphysiotomy
hydro-airplane
hydrocracking
hydrochloride
hydrocephalic
hydrocephalus
hydrodynamics
hybridisation
hybridization
hydroelectric
Tyrrhenian Sea
hydrogenation
hydrokinetics
hydromedusoid
hydromagnetic
hydrometrical
hygrometrical
Hydrangeaceae
hydropathical
hydrarthrosis
hydrostatical
hydrosulphide
hydrosulphite
hydrosomatous
hygroscopical
hydraulically
hydraulic belt
hydraulic jack
hydraulicking
hydroxylamine
hydrazoic acid
hypsophyllary
Tyssetrengane
syntactically
cysticercosis
✧dyotheletical
synthetically
synthetic drug
✧dyothelitical
Myrtle Simpson
mystification
Nyctaginaceae
systemisation
systematician
systematology
systemization
Cyathophyllum
oyster-catcher
oyster-fishery
mystery-monger
hysteranthous
sylvicultural
Sylvie Guillem
Czech Republic
Azteca Stadium
ozone-depleter
ozone-friendly
Czeslaw Milosz

Bahasa Malaysia
Mahayana Sutras
naval architect
salamander-like
banana republic
calabash nutmeg
macadamisation
macadamization
palatalisation
palatalization
Kalahari Desert
banana-fingered
banana solution
paratactically
radar altimeter
radar astronomy
palaeanthropic
Palaeanthropus
palaebiologist
Sarah Bernhardt
balance of power
balance of trade
Kazan Cathedral
Man and Superman
manageableness
Japanese garden
Japanese War God
Japanese vellum
Japanese medlar
vasa deferentia
Japanese beetle
Hamamelidaceae
Pan-Americanism
caramelisation
caramelization
jalapeño pepper
cadaverousness
paraleipomenon
paraphrastical
catachrestical
cataphorically
calamine powder
calamine lotion
paralinguistic
law-abidingness
Gamaliel Pickle
paradigmatical
Canadian dollar
Canadian French
Hawaiian guitar
parasitologist
calamitousness
catadioptrical
salami strategy
karaoke machine
hapax legomenon
parallel-veined
parallel slalom
parallel planes
parallel motion
parallel cousin
parallelepiped
parallelopiped
parallel rulers
savanna-sparrow
pararosaniline
palaeoecologic
palaeopedology
Palaeosiberian
palagonite-tuff
macaroni cheese
palaeobiologic
Patagonian hare
palato-alveolar
palaeoclimatic
paramount chief
palaeobotanist
palaeographist
malacostracous
Malacopterygii
malappropriate
data processing
paragrammatist
data protection
parapsychology
tarantula juice
galactopoietic
galactophorous
savant syndrome
Mahamuni Pagoda
Gaea hypothesis
Gaia hypothesis
lambda particle
garboard strake
Barbican Centre
Barbados cherry
marble-constant
marble-breasted
cabbage-lettuce
cabbage-root fly
cabbage-tree hat
babbling thrush
Cambridgeshire
carbon monoxide
rambunctiously
Man Booker Prize
namby-pambiness
Barbara Dickson
Marburg disease
Bamburgh Castle
Barbara Jackson
Barberton daisy
carburetted gas
Sabbath-breaker
sabbatical year
rabbeting-plane
rabbit-squirrel
Sabbatarianism
barbituric acid
carboxylic acid
Barbizon School
saccharisation
saccharization
sacchariferous
saccharic ester
Marchantiaceae
Watch Committee
narcocatharsis
fancy dress ball
barcode scanner
sauce espagnole
pancreatectomy
Marc Girardelli
marching orders
sanctification
Pancake Tuesday
watch like a hawk
masculine rhyme
Malcolm Rifkind
vascular tissue
vascular plants
vascular bundle
Malcolm Sargent
calculated risk
Catchment board
catchment basin
watchman's clock
parchment paper
Fanconi anaemia
malcontentedly
carcinogenesis
carcinological
carcinomatosis
catch one's death
watch one's mouth
Pancho Gonzales
Marco Polo sheep
cascarilla bark
calcareous tufa
cascara sagrada
Marcgraviaceae
narcosynthesis
Marcus Antonius
Marcus Aurelius
watch the birdie
narcoterrorism
calcium blocker
calcium carbide
Marco Van Basten
lasciviousness
patchwork quilt
cardiac failure
cardiac massage
band-pass filter
handicraftsman
landed interest
handkerchieves
sandwich course
sandwich boards
Sandwich Island
random variable
Random Sketches
paedomorphosis
maidenhair-tree
pardonableness
ward in Chancery
cardinal-deacon
Cardinal Newman
cardinal beetle
cardinal-bishop
cardinal virtue
cardinal flower
cardinal-priest
cardinal number
gardening leave
maiden fortress
pardon my French
cardiovascular
wardrobe master
cardiothoracic
cardiomyopathy
wandering nerve
mandarin collar
mandarin orange
have had a gutful
Dame Janet Baker
Lake Tanganyika
lateralisation
lateralization
lateral incisor
James A Michener
have had one's day
Rabelaisianism
sales assistant
water-breathing
water barometer
James Clark Ross
Pavel Cherenkov
James Callaghan
watercolourist
gated community
parenchymatous
Rajendra Prasad
valet de chambre
dames de la halle
lavender cotton
Dame Edith Evans
sales executive
have been around
pâté de foie gras
lares et penates
take personally
casement window
pavement artist
Cape of Good Hope
rate of exchange
have a great mind
Dame Ngaio Marsh
take the biscuit
take the edge off
Gareth of Orkney
have the goods on
have the jitters
take the liberty
take the michael
take a hammering
catechumenical
catechumenship
water horehound
make the running
catechetically
take the trouble
male chauvinism
male chauvinist
Lake Windermere
make rings round
watering-trough
Cape Finisterre
care killed a cat
valerianic acid
valerianaceous
Babes in Toyland
Lake Okeechobee
have clean hands
Dame Ellen Terry
laser-light show
naked-light mine
canellini beans
satem languages
Waterloo Sunset
patellar reflex
lamellirostral
satellite state
James Mackenzie
tabernacle-work
have an edge over
make a night of it
take one's choice
take one's chance
save one's breath
take one's breath
have one's own way
maternity leave
paternity leave
have one too many
Yale University
Camelopardalis
have come to stay
take for granted
take to the boats
pageboy haircut
categorisation
categorization
Caledonian Club
take to one's toes
have no words for
make so free as to
Cape gooseberry
warehouse party
Harefoot Harold
water on the knee
barefoot doctor
category killer
take up the reins
water privilege
water pimpernel
make up one's mind
make a poor mouth
take up a quarrel
James Parkinson
davenport-trick
galeopithecine
galeopithecoid
water potential
careers adviser
take a raincheck
career diplomat
careers officer
water-repellent
water-resistant
have a roving eye
Hamersley Range
make a song about
Paterson's curse
majesticalness
patent medicine
watertightness
have a thick skin
have a tile loose
Lake Stymphalos
Sarepta mustard
take it on the lam
man-eating shark
have it both ways
paper tape punch

valetudinarian
La Resurrezione
have everything
take by surprise
waifs and strays
Ralf Schumacher
daffadowndilly
Garfield Sobers
half-wellington
halfpennyworth
calf's-foot jelly
malfunctioning
saffron milk cap
Rafferty's rules
half-a-sovereign
bang-tail muster
Maggie Tulliver
baggage reclaim
bargain and sale
sanguinariness
bargain-counter
sanguification
bargaining chip
sanguinivorous
large intestine
Bargello Museum
Hanging Gardens
manganese steel
anguorousness
arger than life
arger-than-life
Margaret Sanger
margaritic acid
Margaret Atwood
Margaret Fuller
Margaret DuPont
arget language
angston Hughes
arget practice
laughterliness
laughters-in-law
angatiratanga
angmuir trough
ashi-Bazoukery
achydactylous
athodographer
achydermatous
athode-ray tube
athleen Turner
athygraphical
achygraphical
aphnis et Chloé
atholic Herald
arhelic circle
anhellenistic
athologically
akhalin Island
achelor of Arts
athematically
athematicised
athematicized
athing costume
athaniel Bliss
ash on delivery
sh-on-delivery
achinegunning
athing machine
ashing machine
shionability
cheometrical
shionmonging

Fathers and Sons
fatherlessness
Catherine-wheel
tachistoscopic
Kathy Whitworth
lachrymal gland
capital account
Vatican Council
habit and repute
laminated glass
palisade tissue
capitalisation
capitalization
radicalisation
radicalization
Vatican Museums
capital offence
Vaticanologist
Davis apparatus
magical realism
magical realist
radioautograph
radio altimeter
radio astronomy
maxima cum laude
sanitary napkin
sanitary cordon
Caribbean Times
variable region
David Baltimore
David Ben-Gurion
radiobiologist
David Berkowitz
Nadia Boulanger
radiochemistry
Mario Chipolini
David Coulthard
ratio decidendi
Basil D'Oliveira
Native Canadian
Native-Canadian
native language
Cabinet Council
cabinet-edition
Galileo Galilei
Maria Edgeworth
Native American
Native-American
Nadine Gordimer
cabinet picture
cabinet pudding
canine appetite
facile princeps
malice prepense
David Fabricius
satisfactorily
tariff reformer
radio frequency
hagiographical
palingenetical
gaming contract
Hamish MacInnes
parish register
parish minister
vanishing cream
vanishing point
lapidification
Basidiomycetes
papilionaceous
Daniel Day-Lewis
radial velocity

Danielle Steele
Jamie Lee Curtis
radiologically
capillary joint
radial symmetry
radiometric age
national school
national church
national anthem
national income
rational number
manifold-writer
Camilo José Cela
facinorousness
calico-printing
lay it on the line
Calippic Period
may it please you
cabin passenger
saxifragaceous
radioresistant
Babinski effect
radiosensitise
radiosensitive
radiosensitize
Dakin's solution
radio-strontium
radiotherapist
man in the street
radiotelegraph
radiotelemeter
radiotelephone
radiotelephony
radio telescope
sagittal suture
radiation belts
Magister Artium
canicular cycle
manipulatively
manipulability
fatiguableness
latitudinarian
family planning
family grouping
Marjorie Proops
cack-handedness
backscratching
dark adaptation
Jackie Robinson
back-seat driver
mark of the Beast
talk of the devil
package holiday
walk the streets
darkling beetle
Jack-in-the-green
Mackenzie Range
Mackenzie River
talking machine
walk one's chalks
backing storage
rack one's brains
walking wounded
hack someone off
talk-down system
Jackson Pollock
jackboot around
mark/space ratio
back-projection
mackerel breeze
market-gardener

marketableness
market research
walk a tightrope
Jack Cunningham
✧jack-by-the-hedge
oak-leaf cluster
Kailyard school
parliament-cake
parliament-heel
palliative care
ballpark figure
hallucinogenic
fallaciousness
Gaelic football
Wallace Stevens
called to the bar
early day motion
ballpeen hammer
Paul Henri Spaak
Earl of Cardigan
Earl of Sandwich
Earl of Aberdeen
cauliflower ear
Earl of Rosebery
calligraphical
daylight-saving
Paul Whitehouse
tabloidisation
tabloidization
tail-end Charlie
fall on deaf ears
Pauline Letters
mailing machine
fall on one's feet
Wayland's Smithy
carline thistle
Sailing Tonight
call in question
balloon barrage
Balliol College
Halldór Laxness
Fallopian tubes
calliper splint
Paula Radcliffe
haplostemonous
tablespoonfuls
ballet-mistress
fault tolerance
parlour-boarder
early-Victorian
Vaslav Nijinsky
tallow chandler
Harley Davidson®
Cadmean letters
Cadmean victory
Karma Chameleon
haemocytometer
haemagglutinin
Macmillan nurse
Naomi Mitchison
Tasmanian devil
Tasmanian tiger
harmonic pencil
harmonic series
harmonic motion
salmon-coloured
harmoniousness
gamma radiation
Balmoral Castle
hammer and tongs
Parmesan cheese

haematogenesis
haematophagous
haematopoiesis
haematopoietic
palmatipartite
Saint Bride's Bay
maintenance-man
Launcelot du Lac
Launcelot Gobbo
painter-stainer
faint-heartedly
Saint-John Perse
Saint Kentigern
magniloquently
vaingloriously
Saint Magnus Bay
Jayne Mansfield
cannonball-tree
rainbow therapy
banner headline
garnishee order
Magnus Albertus
magnetic needle
magnetic mirror
magnetic moment
magnetic bottle
magnetic stripe
magnetic curves
magneto-elastic
cannot be helped
magneto-optical
magnetospheric
pain au chocolat
malnourishment
Saint Valentide
Maundy Thursday
Barney Oldfield
Haloragidaceae
panoramic sight
Day of Atonement
war of attrition
Jacob Bronowski
Harold D Babcock
Baron de Fourier
Harold Nicolson
Mason-Dixon Line
bayonet fitting
eat one's head off
nanotechnology
Napoleonic Wars
barometrically
LA Confidential
major-generalcy
parochial board
Baron Haussmann
vasodilatation
vasodilatatory
Carolina Nairne
canonical hours
✧calorie counter
calorification
saponification
calorific value
Kaposi's sarcoma
Day of Judgement
Jaroslav Drobny
paroemiography
saloon carriage
paronomastical
malodorousness
canon of the mass

law of parsimony
favourableness
vapour pressure
Labour Exchange
Baron Shawcross
War of Secession
man of the moment
law of the jungle
rampageousness
sapphire-quartz
harpsichordist
pamphleteering
campylotropous
campanulaceous
campanological
camphorated oil
capparidaceous
Walpurgis night
carpetbag steak
Jacques Derrida
banqueting-hall
matriarchalism
patriarchalism
marriage-favour
carriage return
marriage-broker
marriage bureau
patrialisation
patrialization
patria potestas
sacrococcygeal
iatrochemistry
Sarraceniaceae
batrachophobia
batrachophobic
capriciousness
fabric softener
macrocephalous
Garrick Theatre
Maurice Utrillo
Maurice Wilkins
macrodactylous
Sagrada Familia
manriding train
labradorescent
sacred mushroom
barrier nursing
macroeconomics
macroevolution
Maarten Schmidt
Gabriel's hounds
Caprifoliaceae
pair of snuffers
barrage-balloon
fairy godmother
cairngorm-stone
harrying of hell
sacrilegiously
Laurel and Hardy
Gavrilo Princip
macromolecular
sacramentalise
sacramentalize
sacramentalism
sacramentarian
sacramentalist
sacramentality
sacrament house
macro-marketing
Matra Mountains
Tatra Mountains
Laurence Binyon
Laurence Sterne
Laurence Eusden
matron of honour
Warren G Harding
Warren Mitchell
warrant officer
carry one's point
matryoshka doll
fair to middling
sauropterygian
pair production
matresfamilias
patresfamilias
barrister-at-law
sacrosanctness
macrosporangia
carrot and stick
narrow-mindedly
Garry Winogrand
raise an eyebrow
Paisley pattern
falsifiability
Wars of Religion
Wars of the Roses
Passifloraceae
sausage bassoon
sausage machine
massage parlour
far-sightedness
caustic ammonia
karstification
caustic surface
balsam of Gilead
parsimoniously
Nansen passport
Hansen's disease
passionateness
caisson disease
raise one's glass
marsupial mouse
false pretences
false pregnancy
basso profundos
mass production
causes célèbres
lapsus memoriae
raise the market
cassette single
cassette player
sansculottides
sansculotterie
danseurs nobles
passive smoking
marsh woundwort
canthaxanthine
castrametation
Martha Gellhorn
Sant Fateh Singh
Dante Alighieri
Santiago de Cuba
São Tiago Island
partial product
past participle
lanthanum glass
Can't Pay? Won't Pay!
tactical voting
particularness
fastidiousness
Matthew Bramble
Cartier-Bresson
Matthew Boulton
canteen culture
maître de ballet
Battle of Naseby
Battle of Harlaw
Battle of Cannae
Battle of Wagram
Battle of Actium
Battle of Verdun
Battle of Shiloh
Battle of Pinkie
Battle of Midway
Battle of Amiens
Battle of Mohács
Battle of Kosovo
Battle of Towton
Battle of Arnhem
Battle of Quebec
Battle of Lützen
Battle of Mycale
castles in Spain
parthenocarpic
saltpetre-paper
castle-building
battle-axe block
salt of the earth
salt of wormwood
Rastafarianism
cartographical
pantographical
mastigophorous
cast a horoscope
Captain Corelli
partridgeberry
captain-general
cartridge-paper
farthingsworth
Captain Marryat
mastoid process
Captain W E Johns
tautologically
Bartolomeu Diaz
dactyliography
pantomimically
pantomime horse
Martin Van Buren
Martin Scorsese
Batten's disease
Battenberg cake
Battonberg cake
cantankerously
fast and furious
Past and Present
Castanospermum
Fastens Tuesday
Battenburg cake
xanthomelanous
cast to the winds
East Coast fever
pantopragmatic
party-political
haute politique
pattypan squash
Latter-day Saint
Easter Saturday
Walter De La Mare
tatterdemalion
Sartor Resartus
master sergeant
matter-of-factly
master of hounds
factory farming
bastardisation
bastardization
Walter Lippmann
castor-oil plant
pastoral letter
martyrological
pastoral charge
Walter Ulbricht
Gasteromycetes
factor analysis
bacteriophobia
bacteriologist
bacteriostasis
battery of tests
bacteriostatic
Walter Cronkite
latter prophets
bastard saffron
pattern therapy
Canterbury lamb
Canterbury bell
Cartesian devil
Cartesian diver
earthshakingly
fantasy cricket
cartes-de-visite
cast a spell upon
cast aspersions
fantastication
fantasticality
cartes blanches
baptism of blood
earth satellite
wait attendance
factitiousness
Pasteurelloses
Pasteurellosis
pasteurisation
pasteurization
natura naturata
natura naturans
natural history
naturalisation
naturalization
tabularisation
tabularization
natural numbers
Hague Agreement
natural science
natural therapy
manufacturable
natural virtues
natural wastage
ranunculaceous
nature printing
capuchin monkey
Baluchitherium
value judgement
casual labourer
Samuel Pickwick
Samuel L Jackson
manual alphabet
manual exercise
vacuum cleaning
vacuum concrete
Palus Nebularum
Papua New Guinea
Ranulph Fiennes
daguerreotyper
salubriousness
Lacus Somniorum
Sauvignon Blanc
marvellousness
Calvin Coolidge
galvanoplastic
galvanized iron
Gatwick Airport
Manx shearwater
Calycanthaceae
lady of the night
laryngological
laryngoscopist
labyrinthodont
dazzle-painting
panzer division
Abraham Hayward
Abraham Lincoln
oblate spheroid
object language
absent-mindedly
obsequiousness
observableness
observation car
I beg your pardon?
obligatoriness
obiit sine prole
abominableness
abundance ratio
Ebenezer Howard
absorbefacient
absorptiveness
absorptiometer
absorptiometry
absquatulation
eburnification
abstractedness
abstractionism
abstractionist
obstreperously
a bit of all right
abstemiousness
obstructionism
obstructionist
abjure the realm
above and beyond
above-mentioned
above suspicion
scratchbuilder
scrape together
Schafer's method
ocean-greyhound
McNaghten rules
oceanic islands
à chacun son goût
iceberg lettuce
acid-house party
schematisation
schematization
science fiction
screaming farce
screen printing
sclerophyllous
sclerotisation
sclerotization
screw propeller
screw-propeller
acceptableness
scientifically
accepting house
schedule tribes
McKenzie Friend

scribbling-book
Schindler's List
active immunity
Schiff's reagent
octingentenary
actinide series
Achille Bazaine
Achilles' tendon
schismatically
action painting
action spectrum
action stations
actinobacillus
schizophyceous
schizognathous
schizomycetous
eclipse plumage
achievement age
acclimatisable
acclimatizable
scaling circuit
scale staircase
ecclesiastical
Ecclesiasticus
ecclesiologist
scombresocidae
Schmitt trigger
candalisation
candalization
candalousness
chnographical
conographical
cenographical
acanthocephala
canning speech
cintillometer
cintillascope
cintilloscope
conomy of scale
conometrician
ing on the cake
cknowledgment
chola cantorum
chocardiogram
cholastically
chondroplasia
ct of Indemnity
choolmasterly
hoolteaching
hool-divinity
hoolmistress
countability
countantship
hooner-rigged
complishable
complishment
ross the board
ross-the-board
ross-the-table
hottky defect
hottky effect
aphocephalic
aphocephalus
ertain person
ore an own goal
orpion spider
urrilousness
aremongering
hromatically
arine disease
ore points off

Acts of Sederunt
scatterbrained
scatter diagram
Scotch bluebell
Scotch woodcock
Scotch attorney
Scottish Office
Scottification
ichthyological
ichthyolatrous
ichthyophagist
ichthyophagous
ichthyosaurian
occupationally
scrubbing-board
scrubbing-brush
scrutin de liste
scrutinisation
scrutinization
scrutinisingly
scrutinizingly
sceuophylacium
occult sciences
acoustic guitar
accustomedness
accumulatively
accumulator bet
scrupulousness
Schwenkfeldian
Advanced Higher
advance factory
advancing years
Edward de Baliol
Edward the Elder
Edward M Kennedy
Edward Woodward
Edward John Eyre
Edward Molyneux
Edward Steichen
adiathermanous
idealistically
Adlai Stevenson
advantage court
advantageously
edible dormouse
odd-come-shortly
educationalist
adscititiously
adventitiously
Oddfellows Club
administrative
administration
administratrix
edriophthalmic
admissibleness
Adolf Butenandt
Adelphi Theatre
Adela Pankhurst
Adolf von Baeyer
I don't believe so
adenocarcinoma
identical rhyme
identical twins
identification
identity parade
identity crisis
advocate-depute
idiopathically
addressability
editio princeps
Edouard Beneden

Separate Tables
separate school
set a game to five
vexata quaestio
geoarchaeology
metal composite
seral community
recalcitration
Gerald Gardiner
rewardableness
Herald's College
Gerald M Edelman
regardlessness
hen-and-chickens
sex-and-shopping
wet-and-dry paper
tea and sympathy
Debateable Land
megatechnology
delayed neutron
megavertebrate
sebaceous gland
telangiectasia
telangiectasis
telangiectatic
pelargonic acid
Seraphic Father
Seraphic Doctor
detached retina
metachromatism
metaphorically
semaphorically
metaphysically
metaphosphoric
set-aside scheme
melamine resins
mesaticephalic
negative equity
negative proton
negative number
metalinguistic
rehabilitative
denazification
desalinisation
desalinization
gelatinisation
gelatinization
keratinisation
keratinization
rehabilitation
relativisation
relativization
semasiological
hepaticologist
legalistically
retaliationist
recapitulative
recapitulation
recapitulatory
remarkableness
dérailleur gear
metallographic
metallographer
metallogenetic
metalloprotein
beta interferon
Leda and the Swan
hexagonal chess
megalomaniacal
devalorisation
devalorization

revalorisation
revalorization
nematodiriasis
Heraion of Samos
dexamphetamine
megasporangium
megasporophyll
mesa transistor
Renaissance man
metapsychology
relapsing fever
penal servitude
Sebastian Cabot
tenants' charter
semantic memory
departmentally
telautographic
melastomaceous
Hexactinellida
senatus consult
Ieyasu Tokugawa
Sézary syndrome
Rembrandtesque
Der Blaue Reiter
Lee Buck Trevino
feeble-mindedly
Wembley Stadium
Leibnitzianism
herbal medicine
red-bloodedness
berberidaceous
Herbert Marcuse
Herbert Spencer
Derbyshire neck
Derbyshire spar
merchandisable
merchandizable
merchant tailor
merchant prince
leucocythaemia
leucocytolysis
leucocytopenia
leucocytopenic
Decca Flight Log
teaching fellow
neocolonialism
neocolonialist
Hercules beetle
Hercules' choice
percentile rank
geocentrically
Redcross Knight
Peace of Utrecht
perceptiveness
perceptibility
cercopithecoid
Leicestershire
percussion-lock
percussion-fuse
fence the tables
percutaneously
reacquaintance
heads and thraws
dead man's handle
headmastership
dead set against
meddlesomeness
lead tetraethyl
Dead Sea Scrolls
dead letter drop
needle exchange

deed of covenant
read the riot act
Seidlitz powder
Mesdemoiselles
leading article
leading counsel
weeding-forceps
wedding garment
dead in the water
lending library
reading-machine
vending machine
Ferdinand Braun
mend one's fences
leading strings
leaden-stepping
reed instrument
read only memory
lead to the altar
dead to the world
send to Coventry
lead up the aisle
lead apes in hell
Jeddart justice
gender-specific
dead as a herring
tendovaginitis
meadow mushroom
general council
general damages
televangelical
telepathically
federalisation
federalization
generalisation
generalization
vegetativeness
Serena Williams
teleradium unit
Père David's deer
generalissimos
general journal
vegetable ivory
vegetable mould
vegetable sheep
general meeting
Geneva movement
general officer
general-purpose
general paresis
general reserve
general servant
beseechingness
telescopically
aerenchymatous
degenerateness
regeneratively
Reverend Mother
Kegel exercises
bene merentibus
venereological
defenestration
Benedetto Croce
Peter Greenaway
revengefulness
genethliacally
genethlialogic
Hemel Hempstead
telephone booth
telephonically
telephone kiosk

what do you say to?
photoperiodism
phytopathology
white quebracho
photorealistic
The Turkish Bath
photosynthesis
photosynthetic
photosensitise
photosensitive
photosensitize
white supremacy
what's the damage?
that's the ticket
phototelegraph
what a vengeance
what-d'you-call-'em
what-d'you-call-it
rheumatic fever
rheumatologist
thaumatography
thaumaturgical
the unconscious
shouldered arch
shoulder-height
shoulder girdle
thoughtfulness
thought process
thought-reading
chaulmoogra oil
shove-halfpenny
chivalrousness
the Virgin Queen
chevaux-de-frise
The White Rabbit
The Winter's Tale
The Woodlanders
the world to come
the worm may turn
The Water-Babies
shawl waistcoat
the Year of Grace
chrysanthemums
Chrysostom John
Rhizophoraceae
vicar-apostolic
disambiguation
Financial Times
finance company
disaccommodate
misacceptation
cigarette paper
disaffiliation
vital functions
disaffirmation
disaggregation
Sir Angus Wilson
viral hepatitis
vitalistically
disacknowledge
viral marketing
simaroubaceous
disapplication
misapplication
vital principle
disappointment
disapprobative
disapprobation
disapprobatory
disapprovingly
disappropriate
misappropriate
Sir Adrian Boult
Linacre College
binaural effect
disarrangement
misarrangement
disassociation
Dirac's constant
disattribution
Sir Anthony Caro
Sir Anthony Eden
Disasters of War
misanthropical
bipartisanship
Sir Arthur Bliss
Sir Arthur Evans
miraculousness
disadventurous
misadventurous
misadvisedness
binary notation
binary munition
Sir Bobby Robson
nimble-fingered
Bix Beiderbecke
Big Bill Broonzy
pit bull terrier
ribbon building
Sir Bernard Katz
Gilbert Islands
Gilbert Sheldon
Sir Basil Spence
Limbus infantum
Sir Charles Bell
aircraftswoman
Sir Cecil Beaton
pisciculturist
pièce d'occasion
discodermolide
kitchen cabinet
discretionally
witches' Sabbath
witches' thimble
Winchester disk
zincographical
bioclimatology
circuit breaker
mischief-making
discriminately
discriminative
discriminating
discrimination
zinckification
discriminatory
circuitousness
his cake is dough
miscellanarian
Lincoln Airport
Lincoln College
circular letter
discolouration
miscalculation
circumnavigate
circumscissile
discommendable
circumbendibus
circumferentor
circumlittoral
circumambience
circumambiency
circumambulate
circumforanean
discomboberate
circumposition
discomfortable
discombobulate
circumlocution
circumvolution
circumlocutory
circumspective
Giacomo Puccini
circumspection
circumstantial
circumnutation
miscomputation
circumnutatory
circumgyration
circumgyratory
disconnectedly
discontentedly
disconcertment
discontentment
miscontentment
air-conditioned
air-conditioner
discontinuance
disconsolately
disconsolation
disconformable
oil-control ring
Vincent's angina
Vincent Van Gogh
cinchonisation
cinchonization
disceptatorial
disciplinarium
disciplinarian
discursiveness
discerpibility
diachronically
pincer movement
discouragement
discouragingly
viscous damping
discount market
Viscount Nelson
discountenance
discourteously
discount-broker
vindictiveness
fiddle-faddling
middle distance
middle-distance
Middle-American
bird of paradise
biodegradation
disdainfulness
Mindanao Island
hidden treasure
Sir Denis Forman
wind instrument
Birds of America
mind-bogglingly
birds of one wing
wild-goose chase
kindergartener
Sir Dirk Bogarde
Sir Derek Jacobi
Sir Derek Barton
finders keepers
nil desperandum
misdescription
mind-numblingly
Sir David Wilkie
window-shopping
window envelope
window-dressing
fire salamander
Cinema Paradiso
line management
fives-and-threes
liberated woman
liberalisation
liberalization
mineralisation
mineralization
mineral kingdom
cinematography
mineral spirits
nine days' wonder
tidewaitership
Tibetan terrier
Literary Review
Five Easy Pieces
literary source
disemboguement
disembogue into
river blindness
disembarkation
disembowelment
disenchantress
disenchantment
disencumbrance
video digitizer
like a dying duck
rites de passage
fire department
fivepence piece
sidereal period
nineteenth hole
River Euphrates
nine men's morris
bioelectricity
disenfranchise
eigen-frequency
video frequency
disengagedness
bioengineering
miles gloriosus
give the heave-ho
give a hammering
give the meeting
vice-chancellor
kinetheodolite
Nigel Hawthorne
like-mindedness
Zinedine Zidane
kinesiological
vicesimo-quarto
vigesimo-quarto
fides implicita
River Irrawaddy
river-jack viper
time immemorial
pigeon-fancying
live and breathe
pile on the agony
live and let live
pigeon-breasted
line one's pocket
Sir Ernst B Chain
give someone gyp
ride someone off
rice polishings
rites of passage
fire-worshipper
vice-consulship
side horse vault
pile up the agony
give up the ghost
linear equation
vice-presidency
miner's phthisis
Riders to the Sea
fixed satellite
licentiateship
direct mailshot
disentrainment
silent majority
diverticulosis
diverticulated
diverticulitis
directed number
videotelephone
directionality
licentiousness
libertarianism
director's chair
director circle
disenthralment
direct drilling
like it or lump it
divertissement
silentium altum
digestive tract
rime suffisante
disequilibrate
disequilibrium
Sir Edward Elgar
Sir Edward Heath
Sir Edward Tylor
Cider with Rosie
life expectancy
Cicely Wedgwood
live by one's wits
livery cupboard
diffractometer
Wilfred Mannion
Wilfred O'Reilly
oil-filled cable
disfurnishment
difference tone
differentiable
differentially
differentiator
diffusion plant
King James Bible
biographically
siege-artillery
piggyback plant
zingiberaceous
Diego de Almagro
single-handedly
single-mindedly
single-breasted
single currency
ring the changes
King Philip's War
Pilgrim Fathers
jingling Johnny
jingoistically
linguistically
Kingsley Martin
siege mentality

king's messenger
ringing chamber
singing-gallery
diagnosability
Siege of Antwerp
Sir George Grove
Sir George Robey
biogeochemical
Singapore Sling
finger-painting
fingers-breadth
finger-alphabet
finger-pointing
gingerbread man
fingerprinting
big girl's blouse
disgustfulness
disgustingness
disgruntlement
Diego Velázquez
misgovernaunce
right as a trivet
right ascension
Highland cattle
high-handedness
right about face
right about face!
night-blindness
Sir Hubert Parry
lithochromatic
Michael Bentine
rich tea biscuit
Michael Brunson
Michael Collins
Michael Denness
Michael Douglas
high-level waste
Michael Faraday
Michael Holding
Michael Holroyd
high technology
Michael Hordern
Michael Jackson
Michael Johnson
Michael Meacher
Michaelmas term
high-resolution
lighter-than-air
rich text format
Michael Tippett
night-flowering
night-fossicker
night-foundered
light flyweight
lithographical
with a good grace
Sir Hugh Walpole
light-heartedly
xiphihumeralis
right-hand drive
Mikhail Bakunin
high-mindedness
fighting chance
lighting-up time
Fighting French
Mikhail Kalinin
xiphoid process
light intensity
Wilhelm Dilthey
pinhole glasses
lithologically

Michel Foucault
diaheliotropic
Michele Platini
Nicholas Ridley
Wilhelmstrasse
Sir Humphry Davy
Nightmare Abbey
niche marketing
with one consent
lithonthryptic
with an ill grace
lightning chess
within an inch of
lithontriptist
with one's tail up
Sir Henry Morgan
Sir Henry Cotton
Sir Henry Irving
withholding tax
right off the bat
High Commission
high-speed steel
light pollution
fisherman's ring
fisherman's luck
Richard Branson
Richard Burbage
Richard Dawkins
Richard Ellmann
high-priesthood
Richard Hoggart
Richard Hakluyt
Richard Ingrams
Sir Harold Kroto
withering-floor
high-principled
Richard Roberts
Richard Rodgers
Richard Strauss
Richard Woolley
Sir Harry Lauder
without compare
without dispute
wish fulfilment
without measure
without more ado
without reserve
with a vengeance
right ventricle
fight windmills
Eighty Years' War
highly-seasoned
Sir Isaac Newton
Sir Isaac Pitman
digitalisation
digitalization
militarisation
militarization
Divina Commedia
viviparousness
digital plotter
military police
disinclination
civil commotion
disincarcerate
disincorporate
limited company
limited edition
limited express
divided highway
citizen's arrest

vivisectionist
Viti Levu Island
disinformation
misinformation
bioinformatics
disinfestation
riding the stang
riding-interest
disingenuously
riding breeches
airing cupboard
finishing touch
disinheritance
dividing-engine
silicification
vitilitigation
libidinousness
sit in judgement
civil liberties
visible exports
visible horizon
visible imports
disillusionary
disillusionise
disillusionize
Sir Ian McKellen
Viviana Durante
Vivian Richards
silicon carbide
die in one's boots
ricinoleic acid
dig in one's heels
die in one's shoes
visitor general
liaison officer
pin it on someone
filiopietistic
Filippino Lippi
misimprovement
disimpassioned
dinitrobenzene
Winifred Holtby
Winifred Atwell
misinstruction
pig-in-the-middle
disintegrative
disintegration
sinistrorsally
ministerialist
misinterpreter
disinteresting
diminutiveness
ridiculousness
disinvestiture
disjecta membra
Sir Jack Brabham
Sir John Gielgud
Sir John Hawkins
Sir John Hawkyns
Sir John Kendrew
Sir John Lubbock
Sir John Tenniel
disjointedness
Sir Joseph Banks
Sir Joseph Lyons
pickaback plant
tickled a th' sere
pickled herring
milk of magnesia
kick in the pants
kick in the teeth

milking machine
milking parlour
lick one's wounds
Vidkun Quisling
hickery-pickery
risk assessment
Rikki-Tikki-Tavi
Kirkstall Abbey
Rickettsiaceae
Rickettsia body
Mickey Spillane
field ambulance
William Barclay
William Barentz
William Bateson
William Cobbett
billiard-marker
William Dampier
William Gilbert
William Golding
William Huggins
William Hogarth
William H Bonney
William Hazlitt
William Ireland
field allowance
William MacEwen
William Nevison
William Russell
William Shatner
William Siemens
field artillery
William Tyndale
William Thomson
William Vickrey
Gillian Wearing
William Wallace
William Wyndham
dialectologist
viola da braccio
fille de chambre
Billie Jean King
Willie Whitelaw
bill of oblivion
Dial M for Murder
bill of exchange
village college
bill-discounter
villainousness
bioluminescent
diplomatically
willing-hearted
Finlandisation
Finlandization
milling machine
millenarianism
filling station
Billings method
bibliomaniacal
Sir Leon Brittan
field preaching
Pillars of Islam
diplostemonous
Willesden paper
Gielgud Theatre
pillow-fighting
Sir Lewis Namier
mismeasurement
sigmoid flexure
sigmoidoscopic
Jimmy Johnstone

diamantiferous
diamondiferous
diamond jubilee
Sigmund Romberg
diamond wedding
sigma particles
Kilmarnock cowl
biomathematics
biometeorology
film supporting
Sir Max Mallowan
Sir Max Beerbohm
Finn mac Cumhail
piano accordion
lignocellulose
pioneer species
sign of the cross
Midnight Cowboy
signal sequence
Lionel Trilling
winning-gallery
Giant's Causeway
pinnatipartite
Sir Nevill F Mott
Disneyfication
Nicolas Fouquet
Nicobar Islands
Nicolas Poussin
minotaur beetle
Nikolai Vavilov
Simon Bar Kokhba
Ripon Cathedral
Ninon de Lenclos
disorderliness
pin one's faith on
dig one's heels in
pin one's hopes on
Simone Signoret
hit one in the eye
win one's worship
bid/offer spread
Timothy Severin
disorientation
risorius muscle
minority waiter
dinoflagellate
lie on one's hands
sit on one's hands
lipogrammatism
lipogrammatist
dip of the needle
Simon the Zealot
sit on the splice
ribonucleotide
dicotyledonous
misogynistical
display cabinet
diaphanousness
Kipp's apparatus
simple sentence
simple-mindedly
displenishment
simple interest
simple fraction
simple fracture
displeasedness
simplificative
simplification
simplistically
dispensatively
dispensability

dispensational
dispensatorily
mispunctuation
diaphototropic
hippopotamuses
airport fiction
dispiritedness
disposableness
dispose towards
disputableness
hippety-hoppety
dispiteousness
disputatiously
Sir P G Wodehouse
disqualifiable
disquisitional
Tierra del Fuego
microaerophile
microbiologist
Sir Robert Ensor
microbarograph
microchemistry
nitrocellulose
microcomponent
microcomputing
microcephalous
fibrocartilage
microcircuitry
microdetection
Pierre de Fermat
microeconomics
microevolution
vibroflotation
hierographical
hierogrammatic
disregardfully
nitroglycerine
hieroglyphical
microinjection
Gibraltar board®
micrologically
microminiature
micromarketing
micrometeorite
vitriolisation
vitriolization
vitreous enamel
vitreous humour
hip replacement
micropegmatite
microprocessor
library binding
library edition
hierarchically
mirror nuclides
mirror symmetry
disrespectable
digressiveness
vitrescibility
microseismical
Hierosolymitan
microsporangia
microstructure
Pier Luigi Nervi
Sir Rex Harrison
Sir Sean Connery
Mies van der Rohe
Miss Jane Marple
Giessbach Falls
dissociability
first-class mail
first-class post
Sir Sidney Nolan
Giosuè Carducci
Miss Jean Brodie
dissolvability
dissolubleness
diesel-electric
tinsel-slipper'd
dissolutionism
dissolutionist
dissymmetrical
kissing disease
Wilson's disease
wigs on the green
Wilson Kipketer
pins and needles
kissing-strings
dioscoreaceous
Ripstone pippin
fission reactor
Giuseppe Giusti
dissertational
disserviceable
biosystematics
Rimsky-Korsakov
Fifth Amendment
virtual reality
mistranslation
distractedness
histochemistry
fifth columnist
listed building
little magazine
tittle-tattling
diathermaneity
Little and Large
little green men
distressed area
distress signal
win the exchange
little by little
Tintagel Castle
histogenically
Pitt the Younger
histrionically
distributively
distributional
mistake one's man
mistake one's way
distilled water
histologically
histolytically
Mittel-European
Mitteleuropean
distemperature
Sir Tom Stoppard
tintinnabulate
tintinnabulant
tintinnabulary
tintinnabulous
Miltonic sonnet
distant healing
distensibility
Sistine Madonna
listen to reason
fitting-out dock
Milton Friedman
distinguishing
Pietro Mascagni
Pietro Badoglio
Sir Thomas Pride
Sir Thomas Wyatt
Pietro Annigoni
virtuous circle
histoplasmosis
dicta probantia
histopathology
Victor Vasarely
Victoria sponge
Victoria Island
historical cost
dipterocarpous
picture gallery
Victor/Victoria
Winter Olympics
Victor Emmanuel
Viktor Korchnoi
Vittorio De Sica
sisters of mercy
historiography
victoriousness
winter solstice
Pieter Brueghel
Pieter Breughel
winter quarters
picture-writing
Nietzscheanism
birth-strangled
virtute officii
simulated pearl
figurativeness
liquid paraffin
liquidity ratio
vituperatively
lieutenantship
figure of speech
liturgiologist
bituminisation
bituminization
bituminous coal
fiduciary issue
Miguel Indurain
Miguel Asturias
liquorice-vetch
simultaneously
Dieu et mon droit
pituitary gland
air vice-marshal
nievie-nick-nack
Giovanni Pisano
silver pheasant
silversmithing
silver quandong
Sir Walter Scott
View on the Stour
Dilwara temples
City Livery Club
Sibylline Books
bicycle ricksha
dizygotic twins
zinziberaceous
piezochemistry
Dizzy Gillespie
piezomagnetism
diazonium salts
Oki Archipelago
skylight filter
skeleton shrimp
skimble-skamble
skunk-blackbird
skate on thin ice
clearance cairn
cloak and dagger
plea bargaining
pleased as Punch
please yourself
bleaching green
floating beacon
floating charge
floating kidney
floating policy
floating bridge
floating island
oleaginousness
Ella Fitzgerald
Altai Mountains
plead not guilty
algae poisoning
Aldabra Islands
clear-starching
clear-sightedly
cleansing-cream
pleasure-seeker
pleasure-giving
pleasure ground
clean up one's act
globe artichoke
global variable
à la belle étoile
global exchange
block and tackle
blockade-runner
glucocorticoid
Plácido Domingo
black-eyed Susan
black guillemot
black horehound
black-hat hacker
blocking motion
electioneering
black in the face
black-marketeer
ill-conditioned
plectognathous
place of worship
Blackpool Tower
electrobiology
electrochemist
electric heater
electric window
electroculture
Electra complex
electric guitar
electrodynamic
electrifyingly
electroforming
electrogilding
electrogenesis
electrokinetic
electrolytical
electromyogram
electromotance
electron camera
electronic mail
electronically
electronic book
electron optics
electro-osmosis
electro-osmotic
electro-optical
electroplating
electrostatics
electrotechnic
electrotherapy
electrothermic
electrothermal
electrovalence
electrovalency
electrowinning
pluck up courage
flock wallpaper
bladder campion
slide projector
Old Deuteronomy
Clyde W Tombaugh
blue ear disease
blueback salmon
alder-buckthorn
elderberry wine
Almeida Theatre
Blue Ribbon Army
illegitimately
illegitimation
Algernon Sidney
Claes Oldenburg
allegorisation
allegorization
allelomorphism
Bluecoat School
blue-green algae
elder statesman
✧elder statesmen
Albert Calmette
old-established
Albert Reynolds
Albert Memorial
Albert the Great
Albert Einstein
Alberto Moravia
Blue Suede Shoes
sleepy sickness
sleepy staggers
fluff one's lines
Flyfishers' Club
sluggardliness
elegiac stanzas
flagrante bello
oligocythaemia
flog a dead horse
plague-stricken
flag of distress
flag-lieutenant
flagelliferous
flagellomaniac
Glagolitic Mass
alignment chart
gleg in the uptak
old-gentlemanly
slug-foot-second
oligopsonistic
oligarchically
flight-recorder
gleg at the uptak
flight envelope
flight engineer
flagitiousness
alphabetically
alphamerically
alphanumerical
alpha particles
alpha radiation
all in a day's work
alligator apple
Alois Alzheimer

 Words marked ✧ can also be spelled with one or more capital letters

plain chocolate
illiterateness
alliteratively
altimetrically
Albigensianism
flying bedstead
flying squirrel
Flying Dutchman
flying buttress
illimitability
fluid mechanics
Elsinore Castle
ultimogeniture
plains wanderer
claims assessor
ill-intentioned
El Misti Volcano
altitudinarian
Clairvaux Abbey
Plumbaginaceae
clumber spaniel
plumbisolvency
elementariness
old man of the sea
alimentiveness
flamboyant-tree
plumbosolvency
flame-retardant
climate control
climatological
Plantaginaceae
plantation song
blank cartridge
slantendicular
planned economy
Blenheim Palace
slanderousness
Flinders Ranges
Flinders Petrie
Alan Dershowitz
blankety-blanky
plant-formation
slantindicular
planning blight
clonal deletion
planing-machine
plane-polarised
plane-polarized
plenipotential
Elinor Dashwood
ill-naturedness
planet-stricken
glandular fever
Alan Rusbridger
glanduliferous
allopathically
pleonastically
blood-bespotted
blood-consuming
blood corpuscle
floor exercises
all-overishness
all over the shop
alcoholisation
alcoholization
alloiostrophos
blood poisoning
blood-sacrifice
bloodthirstily
blepharoplasty
Elephanta caves
alopecia areata
slap on the wrist
clap by the heels
ultracrepidate
clerical collar
floriculturist
Alfred Marshall
Alfred de Musset
Alfred Munnings
altruistically
ultramicrotome
ultramicrotomy
✧ultramontanism
ultramontanist
Clarence Darrow
Florence fennel
Florentine iris
ultroneousness
glory of the snow
ultrasonically
ultrastructure
all-round camera
clergyman's knee
plasma membrane
plasmapheresis
Alastair Burnet
flash blindness
Elisabethville
class-conscious
closed syllable
close encounter
blistered-steel
plaster of Paris
blister-plaster
cluster physics
glass harmonica
classical Latin
classical music
classification
classificatory
plastic surgeon
plastic surgery
clash-ma-clavers
Glastonbury Tor
Elasmobranchii
close the record
close to the bone
glossy magazine
glossy starling
platycephalous
pluto-democracy
bletheranskate
clitter-clatter
slatternliness
blithesomeness
flatbed scanner
clutch at straws
clotting factor
glutaminic acid
platinum blonde
platinum sponge
flat-footedness
all-terrain bike
clitoridectomy
glutaraldehyde
plate tectonics
gluteus maximus
plethysmograph
cloth-yard shaft
pleurapophyses
pleurapophysis
clouded leopard
slaughterhouse
slaughterously
flaughter-spade
plough the sands
eleutheromania
illuminatingly
Pleuronectidae
altum silentium
illustratively
illustrational
claustrophobia
claustrophobic
clavicytherium
Olivier Theatre
Slavonic Dances
pluviometrical
Oliver Plunkett
Oliver Cromwell
sliver building
glove-stretcher
claw-hammer-coat
Aldwych Theatre
blow the whistle
blow hot and cold
flowery-kirtled
blaxploitation
Alexander Balus
Alexander Korda
Alexander Monro
Alexandre Dumas
Alexandr Oparin
alexipharmakon
Lloyd Honeyghan
Elizabeth Arden
Elizabethanism
Elizabeth Bowen
Elizabeth David
Elizabeth Frink
Elizabeth Grant
Elizabeth Kenny
Eliza Doolittle
empathetically
imparidigitate
imparisyllabic
embarrassingly
impassableness
impassibleness
ambassadorship
impacted faeces
impact adhesive
immaculateness
Ummayyad Mosque
Amedeo Avogadro
imperativeness
imperative mood
impercipiently
imperceptively
imperfectively
immethodically
Imperial Palace
imperial gallon
imperial octavo
imperial weight
imperial bushel
embellishingly
impermeability
Emperor Akihito
emperor penguin
imperturbation
imperviability
imperviousness
image converter
imaginableness
image processor
amphibological
amphibiousness
emphaticalness
omnibenevolent
immiserisation
immiserization
ambidextrously
empire-building
immitigability
omnium-gatherum
omnivorousness
omnicompetence
amniotic cavity
omnibus edition
a majori ad minus
smoke abatement
smoking concert
smoke-room story
Smokey Robinson
Emiliano Zapata
Emile Clapeyron
implacableness
Emily Dickinson
smelling bottle
emulsification
small intestine
implementation
emblematically
Emil von Behring
smell of the lamp
I'm all right, Jack
small-tooth comb
implausibility
a minori ad majus
imponderabilia
immoderateness
impoverishment
smoothing plane
immobilisation
immobilization
embolismic year
embourgeoising
imposthumation
impracticality
American Legion
American Beauty
American blight
American Indian
American-Indian
emergency light
impregnability
umbrageousness
emerging market
Amaryllidaceae
amaranthaceous
embryo transfer
impressiveness
impressibility
impressionable
smart sanctions
improvableness
improvvisatore
emission theory
emotionalistic
imitation pearl
amateurishness
ambulancewoman
immune response
immunogenetics
immunogenicity
immunochemical
immunophoresis
immunoglobulin
immunosuppress
empyreumatical
incapacitation
unwatchfulness
Antarctic Ocean
unhandsomeness
incandescently
untameableness
engagement ring
unmaterialised
unmaterialized
intangibleness
unmathematical
antaphrodisiac
insanitariness
inhabitability
insatiableness
invariableness
unsatisfaction
unsatisfactory
kneading-trough
inhabitiveness
unmalleability
and all that jazz
one-armed bandit
enharmonically
inharmoniously
unmaintainable
unearned income
unmannerliness
Anna Howard Shaw
antagonisation
antagonization
unvanquishable
unmarriageable
unmatriculated
unpassableness
enfant terrible
unfaithfulness
incautiousness
endarterectomy
unsaturated fat
unmanufactured
invaluableness
insalubriously
knickerbockers
an ace in the hole
unscripturally
unacknowledged
unaccommodated
unaccounted-for
unaccomplished
knock on the head
anacardiaceous
anachronically
inaccurateness
inscrutability
unacquainted in
unacquaintance
anacoustic zone
unscrupulously
inadvisability
one-dimensional
unidentifiable
inadequateness

double-stopping
double exposure
Tomb of Mausolus
not be having any
Doubting-Castle
doubting Thomas
non-belligerent
Lombardy poplar
morbus gallicus
combustibility
combat trousers
morceau de salon
forcible feeble
concrete poetry
concrete jungle
concretisation
concretization
force force pump
dolce far niente
conceivability
Joschka Fischer
conciliatorily
concelebration
non-comedogenic
non-competitive
non-compearance
coxcombicality
non-committally
non-communicant
non-contentious
volcanological
non-conformance
concentrically
toucan crossing
boa constrictor
non-concurrence
Voice of America
non-co-operation
non-cooperation
porcupine grass
concerti grossi
non-chromosomal
concerto grosso
worcesterberry
Worcester china
Worcestershire
Worcester sauce
concessionaire
concession road
voice synthesis
moccasin flower
vouch to warrant
conclusiveness
concavo-concave
lords and ladies
cold dark matter
Ford Madox Brown
Lord Carrington
Lord Hattersley
conductibility
Tom, Dick, or Harry
loaded question
good neighbours
bowdlerisation
bowdlerization
good fellowship
goodfellowship
Lord of the Flies
Lord of the Rings
gold-of-pleasure
goods for own use

Lord Chancellor
wood nightshade
Good Vibrations
Lord Lieutenant
lords in waiting
hold all the aces
Lord Elwyn-Jones
London Marathon
Golden Pavilion
condensability
holding company
golden pheasant
Gordon Richards
folding-machine
hold in contempt
holding pattern
hold one's whisht
hold one's tongue
hold one's breath
hold one's ground
wooden overcoat
Lord Howe Island
Lord John Fisher
good-for-nothing
hold your horses
good conscience
roadworthiness
food-controller
hold up one's head
powder magazine
word processing
powder one's nose
wonder-stricken
condescendence
condescend upon
Lords Spiritual
non-destructive
job description
nondisjunction
conditional fee
conditionality
Lord Rutherford
good-humouredly
mole salamander
José Capablanca
mover and shaker
Romeo and Juliet
moderate breeze
Coleman Hawkins
José María Aznar
roses all the way
dodecanoic acid
José Ramos-Horta
power-amplifier
dodecasyllabic
dodecasyllable
power breakfast
Roger Bannister
nomenclatorial
lower criticism
honeycomb tripe
fovea centralis
robes-de-chambre
foreseeability
Home Department
non-electrolyte
code of practice
vowel gradation
Joseph P Kennedy
Josephine Baker
something like a

Joseph Goebbels
Joseph Rowntree
foreshortening
Joseph Grimaldi
norethisterone
forethoughtful
Joseph Pulitzer
norepinephrine
covering letter
Comédie humaine
Roderick Random
soteriological
mode dispersion
solecistically
Yoweri Museveni
Modern Painters
fore-and-aft sail
come unfastened
love-in-idleness
governmentally
mose in the chine
hole in the heart
come on the scene
come into effect
someone or other
lose one's tongue
money of account
gone for a Burton
Love Songs in Age
fore-topgallant
come to the front
polemoniaceous
come to one's hand
power of the keys
noteworthiness
con espressione
Józef Pilsudski
cotemporaneous
dose equivalent
Boxer Rebellion
foreordination
come from behind
✧women's movement
power structure
money-scrivener
women's suffrage
Robert Bakewell
Roberts Airport
Robert Schumann
rosette disease
Robert Delaunay
Robert Devereux
Robert Helpmann
Robert Henryson
cover the ground
cover the buckle
moment of a force
lowest of the low
Robert the Bruce
Robert Chambers
Robert Pitcairn
Robert F Kennedy
Robert Koldewey
potentiometric
Robert Robinson
Robert Browning
Robert Guiscard
molecular sieve
come full circle
core curriculum
comedy of menace

Lorenzo Da Ponte
confidentially
Wolfson College
tomfoolishness
conformability
conformational
not for the world
conference call
comfort station
Bob Fitzsimmons
longs and shorts
rough-and-tumble
Douglas Jardine
Long Parliament
longwall system
Golgi apparatus
congratulative
congratulation
congratulatory
rough breathing
✧congregational
long-headedness
Borghese Museum
mongrelisation
mongrelization
Congressperson
Song of Hiawatha
longshore drift
long-windedness
bougainvillaea
jogging bottoms
long in the tooth
morganatically
Songs of ascents
Songs of degrees
conglomeration
for good measure
longhorn beetle
Long John Silver
conglobulation
coign of vantage
longitudinally
dodge the column
conglutinative
conglutination
Joshua Reynolds
for heaven's sake
go the extra mile
Rochelle-powder
Roehampton Club
roche moutonnée
nothing special
Lothar Matthaus
oophorectomise
oophorectomize
mothers' meeting
mother superior
sophistication
nominal account
logical atomism
nominalisation
nominalization
motivationally
Louis Armstrong
solitaire board
Louis Althusser
Colin Blakemore
sociobiologist
Louis Chevrolet
motivelessness
go like hot cakes

vociferousness
non-inflammable
forisfamiliate
moving pavement
loving kindness
moving pictures
dolichocephaly
go with the worse
polishing-paste
polishing-slate
Polish notation
polishers' putty
political verse
comitia curiata
positive action
positive number
politicisation
politicization
solidification
solicitousness
comitia tributa
✧social democrat
social security
social services
social climbing
social engineer
social mobility
social contract
Coriolis effect
sodium benzoate
sodium chlorate
sodium chloride
motion sickness
notional income
Cosimo de' Medici
Sonia O'Sullivan
Boris Pasternak
Rosicrucianism
robin redbreast
holier-than-thou
Tobias Smollett
Robinson Crusoe
société anonyme
dog in the manger
Society Islands
✧sovietological
Society of Jesus
solitudinarian
non-involvement
bodily function
non-judgemental
conjugal rights
conjugate angle
conjoined twins
conjunctivitis
cocktail shaker
cocktail lounge
works committee
cock-a-doodle-doo
mock-heroically
Book of Habakkuk
Book of Jeremiah
Book of Nehemiah
Book of Proverbs
book-mindedness
corkwing wrasse
poikilothermic
poikilothermal
Rocky Mountains
working classes
working capital

Words marked ✧ can also be spelled with one or more capital letters

working drawing
look for trouble
worker director
joukery-pawkery
rocket launcher
mocks the pauses
pocket an insult
mock turtle soup
work experience
monkey business
monkey's wedding
Boolean algebra
hooly and fairly
Coolgardie safe
coeliac disease
collective farm
collective noun
collectivistic
collector's item
woollen-drapery
soul-destroying
not lift a finger
zoological park
Holly Golightly
college pudding
goal difference
coelanaglyphic
pollen analysis
coaling station
polling station
go along with you
soul-confirming
collapsability
collapsibility
colliquescence
noblesse oblige
Colles' fracture
would to God that
toilet training
bouleversement
world-weariness
ollow one's nose
ollow-my-leader
Cooley's anaemia
woolly-hand crab
olly Zuckerman
omma butterfly
omme çi, comme ça
osmochemistry
osmic constant
osmeceuticals
ormidableness
omme d'affaires
oamed plastics
omme de lettres
ommodiousness
orm-referenced
osmographical
ormal solution
ommentatorial
orman Hartnell
ommandantship
ommunications
ommon Serjeant
ommon recovery
ommand economy
ommonsensical
ommon plantain
ommon Entrance
ommunion cloth
ommon toadflax

Norman Conquest
communion table
common-or-garden
common fraction
community chest
community nurse
community radio
commensurately
commensuration
foam insulation
common puffball
common multiple
Wormwood Scrubs
cosmopolitical
commercial bank
commercial room
former prophets
commissaryship
commissionaire
committee stage
committeewoman
foam at the mouth
commit to memory
going-away dress
John Barbirolli
toing and froing
foundation-stop
John Barleycorn
Fountains Abbey
mountain tallow
mountain laurel
mountain marrow
mountaineering
mountain beaver
mountain biking
mountain sorrel
Mount Annapurna
mountain stream
John Jacob Astor
Mount Aconcagua
roundaboutedly
roundaboutness
Joanna Trollope
John Galsworthy
John McLaughlin
bonne compagnie
counterbalance
counter-battery
counterchanged
counterculture
counter-current
counterfactual
counterfeiting
counsel-keeping
counsellorship
countermeasure
Bonnie and Clyde
counter-opening
counter-passant
counter-riposte
countershading
counter-subject
founders' shares
counter-skipper
counter-salient
counter-trading
counter-wrought
John of the Cross
John the Baptist
join the colours
council chamber

coincidentally
founding father
pointing device
sounding rocket
councillorship
Ioannis Metaxas
Council of State
Joan Littlewood
Mount Karisimbi
Mount Kosciusko
Cornelius Nepos
somnambulation
somnambulistic
Downing College
down in the mouth
down on one's luck
morning prayers
John Couch Adams
John Boyd Dunlop
John Logie Baird
loan collection
town councillor
John Von Neumann
Mount Pichincha
Young Pretender
Mount Paricutin
country bumpkin
country dancing
do oneself wrong
do one's homework
joint-stock bank
Mount Stromboli
do one's business
do one's own thing
John Stuart Mill
round the wicket
round the corner
sonnet sequence
Mount Tongariro
point-to-pointer
cornet-à-pistons
connaturalness
Joan Sutherland
John Rutherford
John Duns Scotus
county palatine
monosaccharide
Coromandel wood
Coromandel work
Corona Borealis
Colorado beetle
monocarpellary
coronary artery
coronary bypass
morocco leather
non-operational
holometabolism
holometabolous
Honoré de Balzac
homogenisation
homogenization
colonel-in-chief
Lofoten Islands
do someone proud
do someone right
do someone wrong
for one's own hand
borough-English
motor generator
Dorothea Brooke
Monochlamydeae

go to the country
Dorothy Hodgkin
podophthalmous
monophthongise
monophthongize
monotheistical
Dorothy L Sayers
✧monotheletical
monochromatism
robotic dancing
soporiferously
monolingualism
dolomitisation
dolomitization
Colonial Office
colonial system
Monoplacophora
corolliflorous
go to all lengths
go down the drain
go down the tubes
Bologna sausage
homoeoteleuton
homoeothermous
lobotomisation
lobotomization
monopolisation
monopolization
Solomon Islands
homoeomorphism
homoeomorphous
monotonousness
nolo contendere
nolo episcopari
colour magazine
colour fastness
honourableness
coloured pencil
colour reversal
colour-sergeant
loxodromic line
monoprionidian
colour contrast
monopropellant
Colour Symphony
Zoroastrianism
top of the league
go for the doctor
pococuranteism
coconut matting
comprehensible
comprehensibly
complexionless
morphinomaniac
compulsoriness
compensational
go up in the world
companion hatch
louping-on-stane
non-penetrative
compunctiously
morphophonemic
compurgatorial
comparableness
corpora callosa
non-performance
copper-bottomed
corpora striata
corporation tax
corporate state
copper sulphate

corpus callosum
compossibility
compassionable
composing stick
composite class
corpus striatum
corpuscularian
corpuscularity
compatibleness
hospitableness
hospital corner
hospital doctor
computer dating
compound engine
compound number
porphyrogenite
zoophytologist
mosquito canopy
conquistadores
journalisation
journalization
Konrad Adenauer
corrida de toros
comrades-in-arms
four-leaf clover
Monroe doctrine
four-centre arch
four-letter word
courageousness
corrugated iron
four-wheel drive
four-wheel-drive
fourth official
court holy water
fourth interval
poor white trash
co-ordinateness
boarding school
mourning border
correligionist
Hoare-Laval Pact
roaring forties
horrendousness
Bourbon biscuit
Court of Session
corruptibility
horror-stricken
non-residential
yours sincerely
correspondence
correspondency
non-restrictive
Socratic method
yours to command
you're telling me
House and Garden
horse artillery
Constantinople
roast-beef plant
gooseberry-wine
gooseberry-moth
gooseberry-fool
gooseberry-bush
consubstantial
consociational
✧coxsackie virus
posse comitatus
hop, step and jump
boisterousness
lokshen pudding
toasted teacake

coessentiality
consuetudinary
coastguardsman
horse-godmother
hop, skip and jump
conspiratorial
worshipfulness
boys will be boys
conscienceless
constitutively
constitutional
consuls general
consulting room
Horse Lying Down
horse latitudes
housemaid's knee
nonsensicality
consanguineous
torsion balance
House of Commons
house of ill fame
jobs for the boys
dog's-tooth grass
house of worship
noise pollution
house physician
conservatively
construability
conservational
conservatorium
constructively
✧constructivism
constructivist
constructional
construct state
conscriptional
possessiveness
topsy-turviness
God save the mark
God's own country
contrafagottos
motte and bailey
Portland cement
contrat de vente
bootlace fungus
contradictable
contradictious
Port Jackson Bay
contraindicate
contraindicant
contrapositive
contraposition
South Australia
contractedness
contrast medium
contractionary
contract bridge
postmastership
contrapuntally
contracyclical
contrary motion
horticulturist
cost-accountant
cost-accounting
contact process
corticosteroid
corticosterone
contact tracing
corticotrophin
Pontederiaceae
lost generation
for the hell of it
how the wind lies
for the life of me
for the high jump
don't get me wrong
northern lights
southern lights
root mean square
postmenopausal
for the love of it
röntgenography
for the most part
Port Georgetown
north-eastwards
south-eastwards
for the duration
not the full quid
pop the question
Pontefract cake
pontifical mass
fortifications
cost efficiency
voltage divider
contagiousness
contiguousness
Port Phillip Bay
youth hosteller
container crane
tortoise beetle
post-millennial
fortuitousness
footplatewoman
footplatewomen
hostile witness
contumaciously
contemperation
contemperature
contumeliously
contemporanean
contemporarily
contemptuously
noctambulation
potting compost
soft underbelly
contingent upon
foot-in-the-mouth
continuity girl
Fontana Magiore
continental day
continentalism
continentalist
continuous wave
continuousness
portentousness
north-north-east
north-north-west
fortune-telling
postindustrial
control account
rostrocarinate
controvertible
controvertibly
worth one's while
dogtooth violet
postpositively
postpositional
controlled drug
controllership
foot-pound force
do-it-yourselfer
soft-conscienc'd
control surface
foster-daughter
Doctors' Commons
post-production
forthrightness
conterminously
contesseration
costus arabicus
hostess trolley
south-south-east
south-south-west
Northumberland
contour farming
boatswain's mate
boatswain's call
boatswain's pipe
north-westwards
south-westwards
poetry in motion
North Yorkshire
South Yorkshire
modularisation
modularization
popularisation
popularization
locus classicus
loquaciousness
columella auris
volumetrically
document reader
solubilisation
solubilization
voluminousness
botulinum toxin
not unnaturally
coquettishness
robustiousness
voluptuousness
voluntary chain
Mobutu Seze Seko
Romulus Francis
nouveaux riches
convocationist
Torvill and Dean
convulsiveness
coevolutionary
Convolvulaceae
conventionally
conversational
conversaziones
convertibility
convexo-concave
not worth shucks
woe worth the day
forward-looking
forward pricing
Hogwarts School
hot-water bottle
polysaccharide
polyacrylamide
polymerisation
polymerization
polytheistical
Polyplacophora
polyembryonate
polynorbornene
Holy Cross Abbey
polynucleotide
polysyllabical
polysynthetism
speak by the card
upward mobility
upwardly mobile
a place in the sun
speak in tongues
speak out of turn
splat quenching
sphaerocrystal
special damages
special effects
specialisation
specialization
special licence
spectator sport
spectacularity
special verdict
specific legacy
specific charge
apical meristem
epicontinental
spectrographic
spectrological
spectroscopist
space traveller
apodeictically
epidemiologist
Epidermophyton
spread-eagleism
appendicectomy
Appendicularia
speechlessness
speech-training
spherical angle
apheliotropism
J Presper Eckert
speedway racing
epigraphically
epigrammatical
spaghetti strap
epigenetically
optimalisation
optimalization
optical pumping
upside-down cake
spring-carriage
spring mattress
spring ligament
spring-cleaning
sprightfulness
optimistically
split one's sides
split one's votes
ipsissima verba
splitting image
apple charlotte
spelaeological
applied physics
apologetically
apple of discord
apolipoprotein
apples and pears
open-handedness
spinthariscope
open-mindedness
spindle moulder
spindle-shanked
✧open university
opinionatively
upon conscience
open to question
Spanish bayonet
Spanish customs
Spanish needles
spongy platinum
up to the knocker
a prophetic week
opposite prompt
opposite number
aphoristically
optoelectronic
up to one's ears in
up to one's tricks
uproariousness
apoplectically
apophthegmatic
approach stroke
spermatogenous
spermatothecal
spermatophytic
spermatogonium
spermatorrhoea
appreciatively
spirochaetosis
upgradeability
apprehensively
appraisal wells
sporting chance
spermiogenesis
sparkling water
apartment house
apprenticement
apprenticeship
apprenticehood
sporangiophore
sporangiospore
spironolactone
sports medicine
oppressiveness
spiritualistic
spiritlessness
sporotrichosis
operating table
operationalism
operationalist
spirituousness
spirit-stirring
operative words
approved school
opus latericium
epistemologist
opisthocoelian
opisthocoelous
opisthographic
opisthoglossal
Spasskaya Tower
apostolic vicar
epistolography
ophthalmometer
ophthalmometry
ophthalmoscope
ophthalmoscopy
apothegmatical
spit and sawdust
spatiotemporal
spawning-ground
epexegetically
sphygmographic
square shooting
square brackets
squash racquets
equation of time
squadron leader
squirearchical

equiangularity
equiponderance
aquifoliaceous
squirrel monkey
bread-and-butter
Great Attractor
breakbone fever
Orlando Furioso
Orlando Gibbons
breakdown truck
armamentariums
breakfast-table
urban guerrilla
breathtakingly
wreathed string
breathlessness
wreath filament
preaching-cross
preaching friar
preaching-house
breathing space
breathing-while
organ-harmonium
organisability
organizability
organisational
organizational
erratic boulder
organic disease
organized crime
pro aris et focis
organizer-purse
breaking stress
organismically
broad in the beam
treacle mustard
break no squares
break new ground
organometallic
preadolescence
break one's heart
great prolation
organ-pipe coral
prearrangement
Great Slave Lake
break the record
read the boards
Treasure Island
great white hope
Treaty of Amiens
probabiliorism
probabiliorist
Arabic alphabet
Arabic numerals
brobdingnagian
pribble-prabble
rebendal stall
robanchaceous
ro bono publico
rab-Israeli War
race-and-favour
rocrastinator
recociousness
rocodile tears
rochelminthes
rocken spectre
rockford's Club
racticability
ractical joker
ractical units
uctification

trichinisation
trichinization
brachial artery
brachium civile
traction engine
trochlear nerve
trickle charger
proceleusmatic
precompetitive
preconcertedly
arachnological
try conclusions
triconsonantic
preconsonantal
triconsonantal
trichobacteria
trichophytosis
trichomoniasis
trichotomously
precious metals
gracious living
precipitinogen
precariousness
procuratorship
process control
tricuspid valve
prick-the-garter
grecque meander
cruciverbalism
cruciverbalist
brachydactylic
brachycephalic
brachypinakoid
brachydiagonal
procryptically
Trachypteridae
graduate school
credibility gap
predictability
Traducianistic
productiveness
productibility
production line
predaciousness
producers' goods
cradle-snatcher
grudge a thought
bridge-building
prodigiousness
Freddie Mercury
Fridtjof Nansen
tridimensional
trade paperback
Frédéric Chopin
Frederick Loewe
Frederick Soddy
Frederick Twort
predesignation
predesignatory
predestinative
predestinarian
predestination
predisposition
creditableness
traditionalism
traditionalist
traditionality
traditionarily
predeterminate
predeterminism
credit transfer

credit standing
predevelopment
irreparability
free-handedness
Praeraphaelite
irrelativeness
Green Cross Code
friendlessness
Brief Encounter
breeze concrete
breeder reactor
breech delivery
order in council
breeding ground
arsenic hydride
green labelling
Greenland whale
orderly officer
irreplevisable
free enterprise
irremovability
irrevocability
irreconcilable
irreconcilably
true-lover's knot
freedom fighter
praetorian gate
irrecognisable
irrecognizable
tree worshipper
Order of the Bath
irresoluteness
irresolubility
irrespectively
free-spokenness
irresponsively
armes parlantes
irreproachable
irreproachably
Friedrich Krupp
irreproducible
irrestrainable
Ornette Coleman
Oriental Region
argent comptant
Ernest Starling
irrefutability
irresuscitable
irresuscitably
irreducibility
prefabrication
trifacial nerve
traffic-calming
graffiti artist
traffic manager
traffic pattern
traffic returns
traffic signals
Gräfenberg spot
griffon vulture
preferentially
Griff Rhys Jones
professionally
professorially
profitableness
orographically
pragmatisation
pragmatization
pragmaticality
programme music
program trading

tragicomically
drug resistance
progress chaser
progressionary
progressionism
progressionist
Prague Symphony
dragon-standard
progenitorship
prognosticator
Gregorian chant
Gregorian modes
Gregorian tones
Gregory of Nyssa
gregariousness
Gregory of Tours
Gregory's powder
Bright's disease
Brigitte Bardot
bright and early
prohibitionary
prohibitionism
prohibitionist
orthochromatic
Orthodox Church
Archaebacteria
archgenethliac
archiepiscopal
archaeological
archaeometrist
Archaeornithes
archaeozoology
orthographical
Archbishop Tutu
graham crackers
orthopedically
orthopterology
orthophosphate
Arthur Honegger
Arthur Kornberg
Arthur Koestler
Arthur Griffith
Arthur Sullivan
Brahms and Liszt
architectonics
arrhythmically
archetypically
droit au travail
ordinary seaman
ordinary degree
ordinary shares
Eroica Symphony
greisenisation
greisenization
praiseworthily
brain-fever bird
Irving Langmuir
Ornithodelphia
ornithodelphic
ornithological
ornithomorphic
ornithophilous
prairie chicken
Training Agency
training wheels
trailing vortex
artificialness
artificial silk
article of virtu
artillery-plant
Artium Magister

traitorousness
Mr Mistoffelees
articulateness
projectisation
projectization
projective test
brake parachute
A Rake's Progress
Irek Mukhamedov
Uralian emerald
Brillat-Savarin
frolicsomeness
prolocutorship
drill-husbandry
proletarianise
proletarianize
proletarianism
grammaticality
grammaticaster
from bank to bank
from bad to worse
prima ballerina
crème de la crème
premeditatedly
premier danseur
trumpet-tongued
from time to time
Kremlinologist
premillenarian
criminal lawyer
criminological
tremendousness
Urim and Thummim
Primrose League
gram-equivalent
primary battery
primary colours
primordial soup
primary process
promise-breaker
promise-crammed
promise-keeping
promissory note
bremsstrahlung
aromatherapist
trimethylamine
brand awareness
transamination
transcendental
transcendently
transcutaneous
✧transcaucasian
Frank Churchill
granddad collar
granadilla tree
printed circuit
front-end loaded
front-end system
fringe medicine
prince's feather
Prince of Orange
Prince Charming
grangerisation
grangerization
prince-imperial
grande toilette
orange-coloured
orange-squeezer
cranberry sauce
transformative
transformation

transfer ticket
transformistic
transferential
transfusionist
uranographical
prenegotiation
French-Canadian
French marigold
Bran the Blessed
bronchodilator
French vermouth
bronchiectasis
French knickers
French-polisher
trencher-knight
trencher-friend
French dressing
principal focus
principalities
principal parts
Frankie Dettori
Ironside Edmund
printing office
bringings forth
Bringing Up Baby
drinking-up time
transitiveness
transitionally
Francis Kilvert
fringillaceous
Grenville Davey
Granville Hicks
transitoriness
Francis of Sales
grandiloquence
Francis Picabia
Francis Poulenc
Francis Quarles
frontierswoman
wrong in the head
Grand Jury Prize
crinkle-crankle
drink like a fish
Franklin Pierce
transliterator
transmigrative
transmigration
transmigratory
transmogrified
transmissively
transmissivity
transmissional
Drang nach Osten
Ordnance Survey
pronunciamento
Bruno of Cologne
François Villon
Françoise Sagan
François Guizot
transplantable
transpicuously
transportation
transportingly
transport rider
Grand St Bernard
Vreni Schneider
grand serjeanty
transsexualism
transsexuality
bring to account
Trinity College

bring to justice
trinitrophenol
trinitrotoluol
Trinitarianism
Frank Tarkenton
crinkum-crankum
trinkum-trankum
bring up the rear
Transvaal daisy
transvaluation
transversality
transverse wave
transvestitism
ergocalciferol
arrondissement
preoperational
cry one's eyes out
prioritisation
prioritization
cryobiological
arboricultural
A Room of One's Own
Brooks Robinson
cry out to be done
cry out to be used
A Room with a View
drop handlebars
cryptaesthesia
cryptaesthetic
✧tropic of Cancer
propaedeutical
Triple Alliance
triple-tonguing
triphenylamine
uropygial gland
propagandistic
proprioceptive
graphic formula
graphic granite
graphitisation
graphitization
graphics tablet
proprietorship
propeller-blade
propeller shaft
tropologically
preponderantly
drop one's bundle
cryptorchidism
trophoneurosis
cryptococcosis
cryptosporidia
trapdoor spider
cryptographist
drip irrigation
proportionable
proportionably
proportionless
proportionment
proportionally
tripersonalism
tripersonalist
tripersonality
proper fraction
properispomena
property master
Krapp's Last Tape
preposterously
crêpes suzettes
propitiatorily
propitiousness

trapezohedrons
croque-monsieur
Arbroath smokie
pre-Reformation
Tristan da Cunha
crystal healing
crystal indices
Frisian Islands
crystallomancy
crystallisable
crystallizable
cross assembler
crystal therapy
crossbar switch
cross batteries
trisoctahedron
cross-correlate
brush discharge
trustee account
proscenium arch
Prosper Mérimée
prosperousness
Brussels carpet
✧brussels sprout
cross-fingering
cross-fertilise
cross-fertilize
prosthodontics
prosthodontist
Aristide Briand
cross-infection
crossing-warden
dressing-jacket
Prussification
cross-marketing
presumptuously
presentability
presentational
presence of mind
prosencephalic
prosencephalon
presentiveness
presentimental
prison-breaking
Bristol-diamond
cross one's heart
crossover voter
Bristol fashion
aristocratical
Crossopterygii
cross-pollinate
presupposition
preservability
cross-reference
dress-rehearsal
Tristram Shandy
prescriptively
proscriptively
prescriptivism
prescriptivist
cross-sectional
grass someone up
grasp the nettle
press the button
trust territory
grist to the mill
pressure helmet
pressure vessel
pressure cooker
pressurisation
pressurization

Irish wolfhound
presbyterially
Aretha Franklin
trituberculate
trituberculism
protected state
protectiveness
truth condition
Brother Cadfael
brothel creeper
froth flotation
Mrs Tiggy-Winkle
Crutched-friars
prettification
trithionic acid
gratuitousness
prittle-prattle
arithmetic mean
arithmetically
Britannia metal
prothonotarial
prothonotariat
protoplasmatic
erythroblastic
fraternisation
fraternization
erythropoiesis
erythropoietic
erythropoietin
preterite tense
protospathaire
Arctostaphylos
British bulldog
British cholera
British disease
Fritz Schaudinn
protistologist
Prototracheata
protrusiveness
Protevangelium
pretty-pretties
protozoologist
traumatisation
traumatization
Urquhart Castle
preux chevalier
groundlessness
ground squirrel
groundbreaking
argumenti causa
Crouched-friars
brought forward
draughtsperson
Broughty Castle
group insurance
troubleshooter
group selection
proud-stomached
trivialisation
trivialization
Trivial Pursuit®
provided school
providentially
prevailing wind
Bravais lattice
traveller's tale
Travellers Club
traveller's tree
travelling folk
travel sickness
preventability

preventiveness
provincial rose
driving licence
proventriculus
Trevor McDonald
Trevor Chappell
driver's license
provost marshal
private baptism
private company
private patient
drive to the wall
graveyard shift
crown and anchor
draw the curtain
draw the long bow
growth industry
growth promoter
Brownian motion
proximate cause
proximity talks
crux criticorum
greywacke-slate
grey literature
Greyhound Derby
grey-goose quill
grey-goose shaft
Greyfriars Hall
prayerlessness
fray at the edges
frozen shoulder
as far as I can see
asparagus-stone
Osvaldo Ardiles
Island of Staffa
island universe
Oswald Spengler
escape velocity
escape sequence
Estates General
Islamicisation
Islamicization
escalier dérobé
a stab in the dark
Oskar Kokoschka
Ismail Merchant
espagnole sauce
Isaac Rosenberg
Isabelle Adjani
Isabelita Perón
psychogenetics
psychotechnics
psychometrical
psychoneuroses
psychoneurosis
psychoneurotic
psychochemical
psychophysical
psycholinguist
psychoanalysis
psychoanalytic
psychosomatics
psychodramatic
psychographics
psychodynamics
isodiametrical
osteoarthrosis
osteoarthritic
osteoarthritis
ascending aorta
osteodermatous

asseveratingly
Isle of Anglesey
Isle of Colonsay
Osteoglossidae
esterification
osteologically
as near as dammit
asset-stripping
asbestos cement
ostentatiously
as the crow flies
as the case may be
as who should say
eschatological
as fit as a fiddle
Ustilaginaceae
a stiff upper lip
oscillographic
astigmatically
psyllid yellows
psilanthropism
psilanthropist
Asclepiadaceae
isolated replay
asymmetric bars
asymmetrically
asymptotically
asynchronously
osmoregulation
osmoregulatory
a shot in the dark
associationism
a sop to Cerberus
psephoanalysis
astrochemistry
ostrich-feather
astrogeologist
astrologically
astronomically
a strong stomach
A Shropshire Lad
astrophysicist
sothiocyanate
sotopic number
isque ad nauseam
seudaesthesia
seudepigrapha
seudepigraphy
seudoscorpion
seudomembrane
seudomorphism
seudomorphous
seudosolution
seudo-archaism
seudosymmetry
seudonymously
stuary English
teal a marriage
trawberry mark
trawberry leaf
rawberry roan
rawberry tree
t Kanchenjunga
rand-scouring
raddle-legged
Dabeoc's heath
eamed pudding
range Meeting
daggers drawn
raightjacket
raight ticket
straight as a die
steaming lights
stratification
strabismometer
stratigraphist
straw in the wind
it's a small world
Atlas Mountains
attainableness
strain courtesy
stray radiation
stealth fighter
stick at nothing
stock car racing
stocking filler
stocking stitch
stacking system
stick one's bib in
stick one's oar in
stichometrical
Stockton-on-Tees
sticky-fingered
utter barrister
stretching-bond
stretching iron
steel engraving
stoechiometric
steering column
etherification
steeplechasing
steeple-crowned
attemptability
Uther Pendragon
St George's cross
Ethel Rosenberg
strepsipterous
stress fracture
attention value
street-credible
Stafford Cripps
stigmatisation
stigmatization
stigmatiferous
stigmatophilia
stegocephalian
stegocephalous
stage direction
St Agnes's flower
stagflationary
steganographic
steganographer
et sic de ceteris
strike a balance
strike a bargain
strikebreaking
stoicheiometry
stoichiometric
striking circle
stainless steel
striated muscle
attitudinarian
attitudinising
attitudinizing
Stokesay Castle
Italianisation
Italianization
Stella Kowalski
stalactitiform
Steller's sea-cow
stultification
otolaryngology
Stillson wrench®
stiletto-heeled
utility program
utilitarianise
utilitarianize
utilitarianism
utility vehicle
atomic radiator
atomic mass unit
stomachfulness
stamp collector
stoma-care nurse
stamping-ground
etymologically
stumbling-block
Stamford Bridge
stoma therapist
stomatogastric
standard candle
standard-bearer
Stannary Courts
ethnobotanical
ethnic minority
stone-cold sober
stand confessed
Stanley Baldwin
St Anne's College
Stanley Kubrick
Stanley Spencer
at one fell swoop
ethnographical
St Anthony's fire
stinking badger
stinging nettle
standing orders
stand in the gate
sting in the tail
ethnologically
Stone of Destiny
St Andrew's cross
at one's disposal
stand the racket
stand upon terms
stoope-gallaunt
stroke of genius
strobe lighting
at someone's beck
Ettore Sottsass
strong language
et hoc genus omne
strobilisation
strobilization
Otto Lilienthal
St John's College
attorney in fact
Mt Popocatepetl
Stephen Decatur
Stephen Dedalus
Stephen Dorrell
Stephen Hawking
Stephen Langton
Stephen Spender
step on the juice
stupendousness
staphyloplasty
staphylococcal
staphylococcus
eternalisation
eternalization
Sturmabteilung
attractiveness
yttro-columbite
pteridophilist
star-of-the-earth
storage battery
pterygoid plate
uterogestation
starch hyacinth
storm in a teacup
starting handle
Stirling Castle
starting pistol
starting blocks
Stirling engine
starting stalls
stare in the face
startle colours
pterylographic
ottrelite-slate
stir one's stumps
stereotactical
stereoscopical
stereometrical
star connection
stertorousness
stereospecific
stereoisomeric
St Cross College
yttro-tantalite
at a rate of knots
stirrup leather
static pressure
statuesqueness
at it like knives
Staten-Generaal
state of affairs
stationariness
stationary wave
Stationers' Hall
station-manager
state socialism
states of matter
Staubbach Falls
stout-heartedly
St Hugh's College
a touch of the sun
stouth and routh
Ithuriel's spear
at full throttle
strut one's stuff
St Justin Martyr
structural gene
Steven Weinberg
A Town Like Alice
Mt Ixtaccihuatl
ethylene glycol
it's your funeral
put a call on hold
Musala Mountain
subarborescent
cup-and-ring mark
lunar distances
Sulawesi Island
subaggregation
human guinea pig
subatmospheric
Suzanne Lenglen
put a good face on
human resources
subassociation
subalternation
Lucas van Leyden
Lubbock Airport
rumbledethumps
Hubble constant
rumblegumption
turbofan engine
turbogenerator
tumbling barrel
Tunbridge Wells
rubbing alcohol
turbine steamer
numberlessness
Humbert Humbert
lumbersomeness
Dunbartonshire
rubber solution
number-cruncher
lumbar puncture
purchase system
luncheon-basket
juice extractor
functional food
durchkomponirt
Durchmusterung
subconsciously
subcontinental
vulcanological
subcontracting
subcontrariety
quick on the draw
susceptiveness
susceptibility
successfulness
successiveness
successionless
successionally
succession duty
quicksilvering
quicksilverish
subcutaneously
functus officio
punctuationist
quadragenarian
quadrangularly
subduction zone
muddle-headedly
bundle of laughs
bundle of nerves
hundred-per-cent
purdah carriage
quodlibetarian
quadrigeminate
quadrigeminous
quadrisyllabic
quadrisyllable
✧fundamentalism
fundamentalist
fundamentality
Duc de Richelieu
murdering-piece
muddy the waters
Sunday painters
superambitious
superannuation
Queen Anne's lace
Queen Anne's dead
tuner amplifier
funeral parlour
superabsorbent
superabundance
superciliously
supercelestial

superconfident
supercontinent
superconductor
supercargoship
superexcellent
superelevation
Queen Elizabeth
supereminently
supererogative
supererogation
supererogatory
Eugene Goossens
superessential
Duke of Hamilton
superficialise
superficialize
superficiality
superfoetation
Duke of Portland
cuneiform bones
super flyweight
Jude the Obscure
superincumbent
superinduction
superinfection
Eugenio Montale
Eudemian Ethics
superimportant
superintendent
superintending
Sudeck's atrophy
supernormality
supernaturally
surefootedness
ruse contre ruse
superovulation
superphosphate
Queensland blue
queen substance
supersonically
supersonic boom
supersensitive
superstructive
superstruction
superstructure
superscription
supersaturated
Queen's evidence
superterranean
numerus clausus
bureau de change
rule out of court
supervisorship
suffice it to say
turf accountant
surface tension
ruff and honours
puffin crossing
sufferableness
Kupferschiefer
out for the count
furfuraldehyde
run for one's life
buffer solution
Musgrave Ranges
surgical spirit
luggage-carrier
Jürgen Habermas
subgenerically
surgeon general
vulgar fraction
suggestiveness
suggestibility
Hugh MacDiarmid
push technology
Cuthbert's beads
push the boat out
euphuistically
authentication
rush one's fences
mushroom-anchor
Luther Vandross
euphorbiaceous
musical glasses
audit committee
jurisdictional
businessperson
audio-frequency
subinfeudation
subinfeudatory
municipal court
humidification
judicial factor
judicial review
judicial combat
judicial murder
musicians' cramp
munition-worker
bulimia nervosa
auxiliary nurse
pugilistically
lucid intervals
put in mothballs
numismatically
audiometrician
Julian calendar
luminous energy
Nudibranchiata
nudibranchiate
Julius Dedekind
cubic saltpetre
subinsinuation
Julius von Sachs
Lucius Apuleius
music therapist
run in the family
subject heading
subjectiveness
subjectivistic
Turks and Caicos
huckleberrying
Buckley's chance
Turkish delight
bucket and spade
Turkey merchant
nuclear fission
nuclearisation
nuclearization
Guillaume Dufay
Guillaume Farel
nuclear-powered
nuclear physics
nuclear reactor
nuclear warfare
public defender
Public Image Ltd
public document
public speaking
public spending
public-spirited
public attorney
duplicate ratio
public nuisance
bull-headedness
pull technology
Guillermo Vilas
fully-fashioned
pull the long bow
pull the strings
quilting-cotton
Dublin Bay prawn
Hurlingham Club
outlandishness
burling-machine
pull one's weight
null-modem cable
full-court press
full to bursting
Sully Prudhomme
Guild Socialism
full steam ahead
quality control
Ku Klux Klansman
Muammar Gaddafi
submicroscopic
rummlegumption
cum multis aliis
rummelgumption
subminiaturise
subminiaturize
busman's holiday
pulmonary valve
submergibility
submersibility
summary offence
summer solstice
submissiveness
Sunny Afternoon
pugnaciousness
turnkey package
quintessential
quincentennial
turn the air blue
turn the stomach
quantitatively
quantification
quantity theory
running balance
running banquet
running footman
turn on one's heel
running rigging
running repairs
burn one's faggot
turn one's back on
turn up one's toes
vulnerableness
quinquecostate
quinquefoliate
quinquefarious
quantum gravity
quinquagesimal
quinquennially
quinquevalence
put on a pedestal
automatic drive
autoradiograph
automatic pilot
Euro-Parliament
✧Aurora Borealis
out of character
out of condition
Euroscepticism
put one's shirt on
Eurocentricity
run off one's feet
Rudolf von Laban
mucoviscidosis
tumorigenicity
autobiographic
autobiographer
Ludovic Kennedy
eulogistically
auto-intoxicant
out of one's depth
out of one's skull
autocoprophagy
humoursomeness
autograph album
autocratically
mucous membrane
furor scribendi
put on the market
out of the window
out of this world
put out to tender
Yukon Territory
auto-suggestive
auto-suggestion
autotypography
sulphacetamide
sulphathiazole
sulphanilamide
sulphadimidine
humpback bridge
Rump Parliament
auspiciousness
suspiciousness
supplementally
purple-coloured
suppressor cell
suppressor grid
supplicatingly
surprisingness
turpentine tree
suspensibility
vulpine opossum
suspend payment
Humphry Clinker
outperformance
Humphrey Bogart
purposefulness
surpassingness
suppositionary
supposititious
turpeth mineral
sulphur dioxide
sulphurisation
sulphurization
sulphurous acid
jusqu'auboutist
quaquaversally
turquoise-green
quart and tierce
curricula vitae
puerperal fever
puerperal mania
quarter-binding
quarter-gallery
quarter-pounder
quarter section
outrageousness
Guardian Angels
Supralapsarian
supramolecular
querimoniously
current account
current affairs
current bedding
current density
currente calamo
surrender value
quarantine flag
au grand sérieux
run rings around
eutrophication
suprasegmental
nutritiousness
Murray Gell-Mann
quartz-porphyry
substance abuse
Russianisation
Russianization
substantialise
substantialize
substantialism
substantiation
substantialist
substantiality
Russian thistle
substantivally
Russo-Byzantine
Aussichtspunkt
pulse diagnosis
Burschenschaft
question master
question of fact
substitutively
substitutivity
substitutional
put someone wise
Cuisenaire rods
cuisine minceur
nursing officer
purse-snatching
Tuatha dé Danaan
Australian Alps
rustic capitals
Eustachian tube
multicuspidate
futtock-shrouds
Kurt Schwitters
Curtley Ambrose
run the gauntlet
put the screws on
put the whammy on
put the change on
put the finger on
cuttlefish bone
put the tin hat on
put the tin lid on
put the kibosh on
tug the forelock
further outlook
put the brakes on
rub the wrong way
run their course
turtle graphics
buttress-thread
ductless glands
justifiability
multifactorial
multifoliolate
multiflora rose
multifariously

hunt-the-slipper
sustainability
sustained yield
curtain lecture
quota immigrant
curtain walling
multilaterally
huntsman spider
multum non multa
multinucleated
hunting leopard
hunting-leopard
just intonation
putting the shot
button mushroom
Multnomah Falls
multi-ownership
multiple-choice
multiple cinema
Bustopher Jones
multiplicative
multiplication
multiprocessor
hunter-gatherer
multiracialism
quattrocentism
quattrocentist
gutter-merchant
subterrestrial
buttery fingers
butterfingered
multarticulate
butterfly knife
cultural cringe
butterfly screw
butterfly valve
mustard plaster
culture vulture
quite something
curtate annuity
multithreading
Gustave Courbet
cumulativeness
cumulative dose
cumulative vote
cucurbitaceous
mutual inductor
ugubriousness
Auguste Blanqui
August Weismann
Auguste Lumière
Augustinianism
umultuousness
Auguste Piccard
usumu Tonegawa
Dunvegan Castle
urvilinearity
uf Wiedersehen
utward-sainted
uly Revolution
ury the hatchet
uoyant density
udyard Kipling
uzzle velocity
uizzification
viation spirit
voidable costs
valbard Island
vil-mindedness
volutionarily
volutionistic
even-handedness
evangelicalism
evangelisation
evangelization
avenger of blood
evaporated milk
overcapitalise
overcapitalize
overeat oneself
over-absorption
avariciousness
overscrupulous
overdependence
over-determined
over-refinement
average costing
over-the-counter
overwhelmingly
Dvorak keyboard
overindulgence
overpoweringly
over-confidence
overcommitment
overcompensate
overcorrection
overpopulation
overspecialise
overspecialize
ivory-porcelain
overproduction
overprotective
every second day
Évariste Galois
overestimation
overburdensome
over my dead body
sweating system
two-dimensional
Swedish massage
sweet-and-twenty
sweet horsemint
a week of Sundays
two for his heels
two-for-his-heels
a will of one's own
swallow-shrikes
swimming trunks
swans a-swimming
twinned crystal
twin-lens reflex
swindge-buckler
swingling-stock
Gwyneth Paltrow
twenty-four-hour
swoop-stake-like
swoopstake-like
two-pot screamer
a warm reception
sword-swallower
qwerty keyboard
Swiss army knife
two-start thread
a wise thing to do
'twixt sun and sun
expanding metal
exsanguination
exhaustiveness
exhaustibility
expansion board
expansionistic
expansion joint
exacerbescence
execution error
extended family
extended memory
extended credit
experimentally
experienceable
experienceless
expedientially
experientially
external degree
extemporaneity
extemporaneous
excess capacity
expense account
extensionalism
extensionality
exceptionalism
exceptionality
ex-servicewoman
oxygen cylinder
oxyhaemoglobin
exhilaratingly
extinguishable
extinguishment
excision repair
explorationist
exclusion order
explosive rivet
exclaustration
examine-in-chief
exempt supplies
✧Oxford movement
excommunicable
excommunicator
extortionately
excruciatingly
extractability
extra-condensed
extracanonical
extracorporeal
extraforaneous
excrementitial
extra marmalade
extramaritally
extreme unction
extrinsicality
extraneousness
extraordinaire
extra-parochial
express company
expressiveness
expression mark
expressionless
expression stop
express oneself
express volumes
extravehicular
exasperatingly
existentialism
existentialist
axis of symmetry
ex utraque parte
exothermically
excuse my French
excursion train
pyjama trousers
gynaecological
gynandromorphy
hydatid disease
dynamic geology
pyramidologist
dynamic routing
pyramid selling
tyrannicalness
synaposematism
dynamometrical
dynamo-electric
symbolicalness
myocardiopathy
synchronically
Lyndon B Johnson
hyperaesthesia
hyperaesthesic
hyperaesthetic
hyperacuteness
hyperbolically
hyperbatically
hypercriticise
hypercriticize
hypercriticism
hypercalcaemia
hyperconscious
hypercatalexis
hyperextension
hyperglycaemia
hyperinflation
hyperkeratosis
hyperlipidemia
hypernatraemia
pyrenomycetous
hypersensitise
hypersensitive
hypersensitize
cybersquatting
synectics group
hypertrophical
cyberterrorism
cyberterrorist
hyperventilate
mythical theory
Pythagoreanism
by the holy poker
mythologically
pyrheliometric
by the same token
Lyrical Ballads
Sybille Bedford
Cybill Shepherd
Tyrian cynosure
lyriform organs
Cyril Ramaphosa
Sybil Thorndike
cyclobarbitone
cyclic compound
cyclanthaceous
pyelonephritic
pyelonephritis
cyclopentolate
cycle per second
hyaluronic acid
myrmecological
myrmecophagous
myrmecophilous
dysmenorrhoeic
dysmenorrhoeal
symmetrisation
symmetrization
symmetrophobia
cyanoacetylene
cyanobacterium
cyanocobalamin
Lyon King of arms
by one's lonesome
hypnotherapist
zygomatic fossa
pyrogallic acid
gyroscopically
pyro-acetic acid
pyrometallurgy
cytogeneticist
pyrotechnician
hypodermically
hypomenorrhoea
Syrophoenician
Zygophyllaceae
sycophantishly
hypochondriasm
hypochondriast
hypothyroidism
hypophysectomy
pyrophosphoric
hypothetically
pyrophotograph
cytophotometer
cytophotometry
mylonitisation
mylonitization
hypomixolydian
hypoallergenic
hypocoristical
gynomonoecious
Zygobranchiata
zygobranchiate
hypocritically
gyrostabiliser
gyrostabilizer
hypostatically
xylopyrography
xylotypography
synonymousness
lymphangiogram
lyophilisation
lyophilization
nymphomaniacal
symptomatology
lymphoid tissue
sympathetic ink
sympathy strike
hydro-aeroplane
hydrobiologist
hydrocellulose
hydrocephalous
hydrocortisone
hydrocoralline
hydrodynamical
hybrid computer
hydroextractor
hydrographical
hygrographical
dyer's-greenweed
hydrogeologist
cyproheptadine
Pyrrhic victory
hydrologically
hydromechanics
hydromagnetics
hydronephrosis
hydronephrotic
Hydropterideae
hydropneumatic
hydroponically
hydrophobicity

Words marked ✧ can also be spelled with one or more capital letters

hydrosulphuric
hygroscopicity
by prescription
hydraulic brake
hydraulic press
hydroxyapatite
cystic fibrosis
synthetic resin
hyetographical
nyctaginaceous
Pyotr Kropotkin
dysteleologist
cystolithiasis
systems analyst
systems program
system operator
systematically
system building
Wynton Marsalis
Lytton Strachey
hysterectomise
hysterectomize
mysteriousness
oyster mushroom
Cyrus McCormick
Sylvian fissure
Kyzyl Kum Desert
azidothymidine
ozone-depleting
ozone depletion
azione teatrale
Ozark Mountains

15 – even

Maracana Stadium
Kawasaki disease
Jawaharlal Nehru
Bahasa Indonesia
Kalamazoo® system
Parasaurolophus
Fatal Attraction
Madama Butterfly
balance of nature
managed currency
Japanese lantern
management buy-in
palace of culture
paraheliotropic
Yamabe no Akahito
parametral plane
La Cage aux Folles
Madame Butterfly
katathermometer
parachute troops
salami technique
paralinguistics
parasiticalness
Hawaiian Islands
parabiotic twins
capacity for heat
Papal knighthood
catallactically
parallel imports
parallelepipeda
cataclysmically
✧balaclava helmet
basal metabolism
japanned leather
palaeopathology
palaeomagnetism
palaeoecologist
palaeogeography
palaeophytology
paradoxicalness
paragogic future
palaeobiologist
palaeolimnology
parasol mushroom
palaeoanthropic
Palaeoanthropus
palaeobotanical
palaeozoologist
data compression
palaeographical
palaeontography
palaeontologist
palaeoethnology
malacopterygian
hamadryas baboon
paragraphically
malassimilation
parasympathetic
Barbra Streisand
Barbican Theatre
cabbage palmetto
Kasbah of Algiers
Cambridge roller
carbonic-acid gas
carbon anhydride
Barbara Cartland
Barbara Hepworth
Barbara Stanwyck
Sabbath-breaking
harbour of refuge
harbour porpoise
bacchanalianism
catch-as-catch-can
paschal full moon
dance attendance
fancy dress party
Marchese Marconi
Gaucher's disease
pancreatic juice
sanctimoniously
Malcolm Bradbury
Malcolm Campbell
masculine ending
masculinisation
masculinization
vascular disease
vascularisation
vascularization
Pascal's triangle
carcinogenicity
sarcenchymatous
malconformation
Fanconi's anaemia
catch one's breath
Pasch of the Cross
batch processing
batch production
calcium chloride
calcium sulphate
gaudeamus igitur
landscape-marble
hard act to follow
saddler-corporal
saddle-bill stork
Candle in the Wind
hard-heartedness
saddler-sergeant
Cardiff Arms Park
candelabrum tree
Randall Davidson
Magdalen College
landing-carriage
hard-and-fastness
Cardinal Mazarin
haud one's wheesht
hard-rock geology
cards on the table
cardiopulmonary
mandarin palette
wandering sailor
maldistribution
hand it to someone
lay down one's arms
yadda yadda yadda
Dame Barbara Ward
Lateran Councils
camera-ready copy
Dame Maggie Smith
make fair weather
Dame Laura Knight
lateral thinking
make a clean break
make a clean sweep
maleic hydrazide
take advantage of
make a difference
calendarisation
calendarization
laser disc player
laser disk player
Dame Rebecca West
Mare Serenitatis
Dame Nellie Melba
Bakewell pudding
have seen service
Careless Whisper
casement curtain
water equivalent
Vale of Glamorgan
materfamiliases
paterfamiliases
wages-fund theory
make a good dinner
have the best of it
take the chill off
have the edge over
take their course
make short work of
take the shine off
take the shilling
have what it takes
take the wraps off
Cape nightingale
material fallacy
materialistical
materialisation
materialization
Batesian mimicry
Haleakala Crater
Waterloo cracker
Dame Flora Robson
lamellirostrate
case-insensitive
Capernaitically
take a name in vain
take into account
make inroads into
have one's marbles
make one's manners
have one's end away
have one's knife in
take one's cue from
make one's excuses
maternity rights
Mare Moscoviense
take some beating
have someone's ear
make someone's day
make someone tick
take someone up on
categoricalness
make common cause
Dame Joan Hammond
take to one's heels
take to one's heart
take no prisoners
water on the brain
category mistake
save appearances
take upon oneself
Balearic Islands
take French leave
sales resistance
Dame Iris Murdoch
Haversian canals
Vanessa Redgrave
have a screw loose
water tube boiler
take at advantage
gazetted officer
parenthetically
have itching ears
take it on the chin
paper tape reader
take it or leave it
take it from there
take it lying down
Dame Muriel Spark
make out one's case
maneuverability
have two left feet
have a way with one
have by the throat
San Francisco Bay
half-heartedness
Haffner Symphony
Manfred Symphony
MacFarlane's buat
par for the course
laugh and lay down
laugh and lie down
Marghanita Laski
Vaughan Williams
lay great store by
bargain-basement
laughing jackass
laugh like a drain
hanging buttress
marginal tax rate
marginal revenue
marginalisation
marginalization
manganese bronze
manganese nodule
kangaroo closure
kangaroo justice
Margaret Beckett
Margaret of Anjou
margaritiferous
Margaret Forster
Margaret Drabble
caught and bowled
naughty nineties
Sangster Airport
cache controller
Dashiell Hammett
Kathleen Ferrier
Daphne Du Maurier
Daphnis and Chloe
✧catholicisation
✧catholicization
Rachel Whiteread
Dag Hammarskjöld
mathematisation
mathematization
Aachen Cathedral
Nathanael Greene
machine language
cash in one's chips
Nathan Söderblom
machine-readable
machine-washable
fashionableness
bathroom cabinet
manhood suffrage
pathophysiology
Hay-Herrán Treaty
Father Christmas
Mathurin Régnier
Katherine Graham
gathering-ground
Catherine Howard
Manhattan Island
pathetic fallacy
catheterisation
catheterization
lachryma Christi
capital gains tax
Fatima Whitbread
navigation light
capitation grant
Marie Antoinette
David Cronenberg
manic-depressive
variae lectiones
canine distemper
cabinet minister
marine insurance
native companion
Mariner's Compass

Words marked ✧ can also be spelled with one or more capital letters

radio-gramophone
saving reverence
racing certainty
laying-on of hands
radiogoniometer
Hamish Henderson
basidiomycetous
Kasimir Malevich
Daniel Barenboim
Daniel Bernoulli
Camille Pissarro
radiolarian ooze
capillary action
papillary muscle
lapis lazuli blue
lapis lazuli ware
radio microphone
radium emanation
radiometrically
Valiant-for-Truth
Patient Griselda
National Gallery
national service
National Theatre
rational horizon
National Society
National Lottery
nationalisation
rationalisation
nationalization
rationalization
Californian bees
California poppy
mari complaisant
radioscopically
ladies' companion
radiotelegraphy
magisterialness
canisterisation
canisterization
canicular period
Wasily Kandinsky
cavity radiation
amily allowance
amily fruit tree
San Joaquin River
Sam Jackson Snead
back-calculation
backward-looking
alkland Islands
awksbill turtle
alk a blue streak
ackadaisically
ackney-coachman
ackney carriage
ack-of-all-trades
alk against time
alk like a pen-gun
ankim Chatterji
alking dragline
alk on eggshells
ack-in-the-pulpit
ack on one's heels
Wackford Squeers
ask-conditioned
ack to the Future
ack to square one
anker's envelope
ack translation
ackground tasks
ackground queue
market-gardening
packet switching
bankruptcy order
railway crossing
tableau curtains
railway carriage
parliament-hinge
Parliament clock
parliament-house
parliamentarian
parliamentarily
parliamentarism
tableaux vivants
sail near the wind
hall of residence
Earl of Shelburne
Earl of Liverpool
Earl of Lichfield
Earl of Rochester
Earl of Godolphin
Earl of Strafford
daylight robbery
wall gillyflower
Paul Pierre Broca
wallflower brown
Marlene Dietrich
falling sickness
balloon catheter
fall to the ground
ballroom dancing
Earl Mountbatten
Callippic Period
wallop in a tether
paulo-post-future
Wallis and Futuna
Callitrichaceae
cable television
Karl Guthe Jansky
fall over oneself
Palma de Mallorca
warm-heartedness
haemoglobinuria
warm-bloodedness
Tasmanian myrtle
Raymond Chandler
Raymond Poincaré
Raymond Williams
hammerhead shark
palm-tree justice
Carmarthenshire
✧hammer and sickle
gamma securities
Malmesbury Abbey
maintainability
rain cats and dogs
cannibalisation
cannibalization
Magna est Veritas
magnifying glass
Saint George's Bay
cannellini beans
carnal knowledge
darning mushroom
warning triangle
rainbow-coloured
rainbow dressing
manneristically
Magnus Magnusson
carnassial tooth
magnetic battery
magnetic therapy
magnetic forming
magnetic compass
magnetic equator
magnetic pyrites
magneto-electric
paint the town red
cannot choose but
main purpose rule
day-neutral plant
Raynaud's disease
carnivorousness
panoramic camera
Radovan Karadzic
sadomasochistic
nasogastric tube
Harold Macmillan
Manon des Sources
War of Devolution
lay one's finger on
eat one's heart out
Baroness Kennedy
pay off old scores
panophthalmitis
Bay of Heligoland
masochistically
majority carrier
majority verdict
War of Jenkins' Ear
Mason Locke Weems
Jaroslav Seifert
paroemiographer
law of mass action
Madonna and Child
Madonna del Prato
vasoconstrictor
labour-intensive
War of the Pacific
Aaron Temkin Beck
Jacobus Arminius
Carolus Linnaeus
manoeuvrability
Ralph Abercromby
malpractitioner
Pan-Presbyterian
malpresentation
campaign against
Tadpole and Taper
carpometacarpus
harp on one string
Harpers and Queen
Caspar Bartholin
Ralph Richardson
tamper-resistant
damp-proof course
Macquarie Island
Jacques Cousteau
Marquês de Pombal
Jacqueline du Pré
banqueting-house
Jacquetta Hawkes
Marquis of Granby
marriage partner
marriageability
marriage-licence
Marriage à la Mode
carriage and pair
marriage-portion
carriage-forward
carriage driving
Maurice Johnston
sarraceniaceous
carry conviction
matric potential
macrocosmically
labradorescence
Gabriela Mistral
Maureen Connolly
married quarters
pair of virginals
caprifoliaceous
pair of compasses
carry into effect
sacral vertebrae
Sacramento River
warrantableness
Laurence Olivier
Lawrence Durrell
carry off the bell
madreporic plate
Patripassianism
saprophytically
macrosporangium
macroscopically
Taurus Mountains
Zagros Mountains
walrus moustache
Saorstát Eireann
harrowing of hell
Barrow-in-Furness
mass radiography
Hanseatic league
marshalling yard
Marshall Islands
mass observation
false conception
marsh-cinquefoil
Tay-Sachs disease
Hans Reichenbach
laissez-faireism
Wars of the Vendée
Caesalpiniaceae
Wassily Leontief
Hansel and Gretel
balsamic vinegar
tan someone's hide
tarsometatarsal
tarsometatarsus
Carson McCullers
passenger-pigeon
✧lapsang souchong
Sans Souci Museum
raise one's dander
raise one's sights
pass round the hat
Marsipobranchii
causa sine qua non
raise to the bench
Jan Smuts Airport
passive immunity
passive resister
Ramsay MacDonald
facts and figures
partial fraction
partial pressure
Martha's Vineyard
particle physics
Nantucket Island
Nautical Almanac
particularistic
pantechnicon-van
catted and fished
say the magic word
Battle of Salamis
Battle of Cambrai
Battle of Marengo
Battle of Salerno
Battle of Cassino
Battle of Lepanto
Battle of Leuctra
Walther Flemming
Battle of Leipzig
Battle of the Nile
Battle of the Neva
Battle of Thapsus
Matthew Flinders
Battle of Okinawa
Battle of Flodden
Battle of Plassey
Battle of Colenso
Battle of Cowpens
Battle of Corunna
Battle of Dresden
Battle of Britain
Battle of Dunkirk
Battle of Jutland
Battle of Bull Run
Battle of Iwo Jima
castles in the air
Matthew Meselson
parthenogenesis
parthenogenetic
Walther Rathenau
party-government
Captain Absolute
East Siberian Sea
Captain MacHeath
captain's biscuit
Tantallon Castle
pactum illicitum
Baltimore oriole
casting director
Martin Heidegger
Waiting for Godot
Martin Niemöller
Martin Frobisher
castanospermine
Martínez de Perón
Cautionary Tales
waste one's breath
Hawthorne effect
gastroenteritis
Bartholomew Fair
Bartholomew-tide
pantopragmatics
Tattersall check
tatterdemallion
Easter Rebellion
Easter sepulchre
Easter offerings
Lantern Festival
pastoral address
Pastoral Letters
bacteriological
Walter Greenwood
Canterbury Tales
earthshattering
baptism by desire
fantasy football
fantasticalness
last but not least
lactovegetarian
faithworthiness
natural cycle IVF

natural immunity
saturation point
natural language
natural religion
natural theology
nature knowledge
value in exchange
Samuel Hahnemann
Papua New Guinean
La Aurora Airport
Palus Putredinis
daguerreotypist
Salvador Allende
saeva indignatio
galvanic battery
harvest festival
calves'-foot jelly
canvas-stretcher
Harvey Smith wave
Marxism-Leninism
Lady Margaret Jay
lazy daisy stitch
many-headed beast
Baby One More Time
Baby Doc Duvalier
baby-doll pyjamas
Caryophyllaceae
Tarzan of the Apes
Tarzan the Ape Man
abscission layer
objectification
objective danger
objectivisation
objectivization
observationally
observation post
ebullioscopical
Ebenezer Scrooge
absorbent cotton
abiogenetically
abbot of unreason
absorptiometric
absorption bands
absorption lines
absolute address
absolute ceiling
absolute alcohol
Aberdeen terrier
abstract of title
obstructionally
obstructiveness
Abdullah Ibrahim
about one's person
abruptly pinnate
above the weather
a bowl of cherries
scratchbuilding
scrape the barrel
Accademia Museum
occasional table
occasional cause
oceanographical
éclaircissement
ice contact slope
acid soil complex
screwball comedy
accelerator card
screwing machine
screaming abdabs
screaming meemie
sclerodermatous

scheduled castes
scribaciousness
scribbling-paper
A Child of our Time
scrivener's palsy
occidental topaz
Schiphol Airport
activity holiday
schillerisation
schillerization
action potential
action committee
echinodermatous
schizo-affective
schizophrenetic
acrimoniousness
scripture-reader
schistosomiasis
ochlocratically
ecological niche
acclimatisation
acclimatization
scalene triangle
scolopendriform
ecclesiasticism
ecclesiological
acanthocephalan
scintillatingly
economic refugee
economic migrant
acknowledgeable
acknowledgeably
acknowledgement
echocardiograph
act of contrition
achondroplastic
accordion pleats
acromion process
a crook in one's lot
schoolmastering
schoolmasterish
schoolmistressy
school inspector
accommodatingly
accountableness
act of parliament
across the tracks
scaphocephalous
Schrecklichkeit
scarlet geranium
achromatisation
achromatization
A Christmas Carol
Acts of Adjournal
icositetrahedra
scatter cushions
act the giddy goat
Scott Fitzgerald
scotched collops
Scottish terrier
Scottish Borders
acute rheumatism
ecotoxicologist
ichthyodorulite
ichthyodorylite
Ichthyopterygia
occupation level
scrumptiousness
acquisitiveness
acoustic coupler
acousto-electric

advance workings
Edward V Appleton
Edward the Martyr
Eduardo Paolozzi
Edward G Robinson
ideal transducer
adhesive binding
adventurousness
Admiral Graf Spee
admiralty anchor
ad misericordiam
addition product
Adrian Edmondson
Adriano Olivetti
Addison's disease
edriophthalmian
edriophthalmous
adenocarcinomas
adenohypophyses
adenohypophysis
identity element
odontoid process
odontostomatous
Edinburgh Castle
a drop in the ocean
Ode on Melancholy
ideographically
idiosyncratical
odoriferousness
adjutant-general
Edouard Daladier
Édouard Daladier
set a game to three
metamathematics
decarbonisation
decarbonization
decarburisation
decarburization
decarboxylation
decalcification
melancholically
per ardua ad astra
Gérard Depardieu
Bel and the Dragon
Leland H Hartwell
bed and breakfast
bed-and-breakfast
aerated concrete
New-Age Traveller
Megacheiroptera
Nemathelminthes
nemathelminthic
hexachlorophane
hexachlorophene
relative address
relative density
mesaticephalous
relatively prime
Melanie Griffith
metalinguistics
metasilicic acid
regaliamantling
hepaticological
metallurgically
demagnetisation
demagnetization
hexagonal system
pedagoguishness
desacralisation
desacralization
legal separation

penal settlement
Sebastian Faulks
metastable state
departmentalise
departmentalism
departmentalize
department store
departure lounge
penalty shoot-out
leg before wicket
herb Christopher
Pembroke College
kerbstone-broker
merchant service
merchant of death
Merce Cunningham
peacock-pheasant
teacher-governor
leucaemogenesis
teaching machine
✧reichian therapy
reaction turbine
descriptiveness
pencil-sharpener
pencil moustache
Ten Commandments
new-Commonwealth
neoconservatism
neoconservative
fencing mistress
Deccan Mountains
geochronologist
Neo-Christianity
hendecasyllabic
hendecasyllable
re-education camp
dead men's fingers
readvertisement
deed of accession
verdigris agaric
Hendrik Verwoerd
Wendell M Stanley
geodemographics
leading business
tendentiousness
Ferdinand Marcos
leading question
Weedon Grossmith
head-down display
send round the hat
dead tree edition
tender-heartedly
read-write memory
dead as a doornail
meadow-saxifrage
General Assembly
General Belgrano
Hereward the Wake
Peter and the Wolf
general delivery
general election
Geneva mechanism
general epistles
General Galtieri
vegetable butter
renewable energy
vegetable marrow
vegetable oyster
Helena Blavatsky
senega snakeroot
general practice

General Pinochet
general retainer
federal theology
Genevan theology
general warranty
Rebecca de Winter
defencelessness
telescopic shaft
telescopic sight
Terence Rattigan
Seleucus Nicator
seven deadly sins
dependent clause
serendipitously
degenerationist
deleteriousness
venereal disease
redetermination
New England aster
New English Bible
Berengar of Tours
telephone number
telethermoscope
telephotography
hereditarianism
hereditarianist
repetitiousness
benefit of clergy
Federico Fellini
jewel in the crown
determinability
determinateness
perennial nettle
heterodactylous
heterocercality
heterogeneously
heterosexuality
heterochromatic
heterochromatin
ceremoniousness
development area
developmentally
selenographical
heteroduplex DNA
redemption yield
Peter Paul Rubens
metempsychosist
Père Armand David
deferred payment
deferred annuity
peregrine falcon
Peregrine Pickle
telegraphically
penetrativeness
cerebrovascular
reverse genetics
Secession Church
necessary truths
reverse takeover
desensitisation
necessitousness
desensitization
reverse yield gap
Celestial Empire
fenestra rotunda
dementia praecox
celestial sphere
beneath contempt
seventeen-hunder
desertification
seventh interval

detention centre
reception centre
select committee
Refection Sunday
reception theory
telestereoscope
semesterisation
semesterization
selective mating
desexualisation
desexualization
reserve currency
Received English
receiving-office
receiver general
Helen Wills Moody
Gene Myron Amdahl
self-capacitance
self-sacrificing
self-observation
self-abandonment
perfectionistic
perfect interval
self-advancement
self-resemblance
self-referential
self-determining
self-development
self-registering
self-realisation
self-realization
self-reproachful
self-deprecating
self-degradation
self-centredness
self-certificate
self-fertilizing
self-destruction
self-destructive
self-affirmation
self-disciplined
self-vindication
self-righteously
self-liquidating
self-slaughtered
self-importantly
self-improvement
perfunctoriness
self-indulgently
self-sovereignty
reafforestation
self-confidently
self-forgetfully
self-pollination
self-complacence
self-considering
self-constituted
self-consciously
self-consequence
self-consistency
self-portraiture
self-documenting
self-opinionated
self-approbation
self-approvingly
performance poet
performance test
performing right
self-propagating
self-propagation
self-preparation

Geoffrey Chaucer
Geoffrey Boycott
beefsteak fungus
self-sufficiency
self-humiliation
perfluorocarbon
self-substantial
self-questioning
self-sustainment
self-explication
self-explanatory
self-examination
sergeant-drummer
neighbourliness
League of Nations
set great store by
wedge-heeled shoe
weighing-machine
Sergei Diaghilev
Sergei Prokofiev
pergamentaceous
Newgate Calendar
weighted average
Methodistically
technical writer
Cepheid variable
cephalochordate
methylphenidate
nepheline-basalt
lethal injection
methamphetamine
mechanomorphism
mechanoreceptor
mechanistically
dephlogisticate
technologically
technostructure
Lee Harvey Oswald
Gerhard Schröder
Mephistophelean
Mephistophelian
lexical analysis
pelican crossing
decimal currency
meditate the muse
decimal fraction
hesitation waltz
let it all hang out
decimal notation
Mexican standoff
semimanufacture
semi-latus rectum
reliability test
heliacal setting
behind the scenes
Semi-Pelagianism
Meriwether Lewis
residential area
deliver the goods
sedimentologist
decipherability
periphery camera
legitimate drama
medicine cabinet
feminine caesura
medicine-dropper
Leni Riefenstahl
delirium tremens
meridian passage
Petition of Right
deficit spending

sericiculturist
Cecil James Sharp
serial technique
aerial surveying
medium frequency
semi-independent
regional council
regionalisation
regionalization
semi-logarithmic
meritoriousness
lexicologically
lexicographical
lepidopterology
semidocumentary
Benito Mussolini
menispermaceous
reciprocal cross
reciprocity rule
denitrification
devitrification
semitransparent
hemicrystalline
semicrystalline
Ménière's disease
perissodactylic
res ipsa loquitur
regius professor
perissosyllabic
Begin the Beguine
peristaltically
meristem culture
heliotropically
semilunar valves
semisubmersible
desilverisation
desilverization
devil-worshipper
semicylindrical
Benjamin Britten
leukaemogenesis
peak viewing time
weak interaction
aeolian deposits
belly-button ring
replication fork
Leslie Charteris
mellifluousness
penlight battery
✧sealyham terrier
health-conscious
cellular therapy
well-intentioned
feel in one's bones
Hellenistically
tell one's own tale
well-woman clinic
well-conditioned
well-upholstered
Jelly Roll Morton
depleted uranium
yellow pimpernel
yellow brick road
yellow archangel
fellow traveller
Yellow Submarine
yellow-eyed grass
sell by the candle
Bermuda Triangle
femme incomprise
germ-line therapy

German Catholics
helminthologist
terminal illness
permanent deacon
permanent magnet
German police dog
Herman Hollerith
hermeneutically
Hermione Granger
hermaphroditism
geomorphogenist
geomorphologist
vermis cerebelli
permissible dose
Hermitage Museum
dermatoglyphics
geometrical mean
dermatomyositis
Bernhard Leopold
Bernhard Riemann
Bernabau Stadium
reinterrogation
Meindert Hobbema
Jeannette Rankin
Wernher von Braun
Jean-Michel Jarre
Jean Claude Killy
meaninglessness
Fernando Arrabal
Leonard Cheshire
re-entry corridor
Leonard Hobhouse
Leonor Michaelis
Leonardo da Vinci
Kenneth Williams
deindustrialise
reindustrialise
deindustrialize
reindustrialize
xeroradiography
Rev Obadiah Slope
hen on a hot girdle
reconcilability
second-adventist
second childhood
second-class mail
second-class post
second-in-command
second honeymoon
seconds pendulum
secondary action
secondary colour
secondary causes
secondary modern
secondary picket
secondary school
beyond suspicion
recoverableness
get one's bearings
get one's dander up
recovered memory
before-mentioned
mesonephric duct
let one's hair down
get one's monkey up
Jérôme Bonaparte
get one's rocks off
get one's skates on
set one's sights on
get one's shirt out
get off one's chest

Le Rouge et le Noir
demolition derby
memorial service
memoria technica
recollectedness
meroblastically
renormalisation
renormalization
decommissioning
recognisability
recognizability
below one's breath
get on one's nerves
zero-point energy
decolourisation
decolourization
aerospike nozzle
decomposability
resourcefulness
democratifiable
democratisation
democratization
reconsideration
Devonshire cream
reconstitutable
reconsolidation
remorselessness
demonstrability
reconstructable
reconstructible
remonstratingly
demonstratively
refortification
get out of one's way
Deo Optimo Maximo
decontamination
decontaminative
decontextualise
decontextualize
reconvalescence
revolving credit
aerodynamically
Le Nozze di Figaro
respectableness
People's Assembly
People's Congress
Temple of Hathoor
Temple of Somnath
Temple of Solomon
Temple of Artemis
People's Republic
Neapolitan sixth
Leopold von Ranke
keep a low profile
serpentine verse
responsibleness
perpendicularly
reopening clause
keep one's thumb on
keep one's shirt on
keep good quarter
reapportionment
tempt providence
jeepers creepers
peppermint cream
temperamentally
temperance hotel
reappropriation
tempestuousness
perpetual curate
perpetual motion

perpetuum mobile
sesquicarbonate
sesquicentenary
neuroanatomical
reproachfulness
Tetrabranchiata
tetrabranchiate
neuroblastomata
detribalisation
detribalization
neurobiological
Henry Cabot Lodge
Ferruccio Busoni
Tetractinellida
refractive index
jerry-come-tumble
New Red Sandstone
Pedro de Alvarado
Pedro de Valdivia
George Vancouver
retrievableness
George Santayana
wear several hats
degree of freedom
decree of nullity
Georges Lemaître
George von Hevesy
Georges Pompidou
George Grenville
George Grossmith
George Du Maurier
bear heavily upon
neurofibrillary
retrogressional
retrogressively
ferruginous duck
wear the breeches
neurohypophyses
neurohypophysis
wear the trousers
learning support
near-sightedness
Georgi Plekhanov
neurolinguistic
neural computing
ferro-molybdenum
necromantically
recrementitious
refrangibleness
hearing-impaired
tear one's hair out
beer and skittles
bear down towards
dear to one's heart
near to one's heart
metropolitanise
metropolitanism
metropolitanate
metropolitanize
neuropsychiatry
neuropsychology
neurophysiology
retroreflective
heir presumptive
retrospectively
near as ninepence
tetrasyllabical
refreshment-room
tetrasporangium
retrotransposon
Territorial Army

Debrett's Peerage
rear its ugly head
ferrous sulphate
Henri van de Velde
reprivatisation
reprivatization
re-establishment
sensible horizon
peasecod-bellied
peasecod-cuirass
gens de condition
perspicaciously
perspicuousness
tensile strength
get someone's goat
see someone right
Bessemer process
pessimistically
messenger-at-arms
personification
personal service
personal effects
personal shopper
personal trainer
personal pronoun
personalisation
personality cult
personalization
persona non grata
gemstone therapy
New Scotland Yard
session musician
seismologically
seismographical
feast of trumpets
sense perception
lesser celandine
lesser spearwort
lesser prolation
dessertspoonful
measure strength
sensation-monger
Tess Durbeyfield
Nevsky Alexander
Perth and Kinross
Bertrand Russell
tent caterpillar
centrally-heated
tertiary college
tertiary colours
Tectibranchiata
tectibranchiate
vertebral column
vestibular nerve
destabilization
Deutsches Museum
vertical take-off
tentaculiferous
vested interests
Gentleman-at-arms
gentleman farmer
gentlemanliness
wet the baby's head
feather-boarding
weatherboarding
genteel business
feathered friend
gentlemen ushers
Centre Beaubourg
centre of inertia
weather forecast

centre of gravity
get the finger out
settle old scores
Meet Me in St Louis
weather notation
feather one's nest
get the worst of it
leather on willow
get the drop on one
weather the storm
rent restriction
heath fritillary
heat of formation
vertiginousness
ventriloquially
ventriloquistic
restrictiveness
centrifugal pump
Fertile Crescent
fertile material
de-Stalinisation
de-Stalinization
dental hygienist
centum languages
September people
testament-dative
Teutonic Knights
sententiousness
centinel private
wetting-out agent
meat and potatoes
septentrionally
Weston-super-Mare
neptunium series
Hertford College
beat someone to it
destroying angel
Neath Port Talbot
depth psychology
Venture Air Scout
western blotting
letter of comfort
letters-of-marque
gesture politics
letters rogatory
Venture Sea Scout
venturesomeness
Heathrow Airport
Kentish ragstone
Pentothal sodium
destructibility
destructiveness
Festival Theatre
Keith Waterhouse
regular customer
Beaumaris Castle
Recumbent Figure
secundogeniture
secundum naturam
secundum regulam
secundum ordinem
security blanket
Security Council
sexual selection
sexual therapist
medullary sheath
Return of the Jedi
Jesus of Nazareth
resurrection man
resurrection pie
resurrectionary

resurrectionise
resurrectionism
resurrectionist
resurrectionize
demulsification
Gewürztraminer
demutualisation
demutualization
serviceableness
service contract
service industry
service provider
Belvedere Museum
servomechanical
Kelvin Mackenzie
heaven of heavens
see what one can do
between two fires
between you and me
network computer
Beryl Bainbridge
dehypnotisation
dehypnotization
very approximate
New York Marathon
demystification
mezzanine window
affaire d'honneur
of the first water
offhand grinding
African-American
African elephant
efficaciousness
African mahogany
African marigold
officer of the day
affluent society
a finger in the pie
of one's own accord
of one's own making
of no consequence
affranchisement
A Farewell to Arms
a fish out of water
egg-and-spoon race
agranulocytosis
against the clock
against the grain
agriculturalist
Ggantija temples
agency secretary
age of discretion
ignominiousness
Egyptianisation
Egyptianization
eggs in moonshine
The Age of Anxiety
sheathe the sword
The Annunciation
ahead of one's time
The African Queen
cheat the gallows
The Artful Dodger
The Bicycle Thief
the back of beyond
The Beggar's Opera
the big enchilada
the bright lights
The Birth of Venus
The Boston Herald
the bitch goddess

shabby-gentility
The Charnel House
the coast is clear
the crescent moon
thickheadedness
checking account
chocolate éclair
the common people
the chosen people
the cat's whiskers
chuck-will's-widow
The Cowardly Lion
thick-wittedness
The Death of Marat
The Dead Kennedys
The Dance of Death
the devil's tattoo
The Divine Comedy
shadow pantomime
wheel animalcule
Shwe Dagon Pagoda
wheelbarrow race
the end of the line
the end of the road
three-day eventer
The Eve of St Agnes
threshold lights
Shwezigon Pagoda
three-legged race
Three Men in a Boat
phrenologically
threepenceworth
threepenny piece
threepennyworth
three-ring circus
The Essays of Elia
chief technician
three times three
chrestomathical
The Flagellation
The Faerie Queene
shift for oneself
shifting spanner
The Female Eunuch
shift one's ground
the fatal sisters
the feudal system
the Four Freedoms
the fourth estate
The Grauballe Man
the Greek calends
the gift of the gab
the gloves are off
the Good Shepherd
The Garden of Eden
The Garden of Love
the hale hypothec
the how and the why
Sheila Rowbotham
The Iceman Cometh
shrink-resistant
shrinking violet
The Isle of Avalon
Christmas beetle
Christmas cactus
Christian de Duve
Christmas flower
Christmas Island
Christian Slater
Christadelphian
Christy minstrel

Christ in Majesty
Christopher Dean
Christopher Wren
The Invisible Man
Thojib N J Suharto
Shikibu Murasaki
Thelma and Louise
cholecalciferol
cholecystectomy
cholecystokinin
cholecystostomy
Philadelphaceae
the lady vanishes
Chelsea Arts Club
shilling shocker
chalking the door
a hole in one's coat
philanthropical
cholangiography
chalcographical
Children's Corner
cholesterolemia
Thales of Miletus
child-safety seat
the Last Judgment
thalassotherapy
thalassographer
thalassographic
philosophically
The Little Prince
The Littlest Hobo
he Low Countries
shilly-shallying
hemoattractant
hemical warfare
hemical element
hombencephalon
hamberlainship
hamber practice
hombenporphyry
hamphorhynchus
he Mansion House
humbnail sketch
homson's gazelle
hemopsychiatry
he Marx Brothers
he morning after
e morn's morning
e merry monarch
homas Babington
homas Jefferson
homas De Quincey
homas Middleton
homas Gradgrind
hantasmagorial
e noble science
honocardiogram
ange of address
understricken
hen I Fall In Love
hynchobdellida
hynchocephalia
in-skinnedness
enakistoscope
enylketonuria
enylketonuric
enolphthalein
andler's wobble
onemicisation
onemicization
enomenologist

phenomenalistic
thin on the ground
the nine worthies
phantom material
think on one's feet
chenopodiaceous
chondrification
Chinese checkers
Chinese chequers
Thanksgiving Day
Chinese layering
Chinese pavilion
Chinese whispers
phoneticisation
phoneticization
thanatognomonic
think twice about
phonautographic
The New York Times
thankworthiness
thiobarbiturate
chromatographic
chloramphenicol
thromboembolism
The Old Wives' Tale
theorematically
shoot from the hip
through-composed
through the night
shooting gallery
theolinguistics
throw in one's hand
throw in the cards
throw in the towel
Theodor Billroth
Theodore Roethke
theosophistical
chronologically
Theodor Svedberg
chromoxylograph
shoot tip culture
throw to the winds
throw up the cards
chops and changes
The Pearl Fishers
chapter and verse
shepherd's myrtle
shepherd's needle
shepherd's tartan
ship of the desert
the Principality
shopping-bag lady
chipping sparrow
chapelle ardente
shape one's course
the plot thickens
the Paris Commune
The Potato Eaters
the powers that be
thermal capacity
pharmacotherapy
pharmacokinetic
pharmacognostic
pharmacognosist
therianthropism
thoracocentesis
character sketch
third degree burn
shared ownership
chargé-d'affaires
Charles de Gaulle

Where Eagles Dare
Charles Goodyear
Charles James Fox
Charles Kingsley
Charles Laughton
Shirley MacLaine
charged particle
Shirley Williams
Charles Yanofsky
The Raft of Medusa
third-generation
Church of England
whirling-machine
whirling dervish
whirligig beetle
thermionic valve
thorn in the flesh
churrigueresque
a hard nut to crack
choriocarcinoma
thermobaric bomb
thermochemistry
theriomorphosis
Pharaoh's serpent
Charlotte Amalie
Charlotte Brontë
Charlotte Corday
Charlottesville
Charlotte Sophia
thermodynamical
The Rape of Europa
therapeutically
third-rail system
short sharp shock
pharisaicalness
there's no telling
The Rite of Spring
short-term memory
thoroughgoingly
sharp-wittedness
thirtysomething
physicochemical
The Secret Garden
The Second Coming
Chester-le-Street
The Sleepwalkers
phosphocreatine
phosphorylation
phosphorescence
phosphorous acid
the silver screen
whistle for a wind
whistling kettle
whistle-stop tour
phase modulation
the same old story
chestnut boletus
physiotherapist
physiologically
physiographical
the Supreme Being
The Sorrow of Love
The Sound of Music
the sky's the limit
Shetland Islands
Thatta monuments
Whitechapel cart
photoconducting
photoconductive
whited sepulchre
photodegradable

photoelasticity
chattel mortgage
shutter priority
phytoestrogenic
photogrammetric
phytogeographer
phytogeographic
thatched cottage
photoionization
photojournalism
photojournalist
photolithograph
photomechanical
photomicroscope
photomacrograph
photomicrograph
photomultiplier
white man's burden
that's more like it
The Three Witches
the Three Wise Men
The Three Sisters
photorefractive
whiter than white
white rhinoceros
what is he for a man?
white sandalwood
photosynthesize
photosensitiser
photosensitizer
phototransistor
what's the big idea?
phototelegraphy
phototypesetter
The Tower of Babel
photoxylography
what's your poison?
photozincograph
rheumatological
shout blue murder
shoulder-shotten
shoulder-clapper
shoulder-slipped
thought disorder
thoughtlessness
thrust to the wall
Chavín de Huantar
shiver my timbers
the weaker vessel
the Weird Sisters
The Woman in White
show one's ivories
the worse for wear
Minamata disease
bioavailability
Sir Alan L Hodgkin
bioaccumulation
Sir Alex Ferguson
Sir Alec Guinness
mirabelle brandy
milage allowance
picaresque novel
cigarette holder
disaffectedness
disaffectionate
disafforestment
vitamin B complex
titanium dioxide
misapprehension
misapprehensive
misappreciation

misappreciative
disappointingly
disagreeability
vital statistics
Sir Austen Layard
disassimilation
disassimilative
disarticulation
Sir Astley Cooper
bioastronautics
Sir Arthur Harris
disadvantageous
win by a short head
misbecomingness
pin back one's ears
Liebig condenser
hit below the belt
ribbon parachute
Tim Brooke-Taylor
Limburger cheese
Sir Barnes Wallis
gibberellic acid
discharging arch
Sir Charles Hallé
Sir Charles Barry
aircraft-carrier
viscoelasticity
Sir Clement Freud
kitchen gardener
discretionarily
Winchester rifle®
air-chief-marshal
Sir Cliff Richard
pitching niblick
Pitcairn Islands
circuit training
mischievousness
miscellaneously
Lincoln Memorial
Niccolò Paganini
circular measure
circularisation
circularization
circumnavigable
circumnavigator
circumvallation
Giacomo Agostini
circumscribable
circumscription
circumscriptive
discommendation
circumferential
Giacomo Leopardi
circumambagious
circumincession
circuminsession
circumforaneous
discommodiously
circumspectness
circumstantials
circumstantiate
air-conditioning
disconfirmation
discontinuation
discontinuously
Vincenzo Bellini
misconstruction
piece of one's mind
viscosimetrical
Piscis Austrinus
Liechtensteiner

Viscount Haldane
Viscount Camrose
Viscount Allenby
discovered check
Windward Islands
windfall profits
windscreen-wiper
vindicativeness
Middle-Easterner
Middle Westerner
middle-of-the-road
middle-age spread
Middle Englander
kind-heartedness
middle-stitching
wind-chill factor
Wisdom of Solomon
Sir Donald Sinden
Sir Donald Wolfit
find one's account
mind one's p's and q's
birds of a feather
gird up one's loins
Cinderella dance
Diodorus Siculus
Pindus Mountains
biodestructible
Sir Douglas Bader
Sir David Barclay
window gardening
wind synthesizer
Liberal Democrat
Airedale terrier
like gangbusters
bimetallic strip
mineralogically
cinematographer
cinematographic
videoconference
like a dog's dinner
bigeneric hybrid
fides et justitia
live cell therapy
fivepenny morris
ninepenny morris
wireless station
line of scrimmage
line of flotation
like the clappers
give the game away
dimethylaniline
vice-chamberlain
give the show away
like a house afire
kinesitherapist
cinemicrography
bite on the bridle
bite on the bullet
cineangiography
fire in one's belly
give oneself away
give oneself airs
line one's pockets
time-zone fatigue
time-zone disease
give someone best
give someone five
give someone hell
give someone rope
fine-toothed comb
Lives of the Poets
wide area network
fire-crested wren
River Shenandoah
Life is Beautiful
diversification
disentrancement
direct marketing
Ninette de Valois
direct discourse
direct injection
disentanglement
give it some welly
direction-finder
give it to someone
director-general
disenthrallment
Sir Edwin Lutyens
Sir Edward German
Sir Edward Hulton
riverworthiness
Sir Francis Drake
diffrangibility
Sir Frank Whittle
Sir Freddie Laker
Wilfred Thesiger
Linford Christie
differentiation
disgracefulness
ring-tailed lemur
Ziegler catalyst
single-heartedly
single use camera
king of the castle
king of the forest
King William's War
linguistic atlas
Ringelmann chart
cingulum Veneris
singularisation
singularization
virgin parchment
Virginia creeper
Singin' in the Rain
sing another song
sing another tune
singing telegram
Sir George Cayley
Sir George Stokes
Sir George Thomas
biogeochemistry
biogeographical
ginger beer plant
Sir Geraint Evans
Ringer's solution
Richmal Crompton
Highland costume
with bated breath
high-maintenance
dishearteningly
dishabilitation
Pithecanthropus
lithochromatics
with a difference
Michael Atherton
Michaelmas-daisy
Michael Ondaatje
tighten one's belt
Michael Portillo
Michael Redgrave
tighten the screw
light-headedness
right-handedness
Right Honourable
Mikhail Bulgakov
Nizhniy Novgorod
Michail Saltykov
fish skin disease
fishskin disease
diaheliotropism
with closed doors
Wilhelm Steinitz
Nicholas Wiseman
light literature
light-mindedness
right-mindedness
nightmarishness
Nikhanj Kapil Dev
lightning strike
within arm's reach
Sir Henry Raeburn
Sir Henry Segrave
fight one's corner
wish someone well
right off the reel
with compliments
Sir Hermann Bondi
Richard Crossman
higher education
Richard Dreyfuss
Richard Dimbleby
Richard Dunwoody
Richard Hamilton
Richard Lovelace
dithyrambically
hither and yonder
disharmoniously
Richard P Feynman
tightrope walker
higher criticism
high-gravel-blind
withdrawing-room
night starvation
fight to the ropes
without ceremony
without recourse
wishful thinking
with a wild wanion
Sir Isaiah Berlin
digital computer
Kiribati Islands
military academy
military honours
military two-step
dividend warrant
milites gloriosi
limited monarchy
Citizen's Charter
disinflationary
riding committee
finishing school
finishing stroke
visiting fireman
digitizing table
minimizing glass
digitizing board
Sicilian Vespers
Divisional Court
visible spectrum
disillusionment
Sir Ian Trethowan
lie in one's throat
disimprisonment
vicissitudinous
misintelligence
sinistrodextral
Minister of State
disinterestedly
miniaturisation
miniaturization
Ministry of Works
Sir Jacob Epstein
Sir John Betjeman
Sir John Charnley
Sir John Franklin
Sir John Falstaff
Sir John Herschel
Sir John Marshall
Sir John Mortimer
Sir John Suckling
Sir John Vanbrugh
hip joint disease
Sir Julian Huxley
Sir Jeremy Isaacs
Sir Joseph Paxton
sickle-cell trait
sickness benefit
Wilkins Micawber
pick up the pieces
kick up one's heels
nick translation
ticket collector
William Beaumont
William Chambers
William Congreve
William Christie
William Davenant
William Friedkin
William Faulkner
William Hamilton
William Herschel
William J Brennan
William Kunstler
William Langland
William McKinley
William Marshall
William of Ockham
William Rees-Mogg
Gillian Shephard
William Whitelaw
dialectological
Willie Shoemaker
gillie-white-foot
bill of adventure
millefiori glass
bill of mortality
biological clock
Niels Henrik Abel
Willem De Kooning
Willem Einthoven
bioluminescence
diplomatic pouch
diplomatic corps
Killing Me Softly
violinistically
field naturalist
Giulio Andreotti
bibliographical
Millard Fillmore
field-sequential
Violeta Chamorro
wield the sceptre
yield up the ghost
pillow-structure
Sir Michael Caine
diamagnetically
Ciampino Airport
diamondback moth
Riemannian space
Giant Clothespin
significatively
Lionel Barrymore
Sir Norman Foster
Sir Norman Fowler
Wiener schnitzel
Nikolay Bukharin
Nikolai Bulganin
Fibonacci series
Girolamo Cardano
Nikolaus Pevsner
Simon de Montfort
disorderly house
dig one's own grave
disorganisation
disorganization
binomial theorem
minority carrier
disobligingness
pin on one's sleeve
Sigourney Weaver
kilogram-calorie
tip of the iceberg
dip of the horizon
oil of turpentine
binocular vision
ribonucleic acid
Sir Oswald Mosley
displacement ton
displaced person
Hippocratic face
Hippocratic look
Hippocratic oath
pipped at the post
displeasingness
Sir Philip Sidney
Sir Pelham Warner
dispensableness
diaphototropism
disproportional
misproportioned
dispersal prison
diaphragmatitis
dispassionately
Sir Patrick Moore
Sir Peter Medawar
Sir Peter Ustinov
disputativeness
biopsychosocial
disquisitionary
microanalytical
diurnal parallax
microaerophilic
microbiological
Sir Richard Scott
Sir Richard Stone
citric acid cycle
Microchiroptera
nitric anhydride
microcosmic salt
nitro-derivative
microdissection
Pierre d'Aubusson
Pierre de Ronsard
microelectronic
Pierre Corneille

microfilm reader
hierogrammatist
nitrogen dioxide
nitrogenisation
nitrogen mustard
nitrogenization
Giorgiy Malenkov
micromicrofarad
micromicrocurie
micromillimetre
micromanagement
micrometer gauge
Tigran Petrosian
citronella grass
Sir Ronald Fisher
Hieronymus Bosch
Sir Rhodes Boyson
micropegmatitic
microprocessing
microphotograph
disreputability
disrespectfully
microsporangium
microscopically
microsporophyll
microtechnology
Diprotodontidae
microtunnelling
nitrous bacteria
dissociableness
dissecting table
irst degree burn
diastereoisomer
Kirsten Flagstad
its of the mother
irst generation
irst in, first out
ipstick lesbian
issajous figure
dissolvableness
irst lieutenant
dissolving views
diesel-hydraulic
ir Samuel Cunard
il someone's palm
ssencephalous
igs and whistles
ssion spectrum
rst principles
ssiparousness
ir Seretse Khama
iostratigraphy
issatisfaction
issatisfactory
ctualling-bill
ctualling-ship
ctualling-yard
ift Valley fever
stractibility
otechnologist
rthday honours
t the headlines
ttle Nell Trent
the high spots
tle Englander
istress Quickly
stressfulness
ty-fourth note
h generation
h-generation
ilt Chamberlain

district heating
district visitor
district council
Fifth-monarchism
Fifth-monarchist
Sir Tom Hopkinson
airtime provider
fitting-out basin
distinctiveness
distinguishable
distinguishably
distinguishment
Sir Thomas Browne
fifty pence piece
filterable virus
historical novel
historic pricing
Victorien Sardou
Mister Fezziwigg
picture moulding
Mister Wonderful
historiographer
historiographic
picture postcard
picture-postcard
picture restorer
picturesqueness
distastefulness
tilt at windmills
distrustfulness
mistrustfulness
Titus Andronicus
figurate numbers
biquadratic root
Figure and Clouds
liturgiological
ritualistically
risus sardonicus
situation comedy
situation ethics
Giovanni Cassini
Giovanni Bellini
Giovanni Gentile
Giovanni Agnelli
Giovanni Tiepolo
silver birch tree
Sir William Bragg
Sir William Osler
ribwort plantain
City of Edinburgh
lily of the valley
bicycle rickshaw
Django Reinhardt
Skiddaw Mountain
clean as a whistle
old-age pensioner
bleaching powder
floating capital
floating battery
al-hallown summer
clear one's throat
all along the line
Eleanor Rathbone
Allan Quatermain
pleasurableness
pleasure-seeking
flibbertigibbet
globigerina ooze
globular cluster
glacial deposits
all-changing-word

Blackfriars Hall
Black Forest cake
black nightshade
gluconeogenesis
place of business
Alec Douglas-Home
electroanalysis
electroacoustic
electric battery
electrochemical
electric blanket
electrical storm
electric furnace
electric current
electrodynamics
electrification
black rhinoceros
electrokinetics
electromagnetic
electromyograph
electrometrical
electron capture
electronic piano
electronic flash
electronic organ
electronic brain
electronic music
electronegative
electrophoresis
electrophoretic
electropositive
electrotechnics
electrothermics
clicks and mortar
black-tailed deer
Alec D'Urberville
blackwater fever
Vladimir Nabokov
Wladyslaw Anders
Gladstone sherry
sleeve waistcoat
Elie Metchnikoff
sleeping partner
sleeping draught
Ellesmere Island
alternis vicibus
alternate energy
alternative fuel
alternative host
alternative vote
blue-footed booby
Alberto Fujimori
Albert Chevalier
Albert Nile River
Albertina Museum
ill-favouredness
elegiac couplets
oligonucleotide
slog one's guts out
plagiostomatous
oligosaccharide
Flight into Egypt
plight one's troth
flight attendant
alphabetisation
alphabetization
alpha-chloralose
flehmen reaction
Ilchester cheese
Alcide de Gasperi
flying phalanger

Gleichschaltung
illimitableness
Elsie Stephenson
Cloisters Museum
Aleister Crowley
Aleksandr Tairov
plumbaginaceous
slimmers' disease
slumpflationary
à la maître d'hôtel
alimentary canal
Clemens Brentano
aluminium bronze
flamboyante-tree
Plymouth Brother
blameworthiness
climax community
plantaginaceous
clinical baptism
clinical lecture
clinical convert
clinical surgery
blanket coverage
Blenheim spaniel
blonde bombshell
clandestineness
blunt instrument
Planck's constant
clonal selection
Glencoe Massacre
plenipotentiary
plant succession
along the lines of
planetary nebula
fling to the winds
blood-and-thunder
bloodcurdlingly
fluorescent tube
all over the place
fly off the handle
blood-guiltiness
clootie dumpling
algorithmically
allotriomorphic
Bloomsbury Group
slip of the tongue
slapstick comedy
ultracentrifuge
Old Red Sandstone
Alfred Whitehead
Alfred Hitchcock
Alfred Stieglitz
ultrafiltration
ultra-high vacuum
ultramicroscope
ultramicroscopy
Glorious Twelfth
clerk of the works
clerk of the court
Clermont-Ferrand
Clarissa Harlowe
ultrasonography
ultraviolet star
Alessandro Volta
Alaskan malamute
Alaskan malemute
Alistair Maclean
Alistair Darling
Alastair Dunnett
closed community
clustered column

plasterers' putty
blast-furnaceman
Classical Greats
Flushing Meadows
glossographical
flash photolysis
close to the chest
All Souls College
slotted aerofoil
flutter-tonguing
Platyhelminthes
slotting-machine
cloth-lined board
I'll trouble you to
platitudinarian
Cloudcuckooland
cloud-cuckoo-land
cloud-compelling
Albus Dumbledore
Flaubert's Parrot
Gloucestershire
ploughman's lunch
ploughshare bone
eleutherococcus
eleutherodactyl
eleutherophobia
eleutherophobic
Aleutian Islands
Claudius Dornier
pleuropneumonia
illustriousness
alive and kicking
Olivier Messiaen
Cleve-Garth Falls
Oliver Heaviside
flavor of the week
Oliver Goldsmith
slave-trafficker
flavour enhancer
Flavius Josephus
Blowin' in the Wind
clown's woundwort
flux-gate compass
Alexander Calder
Alexander Dubcek
Alexander Gibson
Alexander Irvine
Alexander Nevski
flex one's muscles
elixir of vitriol
Alexius Comnenus
play first fiddle
Aloys Senefelder
Elizabeth Bennet
Elizabeth Bishop
Elizabeth Taylor
immaterial issue
impassionedness
impact parameter
Emmanuel College
amicable numbers
smack on the wrist
impenetrability
imperfect fungus
imperfect flower
imperishability
emperick qutique
imperial measure
impermeableness
Emperor Concerto
Amiens Cathedral

immersion heater
immensurability
Umberto Boccioni
impecuniousness
imperviableness
imaginary number
imaginativeness
image processing
amphitheatrical
omnifariousness
omnibenevolence
omnidirectional
smoke and mirrors
smoking carriage
Emelyan Pugachev
emblic myrobalan
smelling of roses
smelting-furnace
small-mindedness
implausibleness
amino-acetic acid
amende honorable
a month of Sundays
emancipationist
imponderability
ammonium nitrate
immortalisation
immortalization
importunateness
impracticalness
Americanisation
Americanization
Amerigo Vespucci
amaryllidaceous
G Marconi Airport
embryologically
ambrosia beetles
impressionistic
imprescriptible
improvvisatrice
improvisational
improvisatorial
emission current
amusement arcade
a matter of course
ambulance broker
ambulance-chaser
immunopathology
immunochemistry
immunologically
immunocompetent
incapaciousness
Antarctic Circle
incalculability
unsatisfiedness
unparliamentary
anharmonic ratio
uncanonicalness
unpatriotically
infant mortality
unobjectionable
unobjectionably
inobtrusiveness
unobtrusiveness
knock all of a heap
anacreontically
inaccessibility
knick-knackatory
knuckle sandwich
unaccommodating
onychocryptosis
knockout auction
inscrutableness
inadvisableness
unadvisableness
inadmissibility
unidiomatically
antenatal clinic
inseparableness
interambulacral
interambulacrum
Ingemar Stenmark
interchangeable
interchangeably
interchangement
unpeaceableness
unteachableness
intercollegiate
intercolonially
interconversion
interconnection
under correction
inner dead centre
interdigitation
interdependence
interdependency
Independence Day
indeterministic
indeterminately
indetermination
undetermination
unceremoniously
underemployment
indefeasibility
indefensibility
unnecessariness
in seventh heaven
underestimation
interestingness
unrelentingness
indecent assault
antepenultimate
unselfconscious
interferometric
interference fit
interfascicular
encephalography
encephalisation
encephalization
underhandedness
interim accounts
indefinableness
undesirableness
interim dividend
unverifiability
anterior chamber
inferior planets
unremittingness
interjectionary
interjaculatory
under lock and key
intellectualise
intellectualism
intellectualist
intellectuality
intellectualize
intelligibility
unhealthfulness
interlamination
intermodulation
once in a blue moon
indemnification
infernal machine
internalisation
internal student
internalization
internationally
unreconciliable
interosculation
under one's breath
envelope stuffer
unrecommendable
unreconstructed
undemonstrative
under plain cover
interpretership
underprivileged
interpenetrable
interprovincial
underproduction
interpersonally
intemperateness
Anne Bracegirdle
interrogational
interrogatively
understandingly
undersubscribed
intersubjective
intensification
interscholastic
Anderson shelter
interstratified
insensitiveness
entente cordiale
inverted mordent
ungentlemanlike
insect repellent
under the weather
anaesthetically
anaesthesiology
Under the Volcano
under-the-counter
investment trust
investigational
intertwistingly
intertentacular
intestinal flora
intertanglement
injection string
intention tremor
ancestor-worship
incentivisation
incentivization
intertextualise
intertextuality
intertextualize
unleavened bread
interventionism
interventionist
in between whiles
unseaworthiness
ineffaceability
inoffensiveness
ineffectualness
ineffectiveness
inefficaciously
inofficiousness
knights bachelor
knight of the road
knight of the whip
knight's progress
Knights Templars
on the back burner
on the barrelhead
on the danger list
in the first place
in the first flush
Unchained Melody
unchristianlike
unchallengeable
unchallengeably
unwholesomeness
unphilosophical
in the last resort
in the melting-pot
in the nick of time
unchangeability
one hundred hours
Anthony Trollope
on the never-never
anthropopathism
anthropogenesis
anthropocentric
anthropophagite
anthropophagous
anthropobiology
anthroposophist
anthropological
anthropomorphic
anthropopsychic
on the right track
in this day and age
in the same breath
on the wrong track
On the Waterfront
anti-Gallicanism
undisappointing
uncircumscribed
indisciplinable
undisciplinable
antiperistalsis
antiperistaltic
indirect damages
indigestibility
indirect address
incidental music
Annie Get Your Gun
unrighteousness
antitheft device
antichristianly
insight learning
anticholinergic
annihilationism
infinitesimally
antivivisection
indivisibleness
individualistic
anticlericalism
antiglare switch
Annie Macpherson
insignificantly
insignificative
Indian liquorice
ancient monument
Indian rope-trick
Indian wrestling
antimonarchical
environmentally
oneirocriticism
indisputability
India rubber tree
antitrinitarian
indissolubility
indistributable
indistinctively
undistinguished
antistatic agent
antistatic fluid
snake in the grass
in black and white
in all conscience
inalterableness
unalterableness
inflammableness
English Civil War
inclusion bodies
English ryegrass
English sickness
analytical logic
unimaginatively
animal rationale
animal magnetism
anomalistically
anomalistic year
animal husbandry
onomasiological
animated cartoon
uninterestingly
unintermittedly
uninterpretable
uninterruptedly
unintentionally
enantiomorphism
enantiomorphous
on one's pantables
in one's right mind
on one's high horse
on one's own ground
on another planet
unknown quantity
enforcement work
unconcernedness
unconditionally
intolerableness
ontogenetically
in someone's teeth
in someone's power
one over the eight
incongruousness
unforgivingness
unsophisticated
indomitableness
in totidem verbis
encomiastically
incommunicative
uncommunicative
incommensurable
incommensurably
in forma pauperis
incommutability
informativeness
entomologically
on top of the world
uncomplainingly
uncomplaisantly
uncomprehending
incomprehension
incomprehensive
uncomprehensive
uncomplimentary
uncompanionable
incomparability
unco-operatively
uncooperatively
uncompassionate

incompatibility
Anton Rubinstein
incorrigibility
endocrinologist
nconsecutively
nconsiderately
nconsideration
ınconscientious
ınconsciousness
nconspicuously
nconsolability
nfossiliferous
nconsentaneous
nconsequential
nconstrainable
nconstrainedly
nfortunateness
ncontroversial
voluntariness
nspeakableness
n speaking terms
applicability
ıap one's fingers
opportuneness
apprehensible
ıapprehensible
ne-parent family
appropriately
sportsmanlike
spirationally
operativeness
apostolically
equitableness
ıdreas Vesalius
ractableness
tractableness
precedentedly
practisedness
ra dignitatem
credulousness
profitability
progressively
archistically
drei Vyshinsky
grammatically
dromeda galaxy
dromeda nebula
oremeditation
dromonoecious
amuscularly
ransferrable
ranchisement
insicalness
ansigentism
ansigentist
insic factor
angibleness
ransmigrated
ansmissible
ansmissible
grand seigneur
ronounceable
epreneurial
preneurial
epreneurism
roportionate
repossessing
spectively
ossing a deed
structural
susception

untrustworthily
unprotectedness
unprotestantise
unprotestantize
Andrew Aguecheek
anorexia nervosa
one's native heath
Anastasio Somoza
unascertainable
inestimableness
one's true colours
anisotropically
a nasty bit of work
unsteadfastness
gnotobiotically
gnotobiological
United Provinces
another cup of tea
inattentiveness
knitting machine
installment plan
instantaneously
unitary taxation
unstatesmanlike
institutionally
instrument panel
instrumentalism
instrumentalist
instrumentality
instrument board
instrumentation
instructiveness
insulating board
pneumatic trough
angular momentum
pneumatological
angular velocity
Annunciation Day
infundibuliform
innumerableness
insuperableness
induced abortion
unauthenticated
inauthentically
annus horribilis
unauthoritative
indubitableness
injudiciousness
inducible enzyme
insulin reaction
unqualifiedness
invulnerability
insubordinately
insubordination
pneumonia blouse
infusorial earth
unsuspectedness
insurrectionary
insurrectionism
insurrectionist
unsubstantiated
insubstantially
intussusception
intussusceptive
inquisitorially
inquisitiveness
industriousness
induction course
angustirostrate
unavailableness
unavoidableness

known better days
knowledgability
a new lease of life
know what's o'clock
know one's own mind
know a thing or two
inextensibility
inexpensiveness
unexceptionable
unexceptionably
unexceptionally
inexplicability
inextricability
inexcusableness
inexpugnability
unsymmetrically
Andy Goldsworthy
ankylostomiasis
Royal Albert Hall
total body burden
Jonah Barrington
Monarchianistic
✧royal commission
Donald Pleasence
coram domino rege
Mohamed V Airport
local government
Jonathan Edwards
botanical garden
totalitarianism
logarithmically
logarithmic sine
somatic mutation
polarity therapy
Coralline Oolite
solar microscope
Johann Pachelbel
Johannes Eckhart
Johannes V Jensen
Rosamond Lehmann
coracoid process
woman of the world
moral philosophy
solar prominence
Moral Rearmament
Coral Sea Islands
potassium iodide
Romantic Revival
romanticisation
romanticization
non-attributable
non-attributably
go-faster stripes
bomb calorimeter
forbidden ground
forbidden planet
double-facedness
double-barrelled
hobbledehoyhood
corbie messenger
double indemnity
double pneumonia
God bless the mark
double standards
pot-bellied stove
non-belligerency
combination lock
combination oven
combination room
Lombardic script
combustibleness

cowboy and Indian
coccidiomycosis
douche écossaise
rouche moutonnée
conceivableness
Joachim du Bellay
porcelain cement
cocculus indicus
non-commissioned
non compos mentis
non-conventional
non-contributory
conceptualistic
concert overture
concessionnaire
vouch to warranty
Foucault current
Lord James Mackay
Lord Baden-Powell
good-naturedness
Bordeaux mixture
Tom, Dick, and Harry
conduct disorder
Mordecai Richler
coeducationally
bonded warehouse
folded mountains
Lord Peter Wimsey
cold-heartedness
Lord George-Brown
gold certificate
gold-beater's skin
Lord Beaverbrook
Lord Chamberlain
Lord High Admiral
Lord High Steward
Lord Lieutenants
Lords Lieutenant
cold-bloodedness
hold all the cards
gold import point
goldsmith beetle
golden parachute
golden handshake
golden handcuffs
cordon sanitaire
golden saxifrage
London Palladium
Holden Caulfield
Golden Delicious
golden retriever
golden rectangle
woody nightshade
nodding mandarin
Gordon Greenidge
goods on approval
good for anything
good-conditioned
Lord Hore-Belisha
Cold Comfort Farm
Lord Collingwood
Border Leicester
powdering-closet
wondermongering
condescendingly
non-disciplinary
word association
nondescriptness
road fund licence
gold export point
Dog Day Afternoon

Homes and Gardens
moderate in a call
come rain or shine
covenant of works
covenant of grace
Hotel California
honeycomb stitch
Roger de Coverley
co-determination
core temperature
movement therapy
money for old rope
foreign exchange
hope against hope
lose the exchange
Joseph Whitworth
Joseph Nollekens
bore the pants off
Joseph Priestley
come the raw prawn
Joseph Guillotin
Gone with the Wind
Love without Hope
Homeric laughter
Homeric question
mole-electronics
Moses Maimonides
sober-mindedness
government paper
government stock
José Enrique Rodó
come into one's own
governor-general
lose one's marbles
power of attorney
come someone's way
come home to roost
lower one's sights
cover one's tracks
homecoming queen
power-on self-test
tower of strength
come up to scratch
homeopathically
forensic science
Roget's Thesaurus
Love is all Around
Women's Institute
Somerset Maugham
potential energy
domestic science
domestic economy
Roberto Clemente
Robert Jenkinson
Robert Henry Dick
moment of inertia
Robert A Millikan
Robert S Mulliken
Homerton College
Robert Southwell
poverty-stricken
Coventry Patmore
molecular weight
comedy of manners
comedy of humours
Lorenzo Ghiberti
go off at a tangent
go off at half cock
non-fiction novel
confidence trick
confidentiality

confident person
coffee-table book
configurational
hot foil stamping
Norfolk dumpling
confrontational
comfortableness
comfortlessness
confessionalism
confessionalist
go off the deep end
congealableness
longwall working
tough as old boots
Congratulations
Hoagy Carmichael
tongue-and-groove
how goes the enemy?
tong-test ammeter
long-sightedness
Hodgkin's disease
Jorge Luis Borges
tough-mindedness
song-and-dance act
for goodness sake
zoogeographical
too good to be true
rough puff-pastry
Hoggar Mountains
Vosges Mountains
long-sufferingly
non-governmental
Moog synthesizer®
Joshua Lederberg
lophobranchiate
to the effect that
Loch Ness monster
To the Lighthouse
to the manner born
roche moutonnéed
nothingarianism
cochineal insect
nothing for it but
nothing less than
Koch's postulates
mother of vinegar
Do the Right Thing
Mothering Sunday
jodhpur breeches
Louisa May Alcott
logical analysis
logical designer
logical elements
sociobiological
folie de grandeur
police inspector
Louise Bourgeois
police constable
Robin Goodfellow
moving staircase
dolichocephalic
polishing-powder
Josiah Bounderby
go without saying
political animal
political asylum
dominical letter
political status
positive vetting
Dominion Theatre
social democracy
social secretary
social cleansing
social insurance
sociolinguistic
socialistically
social ownership
social exclusion
sodium carbonate
sodium ascorbate
goniometrically
sodium hydroxide
cosignificative
toxicologically
horizontal scrub
ion implantation
solid propellant
conic projection
posigrade rocket
rosin rosin plant
solid-state light
Robinson College
solipsistically
logistics vessel
Corinthian brass
non-intervention
non-intrusionist
comity of nations
non-judgmentally
conjugate angles
Dow-Jones average
conjunctionally
conjunctive mood
conjunctiveness
Look Back in Anger
pork scratchings
forked lightning
cooked breakfast
cockneyfication
Book of Zephaniah
Book of Zechariah
Book of Leviticus
look the other way
Yorkshire Ripper
look who's talking
working majority
work one's passage
work one's guts out
work double tides
Völkerwanderung
rocket scientist
socket head screw
pocket an affront
pocket one's pride
coal-tar creosote
collaboratively
collective fruit
collector's piece
Roy Lichtenstein
Zöllner's pattern
poulters' measure
Lob-lie-by-the-fire
collegial church
colloidal system
Rollright Stones
bowl a maiden over
noble-mindedness
couldn't care less
collenchymatous
foul-mouthedness
dollar diplomacy
world-shattering
cool as a cucumber
collision course
Toulouse-Lautrec
world without end
world-without-end
cosmic radiation
cosmic abundance
not much the wiser
not much to look at
too much too young
commodification
Commodore Keppel
commodity market
norm-referencing
room temperature
hot-melt adhesive
formularisation
formularization
commendableness
communibus annis
communicability
communi consensu
communicatively
Commonwealth Day
common of pasture
common chickweed
commonplace book
commonplaceness
command language
communalisation
communalization
common in the soil
common knowledge
common logarithm
common spadefoot
community charge
community centre
community health
common stinkhorn
community school
community spirit
community worker
room to swing a cat
cosmopolitanism
Donmar Warehouse
commercial paper
Commercial Court
commercial break
commissary court
commission agent
Cosmas and Damian
cosmetic surgery
dormitory suburb
going-away outfit
foundation-stone
mountain railway
mountain leather
mountain ringlet
mountain bicycle
mountain bramble
roundaboutility
roundaboutation
John Harvey-Jones
Mount Chimborazo
John Schlesinger
corno di bassetto
counter-approach
counteractively
counter-evidence
counterfeisance
counter-flowered
counterfesaunce
counter-irritant
countermandable
countermovement
John Bennet Lawes
counter-pressure
counter-proposal
John Henry Newman
counter-security
countervailable
John Philip Sousa
join the majority
John Wilkes Booth
Council of Europe
Council of States
connoisseurship
cornelian cherry
Count Leo Tolstoy
Cornelis Drebbel
Cornelius Jansen
born in the purple
morning sickness
horns of a dilemma
down to the ground
Bornholm disease
point of no return
go into committee
horns of the altar
Joan Armatrading
loan translation
joint resolution
do one's damnedest
do one's level best
do one's endeavour
to one's knowledge
round-shouldered
coinstantaneity
coinstantaneous
Johnston Islands
Mount Tungurahua
John Quincy Adams
Young Vic Theatre
Johnny-head-in-air
coromandel ebony
go to rack and ruin
Colorado Springs
Holocaust Museum
Corona Australis
for old sake's sake
for old time's sake
homogeneousness
Dolores Ibárruri
do someone reason
to someone's teeth
colonels-in-chief
sow one's wild oats
homochlamydeous
monochlamydeous
colonial animals
monounsaturated
go to one's account
Molotov cocktail
not on one's nellie
locomotor ataxia
Norodom Sihanouk
sonorous figures
Monocotyledones
colour threshold
colour blindness
loxodromic curve
logographically
nomographically
topographically
holocrystalline
monocrystalline
coconsciousness
Toronto blessing
go for the jugular
motorway madness
nobody's business
monosymmetrical
non-prescription
complete annuity
comprehensively
comprehensivise
comprehensivize
complementarily
complementarity
complementation
compressibility
complex sentence
no spring chicken
compendiousness
companion-in-arms
companion ladder
company promoter
non-professional
morphophonemics
non-profit-making
morphologically
doppio movimento
vox populi vox Dei
corporification
compartmentally
copper engraving
corporation sole
corporate raider
co-operativeness
compassionately
colposcopically
composite school
hoppus cubic foot
hospitalisation
hospitalization
computer hacking
computer science
computer-to-plate
computerisation
computerization
compotationship
competitiveness
compound larceny
compound animals
zoophysiologist
zoophytological
conquerableness
torque converter
mosquito curtain
do a roaring trade
poor man of mutto
correcting fluid
correction fluid
Fourier analysis
Mourne Mountain
yours faithfully
Rodrigues Island
corrugated paper
fourth dimension
co-ordinate bonds
four-dimensional
correlativeness
court-martialled

pour cold water on
Court of Requests
corruptibleness
Morrison shelter
correspondently
correspondingly
courts-bouillons
four-stroke cycle
doorstep selling
Norroy and Ulster
horse and hattock
Mössbauer effect
Constant Lambert
dorsibranchiate
gooseberry-stone
consubstantiate
consecratedness
consecutiveness
considerateness
consideratively
mousseline sauce
Monsieur de Paris
orswear oneself
ousehold troops
ow-spiritedness
onscience money
onscience-proof
onscientiously
onstitutionist
onspicuousness
oastline effect
onsolation race
ssil turquoise
onsumer society
onsumptiveness
onsentaneously
oisoned chalice
onsensicalness
onsenting adult
ssing the caber
ouse of Assembly
od's honest truth
g's-tooth violet
ssip columnist
nsequentially
nservation law
nservationist
nservatorship
nstructionism
nstructionist
rseradish tree
nscriptionist
ssession order
se-shoe magnet
ssuth Overture
rsiventrality
d Save the Queen
ntraband of war
travallation
ots and saddles
n't make me laugh
rthanger Abbey
tradictorily
tradictively
trapropeller
trait-gallery
trait-painter
tmanteau word
tractability
tractibility
th Bank Centre
Monte Carlo rally
north-countryman
Comte de Mirabeau
now there's a thing
how the wind blows
for the time being
for the life of her
for the life of him
Southern Comfort®
not the word for it
röntgenotherapy
post-Reformation
north-east-by-east
south-east-by-east
north-eastwardly
south-eastwardly
coat-of-mail shell
mortiferousness
Portuguese shark
cottage hospital
cottage industry
Montagu's harrier
not to have a ghost
doctrinarianism
Gottlieb Daimler
post-millenarian
postfix notation
postulationally
contemplatively
contemporaneity
contemporaneous
Mortimer Wheeler
contemptibility
contempt of court
continuation-day
rooting compound
Nottinghamshire
contentiousness
Hottentot's bread
cost someone dear
controversially
Montgomery Clift
montmorillonite
soft-rock geology
controllability
soft commodities
foot-pound-second
control register
postconsonantal
Götterdämmerung
Gottfried Keller
Gottfried Semper
mortar and pestle
South Seas Island
worth the whistle
Toots Thielemans
fortiter et recte
contour feathers
soft furnishings
tout au contraire
South Uist Island
boatswain's chair
north-west-by-west
south-west-by-west
north-westwardly
south-westwardly
post-synchronise
post-synchronize
softly-sprighted
conus arteriosus
so much the better
volutin granules
go out like a light
go out of business
voluntary muscle
voluntary school
you've got me there
nouvelle cuisine
convolvulaceous
convenience food
conventionalise
conventionalism
conventionalist
conventionality
conventionalize
conversationism
conversationist
convergence zone
loaves and fishes
Joe Willie Namath
forward contract
forward delivery
notwithstanding
Norway saltpetre
Corynebacterium
polychlorinated
polychloroprene
polyphloesboean
body-line bowling
bodyline bowling
polyelectrolyte
polyunsaturated
Holy Roman Empire
roly-poly pudding
polycrystalline
Polyprotodontia
now you're talking
For Your Eyes Only
polysyllabicism
polysynthetical
apparent horizon
sphaerosiderite
aplastic anaemia
speak to the heart
special delivery
spick and span new
special hospital
special pleading
special retainer
special warranty
specific impulse
specific gravity
apocalyptically
speculativeness
spectroscopical
space travelling
epidemiological
upper atmosphere
spread-eaglewise
appendicularian
splendide mendax
spread one's wings
ephemeris second
speech pathology
speechification
speech therapist
speech community
speech synthesis
Sphenisciformes
spheroidisation
spheroidization
J Pierpont Morgan
appearance money
optical activity
optical illusion
optical spectrum
optical splitter
Ophioglossaceae
springer spaniel
split infinitive
spoiling tactics
sprinkler system
split-level house
split-level trust
spoilt for choice
Apollinarianism
spontaneousness
Spencer Perceval
open-heartedness
open aestivation
opinionatedness
spend one's breath
Spanish chestnut
Spanish Civil War
Spanish mackerel
Spanish omelette
Spanish windlass
up to the eyeballs
up to the eyebrows
optoelectronics
appointment book
à propos de bottes
opportunity cost
opportunity shop
apophthegmatist
apophthegmatize
approachability
spermatic artery
spermatogenesis
spermatogenetic
spermatoblastic
opprobriousness
spirochaetaemia
spur of the moment
Ephraim Chambers
sparring partner
spiral staircase
appropriateness
appropinquation
spirit of ammonia
operating system
approved schools
A Passage to India
opus reticulatum
epistemological
Opisthobranchia
opisthognathous
episcopalianism
epistolary novel
Spasmodic School
ophthalmologist
ophthalmoplegia
ophthalmoplegic
ophthalmophobia
ophthalmoscopic
spot advertising
epitheliomatous
Speyer Cathedral
square leg umpire
square kilometre
equalitarianism
equilateral arch
Aquila and Prisca
equine distemper
Squire Trelawney
squish lip system
equinoctial line
equinoctial year
equiprobability
ergatandromorph
Great Bitter Lake
Mr Tambourine Man
crease-resistant
crease-resisting
grease the wheels
greater plantain
Artaxerxes Ochus
great-grandchild
triangular prism
breach of promise
breathe one's last
treacherousness
creative therapy
creation science
irrationalistic
Treaties of Paris
broad-leaved dock
treacle wormseed
Dr Hawley Crippen
broadmindedness
Ariadne auf Naxos
treasonableness
organophosphate
trial of strength
preacquaintance
Friars Preachers
breast screening
creature of habit
great white shark
Arabian numerals
problematically
proboscis monkey
probationership
procrastinating
procrastination
procrastinatory
procrastinative
Crucible Theatre
Frick Collection
Price Commission
Crocodile Dundee
procreativeness
practicableness
practical reason
brachiocephalic
tracking station
friction welding
fractionisation
fractionization
arachidonic acid
brachistochrone
price leadership
trichloroethane
Bracknell Forest
dry construction
preconstruction
precipitousness
processionalist
bricks-and-mortar
prick up one's ears
brachydactylous
brachycephalous
predictableness
cradle-snatching

Frederic Raphael
Frederick Ashton
Frederick Blanda
Frederick Delius
Frédéric Mistral
Frederick Sanger
Frederick Treves
Frederick Temple
dry distillation
grade separation
credit insurance
traditional jazz
predeterminable
irreparableness
green accounting
friendly society
friendly numbers
Orfeo ed Euridice
irrepealability
irredeemability
free-heartedness
true-heartedness
irreversibility
irretentiveness
greenery-yallery
greeting meeting
creeping thistle
freezing mixture
irreligiousness
arterialisation
arterialization
irremissibility
irresistibility
Erlenmeyer flask
irremovableness
irrevocableness
irreconcilement
praetorian guard
irresolvability
pre-emption right
Friedrich Bessel
Friedrich Engels
irrefragability
irreprehensible
irreprehensibly
green revolution
free association
oriented towards
Ernest Hemingway
oriental emerald
arrectis auribus
armed to the teeth
irrefutableness
irreducibleness
irreductibility
green woodpecker
prefect of police
Fra Filippo Lippi
Graf von Zeppelin
preformationism
preformationist
preferred shares
preferentialism
preferentialist
professionalise
professionalism
professionalize
drift transistor
pragmaticalness
programmability
programme trader

drogue parachute
progressiveness
progressive rock
fragmentariness
trigeminal nerve
trigonometrical
prognostication
prognosticative
Gregory's mixture
Gregory the Great
Brighton and Hove
bright as a button
Archibald Garrod
prohibitiveness
Archichlamydeae
orthodontically
archiepiscopacy
archiepiscopate
orthokeratology
orthopaedically
orthophosphoric
orthopsychiatry
Arthur Eddington
Arthur Pendennis
Arthur Wellesley
prehistorically
orchestral music
orchestra stalls
architecturally
orbital motorway
droit du seigneur
ornithodelphian
ornithodelphous
Erziehungsroman
ornithorhynchus
druidical circle
training college
trailing arbutus
prairie schooner
armillary sphere
articles of faith
brake horsepower
Erskine Childers
Erskine Caldwell
broken-heartedly
drilling machine
prolate spheroid
dramma per musica
prima ballerinas
drumhead cabbage
from the shoulder
crimping-machine
prima inter pares
trembling poplar
criminalisation
criminalization
crime prevention
gramophonically
crime passionnel
primary assembly
primary election
primary meristem
Prometheus Bound
from stem to stern
primitive streak
bring and buy sale
truncation error
transactionally
transcriptional
transcriptively
Brandenburg Gate

front-end loading
grande amoureuse
transfigurement
✧transfiguration
transfer machine
Frankfurt am Main
transfer payment
transferability
transgressional
transgressively
wrong-headedness
Frenchification
bronchiodilator
French-polishing
French Polynesia
bronchoscopical
franchise player
principal clause
principal dancer
principal mobile
Francis Beaufort
Francis Beaumont
Francisco de Goya
Francisco Franco
Franciscus Vieta
franking-machine
printing machine
wringing-machine
transition metal
transition point
transilluminate
Francis of Assisi
grandiloquently
Francis Palgrave
Grand Inquisitor
transistor radio
Brinell hardness
translatability
granulated sugar
translationally
transliteration
granulitisation
granulitization
transmogrifying
grant-maintained
transmutability
transmutational
pronunciamentos
François Mauriac
François Fénelon
François Boucher
front of the house
transplantation
Grand Pensionary
transportedness
transparentness
transposability
transpositional
prunes and prisms
Trinity Brethren
grind the faces of
granitification
prenatal therapy
trinitrobenzene
trinitrotoluene
trine to the cheat
tranquilizingly
tranquilization
transubstantial
transverse flute
transverse colon

front-wheel drive
brandy Alexander
Eriocaulonaceae
proof-correcting
proof correction
Arnold of Brescia
Arnold Dolmetsch
cry one's heart out
Arnolfini Museum
arboriculturist
proof of identity
proof of purchase
arrow-poison frog
cryoprecipitate
oreographically
graphic designer
graphite reactor
graphics plotter
proprietorially
propylene glycol
propylitisation
propylitization
drop one's aitches
trypanosomiasis
crypto-Christian
crypto-communist
cryptosporidium
proportionality
proportionately
properispomenon
prepossessingly
prepositionally
trapezius muscle
preregistration
Pre-Raphaelistic
Pre-Raphaelitish
Pre-Raphaelitism
prismatic powder
crystallography
crystalline lens
crystallisation
crystallization
grass characters
trisoctahedrons
press conference
grasscloth plant
cross-curricular
President Marcos
iris recognition
crested screamer
Brussels griffon
prospectiveness
Arts Theatre Club
grasshopper mind
dressing station
crossing-sweeper
prestidigitator
cry stinking fish
gross investment
trisyllabically
bristlecone pine
cross-laterality
gris-amber-steam'd
presentationism
presentationist
presentableness
presence chamber
prosenchymatous
Aristotelianism
Cross of St George
crossopterygian

preservationist
brass someone off
cross the Rubicon
brushtail possum
pressure therapy
Ernst Walter Mayr
crashworthiness
trustworthiness
crossword puzzle
freshwater snail
✧presbyterianise
✧presbyterianism
✧presbyterianize
protection money
critical damping
brothel-creepers
writ of privilege
writ of execution
pretentiousness
preternaturally
fraternity house
protospatharius
British Columbia
protozoological
Arjuna Ranatunga
traumatological
group discussion
argumentum ad rem
argumentatively
Fraunhofer lines
draught-proofing
draughtsmanship
troublesomeness
troubleshooting
Arturo Toscanini
Triumph of Caesar
Artur Rubinstein
provocativeness
✧privy councillor
✧privy counsellor
Aravinda Da Silva
Grover Cleveland
provost-sergeant
private attorney
gravity platform
private practice
gravitationally
growth substance
draw in one's horns
Crown prosecutor
drown someone ou
drawn-thread work
Brown University
proxime accessit
Proxima Centauri
proximate object
X-ray diffraction
X-ray micrography
Army and Navy Clu
greyhound-racing
Greyfriars Bobby
Prayer of Azariah
escalator clause
Island of Molokai
I stand corrected
escape mechanism
escape character
a slap on the wrist
Isabelle Huppert
psychopathology
psychogenetical

psychogeriatric
psychometrician
psychochemistry
psychotherapist
psychophysicist
psychobiography
psychobiologist
psychohistorian
psychologically
psychosomimetic
psychotomimetic
psychographical
sychosynthesis
sychrometrical
idor Isaac Rabi
steochondroses
steochondrosis
scend the throne
steopathically
scension Island
sbert Lancaster
ssential organs
sheet in the wind
sheet to the wind
thick as a plank
cherichia coli
hmus of fauces
similationist
stislav Keldysh
immunisation
immunization
sisted take-off
clepiadaceous
magnetic line
hmolean Museum
emplastically
a matter of fact
long as one's arm
onic medicine
notic pressure
ociation copy
orm in a teacup
ound as a roach
borne Reynolds
ot the Sheriff
perimetrical
rodynamicist
reiculturist
ronomer Royal
onautically
onavigation
ulating orbit
udepigraphic
udoephedrine
udopregnancy
arbara's cress
wberry shrub
ddle carrier
egic metals
alentine's Day
Kangchenjunga
ght talking
ght-talking
ght shooter
ghtforward
chment order
biliousness
igraphical
n locomotive
n hardening
trick's cross
it's a free country
St Lawrence River
straitwaistcoat
Atlantic Charter
St Martin's summer
stable companion
stockbroker belt
sticking-plaster
stocking stuffer
stickit minister
stick in one's craw
stocks and stones
stick to one's guns
Athena Promachos
stretcher-bearer
stretching frame
stretch one's legs
etherealisation
etherealization
St Peter's College
stoechiological
strephosymbolia
atherosclerosis
atherosclerotic
stress of weather
street furniture
stiff-neckedness
Stefan Wyszynski
staff-tree family
stagnation point
St Ignatius's bean
stigmatophilist
steganographist
at the drop of a hat
at the first blush
St Thomas Aquinas
ethical genitive
St Hilda's College
strike a bad patch
strike-slip fault
string orchestra
stoicheiometric
stoichiological
Ethiopian pepper
Ethiopian region
St Kitts and Nevis
Stella McCartney
Italian Concerto
Italian ryegrass
Italian vermouth
stalactitically
stalagmitically
Ptolemaic system
stilpnosiderite
at a loss for words
at close quarters
utility function
stamp collecting
stomach staggers
atomic structure
stemless thistle
stamping machine
stamp of approval
stand and deliver!
standard English
standardisation
standardization
ethnic cleansing
ethnocentricity
Stanley Kowalski
Stanley Matthews
St Anthony's cross
stinking parasol
standing-off dose
standing rigging
standing ovation
ethnolinguistic
ethnomusicology
stand on ceremony
stand one's corner
stand one's ground
standoffishness
St Antony of Padua
stand to one's guns
stand upon points
strombuliferous
strolling player
Attorney-General
Otto von Bismarck
atmospherically
a thousand and one
Utopia Unlimited
Stephen Jay Gould
Stephen Sondheim
stapling machine
stop-frame camera
staphylorrhaphy
Stars and Stripes
eternal triangle
attributiveness
à tort et à travers
star of Bethlehem
storage capacity
stereochemistry
stereoisomerism
Sturt's desert pea
at cross purposes
state capitalism
State Department
Statue of Liberty
St Stephen's House
St Cuthbert's duck
structural steel
Steven Spielberg
stewards' enquiry
Guiana Highlands
put a fast one over
cut and come again
sum and substance
butanedioic acid
Luca della Robbia
run a temperature
humanitarianism
mutatis mutandis
Judas Maccabaeus
put a brave face on
Sugar Ray Leonard
put back the clock
Hubble's constant
bubble and squeak
lumbrical muscle
numbered account
number-crunching
Mulberry harbour
rumbustiousness
Dutch admiral pea
quick-conceiving
Dutch elm disease
luncheon voucher
dulcified spirit
punctiliousness
functional group
durchkomponiert
musculoskeletal
subcommissioner
succinylcholine
vulcanized fibre
quick off the mark
susceptibleness
pulchritudinous
succession house
successlessness
succulent-house
punctuation mark
subcivilisation
subcivilization
quick-wittedness
Hundred Years' War
quadripartition
fundamental unit
Guy de Maupassant
quadruplication
Sunday Telegraph
funeral director
superadditional
pure mathematics
superabundantly
supercalendered
tuberculisation
tuberculization
superconfidence
superconductive
outer dead centre
superexaltation
superexcellence
Eugène Delacroix
superficialness
Duke of Newcastle
superfluousness
superheterodyne
superincumbence
superincumbency
superinducement
juvenile hormone
superimposition
superior planets
superintendence
superintendency
superlativeness
Museum of Mankind
Süleyman Demirel
supernaturalise
supernaturalism
supernaturalist
supernaturalize
superordination
queen of puddings
superplasticity
superpatriotism
queen's messenger
superstitiously
superstructural
supersaturation
Gulf War syndrome
surface activity
Nuffield College
luffing-jib crane
Jurgen Klinsmann
Burgundy mixture
burgh of regality
Luigi Pirandello
Jungermanniales
fungistatically
tungsten carbide
much of a muchness
push the envelope
Durham Cathedral
euphemistically
Cushing's disease
push one's fortune
Luchino Visconti
Sutherland Falls
authoritatively
Hugh Esmor Huxley
luminance signal
musical director
Audit Commission
cubic centimetre
Jupiter Symphony
rudimentariness
Munich Agreement
punitive damages
judicial trustee
pusillanimously
audiometrically
numismatologist
Julian of Norwich
Nubian monuments
jurisprudential
junior flyweight
Julius Rosenberg
Julius Streicher
Juliette Binoche
put in the picture
subintellection
subintelligence
subintelligitur
music to one's ears
put into practice
musique concrète
audiovisual aids
subject-superior
Huckleberry Finn
Buckinghamshire
bunker mentality
Burkitt lymphoma
nuclear-free zone
nuclear medicine
nuclear membrane
dual carriageway
nuclear reaction
nuclear umbrella
public relations
public-relations
public transport
duplicate bridge
public utilities
public ownership
Full Metal Jacket
dual personality
qualifying round
pull the forelock
full-line forcing
fuelling machine
building society
Juilliard School
pull in one's horns
pull one's punches
pull someone's leg
full motion video
full-motion video
full-bottomed wig
nucleosynthesis
Sublapsarianism

pull up one's socks
pullorum disease
full-dress debate
qualis ab incepto
duplex apartment
pulmobranchiate
Summoned by Bells
fulminating gold
submarine canyon
submarine effect
Our Mutual Friend
turntable ladder
funnel-web spider
running headline
burning mountain
turn in on oneself
turn in one's grave
running ornament
burning question
burn one's fingers
burn one's bridges
turn one's stomach
Juan José Arreola
burnet saxifrage
burnt to a frazzle
furniture beetle
quinquagenarian
quintuplication
quantum sufficit
mucosanguineous
autoradiography
humoral immunity
automatic teller
out of all measure
put on a brave face
✧Aurora Australis
autoschediastic
out of commission
subordinateness
put one's back into
cut one's eye teeth
run one's eyes over
put one's finger on
put one's foot down
put one's foot in it
European Council
Europeanisation
Europeanization
autodidacticism
Ludovico Ariosto
out of one's senses
automorphically
autocorrelation
out of proportion
autotransformer
autographically
out of the running
put out to pasture
Eudoxus of Cnidus
out of whole cloth
humpbacked whale
purple gallinule
supplementarily
supplementation
purple of Cassuis
purple of Cassius
suppressor T-cell
jus primae noctis
sulphinpyrazone
Jumpin' Jack Flash
suspense account
jumping-off place
due process of law
supportableness
purposelessness
sub-postmistress
suppositionally
sulphur bacteria
sulphureousness
sulphur trioxide
jusqu'auboutisme
jusqu'auboutiste
curriculum vitae
lubricated water
quartermistress
guerre à outrance
quarrelsomeness
quarter-sessions
autrefois acquit
surrogate mother
guerrilla strike
burr in the throat
surreptitiously
sunrise industry
Aubrey Beardsley
Russian Civil War
Russian dressing
Russian roulette
substantialness
substantiveness
Aussichtspunkte
subspecifically
Russo-Finnish War
questionability
question-begging
substitutionary
rub salt in a wound
pulse modulation
run someone close
puss in the corner
Dunsinane Castle
curse of Scotland
substratosphere
subsistence wage
Sunset Boulevard
Australian crane
Australian rules
multiarticulate
Eustachian valve
multiculturally
justices' justice
put the clock back
put the mockers on
put the squeeze on
justifiableness
sustaining pedal
multilocational
multilingualism
multilateralism
multilateralist
multinucleolate
button accordion
Sutton Coldfield
Burton-upon-Trent
putting the stone
Kurt Vonnegut, Jnr
multiprocessing
juxtapositional
mustard and cress
subterraneously
quatercentenary
Quatorze Juillet
buttery-fingered
butterfly effect
butterfly flower
butterfly orchid
butterfly orchis
butterfly stroke
Hunter S Thompson
Justus von Liebig
custos rotulorum
multitudinously
Gustave Flaubert
suburbanisation
suburbanization
autumnal equinox
mutuus consensus
Auguste Mariette
Augusto Pinochet
Pulver Wednesday
Ludwig Feuerbach
Ludwig von Köchel
Ludwig Boltzmann
puzzle-prize book
avec acharnement
available market
evangelicalness
evangelistarion
Evonne Goolagong
Svante Arrhenius
Ivan the Terrible
evening primrose
Evening Standard
overfamiliarity
everlastingness
overachievement
overhead charges
over head and ears
overdevelopment
overweeningness
overleap oneself
overbearingness
average adjuster
overthrust fault
aversion therapy
overflow meeting
every mother's son
every now and then
over God's forbode
overforwardness
overpreparation
every second week
overuse syndrome
a widow bewitched
sweet Fanny Adams
owner-occupation
a week on Saturday
sweep second hand
two hundred hours
twelve-hour clock
swimming costume
Owen Chamberlain
twenty-four-seven
two-pair-of-stairs
sword-and-sorcery
sword-and-buckler
twirl one's thumbs
swathing-clothes
swathling-clouts
swothling-clouts
exhaust manifold
axial tomography
oxy-calcium light
oxidative stress
experimentalise
experimentalism
experimentalist
experimentalize
experimentation
experimentative
expeditiousness
experientialism
experientialist
exteriorisation
exteriorization
externalisation
external student
external storage
externalization
exteroceptivity
extemporariness
extemporisation
extemporization
extensification
expenses account
extensivization
Expectation Week
exchangeability
exchange teacher
Exchange and Mart
exchange control
exchange student
exhibitionistic
exclamation mark
exclusion clause
exemplification
exemplificative
exemption clause
excommunication
excommunicatory
excommunicative
extracellularly
extra-curricular
exercise bicycle
extra-illustrate
extrajudicially
extreme fighting
excrementitious
extraordinaries
extraordinarily
extra-provincial
express delivery
expressionistic
expressis verbis
axis of incidence
Exeter Cathedral
oxytetracycline
excursion ticket
gynandromorphic
Pyramid of Cheops
Pyramid of the Sun
Pyramids of Egypt
Byzantine Church
Byzantine Empire
synarthrodially
synchronistical
synchronisation
synchronousness
synchronization
synchro swimming
syndical chamber
Fyodor Chaliapin
hyperadrenalism
hypercritically
hypercorrection
hypercatalectic
synecdochically
synergistically
Sydenham's chorea
hyperlipidaemia
synecologically
hyperthyroidism
mythologisation
mythologization
by the short hairs
by the strong hand
myristicivorous
syllabification
dyslogistically
syllogistically
hyaloid membrane
pygmy chimpanzee
by small and small
dysmorphophobia
symmetricalness
pycnodysostosis
pyknodysostosis
hypnagogic image
hypnogogic image
lying-in hospital
hypnotisability
hypnotizability
hypomagnesaemia
cytomegalovirus
cytogenetically
pyrotechnically
pyrometric cones
hypoventilation
zygophyllaceous
sycophantically
hypochondriacal
hypochondriasis
pyrophotography
hyponitrous acid
hypopituitarism
by hook or by crook
pyro-electricity
typographically
Synoptic Gospels
xylotypographic
lymphadenopathy
lymphatic system
sympodial growth
symptomatically
symptomological
sympathetically
sympathomimetic
by trial and error
hydrobiological
hydrocyanic acid
Hydrocorallinae
hydrodynamicist
hydrogen cyanide
hydrometallurgy
oyer and terminer
hydropathically
hydrostatically
hygroscopic salt
hydraulic cement
hydraulic mining
dyer's-yellowwee
synthetic resins
dysteleological
systems analysis
systems software

nyetometrograph
systematisation
systematization
Sylvia Pankhurst
Czechoslovakian
Dzungaria Desert